Y0-BSM-462

Headquarters USA

A Directory of Contact Information for Headquarters and Other Central Offices of Major Businesses & Organizations in the United States and in Canada

2016

38th EDITION

Volume 2: Classification by Subject

Mailing Addresses, Telephone Numbers, Toll-Free Phone Numbers, Fax Numbers, and World Wide Web Addresses for:

- Associations, Foundations, and Similar Organizations
- Businesses, Industries, and Professions of All Types
- Colleges, Universities, Vocational & Technical Schools, and Other Educational Institutions
- Electronic Resources, including Internet Companies, Organizations, and Web Sites
- Embassies, Consulates, and UN Missions & Agencies
- Government Agencies & Offices at All Levels — City, County, State, Federal
- Libraries, Museums & Galleries, Zoos & Botanical Gardens, Performing Arts Organizations & Facilities, and Other Cultural Institutions
- Media Newspapers, Magazines, Newsletters; and Radio & Television Companies, Networks, Stations and Syndicators
- Research Centers & Organizations, including Scientific, Public Policy, and Market Research
- Professional Sports Teams, Other Sports Organizations, and Sports Facilities

and also including an Area/Zip Code Guide Covering more than 12,000 US Cities and Towns, as well as Area Code Tables in State & Numerical Order; and a detailed Index to Classified Headings under which listings are organized in the Directory's Classified Section.

Rich's Business Directories Inc.

Rich's Business Directories Inc.

Pearline Jaikumar, *Editor*
Karthikeyan Ponnambalam, *Research Manager*

⋆ ⋆ ⋆

Keith Jones,
Managing Editor

In collaboration with Omnigraphics Inc.

ISBN 978-0-7808-1432-5

ISSN 1531-2909

Printed in the United States of America

Rich's Business Directories Inc., in collaboration with Omnigraphics Inc.
155 W. Congress, Ste 200 Detroit, MI 48226
Phone Orders: 800-234-1340 • Fax Orders: 800-875-1340
Mail Orders: P.O. Box 8002 • Aston, PA 19014-8002
www.omnigraphics.com

Table of Contents

Volume 1:
Alphabetical by Organization Name

Volume 2:
Classified by Subject

Classified Headings Table

Listed here are all of the headings under which listings are categorized in the Classified Section of this directory. The headings are numbered sequentially, and these numbers correspond to those printed in the "Class' column that accompanies listings in the Alphabetical Section. Just match the number in the "Class" column to the corresponding number printed in this table in order to identify the type of business or organization of any white pages listing. Use this table, too, to locate the page on which that subject category appears in the classified section.

For a more detailed list of classified headings, including "See" and "See also" references, please see the Index to Classified Headings at the back of this book.

A

Still can't find what you're looking for? *For a more detailed subject selection, see the Index to Classified Headings at the back of this directory.*

Still can't find what you're looking for? *For a more detailed subject selection, see the Index to Classified Headings at the back of this directory.*

Still can't find what you're looking for? *For a more detailed subject selection, see the Index to Classified Headings at the back of this directory.*

G

H

Still can't find what you're looking for? *For a more detailed subject selection, see the Index to Classified Headings at the back of this directory.*

Still can't find what you're looking for? *For a more detailed subject selection, see the Index to Classified Headings at the back of this directory.*

Still can't find what you're looking for? *For a more detailed subject selection, see the Index to Classified Headings at the back of this directory.*

Page

Still can't find what you're looking for? *For a more detailed subject selection, see the Index to Classified Headings at the back of this directory.*

Still can't find what you're looking for? *For a more detailed subject selection, see the Index to Classified Headings at the back of this directory.*

Still can't find what you're looking for? *For a more detailed subject selection, see the Index to Classified Headings at the back of this directory.*

Classified Section

Listings in the Classified Section are organized alphabetically (or, where noted, by city or state names) under subject headings denoting a business or organization type. Alphabetizing is on a word-by-word rather than letter-by-letter basis.

For a detailed explanation of the scope and arrangement of listings, please refer to “"How to Use This Directory' at the beginning of this book. Page elements and listing formats are illustrated on the sample pages with accompanying explanatory notes found just inside the back cover.

1 ABRASIVE PRODUCTS

Listing	City	State	Zip	Phone	Fax
Abrasive Technology Inc 8400 Green Meadows Dr. *Web:* www.abrasive-tech.com	Lewis Center	OH	43035	740-548-4100	
Acme Holding Co 24200 Marmon Ave. *Web:* www.acmeabrasive.com	Warren	MI	48089	586-759-3332	759-3334
Agsco Corp 160 W Hintz Rd. *Web:* www.agsco.com	Wheeling	IL	60090	847-520-4455	
Avery Abrasives Inc 2225 Reservoir Ave. **Fax:* Cust Svc ■ *Web:* www.averyabrasives.com	Trumbull	CT	06611	203-372-3513	372-3714*
Basic Carbide Corp 900 Main St. *TF:* 800-426-4291 ■ *Web:* www.basiccarbide.com	Lowber	PA	15660	724-446-1630	446-1656
Bullard Abrasives Inc Six Carol Dr. *TF:* 800-227-4469 ■ *Web:* www.bullardabrasives.com	Lincoln	RI	02865	401-333-3000	
Camel Grinding Wheels 7525 N Oak Pk Ave. *TF:* 800-447-4248 ■ *Web:* www.cgwheels.com	Niles	IL	60714	847-647-5994	647-1861
Comco Inc 2151 N Lincoln St. *TF:* 800-796-6626 ■ *Web:* www.comcoinc.com	Burbank	CA	91504	818-841-5500	955-8365
Composition Materials Company Inc 249 Pepes Farm Rd. *TF:* 800-262-7763 ■ *Web:* compomat.com	Milford	CT	06460	203-874-6500	874-6505
Diagrind Inc 10491 164th Pl. *Web:* www.diagrind.com	Orland Park	IL	60467	708-460-4333	460-8842
Eagle Grinding Wheel Corp 2519 W Fulton St. *Web:* www.eaglegrindingwheel.com	Chicago	IL	60612	312-733-1770	733-5949
Emerald Creek Garnet Ltd 59652 Hwy 3 Rt 4. *Web:* www.emeraldcreekgarnet.com	Fernwood	ID	83830	208-245-2096	
Equipment Development Company Inc 100 Thomas Johnson Dr. *Web:* www.edcoinc.com	Frederick	MD	21702	301-663-1600	
Ervin Industries Inc 3893 Research Pk Dr. *TF:* 800-748-0055 ■ *Web:* www.ervinindustries.com	Ann Arbor	MI	48108	734-769-4600	663-0136
Formax Manufacturing Corp 168 Wealthy St SW. *TF:* 800-242-2833 ■ *Web:* formaxmfg.com	Grand Rapids	MI	49503	616-456-5458	456-7507
Garfield Industries 62 Clinton Rd. *Web:* garfieldbuff.com	Fairfield	NJ	07004	973-575-8800	575-6840
Gemtex Abrasives 60 Belfield Rd. *TF:* 800-387-5100 ■ *Web:* www.gemtexabrasives.com	Toronto	ON	M9W1G1	416-245-5605	245-3723
Glit/Microtron 809 Broad St PO Box 709. **Fax Area Code:* 706 ■ *TF:* 800-325-1051 ■ *Web:* www.continentalcommercialproducts.com	Wrens	GA	30833	314-739-8585	547-6367*
Global Material Technologies 1540 E Dundee Rd Ste 210. *Web:* www.gmt-inc.com	Palatine	IL	60074	847-202-7000	215-4838
Hermes Abrasives Ltd PO Box 2389. *Web:* www.hermesabrasives.com	Virginia Beach	VA	23450	757-486-6623	
Marvel Abrasive Products Inc 6230 S Oak Pk Ave. *TF:* 800-621-0673 ■ *Web:* www.marvelabrasives.com	Chicago	IL	60638	800-621-0673	701-0187
Micro Surface Finishing Products Inc 1217 W Third St. *Web:* www.micro-surface.com	Wilton	IA	52778	563-732-3240	
Modern Abrasive Corp PO Box 219. *Web:* www.modernabrasive.com	Spring Grove	IL	60081	815-675-2352	675-2822
Mosher Co 15 Exchange St. *Web:* www.mocomfg.com	Chicopee	MA	01014	413-598-8341	594-7647
Moyco Technologies Inc 200 Commerce Dr.	Montgomeryville	PA	18936	215-855-4300	362-3809
Norton Sandblasting Equipment 1006 Executive Blvd. *Web:* www.nortonsandblasting.com	Chesapeake	VA	23320	757-548-4842	
Precision H20 Inc 6328 E Utah Ave. *TF:* 800-425-2098 ■ *Web:* www.precisionh2o.com	Spokane	WA	99212	509-536-9214	536-9205
Premix-Marbletite Manufacturing Co 1259 NW 21st St. *Web:* www.premixmarbletite.com	Pompano Beach	FL	33069	954-917-7665	
Radiac Abrasives Inc 1015 S College Ave. **Fax:* Cust Svc ■ *TF:* 800-851-1095 ■ *Web:* www.radiac.com	Salem	IL	62881	618-548-4200	548-4207*
Raytech Industries 475 Smith St. *TF Cust Svc:* 800-243-7163 ■ *Web:* www.raytech-ind.com	Middletown	CT	06457	860-632-2020	632-1699
Red Hill Grinding Wheel 335 Dotts St.	Pennsburg	PA	18073	215-679-7964	
Saint-Gobain Abrasives Inc 2770 W Washington St. *TF:* 800-561-9490 ■ *Web:* www.nortonconstructionproducts.com	Stephenville	TX	76401	254-918-2310	918-2312
Sancap Abrasives 16123 Armour St NE. *TF:* 800-433-6663 ■ *Web:* www.sancapabrasives.com	Alliance	OH	44601	330-821-3510	821-3516
Sandusky-Chicago Abrasive Wheel Co 1100 W Barker Ave. *TF:* 800-843-4980 ■ *Web:* www.sanduskychicago.com	Michigan City	IN	46360	219-879-6601	872-8139
Schaffner Mfg Company Inc 21 Herron Ave Schaffner Ctr. *Web:* www.schaffnermfg.com	Pittsburgh	PA	15202	412-761-9902	761-8998
Shark Industries Ltd 6700 Bleck Dr. *Web:* www.sharkind.com	Rockford	MN	55373	763-565-1900	
Superior Abrasives Inc 4800 Wadsworth Rd. *TF:* 800-235-9123 ■ *Web:* www.superiorabrasives.com	Dayton	OH	45414	937-278-9123	278-7581
Trumbull Industries Inc 400 Dietz Rd NE. *TF:* 800-477-1799 ■ *Web:* www.trumbull.com	Warren	OH	44482	330-393-6624	399-4421
Uneeda Enterprizes Inc 640 Chestnut Ridge Rd Spring Valley. *Web:* www.sandpaper.com	New York	NY	10977	845-426-2800	
United Abrasives Inc 185 Boston Post Rd. *Web:* www.unitedabrasives.com	North Windham	CT	06256	860-456-7131	456-8341
US Technology Corp 4200 Munson St NW. *Web:* www.ustechnology.com	Canton	OH	44718	330-455-1181	
Virginia Materials & Supplies Inc 3306 Peterson St. *Web:* www.sandblaster.com	Norfolk	VA	23509	757-855-0155	
VSM Abrasives 1012 E Wabash St. *TF Cust Svc:* 800-737-0176 ■ *Web:* www.vsmabrasives.com	O'Fallon	MO	63366	636-272-7432	272-7434
Washington Mills Electro Minerals Co 20 N Main St. *Web:* www.washingtonmills.com	North Grafton	MA	01536	508-839-6511	839-7675

2 ACCOUNTING FIRMS

Listing	City	State	Zip	Phone	Fax
A + i Design Corp 125 Fifth Ave. *Web:* www.aplusi.com	New York	NY	10003	212-460-8920	
A D Singleton & Company CPA Inc 441 S Escondido Blvd. *Web:* adscpa.com	Escondido	CA	92025	760-747-4605	
Aarons Grant & Habif LLC 3500 Piedmont Rd Ste 500. *Web:* www.aghllc.com	Atlanta	GA	30305	404-233-5486	
Abbott Company Ltd 345 E Flower St. *Web:* acoabbott.com	Phoenix	AZ	85012	602-224-9092	
Abbott Stringham & Lynch 1550 Leigh Ave. *Web:* www.aslcpa.com	San Jose	CA	95125	408-377-8700	
Abrams Foster Nole & Williams PA West Quadrangle 2 Hamill Rd Ste 241. *Web:* www.afnw.com	Baltimore	MD	21210	410-433-6830	
Accountants in Transition Inc 10509 Vista Sorrento Pkwy Ste 300. *Web:* calltsg.com/	San Diego	CA	92121	858-404-9900	
Accounting Career Consultants 1001 Craig Rd Ste 391. *Web:* www.careeradvancers.com	Saint Louis	MO	63146	314-569-9898	
Accounts Payable Chexs Inc 1829 Ranchlands Blvd Nw. *Web:* www.apchexs.com	Calgary	AB	T3G2A7	403-247-8913	
AccuPay Payroll Inc 50 S Penn St Ste A5. *Web:* www.accupay.net	Hatboro	PA	19040	267-803-1213	
Accurecord Inc 200 Broadhollow Rd Ste 308. *Web:* www.accurecord.com	Melville	NY	11747	631-243-6400	
Accutrack Medical Billing 15703 Freeman Ave.	Lawndale	CA	90260	310-679-2141	
Ace Payroll Services Inc 1860 Walt Whitman Rd Ste 600. *Web:* www.acepayroll.com	Melville	NY	11747	516-420-9500	
Acsel Corp 2876 Guardian Ln. *Web:* acsel.org	Virginia Beach	VA	23452	757-463-5240	
Active Captive Management 16485 Laguna Canyon Rd Ste 200. *TF:* 800-921-0155 ■ *Web:* www.activecaptive.com	Irvine	CA	92618	949-727-0155	
ACU Serve Corp 2020 Front St Ste 205. *Web:* acuservecorp.com	Cuyahoga Fls	OH	44221	330-923-5258	
Adams & Polunsky Ad Valorem Tax Advisors Inc 8000 W Interstate 10 Ste 1600. *Web:* adams-tax.com	San Antonio	TX	78230	210-349-5606	
Adserts Inc 18650 W Corporate Dr Ste 200. *Web:* adserts.com	Brookfield	WI	53045	262-794-9010	
Advanced Payroll Solutions LLC 201 W Passaic St Ste 202A. *Web:* www.advpayrollsolutions.com	Rochelle Park	NJ	07662	201-587-0320	
Advertising Audit International LLC 32663 Red Maple St. *Web:* www.adauditintl.com	Union City	CA	94587	415-828-0779	

				Phone	Fax
Ahern Adcock Devlin LLP 2155 Chicago Ave Ste 100 *Web:* aadcpas.com	Riverside	CA	92507	951-683-0672	
Ahola Corp, The 6820 W Snowville Rd *TF:* 800-727-2849 ■ *Web:* www.ahola.com	Brecksville	OH	44141	440-717-7620	
Akin Doherty Klein & Feuge PC 8610 N New Braunfels Ste 101 *Web:* www.adkf.com	San Antonio	TX	78217	210-829-1300	
Albert R Maccani CPA 1537 S Delsea Dr	Vineland	NJ	08360	856-691-3279	
Albrecht- Viggiano- Zureck & Co 25 Suffolk Ct *Web:* www.avz.com	Hauppauge	NY	11788	631-434-9500	
Aldagen Inc 2810 Meridian Pkwy Ste 148	Durham	NC	27713	919-484-2571	
Alex Alonzo Accountancy Corp 650 N First St	San Jose	CA	95112	408-295-3214	
Alexander X Kuhn & Co 123 W Front St Ste 200 *Web:* www.axk.com	Wheaton	IL	60187	630-681-8100	
Alfred M Shiver Pa 260 E Court St *Web:* shivercpa.com	Marion	NC	28752	828-652-7319	
Alkon & Levine PC 29 Crafts St *Web:* alkon-levine.com	Newton	MA	02458	617-969-6630	
Allan S Feinberg An Acct Corp 16311 Ventura Blvd Ste 610	Encino	CA	91436	818-325-2800	
Allen Gibbs & Houlik LC 301 N Main Ste 1700	Wichita	KS	67202	316-267-7231	
Allison Knapp & Siekmann Ltd 2810 Frank Scott Pkwy W *Web:* akscpa.com	Belleville	IL	62223	618-233-2641	
Almich & Assoc An Accountancy Corp 26463 Rancho Pkwy S *Web:* almichcpa.com	Lake Forest	CA	92630	949-600-7550	
Almquist, Maltzahn, Galloway & Luth PC 1203 W Second St *Web:* www.gicpas.com	Grand Island	NE	68801	308-381-1810	
Altera Payroll Inc 2400 Northside Crossing *TF:* 877-474-6060 ■ *Web:* www.alterapayroll.com	Macon	GA	31210	478-477-6060	
Amani Fahmy-Jensen CPA PC 763 N St	White Plains	NY	10605	914-948-1880	
Ambrico & Company PA 425 W Colonial Dr Ste 305	Orlando	FL	32804	407-316-8900	
Anchin Block & Anchin LLP 1375 Broadway 18th Fl *Web:* www.anchin.com	New York	NY	10018	212-840-3456	840-7066
Andaloro, Smith & Krueger LLP N19W24400 Riverwood Dr Ste 200 *Web:* www.askcpas.com	Waukesha	WI	53188	262-544-2000	
Anderson Satuloff Machado 20700 Ventura Blvd Ste 205 *Web:* asmmcpa.com	Woodland Hills	CA	91364	818-710-0622	
Andrews Hooper Pavlik Plc 5300 Gratiot Rd *Web:* ahpplc.com	Saginaw	MI	48638	989-497-5300	
Angell & Company Pllc 3250 W Big Beaver Rd Ste 139 *Web:* angellcompany.com	Troy	MI	48084	248-649-8720	
Angelo & O'Brien Pa 340 N Ave E	Cranford	NJ	07016	908-276-8300	
Anstiss & Company PC 1115 Westford St *Web:* anstisscpa.com	Lowell	MA	01851	978-452-2500	
Appleone Payroll & Tax Filing 990 Knox St *Web:* appleonepayroll.com	Torrance	CA	90502	310-516-9359	
AppleOne Services Ltd 50 Paxman Rd Ste 8 *Web:* www.appleone.ca	Etobicoke	ON	M9C1B7	416-622-0100	
Arend Laukhuf & Stoller Inc 117 N Main St PO Box 249 *Web:* als-cpa.com	Paulding	OH	45879	419-399-3686	
Arledge & Assoc Inc 309 N Bryant Ave *Web:* www.jmacpas.com	Edmond	OK	73034	405-348-0615	348-0931
Armanino LLP 12667 Alcosta Blvd Ste 500 *Web:* www.amllp.com	San Ramon	CA	94583	925-790-2600	790-2601
Arnold Walker & Arnold & Company PC 915 N Jefferson Ave *Web:* www.awacpa.com	Mount Pleasant	TX	75455	903-572-6606	
Aronson & Co 805 King Farm Blvd Ste 300 *Web:* www.aronsonllc.com	Rockville	MD	20850	301-231-6200	231-7630
Arrone Appel CPA Professional 2425 Balsam Dr *Web:* appel-cpa.com	Boulder	CO	80304	303-545-5755	
Ascend Hr Solutions 450 East 1000 North *Web:* www.inter-mtn.com	North Salt Lake	UT	84054	801-299-6400	
Astra Group Corp 5913 Woodson Rd *Web:* cobaltastra.com	Mission	KS	66202	913-378-1900	
Athey & Company PA 1015 N Pearl St *Web:* www.atheycocpa.com	Bridgeton	NJ	08302	856-451-8277	
Audit Logistics LLC 1172 W Century Dr Ste 245 *Web:* www.auditlogistics.com	Louisville	CO	80027	303-951-9000	
Auerr Zajac & Assoc LLP 29 Dean Ave *Web:* auerr-zajaccpa.com	Franklin	MA	02038	508-528-1305	
Axley & Rode LLP 1307 S First St *Web:* www.axleyrode.com	Lufkin	TX	75901	936-634-6621	634-8183
Babush Neiman Komman Johnson LLP 5909 Peachtree Dunwoody 800 *Web:* www.bnkj.com	Atlanta	GA	30328	770-261-1900	
Baden Gage & Schroeder LLC 6920 Pointe Inverness Way Ste 300 *Web:* badencpa.com	Fort Wayne	IN	46804	260-422-2551	422-7862
Bain Freibaum & Company LLC 3515 N Arnoult Rd *Web:* bfscpa.com	Metairie	LA	70002	504-568-0086	
Baker Tilly 8219 Leesburg Pk Ste 800 *Web:* www.bakertilly.com	Vienna	VA	22182	703-923-8300	923-8330
Bansley & Kiener LLP 8745 W Higgins Rd Ste 200 *Web:* www.bk-cpa.com	Chicago	IL	60631	312-263-2700	
Barfield Murphy Shank & Smith PC 1121 Riverchase Office Rd *Web:* bmss.com	Birmingham	AL	35244	205-982-5500	

				Phone	Fax
Barrett & Company Pllc 4910 NW Camas Meadows Dr	Camas	WA	98607	360-210-5100	
Barson Group Pa 60 E Main St PO Box 8018 *Web:* barsongroup.com	Somerville	NJ	08876	908-203-9800	
Bart Morrill CPA PC 24 S Main *Web:* morrillcpa.com	Roosevelt	UT	200 E	435-725-1900	
Bates Coughtry Reiss LLP 2601 Saturn St Ste 210 *Web:* bcrcpas.com	Brea	CA	92821	714-871-2422	
Batson Acctg & Tax pa 20 Washington Pk *Web:* www.batsontax.net	Greenville	SC	29601	864-235-6824	
Battelle Rippe Kingston LLP 2000 W Dorothy Ln *Web:* www.rippe.com	Dayton	OH	45439	937-298-0201	
Bauman Associates Ltd PO Box 1225 *Web:* baumancpa.com	Eau Claire	WI	54702	715-834-2001	
Beacon Acctg Group LLC Six Pidgeon Hill Dr Ste 300 *Web:* beaconaccountinggroup.com	Sterling	VA	20165	703-430-7666	
Beasley Mitchell Co 509 S Main St Ste A *Web:* www.bmc-cpa.com	Las Cruces	NM	88005	575-528-6700	
Beason & Nalley Inc 101 Monroe St Ne *TF:* 800-416-1946 ■ *Web:* www.beasonnalley.com	Huntsville	AL	35801	256-533-1720	
Belfint Lyons & Shuman Pa 1011 Centre Rd Ste 310 *Web:* belfint.com	Wilmington	DE	19805	302-225-0600	
Bement & Company PC 39 E Eagle Ridge Dr Ste 200 *Web:* bementcompany.com	North Salt Lake	UT	84054	801-936-1900	
BendaGrace Stulz & Company PC 38800 Van Dyke Ave *Web:* bgscpas.com	Sterling Heights	MI	48312	586-883-6240	
BenefitMall 3450 Lakeside Dr Ste 400 *TF:* 877-729-6299 ■ *Web:* www.compupay.com	Miramar	FL	33027	954-874-4800	
Benham, Ichen & Knox LLP 1117 S Milwaukee Ave Ste C11 *Web:* www.bikcpa.com	Libertyville	IL	60048	847-362-4310	
Benjamin H Moore & Company Inc 720 N Maitland Ave Ste 105 *Web:* bhmcpapa.com	Maitland	FL	32751	407-644-3119	
Benko & Piane CPA'S 8301 Florence Ave Ste 316	Downey	CA	90240	562-923-9231	
Bennett & Middendorf Ltd 901 York *Web:* bennettandmiddendorf.com	Quincy	IL	62301	217-222-1142	
Bennett-Thrasher PC 3625 Cumberland Blvd *Web:* btcpa.net	Atlanta	GA	30339	770-396-2200	
Benson Piombo & Co 300 Tamal Plz Ste 180 *Web:* bbensoncpa.com	Corte Madera	CA	94925	415-924-2292	
Berdon LLP 360 Madison Ave Eighth Fl *Web:* www.berdonllp.com	New York	NY	10017	212-832-0400	371-1159
Berger & Company PA 95 Thames Blvd	Bergenfield	NJ	07621	201-384-6667	
Berger Assoc PC 1700 Bedford St Ste 101 *Web:* bergerassociatespc.com	Stamford	CT	06905	203-325-9727	
Bergey & Co 616 Williams St *Web:* bergeycpa.com	Berlin	MD	21811	410-641-1101	
Berkheimer Outsourcing Inc 1530 Vly Ctr Pkwy *Web:* work2berk.com	Bethlehem	PA	18017	610-954-9575	
Berkowitz Dick Pollack & Brant LLP 200 S Biscayne Blvd Sixth Fl *TF:* 800-999-1272 ■ *Web:* www.bpbcpa.com	Miami	FL	33131	305-379-7000	379-8200
Bernard N Ackerman CPA PA 864 Riverview Rd *Web:* www.bnacpa.com	Rock Hill	SC	29730	803-366-8371	
Berry Dunn Mcneil & Parker 100 Middle St 4th Fl *TF:* 800-908-4490 ■ *Web:* www.berrydunn.com/	Portland	ME	04101	207-775-2387	774-2375
Beyer Stagni & Co 1620 Polk St *Web:* bestcocpa.com	Houma	LA	70360	985-851-2433	
Bianchi Kasavan & Pope LLP 243 Sixth St Ste 220 *Web:* www.blhhcpa.com	Hollister	CA	95023	831-638-2111	
Bigelow & Co 500 N Commercial St *Web:* www.bigelowcpa.com	Manchester	NH	03101	603-627-7659	
BiggsKofford & Co 630 Southpointe Ct Ste 200 *Web:* www.biggskofford.com	Colorado Springs	CO	80906	719-579-9090	
Bill Pollard Jr CPA 79 E Eleventh St *Web:* billpollardcpa.com	Tracy	CA	95376	209-832-5110	
Binetti & Feerick CPAs PA 381 Broadway Ste 45	Westwood	NJ	07675	201-664-9151	
Black & Soli PC CPA 81 W Esperanza Blvd Ste E *Web:* blackandsoli.com	Green Valley	AZ	85614	520-625-5988	
Black Bashor & Porsch LLP 270 E Connelly Blvd *Web:* bbpcpa.com	Sharon	PA	16146	724-981-7510	
Blackman Kallick 10 S Riverside Plaza *TF:* 866-939-3921 ■ *Web:* www.plantemoran.com	Chicago	IL	60606	312-207-1040	207-1066
Blanski Peter Kronage & Zoch 7500 Olson Memorial Hwy Ste 200 *Web:* www.bpkz.com	Minneapolis	MN	55427	763-546-6211	
Blinn Farrell & Co 60 Bailey Blvd *Web:* blinnfarrell.com	Haverhill	MA	01830	978-372-8518	
Blue & Co 12800 N Meridian St Ste 400 *TF:* 800-717-2583 ■ *Web:* www.blueandco.com	Carmel	IN	46032	317-848-8920	573-2458
Blum Shapiro 29 S Main St PO Box 272000 *TF:* 866-356-2586 ■ *Web:* www.bshapiro.com	West Hartford	CT	06107	860-561-4000	521-9241
Bohr Dahm Greif & Assoc PC 1845 51st St Ne *Web:* bdgcpas.com	Cedar Rapids	IA	52402	319-366-8400	
Bolden Lipkin PC 3993 Huntingdon Pk *Web:* blicpa.com	Huntingdon Valley	PA	19006	215-947-3750	
Boldt Carlisle & Smith LLC 480 Church St SE *Web:* www.bcsllc.com	Salem	OR	97301	503-585-7751	
Bollus Lynch LLP 89 Shrewsbury St *Web:* bolluslynch.com	Worcester	MA	01604	508-755-7107	755-3896

Firm	City	State	ZIP	Phone	Fax
Bolnick & Snow LLP 39 Old Doansburg Rd *Web:* bolnickandsnow.com	Brewster	NY	10509	845-279-6300	
Bolon Hart & Buehler Inc 100 E Broad St Ste 2450 *Web:* bhbcpa.com	Columbus	OH	43215	614-228-2691	
BoltonSullivanTaylor & WeberLLP 1023 N Mallard *Web:* bstwcpa.com	Palestine	TX	75801	903-729-2229	
Bonadio Group, The 171 Sully's Trail Ste 201 *TF:* 877-917-3077 ■ *Web:* www.bonadio.com	Pittsford	NY	14534	585-381-1000	381-3131
Bonanno, Savino & Davies PC 105 Chestnut St Ste 32 *Web:* www.bsdcpa.com	Needham	MA	02492	781-449-3919	
Bonari & Company CPAs 3724 Lakeside Dr Ste 201 *Web:* bonaricpas.com	Reno	NV	89509	775-322-5850	
Bond Andiola & Company PC 600 Rt 206 S *Web:* www.bac-cpa.com	Raritan	NJ	08869	908-722-5885	
Boohaker Schillaci & Company PC 601 Vestavia Pkwy Ste 300 *Web:* www.bsccpa.com	Birmingham	AL	35216	205-824-1617	
Booker Arceneaux & Laskowski LLP 1100 NW Loop 410 Ste 207	San Antonio	TX	78213	210-341-2538	
Bookkeeping Express Enterprises LLC 671 N. Glebe Rd Ste 1610 *Web:* www.bookkeepingexpress.com	Arlington	VA	22203	703-766-5757	
Botz Deal & Company PC Two Wbury Dr Ste 106 *Web:* www.botzdeal.com	Saint Charles	MO	63301	636-946-2800	
Bowen & Bowen 16 W 445 S Frontage Rd *Web:* bowencpa.com	Burr Ridge	IL	60527	630-325-9800	
Bowman & Company LLP 601 White Horse Rd *Web:* www.bowmanllp.com	Voorhees	NJ	08043	856-435-6200	
Boyarsky Silbert & Silverman PA 6151 Executive Blvd	Rockville	MD	20852	301-231-0535	
Boyle & Stoll CPAs PC 3755 Brickway Blvd *Web:* boyle-stoll.com	Santa Rosa	CA	95403	707-571-1951	
Brabo & Carlsen LLP 1111 E Tahquitz Canyon Way *Web:* brabo-carlsen.com	Palm Springs	CA	92262	760-320-0848	
Bradley J Mcdonough CPA 2645 Frederica St Ste 200	Owensboro	KY	42301	270-852-2733	
Bradshaw- Smith & Co 5851 W Charleston *Web:* www.bradshawsmith.com	Las Vegas	NV	89146	702-878-9788	
Brady Martz & Assoc PC 401 Demers Ave Ste 300 *Web:* bradymartz.com	Grand Forks	ND	58201	701-775-4685	795-7498
Branter Thibodeau & Associate 674 Mt Hope Ave Ste 1 *Web:* btacpa.com	Bangor	ME	04401	207-947-3325	
Brantley Janson Yost & Ellison CPA 1617 S 325th St *Web:* www.brantleyjanson.com	Federal Way	WA	98003	253-838-3484	
Briggs & Veselka Co 9 Greenway Plaza Ste 1700 *Web:* bvccpa.com	Houston	TX	77046	713-667-9147	626-7832
Brimmer Burek & Keelan LLP 5601 Mariner St Ste 200 *Web:* www.bbkm.com	Tampa	FL	33609	813-282-3400	
Brockman Coats Gedelian & Co 1735 Merriman Rd *Web:* bcgcompany.com	Akron	OH	44313	330-864-6661	
Broniec Assoc Inc 4855 Peachtree Industrial Blvd Ste 215 *Web:* www.broniec.com	Norcross	GA	30092	770-729-9664	
Brooks Mcginnis & Company LLC 5871 Glenridge Dr Ste 200 *Web:* brooksmcginnis.com	Atlanta	GA	30328	404-531-4940	
Brown Armstrong Accountancy Corp 4200 Truxtun Ave Ste 300 *Web:* www.bacpas.com	Bakersfield	CA	93309	661-324-4971	
Brown Graham & Company PC 7431 Continental Pkwy *Web:* www.bgc-cpa.com	Amarillo	TX	79114	806-355-8241	
Brown Ronald & Assoc pa 551 Ave K SE *Web:* ronaldbrowncpa.com	Winter Haven	FL	33880	863-299-1500	
Brown Schultz Sheridan & Fritz 210 Grandview Ave *Web:* bssf.com	Camp Hill	PA	17011	717-761-7171	
Bruce Hersh CPA Accountancy Corp 17547 Ventura Blvd	Encino	CA	91316	818-905-0533	
Bruno Skorheim 9665 Chesapeake Dr Ste 470 *Web:* www.brunoskorheim.com	San Diego	CA	92123	858-300-3141	
Bryant Katt & Assoc PC 6211 O St *Web:* bka-cpa.com	Lincoln	NE	68510	402-486-1040	
Bryen & Bryen LLP 100 Centre Blvd Ste A *Web:* www.bryen-bryenllp.com	Marlton	NJ	08053	856-985-8550	
Buckeye Payroll Services 5749 Park Ctr Ct *Web:* www.buckeyepayroll.com	Toledo	OH	43615	419-472-7377	
Buckley Gent Macdonald & Cary PC 100 Great Oaks Blvd Ste 121	Albany	NY	12203	518-437-0430	
Buddy H Coffey CPA PC 201 N Thornton Ave	Dalton	GA	30720	706-226-7924	
Bunker Clark Winnell Nuorala PC 2301 Mitchell Park Dr *Web:* bcwncpa.com	Petoskey	MI	49770	231-347-3963	
Burke & Schindler PLL 901 Adams Crossing *Web:* www.burkecpa.com	Cincinnati	OH	45202	513-455-8200	
Burr Pilger & Mayer LLP (BPMLLP) 600 California St Ste 1300 *TF:* 866-312-4390 ■ *Web:* www.bpmcpa.com	San Francisco	CA	94108	415-421-5757	288-6288
Business Strategy Inc 944 52nd St SE	Grand Rapids	MI	49508	616-261-2200	
C J Schlosser & Company LLC 233 E Ctr Dr PO Box 416 *Web:* www.cjsco.com	Alton	IL	62002	618-465-7717	465-7710
C&I Value Advisors LLC 4805 W Laurel St Ste 100 *Web:* clvalue.com	Tampa	FL	33607	813-286-7373	
Cachet Financial Services 750 E Green St Ste 315 *Web:* www.cachetbanq.com	Pasadena	CA	91101	626-578-9400	
Calegari & Morris 123 Mission St 18th Fl *Web:* calegariandmorris.com	San Francisco	CA	94105	415-981-8766	
Callero & Callero LLP 7800 N Milwaukee Ave *Web:* callero.com	Niles	IL	60714	847-966-2040	
Camp Moring & Cannon LLC 1418 Laurel St *Web:* cmccpas.net	Columbia	SC	29201	803-252-9375	
Campbell Rappold & Yurasits LLP 1033 S Cedar Crest Blvd *Web:* crycpas.com	Allentown	PA	18103	610-435-7489	
Candy & Schonwald Pllc 3116 Live Oak St *Web:* cscpa.com	Dallas	TX	75204	214-826-6660	
Cannon Wright Blount Pllc 756 Ridge Lk Blvd Ste 100 *Web:* www.cannonwrightblount.com	Memphis	TN	38120	901-685-7500	
Cantor & Cantor CPA'S 31550 Northwestern Hwy Ste 110	Farmington Hills	MI	48334	248-851-0664	
Carbis Walker LLP 2599 Wilmington Rd *Web:* carbis.com	New Castle	PA	16105	724-658-1565	
Care Acctg Inc 110 Central Sq Dr	Beaver Falls	PA	15010	724-843-1400	
Carmichael Brasher Tuvell & Co 1647 Mt Vernon Rd *Web:* www.cbtcpa.com	Atlanta	GA	30338	678-443-9200	
Carothers & Vlasman CPA'S PC 3555 Stanford Rd Ste 104	Fort Collins	CO	80525	970-223-7471	
Carr Riggs & Ingram LLC 1117 Boll Weevil Cir PO Box 311070 *Web:* www.cricpa.com	Enterprise	AL	36330	334-347-0088	347-7650
Carver Florek & James LLC 2246 University Park Blvd *Web:* cfjcpa.com	Layton	UT	84041	801-926-1177	
Cascade Billing Center Inc 1001 Cooper Point Rd SW Ste 140 *Web:* cascadebilling.com	Olympia	WA	98502	360-352-2037	
Case Sabatini & Co 470 Sts Run Rd Ste 1 *Web:* www.casesabatini.com	Pittsburgh	PA	15236	412-881-4411	
Casey Neilon & Assoc LLC 503 N Division St *Web:* wealthcarecpas.com	Carson City	NV	89703	775-283-5555	
Cast & Crew Entertainment Services LLC 2300 Empire Ave *Web:* www.castandcrew.com	Burbank	CA	91504	818-848-6022	
Catanese Group PC 307 State St *Web:* catanesegroup.com	Johnstown	PA	15905	814-255-8400	
Caufield & Flood 407 E Congress Pkwy Ste A *Web:* www.cfcpas.com	Crystal Lake	IL	60014	847-669-5950	
CBIZ Tofias PC 500 Boylston St *TF:* 888-761-8835 ■ *Web:* www.cbiz.com	Boston	MA	02116	617-761-0600	761-0601
Cbm Chartered Accountants 152 Jackson St E Ste 200 *Web:* www.cbmca.com	Hamilton	ON	L8N1L3	905-572-7220	
Cerow & Company CPA'S PA 1801 Sarno Rd Ste 3	Melbourne	FL	32935	321-242-2511	
Certified General Accountants Assn of British Columbia 300-1867 W Broadway *TF:* 800-565-1211 ■ *Web:* www.cga-bc.org	Vancouver	BC	V6J5L4	604-732-1211	
Certipay 199 Ave B NW Ste 270 *TF:* 800-422-3782 ■ *Web:* www.certipay.com	Winter Haven	FL	33881	863-299-2400	299-2131
CGA Canada 4200 N Fraser Way *Web:* cga-canada.org	Burnaby	BC	V5J5K7	604-669-3555	
Charles E Reed & AssocPC 3636 Professional Dr	Port Arthur	TX	77642	409-983-3277	
Cherry Bekaert & Holland LLP 200 S 10th St Ste 900 *Web:* www.cbh.com	Richmond	VA	23219	804-673-5700	673-4290
Chiampou Travis Besaw & Kershner LLP 45 Bryant Woods N *Web:* www.chiampou.com	Amherst	NY	14228	716-630-2400	
Cicinelli & Dippolito CPAs PC 1858 Commerce St *Web:* cdcpas.com	Yorktown Heights	NY	10598	914-302-2290	
Citrin Cooperman & Company LLP 529 Fifth Ave Second Fl *Web:* www.citrincooperman.com	New York	NY	10017	212-697-1000	697-1004
CJBS LLC 2100 Sanders Rd Ste 200 *Web:* www.cjbs.com	Northbrook	IL	60062	847-945-2888	
Clark Nuber PS 10900 NE Fourth St Ste 1700 *TF General:* 800-504-8747 ■ *Web:* www.clarknuber.com	Bellevue	WA	98004	425-454-4919	454-4620
Clark Schaefer Hackett & Co One E Fourth St Ste 1200 *Web:* www.cshco.com	Cincinnati	OH	45202	513-241-3111	422-7882
Clausman & Assoc PC 1980 E 116th St	Carmel	IN	46032	317-844-3110	
Clayton & Mckervey PC 2000 Town Ctr Ste 1800 *Web:* www.claytonmckervey.com	Southfield	MI	48075	248-208-8860	208-9115
CliftonLarsonAllen - CLA 301 SW Adams St Ste 1000 *TF:* 800-354-5849 ■ *Web:* www.cliftoncpa.com	Peoria	IL	61602	309-671-4500	671-4508
Clinic Service Corp 3464 S Willow St *Web:* www.clinicservice.com	Denver	CO	80231	303-755-2900	
Cole & Reed PC 531 Couch Dr *Web:* coleandreed.com	Oklahoma City	OK	73102	405-239-7961	
Collins Barrow Calgary LLP 1400 First Alberta Pl 777 - Eighth Ave SW *Web:* www.collinsbarrow.com	Calgary	AB	T2P3R5	403-298-1500	
Colusa Casino & Bingo 3770 Hwy 45 *Web:* www.colusacasino.com	Colusa	CA	95932	530-458-8844	

Firm / Address	City	State	Zip	Phone	Fax
Community hospitals and Wellness centers 6050 Oak Tree Blvd S Ste 500 *NYSE: CBZ* ■ *Web:* www.cbizinc.com	Cleveland	OH	44131	216-447-9000	
Complete Business Consultants 1901 Jefferson Ave Ste 105	Tacoma	WA	98402	253-383-3700	
Complete Payroll Processing Inc 7488 SR- 39 Po Box 190 *TF:* 888-237-5800 ■ *Web:* www.completepayroll.com	Perry	NY	14530	585-237-5800	
Computer Business Applications Inc 507 N Mulberry St *Web:* www.cbatech.com	Elizabethtown	KY	42701	270-737-1888	
ComputerSearch Corp 331 Audubon Pkwy *Web:* www.cspayroll.com	Amherst	NY	14228	716-689-0511	
Comyns, Smith, McCleary & Deaver LLP 3470 Mount Diablo Blvd Ste A110 *Web:* csmllp.com	Lafayette	CA	94549	925-299-1040	
Condley & Co LLP 993 N 3rd St *Web:* www.condley.com	Abilene	TX	79601	325-677-6251	677-0006
Cone & Smith PC 3421 Rainbow Pkwy	Rainbow City	AL	35906	256-413-3057	
Conner Ash PC 12101 Woodcrest Exec Dr 300 *Web:* www.connerash.com	Saint Louis	MO	63141	314-205-2510	
Considine & Considine 1501 Fifth Ave Ste 400 *Web:* www.cccpa.com	San Diego	CA	92101	619-231-1977	
Contingent Workforce Solutions Inc 2430 Meadowpine Blvd Ste 101 *TF:* 866-837-8630 ■ *Web:* cwsolutions.ca	Mississauga	ON	L5N6S2	866-837-8630	
Cooper, Travis & Company PLC 3008 Poston Ave *Web:* www.coopertravis.com	Nashville	TN	37203	615-329-4500	
Corbett Duncan & Hubly PC 100 E Pierce Rd Ste 100 *Web:* www.cdhcpa.com	Itasca	IL	60143	630-285-0215	
Corcoran Ender & Assoc 4010 S California Av *Web:* cpa-chicago.com	Chicago	IL	60632	773-247-7132	
Correll Assoc PC 26026 Telegraph Rd Ste 200 *Web:* correllcpa.com	Southfield	MI	48033	248-355-5151	
Coulter & Justus PC 9717 Cogdill Rd Ste 201 *Web:* cj-pc.com	Knoxville	TN	37932	865-637-4161	
Cowan Bolduc Doherty CPAs & Advisors 231 Sutton St *Web:* www.cbdcpa.com	North Andover	MA	01845	978-620-2000	
CPA Tax Solutions LLC 375 Mather St *Web:* cpataxsolutionsllc.com	Hamden	CT	06514	203-248-8600	
Crisell & Assoc 2199 E Willow St *Web:* crisellcpas.com	Signal Hill	CA	90755	562-595-0501	
Criticaledge Group Inc 2751 Dixwell Ave	Hamden	CT	06518	203-281-0006	
Crowe Horwath LLP One Mid America Plz Ste 700 *Web:* www.crowehorwath.com	Oak Brook	IL	60522	630-574-7878	
Cummings & Carroll PC 175 Great Neck Rd	Great Neck	NY	11021	516-482-3260	
Curtis Blakely & Company PC 2403 Judson Rd *Web:* cbandco.com	Longview	TX	75605	903-758-0734	
Cygan Hayes Ltd 20635 Abbey Woods Ct N *Web:* cyganhayes.com	Frankfort	IL	60423	815-534-5713	534-5523
D'Huyvetter & Swichkow PC 519 Johnson Ferry Rd Ste A-100 *Web:* www.dspccpa.com	Marietta	GA	30068	404-231-3500	
Dahl Hatton Muir & Reese Ltd 217 S Birch Ave PO Box 698 *Web:* dhmrcpa.com	Hallock	MN	56728	218-843-2645	
Dal Poggetto & Company LLP 149 Stony Cir	Santa Rosa	CA	95401	707-545-3311	
Dale M Long PC CPA'S 5945 Ward Rd Ste 200 *Web:* dalelongpc.com	Arvada	CO	80004	303-431-2666	
Dannible & McKee LLP 221 S Warren St *Web:* www.dmconsulting.com	Syracuse	NY	13202	315-472-9127	
Danser Balaam & Frank Five Independence Way	Princeton	NJ	08540	609-987-0300	
Darmody, Merlino & Company LLP 75 Federal St Ste 1500 *Web:* www.darmodymerlino.com	Boston	MA	02110	617-426-7300	
Davis Smith Accounting Associates pa 5582 Milford Harrington Hwy *Web:* www.davis-smithaccounting.com	Harrington	DE	19952	302-398-4020	
Dee J Wolfe CPA PC 818 NW 14th Ave *Web:* deejwolfe.com	Portland	OR	97209	503-295-0366	
Delap LLP 5885 Meadows Rd Ste 200 *Web:* delapcpa.com	Lake Oswego	OR	97035	503-697-4118	
Delisi & Assoc PC 217 S Pennsylvania Ave *Web:* delisiassociates.com	Greensburg	PA	15601	724-832-8585	
Deloitte & Touche USA LLP 1633 Broadway *Web:* www.deloitte.com	New York	NY	10019	212-489-1600	489-1687
Deloitte Touche Tohmatsu 1633 Broadway *Web:* www.deloitte.com	New York	NY	10019	212-489-1600	
Demello Mcauley Mcreynolds & Holland LLP 351 G St *Web:* dmmh-cpa.com	Eureka	CA	95501	707-445-0871	
Deming Malone Livesay & Ostroff 9300 Shelbyville Rd Ste 1100 *Web:* www.dmlo.com	Louisville	KY	40222	502-426-9660	
Denney & Company Chtd 1096 N Eastland Dr Ste 200 *Web:* denneycpa.com	Twin Falls	ID	83301	208-733-3223	
Dent, Baker & Company LLP 2204 Lakeshore Dr Ste 300 *Web:* www.dentbaker.com	Birmingham	AL	35209	205-871-1880	
Dermody, Burke & Brown CPAs LLC 443 N Franklin St *Web:* www.dbbllc.com	Syracuse	NY	13204	315-471-9171	
Desmond & Ahern Ltd 10827 S Western Ave *Web:* www.desmondcpa.com	Chicago	IL	60643	773-779-4720	
DFrank Plater Jr Prof Corp 610 Colcord Dr	Oklahoma City	OK	73102	405-236-3739	
DGL Software Services Ltd 200 1040 - Seventh Ave SW *Web:* www.dglsoftware.com	Calgary	AB	T2P3G9	403-234-9202	
Diclaudio & Kramer LLC 50 Abele Rd Ste 1001	Bridgeville	PA	15017	412-220-7722	
Diebold & Assoc Ltd 1340 Remington Rd *Web:* dieboldcpa.com	Schaumburg	IL	60173	847-755-9000	
Dipietro & Thornton 9550 Prototype Ct Ste 101 *Web:* dipietro-thornton.com	Reno	NV	89521	775-825-1040	
Dix Barrett & Stiltner Pc 5670 Greenwood Plz Blvd Ste 505 *Web:* www.dbs-cpas.com	Greenwood Village	CO	80111	303-689-0844	
Dixon Hughes PLLC 6525 Morrison Blvd Ste 500 *Web:* www.dhgllp.com	Charlotte	NC	28211	704-367-7020	367-7760
Doeren Mayhew 305 West Big Beaver Rd Ste 200 *Web:* www.doeren.com	Troy	MI	48084	248-244-3000	244-3090
Doling Chang Ashmore CPA Inc 430 Sherman Ave *Web:* doling.com	Palo Alto	CA	94306	650-321-8744	
Don Farmer CPA Pa 508 Mulberry St PO Box 1858 *Web:* donfarmercpa.com	Lenoir	NC	28645	828-754-1613	
Donald E Graves CPA LLC 377 Main St Ste 400 *Web:* donaldegravescpa.com	Greenfield	MA	01301	413-774-6036	
Donald T Ostop & Company PC 790 Farmington Ave Bldg 2 *Web:* dtoco.com	Farmington	CT	06032	860-677-0779	
Douglas Daw CPA 1101 California Ave Ste 211	Corona	CA	92881	951-582-9023	
Draper & Mcginley Pa 365 W Patrick St first Fl *Web:* drapermcginleypa.com	Frederick	MD	21701	301-694-7411	694-0954
DS & B Ltd 222 S Ninth St *Web:* dsb-cpa.com	Minneapolis	MN	55402	612-359-9630	
Duggan Joiner & Company PA 334 NW Third Ave *Web:* djcocpa.com	Ocala	FL	34475	352-732-0171	
Dworken-Hillman-LaMorte & Sterczala Four Corporate Dr Ste 488 *Web:* dhls.com	Shelton	CT	06484	203-929-3535	
Eadie & Payne LLP 1839 W Redlands Blvd *Web:* eadiepaynellp.com	Redlands	CA	92373	909-793-2406	
Easter & Stoney Ps 206 E First St	Aberdeen	WA	98520	360-533-7272	
Eckhoff Accountancy Corp 145 N Redwood Dr *Web:* www.eckhoff.com	San Rafael	CA	94903	415-499-9400	
ECS Financial Services Inc 3400 Dundee Rd *Web:* ecsfinancial.com	Northbrook	IL	60062	847-291-1333	
Edmond A Swad P C 38701 Seven Mile Rd *Web:* swadco.com	Livonia	MI	48152	734-462-9333	
Edward D Astrin CPA A P C 16633 Ventura Blvd Ste 1450	Encino	CA	91436	818-501-3022	
Ehrhardt Keefe Steiner & Hottman PC 7979 E Tufts Ave Ste 400 *Web:* www.eksh.com	Denver	CO	80237	303-740-9400	740-9009
Eichen & Di Meglio 1 Dupont St *Web:* eanddcpa.com	Plainview	NY	11803	516-576-3333	
Eide Bailly LLP 4310 17th Ave S *Web:* www.eidebailly.com	Fargo	ND	58103	701-239-8500	239-8600
Eisenberg Group AC CPAs, The 2260 Avenida De La Playa	La Jolla	CA	92037	858-551-5500	
Eisner & Maglione CPA'S LLC 66 Commack Rd Ste 201 *Web:* emcpallc.com	Commack	NY	11725	631-499-4039	
Eisner LLP 750 Third Ave *Web:* www.eisneramper.com	New York	NY	10017	212-949-8700	891-4100
Ekmanian Tax & Acctg A Professional Corp 320 James Way Ste 210 *Web:* ekmaniancpa.com	Pismo Beach	CA	93449	805-556-4512	
Elerick & Elerick PA 265 N Wymore Rd *Web:* elerickandelerick.com	Winter Park	FL	32789	407-629-9995	
Elko & Assoc Ltd Two W Baltimore Ave Ste 210 *Web:* www.elkocpa.com	Media	PA	19063	610-565-3930	
Elliott Davis Decosimo LLC 2 Union Sq Tallan Bldg Ste 1100 *TF:* 800-782-8382 ■ *Web:* www.decosimo.com	Chattanooga	TN	37402	423-756-7100	756-2939
Elliott Davis LLC 200 E Broad St PO Box 6286 *TF:* 800-503-4721 ■ *Web:* www.elliottdavis.com	Greenville	SC	29606	864-242-3370	232-7161
Elliott Lewis Leiber & Stumpf Inc Certif 1611 e Fourth st *Web:* www.ellscpas.com	Santa Ana	CA	92701	714-569-1000	
Engelson Assoc 3317 Mormon Coulee Rd *Web:* eacpas.net	La Crosse	WI	54601	608-788-2181	
Ennis Pellum & Assoc Cpas 5150 Belfort Rd S Bldg 600 *Web:* www.jaxcpa.com	Jacksonville	FL	32256	904-396-5965	399-4094
Ernst & Young Five Times Sq **Fax:* Mail Rm ■ *Web:* www.ey.com	New York	NY	10036	212-773-3000	773-6350*
Ernst Swedean & Assoc PC 4125 Gordon Dr *Web:* esacpaonline.com	Sioux City	IA	51106	712-274-6617	
Erwin & Co 6311 Ranch Dr *Web:* erwinco.com	Little Rock	AR	72223	501-868-7486	
Estep-Doctor & Company PC 3737 W Bethel Ave *Web:* edcpa.com	Muncie	IN	47304	765-289-5366	
Fair Anderson & Langeman 3065 S Jones Blvd Ste 100 *Web:* www.falcpa.com	Las Vegas	NV	89146	702-870-7999	
Fairchild Lebel & Rice PC 5123 W St Joseph	Lansing	MI	48917	517-321-5990	
Faske Lay & Co 3508 Far W Blvd 300 *Web:* www.faskelay.com	Austin	TX	78731	512-346-9623	346-8109
Faust & Assoc 200 Third St *Web:* faustcpa.com	Mccomb	MS	39648	601-684-6382	

	City	State	Zip	Phone	Fax
Federal Management Systems Inc 462 K St NW *TF:* 877-637-8277 ■ *Web:* www.fmshq.com	Washington	DC	20001	202-842-3003	829-4470
Feeley & Driscoll PC 200 Portland St *Web:* fdcpa.com	Boston	MA	02114	617-742-7788	
Feeley Bonaventura & Hyzy CPAsPc 5695 Main St *Web:* fbhcpa.com	Williamsville	NY	14221	716-632-0606	
Fenster & Fenster 1514 S D St *Web:* fensterandfenster.com	San Bernardino	CA	92408	909-889-0288	
Ferguson & Redelsperger PC 1026 Main St	Duncan	OK	73533	580-255-2190	
Ferrarabuckworth LLC 60 Pompton Ave	Verona	NJ	07044	973-857-8800	
Ferrell Wealth Management Inc 1400 W Fairbanks Ave *Web:* ferrellwm.com	Winter Park	FL	32789	407-629-7008	
Fiducial 1370 Ave of the Americas 31st Fl *TF:* 866-343-8242 ■ *Web:* www.fiducial.com	New York	NY	10019	212-207-4700	308-2613
Filomeno & Company PC 80 S Main St *Web:* www.filomeno.com	Hartford	CT	06107	860-561-0020	
Finkler & Company CPAs Inc 16600 Sprague Rd 285 *Web:* finklercpa.com	Middleburg Hts	OH	44130	440-826-1550	
Fischer Cunnane & Assoc Ltd 11 Turner Ln *Web:* www.fischercunnane.com	West Chester	PA	19380	610-431-1003	
Fitts Roberts & Co PC 5718 Westheimer Rd Ste 800 *Web:* www.fittsroberts.com	Houston	TX	77057	713-260-5230	
Flackman Goodman & Potter 106 Prospect St *Web:* www.fgpcpa.com	Ridgewood	NJ	07450	201-445-0500	
Fletcher & Assoc PC 424 E Jackson St *Web:* fletchcpa.com	Thomasville	GA	31792	229-226-2241	
Flex Checks Inc PO Box 141215 *TF:* 866-791-7900 ■ *Web:* www.flexchecks.com	Grand Rapids	MI	49514	616-791-7900	
Flynn Walker Diggin CPA PC 50 Seward St *Web:* flynnwalkerdiggin.com	Saratoga Springs	NY	12866	518-583-1234	
Fontana CPAs Pa 2519 N Mcmullen Booth Rd Ste 5 *Web:* fontanacpas.com	Clearwater	FL	33761	727-799-9533	
Fox CPA Group Ltd 204 E Cherry St	Watseka	IL	60970	815-432-3126	
Frank J Larusso CPA PC 550 Mamaroneck Ave- Ste 509	Harrison	NY	10528	914-698-8303	
Frank Rimerman & Company LLP 1801 Page Mill Rd *Web:* www.frankrimerman.com	Palo Alto	CA	94304	650-845-8100	494-1975
Frank Seringer & Chaney Inc 197 N Leavitt Rd *Web:* fsc-cpa.com	Amherst	OH	44001	440-984-2441	
Frankie Friend & Assoc Inc 2305 E Arapahoe Rd Ste 132 *Web:* www.frankiefriend.com	Centennial	CO	80122	303-768-8577	
Franzen & Franzen LLP 125 E De La Guerra St Ste 201 *Web:* franzencpa.com	Santa Barbara	CA	93101	805-563-0821	
Frasier Dean & Howard PLLC 3310 W End Ave Ste 550 *Web:* www.fdhcpa.com	Nashville	TN	37203	615-383-6592	
Freed Maxick & Battaglia CPAs 800 Liberty Bldg *Web:* www.freedmaxick.com	Buffalo	NY	14202	716-847-2651	
Freedman & Goldberg CPA'S PC 31150 Northwestern Hwy Ste 200 *Web:* freedmangoldberg.com	Farmington Hills	MI	48334	248-626-2400	
Freyberg Hinkle Ashland Powers & Stowell Sc CPA 15420 W Capitol Dr *Web:* www.freyberg-hinkle.com	Brookfield	WI	53005	262-784-6210	
Friedberg Smith & Co PC 855 Main St *TF:* 800-772-1213 ■ *Web:* www.fscocpa.com/	Bridgeport	CT	06604	203-366-5876	366-1924
Friedman & Huey Assoc LLP 1313 W 175th St *Web:* www.fhassoc.com	Homewood	IL	60430	708-799-6800	
Friedman LLP 1700 Broadway *TF:* 800-372-1033 ■ *Web:* www.friedmanllp.com	New York	NY	10019	212-842-7000	842-7001
Frohm Kelley Butler & Ryan PC 333 Ft St	Port Huron	MI	48060	810-987-2727	
Frost PLLC 425 W Capitol Ave Ste 3300 *Web:* www.frostpllc.com	Little Rock	AR	72201	501-376-9241	
Frost Ruttenberg & Rothblatt PC 111 S Pfingsten Rd Ste 300 *Web:* frrcpas.com	Deerfield	IL	60015	847-236-1111	
Fulbright & Fulbright 5410 NC 55 Greenwood Commons #AC *Web:* www.moneyful.com	Durham	NC	27713	919-544-0398	
Fuller Landau LLP 1010 De La Gauchetiere St W Pl du Canada Ste 200 *Web:* www.fullerlandau.com	Montreal	QC	H3B2N2	514-875-2865	
Furst & Jinks PA 170 Changebridge Rd *Web:* furstandjinks.com	Montville	NJ	07045	973-575-9191	
Fust Charles Chambers LLP 5786 Widewaters Pkwy *Web:* www.fcc-cpa.com	Syracuse	NY	13214	315-446-3600	446-3899
G. R. RUSH & COMPANY 5720 Skurlock Rd 6500 Bldg Osborne Office Pk *Web:* www.rushcpa.com	Chattanooga	TN	37411	423-899-5162	
Gable- Peritz- Miskin & Co 323 NORRISTOWN Rd *Web:* gpmllp.net	Spring House	PA	19477	215-628-0500	
Gail Rosen CPA PC 2032 Washington Vly Rd *Web:* gailrosencpa.com	Martinsville	NJ	08836	732-469-4202	
Gallagher Flynn & Company LLP 55 Community Dr *Web:* www.gfc.com	South Burlington	VT	05403	802-863-1331	651-7305
Gallina LLP 2870 Gold Tailings Crt 2nd Fl *TF:* 877-638-1188 ■ *Web:* www.gallina.com	Rancho Cordova	CA	95670	916-638-1188	638-1782
Gardenswartz & Dodds PC 600 17th St Ste 1800 N *Web:* gndpc.com	Denver	CO	80202	303-534-6770	
Gary A Halpert CPA 20335 Ventura Blvd Ste 400	Woodland Hills	CA	91364	818-715-9081	
Gary L Schutz PC 900 NW Joy Ave	Portland	OR	97229	503-520-1120	
Gatewood Hughey & Company CPA 2000 W First St Ste 411	Winston-Salem	NC	27104	336-724-4446	
GBQ Partners LLC 230 W St Ste 700 *Web:* www.gbq.com	Columbus	OH	43215	614-221-1120	
Gekakis & Co 901 Mariners Island Blvd Ste 610	San Mateo	CA	94404	650-349-5700	
Gelfand Rennert & Feldman LLP 1880 Century Park E Ste 1600 *Web:* www.grfllp.com	Los Angeles	CA	90067	310-553-1707	
Gentile Pismeny & Brengel LLP 159 Northern Blvd *Web:* www.gpb.net	Great Neck	NY	11021	516-487-4110	
George Bagley & Company LLC 1315 W 22nd St Ste 305 *Web:* bagleycpa.com	Oak Brook	IL	60523	630-990-0355	
Gerbel & Company PC 830 Pleasant St PO Box 44 *Web:* gerbel.com	St Joseph	MI	49085	269-983-0534	
Ghirardo CPA 7200 Redwood Blvd Ste 403 *Web:* www.ghirardocpa.com	Novato	CA	94945	415-897-5678	
Gibbons & Kawash 707 Virginia St Bank One Ctr Ste 500 *Web:* gandkcpas.com	Charleston	WV	25301	304-345-8400	
Gibgot Willenbacher & Co 310 E Shore Rd *Web:* gw-cpa.com	Great Neck	NY	11023	516-482-3660	
Gilbert & Calabrese LLC 181 Rt 206 *Web:* gcllc-cpa.com	Flanders	NJ	07836	973-448-1099	
Gilbert Associates Inc 2880 Gateway Oaks Dr Ste 100 *Web:* www.gilbertcpa.com	Sacramento	CA	95833	916-646-6464	
Gilbert Metzger & Madigan LLP 6029 Park Dr PO Box 677 *Web:* gmmcpa.com	Charleston	IL	61920	217-345-2128	
Gillispie & Ogilbee Pc 4400 N Meridian Ave *Web:* www.gocpas.com	Oklahoma City	OK	73112	405-947-3030	942-0017
Gilmore Jasion & Mahler Ltd 1715 Indianwood Cir Ste 100 *Web:* www.gjmltd.com	Maumee	OH	43537	419-794-2000	
Gitlin & Assoc LLP 55 S Main St	Liberty	NY	12754	845-292-7780	
Gitomer & Berenholz PC 445 Shady Ln *Web:* gbm-cpa.com	Huntingdon Valley	PA	19006	215-379-3500	
Glass & Company CPAs PC 515 Congress Ave Ste 1900 *Web:* glasscpa.com	Austin	TX	78701	512-480-8182	
Glass, Jacobson & Medallion Financial Services LLC 10711 Red Run Blvd Ste 101 *Web:* www.glassjacobson.com	Owings Mills	MD	21117	410-356-1000	
Glenn m Gelman & Assoc Certified Public Accountants 1940 E 17th St *Web:* www.gmgcpa.com	Santa Ana	CA	92705	714-667-2600	
Gold Meltzer Plasky & Wise PA 505 Pleasant Vly Ave *Web:* www.gmpw.com	Moorestown	NJ	08057	856-727-0100	
Goldberg Harder Adelstein & Co 132 Lincoln St	Boston	MA	02111	617-426-3350	
Gompers & Assoc PLLC 117 Edgington Ln *Web:* gomperscpa.com	Wheeling	WV	26003	304-242-9300	
Gordon Stockman & Waugh PC 8726 Industrial Rd *Web:* gswcpa.com	Peoria	IL	61615	309-692-4030	692-4159
Gorfine Schiller & Gardyn PA 10045 Red Run Blvd Ste 250	Owings Mills	MD	21117	410-356-5900	
Gorman & Assoc PC Certifi 1825 Franklin St Ste B *Web:* gaapc.com	Northampton	PA	18067	610-262-1280	
Gottlieb Flekier & Company PA 12721 Metcalf Ave Ste 201 *Web:* gfccpa.com	Overland Park	KS	66213	913-491-6655	
Grant Bennett Accountants 1375 Exposition Blvd Ste 230 *Web:* www.gbacpa.com	Sacramento	CA	95815	916-922-5109	
Grant J Milleret CPA 10777 W Twain Ave	Las Vegas	NV	89135	702-367-0341	
Grant Thornton (CCRLLP) 1400 Computer Dr *Web:* www.grantthornton.com	Westborough	MA	01581	508-926-2200	616-2972
Grant Thornton International Ltd 175 W Jackson Blvd 20th Fl *Web:* www.grantthornton.com	Chicago	IL	60604	312-856-0200	
Grant Thornton LLP 175 W Jackson Blvd 20th Fl *Web:* www.grantthornton.com	Chicago	IL	60604	312-856-0200	602-8099
Grantham Poole CPAs 1062 Highland Colony Pkwy Ste 201 *Web:* www.granthampoole.com	Ridgeland	MS	39157	601-499-2400	
Grassi & Co 488 Madison Ave *Web:* www.grassicpas.com	New York	NY	10022	212-661-6166	
Graves & Company PC 20550 Vernier Rd *Web:* gravescpa.com	Harper Woods	MI	48225	313-886-8892	
Gray Blodgett & Company Pllc 629 24th Ave SW *Web:* cpagray.com	Norman	OK	73069	405-360-5533	
Gray Callison & Company PA 3813 Forrestgate Dr *Web:* graycallison.com	Winston-Salem	NC	27103	336-760-3210	
Gray Hunter Stenn LLP 500 Maine St *Web:* www.gray-hunter-stenn.com	Quincy	IL	62301	217-222-0304	
Greenberg Ettlin & Assoc PA 109 Bridge St *Fax Area Code: 398 ■ *Web:* ge-cpa.com	Elkton	MD	21921	410-398-1961	381-2618*

Firm	City	State	Zip	Phone	Fax
Greenberg Rosenblatt Kull & Bitsoli PC The Day Bldg 306 Main St Ste 400 *Web:* www.grkb.com	Worcester	MA	01615	508-791-0901	
Greenstein Rogoff Olsen & Company LLP 39159 Paseo Padre Pkwy Ste 315 *Web:* www.groco.com	Fremont	CA	94538	510-797-8661	
Gregory & Assoc Pllc 14 E Tabb St *Web:* gregory-cpas.com	Petersburg	VA	23803	804-733-4511	
Gregory, Sharer & Stuart PA 100 Second Ave S Ste 600 *Web:* www.gsscpa.com	Saint Petersburg	FL	33701	727-821-6161	
Grimbleby Coleman CPA's Inc 200 W Roseburg Ave *Web:* www.grimbleby-coleman.com	Modesto	CA	95350	209-527-4220	
Gross Mendelsohn & Assoc pa 36 S Charles St Ste 1800 *Web:* www.gma-cpa.com	Baltimore	MD	21201	410-685-5512	
Grossman & Grossman LLP Four Executive Park Dr	Albany	NY	12203	518-438-3509	
Guess CPA PC 4000 Eagle Point Corporate Dr	Birmingham	AL	35242	205-259-1905	
Gumbiner Savett Inc 1723 Cloverfield Blvd *TF:* 800-989-9798 ■ *Web:* www.gscpa.com	Santa Monica	CA	90404	310-828-9798	
Habenicht Novak & Birckbichler 287 Pittsburgh Rd Ste 1 *Web:* hnbcpa.net	Butler	PA	16002	724-283-8661	
Habif Arogeti & Wynne LLP 5 Concourse Pkwy NE *Web:* www.hawcpa.com	Atlanta	GA	30328	404-892-9651	
Hacker Johnson & Smith PA 500 N Wshore Blvd Ste 1000 *TF:* 800-366-7126 ■ *Web:* www.hackerjohnson.com	Tampa	FL	33609	813-286-2424	
Haddox Reid Burkes & Calhoun PLLC PO Box 22507 *Web:* www.hrbccpa.com	Jackson	MS	39225	601-948-2924	
Hagen Streiff Newton Oshiro PC 15601 Dallas Pkwy Ste 1050 *Web:* www.hsno.com	Addison	TX	75001	972-980-5060	
Hague Sahady & Company PC 126 President Ave Ste 201 *Web:* hague-sahady.com	Fall River	MA	02720	508-675-7889	
Hall Kistler & Company LLP 220 Market Ave S Ste 700 *Web:* www.hallkistler.com	Canton	OH	44702	330-453-7633	
Ham, Langston & Brezina LLP 11550 Fuqua St Ste 475 *Web:* www.hlb-cpa.com	Houston	TX	77034	281-481-1040	
Hanrahan Carey & Company PLC 306 S Troy *Web:* hccplc.com	Royal Oak	MI	48067	248-544-1484	
Hantzmon Wiebel LLP 818 E Jefferson St *Web:* www.hantzmonwiebel.com	Charlottesville	VA	22902	434-296-2156	
Harding Shymanski & Company PSC 21 SE Third St Ste 500 *Web:* www.hsccpa.com	Evansville	IN	47735	812-464-9161	
Harper & Pearson Company PC One Riverway Ste 1000 *Web:* harperpearson.com	Houston	TX	77056	713-622-2310	
Harshad Kothari CPA Inc 14752 Beach Blvd Ste 205	La Mirada	CA	90638	714-523-9802	
Hartman Blitch & Gartside 4929 Atlantic Blvd *Web:* www.hbgcpa.com	Jacksonville	FL	32207	904-396-9802	396-1528
Haskell & White LLP 8001 Irvine Ctr Dr Ste 300 *Web:* www.hwcpa.com	Irvine	CA	92618	949-450-6200	
Hein & Assoc LLP 1999 Broadway Ste 4000 *Web:* www.heincpa.com	Denver	CO	80202	303-298-9600	298-8118
Heinfeld Meech & Company PC 10120 N Oracle Rd *Web:* heinfeldmeech.com	Tucson	AZ	85704	520-742-2611	
Hellam Varon & Company Inc PS 1750 112th Ave Ne *Web:* hellamvaron.com	Bellevue	WA	98004	425-453-9192	
Henry & Peters PC 3310 S Broadway Ste 100 *Web:* www.henrypeters.com	Tyler	TX	75701	903-597-6311	597-0343
Herbein & Company Inc 2763 Century Blvd *Web:* herbein.com	Reading	PA	19610	610-378-1175	
Hesley Hunt & Assoc Ltd 2607 White Bear Ave N *Web:* heshcpa.com	Maplewood	MN	55109	651-770-8505	
Hicko CPA Group PC, The 310 E 90th Dr	Merrillville	IN	46410	219-738-2863	
Hilburn & Lein CPA'S 5520 S Ft Apache *Web:* hilburn-lein.com	Las Vegas	NV	89148	702-597-1945	
Hill Barth & King LLC 7680 Market St *TF:* 800-733-8613 ■ *Web:* www.hbkcpa.com	Youngstown	OH	44512	330-758-8613	758-0357
Hill Larson Walth & Benda Pa 326 N Main St *Web:* hlwb-cpa.com	Austin	MN	55912	507-433-2264	
Hill Schroderus & Company LLP 923 Spring St *Web:* hs-co.com	Petoskey	MI	49770	231-347-4136	
Hillin & Clark PC 364 S Broadview *Web:* hillinandclark.com	Cape Girardeau	MO	63703	573-334-8200	
Hobe & Lucas One Independence Pl 4807 Rockside Rd Ste 510 *Web:* www.hobe.com	Independence	OH	44131	216-524-8900	
Hocking & Reid LLC 5757 S 34th St Ste 100	Lincoln	NE	68516	402-441-0140	
Holly A Carlin CPA 1912 Sidewinder Dr 211A *Web:* carlincpa.com	Park City	UT	84060	435-649-0909	
Holly C Roundtree 5001 Spring Vly Rd Ste 250E *Web:* hcroundtreecpa.com	Dallas	TX	75244	972-404-4434	
Holthouse Carlin & Van Trigt LLP 11444 W Olympic Blvd Ste 300-S *Web:* www.hcvt.com	Los Angeles	CA	90064	310-566-1900	566-1901
Honegger Ringger & Company Inc 1905 N Main St *Web:* www.hrc-cpa.com	Bluffton	IN	46714	260-824-4107	
Honkamp Krueger & Company PC 2345 JFK Rd PO Box 699 *TF:* 888-556-0123 ■ *Web:* www.honkamp.com	Dubuque	IA	52004	563-556-0123	556-8762
Horizon Business Solutions Inc 1589 Brice Rd *Web:* horizonbiz.com	Reynoldsburg	OH	43068	614-577-1700	
Horne LLP 26 Security Dr **Fax Area Code:* 601 ■ *Web:* www.horne-llp.com	Jackson	TN	38305	731-668-7070	355-6521*
House Park & Dobratz Pc 605 W 47th St Ste 301 *Web:* www.hpdco.com	Kansas City	MO	64112	816-931-3393	931-9636
Howard Cunningham Houchin & Turner LLP 6901 Quaker Ave Ste 100 *Web:* hchtcpa.com	Lubbock	TX	79413	806-799-6699	
Howson & Simon LLP 101 Ygnacio Vly Rd Ste 310	Walnut Creek	CA	94596	925-977-9060	
Hoyman Dobson & Company PA 215 Baytree Dr *Web:* www.hoyman.com	Melbourne	FL	32940	321-255-0088	
HR&P Solutions Inc 14550 Torrey Chase Ste 100 *Web:* www.hrp.net	Houston	TX	77014	281-880-6525	
Huckstep & Assoc LLC 3734 S Ave Ste E *TF:* 800-269-6466 ■ *Web:* www.huckstep.com	Springfield	MO	65807	417-889-8991	
Huggins & Company CPA Pa 6148-D Brookshire Blvd	Charlotte	NC	28216	704-394-2364	
Hulsey Harwood & Sheridan LLC 1900 Roselawn Ave. *Web:* hhcpa.net	Monroe	LA	71201	318-325-6500	
Hulslander SUSAn d CPA PC 24 First Ave E Ste D	Kalispell	MT	59901	406-755-3092	
Hunter Hunter & Hunt Cpa's 1315 Fourth St Ste A *Web:* www.hhh-cpa.com	Eureka	CA	95501	707-476-0674	
Hutchinson & Bloodgood LLP 579 Auto Ctr Dr *Web:* www.hbllp.com	Watsonville	CA	95076	818-637-5000	
Infonaut Inc 255 Consumers Rd Ste 500 *Web:* www.infonaut.ca	Toronto	ON	M2J1R4	416-607-6260	
Iprocess Online Inc 1050 Hull St Ste 100 *Web:* www.iprocessonline.com	Baltimore	MD	21230	410-547-3270	
J a Smith & Associates Inc 2147 Bowen Rd *Web:* www.jasmith.com	Nanaimo	BC	V9S1H8	250-751-3383	
J Hall & Associates Inc: Hall Johnathan W CPA 327 S Market St	Troy	OH	45373	937-339-8417	
James B Mcevoy CPA 280 N Bedford Rd *Web:* jmcevoycpa.com	Mt Kisco	NY	10549	914-241-0460	
James E Raftery CPA PC 606 N Stapley Dr	Mesa	AZ	85203	480-835-1040	
James R Swab 1707 Myrtle Rd	Silver Spring	MD	20902	301-681-7935	
Jankins & Jablonski SC 15400 W Capitol Dr	Brookfield	WI	53005	262-781-2121	
Jannsen & Company SC W239 N3490 Pewaukee Rd *Web:* jannsen.com	Pewaukee	WI	53072	262-513-9292	
Jefferson Urian Doane & Sterner Inc 651 N Bedford St Extn P.O. Box 830 *Web:* juds.com	Georgetown	DE	19947	302-856-3900	
Jeffrey D Stewart & Company CPA'S 6663 Western Row Rd	Mason	OH	45040	513-573-9600	
Jennifer A Jones CPA Ltd 10615 Judicial Dr Ste 701 *Web:* jajonescpa.com	Fairfax	VA	22030	703-352-1587	
JH Cohn LLP Four Becker Farm Rd *TF:* 877-704-3500 ■ *Web:* www.cohnreznick.com	Roseland	NJ	07068	973-228-3500	228-0330
Jobe Hastings & Assoc CPA's 745 S Church St Ste 105 *Web:* jobehastings.com	Murfreesboro	TN	37133	615-893-7777	
John A Culhane CPA 755 Main St Bldg Ste 1 *Web:* culhanecpa.com	Monroe	CT	06468	203-268-4431	
John Gerlach & Co LLP 37 W Broad St Ste 530 *Web:* www.johngerlach.com	Columbus	OH	43215	614-224-2164	224-1391
John Waddell & Company CPAs 3416 American River Dr Ste A *Web:* jwaddell.com	Sacramento	CA	95864	916-488-2460	
Johnson & Mackowiak 70 E Main St *Web:* jma-cpas.com/	Fredonia	NY	14063	716-672-4770	679-1512
Johnson & Shute PS 11130 NE 33rd Pl *Web:* johnsonandshute.com	Bellevue	WA	98004	425-827-5755	
Johnson Lambert & Company LLP 700 Spring Forest Rd *Web:* www.johnsonlambert.com	Raleigh	NC	27609	919-719-6400	
Jones & Kolb Ten Piedmont Ctr Ste 100 *Web:* www.joneskolb.com	Atlanta	GA	30305	404-262-7920	
Jones Accounting 13100 Brooks Dr Ste 111 *Web:* jonesaccountingservice.com	Baldwin Park	CA	91706	626-856-5501	
Jones CPA Group 749 Boush St *Web:* stricklandandjones.com	Norfolk	VA	23510	757-627-7672	
Jones Ham & Cluff P C 14475 SW Allen Blvd Ste A *Web:* itjcpa.com	Beaverton	OR	97005	503-643-6333	
Jones Henle & Schunck 135 Town & Country Dr *Web:* www.jhs.com	Danville	CA	94526	925-820-1821	
Jones Kohanski & Company LLP Six Brookhill Sq S *Web:* jk-cpa.com	Sugarloaf	PA	18249	570-788-7000	
Joseph Crnkovich Jr CPA 1053 Mclaughlin Run Rd	Bridgeville	PA	15017	412-257-0844	
Joyce Swanson CPA 6715 Grover St	Omaha	NE	68106	402-390-2722	
JPMS Cox PLLC 11300 Cantrell Rd Ste 301 *Web:* www.jpmscox.com	Little Rock	AR	72212	501-227-5800	227-5851
JST Enterprises 5120 Summerhill Rd *Web:* www.jstent.com	Texarkana	TX	75503	903-794-3743	

				Phone	Fax
Julian J Rodriguez PA 95 Merrick Way	Coral Gables	FL	33134	305-445-0777	
Web: jjrpa.net					
Junkermier Clark Campanella Stevens PC					
501 Park Dr S Po Box 989	Great Falls	MT	59403	406-761-2820	
Web: www.jccscpa.com					
Kahn Litwin Renza & Company Ltd					
951 N Main St	Providence	RI	02904	401-274-2001	
TF: 888-557-8557 ■ *Web:* www.kahnlitwin.com					
Kalfsbeek & Company Accountancy Corp					
4529 Quail Lakes Dr Ste C	Stockton	CA	95207	209-235-1040	
Kallman & Company LLP					
125 S Barrington Pl	Los Angeles	CA	90049	310-909-1900	
Web: www.kallmanandco.com					
Kalmanowitz & Lee CPAs Pllc					
575 Eighth Ave Ste 1706	New York	NY	10018	212-687-2628	
Katz Abosch Windesheim Gershman & Freedman PA					
9690 Deereco Rd Ste 500	Lutherville Timonium	MD	21093	410-828-2727	
Web: www.katzabosch.com					
Katz Sapper & Miller					
800 E 96th St Ste 500	Indianapolis	IN	46240	317-580-2000	580-2117
Web: www.ksmcpa.com					
Kauffmann & Assoc Pllc					
4350 Brownsboro Rd Ste 170	Louisville	KY	40207	502-893-8067	
Web: kaacpas.com					
Kaufman & Kabani					
800 S Figueroa St Ste 900	Los Angeles	CA	90017	213-488-6180	
Web: kkcpa.com					
Kaufman Rossin & Co PA 2699 S Bayshore Dr	Miami	FL	33133	305-858-5600	856-3284
TF: 866-357-9634 ■ *Web:* www.kaufmanrossin.com					
Keefe McCullough & Co LLP Certified Public Accountants					
6550 N Federal Hwy Ste 410	Fort Lauderdale	FL	33308	954-771-0896	938-9353
Web: www.kmccpa.com					
Keith A Shibou CPA Accountancy Corp					
1900 E Tahquitz Canyon Way	Palm Springs	CA	92262	760-325-1214	
Kellogg & Andelson					
14724 Ventura Blvd Second Fl	Sherman Oaks	CA	91403	818-971-5100	
Web: www.k-a.com					
Kelly Dunn & Nestor 921 Bergen Ave	Jersey City	NJ	07306	201-795-1122	
Kenefick & Company CPA'S PA 2809 Cavan Ct	Charlotte	NC	28270	704-544-6757	
Web: kenefickandco.com					
Kennedy & Coe LLC 3030 Cortland Cir	Salina	KS	67401	785-825-1561	825-5371
Web: www.kcoe.com					
Kenneth Delarbre & Company PA					
1618 S Highland Ave	Clearwater	FL	33756	727-585-4708	
Kernutt Stokes LLP 1600 Executive Pkwy	Eugene	OR	97401	541-687-1170	
Web: kernuttstokes.com					
Kesner, Godes & Morrissey LLC					
15 Pacella Park Dr Ste 200	Randolph	MA	02368	781-961-2900	
Web: www.kesnermorrissey.com					
Kessler Orlean Silver & Company PC					
1101 Lk Cook Rd Ste C	Deerfield	IL	60015	847-580-4100	
Web: koscpa.com					
Kevin J Goering CPA Pa 2201 W 25th St	Lawrence	KS	66047	785-832-8300	
Web: goeringcpa.com					
Keystone Payroll					
355 Colonnade Blvd Ste C	State College	PA	16803	814-234-2272	
Web: www.keystonepayroll.com					
KFMR Katz Ferraro McMurtry PC					
300 Benedum-Trees Bldg 223 Fourth Ave	Pittsburgh	PA	15222	412-471-0200	
Web: www.kfmr.com					
Kieckhafer Dietzler & Hauser LLP					
627 Elm St	West Bend	WI	53095	262-334-2341	
Web: kdhcpa.com					
Kimball & O'Brien PC 465 Washington Ave	Kingston	NY	12401	845-331-5030	
Web: kimballobrien.com					
Kingery & Crouse PA 2801 W Busch Blvd Ste 200	Tampa	FL	33618	813-874-1280	
Web: www.tampacpa.com					
Kirkpatrick Phillips & Miller					
1445 E Republic Rd	Springfield	MO	65804	417-882-4300	882-4343
Web: www.kpmcpa.com					
Kiwi Partners Inc 30 Soundview Ln	Port Washington	NY	11050	516-767-6678	
Web: www.kiwipartners.com					
Klatzkin & Company Jr CPA's					
1670 Whitehorse Hamilton Sq Rd Ste 7	Trenton	NJ	08690	609-890-9189	
Web: www.klatzkin.com					
Klein, Hall & Associates LLC					
3973 75th St Ste 102	Aurora	IL	60504	630-898-5578	
Web: kleinhallcpa.com					
Klingher Nadler LLP					
580 Sylvan Ave Ste Ma	Englewood Cliffs	NJ	07632	201-731-3025	
Web: klinghernadler.com					
Knutte & Assoc PC 7900 S Cass Ave	Darien	IL	60561	630-960-3317	
Web: www.knutte.com					
Koch Group & Company LLP					
333 Seventh Ave Rm 8	New York	NY	10001	212-631-0700	
Web: www.kgcpas.com					
Koller & Company LLP 206 S Iowa Ave	Washington	IA	52353	319-653-6561	
Web: kollerandcompany.com					
Komisar Brady & Company LLP					
135 S 84th St Ste 200	Milwaukee	WI	53214	414-271-3966	
Web: www.komisarbrady.com					
Kositzka Wicks & Co					
5500 Cherokee Ave Ste 400	Alexandria	VA	22312	703-642-2700	
Web: www.kwccpa.com					
Kovash & Dasovick PC 148 W First St	Dickinson	ND	58601	701-483-1156	
KPMG LLP US Three Chestnut Ridge Rd	Montvale	NJ	07645	201-307-7000	307-7575
Web: www.kpmg.com					
KraftCPAs Pllc 555 Great Cir Rd	Nashville	TN	37228	615-242-7351	
Web: kraftcpas.com					
Kramer Accountancy Corp					
120 N Topanga Canyon Blvd Ste 111	Topanga	CA	90290	310-455-9300	
Web: kramercpa.com					
Kramer Fiduciary Services					
1500 Ardmore Blvd Ste 205	Pittsburgh	PA	15221	412-351-2150	
Web: kramerfiduciary.com					
Kruggel Lawton & Company LLC					
210 S Michigan St Ste 200	South Bend	IN	46601	574-289-4011	
Web: klcpas.com					
Kuhn & Company CPAs 1730 Park St	Naperville	IL	60563	630-416-7700	
Web: kuhnandcompany.com					
Kurtz & Hornak PA 354 N Ave E	Cranford	NJ	07016	908-276-3380	
Kutchins, Robbins, & Diamond Ltd					
1101 Perimter Dr Ste 760	Schaumburg	IL	60173	847-240-1040	
Web: krdcpas.com					
L f L Veritas LLC 1086 Teaneck Rd Ste 2C	Teaneck	NJ	07666	201-833-2266	
Web: www.lflveritas.com					
Labenz & Assoc LLC 4535 Normal Blvd Ste 195	Lincoln	NE	68506	402-437-8383	
Web: labenz.com					
Lanaux & Felger CPAs Apc 5779 Hwy 311	Houma	LA	70360	985-851-0883	
Lance Soll & Lunghard LLP					
203 N Brea Blvd Ste 203	Brea	CA	92821	714-672-0022	
Web: www.lslcpas.com					
Lane Gorman Trubitt LLP 2626 Howell St Ste 700	Dallas	TX	75204	214-871-7500	871-0011
Web: www.lgt-cpa.com					
Langdon & Company LLP 223 Us 70 Hwy E Ste 100	Garner	NC	27529	919-662-1001	
Web: www.langdoncpa.com					
Lanigan, Ryan, Malcolm & Doyle PC					
555 Quince Orchard Rd Ste 600	Gaithersburg	MD	20878	301-258-8900	
Web: lrmd-cpa.com					
Lanni Restifo LLC 21-00 Rt 208 S	Fair Lawn	NJ	07410	201-797-1600	
Web: lannirestifo.com					
Lapp, Fatch, Myers & Gallagher Accountants, A Professional Corp					
2401 Professional Pkwy	Santa Maria	CA	93455	805-934-0015	
Web: lfmgcpas.com					
Larry Associates Inc					
6136 170th St Ste M1	Fresh Meadows	NY	11365	718-321-0384	
Web: www.tspl.com					
LarsonAllen LLP 220 S Sixth St Ste 300	Minneapolis	MN	55402	612-376-4500	376-4850
TF: 888-529-2648 ■ *Web:* www.larsonallen.com					
Latta Harris Hanon & Penningroth LLP					
2730 Naples Ave SW Ste 101	Iowa City	IA	52240	319-358-0520	
Web: lattaharris.com					
Lattimore Black Morgan & Cain PC					
5250 Virginia Way	Brentwood	TN	37027	615-377-4600	309-2500
Web: www.lbmc.com					
Lavine Lofgren Morris & Engelberg CPAs					
4180 La Jolla Village Dr Ste 300	La Jolla	CA	92037	858-455-0898	
Web: www.llme.com					
Lazer Grant Inc 309 Mcdermot Ave	Winnipeg	MB	R3A1T3	204-942-0300	957-5611
TF: 800-220-0005 ■ *Web:* www.lazergrant.ca					
Leaf, Saltzman, Manganelli, Pfeil & Tendler PC					
310 Passaic Ave Ste 301	Fairfield	NJ	07004	973-808-9500	
Web: www.njcpafirm.com					
Leffler Accountancy Corp					
16030 Ventura Blvd Ste 490	Encino	CA	91436	818-501-1181	
Lefkowitz Garfinkel Champi & DeRienzo PC					
10 Weybosset St	Providence	RI	02903	401-421-4800	
TF: 800-927-5423 ■ *Web:* www.lgcd.com					
Lenning & Company Inc					
13924 Seal Beach Blvd Ste C	Seal Beach	CA	90740	562-594-9729	
Web: lenning.com					
Leone Mcdonnell & Roberts pa Cpa					
Five Nelson St	Dover	NH	03820	603-749-2700	
Web: www.lmrpa.com					
Lerch Vinci & Higgins 17-17 State Rt 208	Fair Lawn	NJ	07410	201-791-7100	
Web: www.lvhcpa.com					
Lester Halpern & Company PC 14 Bobala Rd	Holyoke	MA	01040	413-536-3970	
Web: halperncpa.com					
Levin, Swedler & Company Inc					
3501 Embassy Pkwy Ste 200	Akron	OH	44333	330-666-4199	
Web: www.levinswedler.com					
Lewellen Accountancy Corp					
23521 Paseo De Valencia 205	Laguna Hills	CA	92653	949-859-4644	
Lewis & Company PC					
3804 Poplar Hill Rd Ste B	Chesapeake	VA	23321	757-638-4566	
Lewis & Knopf CPAs PC					
5206 Gateway Centre Ste 100	Flint	MI	48507	810-238-4617	
Web: www.lewis-knopf.com					
LH Frishkoff & Co 529 Fifth Ave Ste 901	New York	NY	10017	212-808-0070	
Web: www.lhfrishkoff.com					
Libero & Kappel CPAs 57 Old Country Rd	Westbury	NY	11590	516-333-5511	
Limsky Kypriotis & Co 220 Ridgedale Ave	Florham Park	NJ	07932	973-822-3400	
Lindquist Von Husen & Joyce LLP					
90 New Montgomery St 11th Fl	San Francisco	CA	94105	415-957-9999	
Web: lvhj.com					
Lindstrom Sorenson & Assoc LLP					
3815 N Mulford Rd	Rockford	IL	61114	815-282-1288	
Web: lsallp.com					
Linger Peterson Shrum & Co					
575 E Locust Ave Ste 308	Fresno	CA	93720	559-438-8740	
Link Murrel & Co 18831 Bardeen Ave Ste 200	Irvine	CA	92612	949-261-1120	
Web: www.link-murrel.com					
Lipsey Youngren Means Ogren & Sandberg LLP					
525 B St Ste 1400	San Diego	CA	92101	619-234-0877	234-9319
Web: www.lymscpa.com					
LMGW Certified Public Accountants LLP					
20520 Prospect Rd Ste 200	Saratoga	CA	95070	408-252-1800	
Web: www.wheelerco.com					
Lmo Reps LLC 21 Roulston Rd	Windham	NH	03087	603-893-4178	
Web: lmoreps.com					
Lodgen, Lacher, Golditch, Sardi, Saunders, & Howard LLP					
16530 Ventura Blvd Ste 305	Encino	CA	91436	818-783-0570	
Web: www.lgshcpa.com					
Loeb & Loeb LLP 345 Park Ave 12th Fl	New York	NY	10017	212-867-4000	407-4990
Web: www.loeb.com					

Phone | Fax

Logan Simpson Design Inc 51 W Third St Ste 450 ... Tempe AZ 85281 480-967-1343
Web: www.logansimpson.com

Long Chilton LLP 3125 Central Blvd. ... Brownsville TX 78520 956-546-1655 546-0377
Web: www.longchilton.com

Loomis & Company CPA's LLP
267 E Campbell Ave Ste 200 ... Campbell CA 95008 408-385-3400
Web: www.loomiscpas.com

Lopata Flegel & Company LLP
600 Mason Ridge Ctr Dr Ste 100 ... Saint Louis MO 63141 314-514-8881
Web: www.lopataflegel.com

Lott (TE) & Co 221 N Seventh St PO Box 471 ... Columbus MS 39701 662-328-5387
Web: www.telott.com

Louis Plung & Company LLP
444 Liberty Ave Ste 900 ... Pittsburgh PA 15222 412-281-8771
Web: www.louisplung.com

Love Scherle & Bauer PC
310 Grant St Ste 1020 ... Pittsburgh PA 15219 412-281-8270
Web: lovescherlebauer.com

Lucas Horsfall Murphy & Pindroh LLP
100 E Corson St Ste 200 ... Pasadena CA 91103 626-744-5100
Web: www.lhmp.com

Lurie Besikof Lapidus & Co LLP
2501 Wayzata Blvd ... Minneapolis MN 55405 612-377-4404 377-1325
TF: 877-322-8228 ■ *Web:* www.lblco.com

Lutz & Carr 300 E 42nd St. ... New York NY 10017 212-697-2299
Web: www.lutzandcarr.com

Lynn a Sylvester CPA PA 675 S Haywood St ... Waynesville NC 28786 828-456-6505
Web: www.lascpa-nc.com

M & K CPAs PLLC 4100 Nsam Houston Pkwy. ... Houston TX 77086 832-242-9950
Web: mkacpas.com

Maglin Miskiv & Assoc CPA'S PA
299 Cherry Hill Rd Ste 100. ... Parsippany NJ 07054 973-263-3300

Mahoney Ulbrich Christiansen & Russ P A
30 E Plato Blvd ... Saint Paul MN 55107 651-227-6695
Web: www.mucr.com

Mallah Furman & Co
Brickell Bay Office Tower 1001 Brickell Bay Dr
Ste 1400 ... Miami FL 33131 305-371-6200
Web: www.mallahfurman.com

Maloney & Kennedy Pllc 15 Dartmouth Dr Ste 203 ... Auburn NH 03032 603-624-8819
Web: maloneyandkennedy.com

Mann Urrutia Nelson CPA's & Assoc LLP
2901 Douglas Blvd Ste 290 ... Roseville CA 95661 916-774-4208 774-4230
Web: www.muncpas.com

Manning Elliott LLP
1050 W Pender St 11th Fl. ... Vancouver BC V6E3S7 604-714-3600
Web: www.manningelliott.com

Mantyla Mcreynolds LLC
178 S Rio Grande St Ste 200 ... Salt Lake City UT 84101 801-269-1818
Web: www.mmacpa.com

Manzi, Pino & Company PC
1895 Walt Whitman Rd - Ste 5 ... Melville NY 11747 631-420-5620
Web: manzipinocpa.com

Marc B Freedman CPA PC 215 W 95th St Ste 2R. ... New York NY 10025 212-678-2418
Web: mbfcpa.com

Marcheschi Plankis & Pogore
9951 W 190th St Ste A ... Mokena IL 60448 708-479-7333
Web: mppcpa.com

Marcus Errico Emmer & Brooks PC
45 Braintree Hill Pk Ste 107 ... Braintree MA 02184 781-843-5000
Web: www.meeb.com

Margolin Winer & Evens LLP
400 Garden City Plz Fifth Fl ... Garden City NY 11530 516-747-2000 747-6707
Web: www.mwellp.com

Margolis Phipps & Wright PC
1400 Post Oak Blvd Ste 900 ... Houston TX 77056 713-625-3500
Web: mcgladrey.com

Mark Bailey & Co Ltd 1495 Ridgeview Dr Ste 200 ... Reno NV 89519 775-332-4200
Web: www.markbaileyco.com

Marks Paneth & Shron LLP
622 Third Ave 7th Fl ... New York NY 10017 212-503-8800 503-8800
Web: www.markspaneth.com

Martin & Martin CPA'S Ltd
900 N Arlington Heights Rd Ste 360 ... Itasca IL 60143 847-250-5074
Web: mmcpasltd.com

Martin & Orr LLC 127 Peachtree St Ste 500 ... Atlanta GA 30303 404-525-3007
Web: martin-orr.com

Maruji & Raines PS 775 S Main St Ste A ... Colville WA 99114 509-684-5289
Web: www.mrcpas.com

Marvin & Company PC 11 British American Blvd ... Latham NY 12110 518-785-0134
Web: marvincpa.com

Massachusetts Society of Certified Public Accountants
105 Chauncy St 10th Fl ... Boston MA 02111 617-556-4000
Web: www.mscpaonline.org

Mather & Company CPAs LLC
9100 Shelbyville Rd ... Louisville KY 40222 502-429-0800
Web: matherandcompany.com

Matthews Carter & Boyce PC
11320 Random Hills Rd Ste 600. ... Fairfax VA 22030 703-218-3600
Web: www.mcb-cpa.com

Mauldin & Jenkins Certified Public Accountants LLC
200 Galleria Pkwy SE ... Atlanta GA 30339 770-955-8600 446-3664*
**Fax Area Code: 229* ■ *TF:* 800-277-0080 ■ *Web:* www.mjcpa.com

Maxson & Assoc Accountancy Corp
6700 E Pacific Coast Hwy ... Long Beach CA 90803 562-594-4681
Web: maxson-accounting.com

May & Co 110 Monument Pl ... Vicksburg MS 39180 601-636-4762
Web: www.maycpa.com

May Cocagne & King Pc 316 S Charter St ... Monticello IL 61856 217-762-7717
Web: www.mckcpa.com

Mayer, Shanzer, & Mayer PC 918 Maple St ... Conshohocken PA 19428 610-828-0200
Web: www.msmpc.com

Phone | Fax

McConnell Jones Lanier & Murphy LLP
The Lakes On Post Oak 3040 Post Oak Blvd
Ste 1600 ... Houston TX 77056 713-968-1600
TF: 866-908-4650 ■ *Web:* www.mcconnelljones.com

Mccormack Guyette & Assoc PC 66 Grove St ... Rutland VT 05701 802-775-3221
Web: cpa-vermont.com

Mcelrath Geyer Sandler & Fisher
1500 Quail St Ste 450 ... Newport Beach CA 92660 949-252-0252

McGowen Hurst Clark & Smith PC
1601 W Lakes Pkwy Ste 300 ... West Des Moines IA 50266 515-288-3279
Web: www.mhcscpa.com

Mcgreal & Company PC 5740 W 95th St ... Oak Lawn IL 60453 708-422-8600
Web: mcgreal.com

McGregor & Company LLP 1190 Blvd Ne ... Orangeburg SC 29115 803-536-1015
Web: mcgregorcpa.com

Mcguire Peck & Co 630 Silver St ... Agawam MA 01001 413-789-2551

Mckenna & Assoc PC 1515 S Washington St ... Grand Forks ND 58201 701-772-4819
Web: mckennaandassociates.net

McKonly & Asbury LLP 415 Fallowfield Rd ... Camp Hill PA 17011 717-761-7910 761-7944
Web: www.macpas.com

McNair McLemore Middlebrooks & Company LLP
389 Mulberry St ... Macon GA 31202 478-746-6277
Web: www.mmmcpa.com

Mcruer & & Associates Cpas
1251 Nw Briarcliff Pkwy Ste 100 ... Kansas City MO 64116 816-741-7882
Web: kccpa.com

Mcswain & Co PS 612 Woodland Sq Loop SE Ste 300 ... Lacey WA 98503 360-357-9304
Web: mcswaincpa.net

McSweeney & Assoc A Professional Corp
350 Crown Point Cir Ste 200 ... Grass Valley CA 95945 530-272-5555
Web: mcsweeneyandassociates.com

Medical Billing Concepts Inc
16001 Ventura Blvd Ste 135 ... Encino CA 91436 818-817-9832
Web: www.medbillconcepts.com

Medical Billing Unlimited Inc
5959 Gateway Blvd W Ste 120 ... El Paso TX 79925 915-779-1716
Web: mbuinc.com

Medical Management Specialists
4100 Embassy Dr SE Ste 200 ... Grand Rapids MI 49546 616-975-1845
Web: www.mms.med.pro

Medwig & Co 401 Wood St ... Pittsbugh PA 15222 412-562-9061

Melanson Heath & Company PC 102 Perimeter Rd ... Nashua NH 03063 603-882-1111
Web: melansonheath.com

Mellon Johnson & Reardon Certified Public Accountants LLP
3270 Inland Empire Blvd Ste 300 ... Ontario CA 91764 909-985-7286
Web: mjrcpas.com

Messina & Company LLC 1615 Pontiac Ave ... Cranston RI 02920 401-463-6800

Metro Metro & Assoc 3311 Olney Sandy Spring Rd. ... Olney MD 20832 301-929-9700
Web: metrometro.com

Michael Bossy Group 251 James St ... Delhi ON N4B2B2 519-582-1260
Web: www.bnggroup.ca

Michael J Liccar & Co 231 s la salle st ... Chicago IL 60604 708-672-6380
Web: www.liccar.com

Michael R Rubenstein & Assoc
12527 New Brittany Blvd ... Fort Myers FL 33907 239-489-4443
Web: mrubensteincpa.com

Michael S Kaslik PC 1123 Vesper Rd ... Ann Arbor MI 48103 734-995-4455

Michalik & Daniels LLC 934 Western Ave ... Pittsburgh PA 15233 412-322-2662

Mickey Casanova & Sack 1735 - 28th St ... Bakersfield CA 93301 661-325-9451

Millard, Rouse & Rosebrugh LLP
96 Nelson St ... Brantford ON N3T5N3 519-863-3557
Web: www.millards.com

Miller & Company Plc
900 S Shackleford Rd Ste 605 ... Little Rock AR 72211 501-221-3343
Web: millercocpas.net

Miller & Miller Accountancy Corp
1320 E Shaw Ave Ste 167 ... Fresno CA 93710 559-225-6211
Web: millermillerpc.com

Miller Cooper & Company Ltd
1751 Lk Cook Rd Ste 400 ... Deerfield IL 60015 847-205-5000
Web: www.millercooper.com

Miller Giangrande LLP 915 W Imperial Hwy ... Brea CA 92821 714-494-2200
Web: mngcpa.com

Miller Kaplan Arase & Company LLP
4123 Lankershim Blvd ... Hollywood CA 91602 818-769-2010
Web: www.millerkaplan.com

Milluzzo & Company PC 182 Kelsey St ... Newington CT 06111 860-667-9991

MNP LLP 715 Fifth Ave SW Seventh Fl ... Calgary AB T2P2X6 403-444-0150
Web: www.mnp.ca

Mondorf & Fenwick Pllc 523 Columbia Dr ... Johnson City NY 13790 607-797-4339
Web: mfcpas.com

Monroe Shine & Company Inc
222 E Market St ... New Albany IN 47150 812-945-2311
Web: www.monroeshine.com

Mooney & Thomas PC 2111 Plum St Ste 150 ... Aurora IL 60506 630-844-5272
Web: mooneythomas.com

Moore & Company PA
560 Riverside Dr Ste A-102 ... Salisbury MD 21801 410-749-3211
Web: moore-company.com

Moore & Neidenthal Inc 3034 N Wooster Ave ... Dover OH 44622 330-364-7774
Web: mnpinnacle.com

Moore Reichl & Baker P C
11200 Wheimer Ste 410 ... Houston TX 77042 281-558-9800
Web: mrbcpas.com

Moore Stephens Lovelace PA
1201 S Orlando Ave Ste 400 ... Winter Park FL 32789 407-740-5400 740-0012
TF: 800-683-5401 ■ *Web:* www.mslcpa.com

Morrison Brown Argiz & Farra LLP
1001 Brickell Bay Dr Ninth Fl ... Miami FL 33131 305-373-5500 373-0056
TF: 800-239-3843 ■ *Web:* www.mbafcpa.com

Morton Leben 270 N Ave ... New Rochelle NY 10801 914-636-1800

Moss Adams LLP 999 Third Ave Ste 2800 ... Seattle WA 98104 206-302-6500 622-9975
Web: www.mossadams.com

Name / Address	City	State	Zip	Phone	Fax
Mowat Mackie & Anderson LLP 1999 Harrison St Ste 1500 *Web:* www.mowat.com	Oakland	CA	94612	510-893-1120	
Mrasek & Assoc PC 6193 Miller Rd Ste A	Swartz Creek	MI	48473	810-635-2409	
Muckel Anderson CPAs 300 E Second St *Web:* muckelanderson.com	Reno	NV	89501	775-686-3200	
Nagy & Croniser CPA'S LLP 5564 Woodlawn Ave	Lowville	NY	13367	315-376-6518	
Nearman Maynard Vallez CPAs & Consultants pa 205 Brandywine Blvd Ste 200 *Web:* nearman.com	Fayetteville	GA	30214	770-461-5706	
Nethaway & Clausen PC 6000 W St Joseph Ste 101 *Web:* nethawayclausen.com	Lansing	MI	48917	517-321-0019	
Nichols Accounting Group PC, The 230 N Oregon St *Web:* www.nicholsaccounting.com	Ontario	OR	97914	541-881-1433	
Nicholson & Company PA Two Southern Pointe Pkwy Ste 100 *Web:* www.nicholsoncpas.com	Hattiesburg	MS	39402	601-264-3519	
Nietzke & Faupel PC 7274 Hartley St *Web:* nfcpa.com	Pigeon	MI	48755	989-453-3122	
Nightlinger Colavita & Volpa Pa 991 S Black Horse Pk *Web:* colavita.net	Williamstown	NJ	08094	856-629-3111	
Nimensky Gallinson & Buren PA CPAs 316 Eisenhower Pkwy *Web:* ngbcpa.com	Livingston	NJ	07039	973-533-9200	
Nisivoccia & Company LLP 200 Valley Rd Ste 300 *Web:* www.nisivoccia.com	Mt Arlington	NJ	07856	973-328-1825	
Nolan O Luke CPA Pa 830 N Main	Wichita	KS	67203	316-265-0599	
Norman Jones Enlow & Co 226 N Fifth St Ste 500 *Web:* www.nje.com	Columbus	OH	43215	614-228-4000	
Norman W Marcoux CPA Inc 350 University Ave Ste 107 *Web:* marcouxcpa.com	Sacramento	CA	95825	916-927-7772	
Novogradac & Company LLP 246 First St Fifth Fl *Web:* www.novoco.com	San Francisco	CA	94105	415-356-8000	356-8001
Nperspective LLC 5971 Brick Ct Ste 100-B *Web:* www.nperspective.net	Winter Park	FL	32792	407-679-7600	
NSF-GFTC 88 McGilvray St *Web:* www.gftc.ca	Guelph	ON	N1G2W1	519-821-1246	
O'Connor & Drew PC 25 Braintree Hill Office Park Suit *Web:* ocd.com	Braintree	MA	02184	617-471-1120	
O'Connor Davies Munns & Dobbins LLP 665 Fifth Ave *TF:* 800-397-0249 ■ *Web:* www.odpkf.com	New York	NY	10022	212-286-2600	286-4080
Olsen & Thompson Pa 970 Mt Kemble Ave *Web:* otcpa.com	Morristown	NJ	07960	973-425-3212	
Oprs 1615 Ellis St	Kewaunee	WI	54216	920-388-2788	
Opus 21 Management Solutions 3140 Neil Armstrong Blvd *Web:* www.opus21ms.com	Eagan	MN	55121	651-905-0400	
Ostrow Reisin Berk & Abrams Ltd 455 N Cityfront Plz Dr *Web:* www.orba.com	Chicago	IL	60611	312-670-7444	670-8301
Packer Thomas 6601 Westford Pl Ste 101 *Web:* www.packerthomas.com	Canfield	OH	44406	330-533-9777	
Padgett Business Services 160 Hawthorne Pk **Fax Area Code:* 706 ■ *TF:* 800-723-4388 ■ *Web:* www.padgettbusinessservices.com	Athens	GA	30606	800-723-4388	543-8537*
Paduano Di Tommaso & Golda 220 Monmouth Rd *Web:* www.pdgcpa.com	Oakhurst	NJ	07755	732-531-4100	
Pannell Kerr Forster Of Texas Pc 5847 San Felipe St *TF:* 800-829-3676 ■ *Web:* www.pkftexas.com	Houston	TX	77057	713-860-1400	355-3909
Parente Randolph LLC 1650 Market St Ste 4500 *Web:* www.parentenet.com	Philadelphia	PA	19103	215-972-0701	563-4925
ParenteBeard LLC 46 Public Sq Ste 400 *Web:* www.parentebeard.com	Wilkes-Barre	PA	18701	570-820-0100	
Parker Swearngin LLP 215 Se Douglas St *Web:* parkerswearngin.biz	Lees Summit	MO	64063	816-434-6770	
Patel & Assoc 266 17th St Ste 200 *Web:* patelcpa.com	Oakland	CA	94612	510-452-5051	
Patrick & Buzarellos LLP 1900 Point W Way Ste 102 *Web:* pbpcpas.com	Sacramento	CA	95815	916-920-1604	
Patrick J Kozlowski Accountancy 1127 11th St 225	Sacramento	CA	95814	916-448-5191	
Patrick Mcguire Certified Public Accountant 314 W 18th St *Web:* www.mhpllp.com	Cheyenne	WY	82001	307-634-2151	
Patrick T Hsu CPA 7927 Garden Grove Blvd	Garden Grove	CA	92841	714-895-6516	
Paulson Professional Corp 975 Willagillespie Rd Ste 202	Eugene	OR	97401	541-484-1881	
Payday Inc 5011 Indian School Rd NE *Web:* www.paydayinc.com	Albuquerque	NM	87110	505-255-5433	
Paylogic 2843 Brownsboro Rd Ste 111 *Web:* www.epaylogic.com	Louisville	KY	40206	502-894-0088	
Paylogix 1025 Old Country Rd Ste 310 *Web:* paylogix.com	Westbury	NY	11590	516-408-7800	
Paymetric Inc 1225 Northmeadow Pkwy Ste 110 *TF:* 888-445-4901 ■ *Web:* www.paymetric.com	Roswell	GA	30076	678-242-5281	
Payright Payroll Service Inc 468 Great Rd (2A) *Web:* www.payrightpayroll.com	Acton	MA	01720	978-263-5004	
Payroll 1 Inc 34100 Woodward Ave Ste 250 *Web:* www.payroll1.com	Birmingham	MI	48009	248-548-7020	
Payroll Masters 855 Bordeaux Way *Web:* www.payrollmasters.com	Napa	CA	94558	707-226-1428	
PDR Certified Public Accountants Inc 29750 Us Hwy 19 N *Web:* pdr-cpa.com	Clearwater	FL	33761	727-785-4447	
Peachin Schwartz & Weingardt Pc 9449 Priority Way W Dr Ste 150 *Web:* www.psw-cpa.com	Indianapolis	IN	46240	317-574-4280	574-4286
Pearce Bevill Leesburg & Moore Pc 110 Office Pk Dr *TF:* 800-654-1654 ■ *Web:* www.pearcebevill.com	Birmingham	AL	35223	205-323-5440	328-8523
Peck & Peck CPAs PC 312 S Pacific	Dillon	MT	59725	406-683-4254	
Pereira & Azevedo Cpa LLC 52-54 Rome St *Web:* www.njcpas.com	Newark	NJ	07105	973-466-1663	
Perelson Weiner LLP One Dag Hammarskjold Plz 42nd Fl *Web:* www.pwcpa.com	New York	NY	10017	212-605-3100	
Perioperative Services LLC 111 Continental Dr Ste 412 *Web:* periopradonc.com	Newark	DE	19713	302-733-0806	
Perkins Lund Collar & Assoc PLLC 2607 Oberlin Rd #200 *Web:* www.plccpa.com	Raleigh	NC	27608	919-781-1721	
Peter Bell CPA 1735 Dilworth Rd E *Web:* peterbellcpa.com	Charlotte	NC	28203	704-525-9999	
Peter J Bertuglia CPA PC 775 Park Ave *Web:* bertugliacpa.com	Huntington	NY	11743	631-385-7003	
Peters & Company PC 610 S W Alder St 910 *Web:* peterscopc.com	Portland	OR	97205	503-241-8080	
Pfeffer Hanniford & Palka CPA's PC 225 E Grand River Ave Ste 104 *Web:* phpcpa.com	Brighton	MI	48116	810-229-5550	
Phillips Gold & Company LLP 1430 Broadway Rm 1200 *Web:* www.pgcebiz.com	New York	NY	10018	212-730-1112	
Pickens Snodgrass Koch & Company PC 3001 Medlin Dr Ste 100 *Web:* www.pskcpa.com	Arlington	TX	76015	817-664-3000	
Piehl, Hanson, Beckman PA 700 S Grade Rd Sw *Web:* www.phbcpa.com	Hutchinson	MN	55350	320-234-4430	
Piercy Bowler Taylor & Kern 6100 Elton Ave Ste 1000 *Web:* pbtk.com	Las Vegas	NV	89107	702-384-1120	
Pilarski Sinkel & Hankes Ltd 5100 Eden Ave S Ste 304	Edina	MN	55436	952-929-2580	
Piltz Williams Larosa & Co 1077 Tommy Munro Dr *Web:* pwlcpa.com	Biloxi	MS	39532	228-374-4141	
Pinto Mucenski Hooper VanHouse & Company Certified Public Accountants PC 42 Market St *Web:* www.pmhvcpa.com	Potsdam	NY	13676	315-265-6080	
PJ Schneiders & Company LLP 152 Himmelein Rd Village Greene E *Web:* corrugatedcpa.com	Medford	NJ	08055	609-654-8300	
Plante & Moran PLLC 27400 NW Hwy *TF:* 866-639-9991 ■ *Web:* www.plantemoran.com	Southfield	MI	48034	248-352-2500	352-0018
Playfair Planning Services 1640 E 94th St *Web:* playfairplanning.com	Brooklyn	NY	11236	718-629-5898	
PMB Helin Donovan LLP 5918 W Courtyard Dr *Web:* pmbhd.com	Austin	TX	78730	512-258-9670	
Port & Company CPA'S 5730 Commons Park Dr	East Syracuse	NY	13057	315-449-1200	
Port Kashdin & Mcsherry CPAs 111 W Rd *Web:* pkmcpa.com	Cortland	NY	13045	607-756-5681	
Porter & Company PC CPAs 241 Summit Ave Ste 100 *Web:* porterandco.com	Greensboro	NC	27401	336-370-1000	
Porter & Porter PC 1370 Ramar Rd Ste B	Bullhead City	AZ	86442	928-758-4106	
Portnoy CPA 9283 San Jose Blvd *Web:* www.portnoycpa.com	Jacksonville	FL	32257	904-731-8005	
Pradip Patel & Company Ltd Certified Public Accountants 999 Plz Dr *Web:* patel-cpa.com	Schaumburg	IL	60173	847-413-0414	
Presnell Gage Pllc 1216 Idaho St *Web:* www.presnellgage.com/	Lewiston	ID	83501	208-746-8281	746-5174
PRG-Schultz International Inc 600 Galleria Pkwy Ste 100 *TF:* 800-752-5894 ■ *Web:* www.prgx.com	Atlanta	GA	30339	770-779-3900	779-3133
Price Stagner & Company Pllc 501 Darby Creek Rd No 6 *Web:* pricestagner.com	Lexington	KY	40509	859-263-1944	
PricewaterhouseCoopers LLP 300 Madison Ave **Fax Area Code:* 813 ■ *TF:* 800-993-9971 ■ *Web:* www.pwc.com	New York	NY	10017	646-471-4000	286-6000*
Pritchard Bieler Gruver & Willison PC 590 Bethlehem Pk *Web:* www.pbgw.com	Colmar	PA	18915	215-997-6700	
Pro HR Plus 724 Garland St	Little Rock	AR	72201	501-537-7747	
Pro Pay LLC 7450 W 130th St Ste 220	Overland Park	KS	66213	913-826-6300	
Quality Medical Reimbursement Services 6695 Highland Rd Ste 106 *Web:* qualitymedicalreimbursement.com	Waterford	MI	48327	248-666-4266	
Quast Janke & Co 1010 N Johnson St *Web:* qjc.com	Bay City	MI	48708	989-892-4549	
R J Williams 585 Rugh St	Greensburg	PA	15601	724-834-3403	
Radakovich Shaw & Blythe LLP 3220 S Higuera St Ste 201 *Web:* radshaw.com	San Luis Obispo	CA	93401	805-544-1557	
Raffa PC 1899 L St NW Ste 900 *Web:* www.raffa.com	Washington	DC	20036	202-822-5000	
Raimondo Pettit & Glassman 21515 Hawthorne Blvd Ste 1250 *Web:* www.rpgcpa.com	Torrance	CA	90503	310-540-5990	
Ramberg & Assoc Pa 1080 SW Wanamaker Rd *Web:* rambergandassociates.com	Topeka	KS	66604	785-273-7276	

Firm / Address	City	State	ZIP	Phone	Fax
REA & Assoc Inc 419 W High Ave PO Box 1020 *Web:* www.reacpa.com	New Philadelphia	OH	44663	330-339-6651	308-9506
Realty Consulting Services Inc 1628 Colonial Pkwy	Inverness	IL	60067	847-241-2900	
Reed & Brinkman Acctg Inc 208 Sherman St	Jackson	MN	56143	507-847-4222	
Rehmann Group 5800 Gratiot St Ste 201 *TF:* 866-799-9580 ■ *Web:* www.rehmann.com	Saginaw	MI	48638	989-799-9580	799-0227
Reid Hurst Nagy 105-13900 Maycrest Way *Web:* www.rhncga.com	Richmond	BC	V6V3E2	604-273-9338	
Reilly Penner & Benton LLP 1233 N Mayfair Rd *Web:* rpb.biz	Milwaukee	WI	53226	414-271-7800	
Repanich & Clevenger CPA'S 12715 Bel Red Rd Ste 200 *Web:* repanichclevenger.com	Bellevue	WA	98005	425-451-4019	
Revens Revens & St Pierre 946 Centerville Rd *Web:* rrsplaw.com	Warwick	RI	02886	401-822-2900	
Reynolds Hix & Company PA 6729 Academy Rd Ne Ste D *Web:* rhcocpa.com	Albuquerque	NM	87109	505-828-2900	
Reznick Group PC 7501 Wisconsin Ave Ste 400 E *Web:* cohnreznick.com	Bethesda	MD	20814	301-652-9100	
RF Murray & Co CPAs PC 3741 Wilder Rd *TF:* 800-929-3556 ■ *Web:* rfmurraycpa.com	Bay City	MI	48706	989-686-7740	686-7742
RGL Forensic 5619 DTC Pkwy Ste 1010 *Web:* www.rgl.com	Englewood	CO	80111	303-721-8898	721-8936
Rich Gelwarg & Lampf LLP 4 Ethel Rd *Web:* www.rglcpas.com	Edison	NJ	08817	732-287-5565	
Richard L Brown & Company PA 1810 S Macdill Ave	Tampa	FL	33629	813-258-0338	
Richardson Pennington & Skinner Psc 513 S Second St *Web:* www.rps-cpa.com	Louisville	KY	40202	502-583-9587	
Richey May & Company PC 9605 S Kingston Ct Ste 200 *Web:* www.richeymay.com	Englewood	CO	80112	303-721-6131	
Ringold Financial Management Services Inc 850 S Wabash Ave Ste 210 *Web:* www.ringoldfinancial.com	Chicago	IL	60605	312-566-9705	
Ritz, Holman, Butala, Fine LLP 330 E Kilbourn Ave Two Plz E Ste 550 *Web:* www.ritzholman.com	Milwaukee	WI	53202	414-271-1451	
Robert I Goldstein 6507 Wilkins Ave Ste 202	Pittsburgh	PA	15217	412-362-9040	
Robert K Taylor 2890 N Main St Ste 305	Walnut Creek	CA	94597	925-944-7660	
Robert M Grum Jr CPA 4540 Kearny Villa Rd Ste 108	San Diego	CA	92123	858-560-5449	
Roberts & Allan 2824 Park Ave Ste B	Merced	CA	95348	209-383-2442	
Robertson & Assoc CPA'S 55 First St Ste G *Web:* robertsoncpa.com	Lakeport	CA	95453	707-263-9012	
Robinson Hughes & Christopher Psc 459 W Martin Luther King Blvd *Web:* rhccpas.com	Danville	KY	40422	859-236-6628	
Rodefer Moss & Company PLLC 608 Mabry Hood Rd *Web:* www.rodefermoss.com	Knoxville	TN	37932	865-583-0091	
Roger D Perry PC 3050 Business Park Cir	Goodlettsville	TN	37072	615-851-6081	
Roger Sipe CPA Firm LLC 5742 Coventry Ln *Web:* sipecpa.com	Fort Wayne	IN	46804	260-432-9996	
Rogers Huber & Assoc 973 Lycoming Mall Dr *Web:* rogershuber.com	Muncy	PA	17756	570-546-2238	
Ronald T Karpowich CPA 725 Front St	Freeland	PA	18224	570-636-2358	
Roscoe & Swanson Accountancy 3848 W Carson St Ste 215 *Web:* rscpa.com	Torrance	CA	90503	310-540-5300	
Rosen Sapperstein & Friedlander Cht 300 Red Brook Blvd *Web:* rsfchart.com	Owings Mills	MD	21117	410-581-0800	
Rosen Seymour Shapss Martin & Company LLP 757 Third Ave Sixth Fl *Web:* www.rssmcpa.com	New York	NY	10017	212-303-1800	755-5600
RosenbaumRollins & Olah PC 30230 Orchard Lk Rd Ste 200 *Web:* rra-cpas.com	Farmington Hills	MI	48334	248-855-6640	
Rosenblum & Cohen CPAs 100 Merrick Rd	Rockville Centre	NY	11570	516-763-1212	
Ross Buehler Falk & Company LLP (RBF) 1500 Lititz Pk *Web:* www.rbfco.com	Lancaster	PA	17601	717-393-2700	393-1743
Rossmann Macdonald & Benetti Inc 3838 Watt Ave Ste E500 *Web:* www.rmb-cpa.com	Sacramento	CA	95821	916-488-8360	
Rotenberg Meril Solomon Park 80 W Plz 1 250 Pehle Ave Ste 101 *Web:* www.rmsbg.com	Saddle Brook	NJ	07663	201-487-8383	
Roth & Company PC 666 Walnut Ste 1450 *Web:* www.rothcpa.com	Des Moines	IA	50309	515-244-0266	
Roy & Assoc PC 433 Frye Farm Rd Ste 7 *Web:* royandassociates.net	Greensburg	PA	15601	724-834-3900	
Rozovics & Wojocicki Pc 1580 N Northwest Hwy Ste 120 *Web:* rozwoj.com	Park Ridge	IL	60068	847-699-7600	
RubinBrown LLP One N Brentwood Blvd Ste 1100 *Web:* www.rubinbrown.com	Saint Louis	MO	63105	314-290-3300	290-3400
Ruby Stein Wagner 300 Rue Leo-pariseau Ste 1900 *Web:* rsw.ca	Montreal	QC	H2X4B5	514-842-3911	
Ryan & Coscia PC 256 Essex St *Web:* ryancoscia.com	Salem	MA	01970	978-744-1760	
Ryansharkey LLP 12700 Sunrise Vly Dr *Web:* ryansharkey.com	Reston	VA	20191	703-652-1124	
S & p Tax Solutions Ltd 95 Revere Dr Ste A *Web:* www.sandptax.com	Northbrook	IL	60062	847-480-4400	
S R Snodgrass AC 2100 Corporate Dr *TF:* 800-580-7738 ■ *Web:* www.srsnodgrass.com	Wexford	PA	15090	724-934-0344	934-0345
Sackrider & Company Inc 1925 Wabash Ave *Web:* sackrider.com	Terre Haute	IN	47807	812-232-9492	
Sales Tax Resource Group 16882 Bolsa Chica St Ste 206 *Web:* www.salestaxresource.com	Huntington Beach	CA	92649	714-377-2600	
Sanford & Company PA 812 Dequeen *Web:* sanford-cpa.com	Mena	AR	71953	479-394-5414	
Sansiveri Kimball & Company LLP 55 Dorrance St *Web:* sansiveri.com	Providence	RI	02903	401-331-0500	
Santa Monica Partners 1865 Palmer Ave Ste 108 *Web:* www.smplp.com	Larchmont	NY	10538	914-833-0958	
Santora CPA Group 220 Continental Dr Ste 112 Christiana Executive Campus *Web:* www.santoracpagroup.com	Newark	DE	19713	302-737-6200	
Sara E Cooley CPA 2240 Shelter Island Dr Ste 205	San Diego	CA	92106	619-758-9743	
Sarfino & Rhoades LLP 11921 Rockville Pk Ste 501 *Web:* www.sarfinoandrhoades.com	North Bethesda	MD	20852	301-770-5500	
Sartain Fischbein & Co 3010 S Harvard Ave Ste 400 *Web:* www.sfandco.com	Tulsa	OK	74114	918-749-6601	
Sattell Johnson Appel & Co Sc 111 Heritage Reserve Ste 100 *Web:* sattell.com	Menomonee Falls	WI	53051	414-273-0500	
SC&H Group LLC 910 Ridgebrook Rd *TF:* 800-832-3008 ■ *Web:* www.scandh.com	Sparks	MD	21152	410-403-1500	403-1570
Scafidi Cranston & Assoc LLC 42 S Main St *Web:* scafidicranston.com	Medford Lakes	NJ	08055	609-953-8699	
Scheinkman & ScheinkmanPA 18 NE Second Ave	Dania Beach	FL	33004	954-920-6173	
Schenck Business Solutions 200 E Washington St *TF:* 800-236-2246 ■ *Web:* www.schencksc.com	Appleton	WI	54911	920-731-8111	731-8037
Schlenner Wenner & Co 630 Roosevelt Rd *TF:* 877-616-0286 ■ *Web:* www.swcocpas.com	Saint Cloud	MN	56301	320-251-0286	
Schmidt Assoc PC 2530 S Grand Ave Ste C *Web:* schmidt-cpapc.com	Carthage	MO	64836	417-358-6090	
Schmidt Westergard & Company PLLC 77 W University Dr *Web:* sw-cpa.com	Mesa	AZ	85201	480-834-6030	
Schneider Downs & Company Inc 1133 Penn Ave *Web:* www.schneiderdowns.com	Pittsburgh	PA	15222	412-261-3644	261-4876
Schroer & Assoc 300 W Broadway 41 *Web:* schroer-cpa.com	Council Bluffs	IA	51503	712-322-8734	
Schulz & Urbanski PC 6 Forest Park Dr	Farmington	CT	06032	860-678-9042	
Schwartz & Nesbitt PC 281 Farmington Ave	Farmington	CT	06030	860-677-4585	
Schwartz Lasson Harris Ltd Two Walnut Grove Dr Ste100 *Web:* slhcpas.com	Horsham	PA	19044	215-956-9700	
Schwendiman Sutton & Simmons Pllc / Psp Inc 39 Professional Plz *Web:* ssscpa.net	Rexburg	ID	83440	208-356-3452	
Scribner Cohen & Company SC 400 E Mason St Ste 300 *Web:* scribnercohen.com	Milwaukee	WI	53202	414-271-1700	
Seidel Schroeder & Co 304 E Blue Bell Rd *Web:* www.ssccpa.com	Brenham	TX	77833	979-846-8980	830-8131
Seiler LLP Three Lagoon Dr Ste 400 *Web:* www.seiler.com	Redwood City	CA	94065	650-365-4646	368-4055
Selden Fox Ltd 619 Enterprise Dr *Web:* www.seldenfox.com	Oak Brook	IL	60523	630-954-1400	
Self Maples & Copeland Pc 1601 Second Ave E *Web:* cpasmc.com	Oneonta	AL	35121	205-625-3472	
Seligman Friedman & Company PC 235 St Charles Way Ste 250 *Web:* www.sfc-cpa.com	York	PA	17402	717-741-0004	
Serna & Co PC 6031 W Ih-20 Ste 251 *Web:* serna.com	Arlington	TX	76017	817-483-3884	483-3889
Seward & Monde 296 State St *Web:* sewardmonde.com	North Haven	CT	06473	203-248-9341	
Seybold John & Company Ltd 800 Busse Hwy Ste 200 *Web:* www.johnseybold.com	Park Ridge	IL	60068	847-696-1060	
Shajani LLP 5212 48 St *Web:* shajani.ca	Red Deer	AB	T4N7C3	403-347-1384	
Shannon & Assoc LLP 1851 Central Pl S Ste 225 *Web:* www.shannon-cpas.com	Kent	WA	98030	253-852-8500	
Sharpe Kawam Carmosino & Company LLC One Mars Ct Ste 1 *Web:* skcandco.com	Boonton	NJ	07005	973-335-1112	
Sharrard McGee & Company PA 1321 Long St *Web:* www.sharrardmcgee.com	High Point	NC	27262	336-884-0410	
Shaw & Sullivan P C 1221 Cameron St *Web:* shawcpa.com	Alexandria	VA	22314	703-548-2776	
Sherman & Armbruster LLP 609 Treybourne Dr *Web:* shermanandarmbruster.com	Greenwood	IN	46142	317-881-6670	
Siegfried Group LLP, The 1201 Market St *Web:* siegfriedgroup.com	Wilmington	DE	19801	302-984-1800	
Siepert & Company LLP Cpa 1920 W Hart Rd Side Side *Web:* www.siepert.com	Beloit	WI	53511	608-365-2266	

Firm / Address	City	State	Zip	Phone	Fax
Sikich LLP 1415 W Diehl Rd Ste 400 *TF:* 877-279-1900 ■ *Web:* www.sikich.com/sg	Naperville	IL	60563	630-566-8400	566-8401
Silberman Langner Assoc 6050 Santo Rd *Web:* silbermanlangner.com	San Diego	CA	92124	858-268-3330	
Simon Lever & Co 444 Murry Hill Cir *Web:* www.simonlever.com	Lancaster	PA	17601	717-569-7081	
Simons Bitzer & Assoc PC 8350 S Emerson Ave Ste 100 *Web:* www.simonsbitzer.com	Indianapolis	IN	46237	317-782-3070	
Singer Lewak Greenbaum & Goldstein LLP 10960 Wilshire Blvd 7th Fl *TF:* 877-754-4557 ■ *Web:* www.singerlewak.com	Los Angeles	CA	90024	310-477-3924	478-6070
Sini & Reeves LLP CPA 348 Main St Rt 25A	East Setauket	NY	11733	631-751-5225	
SJ Grillo 420 Jericho Tpke	Jericho	NY	11753	516-681-3433	
Slade Quilty & Assoc CPA'S LLP 26619 Carmel Ctr Pl Ste 102	Carmel	CA	93923	831-625-8740	
Smith & Howard PC 271 17th St NW Ste 1600 *Web:* www.smith-howard.com	Atlanta	GA	30363	404-874-6244	874-1658
Smith & Smith CPAs PC 2423 Us Hwy 2 E	Kalispell	MT	59901	406-755-4567	
Smith Anglin & Co 17738 Preston Rd *Web:* www.smithanglin.com	Dallas	TX	75252	972-267-1244	
Smith Brooks Bolshoun & CoLLP 2680 18th St Ste 200 *Web:* sbbllp.com	Denver	CO	80211	303-480-1200	
Smith Goolsby Artis & Reams Psc 1330 Carter Ave	Ashland	KY	41101	606-329-1171	
Smith Koelling Dykstra & Ohm PC 1605 N Convent *Web:* skdocpa.com	Bourbonnais	IL	60914	815-937-1997	
Smith Linden & Basso 5120 Birch St Ste 200 *Web:* www.slb-cpa.com	Newport Beach	CA	92660	949-752-0660	
Smith Schafer & Assoc Ltd 220 S Broadway Ste 102 *Web:* www.smithschafer.com	Rochester	MN	55904	507-288-3277	
Smoak Davis & Nixon LLP 5011 Gate Pkwy Bldg 100 Ste 300 *Web:* www.sdnllp.com	Jacksonville	FL	32256	904-396-5831	
Smoker Smith & Associates Pc 339 W Governor Rd Ste 202 *Web:* www.smokersmith.com	Hershey	PA	17033	717-533-5154	
Smolin, Lupin & Company PA 165 Passaic Ave Fourth Fl *Web:* www.smolin.com	Fairfield	NJ	07004	973-439-7200	
Smoll & Banning CPAs LLC 2410 Central Ave *Web:* smollbanning.com	Dodge City	KS	67801	620-225-6100	
Smythe Ratcliffe LLP 700 - 355 Burrard St *Web:* www.smytheratcliffe.com	Vancouver	BC	V6C2G8	604-687-1231	
Sobel & Company LLC 293 Eisenhower Pkwy Ste 290 *Web:* www.sobel-cpa.com	Livingston	NJ	07039	973-994-9494	
Software Solutions Unlimited Inc 9595 SW Gemini Dr *Web:* www.ssui.com	Beaverton	OR	97008	971-249-5400	
Sol Schwartz & Assoc 7550 W Interstate 10 Ste 1200 *Web:* www.ssacpa.com	San Antonio	TX	78229	210-384-8000	384-8011
Somerset CPAs PC 3925 River Crossing Pkwy Ste 300 *Web:* somersetcpas.com	Indianapolis	IN	46240	317-472-2200	
Sonnabend & Shu CPAS Inc 5832 Melvin Ave	Tarzana	CA	91356	818-776-0060	
Sorensen Vance & Company PC 3115 East Lion Ln Ste 220 *Web:* sorensenvance.com	Salt Lake City	UT	84121	801-733-5055	
Soukup Bush & Assoc CPAs PC 2032 Caribou Dr Ste 200 *Web:* soukupbush.com	Fort Collins	CO	80525	970-223-2727	
Spicer Jeffries & Company LLP 5251 S Quebec St Ste 200 *Web:* spicerjeffries.com	Greenwood Village	CO	80111	303-753-1959	
Spritzer Kaufman LLP 19 W 44th St Ste 1703 *Web:* spritzerkaufman.com	New York	NY	10036	212-593-1040	
Sproles- Woodard- & Co 777 Main St Ste 3250 *Web:* www.sproles.com	Fort Worth	TX	76102	817-332-1328	
Squar Milner Peterson Miranda & Williamson LLP 4100 Newport Pl Dr Ste 600 *Web:* www.squarmilner.com	Newport Beach	CA	92660	949-222-2999	222-2989
Squire & Company PC 1329 South 800 East *Web:* www.squire.com	Orem	UT	84097	801-225-6900	
SS&G Financial Services Inc 32125 Solon Rd *Web:* www.ssandg.com	Solon	OH	44139	440-248-8787	248-0841
Stanisky & Co 2550 Leechburg Rd *Web:* staniskycpa.com	Lower Burrell	PA	15068	724-339-7340	
Stanislawski & Harrison 301 N Lake Ave Ste 900 *Web:* www.snh-cpa.com	Pasadena	CA	91101	626-793-3600	
Stanley Benefit Services Inc 300 E Wendover Ave Ste 101 *Web:* www.stanleybenefits.com	Greensboro	NC	27401	336-271-4450	
Stanley R Hinckley CPA Inc 9292 Cincinnati-Columbus Rd	Cincinnati	OH	45241	513-777-4505	
Stealth Mktg Services 4424 Via De La Plz	Yorba Linda	CA	92886	714-693-3823	
Steinke Vertal Langdon & Drum Inc 3511 Center Rd PO Box 8 *Web:* svldcpa.com	Brunswick	OH	44212	330-225-3377	
Stephen A Kepniss & Assoc PC 211 Mountain Ave	Springfield	NJ	07081	973-921-1250	
Stephen M Meltz & Assoc CPA'S PC 6954 W Touhy Ave	Niles	IL	60714	847-647-6701	
Stephen Wojdowski CPA 8885 Rio San Diego Dr 3215	San Diego	CA	92108	619-296-0150	
Steven A Doyle Ltd 1565 82nd St W	Inver Grove Heights	MN	55077	651-688-8141	
Steven F Thurn CPA Psc 2134 Nicholasville Rd Ste 2 *Web:* thurncpa.com	Lexington	KY	40503	859-276-3782	
Stevenson Jones & Holmaas PC 5920 E Pima Ste 170	Tucson	AZ	85712	520-886-5495	
Stewart Archibald & Barney LLP 7881 W Charleston Blvd Ste 250 *Web:* www.sabcpa.com	Las Vegas	NV	89117	702-579-7000	
Stinnett & Assoc LLC 8801 S Yale Ave Ste 330 *Web:* www.stinnett-associates.com	Tulsa	OK	74137	918-728-3300	
Stockman Kast Ryan & Scruggs PC 102 N Cascade Ste 400 *Web:* www.skrco.com	Colorado Springs	CO	80903	719-630-1186	
Stockton Accountancy Corp 3355 Cerritos Ave	Los Alamitos	CA	90720	562-493-3591	
Stone & Company LLC 57 Bedford St *Web:* stonecpas.com	Lexington	MA	02420	781-863-6300	
Stone Parker & Company CPA Pa 7512 Ridge Rd *Web:* stoneparkercpa.com	Port Richey	FL	34668	727-842-3180	
Strategic Account Management Assn 33 N La Salle St Ste 3700 *Web:* www.strategicaccounts.org	Chicago	IL	60602	312-251-3131	
Stratton & Assoc Pllc 398 S Ninth St Ste 290 *Web:* strattoncpa.com	Boise	ID	83702	208-336-4953	
Strothman & Company PSC 1600 Waterfront Plz *Web:* strothman.com	Louisville	KY	40202	502-585-1600	
Stuedle Spears & Company PSC 2821 S Hurstbourne Pkwy Ste 1	Louisville	KY	40220	502-491-5253	
Suby Von Haden & Assoc SC 1221 John Q Hammons Dr *TF:* 800-279-2616 ■ *Web:* www.sva.com	Madison	WI	53717	608-831-8181	831-4243
Sullivan & Menendez LLP 5510 Merrick Rd	Massapequa	NY	11758	516-795-2500	
Surgent Mccoy Cpe LLC 237 Lancaster Ave *Web:* cpenow.com	Devon	PA	19333	610-688-4477	
Susan Carlisle CPA A Professional 21243 Ventura Blvd Ste 138 *Web:* carlislecpa.com	Woodland Hills	CA	91364	818-888-3223	
Swindon Springer & Company Inc 4130 Gibson Dr Ste A6 *Web:* www.swindonspringer.com	Tipp City	OH	45371	937-667-7771	
Synter Resource Group LLC 5935 Rivers Ave Ste 102 *Web:* www.synterresource.com	Charleston	SC	29406	843-746-2200	
T James Williams & Company AC 7080 N Whitney Ste 103 *Web:* tjwco.com	Fresno	CA	93720	559-322-9100	
Talbot Korvola & Warwick LLP 4800 Meadows Rd Ste 200 *Web:* tkw.com	Lake Oswego	OR	97035	503-274-2849	274-2853
Taylor Polson & Company PSC 101 Mckenna St	Glasgow	KY	42141	270-651-8877	
Teal Becker & Chiramonte (TBC) 7 Washington Sq *TF:* 888-380-9660 ■ *Web:* www.tbccpa.com	Albany	NY	12205	518-456-6663	456-3975
Team Jenn Corp 13323 W Washington Blvd Ste 100 *Web:* teamjenn.com	Los Angeles	CA	90066	310-822-8552	
Telniasoft Inc 1802 Brightseat Rd Ste 101 *Web:* telniasoft.com	Landover	MD	20785	301-918-4011	
Templeton & Company LLP 222 Lakeview Ave Ste 1200 *Web:* www.templetoncpa.com	West Palm Beach	FL	33401	561-798-9988	
Terry Jones & Assoc PC 5910 Grelot Rd *Web:* tjonescpa.com	Mobile	AL	36609	251-341-4593	
Theriot Charles C CPA 306 Grinage St *Web:* theriotaccountingfirm.com	Houma	LA	70360	985-872-9036	
Thomas A Lirot CPA PSC 551 State St *Web:* lirotcpa.com	Radcliff	KY	40160	270-351-1540	
Thomas C Jones CPA 105 S St *Web:* tomjonescpa.com	Elkton	MD	21921	410-398-9382	
Thomas E Holter PC 2730 E Broadway Blvd Ste 130	Tucson	AZ	85716	520-577-8818	
Thomas E Thevenin CPA PC 30 Wapping Rd	Kingston	MA	02364	781-582-1211	
Thomas Gammill & Company Ltd 5026 Old Greenwood St *Web:* gammillcpa.com	Fort Smith	AR	72903	479-648-1121	
Thomas Knight Trent King & Co 141 Senora Rd *Web:* www.tktk.com	Roxboro	NC	27573	336-599-0168	
Thomas W Daniels & Company PC 1310 Eagle Ridge Dr *Web:* thomaswdaniels.com	Schererville	IN	46375	219-864-7010	
Thombley & Simmons PC 78 Cole St Ste 200	Marietta	GA	30060	770-423-1234	
Thompson Greenspon & Company PC 4035 Ridgetop Rd Ste 700 *Web:* www.tgccpa.com	Fairfax	VA	22030	703-385-8888	
Tice Brunell & Baker Cpa Pc 14 Corporate Woods Blvd *Web:* www.tbbcpas.com	Albany	NY	12211	518-482-1887	
Tilton & Company CPA's PC 4015 S Mcclintock Dr Ste 105 *Web:* tiltonco.com	Tempe	AZ	85282	480-897-7708	
TimePlus Payroll Inc 695 Mansell Rd Ste 250 *Web:* www.timeplus.com	Roswell	GA	30076	770-998-5790	
Timmins Kroll & Jacobson LLP 10550 New York Ave Ste 200 *Web:* www.tkjcpa.com	Des Moines	IA	50322	515-270-8080	276-8329
Timpson Garcia 70 Washington St Ste 300 *Web:* www.timpsongarcia.com	Oakland	CA	94607	510-832-2325	
Tipton Marler Garner & Chastain 501 W 19th St *Web:* cpagroup.com	Panama City	FL	32405	850-769-9491	

Firm / Address	City	State	Zip	Phone	Fax
Titus Group Inc, The 1200 N Mayfair Rd Ste 270 *Web:* titus-us.com	Milwaukee	WI	53226	414-727-0400	
TMG Company LLC 1718 Briarcrest Dr Ste 100 *TF:* 800-720-1563 ■ *Web:* www.tmgco.com	Bryan	TX	77802	979-774-4492	
Tobias Financial Advisors 1000 S Pine Island Rd Ste 250 *Web:* www.tobiasfinancial.com	Plantation	FL	33324	954-424-1660	
Todd Rivenbark Puryear Company Inc 2405 Robeson St *Web:* www.trpcpa.com	Fayetteville	NC	28305	910-323-3600	
Tollefson & Clancey CPA'S 151 Callan Ave Ste 310	San Leandro	CA	94577	510-483-0145	
Tomkiewicz Wright LLC 6111 P'Tree Dunwoody Rd Bld E 102 *Web:* twcpaga.com	Atlanta	GA	30328	770-351-0411	
Torosian & Walter Financial Services LLC 7225 N First St Ste 101 *Web:* www.twcpa.com	Fresno	CA	93720	559-256-5600	
Toski & Co PC 300 Essjay Rd Ste 115 *TF:* 800-546-7556 ■ *Web:* www.efprotenberg.com	Williamsville	NY	14221	716-634-0700	634-0764
Toukan & Co 575 Charring Cross Dr Ste 200 *Web:* toukan.com	Westerville	OH	43081	614-901-7100	
Tower Accounting 3435 Blue Mtn Dr *Web:* www.toweraccounting.com	San Jose	CA	95127	408-929-4576	
Trager Kevy & Trager 575 Hempstead Tpke Ste 1 *Web:* tktcpa.com	W Hempstead	NY	11552	516-292-9494	
Trout Ebersole & Groff 1705 Oregon Pk *Web:* www.troutcpa.com	Lancaster	PA	17601	717-569-2900	
Troutt, Beeman & Company PC 1212 Locust St *Web:* www.tbco.net	Harrisonville	MO	64701	816-380-5500	
Truitt Tingle & Paramore LLC 5346 Stadium Trace Pkwy Ste 202 *Web:* ttpcpa.com	Hoover	AL	35244	205-733-8265	
Turlington & Co 509 E Ctr St PO Box 1697 *Web:* www.turlingtonandcompany.com	Lexington	NC	27292	336-249-6856	
Turner Vedrenne & Howard PC 9330 Lbj Fwy Ste 875 *Web:* tvhcpas.com	Dallas	TX	75243	972-644-4131	
Turner Warren Hwang & Conrad 100 N First St Ste 202 *Web:* www.twhc.com	Burbank	CA	91502	818-955-9537	
TYS LLP 3150 Crow Canyon Pl Ste 170 *Web:* tysllp.com	San Ramon	CA	94583	925-498-6200	
UHY Advisors Inc 30 S Wacker Dr *Web:* www.uhyadvisors-us.com	Chicago	IL	60606	312-578-9600	346-6500
UHY Advisors NY Inc 66 S Pearl St *Web:* uhy-us.com	Albany	NY	12207	518-449-3171	449-5832
United Paramount Tax Group Inc 4025 Woodland Park Blvd Ste 310 *Web:* uptg.com	Arlington	TX	76013	817-983-0099	
Unity HR LLC 2400 Meridian St Bldg B *Web:* www.unityhr.com	Bellingham	WA	98225	360-671-0762	
Updegrove Combs Mcdaniel & Wilson Plc 10 Rock Pointe Ln Ste 3 *Web:* ucmcpas.com	Warrenton	VA	20186	540-347-5681	
Urish Popeck & Co Three Gateway Ctr Ste 2400 *Web:* www.urishpopeck.com	Pittsburgh	PA	15222	412-391-1994	
Vanacore Debenedictus Digovanni Waddell LLP 11 Racquet Rd Ste 6 *Web:* www.vddw.com	Newburgh	NY	12550	845-567-9000	
Vavrinek Trine Day & Company LLP 8270 Aspen St *Web:* www.vtdcpa.com	Rancho Cucamonga	CA	91730	909-466-4410	466-4431
Vavro & Company Inc 4725 Grayton Rd Ste 1040	Cleveland	OH	44135	440-886-0400	
Venturity Financial Partners 14131 Midway Rd Ste 112 *Web:* www.venturity.net	Addison	TX	75001	972-692-0380	
Verdolino & Lowey PC 124 Washington St Ste 306 *Web:* vlpc.com	Foxboro	MA	02035	508-543-1720	
Verlyn G Adamson CPA 708 S Second St *Web:* vacpa.cc	Mount Horeb	WI	53572	608-437-6322	
Vestal & Wiler Cpas 201 E Pine St Ste 801 *Web:* vestal-wiler.com	Orlando	FL	32801	407-843-4433	
Vicenti Lloyd & Stutzman LLP 2210 E Rt 66 *Web:* vlsllp.com	Glendora	CA	91740	626-857-7300	
Virginia Society of Certified Public Accountants 4309 Cox Rd *Web:* vscpa.com	Glen Allen	VA	23060	804-270-5344	
W Harold Talley Company Inc 4905 Radford Ave Ste 200	Richmond	VA	23230	804-359-5313	
Wakoff Andriulli & Company LLC 100 Craig Rd Ste 109 *Web:* njcpa.com	Manalapan	NJ	07726	732-866-8882	
Walker & Armstrong LLP 3838 N Central Ave *Web:* wa-cpas.com	Phoenix	AZ	85012	602-230-1040	
Walker & Massey CPAs 150 W Rialto Ave	Rialto	CA	92376	909-875-0244	
Wall, Einhorn & Chernitzer PC 555 E Main St Ste 1600 *Web:* www.wec-cpa.com	Norfolk	VA	23510	757-625-4700	
Walsh Kelliher & Sharp Apc 1292 Sadler Way Ste 220 *Web:* wkscpa.com	Fairbanks	AK	99701	907-456-2222	
Walter G Grady CPA 2843 Johnson Ave	Alameda	CA	94501	510-523-2310	
Walter L Weisman CPA 8911 La Mesa Blvd 201	La Mesa	CA	91942	619-697-7878	
Warady & Davis LLP 1717 Deerfield Rd *Web:* waradydavis.com	Deerfield	IL	60015	847-267-9600	
Warren Averett Kimbrough & Marino LLC 2500 Acton Rd *Web:* warrenaverett.com	Birmingham	AL	35243	205-979-4100	979-6313
Watson Rice & Co 301 Rt 17 N 4th Fl *TF:* 800-945-5985 ■ *Web:* watsonrice.com	Rutherford	NJ	07070	201-460-4590	460-7224
Weber Obrien Ltd 5580 Monroe St *Web:* www.weberobrien.com	Sylvania	OH	43560	419-885-8338	
Weinstein & Anastasio PC 2319 Whitney Ave Ste 2a	Hamden	CT	06518	203-397-2525	
Weiser LLP 135 W 50th St *Web:* weisermazars.com	New York	NY	10020	212-812-7000	375-6888
Weissberg & Speller CPA'S PC 3601 Hempstead Tpke *Web:* weissbergandspeller.com	Levittown	NY	11756	516-796-2727	
Wells Coleman & Co 3800 Patterson Ave *Web:* www.wellscoleman.com	Richmond	VA	23221	804-358-1150	
West & Company CPAs PC 97 N Main St *Web:* westcpapc.com	Gloversville	NY	12078	518-725-7127	
Whiteman & Co PA 111 2nd Avenue Northeast Ste 1600	St Petersburg	FL	33701	727-896-2727	
Whitley Penn 3411 Richmond Ave Ste 500 *Web:* www.whitleypenn.com	Houston	TX	77046	713-621-1515	621-1570
Wiebe & Assoc 377 N Central Ave *Web:* www.wiebecpas.com	Upland	CA	91786	909-985-5357	
Wilcoxon Research Inc 20511 Seneca Meadows Pkwy *TF:* 800-945-2696 ■ *Web:* www.wilcoxon.com	Germantown	MD	20876	301-330-8811	
Wilkin & Guttenplan PC 1200 Tices Ln *Web:* wgcpas.com	East Brunswick	NJ	08816	732-846-3000	
William Burton & Company Inc 99 Walnut St *Web:* cpaburton.com	Saugus	MA	01906	781-233-2204	
William G Koch & Assoc 2650 Wview Dr *Web:* wgkcpa.com	Wyomissing	PA	19610	610-678-9700	
William H Bunch Cpa pa 102 Market St Ste 200 *Web:* williamhbunchcpa.com	Chapel Hill	NC	27516	919-929-0595	
Williams Benator & Libby LLP 1040 Crown Pinte Pkwy NE Ste 400 *Web:* www.wblcpa.com	Atlanta	GA	30338	770-512-0500	512-0200
Williamson Employment Services Inc 213 Hilltop Rd *Web:* www.williamsonemployment.com	St. Joseph	MI	49085	269-983-0142	
Willis Boatner & Whiteside LLC 200 Broad St *Web:* wbw-cpa.com	Gadsden	AL	35901	256-543-8902	
Wilson Harris & Co 1602 W Franklin St *Web:* wilsonharris.com	Boise	ID	83702	208-344-1355	
Windham Brannon PC 3630 Peachtree Rd Ne *Web:* windhambrannon.com	Atlanta	GA	30326	404-898-2000	
Winer & Bevilacqua Inc 82 N Miller Rd *Web:* wb-cpa.com	Fairlawn	OH	44333	330-867-3578	
Winkler & Whittenberg Inc CPA'S 15446 E Valley Blvd *Web:* whittenbergcpa.com	City Of Industry	CA	91746	626-330-2224	961-0156
Winther Stave & Company LLP 1316 W 18th St *Web:* www.winther-stave.com	Spencer	IA	51301	712-262-3117	
Wipfli LLP 10000 Innovation Dr Ste 250 *Web:* www.wipfli.com	Milwaukee	WI	53226	414-431-9300	431-9303
Wireless Watchdogs LLC 5800 Hannum Ave Ste B *Web:* www.wirelesswatchdogs.com	Culver City	CA	90230	310-622-0688	
Wishnow Ross Warsavsky & Co 16130 Ventura Blvd	Encino	CA	91436	818-981-2240	
WithumSmith+Brown 5 Vaughn Dr *TF:* 866-455-7438 ■ *Web:* www.withum.com	Princeton	NJ	08540	609-520-1188	520-9882
Wojteczko Snyder Group PC 5583 S Prince St *Web:* wsgrouppc.com	Littleton	CO	80120	303-730-7999	
Wolf Tesar & Company PC 133 N Pkwy Dr *Web:* wolftesar.com	Pekin	IL	61554	309-346-4106	
Wong & Knowles CPA PC 340 W Butterfield Rd *TF:* 866-966-4272 ■ *Web:* wongknowles.com	Elmhurst	IL	60126	630-993-2223	993-2229
Woodfield Fund Admin LLC 3601 Algonquin Rd Ste 900 *Web:* www.woodfieldllc.com	Rolling Meadows	IL	60008	847-255-3500	
Woronoff Hyman Levenson & Sweet PC 30600 Northwestern Hwy Ste 302 *Web:* whls.com	Farmington Hills	MI	48334	248-487-2600	
Wyatt & Company Inc 6846 S Trenton Ave *Web:* wyattandcompany.com	Tulsa	OK	74136	918-488-0311	
XPS Group Inc 888 Ft St Second Fl *Web:* www.xpsgroup.net	Victoria	BC	V8W1H8	250-383-4135	
Yeo & Yeo PC 3023 Davenport Ave *Web:* yeoandyeo.com	Saginaw	MI	48602	989-793-9830	
YFF & Scholma PC 688 Cascade W Pkwy SE *Web:* yffandscholma.com	Grand Rapids	MI	49546	616-942-6530	
Yodice & Co PC 1259 Rt # 46 *Web:* yodiceco.com	Parsippany	NJ	07054	973-263-8228	263-2515
Young & Company LLC 11200 SW Allen Blvd Ste 100 *Web:* youngcocpas.com	Beaverton	OR	97005	503-646-4800	
Yount Hyde & Barbour PC 50 S Cameron St *Web:* www.yhbcpa.com	Winchester	VA	22601	540-662-3417	
Zeisler, Zeisler, Rawson & Johnson LLP 901 A St Ste C *Web:* zzrllp.com	San Rafael	CA	94901	415-451-1703	
Zisook & Greenberg Ltd 208 S Lasalle St Ste 1600	Chicago	IL	60604	312-641-1090	

3 ADHESIVES & SEALANTS

Phone *Fax*

Adco Global Inc
100 Tri State International Ste 135 . . . Lincolnshire IL 60069 847-282-3485 282-3481
Web: www.adcoglobal.com

Adhesives Research Inc
400 Seaks Run Rd PO Box 100 . . . Glen Rock PA 17327 717-235-7979 235-8320
TF: 800-445-6240 ■ *Web:* www.adhesivesresearch.com

Arclin 5865 McLaughlin Rd Ste 3 . . . Mississauga ON L5R1B8 905-712-0900
Web: www.dynea.com

Arlon Graphics 2811 S Harbor Blvd . . . Santa Ana CA 92704 714-540-2811 329-2756*
**Fax Area Code:* 800 ■ *TF:* 800-232-7161 ■ *Web:* www.arlon.com

Atlas Minerals & Chemicals Inc
1227 Valley Rd . . . Mertztown PA 19539 610-682-7171 682-9200
TF Cust Svc: 800-523-8269 ■ *Web:* www.atlasmin.com

Axson North America Inc 1611 Hults Dr . . . Eaton Rapids MI 48827 517-663-8191 663-0523
Web: www.axson-na.com

BASF Corp/Bldg Systems 889 Valley Pk Dr . . . Shakopee MN 55379 952-496-6000 *
**Fax:* Cust Svc ■ *TF Cust Svc:* 800-433-9517 ■ *Web:* www.buildingsystems.basf.com

Basic Adhesives Inc 60 Webro Rd . . . Clifton NJ 07012 973-614-9000
Web: www.elektromek.com

Bemis Assoc Inc One Bemis Way . . . Shirley MA 01464 978-425-6761 425-2278
Web: www.bemisworldwide.com

Bestolife Corp 2777 Stemmons Fwy Ste 1800 . . . Dallas TX 75207 214-583-0271 631-3047
TF: 855-243-9164 ■ *Web:* www.bestolife.com

Bonstone Materials Corp 707 Swan Dr . . . Mukwonago WI 53149 262-363-9877
Web: bonstone.com

Bostik Inc 11320 Watertown Plank Rd . . . Wauwatosa WI 53226 414-774-2250 774-8075
TF: 800-726-7845 ■ *Web:* www.bostik-us.com

BR 111 Exotic Hardwood Flooring 1 NE 40th St . . . Miami FL 33137 800-525-2711 882-8142*
**Fax Area Code:* 305 ■ *TF:* 800-525-2711 ■ *Web:* www.br111.com

Brady Coated Products 6555 W Good Hope Rd . . . Milwaukee WI 53223 414-358-6600 541-1686*
**Fax Area Code:* 800 ■ *TF:* 800-662-1191 ■ *Web:* www.coatedproducts.com

CFC International Inc 500 State St . . . Chicago Heights IL 60411 708-891-3456 758-5989
TF: 800-393-4505 ■ *Web:* www.cfcintl.com

Chase Corp 26 Summer St . . . Bridgewater MA 02324 781-332-0700 697-6419*
NYSE: CCF ■ **Fax Area Code:* 508 ■ *Web:* www.chasecorp.com

Chemence Inc 185 Bluegrass Valley Pkwy . . . Alpharetta GA 30005 770-664-6624 664-6620
Web: www.chemence.com

Colloid Environmental Technologies Co (CETCO)
2870 Forbs Ave . . . Hoffman Estates IL 60192 847-851-1899 527-9948*
**Fax Area Code:* 800 ■ *TF:* 800-527-9948 ■ *Web:* www.cetco.com

Concrete Sealants Inc 9325 SR- 201 . . . Tipp City OH 45371 937-845-8776
Web: www.conseal.com

Covalent Medical Inc
4750 S State St Ste 301 . . . Ann Arbor MI 48108 734-429-2451
Web: www.covamed.com

Custom Bldg Products
13001 Seal Beach Blvd . . . Seal Beach CA 90740 562-598-8808 598-4008
TF: 800-272-8786 ■ *Web:* www.custombuildingproducts.com

DAP Products Inc 2400 Boston St Ste 200 . . . Baltimore MD 21224 410-675-2100 558-1068*
**Fax:* Cust Svc ■ *TF Cust Svc:* 800-543-3840 ■ *Web:* www.dap.com

Dehco Inc 58263 Charlotte Ave . . . Elkhart IN 46517 574-294-2684
Web: www.dehco.com

Devcon Inc 30 Endicott St . . . Danvers MA 01923 855-489-7262 774-0516*
**Fax Area Code:* 978 ■ *TF:* 800-626-7226 ■ *Web:* www.devcon.com

Dymax Corp 318 Industrial Ln Ste 2 . . . Torrington CT 06790 860-482-1010 496-0608
TF: 877-396-2963 ■ *Web:* www.dymax.com

Eclectic Products Inc
1075 Arrowsmith St PO Box 2280 . . . Eugene OR 97402 541-284-9621 746-1983
TF: 800-693-4667 ■ *Web:* www.eclecticproducts.com

EFTEC North America LLC 20219 Northline Rd . . . Taylor MI 48180 248-585-2200 374-2050*
**Fax Area Code:* 734 ■ *Web:* www.eftec.ch

Elmer's Products Inc One Easton Oval . . . Columbus OH 43219 888-435-6377 985-2605*
**Fax Area Code:* 614 ■ *TF:* 888-435-6377 ■ *Web:* www.elmers.com

Euclid Chemical Co 19218 Redwood Rd . . . Cleveland OH 44110 216-531-9222 531-9596
TF: 800-321-7628 ■ *Web:* www.euclidchemical.com

Foster Construction Products Inc
1105 S Frontenac St . . . Aurora IL 60504 800-231-9541 942-6856
TF: 800-231-9541 ■ *Web:* www.fosterproducts.com

Fox Industries Inc 3100 Falls Cliff Rd . . . Baltimore MD 21211 410-243-8856 243-2701
TF: 888-760-0369 ■ *Web:* strongtie.com

Franklin International 2020 Bruck St . . . Columbus OH 43207 614-443-0241 445-1813
TF: 800-877-4583 ■ *Web:* www.franklininternational.com

Geocel Corp PO Box 398 . . . Elkhart IN 46515 574-264-0645 348-7009*
**Fax Area Code:* 800 ■ *TF:* 800-348-7615 ■ *Web:* www.geocelusa.com

Grace Darex Packaging Technologies
62 Whittemore Ave . . . Cambridge MA 02140 617-498-4987 498-4433
TF: 866-333-3726 ■ *Web:* grace.com/packaging/en-us

H B Fuller Construction Products Inc
1105 S Frontenac Rd . . . Aurora IL 60504 800-832-9002 942-6856
TF: 800-832-9002 ■ *Web:* www.tecspecialty.com

HB Fuller Co
1200 Willow Lk Blvd PO Box 64683 . . . Saint Paul MN 55164 651-236-5900 236-5898
NYSE: FUL ■ *TF:* 888-423-8553 ■ *Web:* www.hbfuller.com

Henkel Corp One Henkel Way . . . Rocky Hill CT 06067 860-571-5100 571-5465
TF Cust Svc: 800-243-4874 ■ *Web:* www.henkel.com

Hercules Chemical Company Inc 111 S St . . . Passaic NJ 07055 973-778-5000 777-4115
TF: 800-221-9330 ■ *Web:* www.oatey.com

Hexion Specialty Chemicals Inc
180 E Broad St . . . Columbus OH 43215 614-225-4000
Web: www.momentive.com

Houghton International Inc
945 Madison Ave PO Box 930 . . . Valley Forge PA 19482 610-666-4000 666-0174
TF: 888-459-9844 ■ *Web:* www.houghtonintl.com

IDQ Holdings Inc 2901 W Kingsley Rd . . . Garland TX 75041 214-778-4600
Web: www.idqusa.com

Illinois Tool Works Inc TACC Div
56 Air Stn Industrial Pk . . . Rockland MA 02370 888-751-0409 231-8222*
**Fax Area Code:* 800 ■ *TF Hotline:* 888-751-0409 ■ *Web:* www.itwtacc.com

Phone *Fax*

Inovex Industries Inc
45681 Oakbrook Ct Ste 102 . . . Sterling VA 20166 703-421-9778 421-1967
TF: 888-374-3366 ■ *Web:* www.ride-on.com

Integral Products Inc 24030 Frampton Ave . . . Harbor City CA 90710 310-326-8889
Web: www.integralproducts.com

IPS Corp 455 W Victoria St . . . Compton CA 90220 310-898-3300 853-5008*
**Fax Area Code:* 901 ■ *TF:* 800-888-8312 ■ *Web:* www.ipscorp.com

Key Polymer Corp 17 Shepherd St . . . Lawrence MA 01843 978-683-9411 686-7729
Web: www.keypolymer.com

L & L Products Inc 160 McLean Dr . . . Romeo MI 48065 586-336-1700 336-1699
Web: www.llproducts.com

LaPolla Industries Inc
15402 Vantage Pkwy E Ste 322 . . . Houston TX 77032 281-219-4700 219-4102
OTC: LPAD ■ *Web:* lapolla.com/investor-relations/

Laticrete International Inc 91 Amity Rd . . . Bethany CT 06524 203-393-0010 393-1684
TF: 800-243-4788 ■ *Web:* www.laticrete.com

Light Fabrications Inc 40 Hytec Cir . . . Rochester NY 14606 585-426-5330 426-5239
TF: 800-836-6920 ■ *Web:* www.lightfab.com

Lord Corp 111 Lord Dr . . . Cary NC 27511 919-468-5979
TF: 877-275-5673 ■ *Web:* www.lord.com

Manus Products of Minnesota Inc
866 Industrial Blvd . . . Waconia MN 55387 952-442-3323 442-3327
Web: www.manus.net

MAPEI Corp 1144 E Newport Ctr Dr . . . Deerfield Beach FL 33442 954-246-8888 246-8800
TF: 800-426-2734 ■ *Web:* www.mapei.com

Mask-Off Company Inc 345 W Maple Ave . . . Monrovia CA 91016 626-359-3261 359-7160
Web: www.mask-off.com

Morgan Adhesives Co 4560 Darrow Rd . . . Stow OH 44224 330-688-1111 688-2540
TF: 866-262-2822 ■ *Web:* www.mactac.com

Multiseal Inc 4320 Hitch Peters Rd . . . Evansville IN 47711 812-428-3422 428-3432
Web: www.multiseal-usa.com

National Casein Co 601 W 80th St . . . Chicago IL 60620 773-846-7300 487-5709
Web: www.nationalcasein.com

Nylok Corp 15260 Hallmark Dr . . . Macomb MI 48042 586-786-0100 786-0598
TF: 800-826-5161 ■ *Web:* www.nylok.com

Pacific Polymers Inc 12271 Monarch St . . . Garden Grove CA 92841 714-898-0025
TF: 800-888-8340 ■ *Web:* www.pacpoly.com

Para-Chem Southern Inc
863 SE Main St PO Box 127 . . . Simpsonville SC 29681 864-967-7691 963-1241
TF: 800-763-7272 ■ *Web:* www.parachem.com

Pecora Corp 165 Wambold Rd . . . Harleysville PA 19438 215-723-6051 799-2518
TF: 800-523-6688 ■ *Web:* www.pecora.com

Red Devil Inc 1437 S Boulder . . . Tulsa OK 74119 800-423-3845 585-8120*
**Fax Area Code:* 918 ■ *TF:* 800-423-3845 ■ *Web:* www.reddevil.com

Ritrama 800 Kasota Ave SE . . . Minneapolis MN 55414 612-378-2277 378-9327
TF: 800-328-5071 ■ *Web:* www.ritrama.com

Solar Compounds Corp 1201 W Blancke St . . . Linden NJ 07036 908-862-2813 862-8061
Web: www.solarcompounds.com

Southern Grouts & Mortars Inc
1502 SW Second Pl . . . Pompano Beach FL 33069 954-943-2288 943-2402
TF: 800-641-9247 ■ *Web:* www.sgm.cc

Super Glue Corp
9420 Santa Anita Ave . . . Rancho Cucamonga CA 91730 909-987-0550 987-0490
TF: 800-538-3091 ■ *Web:* www.supergluecorp.com

Super-Tek Products Inc 25-44 Borough Pl . . . Woodside NY 11377 718-278-7900
Web: www.super-tek.com

Surteco USA Inc 7104 Cessna Dr . . . Greensboro NC 27409 336-668-9555 668-7795
Web: www.canplast.com

Tailored Chemical Products Inc
700 12th St Dr NW . . . Hickory NC 28601 828-322-6512 322-7688
TF: 800-627-1687 ■ *Web:* www.tailoredchemical.com

Tremco Inc Roofing Div 3735 Green Rd . . . Beachwood OH 44122 216-292-5000 760-3070*
**Fax Area Code:* 800 ■ **Fax:* Cust Svc ■ *TF:* 800-852-6013 ■ *Web:* www.tremcoroofing.com

Uniseal Inc 1800 W Maryland St . . . Evansville IN 47712 812-436-4840 429-1831
TF: 800-443-9081 ■ *Web:* www.uniseal.com

W.F. Taylor Company Inc 11545 Pacific Ave . . . Fontana CA 92337 951-360-6677 360-1177
TF: 800-397-4583 ■ *Web:* www.wftaylor.com

Western American National Bank
1518 Taney St . . . Kansas City MO 64116 816-421-3000 421-3122

Worthen Industries Inc Three E Spit Brook Rd . . . Nashua NH 03060 603-888-5443 888-7945
TF: 800-444-5988 ■ *Web:* www.worthenindustries.com

&Barr 600 E Washington St . . . Orlando FL 32801 407-849-0100
Web: www.fhbnet.com

4 ADVERTISING AGENCIES

SEE ALSO Public Relations Firms p. 2981

Phone *Fax*

160 Over 90 One S Broad St Fl 10 . . . Philadelphia PA 19107 215-732-3200
Web: www.160over90.com

22 Squared 1170 Peachtree St NE 14th Fl . . . Atlanta GA 30309 404-347-8700
Web: www.22squared.com

2B Productions Inc 1674 Broadway Ste 902 . . . New York NY 10019 212-765-8202
Web: www.2binc.com

3marketeers Advertising Inc 785 The Almeda . . . San Jose CA 95126 408-293-3233 293-2433
Web: www.3marketeers.com

5 Star Sports Calendar LLC
3340 N College Ave . . . Fayetteville AR 72703 479-444-8428
Web: www.fivestarsports.com

9summer LLC Seven Research Dr . . . Woodbridge CT 06525 203-397-0500

A Bright Idea LLC 210 Archer St . . . Bel Air MD 21014 410-836-7180
Web: www.abrightideaonline.com

A Web That Works 2733 Concession Rd 7 . . . Bowmanville ON L1C3K6 905-263-2666 263-8989
TF: 800-579-9253 ■ *Web:* www.awebthatworks.com

Abelson-Taylor Inc 33 W Monroe St . . . Chicago IL 60603 312-894-5500 894-5658
Web: abelsontaylor.com

Acento Adv Inc 2254 S Sepulveda Blvd . . . Los Angeles CA 90064 310-943-8300 829-2424
Web: www.acento.com

Ackerman McQueen Inc (AM)
1601 NW Expy Ste 1100 . . . Oklahoma City OK 73118 405-843-7777 848-8034
Web: www.am.com

Agency	City	State	ZIP	Phone	Fax
Ad Partners Inc 4631 Woodland Corporate Blvd Ste 109 *Web:* www.theadpartners.com	Tampa	FL	33614	813-418-4645	
Adams & Knight Inc 80 Avon Meadow Ln *Web:* www.adamsknight.com	Avon	CT	06001	860-676-2300	
Adasia Communications Inc 400 Sylvan Ave Fl 7 *Web:* www.adasia-us.com	Englewood Cliffs	NJ	07632	201-608-0388	
Addwater2 Inc 383 First St W *Web:* addwater2.com	Sonoma	CA	95476	707-938-1223	
AdMasters 16901 Dallas Pkwy Ste 204 *Web:* www.admasters.com	Addison	TX	75001	972-866-9300	
Adnet Adv Agency Inc 116 John St Fl 35 *Web:* www.adnet-nyc.com	New York	NY	10038	212-587-3164	
Advertising Premium Sales Inc 11675 Lilburn Park Rd *Web:* apspromos.com	Saint Louis	MO	63146	314-872-7000	
Agent 16 79 Fifth Ave	New York	NY	10003	212-367-3800	
Aj Ross Creative Media 1149 NY 17M *Web:* www.ajross.com	Chester	NY	10918	845-783-5770	
AKQA Inc 360 Third St 5th Fl *Web:* www.akqa.com	San Francisco	CA	94107	415-645-9400	645-9420
Alesco Data Group LLC 5276 Summerlin Commons Way *TF:* 800-701-6531 ■ *Web:* www.alescodata.com	Fort Myers	FL	33907	239-275-5006	
Alison Group Inc, The 2090 NE 163rd St *Web:* www.alisongroup.com	North Miami Beach	FL	33162	305-893-6255	
All-Ways Adv Co 1442 Broad St *TF:* 800-255-9291 ■ *Web:* www.awadv.com	Bloomfield	NJ	07003	973-338-0700	338-1410
Allen & Gerritsen Two Seaport Ln *Web:* www.a-g.com	Boston	MA	02210	857-300-2000	
Alliance Communications Inc 15310 Amberly Dr Ste 215 *Web:* www.alliancecommunications.net	Tampa	FL	33647	813-978-1992	
American Telecast Corp 835 Springdale Dr Ste 206 *Web:* www.americantelecast.com	Exton	PA	19341	610-430-7800	
AMP Agency 77 N Washington St *Web:* www.ampagency.com	Boston	MA	02114	617-723-8929	723-2188
Anderson Communications 1691 Phoenix Blvd Ste 390 *Web:* www.andercom.com	Atlanta	GA	30349	404-766-8000	767-5264
Anderson Partners Inc 6919 Dodge St *Web:* www.andersonpartners.com	Omaha	NE	68132	402-341-4807	
Animated Designs LLC 31336 Via Colinas Ste 103 *Web:* www.anides.com	Westlake Village	CA	91362	818-889-2348	
Apple Rock Adv & Promotion 7602 Business Park Dr *Web:* www.applerock.com	Greensboro	NC	27409	336-232-4800	
Archer/Malmo Adv Inc 65 Union Ave Ste 500 *Web:* www.archermalmo.com	Memphis	TN	38103	901-523-2000	523-7654
Argus Communications Inc 280 Summer St Fl 4 *Web:* www.argus-online.com	Boston	MA	02210	617-261-7676	
Arrowhead Adv 16155 N 83rd Ave Ste 205 *Web:* www.arrowheadadv.com	Peoria	AZ	85382	623-979-3000	
Arvizu Adv & Promotions Inc 3111 N Central Ave Ste 1240 *Web:* www.arvizu.com	Phoenix	AZ	85012	602-279-4669	
AskMencom Solutions Canada Inc 4200 St Laurent Ste 801	Montreal	QC	H2W2R2	514-908-2552	
Aspen Marketing Services 1240 N Ave *TF:* 800-848-0212 ■ *Web:* www.aspenms.com	West Chicago	IL	60185	630-293-9600	293-9600
ATD Austin 174 S Guadalupe St Ste 103 *Web:* theredphonebook.com	San Marcos	TX	78666	512-395-8101	
Augie Leopold Adv Specialties Inc 3214 Roman St *Web:* augieleopold.com	Metairie	LA	70001	504-836-0525	
Automated Presort Inc 1400 Centre Cir Dr *Web:* www.automatedpresort.com	Downers Grove	IL	60515	630-620-7678	
Avid Neo Geo 108 Lake Ave *Web:* www.avidneogeo.com	Orlando	FL	32801	407-246-0092	
Avrett Free Ginsberg (AFG) 885 Second Ave Dag Hammarskjold Plz *Web:* avrettfreeginsberg.com	New York	NY	10017	212-832-3800	
Azul 7 Inc 800 Hennepin Ave Ste 700 *Web:* azul7.com	Minneapolis	MN	55403	612-767-4335	
Bader Rutter & Assoc Inc 13845 Bishops Dr *Web:* www.baderrutter.com	Brookfield	WI	53005	262-784-7200	938-5595
Bailey Lauerman & Assoc Inc 1248 O St Ste 900 *TF:* 800-869-0411 ■ *Web:* www.baileylauerman.com	Lincoln	NE	68508	402-475-2800	475-5115
Bakersfield Californian Inc 1707 Eye St *Web:* www.bakersfield.com	Bakersfield	CA	93301	661-395-7500	
Balcom Agency, The 1500 Ballinger St *Web:* www.balcomagency.com	Fort Worth	TX	76102	817-877-9933	
Barkley 1740 Main St *Web:* barkleyus.com	Kansas City	MO	64108	816-842-1500	
Barnhart 1732 Champa St *Web:* www.barnhartusa.com	Denver	CO	80202	303-626-7200	
Bbdo Atlanta Inc 3500 Lenox Rd Ne Ste 1900 *Web:* bbdoatl.com	Atlanta	GA	30326	404-231-1700	
BBDO Worldwide Inc 1285 Ave of the Americas *Web:* www.bbdo.com	New York	NY	10019	212-459-5000	459-6645
Beehive Specialty Co 8701 Wall St Ste 900 *Web:* www.beehivespecialty.com	Austin	TX	78754	512-912-7940	997-7944
Bemis Balkind LLC 6135 Wilshire Blvd *Web:* www.bemisbalkind.com	Los Angeles	CA	90048	323-965-4800	
Bernard Hodes Group 220 E 42 St *TF:* 888-438-9911 ■ *Web:* findly.com/hodesredirect/	New York	NY	10017	212-999-9000	999-9484
Bernstein-Rein 4600 Madison Ave Ste 1500 *Web:* www.b-r.com	Kansas City	MO	64112	816-756-0640	399-6000
Beyond Spots & Dots 1034 Fifth Ave *Web:* www.beyondspotsanddots.com	Pittsburgh	PA	15219	412-281-6215	
Binary Pulse Inc 3545 Harbor Gateway S Ste 102 *Web:* www.binarypulse.com	Costa Mesa	CA	92626	714-429-0110	
Birdsong Gregory LLC 715 N Church St Ste 101 *Web:* www.birdsonggregory.com	Charlotte	NC	28202	704-332-2299	
Blue Sky Agency 950 Joseph E Lowery Blvd Ste 30 *Web:* www.bluesky-agency.com	Atlanta	GA	30318	404-876-0202	
Bonnie Heneson Communications Inc 9199 Reisterstown Rd Ste 212C *Web:* www.bonnieheneson.com	Owings Mills	MD	21117	410-654-0000	
Borden Agency, The 1975 Pioneer Rd *Web:* aardvarkel.com	Huntingdon Valley	PA	19006	215-442-0590	
Boyden & Youngblutt Adv & Mktg Inc 120 W Superior St *Web:* b-y.net	Fort Wayne	IN	46802	260-422-4499	
Brand Pharm 79 Madison Ave	New York	NY	10016	212-684-0909	
Bromley Communications LLC 401 E Houston St *Web:* bromley.biz	San Antonio	TX	78205	210-244-2000	
Bros & Co 4860 S Lewis Ave Ste 100 *Web:* www.broco.com	Tulsa	OK	74105	918-743-8822	
Brown Parker & Demarinis Adv Inc 3333 S Congress Ave Ste 305b *Web:* bpdadvertising.com	Delray Beach	FL	33445	561-276-7701	
Bryan Mills Iradesso Inc 1129 Leslie St *Web:* www.bmir.com	Toronto	ON	M3C2K5	416-447-4740	
Buntin Group, The 1001 Hawkins St *Web:* www.buntingroup.com	Nashville	TN	37203	615-244-5720	244-6511
Burgess Adv & Assoc Inc 1290 Congress St *Web:* www.burgessadv.com	Portland	ME	04102	207-775-5227	
Burrell 233 N Michigan Ave Ste 2900 *Web:* www.burrell.com	Chicago	IL	60601	312-297-9600	297-9601
Cade & Assoc Adv Inc 1645 Metropolitan Blvd *TF:* 800-715-2233 ■ *Web:* www.cade1.com	Tallahassee	FL	32308	850-385-0300	
Cambridge BioMarketing Group LLC 245 First St 12th Fl *Web:* www.cambridgebmg.com	Cambridge	MA	02142	617-225-0001	
Cameron Christopher Thomas Adv Inc 1441 29th St *Web:* www.cctadvertising.com	Denver	CO	80205	303-531-7180	
Camnet Inc 3201 Fourth St NW *Web:* camnet.us	Albuquerque	NM	87107	505-761-4500	
Campbell-Ewald 2000 Brush St Ste 601 *Web:* www.lowecampbellewald.com	Detroit	MI	48226	586-574-3400	
Carmichael Lynch 110 Fifth St N *Web:* www.carmichaellynch.com	Minneapolis	MN	55403	612-334-6000	
Carol H Williams Adv 555 12th St Ste 1700 *Web:* www.carolhwilliams.com	Oakland	CA	94607	510-763-5200	763-9266
Carton Donofrio Partners Inc 100 N Charles St *Web:* www.cartondonofrio.com	Baltimore	MD	21201	410-576-9000	
Celtic Inc 330 S Executive Dr Ste 206 *Web:* www.celticinc.com	Brookfield	WI	53005	262-789-7630	
Charles Tombras Adv Inc 630 Concord St *Web:* www.tombras.com	Knoxville	TN	37919	865-524-5376	
Ciceron Inc 126 N Third St Ste 309 *Web:* www.ciceron.com	Minneapolis	MN	55401	612-204-1919	
Clarity Coverdale Fury (CCF) 120 S Sixth St 1 Financial Plz Ste 1300 *Web:* www.claritycoverdalefury.com	Minneapolis	MN	55402	612-339-3902	359-4392
Clean Design Inc 8081 Arco Corporate Dr Ste 100 *Web:* www.cleandesign.com	Raleigh	NC	27617	919-544-2193	
Cline Davis & Mann Inc (CDM) 220 E 42nd St *Web:* www.clinedavis.com	New York	NY	10017	212-907-4300	687-5411
CMD 1631 NW Thurman St *Web:* www.cmdpdx.com	Portland	OR	97209	503-223-6794	223-2430
Cole & Weber United 221 Yale Ave N Ste 600 *Web:* www.coleweber.com	Seattle	WA	98109	206-447-9595	233-0178
Colle & McVoy Inc 400 First Ave N Ste 700 *Web:* www.collemcvoy.com	Minneapolis	MN	55401	612-305-6000	305-6500
Commercial Mailing Accessories Inc 28220 Playmor Beach Rd *TF:* 800-325-7303 ■ *Web:* www.dispensamatic.com	Rocky Mount	MO	65072	800-325-7303	
Communications Media Inc 2200 Renaissance Blvd *Web:* www.cmimedia.com	King Of Prussia	PA	19406	484-322-0880	
Compas Inc 4300 Haddonfield Rd Ste 200 *Web:* www.compasonline.com	Pennsauken	NJ	08109	856-667-8577	667-6112
Concept Group Inc 190 Fifth St E Ste 200 *Web:* conceptgroup.com	Saint Paul	MN	55101	651-221-9710	
Connelly Partners LLC 46 Waltham St Fourth Fl *Web:* www.connellypartners.com	Boston	MA	02118	617-521-5400	
Cooper-smith Adv LLC 4444 Bennett Rd *Web:* cooper-smith.com	Toledo	OH	43612	419-470-5900	
Corbett Accel Healthcare Group 211 E Chicago Ave	Chicago	IL	60611	312-475-2500	649-7232
Cormark Securities Inc 200 Bay St Royal Bank Plz S Tower Ste 2800 *Web:* www.cormark.com	Toronto	ON	M5J2J2	416-362-7485	
Cotton & Co 633 SE Fifth St *TF:* 800-266-9076 ■ *Web:* www.thecottonsolution.com	Stuart	FL	34994	772-287-6612	
Cramer 425 University Ave *Web:* www.cramer.com	Norwood	MA	02062	781-278-2300	278-8464
Cramer-Krasselt 246 E Chicago St *Web:* www.c-k.com	Milwaukee	WI	53202	414-227-3500	

Phone Fax

Cranford Johnson Robinson Woods
303 W Capitol Ave Little Rock AR 72201 501-975-6251 975-4241
Web: www.cjrw.com
Crawford Strategy 200 E Camperdown Way Greenville SC 29601 864-232-2302
Web: www.crawfordstrategy.com
Create Adv Group LLC
6022 Washington Blvd Culver City CA 90232 310-280-2999
Web: createadvertising.com
Creative Alliance Inc 437 W Jefferson St Louisville KY 40202 502-584-8787 589-9900
TF: 800-525-0294 ■ *Web:* www.cre8.com
Creative Broadcast Concepts
56 Industrial Park Rd Saco ME 04072 207-283-9191
Web: www.cbcads.com
Creative Fire 313 Ontario Ave Saskatoon SK S7K3J7 306-934-3337
Web: creative-fire.com
Creative Marketing Alliance Inc
191 Clarksville Rd Princeton Junction NJ 08550 609-799-6000 799-7032
Web: www.cmasolutions.com
Creative Producers Group Inc
1220 Olive St Ste 210 Saint Louis MO 63103 314-367-2255
Web: www.creativeworks.com
Customized Newspaper Advertising
319 E Fifth St Fl 2nd Des Moines IA 50309 515-244-2145
Web: www.inanews.com
Dailey & Assoc 8687 Melrose Ave West Hollywood CA 90069 310-360-3100 360-3100*
**Fax:* Acctg ■ *Web:* www.daileyideas.com
Dalton Agency Inc, The
140 W Monroe St Ste 200 Jacksonville FL 32202 904-398-5222 398-5220
Web: www.daltonagency.com
Dana Communications Inc Two E Broad St Hopewell NJ 08525 609-466-9187 466-0285
Web: www.danacommunications.com
Dastmalchi Enterprises Inc
31 East Macarthur Crescent Ste 111 Santa Ana CA 92707 949-270-2660
Web: dastmalchi.com
Davis Elen Adv 865 S Figueroa St Ste 1200 Los Angeles CA 90017 213-688-7236 688-7288
TF: 800-729-4322 ■ *Web:* www.daviselen.com
Daxon Mktg 679 Buttonwood Dr Brea CA 92821 714-529-1218
DDB Worldwide 437 Madison Ave New York NY 10022 212-415-2000 415-3414
Web: www.ddb.com
Dealer Impact Systems LLC 7733 Douglas Ave Urbandale IA 50322 515-334-9638
Web: flickfusion.com
Della Femina/Rothschild/Jeary & Partners
902 Broadway 15th Fl New York NY 10010 212-506-0700 506-0751
Web: www.dfjp.com
Dentsu America Inc 32 Ave of the Americas New York NY 10013 212-397-3333
Web: 360i.com/
Design 446 Inc 2411 Atlantic Ave Manasquan NJ 08736 732-292-2400
Web: www.design446.com
Detrow & Underwood Inc 12 W Main St Ashland OH 44805 419-289-0265
Web: www.detrowunderwood.com
Deutsch Inc 111 Eigth Ave 14th Fl New York NY 10011 212-981-7600 981-7525
Web: www.deutschinc.com
DGWB Inc 217 N Main St Ste 200 Santa Ana CA 92701 714-881-2300
Web: www.dgwb.com
Diablo Media LLC 1809 Blake St Denver CO 80202 303-305-4052
Web: www.diablomedia.com
Dieste 1999 Bryan St Ste 2700 Dallas TX 75201 214-259-8000 259-8040
Web: www.dieste.com
Dillon Works! Inc 11775 Harbour Reach Dr Mukilteo WA 98275 425-493-8309
Web: www.dillonworks.com
Doe Anderson Inc 620 W Main St Louisville KY 40202 502-589-1700
Web: www.doeanderson.com
Doner Adv 25900 NW Hwy Southfield MI 48075 248-354-9700 827-0880*
**Fax:* PR ■ *Web:* doner.com
Doremus 200 Varick St New York NY 10014 212-366-3000 366-3060
Web: www.doremus.com
Dudnyk 5 Walnut Grove Dr Ste 280 Horsham PA 19044 215-443-9406 443-0207
TF: 800-767-3263 ■ *Web:* www.dudnyk.com
Dudnyk Exchange 5 Walnut Grove Horsham PA 19044 267-532-1046
Web: dudnyk.com/
Duffy & Shanley Inc 10 Charles St Providence RI 02904 401-274-0001 274-3535
Web: www.duffyshanley.com
DW Green Co 8100 S Priest Dr Tempe AZ 85284 480-491-8483
Web: www.dwgreen.com
Dynamic Digital Adv 1265 Industrial Blvd Southampton PA 18966 215-355-6442
Web: www.zeroonezero.com
E Morris Communications Inc 820 N Orleans Chicago IL 60610 312-943-2900 943-5856
Web: www.emorris.com
Easterly & Co 1177 W Loop S Ste 950 Houston TX 77027 713-529-2949
Web: www.easterly.com
Educationdynamics LLC
5 Marine View Plaza Ste 212 Hoboken NJ 07030 201-377-3000 377-3081
Web: www.educationdynamics.com
Edward Howard & Co
1100 Superior Ave Ste 1600 Cleveland OH 44114 216-781-2400 781-8810
Web: www.edwardhoward.com
Elad National Properties LLC
1301 International Pkwy Ste 200 Sunrise FL 33323 954-846-7800
Web: www.eladnational.com
Elevate Group Holdings LLC 615 Regal Row Dallas TX 75247 214-951-9502
Web: www.elevate-group.com
Elevation B2B Marketing
1955 S Val Vista Dr Ste 101 Mesa AZ 85204 480-775-8880
Web: www.canyoncomm.com
Epoch Adv Agency Inc
888 E Brighton Ave Ste 3 Syracuse NY 13205 315-492-3270
Web: www.epoch-adv.com
Eric Mower & Assoc 211 W Jefferson St Syracuse NY 13202 315-466-1000 466-2000
Web: www.mower.com
Ernst-Van Praag Inc 433 Plaza Real Ste 275 Boca Raton FL 33432 561-447-0557 447-0527
Web: www.evpconsulting.com
Euro RSCG Life 200 Madison Ave Second Fl New York NY 10016 212-251-8800 251-8819
Web: www.havaslife.com

Phone Fax

Euro RSCG Life Chelsea 75 Ninth Ave New York NY 10011 212-299-5000 299-5050
Web: www.havasworldwide.com
Euro RSCG Worldwide 350 Hudson St Sixth Fl New York NY 10014 212-886-2000 886-5013
Web: www.havasworldwide.com
Evans Hardy & Young Inc
829 De La Vina St Santa Barbara CA 93101 805-963-5841
Web: www.ehy.com
Exclaim Inc 220 N Smith St Ste 204 Palatine IL 60067 847-392-0008
Web: www.exclaim-inc.com
Explore Communications Inc 3213 Zuni St Denver CO 80211 303-393-0567
Web: www.explorehq.com
Fahlgren Inc 4030 Easton Station Ste 300 Columbus OH 43219 614-383-1500 383-1501
TF: 800-731-8927 ■ *Web:* www.fahlgrenmortine.com
Fallon 901 Marquette Ave Ste 2400 Minneapolis MN 55402 612-758-2345 758-2346
TF: 888-758-2345 ■ *Web:* www.fallon.com
Finelight Inc 1801 S Liberty Dr Ste 300 Bloomington IN 47403 812-339-6700
Fire & Rain LLC 40 N First Ave Evansville IN 47710 812-464-5244
Web: www.firerain.com
Fitzgerald & Co 3333 Piedmont Rd 11th Fl Atlanta GA 30305 404-504-6900 239-0548
Web: www.fitzco.com
Fitzmartin Inc 2826 6th Ave S Ste 200 Birmingham AL 35233 205-322-1010
Web: fitzmartin.com
Fleming & Van Metre Adv
600 W Germantown Pk Plymouth Meeting PA 19462 610-941-0395
Web: thinkfvm.com
Flying Bridge Technologies
2709 Water Ridge Pkwy Ste 480 Charlotte NC 28217 704-357-8011
Web: www.flyingbridge.net
Frogdesign Inc 660 Third St 4th Fl San Francisco CA 94107 415-442-4804 442-4803
Web: www.frogdesign.com
G s Design 6665 N Sidney Pl Milwaukee WI 53209 414-228-9666
Web: www.gsdesign.com
G2 USA 200 Fifth Ave New York NY 10010 212-546-2222
Web: www.geometry.com
Garza Communications Inc
2601 Hibernia St Ste 200 Dallas TX 75204 214-720-3888
Web: www.garzacommunications.com
Get a Clue Design 1026 14th Ave Dr NW Hickory NC 28601 828-324-4262
Gigante Vaz Partners Inc
The Puck Bldg 295 Lafayette St New York NY 10012 212-343-0004
Web: www.gigantevaz.com
Gilmour Craves 455 Irwin St Ste 201 San Francisco CA 94107 415-431-9955
Web: gilmourcraves.com
Gish Sherwood & Friends Inc
209 10th Ave S Ste 222 Nashville TN 37203 615-385-1100
Web: www.gsandf.com
GKV 1500 Whetstone Way Fourth Fl Baltimore MD 21230 410-539-5400 234-2441
Web: www.gkv.com
Global Hue 4000 Town Ctr Ste 1600 Southfield MI 48075 248-223-8900 871-6216*
**Fax Area Code:* 646 ■ *Web:* www.globalhue.com
GlobalWorks Group LLC 220 Fifth Ave New York NY 10001 212-252-8800 252-0002
Web: www.globalworks.com
Glynndevins Adv & Mktg
11230 College Blvd Overland Park KS 66210 913-491-0600
Web: www.glynndevins.com
Godfrey Adv Inc 40 N Christian St Lancaster PA 17602 717-393-3831
Web: www.godfrey.com
Goodby Silverstein & Partners
720 California St San Francisco CA 94108 415-392-0669
Web: www.goodbysilverstein.com
Graham Group Inc, The
2014 W Pinhook Rd Ste 210 Lafayette LA 70508 337-232-8214 235-3787
Web: www.graham-group.com
Graphica 4501 Lyons Rd Miamisburg OH 45342 937-866-4013
Web: www.graphicadesign.com
GREENCREST Marketing Inc
120 Northwoods Blvd Columbus OH 43235 614-885-7921
Web: www.greencrest.com
Grey Group 200 Fifth Ave New York NY 10010 212-546-2000 546-1495
Web: www.grey.com
Grey Healthcare Group Inc 200 Fifth Ave New York NY 10010 212-886-3000
Web: www.ghgroup.com
GSD & M Idea City 828 W Sixth St Austin TX 78703 512-242-4736 242-4700
Web: www.gsdm.com
GSW Worldwide 500 Old Worthington Rd Westerville OH 43082 614-848-4848 848-3477
Web: www.gsw-w.com
Hal Lewis Group 1700 Market St Sixth Fl Philadelphia PA 19103 215-563-4461 563-1148
Web: www.hlg.com
Haley Miranda Group 8654 Washington Blvd Culver City CA 90232 310-842-7369
Web: www.haleymiranda.com
Hamilton Communications Group 20 N Wacker Dr Chicago IL 60606 312-321-5000
Web: hamiltongrp.com
Hammer Creative Inc
6311 Romaine St Third Fl Hollywood CA 90038 323-606-4700
Web: www.hammercreative.com
Hanson Directory Service Inc
1501 N 15th Ave E Newton IA 50208 641-792-2855
Web: www.hansondirectory.com
Hanson Watson Assoc 1411 15th St Moline IL 61265 309-764-8315
Web: www.hansonwatson.com
Harrison & Star 75 Varick St New York NY 10013 212-727-1330 822-6590
Web: www.harrisonandstar.com
Hart Associates Inc 1915 Indian Wood Cir Maumee OH 43537 419-893-9600
Web: www.hartinc.com
Harvey & Company LLC
5000 Birch St Ste 9200 Newport Beach CA 92660 949-757-0400
Web: www.harveyllc.com
Healthcare Consultancy Group
711 Third Ave 17th Fl New York NY 10017 212-849-7935
Web: www.hcgrp.com
HealthSTAR Communications Inc
1000 Wyckoff Ave Mahwah NJ 07430 201-560-5370
Web: www.healthstarcom.com

Company	City	State	ZIP	Phone	Fax
HEILBrice Inc 9840 Irvine Ctr Dr *Web:* www.heilbrice.com	Irvine	CA	92618	949-336-8800	336-8819
High Velocity Communications LLC 1720 Dolphin Dr Ste D *Web:* www.highvelocityllc.com	Waukesha	WI	53186	262-544-6600	
Hudson Fusion 30 State St Ste 204 *Web:* www.hudsonfusion.com	Ossining	NY	10562	914-762-0900	
Hunter Barth Adv Inc 2043 Wcliff Dr Ste 303 *TF:* 877-524-2732 ■ *Web:* www.hunterbarth.com	Newport Beach	CA	92660	949-631-9900	
Hunter Hamersmith 725 NE 125th St *Web:* www.hhadvertising.net	North Miami	FL	33161	305-895-8430	892-9611
Hyphen 711 Third Ave 17th Fl *Web:* hyphendigital.com	New York	NY	10017	212-856-8700	
Ideal Adv & Printing 116 N Winnebago St *TF:* 800-208-0294 ■ *Web:* www.idealad.com	Rockford	IL	61101	815-965-1713	
Image Group 31 E Eighth St Ste 200 *Web:* www.imagegroup.com	Holland	MI	49423	616-393-9588	
Image Makers Adv LLC 140 S Beach St Ste 202 *Web:* imdaytona.com	Daytona Beach	FL	32114	386-236-1200	
Imaginasium Inc 110 S Washington St *Web:* www.imaginasium.biz	Green Bay	WI	54301	920-431-7872	
Impact - Proven Solutions 4600 Lyndale Ave N *Web:* www.impact-ps.com	Minneapolis	MN	55412	612-521-6245	
In Focus Adv Inc 29219 Canwood St Ste 101 *Web:* infocusadv.com	Agoura Hills	CA	91301	818-889-1342	
Innis Maggiore Group Inc 4715 Whipple Ave NW *TF:* 800-460-4111 ■ *Web:* www.innismaggiore.com	Canton	OH	44718	330-492-5500	492-5568
Innovage LLC 19511 Pauling *Web:* www.innovage.net	Foothill Ranch	CA	92610	949-587-9207	
Integrative Logic Inc 2397 Huntcrest Way Ste 200 *Web:* www.integrativelogic.com	Lawrenceville	GA	30043	678-638-2600	
Intermark Group Inc 101 25th St N *TF:* 800-624-9239 ■ *Web:* www.intermarkgroup.com	Birmingham	AL	35243	205-803-0000	870-3843
Internet Business Systems Inc 595 Millich Dr Ste 210 *Web:* www.ibsystems.com	Campbell	CA	95008	408-850-9202	
Interpublic Group 1114 Ave of the Americas *NYSE: IPG* ■ *Web:* www.interpublic.com	New York	NY	10036	212-704-1200	
Iris Group Inc, The 1675 Faraday Ave *Web:* www.irisgroup.com	Carlsbad	CA	92008	760-431-1103	
J Walter Thompson 466 Lexington Ave *Web:* www.jwt.com	New York	NY	10017	212-210-7000	
James Group Inc, The 19 W 21st St Ste 202 *Web:* www.thejamesgroup.com	New York	NY	10010	212-243-2022	
Jeff Scott & Assoc 4604 137th St Ste 101sf *Web:* www.jeffscottassociates.com	Crestwood	IL	60445	708-489-2050	
Jennings & Assoc 2121 Palomar Airport Rd Ste 220 *Web:* jandacommunications.com	Carlsbad	CA	92011	760-431-7466	
JH&A Adv Inc 2312 Western Trls Ste 303-C *Web:* www.jhaadvertising.com	Austin	TX	78745	512-444-0716	
Johnson Group, The 436 Market St *Web:* www.johngroup.com	Chattanooga	TN	37402	423-756-2608	
Keiler & Co 304 Main St *Web:* www.keiler.com	Farmington	CT	06032	860-677-8821	676-8164
Keller Crescent Co Inc 6454 Saguaro Ct **Fax:* Cust Svc ■ *Web:* www.kellercrescent.com	Indianapolis	IN	46268	812-464-2461	426-7601*
King Agency Inc, The Three N Lombardy St *Web:* thekingagency.com	Richmond	VA	23220	804-249-7500	
Kirshenbaum Bond Senecal & Partners LLC 160 Varick St Fl 4 *Web:* www.kbsp.com	New York	NY	10013	212-633-0080	
Kleber & Assoc 1215 Hightower Trial Bldg C *Web:* www.kleberandassociates.com	Atlanta	GA	30350	770-518-1000	518-2700
Koopman Ostbo Inc 412 NW Eighth Ave *Web:* koopmanostbo.com	Portland	OR	97209	503-223-2168	
Korey Kay & Partners 130 Fifth Ave *Web:* www.koreykay.com	New York	NY	10011	212-620-4300	
Kovel/Fuller LLC 9925 Jefferson Blvd *Web:* www.kovelfuller.com	Culver City	CA	90232	310-841-4444	841-4599
KSC Adv & PR 40 Sarasota Ctr Blvd Ste 107 *Web:* kscadvpr.com	Sarasota	FL	34240	941-906-1555	
Kuno Creative Group LLC 36901 American Wy Ste 2A *TF:* 800-303-0806 ■ *Web:* www.kunocreative.com	Avon	OH	44011	800-303-0806	
KW Adv 333 Bishops Way Ste 148 *Web:* mgicommunications.com/	Brookfield	WI	53005	262-786-4402	
Laird Partners LLC 475 Tenth Ave Seventh Fl *Web:* www.lairdandpartners.com	New York	NY	10018	212-478-8181	478-8210
Laplaca Cohen Adv Inc 43 W 24th St Fl 10 *Web:* www.laplacacohen.com	New York	NY	10010	212-675-4106	
Latorra Paul & Mccann Inc 120 E Washington St University Bldg 10th Fl *Web:* www.lpm-adv.com/Home.aspx	Syracuse	NY	13202	315-476-1646	476-1611
Laughlin/Constable Inc 207 E Michigan St *TF:* 800-432-8747 ■ *Web:* www.laughlin.com	Milwaukee	WI	53202	414-272-2400	272-3056
Launch Agency LP 4100 Midway Rd Ste 2110 *Web:* launchagency.com	Carrollton	TX	75007	972-818-4100	
Launchpad Adv LLC 149 Fifth Ave Ninth Fl *Web:* www.lpnyc.com	New York	NY	10010	212-303-7650	
Lawrence & Schiller Inc 3932 S Willow Ave *TF:* 800-356-9377 ■ *Web:* www.l-s.com	Sioux Falls	SD	57105	605-338-8000	338-8892
Leader Promotions Inc 790 E Johnstown Rd *Web:* www.leaderpromos.com	Columbus	OH	43230	614-416-6565	
Lehman Millet Inc Two Atlantic Ave *TF:* 800-634-5315 ■ *Web:* www.lehmanmillet.com	Boston	MA	02110	800-634-5315	
Leibold Assoc 983 Ehlers Rd *Web:* www.leibold.com	Neenah	WI	54956	920-725-5328	
Leo Burnett Company Inc 35 W Wacker Dr *Web:* www.leoburnett.com	Chicago	IL	60601	312-220-5959	220-3299
Lessing-flynn Adv Co 3106 Ingersoll Ave *Web:* www.lessingflynn.com	Des Moines	IA	50312	515-274-9271	
Lewis Communications Inc 600 Meadow Brook Corp 2 *Web:* www.lewiscommunications.com	Birmingham	AL	35242	205-980-0774	437-0250
Lindsay Stone & Briggs Inc One South Pinckney St Suite 500 *TF:* 866-403-8838 ■ *Web:* www.lsb.com	Madison	WI	53703	608-251-7070	251-8989
Linnihan Foy Adv 615 First Ave Ne Ste 320 *Web:* www.linnihanfoy.com	Minneapolis	MN	55413	612-331-3586	
Liquid Adv Inc 499 Santa Clara Ave *Web:* www.liquidadvertising.com	Venice	CA	90291	310-450-2653	
Lopez Negrete Communications Inc 3336 Richmond Ave Ste 200 *Web:* www.lopeznegrete.com	Houston	TX	77098	713-877-8777	877-8796
Losasso Adv Inc 4853 N Ravenswood Ave *Web:* www.losasso.com	Chicago	IL	60640	773-271-2100	
Lost Planet Editorial 113 Spring St Fl 4 *Web:* www.quakebasket.com	New York	NY	10012	212-226-5678	
Love Adv Inc 770 S Post Oak Ln Ste 101 *Web:* www.loveadv.com	Houston	TX	77056	713-552-1055	552-9155
Lucid Fusion Inc 8935 Research Dr Ste 200 *Web:* www.lucidfusion.com	Irvine	CA	92618	949-502-7750	
Luckie & Co 600 Luckie Dr PO Box 530584 *Web:* www.luckie.com	Birmingham	AL	35223	205-879-2121	877-9713
Luquire George Andrews Inc 4201 Congress St Ste 400 *Web:* www.lgaadv.com	Charlotte	NC	28209	704-552-6565	552-1972
LyonHeart Communications Inc 220 E 42nd St Third Fl	New York	NY	10017	212-771-3000	771-3010
Mangan Holcomb Partners 2300 Cottondale Ln *Web:* www.manganholcomb.com	Little Rock	AR	72202	501-376-0321	376-6127
MARC USA 225 W Stn Sq Dr Ste 500 *Web:* www.marcusa.com	Pittsburgh	PA	15219	412-562-2000	562-2022
Marca Hispanic LLC 1320 S Dixie Hwy Ste 385 *Web:* marcamiami.com	Coral Gables	FL	33146	305-665-5410	
Marcel Media LLC 445 W Erie St Ste 211 *Web:* www.marcelmedia.com	Chicago	IL	60654	312-255-8044	
Maricich Brand Communications 18201 McDurmott W Ste A *Web:* www.maricich.com	Irvine	CA	92614	949-223-6455	
Maris West & Baker Inc 18 Northtown Dr *Web:* www.mwb.com	Jackson	MS	39211	601-977-9200	
Marketing Directions 28005 Clemens Rd *Web:* ideaswithapoint.com	Westlake	OH	44145	440-835-5550	
Marketing Support Inc 200 E Randolph Dr Ste 5000 *Web:* agencymsi.com/	Chicago	IL	60601	312-565-0044	946-6100
Mars Adv Company Inc 25200 Telegraph Rd *Web:* themarsagency.com	Southfield	MI	48034	248-936-2200	936-2501
Marshad Technology Group 99 Hudson St Fl 5 *Web:* www.marshad.com	New York	NY	10013	212-925-8656	292-8912
Marshall Adv & Design 2729 Bristol St	Costa Mesa	CA	92626	714-545-5757	
Martin Agency Inc One Shockoe Plz *Web:* www.martinagency.com	Richmond	VA	23219	804-698-8000	698-8001
Martin Thomas Inc 42 Riverside Dr **Fax Area Code:* 866 ■ *Web:* www.martinthomas.com	Barrington	RI	02806	401-245-8500	899-2710*
Martin-Williams Adv 150 S 5th st Ste 900 *TF:* 800-632-1388 ■ *Web:* www.martinwilliams.com	Minneapolis	MN	55402	612-340-0800	342-9700
Matlock Adv & Public Relations 107 Luckie St *Web:* www.matlock-adpr.com	Atlanta	GA	30303	404-872-3200	876-4929
Matthews Group Inc, The 400 Lake St *Web:* www.thematthewsgroup.com	Bryan	TX	77801	979-823-3600	
May Adv 718 Washington Ave N Ste 306 *Web:* www.mayads.com	Minneapolis	MN	55401	612-332-2450	
Mcdougall & Duval Adv Inc 24 Millyard Ste 8 *Web:* mcdougallduval.com	Amesbury	MA	01913	978-388-3100	
McKee Wallwork Cleveland LLC 1030 18th St NW *Web:* mckeewallwork.com	Albuquerque	NM	87104	505-821-2999	821-0006
McKinney 318 Blackwell St *Web:* www.mckinney.com	Durham	NC	27701	919-313-0802	313-0805
Media Buying Services Inc 4545 E Shea Blvd Ste 162 *Web:* www.mediabuyingservices.com	Phoenix	AZ	85028	602-996-2232	
Media Logic USA LLC 59 Wolf Rd *TF:* 866-353-3011 ■ *Web:* medialogic.com/	Albany	NY	12205	518-456-3015	456-4279
Media Storm LLC 99 Washington St *Web:* www.mediastorm.biz	South Norwalk	CT	06854	203-852-8001	852-0746
Media Two Interactive LLC 111 E Hargett St Ste 200 *Web:* www.mediatwo.net	Raleigh	NC	27601	919-553-1246	
Media-Max Inc 12 N Washington St *Web:* www.mediamaxinc.net	Montoursville	PA	17754	570-368-7633	
MedPoint Digital Inc 909 Davis St Ste 500 *Web:* www.medpt.com	Evanston	IL	60201	847-869-4700	
Merkley & Partners 200 Varick St 12th Fl *Web:* www.merkleyandpartners.com	New York	NY	10014	212-805-7500	
MGH Adv Inc 100 Painters Mill Rd Ste 600 *Web:* www.mghus.com	Owings Mills	MD	21117	410-902-5000	902-8712
Miller Brooks Inc 11712 N Michigan Rd *Web:* millerbrooks.com/	Zionsville	IN	46077	317-873-8100	
Mindgrub Technologies LLC 1215 E Ft Ave Ste 200 *Web:* www.mindgrub.com	Baltimore	MD	21230	410-988-2444	

Company / Address	City	State	Zip	Phone	Fax
MindShare 498 Seventh Ave *Web:* www.mindshareworld.com	New York	NY	10018	212-297-7000	297-7777
Mindstorm Communications Group Inc 10316 Feld Farm Ln Ste 200 *Web:* www.gomindstorm.com	Charlotte	NC	28210	704-331-0870	
Minnow Project a Creative Lab 815 O St Ste 3 *Web:* www.minnowproject.com	Lincoln	NE	68508	402-475-3322	
MKTG Inc 75 Ninth Ave Third Fl *OTC: CMKG* ■ *Web:* www.mktg.com	New York	NY	10011	212-366-3400	
MMG Worldwide 4601 Madison Ave *Web:* www.mmgyglobal.com	Kansas City	MO	64112	816-472-5988	471-5395
Mob Media Inc 27121 Towne Centre Dr Ste 260 *Web:* mobmedia.com	Foothill Ranch	CA	92610	949-222-0220	
Momentum Worldwide 250 Hudson St 2nd Fl *Web:* www.momentumww.com	New York	NY	10013	646-638-5400	638-5401
Moroch Partners 3625 N Hall St Ste 1100 *Web:* www.moroch.com	Dallas	TX	75219	214-520-9700	520-5611
Moses Anshell Inc 20 W Jackson St *Web:* mosesinc.com/	Phoenix	AZ	85003	602-254-7312	
MRM//McCANN 622 Third Ave *Web:* mrm-mccann.com/en/index.html	New York	NY	10017	646-865-6230	
Mthink 55 New Montgomery St Ste 617 *Web:* www.mthink.com	San Francisco	CA	94105	415-371-8800	
Mullen 40 Broad St *Web:* www.mullen.com	Boston	MA	02109	617-226-9000	226-9100
Muse Communications Inc 9543 Culver Blvd 2nd Fl **Fax Area Code:* 323 ■ *Web:* www.museusa.com	Culver City	CA	90232	310-945-4100	960-4081*
Nap I Inc 2154 W Northwest Hwy *Web:* www.napiinc.com	Dallas	TX	75220	972-401-7488	
NAS Recruitment Communications 9700 Rockside Rd Ste 170 **Fax Area Code:* 216 ■ *TF:* 866-627-7327 ■ *Web:* www.nasrecruitment.com	Cleveland	OH	44125	866-627-7327	468-8280*
Nasuti & Hinkle 7768 Woodmont Ave Ste 202 *Web:* nasuti.com	Bethesda	MD	20814	301-222-0010	
Neathawk Dubuque & Packett One E Cary St *Web:* ndp.agency	Richmond	VA	23219	804-783-8140	
Network Journal, The 39 Broadway Rm 2120 *Web:* www.tnj.com	New York	NY	10006	212-962-3791	
New Millenium Directories 1630 S Galena Ave *Web:* www.bigprintphonebook.com	Freeport	IL	61032	815-233-5797	
Newman Grace Inc 6133 Fallbrook Ave Ste 100 *Web:* www.newmangrace.com	Woodland Hls	CA	91367	818-713-1678	
Next Communications Inc 10249 Yellow Cir Dr Ste 100 *Web:* www.nextcom.com	Minnetonka	MN	55343	952-934-8220	
Norm Marshall & Assoc Inc 11059 Sherman Way *Web:* normmarshall.com	Sun Valley	CA	91352	818-982-3505	
North Charles Street Design Organization 222 W Saratoga St *Web:* www.ncsdo.com	Baltimore	MD	21201	410-539-4040	
Northlich 720 E Pete Rose Way Ste 120 *Web:* www.northlich.com	Cincinnati	OH	45202	513-421-8840	287-1858
Nowak Assoc Inc 6075 E Molloy Rd Bldg 7 *Web:* www.nowakagency.com	Syracuse	NY	13211	315-463-1001	463-7933
O'Leary & Partners 5000 Birch St Ste 1000 *Web:* www.olearyandpartners.com	Newport Beach	CA	92660	949-833-8006	833-9155
Ocean Bridge Group 1714 16th St *Web:* www.oceanbridgegroup.com	Santa Monica	CA	90404	310-392-3200	
Off Madison Ave Inc 5555 E Van Buren St Ste 215 *Web:* www.offmadisonave.com	Phoenix	AZ	85008	480-505-4500	
Ogden Publications Inc 1503 SW 42nd St *Web:* www.ogdenpubs.com	Topeka	KS	66609	785-274-4300	
Ogilvy & Mather Worldwide 636 11th Ave *Web:* www.ogilvy.com	New York	NY	10036	212-237-4000	237-5123
Ogilvy One Worldwide 636 11th Ave *Web:* www.ogilvy.com	New York	NY	10036	212-237-6000	237-6757
Olson 420 N Fifth St *Web:* olson.com	Minneapolis	MN	55401	612-215-9800	
Orange Label Art & Advrtg 4000 MacArthur Blvd Ste 520 *Web:* www.orangelabeladvertising.com	Newport Beach	CA	92660	949-631-9900	
Orangeseed Design Inc 901 N Third St Ste 305 *Web:* www.orangeseed.com	Minneapolis	MN	55401	612-252-9757	
Osborn & Barr 914 Spruce St *Web:* www.osborn-barr.com	Saint Louis	MO	63102	314-726-5511	726-6350
Overlay TV Inc 80 Aberdeen St Ste 401 *Web:* www.overlay.tv	Ottawa	ON	K1S5R5	613-761-6152	
Pacific Communications 575 Anton Blvd Ste 900 *Web:* www.pacificcommunications.com/	Costa Mesa	CA	92626	714-427-1900	
Pacifico Inc 1190 Coleman Ave Ste 110 *Web:* www.pacifico.com	San Jose	CA	95110	408-327-8888	
Page 1 Solutions LLC 17301 W Colfax Ave Ste 275 *Web:* www.page1solutions.com	Golden	CO	80401	303-233-3886	
Paradise Adv & Mktg Inc 150 Second Ave N Ste 800 *Web:* www.paradiseadv.com	Saint Petersburg	FL	33701	727-821-5155	
Parkerwhite Inc 230 Birmingham Dr *Web:* www.parkerwhite.com	Cardiff By The Sea	CA	92007	760-783-2020	
Partners Riley 1375 Euclid Ave Ste 410 *Web:* www.mradvertising.com	Cleveland	OH	44115	216-241-2141	
Patient Recruiting Agency LLC, The 6207 Bee Cave Rd Ste 288 *Web:* tpra.com	Austin	TX	78746	512-345-7788	
Pavone Inc 1006 Market St *Web:* www.pavone.net	Harrisburg	PA	17101	717-234-8886	
Pedone 49 W 27th St *Web:* www.pedonepartners.com	New York	NY	10001	212-627-3300	627-3966
Penna Powers Brian Haynes Inc 1706 S Major St *Web:* www.ppbh.com	Salt Lake City	UT	84115	801-487-4800	
Penny Ohlmann Neiman Inc 1605 N Main St *Web:* ohlmanngroup.com	Dayton	OH	45405	937-278-0681	277-1723
Periscope Inc 921 Washington Ave S *Web:* www.periscope.com	Minneapolis	MN	55415	612-399-0500	399-0600
Peterson Milla Hooks 1315 Harmon Pl *Web:* www.pmhadv.com	Minneapolis	MN	55403	612-349-9116	349-9141
Petrol Adv Inc 443 N Varney St *Web:* petrolad.com	Burbank	CA	91502	323-644-3720	
Phelps Group, The 901 Wilshire Blvd *Web:* phelpsagency.com	Santa Monica	CA	90401	310-752-4400	752-4444
PJA Adv & Mktg 12 Arrow St *Web:* www.agencypja.com	Cambridge	MA	02138	617-492-5899	
PKA Marketing 1009 W Glen Oaks Ln Ste 107 *Web:* pkamar.publishpath.com/	Mequon	WI	53092	262-241-9414	241-9454
Plan b 116 W Illinois St Fl 2W *Web:* www.thisisplanb.com	Chicago	IL	60654	312-222-0303	
Plowshare Group Inc One Dock St *Web:* www.plowsharegroup.com	Stamford	CT	06902	203-425-3949	
Pm Group Inc, The 7550 W Interstate 10 Ste 500 *Web:* thepmgrp.com	San Antonio	TX	78229	210-490-2554	490-5496
Point to Point Inc 23240 Chagrin Blvd Ste 200 *Web:* www.p2pcom.com	Cleveland	OH	44122	216-831-4421	
Posner Adv 30 Broad St *Web:* www.posneradv.com	New York	NY	10004	212-867-3900	480-3440
Post No Bills Inc 801 Gervais St *Web:* www.postnobills.com	Columbia	SC	29201	803-254-4334	
Power Creative 11701 Commonwealth Dr *Web:* www.powercreative.com	Louisville	KY	40299	502-267-0772	
Prime Adv & Design Inc 7351 Kirkwood Ln N Ste 144 *Web:* www.primeadvertising.com	Maple Grove	MN	55369	763-424-9406	
Princeton Partners Inc 205 Rockingham Row *Web:* www.princetonpartners.com	Princeton	NJ	08540	609-452-8500	452-7212
Proact Marketing Group Inc 2604 Ne Industrial Dr Ste 270 *Web:* www.proactmarketing.com	Kansas City	MO	64117	816-472-9898	
Product Mktg Group Inc 978 Douglas Ave *Web:* eternalmessage.com	Altamonte Springs	FL	32714	407-774-6363	
ProEd Communications Inc 25101 Chagrin Blvd Ste 230 *Web:* www.proedcom.com	Beachwood	OH	44122	216-595-7919	
Publicis & Hal Riney 2001 Embarcadero *Web:* www.hrp.com	San Francisco	CA	94133	415-293-2001	
Publicis Touchpoint Solutions Inc 1000 Floral Vale Blvd Ste 400 *Web:* www.touchpointsolutions.com	Yardley	PA	19067	215-525-9800	
Publicis USA 950 Sixth Ave *Web:* publicisna.com/	New York	NY	10001	212-279-5550	
Purchase Planners Group Inc 801 S Grand Ave Ste 425 *Web:* www.ppg-la.com	Los Angeles	CA	90017	213-687-4206	
Purematter 350 W Julian St Bldg 3 *Web:* www.purematter.com	San Jose	CA	95110	408-297-7800	
R2c Group Inc 207 NW Pk Ave *Web:* www.r2cgroup.com	Portland	OR	97209	503-222-0025	276-4096
Rabinovici & Assoc Inc 800 Silks Run Ste 2320 *Web:* www.rabinovicionline.com	Hallandale	FL	33009	305-655-0021	
Rare Method 1812 Fourth St SW Ste 500 *Web:* rareresults.ca	Calgary	AB	T2S1W1	403-543-4500	532-3004
Rdw Group Inc 125 Holden St *Web:* www.rdwgroup.com	Providence	RI	02908	401-521-2700	521-0014
Re Group Inc 213 W Liberty St Ste 100 *Web:* www.regroup.us	Ann Arbor	MI	48104	734-213-0200	
ReachLocal Inc 21700 Oxnard St Ste 1600 *NASDAQ: RLOC* ■ *Web:* www.reachlocal.com	Woodland Hills	CA	91367	818-274-0260	
Red Tettemer Inc One S Broad St 24th Fl *Web:* rtop.com/	Philadelphia	PA	19107	267-402-1410	
Redstone Communications Group Inc 10031 Maple St *Web:* www.redstoneweb.com	Omaha	NE	68134	402-393-5435	
Redux Media Inc 468 St-Jean St Ste 301 *Web:* www.reduxmedia.com	Montreal	QC	H2Y2S1	514-866-4343	
Regan Group, The 4895 W 147th St *Web:* www.therегangroup.com	Hawthorne	CA	90250	310-675-6161	
Regency Outdoor Adv Inc 8820 Sunset Blvd Second Fl *Web:* www.regencyoutdoor.com	West Hollywood	CA	90069	310-657-8883	
Regina Villa Associates Inc 51 Franklin St Ste 400 *Web:* www.reginavilla.com	Boston	MA	02110	617-357-5772	
Register Tapes Unlimited Inc 1445 Langham Creek *TF:* 800-247-4793 ■ *Web:* www.rtui.com	Houston	TX	77084	281-206-2500	492-6390
Reply Inc 12667 Alcosta Blvd Ste 200 *TF:* 888-466-8677 ■ *Web:* www.reply.com	San Ramon	CA	94583	925-983-3400	
Research Horizons LLC 6423 Montgomery St Ste 12 *Web:* www.phoenixmi.com	Rhinebeck	NY	12572	845-876-8228	
Resource Interactive 343 N Front St *Web:* www.resource.com	Columbus	OH	43215	614-621-2888	621-2873

Company	City	State	Zip	Phone	Fax
Revolution Agency Inc 1210 E Windsor Ave *Web:* revolutionagency.com	Phoenix	AZ	85006	602-956-5465	
Rhea & Kaiser 400 E Diehl Rd Ste 500 *Web:* www.rkconnect.com	Naperville	IL	60563	630-505-1100	505-1109
RHR Adpro Adv LLC 105 Library Rd *Web:* adpro-ads.com	Dover	AR	72837	479-331-2526	
Richard Harrison Bailey Inc 121 S Niles Ave *Web:* www.rhb.com	South Bend	IN	46617	574-287-8333	
Richards Group 8750 N Central Expy Ste 1200 *Web:* www.richards.com	Dallas	TX	75231	214-891-5700	891-5230
Richards/Carlberg 1900 W Loop S Ste 1100 *Web:* www.richardscarlberg.com	Houston	TX	77027	713-965-0764	965-0135
Riley Hayes Adv 333 S First St *Web:* www.rileyhayes.com	Minneapolis	MN	55401	612-338-7161	
Risdall Adv Agency 550 Main St *TF:* 888-747-3255 ■ *Web:* www.risdall.com	New Brighton	MN	55112	651-286-6700	631-2561
Ritta & Assoc 568 Grand Ave *Web:* www.ritta.com	Englewood	NJ	07631	201-567-4400	
RMD Adv 6116 Cleveland Ave *Web:* www.rmdadvertising.com	Columbus	OH	43231	614-794-2008	
Roberts Communications Inc 64 Commercial St *Web:* www.robertscomm.com	Rochester	NY	14614	585-325-6000	325-6001
Ron Foth Adv 8100 N High St *TF:* 888-766-3684 ■ *Web:* www.ronfoth.com	Columbus	OH	43235	614-888-7771	888-5933
Rubin Postaer & Assoc 2525 Colorado Ave *Web:* www.rpa.com	Santa Monica	CA	90404	310-394-4000	
Saatchi & Saatchi 375 Hudson St *Web:* www.saatchiny.com	New York	NY	10014	212-463-2000	463-9856
Sagon Phior 2107 Sawtelle Blvd *Web:* sagonphior.com	Los Angeles	CA	90025	310-575-4441	
Salva O'renick 1810 Cherry St *Web:* www.uncommonsense.com	Kansas City	MO	64108	816-842-6996	
Sanders/Wingo Adv Inc 221 N Kansas Ste 900 *Web:* www.sanderswingo.com	El Paso	TX	79901	915-533-9583	533-3601
Sawtooth Group 141 W Front St *Web:* www.sawtoothgroup.com	Red Bank	NJ	07701	732-945-1004	
SBC Adv Ltd 333 W Nationwide Blvd *Web:* www.sbcadvertising.com	Columbus	OH	43215	614-255-2333	255-2600
Scott Howell & Company Inc 3900 Willow St Ste 200 *Web:* www.scott-howell.com	Dallas	TX	75226	214-951-9494	688-0555
Seiden Group 112 Madison Ave *Web:* www.seidenadvertising.com	New York	NY	10016	212-223-8700	
Serino Coyne Inc 1515 Broadway 36th Fl *Web:* www.serinocoyne.com	New York	NY	10036	212-626-2700	626-2799
Seven Dials Media 2449 Wendover Dr	Naperville	IL	60565	630-355-6199	
Shaker Recruitment Adv & Communications 1100 Lake St Third Fl *TF:* 800-323-5170 ■ *Web:* www.shaker.com	Oak Park	IL	60301	708-383-5320	
Sheehy & Assoc 2297 Lexington Rd *Web:* www.sheehy1.com	Louisville	KY	40206	502-456-9007	
Sherry Matthews Inc 200 S Congress Ave *TF:* 877-478-4397 ■ *Web:* www.sherrymatthews.com	Austin	TX	78704	512-478-4397	478-4978
Shumsky Enterprises Inc 811 E Fourth St *TF:* 800-223-2203 ■ *Web:* www.shumsky.com	Dayton	OH	45402	937-223-2203	223-2252
SIDES & Assoc Inc 222 Jefferson St Ste B PO Box 3267 *Web:* www.sides.com	Lafayette	LA	70501	337-233-6473	233-6485
Siegel & Gale 625 Ave of the Americas 4th Fl *TF:* 800-356-9377 ■ *Web:* siegelgale.com	New York	NY	10011	212-453-0400	453-0401
Sierra Select Distributors 4320 Roseville Rd *Web:* www.sierraselect.com	North Highlands	CA	95660	916-483-9295	
Simon Group Inc, The 1506 Old Bethlehem Pk *Web:* www.simongroup.com	Sellersville	PA	18960	215-453-8700	
Sksw Adv 1255 W 15th St Ste 800 *Web:* sksw.com	Plano	TX	75075	972-424-3000	424-3011
Sky Adv Inc 14 E 33rd St APT 7s *Web:* www.skyad.com	New York	NY	10016	212-677-2500	677-2791
Slingshot LLC 208 N Market St Ste 500 *Web:* www.slingshotllc.com	Dallas	TX	75202	214-634-4411	634-5511
Source Communications Inc 433 Hackensack Ave 8th Fl *Web:* www.sourcead.com	Hackensack	NJ	07601	201-343-5222	343-5710
SPAR Group Inc 560 White Plains Rd *NASDAQ: SGRP* ■ *TF:* 800-314-7727 ■ *Web:* www.sparinc.com	Tarrytown	NY	10591	914-332-4100	332-0741
Spawn Ideas Inc 808 E St *Web:* spawnak.com/	Anchorage	AK	99501	907-274-9553	
SPM Marketing & Communications 15 W Harris Ave Ste 300 *Web:* www.spmadvertising.com	La Grange	IL	60525	708-246-7700	
Springer Mktg & Adv 65 Wilkie Way *Web:* www.springermktadv.com	Fletcher	NC	28732	828-687-0334	
Stackpole & Partners Ltd 222 Merrimac St *Web:* www.stackpolepartners.com	Newburyport	MA	01950	978-463-6600	
Stephan & Brady Inc 1850 Hoffman St PO Box 1588 *Web:* www.stephanbrady.com	Madison	WI	53704	608-241-4141	241-4246
Stephenz Group Inc, The 75 E Santa Clara St Ste 900 *Web:* www.stephenz.com	San Jose	CA	95113	408-286-9899	
Sterling-Rice Group, The (SRG) 1801 13th St Ste 400 *Web:* www.srg.com	Boulder	CO	80302	303-381-6400	444-6637
Stern Adv Inc 29125 Chagrin Blvd Ste 300 *Web:* www.sternadvertising.com	Cleveland	OH	44113	216-464-4850	464-4512
Stone & Ward Inc 225 E Markham St *Web:* www.stoneward.com	Little Rock	AR	72201	501-375-3003	375-8314

Company	City	State	Zip	Phone	Fax
Streamworks LLC 3770 Dunlap St N *Web:* www.expedite-dmf.com	Arden Hills	MN	55112	651-486-0252	
Sudler & Hennessey 230 Pk Ave S **Fax:* Hum Res ■ *Web:* www.sudler.com	New York	NY	10003	212-614-4100	598-6907*
Sullivan Higdon & Sink Inc 255 N Mead *Web:* www.wehatesheep.com	Wichita	KS	67202	316-263-0124	263-7017
Swanson Russell 1222 P St *Web:* www.swansonrussell.com	Lincoln	NE	68508	402-437-6400	437-6401
TBWA Chiat/Day Inc 488 Madison Ave *Web:* tbwachiatday.com	New York	NY	10022	212-804-1000	804-1200
TDG Communications Inc 93 Sherman St *Web:* www.tdgcommunications.com	Deadwood	SD	57732	605-722-7111	
Team One 13031 W Jefferson Blvd Ste 700 *Web:* www.teamone-usa.com	Los Angeles	CA	90094	310-437-2500	322-7565
Thayer Media Inc 9000 E Nichols Ave Ste 202 *Web:* www.thayermedia.com	Centennial	CO	80112	303-221-2221	
Thomasarts Inc 240 South 200 West *Web:* www.thomasarts.com	Farmington	UT	84025	801-451-5365	
Thompson Marketing 70 NE Loop 410 Ste 1050 *Web:* www.thompsonmarketinginc.com	San Antonio	TX	78216	210-349-9925	
Tinsley Adv 2000 S Dixie Hwy *TF:* 800-432-2242 ■ *Web:* www.tinsley.com	Miami	FL	33133	305-856-6060	858-3877
Topin & Associates Inc 205 N Michigan Ave Ste 2315 *Web:* www.topin.com	Chicago	IL	60601	312-645-0100	
Trahan Burden & Charles Inc (TBC) 900 S Wolfe St *Web:* www.tbc.us	Baltimore	MD	21231	410-347-7500	986-1299
Treasure Valley Reminder 1160 Sw Fourth St *Web:* www.argusobserver.com	Ontario	OR	97914	541-889-5387	
Tribal DDB Worldwide 437 Madison Ave Eighth Fl *Web:* tribalworldwide.com	New York	NY	10022	212-515-8600	515-8660
Trolex Corp 55-57 Bushes Ln *Web:* www.trolexcorp.com	Elmwood Park	NJ	07407	201-794-8004	
Trone 1823 Eastchester Dr *TF:* 877-493-3043 ■ *Web:* www.tronebrandenergy.com	High Point	NC	27265	336-886-1622	886-4242
Unit 7 30 Irving Pl Fl 11	New York	NY	10003	212-209-1600	
UniWorld Group Inc 1 Metro Ctr N *TF:* 800-900-2958 ■ *Web:* uwg.is	Brooklyn	NY	11201	212-219-1600	219-6395
Verso Adv Inc 50 W 17th St Fl 5	New York	NY	10011	212-292-2990	
VIA Agency 619 Congress St *Web:* www.theviaagency.com	Portland	ME	04101	207-221-3000	761-9422
Vidal Partnership Inc, The 228 E 45th St Fl 14 *Web:* www.vidalpartnership.com	New York	NY	10017	212-867-5185	
Vistacomm 1401 N C Ave	Sioux Falls	SD	57104	605-977-2100	
VML Inc 250 NW RichaRds Rd *TF:* 800-990-2468 ■ *Web:* www.vml.com	Kansas City	MO	64116	816-283-0700	283-0954
Vox Medica Inc 601 Walnut St Ste 250-S *TF:* 800-842-6482 ■ *Web:* www.voxmedica.com	Philadelphia	PA	19106	215-238-8500	592-7748
Walker Brand Communication 1810 W Kennedy Blvd *Web:* www.walkerbrands.com	Tampa	FL	33606	813-875-3322	
Wasserman Media Group LLC 10960 Wilshire Blvd Ste 2200 *Web:* www.wmgllc.com	Los Angeles	CA	90024	310-407-0200	407-0300
Weintraub Adv Inc 7745 Carondelet Ave *Web:* www.weintraubadv.com	Saint Louis	MO	63105	314-721-5050	721-6850
West Orange Times, The 720 S Dillard St *Web:* www.wotimes.com	Winter Garden	FL	34787	407-656-2121	
White & Partners Inc 13665 Dulles Tech Dr Ste 150 *Web:* white64.com/	Herndon	VA	20171	703-793-3000	793-1495
Whitespace Creative Inc 24 N High St Ste 200 *Web:* www.whitespace-creative.com	Akron	OH	44308	330-762-9320	
Wieden & Kennedy 224 NW 13th Ave *Web:* www.wk.com	Portland	OR	97209	503-937-7000	937-8000
Williams & Assoc Inc 247 S Wilmot Rd *Web:* www.wasoc.com	Tucson	AZ	85711	520-745-8500	
Williams Whittle Assoc Inc 711 Princess St *Web:* www.williamswhittle.com	Alexandria	VA	22314	703-836-9222	684-3285
Wingate Healthcare Inc 63 Kendrick St *Web:* www.wingate.com	Needham	MA	02494	781-707-9500	
WM Martin Adv Inc 6705 Levelland Rd Ste A *Web:* www.wmmadv.com	Dallas	TX	75252	972-732-8040	
World 50 Inc 3525 Piedmont Rd NE Bldg 7-600 *Web:* www.w50.com	Atlanta	GA	30305	404-816-5559	
WPP Group USA Inc 125 Pk Ave Fourth Fl *Web:* www.wpp.com	New York	NY	10017	212-632-2200	632-2222
WYSE Adv 668 Euclid Ave *Web:* wyseadv.com	Cleveland	OH	44114	216-696-2424	
Zazoom 7600 E Doubletree Ranch Rd Ste 1	Scottsdale	AZ	85258	480-998-3200	
Zubi Adv Services Inc 2990 Ponce De Leon Blvd Sixth Fl *Web:* www.zubiad.com	Coral Gables	FL	33134	305-448-9824	

ADVERTISING DISPLAYS

SEE Signs p. 3174; Displays - Exhibit & Trade Show p. 2202; Displays - Point-of-Purchase p. 2203

5 ADVERTISING SERVICES - DIRECT MAIL

Company	City	State	Zip	Phone	Fax
29 Prime Inc 9701 Jeronimo Rd *TF:* 888-513-7746 ■ *Web:* www.29prime.com	Irvine	CA	92618	888-513-7746	

Phone Fax

3D2B Inc 80-02 Kew Gardens Rd Ste 903 Kew Gardens NY 11415 718-709-0900
Web: www.3d2b.com

3DShopping.com 28th Fl US Bank Tower Los Angeles CA 90071 800-442-5299
TF: 800-442-5299 ■ *Web:* www.3dshopping.com

4Mads 834 Bush St Ste A San Francisco CA 94108 415-795-3686
Web: 4mads.com

614 Media Group Inc 458 E Main St Columbus OH 43215 614-488-4400
Web: www.614mediagroup.com

A m Mailing Services Inc
100 Interstate Blvd Edgerton WI 53534 608-884-3452
Web: www.ammailing.com

Aa Temps Inc 7002 little river tpke Annandale VA 22003 703-642-9050
Web: www.ardelle.com

Access Direct Systems Inc
91 Executive Blvd Farmingdale NY 11735 631-420-0770 420-1647
Web: accessdirect.com

Access Worldwide Inc
5192 Southridge Pkwy Ste 112 Atlanta GA 30349 404-675-0633
Web: www.accessworldwide.net

Accurate Mailings Inc 215 O'Neill Ave Belmont CA 94002 650-508-8885
TF: 800-732-3290 ■ *Web:* www.accuratemailings.com

Accutrend Data Corp
7860 E Berry Pl Ste 200 Greenwood Village CO 80111 303-488-0011
Web: www.newbusinessreporter.com

Action Mailing Corp 3165 W Heartland Dr Liberty MO 64068 816-415-9000
Web: action-mailing.com

Acxiom Corp 601 E Third St Little Rock AR 72201 501-342-7799
NASDAQ: ACXM ■ *TF:* 888-337-7699 ■ *Web:* www.acxiom.com

Ad-mail Inc 905 Nw 17th Ave Portland OR 97209 503-223-1101
Web: www.admailinc.com

adhesive.co LLC
7272 E Indian School Rd Ste 102 Scottsdale AZ 85251 480-339-4700
Web: adhesive.co

AdKarma LLC 3806 Buttonwood Dr Ste 101 Columbia MO 65201 573-446-7366
Web: adkarma.net

ADS Media Group Inc
15265 Capital Port Ste 100 San Antonio TX 78249 210-655-6613
Web: www.adsmediagroup.com

Adtron Inc 1700 Morrissey Dr Bloomington IL 61704 309-662-1221 663-6691

Advance Design Inc
7100 E Vly Green Rd Fort Washington PA 19034 215-774-1000
Web: www.advancewebdesign.com

Advanced Distributor Products LLC
2175 W Park Pl Blvd Stone Mountain GA 30087 770-465-5560
Web: www.adpnow.com

Adventist Media Center Inc
101 W Cochran St Simi Valley CA 93065 805-955-7777
Web: www.adventistmediacenter.com

Adviso Consulting Inc 909 Mont-Royal E Montreal QC H2J1X3 514-598-1881
Web: www.adviso.ca

Adwerx Inc 307 W Main St Durham NC 27701 888-746-5678
TF: 888-746-5678 ■ *Web:* www.adwerx.com

Adzzup LLC 8240 S Kyrene Rd Ste 101 Tempe AZ 85284 888-723-9987
TF: 888-723-9987 ■ *Web:* adzzup.com

Agency Revolution 698 NW Bend OR 97701 800-606-0477
TF: 800-606-0477 ■ *Web:* www.agencyrevolution.com

Aid Mailing & Fulfillment
2594 Leghorn St Mountain View CA 94043 650-919-1999
Web: aidmail.com

Airbrush Action Inc PO Box 438 Allenwood NJ 08720 732-223-7878
Web: www.airbrushaction.com

AKT Enterprises 6424 Forest City Rd Orlando FL 32810 877-306-3651
TF: 877-306-3651 ■ *Web:* www.aktenterprises.com

Alaska Laser Printing & Mailing Services
165 E 56th Ave Anchorage AK 99518 907-561-8000
Web: www.alaskalaserprint.com

All Direct Mail Services Inc 15392 Cobalt St Sylmar CA 91342 818-833-7773

All Needs Computer & Mailing Services Inc
8100 S 13th St Lincoln NE 68512 402-421-1083
Web: www.ancms.com

Allstyle Coil Company LP 7037 Brittmore Dr Houston TX 77041 713-466-6333
Web: www.allstyle.com

American List Counsel Inc 4300 US Hwy 1 Princeton NJ 08543 609-580-2800 580-2888
Web: www.alc.com

American Mailers - Illinois Inc
820 Frontenac Rd Naperville IL 60563 630-579-8800
Web: anetorder.us

American Target Advertising Inc
9625 Surveyor Ct Ste 400 Manassas VA 20110 703-396-6940
Web: www.nonprofitprosperity.com

Americomm 804 Greenbrier Cir Chesapeake VA 23320 757-622-2724 624-5713
TF: 800-527-6757 ■ *Web:* americommllc.com/

Ameripack Inc 107 N Gold Dr Robbinsville NJ 08691 609-259-7004 259-8975
TF: 800-456-7963 ■ *Web:* www.ameripack.com

Ami 4407 Wheeler Ave Alexandria VA 22304 703-370-4606
Web: amidirect.com

Andrew Associates Inc Six Pearson Way Enfield CT 06082 860-253-0000
Web: www.andrewmail.com

Ansira Inc 2300 Locust St Saint Louis MO 63103 314-783-2300
Web: www.thenationalsystem.com

AnswersMedia Inc 30 N Racine Ave Ste 300 Chicago IL 60607 312-421-0113
Web: www.answersmediainc.com

Argonaut Inc 576 Folsom St San Francisco CA 94105 415-633-8200
Web: www.argonautinc.com

Arista Information Systems Inc
1105 Fairchild Rd Winston-Salem NC 27105 336-776-1105 776-1104
Web: www.aristainfo.com

Ballantine Corp, The 1700 State Rt 23 Ste 350 Wayne NJ 07470 973-305-1500
Web: ballantine.com

Bancroft & Sons Transportation Inc
3390 High Prairie Rd Grand Prairie TX 75050 972-790-3777 986-0347
Web: www.bancroftandsons.com

BBDO Chicago Inc 410 N Michigan Ave Chicago IL 60611 312-337-7860
Web: www.energybbdo.com

Bindery Associates Inc 2025 Horseshoe Rd Lancaster PA 17602 717-295-7443
Web: www.binderyassociates.com

Blow Me Away Media Corp 229 N Sherman Ave Corona CA 92882 951-299-6595
Web: www.blowmeawaymedia.tv

Blue Interactive Agency
608 SW Fourth Ave Fort Lauderdale FL 33315 954-779-2801
Web: www.blueinteractiveagency.com

BlueSpire Strategic Marketing
7650 Edinborough Way Ste 500 Minneapolis MN 55435 800-727-6397
TF: 800-727-6397 ■ *Web:* bluespiremarketing.com

Boostability Inc
2600 West Executive Pkwy Ste 200 Lehi UT 84043 800-261-1537
TF: 800-261-1537 ■ *Web:* www.boostability.com

Booth 4004 Los Feliz Blvd Los Angeles CA 90027 323-805-0150
Web: www.boothco.com

Brand.net Inc 208 Utah St Ste 210 San Francisco CA 94103 415-216-4152
Web: www.brand.net

Brierley & Partners 5465 Legacy Dr Ste 300 Plano TX 75024 214-760-8700 743-5511
TF: 800-899-8700 ■ *Web:* www.brierley.com

Bruen Productions International Inc
5235 Gulf Stream Court Second Fl Loveland CO 80538 970-593-6300
Web: www.bruen.com

BuildCentral Inc 200 W Madison St Ste 1110 Chicago IL 60606 312-223-1600
Web: www.buildcentral.com

Bulldog Solutions LLC
7600 N Capital of Texas Hwy Bldg C Ste 250 Austin TX 78731 877-402-9199
TF: 877-402-9199 ■ *Web:* www.bulldogsolutions.com

Burdiss Lettershop Services Co 9765 Widmer Rd Lenexa KS 66215 913-492-0545
Web: www.burdiss.com

Cactus Mailing Co 16121 N 78th St Ste 103 Scottsdale AZ 85260 480-443-1442
Web: www.cactusmailing.com

Calmark Inc 1400 W 44th St Chicago IL 60609 773-247-7200

Cardenas Marketing Network Inc
1459 W Hubbard St Chicago IL 60642 312-492-6424
Web: www.cmnevents.com

Cardlytics Inc
675 Ponce de Leon Ave NE Ste 6000 Atlanta GA 30308 888-798-5802
TF: 888-798-5802 ■ *Web:* www.cardlytics.com

Carl Bloom Assoc Inc 81 Main St Ste 126 White Plains NY 10601 914-761-2800 761-2744
Web: www.carlbloom.com

Cass Data & Mailing Services Inc
26 Eglin Pkwy Se Ste 4 Fort Walton Beach FL 32548 850-862-5110
Web: cassdata.com

Catalina Marketing Corp
200 Carillon Pkwy Saint Petersburg FL 33716 727-579-5000 556-2700
TF: 888-322-3814 ■ *Web:* www.catalinamarketing.com

Catawba Print & Mail Inc 1215 15th St Dr Ne Hickory NC 28601 828-324-2021
Web: www.catawbamail.com

Centron Data Services Inc
1175 Devin Dr Norton Shores MI 49441 800-732-8787 799-0092*
**Fax Area Code:* 231 ■ *TF Cust Svc:* 800-732-8787 ■ *Web:* www.centrondata.com

Century Direct LLC
30-00 47th Ave Third Fl Long Island City NY 11101 212-763-0600 349-9528*
**Fax Area Code:* 718 ■ *Web:* www.centurydirect.net

Cenveo Inc 201 Broad St 1 Canterberry Green Stamford CT 06901 203-595-3000 595-3070
NYSE: CVO ■ *Web:* www.cenveo.com

Ces Mail Communications Inc
2319 Atlantic Ave Raleigh NC 27604 919-833-5785
Web: www.cesmail.com

Ciplex 6121 Santa Monica Blvd Ste A Los Angeles CA 90038 310-461-0330
Web: www.ciplex.com

Club Marketing Services Inc
101 W Central Bentonville AR 72712 479-696-3100
Web: www.clubmarketing.com

Cohen & Company Creative Inc
12002 Miramar Pkwy Ste C Miramar FL 33025 954-923-8133
Web: www.cohenadv.com

Colorado Data Mail Inc 2525 W Fourth Ave Denver CO 80219 303-629-6155
Web: www.coloradodatamail.com

Comark Direct 507 S Main St Ft. Worth TX 76104 888-742-0405
TF: 888-742-0405 ■ *Web:* comarkdirect.com

Crispin Porter & Bogusky LLC
3390 Mary St Ste 300 Coconut Grove Miami FL 33133 305-859-2070
Web: www.cpbgroup.com

Critical Mass Inc 1011 Ninth Ave SE Ste 300 Calgary AB T2G0H7 403-262-3006
Web: www.criticalmass.com

Cruising Gide Publications Inc
1130 Pinehurst Rd Ste B Dunedin FL 34698 727-733-5322
Web: www.cruisingguides.com

CSE, Inc. 5400 S Wridge Dr New Berlin WI 53151 262-786-8400
Web: www.csepromo.com

CSG Direct Inc 640 Maestro Dr Ste 100 Reno NV 89511 775-852-9777
Web: www.csgdirect.com

CTM Media Group Inc 11 Largo Dr S Stamford CT 06907 203-323-5161
Web: www.ctmmediagroup.com

CTRAC Computer Services Inc
16855 Foltz Pkwy Strongsville OH 44149 440-572-1000 572-3330
Web: www.ctrac.com

Current360 1324 E Washington St Louisville KY 40206 502-589-3567
Web: current360.com

Custom Direct Inc 715 E Irving Park Rd Roselle IL 60172 630-529-1936
Web: www.customdirect.com

Data & Mailing Resources Inc 4929 Blalock Rd Houston TX 77041 713-426-1550
Web: www.dmr-inc.net

DB Studios Inc 17032 Murphy Ave Irvine CA 92614 949-833-0100
Web: dbstudios.com

DB5 202 N Ave 64 Los Angeles CA 90042 646-884-3940
Web: www.dogsbollocks5.com

Deans Mailing & List Services Inc
3015 W Weldon Ave Phoenix AZ 85017 602-272-2100
Web: www.deansmailing.com

Phone Fax

Delucchi Plus LLC 2101 L St NW Ste 650 .... Washington DC 20037 202-349-4000
Web: www.delucchiplus.com
Digital Operative
3990 Old Town Ave Ste C300 .... San Diego CA 92110 619-795-0630
Web: www.digitaloperative.com
Diji Integrated Press 4920 W Cypress St Ste 100 .... Tampa FL 33607 813-289-1660
Web: www.dijipress.com
Direct Mail Processors Inc 1150 Conrad Ct .... Hagerstown MD 21740 301-714-4700
Web: www.directmailprocessors.com
Direct Resource Solutions LLC 6912 N 97th Cir .... Omaha NE 68122 402-991-2810
Web: www.uaaclearinghouse.com
DirectMailcom 201 Skipjack Rd .... Prince Frederick MD 20678 301-855-1700
TF: 866-284-5816 ■ *Web:* www.directmail.com
DL Blair Inc 400 Post Ave Ste 400 .... Westbury NY 11590 516-746-3700 746-3889
Web: www.dlblair.com
DMG|Bluegill
920 Volunteer Landing Ln Ste 201 .... Knoxville TN 37915 865-584-9740
Web: www.dmgbluegill.com
DMNmedia 508 Young St .... Dallas TX 75202 214-842-6864
Web: dmnmedia.com
Dms 100 S Keowee St .... Dayton OH 45402 937-222-5056
Web: www.daytonmailing.com
DMW Worldwide LLC 701 Lee Rd Ste 103 .... Chesterbrook PA 19087 610-407-0407 407-0410
Web: www.dmwdirect.com
DogTime Media Inc 27 Maiden Ln Ste 700 .... San Francisco CA 94108 415-830-9300
Web: dogtimemedia.com
DOMOREGOOD 25 Ottawa Ave SW Ste 600 .... Grand Rapids MI 49503 616-776-1111
Web: www.hanon-mckendry.com
Dove Mailing Inc
5601 Fulton Industrial Blvd Sw .... Atlanta GA 30336 404-629-0122
Web: www.dovemailing.com
Dp Murphy Company Inc 945 Grand Blvd .... Deer Park NY 11729 631-673-9400
Web: dpmurphy.com
Dynamicard 10085 Carroll Canyon Rd Ste 101 .... San Diego CA 92131 858-928-7670
Web: www.dynamicard.com
egc group Inc, The
1175 Walt Whitman Rd Ste 200 .... Melville NY 11747 516-935-4944
Web: www.egcgroup.com
eLocal Listing LLC
28765 Single Oak Dr Ste 250 .... Temecula CA 92590 800-285-0484
TF: 800-285-0484 ■ *Web:* www.elocallisting.com
ELS Marketing Inc 3133 Orlando Dr .... Mississauga ON L4V1C5 905-612-1060
Web: www.corelogistics.net
Encompass Media Inc 28 E 28th St Ninth Fl .... New York NY 10016 212-993-9429
Web: emgmediainc.com
Engageclick 430 Sherman Ave .... Palo Alto CA 94306 650-328-2000
Web: engageclick.com
Envoy Inc 6910 Pacific St Ste 102 .... Omaha NE 68106 402-558-0637
Web: www.envoyinc.com
EQ Inc 1255 Bay St Ste 400 .... Toronto ON M5R2A9 416-597-8889
Web: www.cyberplex.com
EventPro Strategies LLC
7373 E Stetson Dr Ste B120 .... Scottsdale AZ 85251 480-449-4100 283-1190
Web: www.eventprostrategies.com
eVision LLC 179 E Main St .... Branford CT 06405 203-481-8005
Web: www.evisionsem.com
EWI Worldwide Inc 13211 Merriman Rd .... Livonia MI 48150 734-525-9010
Web: www.ewiworldwide.com
eWinery Solutions 1700 Soscol Ave Ste 3 .... Napa CA 94559 707-253-7400
Web: www.ewinerysolutions.com
eyeReturn Marketing
110 Eglinton Ave E Ste 705 .... Toronto ON M4P2Y1 416-929-4834
Web: www.eyereturnmarketing.com
Family Benefits Marketing Co
3403 N Ridge Ave .... Arlington Heights IL 60004 847-368-1423
Web: www.fbmc-usa.com
Farmer, Lumpe & Mcclelland Advertising Agency Ltd
500 W Wilson Bridge Rd Ste 316 .... Worthington OH 43085 614-601-5195
Web: www.wideopenthinking.com
FFF Enterprises Inc 41093 County Ctr Dr .... Temecula CA 92591 951-296-2500
TF: 800-843-7477 ■ *Web:* www.fffenterprises.com
Focus Direct LLC 9707 Broadway .... San Antonio TX 78217 210-805-9185 247-1691
TF: 800-555-1551 ■ *Web:* mysanantonio.com
Forthea 3355 W Alabama St Ste 1230 .... Houston TX 77098 713-568-2763
Web: www.forthea.com
Frampton Mailing Systems 450 Horton St E .... London ON N6B1M3 519-680-6245
Web: fms.ca
Franklin Press Inc 1391 Highland Rd .... Baton Rouge LA 70802 225-387-0504
Web: gofranklingo.com/
FUEL Digital Marketing & Branding
25 E Court St Ste 202 .... Greenville SC 29601 864-627-1676
Web: www.fuelingbrands.com
Full E-media Marketing Inc PO Box 1446 .... San Clemente CA 92674 949-940-0198
Web: www.fullemedia.com
Funnel Science Internet Marketing LLC
1802 N Carson St .... Carson City NV 89701 877-301-0001
TF: 877-301-0001 ■ *Web:* www.funnelscience.com
Fusion Imaging inc 601 Boro St .... Kaysville UT 84037 801-546-4567
Web: www.fusion-imaging.com
G2 USA 200 Fifth Ave .... New York NY 10010 212-546-2222
Web: www.geometry.com
Gannett Direct Marketing Services Inc
3400 Robards Ct .... Louisville KY 40218 502-454-6660 452-8518*
Gate6 Inc 23460 N 19th Ave Ste 110 .... Phoenix AZ 85027 623-572-7725
Web: www.gate6.com
Genesis Direct 8514 Sunstate St .... Tampa FL 33634 813-855-4274
Web: www.genesisdirect.com
Graham Advertising
525 Communication Cir .... Colorado Springs CO 80905 719-635-7335
Web: www.grahamoleson.com
Graphics & Mailing Service Inc
2026 Locust St .... Montgomery AL 36107 334-263-3419
Web: www.graphicsandmailing.com

Phone Fax

Greater Data & Mailing Inc 551 Acorn St .... Deer Park NY 11729 631-667-1450
Web: greaterdata.com
Gregory Welteroth Advertising Inc
356 Laurens Rd .... Montoursville PA 17754 570-433-3366
Web: www.gwa-inc.com
Griffin Tabor Communications
8445 camino santa fe .... San Diego CA 92121 858-625-0070
Web: www.taborcommunications.com
Grow (Norfolk, VA) 427 Granby St .... Norfolk VA 23510 757-248-5274
Web: www.thisisgrow.com
Guest Communications Corp
15009 W 101st Ter .... Shawnee Mission KS 66215 913-888-1217
Web: www.gcckc.com
Guidemark Health Inc Six Campus Dr .... Parsippany NJ 07054 201-740-6160
Web: www.guidemarkhealth.com
Guthrie & Associates Meeting & Event Management Inc
10889 La Alberca Ave .... San Diego CA 92127 858-487-7759
Web: www.guthrie-meetings-events.com
Gyro Creative Group 400 Grand River Ave .... Detroit MI 48226 313-964-0100
Web: www.gyrocreative.com
Haines & Company Inc 8050 Freedom Ave .... North Canton OH 44720 800-843-8452 494-3862*
**Fax Area Code: 330* ■ *TF:* 800-843-8452 ■ *Web:* www.haines.com
Hallmark Data Systems 7300 Linder Ave .... Skokie IL 60077 847-983-2000 763-9593
Web: www.halldata.com
Hands on Mailing & Fulfillment Inc
6840 Orangethorpe Ave Ste E .... Buena Park CA 90620 714-522-3979
Web: handsonmailing.com
Harte-Hanks Inc
9601 McAllister Fwy Ste 610 .... San Antonio TX 78216 210-829-9000 829-9403
NYSE: HHS ■ *TF:* 800-456-9748 ■ *Web:* hartehanks.com/
Hawkeye 325 Arlington Ave Ste 700 .... Charlotte NC 28203 704-344-7900 344-7920
Web: www.hawkeyeww.com
Headrick Companies Inc, The One Freedom Sq .... Laurel MS 39440 601-649-1977
Web: www.headricks.com
Heartbeat Ideas 200 Hudson St Ninth Fl .... New York NY 10013 212-812-2233
Web: www.heartbeatdigital.com
Hecks Direct Mail & Printing Service Inc
202 W Florence Ave .... Toledo OH 43605 419-661-6000 661-6036
Web: www.hecksprinting.com
Heritage Co, The
2402 Wildwood Ave Ste 500 .... North Little Rock AR 72120 501-835-5000
TF: 800-643-8822 ■ *Web:* www.theheritagecompany.com
HERO Entertainment Marketing Inc
4590 Ish Dr Ste 140 .... Simi Valley CA 93063 805-527-2000
Web: www.heropp.com
Hkm Direct Market Communications Inc
5501 Cass Ave .... Cleveland OH 44102 216-651-9500 961-6330
TF General: 800-860-4456 ■ *Web:* www.hkmdirectmarket.com
Hobart Group Holdings LLC 240 Main St .... Gladstone NJ 07934 908-470-1780
Web: thehobartgroup.com
Hooker & Company Inc
165 Western Ave N Ste 12 .... Saint Paul MN 55102 651-659-9648
Web: hookerandcompany.com
Houston Production Guide Film 2054 W Main St .... Houston TX 77098 713-523-5387
Web: www.houstonproductionguide.com
Huntsinger & Jeffer Inc 809 Brook Hill Cir .... Richmond VA 23227 804-266-2499
Web: huntsinger-jeffer.com
I Imagine Studio Inc 152 W Huron Ste 100 .... Chicago IL 60654 847-467-0308
Web: www.iimaginestudio.com
Icon Media Direct Inc 5910 Lemona Ave .... Van Nuys CA 91411 818-995-6400
Web: www.iconmediadirect.com
iConnected Marketing Corp 125 Tech Park Dr .... Rochester NY 14623 585-444-8500
Web: www.iconnectedmarketing.com
iDirect Marketing Inc
6789 Quail Hill Pkwy Ste 550 .... Irvine CA 92603 949-753-7300 269-0198
Web: www.idirectmarketing.com
IGT Media Holdings Inc
21 SE First Ave Third Fl .... Miami FL 33131 305-573-2800
Web: www.igtmh.com
Image Printing Solutions 60 Bunsen .... Irvine CA 92618 949-754-9000
Web: www.imageprintingsolutions.com
Immediate Mailing Services Inc
245 Commerce Blvd .... Liverpool NY 13088 315-437-4189
Web: imsdirect.com
Impact Directories 1251 N Cole Rd .... Boise ID 83704 208-375-2220
Web: www.impactyp.com
Impact Mailing Services Inc
100 Forsyth Hall Dr Ste A1 .... Charlotte NC 28273 704-583-9490
Web: impactmailingservices.com
infoGroup Inc 1020 E First St .... Papillion NE 68046 402-836-5290
TF: 866-414-7848 ■ *Web:* www.infousacity.com
Innocean USA Ste 200 180 Fifth St .... Huntington Beach CA 92648 714-861-5200
Web: www.innocean.com
Insegment Inc 313 Washington St Ste 401 .... Newton MA 02458 617-965-0800
Web: www.insegment.com
International Delivery Solutions LLC
7340 S Howell Ave .... Milwaukee WI 53154 877-437-8722
Web: www.idstrac.com
Interrupt Marketing 6622 Maplewood Ave .... Sylvania OH 43560 419-724-9900
Web: www.interruptdelivers.com
Intrigue Media Solutions Inc 151 Westmount Rd .... Guelph ON N1H5J3 519-265-4933
Web: www.intrigueme.ca
Involve LLC 16 E Poplar Ave .... Columbus OH 43215 614-545-3464
Web: www.getinvolve.com
Jack Nadel International Inc
8701 Bellanca Ave .... Los Angeles CA 90045 310-815-2600
Web: www.nadel.com
Jacobs & Clevenger Inc
515 N State St Ste 1700 .... Chicago IL 60654 312-894-3000 894-3005
Web: www.jacobsclevenger.com
JLS Mailing Services Inc 672 Crescent St .... Brockton MA 02302 508-313-1000
Web: www.jlsms.com

Company / Address	City	State	ZIP	Phone	Fax
Johnson & Quin Inc 7460 N Lehigh Ave *Web:* www.j-quin.com	Niles	IL	60714	847-588-4800	647-6949
JUICE Mobile 365 Bloor St E Ste 1001 *Web:* www.juicemobile.com	Toronto	ON	M4W3L4	647-343-6300	
Karcher Group Inc, The 5590 Lauby Rd Ste 8 *Web:* karchergroup.com	North Canton	OH	44720	330-493-6141	
Kepler Group LLC Six E 32nd St Sixth Fl *Web:* www.keplergrp.com	New York	NY	10016	646-524-6896	
Kirk Integrated Marketing Services Ltd 11388 No 5 Rd Ste 110 *Web:* www.kirkmarketing.com	Richmond	BC	V7A4E7	604-279-8484	
Kroll Direct Marketing Inc 101 Morgan Ln Ste 120 *Web:* www.krolldirect.com	Plainsboro	NJ	08536	609-275-2900	
KTC Media Group 9891 Hamilton Ave *Web:* www.ktcmediagroup.com	Huntington Beach	CA	92646	714-378-1660	
L & D Mail Masters Inc 110 Security Pkwy *Web:* www.ldmailmasters.com	New Albany	IN	47150	812-981-7161	
Lake Group Media Inc 1 Byram Brook Pl Ste 2-N *Web:* www.lakegroupmedia.com	Armonk	NY	10504	914-925-2400	925-2499
Lake Michigan Mailers 3777 Sky King Blvd *Web:* www.lakemichiganmailers.com	Kalamazoo	MI	49009	269-383-9333	
LeadDog Marketing Group 159 W 25th St Second Fl *Web:* www.leaddogmarketing.com	New York	NY	10001	212-488-6530	
LeadRival 1207 S White Chapel Blvd Ste 250 *TF:* 800-332-8017 ■ *Web:* www.leadrival.com	Southlake	TX	76092	800-332-8017	
LEAP 2500 Technology Dr *Web:* www.leapagency.com	Louisville	KY	40299	502-212-1390	
Lemon Peak Marketing Services 500 W Putnam Ave Ste 400 *TF:* 888-253-7348 ■ *Web:* www.lemonpeak.com	Greenwich	CT	06831	888-253-7348	
Leon Henry Inc 200 N Central Ave Ste 220 *Web:* www.leonhenryinc.com	Hartsdale	NY	10530	914-285-3456	
Leonie Industries LLC 17383 Sunset Blvd Ste 420A *Web:* www.leoniegroup.com	Pacific Palisades	CA	90272	310-573-9505	
LetterLogic Inc 1209 Fourth Ave S *Web:* www.letterlogic.com	Nashville	TN	37210	615-783-0070	
Level Interactive 241 Fourth Ave *TF:* 877-733-8625 ■ *Web:* www.level-interactive.com	Pittsburgh	PA	15222	877-733-8625	
Lewis Direct Marketing 325 E Oliver St *TF:* 800-533-5394 ■ *Web:* www.lewisdirect.com	Baltimore	MD	21202	410-539-5100	685-5144
Lewis Media Partners LLC 500 Libbie Ave Ste 2-C *Web:* www.lewismediapartners.com	Richmond	VA	23226	804-741-7115	
Lexinet Corp, The 701 N Union St *Web:* www.lexinetcorporation.com	Council Grove	KS	66846	620-767-7000	
Licher Direct Mail Inc 980 Seco St *Web:* www.licherdm.com	Pasadena	CA	91103	626-795-3333	
List Services Corp Six Trowbridge Dr *Web:* www.listservices.com	Bethel	CT	06810	203-743-2600	
Lodestone Social 1011 Westlake Dr *Web:* lodestonesocial.com	Austin	TX	78746	512-410-1204	
Loyalty 360 Inc 4120 Dumont St *Web:* loyalty360.org	Cincinnati	OH	45226	513-800-0360	
Lunchbox LP 2920 S Sepulveda Blvd *Web:* www.lbox.com	Los Angeles	CA	00064	310-559-9222	
Lynden Tribune 113 Sixth St *Web:* lyndentribune.com	Lynden	WA	98264	360-354-4444	
M5 Marketing Communications Inc 42 O'Leary Ave *Web:* www.m5.ca	St. John's	NL	A1B4B7	709-753-5559	
Magnetic Media Online Inc 311 W 43rd St Ste 1406 *Web:* www.magnetic.com	New York	NY	10036	212-757-3189	
Mail America Communications Inc 1174 Elkton Farm Rd *Web:* www.mail-america.com	Forest	VA	24551	434-534-8000	
Mail Bag Inc 201 Commerce Dr *Web:* www.mailbaginc.com	Upper Marlboro	MD	20774	301-249-7800	
Mail Haus, The 1745 Suburban Dr *Web:* www.themailhaus.com	De Pere	WI	54115	920-338-9198	
Mail Right Inc 4470 Yankee Hill Rd *Web:* mailright.com	Rocklin	CA	95677	916-315-8235	
Mail Source Inc 111 Boardwalk *Web:* mailsourceinc.com	Fall Creek	WI	54742	715-877-3711	
Mail Unlimited Inc 4607 Metric Dr *Web:* mailunlimited.com	Winter Park	FL	32792	407-657-9333	
Mailer's Choice Inc 1504 Elm Hill Pk *Web:* www.mailerschoice.com	Nashville	TN	37210	615-883-0070	
Mailing Services of Pittsburgh Inc 155 Commerce Dr *Web:* msp-pgh.com	Freedom	PA	15042	724-774-3244	
Mailing Systems Inc 2431 Mercantile Dr Ste A *Web:* www.msimail.net	Rancho Cordova	CA	95742	916-674-2035	
Mailings Unlimited 116 Riverside Industrial Pkwy *Web:* www.growwithmail.com	Portland	ME	04103	207-347-5000	
Mailmark Enterprises LLC 8587 Canoga Ave *Web:* mailmark.com	Canoga Park	CA	91304	818-407-0660	
Mailrite Print & Mail Inc 834 Striker Ave Ste C *Web:* www.mailritemail.com	Sacramento	CA	95834	916-927-6245	
Mailroom Service Center Inc 3075 Shattuck Rd *Web:* www.mailroomservicecenter.com	Saginaw	MI	48603	989-790-2166	
Mailways Enterprises Inc 6105 Factory Rd Ste 1 *Web:* www.mailways.com	Crystal Lake	IL	60014	815-455-4850	
Major Fulfillment Inc 1455 W 139th St *Web:* www.majorfulfillment.com	Gardena	CA	90249	310-204-1874	
Maple Direct Inc 2349 Haddonfield Rd *Web:* www.mapledirect.com	Pennsauken	NJ	08110	856-488-4700	
Market Data Retrieval Six Armstrong Rd *TF:* 800-333-8802 ■ *Web:* www.schooldata.com	Shelton	CT	06484	203-926-4800	926-0784
Marketing Drive LLC 800 Connecticut Ave *Web:* www.matchmg.com	Norwalk	CT	06854	203-857-6100	857-1786
Marketing Resource Group Inc (MRG) 225 S Washington Sq *Web:* mrgmi.com	Lansing	MI	48933	517-372-4400	372-4045
Marketsmith Inc Two Wing Dr *Web:* www.marketsmithinc.com	Cedar Knolls	NJ	07927	973-889-0006	
Mason Inc 23 Amity Rd *Web:* www.mason-madison.com	Bethany	CT	06524	203-393-1101	
Maxmedia Inc 2160 Hills Ave Ste A *Web:* www.maxmedia.com	Atlanta	GA	30318	404-564-0063	
McCann WorldGroup Inc 622 Third Ave *Web:* www.mccannworldgroup.com	New York	NY	10017	646-865-2000	487-9610
McGuffin Creative Group 566 W Adams St *Web:* mcguffincg.com	Chicago	IL	60661	312-715-9812	
McMurry Inc 1010 E Missouri Ave McMurry Campus Center *Web:* www.mcmurry.com	Phoenix	AZ	85014	602-395-5850	
MedTera Solutions 40 W 37th St Ste 1203 *Web:* www.medterasolutions.com	New York	NY	10018	212-488-2130	
Meridian Display & Merchandising Inc 162 York Ave E *TF:* 800-786-2501 ■ *Web:* www.meridiandisplay.com	St Paul	MN	55117	651-227-3020	
Merrick Towle Associates Inc 5801-F Ammendale Rd *Web:* www.merricktowle.com	Beltsville	MD	20705	301-974-6000	
MetaResponse Group Inc 700 W Hillsboro Blvd Ste 4-107 *Web:* www.metaresponse.com	Deerfield Beach	FL	33441	954-360-0644	
Metro Mailing Service Inc 4251 Gateway Park Blvd *Web:* www.mmsmail.com	Sacramento	CA	95834	916-928-0801	
Mila Displays Inc 1315B Broadway Ste 108 *TF:* 800-295-6452 ■ *Web:* www.miladisplays.com	Hewlett	NY	11557	516-791-2643	
Miller's Presort Inc 1147 Sweitzer Ave *Web:* millerspresort.com	Akron	OH	44301	330-434-9200	
MineAfrica Inc 769 Euclid Ave *Web:* www.mineafrica.com	Toronto	ON	M6G2V3	416-588-7749	
Mobivity Inc 58 W Buffalo Ste 200 *TF:* 877-282-7660 ■ *Web:* mobivity.com	Chandler	AZ	85225	877-282-7660	
Mohan Group, The 866 The Queensway Ste 200 *Web:* www.mohangroup.com	Toronto	ON	M8Z1N7	416-255-2500	
Money Mailer LLC 12131 Western Ave **Fax Area Code:* 847 ■ *TF:* 800-468-5865 ■ *Web:* www.moneymailer.com	Garden Grove	CA	92841	714-889-3800	265-7624*
Monigle Associates Inc 150 Adams St *Web:* www.monigle.com	Denver	CO	80206	303-388-9358	
Move Networks Inc 796 E Utah Vly Dr	American Fork	UT	84003	801-756-5805	
Mpress Inc 4100 Howard Ave *Web:* www.mpressnow.com	New Orleans	LA	70125	504-524-8248	
MUNDO Media Inc 120 E Beaver Creek Rd Ste 200 *Web:* www.mundomedia.com	Richmond Hill	ON	L4B4V1	416-342-5646	
Nationwide Biweekly Administration Inc 855 Lower Bellbrook Rd *TF:* 888-802-1296 ■ *Web:* www.nbabiweekly.com	Xenia	OH	45385	888-802-1296	
New Channel Direct 2659 Center Rd *Web:* www.newchanneldirect.com	Hinckley	OH	44233	330-225-8950	
New Idea Engineering Inc 2784 Homestead Rd Ste 173 *Web:* www.ideaeng.com	Santa Clara	CA	95051	408-446-3460	
NewClients Inc 3900 Gaskins Rd *Web:* www.newclients.com	Richmond	VA	23233	804-560-7000	
News America Marketing 1185 Ave of the Americas 27 *TF:* 800-462-0852 ■ *Web:* www.newsamerica.com	New York	NY	10036	212-782-8000	575-5845
Next Day Flyers 18711 S Broadwick St *TF:* 800-251-9948 ■ *Web:* www.nextdayflyers.com	Rancho Dominguez	CA	90220	800-251-9948	
North Georgia Brick Company Inc 2405 Oak St W *Web:* www.northgeorgiabrick.com	Cumming	GA	30041	770-886-6555	
O'Halloran Adv Inc 270 Saugatuck Ave *TF:* 877-466-6616 ■ *Web:* www.ohalloranagency.com	Westport	CT	06880	203-341-9400	341-9422
Oboxmedia Inc 4200 St Laurent Blvd Ste 900 *Web:* oboxmedia.com	Montreal	QC	H2W2R2	514-282-5020	
Odell Simms & Lynch Inc 7704 Leesburg Pk *Web:* www.odellsimms.com	Falls Church	VA	22043	703-903-9797	903-8850
Ogilvy One Worldwide 636 11th Ave *Web:* www.ogilvy.com	New York	NY	10036	212-237-6000	237-6757
OneKreate Inc 3850 N 29th Terrace *Web:* www.onekreate.com	Hollywood	FL	33020	954-322-7600	
OnMedia Communications Company Inc 4400 College Blvd Ste 195 *Web:* www.onmediaadsales.com	Overland Park	KS	66211	913-491-4030	
Onsite Management Group 4400 Bishop Ln Ste 214 *Web:* omgservices.com	Louisville	KY	40218	502-583-1664	
Orlandi Inc 131 Executive Blvd *Web:* www.orlandi-usa.com	Farmingdale	NY	11735	631-756-0110	
PARA Marketing 227 Bellevue Way NE Ste 605 *Web:* paramarketing.com	Bellevue	WA	98004	425-605-9558	
Passkey Systems 4395 Polaris Ave *Web:* www.passkeysys.com	Las Vegas	NV	89103	702-798-7999	
Perfekt Marketing Inc 3015 S 48th St *Web:* www.perfektmarketing.com	Tempe	AZ	85282	602-453-3333	
Pitch 8825 National Blvd *Web:* www.thepitchagency.com	Culver City	CA	90232	424-603-6000	

Phone Fax

PolyQuest Inc 1985 Eastwood Rd Ste 206 .... Wilmington NC 28403 910-342-9554
Web: www.polyquest.com
POP Displays USA LLC 555 Tuckahoe Rd. .... Yonkers NY 10710 914-771-4200
Web: www.diam-int.com
Postal Presort Inc 820 W Second St N .... Wichita KS 67203 316-262-3333
Web: www.postalpresort.com
PowerChord Inc
100 Second Ave S Ste 200 S Twr .... Saint Petersburg FL 33701 727-823-1530
Web: www.powerchordsystem.com
Precise Resource Group Inc 3016 Skyway Cir S .... Irving TX 75038 972-570-0121
Web: preciseresourcegroup.com
Primadata Inc 1228 W Scyene Rd Ste 134 .... Mesquite TX 75149 972-216-9910
Web: eprimadata.com
PrimeNet Direct Mktg Solutions LLC
7320 Bryan Dairy Rd. .... Largo FL 33777 727-447-6245
Web: www.primenet.com
Promotions Unlimited 7601 Durand Ave .... Mount Pleasant WI 53177 262-681-7000 681-7001
TF: 800-992-9307 ■ *Web:* www.promot.com
Prompt Mailers Inc 66 Willow Ave .... Staten Island NY 10305 718-447-6206
Web: www.promptmailers.com
Prospectr Marketing 3508 W 22nd St. .... Minneapolis MN 55416 800-908-3523
TF: 800-908-3523 ■ *Web:* www.prospectrs.com
Purple Strategies LLC 815 Slaters Ln. .... Alexandria VA 22314 703-548-7877
Web: www.purplestrategies.com
QuadW International Inc
333 N Wood Dale Rd Ste D. .... Wood Dale IL 60191 630-694-4444
Web: www.quadwinc.com
QuantumDigital Inc 8702 Cross Park Dr Ste 200 .... Austin TX 78754 512-837-2300 837-2777
Web: quantumdigital.com
R.W. Lynch Company Inc
2333 San Ramon Vly Blvd .... San Ramon CA 94583 925-837-3877
Web: www.rwlynch.com
Radius Advertising
10883 Pearl Rd Ste 100 .... Strongsville OH 44136 440-638-3800
Web: www.radiuscleveland.com
RAJ Manufacturing Inc 2692 Dow Ave. .... Tustin CA 92780 714-838-3110
Web: www.rajman.com
Ratespecial LLC 35 N Arroyo Pkwy Ste 250 .... Pasadena CA 91103 626-376-4702
Web: www.ratespecial.com
Rauxa Direct LLC 275 McCormick Ave A. .... Costa Mesa CA 92626 714-427-1271 427-0661
Web: www.rauxa.com
RDI Marketing Services
4350 Glendale Milford Rd Ste 250 .... Cincinnati OH 45242 513-984-5927 984-9735
TF: 800-388-7636 ■ *Web:* www.rdimarketing.com
ReadyPulse 1600 A El Camino Real. .... San Carlos CA 94070 888-998-7412
TF: 888-998-7412 ■ *Web:* www.readypulse.com
Redfin 9890 S Maryland Pkwy Ste 200 .... Las Vegas NV 89183 877-973-3346 313-9320*
**Fax Area Code:* 702 ■ *TF:* 800-561-5463 ■ *Web:* redfin.com
Renkim Corp 13333 Allen Rd .... Southgate MI 48195 734-374-8300
Web: www.renkim.com
Results:Digital LLC 91 Montvale Ave Ste 104 .... Stoneham MA 02180 617-250-8580
Web: resultsdigital.com
Rich Ltd 3809 Ocean Ranch Blvd Ste 110 .... Oceanside CA 92056 760-722-2300
Web: www.richltd.com
RME360 4805 Independence Pkwy Ste 250. .... Tampa FL 33634 888-383-8770
TF: 888-383-8770 ■ *Web:* www.rme360.com
RR Donnelley Logistics 1000 Windham Pkwy .... Bolingbrook IL 60490 630-226-6100 226-6555
TF: 888-744-7773 ■ *Web:* www.rrdonnelley.com
RR Donnelley Response Marketing Services
4101 Winfield Rd .... Warrenville IL 60555 630-963-9494
TF: 800-722-9001 ■ *Web:* www.rrdonnelley.com
RSVP Publications 6730 W Linebaugh Ave Ste 201 .... Tampa FL 33625 813-960-7787 549-3306
TF: 800-360-7787 ■ *Web:* www.rsvppublications.com
Rtc Direct Mailing Inc 56 Seip Ln .... Shoemakersville PA 19555 610-562-5122
Web: rtcdirect.net
RTC Relationship Marketing
1055 Thomas Jefferson St NW Ste 200 .... Washington DC 20007 202-625-2111 424-7900
Web: www.rtcdirect.com
Russ Reid Company Inc Two N Lake Ave Ste 600. ...... Pasadena CA 91101 626-449-6100 449-6190
Web: www.russreid.com
Russell Johns Associates LLC
5020 W Linebaugh Ave Ste 210 .... Tampa FL 33624 727-443-7667
Web: russelljohns.com
Sage Direct Inc 3400 Raleigh Dr Se. .... Grand Rapids MI 49512 616-940-8311
Web: www.sagedirect.com
Sales Benchmark Index
1595 Peachtree Pkwy Ste 204-328. .... Cumming GA 30041 888-556-7338
TF: 888-556-7338 ■ *Web:* www.salesbenchmarkindex.com
San Jose Mailing & Printing
1445 Monterey Hwy .... San Jose CA 95110 408-971-1911
Web: sanjosemailing.com
Sanctuary Marketing Group Inc
219 E Maple St Ste 125 .... North Canton OH 44720 330-266-1188
Web: www.sanctuarymg.com
Scann Sort Inc 920 Brenner St. .... Winston Salem NC 27101 336-773-1100
Web: www.scannsort.com
Sebis Direct Inc 6516 W 74th St .... Bedford IL 60638 312-243-9300
Web: www.sebis.com
Selectable Media Inc 168 Fifth Ave Ste 302 .... New York NY 10010 212-796-6214
Web: selectablemedia.com
Semcasting Inc 41 High St. .... North Andover MA 01845 978-684-7580
Web: semcasting.com
Senior Alternatives For Living
26211 Central Park Blvd. .... Southfield MI 48076 888-932-7747
Web: www.alternativesforseniors.com
Sherman & Assoc 333 Harmon Ave NW .... Warren OH 44483 330-399-4500 399-6747
Web: www.shermanexperience.com
ShiftCentral Inc 210 John St Ste 100. .... Moncton NB E1C0B8 866-551-5533
TF: 866-551-5533 ■ *Web:* www.shiftcentral.com
Shikatani Lacroix Design Inc 387 Richmond E .... Toronto ON M5A1P6 416-367-1999
Web: www.sld.com
SightWorks Inc 5200 SW Macadam Blvd Ste 500. .... Portland OR 97239 503-223-4184
Web: www.sightworks.com

Phone Fax

SmithGifford Inc 106 W Jefferson St .... Falls Church VA 22046 703-532-5992
Web: www.smithgifford.com
SMS Marketing Services Inc
777 Terrace Ave Ste 401 .... Hasbrouck Heights NJ 07604 201-865-5800
Web: www.sms-inc.com
SocialCode LLC 302 Fifth Ave Fourth Fl .... New York NY 10001 917-261-3045
Web: www.socialcode.com
Soloflight Design 126 Sloan St. .... Roswell GA 30075 770-925-1115
Web: www.soloflightdesign.com
Source One Distribution Services
1220 Morse Ave .... Royal Oak MI 48067 248-399-5060
Web: www.sourceone-dist.com
SourceLink Inc 500 Pk Blvd Ste 415. .... Itasca IL 60143 866-947-6872 350-0491*
**Fax Area Code:* 847 ■ *TF:* 866-947-6872 ■ *Web:* www.sourcelink.com
Spectra Products LLC 1364 Reynolds Rd. .... Johnson City NY 13760 607-770-1985
Web: www.spectraproducts.com
Speedy Automated Mailers Inc
2200 Queen St Ste 15. .... Bellingham WA 98229 360-676-4775
Web: speedy-inc.com
SproutLoud Media Networks LLC
15431 SW 14th St .... Sunrise FL 33326 954-476-6211
Web: www.sproutloud.com
Spyder Trap Inc 1625 hennepin ave. .... Minneapolis MN 55403 612-871-2270
Web: m.spydertrap.com
Square 2 Marketing Inc
Valley Sq 1501 Main St
Ste 210 Above LensCrafters .... Warrington PA 18976 215-491-0100
Web: www.square2marketing.com
Stagnito Media LLC 570 Lk Cook Rd Ste 310. .... Deerfield IL 60015 224-632-8200
Web: www.stagnitomedia.com
Starshot Ventures Inc 3555 Lakeshore Blvd W .... Toronto ON M8W1P4 416-503-8362
Web: www.starshot.com
Statlistics Inc 69 Kenosia Ave. .... Danbury CT 06810 203-778-8700
Web: www.statlistics.com
Steel House Inc 3644 Eastham Dr .... Culver City CA 90232 888-978-3354
TF: 888-978-3354 ■ *Web:* www.steelhouse.com
Step Saver Inc 213 Spring St. .... Southington CT 06489 860-628-9645 621-1841
Web: www.stepsaver.com
STIR LLC 135 W Wells St Ste 800 .... Milwaukee WI 53203 414-278-0040
Web: www.stirmarketing.com
Stoltz Marketing Group LLC
913 W River St Ste 410. .... Boise ID 83702 208-388-0766
Web: www.stoltzgroup.com
Storeimage Programs Inc 141 Jean-Proulx St .... Gatineau QC J8Z1T4 819-778-0114
Web: www.storeimage.com
Straightforward Media LLC 8088 N 110th Dr .... Peoria AZ 85345 623-266-3962
Web: www.straightforwardmedia.com
StreamTrack Media Inc 345 Chapala St .... Santa Barbara CA 93101 805-308-9190
Web: streamtrackmedia.com
Struck Axiom Inc
159 West Broadway Ste 200. .... Salt Lake City UT 84101 801-531-0122
Web: www.struck.com
StudioGood
1880 Santa Barbara St Ste 260. .... San Luis Obispo CA 93401 805-455-9044
Web: www.studiogood.com
Sub Rosa 353 W 12Th St .... New York NY 10014 212-414-8605
Web: www.wearesubrosa.com
SuperCoups 350 Revolutionary Dr .... East Taunton MA 02718 508-977-2000 977-0644
TF: 800-626-2620 ■ *Web:* www.supercoups.com
Sussex Publishers LLC 115 E 23rd St Ninth Fl. .... New York NY 10010 212-260-7210
Web: www.sussexpub.com
Target Direct Mailing Services
1206 Esi Dr. .... Springdale AR 72764 479-750-4900
Web: www.targetdm.com
Tel-e Technologies 7 Kodiak Crescent .... Toronto ON M3J3E5 416-631-1300 635-1711
TF: 800-661-2340 ■ *Web:* www.tel-e-technologies.com
Tension Envelope Corp 819 E 19th St .... Kansas City MO 64108 800-388-5122 283-1498*
**Fax Area Code:* 816 ■ *TF:* 800-388-5122 ■ *Web:* tensionenvelope.com
Texas Mailhouse Inc 8606 Wall St Ste 1740 .... Austin TX 78754 512-837-2046
Web: texasmailhouse.com
Tgi Direct 5365 Hill 23 Dr. .... Flint MI 48507 800-337-2237
TF: 800-337-2237 ■ *Web:* www.tgidirect.com
thelab LLC 637 W 27th St Eighth Fl .... New York NY 10001 212-209-1333
Web: www.thelabnyc.com
Thorburn Group, The
706 N First St Ste 121 .... Minneapolis MN 55401 612-866-2593
Web: www.thethorburngroup.com
TINK Profitabilite numerique Inc
87 Prince Ste 140. .... Montreal QC H3C2M7 514-866-0995
Web: www.tink.ca
Tk Media Direct Inc
5062 Lankershim Blvd Ste 3033. .... N. Hollywood CA 91601 818-851-1483
Web: tkmediadirect.com
Tmr Mailing Services Inc
506 Manchester Expy Ste A1 .... Columbus GA 31904 706-653-2090
Web: www.tmrmailing.com
Total Outdoor Corp 414 Stewart St Ste 204 .... Seattle WA 98101 206-430-6080
Web: www.totaloutdoor.com
Totem Communications Group Inc 37 Front St E. ...... Toronto ON M5E1B3 416-360-7339
Web: totem.tc
Towne AllPoints Communications Inc
3441 W MacArthur Blvd .... Santa Ana CA 92704 714-540-3095
Web: www.towne.com
Towne Mailer 2424 S Garfield St .... Missoula MT 59801 406-541-6245
Web: www.townemailer.com
TriMax Direct 106 W Water St Ste 201. .... St. Paul MN 55107 651-292-0165
Web: www.trimaxdirect.com
Trinity Direct LLC 10 Park Pl .... Butler NJ 07405 973-283-3600
Web: www.trinitydirect.net
TrustWorkz 2449 Towne Lk Pkwy .... Woodstock GA 30189 770-615-3275
Web: trustworkz.com
Tutor Universe Inc 316 E Court Ste 7 .... Iowa City IA 52240 319-855-1595
Web: www.tutoruniverse.com

				Phone	Fax
Two West Inc 514 W 26th St *Web:* www.twowest.com	Kansas City	MO	64108	816-471-3255	
U s Monitor 86 Maple Ave *Web:* usmonitor.com	New City	NY	10956	845-634-1331	
Underdog Media 10 E Yanonali St Ste 2C *Web:* www.underdogmedia.com	Santa Barbara	CA	93101	805-880-6910	
Uniguest Inc 1035 Acorn Dr *Web:* www.ushospitality.com	Nashville	TN	37210	615-259-4500	
Unique Mailing Services Inc 325 Marmon Dr	Bolingbrook	IL	60440	630-739-4848	
United Letter Service Inc 2200 Estes Ave *Web:* www.unitedgmg.com	Elk Grove Village	IL	60007	312-427-3537	
Universal Wilde 26 Dartmouth St *TF:* 866-825-5515 ■ *Web:* www.universalwilde.com	Westwood	MA	02090	781-251-2700	251-2613
UpClose Marketing & Printing 120 W White St *Web:* www.upcloseprinting.com	Champaign	IL	61820	217-359-3200	
Valassis One Targeting Ctr *Web:* www.valassis.com	Windsor	CT	06095	860-285-6100	
Valassis Canada Inc 47 Jutland Rd Etobicoke *Web:* www.valassis.ca	Toronto	ON	M8Z2G6	416-259-3600	
Valpak Direct Marketing Systems Inc 8605 Largo Lakes Dr *TF:* 800-237-6266 ■ *Web:* www.valpak.com	Largo	FL	33773	800-237-6266	
Varvid Inc 1319 Commercial St Ste 201 *Web:* www.varvid.com	Bellingham	WA	98225	360-738-7168	
Verso Group Enterprises LLC 148 Main St *Web:* www.versogroup.com	Toledo	OH	43605	419-693-5302	
Vertical Vision Financial Marketing LLC 145 Towne Lk Pkwy *TF:* 866-984-1585 ■ *Web:* www.v2fm.com	Woodstock	GA	30188	866-984-1585	
Viamedia Inc 220 Lexington Green Cir Ste 300 *Web:* www.viamediatv.com	Lexington	KY	40503	859-977-9000	
Vijayeswari Usa LLC 26 Plz Dr *Web:* www.asico.com	Westmont	IL	60559	630-789-1291	
Voltage Ltd 901 Front St Ste B115 *Web:* voltagead.com	Louisville	CO	80027	303-664-1687	
Walls+Forms Inc 204 Airline Dr Ste 200 *Web:* www.wallsforms.com	Coppell	TX	75019	972-745-0800	
Walts Mailing Service Ltd 9610 E First Ave *Web:* waltsmailing.com	Spokane Valley	WA	99206	509-924-5939	
Weekleys Mailing Service Inc 1420 W Bagley Rd *Web:* www.weekleysmailing.com	Berea	OH	44017	440-234-4325	
Weinberg Capital Group 5005 Rockside Rd Ste 1140 *Web:* www.weinbergcap.com	Cleveland	OH	44131	216-503-8303	
Welded Fixtures Inc 8155 Byron Rd *Web:* www.weldedfixtures.com	Whittier	CA	90606	562-907-7007	
WiderFunnel Marketing Inc Ste 551 409 Granville St *Web:* www.widerfunnel.com	Vancouver	BC	V6C1T2	604-800-6450	
Wilkins Media Co 8010 Roswell Rd Ste 120 *Web:* outofhomeamerica.com	Atlanta	GA	30350	770-804-1818	
WireBuzz LLC 7762 E Gray Rd Ste 200 *Web:* www.wirebuzz.com	Scottsdale	AZ	85260	480-699-8053	
Woodbine Agency Inc 210 S Cherry St *Web:* www.woodbine.com	Winston-salem	NC	27101	336-724-0450	
Words, Data & Images LLC 3190 Rider Trl South *Web:* www.gabrielgroup.com	Earth City	MO	63045	314-743-5700	
World Innovators Inc 22 Bacon Rd Ste 275 *Web:* www.worldinnovators.com	Roxbury	CT	06783	860-210-8088	
World Marketing 7950 Joliet Rd Ste 200 *Web:* www.worldmarkinc.com	McCook	IL	60525	708-871-6000	871-6245
Yeck Bros Co 2222 Arbor Blvd *TF:* 800-417-2767 ■ *Web:* www.yeck.com	Dayton	OH	45439	937-294-4000	294-6985
Yiftee Inc 565 Middlefield Rd *Web:* yiftee.com	Menlo Park	CA	94025	650-564-4438	
YP Intellectual Property LLC 611 N Brand Blvd Fifth Fl Ste 500 *Web:* corporate.yp.com	Glendale	CA	91203	818-937-5500	
Zambezi 248 Westminster Ave *Web:* www.zambezi-la.com	Venice	CA	90291	310-450-6800	
ZOG Digital Inc 18835 Thompson Peak Pkwy *Web:* www.zogdigital.com	Scottsdale	AZ	85255	480-426-9952	

6 ADVERTISING SERVICES - MEDIA BUYERS

				Phone	Fax
Allan Hackel Organization Inc 1330 Ctr St *Web:* www.hackelbarter.com	Newton Center	MA	02459	617-965-4400	527-6005
Anvil Media Inc 310 NE Failing St *Web:* www.anvilmediainc.com	Portland	OR	97212	503-595-6050	
ARS Adv Inc 1001 Reads Lk Rd *Web:* aislerocket.com	Chattanooga	TN	37415	423-875-3743	875-5346
Beachbody LLC 3301 Exposition Blvd *Web:* www.beachbody.com	Santa Monica	CA	90404	310-883-9000	
Billups Inc 340 Oswego Pointe Dr Ste 101 *Web:* billupsww.com	Lake Oswego	OR	97034	503-454-0714	
Corinthian Media 500 Eigth Ave Fifth Fl *Web:* www.mediabuying.com	New York	NY	10018	212-279-5700	
CRN International Inc One Circular Ave *Web:* www.skiwatchca.com	Hamden	CT	06514	203-288-2002	
EFX Media 2300 S Ninth St Ste 136 *Web:* www.efxmedia.com	Arlington	VA	22204	703-486-2303	
Ektron Inc 542 Amherst St (Rt 101A) *TF:* 866-435-8766 ■ *Web:* www.ektron.com	Nashua	NH	03063	603-594-0249	594-0258
EMC Outdoor 5074 W Chester Pike Second Fl *Web:* www.emcoutdoor.com	Newtown Square	PA	19073	610-353-9300	
Envision Creative Group 3400 Northland Dr *Web:* www.envisioncreativegroup.com	Austin	TX	78731	512-292-1049	
Harmelin Media 525 Righters Ferry Rd *Web:* www.harmelin.com	Bala Cynwyd	PA	19004	610-668-7900	
MAGNA Global USA 100 W 33rd St 9th Fl *Web:* www.magnaglobal.com	New York	NY	10001	212-883-4751	
Media Brokers International Inc 11720 Amberpark Dr Ste 600 *Web:* www.media-brokers.com	Alpharetta	GA	30009	678-514-6200	
Media Space Solutions 904 MainSt *TF:* 888-672-2100 ■ *Web:* www.mediaspacesolutions.com	Hopkins	MN	55343	612-253-3900	454-2848
Media Works Ltd 1425 Clarkview Rd Ste 500 *Web:* www.medialtd.com	Baltimore	MD	21209	443-470-4400	
Mediaedge:cia LLC 825 Seventh Ave *Web:* www.mecglobal.com	New York	NY	10019	212-474-0000	
Mediaspot Inc 1550 Bayside Dr *Web:* www.mediaspot.com	Corona Del Mar	CA	92625	949-721-0500	
Newton Media Associates Inc 824 Greenbrier Pkwy Ste 200 *Web:* www.newtonmedia.com	Chesapeake	VA	23320	757-547-5400	
Oceanos Inc 892 Plain St *Web:* www.oceanosinc.com	Marshfield	MA	02050	781-804-1010	
Petry Media Corp 200 Pk Ave Ste 1700 *Web:* www.petrymedia.com	New York	NY	10166	212-230-5600	
PGR Media 34 Farnsworth St Second Fl *Web:* www.pgrmedia.com	Boston	MA	02210	617-502-8400	451-0451
TaigMarks Inc 223 S Main St Ste 100 *Web:* www.taigmarks.com	Elkhart	IN	46516	574-294-8844	294-8855
Telerep Inc One Dag Hammarskjold Plz *Web:* www.telerepinc.com	New York	NY	10017	212-759-8787	
Transvideo Studios 990 Villa St *Web:* www.transvideo.com	Mountain View	CA	94041	650-965-4898	962-1753
True Media 29 S Ninth St Ste 201 *Web:* www.truemediaservices.com	Columbia	MO	65203	573-443-8783	
Universal McCann 100 W 33rd St Eighth Fl *Web:* www.umww.com	New York	NY	10001	212-883-4700	
Winstar Interactive Media (WIMS) 1675 Palm Beach Lakes Blvd Ste 1000 *Web:* www.winstarinteractive.com	West Palm Beach	Fl	33401	561-227-0626	
Worldata 3000 N Military Trl *TF:* 800-331-8102 ■ *Web:* www.worldata.com	Boca Raton	FL	33431	561-393-8200	368-8345

7 ADVERTISING SERVICES - ONLINE

				Phone	Fax
1938 Media One Astor Pl Ph J *Web:* 1938media.com	New York	NY	10003	917-407-7600	
2Advanced Studios LLC 32 Journey Ste 200 *Web:* www.2advanced.com	Aliso Viejo	CA	92656	949-521-7000	
5 Metacom Inc 630 W Carmel Dr Ste 180 *Web:* www.5metacom.com	Carmel	IN	46032	317-580-7540	
A-Team Advertising Advisors LLC Four Park Ave Ste 15R *Web:* www.a-teamadvisors.com	New York	NY	10016	646-530-8670	
Absolute Media Inc 1150 Summer St *Web:* www.absolutemediainc.com	Stamford	CT	06905	203-327-9090	
Absorbent Ink 5812 Trade Ctr Dr Ste 100 *TF:* 866-618-3471 ■ *Web:* www.absorbentprinting.com	Austin	TX	78744	866-618-3471	
Access To Media 432 Front St *TF:* 866-612-0034 ■ *Web:* www.accesstomedia.com	Chicopee	MA	01013	866-612-0034	
Active Network 10182 Telesis Ct Ste 100 *TF:* 888-543-7223 ■ *Web:* www.activenetwork.com	San Diego	CA	92121	858-964-3800	551-7619
Adams & Longino Advertising Inc 605 Lynndale Ct Ste F *Web:* www.adamsadv.com	Greenville	NC	27858	252-355-5566	
Adease 170 Laurel St *Web:* adease.com	San Diego	CA	92101	619-243-2290	
ADFLOW Networks Inc 3170 Harvester Rd Ste 102 *Web:* adflownetworks.com	Burlington	ON	L7N3W8	905-333-0200	
Adler Display Studio Inc 7140 Windsor Blvd *Web:* www.adlerdisplay.com	Baltimore	MD	21244	410-281-1200	
Admerasia Inc 159 W 25th St Sixth Fl *Web:* www.admerasia.com	New York	NY	10001	212-686-3333	
Adsport Inc 389 E Palm Ln *Web:* www.adsport.com	Phoenix	AZ	85004	602-262-0500	
Adstrategies Inc 101 Bay St Ste 201 *Web:* www.adstrategies.com	Easton	MD	21601	410-822-2450	
Advance Digital Inc 185 Hudson St *Web:* www.advancedigital.com	Jersey City	NJ	07302	201-459-2888	
Adwerks Inc 512 N Main Ave *Web:* www.adwerks.com	Sioux Falls	SD	57104	605-357-3690	
Adz Etc Inc N88w16749 Main St Ste 3 *Web:* www.adzetc.com	Menomonee Fls	WI	53051	262-502-0507	
Affinitive LLC 135 W 26th St Eighth Fl *Web:* www.beaffinitive.com	New York	NY	10001	212-684-9100	
Agency Mabu 1003 Gateway Ave *Web:* www.agencymabu.com	Bismarck	ND	58503	701-250-0728	
Alamo Tee's & Advertising 12814 Cogburn *Web:* alamotees.com	San Antonio	TX	78249	210-699-3800	
Allis Information Management Inc 204 W Wackerly St *Web:* www.allisinfo.com	Midland	MI	48640	989-835-5811	
Almighty LLC 300 Western Ave Fl 2 *Web:* www.bealmighty.com	Boston	MA	02134	617-782-1511	
Aloft Group Inc 26 Parker St *Web:* www.aloftgroup.com	Newburyport	MA	01950	978-462-0002	

Company / Address	City	State	Zip	Phone	Fax
AMCI 4755 Alla Rd Ste 1000	Marina Del Rey	CA	90292	310-765-4100	
Web: www.amciglobal.com					
Ammirati Ready Inc 19 Union Sq W 11th Fl	New York	NY	10003	212-925-2111	
Web: www.ammirati.com					
Anderson Marketing Group 7420 Blanco Rd Ste 200	San Antonio	TX	78216	210-223-6233	
Web: www.andersonmarketing.com					
Anson-Stoner Inc 111 E Fairbanks Ave	Winter Park	FL	32789	407-629-9484	
Web: www.anson-stoner.com					
Apex Advertising Inc 2959 Old Tree Dr	Lancaster	PA	17603	717-396-7100	
Web: www.apexadv.com					
Apple Printing & Advertising Specialties Inc 5055 Nw 10th Ter	Fort Lauderdale	FL	33309	954-776-5691	
Web: appleprinting.com					
Arc Worldwide 35 W Wacker Dr 15th Fl	Chicago	IL	60601	312-220-5959	220-6212
Web: www.arcww.com					
Archer Communications Inc 252 Alexander St	Rochester	NY	14607	585-461-1570	
Web: www.archercom.com					
Archer Group, The 233 N King St First Fl	Wilmington	DE	19801	302-429-9120	
Web: www.archer-group.com					
Archmill House Inc 1276 Osprey Dr	Ancaster	ON	L9G4V5	905-648-7330	
Web: www.archmillhouse.com					
Archrival Inc 720 O St	Lincoln	NE	68508	402-435-2525	
Web: www.archrival.com					
Atlas Advertising LLC 1128 Grant St	Denver	CO	80203	303-292-3300	
Web: www.atlas-advertising.com					
Atomic Direct LLC 1219 Se Lafayette St	Portland	OR	97202	503-296-6131	
Web: atomicdirect.com					
Austin & Williams 125 Kennedy Dr Ste 100	Hauppauge	NY	11788	631-231-6600	
Web: www.austin-williams.com					
Ayzenberg Group Inc 49 E Walnut St	Pasadena	CA	91103	626-584-4070	
Web: www.ayzenberg.com					
Babcock & Jenkins Inc 711 S W Alder Ste 200	Portland	OR	97205	503-382-8613	
Web: www.bnj.com					
Barber Martin & Associates 7400 beaufont springs Dr	Richmond	VA	23225	804-320-3232	
Web: www.barbermartin.com					
BARD Advertising Inc 4900 Lincoln Dr	Edina	MN	55436	952-345-8000	
Web: www.bardadvertising.com					
Barnes Advertising Corp 1580 Fairview Rd	Zanesville	OH	43701	740-453-6836	
Web: barnesadvertisingcorp.com					
Barnett & Murphy Inc 1323 Brookhaven Dr	Orlando	FL	32803	407-650-0264	
Web: www.bmdm.com					
Barnett Cox & Associates 711 Tank Farm Rd Ste 210	San Luis Obispo	CA	93401	805-545-8887	
Web: www.barnettcox.com					
Bazzirk Inc 1027 E Riverside Dr	Austin	TX	78704	512-418-8500	
Web: www.bazzirk.com					
Beber Silverstein Group 89 Ne 27th St Unit 119	Miami	FL	33137	305-856-9800	
Web: www.thinkbsg.com					
Benchworks Inc 860 High St	Chestertown	MD	21620	410-810-8862	
Web: www.benchworks.com					
Bensimon Byrne Inc 420 Wellington St W	Toronto	ON	M5V1E3	416-922-2211	
Web: bensimonbyrne.com					
Bfg Communications Six Anolyn Ct	Bluffton	SC	29910	843-837-9115	
Web: www.bfgcom.com					
Biggs/Gilmore Communications 261 E Kalamazoo Ave	Kalamazoo	MI	49007	269-349-7711	349-3051
Blaine Warren Advertising LLC 7120 Smoke Ranch Rd	Las Vegas	NV	89128	702-435-6947	
Web: www.blainewarren.com					
Blast Radius Inc 1146 Homer St	Vancouver	BC	V6B2X6	604-647-6500	
Web: www.blastradius.com					
Blf Marketing LLC 220 Athens Way Ste 110	Nashville	TN	37228	615-726-2360	
Web: blfmarketing.com					
Blohm Creative Partners 1331 E Grand River Ave Ste 210	East Lansing	MI	48823	517-333-4900	
Web: www.blohmcreative.com					
Bloom Agency Inc, The 939 Burke St Ste D	Winston Salem	NC	27101	336-724-1766	
Web: www.thebloomagency.com					
Blue Cat Design Mastwoods Rd	Welcome	ON	L1A3V5	905-753-1017	753-2777
TF: 888-258-3228 ■ *Web:* www.bluecatdesign.com					
Blue Iceberg LLC 146 W 29th St Studio 11W	New York	NY	10001	212-337-9920	
Web: www.blue-iceberg.com					
Blue State Digital LLC 406 Seventh St NW Third Fl	Washington	DC	20004	202-449-5600	
Web: bluestatedigital.com					
boathouse group Inc 260 Charles St	Waltham	MA	02453	781-663-6600	
Web: www.boathouseinc.com					
Bolin Marketing & Advertising 2523 Wayzata Blvd Ste 300	Minneapolis	MN	55405	612-374-1200	
Web: www.bolinmarketing.com					
Bon Advertising Inc 307 W Muhammad Ali Blvd	Louisville	KY	40202	502-589-7711	
Web: www.bch.com					
Bond Group The Inc 2419 N Ashland Ave	Chicago	IL	60614	773-549-2710	
Web: www.bondgrp.com					
Boscobel Marketing Communications Inc 8606 Second ave	Silver Spring	MD	20910	301-588-2900	
Web: www.boscobel.com					
Brand Launcher Inc 4703 Falls Rd	Baltimore	MD	21209	410-235-7070	
Web: www.brandlauncher.com					
Brandon Advertising 3023 Church St	Myrtle Beach	SC	29577	843-916-2000	
Web: www.thebrandonagency.com					
Brandt Ronat & Co 60 Mcleod St	Merritt Island	FL	32953	321-453-3101	
Web: brc60.com					
Brandtailers 17838 Fitch	Irvine	CA	92614	949-442-0500	
Web: www.brandtailers.com					
Bravado International Group Merchandising Services Inc 1755 Broadway Second Fl	New York	NY	10019	212-445-3400	
Web: www.bravadousa.com					
Brownstein Group Inc 215 S Broad St Ste 900	Philadelphia	PA	19107	215-735-3470	
Web: m.brownsteingroup.com					
Brunet-Garcia Advertising Inc 1510 Hendricks Ave	Jacksonville	FL	32207	904-346-1977	
Web: www.brunetgarcia.com					
Brunner Inc 11 Stanwix St 5th Fl	Pittsburgh	PA	15222	412-995-9500	995-9501
Web: www.brunnerworks.com					
Brush Art Corp 343 W Us Hwy 24	Downs	KS	67437	785-454-3383	
Web: www.brushart.com					
Burkhart Advertising Inc 1335 Mishawaka Ave	South Bend	IN	46615	574-233-2101	
Web: www.burkhartadv.com					
Burst Media 8 New England Executive Pk	Burlington	MA	01803	781-272-5544	852-8676
Web: www.burstmedia.com					
Business Direct Inc 5620 Old Bullard Rd Ste 128	Tyler	TX	75703	903-593-9399	
Web: businessdirect.com					
Buster Creative 901 Martin Luther King Jr Dr	North Chicago	IL	60064	847-775-1525	
Web: www.bustercreative.com					
Butler Shine Stern & Partners 20 Liberty Ship Way	Sausalito	CA	94965	415-331-6049	331-3524
Web: bssp.com					
BVK Inc 250 W Coventry Ct Ste 300	Milwaukee	WI	53217	414-228-1990	
Web: www.bvk.com					
C L Graphics Inc 134 Virginia Rd Ste A	Crystal Lake	IL	60014	815-455-0900	
Web: www.clgraphics.com					
Campus Media Group Inc Two Appletree Sq Fourth Fl	Bloomington	MN	55425	952-854-3100	
Web: www.campusmediagroup.com					
Carson Group Advertising, The 1708 Hwy 6 S	Houston	TX	77077	281-496-2600	
Web: www.carsongroupadvertising.com					
Casanova Pendrill Publicidad Inc 275-A McCormick Ave Ste 100	Costa Mesa	CA	92626	714-918-8200	
Web: casanova.com					
Catalpha Advertising & Design Inc 6801 Loch Raven Blvd	Towson	MD	21286	410-337-0066	
Web: www.catalpha.com					
Catalyst Direct Inc 110 Marina Dr	Rochester	NY	14626	585-453-8300	
Web: www.catalystinc.com					
Catral Doyle Creative Co 231 E Buffalo St Ste 301	Milwaukee	WI	53202	414-276-3075	
Web: www.cdcreative.com					
Central Address Systems Inc 10303 Crown Point Ave	Omaha	NE	68134	402-964-9998	
Web: www.cas-online.com					
ChemPetitive Group, The 730 W Randolph St Fifth Fl	Chicago	IL	60661	312-997-2436	
Web: chempetitive.com					
Cheryl Andrews Marketing Communications 331 Almeria Ave	Coral Gables	FL	33134	305-444-4033	
Web: www.cam-pr.com					
Cheshire Center Pediatric Comm 2500 N Church St	Greensboro	NC	27405	336-375-2240	
Web: www.cheshirecenter.net					
Chrisad Inc 11 Professional Ctr Pkwy	San Rafael	CA	94903	415-924-8575	
Web: www.chrisad.com					
Chumney & Associates 742 US Hwy 1	North Palm Beach	FL	33408	561-882-0066	
Web: chumneyads.com					
Circle s Studio LLC 201 W Seventh St	Richmond	VA	23224	804-232-2908	
Web: www.circlesstudio.com					
CKR Interactive Inc 399 NThird St	Campbell	CA	95008	408-517-1400	
Web: www.ckrinteractive.com					
CMG Worldwide Inc 10500 Crosspoint Blvd	Indianapolis	IN	46256	317-570-5000	
Web: www.cmgworldwide.com					
Colangelo Synergy Marketing Inc 120 Tokeneke Rd	Darien	CT	06820	203-662-6600	
Web: www.colangelo-sm.com					
Cold Open Inc 1313 Innes Pl	Venice	CA	90291	310-399-3307	
Web: www.coldopen.com					
Colsky Media 2740 Van Ness Ave Ste 220	San Francisco	CA	94109	415-673-5400	
Web: www.colskymedia.com					
Commission Junction Inc 530 E Montecito St	Santa Barbara	CA	93103	805-730-8000	730-8001
TF: 800-761-1072 ■ *Web:* www.cj.com					
Concerto Marketing Group Inc 128 Hastings St W	Vancouver	BC	V6B1G8	604-684-8933	
Web: www.concertomarketing.com					
Concussion LLP 707 W Vickery Blvd #103	Fort Worth	TX	76104	817-336-6824	
Web: www.pavlovagency.com					
Confluent Translations LLC 340 Mansfield Ave	Pittsburgh	PA	15220	412-539-1410	
Web: www.ncs-pubs.com					
Conroy Media Ltd 6713 Kingery Hwy	Willowbrook	IL	60527	630-920-7800	
Web: www.conroymedialtd.com					
Conway Marketing Communications 6400 Baum Dr	Knoxville	TN	37919	865-588-5731	
Web: www.conwaymktg.com					
Core Twelve Inc 600 W Van Buren #1010	Chicago	IL	60607	312-274-1270	
Web: www.core12.com					
Creative Outdoor Advertising 2402 Stouffville Rd	Gormley	ON	L0H1G0	800-661-6088	
TF: 800-661-6088 ■ *Web:* www.creativeoutdoor.com					
Cronin & Company LLC 50 Nye Rd	Glastonbury	CT	06033	860-659-0514	
Web: www.cronin-co.com					
Crosby Marketing Communications Inc The Crosby Bldg 705 Melvin Ave Ste 200	Annapolis	MD	21401	410-626-0805	
Web: www.crosbymarketing.com					
Crosby-wright 5907 N Rocking Rd	Scottsdale	AZ	85250	480-367-1112	
Web: www.crosby-wright.com					
Crouch Group Inc, The 300 N Carroll Blvd Ste 103	Denton	TX	76201	940-383-1990	
Web: thecrouchgroup.com					

Company / Address	City	State	ZIP	Phone	Fax
D m 2 Design Consultancy 115 River Rd Ste 1030 *Web:* thinkdm2.com	Edgewater	NJ	07020	201-840-8910	
D&S Creative Communications Inc 140 Park Ave E *Web:* www.blackriverdisplay.com	Mansfield	OH	44902	419-524-4312	
D2 Creative 28 World's Fair Dr *Web:* www.d2creative.com	Somerset	NJ	08873	732-507-7300	805-0637
Dailey Marketing Group Inc 29829 Santa Margarita Pkwy Ste 100 *Web:* www.daileymarketing.com	Rancho Santa Margarita	CA	92688	949-454-0751	
Daniels & Roberts Inc 209 N Seacrest Blvd Ste 2 *Web:* www.danielsandroberts.com	Boynton Beach	FL	33435	561-241-0066	
Datamine Internet Marketing Solutions Inc 330 S Lake St *Web:* www.datamine.net	Gary	IN	46403	219-939-9987	
Davco Advertising Inc 89 N Kinzer Rd *Web:* davcoadvertising.com	Kinzers	PA	17535	717-442-4155	
Decker Advertising 99 Citizens Dr *Web:* www.deckerdoesit.com	Glastonbury	CT	06033	860-659-1311	
Definition 6 LLC 2115 Monroe Dr Ste 100 *Web:* www.definition6.com	Atlanta	GA	30324	404-870-0323	
Denmark Group Inc, The 6000 Lk Forrest Dr Ste 260 *Web:* www.denmarktheagency.com	Atlanta	GA	30328	404-256-3681	
DeSantis Breindel Inc 30 W 21 St *Web:* www.desantisbreindel.com	New York	NY	10010	212-994-7680	
Designsensory Inc 1740 Commons Point Dr Centerpoint Commons Bldg 1 *Web:* www.designsensory.com	Knoxville	TN	37932	865-690-2249	
Dhx Advertising Inc 217 Ne Eighth Ave *Web:* www.dhxadv.com	Portland	OR	97232	503-872-9616	
Dicom Inc 1650 Des Peres Rd Ste 100 *Web:* dicominc.com	St. Louis	MO	63131	314-909-0900	
Digital Lightbridge LLC 11902 Little Rd *Web:* www.digitallightbridge.com	New Port Richey	FL	34654	727-863-7806	
Digital Pulp Inc 220 E 23rd St Ste 900 *Web:* www.digitalpulp.com	New York	NY	10010	212-679-0676	679-6217
Dinkel r a & Associates Inc 4641 Willoughby Rd *Web:* ideasideas.com	Holt	MI	48842	517-699-7000	
Dky Inc 6009 Penn Ave S *Web:* dkyinc.com	Minneapolis	MN	55419	612-798-4070	
Dogwood Productions Inc 757 Government St *Web:* www.dogwoodproductions.com	Mobile	AL	36602	251-476-0858	
DoublePositive Marketing Group Inc 1501 S Clinton St Ste 1520 *Web:* www.doublepositive.com	Baltimore	MD	21224	410-332-0464	
Downtown Partners Chicago 200 E Randolph St 34th Fl *Web:* www.downtownpartners.com	Chicago	IL	60601	312-552-5800	
Dreamentia Inc 453 S Spring St Ste 808 *Web:* www.dreamentia.com	Los Angeles	CA	90013	213-347-6000	
E t Mktg. Solutions Ltd 207-3833 Henning Dr *Web:* www.etmarketingsolutions.com	Burnaby	BC	V5C6N5	604-801-6168	
eBay Enterprise Inc 935 First Ave *NASDAQ: EBAY* ■ *TF:* 877-255-2857 ■ *Web:* www.ebayenterprise.com	King of Prussia	PA	19406	610-491-7000	491-7366
Elkins Retail Advertising Inc 6040 Hellyer Ave Ste 100 *Web:* elkinsadvertising.com	San Jose	CA	95138	408-249-1411	
Ellison Advertising 3410 Se 20th Ave *Web:* www.ellisonadvertising.com	Portland	OR	97202	503-236-8400	
Ellison Media Co 14804 N Cave Creek Rd *Web:* www.ellisonmedia.com	Phoenix	AZ	85032	602-404-4000	
Emanate PR 711 Third Ave 12th Fl *Web:* www.emanatepr.com	New York	NY	10017	212-805-8000	
Engauge Marketing LLC 375 N Front St Ste 400 *Web:* www.engauge.com	Columbus	OH	43215	614-573-1010	
Ervin & Smith Advertising & Public Relations Inc 16934 Frances St *Web:* www.ervinandsmith.com	Omaha	NE	68130	402-334-6969	
Everett Studios Inc Five N Greenwich Rd *Web:* www.goeverett.com	Armonk	NY	10504	914-997-2200	
Evo Exhibits 399 Wegner Dr *Web:* www.evoexhibits.com	West Chicago	IL	60185	630-520-0710	
Evok Advertising Inc 2500 Kunze Ave *Web:* www.evokad.com	Orlando	FL	32806	407-302-4416	
Exl Media Corp 803 Tahoe Blvd Ste 7 *Web:* www.exlmedia.com	Incline Village	NV	89451	775-832-0202	
Expert Communications Inc 394 Pacific Ave *Web:* www.eciww.com	San Francisco	CA	94111	415-981-9900	
ExpoPlus 1055 Research Ctr Atlanta Dr Sw *Web:* www.expoplus.com	Atlanta	GA	30331	404-699-0650	
Extreme Communications Ltd 47 Fraser Ave N Entrance Second Fl *Web:* www.extremegroup.com	Toronto	ON	M6K1Y7	416-607-6665	
Extreme Packing Solutions Five Dodge St *Web:* extremepackingsolutions.com	Beverly	MA	01915	978-232-9190	
F p i s Inc 220 Story Rd *Web:* www.fpis.com	Ocoee	FL	34761	407-656-8818	
Faction Media LLP 1730 Blake St Ste 200 *TF:* 866-788-5306 ■ *Web:* www.factionmedia.com	Denver	CO	80202	866-788-5306	
Flourish Inc 1001 Huron Rd E Ste 102 *Web:* www.eflourish.com	Cleveland	OH	44115	216-696-9116	
Foster Marketing LLC 3909-F Ambassador Caffery *Web:* www.fostermarketing.com	Lafayette	LA	70503	337-235-1848	
Foundry 9 LLC 44 W 28th St Sixth Fl *Web:* www.foundry9.com	New York	NY	10001	212-989-7999	
Freed Advertising LP 1650 Hwy 6 Ste 400 *Web:* www.freedadvertising.com	Sugar Land	TX	77478	281-240-4949	
Fuse Inc 802 N First St *Web:* www.fuseadvertising.com	St. Louis	MO	63102	314-421-4040	
FUSION b2b Inc 1548 Bond St Ste 114 *Web:* www.fusionb2b.com	Naperville	IL	60563	630-579-8300	
Fusionary Media 220 Grandville SW *Web:* www.fusionary.com	Grand Rapids	MI	49503	616-454-2357	
Fusionbox Inc 2031 Curtis St *Web:* www.fusionbox.com	Denver	CO	80205	303-952-7490	
Gabriel deGrood Bendt LLC 608 Second Ave S Ste 129 *Web:* www.gdbagency.com	Minneapolis	MN	55402	612-547-5000	
Garrigan Lyman Group Inc, The 1524 Fifth Ave Ste 400 *Web:* www.glg.com	Seattle	WA	98101	206-223-5548	
Gauger & Associates 360 Post St Ste 901 *Web:* www.gauger-associates.com	San Francisco	CA	94108	415-434-0303	
Gbsa Inc 2710 N ave *Web:* www.graystoneadv.com	Bridgeport	CT	06604	203-549-0060	
Giovatto Advertising & Consulting Inc 95 N State Rt 17 *Web:* www.giovatto.com	Paramus	NJ	07652	201-226-9700	
Global TV Concepts Ltd 676 S Military Trl *Web:* www.globaltvconcepts.com	Deerfield Beach	FL	33442	954-570-9999	
Global Village Marketing & Data Services Inc 2710 Thomes Ave *Web:* www.globalvillagemktg.com	Cheyenne	WY	82001	307-222-4135	
goodness Mfg. LLC 6922 Hollywood Blvd 12th Fl *Web:* www.goodnessmfg.com	Hollywood	CA	90028	310-845-3035	
Gragg Advertising Inc 450 E Fourth St Ste 100 *Web:* www.graggadv.com	Kansas City	MO	64106	816-931-0050	
Grapevine Communications International Inc 5201 Paylor Ln *Web:* www.grapeinc.com	Sarasota	FL	34240	941-351-0024	
Gray & Associates Diversity Advertising & Public Relations Inc 2677 Tritt Springs Trce Ne *Web:* www.grayassoc.net	Marietta	GA	30062	678-560-9272	
Greenhaus Inc 2660 First Ave *Web:* greenhaus.com	San Diego	CA	92103	619-744-4024	
Grip Ltd 179 John St Sixth Fl *Web:* www.griplimited.com	Toronto	ON	M5T1X4	416-340-7111	
Hacker Group Inc 1215 Fourth Ave Ste 2100 *Web:* hal2l.com/	Seattle	WA	98161	206-805-1500	805-1599
Harmonic International LLC 10 E Lee St Ste 2704 *Web:* www.harmonicinternational.com	Baltimore	MD	21202	410-727-3554	
Harris D. McKinney Inc 55 W Wacker Dr *Web:* www.harrisdmckinney.com	Chicago	IL	60601	312-506-5200	
Hart-Boillot LLC 134 Rumford Ave Ste 307 *Web:* www.hbagency.com	Newton	MA	02466	781-893-0053	
Helgeson Enterprises Inc 4461 White Bear Pkwy *Web:* www.helgesonent.com	White Bear Lake	MN	55110	651-762-9700	
Hellman Associates Inc 1225 W Fourth St PO Box 627 *Web:* www.hellman.com	Waterloo	IA	50704	319-234-7055	
HelloWorld One ePrize Dr *TF:* 877-837-7493 ■ *Web:* www.eprize.com	Pleasant Ridge	MI	48069	877-837-7493	
Hitchcock Fleming & Associates Inc 500 Wolf Ledges Pkwy *Web:* www.teamhfa.com	Akron	OH	44311	330-376-2111	
Hub Strategy & Communication 39 Mesa St Ste 212 *Web:* hubstrategy.com	San Francisco	CA	94129	415-561-4345	
HY Connect 142 E Ontario St Ste 13 *Web:* www.hoffmanyork.com	Chicago	IL	60611	312-787-2330	
Hyperquake LLC 205 W Fourth St Ste 1010 *Web:* www.hyperquake.com	Cincinnati	OH	45202	513-563-6555	
IBIS Communications 1024 17th Ave South *Web:* www.ibiscommunications.com	Nashville	TN	37212	615-777-1900	
Ideaology Advertising Inc 4223 Glencoe Ave Ste A127 *Web:* www.ideaology.biz	Marina Del Rey	CA	90292	310-306-6501	
Ideaworks 1110 N Palafox St *Web:* www.ideaworksusa.com	Pensacola	FL	32501	850-434-9095	
Identity Group, The 440 W First St Ste 204 *Web:* theidgroup.com	Tustin	CA	92780	714-573-0010	
Ignited LLC 2221 Park Pl *Web:* www.ignitedla.com	El Segundo	CA	90245	310-773-3100	
Images Usa 1320 Ellsworth Industrial Blvd *Web:* www.imagesusa.net	Atlanta	GA	30318	404-892-2931	
inferno LLC 505 Tennessee St Ste 108 *Web:* www.creativeinferno.com	Memphis	TN	38103	901-278-3773	
Intech Direct 105 E Marquardt Dr *Web:* intechdirect.com	Wheeling	IL	60090	847-850-5999	
Interbrand Design Forum LLC 7575 Paragon Rd *Web:* www.interbranddesignforum.com	Dayton	OH	45459	937-439-4400	
Interlex Communications 4005 Broadway St Ste B *Web:* www.interlexusa.com	San Antonio	TX	78209	210-930-3339	
Interline Creative Group 553 North N Ct Ste 160 *Web:* www.interlinegroup.com	Palatine	IL	60067	847-358-4848	
Internet Matrix Inc 10179 Huennekens St *Web:* www.imatrix.com	San Diego	CA	92121	858-444-4200	
iProspect 200 Clarendon St 23rd Fl *Web:* www.iprospect.com	Boston	MA	02116	617-449-4300	
IZEA Inc 480 N Orlando Ave Ste 200 *Web:* www.izea.com	Winter Park	FL	32789	407-674-6911	

Company / Address	City	State	ZIP	Phone	Fax
J & L Mail Services Inc 2100 Nelson Miller Pkwy *Web:* www.jandlmarketing.com	Louisville	KY	40223	502-261-9292	
J m Fox Associates Inc 616 Dekalb St *Web:* jmfox.com	Norristown	PA	19401	610-275-5957	
J r Thompson Co 26970 Haggerty Rd Ste 100 *Web:* www.jrthompson.com	Farmington Hills	MI	48331	248-553-4566	
Jackson Marketing Group Inc Two Task Industrial Ct *Web:* www.jacksonmg.com	Greenville	SC	29607	864-272-3000	
Jacobs Agency Inc 430 W Erie St Ste 403 *Web:* www.jacobsagency.com	Chicago	IL	60610	312-664-5000	
Jacobson Rost Inc 233 N Water St Fl 6 *Web:* www.jacobsonrost.com	Milwaukee	WI	53202	414-220-4888	
Jajo Inc 200 N Broadway St Ste 110 *Web:* www.jajo.net	Wichita	KS	67202	316-267-6700	
Jarrard Phillips Cate & Hancock Inc 219 Ward Cir Ste 3 *Web:* www.jarrardinc.com	Brentwood	TN	37027	615-254-0575	
Jay Advertising Inc 170 Linden Oaks Ste A *Web:* www.jayww.com	Rochester	NY	14625	585-264-3600	
Jayray Ads & Pr Inc 535 Dock St Ste 205 *Web:* www.jayray.com	Tacoma	WA	98402	253-627-9128	
Jeffrey Scott Agency Inc 670 P St *Web:* jsaweb.com	Fresno	CA	93721	559-268-9741	
Jobelephantcom Inc 5443 Fremontia Ln *Web:* www.jobelephant.com	San Diego	CA	92115	619-795-0837	
John St 172 John St *Web:* www.johnst.com	Toronto	ON	M5T1X5	416-348-0048	
JT Mega 4020 Minnetonka Blvd *Web:* www.jtmega.com	Minneapolis	MN	55416	952-929-1370	
Juice Studios 1648 10th St *Web:* www.juicewest.com	Santa Monica	CA	90404	310-460-7830	
Kathy Floam Pomerantz Agency 914 Bay Ridge Rd Ste 180 *Web:* www.pomagency.com	Annapolis	MD	21403	410-216-9447	
Kelley Advertising Co 3408 Nw 46th St *Web:* kellyadvertising.com	Oklahoma City	OK	73112	405-946-2222	
Klondike Advertising Specialty House 1900 w benson blvd *Web:* www.klondikeadv.com	Anchorage	AK	99517	907-274-3535	
Knoodle Sales & Marketing Corp 4450 N 12th St Ste 120 *Web:* www.knoodleshop.com	Phoenix	AZ	85014	602-530-9900	
Koeppel Direct Inc 16200 Dallas Pkwy Ste 270 *Web:* koeppeldirect.com	Dallas	TX	75248	972-732-6110	
Kuhn & Wittenborn Advertising 2405 Grand Blvd Ste 600 *Web:* kuhnwitt.com	Kansas City	MO	64108	816-471-7888	
Kutoka Interactive Inc 3689 St-Hubert St *Web:* www.kutoka.com	Montreal	QC	H2L3Z9	514-849-4800	
Labov & Beyond Inc 609 E Cook Rd *Web:* labov.com	Fort Wayne	IN	46825	260-497-0111	
LaneTerralever LLC 725 W McDowell rd *Web:* www.eblane.com	Phoenix	AZ	85007	602-258-5263	
Lapiz Hispanic Marketing 35 W Wacker Dr Fl Twelve *Web:* www.lapizusa.com	Chicago	IL	60601	312-220-5000	
Lavidge Co, The 2777 E Camelback Rd Ste 300 *Web:* www.lavidge.com	Phoenix	AZ	85016	480-998-2600	
Lazbro Inc 12840 Bonaparte Ave *Web:* www.lazbro.com	Los Angeles	CA	90066	310-989-6111	
LeapFrog Solutions Inc 3201 Jermantown Rd Ste 350 *Web:* www.leapfrogit.com	Fairfax	VA	22030	703-273-7900	
Leone Advertising 2024 Santa Cruz Ave *Web:* leonead.com	Menlo Park	CA	94025	650-854-5895	
Lewis Advertising Inc 1050 Country Club Rd PO Drawer L *Web:* www.lewisadvertising.com	Rocky Mount	NC	27802	252-443-5131	
LiveWorld Inc 4340 Stevens Creek Blvd Ste 101 *Web:* www.liveworld.com	San Jose	CA	95129	408-871-5200	871-5300
Lmi Advertising 24e E Roseville Rd *Web:* lmiadvertising.com	Lancaster	PA	17601	717-569-8826	
Local Pages of New Mexico LLC, The 4910 West Amelia Earhart Dr Ste 1 *Web:* localpagesonline.com	Salt Lake City	UT	84116	801-963-1702	
Lockard & Wechsler Inc Two Bridge St Ste 200 *Web:* www.lwdirect.com	Irvington	NY	10533	914-591-6600	
Loomis Agency LLC, The 17120 Dallas Pkwy Ste 200 *Web:* www.theloomisagency.com	Dallas	TX	75248	972-331-7000	
Lopez Marketing Group Inc 11169 La Quinta Pl *Web:* www.lopezgroup.com	El Paso	TX	79936	915-772-8018	
M&C Saatchi LA Inc 2032 Broadway *Web:* mcsaatchi-la.com	Santa Monica	CA	90404	310-401-6070	
Macquarium Intelligent Communications 1800 Peachtree St NW Ste 250 *Web:* www.macquarium.com	Atlanta	GA	30309	404-554-4000	554-4001
Mad 4 Marketing Inc 5203 NW 33rd Ave *Web:* www.mad4marketing.com	Fort Lauderdale	FL	33309	954-485-5448	
Maddock Douglas Inc 111 Adell Pl *Web:* www.maddockdouglas.com	Elmhurst	IL	60126	630-279-3939	
MadeToOrder 1244-A Quarry Ln *Web:* www.madetoorder.com	Pleasanton	CA	94566	925-484-0600	
Magner Sanborn 111 N Post Ste 400 *Web:* www.magnersanborn.com	Spokane	WA	99201	509-688-2200	
Mallof, Abruzino & Nash Marketing 765 Kimberly Dr *Web:* www.manmarketing.com	Carol Stream	IL	60188	630-929-5200	
Mandala Agency, The 2855 Nw Crossing Dr *Web:* www.mandala-agency.com	Bend	OR	97701	541-389-6344	
Mangos Graphics Inc 10 Great Vly Pkwy *Web:* www.mangosinc.com	Malvern	PA	19355	610-296-2555	
Marchex Inc 520 Pike St Ste 2000 *NASDAQ: MCHX* ■ *TF:* 800-840-1012 ■ *Web:* www.marchex.com	Seattle	WA	98101	206-331-3300	331-3695
Marco Corp, The 470 Hardy Rd *Web:* www.themarcocorporation.ca	Brantford	ON	N3V6T1	519-751-2227	
MarketLauncher Inc 1800 Pembroke Dr Ste 300 *TF:* 800-901-3803 ■ *Web:* www.marketlauncher.com	Orlando	FL	32810	800-901-3803	
Marriner Marketing Communications Inc 6731 Columbia Gateway Dr Ste 250 *Web:* www.marriner.com	Columbia	MD	21046	410-715-1500	
Mary Pomerantz Advertising 300 Route 27 *Web:* www.marypomerantzadvertising.com	Highland Park	NJ	08904	732-214-9600	
MasonBaronet Inc 1801 N Lamar St Ste 250 *Web:* www.masonbaronet.com	Dallas	TX	75202	214-954-0316	
MatchCraft Inc 2701 Ocean Park Blvd Ste 220 *Web:* www.matchcraft.com	Santa Monica	CA	90405	310-314-3320	
McGill Buckley Inc 2206 Anthony Ave *Web:* www.mcgillbuckley.com	Ottawa	ON	K2B6V2	613-728-4199	
Media Fusion Inc 4951 Century St *Web:* www.fusiononline.com	Huntsville	AL	35816	256-532-3874	
Mediabidscom Inc 448 Main St *Web:* www.mediabids.com	Winsted	CT	06098	860-379-9602	
Mekanism Inc 640 Second St Fl 3 *Web:* www.mekanism.com	San Francisco	CA	94107	415-908-4000	
Mercury Communication Partners 13414 Watertown Plank Rd *Web:* www.mercuryww.com	Elm Grove	WI	53122	262-782-4637	
Meringcarson 1700 I St Ste 210 *Web:* www.meringcarson.com	Sacramento	CA	95811	916-340-2200	
Merlot Marketing 4430 Duckhorn Dr *Web:* www.merlotmarketing.com	Sacramento	CA	95834	916-285-9835	
Merz Group, The 1570 Mcdaniel Dr *Web:* www.themerzgroup.com	West Chester	PA	19380	610-429-3160	
MetaDesign North America 615 Battery St Sixth Fl *Web:* www.metadesign.com	San Francisco	CA	94111	415-627-0790	627-0795
Meyocks Group Inc, The 6800 Lk Dr Ste 150 *Web:* www.meyocks.com	West Des Moines	IA	50266	515-225-1200	
Minimus LLC 914 tourmaline dr *Web:* www.minimus.biz	Newbury Park	CA	91320	805-376-6352	
Mintz & Hoke Inc 40 Tower Ln *Web:* www.mintz-hoke.com	Avon	CT	06001	860-678-0473	
Mitchell & Resnikoff 8003 Old York Rd *Web:* mitch-res.com	Elkins Park	PA	19027	215-635-1000	
Mjs Advertising Marketing Consulting LLC 1801 Clint Moore Rd Ste 201 *Web:* www.mjsadvertising.com	Boca Raton	FL	33487	561-443-0440	
Modern Marketing Partners 1220 Iroquois Ave Ste 210 *Web:* www.modernmarketingpartners.com	Naperville	IL	60563	630-868-5060	
Mogo Marketing 14 Crystal Creek Dr *Web:* www.mogomarketing.com	Larkspur	CA	94939	415-573-9490	
Monarch Creative 309 N Water St Ste 360 *Web:* monarchcreative.net	Milwaukee	WI	53202	414-277-0077	
Moore & Scarry Advertising Inc 12601 Westlinks Dr Ste 7 *Web:* www.mooreandscarry.com	Fort Myers	FL	33913	239-689-4000	
Moore Communications Group Inc 2011 Delta Blvd *Web:* www.moore-pr.com	Tallahassee	FL	32303	850-224-0174	
n-tara Inc 2214 E Fairview Ave *Web:* www.ntarainteractive.com	Johnson City	TN	37601	423-926-8272	
Nail Communications Inc 63 Eddy St *Web:* nail.cc	Providence	RI	02903	401-331-6245	
Neal Advertising LLC 175 Andover St Ste 301 *Web:* nealadv.com	Danvers	MA	01923	978-774-4444	
Nelson Schmidt Inc 600 E Wisconsin Ave *Web:* www.n-s.com	Milwaukee	WI	53202	414-224-0210	
NetGain Technology Inc 720 W St Germain St *Web:* www.netgainhosting.com	Saint Cloud	MN	56301	320-251-4700	251-5030
New Day Marketing Ltd 923 Olive St *Web:* www.newdaymarketing.com	Santa Barbara	CA	93101	805-965-7833	
NOBLE 2215 W Chesterfield Blvd *Web:* www.noble.net	Springfield	MO	65807	417-875-5000	
non-linear creations Inc 987 Wellington St Ste 201 *TF:* 866-915-2997 ■ *Web:* www.nonlinearcreations.com	Ottawa	ON	K1Y2Y1	613-241-2067	241-3086
Obrien et Al Advertising Inc 3113 Pacific Ave *Web:* www.obrienetal.com	Virginia Beach	VA	23451	757-422-3231	
Okeeffe & Company Marketing Inc 921 King St *Web:* www.ikco.com	Alexandria	VA	22314	703-883-9000	
Olson Communications Inc 15205 N Kierland Blvd Ste 210 *Web:* www.olsoncomm.com	Scottsdale	AZ	85254	480-368-7999	
Openjar Concepts Inc 27710 jefferson ave *Web:* www.openjar.com	Temecula	CA	92590	951-296-9222	
Organic Inc 555 Market St Fourth Fl *Web:* www.organic.com	San Francisco	CA	94105	415-581-5300	581-5400
Ostler Group Inc, The 7430 South Creek Rd Ste 204 *Web:* www.ostlergroup.com	Sandy	UT	84093	801-566-6081	
Out There Advertising Inc 22 E Second St *Web:* outthereadvertising.com	Duluth	MN	55802	218-720-6002	

Company	City	State	ZIP	Phone	Fax
Owen Media Inc 3130 E Madison St Ste 206 *Web:* www.owenmedia.com	Seattle	WA	98112	206-322-1167	
Oxiem LLC One S Limestone *TF:* 866-432-8235 ■ *Web:* oxiem.com	Springfield	OH	45502	866-432-8235	
Pace & Partners 1223 Turner St Ste 101 *Web:* www.gudmarketing.com	Lansing	MI	48906	517-267-9800	
Pacifico Inc 1190 Coleman Ave Ste 110 *Web:* www.pacifico.com	San Jose	CA	95110	408-327-8888	
Palio Communications LLC 260 Broadway *Web:* www.palio.com	Saratoga Springs	NY	12866	518-584-8924	
Palmer Advertising 466 Geary St Ste 301 *Web:* www.palmeradvertising.com	San Francisco	CA	94102	415-771-2327	
PAPA Advertising Inc 1673 W Eighth St *Web:* www.papaadvertising.com	Erie	PA	16505	814-454-6236	
Partners Napier Inc 192 Mill St Ste 600 *Web:* www.partnersandnapier.com	Rochester	NY	14614	585-454-1010	
Payne, Ross & Associates Advertising Inc 206 E Jefferson St *Web:* www.payneross.com	Charlottesville	VA	22902	434-977-7607	
PCF. Virtual 4224 Waialae Ave Ste 5 *Web:* www.kokomarinacenter.net	Honolulu	HI	96816	808-737-4676	
Peter A. Mayer Advertising Inc 324 Camp St *Web:* www.peteramayer.com	New Orleans	LA	70130	504-581-7191	
Pickering Creative Group 8001 S 13th St *Web:* www.pickeringcreative.com	Lincoln	NE	68512	402-423-5447	
Pierce-Cote Advertising 683 Main St *Web:* www.pierce-cote.com	Osterville	MA	02655	508-420-5566	
Pinckney Hugo Group 760 W Genesee St *Web:* www.pinckneyhugo.com	Syracuse	NY	13204	315-478-6700	
Pinnacle Exhibits Inc 22400 NW Westmark Dr *Web:* www.pinnacle-exhibits.com	Hillsboro	OR	97124	503-844-4848	
Planet Propaganda 605 Williamson St *Web:* planetpropaganda.com	Madison	WI	53703	608-256-0000	
PlattForm Advertising Inc 15500 W 113th St Ste 200 *Web:* www.plattformad.com	Lenexa	KS	66219	913-254-6000	
Play Advertising Inc 1455 Lakeshore Rd *Web:* playadvertising.com	Burlington	ON	L7S2J1	905-631-8299	
Poretta & Orr Inc 450 East St *Web:* porettaorr.com	Doylestown	PA	18901	215-345-1515	
Powers Agency Inc One W Fourth St Fifth Fl *Web:* www.powersagency.com	Cincinnati	OH	45202	513-721-5353	
Prairie Dog LLC 6155 Oak St *Web:* www.pdog.com	Kansas City	MO	64113	816-822-3636	
Precise Mailing Inc 168 Beacon St *Web:* www.precisemailing.com	South San Francisco	CA	94080	650-589-4000	
PriceWeber Marketing Communications Inc 10701 Shelbyville Rd *Web:* www.priceweber.com	Louisville	KY	40243	502-499-9220	
Primacy 1577 New Britain Ave *TF:* 866-497-3725 ■ *Web:* www.theprimacy.com	Farmington	CT	06032	860-679-9332	679-9344
Primary Media Outdoor Advertising 2511 Boll St *Web:* primarymedia.com	Dallas	TX	75204	214-880-0440	
Priority Marketing 8200 College Pkwy Ste 201 *Web:* www.prioritymarketing.com	Fort Myers	FL	33919	239-267-2638	
Proof Advertising LLC 114 W Seventh St Ste 500 *Web:* www.proof-advertising.com	Austin	TX	78701	512-345-6658	
Propaganda Inc 3115 S Grand Blvd Ste 500 *Web:* www.propaganda-inc.com	St. Louis	MO	63118	314-664-8516	
Publipage Inc 2055 Rue Peel *Web:* publipage.com	Montreal	QC	H3A1V4	514-286-8154	
Push Inc 101 Ernestine St *Web:* www.pushhere.com	Orlando	FL	32801	407-841-2299	
Q Interactive Inc 1601 NW 136th Ave **Fax Area Code:* 312	Sunrise	FL	33323	954-653-9000	469-1744*
Quenzel Associates Inc 12801 University Dr Ste 2 *Web:* www.denmarkinteriors.com	Fort Myers	FL	33907	239-226-0040	
Quest Companies Inc 8011 N Point Blvd Ste 201 *TF:* 800-467-9409 ■ *Web:* www.questcompaniesinc.com	Winston-salem	NC	27106	800-467-9409	
Questus Inc 675 Davis St *Web:* www.questus.com	San Francisco	CA	94111	415-677-5700	
Quiet Light Communications Inc 220 E State St *Web:* www.quietlightcom.com	Rockford	IL	61104	815-398-6860	
R C Romine Advertising & Marketing 1250 Executive Pl Ste 601 *Web:* www.rcromine.com	Geneva	IL	60134	630-208-1020	
R/GA 350 W 39th St *Web:* www.rga.com	New York	NY	10018	212-946-4000	946-4010
Rainbow Advertising Lp 3904 W Vickery Blvd *Web:* www.rainbowadvertising.com	Fort Worth	TX	76107	817-738-3838	
Rakuten Marketing LLC 215 Pk Ave S 9th Fl *TF:* 888-880-8430 ■ *Web:* www.linkshareuk.com	New York	NY	10003	646-943-8200	943-8204
Rapp Advertising 30 Commerce St Ste 2 *Web:* www.rappadv.com	Springfield	NJ	07081	973-467-5570	
Rare Bird Inc 8555 Cedar Pl Dr Ste 114 *Web:* rarebirdinc.com	Indianapolis	IN	46240	317-251-6744	
Rc Productions Inc 1756 Lakeshore Dr *Web:* www.rcproductions.com	Muskegon	MI	49441	231-759-3160	
Real Integrated 40900 woodward ave *Web:* www.realintegrated.com	Bloomfield Hills	MI	48304	248-540-0660	
Real World Inc 8098 N Via De Negocio *Web:* www.realworldinc.com	Scottsdale	AZ	85258	480-296-0160	
Red Door Interactive Inc 350 10th Ave Ste 1100 *Web:* www.reddoor.biz	San Diego	CA	92101	619-398-2670	
Red Square Agency Inc 54 Saint Emanuel St *Web:* redsquaregaming.com	Mobile	AL	36602	251-476-1283	
RedPeg Marketing 727 N Washington St *Web:* www.redpegmarketing.com	Alexandria	VA	22314	703-519-9000	
Remer Inc 205 Marion St *Web:* www.remerinc.com	Seattle	WA	98104	206-624-1010	
Renegade LLC 437 Fifth Ave Fourth Fl *Web:* www.renegade.com	New York	NY	10016	646-486-7702	486-7800
Republica LLC 2153 Coral Way The Republica Bldg *Web:* republica.net	Miami	FL	33145	786-347-4700	
Republik, The 211 Rigsbee Ave *Web:* therepublik.net	Durham	NC	27701	919-956-9400	
RES Exhibit Services LLC 435 Smith St *Web:* www.res-exhibits.com	Rochester	NY	14608	585-546-2040	
Return Path Inc 304 Pk Ave S Seventh Fl *Web:* www.returnpath.com	New York	NY	10010	212-905-5500	905-5501
Riester Corp 802 N Third Ave *Web:* www.riester.com	Phoenix	AZ	85003	602-462-2200	
Robert Michael Communications Inc 101 Laurel Rd *Web:* www.rmei.com	Voorhees	NJ	08043	856-547-4141	
Room 214 Inc 3390 Valmont Rd Ste 214 *TF:* 866-624-1851 ■ *Web:* room214.com	Boulder	CO	80301	866-624-1851	
Rosenberg Advertising 12613 Detroit Ave *Web:* rosenbergadv.com	Lakewood	OH	44107	216-529-7910	
Royal Industries Inc 225 25th St *Web:* www.royalindustries.com	Brooklyn	NY	11232	718-369-3046	
Schnake Turnbo Frank Inc 20 E Fifth St Ste 1500 *Web:* www.stfpr.com	Tulsa	OK	74103	918-582-9151	
Schubert Communications Inc 112 Schubert Dr *Web:* www.schubert.com	Downingtown	PA	19335	610-269-2100	
Scream Agency LLC 1501 Wazee St Ste 1b *Web:* www.screamagency.com	Denver	CO	80202	303-893-8608	
Screamer Design LLC 107 Leland St Ste 3 *Web:* screamerco.com	Austin	TX	78704	512-691-7894	
ScreenScape Networks Inc 133 Queen St Third Fl *Web:* screenscape.net	Charlottetown	PE	C1A7K4	902-368-1975	
Secret Weapon Marketing 1658 10th St *Web:* www.secretweapon.net	Santa Monica	CA	90404	310-656-5999	
SEOP Inc 1720 E Garry St Ste 103 *TF:* 877-231-1557 ■ *Web:* www.seop.com	Santa Ana	CA	92705	877-231-1557	
SGW Integrated Marketing Communications Inc 219 Changebridge Rd *Web:* www.sgw.com	Montville	NJ	07045	973-299-8000	
Shine Advertising 612 W Main St Ste 105 *Web:* shineunited.com	Madison	WI	53703	608-442-7373	
Siegel & Gale 625 Ave of the Americas 4th Fl *TF:* 800-356-9377 ■ *Web:* siegelgale.com	New York	NY	10011	212-453-0400	453-0401
Simantel Group 321 SW Water St *Web:* www.simantel.com	Peoria	IL	61602	309-674-7747	
Simmonsflint 33 S Third St Ste D *Web:* www.simmonsflint.com	Grand Forks	ND	58201	701-746-4573	
Siquis Ltd 1340 Smith Ave Ste 300 *Web:* www.siquis.com	Baltimore	MD	21209	410-323-4800	
Smith, Kaplan, Allen & Reynolds Advertising Agency Inc 111 S 108th Ave *Web:* skar.com	Omaha	NE	68154	402-330-0110	
Source Marketing LLC 761 Main Ave *Web:* www.source-marketing.com	Norwalk	CT	06851	203-291-4000	
Spear Marketing Group 1630 N Main St Ste 200 *Web:* www.spearmarketing.com	Walnut Creek	CA	94596	925-891-9050	
Springbox Ltd 708 Congress Ave Ste A *Web:* www.springbox.com	Austin	TX	78701	512-391-0065	
Stealth 1617 locust st *Web:* stlautos.com	Saint Louis	MO	63103	314-480-3606	
Stein + Partners Brand Activation (SPBA) 432 Pk Ave S *Web:* www.steinias.com	New York	NY	10016	212-213-1112	779-7305
Steinreich Communications LLC 2125 Center Ave *Web:* www.scompr.com	Fort Fee	NJ	07024	201-498-1600	
Stephens Advertising Inc 417 E Stroop Rd *Web:* www.stephensdirect.com	Dayton	OH	45429	937-299-4993	
Stonearch Creative 710 S Second St Fl 7 *Web:* www.stonearchcreative.com	Minneapolis	MN	55401	612-200-5000	
Straight North LLC 1001 W 31st St *TF:* 866-353-3953 ■ *Web:* www.straightnorth.com	Downers Grove	IL	60515	866-353-3953	
Stream Companies Inc 400 Lapp Rd *Web:* www.streamcompanies.com	Malvern	PA	19355	610-644-8637	
Streng Design & Advertising Inc 244 W River Dr *Web:* www.strengdesign.com	Saint Charles	IL	60174	630-584-3887	
StrongView Systems Inc 1300 Island Dr Ste 200 *Web:* www.strongview.com	Redwood City	CA	94065	650-421-4200	
Sundin Associates Inc 34 Main St Fl 3 *Web:* www.sundininc.com	Natick	MA	01760	508-650-3972	
Taglairino Advertising Group Ny Inc 75 Sw 15th Rd *Web:* www.tagad.com	Miami	FL	33129	305-577-9988	
Taxi Canada Inc 495 Wellington St W Ste 102 *Web:* taxi.ca	Toronto	ON	M5V1E9	416-342-8294	
Team Detroit Inc 550 Town Ctr Dr *Web:* www.teamdetroit.com	Dearborn	MI	48126	313-615-2000	
Ten Adams Corp 1112 Se First St *Web:* www.tenadams.com	Evansville	IN	47713	812-422-7440	

Phone Fax

Teplow Cucurillo Communications LLC
68 Harvard St . . . . . Brookline MA 02445 617-566-6710
Web: tepcuc.com

Texas Press Association 718 W Fifth St Ste 100 . . . . . Austin TX 78701 512-477-6755
Web: www.texaspress.com

Third Rail Creative 112 E Seventh St . . . . . Austin TX 78701 512-358-9907
Web: thirdrailcreative.com

Thunder Tech Inc
3635 Perkins Ave Studio 5 SW . . . . . Cleveland OH 44114 216-391-2255
Web: www.thundertech.com

Timmons & Company Inc 1753 Kendarbren Dr . . . . . Jamison PA 18929 267-483-8220
Web: www.timmonsandcompany.com

Tiziani Whitmyre Inc Two Commercial St . . . . . Sharon MA 02067 781-793-9380
Web: www.tizinc.com

Tobe Direct 9700 Park Plz Ave Ste 210 . . . . . Louisville KY 40241 866-820-7313
TF: 866-820-7313 ■ *Web:* www.tobedirect.com

Topica Inc 1 Post Street Suite 875 . . . . . San Francisco CA 94104 415-344-0800 344-0900
TF: 888-728-2465 ■ *Web:* www.topica.com

Total Promotions 1340 Old Skokie Rd . . . . . Highland Park IL 60035 847-831-9500
Web: www.totalpromote.com

TPG Direct
Seven N Columbus Blvd The Piers at Penn's Landing
. . . . . Philadelphia PA 19106 215-592-8381
Web: www.tpgdirect.com

Traction Corp 1349 Larkin St . . . . . San Francisco CA 94109 415-962-5800
Web: www.tractionco.com

Trademark Media Corp 1601 E Seventh St Ste 200 . . . . . Austin TX 78702 512-459-7000
Web: www.trademarkmedia.com

Transcontinental Inc
1100 Rene-Levesque Blvd W 24th Fl . . . . . Montreal QC H3B4X9 514-392-9000
TF: 800-361-5479 ■ *Web:* tctranscontinental.com

Tri-Auto Enterprises LLC
7225 Georgetown Rd . . . . . Indianapolis IN 46268 317-644-5700
Web: perq.com

Tri-Media Integrated Marketing Technologies Inc (Prior to the acquisition by Andromeda Media)
517 Niagara St . . . . . Welland ON L3C1L7 905-732-6431
Web: www.tri-media.com

Truth & Advertising 454 N Broadway Ste 200 . . . . . Santa Ana CA 92701 714-542-8778
Web: truthemail.com

Tukaiz Communications LLC
2917 N Latoria Ln . . . . . Franklin Park IL 60131 847-455-1588
Web: www.tukaiz.com

Twist Image 407 rue McGill Second Fl . . . . . Montreal QC H2Y2G3 514-987-9992
Web: www.twistimage.com

Two by Four Ltd 10 N Dearborn St Ste 1000 . . . . . Chicago IL 60602 312-382-0100
Web: twoxfour.com

Unleaded Communications Inc 1701 Commerce St . . . . . Houston TX 77002 713-874-8200
Web: ulcomm.com

Uri Inc 3542 Hayden Ave Ste A . . . . . Culver City CA 90232 310-360-1212
Web: uriglobal.com

US Media Consulting
1801 SW Third Ave Third Fl . . . . . Miami FL 33129 305-722-5500
Web: www.usmediaconsulting.com

ValueClick Inc
30699 Russell Ranch Rd Ste 250 . . . . . Westlake Village CA 91362 818-575-4500 575-4501
NASDAQ: VCLK ■ *TF:* 877-361-3316 ■ *Web:* conversantmedia.com/valueclick/

ValueClick Media 530 E Montecito St . . . . . Santa Barbara CA 93103 805-879-1600 456-6611
TF: 877-361-3316 ■ *Web:* conversantmedia.com/valueclickmedia/

Vermont Media Publishing Company Ltd
Rt 100 PO Box 310 . . . . . West Dover VT 05356 802-464-3388 464-7255
Web: www.dvalnews.com

Versant Inc 11000 W Park Pl Ste A . . . . . Milwaukee WI 53224 414-410-0500
Web: www.versantsolutions.com

Vibrant Media Inc 565 Fifth Ave 15th Fl . . . . . New York NY 10017 646-312-6100
Web: www.vibrantmedia.com

Villing & Company Inc 5909 Nimtz Pkwy . . . . . South Bend IN 46628 574-277-0215
Web: villing.com

Vision Creative Group Inc 16 Wing Dr . . . . . Cedar Knolls NJ 07927 973-984-3454
Web: www.visioncreativegroup.com

VisionMAX Solutions Inc
Skymark Tower 2680 Skymark Ave Ste 600 . . . . . Mississauga ON L4W5L6 905-282-0503
Web: www.visionmax.com

Walker Advertising Inc 1010 S Cabrillo Ave . . . . . San Pedro CA 90731 310-519-4050
Web: www.losdefensores.com

Walsh & Sheppard Inc 111 W Ninth Ave . . . . . Anchorage AK 99501 907-338-3857
Web: www.walshsheppard.com

Walter F. Cameron Advertising Inc
350 Motor Pkwy Ste 410 . . . . . Hauppauge NY 11788 631-232-3033
Web: www.cameronadv.com

Wasserman & Partners Advertising Inc
1020 Mainland St Ste 160 . . . . . Vancouver BC V6B2T4 604-684-1111
Web: wasserman-partners.com

WebMetro 160 E Via Verde Ave Ste 220 . . . . . San Dimas CA 91773 909-599-8885
Web: www.webmetro.com

WebsiteBiz Inc 1713 Cleveland Ave . . . . . Charlotte NC 28203 704-338-1794
Web: www.websitebiz.com

Weinrib & Connor 297 Knollwood Rd . . . . . White Plains NY 10607 914-686-3900
Web: www.studio23.com

Williams & Helde Inc 711 Sixth Ave N Ste 200 . . . . . Seattle WA 98109 206-285-1940
Web: www.williams-helde.com

Words at Work 403 W Ponce De Leon Ave Ste 113 . . . . . Decatur GA 30030 404-270-9200
Web: wordsatwork.com

Working Media Group LLC 21 W 38th St 13th Fl . . . . . New York NY 10018 212-679-2681
Web: www.workingmediagroup.com

Worldwide Partners Inc 100 Spruce St Ste 203 . . . . . Denver CO 80230 303-577-9760
Web: www.worldwidepartners.com

Wowza Inc 2601 Second Ave S Studio One . . . . . Minneapolis MN 55408 612-435-7100
Web: wowzamade.com

Wray Ward Marketing Communications
900 Baxter St . . . . . Charlotte NC 28204 704-332-9071
Web: www.wrayward.com

WRL Advertising Inc 4470 Dressler Rd NW . . . . . Canton OH 44718 330-493-8866
Web: www.wrladv.com

X-15 Creative Marketing LLC
300 S Madison Ave . . . . . La Grange IL 60525 708-579-1623
Web: x-15marketing.com

Xperience Interactive
2601 Ocean Park Blvd Ste 116 . . . . . Santa Monica CA 90405 424-214-1471
Web: www.xperienceinteractive.com

Yearick-Millea 100 First Ave Ste 525 . . . . . Pittsburgh PA 15222 412-323-9320
Web: www.yearick-millea.com

Yellowhammer Media Group Inc
111-113-West 28th St . . . . . New York NY 10001 646-490-9841
Web: www.yhmg.com

Yesmail 309 SW Sixth Ave Ste 700 . . . . . Portland OR 97204 503-241-4185 241-4279
TF: 877-937-6245 ■ *Web:* www.yesmail.com

YuMe Inc 1204 Middlefield Rd . . . . . Redwood City CA 94063 650-591-9400
Web: www.yume.com

Zachry Associates Inc
500 Chestnut St Ste 2000 . . . . . Abilene TX 79602 325-677-1342
Web: www.zachryinc.com

8 ADVERTISING SERVICES - OUTDOOR ADVERTISING

Phone Fax

A & A Safety Inc 1126 Ferris Rd . . . . . Amelia OH 45102 513-943-6100
Web: www.aasafetyinc.com

Aarrow Advertising 4312 Valeta St . . . . . San Diego CA 92107 619-222-3770
Web: aarrowsignspinners.com

Adams Outdoor Adv Co 911 SW Adams St . . . . . Peoria IL 61602 309-692-2482 692-8452
Web: www.adamsoutdoor.com

Advanced Sign Co 2024 Fifth St NW . . . . . Albuquerque NM 87102 505-246-8458
Web: www.advancedsignco.com

Affiliate Traction 2125 Delaware Ave Ste E . . . . . Santa Cruz CA 95060 831-464-1441
Web: www.affiliatetraction.com

Alpak Display Group 575 N Midland Ave . . . . . Saddle Brook NJ 07663 201-797-1411
Web: www.alpak.com

Barrett Outdoor Communications Inc
381 Highland St . . . . . West Haven CT 06516 203-932-4601
Web: www.barrettoc.com

Blue Hive Inc Seven Coppage Dr . . . . . Worcester MA 01603 508-581-9560
Web: www.blue-hive.com

Bowlin Travel Centers Inc
150 Louisiana NE . . . . . Albuquerque NM 87108 505-266-5985
OTC: BWTL ■ *Web:* www.bowlintc.com

Chicago Scenic Studios Inc
1315 N North Branch St . . . . . Chicago IL 60642 312-274-9900
Web: www.chicagoscenic.com

Cineplex Digital Networks 369 York St Ste 2C . . . . . London ON N6B3R4 519-438-0111
Web: ek3.com

Clear Ch Outdoor Inc
2325 E Camelback Rd Ste 400 . . . . . Phoenix AZ 85016 602-381-5700 381-5782
Web: www.clearchanneloutdoor.com

Compass Collective 165 Ottley Dr Ne . . . . . Atlanta GA 30324 404-875-6543
Web: www.compasscollective.com

Display Works Inc 335 Gordons Corner Rd . . . . . Manalapan NJ 07726 732-536-0800
Web: www.displayworks.com

Dodd Technologies Inc 7979 W Fall Creek Dr . . . . . Pendleton IN 46064 317-485-4604
Web: doddtechnologies.com

Fairway Outdoor Advertising Inc
814 Duncan-Reidville Rd . . . . . Duncan SC 29334 864-439-6371
Web: fairwayoutdoor.com

Impac International 11445 Pacific Ave . . . . . Fontana CA 92337 951-685-9660
Web: impacpanel.com

Ion Art Inc 407 Radam Ln Ste A100 . . . . . Austin TX 78745 512-326-9333
Web: ionart.com

Kegerreis Outdoor Advertising LLC
1310 Lincoln Way E . . . . . Chambersburg PA 17202 717-263-6700
Web: www.kegerreis.com

Kubin-Nicholson Corp 8440 N 87th St . . . . . Milwaukee WI 53224 414-586-4300 586-6802
TF: 800-858-9557 ■ *Web:* www.kubin.com

Lamar Adv Co 5321 Corporate Blvd . . . . . Baton Rouge LA 70808 225-926-1000 923-0658
NASDAQ: LAMR ■ *TF:* 800-235-2627 ■ *Web:* www.lamar.com

Metro Bench Advertisers 3014 W Horatio St . . . . . Tampa FL 33609 813-872-8502
Web: www.metrobench.com

Midway Displays Inc 6554 S Austin Ave . . . . . Bedford Park IL 60638 708-563-2323
Web: www.midwaydisplays.com

NextMedia Group Inc
6312 S Fiddlers Green Cir Ste 205E . . . . . Greenwood Village CO 80111 303-694-9118 694-4940

Norton Outdoor Advertising
5280 Kennedy Ave . . . . . Cincinnati OH 45213 513-631-4864
Web: www.norton-outdoor.com

Origin LLC 119 E Graham Pl . . . . . Burbank CA 91502 818-848-1648
Web: www.originpop.com

OUTFRONT Media Inc 405 Lexington Ave . . . . . New York NY 10174 212-297-6400
TF: 800-926-8834 ■ *Web:* www.cbsoutdoor.com

Peachtree Packaging Inc
770 Marathon Pkwy . . . . . Lawrenceville GA 30046 770-822-1304 995-8447
Web: www.peachtreepackaging.com

PG Exhibits 3510 Himalaya Rd . . . . . Aurora CO 80011 303-722-6565
Web: www.pgexhibits.com

R.O.A. General Inc
1775 N Warm Springs Rd . . . . . Salt Lake City UT 84116 801-521-1775
Web: reaganoutdoor.com

RCS Enterprises Inc 7075 W Parkland Ct . . . . . Milwaukee WI 53223 414-354-6900
Web: www.rcsinnovations.com

Redstar Media Group LLC
7685 Williamsport Pk . . . . . Falling Waters WV 25419 304-274-6943

Reynolds Sign 1336 S Irving Heights Dr . . . . . Irving TX 75060 972-870-1594
Web: reynoldssign.com

Skyline Displays Bay Area Inc
44111 Fremont Blvd . . . . . Fremont CA 94538 510-490-9900
Web: www.skybay.com

Phone Fax

Skyline Exhibits Metro Chicago
2140 W Walnut St. . . . . Chicago IL 60612 312-733-0660
Web: skylinemetrochicago.com

Spec Personnel LLC 25 Walls Dr. . . . . Fairfield CT 06824 203-254-9935
Web: www.speconthejob.com

Stott Outdoor Advertising Po Box 7209. . . . . Chico CA 95927 530-342-3235
Web: stottoutdoor.com

Studio y Creations Inc 1-6204 29 St Se. . . . . Calgary AB T2C1W3 403-253-5447
Web: www.studioycreations.com

Suite 66 366 Adelaide St W Ste 600 . . . . . Toronto ON M5V1R9 416-628-5565
Web: www.suite66.com

Vestcom International Inc 7302 Kanis Rd . . . . . Little Rock AR 72204 501-663-0100
Web: www.vestcom.com

Witt Sign Company Inc 306 McCowan Dr. . . . . Lebanon TN 37087 615-444-3898 444-3980
Web: wittsigns.com

Woodlands Academy Preparatory School, The
27440 Kuykendahl Rd. . . . . Tomball TX 77375 281-516-0600
Web: woodlandsprep.org

WSOS Community Action Commission Inc
109 S Front St . . . . . Fremont OH 43420 419-334-8911
Web: www.wsos.org

9 ADVERTISING SPECIALTIES

SEE Farm Machinery & Equipment - Mfr p. 2282; Farm Machinery & Equipment - Whol p. 2284

Phone Fax

Adco Litho Line Inc 2700 W Roosevelt Rd . . . . . Broadview IL 60155 708-345-8200

ADG Promotional Products 2300 Main St . . . . . Hugo MN 55038 800-852-5208 886-6790
TF: 800-852-5208 ■ *Web:* www.adgpromo.com

AIA Corporation (AIA) 800 Winneconne Ave . . . . . Neenah WI 54956 920-886-3700 886-3733
TF: 800-460-7836 ■ *Web:* www.aiagearedforgrowth.com

Airmate Co Inc 16280 County Rd D. . . . . Bryan OH 43506 419-636-3184 636-4210
TF: 800-544-3614 ■ *Web:* www.airmatecompany.com

Alexander Mfg Co 12978 Tesson Ferry Rd . . . . . Sappington MO 63128 314-842-3344
TF General: 800-258-2743 ■ *Web:* www.alexandermc.com

Allen Co 712 E Main St . . . . . Blanchester OH 45107 937-783-2491 783-4831
TF: 800-329-2491 ■ *Web:* www.allenmugs.com

Americanna Co 29 Aldrin Rd. . . . . Plymouth MA 02360 508-747-5550 747-5578
TF Cust Svc: 888-747-5550 ■ *Web:* www.americanna.com

Amsterdam Printing & Litho Corp
166 Wallins Corners Rd . . . . . Amsterdam NY 12010 518-842-6000 843-5204
TF Cust Svc: 800-833-6231 ■ *Web:* www.amsterdamprinting.com

Arthur Blank & Co Inc 225 Rivermoor St . . . . . Boston MA 02132 617-325-9600 327-1235
TF: 800-776-7333 ■ *Web:* www.abnote.com

Atlas Match LLC 1801 S Airport Cir. . . . . Euless TX 76040 817-267-1500 354-7478
TF: 800-628-2426 ■ *Web:* www.atlasmatch.com

Bastian Co 15 Eagle St . . . . . Phelps NY 14532 315-548-2300 548-2310
Web: www.bastiancompany.com

Belaire Products Inc 763 S Broadway St . . . . . Akron OH 44311 330-253-3116 376-7790
TF: 800-886-3224 ■ *Web:* www.belaireproducts.com

Bergamot Inc 820 E Wisconsin St. . . . . Delavan WI 53115 262-728-5572 728-3750*
**Fax:* Sales ■ *TF Cust Svc:* 800-922-6733 ■ *Web:* www.bergamot.net

Brown & Bigelow Inc 345 Plato Blvd E. . . . . Saint Paul MN 55107 651-293-7000 293-7025*
**Fax:* Hum Res ■ *TF Cust Svc:* 800-628-1755 ■ *Web:* www.brownandbigelow.com

Churchwell Co 814 S Edgewood Ave. . . . . Jacksonville FL 32205 904-356-5721 354-2436
TF: 877-537-6166 ■ *Web:* www.churchwellcompany.com

Crown Products LLC 3107 Halls Mill Rd. . . . . Mobile AL 36606 251-665-3600 471-2095
Web: www.crownprod.com

Dard Products Inc 912 Custer Ave. . . . . Evanston IL 60202 847-328-5000 328-7835
Web: www.tagmaster.net

Dunn Manufacturing Inc 1400 Goldmine Rd . . . . . Monroe NC 28110 704-283-2147 289-6857
TF: 800-868-7111 ■ *Web:* facebook.com

EBSCO Creative Concepts
3500 Blue Lake Dr Ste 150. . . . . Birmingham AL 35243 205-262-2696 262-2693
TF: 800-756-7023 ■ *Web:* www.ebscocreativeconcepts.com

Ever-Lite Company Inc 1717 N Bayshore Dr . . . . . Miami FL 33132 305-577-0819
Web: www.ever-lite.com

Flair Communications Agency Inc
214 W Erie St . . . . . Chicago IL 60654 312-943-5959 943-6049
TF: 800-621-8317 ■ *Web:* flairagency.com

Geiger 70 Mt Hope Ave . . . . . Lewiston ME 04240 207-755-2000 755-2422
Web: www.geiger.com

Gold Bond Inc 5485 Hixson Pike . . . . . Hixson TN 37343 423-842-5844 842-7934
Web: www.goldbondinc.com

Hit Promotional Products Inc
7150 Bryan Dairy Rd. . . . . Largo FL 33777 727-541-5561 541-5130
TF: 800-237-6305 ■ *Web:* www.hitpromo.net

Imageworks Manufacturing Inc 49 S St . . . . . Park Forest IL 60466 708-503-1122 503-1133
Web: www.imageworksmfg.com

Instant Imprints 5897 Oberlin Dr Ste 200 . . . . . San Diego CA 92121 858-642-4848 453-6513
TF: 800-542-3437 ■ *Web:* www.instantimprints.com

Lewtan Industries Corp 30 High St . . . . . Hartford CT 06103 860-278-9800
Web: www.lewtan123.com

Marco Promotional Products
2640 Commerce Dr . . . . . Harrisburg PA 17110 877-545-9322 545-5672*
**Fax Area Code:* 866 ■ *TF:* 877-545-9322 ■ *Web:* www.marcopromotionalproducts.com

Marietta Hospitality 37 Huntington St. . . . . Cortland NY 13045 607-753-6746 756-0658*
**Fax:* Cust Svc ■ *TF:* 800-950-7772 ■ *Web:* www.mariettacorp.com

Maryland Match Corp 605 Alluvion St. . . . . Baltimore MD 21230 410-752-8164 752-3441
TF: 800-423-0013 ■ *Web:* www.marylandmatch.com

Mid-America Merchandising Inc
204 W Third St . . . . . Kansas City MO 64105 816-471-5600 842-0952
TF: 800-333-6737 ■ *Web:* www.mmipromo.com

MMG Works/Status Promotions
4601 Madison Ave . . . . . Kansas City MO 64112 816-472-5988 472-7107
TF: 800-945-4044 ■ *Web:* www.mmgworks.com

Myron Corp 205 Maywood Ave . . . . . Maywood NJ 07607 877-803-3358
TF: 877-803-3358 ■ *Web:* www.myron.com

National Pen Corp (NPC)
12121 Scripps Summit Dr Ste 200. . . . . San Diego CA 92131 858-675-3000 675-0890
TF: 800-854-1000 ■ *Web:* www.pens.com

Phone Fax

Nationwide Adv Specialty Co
2025 S Cooper St . . . . . Arlington TX 76010 817-275-2678 274-4301
Web: www.nationwideadvertising.net

Neely Mfg 2178 Hwy 2 . . . . . Corydon IA 50060 641-872-1100
Web: www.neelymfg.com

Newton Mfg Co 1123 First Ave E . . . . . Newton IA 50208 641-792-4121 792-6261
TF: 800-500-7227 ■ *Web:* www.newtonmfg.net

Norscot Group Inc
1000 W Donges Bay Rd PO Box 998 . . . . . Mequon WI 53092 262-241-3313 241-4904
TF: 800-653-3313 ■ *Web:* www.norscot.com

Norwood Promotional Products Inc
14421 Myerlake Cir . . . . . Clearwater IN 33760 727-538-3527 275-2570*
**Fax Area Code:* 317 ■ *TF:* 877-555-2223 ■ *Web:* www.norwood.com

Numo Manufacturing Co 1072 E Hwy 175. . . . . Kaufman TX 75142 972-962-5400
Web: www.numomfg.com

Pilgrim Plastic Products Co
1200 W Chestnut St . . . . . Brockton MA 02301 508-583-9046 257-3955*
**Fax Area Code:* 651 ■ *TF:* 877-343-7810 ■ *Web:* www.pilgrimplastics.com

Prime Resources Corp 1100 Boston Ave . . . . . Bridgeport CT 06610 203-331-9100 330-0123
TF: 800-621-5463 ■ *Web:* www.primeline.com

Quick Point Inc 1717 Fenpark Dr. . . . . Fenton MO 63026 636-343-9400 343-3587
Web: www.quickpoint.com

Quikey Manufacturing Co 1500 Industrial Pkwy . . . . . Akron OH 44310 330-633-8106 633-6670
TF: 877-901-1200 ■ *Web:* www.quikey.com

Slack & Company Inc
233 N Michigan Ave Ste 3050 . . . . . Chicago IL 60601 312-970-5800 970-5850
Web: www.slackandcompany.com

Staples Promotional Products
7500 W 110th St. . . . . Overland Park KS 66210 913-319-3100
TF: 800-369-4669 ■ *Web:* www.staplespromotionalproducts.com

Universal Creative Concepts Corp
10143 Royalton Rd Unit E. . . . . North Royalton OH 44133 440-230-1366 230-1919
TF: 800-876-8626 ■ *Web:* www.uccpromo.com

Vanguard East 1172 Azalea Garden Rd . . . . . Norfolk VA 23502 800-221-1264 857-0222*
**Fax Area Code:* 757 ■ *TF:* 800-221-1264 ■ *Web:* www.vanguardmil.com

VATEX America 2395 Hermitage Rd. . . . . Richmond VA 23220 804-353-9010 353-8939
Web: www.vatex.com

Western Plastic Products Inc 8441 Monroe Ave. . . . . Stanton CA 90680 800-453-1881 495-2232*
**Fax Area Code:* 562 ■ *TF:* 800-453-1881 ■ *Web:* www.wbadges.com

Zebra Marketing
7119 Laurel Canyon Blvd Suite 3 . . . . . North Hollywood CA 91605 818-765-6442
TF: 800-348-2422 ■ *Web:* www.zebramerchandise.blogspot.in

AGRICULTURAL CHEMICALS

AGRICULTURAL MACHINERY & EQUIPMENT

SEE Farm Machinery & Equipment - Mfr p. 2282; Farm Machinery & Equipment - Whol p. 2284

10 AGRICULTURAL PRODUCTS

SEE ALSO Fruit Growers p. 2338; Horse Breeders p. 2478; Horticultural Products Growers p. 2478; Seed Companies p. 3165

Phone Fax

Border Valley Trading Ltd 604 E Mead Rd. . . . . Brawley CA 92227 760-344-6700 344-4305
Web: www.bordervalley.com

United Farmers Co-op (UFC)
705 E Fourth St PO Box 461. . . . . Winthrop MN 55396 507-647-6600 647-6620
TF: 866-998-3266 ■ *Web:* www.ufcmn.com

10-1 Cattle Ranches, Farms, Feedlots (Beef Cattle)

Phone Fax

A Duda & Sons Inc 1200 Duda Trail . . . . . Oviedo FL 32765 407-365-2111 365-2147
Web: www.duda.com

Agri Beef Co 1555 Shoreline Dr Ste 320. . . . . Boise ID 83702 208-338-2500 338-2605
TF: 800-657-6305 ■ *Web:* www.agribeef.com

AzTx Cattle Co PO Box 390 . . . . . Hereford TX 79045 806-364-8871 364-3842
TF: 800-999-5065 ■ *Web:* www.aztx.com

Bar G Feed Yard 275 FM 1057 Rd . . . . . Summerfield TX 79085 806-357-2241 357-2325
Web: bar-g.com

Barton County Feeders Inc 1164 SE 40th Rd . . . . . Ellinwood KS 67526 620-564-2200 564-2253
Web: bartoncountyfeeders.com

Beef Belt Feeders Inc 1350 E Rd 70 . . . . . Scott City KS 67871 620-872-5306

Beef Northwest Feeders Inc 3455 Victorio Rd . . . . . Nyssa OR 97913 541-372-2101 372-5661
Web: www.beefnw.com

Bledsoe Cattle Co 41726 US 385. . . . . Wray CO 80758 970-332-4955

Boise Valley Feeders LLC
1555 Shoreline Dr Suite 320 . . . . . Boise ID 83702 208-338-2605 657-6305*
**Fax Area Code:* 800 ■ *Web:* www.agribeef.com

Buffalo Feeders LLC E US Hwy 64 PO Box 409 . . . . . Buffalo OK 73834 580-735-2511 735-6035
Web: www.buffalofeeders.com

Cactus Feeders Inc 2209 W Seventh Ave. . . . . Amarillo TX 79106 806-373-2333 371-4767
TF: 877-698-7355 ■ *Web:* www.cactusfeeders.com

Coyote Lake Feedyard Inc 1287 FM 1731 . . . . . Muleshoe TX 79347 806-946-3321 946-3329
TF: 800-299-3321 ■ *Web:* www.coyotelakefeedyard.com

Darr Feedlot Inc 42826 Rd 759 . . . . . Cozad NE 69130 308-324-2363 324-2365
Web: www.darrfeedlot.com

Dean Cluck Feedyard Inc 105 Dean Cluck Ave . . . . . Gruver TX 79040 806-733-5021 733-2244
TF: 888-458-4787 ■ *Web:* deancluckfeedyard.com

Dinklage Feedyards PO Box 274 . . . . . Sidney NE 69162 308-254-5940 254-6260
TF: 888-343-5940 ■ *Web:* www.dinklagefeedyards.com

Fall River Feedyard LLC
27962 Angostura Rd. . . . . Hot Springs SD 57747 605-745-4109
Web: aranch.d-cs2.net

Ford County Feed Yard Inc 12466 US Hwy 400. . . . . Ford KS 67842 620-369-2252

Phone | Fax

Friona Feedyard 2370 FM 3140 .... Friona TX 79035 806-265-3574 265-3577
TF: 800-658-6014 ■ *Web:* www.frionaind.com

Friona Industries LP
500 S Taylor St Ste 601 PO Box 15568 .... Amarillo TX 79101 806-374-1811 374-1324
TF: 800-658-6014 ■ *Web:* www.frionaind.com

Garden City Feed Yard
1805 W Annie Scheer Rd .... Garden City KS 67846 620-275-4191
TF: 800-272-4191 ■ *Web:* www.aztx.com

Gottsch Feeding Corp
20507 Nicholas Cir Ste 100 .... Elkhorn NE 68022 402-463-6215
Web: gottschcattlecompany.com

Gray County Feed Yard Inc 23405 SR 23 .... Cimarron KS 67835 620-855-3486 855-7739
Web: graycountyfeed.com

Great Bend Feeding Inc 2006 Broadway Ave .... Great Bend KS 67530 620-793-9200
Web: www.ilsbeef.com

Hansford County Feeders LP
13800 County Rd 19 .... Spearman TX 79081 806-477-1900 477-1910
Web: hcflp.com

Hays Feeders LLC 1174 Feedlot Rd .... Hays KS 67601 785-625-3415 625-0074
Web: www.prattfeeders.com

Herd Company Cattle Co 83973 489th Ave .... Bartlett NE 68622 402-482-5931 482-5971

High Choice Feeders LLC 553 W Rd 40 .... Scott City KS 67871 620-872-7271 872-5763
Web: highchoicefeeders.com

Ingalls Feed Yard 10505 US Hwy 50 .... Ingalls KS 67853 620-335-5174
Web: www.irsikanddoll.com

Irsik & Doll Co PO Box 847 .... Cimarron KS 67835 620-855-3111 855-3748
Web: www.irsikanddoll.com

JR Simplot Co 999 W Main St Ste 1300 .... Boise ID 83702 208-336-2110 389-7515
TF: 800-832-8893 ■ *Web:* www.simplot.com

King Ranch Inc Three Riverway Ste 1600 .... Houston TX 77056 832-681-5700
Web: www.king-ranch.com

Knight Feedlot Inc 1768 Ave J .... Lyons KS 67554 620-257-5106 257-3347

Littlefield Feedyard Farm to Market 37 .... Littlefield TX 79339 806-385-5141
TF: 800-658-6014 ■ *Web:* www.frionaind.com

Midwest Feeders Inc 5013 13 Rd .... Ingalls KS 67853 620-335-5790 335-5636
Web: www.midwest-feeders.com

Morrison Enterprises 3303 W 12th St .... Hastings NE 68901 402-463-3191 462-8542

North Platte Livestock Feeders Inc
3303 W 12th St .... Hastings NE 68901 402-463-6215
Web: www.gottschcattlecompany.com

PM Beef Group LLC 2850 Hwy 60 E .... Windom MN 56101 507-831-2761 831-6216
TF: 800-622-5213 ■ *Web:* www.pmbeef.com

Pratt Feeders LLC PO Box 945 .... Pratt KS 67124 620-672-6448 672-7797
Web: www.prattfeeders.com

Premium Feeders Inc 705 US Hwy 36 .... Scandia KS 66966 785-335-2221
Web: www.premiumfeeders.com

Quality Beef Producers 5000 IH- 40 .... Wildorado TX 79098 806-426-3325 426-3582

Randall County Feedyard 15000 FM 2219 .... Amarillo TX 79119 806-499-3701
TF: 800-658-6014 ■ *Web:* www.frionaind.com

Red Rock Feeding Co 35415 E Sasco Cir .... Red Rock AZ 85245 520-682-3448

Royal Beef Feed Yard 11060 N Falcon Rd .... Scott City KS 67871 620-872-5371 872-3380
Web: www.irsikanddoll.com

Sparrowk Livestock 18780 E Hwy 88 .... Clements CA 95227 209-759-3530 759-3831
Web: www.sparrowk.com

Sublette Feeders 1535 Uu Rd .... Sublette KS 67877 620-668-5501

Swisher County Cattle Co Farm Market 214 Rd .... Tulia TX 79088 806-627-4231
TF: 800-658-6014 ■ *Web:* www.frionaind.com

Tejas Feeders Ltd PO Box 1782 .... Pampa TX 79066 806-665-2030 669-0210
Web: www.tejasfeeders.com

Tejon Ranch Co 4436 Lebec Rd PO Box 1000 .... Lebec CA 93243 661-248-3000 248-3100
NYSE: TRC ■ *Web:* www.tejonranch.com

Tri-State Feeders Inc Three Mile S Hwy 83 .... Turpin OK 73950 580-778-3600

Weborg Feeding Co 1737 V Rd .... Pender NE 68047 402-385-3441 385-2441
Web: www.weborgfeeding.com

Western Feed Yard Inc 548 S Rd I .... Johnson KS 67855 620-492-6256 492-6239

10-2 Cotton Farms

Phone | Fax

JG Boswell Co 101 W Walnut St .... Pasadena CA 91103 626-583-3000 583-3090
NYSE: BWEL

Wesson Farms Inc 25 Victoria Rd .... Osceola AR 72370 870-563-2674 563-6927

Westlake Farms Inc 23311 Newton Ave .... Stratford CA 93266 559-947-3348

10-3 Dairy Farms

Phone | Fax

Astia Inc 833 Market St Ste 605 .... San Francisco CA 94103 415-421-5500
Web: www.astia.org

Avid Identification Systems Inc
3185 Hamner Ave .... Norco CA 92860 951-371-7505
Web: www.avidid.com

Berry Bros General Contractors Inc
1414 River Rd .... Berwick LA 70342 985-384-8770

Big D Ranch 7590 S 10 Mile Rd .... Meridian ID 83642 208-888-1710 888-0075
Web: www.bigdranch.com

Biomedical Research Models Inc
67 Millbrook St .... Worcester MA 01606 508-459-7544
Web: brmcro.com/

DNA LandMarks Inc
84 Richelieu St .... Saint Jean-Sur-Richelieu QC J3B6X3 450-358-2621
Web: www.dnalandmarks.com

Fred Rau Dairy 10255 W Manning Ave .... Fresno CA 93706 559-237-3393 237-3879

G & R Foods Inc PO Box 610 .... Reedsburg WI 53959 608-524-3776 524-1752
Web: www.grfoodsinc.com

Hollandia Dairy Inc 622 E Mission Rd .... San Marcos CA 92069 760-744-3222 744-2789
TF: 888-883-2479 ■ *Web:* www.hollandiadairy.com

Kreider Farms 1461 Lancaster Rd .... Manheim PA 17545 717-665-4415 665-9614
TF: 888-665-4415 ■ *Web:* www.kreiderfarms.com

Phone | Fax

Marburger Farm Dairy Inc
1506 Mars Evans City Rd .... Evans City PA 16033 724-538-4800 538-3250
TF: 800-331-1295 ■ *Web:* www.marburgerdairy.com

Maytag Dairy Farms Inc 2282 E Eighth St N .... Newton IA 50208 641-792-1133 792-1567
Web: iowabackroads.com

McClellan Park LLC 3140 Peacekeeper Way .... Mcclellan CA 95652 916-965-7100
Web: www.mcclellanpark.com

Meadow Gold Dairy 55 S Wakea Ave .... Kahului HI 96732 808-877-5541
Web: www.lanimoo.com

Provimi Foods Inc W2103 County Rd W .... Seymour WI 54165 920-833-6861
Web: www.provimi-veal.com

Ronnybrook Farm Dairy Inc
310 Prospect Hill Rd .... Ancramdale NY 12503 518-398-6455
Web: www.ronnybrook.com

Shamrock Farms Co 40034 W Clayton Rd .... Stanfield AZ 85172 480-988-1452
Web: www.shamrockfarms.net

Tree Top Ranches LP PO Box 8126 .... Boise ID 83707 208-377-0998

Virginia Poultry Growers Co-op Inc
6349 Rawley Pk .... Hinton VA 22831 540-867-4000
Web: www.vapoultrygrowers.com

10-4 General Farms

Phone | Fax

ABF Farm Services Inc 7761 W Undine Rd .... Stockton CA 95206 209-462-0208 462-9429

Agrex Inc 10975 Grandview Dr St Ste 200 .... Overland Park KS 66210 913-851-6300 851-6210
TF: 800-334-6788 ■ *Web:* www.agrexinc.com

Amana Colonies 622 46th Ave .... Amana IA 52203 319-622-7622
TF: 800-579-2294 ■ *Web:* www.amanacolonies.com

Belk Farms 57300 Desert Cactus Dr .... Thermal CA 92274 760-399-5951

Burford Ranch 1443 W Sample Ave .... Fresno CA 93711 559-431-0902 431-1625

DM Camp & Sons 31798 Merced Ave .... Bakersfield CA 93308 661-399-5511
Web: www.dmcampandsons.com

farmers win coop (FFC) 110 N Jefferson .... Fredericksburg IA 50630 563-237-5324 237-6123
TF: 800-562-8389 ■ *Web:* www.fburgcoop.com

FarmTek 1440 Field of Dreams Way .... Dyersville IA 52040 563-875-2288
TF: 800-327-6835 ■ *Web:* www.farmtek.com

Gold-eagle Co-op 515 N Locust St PO Box 280 .... Goldfield IA 50542 800-825-3331
TF: 800-825-3331 ■ *Web:* www.goldeaglecoop.com

Great American Farms Inc
1255 W Atlantic Blvd Ste 218 .... Pompano Beach FL 33069 954-785-9400 941-2977

Mercer Canyons Inc 46 Sonova Rd .... Prosser WA 99350 509-894-4773 894-4965
Web: mercercanyons.com

Mid Valley Agricultural Services Inc
16401 E Hwy 26 PO Box 593 .... Linden CA 95236 209-931-7600 931-0747
Web: www.midvalleyag.com

Morrison Enterprises 3303 W 12th St .... Hastings NE 68901 402-463-3191 462-8542

Oji Bros Farms Inc 8547 Sawtelle Ave .... Yuba City CA 95991 530-673-0845 673-8742

OPC Farms Inc 22300 Railroad Ave .... San Joaquin CA 93660 559-693-2700

Plains Grain & Agronomy LLC
109 Third Ave PO Box 6 .... Enderlin ND 58027 701-437-2400
TF: 800-950-2219 ■ *Web:* www.plainsgrain.com

River Garden Farms Co
41758 County Rd 112 .... Knights Landing CA 95645 530-735-6274 735-6734

Star of the West Milling Co
121 E Tuscola St .... Frankenmuth MI 48734 989-652-9971 652-6358
TF: 888-281-4161 ■ *Web:* www.starofthewest.com

Sumner Peck Ranch Inc (SPR) 14860 N Hwy 41 .... Madera CA 93636 559-822-3301
Web: www.sumnerpeckranch.com

Tosh Farms 1586 Atlantic Ave .... Henry TN 38231 731-243-4861 243-4860
Web: www.toshfarms.net

10-5 Grain Farms

Phone | Fax

AgriNorthwest 7404 W Hood Pl Ste B .... Kennewick WA 99336 509-734-1195 783-5438
TF: 888-632-5511 ■ *Web:* tricityregionalchamber.com

Alger Farms Inc 950 NW Eigth St .... Homestead FL 33030 305-247-4334
Web: www.algerfarms.com

Big River Resources West Burlington LLC
15210 103rd St .... West Burlington IA 52655 319-753-1100 753-1103
Web: www.bigriverresources.com

Busch Agricultural Resources Inc
2101 26th St S .... Moorhead MN 56560 218-233-8531
Web: www.anheuser-busch.com

Colusa Elevator Co 2531 N County Rd .... Colusa IL 62329 217-755-4221 755-4202
Web: www.colusaelevator.com

Country Pride Co-op (CPC)
648 W Second St PO Box 529 .... Winner SD 57580 605-842-2711 842-2715
TF: 888-325-7743 ■ *Web:* www.countrypridecoop.com

Erwin-Keith Inc 1529 Hwy 193 .... Wynne AR 72396 870-238-2079 238-8621
Web: progenyag.com

Golden Grain Energy LLC 1822 43rd St SW .... Mason City IA 50401 641-423-8525 421-8457
TF: 888-443-2676 ■ *Web:* www.goldengrainenergy.com

Hoegemeyer Hybrids Inc 1755 Hoegemeyer Rd .... Hooper NE 68031 402-654-3399
TF: 800-245-4631 ■ *Web:* www.therightseed.com

Illinois Foundation Seeds Inc (IFSI)
1083 County Rd 900 N .... Tolono IL 61880 217-485-6260 485-3687
Web: www.ifsi.com

MFA Inc 201 Ray Young Dr .... Columbia MO 65201 573-874-5111 876-5505
Web: www.mfaincorporated.com

Midwest Co-op PO Box 787 .... Pierre SD 57501 605-224-5935 224-9550
Web: www.midwestcooperatives.com

Minn-Dak Growers Ltd 4034 40th Ave N .... Grand Forks ND 58203 701-746-7453 780-9050
Web: www.minndak.com

Moews Seed Co Inc 9821 IL Hwy 89 .... Granville IL 60640 815-339-2201
TF: 800-663-9795 ■ *Web:* www.moews.com

	City	State	ZIP	Phone	Fax
Morrow County Grain Growers Inc (MCGG) 350 N Main St *TF:* 800-452-7396 ■ *Web:* www.mcgg.net	Lexington	OR	97839	541-989-8221	989-8229
Pioneer Hi-Bred International Inc PO Box 1000 *TF:* 800-247-6803 ■ *Web:* www.pioneer.com	Johnston	IA	50131	515-535-3200	535-4415
Remington Seeds 4746 W US Hwy 24 PO Box 9 *Web:* www.remingtonseeds.com	Remington	IN	47977	219-261-3444	261-2220
Richard Gumz Farms 8905 S Gumz Rd	North Judson	IN	46366	574-896-5441	
Stonington Co-op Grain 402 Walnut St PO Box 350	Stonington	IL	62567	217-325-3211	
Sunray Co-op 201 N Main PO Box 430 *TF:* 800-621-3570 ■ *Web:* www.sunraycoop.com	Sunray	TX	79086	806-948-4121	948-1991
Wesson Farms Inc 25 Victoria Rd	Osceola	AR	72370	870-563-2674	563-6927
Westlake Farms Inc 23311 Newton Ave	Stratford	CA	93266	559-947-3348	
William F Renk & Sons Inc 6809 Wilburn Rd **Fax Area Code:* 608 ■ *TF:* 800-289-7365 ■ *Web:* www.renkseed.com	Sun Prairie	WI	53590	800-289-7365	825-6143*
Wyffels Hybrids Inc 13344 US Hwy 6 *TF:* 800-369-7833 ■ *Web:* www.wyffels.com	Geneseo	IL	61254	309-944-8334	944-8338

10-6 Hog Farms

	City	State	ZIP	Phone	Fax
Cargill Inc 15407 McGinty Rd W **Fax:* Cust Svc ■ *TF:* 800-227-4455 ■ *Web:* www.cargill.com	Wayzata	MN	55391	952-742-7575	742-7209*
Christensen Farms 23971 County Rd 10 *Web:* www.christensenfarms.com	Sleepy Eye	MN	56085	507 794 5310	794 2471
Goschie Farms Inc 7365 Meridian Rd NE *Web:* goschiefarms.com	Silverton	OR	97381	503-873-5638	
Hanor Co E 4614 Hwy 14-60 *Web:* hanorcompany.com	Spring Green	WI	53588	608-588-9170	588-2308
Hastings Pork 301 S Burlington Avenue *Web:* www.hastingschamber.com	Hastings	NE	68901	402-461-8400	
Hog Slat Inc PO Box 300 *TF:* 800-949-4647 ■ *Web:* www.hogslat.com	Newton Grove	NC	28366	910-594-0219	594-1392
Iowa Select Farms LP 811 S Oak St PO Box 400 *Web:* www.iowaselect.com	Iowa Falls	IA	50126	641-648-4479	648-4251
Jeckel Pork Farm Inc 600 N Sherman	Delavan	IL	61734	309-244-7281	
NG Purvis Farms Inc 2504 Spies Rd	Robbins	NC	27325	910-948-2297	948-3213
PIC USA 100 Bluegrass Commons Blvd Ste 2200 *TF:* 800-325-3398 ■ *Web:* www.pic.com/usa	Hendersonville	TN	37075	615-265-2700	
Prestage Farms 4651 Taylors Bridge Hwy *Web:* www.prestagefarms.com	Clinton	NC	28329	910-596-5700	592-9552
Schwartz Farms Inc 32296 190th St *Web:* schwartzfarms.com	Sleepy Eye	MN	56085	507-794-5779	
Seaboard Foods 9000 W 67th St Ste 200 *TF:* 800-262-7907 ■ *Web:* www.seaboardfoods.com	Shawnee Mission	KS	66202	913-261-2600	261-2626
Smithfield Foods Inc 200 Commerce St *NYSE: SFD* ■ *TF:* 800-276-6158 ■ *Web:* www.smithfieldfoods.com	Smithfield	VA	23430	757-365-3000	365-3017
Swine Graphics Enterprises LP 1620 Superior St PO Box 668 *Web:* sgepork.com	Webster City	IA	50595	515-832-5481	832-2237
Texas Farm LLC 4200 S Main St *Web:* texasfarmpork.com	Perryton	TX	79070	806-435-5935	435-3656
Tyson Foods Inc 2210 W Oaklawn Dr PO Box 2020 *NYSE: TSN* ■ *TF:* 800-643-3410 ■ *Web:* www.tyson.com	Springdale	AR	72762	479-290-4000	
Wakefield Pork Inc 410 Main Ave E *Web:* www.wakefieldpork.com	Gaylord	MN	55334	507-237-5581	237-5584
Whole Hog Health 88155 Hwy 57 *Web:* wholehogai.com	Hartington	NE	68739	402-254-2444	

10-7 Mushroom Growers

	City	State	ZIP	Phone	Fax
Monterey Mushrooms Inc 260 Westgate Dr **Fax Area Code:* 610 ■ *TF:* 800-333-6874 ■ *Web:* www.montereymushrooms.com	Watsonville	CA	95076	831-763-5300	929-0271*
Ostrom Mushroom Farms 8322 Steilacoom Rd SE *Web:* www.ostrommushrooms.com	Olympia	WA	98513	360-491-1410	
Phillips Mushroom Farms Inc 1011 Kaolin Rd *TF:* 800-722-8818 ■ *Web:* www.phillipsmushroomfarms.com	Kennett Square	PA	19348	610-925-0520	925-0527
Sylvan Inc 90 Glade Dr *TF:* 866-352-7520 ■ *Web:* www.sylvaninc.com	Kittanning	PA	16201	724-543-3900	543-7583

10-8 Poultry & Eggs Production

	City	State	ZIP	Phone	Fax
Allen's Hatchery Inc 126 N Shipley St *Web:* allenharimllc.com/index.cfm	Seaford	DE	19973	302-629-9163	629-0514
Amick Farms Inc 2079 Batesburg Hwy **Fax:* Sales ■ *TF:* 800-926-4257 ■ *Web:* www.amickfarms.com	Batesburg	SC	29006	803-532-1400	*
Aviagen Group 5015 Bradford Dr *TF:* 800-826-9685 ■ *Web:* aviagen.com	Huntsville	AL	35805	256-890-3800	890-3919
Cagle's Farms Inc 1385 Collier Rd NW	Atlanta	GA	30318	404-355-2820	350-9605
Cobb-Vantress Inc PO Box 1030 *TF:* 800-748-9719 ■ *Web:* www.cobb-vantress.com	Siloam Springs	AR	72761	479-524-3166	524-3043
Cooper Farms 22348 County Rd 140 PO Box 547 *TF:* 800-423-2765 ■ *Web:* www.cooperfarms.com	Oakwood	OH	45873	419-594-3325	594-3372
Creighton Bros LLC PO Box 220 *Web:* www.creightonbrothersllc.com	Atwood	IN	46502	574-267-3101	267-6446
Culver Duck Farms Inc PO Box 910 *TF:* 800-825-9225 ■ *Web:* www.culverduck.com	Middlebury	IN	46540	574-825-9537	825-2613
Demler Egg Ranch 1455 N Warren Rd	San Jacinto	CA	92582	951-654-8166	487-9766
Diestel Turkey Ranch 22200 Lyons Bald Mtn Rd *Web:* www.diestelturkey.com	Sonora	CA	95370	209-532-4950	532-5059
Dorothy Egg Farms LLC 271 Turkey Ln	Winthrop	ME	04364	207-377-9927	
Echo Lake Farm Produce Co PO Box 279 *Web:* www.echolakefoods.com	Burlington	WI	53105	800-888-3447	
Esbenshade Farms 220 Eby Chiques Rd *Web:* esbenshadefarmmill.com	Mount Joy	PA	17552	717-653-8061	653-6922
Foster Farms Inc 1000 Davis St PO Box 457 **Fax Area Code:* 209 ■ *TF:* 800-255-7227 ■ *Web:* www.fosterfarms.com	Livingston	CA	95334	800-255-7227	394-6362*
Glenwood Foods LLC 20850 Jackson Ln	Jetersville	VA	23083	804-561-3447	561-3228
Hubbard ISA 195 Main St *Web:* www.hubbardbreeders.com	Walpole	NH	03608	603-756-3311	756-9034
Hy-Line International 1755 W Lakes Pkwy *Web:* www.hyline.com	West Des Moines	IA	50266	515-225-6030	225-6425
Maple Leaf Farms Inc PO Box 308 *TF:* 800-348-2812 ■ *Web:* www.mapleleaffarms.com	Milford	IN	46542	574-658-4121	658-2208
Mar-Jac Poultry Inc 1020 Aviation Blvd PO Box 1017 *Web:* www.marjacpoultry.com	Gainesville	GA	30501	770-531-5007	531-5049
Michael Foods Inc 301 Carlson Pkwy Ste 400 *TF:* 800-328-5474 ■ *Web:* www.michaelfoods.com	Minnetonka	MN	55305	952-258-4000	258-4911
PECO Foods Inc 3701 Kauloosa Ave *Web:* www.pecofoods.com	Tuscaloosa	AL	35401	205-345-3955	343-2401
Perdue Farms Inc 31149 Old Ocean City Rd *TF:* 800-473-7383 ■ *Web:* www.perdue.com	Salisbury	MD	21804	410-543-3000	543-3532
Pilgrim's Corp 1770 Promontory Cir *NASDAQ: PPC* ■ *TF:* 800-321-1470 ■ *Web:* www.pilgrimspride.com	Greeley	CO	80634	800-321-1470	
Plainville Farms Inc 304 S Water St PO Box 38 **Fax Area Code:* 315 ■ *Web:* www.plainvillefarms.com	New Oxford	PA	17350	717-624-2191	701-1354*
Puglisi Egg Farms Inc 75 Easy St	Howell	NJ	07731	732-938-2373	938-2232
Ritewood Inc 3643 S 4000 E PO Box 120	Franklin	ID	83237	208-646-2213	646-2217
Simpson's Eggs Inc 5015 Hwy 218 E *TF:* 800-726-1330 ■ *Web:* www.simpsonseggs.com	Monroe	NC	28110	704-753-1478	753-4762
Tyson Foods Inc 2210 W Oaklawn Dr PO Box 2020 *NYSE: TSN* ■ *TF:* 800-643-3410 ■ *Web:* www.tyson.com	Springdale	AR	72762	479-290-4000	
Wayne Farms LLC 4110 Continental Dr **Fax Area Code:* 770 ■ *TF:* 800-392-0844 ■ *Web:* www.waynefarms.com	Oakwood	GA	30566	800-392-0844	531-0858*
Weiss Lake Egg Company Inc 9602 County Rd 59	Centre	AL	35960	256-927-5546	
Wilcox Farms Inc 40400 Harts Lake Valley Rd *Web:* www.wilcoxfarms.com	Roy	WA	98580	360-458-7774	458-3995
Willmar Poultry Co, The (WPC) 3735 County Rd 5 SW *TF:* 800-328-8849	Willmar	MN	56201	320-235-8850	
Zacky Farms Inc 2020 SE Ave *TF:* 800-888-0235 ■ *Web:* www.zacky.com	Fresno	CA	93721	562-641-2020	641-2040
Zephyr Egg Co Inc 4622 Gall Blvd *TF:* 800-333-4415 ■ *Web:* refrigeratedtransporter.com	Zephyrhills	FL	33542	813-782-1521	

10-9 Sugarcane & Sugarbeets Growers

	City	State	ZIP	Phone	Fax
A Duda & Sons Inc 1200 Duda Trail *Web:* www.duda.com	Oviedo	FL	32765	407-365-2111	365-2147
Alico Inc (ALCO) 10070 Daniels Interstate Ct Ste 100 *NASDAQ: ALCO* ■ *Web:* www.alicoinc.com	Fort Myers	FL	33913	863-675-2966	
Florida Crystals Corp 1 N Clematis St Ste 200 *Web:* www.floridacrystals.com	West Palm Beach	FL	33401	561-366-5100	366-5158
Gay & Robinson Inc PO Box 156	Kaumakani	HI	96747	808-335-3133	335-6424
Sugar Cane Growers Co-op of Florida PO Box 666 *Web:* www.scgc.org	Belle Glade	FL	33430	561-996-5556	996-4747
US Sugar Corp 111 Ponce de Leon Ave *Web:* www.ussugar.com	Clewiston	FL	33440	863-983-8121	983-9827
Wedgworth Farms Inc 300 North Dixie Hwy Ste 471 *TF:* 800-477-2077 ■ *Web:* pbchistoryonline.org	West Palm Beach	FL	33401	561-832-4164	832-7965

10-10 Tree Nuts Growers

	City	State	ZIP	Phone	Fax
Agri-World Co-op 31545 Donald Ave	Madera	CA	93636	559-673-1306	673-1318
Blue Diamond Growers 1802 C St *Web:* www.bluediamond.com	Sacramento	CA	95811	916-442-0771	446-8461
Braden Farms Inc 6940 Hughson Ave	Hughson	CA	95326	209-883-4061	
Columbia Empire Farms 31461 NE Bell Rd *Web:* www.columbiaempirefarms.com	Sherwood	OR	97140	503-538-2156	
Cummings Violich Inc 1750 Dayton Rd	Chico	CA	95928	530-894-5494	891-4946
Farmland Management Services 301 E Main St **Fax Area Code:* 785	Turlock	CA	95380	209-669-0742	243-1873*
Green Valley Pecan Co 1625 E Sahuarita Rd *Web:* greenvalleypecan.com	Sahuarita	AZ	85629	520-791-2852	791-2853
Hammons Products Co 105 Hammons Dr PO Box 140 **Fax Area Code:* 417 ■ *TF:* 888-429-6887 ■ *Web:* www.hammonsproducts.com	Stockton	MO	65785	888-429-6887	276-5187*
Lassen Land Co 320 E S St PO Box 607	Orland	CA	95963	530-865-7676	865-8085
MacFarms of Hawaii LLC 89-406 Mamalahoa Hwy **Fax Area Code:* 808 ■ *Web:* www.macfarms.com	Captain Cook	HI	96704	415-399-1211	328-8081*
Mauna Loa Macadamia Nut Corp 16-701 Macadamia Rd **Fax:* Cust Svc ■ *TF Cust Svc:* 888-628-6256 ■ *Web:* www.maunaloa.com	Keaau	HI	96749	808-966-8618	966-8410*
ML Macadamia Orchards LP 26-238 Hawaii Belt Rd *NYSE: NNUT*	Hilo	HI	96720	808-969-8057	969-8123

Phone *Fax*

Spycher Bros Farms 14827 W HaRding Rd.... Turlock CA 95380 209-668-2471 668-4988
Web: www.spycherbros.com
Sunnyland Farms Inc PO Box 8200.... Albany GA 31706 800-999-2488 888-4979*
**Fax Area Code:* 229 ■ *TF:* 800-999-2488 ■ *Web:* www.sunnylandfarms.com
Tejon Ranch Co 4436 Lebec Rd PO Box 1000.... Lebec CA 93243 661-248-3000 248-3100
NYSE: TRC ■ *Web:* www.tejonranch.com

10-11 Vegetable Farms

Phone *Fax*

A Duda & Sons Inc 1200 Duda Trail.... Oviedo FL 32765 407-365-2111 365-2147
Web: www.duda.com
Abe-El Produce 42143 Rd 120.... Orosi CA 93647 559-528-3030 528-6772
Agri-Empire Corp 630 W Seventh St.... San Jacinto CA 92583 951-654-7311 654-7639
Web: www.agri-empire.com
Amigo Farms Inc 4245 E Hwy 80.... Yuma AZ 85365 928-726-3738 726-3744
Web: www.amigofarms.com
Anderson Farms Inc 4600 Second St.... Davis CA 95618 530-753-5695
Barkley Co PO Box 5540.... Yuma AZ 85365 928-782-2571 782-4656
Web: www.barkleycompany.com
Barnes Farming Corp 7840 Old Bailey Hwy.... Spring Hope NC 27882 800-367-2799 459-9020*
**Fax Area Code:* 252 ■ *TF:* 800-367-2799 ■ *Web:* www.farmpak.com
Bergin Fruit & Nut Company Inc
2000 Energy Park Dr.... St Paul MN 55108 651-642-1234
Web: berginfruit.com
Black Gold 4320 18th Ave S Grand Forks.... Grand Forks ND 58201 701-792-3414 772-0749
Web: www.blackgoldpotato.com
Bo-Jac Seed Co 245 County Rd 1500 E.... Mount Pulaski IL 62548 217-792-5001 792-5006
Bolthouse Farms 7200 E Brundage Ln.... Bakersfield CA 93307 800-467-4683 366-2834*
**Fax Area Code:* 661 ■ **Fax:* Sales ■ *TF:* 800-467-4683 ■ *Web:* www.bolthouse.com
Bonipak 1850 W Stowell Rd.... Santa Maria CA 93458 805-925-2585 922-7982
Web: www.bonipak.com
Borzynski Bros Distributing Inc
10508 Kraut Rd.... Franksville WI 53126 262-886-1623
Web: apps.bluebookservices.com
Boskovich Farms Inc 711 Diaz Ave.... Oxnard CA 93030 805-487-2299 487-5189
Web: www.boskovichfarms.com
Buurma Farms Inc 3909 Kok Rd.... Willard OH 44890 419-935-6411 935-1918
TF: 888-428-8762 ■ *Web:* www.buurmafarms.com
Caruso Inc 3465 Hauck Rd.... Cincinnati OH 45241 513-860-9200
TF: 800-759-7659 ■ *Web:* carusologistics.com
Charles H West Farms Inc
2953 Tub Mill Pond Rd.... Milford DE 19963 302-335-3936 335-0438
Christopher Ranch 305 Bloomfield Ave.... Gilroy CA 95020 408-847-1100 847-5488
TF: 800-779-1156 ■ *Web:* primuslabs.com
Coast Produce Co 1791 Bay St.... Los Angeles CA 90021 213-955-4900 955-4949
Web: www.coastproduce.com
CROPP Co-op One Organic Way.... LaFarge WI 54639 888-444-6455 625-3025*
**Fax Area Code:* 608 ■ *TF:* 888-444-6455 ■ *Web:* www.organicvalley.coop
D'Arrigo Bros Company of California Inc
PO Box 850.... Salinas CA 93902 831-455-4500 455-4445
TF Cust Svc: 800-995-5939 ■ *Web:* www.andyboy.com
Dean Kincaid Inc Wisconsin 106.... Palmyra WI 53156 262-495-3000
Dresick Farms Inc PO Box 1260.... Huron CA 93234 559-945-2513 945-9627
Earthbound Farm 1721 San Juan Hwy.... San Juan Bautista CA 95045 831-623-7880 623-4988
TF: 800-690-3200 ■ *Web:* www.ebfarm.com
Everkrisp Vegetables Inc 9202 W Harrison St.... Tolleson AZ 85353 623-936-3321 936-1008
Web: everkrispvegetables.com
Far Niente Winery Inc 1350 Acacia Dr.... Oakville CA 94562 707-944-2861
Web: www.farniente.com
Frank Capurro & Son LLC
2250 Hwy 1 PO Box 410.... Moss Landing CA 95039 831-786-0731
Fresh Express Inc
550 South Caldwell St Ste 1212.... Charlotte NC 28202 800-242-5472 636-5000*
**Fax Area Code:* 980 ■ *TF Cust Svc:* 800-242-5472 ■ *Web:* www.freshexpress.com
George Wood Farms Inc 113 N Carolina 343.... Camden NC 27921 252-335-4357
Gilead Group LLC
12444 Powerscourt Dr Ste 375.... St Louis MO 63131 314-821-2500
Web: www.gileadgroup.net
Grant Family Farms 12155 NCR 15.... Wellington CO 80549 970-568-7654 568-7655
Web: www.grantfarms.com
Greenheart Farms Inc
902 Zenon Way PO Box 1510.... Arroyo Grande CA 93420 805-481-2234 481-7374
TF: 800-549-5531 ■ *Web:* www.greenheartfarms.com
Griffin Ranches Inc 9490 W County 19th St.... Somerton AZ 85350 928-627-8809
Grimmway Farms Inc PO Box 81498.... Bakersfield CA 93380 800-301-3101 845-9750*
**Fax Area Code:* 661 ■ *TF:* 800-301-3101 ■ *Web:* www.grimmway.com
Harris Farms Inc 27366 W Oakland Ave.... Coalinga CA 93210 559-884-2859 884-2855
TF: 800-311-6211 ■ *Web:* www.harrisfarms.com
Hartung Bros Inc 708 Heartland Trl Ste 2000.... Madison WI 53717 608-829-6000 829-6001
TF: 800-362-2522 ■ *Web:* www.hartungbrothers.com
HFM FoodService Inc 716 Umi St.... Honolulu HI 96819 808-843-3200
Web: www.hfmfoodservice.com
Hundley Farms Inc 28200 Florida 80.... Belle Glade FL 33430 561-996-6855
Jack Bros Co 551 W Main St.... Brawley CA 92227 760-344-3781
Leach Farms Inc
W1102 Buttercup Ct P.O. Box 192.... Berlin WI 54923 920-361-1880 361-4474
Web: www.leachfarms.com
Long Farms Inc 2849 Lust Rd.... Apopka FL 32703 407-889-4141 889-5069
Major Farms Inc 1060 Growers St.... Salinas CA 93901 831-422-9616
Martori Farms 7332 E Butherus Dr.... Scottsdale AZ 85260 480-998-1444
Web: www.martorifarms.com
McEntire Produce Inc
2040 American Italian Way.... Columbia SC 29209 803-799-3388
Web: www.mcentireproduce.com
Mount Dora Farms 16398 Jacinto Ft Blvd.... Houston TX 77015 713-821-7439 821-7342
Web: www.mountdorafarms.com
Mountain King 6950 Neuhaus St.... Houston TX 77061 713-923-5807 921-3565
My-T Acres Inc 8127 Lewiston Rd.... Batavia NY 14020 585-343-1026 343-2051

Phone *Fax*

Nash Produce Co 6160 S N Carolina 58.... Nashville NC 27856 252-443-6011 443-6746
TF: 800-334-3032 ■ *Web:* www.nashproduce.com
Navajo Agricultural Products Industry
PO Drawer 1318.... Farmington NM 87499 505-566-2600 324-9458
Web: www.navajopride.com
Ocean Mist Farms
10855 Ocean Mist Pkwy Ste A.... Castroville CA 95012 831-633-2144 633-0561
Web: www.oceanmist.com
Pacific Tomato Growers 503 Tenth St W.... Palmetto FL 34221 941-722-3291 729-4707
Web: www.sunripeproduce.com
Pacific Triple E 8690 W Linne Rd.... Tracy CA 95304 209-835-5123
Web: www.sunripeproduce.com
Papen Farms Inc 847 Papen Ln.... Dover DE 19904 302-697-3291 697-2380
Paramount Farms Inc PO Box 188.... Bancroft WI 54921 715-335-6357 335-6091
Web: www.paramountfarmsinc.com
Peri & Sons Farms Inc PO Box 35.... Yerington NV 89447 775-463-4444 463-4028
Web: www.periandsons.com
Petrocco Farms 14110 Brighton Rd.... Brighton CO 80601 303-659-6498 659-7645
TF: 888-876-2207 ■ *Web:* www.petroccofarms.com
Prime Time International
86-705 Ave 54 Ste A.... Coachella CA 92236 760-399-4278 399-4281
Web: www.primetimeproduce.com
Roth Farms Inc 27502 CR 880 PO Box 1300.... Belle Glade FL 33430 561-996-2991 996-8501
Web: www.rothfarms.com
Rousseau Farming Co 9601 W Harrison Ave.... Tolleson AZ 85353 623-936-7100
Russo Farms Inc 1962 SE Ave.... Vineland NJ 08360 856-692-5942 692-8534
Web: russofarms.com
Sackett Ranch Inc 2939 Neff Rd NE.... Stanton MI 48888 989-762-5049 762-5500
Sakata Farms Inc E Bromley Ln.... Brighton CO 80601 303-659-1559
Sam S Accursio Farms & Well
1225 NW Second St.... Homestead FL 33030 305-246-3455
San Miguel Produce Inc 4444 Naval Air Rd.... Oxnard CA 93033 805-488-0981 488-2103
TF: 888-347-3367 ■ *Web:* www.cutnclean.com
Sea Mist Farms
10855 Ocean Mist Pkwy Ste C.... Castroville CA 95012 831-633-2144 633-8163
Web: www.oceanmist.com
SMT Farms 8420 US 95.... Yuma AZ 85365 928-341-9616
Sun World International Inc
16350 Drive Rd.... Bakersfield CA 93308 661-392-5000
Web: www.sun-world.com
Tanimura & Antle Inc PO Box 4070.... Salinas CA 93912 800-772-4542 455-4112*
**Fax Area Code:* 831 ■ *TF:* 800-772-4542 ■ *Web:* www.taproduce.com
Taylor & Fulton Inc 932 Fifth Ave W.... Palmetto FL 34221 941-729-3883 723-2969
TF: 800-457-5577 ■ *Web:* www.taylorfulton.com
Teixeira Farms Inc
2600 Bonita Lateral Rd.... Santa Maria CA 93458 805-928-3801 928-9405
Web: www.teixeirafarms.com
Thomas Produce Co 9905 Clint Moore Rd.... Boca Raton FL 33496 561-482-1111 852-0018
Web: www.thomasproduce.com
Tom Bengard Ranch Inc 634 W Market.... Salinas CA 93901 831-758-5770
Web: bengardranch.com
Torrey Farms Inc Maltby Rd.... Elba NY 14058 585-757-9941
Web: www.torreyfarms.com
Tri-Campbell Farms 15111 Hwy 17.... Grafton ND 58237 701-352-3116 352-2008
TF: 800-222-7783 ■ *Web:* www.tricampbellfarms.com
Turek Farms 8558 State Rt 90.... King Ferry NY 13081 315-364-8735 364-5257
Web: www.turekfarms.com
Twin Garden Farms 23017 Illinois 173.... Harvard IL 60033 815-943-7448 943-8024
Web: www.twingardenfarms.com
Village Farms LP 7 Christopher Way.... Eatontown NJ 07724 732-676-3000 936-1187*
**Fax Area Code:* 407 ■ *Web:* www.villagefarms.com
Wada Farms Potatoes Inc 326 S 1400 W.... Pingree ID 83262 208-684-9801 684-4157
Web: www.wadafarms.com
Weber Farms 3559 Rd 'K' NW.... Quincy WA 98848 509-787-3620 787-4465
West Coast Distributing Inc
Commerce Pl 350 Main St.... Boston MA 02148 781-665-9393
TF: 800-235-3730 ■ *Web:* www.wcd-network.com
Wiers Farm Inc 4465 St Rt 103 S PO Box 385.... Willard OH 44890 419-935-0131 933-2017
TF: 800-777-6243 ■ *Web:* wiersfarm.com
Wilson Farm Inc 10 Pleasant St.... Lexington MA 02421 781-862-3900 863-0469
Web: www.wilsonfarm.com
Wolfsen Inc 1269 W 'I' St.... Los Banos CA 93635 209-827-7700 827-7780
Web: wolfseninc.com/
Worzella & Sons Inc 2801 Hoover Ave.... Plover WI 54467 715-344-4098 344-4803
Web: worzellaandsons.com
Wysocki Produce Farm Inc 6320 Third Ave.... Plainfield WI 54966 715-366-7175

11 AGRICULTURAL SERVICES

11-1 Crop Preparation Services

Phone *Fax*

AG Plus Inc 401 N Main PO Box 306.... South Whitley IN 46787 260-723-5141 273-5143
Web: www.agplusinc.com
Agricor Inc PO Box 807.... Marion IN 46952 765-662-0606 662-7189
Web: www.agricor.org
American Raisin Packers Inc
2335 Chandler St PO Box 30.... Selma CA 93662 559-896-4760 896-8942
Web: americanraisinpacking.com
Andrews Distribution Co 13650 Copus Rd.... Bakersfield CA 93313 661-858-2266 858-2965
Web: www.andrewsag.com
Baird-Neece Packing Corp 60 SE St.... Porterville CA 93257 559-784-3393
Borg Produce Co
1601 E Olympic Blvd Bldg 100.... Los Angeles CA 90021 213-688-9388 688-9381
Web: www.borgproduce.com
Cecelia Packing Corp 24780 E S Ave.... Orange Cove CA 93646 559-626-5000 626-7561
Web: ceceliapack.com
Chooljian Bros Packing Company Inc
3192 S Indianola St.... Sanger CA 93657 559-875-5501 875-1582
Web: www.chooljianbrothers.com

Phone Fax

Cummins Family Produce Inc
2570 Eldridge Ave. . . . . Twin Falls ID 83301 208-733-5371
Deardorff-Jackson Company Inc PO Box 1188 . . . . . Oxnard CA 93032 805-487-7801 483-1286
Web: www.deardorfffamilyfarms.com
Delta Packing Co 6021 E Kettleman Ln . . . . . Lodi CA 95240 209-334-1023 334-0811
Web: www.deltapacking.com
Diamond Fruit Growers Inc 3515 Chevron Dr. . . . . Hood River OR 97031 541-354-5300 354-5394
Web: www.diamondfruit.com
DiMare Bros/New England Farms Packing Co
84 New England Produce Ctr . . . . . Chelsea MA 02150 617-889-3800
Web: dimarefresh.com
Dundee Citrus Growers Assn 111 First St N . . . . . Dundee FL 33838 863-439-1574 439-1535
Web: www.dun-d.com
Emerald Packing 2823 N Orange Blossom Trl . . . . . Orlando FL 32804 407-420-9534
Erwin-Keith Inc 1529 Hwy 193 . . . . . Wynne AR 72396 870-238-2079 238-8621
Web: progenyag.com
Farmers Co-op Union, The
225 S Broadway PO Box 159 . . . . . Sterling KS 67579 620-278-2141
TF: 800-238-1843 ■ *Web:* cpcoop.us
Fillmore-Piru Citrus Assn (FPCA)
357 N Main St PO Box 350. . . . . Piru CA 93040 805-521-1781 521-0990
Web: www.fillmorepirucitrus.com
Fresh Express Inc
550 South Caldwell St Ste 1212. . . . . Charlotte NC 28202 800-242-5472 636-5000*
**Fax Area Code:* 980 ■ *TF Cust Svc:* 800-242-5472 ■ *Web:* www.freshexpress.com
Golden Peanut Company LLC
100 N Pt Ctr E Ste 400 . . . . . Alpharetta GA 30022 770-752-8160 752-8308
Web: www.goldenpeanut.com
Great Lakes Packers Inc
400 Great Lakes Pkwy. . . . . Bellevue OH 44811 419-483-2956
Gruma Corp 1159 Cottonwood L Ste 200 . . . . . Irving TX 75038 972-232-5000 232-5176
TF: 800-627-3221 ■ *Web:* www.gruma.com
GTC-GTC LLC 14574 Weld County Rd 64 . . . . . Greeley CO 80631 970-351-6000 351-6003
Haines City Citrus Growers Assn (HCCGA)
Eight Railroad Ave PO Box 337. . . . . Haines City FL 33844 863-422-1174 422-6544
TF Sales: 800-327-6676 ■ *Web:* www.hilltopcitrus.com
Harllee Packing Inc 2308 US 301 N. . . . . Palmetto FL 34221 941-722-7747 723-3027
Web: www.harlleepacking.com
Harris Woolf California Almonds
26060 Colusa Rd . . . . . Coalinga CA 93210 559-884-2147 884-2746
Web: goldhills.com
Hazelnut Growers of Oregon 401 N 26th Ave . . . . . Cornelius OR 97113 503-648-4176 648-9515
TF: 800-273-4676 ■ *Web:* www.westnut.com
Hunt Bros 2404 Hunt Bros Rd SE . . . . . Lake Wales FL 33898 863-676-9471 676-8362
Index Fresh Inc 18184 Slover Ave . . . . . Bloomington CA 92316 909-877-0999 877-0495
TF: 800-352-6931 ■ *Web:* www.indexfresh.com
Indian River Exchange Packers Inc
7355 Ninth St SW. . . . . Vero Beach FL 32968 772-562-2252
Web: irexp.com
JLG Harvesting Inc 1450 S Atlantic Ave. . . . . Yuma AZ 85365 928-329-7548 329-7551
Kingsburg Apple Packers Inc
10363 E Davis Ave PO Box 38 . . . . . Kingsburg CA 93631 559-897-5132 897-4532
Web: www.kingsburgorchards.com
Kingston Cos 477 Shoup Ave Ste 207 . . . . . Idaho Falls ID 83402 208-522-2365 522-7488
Web: kingstoncorp.com
Klink Citrus Assn 32921 Rd 159 PO Box 188 . . . . . Ivanhoe CA 93235 559-798-1881 798-0182
LA Hearne Company Inc 512 Metz Rd. . . . . King City CA 93930 831-385-5441 385-4377
Web: www.hearneco.com
Lake Region Packing Assn Inc
1293 S Duncan Dr . . . . . Tavares FL 32778 352-343-3111 448-3441*
**Fax Area Code:* 952
Mann Packing Company Inc PO Box 690 . . . . . Salinas CA 93902 831-422-7405 422-1131
TF: 800-285-1002 ■ *Web:* www.veggiesmadeeasy.com
Mariani Nut Co 709 Dutton St . . . . . Winters CA 95694 530-662-3311 949-4042
Web: www.marianinut.com
Mariani Packing Company Inc 500 Crocker Dr . . . . . Vacaville CA 95688 707-452-2800 452-2973
TF: 800-231-1287 ■ *Web:* www.marianifruit.com
Mesa Citrus Growers Assn 254 W Broadway Rd . . . . . Mesa AZ 85210 480-964-8615
Mooney Farms 1220 Fortress St . . . . . Chico CA 95973 530-899-2661 899-7746
Web: www.mooneyfarms.com
Northern Fruit Co 220 2nd St NE . . . . . East Wenatchee WA 98802 509-884-6651 884-1990
Web: www.northernfruit.org
Packers of Indian River Ltd
5700 W Midway Rd . . . . . Fort Pierce FL 34981 772-464-6575
Phelan & Taylor Produce Co 1860 Front St . . . . . Oceano CA 93445 805-489-2413
Pleasant Valley Potato Inc 275 E Elmore Ave . . . . . Aberdeen ID 83210 208-397-4194 397-4841
Web: www.pleasantvalleypotato.com
River Ranch Fresh Foods 1156 Abbott St . . . . . Salinas CA 93901 831-758-1390 755-8270
TF: 800-538-5868
Rivermaid Travelling Co PO Box 350 . . . . . Lodi CA 95240 209-369-3586 369-5465
Web: www.rivermaid.com
RPAC LLC 21490 S Ortigalita Rd . . . . . Los Banos CA 93635 209-826-0272 826-3882
Web: www.rpacalmonds.com
Tracy-Luckey Company Inc
110 N Hicks St PO Box 880 . . . . . Harlem GA 30814 706-556-6216 556-6210
TF: 800-476-4796 ■ *Web:* www.tracy-luckey.com
Veg-Pro Inc 11800 Gordon Ave PO Box 635 . . . . . Grant MI 49327 231-834-5634
Wilco Peanut Co 3391 US Hwy 281 N. . . . . Pleasanton TX 78064 830-569-3808 569-2743

11-2 Livestock Improvement Services

Phone Fax

ABS Global Inc 1525 River Rd PO Box 459. . . . . DeForest WI 53532 608-846-3721 846-6442
TF Cust Svc: 800-356-5331 ■ *Web:* www.absglobal.com
Accelerated Genetics E 10890 Penny Ln . . . . . Baraboo WI 53913 608-356-8357 356-4387
TF: 800-451-9275 ■ *Web:* www.accelgen.com
Alta California N8350 High Road. . . . . Watertown WI 53094 920-261-5065 262-8022
TF: 800-932-2855 ■ *Web:* web.altagenetics.com
AMS Genetics Inc
7441 Sharpsburg Pk PO Box 12. . . . . Boonsboro MD 21713 240-329-0169 469-4231
Web: www.amsgenetics.com

Phone Fax

Certified Semen Services
401 Bernadette Dr PO Box 1033. . . . . Columbia MO 65203 573-445-4406 446-2279
Web: www.naab-css.org
COBA/Select Sires Inc
1224 Alton Darby Creek Rd . . . . . Columbus OH 43228 614-878-5333 870-2622
TF: 800-837-2621 ■ *Web:* www.cobaselect.com
Cobb-Vantress Inc PO Box 1030. . . . . Siloam Springs AR 72761 479-524-3166 524-3043
TF: 800-748-9719 ■ *Web:* www.cobb-vantress.com
Dairy One 730 Warren Rd . . . . . Ithaca NY 14850 607-257-1272 257-6808
TF: 800-344-2697 ■ *Web:* www.dairyone.com
Flatness International Inc
104 Stony Mtn Rd. . . . . Tunkhannock PA 18657 570-836-3527 836-1549
Web: www.flatnessintl.com
Genex Co-op Inc/CRI 117 E Green Bay St . . . . . Shawano WI 54166 715-526-2141 526-4511
TF: 888-333-1783 ■ *Web:* genex.crinet.com
Hagyard-Davidson-McGee Assoc PSC
4250 Iron Works Pike. . . . . Lexington KY 40511 859-255-8741 253-0196
Web: www.hagyard.com
NA of Animal Breeders (NAAB) 401 Bernadette Dr. . . . . Columbia MO 65203 573-445-4406 446-2279
Web: www.naab-css.org
National Dairy Herd Improvement Assn Inc
421 S 9 Mound Rd PO Box 930399 . . . . . Verona WI 53593 608-848-6455 848-7675
Web: www.dhia.org
Newsham Choice Genetics LC
5058 Grand Ridge Dr Ste 200. . . . . West Des Moines IA 50265 515-225-9420
Web: choice-genetics.com
Reproduction Enterprises Inc
908 N Prairie Rd. . . . . Stillwater OK 74075 405-377-8037 377-4541
TF: 866-734-2855 ■ *Web:* www.reproductionenterprises.com
SEK Genetics 9525 70th Rd . . . . . Galesburg KS 66740 800-443-6389 763-2231*
**Fax Area Code:* 620 ■ *TF:* 800-443-6389 ■ *Web:* www.sekgenetics.com
Select Sires Inc 11740 US Hwy 42 N . . . . . Plain City OH 43064 614-873-4683 873-5751
Web: www.selectsires.com
Simonsen Laboratories Inc 1180-C Day Rd . . . . . Gilroy CA 95020 408-847-2002 847-4176
Web: www.simlab.com

12 AIR CARGO CARRIERS

Phone Fax

ABX Air Inc 145 Hunter Dr. . . . . Wilmington OH 45177 937-382-5591
TF: 800-736-3973 ■ *Web:* www.abxair.com
Aeronet Worldwide 42 Corporate Pk. . . . . Irvine CA 92606 949-474-3000 559-7090*
**Fax Area Code:* 800 ■ *TF:* 800-552-3869 ■ *Web:* www.aeronet.com
Agility Holdings Inc 240 Commerce. . . . . Irvine CA 92602 714-617-6300
Web: www.geo-logistics.com
Air Creebec Inc 101 Fecteau St . . . . . Val-d'or QC J9P0G4 819-825-8375
Web: www.aircreebec.ca
Air North Charter & Training Ltd
150 Condor Rd. . . . . Whitehorse YT Y1A6E6 867-668-2228
Web: www.flyairnorth.com
Air-Sea Forwarders Inc PO Box 90637 . . . . . Los Angeles CA 90009 310-216-1616 216-2625
Web: www.airseainc.com
Alex Nichols Agency 3800 Hampton Rd . . . . . Oceanside NY 11572 516-678-9100 678-1344
Web: www.anaht.com
Alpine Air Express 1177 Alpine Air Way . . . . . Provo UT 84601 801-373-1508 377-3781
Web: www.alpine-air.com
Ameriflight Inc 4700 Empire Ave Hngr 1. . . . . Burbank CA 91505 818-847-0000 847-0305*
**Fax:* Cust Svc ■ *TF:* 800-800-4538 ■ *Web:* www.ameriflight.com
Amerijet International Inc
2800 S Andrews Ave. . . . . Fort Lauderdale FL 33316 954-320-5300 765-3521
TF: 800-927-6059 ■ *Web:* www.amerijet.com
Atlas Air Worldwide Holdings Inc
2000 Westchester Ave. . . . . Purchase NY 10577 914-701-8000 701-8001
NASDAQ: AAWW ■ *TF:* 866-434-1617 ■ *Web:* www.atlasair.com
Cathay Pacific Cargo
6040 Avion Dr Ste 338 . . . . . Los Angeles CA 90045 310-417-0052 348-9789
TF: 800-628-6960 ■ *Web:* www.cathaypacificcargo.com
Cayman Airways Cargo Services 6103 NW 72nd Ave . . . . . Miami FL 33166 305-526-3190 455-5616
TF: 800-252-2746 ■ *Web:* www.caymanairways.com
Central Airlines Inc
411 NW Lou Holland Dr. . . . . Kansas City MO 64116 816-472-7711 472-1682
Web: www.centralairsouthwest.com
Centurion Cargo 4500 NW36th St. . . . . Miami FL 33166 305-871-0130 871-0118
Web: www.centurioncargo.com
China Airlines Cargo Sales & Service
11201 Aviation Blvd . . . . . Los Angeles CA 90045 310-646-4293 248-4176*
**Fax Area Code:* 907 ■ *TF:* 800-778-4838 ■ *Web:* www.china-airlines.com
Delta Air Cargo PO Box 20559 Dept 670. . . . . Atlanta GA 30320 800-352-2737 714-5022*
**Fax Area Code:* 404 ■ *TF:* 800-352-2737 ■ *Web:* deltacargo.com
Eagle Air Freight Inc 140 Eastern Ave Ste 1b. . . . . Chelsea MA 02150 617-884-4436
Web: www.eagle-freight.com
Empire Airlines Inc 11559 N Atlas Rd. . . . . Hayden ID 83835 208-292-3850 292-3851
Web: www.empireairlines.com
ICL Express 2307 Coney Island Ave. . . . . Brooklyn NY 11223 718-376-1023 376-1073
Web: www.icl-express.com
Kalitta Flying Service
818 Willow Run Airport . . . . . Ypsilanti MI 48198 734-484-0088 484-3640
TF: 800-521-1590 ■ *Web:* www.kalittaair.com
Lan Cargo 6500 NW 22nd St. . . . . Miami FL 33122 786-265-6000 871-4981*
**Fax Area Code:* 305 ■ *Web:* www.lancargo.com
LOT Polish Airlines Cargo
JFK International Airport 11835 Queens Blvd . . . . . Flushing NY 11375 212-789-0970 656-6063*
**Fax Area Code:* 718 ■ *Web:* www.lot.com
Lynden Air Cargo LLC 6441 S Airpark Pl. . . . . Anchorage AK 99502 907-243-7248 257-5124
TF: 888-243-7248 ■ *Web:* www.lynden.com
MartinAire Aviation LLC
4553 Glenn Curtiss Dr . . . . . Addison TX 75001 972-349-5700 349-5750
TF: 866-557-1861 ■ *Web:* www.martinaire.com
Polar Air Cargo 2000 Westchester Ave. . . . . Purchase NY 10577 914-701-8000 701-8001
Web: www.polaraircargo.com

				Phone	Fax
Qantas Airways Cargo 6555 W Imperial Hwy	Los Angeles	CA	90045	310-665-2280	665-2201
TF General: 800-227-0290 ■ *Web:* www.qantas.com.au					
Rhoades Aviation Inc 4770 Ray Boll Blvd	Columbus	IN	47203	812-372-1819	
Web: rhoadesaircenter.com					
Ryan International Airlines Inc 4949 Harrison Ave	Rockford	IL	61108	815-316-5420	398-0192
Service by Air Inc 222 Crossways Pk Dr	Woodbury	NY	11797	800-243-5545	921-4304*
**Fax Area Code:* 516 ■ *TF:* 800-243-5545 ■ *Web:* www.sbaglobal.com					
Southwest Airlines Air Cargo 2702 Love Field Dr	Dallas	TX	75235	800-533-1222	792-5594*
**Fax Area Code:* 214 ■ *TF:* 800-533-1222 ■ *Web:* www.swacargo.com					
Tampa Airlines Cargo 1650 NW 66th Ave Bldg 708	Miami	FL	33126	305-526-6720	871-6913
Web: aviancacargo.com					
Thai Airways International Cargo 6501 W Imperial Hwy	Los Angeles	CA	90045	310-670-8591	670-1057
Web: www.thaicargo.com					
United Airlines Cargo PO Box 66100	Chicago	IL	60666	800-822-2746	
TF: 800-822-2746 ■ *Web:* www.unitedcargo.com					
Virgin Atlantic Cargo JFK International Airport Bldg 15	Jamaica	NY	11430	516-775-2600	354-3760
TF: 800-828-6822 ■ *Web:* www.virgin-atlantic.com					

13 AIR CHARTER SERVICES

SEE ALSO Helicopter Transport Services p. 2458; Aviation - Fixed-Base Operations p. 1844

				Phone	Fax
Active Aero Group 2068 E St	Belleville	MI	48111	734-547-7200	547-7222*
**Fax:* Hum Res ■ *TF Cust Svc:* 800-872-5387 ■ *Web:* www.activeaero.com					
Aero Air LLC 2050 NE 25th Ave	Hillsboro	OR	97124	503-640-3711	681-6514
TF: 800-448-2376 ■ *Web:* www.aeroair.com					
Air Charter Team 4151 N Mulberry Dr Ste 250	Kansas City	MO	64116	816-283-3280	283-3185
TF: 800-205-6610 ■ *Web:* www.aircharterteam.com					
Air Palm Springs 145 S Gene Autry Trl Ste 14	Palm Springs	CA	92262	760-322-1104	322-1204
TF: 800-760-7774 ■ *Web:* www.airps.com					
Airbus Helicopters Canada 1100 Gilmore Rd PO Box 250	Fort Erie	ON	L2A5M9	905-871-7772	
Web: www.airbushelicopters.ca					
AirFlite Inc 3250 AirFlite Way	Long Beach	CA	90807	562-490-6200	490-6290
TF: 800-241-3548 ■ *Web:* www.airflight.com					
Airship Ventures Inc NASA Research Park Bldg 156	Moffett Field	CA	94035	650-969-8100	
Web: www.airshipventures.com					
Alpine Helicopters Ltd 1295 Industrial Rd	Kelowna	BC	V1Z1G4	250-769-4111	
Web: www.alpinehelicopter.com					
American Air Charter Inc 577 Bell Ave	Chesterfield	MO	63005	636-532-2707	532-1486
TF: 888-532-2710 ■ *Web:* www.americanaircharter.com					
Avstar Aviation Ltd 12 N Haven Ln	East Northport	NY	11731	631-499-0048	499-0051
TF: 800-575-2359 ■ *Web:* www.avstaraviation.com					
Berry Aviation Inc 1807 Airport Dr	San Marcos	TX	78666	512-353-2379	353-2593
TF: 800-229-2379 ■ *Web:* www.berryaviation.com					
Bighorn Airways Inc 912 W Brundage Ln	Sheridan	WY	82801	307-672-3421	672-8580
Web: www.bighornairways.com					
Bluffton Flying Service Co 1080 Navajo Dr	Bluffton	OH	45817	419-358-7045	358-6851
TF: 800-468-6359 ■ *Web:* www.blufftonflyingservice.com					
Charter Flight Inc 1928 S Blvd	Charlotte	NC	28208	704-359-9124	
TF: 800-521-3148 ■ *Web:* www.charterflightinc.com					
Charter Services Inc 8400 Airport Rd W	Mobile	AL	36608	251-633-6090	
Web: www.csijets.com					
Chrysler Aviation Inc (CAI) 7120 Hayvenhurst Ave Ste 309	Van Nuys	CA	91406	818-989-7900	
TF: 800-995-0825 ■ *Web:* www.chrysleraviation.com					
Clay Lacy Aviation 7435 Valjean Ave	Van Nuys	CA	91406	818-989-2900	904-3450
TF: 800-423-2904 ■ *Web:* www.claylacy.com					
Clintondale Aviation Inc 652 Rt Highland Ste 201	New York	NY	12528	845-883-9657	883-5277
Web: www.clintondale.com					
Corporate Flight Inc 6150 Highland Rd	Waterford	MI	48327	248-666-8800	666-8804
Web: corporateflight.com					
CSI Aviation Services Inc 3700 Rio Grand Blvd NW	Albuquerque	NM	87107	505-761-9000	
TF: 800-765-9464 ■ *Web:* csiaviation.com					
Custom Helicopters Ltd 401 Helicopter Dr	St. Andrews	MB	R1A3P7	204-338-7953	
Web: www.customheli.com					
Elite Aviation LLC 7501 Hayvenhurst Pl	Van Nuys	CA	91406	818-988-5387	988-2111
Web: www.eliteaviation.com					
Era Helicopters LLC 600 Airport Service Rd PO Box 6550	Lake Charles	LA	70606	337-478-6131	474-3918
TF: 800-256-2372 ■ *Web:* www.erahelicopters.com					
Exec Air Montana Inc 2430 Airport Rd	Helena	MT	59601	406-442-2190	442-2199
TF: 800-513-2190 ■ *Web:* www.execairmontana.com					
Executive Jet 4556 Airport Rd	Cincinnati	OH	45226	513-979-6600	979-6600
TF: 877-356-5387 ■ *Web:* www.executivejetmanagement.com					
Fair Winds Air Charter Inc 2525 SE Witham Field Hngr 7	Stuart	FL	34996	772-288-4130	288-4230
TF: 800-989-9665 ■ *Web:* www.flyfairwind.com					
Flightstar Corp Seven Airport Rd Willard Airport	Savoy	IL	61874	217-351-7700	351-9843
TF: 800-747-4777 ■ *Web:* www.flightstar.com					
Hop-A-Jet Inc 5525 NW 15th Ave Ste 150	Fort Lauderdale	FL	33309	954-771-5779	772-6981
TF: 800-556-6633 ■ *Web:* www.hopajetworldwide.com					
International Jet Aviation Services 8511 Aviator Ln	Centennial	CO	80112	303-790-0414	790-4144
TF: 800-858-5891 ■ *Web:* www.internationaljet.com					
Jet Aviation Business Jets Inc 112 Charles A Lindbergh Dr	Teterboro	NJ	07608	201-462-4100	462-4136
TF: 800-736-8538 ■ *Web:* www.jetaviation.com					
Jet Resource Inc 455 Wilmer Ave Lunken Airport Hngr 27	Cincinnati	OH	45226	513-871-1554	871-4181
TF: 800-404-5387 ■ *Web:* www.jetresource.com					
JetSuite 18952 MacArthur Blvd	Irvine	CA	92612	866-779-7770	
Web: www.jetsuite.com					
KaiserAir Inc 8735 Earhart Rd PO Box 2626	Oakland	CA	94621	510-569-9622	255-5017
TF: 800-538-2625 ■ *Web:* www.kaiserair.com					
Key Air LLC Three Juliano Dr Ste 201	Oxford	CT	06478	203-264-0605	264-0218
TF: 888-539-2471 ■ *Web:* www.keyair.com					
Key Lime Air Corp 13252 E Control Tower Rd	Englewood	CO	80112	303-768-9626	
Web: www.keylimeair.com					
Kucera International Inc 38133 Western Pkwy	Willoughby	OH	44094	440-975-4230	
Web: www.kucerainternational.com					
Life Flight Network LLC 22285 Yellow Gate Ln NE	Aurora	OR	97002	503-678-4364	
TF: 800-232-0911 ■ *Web:* www.lifeflight.org					
LR Services 602 Hayden Cir	Allentown	PA	18109	610-266-2500	266-3100
TF: 888-675-9650 ■ *Web:* www.lrservices.com					
Mayo Aviation Inc 7735 S Peoria St	Englewood	CO	80112	303-792-4020	790-4909
TF: 800-525-0194 ■ *Web:* www.mayoaviation.com					
Miami Air International Inc 5000 NW 36 St Ste 307	Miami	FL	33122	305-876-3600	871-4222
Web: www.miamiair.com					
Million Air Interlink Inc 8501 Telephone Rd	Houston	TX	77061	713-640-4000	283-8274*
**Fax Area Code:* 866 ■ *TF:* 888-589-9059 ■ *Web:* www.millionair.com					
Nashville Jet 635 Hangar Ln	Nashville	TN	37217	615-350-8400	350-8408
TF: 800-824-4778 ■ *Web:* www.nashvillejetcharters.com					
New England Life Flight Inc 1727 Robins St Hangar	Bedford	MA	01730	781-863-2213	
TF: 800-233-8998 ■ *Web:* www.bostonmedflight.org					
New World Aviation Inc 987 Postal Rd	Allentown	PA	18109	610-231-9555	
Web: www.newworldaviation.com					
Ohio Medical Transportation Inc 2827 W Dblin Granville Rd	Columbus	OH	43235	614-734-8001	
TF: 877-633-3598 ■ *Web:* www.medflight.com					
Pacific Coast Jet Charter Inc 10600 White Rock Rd	Rancho Cordova	CA	95670	916-631-6507	631-6687
TF: 800-655-3599 ■ *Web:* www.pacificjet.com					
Pentastar Aviation 7310 Highland Rd	Waterford	MI	48327	248-666-3630	666-9657*
**Fax:* Mktg ■ *TF:* 800-662-9612 ■ *Web:* www.pentastaraviation.com					
Planemasters Ltd 32 W 611 Tower Rd DuPage Airport	West Chicago	IL	60185	630-513-2100	377-3283
TF: 800-994-6400 ■ *Web:* www.planemasters.com					
Premier Jets 2140 NE 25th Ave	Hillsboro	OR	97124	503-640-2927	681-3064
TF: 800-635-8583 ■ *Web:* www.premierjets.com					
Presidential Aviation 1725 NW 51st Pl Ft Lauderdale Executive Airport Hngr 71	Fort Lauderdale	FL	33309	954-772-8622	
Web: presidential-aviation.com/					
Priester Aviation 1061 S Wolf Rd	Wheeling	IL	60090	847-537-1133	459-0778
TF: 888-323-7887 ■ *Web:* www.priesterav.com					
Ryan International Airlines Inc 4949 Harrison Ave	Rockford	IL	61108	815-316-5420	398-0192
S Jet 1251 W Blee Rd	Springfield	OH	45502	937-323-5804	323-8168
Web: www.spectrajetinc.com					
San Juan Airlines Co 4000 Airport Rd Ste A	Anacortes	WA	98221	360-293-4691	299-0981
TF: 800-874-4434 ■ *Web:* www.sanjuanairlines.com					
Seneca Flight Operations 2262 Airport Dr	Penn Yan	NY	14527	315-536-4471	536-4558
Web: www.senecaflight.com					
Sentient Jet LLC 100 Grossman Dr Ste 400	Braintree	MA	02184	781-763-0200	
TF: 866-602-0044 ■ *Web:* www.sentient.com					
Skyservice Airlines Inc 9785 Ryan Ave	Dorval	QC	H9P1A2	514-636-3300	636-4855
TF: 888-985-1402 ■ *Web:* skyservice.com					
Tavaero Jet Charter 7930 Airport Blvd	Houston	TX	77061	713-644-6431	643-5398
TF: 800-343-3771 ■ *Web:* www.tavaero.com					
Thunder Airlines Ltd 310 Hector Dougall Way	Thunder Bay	ON	P7E6M6	807-475-4211	
Web: www.thunderair.com					
Trans-Exec Air Service Inc 7240 Hayvenhurst Pl Ste 200	Van Nuys	CA	91406	818-904-6900	904-6909
Web: www.transexec.com					
Tulip City Air Service Inc 1581 S Washington Ave	Holland	MI	49423	616-392-7831	392-1841
TF: 800-748-0515 ■ *Web:* www.tulipcityair.com					
Twin Cities Air Service 81 Airport Dr	Auburn	ME	04210	800-564-3882	784-5326*
**Fax Area Code:* 207 ■ *TF:* 800-564-3882 ■ *Web:* www.twincitiesairservice.com					
West Coast Aviation Services 19711 Campus Dr Ste 150	Santa Ana	CA	92707	949-852-8340	260-3999
TF: 800-352-6153 ■ *Web:* www.westcoastaviationservices.net					

AIR CONDITIONING EQUIPMENT - AUTOMOTIVE

AIR CONDITIONING EQUIPMENT - WHOL

SEE Plumbing, Heating, Air Conditioning Equipment & Supplies - Whol p. 2947

14 AIR CONDITIONING & HEATING EQUIPMENT - COMMERCIAL/INDUSTRIAL

SEE ALSO Air Conditioning & Heating Equipment - Residential p. 1728; Refrigeration Equipment - Mfr p. 3047

				Phone	Fax
AAON Inc 2425 S Yukon Ave	Tulsa	OK	74107	918-583-2266	583-6094
NASDAQ: AAON ■ *Web:* www.aaon.com					
Absolut Aire Inc 5496 N Riverview Dr	Kalamazoo	MI	49004	269-382-1875	382-5291
TF: 800-804-4000 ■ *Web:* www.absolutaire.com					
ACS Group 1100 E Woodfield Rd Ste 588	Schaumburg	IL	60173	847-273-7700	273-7804
TF: 800-783-7835 ■ *Web:* www.aecinternet.com					

				Phone	*Fax*
ACS Group, The 2900 S 160th St / *Web:* www.acscorporate.com	New Berlin	WI	53151	262-641-8600	
Advantage Engineering Inc 525 E S- 18 Rd / *TF:* 800-669-1282 ■ *Web:* www.advantageengineering.com	Greenwood	IN	46142	317-887-0729	881-1277
Afcon Products Inc Elec Equip 35 Sargent Dr / *Web:* www.afconproducts.com	Bethany	CT	06524	203-393-9301	
Airco Mechanical Inc 8210 Demetre Ave / *Web:* www.aircomech.com	Sacramento	CA	95828	916-381-4523	386-0350
Aitken Products Inc 566 N Eagle St PO Box 151 / *TF:* 800-569-9341 ■ *Web:* www.aitkenproducts.com	Geneva	OH	44041	440-466-5711	466-5716
American Coolair Corp 3604 Mayflower St / *TF:* 877-250-2822 ■ *Web:* www.coolair.com	Jacksonville	FL	32205	904-389-3646	387-3449
Aqua Cal Inc 2737 24th St N / *Web:* www.aquacal.com	Saint Petersburg	FL	33713	727-823-5642	
Arctic Industries Inc 9731 NW 114th Way / *TF:* 800-325-0123 ■ *Web:* arcticwalkins.com/	Miami	FL	33178	305-883-5581	883-4651
Armstrong International Inc 2081 SE Ocean Blvd 4th Fl / *TF:* 866-738-5125 ■ *Web:* www.armstronginternational.com	Stuart	FL	34996	772-286-7175	286-1001
Auer Steel & Heating Supply Co 2935 W Silver Spring Dr / *TF:* 800-242-0406 ■ *Web:* www.auersteel.com	Milwaukee	WI	53209	414-463-1234	463-0303
Bally Refrigerated Boxes Inc 135 Little Nine Rd / *Web:* www.ballyrefboxes.com	Morehead City	NC	28557	252-240-2829	240-0384
Birk Manufacturing 14 Capitol Dr Colton Rd Industrial Park Exit 71 off I-95 / *Web:* www.birkmfg.com	East Lyme	CT	06333	860-739-4170	
Blissfield Manufacturing Co 626 Depot St / *TF Cust Svc:* 800-626-1772 ■ *Web:* www.blissfield.com	Blissfield	MI	49228	517-486-2121	486-2128
Brainerd Compressor Rebuilders Inc 3034 Sandbrook St / *TF:* 800-228-4138 ■ *Web:* www.brainerdcompressor.com	Memphis	TN	38116	800-228-4138	
Bristol Compressors Inc 15185 Industrial Pk Rd / *Web:* www.bristolcompressors.com	Bristol	VA	24202	276-466-4121	645-7500
Brooks Automation Inc Polycold Systems 3800 Lakeville Hwy / *TF:* 800-698-6149 ■ *Web:* www.brooks.com	Petaluma	CA	94954	707-769-7000	769-1380
Bruner Corp 3637 Lacon Rd / *Web:* www.brunercorp.com	Hilliard	OH	43026	614-334-9000	334-9001
Bry-Air Inc 10793 SR 37 W / *TF:* 877-427-9247 ■ *Web:* www.bry-air.com	Sunbury	OH	43074	740-965-2974	965-5470
Buckley Associates Inc 385 King St / *Web:* www.buckleyonline.com	Hanover	MA	02339	781-878-5000	
Carnes Co 448 S Main St / *Web:* www.carnes.com	Verona	WI	53593	608-845-6411	845-6470
Carrier Corp 1 Carrier Pl / **Fax:* Hum Res ■ *TF:* 800-227-7437 ■ *Web:* www.carrier.com	Farmington	CT	06034	860-674-3000	674-3139*
CEI Enterprises Inc 245 WoodwaRd Rd SE / **Fax Area Code:* 505 ■ *TF:* 800-545-4034 ■ *Web:* www.ceienterprises.com	Albuquerque	NM	87102	800-545-4034	243-1422*
Cembell Industries Inc 740 CCC Rd (Hwy 628) / *Web:* www.cembell.com	Montz	LA	70068	985-652-1188	
Central Products LLC 7750 Georgetown Rd / *Web:* www.centralrestaurant.com	Indianapolis	IN	46268	317-876-1010	
Champion Energy Corp One Radisson Plz Ste 801 / *Web:* www.championenergy.com	New Rochelle	NY	10801	914-576-6190	576-6126
Chiller Solutions LLC 101 Alexander Ave / *Web:* www.edwards-eng.com	Pompton Plains	NJ	07444	973-835-2800	
Chromalox Inc 103 Gamma Dr Ext / *Web:* www.chromalox.com	Pittsburgh	PA	15238	412-967-3800	
ClimaCool Corp 15 S Virginia / *Web:* www.climacoolcorp.com	Oklahoma City	OK	73106	405-815-3000	
ClimateMaster Inc 7300 SW 44th St / **Fax:* Cust Svc ■ *TF:* 800-299-9747 ■ *Web:* www.climatemaster.com	Oklahoma City	OK	73179	405-745-6000	745-2006*
Cold Shot Chillers 14020 InterDr W / *Web:* www.waterchillers.com	Houston	TX	77032	281-227-8400	
Colmac Coil Manufacturing Inc 370 N Lincoln St PO Box 571 / *TF:* 800-845-6778 ■ *Web:* www.colmaccoil.com	Colville	WA	99114	509-684-2595	684-8331
Colonial Commercial Corp 275 Wagaraw Rd / *OTC: CCOM* ■ *Web:* www.colonialcomm.com	Hawthorne	NJ	07506	973-427-8224	427-6981
Cummins Northwest LLC 811 SW Grady Way / *Web:* www.cumminsnorthwest.com	Renton	WA	98055	425-235-3400	
Dais Analytic Corp 11552 Prosperous Dr / *Web:* www.daisanalytic.com	Odessa	FL	33556	727-375-8484	
Data Aire Inc 230 W BlueRidge Ave / *Web:* www.dataaire.com	Orange	CA	92865	714-921-6000	
Dehumidification Manufacturing Gp LLC 6609 Ave U / *Web:* www.rentdh.com	Houston	TX	77011	713-939-1166	
Desert Aire Corp N120 W18485 Freistadt Rd / *Web:* www.desert-aire.com	Germantown	WI	53022	262-946-7400	
DiversiTech Inc 6650 Sugarloaf Pkwy Ste 100 / *TF:* 800-995-2222 ■ *Web:* www.diversitech.com	Duluth	GA	30097	678-542-3600	542-3700
Dometic Corp 2320 Industrial Pkwy PO Box 490 / *TF:* 800-544-4881 ■ *Web:* www.dometic.com	Elkhart	IN	46516	574-294-2511	293-9686
Doucette Industries Inc (DII) 20 Leigh Dr / *TF:* 800-445-7511 ■ *Web:* www.doucetteindustries.com	York	PA	17406	717-845-8746	845-2864
Drink More Water Store 7595-A Rickenbacker Dr / *TF:* 800-697-2070 ■ *Web:* www.drinkmorewater.com	Gaithersburg	MD	20879	800-697-2070	
DRISTEEM Corp 14949 Technology Dr / *TF:* 800-328-4447 ■ *Web:* www.dristeem.com	Eden Prairie	MN	55344	952-949-2415	229-3200
DRS Sustainment Systems Inc 7375 Industrial Rd / *TF:* 800-694-5005 ■ *Web:* www.drs.com	Florence	KY	41042	859-372-8204	795-1475
Duro Dyne Corp 81 Spence St / *TF:* 800-899-3876 ■ *Web:* www.durodyne.com	Bay Shore	NY	11706	631-249-9000	249-9000
EGS Electrical Group LLC EasyHeat Div 9377 W Higgins Rd / **Fax Area Code:* 800 ■ *TF:* 800-621-1506 ■ *Web:* www.emersonindustrial.com	Rosemont	IL	60018	847-268-6000	356-4714*
Electro Impulse Laboratory Inc 1805 Rte 33 PO Box 278 / *Web:* www.electroimpulse.com	Neptune	NJ	07753	732-776-5800	776-6793
Elliott-lewis Corp 2900 Black Lk Pl / *Web:* www.elliottlewis.com	Philadelphia	PA	19154	215-698-4400	698-4436
Ellis & Watts Inc 4400 Glen Willow Lake Ln / *Web:* www.elliswatts.com	Batavia	OH	45103	513-752-9000	752-4983
Emerson Climate Technologies 1675 Campbell Rd / *Web:* www.emersonclimate.com	Sidney	OH	45365	937-498-3011	498-3334
Energy Labs Inc 9651 Airway Rd Ste E / *Web:* www.cafepatterson.com	San Diego	CA	92154	619-671-0100	
Environmental Air Systems Inc 521 Banner Ave / *Web:* www.easinc.net	Greensboro	NC	27401	336-273-1975	273-1975
EST Group Inc 2701 Township Line Rd / *Web:* estgroup.cwfc.com	Hatfield	PA	19440	215-721-1100	
Evapco Inc 5151 Allendale Ln / *Web:* www.evapco.com	Taneytown	MD	21787	410-756-2600	756-6450
Fidelity Engineering Corp 25 Loveton Cir PO Box 2500 / *TF:* 800-787-6000 ■ *Web:* www.fidelityengineering.com	Sparks	MD	21152	410-771-9400	771-9412
First Operations LP 8273 Moberly Ln / *Web:* www.firstco.com	Dallas	TX	75227	214-388-5751	388-2255
Focal Point Energy Inc 1650 Las Plumas Ave Ste C / *Web:* www.focalpointenergy.com	San Jose	CA	95133	408-923-1541	
Friedrich 10001 Reunion Pl Ste 500 / *TF:* 800-541-6645 ■ *Web:* www.friedrich.com	San Antonio	TX	78216	210-546-0500	357-4480
Fulton Precision Industries 300 Success Dr / *Web:* www.fultonprecision.com	Mcconnellesburg	PA	17233	717-485-5158	
GHC Mechanical Inc 990 Pauly Dr / *Web:* www.ghcmech.com	Elk Grove Village	IL	60007	847-593-0123	
GlassPoint Solar Inc 46485 Landing Pkwy / *Web:* www.glasspoint.com	Fremont	CA	94538	415-778-2800	
Governair Corp 4841 N Sewell Ave / *Web:* governair.com	Oklahoma City	OK	73118	405-525-6546	
Great Lakes Plumbing & Heating Company Inc 4521 W Diversey Ave / *Web:* www.glph.com	Chicago	IL	60639	773-489-0400	489-1492
Gusmer Enterprises Inc 1165 Globe Ave / *Web:* www.gusmerenterprises.com	Mountainside	NJ	07092	908-301-1811	
Haakon Industries (Canada) Ltd 11851 Dyke Rd / *Web:* www.haakon.com	Richmond	BC	V7A4X8	604-273-0161	273-8397
Halton Group Americas Inc 2413 Nashville Rd Ste C4 / *Web:* www.halton.com	Bowling Green	KY	42101	270-393-7214	
Hankison International 1000 Philadelphia St / *Web:* www.spx.com	Canonsburg	PA	15317	724-745-1555	745-6040
Haskris Co 100 Kelly St / *Web:* www.haskris.com	Elk Grove Village	IL	60007	847-956-6420	
Hastings HVAC Inc 3606 Yost Ave PO Box 669 / *TF Cust Svc:* 800-228-4243 ■ *Web:* www.hastingshvac.com	Hastings	NE	68902	402-463-9821	463-6273
Heat Controller Inc 1900 Wellworth Ave / *Web:* www.heatcontroller.com	Jackson	MI	49203	517-787-2100	787-9341
Heat Pipe Technology Inc 4340 NE 49th Ave / *Web:* www.heatpipe.com	Gainesville	FL	32609	352-367-0999	367-1688
Heateflex Corp 405 Santa Clara St / *Web:* www.heateflex.com	Arcadia	CA	91006	626-599-8566	
Henry Technologies 701 S Main St / *TF:* 800-964-3679 ■ *Web:* www.henrytech.com	Chatham	IL	62629	217-483-2406	483-2408
Howden Buffalo Inc 7909 Parklane Rd Ste 300 / **Fax Area Code:* 866 ■ *Web:* www.howden.com	Columbia	SC	29223	803-741-2700	757-0908*
Hunton Group, The 10555 Westpark Dr / *Web:* www.huntongroup.com	Houston	TX	77042	713-266-3900	267-5753
International Environmental Corp (IEC) PO Box 2598 / *Web:* www.iec-okc.com	Oklahoma City	OK	73101	405-605-5000	605-5001
ITT Corp 1133 Westchester Ave / **Fax:* Mktg ■ *Web:* www.bellgossett.com	White Plains	NY	10604	914-641-2000	696-2950*
ITW Vortec 10125 Carver Rd / *TF:* 800-441-7475 ■ *Web:* www.itw-air.com	Cincinnati	OH	45242	513-891-7485	891-4092
Jensen USA Inc 99 Aberdeen Loop / *Web:* www.jensen-group.com	Panama City	FL	32405	850-271-5959	
Kobelco Compressors (America) Inc 3000 Hammond Ave / *Web:* www.kobelcocompressors.com	Elkhart	IN	46516	574-295-3145	293-1641
Kooltronic Inc 30 Pennington-Hopewell Rd / *Web:* www.kooltronic.com	Pennington	NJ	08534	609-466-3400	466-1114
Krack Corp 1300 N Arlington Heights Rd Ste 130 / *Web:* www.krack.com	Itasca	IL	60143	630-629-7500	250-3537
Lawler Manufacturing Corp Seven Kilmer Ct / *Web:* www.lawlercorp.com	Edison	NJ	08817	732-777-2040	777-4828
Layton Manufacturing Corp 825 Remsen Ave / *TF:* 800-545-8002 ■ *Web:* www.laytonmfg.com	Brooklyn	NY	11236	718-498-6000	498-6003
Lintern Corp 8685 Stn St / *TF:* 800-321-3638 ■ *Web:* www.lintern.com	Mentor	OH	44060	440-255-9333	255-6427
Lomanco Inc 2101 W Main St / *TF:* 800-643-5596 ■ *Web:* www.lomanco.com	Jacksonville	AR	72076	501-982-6511	982-1258
Mammoth Inc 13200 Pioneer Trl Ste 150 / *Web:* www.mammoth-inc.com	Chaska	MN	55318	952-358-6600	358-6700
Maradyne Corp 4540 W 160th St / *TF:* 800-537-7444 ■ *Web:* www.maradyne.com	Cleveland	OH	44135	216-362-0755	362-0799
Marvair Airxcel Inc 156 Seedling Dr / *Web:* www.marvair.com	Cordele	GA	31015	912-273-3636	
Master-Bilt Products 908 Hwy 15 N / *TF:* 800-647-1284 ■ *Web:* www.master-bilt.com	New Albany	MS	38652	662-534-9061	534-6049

Company	City	State	Zip	Phone	Fax
Mee Industries Inc 16021 Adelante St *Web:* www.meefog.com	Irwindale	CA	91702	626-359-4550	
Mermaid Manufacturing 2651 Park Windsor Dr Ste 203 *Web:* www.mmair.com	Fort Myers	FL	33901	239-418-0535	
Mestek Inc 260 N Elm St *Web:* www.mestek.com	Westfield	MA	01085	413-568-9571	
Midwest Towers Inc 1156 Hwy 19 East *TF:* 800-900-2190 ■ *Web:* www.midwesttowers.com	Chickasha	OK	73018	405-224-4622	224-4625
Mobile Climate Control Corp 17103 State Rd 4 E PO Box 150 *TF:* 800-450-2211 ■ *Web:* www.mcc-hvac.com	Goshen	IN	46528	574-534-1516	533-4452
Multistack LLC 1065 Maple Ave *Web:* www.multistack.com	Sparta	WI	54656	608-366-2400	
Munters Corp 210 Sixth St PO Box 6428 **Fax:* Cust Svc ■ *TF:* 800-843-5360 ■ *Web:* www.munters.com	Fort Myers	FL	33907	239-936-1555	278-8790*
Munters Corp DHI 79 Monroe St *TF Sales:* 800-843-5360 ■ *Web:* www.munters.com	Amesbury	MA	01913	978-241-1100	241-1215
National Refrigeration & Air Conditioning Canada Corp 159 Roy Blvd *Web:* www.trentonrefrigeration.com	Brantford	ON	N3T5Y6	519-751-0444	
Niagara Blower Co Inc 673 Ontario St *TF:* 800-426-5169 ■ *Web:* www.niagarablower.com	Buffalo	NY	14207	716-875-2000	875-1077
Nordyne Inc 8000 Phoenix Pkwy **Fax:* Sales ■ *TF:* 800-422-4328 ■ *Web:* www.nordyne.com	O'Fallon	MO	63368	636-561-7300	561-7323*
Nortek Air Solutions LLC 13200 Pioneer Trl Ste 150 *Web:* www.ces-group.com	Eden Prairie	MN	55347	952-358-6600	
North American Filter Corp 200 W Shore Blvd *Web:* www.nafcoinc.com	Newark	NY	14513	315-331-7000	
Novelaire Technologies LLC 10132 Mammoth Ave *Web:* www.novelaire.com	Baton Rouge	LA	70814	225-924-0427	
Pacific Rim Mechanical 7655 Convoy Ct *TF:* 800-891-4822 ■ *Web:* www.prmech.com	San Diego	CA	92111	858-974-6500	974-6501
Packless Metal Hose Inc PO Box 20668 *TF:* 800-347-4859 ■ *Web:* www.packless.com	Waco	TX	76702	254-666-7700	666-7893
Peerless of America Inc 1201 Wabash Ave *Web:* www.peerlessofamerica.com	Effingham	IL	62401	217-342-0400	342-0412
Perry Products Corp 25 Mount Laurel Rd *Web:* www.perryproducts.com	Hainesport	NJ	08036	609-267-1600	267-8724
PH Windsolutions Inc 642 De Courcelle Ste 304 *Web:* www.phwindsolutions.com	Montreal	QC	H4C3C5	514-522-6329	
Phelps Fan LLC 10701 I-30 *Web:* www.phelpsfan.com	Little Rock	AR	72209	501-568-5550	568-3363
Phoenix Manufacturing Inc 3655 E Roeser Rd *TF Cust Svc:* 800-325-6952 ■ *Web:* www.evapcool.com	Phoenix	AZ	85040	602-437-1034	437-4833
Pittsburgh Plumbing Heating & Industrial (PPHI) 434 Melwood Ave *TF:* 800-445-4155 ■ *Web:* www.pphind.com	Pittsburgh	PA	15213	412-622-8100	622-8145
Polar King International Inc 4424 New Haven Ave *Web:* www.polarking.com	Fort Wayne	IN	46803	260-428-2530	
Precision Pump & Valve Service Inc 517 Old Goff Mtn Rd *Web:* www.ppvs.com	Cross Lanes	WV	25313	304-776-1710	
Proair LLC 28731 County Rd 6 *TF:* 800-338-8544 ■ *Web:* www.proairllc.com	Elkhart	IN	46514	574-264-5494	264-2194
RAE Corp Technical Systems Div 4492 Hunt St *Web:* rae-corp.com	Pryor	OK	74361	918-825-7222	825-0723
Rama Corp 600 W Esplanade Ave *TF:* 800-472-5670 ■ *Web:* ramacorporation.com/	San Jacinto	CA	92583	951-654-7351	654-3748
Refrigeration Research Inc 525 N Fifth St *Web:* www.refresearch.com	Brighton	MI	48116	810-227-1151	227-3700
Refrigerator Manufacturers Inc 17018 Edwards Rd *Web:* www.rmi-econocold.com	Cerritos	CA	90703	562-926-2006	
Rheem Mfg Company Air Conditioning Div 5600 Old Greenwood Rd *Web:* www.rheem.com	Fort Smith	AR	72903	479-646-4311	
Rink Systems Inc 1103 Hershey St *TF:* 800-944-7930 ■ *Web:* www.rinksystems.com	Albert Lea	MN	56007	507-373-9175	377-1060
Ritchie Engineering Company Inc 10950 Hampshire Ave S *Web:* www.yellowjacket.com	Bloomington	MN	55438	952-943-1300	
Ruskin Rooftop Systems 1625 Diplomat Dr *Web:* www.rooftopsystems.com	Carrollton	TX	75006	972-247-7447	
Russell Food Equipment Ltd 1255 Venables St *Web:* www.russellfood.ca	Vancouver	BC	V6A3X6	604-253-6611	
San Jamar Inc 555 Koopman Ln *Web:* www.sanjamar.com	Elkhorn	WI	53121	262-723-6133	
Schaefer Ventilation Equipment LLC One Industrial Blvd Ste 101 *Web:* www.schaeferfan.com	Sauk Rapids	MN	56379	320-251-8696	
Sealed Unit Parts Company Inc 2230 Landmark Pl *TF:* 800-333-9125 ■ *Web:* www.supco.com	Allenwood	NJ	08720	732-223-6644	223-1617
Seasons-4 Inc 4500 Industrial Access Rd *TF:* 800-888-9900 ■ *Web:* www.seasons4.net	Douglasville	GA	30134	770-489-0716	489-2938
Shield Air Solutions Inc 3708 Greenhouse Rd *TF:* 800-237-2095 ■ *Web:* shieldair.com	Houston	TX	77084	281-944-4300	
Skuttle Manufacturing Co 101 Margaret St *TF:* 800-848-9786 ■ *Web:* www.skuttle.com	Marietta	OH	45750	740-373-9169	373-9565
Slant Fin Corp 100 Forest Dr *Web:* www.slantfin.com	Greenvale	NY	11548	516-484-2600	484-2600
Snyder Capital Corp 5110 Pk Ln	Dallas	TX	75220	214-754-0500	
So Low Environmental Equipment Company Inc 10310 Spartan Dr *Web:* www.so-low.com	Cincinnati	OH	45215	513-772-9410	
Standard Refrigeration Co 2050 N Ruby St *Web:* www.stanref.com	Melrose Park	IL	60160	708-345-5400	345-3513
T Rad North America Inc 210 Bill Bryan Blvd PO Box 2300 *Web:* www.copar.net	Hopkinsville	KY	42240	270-885-9116	
Tecumseh Power Co 900 N St *Web:* www.tecumsehpower.com	Grafton	WI	53024	262-377-2700	
Tecumseh Products Company PAris Div 2700 W Wood St *Web:* tecumseh.com	Paris	TN	38242	731-642-6394	644-8181
Tekgard Inc 3390 Farmtrail Rd *Web:* www.tekgard.com	York	PA	17406	717-854-0005	
Temp-Control Mechanical Corp (TCM) 4800 N Ch Ave *TF:* 877-826-3828 ■ *Web:* www.tcmcorp.com	Portland	OR	97217	503-285-9851	285-9978
Temtrol LLC 106 N Industrial Blvd *Web:* www.temtrol.com	Okarche	OK	73762	405-263-7286	263-4924
Texas Air Systems Inc 6029 W Campus Cir Dr *Web:* www.texasairsystems.com	Irving	TX	75063	972-570-4700	
Therma-Flite Inc 849 Jackson St *Web:* www.therma-flite.com	Benicia	CA	94510	707-747-5949	
Thermal Care Inc 7720 N Lehigh Ave *TF:* 888-828-7387 ■ *Web:* www.thermalcare.com	Niles	IL	60714	847-966-2260	966-9358
Thermo King Corp 314 W 90th St *Web:* www.thermoking.com	Minneapolis	MN	55420	952-887-2200	887-2615
ThermoElectric Cooling America Corp 4048 W Schubert Ave *TF:* 888-832-2872 ■ *Web:* www.thermoelectric.com	Chicago	IL	60639	773-342-4900	342-0191
Tom Barrow Co (TBC) 2800 Plant Atkinson Rd *TF:* 800-229-8226 ■ *Web:* www.tombarrow.com	Smyrna	GA	30080	404-351-1010	350-9121
Tom Richards Inc 7010 Lindsay Dr *Web:* www.process-technology.com	Mentor	OH	44060	440-974-1300	
Transitair Inc 27 Bank St *Web:* www.transitairusa.com	Hornell	NY	14843	607-324-7860	
Traulsen & Company Inc 4401 Blue Mound Rd **Fax Area Code:* 817 ■ **Fax:* Cust Svc ■ *TF:* 800-825-8220 ■ *Web:* www.traulsen.com	Fort Worth	TX	76106	800-825-8220	624-4302*
Tulsa Heaters Inc 1215 S Boulder Ste 1200 *Web:* www.tulsaheaters.com	Tulsa	OK	74119	918-582-9918	582-9916
Tutco Inc 500 Gould Dr *TF:* 877-262-4533 ■ *Web:* www.tutco.com	Cookeville	TN	38506	931-432-4141	432-4140
United CoolAir Corp 491 E Princess St *TF:* 877-905-1111 ■ *Web:* www.unitedcoolair.com	York	PA	17403	717-843-4311	854-4462
United Electric Company LP 501 Galveston St *Web:* www.magicaire.com	Wichita Falls	TX	76301	940-397-2100	397-2166
Vinotheque Wine Cellars 1738 E Alpine Ave *Web:* www.vinotheque.com	Stockton	CA	95205	209-466-9463	
Watsco Inc 2665 S Bayshore Dr Ste 901 *NYSE:* WSO ■ *Web:* www.watsco.com	Miami	FL	33133	305-714-4100	858-4492
Watts Radiant Inc 4500 E Progress Pl *TF:* 800-276-2419 ■ *Web:* www.wattsradiant.com	Springfield	MO	65803	417-864-6108	864-8161
WEBCO Inc 3300 E Pythian St *Web:* www.webco-inc.com	Springfield	MO	65802	417-866-7231	
Whalen Co, The PO Box 1390 *Web:* www.whalencompany.com	Easton	MD	21601	410-822-9200	822-8926
Williams Distributing Co 658 Richmond NW *Web:* www.wmsdist.com	Grand Rapids	MI	49504	616-456-1613	
Williams Furnace Co 250 W Laurel St *Web:* www.wfc-fc.com	Colton	CA	92324	909-825-0993	
WSA Engineered Systems 2018 S First St *Web:* www.wsaes.com	Milwaukee	WI	53207	414-481-4120	481-4121

15 AIR CONDITIONING & HEATING EQUIPMENT - RESIDENTIAL

SEE ALSO Air Conditioning & Heating Equipment - Commercial/Industrial p. 1726

Company	City	State	Zip	Phone	Fax
Airefco Inc 18755 SW Teton Ave PO Box 1349 *TF:* 800-869-1349 ■ *Web:* www.airefco.com	Tualatin	OR	97062	503-692-3210	691-2392
Allied Air Enterprises 215 Metropolitan Dr **Fax Area Code:* 803 ■ *TF:* 800-448-5872 ■ *Web:* www.alliedair.com	West Columbia	SC	29170	800-448-5872	738-4001*
Amana Appliances Inc 2800 220th Trl *TF Cust Svc:* 800-843-0304 ■ *Web:* www.amana.com	Amana	IA	52204	319-622-5511	622-2180
Bard Mfg Co Inc 1914 Randolph Dr *TF:* 877-347-6456 ■ *Web:* www.bardhvac.com	Bryan	OH	43506	419-636-1194	636-2640
Behr Climate Systems 5020 Augusta Dr *Web:* www.mahle.com	Fort Worth	TX	76106	817-624-7273	624-3328
Bergstrom Manufacturing Co 2390 Blackhawk Rd *Web:* www.bergstrominc.com	Rockford	IL	61125	815-874-7821	874-2144
CalsonicKansei North America Inc One Calsonic Way *Web:* www.calsonic.com	Shelbyville	TN	37160	931-684-4490	684-2724
Delphi Harrison Thermal Systems 200 Upper Mtn Rd *Web:* delphi.com	Lockport	NY	14094	716-439-2011	
Evans Tempcon Inc 701 Ann St NW *Web:* www.evanstempcon.com	Grand Rapids	MI	49504	616-361-2681	361-9646
Friedrich 10001 Reunion Pl Ste 500 *TF:* 800-541-6645 ■ *Web:* www.friedrich.com	San Antonio	TX	78216	210-546-0500	357-4480
Goodman Mfg Company LP 5151 San Felipe St Ste 500 *Web:* www.goodmanmfg.com	Houston	TX	77056	713-861-2500	
HDT Global 30500 Aurora Rd Ste 100 **Fax Area Code:* 440 ■ *Web:* www.hdtglobal.com	Solon	OH	44139	216-438-6111	248-1691*
International Comfort Products Corp (ICP) 650 Heil Quaker Ave **Fax Area Code:* 860 ■ *TF:* 800-458-6650 ■ *Web:* www.icpusa.com	Lewisburg	TN	37091	931-359-3511	660-7964*

	City	State	Zip	Phone	Fax
Johnson Controls Inc - YORK 5757 N Green Bay Ave *Web:* www.johnsoncontrols.com	Milwaukee	WI	53201	414-524-1200	
Kim Hotstart Manufacturing Co 5723 E Alki Ave *TF:* 800-224-5550 ■ *Web:* www.hotstart.com	Spokane	WA	99212	509-536-8660	563-4216
Lennox Industries Inc 2100 Lake Pk Blvd *TF Cust Svc:* 800-953-6669 ■ *Web:* www.lennox.com	Richardson	TX	75080	800-953-6669	572-4001
Lennox International Inc 2140 Lake Pk Blvd *NYSE:* LII ■ **Fax:* Mail Rm ■ *TF:* 800-953-6669 ■ *Web:* www.lennoxinternational.com	Richardson	TX	75080	972-497-5000	497-5292*
Modine Manufacturing Co 1500 De Koven Ave *NYSE:* MOD ■ *Web:* www.modine.com	Racine	WI	53403	262-636-1200	636-1424
National System of Garage Ventilation Inc 714 N Church St PO Box 1186 *TF:* 800-728-8368 ■ *Web:* www.nsgv.com	Decatur	IL	62525	217-423-7314	422-5387
Nortek Inc 50 Kennedy Plz *NASDAQ:* NTK ■ *Web:* www.nortekinc.com	Providence	RI	02903	401-751-1600	751-4610
Simpson Mfg Company Inc 5956 W Las Positas Blvd *NYSE:* SSD ■ *TF:* 800-925-5099 ■ *Web:* www.simpsonmfg.com	Pleasanton	CA	94588	925-560-9000	847-3871
Takagi Industrial Company USA Inc Five Whatney *TF:* 888-882-5244 ■ *Web:* www.takagi.com	Irvine	CA	92618	949-770-7171	770-3171
TPI Corp PO Box 4973 *TF:* 800-682-3398 ■ *Web:* www.tpicorp.com	Johnson City	TN	37602	423-477-4131	
Trane Company Unitary Products Group 6200 Troup Hwy *Web:* www.trane.com	Tyler	TX	75707	903-581-3200	581-3482
Van Natta Mechanical Corp 25 Whitney Rd *Web:* www.vannattamechanical.com	Mahwah	NJ	07430	201-391-3700	930-0295
Ventamatic Ltd 100 Washington Rd **Fax Area Code:* 940 ■ *TF:* 800-433-1626 ■ *Web:* www.bvc.com	Mineral Wells	TX	76067	800-433-1626	325-9311*
Whirlpool Corp 2000 N M-63 *NYSE:* WHR ■ *TF:* 800-253-1301 ■ *Web:* www.whirlpoolcorp.com	Benton Harbor	MI	49022	269-923-5000	
Young Touchstone Inc 200 Smith Ln *TF Sales:* 800-238-8230 ■ *Web:* www.youngtouchstone.com	Jackson	TN	38301	731-424-5045	424-4625

16 AIR FARE CONSOLIDATORS

	City	State	Zip	Phone	Fax
Airline Tariff Publishing Co (ATPCO) 45005 Aviation Dr Ste 400 *Web:* www.atpco.net	Dulles	VA	20166	703-471-7510	471-6584
Brazilian Travel Service (BTS) 16 W 46th St Second Fl *TF:* 800-342-5746 ■ *Web:* www.btstravelonline.com	New York	NY	10036	212-764-6161	719-4142
C & H International 4751 Wilshire Blvd Ste 201 *TF:* 800-833-8888 ■ *Web:* www.cnhintl.com	Los Angeles	CA	90010	323-933-2288	939-2286
Centrav Inc 511 E Travelers Trl *TF:* 800-874-2033 ■ *Web:* www.centrav.com	Burnsville	MN	55337	952-886-7650	886-7640
GTT Global 4100 Spring Valley Rd Ste 202 *TF:* 888-288-7182 ■ *Web:* www.gttglobal.com	Dallas	TX	75244	972-239-5069	
International Travel Systems Inc 64 Madison Ave 2nd Fl *TF:* 800-258-0135 ■ *Web:* international-travel-systems.com	Wood-Ridge	NJ	07075	201-727-0470	727-0473
Mill-Run Inc 424 Madison Ave 12th Fl *Web:* www5.millrun.com	New York	NY	10017	212-486-9840	223-8129
Picasso Travel 300 N Continental Blvd Ste 310 *Web:* picassotravel.com	El Segundo	CA	90245	310-645-4400	
Sky Bird Travel & Tours Inc 24701 Swanson *TF:* 888-759-2473 ■ *Web:* www.skybirdtravel.com	Southfield	MI	48033	248-372-4800	372-4810
Skylink Travel 980 Ave of the Americas *TF:* 800-247-6659 ■ *Web:* www.skylinkus.com	New York	NY	10018	212-573-8980	573-8878
Solar Tours 1629 K St NW Ste 604 *TF:* 800-388-7652 ■ *Web:* www.solartours.com	Washington	DC	20006	202-861-5864	452-0905
Trans Am Travel 4222 King St Ste 130 *TF:* 800-822-7600 ■ *Web:* www.transamtravel.com	Alexandria	VA	22302	703-998-7676	824-8190

17 AIR PURIFICATION EQUIPMENT - HOUSEHOLD

SEE ALSO Appliances - Small - Mfr p. 1744

	City	State	Zip	Phone	Fax
Air Quality Engineering Inc 7140 Northland Dr N *TF:* 800-328-0787 ■ *Web:* www.air-quality-eng.com	Brooklyn Park	MN	55428	763-531-9823	531-9900
Airguard Industries Inc 100 River Ridge Cir *TF:* 800-999-3458 ■ *Web:* clcair.com/brands-products/airguard	Jeffersonville	IN	47130	866-247-4827	
Dayton Reliable Air Filter Inc 2294 N Moraine Dr **Fax Area Code:* 937 ■ *TF Orders:* 800-699-0747 ■ *Web:* www.reliablefilter.com	Dayton	OH	45439	800-699-0747	293-3975*
Field Controls LLC 2630 Airport Rd *Web:* www.fieldcontrols.com	Kinston	NC	28504	252-522-3031	522-0214
Gaylord Industries Inc 10900 SW Avery St *TF:* 800-547-9696 ■ *Web:* gaylordventilation.com	Tualatin	OR	97062	503-691-2010	692-6048
General Filters Inc 43800 Grand River Ave **Fax Area Code:* 248 ■ *TF:* 866-476-5101 ■ *Web:* www.generalfilters.com	Novi	MI	48375	866-476-5101	349-2366*
HEPA Corp 3071 E Coronado St *Web:* www.hepa.com	Anaheim	CA	92806	714-630-5700	630-2894
Home Care Industries Inc ALFCO Div One Lisbon St *TF Cust Svc:* 800-325-1908 ■ *Web:* www.homecareind.com	Clifton	NJ	07013	973-365-1600	365-1770
Indoor Purification Systems Inc *Surround Air Div* 334 N Marshall Way Ste C *TF:* 888-812-1516 ■ *Web:* surroundair.com	Layton	UT	84041	801-547-1162	991-4838
Kaz Home Environment 250 Tpke Rd *Web:* www.kaz.com	Southborough	MA	01772	508-490-7000	
Koch Filter Corp 625 W Hill St *TF:* 800-757-5624 ■ *Web:* www.kochfilter.com	Louisville	KY	40208	502-634-4796	637-2280
Permatron Group 2020 Touhy Ave *TF:* 800-882-8012 ■ *Web:* www.permatron.com	Elk Grove Village	IL	60007	847-434-1421	451-1811
PuriTec 4705 S Durango Dr Ste 100-102 **Fax Area Code:* 888 ■ *TF:* 888-491-4100 ■ *Web:* www.puriteam.com	Las Vegas	NV	89147	610-268-5420	759-8905*
Rena Ware International Inc 15885 NE 28th St *Web:* www.renaware.com	Bellevue	WA	98008	425-881-6171	882-7500
Research Products Corp 1015 E Washington Ave *TF:* 800-334-6011 ■ *Web:* www.aprilaire.com	Madison	WI	53703	608-257-8801	257-4357
RPS Products Inc 281 Keyes Ave *TF:* 800-683-7030 ■ *Web:* www.rpsproducts.com	Hampshire	IL	60140	847-683-3400	683-3939
Spencer Turbine Co 600 Day Hill Rd *TF:* 800-232-4321 ■ *Web:* www.spencerturbine.com	Windsor	CT	06095	860-688-8361	688-0098
Tjernlund Products Inc 1601 Ninth St *TF:* 800-255-4208 ■ *Web:* www.tjernlund.com	White Bear Lake	MN	55110	651-426-2993	426-9547
United Air Specialists Inc (UAS) 4440 Creek Rd *TF:* 800-252-4647 ■ *Web:* www.uasinc.com	Cincinnati	OH	45242	513-891-0400	891-4171
Vornado Air Circulation Systems Inc 415 E 13th St *TF:* 800-234-0604 ■ *Web:* www.vornado.com	Andover	KS	67002	316-733-0035	733-1544

18 AIR PURIFICATION EQUIPMENT - INDUSTRIAL

	City	State	Zip	Phone	Fax
AAF International Corp 10300 Ormsby Pk Pl Ste 600 **Fax Area Code:* 888 ■ *TF:* 888-223-2003 ■ *Web:* www.aafintl.com	Louisville	KY	40223	502-637-0011	223-6500*
Acme Engineering & Manufacturing Corp PO Box 978 *Web:* www.acmefan.com	Muskogee	OK	74402	918-682-7791	682-0134
Advantec MFS Inc 6723 Sierra Ct Ste A *TF:* 800-334-7132 ■ *Web:* www.advantecmfs.com	Dublin	CA	94568	925-479-0625	479-0630
Aerovent Inc 5959 Trenton Ln *Web:* www.aerovent.com	Plymouth	MN	55442	763-551-7500	551-7501
Aget Manufacturing Co 1408 E Church St *TF:* 800-832-2438 ■ *Web:* www.agetmfg.com	Adrian	MI	49221	517-263-5781	263-7154
Air Quality Engineering Inc 7140 Northland Dr N *TF:* 800-328-0787 ■ *Web:* www.air-quality-eng.com	Brooklyn Park	MN	55428	763-531-9823	531-9900
Airflow Systems Inc 11221 Pagemill Rd *TF:* 800-818-6185 ■ *Web:* www.airflowsystems.com	Dallas	TX	75243	214-503-8008	503-9596
Airfoil Impellers Corp PO Box 9966 *Web:* www.airfoil.com	College Station	TX	77842	979-822-6418	775-5588
Airguard Industries Inc 100 River Ridge Cir *TF:* 800-999-3458 ■ *Web:* clcair.com/brands-products/airguard	Jeffersonville	IN	47130	866-247-4827	
Airmaster Fan Co 1300 Falahee Rd *Web:* www.airmasterfan.com	Jackson	MI	49203	517-764-2300	764-3838
Alanco Technologies Inc 15575 N 83rd Way Ste 3 *OTC:* ALAN ■ *Web:* www.alanco.com	Scottsdale	AZ	85260	480-607-1010	607-1515
American Fan Company Inc 2933 Symmes Rd *TF:* 866-771-6266 ■ *Web:* www.americanfan.com	Fairfield	OH	45014	513-874-2400	870-6249
AMETEK Rotron Mil-Aero Products Div 55 Hasbrouck Ln *Web:* www.ametekaerodefense.com	Woodstock	NY	12498	845-679-1371	679-1371
AMETEK Technical & Industrial Products 100 E Erie St *Web:* www.ametektip.com	Kent	OH	44240	330-673-3452	677-3306
Anguil Environmental Systems Inc 8855 N 55th St *TF:* 800-488-0230 ■ *Web:* www.anguil.com	Milwaukee	WI	53223	414-365-6400	365-6410
Arrow Pneumatics Inc 2111 W 21st St *Web:* www.arrowpneumatics.com	Broadview	IL	60155	708-343-9595	343-1907
Baghouse & Industrial Sheet Metal Services Inc 1731 Pomona Rd *TF:* 888-224-4687 ■ *Web:* www.1888baghouse.com	Corona	CA	92880	951-272-6610	272-1241
Beckett Air Inc 37850 Beckett Pkwy *TF:* 800-831-7839 ■ *Web:* www.beckettair.com	North Ridgeville	OH	44039	440-327-9999	327-3569
Bruning & Federle Mfg Co 2503 Northside Dr *Web:* www.bruning-federle.com	Statesville	NC	28625	704-873-7237	
Buffalo Air Handling Co 467 Zane Snead Dr *Web:* www.buffaloair.com	Amherst	VA	24521	434-946-7455	946-7941
Cincinnati Fan & Ventilator 7697 Snider Rd *Web:* www.cincinnatifan.com	Mason	OH	45040	513-573-0600	573-0640
Clarcor Inc 840 Crescent Ctr Dr Ste 600 *NYSE:* CLC ■ *TF:* 800-252-7267 ■ *Web:* www.clarcor.com	Franklin	TN	37067	615-771-3100	771-5616
Cleanroom Systems 7000 Performance Dr *TF:* 800-825-3268 ■ *Web:* www.cleanroomsystems.com	North Syracuse	NY	13212	315-452-7400	452-7420
Clements National Co 6650 S Narragansett Ave *TF:* 800-966-0016 ■ *Web:* www.cadillacproducts.com	Chicago	IL	60638	708-594-5890	594-2481
Columbus Industries Inc 2938 SR-752 *TF:* 800-766-2552 ■ *Web:* www.colind.com	Ashville	OH	43103	740-983-2552	983-4622
Corning Environmental Technologies One Riverfront Plz *Web:* corning.com:80/environmentaltechnologies/index.aspx	Corning	NY	14831	607-974-9000	974-8776
CSM Worldwide Inc 269 Sheffield St *Web:* www.csmworldwide.com	Mountainside	NJ	07092	908-233-2882	233-1064
CUNO Inc 400 Research Pkwy *TF:* 800-243-6894 ■ *Web:* solutions.3m.com	Meriden	CT	06450	203-237-5541	238-8701
Daw Technologies Inc 1600 West 2200 South Ste 201 *Web:* www.dawtech.com	Salt Lake City	UT	84119	801-977-3100	973-6640
Disa Systems Inc 150 Transit Ave *TF:* 800-845-8508 ■ *Web:* www.disagroup.com	Thomasville	NC	27360	336-889-9187	
Donaldson Company Inc 1400 W 94th St *NYSE:* DCI ■ *Web:* www.donaldson.com	Bloomington	MN	55431	952-887-3131	

Phone | Fax

Ducon Technologies Inc 19 Engineers Ln .... Farmingdale NY 11735 631-694-1700 420-4985
Web: www.ducon.com
Dustex Corp 100 Chastain Ctr Blvd Ste 195 .... Kennesaw GA 30144 770-429-5575 429-5556
Web: www.dustex.com
Dynamic Air Engineering Inc 620 E Dyer Rd .... Santa Ana CA 92705 714-540-1000 545-9145
Web: www.dynamic-air.com
EBM Industries Inc
EBM-papst Inc 100 & 110 Hyde Rd .... Farmington CT 06034 860-674-1515 674-8536
Web: www.ebmpapst.us
Epcon Industrial Systems Inc 17777 IH- 45 S .... Conroe TX 77385 936-273-1774 273-4600
Filtertech Inc 113 Fairgrounds Dr PO Box 527 .... Manlius NY 13104 315-682-8815 682-8825
Web: www.filtertech.com
Filtration Group Inc 912 E Washington St .... Joliet IL 60433 815-726-4600 518-1162*
**Fax Area Code:* 800 ■ *TF:* 800-739-4600 ■ *Web:* www.filtrationgroup.com
Flanders Corp 531 Flanders Filters Rd .... Washington NC 27889 252-946-8081 946-3425
OTC: FLDR ■ *TF:* 800-637-2803 ■ *Web:* www.flanderscorp.com
Fuel Tech Inc 27601 Bella Vista Pkwy .... Warrenville IL 60555 630-845-4500 845-4502
NASDAQ: FTEK ■ *TF General:* 800-666-9688 ■ *Web:* www.ftek.com
Gaylord Industries Inc 10900 SW Avery St .... Tualatin OR 97062 503-691-2010 692-6048
TF: 800-547-9696 ■ *Web:* gaylordventilation.com
General Filters Inc 43800 Grand River Ave .... Novi MI 48375 866-476-5101 349-2366*
**Fax Area Code:* 248 ■ *TF:* 866-476-5101 ■ *Web:* www.generalfilters.com
Glasfloss Industries Inc PO Box 150469 .... Dallas TX 75315 214-741-7056 435-8377*
**Fax Area Code:* 800 ■ *Web:* www.glasfloss.com
Great Lakes Filters 301 Arch Ave .... Hillsdale MI 49242 800-521-8565 437-8942*
**Fax Area Code:* 517 ■ *TF:* 800-521-8565 ■ *Web:* www.greatlakesfilters.com
Greenheck Fan Corp
1100 Industrial Ave PO Box 410 .... Schofield WI 54476 715-359-6171 355-2399
Web: www.greenheck.com
Griffin Filters 106 Metropolitan Pk Dr .... Liverpool NY 13088 315-451-5300 451-2338
Web: www.griffinfilters.com
Hardie-Tynes Company Inc PO Box 12166 .... Birmingham AL 35202 205-252-5191 252-3254
Web: www.hardie-tynes.com
Hartzell Fan Inc 910 S Downing St .... Piqua OH 45356 937-773-7411 773-8994
TF: 800-336-3267 ■ *Web:* www.hartzellairmovement.com
HEPA Corp 3071 E Coronado St .... Anaheim CA 92806 714-630-5700 630-2894
Web: www.hepa.com
Home Care Industries Inc ALFCO Div
One Lisbon St .... Clifton NJ 07013 973-365-1600 365-1770
TF Cust Svc: 800-325-1908 ■ *Web:* www.homecareind.com
Honeyville Metal Inc 4200 S 900 W .... Topeka IN 46571 260-593-2266 593-2486
TF: 800-593-8377 ■ *Web:* www.honeyvillemetal.com
Houston Service Industries Inc
7901 Hansen Rd .... Houston TX 77061 713-947-1623 947-6409
TF: 800-725-2291 ■ *Web:* www.hsiblowers.com
Howden Buffalo Inc 7909 Parklane Rd Ste 300 .... Columbia SC 29223 803-741-2700 757-0908*
**Fax Area Code:* 866 ■ *Web:* www.howden.com
King Engineering Corp 3201 S State St .... Ann Arbor MI 48106 734-662-5691 662-6652
TF Cust Svc: 800-242-8871 ■ *Web:* www.king-gage.com
Koch Filter Corp 625 W Hill St .... Louisville KY 40208 502-634-4796 637-2280
TF: 800-757-5624 ■ *Web:* www.kochfilter.com
La Calhene Inc 1325 Field Ave S .... Rush City MN 55069 320-358-4713 358-4713
Web: getinge.com/nuclear/
Loren Cook Co 2015 E Dale St .... Springfield MO 65803 417-869-6474 862-3820
Web: www.lorencook.com
Lydall Inc One Colonial Rd .... Manchester CT 06042 860-646-1233 646-4917
NYSE: LDL ■ *Web:* www.lydall.com
Marsulex Environmental Technology
200 N Seventh St .... Lebanon PA 17046 717-274-7000 274-7103
Web: www.met-apc.com
McIntire Co 745 Clark Ave .... Bristol CT 06010 860-585-0050 314-4500
TF: 800-437-9247 ■ *Web:* www.mcintireco.com
Met-Pro Corp Duall Div 1550 Industrial Dr .... Owosso MI 48867 989-725-8184 725-8188
Web: www.mpeas.com
Met-Pro Corp Systems Div
160 Cassell Rd PO Box 144 .... Harleysville PA 19438 215-723-9300 723-8501
TF: 800-621-0734 ■ *Web:* www.mpeas.com
Midwesco Filter Resources Inc
385 Battaile Dr .... Winchester VA 22601 540-667-8500 504-8051
TF: 800-336-7300 ■ *Web:* www.midwesco-tdcfilter.com
Midwest International Standard Products Inc
105 Stover Rd .... Charlevoix MI 49720 231-547-4000 547-9453
Web: www.midwestmagic.com
NAO Inc 1284 E Sedgley Ave .... Philadelphia PA 19134 215-743-5300 743-3018
TF Cust Svc: 800-523-3495 ■ *Web:* www.nao.com
National Filter Media Corp
691 North 400 West .... Salt Lake City UT 84103 801-363-6736 531-1293
TF: 800-777-4248 ■ *Web:* www.nfm-filter.com
New York Blower Co 7660 Quincy St .... Willowbrook IL 60527 630-794-5700 794-5776
Web: www.nyb.com
Parker Hannifin Corp Finite Filtratio & Separation Div
500 Glaspie St .... Oxford MI 48371 248-628-6400 628-1850
TF: 800-521-4357 ■ *Web:* www.parker.com
Pneumech Systems Mfg LLC
201 Pneu Mech Dr .... Statesville NC 28625 704-873-2475 871-2780
TF: 800-358-7374 ■ *Web:* www.pneu-mech.com
Precipitator Services Group Inc
1625 Broad St .... Elizabethton TN 37643 423-543-7331 543-8737
Process Equipment Inc
2770 Welborn St PO Box 1607 .... Pelham AL 35124 205-663-5330 663-6037
TF: 888-663-2028 ■ *Web:* www.processbarron.com
Purafil Inc 2654 Weaver Way .... Doraville GA 30340 770-662-8545 263-6922
TF: 800-222-6367 ■ *Web:* www.purafil.com
Revcor Inc 251 E Edwards Ave .... Carpentersville IL 60110 847-428-4412 426-4630
TF: 800-323-8261 ■ *Web:* www.revcor.com
RP Fedder Corp 740 Driving Pk Ave .... Rochester NY 14613 585-288-1600 288-2481
Web: www.rpfedder.com
RPS Products Inc 281 Keyes Ave .... Hampshire IL 60140 847-683-3400 683-3939
TF: 800-683-7030 ■ *Web:* www.rpsproducts.com
Sly Inc 8300 Dow Cir .... Strongsville OH 44136 440-891-3200 891-3210
TF: 800-334-2957 ■ *Web:* www.slyinc.com

Sonic Air Systems Inc 1050 Beacon St .... Brea CA 92821 714-255-0124 255-8366
TF: 800-827-6642 ■ *Web:* www.sonicairsystems.com
SPE Amerex 201 Houston St Ste 200 .... Batavia IL 60510 630-406-7756
Web: amerextech.com
Spencer Turbine Co 600 Day Hill Rd .... Windsor CT 06095 860-688-8361 688-0098
TF: 800-232-4321 ■ *Web:* www.spencerturbine.com
Standard Filter Corp 5928 Balfour Ct .... Carlsbad CA 92008 760-929-8559 929-1901
TF: 800-634-5837 ■ *Web:* www.standardfilter.com
Sterling Blower Co 135 Vista Ctr Dr .... Forest VA 24551 434-316-5310 316-5910
Web: www.sterlingblower.com
Strobic Air Corp
160 Cassell Rd PO Box 144 .... Harleysville PA 19438 215-723-4700 723-7401
Web: www.strobicair.com
Tek Air Systems Inc 41 Eagle Rd .... Danbury CT 06810 203-791-1400 798-6534
Web: www.tek-air.com
Terra Universal Inc 800 S Ramon Ave .... Fullerton CA 92831 714-578-6000 578-6020
Web: www.terrauni.com
Tjernlund Products Inc 1601 Ninth St .... White Bear Lake MN 55110 651-426-2993 426-9547
TF: 800-255-4208 ■ *Web:* www.tjernlund.com
Tri-Dim Filter Corp 93 Industrial Dr Bldg 2 .... Louisa VA 23093 540-967-2600 967-2835
TF: 800-458-9835 ■ *Web:* www.tridim.com
Tri-Mer Corp 1400 Monroe St PO Box 730 .... Owosso MI 48867 989-723-7838 723-7844
Web: www.tri-mer.com
Trion Inc 101 McNeill Rd .... Sanford NC 27330 919-775-2201 774-8771
Web: www.trioniaq.com
Tuthill Vacuum & Blower Systems
4840 W Kearney St .... Springfield MO 65803 417-865-8715 865-2950
TF: 800-825-6937 ■ *Web:* www.tuthill.com
Twin City Fan Cos Ltd 5959 Trenton Ln N .... Minneapolis MN 55442 763-551-7600 551-7601
Web: www.tcf.com
United Air Specialists Inc (UAS)
4440 Creek Rd .... Cincinnati OH 45242 513-891-0400 891-4171
TF: 800-252-4647 ■ *Web:* www.uasinc.com
Venturedyne Ltd 600 College Ave .... Pewaukee WI 53072 262-691-9900 691-9901
Web: www.venturedyne.com
Waco 2546 Gen Armistead Ave .... Norristown PA 19403 610-630-4800 630-4904
TF: 800-928-7159 ■ *Web:* www.wacofilters.com

19 AIR TRAFFIC CONTROL SERVICES

The Federal Aviation Administration (a US government agency) and NAV CANADA (a private, not-for-profit Canadian firm) provide air traffic services nationwide in the US and Canada, respectively. The types of services provided include aircraft routing, approach and departure instruction, and weather information.

Phone | Fax

Great Lakes Region 2300 E Devon Ave .... Des Plaines IL 60018 847-294-7272 294-7036
Web: www.faa.gov
Federal Aviation Administration Northwest Mountain Region
1601 Lind Ave SW .... Renton WA 98057 425-227-2001
TF: 800-220-5715 ■ *Web:* www.faa.gov
Alaskan Region 222 W Seventh Ave Ste 14 .... Anchorage AK 99513 907-271-5438 271-2851
Web: www.faa.gov
Central Region Federal Bldg 901 Locust St ...... Kansas City MO 64106 816-329-3050
Web: www.faa.gov
Eastern Region 159-30 Rockaway Blvd .... Jamaica NY 11434 718-553-3001
Web: www.faa.gov
Federal Aviation Administration Regional Offices
New England Region
12 New England Executive Pk .... Burlington MA 01803 781-238-7020 238-7608
Web: www.faa.gov/airports/new_england
Western Pacific Region 15000 Aviation Blvd .... Lawndale CA 90261 310-725-7800 725-6811
Web: www.faa.gov/airports/western_pacific
Federal Aviation Administration Southern Region
1701 Columbia Ave .... College Park GA 30337 404-305-5000
Web: www.faa.gov
FlightAware Eight Greenway Plz Ste 1300 .... Houston TX 77046 713-877-9010
Web: www.flightaware.com
mPower Software Services LLC
770 Newtown-Yardley Rd Ste 225 .... Newtown PA 18940 215-497-9730
Web: www.mpowerss.com
NAV CANADA 77 Metcalfe St PO Box 3411 Stn D .... Ottawa ON K1P5L6 613-563-5588 563-3426
TF: 800-876-4693 ■ *Web:* www.navcanada.ca
Veracity Engineering
600 Maryland Ave Sw Ste 600e .... Washington DC 20024 202-488-0975
Web: www.veracity-eng.com

20 AIRCRAFT

SEE ALSO Airships p. 1740

Phone | Fax

ACR Aircraft Component Repair Inc
25058 Anza Dr .... Valencia CA 91355 661-295-6677 295-6679
Web: www.acr.aero
Aeronautical Accessories Inc
Tri-County Industrial Park 423 Century Ct
.... Piney Flats TN 37686 423-538-5151
Web: www.edwardsassociates.com
Aerospace Technologies Group Inc
620 NW 35th St .... Boca Raton FL 33431 561-244-7400
Web: www.atgshades.com
AeroVironment Inc
181 W Huntington Dr Ste 202 .... Monrovia CA 91016 626-357-9983 359-9628
NASDAQ: AVAV ■ *TF:* 888-833-2148 ■ *Web:* www.avinc.com
Air Tractor Inc 1524 Lelind Snow Way .... Olney TX 76374 940-564-5616 564-5625
Web: www.airtractor.com
Airbus Helicopters Inc 2701 Forum Dr .... Grand Prairie TX 75052 972-641-0000 641-3550
TF: 800-873-0001 ■ *Web:* airbushelicoptersinc.com/
AvCraft Technical Services Inc
3301 Mustang St .... Myrtle Beach SC 29577 843-232-1338
Web: www.avcrafttechnical.com

				Phone	Fax
Axiam Inc 58 Blackburn Ctr	Gloucester	MA	01930	978-281-3550	
Web: www.axiam.com					
Ballistic Recovery Systems Inc 380 Airport Rd	South St. Paul	MN	55075	651-457-7491	
Web: www.brsparachutes.com					
Bell Helicopter Textron Inc 600 E Hurst Blvd (State Hwy 10)	Hurst	TX	76053	817-280-2011	280-2321
TF: 888-874-5884 ■ *Web:* www.bellhelicopter.com					
Boeing Co, The 100 N Riverside Plz	Chicago	IL	60606	312-544-2000	
NYSE: BA ■ *Web:* www.boeing.com					
Boeing Company Commercial Airplane Group PO Box 3707	Seattle	WA	98124	206-655-2121	
Web: www.boeing.com/commercial					
Bombardier Aerospace 400 Cote-Vertu Rd W	Dorval	QC	H4S1Y9	514-855-5000	855-7401
TF General: 866-855-5001 ■ *Web:* www.bombardier.com					
Bombardier Aerospace Learjet One Learjet Way	Wichita	KS	67209	316-946-2000	946-2220
Web: businessaircraft.bombardier.com					
Bombardier Inc 800 RenT-LTvesque Blvd W	Montreal	QC	H3B1Y8	514-861-9481	861-7769
TSE: BBD/B ■ *Web:* www.bombardier.com					
Cessna Aircraft Co One Cessna Blvd	Wichita	KS	67215	316-517-6000	517-7250
Web: www.cessna.com					
Composite Resources Inc 485 Lakeshore Pkwy	Rock Hill	SC	29730	803-366-9700	
Web: www.composite-resources.com					
Conair Group Inc 1510 Tower St	Abbotsford	BC	V2T6H5	604-855-1171	855-1185
Web: conair.ca					
Concorde Battery Corp 2009 W San Bernardino Rd	West Covina	CA	91790	626-813-1234	
Web: www.concordebattery.com					
CPI Manufacturing LLC 108 Ledyard St	Hartford	CT	06114	860-296-7980	
Web: www.cpimanufacturing.com					
Dallas Airmotive Inc 900 Nolen Dr Ste 100	Grapevine	TX	76051	214-956-3001	956-2825*
**Fax Area Code:* 817 ■ *Web:* www.dallasairmotive.com					
Dassault Falcon Jet Corp PO Box 2000	South Hackensack	NJ	07606	201-440-6700	322-7221*
**Fax Area Code:* 302 ■ **Fax:* Hum Res ■ *TF:* 800-527-2463 ■ *Web:* www.dassaultfalcon.com					
Defense Support Services LLC 901 Lincoln Dr W Ste 200	Marlton	NJ	08053	856-866-2200	
Web: www.ds2.com					
Diamond Aircraft Industries Inc 1560 Crumlin Sideroad	London	ON	N5V1S2	519-457-4000	
Web: www.diamondaircraft.com					
Embraer Aircraft Corp 276 SW 34th St	Fort Lauderdale	FL	33315	954-359-3700	359-3701
Web: www.embraer.com.br					
Enstrom Helicopter Corp USA 2209 22nd St	Menominee	MI	49858	906-863-1200	863-6244
Web: www.enstromhelicopter.com					
Epic AIR LLC 22590 Nelson Rd	Bend	OR	97701	541-318-8849	
Web: www.epicaircraft.com					
Erickson Air-Crane Co 5550 SW Macadam Ave Ste 200	Portland	OR	97239	503-505-5800	
TF: 800-424-2413 ■ *Web:* www.ericksonaircrane.com					
First Wave Aviation LLC 5440 S 101st E Ave	Tulsa	OK	74146	918-622-0007	
Web: www.firstwave.aero					
Gulfstream Aerospace Corp 500 Gulfstream Rd	Savannah	GA	31408	912-965-3000	395-8222
Web: www.gulfstream.com					
Heli-One American Support LLC 120 NE Frontage Rd	Fort Collins	CO	80524	970-492-1000	
Web: www.heli-one.ca					
Honda Aircraft Company Inc 6430 Ballinger RdGreensboro	Greensboro	NC	27410	336-662-0246	
Web: hondajet.honda.com					
Kaman Aerospace Corp Old Windsor Rd PO Box 2	Bloomfield	CT	06002	860-242-4461	243-7514
Web: www.kaman.com					
Kaman Aerospace International Corp PO Box 2	Bloomfield	CT	06002	860-242-4461	243-7514
Web: www.kaman.com					
Kay & Associates Inc 165 N Arlington Heights Rd Ste 150	Buffalo Grove	IL	60089	847-255-8444	
Web: www.kayinc.com					
Lockheed Martin Aeronautics Co 1 Lockheed Blvd	Fort Worth	TX	76108	817-777-2000	777-2115
Web: www.lockheedmartin.com					
Lockheed Martin Corp 6801 Rockledge Dr	Bethesda	MD	20817	301-897-6000	897-6083
NYSE: LMT ■ *TF:* 866-562-2363 ■ *Web:* www.lockheedmartin.com					
M7 Aerospace 10823 NE Entrance Rd	San Antonio	TX	78216	210-824-9421	
Web: www.m7aerospace.com					
Maule Air Inc 2099 GA Hwy 133 S	Moultrie	GA	31788	229-985-2045	890-2402
Web: www.mauleairinc.com					
Moller International Inc 1222 Research Park Dr	Davis	CA	95618	530-756-5086	
Web: www.moller.com					
Mooney Aircraft Corp 165 Al Mooney Rd	Kerrville	TX	78028	800-456-3033	
TF: 800-456-3033 ■ *Web:* www.mooney.com					
New Piper Aircraft Inc 2926 Piper Dr	Vero Beach	FL	32960	772-567-4361	978-6584
Web: www.piper.com					
North American Aircraft Services Inc 11502 Jones Maltsberger	San Antonio	TX	78216	210-805-0049	
Web: www.naasinc.com					
Northrop Grumman Corp 2980 Fairview Park Dr	Falls Church	VA	22042	703-280-2900	201-3023*
NYSE: NOC ■ **Fax Area Code:* 310 ■ *Web:* www.northropgrumman.com					
Northrop Grumman Corp Military Aircraft Systems Div One Hornet Way	El Segundo	CA	90245	310-332-1000	
Web: northropgrumman.com					
Piedmont Aviation Component Services LLC 1031 E Mtn St Bldg 320	Kernersville	NC	27284	336-776-6300	
Web: www.piedmontaviation.com					
Quicksilver Manufacturing Inc 42214 Sarah Way	Temecula	CA	92590	951-506-0061	
Web: www.quicksilveraircraft.com					
Robinson Helicopter Co 2901 Airport Dr	Torrance	CA	90505	310-539-0508	539-5198
TF: 800-905-0655 ■ *Web:* www.robinsonheli.com					
Rockland Aerospace Inc 2111 Baldwin Ave Ste 8	Crofton	MD	21114	410-451-0969	
Web: www.mhdrockland.com					
Sabreliner Corp 1390 Hwy H Ste 1500	Perryville	MO	63775	573-543-2212	
Web: www.sabrelineraviation.com					
Scaled Composites Inc 1624 Flight Line Rd	Mojave	CA	93501	661-824-4541	824-4174
Web: www.scaled.com					
Sikorsky Aircraft Corp 6900 Main St PO Box 9729	Stratford	CT	06615	203-386-4000	
Web: www.sikorsky.com					
Spirit AeroSystems Inc 3801 S Oliver St	Wichita	KS	67210	316-526-9000	
Web: www.spiritaero.com					
TDG Aerospace Inc 545 Corporate Dr	Escondido	CA	92029	760-466-1040	
Web: www.tdgaerospace.com					
Teledyne Continental Motors Inc 2039 Broad St	Mobile	AL	36615	251-438-3411	
Web: www.continentalmotors.aero					
Texas Pneumatics Systems Inc 2404 Superior Dr	Pantego	TX	76013	817-794-0068	
Web: www.txps.com					
Thrush Aircraft Inc 300 Old Pretoria Rd	Albany	GA	31721	229-883-1440	439-9790
Web: www.thrushaircraft.com					
Valair Aviation 7301 NW 50th St	Oklahoma City	OK	73132	405-789-5000	
Web: www.valairaviation.com					
Van Horn Aviation LLC 1000 E Vista Del Cerro Dr	Tempe	AZ	85281	480-483-4202	
Web: www.vanhornaviation.com					
Vantage Associates Inc 900 Civic Ctr Dr	National City	CA	91950	619-477-6940	
Web: www.vantagemmc.com					

21 AIRCRAFT ENGINES & ENGINE PARTS

				Phone	Fax
A & B Aerospace Inc 612 Ayon Ave	Azusa	CA	91702	626-334-2976	334-6539
Web: abaerospace.com					
AAR Corp 1100 N Wood Dale Rd 1 AAR Pl	Wood Dale	IL	60191	630-227-2000	227-2019
NYSE: AIR ■ *TF:* 800-422-2213 ■ *Web:* www.aarcorp.com					
Aberdeen Regional Airport 123 S Lincoln St	Aberdeen	SD	57402	605-626-7020	
Web: www.aberdeen.sd.us					
Abipa Canada Inc 2000, Blvd Dagenais ouest	Laval	QC	H7L5W2	450-963-6888	963-8881
TF: 877-963-6888 ■ *Web:* www.abipa.com					
Able Engineering & Component Services Inc 2920 E Chambers St	Phoenix	AZ	85040	602-304-1227	
Web: www.ableengineering.com					
Acme Aerospace Inc 528 W 21st St	Tempe	AZ	85282	480-894-6864	
Web: www.acme-aero.com					
Action Aircraft Lp 10570 Olympic Dr	Dallas	TX	75220	214-351-1284	
Web: www.actionaircraft.com					
ADEPT Technologies LLC 2865 Wall Triana Hwy	Huntsville	AL	35824	256-851-2932	
Web: www.adept-technologies.com					
Aerex Manufacturing Inc 34 S Satellite Rd	South Windsor	CT	06074	860-291-9468	
Web: www.aerexmfg.com					
Aero manufacturing Corp 100 Sam Fonzo Dr	Beverly	MA	01915	978-720-1000	
Web: www.aeromanufacturing.com					
Aerospace & Commercial Technologies Inc 970 Fm 2871	Fort Worth	TX	76126	817-560-6600	
Web: www.aero-com-tech.com					
Aerotec International Inc 3007 E Chambers St	Phoenix	AZ	85040	602-253-4540	
Web: www.aerotecinternational.com					
Aerotron AirPower Inc 456 Aerotron Pkwy	Lagrange	GA	30240	706-812-1700	
Web: www.aerotron.com					
Agilis Engineering Inc 3930 Rca Blvd Ste 3000	Palm Beach Gardens	FL	33410	561-626-8900	
Web: www.agilis.com					
Agusta Aerospace Corp 3050 Red Lion Rd	Philadelphia	PA	19114	215-281-1400	
Web: us.agustawestland.com					
Aimpoint Inc 14103 Mariah Ct	Chantilly	VA	20151	703-263-9795	
Web: www.aimpoint.com					
Air Georgian Ltd 2450 Derry Rd E Shell Aerocentre	Mississauga	ON	L5S1B2	905-676-1221	
Web: www.airgeorgian.ca					
Airbus Group Inc 2550 Wasser Ter Ste 9000	Herndon	VA	20171	703-466-5600	
Web: northamerica.airbus-group.com					
Airista LLC 913 Ridgebrook Rd	Sparks Glencoe	MD	21152	410-878-2700	
Web: www.airista.com					
All Power Mfg Company Inc 13141 Molette St	Santa Fe Springs	CA	90670	562-802-2640	
Web: www.allpowermfg.com					
Alpha Q Inc 87 Upton Rd	Colchester	CT	06415	860-537-4681	537-4332
Web: alphaqinc.com					
American Dynamics Flight Systems Inc 8264 Preston Ct Ste A	Jessup	MD	20794	301-358-0747	
Web: www.adflightsystems.com					
Arnprior Aerospace Inc 107 Baskin Dr E	Arnprior	ON	K7S3M1	613-623-4267	
Web: www.arnprioraerospace.com					
AV & R 269 Prince St	Montreal	QC	H3C2N4	514-788-1420	
Web: www.avr-vr.com					
Avalex Technologies Corp 2665 Gulf Breeze Pkwy	Gulf Breeze	FL	32563	850-470-8464	
Web: www.avalex.com					
Aventure International Aviation Services LLC 108 International Dr Ste 300	Peachtree Cty	GA	30269	770-632-7930	
Web: aventureaviation.com					
Averitt Air Inc 625 Hngr Ln Hngr 4 Nashville International Airport	Nashville	TN	37217	615-399-8077	
Web: www.averittair.com					
Aviation Systems of Northwest Florida Inc 175 E Olive Rd	Pensacola	FL	32514	800-759-0953	
Web: lsijax.com					
Avior Integrated Products Inc 1001 Autoroute 440 Ouest	Laval	QC	H7L3W3	450-629-6200	
Web: www.avior.ca					

	City	State	ZIP	Phone	Fax
Avtron Aerospace Inc 7900 E Pleasant Vly Rd *Web:* www.avtronaero.com	Cleveland	OH	44131	216-750-5152	
Azmark Aero Systems LLC 944 Guadalupe Rd *Web:* www.azmark.aero	Gilbert	AZ	85233	480-926-8969	926-8970
BAE Systems Aerospace & Defense Group Inc 7822 S 46th St *Web:* www.baesystems.com	Phoenix	AZ	85044	602-643-7233	
BAE Systems Electronics & Integrated Solutions 65 Spit Brook Rd *Web:* www.eis.na.baesystems.com	Nashua	NH	03060	603-885-4321	
BAE Systems Simula Inc 7822 S 46th St	Phoenix	AZ	85044	602-643-7233	
Barnes Aerospace 169 Kennedy Rd *Web:* www.barnesaerospace.com	Windsor	CT	06095	860-298-7740	298-7738
Beacon Industries Inc 12300 Old Tesson Rd *TF:* 800-454-7159 ■ *Web:* www.beacontechnology.com	Saint Louis	MO	63128	314-487-7600	487-0100
BH Aircraft Company Inc 2230 Smithtown Ave *Web:* www.bhaircraft.com	Ronkonkoma	NY	11779	631-981-4200	981-0221
Big Fly Inc 13940 Cedar Rd Ste 227 *Web:* www.bigflyaviation.com	Cleveland	OH	44118	216-906-0022	
Blackcomb Aviation LP Vancouver International Airport 4360 Agar Dr *Web:* www.blackcombaviation.com	Richmond	BC	V7B1A3	604-273-5311	
Brown Precision Inc 90 Shields Rd *Web:* www.brownprecisioninc.com	Huntsville	AL	35811	256-746-0533	
Budney Industries Inc PO Box 8316 *Web:* www.budney.com	Berlin	CT	06037	860-828-1950	828-7528
Cadence Aerospace LLC 610 Newport Ctr Dr Ste 950 *Web:* www.prvaerospace.com	Newport Beach	CA	92660	949-877-3630	
California Amforge Corp 750 N Vernon Ave *Web:* www.cal-amforge.com	Azusa	CA	91702	626-334-4931	
Cbol Corp 19850 Plummer St *Web:* www.cbol.com	Chatsworth	CA	91311	818-704-8200	704-4336
CBS Manufacturing Co, The 35 Kripes Rd *Web:* www.cbsmfg.com	East Granby	CT	06026	860-653-8100	844-8150
Centra Industries Inc 24 Cherry Blossom Rd *Web:* www.centra-ind.com	Cambridge	ON	N3H4R7	519-650-2828	650-7474
Chromalloy Gas Turbine LLC 330 Blaisdell Rd *Web:* www.chromalloy.com	Orangeburg	NY	10962	845-359-4700	
Chromalloy Nevada 3636 Arrowhead Dr *Web:* chromalloy.com	Carson City	NV	89706	775-687-8833	
Cobham Electronic Systems Inc 1001 Pawtucket Blvd	Lowell	MA	01854	978-442-4700	
Continental Motors Inc 2039 Broad St *TF:* 800-718-3411 ■ *Web:* www.tcmlink.com	Mobile	AL	36615	251-438-3411	432-7352
Corporate Eagle Management Services Inc 6320 Highland Rd *Web:* corporateeagle.com	Waterford	MI	48327	248-461-9000	
Dakota Air Parts International Inc 1801 23rd Ave N Ste 119 *Web:* www.dakotaairparts.com	Fargo	ND	58102	701-297-9999	
Danbury Aerospace 9503 Middlex Dr *Web:* www.danbury.aero	San Antonio	TX	78217	210-820-2400	
Dart Aerospace Ltd 1270 Aberdeen St *Web:* www.dartaerospace.com	Hawkesbury	ON	K6A1K7	613-632-3336	
Data Link Solutions LLC 350 Collins Rd NE *Web:* www.datalinksolutions.net	Cedar Rapids	IA	52498	319-295-5100	
Davidson Technologies Inc 530 Discovery Drive Cummings Research Park *Web:* www.davidson-tech.com	Huntsville	AL	35806	256-922-0720	971-6861
Delta Industries 39 Bradley Pk Rd *Web:* mbaerospace.com	East Granby	CT	06026	860-653-5041	653-5792
DNE Systems Inc 50 Barnes Industrial Park N *Web:* www.dne.com	Wallingford	CT	06492	203-265-7151	
Doncasters Inc 36 Spring Ln *Web:* www.doncasters.com	Farmington	CT	06032	860-677-1376	
Eaton Aerospace LLC 9650 Jeronimo Rd Ste 1200 *Web:* www.aerospace.eaton.com	Irvine	CA	92618	949-452-9500	
EFW Inc 4700 Marine Creek Pkwy *Web:* www.efw.com	Fort Worth	TX	76136	817-234-6600	234-6768
Electro-Methods Inc 330 Governors Hwy *Web:* electro-methods.com	South Windsor	CT	06074	860-289-8661	
Electroimpact Inc 4413 Chennault Beach Rd *Web:* www.electroimpact.com	Mukilteo	WA	98275	425-348-8090	
Engine Components Inc (ECI) 9503 Middlex *TF:* 800-324-2359 ■ *Web:* eci.aero	San Antonio	TX	78217	210-820-8101	820-8102
Essner Manufacturing LP 6651 Will Rogers Blvd *Web:* www.essner.com	Fort Worth	TX	76140	817-551-5511	
Esterline Defense Group 85901 Ave 53 *Web:* www.armtecdefense.com	Coachella	CA	92236	760-398-0143	
Ferco Tech Corp 291 Conover Dr *Web:* www.fercotech.com	Franklin	OH	45005	937-746-6696	
FIELD AVIATION COMPANY Inc 2450 Derry Rd E Hngr 2 *Web:* www.fieldav.com	Mississauga	ON	L5S1B2	905-676-1540	
Flight Dimensions International Inc 4835 Cordell Ave Ste 150 *TF:* 866-235-6870 ■ *Web:* www.flightexplorer.com	Bethesda	MD	20814	301-634-8201	
Flightsafety Services Corp 10770 E Briarwood Ave Ste 100 *Web:* www.flightsafety.com	Centennial	CO	80112	303-783-1023	
G2 Solutions LLC 11410 Ne 124Th St *Web:* g2globalsolutions.com	Kirkland	WA	98034	425-789-0200	
GA Telesis LLC 1850 NW 49th St *Web:* www.gatelesis.com	Fort Lauderdale	FL	33309	954-676-3111	676-9998
Gama Aviation Inc 2 Corporate Dr Ste 1050 *Web:* www.gamagroupusa.com	Shelton	CT	06484	203-337-4600	
Garsite LLC 539 S Tenth St *TF:* 888-427-7483 ■ *Web:* www.garsite.com	Kansas City	KS	66105	913-342-5600	342-0638
GE Aircraft Engines 1 Neumann Way **Fax:* Sales ■ *Web:* www.geaviation.com	Cincinnati	OH	45215	513-243-2000	243-9494*
GE Aviation One Neumann Way *Web:* www.geaviation.com	Cincinnati	OH	45215	513-243-2000	
General Dynamics Armament & Technical Products Inc 2118 Water Ridge Pkwy Ste 300 *Web:* www.gdatp.com	Charlotte	NC	28217	704-714-8000	
General Kinetics Engineering Corp 110 E Dr *Web:* www.kinetics.ca	Brampton	ON	L6T1C1	905-458-0888	458-7566
Geospatial Systems Inc 150 Lucius Gordon Dr *Web:* www.geospatialsystems.com	West Henrietta	NY	14586	585-427-8310	
Graco Supply Co 1001 Miller Ave *Web:* www.gracosupply.com	Fort Worth	TX	76105	817-535-3200	
Gros-Ite Industries 1790 New Britain Ave *TF:* 877-777-4778 ■ *Web:* www.edactechnologies.com	Farmington	CT	06032	860-677-2603	
Haley Industries Ltd 634 Magnesium Rd	Haley	ON	K0J1Y0	613-432-8841	
Hartzell Engine Technologies LLC 2900 Selma Hwy *TF:* 877-359-5355 ■ *Web:* www.hartzellenginetech.com	Montgomery	AL	36108	334-386-5400	
HEICO Corp 3000 Taft St *NYSE:* HEI ■ *Web:* www.heico.com	Hollywood	FL	33021	954-987-4000	987-8228
Imagine Air Jet Services LLC 460 Briscoe Blvd Ste 210 *Web:* www.flyimagineair.com	Lawrenceville	GA	30046	678-226-2329	
Indal Technologies Inc 3570 Hawkestone Rd *Web:* www.indaltech.cwfc.com	Mississauga	ON	L5C2V8	905-275-5300	
Innotech-Execaire Aviation Group 10225 Ryan Ave Montreal International Airport *Web:* www.innotech-execaire.com	Dorval	QC	H9P1A2	514-636-8484	636-8573
Insight Technology Inc Nine Akira Way *TF:* 866-509-2040 ■ *Web:* www.insighttechnology.com	Londonderry	NH	03053	603-626-4800	
Institute For Natural Resources 2354 Stanwell Dr *Web:* www.inrseminars.com	Concord	CA	94520	925-609-2820	
International Enterprises Inc 108 Allen St *Web:* www.ieionline.com	Talladega	AL	35160	256-362-8562	
ION Corp 7500 Equitable Dr *Web:* www.ioncorp.com	Eden Prairie	MN	55344	952-936-9490	
Jet Source Inc 2056 Palomar Airport Rd *Web:* www.jetsource.com	Carlsbad	CA	92011	760-438-0877	
Jetlease Inc 5718 Westheimer 17th Fl *Web:* www.jetleaseinc.com	Houston	TX	77057	713-952-5100	
Jupitor Corporation USA 55 Fairbanks *Web:* www.jupitor.co.jp	Irvine	CA	92718	949-588-0505	
Kalitta Charters LLC 843 Willow Run Airport *TF:* 800-525-4882 ■ *Web:* www.kalittacharters.com	Ypsilanti	MI	48198	734-544-3400	
Kalogridis International Ltd 4819 Maple Ave *Web:* www.kalogridis.com	Dallas	TX	75219	214-637-0519	
Keddeg Co 10700 Pflumm Rd *Web:* www.keddeg.com	Lenexa	KS	66215	913-492-1222	
Kelly Aerospace Turbine Rotables Inc 3414 W 29th St S *TF:* 866-359-5287 ■ *Web:* www.turbinerotables.com	Wichita	KS	67217	316-943-6100	
KING AEROSPACE Inc 4444 Westgrove Ste 250 *Web:* www.kingaerospaceinc.com	Addison	TX	75001	972-248-4886	
Kreisler Industrial Corp 180 Van Riper Ave *Web:* www.kreislermfg.com	Elmwood Park	NJ	07407	201-791-0700	791-8015
Kreisler Mfg Corp 180 Van Riper Ave *TF:* 888-750-5834 ■ *Web:* www.kreislermfg.com	Elmwood Park	NJ	07407	201-791-0700	791-8015
L-3 Fuzing & Ordnance Systems 3975 Mcmann Rd	Cincinnati	OH	45245	513-943-2000	
Lancair International Inc 250 SE Timber Ave *Web:* www.aerocraftparts.com	Redmond	OR	97756	541-923-2233	
Le Bas International Air Division Inc 3440 Empresa Dr *Web:* www.lebas.com	San Luis Obispo	CA	93401	805-593-0510	
Lear Romec Crane Corp 241 S Abbe Rd PO Box 4014 *Web:* www.craneae.com	Elyria	OH	44036	440-323-3211	322-3378
Leesta Industries Ltd Six Plateau *Web:* www.leesta.com	Pointe-Claire	QC	H9R5W2	514-694-3930	
McNally Group 5445 DTC Pkwy P4 *Web:* www.mcnally-group.com	Greenwood Village	CO	80111	303-846-3035	
Meco Inc 2121 S Main St **Fax Area Code:* 281	Paris	IL	61944	217-465-7575	313-0643*
Mesotec Inc 3575 Industrial Blvd *Web:* www.mesotec.ca	Sherbrooke	QC	J1L1X7	819-822-2777	822-4117
Mint Turbines LLC 2915 N State Hwy 99 *Web:* www.mintturbines.com	Stroud	OK	74079	918-968-9561	
Mist Mobility Integrated Systems Technology Inc 3 Iber Rd *Web:* www.mmist.ca	Ottawa	ON	K2S1E6	613-723-0403	723-8925
Moeller Mfg Company Inc Aircraft Div 30100 Beck Rd *Web:* www.moelleraircraft.com	Wixom	MI	48393	248-960-3999	960-1593
MTU Aero Engines North America Inc 795 Brook St Bldg 5 *Web:* www.mtu.de	Rocky Hill	CT	06067	860-258-9700	258-9797
National Board for Certified Counselors Inc Three Terrace Way Ste D *Web:* www.nbcc.org	Greensboro	NC	27403	336-547-0607	

Company	City	State	Zip	Phone	Fax
Navhouse Corp 10 Loring Dr *Web:* www.navhouse.com	Bolton	ON	L7E1J9	905-857-8102	
Near Space Systems Inc 2375 Telstar Dr Ste 115 *Web:* www.globalnearspace.com	Colorado Springs	CO	80920	719-685-8108	
Neptec Design Group Ltd 302 Legget Dr Ste 202 *Web:* www.neptec.com	Kanata	ON	K2K1Y5	613-599-7602	
Nexcelle LLC 30 Merchant St Mail Drop W28 Princeton Hill *Web:* www.nexcelle.com	Cincinnati	OH	45246	513-552-6659	
Nextant Aerospace LLC 355 Richmond Rd *Web:* www.nextantaerospace.com	Cleveland	OH	44143	216-261-9000	
Niles Precision Co PO Box 548 *Web:* www.nilesprecision.com	Niles	MI	49120	269-683-0585	683-7762
Noel-Smyser Engineering Corp 4005 Industrial Blvd *Web:* www.noel-smyser.com	Indianapolis	IN	46254	317-293-2215	
Northstar Aerospace Inc 6006 W 73rd St *TSE: NAS* ■ *TF:* 800-362-3907 ■ *Web:* www.nsaero.com	Bedford Park	IL	60638	708-728-2000	728-2009
Northwest Uav Propulsion Systems 2717 Ne Bunn Rd *Web:* www.nwuav.com	Mcminnville	OR	97128	503-434-6845	
Novaria Group Inc 306 W Seventh St Ste 310 *Web:* www.novariagroup.com	Fort Worth	TX	76102	817-381-3810	
Ordnance Technologies (NA) Inc 7380 Sand Lk Rd Ste 360 *Web:* www.otnausa.com	Orlando	FL	32819	407-354-3827	
Pacific Scientific Energetic Materials Company Inc 7073 W Willis Dr *Web:* www.psemc.com	Chandler	AZ	85226	480-763-3000	
Pankl Aerospace Systems Inc 16615 Edwards Rd *Web:* www.pankl.com	Cerritos	CA	90703	562-207-6300	
Paradigm Precision Holdings LLC 3651 SE Commerce Ave *Web:* www.paradigmprecision.com	Stuart	FL	34997	772-287-7770	
Parker Gas Turbine Fuel Systems Div (GTFSD) 8940 Tyler Blvd. *Web:* parker.com	Mentor	OH	44060	440-266-2300	266-2311
Parker Hannifin Corp Control System Div 14 Robbins Pond Rd. *Web:* parker.com	Devens	MA	01434	978-784-1200	
Phoenix Aerospace Inc 61B Industrial Pkwy *Web:* www.phxaero.com	Mound House	NV	89706	775-882-9700	
Powill Manufacturing & Engineering Inc 21039 N 27th Ave *Web:* powill.com	Phoenix	AZ	85027	623-780-4100	
Pratt & Whitney 400 Main St. **Fax:* Sales ■ *Web:* www.pratt-whitney.com	East Hartford	CT	06108	860-565-4321	565-6609*
Pratt & Whitney Canada Inc 1000 Marie-Victorin Blvd *TF:* 800-268-8000 ■ *Web:* www.pwc.ca	Longueuil	QC	J4G1A1	450-677-9411	647-3620
Preece Inc 26845 Vista Ter *Web:* www.preeceinc.com	Lake Forest	CA	92630	949-770-9411	
Prime Industries Inc 406 Dividend Dr *Web:* www.primeindustriesusa.com	Peachtree City	GA	30269	770-632-1851	
Primus International - Walden's Machine LLC 3030 N Erie Ave *Web:* www.wmitulsa.com	Tulsa	OK	74115	918-836-6317	
QED Instruments Inc 2920 S Halladay St *Web:* www.qedinstruments.com	Santa Ana	CA	92705	714-546-6010	
Quality Honeycomb LP 624 107th St *Web:* www.qualityhoneycomb.com	Arlington	TX	76011	817-640-1190	
RedXDefense LLC 7642 Standish Pl *Web:* www.redxdefense.com	Rockville	MD	20855	301-279-7970	
Robertson Fuel Systems LLC 800 W Carver Rd Ste 101 *Web:* www.robbietanks.com	Tempe	AZ	85284	480-337-7050	
Rogerson Kratos Corp 403 S Raymond *Web:* www.rogersonkratos.com	Pasadena	CA	91109	626-449-3090	
Rolls-Royce North America 1875 Explorer St Ste 200 *TF:* 888-269-2377 ■ *Web:* www.rolls-royce.com/northamerica/na	Reston	VA	20190	703-834-1700	709-6086
Saab Barracuda LLC 608 E Mcneill St. *Web:* www.saabgroup.com	Lillington	NC	27546	910-893-2094	
Sandel Avionics Inc 2401 Dogwood Way *TF:* 877-726-3357 ■ *Web:* www.sandel.com	Vista	CA	92081	760-727-4900	
Senior Aerospace Ketema Div 790 Greenfield Dr *TF:* 800-669-6820 ■ *Web:* www.sfketema.com	El Cajon	CA	92021	619-442-3451	440-1456
SGB Enterprises Inc 24844 Anza Dr Ste A. *Web:* www.sgbent.com	Valencia	CA	91355	661-294-8306	
Sheffield Manufacturing Inc 9131 Glenoaks Blvd *Web:* www.sheffield-mfg.com	Sun Valley	CA	91352	818-767-4948	
Shur-Lok Corp 2541 White Rd *Web:* www.shur-lok.com	Irvine	CA	92614	949-474-6000	
Sifco Industries Inc 970 E 64th St *NYSE: SIF* ■ *Web:* www.sifco.com	Cleveland	OH	44103	216-881-8600	432-6281
Spatial & Spectral Research LLC 13 Beech St. *Web:* www.ssrllc.us	Bedford	NH	03110	603-472-2575	
ST Aerospace San Antonio LP 9800 John Saunders Rd *Web:* www.stasaa.com	San Antonio	TX	78216	210-293-3200	293-3680
Tactical Support Equipment Inc 4039 Barefoot Rd *Web:* www.tserecon.com	Fayetteville	NC	28306	910-425-3360	
Teledyne Technologies Inc 1049 Camino Dos Rios *NYSE: TDY* ■ *TF:* 877-666-6968 ■ *Web:* www.teledynetechnologies.com	Thousand Oaks	CA	91360	805-373-4545	
Trident Systems Inc 10201 Fairfax Blvd Ste 300 *Web:* www.tridsys.com	Fairfax	VA	22030	703-273-1012	
Tulmar Safety Systems Inc 1123 Cameron St *Web:* www.tulmar.com	Hawkesbury	ON	K6A2B8	613-632-1282	632-2030
Turbomeca USA Inc 2709 N Forum Dr *TF:* 800-662-6322 ■ *Web:* www.turbomeca.com	Grand Prairie	TX	75052	972-606-7600	
Universal Asset Management Inc 5350 Poplar Ave Ste 150 *Web:* www.uaminc.com	Memphis	TN	38119	901-682-4064	
Universal Avionics Systems Corp 3260 E Universal Way *Web:* www.uasc.com	Tucson	AZ	85756	520-295-2300	
Vector Aerospace Helicopter Services Inc 4551 Agar Dr Ste 2100 *Web:* www.vectoraerospace.com	Richmond	BC	V7B1A4	604-276-7600	276-7675
VerTechs Enterprises Inc 788 Greenfield Dr *Web:* www.luchner.com	El Cajon	CA	92021	253-252-3914	
Visioneering Inc 31985 Groesbeck Hwy *Web:* www.vistool.com	Fraser	MI	48026	586-293-1000	
VT Systems Inc 99 Canal Ctr Plz Ste 220 *Web:* www.vt-systems.com	Alexandria	VA	22314	703-739-2610	
Wall Colmonoy Corp 101 W Girard Ave *Web:* www.wallcolmonoy.com	Madison Heights	MI	48071	248-585-6400	585-7960
Wesco Aircraft Hardware Corp 27727 Ave Scott *Web:* www.wescoair.com	Valencia	CA	91355	661-775-7200	
Whitcraft LLC 76 County Rd *Web:* www.whitcraft.com	Eastford	CT	06242	860-974-0786	
Williams International 2280 E W Maple Rd PO Box 200 *Web:* www.williams-int.com	Walled Lake	MI	48390	248-624-5200	624-5345
Woodward HRT Inc 25200 W Rye Canyon Rd *Web:* www.hrtextron.com	Santa Clarita	CA	91355	661-294-6000	
XOJET Inc 2000 Sierra Point Pkwy *Web:* www.xojet.com	Brisbane	CA	94005	650-676-4700	

22 AIRCRAFT PARTS & AUXILIARY EQUIPMENT

SEE ALSO Precision Machined Products p. 2953

Company	City	State	Zip	Phone	Fax
A G H Industries Inc 7420 Whitehall St *Web:* www.aghindustries.com	Richland Hills	TX	76118	817-284-1742	
AAR Cargo Systems 500 Gateway Dr *Web:* www.aarcorp.com	Goldsboro	NC	27534	919-705-2400	705-2499
AAR Composites 14201 Myerlake Cir. *TF:* 800-422-2213 ■ *Web:* aarcorp.com	Clearwater	FL	33760	727-539-8585	539-0316
AAR Corp 1100 N Wood Dale Rd 1 AAR Pl. *NYSE: AIR* ■ *TF:* 800-422-2213 ■ *Web:* www.aarcorp.com	Wood Dale	IL	60191	630-227-2000	227-2019
Ace Clearwater Enterprises 19815 Magellan Dr *Web:* www.aceclearwater.com	Torrance	CA	90502	310-538-5380	323-2137
Acromil Corp 18421 Railroad St *Web:* www.acromil.com	City of Industry	CA	91748	626-964-2522	810-6100
Advanced Technology Co 2858 E Walnut St *TF:* 800-447-2442 ■ *Web:* www.at-co.com	Pasadena	CA	91107	626-449-2696	793-9442
Aereon Corp 20 Nassau St Ste 223 *Web:* www.aereon.com	Princeton	NJ	08542	609-921-2131	
Aero Controls Inc 1610 20th St NW *Web:* www.aerocontrols.com	Auburn	WA	98001	253-269-3000	
Aero Gear Inc 1050 Day Hill Rd *Web:* www.aerogear.com	Windsor	CT	06095	860-688-0888	285-8514
Aero Parts Mfg & Repair Inc 431 Rio Rancho Blvd NE *Web:* www.aeroparts.aero	Rio Rancho	NM	87124	505-891-6600	891-6650
Aero Seating Technologies LLC 5079 Walnut Grove Ave *Web:* www.aeroseating.com	San Gabriel	CA	91776	626-286-1130	
Aero-mach Laboratories Inc 7707 E Funston St *Web:* www.aeromach.com	Wichita	KS	67207	316-682-7707	
Aerofit Inc 1425 S Acacia Ave *Web:* www.aerofit.com	Fullerton	CA	92831	714-521-5060	
Aerosource Inc 390 Campus Dr *Web:* www.aerosourceinc.com	Somerset	NJ	08873	732-469-9300	
Aerospace Products International (API) 3778 Distriplex Dr N **Fax Area Code:* 800 ■ *TF:* 888-274-2497 ■ *Web:* www.apiworldwide.com	Memphis	TN	38118	901-365-3470	950-1411*
Aircraft Belts Inc 1176 Telecom Dr. *Web:* www.aircraftbelts.com	Creedmoor	NC	27522	919-956-4395	
Airline Hydraulics Corp 3557 Progress Dr *Web:* www.airlinehyd.com	Bensalem	PA	19020	215-638-4700	
Airtex Manufacturing Inc 259 Lower Morrisville Rd *Web:* www.airtexinteriors.com	Fallsington	PA	19054	215-295-4115	
Alken Industries Inc 2175 Fifth Ave *Web:* www.alkenind.com	Ronkonkoma	NY	11779	631-467-2000	
Ametek Advanced Industries Inc 4550 Southeast Blvd. *Web:* www.advancedindustries.com	Wichita	KS	67210	316-522-0424	
Ametek HSA Inc 7841 NW 56th St *Web:* www.highstandardaviation.com	Miami	FL	33166	305-599-8855	
Apex Composites LLC 5322 John Lucas Dr. *Web:* www.apexcomposites.com	Burlington	ON	L7L6A6	905-331-8042	
Apex Engineering International LLC 1234 Wellington Pl. *Web:* www.aeillc.com	Wichita	KS	67203	316-262-1494	262-8659
Arden Engineering Inc 1878 N Main St *Web:* www.arden-engr.com	Orange	CA	92865	714-998-6410	998-0956
Arkwin Industries Inc 686 Main St. **Fax:* Sales ■ *TF:* 800-284-2551 ■ *Web:* www.arkwin.com	Westbury	NY	11590	516-333-2640	334-6786*

Phone Fax

Arrow Gear Company Inc 2301 Curtiss St Downers Grove IL 60515 630-969-7640 969-0253
Web: www.arrowgear.com

Arrowhead Products Corp
4411 Katella Ave Los Alamitos CA 90720 714-828-7770 995-3452
Web: www.arrowheadproducts.net

Arvan Inc 14083 S Normandie Ave Gardena CA 90249 310-327-1818 324-6634
Web: www.arvaninc.com

Aurora Flight Sciences Corp 9950 Wakeman Dr Manassas VA 20110 703-369-3633 369-4514
Web: www.aurora.aero

Avcorp Industries Inc 10025 River Way Delta BC V4G1M7 604-582-6677 582-2620
TF: 866-781-3111 ■ *Web:* www.avcorp.com

Avidyne Corp 55 Old Bedford Rd Ste 101 Lincoln MA 01773 781-402-7400
Web: www.avidyne.com

Avox Systems Inc 225 Erie St Lancaster NY 14086 716-683-5100 681-1089
TF: 866-278-3237 ■ *Web:* www.avoxsys.com

Bauer Howden Inc 175 Century Dr Bristol CT 06010 860-583-9100
Web: www.bauerct.com

Blair-HSM Group of Cos 3671 Horseblock Rd Medford NY 11763 631-924-6600
Web: www.blair-hsm.com

Boeing Company Commercial Airplane Group
PO Box 3707 Seattle WA 98124 206-655-2121
Web: www.boeing.com/commercial

Bowhead 4900 Seminary Rd Ste 1200 Alexandria VA 22311 703-413-4226
Web: www.bowheadsupport.com

Burnham Composite Structures Inc
6262 W 34th St S Wichita KS 67215 316-946-5900
Web: www.burnhamcs.com

C&D Zodiac 7330 Lincoln Way Garden Grove CA 92841 714-891-1906
Web: www.cdzodiac.com

Capps Manufacturing Inc 2121 S Edwards Wichita KS 67213 316-942-9351
Web: www.cappsmfg.com

Carleton Life Support Systems Inc
2734 Hickory Grove Rd Davenport IA 52804 563-383-6000 383-6430
Web: www.cobham.com

CEF Industries Inc 320 S Church St Addison IL 60101 630-628-2299 628-1386
TF: 800-888-6419 ■ *Web:* www.cefindustries.com

Cfan Co 1000 Technology Way San Marcos TX 78666 512-353-2832 353-2838
Web: www.cfan.com/

Champion Aerospace LLC 1230 Old Norris Rd Liberty SC 29657 864-843-1162
Web: www.championaerospace.com

Conrad Co, The 1304 Farmville Rd Memphis TN 38122 901-323-5926
Web: www.theconradcompany.com

Coronado Manufacturing Inc
8991 Glenoaks Boulvard Sun Valley CA 91352 818-768-5010
Web: www.coronadomfg.com

Cox & Company Inc 200 Varick St New York NY 10014 212-366-0200 366-0222
Web: www.coxandco.com

Craft Manufacturing & Tooling Inc
7152 Central Ave Hot Springs National Park AR 71913 501-525-0268
Web: www.cmtaerospaceproducts.com

CRS Jet Spares Inc 6701 NW 12th Ave Fort Lauderdale FL 33309 954-972-2807 972-2708
TF: 800-338-5387 ■ *Web:* www.crsjetspares.com

CTL Aerospace Inc 5616 Spellmire Dr Cincinnati OH 45246 513-874-7900 874-2499
Web: www.ctlaerospace.com

Curtiss-Wright Corp
10 Waterview Blvd 2nd Fl Parsippany NJ 07054 973-541-3700 541-3699
NYSE: CW ■ *TF:* 855-449-0995 ■ *Web:* www.curtisswright.com

Curtiss-Wright Flight Systems
201 Old Boiling Springs Rd Shelby NC 28152 704-481-1150 482-1903*
**Fax:* Cust Svc ■ *Web:* www.curtisswright.com

Davis Aircraft Products Company Inc
1150 Walnut Ave Bohemia NY 11716 631-563-1500
Web: www.davisaircraftproducts.com

Disan Engineering Corp 101 Mohawk Dr Nowata OK 74048 918-273-1636
Web: www.disancorp.com

Ducommun AeroStructures Inc
268 E Gardena Blvd Gardena CA 90248 310-380-5390
Web: www.ducommunaero.com

Dukes Aerospace 9060 Winnetka Ave Northridge CA 91324 818-998-9811 998-9811
Web: www.dukesaerospace.com

Electromech Technologies Inc 2600 S Custer Wichita KS 67217 316-941-0400
Web: www.electromech.com

Enflite Inc 105 Cooperative Way Georgetown TX 78626 512-868-3399 868-3320
Web: www.enflite.com

Enviro Systems Inc 12037 N Hwy 99 Seminole OK 74868 405-382-0731 382-0737
Web: www.enviro-ok.com

Esterline Interface Technologies
600 W Wilbur Ave Coeur d'Alene ID 83815 208-765-8000 292-2275
TF: 800-444-5923 ■ *Web:* www.esterline.com

Exotic Metals Forming Company LLC
5411 S 226th St Kent WA 98032 253-395-3710 872-8033
Web: www.exoticmetals.com

Fairchild Controls Corp 540 Highland St Frederick MD 21701 301-228-3400 682-6885
TF: 800-695-5378 ■ *Web:* www.fairchildcontrols.com

FFC Inc 4010 Pilot Dr Ste 103 Memphis TN 38118 901-842-7110
Web: www.ffcfuelcells.com

Fiber Art Inc 124 Industrial Dr Cibolo TX 78108 210-658-8866
Web: www.fiberartinc.com

First Call International Inc
6329 Airport Fwy Fort Worth TX 76117 817-831-2220
Web: www.firstcallintl.com

FletchAir Inc 103 Turkey Run Ln Comfort TX 78013 830-995-5900 995-5903
TF: 800-329-4647 ■ *Web:* www.fletchair.com

GE Aviation Systems Div
3290 Patterson Ave SE Grand Rapids MI 49512 616-241-8274
Web: www.geaviation.com

General Aviation Industries Inc
415 Jones Rd Weatherford TX 76088 817-598-4848
Web: www.gaiinc.net

General Electrodynamics Corporation Inc
8000 Calendar Rd Arlington TX 76001 817-572-0366
Web: www.gecscales.com

Phone Fax

GKN Aerospace Bandy Machining Inc
3420 N San Fernando Blvd Burbank CA 91504 818-846-9020
Web: www.gkn.com

GKN Aerospace Chem-tronics Inc
1150 W Bradley Ave El Cajon CA 92020 619-448-2320 258-5270
Web: www.gkn.com

Global Ground Support LLC 540 Old Hwy 56 Olathe KS 66061 913-780-0300 780-0829
TF: 888-780-0303 ■ *Web:* www.globalgroundsupport.com

Globe Engineering Company Inc PO Box 12407 Wichita KS 67277 316-943-1266 943-3089
Web: www.globeeng.com

Goodrich Corp Aircraft Interior Products Div
3420 S Seventh St Phoenix AZ 85040 602-243-2200 243-2300
TF: 877-808-7575 ■ *Web:* utcaerospacesystems.com

Goodrich Corp Landing Gear Div
6225 Oak Tree Blvd Independence OH 44131 216-341-1700 429-4806
Web: utcaerospacesystems.com

Goodrich Landing Gear Div
1400 S Service Rd W Oakville ON L6L5Y7 905-827-7777
Web: customers.goodrich.com

Growth Industries Inc
12523 Third St PO Box 900 Grandview MO 64030 816-763-7676 765-4925
Web: www.growthind.com

GSE Dynamics Inc 25 Corporate Dr Hauppauge NY 11788 631-231-1044
Web: www.gsedynamics.com

Hansen Engineering Company Inc
24050 Frampton Ave Harbor City CA 90710 310-534-3870
Web: www.hansenengineering.com

Harlow Aerostructures LLC 1501 McLean Blvd S Wichita KS 67213 316-265-5268
Web: www.harlowair.com

Harter Industries Inc 401 W Gemini Dr Tempe AZ 85283 480-345-9595
Web: www.harter.aero

Hartwell Corp 900 Richfield Rd Placentia CA 92870 714-993-4200 579-4419
Web: www.hartwellcorp.com

Hartzell Propeller Inc 1 Propeller Pl Piqua OH 45356 937-778-4200 778-4321
Web: www.hartzellprop.com

Heizer Aerospace Inc
8750 Pevely Industrial Dr Pevely MO 63070 636-475-6300 464-4206
Web: www.haiusa.com

Hiller Inc 630 N Washington Wichita KS 67214 316-264-8022
Web: www.hillerinc.com

Honeywell Aerospace 3520 Westmoor St South Bend IN 46628 574-231-2000 231-2020
TF: 800-707-4555 ■ *Web:* honeywell.com

Hydro-Aire Inc 3000 Winona Ave Burbank CA 91504 818-526-2600 842-6117
Web: www.craneae.com

Inair Aviation Services Co
8225 Country Club Pl Indianapolis IN 46214 317-271-0195
Web: www.inairaviation.com

Jamco America Inc 1018 80th St SW Everett WA 98203 425-347-4735 353-2343
Web: www.jamcoamerica.com

Jarvis Airfoil Inc 528 Glastonbury Tpke Portland CT 06480 860-342-5000
Web: www.jarvisairfoil.com

Jeff Bonner R & D Inc 10525 Mopac Dr San Antonio TX 78217 210-590-3133 590-3155
Web: www.jbrnd.com

Kaman Aerospace Corp
Old Windsor Rd PO Box 2 Bloomfield CT 06002 860-242-4461 243-7514
Web: www.kaman.com

Keith Products Inc 4554 Claire Chennault Addison TX 75001 972-407-1234
Web: www.keithproducts.com

L-3 Communications Integrated Systems
10001 Jack Finney Blvd Greenville TX 75402 903-455-3450 457-4413
TF: 877-282-1168 ■ *Web:* www.l-3com.com

LMI Aerospace Inc (LMIA)
411 Fountain Lakes Blvd Saint Charles MO 63301 636-946-6525 949-1576
NASDAQ: LMIA ■ *Web:* www.lmiaerospace.com

Magellan Aerospace 2320 Wedekind Dr Middletown OH 45042 513-422-2751 422-0812
Web: www.aeroncainc.com

Magellan Aerospace Corp
3160 Derry Rd East Mississauga ON L4T1A9 905-673-3250
Web: www.magellan.aero

Mayday Manufacturing Co 3100 Jim Christal Rd Denton TX 76207 940-898-8301 898-8305
Web: www.maydaymfg.com

MC Gill Corp 4056 Easy St El Monte CA 91731 626-443-6094 350-5880
Web: www.mcgillcorp.com

Mecaer America Inc 3205 Rue Delaunay Laval QC H7L5A4 450-682-7117 682-8152
Web: www.mecaer.ca

Middle River Aircraft Systems (MRAS)
103 Chesapeake Pk Plaza Baltimore MD 21220 410-682-1500 682-1230
TF: 877-432-3272 ■ *Web:* www.mras-usa.com

Miltec Corp 678 Discovery Dr Huntsville AL 35806 256-428-1300
Web: www.mil-tec.com

Mnemonics Inc 3900 Dow Rd Melbourne FL 32934 321-254-7300 242-0862
Web: www.mnemonicsinc.com

MSA Aircraft Products Inc 10000 Iota Dr San Antonio TX 78217 210-590-6100 590-6884
Web: www.msaaircraft.com

Nasco Aircraft Brake Inc 13300 Estrella Ave Gardena CA 90248 310-532-4430 532-6014
Web: www.nascoaircraft.com

Neill Aircraft Co 1260 W 15th St Long Beach CA 90813 562-432-7981 491-0483
Web: www.neillaircraft.com

NMG Aerospace 4880 Hudson Dr Stow OH 44224 330-688-6494
Web: www.nationalmachinegroup.com

NORDAM Group 6911 N Whirlpool Dr PO Box 3365 Tulsa OK 74117 918-878-4000 878-4808*
**Fax:* Sales ■ *Web:* www.nordam.com

North American Aviation 7330 N Broadway St Park City KS 67219 316-744-6450
Web: www.naavinc.com

Northrop Grumman Corp
2980 Fairview Park Dr Falls Church VA 22042 703-280-2900 201-3023*
NYSE: NOC ■ **Fax Area Code:* 310 ■ *Web:* www.northropgrumman.com

Oakridge Holdings Inc 1003 400 W ONTARIO St Chicago IL 60654 312-505-9267
Web: www.oakridgeholdingsinc.com

Pacific Precision Products Manufacturing
9671 Irvine Ctr Dr Koll Ctr II Bldg 6 Irvine CA 92618 949-727-3844
Web: www.ppp.aero

	City	State	ZIP	Phone	Fax
Paramount Panels Inc 1531 E Cedar *Web:* www.paramountpanels.com	Ontario	CA	91761	909-947-8008	947-8012
Parker Aerospace Group 14300 Alton Pkwy *Web:* parker.com	Irvine	CA	92618	949-833-3000	
Precise Flight Inc 63354 Powell Butte Hwy *Web:* www.preciseflight.com	Bend	OR	97701	541-382-8684	
Precision Components International Inc 8801 Macon Rd *Web:* www.pciga.com	Midland	GA	31820	706-568-5900	
R&B Electronics Inc 1520 Industrial Park Dr Sault *Web:* www.randbelectronics.com	Marie	MI	49783	906-632-1542	
RECARO Aircraft Seating Americas Inc 2275 Eagle Pkwy *Web:* www.recaro-as.com	Fort Worth	TX	76177	817-490-9160	
Rogerson Aircraft Corp 2201 Alton Pkwy *Web:* www.rogerson.com	Irvine	CA	92606	949-660-0666	
Rotair Industries Inc 964 Crescent Ave *Web:* www.rotair.com	Bridgeport	CT	06607	203-576-6545	
S-TEC Corp 1 S-TEC Way Municipal Airport *Web:* www.s-tec.com	Mineral Wells	TX	76067	940-325-9406	325-3904
Senior Aerospace Composites 2700 S Custer Ave *Web:* www.seniorcomposites.com	Wichita	KS	67217	316-942-3208	
Shimadzu Precision Instruments inc 3111 Lomita Blvd *Web:* www.shimadzu.com	Torrance	CA	90505	310-517-9910	517-9180
Sigma Tek Inc 1001 Industrial Rd *Web:* www.sigmatek.com	Augusta	KS	67010	316-775-6373	
Soundair Inc 1826 Bickford Ave *Web:* www.soundair.com	Snohomish	WA	98290	360-453-2300	
Spectrum Aerospace Inc 609 W Knox Rd *Web:* www.spectrum-aero.com	Tempe	AZ	85284	480-966-0077	
SPP Canada Aircraft Inc 2025 Meadowvale Blvd Unit 1 *Web:* www.mhi.co.jp	Mississauga	ON	L5N5N1	905-821-9339	
SPX Corp 300 Fenn Rd *Web:* www.spx.com	Newington	CT	06111	860-666-2471	666-2471
Star Aviation Inc 2150 Michigan Ave Brookley Complex *Web:* www.staraviation.com	Mobile	AL	36615	251-650-0600	
STS Component Solutions LLC 2910 SW 42 Ave *TF:* 888-777-2960 ■ *Web:* www.stsaviationgroup.com	Palm City	FL	34990	888-777-2960	
Styles Logistics Inc 30 Airway Dr Ste 2 *Web:* www.skygeek.com	Lagrangeville	NY	12540	845-677-8185	
Supracor Inc 2050 Corporate Ct *Web:* www.supracor.com	San Jose	CA	95131	408-432-1616	
Symbolic Displays Inc 1917 E St Andrew Pl *Web:* www.symbolicdisplays.com	Santa Ana	CA	92705	714-258-2811	258-2810
Transaero Inc 35 Melville Park Rd Ste 100 *Web:* www.transaeroinc.com	Melville	NY	11747	631-752-1240	
Triumph Fabrications 1923 Central Ave *Web:* www.triumphgroup.com	Hot Springs	AR	71901	501-321-9325	
Triumph Gear Systems Inc 6125 Silver Creek Dr	Park City	UT	84098	435-649-1900	
Triumph Structures-Long Island LLC 717 Main St *Web:* www.triumphgrp.com	Westbury	NY	11590	516-997-5757	
Triumph Thermal Systems Inc 200 Railroad St *Web:* www.triumphgroup.com	Forest	OH	45843	419-273-2511	273-3285
Tronair Inc 1740 Eber Rd Ste E *TF:* 800-426-6301 ■ *Web:* www.tronair.com	Holland	OH	43528	419-866-6301	867-0634
United Tool & Die Co One Carney Rd *Web:* www.utdco.com	West Hartford	CT	06110	860-246-6531	
UTC Aerospace Systems 14300 Judicial Rd *NYSE:* GR	Burnsville	MN	55306	952-892-4000	
Vibro-Meter Inc 144 Harvey Rd *TF:* 800-842-4291 ■ *Web:* www.vibro-meter.com	Londonderry	NH	03053	603-669-0940	669-0931
Vought Aircraft Div 300 Austin Blvd *Web:* www.triumphgroup.com/companies/triumph-aerostructures-vought-aircraft-division	Red Oak	TX	75154	972-946-2011	
WestWind Technologies Inc 2901 Wall Triana Hwy Ste 124 *Web:* www.westwindcorp.com	Huntsville	AL	35824	256-319-0137	
Wittenstein Inc 1249 Humbracht Cir *Web:* www.wittenstein-us.com	Bartlett	IL	60103	630-540-5300	
Zee Systems Inc 406 W Rhapsody Dr *Web:* www.zeeco-zeesys.com	San Antonio	TX	78216	210-342-9761	341-2609

23 AIRCRAFT RENTAL

SEE ALSO Aviation - Fixed-Base Operations p. 1844

	City	State	ZIP	Phone	Fax
Adler Tank Rentals LLC 260 Mack Pl *Web:* m.adlertankrentals.com	South Plainfield	NJ	07080	908-462-9800	
AeroCentury Corp 1440 Chapin Ave Ste 310 *NYSE:* ACY ■ *Web:* www.aerocentury.com	Burlingame	CA	94010	650-340-1888	696-3929
AeroTurbine Inc 2323 NW 82nd Ave **Fax Area Code:* 281 ■ **Fax:* Cust Svc ■ *TF Cust Svc:* 877-747-2370 ■ *Web:* www.aeroturbine.com	Miami	FL	33122	305-590-2600	396-1903*
Aircastle Ltd 300 First Stamford Pl Fifth Fl *NYSE:* AYR ■ *Web:* www.aircastle.com	Stamford	CT	06902	203-504-1020	504-1021
AmQuip Crane Rental LLC 1150 Northbrook Dr Ste 100 *Web:* www.amquip.com	Trevose	PA	19053	215-639-9200	
Apple Discount Drugs 404 N Fruitland Blvd *Web:* www.appledrugs.com	Salisbury	MD	21801	410-749-8401	
Argus Supply Co 46400 Continental Dr *Web:* argus-hazco.com	Chesterfield	MI	48047	586-840-3200	
Armour Transportation Systems Inc 689 Edinburgh Dr *Web:* www.armour.ca	Moncton	NB	E1E2L4	506-857-0205	

	City	State	ZIP	Phone	Fax
Atlas Aircraft Center 115 Flight Line Ave *Web:* www.planesense.org	Portsmouth	NH	03801	603-501-7700	
ATT Metrology Services Inc 30210 SE 79th St Ste 100 *Web:* www.attinc.com	Issaquah	WA	98027	425-867-5356	
Aviation Capital Group Corp 840 Newport Ctr Dr Ste 300 *Web:* www.aviationcapitalgroup.com	Newport Beach	CA	92660	949-219-4600	759-5675
Aviation Leasing Group 8080 Ward Pkwy Ste 407	Kansas City	MO	64114	816-931-7300	931-8200
Avsi Group 4464 w 12th st *Web:* www.avsigroup.com	Houston	TX	77055	713-290-8300	
Bar XH Air Inc 575 Palmer Rd NE (Esso Avitat) *Web:* www.barxh.com	Calgary	AB	T2E7G4	403-291-3227	
Bartha Visual 600 N Cassady Ave *Web:* bartha.com	Columbus	OH	43219	614-252-7455	
Blue Dot Energy Services LLC Route 76 E *Web:* www.bluedotinc.com	Bridgeport	WV	26330	304-842-3829	
Boucher Brothers Management Inc 1451 Ocean Dr Ste 205 *Web:* www.boucherbrothers.com	Miami Beach	FL	33139	305-535-8177	
BSM 2nd Street LLC 5405 Wilshire Blvd *Web:* www.blankspaces.com	Los Angeles	CA	90036	323-330-9505	
Eagle Helicopters Inc 4130 Heliport Dr *Web:* www.kachinaaviation.com	Nampa	ID	83687	208-318-0100	
Equipment Corporation of America 1000 Sta St PO Box 306 *Web:* www.ecanet.com	Coraopolis	PA	15108	412-264-4480	
Excel Railcar Corp 28367 Davis Pkwy Cantera Lakes Office Campus Ste 300 *Web:* excelrailcar.com	Warrenville	IL	60555	630-657-1100	
FlexShopper Inc 2700 N Military Trl Ste 200 *Web:* www.flexshopper.com	Boca Raton	FL	33431	561-367-1504	
Frain Group Inc, The 9377 W Grand Ave *Web:* www.fraingroup.com	Franklin Park	IL	60131	630-629-9900	
G p Aviation Services 95 Round Hill Rd *Web:* gpaviation.com	Armonk	NY	10504	914-273-0123	
GE Aviation Services 777 Long Ridge Rd *Web:* www.gecas.com	Stamford	CT	06927	203-585-2700	
Host t Parker of Maryland Inc 2200 Broening Hwy Ste 230 *Web:* www.tparkerhost.com	Baltimore	MD	21224	410-633-4666	
International Lease Finance Corp (ILFC) 10250 Constellation Blvd Ste 3400 *Web:* www.ilfc.com	Los Angeles	CA	90067	310-788-1999	788-1990
J.A. Riggs Tractor Company Inc 9125 Interstate 30 *Web:* www.riggs-cat.com	Little Rock	AR	72209	501-570-3100	
Jetscape Inc 10 S New River Dr E Ste 200 *TF:* 800-355-5387 ■ *Web:* www.jetscape.aero	Fort Lauderdale	FL	33301	954-763-4737	763-4757
Martin Tractor Company Inc 1737 SW 42nd St *Web:* www.martintractor.com	Topeka	KS	66609	785-266-5770	
Moncton Flight College Moncton Airport *Web:* www.mfc.nb.ca	Moncton	NB	E1A1R9	506-857-3080	
NCSG Crane & Heavy Haul Services Ltd 11466 Winterburn Rd *Web:* www.ncsg.com	Edmonton	AB	T5S2Y3	780-455-1075	
Northern Jet Management 5500 44th St SE *Web:* www.northernjet.net	Grand Rapids	MI	49512	616-336-4800	
Peterson Power Systems Inc 2828 Teagarden St *Web:* www.petersonpower.com	San Leandro	CA	94577	510-895-8400	
Prive Jets LLC 1250 E Hallandale Beach Blvd Ste 505 *Web:* www.privejets.com	Hallandale	FL	33009	305-917-1600	
Red-D-Arc Inc 667 S Service Rd PO Box 40 *Web:* www.red-d-arc.com	Grimsby	ON	L3M4G1	905-643-4212	
RobotWorx Inc 370 W Fairground St *Web:* www.robots.com	Marion	OH	43302	740-251-4312	
Simplex Equipment Rental 9740 Boul de l'Acadie *Web:* www.simplex.ca	Montreal	QC	H4N1L8	514-331-7777	
Sonsray Machinery LLC 1475 Pioneer Way *Web:* www.sonsraymachinery.com	El Cajon	CA	92020	619-873-0123	
Sound Image 2415 W Vineyard Ave *Web:* www.sound-image.com	Escondido	CA	92029	760-737-3900	
Sunwest Aviation Ltd 230 Aviation Pl Ne *Web:* www.sunwestaviation.ca	Calgary	AB	T2E7G1	403-275-8121	
Swiftlift Inc 820 Phillips Rd *Web:* www.swiftlift.com	Victor	NY	14564	585-742-2160	
Total Oilfield Rentals Partnership 6517 51 Ave *Web:* www.totaloilfield.ca	Whitecourt	AB	T7S1N3	780-778-6222	
Trench Plate Rental Co 13217 Laureldale Ave *TF:* 800-821-4478 ■ *Web:* www.tprco.com	Downey	CA	90242	800-821-4478	
Tri-state Aero Inc 6101 Flight Line Dr *Web:* www.tristateaero.com	Evansville	IN	47725	812-426-1221	
Twin Otter International Ltd 2806 Perimeter Rd *Web:* www.twinotter.com	North Las Vegas	NV	89032	702-646-8837	
Us Adventure Rv 5120 n brady st *TF:* 877-768-4678 ■ *Web:* www.usadventurerv.com	Davenport	IA	52806	877-768-4678	
Warren Power & Machinery LP 4501 W Reno Ave *Web:* www.warrencat.com	Oklahoma City	OK	73127	405-947-6771	
Wood's CRW Corp 795 Marshall Ave PO Box 1099 *Web:* www.woodscrw.com	Williston	VT	05495	802-658-1700	

Phone *Fax*

Wright Air Service Inc
3842 University Ave S PO Box 60142 Fairbanks AK 99706 907-474-0502 474-0375
Web: www.wrightairservice.com

24 AIRCRAFT SERVICE & REPAIR

Phone *Fax*

AAR Aircraft Component Services
747 Zeckendorf Blvd Garden City NY 11530 516-222-9000 222-0987
TF: 800-422-2213 ■ *Web:* www.aarcorp.com

AAR Aircraft Services
6611 S Meridian Ave Oklahoma City OK 73159 405-218-3000 218-3610
Web: www.aarcorp.com

AAR Corp 1100 N Wood Dale Rd 1 AAR Pl Wood Dale IL 60191 630-227-2000 227-2019
NYSE: AIR ■ *TF:* 800-422-2213 ■ *Web:* www.aarcorp.com

AAR Landing Gear Services 9371 NW 100th St Miami FL 33178 305-887-4027 887-9437
TF: 800-422-2213 ■ *Web:* www.aarcorp.com

Aero Twin Inc 2403 Merrill Field Dr Anchorage AK 99501 907-274-6166 274-4285
Web: www.aerotwin.com

Alabama Aircraft Industries
1943 50th St N Birmingham AL 35212 205-592-0011 592-0195

American Avionics 7023 Perimeter Rd S Seattle WA 98108 206-763-8530 763-2036
TF Sales: 800-518-5858 ■ *Web:* www.americanavionics.com

Barfield Inc 4101 NW 29th St Miami FL 33142 305-894-5300 894-5301
TF: 800-321-1039 ■ *Web:* www.barfieldinc.com

Basler Turbo Conversions LLC 255 W 35th St Oshkosh WI 54902 920-236-7820 235-0381
Web: www.baslerturbo.com

Bridgestone Aircraft Tire USA Inc
802 S Ayersville Rd Mayodan NC 27027 336-548-8100 548-7441
Web: bridgestone.com

Byerly Aviation 6100 EM Dirkson Pkwy Peoria IL 61607 309-697-6300 697-2779
Web: www.byerlyaviation.com

Christiansen Aviation Inc 200 Lear Jet Ln Tulsa OK 74132 918-299-2646 298-6656
Web: www.christiansenaviation.com

Cutter Aviation 2802 E Old Tower Rd Phoenix AZ 85034 602-273-1237 275-4010
TF: 800-234-5382 ■ *Web:* cutteraviation.com/

Duncan Aviation Inc 3701 Aviation Rd Lincoln NE 68524 402-475-2611 475-5541
TF: 800-228-4277 ■ *Web:* www.duncanaviation.aero

Elbit Systems of America
4700 Marine Creek Pkwy Fort Worth TX 76179 817-234-6600
Web: www.elbitsystems-us.com

Elliott Aviation Inc 6601 74th Ave PO Box 100 Milan IL 61264 309-799-3183 799-2014
TF: 800-447-6711 ■ *Web:* www.elliottaviation.com

Emteq Inc 5349 S Emmer Dr New Berlin WI 53151 262-679-6170 679-6175
TF: 888-679-6170 ■ *Web:* www.emteq.com

GKN Aerospace Chem-tronics Inc
1150 W Bradley Ave El Cajon CA 92020 619-448-2320 258-5270
Web: www.gkn.com

Hawker Pacific Aerospace
11240 Sherman Way Sun Valley CA 91352 818-765-6201 765-8073
Web: www.hawker.com

Helicomb International Inc 1402 S 69th E Ave Tulsa OK 74112 918-835-3999 834-4451
Web: www.syncaero.com

Honeywell Aerospace 3520 Westmoor St South Bend IN 46628 574-231-2000 231-2020
TF: 800-707-4555 ■ *Web:* honeywell.com

Jet Aviation 112 Charles A Lindbergh Dr Teterboro NJ 07608 201-288-8400 462-4005
TF: 800-538-0832 ■ *Web:* www.jetaviation.com

Kfs Inc 1840 West Airfield Dr Dallas TX 75261 817-488-4115 488-4350
TF: 800-364-4115 ■ *Web:* www.kfsinc.com

L-3 Communications Flight International Aviation LLC
One Lear Dr Newport News VA 23602 757-886-5500 874-7481
TF: 800-358-4685 ■ *Web:* www.l-3com.com/fi

Martin Aviation 19300 Ike Jones Rd Santa Ana CA 92707 714-210-2945 557-0637
Web: martin-aviation.com

McKinley Air Transport Inc
5430 Lauby Rd North Canton OH 44720 330-499-3316 499-0444
TF General: 800-225-6446

Mercury Air Group Inc 5456 McConnell Ave Los Angeles CA 90066 310-827-2737 827-8921
Web: www.mercuryairgroup.com

Million Air Interlink Inc 8501 Telephone Rd Houston TX 77061 713-640-4000 283-8274*
**Fax Area Code:* 866 ■ *TF:* 888-589-9059 ■ *Web:* www.millionair.com

NORDAM Group 6911 N Whirlpool Dr PO Box 3365 Tulsa OK 74117 918-878-4000 878-4808*
**Fax:* Sales ■ *Web:* www.nordam.com

Pemco World Air Services 4102 N Westshore Blvd Tampa FL 33614 813-322-9600
Web: www.pemcoair.com

Precision Airmotive LLC 14800 40th Ave NE Marysville WA 98271 360-651-8282 651-8080*
**Fax:* Sales ■ *Web:* www.precisionairmotive.com

Priester Aviation 1061 S Wolf Rd Wheeling IL 60090 847-537-1133 459-0778
TF: 888-323-7887 ■ *Web:* www.priesterav.com

Rolls-Royce Engine Services Inc
7200 Earhart Rd Oakland CA 94621 510-613-1000 635-3221
TF: 866-793-4273 ■ *Web:* www.rolls-royce.com

Serco Inc 1818 Library St Ste 1000 Reston VA 20190 703-939-6000 939-6000
TF: 866-628-6458 ■ *Web:* www.serco-na.com

Servisair 151 Northpoint Dr Houston TX 77060 281-260-3900 999-3740
Web: www.servisair.com

SGT Inc 7701 Greenbelt Rd Ste 400 Greenbelt MD 20770 301-614-8600 614-8601
Web: www.sgt-inc.com

Sierra Industries Ltd 122 Howard Langford Dr Uvalde TX 78801 830-278-4481 278-7649
TF: 888-835-9377 ■ *Web:* www.sijet.com

Sifco Industries Inc 970 E 64th St Cleveland OH 44103 216-881-8600 432-6281
NYSE: SIF ■ *Web:* www.sifco.com

Southern California Aviation Inc
18438 Readiness St Victorville CA 92394 760-530-2400 246-1186
Web: comav.com/services/technical-services

Summit Aviation Inc
4200 Summit Bridge Rd PO Box 258 Middletown DE 19709 302-834-5400 378-7035
TF: 800-441-9343 ■ *Web:* www.summit-aviation.com

Triumph Accessory Services 411 NW Rd Wellington KS 67152 620-326-2235 326-3761
Web: www.triumphgroup.com

Phone *Fax*

Triumph Group Inc 1550 Liberty Ridge Dr Ste 100 Wayne PA 19087 610-251-1000 251-1555
NYSE: TGI ■ *Web:* www.triumphgroup.com

Tulsair Beechcraft Inc 3207 N Sheridan Rd Tulsa OK 74115 918-835-7651 835-7413
TF: 800-331-4071 ■ *Web:* www.tulsair.com

West Star Aviation Inc
796 Heritage Way Grand Junction CO 81506 970-243-7500 248-5243
TF: 800-255-4193 ■ *Web:* www.weststaraviation.com

Windsor Airmotive 68 Deming St Newington CT 06111 860-666-1777

25 AIRLINES - COMMERCIAL

SEE ALSO Air Cargo Carriers p. 1725; Air Charter Services p. 1726; Airlines - Frequent Flyer Programs p. 1737

Phone *Fax*

Aeroflot Russian International Airlines
10 Rockefeller Plaza Ste 1015 New York NY 10020 212-944-2300 220-5403*
**Fax Area Code:* 423 ■ *TF:* 866-879-7647 ■ *Web:* www.aeroflot.com

Air India 570 Lexington Ave 15th Fl New York NY 10022 800-223-7776 407-1416*
**Fax Area Code:* 212 ■ *TF:* 800-223-7776 ■ *Web:* www.airindia.com

Air New Zealand Ltd
1960 E Grand Ave Ste 300 El Segundo CA 90245 310-648-7104 272-9494*
**Fax Area Code:* 800 ■ *TF:* 800-262-1234 ■ *Web:* www.airnewzealand.com

Air Sunshine Inc PO Box 22237 Fort Lauderdale FL 33335 954-434-8900
TF: 800-435-8900 ■ *Web:* www.airsunshine.com

Air Tahiti Nui 1990 E Grand Ave El Segundo CA 90245 310-662-1860 640-3683
TF Cust Svc: 877-824-4846 ■ *Web:* www.airtahitinui-usa.com

Air Wisconsin Airlines Corp
W6390 Challenger Dr Ste 203 Appleton WI 54914 920-739-5123 749-7588
Web: www.airwis.com

All Nippon Airways Company Ltd
2050 W 190th St Ste 100 Torrance CA 90504 800-235-9262
TF: 800-235-9262 ■ *Web:* www.ana.co.jp

Allegiant Air 8360 S Durango Dr Las Vegas NV 89113 702-851-7300 851-7301
NASDAQ: ALGT ■ *Web:* www.allegiantair.com

American Airlines Inc
4333 Amon Carter Blvd Fort Worth TX 76155 817-963-1234 967-4162*
**Fax:* Cust Svc ■ *TF:* 800-433-7300 ■ *Web:* www.aa.com

Atlanta Airlines Terminal Corp
Hartsfield-Jackson Atlanta International Airport
PO Box 45170 Atlanta GA 30320 404-530-2100
Web: www.aatc.org

Bearskin Airlines 1475 W Walsh St Thunder Bay ON P7E4X6 807-577-1141 474-2647
TF: 800-465-2327 ■ *Web:* www.bearskinairlines.com

Bering Air 1470 Sepalla Dr PO Box 1650 Nome AK 99762 907-443-5464 443-5919
TF: 800-478-5422 ■ *Web:* www.beringair.com

British Airways PLC (BA) 75-20 Astoria Blvd Flushing NY 11370 347-418-4000 418-4081
TF: 800-403-0882 ■ *Web:* www.britishairways.com

Bulloch & Bulloch Inc
309 Cash Memorial Blvd Forest Park GA 30297 404-762-5063
TF: 800-339-8177 ■ *Web:* www.jphallexpress.com

Cape Air 660 Barnstable Rd Hyannis MA 02601 508-771-6944 227-3247*
**Fax Area Code:* 800 ■ *TF:* 866-227-3247 ■ *Web:* www.capeair.com

Cayman Airways Ltd 91 Owen Roberts Dr Grand Cayman KY 10092 345-949-8200 949-7607
TF: 800-422-9626 ■ *Web:* www.caymanairways.com

Chautauqua Airlines Inc
8909 PuRdue Rd Ste 300 Indianapolis IN 46268 317-484-6000 484-6040
Web: www.flychautauqua.com

Commutair Inc 240 Valley Rd South Burlington VT 05403 802-951-2500
Web: www.commutair.com

Czech Airlines 1 Penn Plaza Ste 1416 New York NY 10001 855-359-2932 279-6602*
**Fax Area Code:* 212 ■ *TF:* 855-359-2932 ■ *Web:* www.csa.cz

Delta Air Lines Inc 1030 Delta Blvd Atlanta GA 30354 404-715-2600 773-2108
NYSE: DAL ■ *TF:* 800-221-1212 ■ *Web:* www.delta.com

EgyptAir 19 W 44th St Ste 1701 New York NY 10036 212-581-5600
Web: egyptair.com/

El Al Israel Airlines Ltd
15 E 26th St Sixth Fl New York NY 10010 212-852-0600 852-0797
TF: 800-223-6700 ■ *Web:* www.elal.co.il

EVA Airways 200 N Sepulveda Blvd Ste 1600 El Segundo CA 90245 310-362-6600 362-6660
TF: 800-695-1188 ■ *Web:* www.evaair.com

ExpressJet Airlines Inc 990 Toffie Terr Atlanta GA 30354 404-856-1000
Web: www.expressjet.com

Great Lakes Aviation Ltd 1022 Airport Pkwy Cheyenne WY 82001 307-432-7000 432-7071*
OTC: GLUX ■ **Fax:* Hum Res ■ *TF:* 800-554-5111 ■ *Web:* www.greatlakesav.com

Hawaiian Airlines Inc
3375 Koapaka St Ste G350 Honolulu HI 96819 808-835-3700 835-3690
TF: 800-367-5320 ■ *Web:* www.hawaiianairlines.com

Helicopter Tech Inc 452 Swedeland Rd King Of Prussia PA 19406 610-272-8090
Web: www.helicoptertechinc.com

Horizon Air Industries Inc
19300 International Blvd PO Box 68977 Seattle WA 98188 206-241-6757 431-4624
Web: www.alaskaair.com

JetBlue Airways 29 Queens Blvd Ste 118 Forest Hills NY 11375 718-286-7900 709-3621
NASDAQ: JBLU ■ *TF:* 800-538-2583 ■ *Web:* www.jetblue.com

Kenmore Air Harbor Inc 6321 NE 175th St Kenmore WA 98028 425-486-1257 485-4774
TF: 866-435-9524 ■ *Web:* www.kenmoreair.com

Korean Air 6101 W Imperial Hwy Los Angeles CA 90045 310-417-5200 417-3051
TF: 800-438-5000 ■ *Web:* www.koreanair.com

Malaysia Airlines
100 N Sepulveda Blvd Ste 1710 El Segundo CA 90245 310-535-9288 535-9088
TF Resv: 800-552-9264 ■ *Web:* www.malaysiaairlines.com

MD Helicopters Inc 4555 E Mcdowell Rd Mesa AZ 85215 480-346-6344
Web: www.mdhelicopters.com

New England Airlines Inc 56 Airport Rd Westerly RI 02891 800-243-2460 596-7366*
**Fax Area Code:* 401 ■ *TF:* 800-243-2460 ■ *Web:* www.block-island.com/nea

Olympic Airways 7000 Austin St Forest Hills NY 11375 718-269-2200
Web: patch.com/foresthills

Pacific Air Cargo 5761 W Imperial Hwy Los Angeles CA 90045 310-645-2178
Web: www.pacificaircargo.com

Pacific Wings One Keolani Pl Ste 30 Kahului HI 96732 808-873-0877 873-7920
TF: 888-575-4546 ■ *Web:* www.pacificwings.com

Phone Fax

Pakistan International Airlines Corp (PIA)
1200 New Jersey Ave SE........................Washington DC 20590 800-578-6786
TF: 800-578-6786 ■ *Web:* www.piac.com.pk

Peninsula Airways Inc 6100 Boeing Ave...........Anchorage AK 99502 907-771-2500 771-2661
TF: 800-448-4226 ■ *Web:* www.penair.com

Phoenix Air Group Inc
100 Phoenix Air Dr SW.......................... Cartersville GA 30120 770-387-2000 387-4545
Web: www.phoenixair.com

Piedmont Airlines Inc
5443 Airport Terminal Rd..........................Salisbury MD 21804 410-742-2996 693-2300*
**Fax Area Code:* 480 ■ *TF:* 800-354-3394 ■ *Web:* www.piedmont-airlines.com

Pinnacle Airlines Corp
40 S Main St 1 Commerce Sq ....Memphis TN 38103 901-348-4100 348-4130
OTC: PNCLQ ■ *Web:* www.flypinnacle.com

PSA Airlines Inc 3400 Terminal Dr....................Vandalia OH 45377 937-454-1116 264-3911
TF Resv: 800-235-0986 ■ *Web:* www.psaairlines.net

Qantas Airways Ltd 6080 Ctr Dr Ste 400 ....Los Angeles CA 90045 310-726-1400 726-1485
TF: 800-227-4500 ■ *Web:* www.qantas.com.au

Scandinavian Airlines System (SAS)
301 Route 17 N Ste 500..........................Rutherford NJ 07070 800-437-5807 896-3735*
**Fax Area Code:* 201 ■ *TF:* 800-221-2350 ■ *Web:* www.flysas.com

Silver Airways Corp
1100 Lee Wagener Blvd Ste 201................Fort Lauderdale FL 33315 954-985-1500
TF: 844-674-5837 ■ *Web:* www.silverairways.com

Singapore Airlines Ltd
222 N Sepulveda Blvd Ste 1600................... El Segundo CA 90245 310-647-1922
TF: 800-742-3333 ■ *Web:* www.singaporeair.com

Skyservice Airlines Inc 9785 Ryan Ave................ Dorval QC H9P1A2 514 636 3300 636-4855
TF: 888-985-1402 ■ *Web:* skyservice.com

SkyWest Airlines 444 S River Rd .... Saint George UT 84790 435-634-3000 634-3105
Web: www.skywest.com

South African Airways
515 E Las Olas Blvd 16th Fl...................Fort Lauderdale FL 33301 954-769-5000 769-5079*
**Fax:* Sales ■ *TF:* 800-722-9675 ■ *Web:* www.flysaa.com

Southwest Airlines Co
2702 Love Field Dr PO Box 36611..................... Dallas TX 75235 214-792-4000 792-4011
NYSE: LUV ■ *TF:* 800-435-9792 ■ *Web:* www.southwest.com

Spirit Airlines Inc 2800 Executive Way ....Miramar FL 33025 800-772-7117
NASDAQ: SAVE ■ *TF:* 800-772-7117 ■ *Web:* www.spirit.com

SriLankan Airlines 379 Thornall St 6th Fl...............Edison NJ 08837 732-205-0017 205-0299
TF: 877-915-2652 ■ *Web:* www.srilankanusa.com

Sun Country Airlines Inc
1300 Mendota Heights Rd ....Mendota Heights MN 55120 651-681-3900 681-3970
TF: 800-359-6786 ■ *Web:* www.suncountry.com

Thai Airways International Ltd
222 N Sepulveda Blvd Ste 100.................... El Segundo CA 90245 310-640-0097 322-8728*
**Fax:* Sales ■ *TF:* 800-426-5204 ■ *Web:* www.thaiairwaysusa.com

US Airways Express 111 W Rio Salado Pkwy............ Tempe AZ 85281 480-693-0800
TF: 800-679-8215 ■ *Web:* www.usairways.com

USA 3000 Airlines
335 Bishop Hollow Rd ....Newtown Square PA 19073 610-325-1280
Web: usa3000.com

Virgin Atlantic Airways Ltd 747 Belden Ave...........Norwalk CT 06850 800-821-5438 750-6430*
**Fax Area Code:* 203 ■ **Fax:* Mktg ■ *TF:* 888-747-7474 ■ *Web:* www.virgin-atlantic.com

WestJet Airlines Ltd 22 Aerial Pl NE .... Calgary AB T2E3J1 403-444-2600 253-0131*
TSE: WJA ■ **Fax Area Code:* 844 ■ *TF:* 888-293-7853 ■ *Web:* www.westjet.com

26 AIRLINES - FREQUENT FLYER PROGRAMS

Phone Fax

Aer Lingus Airlines Gold Cir Club
300 Jericho Quad Ste 130 .... Jericho NY 11753 800-474-7424 622-4287*
**Fax Area Code:* 516 ■ *TF:* 800-474-7424 ■ *Web:* www.aerlingus.com

Air Jamaica 7th Heaven 9200 S Dadeland Blvd.......... Miami FL 33156 305-670-3222 669-6631
TF: 800-523-5585 ■ *Web:* www.airjamaica.com

British Airways Executive Club PO Box 300743 ....Jamaica NY 11430 800-452-1201 251-6767*
**Fax Area Code:* 212 ■ *TF:* 800-452-1201 ■ *Web:* www.britishairways.com

Continental Airlines Inc 900 Grand Plz Dr...........Houston TX 77067 713-952-1630
TF: 800-621-7467 ■ *Web:* www.united.com

Czech Airlines OK Plus
147 W 35th St Ste 1505...........................New York NY 10001 855-359-2932 279-6602*
**Fax Area Code:* 212 ■ *TF:* 855-359-2932 ■ *Web:* www.csa.cz

Hawaiian Airlines HawaiianMiles
PO Box 30008 ....Honolulu HI 96820 877-426-4537 838-6777*
**Fax Area Code:* 808 ■ *TF:* 877-426-4537 ■ *Web:* www.hawaiianairlines.com

Icelandair North America 1900 Crown Colony Dr ....Quincy MA 02169 800-223-5500
TF: 800-223-5500 ■ *Web:* www.icelandair.com

Korean Air Skypass
1813 Wilshire Blvd Ste 300 ....Los Angeles CA 90057 213-484-1900 417-5678*
**Fax Area Code:* 310 ■ *TF:* 800-438-5000 ■ *Web:* www.koreanair.com

Kuwait Airways Oasis Club 400 Kelby St ....Fort Lee NJ 07024 201-582-9222 947-8113
TF: 800-458-9248 ■ *Web:* www.kuwaitairways.com

Miles & More PO Box 946 .... Santa Clarita CA 91380 800-581-6400 244-4950*
**Fax Area Code:* 661 ■ *TF:* 800-581-6400 ■ *Web:* www.miles-and-more.com

REACH Air Medical Services
451 Aviation Blvd .... Santa Rosa CA 95403 707-324-2400 324-2478
Web: reachair.com/

Singapore Airlines KrisFlyer
380 World Way Ste 336B ....Los Angeles CA 90045 310-646-6221
TF: 800-742-3333 ■ *Web:* www.singaporeair.com

SriLankan Travel Inc 379 Thornall St Sixth Fl ....Edison NJ 08837 732-205-0017 205-0299
TF: 877-915-2652 ■ *Web:* www.srilankanusa.com

US Airways Dividend Miles Program
4000 E Sky Harbor Blvd ....Phoenix AZ 85034 480-693-0800 693-5546
Web: www.usairways.com

Virgin Atlantic Flying Club 747 Belden Ave ....Norwalk CT 06850 800-365-9500
TF: 800-365-9500 ■ *Web:* virgin-atlantic.com/us/en/flying-club.html

27 AIRPORTS

SEE ALSO Ports & Port Authorities p. 2954

Listings for airports in the US and Canada are organized by states and provinces, and then by city names within those groupings.

Phone Fax

Birmingham International Airport
5900 Messer Airport Hwy.......................Birmingham AL 35212 205-595-0533 599-0538
Web: flybirmingham.com

Huntsville International Airport
1000 Glenn Hearn Blvd Ste 20008................. Huntsville AL 35824 256-772-9395
Web: www.flyhuntsville.com

Mobile Regional Airport 8400 Airport Blvd.............Mobile AL 36608 251-633-4510 639-7437
TF: 800-357-5373 ■ *Web:* www.mobairport.com

Montgomery Regional Airport
4445 Selma Hwy................................ Montgomery AL 36108 334-281-5040 281-5041
Web: www.iflymontgomery.com

Ted Stevens Anchorage International Airport
5000 W International Airport Rd...................Anchorage AK 99502 907-266-2526
Web: dot.state.ak.us

Fairbanks International Airport
6450 Airport Way ....Fairbanks AK 99709 907-474-2500 474-2513
Web: www.dot.state.ak.us/faiiap

Juneau International Airport
1873 Shell Simmons Dr Ste 200 ....Juneau AK 99801 907-789-7821 789-1227
TF: 800-478-4176 ■ *Web:* www.juneau.org/airport

Calgary International Airport
2000 Airport Rd NE................................ Calgary AB T2E6W5 403-735-1200 735-1281
TF: 877-254-7427 ■ *Web:* www.calgaryairport.com

Edmonton International Airport
8340 Sparrow Crescent .... Edmonton AB T9E8B7 780-980-0986
TF: 800-854-9517 ■ *Web:* ramada.com

Flagstaff Pulliam Airport
6200 S Pulliam Dr ....Flagstaff AZ 86001 928-556-1234 556-1288
TF: 800-463-1389 ■ *Web:* www.flagstaff.az.gov

Phoenix Sky Harbor International Airport
3400 E Sky Harbor Blvd Ste 3300.....................Phoenix AZ 85034 602-273-3300
Web: skyharbor.com

Tucson International Airport
7250 S Tucson Blvd ....Tucson AZ 85706 520-573-8100 573-8008
TF: 800-758-1874 ■ *Web:* www.flytucson.com

Northwest Arkansas Regional Airport
One Airport Blvd Ste 100 .... Bentonville AR 72712 479-205-1000 205-1001
Web: www.flyxna.com

Fort Smith Regional Airport
6700 McKennon Blvd Ste 200 ....Fort Smith AR 72903 479-452-7000 452-7008
TF: 800-992-7433 ■ *Web:* www.fortsmithairport.com

Hot Springs Memorial Field
525 Airport Rd ....Hot Springs AR 71913 501-321-6750 321-6754
TF: 800-992-7433 ■ *Web:* cityhs.net/442/flight-information

Bill & Hillary Clinton National Airport
1 Airport Dr.................................... Little Rock AR 72202 501-372-3439 372-0612
Web: www.fly-lit.com

Vancouver International Airport
Airport Postal Outlet PO Box 23750................. Richmond BC V7B1Y7 604-207-7077
Web: www.yvr.ca

Meadows Field Airport
3701 Wings Way Ste 300.........................Bakersfield CA 93308 661-391-1800 391-1801
Web: www.meadowsfield.com

Bob Hope Airport 2627 N Hollywood Way ....Burbank CA 91505 818-840-8840 848-1173
Web: www.bobhopeairport.com

Fresno Yosemite International Airport
5175 E Clinton Way ....Fresno CA 93727 559-621-4500 251-4825
TF: 800-244-2359 ■ *Web:* www.fresno.gov

Long Beach Airport LGB
4100 Donald Douglas Dr ....Long Beach CA 90808 562-570-2600 570-2601
TF: 800-331-1212 ■ *Web:* www.lgb.org

Modesto City Airport 617 Airport Way............... Modesto CA 95354 209-577-5319 576-1985
Web: www.modestogov.com

Monterey Peninsula Airport
200 Fred Kane Dr Ste 200..........................Monterey CA 93940 831-648-7000 373-2625
Web: www.montereyairport.com

Ontario International Airport
1923 E Avion St .... Ontario CA 91761 909-937-2700 937-2743
Web: www.lawa.org/welcomeont.aspx

Oxnard Airport 2889 W Fifth St ....Oxnard CA 93030 805-382-3022
Web: iflyoxnard.com

Palm Springs International Airport
3200 E Tahquitz Canyon Way ....Palm Springs CA 92262 760-318-3800 318-3815
TF: 800-847-4389 ■ *Web:* www.palmspringsca.gov

Palo Alto Airport 1925 Embarcadero Rd .... Palo Alto CA 94303 408-918-7700
Web: www.countyairports.org

Sacramento International Airport
6900 Airport Blvd................................Sacramento CA 95837 916-929-5411
Web: www.sacairports.org

San Diego International Airport - Lindbergh Field
3225 N Harbor Dr San Diego
County Regl Airport Authority Third Fl............... San Diego CA 92101 619-400-2404 400-2866
Web: www.san.org

San Francisco International Airport
PO Box 8097 .... San Francisco CA 94128 650-821-8211 821-5005
TF: 800-435-9736 ■ *Web:* www.flysfo.com

Norman Y Mineta San Jose International Airport
1701 Airport Blvd Ste B-1130....................... San Jose CA 95110 408-501-7600 441-4591
Web: www.flysanjose.com

John Wayne Airport 18601 Airport Way .... Santa Ana CA 92707 949-252-5200 252-5290
Web: www.ocair.com

Colorado Springs Municipal Airport
7770 Milton E Proby Pkwy .... Colorado Springs CO 80916 719-550-1900 550-1901
Web: www.springsgov.com

Denver International Airport 8500 Pena Blvd...........Denver CO 80249 303-342-2000 342-2215
TF: 800-247-2336 ■ *Web:* www.flydenver.com

Phone | Fax

Fort Collins/Loveland Municipal Airport
4900 Earhart Rd . . . Loveland CO 80538 970-962-2850 962-2855
Web: www.fortloveair.com

Tweed New Haven Regional Airport
155 Burr St . . . New Haven CT 06512 203-466-8833 466-1199
Web: www.flytweed.com

Ronald Reagan Washington National Airport
One Aviation Cir . . . Washington DC 20001 703-417-8000 417-8371*
**Fax:* PR ■ *Web:* www.mwaa.com

Washington Dulles International Airport
Dulles Airport Access Rd . . . Washington DC 20041 703-572-2700 572-5718
Web: www.metwashairports.com/dulles

Daytona Beach International Airport
700 Catalina Dr Ste 300 . . . Daytona Beach FL 32114 386-248-8030 248-8038
Web: www.flydaytonafirst.com

Fort Lauderdale Executive Airport
5101 NW 21st Ave . . . Fort Lauderdale FL 33309 954-828-4955 938-4974
Web: fortlauderdale.gov

Fort Lauderdale/Hollywood International Airport
100 Aviation Blvd . . . Fort Lauderdale FL 33315 954-359-1200 359-0027
TF: 866-682-2258 ■ *Web:* www.broward.org

Southwest Florida International Airport
11000 Terminal Access Rd Ste 8671 . . . Fort Myers FL 33913 239-590-4800 590-4511
TF: 800-359-6786 ■ *Web:* www.flylcpa.com

Jacksonville International Airport
2400 Yankee Clipper Dr . . . Jacksonville FL 32218 904-741-4902 741-2224
Web: www.flyjacksonville.com

Key West International Airport
3491 S Roosevelt Blvd . . . Key West FL 33040 305-809-5200 292-3578
Web: keywestinternationalairport.com

Miami International Airport
2261 NW 66th Ave Bldg 702 Ste 217 . . . Miami FL 33122 305-876-7000 876-8077
Web: www.miami-airport.com

Naples Municipal Airport 160 Aviation Dr N . . . Naples FL 34104 239-643-0733 643-4084
Web: www.flynaples.com

Orlando International Airport
One Jeff Fuqua Blvd . . . Orlando FL 32827 407-825-2001 825-2202
Web: www.orlandoairports.net

Pensacola Gulf Coast Regional Airport
2430 Airport Blvd Ste 225 . . . Pensacola FL 32504 850-436-5000 436-5006
TF: 800-874-6580 ■ *Web:* www.flypensacola.com

Sarasota-Bradenton International Airport
6000 Airport Cir . . . Sarasota FL 34243 941-359-5200 359-5054
TF: 800-711-1712 ■ *Web:* www.srq-airport.com

Tallahassee Regional Airport
3300 Capital Cir SW . . . Tallahassee FL 32310 850-891-7800 891-7837
Web: talgov.com

Tampa International Airport
4100 George J Bean Pkwy PO Box 22287 . . . Tampa FL 33607 813-870-8700 875-6670
TF: 866-289-9673 ■ *Web:* www.tampaairport.com

Palm Beach International Airport
1000 Turnage Blvd . . . West Palm Beach FL 33406 561-471-7420 471-7427
Web: www.pbia.org

Hartsfield-Jackson Atlanta International Airport
6000 N Terminal Pkwy Ste 4000 . . . Atlanta GA 30320 404-530-6600 530-6803
TF: 800-897-1910 ■ *Web:* www.atlanta-airport.com

Augusta Regional Airport - Bush Field (AGS)
1501 Aviation Way . . . Augusta GA 30906 706-798-3236 798-1551
TF: 866-289-9673 ■ *Web:* flyags.com

Columbus Metropolitan Airport
3250 W Britt David Rd . . . Columbus GA 31909 706-324-2449
Web: flycolumbusga.com

Middle Georgia Regional Airport
1000 Airport Dr . . . Macon GA 31216 478-788-3760
Web: iflymacon.com

Savannah/Hilton Head International Airport
400 Airways Ave . . . Savannah GA 31408 912-964-0514 964-0877
Web: www.savannahairport.com

Honolulu International Airport
300 Rodgers Blvd . . . Honolulu HI 96819 808-831-3600
Web: www.honoluluairport.com

Kahului Airport 1 Kahului Airport Rd . . . Kahului HI 96732 808-872-3830 872-3829
TF: 800-321-3712 ■ *Web:* www.hawaii.gov/ogg

Kona International Airport
73-200 Kupipi St . . . Kailua-Kona HI 96740 808-327-9520 838-8067
TF: 800-321-3712 ■ *Web:* www.hawaii.gov/koa

Boise Airport 3201 Airport Way . . . Boise ID 83705 208-383-3110 343-9667
Web: www.cityofboise.org

Pocatello Regional Airport
1950 Airport Way PO Box 4169 . . . Pocatello ID 83205 208-234-6154 233-8418
Web: www.pocatello.us

Chicago Midway Airport 5700 S Cicero Ave . . . Chicago IL 60638 773-838-0600 838-0588
TF: 800-832-6352 ■ *Web:* www.flychicago.com

O'Hare International Airport
Dept of Aviation PO Box 66142 . . . Chicago IL 60666 773-686-3700
TF: 800-832-6352 ■ *Web:* www.flychicago.com

Prospect Airport Services Inc
2130 S Wolf Rd . . . Des Plaines IL 60018 847-299-3636 299-3638
Web: www.prospectair.com

Peoria Regional Airport
6100 W Everett McKinley Dirksen Pkwy . . . Peoria IL 61607 309-697-8272 697-8132
Web: www.flypia.com

Greater Rockford Airport 60 Airport Dr . . . Rockford IL 61109 815-969-4000 969-4001
TF: 800-517-2000 ■ *Web:* www.flyrfd.com

Willard Airport 11 Airport Rd . . . Savoy IL 61874 217-244-8618 244-8644
Web: www.flycmi.com

Abraham Lincoln Capital Airport
1200 Capital Airport Dr . . . Springfield IL 62707 217-788-1060 788-8056
Web: www.flyspi.com

Du Page Airport Authority
2700 International Dr Ste 200 . . . West Chicago IL 60185 630-584-2211 584-3022
TF: 800-208-5690 ■ *Web:* www.dupageairport.com

Phone | Fax

Evansville Regional Airport
7801 Bussing Dr . . . Evansville IN 47725 812-421-4401 421-4412
Web: flyevv.com

Fort Wayne International Airport
3801 W Ferguson Rd Ste 209 . . . Fort Wayne IN 46809 260-747-4146 747-1762
Web: www.fwairport.com

South Bend Regional Airport
4477 Progress Dr . . . South Bend IN 46628 574-282-4590 239-2585
Web: www.flysbn.com

Eastern Iowa Airport, The
2515 Arthur Collins PkwySW . . . Cedar Rapids IA 52404 319-362-8336 362-1670
Web: www.eiairport.org

Des Moines International Airport
5800 Fleur Dr . . . Des Moines IA 50321 515-256-5050 256-5025
TF: 877-686-0029 ■ *Web:* www.dsmairport.com

Dubuque Regional Airport 11000 Airport Rd . . . Dubuque IA 52003 563-589-4127 589-4108
Web: www.flydbq.com

Midcontinent Airport 2173 Air Cargo Rd . . . Wichita KS 67209 316-946-4700 946-4793
Web: www.flywichita.com

Blue Grass Airport 4000 Terminal Dr . . . Lexington KY 40510 859-425-3100 233-1822
Web: www.bluegrassairport.com

Louisville International Airport
700 Administration Dr PO Box 9129 . . . Louisville KY 40209 502-368-6524 367-0199
Web: flylouisville.com

Baton Rouge Metropolitan Airport
9430 Jackie Cochran Dr Ste 300 . . . Baton Rouge LA 70807 225-355-0333 355-2334
TF: 877-359-2538 ■ *Web:* www.flybtr.com

Lafayette Regional Airport 222 Tower Dr . . . Lafayette LA 70508 337-266-4400
Web: www.lftairport.com

Shreveport Regional Airport
5103 Hollywood Ave . . . Shreveport LA 71109 318-673-5370 673-5377
Web: www.shreveportla.gov

Augusta State Airport 75 Airport Rd . . . Augusta ME 04330 207-626-2306 626-2309
TF: 800-654-3131 ■ *Web:* www.augustamaine.gov

Bangor International Airport 287 Godfrey Blvd . . . Bangor ME 04401 207-992-4600 945-3607
TF: 866-359-2264 ■ *Web:* www.flybangor.com

Portland International Jetport
1001 Westbrook St . . . Portland ME 04102 207-874-8877 774-7740
Web: www.portlandjetport.org

Hancock County-Bar Harbor Airport
115 Caruso Dr . . . Trenton ME 04605 207-667-7329 667-0218
Web: www.bhbairport.com

Winnipeg James Armstrong Richardson International Airport
2000 Wellington Ave
Rm 249 Administration Bldg . . . Winnipeg MB R3H1C2 204-987-9400 987-9401
Web: www.waa.ca

Baltimore/Washington International Thurgood Marshall Airport (BWI)
PO Box 8766 . . . Baltimore MD 21240 410-859-7111 768-9452
TF: 800-435-9294 ■ *Web:* www.bwiairport.com

Salisbury Ocean City-Wicomico County Regional Airport
5485 Airport Terminal Rd . . . Salisbury MD 21804 410-548-4827 548-4945
Web: flysbyairport.com

Worcester Regional Airport 375 Airport Dr . . . Worcester MA 01602 508-799-1350 799-1866
Web: www.worcesterma.gov

Alpena County Regional Airport
1617 Airport Rd . . . Alpena MI 49707 989-354-2907 358-9988
Web: www.alpenaairport.com

Coleman A Young International Airport
11499 Conner . . . Detroit MI 48213 313-628-2146 372-2448
Web: www.detroitmi.gov

Detroit Metropolitan Airport
Smith Terminal - Mezzanine Level . . . Detroit MI 48242 734-942-3550
Web: www.metroairport.com

Bishop International Airport
G-3425 W Bristol Rd . . . Flint MI 48507 810-235-6560 233-3065
TF: 800-433-7300 ■ *Web:* www.bishopairport.org

Gerald R Ford International Airport
5500 44th St SE . . . Grand Rapids MI 49512 616-233-6000 233-6025
TF: 866-289-9673 ■ *Web:* www.grr.org

Capital Region International Airport
4100 Capital City Blvd . . . Lansing MI 48906 517-321-6121 321-6197
TF: 866-841-4900 ■ *Web:* www.flylansing.com

Duluth International Airport 4701 Grinden Dr . . . Duluth MN 55811 218-727-2968 727-2960
TF: 855-787-2227 ■ *Web:* www.duluthairport.com

Rochester International Airport (RST)
7600 Helgerson Dr SW . . . Rochester MN 55902 507-282-2328 282-2346
Web: flyrst.com

Gulfport/Biloxi International Airport
14035 - L Airport Rd . . . Gulfport MS 39503 228-863-5951 863-5953
Web: www.flygpt.com

Jackson International Airport
100 International Dr Ste 300 . . . Jackson MS 39208 601-939-5631 939-3713
TF: 800-227-7368 ■ *Web:* www.jmaa.com

Hattiesburg-Laurel Regional Airport
1002 Terminal Dr . . . Moselle MS 39459 601-649-2444 545-3155
TF: 800-433-7300 ■ *Web:* www.flypib.com

Tupelo Regional Airport 105 Lemons Dr . . . Tupelo MS 38801 662-823-4359 823-8329
TF: 877-777-4778 ■ *Web:* www.flytupelo.com

Columbia Regional Airport
11300 S Airport Dr . . . Columbia MO 65201 573-874-7508 874-0105
Web: flymidmo.com

Kansas City International Airport
601 Brasilia Ave PO Box 20047 . . . Kansas City MO 64153 816-243-5237 243-3171
Web: www.flykci.com

Lambert Saint Louis International Airport
10701 Lambert International Blvd
PO Box 10212 . . . Saint Louis MO 63145 314-426-8000 426-1221
TF: 855-787-2227 ■ *Web:* www.flystl.com

Springfield-Branson National Airport
2300 N Airport Blvd . . . Springfield MO 65802 417-868-0500 869-1031
Web: www.flyspringfield.com

Billings Logan International Airport
1901 Terminal Cir . . . Billings MT 59105 406-657-8495 657-8438
Web: www.ci.billings.mt.us

Airport / Address	City	State	ZIP	Phone	Fax
Great Falls International Airport 2800 Terminal Dr	Great Falls	MT	59404	406-727-3404	727-6929
Web: flygtf.com					
Helena Regional Airport 2850 Skyway Dr	Helena	MT	59601	406-442-2821	449-2340
Web: www.helenaairport.com					
Lincoln Airport 2400 W Adams St	Lincoln	NE	68524	402-458-2480	458-2490
Web: www.lincolnairport.com					
Eppley Airfield 4501 Abbott Dr Ste 2300	Omaha	NE	68110	402-661-8000	661-8000
Web: flyoma.com					
McCarran International Airport 5757 Wayne Newton Blvd PO Box 11005	Las Vegas	NV	89119	702-261-5211	597-9553
TF: 888-261-4414 ■ *Web:* www.mccarran.com					
Reno-Tahoe International Airport 2001 E Plumb Ln	Reno	NV	89502	775-328-6400	328-6510
TF: 877-736-6359 ■ *Web:* www.renoairport.com					
Atlantic City International Airport (ACY) 101 Atlantic City International Airport Ste 106	Egg Harbor Township	NJ	08234	609-645-7895	641-4348
Web: www.sjta.com					
Newark Liberty International Airport One Hotel Rd	Newark	NJ	07114	973-961-6007	961-6259
TF: 888-397-4636 ■ *Web:* www.panynj.gov					
Albuquerque International Sunport 2200 Sunport Blvd	Albuquerque	NM	87106	505-244-7700	842-4278
Web: cabq.gov					
Las Cruces International Airport 8990 Zia Blvd	Las Cruces	NM	88007	575-541-2471	527-6470
Web: www.las-cruces.org					
Santa Fe Municipal Airport (SAF) 121 Aviation Dr PO Box 909	Santa Fe	NM	87504	505-955-2900	955-2905
TF: 866-773-2587 ■ *Web:* santafenm.gov/airport					
Buffalo Niagara International Airport 4200 Genesee St	Cheektowaga	NY	14225	716-630-6000	630-6070
Web: www.buffaloairport.com					
John F Kennedy International Airport (JFK) 150 Greenwich St	New York	NY	10007	212-435-7000	244-3505*
**Fax Area Code:* 718 ■ *Web:* panynj.gov					
Greater Rochester International Airport 1200 Brooks Ave	Rochester	NY	14624	585-753-7020	753-7008
Web: www.monroecounty.gov					
Long Island MacArthur Airport 100 Arrival Ave Ste 100	Ronkonkoma	NY	11779	631-467-3300	467-3348
TF: 888-542-4776 ■ *Web:* www.macarthurairport.com					
Syracuse Hancock International Airport 1000 Colonel Eileen Collins Blvd	Syracuse	NY	13212	315-454-4330	454-8757
Web: www.syrairport.org					
Westchester County Airport 240 Airport Rd Ste 202	White Plains	NY	10604	914-995-4860	995-3980
Web: www.co.westchester.ny.us/airport					
Asheville Regional Airport 61 Terminal Dr Ste 1	Fletcher	NC	28732	828-684-2226	684-3404
TF: 866-719-3910 ■ *Web:* www.flyavl.com					
Piedmont Triad International Airport 1000 A Ted Johnson Pkwy	Greensboro	NC	27409	336-665-5600	665-1425
Web: www.flyfrompti.com					
Raleigh-Durham International Airport PO Box 80001	Raleigh	NC	27623	919-840-2123	840-0175
TF: 800-252-7522 ■ *Web:* www.rdu.com					
Smith Reynolds Airport 3801 N Liberty St	Winston-Salem	NC	27105	336-767-6361	767-8556
Web: www.smithreynolds.org					
Bismarck Municipal Airport 2301 University Dr Bldg 17 PO Box 991	Bismarck	ND	58502	701-355-1800	221-6886
Web: www.bismarckairport.com					
Hector International Airport 2801 32nd Ave NW	Fargo	ND	58102	701-241-1501	241-1538
Web: www.fargoairport.com					
Halifax Stanfield International Airport (HIAA) 1 Bell Blvd	Enfield	NS	B2T1K2	902-873-4422	873-4750
TF: 800-565-5359 ■ *Web:* www.hiaa.ca					
Cincinnati-Northern Kentucky International Airport PO Box 752000	Cincinnati	OH	45275	859-767-3151	767-3080
Web: www.cvgairport.com					
Cleveland Hopkins International Airport 5300 Riverside Dr	Cleveland	OH	44135	216-265-6000	265-6021
Web: www.clevelandairport.com					
Port Columbus International Airport 4600 International Gateway	Columbus	OH	43219	614-239-4000	239-2219
Web: www.columbusairports.com					
Akron-Canton Airport 5400 Lauby Rd NW	North Canton	OH	44720	330-499-4221	499-5176
TF: 888-434-2359 ■ *Web:* www.akroncantonairport.com					
Toledo Express Airport 11013 Airport Hwy	Swanton	OH	43558	419-865-2351	867-8245
TF: 888-381-8294 ■ *Web:* www.toledoexpress.com					
Dayton International Airport 3600 Terminal Dr Ste 300	Vandalia	OH	45377	937-454-8200	454-8284
TF: 800-433-7300 ■ *Web:* www.flydayton.com					
Youngstown-Warren Regional Airport 1453 Youngstown-Kingsville Rd NE	Vienna	OH	44473	330-856-1537	609-5371
TF: 800-444-1440 ■ *Web:* www.yngwrnair.com					
Will Rogers World Airport 7100 Terminal Dr PO Box 937	Oklahoma City	OK	73159	405-680-3200	680-3311
Web: www.flyokc.com					
Tulsa International Airport 7777 E Apache PO Box 581838	Tulsa	OK	74115	918-838-5000	838-5199
Web: www.tulsaairports.com					
Ottawa Macdonald-Cartier International Airport 1000 Airport PkwyPrivate Ste 2500	Ottawa	ON	K1V9B4	613-248-2000	248-2012
TF: 888-901-6222 ■ *Web:* www.ottawa-airport.ca					
Eugene Airport 28801 Douglas Dr	Eugene	OR	97402	541-682-5430	682-6838
Web: www.eugene-or.gov					
Portland International Airport 7000 NE Airport Way	Portland	OR	97218	503-460-4234	460-4124
TF: 800-547-8411 ■ *Web:* www.portofportland.com					
Lehigh Valley International Airport 3311 Airport Rd	Allentown	PA	18109	610-266-6000	264-0115
TF: 800-359-5842 ■ *Web:* www.flylvia.com					
Wilkes-Barre/Scranton International Airport 100 Terminal Dr Ste 1	Avoca	PA	18641	570-602-2000	602-2010
TF: 877-235-9287 ■ *Web:* www.flyavp.com					
Erie International Airport 4411 W 12th St	Erie	PA	16505	814-833-4258	833-0393
Web: www.erieairport.org					
Harrisburg International Airport One Terminal Dr Ste 300	Middletown	PA	17057	717-948-3900	948-4636
TF: 888-235-9442 ■ *Web:* www.flyhia.com					
Philadelphia International Airport 8000 Essington Ave	Philadelphia	PA	19153	215-937-6937	937-6497
TF: 800-514-0301 ■ *Web:* www.phl.org					
Pittsburgh International Airport Landside Terminal Fourth Fl Mezz PO Box 12370	Pittsburgh	PA	15231	412-472-3525	472-3636
TF: 888-429-5377 ■ *Web:* www.pitairport.com					
Rhode Island Airport Corp 2000 Post Rd Warwick	Warwick	RI	02886	401-691-2000	732-3034
TF: 888-268-7222 ■ *Web:* www.pvdairport.com					
Charleston International Airport 5500 International Blvd Ste 101	Charleston	SC	29418	843-767-7000	760-3020
Web: www.chs-airport.com					
Columbia Metropolitan Airport 3000 Aviation Way W PO Box 280037	Columbia	SC	29170	803-822-5010	
TF: 888-562-5002 ■ *Web:* www.columbiaairport.com					
Greenville-Spartanburg Airport (GSP) 2000 GSP Dr Ste 1	Greer	SC	29651	864-877-7426	848-6225
TF: 800-331-1212 ■ *Web:* www.gspairport.com					
Hilton Head Island Airport 120 Beach City Rd	Hilton Head Island	SC	29926	843-255-2950	689-5411
Web: bcgov.net					
Myrtle Beach International Airport 1100 Jetport Rd	Myrtle Beach	SC	29577	843-448-1589	626-9096
Web: www.flymyrtlebeach.com					
Pierre Regional Airport 4001 Airport Rd	Pierre	SD	57501	605-773-7447	
Web: www.pierreairport.com					
Rapid City Regional Airport 4550 Terminal Rd Ste 102	Rapid City	SD	57703	605-393-9924	394-6190
TF: 800-357-9998 ■ *Web:* www.rcgov.org/airport					
Sioux Falls Regional Airport 2801 Jaycee Ln	Sioux Falls	SD	57104	605-336-0762	367-7374
Web: www.sfairport.com					
McGhee Tyson Airport 2055 Alcoa Hwy	Alcoa	TN	37701	865-342-3000	342-3050
Web: www.tys.org					
Tri-Cities Regional Airport 2525 Hwy 75 PO Box 1055	Blountville	TN	37617	423-325-6000	325-6060
Web: triflight.com					
Chattanooga Metropolitan Airport 1001 Airport Rd Ste 14	Chattanooga	TN	37421	423-855-2202	855-2212
Web: www.chattairport.com					
Memphis International Airport 2491 Winchester Rd Ste 113	Memphis	TN	38116	901-922-8000	922-8099
Web: www.memphisairport.org					
Metropolitan Nashville Airport Authority 1 Terminal Dr Ste 501	Nashville	TN	37214	615-275-1675	275-1784*
**Fax:* Hum Res ■ *Web:* www.flynashville.com					
Abilene Regional Airport 2933 Airport Blvd	Abilene	TX	79602	325-676-6367	676-6317
Web: www.abilenetx.com/airport					
Rick Husband Amarillo International Airport 10801 Airport Blvd	Amarillo	TX	79111	806-335-1671	335-1672
Web: airport.amarillo.gov					
Austin-Bergstrom International Airport (ABIA) 3600 Presidential Blvd	Austin	TX	78719	512-530-2242	530-7686
Web: www.ci.austin.tx.us					
Corpus Christi International Airport 1000 International Dr	Corpus Christi	TX	78406	361-289-0171	289-0251
Web: www.corpuschristiairport.com					
Dallas Love Field 8008 Cedar Springs Rd LB 16	Dallas	TX	75235	214-670-5683	670-6051
Web: www.dallas-lovefield.com					
Dallas-Fort Worth International Airport (DFW) 3200 E Airfield Dr PO Box 619428	Dallas	TX	75261	972-973-8888	574-5509
TF: 800-252-7522 ■ *Web:* www.dfwairport.com					
El Paso International Airport 6701 Convair Rd	El Paso	TX	79925	915-780-4749	
Web: www.elpasointernationalairport.com					
Bush Intercontinental Airport 2800 N Terminal Rd	Houston	TX	77032	281-233-3000	233-3108
Web: www.fly2houston.com/iah					
William P Hobby Airport (HOU) 7800 Airport Blvd	Houston	TX	77061	713-640-3000	641-7703
Web: fly2houston.com/hobbyhome					
Lubbock Preston Smith International Airport 5401 N Martin Luther King Blvd	Lubbock	TX	79403	806-775-2044	775-3133
Web: www.mylubbock.us/departmental-websites/departments/lubbock-airport/home					
Midland International Airport 9506 Laforce Blvd PO Box 60305	Midland	TX	79711	432-560-2200	560-2237
Web: www.midlandinternational.com					
San Antonio International Airport (SAT) 9800 Airport Blvd Rm 2041	San Antonio	TX	78216	210-207-3411	207-3500*
**Fax:* PR ■ *TF:* 800-237-6639 ■ *Web:* www.sanantonio.gov/aviation					
Ogden-Hinckley Airport 3909 Airport Rd	Ogden	UT	84405	801-629-8251	627-8104
Web: www.ogdencity.com					
Salt Lake City International Airport 776 N Terminal Dr PO Box 145550	Salt Lake City	UT	84116	801-575-2400	575-2645
TF: 800-595-2442 ■ *Web:* www.slcairport.com					
Burlington International Airport 1200 Airport Dr	South Burlington	VT	05403	802-863-1889	863-7947
Web: www.burlingtonintlairport.com					
Newport News/Williamsburg International Airport 900 Bland Blvd Ste G	Newport News	VA	23602	757-877-0221	877-6369
Web: flyphf.com					

	City	State	Zip	Phone	Fax
Norfolk International Airport 2200 Norview Ave. *Web:* www.norfolkairport.com	Norfolk	VA	23518	757-857-3351	857-3265
Richmond International Airport One Richard E Byrd Terminal D Ste C **Fax:* Mail Rm ■ *Web:* www.flyrichmond.com	Richmond	VA	23250	804-226-3000	652-2606*
Roanoke Regional Airport 5202 Aviation Dr NW. *Web:* flyroa.com/	Roanoke	VA	24012	540-362-1999	563-4838
Seattle-Tacoma International Airport (SEA-TAC) 17801 International Blvd PO Box 68727 *Web:* portseattle.org/sea-tac	Seattle	WA	98158	206-787-5388	
Spokane International Airport 9000 W Airport Dr *TF:* 855-787-2227 ■ *Web:* www.spokaneairports.net	Spokane	WA	99224	509-455-6455	624-6633
Yeager Airport 100 Airport Rd Ste 175 *Web:* www.yeagerairport.com	Charleston	WV	25311	304-344-8033	344-8034
Morgantown Municipal Airport 100 Hartfield Rd *Web:* morgantownairport.com	Morgantown	WV	26505	304-291-7461	291-7463
Austin Straubel International Airport 2077 Airport Dr Ste 18 *Web:* www.co.brown.wi.us	Green Bay	WI	54313	920-498-4800	498-8799
Dane County Regional Airport 4000 International Ln *Web:* www.msnairport.com	Madison	WI	53704	608-246-3380	246-3385
General Mitchell International Airport 5300 S Howell Ave *Web:* www.mitchellairport.com	Milwaukee	WI	53207	414-747-5300	747-4525
Natrona County International Airport 8500 Airport Pkwy *Web:* www.iflycasper.com	Casper	WY	82604	307-472-6688	472-1805
Cheyenne Regional Airport 4000 Airport Pkwy PO Box 2210 *Web:* www.cheyenneairport.com	Cheyenne	WY	82001	307-634-7071	632-1206
Jackson Hole Airport 1250 E Airport Rd PO Box 159 *Web:* www.jacksonholeairport.com	Jackson	WY	83001	307-733-7682	733-9270

28 AIRSHIPS

SEE ALSO Aircraft p. 1730

	City	State	Zip	Phone	Fax
Boland Balloon Post Mills Airport PO Box 51 *Web:* www.myairship.com	Post Mills	VT	05058	802-333-9254	333-9254
Cameron Balloons US PO Box 3672 *TF:* 866-423-6178 ■ *Web:* www.cameronballoons.com	Ann Arbor	MI	48106	734-426-5525	426-5026
FireFly Balloons 850 Meacham Rd *Web:* www.fireflyballoons.net	Statesville	NC	28677	704-878-9501	878-9505
ILC Dover Inc One Moonwalker Rd *TF:* 800-631-9567 ■ *Web:* www.ilcdover.com	Frederica	DE	19946	302-335-3911	335-0762
ISL Information Systems Labs 10070 Barnes Canyon Rd *Web:* www.islinc.com	San Diego	CA	92121	858-535-9680	535-9848
Lindstrand Balloons USA 11440 Dandar St *Web:* www.lindstrand.com	Galena	IL	61036	815-777-6006	777-6004
Millennium Airship Inc Bremerton National Airport PO Box 1972 *Web:* www.millenniumairship.com	Belfair	WA	98528	360-674-2488	674-2494
TCOM LP 7115 Thomas Edison Dr *Web:* www.tcomlp.com	Columbia	MD	21046	410-312-2400	312-2455
Worldwide Aeros Corp 1734 Gage Rd **Fax Area Code:* 323 ■ *Web:* aeroscraft.com	Montebello	CA	90640	818-344-3999	201-8383*

29 ALL-TERRAIN VEHICLES

SEE ALSO Sporting Goods p. 3182

	City	State	Zip	Phone	Fax
American Honda Motor Company Inc 1919 Torrance Blvd *TF:* 800-999-1009 ■ *Web:* www.honda.com	Torrance	CA	90501	310-783-3170	
American Suzuki Motor Corp 3251 Imperial Hwy *Web:* www.suzuki.com	Brea	CA	92821	714-996-7040	524-2512
Cycle Country Access Corp 205 N Depot St PO Box 107 *TF Sales:* 800-841-2222 ■ *Web:* www.cyclecountry.com	Fox Lake	WI	53933	800-841-2222	
Kawasaki Motors Corp USA PO Box 25252 *Web:* www.kawasaki.com	Santa Ana	CA	92799	949-770-0400	460-5600
Ontario Drive & Gear Ltd (ODG) 220 Bergey Ct *TF:* 877-274-6288 ■ *Web:* www.argoatv.com	New Hamburg	ON	N3A2J5	519-662-2840	
Polaris Industries Inc 2100 Hwy 55 *NYSE:* PII ■ *Web:* www.polaris.com	Medina	MN	55340	763-542-0500	542-0599
Recreatives Industries Inc 60 Depot St *TF:* 800-255-2511 ■ *Web:* www.maxatvs.com	Buffalo	NY	14206	716-855-2226	855-1094
Yamaha Motor Corp USA 6555 Katella Ave *TF Cust Svc:* 800-656-7695 ■ *Web:* www.yamaha-motor.com	Cypress	CA	90630	800-656-7695	

30 AMBULANCE SERVICES

	City	State	Zip	Phone	Fax
Abbott Ambulance Inc 2500 Abbott Pl *TF:* 888-974-7035 ■ *Web:* www.abbottems.org	Saint Louis	MO	63143	314-768-1000	781-3595
Acadian Ambulance Service Inc 300 Hopkins St **Fax Area Code:* 337 ■ *TF:* 800-259-3333 ■ *Web:* www.acadian.com	Lafayette	LA	70501	800-259-3333	291-2211*
Air Trek Inc 28000 A-5 Airport Rd *Web:* www.medjets.com	Punta Gorda	FL	33982	941-639-7855	
American Ambulance Service Inc One American Way *Web:* www.americanamb.com	Norwich	CT	06360	860-886-1463	
American Medical Response (AMR) 6200 S Syracuse Way Ste 200 *TF:* 877-244-4890 ■ *Web:* www.amr.net	Greenwood Village	CO	80111	303-495-1200	495-1811
Area Metropolitan Ambulance Authority 551 E Berry St *Web:* www.medstar911.org	Fort Worth	TX	76110	817-923-3700	
Armstrong Ambulance Service Inc 87 Mystic St *Web:* armstrongambulance.com	Arlington	MA	02474	781-648-0612	
ATI Ambulance 8400 183rd Pl Ste 4500 *Web:* www.traceambulance.com	Tinley Park	IL	60487	708-802-8101	
Bangs Ambulance Service Inc 205 W Green St *Web:* www.bangsambulance.com	Ithaca	NY	14850	607-273-1161	
CareFlite 3110 S Great Southwest Pkwy *Web:* www.careflite.org	Grand Prairie	TX	75052	972-339-4200	
Carrier Coach Inc 271 Buffalo St *Web:* www.coach.com	Gowanda	NY	14070	716-532-2600	
Cataldo Ambulance Service Inc 137 Washington St *Web:* www.cataldoambulance.com	Somerville	MA	02143	617-625-0126	
County Rescue Services 1765 Allouez Ave *Web:* www.countyrescue.com	Green Bay	WI	54311	920-469-9779	
Critical Care Services Inc 3010 Broadway St NE *Web:* www.lifelinkiii.com	Minneapolis	MN	55413	612-638-4900	
Danville Ambulance Service Office 12 A St *Web:* www.danvilleambulance.com	Danville	PA	17821	570-275-3031	
Emergency Ambulance Service International Inc 3200 E Birch St Ste A *Web:* www.emergencyambulance.com	Brea	CA	92821	714-990-1331	
Emergycare Inc 1701 Sassafras St *Web:* www.emergycare.org	Erie	PA	16502	814-870-1010	
Excellance Inc 453 Lanier Rd *Web:* www.excellance.com	Madison	AL	35758	256-772-9321	
Global Air Response 5919 Approach Rd **Fax Area Code:* 941 ■ *TF:* 800-631-6565 ■ *Web:* www.airresponse.net	Sarasota	FL	34238	800-631-6565	926-7690*
Hunters Ambulance Service Inc 47 N Plains Industrial Rd Ste A *Web:* www.huntersamb.com	Wallingford	CT	06492	203-269-6586	
Industrial Paramedic Services Ltd 630 Fourth Ave SW Ste 100 *Web:* ipsems.com	Calgary	AB	T2P0J9	403-264-6435	
Keystone Quality Transport Co 1260 E Woodland Ave *Web:* keystonequalitytransport.com	Springfield	PA	19064	610-604-1421	
Lake EMS 2761 W Old U.S. Hwy 441 *Web:* www.lakesumterems.org	Mount Dora	FL	32757	352-383-4554	
Lifenet Inc 6225 St Michaels Dr *Web:* www.lifenetems.org	Texarkana	TX	75503	903-832-8531	
LifeStar Response Corp 3710 Commerce Dr Ste 1006 *Web:* www.lifestarcompanies.com	Halethorpe	MD	21227	410-247-1178	
Medic Rescue for Your Convenience You May Dial 313 Bridge St *Web:* www.medicrescue.org	Beaver	PA	15009	724-728-3620	
MedjetAssist 3500 Colonnade Pkwy Ste 500 PO Box 43099 *TF:* 800-527-7478 ■ *Web:* www.medjetassist.com	Birmingham	AL	35243	205-595-6626	595-6658
Mercy Flights Inc 2020 Milligan Way *Web:* www.mercyflights.com	Medford	OR	97504	541-858-2600	
Metro Aviation Inc 1214 Hawn Ave PO Box 7008 *Web:* www.metroaviation.com	Shreveport	LA	71137	318-222-5529	222-0503
Metro West Ambulance Service Inc 5475 Ne Dawson Creek Dr *Web:* www.metrowest.fm	Hillsboro	OR	97124	503-648-6658	
Midwest Ambulance Service of Iowa 2535 106th St *Web:* www.midwestambulance.com	Urbandale	IA	50322	515-222-2222	252-1725
Midwood Ambulance & Oxygen Service Inc 2593 W 13th St *Web:* www.midwoodambulance.com	Brooklyn	NY	11223	718-645-1000	
Mission Ambulance 1055 E Third St *TF:* 800-899-9100 ■ *Web:* www.missionambulance.com	Corona	CA	92879	800-899-9100	
Mobile Life Support Services Inc 3188 Us Rt 9w *Web:* www.mobilelife.com	New Windsor	NY	12553	845-562-4368	
Monroe Medi-Trans Inc 1669 Lyell Ave *Web:* www.monroeambulance.com	Rochester	NY	14606	585-454-6910	
MTS Ambulance 2431 Greenup Ave *Web:* www.mtsambulance.com	Ashland	KY	41101	606-324-3286	
NES Healthcare Group Inc 39 Main St PO Box 156 *Web:* www.neshealth-care.com	Tiburon	CA	94920	631-265-7450	
Paramedics Plus LLC 352 Glenwood *Web:* www.paramedicsplus.com	Tyler	TX	75702	903-535-5802	
Paratech Ambulance Service 9401 W Brown Deer Rd *Web:* www.paratechambulance.com	Milwaukee	WI	53224	414-358-1111	
Peach State Ambulance Inc 105 Peach State Ct *Web:* www.peachstateambulance.com	Tyrone	GA	30290	678-364-0003	
PL Custom Body & Equipment Company Inc 2201 Atlantic Ave *Web:* www.plcustom.com	Manasquan	NJ	08736	732-223-1411	
Professional Ambulance & Oxygen Service Inc 31 Smith Pl *Web:* www.proems.com	Cambridge	MA	02138	617-492-2700	
PROMPT Ambulance Central Inc 9835 Express Dr *Web:* www.promptambulance.com	Highland	IN	46322	219-934-1010	

Phone *Fax*

REVA Air Ambulance Inc
1745 NW 51 Pl Hngr 73 Fort Lauderdale FL 33309 954-730-9300
Web: www.flyreva.com

Rural/Metro Corp 9221 E Via de Ventura Scottsdale AZ 85258 800-352-2309 606-3268*
**Fax Area Code:* 480 ■ **Fax:* Hum Res ■ *TF:* 800-352-2309 ■ *Web:* www.ruralmetro.com

Schaefer Ambulance Service Inc
4627 Beverly Blvd Los Angeles CA 90004 323-468-1600
Web: www.schaeferamb.com

Shock Trauma Air Rescue Society (STARS)
1441 Aviation Pk NE Calgary AB T2E8M7 403-295-1811 275-4891
Web: www.stars.ca

Skyservice Airlines Inc 9785 Ryan Ave Dorval QC H9P1A2 514-636-3300 636-4855
TF: 888-985-1402 ■ *Web:* skyservice.com

Transcare Pennsylvania 400 Seco Rd Monroeville PA 15146 412-373-6300 373-8263
Web: transcare.com

Westlog Aviation 311 Cove Rd Brookings OR 97415 541-469-7911
Web: www.cal-ore.com

31 AMUSEMENT PARK COMPANIES

SEE ALSO Circus, Carnival, Festival Operators p. 1949

Phone *Fax*

AAF Rose Bowl Aquatics Center
360 N Arroyo Blvd Pasadena CA 91103 626-564-0330
Web: www.rosebowlaquatics.org

Ada Community Library 10664 W Victory Rd Boise ID 83709 208-362-0181
Web: www.adalib.org

All Star Adventures 1010 N Webb Rd Wichita KS 67206 316-682-3700
Web: www.allstarwichita.com

Austins Entertainment LLC 16231 N Ih-35 Pflugerville TX 78660 512-670-9600
Web: www.austinspark.com

Bay Tek Games Inc 1077 E Glenbrook Dr Pulaski WI 54162 920-822-3951
Web: www.bay-tek.com

Belle Haven Country Club Inc
6023 Ft Hunt Rd Alexandria VA 22307 703-329-1448
Web: www.bellehavencc.com

Bend Metro Parks & Recreation District
200 NW Pacific Park Ln Bend OR 97701 541-389-7275
Web: bendparksandrec.org

BounceU 1166 S Gilbert Rd Gilbert AZ 85296 480-632-9663
Web: www.bounceu.com

Bowlmor Holdings LLC 222 W 44th St New York NY 10036 212-777-2214
Web: www.bowlmor.com

Buffalo Grove Park District
530 Bernard Dr Buffalo Grove IL 60089 847-850-2100
Web: bgparks.org

California Exposition & State Fair
PO Box 15649 Sacramento CA 95852 916-263-4041
Web: www.calexpo.com

CAMELBACK MOUNTAIN 301 Resort Dr Tannersville PA 18372 570-629-1661 629-2388
TF: 888-337-6966 ■ *Web:* www.skicamelback.com

Casino Pauma
777 Pauma Reservation Rd PO Box 1067 Pauma Valley CA 92061 760-742-2177
Web: www.casinopauma.com

Castles n Coasters 9445 N Metro Pkwy E Phoenix AZ 85051 602-997-7575
Web: www.castlesncoasters.com

Cedar Fair LP One Cedar Pt Dr Sandusky OH 44870 419-627-2233 627-2260
NYSE: FUN ■ *Web:* www.cedarfair.com

City of Dearborn 1300 S Telegraph Rd Dearborn MI 48124 313-563-4653
Web: www.cityofdearborn.org

Clementon Amusement Park & Splash World Waterpark
144 Berlin Rd Clementon NJ 08021 856-783-0263
Web: www.clementonpark.com

Cliff's Amusement Park Inc
4800 Osuna Rd NE Albuquerque NM 87109 505-881-9373
Web: www.cliffsamusementpark.com

Cordova Recreation & Park District
2197 Chase Dr Rancho Cordova CA 95670 916-362-1841
Web: www.crpd.com

Des Plaines Park District 2222 Birch St Des Plaines IL 60018 847-391-5700
Web: dpparks.org

Dorney Park Coaster Company Inc
3830 Dorney Park Rd Allentown PA 18104 610-395-3724
Web: www.dorneypark.com

Downers Grove Park District
2455 Warrenville Rd Downers Grove IL 60516 630-960-7500
Web: www.dgparks.org

Flagship Marinas Acquisitions LLC
950 E Paces Ferry Rd Ste 820 Atlanta GA 30320 770-965-7605
Web: www.flagshipmarinas.com

Freedom Station Family Fun Center
2992 N Park Ave Ste A Prescott Valley AZ 86314 928-775-4040
Web: www.freedomstationfun.com

Georgia Public Library
1800 Century Pl NE Ste 150 Atlanta GA 30345 404-235-7200
Web: www.georgialibraries.org

Going Bonkers Inc 229 N 48th St Quincy IL 62305 217-223-6331
Web: www.goingbonkers.com

Golfland Entertainment Centers Inc
155 W Hampton Ave Mesa AZ 85210 480-834-8319
Web: www.golfland.com

Harris Goldman Productions Inc
8885 Rio San Diego Dr Ste 335 San Diego CA 92108 619-299-7951
Web: www.harrisgoldman.com

Hawaiian Falls Waterparks 4550 N Garland Ave Garland TX 75040 972-675-8888
Web: hfalls.com

Herschend Family Entertainment Corp (HFE)
5445 Triangle Pkwy Ste 200 Norcross GA 30092 770-441-1940
Web: hfecorp.com

HITS Inc 319 Main St Saugerties NY 12477 845-246-8833
Web: www.hitsshows.com

Phone *Fax*

iFly USA LLC 31310 Alvarado-Niles Rd Union City CA 94587 510-489-4359
Web: www.iflysfbay.com

International Training Inc
1045 Ne Industrial Blvd Jensen Beach FL 34957 207-729-4201
Web: www.tdisdi.com

Island Global Yachting Ltd
515 E Las Olas Blvd Ste 900 Fort Lauderdale FL 33301 954-302-6000
Web: www.igymarinas.com

Island Windjammers Inc 165 Shaw Dr Acworth GA 30102 877-772-4549
TF: 877-772-4549 ■ *Web:* www.islandwindjammers.com

Kennywood Entertainment Corp
4800 Kennywood Blvd West Mifflin PA 15122 412-461-8127
TF: 800-213-5861

Kids Play Today LLC 837 Route 6 Unit 5 Shohola PA 18458 570-296-2313
Web: www.kidsplaytoday.com

Lake Quassapaug Park 2132 Middlebury Rd Middlebury CT 06762 203-758-2913
Web: www.quassy.com

Laserdome 2050 Auction Rd Manheim PA 17545 717-492-0002
Web: laserdome.com

Leesburg Animal Park 19270 James Monroe Hwy Leesburg VA 20175 703-669-0010
Web: www.leesburganimalpark.com

Lisle Park District 1825 Short St Lisle IL 60532 630-964-3410
Web: www.lisleparkdistrict.org

Magic Mountain Fun Centers
5890 Scarborough Blvd Columbus OH 43232 614-840-9600
Web: www.magicmountainfuncenter.com

Michigan's Adventure Inc 4750 Whitehall Rd Muskegon MI 49445 231-766-3377
Web: www.miadventure.com

Mundelein Park & Recreation District
1401 N Midlathian Rd Mundelein IL 60060 847-566-0650
Web: mundeleinparks.org

New Lenox Community Park District
1 Manor Dr New Lenox IL 60451 815-485-3584
Web: www.newlenoxparks.org

New York Botanical Garden, The
2900 Southern Blvd Bronx NY 10458 718-817-8700
Web: www.nybg.org

Northbrook Park District 545 Academy Dr Northbrook IL 60062 847-897-6200
Web: www.nbparks.org

Oak Lawn Park District 9400 S Kenton Ave Oaklawn IL 60453 708-857-2222
Web: www.olparks.com

Oak Park Park District 218 Madison St Oak Park IL 60302 708-383-0002
Web: pdop.org

Ober Gatlinburg Inc 1001 Pkwy Ste 2 Gatlinburg TN 37738 865-436-5423
Web: obergatlinburg.com

Ocean Breeze Waterpark
849 General Booth Blvd Virginia Beach VA 23451 757-422-4444
Web: www.oceanbreezewaterpark.com

Odyssey Fun World 3440 Odyssey Ct Naperville IL 60563 630-416-2222
Web: www.odysseyfunworld.com

Optical Discount Corp
10415 Slusher Dr Santa Fe Springs CA 90670 562-946-3050
Web: www.odc-nimbus.com

Park Ridge Recreation & Park District
2701 Sibley Ave Park Ridge IL 60068 847-692-5127
Web: prparks.org

Paul Gauguin Cruises Inc
11100 Main St Ste 300 Bellevue WA 98004 425-440-6171
Web: www.pgcruises.com

Pennsylvania Renaissance Faire
2775 Lebanon Rd Manheim PA 17545 717-665-7021
Web: www.parenfaire.com

Q Center 1405 N Fifth Ave Saint Charles IL 60174 630-377-3100
Web: www.qcenter.com

Rentschler Field 615 Silver Ln East Hartford CT 06118 860-610-4700
Web: www.rentschlerfield.com

Ripley Entertainment Inc
7576 Kingspointe Pkwy Ste 188 Orlando FL 32819 407-345-8010 345-0801
Web: www.ripleys.com

Sage YMCA of Metro Chicago 701 Manor Rd Crystal Lake IL 60014 815-459-4455
Web: www.ymcachicago.org

Santa Cruz Seaside Co 400 Beach St Santa Cruz CA 95060 831-423-5590
Web: www.beachboardwalk.com

Schaumburg Park District 235 E Beech Dr Schaumburg IL 60193 847-985-2115
Web: www.parkfun.com

Sea Research Foundation Inc 55 Coogan Blvd Mystic CT 06355 860-572-5955
Web: www.searesearch.com

Seven Hills Sky Divers Club Inc
2110 Sunnyside Cres Madison WI 53704 608-244-5252
Web: www.sevenhillsskydivers.org

Ski Shawnee Inc 339 Hollow Rd Shawnee On Delaware PA 18356 570-421-7231
Web: www.shawneemt.com

Splash Lagoon Water Pk Resort 8091 Peach St Erie PA 16509 814-217-1111
Web: www.splashlagoon.com

Taos Ski Valley Inc 116 Sutton Pl Taos Ski Valley NM 87525 575-776-2291
Web: www.skitaos.org

Tweetsie Railroad Inc
300 Tweetsie Railroad Ln Blowing Rock NC 28605 828-264-9061
Web: www.tweetsie-railroad.com

Universal City Development Partners Ltd
1000 Universal Studios Plz Orlando FL 32819 407-363-8000
Web: www.universalorlando.com

Universal Parks & Resorts
100 Universal City Plz Universal City CA 91608 818-777-1000
Web: nbcuni.com

Ville De Riviere-Du-Loup
65 Rue De Lehetel-De-Ville Riviere-du-loup QC G5R1L4 418-867-6700
Web: www.ville.riviere-du-loup.qc.ca

Walt Disney Parks & Resorts
500 S Buena Vista St Burbank CA 91521 818-560-1000 560-1930
Web: thewaltdisneycompany.com/

	City	State	ZIP	Phone	Fax
Walt Disney Parks & Resorts LLC 500 S Buena Vista St	Burbank	CA	91521	818-560-1000	
Web: disneyparks.disney.go.com					
West Point Thoroughbreds Inc Two Smith Bridge Rd	Saratoga Springs	NY	12866	518-583-6638	
Web: www.westpointtb.com					
West Suburban Special Recreation Association 2915 Maple St	Franklin Park	IL	60131	847-455-2100	
Web: www.wssra.net					
Westchester Park District 10201 Bond St	Westchester	IL	60154	708-865-8200	
Web: www.wpdparks.org					
Wet 'n' Wild Hawaii 400 Farrington Hwy	Kapolei	HI	96707	808-674-9283	
Web: wetnwildhawaii.com					
Wheaton Park District 102 E Wesley St	Wheaton	IL	60187	630-665-4710	
Web: www.wheatonparkdistrict.com					
Wheeling Park District 333 W Dundee Rd	Wheeling	IL	60090	847-465-3333	
Web: www.wheelingparkdistrict.com					
Wild Adventures Valdosta LLC 3766 Old Clyattville Rd	Valdosta	GA	31601	229-219-7080	
Web: www.wildadventures.com					
Wisconsin Center District 500 W Kilbourn	Milwaukee	WI	53203	414-908-6000	
Web: www.wcd.org					
Woodridge Park District 2600 Center Dr	Woodridge	IL	60517	630-353-3300	
Web: www.woodridgeparks.org					
World Poker Tour 5700 Wilshire Blvd	Los Angeles	CA	90036	323-330-9900	
Web: www.wptmag.com					
YMCA of Pikes Peak Region Inc 207 N Nevada Ave	Colorado Springs	CO	80903	719-473-9622	
Web: www.ppymca.org					
YMCA of Triangle Area 801 Corporate Ctr Dr	Raleigh	NC	27607	919-719-9622	
Web: www.ymcatriangle.org					

32 AMUSEMENT PARKS

	City	State	ZIP	Phone	Fax
Adventure Landing 3311 Capital Blvd	Raleigh	NC	27604	919-872-1688	872-3408
Web: www.adventurelanding.com					
Adventuredome 2880 Las Vegas Blvd S	Las Vegas	NV	89109	702-691-5861	794-3906
TF: 866-456-8894 ■ *Web:* www.adventuredome.com					
Adventureland Park 305 34th Ave NW	Altoona	IA	50009	515-266-2121	266-9831
TF: 800-532-1286 ■ *Web:* www.adventurelandpark.com					
Busch Gardens Williamsburg 1 Busch Gardens Blvd	Williamsburg	VA	23185	800-343-7946	253-3399*
**Fax Area Code:* 757 ■ **Fax:* Mktg ■ *TF:* 800-343-7946 ■ *Web:* www.buschgardens.com					
California's Great America 4701 Great America Pkwy	Santa Clara	CA	95054	408-988-1776	986-5855*
**Fax:* Sales ■ *Web:* www.cagreatamerica.com					
Camelbeach Mountain Waterpark One Camelback Rd PO Box 168	Tannersville	PA	18372	570-629-1661	629-0942
Web: www.camelbeach.com					
Casino Pier & Water Works 800 Ocean Terr	Seaside Heights	NJ	08751	732-793-6488	793-0461
Web: www.casinopiernj.com					
Castle Park 3500 Polk St	Riverside	CA	92505	951-785-3000	785-3075
Web: www.castlepark.com					
Cedar Fair Parks 14523 Carowinds Blvd	Charlotte	NC	28273	704-588-2600	587-9034
TF: 800-888-4386 ■ *Web:* www.carowinds.com					
Cedar Point Amusement Park One Cedar Pt Dr	Sandusky	OH	44870	419-626-0830	627-2200*
**Fax:* Mktg ■ *Web:* www.cedarpoint.com					
Children's Fairyland Theme Park 699 Bellevue Ave	Oakland	CA	94610	510-452-2259	452-2261
Web: www.fairyland.org					
Coney Island Park 6201 Kellogg Ave	Cincinnati	OH	45230	513-232-8230	231-1352
Web: www.coneyislandpark.com					
Darien Lake Theme Park Resort 9993 Allegheny Rd PO Box 91	Darien Center	NY	14040	585-599-4641	599-4053
TF: 866-640-0652 ■ *Web:* www.darienlake.com					
Disney's Animal Kingdom 2901 Osceola Pkwy	Lake Buena Vista	FL	32830	407-938-3000	938-4799
Web: disneyworld.disney.go.com/parks/animal-kingdom					
Disney's Blizzard Beach 1534 Blizzard Beach Dr	Lake Buena Vista	FL	32830	407-560-3400	
Web: www.disneyworld.disney.go.com					
Disney's California Adventure 1313 S Disneyland Dr	Anaheim	CA	92802	714-781-7290	
TF: 800-225-2024 ■ *Web:* disneyland.disney.go.com					
Disney's Hollywood Studios 3111 World Dr	Orlando	FL	32836	407-824-4321	
Web: disneyworld.disney.go.com/parks/hollywood-studios					
Disney's Typhoon Lagoon 1145 E Buena Vista Blvd	Lake Buena Vista	FL	32830	407-560-7223	
Web: disneyworld.disney.go.com					
Disneyland 1313 S Harbor Blvd	Anaheim	CA	92802	714-781-7290	
Dollywood 2700 Dollywood Parks Blvd	Pigeon Forge	TN	37863	800-365-5996	428-9743*
**Fax Area Code:* 865 ■ **Fax:* Mktg ■ *TF:* 800-365-5996 ■ *Web:* www.dollywood.com					
Dorney Park & Wildwater Kingdom 3830 Dorney Pk Rd	Allentown	PA	18104	610-395-3724	
TF: 800-747-0561 ■ *Web:* dorneypark.com					
Dutch Wonderland Family Amusement Park 2249 Lincoln Hwy E	Lancaster	PA	17602	717-291-1888	291-1595
TF: 866-386-2839 ■ *Web:* www.dutchwonderland.com					
Elitch Gardens 2000 Elitch Cir	Denver	CO	80204	303-595-4386	629-0740
Web: www.elitchgardens.com					
EPCOT 1200 Epcot Resort Blvd	Lake Buena Vista	FL	32830	407-824-4321	
Web: disneyworld.disney.go.com					
Family Kingdom Amusement Park & Oceanfront Water Park 300 S Ocean Blvd	Myrtle Beach	SC	29577	843-626-3447	448-4548
Web: www.familykingdomfun.com					
Frontier City Theme Park 11501 NE Expy	Oklahoma City	OK	73131	405-478-2140	478-2118
Web: www.frontiercity.com					
Fun Town Splash Town USA Inc US Rt 1 774 Portland Rd PO Box 29	Saco	ME	04072	207-284-5139	283-4716
Web: www.funtownsplashtownusa.com					
Geauga Lake Wildwater Kingdom 1100 Squires Rd	Aurora	OH	44202	330-562-8303	
Web: www.wildwaterfun.com					
Grand Harbor Resort & Waterpark 350 Bell St	Dubuque	IA	52001	563-690-4000	690-0558
TF: 866-690-4006 ■ *Web:* www.grandharborresort.com					
Great Escape & Splashwater Kingdom Po Box 511	Lake George	NY	12845	518-792-3500	792-3404
Web: www.sixflags.com					
Hersheypark 100 Hershey Pk Dr	Hershey	PA	17033	717-534-3900	534-3153
TF: 800-437-7439 ■ *Web:* www.hersheypark.com					
Holiday World & Splashin' Safari 452 E Christmas Blvd	Santa Claus	IN	47579	812-937-4401	937-4405
TF: 877-463-2645 ■ *Web:* www.holidayworld.com					
Idlewild & Soak Zone Rt 30 E PO Box C	Ligonier	PA	15658	724-238-3666	238-6544
Web: www.idlewild.com					
Indiana Beach 5224 E Indiana Beach Rd	Monticello	IN	47960	574-583-4141	583-4125
TF: 800-583-4306 ■ *Web:* www.indianabeach.com					
Kennywood Park 4800 Kennywood Blvd	West Mifflin	PA	15122	412-461-0500	464-0719
Web: www.kennywood.com					
Knight's Action Park & Caribbean Water Adventure 1700 Recreation Dr	Springfield	IL	62711	217-546-8881	546-8995
Web: www.knightsactionpark.com					
Knoebels Amusement Resort 391 Knoebels Blvd	Elysburg	PA	17824	570-672-2572	672-3293
TF: 800-487-4386 ■ *Web:* www.knoebels.com					
Knott's Berry Farm 8039 Beach Blvd	Buena Park	CA	90620	714-220-5220	220-5124
TF: 800-742-6427 ■ *Web:* www.knotts.com					
Knott's Soak City Orange County 8039 Beach Blvd	Buena Park	CA	90620	714-220-5200	
Web: www.knotts.com/public/park/soakcity/orange_county					
Knott's Soak City San Diego 2052 Entertainment Cir	Chula Vista	CA	91911	714-220-5200	661-7393*
**Fax Area Code:* 619 ■ *Web:* www.knotts.com					
Lagoon & Pioneer Village 375 N Lagoon Dr	Farmington	UT	84025	801-451-8000	451-8015
TF: 800-748-5246 ■ *Web:* www.lagoonpark.com					
Lake Compounce Family Theme Park 822 Lake Ave	Bristol	CT	06010	860-583-3300	589-7974
Web: www.lakecompounce.com					
Lake Winnepesaukah Amusement Park 1730 Lakeview Dr	Rossville	GA	30741	706-866-5681	858-0497
Web: www.lakewinnie.com					
LEGOLAND California 1 Legoland Dr	Carlsbad	CA	92008	760-438-5346	918-5459
TF: 877-534-6526 ■ *Web:* www.legoland.com					
Magic Kingdom Park 3111 World Dr	Lake Buena Vista	FL	32836	407-824-4321	
Web: disneyworld.disney.go.com/parks/magic-kingdom					
Magic Springs Theme Park & Crystal Falls Water Park 1701 E Grand Ave	Hot Springs	AR	71901	501-624-0100	318-5367
Web: www.magicsprings.com					
Marineland 7657 Portage Rd	Niagara Falls	ON	L2E6X8	905-356-9565	374-6652
Web: www.marinelandcanada.com					
Morey's Piers & Raging Waters Waterparks 3501 Boardwalk	Wildwood	NJ	08260	609-522-3900	522-0788
Web: www.moreyspiers.com					
Myrtle Waves Water Park 3000 Tenth Ave N Ext	Myrtle Beach	SC	29577	843-913-9250	
Web: www.myrtlewaves.com					
NASCAR SpeedPark 1545 Pkwy Vaughan Mills Mall Space E-2	Sevierville	TN	37862	865-908-5500	669-7371*
**Fax Area Code:* 905 ■ *Web:* www.nascarspeedpark.com					
Oaks Amusement Park 7805 SE Oaks PkWy	Portland	OR	97202	503-233-5777	236-9143
Web: www.oakspark.com					
Paramount Canada's Wonderland 9580 Jane St	Vaughan	ON	L6A1S6	905-832-8131	832-7519
Web: www.canadaswonderland.com					
Paramount's Kings Dominion 16000 Theme Pkwy	Doswell	VA	23047	804-876-5000	876-5864
TF: 800-367-7623 ■ *Web:* www.kingsdominion.com					
Raging Waters 2333 S White Rd	San Jose	CA	95148	408-238-9900	270-2022
Web: www.rwsplash.com					
Raging Waters Sacramento 1600 Exposition Blvd	Sacramento	CA	95815	916-924-3747	924-1314
Web: www.rwsac.com					
Sandcastle Water Park 1000 Sandcastle Dr	Homestead	PA	15120	412-462-6666	462-0827
Web: www.sandcastlewaterpark.com					
Santa Cruz Beach Boardwalk 400 Beach St	Santa Cruz	CA	95060	831-423-5590	460-3335
Web: www.beachboardwalk.com					
Schlitterbahn Beach Waterpark 33261 State Pk Rd Hwy 100	South Padre Island	TX	78597	956-772-7873	761-3960
Web: www.schlitterbahn.com					
Schlitterbahn Waterpark Resort 381 E Austin St	New Braunfels	TX	78130	830-625-2351	625-3515
Web: www.schlitterbahn.com					
SeaWorld Orlando 7007 Sea World Dr	Orlando	FL	32821	407-351-3600	363-2409*
**Fax:* Cust Svc ■ *TF:* 800-327-2424 ■ *Web:* seaworldparks.com					
SeaWorld San Diego 500 SeaWorld Dr	San Diego	CA	92109	619-226-3901	
TF: 800-257-4268 ■ *Web:* www.seaworld.com					
Sesame Place 100 Sesame Rd	Langhorne	PA	19047	215-752-7070	741-5307
Web: www.sesameplace.com					
Seven Peaks Water Park 1330 East 300 North	Provo	UT	84606	801-373-8777	373-8791
Web: www.sevenpeaks.com					
Silver Springs State Park 5656 E Silver Springs Blvd	Silver Springs	FL	34488	352-236-7148	
Web: www.floridastateparks.org					
Six Flags America 13710 Central Ave	Mitchellville	MD	20721	301-249-1500	
Web: www.sixflags.com/parks/america					
Six Flags Discovery Kingdom 1001 Fairgrounds Dr	Vallejo	CA	94589	707-644-4000	644-0241
Web: www.sixflags.com					
Six Flags Fiesta Texas 17000 IH-10 W	San Antonio	TX	78257	210-697-5000	697-5415
TF: 800-370-7488 ■ *Web:* www.sixflags.com					
Six Flags Great Adventure One Six Flags Blvd	Jackson	NJ	08527	732-928-1821	
TF: 800-772-2287 ■ *Web:* www.sixflags.com/parks/greatadventure					
Six Flags Great America 542 N Rt 21	Gurnee	IL	60031	847-249-2133	
Web: www.sixflags.com					
Six Flags Hurricane Harbor Dallas 1800 E Lamar Blvd	Arlington	TX	76006	817-265-3356	
Web: www.sixflags.com/parks/hurricaneharbordallas					

Phone | Fax

Six Flags Hurricane Harbor Los Angeles
26101 Magic Mtn Pkwy .... Valencia CA 91355 661-255-4527
Web: www.sixflags.com/parks/hurricaneharborla

Six Flags Magic Mountain
26101 Magic Mtn Pkwy .... Valencia CA 91355 661-255-4100 255-4170
Web: www.sixflags.com

Six Flags New England 1623 Main St .... Agawam MA 01001 413-786-9300 821-2402*
**Fax:* Mktg ■ *TF:* 800-370-7488 ■ *Web:* www.sixflags.com

Six Flags Over Georgia 275 Riverside PkwySW .... Austell GA 30168 770-948-9290
Web: www.sixflags.com

Six Flags Over Texas 2201 Rd to Six Flags .... Arlington TX 76011 817-640-8900 607-6148
Web: www.sixflags.com/parks/overtexas

Six Flags Saint Louis
4900 Six Flags Rd PO Box 60 .... Eureka MO 63025 636-938-5300
Web: www.sixflags.com/parks/stlouis

Six Flags White Water Park
250 Cobb Pkwy N Ste 100 .... Marietta GA 30062 770-948-9290 587-2753*
**Fax Area Code:* 636 ■ *Web:* www.sixflags.com

Six Flags Wild Safari One Six Flags Blvd .... Jackson NJ 08527 732-928-1821 928-2775
TF: 800-772-2287 ■ *Web:* www.sixflags.com/parks/wildsafari

Splashtown Water Park 21300 IH-45 N .... Spring TX 77373 281-355-3300 353-7946
Web: www.wetnwildsplashtown.com/

Splish Splash 2549 Splish Splash Dr .... Calverton NY 11901 631-727-3600
Web: www.splishsplash.com

Universal Orlando 6000 Universal Blvd .... Orlando FL 32819 407-363-8000 363-8006
TF: 877-801-9720 ■ *Web:* universalorlando.com

Universal Studios Hollywood
100 Universal City Plaza .... Universal City CA 91608 800-864-8377
TF: 800-864-8377 ■ *Web:* www.universalstudioshollywood.com

Universal's Islands of Adventure
6000 Universal Studios Plz .... Orlando FL 32819 407-363-8000 224-6942
TF: 877-801-9720 ■ *Web:* universalorlando.com

Valleyfair One Valleyfair Dr .... Shakopee MN 55379 952-445-7600 445-1539
Web: www.valleyfair.com

Village Vacances Valcartier
1860 Valcartier Blvd .... Valcartier QC G0A4S0 418-844-2200 844-1239
TF: 888-384-5524 ■ *Web:* www.valcartier.com

Water Country USA
176 Water Country Pkwy .... Williamsburg VA 23185 800-343-7946 253-3216*
**Fax Area Code:* 757 ■ *TF:* 800-343-7946 ■ *Web:* www.watercountryusa.com

Waterworld California 1950 Waterworld Pkwy .... Concord CA 94520 925-609-1364 609-1360
Web: www.waterworldcalifornia.com

Western Playland Amusement Park
1249 Futurity Dr .... Sunland Park NM 88063 575-589-3410 589-0877
Web: www.westernplayland.com

Wet 'n Wild Emerald Pointe
3910 S Holden Rd .... Greensboro NC 27406 336-852-9721 852-2391
TF: 800-555-5900 ■ *Web:* www.emeraldpointe.com

Wet 'n Wild Orlando 6200 International Dr .... Orlando FL 32819 407-351-1800 363-1147
TF General: 800-992-9453 ■ *Web:* www.wetnwild.com

White Water Bay 3908 W Reno Ave .... Oklahoma City OK 73107 405-943-9687
Web: www.whitewaterbay.com

Wild Waves/Enchanted Village
36201 Enchanted Pkwy S .... Federal Way WA 98003 253-661-8000
Web: wildwaves.com

Wonderland Amusement Park 2601 Dumas Dr .... Amarillo TX 79107 806-383-0832 383-8737
TF: 800-383-4712 ■ *Web:* www.wonderlandpark.com

Worlds of Fun & Oceans of Fun
4545 NE Worlds of Fun Dr .... Kansas City MO 64161 816-454-4545 454-4655
Web: www.worldsoffun.com

33 ANIMATION COMPANIES

SEE ALSO Motion Picture Production - Special Interest p. 2768; Motion Picture & Television Production p. 2768

Phone | Fax

Advanced Animations PO Box 34 .... Stockbridge VT 05772 802-746-8974 746-8971
Web: www.advancedanimations.com

Atomic Cartoons Inc 112 W Sixth Sve .... Vancouver BC V5Y1K6 604-734-2866
Web: www.atomiccartoons.com

Bix Pix Entertainment Inc
11630 Tuxford St .... Sun Valley CA 91352 818-252-7474 252-7410
Web: www.bixpix.com

Blue Sky Studios Inc One American Ln .... Greenwich CT 06831 203-992-6000 992-6001
Web: www.blueskystudios.com

Blur Studio 3960 Ince Blvd .... Culver City CA 90232 424-298-4800 298-4801
Web: www.blur.com

Brilliant Digital Entertainment Inc
14011 Ventura Blvd Ste 501 .... Sherman Oaks CA 91423 818-386-2179
Web: www.globalfileregistry.com

DUCK 2205 Stoner Ave .... Los Angeles CA 90064 310-478-0771 478-0773
Web: www.duckstudios.com

Film Roman Inc 2950 N Hollywood Way Third Fl .... Burbank CA 91505 818-748-4000
Web: www.filmroman.com

Hash Inc 10411 NE 110th Cir .... Vancouver WA 98662 360-750-0042 750-0451
Web: www.hash.com

Jim Henson's Creature Shop
1416 N LaBrea Ave .... Hollywood CA 90028 323-802-1557 802-1891
Web: www.creatureshop.com

Klasky Csupo Inc 1238 N Highland Ave .... Los Angeles CA 90038 323-468-2600 468-3021
Web: www.klaskycsupo.com

Laika 1400 NW 22nd Ave .... Portland OR 97210 503-225-1130 226-3746
Web: www.laika.com

NestFamily 1461 S Beltline Rd Ste 500 .... Coppell TX 75019 972-402-7100 629-7181
TF: 800-596-7386 ■ *Web:* www.nestlearning.com

Pixar Animation Studios 1200 Pk Ave .... Emeryville CA 94608 510-922-3000 752-3151
Web: www.pixar.com

Rhythm & Hues Inc 2100 E Grand Ave .... El Segundo CA 90245 310-448-7500 448-7600
Web: www.rhythm.com

Phone | Fax

Sony Pictures Animation
9050 W Washington Blvd .... Culver City CA 90232 310-840-8000
Web: sonypicturesanimation.com

Topix 35 McCaul St Ste 200 .... Toronto ON M5T1V7 416-971-7711 971-9277
Web: www.topix.com

34 APPAREL FINDINGS

Phone | Fax

Blind Center, The 1001 N Bruce St .... Las Vegas NV 89101 702-642-6000
Web: www.blindcenter.org

Cushman & Marden Inc
56 Pulaski St PO Box 3001 .... Peabody MA 01960 978-532-1670 532-1670
Web: www.cushmanandmarden.com

Dallas Bias Fabrics Inc 1401 N Carroll Ave .... Dallas TX 75204 214-824-2036 824-2036
Web: www.dallasbias.com

Metric Products Inc 4630 Leahy St .... Culver City CA 90232 310-815-9000
Web: www.metric-products.com

Modern Quilters Inc
62038 Minnesota Hwy 24 PO Box 66 .... Litchfield MN 55355 320-693-7987 693-2288
Web: modernquilters.com

QST Industries Inc 550 W Adams St Ste 200 .... Chicago IL 60661 312-930-9400 648-0312
Web: www.qst.com

TeamWorld Inc 498 Conklin Ave .... Binghamton NY 13903 607-770-1005
Web: www.teamworld.com

35 APPLIANCE & HOME ELECTRONICS STORES

SEE ALSO Computer Stores p. 2051; Department Stores p. 2197; Furniture Stores p. 2348; Home Improvement Centers p. 2475

Phone | Fax

A & A Mechanical Inc 1111 Ulrich Ave .... Louisville KY 40219 502-968-0164
Web: aamechanical.com

Aaca Parts & Supplies
1502 S Interstate 35 E Ste 244 .... Lancaster TX 75146 972-223-8484
Web: www.aacapartsandsupplies.com

ABC Appliance Inc 1 Silverdome Industrial Pk .... Pontiac MI 48343 248-335-4222 335-2568*
**Fax:* Hum Res ■ *TF:* 800-981-3866 ■ *Web:* www.abcwarehouse.com

Acs of Texas 16622 Sperry Gardens Dr .... Houston TX 77095 832-593-9990
Web: www.acsoftexas.com

Air Cleaning Technologies Inc
1300 W Detroit .... Broken Arrow OK 74012 918-251-8000
Web: www.aircleaningtech.com

Air Systems of Sacramento Inc
3850 Happy Ln .... Sacramento CA 95827 916-368-0336
Web: www.airsystems1.com

American TV & Appliance of Madison Inc
2404 W Beltline Hwy .... Madison WI 53713 608-271-1000 275-7439
Web: www.americantv.com

Arthur F Schultz Co 939 W 26th St .... Erie PA 16508 814-454-8171 454-3052
Web: www.arthurfschultz.com

Audio Direct 2004 E Irvington Rd Ste 264 .... Tucson AZ 85714 888-628-3467
TF Cust Svc: 888-628-3467 ■ *Web:* www.audio-direct.com

Best Buy Company Inc 7601 Penn Ave S .... Minneapolis MN 55423 612-291-1000 292-2323*
NYSE: BBY ■ **Fax:* Cust Svc ■ *TF:* 888-237-8289 ■ *Web:* www.bestbuy.com

Blencowe Group Inc, The 915 Lady St Ste 444 .... Columbia SC 29201 803-779-5866
Web: blencowe.com

Blume Mechanical LLC 11300 43rd St N .... Clearwater FL 33762 727-544-5993
Web: www.blume-mechanical.com

BrandsMart USA Corp 3200 SW 42nd St .... Fort Lauderdale FL 33312 800-432-8579 797-4061*
**Fax Area Code:* 954 ■ *TF:* 800-432-8579 ■ *Web:* www.brandsmartusa.com

Carey Sales & Services Inc
3141-47 Frederick Ave .... Baltimore MD 21229 410-945-7878
Web: www.careysales.com

Clay Dunn Enterprises Inc 1606 E Carson St .... Carson CA 90745 310-549-1698
Web: www.airtecperforms.com

Coilmaster Corp 440 Industrial Dr .... Moscow TN 38057 901-877-3333
Web: coilmastercorp.com

Conn's Inc 3295 College St .... Beaumont TX 77701 409-832-1696 832-4344
NASDAQ: CONN ■ *TF Cust Svc:* 800-511-5750 ■ *Web:* www.conns.com

EarthLinked Technologies Inc
4151 S Pipkin Rd .... Lakeland FL 33811 863-701-0096
Web: earthlinked.com

East Coast Appliance Sales, Service & Parts Inc
2053 Laskin Rd .... Virginia Beach VA 23454 757-425-2883
Web: www.eastcoastappliance.com

Eklund's Appliance & TV Co
1007 Central Ave W .... Great Falls MT 59404 406-761-3430 453-6942
Web: www.eklundsappliance.com

Farley Appliance 814 W Main St .... League City TX 77573 281-332-8000
Web: farleyappliance.com

Fry's Electronics 600 E Brokaw Rd .... San Jose CA 95112 408-350-1484 487-4700*
**Fax:* PR ■ *Web:* www.frys.com

GeoMicro Inc 3200 El Camino Real Ste 140 .... Irvine CA 92602 714-505-8868
Web: www.geomicro.com

GNP Audio Video Inc
122-A Foothill Blvd Ste 326 .... Arcadia CA 91006 626-577-7767 584-6994
Web: www.gnpaudiovideo.com

Gregg Appliances Inc 4151 E 96th St .... Indianapolis IN 46240 317-848-8710 848-8723
NYSE: HGG ■ *TF:* 800-284-7344 ■ *Web:* www.hhgregg.com

Guardian Technologies LLC
7700 Saint Clair Ave .... Mentor OH 44060 440-942-6995
Web: www.guardiantechnologies.com

Harco Company Ltd 5915 Coopers Ave .... Mississauga ON L4Z1R9 905-890-1220
Web: www.harcoco.com

Howard's Appliance & Big Screen Superstores
901 E Imperial Hwy .... La Habra CA 90631 714-871-2700 871-5840
Web: www.howards.com

Phone Fax

Interbond Corp of America
3200 SW 42nd St Fort Lauderdale FL 33312 800-432-8579 797-4061*
*Fax Area Code: 954 ■ *Fax: Hum Res ■ TF: 800-432-8579 ■ Web: www.brandsmartusa.com
JCM Associates Inc
301C Prince Georges Blvd Upper Marlboro MD 20774 301-390-5500
Web: www.gojcm.com
Midland Radio Corp 5900 Parretta Dr Kansas City MO 64120 816-241-8500 241-5713
Web: midlandusa.com
Mintie Corp 14264 Doolittle Dr San Leandro CA 94577 510-351-5868
Web: www.mintie.com
National Auto Sound Inc 11001 E Hwy 40 Independence MO 64055 816-356-8700 356-7230
Web: www.nationalautosound.com
Niederauer Inc 1976 W San Carlos St San Jose CA 95128 408-297-2440 286-9436
Web: westernappliance.com
PC Richard & Son Inc 150 Price Pkwy Farmingdale NY 11735 631-843-4300
TF: 800-696-2000 ■ Web: www.pcrichard.com
Pieratt's 110 Mt Tabor Rd Lexington KY 40517 859-268-6000 268-9065
TF: 855-743-7288 ■ Web: www.pieratts.com
Queen City TV & Appliance Company Inc
2430 Queen City Dr Charlotte NC 28208 704-391-6000 391-6038
TF All: 800-365-6665 ■ Web: www.queencityonline.com
QuestSoft Corp 23441 S Pointe Dr Ste 270 Laguna Hills CA 92653 949-837-9506
Web: www.questsoft.com
RadioShack Corp 300 RadioShack Cir Fort Worth TX 76102 800-442-7221 415-2303*
NYSE: RSH ■ *Fax Area Code: 817 ■ TF: 800-843-7422 ■ Web: www.radioshack.com
Radon Control Systems Inc 160 US Route 1 Freeport ME 04032 207-865-9200
Web: awqinc.com
Sherman Mechanical Inc 1075 Alexander Ct Cary IL 60013 847-458-0200
Web: www.shermanmech.com
Simutek Inc 3136 E Ft Lowell Rd Tucson AZ 85716 520-321-9077 321-9078
Web: www.simutek.com
Sparkle Solutions LP
2700 Steeles Ave W Unit 4 Concord ON L4K3C8 905-660-2282
Web: www.sparklesolutions.ca
Starsound Audio Inc 2679 Oddie Blvd Reno NV 89512 775-331-1010 331-1030
Web: www.starsound.com
Synaptec Software Inc
4155 E Jewell Ave Ste 600 Denver CO 80222 303-320-4420
Web: www.lawbase.com
Valu Home Centers Inc 45 S Rossler Ave Buffalo NY 14206 716-825-7377
Web: valuhomecenters.com
Videoland Inc 6808 Hornwood Dr Houston TX 77074 800-877-2900 772-0500*
*Fax Area Code: 713 ■ TF: 800-877-2900 ■ Web: www.hometheaterstore.com
Wireless Zone 34 Industrial Pk Pl Middletown CT 06457 860-632-9494 652-0520*
*Fax Area Code: 989 ■ TF: 888-881-2622 ■ Web: www.wirelesszone.com
Yale Appliance 296 Freeport St Dorchester MA 02122 617-825-9253 825-6541
TF: 800-565-6435 ■ Web: www.yaleappliance.com

36 APPLIANCES - MAJOR - MFR

SEE ALSO Air Conditioning & Heating Equipment - Residential p. 1728

Phone Fax

Anaheim Mfg Co 2680 Orbiter St PO Box 4146 Brea CA 92821 310-542-5259 996-7073*
*Fax Area Code: 714 ■ TF Cust Svc: 800-854-3229 ■ Web: www.anaheimmfg.com
AO Smith Corp
11270 W Pk Pl Ste 170 PO Box 245008 Milwaukee WI 53224 414-359-4000 359-4180
NYSE: AOS ■ TF: 800-359-4065 ■ Web: www.aosmith.com
AO Smith Water Products Co
500 Tennessee Waltz Pkwy Ashland City TN 37015 800-527-1953 792-2163*
*Fax Area Code: 615 ■ TF: 800-527-1953 ■ Web: www.hotwater.com
ASKO Appliances Inc PO Box 44848 Madison WI 53744 800-898-1879 260-0631
TF: 800-898-1879 ■ Web: askona.com/
Atlanta Attachment Co Inc
362 Industrial Pk Dr Lawrenceville GA 30045 770-963-7369 963-7641
TF: 877-206-5116 ■ Web: www.atlatt.com
Bock Water Heaters Inc 110 S Dickinson St Madison WI 53703 608-257-2225
Web: www.bockwaterheaters.com
Bradford White Corp 725 Talamore Dr Ambler PA 19002 215-641-9400 641-1612
TF: 800-523-2931 ■ Web: www.bradfordwhite.com
Brown Stove Works Inc 1422 Carolina Ave Cleveland TN 37320 423-476-6544 476-6599
TF All: 800-251-7485 ■ Web: www.brownstoveworksinc.com
Cemline Corp PO Box 55 Cheswick PA 15024 724-274-5430 274-5448
TF: 800-245-6268 ■ Web: www.cemline.com
Char-Broil 1442 Belfast Ave Columbus GA 31902 706-571-7000 576-6355*
*Fax: Cust Svc ■ TF Cust Svc: 866-239-6777 ■ Web: www.charbroil.com
CookTek LLC 156 N Jefferson St Ste 300 Chicago IL 60661 312-563-9600 432-6220
TF: 888-266-5835 ■ Web: www.cooktek.com
Dwyer Products Corp 1226 Michael Dr Ste F Wood Dale IL 60191 630-741-7900 741-7974
TF: 800-822-0092 ■ Web: www.dwyerproducts.com
Ecosmart US LLC 3315 NW 167th St Miami Gardens FL 33056 305-623-7900
Web: www.ecosmartus.com
Electric Heater Co 45 Seymour St Stratford CT 06615 203-378-2659 378-3593
TF: 800-647-3165 ■ Web: www.hubbellheaters.com
Electrolux 20445 Emerald Pkwy Ste 250 Cleveland OH 44135 216-898-1800
Web: electrolux.com
Electrolux Appliances PO Box 212237 Augusta GA 30907 877-435-3287 228-6615*
*Fax Area Code: 706 ■ TF: 877-435-3287 ■ Web: www.electroluxappliances.com
Fisher & Paykel Appliances Inc
5900 Skylab Rd Huntington Beach CA 92647 888-936-7872 547-1971*
*Fax Area Code: 800 ■ TF: 888-936-7872 ■ Web: www.fisherpaykel.com
In-Sink-Erator 4700 21st St Racine WI 53406 262-554-5432
TF: 800-558-5712 ■ Web: www.insinkerator.com
LG Electronics USA Inc
1000 Sylvan Ave Englewood Cliffs NJ 07632 201-816-2000
TF Tech Supp: 800-180-9999 ■ Web: www.lg.com
Lochinvar Corp 300 Maddox Simpson Pkwy Lebanon TN 37090 615-889-8900 547-1000
TF: 800-722-2101 ■ Web: www.lochinvar.com
Maytag Appliances 403 W Fourth St N Newton IA 50208 800-344-1274
TF Cust Svc: 800-344-1274 ■ Web: www.maytag.com
Miele Inc 9 Independence Way Princeton NJ 08540 609-419-9898 419-4298
TF: 800-843-7231 ■ Web: www.miele.com

Phone Fax

Multi-Pak Corp 180 Atlantic St Hackensack NJ 07601 201-342-7474 342-6525
Web: www.multipakcorp.com
Northland Corp 1260 E Van Deinse St Greenville MI 48838 800-223-3900 754-0970*
*Fax Area Code: 616 ■ TF: 800-223-3900 ■ Web: www.northlandnka.com
Peerless Premier Appliance Co
119 S 14th St Belleville IL 62222 941-763-3915 235-1771*
*Fax Area Code: 618 ■ TF: 800-858-5844 ■ Web: www.premierrange.com
Roper Corp 1507 Broomtown Rd La Fayette GA 30728 706-638-5100
Web: roperappliances.com
Sanyo Fisher Co 21605 Plummer St Chatsworth CA 91311 818-998-7322
Web: us.sanyo.com
Sharp Electronics Corp One Sharp Plz Mahwah NJ 07430 201-529-8200 529-8413
TF: 800-237-4277 ■ Web: www.sharpusa.com
Vaughn Manufacturing Corp
26 Old Elm St PO Box 5431 Salisbury MA 01952 978-462-6683 462-6497
TF: 800-282-8446 ■ Web: www.vaughncorp.com
Weber-Stephen Products Co 200 E Daniels Rd Palatine IL 60067 800-446-1071 934-3153*
*Fax Area Code: 847 ■ TF Cust Svc: 800-446-1071 ■ Web: www.weber.com
Whirlpool Corp 2000 N M-63 Benton Harbor MI 49022 269-923-5000
NYSE: WHR ■ TF: 800-253-1301 ■ Web: www.whirlpoolcorp.com
Whirlpool Corp North American Region
2000 N M-63 Benton Harbor MI 49022 269-923-5000 923-3525*
*Fax: Hum Res ■ TF: 800-253-1301 ■ Web: www.whirlpoolcorp.com
Wisco Industries Inc 736 Janesville St Oregon WI 53575 608-835-3106 835-7399
TF: 800-999-4726 ■ Web: www.wiscoind.com

37 APPLIANCES - SMALL - MFR

SEE ALSO Air Purification Equipment - Household p. 1729; Vacuum Cleaners - Household p. 3273

Phone Fax

Abatement Technologies
605 Satellite Blvd Ste 300 Suwanee GA 30024 678-889-4200 358-2394*
*Fax Area Code: 800 ■ TF: 800-634-9091 ■ Web: www.abatement.com
Adams Mfg Company Inc 9790 Midwest Ave Cleveland OH 44125 216-587-6801 587-6807
Web: www.adamsmanufacturing.com
Aisin Holdings of America Inc
1665 E Fourth St Seymour IN 47274 812-524-8144 524-8146
Web: www.aisinworld.com
Andis Co 1800 County Rd H Sturtevant WI 53177 262-884-2600 884-1100
TF: 800-558-9441 ■ Web: www.andis.com
Bernina of America Inc 3702 Prairie Lake Ct Aurora IL 60504 630-978-2500 978-8214
Web: www.bernina.com
Broan-NuTone LLC 926 W State St PO Box 140 Hartford WI 53027 262-673-4340 673-8709
TF Cust Svc: 800-558-1711 ■ Web: www.broan.com
Bunn-O-Matic Corp 1400 Stevenson Dr Springfield IL 62703 217-529-6601
TF: 800-637-8606 ■ Web: www.bunn.com
Cadet Mfg Company Inc
2500 W Fourth Plain Blvd Vancouver WA 98660 360-693-2505 694-6939
TF: 800-442-2338 ■ Web: cadetheat.com
Casablanca Fan Co 761 Corporate Ctr Dr Pomona CA 91768 909-689-1477 629-0958
TF: 888-227-2178 ■ Web: www.casablancafanco.com
City of Chula Vista 276 Fourth Ave Chula Vista CA 91910 619-691-5047
TF: 877-478-5478 ■ Web: chulavistaca.gov
Conair Corp One Cummings Pt Rd Stamford CT 06902 203-351-9000 351-9180
OTC: CNGA ■ TF: 800-326-6247 ■ Web: www.conair.com
Craftmade International Inc 650 S Royal Ln Coppell TX 75019 972-393-3800 304-1728
OTC: CRFT ■ TF: 800-486-4892 ■ Web: www.craftmade.com
Cuisinart 1 Cummings Pt Rd Stamford CT 06902 203-975-4609 975-4660
TF: 800-726-0190 ■ Web: www.cuisinart.com
El Electronics LLC 1800 Shames Dr Westbury NY 11590 516-334-0870 338-4741
TF: 877-346-3837 ■ Web: www.electroind.com
Electro Industries Inc 2150 W River St Monticello MN 55362 763-295-4138
Web: www.electromn.com
Electrolux 20445 Emerald Pkwy Ste 250 Cleveland OH 44135 216-898-1800
Web: electrolux.com
Fan-Tastic Vent Corp 2083 S Almont Ave Imlay City MI 48444 810-724-3818 724-3460
TF: 800-521-0298 ■ Web: www.fantasticvent.com
Hamilton Beach/Proctor-Silex Inc
4421 Waterfront Dr Glen Allen VA 23060 804-273-9777 527-7142
TF Cust Svc: 800-851-8900 ■ Web: www.hamiltonbeach.com
Hotronic USA Inc 25 Omega Dr Williston VT 05495 802-862-7403 863-6519
Web: www.hotronic.com
Hunter Fan Co
7130 Goodlett Farms Pkwy Ste 400 Memphis TN 38016 901-743-1360
TF: 888-830-1326 ■ Web: www.hunterfan.com
Jarden Consumer Solutions
2381 Executive Ctr Dr Boca Raton FL 33431 561-912-4100
TF: 800-777-5452 ■ Web: www.jardencs.com
Kaz Home Environment 250 Tpke Rd Southborough MA 01772 508-490-7000
Web: www.kaz.com
KAZ Inc 250 Tpke Rd Southborough MA 01772 800-477-0457
TF: 800-477-0457 ■ Web: www.kaz.com
King Electrical Manufacturing Co
9131 Tenth Ave S Seattle WA 98108 206-762-0400 763-7738
TF: 800-603-5464 ■ Web: www.king-electric.com
Lasko Metal Products Inc
820 Lincoln Ave West Chester PA 19380 610-692-7400 696-4648
TF: 800-233-0268 ■ Web: www.laskoproducts.com
LG Electronics USA Inc
1000 Sylvan Ave Englewood Cliffs NJ 07632 201-816-2000
TF Tech Supp: 800-180-9999 ■ Web: www.lg.com
Lifetime Brands Inc Farberware Div
1000 Stewart Ave Garden City NY 11530 516-683-6000 555-0101
TF: 800-999-2811 ■ Web: www.lifetimebrands.com
Marley Engineered Products
470 Beauty Spot Rd E Bennettsville SC 29512 843-479-4006 479-8912
TF: 800-452-4179 ■ Web: www.marleymep.com
National Presto Industries Inc
3925 N Hastings Way Eau Claire WI 54703 715-839-2121 839-2148
NYSE: NPK ■ TF: 800-877-0441 ■ Web: www.gopresto.com

Phone Fax

Nesco/American Harvest
1700 Monroe St PO Box 237 ...... Two Rivers WI 54241 920-793-1368 793-1086
TF Cust Svc: 800-288-4545 ■ *Web:* www.nesco.com

Schawbel Corp 26 Crosby Dr ...... Bedford MA 01730 781-541-6900
TF: 866-753-3837 ■ *Web:* www.schawbelcorporation.com

Sharp Electronics Corp One Sharp Plz ...... Mahwah NJ 07430 201-529-8200 529-8413
TF: 800-237-4277 ■ *Web:* www.sharpusa.com

Singer Sewing Co
1224 Hill Quaker Blvd PO Box 7017 ...... La Vergne TN 37086 615-213-0880 213-0994
TF: 877-738-9869 ■ *Web:* www.singerco.com

Vita-Mix Corp 8615 Usher Rd ...... Cleveland OH 44138 440-235-4840 235-3726
TF: 800-848-2649 ■ *Web:* www.vitamix.com

West Bend Housewares LLC
2845 Wingate St PO Box 2780 ...... West Bend WI 53095 866-290-1851 513-2498*
**Fax Area Code:* 224 ■ *TF:* 866-290-1851 ■ *Web:* www.westbend.com

Whirlpool Corp KitchenAid Div
553 Benson Rd ...... Benton Harbor MI 49022 800-422-1230
TF: 800-422-1230 ■ *Web:* www.kitchenaid.com

World Dryer Corp 5700 McDermott Dr ...... Berkeley IL 60163 708-449-6950 449-6958
TF: 800-323-0701 ■ *Web:* www.worlddryer.com

38 APPLIANCES - WHOL

Phone Fax

All Inc 185 Plato Blvd W ...... Saint Paul MN 55107 651-227-6331 292-0541
TF: 800-829-2127 ■ *Web:* www.allinc.com

Almo Corp 2709 Commerce Way ...... Philadelphia PA 19154 215-698-4000 698-4080*
**Fax:* Hum Res ■ *TF:* 800-345-2566 ■ *Web:* www.almo.com

Aves Audio Visual Systems Inc PO Box 500 ...... Sugar Land TX 77487 281-295-1300 295-1310
TF: 800-365-2837 ■ *Web:* www.avesav.com

Better Bathrooms Ltd 822 Henderson Ave ...... Coquitlam BC V3K1P2 604-939-4322
Web: www.better-bathrooms.ca

Blodgett Supply Co Inc 100 Ave D PO Box 759 ...... Williston VT 05495 802-864-9831 229-5105
TF: 888-888-3424 ■ *Web:* www.blodgettsupply.com

Brady Marketing Co
1331N California Blvd Ste 320 ...... Walnut Creek CA 94596 925-676-1300 676-3082
TF: 800-326-6080 ■ *Web:* www.bradymarketing.com

Brooke Distributors Inc 16250 NW 52nd Ave ...... Hialeah FL 33014 305-624-9752 620-3988
TF: 800-275-8792 ■ *Web:* www.brooke.com

Bursma Electronic Distributing Inc
2851 Buchanan Ave SW ...... Grand Rapids MI 49548 616-831-0080 831-9400
TF: 800-777-2604 ■ *Web:* www.bursma.com

C & L Supply Co PO Box 578 ...... Vinita OK 74301 918-256-6411 256-3836
TF: 800-256-6411 ■ *Web:* www.clsupplyinc.com

Carl Schaedel & Company Inc Four Sperry Rd ...... Fairfield NJ 07004 973-244-1311 244-0822
Web: www.carlschaedel.com

Ceavco Audio-visual Co 6240 W 54th Ave ...... Arvada CO 80002 303-539-3400 539-3401
Web: www.ceavco.com

Cowboy Maloney's Electric City
1313 Harding St ...... Jackson MS 39202 601-948-5600
Web: cowboy-maloney.com

Cunningham Distributing Inc 2015 Mills Ave ...... El Paso TX 79901 915-533-6993 545-1320

DAS Inc 724 Lawn Rd ...... Palmyra PA 17078 717-964-3642 437-3659*
**Fax Area Code:* 800 ■ *TF:* 866-622-7979 ■ *Web:* www.das-roadpro.com

E&S International Enterprises Inc
7801 Hayvenhurst Ave ...... Van Nuys CA 91406 818-887-0700
Web: www.esintl.com

Eagle Distributors LLC 2439 Albany St ...... Kenner LA 70062 504-464-5991
Web: www.eagledistributors.com

Electrical Distributing Inc
4600 NW St Helens Rd ...... Portland OR 97210 503-226-4044 226-4040
TF: 800-877-4229 ■ *Web:* www.edinw.com

Erb Company Inc 1400 Seneca St ...... Buffalo NY 14210 716-825-1400
Web: erbco.com

Factory Direct Appliance Inc
14105 Marshall Dr ...... Lenexa KS 66215 913-888-8028 888-7570
Web: www.kcfda.com

Felix Storch Inc 770 Garrison Ave ...... Bronx NY 10474 718-893-3900
Web: www.summitappliance.com

Gamla Enterprises North America Inc
875 Ave of The Americas Ste 205 ...... New York NY 10001 212-947-3790 947-3559
TF: 800-442-6526 ■ *Web:* www.gamlaphoto.com

Gerhard's Appliances 290 N Keswick Ave ...... Glenside PA 19038 215-884-8650 884-0349
Web: www.gerhardsappliance.com

Gotham Sales Co 302 Main St ...... Millburn NJ 07041 973-912-8412 912-0814
TF: 800-292-7726 ■ *Web:* www.gothamsales.com

H Schultz & Sons Inc 777 Lehigh Ave ...... Union NJ 07083 908-687-5400 687-1788
Web: www.housewaresandthings.com

Hall Electric Supply Company Inc
263 Main St ...... Stoneham MA 02180 781-438-3800 438-3833
TF: 800-444-3726 ■ *Web:* www.hescoapplianceparts.com

HB Communications Inc 60 Dodge Ave ...... North Haven CT 06473 203-234-9246 234-2013
TF: 800-243-4414 ■ *Web:* www.hbcommunications.com

Helen of Troy Ltd One Helen of Troy Plz ...... El Paso TX 79912 915-225-8000 225-8004
NASDAQ: HELE ■ *Web:* www.hotus.com

Home Entertainment Distribution Inc
120 Shawmut Rd ...... Canton MA 02021 781-821-0087 200-3764*
**Fax Area Code:* 866 ■ *TF:* 800-343-9619 ■ *Web:* www.insurersworld.com

John m Hartel & Company Inc
10 Jefferson Ave ...... Pearl River NY 10965 845-735-3666
Web: jmhartel.com

Klaus Cos 8400 N Allen Rd ...... Peoria IL 61615 309-691-4840
Web: www.klausco.com

M.d.m. Commercial Enterprises Inc
1102 A1a N Ste 205 ...... Ponte Vedra FL 32082 800-359-6741 241-3133*
**Fax Area Code:* 904 ■ *TF:* 800-359-6741 ■ *Web:* www.mdmcommercial.com

Midwest Sales & Service Inc
917 S Chapin St ...... South Bend IN 46601 574-287-3365
TF: 800-772-7262 ■ *Web:* midwestsales.org

Molok North America Ltd 179 Norpark Ave ...... Mount Forest ON N0G2L0 519-323-9909
Web: molokna.com

Phone Fax

Nelson & Small Inc 212 Canco Rd ...... Portland ME 04103 207-775-5666 775-4303
TF: 800-341-0780 ■ *Web:* www.nelsonsmall.com

Next Plumbing Supply
1839 Old Okeechobee Rd ...... West Palm Beach FL 33409 561-689-9060
Web: nextps.com

O'Rourke Sales Co 3885 Elmore Ave Ste 100 ...... Davenport IA 52807 563-823-1501 823-1534
Web: www.orourkesales.com

Oregon Scientific Inc 19861 SW 95th Pl ...... Tualatin OR 97062 503-783-5100 691-6208
Web: global.oregonscientific.com

Peirce-Phelps Inc 2000 N 59th St ...... Philadelphia PA 19131 215-879-7000 879-5141
TF: 800-222-2742 ■ *Web:* www.peirce.com

Potter Distributing Inc
4037 Roger B Chaffee Blvd ...... Grand Rapids MI 49548 616-531-6860 531-9578
TF: 800-748-0568 ■ *Web:* www.potterdistributing.com

Power Plus Sound & Lighting Inc 2460 Grand Ave ...... Vista CA 92081 760-727-1717
Web: www.powerpluscorp.com

Precision Trading Corp
15800 NW 48th Ave ...... Miami Gardens FL 33014 305-592-4500 593-6169
Web: www.precisiontrading.com

Prudential Builders Ctr 3304 E Ferry ...... Spokane WA 99202 509-535-2401
Web: mystore411.com

R & B Wholesale Distributors Inc
2350 S Milliken Ave ...... Ontario CA 91761 909-230-5400 230-5405
Web: www.rbdist.com

Radio Distributing Company Inc
27015 Trolley Industrial Dr ...... Taylor MI 48180 313-295-4500 295-3710
TF: 800-462-1544 ■ *Web:* www.radiodistributing.com

Roth Distributing Co 11300 W 47th St ...... Minnetonka MN 55343 952-933-4428
TF: 800 363 3818 ■ *Web:* www.rothliving.com

Servall Co 6761 E Ten Mile Rd ...... Center Line MI 48015 586-754-9985 754-2260
TF: 800-856-9874 ■ *Web:* 1stsourceservall.com

Siano Appliance Distributors Inc
5372 Pleasant View Rd ...... Memphis TN 38134 901-382-5833 372-3621
TF: 800-742-6699 ■ *Web:* www.sianoappliance.com

Speco Technologies 200 New Hwy ...... Amityville NY 11701 631-957-8700 957-9142
TF: 800-645-5516 ■ *Web:* www.specotech.com

Tacony Corp 1760 Gilsinn Ln ...... Fenton MO 63026 636-349-3000 349-2333
Web: www.tacony.com

Telerent Leasing Corp 4191 Fayetteville Rd ...... Raleigh NC 27603 919-772-8604
TF: 800-626-0682 ■ *Web:* www.telerent.com

Tri-State Video Services Inc
1379 Pittsburgh Rd ...... Valencia PA 16059 724-898-1630 898-2330
TF: 888-382-7768 ■ *Web:* www.tristatevideo.com

WASH Multifamily Laundry Systems
100 N Sepulveda Blvd 12th Fl ...... El Segundo CA 90245 800-421-6897
TF General: 800-421-6897 ■ *Web:* www.washlaundry.com

Westland Sales PO Box 427 ...... Clackamas OR 97015 503-655-2563 656-8829
TF: 800-356-0766 ■ *Web:* www.splendide.com

Whirlpool Canada 200-6750 Century Ave ...... Mississauga ON L5N0B7 905-821-6400 821-7871
TF: 800-807-6777

Williams Kitchen & Bath 658 Richmond NW ...... Grand Rapids MI 49504 616-771-0505 882-0983*
**Fax Area Code:* 517 ■ *TF:* 800-968-3718 ■ *Web:* www.williamskitchen.com

Woodson & Bozeman Inc 3870 New Getwell Rd ...... Memphis TN 38118 901-362-1500 362-1509
TF: 800-876-4243 ■ *Web:* www.woodsonbozeman.com

39 APPLICATION SERVICE PROVIDERS (ASPS)

Application Service Providers rent, deliver, license, manage, and/or host proprietary and/or third-party business software ("applications") and/or computer services to multiple users (customers). Included here are companies that host software applications as well as companies that provide the equipment necessary to do so.

Phone Fax

Access Data Corp 2 Chatham Ctr 2nd Fl ...... Pittsburgh PA 15219 412-201-6000 201-6060
Web: access-data.broadridge.com

AllMeds Inc 151 Lafayette Dr Ste 401 ...... Oak Ridge TN 37830 865-482-1999 481-0921
TF: 888-343-6337 ■ *Web:* www.allmeds.com

Amber Road Inc One Meadowlands Plz ...... East Rutherford NJ 07073 201-935-8588 935-5187
Web: www.amberroad.com

Application Consulting Group
1639 NJ-10 Ste 107 ...... Parsippany NJ 07054 973-898-0012 898-6647
Web: www.acgi.com

Ariba Inc 807 11th Ave ...... Sunnyvale CA 94089 650-390-1000
NASDAQ: ARBA ■ *TF:* 866-772-7422 ■ *Web:* www.ariba.com

Avanade Inc 818 Stewart St ...... Seattle WA 98101 206-239-5600 239-5605
Web: www.avanade.com

Avazpour Networking Services Inc
10895 Grandview Dr Ste 250 ...... Overland Park KS 66210 913-498-8777

Baillio's Inc 5301 Menaul Blvd NE ...... Albuquerque NM 87110 505-883-7511
TF: 800-540-7511 ■ *Web:* baillios.com

BizLand Inc 70 BlanchaRd Rd ...... Burlington MA 01803 800-249-5263 272-2915*
**Fax Area Code:* 781 ■ *TF:* 800-249-5263 ■ *Web:* www.bizland.com

BroadVision Inc
1600 Seaport Blvd Ste 550 ...... Redwood City CA 94063 650-295-0716 364-3425
NASDAQ: BVSN ■ *Web:* www.broadvision.com

Cayenta Canada Corp 4200 N Fraser Way Ste 201 ...... Burnaby BC V5J5K7 604-570-4300 291-0742
TF: 866-229-3682 ■ *Web:* www.cayenta.com

Centric Software Inc
655 Campbell Technology Pkwy Ste 200 ...... Campbell CA 95008 408-574-7802 866-5869
Web: www.centricsoftware.com

Chemical Safety Corp
5901 Christie Ave Ste 502 ...... Emeryville CA 94608 510-594-1000 594-1100
TF: 888-594-1100 ■ *Web:* www.chemicalsafety.com

Cision Inc 12051 Indian Creek Ct ...... Beltsville MD 20705 301-459-2590 459-2827
NASDAQ: VOCS ■ *TF:* 866-639-5087 ■ *Web:* www.vocus.com

CliniComp International 9655 Towne Ctr Dr ...... San Diego CA 92121 858-546-8202 546-1801
TF: 800-350-8202 ■ *Web:* www.clinicomp.com

Cogency Software Inc
500 Airport Blvd Ste 152 ...... Burlingame CA 94010 650-685-2500 685-2515
Web: www.cogencysoftware.com

				Phone	Fax
Computer Programs & Systems Inc (CPSI) 6600 Wall St *NASDAQ: CPSI* ■ *TF:* 800-711-2774 ■ *Web:* www.cpsi.com	Mobile	AL	36695	251-639-8100	639-8214
Connectria Corp 10845 Olive Blvd Ste 300 *TF:* 800-781-7820 ■ *Web:* www.connectria.com	Saint Louis	MO	63141	314-587-7000	587-7090
Crexendo Inc 1615 S 52nd St *OTC: CXDO* ■ *Web:* crexendo.com/	Tempe	AZ	85281	801-431-4695	
Critical Path Inc 2655 Campus Dr Ste 250 *TF:* 800-353-8437 ■ *Web:* owmessaging.com	San Mateo	CA	94403	650-480-7300	356-8501
CyberData Inc 20 Max Ave *Web:* cyberdata.com	Hicksville	NY	11801	516-942-8000	942-0800
Cyveillance Inc 11091 Sunset Hills Rd Ste 210 *TF:* 888-243-0097 ■ *Web:* www.cyveillance.com	Reston	VA	20190	703-351-1000	560-2506
Daptiv 1008 Western Ave Suite 700 *TF:* 888-621-8361 ■ *Web:* www.daptiv.com	Seattle	WA	98101	206-341-9117	341-9123
Digital River Inc 10380 Bren Rd W Ste 150 *NASDAQ: DRIV* ■ **Fax Area Code:* 952 ■ *TF:* 800-598-7450 ■ *Web:* www.digitalriver.com	Minnetonka	MN	55343	800-598-7450	253-8497*
DigitalWork Inc 2345 S Alma School Rd Suite 105 **Fax Area Code:* 480 ■ *TF:* 877-496-7571 ■ *Web:* www.digitalwork.com	Mesa	AZ	85210	877-496-7571	272-6923*
DocMan Technologies 31300 Bainbridge Rd **Fax Area Code:* 440 ■ *TF:* 888-636-2626 ■ *Web:* www.docmantech.com	Cleveland	OH	44122	888-636-2626	542-9668*
E-Builder Inc 1800 NW 69 Ave Ste 201 *TF:* 800-580-9322 ■ *Web:* www.e-builder.net	Plantation	FL	33313	954-556-6701	792-5949
E-Markets Inc 807 Mountain Ave Ste 200 *TF:* 877-674-7419 ■ *Web:* www.e-markets.com	Berthoud	CO	80513	877-674-7419	
eGain Communications Corp 345 E Middlefield Rd *NASDAQ: EGAN* ■ *TF:* 888-603-4246 ■ *Web:* www.egain.com	Mountain View	CA	94043	650-230-7500	230-7600
Electric Mail Company Inc 3999 Henning Dr Ste 300 *TF:* 800-419-7463 ■ *Web:* www.electricmail.com	Burnaby	BC	V5C6P9	604-482-1111	482-1110
Emdeon Business Services LLC 3055 Lebanon Pk *Web:* www.emdeon.com	Nashville	TN	37214	615-932-3000	
ePlus Inc 13595 Dulles Technology Dr *NASDAQ: PLUS* ■ *TF:* 888-482-1122 ■ *Web:* www.eplus.com	Herndon	VA	20171	703-984-8400	984-8600
FinancialCAD Corp 13450 102nd Ave Ste 1750 *TF:* 800-304-0702 ■ *Web:* www.fincad.com	Surrey	BC	V3T5X3	604-957-1200	957-1201
Flying Aces Technology LLC 305 N Westgate Rd Ste 100 *Web:* www.flying-aces.com	Mount Prospect	IL	60056	847-299-7815	
HealthMEDX 5100 N Towne Ctr Dr *TF:* 877-875-1200 ■ *Web:* www.healthmedx.com	Ozark	MO	65721	417-582-1816	582-0296
Horseman's Guarantee Corp of America 25 W Palatine Rd *Web:* www.hgcaonline.com	Palatine	IL	60067	847-394-4210	358-7635
I-Business Network LLC 2617 Sandy Plains Rd Ste B *Web:* www.i-bn.net	Marietta	GA	30066	678-627-0646	627-0688
Infogain Corp 485 Alberto Way *Web:* www.infogain.com	Los Gatos	CA	95032	408-355-6000	355-7000
Intacct Corp 125 S Market St Ste 600 *TF:* 877-437-7765	San Jose	CA	95113	408-878-0900	
Integrity eLearning Inc 751 S Weir Canyon Rd Ste 157451 *Web:* www.ielearning.com	Anaheim Hills	CA	92808	714-637-9480	
Internap Network Services Corp 250 Williams St Ste E-100 *NASDAQ: INAP* ■ *TF:* 877-843-7627 ■ *Web:* www.internap.com	Atlanta	GA	30303	404-302-9700	475-0520
IntraLinks Inc 150 E 42nd St Ste 8 *TF:* 888-546-5383 ■ *Web:* www.intralinks.com	New York	NY	10017	212-543-7700	543-7978
Jamcracker Inc 4677 Old Ironsides Dr Ste 450 *Web:* www.jamcracker.com	Santa Clara	CA	95054	408-496-5500	496-9944
Journyx Inc 7600 Burnet Rd Ste. 300 *TF:* 800-755-9878 ■ *Web:* www.journyx.com	Austin	TX	78757	512-834-8888	834-8858
Kleinschmidt Inc 450 Lake Cook Rd *TF:* 800-824-2330 ■ *Web:* www.kleinschmidt.com	Deerfield	IL	60015	847-945-1000	945-4619
LearningStation Inc 8008 Corporate Ctr Dr Ste 210 *TF:* 888-679-7058 ■ *Web:* www.learningstation.com	Charlotte	NC	28226	888-679-7058	
LivePerson Inc 462 Seventh Ave 3rd Fl *NASDAQ: LPSN* ■ *Web:* www.liveperson.com	New York	NY	10018	212-609-4200	609-4201
MetraTech Corp 200 W St *Web:* www.metratech.com	Waltham	MA	02451	781-839-8300	839-8301
NeoMedia Technologies Inc 1515 Walnut St Ste 100 **Fax Area Code:* 636 ■ *Web:* www.neom.com	Boulder	CO	80302	678-638-0460	648-9922*
NetBase Corp 7960 Donegan Dr Ste 225 *Web:* netbasecorp.net	Manassas	VA	20109	703-396-7909	
onProject Inc PO Box 104 *TF:* 877-936-6776 ■ *Web:* www.onproject.com	Franklin Lakes	NJ	07417	973-971-9970	971-9970
Oracle Corp 500 Oracle Pkwy *NYSE: ORCL* ■ *TF Sales:* 800-392-2999 ■ *Web:* www.oracle.com	Redwood Shores	CA	94065	650-506-7000	506-7200
Outstart Inc 745 Atlantic Ave 4th Fl *TF:* 877-971-9171 ■ *Web:* www.outstart.com	Boston	MA	02111	617-897-6800	897-6801
Paramount Technologies Inc 1374 EW Maple Rd *TF:* 800-725-4408 ■ *Web:* paramounttechnologies.com	Walled Lake	MI	48390	248-960-0909	960-1919
Passkey International 180 Old Colony Ave Third Fl **Fax Area Code:* 617 ■ *TF:* 866-649-1539 ■ *Web:* www.passkey.com	Quincy	MA	02170	866-649-1539	328-1461*
PBM Corp 20600 Chagrin Blvd Ste 450 *TF:* 800-341-5809 ■ *Web:* www.pbmcorp.com	Cleveland	OH	44122	216-283-7999	283-7931
Perfect Commerce Inc One Compass Way Ste 120 *TF Sales:* 877-871-3788 ■ *Web:* perfect.com	Newport News	VA	23606	757-766-8211	
PhDx Systems Inc 1001 University Blvd SE Ste 103 *TF:* 888-999-7439 ■ *Web:* www.phdx.com	Albuquerque	NM	87106	505-764-0174	764-0074
PicoSearch LLC 10 Fawcett St *Web:* sas.com/en_us/company-information/picosearch.html	Cambridge	MA	02138	617-547-4020	576-7227
Pointivity 5355 Mira Sorrento Pl # 600 *Web:* www.pointivity.com	San Diego	CA	92121	858-777-6900	777-6915
Premiere Global Services Inc (PGI) 3280 Peachtree Rd NE Ste 1000 Terminus Bldg *NYSE: PGI* ■ *TF:* 866-548-3203 ■ *Web:* www.pgi.com	Atlanta	GA	30305	719-457-6901	
Prodata Systems Inc 11007 Slater Ave NE *TF:* 866-582-7485 ■ *Web:* www.prodata.com	Kirkland	WA	98033	425-296-4168	822-3443
Prosum technology services 2321 Rosecrans Ave Ste 4225 *TF:* 888-477-6786 ■ *Web:* www.prosum.com	El Segundo	CA	90245	310-426-0600	426-0690
PureWorks Inc 5000 Meridian Blvd Ste 600 *TF:* 888-202-3016 ■ *Web:* www.ulworkplace.com	Franklin	TN	37067	615-367-4404	367-3887
Radware Inc 575 Corporate Dr Lobby 2 *TF:* 888-234-5763 ■ *Web:* www.radware.com	Mahwah	NJ	07430	201-512-9771	512-9774
Resource Development Corp 280 Daines St Ste 200 *TF:* 800-360-7222 ■ *Web:* www.resourcedev.com	Birmingham	MI	48009	248-646-2300	646-0789
Salesforce.com Inc One Market St The Landmark Ste 300 *NYSE: CRM* ■ *TF:* 800-667-6389 ■ *Web:* www.salesforce.com	San Francisco	CA	94105	415-901-7000	901-7040
Salesnet 3296 Summit Ridge Pkwy Ste 210 *TF:* 866-732-8632 ■ *Web:* www.salesnet.com	Duluth	GA	30096	866-732-8632	
Smart Online Inc 4505 Emperor Blvd Ste 320 **Fax Area Code:* 919 ■ *TF:* 800-578-9000 ■ *Web:* www.mobilesmith.com	Durham	NC	27703	800-578-9000	765-5020*
Strategic Systems Consulting Inc 7742 Spalding Dr Ste 363 **Fax Area Code:* 404 ■ *Web:* www.eapps.com	Norcross	GA	30092	770-448-2100	601-7454*
Streamline Health Solutions Inc 10200 Alliance Rd Ste 200 *NASDAQ: STRM* ■ *TF:* 800-878-5269 ■ *Web:* streamlinehealth.net	Cincinnati	OH	45242	513-794-7100	794-9770
Syntrio 50 California St Ste 3260 *Web:* www.syntrio.com	San Francisco	CA	94111	415-951-7913	951-7915
Talisma Corp 777 Yamato Rd *TF:* 866-397-2537 ■ *Web:* www.talisma.com	Boca Raton	FL	33431	561-923-2500	999-0096
TALX Corp 11432 Lackland Dr *TF:* 800-888-8277 ■ *Web:* www.talx.com	Saint Louis	MO	63146	314-214-7000	214-7588
Thoughtworks Inc 200 E Randolph St 25th Fl *Web:* www.thoughtworks.com	Chicago	IL	60601	312-373-1000	373-1001
Toolwire Inc 7031 Koll Ctr Pkwy Ste 220 *TF:* 866-935-8665 ■ *Web:* www.toolwire.com	Pleasanton	CA	94566	925-227-8500	227-8501
UnicornHRO 25 Hanover Rd Ste B *TF:* 800-368-8149 ■ *Web:* www.unicornhro.com	Florham Park	NJ	07932	973-360-0688	360-0699
USA.NET Inc 1155 Kelly Johnson Blvd Ste 305 *TF:* 800-234-2175 ■ *Web:* www.silversky.com	Colorado Springs	CO	80920	719-265-2930	
WebMD Health Holdings Inc 111 Eigth Ave Seventh Fl *NASDAQ: WBMD* ■ *Web:* www.webmd.com	New York	NY	10011	212-624-3700	624-3800
Wizmo Inc 6300 W Old Shakopee Rd Ste 140 *Web:* www.wizmo.com	Bloomington	MN	55438	952-983-3300	983-3600
Workscape Inc 123 Selton St *TF:* 888-605-9620 ■ *Web:* www.workscape.com	Marlborough	MA	01752	508-861-5500	573-9500

40 AQUARIUMS - PUBLIC

SEE ALSO Zoos & Wildlife Parks p. 3302; Botanical Gardens & Arboreta p. 1880

				Phone	Fax
Adventure Aquarium 1 Riverside Dr *TF:* 800-616-5297 ■ *Web:* www.adventureaquarium.com	Camden	NJ	08103	856-365-3300	365-3311
Aquarium of the Bay The Embarcadero at Beach St Pier 39 *Web:* www.aquariumofthebay.com	San Francisco	CA	94133	415-623-5300	623-5324
Aquarium of the Pacific 100 Aquarium Way *Web:* www.aquariumofpacific.org	Long Beach	CA	90802	562-590-3100	950-3109
Atlantic City Aquarium 800 N New Hampshire Ave *Web:* acaquarium.com	Atlantic City	NJ	08401	609-348-2880	
Audubon Aquarium of the Americas 6500 Magazine St *TF:* 800-774-7394 ■ *Web:* www.auduboninstitute.org	New Orleans	LA	70118	504-581-4629	
Birch Aquarium at Scripps 2300 Expedition Way *Web:* www.aquarium.ucsd.edu	La Jolla	CA	92037	858-534-3474	534-7114
Cabrillo Marine Aquarium 3720 Stephen M White Dr *Web:* www.cabrillomarineaquarium.org	San Pedro	CA	90731	310-548-7562	548-2649
Clearwater Marine Aquarium 249 Windward Passage *Web:* www.cmaquarium.org	Clearwater	FL	33767	727-441-1790	447-4922
Dallas World Aquarium 1801 N Griffin St *Web:* www.dwazoo.com	Dallas	TX	75202	214-720-2224	720-2242
Dauphin Island Sea Lab Estuarium 101 Bienville Blvd *Web:* www.disl.org	Dauphin Island	AL	36528	251-861-2141	861-4646
Downtown Aquarium 410 Bagby St & Memorial Dr *Web:* www.aquariumrestaurants.com	Houston	TX	77002	713-223-3474	315-5039
Downtown Aquarium - Denver 700 Water St *Web:* www.aquariumrestaurants.com	Denver	CO	80211	303-561-4450	561-4650
Florida Aquarium 701 Channelside Dr *TF:* 800-353-4741 ■ *Web:* www.flaquarium.org	Tampa	FL	33602	813-273-4000	273-4160
Georgia Aquarium 225 Baker St *Web:* www.georgiaaquarium.org	Atlanta	GA	30313	404-581-4000	
Great Lakes Aquarium 353 Harbor Dr *Web:* www.glaquarium.org	Duluth	MN	55802	218-740-3474	740-2020
Gulf Coast Research Laboratory 703 E Beach Dr	Ocean Springs	MS	39564	228-872-4200	
John G Shedd Aquarium 1200 S Lk Shore Dr *Web:* www.sheddaquarium.org	Chicago	IL	60605	312-939-2438	939-3793
Key West Aquarium One Whitehead St *TF:* 888-544-5927 ■ *Web:* www.keywestaquarium.com	Key West	FL	33040	305-296-2051	293-7094

	City	State	Zip	Phone	Fax
Maria Mitchell Assn Aquarium Four Vestal St *Web:* mariamitchell.org	Nantucket	MA	02554	508-228-9198	228-1031
Marineland of Florida 9600 Ocean Shore Blvd *TF:* 877-933-3402 ■ *Web:* www.marineland.net	Saint Augustine	FL	32080	904-460-1275	471-1111
Marinelife Ctr of Juno Beach 14200 US Hwy 1 Loggerhead Pk *TF:* 800-843-5451 ■ *Web:* www.marinelife.org	Juno Beach	FL	33408	561-627-8280	627-8305
Maritime Aquarium at Norwalk 10 N Water St *Web:* www.maritimeaquarium.org	Norwalk	CT	06854	203-852-0700	838-5416
Maui Ocean Ctr 192 Maalaea Rd *TF:* 800-350-5634 ■ *Web:* www.mauioceancenter.com	Wailuku	HI	96793	808-270-7000	270-7070
Miami Seaquarium 4400 Rickenbacker Cswy *Web:* www.miamiseaquarium.com	Miami	FL	33149	305-361-5705	361-6077
Monterey Bay Aquarium 886 Cannery Row *TF:* 866-963-9645 ■ *Web:* www.montereybayaquarium.org	Monterey	CA	93940	831-648-4800	648-4810
Mystic Aquarium & Institute for Exploration 55 Coogan Blvd *Web:* www.mysticaquarium.org	Mystic	CT	06355	860-572-5955	572-5969
National Aquarium 14th & Constitution Ave NW Dept of Commerce Bldg Rm B-077 *Web:* aqua.org	Washington	DC	20230	202-482-2825	482-4946
National Aquarium in Baltimore 501 E Pratt St Pier 3 *Web:* www.aqua.org	Baltimore	MD	21202	410-576-3800	576-8641
National Park Aquarium 209 Central Ave *Web:* nationalparkaquarium.org	Hot Springs	AR	71901	501-624-3474	
New England Aquarium One Central Wharf *Web:* www.neaq.org	Boston	MA	02110	617-973-5200	720-5098
Newport Aquarium One Aquarium Way *TF:* 800-406-3474 ■ *Web:* www.newportaquarium.com	Newport	KY	41071	859-261-7444	261-5888
North Carolina Aquarium at Fort Fisher 900 Loggerhead Rd *TF:* 800-832-3474 ■ *Web:* www.ncaquariums.com	Kure Beach	NC	28449	910-458-8257	458-6812
North Carolina Aquarium on Roanoke Island 374 Airport Rd PO Box 967 *TF:* 866-332-3475 ■ *Web:* www.ncaquariums.com	Manteo	NC	27954	252-473-3493	473-1980
Oklahoma Aquarium 300 S Aquarium Dr *Web:* www.okaquarium.org	Jenks	OK	74037	918-296-3474	296-3467
Oregon Coast Aquarium 2820 SE Ferry Slip Rd *TF:* 800-452-7888 ■ *Web:* www.aquarium.org	Newport	OR	97365	541-867-3474	867-6846
Pacific Undersea Gardens 490 Belleville St *Web:* www.pacificunderseagardens.com	Victoria	BC	V8V1W9	250-382-5717	382-5210
Parc Aquarium du Quebec 1675 des Hotels Ave *TF:* 866-659-5264 ■ *Web:* www.sepaq.com	Quebec	QC	G1W4S3	418-659-5264	646-9238
Pittsburgh Zoo & PPG Aquarium 1 Wild Pl *TF:* 800-732-0999 ■ *Web:* pittsburghzoo.com	Pittsburgh	PA	15206	412-665-3640	665-3661
Point Defiance Zoo & Aquarium 5400 N Pearl St *Web:* www.pdza.org	Tacoma	WA	98407	253-591-5337	591-5448
Ripley's Aquarium 1110 Celebrity Cir *TF:* 800-734-8888 ■ *Web:* www.ripleys.com	Myrtle Beach	SC	29577	843-916-0888	916-0752
Sea Life Park 41-202 Kalanianaole Hwy *TF:* 866-365-7446 ■ *Web:* www.sealifeparkhawaii.com	Waimanalo	HI	96795	808-259-2500	259-7373
Seattle Aquarium 1483 Alaskan Way Pier 59 *Web:* www.seattleaquarium.org	Seattle	WA	98101	206-386-4300	386-4328
SeaWorld Orlando 7007 Sea World Dr **Fax:* Cust Svc ■ *TF:* 800-327-2424 ■ *Web:* seaworldparks.com	Orlando	FL	32821	407-351-3600	363-2409*
South Carolina Aquarium 100 Aquarium Wharf **Fax Area Code:* 866 ■ *TF:* 800-722-6455 ■ *Web:* www.scaquarium.org	Charleston	SC	29401	843-577-3474	210-1059*
Steinhart Aquarium *California Academy of Sciences* 55 Music Concourse Dr Golden Gate Park *Web:* www.calacademy.org/aquarium	San Francisco	CA	94118	415-379-8000	
Tennessee Aquarium 1 Broad St *TF:* 800-262-0695 ■ *Web:* www.tennis.org	Chattanooga	TN	37402	423-802-6768	265-2871
Texas State Aquarium 2710 N Shoreline Blvd *TF General:* 800-477-4853 ■ *Web:* www.texasstateaquarium.org	Corpus Christi	TX	78402	361-881-1200	881-1257
University of Georgia Aquarium 30 Ocean Science Cir *Web:* www.marex.uga.edu/aquarium	Savannah	GA	31411	912-598-2496	598-2302
Vancouver Aquarium Marine Science Ctr 845 Avison Way *TF:* 800-931-1186 ■ *Web:* www.vanaqua.org	Vancouver	BC	V6G3E2	604-659-3474	659-3515
Waikiki Aquarium 2777 Kalakaua Ave *Web:* waikikiaquarium.org/	Honolulu	HI	96815	808-923-9741	923-1771

41 ARBITRATION SERVICES - LEGAL

	City	State	Zip	Phone	Fax
Aaron Riechert Carpol & Riffle APC 900 Veterans Blvd Ste 600 *Web:* www.arcr.com	Redwood City	CA	94063	650-368-4662	
Acceleros 11900 Metric Blvd Ste J-163 *Web:* www.acceleros.com	Austin	TX	78758	512-736-8385	
Advance Case Loans LLC 205 W Wacker Dr Ste 901 *Web:* www.advancecaseloans.com	Chicago	IL	60606	312-332-4100	
Advanced Medical Systems 820 Bear Tavern Rd *Web:* www.advmedsys.com	Ewing	NJ	08628	609-882-6889	
Advanced Practice Strategies Inc 470 Atlantic Ave 14th Fl *Web:* www.aps-web.com	Boston	MA	02210	617-275-7300	
Alan Jones Auctioneers 2470 Nw Dallas St *Web:* antiqueauctioncenter.com	Grand Prairie	TX	75050	972-641-7115	
Albany Door Systems 975A Old Norcross Rd *Web:* www.albanydoorsystems.com	Lawrenceville	GA	30046	770-338-5000	
Alex Lyon & Son Sales Managers & Auctioneers Inc 7697 Route 31 *Web:* www.lyonauction.com	Bridgeport	NY	13030	315-633-2944	
Allerair Industries Inc 9600 Rte Transcanadienne *Web:* www.allerair.com	Saint-laurent	QC	H4S1V9	514-335-4277	
Alliance Abroad Group LP 1221 S Mo Pac Expy Ste 250 *Web:* www.allianceabroad.com	Austin	TX	78746	512-457-8062	
Alliance Credit Counseling Inc 13777 Ballantyne Corporate Pl Ste 100 *Web:* www.knowdebt.org	Charlotte	NC	28277	704-341-1010	
AmbioPharm Inc 1024 Dittman Ct *Web:* www.ambiopharm.com	North Augusta	SC	29842	415-921-3593	
Amerge Corp 1406 W Sixth St Ste 200 *Web:* www.acquisitions-mergers.com	Cleveland	OH	44113	216-928-6007	
Americall 1502 Tacoma Ave S *Web:* www.americall.com	Tacoma	WA	98402	253-272-4111	
American Arbitration Assn Inc (AAA) 1633 Broadway 10th Fl *TF:* 800-778-7879 ■ *Web:* www.adr.org	New York	NY	10019	212-716-5800	716-5905
Amirsys Inc 2180 South 1300 East Ste 405 *Web:* www.amirsys.com	Salt Lake City	UT	84106	801-485-6500	
Anderson Brule Architects Inc 325 S First St Fl 4 *Web:* www.aba-arch.com	San Jose	CA	95113	408-298-1885	
Angelo Gordon & Co 245 Park Ave *Web:* www.angelogordon.com	New York	NY	10167	212-692-2000	
Anresco Inc 1370 Van Dyke Ave *Web:* anresco.com	San Francisco	CA	94124	415-822-1100	
APEX Financial Services Inc 11800 Singletree Ln Ste 314 *Web:* www.apexfsi.com	Eden Prairie	MN	55344	952-238-1315	
Arbitration Forums Inc 3350 Buschwood Pk Dr Ste 295 *TF Cust Svc:* 800-967-8889 ■ *Web:* www.arbfile.org	Tampa	FL	33618	813-931-4004	931-4618
Assemblies Unlimited Inc 143 Covington Dr *Web:* www.assemblies.com	Bloomingdale	IL	60108	630-980-0200	
Asset Appraisal Services Inc 344 N 115th St *Web:* www.assetappraisalservices.com	Omaha	NE	68154	402-390-0505	
Asset Sales Inc 301 Post Office Dr Ste C *Web:* www.asset-sales.com	Indian Trail	NC	28079	704-821-4315	
Asynchrony Solutions Inc 900 Spruce St Ste 700 *Web:* www.asolutions.com	St. Louis	MO	63102	314-678-2200	
Atwood & Cherny PC 101 Huntington Ave 25th Fl *Web:* www.atwoodcherny.com	Boston	MA	02199	617-262-6400	
August Law Group PC 19200 Von Karman Ste 900 *Web:* www.augustlawgroup.com	Irvine	CA	92612	949-752-7772	
Avant Business Services 60 E 42nd St Lowr Level *Web:* www.nymessenger.com	New York	NY	10165	212-687-5145	
Balasa Dinverno Foltz LLC 500 Park Blvd Ste 1400 *Web:* www.bdfllc.com	Itasca	IL	60143	630-875-4900	
Bandit Lites Inc 2233 Sycamore Dr *Web:* www.banditlites.com	Knoxville	TN	37921	865-971-3071	
Bass & Associates PC 3936 E Ft Lowell Rd Ste 200 *Web:* www.bass-associates.com	Tucson	AZ	85712	520-577-1544	
Bass Doherty & Finks PC 40 Soldiers Field Pl *Web:* www.bassdoherty.com	Boston	MA	02135	617-787-5551	
Beacon Application Services Corp 959 Concord St Ste 250 *Web:* www.beaconservices.com	Framingham	MA	01701	508-663-4433	
Bexar Appraisal District 411 N Frio St *Web:* www.bcad.org	San Antonio	TX	78207	210-224-8511	
Bird Marella Boxer Wolpert Nessim Drooks & Lincenberg PC 1875 Century Park E 23rd Fl *Web:* www.birdmarella.com	Los Angeles	CA	90067	310-201-2100	
Bluewater Industries Inc 5300 Memorial Ste 550	Houston	TX	77007	713-802-2060	
Bluteau DeVenney & Company Inc 5670 Spring Garden Rd Ste 901A *Web:* www.bluteaudevenney.com	Halifax	NS	B3J1H6	902-425-0467	
Borden Ladner Gervais LLP 40 King St W *Web:* www.blg.com	Toronto	ON	M5H3Y4	416-367-6000	
Braverman & Co 331 Madison Ave *Web:* www.braverlaw.net	New York	NY	10017	212-682-2900	
Brock Capital Group LLC 622 Third Ave Fl 12 *Web:* www.brockcapital.com	New York	NY	10017	212-209-3000	
Brown & Streza LLP 40 Pacifica 15th Fl *Web:* www.brownandstreza.com	Irvine	CA	92618	949-453-2900	
Brunswick School Inc 100 Maher Ave *Web:* www.brunswickschool.org	Greenwich	CT	06830	203-625-5800	
Burr & Forman LLP 420 N 20th St Ste 3400 *Web:* www.burr.com	Birmingham	AL	35203	205-251-3000	
Butzel Long PC 150 W Jefferson Ste 900 *Web:* www.butzel.com	Detroit	MI	48226	313-225-7000	
Buy Rite Liquidators 1076 Park Rd *Web:* buyriteliquidators.com	Blandon	PA	19510	610-926-4444	
California District Attorneys Association 921 11th St *Web:* www.cdaa.org	Sacramento	CA	95814	916-443-2017	
Capital Valuation Group Inc 10 E Doty St Ste 1002 *Web:* www.capvalgroup.com	Madison	WI	53703	608-257-2757	
Careerpros LLC 3392 Hillcrest Rd *Web:* www.careerpros.com	Dubuque	IA	52002	563-556-3040	

Phone Fax

Carlson & Messer LLP
5959 W Century Blvd Ste 1214 . . . Los Angeles CA 90045 310-242-2200
Web: www.cmtlaw.com

Cauldwell Wingate Company LLC
380 Lexington Ave 53rd Fl . . . New York NY 10168 212-983-7150
Web: www.cauldwellwingate.com

Certified Business Brokers Ltd
10301 Northwest Fwy Ste 200 . . . Houston TX 77092 713-680-1200
Web: www.certifiedbb.com

Chapman Associates
16 E Schaumburg Rd Ste 3 . . . Schaumburg IL 60194 847-884-0010
Web: www.chapman-usa.com

CIR Law Offices LLP 8665 Gibbs Dr Ste 150 . . . San Diego CA 92123 800-496-8909
TF: 800-496-8909 ■ *Web:* www.cirlaw.com

Clark Wilson LLP 900 885 W Georgia St . . . Vancouver BC V6C3H1 604-687-5700 687-6314
Web: www.cwilson.com

Classic Die Services Inc
6926 Trafalgar Dr Ste D . . . Fort Wayne IN 46803 260-748-6907
Web: www.classicdieservices.com

Clean Air Engineering Inc 500 W Wood St . . . Palatine IL 60067 847-991-3300
Web: www.cleanair.com

Clearinghouse Community Development Financial Institution
23861 El Toro Rd Ste 401 . . . Lake Forest CA 92630 949-859-3600
Web: www.clearinghousecdfi.com

CMC-KUHNKE 250 Falls Rd . . . Hudson NY 12534 518-828-9345
Web: www.cmc-kuhnke.com

Coblentz Patch Duffy & Bass LLP
One Ferry Bldg Ste 200 . . . San Francisco CA 94111 415-391-4800
Web: www.coblentzlaw.com

Conestoga Energy Partners LLC
300 N Lincoln Ave . . . Liberal KS 67901 620-624-2901
Web: www.conestogaenergy.net

Conference Technologies Inc
11653 Adie Rd . . . Maryland Heights MO 63043 314-993-1400
Web: www.conferencetech.com

Consensus Advisors LLC 73 Newbury St . . . Boston MA 02116 617-437-6500
Web: www.consensusadvisors.com

Cotchett Pitre & McCarthy LLP
San Francisco Airport Office Ctr 840 Malcolm Rd
Ste 200 . . . Burlingame CA 94010 650-697-6000
Web: www.cpmlegal.com

Council of Better Business Bureaus Inc
Dispute Resolution Services & Mediation Training
4200 Wilson Blvd Ste 800 . . . Arlington VA 22203 703-276-0100 525-8277
TF: 800-537-4600 ■ *Web:* www.bbb.org

Cox & Palmer LLP
1100-1959 Upper Water St Purdy's Wharf Tower I
. . . Halifax NS B3J3N2 902-421-6262
Web: www.coxandpalmerlaw.com

CPR Institute for Dispute Resolution
575 Lexington Ave 21st Fl . . . New York NY 10022 212-949-6490 949-8859
TF: 866-723-1781 ■ *Web:* www.cpradr.org

Crowley Barrett & Karaba
20 S Clark St Ste 2310 . . . Chicago IL 60603 312-726-2468
Web: cbklaw.com

D W Hammer & Company Inc
17480 Dallas Pkwy Ste 100 . . . Dallas TX 75287 972-250-2547
Web: www.dwhammerco.com

D'Arcangelo & Co 510 Haight Ave . . . Poughkeepsie NY 12603 845-473-7774
Web: www.darcangelo.com

David A Noyes & Co 209 S LaSalle St . . . Chicago IL 60604 312-782-0400
Web: www.danoyes.com

Davies Ward Phillips & Vineberg LLP
155 Wellington St W . . . Toronto ON M5V3J7 416-863-0900
Web: www.dwpv.com

DB Squared LLC 2928 N McKee Cir . . . Fayetteville AR 72703 479-587-0151
Web: www.dbsquared.biz

Devicix LLC 7680 Executive Dr . . . Eden Prairie MN 55344 952-368-0073
Web: www.devicix.com

E Tech Systems Inc 1900 E Golf Rd Ste 950 . . . Schaumburg IL 60173 847-352-4770
Web: www.etechsys.com

EBG Consulting 419 Hudson Rd . . . Sudbury MA 01776 978-261-5552
Web: www.ebgconsulting.com

Emerald Technology Valuations LLC
231 Sansome St Fifth Fl . . . San Francisco CA 94104 415-773-6310
Web: www.emerald-tech.com

EmpXtrack 134 N Manchester Ln . . . Bloomingdale IL 60108 630-339-4155
Web: www.empxtrack.com

Epixx 3915 Heritage Colony Dr . . . Missouri City TX 77459 281-208-1989
Web: www.epixx.com

Estabrook Capital Management LLC
875 Third Ave 15th Fl . . . New York NY 10022 212-605-5595
Web: www.estabrookcap.com

Eye-To-Eye Communications Inc
2624 W Canyon Ave . . . San Diego CA 92123 858-565-9800
Web: www.eyetoeyepr.com

Family Credit Counseling Service
111 N Wabash Ste 1408 . . . Chicago IL 60602 800-994-3328
TF: 800-994-3328 ■ *Web:* www.familycredit.org

Farris Vaughan Wills & Murphy
700 W Georgia St Pacific Centre S 25th Fl
PO Box 10026 . . . Vancouver BC V7Y1B3 604-684-9151
Web: www.farris.com

Fasken Martineau DuMoulin LLP
333 Bay St Bay Adelaide Centre
Ste 2400 PO Box 20 . . . Toronto ON M5H2T6 416-366-8381 364-7813
TF: 800-268-8424 ■ *Web:* www.fasken.com

Federal Mediation & Conciliation Service
2100 K St NW . . . Washington DC 20427 202-606-8100 606-4251
Web: www.fmcs.gov

Fennebresque & Company LLC
550 S Caldwell St NASCAR Plz Ste 755 . . . Charlotte NC 28202 704-295-8900
Web: www.fennebresque.com

Florida Council Against Sexual Violence Inc
1820 E Park Ave Ste 100 . . . Tallahassee FL 32301 850-297-2000
Web: www.fcasv.org

Florida Surplus Lines Service Office
1441 Maclay Commerce Dr . . . Tallahassee FL 32312 850-224-7676
Web: www.fslso.com

Folger Levin LLP 199 Fremont St 20th Fl . . . San Francisco CA 94105 415-625-1050
Web: www.folgerlevin.com

Fossil Energy Research Corp
23342 S Pointe Dr Ste C . . . Laguna Hills CA 92653 949-859-4466
Web: www.ferco.com

Fraser Yachts Florida Inc
1800 Southeast 10th Ave Ste 400 . . . Fort Lauderdale FL 33316 954-463-0600
Web: www.fraseryachts.com

Freedom Cad Services Inc 20 Cotton Rd Ste 201 . . . Nashua NH 03063 603-864-1300
Web: www.freedomcad.com

Garland Power & Light PO Box 469002 . . . Garland TX 75046 972-205-2650
Web: www.garlandpower-light.org

Global Imaging Inc 2011 Cherry St Ste 116 . . . Louisville CO 80027 303-673-9773
Web: www.globalimaginginc.com

Gokeyless 3646 Cargo Rd . . . Vandalia OH 45377 937-890-2333
Web: www.gokeyless.com

Goldman Sloan Nash & Haber LLP
480 University Ave Ste 1600 . . . Toronto ON M5G1V2 416-597-9922
Web: www.gsnh.com

Goodmans LLP 333 Bay St Ste 3400 . . . Toronto ON M5H2S7 416-979-2211
Web: www.goodmans.ca

Goodmind LLC 41 E 11Th St 11Th Fl . . . New York NY 10003 212-660-0110
Web: www.goodmind.net

Gordon & Rees LLP
275 Battery St Ste 2000 . . . San Francisco CA 94111 415-986-5900
Web: www.gordonrees.com

Gould & Ratner 222 N LaSalle Ste 800 . . . Chicago IL 60601 312-236-3003
Web: www.gouldratner.com

Gowling Lafleur Henderson LLP
100 King St W 1 First Canadian Pl Ste 1600 . . . Toronto ON M5X1G5 416-862-7525 862-7661
Web: www.gowlings.com

Gray Rust St Amand Moffett & Brieske LLP
950 E Paces Ferry Rd Ne . . . Atlanta GA 30326 404-870-7373
Web: www.grsmb.com

Groundwire PO Box 1323 . . . Castle Rock CO 80104 303-660-3582
Web: www.groundwire.net

Guidesoft Inc
5875 Castle Creek Pkwy Ste 400 . . . Indianapolis IN 46250 317-578-1700
Web: www.knowledgeservices.com

Gunderson Dettmer Stough Villeneuve Franklin & Hachigian LLP
1200 Seaport Blvd . . . Redwood City CA 94063 650-321-2400
Web: www.gunder.com

GWAVA Inc 100 Alexis Nihon Rd Ste 500 . . . Montreal QC H4M2P1 514-639-4850
Web: www.gwava.com

Hammerman & Hultgren PC
3101 N Central Ave Ste 500 . . . Phoenix AZ 85012 602-264-2566
Web: www.hammerman-hultgren.com

Herzog & Co
4640 Lankershim Blvd Ste 400 . . . North Hollywood CA 91602 818-762-4640
Web: www.herzogcompany.com

Higgins, Marcus & Lovett Inc
800 S Figueroa St Ste 710 . . . Los Angeles CA 90017 213-617-7775
Web: www.hmlinc.com

Holland & Knight LLP 2115 Harden Blvd . . . Lakeland FL 33803 863-682-1161
Web: www.hklaw.com

Honigman Miller Schwartz & Cohn LLP
660 Woodward Ave Ste 2290 . . . Detroit MI 48226 313-465-7000
Web: www.honigman.com

Hrv Conformance Verification Associates Inc
200 Hightower Blvd Ste 400 . . . Pittsburgh PA 15205 412-788-2522
Web: www.hrvinc.com

Hughes Design Associates 7160 Beneva Rd . . . Sarasota FL 34238 941-922-4767
Web: www.hughesdes.com

Huntzinger Management Group Inc, The
670 N River St Ste 401 . . . Plains PA 18705 570-824-4721
Web: huntzingergroup.com

I-Safe America Inc
5900 Pasteur Court Ste 100 . . . Carlsbad CA 92008 760-603-7911
Web: www.isafe.org

Infinity Direct Inc
13220 County Rd 6 Ste 200 . . . Plymouth MN 55441 763-559-1111
Web: www.infinitydirect.com

Inland Valley Arbitration & Mediation Service (IVAMS)
8287 White Oak Ave . . . Rancho Cucamonga CA 91730 909-466-1665 466-1796
Web: www.ivams.com

J p King Auction Company Texas Ltd
108 Fountain Ave . . . Gadsden AL 35901 256-546-5217
Web: www.jpking.com

JAMS/Endispute
500 N State College Blvd 14th Fl . . . Orange CA 92868 714-939-1300 939-8710
TF: 800-352-5267 ■ *Web:* www.jamsadr.com

JDC Group Inc 990 Hammond Dr Ste 750 . . . Atlanta GA 30328 404-601-3310
Web: www.jdc-group.com

Jeffrey Byrne & Associates
4042 Central St . . . Kansas City MO 64111 800-222-9233
TF: 800-222-9233 ■ *Web:* www.fundraisingjba.com

Johanson & Yau Accountancy Corp
160 W Santa Clara St Ste 900 . . . San Jose CA 95113 408-288-5111
Web: www.jyac.com

JS Paluch Company Inc
3708 River Rd Ste 400 . . . Franklin Park IL 60131 847-678-9300
Web: www.jspaluch.com

Judge Organization Companies, The
201A Export St . . . Newark NJ 07114 973-491-0600
Web: www.judgeorg.com

Judicate West 1851 E First St Ste 1450 . . . Santa Ana CA 92705 714-834-1340 834-1344
TF: 800-488-8805 ■ *Web:* www.judicatewest.com

Company	City	State	Zip	Phone	Fax
July Business Services 215 Mary Ave Ste 302 *TF:* 888-333-5859 ■ *Web:* www.julyservices.com	Waco	TX	76701	888-333-5859	
JumpSport Inc 2055 S Seventh St Ste A *Web:* www.jumpsport.com	San Jose	CA	95112	408-213-2551	
Kaufman Company Inc 19 Walkhill Rd *Web:* www.kaufmanco.com	Norwood	MA	02062	508-786-9777	
Keais Records Service Inc 1010 Lamar Ste 300 *Web:* keais.com	Houston	TX	77002	713-224-6865	
Kelley Executive Partners 1275 E 10th St *Web:* www.kelley.iu.edu	Bloomington	IN	47405	812-855-0229	
KLS Professional Advisors Group LLC 111 Fifth Ave Eighth Fl *Web:* www.caravan-ny.com	New York	NY	10003	212-355-0346	
Koster Industries Inc 40 Daniel St Ste 2 *Web:* www.kosterindustries.com	Farmingdale	NY	11735	631-454-1766	
Kynikos Associates LP 20 W 55th St Eighth Fl *Web:* www.kynikos.com	New York	NY	10019	212-649-0200	
Lake Court Medical Supplies Inc 27733 Groesbeck Hwy *Web:* www.lakecourt.com	Roseville	MI	48066	586-771-3100	
Land Information Access Association Land Information Access Association 324 Munson Ave *Web:* www.liaa.org	Traverse City	MI	49686	231-929-3696	
Lang Richert & Patch 5200 N Palm Ave Fig Garden Financial Ctr Fourth Fl *Web:* www.lrp.org	Fresno	CA	93704	559-228-6700	
Larwin Co 16633 Ventura Blvd Ste 1300	Encino	CA	91436	818-986-8890	
Lasership Inc 1912 Woodford Rd *Web:* www.lasership.com	Vienna	VA	22182	703-761-9030	
Leader's Edge Two Bala Plz Ste 300 *Web:* www.the-leaders-edge.com	Bala Cynwyd	PA	19004	610-660-6684	
LEADERS Magazine Inc 59 E 54Th St *Web:* www.leadersmag.com	New York	NY	10022	212-758-0740	
Lenczner Slaght Royce Smith Griffin LLP 130 Adelaide St W Ste 2600 *Web:* www.lsrsg.com	Toronto	ON	M5H3P5	416-865-9500	
Living Color Enterprises Inc 6850 NW 12th Ave *Web:* www.livingcolor.com	Fort Lauderdale	FL	33309	954-970-9511	
Loeb Equipment & Appraisal Co 4131 S State St *Web:* www.loebequipment.com	Chicago	IL	60609	773-548-4131	
London Company Investment Counsel, The 1801 Bayberry Ct Ste 301 *Web:* www.tlcadvisory.com	Richmond	VA	23226	804-775-0317	
Luan Enterprises 5624 W 79th St *Web:* www.alltite.com	Burbank	IL	60459	708-423-4547	
Lush Group Inc 24 Southwest Ave *Web:* www.lgisoftware.com	Jamestown	RI	02835	401-423-9111	
Manomet Center for Conservation Sciences 81 Stage Point Rd *Web:* www.manomet.org	Manomet	MA	02345	508-224-6521	
Mark IV Capital Inc 100 Bayview Cir Ste 4500 *Web:* www.markiv.com	Newport Beach	CA	92660	949-509-1444	
Marks Nelson Vohland & Campbel 7701 College Blvd Ste 150 *Web:* www.marksnelsoncpa.com	Overland Park	KS	66210	913-498-9000	
Mater Dei Academy 3695 Elm St *Web:* www.materdeiacademy.org	Columbus	OH	43213	614-231-1984	
McDonald Carano Wilson LLP 100 W Liberty St 10th Fl *Web:* www.mcdonaldcarano.com	Reno	NV	89505	775-788-2000	
Meals for Homebound 10824 Topanga Canyon Blvd # 7 *Web:* www.vic-la.org	Chatsworth	CA	91311	818-718-6460	
Mecham Co, The 4107 S Forest Meadows *Web:* www.mechamcompany.com	Spokane	WA	99206	509-922-0535	
Medicount Management Inc 10361 Spartan Dr *Web:* www.medicount.com	Cincinnati	OH	45215	513-772-4465	
Merchant Law Group LLP 2401 Saskatchewan Dr Saskatchewan Dr Plz *Web:* www.merchantlaw.com	Regina	SK	S4P4H8	306-359-7777	
Meristem LLP 601 Carlson Pkwy Ste 800 *Web:* www.meristemmfo.com	Minnetonka	MN	55305	952-835-2577	
Meriwether Capital LLC 30 Rockefeller Plz Rm 5600 *Web:* www.meriwethercapital.net	New York	NY	10112	212-649-5890	
Merlin Law Group PA 777 S Harbour Island Blvd *Web:* www.merlinlawgroup.com	Tampa	FL	33602	813-229-1000	
Michael Best & Friedrich LLP 100 E Wisconsin Ave Ste 3300 *Web:* www.michaelbest.com	Milwaukee	WI	53202	414-271-6560	
Middleton & Company Inc 600 Atlantic Ave 18th Fl *Web:* www.middletonco.com	Boston	MA	02210	617-357-5101	
Miller Thomson LLP Scotia Plz 40 King St W Ste 5800 *Web:* www.millerthomson.com	Toronto	ON	M5H3S1	416-595-8500	
Missouri Protection & Advocacy Services 925 S Country Club Dr Ste 3 *Web:* www.moadvocacy.org	Jefferson City	MO	65109	573-893-3333	
MovieTickets.com Inc 2255 Glades Rd Ste 100E *Web:* www.movietickets.com	Boca Raton	FL	33431	561-322-3200	
mSnap Inc 388 Market St Ste 854 *Web:* www.msnapinc.com	San Francisco	CA	94111	415-981-0812	
Mueller Law Office, The 404 W Seventh St *Web:* www.muellerlaw.com	Austin	TX	78701	512-478-1236	
Nathan Sommers Jacobs PC 2800 Post Oak Blvd 61st Fl *Web:* www.nathansommers.com	Houston	TX	77056	713-960-0303	
National Arbitration & Mediation 990 Stewart Ave *TF:* 800-358-2550 ■ *Web:* www.namadr.com	Garden City	NY	11530	516-794-8950	794-8518
NBS Technologies Inc 703 Evans Ave Ste 402 *Web:* www.nbstech.com	Toronto	ON	M9C5E9	416-621-1911	
Ncs Subsea Inc 3928 Bluebonnet Dr *Web:* ncs-subsea.com	Stafford	TX	77477	281-491-3123	
Neat Oh International 790 W Frontage Rd Ste 303 *Web:* www.neat-oh.com	Northfield	IL	60093	847-441-4290	
Neovia 90 Castilian Dr Ste 110 *Web:* www.neoviainsurance.com	Goleta	CA	93117	805-961-3111	
Nexus World Services Inc 7114 W Jefferson Ste 110 *Web:* www.nexusworldservices.com	Denver	CO	80235	303-988-1243	
Nichols Jackson Dillard Hager & Smith LLP 500 N Akard St Ste 1800 *Web:* www.njdhs.com	Dallas	TX	75201	214-965-9900	
Nines Hotel, The 525 SW Morrison *TF:* 877-229-9995 ■ *Web:* www.thenines.com	Portland	OR	97204	877-229-9995	
Notus Career Management Five Centerpointe Dr Ste 400 *TF:* 800-431-1990 ■ *Web:* www.getnotus.com	Lake Oswego	OR	97035	800-431-1990	
O'connor Company Inc 14851 W 99th St *Web:* www.oconnor-hvac.com	Lenexa	KS	66215	913-894-8788	
OCTG LLP 9200 Sheldon Rd *Web:* www.octg.org	Houston	TX	77049	281-456-9057	
OnCell Systems Inc 1160D Pittsford-Victor Rd *Web:* oncell.com	Pittsford	NY	14534	585-419-9844	
OneTouch Direct LLC 4902 W Sligh Ave *TF:* 866-948-4005 ■ *Web:* www.onetouchdirect.com	Tampa	FL	33634	866-948-4005	
Optimal Outsource Seven Rancho Cir *Web:* optimaloutsource.com	Lake Forest	CA	92630	949-916-3700	
ORC ProTel Inc 17233 Continental Dr *Web:* www.orcprotel.com	Lansing	IL	60438	708-418-7400	
Osler Hoskin & Harcourt LLP 100 King St W 1 First Canadian Pl Ste 6100 *Web:* www.osler.com	Toronto	ON	M5X1B8	416-362-2111	
OTS 3924 Clock Pointe Trl *TF:* 877-445-2058 ■ *Web:* www.ots.net	Stow	OH	44224	877-445-2058	
P.W. Gillibrand Company Inc 4537 Ish Dr *Web:* www.pwgillibrand.com	Simi Valley	CA	93063	805-526-2195	
Paging Network of Canada Inc 1-1685 Tech Ave *Web:* www.pagenet.ca	Mississauga	ON	L4W0A7	905-614-3100	
Pamlico Capital 150 N College St Ste 2400 *Web:* www.pamlicocapital.com	Charlotte	NC	28202	704-414-7150	
Parker Rose Design Inc 10075 Mesa Rim Rd Ste A *TF:* 800-403-2711 ■ *Web:* www.parker-rose.com	San Diego	CA	92121	800-403-2711	
Parnell & Crum PA 641 S Lawrence St *Web:* www.parnellcrum.com	Montgomery	AL	36104	334-832-4200	
Patpro Inc 2111 Eisenhower Ave Ste 404 *Web:* www.epatpro.com	Alexandria	VA	22314	703-299-8500	
Pearl Law Group 315 Montgomery St Seventh Fl *Web:* www.immigrationlaw.com	San Francisco	CA	94104	415-771-7500	
Pennsylvania Employees Benefit Trust Fund 150 S 43rd St *Web:* www.pebtf.org	Harrisburg	PA	17111	717-561-4750	
Perkins Investment Management LLC 1 S Wacker Dr Ste 2920 *Web:* pwmco.com	Chicago	IL	60606	312-341-9727	341-9737
Pine Tree Equity Management LP 777 Brickell Ave Ste 1070 *Web:* www.pinetreeequity.com	Miami	FL	33131	305-808-9820	
Pite Duncan LLP 4375 Jutland Dr Ste 200 *Web:* www.piteduncan.com	San Diego	CA	92117	858-750-7600	
PMA Canada Ltd 231 Oak Park Blvd *Web:* www.pmacanada.com	Oakville	ON	L6H7S8	905-257-2116	
Polaris Capital Management LLC 121 High St *Web:* www.polariscapital.com	Boston	MA	02110	617-951-1365	
Prima Civitas Foundation 1614 E Kalamazoo St *Web:* primacivitas.org	Lansing	MI	48912	517-999-3382	
Prime NDT Services Inc 5260 W Coplay Rd *Web:* www.primendt.com	Whitehall	PA	18052	610-262-4954	
Print Resources Inc 1500 E Riverside Dr *Web:* www.printindy.com	Indianapolis	IN	46202	317-833-7000	
PrismOne Group Inc 37 N Boyd St *Web:* www.prismone.net	Winter Garden	FL	34787	321-293-1000	
Prodo Laboratories 32 Mauchly Ste A *Web:* prodolabs.com	Irvine	CA	92618	949-727-1972	
Project Access Inc 4029 Westerly Pl Ste 113 *Web:* www.project-access.org	Newport Beach	CA	92660	949-253-6200	
Promotion Fulfillment Center 311 21st St *Web:* www.pfcfulfills.com	Camanche	IA	52730	563-259-0105	
Quatred LLC 532 Fourth Range Rd *TF:* 888-395-8534 ■ *Web:* www.quatred.com	Pembroke	NH	03275	888-395-8534	
Quiktrak Inc 9700 SW Nimbus Ave *Web:* www.quiktrak.com	Beaverton	OR	97008	503-968-9800	
Rachman Group, The 33 Walt Whitman Rd Ste 232 *Web:* www.mrhuntington.com	Huntington Station	NY	11746	631-547-5464	
Randall S Miller & Associates PC 43252 Woodward Ave Ste 180 *Web:* www.millerlaw.biz	Bloomfield Hills	MI	48302	248-335-9200	
Realty Capital Partners LLC 8333 Douglas Ave *Web:* www.rcpinvestments.com	Dallas	TX	75225	469-533-4000	

	City	State	ZIP	Phone	Fax
Resolute Systems Inc 1550 N Prospect Ave. *TF:* 800-776-6060 ■ *Web:* www.resolutesystems.com	Milwaukee	WI	53202	414-276-4774	270-0932
RESOLVE Partners LLC 2010 New Garden Rd *Web:* www.resolve-partners.com	Greensboro	NC	27410	336-346-3095	
Resume Solutions 1033 Bay St *Web:* www.resumesolutions.ca	Toronto	ON	M5S3A5	416-361-1290	
Reyes | Browne | Reilley 5950 Berkshire Ln Ste 410 *Web:* www.reyeslaw.com	Dallas	TX	75225	214-526-7900	
RICHARD HENRY GROUP LLC P O Box 45422 *Web:* www.rhgsolutions.com	Westlake	OH	44145	440-724-2658	
Roda Group, The 918 Parker St *Web:* www.rodagroup.com	Berkeley	CA	94710	510-649-1900	
Ronald Mark Associates Inc 1227 Central Ave. *Web:* www.ronaldmark.com	Hillside	NJ	07205	908-558-0011	
Rosenthal Appraisal Company Inc Six W Railroad Ave *Web:* www.rosappraisal.com	Tenafly	NJ	07670	201-567-4300	
Russ Blakely & Associates 620 Lindsay St Ste 201 *Web:* www.russblakelyassoc.net	Chattanooga	TN	37403	423-266-8306	
Safer Healthcare 4200 E Eighth Ave Ste 005 *Web:* www.saferhealthcare.com	Denver	CO	80220	303-298-8083	
Safety First Systems LLC 65 Route 4 E *Web:* nationwideagribusiness.safetyfirst.com	River Edge	NJ	07661	201-267-8900	
Safety Management Systems Inc 2916 N University Ave *Web:* www.safetyms.com	Lafayette	LA	70507	337-521-3400	
San Pasqual Fiduciary Trust Co 550 S Hope St Ste 550 *Web:* www.spftc.com	Los Angeles	CA	90071	213-452-8500	
SCF Partners 600 Travis Ste 6600 *Web:* www.scfpartners.com	Houston	TX	77002	713-227-7888	227-7850
Schiller Ducanto & Fleck 225 E Deerpath Ste 270 *Web:* www.sdflaw.com	Lake Forest	IL	60045	847-615-8300	
Sector3 Appraisals Inc 8802 69th Rd *Web:* www.sector3appraisals.com	Forest Hills	NY	11375	718-268-4376	
Sedona Staffing 7380 Clairemont Mesa Blvd Ste 209 *Web:* www.sedonastaffing.com	San Diego	CA	92111	858-268-9844	
Sensor Geophysical Ltd 736-6 Ave SW Ste 1300 *Web:* sensorgeo.com	Calgary	AB	T2P3T7	403-237-7711	
Service Brands International LLC 3948 Ranchero Dr *Web:* www.servicebrands.com	Ann Arbor	MI	48108	734-822-6697	
shopgoodwill.com 210 Liberty St *Web:* www.shopgoodwill.com	Powell	OH	43065	614-985-9675	
Smith Gambrell & Russell LLP 1230 Peachtree St NE Promenade II Ste 3100 *Web:* www.sgrlaw.com	Atlanta	GA	30309	404-815-3500	
Sperry Rail Inc 46 Shelter Rock Rd *Web:* www.sperryrail.com	Danbury	CT	06810	203-791-4500	
Sports Management Network Inc 1668 S Telegraph Rd Ste 200 *Web:* www.sportsmanagementnetwork.com	Bloomfield Hills	MI	48302	248-335-3535	
Spotts Fain PC 411 E Franklin St Ste 600 *Web:* www.spottsfain.com	Richmond	VA	23219	804-697-2000	
Stacey Braun Associates Inc 377 Broadway *Web:* www.staceybraun.com	New York	NY	10013	212-226-7707	
Summa Strategies Canada Inc 100 Sparks St Ste 1000 *Web:* www.summa.ca	Ottawa	ON	K1P5B7	613-235-1400	
Tab Services Inc 2065 S Raritan St Unit A *Web:* tabservices.com	Denver	CO	80223	303-649-1213	
Tarter Krinsky & Drogin LLP 1350 Broadway *Web:* www.tarterkrinsky.com	New York	NY	10018	212-216-8000	
Tech Networks of Boston 574 Dorchester Ave *Web:* techboston.com	Boston	MA	02127	617-269-0299	
Technomics Inc 201 12th St S Ste 612 *Web:* www.technomics.net	Arlington	VA	22202	571-366-1400	
Timber Products Inspection Inc 1641 Sigman Rd NW *Web:* www.tpinspection.com	Conyers	GA	30012	770-922-8000	
Torys LLP 79 Wellington St W TD Centre 30th Fl 30th Fl *Web:* www.torys.com	Toronto	ON	M5K1N2	416-865-0040	
Total Safety Consulting LLC 751 Broadway *Web:* www.totalsafety.org	Bayonne	NJ	07002	201-437-5150	
Tranzon LLC 7204 Glen Forest Dr Ste 105 *Web:* www.tranzon.com	Richmond	VA	23226	207-775-4300	
Tri-Starr Investigations Inc 3525 Hwy 138 SW *Web:* www.tristarr.com	Stockbridge	GA	30281	770-388-9841	
Triton Diving Services LLC 3421 N Causeway Blvd Ste 601 *Web:* www.tritondiving.net	Metairie	LA	70002	504-846-5056	
Tti Environmental Inc 1253 N Church St *Web:* www.ttienvinc.com	Moorestown	NJ	08057	856-840-8800	
Turbo Mechanical Inc 515 McPhee Rd SW *Web:* www.turbomechanical.com	Olympia	WA	98502	360-943-1888	
UbiCare 284 Amory St G-101 *Web:* www.ubicare.com	Boston	MA	02130	617-524-8861	
UMIAQ LLC 6700 Arctic Spur Rd *Web:* www.uicprofessionalservices.com	Anchorage	AK	99518	907-677-8220	
University Physicians Inc 13199 E Montview Blvd *Web:* www.upicolo.org	Aurora	CO	80045	303-493-7000	
Usherwood Office Technology Inc Rockwest Ctr 1005 W Fayette St *Web:* www.usherwood.com	Syracuse	NY	13204	315-472-0050	
Valley Internet Inc 102 Maple St East **Fax Area Code:* 615 ■ *TF:* 888-433-1924 ■ *Web:* vallnet.com	Fayetteville	TN	37334	931-433-1921	221-0119*
Vanguard Dealer Services L.L.C 30 Two Bridges Rd Ste 350 *Web:* www.vanguarddealerservices.com	Fairfield	NJ	07004	973-575-7171	
Varnum LLP Bridgewater Pl PO Box 352 *Web:* www.varnumlaw.com	Grand Rapids	MI	49501	616-336-6000	
Vehtech Inc 40 Cranbrook Way *Web:* www.vehtech.com	Covington	GA	30016	770-788-2032	
Veritas Capital 590 Madison Ave 41st Fl *Web:* www.veritascapital.com	New York	NY	10022	212-415-6700	
Viant Group LLC 500 Washington St Ste 325 *Web:* www.viantgroup.com	San Francisco	CA	94111	415-820-6100	
Webb; County Appraisal Distric 3302 Clark Blvd *Web:* www.webbcad.org	Laredo	TX	78043	956-718-4091	
WelcomeMat Services Inc 3348 Peachtree Rd 200 Tower Pl Ste 1095 *Web:* www.welcomematservices.com	Atlanta	GA	30326	404-841-2226	
Wetherby Asset Management 417 Montgomery St Third Fl *Web:* www.wetherby.com	San Francisco	CA	94104	415-399-9159	
Whitham Curtis Christofferson & Cook PC 11491 Sunset Hills Rd Ste 340 *Web:* www.wcc-ip.com	Reston	VA	20190	703-787-9400	
Wikibon Project, The Four Mount Royal Ave Ste 220 *Web:* www.wikibon.org	Marlborough	MA	01752	774-463-3400	
WLC 200 Pronghorn St *Web:* www.wlcwyo.com	Casper	WY	82601	307-266-2524	
Wolfe Industrial Auctions Inc 9801 Hansonville Rd *Web:* wolfeauctions.com	Frederick	MD	21702	301-898-0340	
Workforce Board, The 2604 Dempster St Ste 305 *Web:* workforceboard.org	Park Ridge	IL	60068	847-699-9155	
Xerces Society, The 4828 Se Hawthorne Blvd *Web:* xerces.org	Portland	OR	97215	503-232-6639	
Zarzaur & Cunningham PC 2209 Morris Ave PO Box 11366 *Web:* www.zsattorneys.com	Birmingham	AL	35203	205-250-8437	

ARCHITECTS

SEE Engineering & Design p. 2256

ART - COMMERCIAL

SEE Graphic Design p. 2437

42 ART DEALERS & GALLERIES

	City	State	ZIP	Phone	Fax
Abbozzo Gallery 401 Richmond Stt W Ste 128 **Fax Area Code:* 905 ■ *TF:* 866-844-4481 ■ *Web:* www.abbozzogallery.com	Toronto	ON	M5V3A8	416-260-2220	844-2036*
ACA Galleries 529 W 20th St Fifth Fl *Web:* www.acagalleries.com	New York	NY	10011	212-206-8080	206-8498
Acquavella Galleries Inc 18 E 79th St *Web:* www.acquavellagalleries.com	New York	NY	10075	212-734-6300	794-9394
Airway Surgical Appliances Ltd 189 Colonnade Rd *Web:* www.airwaysurgical.ca	Nepean	ON	K2E7J4	613-723-4790	
Alexander & Bonin LLC 132 Tenth Ave. *Web:* www.alexanderandbonin.com	New York	NY	10011	212-367-7474	367-7337
Allan Stone Projects 535 W 22nd St Third Fl **Fax Area Code:* 917 ■ *Web:* www.allanstoneprojects.com	New York	NY	10011	212-987-4997	421-9895*
Alpha Gallery 37 Newbury St *Web:* www.alphagallery.com	Boston	MA	02116	617-536-4465	536-5695
Angles Gallery 2754 S La Cienega Blvd. *Web:* www.anglesgallery.com	Los Angeles	CA	90034	310-396-5019	202-6330
Anna Kustera Gallery 520 W 21st St *Web:* www.annakustera.com	New York	NY	10011	212-989-0082	
Army & Navy Club, The 901 17th St NW *Web:* www.armynavyclub.org	Washington	DC	20006	202-628-8400	
Art Emporium 2928 Granville St *Web:* www.theartemporium.ca	Vancouver	BC	V6H3J7	604-738-3510	733-5427
Art Placement Inc 228 Third Ave S Ste 228 *Web:* www.artplacement.com	Saskatoon	SK	S7K1L9	306-664-3385	933-2521
Aspen Hill Club 14501 Homecrest Rd *Web:* www.aspenhillclub.com	Silver Spring	MD	20906	301-598-5200	
Babcock Galleries 724 Fifth Ave 11th Fl *Web:* www.artnet.com	New York	NY	10019	212-767-1852	767-1857
Barbara Gladstone Gallery 515 W 24th St *Web:* www.gladstonegallery.com	New York	NY	10011	212-206-9300	206-9301
Barbara Krakow Gallery 10 Newbury St Fifth Fl *Web:* www.barbarakrakowgallery.com	Boston	MA	02116	617-262-4490	262-8971
Barbara Mathes Gallery 22 E 80th St *Web:* barbaramathesgallery.com	New York	NY	10075	212-570-4190	570-4191
Bau-Xi Gallery 3045 Granville St *Web:* www.bau-xi.com	Vancouver	BC	V6H3J9	604-733-7011	733-3211
Beckett Fine Art Ltd 33 Hazelton Ave Ste 212 *Web:* www.beckettfineart.com	Toronto	ON	M5R2E3	416-922-5582	
Berry-Hill Galleries Inc 11 E 70th St *Web:* www.berry-hill.com	New York	NY	10021	212-744-2300	744-2838
Brooke Alexander Editions 59 Wooster St *Web:* www.baeditions.com	New York	NY	10012	212-925-4338	941-9565
Catriona Jeffries Gallery 274 E First Ave *Web:* www.catrionajeffries.com	Vancouver	BC	V5T1A6	604-736-1554	736-1054
Chamber Music Society of Lincoln Center 70 Lincoln Ctr Plz *Web:* www.chambermusicsociety.org	New York	NY	10023	212-875-5788	
Cheim & Read 547 W 25th St *Web:* www.cheimread.com	New York	NY	10001	212-242-7727	242-7737

Name / Address	City	State	ZIP	Phone	Fax
Christopher Cutts Gallery 21 Morrow Ave *Web:* www.cuttsgallery.com	Toronto	ON	M6R2H9	416-532-5566	532-7272
Conner Rosenkranz LLC 19 E 74th St *Web:* www.crsculpture.com	New York	NY	10021	212-517-3710	
Corkin Shopland Gallery 55 Mill St Bldg 61 *Web:* www.corkingallery.com	Toronto	ON	M5A3C4	416-979-1980	979-7018
Courts Plus Fitness Center 3491 University Dr S *Web:* www.courtsplus.org	Fargo	ND	58104	701-237-4805	
CRG Gallery 548 W 22nd St *Web:* crggallery.com	New York	NY	10011	212-229-2766	229-2788
D'Amelio Terras 525 W 22nd St *Web:* www.damelioterras.com	New York	NY	10011	212-352-9460	352-9464
Danese 535 W 24th St Sixth Fl *Web:* danesecorey.com	New York	NY	10011	212-223-2227	605-1016
David Findlay Jr Fine Art 724 Fifth Ave *Web:* www.davidfindlayjr.com	New York	NY	10019	212-486-7660	486-6377
David Nolan Gallery 527 W 29th St *Web:* www.davidnolangallery.com	New York	NY	10001	212-925-6190	334-9139
David Zwirner Gallery 525 W 19th St *Web:* www.davidzwirner.com	New York	NY	10011	212-727-2070	727-2072
Davis & Langdale Company Inc 231 E 60th St *Web:* davisandlangdale.com	New York	NY	10022	212-838-0333	752-7764
Dickinson Roundell Inc 19 E 66th St *Web:* www.simondickinson.com	New York	NY	10065	212-772-8083	772-8186
Didier Aaron Inc 32 E 67th St *Web:* www.didieraaron.com	New York	NY	10065	212-988-5248	
Douglas Udell Gallery 10332 124th St *Web:* www.douglasudellgallery.com	Edmonton	AB	T5N1R2	780-488-4445	488-8335
Drabinsky Gallery 114 Yorkville Ave	Toronto	ON	M5R1B9	416-324-5766	324-5770
Edward Day Gallery Inc 952 Queen St W *Web:* www.edwarddaygallery.com	Toronto	ON	M6J1G8	416-921-6540	
Edwynn Houk Gallery 745 Fifth Ave Fourth Fl *Web:* www.houkgallery.com	New York	NY	10151	212-750-7070	688-4848
Elkon Gallery Inc 18 E 81st St Ste 2-A	New York	NY	10028	212-535-3940	737-8479
Equinox Gallery 2321 Granville St *Web:* www.equinoxgallery.com	Vancouver	BC	V6H3G4	604-736-2405	736-0464
Feheley Fine Arts 65 George St **Fax Area Code:* 647 ■ *TF:* 877-904-9114 ■ *Web:* www.feheleyfinearts.com	Toronto	ON	M5A4L8	416-323-1373	361-7667*
Fischbach Gallery 210 11th Ave *Web:* www.fischbachgallery.com	New York	NY	10001	212-759-2345	366-1783
Forum Gallery 730 Fifth Ave *Web:* www.forumgallery.com	New York	NY	10019	212-355-4545	355-4547
Fraenkel Gallery 49 Geary St *Web:* www.artnet.com	San Francisco	CA	94108	415-981-2661	981-4014
Galerie Lelong 528 W 26th St *Web:* www.galerie-lelong.com	New York	NY	10001	212-315-0470	262-0624
Galerie Saint Etienne 24 W 57th St *Web:* www.gseart.com	New York	NY	10019	212-245-6734	765-8493
Galerie Valentin 1490 Sherbrooke Quest Ste 200 *Web:* www.galerievalentin.com	Montreal	QC	H3G1L3	514-939-0500	939-0413
Gallery 78 Inc 796 Queen St *TF:* 888-883-8322 ■ *Web:* www.gallery78.com	Fredericton	NB	E3B1C6	506-454-5192	443-0199
Gallery Moos Ltd 622 Richmond St W *Web:* www.gallerymoos.com	Toronto	ON	M5V1Y9	416-504-5445	504-5446
Gallery One 121 Scollard St *Web:* www.artgalleryone.com	Toronto	ON	M5R1G4	416-929-3103	
Gallery Paule Anglim 14 Geary St *Web:* www.gallerypauleanglim.com	San Francisco	CA	94108	415-433-2710	433-1501
George Adams Gallery 525 W 26th St *Web:* www.artnet.com	New York	NY	10001	212-564-8480	564-8485
Gotham Growth Group 301 Tory Turn *Web:* www.gothamgrowth.com	Radnor	PA	19087	484-433-9806	
Granite Links Golf Club 100 Quarry Hills Dr *Web:* www.granitelinksgolfclub.com	Quincy	MA	02169	617-689-1900	
Hans P Kraus Jr Inc 962 Pk Ave *Web:* www.sunpictures.com	New York	NY	10028	212-794-2064	744-2770
Harlow's Casino 4280 Harlow Blvd *Web:* www.harlowscasino.com	Greenville	MS	38701	662-335-9797	
Heffel Gallery Ltd 2247 Granville St *TF:* 800-528-9608 ■ *Web:* www.heffel.com/gallery	Vancouver	BC	V6H3G1	604-732-6505	732-4245
Hirschl & Adler Galleries Inc 730 Fifth Ave *Web:* www.hirschlandadler.com	New York	NY	10019	212-535-8810	772-7237
Inuit Gallery of Vancouver Ltd 206 Cambie St Gastown *TF:* 888-615-8399 ■ *Web:* www.inuit.com	Vancouver	BC	V6B2M9	604-688-7323	
Jack Kilgore & Company Inc 154 E 71st St Third Fl	New York	NY	10021	212-650-1149	650-1389
Jack Tilton Gallery Eight E 76th St *Web:* www.jacktiltongallery.com	New York	NY	10021	212-737-2221	396-1725
James Goodman Gallery 41 E 57th St Ste 802 *Web:* www.jamesgoodmangallery.com	New York	NY	10022	212-593-3737	980-0195
James Graham & Sons Inc 32 E 67th St *Web:* www.graham1857.com	New York	NY	10065	212-535-5767	794-2454
Jason McCoy Inc 41 E 57th St 11th Fl *Web:* www.jasonmccoyinc.com	New York	NY	10022	212-319-1996	319-4799
Jill Newhouse Gallery Four E 81st St *Web:* www.jillnewhouse.com	New York	NY	10028	212-249-9216	734-4098
John Berggruen Gallery 228 Grant Ave *Web:* www.berggruen.com	San Francisco	CA	94108	415-781-4629	781-0126
June Kelly Gallery 166 Mercer St # 3C *Web:* www.junekellygallery.com	New York	NY	10012	212-226-1660	226-2433
Kinsman Robinson Galleries 108 Cumberland St *Web:* www.kinsmanrobinson.com	Toronto	ON	M5R1A6	416-964-2374	964-9042
Kraushaar Galleries Inc 15 E 71 St Ste 2B *Web:* www.kraushaargalleries.com	New York	NY	10021	212-288-2558	288-2557
LA Louver Inc 45 N Venice Blvd *Web:* www.lalouver.com	Venice	CA	90291	310-822-4955	821-7529
Laurence Miller Gallery 20 W 57th St 3rd Fl *Web:* www.laurencemillergallery.com	New York	NY	10019	212-397-3930	397-3932
Lennon Weinberg Inc 514 W 25th St *Web:* www.lennonweinberg.com	New York	NY	10001	212-941-0012	929-3265
Leo Castelli Gallery 18 E 77th St *Web:* www.castelligallery.com	New York	NY	10075	212-249-4470	
Leonard Hutton Galleries 790 Madison Ave Ste 506 *Web:* www.leonardhuttongalleries.com	New York	NY	10065	212-751-7373	832-2261
Leslie Tonkonow Artworks & Projects 535 W 22nd St Sixth Fl *Web:* www.tonkonow.com	New York	NY	10011	212-255-8450	414-8744
Locks Gallery 600 Washington Sq S *Web:* www.locksgallery.com	Philadelphia	PA	19106	215-629-1000	629-3868
Luhring Augustine Gallery 531 W 24th St *Web:* www.luhringaugustine.com	New York	NY	10011	212-206-9100	206-9055
Manny Silverman Gallery 619 N Almont Dr *Web:* mannysilvermangallery.com	Los Angeles	CA	90069	310-659-8256	659-1001
Margo Leavin Gallery 812 N Robertson Blvd *Web:* www.margoleavingallery.com	Los Angeles	CA	90069	310-273-0603	273-9131
Marian Goodman Gallery 24 W 57th St *Web:* www.mariangoodman.com	New York	NY	10019	212-977-7160	581-5187
Mary Ryan Gallery 515 W 26th St *Web:* www.maryryangallery.com	New York	NY	10001	212-397-0669	397-0766
Mary-Anne Martin Fine Art 23 E 73rd St 4th Fl *Web:* www.mamfa.com	New York	NY	10021	212-288-2213	861-7656
Masters Gallery Ltd 2115 Fourth St SW *TF:* 866-245-0616 ■ *Web:* www.mastersgalleryltd.com	Calgary	AB	T2S1W8	403-245-2064	244-1636
Matthew Marks Gallery 523 W 24th St *Web:* www.matthewmarks.com	New York	NY	10011	212-243-0200	243-0047
Maxwell Davidson Gallery 724 Fifth Ave 4th Fl *Web:* www.davidsongallery.com	New York	NY	10001	212-759-7555	759-5824
Mayberry Fine Art Inc 212 Mcdermot Ave *Web:* www.mayberryfineart.com	Winnipeg	MB	R3B0S3	204-255-5690	
McKee Gallery 745 Fifth Ave 4th Fl *Web:* www.mckeegallery.com	New York	NY	10151	212-688-5951	752-5638
Meredith Long & Co 2323 San Felipe *Web:* www.meredithlonggallery.com	Houston	TX	77019	713-523-6671	523-2355
Metro Pictures Gallery 519 W 24th St *Web:* metropicturesgallery.com	New York	NY	10011	212-206-7100	337-0070
Meyer East Gallery 225 Canyon Rd *Web:* www.meyereastgallery.com	Santa Fe	NM	87501	505-983-1657	988-9867
Michael Gibson Gallery 157 Carling St *TF:* 866-644-2766 ■ *Web:* www.gibsongallery.com	London	ON	N6A1H5	519-439-0451	439-2842
Michael Rosenfeld Gallery 24 W 57th St Seventh Fl *Web:* www.michaelrosenfeldart.com	New York	NY	10019	212-247-0082	247-0402
Michael Werner Gallery Four E 77th St Second Fl *Web:* www.michaelwerner.com	New York	NY	10075	212-988-1623	988-1774
Mira Godard Gallery 22 Hazelton Ave *Web:* www.godardgallery.com	Toronto	ON	M5R2E2	416-964-8197	964-5912
Miriam Shiell Fine Art Ltd 16-A Hazelton Ave *Web:* www.miriamshiell.com	Toronto	ON	M5R2E2	416-925-2461	925-2471
Mitchell-Iness & Nash Gallery 1018 Madison Ave *Web:* www.miandn.com	New York	NY	10075	212-744-7400	744-7401
Modernism Inc 685 Market St Ste 290 *Web:* www.modernisminc.com	San Francisco	CA	94105	415-541-0461	541-0425
Moeller Fine Art Ltd 36 E 64th St *Web:* www.moellerfineart.com	New York	NY	10065	212-644-2133	644-2134
Montgomery Gallery 406 Jackson St *Web:* www.montgomerygallery.com	San Francisco	CA	94111	415-788-8300	788-5469
Nancy Hoffman Gallery 520 W 27th St *Web:* www.nancyhoffmangallery.com	New York	NY	10001	212-966-6676	334-5078
Newzones Gallery of Contemporary Art 730 11th Ave SW *Web:* www.newzones.com	Calgary	AB	T2R0E4	403-266-1972	266-1987
Nouveau Gallery 2146 Albert St *Web:* www.nouveaugallery.com	Regina	SK	S4P2T9	306-569-9279	352-2453
O'Hara Gallery 595 Madison Ave *Web:* www.johg.com	New York	NY	10022	212-644-3533	
Odon Wagner Gallery 196 Davenport Rd *TF:* 800-551-2465 ■ *Web:* www.odonwagnergallery.com	Toronto	ON	M5R1J2	416-962-0438	962-1581
Olga Korper Gallery 17 Morrow Ave *Web:* www.olgakorpergallery.com	Toronto	ON	M6R2H9	416-538-8220	538-8772
Otto Naumann Ltd 22 E 80th St Second Fl *Web:* www.dutchpaintings.com	New York	NY	10075	212-734-4443	535-0617
Pace Gallery, The 32 E 57th St 2th Fl *Web:* www.pacegallery.com	New York	NY	10022	212-421-3292	421-0835
Pace Prints 32 E 57th St Third Fl *Web:* www.paceprints.com	New York	NY	10022	212-421-3237	832-5162
Paul Kuhn Gallery 724 11th Ave SW *Web:* www.paulkuhngallery.com	Calgary	AB	T2R0E4	403-263-1162	262-9426
Paula Cooper Gallery 534 W 21st St *Web:* www.paulacoopergallery.com	New York	NY	10011	212-255-1105	255-5156
Peter Findlay Gallery 16 E 79th St *Web:* www.findlay.com	New York	NY	10075	212-644-4433	644-1675
Phyllis Kind Gallery 236 W 26th St Ste 503 *Web:* www.phylliskindgallery.com	New York	NY	10001	212-925-1200	941-7841
Rhona Hoffman Gallery 118 N Peoria St *Web:* www.artnet.com	Chicago	IL	60607	312-455-1990	455-1727
Richard Gray Gallery 875 N Michigan Ave Ste 2503 *Web:* www.richardgraygallery.com	Chicago	IL	60611	312-642-8877	642-8488
Richard L Feigen & Co 34 E 69th St *Web:* www.rlfeigen.com	New York	NY	10021	212-628-0700	249-4574
Riva Yares Gallery 3625 Bishop Ln **Fax Area Code:* 505 ■ *Web:* www.rivayaresgallery.com	Scottsdale	AZ	85251	480-947-3251	986-8661*
Robert Miller Gallery 524 W 26th St *Web:* www.robertmillergallery.com	New York	NY	10001	212-366-4774	366-4454

	City	State	Zip	Phone	Fax
Roberts Gallery Ltd 641 Yonge St *Web:* www.robertsgallery.net	Toronto	ON	M4Y1Z9	416-924-8731	
Ronald Feldman Fine Arts Inc 31 Mercer St *Web:* www.feldmangallery.com	New York	NY	10013	212-226-3232	941-1536
Schwarz Gallery 1806 Chestnut St *Web:* www.schwarzgallery.com	Philadelphia	PA	19103	215-563-4887	561-5621
Sikkema Jenkins & Co 530 W 22nd St *Web:* www.sikkemajenkinsco.com	New York	NY	10011	212-929-2262	929-2340
Sperone Westwater 257 Bowery *Web:* www.speronewestwater.com	New York	NY	10002	212-999-7337	999-7338
Stephen Bulger Gallery 1026 Queen St W *Web:* www.bulgergallery.com	Toronto	ON	M6J1H6	416-504-0575	504-8929
Stephen Mazoh & Company Inc 19 Pink Ln	Rhinebeck	NY	12572	845-876-2723	876-5838
Susan Hobbs Gallery Inc 137 Tecumseth St *Web:* www.susanhobbs.com	Toronto	ON	M6J2H2	416-504-3699	504-8064
Susan Sheehan Gallery 136 E 16th St *Web:* www.susansheehangallery.com	New York	NY	10003	212-489-3331	489-4009
Tasende Gallery 820 Prospect St *Web:* www.tasendegallery.com	La Jolla	CA	92037	858-454-3691	454-0589
Tatar Art Projects 300 King St E *Web:* tatarartprojects.ca	Toronto	ON	M5A1K4	416-360-3822	362-3843
Thielsen Gallery 1038 Adelaide St N *Web:* www.thielsengallery.com	London	ON	N5Y2M9	519-434-7681	434-8814
Tibor de Nagy Gallery 724 Fifth Ave 12th Fl *Web:* www.tibordenagy.com	New York	NY	10019	212-262-5050	262-1841
TrepanierBaer Gallery 999 Eigth St SW Ste 105 *Web:* www.trepanierbaer.com	Calgary	AB	T2R1J5	403-244-2066	244-2094
Ubu Gallery 416 E 59th St *Web:* www.ubugallery.com	New York	NY	10022	212-753-4444	753-4470
Uno Langmann Ltd 2117 Granville St *TF:* 800-730-8825 ■ *Web:* www.langmann.com	Vancouver	BC	V6H3E9	604-736-8825	
Valley House Gallery Inc 6616 Spring Vly Rd *Web:* www.valleyhouse.com	Dallas	TX	75254	972-239-2441	239-1462
Vivian Horan Fine Art 35 E 67th St 2nd Fl *Web:* vivianhoran.com	New York	NY	10065	212-517-9410	772-6107
Wallace Galleries Ltd 500 Fifth Ave SW *Web:* www.wallacegalleries.com	Calgary	AB	T2P3L5	403-262-8050	264-7112
West End Gallery Ltd 12308 Jasper Ave *Web:* www.westendgalleryltd.com	Edmonton	AB	T5N3K5	780-488-4892	488-4893
Winchester Galleries Ltd 2260 Oak Bay Ave *Web:* www.winchestergalleriesltd.com	Victoria	BC	V8R1G7	250-595-2777	595-2310
WM Brady & Company Inc 22 E 80th St Fourth Fl	New York	NY	10075	212-249-7212	628-6587
Wynick Tuck Gallery 401 Richmond St W Ground Fl *Web:* www.wynicktuckgallery.ca	Toronto	ON	M5V3A8	416-504-8716	504-8699
Zabriskie Gallery 41 E 57th St Fourth Fl *Web:* www.zabriskiegallery.com	New York	NY	10022	212-752-1223	752-1224
Zolla Lieberman Gallery 325 W Huron St *Web:* www.zollaliebermangallery.com	Chicago	IL	60654	312-944-1990	944-8967
Zwickers Gallery 5415 Doyle St *Web:* www.zwickersgallery.ca	Halifax	NS	B3J1H9	902-423-7662	422-3870

43 ART MATERIALS & SUPPLIES - MFR

SEE ALSO Pens, Pencils, Parts p. 2899

	City	State	Zip	Phone	Fax
Alvin & Company Inc 1335 Blue Hills Ave **Fax Area Code:* 800 ■ *TF:* 800-444-2584 ■ *Web:* www.alvinco.com	Bloomfield	CT	06002	860-243-8991	777-2896*
American Art Clay Co (AMACO) 6060 Guion Rd *TF:* 800-374-1600 ■ *Web:* www.amaco.com	Indianapolis	IN	46254	317-244-6871	248-9300
American Metalcraft Inc 2074 George St *TF:* 800-333-9133 ■ *Web:* www.amnow.com	Melrose Park	IL	60160	708-345-1177	345-5758
Ampersand Art Supply 1235 S Loop 4 Ste 400 *TF:* 800-822-1939 ■ *Web:* www.ampersandart.com	Buda	TX	78610	512-322-0278	322-9928
ART Studio Clay Co 9320 Michigan Ave *TF:* 800-323-0212 ■ *Web:* www.artclay.com	Sturtevant	WI	53177	262-884-4278	884-4343
Artist Brand Canvas 2448 Loma Ave **Fax Area Code:* 323 ■ *TF Orders:* 888-579-2704 ■ *Web:* www.artistbrandcanvas.com	South El Monte	CA	91733	626-579-2740	686-2658*
Badger Air Brush Co 9128 Belmont Ave *TF:* 800-247-2787 ■ *Web:* www.badgerairbrush.com	Franklin Park	IL	60131	847-678-3104	671-4352
Canson Inc 21 Industrial Dr *TF:* 800-628-9283 ■ *Web:* www.cansonstudio.com	South Hadley	MA	01075	413-538-9250	534-7692
Chartpak Inc 1 River Rd *TF:* 800-628-1910 ■ *Web:* www.chartpak.com	Leeds	MA	01053	413-584-5446	584-6781
Daler-Rowney USA Ltd Two Corporate Dr *Web:* www.daler-rowney.com	Cranbury	NJ	08512	609-655-5252	655-5852
DecoArt Inc 49 Cotton Ave *TF:* 800-367-3047 ■ *Web:* www.decoart.com	Stanford	KY	40484	606-365-3193	365-2997
Duncan Enterprises 5673 E Shields Ave *TF:* 800-438-6226 ■ *Web:* www.ilovetocreate.com	Fresno	CA	93727	559-291-4444	291-4444
Duro Art Industries Inc 1832 Juneway Terr *Web:* www.duroart.com	Chicago	IL	60626	773-743-3430	743-3882
Gare Inc 165 Rosemont St **Fax Area Code:* 800 ■ *TF:* 888-289-4273 ■ *Web:* www.gare.com	Haverhill	MA	01832	978-373-9131	292-0885*
General Pencil Co Inc 3160 Bay Rd *Web:* www.generalpencil.com	Redwood City	CA	94063	650-369-4889	369-7169
Georgie's Ceramic & Clay Company Inc 756 NE Lombard St *TF:* 800-999-2529 ■ *Web:* www.georgies.com	Portland	OR	97211	503-283-1353	283-1387
Golden Artists Colors Inc 188 Bell Rd *TF:* 800-959-6543 ■ *Web:* www.goldenpaints.com	New Berlin	NY	13411	607-847-6154	847-6767
Jack Richeson & Company Inc 557 Marcella Dr *TF:* 800-233-2404 ■ *Web:* www.richesonart.com	Kimberly	WI	54136	920-738-0744	738-9156
Martin/F Weber Co 2727 Southampton Rd *TF:* 800-876-8076 ■ *Web:* www.weberart.com	Philadelphia	PA	19154	215-677-5600	677-3336
National Artcraft Supply Co 300 Campus Dr *TF:* 888-937-2723 ■ *Web:* www.nationalartcraft.com	Aurora	OH	44202	330-562-3500	562-3507
Paasche Airbrush Co 4311 N Normandy *TF Sales:* 800-621-1907 ■ *Web:* www.paascheairbrush.com	Chicago	IL	60634	773-867-9191	867-9198
Plaid Enterprises Inc 3225 Westech Dr **Fax:* Mktg ■ *TF:* 800-842-4197 ■ *Web:* www.plaidonline.com	Norcross	GA	30092	678-291-8100	291-8368*
Sargent Art Inc 100 E Diamond Ave *TF:* 800-424-3596 ■ *Web:* www.sargentart.com	Hazleton	PA	18201	570-454-3596	459-1752
Sinopia Pigments 2349 Third St PO Box 884354 *Web:* www.sinopia.com	San Francisco	CA	94107	415-824-3180	
Smooth-On Inc 2000 St John St *TF:* 800-766-6841 ■ *Web:* www.smooth-on.com	Easton	PA	18042	610-252-5800	252-6200
Testor Corp 440 Blackhawk Pk Ave *TF:* 800-837-8677 ■ *Web:* www.testors.com	Rockford	IL	61104	815-962-6654	962-7401
Tri-Chem 681 Main St Bldg 24 *Web:* www.trichem.com	Belleville	NJ	07109	973-751-9200	450-1260
Utrecht Art Supplies PO Box 1769 **Fax Area Code:* 800 ■ *TF:* 888-336-3114 ■ *Web:* www.utrechtart.com	Galesburg	IL	61402	609-409-8001	382-1979*

44 ART MATERIALS & SUPPLIES - WHOL

	City	State	Zip	Phone	Fax
American Hobby Craft Distributors Inc 2040 W N Ln	Phoenix	AZ	85021	602-861-1239	944-7124
Creative Hobbies Inc 900 Creek Rd Ste A *TF:* 800-843-5456 ■ *Web:* www.creative-hobbies.com	Bellmawr	NJ	08031	856-933-2540	
CWI Gifts & Crafts 77 Cypress St SW *TF:* 800-666-5858 ■ *Web:* www.shopcwi.com	Reynoldsburg	OH	43068	740-964-6210	964-6212
D&L Art Glass Supply 1440 W 52nd Ave *TF:* 800-525-0940 ■ *Web:* www.dlstainedglass.com	Denver	CO	80221	303-449-8737	442-3429
Darice Inc 13000 Darice Pkwy **Fax Area Code:* 440 ■ *TF:* 800-321-1494 ■ *Web:* www.darice.com	Strongsville	OH	44149	866-432-7433	238-1680*
Decorator & Craft Corp (DC & C) 428 S Zelta St *Web:* www.dcccrafts.com	Wichita	KS	67207	316-685-6265	685-7606
Dumouchelle Art Gallery 409 E Jefferson Ave *Web:* www.dumouchelles.com	Detroit	MI	48226	313-963-6255	963-8199
Howell's Craftand Imports 6030 NE 112th Ave **Fax Area Code:* 503 ■ *TF:* 800-547-0368 ■ *Web:* www.howells-craftland.com	Portland	OR	97220	800-547-0368	255-6878*
King Craft Co 142 N Main St PO Box 671 *Web:* www.kingcraftco.com	Herkimer	NY	13350	315-866-5500	866-8062
Pioneer Wholesale Co 500 W Bagley Rd *TF:* 888-234-5400 ■ *Web:* www.pioneerwholesaleco.com	Berea	OH	44017	440-234-5400	234-5403
Sbar's Inc 14 Sbar Blvd *TF:* 800-989-7227 ■ *Web:* www.sbarsonline.com	Moorestown	NJ	08057	856-234-8220	234-9159
Sepp Leaf Products Inc 381 Pk Ave S Ste 1301 *TF:* 800-971-7377 ■ *Web:* www.seppleaf.com	New York	NY	10016	212-683-2840	725-0308
Shop Hobby Lobby 7717 SW 44th St *TF:* 800-888-0321 ■ *Web:* shop.hobbylobby.com	Oklahoma City	OK	73179	405-745-1275	

45 ART SUPPLY STORES

	City	State	Zip	Phone	Fax
Aaron Bros Inc 1221 S Beltline Rd Ste 500 *Web:* www.aaronbrothers.com	Coppell	TX	75019	214-492-6200	
Able Infosat Communications Inc 5906 Broadway St *Web:* www.able-usa.com	Pearland	TX	77581	281-485-8800	
AC Moore Arts & Crafts Inc 130 AC Moore Dr *NASDAQ: ACMR* ■ *Web:* www.acmoore.com	Berlin	NJ	08009	888-226-6673	
Accord Carton 6155 W 115th St *Web:* accordcarton.com	Alsip	IL	60803	708-388-7070	
Al Friedman Company Inc 44 W 18th St Fourth Fl *TF:* 800-204-6352 ■ *Web:* www.aifriedman.com	New York	NY	10011	212-243-9000	929-7320
Alabama Art Supply Inc 1006 23rd St S *TF Cust Svc:* 800-749-4741 ■ *Web:* www.alabamaart.com	Birmingham	AL	35205	205-322-4741	254-3116
All Copy Products LLC 4141 Colorado Blvd *Web:* www.allcopyproducts.com	Denver	CO	80216	303-295-0741	
All in One Poster Co 8521 Whitaker St *Web:* www.allinoneposters.com	Buena Park	CA	90621	714-521-7720	
All Media Art Supply 417 E Main St *Web:* allmediaartsupply.com	Kent	OH	44240	330-678-8078	678-0794
All-Fab Building Components Inc 1755 Dugald Rd *Web:* www.all-fab.com	Winnipeg	MB	R2J0H3	204-661-8880	
Alpina Manufacturing LLC 3418 N Knox Ave *Web:* www.fastchangeframes.com	Chicago	IL	60641	773-202-8887	
AmeriWater Inc 1303 Stanley Ave *Web:* ameriwater.com	Dayton	OH	45404	937-461-8833	
Aquinas & More Catholic Goods Inc 4727 N Academy Blvd Ste A *Web:* www.aquinasandmore.com	Colorado Springs	CO	80918	719-495-7493	
Arizona Art Supply 4025 N 16th St *TF:* 877-264-9514 ■ *Web:* www.arizonaartsupply.com	Phoenix	AZ	85016	602-264-9514	
Armor Security Inc 2601 Stevens Ave South *Web:* www.armorsecurity.com	Minneapolis	MN	55408	612-870-4142	
Art Corner, The 264 Washington St *Web:* artcornersalem.com	Salem	MA	01970	978-745-9524	
Art Essentials 32 E Victoria St *Web:* www.sbartessentials.com	Santa Barbara	CA	93101	805-965-5456	965-3347
Art Hardware 119 E Costilla *Web:* art-hardware.com	Colorado Springs	CO	80903	719-635-2348	
Art Supply Warehouse 6672 Westminster Blvd *TF:* 800-854-6467 ■ *Web:* www.artsupplywarehouse.com	Westminster	CA	92683	714-891-3626	895-6701
Artmart 2355 S Hanley Rd *Web:* www.artmartstl.com	Saint Louis	MO	63144	314-781-9999	781-3121
Asel Art Supply 2701 Cedar Springs *TF:* 888-273-5278 ■ *Web:* www.aselart.com	Dallas	TX	75201	214-871-2425	871-0007
Backblaze Inc 500 Ben Franklin Ct *Web:* www.backblaze.com	San Mateo	CA	94401	650-352-3738	

Phone Fax

Best Banner Sign Graphics Inc 630 Canion St ... Austin TX 78752 512-458-5348
Web: www.bannersigngraphics.com

Bestronics Inc 2060 Ringwood Ave ... San Jose CA 95131 408-432-3222
Web: www.bestronics.com

Bettendorf Office Products Inc
3280 Middle Rd ... Bettendorf IA 52722 563-359-3487 359-8901
Web: www.bettoffice.com

Blaine's Art Supply 1025 Photo Ave ... Anchorage AK 99503 907-561-5344 562-5988
TF: 866-561-4278 ■ *Web:* www.blainesart.com

Bliss Industries Inc 386 Railroad Ct ... Milpitas CA 95035 408-945-8401
Web: www.blissindustries.com

Business Systems & Consultants Inc
113 Little Vly Ct ... Birmingham AL 35244 205-988-3300
Web: bscsolutions.com

Care Wise Medical Products Corp
16110 Caputo Dr ... Morgan Hill CA 95038 408-779-5531
Web: www.carewise.com

Cashman Equipment Co 3300 St Rose Pkwy ... Henderson NV 89052 702-649-8777
Web: www.cashmanequipment.com

Cazenovia Equipment Company Inc
Two Remington Park Dr ... Cazenovia NY 13035 315-655-8620
Web: www.cazenoviaequipment.com

Cody Pools Inc 2300 W Parmer Ln ... Austin TX 78727 512-835-4966
Web: www.codypools.com

Condor Reliability Services Inc
3400 De La Cruz Blvd Unit R ... Santa Clara CA 95054 408-486-9600
Web: www.crsigroup.com

Congdon's Aids To Daily Living Ltd
100 A Ave Ste 15830 ... Edmonton AB T5P0L8 780-483-1762
Web: congdons.ab.ca

Continental Art Supplies 7041 Reseda Blvd ... Reseda CA 91335 818-345-1044
Web: www.continentalart.com

Controls Corporation of America
1501 Harpers Rd ... Virginia Beach VA 23454 757-422-8330
Web: www.concoa.com

Crafts Frames & Things 108 Owen Dr ... Fayetteville NC 28304 910-485-4833
Web: www.craftsframesandthings.com

Dick Blick Co PO Box 1267 ... Galesburg IL 61402 309-343-6181
TF Orders: 800-447-8192 ■ *Web:* www.dickblick.com

Douglas & Sturgess Inc 1023 Factory St ... Richmond CA 94801 510-235-8411 235-4211
TF: 800-762-0744 ■ *Web:* www.artstuf.com

Esna Technologies Inc
30 W Beaver Creek Rd Ste 101 ... Richmond Hill ON L4B3K1 905-707-9700
Web: www.esnatech.com

EverGlow NA Inc 1122 Industrial Dr ... Matthews NC 28105 704-841-2580
Web: www.everglow.us

Fastframe USA Inc
1200 Lawrence Dr Ste 300 ... Newbury Park CA 91320 805-498-4463 498-8983
TF: 888-863-7263 ■ *Web:* www.fastframe.com

Flax Art & Design 1699 Market St ... San Francisco CA 94103 415-552-2355
TF: 844-352-9278 ■ *Web:* www.flaxart.com

Flying Colors, Powered by Moss
1336 Seventh St ... Berkeley CA 94710 510-526-9100
Web: www.moss-sports.com

G & H Art Co 4300 Hamilton Rd ... Columbus GA 31904 706-576-5551

Georgie's Ceramic & Clay Company Inc
756 NE Lombard St ... Portland OR 97211 503-283-1353 283-1387
TF: 800-999-2529 ■ *Web:* www.georgies.com

Haber Vision LLC 15710 W Colfax Ave Ste 204 ... Golden CO 80401 303-459-2220
Web: www.habervision.com

Herweck's Art & Drafting Supplies
300 Broadway St ... San Antonio TX 78205 210-227-1349 227-8533
TF: 800-725-1349 ■ *Web:* www.herwecks.com

Hobby Lobby Creative Centers
7707 SW 44th St ... Oklahoma City OK 73179 405-745-1100 745-1547
Web: www.hobbylobby.com

Hobbytown USA 1233 Libra Dr ... Lincoln NE 68512 402-434-5050
Web: www.hobbytown.com

Imaging Office Systems Inc
4505 E Park 30 Dr ... Columbia City IN 46725 260-248-9696
Web: www.imagingoffice.com

Insight Instruments Inc
2580 SE Willoughby Blvd ... Stuart FL 34994 772-219-9393
Web: www.insightinstruments.com

J. D. Young Company Inc 116 W Third St ... Tulsa OK 74103 918-582-9955
Web: www.jdyoung.com

Kanson Electronics Inc 245 Forrest Ave ... Hohenwald TN 38462 931-796-3050
Web: www.issc-kanson.com

Lantana Communications Corp
1700 Tech Centre Pkwy Ste 100 ... Arlington TX 76014 800-345-4211
TF: 800-345-4211 ■ *Web:* www.lantanacom.com

Lee's Art Shop Inc 220 W 57th St ... New York NY 10019 212-247-0110 581-7023
Web: www.leesartshop.com

Legend Data Systems Inc 18024 72nd Ave South ... Kent WA 98032 425-251-1670
Web: www.legendid.com

Longwall Associates Inc 212 Kendall Ave ... Chilhowie VA 24319 276-646-2004
Web: www.longwall.com

M C Electronics Inc 1891 Airway Dr ... Hollister CA 95023 831-637-1651
Web: www.mcelectronics.com

MarketFrames Group LLC
1231 NW Hoyt St Ste 101 ... Portland OR 97209 503-892-0160
Web: www.marketframes.com

Michaels Stores Inc 8000 Bent Branch Dr ... Irving TX 75063 972-409-1300 409-7570*
**Fax:* Hum Res ■ *TF Cust Svc:* 800-642-4235 ■ *Web:* www.michaels.com

Micron Industries Corp 1211 22nd St Ste 200 ... Oak Brook IL 60523 630-516-1222
Web: micronpower.com

Millers Artist Supplies Co
33332 W 12 Mile Rd ... Farmington Hills MI 48334 248-489-8070 489-8643
Web: www.millersart.com

Modern Farm Equipment Co 2929 N Bluff St ... Fulton MO 65251 573-642-5777
Web: www.modernfarmequip.com

Motion Specialties Inc 7413 Macleod Trl SW ... Calgary AB T2H0L8 403-247-2222
Web: www.motionspecialties.com

Phone Fax

National Art Shop 509 S National Ave ... Springfield MO 65802 417-866-3743 866-3748
TF: 800-949-3743 ■ *Web:* nationalartshop.com

Nelson White Systems Inc
8725-A Loch Raven Blvd ... Baltimore MD 21286 410-668-9628
Web: www.nelsonwhite.com

New York Central Art Supply 62 Third Ave ... New York NY 10003 800-950-6111 475-2513*
**Fax Area Code:* 212 ■ *TF:* 800-950-6111 ■ *Web:* www.nycentralart.com

NovaMed Corp 30 Nutmeg Dr ... Trumbull CT 06611 203-380-6682
Web: www.novamedcorp.com

Omnipure Filter Company Inc
1904 Industrial Way ... Caldwell ID 83605 208-454-2597
Web: www.omnipure.com

Orbit Medical Enterprises Inc
716 East 4500 South Ste 260 S ... Salt Lake City UT 84107 801-713-2020
Web: www.orbitmedical.com

Orthotic Prosthetic Center Inc
8330 Professional Hill Dr ... Fairfax VA 22031 703-698-5007
Web: opc1.com

Pantronix Corp 2710 Lakeview Ct ... Fremont CA 94538 510-656-5898
Web: www.pantronix.com

Pat Catan's Craft Centers
21160 Drake Rd ... Strongsville OH 44149 440-238-7318 238-3536
TF: 800-321-1494 ■ *Web:* www.patcatans.com

Patten Monument Co 3980 W River Dr NE ... Comstock Park MI 49321 616-785-4141
Web: www.pattenmonument.com

Petersen Industries Inc 4000 SR 60 W ... Lake Wales FL 33859 863-676-1493
Web: www.petersenind.com

Plaza Art 633 Middleton St ... Nashville TN 37203 615-254-3368 254-1814
TF: 866-668-6714 ■ *Web:* www.plazaart.com

Plaza Artists Materials of the MidAtlantic Inc
1990 K Str NW ... Washington DC 20006 202-331-7090 331-3004
TF: 866-668-6714 ■ *Web:* www.plazaart.com

Premier Pyrotechnics Inc 25255 Hwy K ... Richland MO 65556 888-647-6863
TF: 888-647-6863 ■ *Web:* www.premierpyro.com

Proline Supply Co 6711 Bingle Rd ... Houston TX 77092 713-939-9730
Web: www.prolinesupplyco.com

Provisio Group Ltd, The
10910 W Sam Houston Pkwy N Ste 500 ... Houston TX 77064 281-894-7700
Web: www.provisiogroup.com

Quality Filtration LLC
5215 Linbar Dr Ste 204 ... Nashville TN 37211 615-833-2400
Web: www.qualityfiltration.com

Rabbit Air 9242 1/2 Hall Rd ... Downey CA 90241 562-861-4688
Web: www.rabbitair.com

Ready Set Go Po Box 856 ... Ukiah CA 95482 707-468-0213
Web: rdysetgo.com

Regali Inc 518 N Interurban St ... Richardson TX 75081 972-726-8830
Web: www.regaliinc.com

Repeat Business Systems Inc Four Fritz Blvd ... Albany NY 12205 518-869-8116
Web: www.repeatbusinesssystems.com

Restaurant Solutions Inc 1423 Austell Rd ... Marietta GA 30008 770-421-1999
Web: www.restaurantsolutionsinc.com

Rex Artist Supplies 3160 SW 22 St ... Miami FL 33145 305-445-1413 445-1412
TF: 800-739-2782 ■ *Web:* www.rexart.com

RISD Store Art Supplies 30 N Main St ... Providence RI 02903 401-454-6464 454-6453
Web: risdstore.com

Riverside Art Shop 1600 Grand Army Hwy ... Somerset MA 02726 508-672-6735 672-6797
Web: www.riversideart.com

Santa Fe Partners LLC
1512 Pacheco St Ste D202 ... Santa Fe NM 87505 505-989-8180
Web: santafepartnersllc.com

Savoir-Faire 40 Leveroni Ct ... Novato CA 94949 415-884-8090
Web: www.savoirfaire.com

Schulz Electric Co 30 Gando Dr ... New Haven CT 06513 203-562-5811
Web: schulzelectric.com

Short Order Lp 12521 Amherst Dr ... Austin TX 78727 512-610-3600
Web: www.shortorder.com

Spokane Art Supply Inc 1303 N Monroe St ... Spokane WA 99201 509-327-6622 327-6629
TF: 800-556-5568 ■ *Web:* www.spokaneartsupply.com

Stagecraft Industries Inc 5051 N Lagoon Ave ... Portland OR 97217 503-286-1600
Web: www.stagecraftindustries.com

Starvin' Artist Supplies 802 S Oak Pk ... Oak Park IL 60304 708-358-3600
TF: 800-427-8478 ■ *Web:* www.starvinartistsupply.com

Stewart Business Systems LLC
105 Connecticut Dr ... Burlington NJ 08016 609-589-4800
Web: www.stewartnj.com

Suder's Art Store 1309 Vine St ... Cincinnati OH 45202 513-241-0800
Web: sudersartstore.com

SVTRONICS INC 3465 Technology ... Plano TX 75074 214-440-1234
Web: www.svtronics.com

Symon's Fire Protection Inc
1050 Pioneer Way Ste R ... El Cajon CA 92020 619-588-6364
Web: www.symonsfp.com

Texas Art Supply 2001 Montrose Blvd ... Houston TX 77006 713-526-5221 526-4062
TF: 800-888-9278 ■ *Web:* www.texasart.com

Texas Deer Association
403 E Ramsey Rd Ste 204 ... San Antonio TX 78216 210-767-8300
Web: www.texasdeerassociation.com

Thomsons Art Supply Inc
184 Mamaroneck Ave ... White Plains NY 10601 914-949-4885 949-4978
TF: 800-287-4885 ■ *Web:* www.thomsonsart.com

Top Notch Art Ctr 411 S Craig St ... Pittsburgh PA 15213 412-683-4444
Web: tnartsupply.com

Trinity Ceramic Supply Inc 9016 Diplomacy Row ... Dallas TX 75247 214-631-0540 637-6463
Web: www.trinityceramic.com

Tristar Electronics Corp
3610 Willowbend Blvd Ste 1020 ... Houston TX 77054 713-667-7200
Web: www.tristareca.com

Versalift East Inc 2706 Brodhead Rd ... Bethlehem PA 18020 610-866-1400
Web: www.versalifteast.com

Village Art Supply 715 Hahman Dr ... Santa Rosa CA 95405 707-575-4501 568-2112

VMI Inc 211 E Weddell Dr ... Sunnyvale CA 94089 408-745-1700
Web: www.vmivideo.com

Phone Fax

Walden Equipment Ltd 106 Fielding Rd .... Lively ON P3Y1L5 705-682-2084
Web: www.waldenequipment.ca

Wasatch Container Inc
645 North 400 West .... North Salt Lake UT 84054 801-295-8888
Web: www.wasatchcontainer.com

Wet Paint Inc 1684 W Grand Ave .... Saint Paul MN 55105 651-698-6431 698-8041
Web: www.wetpaintart.com

Wire & Plastic Machinery Co 800 E Second St .... Bonham TX 75418 903-583-2183
Web: www.wireandplastic.com

Woodcraft Supply LLC
1177 Rosemar Rd PO Box 1686 .... Parkersburg WV 26105 800-535-4482 428-8271*
*Fax Area Code: 304 ■ TF: 800-535-4482 ■ Web: www.woodcraft.com

Zistos Corp 1736 Church St .... Holbrook NY 11741 631-434-1370
Web: www.zistos.com

46 ASPHALT PAVING & ROOFING MATERIALS

Phone Fax

AE Stone Inc 1435 Doughty Rd .... Egg Harbor Township NJ 08234 609-641-2781 641-0374
Web: www.aestone.com

American Asphalt Paving Co 500 Chase Rd .... Shavertown PA 18708 570-696-1181 696-3486
Web: www.amerasphalt.com

Asphalt Materials Inc PO Box 5 .... West Jordan UT 84084 801-561-4231 561-7795
Web: asphaltmaterials.net

Atlas Roofing Corp 2322 Valley Rd .... Meridian MS 39307 601-483-7111 483-7344
TF Cust Svc: 800-478-0258 ■ Web: www.atlasroofing.com

Baker Rock Resources
21880 SW Farmington Rd .... Beaverton OR 97007 503-642-2531 642-2534
TF: 800-340-7625 ■ Web: www.baker-rock.com

Brannan Sand & Gravel Co 2500 Brannan Way .... Denver CO 80229 303-534-1231 534-1231
Web: www.brannan1.com

Brewer Co 1354 US Hwy 50 .... Milford OH 45150 513-576-6300 576-1414
TF: 800-394-0017 ■ Web: www.brewercote.com

Brox Industries Inc 1471 Methuen St .... Dracut MA 01826 978-454-9105 805-9720
Web: www.broxindustries.com

Burkholder Paving 621 Martindale Rd .... Ephrata PA 17522 717-354-1340 428-7469*
*Fax Area Code: 888 ■ TF: 866-839-3426 ■ Web: www.burkholderpaving.com

Capitol Aggregates Ltd
12625 Wetmore Rd Ste 301 .... San Antonio TX 78247 210-871-6100 599-1709
TF: 800-292-5315 ■ Web: www.capitolaggregates.com

CertainTeed Corp 750 E Swedesford Rd .... Valley Forge PA 19482 610-341-7000 341-7777
TF Prod Info: 800-782-8777 ■ Web: www.certainteed.com

Coastal Bridge Company LLC
4825 Jamestown Ave PO Box 14715 .... Baton Rouge LA 70898 225-766-0244 766-0423
Web: www.coastalbridge.com

Community Asphalt Corp 9675 NW 117 Ave Ste 108 .... Miami FL 33178 305-884-9444 884-9448
TF General: 800-741-0806 ■ Web: www.cacorp.net

Consolidated Fiberglass Products Co
3801 Standard St .... Bakersfield CA 93308 661-323-6026 324-2635
Web: www.conglas.com

Coopers Creek Chemical Corp
884 River Rd .... West Conshohocken PA 19428 610-828-0375 828-9720
Web: www.cooperscreekchemical.com

Crafco Inc 420 N Roosevelt Ave .... Chandler AZ 85226 602-276-0406 961-0513*
*Fax Area Code: 480 ■ TF: 800-528-8242 ■ Web: www.crafco.com

Dalrymple Gravel & Contracting Company Inc
2105 S Broadway .... Pine City NY 14871 607-737-6200 737-1056
Web: www.dalrymplecompanies.com

Dalton Enterprises Inc 131 Willow St .... Cheshire CT 06410 203-272-3221 271-3396
TF: 800-851-5606 ■ Web: www.latexite.com

Dewitt Products Co 5860 Plumer Ave .... Detroit MI 48209 313-554-0575 554-2171
TF Cust Svc: 800-962-8599 ■ Web: www.dewittproducts.com

Fields Company LLC 2240 Taylor Way .... Tacoma WA 98421 800-627-4098 383-2181*
*Fax Area Code: 253 ■ TF: 800-627-4098 ■ Web: www.fieldscorp.com

GAF Materials Corp 1361 Alps Rd .... Wayne NJ 07470 973-628-3000
TF: 800-365-7353 ■ Web: www.gaf.com

Gardner-Gibson PO Box 5449 .... Tampa FL 33675 813-248-2101 248-6768
TF: 800-237-1155 ■ Web: www.gardner-gibson.com

Garland Company Inc 3800 E 91st St .... Cleveland OH 44105 216-641-7500 641-0633
TF: 800-321-9336 ■ Web: www.garlandco.com

General Asphalt Co Inc 4850 NW 72nd Ave .... Miami FL 33166 305-592-3480 477-4675

Glenn O Hawbaker Inc
1952 Waddle Rd Ste 203 .... State College PA 16803 814-237-1444
TF: 800-221-1355 ■ Web: www.goh-inc.com

Granite Construction Inc 585 W Beach St .... Watsonville CA 95076 831-724-1011 722-9657
NYSE: GVA ■ Web: www.graniteconstruction.com

Heely-Brown Company Inc
1280 Chattahoochee Ave .... Atlanta GA 30318 404-352-0022 350-2693
TF: 800-241-4628 ■ Web: www.heelybrown.com

Hempt Bros Inc 205 Creek Rd .... Camp Hill PA 17011 717-737-3411 761-5019
Web: hemptbros.com

Henry Co 909 N Sepulveda Blvd Ste 650 .... El Segundo CA 90245 310-955-9200 223-1285*
*Fax Area Code: 866 ■ *Fax: Cust Svc ■ TF: 800-598-7663 ■ Web: www.henry.com

HRI Inc 1750 W College Ave .... State College PA 16801 877-474-9999 238-0131*
*Fax Area Code: 814 ■ TF: 877-474-9999 ■ Web: www.hrico.com

Innovative Metals Company Inc (IMETCO)
4648 S Old Peachtree Rd .... Norcross GA 30084 770-908-1030 908-2264
TF: 800-646-3826 ■ Web: www.imetco.com

Jax Asphalt Co 1800 Waterworks Rd .... Mount Vernon IL 62864 618-244-0500

Karnak Corp, The 330 Central Ave .... Clark NJ 07066 732-388-0300 388-9422
TF: 800-526-4236 ■ Web: www.karnakcorp.com

Koppers Inc 436 Seventh Ave .... Pittsburgh PA 15219 412-227-2001 227-2333
NYSE: KOP ■ TF: 800-321-9876 ■ Web: www.koppers.com

Lunday-Thagard Co 9302 Garfield Ave .... South Gate CA 90280 562-928-7000 806-4032
TF: 800-266-6551 ■ Web: lundaythagard.com

Malarkey Roofing Products PO Box 17217 .... Portland OR 97217 503-283-1191 289-7644
TF: 800-545-1191 ■ Web: www.malarkeyroofing.com

Marathon Petroleum LLC PO Box 1 .... Findlay OH 45839 419-422-2121 425-7040
Web: www.marathonpetroleum.com

Phone Fax

Martin Asphalt Co
Three Riverway Ste 400 .... South Houston TX 77056 713-350-6800 350-6801
TF: 800-662-0987 ■ Web: www.themartincompanies.com

Midland Asphalt Materials Inc 640 Young St .... Tonawanda NY 14150 716-692-0730 692-0613
Web: www.midlandasphalt.com

Neyra Industries 10700 Evendale Dr .... Cincinnati OH 45241 513-733-1000 733-3989
TF: 800-543-7077 ■ Web: www.neyra.com

Oldcastle Materials Inc
900 Ashwood Pkwy Ste 700 .... Atlanta GA 30338 770-522-5600 522-5608
Web: www.apac.com

Pace Products Inc
4510 W 89th St Ste 110 .... Prairie Village KS 66207 888-389-8203 469-4067*
*Fax Area Code: 913 ■ TF: 888-389-8203 ■ Web: www.paceproducts.com

Package Pavement Company Inc PO Box 408 .... Stormville NY 12582 845-221-2224 221-0433
TF: 800-724-8193 ■ Web: www.packagepavement.com

Palmer Asphalt Co 196 W Fifth St PO Box 58 .... Bayonne NJ 07002 201-339-0855 339-8320
TF: 800-352-9898 ■ Web: www.palmerasphalt.com

Peckham Industries Inc 20 Haarlem Ave .... White Plains NY 10603 914-949-2000 949-2075
Web: www.peckham.com

PetersenDean Roofing and Solar
707 Aldridge Rd Ste A .... Vacaville CA 95688 877-552-4418 469-6248*
*Fax Area Code: 707 ■ Web: petersendean.com

Pike Industries Inc 3 Eastgate Pk Rd .... Belmont NH 03220 603-527-5100 527-5101
TF: 800-283-0803 ■ Web: pikeindustries.com

Rason Asphalt Inc 44 Morris Ave .... Glen Cove NY 11542 516-671-1500

Russell Standard Corp 285 Kappa Dr Ste 300 .... Pittsburgh PA 15238 800-323-3053
TF General: 800-323-3053 ■ Web: www.russellstandard.com

Seaboard Asphalt Products Co
3601 Fairfield Rd .... Baltimore MD 21226 410-355-0330 355-5864
TF: 800-536-0332 ■ Web: www.seaboardasphalt.com

Sika Sarnafil Inc 100 Dan Rd .... Canton MA 02021 781-828-5400 828-5365
TF: 800-451-2504 ■ Web: usa.sarnafil.sika.com

Simon Roofing & Sheet Metal Corp
70 Karago Ave .... Youngstown OH 44512 330-629-7663 629-7399
TF: 800-523-7714 ■ Web: www.simonroofing.com

South State Inc 202 Reeves Rd .... Bridgeton NJ 08302 856-451-5300 455-3461
Web: southstateinc.com

Stavola Contracting PO Box 482 .... Red Bank NJ 07701 732-542-2328 389-6083
Web: www.stavola.com

Suit-Kote Corp 1911 Lorings Crossing Rd .... Cortland NY 13045 607-753-1100 756-8611
TF: 800-622-5636 ■ Web: www.suit-kote.com

Tilcon Connecticut Inc PO Box 1357 .... New Britain CT 06050 860-224-6010 225-1865
TF: 888-845-2666 ■ Web: www.tilconct.com

Vance Bros Inc
5201 Brighton PO Box 300107 .... Kansas City MO 64130 816-923-4325 923-6472
TF: 800-821-8549 ■ Web: www.vancebrothers.com

Vulcan Materials Co
1200 Urban Ctr Dr PO Box 385014 .... Birmingham AL 35238 205-298-3000 298-2942
NYSE: VMC ■ TF: 800-615-4331 ■ Web: www.vulcanmaterials.com

Weldon Materials 141 Central Ave .... Westfield NJ 07090 908-233-4444 233-4215
Web: www.weldonmat.com

47 ASSOCIATION MANAGEMENT COMPANIES

Phone Fax

ABEO Group, The 212 S Tryon St Ste 1150 .... Charlotte NC 28281 704-365-3622
Web: www.associationoffices.com

Able Management Solutions Inc
5310 E Main St Ste 104 .... Columbus OH 43213 614-868-1144 868-1177
Web: www.ablemgt.com

Administrative Systems Inc
5204 Fairmount Ave .... Downers Grove IL 60515 630-655-0112 493-0798

Advanced Management Concepts 136 S Keowee St .... Dayton OH 45402 937-222-1024 222-5794
Web: www.advmgtconcepts.com

Allen Press Inc 810 E Tenth St PO Box 1897 .... Lawrence KS 66044 785-843-1235 843-1274
TF: 800-627-0932 ■ Web: allenpress.com

Alliance Management Group
1901 Pennsylvania Ave NW Ste 804 .... Washington DC 20006 202-293-7642 293-0495
Web: www.alliancemg.com

Amber Assn Partners LLC
801 N Fairfax St Ste 211 .... Alexandria VA 22314 703-299-0000 299-9233
Web: amberllc.com

AMR Management Services
201 E Main St Ste 1405 .... Lexington KY 40507 859-514-9150 514-9207
Web: www.amrms.com

Applied Measurement Professionals Inc (AMP)
18000 W 105th St .... Olathe KS 66061 913-895-4600 895-4650
Web: www.goamp.com

Association & Society Management International Inc
201 Pk Washington Ct .... Falls Church VA 22046 703-533-0251 241-5603
Web: www.asmii.com

Association Assoc Inc
Mercerville Rd Bldg B Ste 514 .... Trenton NJ 08619 609-890-9207 581-8244
Web: www.hq4u.com

Association Enterprise Inc (AE)
1601 N Bond St Ste 303 .... Naperville IL 60563 630-369-7786 369-3773
Web: incentivemarketing.org

Association Headquarters Inc
1120 Rt 73 Ste 200 .... Mount Laurel NJ 08054 856-439-0500 439-0525
Web: ahredchair.com

Association Management & Communications
349 Granada Rd .... West Palm Beach FL 33401 561-802-4310

Association Management Ctr 4700 W Lake Ave .... Glenview IL 60025 847-375-4700 374-9143*
*Fax Area Code: 888 ■ Web: www.connect2amc.com

Association Management Group Inc (AMG)
8400 Westpark Dr Second Fl .... McLean VA 22102 703-610-9000 610-9005
Web: www.amg-inc.com

Association Management Resources
2810 Industrial Plz Dr Bldg C .... Tallahassee FL 32301 850-656-8848
Web: www.mgmtresources.org

Association Management Solutions LLC (AMSL)
48377 Fremont Blvd Ste 117 .... Fremont CA 94538 510-492-4000 492-4001
Web: www.amsl.com

Phone Fax

Association Management Specialists
275 E Hillcrest Dr Ste 215 .... Thousand Oaks CA 91360 805-557-1111 557-1133
Web: www.assoc-mgmt.net

Association Management Systems Inc
214 N Hale St .... Wheaton IL 60187 630-510-4500 510-4501
Web: www.association-mgmt.com

Association Managers Inc
12427 Hedges Run Dr Ste 104 .... Lake Ridge VA 22192 703-426-8100 426-8400
TF: 800-403-3374 ■ *Web:* www.assnmgrs.com

Association Resource Ctr (ARC)
555 Capitol Mall Ste 755 PO Box 276567 .... Sacramento CA 95814 916-932-2200 932-2209
Web: www.4arc.com

Association Resources Inc
342 N Main St .... West Hartford CT 06117 860-586-7500 586-7550
Web: www.associationresources.com

Association Solutions Ltd
1111 Burlington Ave Ste 102 .... Lisle IL 60532 630-241-3100 241-0142

Bannister & Assoc Inc 34 N High St .... New Albany OH 43054 614-895-1355 895-3466
TF: 800-995-3579 ■ *Web:* www.bannister.com

BTF Enterprises Inc 3540 Soquel Ave Ste A .... Santa Cruz CA 95062 831-464-4880 464-4881
Web: www.btfenterprises.com

Calabrese Management
4305 N Sixth St Ste A-2 .... Harrisburg PA 17110 717-238-9989 238-9985
Web: www.calabresemgt.com

Center for Assn Growth
1926 Waukegan Rd Ste 1 .... Glenview IL 60025 847-657-6700 657-6819
TF: 800-492-6462 ■ *Web:* tcag.us

Center for Assn Resources Inc
1901 N Roselle Rd Ste 920 .... Schaumburg IL 60195 888-705-1434 885-8393*
**Fax Area Code:* 847 ■ *TF:* 888-705-1434 ■ *Web:* www.association-resources.com

Challenge Management Inc (CMI)
4230 LBJ Fwy Ste 414 .... Dallas TX 75244 972-755-2560 755-2561
Web: www.challenge-management.com

CM Services Inc
800 Roosevelt Rd Bldg C Ste 312 .... Glen Ellyn IL 60137 630-858-7337 790-3095
TF: 800-613-6672 ■ *Web:* www.cmservices.com

Coulter Cos 7918 Jones Branch Dr Ste 300 .... McLean VA 22102 703-506-3260 506-3266
Web: www.coultercos.com

Crow-Segal Management Co
341 N Maitland Ave Ste 130 .... Maitland FL 32751 407-647-8839 629-2502
Web: www.crowsegal.com

Custom Management Group LLC
154 Hansen Rd .... Charlottesville VA 22911 434-971-4788 977-1856
Web: www.custommanagement.com

Degnon Assoc Inc 6728 Old McLean Village Dr .... McLean VA 22101 703-556-9222 556-8729
Web: degnon.org

DeSantis Management Group
1950 Old Tustin Ave .... Santa Ana CA 92705 714-550-9155 550-9234
Web: www.desantisgroup.com

Diversified Management Services
525 SW Fifth St Ste A .... Des Moines IA 50309 515-282-8192 282-9117
Web: www.assoc-mgmt.com

Drake & Co
16020 Swingley Ridge Rd Ste 300 .... Chesterfield MO 63017 636-449-5050 449-5051
Web: www.drakeco.com

Drohan Management Group (DMG)
12100 Sunset Hills Rd Ste 130 .... Reston VA 20190 703-437-4377 435-4390
Web: www.drohanmgmt.com

Ewald Consulting Group Inc
1000 Westgate Dr Ste 252 .... Saint Paul MN 55114 651-290-6260 290-2266
Web: www.ewald.com

Executive Administration Inc
85 W Algonquin Rd Ste 550 .... Arlington Heights IL 60005 847-427-9600 427-9656
Web: www.execadmin.com

Executive Director Inc
555 E Wells St Ste 1100 .... Milwaukee WI 53202 414-276-6445 276-3349
Web: www.execinc.com

Executive Management Assoc
210 N Glenoaks Blvd Ste C .... Burbank CA 91502 818-843-5660 843-7423
Web: www.emaoffice.com

Fanning Group Inc
1280 Main St Second Fl PO Box 479 .... Hanson MA 02341 781-293-4100 294-0808
Web: www.fanningnet.com

Fernley & Fernley Inc
100 N 20th St Fourth Fl .... Philadelphia PA 19103 215-564-3484 564-2175
Web: www.fernley.com

Giuffrida Assoc Inc 204 E St NE .... Washington DC 20002 202-547-6340 547-6348
Web: www.giuffrida.org

Grassley Group, The (FMCI)
409 Washington St Ste A .... Cedar Falls IA 50613 866-619-5580 342-0411*
**Fax Area Code:* 703 ■ *TF:* 866-619-5580 ■ *Web:* www.grassleygroup.com

Guild Assoc Inc, The 389 Main St Ste 202 .... Malden MA 02148 781-397-8870 397-8887
Web: www.guildassoc.com

Harrington Co 4248 Pk Glen Rd .... Minneapolis MN 55416 952-928-7477 929-1318
Web: www.harringtoncompany.com

Hauck & Assoc Inc 1255 23rd St NW Ste 200 .... Washington DC 20037 202-452-8100 833-3636
TF: 800-767-7777 ■ *Web:* www.hauck.com

IMI Assn Executives Inc
2501 Aerial Ctr Pkwy Ste 103 .... Morrisville NC 27560 919-459-2070 459-2075
Web: www.imiae.com

Interactive Management Inc
12011 Tejon St Ste 700 .... Westminster CO 80234 303-433-4446 458-0002
Web: www.imigroup.org

J Edgar Eubanks & Assoc
One Windsor Cove Ste 305 .... Columbia SC 29223 803-252-5646 765-0860
TF: 800-445-8629 ■ *Web:* www.jee.com

Kellen Co
National Press Bldg 529 14th St NW
Ste 750 .... Washington DC 20045 404-252-3663 252-0774
Web: www.kellencompany.com

King Stringfellow Group
2105 Laurel Bush Rd Ste 200 .... Bel Air MD 21015 443-640-1030 640-1031
Web: stringfellowgroup.net

Phone Fax

LoBue & Majdalany Management Group
572B Ruger St PO Box 29920 .... San Francisco CA 94129 415-561-6110 561-6120
TF: 800-820-4690 ■ *Web:* www.lm-mgmt.com

Madeleine Crouch & Company Inc
14070 Proton Rd Ste 100 .... Dallas TX 75244 972-233-9107 490-4219
Web: www.madcrouch.com

Management Solutions Plus Inc
9707 Key W Ave Ste 100 .... Rockville MD 20850 301-258-9210 990-9771
Web: www.mgmtsol.com

McBride & Assoc Inc
1633 Normandy Ct Ste A-200 .... Lincoln NE 68512 402-476-3852 476-6547
Web: www.mcbridemanagement.com

Melby Cameron & Hull Co
23607 Hwy 99 Ste 2C Ste 2C .... Edmonds WA 98026 425-774-7479
Web: www.mcamgmt.com/

Multiservice Management Co
994 Old Eagle School Rd Ste 1019 .... Wayne PA 19087 610-971-4850 971-4859
Web: www.mmco1.com

NeuStar Inc 21575 Ridgetop Cir .... Sterling VA 20166 571-434-5400
TF: 855-638-2677 ■ *Web:* www.neustar.biz

Offinger Management Co
1100-H Brandywine Blvd .... Zanesville OH 43701 740-452-4541 452-2552
Web: www.offinger.com

Organization Management Group
638 Independence Pkwy Ste 100 .... Chesapeake VA 23320 757-473-8701 473-9897
Web: www.managegroup.com

PAI Management Corp 5272 River Rd Ste 630 .... Bethesda MD 20816 301-656-4224 656-0989
Web: www.paimgmt.com

Pathfinder Group 6009 Quinpool Rd .... Halifax NS B3K5S3 902-425-2445
Web: www.pathfinder-group.com

Prime Management Services 3416 Primm Ln ...... Birmingham AL 35216 205-823-6106 823-2760
TF: 866-609-1599 ■ *Web:* primemanagement.net

Professional Management Assoc LLC
390 Amwell Rd Ste 403 .... Hillsborough NJ 08844 908-359-1184 359-7619
Web: www.association-partners.com

Queen Communications LLC 1215 Anthony Ave .... Columbia SC 29201 803-779-0340 254-3773
Web: www.queencommunicationsllc.com

R W Armstrong 300 S Meridian St .... Indianapolis IN 46225 317-786-0461 788-0957
Web: www.rwa.com

Raybourn Group International
9100 PuRdue Rd Ste 200 .... Indianapolis IN 46268 317-328-4636 280-8527
TF: 800-362-2546 ■ *Web:* www.raybourn.com

REM Assn Services
2001 Jefferson Davis Hwy Ste 1004 .... Arlington VA 22202 703-416-0010 416-0014
Web: www.remservices.biz

Resource Ctr for Assns
10200 W 44th Ave Ste 304 .... Wheat Ridge CO 80033 303-422-2615 422-8894

Robstan Group Inc 400 Admiral Blvd .... Kansas City MO 64106 816-472-8870 472-7765
Web: www.robstan.com

Ruggles Service Corp 2209 Dickens Rd .... Richmond VA 23230 804-282-0062 282-0090
Web: www.societyhq.com

S & S Management Services Inc
One Regency Dr .... Bloomfield CT 06002 860-243-3977 286-0787
Web: www.ssmgt.com

Sanford Organization Inc, The (TSO)
1000 N Rand Rd Ste 214 .... Wauconda IL 60084 847-526-2010 526-3993
Web: www.tso.net

Sherwood Group Inc 111 Deer Lk Rd Ste 100 .... Deerfield IL 60015 847-480-9080 480-9282
Web: www.sherwood-group.com

Solutions for Assns Inc
140 N Bloomingdale Rd .... Bloomingdale IL 60108 630-351-8669 351-8490
Web: www.solutions-for-assoc.com

STAT Assn Marketing & Management Inc
11240 Waples Mill Rd Ste 200 .... Fairfax VA 22030 703-934-0160 359-7562
Web: www.statmarketing.com

Talley Management Group Inc 19 Mantua Rd ...... Mount Royal NJ 08061 856-423-7222 423-3420
Web: www.talley.com

Technical Enterprises Inc 7044 S 13th St .... Oak Creek WI 53154 414-768-8000 768-8001
Web: www.techenterprises.net

Thomas Assoc Inc 1300 Sumner Ave .... Cleveland OH 44115 216-241-7333 241-0105
Web: www.taol.com

Total Management Solutions Inc
55 Harristown Rd .... Glen Rock NJ 07452 201-447-0707 447-3831
TF: 866-544-0707 ■ *Web:* www.totmgtsol.com

Verto Solutions 1620 'I' St NW Ste 925 .... Washington DC 20006 202-293-5800 463-8998
Web: www.vertosolutions.net

Virtual Inc 401 Edgewater Pl Ste 600 .... Wakefield MA 01880 781-246-0500 224-1239
Web: www.virtualmgmt.com

Wanner Assoc Inc 908 N Second St .... Harrisburg PA 17102 717-236-2050 236-2046
Web: www.wannerassoc.com

Ward Management Group Inc
10293 N Meridian St Ste 175 .... Indianapolis IN 46290 317-816-1619 816-1633
Web: www.wardmanage.com

Wherry Assoc Inc 30200 Detroit Rd .... Cleveland OH 44145 440-899-0010 892-1404
Web: www.wherryassoc.com

Williams Management Resources Inc (WMR)
1717 N Naper Blvd Ste 102 .... Naperville IL 60563 630-416-1166 416-9798
Web: www.wmrhq.com

Willow Group 1485 Laperriere Ave .... Ottawa ON K1Z7S8 613-722-8796 729-6206
Web: www.thewillowgroup.com

48 ASSOCIATIONS & ORGANIZATIONS - GENERAL

SEE ALSO Performing Arts Organizations p. 2907; Political Action Committees p. 2951; Political Parties (Major) p. 2953

48-1 Accreditation & Certification Organizations

Phone Fax

AACSB International - Assn to Advance Collegiate Schools of Business
777 S Harbour Island Blvd Ste 750 .... Tampa FL 33602 813-769-6500 769-6559
Web: www.aacsb.edu

Phone | Fax

ABET Inc 111 Market Pl Ste 1050 ... Baltimore MD 21202 410-347-7700 625-2238
Web: www.abet.org

Accreditation Assn for Ambulatory Health Care (AAAHC)
5250 Old OrchaRd Rd Ste 200 ... Skokie IL 60077 847-853-6060 853-9028
Web: www.aaahc.org

Accreditation Commission for Acupuncture & Oriental Medicine (ACAOM)
7501 Greenway Ctr Dr Ste 760 ... Greenbelt MD 20770 301-313-0855 313-0912
TF: 800-735-2968 ■ *Web:* www.acaom.org

Accreditation Council for Accountancy & Taxation (ACAT)
1010 N Fairfax St ... Alexandria VA 22314 703-549-2228 549-2984
TF: 888-289-7763 ■ *Web:* www.acatcredentials.org

Accreditation Council for Graduate Medical Education (ACGME)
515 N State St Ste 2000 ... Chicago IL 60610 312-755-5000 755-7498
Web: www.acgme.org

Accreditation Council for Pharmacy Education
20 N Clark St Ste 2500 ... Chicago IL 60602 312-664-3575 664-4652
Web: www.acpe-accredit.org

Accreditation Review Commission on Education for the Physician Assistant Inc (ARC-PA)
12000 Findley Rd Ste 240 ... Duluth GA 30097 770-476-1224 476-1738
Web: www.arc-pa.org

Accrediting Bureau of Health Education Schools (ABHES)
7777 Leesburg Pike Ste 314 N ... Falls Church VA 22043 703-917-9503 917-4109
TF: 800-228-9290 ■ *Web:* www.abhes.org

Accrediting Commission of Career Schools & Colleges of Technology (ACCSCT)
2101 Wilson Blvd Ste 302 ... Arlington VA 22201 703-247-4212 247-4533
Web: www.accsc.org

Accrediting Council for Continuing Education & Training (ACCET)
1722 N St NW ... Washington DC 20036 202-955-1113 955-1118
Web: www.accet.org

Accrediting Council for Independent Colleges & Schools (ACICS)
750 First St NE Ste 980 ... Washington DC 20002 202-336-6780 842-2593
TF: 800-258-3826 ■ *Web:* www.acics.org

Accrediting Council on Education in Journalism & Mass Communications (ACEJMC)
Univ of Kansas School of Journalism Stauffer-Flint Hall
1435 Jayhawk Blvd ... Lawrence KS 66045 785-864-3973 864-5225
Web: www2.ku.edu

American Academy for Liberal Education (AALE)
127 S. Peyton St Ste 200 ... Alexandria VA 22314 202-452-8611 452-8620
Web: www.aale.org

American Assn for Accreditation of Ambulatory Surgery Facilities Inc (AAAASF)
5101 Washington St Ste 2F PO Box 9500 ... Gurnee IL 60031 847-775-1985 775-1985
TF: 888-545-5222 ■ *Web:* www.aaaasf.org

American Assn for Laboratory Accreditation (A2LA)
5301 Buckeystown Pike Ste 350 ... Frederick MD 21704 301-644-3248 662-2974
TF: 888-627-8318 ■ *Web:* www.a2la.org

American Board of Internal Medicine (ABIM)
510 Walnut St Ste 1700 ... Philadelphia PA 19106 215-446-3500 446-3590
TF: 800-441-2246 ■ *Web:* www.abim.org

American Board of Medical Specialties (ABMS)
353 N Clark St Ste 1400 ... Chicago IL 60654 312-436-2600 328-3596*
**Fax Area Code:* 847 ■ *Web:* www.abms.org

American College of Nurse-Midwives Div of Accreditation
8403 Colesville Rd Ste 1550 ... Silver Spring MD 20910 240-485-1800 485-1818
Web: www.midwife.org

American Council for Construction Education (ACCE)
1717 N Loop 1604 E Ste 320 ... San Antonio TX 78232 210-495-6161 495-6168
Web: www.acce-hq.org

American Culinary Federation Inc (ACF)
180 Ctr Pl Way ... Saint Augustine FL 32095 904-824-4468 825-4758
TF: 800-624-9458 ■ *Web:* www.acfchefs.org

American Library Assn Committee on Accreditation
50 E Huron St ... Chicago IL 60611 312-944-6780 280-2433
TF: 800-545-2433 ■ *Web:* americanlibrariesmagazine.org

American National Standards Institute (ANSI)
25 W 43rd St 4th fl ... New York NY 10036 212-642-4900 398-0023
TF: 800-374-3818 ■ *Web:* www.ansi.org

American Osteopathic Assn (AOA)
142 E Ontario St ... Chicago IL 60611 312-202-8000 202-8200
TF: 800-621-1773 ■ *Web:* www.osteopathic.org

American Psychological Assn Committee on Accreditation
750 First St NE ... Washington DC 20002 202-336-5979 336-5978
Web: www.apa.org/ed

American Veterinary Medical Assn Council on Education
1931 N Meacham Rd Ste 100 ... Schaumburg IL 60173 847-925-8070 925-1329
TF: 800-248-2862 ■ *Web:* www.avma.org

Association for Assessment & Accreditation of Laboratory Animal Care International
5283 Corporate Dr Ste 203 ... Frederick MD 21703 301-696-9626 696-9627
TF: 800-926-0066 ■ *Web:* www.aaalac.org

Association for Biblical Higher Education (AABC)
5850 T G Lee Blvd Ste 130 ... Orlando FL 32822 407-207-0808 207-0840
Web: www.abhe.org

Association for Clinical Pastoral Education (ACPE)
1549 Clairmont Rd Ste 103 ... Decatur GA 30033 404-320-1472 320-0849
Web: www.acpe.edu

Association of Advanced Rabbinical & Talmudic Schools (AARTS)
11 Broadway ... New York NY 10004 212-363-1991 533-5335

Association of Collegiate Business Schools & Programs (ACBSP)
11520 W 119th St ... Overland Park KS 66213 913-339-9356 339-6226
Web: www.acbsp.org

Association of Specialized & Professional Accreditors (ASPA)
3304 N Broadway St Ste 214 ... Chicago IL 60657 773-857-7900 857-7901
Web: www.aspa-usa.org

Canadian Architectural Certification Board
One Nicholas St Ste 710 ... Ottawa ON K1N7B7 613-241-8399 241-7991
Web: www.cacb-ccca.ca

Canadian Assn of Occupational Therapists (CAOT)
1125 Colonel By Dr ... Ottawa ON K1S5R1 613-523-2268 523-2552
TF: 800-434-2268 ■ *Web:* www.caot.ca

Canadian Assn of Speech-Language Pathologists & Audiologists (CASLPA)
One Nicholas St Ste 1000 ... Ottawa ON K1N7B7 613-567-9968 567-2859
TF: 800-259-8519 ■ *Web:* sac-conference.ca/

Canadian Forestry Accreditation Board
18 Pommel Crescent ... Kanata ON K2M1A2 613-599-7259 599-8107
Web: www.cfab.ca

Canadian Information Processing Society (CIPS)
5090 Explorer Dr Ste 801 ... Mississauga ON L4W4T9 905-602-1370 602-7884
TF: 877-275-2477 ■ *Web:* www.cips.ca

Certified Financial Planner Board of Standards Inc
1425 K St NW Ste 500 ... Washington DC 20005 202-379-2200 379-2299
TF: 800-487-1497 ■ *Web:* www.cfp.net

CoAEMSP 8301 Lakeview Pkwy Ste 111-312 ... Rowlett TX 75088 817-330-0080 330-0089
Web: www.coaemsp.org

COLA 9881 Broken Land Pkwy Ste 200 ... Columbia MD 21046 410-381-6581 381-8611*
**Fax:* Hum Res ■ *TF:* 800-981-9883 ■ *Web:* www.cola.org

Commission on Accreditation for Dietetics Education (CADE)
120 S Riverside Plz Ste 2000 ... Chicago IL 60606 312-899-0040
TF: 800-877-1600 ■ *Web:* www.eatright.org

Commission on Accreditation for Law Enforcement Agencies (CALEA)
13575 Heathcote Blvd Ste 320 ... Gainesville VA 20155 703-352-4225 890-3126
TF: 877-789-6904 ■ *Web:* www.calea.org

Commission on Accreditation in Physical Therapy Education (CAPTE)
1111 N Fairfax St ... Alexandria VA 22314 703-706-3245 838-8910
TF: 800-999-2782 ■ *Web:* www.capteonline.org/home.aspx

Commission on Accreditation of Allied Health Education Programs (CAAHEP)
1361 Pk St ... Clearwater FL 33756 727-210-2350 210-2354
TF: 800-228-2262 ■ *Web:* www.caahep.org

Commission on Accreditation of Healthcare Management Education
2111 Wilson Blvd Ste 700 ... Arlington VA 22201 703-351-5010 991-5989
Web: www.cahme.org

Commission on Accreditation of Rehabilitation Facilities International (CARF)
6951 E Southpoint Rd ... Tucson AZ 85756 520-325-1044 318-1129
TF: 888-281-6531 ■ *Web:* www.carf.org

Commission on Collegiate Nursing Education
1 Dupont Cir NW Ste 530 ... Washington DC 20036 202-887-6791 887-8476
TF: 800-441-1414 ■ *Web:* www.aacn.nche.edu

Commission on Dental Accreditation of Canada
1815 Alta Vista Dr ... Ottawa ON K1G3Y6 613-523-7114 523-7736
TF: 866-521-2322 ■ *Web:* www.cda-adc.ca

Commission on English Language Program Accreditation (CEA)
801 N Fairfax St Ste 402A ... Alexandria VA 22314 703-665-3400 519-2071
Web: www.cea-accredit.org

Commission on Massage Therapy Accreditation (COMTA)
5335 Wisconsin Ave NW Ste 440 ... Washington DC 20015 202-895-1518 895-1519
Web: www.comta.org

Community Health Accreditation Program Inc (CHAP)
1275 K St NW Ste 800 ... Washington DC 20005 202-862-3413 862-3419
TF: 800-656-9656 ■ *Web:* www.chapinc.org

Continuing Care Accreditation Commission (CARF-CCAC)
1730 Rhode Island Ave NW Ste 209 ... Washington DC 20036 202-587-5001 587-5009
TF: 866-888-1122 ■ *Web:* www.carf.org

Council for Higher Education Accreditation (CHEA)
One Dupont Cir NW Ste 510 ... Washington DC 20036 202-955-6126 955-6129
Web: www.chea.org

Council for Interior Design Accreditation (CIDA)
206 Grandville Ave Ste 350 ... Grand Rapids MI 49503 616-458-0400 458-0460
Web: www.accredit-id.org

Council of the Section of Legal Education & Admissions to the Bar
321 N Clark St 21st Fl ... Chicago IL 60654 312-988-6738 988-5681
Web: www.americanbar.org

Council on Academic Accreditation in Audiology & Speech-Language Pathology
2200 Research Blvd ... Rockville MD 20850 301-296-5700
TF: 800-498-2071 ■ *Web:* www.asha.org

Council on Accreditation (COA)
45 Broadway 29th Fl ... New York NY 10006 212-797-3000 797-1428
TF: 866-262-8088 ■ *Web:* www.coanet.org

Council on Accreditation of Nurse Anesthesia Educational Programs
222 S Prospect Ave ... Park Ridge IL 60068 847-692-7050 692-6968
TF: 855-526-2262 ■ *Web:* www.aana.com

Council on Aviation Accreditation (CAA)
Aviation Accreditation Board International
3410 Skyway Dr ... Auburn AL 36830 334-844-2431 844-2432
TF: 800-767-4767 ■ *Web:* www.aabi.aero

Council on Chiropractic Education Commission on Accreditation
8049 N 85th Way ... Scottsdale AZ 85258 480-443-8877 483-7333
TF: 888-443-3506 ■ *Web:* www.cce-usa.org

Council on Education for Public Health
800 I St NW Ste 202 ... Washington DC 20001 202-789-1050 789-1895
Web: www.ceph.org

Council on Naturopathic Medical Education
342 Main St ... Great Barrington MA 01230 413-528-8877 528-8880
Web: www.cnme.org

Council on Occupational Education
7840 Roswell Rd Bldg 300 Ste 325 ... Atlanta GA 30350 770-396-3898 396-3790
TF: 800-917-2081 ■ *Web:* www.council.org

Council on Quality & Leadership, The (CQL)
100 W Rd Ste 300 ... Towson MD 21204 410-583-0060 583-0063
Web: www.cql.org

Distance Education & Training Council (DETC)
1601 18th St NW Ste 2 ... Washington DC 20009 202-234-5100 332-1386
Web: www.detc.org

Emergency Management Accreditation Program Inc (EMAP)
PO Box 11910 ... Lexington KY 40578 859-244-8222 244-8239
Web: www.emaponline.org

Engineers Canada 180 Elgin St Ste 1100 ... Ottawa ON K2P2K3 613-232-2474 230-5759
TF: 877-408-9273 ■ *Web:* www.engineerscanada.ca

Joint Commission on Accreditation of Healthcare Organizations (JCAHO)
One Renaissance Blvd ... Oakbrook Terrace IL 60181 630-792-5000 792-5005
Web: www.jointcommission.org

Joint Review Committee on Education in Radiologic Technology (JRCERT)
20 N Wacker Dr Ste 2850 ... Chicago IL 60606 312-704-5300 704-5304
Web: www.jrcert.org

Joint Review Committee on Educational Programs in Nuclear Medicine Technology (JRCNMT)
2000 W Danforth Rd Ste 130 203 ... Edmond OK 73003 405-285-0546 285-0579
Web: www.jrcnmt.org

Landscape Architectural Accreditation Board (LAAB)
636 'I' St NW ... Washington DC 20001 202-898-2444 898-1185
Web: www.asla.org/nonmembers/education.cfm

Phone Fax

Liaison Committee on Medical Education (LCME)
American Medical Assn 515 N State St................Chicago IL 60610 312-464-4933 464-5830
Web: www.lcme.org

Middle States Commission on Higher Education
3624 Market St................................Philadelphia PA 19104 267-284-5000 662-5501*
**Fax Area Code:* 215 ■ *Web:* www.msche.org

Montessori Accreditation Council for Teacher Education (MACTE)
313 Second St SE Ste 112 ....Charlottesville VA 22902 434-202-7793 525-8838*
**Fax Area Code:* 888 ■ *Web:* www.macte.org

NA of Nurse Practitioners in Women's Health Council on Accreditation
505 C St NE ....Washington DC 20002 202-543-9693 543-9858
Web: www.npwh.org

National Accrediting Agency for Clinical Laboratory Sciences (NAACLS)
8410 W Bryn Mawr Ave Ste 670.....................Chicago IL 60631 773-714-8880 714-8886
Web: www.naacls.org

National Accrediting Commission of Cosmetology Arts & Sciences (NACCAS)
4401 Ford Ave Ste 1300..........................Alexandria VA 22302 703-600-7600 379-2200
TF: 877-212-5752 ■ *Web:* www.naccas.org

National Architectural Accrediting Board (NAAB)
1735 New York Ave NW ....Washington DC 20006 202-783-2007 783-2822
Web: www.naab.org

National Certification Commission for Acupuncture & Oriental Medicine (NCCAOM)
76 S Laura St Ste 1290.........................Jacksonville FL 32202 904-598-1005 598-5001
Web: www.nccaom.org

National Commission on Certification of Physician Assistants
12000 Findley Rd Ste 200 ....Duluth GA 30097 678-417-8100 417-8135
Web: www.nccpa.net

National Council for Accreditation of Teacher Education (NCATE)
2010 Massachusetts Ave NW Ste 500 ....Washington DC 20036 202-466-7496 296-6620
TF: 800-255-8664 ■ *Web:* www.ncate.org

National Recreation & Park Assn
22377 Belmont Ridge Rd ....Ashburn VA 20148 703-858-0784 858-0794
TF: 800-626-6772 ■ *Web:* www.nrpa.org

New England Assn of Schools & Colleges (NEASC)
209 Burlington Rd ....Bedford MA 01730 781-271-0022 541-5400
Web: www.neasc.org

North Central Assn Commission on Accreditation & School Improvement (NCA CASI)
9115 Westside Pkwy.............................Alpharetta GA 30009 888-413-3669
TF: 888-413-3669 ■ *Web:* advanc-ed.org/

North Central Assn Higher Learning Commission
230 S LaSalle St................................Chicago IL 60604 312-263-0456 263-7462
TF: 800-621-7440 ■ *Web:* www.ncacihe.org

Northwest Assn of Accredited Schools (NAAS)
1510 Robert St Ste 103...............................Boise ID 83705 208-493-5077 334-3228
Web: advanc-ed.org/

Northwest Commission on Colleges & Universities (NWCCU)
8060 165th Ave NE Ste 100 ....Redmond WA 98052 425-558-4224 376-0596
Web: www.nwccu.org

Office of Social Work Accreditation & Education Excellence
1725 Duke St Ste 500...........................Alexandria VA 22314 703-683-8080 683-8099
Web: www.cswe.org

Society of Accredited Marine Surveyors Inc (SAMS)
7855 Argyle Forest Blvd Ste 203 ....Jacksonville FL 32244 904-384-1494 388-3958
TF: 800-344-9077 ■ *Web:* www.marinesurvey.org

Society of American Foresters (SAF)
5400 Grosvenor Ln...............................Bethesda MD 20814 301-897-8720 897-3690
Web: www.safnet.org

Southern Assn of Colleges & Schools
1866 Southern Ln.................................Decatur GA 30033 404-679-4500 679-4558
TF: 888-413-3669 ■ *Web:* www.sacs.org

Teacher Education Accreditation Council (TEAC)
One Dupont Cir Ste 320 ....Washington DC 20036 202-466-7236
Web: www.teac.org

TransNational Assn of Christian Colleges & Schools (TRACS)
15935 Forest Rd PO Box 328.........................Forest VA 24551 434-525-9539 525-9538
TF: 800-669-4000 ■ *Web:* www.tracs.org

URAC 1220 L St NW Ste 400 ....Washington DC 20005 202-216-9010 216-9006
Web: www.urac.org

Western Assn of Schools & Colleges (WASC)
985 Atlantic Ave ....Alameda CA 94501 510-748-9001
Web: wascsenior.org/

48-2 Agricultural Organizations

Phone Fax

Agricultural Retailers Assn (ARA)
1156 15th St NW Ste 500........................Washington DC 20005 202-457-0825 457-0864
Web: www.aradc.org

Agriculture Council of America (ACA)
11020 King St Ste 205........................Overland Park KS 66210 913-491-1895 491-6502
Web: www.agday.org

American Agricultural Economics Assn (AAEA)
555 E Wells St Ste 1100..........................Milwaukee WI 53202 414-918-3190 272-6070
Web: www.aaea.org

American Angus Assn (AAA)
3201 Frederick Ave...........................Saint Joseph MO 64506 816-383-5100 233-9703
TF: 800-821-5478 ■ *Web:* www.angus.org

American Assn of Bovine Practitioners (AABP)
3320 Skyway Dr Ste 802 PO Box 3610..................Auburn AL 36831 334-821-0442 821-9532
TF: 800-269-2227 ■ *Web:* www.aabp.org

American Dairy Goat Assn (ADGA)
209 W Main St PO Box 865 ....Spindale NC 28160 828-286-3801 287-0476
Web: www.adga.org

American Dairy Science Assn (ADSA)
1111 N Dunlap Ave...................................Savoy IL 61874 217-356-5146 398-4119
TF: 888-670-2250 ■ *Web:* www.adsa.org

American Egg Board (AEB)
1460 Renaissance Dr Ste 301.....................Park Ridge IL 60068 847-296-7043 296-7007
TF: 888-549-2140 ■ *Web:* www.aeb.org

American Farm Bureau Federation
600 Maryland Ave SW Ste 1000-W ....Washington DC 20024 202-406-3600 406-3606
Web: www.fb.org

Phone Fax

American Farmland Trust (AFT) 1200 18th St ......Washington DC 20036 202-331-7300 659-8339
TF: 800-431-1499 ■ *Web:* www.farmland.org

American Feed Industry Assn (AFIA)
2101 Wilson Blvd Ste 916 ....Arlington VA 22201 703-524-0810 524-1921
Web: www.afia.org

American Fisheries Society (AFS)
5410 Grosvenor Ln Ste 110 ....Bethesda MD 20814 301-897-8616 897-8096
Web: www.fisheries.org

American Forest & Paper Assn (AF&PA)
1111 19th St NW Ste 800.........................Washington DC 20036 202-463-2700 463-2785
TF: 800-878-8878 ■ *Web:* www.afandpa.org

American Forest Foundation (AFF)
1111 19th St NW Ste 780.........................Washington DC 20036 202-463-2462 463-2461
Web: www.forestfoundation.org

American Gelbvieh Assn 10900 Dover St ....Westminster CO 80021 303-465-2333 465-2339
TF: 877-279-2195 ■ *Web:* www.gelbvieh.org

American Hereford Assn 1501 Wyandotte St........Kansas City MO 64108 816-842-3757 842-6931
Web: www.hereford.org

American Jersey Cattle Assn
6486 E Main St.............................Reynoldsburg OH 43068 614-861-3636 861-8040
Web: www.usjersey.com

American Land Rights Assn (ALRA)
30218 NE 82nd Ave PO Box 400 ....Battle Ground WA 98604 360-687-3087 687-2973
Web: www.landrights.org

American National CattleWomen Inc (ANCW)
PO Box 3881 ....Englewood CO 80155 303-694-0313 694-2390
Web: www.ancw.org

American Nursery & Landscape Assn (ANLA)
1000 Vermont Ave NW Ste 300....................Washington DC 20005 202-789-2900 789-1893
Web: americanhort.org

American Royal Assn
1701 American Royal Ct...........................Kansas City MO 64102 816-221-9800 221-8189
TF: 800-767-8487 ■ *Web:* www.americanroyal.com

American Seed Trade Assn (ASTA)
225 Reinekers Ln Ste 650.........................Alexandria VA 22314 703-837-8140 837-9365
TF: 888-890-7333 ■ *Web:* www.amseed.org

American Sheep Industry Assn (ASI)
9785 Maroon Cir Ste 360.........................Englewood CO 80112 303-771-3500 771-8200
Web: www.sheepusa.org

American Simmental Assn (ASA) One Simmental Way . Bozeman MT 59715 406-587-4531 587-9301
Web: www.simmental.org

American Society for Horticultural Science (ASHS)
1018 Duke St ....Alexandria VA 22314 703-836-4606 836-2024
TF: 800-331-1600 ■ *Web:* www.ashs.org

American Society of Agricultural Consultants (ASAC)
N78W14573 Appleton Ave ....Menomonee Falls WI 53051 262-253-6902 253-6903
TF: 800-327-6789 ■ *Web:* www.agconsultants.org

American Society of Agronomy (ASA)
5585 Guilford Rd ....Madison WI 53711 608-273-8080 273-2021
TF: 866-359-9161 ■ *Web:* www.agronomy.org

American Society of Animal Science (ASAS)
1111 N Dunlap Ave.................................Savoy IL 61874 217-356-9050 398-4119
Web: www.asas.org

American Society of Farm Managers & Rural Appraisers (ASFMRA)
950 S Cherry St Ste 508.............................Denver CO 80246 303-758-3513 758-0190
Web: www.asfmra.org

American Society of Landscape Architects (ASLA)
636 'I' St NW..................................Washington DC 20001 202-898-2444 898-1185
TF: 888-999-2752 ■ *Web:* www.asla.org

American Soybean Assn (ASA)
12125 Woodcrest Executive Dr Ste 100 ....Saint Louis MO 63141 314-576-1770 576-2786
TF: 800-688-7692 ■ *Web:* www.soygrowers.com

American-International Charolais Assn (AICA)
11700 NW Plaza Cir ....Kansas City MO 64153 816-464-5977 464-5759
TF: 800-270-7711 ■ *Web:* www.charolaisusa.com

Association of Consulting Foresters of America (ACF)
312 Montgomery St Ste 208.......................Alexandria VA 22314 703-548-0990 548-6395
TF: 888-540-8733 ■ *Web:* www.acf-foresters.org

Association of Farmworker Opportunity Programs (AFOP)
1726 M St NW Ste 602.........................Washington DC 20036 202-828-6006 828-6005
TF: 866-487-9243 ■ *Web:* afop.org

Association of Water Technologies (AWT)
15245 Shady Grove Rd Ste 130 ....Rockville MD 20850 301-740-1421 990-9771
TF: 800-858-6683 ■ *Web:* www.awt.org

Beattie Farmers Union Co-op Assn PO Box 79.........Beattie KS 66406 785-353-2237 353-2236
Web: www.beattiecoop.com

Beefmaster Breeders United (BBU)
6800 Pk Ten Blvd Ste 290-W ....San Antonio TX 78213 210-732-3132 732-7711
Web: www.beefmasters.org

Beet Sugar Development Foundation
800 Grant St Ste 300 ....Denver CO 80203 303-832-4460 832-4468
Web: www.bsdf-assbt.org

Breg Inc 2611 Commerce Way Ste C.....................Vista CA 92081 760-599-3000 329-2734*
**Fax Area Code:* 800 ■ *TF:* 800-897-2734 ■ *Web:* www.breg.com

Brown Swiss Cattle Breeders Assn of the USA
800 Pleasant St......................................Beloit WI 53511 608-365-4474 365-5577
Web: www.brownswissusa.com

Burley Tobacco Growers Co-op Assn
620 S Broadway ....Lexington KY 40508 859-252-3561 231-9804
Web: www.burleytobacco.com

California Redwood Assn (CRA)
818 Grayson Rd Ste 201.........................Pleasant Hill CA 94523 925-935-1499 935-1496
Web: californiaredwoodco.com

Corn Refiners Assn Inc (CRA)
1701 Pennsylvania Ave..........................Washington DC 20006 202-331-1634 331-2054
TF: 800-284-5779 ■ *Web:* www.corn.org

Cotton Council International
1521 New Hampshire Ave NW ....Washington DC 20036 202-745-7805 483-4040
Web: www.cottonusa.org

Cotton Inc 6399 Weston Pkwy ....Cary NC 27513 919-678-2220 678-2230
TF: 800-334-5868 ■ *Web:* www.cottoninc.com

Organization	City	State	Zip	Phone	Fax
Crop Science Society of America (CSSA) 677 S Segoe Rd *Web:* www.crops.org	Madison	WI	53711	608-273-8080	273-2021
CropLife America 1156 15th St NW Ste 400 *TF:* 800-266-9432 ■ *Web:* www.croplifeamerica.org	Washington	DC	20005	202-296-1585	463-0474
Dairy Management Inc (DMI) 10255 W Higgins Rd Ste 900 *TF:* 800-853-2479 ■ *Web:* www.dairy.org	Rosemont	IL	60018	800-853-2479	
Decatur Co-op Assn 305 S York Ave PO Box 68 *TF:* 800-886-2293 ■ *Web:* www.decaturcoop.net	Oberlin	KS	67749	785-475-2234	475-3469
Farm Equipment Manufacturers Assn (FEMA) 1000 Executive Pkwy Ste 100 *Web:* www.farmequip.org	Saint Louis	MO	63141	314-878-2304	732-1480
Farmer's Co-op Assn 110 S Keokuk Wash Rd *TF:* 877-843-4893 ■ *Web:* www.keotafarmerscoop.com	Keota	IA	52248	641-636-3748	636-2460
Farmers Co-op PO Box 1640 *Web:* www.farmercoop.com	Van Buren	AR	72957	479-474-6622	474-4787
Farmers Co-op Society 317 Third St NW *Web:* www.farmerscoopsociety.com	Sioux Center	IA	51250	712-722-2671	722-2674
Farmers Educational & Co-op Union of America 20 F St NW Ste 300 *TF:* 800-331-1212 ■ *Web:* www.nfu.org	Washington	DC	20001	202-554-1600	554-1654
Fertilizer Institute, The (TFI) 425 Third St SW Ste 950 *Web:* www.tfi.org	Washington	DC	20024	202-962-0490	962-0577
Forest Products Society 2801 Marshall Ct *Web:* www.forestprod.org	Madison	WI	53705	608-231-1361	231-2152
Golf Course Superintendents Assn of America (GCSAA) 1421 Research Pk Dr *TF:* 800-472-7878 ■ *Web:* www.gcsaa.org	Lawrence	KS	66049	785-841-2240	832-4455
Herb Growing & Marketing Network (HGMN) PO Box 245 *Web:* www.herbworld.com	Silver Spring	PA	17575	717-393-3295	393-9261
Hohman Assoc Inc (HAI) 6951 W Little York *TF:* 800-324-0978 ■ *Web:* www.hohmanassociates.com	Houston	TX	77040	713-896-0978	896-9419
Holstein Assn USA Inc One Holstein Pl *TF Orders:* 800-952-5200 ■ *Web:* www.holsteinusa.com	Brattleboro	VT	05302	802-254-4551	254-8251
Humane Farming Assn (HFA) PO Box 3577 *Web:* www.hfa.org	San Rafael	CA	94912	415-485-1495	485-0106
International Brangus Breeders Assn (IBBA) 5750 Epsilon Dr *Web:* www.gobrangus.com	San Antonio	TX	78249	210-696-8231	696-8718
International Order-Hoo-Hoo 207 E Main St	Gurdon	AR	71743	870-353-4997	
International Plant Nutrition Institute (IPNI) 3500 PkwyLn Ste 550 *TF:* 800-521-3044 ■ *Web:* www.ipni.net	Norcross	GA	30092	770-447-0335	448-0439
International Society of Arboriculture (ISA) PO Box 3129 *TF:* 888-472-8733 ■ *Web:* www.isa-arbor.com	Champaign	IL	61826	217-355-9411	355-9516
Irrigation Assn (IA) 6540 Arlington Blvd *Web:* www.irrigation.org	Falls Church	VA	22042	703-536-7080	536-7019
Livestock Marketing Assn (LMA) 10510 N Ambassador Dr *TF:* 888-484-8477 ■ *Web:* www.lmaweb.com	Kansas City	MO	64153	816-891-0502	891-7108
Mid-Kansas Co-op Assn (MKC) 117 N Edwards Ave *TF:* 800-864-4428 ■ *Web:* mkcoop.com	Moundridge	KS	67107	620-345-6361	
Milk Industry Foundation (MIF) 1250 H St NW Ste 900 *TF:* 866-225-4821 ■ *Web:* www.idfa.org	Washington	DC	20005	202-737-4332	331-7820
Mohair Council of America 233 W Twohig Rd *TF:* 800-583-3161 ■ *Web:* www.mohairusa.com	San Angelo	TX	76903	325-655-3161	
National Agri-Marketing Assn (NAMA) 11020 King St Ste 205 *TF:* 800-530-5646 ■ *Web:* www.nama.org	Overland Park	KS	66210	913-491-6500	491-6502
National Agricultural Aviation Assn (NAAA) 1005 E St SE *Web:* www.agaviation.org	Washington	DC	20003	202-546-5722	546-5726
National Association of Landscape Professionals Inc (PLANET) 950 Herndon Pkwy Ste 450 *TF:* 800-395-2522 ■ *Web:* www.landcarenetwork.org	Herndon	VA	20170	703-736-9666	736-9668
National Cattlemen's Beef Assn (NCBA) 9110 E Nichols Ave Ste 300 *TF:* 866-233-3872 ■ *Web:* www.beefusa.org	Centennial	CO	80112	303-694-0305	694-2851
National Chicken Council 1015 15th St NW Ste 930 *Web:* www.eatchicken.com	Washington	DC	20005	202-296-2622	293-4005
National Christmas Tree Assn (NCTA) 16020 Swingley Ridge Rd Ste 300 *Web:* www.realchristmastrees.org	Chesterfield	MO	63017	636-449-5070	449-5051
National Corn Growers Assn (NCGA) 632 Cepi Dr *Web:* www.ncga.com	Chesterfield	MO	63005	636-733-9004	733-9005
National Cotton Council of America 7193 Goodlett Farms Pkwy *TF:* 888-232-1738 ■ *Web:* www.cotton.org	Memphis	TN	38016	901-274-9030	725-0510
National Cottonseed Products Assn (NCPA) 866 Willow Tree Cir Ste 200 *Web:* www.cottonseed.com	Cordova	TN	38018	901-682-0800	682-2856
National Council of Farmer Co-ops (NCFC) 50 F St NW Ste 900 *Web:* www.ncfc.org	Washington	DC	20001	202-626-8700	626-8722
National Crop Insurance Services (NCIS) 8900 Indian Creek Pkwy Ste 600 *TF:* 800-951-6247 ■ *Web:* www.ag-risk.org	Overland Park	KS	66210	913-685-2767	685-3080
National Dairy Council (NDC) 10255 W Higgins Rd Suite 900 *Web:* www.nationaldairycouncil.org	Rosemont	IL	60018	847-803-2479	803-2077
National Endangered Species Act Reform Coalition (NESARC) 1050 Thomas Jefferson St NW Sixth Fl *Web:* www.nesarc.org	Washington	DC	20007	202-333-7481	338-2416
National Family Farm Coalition (NFFC) 110 Maryland Ave NE Ste 307 *Web:* www.nffc.net	Washington	DC	20002	202-543-5675	543-0978
National Farmers Organization (NFO) 528 Billy Sunday Rd Ste 100 PO Box 2508 *TF:* 800-247-2110 ■ *Web:* www.nfo.org	Ames	IA	50010	515-292-2000	292-7106
National FFA Organization 6060 FFA Dr *TF:* 800-772-0939 ■ *Web:* www.ffa.org	Indianapolis	IN	46268	317-802-6060	802-6061
National Fisheries Institute Inc 7918 Jones Branch Dr Ste 700 *Web:* www.aboutseafood.com	McLean	VA	22102	703-752-8880	752-7583
National Grain & Feed Assn (NGFA) 1250 'I' St NW Ste 1003 *Web:* www.ngfa.org	Washington	DC	20005	202-289-0873	289-5388
National Grange 1616 H St NW *TF:* 888-447-2643 ■ *Web:* www.nationalgrange.org	Washington	DC	20006	202-628-3507	347-1091
National Oilseed Processors Assn 1300 L St NW Ste 1020 *Web:* www.nopa.org	Washington	DC	20005	202-842-0463	842-9126
National Onion Assn (NOA) 822 Seventh St Ste 510 *Web:* www.onions-usa.org	Greeley	CO	80631	970-353-5895	353-5897
National Renderers Assn (NRA) 801 N Fairfax St Ste 205 *Web:* www.nationalrenderers.org	Alexandria	VA	22314	703-683-0155	683-2626
National Turkey Federation (NTF) 1225 New York Ave NW Ste 400 *TF:* 866-536-7593 ■ *Web:* www.eatturkey.com	Washington	DC	20005	202-898-0100	898-0203
National Woodland Owners Assn (NWOA) 374 Maple Ave E Ste 310 *TF:* 800-476-8733 ■ *Web:* www.woodlandowners.org	Vienna	VA	22180	703-255-2700	
North American Blueberry Council (NABC) 80 Iron Pt Cir Dr *Web:* www.blueberry.org	Folsom	CA	95630	916-983-0111	983-9370
North American Limousin Foundation (NALF) 7383 S Alton Way Ste 100 *Web:* www.nalf.org	Englewood	CO	80112	303-220-1693	220-1884
Red Angus Assn of America 4201 N IH- 35 **Fax Area Code:* 888 ■ *Web:* www.redangus.org	Denton	TX	76207	940-387-3502	829-6069*
River Country Co-op 425 Clinton Ave *Web:* www.rivercountry.coop	South Saint Paul	MN	55075	651-451-1151	451-8582
Rural Coalition 1029 Vermont Ave NW Ste 601 *Web:* www.ruralco.org	Washington	DC	20005	202-628-7160	393-1816
Santa Gertrudis Breeders International PO Box 1257 *TF:* 800-500-8242 ■ *Web:* www.santagertrudis.com	Kingsville	TX	78364	361-592-9357	592-8572
Shelburne Farms 1611 Harbor Rd *TF:* 800-286-6022 ■ *Web:* www.shelburnefarms.org	Shelburne	VT	05482	802-985-8686	985-8123
Skagit Farmers Supply 1833 Pk Ln PO Box 266 *Web:* www.skagitfarmers.com	Burlington	WA	98233	360-757-6053	757-4143
Society of American Foresters (SAF) 5400 Grosvenor Ln *Web:* www.safnet.org	Bethesda	MD	20814	301-897-8720	897-3690
Soil Science Society of America (SSSA) 677 S Segoe Rd *Web:* www.soils.org	Madison	WI	53711	608-273-8080	273-2021
Southern Forest Products Assn (SFPA) 2900 Indiana Ave *TF:* 866-574-4155 ■ *Web:* www.sfpa.org	Kenner	LA	70065	504-443-4464	443-6612
Sugar Assn 1300 L St NW Ste 1001 *Web:* www.sugar.org	Washington	DC	20005	202-785-1122	785-5019
Supima 4141 E Broadway Rd *Web:* www.supima.com	Phoenix	AZ	85040	602-792-6002	792-6004
Texas Longhorn Breeders Assn of America (TLBAA) 2315 N Main St Ste 402 *Web:* www.tlbaa.org	Fort Worth	TX	76164	817-625-6241	625-1388
Tobacco Assoc Inc 1306 Annapolis Dr Ste 102 *Web:* www.tobaccoassociatesinc.org	Raleigh	NC	27608	919-821-7670	821-7674
Tobacco Merchants Assn (TMA) PO Box 8019 *TF:* 888-672-4991 ■ *Web:* www.tma.org	Princeton	NJ	08543	609-275-4900	275-8379
United Fresh Produce Assn 1901 Pennsylvania Ave NW Ste 1100 *Web:* www.unitedfresh.org	Washington	DC	20006	202-303-3400	303-3433
United Producers Inc 8351 N High St Ste 250 *TF:* 800-456-3276 ■ *Web:* www.uproducers.com	Columbus	OH	43235	800-456-3276	
United Soybean Board (USB) 16305 Swingley Ridge Rd Ste 150 *TF:* 800-989-8721 ■ *Web:* www.unitedsoybean.org	Chesterfield	MO	63017	636-530-1777	530-1560
US Apple Assn 8233 Old Courthouse Rd Ste 200 *TF:* 800-781-4443 ■ *Web:* www.usapple.org	Vienna	VA	22182	703-442-8850	790-0845
US Grains Council 1400 K St NW Ste 1200 *Web:* www.grains.org	Washington	DC	20005	202-789-0789	898-0522
US Potato Board (USPB) 7555 E Hampden Ave Ste 412 *TF:* 866-632-9992 ■ *Web:* www.uspotatoes.com	Denver	CO	80231	303-369-7783	369-7718
US Poultry & Egg Assn 1530 Cooledge Rd *Web:* www.uspoultry.org	Tucker	GA	30084	770-493-9401	493-9257
US Wheat Assoc (USW) 3103 Tenth St N Ste 300 **Fax Area Code:* 703 ■ *Web:* www.uswheat.org	Arlington	VA	22201	202-463-0999	524-4399*
Western Wood Products Assn (WWPA) 522 SW Fifth Ave Ste 500 *Web:* www2.wwpa.org	Portland	OR	97204	503-224-3930	224-3934
Wheat Quality Council 1814 Abbey Rd *Web:* www.wheatqualitycouncil.org	Pierre	SD	57501	605-224-5187	224-0517
Wild Blueberry Assn of North America (WBANA) PO Box 100 *Web:* www.wildblueberries.com	Old Town	ME	04468	207-570-3535	581-3499

48-3 Animals & Animal Welfare Organizations

Organization	City	State	Zip	Phone	Fax
African Wildlife Foundation (AWF) 1400 16th St NW Ste 120 *TF:* 888-494-5354 ■ *Web:* www.awf.org	Washington	DC	20036	202-939-3333	939-3332
Alaska Wildlife Alliance 308 G St Ste 308 *Web:* www.akwildlife.org	Anchorage	AK	99501	907-277-0897	
American Animal Hospital Assn (AAHA) 12575 W Bayaud Ave *TF:* 800-252-2242 ■ *Web:* www.aahanet.org	Lakewood	CO	80228	303-986-2800	986-1700
American Assn of Equine Practitioners (AAEP) 4075 Iron Works Pkwy *TF:* 800-443-0177 ■ *Web:* www.aaep.org	Lexington	KY	40511	859-233-0147	233-1968
American Buckskin Registry Assn Inc (ABRA) 1141 Hartnell Ave *Web:* www.americanbuckskin.org	Redding	CA	96002	530-223-1420	
American Cetacean Society (ACS) 745 W Paseo Del Mar *Web:* www.acsonline.org	San Pedro	CA	90731	310-548-6279	548-6950
American Donkey & Mule Society (ADMS) 1346 Morningside Ave *TF:* 877-752-4068 ■ *Web:* www.lovelongears.com	Lewisville	TX	75057	972-219-0781	420-9980
American Horse Council (AHC) 1616 H St NW Seventh Fl *Web:* www.horsecouncil.org	Washington	DC	20006	202-296-4031	296-1970
American Humane Assn (AHA) 63 Inverness Dr E *TF:* 800-227-4645 ■ *Web:* www.americanhumane.org	Englewood	CO	80112	303-792-9900	792-5333
American Miniature Horse Assn (AMHA) 5601 S IH- 35 W *Web:* www.amha.org	Alvarado	TX	76009	817-783-5600	783-6403
American Morgan Horse Assn (AMHA) 4066 Shelburne Rd Ste 5 *TF:* 888-436-3700 ■ *Web:* www.morganhorse.com	Shelburne	VT	05482	802-985-4944	985-8897
American Paint Horse Assn (APHA) 2800 Meacham Blvd *Web:* www.apha.com	Fort Worth	TX	76137	817-834-2742	834-3152
American Quarter Horse Assn (AQHA) 1600 Quarter Horse Dr *TF:* 800-291-7323 ■ *Web:* www.aqha.com	Amarillo	TX	79104	806-376-4811	349-6411
American Rabbit Breeders Assn (ARBA) Eight Westport Ct *Web:* www.arba.net	Bloomington	IL	61704	309-664-7500	664-0941
American Saddlebred Horse Assn (ASHA) 4083 Iron Works Pkwy *Web:* www.saddlebred.com	Lexington	KY	40511	859-259-2742	259-1628
American Shetland Pony Club (ASPC) 81B E Queenwood Rd Ste 2 *Web:* shetlandminiature.com	Morton	IL	61550	309-263-4044	263-5113
American Shorthorn Assn 8288 Hascall St *Web:* www.shorthorn.org	Omaha	NE	68124	402-393-7200	393-7203
American Society for the Prevention of Cruelty to Animals (ASPCA) 424 E 92nd St *Web:* www.aspca.org	New York	NY	10128	212-876-7700	
American Warmblood Registry (AWR) PO Box 197 **Fax Area Code:* 775 ■ *Web:* www.americanwarmblood.com	Carter	MT	59420	406-734-5499	667-0516*
Animal Alliance of Canada 221 Broadview Ave *Web:* www.animalalliance.ca	Toronto	ON	M4M2G3	416-462-9541	462-9647
Animal Health Institute (AHI) 1325 G St NW Ste 700 *Web:* www.ahi.org	Washington	DC	20005	202-637-2440	
Appaloosa Horse Club (ApHC) 2720 W Pullman Rd *TF:* 888-304-7768 ■ *Web:* www.appaloosa.com	Moscow	ID	83843	208-882-5578	882-8150
Arabian Horse Assn (AHA) 10805 E Bethany Dr *Web:* www.arabianhorses.org	Aurora	CO	80014	303-696-4500	696-4599
ASPCA Animal Poison Control Ctr 424 E 92nd St **Fax Area Code:* 217 ■ *TF:* 888-426-4435 ■ *Web:* www.aspca.org	New York	NY	10128	212-876-7700	337-0599*
Association of Zoos & Aquariums (AZA) 8403 Colesville Rd Ste 710 *TF:* 800-821-4557 ■ *Web:* www.aza.org	Silver Spring	MD	20910	301-562-0777	562-0888
Atlantic Salmon Federation (ASF) PO Box 5200 *TF:* 800-565-5666 ■ *Web:* www.asf.ca	Saint Andrews	NB	E5B3S8	506-529-1033	529-4438
Bat Conservation International (BCI) 500 N Capital of Texas Hwy *TF:* 800-538-2287 ■ *Web:* batcon.org	Austin	TX	78746	512-327-9721	327-9724
Belgian Draft Horse Corp of America 125 Southwood Dr *Web:* www.belgiancorp.com	Wabash	IN	46992	260-563-3205	
Bird Studies Canada 115 Front St PO Box 160 *TF:* 888-448-2473 ■ *Web:* www.bsc-eoc.org	Port Rowan	ON	N0E1M0	519-586-3531	586-3532
Born Free USA United with Animal Protection Institute 1122 S St *TF:* 800-348-7387 ■ *Web:* bornfreeusa.org	Sacramento	CA	95814	916-447-3085	447-3070
Canadian Federation of Humane Societies (CFHS) 30 Concourse Gate Ste 102 *TF:* 888-678-2347 ■ *Web:* cfhs.ca	Ottawa	ON	K2E7V7	613-224-8072	723-0252
Canadian Kennel Club (CKC) 200 Ronson Dr Ste 400 *TF:* 800-250-8040 ■ *Web:* www.ckc.ca	Etobicoke	ON	M9W5Z9	416-675-5511	675-6506
Canadian Peregrine Foundation 1450 O'Connor Dr Bldg B Ste 214 *TF:* 888-709-3944 ■ *Web:* www.peregrine-foundation.ca	Toronto	ON	M4B2T8	416-481-1233	481-7158
Certified Horsemanship Assn (CHA) 1795 Alysheba Way Ste 7102 *TF:* 800-399-0138 ■ *Web:* www.cha-ahse.org	Lexington	KY	40509	859-259-3399	255-0726
Defenders of Wildlife 1130 17th St NW *TF:* 800-385-9712 ■ *Web:* www.defenders.org	Washington	DC	20036	202-682-9400	682-1331
Delta Waterfowl Foundation PO Box 3128 *TF:* 888-987-3695 ■ *Web:* www.deltawaterfowl.org	Bismarck	ND	58502	701-222-8857	224-1924
Dian Fossey Gorilla Fund International 800 Cherokee Ave SE *TF:* 800-851-0203 ■ *Web:* www.gorillafund.org	Atlanta	GA	30315	404-624-5881	624-5867
Ducks Unlimited Inc One Waterfowl Way *TF:* 800-453-8257 ■ *Web:* www.ducks.org	Memphis	TN	38120	901-758-3825	758-3850
Friends of Animals Inc (FOA) 777 Post Rd Ste 205 *TF:* 800-321-7387 ■ *Web:* www.friendsofanimals.org	Darien	CT	06820	203-656-1522	656-0267
Fund for Animals, The 200 W 57th St *Web:* www.fundforanimals.org	New York	NY	10019	212-246-2096	246-2633
Greyhound Friends Inc 167 Saddle Hill Rd *Web:* www.greyhound.org	Hopkinton	MA	01748	508-435-5969	435-0547
Hawk Mountain Sanctuary (HMS) 1700 Hawk Mtn Rd *Web:* www.hawkmountain.org	Kempton	PA	19529	610-756-6961	756-4468
Humane Farming Assn (HFA) PO Box 3577 *Web:* www.hfa.org	San Rafael	CA	94912	415-485-1495	485-0106
Humane Society of the US (HSUS) 2100 L St NW *Web:* www.humanesociety.org	Washington	DC	20037	202-452-1100	778-6132
In Defense of Animals (IDA) 3010 Kerner Blvd *TF:* 800-705-0425 ■ *Web:* www.idausa.org	San Rafael	CA	94901	415-448-0048	454-1031
International Fund for Animal Welfare (IFAW) 290 Summer St *TF:* 800-932-4329 ■ *Web:* www.ifaw.org	Yarmouth Port	MA	02675	508-744-2000	744-2009
International Primate Protection League (IPPL) 120 Primate Ln *Web:* www.ippl.org	Summerville	SC	29483	843-871-2280	871-7988
International Society for Animal Rights (ISAR) PO Box F *TF:* 888-589-6397 ■ *Web:* www.isaronline.org	Clarks Summit	PA	18411	570-586-2200	586-9580
International Veterinary Acupuncture Society (IVAS) 1730 S College Ave Ste 301 *Web:* www.ivas.org	Fort Collins	CO	80525	970-266-0666	266-0777
Jane Goodall Institute for Wildlife Research Education & Conservation (JGI) 4245 N Fairfax Dr Ste 600 *TF:* 800-592-5263 ■ *Web:* www.janegoodall.org	Arlington	VA	22203	703-682-9220	682-9312
Missouri Fox Trotting Horse Breed Assn Inc PO Box 1027 *TF:* 877-663-4203 ■ *Web:* www.mfthba.com	Ava	MO	65608	417-683-2468	683-6144
Mountain Lion Foundation PO Box 1896 *TF:* 800-319-7621 ■ *Web:* www.mountainlion.org	Sacramento	CA	95812	916-442-2666	442-2871
NA of Animal Breeders (NAAB) 401 Bernadette Dr *Web:* www.naab-css.org	Columbia	MO	65203	573-445-4406	446-2279
National Animal Control Assn 101 N Church St Ste C *Web:* www.nacanet.org	Olathe	KS	66061	913-768-1319	768-1378
National Anti-Vivisection Society (NAVS) 53 W Jackson Blvd Ste 1552 *TF:* 800-888-6287 ■ *Web:* www.navs.org	Chicago	IL	60604	312-427-6065	427-6524
National Cutting Horse Assn (NCHA) 260 Bailey Ave *Web:* www.nchacutting.com	Fort Worth	TX	76107	817-244-6188	244-2015
National Disaster Search Dog Foundation 501 E Ojai Ave *TF:* 888-459-4376 ■ *Web:* www.searchdogfoundation.org	Ojai	CA	93023	805-646-1015	640-1848
National Reining Horse Assn (NRHA) 3000 NW Tenth St *Web:* nrha1.com	Oklahoma City	OK	73107	405-946-7400	946-8425
National Wild Turkey Federation (NWTF) 770 Augusta Rd PO Box 530 *TF Cust Svc:* 800-843-6983 ■ *Web:* www.nwtf.com	Edgefield	SC	29824	803-637-3106	637-0034
National Wildlife Federation (NWF) 11100 Wildlife Ctr Dr *TF:* 800-822-9919 ■ *Web:* www.nwf.org	Reston	VA	20190	703-438-6000	438-3570
Paso Fino Horse Assn 4047 Iron Works Pkwy Ste 1 *Web:* www.pfha.org	Lexington	KY	40511	859-825-6000	258-2125
People for the Ethical Treatment of Animals (PETA) 501 Front St *TF:* 800-248-7729 ■ *Web:* www.peta.org	Norfolk	VA	23510	757-622-7382	622-0457
Performing Animal Welfare Society (PAWS) 11435 Simmerhorn Rd *TF:* 800-513-6560 ■ *Web:* www.pawsweb.org	Galt	CA	95632	209-745-2606	745-1809
Pet Sitters International (PSI) 201 E King St *TF:* 800-325-7353 ■ *Web:* www.petsit.com	King	NC	27021	336-983-9222	983-5266
Pinto Horse Assn of America 7330 NW 23rd St *Web:* www.pinto.org	Bethany	OK	73008	405-491-0111	787-0773
Racking Horse Breeders Assn of America (RHBAA) 67 Horse Ctr Rd *Web:* www.rackinghorse.com	Decatur	AL	35603	256-353-7225	353-7266
Ruffed Grouse Society (RGS) 451 McCormick Rd *TF:* 888-564-6747 ■ *Web:* www.ruffedgrousesociety.org	Coraopolis	PA	15108	412-262-4044	262-9207
Save the Manatee Club (SMC) 500 N Maitland Ave Ste 210 *TF:* 800-432-5646 ■ *Web:* www.savethemanatee.org	Maitland	FL	32751	407-539-0990	539-0871
Tennessee Walking Horse Breeders' & Exhibitors' Assn (TWHBEA) 250 N Ellington Pkwy PO Box 286 *Web:* www.twhbea.com	Lewisburg	TN	37091	931-359-1574	359-7530
Thoroughbred Owners & Breeders Assn (TOBA) PO Box 910668 *TF:* 888-606-8622 ■ *Web:* www.toba.org	Lexington	KY	40591	859-276-2291	276-2462
Trout Unlimited (TU) 1300 N 17th St Ste 500 *TF:* 800-834-2419 ■ *Web:* www.tu.org	Arlington	VA	22209	703-522-0200	284-9400
Wildlife Conservation Society (WCS) 2300 Southern Blvd *Web:* www.wcs.org	Bronx	NY	10460	718-220-5100	
Wildlife Forever 2700 Fwy Blvd Ste 1000 *Web:* www.wildlifeforever.org	Brooklyn Center	MN	55430	763-253-0222	560-9961
Wildlife Management Institute (WMI) 1440 Upper Bermudian Rd **Fax Area Code:* 802 ■ *Web:* www.wildlifemanagementinstitute.org	Gardners	PA	17324	717-677-4480	563-2157*
World Animal Protection (WSPA) 450 Seventh Avenue 31st Floor **Fax Area Code:* 212 ■ *TF:* 800-883-9772 ■ *Web:* www.wspa-usa.org	New York	NY	10123	800-883-9772	564-4250*

Phone | Fax

World Wildlife Fund (WWF)
1250 24th St NW PO Box 97180 .... Washington DC 20090 202-293-4800 293-9211
TF: 800-225-5993 ■ *Web:* www.worldwildlife.org

World Wildlife Fund Canada (WWF)
245 Eglinton Ave E Ste 410 .... Toronto ON M4P3J1 416-489-8800 489-3611
TF: 800-267-2632 ■ *Web:* www.wwf.ca

Zoocheck Canada 788 1/2 O'Connor Dr............... Toronto ON M4B2S6 416-285-1744 285-4670
TF: 888-801-3222 ■ *Web:* www.zoocheck.com

48-4 Arts & Artists Organizations

Phone | Fax

Academy of Motion Picture Arts & Sciences
8949 Wilshire Blvd............................ Beverly Hills CA 90211 310-247-3000 859-9619
Web: www.oscars.org

Actors' Equity Assn 1560 Broadway................. New York NY 10036 212-869-8530 719-9815
Web: www.actorsequity.org

Alliance of Motion Picture & Television Producers (AMPTP)
15301 Ventura Blvd Bldg E..................... Sherman Oaks CA 91403 818-995-3600
Web: www.amptp.org

American Academy of Arts & Letters
633 W 155th St.................................. New York NY 10032 212-368-5900 212-4615
Web: www.artsandletters.org

American Academy of Arts & Sciences
136 Irving St.................................... Cambridge MA 02138 617-576-5000 576-5050
TF: 800-666-2211 ■ *Web:* www.amacad.org

American Antiquarian Society (AAS)
185 Salisbury St................................ Worcester MA 01609 508-755-5221 753-3311
Web: www.americanantiquarian.org

American Arts Alliance
Performing Arts Alliance
1211 Connecticut Ave NW Ste 200 .... Washington DC 20036 202-207-3850 833-1543
Web: www.theperformingartsalliance.org

American Assn for State & Local History (AASLH)
1717 Church St .... Nashville TN 37203 615-320-3203 327-9013
Web: www.aaslh.org

American Assn of Museums (AAM)
1575 Eye St NW Ste 400......................... Washington DC 20005 202-289-1818 289-6578
TF: 866-226-2150 ■ *Web:* www.aam-us.org

American Ceramic Society (ACerS)
600 N Cleveland Ave # 210....................... Westerville OH 43082 614-890-4700 899-6109
Web: www.ceramics.org

American Choral Directors Assn (ACDA)
545 Couch Dr.............................. Oklahoma City OK 73102 405-232-8161 232-8162
TF: 800-624-0166 ■ *Web:* www.acda.org

American College of Musicians
808 Rio Grande St .... Austin TX 78701 512-478-5775 478-5843
Web: www.pianoguild.com

American Composers Alliance Inc (ACA)
802 W 190th St Ste 1B.......................... New York NY 10040 212-925-0458
Web: www.composers.com

American Craft Council 72 Spring St Sixth Fl......... New York NY 10012 212-274-0630
TF: 800-836-3470 ■ *Web:* www.craftcouncil.org

American Design Drafting Assn (ADDA)
105 E Main St.................................... Newbern TN 38059 731-627-0802 627-9321
Web: www.adda.org

American Federation of Arts (AFA)
305 E 47th St 10th Fl .... New York NY 10017 212-988-7700 861-2487
Web: www.afaweb.org

American Federation of Musicians of the US & Canada (AFM)
1501 Broadway Ste 600 .... New York NY 10036 212-869-1330 764-6134
TF: 800-762-3444 ■ *Web:* www.afm.org

American Film Institute (AFI)
2021 N Western Ave........................... Los Angeles CA 90027 323-856-7600 467-4578
Web: www.afi.com

American Guild of Musical Artists (AGMA)
1430 Broadway 14th Fl........................... New York NY 10018 212-265-3687 262-9088
TF: 800-543-2462 ■ *Web:* www.musicalartists.org

American Guild of Organists (AGO)
475 Riverside Dr Ste 1260 .... New York NY 10115 212-870-2310 870-2163
Web: www.agohq.org

American Guild of Variety Artists (AGVA)
363 Seventh Ave 17th Fl.......................... New York NY 10001 212-675-1003 633-0097
TF: 800-331-0890 ■ *Web:* agvausa.com

American Institute for Conservation of Historic & Artistic Works (AIC)
1156 15th St NW Ste 320....................... Washington DC 20005 202-452-9545 452-9328
Web: www.conservation-us.org

American Institute of Architects (AIA)
1735 New York Ave NW .... Washington DC 20006 202-626-7300 626-7547
TF Orders: 800-242-3837 ■ *Web:* www.aia.org

American Institute of Graphic Arts (AIGA)
164 Fifth Ave.................................... New York NY 10010 212-807-1990 807-1799
TF: 800-548-1634 ■ *Web:* www.aiga.org

American Musicological Society (AMS)
6010 College Stn .... Brunswick ME 04011 207-798-4243 798-4254
TF: 888-421-1442 ■ *Web:* www.ams-net.org

American Society of Artists PO Box 1326............ Palatine IL 60078 312-751-2500
Web: americansocietyofartists.us

American Society of Cinematographers (ASC)
1782 N Orange Dr................................ Hollywood CA 90028 323-969-4333 882-6391
TF: 800-448-0145 ■ *Web:* www.theasc.com

American Society of Interior Designers (ASID)
608 Massachusetts Ave .... Washington DC 20002 202-546-3480 546-3240
Web: www.asid.org

Americans for the Arts
1000 Vermont Ave NW 6th Fl..................... Washington DC 20005 202-371-2830 371-0424
TF: 866-471-2787 ■ *Web:* americansforthearts.org/

Archives of American Art
750 Ninth St NW Ste 2200....................... Washington DC 20001 202-633-7940 633-7994
Web: www.aaa.si.edu

Phone | Fax

Art Dealers Assn of America (ADAA)
205 Lexington Ave Ste 901......................... New York NY 10016 212-488-5550 688-6809*
**Fax Area Code:* 646 ■ *Web:* www.artdealers.org

Art Directors Guild (ADG)
11969 Ventura Blvd Ste 200...................... Studio City CA 91604 818-762-9995 762-9997
Web: www.adg.org

Arts & Business Council of Americans for the Arts
1 E 53rd St 2nd Fl................................ New York NY 10022 212-223-2787 980-4857
TF: 866-471-2787 ■ *Web:* americansforthearts.org/

Association for Information Media & Equipment (AIME)
PO Box 9844 .... Cedar Rapids IA 52409 319-654-0608 654-0609
Web: www.aime.org

Association for Recorded Sound Collections (ARSC)
PO Box 543 .... Annapolis MD 21404 410-757-0488
Web: www.arsc-audio.org

Association of Children's Museums (ACM)
2711 Jefferson Davis Hwy Ste 600.................. Arlington VA 22202 703-224-3100 898-1086*
**Fax Area Code:* 202 ■ *Web:* www.childrensmuseums.org

Association of Film Commissioners International (AFCI)
109 E 17th St .... Cheyenne WY 82001 307-637-4422 375-2903*
**Fax Area Code:* 413 ■ *TF:* 888-765-5777 ■ *Web:* www.afci.org

Association of Performing Arts Presenters
1211 Connecticut Ave NW Ste 200................. Washington DC 20036 202-833-2787 833-1543
TF: 888-820-2787 ■ *Web:* www.apap365.org

Association of Talent Agents
9255 Sunset Blvd Ste 930 .... Los Angeles CA 90069 310-274-0628 274-5063
Web: www.agentassociation.com

Authors Guild 31 E 32nd St Seventh Fl .... New York NY 10016 212-563-5904 564-5363
Web: www.authorsguild.org

Ballet Theatre Foundation
American Ballet Theatre
890 Broadway Third Fl .... New York NY 10003 212-477-3030 254-5938
Web: www.abt.org

Bix Beiderbecke Memorial Society
PO Box 3688 Ste 201............................ Davenport IA 52808 563-324-7170 326-1732
TF: 888-249-5487 ■ *Web:* www.bixsociety.org

Broadcast Music Inc (BMI)
250 Greenwich St 7 World Trade Ctr................. New York NY 10007 212-220-3000 220-4474
Web: www.bmi.com

Broadway League, The 729 Seventh Ave 5th Fl........ New York NY 10019 212-764-1122 944-2136
TF: 866-442-9878 ■ *Web:* www.broadwayleague.com

Chamber Music America (CMA)
305 Seventh Ave 5th Fl............................ New York NY 10001 212-242-2022 242-7955
TF: 888-221-9836 ■ *Web:* www.chamber-music.org

Choristers Guild 2834 W Kingsley Rd................. Garland TX 75041 972-271-1521 398-3611
TF: 800-246-7478 ■ *Web:* www.choristersguild.org

Chorus America 1156 15th St NW Ste 310 .... Washington DC 20005 202-331-7577 331-7599
Web: www.chorusamerica.org

Clowns of America International (COAI)
PO Box 1171 .... Englewood FL 34295 941-474-4351
TF: 877-816-6941 ■ *Web:* www.coai.org

Conductors Guild 719 Twinridge Ln .... Richmond VA 23235 804-553-1378 553-1876
Web: www.conductorsguild.org

Country Music Assn Inc (CMA) 1 Music Cir S .... Nashville TN 37203 615-244-2840 726-0314
TF: 800-788-3045 ■ *Web:* cmaworld.com

Dance/USA 1111 16 St NW Ste 300................ Washington DC 20036 202-833-1717 833-2686
Web: www.danceusa.org

Design Management Institute (DMI)
38 Chauncy St Ste 800.............................. Boston MA 02111 617-338-6380 338-6570
TF: 800-200-5909 ■ *Web:* www.dmi.org

Dramatists Guild of America Inc
1501 Broadway Ste 701............................ New York NY 10036 212-398-9366 944-0420
Web: www.dramatistsguild.com

Drum Corps International (DCI) PO Box 3129....... Indianapolis IN 46206 317-275-1212 713-0690
TF Orders: 800-495-7469 ■ *Web:* www.dci.org

Earshot Jazz 3429 Fremont Pl Ste 309.................. Seattle WA 98103 206-547-6763 547-6286
Web: www.earshot.org

Educational Theatre Assn 2343 Auburn Ave .... Cincinnati OH 45219 513-421-3900 421-7077
Web: www.schooltheatre.org

Folk Alliance International 510 S Main St........... Memphis TN 38103 901-522-1170 522-1172
Web: www.folk.org

Glass Art Society (GAS) 6512 23rd Ave NW Ste 329 ...... Seattle WA 98121 206-382-1305 382-2630
TF: 800-636-2377 ■ *Web:* www.glassart.org

Gold Coast Jazz Society
1350 E Sunrise Blvd......................... Fort Lauderdale FL 33304 954-524-0805 525-7880
Web: www.goldcoastjazz.org

Gospel Music Assn (GMA) 741 Cool Springs Blvd....... Franklin TN 37067 615-242-0303 254-9755
Web: www.gospelmusic.org

Graphic Artists Guild Inc
32 Broadway Ste 1114............................ New York NY 10004 212-791-3400 791-0333
Web: www.graphicartistsguild.org

Guild of American Luthiers 8222 S Pk Ave............ Tacoma WA 98408 253-472-7853
Web: www.luth.org

Hollywood Foreign Press Assn (HFPA)
646 N Robertson Blvd....................... West Hollywood CA 90069 310-657-1731
Web: www.hfpa.org

Independent Film & Television Alliance (IFTA)
10850 Wilshire Blvd Ninth Fl.................... Los Angeles CA 90024 310-446-1047 446-1600
Web: www.ifta-online.org

Indian Arts & Crafts Assn (IACA)
4010 Carlisle Blvd NE Ste C.................... Albuquerque NM 87107 505-265-9149 265-8251
Web: www.iaca.com

International Ctr of Medieval Art (ICMA)
The Cloisters Fort Tryon Pk .... New York NY 10040 212-928-1146 928-9946
Web: www.medievalart.org

International Interior Design Assn (IIDA)
222 Merchandise Mart Plz Ste 567.................... Chicago IL 60654 312-467-1950 467-0779
TF: 888-799-4432 ■ *Web:* www.iida.org

International Society of Bassists (ISB)
14070 Proton Rd Ste 100 .... Dallas TX 75244 972-233-9107 490-4219
Web: www.isbworldoffice.com

Phone | Fax

International Ticketing Assn (INTIX)
5868 E 71st St Ste E367 .... Indianapolis IN 46220 212-629-4036 629-4036
Web: www.intix.org

Kansas City Jazz Ambassadors (KCJA)
PO Box 36181 .... Kansas City MO 64171 913-967-6767
Web: www.kcjazzambassadors.com

League of American Orchestras
33 W 60th St Fifth Fl. .... New York NY 10023 212-262-5161 262-5198
Web: www.americanorchestras.org

League of Resident Theatres (LORT)
1501 Broadway Ste 2401 .... New York NY 10036 212-944-1501 768-0785
Web: www.lort.org

Motion Picture & Television Fund
23388 Mulholland Dr. .... Woodland Hills CA 91364 781-314-0800
Web: www.mptf.com

Motion Picture Assn (MPA)
15301 Ventura Blvd Bldg E Sherman Oaks .... Sherman Oaks CA 91403 818-995-6600 285-4403
Web: www.mpaa.org

Motion Picture Assn of America
1600 Eye St NW .... Washington DC 20006 202-293-1966 296-7410
Web: www.mpaa.org

Mystery Writers of America Inc (MWA)
1140 Bdwy Ste 1507. .... New York NY 10001 212-888-8171 888-8107
Web: www.mysterywriters.org

National Academy of Recording Arts & Sciences
3030 Olympic Blvd. .... Santa Monica CA 90404 310-392-3777 392-2306
TF: 800-423-2017 ■ *Web:* www.grammy.com

National Academy of Television Arts & Sciences
111 W 57th St Ste 600 .... New York NY 10019 212-586-8424 246-8129
Web: www.emmyonline.org

National Association of Theatre Owners. (NATO)
750 First St NE Ste 1130 .... Washington DC 20002 202-962-0054 962-0370
TF General: 800-365-5701 ■ *Web:* www.natoonline.org

National Council for the Traditional Arts (NCTA)
1320 Fenwick Ln Ste 200 .... Silver Spring MD 20910 301-565-0654 565-0472
Web: www.ncta.net

National Guild of Piano Teachers PO Box 1807 .... Austin TX 78767 512-478-5775 478-5843
Web: pianoguild.com

National Humanities Alliance (NHA)
21 Dupont Cir NW Ste 604 .... Washington DC 20036 202-296-4994 872-0884
Web: www.nhalliance.org

National League of American Pen Women Inc
1300 17th St NW .... Washington DC 20036 202-785-1997 452-6868
Web: www.nlapw.org

National Music Publishers' Assn (NMPA)
975 F St NW Ste 375 .... Washington DC 20004 202-393-6672 393-6673
Web: www.nmpa.org

National Speakers Assn (NSA) 1500 S Priest Dr. .... Tempe AZ 85281 480-968-2552 968-0911
Web: www.nsaspeaker.org

Percussive Arts Society (PAS)
110 W Washington St. .... Indianapolis IN 46204 317-974-4488 974-4499
TF: 888-990-6663 ■ *Web:* www.pas.org

PLASA North America 630 Ninth Ave Ste 609. .... New York NY 10036 212-244-1505 244-1502
Web: www.plasa.org

Professional Photographers of America Inc (PPA)
229 Peachtree St NE Ste 2200 .... Atlanta GA 30303 404-522-8600 614-6400
TF: 800-786-6277 ■ *Web:* www.ppa.com

Professional Picture Framers Assn (PPFA)
2282 Springport Rd Ste F .... Jackson MI 49202 517-788-8100 788-8371
TF: 800-762-9287 ■ *Web:* www.pmai.org/ppfa

Recording Industry Assn of America Inc (RIAA)
1025 F St NW 10th Fl .... Washington DC 20004 202-775-0101 775-7253
Web: www.riaa.com

Screen Actors Guild (SAG)
5757 Wilshire Blvd. .... Los Angeles CA 90036 323-954-1600 549-6775
TF: 800-724-0767 ■ *Web:* www.sagaftra.org

SESAC Inc 55 Music Sq E .... Nashville TN 37203 615-320-0055 963-3527
TF: 800-826-9996 ■ *Web:* www.sesac.com

SITE Santa Fe 1606 Paseo de Peralta .... Santa Fe NM 87501 505-989-1199 989-1188
Web: www.sitesantafe.org

Society for Ethnomusicology (SEM)
Indiana University
1165 E 3rd St Morrison Hall 005 .... Bloomington IN 47405 812-855-6672 855-6673
TF: 800-933-9330 ■ *Web:* www.ethnomusicology.org

Society of American Archivists (SAA)
17 N State St Ste 1425 .... Chicago IL 60602 312-606-0722 606-0728
TF: 866-722-7858 ■ *Web:* www2.archivists.org

Society of Animal Artists Inc
5451 Sedona Hills Dr .... Berthoud CO 80513 970-532-3127 532-2537
Web: www.societyofanimalartists.com

Society of Glass & Ceramic Decorators (SGCD)
PO Box 2489 .... Zanesville OH 43702 740-588-9882 588-0245
Web: www.sgcd.org

Society of Motion Picture & Television Engineers (SMPTE)
Three Barker Ave. .... White Plains NY 10601 914-761-1100 761-3115
Web: www.smpte.org

Songwriters Guild of America
209 Tenth Ave S Ste 321. .... Nashville TN 37203 615-742-9945 742-9948
Web: www.songwritersguild.com

Stuntwomen's Association of Motion Pictures, Inc.
3760 Cahuenga Blvd Ste 104 .... Studio City CA 91604 818-762-0907
Web: www.stuntwomen.com

Tucson Jazz Society (TJS) PO Box 41071 Ste 206. .... Tucson AZ 85717 520-903-1265
Web: www.tucsonjazz.org

Women in Film (WIF)
6100 Wilshire Blvd Ste 710 .... Los Angeles CA 90048 323-935-2211 935-2212
Web: www.wif.org

World Monuments Fund (WMF)
350 Fifth Ave Ste 2412. .... New York NY 10118 646-424-9594 424-9593
TF: 800-547-9171 ■ *Web:* www.wmf.org

Young Audiences Inc 171 Madison Ave Ste 200 .... New York NY 10016 212-831-8110 289-1202
Web: www.youngaudiences.org

48-5 Charitable & Humanitarian Organizations

Phone | Fax

ACDI/VOCA 50 F St NW Ste 1075 .... Washington DC 20001 202-638-4661 783-7204
TF: 800-929-8622 ■ *Web:* www.acdivoca.org

Action Against Hunger 247 W 37th St 10th Fl .... New York NY 10018 212-967-7800 967-5480
TF: 877-777-1420 ■ *Web:* www.actionagainsthunger.org

Adventist Community Services
12501 Old Columbia Pk .... Silver Spring MD 20904 301-680-6438 680-6125
TF: 877-227-2702 ■ *Web:* www.communityservices.org

Adventist Development & Relief Agency International (ADRA)
12501 Old Columbia Pk .... Silver Spring MD 20904 301-680-6380 680-6370
TF: 800-424-2372 ■ *Web:* www.adra.org

Africare Inc 440 R St NW .... Washington DC 20001 202-462-3614 387-1034
Web: www.africare.org

Aga Khan Foundation USA (AKF)
1825 K St NW Ste 901 .... Washington DC 20006 202-293-2537 423-4216*
**Fax Area Code:* 416 ■ *TF:* 800-267-2532

Air Serv International
410 Rosedale Ct Ste 100 .... Warrenton VA 20186 540-428-2323 428-2326
Web: www.airserv.org

Alan Guttmacher Institute (AGI)
125 Maiden Ln Seventh Fl .... New York NY 10038 212-248-1111 248-1951
TF: 800-355-0244 ■ *Web:* www.guttmacher.org

America's Second Harvest
35 E Wacker Dr Ste 2000 .... Chicago IL 60601 312-263-2303 263-5626
TF: 800-771-2303 ■ *Web:* www.feedingamerica.org

American Anti-Slavery Group, The
198 Tremont St. .... Boston MA 02116 617-426-8161 964-2716*
**Fax Area Code:* 270 ■ *TF:* 800-884-0719 ■ *Web:* www.iabolish.org

American Council for Voluntary International Action
1400 16th St NW Ste 210 .... Washington DC 20036 202-667-8227 667-8236
Web: www.interaction.org

American Friends Service Committee (AFSC)
1501 Cherry St. .... Philadelphia PA 19102 215-241-7000
Web: www.afsc.org

American Institute of Philanthropy (AIP)
3450 N Lk Shore Dr .... Chicago IL 60657 773-529-2300 529-0024
Web: www.charitywatch.org

American Jewish Joint Distribution Committee (JDC)
711 Third Ave 10th Fl .... New York NY 10017 212-687-6200 370-5467
Web: www.jdc.org

American Jewish World Service (AJWS)
45 W 36th St. .... New York NY 10018 212-792-2900 792-2930
TF: 800-889-7146 ■ *Web:* www.ajws.org

American Lebanese Syrian Associated Charities (ALSAC)
501 St Jude Pl .... Memphis TN 38105 901-578-2000 578-2805
TF: 800-822-6344 ■ *Web:* www.stjude.org

American Near East Refugee Aid (ANERA)
1111 14th St NW Ste 400. .... Washington DC 20005 202-842-2766 266-9701
Web: www.anera.org

American Red Cross 2025 E St NW .... Washington DC 20006 202-303-4498 303-0044
Web: www.redcross.org

American Refugee Committee (ARC)
430 Oak Grove St Ste 204. .... Minneapolis MN 55403 612-872-7060 607-6499
TF: 800-875-7060 ■ *Web:* www.arcrelief.org

AmeriCares Foundation 88 Hamilton Ave .... Stamford CT 06902 203-658-9500 327-5200
TF: 800-486-4357 ■ *Web:* www.americares.org

Amigos de las Americas 5618 Star Ln. .... Houston TX 77057 713-782-5290 782-9267
TF: 800-231-7796 ■ *Web:* www.amigoslink.org

Amnesty International USA (AIUSA)
5 Penn Plaza 16th Fl. .... New York NY 10001 212-807-8400 627-1451
TF: 866-273-4466 ■ *Web:* www.amnestyusa.org

Arms Control Assn 1313 L St NW Ste 130. .... Washington DC 20005 202-463-8270 463-8273
Web: www.armscontrol.org

Association of Fundraising Professionals (AFP)
4300 Wilson Blvd Ste 300 .... Arlington VA 22203 703-684-0410 684-0540
TF: 800-666-3863 ■ *Web:* www.afpnet.org

Bread for the World 50 F St NW Ste 500 .... Washington DC 20001 202-639-9400 639-9401
TF Cust Svc: 800-822-7323 ■ *Web:* www.bread.org

Brother's Brother Foundation (BBF)
1200 Galveston Ave .... Pittsburgh PA 15233 412-321-3160 321-3325
Web: www.brothersbrother.org

Canadian Council for International Cooperation (CCIC)
450 Rideau St Ste 200 .... Ottawa ON K1N5Z4 613-241-7007 241-5302
Web: www.ccic.ca

CARE USA 151 Ellis St NE .... Atlanta GA 30303 404-681-2552 577-5977*
**Fax:* Hum Res ■ *TF:* 800-521-2273 ■ *Web:* www.care.org

Catholic Charities USA
2050 Ballenger Ave Ste 400 .... Alexandria VA 22314 703-549-1390 549-1656
Web: www.catholiccharitiesusa.org

Catholic Medical Mission Board (CMMB)
10 W 17th St. .... New York NY 10011 212-242-7757 645-1485
TF: 800-678-5659 ■ *Web:* www.cmmb.org

Catholic Relief Services (CRS)
228 W Lexington St .... Baltimore MD 21201 410-625-2220 685-1635
TF: 800-235-2772 ■ *Web:* www.crs.org

Center for Community Change (CCC)
1536 U St NW. .... Washington DC 20009 202-339-9300 387-4891
Web: www.communitychange.org

Center for Human Services
7200 Wisconsin Ave Ste 600 .... Bethesda MD 20814 301-654-8338 941-8427
Web: www.chs-urc.org

Centre for Development & Population Activities (CEDPA)
1133 21st St NW Ste 800 .... Washington DC 20036 202-667-1142 332-4496
Web: www.cedpa.org

Child Health Foundation
10630 Little Patuxent Pkwy
Century Plz Ste 126 .... Columbia MD 21044 410-992-5512 992-5641
Web: www.childhealthfoundation.org

				Phone	Fax
Children International 2000 E Red Bridge Rd *TF:* 800-888-3089 ■ *Web:* www.children.org	Kansas City	MO	64131	816-942-2000	942-3714
Children's Miracle Network 4220 Steeles Ave W Ste C18 *Web:* www.childrensmiraclenetwork.ca	Woodbridge	ON	L4L3S8	905-265-9750	265-9749
Christian Appalachian Project 6550 S KY Rt 321 PO Box 459 *TF:* 800-755-5322 ■ *Web:* www.christianapp.org	Hagerhill	KY	41222	800-755-5322	
Christian Blind Mission (CBM) 450 E Pk Ave *TF:* 800-937-2264 ■ *Web:* www.cbmus.org	Greenville	SC	29601	864-239-0065	239-0069
Christian Disaster Response International PO Box 3339 *Web:* www.cdresponse.org	Winter Haven	FL	33885	863-967-4357	
Christian Reformed World Relief Committee (CRWRC) 2850 Kalamazoo Ave SE *TF:* 800-552-7972 ■ *Web:* www.worldrenew.net	Grand Rapids	MI	49560	616-241-1691	224-0806
Church World Service 28606 Phillips St PO Box 968 *TF:* 800-297-1516 ■ *Web:* www.cwsglobal.org	Elkhart	IN	46515	574-264-3102	262-0966
Church World Service Emergency Response Program 475 Riverside Dr Ste 700 *TF:* 888-297-2767 ■ *Web:* www.cwserp.org	New York	NY	10115	212-870-3151	870-2236
Citizens Network for Foreign Affairs (CNFA) 1828 L St NW Ste 710 *Web:* www.cnfa.org	Washington	DC	20036	202-296-3920	296-3948
Coalition on Human Needs (CHN) 1120 Connecticut Ave NW *TF:* 800-822-7323 ■ *Web:* www.chn.org	Washington	DC	20036	202-223-2532	223-2538
Community Action Partnership 1140 Connecticut Ave NW Ste 1210 *Web:* www.communityactionpartnership.com	Washington	DC	20036	202-265-7546	265-5048
Community Food Bank of New Jersey Inc 31 Evans Terminal *TF:* 866-527-1087 ■ *Web:* www.cfbnj.org	Hillside	NJ	07205	908-355-3663	355-0270
Community Health Charities 200 N Glebe Rd Ste 801 *TF:* 800-654-0845 ■ *Web:* www.healthcharities.org	Arlington	VA	22203	703-528-1007	528-1365
Community Renewal Team Inc 555 Windsor St *Web:* www.crtct.org	Hartford	CT	06120	860-560-5600	
Compassion International 12290 Voyager Pkwy **Fax:* Hum Res ■ *TF:* 800-336-7676 ■ *Web:* www.compassion.com	Colorado Springs	CO	80921	719-487-7000	481-1893*
Concern America 2015 N Broadway *TF:* 800-266-2376 ■ *Web:* www.concernamerica.org	Santa Ana	CA	92706	714-953-8575	953-1242
Council on Foundations 2121 Crystal Dr Ste 700 *TF:* 800-673-9036 ■ *Web:* www.cof.org	Arlington	VA	22202	703-879-0600	879-0800
CRISTA Ministries 19303 Fremont Ave N *TF Cust Svc:* 800-346-9140 ■ *Web:* www.crista.org	Seattle	WA	98133	206-546-7200	546-7458
Direct Relief International 27 S La Patera Ln *TF:* 800-676-1638 ■ *Web:* www.directrelief.org	Goleta	CA	93117	805-964-4767	681-4838
Doctors Without Borders USA Inc 333 Seventh Ave Second Fl *TF:* 888-392-0392 ■ *Web:* www.doctorswithoutborders.org	New York	NY	10001	212-679-6800	679-7016
Dress for Success Worldwide 32 E 31st St Seventh Fl *Web:* www.dressforsuccess.org	New York	NY	10016	212-532-1922	684-9563
Enterprise Community Partners Inc 10227 Wincopin Cir *TF:* 800-624-4298 ■ *Web:* www.enterprisecommunity.com	Columbia	MD	21044	410-964-1230	964-1918
EnterpriseWorks/VITA 1100 H StNW Ste 1200 *Web:* www.enterpriseworks.org	Washington	DC	20005	202-639-8660	639-8664
Episcopal Migration Ministries (EMM) 815 Second Ave *TF:* 800-334-7626 ■ *Web:* episcopalchurch.org/page/episcopal-migration-ministries	New York	NY	10017	212-716-6258	972-0860
Episcopal Relief & Development 815 Second Ave **Fax Area Code:* 212 ■ *TF:* 800-334-7626 ■ *Web:* www.episcopalrelief.org	New York	NY	10017	855-312-4325	687-5302*
Ethiopian Community Development Council Inc (ECDC) 901 S Highland St *Web:* www.ecdcus.org	Arlington	VA	22204	703-685-0510	685-0529
Evangelical Council for Financial Accountability (ECFA) 440 W Jubal Early Dr Ste 130 *TF:* 800-323-9473 ■ *Web:* www.ecfa.org	Winchester	VA	22601	540-535-0103	535-0533
Fair Labor Assn (FLA) 1111 19th St NW Ste 401 *Web:* www.fairlabor.org	Washington	DC	20036	202-898-1000	898-9050
Feed the Children (FTC) PO Box 36 *TF:* 800-627-4556 ■ *Web:* www.feedthechildren.org	Oklahoma City	OK	73101	405-942-0228	945-4177
First Book 1319 F St NW Ste 1000 *Web:* www.firstbook.org	Washington	DC	20004	202-393-1222	628-1258
Food for the Poor Inc (FFP) 6401 Lyons Rd *TF:* 800-427-9104 ■ *Web:* www.foodforthepoor.org	Coconut Creek	FL	33073	954-427-2222	570-7654
Foundation for International Community Assistance (FINCA) 1101 14th St NW 11th Fl *Web:* www.finca.org	Washington	DC	20005	202-682-1510	682-1535
Freedom from Hunger 1644 DaVinci Ct *TF:* 800-708-2555 ■ *Web:* www.freedomfromhunger.org	Davis	CA	95618	530-758-6200	758-6241
Fund for Peace, The 1101 14th St Ste 1020 *Web:* global.fundforpeace.org	Washington	DC	20006	202-223-7940	223-7947
Giving Institute 303 W Madison St Ste 2650 *Web:* givinginstitute.org	Chicago	IL	60606	312-981-6794	
Global Children's Organization 3580 Wilshire Blvd # 1800 *Web:* www.globalchild.org	Los Angeles	CA	90010	213-368-8385	389-1237
Goodwill Industries International Inc 15810 Indianola Dr *TF:* 800-741-0197 ■ *Web:* www.goodwill.org	Rockville	MD	20855	301-530-6500	530-1516
Grantmakers in Health (GIH) 1100 Connecticut Ave NW Ste 1200 *Web:* www.gih.org	Washington	DC	20036	202-452-8331	452-8340
Habitat for Humanity International Inc 121 Habitat St *TF:* 800-422-4828 ■ *Web:* www.habitat.org	Americus	GA	31709	229-924-6935	924-6541
Healing the Children (HTC) 2624 W Beacon Ave *TF:* 888-233-9527 ■ *Web:* www.healingthechildren.org	Spokane	WA	99208	509-327-4281	327-4284
Healthrite International 80 Maiden Ln *Web:* www.healthright.org	New York	NY	10038	212-226-9890	226-7026
Heart to Heart International 401 S Clairborne Rd Ste 302 *Web:* www.hearttoheart.org	Olathe	KS	66062	913-764-5200	764-0809
Hebrew Immigrant Aid Society (HIAS) 333 Seventh Ave 16th Fl *TF:* 800-442-7714 ■ *Web:* www.hias.org	New York	NY	10001	212-967-4100	967-4483
Heifer International One World Ave *TF:* 800-422-0474 ■ *Web:* www.heifer.org	Little Rock	AR	72202	501-907-2600	907-2902
Helen Keller International 352 Pk Ave S Ste 1200 *TF:* 877-535-5374 ■ *Web:* www.hki.org	New York	NY	10010	212-532-0544	532-6014
HELP USA 5 Hanover Sq *Web:* www.helpusa.org	New York	NY	10004	212-400-7000	400-7005
Hole in the Wall Gang Camps Inc 265 Church St Ste 503 *Web:* www.seriousfunnetwork.org	New Haven	CT	06510	203-562-1203	562-1207
HOPE Worldwide 1285 Drummers Ln Ste 105 *Web:* www.hopeww.org	Wayne	PA	19087	610-254-8800	254-8989
Housing Assistance Council (HAC) 1025 Vermont Ave NW Ste 606 *TF:* 866-234-2689 ■ *Web:* www.ruralhome.org	Washington	DC	20005	202-842-8600	347-3441
Hunger Project, The Five Union Sq W *TF:* 800-228-6691 ■ *Web:* www.thp.org	New York	NY	10003	212-251-9100	532-9785
I Have a Dream Foundation (IHAD) 330 Seventh Ave 20th Fl *Web:* www.ihaveadreamfoundation.org	New York	NY	10001	212-293-5480	293-5478
Independent Charities of America (ICA) 1100 Larkspur Landing Cir Ste 340 *TF:* 800-477-0733 ■ *Web:* www.independentcharities.org	Larkspur	CA	94939	415-925-2600	925-2650
Independent Order of Foresters (IOF) 789 Don Mills Rd *TF:* 800-828-1540 ■ *Web:* www.foresters.com	Toronto	ON	M3C1T9	416-429-3000	429-3896
Independent Sector 1602 L St NW Ste 900 *TF:* 888-737-9477 ■ *Web:* www.independentsector.org	Washington	DC	20036	202-467-6100	467-6101
INMED Partnerships for Children 20110 Ashbrook Pl Ste 260 *Web:* www.inmed.org	Ashburn	VA	20147	703-729-4951	858-7253
Interchurch Medical Assistance Inc (IMA) 500 Main St PO Box 429 *Web:* www.imaworldhealth.org	New Windsor	MD	21776	410-635-8720	635-8726
International Aid Inc 17011 W Hickory St *TF:* 800-968-7490 ■ *Web:* www.internationalaid.org	Spring Lake	MI	49456	616-846-7490	846-3842
International Eye Foundation (IEF) 10801 Connecticut Ave *Web:* www.iefusa.org	Kensington	MD	20895	240-290-0263	290-0269
International Institute of Rural Reconstruction (IIRR) 40 Exchange Pl Ste 1205 *Web:* www.iirr.org	New York	NY	10005	212-880-9147	880-9148
International Medical Corps (IMC) 1919 Santa Monica Blvd Ste 400 *TF:* 800-481-4462 ■ *Web:* www.internationalmedicalcorps.org	Santa Monica	CA	90404	310-826-7800	442-6622
International Orthodox Christian Charities (IOCC) 110 W Rd Ste 360 *TF:* 877-803-4622 ■ *Web:* www.iocc.org	Towson	MD	21204	410-243-9820	243-9824
International Planned Parenthood Federation - Western Hemisphere Region (IPPF/WHR) 120 Wall St 9th Fl *TF:* 866-477-3947 ■ *Web:* www.ippfwhr.org	New York	NY	10005	212-248-6400	248-4221
International Rescue Committee (IRC) 122 E 42nd St 12th Fl *TF:* 800-435-7352 ■ *Web:* www.rescue.org	New York	NY	10168	212-551-3000	551-3179
Jesuit Refugee Service North America (JRS) 1016 16th St NW Ste 500	Washington	DC	20036	202-462-0400	
Lutheran Disaster Response 8765 W Higgins Rd **Fax Area Code:* 773 ■ *TF:* 800-638-3522 ■ *Web:* www.elca.org	Chicago	IL	60631	800-638-3522	380-2707*
Lutheran Immigration & Refugee Service (LIRS) 700 Light St *Web:* www.lirs.org	Baltimore	MD	21230	410-230-2700	230-2890
Make-A-Wish Foundation of America 4742 N 24th St Ste 400 *TF:* 800-722-9474 ■ *Web:* www.wish.org	Phoenix	AZ	85016	602-279-9474	279-0855
MAP International 4700 Glynco Pkwy *TF:* 800-225-8550 ■ *Web:* www.map.org	Brunswick	GA	31525	912-265-6010	265-6170
Marine Toys for Tots Foundation 18251 Quantico Gateway Dr *Web:* www.toysfortots.org	Triangle	VA	22172	703-640-9433	649-2054
Medical Care Development International (MCDI) 8401 Colesville Rd Ste 425 *Web:* www.mcd.org	Silver Spring	MD	20910	301-562-1920	562-1921
Medical Teams International (MTI) PO Box 10 *TF:* 800-959-4325 ■ *Web:* www.medicalteams.org	Portland	OR	97207	503-624-1000	624-1001
Mennonite Central Committee (MCC) 21 S 12th St PO Box 500 *TF:* 888-563-4676 ■ *Web:* www.mcc.org	Akron	PA	17501	717-859-1151	859-2171
Mennonite Disaster Service (MDS) 583 Airport Rd *TF:* 800-241-8111 ■ *Web:* www.mds.mennonite.net	Lititz	PA	17543	717-735-3536	859-4910
MENTOR/National Mentoring Partnership 1600 Duke St Ste 300 *TF:* 877-333-2464 ■ *Web:* www.mentoring.org	Alexandria	VA	22314	703-224-2200	226-2581
Mercy Corps 3015 SW First Ave *TF:* 800-292-3355 ■ *Web:* www.mercycorps.org	Portland	OR	97201	503-796-6800	796-6844
Mercy-USA for Aid & Development Inc (M-USA) 44450 Pinetree Dr Ste 201 *TF:* 800-556-3729 ■ *Web:* www.mercyusa.org	Plymouth	MI	48170	734-454-0011	454-0303
Michigan Municipal League 1675 Green Rd PO Box 1487 *TF:* 800-653-2483 ■ *Web:* www.mml.org	Ann Arbor	MI	48105	734-662-3246	662-8083

Phone Fax

Migration & Refugee Services
US Conference of Catholic Bishops
3211 Fourth St NE ... Washington DC 20017 202-541-3000 722-8755
Web: origin.usccb.org

NA for the Exchange of Industrial Resources (NAEIR)
560 McClure St ... Galesburg IL 61401 309-343-0704 343-7316
TF: 800-562-0955 ■ *Web:* www.naeir.org

National Alliance to End Homelessness
1518 K St NW Ste 410 ... Washington DC 20005 202-638-1526 638-4664
TF: 800-657-3769 ■ *Web:* www.endhomelessness.org

National AMBUCS Inc (AMBUCS)
4285 Regency Ct PO Box 5127 ... High Point NC 27265 336-852-0052 852-6830
TF: 800-838-1845 ■ *Web:* www.ambucs.org

National Benevolent Assn (NBA)
149 Weldon Pkwy Ste 115 ... Maryland Heights MO 63043 314-993-9000 993-9018
Web: www.nbacares.org

National Children's Advocacy Ctr (NCAC)
210 Pratt Ave ... Huntsville AL 35801 256-533-5437 534-6883
Web: www.nationalcac.org

National Coalition for the Homeless (NCH)
2201 P St NW ... Washington DC 20037 202-462-4822 462-4823
TF: 877-243-1576 ■ *Web:* www.nationalhomeless.org

National Committee for Responsive Philanthropy (NCRP)
2001 S St NW Ste 620 ... Washington DC 20009 202-387-9177 332-5084
Web: www.ncrp.org

National Peace Corps Assn (NPCA)
1900 L St NW Ste 610 ... Washington DC 20036 202-293-7728 293-7554
TF: 800-424-8580 ■ *Web:* peacecorpsconnect.org

National Student Campaign Against Hunger & Homelessness (NSCAHH)
328 S Jefferson St Ste 620 ... Chicago IL 60661 312-544-4436 275-7150
Web: www.studentsagainsthunger.org

Near East Foundation
230 Euclid Ave 900 S Crouse Ave ... Syracuse NY 13210 315-428-8670 425-2350*
**Fax Area Code:* 212 ■ *Web:* www.neareast.org

Neighborhood Service Organization Inc
220 Bagley St Ste 1200 ... Detroit MI 48226 313-961-4890 961-5120
Web: www.nso-mi.org

North American Mission Board SBC
4200 N Pt Pkwy ... Alpharetta GA 30022 770-410-6000 410-6133
TF: 800-634-2462 ■ *Web:* namb.net

Nuclear Age Peace Foundation (NAPF)
1187 Coast Village Rd Ste 1 PO Box 121 ... Santa Barbara CA 93108 805-965-3443 568-0466
Web: www.wagingpeace.org

OIC International
1500 Walnut St Ste 1304 ... Philadelphia PA 19102 215-842-0220 842-2276
TF: 800-653-6424 ■ *Web:* www.oici.org/

Operation USA 3617 Hayden Ave Ste A ... Culver City CA 90232 310-838-3455 838-3477
TF: 800-678-7255 ■ *Web:* www.opusa.org

ORBIS International Inc
520 Eigth Ave 11th Fl ... New York NY 10018 646-674-5500 674-5599
TF: 800-672-4787 ■ *Web:* www.orbis.org

Oregon Food Bank Inc PO Box 55370 ... Portland OR 97238 503-282-0555 282-0922
TF: 888-398-8702 ■ *Web:* www.oregonfoodbank.org

ORT American Inc 75 Maiden Ln 10th Fl ... New York NY 10038 212-505-7700 674-3057
TF: 800-519-2678 ■ *Web:* www.ortamerica.org

Outreach International
129 W Lexington PO Box 210 ... Independence MO 64050 816-833-0883 833-0103
TF: 888-833-1235 ■ *Web:* www.outreach-international.org

Oxfam America 226 Cswy St Fifth Fl ... Boston MA 02114 617-482-1211 728-2594
TF: 800-776-9326 ■ *Web:* www.oxfamamerica.org

Pan American Development Foundation (PADF)
1889 F St NW 2nd Fl ... Washington DC 20006 202-458-3969 458-6316
TF: 877-572-4484 ■ *Web:* www.padf.org

Partners of the Americas
1424 K St NW Ste 700 ... Washington DC 20005 202-628-3300 628-3306
TF: 800-322-7844 ■ *Web:* www.partners.net

Partnership for Philanthropic Planning (NCPG)
233 McCrea St Ste 400 ... Indianapolis IN 46225 317-269-6274 269-6276
Web: www.pppnet.org

Pathfinder International
Nine Galen St Ste 217 ... Watertown MA 02472 617-924-7200 924-3833
Web: www.pathfind.org

Peace Action 8630 Fenton St ... Silver Spring MD 20910 301-565-4050 565-0850
Web: www.peace-action.org

People-to-People Health Foundation
255 Carter Hall Ln ... Millwood VA 22646 540-837-2100 837-1813
TF: 800-544-4673 ■ *Web:* www.projecthope.org

Physicians for Human Rights (PHR)
185 Devonshire St Ste M102 ... Boston MA 02110 617-301-4200 301-4250
Web: physiciansforhumanrights.org

Physicians for Social Responsibility (PSR)
1875 Connecticut Ave NW Ste 1012 ... Washington DC 20009 202-667-4260 667-4201
TF: 800-459-1887 ■ *Web:* www.psr.org

Points of Light Foundation & Volunteer Ctr National Network
1400 'I' St NW Ste 800 ... Washington DC 20005 202-729-8000 729-8100
TF: 866-269-0510 ■ *Web:* www.pointsoflight.org

Population Action International (PAI)
1300 19th St NW Ste 200 ... Washington DC 20036 202-557-3400 728-4177
Web: pai.org

Population Communication
1250 E Walnut St Ste 220 ... Pasadena CA 91106 626-793-4750 793-4791
Web: populationcommunication.com

Population Connection 2120 L St NW Ste 500 ... Washington DC 20037 202-332-2200 332-2302
TF: 800-767-1956 ■ *Web:* www.populationconnection.org

Population Resource Ctr (PRC) 1725 K St NW ... Washington DC 20006 202-467-5030 467-5034
Web: prcdc.org

Presbyterian Disaster Assistance (PDA)
100 Witherspoon St ... Louisville KY 40202 800-728-7228 569-8039*
**Fax Area Code:* 502 ■ *TF:* 800-728-7228 ■ *Web:* www.presbyterianmission.org

Project Concern International (PCI)
5151 Murphy Canyon Rd Ste 320 ... San Diego CA 92123 858-279-9690 694-0294
TF: 877-724-4673 ■ *Web:* www.pciglobal.org

ProLiteracy Worldwide 1320 Jamesville Ave ... Syracuse NY 13210 315-422-9121 422-6369
TF: 800-448-8878 ■ *Web:* www.proliteracy.org

Phone Fax

Rainbow/PUSH Coalition Inc 930 E 50th St ... Chicago IL 60615 773-373-3366 373-3571
Web: www.rainbowpush.org

Rebuilding Together Inc
1899 L St NW Ste 1000 ... Washington DC 20036 800-473-4229 483-9081*
**Fax Area Code:* 202 ■ *TF:* 800-473-4229 ■ *Web:* www.rebuildingtogether.org

Refugees International (RI)
2001 S St NW Ste 700-K ... Washington DC 20009 202-828-0110 828-0819
TF: 800-733-8433 ■ *Web:* www.refugeesinternational.org

Research!America 1101 King St Ste 520 ... Alexandria VA 22314 703-739-2577 739-2372
Web: www.researchamerica.org

Resource Foundation, The
237 W 35th St Ste 1203 ... New York NY 10001 212-675-6170 268-5325
Web: www.resourcefnd.org

Resource Inc 1900 Chicago Ave S ... Minneapolis MN 55404 612-752-8000 752-8001
Web: www.resource-mn.org

RESULTS 750 First St NE Ste 1040 ... Washington DC 20002 202-783-7100 783-2818
Web: www.results.org

Rotary Foundation, The 1560 Sherman Ave ... Evanston IL 60201 847-866-3000 328-8554
TF: 800-435-7352 ■ *Web:* www.rotary.org

Second Harvest Food Bank of Central Florida
2008 Brengle Ave ... Orlando FL 32808 407-295-1066 292-4758
Web: www.foodbankcentralflorida.org

Sertoma International 1912 E Meyer Blvd ... Kansas City MO 64132 816-333-8300 333-4320
TF: 800-593-5646 ■ *Web:* www.sertoma.org

SHARE El Salvador 2425 College Ave ... Berkeley CA 94704 510-848-8487
Web: www.share-elsalvador.org

Share Our Strength 1730 M St NW Ste 700 ... Washington DC 20036 202-393-2925 347-5868
TF: 800-969-4767 ■ *Web:* www.nokldhungry.org

Smile Train Inc 41 Madison Ave Ste 28 ... New York NY 10010 212-689-9199 689-9299
TF: 877-543-7645 ■ *Web:* www.smiletrain.org

Society of Saint Andrew (SoSA)
3383 Sweet Hollow Rd ... Big Island VA 24526 434-299-5956 299-5949
TF: 800-333-4597 ■ *Web:* www.endhunger.org

Soroptimist International of the Americas
1709 Spruce St ... Philadelphia PA 19103 215-893-9000 893-5200
Web: www.soroptimist.org

Southeast Asia Resource Action Ctr (SEARAC)
1628 16th St NW Third Fl ... Washington DC 20009 202-667-4690 667-6449
TF: 888-907-1485 ■ *Web:* www.searac.org

Special Wish Foundation Inc
1250 Memory Ln N Ste B ... Columbus OH 43209 614-258-3186
TF: 800-486-9474 ■ *Web:* www.spwish.org

TechnoServe 49 Day St ... Norwalk CT 06854 203-852-0377 838-6717
TF: 800-999-6757 ■ *Web:* www.technoserve.org

Trickle Up Program Inc 104 W 27th St 12th Fl ... New York NY 10001 212-255-9980 255-9974
TF: 866-246-9980 ■ *Web:* www.trickleup.org

Turning Point Community Programs
3440 Viking Dr Ste 114 ... Sacramento CA 95827 916-364-8395
Web: www.tpcp.org

Unitarian Universalist Service Committee (UUSC)
689 Massachusetts Ave ... Cambridge MA 02139 617-868-6600 868-7102
TF: 800-388-3920 ■ *Web:* www.uusc.org

United Nations Children's Fund (UNICEF)
Three United Nations Plz ... New York NY 10017 212-326-7000 888-7465
Web: www.unicef.org

United Nations Foundation (UNF)
1800 Massachusetts Ave NW Ste 400 ... Washington DC 20036 202-887-9040 887-9021
Web: www.unfoundation.org

United Way of America 701 N Fairfax St ... Alexandria VA 22314 703-836-7100 683-7840
TF: 800-892-2757 ■ *Web:* www.unitedway.org

US Committee for Refugees & Immigrants (USCRI)
2231 Crystal Dr Ste 350 ... Arlington VA 22202 703-310-1130 769-4241
Web: www.refugees.org

US Fund for UNICEF 125 Maiden Ln ... New York NY 10038 800-367-5437 779-1679*
**Fax Area Code:* 212 ■ *TF:* 800-367-5437 ■ *Web:* www.unicefusa.org

USA for UNHCR 1775 K St NW Ste 580 ... Washington DC 20006 202-296-1115 296-1081
TF: 800-770-1100 ■ *Web:* www.unrefugees.org

Veterans for Peace Inc (VFP)
216 S Meramec Ave ... Saint Louis MO 63105 314-725-6005 725-7103
TF: 877-429-0678 ■ *Web:* www.veteransforpeace.org

Voices of September 11th 161 Cherry St ... New Canaan CT 06840 203-966-3911 966-5701
TF: 866-505-3911 ■ *Web:* www.voicesofseptember11.org

Volunteers of America 1660 Duke St ... Alexandria VA 22314 703-341-5000 341-7000
TF: 800-899-0089 ■ *Web:* www.voa.org

War Resisters League 339 Lafayette St ... New York NY 10012 212-228-0450 228-6193
TF: 800-975-9688 ■ *Web:* www.warresisters.org

Women's Action for New Directions (WAND)
691 Massachusetts Ave ... Arlington MA 02476 781-643-6740 643-6744
Web: www.wand.org

World Concern 19303 Fremont Ave N ... Seattle WA 98133 206-546-7201 546-7269
TF: 800-755-5022 ■ *Web:* www.worldconcern.org

World Education Inc 44 Farnsworth St ... Boston MA 02210 617-482-9485 482-0617
Web: www.worlded.org

World Food Program USA (WFP)
1725 Eye St NW Ste 510 ... Washington DC 20036 202-530-1694 530-1698
TF: 888-454-0555 ■ *Web:* wfpusa.org

World Hunger Year Inc (WHY)
505 Eigth Ave Ste 2100 ... New York NY 10018 212-629-8850 465-9274
TF: 800-548-6479 ■ *Web:* www.whyhunger.org

World Learning 1 Kipling Rd PO Box 676 ... Brattleboro VT 05302 802-257-7751 258-3248
TF: 800-257-7751 ■ *Web:* www.worldlearning.org

World Neighbors Inc (WN) 4127 NW 122nd St ... Oklahoma City OK 73120 405-752-9700
TF: 800-242-6387 ■ *Web:* www.wn.org

World Peace Prayer Society 26 Benton Rd ... Wassaic NY 12592 845-877-6093 877-6862
Web: www.worldpeace.org

World Relief Seven E Baltimore St ... Baltimore MD 21202 443-451-1900 451-1995
TF: 800-535-5433 ■ *Web:* www.worldrelief.org

World Vision Inc
34834 Weyerhaeuser Way S PO Box 9716 ... Federal Way WA 98001 253-815-1000
TF: 888-511-6548 ■ *Web:* www.worldvision.org

48-6 Children & Family Advocacy Organizations

Organization	City	State	Zip	Phone	Fax
AARP 601 E St NW *TF:* 888-687-2277 ■ *Web:* www.aarp.org	Washington	DC	20049	202-434-2277	434-7597
AARP Grandparent Information Ctr 601 E St NW *TF:* 888-687-2277 ■ *Web:* aarp.org/relationships/grandparenting/	Washington	DC	20049	202-434-3525	434-6474
Adoption ARC Inc 4701 Pine St Ste J-7 *TF:* 800-884-4004 ■ *Web:* www.adoptionarc.com	Philadelphia	PA	19143	215-748-1441	842-9881
Alliance for Aging Research (AAR) 750 17th St NW Ste 1100 *Fax Area Code: 770 ■ *TF:* 866-840-6283 ■ *Web:* www.agingresearch.org	Washington	DC	20006	202-293-2856	234-5030*
Alliance for Children & Families Inc 11700 W Lk Pk Dr *TF:* 800-221-3726 ■ *Web:* www.alliance1.org	Milwaukee	WI	53224	414-359-1040	359-1074
Alliance for Retired Americans 815 16th St NW Fourth Fl *TF:* 888-373-6497 ■ *Web:* www.retiredamericans.org	Washington	DC	20006	202-637-5399	637-5398
America's Promise - the Alliance for Youth 909 N Washington St Ste 400 *Web:* www.americaspromise.org	Alexandria	VA	22314	703-684-4500	
American Academy of Pediatrics (AAP) 141 NW Pt Blvd *TF:* 800-433-9016 ■ *Web:* www.aap.org	Elk Grove Village	IL	60007	847-434-4000	434-8000
American Adoption Congress (AAC) PO Box 42730 *Web:* www.americanadoptioncongress.org	Washington	DC	20015	202-483-3399	
American Assn for Marriage & Family Therapy (AAMFT) 112 S Alfred St *Web:* www.aamft.org	Alexandria	VA	22314	703-838-9808	838-9805
American Coalition for Fathers & Children (ACFC) 1718 M St NW Ste 1187 *TF:* 800-978-3237 ■ *Web:* www.acfc.org	Washington	DC	20036	800-978-3237	
American Culinary Federation Chef & Child Foundation 180 Ctr Pl Way *TF:* 800-624-9458 ■ *Web:* www.acfchefs.org/content/acfprograms/chefandchild	Saint Augustine	FL	32095	904-824-4468	825-4758
American Humane Assn (AHA) 63 Inverness Dr E *TF:* 800-227-4645 ■ *Web:* www.americanhumane.org	Englewood	CO	80112	303-792-9900	792-5333
American Seniors Housing Assn (ASHA) 5225 Wisconsin Ave NW # 502 *Web:* www.seniorshousing.org	Washington	DC	20015	202-237-0900	237-1616
American SIDS Institute 528 Raven Way *Web:* www.sids.org	Naples	FL	34110	239-431-5425	431-5536
American Society on Aging (ASA) 71 Stevenson St Ste 1450 *TF:* 800-537-9728 ■ *Web:* www.asaging.org	San Francisco	CA	94105	415-974-9600	974-0300
Association for Couples in Marriage Enrichment (ACME) PO Box 21374 *TF:* 800-634-8325 ■ *Web:* www.bettermarriages.org	Winston-Salem	NC	27120	336-724-1526	721-4746
Athletes & Entertainers for Kids (AEFK) 14340 Bolsa Chica Rd Unit C	Westminster	CA	92683	562-438-5905	
Believe In Tomorrow National Children's Foundation 6601 Frederick Rd *TF:* 800-933-5470 ■ *Web:* www.believeintomorrow.org	Baltimore	MD	21228	410-744-1032	744-1984
Blue Grass Regional Mental Health-Mental Retardation Board Inc 1351 Newtown Pike Bldg 1 *TF:* 800-928-8000 ■ *Web:* www.bluegrass.org	Lexington	KY	40511	859-253-1686	255-4866
Boys Town 14100 Crawford St *TF:* 800-448-3000 ■ *Web:* www.boystown.org	Boys Town	NE	68010	402-498-1300	498-1348
Buckner International 600 N Pearl St Ste 2000 20th Fl *TF:* 800-442-4800 ■ *Web:* www.buckner.org	Dallas	TX	75201	214-758-8000	758-8159
Cal Farley's Boys Ranch 600 W 11th St PO Box 1890 *TF:* 800-687-3722 ■ *Web:* www.calfarley.org	Amarillo	TX	79174	806-372-2341	372-6638
Camelot Community Care Inc 4910 D Creekside Dr *TF:* 866-343-8606 ■ *Web:* www.camelotcommunitycare.org	Clearwater	FL	33760	727-593-0003	595-0735
Child Find Canada 212-2211 McPhillips St *TF:* 800-387-7962 ■ *Web:* www.childfind.ca	Winnipeg	MB	R2V3M5	204-339-5584	339-5587
Child Lures Prevention 5166 Shelburne Rd *TF:* 800-552-2197 ■ *Web:* www.childluresprevention.com	Shelburne	VT	05482	802-985-8458	985-8418
Child Trends 4301 Connecticut Ave NW Ste 100 *Web:* www.childtrends.org	Washington	DC	20008	240-223-9200	200-1238
Child Welfare League of America (CWLA) 2345 Crystal Dr Ste 250 *Fax Area Code: 703 ■ *Web:* www.cwla.org	Arlington	VA	22202	202-688-4200	412-2401*
Childhelp USA 4350 E Camelback Rd Bldg F250 *TF:* 800-422-4453 ■ *Web:* www.childhelp.org	Phoenix	AZ	85018	480-922-8212	922-7061
Children Awaiting Parents Inc (CAP) 595 Blossom Rd Ste 306 *TF:* 888-835-8802 ■ *Web:* www.capbook.org	Rochester	NY	14610	585-232-5110	232-2634
Children Inc 4205 Dover Rd *TF:* 800-538-5381 ■ *Web:* childrenincorporated.org	Richmond	VA	23221	804-359-4562	
Children of Deaf Adults Inc (CODA) 3131 Calle Mariposa *Web:* coda-international.wildapricot.org/	Santa Barbara	CA	93105	805-682-0997	
Children of the Night 14530 Sylvan St *TF:* 800-551-1300 ■ *Web:* www.childrenofthenight.org	Van Nuys	CA	91411	818-908-4474	908-1468
Children's Defense Fund (CDF) 25 E St NW *TF:* 800-233-1200 ■ *Web:* www.childrensdefense.org	Washington	DC	20001	202-628-8787	662-3510
Christian Foundation for Children & Aging (CFCA) One Elmwood Ave *TF:* 800-875-6564 ■ *Web:* unbound.org/	Kansas City	KS	66103	913-384-6500	384-2211
CityKids Foundation 57 Leonard St *Web:* www.citykids.com	New York	NY	10013	212-925-3320	925-0128
Community Options Inc 16 Farber Rd *Web:* www.comop.org	Princeton	NJ	08540	609-951-9900	951-9112
Connecting Generations 100 W Tenth St Ste 1115 *TF:* 877-202-9050 ■ *Web:* www.connecting-generations.org	Wilmington	DE	19801	302-656-2122	656-2123
Consortium for Citizens with Disabilities (CCD) 1660 L St NW Ste 701 *Web:* www.c-c-d.org	Washington	DC	20036	202-783-2229	783-8250
Corps Network, The 1100 G St NW Ste 1000 *TF:* 800-245-5627 ■ *Web:* www.corpsnetwork.org	Washington	DC	20005	202-737-6272	737-6277
Council for Equal Rights in Adoption 444 E 76th St *Web:* www.adoptionhealing.com	New York	NY	10021	212-988-0110	988-0291
Covenant House Five Penn Plz Third Fl *Fax: Hum Res ■ *TF:* 800-999-9999 ■ *Web:* www.covenanthouse.org	New York	NY	10001	212-727-4000	727-6516*
Crossroads For Youth 930 E Drahner PO Box 9 *Web:* www.crossroadsforyouth.org	Oxford	MI	48371	248-628-2561	628-3080
DePelchin Children's Ctr 4950 Memorial Dr *TF:* 888-730-2335 ■ *Web:* www.depelchin.org	Houston	TX	77007	713-730-2335	802-3801
Envision Inc 610 N Main St *TF:* 888-425-7072 ■ *Web:* www.envisionus.com	Wichita	KS	67203	316-440-1500	440-1540
Evan B Donaldson Adoption Institute 120 E 38th St *Fax Area Code: 775 ■ *TF:* 800-837-2655 ■ *Web:* www.adoptioninstitute.org	New York	NY	10016	212-925-4089	796-6592*
Experience Works Inc 2200 Clarendon Blvd Ste 1000 *TF:* 866-397-9757 ■ *Web:* www.experienceworks.org	Arlington	VA	22203	703-522-7272	522-0141
Family Research Council (FRC) 801 G St NW *TF:* 800-225-4008 ■ *Web:* www.frc.org	Washington	DC	20001	202-393-2100	393-2134
Federation of Families for Children's Mental Health (FFCMH) 9605 Medical Ctr Dr Ste 280 *Web:* www.ffcmh.org	Rockville	MD	20850	240-403-1901	403-1909
Find the Children 2656 29th St Ste 203 *TF:* 888-477-6721 ■ *Web:* www.findthechildren.com	Santa Monica	CA	90405	310-314-3213	314-3169
First Candle 1314 Bedford Ave Ste 210 *TF:* 800-221-7437 ■ *Web:* www.firstcandle.org	Baltimore	MD	21208	410-653-8226	653-8709
Focus on the Family 8605 Explorer Dr *TF Sales:* 800-232-6459 ■ *Web:* www.focusonthefamily.com	Colorado Springs	CO	80920	719-531-3400	531-3424
Food Research & Action Ctr (FRAC) 1875 Connecticut Ave NW Ste 540 *Web:* www.frac.org	Washington	DC	20009	202-986-2200	986-2525
Generations United (GU) 1333 H St NW Ste 500-W *TF:* 800-677-1116 ■ *Web:* www.gu.org	Washington	DC	20005	202-289-3979	289-3952
Girls Inc 120 Wall St Third Fl *TF:* 800-374-4475 ■ *Web:* www.girlsinc.org	New York	NY	10005	212-509-2000	509-8708
Grandparents Rights Organization (GRO) 100 W Long Lk Rd Ste 250 *Web:* www.grandparentsrights.org	Bloomfield Hills	MI	48304	248-646-7177	646-9722
Head Start Child Development Council Inc 2451 Country Club Blvd *Web:* www.hscdc.org	Stockton	CA	95204	209-466-5541	
Healthy Teen Network 1501 St Paul St Ste 124 *Web:* www.healthyteennetwork.org	Baltimore	MD	21202	410-685-0410	685-0481
Human Life International (HLI) Four Family Life Ln *TF Orders:* 800-549-5433 ■ *Web:* www.hli.org	Front Royal	VA	22630	540-635-7884	622-6247
Ignitus Worldwide 9200 S Dadeland Blvd Ste 417 *Web:* www.ignitusworldwide.org	Miami	FL	33156	305-670-2409	
International Soundex Reunion Registry 901 E Second St *Web:* www.isrr.net	Carson City	NV	89701	775-882-7755	
Jewish Assn for Services for the Aged (JASA) 247 W 37th St *Web:* www.jasa.org	New York	NY	10018	212-273-5272	695-9070
Jewish Board of Family & Children Services (JBFCS) 120 W 57th St *TF:* 888-523-2769 ■ *Web:* www.jbfcs.org	New York	NY	10019	212-582-9100	956-5676
Justice in Aging (NSCLC) 1444 'I' St Ste 1100 *Web:* nsclc.org	Washington	DC	20005	202-289-6976	289-7224
Kansas Children's Service League (KCSL) 3545 SW 5th *TF:* 877-530-5275 ■ *Web:* www.kcsl.org	Topeka	KS	66606	785-274-3100	
Kempe Children's Ctr 13123 E 16th Ave *Web:* www.kempe.org	Aurora	CO	80045	303-864-5250	864-5302
KlaasKids Foundation PO Box 925 *Web:* www.klaaskids.org	Sausalito	CA	94966	415-331-6867	331-5633
Leading Age 2519 Connecticut Ave NW *TF:* 866-702-3278 ■ *Web:* www.leadingage.org	Washington	DC	20008	202-783-2242	783-2255
Little Flower Children & Family Services of New York 2450 N Wading River Rd *Web:* www.littleflowerny.org	Wading River	NY	11792	631-929-6200	929-6121
Margaret Sanger Ctr International (MSCI) 26 Bleecker St *Web:* www.plannedparenthood.org	New York	NY	10012	212-965-7000	274-7299
May Institute Inc 41 Pacella Pk Dr *TF:* 800-778-7601 ■ *Web:* www.mayinstitute.org	Randolph	MA	02368	781-440-0400	
Men Against Destruction Defending Against Drugs & Social Disorder Inc (MAD DADS) 3026 4th Ave S *Web:* www.maddads.com	Minneapolis	MN	55408	612-822-0802	253-0663
MENTOR/National Mentoring Partnership 1600 Duke St Ste 300 *TF:* 877-333-2464 ■ *Web:* www.mentoring.org	Alexandria	VA	22314	703-224-2200	226-2581
Mentoring USA Five Hanover Sq *Web:* www.helpusa.org	New York	NY	10004	212-400-8294	400-8278
MOPS International 2370 S Trenton Way *TF General:* 888-910-6677 ■ *Web:* www.mops.org	Denver	CO	80231	303-733-5353	733-5770
Mothers Against Drunk Driving (MADD) 511 E John Carpenter Fwy Ste 700 *TF:* 877-275-6233 ■ *Web:* www.madd.org	Irving	TX	75062	214-744-6233	869-2206
Mothers of Supertwins (MOST) 116 Yuma Ln *Fax Area Code: 618 ■ *Web:* www.mostonline.org	East Islip	NY	11730	631-859-1110	593-0480*

Phone Fax

NA for Home Care & Hospice (NAHC)
228 Seventh St SE ....Washington DC 20003 202-547-7424 547-3540
Web: www.nahc.org

National Adoption Ctr
1500 Walnut St Ste 701 .... Philadelphia PA 19102 215-735-9988 735-9410
Web: www.adopt.org

National Alliance for Caregiving
4720 Montgomery Ln Fifth Fl.......................Bethesda MD 20814 301-718-8444 652-7711
Web: caregiving.org

National Caregiving Foundation
801 N Pitt St...................................Alexandria VA 22314 703-299-9300 299-9304
TF: 800-930-1357 ■ *Web:* www.caregivingfoundation.org

National Caucus & Ctr on Black Aged Inc (NCBA)
1220 L St NW Ste 800 ....Washington DC 20005 202-637-8400 347-0895
Web: www.ncba-aged.org

National Child Care Assn (NCCA)
1325 G St NW Ste 500 ....Washington DC 20005 866-536-1945
TF: 866-536-1945 ■ *Web:* www.nccanet.org

National Child Support Enforcement Assn (NCSEA)
1760 Old Meadow Rd Ste 500 ....McLean VA 22102 703-506-2880 506-3266
Web: www.ncsea.org

National Coalition Against Domestic Violence (NCADV)
One Broadway Ste B210..............................Denver CO 80203 303-839-1852 831-9251
TF: 800-799-7233 ■ *Web:* www.ncadv.org

National Coalition for the Protection of Children & Families (NCPCF)
800 Compton Rd Ste 9224........................ Cincinnati OH 45231 513-521-6227 521-6337
Web: www.eos.net

National Council for Adoption (NCFA)
225 N Washington St ....Alexandria VA 22314 703-299-6633 299-6004
Web: www.adoptioncouncil.org

National Council on Family Relations (NCFR)
1201 W River Pkwy Ste 200 .... Minneapolis MN 55454 888-781-9331
TF: 888-781-9331 ■ *Web:* www.ncfr.org

National Council on the Aging (NCOA)
1901 L St NW Fourth Fl ....Washington DC 20036 202-479-1200 479-0735
TF: 800-677-1116 ■ *Web:* www.ncoa.org

National Court Appointed Special Advocate Assn (CASA)
100 W Harrison St N Twr Ste 500......................Seattle WA 98119 206-270-0072 270-0078
TF: 800-628-3233 ■ *Web:* www.casaforchildren.org

National Ctr for Children in Poverty (NCCP)
215 W 125th St Third Fl...........................New York NY 10027 646-284-9600 284-9623
Web: www.nccp.org

National Ctr for Family Literacy (NCFL)
325 W Main St Ste 300..............................Louisville KY 40202 502-584-1133 584-0172
TF: 877-326-5481 ■ *Web:* familieslearning.org/

National Ctr for Missing & Exploited Children (NCMEC)
699 Prince St ....Alexandria VA 22314 703-274-3900 274-2200
TF: 800-843-5678 ■ *Web:* www.missingkids.com

National Domestic Violence Hotline (NDVH)
PO Box 161810 .... Austin TX 78716 512-794-1133 453-8541
TF: 800-799-7233 ■ *Web:* www.thehotline.org

National Family Caregivers Assn (NFCA)
10400 Connecticut Ave Ste 500 .... Kensington MD 20895 301-942-6430 942-2302
TF: 800-896-3650 ■ *Web:* caregiveraction.org

National Healthy Mothers Healthy Babies Coalition (HMHB)
4401 Ford Ave Ste 300..........................Alexandria VA 22302 703-837-4792 664-0485
Web: www.hmhb.org

National Hispanic Council on Aging (NHCOA)
734 15th St NW Ste 1050.......................Washington DC 20005 202-347-9733 347-9735
TF: 800-633-4227 ■ *Web:* www.nhcoa.org

National Interfaith Coalition on Aging (NICA)
1901 L St NW Fourth Fl ....Washington DC 20036 202-479-1200 479-0735
Web: www.ncoa.org

National Network for Youth, The
741 Eigth St SE..................................Washington DC 20003 202-783-7949 783-7955
Web: www.nn4youth.org

National Organization of Mothers of Twins Clubs Inc (NOMOTC)
PO Box 700860 ....Plymouth MI 48170 248-231-4480
Web: www.nomotc.org

National Resource Ctr on Domestic Violence (NRCDV)
6400 Flank Dr Ste 1300 ....Harrisburg PA 17112 800-799-7233 545-9456*
**Fax Area Code:* 717 ■ *TF:* 800-799-7233 ■ *Web:* www.nrcdv.org

National Resource Ctr on Native American Aging (NRCNAA)
501 N Columbia Rd Rm 4535....................Grand Forks ND 58202 701-777-6780 777-6779
TF: 800-896-7628 ■ *Web:* ruralhealth.und.edu

National Resource Ctr on Nutrition Physical Activity & Aging
Florida International Univ
11200 SW Eighth St Bldg OE200 .... Miami FL 33199 305-348-1517 348-1518
Web: nutritionandaging.fiu.edu

National Runaway Switchboard (NRS)
3080 N Lincoln Ave ....Chicago IL 60657 773-880-9860 929-5150
TF: 800-786-2929 ■ *Web:* www.1800runaway.org

National SAFE KIDS Campaign
1301 Pennsylvania Ave NW Ste 1000...............Washington DC 20004 202-662-0600 393-2072
Web: www.safekids.org

National Urban Technology Ctr
80 Maiden Ln Ste 606 ....New York NY 10038 212-528-7350 528-7355
TF: 800-998-3212 ■ *Web:* www.urbantech.org

National WIC Assn (NWA) 2001 S St NW Ste 580 ....Washington DC 20009 202-232-5492 387-5281
TF: 866-782-6246 ■ *Web:* www.nwica.org

North America Missing Children Assn Inc (NAMCA)
201 Brownlow Ave ....Dartmouth NS B3B1W2 902-494-2449 468-2803
TF: 800-260-0753 ■ *Web:* www.chebucto.ns.ca

North American Council on Adoptable Children (NACAC)
970 Raymond Ave Ste 106 ....Saint Paul MN 55114 651-644-3036 644-9848
TF: 877-823-2237 ■ *Web:* www.nacac.org

Orphan Foundation of America (OFA)
21351 Gentry Dr Ste 130 ....Sterling VA 20166 571-203-0270 203-0273
TF: 800-950-4673 ■ *Web:* www.fc2success.org

Parents Helping Parents (PHP)
1400 Parkmoor Ave Ste 100........................ San jose CA 95126 408-727-5775 286-1116
TF: 855-727-5775 ■ *Web:* www.php.com

Phone Fax

Parents of Murdered Children (POMC)
4960 Ridge Ave Ste 2 .... Cincinnati OH 45209 513-721-5683 345-4489
TF: 888-818-7662 ■ *Web:* www.pomc.com

Parsons Child & Family Ctr 60 Academy Rd............Albany NY 12208 518-426-2600 447-5234
TF: 800-342-3009 ■ *Web:* www.parsonscenter.org

Pension Rights Ctr
1350 Connecticut Ave NW Ste 206................Washington DC 20036 202-296-3776 833-2472
TF: 866-735-7737 ■ *Web:* www.pensionrights.org

Plan USA 155 Plan Way............................Warwick RI 02886 401-738-5600 738-5608
TF: 800-556-7918 ■ *Web:* www.planusa.org

Planned Parenthood Federation of America
434 W 33rd St ....New York NY 10001 212-541-7800 245-1845
TF: 800-230-7526 ■ *Web:* www.plannedparenthood.org

Pressley Ridge 5500 Corporate Dr Ste 400........... Pittsburgh PA 15237 412-872-9400 872-9478
TF: 800-718-0356 ■ *Web:* www.pressleyridge.org

Promise Keepers (PK) PO Box 11798..................Denver CO 80211 866-776-6473 433-1036*
**Fax Area Code:* 303 ■ *TF:* 866-776-6473 ■ *Web:* promisekeepers.org

Rainbows 1360 Hamilton Pkwy...........................Itasca IL 60143 847-952-1770 952-1774
TF: 800-266-3206 ■ *Web:* www.rainbows.org

Rape Abuse & Incest National Network (RAINN)
2000 L St NW Ste 406 ....Washington DC 20036 202-544-1034 544-3556
TF: 800-656-4673 ■ *Web:* www.rainn.org

Safer Foundation 571 W Jackson Blvd ....Chicago IL 60661 312-922-2200 922-0839
Web: www.saferfoundation.org

SOS Children's Villages-USA
1001 Connecticut Ave NW Ste 1250................Washington DC 20036 202-347-7920
TF General: 888-767-4543 ■ *Web:* www.sos-usa.org

Spaulding for Children
16250 Northland Dr Ste 120....................... Southfield MI 48075 248-443-7080 443-7099
Web: www.spaulding.org

Stepfamily Foundation 310 W 85th St...............New York NY 10024 212-877-3244
Web: www.stepfamily.org

Students Against Destructive Decisions (SADD)
255 Main St ....Marlborough MA 01752 508-481-3568 481-5759
TF: 877-723-3462 ■ *Web:* www.sadd.org

Triplet Connection PO Box 429.................. Spring City UT 84662 435-851-1105 462-7466
Web: www.tripletconnection.org

United Way of Greater Cincinnati
2400 Reading Rd .... Cincinnati OH 45202 513-762-7100 762-7146
Web: www.uwgc.org

Voices for America's Children
1000 Vermont Ave NW Ste 700....................Washington DC 20005 202-289-0777
Web: www.voicesforamericaschildren.org

Well Spouse Assn 63 W Main St Ste H .... Freehold NJ 07728 732-577-8899 577-8644
TF: 800-838-0879 ■ *Web:* www.wellspouse.org

YMCA of the USA (YMCA) 101 N Wacker Dr 14th Fl......Chicago IL 60606 312-977-0031 977-9063
TF: 800-872-9622 ■ *Web:* www.ymca.net

YWCA USA (YWCA) 2025 M St NW Ste 550.........Washington DC 20036 202-467-0801 467-0802
TF: 888-872-9259 ■ *Web:* www.ywca.org

48-7 Civic & Political Organizations

Phone Fax

Advocates for Self-Government
1010 N Tennessee St Ste 215..................... Cartersville GA 30120 770-386-8372
TF: 800-932-1776 ■ *Web:* theadvocates.org

AIDS United 1424 K St NW Ste 200................Washington DC 20005 202-408-4848 408-1818
Web: www.aidsunited.org

Alliance for Justice (AFJ)
11 Dupont Cir NW Second Fl......................Washington DC 20036 202-822-6070 822-6068
Web: www.afj.org

Alliance of Nonprofit Mailers (ANM)
1211 Connecticut Ave NW Ste 610.................Washington DC 20036 202-462-5132 462-0423
Web: www.nonprofitmailers.org

American Assn of Political Consultants (AAPC)
600 Pennsylvania Ave SE Ste 330 ....Washington DC 20003 703-245-8020 544-9816*
**Fax Area Code:* 202 ■ *Web:* www.theaapc.org

American Cause, The 501 Church St Ste 315 ....Vienna VA 22180 703-255-2632 255-2219
Web: www.theamericancause.org

American Conservative Union, The (ACU)
1331 H St NW Ste 500 ....Washington DC 20005 202-347-9388 836-8606*
**Fax Area Code:* 703 ■ *Web:* www.conservative.org

American Council for an Energy-Efficient Economy (ACEEE)
529 14th St NW Ste 600.........................Washington DC 20045 202-507-4000 429-2248
Web: www.aceee.org

American Israel Public Affairs Committee (AIPAC)
251 H St...Washington DC 20001 202-639-5200
Web: aipac.org

American Jewish Congress
260 Madison Ave Second Fl........................New York NY 10016 212-879-4500 758-1633
Web: www.ajcongress.org

American Legislative Exchange Council (ALEC)
1101 Vermont Ave NW 11th Fl.....................Washington DC 20005 202-466-3800 466-3801
Web: www.alec.org

Americans for Democratic Action (ADA)
1625 K St NW Ste 210 ....Washington DC 20006 202-785-5980 785-5969
TF: 855-712-8441 ■ *Web:* www.adaction.org

Americans for Fair Taxation PO Box 27487...........Houston TX 77027 713-963-9023 963-8403
Web: www.fairtax.org

Americans for Peace Now (APN)
1101 14th St NW 6th Fl ....Washington DC 20005 202-728-1893 728-1895
TF: 877-429-0678 ■ *Web:* www.peacenow.org

Americans United for Separation of Church & State
518 C St NE ....Washington DC 20002 202-466-3234 466-2587
TF: 800-875-3707 ■ *Web:* www.au.org

Brady Campaign to Prevent Gun Violence
1225 'I' St NW Ste 1100..........................Washington DC 20005 202-898-0792 371-9615
TF: 800-732-0999 ■ *Web:* www.bradycampaign.org

Cair National (CAIR) 453 New Jersey Ave SE ....Washington DC 20003 202-488-8787 488-0833
Web: www.cair.com

Organization	City	State	Zip	Phone	Fax
Campaign Legal Ctr Media Policy Program Campaign Legal Ctr *TF:* 877-855-5007 ■ *Web:* www.campaignlegalcenter.org	Washington	DC	20036	202-736-2200	736-2222
CapitolWatch PO Box 650911 *Web:* www.capitolwatch.org	Potomac Falls	VA	20165	703-430-6617	430-6623
Center for Democracy & Technology (CDT) 1634 'I' St NW 11th Fl *TF:* 800-869-4499 ■ *Web:* www.cdt.org	Washington	DC	20006	202-637-9800	637-0968
Christian Coalition of America PO Box 37030 **Fax Area Code:* 808 ■ *TF:* 888-999-6778 ■ *Web:* www.cc.org	Washington	DC	20013	202-479-6900	586-0006*
Citizens Against Government Waste (CAGW) 1301 Pennsylvania Ave NW Ste 1075 *TF:* 800-232-6479 ■ *Web:* www.cagw.org	Washington	DC	20004	202-467-5300	467-4253
Citizens Committee for the Right to Keep & Bear Arms (CCRKBA) 12500 NE Tenth Pl *TF:* 800-426-4302 ■ *Web:* www.ccrkba.org	Bellevue	WA	98005	425-454-4911	451-3959
Citizens for Tax Justice (CTJ) 1616 P St NW Ste 200-B *TF:* 888-626-2622 ■ *Web:* www.ctj.org	Washington	DC	20036	202-299-1066	299-1065
Close Up Foundation 1330 Braddock Pl Ste 400 *TF:* 800-256-7387 ■ *Web:* www.closeup.org	Alexandria	VA	22314	703-706-3300	
Coalition to Stop Gun Violence 1023 15th St NW Ste 301 *Web:* www.csgv.org	Washington	DC	20005	202-408-0061	
Common Cause 1133 19th St NW Ninth Fl *Web:* www.commoncause.org	Washington	DC	20036	202-833-1200	659-3716
Community Assns Institute (CAI) 6402 Arlington Blvd Ste 500 *TF:* 888-224-4321 ■ *Web:* www.caionline.org	Falls Church	VA	22042	703-970-9220	970-9558
Concord Coalition 1011 Arlington Blvd Ste 300 *TF:* 888-333-4248 ■ *Web:* www.concordcoalition.org	Arlington	VA	22209	703-894-6222	894-6231
Congress Watch 215 Pennsylvania Ave SE *TF:* 800-289-3787 ■ *Web:* www.citizen.org/congress	Washington	DC	20003	202-546-4996	547-7392
Constitutional Rights Foundation 601 S Kingsley Dr *TF:* 800-488-4273 ■ *Web:* www.crf-usa.org	Los Angeles	CA	90005	213-487-5590	386-0459
Council of Canadians 170 Laurier Ave W Ste 700 *Web:* www.canadians.org	Ottawa	ON	K1P5V5	613-233-2773	233-6776
Council of the Americas 680 Pk Ave *Web:* as-coa.org	New York	NY	10065	212-628-3200	249-5868
Democracy 21 1825 I St NW *Web:* www.democracy21.org	Washington	DC	20006	202-429-2008	429-9574
Democratic Congressional Campaign Committee (DCCC) 430 S Capitol St SE *Web:* www.dccc.org	Washington	DC	20003	202-863-1500	485-3536
Democratic Governors Assn (DGA) 1401 K St NW Ste 200 *Web:* www.democraticgovernors.org	Washington	DC	20005	202-772-5600	772-5602
Democratic Senatorial Campaign Committee (DSCC) 120 Maryland Ave NE *Web:* www.dscc.org	Washington	DC	20002	202-224-2447	969-0354
EMILY's List 1800 M St NW Ste 375N *TF:* 800-683-6459 ■ *Web:* www.emilyslist.org	Washington	DC	20036	202-326-1400	326-1415
Evangelicals for Social Action (ESA) PO Box 367 *TF:* 800-650-6600 ■ *Web:* www.evangelicalsforsocialaction.org	Wayne	PA	19087	484-384-2990	493-1528
Families USA 1201 New York Ave NW Ste 1100 *TF:* 888-392-5132 ■ *Web:* www.familiesusa.org	Washington	DC	20005	202-628-3030	347-2417
Federation for American Immigration Reform (FAIR) 25 Massachusetts Ave NW Ste 330 *TF:* 877-627-3247 ■ *Web:* www.fairus.org	Washington	DC	20009	202-328-7004	387-3447
Foreign Policy Assn (FPA) 470 Pk Ave S *TF:* 800-628-5754 ■ *Web:* www.fpa.org	New York	NY	10016	212-481-8100	481-9275
Foundation for Moral Law PO Box 4086 *Web:* www.morallaw.org	Montgomery	AL	36103	334-262-1245	262-1708
Freedom Forum 555 Pennsylvania Ave NW *Web:* www.newseuminstitute.org	Washington	DC	20001	202-639-0537	
FreedomWorks 601 Pennsylvania Ave NW Ste 700-N *TF:* 888-564-6273 ■ *Web:* www.freedomworks.org	Washington	DC	20004	202-783-3870	942-7649
Girls Nation *American Legion Auxiliary* 8945 N Meridian St *Web:* www.alaforveterans.org	Indianapolis	IN	46260	317-569-4500	569-4502
Global Exchange 2017 Mission St Ste 303 *TF:* 800-497-1994 ■ *Web:* www.globalexchange.org	San Francisco	CA	94110	415-255-7296	255-7498
Interfaith Alliance 1212 New York Ave NW Ste 1250 *TF:* 800-510-0969 ■ *Web:* www.interfaithalliance.org	Washington	DC	20005	202-238-3300	238-3301
International Society of Political Psychology (ISPP) 126 Ward St Ste 1213 PO Box 1213 *Web:* www.ispp.org	Columbus	NC	28722	828-894-5422	894-5422
Interreligious Foundation for Community Organization (IFCO) 418 W 145th St *Web:* www.ifconews.org	New York	NY	10031	212-926-5757	926-5842
Judicial Watch Inc 425 Third St SW Ste 800 *TF:* 888-593-8442 ■ *Web:* www.judicialwatch.org	Washington	DC	20024	202-646-5172	646-5199
Junior Chamber International (JCI) 15645 Olive Blvd *TF:* 800-905-5499 ■ *Web:* www.jci.cc	Chesterfield	MO	63017	636-449-3100	449-3107
Keep America Beautiful Inc 1010 Washington Blvd *Web:* www.kab.org	Stamford	CT	06901	203-323-8987	325-9199
Landmark Volunteers 800 N Main St	Sheffield	MA	01257	413-229-0255	229-2050
League of Conservation Voters 1920 L St NW Ste 800 *Web:* www.lcv.org	Washington	DC	20036	202-785-8683	835-0491
League of Women Voters (LWV) 1730 M St NW Ste 1000 *Web:* www.lwv.org	Washington	DC	20036	202-429-1965	429-0854
NA of Town Watch (NATW) 308 E Lancaster Ave Ste 115 *Web:* www.nationaltownwatch.org	Wynnewood	PA	19096	610-649-7055	649-5456
National Civic League (NCL) 1889 York St **Fax Area Code:* 888 ■ *Web:* www.ncl.org	Denver	CO	80206	303-571-4343	314-6053*
National Coalition on Black Civic Participation Inc (NCBCP) 1050 Connecticut Ave NW Ste 700 *Web:* ncbcp.org/	Washington	DC	20036	202-659-4929	659-5025
National Committee to Preserve Social Security & Medicare (NCPSSM) 10 G St NE Ste 600 *TF:* 800-966-1935 ■ *Web:* www.ncpssm.org	Washington	DC	20002	202-216-0420	216-0451
National Community Action Foundation (NCAF) 1 Massachusetts Ave NW # 310 *Web:* ncaf.org	Washington	DC	20001	202-842-2092	842-2095
National Council of Women of the US Inc (NCWO) 777 UN Plz *Web:* ncwus.org	New York	NY	10017	212-697-1278	972-0164
National Council on Public History (NCPH) 425 University Blvd 327 Cavanaugh Hall *TF:* 800-554-5542 ■ *Web:* www.ncph.org	Indianapolis	IN	46202	317-274-2716	278-5230
National Ctr for Neighborhood Enterprise (NCNE) 1625 K St Ste 1200 *TF:* 866-518-1263 ■ *Web:* www.cneonline.org	Washington	DC	20006	202-518-6500	588-0314
National Endowment for Democracy (NED) 1025 F St NW Ste 800 *Web:* www.ned.org	Washington	DC	20004	202-378-9700	
National Federation of Democratic Women (NFDW) 7211 E Lincoln *Web:* www.nfdw.com	Wichita	KS	67207	316-612-9709	
National Federation of Republican Women (NFRW) 124 N Alfred St *TF:* 800-373-9688 ■ *Web:* www.nfrw.org	Alexandria	VA	22314	703-548-9688	548-9836
National Taxpayers Union (NTU) 108 N Alfred St *TF:* 800-680-7289 ■ *Web:* www.ntu.org	Alexandria	VA	22314	703-683-5700	683-5722
National Women's Political Caucus (NWPC) PO Box 50476 *Web:* www.nwpc.org	Washington	DC	20091	202-785-1100	370-6306
Native American Community Board (NACB) PO Box 572 *Web:* www.nativeshop.org	Lake Andes	SD	57356	605-487-7072	487-7964
OMB Watch 1742 Connecticut Ave NW *TF:* 866-483-5137 ■ *Web:* www.foreffectivegov.org	Washington	DC	20009	202-234-8494	234-8584
Organization of American States (OAS) 1889 F St NW *TF:* 888-442-4887 ■ *Web:* www.oas.org	Washington	DC	20006	202-458-3000	458-3967
People for the American Way (PFAW) 2000 M St NW Ste 400 *TF:* 800-326-7329 ■ *Web:* www.pfaw.org	Washington	DC	20036	202-467-4999	293-2672
Population Reference Bureau (PRB) 1875 Connecticut Ave NW Ste 520 *TF:* 800-877-9881 ■ *Web:* www.prb.org	Washington	DC	20009	202-483-1100	328-3937
Population-Environment Balance Inc 2000 P St NW Ste 600 *TF:* 800-866-6269 ■ *Web:* www.balance.org	Washington	DC	20036	202-955-5700	955-6161
Preservation Action 401 F St NW 3rd Fl *Web:* www.preservationaction.org	Washington	DC	20001	202-637-7873	637-7874
Project Vote 1350 I St NW Ste 1250 *TF:* 888-546-4173 ■ *Web:* www.projectvote.org	Washington	DC	20005	202-546-4173	
Public Affairs Council (PAC) 2033 K St NW Ste 700 *Web:* www.pac.org	Washington	DC	20006	202-872-1790	
Public Citizen 1600 20th St NW *Web:* www.citizen.org	Washington	DC	20009	202-588-1000	588-7796
Public Forum Institute 2300 M St NW Ste 900 *Web:* www.publicforuminstitute.org	Washington	DC	20037	202-467-2774	
Public Service Research Foundation 320-D Maple Ave E *Web:* www.psrf.org	Vienna	VA	22180	703-242-3575	242-3579
Republican Governors Assn (RGA) 1747 Pennsylvania Ave NW Ste 250 *Web:* www.rga.org	Washington	DC	20006	202-662-4140	662-4925
Ripon Society 1300 L St NW Ste 900 *Web:* www.riponsociety.org	Washington	DC	20005	202-216-1008	216-0036
Rock the Vote (RTV) 1001 Connecticut Ave NW Ste 640 *Web:* www.rockthevote.com	Washington	DC	20036	202-719-9910	
Secure America's Future Economy (SAFE) 214 N Spring Vly Rd *Web:* www.s-a-f-e.org	Wilmington	DE	19807	302-478-0676	
Sister Cities International (SCI) 1301 Pennsylvania Ave NW Ste 850 *Web:* www.sister-cities.org	Washington	DC	20004	202-347-8630	393-6524
US Junior Chamber of Commerce 7447 S Lewis Ave *TF:* 800-905-5499 ■ *Web:* www.jci.cc	Tulsa	OK	74136	636-681-1857	681-1401
US Term Limits (USTL) 1250 Connecticut Ave NW Ste 200 **Fax Area Code:* 703 ■ *Web:* www.termlimits.org	Washington	DC	20036	202-261-3532	383-5288*
Violence Policy Ctr (VPC) 1730 Rhode Island Ave NW Ste 1014 *Web:* www.vpc.org	Washington	DC	20036	202-822-8200	
WISH List 333 N Fairfax St Ste 302 *Web:* www.thewishlist.org	Alexandria	VA	22314	703-778-5550	778-5554
Women's Campaign Fund (WCF) 1900 L St NW Ste 500 *Web:* www.wcfonline.org	Washington	DC	20036	202-393-8164	393-0649
Young America's Foundation 110 Elden St **Fax Area Code:* 703 ■ *TF:* 800-292-9231 ■ *Web:* www.yaf.org	Herndon	VA	20170	800-872-1776	318-9122*
Young Democrats of America (YDA) PO Box 77496 *Web:* www.yda.org	Washington	DC	20013	202-639-8585	318-3221

48-8 Civil & Human Rights Organizations

				Phone	Fax
ACT UP 12 Wooster St ... *Web:* www.actupny.org	New York	NY	10013	212-966-4873	
American Civil Liberties Union (ACLU) 125 Broad St 18th Fl. *TF:* 877-867-1025 ■ *Web:* www.aclu.org	New York	NY	10004	212-549-2500	549-2580
American Jewish Committee (AJC) 165 E 56th St *Web:* www.ajc.org	New York	NY	10022	212-751-4000	750-0326
American Society of Access Professionals (ASAP) 1444 'I' St NW Ste 700 *Web:* www.accesspro.org	Washington	DC	20005	202-712-9054	216-9646
American-Arab Anti Discrimination Committee (ADC) 1732 Wisconsin Ave. *Web:* www.adc.org	Washington	DC	20007	202-244-2990	244-3196
Americans for Effective Law Enforcement (AELE) 841 W Touhy Ave *TF:* 800-763-2802 ■ *Web:* www.aele.org	Park Ridge	IL	60068	847-685-0700	685-9700
Americans for Tax Reform (ATR) 722 12th St NW Ste 4 *Web:* www.atr.org	Washington	DC	20005	202-785-0266	785-0261
Anti-Defamation League (ADL) 605 Third Ave. *TF:* 866-386-3235 ■ *Web:* www.adl.org	New York	NY	10158	212-885-7700	867-0779
Arab American Institute (AAI) 1600 K St NW Ste 601 *Web:* www.aaiusa.org	Washington	DC	20006	202-429-9210	429-9214
Asian American Legal Defense & Education Fund (AALDEF) 99 Hudson St 12th Fl *TF:* 800-966-5946 ■ *Web:* www.aaldef.org	New York	NY	10013	212-966-5932	966-4303
Association for Women's Rights in Development (AWID) 215 Spadina Ave Ste 150 *Web:* www.awid.org	Toronto	ON	M5T2C7	416-594-3773	594-0330
Becket Fund for Religious Liberty 1350 Connecticut Ave NW Ste 605 *TF:* 800-743-7734 ■ *Web:* www.becketfund.org	Washington	DC	20036	202-955-0095	955-0090
Center for Individual Rights (CIR) 1233 20th St NW Ste 300 *TF:* 877-426-2665 ■ *Web:* www.cir-usa.org	Washington	DC	20036	202-833-8400	833-8410
Center for Reproductive Rights 120 Wall St 14th Fl *Web:* www.reproductiverights.org	New York	NY	10005	917-637-3600	637-3666
Congress of Racial Equality (CORE) 817 Broadway Third Fl *Web:* www.core-online.org	New York	NY	10003	212-598-4000	
Corporate Accountability International 10 Milk St Ste 610 *TF:* 800-688-8797 ■ *Web:* www.stopcorporateabuse.org	Boston	MA	02108	617-695-2525	695-2626
Cultural Survival Inc 215 Prospect St *Web:* www.culturalsurvival.org	Cambridge	MA	02139	617-441-5400	441-5417
Disability Rights Ctr Inc 18 Low Ave. *TF:* 800-834-1721 ■ *Web:* www.drcnh.org	Concord	NH	03301	603-228-0432	225-2077
Drug Policy Alliance 70 W 36th St 16th Fl *Web:* www.drugpolicy.org	New York	NY	10018	212-613-8020	613-8021
Ethics Resource Ctr 2345 Crystal Dr Ste 201 *Web:* www.ethics.org	Arlington	VA	22202	703-647-2185	647-2180
Families Against Mandatory Minimums (FAMM) 1612 K St NW Ste 700 *TF:* 800-435-7352 ■ *Web:* www.famm.org	Washington	DC	20006	202-822-6700	822-6704
Gay & Lesbian Alliance Against Defamation (GLAAD) 104 W 29th St Fourth Fl *Web:* www.glaad.org	New York	NY	10001	212-629-3322	629-3225
Grandparents Rights Organization (GRO) 100 W Long Lk Rd Ste 250 *Web:* www.grandparentsrights.org	Bloomfield Hills	MI	48304	248-646-7177	646-9722
Human Rights Campaign 1640 Rhode Island Ave NW *TF:* 800-777-4723 ■ *Web:* www.hrc.org	Washington	DC	20036	202-628-4160	347-5323
Human Rights Watch 350 Fifth Ave 34th Fl *Web:* www.hrw.org	New York	NY	10118	212-290-4700	736-1300
Institute for Health Freedom 1875 Eye St NW Ste 500 *Web:* www.forhealthfreedom.org	Washington	DC	20006	202-429-6610	861-1973
International Gay & Lesbian Human Rights Commission (IGLHRC) 80 Maiden Ln Ste 1505 *Web:* www.iglhrc.org	New York	NY	10038	212-268-8040	430-6060
International Organization for Migration 1752 N St NW Ste 700 *Web:* www.iom.int	Washington	DC	20036	202-862-1826	862-1879
King Ctr, The 449 Auburn Ave NE *Web:* www.thekingcenter.org	Atlanta	GA	30312	404-526-8900	
La Causa Inc PO Box 4188 *Web:* www.lacausa.org	Milwaukee	WI	53204	414-647-8750	647-8797
Lambda Legal Defense & Education Fund 120 Wall St Ste 1500 *TF:* 866-542-8336 ■ *Web:* www.lambdalegal.org	New York	NY	10005	212-809-8585	809-0055
Leadership Conference on Civil Rights (LCCR) 1629 K St NW Ste 1000 *TF:* 888-460-0813 ■ *Web:* www.civilrights.org	Washington	DC	20006	202-466-3311	466-3435
Legal Counsel for the Elderly 601 E St NW Bldg A Fourth Fl *Web:* www.aarp.org	Washington	DC	20049	202-434-2170	434-6464
Media Watch PO Box 618 *TF:* 800-631-6355 ■ *Web:* www.mediawatch.com	Santa Cruz	CA	95061	831-423-6355	
Medicare Rights Ctr (MRC) 520 Eigth Ave N Wing Third Fl *TF Hotline:* 800-333-4114 ■ *Web:* www.medicarerights.org	New York	NY	10018	212-869-3850	869-3532
Migrant Legal Action Program (MLAP) 1001 Connecticut Ave NW Ste 915 *Web:* www.mlap.org	Washington	DC	20036	202-775-7780	775-7784
NA for the Advancement of Colored People (NAACP) 4805 Mt Hope Dr *TF:* 877-622-2798 ■ *Web:* www.naacp.org	Baltimore	MD	21215	410-580-5777	486-9255
NARAL Pro-Choice America 1156 15th St NW Ste 700 *Web:* www.naral.org	Washington	DC	20005	202-973-3000	973-3096
National Abortion Federation (NAF) 1755 Massachusetts Ave NW *TF:* 800-772-9100 ■ *Web:* www.prochoice.org	Washington	DC	20036	202-667-5881	667-5890
National Coalition Against Censorship (NCAC) 275 Seventh Ave Ninth Fl *Web:* www.ncac.org	New York	NY	10001	212-807-6222	807-6245
National Coalition Against Domestic Violence (NCADV) One Broadway Ste B210 *TF:* 800-799-7233 ■ *Web:* www.ncadv.org	Denver	CO	80203	303-839-1852	831-9251
National Coalition to Abolish the Death Penalty (NCADP) 1620 L St Ste 250 *Web:* www.ncadp.org	Washington	DC	20036	202-331-4090	
National Conference on Citizenship (NCOC) 1875 K St NW 5th Fl *TF:* 800-745-7275 ■ *Web:* www.ncoc.net	Washington	DC	20006	202-729-8038	449-8276
National Consumer Law Ctr (NCLC) Seven Winthrop Sq *Web:* www.nclc.org	Boston	MA	02110	617-542-8010	542-8028
National Council on Crime & Delinquency (NCCD) 1970 Broadway Ste 500 *TF:* 800-306-6223 ■ *Web:* www.nccdglobal.org	Oakland	CA	94612	510-208-0500	208-0511
National Crime Prevention Council (NCPC) 2345 Crystal Dr Ste 500 *Web:* www.ncpc.org	Arlington	VA	22202	202-466-6272	296-1356
National Ctr for Juvenile Justice (NCJJ) 3700 S Water St Ste 200 *Web:* ncjj.org	Pittsburgh	PA	15203	412-227-6950	227-6955
National Ctr for Victims of Crime, The 2000 M St NW Ste 480 *TF:* 800-394-2255 ■ *Web:* www.victimsofcrime.org	Washington	DC	20036	202-467-8700	467-8701
National Freedom of Information Coalition Univ of Missouri *TF:* 866-682-6663 ■ *Web:* www.nfoic.org	Columbia	MO	65211	573-882-4856	884-6204
National Gay & Lesbian Task Force (NGLTF) 1325 Massachusetts Ave NW Ste 600 *Web:* www.thetaskforce.org	Washington	DC	20005	202-393-5177	393-2241
National Immigration Forum 50 F St NW Ste 300 *Web:* www.immigrationforum.org	Washington	DC	20001	202-347-0040	347-0058
National Organization for the Reform of Marijuana Laws (NORML) 1600 K St NW Ste 501 *TF:* 888-676-6765 ■ *Web:* www.norml.org	Washington	DC	20006	202-483-5500	483-0057
National Organization for Victim Assistance (NOVA) 510 King St Ste 424 *TF:* 800-879-6682 ■ *Web:* trynova.org	Alexandria	VA	22314	703-535-6682	535-5500
National Right to Life Committee Inc (NRLC) 512 Tenth St NW *Web:* www.nrlc.org	Washington	DC	20004	202-626-8800	737-9189
National Urban League Inc 120 Wall St Eighth Fl *Web:* nul.iamempowered.com	New York	NY	10005	212-558-5300	558-5332
No Peace Without Justice (NPWJ) 866 UN Plz Ste 408 *Web:* www.npwj.org	New York	NY	10017	212-980-2558	980-1072
Nuclear Information & Resource Service (NIRS) 6930 Carroll Ave Ste 340 *Web:* www.nirs.org	Takoma Park	MD	20912	301-270-6477	270-4291
Osborne Assn 809 Westchester Ave *Web:* www.osborneny.org	Bronx	NY	10455	718-707-2600	707-3103
Parents Families & Friends of Lesbians & Gays (PFLAG) 1828 L St NW Ste 660 *Web:* community.pflag.org/page.aspx?pid=194&srcid=-2	Washington	DC	20036	202-467-8180	349-0788
Patients Rights Council (PRC) PO Box 760 *TF:* 800-958-5678 ■ *Web:* www.patientsrightscouncil.org	Steubenville	OH	43952	740-282-3810	
PEN American Ctr 588 Broadway *Web:* www.pen.org	New York	NY	10012	212-334-1660	334-2181
Pro-Life Action League 6160 N Cicero Ave Ste 600 *Web:* www.prolifeaction.org	Chicago	IL	60646	773-777-2900	777-3061
Rutherford Institute PO Box 7482 *TF:* 800-225-1791 ■ *Web:* www.rutherford.org	Charlottesville	VA	22906	434-978-3888	978-1789
Second Amendment Foundation 12500 NE Tenth Pl *TF:* 800-426-4302 ■ *Web:* www.saf.org	Bellevue	WA	98005	425-454-7012	451-3959
Sentencing Project 1705 DeSales St NW Eighth Fl *Web:* sentencingproject.org	Washington	DC	20036	202-628-0871	628-1091
Simon Wiesenthal Ctr 1399 Roxbury Dr Ste 100 *TF:* 800-900-9036 ■ *Web:* www.wiesenthal.com	Los Angeles	CA	90035	310-553-9036	772-7655
Southern Poverty Law Ctr (SPLC) 400 Washington Ave. *Web:* www.splcenter.org	Montgomery	AL	36104	334-956-8200	956-8483
Thomas Jefferson Ctr for the Protection of Free Expression 400 Worrell Dr *Web:* www.tjcenter.org	Charlottesville	VA	22911	434-295-4784	296-3621
Urban Land Institute (ULI) 1025 Thomas Jefferson St NW Ste 500W *TF Orders:* 800-321-5011 ■ *Web:* www.uli.org	Washington	DC	20007	202-624-7000	624-7140
WeTip Inc PO Box 1296 *TF:* 800-782-7463 ■ *Web:* www.wetip.com	Rancho Cucamonga	CA	91729	909-987-5005	987-2477

48-9 Computer & Internet Organizations

Phone Fax

1394 Trade Assn 23117 39th Ave SE Ste E Bothell WA 98021 425-870-6574 320-3897
Web: www.1394ta.org

American Registry for Internet Numbers (ARIN)
3635 Concorde Pkwy Ste 200 PO Box 79010 Chantilly VA 20151 703-227-9840 997-6200
Web: www.arin.net

American Society for Information Science & Technology (ASIS&T)
8555 16th St Ste 850 Silver Spring MD 20910 301-495-0900 495-0810
Web: www.asis.org

Apache Software Foundation (ASF)
1901 Munsey Dr Forest Hill MD 21050 410-420-0140 803-2258
Web: www.apache.org

Association for Computing Machinery (ACM)
Two Penn Plz Ste 701 New York NY 10121 212-626-0500 944-1318
TF: 800-342-6626 ■ *Web:* www.acm.org

Association For Data Ctr Management Professionals (AFCOM)
742 E Chapman Ave Orange CA 92866 714-997-7966 997-9743
Web: www.afcom.com

Association for the Advancement of Artificial Intelligence (AAAI)
445 Burgess Dr Ste 100 Menlo Park CA 94025 650-328-3123 321-4457
Web: www.aaai.org

Association of Service & Computer Dealers International (ASCDI)
131 NW First Ave Delray Beach FL 33444 561-266-9016 431-6302
Web: www.ascdi.com

Association of Shareware Professionals (ASP)
PO Box 1522 Martinsville IN 46151 765-349-4740 301-3756*
**Fax Area Code:* 815 ■ *Web:* www.asp-software.org

Association of Support Professionals, The
122 Barnard Ave Watertown MA 02472 617-924-3944 924-7288
Web: www.asponline.com

Broadband Forum 48377 Fremont Blvd Ste 117 Fremont CA 94538 510-492-4020
Web: www.broadband-forum.org

CANARIE 110 O'Connor St Fourth Fl Ottawa ON K1P5M9 613-943-5454 943-5443
Web: www.canarie.ca

Coalition for Networked Information
21 Dupont Cir NW Euram Bldg Ste 800 Washington DC 20036 202-296-5098 872-0884
Web: www.cni.org

CommerceNet 169 University Ave Palo Alto CA 94301 650-289-4040 289-4041
Web: commerce.net

Computer Assisted Language Instruction Consortium (CALICO)
214 Centennial Hall San Marcos TX 78666 512-245-1417 245-8298
Web: www.calico.org

Computer Measurement Group (CMG)
151 Fries Mill Rd Ste 104 Turnersville NJ 08012 856-401-1700 401-1708
TF: 800-436-7264 ■ *Web:* www.cmg.org

Computing Research Assn 1828 L St NW Washington DC 20036 202-234-2111 667-1066
Web: www.cra.org

Computing Technology Industry Assn (CompTIA)
3500 Lacey Rd Ste 100 Downers Grove IL 60515 630-678-8300 678-8384
Web: www.comptia.org

Consortium for School Networking (CoSN)
1025 Vermont Ave NW Ste 1010 Washington DC 20005 202-861-2676 393-2011
TF: 866-267-8747 ■ *Web:* www.cosn.org

Data Interchange Standards Assn (DISA)
7600 Leesburg Pike Ste 430 Falls Church VA 22043 703-970-4480 970-4488
TF: 866-205-5001 ■ *Web:* www.disa.org

EDUCAUSE 1150 18th St NW Ste 1010 Washington DC 20036 202-872-4200 872-4318
Web: www.educause.edu

Electronic Frontier Foundation Inc (EFF)
454 Shotwell St San Francisco CA 94110 415-436-9333 436-9993
Web: www.eff.org

Electronic Privacy Information Ctr (EPIC)
1718 Connecticut Ave NW Ste 200 Washington DC 20009 202-483-1140 483-1248
Web: www.epic.org

Entertainment Software Assn (ESA)
575 Seventh St NW Ste 300 Washington DC 20004 202-223-2400 223-2401
Web: www.theesa.com

Information Systems Audit & Control Assn (ISACA)
3701 Algonquin Rd Ste 1010 Rolling Meadows IL 60008 847-253-1545 253-1443
TF: 888-491-8833 ■ *Web:* www.isaca.org

Information Technology Industry Council (ITI)
1101 K St NW Ste 610 Washington DC 20005 202-737-8888 638-4922
Web: www.itic.org

Institute for Certification of Computing Professionals (ICCP)
2400 E Devon Ave Ste 281 Des Plaines IL 60018 847-299-4227 299-4280
TF: 800-843-8227 ■ *Web:* www.iccp.org

Institute for Women & Technology (IWT)
1501 Page Mill Rd MS 1105 Palo Alto CA 94304 650-236-4756 852-8172

International Webmasters Assn (IWA)
119 E Union St Ste A Pasadena CA 91103 626-449-3709
Web: www.iwanet.org

Internet Assigned Numbers Authority (IANA)
4676 Admiralty Way Ste 330 Marina del Rey CA 90292 310-823-9358 823-8649
Web: www.iana.org

Internet Corp for Assigned Names & Numbers (ICANN)
4676 Admiralty Way Ste 330 Marina del Rey CA 90292 310-823-9358 823-8649
Web: www.icann.org

Internet Society (ISOC) 1775 Wiehle Ave Ste 102 Reston VA 20190 703-439-2120 326-9881
Web: www.internetsociety.org

Internet2 1000 Oakbrook Dr Ste 300 Ann Arbor MI 48108 734-913-4250 913-4255
Web: www.internet2.edu

ITechLaw Assn 401 Edgewater Pl Ste 600 Wakefield MA 01880 703-506-2895 224-1239*
**Fax Area Code:* 781 ■ *Web:* www.itechlaw.org

National Urban Technology Ctr
80 Maiden Ln Ste 606 New York NY 10038 212-528-7350 528-7355
TF: 800-998-3212 ■ *Web:* www.urbantech.org

Network & Systems Professionals Assn Inc (NaSPA)
7044 S 13th St Oak Creek WI 53154 414-768-8000 768-8001
TF: 877-777-3520 ■ *Web:* www.naspa.com

Phone Fax

Object Management Group (OMG)
140 Kendrick St Ste 300 Needham MA 02494 781-444-0404 444-0320
Web: www.omg.org

Open Group 44 Montgomery St Ste 960 San Francisco CA 94104 415-374-8280 374-8293
TF: 800-433-6611 ■ *Web:* www.opengroup.org

Portable Computer & Communications Assn (PCCA)
PO Box 680 Hood River OR 97031 541-490-5140 410-8447*
**Fax Area Code:* 413 ■ *TF:* 877-323-8888 ■ *Web:* www.pcca.org

Print Services & Distribution Assn (PSDA)
330 N. Wabash Ave Ste 2000 Chicago IL 60611 800-230-0175
TF: 800-336-4641 ■ *Web:* www.psda.org

Society for Information Display (SID)
1475 S Bascom Ave Ste 114 Campbell CA 95008 408-879-3901 879-3833
Web: www.sid.org

Society for Information Management (SIM)
401 N Michigan Ave Ste 2400 Chicago IL 60611 312-527-6734
TF: 800-387-9746 ■ *Web:* www.simnet.org

Society for Modeling & Simulation International (SCS)
4838 Ronson Ct Ste L PO Box 17900 San Diego CA 92111 858-277-3888 277-3930
Web: www.scs.org

Software & Information Industry Assn (SIIA)
1090 Vermont Ave NW Sixth Fl Washington DC 20005 202-289-7442 289-7097
Web: www.siia.net

TechNet 805 15th St NW Ste 708 Washington DC 20005 202-650-5100
Web: www.technet.org

TechServe Alliance 1420 King St Ste 610 Alexandria VA 22314 703-838-2050 838-3610
TF: 888-421-1442 ■ *Web:* www.techservealliance.org

Transaction Processing Performance Council (TPC)
572 Ruger St San Francisco CA 94129 415-561-6272 561-6120
Web: www.tpc.org

USENIX Assn 2560 Ninth St Ste 215 Berkeley CA 94710 510-528-8649 548-5738
Web: www.usenix.org

World Wide Web Consortium (W3C)
32 Vassar St Rm 32-G515 Cambridge MA 02139 617-253-2613 258-5999
Web: www.w3.org

48-10 Consumer Interest Organizations

Phone Fax

Accuracy in Media Inc (AIM)
4455 Connecticut Ave NW Ste 330 Washington DC 20008 202-364-4401 364-4098
TF: 800-787-4567 ■ *Web:* www.aim.org

Advocates for Highway & Auto Safety
750 First St NE Ste 901 Washington DC 20002 202-408-1711 408-1699
TF: 877-366-0711 ■ *Web:* www.saferoads.org

American Council on Science & Health (ACSH)
1995 Broadway Second Fl New York NY 10023 212-362-7044 362-4919
TF: 866-905-2694 ■ *Web:* www.acsh.org

Call for Action 11820 Parklawn Dr Ste 340 Rockville MD 20852 240-747-0225
Web: www.callforaction.org

Carpet & Rug Institute (CRI)
100 S Hamilton St PO Box 2048 Dalton GA 30720 706-278-3176 278-8835
Web: www.carpet-rug.org

Center for Auto Safety (CAS)
1825 Connecticut Ave NW Ste 330 Washington DC 20009 202-328-7700 387-0140
TF: 800-424-9393 ■ *Web:* www.autosafety.org

Center for Science in the Public Interest (CSPI)
1875 Connecticut Ave NW Ste 300 Washington DC 20009 202-332-9110 265-4954
Web: www.cspinet.org

Consumer Federation of America (CFA)
1620 I St NW Ste 200 Washington DC 20006 202-387-6121 265-7989
TF: 877-382-4357 ■ *Web:* www.consumerfed.org

Consumers' Research Council of America (CRCA)
2020 Pennsylvania Ave NW Ste 300-A Washington DC 20006 202-835-9698 835-9739
TF: 800-675-5376 ■ *Web:* www.consumersresearchcncl.org

Council of Better Business Bureaus Inc Wise Giving Alliance
4200 Wilson Blvd Ste 800 Arlington VA 22203 703-276-0100 525-8277
Web: www.bbb.org

Funeral Consumers Alliance
33 Patchen Rd South Burlington VT 05403 802-865-8300 865-2626
TF: 800-765-0107 ■ *Web:* www.funerals.org

Green Seal 1001 Connecticut Ave NW Ste 827 Washington DC 20036 202-872-6400 872-4324
Web: www.greenseal.org

Insurance Information Institute Inc (III)
110 William St New York NY 10038 212-346-5500 732-1916
TF: 877-263-7995 ■ *Web:* www.iii.org

Internet Fraud Watch
1701 K St NW Suite 1200 Ste 1200 Washington DC 20006 202-835-3323 835-0747
Web: fraud.org/scams/internet-fraud

National Committee for Quality Assurance (NCQA)
1100 13th St Washington DC 20005 202-955-3500 955-3599
TF: 888-275-7585 ■ *Web:* www.ncqa.org

National Consumers League (NCL)
1701 K St NW Ste 1200 Washington DC 20006 202-835-3323 835-0747
TF: 800-388-2227 ■ *Web:* www.natlconsumersleague.org

National Ctr for Employee Ownership (NCEO)
1736 Franklin St Eighth Fl Oakland CA 94612 510-208-1300 272-9510
Web: www.nceo.org

National Endowment for Financial Education (NEFE)
1331 17th St Ste 1200 Denver CO 80202 303-741-6333 220-0838
Web: www.nefe.org

National Fireworks Assn (NFA)
8224 NW Bradford Ct Kansas City MO 64151 816-741-1826 741-1348
Web: www.nationalfireworks.org

National Fraud Information Ctr (NFIC)
1701 K St NW Ste 1200 Washington DC 20006 202-835-3323 835-0747
TF: 800-333-4636 ■ *Web:* www.fraud.org

NeighborWorks America
999 N Capitol St NE Ste 900 Washington DC 20002 202-760-4000 376-2600
Web: www.nw.org

Organization	City	State	ZIP	Phone	Fax
Philanthropic Research Inc 4801 Courthouse St Ste 220 — TF: 800-784-9378 ■ Web: find.hamptonroads.com	Williamsburg	VA	23188	757-229-4631	229-8912
Privacy Rights Clearinghouse 3100 Fifth Ave Ste B — Web: www.privacyrights.org	San Diego	CA	92103	619-298-3396	298-5681
Private Citizen Inc PO Box 233 — TF: 888-382-1222 ■ Web: www.privatecitizen.com	Naperville	IL	60566	630-393-1555	
Public Citizen 1600 20th St NW — Web: www.citizen.org	Washington	DC	20009	202-588-1000	588-7796
Public Citizen Health Research Group 1600 20th St NW — Web: www.citizen.org/hrg	Washington	DC	20009	202-588-1000	588-7796
SOCAP International 625 N Washington St Ste 304 — Web: www.socap.org	Alexandria	VA	22314	703-519-3700	549-4886
US Metric Assn Inc (USMA) 10245 Andasol Ave	Northridge	CA	91325	818-363-5606	

48-11 Educational Associations & Organizations

Organization	City	State	ZIP	Phone	Fax
A Better Chance Inc 253 W 35th St 6th Fl — *Fax Area Code: 913 ■ TF: 800-562-7865 ■ Web: www.abetterchance.org	New York	NY	10001	646-346-1310	663-3766*
AACSB International - Assn to Advance Collegiate Schools of Business 777 S Harbour Island Blvd Ste 750 — Web: www.aacsb.edu	Tampa	FL	33602	813-769-6500	769-6559
Academy for Educational Development (AED) 1825 Connecticut Ave NW Ste 800 — Web: www.fhi360.org	Washington	DC	20009	202-884-8000	884-8400
Academy of Political Science 475 Riverside Dr Ste 1274 — Web: www.psqonline.org	New York	NY	10115	212-870-2500	870-2202
AFS International Inc 71 W 23rd St 6th Fl — Web: www.afs.org	New York	NY	10010	212-807-8686	
Alliance for Excellent Education 1201 Connecticut Ave Ste 901 — TF: 800-695-0285 ■ Web: www.all4ed.org	Washington	DC	20036	202-828-0828	828-0821
Alliance for International Educational & Cultural Exchange 1776 Massachusetts Ave NW Ste 620 — TF: 888-304-9023 ■ Web: www.alliance-exchange.org	Washington	DC	20036	202-293-6141	293-6144
American Indian College Fund 8333 Greenwood Blvd — TF: 800-776-3863 ■ Web: www.collegefund.org	Denver	CO	80221	303-426-8900	426-1200
American Montessori Society (AMS) 281 Pk Ave S Sixth Fl — Web: www.amshq.org	New York	NY	10010	212-358-1250	358-1256
American Philosophical Society (APS) 104 S Fifth St — Web: www.amphilsoc.org	Philadelphia	PA	19106	215-440-3400	440-3436
Americas Society 680 Pk Ave 68th St — Web: www.as-coa.org	New York	NY	10065	212-628-3200	628-3200
Archaeological Institute of America (AIA) 656 Beacon St 4th Fl — TF: 877-524-6300 ■ Web: www.archaeological.org	Boston	MA	02215	617-353-9361	353-6550
Associated Collegiate Press (ACP) 2221 University Ave SE Ste 121 — Web: www.studentpress.org	Minneapolis	MN	55414	612-625-8335	626-0720
Association for Asian Studies (AAS) 825 Victors Way Ste 310 — Web: www.asian-studies.org	Ann Arbor	MI	48108	734-665-2490	665-3801
Association of Jesuit Colleges & Universities (AJCU) 1 Dupont Cir NW Ste 405 — Web: www.ajcunet.edu	Washington	DC	20036	202-862-9893	862-8523
Association of Writers & Writing Programs (AWP) George Mason Univ MS 1E3 — Web: awpwriter.org	Fairfax	VA	22030	703-993-4301	993-4302
Astronomical Society of the Pacific 390 Ashton Ave — Web: www.astrosociety.org	San Francisco	CA	94112	415-337-1100	337-5205
Braille Institute of America Inc 741 N Vermont Ave — TF: 800-272-4553 ■ Web: www.brailleinstitute.org	Los Angeles	CA	90029	323-663-1111	663-0867
Breakthrough Collaborative 545 Sansome St Ste 700 — Web: www.breakthroughcollaborative.org	San Francisco	CA	94111	415-442-0600	442-0609
Bryan City School District 1350 Fountain Grove Dr — Web: www.bryan.k12.oh.us	Bryan	OH	43506	419-636-6973	633-6280
Challenger Ctr for Space Science Education 422 First St SE Third Fl — *Fax Area Code: 800 ■ TF General: 800-969-5747 ■ Web: www.challenger.org	Washington	DC	20003	202-827-1580	969-5747*
Chickasaw Nation, The 520 Arlington St PO Box 1548 — TF: 866-466-1481 ■ Web: www.chickasaw.net	Ada	OK	74821	580-436-2603	436-7297
College Board 45 Columbus Ave — *Fax: PR ■ TF: 800-927-4302 ■ Web: www.collegeboard.org	New York	NY	10023	212-713-8000	713-8282*
College Parents of America (CPA) 2200 Wilson Blvd Ste 102-396 — TF: 888-761-6702 ■ Web: www.collegeparents.org	Arlington	VA	22201	888-761-6702	
Columbia Scholastic Press Assn (CSPA) Columbia University MC 5711 — Web: cspa.columbia.edu	New York	NY	10027	212-854-9400	854-9401
Committee for Education Funding (CEF) 1640 Rhode Island Ave NW # 600 — Web: www.cef.org	Washington	DC	20036	202-383-0083	383-0097
Comstar Enterprises Inc PO Box 6698 — TF: 800-533-2343 ■ Web: comstar-inc.com	Springdale	AR	72766	479-361-2111	361-1069
Council For Economic Opportunities In Greater Cleveland 1228 Euclid Ave Ste 700 — TF: 888-262-3226 ■ Web: www.ceogc.org	Cleveland	OH	44115	216-696-9077	696-0770
Council for Opportunity in Education 1025 Vermont Ave NW Ste 900 — TF: 800-633-7313 ■ Web: www.coenet.us	Washington	DC	20005	202-347-7430	347-0786
Education Development Ctr Inc (EDC) 55 Chapel St — TF: 800-225-4276 ■ Web: www.edc.org	Newton	MA	02458	617-969-7100	969-5979
Education Trust 1250 H St NW Ste 700 — Web: www.edtrust.org	Washington	DC	20005	202-293-1217	293-2605
Facing History & Ourselves 16 HuRd Rd — TF: 800-856-9039 ■ Web: www.facinghistory.org/	Brookline	MA	02445	617-232-1595	232-0281
Family Career & Community Leaders of America (FCCLA) 1910 Assn Dr — TF: 800-234-4425 ■ Web: www.fcclainc.org	Reston	VA	20191	703-476-4900	860-2713
FIRST 200 Bedford St — TF: 800-871-8326 ■ Web: www.usfirst.org	Manchester	NH	03101	603-666-3906	666-3907
Foundation Ctr 79 Fifth Ave Second Fl — TF: 800-424-9836 ■ Web: www.foundationcenter.org	New York	NY	10003	212-620-4230	807-3691
Future Business Leaders of America-Phi Beta Lambda Inc (FBLA-PBL) 1912 Assn Dr — *Fax Area Code: 866 ■ TF: 800-325-2946 ■ Web: www.fbla-pbl.org	Reston	VA	20191	800-325-2946	500-5610*
German Academic Exchange Service (DAAD) 871 United Nations Plz — Web: www.daad.org	New York	NY	10017	212-758-3223	755-5780
Graduate Management Admission Council (GMAC) 11921 Freedom Dr Ste 300 — TF: 866-505-6559 ■ Web: www.gmac.com	Reston	VA	20190	703-668-9600	668-9601
Great Books Foundation 35 E Wacker Dr Ste 400 — TF: 800-222-5870 ■ Web: www.greatbooks.org	Chicago	IL	60601	312-332-5870	407-0334
Institute for Education & the Arts 1156 15th St NW Ste 600 — Web: www.edartsinstitute.org	Washington	DC	20005	202-223-9721	659-8621
Institute of Consumer Financial Education PO Box 34070 — Web: www.financial-education-icfe.org	San Diego	CA	92163	619-239-1401	923-3284
Institute of General Semantics (IGS) 72-11 Austin St — *Fax Area Code: 718 ■ TF: 800-346-1359 ■ Web: www.generalsemantics.org	Forest Hills	NY	11375	212-729-7973	793-2527*
Institute of International Education (IIE) 809 United Nations Plaza # 1 — Web: www.iie.org	New York	NY	10017	212-883-8200	984-5358
Intercollegiate Studies Institute (ISI) 3901 Centerville Rd — TF: 800-526-7022 ■ Web: home.isi.org	Wilmington	DE	19807	302-652-4600	652-1760
Intercultural Development Research Assn (IDRA) 5815 Callaghan Rd Ste 101 — Web: www.idra.org	San Antonio	TX	78228	210-444-1710	444-1714
International Montessori Council & The Montessori Foundation 2400 Miguel Bay Dr PO Box 130 — TF: 800-655-5843 ■ Web: www.montessori.org	Terra Ceia Island	FL	34250	941-729-9565	729-9594
International Studies Assn (ISA) 324 Social Sciences University of Arizona — *Fax Area Code: 520 ■ Web: www.isanet.org	Tucson	AZ	85721	860-486-5850	621-5780*
Junior Achievement of Canada (JACAN) 1 Eva Rd Ste 218 — TF: 800-265-0699 ■ Web: www.jacan.org	Toronto	ON	M9C4Z5	416-622-4602	622-6861
Junior State of America (JSA) 400 S El Camino Real Ste 300 — TF: 800-334-5353 ■ Web: www.jsa.org	San Mateo	CA	94402	650-347-1600	347-7200
League for Innovation in the Community College 4505 E Chandler Blvd Ste 250 — Web: www.league.org	Phoenix	AZ	85048	480-705-8200	705-8201
Linguistic Society of America (LSA) 1325 18th St NW Ste 211 — Web: www.linguisticsociety.org	Washington	DC	20036	202-835-1714	835-1717
Medieval Academy of America, The 17 Dunster St Ste 202 — Web: www.medievalacademy.org	Cambridge	MA	02138	617-491-1622	492-3303
Music for All 39 W Jackson Pl Ste 150 — TF: 800-848-2263 ■ Web: www.musicforall.org	Indianapolis	IN	46225	317-636-2263	524-6200
National Ctr for Education Information (NCEI) 4401-A Connecticut Ave NW Ste 212 — Web: www.ncei.com	Washington	DC	20008	202-822-8280	822-8284
National Ctr for Family Literacy (NCFL) 325 W Main St Ste 300 — TF: 877-326-5481 ■ Web: familieslearning.org/	Louisville	KY	40202	502-584-1133	584-0172
National Head Start Assn (NHSA) 1651 Prince St — TF: 866-677-8724 ■ Web: www.nhsa.org	Alexandria	VA	22314	703-739-0875	739-0878
National Honor Society (NHS) 1904 Assn Dr — TF: 800-253-7746 ■ Web: www.nhs.us	Reston	VA	20191	703-860-0200	476-5432
National Research Council (NRC) 500 Fifth St NW — Web: www.nationalacademies.org/nrc	Washington	DC	20001	202-334-2000	
National Scholastic Press Assn (NSPA) 2221 University Ave SE Ste 121 — Web: www.studentpress.org/nspa	Minneapolis	MN	55414	612-625-8335	626-0720
National Speech and Debate Association's (NFL) 125 Watson St PO Box 38 — Web: www.nflonline.org	Ripon	WI	54971	920-748-6206	748-9478
North-American Interfraternity Conference (NIC) 3901 W 86th St Ste 390 — Web: www.nicindy.org	Indianapolis	IN	46268	317-872-1112	872-1134
Northwestern Illinois Assn 245 W Exchange St Ste 4 — Web: www.thenia.org	Sycamore	IL	60178	815-895-9227	895-2971
Panhandle-Plains Higher Education Authority Inc (PPHEA) 1303 23rd St PO Box 839 — TF: 877-629-3669 ■ Web: www.pphea.org	Canyon	TX	79015	806-324-4100	655-3669
Public Education Network (PEN) 601 13th St NW Ste 710-S — Web: www.publiceducation.org	Washington	DC	20005	202-628-7460	
Reading Is Fundamental Inc (RIF) 1825 Connecticut Ave NW Ste 400 — TF: 877-743-7323 ■ Web: www.rif.org	Washington	DC	20009	202-536-3400	287-3196

Phone Fax

Rolling Readers USA
2515 Camino del Rio S Ste 330 .... San Diego CA 92108 619-516-4095 516-4096
Web: www.rollingreaders.org

Scholarship America
One Scholarship Way PO Box 297 .... Saint Peter MN 56082 507-931-1682 931-9168
TF: 800-537-4180 ■ *Web:* www.scholarshipamerica.org

SkillsUSA 14001 James Monroe Hwy .... Leesburg VA 20176 703-777-8810 777-8999
TF: 800-321-8422 ■ *Web:* www.skillsusa.org

White House Historical Assn
740 Jackson Pl NW .... Washington DC 20006 202-737-8292 789-0440
Web: www.whitehousehistory.org

Woodrow Wilson National Fellowship Foundation
5 Vaughn Dr # 300 .... Princeton NJ 08540 609-452-7007 452-0066
TF: 800-899-9963 ■ *Web:* www.woodrow.org

World Learning International Development Programs
1015 15th St NW Ste 750 .... Washington DC 20005 202-408-5420 408-5397
TF: 800-345-2929 ■ *Web:* www.worldlearning.org

Young Astronaut Council 5200 27th St NW .... Washington DC 20015 301-617-0923
Web: youngastronauts.org

Youth For Understanding USA
6400 Goldsboro Rd Ste 100 .... Bethesda MD 20817 240-235-2100 235-2104
TF: 800-424-3691 ■ *Web:* www.yfuusa.org

48-12 Energy & Natural Resources Organizations

Phone Fax

Air & Waste Management Assn (A&WMA)
420 Fort Duquesne Blvd
1 Gateway Ctr 3rd Fl .... Pittsburgh PA 15222 412-232-3444 232-3450
TF: 800-270-3444 ■ *Web:* www.awma.org

Alliance to Save Energy (ASE)
1850 M St NW Ste 600 .... Washington DC 20036 202-857-0666 331-9588
TF: 800-862-2086 ■ *Web:* www.ase.org

American Academy of Environmental Engineers
130 Holiday Ct Ste 100 .... Annapolis MD 21401 410-266-3311 266-7653

American Assn of Petroleum Geologists (AAPG)
1444 S Boulder Ave PO Box 979 .... Tulsa OK 74119 918-584-2555 560-2665
TF: 800-364-2274 ■ *Web:* www.aapg.org

American Assn of Professional Landmen (AAPL)
4100 Fossil Creek Blvd .... Fort Worth TX 76137 817-847-7700 847-7704
Web: www.landman.org

American Coal Ash Assn (ACAA)
15200 E Girard Ave Ste 3050 .... Aurora CO 80014 720-870-7897 870-7889
Web: www.acaa-usa.org

American Coalition for Clean Coal Electricity (ACCCE)
1152 15th St NW Ste 400 .... Washington DC 20005 202-459-4800
Web: americaspower.org

American Coke & Coal Chemicals Institute (ACCCI)
1140 Connecticut Ave NW Ste 705 .... Washington DC 20036 202-452-7198 463-6573
Web: www.accci.org

American Gas Assn (AGA)
400 N Capitol St NW Fourth Fl .... Washington DC 20001 202-824-7000 824-7115
Web: www.aga.org

American Hydrogen Assn (AHA) 2350 W Shangri La .... Phoenix AZ 85029 602-328-4238
Web: www.clean-air.org

American Institute of Mining Metallurgical & Petroleum Engineers (AIME)
12999 E Adam Aircraft Cir PO Box 270728 .... Englewood CO 80112 303-325-5185 702-0049*
**Fax Area Code:* 888 ■ *Web:* www.aimehq.org

American Oil Chemists Society (AOCS)
2710 S Boulder PO Box 17190 .... Urbana IL 61802 217-359-2344 351-8091
TF: 866-535-2730 ■ *Web:* www.aocs.org

American Petroleum Institute (API)
1220 L St NW .... Washington DC 20005 202-682-8000
Web: www.api.org

American Public Gas Assn (APGA)
201 Massachusetts Ave NE Ste C-4 .... Washington DC 20002 202-464-2742 464-0246
TF: 800-927-4204 ■ *Web:* www.apga.org

American Public Power Assn (APPA)
1875 Connecticut Ave Ste 1200 .... Washington DC 20009 202-467-2900 467-2910
TF: 800-515-2772 ■ *Web:* www.publicpower.org

American Solar Energy Society (ASES)
4760 Walnut St Ste 106 .... Boulder CO 80301 303-443-3130 443-3212
Web: www.ases.org

American Water Works Assn (AWWA)
6666 W Quincy Ave .... Denver CO 80235 303-794-7711 347-0804
TF: 800-926-7337 ■ *Web:* www.awwa.org

American Wind Energy Assn (AWEA)
1501 M St NW Ste 1000 .... Washington DC 20005 202-383-2500 383-2505
Web: www.awea.org

Association of Energy Engineers (AEE)
4025 Pleasantdale Rd Ste 420 .... Atlanta GA 30340 770-447-5083 446-3969
TF: 877-407-0784 ■ *Web:* www.aeecenter.org

Association of Energy Service Cos (AESC)
14531 Fm 529 Ste 250 .... Houston TX 77095 713-781-0758 781-7542
TF: 800-692-0771 ■ *Web:* www.aesc.net

Cooling Technology Institute (CTI)
2611 FM 1960 Rd W Ste A-101 .... Houston TX 77068 281-583-4087 537-1721
Web: www.cti.org

Edison Electric Institute (EEI)
701 Pennsylvania Ave NW .... Washington DC 20004 202-508-5000 508-5051
TF: 800-649-1202 ■ *Web:* www.eei.org

Electric Power Supply Assn (EPSA)
1401 New York Ave NW 11th Fl .... Washington DC 20005 202-628-8200 628-8260
Web: www.epsa.org

Electricity Consumers Resource Council (ELCON)
1333 H St NW W Twr Eighth Fl .... Washington DC 20005 202-682-1390 289-6370
Web: www.elcon.org

Energy Recovery Council (IWSA)
1730 Rhode Island Ave NW Ste 700 .... Washington DC 20036 202-467-6240
Web: www.wte.org

Environmental Industry Assn
4301 Connecticut Ave NW Ste 300 .... Washington DC 20008 202-244-4700 966-4824
TF: 800-424-2869 ■ *Web:* www.environmentalistseveryday.org

Environmental Technology Council (ETC)
1112 16th St NW Ste 420 .... Washington DC 20036 202-783-0870 737-2038
Web: www.etc.org

Gas Processors Assn (GPA) 6526 E 60th St .... Tulsa OK 74145 918-493-3872 493-3875
Web: www.gpaglobal.org

Gas Processors Suppliers Assn (GPSA)
6526 E 60th St .... Tulsa OK 74145 918-493-3872
Web: www.gpaglobal.org

Independent Petroleum Assn of America (IPAA)
1201 15th St NW Ste 300 .... Washington DC 20005 202-857-4722 857-4799
TF: 800-433-2851 ■ *Web:* www.ipaa.org

Institute of Clean Air Cos (ICAC)
1730 M St NW Ste 206 .... Washington DC 20036 202-457-0911 367-2114
TF: 888-383-5726 ■ *Web:* www.icac.com

Institute of Hazardous Materials Management (IHMM)
11900 Parklawn Dr Ste 450 .... Rockville MD 20852 301-984-8969 984-1516
TF: 800-437-0137 ■ *Web:* www.ihmm.org

Institute of Nuclear Power Operations
700 Galleria Pkwy SE Ste 100 .... Atlanta GA 30339 770-644-8000 644-8549
Web: www.inpo.info

Institute of Scrap Recycling Industries Inc (ISRI)
1615 L St NW Ste 600 .... Washington DC 20036 202-662-8500 626-0900
Web: www.isri.org

Interstate Oil & Gas Compact Commission (IOGCC)
900 NE 23rd St PO Box 53127 .... Oklahoma City OK 73152 405-525-3556 525-3592
TF: 800-822-4015 ■ *Web:* iogcc.publishpath.com/

Methanol Institute (MI)
4100 Fairfax Dr Ste 740 .... Arlington VA 22203 703-248-3636 248-3997
TF: 888-275-0768 ■ *Web:* www.methanol.org

National Ground Water Assn (NGWA)
601 Dempsey Rd .... Westerville OH 43081 614-898-7791 898-7786
TF: 800-551-7379 ■ *Web:* www.ngwa.org

National Mining Assn (NMA)
101 Constitution Ave NW Ste 500-E .... Washington DC 20001 202-463-2600 463-2666
Web: www.nma.org

National Ocean Industries Assn (NOIA)
1120 G St NW Ste 900 .... Washington DC 20005 202-347-6900 347-8650
TF: 800-558-9994 ■ *Web:* www.noia.org

National Petrochemical & Refiners Assn (NPRA)
1667 K St NW Ste 700 .... Washington DC 20006 202-457-0480 457-0486
Web: www.afpm.org

National Propane Gas Assn (NPGA)
1899 L St NW Ste 350 .... Washington DC 20036 202-466-7200 466-7205
Web: www.npga.org

National Rural Electric Co-op Assn (NRECA)
4301 Wilson Blvd .... Arlington VA 22203 703-907-5939 907-6885
TF: 866-759-2619 ■ *Web:* www.nreca.coop

National Rural Water Assn (NRWA) 2915 S 13th St ..... Duncan OK 73533 580-252-0629 255-4476
Web: www.nrwa.org

National Water Resources Assn (NWRA)
3800 Fairfax Dr # 4 .... Arlington VA 22203 703-524-1544 343-9483*
**Fax Area Code:* 928 ■ *TF:* 800-468-3533 ■ *Web:* www.nwra.org

Natural Gas Supply Assn (NGSA)
805 15th St NW Ste 510 .... Washington DC 20005 202-326-9300 326-9330
Web: www.ngsa.org

North American Electric Reliability Council (NERC)
1325 G St NW Ste 600 .... Washington DC 20005 609-452-8060 452-9550
TF: 877-668-4493 ■ *Web:* www.nerc.com

Nuclear Energy Institute (NEI)
1776 'I' St NW Ste 400 .... Washington DC 20006 202-739-8000 785-4019
Web: www.nei.org

Renewable Fuels Assn (RFA) 425 Third St SW ...... Washington DC 20024 202-289-3835 289-7519
TF: 800-433-8850 ■ *Web:* www.ethanolrfa.org

Society of Exploration Geophysicists (SEG)
8801 S Yale Ave Ste 500 PO Box 702740 .... Tulsa OK 74137 918-497-5500 497-5557
Web: www.seg.org

Society of Petroleum Engineers (SPE)
222 Palisades Creek Dr .... Richardson TX 75080 972-952-9393 952-9435
TF: 800-456-6863 ■ *Web:* www.spe.org

Society of Petrophysicists & Well Log Analysts (SPWLA)
8866 Gulf Fwy Ste 320 .... Houston TX 77017 713-947-8727 947-7181
Web: www.spwla.org

Solar Energy Industries Assn (SEIA)
505 Ninth St NW Ste 800 .... Washington DC 20004 202-682-0556 682-0559
Web: www.seia.org

U.S. Lumber Coalition 1750 K St NW .... Washington DC 20006 202-582-0021
Web: www.uslumbercoalition.org

US Energy Assn (USEA)
1300 Pennsylvania Ave NW Ste 550 .... Washington DC 20004 202-312-1230
Web: www.usea.org

Water Quality Assn (WQA) 4151 Naperville Rd .... Lisle IL 60532 630-505-0160 505-9637
Web: www.wqa.org

Western Forestry & Conservation Assn
4033 SW Canyon Rd .... Portland OR 97221 503-226-4562 226-2515
TF: 888-722-9416 ■ *Web:* www.westernforestry.org

48-13 Environmental Organizations

Phone Fax

Adirondack Council
103 Hand Ave Ste 3 PO Box 2 .... Elizabethtown NY 12932 518-873-2240 873-6675
TF: 877-873-2240 ■ *Web:* www.adirondackcouncil.org

Alaska Wilderness League
122 C St NW Ste 240 .... Washington DC 20001 202-544-5205 544-5197
Web: www.alaskawild.org

Alliance for Responsible Atmospheric Policy
2111 Wilson Blvd Eighth Fl .... Arlington VA 22201 703-243-0344 243-2874
Web: www.alliancepolicy.org

Organization	City	State	Zip	Phone	Fax
American Cave Conservation Assn 119 E Main St PO Box 409 *Web:* www.hiddenrivercave.com	Horse Cave	KY	42749	270-786-1466	786-1467
American Farmland Trust (AFT) 1200 18th St *TF:* 800-431-1499 ■ *Web:* www.farmland.org	Washington	DC	20036	202-331-7300	659-8339
American Forests 734 15th St NW *TF:* 800-368-5748 ■ *Web:* www.americanforests.org	Washington	DC	20005	202-737-1944	737-2457
American Lands Alliance 726 Seventh St SE *Web:* www.americanlands.org	Washington	DC	20003	202-547-9400	
American Littoral Society (ALS) 18 Hartshorne Dr Ste 1 *TF:* 800-424-8802 ■ *Web:* www.littoralsociety.org	Highlands	NJ	07732	732-291-0055	291-3551
American Rivers 1101 14th St NW Ste 1400 *TF:* 877-347-7550 ■ *Web:* www.americanrivers.org	Washington	DC	20005	202-347-7550	347-9240
American Shore & Beach Preservation Assn (ASBPA) 5460 Beaujolais Ln *TF:* 800-331-1600 ■ *Web:* www.asbpa.org	Fort Myers	FL	33919	239-489-2616	489-9917
Appalachian Mountain Club (AMC) Five Joy St *TF Orders:* 800-262-4455 ■ *Web:* www.outdoors.org	Boston	MA	02108	617-523-0655	523-0722
APVA Preservation Virginia 204 W Franklin St *Web:* apva.org	Richmond	VA	23220	804-648-1889	775-0802
Audubon Naturalist Society 8940 Jones Mill Rd *TF:* 888-744-4723 ■ *Web:* www.audubonnaturalist.org	Chevy Chase	MD	20815	301-652-9188	951-7179
Beyond Pesticides 701 E St SE Ste 200 *TF:* 866-260-6653 ■ *Web:* www.beyondpesticides.org	Washington	DC	20003	202-543-5450	543-4791
Big Bend Natural History Assn PO Box 196 *Web:* www.bigbendbookstore.org	Big Bend National Park	TX	79834	432-477-2236	477-2234
Canadian Parks & Wilderness Society (CPAWS) 250 City Ctr Ave Ste 506 *TF:* 800-333-9453 ■ *Web:* www.cpaws.org	Ottawa	ON	K1R6K7	613-569-7226	569-7098
Canadian Water Resources Assn (CWRA) 9 Corvus Ct *Web:* www.cwra.org	Ottawa	ON	K2E7Z4	613-237-9363	594-5190
Canadian Wildlife Federation (CWF) 350 Michael Cowpland Dr *TF:* 800-563-9453 ■ *Web:* www.cwf-fcf.org	Kanata	ON	K2M2W1	613-599-9594	599-4428
Charles A & Anne Morrow Lindbergh Foundation 2150 Third Ave N Ste 310 *Web:* www.lindberghfoundation.org	Anoka	MN	55303	763-576-1596	576-1664
Citizens Network for Sustainable Development (CitNet) PO Box 7458 *Web:* www.citnet.org	Silver Spring	MD	20907	301-588-5550	
Civil War Preservation Trust (CWPT) 1331 H St NW Ste 1001 *TF:* 888-606-1400 ■ *Web:* www.civilwar.org	Washington	DC	20005	202-367-1861	367-1865
Clean Water Action 4455 Connecticut Ave NW *TF:* 800-234-7284 ■ *Web:* www.cleanwateraction.org	Washington	DC	20008	202-895-0420	895-0438
Co-op America 1612 K St NW Ste 600 *TF:* 800-584-7336 ■ *Web:* www.greenamerica.org	Washington	DC	20006	202-872-5307	331-8166
Coalition for Responsible Waste Incineration (CRWI) 1615 L St NW Ste 1350 *Web:* www.crwi.org	Washington	DC	20036	202-452-1241	887-8044
Coastal Conservation Assn (CCA) 6919 Portwest Dr Ste 100 *TF:* 800-201-3474 ■ *Web:* www.joincca.org	Houston	TX	77024	713-626-4234	626-5852
Conservation Fund 1655 N Fort Myer Dr Ste 1300 *TF:* 800-672-5839 ■ *Web:* www.conservationfund.org	Arlington	VA	22209	703-525-6300	525-4610
Conservation International (CI) 2011 Crystal Dr Ste 500 *TF:* 800-406-2306 ■ *Web:* www.conservation.org	Arlington	VA	22202	703-341-2400	553-0654
Conservation Treaty Fund (CTSF) 3705 CaRdiff Rd	Chevy Chase	MD	20815	301-652-6390	
Earth Day Network (EDN) 1616 P St NW Ste 340 *Web:* www.earthday.org	Washington	DC	20036	202-518-0044	518-8794
Earth Island Institute 300 Broadway Ste 28 *Web:* www.earthisland.org	San Francisco	CA	94133	415-788-3666	788-7324
Earth Share 7735 Old Georgetown Rd Ste 900 *TF:* 800-875-3863 ■ *Web:* www.earthshare.org	Bethesda	MD	20814	240-333-0300	333-0301
EarthRights International 1612 K St NW Ste 401 *TF:* 888-224-9043 ■ *Web:* www.earthrights.org	Washington	DC	20006	202-466-5188	466-5189
Earthwatch Institute 114 Western Ave *TF:* 800-776-0188 ■ *Web:* www.earthwatch.org	Boston	MA	02134	978-461-0081	461-2332
Ecojustice Canada 131 Water St Ste 214 *TF:* 800-926-7744 ■ *Web:* www.ecojustice.ca	Vancouver	BC	V6B4M3	604-685-5618	685-7813
Educational Communications Inc PO Box 351419 *Web:* www.ecoprojects.org	Los Angeles	CA	90035	310-559-9160	559-9160
Environmental Defense 257 Pk Ave S *TF:* 800-505-0703 ■ *Web:* www.edf.org	New York	NY	10010	212-505-2100	505-2100
Environmental Information Assn (EIA) 6935 Wisconsin Ave Ste 306 *TF:* 888-343-4342 ■ *Web:* www.eia-usa.org	Chevy Chase	MD	20815	301-961-4999	961-3094
Environmental Law Institute (ELI) 2000 L St NW Ste 620 *TF:* 800-433-5120 ■ *Web:* www.eli.org	Washington	DC	20036	202-939-3800	939-3868
Environmental Protection Information Ctr (EPIC) 145 G St Ste A *Web:* www.wildcalifornia.org	Arcata	CA	95521	707-822-7711	822-7712
Forest Guild 80 E San Francisco PO Box 519 *Web:* forestguild.org	Santa Fe	NM	87504	505-983-8992	986-0798
Forest History Society 701 William Vickers Ave *Web:* www.foresthistory.org	Durham	NC	27701	919-682-9319	682-2349
Forest Landowners Assn (FLA) 900 Cir 75 Pkwy Ste 205 *TF:* 800-325-2954 ■ *Web:* www.forestlandowners.com	Atlanta	GA	30339	404-325-2954	325-2955
Freshwater Society 2500 Shadywood Rd *TF:* 888-471-9773 ■ *Web:* www.freshwater.org	Excelsior	MN	55331	952-471-9773	471-7685
Friends of the Earth 1717 Massachusetts Ave NW Ste 600 *TF:* 877-843-8687 ■ *Web:* www.foe.org	Washington	DC	20036	202-783-7400	783-0444
Friends of the Everglades 11767 S Dixie Hwy Ste 232 *Web:* www.everglades.org	Miami	FL	33156	305-669-0858	669-4108
Friends of the River 1418 20th St Ste 100 *TF:* 888-464-2477 ■ *Web:* www.friendsoftheriver.org	Sacramento	CA	95811	916-442-3155	442-3396
Grand Canyon Trust 2601 N Fort Valley Rd *Web:* www.grandcanyontrust.org	Flagstaff	AZ	86001	928-774-7488	774-7570
Greater Yellowstone Coalition (GYC) 13 S Willson Ave Ste 2 *TF:* 800-775-1834 ■ *Web:* www.greateryellowstone.org	Bozeman	MT	59715	406-586-1593	556-2839
Greenpeace Canada 33 Cecil St *TF:* 800-320-7183 ■ *Web:* www.greenpeace.org	Toronto	ON	M5T1N1	416-597-8408	597-8422
Greenpeace USA 702 H St NW Ste 300 *TF:* 800-326-0959 ■ *Web:* www.greenpeace.org	Washington	DC	20001	202-462-1177	462-4507
Ground Water Protection Council (GWPC) 13308 N MacArthur Blvd *Web:* www.gwpc.org	Oklahoma City	OK	73142	405-516-4972	516-4973
Hells Canyon Preservation Council 105 Fir St Ste 327 PO Box 2768 *Web:* www.hellscanyon.org	La Grande	OR	97850	541-963-3950	963-0584
Heritage Canada Foundation Five Blackburn Ave *TF:* 866-964-1066 ■ *Web:* www.heritagecanada.org	Ottawa	ON	K1N8A2	613-237-1066	237-5987
Historic New England 141 Cambridge St *TF:* 800-722-2256 ■ *Web:* www.historicnewengland.org	Boston	MA	02114	617-227-3956	227-9204
International Assn of Wildland Fire (IAWF) 3416 Primm Ln *Web:* www.iawfonline.org	Birmingham	AL	35216	205-824-7614	
International Society of Tropical Foresters (ISTF) 5400 Grosvenor Ln **Fax Area Code:* 877 ■ *TF:* 866-897-8720 ■ *Web:* www.istf-bethesda.org	Bethesda	MD	20814	301-530-4514	665-6473*
Island Nature Trust PO Box 265 *Web:* www.islandnaturetrust.ca	Charlottetown	PE	C1A7K4	902-566-9150	628-6331
Izaak Walton League of America (IWLA) 707 Conservation Ln *TF:* 800-453-5463 ■ *Web:* www.iwla.org	Gaithersburg	MD	20878	301-548-0150	548-0146
Land Trust Alliance (LTA) 1660 L St NW Ste 1100 *Web:* www.landtrustalliance.org	Washington	DC	20036	202-638-4725	638-4730
League to Save Lake Tahoe 2608 Lake Tahoe Blvd *TF:* 888-844-9904 ■ *Web:* www.keeptahoeblue.org	South Lake Tahoe	CA	96150	530-541-5388	541-5454
Montana Wilderness Assn (MWA) 30 S Ewing St *TF:* 855-406-4483 ■ *Web:* www.wildmontana.org	Helena	MT	59601	406-443-7350	443-0750
Mount Rushmore Society 711 N Creek Dr *Web:* www.mountrushmoresociety.com	Rapid City	SD	57703	605-341-8883	341-0433
National Alliance of Preservation Commissions 1242 1/2 S Lumpkin St University of Georgia *Web:* www.uga.edu/sed/pso/programs/napc/napc.htm	Athens	GA	30602	706-542-8924	
National Arbor Day Foundation 100 Arbor Ave *TF:* 888-448-7337 ■ *Web:* www.arborday.org	Nebraska City	NE	68410	402-474-5655	474-0820
National Audubon Society (NAS) 225 Varick St *TF:* 800-274-4201 ■ *Web:* www.audubon.org	New York	NY	10014	212-979-3000	979-3188
National Council for Air & Stream Improvement Inc (NCASI) PO Box 13318 *TF:* 888-448-2473 ■ *Web:* www.ncasi.org	Research Triangle Park	NC	27709	919-941-6400	941-6401
National Fish & Wildlife Foundation 1133 15th St NW Ste 1100 *Web:* www.nfwf.org	Washington	DC	20005	202-857-0166	857-0162
National Forest Foundation 27 Ft Missoula Rd Bldg 27 Ste 3 *Web:* www.nationalforests.org	Missoula	MT	59804	406-542-2805	542-2810
National Marine Sanctuary Foundation 8601 Georgia Ave Ste 501 *Web:* www.nmsfocean.org	Silver Spring	MD	20910	301-608-3040	608-3044
National Park Foundation (NPF) 1201 Eye St NW Ste 550-B *Web:* www.nationalparks.org	Washington	DC	20005	202-354-6460	371-2066
National Park Trust (NPT) 401 E Jefferson St Ste 102 *Web:* www.parktrust.org	Rockville	MD	20850	301-279-7275	279-7211
National Parks Conservation Assn (NPCA) 1300 19th St NW Ste 300 *TF:* 800-628-7275 ■ *Web:* www.npca.org	Washington	DC	20036	202-223-6722	
National Trust for Historic Preservation 1785 Massachusetts Ave NW *TF:* 800-944-6847 ■ *Web:* www.preservationnation.org	Washington	DC	20036	202-588-6000	588-6038
National Wildlife Refuge Assn (NWRA) 1250 Connecticut Ave NW Ste 600 *Web:* www.refugeassociation.org	Washington	DC	20036	202-292-2402	292-2435
Natural Areas Assn (NAA) PO Box 1504 *Web:* www.naturalareas.org	Bend	OR	97709	541-317-0199	317-0140
Natural Resources Defense Council (NRDC) 40 W 20th St *Web:* www.nrdc.org	New York	NY	10011	212-727-2700	727-1773
Nature Conservancy 4245 N Fairfax Dr Ste 100 *TF Cust Svc:* 800-628-6860 ■ *Web:* www.nature.org	Arlington	VA	22203	703-841-5300	841-1283
Nature Conservancy of Canada 36 Eglinton Ave W Ste 400 *TF:* 800-465-8005 ■ *Web:* www.natureconservancy.ca	Toronto	ON	M4R1A1	416-932-3202	932-3208
Negative Population Growth (NPG) 2861 Duke St Ste 36 *Web:* www.npg.org	Alexandria	VA	22314	703-370-9510	370-9514
New England Wild Flower Society 180 Hemenway Rd *TF:* 888-636-0033 ■ *Web:* www.newfs.org	Framingham	MA	01701	508-877-7630	877-3658

				Phone	Fax
Ocean Conservancy 1300 19th St NW Eighth Fl *TF:* 800-519-1541 ■ *Web:* www.oceanconservancy.org	Washington	DC	20036	202-429-5609	872-0619
Ocean Futures Society 325 Chapala St *TF:* 800-477-7500 ■ *Web:* www.oceanfutures.org	Santa Barbara	CA	93101	805-899-8899	899-8898
Open Space Institute (OSI) 1350 Broadway Ste 201 *Web:* www.osiny.org	New York	NY	10018	212-290-8200	244-3441
Pacific Rivers Council (PRC) 1326 SW 16th Ave *Web:* www.pacificrivers.org	Portland	OR	97201	503-228-3555	228-3556
Pew Charitable Trust 1200 18th St NW Fifth Fl *Web:* www.pewtrusts.org	Washington	DC	20036	202-887-8800	887-8877
Pollution Probe 150 Ferrand Dr Ste 208 *Web:* www.pollutionprobe.org	Toronto	ON	M3C3E5	416-926-1907	926-1601
Project for Public Spaces 700 Broadway Fourth Fl *Web:* www.pps.org	New York	NY	10003	212-620-5660	620-3821
Public Lands Foundation (PLF) PO Box 7226 *TF:* 866-985-9636 ■ *Web:* www.publicland.org	Arlington	VA	22207	703-790-1988	821-3490
Rails-to-Trails Conservancy (RTC) 2121 Ward Ct NW 5th Fl *Web:* www.railstotrails.org	Washington	DC	20037	202-331-9696	223-9257
Rainforest Action Network (RAN) 221 Pine St Fifth Fl *TF:* 800-368-1819 ■ *Web:* www.ran.org	San Francisco	CA	94104	415-398-4404	398-2732
Renewable Natural Resources Foundation (RNRF) 5430 Grosvenor Ln *Web:* www.rnrf.org	Bethesda	MD	20814	301-493-9101	493-6148
Royal Oak Foundation, The 35 W 35th St Ste 1200 *TF:* 800-913-6565 ■ *Web:* www.royal-oak.org	New York	NY	10001	212-480-2889	785-7234
Save America's Forests 4 Library Ct SE *TF:* 800-729-1363 ■ *Web:* www.saveamericasforests.org	Washington	DC	20003	202-544-9219	544-7462
Sea Grant Assn (SGA) 5784 York Complex University of Maine *Web:* www.sga.seagrant.org	Orono	ME	04469	207-581-1435	581-1426
Shelburne Farms 1611 Harbor Rd *TF:* 800-286-6022 ■ *Web:* www.shelburnefarms.org	Shelburne	VT	05482	802-985-8686	985-8123
Sierra Club 85 Second St Second Fl *Web:* www.sierraclub.org	San Francisco	CA	94105	415-977-5500	977-5799
Sierra Club Canada 412-1 Nicholas St *TF:* 888-810-4204 ■ *Web:* www.sierraclub.ca	Ottawa	ON	K1N7B7	613-241-4611	241-2292
Society for Ecological Restoration International (SERI) 1017 O St NW **Fax Area Code:* 270 ■ *TF:* 866-895-4735 ■ *Web:* ser.org	Washington	DC	20001	202-299-9518	626-5485*
Society of Architectural Historians (SAH) 1365 N Astor St *Web:* www.sah.org	Chicago	IL	60610	312-573-1365	573-1141
Soil & Water Conservation Society (SWCS) 945 SW Ankeny Rd *TF:* 800-843-7645 ■ *Web:* www.swcs.org	Ankeny	IA	50023	515-289-2331	289-1227
Southern Utah Wilderness Alliance (SUWA) 425 East 100 South *Web:* www.suwa.org	Salt Lake City	UT	84111	801-486-3161	
Student Conservation Assn (SCA) 689 River Rd PO Box 550 *TF:* 888-722-9675 ■ *Web:* www.thesca.org	Charlestown	NH	03603	603-543-1700	543-1828
Tall Timbers 13093 Henry Beadel Dr *Web:* www.talltimbers.org	Tallahassee	FL	32312	850-893-4153	893-6470
Thornton W Burgess Society 6 Discovery Hill Rd *TF:* 800-844-4542 ■ *Web:* www.thorntonburgess.org	East Sandwich	MA	02537	508-888-6870	888-1919
Tongass Conservation Society (TCS) PO Box 23377 *Web:* www.tongassconservation.org	Ketchikan	AK	99901	907-225-3275	
Tree Care Industry Assn (TCIA) 136 Harvey Rd Ste 101 *TF:* 800-733-2622 ■ *Web:* tcia.org	Londonderry	NH	03053	603-314-5380	314-5386
Trust for Public Land (TPL) 116 New Montgomery St Fourth Fl *TF:* 800-714-5263 ■ *Web:* www.tpl.org	San Francisco	CA	94105	415-495-4014	495-4103
Union of Concerned Scientists (UCS) Two Brattle Sq Sixth Fl *TF:* 800-666-8276 ■ *Web:* www.ucsusa.org	Cambridge	MA	02238	617-547-5552	864-9405
Upper Mississippi River Conservation Committee (UMRCC) 555 Lester Ave *Web:* www.umrcc.org	Onalaska	WI	54650	608-783-8432	783-8450
Walden Woods Project, The 44 Baker Farm Rd *TF:* 800-554-3569 ■ *Web:* www.walden.org	Lincoln	MA	01773	781-259-4700	259-4710
Water Environment Federation (WEF) 601 Wythe St *TF:* 800-666-0206 ■ *Web:* www.wef.org	Alexandria	VA	22314	703-684-2400	684-2492
Western Canada Wilderness Committee (WCWC) 227 Abbott St *TF:* 800-661-9453 ■ *Web:* www.wildernesscommittee.org	Vancouver	BC	V6B2K7	604-683-8220	683-8229
Wilderness Society 1615 M St NW *Web:* www.wilderness.org	Washington	DC	20036	202-833-2300	429-3958
Wildlife Habitat Council (WHC) 8737 Colesville Rd Ste 800 *Web:* www.wildlifehc.org	Silver Spring	MD	20910	301-588-8994	588-4629
World Forestry Ctr 4033 SW Canyon Rd *Web:* www.worldforestry.org	Portland	OR	97221	503-228-1367	228-4608
World Resources Institute (WRI) 10 G St NE Ste 800 *Web:* www.wri.org	Washington	DC	20002	202-729-7600	729-7610
Yosemite Assn *Yosemite Conservancy* 5020 El Portal Rd PO Box 230 *TF:* 800-469-7275 ■ *Web:* www.yosemiteconservancy.org	El Portal	CA	95318	209-379-2317	379-2486

48-14 Ethnic & Nationality Organizations

				Phone	Fax
Africa-America Institute (AAI) 420 Lexington Ave Ste 1706 *Web:* www.aaionline.org	New York	NY	10170	212-949-5666	682-6174
American Folklore Society (AFS) Ohio State Univ Mershon Ctr 1501 Neil Ave *TF:* 866-311-1200 ■ *Web:* www.afsnet.org	Columbus	OH	43201	614-292-4715	292-2407
American Hellenic Educational Progressive Assn (AHEPA) 1909 Q St NW Ste 500 *TF:* 855-473-3512 ■ *Web:* www.ahepa.org	Washington	DC	20009	202-232-6300	232-2140
American Historical Society of Germans from Russia 631 D St *Web:* www.ahsgr.org	Lincoln	NE	68502	402-474-3363	474-7229
American Latvian Assn Inc 400 Hurley Ave *Web:* www.alausa.org	Rockville	MD	20850	301-340-1914	340-8732
Arab American Institute (AAI) 1600 K St NW Ste 601 *Web:* www.aaiusa.org	Washington	DC	20006	202-429-9210	429-9214
Armenian Assembly of America 1334 G St NW *Web:* www.aaainc.org	Washington	DC	20005	202-393-3434	638-4904
Armenian General Benevolent Union (AGBU) 55 E 59th St 7th Fl *TF:* 800-368-4262 ■ *Web:* www.agbu.org	New York	NY	10022	212-319-6383	319-6507
ASPIRA Assn Inc 1444 'I' St NW Ste 800 *Web:* www.aspira.org	Washington	DC	20005	202-835-3600	835-3613
Assembly of Turkish American Assn (ATAA) 1526 18th St NW *TF:* 800-627-7692 ■ *Web:* www.ataa.org	Washington	DC	20036	202-483-9090	483-9092
Center for Cuban Studies 231 W 29th St Ste 401 *Web:* www.cubaupdate.org	New York	NY	10001	212-242-0559	242-1937
China Institute in America 125 E 65th St *Web:* www.chinainstitute.org	New York	NY	10065	212-744-8181	628-4159
Congress of Russian-Americans 2460 Sutter St *Web:* www.russian-americans.org	San Francisco	CA	94115	415-928-5841	928-5831
Croatian Fraternal Union of America (CFU) 100 Delaney Dr *Web:* www.croatianfraternalunion.org	Pittsburgh	PA	15235	412-843-0380	823-1594
Cuban American National Council 1223 SW Fourth St *Web:* www.cnc.org	Miami	FL	33135	305-642-3484	642-9122
First Nations Development Institute 2217 Princess Anne St Ste 111-1 **Fax Area Code:* 888 ■ *Web:* www.firstnations.org	Fredericksburg	VA	22401	540-371-5615	371-3686*
Foundation for Jewish Culture 330 Seventh Ave 21st Fl PO Box 489	New York	NY	10001	212-629-0500	629-0508
French Institute Alliance Francaise (FIAF) 22 E 60th St *Web:* www.fiaf.org	New York	NY	10022	212-355-6100	935-4119
German-American National Congress (DANK) 4740 N Western Ave Ste 206 *TF:* 888-872-3265 ■ *Web:* www.dank.org	Chicago	IL	60625	773-275-1100	275-4010
Hispanic Society of America 613 W 155th St *Web:* www.hispanicsociety.org	New York	NY	10032	212-926-2234	
Ibero-American Action League Inc 817 E Main St *Web:* www.iaal.org	Rochester	NY	14605	585-256-8900	256-0120
Japan Society 333 E 47th St *Web:* www.japansociety.org	New York	NY	10017	212-832-1155	755-6752
Japanese American Citizens League (JACL) 1765 Sutter St *Web:* www.jacl.org	San Francisco	CA	94115	415-921-5225	931-4671
Korean American Coalition (KAC) 3727 W Sixth St Ste 305 *Web:* www.kacla.org	Los Angeles	CA	90020	213-365-5999	380-7990
Mexican American Legal Defense & Educational Fund (MALDEF) 634 S Spring St *Web:* www.maldef.org	Los Angeles	CA	90014	213-629-2512	629-0266
Mexican-American Opportunity Foundation (MAOF) 401 N Garfield Ave *Web:* www.maof.org	Montebello	CA	90640	323-890-9600	890-9637
National Congress of American Indians (NCAI) 1516 P St NW *TF:* 800-503-3330 ■ *Web:* www.ncai.org	Washington	DC	20005	202-466-7767	466-7797
National Council of La Raza (NCLR) 1126 16th St NW 6th Fl *TF:* 800-821-7060 ■ *Web:* www.nclr.org	Washington	DC	20036	202-785-1670	776-1792
National Hispanic Institute (NHI) 472 FM 1966 Rd *Web:* www.nhi-net.org	Maxwell	TX	78656	512-357-6137	357-2206
National Slovak Society of the USA (NSS) 351 Vly Brook Rd *TF:* 800-488-1890 ■ *Web:* www.nsslife.org	McMurray	PA	15317	724-731-0094	731-0145
Order Sons of Italy in America (OSIA) 219 E St NE *TF:* 800-552-6742 ■ *Web:* www.osia.org	Washington	DC	20002	202-547-2900	546-8168
Organization of Chinese Americans (OCA) 1322 18th St NW *Web:* www.ocanational.org	Washington	DC	20036	202-223-5500	296-0540
Polish American Congress 5711 N Milwaukee Ave *Web:* www.pac1944.org	Chicago	IL	60646	773-763-9944	763-7114
Scottish Heritage USA 315 Page Rd Ste 10 *Web:* www.scottishheritageusa.org	Pinehurst	NC	28374	910-295-4448	295-3147
Sons of Norway 1455 W Lake St Second Fl *TF:* 800-945-8851 ■ *Web:* www.sofn.com	Minneapolis	MN	55408	612-827-3611	827-0658
Swedish Council of America 2600 Pk Ave *TF:* 800-380-2711 ■ *Web:* www.swedishcouncil.org	Minneapolis	MN	55407	612-871-0593	871-0687

Phone Fax

Tolstoy Foundation Inc
104 Lake Rd PO Box 578 Valley Cottage NY 10989 845-268-6722 268-6937
Web: www.tolstoyfoundation.org

Ukrainian NA Inc (UNA) 2200 Rt 10 Parsippany NJ 07054 800-253-9862 292-0900*
**Fax Area Code:* 973 ■ *TF:* 800-253-9862 ■ *Web:* www.ukrainiannationalassociation.org

US Pan Asian American Chamber of Commerce (US PAACC)
1329 18th St NW Washington DC 20036 202-296-5221 296-5225
TF: 800-696-7818 ■ *Web:* www.uspaacc.com

Venezuelan-American Assn of the US
641 Lexington Ave Ste 1430 New York NY 10022 212-233-7776 233-7779
Web: www.venezuelanamerican.org

48-15 Fraternal & Social Organizations

Phone Fax

American Mensa Ltd 1229 Corporate Dr W Arlington TX 76006 817-607-0060 649-5232
TF: 800-666-3672 ■ *Web:* www.us.mensa.org

Association of Junior Leagues International Inc (AJLI)
80 Maiden Ln Ste 305 New York NY 10038 212-951-8300 481-7196
TF: 800-955-3248 ■ *Web:* www.ajli.org

Astor Home For Children, The
6339 Mill St PO Box 5005 Rhinebeck NY 12572 845-871-1000
Web: www.astorservices.org

Athletes in Action 651 Taylor Dr. Xenia OH 45385 937-352-1000
Web: www.athletesinaction.org

Benevolent & Protective Order of Elks of the USA
2750 N Lakeview Ave Chicago IL 60614 773-755-4700 755-4790
Web: www.elks.org

Boy Scouts of America (BSA)
1325 W Walnut Hill Ln PO Box 152079 Irving TX 75015 972-580-2000 580-2502
Web: www.scouting.org

Boys & Girls Clubs of America
1230 W Peachtree St NW Atlanta GA 30309 404-487-5700 487-5757
TF: 800-995-3579 ■ *Web:* www.bgca.org

Citizens For Citizens Inc 264 Griffin St Fall River MA 02724 508-679-0041 324-7503
Web: www.cfcinc.org

Civitan International PO Box 130744 Birmingham AL 35213 205-591-8910 591-8910
TF: 800-248-4826 ■ *Web:* www.civitan.org

Community Counseling & Correctional Service (CCCS)
471 E Mercury St Butte MT 59701 406-782-0417 782-6964
Web: www.cccscorp.com

Cosmopolitan International
7341 W 80th St PO Box 4588 Shawnee Mission KS 66204 913-648-4330 648-4330
TF: 800-648-4331 ■ *Web:* www.cosmopolitan.org

DeMolay International
10200 NW Ambassabor Dr Kansas City MO 64153 816-891-8333 891-9062
TF Orders: 800-336-6529 ■ *Web:* www.demolay.org

English-Speaking Union of the US
144 E 39th St New York NY 10016 212-818-1200 818-1200
Web: www.esuus.org

Fraternal Order of Police (FOP)
701 Marriott Dr Nashville TN 37214 615-399-0900 399-0400
TF: 800-451-2711 ■ *Web:* www.fop.net

Friars Club 57 E 55th St New York NY 10022 212-751-7272 355-0217
Web: www.friarsclub.com

General Grand Chapter Order of the Eastern Star
1618 New Hampshire Ave NW Washington DC 20009 202-667-4737 462-5162
TF: 800-648-1182 ■ *Web:* www.easternstar.org

Girl Scouts of the USA 420 Fifth Ave New York NY 10018 212-852-8000 852-6517
TF: 800-223-0624 ■ *Web:* www.girlscouts.org

Goodwill Industries of Central Texas
1015 Norwood Pk Blvd Austin TX 78753 512-637-7100 637-7400
TF: 800-735-2989 ■ *Web:* www.goodwillcentraltexas.org

Grand Aerie Fraternal Order of Eagles
1623 Gateway Cir S Grove City OH 43123 614-883-2200 883-2201
TF: 877-829-5500 ■ *Web:* www.foe.com

House of, The Good Shepherd, The
1550 Champlin Ave Utica NY 13502 315-235-7600 235-7609
Web: www.hgs-utica.com

Independent Order of Odd Fellows
422 N Trade St Winston-Salem NC 27101 336-725-5955 722-7317
TF: 800-235-8358 ■ *Web:* www.ioof.org

International Assn of Lions Clubs
300 W 22nd St Oak Brook IL 60523 630-571-5466 571-8890
Web: www.lionsclubs.org

KenCrest Services Inc
502 W Germantown Pk Ste 200 Plymouth Meeting PA 19462 610-825-9360
Web: www.kencrest.org

Key Club International
3636 Woodview Trace Indianapolis IN 46268 317-875-8755 879-0204
TF: 800-549-2647 ■ *Web:* www.keyclub.org

Klingberg Family Centers Inc
370 Linwood St New Britain CT 06052 860-224-9113 832-8221
TF: 877-696-6775 ■ *Web:* www.klingberg.org

Knights of Columbus One Columbus Plz New Haven CT 06510 203-752-4000 752-4100
TF Cust Svc: 800-380-9995 ■ *Web:* www.kofc.org

Life Inc 2609 Royall Ave Goldsboro NC 27534 919-778-1900 778-1911
Web: www.lifeincorporated.com

Life's WORC 1501 Franklin Ave PO Box 8165 Garden City NY 11530 516-741-9000 741-5560
Web: www.lifesworc.org

Lifestream Inc PO Box 50487 New Bedford MA 02745 508-993-1991 991-5228
Web: www.lifestreaminc.com

Louisiana Baptist Children's Home Inc (LBCH)
7200 DeSiard St Monroe LA 71203 318-343-2244
Web: www.lbch.org

Lutheran Homes Society Inc 2021 N McCord Rd Toledo OH 43615 419-861-4990 861-4949
TF: 877-646-4050 ■ *Web:* www.lutheranhomessociety.org

Lutheran Social Services of Illinois
1001 E Touhy Ave Ste 50 Des Plaines IL 60018 847-635-4600
TF: 888-671-0300 ■ *Web:* www.lssi.org

Phone Fax

Masonic Service Assn of North America (MSANA)
8120 Fenton St Ste 203 Silver Spring MD 20910 301-588-4010 608-3457
TF: 855-476-4010 ■ *Web:* www.msana.com

Mennonite Home 1520 Harrisburg Pk Lancaster PA 17601 717-393-1301 393-1389
Web: www.mennonitehome.org

Mesa Developmental Services
950 Grand Ave Grand Junction CO 81501 970-243-3702 243-7751
Web: www.mesadev.org

Mile High United Way Inc 2505 18th St Denver CO 80211 303-433-8383 455-6462
Web: www.unitedwaydenver.org

Moose International Inc
155 S International Dr Mooseheart IL 60539 630-859-2000 859-6616
Web: www.mooseintl.org

National Exchange Club 3050 W Central Ave Toledo OH 43606 419-535-3232 535-1989
TF: 800-924-2643 ■ *Web:* www.nationalexchangeclub.org

Neighbor To Family Inc
220 S Ridgewood Ave Ste 260 Daytona Beach FL 32114 386-523-1440 523-1459
Web: www.neighbortofamily.org

Optimist International 4494 Lindell Blvd Saint Louis MO 63108 314-371-6000 371-6006
TF: 800-500-8130 ■ *Web:* www.optimist.org

Oswego County Opportunities Inc 239 Oneida St Fulton NY 13069 315-598-4717 592-7533
TF: 877-342-7618 ■ *Web:* www.oco.org

Partnerships In Community Living Inc
480 Main St E PO Box 129 Monmouth OR 97361 503-838-2403 838-5815
TF: 800-222-1222 ■ *Web:* www.pclpartnership.org

Presbyterian Homes Inc, The
2109 Sandy Ridge Rd Colfax NC 27235 336-886-6553 886-4102
TF: 800-225-9573 ■ *Web:* www.presbyhomesinc.org

Professional Bull Riders Inc (PBR)
101 W Riverwalk Pueblo CO 81003 719-242-2800 242-2855
TF: 800-366-8538 ■ *Web:* www.pbr.com

Quota International 1420 21st St NW Washington DC 20036 202-331-9694 331-4395
Web: quota.org

Rotary International
1560 Sherman Ave 1 Rotary Ctr Evanston IL 60201 847-866-3000 328-8554
Web: www.rotary.org

Ruritan National 5451 Lyons Rd PO Box 487 Dublin VA 24084 540-674-5431 674-2304
TF: 877-787-8727 ■ *Web:* www.ruritan.org

Skill Creations Inc
2101 Royall Ave PO Box 10628 Goldsboro NC 27532 919-734-7398 735-5064
Web: www.skillcreations.com

Spectrum Health Systems Inc
10 Mechanic St Ste 302 Worcester MA 01608 508-792-5400
TF: 800-464-9555 ■ *Web:* www.spectrumhealthsystems.org

Starr Commonwealth
13725 Starr Commonwealth Rd Albion MI 49224 517-629-5591 630-2400
TF: 800-837-5591 ■ *Web:* www.starr.org

Sunnyvale Lumber Inc 870 W Evelyn Ave Sunnyvale CA 94086 408-736-5411 736-6738
Web: www.sunnyvalelumber.com

TelecomPioneers 1801 California St 44th Fl Denver CO 80202 303-571-1200 572-0520
TF: 800-872-5995 ■ *Web:* www.telecompioneers.org

TERI Inc 251 Airport Rd Oceanside CA 92058 760-721-1706
Web: www.teriinc.org

Toastmasters International
23182 Arroyo Vista Rancho Santa Margarita CA 92688 949-858-8255 858-1207
TF: 877-738-8118 ■ *Web:* www.toastmasters.org

Uhlich Children's Advantage Network (UCAN)
3737 N Mozart St Chicago IL 60618 773-588-0180 588-7762
Web: ucanchicago.org

Up With People 6830 Broadway Denver CO 80221 303-460-7100 225-4649
TF: 877-264-8856 ■ *Web:* www.upwithpeople.org

Wabash Ctr Inc 2000 Greenbush St Lafayette IN 47904 765-423-5531
Web: www.wabashcenter.com

Way Station Inc
230 W Patrick St PO Box 3826 Frederick MD 21705 301-662-0099 694-9932
TF: 888-549-0629 ■ *Web:* www.waystationinc.org

48-16 Greek Letter Societies

Phone Fax

Alpha Beta Gamma International Business Honor Society
75 Grasslands Rd Valhalla NY 10595 914-606-6877 606-6331
Web: www.abg.org

Alpha Chi National College Honor Scholarship Society
915 E Market Ave Searcy AR 72143 501-279-4443 279-5438
Web: www.harding.edu

Alpha Chi Omega
5939 Castle Creek Pkwy N Dr Indianapolis IN 46250 317-579-5050 579-5051
TF: 800-328-0522 ■ *Web:* www.alphachiomega.org

Alpha Chi Rho Fraternity Inc 109 Oxford Way Neptune NJ 07753 732-869-1895 988-5357
Web: www.alphachirho.org

Alpha Chi Sigma 2141 N Franklin Rd Indianapolis IN 46219 317-357-5944 351-9702
TF: 800-252-4369 ■ *Web:* www.alphachisigma.org

Alpha Delta Phi International Fraternity
6126 Lincoln Ave Morton Grove IL 60053 847-965-1832 965-1871
Web: www.alphadeltaphi.org

Alpha Delta Pi 1386 Ponce de Leon Ave NE Atlanta GA 30306 404-378-3164 373-0084
Web: www.alphadeltapi.org

Alpha Epsilon Delta (AED)
Texas Christian University
PO Box BOX 298810 Fort Worth TX 76129 817-257-4550 257-0201
Web: aednational.tcu.edu/

Alpha Epsilon Phi Sorority (AEPhi)
11 Lake Ave Ext Ste 1-A Danbury CT 06811 203-748-0029 748-0039
TF: 888-668-4293 ■ *Web:* www.aephi.org

Alpha Epsilon Pi Fraternity Inc
8815 Wesleyan Rd Indianapolis IN 46268 317-876-1913 876-1057
TF: 800-684-3608 ■ *Web:* www.aepi.org

Alpha Gamma Delta 8701 Founders Rd Indianapolis IN 46268 317-872-2655 875-5824
Web: www.alphagammadelta.org

Alpha Gamma Rho 10101 NW Ambassador Dr Kansas City MO 64153 816-891-9200 891-9401
TF: 888-241-4546 ■ *Web:* www.alphagammarho.org

	Phone	Fax
Alpha Kappa Alpha Sorority Inc 5656 S Stony Island Ave. .... Chicago IL 60637	773-684-1282	288-8251
Web: www.aka1908.com		
Alpha Kappa Psi (AKPsi) 7801 E 88th St .... Indianapolis IN 46256	317-872-1553	872-1567
Web: www.akpsi.com		
Alpha Omega International Dental Fraternity 50 W Edmonston Dr .... Rockville MD 20852	301-738-6400	738-6403
TF: 877-368-6326 ■ *Web:* www.ao.org		
Alpha Omicron Pi International 5390 Virginia Way .... Brentwood TN 37027	615-370-0920	371-9736
TF: 855-230-1183 ■ *Web:* www.alphaomicronpi.org		
Alpha Phi Alpha Fraternity Inc 2313 St Paul St. .... Baltimore MD 21218	410-554-0040	554-0054
Web: www.alpha-phi-alpha.com		
Alpha Phi Delta Fraternity Inc 257E Camden-Wyoming Ave Ste A. .... Camden DE 19934	302-531-7854	
Web: www.apd.org		
Alpha Phi International Fraternity 1930 Sherman Ave .... Evanston IL 60201	847-475-0663	475-6820
Web: www.alphaphi.org		
Alpha Phi Omega (APO) 14901 E 42nd St. .... Independence MO 64055	816-373-8667	373-5975
Web: www.apo.org		
Alpha Sigma Alpha (ASA) 9002 Vincennes Cir .... Indianapolis IN 46268	317-871-2920	871-2924
Web: www.alphasigmaalpha.org		
Alpha Sigma Phi National Fraternity 710 Adams St .... Carmel IN 46032	317-843-1911	843-2966
TF: 866-515-4747 ■ *Web:* www.alphasigmaphi.org		
Alpha Tau Omega Fraternity (ATO) One N Pennsylvania St 12th Fl .... Indianapolis IN 46204	317-684-1865	684-1862
TF: 800-798-9286 ■ *Web:* www.ato.org		
Alpha Xi Delta Women's Fraternity 8702 Founders Rd .... Indianapolis IN 46268	317-872-3500	872-2947
Web: www.alphaxidelta.org		
Beta Alpha Psi 220 Leigh Farm Rd. .... Durham NC 27707	919-402-4044	402-4040
Web: www.bap.org		
Beta Beta Beta National Biological Honor Society Univ of N Alabama PO Box 5079 .... Florence AL 35632	256-765-6220	765-6221
Web: www.tri-beta.org		
Beta Gamma Sigma Inc (BGS) 125 Weldon Pkwy .... Maryland Heights MO 63043	314-432-5650	432-7083
TF: 800-337-4677 ■ *Web:* www.betagammasigma.org		
Beta Phi Mu *Florida State Univ College of Information* 3141 Chestnut Street .... Philadelphia PA 19104	215-895-2492	895-2494
Web: beta-phi-mu.org/		
Beta Theta Pi 5134 Bonham Rd PO Box 6277 .... Oxford OH 45056	513-523-7591	523-2381
TF: 800-800-2382 ■ *Web:* www.betathetapi.org		
Chi Alpha Campus Ministries USA 1445 Booneville Ave .... Springfield MO 65802	417-862-2781	865-9947
Web: www.chialpha.com		
Chi Omega Fraternity 3395 Players Club Pkwy. .... Memphis TN 38125	901-748-8600	748-8686
Web: www.chiomega.com		
Chi Phi Fraternity 1160 Satellite Blvd .... Suwanee GA 30024	404-231-1824	389-4457*
**Fax Area Code:* 678 ■ *TF:* 800-849-1824 ■ *Web:* www.chiphi.org		
Chi Psi Fraternity 45 Rutledge St. .... Nashville TN 37210	615-736-2520	736-2366
Web: www.chipsi.org		
Delta Chi Fraternity Inc 314 Church St .... Iowa City IA 52245	319-337-4811	
TF: 888-827-9702 ■ *Web:* www.deltachi.com		
Delta Delta Delta Fraternity 2331 Brookhollow Plz Dr .... Arlington TX 76006	817-633-8001	652-0212
Web: www.tridelta.org		
Delta Gamma 3250 Riverside Dr PO Box 21397 .... Columbus OH 43221	614-481-8169	481-0133
Web: www.deltagamma.org		
Delta Kappa Epsilon Fraternity (DKE) 611 1/2 E William St. .... Ann Arbor MI 48104	734-302-4210	478-0374*
**Fax Area Code:* 202 ■ *Web:* www.dke.org		
Delta Nu Alpha Transportation Fraternity (DNA) 435 Pennsylvania Ave Ste 102 .... Glen Ellyn IL 60137	630-653-3622	653-3632
Web: www.deltanualpha.org		
Delta Phi Epsilon International Sorority 251 S Camac St .... Philadelphia PA 19107	215-732-5901	732-5906
Web: www.dphie.org		
Delta Pi Epsilon (DPE) 1914 Association Dr .... Reston VA 20191	501-219-1866	620-4483*
**Fax Area Code:* 703 ■ *Web:* www.dpe.org		
Delta Sigma Phi Fraternity 1331 N Delaware St .... Indianapolis IN 46202	317-634-1899	634-1410
Web: www.deltasig.org		
Delta Sigma Pi 330 S Campus Ave. .... Oxford OH 45056	513-523-1907	523-7292
Web: www.dspnet.org		
Delta Sigma Theta Sorority Inc 1707 New Hampshire Ave NW .... Washington DC 20009	202-986-2400	986-2513
TF: 866-615-6464 ■ *Web:* www.deltasigmatheta.org		
Delta Tau Delta Fraternity 10000 Allisonville Rd .... Fishers IN 46038	317-284-0203	284-0214
TF: 800-335-8795 ■ *Web:* www.delts.org		
Delta Theta Phi 225 Hillsborough St Ste 432 .... Raleigh NC 27603	800-783-2600	
TF: 800-783-2600 ■ *Web:* www.deltathetaphi.org		
Delta Upsilon International Fraternity 8705 Founders Rd PO Box 68942 .... Indianapolis IN 46268	317-875-8900	876-1629
Web: www.deltau.org		
Delta Zeta Sorority 202 E Church St .... Oxford OH 45056	513-523-7597	523-1921
Web: www.deltazeta.org		
Epsilon Sigma Phi Inc 450 Falls Ave Ste 106 .... Twin Falls ID 83301	208-736-4495	736-6081
Web: www.espnational.org		
Eta Sigma Gamma 2000 University Ave .... Muncie IN 47306	765-285-2258	285-3210
TF: 800-715-2559 ■ *Web:* www.etasigmagamma.org		
Fraternity of Alpha Kappa Lambda 354 Gradle Dr .... Carmel IN 46032	317-564-8003	556-8719*
**Fax Area Code:* 866 ■ *Web:* www.akl.org		
Gamma Beta Phi Society 78 Mitchell Rd Ste A .... Oak Ridge TN 37830	865-483-6212	483-9801
TF: 800-628-9920 ■ *Web:* www.gammabetaphi.org		
Gamma Phi Beta International Sorority (GPB) 12737 E Euclid Dr .... Centennial CO 80111	303-799-1874	799-1876
Web: www.gammaphibeta.org		
International Fraternity of Phi Gamma Delta 1201 Red Mile Rd PO Box 4599 .... Lexington KY 40544	859-255-1848	253-0779
TF: 888-668-4293 ■ *Web:* www.phigam.org		
Kappa Alpha Order 115 Liberty Hall Rd .... Lexington VA 24450	540-463-1865	463-2140
TF: 888-922-6335 ■ *Web:* www.kappaalphaorder.org		
Kappa Alpha Psi Fraternity Inc 2322-24 N Broad St .... Philadelphia PA 19132	215-228-7184	228-7181
Web: www.kappaalphapsi1911.com		
Kappa Alpha Theta Fraternity 8740 Founders Rd .... Indianapolis IN 46268	317-876-1870	876-1925
TF: 800-526-1870 ■ *Web:* www.kappaalphatheta.org		
Kappa Delta Pi 3707 Woodview Trace .... Indianapolis IN 46268	317-871-4900	704-2323
TF: 800-284-3167 ■ *Web:* www.kdp.org		
Kappa Delta Sorority 3205 Players Ln .... Memphis TN 38125	901-748-1897	748-0949
TF: 800-536-1897 ■ *Web:* www.kappadelta.org		
Kappa Kappa Gamma PO Box 38 .... Columbus OH 43216	614-228-6515	228-7809
TF: 866-554-1870 ■ *Web:* www.kappakappagamma.org		
Kappa Sigma Fraternity 1610 Scottsville Rd .... Charlottesville VA 22902	434-295-3193	296-9557
Web: www.kappasigma.org		
Lambda Chi Alpha International Fraternity 8741 Founders Rd .... Indianapolis IN 46268	317-872-8000	875-3828
TF: 800-209-6837 ■ *Web:* www.lambdachi.org		
Mu Phi Epsilon International Music Fraternity 4705 N Sonora Ave Ste 114 .... Fresno CA 93722	559-277-1898	277-2825
TF: 888-259-1471 ■ *Web:* www.muphiepsilon.org		
National Alpha Lambda Delta 328 Orange St .... Macon GA 31201	478-744-9595	744-9924
TF: 800-925-7421 ■ *Web:* www.nationalald.org		
National Fraternity of Kappa Delta Rho (KDR) 331 S Main St .... Greensburg PA 15601	724-838-7100	838-7101
TF: 800-536-5371 ■ *Web:* www.kdr.com		
National Kappa Kappa Iota Inc 1875 E 15th St .... Tulsa OK 74104	918-744-0389	744-0578
TF: 800-678-0389 ■ *Web:* www.nationalkappakappaiota.org		
Omega Psi Phi Fraternity Inc 3951 Snapfinger Pkwy .... Decatur GA 30035	404-284-5533	284-0333
Web: www.oppf.org		
Phi Alpha Theta *National History Honor Society* 4202 E Fowler Ave SOC 107 .... Tampa FL 33620	800-394-8195	974-8215*
**Fax Area Code:* 813 ■ *TF:* 800-394-8195 ■ *Web:* www.phialphatheta.org		
Phi Beta Kappa Society 1606 New Hampshire Ave NW .... Washington DC 20009	202-265-3808	986-1601
Web: www.pbk.org/home		
Phi Beta Sigma Fraternity Inc 145 Kennedy St NW .... Washington DC 20011	202-726-5434	882-1681
Web: pbs1914.org		
Phi Chi Theta 1508 E Beltline Rd Ste 104 .... Carrollton TX 75006	972-245-7202	
Web: www.phichitheta.org		
Phi Delta Kappa International (PDK) 408 N Union St .... Bloomington IN 47407	812-339-1156	339-0018
TF: 800-766-1156 ■ *Web:* www.pdkintl.org		
Phi Delta Phi International Legal Fraternity 1426 21st St NW .... Washington DC 20036	202-223-6801	223-6808
TF: 800-368-5606 ■ *Web:* www.phideltaphi.org		
Phi Delta Theta 2 S Campus Ave .... Oxford OH 45056	513-523-6345	523-9200
TF: 888-373-9855 ■ *Web:* www.phideltatheta.org		
Phi Eta Sigma National Honor Society One Big Red Way .... Bowling Green KY 42101	270-745-6540	745-3893
Web: www.phietasigma.org		
Phi Kappa Psi 5395 Emerson Way .... Indianapolis IN 46226	317-632-1852	
TF: 800-486-1852 ■ *Web:* www.phikappapsi.com		
Phi Kappa Sigma International Fraternity Inc Two Timber Dr .... Chester Springs PA 19425	610-469-3282	469-3286
Web: www.pks.org		
Phi Kappa Tau 5221 Morning Sun Rd. .... Oxford OH 45056	513-523-4193	523-9325
TF: 800-758-1906 ■ *Web:* www.phikappatau.org		
Phi Kappa Theta National Fraternity 9640 N Augusta Dr Ste 420 .... Carmel IN 46032	317-872-9934	879-1889
Web: www.phikaps.org		
Phi Mu Alpha Sinfonia Fraternity of America Inc 10600 Old State Rd. .... Evansville IN 47711	812-867-2433	867-0633
TF: 800-473-2649 ■ *Web:* www.sinfonia.org		
Phi Mu Fraternity 400 Westpark Dr .... Peachtree City GA 30269	770-632-2090	632-2136
Web: www.phimu.org		
Phi Sigma Kappa International 2925 E 96th St .... Indianapolis IN 46240	317-573-5420	573-5430
TF: 888-846-6851 ■ *Web:* www.phisigmakappa.org		
Phi Sigma Pi National Honor Fraternity Inc 2119 Ambassador Cir .... Lancaster PA 17603	717-299-4710	390-3054
TF: 800-366-1916 ■ *Web:* www.phisigmapi.org		
Phi Sigma Sigma Fraternity Inc 8178 Lark Brown Rd Ste 202 .... Elkridge MD 21075	410-799-1224	799-9186
Web: www.phisigmasigma.org		
Phi Theta Kappa International Honor Society 1625 Eastover Dr .... Jackson MS 39211	601-984-3504	984-3550
TF: 800-946-9995 ■ *Web:* www.ptk.org		
Pi Beta Phi Fraternity for Women 1154 Town & Country Commons Dr. .... Town and Country MO 63017	636-256-0680	256-8095
Web: www.pibetaphi.org		
Pi Kappa Alpha Fraternity 8347 W Range Cove .... Memphis TN 38125	901-748-1868	748-3100
Web: pikes.org		
Pi Kappa Phi Fraternity 2015 Ayrsley Town Blvd Ste 200 .... Charlotte NC 28273	704-504-0888	504-0880
Web: www.pikapp.org		
Pi Lambda Phi Fraternity Inc 60 Newtown Rd Ste 118 .... Danbury CT 06810	203-740-1044	740-1644
TF: 800-395-4724 ■ *Web:* www.pilambdaphi.org		
Pi Sigma Alpha 1527 New Hampshire Ave NW .... Washington DC 20036	202-483-2512	483-2657
Web: www.apsanet.org/~psa		

Organization	City	State	ZIP	Phone	Fax
Pi Sigma Epsilon (PSE) 3747 S Howell Ave *Web:* www.pse.org	Milwaukee	WI	53207	414-328-1952	328-1953
Psi Chi National Honor Society in Psychology 825 Vine St **Fax Area Code:* 877 ■ *Web:* www.psichi.org	Chattanooga	TN	37403	423-756-2044	774-2443*
PSI Upsilon Fraternity 3003 E 96th St *TF:* 800-394-1833 ■ *Web:* www.psiu.org	Indianapolis	IN	46240	317-571-1833	844-5170
Sigma Alpha Epsilon Fraternity (SAE) 1856 Sheridan Rd *TF:* 800-233-1856 ■ *Web:* www.sae.net	Evanston	IL	60201	847-475-1856	475-2250
Sigma Alpha Iota (SAI) One Tunnel Rd *Web:* www.sai-national.org	Asheville	NC	28805	828-251-0606	251-0644
Sigma Chi Fraternity 1714 Hinman Ave *TF:* 877-829-5500 ■ *Web:* www.sigmachi.org	Evanston	IL	60201	847-869-3655	869-4906
Sigma Delta Tau 714 Adams St *Web:* sigmadeltatau.com	Carmel	IN	46032	317-846-7747	575-5562
Sigma Gamma Rho Sorority Inc 1000 Southhill Dr Ste 200 *TF:* 888-747-1922 ■ *Web:* www.sgrho1922.org	Cary	NC	27513	919-678-9720	678-9721
Sigma Kappa Sorority 8733 Founders Rd *Web:* www.sigmakappa.org	Indianapolis	IN	46268	317-872-3275	872-0716
Sigma Nu Fraternity Inc Nine Lewis St PO Box 1869 *Web:* www.sigmanu.org	Lexington	VA	24450	540-463-1869	463-1669
Sigma Phi Epsilon Fraternity 310 S Blvd *TF:* 800-767-1901 ■ *Web:* www.sigep.org	Richmond	VA	23220	804-353-1901	359-8160
Sigma Pi Fraternity 106 N Castle Heights Ave *TF:* 800-332-1897 ■ *Web:* www.sigmapi.org	Lebanon	TN	37087	615-373-5728	373-8949
Sigma Tau Gamma 101 Ming St PO Box 54 *Web:* websites.omegafi.com/omegaws/sigmataugamma//	Warrensburg	MO	64093	660-747-2222	
Sigma Theta Tau International 550 W N St *TF:* 888-634-7575 ■ *Web:* www.nursingsociety.org	Indianapolis	IN	46202	317-634-8171	634-8188
Sigma Xi Scientific Research Society 3106 E NC Hwy 54 PO Box 13975 *TF:* 800-243-6534 ■ *Web:* www.sigmaxi.org	Research Triangle Park	NC	27709	919-549-4691	549-0090
Tau Alpha Chi 82 Thompson St	Alpharetta	GA	30009	770-475-4253	475-4408
Tau Beta Pi Assn 1512 Middle Dr *TF:* 877-829-5500 ■ *Web:* www.tbp.org	Knoxville	TN	37996	865-546-4578	546-4579
Tau Beta Sigma National Honorary Band Sorority PO Box 849 *TF Cust Svc:* 800-543-6505 ■ *Web:* www.tbsigma.org	Stillwater	OK	74076	405-372-2333	372-2363
Tau Kappa Epsilon (TKE) 8645 Founders Rd *Web:* www.tke.org	Indianapolis	IN	46268	317-872-6533	875-8353
Theta Delta Chi Inc 214 Lewis Wharf *TF:* 800-999-1847 ■ *Web:* www.thetadeltachi.net	Boston	MA	02110	617-742-8886	742-8868
Theta Phi Alpha Fraternity Inc 27025 Knickerbocker Rd *Web:* www.thetaphialpha.org	Bay Village	OH	44140	440-899-9282	899-9293
Theta Tau Professional Engineering Fraternity 1011 San Jacinto Ste 205 *TF:* 800-264-1904 ■ *Web:* www.thetatau.org	Austin	TX	78701	512-472-1904	472-4820
Zeta Beta Tau Fraternity Inc (ZBT) 3905 Vincennes Rd Ste 100 *Web:* www.zbt.org	Indianapolis	IN	46268	317-334-1898	334-1899
Zeta Phi Beta Sorority Inc 1734 New Hampshire Ave NW *TF:* 800-393-2503 ■ *Web:* zphib1920.org	Washington	DC	20009	202-387-3103	232-4593
Zeta Psi Fraternity of North America 15 S Henry St *TF:* 800-477-1847 ■ *Web:* www.zetapsi.org	Pearl River	NY	10965	845-735-1847	735-1989
Zeta Tau Alpha Fraternity (ZTA) 3450 Founders Rd *Web:* www.zetataualpha.org	Indianapolis	IN	46268	317-872-0540	876-3948

48-17 Health & Health-Related Organizations

Organization	City	State	ZIP	Phone	Fax
Acoustic Neuroma Assn (ANA) 600 Peachtree Pkwy Ste 108 *TF:* 877-200-8211 ■ *Web:* www.anausa.org	Cumming	GA	30041	770-205-8211	205-0239
Alliance for Aging Research (AAR) 750 17th St NW Ste 1100 **Fax Area Code:* 770 ■ *TF:* 866-840-6283 ■ *Web:* www.agingresearch.org	Washington	DC	20006	202-293-2856	234-5030*
Alliance for Lupus Research (ALA) 28 W 44th St Ste 501 *TF:* 800-867-1743 ■ *Web:* www.lupusresearch.org	New York	NY	10036	212-218-2840	218-2848
Alzheimer's Assn 225 N Michigan Ave Ste 1700 **Fax Area Code:* 866 ■ *TF:* 800-272-3900 ■ *Web:* www.alz.org	Chicago	IL	60601	312-335-8700	699-1246*
American Academy for Cerebral Palsy & Developmental Medicine (AACPDM) 555 E Wells St Ste 1100 *Web:* www.aacpdm.org	Milwaukee	WI	53202	414-918-3014	276-2146
American Academy of Medical Acupuncture (AAMA) 1970 E Grand Ave Ste 330 *Web:* www.medicalacupuncture.org	El Segundo	CA	90245	310-364-0193	
American Academy of Sleep Medicine (AASM) 2510 N Frontage Rd Ste 920 *Web:* www.aasmnet.org	Darien	IL	60561	708-492-0930	492-0943
American Assn of Acupunture & Oriental Medicine (AAAOM) PO Box 162340 *TF:* 866-455-7999 ■ *Web:* www.aaaomonline.org	Sacramento	CA	95816	916-443-4770	443-4766
American Assn of Drugless Practitioners (AADP) 2200 Market St Ste 803 *TF:* 888-764-2237 ■ *Web:* www.aadp.net	Galveston	TX	77550	409-621-2600	
American Assn of Naturopathic Physicians (AANP) 4435 Wisconsin Ave NW Ste 403 *TF:* 866-538-2267 ■ *Web:* www.naturopathic.org	Washington	DC	20016	202-237-8150	237-8152
American Assn of Suicidology (AAS) 5221 Wisconsin Ave NW Second Fl *Web:* www.suicidology.org	Washington	DC	20015	202-237-2280	237-2282
American Assn on Intellectual & Developmental Disabilities (AAIDD) 444 N Capitol St NW Ste 846 *TF:* 800-424-3688 ■ *Web:* www.aaidd.org	Washington	DC	20001	202-387-1968	387-2193
American Autoimmune Related Disease Assn (AARDA) 22100 Gratiot Ave *TF:* 800-598-4668 ■ *Web:* www.aarda.org	Eastpointe	MI	48021	586-776-3900	776-3903
American Botanical Council 6200 Manor Rd PO Box 144345 *TF:* 800-373-7105 ■ *Web:* www.abc.herbalgram.org	Austin	TX	78723	512-926-4900	926-2345
American Brain Tumor Assn (ABTA) 2720 River Rd *TF:* 800-886-2282 ■ *Web:* www.abta.org	Des Plaines	IL	60018	847-827-9910	827-9918
American Cancer Society (ACS) 250 William St NW Ste 6001 *TF:* 800-227-2345 ■ *Web:* www.cancer.org	Atlanta	GA	30303	404-320-3333	
American Chronic Pain Assn (ACPA) PO Box 850 *TF:* 800-533-3231 ■ *Web:* www.theacpa.org	Rocklin	CA	95677	916-632-0922	632-3208
American Council for Headache Education (ACHE) 19 Mantua Rd *Web:* www.achenet.org	Mount Royal	NJ	08061	856-423-0043	423-0082
American Council of the Blind (ACB) 1155 15th St NW Ste 1004 *TF:* 800-424-8666 ■ *Web:* www.acb.org	Washington	DC	20005	202-467-5081	467-5085
American Council on Alcoholism (ACA) 1000 E Indian School Rd *TF:* 800-527-5344 ■ *Web:* www.aca-usa.com	Phoenix	AZ	85014	800-527-5344	
American Council on Exercise (ACE) 4851 Paramount Dr *TF:* 800-825-3636 ■ *Web:* www.acefitness.org	San Diego	CA	92123	858-576-6500	576-6564
American Diabetes Assn (ADA) 1701 N Beauregard St *TF:* 800-232-3472 ■ *Web:* www.diabetes.org	Alexandria	VA	22311	703-549-1500	836-2464
American Dietetic Assn (ADA) 120 S Riverside Plz Ste 2000 *TF:* 800-877-1600 ■ *Web:* www.eatright.org	Chicago	IL	60606	312-899-0040	899-4899
American Epilepsy Society (AES) 342 N Main St *TF:* 888-233-2334 ■ *Web:* www.aesnet.org	West Hartford	CT	06117	860-586-7505	586-7550
American Foundation for AIDS Research (AmFAR) 120 Wall St 13th Fl *Web:* www.amfar.org	New York	NY	10005	212-806-1600	806-1601
American Foundation for Suicide Prevention (AFSP) 120 Wall St 22nd Fl *TF:* 888-333-2377 ■ *Web:* www.afsp.org	New York	NY	10005	212-363-3500	363-6237
American Foundation for the Blind (AFB) 2 Penn Plaza *TF:* 800-232-5463 ■ *Web:* www.afb.org	New York	NY	10001	212-502-7600	502-7777
American Hearing Research Foundation Eight S Michigan Ave Ste 814 *Web:* www.american-hearing.org	Chicago	IL	60603	312-726-9670	
American Heart Assn (AHA) 7272 Greenville Ave *TF:* 800-242-8721 ■ *Web:* www.heart.org	Dallas	TX	75231	214-373-6300	706-1191
American Holistic Health Assn (AHHA) PO Box 17400 *Web:* www.ahha.org	Anaheim	CA	92817	714-779-6152	
American Holistic Nurses' Assn (AHNA) 323 N San Francisco St Ste 201 *TF:* 800-278-2462 ■ *Web:* www.ahna.org	Flagstaff	AZ	86001	928-526-2196	526-2752
American Institute of Stress, The (AIS) 124 Pk Ave *Web:* www.stress.org	Yonkers	NY	10703	914-963-1200	965-6267
American Kidney Fund (AKF) 6110 Executive Blvd Ste 1010 **Fax Area Code:* 301 ■ *TF:* 800-638-8299 ■ *Web:* www.akfinc.org	Rockville	MD	20852	800-638-8299	881-0898*
American Liver Foundation (ALF) 39 Broadway *TF:* 800-465-4837 ■ *Web:* www.liverfoundation.org	New York	NY	10006	212-668-1000	483-8179
American Lung Assn (ALA) 14 Wall St *TF:* 800-586-4872 ■ *Web:* www.lung.org	New York	NY	10005	212-315-8700	
American Massage Therapy Assn (AMTA) 500 Davis St Ste 900 *TF:* 877-905-2700 ■ *Web:* www.amtamassage.org	Evanston	IL	60201	847-864-0123	864-1178
American Music Therapy Assn Inc (AMTA) 8455 Colesville Rd Ste 1000 *Web:* www.musictherapy.org	Silver Spring	MD	20910	301-589-3300	589-5175
American Naturopathic Medical Assn (ANMA) 150 S Hwy 160 Ste 8-528 **Fax Area Code:* 888 ■ *TF:* 888-202-4440 ■ *Web:* www.anma.org	Pahrump	NV	89048	702-897-7053	502-3385*
American Organization for Bodywork Therapies of Asia (AOBTA) 1010 Haddonfield-Berlin Rd Ste 408 *Web:* www.aobta.org	Voorhees	NJ	08043	856-782-1616	782-1653
American Orthotic & Prosthetic Assn (AOPA) 330 John Carlyle St Ste 200 *Web:* www.aopanet.org	Alexandria	VA	22314	571-431-0876	431-0899
American Pain Society (APS) 4700 W Lake Ave *TF:* 877-752-4754 ■ *Web:* www.americanpainsociety.org	Glenview	IL	60025	847-375-4715	375-6479
American Parkinson Disease Assn (APDA) 135 Parkinson Ave *TF:* 800-223-2732 ■ *Web:* www.apdaparkinson.org	Staten Island	NY	10305	718-981-8001	981-4399
American Polarity Therapy Assn (APTA) 122 N Elm St Ste 512 *Web:* www.polaritytherapy.org	Greensboro	NC	27401	336-574-1121	574-1151
American SIDS Institute 528 Raven Way *Web:* www.sids.org	Naples	FL	34110	239-431-5425	431-5536
American Sleep Apnea Assn (ASAA) 6856 Eastern Ave NW #203 *TF:* 888-292-6522 ■ *Web:* www.sleepapnea.org	Washington	DC	20012	202-293-3650	293-3656
American Social Health Assn (ASHA) PO Box 13827 *Web:* www.ashastd.org	Research Triangle Park	NC	27709	919-361-8400	361-8425
American Therapeutic Recreation Assn (ATRA) 629 N Main St *TF:* 800-433-5255 ■ *Web:* www.atra-online.com	Hattiesburg	MS	39401	601-450-2872	582-3354

Phone | Fax

American Tinnitus Assn (ATA)
522 SW Fifth Ave Ste 825 .... Portland OR 97204 503-248-9985 248-0024
TF: 800-634-8978 ■ Web: www.ata.org

Americans for Nonsmokers' Rights (ANR)
2530 San Pablo Ave Ste J .... Berkeley CA 94702 510-841-3032 841-3071
Web: www.no-smoke.org

Anxiety Disorders Assn of America (ADAA)
8730 Georgia Ave Ste 600 .... Silver Spring MD 20910 240-485-1001 485-1035
Web: www.adaa.org

Arc of the US 1010 Wayne Ave Ste 650 .... Silver Spring MD 20910 301-565-3842 565-3843
TF: 800-433-5255 ■ Web: www.thearc.org

Arthritis Foundation
1330 W Peachtree St Ste 100 .... Atlanta GA 30309 404-872-7100 872-0457
TF: 800-283-7800 ■ Web: www.arthritis.org

Associated Bodywork & Massage Professionals (ABMP)
25188 Genesee Trl Rd Ste 200 .... Golden CO 80401 303-674-8478 667-8260*
*Fax Area Code: 800 ■ TF: 800-458-2267 ■ Web: www.abmp.com

Association for Applied & Therapeutic Humor (AATH)
65 Enterprise .... Aliso Viejo CA 92656 815-708-6587 715-6931*
*Fax Area Code: 949 ■ TF: 888-747-2284 ■ Web: www.aath.org

Association for Children with Down Syndrome Inc (ACDS)
Four Fern Pl .... Plainview NY 11803 516-933-4700 933-9524
Web: www.acds.org

Association for Macular Diseases Inc
210 E 64th St 8th Fl .... New York NY 10065 212-605-3719
Web: www.macula.org

Association for Research & Enlightenment (ARE)
215 67th St .... Virginia Beach VA 23451 757-428-3588 422-6921
TF: 800-333-4499 ■ Web: www.edgarcayce.org

Association for the Advancement of the Blind & Retarded (AABR)
1508 College Pt Blvd .... College Point NY 11356 718-321-3800
Web: www.aabr.org

Asthma & Allergy Foundation of America (AAFA)
8201 Corporate Dr Ste 1000 .... Landover MD 20785 202-466-7643 466-8940
TF: 800-727-8462 ■ Web: www.aafa.org

Autism Research Institute (ARI)
4182 Adams Ave .... San Diego CA 92116 619-281-7165 563-6840
Web: www.autism.com

Autism Society of America (ASA)
7910 Woodmont Ave Ste 300 .... Bethesda MD 20814 301-657-0881 657-0869
TF: 800-328-8476 ■ Web: www.autism-society.org

BACCHUS Network, The PO Box 100430 .... Denver CO 80250 303-871-0901 871-0907
Web: www.bacchusnetwork.org

BEGINNINGS for Parents of Children Who Are Deaf or Hard of Hearing Inc
302 Jefferson St Ste 110 .... Raleigh NC 27605 919-715-4092 715-4093
TF: 800-541-4327 ■ Web: www.ncbegin.org

Better Hearing Institute (BHI)
1444 I St NW Ste 700 .... Washington DC 20005 202-449-1100
Web: www.betterhearing.org

Better Sleep Council 501 Wythe St .... Alexandria VA 22314 703-683-8371 683-4503
Web: www.bettersleep.org

Better Vision Institute, The (BVI)
Vision Council, The
225 Reinekers Ln Ste 700 .... Alexandria VA 22314 703-548-4560
TF: 800-372-3937

Brain Injury Assn of America
1608 Spring Hill Rd Ste 110 .... Vienna VA 22182 703-761-0750 761-0755
TF: 800-444-6443 ■ Web: www.biausa.org

Campaign for Tobacco-Free Kids
1400 'I' St NW Ste 1200 .... Washington DC 20005 202-296-5469 296-5427
Web: www.tobaccofreekids.org

Cancer Care Inc 275 Seventh Ave 22nd Fl .... New York NY 10001 212-712-8400 712-8495
TF: 800-813-4673 ■ Web: www.cancercare.org

Candlelighters Childhood Cancer Foundation
10920 Connecticut Ave Suuite A PO Box 498 .... Kensington MD 20895 301-962-3520 962-3521
TF: 800-366-2223 ■ Web: www.acco.org

Canine Companions for Independence Inc (CCI)
2965 Dutton Ave PO Box 446 .... Santa Rosa CA 95402 707-577-1700
TF: 800-572-2275 ■ Web: www.cci.org

Carcinoid Cancer Foundation Inc
333 Mamaroneck Ave Ste 492 .... White Plains NY 10605 212-722-3132
TF: 888-722-3132 ■ Web: www.carcinoid.org

Center for Practical Bioethics
1111 Main St Ste 500 .... Kansas City MO 64105 816-221-1100 221-2002
TF: 800-344-3829 ■ Web: www.practicalbioethics.org

Center on Human Policy 805 S Crouse Ave .... Syracuse NY 13244 315-443-3851
Web: www.thechp.syr.edu

CFIDS Assn of America Inc
6827 Fairview Rd PO Box 220398 .... Charlotte NC 28222 704-365-2343 365-9755
Web: solvecfs.org/

Children & Adults with Attention-Deficit/Hyperactivity Disorder (CHADD)
8181 Professional Pl Ste 150 .... Landover MD 20785 301-306-7070 306-7090
TF: 800-233-4050 ■ Web: www.chadd.org

Children's Eye Foundation
1631 Lancaster Dr Ste 200 .... Grapevine TX 76051 817-310-2641
Web: www.childrenseyefoundation.org

Children's Leukemia Research Assn
585 Stewart Ave Ste 18 .... Garden City NY 11530 516-222-1944 222-0457
Web: www.childrensleukemia.org

Children's Organ Transplant Assn (COTA)
2501 W Cota Dr .... Bloomington IN 47403 812-336-8872 336-8885
TF: 800-366-2682 ■ Web: www.cota.org

Children's Tumor Foundation
95 Pine St 16th Fl .... New York NY 10005 212-344-6633 747-0004
TF: 800-323-7938 ■ Web: www.ctf.org

Children's Wish Foundation International
8615 Roswell Rd .... Atlanta GA 30350 770-393-9474 393-0683
TF: 800-323-9474 ■ Web: www.childrenswish.org

Christopher Reeve Foundation
636 Morris Tpke Ste 3A .... Short Hills NJ 07078 973-379-2690 912-9433
TF: 800-225-0292 ■ Web: www.christopherreeve.org

CJE SeniorLife 3003 W Touhy Ave .... Chicago IL 60645 773-508-1000 508-1028
Web: www.cje.net

Cleft Palate Foundation (CPF)
1504 E Franklin St Ste 102 .... Chapel Hill NC 27514 919-933-9044 933-9604
TF: 800-242-5338 ■ Web: www.cleftline.org

Compassion & Choices PO Box 101810 .... Denver CO 80250 303-639-1202 312-2690*
*Fax Area Code: 866 ■ TF: 800-247-7421 ■ Web: www.compassionandchoices.org

Cornelia de Lange Syndrome Foundation Inc (CdLS)
302 W Main St Ste 100 .... Avon CT 06001 860-676-8166 676-8337
TF: 800-753-2357 ■ Web: www.cdlsusa.org

Council for Affordable Health Insurance (CAHI)
127 S Peyton St Ste 210 .... Alexandria VA 22314 703-836-6200 836-6550
Web: www.cahi.org

Council on Size & Weight Discrimination (CSWD)
PO Box 305 .... Mount Marion NY 12456 845-679-1209 679-1206
Web: www.cswd.org

Creutzfeldt-Jakob Disease Foundation Inc
341 W 38th St Ste 501 .... New York NY 10018 212-719-5900 256-0359
TF: 800-659-1991 ■ Web: www.cjdfoundation.org

Crohn's & Colitis Foundation of America (CCFA)
386 Pk Ave S 17th Fl .... New York NY 10016 212-685-3440 779-4098
TF: 800-932-2423 ■ Web: www.ccfa.org

Cystic Fibrosis Foundation
6931 Arlington Rd Ste 200 .... Bethesda MD 20814 301-951-4422 951-6378
TF: 800-344-4823 ■ Web: www.cff.org

Deafness Research Foundation (DRF)
641 Lexington Ave 15th Fl .... New York NY 10022 212-328-9480
Web: hearinghealthfoundation.org

Delta Society 875 124th Ave NE Ste 101 .... Bellevue WA 98005 425-679-5500 679-5539
Web: www.petpartners.org

Dental Lifeline Network 1800 15th St Unit 100 .... Denver CO 80202 303-534-5360 534-5290
TF: 888-471-6334 ■ Web: nfdh.org

Depression & Bipolar Support Alliance (DBSA)
730 N Franklin St Ste 501 .... Chicago IL 60610 312-642-0049 642-7243
TF: 800-826-3632 ■ Web: www.dbsalliance.org

Disability Rights Ctr Inc 18 Low Ave .... Concord NH 03301 603-228-0432 225-2077
TF: 800-834-1721 ■ Web: www.drcnh.org

Disabled & Alone/Life Services for the Handicapped
1440 Broadway 23rd Floor .... New York NY 10018 212-532-6740 532-6740
TF: 800-995-0066 ■ Web: www.disabledandalone.org

Dystonia Medical Research Foundation
One E Wacker Dr Ste 2810 .... Chicago IL 60601 312-755-0198 803-0138
TF General: 800-377-3978 ■ Web: www.dystonia-foundation.org

Easter Seals 230 W Monroe St Ste 1800 .... Chicago IL 60606 312-726-6200 726-1494
TF: 800-221-6827 ■ Web: www.easterseals.com

ECRI Institute 5200 Butler Pike .... Plymouth Meeting PA 19462 610-825-6000 834-1275
TF: 866-247-3004 ■ Web: www.ecri.org

El Paso First Health Plans Inc
1145 Westmoreland Dr .... El Paso TX 79925 915-532-3778 532-2877
TF: 877-532-3778 ■ Web: www.epfirst.com

Elder Service Plan of The North Shore Inc
37 Friend St Ste 3 .... Lynn MA 01902 781-715-6608 715-6699
Web: www.pacenorthshore.org

Elizabeth Glaser Pediatric AIDS Foundation
1140 Connecticut Ave NW Ste 200 .... Washington DC 20036 202-296-9165 296-9185
TF: 888-499-4673 ■ Web: www.pedaids.org

Endometriosis Assn 8585 N 76th Pl .... Milwaukee WI 53223 414-355-2200 355-6065
TF: 800-992-3636 ■ Web: www.endometriosisassn.org

EngenderHealth 440 Ninth Ave 13th Fl .... New York NY 10001 212-561-8000 561-8067
TF: 800-564-2872 ■ Web: www.engenderhealth.org

Epilepsy Foundation 8301 Professional Pl E .... Landover MD 20785 301-459-3700 577-2684
TF: 800-332-1000 ■ Web: epilepsy.com/

Euthanasia Research & Guidance Organization (ERGO)
24829 Norris Ln .... Junction City OR 97448 541-998-1873
Web: www.finalexit.org

FaithTrust Institute 2400 N 45th St Ste 101 .... Seattle WA 98103 206-634-1903 634-0115
TF: 877-860-2255 ■ Web: www.faithtrustinstitute.org

Family Caregiver Alliance (FCA)
180 Montgomery St Ste 900 .... San Francisco CA 94104 415-434-3388 434-3508
TF: 800-445-8106 ■ Web: www.caregiver.org

Family of the Americas Foundation
PO Box 1170 .... Dunkirk MD 20754 301-627-3346 627-0847
TF: 800-443-3395 ■ Web: www.familyplanning.net

Feingold Assn of the US
37 Shell Rd Second Fl .... Rocky Point NY 11778 631-369-9340 369-2988
TF: 800-321-3287 ■ Web: www.feingold.org

First Candle 1314 Bedford Ave Ste 210 .... Baltimore MD 21208 410-653-8226 653-8709
TF: 800-221-7437 ■ Web: www.firstcandle.org

Food Allergy & Anaphylaxis Network (FAAN)
11781 Lee Jackson Hwy Ste 160 .... Fairfax VA 22033 703-691-3179 691-2713
TF: 800-929-4040 ■ Web: www.foodallergy.org

Foundation Fighting Blindness
11435 Cron Hill Dr .... Owings Mills MD 21117 410-568-0150 363-2393
TF: 800-683-5555 ■ Web: www.blindness.org

Freedom From Fear (FFF) 308 Seaview Ave .... Staten Island NY 10305 718-351-1717 980-5022
Web: www.freedomfromfear.org

Gay Men's Health Crisis (GMHC) 119 W 24th St .... New York NY 10011 212-367-1000
TF: 800-243-7692 ■ Web: www.gmhc.org

Genetic Alliance Inc
4301 Connecticut Ave NW Ste 404 .... Washington DC 20008 202-966-5557 966-8553
Web: www.geneticalliance.org

Gift of Life Bone Marrow Foundation
800 Yamato Rd Ste 101 .... Boca Raton FL 33431 561-982-2900 982-2902
TF: 800-962-7769 ■ Web: www.giftoflife.org

Glaucoma Foundation (TGF) 80 Maiden Ln Ste 700 .... New York NY 10038 212-285-0080 651-1888
Web: www.glaucomafoundation.org

Glaucoma Research Foundation
251 Post St Ste 600 .... San Francisco CA 94108 415-986-3162 986-3763
TF: 800-826-6693 ■ Web: www.glaucoma.org

Gluten Intolerance Group (GIG)
31214 124th Ave SE .... Auburn WA 98092 253-833-6655 833-6675
Web: www.gluten.net

Guide Dog Foundation for the Blind Inc
371 E Jericho Tkpe .... Smithtown NY 11787 800-548-4337
TF: 800-548-4337 ■ Web: www.guidedog.org

	City	State	ZIP	Phone	Fax
Guide Dogs for the Blind 350 Los Ranchitos Rd *TF:* 800-295-4050 ■ *Web:* www.guidedogs.com	San Rafael	CA	94903	415-499-4000	499-4035
Guide Dogs of America 13445 Glenoaks Blvd *TF:* 800-459-4843 ■ *Web:* www.guidedogsofamerica.org	Sylmar	CA	91342	818-362-5834	362-6870
Head Injury Hotline 212 Pioneer Bldg *Web:* www.headinjury.com	Seattle	WA	98104	206-621-8558	329-4355
Health Physics Society 1313 Dolley Madison Blvd Ste 402 *TF:* 888-624-8373 ■ *Web:* www.hps.org	McLean	VA	22101	703-790-1745	790-2672
Healthcare Leadership Council (HLC) 750 Ninth St NW Ste 500 *Web:* hlc.org	Washington	DC	20001	202-452-8700	296-9561
Hearing Loss Assn of America 7910 Woodmont Ave Ste 1200 *TF:* 800-221-6827 ■ *Web:* www.hearingloss.org	Bethesda	MD	20814	301-657-2248	913-9413
Hepatitis Foundation International (HFI) 504 Blick Dr *TF:* 800-891-0707 ■ *Web:* www.hepfi.org	Silver Spring	MD	20904	301-622-4200	622-4702
Herb Research Foundation (HRF) 4140 15th St *TF:* 800-748-2617 ■ *Web:* www.herbs.org	Boulder	CO	80304	303-449-2265	449-7849
Hereditary Disease Foundation (HDF) 3960 Broadway Sixth Fl *Web:* www.hdfoundation.org	New York	NY	10032	212-928-2121	928-2172
Hospice Education Institute Three Unity Sq PO Box 98 *TF:* 800-331-1620 ■ *Web:* www.hospiceworld.org	Machiasport	ME	04655	207-255-8800	255-8008
Human Factors & Ergonomics Society (HFES) 1124 Montana Ave Ste B PO Box 1369 *TF:* 800-233-1234 ■ *Web:* www.hfes.org	Santa Monica	CA	90406	310-394-1811	394-2410
Human Growth Foundation 997 Glen Cove Ave Ste 5 *TF:* 800-451-6434 ■ *Web:* www.hgfound.org	Glen Head	NY	11545	516-671-4041	671-4055
Huntington's Disease Society of America (HDSA) 505 Eigth Ave Ste 902 *TF:* 800-345-4372 ■ *Web:* www.hdsa.org	New York	NY	10018	212-242-1968	239-3430
Hysterectomy Educational Resources & Services Foundation (HERS) 422 Bryn Mawr Ave *TF:* 888-750-4377 ■ *Web:* www.hersfoundation.com	Bala Cynwyd	PA	19004	610-667-7757	667-8096
Icahn School of Medicine at Mount Sinai 1 Gustave L Levy Pl *Web:* www.nfjgd.org	New York	NY	10029	212-241-6500	
Immune Deficiency Foundation (IDF) 40 W Chesapeake Ave Ste 308 *TF:* 800-296-4433 ■ *Web:* www.primaryimmune.org	Towson	MD	21204	410-321-6647	321-9165
International Assn for the Study of Pain (IASP) 111 Queen Anne Ave N Ste 501 *TF:* 866-574-2654 ■ *Web:* www.iasp-pain.org	Seattle	WA	98109	206-283-0311	283-9403
International Ctr for the Disabled (ICD) 340 E 24th St *Web:* www.icdnyc.org	New York	NY	10010	212-585-6020	
International Dyslexia Assn, The (IDA) 40 York Rd Fourth Fl *TF:* 800-222-3123 ■ *Web:* www.interdys.org	Towson	MD	21204	410-296-0232	321-5069
International Hearing Society (IHS) 16880 Middlebelt Rd Ste 4 *TF:* 800-521-5247 ■ *Web:* www.ihsinfo.org	Livonia	MI	48154	734-522-7200	522-0200
International OCD Foundation (OCF) PO Box 961029 *Web:* www.ocfoundation.org	Boston	MA	02196	617-973-5801	973-5803
Jannus Inc (MSG) 1607 W Jefferson St *Web:* www.mtnstatesgroup.org	Boise	ID	83702	208-336-5533	336-0880
Juvenile Diabetes Research Foundation International (JDRF) 120 Wall St *TF:* 800-533-2873 ■ *Web:* www.jdrf.org	New York	NY	10005	212-785-9500	785-9595
Kristin Brooks Hope Ctr (KBHC) 1250 24th St NW *TF:* 800-784-2433 ■ *Web:* www.hopeline.com	Washington	DC	20037	202-536-3200	536-3206
La Leche League International Inc (LLLI) 957 N Plum Grove Rd *TF:* 800-525-3243 ■ *Web:* www.lalecheleague.org	Schaumburg	IL	60173	847-519-7730	969-0460
Lamaze International 2025 M St NW Ste 800 *TF:* 800-368-4404 ■ *Web:* www.lamaze.org	Washington	DC	20036	202-367-1128	367-2128
Laurent Clerc National Deaf Education Ctr 800 Florida Ave NE *TF:* 866-637-0102 ■ *Web:* www.gallaudet.edu	Washington	DC	20002	202-651-5050	651-5708
Learning Disabilities Assn of America (LDA) 4156 Library Rd *TF:* 888-300-6710 ■ *Web:* ldaamerica.org	Pittsburgh	PA	15234	412-341-1515	344-0224
Lifespire 350 Fifth Ave Ste 301 *TF:* 800-221-5594 ■ *Web:* www.lifespire.org	New York	NY	10118	212-741-0100	242-0696
Light for Life Foundation International PO Box 644 *TF:* 800-273-8255 ■ *Web:* www.yellowribbon.org	Westminster	CO	80036	303-429-3530	426-4496
Lighthouse International 111 E 59th St *Fax: Hum Res ■ *TF:* 800-829-0500 ■ *Web:* www.lighthouse.org	New York	NY	10022	212-821-9200	821-9707*
Living Bank PO Box 6725 *TF:* 800-528-2971 ■ *Web:* www.livingbank.org	Houston	TX	77027	713-961-9431	961-0979
Lupus Foundation of America Inc (LFA) 2000 L St NW Ste 410 *TF:* 800-558-0121 ■ *Web:* www.lupus.org	Washington	DC	20036	202-349-1155	349-1156
Lymphoma Research Foundation (LRF) 115 Broadway Ste 1301 *TF:* 800-500-9976 ■ *Web:* www.lymphoma.org	New York	NY	10006	212-349-2910	349-2886
Macula Foundation Inc 210 E 64th St 8th Fl *TF:* 800-622-8524 ■ *Web:* www.maculafoundation.org	New York	NY	10065	212-605-3777	605-3795
Male Survivor 5505 Connecticut Ave NW PO Box 103 *TF:* 800-738-4181 ■ *Web:* www.malesurvivor.org	Washington	DC	20015	800-738-4181	
March of Dimes Foundation 1275 Mamaroneck Ave *Web:* www.marchofdimes.com	White Plains	NY	10605	914-428-7100	
MCS Referral & Resources Inc 6101 Gentry Ln *Web:* www.mcsrr.org	Baltimore	MD	21210	410-889-6666	889-4944
MedicAlert Foundation International 2323 Colorado Ave *TF Cust Svc:* 800-432-5378 ■ *Web:* www.medicalert.org	Turlock	CA	95382	209-668-3333	669-2495
Medicare Rights Ctr (MRC) 520 Eigth Ave N Wing Third Fl *TF Hotline:* 800-333-4114 ■ *Web:* www.medicarerights.org	New York	NY	10018	212-869-3850	869-3532
Mended Hearts Inc, The 8150 N Central Expy M2075 *TF:* 888-432-7899 ■ *Web:* www.mendedhearts.org	Dallas	TX	75206	214-296-9252	295-9552
Mental Health America (MHA) 2000 N Beauregard St Sixth Fl *TF Help Line:* 800-969-6642 ■ *Web:* mentalhealthamerica.net/	Alexandria	VA	22311	703-684-7722	684-5968
Mothers Supporting Daughters with Breast Cancer (MSDBC) 25235 Fox Chase Dr *Web:* www.mothersdaughters.org	Chestertown	MD	21620	410-778-1982	778-1411
Multiple Sclerosis Foundation (MSF) 6350 N Andrews Ave *TF:* 800-225-6495 ■ *Web:* www.msfocus.org	Fort Lauderdale	FL	33309	954-776-6805	938-8708
Muscular Dystrophy Assn (MDA) 3300 E Sunrise Dr *TF:* 800-572-1717 ■ *Web:* www.mda.org	Tucson	AZ	85718	520-529-2000	529-5300
NA of People with AIDS (NAPWA) 8401 Colesville Rd Ste 505 *TF:* 866-846-9366	Silver Spring	MD	20910	240-247-0880	
Narcolepsy Network Inc 129 Waterwheel Ln *TF:* 888-292-6522 ■ *Web:* www.narcolepsynetwork.org	North Kingstown	RI	02852	401-667-2523	633-6567
National Adrenal Diseases Foundation (NADF) 505 Northern Blvd *Web:* www.nadf.us	Great Neck	NY	11021	516-487-4992	
National Allergy Bureau (NAB) 555 E Wells St 11th Fl *Web:* aaaai.org/global/nab-pollen-counts.aspx	Milwaukee	WI	53202	414-272-6071	272-6070
National Alliance for Hispanic Health 1501 16th St NW *Web:* www.hispanichealth.org	Washington	DC	20036	202-387-5000	797-4353
National Alliance on Mental Illness (NAMI) 3803 N Fairfax Dr Ste 100 *TF:* 800-950-6264 ■ *Web:* www.nami.org	Arlington	VA	22203	703-524-7600	524-9094
National Alopecia Areata Foundation (NAAF) 14 Mitchell Blvd *Web:* www.naaf.org	San Rafael	CA	94903	415-472-3780	472-5343
National Amputation Foundation 40 Church St *Web:* www.nationalamputation.org	Malverne	NY	11565	516-887-3600	887-3667
National Breast Cancer Coalition (NBCC) 1101 17th St NW Ste 1300 *TF:* 800-622-2838 ■ *Web:* www.breastcancerdeadline2020.org	Washington	DC	20036	202-296-7477	265-6854
National Cancer Registrars Assn (NCRA) 1340 Braddock Pl Ste 203 *TF:* 800-621-4111 ■ *Web:* www.ncra-usa.org	Alexandria	VA	22314	703-299-6640	299-6620
National Citizens' Coalition for Nursing Home Reform (NCCNHR) *National Consumer Voice for Quality Long-Term Care, The* 1828 L St NW Ste 801 *Web:* www.theconsumervoice.org	Washington	DC	20036	202-332-2275	332-2949
National Coalition for Cancer Survivorship (NCCS) 1010 Wayne Ave Ste 315 *TF:* 877-622-7937 ■ *Web:* www.canceradvocacy.org	Silver Spring	MD	20910	877-622-7937	
National Coalition on Health Care 1120 G St NW Ste 810 *Web:* www.nchc.org	Washington	DC	20005	202-638-7151	638-7166
National Committee for Quality Assurance (NCQA) 1100 13th St *TF:* 888-275-7585 ■ *Web:* www.ncqa.org	Washington	DC	20005	202-955-3500	955-3599
National Council on Alcoholism & Drug Dependence Inc (NCADD) 217 Broadway Ste 712 *TF:* 800-622-2255 ■ *Web:* www.ncadd.org	New York	NY	10007	212-269-7797	269-7510
National Ctr for Homeopathy (NCH) 101 S Whiting St *Web:* www.nationalcenterforhomeopathy.org	Alexandria	VA	22304	703-548-7790	
National Dissemination Ctr for Children with Disabilities 1825 Connecticut Ave *TF:* 800-695-0285 ■ *Web:* nichcy.org	Washington	DC	20009	202-884-8200	884-8441
National Down Syndrome Congress (NDSC) 1370 Ctr Dr Ste 102 *TF:* 800-232-6372 ■ *Web:* www.ndsccenter.org	Atlanta	GA	30338	770-604-9500	604-9898
National Down Syndrome Society (NDSS) 666 Broadway 8th Fl *Fax Area Code:* 212 ■ *TF:* 800-221-4602 ■ *Web:* www.ndss.org	New York	NY	10012	800-221-4602	979-2873*
National Eating Disorders Assn 603 Stewart St Ste 803 *Fax Area Code:* 206 ■ *TF:* 800-931-2237 ■ *Web:* www.nationaleatingdisorders.org	Seattle	WA	98101	800-931-2237	829-8501*
National Federation of the Blind (NFB) 1800 Johnson St *TF:* 800-392-5671 ■ *Web:* www.nfb.org	Baltimore	MD	21230	410-659-9314	685-5653
National Fibromyalgia Partnership Inc (NFP) 140 Zinn Way *TF:* 866-725-4404 ■ *Web:* www.fmpartnership.org	Linden	VA	22642	866-725-4404	666-2727
National Fire Protection Assn (NFPA) One Batterymarch Pk *TF:* 800-344-3555 ■ *Web:* www.nfpa.org	Quincy	MA	02169	617-770-3000	770-0700
National Gaucher Foundation (NGF) 2227 Idlewood Rd Ste 6 *TF:* 800-504-3189 ■ *Web:* www.gaucherdisease.org	Tucker	GA	30084	770-934-2910	934-2911
National Headache Foundation (NHF) 820 N Orleans St Ste 217 *Fax Area Code:* 312 ■ *TF:* 888-643-5552 ■ *Web:* www.headaches.org	Chicago	IL	60610	888-643-5552	640-9049*
National Health Council (NHC) 1730 M St NW Ste 500 *Web:* www.nhcouncil.org	Washington	DC	20036	202-785-3910	785-5923
National Healthy Mothers Healthy Babies Coalition (HMHB) 4401 Ford Ave Ste 300 *Web:* www.hmhb.org	Alexandria	VA	22302	703-837-4792	664-0485

Phone | Fax

National Hearing Conservation Assn (NHCA)
3030 W 81st Ave. ... Westminster CO 80031 303-224-9022 458-0002
TF: 800-445-8667 ■ *Web:* www.hearingconservation.org

National Hemophilia Foundation (NHF)
116 W 32nd St 11th Fl ... New York NY 10001 212-328-3700 328-3777
TF: 800-424-2634 ■ *Web:* www.hemophilia.org

National Herpes Resource Ctr (HRC)
PO Box 13827 ... Research Triangle Park NC 27709 919-361-8400 361-8425
TF: 877-478-5868 ■ *Web:* www.ashastd.org/std-sti/Herpes.html

National HPV & Cervical Cancer Prevention Resource Ctr
PO Box 13827 ... Research Triangle Park NC 27709 919-361-8400 361-8425
Web: www.ashastd.org

National Industries for the Blind (NIB)
1310 Braddock Pl ... Alexandria VA 22314 703-310-0500
TF Cust Svc: 800-433-2304 ■ *Web:* www.nib.org

National Inhalant Prevention Coalition (NIPC)
318 Lindsay St ... Chattanooga TN 37403 423-265-4662 265-4889
TF: 800-269-4237 ■ *Web:* www.inhalants.org

National Kidney Foundation (NKF)
30 E 33rd St Eighth Fl ... New York NY 10016 212-889-2210 779-8056
TF: 800-622-9010 ■ *Web:* www.kidney.org

National Marfan Foundation (NMF)
22 Manhasset Ave ... Port Washington NY 11050 516-883-8712 883-8040
TF: 800-862-7326 ■ *Web:* www.marfan.org

National Marrow Donor Program (NMDP)
3001 Broadway St NE Ste 100 ... Minneapolis MN 55413 612-627-5800 627-5877
TF: 800-526-7809 ■ *Web:* bethematch.org

National Multiple Sclerosis Society
733 Third Ave Third Fl ... New York NY 10017 212-986-3240 986-7981
TF: 800-344-4867 ■ *Web:* www.nationalmssociety.org

National Niemann-Pick Disease Foundation Inc (NNPDF)
401 Madison Ave Ste B PO Box 49 ... Fort Atkinson WI 53538 920-563-0930 563-0931
TF: 877-287-3672 ■ *Web:* www.nnpdf.org

National Odd Shoe Exchange PO Box 1120 ... Chandler AZ 85244 480-892-3484
Web: www.oddshoe.org

National Oral Health Information Clearinghouse (NIDCR)
One NOHIC Way ... Bethesda MD 20892 301-496-4261 480-4098
TF: 866-232-4528 ■ *Web:* www.nidcr.nih.gov

National Organization for Albinism & Hypopigmentation (NOAH)
PO Box 959 ... East Hampstead NH 03826 603-887-2310
TF: 800-648-2310 ■ *Web:* www.albinism.org

National Organization for Rare Disorders (NORD)
55 Kenosia Ave PO Box 1968 ... Danbury CT 06813 203-744-0100 798-2291
TF: 800-999-6673 ■ *Web:* www.rarediseases.org

National Organization of Circumcision Information Resource Centers (NOCIRC)
PO Box 2512 ... San Anselmo CA 94979 415-488-9883 488-9660
TF: 800-727-8622 ■ *Web:* www.nocirc.org

National Organization of Restoring Men (NORM)
3205 Northwood Dr Ste 209 ... Concord CA 94520 925-827-4077 827-4119
Web: www.norm.org

National Organization on Disability (NOD)
910 16th St NW Ste 410 ... Washington DC 20006 202-293-5960 293-7999
Web: www.nod.org

National Osteoporosis Foundation (NOF)
1232 22nd St NW ... Washington DC 20037 202-223-2226 223-2237
TF: 800-231-4222 ■ *Web:* www.nof.org

National Ovarian Cancer Coalition (NOCC)
2501 Oak Lawn Ave Ste 435 ... Dallas TX 75219 888-682-7426 273-4201*
**Fax Area Code:* 214 ■ *TF:* 888-682-7426 ■ *Web:* www.ovarian.org

National Pesticide Information Ctr (NPIC)
333 Weniger Hall ... Corvallis OR 97331 800-858-7378 737-0761*
**Fax Area Code:* 541 ■ *TF:* 800-858-7378 ■ *Web:* www.npic.orst.edu

National Psoriasis Foundation (NPF)
6600 SW 92nd Ave Ste 300 ... Portland OR 97223 503-244-7404 245-0626
TF: 800-723-9166 ■ *Web:* www.psoriasis.org

National Rehabilitation Assn (NRA)
633 S Washington St ... Alexandria VA 22314 703-836-0850 836-0848
TF: 888-258-4295 ■ *Web:* www.nationalrehab.org

National Rehabilitation Information Ctr (NARIC)
8201 Corporate Dr Ste 600 ... Landover MD 20785 301-459-5900 459-4263
TF: 800-346-2742 ■ *Web:* www.naric.com

National Reye's Syndrome Foundation (NRSF)
426 N Lewis St ... Bryan OH 43506 419-924-9000 924-9999
TF: 800-233-7393 ■ *Web:* www.reyessyndrome.org

National Rosacea Society
800 S NW Hwy Ste 200 ... Barrington IL 60010 847-382-8971 382-5567
TF: 888-662-5874 ■ *Web:* www.rosacea.org

National SAFE KIDS Campaign
1301 Pennsylvania Ave NW Ste 1000 ... Washington DC 20004 202-662-0600 393-2072
Web: www.safekids.org

National Safety Council (NSC) 1121 Spring Lk Dr ... Itasca IL 60143 630-285-1121 285-1315
TF: 800-621-7615 ■ *Web:* www.nsc.org

National Sleep Foundation (NSF)
1522 K St NW Ste 500 ... Washington DC 20005 202-347-3471 347-3472
Web: www.sleepfoundation.org

National Society of Genetic Counselors (NSGC)
330 N Wabash Ave Ste 2000 ... Chicago IL 60611 312-321-6834 673-6972
Web: www.nsgc.org

National Spinal Cord Injury Assn (NSCIA)
75-20 Astoria Blvd Ste 120 ... East Elmhurst NY 11370 718-512-0010 387-2197*
**Fax Area Code:* 866 ■ *TF:* 800-962-9629 ■ *Web:* www.spinalcord.org

National Stroke Assn (NSA) 9707 E Easter Ln ... Centennial CO 80112 800-787-6537 649-1328*
**Fax Area Code:* 303 ■ *TF Cust Svc:* 800-787-6537 ■ *Web:* www.stroke.org

National Stuttering Assn (NSA)
119 W 40th St 14th Fl ... New York NY 10018 212-944-4050 944-8244
TF: 800-937-8888 ■ *Web:* www.westutter.org

National Tay-Sachs & Allied Diseases Assn (NTSAD)
2001 Beacon St Ste 204 ... Brighton MA 02135 617-277-4463 277-0134
TF: 800-906-8723 ■ *Web:* www.ntsad.org

National Vaccine Information Ctr (NVIC)
407 Church St Ste H ... Vienna VA 22180 703-938-0342 938-5768
Web: www.nvic.org

National Wellness Institute (NWI)
1300 College Ct PO Box 827 ... Stevens Point WI 54481 715-342-2969 342-2979
TF: 877-800-2729 ■ *Web:* www.nationalwellness.org

New West Health Services 130 Neill Ave ... Helena MT 59601 406-457-2200 457-2299
TF: 888-500-3355 ■ *Web:* www.newwestmedicare.com

NISH 8401 Old Courthouse Rd ... Vienna VA 22182 703-560-6800 849-8916
Web: www.sourceamerica.org

North American Menopause Society, The (NAMS)
5900 Landerbrook Dr Ste 390 ... Mayfield Heights OH 44124 440-442-7550 442-2660
Web: www.menopause.org

Oley Foundation
214 Hun Memorial MC-28 Albany Medical Ctr ... Albany NY 12208 518-262-5079 262-5528
TF: 800-776-6539 ■ *Web:* www.oley.org

Oral Health America
410 N Michigan Ave Ste 352 ... Chicago IL 60611 312-836-9900 836-9986
TF: 800-523-3438 ■ *Web:* www.oralhealthamerica.org

Parkinson's Disease Foundation (PDF)
1359 Broadway ... New York NY 10018 212-923-4700 923-4778
TF: 800-457-6676 ■ *Web:* www.pdf.org

Partnership for a Drug-Free America
405 Lexington Ave Ste 1601 ... New York NY 10174 212-922-1560 922-1570
TF: 855-378-4373 ■ *Web:* www.drugfree.org

Pedorthic Footwear Assn (PFA)
2025 M St NW Ste 800 ... Washington DC 20036 202-367-1145 367-2145
TF: 800-673-8447 ■ *Web:* www.pedorthics.org

Phoenix Society for Burn Survivors Inc
1835 RW Berends Dr SW ... Grand Rapids MI 49519 616-458-2773 458-2831
TF: 800-888-2876 ■ *Web:* www.phoenix-society.org

Population Services International (PSI)
1120 19th St NW Ste 600 ... Washington DC 20036 202-785-0072 785-0120
Web: www.psi.org

Postpartum Support International
2200 Pacific Coast Hwy Ste 304A ... Hermosa Beach CA 90254 800-944-4773 204-0635*
**Fax Area Code:* 323 ■ *TF:* 800-944-4773 ■ *Web:* www.postpartum.net

Prader-Willi Syndrome Assn (USA)
8588 Potter Pk Dr Ste 500 ... Sarasota FL 34238 941-312-0400 312-0142
TF: 800-926-4797 ■ *Web:* www.pwsausa.org

Prevent Blindness America
211 W Wacker Dr Ste 1700 ... Chicago IL 60606 800-331-2020
TF: 800-331-2020 ■ *Web:* www.preventblindness.org

Prevent Cancer Foundation (PCF)
1600 Duke St Ste 500 ... Alexandria VA 22314 703-836-4412 836-4413
TF: 800-227-2732 ■ *Web:* preventcancer.org

Program for Appropriate Technology in Health (PATH)
1455 NW Leary Way ... Seattle WA 98107 206-285-3500 285-6619
Web: www.path.org

Project Inform 273 Ninth St ... San Francisco CA 94103 415-558-8669 558-0684
TF: 877-435-7443 ■ *Web:* www.projectinform.org

Public Health Institute 555 12th St 10th Fl ... Oakland CA 94607 510-285-5500 285-5501
TF: 866-632-9992 ■ *Web:* www.phi.org

Recording for the Blind & Dyslexic (RFB&D)
20 Roszel Rd ... Princeton NJ 08540 800-221-4792 987-8116*
**Fax Area Code:* 609 ■ *TF:* 800-221-4792 ■ *Web:* www.rfbd.org

Registry of Interpreters for the Deaf Inc (RID)
333 Commerce St ... Alexandria VA 22314 703-838-0030 838-0454
Web: www.rid.org

Rehabilitation Engineering & Assistive Technology Society of North America (RESNA)
1700 N Moore St Ste 1540 ... Arlington VA 22209 703-524-6686 524-6630
Web: www.resna.org

Research to Prevent Blindness Inc (RPB)
645 Madison Ave 21st Fl ... New York NY 10022 212-752-4333 688-6231
TF: 800-621-0026 ■ *Web:* www.rpbusa.org

RESOLVE: National Infertility Assn
1760 Old Meadow Rd Ste 500 ... McLean VA 22102 703-556-7172 506-3266
TF: 888-592-4449 ■ *Web:* www.resolve.org

Restless Legs Syndrome Foundation Inc
1610 14th St NW Ste 300 ... Rochester MN 55901 507-287-6465 287-6312
TF: 877-463-6757 ■ *Web:* www.rls.org

Rocky Mountain Health Foundation
2775 Crossroads Blvd ... Grand Junction CO 81506 970-248-5027 244-7880
TF: 800-843-0719 ■ *Web:* www.rmhp.org

Rolf Institute of Structural Integration
5055 Chaparral Ct Ste 103 ... Boulder CO 80301 303-449-5903 449-5978
TF: 800-530-8875 ■ *Web:* www.rolf.org

RP International PO Box 900 ... Woodland Hills CA 91365 818-992-0500 992-3265
TF: 877-999-8322 ■ *Web:* www.rpinternational.org

Scleroderma Foundation
300 Rosewood Dr Ste 105 ... Danvers MA 01923 978-463-5843 463-5809
TF: 800-722-4673 ■ *Web:* www.scleroderma.org

Scoliosis Assn Inc 2500 N Military Trail ... Boca Raton FL 33431 561-994-4435

Sickle Cell Disease Assn of America (SCDAA)
3700 Koppers St Ste 570 ... Baltimore MD 21202 410-528-1555 528-1495
TF: 800-421-8453 ■ *Web:* www.sicklecelldisease.org

Simon Foundation for Incontinence
PO Box 815 ... Wilmette IL 60091 847-864-3913 864-9758
Web: www.simonfoundation.org

Skin Cancer Foundation
149 Madison Ave Ste 901 ... New York NY 10016 212-725-5176 725-5751
Web: www.skincancer.org

Society for Women's Health Research
1025 Connecticut Ave NW Ste 701 ... Washington DC 20036 202-223-8224 833-3472
Web: www.womenshealthresearch.org

Spina Bifida Assn (SBAA)
4590 MacArthur Blvd NW Ste 250 ... Washington DC 20007 202-944-3285
TF: 866-546-8372 ■ *Web:* www.spinabifidaassociation.org

Stuttering Foundation of America
3100 Walnut Grove Rd Ste 603 ... Memphis TN 38111 901-452-7343 452-3931
TF: 800-992-9392 ■ *Web:* www.stutteringhelp.org

Support Dogs Inc 11645 Lilburn Pk Rd ... Saint Louis MO 63146 314-997-2325 997-7202
Web: www.supportdogs.org

Susan G Komen for the Cure
5005 LBJ Fwy Ste 250 ... Dallas TX 75244 972-855-1600
TF: 800-227-2345 ■ *Web:* ww5.komen.org

Organization	City	State	ZIP	Phone	Fax
TASH 1001 Connecticut Ave NW Ste 235 *Web:* www.tash.org	Washington	DC	20006	202-540-9020	540-9019
TOPS Club Inc 4575 S Fifth St *TF:* 800-932-8677 ■ *Web:* www.tops.org	Milwaukee	WI	53207	414-482-4620	482-1655
Tourette Syndrome Assn Inc 42-40 Bell Blvd Ste 205 *TF:* 888-486-8738 ■ *Web:* www.tsa-usa.org	Bayside	NY	11361	718-224-2999	279-9596
Trichotillomania Learning Ctr Inc (TLC) 207 McPherson St Ste H *Web:* www.trich.org	Santa Cruz	CA	95060	831-457-1004	426-4383
UCare Minnesota 500 Stinson Blvd NE PO Box 52 *TF:* 866-457-7144 ■ *Web:* www.ucare.org	Minneapolis	MN	55413	612-676-6500	676-6501
Undersea & Hyperbaric Medical Society (UHMS) 21 W Colony Pl Ste 280 *TF:* 877-533-8467 ■ *Web:* membership.uhms.org	Durham	NC	27705	919-490-5140	490-5140
United Network for Organ Sharing (UNOS) 700 N Fourth St *TF:* 888-894-6361 ■ *Web:* www.unos.org	Richmond	VA	23219	804-782-4800	782-4817
Vegan Action PO Box 4288 *Web:* vegan.org/	Richmond	VA	23220	804-577-8341	
Vegetarian Resource Group, The (VRG) PO Box 1463 *Web:* www.vrg.org	Baltimore	MD	21203	410-366-8343	366-8804
Virginia Hospital & Healthcare Assn (VHHA) 4200 Innslake Dr *Web:* www.vhha.com	Glen Allen	VA	23060	804-747-8600	865-5764
Washington Business Group on Health (WBGH) 50 F St NW Ste 600 *Web:* www.businessgrouphealth.org	Washington	DC	20001	202-628-9320	628-9244
Well Spouse Assn 63 W Main St Ste H *TF:* 800-838-0879 ■ *Web:* www.wellspouse.org	Freehold	NJ	07728	732-577-8899	577-8644
Women Alive 1566 Burnside Ave *TF:* 800-554-4876 ■ *Web:* www.women-alive.org	Los Angeles	CA	90019	323-965-1564	965-9886

48-18 Hobby Organizations

Organization	City	State	ZIP	Phone	Fax
Academy of Model Aeronautics (AMA) 5161 E Memorial Dr *TF:* 800-435-9262 ■ *Web:* www.modelaircraft.org	Muncie	IN	47302	765-287-1256	289-4248
American Bonanza Society (ABS) 1922 Midfield Rd *Web:* www.bonanza.org	Wichita	KS	67206	316-945-1700	945-1710
American Contract Bridge League (ACBL) 6575 Windchase Blvd *TF Sales:* 800-264-2743 ■ *Web:* www.acbl.org	Horn Lake	MS	38637	662-253-3100	253-3187
American Craft Council 72 Spring St Sixth Fl *TF:* 800-836-3470 ■ *Web:* www.craftcouncil.org	New York	NY	10012	212-274-0630	
American Federation of Astrologers (AFA) 6535 S Rural Rd *TF:* 888-301-7630 ■ *Web:* www.astrologers.com	Tempe	AZ	85283	480-838-1751	838-8293
American Horticultural Society (AHS) 7931 E Blvd Dr *TF:* 800-777-7931 ■ *Web:* www.ahs.org	Alexandria	VA	22308	703-768-5700	768-8700
American Kennel Club (AKC) 260 Madison Ave Fourth Fl *Web:* www.akc.org	New York	NY	10016	212-696-8200	696-8299
American Philatelic Society (APS) 100 Match Factory Pl *Web:* www.stamps.org	Bellefonte	PA	16823	814-933-3803	933-6128
American Radio Relay League (ARRL) 225 Main St *TF:* 888-277-5289 ■ *Web:* www.arrl.org	Newington	CT	06111	860-594-0200	594-0259
American Rose Society (ARS) 8877 Jefferson Paige Rd *TF:* 800-637-6534 ■ *Web:* rose.org/	Shreveport	LA	71119	318-938-5402	938-5405
Antique Automobile Club of America (AACA) 501 W Governor Rd PO Box 417 *Web:* www.aaca.org	Hershey	PA	17033	717-534-1910	534-9101
Art & Creative Materials Institute Inc (ACMI) 1280 Main St PO Box 479 *Web:* www.acminet.org	Hanson	MA	02341	781-293-4100	294-0808
Barbershop Harmony Society 110 Seventh Ave N *TF:* 800-876-7464 ■ *Web:* www.barbershop.org	Nashville	TN	37203	615-823-3993	313-7619
BMW Motorcycle Owners of America PO Box 3982 *Web:* www.bmwmoa.org	Ballwin	MO	63022	636-394-7277	391-1811
Craft & Hobby Assn (CHA) 319 E 54th St *TF:* 800-822-0494 ■ *Web:* www.craftandhobby.org	Elmwood Park	NJ	07407	201-835-1200	797-0657
Embroiderers Guild of America (EGA) 426 W Jefferson St *Web:* www.egausa.org	Louisville	KY	40202	502-589-6956	584-7900
Experimental Aircraft Assn (EAA) 3000 Poberezny Rd *TF:* 800-236-4800 ■ *Web:* www.eaa.org	Oshkosh	WI	54902	920-426-4800	426-4828
Handweavers Guild of America (HGA) 1255 Hwy 23 NW Ste 211 *Web:* www.weavespindye.org	Suwanee	GA	30024	678-730-0010	730-0836
Knitting Guild of America, The (TKGA) 1100-H Brandywine Blvd *Web:* www.tkga.com	Zanesville	OH	43701	740-452-4541	452-2552
National Garden Clubs Inc (NGC) 4401 Magnolia Ave *TF:* 800-550-6007 ■ *Web:* www.gardenclub.org	Saint Louis	MO	63110	314-776-7574	776-5108
National Gardening Assn (NGA) 1100 Dorset St *TF:* 800-538-7476 ■ *Web:* www.garden.org	South Burlington	VT	05403	802-863-5251	864-6889
National Genealogical Society (NGS) 3108 Columbia Pk Ste 300 *TF:* 800-473-0060 ■ *Web:* www.ngsgenealogy.org	Arlington	VA	22204	703-525-0050	525-0052
National Model Railroad Assn (NMRA) 4121 Cromwell Rd *TF:* 800-654-2256 ■ *Web:* www.nmra.org	Chattanooga	TN	37421	423-892-2846	899-4869
National NeedleArts Assn, The (TNNA) 1100-H Brandywine Blvd *TF:* 800-889-8662 ■ *Web:* www.tnna.org	Zanesville	OH	43701	740-455-6773	452-2552
National Scrabble Assn 403 Front St PO Box 700 *Web:* www2.scrabble-assoc.com	Greenport	NY	11944	631-477-0033	
National Wood Carvers Assn (NWCA) 7424 Miami Ave *Web:* chipchats.org	Cincinnati	OH	45243	513-561-9051	
Philatelic Foundation 341 W 38th St Fifth Fl *Web:* www.philatelicfoundation.org	New York	NY	10018	212-221-6555	221-6208
Society of Decorative Painters 393 N McLean Blvd *Web:* www.decorativepainters.org	Wichita	KS	67203	316-269-9300	269-9191
Sports Car Club of America (SCCA) 6700 SW Topeka Blvd Ste 300 *TF:* 800-770-2055 ■ *Web:* www.scca.com	Topeka	KS	66619	785-357-7222	232-7228
Sweet Adelines International 9110 S Toledo Ave *TF:* 800-992-7464 ■ *Web:* www.sweetadelineintl.org	Tulsa	OK	74137	918-622-1444	665-0894
US Chess Federation (USCF) PO Box 3967 *TF:* 800-903-8723 ■ *Web:* www.uschess.org	Crossville	TN	38557	931-787-1234	787-1200

48-19 Military, Veterans, Patriotic Organizations

Organization	City	State	ZIP	Phone	Fax
Air Force Assn (AFA) 1501 Lee Hwy Fourth Fl *TF:* 800-727-3337 ■ *Web:* www.afa.org	Arlington	VA	22209	703-247-5800	247-5853
American Legion Auxiliary 8945 N Meridian St Second Fl *Web:* www.alaforveterans.org	Indianapolis	IN	46260	317-569-4500	569-4502
American Legion, The 700 N Pennsylvania St *TF Cust Svc:* 800-433-3318 ■ *Web:* www.legion.org	Indianapolis	IN	46204	317-630-1200	630-1223
American Logistics Assn (ALA) 1133 15th St NW Ste 640 *TF:* 800-791-7146 ■ *Web:* www.ala-national.org	Washington	DC	20005	202-466-2520	296-4419
American Society of Military Comptrollers (ASMC) 415 N Alfred St *TF:* 800-462-5637 ■ *Web:* www.asmconline.org	Alexandria	VA	22314	703-549-0360	549-3181
AMVETS 4647 Forbes Blvd *TF:* 877-726-8387 ■ *Web:* www.amvets.org	Lanham	MD	20706	301-459-9600	459-7924
Armed Forces Communications & Electronics Assn (AFCEA) 4400 Fair Lakes Ct *TF:* 800-336-4583 ■ *Web:* www.afcea.org	Fairfax	VA	22033	703-631-6100	631-4693
Armed Services Mutual Benefit Assn (ASMBA) PO Box 160384 *TF:* 800-251-8434 ■ *Web:* www.asmba.com	Nashville	TN	37216	615-851-0800	851-9484
Army Aviation Assn of America (AAAA) 593 Main St *Web:* www.quad-a.org	Monroe	CT	06468	203-268-2450	268-5870
Army Distaff Foundation 6200 Oregon Ave NW *TF:* 800-541-4255 ■ *Web:* www.armydistaff.org	Washington	DC	20015	202-541-0149	541-0128
Association of Civilian Technicians (ACT) 12620 Lk Ridge Dr *Web:* www.actnat.com	Woodbridge	VA	22192	703-494-4845	494-0961
Association of Old Crows (AOC) 1000 N Payne St Ste 300 *TF:* 800-247-5626 ■ *Web:* www.crows.org	Alexandria	VA	22314	703-549-1600	549-2589
Association of the US Army (AUSA) 2425 Wilson Blvd *TF:* 800-336-4570 ■ *Web:* www.ausa.org	Arlington	VA	22201	703-841-4300	525-9039
Disabled American Veterans (DAV) 3725 Alexandria Pike *TF:* 877-426-2838 ■ *Web:* www.dav.org	Cold Spring	KY	41076	859-441-7300	441-1416
Enlisted Assn of the National Guard of the US (EANGUS) 3133 Mt Vernon Ave *TF:* 800-234-3264 ■ *Web:* www.memberconnections.com	Alexandria	VA	22305	703-519-3846	519-3849
Fleet Reserve Assn (FRA) 125 NW St *TF:* 800-372-1924 ■ *Web:* www.fra.org	Alexandria	VA	22314	703-683-1400	549-6610
Marine Corps Assn (MCA) PO Box 1775 *TF:* 800-336-0291 ■ *Web:* www.mca-marines.org	Quantico	VA	22134	703-640-6161	640-0823
Military Benefit Assn (MBA) 14605 Avion Pkwy PO Box 221110 *TF:* 800-336-0100 ■ *Web:* www.militarybenefit.org	Chantilly	VA	20153	703-968-6200	968-6423
Military Officers Assn of America (MOAA) 201 N Washington St *TF:* 800-234-6622 ■ *Web:* www.moaa.org	Alexandria	VA	22314	703-549-2311	838-8173
NA for Uniformed Services (NAUS) 5535 Hempstead Way *TF:* 800-842-3451 ■ *Web:* www.naus.org	Springfield	VA	22151	703-750-1342	354-4380
National Committee for Employer Support of the Guard & Reserve (ESGR) 1555 Wilson Blvd Ste 319 *TF:* 800-336-4590 ■ *Web:* www.esgr.mil	Arlington	VA	22209	703-696-1386	696-1411
National Defense Industrial Assn (NDIA) 2111 Wilson Blvd Ste 400 *Web:* www.ndia.org	Arlington	VA	22201	703-522-1820	522-1885
National Fallen Firefighters Foundation PO Box 498 *TF:* 888-744-6513 ■ *Web:* www.firehero.org	Emmitsburg	MD	21727	301-447-1365	447-1645
National Guard Assn of the US (NGAUS) One Massachusetts Ave NW Ste 200 *TF:* 888-226-4287 ■ *Web:* www.ngaus.org	Washington	DC	20001	202-789-0031	682-9358
National League of Families of American Prisoners & Missing in Southeast Asia 5673 Columbia Pk Ste 100 *Web:* www.pow-miafamilies.org	Falls Church	VA	22041	703-465-7432	465-7433
National Society Daughters of the American Revolution (DAR) 1776 D St NW *Web:* www.dar.org	Washington	DC	20006	202-628-1776	879-3252

Phone | Fax

National Society of the Sons of the American Revolution (NSSAR)
1000 S Fourth St Louisville KY 40203 502-589-1776 589-1671
Web: www.sar.org

Naval Enlisted Reserve Assn (NERA)
6703 Farragut Ave. Falls Church VA 22042 703-534-1329 534-3617
TF: 800-776-9020 ■ *Web:* www.nera.org

Naval Reserve Assn (NRA) 1619 King St Alexandria VA 22314 703-548-5800 683-3647*
**Fax Area Code:* 866 ■ *Web:* ausn.org

Navy League of the US 2300 Wilson Blvd. Arlington VA 22201 703-528-1775 528-2333
TF: 800-356-5760 ■ *Web:* www.navyleague.org

Navy-Marine Corps Relief Society (NMCRS)
875 N Randolph St Ste 225 Arlington VA 22203 703-696-4904 696-0144
TF: 800-654-8364 ■ *Web:* www.nmcrs.org

Non Commissioned Officers Assn (NCOA)
9330 Corporate Dr Ste 701 Selma TX 78154 210-653-6161 637-3337
TF: 800-662-2620 ■ *Web:* www.ncoausa.org

Reserve Officers Assn of the US (ROA)
One Constitution Ave NE. Washington DC 20002 202-479-2200 547-1641
TF: 800-809-9448 ■ *Web:* www.roa.org

Retired Enlisted Assn (TREA)
15821 E Centre Tech Cir Aurora CO 80011 303-340-3939 340-4516
Web: www.trea.org

Society of American Military Engineers (SAME)
607 Prince St Alexandria VA 22314 703-549-3800 684-0231
TF: 800-336-3097 ■ *Web:* www.same.org

Tailhook Assn 9696 Businesspark Ave. San Diego CA 92131 858-689-9223 578-8839
TF: 800-322-4665 ■ *Web:* www.tailhook.net

United Service Organizations (USO)
2111 Wilson Blvd Ste 1200 Arlington VA 22201 703-908-6400 908-6401
Web: www.uso.org

US Coast Guard Chief Petty Officers Assn
5520-G Hempstead Way Springfield VA 22151 703-941-0395 941-0397
Web: www.uscgcpoa.org

US Naval Institute 291 Wood Rd Annapolis MD 21402 410-268-6110 295-1084
TF: 800-233-8764 ■ *Web:* www.usni.org

Veterans for Peace Inc (VFP)
216 S Meramec Ave Saint Louis MO 63105 314-725-6005 725-7103
TF: 877-429-0678 ■ *Web:* www.veteransforpeace.org

Veterans of Foreign Wars of the US (VFW)
406 W 34th St. Kansas City MO 64111 816-756-3390 968-1149
TF: 800-963-3180 ■ *Web:* www.vfw.org

Women in Military Service for America Memorial Foundation Inc
Dept 560. Washington DC 20042 703-533-1155 931-4208
TF: 800-222-2294 ■ *Web:* www.womensmemorial.org

48-20 Religious Organizations

Phone | Fax

92nd St Young Men's & Young Women's Hebrew Assn
1395 Lexington Ave New York NY 10128 212-415-5500 415-5788
Web: www.92y.org

Aberdeen Alliance Church of The Christian & Missionary Alliance, The
1106 S Roosevelt St Aberdeen SD 57401 605-225-9724

Abiding Faith Free Lutheran Church
433 Crestview Ave Ortonville MN 56278 320-839-3949
Web: aflc.org

Abundant Life Tabernacle Upci 591 Broadway Kingston NY 12401 845-338-9883

Abundant Love Church Inc
2615 New Haven Ave Fort Wayne IN 46803 260-420-5683
Web: abundantlove.faithweb.com

Adrian Dominican Sisters
1257 E Siena Heights Dr. Adrian MI 49221 517-266-3400

Aldersgate United Methodist Church
3702 S 90th E Ave Tulsa OK 74145 918-627-4165
Web: aldersgatechurch.com

Allegheny West Conference of Seventh Day Adventists
1339 E Broad St Columbus OH 43205 614-252-5271
Web: www.awconf.org

American Academy of Religion (AAR)
825 Houston Mill Rd NE Ste 300 Atlanta GA 30329 404-727-3049 727-7959
TF: 800-282-6632 ■ *Web:* www.aarweb.org

American Baptist Assn (ABA)
4605 N State Line Ave. Texarkana TX 75503 903-792-2783 792-8128
TF: 800-264-2482 ■ *Web:* www.abaptist.org

American Baptist Churches USA
PO Box 851 Valley Forge PA 19482 610-768-2000 768-2275
TF: 800-222-3872 ■ *Web:* www.abc-usa.org

American Theological Library Assn (ATLA)
300 S Wacker Dr Ste 2100 Chicago IL 60606 312-454-5100 454-5505
TF: 888-665-2852 ■ *Web:* www.atla.com

Answers in Genesis Ky Inc
2800 Bullittsburg Church Rd Petersburg KY 41080 859-727-2222
Web: www.answersingenesis.org

Antiochian Orthodox Christian Archdiocese of North America
358 Mountain Rd Englewood NJ 07631 201-871-1355 871-7954
TF: 888-421-1442 ■ *Web:* www.antiochian.org

Apostolic Assembly of The Faith In Christ Jesus
10807 Laurel St Rancho Cucamonga CA 91730 909-987-3013 481-5691
Web: www.apostolicassembly.org

Archdiocese of Louisville
212 E College St. Louisville KY 40203 502-585-3291
Web: www.archlou.org

Archdiocese of Newark 171 Clifton Ave Newark NJ 07104 973-497-4126
Web: www.rcan.org

Archdiocese of Philadelphia
222 N 17th St. Philadelphia PA 19103 215-965-4636
Web: archphila.org

Archdiocese of Portland in Oregon
2838 E Burnside St. Portland OR 97214 503-234-5334
TF: 800-235-8722 ■ *Web:* www.archdpdx.org

Archdiocese of Saint Paul & Minneapolis
226 Summit Ave Saint Paul MN 55102 651-291-4411
TF: 877-290-1605 ■ *Web:* www.archspm.org

Archdiocese of San Francisco
One Peter Yorke Way San Francisco CA 94109 415-614-5500
Web: www.sfarchdiocese.org

Arkansas Baptist Foundation
10117 Kanis Rd Little Rock AR 72205 501-376-0732
Web: abf.org

Armenian Church of America 630 Second Ave. New York NY 10016 212-686-0710 779-3558
Web: www.armenianchurch.org

Artman Lutheran Home 250 N Bethlehem Pk Ambler PA 19002 215-643-6335
Web: www.libertylutheran.org

Assemblies of God (A/G)
1445 N Boonville Ave Springfield MO 65802 417-862-2781 862-8558
TF: 800-641-4310 ■ *Web:* www.ag.org

Association of Professional Chaplains (APC)
1701 E Woodfield Rd Ste 400 Schaumburg IL 60173 847-240-1014 240-1015
Web: www.professionalchaplains.org

Association of Vineyard Churches
5115 Grove W Blvd. Stafford TX 77477 281-313-8463
Web: www.vineyardusa.org

Automated Assembly Corp
20777 Kensington Blvd Lakeville MN 55044 952-469-6556
Web: www.autoassembly.com

Avant Ministries 10000 N Oak Trafficway Kansas City MO 64155 816-734-8500 734-4601
TF: 800-468-1892 ■ *Web:* www.avantministries.org

B'nai B'rith International
2020 K St NW Seventh Fl Washington DC 20006 202-857-6600 857-6609
TF: 888-388-4224 ■ *Web:* www.bnaibrith.org

B'nai B'rith Youth Organization (BBYO)
2020 K St NW Washington DC 20006 202-857-6633 857-6568
Web: www.bbyo.org

Bannockburn Baptist Church 7100 Brodie Ln Austin TX 78745 512-892-2703 892-7660
Web: bbcfamily.com

Bapitst Campus Ministry Unc Charlotte
1328 John Kirk Dr Charlotte NC 28262 704-547-7472
Web: bcmcharlotte.org

Baptist Bible Fellowship International (BBFI)
720 E Kearney St Springfield MO 65803 417-862-5001 865-0794
Web: www.bbfi.org

Baptist General Convention of Texas
333 N Washington Ave Dallas TX 75246 214-828-5100
Web: texasbaptists.org/

Baptist Mid-Missions 7749 Webster Rd. Cleveland OH 44130 440-826-3930 826-4457
Web: www.bmm.org

Baptist Missionary Assn of America (BMA)
9219 Sibley Hole Rd PO Box 30910 Little Rock AR 72209 501-455-4977 455-3636
Web: bmamissions.org

Baptist Village of Hugo 1200 W Finley St Hugo OK 74743 580-326-8383
Web: baptistvillage.org

Baptist World Alliance
405 N Washington St Falls Church VA 22046 703-790-8980 790-5719
TF: 866-291-7809 ■ *Web:* www.bwanet.org

Bell Shoals Baptist Church of Brandon Inc
2102 Bell Shoals Rd Brandon FL 33511 813-689-4229
Web: bellshoals.com

Benny Hinn Ministries PO Box 162000 Irving TX 75016 817-722-2000
TF: 800-433-1900 ■ *Web:* www.bennyhinn.org

Berean Baptist Church Unaffiliated Inc
517 Glensford Dr Fayetteville NC 28314 910-868-5156
Web: bereanbaptistchurch.org

Beth Medrash Govoha of America Inc
617 Sixth St Lakewood NJ 08701 732-367-1060

Bethel Baptist Church 1196 N Academy St Galesburg IL 61401 309-342-3166
Web: www.mybethel.com

Bethel World Outreach Ministries International Inc
8252 Georgia Ave Silver Spring MD 20910 301-588-8099
Web: cityofhope.bwomi.org

Bethesda Ministries 2200 Peacock Rd Richmond IN 47374 765-939-2975
Web: mybwc.org

Bible League PO Box 28000 Chicago IL 60628 817-595-1664 367-8600*
**Fax Area Code:* 708 ■ *TF:* 866-825-4636 ■ *Web:* www.bibleleague.org

Bible Way Fellowship Baptist Church
10120 Hartsook St Houston TX 77034 713-943-2215
Web: www.bibleway1.org

Billy Graham Evangelistic Assn
One Billy Graham Pkwy PO Box 1270 Charlotte NC 28201 704-401-2432 401-2140
TF: 877-247-2426 ■ *Web:* www.billygraham.org

Brainerd Baptist Church
212 Brookfield Ave Chattanooga TN 37411 423-629-4202
Web: brainerdbaptist.org

Brandywine Valley Baptist Church
Seven Mt Lebanon Rd. Wilmington DE 19803 302-478-4255
Web: www.bvbcnet.org

Breakthrough Urban Ministries
3330 W Carroll Ave. Chicago IL 60624 773-722-1144
Web: breakthrough.org

Brooklyn Tabernacle 17 Smith St. Brooklyn NY 11201 718-290-2000
Web: www.brooklyntabernacle.org

Buddhist Churches of America (BCA)
1710 Octavia St San Francisco CA 94109 415-776-5600 771-6293
Web: buddhistchurchesofamerica.org

California Southern Baptist Convention
678 E Shaw Ave Fresno CA 93710 559-229-9533 229-2824
TF: 888-462-7729 ■ *Web:* www.csbc.com

Calvary Baptist Christian Academy
543 Randolph St. Meadville PA 16335 814-724-8099
Web: cbcmeadville.org

Calvary Chapel 13500 Philmont Ave Philadelphia PA 19116 215-969-1520
Web: www.ccphilly.org

Organization	City	State	Zip	Phone	Fax
Calvary Chapel of Costa Mesa Inc 3800 S Fairview St *Web:* www.calvarychapelcostamesa.com	Santa Ana	CA	92704	714-979-4422	
Camp Hill Presbyterian Church 101 N 23rd St *Web:* www.thechpc.org	Camp Hill	PA	17011	717-737-0488	
Campus Crusade for Christ International 100 Lk Hart Dr *TF:* 888-278-7233 ■ *Web:* www.cru.org	Orlando	FL	32832	407-826-2500	
Campus Outreach 2200 Briarwood Way *Web:* campusoutreach.org	Birmingham	AL	35243	205-776-5500	
Canon Law Society of America (CLSA) 3025 Fourth St NE Ste 111 *Web:* www.clsa.org	Washington	DC	20017	202-832-2350	832-2331
Canyon Ridge Christian Church 6200 W Lone Mtn Rd *Web:* www.canyonridge.org	Las Vegas	NV	89130	702-658-2722	
Capital Christian Center 9470 Micron Ave *Web:* capitalonline.cc/	Sacramento	CA	95827	916-856-5683	
Cathedral School for Boys 1275 Sacramento St *Web:* www.cathedralschool.net	San Francisco	CA	94108	415-771-6600	
Catholic Biblical Assn of America 433 Caldwell Hall *Web:* www.catholicbiblical.org	Washington	DC	20064	202-319-5519	319-4799
Catholic Church Extension Society of the USA 150 S Wacker Dr 20th Fl **Fax Area Code:* 312 ■ *TF:* 800-842-7804 ■ *Web:* www.catholicextension.org	Chicago	IL	60606	800-842-7804	236-5276*
Catholic Social Services 8815 99 St *Web:* www.catholicsocialservices.ab.ca	Edmonton	AB	T6E3V3	780-432-1137	
Catholic Supply of st Louis Inc 6759 Chippewa St *TF:* 800-325-9026 ■ *Web:* www.catholicsupply.com	Saint Louis	MO	63109	314-644-0643	
Catholic Transcript Inc, The 467 Bloomfield Ave *Web:* www.catholictranscript.org	Bloomfield	CT	06002	860-286-2828	
CE National Inc 1003 Presidential Dr *Web:* cenational.org	Winona Lake	IN	46590	574-267-6622	
Center for Action & Contempla 1823 Five Points Rd SW *Web:* www.cac.org	Albuquerque	NM	87105	505-242-9588	
Central Baptist Village 4747 N Canfield Ave *Web:* www.cbvillage.org	Norridge	IL	60706	708-583-8500	
Central Conference of American Rabbis (CCAR) 355 Lexington Ave *Web:* www.ccarnet.org	New York	NY	10017	212-972-3636	692-0819
Centre Street United Methodist Church 217 N Centre St *Web:* centrestreetumc.com	Cumberland	MD	21502	301-722-5370	
Child Evangelism Fellowship Inc 17482 Hwy M *TF:* 800-748-7710 ■ *Web:* www.cefonline.com	Warrenton	MO	63383	636-456-4321	456-2078
Childrens Hopechest PO Box 63842 *Web:* www.hopechest.org	Colorado Springs	CO	80962	719-487-7800	487-7799
Christ & Grace Episcopal Church 1545 S Sycamore St *Web:* christandgrace.org	Petersburg	VA	23805	804-733-7202	
Christ Church of Universal Love, The 11699 130th Ave	Largo	FL	33778	727-585-5088	
Christ Church Xp 8800 Vaughn Rd *Web:* christchurchxp.net	Montgomery	AL	36117	334-387-0566	
Christ in Youth Inc PO Box B *TF:* 800-693-9653 ■ *Web:* ciy.com	Joplin	MO	64801	417-781-2273	781-5958
Christ Universal Temple 11901 S Ashland Ave Apt S *Web:* www.cutemple.org	Chicago	IL	60643	773-568-2282	
Christian & Missionary Alliance 8595 Explorer Dr *TF:* 800-700-2651 ■ *Web:* www.cmalliance.org	Colorado Springs	CO	80920	719-599-5999	
Christian Aid Ministries PO Box 360 *Web:* christianaidministries.org	Berlin	OH	44610	330-893-2428	893-2305
Christian Church (Disciples of Christ) 130 E Washington St *Web:* www.disciples.org	Indianapolis	IN	46204	317-635-3100	635-3700
Christian Fellowship Church Foundation 21673 Beaumeade Cir *Web:* www.cfellowshipc.org	Ashburn	VA	20147	703-729-3900	
Christian Reformed Church in North America (CRC) 2850 Kalamazoo Ave SE *TF:* 800-272-5125 ■ *Web:* www.crcna.org	Grand Rapids	MI	49560	616-241-1691	224-0834
Christophers, The Five Hanover Sq 11th Fl *TF:* 888-298-4050 ■ *Web:* www.christophers.org	New York	NY	10004	212-759-4050	838-5073
Christus Victor Lutheran Church Inc of Knox County Tennessee 4110 Central Ave Pike *Web:* christusvictorknoxville.org	Knoxville	TN	37912	865-687-6622	
Church of God in Christ Inc 930 Mason St *TF:* 877-746-8578 ■ *Web:* www.cogic.org	Memphis	TN	38126	901-947-9300	947-9359
Church of God Ministries 1201 E Fifth St *TF:* 800-848-2464 ■ *Web:* jesusisthesubject.org/	Anderson	IN	46012	765-642-0256	642-5652
Church of God World Missions (COGWM) 2490 Keith St PO Box 8016 *TF:* 800-345-7492 ■ *Web:* www.cogwm.org	Cleveland	TN	37320	423-478-7190	478-7155
Church of Jesus Christ of Latter-Day Saints 50 E N Temple St *Web:* www.lds.org	Salt Lake City	UT	84150	801-240-1000	240-2033
Church of Our Lady of Lourdes 901 Atwells Ave *Web:* parishesonline.com	Providence	RI	02909	401-272-8127	
Church of Scientology Flag Service Organization 503 Cleveland St *Web:* scientology-fso.org	Clearwater	FL	33755	727-445-4387	
Church of the Brethren 1451 Dundee Ave *TF:* 800-323-8039 ■ *Web:* www.brethren.org	Elgin	IL	60120	847-742-5100	742-1407
Church of The Holy Communion 218 Ashley Ave *Web:* www.holycomm.org	Charleston	SC	29403	843-722-2024	
Church of the Nazarene 17001 Prairie Star Pkwy *Web:* www.nazarene.org	Lenexa	KS	66220	913-577-0500	
Church Women United (CWU) 475 Riverside Dr Ste 243 *TF:* 800-298-5551 ■ *Web:* www.churchwomen.org	New York	NY	10115	212-870-2347	870-2338
City of Truth or Consequences 685 Marie St *Web:* www.torcnm.org	Truth Or Consequences	NM	87901	575-894-2603	
City Union Mission Inc 1100 E 11th St *Web:* cityunionmission.org	Kansas City	MO	64106	816-474-9380	
Colonial Hills Baptist Church 5375 W Mt Morris Rd	Mount Morris	MI	48458	810-687-1570	
Columbia Lutheran Home 4700 Phinney Ave N *Web:* www.columbialutheranhome.com	Seattle	WA	98103	206-632-7400	
Commons at Orlando Lutheran Towers, The 300 E Church St *Web:* orlandoseniorhealth.org	Orlando	FL	32801	407-872-7088	
Community of Christ 1001 W Walnut St **Fax:* Hum Res ■ *TF:* 800-825-2806 ■ *Web:* www.cofchrist.org	Independence	MO	64050	816-833-1000	521-3085*
Compassion Canada 985 Adelaide St S *Web:* compassion.ca	London	ON	N6E4A3	519-668-0224	
Congregation Rodeph Sholom Seven W 83rd St *Web:* www.rodephsholom.org	New York	NY	10024	212-362-8800	
Connecting Businessmen to Christ (CBMC) 5746 Marlin Rd Ste 602 Osborne Ctr *TF:* 800-566-2262 ■ *Web:* www.cbmc.com	Chattanooga	TN	37411	423-698-4444	629-4434
Connection Pointe Christian Church of Brownsburg 1800 N Green St *Web:* cpccweb.org	Brownsburg	IN	46112	317-852-2221	
Coral Ridge Presbyterian Church Inc 5555 N Federal Hwy *Web:* www.crpc.org	Fort Lauderdale	FL	33308	954-771-8840	
Cornerstone United Methodist Church Inc 8200 Immokalee Rd *Web:* cornerstonenaples.org	Naples	FL	34119	239-354-9160	
Coupland-Moran Engineers Inc 6001 Indian School Rd Ne Ste 200 *Web:* www.cmenm.com	Albuquerque	NM	87110	505-314-7500	
Covenant United Methodist Church 6824 Tuckaseegee Rd *Web:* www.gbgm-umc.org	Charlotte	NC	28214	704-392-3925	
Crestview Baptist Church Georgetown Texas 2300 Williams Dr *Web:* peoplesharingjesus.com	Georgetown	TX	78628	512-863-6576	
Crossgates Baptist Church Inc Eight Crosswoods Rd *Web:* crossgates.org	Brandon	MS	39042	601-825-2562	
Crossings Community Church 14600 N Portland Ave *Web:* crossingsokc.org	Oklahoma City	OK	73134	405-755-2227	
Crossway Community Church 13905 75th St *Web:* www.crosswayonline.org	Bristol	WI	53104	262-857-4488	
Crossworld 306 Bala Ave *Web:* www.crossworld.org	Bala Cynwyd	PA	19004	888-785-0087	
Crowes Mortuary & Chapel 118 Us Hwy 74A *Web:* crowemortuary.com	Rutherfordton	NC	28139	828-286-2304	
Crux, The 2216 E S St	Anaheim	CA	92806	714-563-2024	
Dane Street Congregational Church 10 Dane St *Web:* www.danestchurch.org	Beverly	MA	01915	978-922-4325	
Dare 2 Share Ministries International PO Box 745323 Ste 101 *Web:* dare2share.org	Arvada,	CO	80006	303-425-1606	
Destination America Inc 2255 Kuhio Ave Ste 1002	Honolulu	HI	96815	808-971-0500	
Diocese of Davenport 2706 N Gaines St *Web:* www.davenportdiocese.org	Davenport	IA	52804	563-324-1911	
Diocese of Greensburg 723 E Pittsburgh St *TF:* 866-409-6455 ■ *Web:* www.dioceseofgreensburg.org	Greensburg	PA	15601	724-837-0901	837-0857
Diocese of Harrisburg 4800 Union Deposit Rd *Web:* hbgdiocese.org	Harrisburg	PA	17111	717-657-4804	
Diocese of La Crosse 3710 E Ave S *Web:* www.dioceseoflacrosse.com	La Crosse	WI	54601	608-788-7700	
Diocese of Metuchen PO Box 191 *Web:* www.diometuchen.org	Metuchen	NJ	08840	732-562-1990	
Diocese of Nashville 2400 21st Ave S *Web:* www.dioceseofnashville.com	Nashville	TN	37212	615-383-6393	
Diocese of Phoenix 400 E Monroe St *Web:* www.diocesephoenix.org	Phoenix	AZ	85004	602-257-0030	
Diocese of Rochester 1150 Buffalo Rd *Web:* www.dor.org	Roch	NY	14624	585-328-3210	
Diocese of San Bernardino Education & Welfare Corp 1201 E Highland Ave *Web:* sbdiocese.org	San Bernardino	CA	92404	909-475-5300	
Diocese of St. Augustine Inc 11625 Old St Augustine *TF:* 800-775-4659 ■ *Web:* www.dosafl.com	Jacksonville	FL	32258	904-262-3200	
Divine Redeemer United Presbyterian Church 407 N Calaveras *Web:* divineredeemersa.org	San Antonio	TX	78207	210-433-9551	
Door Creek Church 6602 Dominion Dr *Web:* www.doorcreekchurch.org	Madison	WI	53718	608-222-8586	
E3 Partners Ministry 16787 Bernardo Ctr Dr Ste 7 *Web:* e3partners.org	San Diego	CA	92128	858-485-9904	
Eagle Rock Baptist Church 1499 Colorado Blvd *Web:* eaglerockbaptist.com	Los Angeles	CA	90041	323-255-4611	

Phone Fax

Eastern Star Church 5750 E 30th St .... Indianapolis IN 46218 317-591-5050
Web: www.easternstarchurch.org

Emmanuel Gospel Center Inc Two San Juan St .... Boston MA 02118 617-262-4567
Web: egc.org

Episcopal Church USA 815 Second Ave .... New York NY 10017 212-716-6000 867-0395
TF: 800-334-7626 ■ *Web:* www.episcopalchurch.org

Episcopal Diocese of West Texas
111 Torcido Dr .... San Antonio TX 78209 210-824-5387
Web: dwtx.org

Evangelical Church Alliance (ECA)
205 W Broadway St PO Box 9 .... Bradley IL 60915 815-937-0720 937-0720
TF: 888-855-6060 ■ *Web:* www.ecainternational.org

Evangelical Fellowship of Canada (EFC)
600 Alden Rd Ste 300 Markham Industrial Pk .... Markham ON L3R0E7 905-479-5885 479-4742
TF: 866-302-3362 ■ *Web:* www.evangelicalfellowship.ca

Evangelical Free Church of America, The
901 E 78th St .... Minneapolis MN 55420 952-854-1300
Web: www.efca.org

Evangelical Lutheran Church in America (ELCA)
8765 W Higgins Rd .... Chicago IL 60631 773-380-2700 380-1465
TF: 800-638-3522 ■ *Web:* www.elca.org

Evangelical Presbyterian Church of Plant City
1107 Charlie Griffin Rd .... Plant City FL 33566 813-759-9383
Web: epcpc.org

Evangelical Training Assn (ETA) PO Box 327 .... Wheaton IL 60187 630-384-6920 384-6927
TF General: 800-369-8291 ■ *Web:* www.etaworld.org

Faith Tabernacle Pentecostal Church of Montgomery County Mo
121 W Fourth St .... Montgomery City MO 63361 573-564-3700

Faithbridge United Methodist Church
18000 Stuebner Airline Rd .... Spring TX 77379 281-320-7588
Web: faithbridge.org

Family Life Worship Center Worldwide Ministries Inc
1517 Joyner Pond Rd .... Aiken SC 29803 803-641-0218

Felician Sisters Cssf 1600 W Oklahoma Ave .... Milwaukee WI 53215 414-645-5329

Fellowship Community 3000 Fellowship Dr .... Whitehall PA 18052 610-799-3000
Web: www.fellowshipcommunity.com

Fellowship Village Dining Service Dept
8000 Fellowship Rd .... Basking Ridge NJ 07920 908-580-3806
Web: fellowshipseniorliving.org/

Fifth Baptist Church of The City of st Louis Mo
3736 Natural Bridge Ave .... Saint Louis MO 63107 314-531-2602

First Assembly of God 1701 N E Ave .... Panama City FL 32405 850-769-3558
Web: firstassemblypc.org

First Baptist Church Dallas
1707 San Jacinto St .... Dallas TX 75201 214-969-0111 969-7720
Web: www.firstdallas.org

First Baptist Church of Orlando Inc, The
3000 S John Young Pkwy .... Orlando FL 32805 407-425-2555 425-2954
Web: www.firstorlando.com

First Christian Church 531 Fifth St .... Columbus IN 47201 812-379-4491
Web: www.fccoc.org

First Church of Christ Scientist
210 Massachusetts Ave P05-10 .... Boston MA 02115 617-450-2000
TF: 800-288-7155 ■ *Web:* www.christianscience.com

First Evangelical Free Church of st Louis County
1375 Carman Rd .... Manchester MO 63021 636-227-0125
Web: efree.org

Focus 603 Park Point Dr Ste 200 .... Genesee CO 80401 303-962-5750
Web: www.focus.org

Fourth Presbyterian Church
3016 Preston Hwy .... Louisville KY 40217 502-634-8021
Web: fourthpc.org

Franciscan Sisters of Chicago Inc
1055 175th St Ste 202 .... Homewood IL 60430 708-647-6500
TF: 800-524-6126 ■ *Web:* www.franciscancommunities.com

Friends General Conference
1216 Arch St Ste 2B .... Philadelphia PA 19107 215-561-1700
Web: www.fgcquaker.org

General Assn of Regular Baptist Churches (GARBC)
1300 N Meacham Rd .... Schaumburg IL 60173 847-585-0816
TF: 888-588-1600 ■ *Web:* www.garbcinternational.org

Glad Tidings Assembly of God Church
1110 Snyder Rd .... Reading PA 19609 610-678-0266
Web: www.gladtidingsonline.com

Glori Energy Inc 4315 S Dr .... Houston TX 77053 713-237-8880
Web: www.glorienergy.com

God Owns This Company Inc 777 Hill Ave .... Muskegon MI 49442 231-727-3333
Web: godownsthiscompany.com

Good Hope Lutheran Church
3359 New Zoarville Rd Ne .... Zoarville OH 44656 330-859-2480
Web: www.nclutheran.org

Grace Church 802 Broadway .... New York NY 10003 212-254-2000
Web: www.gracechurchnyc.org

Grace Episcopal Church 33 Church St .... White Plains NY 10601 914-949-3098 761-2105
Web: www.gracecommunitycenter.org

Grace Place Lutheran Retreats
8460 Watson Rd Ste 225 .... Saint Louis MO 63119 314-842-3077
Web: graceplacewellness.org

Graceworks Church Inc 16131 Hwy 44 .... Prairieville LA 70769 225-622-7805

Greater Atlanta Christian
1575 Indian Trl Lilburn Rd .... Norcross GA 30093 770-243-2000
TF: 800-450-1327 ■ *Web:* www.greateratlantachristian.org

Green Acres Baptist Church
16163 N Peninsula Rd .... Whitehouse TX 75791 903-566-2515
Web: www.gabc.org

Guild Shop of The Church of st John The Divine, The
2009 Dunlavy St .... Houston TX 77006 713-528-5095
Web: theguildshop.org

Harvest Christian Fellowship
6115 Arlington Ave .... Riverside CA 92504 951-687-6902
Web: harvest.org

Harvest Word of Life Ministries International Inc
2260 Lake Ave .... Fort Wayne IN 46805 260-422-5750

Heathwood Hall Episcopal School
3000 S Beltline Blvd .... Columbia SC 29201 803-765-2309
Web: www.heathwood.org

Hella Corporate Center USA Inc
43811 Plymouth Oaks Blvd .... Plymouth MI 48170 734-414-0900
Web: www.hella.com

Henderson Hills Baptist Church
1200 E I 35 Frontage Rd .... Edmond OK 73034 405-341-4639
TF: 877-901-4639 ■ *Web:* www.hhbc.com

Highline United Methodist Church
13015 First Ave S .... Burien WA 98168 206-241-5520
Web: highlineunitedmethodistchurch.org

Hillcrest Church of Christ 307 Oak St .... Tunnel Hill GA 30755 706-673-2234

Hilldale Church of Christ Inc 501 Hwy 76 .... Clarksville TN 37043 931-647-5264
Web: hilldalecc.org

Hillel: The Foundation for Jewish Campus Life
800 Eighth St NW .... Washington DC 20001 202-449-6500
Web: www.hillel.org

Holy Cross Family Ministries
518 Washington St .... North Easton MA 02356 508-238-4095
TF: 800-299-7729 ■ *Web:* www.hcfm.org

Holy Spirit Catholic School
540 N Seventh Ave .... Pocatello ID 83201 208-232-5763
Web: www.hscssa.org

Horizon Christian Fellowship PO Box 17480 .... San Diego CA 92177 858-277-4991
Web: www.horizonchristianfellowship.org

Hunter Memorial Presbyterian Church Inc
109 Rosemont Gdn .... Lexington KY 40503 859-277-5126
Web: hunterlex.org

IFCA International 3520 Fairlane Ave SW .... Grandville MI 49418 616-531-1840 531-1814
TF: 800-347-1840 ■ *Web:* www.ifca.org

Iglesia Adventista Del Septimo Dia
9735 N Houston Rosslyn Rd .... Houston TX 77040 713-937-1200

Iglesia Ni Cristo Church of Christ
505 E 36th St .... Long Beach CA 90807 562-490-9757
Web: incmedia.org

Immanuel Lutheran Church 2120 Lakewood Ave .... Lima OH 45805 419-222-2541
Web: www.wcoil.com

Immanuel Lutheran Communities
185 Crestline Ave .... Kalispell MT 59901 406-752-9622
Web: ilcorp.org

Incarnation Lutheran Church
4880 Hodgson Rd .... Saint Paul MN 55126 651-766-0723
Web: www.incarnationmn.org

Interfaith Action of Greater Saint Paul
1671 Summit Ave .... Saint Paul MN 55105 651-646-8805
Web: www.spacc.org

Interfaith Ministries for Greater Houston
3217 Montrose Blvd .... Houston TX 77006 713-533-4900
Web: www.imgh.org

International Bible Society (IBS)
Biblica 1820 Jet Stream Dr .... Colorado Springs CO 80921 719-488-9200 867-2870
TF Cust Svc: 800-524-1588 ■ *Web:* www.biblica.com

International Centers for Spiritual Living
2825 E 33rd Ave Ste 301 .... Spokane WA 99223 509-534-1011 624-9322
Web: www.cslspokane.org

International Church of the Foursquare Gospel (ICFG)
1910 W Sunset Blvd PO Box 26902 .... Los Angeles CA 90026 213-989-4234 989-4590
TF: 888-635-4234 ■ *Web:* www.foursquare.org

International Pentecostal Holiness Church (IPHC)
PO Box 12609 .... Oklahoma City OK 73157 405-787-7110 789-3957
Web: www.iphc.org

Interserve USA 7000 Ludlow St .... Upper Darby PA 19082 610-352-0581
TF: 800-809-4440 ■ *Web:* www.interserveusa.org

InterVarsity Christian Fellowship/USA
6400 Schroeder Rd .... Madison WI 53711 608-274-9001 274-7882
TF: 866-734-4823 ■ *Web:* www.intervarsity.org

Jericho Road Ministries Inc
1090 Mondon Hill Rd .... Brooksville FL 34601 352-799-2912
Web: www.jericho-road.net

Jesse Duplantis Ministries
1973 Ormond Blvd .... Destrehan LA 70047 985-764-2000

Jewish Community Centers Assn of North America
520 Eigth Ave .... New York NY 10018 212-532-4949 481-4174
Web: www.jcca.org

Jewish National Fund (JNF) 42 E 69th St .... New York NY 10021 212-879-9300
TF: 800-542-8733 ■ *Web:* www.jnf.org

Jewish Reconstructionist Federation (JRF)
101 Greenwood Ave .... Jenkintown PA 19046 215-885-5601 885-5603
TF: 877-226-7573 ■ *Web:* archive.jewishrecon.org

Jewish United Fund/Jewish Federation of Metropolitan Chicago (JUF)
30 S Wells St .... Chicago IL 60606 312-346-6700 444-2086
TF: 855-275-5237 ■ *Web:* www.juf.org

Jews for Jesus 60 Haight St .... San Francisco CA 94102 415-864-2600 552-8325
TF: 800-366-5521 ■ *Web:* jewsforjesus.org

Jimmy Swaggart Ministries (JSM)
8919 World Ministry Blvd PO Box 262550 .... Baton Rouge LA 70810 225-768-8300 769-2244
TF Orders: 800-288-8350 ■ *Web:* www.jsm.org

Kalamazoo Community Foundation
151 S Rose St Ste 332 .... Kalamazoo MI 49007 269-381-4416
Web: www.kalfound.org

Kalamazoo Gospel Mission 448 N Burdick St .... Kalamazoo MI 49007 269-345-2974
Web: kzoogospel.org

Kensington Community Church 1825 E Sq Lake Rd .... Troy MI 48085 248-786-0600
Web: kensingtonchurch.org

Kingsway Charities 1119 Commonwealth Ave .... Bristol VA 24201 276-466-3014 466-0955
TF: 800-321-9234 ■ *Web:* www.kingswaycharities.org

Lake Junaluska Assembly
Lake Junaluska Conference
Retreat Ctr 689 N Lakeshore Dr .... Lake Junaluska NC 28745 828-452-2881
Web: www.lakejunaluska.com

Organization	City	State	ZIP	Phone	Fax
Lakewood United Methodist Church of North Little Rock 1922 Topf Rd *Web:* www.lakewood-umc.org	North Little Rock	AR	72116	501-753-6186	
Life Baptist Church Mission Cottage 158 Sandy Acres Way	Saint Stephen	SC	29479	843-567-4775	
Life of Learning Foundation 459 Galice Rd *Web:* guyfinley.org	Merlin	OR	97532	541-476-1200	
Life Outreach International 1801 W Euless Blvd *Web:* www.lifetoday.org	Euless	TX	76040	817-267-4211	
Lifechurch-tv 4600 E Second St *Web:* www.lifechurch.tv	Edmond	OK	73034	405-478-5433	
Lincoln Lutheran of Racine Inc 2132 Center St *Web:* www.lincolnlutheran.com	Racine	WI	53403	262-833-0141	
Little Promise Keepers 12320 Cypress N Houston Rd *Web:* littlepromisekeepers.com	Cypress	TX	77429	281-807-0009	807-0009
Living Faith Christian Church 19503 Business Ctr Dr *Web:* living.org	Northridge	CA	91324	818-709-8532	
Lone Oak First Baptist Church Inc 3601 Lone Oak Rd *Web:* loneoakfbc.org	Paducah	KY	42003	270-554-1441	
Lord of Life Lutheran Church Lcms 3601 W 15th St *Web:* www.lol-plano.org	Plano	TX	75075	972-867-5588	
Lutheran Church Missouri Synod (LCMS) 1333 S Kirkwood Rd *TF:* 888-843-5267 ■ *Web:* www.lcms.org	Saint Louis	MO	63122	314-965-9000	996-1016
Lutheran Church of Hope 925 Jordan Creek Pkwy *Web:* www.hopewdm.org	West Des Moines	IA	50266	515-222-1520	
Lutheran Home at Hollidaysburg, The 916 Hickory St *TF:* 800-400-2285 ■ *Web:* www.alsm.org	Hollidaysburg	PA	16648	814-696-4527	
Lutheran Home of The Cannon Valley Inc 900 Cannon Vly Dr *Web:* www.northfieldretirement.org	Northfield	MN	55057	507-645-9511	
Lutheran Metropolitan Ministry Admin 1468 W 25th St *Web:* www.lutheranmetro.org	Cleveland	OH	44113	216-696-5507	
Lutheran Social Services of The South Inc (LSS) 8305 Cross Pk Dr PO Box 140767 *TF:* 800-938-5777 ■ *Web:* www.lsss.org	Austin	TX	78754	512-459-1000	467-2746
Mandarin Presbyterian Church Inc, The 11844 Mandarin Rd	Jacksonville	FL	32223	904-680-9944	
Mel Trotter Ministries 363 E State St *Web:* meltrotter.org	Belding	MI	48809	616-794-9844	
Messiah Lutheran Church 303 Rt- 101 PO Box 488 *Web:* www.messiahnh.org	Amherst	NH	03031	603-673-2011	
Messiah Village 100 Mt Allen Dr Ofc *Web:* messiahlifeways.org/residential-communities/messiah-village/	Mechanicsburg	PA	17055	717-790-8232	
Mission Aviation Fellowship (MAF) 112 N Pilatus Ln *TF:* 800-359-7623 ■ *Web:* www.maf.org	Nampa	ID	83687	208-498-0800	498-0801
Mission Springs Community Church of Fremont Inc 48989 Milmont Dr *Web:* msccfremont.org	Fremont	CA	94538	510-490-0446	
Missouri Slope Lutheran Care Center Foundation 2425 Hillview Ave *Web:* www.mslcc.com	Bismarck	ND	58501	701-223-9407	
Morningside Ministries 700 Babcock Rd *Web:* mmliving.org	San Antonio	TX	78201	210-734-1000	734-1111
Morris Cerullo World Evangelism 3545 Aero Ct Frnt *Web:* www.mcwe.com	San Diego	CA	92123	858-277-2200	
Muslim Community Assn 2301 Plymouth Rd *Web:* www.mca-aa.org	Ann Arbor	MI	48105	734-665-6772	
NA of Congregational Christian Churches (NACCC) 8473 S Howell Ave *TF:* 800-262-1620 ■ *Web:* www.naccc.org	Oak Creek	WI	53154	414-764-1620	764-0319
NA of Free Will Baptists (NAFWB) 5233 Mt View Rd *TF:* 877-767-7659 ■ *Web:* www.nafwb.org	Antioch	TN	37013	615-731-6812	731-0771
Nashville Rescue Mission 639 Lafayette St *Web:* www.nashvillerescuemission.org	Nashville	TN	37203	615-255-2475	
Nation of Islam 7351 S Stony Island *Web:* www.noi.org	Chicago	IL	60649	773-324-6000	
National Baptist Convention of America Inc 777 SRL Thornton Fwy *Web:* www.nbcainc.com	Dallas	TX	75203	214-942-3311	942-4696
National Baptist Convention USA Inc 1700 Baptist World Ctr Dr *TF:* 866-531-3054 ■ *Web:* www.nationalbaptist.com	Nashville	TN	37207	615-228-6292	262-3917
National Spiritual Assembly of the Baha'is of the US 1233 Central St *Web:* www.bahai.us	Evanston	IL	60201	847-733-3400	869-0247
Navigators of Canada 11 St John'S Dr *TF:* 866-202-6287 ■ *Web:* www.navigators.ca	Arva	ON	N0M1C0	519-660-8300	
Navigators, The 3820 N 30th St PO Box 6000 *TF:* 866-568-7827 ■ *Web:* www.navigators.org	Colorado Springs	CO	80934	719-598-1212	260-0479
Nebraska Synod Evangelical Lutheran Church in America 4980 S 118th St Ste D *Web:* nebraskasynod.org	Omaha	NE	68137	402-896-5311	
New Covenant Fellowship Church 18901 Waring Stn Rd *Web:* www.fellowshipusa.com	Germantown	MD	20874	301-444-3100	
New Hampshire Catholic Charities Inc 215 Myrtle St PO Box 686 *TF:* 800-562-5249 ■ *Web:* www.nh-cc.org	Manchester	NH	03104	603-669-3030	626-1252
New Hope Housing Inc 8407-E Richmond Hwy *Web:* www.newhopehousing.org	Alexandria	VA	22309	703-799-2293	
New Tribes Mission (NTM) 1000 E First St *TF:* 800-321-5375 ■ *Web:* ntm.org	Sanford	FL	32771	407-323-3430	
Oak Cliff Bible Fellowship 1808 W Camp Wisdom Rd **Fax Area Code:* 214 ■ *Web:* www.ocbfchurch.org	Dallas	TX	75232	972-228-1281	672-9182*
Oklahoma Methodist Manor Inc 4134 E 31st St *Web:* www.ommtulsa.org	Tulsa	OK	74135	918-743-2565	
Open Door Mission 5803 Harrisburg Blvd *Web:* www.opendoorhouston.org	Houston	TX	77011	713-923-8743	921-4206
Orgill Singer 8360 W Sahara Ave Ste 110 *Web:* www.orgillsinger.com	Las Vegas	NV	89117	702-796-9100	
Orlando Union Rescue Mission 1525 W Washington St *Web:* www.ourm.org	Orlando	FL	32805	407-423-2131	
Orthodox Union (OU) 11 Broadway *TF:* 855-505-7500 ■ *Web:* www.ou.org	New York	NY	10004	212-563-4000	564-9058
Oshkosh Convention & Visitors Bureau 2401 W Waukau Ave *TF:* 877-303-9200 ■ *Web:* www.visitoshkosh.com	Oshkosh	WI	54904	920-303-9200	
Palma Ceia United Methodist Church Day School & Day Care 3723 W Bay To Bay Blvd *Web:* palmaceiaumc.org	Tampa	FL	33629	813-837-1541	837-3600
Pathway to Peace Christian Church 5808 Lynn Rd	Tampa	FL	33624	813-908-0893	
Pentecostal Assemblies 3214 S Service Rd *TF:* 800-295-6368 ■ *Web:* www.paoc.org	Burlington	ON	L7N3J2	905-637-7558	
Perimeter Church 9500 Medlock Bridge Rd *Web:* www.perimeter.org	Johns Creek	CO	30097	678-405-2000	405-2009
Pioneers 10123 William Carey Dr *TF:* 800-359-9297 ■ *Web:* www.pioneers.org	Orlando	FL	32832	407-382-6000	382-1008
Potomac Conference Corp of Seventh Day Adventists 606 Greenville Ave *TF:* 800-732-1844 ■ *Web:* www.pcsda.org	Staunton	VA	24401	540-886-0771	886-5734
Presby's Inspired Life 2000 Joshua Rd *Web:* www.presbysinspiredlife.org	Lafayette Hill	PA	19444	610-834-1001	
Presbyterian Childrens Services Inc 1220 N Lindbergh Blvd *TF:* 800-383-8147 ■ *Web:* missouri.pchas.org	St. Louis	MO	63132	314-989-9727	427-2682
Presbyterian Church in America (PCA) 1700 N Brown Rd Ste 105 *Web:* pcanet.org	Lawrenceville	GA	30043	678-825-1000	825-1001
Presbyterian Church (USA) 100 Witherspoon St *TF:* 888-728-7228 ■ *Web:* www.pcusa.org	Louisville	KY	40202	502-569-5000	569-5018
Prince of Peace United Methodist Church of Elk Grove Village 1400 S Arlington Heights Rd *Web:* princeofpeaceumc.org	Elk Grove Village	IL	60007	847-439-0668	439-0715
Progressive National Baptist Convention Inc (PNBC) 601 50th St NE *TF:* 800-876-7622 ■ *Web:* www.pnbc.org	Washington	DC	20019	202-396-0558	398-4998
Promise Keepers (PK) PO Box 11798 **Fax Area Code:* 303 ■ *TF:* 866-776-6473 ■ *Web:* promisekeepers.org	Denver	CO	80211	866-776-6473	433-1036*
Rabbinical Assembly 3080 Broadway *Web:* www.rabbinicalassembly.org	New York	NY	10027	212-280-6000	
Reconstructionist Rabbinical Assn (RRA) 1299 Church Rd *Web:* www.therra.org	Wyncote	PA	19095	215-576-5210	576-8051
Redeemer Lutheran Church of Waverly Bremer County Iowa 2001 W Bremer Ave *Web:* redeemerwaverly.org	Waverly	IA	50677	319-352-1325	
Redemptorist, The One Liguori Dr *Web:* www.liguori.org	Liguori	MO	63057	636-464-2500	
Reformed Church in America 475 Riverside Dr 18th Fl *TF:* 800-722-9977 ■ *Web:* www.rca.org	New York	NY	10115	212-870-3071	870-2499
Reid Temple African Methodist Episcopal Church 11400 Glenn Dale Blvd *Web:* reidtemple.org	Glenn Dale	MD	20769	301-352-0320	
Revival Slavic Christian Center of The Assemblies of God 5601 Hemlock St *Web:* revivalscc.com	Sacramento	CA	95841	916-332-2897	
Rio Grande Bible Institute & Language School 4300 S Us Hwy 281 *Web:* www.riogrande.edu	Edinburg	TX	78539	956-380-8100	
Rock Family Worship Center, The 2300 Memorial Pkwy SW *Web:* www.therockfwc.org	Huntsville	AL	35801	256-533-9292	
Saint Luke Baptist Church 476 Glen Iris Dr Ne	Atlanta	GA	30308	404-688-0528	
Seat of the Soul Foundation PO Box 3310 *TF:* 877-733-4279 ■ *Web:* www.seatofthesoul.com	Ashland	OR	97520	541-482-1515	482-9417
Seventh-day Adventist World Church 12501 Old Columbia Pike *TF:* 800-226-1119 ■ *Web:* www.adventist.org	Silver Spring	MD	20904	301-680-6000	680-6090
Shandon Baptist Church 5250 Forest Dr *Web:* www.shandon.org	Columbia	SC	29206	803-782-1300	
Sim USA Inc PO Box 7900 **Fax Area Code:* 704 ■ *TF:* 800-521-6449 ■ *Web:* www.simusa.org	Charlotte	NC	28241	800-521-6449	587-1518*
Sisters of Mercy of The Americas Northeast Community Inc 55 E Cedar St	Newington	CT	06111	860-594-8619	
Sisters of Saint Francis 1545 S Layton Blvd *Web:* www.lbwn.org	Milwaukee	WI	53215	414-383-9038	
Sisters of st Francis of Assisi of 3221 S Lake Dr *Web:* lakeosfs.org	Saint Francis	WI	53235	414-744-1160	
Sisters of The Presentation 281 Masonic Ave *Web:* www.presentationsisterssf.org	San Francisco	CA	94118	415-422-5001	
Sixth & i Historic Synagogue 600 I St NW *Web:* sixthandi.org	Washington	DC	20001	202-408-3100	

Phone | Fax

Smith Chapel Free Will Baptist Church
519 Boundary Ln ... Fayetteville NC 28301 910-483-4437

Society of Biblical Literature (SBL)
The Luce Ctr 825 Houston Mill Rd ... Atlanta GA 30329 404-727-3100 727-3101
TF: 866-727-9955 ■ *Web:* www.sbl-site.org

Southern Baptist Convention (SBC)
901 Commerce St ... Nashville TN 37203 615-244-2355 742-8919
Web: www.sbc.net

St Athanasius Rectory 2050 E Walnut Ln ... Philadelphia PA 19138 215-548-2700
Web: stathanasiuschurch.us

St Barnabas Episcopal Church in The City of Lafayette
400 Camellia Blvd ... Lafayette LA 70503 337-984-3848
Web: saintbarnabas.us

St Benedict's Monastery 104 Chapel Ln ... St Joseph MN 56374 320-363-7116
Web: sbm.osb.org

St Brendans Church 333 E 206th St ... Bronx NY 10467 718-547-6655
Web: saintbrendanchurch.org

St David's Episcopal Church & School
1300 Wiltshire Ave ... San Antonio TX 78209 210-824-2481
Web: saintdavids.net

St George Greek Orthodox Church
1200 Klockner Rd ... Trenton NJ 08619 609-586-4448
Web: stgeorgetrenton.nj.goarch.org

St John Lutheran Church 1140 W River Rd N ... Elyria OH 44035 440-324-4070
Web: stjohnlutheran-elyria.org

St Johns Ev Lutheran Church & School
20801 W Forest View Dr ... Lannon WI 53046 262-251-2910

St Marks Evangelical Lutheran Church of North st Paul Minnesota Paul Minn
2499 Helen St N ... Saint Paul MN 55109 651-777-7451
Web: stmarks-nsp.org

St Mary Missionary Baptist Church of Plant City
1840 E State Rd 60 ... Plant City FL 33567 813-737-3668

St Mary's Catholic Church 120 E Miller St ... Alpena MI 49707 989-354-2322

St Matthews Parish School
1031 Bienveneda Ave ... Pacific Palisades CA 90272 310-454-1350
Web: www.stmatthewsschool.com

St Peter The Apostle Church
19851 Anita St ... Harper Woods MI 48225 313-886-1770

St Stephens Episcopal Church 351 Main St ... Ridgefield CT 06877 203-438-3789
Web: www.ststephens-ridgefield.org

St Thomas Aquinas Catholic Newman Center at Unlv
4765 Brussels St ... Las Vegas NV 89119 702-736-0887

Sun Valley Community Church 456 E Ray Rd ... Gilbert AZ 85296 480-632-8920
Web: www.sunvalleycc.com

Sunrise Community Evangelical Free Church Inc
298 Aquatic Dr ... Atlantic Beach FL 32233 904-249-3030
Web: sccjax.org

TD Jakes Ministries 3635 Dan Morton Dr ... Dallas TX 75236 972-780-9621
Web: tdjakes.org

Tennessee Baptist Convention
5001 Maryland Way ... Brentwood TN 37027 615-371-2029
TF: 800-558-2090 ■ *Web:* www.tnbaptist.org

Texas Presbyterian Foundation
3500 Oak Lawn Ave Ste 300 ... Dallas TX 75219 214-522-3155 522-3157
TF: 800-955-3155 ■ *Web:* www.tpf.org

Thankful Baptist Church
1608 W Allegheny Ave ... Philadelphia PA 19132 215-229-5024

Third Millennium Ministries
316 Live Oaks Blvd ... Casselberry FL 32707 407-830-0222
Web: www.thirdmill.org

Traditional Values Coalition (TVC)
139 C St SE ... Washington DC 20003 202-547-8570 546-6403
Web: www.traditionalvalues.org

Union for Reformed Judaism 633 Third Ave ... New York NY 10017 212-650-4000 650-4159
Web: www.urj.org

Unitarian Universalist Assn (UUA) 25 Beacon St ... Boston MA 02108 617-742-2100 367-3237
Web: www.uua.org

United Church of Christ (UCC)
700 Prospect Ave ... Cleveland OH 44115 216-736-2100 736-2103
TF: 866-822-8224 ■ *Web:* www.ucc.org

United Church of God an International Assocation
555 Techne Ctr Dr ... Milford OH 45150 513-576-9796
Web: www.ucg.org

United Methodist Retirement & Health Care Center Inc, The
2316 W Modelle Ave ... Clinton OK 73601 580-323-0912
Web: umhcc-clinton.com

United Pentecostal Church International (UPCI)
8855 Dunn Rd ... Hazelwood MO 63042 314-837-7300 837-4503
Web: www.upci.org

United Synagogue of Conservative Judaism (USCJ)
820 Second Ave ... New York NY 10017 212-533-7800 353-9439
Web: www.uscj.org

Urban Alternative PO Box 4000 ... Dallas TX 75208 214-943-3868 943-2632
TF: 800-800-3222 ■ *Web:* www.tonyevans.org

US Conference of Catholic Bishops (USCCB)
3211 Fourth St NE ... Washington DC 20017 202-541-3000 541-3322
TF: 866-582-0943 ■ *Web:* www.usccb.org

US National Committee to the International Dairy Federation
PO Box 930398 ... Verona WI 53593 608-219-4115 262-1278
Web: www.usnac.org

Vanguard Communications of Falls Church Inc
2121 K St NW Ste 650 ... Washington DC 20037 202-331-4323
Web: www.vancomm.com

Voice of God Recordings Inc, The
5911 Charlestown Pk ... Jeffersonville IN 47130 812-256-1177
Web: www.branham.org

Watchtower Bible & Tract Society Inc
25 Columbia Heights ... Brooklyn NY 11201 718-560-5000
Web: www.jw.org

Welborn Baptist Foundation Inc
21 SE 3rd St Ste 610 ... Evansville IN 47708 812-437-8260 437-8269
Web: welbornfdn.org

Wesbury United Methodist Community
31 N Park Ave ... Meadville PA 16335 814-332-9000
Web: www.wesbury.com

Westside Baptist Church Inc of Haines City
1416 Polk City Rd ... Haines City FL 33844 863-422-4720

Westwood Baptist Church 41 State Farm Rd ... Alexandria AL 36250 256-820-2211
Web: www.westwoodbaptist.net

Westwood Community Church 401 Wwood Dr ... Winnipeg MB R3K1G4 204-888-1771
Web: westwood.mb.ca

Wheat Ridge Ministries One Pierce Pl Ste 250E ... Itasca IL 60143 630-766-9066 766-9622
TF: 800-762-6748 ■ *Web:* www.wheatridge.org

White Chapel Church of God Inc
1730 S Ridgewood Ave ... South Daytona FL 32119 386-760-6834
Web: www.wcaeagles.org

Wider Church Ministries
700 Prospect Ave Seventh Fl ... Cleveland OH 44115 216-736-3200 736-3203
TF: 866-822-8224 ■ *Web:* www.ucc.org

Wisconsin Evangelical Lutheran Synod (WELS)
2929 N Mayfair Rd ... Milwaukee WI 53222 414-256-3888 256-3899
Web: www.wels.net

Woman's Missionary Union (WMU)
100 Missionary Ridge ... Birmingham AL 35242 205-991-8100 991-4990
TF: 800-968-7301 ■ *Web:* www.wmu.com

Women in Touch Ministries Wit Inc
1044 W 37th St ... Indianapolis IN 46208 317-925-4177

Word of Faith Family Worship Cathedral
212 Riverside Pkwy ... Austell GA 30168 770-874-8400
Web: woffamily.org

Word of Life Fellowship Church Inc, The
3650 Greenbush St ... Lafayette IN 47905 765-449-4008

World Gospel Mission (WGM)
3783 E State Rd 18 PO Box 948 ... Marion IN 46952 765-664-7331 671-7230
TF: 800-426-0846 ■ *Web:* www.wgm.org

World Literature CrUSAde
640 Chapel Hills Dr ... Colorado Springs CO 80920 719-260-8888
Web: ehc.org

World Methodist Council PO Box 518 ... Lake Junaluska NC 28745 828-456-9432 456-9433
Web: www.worldmethodistcouncil.org

WorldVenture 1501 W Mineral Ave ... Littleton CO 80120 720-283-2000 283-9383
TF: 800-487-4224 ■ *Web:* www.worldventure.com

Worship Center Christian Church, The
9553 Pkwy E ... Birmingham AL 35215 205-451-1750
Web: www.theworshipcentercc.org

Wycliffe Bible Translators
11221 John Wycliffe Blvd ... Orlando FL 32832 407-852-3600 852-3601
TF: 800-992-5433 ■ *Web:* www.wycliffe.org

Yogi Divine Society 2437 Yeoman St ... Waukegan IL 60087 847-336-6451

Young Israel of New Rochelle 1149 N Ave ... New Rochelle NY 10804 914-636-2215
TF: 888-942-3638 ■ *Web:* www.youngisrael.org

Young Life 420 N Cascade Ave ... Colorado Springs CO 80903 719-381-1800
Web: www.younglife.org

Youth for Christ/USA 7670 S Vaughn Ct ... Englewood CO 80112 303-843-9000 843-9002
Web: securegive.yfc.net

48-21 Self-Help Organizations

Phone | Fax

Adult Children of Alcoholics World Service Organization Inc (ACAWSO)
PO Box 3216 ... Torrance CA 90510 562-595-7831
Web: www.adultchildren.org

Al-Anon Family Group Inc
1600 Corporate Landing Pkwy ... Virginia Beach VA 23454 757-563-1600 563-1655
TF: 888-425-2666 ■ *Web:* www.al-anon.org

Alcoholics Anonymous (AA)
475 Riverside Dr 11th Fl ... New York NY 10115 212-870-3400 870-3003
Web: www.aa.org

ARTS Anonymous PO Box 230175 ... New York NY 10023 718-251-3828
Web: www.artsanonymous.org

Bereaved Parents of the USA PO Box 95 ... Park Forest IL 60466 708-748-7866
Web: www.bereavedparentsusa.org

Calix Society, The 3881 Highland Ave Ste 201 ... St Paul MN 55110 651-773-3117
TF: 800-398-0524 ■ *Web:* www.calixsociety.org

Candlelighters Childhood Cancer Foundation
10920 Connecticut Ave Suuite A PO Box 498 ... Kensington MD 20895 301-962-3520 962-3521
TF: 800-366-2223 ■ *Web:* www.acco.org

Chemically Dependent Anonymous (CDA)
PO Box 423 ... Severna Park MD 21146 888-232-4673
TF: 888-232-4673 ■ *Web:* cdawebsitedev.com

Children of Lesbians & Gays Everywhere (COLAGE)
1550 Bryant St Ste 830 ... San Francisco CA 94103 415-861-5437 255-8345
TF: 855-426-5243 ■ *Web:* www.colage.org

Co-Anon Family Groups PO Box 12722 ... Tucson AZ 85732 520-513-5028
TF: 800-898-9985 ■ *Web:* www.co-anon.org

Co-Dependents Anonymous Inc (CODA) PO Box 33577 Phoenix AZ 85067 602-277-7991
Web: www.codependents.org

Cocaine Anonymous World Services Inc (CA)
3740 Overland Ave Ste C ... Los Angeles CA 90034 310-559-5833 559-2554
TF: 800-347-8998 ■ *Web:* www.ca.org

Community Teamwork Inc 155 Merrimack St ... Lowell MA 01852 978-459-0551
Web: www.comteam.org

Compassionate Friends PO Box 3696 ... Oak Brook IL 60522 630-990-0010 990-0246
TF: 877-969-0010 ■ *Web:* www.compassionatefriends.org

Compulsive Eaters Anonymous - HOW (CEA-HOW)
5500 E Atherton St Ste 227B ... Long Beach CA 90815 562-342-9344
Web: www.ceahow.org

Concerned United Birthparents Inc (CUB)
PO Box 503475 ... San Diego CA 92150 800-822-2777 712-3317*
**Fax Area Code: 858* ■ *TF:* 800-822-2777 ■ *Web:* www.cubirthparents.org

Concerns of Police Survivors Inc (COPS)
846 Old S 5 PO Box 3199 ... Camdenton MO 65020 573-346-4911 346-1414
TF: 800-784-2677 ■ *Web:* www.nationalcops.org

				Phone	Fax

Crystal Meth Anonymous General Service Organization (CMA)
4470 W Sunset Blvd Ste 107 PO Box 555 ... Los Angeles CA 90027 877-262-6691
TF: 877-262-6691 ■ *Web:* www.crystalmeth.org

Debtors Anonymous (DA) PO Box 920888 ... Needham MA 02492 781-453-2743 453-2745
TF: 800-421-2383 ■ *Web:* www.debtorsanonymous.org

Depressed Anonymous PO Box 17414 ... Louisville KY 40217 502-569-1989
Web: www.depressedanon.com

DignityUSA Inc PO Box 376 ... Medford MA 02155 202-861-0017 397-0584*
**Fax Area Code:* 781 ■ *TF:* 800-877-8797 ■ *Web:* www.dignityusa.org

Food Addicts In Recovery Anonymous (FA)
400 W Cummings Pk Ste 1700 ... Woburn MA 01801 781-932-6300 932-6322
Web: www.foodaddicts.org

Gam-Anon International Service Office Inc
PO Box 157 ... Whitestone NY 11357 718-352-1671 746-2571
Web: www.gam-anon.org

Gamblers Anonymous (GA) PO Box 17173 ... Los Angeles CA 90017 626-960-3500 960-3501
TF: 888-424-3577 ■ *Web:* www.gamblersanonymous.org

GROW Inc 2403 W Springfield Ave PO Box 3667 ... Champaign IL 61826 217-352-6989 352-8530
Web: www.growinamerica.org

HEARTBEAT/Survivors After Suicide Inc
2015 Devon St ... Colorado Springs CO 80909 719-596-2575
Web: www.heartbeatsurvivorsaftersuicide.org

Incest Survivors Anonymous (ISA)
PO Box 17245 ... Long Beach CA 90807 562-428-5599
Web: www.lafn.org/medical/isa

International Lawyers in Alcoholics Anonymous (ILAA)
415-1080 Mainland St ... Vancouver BC V6B2T4 604-685-2171
Web: www.ilaa.org

Jewish Alcoholics Chemically Dependent Persons & Significant Others
135 W 50th St 6th Fl ... New York NY 10020 212-632-4600 399-3525
Web: www.jacsweb.org

LifeRing Secular Recovery
1440 Broadway Ste 312 ... Oakland CA 94612 510-763-0779 763-1513
TF: 800-811-4142 ■ *Web:* www.lifering.org

Lightning Strike & Electric Shock Survivors International Inc (LSESSI)
PO Box 1156 ... Jacksonville NC 28541 910-346-4708
Web: www.lightning-strike.org

Marijuana Anonymous World Services (MAWS)
PO Box 7807 ... Torrance CA 90504 800-766-6779
TF: 800-766-6779 ■ *Web:* www.marijuana-anonymous.org

MISS Foundation PO Box 5333 ... Peoria AZ 85385 623-979-1000 979-1001
TF: 888-455-6477 ■ *Web:* www.missfoundation.org

Moderation Management Network Inc (MM)
22 W 27th St Fifth Fl ... New York NY 10001 212-871-0974 213-6582
Web: www.moderation.org

Native American Indian General Service Office of Alcoholics Anonymous (NAIGSO-AA)
PO Box 1253 ... Lakeside CA 92040 951-927-2626
Web: www.naigso-aa.org

Overcomers in Christ PO Box 34460 ... Omaha NE 68134 402-573-0966
TF: 866-573-0966 ■ *Web:* www.overcomersinchrist.org

Overcomers Outreach PO Box 922950 ... Sylmar CA 91392 818-833-1803 833-1546
TF: 800-310-3001 ■ *Web:* www.overcomersoutreach.org

Overeaters Anonymous Inc (OA) PO Box 44020 ... Rio Rancho NM 87174 505-891-2664 891-4320
TF: 866-505-4966 ■ *Web:* www.oa.org

Rest Ministries Inc PO Box 502928 ... San Diego CA 92150 858-486-4685 933-1078*
**Fax Area Code:* 800 ■ *Web:* www.restministries.com

S-Anon International Family Groups Inc
PO Box 111242 ... Nashville TN 37222 615-833-3152
TF: 800-210-8141 ■ *Web:* www.sanon.org

Secular Organizations for Sobriety (SOS)
4773 Hollywood Blvd ... Hollywood CA 90027 323-666-4295 666-4271
Web: www.cfiwest.org/sos

Sex & Love Addicts Anonymous (SLAA)
1550 NE Loop 410 Ste 118 ... San Antonio TX 78209 210-828-7900 828-7922
Web: www.slaafws.org

Sex Addicts Anonymous (SAA) PO Box 70949 ... Houston TX 77270 713-869-4902 692-0105
TF: 800-477-8191 ■ *Web:* www.saa-recovery.org

Sexaholics Anonymous (SA) PO Box 3565 ... Brentwood TN 37024 615-370-6062 370-0882
TF: 866-424-8777 ■ *Web:* www.sa.org

SHARE Pregnancy & Infant Loss Support Inc
402 Jackson St ... Saint Charles MO 63301 636-947-6164 947-7486
TF: 800-821-6819 ■ *Web:* www.nationalshare.org

Single Mothers by Choice Inc (SMC) PO Box 1642 ... New York NY 10028 212-988-0993
Web: www.singlemothersbychoice.org

Sisters Network Inc 2922 Rosedale St ... Houston TX 77004 713-781-0255 780-8998
TF: 866-781-1808 ■ *Web:* www.sistersnetworkinc.org

SMART Recovery 7304 Mentor Ave Ste F ... Mentor OH 44060 440-951-5357 951-5358
TF: 866-951-5357 ■ *Web:* www.smartrecovery.org

Straight Spouse Network (SSN) PO Box 507 ... Mahwah NJ 07430 773-413-8213
Web: www.straightspouse.org

Survivors Network of Those Abused by Priests (SNAP)
PO Box 6416 ... Chicago IL 60680 312-455-1499
TF: 877-762-7432 ■ *Web:* www.snapnetwork.org

Survivors of Incest Anonymous (SIA) PO Box 190 ... Benson MD 21018 410-893-3322
Web: www.siawso.org/

TOPS Club Inc 4575 S Fifth St ... Milwaukee WI 53207 414-482-4620 482-1655
TF: 800-932-8677 ■ *Web:* www.tops.org

Twinless Twins Support Group International (TTSG)
PO Box 980481 ... Ypsilanti MI 48198 888-205-8962
TF: 888-205-8962 ■ *Web:* www.twinlesstwins.org

Valley of the Sun United Way
1515 E Osborn Rd ... Phoenix AZ 85014 602-631-4800 631-4809
TF: 877-322-8228 ■ *Web:* www.vsuw.org

White Bison Inc 701 N 20th St ... Colorado Springs CO 80904 719-548-1000 548-9407
TF: 877-871-1495 ■ *Web:* www.whitebison.org

Wings Foundation (WINGS)
7550 W Yale Ave Ste B 201 ... Denver CO 80227 303-238-8660 238-4739
TF: 800-373-8671 ■ *Web:* www.wingsfound.org

Women for Sobriety Inc (WFS) PO Box 618 ... Quakertown PA 18951 215-536-8026 538-9026
Web: www.womenforsobriety.org

Workaholics Anonymous World Service Organization
PO Box 289 ... Menlo Park CA 94026 510-273-9253
Web: www.workaholics-anonymous.org

48-22 Sports Organizations

				Phone	Fax

Adventure Cycling Assn
150 E Pine St PO Box 8308 ... Missoula MT 59807 406-721-1776 721-8754
TF: 800-755-2453 ■ *Web:* www.adventurecycling.org

Aerobics & Fitness Assn of America (AFAA)
15250 Ventura Blvd Ste 200 ... Sherman Oaks CA 91403 818-905-0040 990-5468
TF: 877-968-7263 ■ *Web:* www.afaa.com

Amateur Athletic Union of the US (AAU)
1910 Hotel Plaza Blvd ... Lake Buena Vista FL 32830 407-934-7200 934-7242
TF: 800-228-4872 ■ *Web:* www.aausports.org

Amateur Softball Assn of America Inc (ASA)
2801 NE 50th St ... Oklahoma City OK 73111 405-424-5266 424-3855
TF: 800-654-8337 ■ *Web:* www.asasoftball.com

Amateur Trapshooting Assn (ATA)
601 W National Rd ... Vandalia OH 45377 937-898-4638 898-5472
TF: 800-671-8042 ■ *Web:* www.shootata.com

American Alliance for Health Physical Education Recreation & Dance (AAH-PERD)
1900 Assn Dr ... Reston VA 20191 703-476-3400 476-9527
TF: 800-213-7193 ■ *Web:* shapeamerica.org

American Amateur Baseball Congress (AABC)
100 W Broadway ... Farmington NM 87401 505-327-3120 327-3132
TF: 800-853-2414 ■ *Web:* www.aabc.us

American Baseball Coaches Assn (ABCA)
108 S University Ave Ste 3 ... Mount Pleasant MI 48858 989-775-3300 775-3600
Web: www.abca.org

American Bicycle Assn (ABA) 1645 W Sunrise Blvd ... Gilbert AZ 85233 480-961-1903 961-1842
TF: 866-650-4867 ■ *Web:* www.usabmx.com

American Canoe Assn (ACA)
503 Sophia St Ste 100 ... Fredericksburg VA 22401 540-907-4460 229-3792*
**Fax Area Code:* 888 ■ *Web:* www.americancanoe.org

American Council on Exercise (ACE)
4851 Paramount Dr ... San Diego CA 92123 858-576-6500 576-6564
TF: 800-825-3636 ■ *Web:* www.acefitness.org

American Football Coaches Assn (AFCA)
100 Legends Ln ... Waco TX 76706 254-754-9900 754-7373
TF: 877-557-5338 ■ *Web:* www.afca.com

American Poolplayers Assn Inc (APA)
1000 Lk St Louis Blvd Ste 325 ... Lake Saint Louis MO 63367 636-625-8611 625-2975
Web: www.poolplayers.com

American Running Assn 4405 E W Hwy Ste 405 ... Bethesda MD 20814 301-913-9517 913-9520
TF: 800-776-2732 ■ *Web:* www.americanrunning.org

American Society of Golf Course Architects (ASGCA)
125 N Executive Dr Ste 106 ... Brookfield WI 53005 262-786-5960 786-5919
Web: www.asgca.org

American Sportfishing Assn (ASA)
1001 N Fairfax St Ste 501 ... Alexandria VA 22314 703-519-9691 519-1872
Web: www.asafishing.org

American Sports Institute (ASI)
116 E Blithedale Ave ... Mill Valley CA 94941 415-383-5750
Web: www.amersports.org

American Volkssport Assn (AVA)
1001 Pat Booker Rd Ste 101 ... Universal City TX 78148 210-659-2112 659-1212
TF: 855-999-5200 ■ *Web:* www.ava.org

American Youth Soccer Organization (AYSO)
19750 S Vermont Ave Ste 200 ... Torrance CA 90502 800-872-2976 525-1155*
**Fax Area Code:* 310 ■ *TF:* 800-872-2976 ■ *Web:* ayso.org

AMOA-National Dart Assn (NDA)
9100 PuRdue Rd Ste 200 ... Indianapolis IN 46268 317-387-1299 387-0999
TF: 800-808-9884 ■ *Web:* www.ndadarts.com

Association of Professional Ball Players of America
101 S Kraemer Ave Ste 112 ... Placentia CA 92870 714-528-2012 528-2037
Web: www.apbpa.org

Association of Surfing Professionals (ASP)
PO Box 309 ... Huntington Beach CA 92648 714-536-3500 536-4482
Web: www.aspworldtour.com

ATP Tour Inc 201 ATP Tour Blvd ... Ponte Vedra Beach FL 32082 904-285-8000 285-5966
Web: www.atpworldtour.com

Babe Ruth League Inc
1770 Brunswick Pk PO Box 5000 ... Trenton NJ 08638 609-695-1434 695-2505
TF: 800-880-3142 ■ *Web:* www.baberuthleague.org

Billiard Congress of America
12303 Airport Way Ste 140 ... Broomfield CO 80021 303-243-5070 243-5075
Web: bca-pool.com/?

Boat Owners Assn of the US
880 S Pickett St ... Alexandria VA 22304 703-823-9550 461-2847
TF: 800-395-2628 ■ *Web:* www.boatus.com

Cross Country Ski Areas Assn (CCSAA)
259 Bolton Rd ... Winchester NH 03470 603-239-4341 239-6387
TF: 877-779-2754 ■ *Web:* www.xcski.org

Disabled Sports USA (DS/USA)
451 Hungerford Dr Ste 100 ... Rockville MD 20850 301-217-0960 217-0968
TF: 800-543-2754 ■ *Web:* www.disabledsportsusa.org

Fellowship of Christian Athletes (FCA)
8701 Leeds Rd ... Kansas City MO 64129 816-921-0909 921-8755
TF: 800-289-0909 ■ *Web:* www.fca.org

Hockey North America (HNA) 45570 Shepard Dr ... Sterling VA 20164 703-430-8100 421-9205
TF: 800-446-2539 ■ *Web:* www.hna.com

Ice Skating Institute (ISI) 6000 Custer Rd Bldg 9 ... Plano TX 75023 972-735-8800 735-8815
Web: www.skateisi.com

IDEA Inc 10455 Pacific Ctr Ct ... San Diego CA 92121 858-535-8979 535-8234
TF: 800-999-4332 ■ *Web:* www.ideafit.com

International Assn of Approved Basketball Officials (IAABO)
PO Box 355 ... Carlisle PA 17013 717-713-8129 718-6164
TF: 800-526-1379 ■ *Web:* www.iaabo.org

International Collegiate Licensing Assn (ICLA)
24651 Detroit Rd ... Westlake OH 44145 440-892-4000 892-4007
TF: 877-887-2261 ■ *Web:* www.nacda.com/icla/nacda-icla.html

International Health Racquet & Sportsclub Assn (IHRSA)
70 Fargo St ... Boston MA 02210 617-951-0055 951-0056
TF: 800-228-4772 ■ *Web:* www.ihrsa.org

Phone | Fax

International Professional Rodeo Assn (IPRA)
1412 South Agnew .... Oklahoma City OK 73108 405-235-6540
Web: www.iprarodeo.com

Jockey Club 40 E 52nd St 15th Fl .... New York NY 10022 212-371-5970 371-6123
Web: www.jockeyclub.com

Jockeys' Guild Inc
103 Wind Haven Dr Ste 200 .... Nicholasville KY 40356 859-305-0606 219-9892
TF: 866-465-6257 ■ *Web:* www.jockeysguild.com

Ladies Professional Golf Assn (LPGA)
100 International Golf Dr .... Daytona Beach FL 32124 386-274-6200 274-1099
Web: www.lpga.com

League of American Bicyclists
1612 K St NW Ste 800 .... Washington DC 20006 202-822-1333 822-1334
Web: www.bikeleague.org

Little League Baseball Inc
539 US Rt 15 Hwy PO Box 3485 .... Williamsport PA 17701 570-326-1921 326-1074
Web: www.littleleague.org

Maccabi USA/Sports for Israel
1926 Arch St Ste 4R .... Philadelphia PA 19103 215-561-6900 561-5470
Web: www.maccabiusa.com

Major League Baseball Players Assn
12 E 49th St 24th Fl .... New York NY 10017 212-826-0808 752-4378
Web: mlbplayers.mlb.com/nasapp/mlb/pa

Minor League Baseball
201 Bayshore Dr SE .... Saint Petersburg FL 33701 727-822-6937 821-5819
Web: www.milb.com

NA for Stock Car Auto Racing (NASCAR)
1801 W International Speedway Blvd .... Daytona Beach FL 32114 386-253-0611 252-8804*
**Fax:* Mktg ■ *Web:* www.nascar.com

NA of Collegiate Directors of Athletics (NACDA)
24651 Detroit Rd .... Westlake OH 44145 440-892-4000 892-4007
TF: 877-887-2261 ■ *Web:* www.nacda.com

NA of Intercollegiate Athletics (NAIA)
1200 Grand Blvd .... Kansas City MO 64106 816-595-8000 595-8200
Web: www.naia.org

National Aeronautic Assn
Hanger 7 1 S Smith Blvd Ste 202 .... Arlington VA 22202 703-416-4888
TF: 800-644-9777 ■ *Web:* naa.aero

National Alliance for Youth Sports
2050 Vista Pkwy .... West Palm Beach FL 33411 561-684-1141 684-2546
TF: 800-729-2057 ■ *Web:* www.nays.org

National Athletic Trainers Assn (NATA)
2952 N Stemmons Fwy Ste 200 .... Dallas TX 75247 214-637-6282 637-2206
TF: 800-879-6282 ■ *Web:* www.nata.org

National Basketball Players Assn (NBPA)
310 Malcolm X Blvd .... New York NY 10027 212-655-0880 655-0881
Web: www.nbpa.com

National Collegiate Athletic Assn (NCAA)
700 W Washington St PO Box 6222 .... Indianapolis IN 46206 317-917-6222 917-6888
Web: www.ncaa.org

National Ctr for Bicycling & Walking (NCBW)
8120 Woodmont Ave Ste 520 .... Bethesda MD 20814 202-223-3621 656-4225*
**Fax Area Code:* 301 ■ *Web:* www.bikewalk.org

National Federation of State High School Assn (NFHS)
PO Box 690 .... Indianapolis IN 46206 317-972-6900 822-5700
TF Cust Svc: 800-776-3462 ■ *Web:* www.nfhs.org

National Football League Players (NFLPA)
1133 20th St NW .... Washington DC 20036 202-463-2200
Web: www.nflplayers.com

National Golf Foundation (NGF)
1150 S US Hwy 1 Ste 401 .... Jupiter FL 33477 561-744-6006 744-6107
TF: 800-733-6006 ■ *Web:* www.ngf.org

National Greyhound Assn (NGA) 729 Old US 40 .... Abilene KS 67410 785-263-4660 263-4689
Web: www.ngagreyhounds.com

National Hockey League Players Assn (NHLPA)
20 Bay St Ste 1700 .... Toronto ON M5J2N8 416-907-9801 313-2301
Web: www.nhlpa.com

National Intramural-Recreational Sports Assn (NIRSA)
4185 SW Research Way .... Corvallis OR 97333 541-766-8211 766-8284
Web: www.nirsa.org

National Junior College Athletic Assn (NJCAA)
1755 Telstar Dr Ste 103 .... Colorado Springs CO 80920 719-590-9788 590-7324
Web: www.njcaa.org

National Little Britches Rodeo Assn (NLBRA)
5050 Edison Ave Ste 105 .... Colorado Springs CO 80915 719-389-0333 578-1367
TF: 800-763-3694 ■ *Web:* www.nlbra.org

National Senior Golf Assn (NSGA)
200 Perrine Rd Ste 201 .... Old Bridge NJ 08857 800-282-6772 525-9590*
**Fax Area Code:* 732 ■ *TF:* 800-282-6772 ■ *Web:* www.nationalseniorgolf.com

National Shooting Sports Foundation (NSSF)
11 Mile Hill Rd .... Newtown CT 06470 203-426-1320 426-1087
Web: www.nssf.org

National Soccer Coaches Assn of America (NSCAA)
800 Ann Ave .... Kansas City KS 66101 913-362-1747 362-3439
TF: 800-458-0678 ■ *Web:* www.nscaa.com

National Strength & Conditioning Assn (NSCA)
1885 Bob Johnson Dr .... Colorado Springs CO 80906 719-632-6722 632-6367
TF: 800-815-6826 ■ *Web:* www.nsca.com

National Thoroughbred Racing Assn (NTRA)
2525 Harrodsburg Rd Ste 500 .... Lexington KY 40504 859-223-5444 223-3945
TF: 800-792-6872 ■ *Web:* www.ntra.com

National Tractor Pullers Assn (NTPA)
6155-B Huntley Rd .... Columbus OH 43229 614-436-1761 436-0964
Web: www.ntpapull.com

National Youth Sports Coaches Assn (NYSCA)
2050 Vista Pkwy .... West Palm Beach FL 33411 561-684-1141 684-2546
TF: 800-729-2057 ■ *Web:* www.nays.org

New York Arm Wrestling Assn (NYAWA)
PO Box 670952 .... Flushing NY 11367 718-544-4592 261-8111
Web: www.nycarms.com

PGA of America
100 Ave of the Champions .... Palm Beach Gardens FL 33418 561-624-8400 624-8439
TF: 800-477-6465 ■ *Web:* www.pga.com

PGA Tour Inc 112 PGA Tour Blvd .... Ponte Vedra Beach FL 32082 904-285-3700
Web: www.pgatour.com

PONY Baseball/Softball Inc
1951 Pony Pl PO Box 225 .... Washington PA 15301 724-225-1060 225-9852
TF: 800-321-4473 ■ *Web:* www.pony.org

Pop Warner Little Scholars Inc
586 Middletown Blvd Ste C-100 .... Langhorne PA 19047 215-752-2691 752-2879
TF: 800-257-4268 ■ *Web:* www.popwarner.com

Professional Assn of Diving Instructors International (PADI)
30151 Tomas St .... Rancho Santa Margarita CA 92688 949-858-7234 267-1267
TF Sales: 800-729-7234 ■ *Web:* www.padi.com

Professional Bowlers Assn (PBA)
719 Second Ave Ste 701 .... Seattle WA 98104 206-332-9688 654-6030
TF: 877-910-2695 ■ *Web:* www.pba.com

Professional Rodeo Cowboys Assn (PRCA)
101 Pro Rodeo Dr .... Colorado Springs CO 80919 719-593-8840 548-4876
Web: www.prorodeo.com

Professional Tennis Registry
PO Box 4739 .... Hilton Head Island SC 29938 843-785-7244 686-2033
TF: 800-421-6289 ■ *Web:* www.ptrtennis.org

Roller Skating Assn International (RSAI)
6905 Corporate Dr .... Indianapolis IN 46278 317-347-2626 347-2636
Web: rollerskating.com

Senior Softball USA 2701 K St Ste 101A .... Sacramento CA 95816 916-326-5303 326-5304
TF: 888-244-9499 ■ *Web:* www.seniorsoftball.com

Special Olympics Inc
1133 19th St NW 11th Fl .... Washington DC 20036 202-628-3630 824-0200
TF: 800-700-8585 ■ *Web:* www.specialolympics.org

Sports Turf Managers Assn (STMA)
805 New Hampshire Ste E .... Lawrence KS 66044 785-843-2549 843-2977
TF: 800-323-3875 ■ *Web:* www.stma.org

Thoroughbred Racing Assn (TRA)
420 Fair Hill Dr Ste 1 .... Elkton MD 21921 410-392-9200 398-1366
Web: www.tra-online.com

United States Olympic Committee
1 Olympic Plaza .... Colorado Springs CO 80909 719-866-4567 632-0979
Web: www.teamusa.org

US Biathlon Assn
49 Pineland Dr Ste 301-A .... New Gloucester ME 04260 207-688-6500 688-6505
TF General: 800-242-8456 ■ *Web:* www.teamusa.org

US Bobsled & Skeleton Federation (USBSF)
196 Old Military Rd .... Lake Placid NY 12946 518-523-1842 523-9491
TF: 888-431-3598 ■ *Web:* www.teamusa.org

US Curling Assn (USCA) 5525 Clem's Way .... Stevens Point WI 54482 715-344-1199 344-2279
TF: 888-287-5377 ■ *Web:* teamusa.org/usa-curling

US Equestrian Federation Inc
4047 Iron Works Pkwy .... Lexington KY 40511 859-258-2472 231-6662
Web: www.usef.org

US Equestrian Team Foundation Inc (USET)
1040 Pottersville Rd PO Box 355 .... Gladstone NJ 07934 908-234-1251 234-0670
Web: www.uset.org

US Fencing Assn (USFA) 1 Olympic Plaza .... Colorado Springs CO 80909 719-866-4511 632-5737
TF: 888-431-3598 ■ *Web:* www.usfencing.org

US Figure Skating Assn (USFSA)
20 First St .... Colorado Springs CO 80906 719-635-5200 635-9548
Web: www.usfsa.org

US Golf Assn (USGA) 77 Liberty Corner Rd .... Far Hills NJ 07931 908-234-2300 234-9687
TF Orders: 800-336-4446 ■ *Web:* www.usga.org

US Luge Assn 57 Church St .... Lake Placid NY 12946 518-523-2071 523-4106
Web: www.usaluge.org

US Olympic Committee (USOC)
One Olympic Plz .... Colorado Springs CO 80909 719-632-5551 866-4677
Web: www.teamusa.org

US Parachute Assn (USPA)
5401 Southpoint Ctr Blvd .... Fredericksburg VA 22407 540-604-9740 604-9741
TF: 800-765-2336 ■ *Web:* www.uspa.org

US Professional Tennis Assn (USPTA)
3535 Briarpark Dr Ste 1 .... Houston TX 77042 713-978-7782 978-7780
TF: 800-877-8248 ■ *Web:* uspta.com

US Racquetball Assn (USRA)
1685 W Uintah St .... Colorado Springs CO 80904 719-635-5396 635-0685
Web: www.teamusa.org

US Rowing Assn Two Wall St .... Princeton NJ 08540 609-924-1578 924-1578
TF: 800-314-4769 ■ *Web:* www.usrowing.org

US Sailing Assn 15 Maritime Dr PO Box 1260 .... Portsmouth RI 02871 401-683-0800 683-0840
Web: ussailing.org

US Soccer Federation 1801 S Prairie Ave .... Chicago IL 60616 312-808-1300 808-1301
TF: 800-745-3000 ■ *Web:* www.ussoccer.com

US Synchronized Swimming
132 E Washington St Ste 800 .... Indianapolis IN 46204 317-237-5700 237-5705
TF: 800-775-8762 ■ *Web:* www.teamusa.org

US Taekwondo Union
One Olympic Plz Ste 104C .... Colorado Springs CO 80909 719-866-4632 866-4642
Web: www.teamusa.org

US Trotting Assn (USTA) 750 Michigan Ave .... Columbus OH 43215 614-224-2291 224-4575
TF: 877-800-8782 ■ *Web:* www.ustrotting.com

USA Archery (NAA) One Olympic Plz .... Colorado Springs CO 80909 719-866-4576 632-4733
Web: www.teamusa.org

USA Baseball 403 Blackwell St .... Durham NC 27701 919-474-8721 474-8822
Web: usabaseball.com

USA Basketball
5465 Mark Dabling Boulevard .... Colorado Springs CO 80918 719-590-4800 590-4811
TF: 888-284-5383 ■ *Web:* www.usab.com

USA Boxing Inc 1 Olympic Plz .... Colorado Springs CO 80909 719-228-6800 866-2132
Web: www.teamusa.org/USA-Boxing

USA Canoe/Kayak (USACK)
725 S Lincoln Blvd .... Oklahoma City OK 73129 405-552-4040
Web: www.teamusa.org

USA Cycling Inc One Olympic Plz .... Colorado Springs CO 80909 719-866-4581 866-4628
Web: www.usacycling.org

USA Diving Inc
132 E Washington St Ste 850 .... Indianapolis IN 46204 317-237-5252 237-5257
Web: www.usadiving.org

Organization / Address	City	State	Zip	Phone	Fax
USA Gymnastics 201 S Capitol Ave Ste 300	Indianapolis	IN	46225	317-237-5050	237-5069
TF: 800-345-4719 ■ *Web:* usagym.org					
USA Hockey 1775 Bob Johnson Dr	Colorado Springs	CO	80906	719-576-8724	538-1160
TF: 800-566-3288 ■ *Web:* www.usahockey.com					
USA Judo Inc 1 Olympic Plaza Ste 505	Colorado Springs	CO	80909	719-866-4730	866-4733
TF: 800-775-8762 ■ *Web:* www.teamusa.org					
USA Roller Sports 4730 S St	Lincoln	NE	68506	402-483-7551	483-1465
Web: www.teamusa.org					
USA Swimming 1 Olympic Plaza	Colorado Springs	CO	80909	719-866-4578	866-4669
TF: 800-333-3333 ■ *Web:* www.usaswimming.org					
USA Table Tennis 1 Olympic Plaza	Colorado Springs	CO	80909	719-866-4583	632-6071
TF: 800-775-8762 ■ *Web:* www.teamusa.org					
USA Track & Field (USATF)					
132 E Washington St Ste 800	Indianapolis	IN	46204	317-261-0500	261-0481
TF: 800-365-4663 ■ *Web:* www.usatf.org					
USA Triathlon 5825 Delmonico Dr	Colorado Springs	CO	80919	719-597-9090	597-2121
Web: www.usatriathlon.org					
USA Water Polo 2124 Main St Ste 210	Huntington Beach	CA	92648	714-500-5445	960-2431
TF: 888-712-2166 ■ *Web:* usawaterpolo.org/					
USA Water Ski 1251 Holy Cow Rd	Polk City	FL	33868	863-324-4341	325-8259
TF: 800-533-2972 ■ *Web:* www.usawaterski.org					
USA Weightlifting (USAW)					
1 Olympic Plaza	Colorado Springs	CO	80909	719-866-4508	866-4741
TF: 800-775-8762 ■ *Web:* www.teamusa.org					
USA Wrestling 6155 Lehman Dr	Colorado Springs	CO	80918	719-598-8181	598-9440
TF: 888-431-3598 ■ *Web:* teamusa.org/usa-wrestling/					
USAC Racing (USAC) 4910 W 16th St	Speedway	IN	46224	317-247-5151	
Web: www.usacracing.com					
Wheelchair & Ambulatory Sports USA					
PO Box 5266	Kendall Park	NJ	08824	732-266-2634	355-6500
Web: www.wasusa.org					
Women's Sports Foundation					
1899 Hempstead Tpke					
Ste 400 Eisenhower Pk	East Meadow	NY	11554	516-542-4700	542-4716
TF: 800-227-3988 ■ *Web:* www.womenssportsfoundation.org					
WTA Tour Inc					
One Progress Plz Ste 1500	Saint Petersburg	FL	33701	727-895-5000	894-1982
Web: www.wtatennis.com					

48-23 Travel & Recreation Organizations

Organization / Address	City	State	Zip	Phone	Fax
Adirondack Mountain Club 814 Goggins Rd	Lake George	NY	12845	518-668-4447	668-3746
TF Orders: 800-395-8080 ■ *Web:* www.adk.org					
Alberta Hotel & Lodging Assn (AHLA)					
2707 Ellwood Dr	Edmonton	AB	T6X0P7	780-436-6112	436-5404
TF: 888-436-6112 ■ *Web:* www.ahla.ca					
America Outdoors 5816 Kingston Pk	Knoxville	TN	37919	865-558-3595	558-3598
TF: 800-524-4814 ■ *Web:* www.americaoutdoors.org					
American Amusement Machine Assn (AAMA)					
450 E Higgins Rd Ste 201	Elk Grove Village	IL	60007	847-290-9088	290-9121
TF: 866-372-5190 ■ *Web:* www.coin-op.org					
American Assn for Physical Activity & Recreation (AAPAR)					
1900 Assn Dr	Reston	VA	20191	703-476-3400	476-9527
TF: 800-213-7193 ■ *Web:* shapeamerica.org/aapar					
American Automobile Assn Inc (AAA) 1000 AAA Dr	Heathrow	FL	32746	407-444-4240	444-4247
Web: www.aaa.com					
American Camp Assn (ACA)					
5000 State Rd 67 N	Martinsville	IN	46151	765-342-8456	342-2065
TF: 800-428-2267 ■ *Web:* www.acacamps.org					
American Gaming Assn (AGA)					
1299 Pennsylvania Ave NW Ste 1175	Washington	DC	20004	202-552-2675	552-2676
Web: www.americangaming.org					
American Hiking Society (AHS)					
1422 Fenwick Ln	Silver Spring	MD	20910	301-565-6704	565-6714
Web: www.americanhiking.org					
American Hotel & Lodging Assn (AH&LA)					
1201 New York Ave NW Ste 600	Washington	DC	20005	202-289-3100	289-3185
Web: www.ahla.com					
American Park & Recreation Society (APRS)					
22377 Belmont Ridge Rd	Ashburn	VA	20148	703-858-0784	858-0794
TF: 800-765-3110 ■ *Web:* www.arcat.com					
American Recreation Coalition (ARC)					
1225 New York Ave NW Ste 450	Washington	DC	20005	202-682-9530	682-9529
Web: www.funoutdoors.com					
American Society of Travel Agents (ASTA)					
1101 King St Ste 200	Alexandria	VA	22314	703-739-2782	684-8319
TF: 800-275-2782 ■ *Web:* www.asta.org					
American Trails PO Box 491797	Redding	CA	96049	530-547-2060	547-2035
TF: 866-363-7226 ■ *Web:* www.americantrails.org					
American Whitewater (AW) PO Box 1540	Cullowhee	NC	28723	828-586-1930	586-2840
TF: 866-262-8429 ■ *Web:* americanwhitewater.org					
Amusement & Music Operators Assn (AMOA)					
600 Spring Hill Ring Rd Ste 111	West Dundee	IL	60118	847-428-7699	428-7719
TF: 800-937-2662 ■ *Web:* www.amoa.com					
Appalachian Mountain Club (AMC) Five Joy St	Boston	MA	02108	617-523-0655	523-0722
TF Orders: 800-262-4455 ■ *Web:* www.outdoors.org					
Appalachian Trail Conservancy (ATC)					
799 Washington St PO Box 807	Harpers Ferry	WV	25425	304-535-6331	535-2667
TF Sales: 888-287-8673 ■ *Web:* appalachiantrail.org					
Association of Corporate Travel Executives (ACTE)					
515 King St Ste 440	Alexandria	VA	22314	703-683-5322	683-2720
TF: 800-375-2283 ■ *Web:* www.acte.org					
Association of Destination Management Executives (ADME)					
11 W Monument Ave	Dayton	OH	45402	937-586-3727	586-3699
Web: www.adme.org					
Back Country Horsemen of America (BCHA)					
PO Box 1367	Graham	WA	98338	360-832-2461	832-2471
TF: 888-893-5161 ■ *Web:* www.backcountryhorse.com					
Bowling Proprietors' Assn of America (BPAA)					
621 Six Flags Dr PO Box 5802	Arlington	TX	76011	817-649-5105	633-2940
TF: 800-343-1329 ■ *Web:* www.bpaa.com					
Canadian Automobile Assn (CAA)					
2151 Thurston Dr Ste 200	Ottawa	ON	K1G6C9	613-820-1890	247-0118
TF: 800-267-8713 ■ *Web:* www.caa.ca					
Canadian Parks & Recreation Assn (CPRA)					
1180 Walkley Rd PO Box 83069	Ottawa	ON	K1V2M5	613-523-5315	523-1182
Web: www.cpra.ca					
Colorado Dude & Guest Ranch Assn (CDGRA)					
PO Box D	Shawnee	CO	80475	866-942-3472	
TF: 866-942-3472 ■ *Web:* www.coloradoranch.com					
Continental Divide Trail Society (CDT)					
3704 N Charles St Ste 601	Baltimore	MD	21218	410-235-9610	243-1960
Web: www.cdtsociety.org					
Cruise Lines International Assn (CLIA)					
910 SE 17th St Ste 400	Fort Lauderdale	FL	33316	754-224-2200	224-2250
TF: 877-486-9222 ■ *Web:* www.cruising.org					
Dude Ranchers' Assn 1122 12th St PO Box 2307	Cody	WY	82414	307-587-2339	587-2776
TF: 866-399-2339 ■ *Web:* www.duderanch.org					
Elderhostel Inc 11 Ave de Lafayette	Boston	MA	02111	800-454-5768	426-2166*
**Fax Area Code:* 877 ■ *TF:* 800-454-5768 ■ *Web:* www.roadscholar.org					
Environmental Traveling Companions (ETC)					
Two Marina Blvd Bldg C	San Francisco	CA	94123	415-474-7662	474-3919
Web: www.etctrips.org					
Escapees RV Club 100 Rainbow Dr	Livingston	TX	77399	936-327-8873	327-4388
TF: 800-231-9896 ■ *Web:* www.escapees.com					
Family Campers & RVers (FCRV)					
4804 Transit Rd Bldg 2	Depew	NY	14043	716-668-6242	
Web: www.fcrv.org					
Family Motor Coach Assn (FMCA)					
8291 Clough Pk	Cincinnati	OH	45244	513-474-3622	474-2332
TF: 800-543-3622 ■ *Web:* www.fmca.com					
Global Business Travel Assn, The (GBTA)					
123 N Pitt St	Alexandria	VA	22314	703-684-0836	684-0263
TF: 888-574-6447 ■ *Web:* www.gbta.org					
Good Sam Club PO Box 6888	Englewood	CO	80155	800-234-3450	728-7306*
**Fax Area Code:* 303 ■ *TF:* 800-234-3450 ■ *Web:* www.goodsamclub.com					
Hostelling International USA - American Youth Hostels (HI-AYH)					
8401 Colesville Rd Ste 600	Silver Spring	MD	20910	301-495-1240	495-6697
TF: 800-725-2331 ■ *Web:* www.hiusa.org					
International Airline Passengers Assn (IAPA)					
PO Box 700188	Dallas	TX	75370	972-404-9980	233-5348
TF: 800-821-4272 ■ *Web:* www.iapa.com					
International Assn for Medical Assistance to Travellers (IAMAT)					
2162 Gordon St	Guelph	ON	N1L1G6	519-836-0102	836-3412
Web: www.iamat.org					
International Assn of Amusement Parks & Attractions (IAAPA)					
1448 Duke St	Alexandria	VA	22314	703-836-4800	836-6742
Web: www.iaapa.org					
International Assn of Fairs & Expositions, The (IAFE)					
3043 E Cairo	Springfield	MO	65802	417-862-5771	862-0156
TF: 800-516-0313 ■ *Web:* www.fairsandexpos.com					
International Festivals & Events Assn (IFEA)					
2603 W Eastover Terr	Boise	ID	83706	208-433-0950	433-9812
Web: www.ifea.com					
International Gay & Lesbian Travel Assn (IGLTA)					
1201 NE 26th St Ste 103	Fort Lauderdale	FL	33305	954-630-1637	630-1652
TF: 866-845-4472 ■ *Web:* www.iglta.org					
International Mountain Bicycling Assn (IMBA)					
207 Canyon Blvd Ste 301 PO Box 7578	Boulder	CO	80306	303-545-9011	545-9026
TF: 888-442-4622 ■ *Web:* www.imba.com					
Leave No Trace Ctr for Outdoor Ethics Inc					
1830 17th St	Boulder	CO	80302	303-442-8222	442-8217
TF: 800-332-4100 ■ *Web:* www.lnt.org					
Lewis & Clark Trail Heritage Foundation					
4201 Giant Springs Rd	Great Falls	MT	59405	406-454-1234	771-9237
TF: 888-701-3434 ■ *Web:* www.lewisandclark.org					
Lincoln Highway Assn 136 N Elm St	Franklin Grove	IL	61031	815-456-3030	
Web: www.lincolnhighwayassoc.org					
Loners on Wheels (LOW) 1795 O'Kelley Rd SE	Deming	NM	88030	575-544-7303	546-1350
Web: www.lonersonwheels.com					
Mountaineers, The 7700 Sand Pt Way NE	Seattle	WA	98115	206-521-6000	523-6763
TF: 800-573-8484 ■ *Web:* www.mountaineers.org					
National Club Assn (NCA)					
1201 15th St NW Ste 450	Washington	DC	20005	202-822-9822	822-9808
TF: 800-625-6221 ■ *Web:* nationalclub.org					
National Forest Recreation Assn (NFRA)					
PO Box 488	Woodlake	CA	93286	559-564-2365	564-2048
TF: 800-282-2444 ■ *Web:* www.nfra.org					
National Golf Course Owners Assn (NGCOA)					
291 Seven Farms Dr Second Fl	Charleston	SC	29492	843-881-9956	881-9958
TF: 800-933-4262 ■ *Web:* www.ngcoa.org					
National Indian Gaming Assn (NIGA)					
224 Second St SE	Washington	DC	20003	202-546-7711	546-1755
TF: 866-694-3937 ■ *Web:* www.indiangaming.org					
National Recreation and Park Association (NSPR)					
22377 Belmont Ridge Rd					
22377 Belmont Ridge Rd	Ashburn	VA	20148	703-858-0784	858-0794
TF: 800-626-6772 ■ *Web:* www.nrpa.org					
National Ski Areas Assn (NSAA)					
133 S Van Gordon St Ste 300	Lakewood	CO	80228	303-987-1111	986-2345
Web: www.nsaa.org					
National Tour Assn (NTA) 546 E Main St	Lexington	KY	40508	859-226-4444	226-4404
TF: 800-682-8886 ■ *Web:* www.ntaonline.com					
North Country Trail Assn 229 E Main St	Lowell	MI	49331	616-897-5987	897-6605
TF: 866-445-3628 ■ *Web:* www.northcountrytrail.org					
Oregon-California Trails Assn					
524 S Osage St PO Box 1019	Independence	MO	64051	816-252-2276	836-0989
TF: 888-811-6282 ■ *Web:* www.octa-trails.org					
Pacific Crest Trail Assn (PCTA)					
1331 Garden Hwy	Sacramento	CA	95833	916-285-1846	285-1865
TF: 888-728-7245 ■ *Web:* www.pcta.org					
Pennsylvania AAA Federation					
600 N Third St	Harrisburg	PA	17101	717-238-7192	238-6574
Web: www.aaapa.org					

Organization	City	State	Zip	Phone	Fax
Relais & Chateaux Assn 10 E 53rd St *TF:* 800-735-2478 ■ *Web:* relaischateaux.com	New York	NY	10022	212-319-4880	319-4666
RVing Women (RVW) 879 N Plaza Dr Ste B103 *Web:* rvingwomen.org	Apache Junction	AZ	85120	480-671-6226	671-6230
Santa Fe Trail Assn 1349 K-156 Hwy *Web:* www.santafetrail.org	Larned	KS	67550	620-285-2054	
Society of Incentive & Travel Executives (SITE) 401 N Michigan Ave *Web:* www.siteglobal.com	Chicago	IL	60611	312-321-5148	527-6783
Special Military Active Retired Travel Club (SMART) 600 University Office Blvd Ste 1A *TF:* 800-354-7681 ■ *Web:* www.smartrving.net	Pensacola	FL	32504	850-478-1986	
Statue of Liberty-Ellis Island Foundation Inc, The 17 Battery Pl Ste 210 *Web:* www.statueofliberty.org	New York	NY	10004	212-561-4500	779-1990
Travel Institute 148 Linden St Ste 305 *TF:* 800-542-4282 ■ *Web:* www.thetravelinstitute.com	Wellesley	MA	02482	781-237-0280	237-3860
Washington Trails Assn (WTA) 705 Second Ave Ste 300 *Web:* www.wta.org	Seattle	WA	98121	206-625-1367	625-9249
Western National Parks Assn (WNPA) 12880 N Vistoso Village Dr *Web:* www.wnpa.org	Tucson	AZ	85755	520-622-1999	623-9519
Wilderness Inquiry (WI) 808 14th Ave SE *TF:* 800-728-0719 ■ *Web:* www.wildernessinquiry.org	Minneapolis	MN	55414	612-676-9400	676-9401

48-24 Women's Organizations

Organization	City	State	Zip	Phone	Fax
Association for Women's Rights in Development (AWID) 215 Spadina Ave Ste 150 *Web:* www.awid.org	Toronto	ON	M5T2C7	416-594-3773	594-0330
Center for Women Policy Studies 1776 Masachusetts Ave NW Ste 450 *Web:* www.centerwomenpolicy.org	Washington	DC	20036	202-872-1770	296-8962
Coalition of Labor Union Women (CLUW) 815 16th St NW Second Fl *Web:* www.cluw.org	Washington	DC	20006	202-508-6969	508-6968
Equal Rights Advocates (ERA) 1170 Market St Ste 700 *TF:* 800-839-4372 ■ *Web:* www.equalrights.org	San Francisco	CA	94102	415-621-0672	621-6744
Feminist Majority Foundation-East Coast (FMF) 1600 Wilson Blvd Ste 801 *Web:* www.feminist.org	Arlington	VA	22209	703-522-2214	522-2219
General Federation of Women's Clubs (GFWC) 1734 N St NW *TF:* 800-443-4392 ■ *Web:* www.gfwc.org	Washington	DC	20036	202-347-3168	835-0246
Girls Inc 120 Wall St Third Fl *TF:* 800-374-4475 ■ *Web:* www.girlsinc.org	New York	NY	10005	212-509-2000	509-8708
Inter-American Commission of Women (CIM) 1889 F St NW *Web:* www.oas.org/cim	Washington	DC	20006	202-458-6084	458-6094
International Alliance for Women (TIAW) 1101 Pennsylvania Ave NW Fl 6 *TF:* 888-712-5200 ■ *Web:* www.tiaw.org	Washington	DC	20004	888-712-5200	
International Ctr for Research on Women (ICRW) 1120 20th St NW Ste 500-N *Web:* www.icrw.org	Washington	DC	20036	202-797-0007	797-0020
MS Foundation for Women 12 MetroTech Ctr 26th Fl *Web:* forwomen.org	Brooklyn	NY	11201	212-742-2300	742-1653
National Congress of Neighborhood Women 249 Manhattan Ave *Web:* neighborhoodwomen.org	Brooklyn	NY	11211	718-388-8915	
National Council of Jewish Women (NCJW) 475 Riverside Dr Ste 1901 *TF:* 800-829-6259 ■ *Web:* www.ncjw.org	New York	NY	10115	212-645-4048	645-7466
National Council of Negro Women Inc (NCNW) 633 Pennsylvania Ave NW *TF:* 800-462-6420 ■ *Web:* www.ncnw.org	Washington	DC	20004	202-737-0120	737-0476
National Organization for Women (NOW) 1100 H St NW 3rd Fl *TF:* 855-212-0212 ■ *Web:* www.now.org	Washington	DC	20005	202-628-8669	785-8576
National Partnership for Women & Families 1875 Connecticut Ave NW Ste 650 *Web:* www.nationalpartnership.org	Washington	DC	20009	202-986-2600	986-2539
National Woman's Party 144 Constitution Ave NE *Web:* www.sewallbelmont.org	Washington	DC	20002	202-546-1210	546-3997
National Women's Law Ctr (NWLC) 11 Dupont Cir NW Ste 800 *Web:* www.nwlc.org	Washington	DC	20036	202-588-5180	588-5185
New Ways to Work Inc 103 Morris St Ste A *Web:* www.newwaystowork.org	Sebastopol	CA	95472	707-824-4000	824-4410
Ninety-Nines Inc 4300 Amelia Earhart Rd *TF:* 800-994-1929 ■ *Web:* www.ninety-nines.org	Oklahoma City	OK	73159	405-685-7969	685-7985
Wider Opportunities for Women (WOW) 1001 Connecticut Ave NW Ste 930 *Web:* www.wowonline.org	Washington	DC	20036	202-464-1596	464-1660
Women Employed 65 E Wacker Pl *Web:* www.womenemployed.org	Chicago	IL	60601	312-782-3902	782-5249
Women's Economic Agenda Project (WEAP) 160 Franklin St Ste 208 *Web:* www.weap.org	Oakland	CA	94607	510-986-8620	986-8628
Women's Research & Education Institute (WREI) 714 G St SE Ste 200 *Web:* www.wrei.org	Washington	DC	20003	703-812-7990	812-0687
Women's Sports Foundation 1899 Hempstead Tpke Ste 400 Eisenhower Pk *TF:* 800-227-3988 ■ *Web:* www.womenssportsfoundation.org	East Meadow	NY	11554	516-542-4700	542-4716
Zonta International 1211 W 22nd St Ste 900 *Web:* www.zonta.org	Oak Brook	IL	60523	630-928-1400	928-1559

49 ASSOCIATIONS & ORGANIZATIONS - PROFESSIONAL & TRADE

SEE ALSO Dental Associations - State p. 2195; Labor Unions p. 2612; Library Associations - State & Province p. 2666; Medical Associations - State p. 2724; Nurses Associations - State p. 2831; Pharmacy Associations - State p. 2925; Realtor Associations - State p. 3044; Bar Associations - State p. 1859; Veterinary Medical Associations - State p. 3284

49-1 Accountants Associations

Organization	City	State	Zip	Phone	Fax
AACE International - Assn for the Advancement of Cost Engineering 209 Prairie Ave Ste 100 *TF:* 800-858-2678 ■ *Web:* www.aacei.org	Morgantown	WV	26501	304-296-8444	291-5728
AGN International-North America 2851 S Parker Rd Ste 850 *TF:* 800-782-2272 ■ *Web:* www.agn-na.org	Aurora	CO	80014	303-743-7880	743-7660
American Acctg Assn 5717 Bessie Dr *Web:* www.aaahq.org	Sarasota	FL	34233	941-921-7747	923-4093
American Institute of Certified Public Accountants (AICPA) 1211 Ave of the Americas *TF:* 888-777-7077 ■ *Web:* www.aicpa.org	New York	NY	10036	212-596-6200	596-6213
American Institute of Professional Bookkeepers (AIPB) 6001 Montrose Rd Ste 500 *TF:* 800-622-0121 ■ *Web:* www.aipb.org	Rockville	MD	20852	800-622-0121	541-0066
American Woman's Society of Certified Public Accountants (AWSCPA) 136 S Keowee St *TF:* 800-297-2721 ■ *Web:* www.awscpa.org	Dayton	OH	45402	937-222-1872	222-5794
Association for Acctg Administration (AAA) 136 S Keowee St *Web:* www.cpaadmin.org	Dayton	OH	45402	937-222-0030	222-5794
Association of Certified Fraud Examiners (ACFE) 716 W Ave *TF:* 800-245-3321 ■ *Web:* www.acfe.com	Austin	TX	78701	512-478-9000	478-9297
Association of Chartered Accountants in the US (ACAUS) 19 Betony Pl *Web:* www.acaus.org	The Woodlands	TX	77382	713-205-3890	
Association of Government Accountants (AGA) 2208 Mt Vernon Ave *TF:* 800-242-7211 ■ *Web:* www.agacgfm.org	Alexandria	VA	22301	703-684-6931	548-9367
Association of Healthcare Internal Auditors (AHIA) 10200 W 44th Ave Ste 304 *TF:* 888-275-2442 ■ *Web:* www.ahia.org	Wheat Ridge	CO	80033	303-327-7546	422-8894
BKR International 19 Fulton St Ste 401 *TF:* 800-257-4685 ■ *Web:* www.bkr.com	New York	NY	10038	212-964-2115	964-2133
Construction Financial Management Assn (CFMA) 100 Village Blvd Ste 200A *TF:* 877-462-7827 ■ *Web:* www.cfma.org	Princeton	NJ	08540	609-452-8000	452-0474
CPA Assoc International Inc 301 Rt 17 N *Web:* www.cpaai.com	Rutherford	NJ	07070	201-804-8686	804-9222
CPA Auto Dealer Consultants Assn (CADCA) 624 Grassmere Pk Dr Ste 15 *TF:* 800-231-2524 ■ *Web:* www.autodealercpas.net	Nashville	TN	37211	615-373-9880	377-7092
CPAmerica International 11801 Research Dr *TF:* 800-992-2324 ■ *Web:* www.cpamerica.org	Alachua	FL	32615	386-418-4001	418-4002
Financial Acctg Foundation (FAF) 401 Merritt 7 PO Box 5116 *Web:* fasb.org	Norwalk	CT	06856	203-847-0700	849-9714
Financial Acctg Standards Board (FASB) 401 Merritt 7 PO Box 5116 *TF:* 800-748-0659 ■ *Web:* www.fasb.org	Norwalk	CT	06856	203-847-0700	849-9714
Hospitality Financial & Technology Professionals (HFTP) 11709 Boulder Ln Ste 110 *TF:* 800-646-4387 ■ *Web:* www.hftp.org	Austin	TX	78726	512-249-5333	249-1533
IGAF Worldwide 3235 Satellite Blvd NW	Duluth	GA	30097	678-417-7730	
Institute of Internal Auditors (IIA) 247 Maitland Ave *Web:* na.theiia.org	Altamonte Springs	FL	32701	407-937-1100	937-1101
Institute of Management Accountants Inc (IMA) 10 Paragon Dr Ste 1 *TF:* 800-638-4427 ■ *Web:* www.imanet.org	Montvale	NJ	07645	201-573-9000	474-1600
International Federation of Accountants 545 Fifth Ave 14th Fl *TF:* 888-272-2001 ■ *Web:* www.ifac.org	New York	NY	10017	212-286-9344	286-9570
National Acctg & Finance Council (NAFC) American Trucking Assn 950 N Glebe Rd *Web:* www.trucking.org	Arlington	VA	22203	703-838-1700	
National Association of Nonprofit Accountants & Consultants (NSA) 624 Grassmere Park Dr Ste 15 *TF:* 800-231-2524 ■ *Web:* www.nonprofitcpas.com	Nashville	TN	37211	615-373-9880	377-7092
National CPA Health Care Advisors Assn (HCAA) 624 Grassmere Pk Ste 15 *TF:* 800-231-2524 ■ *Web:* www.hcaa.com	Nashville	TN	37211	615-373-9880	377-7092
National Society of Accountants (NSA) 1010 N Fairfax St *TF:* 800-966-6679 ■ *Web:* www.nsacct.org	Alexandria	VA	22314	703-549-6400	549-2984
New York State Society of Certified Public Accountant (FAE) 14 Wall St 19th Fl *TF General:* 800-537-3635 ■ *Web:* www.nysscpa.org/page/continuing-education/fae-conferences	New York	NY	10005	212-719-8300	719-3365
Tax Executives Institute (TEI) 1200 G St NW Ste 300 *TF:* 877-244-7711 ■ *Web:* www.tei.org	Washington	DC	20005	202-638-5601	638-5607

49-2 Banking & Finance Professionals Associations

Phone | Fax

ABA Marketing Network
1120 Connecticut Ave NW . . . Washington DC 20036 202-663-5000 828-5053
TF: 800-226-5377 ■ *Web:* www.aba.com/marketingnetwork

ACA International - Assn of Credit & Collection Professionals
4040 W 70th St PO Box 390106 . . . Minneapolis MN 55439 952-926-6547 926-1624
TF: 800-844-5654 ■ *Web:* www.acainternational.org

Accuplan Benefits Services
515 East 4500 South Ste G200 . . . Salt Lake City UT 84107 801-266-9900 890-0929*
*Fax Area Code: 877 ■ *TF:* 800-454-2649 ■ *Web:* www.accuplan.net

America's Community Bankers (ACB)
1120 Connecticut Ave NW . . . Washington DC 20036 800-226-5377 296-8716*
*Fax Area Code: 202 ■ *TF:* 800-226-5377 ■ *Web:* www.aba.com

American Assn of Daily Money Managers (AADMM)
174 Crestview Dr . . . Bellefonte PA 16823 877-326-5991 355-2452*
*Fax Area Code: 814 ■ *TF:* 877-326-5991 ■ *Web:* www.aadmm.com

American Assn of Individual Investors (AAII)
625 N Michigan Ave Ste 1900 . . . Chicago IL 60611 312-280-0170 280-9883
TF: 800-428-2244 ■ *Web:* www.aaii.com

American Bankers Assn (ABA)
1120 Connecticut Ave NW . . . Washington DC 20036 202-663-5000 828-5045*
*Fax: Hum Res ■ *TF Cust Svc:* 800-226-5377 ■ *Web:* www.aba.com

American Benefits Council
1501 M St NW Ste 600 . . . Washington DC 20005 202-289-6700 289-4582
TF: 877-829-5500 ■ *Web:* www.americanbenefitscouncil.org

American Council for Capital Formation (ACCF)
1750 K St NW Ste 400 . . . Washington DC 20006 202-293-5811 785-8165
Web: www.accf.org

American Economic Assn (AEA)
2014 Broadway Ste 305 . . . Nashville TN 37203 615-322-2595 343-7590
Web: www.aeaweb.org

American Finance Assn (AFA) 350 Main St . . . Malden MA 02148 781-388-8599 388-8232
TF: 800-835-6770 ■ *Web:* www.afajof.org

American Institute of Certified Planners (AICP)
1776 Massachusetts Ave NW Ste 400 . . . Washington DC 20036 202-872-0611 872-0643
Web: www.planning.org/aicp

Association for Financial Professionals (AFP)
4520 E W Hwy Ste 750 . . . Bethesda MD 20814 301-907-2862 907-2864
Web: www.afponline.org

Bank Administration Institute (BAI)
115 S LaSalle St Ste 3300 . . . Chicago IL 60603 312-683-2464 683-2373*
*Fax: Cust Svc ■ *TF Cust Svc:* 800-224-9889 ■ *Web:* www.bai.org

Better Investing PO Box 220 . . . Royal Oak MI 48068 248-583-6242 583-4880
TF: 877-275-6242 ■ *Web:* www.betterinvesting.org

Certified Financial Planner Board of Standards Inc
1425 K St NW Ste 500 . . . Washington DC 20005 202-379-2200 379-2299
TF: 800-487-1497 ■ *Web:* www.cfp.net

CFA Institute
915 E High St PO Box 3668 . . . Charlottesville VA 22903 434-951-5499 951-5262
TF: 800-247-8132 ■ *Web:* www.cfainstitute.org

Community Banking Advisory Network (CBAN)
624 Grassmere Pk Dr Ste 15 . . . Nashville TN 37211 615-373-9880 377-7092
TF: 800-231-2524 ■ *Web:* www.bankingcpas.com

Consumer Data Industry Assn (CDIA)
1090 Vermont Ave NW Ste 200 . . . Washington DC 20005 202-371-0910 371-0134
Web: www.cdiaonline.org

Council of Institutional Investors
888 17th St NW Ste 500 . . . Washington DC 20006 202-822-0800 822-0801
Web: www.cii.org

Credit Professionals International
10726 Manchester Rd . . . Saint Louis MO 63122 314-821-9393 821-7171
Web: www.creditprofessionals.org

Credit Research Foundation (CRF)
8840 Columbia 100 Pkwy . . . Columbia MD 21045 410-740-5499 740-4620
TF: 866-265-3298 ■ *Web:* www.crfonline.org

Credit Union Executives Society (CUES)
5510 Research Pk Dr . . . Madison WI 53711 608-271-2664 271-2303
TF: 800-252-2664 ■ *Web:* www.cues.org

Electronic Funds Transfer Assn (EFTA)
11350 Random Hills Rd Ste 800 . . . Fairfax VA 22030 703-934-6052 934-6058
Web: www.efta.org

Emerging Markets Traders Assn (EMTA)
360 Madison Ave 18th Fl . . . New York NY 10017 212-313-1100 313-1016
Web: www.emta.org

Farm Credit Council 50 F St NW Ste 900 . . . Washington DC 20001 202-626-8710 626-8718
TF: 866-632-9992 ■ *Web:* www.fccouncil.com

Financial Executives International (FEI)
200 Campus Dr PO Box 674 . . . Florham Park NJ 07932 973-765-1000 765-1018
Web: www.financialexecutives.org

Financial Industry Regulatory Authority (FINRA)
9509 Key W Ave . . . Rockville MD 20850 301-590-6500
Web: www.finra.org

Financial Management Assn International (FMA)
4202 E Fowler Ave . . . Tampa FL 33620 813-974-2084 974-3318
Web: www.fma.org

Financial Managers Society (FMS)
100 W Monroe St Ste 810 . . . Chicago IL 60603 312-578-1300 578-1308
TF Cust Svc: 800-275-4367 ■ *Web:* www.fmsinc.org

Financial Planning Assn (FPA)
7535 E Hampden Ave Ste 400 . . . Denver CO 80231 303-759-4900 759-0749
TF: 800-322-4237 ■ *Web:* www.fpanet.org

Financial Service Centers of America Inc (FiSCA)
21 Main St First Fl . . . Hackensack NJ 07602 201-487-0412 487-3954
Web: www.fisca.org

Financial Services Roundtable
1001 Pennsylvania Ave NW Ste 500 . . . Washington DC 20005 202-289-4322 628-2507
Web: www.fsround.org

FINRA 1735 K St NW . . . Washington DC 20006 202-728-8000
TF: 800-289-9999 ■ *Web:* www.finra.org

Futures Industry Assn (FIA)
2001 Pennsylvania Ave NW Ste 600 . . . Washington DC 20006 202-466-5460 296-3184
Web: www.futuresindustry.org

Independent Community Bankers of America (ICBA)
1615 L St NW Ste 900 . . . Washington DC 20036 202-659-8111
TF: 800-422-8439 ■ *Web:* www.icba.org

Industry Council for Tangible Assets (ICTA)
1510 Circle Dr . . . Annapolis MD 21409 410-626-7005 586-0822*
*Fax Area Code: 727 ■ *Web:* www.ictaonline.org

Institute of International Bankers (IIB)
299 Pk Ave 17th Fl . . . New York NY 10171 212-421-1611 421-1119
Web: www.iib.org

Institute of International Finance (IIF)
1333 H St NW Ste 800-E . . . Washington DC 20005 202-857-3600 775-1430
Web: www.iif.com

International Swaps & Derivatives Assn (ISDA)
360 Madison Ave 16th Fl . . . New York NY 10017 212-901-6000 901-6001
Web: www2.isda.org

Investment Company Institute (ICI)
1401 H St NW Ste 1200 . . . Washington DC 20005 202-326-5800 326-5841
Web: www.ici.org

Investment Management Consultants Assn (IMCA)
5619 DTC Pkwy Ste 500 . . . Greenwood Village CO 80111 303-770-3377 770-1812
TF: 800-250-9083 ■ *Web:* www.imca.org

Investor Protection Trust
919 18th St NW Ste 300 . . . Washington DC 20006 202-775-2111
Web: www.investorprotection.org

Mortgage Bankers Assn (MBA)
1919 M St NW 5th Fl . . . Washington DC 20036 202-557-2700 721-0245*
*Fax: Cust Svc ■ *TF:* 800-793-6222 ■ *Web:* www.mortgagebankers.org

Municipal Securities Rulemaking Board (MSRB)
1900 Duke St Ste 600 . . . Alexandria VA 22314 703-797-6600 797-6700
TF: 888-475-8376 ■ *Web:* www.msrb.org

NA of Credit Management (NACM)
8840 Columbia 100 Pkwy . . . Columbia MD 21045 410-740-5560 740-5574
TF: 800-955-8815 ■ *Web:* www.nacm.org

NA of Federal Credit Unions (NAFCU)
3138 Tenth St N . . . Arlington VA 22201 703-522-4770 524-1082
TF: 800-336-4644 ■ *Web:* www.nafcu.org

NA of Government Guaranteed Lenders (NAGGL)
215 E Ninth Ave . . . Stillwater OK 74074 405-377-4022 377-3931
Web: www.naggl.org

NACHA - Electronic Payments Assn
13665 Dulles Technology Dr Ste 300 . . . Herndon VA 20171 703-561-1100 787-0996
TF: 800-487-9180 ■ *Web:* www.nacha.org

National Federation of Community Development Credit Unions (NFCDCU)
39 Broadway Ste 2140 . . . New York NY 10006 212-809-1850 809-3274
TF: 800-437-8711 ■ *Web:* www.cdcu.coop

National Futures Assn (NFA)
300 S Riverside Plz Ste 1800 . . . Chicago IL 60606 312-781-1300 781-1467
TF: 800-621-3570 ■ *Web:* www.nfa.futures.org

National Investment Co Service Assn (NICSA)
8400 Westpark Dr 2nd Fl . . . McLean VA 22102 508-485-1500 485-1560
TF: 800-426-1122 ■ *Web:* www.nicsa.org

National Investor Relations Institute (NIRI)
8020 Towers Crescent Dr Ste 250 . . . Vienna VA 22182 703-506-3570 506-3571
Web: www.niri.org

North American Securities Administrators Assn (NASAA)
750 First St NE Ste 1140 . . . Washington DC 20002 202-737-0900 783-3571
TF: 800-222-1253 ■ *Web:* www.nasaa.org

Pension Real Estate Assn (PREA)
100 Pearl St 13th Fl . . . Hartford CT 06103 860-692-6341 692-6351
Web: www.prea.org

Risk Management Assn (RMA)
1801 Market St Ste 300 . . . Philadelphia PA 19103 215-446-4000 446-4101
TF Cust Svc: 800-677-7621 ■ *Web:* www.rmahq.org

Securities Industry & Financial Markets Assn (SIFMAA)
120 Broadway 35th Fl . . . New York NY 10271 212-313-1200 313-1301
TF: 888-367-7966 ■ *Web:* www.sifma.org

Security Traders Assn 80 Broad St . . . New York NY 10004 212-837-7765 659-5249*
*Fax Area Code: 202 ■ *Web:* www.securitytraders.org

Smart Card Alliance Inc
191 Clarkville Rd . . . Princeton Junction NJ 08550 609-799-5654 799-7032
TF: 800-556-6828 ■ *Web:* www.smartcardalliance.org

Western Economic Assn International (WEAI)
18837 Brookhurst St Ste 304 . . . Fountain Valley CA 92708 714-965-8800 965-8829
Web: www.weai.org

Winter Kloman Moter & Repp SC (WKMR)
235 N Executive Dr Ste 160 . . . Brookfield WI 53005 262-797-9050 797-8251
Web: www.wkmr.com

World Council of Credit Unions Inc (WOCCU)
5710 Mineral Pt Rd . . . Madison WI 53705 608-395-2000 395-2001
Web: www.woccu.org

49-3 Construction Industry Associations

Phone | Fax

Air Conditioning Contractors of America (ACCA)
2800 S Shirlington Rd Ste 300 . . . Arlington VA 22206 703-575-4477 575-8107
Web: www.acca.org

Air Movement & Control Assn International Inc (AMCA)
30 W University Dr . . . Arlington Heights IL 60004 847-394-0150 253-0088
Web: www.amca.org

American Architectural Manufacturers Assn (AAMA)
1827 Walden Office Sq Ste 550 . . . Schaumburg IL 60173 847-303-5664 303-5774
Web: www.aamanet.org

American Concrete Institute International (ACI)
38800 Country Club Dr PO Box 9094 . . . Farmington Hills MI 48331 248-848-3700 848-3701
Web: www.concrete.org

American Concrete Pavement Assn (ACPA)
5420 Old OrchaRd Rd Ste A-100 . . . Skokie IL 60077 847-966-2272 966-9970
Web: www.pavement.com

Organization	City	State	Zip	Phone	Fax
American Concrete Pipe Assn 8445 Freeport Pkwy Ste 350 *Web:* www.concrete-pipe.org	Irving	TX	75063	972-506-7216	506-7682
American Fence Assn (AFA) 800 Roosevelt Rd Bldg C-312 *TF:* 800-822-4342 ■ *Web:* www.americanfenceassociation.com	Glen Ellyn	IL	60137	630-942-6598	790-3095
American Fire Sprinkler Assn (AFSA) 12750 Merit Dr Ste 350 *Web:* www.firesprinkler.org	Dallas	TX	75251	214-349-5965	343-8898
American Institute of Constructors (AIC) 700 N Fairfax St Ste 510 **Fax Area Code:* 571 ■ *Web:* www.professionalconstructor.org	Alexandria	VA	22314	703-683-4999	527-3105*
American Institute of Steel Construction (AISC) One E Wacker Dr Ste 3100 *Web:* www.aisc.org	Chicago	IL	60601	312-670-2400	670-5403
American Institute of Timber Construction (AITC) 7012 S Revere Pkwy Ste 140 *Web:* www.aitc-glulam.org	Centennial	CO	80112	303-792-9559	792-0669
American Road & Transportation Builders Assn (ARTBA) 1219 28th St NW *TF:* 800-636-2377 ■ *Web:* www.artba.org	Washington	DC	20007	202-289-4434	289-4435
American Society of Heating Refrigerating & Air-Conditioning Engineers Inc (ASHRAE) 1791 Tullie Cir NE *TF Cust Svc:* 800-527-4723 ■ *Web:* www.ashrae.org	Atlanta	GA	30329	404-636-8400	321-5478
American Society of Home Inspectors (ASHI) 932 Lee St Ste 101 *TF:* 800-743-2744 ■ *Web:* www.ashi.org	Des Plaines	IL	60016	847-759-2820	759-1620
American Society of Professional Estimators (ASPE) 2525 Perimeter Pl Dr Ste 103 *TF:* 888-378-6283 ■ *Web:* www.aspenational.org	Nashville	TN	37214	615-316-9200	316-9800
American Subcontractors Assn Inc (ASA) 1004 Duke St *TF:* 866-378-8866 ■ *Web:* www.asaonline.com	Alexandria	VA	22314	703-684-3450	836-3482
American Welding Society (AWS) 550 NW 42nd Ave *TF:* 800-443-9353 ■ *Web:* www.aws.org	Miami	FL	33126	305-443-9353	443-7559
APA - Engineered Wood Assn 7011 S 19th St *Web:* www.apawood.org	Tacoma	WA	98466	253-565-6600	565-7265
Architectural Precast Assn (APA) 6710 Winkler Rd Ste 8 *Web:* www.archprecast.org	Fort Myers	FL	33919	239-454-6989	454-6787
Architectural Woodwork Institute (AWI) 46179 Westlake Dr Ste 120 *TF:* 866-877-6933 ■ *Web:* www.awinet.org	Potomac Falls	VA	20165	571-323-3636	323-3630
Asphalt Institute 2696 Research Pk Dr *Web:* www.asphaltinstitute.org	Lexington	KY	40511	859-288-4960	288-4999
Asphalt Roofing Manufacturers Assn (ARMA) 529 14th St NW Ste 750 *TF:* 800-247-6637 ■ *Web:* www.asphaltroofing.org	Washington	DC	20045	202-207-0917	223-9741
Associated Builders & Contractors Inc (ABC) 4250 Fairfax Dr *TF:* 866-262-0540 ■ *Web:* www.abc.org	Arlington	VA	22203	703-812-2000	812-8235
Associated General Contractors of America (AGC) 2300 Wilson Blvd Ste 400 *TF:* 800-242-1766 ■ *Web:* www.agc.org	Arlington	VA	22201	703-548-3118	548-3119
Associated Locksmiths of America (ALOA) 3500 Easy St *TF:* 800-532-2562 ■ *Web:* www.aloa.org	Dallas	TX	75247	214-819-9733	819-9736
Association for Retail Environment (ARE) 4651 Sheridan St Ste 470 *TF:* 800-421-3483 ■ *Web:* www.retailenvironments.org	Hollywood	FL	33021	954-893-7300	893-7500
Association of the Wall & Ceiling Industries International (AWCI) 513 W Broad St Ste 210 *Web:* www.awci.org	Falls Church	VA	22046	703-538-1600	534-8307
Brick Industry Assn (BIA) 1850 Centennial Pk Dr Ste 301 *TF:* 866-644-1293 ■ *Web:* www.gobrick.com	Reston	VA	20191	703-620-0010	620-3928
Building & Construction Trades Dept AFL-CIO 815 16th St NW Ste 600 *TF:* 800-772-1213 ■ *Web:* www.bctd.org	Washington	DC	20006	202-347-1461	628-0724
Building Material Dealers Assn (BMDA) 1006 SE Grand Ave Ste 301 *Web:* www.bmda.com	Portland	OR	97214	503-208-3763	620-1016
Cedar Shake & Shingle Bureau 7101 Horne St Ste 2 *Web:* www.cedarbureau.org	Mission	BC	V2V7A2	604-820-7700	820-0266
Ceilings & Interior Systems Construction Assn (CISCA) 1010 Jorie Blvd Ste 30 **Fax Area Code:* 866 ■ *Web:* cisca.org	Oak Brook	IL	60523	630-584-1919	560-8537*
Cement Assn of Canada (CAC) 502-350 Sparks St *Web:* www.cement.ca	Ottawa	ON	K1R7S8	613-236-9471	563-4498
Central Station Alarm Assn (CSAA) 8150 Leesburg Pk Ste 700 *Web:* www.csaaintl.org	Vienna	VA	22180	703-242-4670	242-4675
Composite Panel Assn 19465 Deerfield Ave Ste 306 *TF:* 866-426-6767 ■ *Web:* compositepanel.org	Leesburg	VA	20176	703-724-1128	274-1588
Concrete Reinforcing Steel Institute (CRSI) 933 N Plum Grove Rd *Web:* www.crsi.org	Schaumburg	IL	60173	847-517-1200	517-1206
Construction Financial Management Assn (CFMA) 100 Village Blvd Ste 200A *TF:* 877-462-7827 ■ *Web:* www.cfma.org	Princeton	NJ	08540	609-452-8000	452-0474
Distribution Contractors Assn (DCA) 101 W Renner Rd Ste 460 *Web:* www.dca-online.org	Richardson	TX	75082	972-680-0261	680-0461
Door & Hardware Institute (DHI) 14150 Newbrook Dr Ste 200 *Web:* www.dhi.org	Chantilly	VA	20151	703-222-2010	222-2410
Electronic Security Assn Inc (ESA) 2300 Vly View Ln Ste 230 *TF:* 888-447-1689 ■ *Web:* www.esaweb.org	Irving	TX	75062	214-260-5970	260-5979
Forest Resources Assn Inc 600 Jefferson Plz Ste 350 *Web:* www.forestresources.org	Rockville	MD	20852	301-838-9385	838-9481
Hardwood Plywood & Veneer Assn (HPVA) 1825 Michael Faraday Dr *Web:* www.hpva.org	Reston	VA	20190	703-435-2900	435-2537
Interlocking Concrete Pavement Institute (ICPI) 1444 'I' St NW Ste 700 *TF:* 800-241-3652 ■ *Web:* www.icpi.org	Washington	DC	20005	202-712-9036	408-0285
International Assn of Drilling Contractors (IADC) 10370 Richmond Ave Ste 760 *Web:* www.iadc.org	Houston	TX	77042	713-292-1945	292-1946
International Assn of Electrical Inspectors (IAEI) 901 Waterfall Way Ste 602 *TF:* 800-786-4234 ■ *Web:* www.iaei.org	Richardson	TX	75080	972-235-1455	235-6858
International Code Council (ICC) 500 New Jersey Ave NW 6th Fl *TF:* 888-422-7233 ■ *Web:* www.iccsafe.org	Washington	DC	20001	202-370-1800	783-2348
International Council of Shopping Centers (ICSC) 1221 Ave of the Americas 41st Fl **Fax Area Code:* 212 ■ *Web:* www.icsc.org	New York	NY	10020	646-728-3800	589-5555*
International District Energy Assn (IDEA) 24 Lyman St Ste 230 *Web:* www.districtenergy.org	Westborough	MA	01581	508-366-9339	366-0019
International Institute of Ammonia Refrigeration 1001 N Fairfax St Ste 503 *TF:* 800-937-8461 ■ *Web:* www.iiar.org	Alexandria	VA	22314	703-312-4200	312-0065
International Masonry Institute (IMI) 42 E St **Fax Area Code:* 301 ■ *TF:* 800-803-0295 ■ *Web:* www.imiweb.org	Annapolis	MD	21401	410-280-1305	261-2855*
International Road Federation (IRF) 500 Mongomery St Fifth Fl *Web:* www.irfnet.org	Alexandria	VA	22314	703-535-1001	535-1007
International Union of Elevator Constructors (IUEC) 7154 Columbia Gateway Dr *Web:* www.iuec.org	Columbia	MD	21046	410-953-6150	953-6169
International Wood Products Assn (IWPA) 4214 King St *TF:* 855-435-0005 ■ *Web:* www.iwpawood.org	Alexandria	VA	22302	703-820-6696	820-8550
Manufactured Housing Institute (MHI) 2101 Wilson Blvd Ste 610 *TF:* 800-505-5500 ■ *Web:* www.manufacturedhousing.org	Arlington	VA	22201	703-558-0400	558-0401
Marble Institute of America (MIA) 28901 Clemens Rd Ste 100 *TF:* 800-433-4903 ■ *Web:* www.marble-institute.com	Westlake	OH	44145	440-250-9222	250-9223
Mason Contractors Assn of America (MCAA) 33 S Roselle Rd *TF:* 800-536-2225 ■ *Web:* www.masoncontractors.org	Schaumburg	IL	60193	224-678-9709	678-9714
Mechanical Contractors Assn of America (MCAA) 1385 Piccard Dr *TF:* 800-556-3653 ■ *Web:* www.mcaa.org	Rockville	MD	20850	301-869-5800	990-9690
Monument Builders of North America (MBNA) 136 S Keowee St **Fax Area Code:* 937 ■ *TF:* 800-233-4472 ■ *Web:* www.monumentbuilders.org	Dayton	OH	45402	800-233-4472	222-5794*
NA of Home Builders (NAHB) 1201 15th St NW *TF:* 800-368-5242 ■ *Web:* www.nahb.org	Washington	DC	20005	202-266-8200	266-8586
NA of Women in Construction (NAWIC) 327 S Adams St *TF:* 800-552-3506 ■ *Web:* www.nawic.org	Fort Worth	TX	76104	817-877-5551	877-0324
National Association of Tower Erectors (NATE) Eight Second St SE *TF:* 888-882-5865 ■ *Web:* natehome.com	Watertown	SD	57201	605-882-5865	886-5184
National Community Renaissance of California 9421 Haven Ave *Web:* www.nationalcore.org	Rancho Cucamonga	CA	91730	909-483-2444	483-2448
National Concrete Masonry Assn 13750 Sunrise Vly Dr *Web:* www.ncma.org	Herndon	VA	20171	703-713-1900	713-1910
National Corrugated Steel Pipe Assn (NCSPA) 14070 Proton Rd Ste 100 *Web:* www.ncspa.org	Dallas	TX	75244	972-850-1907	490-4219
National Council of Examiners for Engineering & Surveying (NCEES) 280 Seneca Creek Rd *TF:* 800-250-3196 ■ *Web:* www.ncees.org	Seneca	SC	29678	864-654-6824	654-6033
National Electrical Contractors Assn (NECA) 3 Bethesda Metro Ctr Ste 1100 *TF:* 800-214-0585 ■ *Web:* www.necanet.org	Bethesda	MD	20814	301-657-3110	215-4500
National Elevator Industry Inc 1677 County Rd 64 PO Box 838 *Web:* www.neii.org	Salem	NY	12865	518-854-3100	854-3257
National Fire Sprinkler Assn (NFSA) 40 Jon Barrett Rd *Web:* www.nfsa.org	Patterson	NY	12563	845-878-4200	878-4215
National Frame Builders Assn (NFBA) 8735 W Higgins Rd Ste 300 **Fax Area Code:* 847 ■ *TF:* 800-557-6957 ■ *Web:* www.nfba.org	Chicago	IL	60631	800-557-6957	375-6495*
National Hardwood Lumber Assn (NHLA) 6830 Raleigh-LaGrange Rd *TF:* 800-933-0318 ■ *Web:* www.nhla.com	Memphis	TN	38134	901-377-1818	382-6419
National Housing Conference (NHC) 1801 K St NW Ste M-100 *Web:* www.nhc.org	Washington	DC	20006	202-466-2121	466-2122
National Institute of Bldg Sciences (NIBS) 1090 Vermont Ave NW Ste 700 *Web:* www.nibs.org	Washington	DC	20005	202-289-7800	289-1092
National Insulation Assn (NIA) 99 Canal Ctr Plz Ste 222 *TF:* 877-968-7642 ■ *Web:* www.insulation.org	Alexandria	VA	22314	703-683-6422	549-4838
National Kitchen & Bath Assn (NKBA) 687 Willow Grove St **Fax Area Code:* 908 ■ *TF:* 800-843-6522 ■ *Web:* www.nkba.org	Hackettstown	NJ	07840	800-843-6522	852-1695*
National Parking Assn (NPA) 1112 16th St NW Ste 840 *TF:* 800-647-7275 ■ *Web:* www.npapark.org	Washington	DC	20036	202-296-4336	296-3102
National Precast Concrete Assn (NPCA) 10333 N Meridian St Ste 272 *TF:* 800-366-7731 ■ *Web:* www.precast.org	Indianapolis	IN	46290	317-571-9500	571-0041

Phone | Fax

National Ready Mixed Concrete Assn (NRMCA)
900 Spring St ... Silver Spring MD 20910 301-587-1400 585-4219
TF: 888-846-7622 ■ *Web:* www.nrmca.org

National Roofing Contractors Assn (NRCA)
10255 W Higgins Rd Ste 600 ... Rosemont IL 60018 847-299-9070 299-1183
TF Cust Svc: 800-323-9545 ■ *Web:* www.nrca.net

National Stone Sand & Gravel Assn (NSSGA)
1605 King St ... Alexandria VA 22314 703-525-8788 525-7782
TF: 800-342-1415 ■ *Web:* www.nssga.org

National Wood Flooring Assn (NWFA)
111 Chesterfield Industrial Blvd ... Chesterfield MO 63005 636-519-9663
TF: 800-422-4556 ■ *Web:* www.woodfloors.org

North American Bldg Material Distribution Assn (NBMDA)
330 N Wabash Ave Ste 2000 ... Chicago IL 60611 312-321-6845 644-0310
TF: 888-747-7862 ■ *Web:* www.nbmda.org

North American Insulation Manufacturers Assn (NAIMA)
44 Canal Ctr Plz Ste 310 ... Alexandria VA 22314 703-684-0084 684-0427
Web: www.naima.org

Operative Plasterers' & Cement Masons' International Assn of the US & Canada (OPCMIA)
11720 Beltsville Dr Ste 700 ... Beltsville MD 20705 301-623-1000 623-1032
TF: 888-379-1558 ■ *Web:* www.opcmia.org

Painting & Decorating Contractors of America (PDCA)
2316 Millpark Dr Ste 220 ... Maryland Heights MO 63043 314-514-7322 514-9417
TF Cust Svc: 800-332-7322 ■ *Web:* www.pdca.org

Plumbing Manufacturers International (PMI)
1921 Rohlwing Rd Unit G ... Rolling Meadows IL 60008 847-481-5500 481-5501
Web: www.pmihome.org

Plumbing-Heating-Cooling Contractors NA (PHCC)
100 S Washington St ... Falls Church VA 22040 703-237-8100 237-7442
TF: 800-533-7694 ■ *Web:* www.phccweb.org

Portland Cement Assn (PCA) 5420 Old OrchaRd Rd ... Skokie IL 60077 847-966-6200 966-9781
Web: www.cement.org

Precast/Prestressed Concrete Institute (PCI)
200 W Adams St Ste 2100 ... Chicago IL 60606 312-786-0300 786-0353
Web: www.pci.org

Precision Metalforming Assn (PMA)
6363 Oak Tree Blvd ... Independence OH 44131 216-901-8800 901-9190
Web: www.pma.org/home

Refrigeration Service Engineers Society (RSES)
1666 Rand Rd ... Des Plaines IL 60016 847-297-6464 297-5038
TF: 800-297-5660 ■ *Web:* www.rses.org

Sheet Metal & Air Conditioning Contractors' NA (SMACNA)
4201 Lafayette Ctr Dr ... Chantilly VA 20151 703-803-2980 803-3732
Web: www.smacna.org

Sheet Metal Workers International Assn (SMWIA)
1750 New York Ave NW Sixth Fl ... Washington DC 20006 202-783-5880 662-0894
TF: 800-251-7045 ■ *Web:* www.smwia.org

Single Ply Roofing Institute (SPRI)
411 Waverly Oaks Rd Ste 331-B ... Waltham MA 02452 781-647-7026 647-7222
Web: www.spri.org

Steel Framing Alliance
25 Massachusetts Ave NW Ste 800 ... Washington DC 20001 202-785-2022 452-1039
Web: www.steelframingalliance.com

Tile Council of America Inc (TCA)
100 Clemson Research Blvd ... Anderson SC 29625 864-646-8453 646-2821
Web: www.tcnatile.com

Tilt-up Concrete Assn (TCA)
113 First St NW ... Mount Vernon IA 52314 319-895-6911 213-5555*
**Fax Area Code:* 320 ■ *Web:* www.tilt-up.org

US Society on Dams (USSD) 1616 17th St Ste 483 ... Denver CO 80202 303-628-5430 628-5431
Web: www.ussdams.org

Window & Door Manufacturers Assn (WDMA)
330 N Wabash Ave Ste 2000 ... Chicago IL 60611 847-299-5200 264-5150*
**Fax Area Code:* 651 ■ *TF:* 800-223-2301 ■ *Web:* www.wdma.com

Wood Moulding & Millwork Producers Assn (WMMPA)
507 First St ... Woodland CA 95695 530-661-9591 661-9586
TF: 800-550-7889 ■ *Web:* www.wmmpa.com

Wood Products Manufacturers Assn (WPMA)
PO Box 761 ... Westminster MA 01473 978-874-5445 874-9946
Web: www.wpma.org

Wood Truss Council of America (WTCA)
6300 Enterprise Ln ... Madison WI 53719 608-274-4849 274-3329
Web: www.sbcindustry.com

World Millwork Alliance (AMD)
10047 Robert Trent Jones Pkwy ... New Port Richey FL 34655 727-372-3665 372-2879
Web: worldmillworkalliance.com

49-4 Consumer Sales & Service Professionals Associations

Phone | Fax

Advanced Medical Technology Assn
701 Pennsylvania Ave NW Ste 800 ... Washington DC 20004 202-783-8700 783-8750
Web: www.advamed.org

AHRI - Air-Conditioning Heating & Refrigeration Institute
4100 N Fairfax Dr Ste 200 ... Arlington VA 22203 703-524-8800 528-3816
Web: www.ahrinet.org

American Apparel & Footwear Assn (AAFA)
1601 N Kent St Ste 1200 ... Arlington VA 22209 703-524-1864 522-6741
TF: 800-520-2262 ■ *Web:* www.wewear.org

American Boat & Yacht Council Inc (ABYC)
613 Third St Ste 10 ... Annapolis MD 21403 410-990-4460 990-4466
Web: www.abycinc.org

American Gem Society (AGS) 8881 W Sahara Ave ... Las Vegas NV 89117 702-255-6500 255-7420
TF: 866-805-6500 ■ *Web:* www.americangemsociety.org

American Gem Trade Assn (AGTA)
3030 LBJ Fwy Ste 840 ... Dallas TX 75234 214-742-4367 742-7334
TF: 800-972-1162 ■ *Web:* www.agta.org

American Hardware Manufacturers Assn (AHMA)
801 N Plz Dr ... Schaumburg IL 60173 847-605-1025 605-1030
Web: www.ahma.org

Phone | Fax

American Institute of Floral Designers (AIFD)
720 Light St ... Baltimore MD 21230 410-752-3318 752-8295
TF: 877-865-5320 ■ *Web:* www.aifd.org

American Lighting Assn (ALA)
2050 Stemmons Fwy Ste 10046 ... Dallas TX 75207 214-698-9898 698-9899
TF: 800-605-4448 ■ *Web:* www.americanlightingassoc.com

American Pet Products Manufacturers Assn (APPMA)
255 Glenville Rd ... Greenwich CT 06831 203-532-0000 532-0551
TF: 800-452-1225 ■ *Web:* www.americanpetproducts.org

American Rental Assn (ARA) 1900 19th St ... Moline IL 61265 309-764-2475 764-1533
TF: 800-334-2177 ■ *Web:* www.ararental.org

American Sportfishing Assn (ASA)
1001 N Fairfax St Ste 501 ... Alexandria VA 22314 703-519-9691 519-1872
Web: www.asafishing.org

American Watchmakers-Clockmakers Institute (AWI)
701 Enterprise Dr ... Harrison OH 45030 513-367-9800 367-1414
TF: 866-367-2924 ■ *Web:* awci.com

Association for Linen Management
2161 Lexington Rd Ste 2 ... Richmond KY 40475 859-624-0177 624-3580
TF: 800-669-0863 ■ *Web:* www.almnet.org

Association of Home Appliance Manufacturers (AHAM)
1111 19th St NW Ste 402 ... Washington DC 20036 202-872-5955 872-9354
TF: 888-258-3247 ■ *Web:* www.aham.org

Association of Pool & Spa Professionals (APSP)
2111 Eisenhower Ave Ste 500 ... Alexandria VA 22314 703-838-0083 549-0493
TF: 800-323-3996 ■ *Web:* www.apsp.org

Automotive Recyclers Assn (ARA)
3975 Fair Ridge Dr Ste 20N ... Fairfax VA 22033 703-385-1001 385-1494
TF: 888-385-1005 ■ *Web:* www.a-r-a.org

Awards & Recognition Assn (ARA)
4700 W Lake Ave ... Glenview IL 60025 847-375-4800 375-6480
TF: 800-344-2148 ■ *Web:* www.ara.org

Carpet & Rug Institute (CRI)
100 S Hamilton St PO Box 2048 ... Dalton GA 30720 706-278-3176 278-8835
Web: www.carpet-rug.org

Coin Laundry Assn (CLA)
1s660 Midwest Rd Ste 205 ... Oakbrook Terrace IL 60181 630-953-7920
TF: 800-570-5629 ■ *Web:* www.coinlaundry.org

Consumer Healthcare Products Assn (CHPA)
1150 Connecticut Ave NW # 700 ... Washington DC 20036 202-429-9260 223-6835
Web: www.chpa.org

Contact Lens Manufacturers Assn PO Box 29398 ... Lincoln NE 68529 402-465-4122 465-4187
TF: 800-344-9060 ■ *Web:* www.clma.net

Cremation Assn of North America (CANA)
499 Northgate Pkwy ... Wheeling IL 60090 312-245-1077 321-4098
Web: www.cremationassociation.org

Dental Trade Alliance (DTA)
4350 N Fairfax Dr Ste 220 ... Arlington VA 22203 703-379-7755 931-9429
Web: www.dentaltradealliance.org

Diamond Council of America (DCA)
3212 W End Ave Ste 202 ... Nashville TN 37203 615-385-5301 385-4955
TF: 877-283-5669 ■ *Web:* www.diamondcouncil.org

Diving Equipment & Marketing Assn (DEMA)
3750 Convoy St Ste 310 ... San Diego CA 92111 858-616-6408 616-6495
TF: 800-862-3483 ■ *Web:* www.dema.org

Drycleaning & Laundry Institute
14700 Sweitzer Ln ... Laurel MD 20707 301-622-1900 295-0685*
**Fax Area Code:* 240 ■ *TF:* 800-638-2627 ■ *Web:* www.dlionline.org

Envelope Manufacturers Assn (EMA)
500 Montgomery St Ste 550 ... Alexandria VA 22314 703-739-2200 739-2209
TF: 800-354-5892 ■ *Web:* www.envelope.org

Fashion Group International Inc (FGI)
Eight W 40th St Seventh Fl ... New York NY 10018 212-302-5511 302-5533
Web: www.fgi.org

Footwear Distributors & Retailers of America (FDRA)
1319 F St NW Ste 700 ... Washington DC 20004 202-737-5660 638-2615
Web: www.fdra.org

Fragrance Foundation 621 2nd Ave 2nd Fl ... New York NY 10016 212-725-2755 786-3260*
**Fax Area Code:* 646 ■ *Web:* fragrance.org

Gemological Institute of America (GIA)
5345 Armada Dr ... Carlsbad CA 92008 760-603-4000 603-4003
TF: 800-421-7250 ■ *Web:* www.gia.edu

Hearth Patio & Barbecue Assn (HPBA)
1901 N Moore St Ste 600 ... Arlington VA 22209 703-522-0086 522-0548
Web: www.hpba.org

Home Furnishings Independents Assn (HFIA)
2050 Stemmons World Fwy Ste 292 ... Dallas TX 75207 214-741-7632
TF: 800-422-3778 ■ *Web:* www.nahfa.org

Hosiery Assn
7421 Carmel Executive Pk Ste 200-B ... Charlotte NC 28226 704-365-0913 362-2056
Web: www.hosieryassociation.com

Independent Jewelers Organization (IJO)
136 Old Post Rd ... Southport CT 06890 800-624-9252 254-7429*
**Fax Area Code:* 203 ■ *TF:* 800-624-9252 ■ *Web:* www.ijo.com

Independent Office Products & Furniture Dealers Assn (IOPFDA)
3601 E Joppa Rd Ste 200 ... Baltimore MD 21234 410-931-8100 931-8111
Web: www.nopanet.org

Institute of Inspection Cleaning & Restoration Certification (IICRC)
2715 E Mill Plain Blvd ... Vancouver WA 98661 360-693-5675 693-4858
Web: www.iicrc.org

International Assn of Lighting Designers (IALD)
200 World Trade Ctr
Merchandise Mart Ste 9-104 ... Chicago IL 60654 312-527-3677 527-3680
Web: www.iald.org

International Card Manufacturers Assn (ICMA)
191 Clarksville Rd ... Princeton Junction NJ 08550 609-799-4900 799-7032
Web: www.icma.com

International Cemetery Cremation & Funeral Assn (ICCFA)
107 Carpenter Dr Ste 100 ... Sterling VA 20164 703-391-8400 391-8416
TF: 800-645-7700 ■ *Web:* www.iccfa.com

International Engraved Graphics Assn
305 Plus Pk Blvd ... Nashville TN 37217 800-821-3138 366-4192*
**Fax Area Code:* 615 ■ *TF:* 800-821-3138 ■ *Web:* www.iega.org

Organization	City	State	ZIP	Phone	Fax
International Executive Housekeepers Assn (IEHA) 1001 Eastwind Dr Ste 301 — *TF:* 800-200-6342 ■ *Web:* www.ieha.org	Westerville	OH	43081	614-895-7166	895-1248
International Furniture Rental Assn (IFRA) 950 F St NW 10th Fl — *Web:* www.ifra.org	Washington	DC	20004	202-239-3818	654-4818
International Housewares Assn (IHA) 6400 Shafer Ct Ste 650 — *TF:* 888-689-2838 ■ *Web:* www.housewares.org	Rosemont	IL	60018	847-292-4200	292-4211
International Order of the Golden Rule (OGR) 3520 Executive Ctr Dr Ste 300 — *TF:* 800-637-8030 ■ *Web:* www.ogr.org	Austin	TX	78731	512-334-5504	334-5514
International Precious Metals Institute (IPMI) 5101 N 12th Ave Ste C — *Web:* www.ipmi.org	Pensacola	FL	32504	850-476-1156	476-1548
International Sign Assn (ISA) 1001 N Fairfax St Ste 301 — *TF:* 866-949-7446 ■ *Web:* www.signs.org	Alexandria	VA	22314	703-836-4012	836-8353
International Sleep Products Assn (ISPA) 501 Wythe St — *Web:* www.sleepproducts.org	Alexandria	VA	22314	703-683-8371	683-4503
Jewelers Board of Trade (JBT) 95 Jefferson Blvd — *Web:* www.jewelersboard.com	Warwick	RI	02888	401-467-0055	467-6070
Jewelers of America (JA) 52 Vanderbilt Ave 19th Fl — *TF:* 800-223-0673 ■ *Web:* www.jewelers.org	New York	NY	10017	646-658-0246	658-0256
Leather Industries of America (LIA) 3050 K St NW Ste 400 — *TF:* 800-635-0617 ■ *Web:* www.leatherusa.com	Washington	DC	20007	202-342-8497	342-8583
Manufacturing Jewelers & Suppliers of America Inc (MJSA) 57 John L Dietsch Sq — *TF:* 800-444-6572 ■ *Web:* www.mjsa.org	Attleboro Falls	MA	02763	401-274-3840	274-0265
National Beauty Culturists' League Inc (NBCL) 25 Logan Cir NW — *Web:* www.nbcl.org	Washington	DC	20005	202-332-2695	332-0940
National Bicycle Dealers Assn (NBDA) 777 W 19th St Ste O — *Web:* www.nbda.com	Costa Mesa	CA	92627	949-722-6909	722-1747
National Cleaners Assn 252 W 29th St Second Fl — *TF General:* 800-888-1622 ■ *Web:* www.nca-i.com	New York	NY	10001	212-967-3002	967-2240
National Funeral Directors & Morticians Assn (NFDMA) 6290 Shannon Pkwy — **Fax Area Code:* 404 ■ *TF:* 800-434-0958 ■ *Web:* www.nfdma.com	Union City	GA	30291	770-969-0064	286-6573*
National Funeral Directors Assn (NFDA) 13625 Bishop's Dr — *TF:* 800-228-6332 ■ *Web:* nfda.org	Brookfield	WI	53005	262-789-1880	789-6977
National Home Furnishings Assn (NHFA) 3910 Tinsley Dr Ste 101 — *TF:* 800-422-3778 ■ *Web:* www.nahfa.org	High Point	NC	27265	336-886-6100	801-6102
National Pest Management Assn Inc (NPMA) 10460 N St — *Web:* www.pestworld.org	Fairfax	VA	22030	703-352-6762	352-3031
National Shoe Retailers Assn (NSRA) 7386 N La Cholla Blvd — *TF:* 800-673-8446 ■ *Web:* www.nsra.org	Tucson	AZ	85741	520-209-1710	
National Sporting Goods Assn (NSGA) 1601 Feehanville Dr Ste 300 — *TF:* 800-815-5422 ■ *Web:* www.nsga.org	Mount Prospect	IL	60056	847-296-6742	391-9827
National Volunteer Fire Council (NVFC) 7852 Walker Dr Ste 450 — *TF:* 888-275-6832 ■ *Web:* www.nvfc.org	Greenbelt	MD	20770	202-887-5700	887-5291
Outdoor Industry Assn (OIA) 4909 Pearl E Cir Ste 200 — *Web:* www.outdoorindustry.org	Boulder	CO	80301	303-444-3353	444-3284
Outdoor Power Equipment Institute Inc (OPEI) 341 S Patrick St — *Web:* www.opei.org	Alexandria	VA	22314	703-549-7600	549-7604
Pet Food Institute (PFI) 2025 M St NW Ste 800 — *Web:* www.petfoodinstitute.org	Washington	DC	20036	202-367-1120	367-2120
Pet Industry Joint Advisory Council (PIJAC) 1220 19th St NW Ste 400 — *TF:* 800-553-7387 ■ *Web:* www.pijac.org	Washington	DC	20036	202-452-1525	293-4377
Piano Technicians Guild 4444 Forest Ave — *Web:* www.ptg.org	Kansas City	KS	66106	913-432-9975	432-9986
Professional Assn of Innkeepers International (PAII) 207 White Horse Pk — *TF:* 800-468-7244 ■ *Web:* www.innkeeping.org	Haddon Heights	NJ	08035	856-310-1102	895-0432
Recreation Vehicle Industry Assn (RVIA) 1896 Preston White Dr — *TF:* 800-336-0154 ■ *Web:* www.rvia.org	Reston	VA	20191	703-620-6003	620-5071
Security Industry Assn (SIA) 635 Slaters Ln Ste 110 — *TF:* 866-817-8888 ■ *Web:* www.siaonline.org	Alexandria	VA	22314	703-683-2075	683-2469
Selected Independent Funeral Homes 500 Lake Cook Rd Ste 205 — *TF:* 800-323-4219 ■ *Web:* www.selectedfuneralhomes.org	Deerfield	IL	60015	847-236-9401	236-9968
Shoe Service Institute of America (SSIA) 18 School St — **Fax Area Code:* 410 ■ *Web:* www.ssia.info	North Brookfield	MA	01535	508-867-7731	569-8333*
Silver Institute 888 16th St NW Ste 303 — *Web:* www.silverinstitute.org	Washington	DC	20006	202-835-0185	835-0155
SnowSports Industries America (SIA) 8377 Greensboro Dr # B — *Web:* www.snowsports.org	McLean	VA	22102	703-556-9020	821-8276
Society of American Florists (SAF) 1601 Duke St — *TF:* 800-336-4743 ■ *Web:* www.safnow.org	Alexandria	VA	22314	703-836-8700	836-8705
Specialty Sleep Assn (SSA) 46639 Jones Ranch Rd — *Web:* www.sleepinformation.org	Friant	CA	93626	559-868-4187	868-4185
Sports & Fitness Industry Association, The 1150 17th St NW Ste 850 — *Web:* www.sfia.org	Washington	DC	20036	202-775-1762	296-7462
Textile Rental Services Assn (TRSA) 1800 Diagonal Rd Ste 200 — *TF:* 877-770-9274 ■ *Web:* www.trsa.org	Alexandria	VA	22314	703-519-0029	519-0026
Tire Industry Assn (TIA) 1532 Pointer Ridge Pl Ste G — *TF:* 800-876-8372 ■ *Web:* www.tireindustry.org	Bowie	MD	20716	301-430-7280	430-7283
Toy Industry Assn 1115 Broadway Ste 400 — *TF:* 800-541-1345 ■ *Web:* www.toyassociation.org	New York	NY	10010	212-675-1141	633-1429
Uniform & Textile Service Assn (UTSA) 1300 N 17th St Ste 750 — *TF:* 800-996-3426 ■ *Web:* www.glrppr.org	Arlington	VA	22209	703-247-2600	
Vision Council, The 225 Reinekers Ln Ste 700 — *TF:* 866-826-0290 ■ *Web:* www.thevisioncouncil.org	Alexandria	VA	22314	703-548-4560	548-4580
Wallcoverings Assn 401 N Michigan Ave Ste 2200 — *TF:* 800-575-8016 ■ *Web:* www.wallcoverings.org	Chicago	IL	60611	312-644-6610	527-6705
World Floor Covering Assn (WFCA) 2211 Howell Ave — *TF:* 800-624-6880 ■ *Web:* www.wfca.org	Anaheim	CA	92806	714-978-6440	978-6066
World Gold Council 444 Madison Ave Ste 301 — *Web:* www.gold.org	New York	NY	10022	212-317-3800	688-0410

49-5 Education Professionals Associations

Organization	City	State	ZIP	Phone	Fax
American Anthropological Assn (AAA) 2200 Wilson Blvd Ste 600 — *Web:* www.aaanet.org	Arlington	VA	22201	703-528-1902	528-3546
American Assn for Adult & Continuing Education (AAACE) 10111 ML King Jr Hwy Ste 200-C — *Web:* www.aaace.org	Bowie	MD	20720	301-459-6261	459-6241
American Assn of Colleges for Teacher Education (AACTE) 1307 New York Ave NW Ste 300 — *Web:* www.aacte.org	Washington	DC	20005	202-293-2450	457-8095
American Assn of Colleges of Nursing (AACN) One Dupont Cir NW Ste 530 — *Web:* www.aacn.nche.edu	Washington	DC	20036	202-463-6930	785-8320
American Assn of Collegiate Registrars & Admissions Officers (AACRAO) 1 Dupont Cir NW Ste 520 — *TF:* 800-222-4922 ■ *Web:* www.aacrao.org	Washington	DC	20036	202-293-9161	872-8857
American Assn of Community Colleges (AACC) One Dupont Cir NW Ste 410 — *Web:* www.aacc.nche.edu	Washington	DC	20036	202-728-0200	833-2467
American Assn of Family & Consumer Sciences (AAFCS) 400 N Columbus St Ste 202 — *TF:* 800-424-8080 ■ *Web:* www.aafcs.org	Alexandria	VA	22314	703-706-4600	706-4663
American Assn of Physics Teachers (AAPT) One Physics Ellipse — *Web:* www.aapt.org	College Park	MD	20740	301-209-3311	209-0845
American Assn of School Administrators (AASA) 801 N Quincy St Ste 700 — *TF:* 800-771-1162 ■ *Web:* www.aasa.org	Arlington	VA	22203	703-528-0700	841-1543
American Assn of State Colleges & Universities (AASCU) 1307 New York Ave NW Fifth Fl — *TF:* 800-558-3417 ■ *Web:* www.aascu.org	Washington	DC	20005	202-293-7070	296-5819
American Assn of Teachers of French (AATF) Southern Illinois Univ MC 4510 — *Web:* www.frenchteachers.org	Carbondale	IL	62901	618-453-5731	453-5733
American Assn of Teachers of German (AATG) 112 Haddontowne Ct Ste 104 — *TF:* 800-835-6770 ■ *Web:* www.aatg.org	Cherry Hill	NJ	08034	856-795-5553	795-9398
American Assn of Teachers of Spanish & Portuguese (AATSP) 900 Ladd Rd — *TF:* 877-832-2457 ■ *Web:* www.aatsp.org	Walled Lake	MI	48390	248-960-2180	960-9570
American Assn of University Professors (AAUP) 1133 Nineteenth St Ste 200 — *TF:* 800-424-2973 ■ *Web:* www.aaup.org	Washington	DC	20036	202-737-5900	737-5526
American Assn of University Women (AAUW) 1111 16th St NW — *TF:* 800-326-2289 ■ *Web:* www.aauw.org	Washington	DC	20036	202-785-7700	872-1425
American College Personnel Assn (ACPA) One Dupont Cir NW Ste 300 — *Web:* www.acpa.nche.edu/	Washington	DC	20036	202-835-2272	296-3286
American Council on Education (ACE) 1 Dupont Cir NW Ste 800 — *Web:* www.acenet.edu	Washington	DC	20036	202-939-9300	833-4760
American Council on the Teaching of Foreign Languages (ACTFL) 1001 N Fairfax St Ste 200 — *TF:* 844-685-4373 ■ *Web:* www.actfl.org	Alexandria	VA	22314	703-894-2900	894-2905
American Councils for International Education 1776 Massachusetts Ave NW Ste 700 — *Web:* www.americancouncils.org	Washington	DC	20036	202-833-7522	833-7523
American Dental Education Assn (ADEA) 1400 K St NW Ste 1100 — *TF:* 800-353-2237 ■ *Web:* www.adea.org	Washington	DC	20005	202-289-7201	289-7204
American Educational Research Assn (AERA) 1430 K St NW Ste 1200 — *TF:* 800-893-7950 ■ *Web:* www.aera.net	Washington	DC	20005	202-238-3200	238-3250
American Federation of School Administrators (AFSA) 1101 17th St NW Ste 408	Washington	DC	20036	202-986-4209	986-4211
American Historical Assn (AHA) 400 A St SE — *TF:* 888-444-6664 ■ *Web:* www.historians.org	Washington	DC	20003	202-544-2422	544-8307
American Library Assn (ALA) 50 E Huron St — *TF:* 800-545-2433 ■ *Web:* www.ala.org	Chicago	IL	60611	312-944-6780	944-2641
American Medical Student Assn (AMSA) 1902 Assn Dr — *TF:* 800-767-2266 ■ *Web:* www.amsa.org	Reston	VA	20191	703-620-6600	620-5873
American Political Science Assn (APSA) 1527 New Hampshire Ave NW — *Web:* www.apsanet.org	Washington	DC	20036	202-483-2512	483-2657

				Phone	Fax
American School Counselor Assn (ASCA) 1101 King St Ste 625 *TF:* 800-306-4722 ■ *Web:* www.schoolcounselor.org	Alexandria	VA	22314	703-683-2722	683-1619
American School Health Assn (ASHA) 7263 State Rt 43 PO Box 708 *Web:* netforum.avectra.com/eweb/startpage.aspx?site=asha1&webcode=homepage	Kent	OH	44240	703-506-7675	506-3266
American Society for Engineering Education (ASEE) 1818 N St NW Ste 600 *Web:* www.asee.org	Washington	DC	20036	202-331-3500	265-8504
American Society for Training & Development (ASTD) 1640 King St Third Fl PO Box 1443 *TF:* 800-628-2783 ■ *Web:* www.astd.org	Alexandria	VA	22313	703-683-8100	683-1523
American Sociological Assn (ASA) 1307 New York Ave. *TF:* 800-524-9400 ■ *Web:* www.asanet.org	Washington	DC	20005	202-383-9005	638-0882
American String Teachers Assn (ASTA) 4155 Chain Bridge Rd *TF:* 800-821-7303 ■ *Web:* www.astaweb.com	Fairfax	VA	22030	703-279-2113	279-2114
American Studies Assn (ASA) 1120 19th St NW Ste 301 *TF:* 800-468-3571 ■ *Web:* www.theasa.net	Washington	DC	20036	202-467-4783	467-4786
American Translators Assn (ATA) 225 Reinekers Ln Ste 590 *TF:* 800-253-2252 ■ *Web:* www.atanet.org	Alexandria	VA	22314	703-683-6100	683-6122
Association for Advanced Training in the Behavioral Sciences (AATBS) 5126 Ralston St *TF:* 800-472-1931 ■ *Web:* aatbs.com	Ventura	CA	93003	805-676-3030	676-3033
Association for Career & Technical Education (ACTE) 1410 King St. *TF:* 800-826-9972 ■ *Web:* www.acteonline.org	Alexandria	VA	22314	703-683-3111	683-7424
Association for Childhood Education International (ACEI) 1101 16th St NW Ste 300 **Fax Area Code:* 301 ■ *TF:* 800-423-3563 ■ *Web:* www.acei.org	Washington	DC	20036	202-372-9986	570-2212*
Association for Communications Technology Professionals in Higher Education (ACUTA) 152 W Zandale Dr Ste 200 *Web:* www.acuta.org	Lexington	KY	40503	859-278-3338	278-3268
Association for Continuing Higher Education (ACHE) 1700 Asp Ave **Fax Area Code:* 843 ■ *TF:* 800-807-2243 ■ *Web:* www.acheinc.org	Norman	OK	73072	800-807-2243	574-6470*
Association for Gerontology in Higher Education (AGHE) 1220 L St NW Ste 901 *Web:* www.aghe.org	Washington	DC	20005	202-289-9806	289-9824
Association for Practical & Professional Ethics 618 E Third St. *Web:* www.indiana.edu	Bloomington	IN	47405	812-855-4848	
Association for Supervision & Curriculum Development (ASCD) 1703 N Beauregard St. *TF:* 800-933-2723 ■ *Web:* www.ascd.org	Alexandria	VA	22311	703-578-9600	575-5400
Association for the Advancement of Computing in Education (AACE) PO Box 1545 **Fax Area Code:* 703 ■ *TF:* 800-352-5397 ■ *Web:* www.aace.org	Chesapeake	VA	23327	757-366-5606	997-8760*
Association of Advanced Rabbinical & Talmudic Schools (AARTS) 11 Broadway	New York	NY	10004	212-363-1991	533-5335
Association of American Colleges & Universities (AAC&U) 1818 R St NW *Web:* www.aacu.org	Washington	DC	20009	202-387-3760	265-9532
Association of American Law Schools (AALS) 1201 Connecticut Ave NW Ste 800 *Web:* www.aals.org	Washington	DC	20036	202-296-8851	296-8869
Association of American Medical Colleges (AAMC) 2450 N St NW *TF:* 800-273-8255 ■ *Web:* www.aamc.org	Washington	DC	20037	202-828-0400	828-1125
Association of American Universities (AAU) 1200 New York Ave NW Ste 550 *Web:* www.aau.edu	Washington	DC	20005	202-408-7500	408-8184
Association of Christian Schools International (ACSI) 731 Chapel Hills Dr *TF Cust Svc:* 800-367-0798 ■ *Web:* www.acsi.org	Colorado Springs	CO	80920	719-528-6906	
Association of College & University Housing Officers International (ACUHO-I) 941 Chatham Ln Ste 318 *Web:* www.acuho-i.org	Columbus	OH	43221	614-292-0099	292-3205
Association of College Unions International (ACUI) 120 W Seventh St 1 City Ctr Ste 200 *Web:* www.acui.org	Bloomington	IN	47404	812-245-2284	245-6710
Association of Collegiate Schools of Architecture (ACSA) 1735 New York Ave NW 3rd Fl *TF:* 877-426-6323 ■ *Web:* www.acsa-arch.org	Washington	DC	20006	202-785-2324	628-0448
Association of Community College Trustees (ACCT) 1233 20th St NW Ste 605 *TF:* 866-895-2228 ■ *Web:* www.acct.org	Washington	DC	20036	202-775-4667	223-1297
Association of Governing Boards of Universities & Colleges (AGB) 1133 20th St NW Ste 300 *TF:* 800-356-6317 ■ *Web:* www.agb.org	Washington	DC	20036	202-296-8400	223-7053
Association of Higher Education Facilities Officers (APPA) 1643 Prince St *Web:* www.appa.org	Alexandria	VA	22314	703-684-1446	549-2772
Association of Public & Land-grant Universities (APLU) 1307 New York Ave NW Ste 400 *Web:* www.aplu.org	Washington	DC	20005	202-478-6040	478-6046
Association of Research Libraries (ARL) 21 Dupont Cir NW Ste 800 *Web:* www.arl.org	Washington	DC	20036	202-296-2296	872-0884
Association of School Business Officials International (ASBO) 11401 N Shore Dr. **Fax Area Code:* 703 ■ *TF:* 866-682-2729 ■ *Web:* asbointl.org	Reston	VA	20190	866-682-2729	478-0205*
Association of Schools of Public Health (ASPH) 1900 M St NW Ste 710 *Web:* www.asph.org	Washington	DC	20036	202-296-1099	296-1252
Association of Test Publishers 601 Pennsylvania Ave NW Ste 900 *TF:* 866-240-7909 ■ *Web:* www.testpublishers.org	Washington	DC	20004	866-240-7909	
Association of Theological Schools in the US & Canada (ATS) 10 Summit Pk Dr *Web:* www.ats.edu	Pittsburgh	PA	15275	412-788-6505	788-6510

				Phone	Fax
Association of Universities for Research in Astronomy (AURA) 1200 New York Ave NW Ste 350 *TF:* 888-624-8373 ■ *Web:* www.aura-astronomy.org	Washington	DC	20005	202-483-2101	483-2106
Association of University Centers on Disabilities (AUCD) 1100 Wayne Avenue Suite 1000 *TF:* 888-572-2249 ■ *Web:* www.aucd.org	Silver Spring	MD	20910	301-588-8252	588-2842
Broadcast Education Assn (BEA) 1771 N St NW *TF:* 888-326-1415 ■ *Web:* www.beaweb.org	Washington	DC	20036	202-429-3935	775-2981
Business Professionals of America 5454 Cleveland Ave *TF:* 800-334-2007 ■ *Web:* www.bpa.org	Columbus	OH	43231	614-895-7277	895-1165
Business-Higher Education Forum 2025 M St NW Ste 800 *Web:* www.bhef.com	Washington	DC	20036	202-367-1189	367-2269
Career College Assn (CCA) 1101 Connecticut Ave NW Ste 900 *Web:* www.career.org	Washington	DC	20036	202-336-6700	336-6828
Christian Schools International (CSI) 3350 E Paris Ave SE *TF:* 800-635-8288 ■ *Web:* www.csionline.org	Grand Rapids	MI	49512	616-957-1070	957-5022
College & University Professional Assn for Hum Res (CUPA-HR) 1811 Commons Pt Dr *TF:* 877-287-2474 ■ *Web:* www.cupahr.org	Knoxville	TN	37932	865-637-7673	637-7674
College Music Society (CMS) 312 E Pine St. *TF:* 800-729-0235 ■ *Web:* www.music.org	Missoula	MT	59802	406-721-9616	721-9419
Conference on College Composition & Communication (CCCC) 1111 W Kenyon Rd. *TF:* 877-369-6283 ■ *Web:* www.ncte.org/cccc	Urbana	IL	61801	217-328-3870	278-3763
Council for Advancement & Support of Education (CASE) 1307 New York Ave NW Ste 1000 *TF Orders:* 800-554-8536 ■ *Web:* www.case.org	Washington	DC	20005	202-328-5900	387-4973
Council for Christian Colleges & Universities (CCCU) 321 Eigth St NE *Web:* www.cccu.org	Washington	DC	20002	202-546-8713	546-8913
Council for International Exchange of Scholars (CIES) 3007 Tilden St NW Ste 5L *Web:* www.cies.org	Washington	DC	20008	202-686-4000	362-3442
Council for Professional Recognition 2460 16th St NW *TF:* 800-424-4310 ■ *Web:* www.cdacouncil.org	Washington	DC	20009	202-265-9090	265-9161
Council of Administrators of Special Education (CASE) Osigian Office Centre 101 Katelyn Cir Ste E *TF:* 800-585-1753 ■ *Web:* www.casecec.org	Warner Robins	GA	31088	478-333-6892	333-2453
Council of Chief State School Officers (CCSSO) One Massachusetts Ave NW Ste 700 *Web:* www.ccsso.org	Washington	DC	20001	202-336-7000	408-8072
Council of Graduate Schools (CGS) One Dupont Cir NW Ste 230 *Web:* www.cgsnet.org	Washington	DC	20036	202-223-3791	331-7157
Council of Independent Colleges (CIC) One Dupont Cir NW Ste 320 *Web:* www.cic.edu	Washington	DC	20036	202-466-7230	466-7238
Council of the Great City Schools 1301 Pennsylvania Ave NW Ste 702 *TF:* 888-280-7903 ■ *Web:* www.cgcs.org	Washington	DC	20004	202-393-2427	393-2400
Council on International Educational Exchange (CIEE) 300 Fore St Second Fl *TF Cust Svc:* 888-268-6245 ■ *Web:* www.ciee.org	Portland	ME	04101	207-553-4000	553-5272
Council on Social Work Education (CSWE) 1701 Duke St *Web:* www.cswe.org	Alexandria	VA	22314	703-683-8080	683-8099
Distance Education & Training Council (DETC) 1601 18th St NW Ste 2 *Web:* www.detc.org	Washington	DC	20009	202-234-5100	332-1386
Distributive Education Clubs of America (DECA) 1908 Assn Dr *Web:* www.deca.org	Reston	VA	20191	703-860-5000	860-4013
Econometric Society New York Univ Dept of Economics 19 W Fourth St Sixth Fl *Web:* www.econometricsociety.org	New York	NY	10012	212-998-3820	995-4487
Education Commission of the States (ECS) 700 Broadway Ste 810 *TF:* 877-584-8642 ■ *Web:* www.ecs.org	Denver	CO	80203	303-299-3600	296-8332
Educational Housing Services Inc 55 Clark St *TF:* 800-385-1689 ■ *Web:* www.studenthousing.org	Brooklyn	NY	11201	212-977-7622	307-0701
Hispanic Assn of Colleges & Universities (HACU) 8415 Datapoint Dr Ste 400 *TF:* 800-780-4228 ■ *Web:* www.hacu.net	San Antonio	TX	78229	210-692-3805	692-0823
Independent Educational Consultants Assn (IECA) 3251 Old Lee Hwy Ste 510 *Web:* iecaonline.com/	Fairfax	VA	22030	703-591-4850	591-4860
International Council on Hotel Restaurant & Institutional Education (CHRIE) 2810 N Parham Rd Ste 230 *Web:* www.chrie.org	Richmond	VA	23294	804-346-4800	346-5009
International Reading Assn (IRA) 800 Barksdale Rd PO Box 6021 *TF:* 800-336-7323 ■ *Web:* www.reading.org	Newark	DE	19714	302-731-1600	737-0878
International Society for Technology in Education (ISTE) 1710 Rhode Island Ave NW Ste 900 *TF General:* 800-336-5191 ■ *Web:* www.iste.org	Washington	DC	20036	202-861-7777	861-0888
International Technology Education Assn (ITEA) 1914 Assn Dr Ste 201 *Web:* www.iteaconnect.org	Reston	VA	20191	703-860-2100	860-0353
Languages Canada 5886 169 A St **Fax Area Code:* 888 ■ *Web:* www.languagescanada.ca	Surrey	BC	V3S6Z8	604-574-1532	277-0522*
MENC: NA for Music Education 1806 Robert Fulton Dr *TF:* 800-336-3768 ■ *Web:* nafme.org	Reston	VA	20191	703-860-4000	860-1531
Middle States Commission on Higher Education 3624 Market St **Fax Area Code:* 215 ■ *Web:* www.msche.org	Philadelphia	PA	19104	267-284-5000	662-5501*

Phone Fax

Modern Language Assn (MLA) 26 Broadway 3rd Fl ... New York NY 10004 646-576-5000 458-0030
TF: 800-323-4900 ■ *Web:* mla.org
Music Teachers NA (MTNA) 441 Vine St Ste 3100 ... Cincinnati OH 45202 513-421-1420 421-2503
TF: 888-512-5278 ■ *Web:* www.mtna.org
NA of College Auxiliary Services (NACAS)
Three Boar's Head Ln Ste B ... Charlottesville VA 22903 434-245-8425 245-8453
Web: www.nacas.org
NA of Colleges & Employers (NACE)
62 Highland Ave ... Bethlehem PA 18017 610-868-1421 868-1421
TF: 800-544-5272 ■ *Web:* www.naceweb.org
NA of Elementary School Principals (NAESP)
1615 Duke St ... Alexandria VA 22314 703-684-3345 548-6021
TF: 800-386-2377 ■ *Web:* www.naesp.org
NA of Independent Colleges & Universities (NAICU)
1025 Connecticut Ave NW Ste 700 ... Washington DC 20036 202-785-8866 835-0003
Web: www.naicu.edu
NA of State Boards of Education (NASBE)
2121 Crystal Dr Ste 350 ... Arlington VA 22202 703-684-4000
Web: www.nasbe.org
NAFSA: Assn of International Educators
1307 New York Ave NW Eighth Fl ... Washington DC 20005 202-737-3699 737-3657
Web: www.nafsa.org
National Academy of Education
500 Fifth St NW Ste 333 ... Washington DC 20001 202-334-2341 334-2350
Web: www.naeducation.org
National Art Education Assn (NAEA)
1806 Robert Fulton Dr ... Reston VA 20191 703-860-8000 860-2960
TF: 800-299-8321 ■ *Web:* www.arteducators.org
National Assn of Student Financial Aid Administrators (NASFAA)
1101 Connecticut Ave Ste 1100 ... Washington DC 20036 202-785-0453 785-1487
TF: 800-877-8339 ■ *Web:* www.nasfaa.org
National Business Education Assn (NBEA)
1914 Assn Dr ... Reston VA 20191 703-860-8300 620-4483
Web: www.nbea.org
National Catholic Educational Assn (NCEA)
1077 30th St NW Ste 100 ... Washington DC 20007 202-337-6232 333-6706
TF: 800-711-6232 ■ *Web:* www.ncea.org
National Coalition of Girls' Schools (NCGS)
50 Leonard St Ste 2C ... Belmont MA 02478 617-489-0013 489-0024
Web: www.ncgs.org
National Communication Assn (NCA)
1765 N St NW ... Washington DC 20036 202-464-4622 464-4600
Web: www.natcom.org
National Council for the Social Studies (NCSS)
8555 16th St Ste 500 ... Silver Spring MD 20910 301-588-1800 588-2049
TF Orders: 800-683-0812 ■ *Web:* socialstudies.org/
National Council of Supervisors of Mathematics (NCSM)
6000 E Evans Ave Ste 3-205 ... Denver CO 80222 303-758-9611 758-9616
Web: www.mathedleadership.org
National Council of Teachers of English (NCTE)
1111 W Kenyon Rd ... Urbana IL 61801 217-328-3870 328-0977
TF: 877-369-6283 ■ *Web:* www.ncte.org
National Council of Teachers of Mathematics (NCTM)
1906 Assn Dr ... Reston VA 20191 703-620-9840 476-2970
TF Orders: 800-235-7566 ■ *Web:* www.nctm.org
National Council on Economic Education (NCEE)
122 E 42nd St Ste 2600 ... New York NY 10168 212-730-7007 730-1793
TF: 800-338-1192 ■ *Web:* www.councilforeconed.org
National Education Assn (NEA)
1201 16th St NW ... Washington DC 20036 202-833-4000 822-7974
TF: 888-552-0624 ■ *Web:* www.nea.org
National Environmental Safety & Health Training Assn (NESHTA)
2700 N Central Ave Ste 900 ... Phoenix AZ 85004 602-956-6099 234-1867
Web: www.neshta.org
National Guild of Community Schools of the Arts
520 Eigth Ave Ste 302 ... New York NY 10018 212-268-3337 268-3995
Web: www.nationalguild.org
National Middle School Assn (NMSA)
4151 Executive Pkwy Ste 300 ... Westerville OH 43081 614-895-4730 895-4750
TF: 800-528-6672 ■ *Web:* www.amle.org
National School Boards Assn (NSBA)
1680 Duke St ... Alexandria VA 22314 703-838-6722 683-7590
Web: www.nsba.org
National School Public Relations Assn (NSPRA)
15948 Derwood Rd ... Rockville MD 20855 301-519-0496 519-0494
Web: www.nspra.org
National Science Teachers Assn (NSTA)
1840 Wilson Blvd ... Arlington VA 22201 703-243-7100 243-7177
TF Sales: 800-722-6782 ■ *Web:* www.nsta.org
National Staff Development Council (NSDC)
504 S Locust St ... Oxford OH 45056 513-523-6029 523-0638
TF: 800-727-7288 ■ *Web:* www.learningforward.org
North Central Assn Higher Learning Commission
230 S LaSalle St ... Chicago IL 60604 312-263-0456 263-7462
TF: 800-621-7440 ■ *Web:* www.ncacihe.org
Oak Ridge Associated Universities (ORAU)
130 Badger Ave PO Box 117 ... Oak Ridge TN 37831 865-576-3000 576-3643
Web: www.orau.org
Organization for Tropical Studies (OTS)
410 Swift Ave PO Box 90630 ... Durham NC 27705 919-684-5774 684-5661
TF: 877-572-4484 ■ *Web:* www.ots.ac.cr
Organization of American Historians (OAH)
112 N Bryan Ave ... Bloomington IN 47408 812-855-7311 855-0696
TF: 888-737-7006 ■ *Web:* www.oah.org
Registry of Interpreters for the Deaf Inc (RID)
333 Commerce St ... Alexandria VA 22314 703-838-0030 838-0454
Web: www.rid.org
Society for American Archaeology (SAA)
900 Second St NE Ste 12 ... Washington DC 20002 202-789-8200 789-0284
TF: 800-759-5219 ■ *Web:* www.saa.org
Society for College & University Planning (SCUP)
339 E Liberty St Ste 300 ... Ann Arbor MI 48104 734-669-3270 998-6532
TF: 800-257-2578 ■ *Web:* www.scup.org

Phone Fax

Society for Research in Child Development (SRCD)
2950 S State St Ste 401 ... Ann Arbor MI 48104 734-926-0600 926-0601
Web: www.srcd.org
Southern Assn of Colleges & Schools
1866 Southern Ln ... Decatur GA 30033 404-679-4500 679-4558
TF: 888-413-3669 ■ *Web:* www.sacs.org
Teach For America 315 W 36th St Seventh Fl ... New York NY 10018 212-279-2080 279-2081
TF: 800-832-1230 ■ *Web:* www.teachforamerica.org
Teachers of English to Speakers of Other Languages (TESOL)
700 S Washington St Ste 200 ... Alexandria VA 22314 703-836-0774 836-7864
TF: 888-547-3369 ■ *Web:* www.tesol.org
Teaching & Mentoring Communities (TMC)
PO Box 2579 ... Laredo TX 78044 956-722-5174 725-0907
TF: 888-836-5151 ■ *Web:* www.tmccentral.org
Torah Umesorah-National Society for Hebrew Day Schools
620 Foster Ave ... Brooklyn NY 11230 212-227-1000 406-6934
Web: torah-umesorah.com
Trees for Tomorrow (TFT)
519 Sheridan St E PO Box 609 ... Eagle River WI 54521 715-479-6456 479-2318
TF: 800-838-9472 ■ *Web:* www.treesfortomorrow.com
Washington Education Assn Inc
32032 Weyerhaeuser Way S PO Box 9100 ... Federal Way WA 98001 253-941-6700
TF: 800-622-3393 ■ *Web:* www.washingtonea.org
Western Assn of Schools & Colleges (WASC)
985 Atlantic Ave ... Alameda CA 94501 510-748-9001
Web: wascsenior.org/
Women's College Coalition (WCC)
PO Box 3983 PO Box 1952 ... Decatur GA 30031 404-234-8715
Web: www.womenscolleges.org

49-6 Food & Beverage Industries Professional Associations

Phone Fax

American Assn of Cereal Chemists Inc (AACC)
3340 Pilot Knob Rd ... Saint Paul MN 55121 651-454-7250 454-0766
Web: www.aaccnet.org/default.aspx
American Beverage Assn 1101 16th St NW ... Washington DC 20036 202-463-6732 659-5349
Web: www.ameribev.org
American Beverage Licensees (ABL)
5101 River Rd Ste 108 ... Bethesda MD 20816 301-656-1494 656-7539
TF: 800-656-3241 ■ *Web:* www.ablusa.org
American Culinary Federation Inc (ACF)
180 Ctr Pl Way ... Saint Augustine FL 32095 904-824-4468 825-4758
TF: 800-624-9458 ■ *Web:* www.acfchefs.org
American Dairy Products Institute (ADPI)
116 N York St Ste 200 ... Elmhurst IL 60126 630-530-8700 530-8707
Web: www.adpi.org
American Malting Barley Assn (AMBA)
740 N Plankinton Ave Ste 830 ... Milwaukee WI 53203 414-272-4640
Web: www.ambainc.org
American Peanut Shellers Assn 2336 Lk Pk Dr ... Albany GA 31707 229-888-2508 888-5150
Web: www.peanut-shellers.org
American Society for Nutrition (ASNS)
9650 Rockville Pike Ste L3503A ... Bethesda MD 20814 301-634-7050 634-7894
TF: 800-627-8723 ■ *Web:* www.nutrition.org
American Spice Trade Assn (ASTA)
1101 17th St NW Ste 700 ... Washington DC 20036 202-331-2460 463-8998
Web: www.astaspice.org
Association of Food Industries Inc (AFI)
3301 Rt 66 Bldg C Ste 205 ... Neptune NJ 07753 732-922-3008 922-3590
Web: afius.org
At-sea Processors Assn (APA)
4039 21st Ave W Ste 400 ... Seattle WA 98199 206-285-5139 285-1841
Web: www.atsea.org
Beer Institute 122 C St NW Ste 350 ... Washington DC 20001 202-737-2337 737-7004
TF: 800-379-2739 ■ *Web:* www.beerinstitute.org
Biscuit & Cracker Manufacturers Assn (B&CMA)
6325 Woodside Ct Ste 125 ... Columbia MD 21046 443-545-1645 290-8585*
**Fax Area Code:* 410 ■ *TF:* 877-701-8111 ■ *Web:* www.thebcma.org
Confrerie de la Chaine des Rotisseurs
285 Madison Ave ... Madison NJ 07940 973-360-9200 360-9330
Web: www.chaineus.org
Council for Responsible Nutrition (CRN)
1828 L St NW Ste 900 ... Washington DC 20036 202-776-7929 204-7980
Web: www.crnusa.org
Distilled Spirits Council of the US Inc
1250 'I' St NW Ste 400 ... Washington DC 20005 202-628-3544 682-8888
Web: www.discus.org
Flavor & Extract Manufacturers Assn of the US (FEMA)
1101 17th St NW Ste 700 ... Washington DC 20036 202-293-5800 463-8998
Web: www.femaflavor.org
Food Institute One Broadway ... Elmwood Park NJ 07407 201-791-5570 791-5222
Web: www.foodinstitute.com
Food Marketing Institute (FMI)
2345 Crystal Dr Ste 800 ... Arlington VA 22202 202-220-0600 429-4519
TF: 800-732-2639 ■ *Web:* www.fmi.org
Institute of Food Technologists (IFT)
525 W Van Buren St Ste 1000 ... Chicago IL 60607 312-782-8424 782-8348
TF: 800-438-3663 ■ *Web:* www.ift.org
International Assn for Food Protection (IAFP)
6200 Aurora Ave Ste 200W ... Des Moines IA 50322 515-276-3344 276-8655
TF General: 800-369-6337 ■ *Web:* www.foodprotection.org
International Assn of Culinary Professionals (IACP)
1221 Ave of the Americas 42nd fl ... New York NY 10020 866-358-2524 358-2524
TF: 800-928-4227 ■ *Web:* www.iacp.com
International Bottled Water Assn (IBWA)
1700 Diagonal Rd Ste 650 ... Alexandria VA 22314 703-683-5213 683-4074
TF: 800-928-3711 ■ *Web:* www.bottledwater.org
International Dairy Foods Assn (IDFA)
1250 H St NW Ste 900 ... Washington DC 20005 202-737-4332 331-7820
Web: www.idfa.org

				Phone	Fax
International Dairy-Deli-Bakery Assn (IDDBA) 636 Science Dr *TF:* 877-399-4925 ■ *Web:* www.iddba.org	Madison	WI	53705	608-238-7908	238-6330
International Food Information Council Foundation (IFIC) 1100 Connecticut Ave NW Ste 430 *TF:* 888-723-3366 ■ *Web:* www.foodinsight.org	Washington	DC	20036	202-296-6540	296-6547
International Foodservice Distributors Assn (IFDA) 1410 Spring Hill Rd Ste 210 *Web:* www.ifdaonline.org	McLean	VA	22102	703-532-9400	538-4673
International Foodservice Manufacturers Assn (IFMA) 180 N Stetson Ave 2 Prudential Plz Ste 4400 *Web:* www.ifmaworld.com	Chicago	IL	60601	312-540-4400	540-4401
International Ice Cream Assn 1250 H St NW Ste 900 *Web:* www.idfa.org	Washington	DC	20005	202-737-4332	331-7820
Master Brewers Assn of the Americas (MBAA) 3340 Pilot Knob Rd *TF:* 800-328-7560 ■ *Web:* www.mbaa.com	Saint Paul	MN	55121	651-454-7250	454-0766
NA of Catering And Events (NACE) 9891 Broken Land Pkwy Suite 301 *Web:* www.nace.net	Columbia	MD	21046	410-290-5410	290-5460
National Beer Wholesalers Assn (NBWA) 1101 King St Ste 600 *TF:* 800-300-6417 ■ *Web:* www.nbwa.org	Alexandria	VA	22314	703-683-4300	683-8965
National Coffee Assn of USA Inc (NCA) 45 Broadway Ste 1140 *TF:* 800-247-6755 ■ *Web:* www.ncausa.org	New York	NY	10006	212-766-4007	766-5815
National Confectioners Assn (NCA) 1101 30th St NW Ste 200 *TF:* 800-433-1200 ■ *Web:* www.candyusa.com	Washington	DC	20007	202-534-1440	337-0637
National Frozen & Refrigerated Foods Assn (NFRA) 4755 Linglestown Rd Ste 300 PO Box 6069 *Web:* www.nfraweb.org	Harrisburg	PA	17112	717-657-8601	657-9862
National Grocers Assn (NGA) 1005 N Glebe Rd Ste 250 *Web:* www.nationalgrocers.org	Arlington	VA	22201	703-516-0700	516-0115
National Meat Assn (NMA) 1970 Broadway Ste 825 *Web:* meatassociation.com	Oakland	CA	94612	510-763-1533	763-6186
National Milk Producers Federation (NMPF) 2101 Wilson Blvd Ste 400 *TF:* 888-723-3366 ■ *Web:* www.nmpf.org	Arlington	VA	22201	703-243-6111	841-9328
National Pork Producers Council (NPPC) 122 C St NW Ste 875 *Web:* www.nppc.org	Washington	DC	20001	202-347-3600	347-5265
National Restaurant Assn (NRA) 2055 L St NW Ste 700 *TF:* 800-424-5156 ■ *Web:* www.restaurant.org	Washington	DC	20036	202-331-5900	331-2429
North American Meat Processors Assn (NAMP) 1910 Assn Dr **Fax Area Code:* 202 ■ *TF:* 800-535-4555 ■ *Web:* meatassociation.com	Reston	VA	20191	703-758-1900	662-4643*
North American Millers Assn (NAMA) 600 Maryland Ave SW Ste 825-W *Web:* www.namamillers.org	Washington	DC	20024	202-484-2200	488-7416
Popcorn Board 401 N Michigan Ave *Web:* www.popcorn.org	Chicago	IL	60611	312-644-6610	527-6658
Produce Marketing Assn (PMA) 1500 Casho Mill Rd *TF:* 800-872-7245 ■ *Web:* www.pma.com	Newark	DE	19711	302-738-7100	731-2409
Retail Confectioners International (RCI) 2053 S Waverly Ste C *TF:* 800-545-5381 ■ *Web:* www.retailconfectioners.org	Springfield	MO	65804	417-883-2775	883-1108
Salt Institute 700 N Fairfax St Ste 600 *Web:* www.saltinstitute.org	Alexandria	VA	22314	703-549-4648	548-2194
School Nutrition Assn (SNA) 700 S Washington St Ste 300 *TF:* 800-877-8822 ■ *Web:* www.schoolnutrition.org	Alexandria	VA	22314	703-739-3900	739-3915
Snack Food Assn 1600 Wilson Blvd Ste 650 *TF:* 800-628-1334 ■ *Web:* www.sfa.org	Arlington	VA	22209	703-836-4500	836-8262
Specialty Coffee Assn of America (SCAA) 330 Golden Shore Ave Ste 50 *TF:* 800-995-9019 ■ *Web:* www.scaa.org	Long Beach	CA	90802	562-624-4100	624-4101
Tea Assn of the USA Inc 362 Fifth Ave Ste 801 *Web:* www.teausa.com	New York	NY	10001	212-986-9415	697-8658
Tea Council of the USA Inc 362 Fifth Ave Ste 801 *TF:* 877-212-5752 ■ *Web:* www.teausa.com	New York	NY	10001	212-986-9415	697-8658
US Dairy Export Council 2101 Wilson Blvd Ste 400 *Web:* www.usdec.org	Arlington	VA	22201	703-528-3049	528-3705
US Meat Export Federation Inc (USMEF) 1050 17th St Ste 2200 *Web:* www.usmef.org	Denver	CO	80265	303-623-6328	623-0297
USA Poultry & Egg Export Council (USAPEEC) 2300 W Pk Pl Blvd Ste 100 *Web:* www.usapeec.org	Stone Mountain	GA	30087	770-413-0006	413-0007
Wheat Foods Council 10841 S Crossroads Dr Ste 105 *Web:* www.wheatfoods.org	Parker	CO	80134	303-840-8787	840-6877
Wine & Spirits Shippers Assn Inc (WSSA) 11800 Sunrise Vly Dr *TF General:* 800-368-3167 ■ *Web:* www.wssa.com	Reston	VA	20191	703-860-2300	860-2422
Wine & Spirits Wholesalers of America Inc (WSWA) 805 15th St NW Ste 430 *Web:* www.wswa.org	Washington	DC	20005	202-371-9792	789-2405
Wine Institute 425 Market St Ste 1000 *Web:* www.wineinstitute.org	San Francisco	CA	94105	415-512-0151	442-0742
WineAmerica 1015 18th St NW Ste 500 *TF:* 800-824-5419 ■ *Web:* www.wineamerica.org	Washington	DC	20036	202-783-2756	347-6341
World Cocoa Foundation (WCF) 1411 K St NW Ste 1300 *Web:* www.worldcocoafoundation.org	Washington	DC	20005	202-737-7870	737-7832

49-7 Government & Public Administration Professional Associations

				Phone	Fax
American Assn of Motor Vehicle Administrators (AAMVA) 4301 Wilson Blvd Ste 400 *Web:* www.aamva.org	Arlington	VA	22203	703-522-4200	522-1553
American Assn of State Highway & Transportation Officials (AASHTO) 444 N Capitol St NW Ste 249 *TF:* 800-880-4117 ■ *Web:* www.transportation.org	Washington	DC	20001	202-624-5800	624-5806
American Conference of Governmental Industrial Hygienists (ACGIH) 1330 Kemper Meadows Dr *Web:* www.acgih.org	Cincinnati	OH	45240	513-742-2020	742-3355
American Correctional Assn (ACA) 206 N Washington St Ste 200 *TF:* 800-222-5646 ■ *Web:* www.aca.org	Alexandria	VA	22314	703-224-0000	224-0010
American Federation of Police & Concerned Citizens 6350 Horizon Dr *TF:* 800-435-7352 ■ *Web:* www.afp-cc.org	Titusville	FL	32780	321-264-0911	264-0033
American Foreign Service Assn (AFSA) 2101 E St NW *TF:* 800-704-2372 ■ *Web:* www.afsa.org	Washington	DC	20037	202-338-4045	338-6820
American Foreign Service Protective Assn 1716 N St NW *Web:* www.afspa.org	Washington	DC	20036	202-833-4910	833-4918
American Jail Assn (AJA) 1135 Professional Ct *Web:* www.americanjail.org	Hagerstown	MD	21740	301-790-3930	790-2941
American Public Human Services Assn (APHSA) 1133 19th St NW Ste 400 *Web:* www.aphsa.org	Washington	DC	20036	202-682-0100	289-6555
American Public Works Assn (APWA) 2345 Grand Blvd Ste 700 *TF:* 800-848-2792 ■ *Web:* www.apwa.net	Kansas City	MO	64108	816-472-6100	472-1610
American Society for Public Administration (ASPA) 1301 Pennsylvania Ave NW Ste 840 *Web:* www.aspanet.org	Washington	DC	20004	202-393-7878	638-4952
Association of Conservation Engineers (ACE) Missouri Dept of Conservation PO Box 180 *TF:* 866-633-8110 ■ *Web:* www.conservationengineers.org	Jefferson City	MO	65102	573-522-4115	522-2324
Association of Maternal & Child Health Programs (AMCHP) 2030 M St NW Ste 350 *Web:* www.amchp.org	Washington	DC	20036	202-775-0436	466-5471
Association of Public Health Laboratories (APHL) 8515 Georgia Ave Ste 700 *TF:* 800-899-2278 ■ *Web:* www.aphl.org	Silver Spring	MD	20910	240-485-2745	485-2700
Association of Public-Safety Communications Officials International Inc 351 N Williamson Blvd *TF:* 888-272-6911 ■ *Web:* www.apcointl.org	Daytona Beach	FL	32114	386-322-2500	322-2501
Association of Racing Commissioners International (ARCI) 1510 Newtown Pike # 210 *Web:* www.arci.com	Lexington	KY	40511	859-224-7070	224-7071
Association of Social Work Boards (ASWB) 400 S Ridge Pkwy Ste B *TF:* 800-225-6880 ■ *Web:* www.aswb.org	Culpeper	VA	22701	540-829-6880	829-0142
Association of State & Interstate Water Pollution Control Administrators (ASIWPCA) 1221 Connecticut Ave NW Second Fl *Web:* www.acwa-us.org	Washington	DC	20036	202-756-0600	898-0929
Association of State & Territorial Health Officials (ASTHO) 2231 Crystal Dr Ste 450 **Fax Area Code:* 571 ■ *Web:* www.astho.org	Arlington	VA	22202	202-371-9090	527-3189*
Association of State & Territorial Solid Waste Management Officials (ASTSWMO) 444 N Capitol St NW Ste 315 *Web:* www.astswmo.org	Washington	DC	20001	202-624-5828	624-7875
Association of State Wetland Managers 32 Tandberg Trail Suite 2A *TF:* 800-451-6027 ■ *Web:* www.aswm.org	Windham	ME	04062	207-892-3399	892-3089
Commission on Accreditation for Law Enforcement Agencies (CALEA) 13575 Heathcote Blvd Ste 320 *TF:* 877-789-6904 ■ *Web:* www.calea.org	Gainesville	VA	20155	703-352-4225	890-3126
Conference of Radiation Control Program Directors (CRCPD) 1030 Burlington Ln # 4B *Web:* www.crcpd.org	Frankfort	KY	40601	502-227-4543	227-7862
Conference of State Bank Supervisors (CSBS) 1129 20th St NW Fifth Fl *TF:* 800-886-2727 ■ *Web:* www.csbs.org	Washington	DC	20036	202-296-2840	296-1928
Council of State & Territorial Epidemiologists (CSTE) 2872 Woodcock Blvd Ste 303 *TF:* 866-577-9956 ■ *Web:* www.cste.org	Atlanta	GA	30341	770-458-3811	458-8516
Council of State Governments (CSG) 2760 Research Pk Dr *TF Sales:* 800-800-1910 ■ *Web:* www.csg.org	Lexington	KY	40511	859-244-8000	244-8001
Council on Licensure Enforcement & Regulation (CLEAR) 403 Marquis Ave *Web:* www.clearhq.org/	Lexington	KY	40502	859-269-1289	
Federal Bureau of Investigation Agents Assn (FBIAA) PO Box 12650 *Web:* www.fbiaa.org	Arlington	VA	22219	703-247-2173	247-2175
Federal Law Enforcement Officers Assn (FLEOA) 1100 Connecticut Ave NW Ste 900 **Fax Area Code:* 717 ■ *Web:* www.fleoa.org	Washington	DC	20036	202-293-1550	932-2262*
Federal Managers Assn (FMA) 1641 Prince St *Web:* www.fedmanagers.org	Alexandria	VA	22314	703-683-8700	683-8707
Federally Employed Women (FEW) 455 Massachusetts Ave NW Ste 306 **Fax Area Code:* 703 ■ *Web:* www.few.org	Washington	DC	20001	202-898-0994	299-9233*
Federation of State Medical Boards of the US Inc (FSMB) 400 Fuller Wiser Rd Ste 300 *TF:* 800-793-7939 ■ *Web:* www.fsmb.org	Euless	TX	76039	817-868-4000	868-4098

Phone Fax

Federation of Tax Administrators (FTA)
444 N Capitol St NW Ste 348 ... Washington DC 20001 202-624-5890 624-7888
Web: www.taxadmin.org

Forest Service Employees for Environmental Ethics (FSEEE)
PO Box 11615 ... Eugene OR 97440 541-484-2692 484-3004
TF: 800-270-7504 ■ *Web:* www.fseee.org

Government Finance Officers Assn (GFOA)
203 N LaSalle St Ste 2700 ... Chicago IL 60601 312-977-9700 977-4806
Web: www.gfoa.org

International Assn of Arson Investigators (IAAI)
2111 Baldwin Ave # 203 ... Crofton MD 21114 410-451-3473 451-9049
Web: www.firearson.com

International Assn of Assessing Officers (IAAO)
314 W Tenth St ... Kansas City MO 64105 816-701-8100 701-8149
TF: 800-616-4226 ■ *Web:* www.iaao.org

International Assn of Auto Theft Investigators (IAATI)
PO Box 223 ... Clinton NY 13323 315-853-1913 793-0048
Web: www.iaati.org

International Assn of Chiefs of Police (IACP)
515 N Washington St ... Alexandria VA 22314 703-836-6767 836-4543
TF: 800-843-4227 ■ *Web:* www.theiacp.org

International Assn of Fire Chiefs (IAFC)
4025 Fair Ridge Dr Ste 300 ... Fairfax VA 22033 703-273-0911 273-9363
TF: 866-385-9110 ■ *Web:* www.iafc.org

International Assn of Fish & Wildlife Agencies (IAFWA)
444 N Capitol St NW Ste 725 ... Washington DC 20001 202-624-7890 624-7891
Web: www.fishwildlife.org

International Assn of Plumbing & Mechanical Officials (IAPMO)
4755 E Philadelphia St ... Ontario CA 91761 909-472-4100 472-4150
TF: 877-427-6601 ■ *Web:* www.iapmo.org

International Bridge Tunnel & Turnpike Assn (IBTTA)
1146 19th St NW Ste 600 ... Washington DC 20036 202-659-4620 659-0500
Web: www.ibtta.org

International City/County Management Assn (ICMA)
777 N Capitol St NE Ste 500 ... Washington DC 20002 202-289-4262 962-3500
TF: 800-745-8780 ■ *Web:* www.icma.org

International Conference of Funeral Service Examining Boards Inc
1885 Shelby Ln ... Fayetteville AR 72704 479-442-7076 442-7090
TF: 800-709-0180 ■ *Web:* www.theconferenceonline.org

International Institute of Municipal Clerks (IIMC)
8331 Utica Ave Ste 200 ... Rancho Cucamonga CA 91730 909-944-4162 944-8545
TF: 800-251-1639 ■ *Web:* www.iimc.com

International Municipal Signal Assn (IMSA)
165 E Union St PO Box 539 ... Newark NY 14513 315-331-2182 331-8205
TF: 800-723-4672 ■ *Web:* www.imsasafety.org

International Society of Fire Service Instructors (ISFSI)
14001C St Germain Dr ... Centreville VA 20121 800-435-0005 435-0005
TF: 800-435-0005 ■ *Web:* www.isfsi.org

Kansas Assn of Counties (KAC)
300 SW Eigth St Third Fl ... Topeka KS 66603 785-272-2585 272-3585
Web: www.kansascounties.org

Maryland Assn of Counties (MACo)
169 Conduit St ... Annapolis MD 21401 410-269-0043 268-1775
Web: www.mdcounties.org

NA of Clean Water Agencies (NACWA)
1816 Jefferson Pl NW ... Washington DC 20036 202-833-2672 833-4657
Web: www.nacwa.org

NA of Conservation Districts (NACD)
509 Capitol Ct NE ... Washington DC 20002 202-547-6223 547-6450
TF: 888-695-2433 ■ *Web:* www.nacdnet.org

NA of Housing & Redevelopment Officials (NAHRO)
630 'I' St NW ... Washington DC 20001 202-289-3500 289-8181
TF: 877-866-2476 ■ *Web:* www.nahro.org

NA of Postmasters of the US (NAPUS)
Eight Herbert St ... Alexandria VA 22305 703-683-9027 683-6820
Web: www.napus.org

NA of State Mental Health Program Directors (NASMHPD)
66 Canal Ctr Plz Ste 302 ... Alexandria VA 22314 703-739-9333 548-9517
Web: www.nasmhpd.org

National Academy of Public Administration
900 Seventh St NW Ste 600 ... Washington DC 20001 202-347-3190 393-0993
TF: 800-883-3190 ■ *Web:* www.napawash.org

National Alcohol Beverage Control Assn (NABCA)
4401 Ford Ave Ste 700 ... Alexandria VA 22302 703-578-4200 820-3551
Web: www.nabca.org

National American Indian Housing Council (NAIHC)
50 F St NW Ste 3300 ... Washington DC 20001 202-789-1754 789-1758
TF: 800-284-9165 ■ *Web:* www.naihc.net

National Assembly of State Arts Agencies (NASAA)
1029 Vermont Ave NW Second Fl ... Washington DC 20005 202-347-6352 737-0526
Web: www.nasaa-arts.org

National Assn on Aging
1201 15th St NW Ste 350 ... Washington DC 20005 202-898-2578
Web: www.nasuad.org

National Board of Boiler & Pressure Vessel Inspectors
1055 Crupper Ave ... Columbus OH 43229 614-888-8320 847-1147*
**Fax:* Cust Svc ■ *TF:* 877-682-8772 ■ *Web:* www.nationalboard.org

National Conference of State Historic Preservation Officers
444 N Capitol St NW Ste 342 ... Washington DC 20001 202-624-5465 624-5419
Web: www.ncshpo.org

National Conference of State Legislatures
7700 E First Pl ... Denver CO 80230 303-364-7700 364-7800
TF: 866-229-2386 ■ *Web:* www.ncsl.org

National Council of Architectural Registration Boards (NCARB)
1801 K St NW Ste 700-K ... Washington DC 20006 202-783-6500 783-0290
Web: www.ncarb.org

National Council of State Housing Agencies (NCSHA)
444 N Capitol St NW Ste 438 ... Washington DC 20001 202-624-7710 624-5899
Web: www.ncsha.org

National Ctr for State Courts (NCSC)
300 Newport Ave ... Williamsburg VA 23185 757-259-1525 220-0449
TF: 800-616-6164 ■ *Web:* www.ncsc.org

Phone Fax

National District Attorneys Assn (NDAA)
99 Canal Ctr Plaza Ste 510 ... Alexandria VA 22314 703-549-9222 836-3195
TF: 888-325-9943 ■ *Web:* www.ndaa.org

National Emergency Management Assn (NEMA)
PO Box 11910 ... Lexington KY 40578 859-244-8000 244-8239
Web: www.nemaweb.org

National Environmental Health Assn (NEHA)
720 S Colorado Blvd Ste 1000-N ... Denver CO 80246 303-756-9090 691-9490
TF: 866-956-2258 ■ *Web:* www.neha.org

National Fire Protection Assn (NFPA)
One Batterymarch Pk ... Quincy MA 02169 617-770-3000 770-0700
TF: 800-344-3555 ■ *Web:* www.nfpa.org

National Forum for Black Public Administrators (NFBPA)
777 N Capitol St NE Ste 807 ... Washington DC 20002 202-408-9300 408-8558
Web: www.nfbpa.org

National Governors Assn (NGA)
444 N Capitol St NW Ste 267 ... Washington DC 20001 202-624-5300 624-5313
Web: www.nga.org

National Institute of Governmental Purchasing Inc (NIGP)
151 Spring St ... Herndon VA 20170 703-736-8900 736-2818
TF: 800-367-6447 ■ *Web:* www.nigp.org

National League of Cities (NLC)
1301 Pennsylvania Ave NW Ste 550 ... Washington DC 20004 202-626-3000 626-3043
Web: www.nlc.org

National Organization of Black Law Enforcement Executives (NOBLE)
4609 Pinecrest Office Pk Dr Ste F ... Alexandria VA 22312 703-658-1529 658-9479
Web: www.noblenatl.org

National Sheriffs' Assn (NSA) 1450 Duke St ... Alexandria VA 22314 703-836-7827 683-6541
TF: 800-424-7827 ■ *Web:* www.sheriffs.org

National Ski Patrol System Inc (NSP)
133 S Van Gordon St Ste 100 ... Lakewood CO 80228 303-988-1111 988-3005
Web: www.nsp.org

National Volunteer Fire Council (NVFC)
7852 Walker Dr Ste 450 ... Greenbelt MD 20770 202-887-5700 887-5291
TF: 888-275-6832 ■ *Web:* www.nvfc.org

Opportunity Finance Network
620 Chestnut St Ste 572 ... Philadelphia PA 19106 215-923-4754 923-4755
Web: www.opportunityfinance.net

Police Executive Research Forum (PERF)
1120 Connecticut Ave NW Ste 930 ... Washington DC 20036 202-466-7820 466-7826
Web: www.policeforum.org

Public Employees Roundtable (PER)
PO Box 75248 ... Washington DC 20013 202-927-4926 927-4920
Web: www.keyinsurancequotes.com

Public Risk Management Assn (PRIMA)
700 S Washington St Ste 218 ... Alexandria VA 22314 703-528-7701 739-0200
Web: www.primacentral.org

Public Technology Inc
1420 Prince St Ste 200 ... Alexandria VA 22314 202-626-2400
Web: www.pti.org

United Federations of Security
540 N State Rd ... Briarcliff Manor NY 10510 914-941-4103 941-4472
TF: 800-227-4291 ■ *Web:* www.policefederation.com

US Conference of Mayors
1620 'I' St NW Ste 400 ... Washington DC 20006 202-293-7330 293-2352
Web: www.usmayors.org

US Travel Assn
1100 New York Ave NW Ste 450 ... Washington DC 20005 202-408-8422 408-1255
TF: 877-212-5752 ■ *Web:* www.ustravel.org

West Virginia Assn of Counties (WVACO)
2211 Washington St ... Charleston WV 25311 304-346-0591 346-0592
Web: www.wvaco.org

49-8 Health & Medical Professionals Associations

Phone Fax

Academy of General Dentistry (AGD)
211 E Chicago Ave Ste 900 ... Chicago IL 60611 312-440-4300 440-0559
TF: 888-243-3368 ■ *Web:* www.agd.org

Academy of Managed Care Pharmacy (AMCP)
100 N Pitt St Ste 400 ... Alexandria VA 22314 703-683-8416 683-8417
TF: 800-827-2627 ■ *Web:* www.amcp.org

Academy of Osseointegration
85 W Algonquin Rd Ste 550 ... Arlington Heights IL 60005 847-439-1919 439-1569
TF: 800-656-7736 ■ *Web:* www.osseo.org

Academy of Pharmacy Practice & Management
American Pharmacists Assn
1100 15th St NW Ste 400 ... Washington DC 20005 202-628-4410 783-2351
TF: 800-237-2742 ■ *Web:* www.pharmacist.com

Academy of Students of Pharmacy
American Pharmacists Assn
1100 15th St NW Ste 400 ... Washington DC 20005 202-628-4410 783-2351
TF: 800-237-2742 ■ *Web:* www.pharmacist.com

AcademyHealth 1801 K St NW Ste 701 ... Washington DC 20006 202-292-6700 292-6800
Web: www.academyhealth.org

Aerospace Medical Assn (AMA) 320 S Henry St ... Alexandria VA 22314 703-739-2240 739-9652
Web: www.asma.org

Aging Life Care Association (GCM)
3275 W Ina Rd Ste 130 ... Tucson AZ 85741 520-881-8008 325-7925
Web: www.caremanager.org

America's Blood Centers (ABC)
725 15th St NW Ste 700 ... Washington DC 20005 202-393-5725 393-1282
TF: 888-872-5663 ■ *Web:* www.americasblood.org

AMERICA'S ESSENTIAL HOSPITALS (NAPH)
1301 Pennsylvania Ave NW Ste 950 ... Washington DC 20004 202-585-0100 585-0101
Web: www.naph.org

American Academy of Allergy Asthma & Immunology (AAAAI)
555 E Wells St Ste 1100 ... Milwaukee WI 53202 414-272-6071 272-6070
TF: 800-654-2452 ■ *Web:* www.aaaai.org

American Academy of Audiology (AAA)
11730 Plz America Dr Ste 300 ... Reston VA 20190 703-790-8466 790-8631
TF: 800-222-2336 ■ *Web:* www.audiology.org

Phone Fax

American Academy of Cosmetic Dentistry (AACD)
402 W Wilson St. Madison WI 53703 608-222-8583 222-9540
TF: 800-543-9220 ■ *Web:* www.aacd.com

American Academy of Cosmetic Surgery (AACS)
737 N Michigan Ave Ste 2100 Chicago IL 60611 312-981-6760 981-6787
Web: www.cosmeticsurgery.org

American Academy of Dental Group Practice (AADGP)
2525 E Arizona Biltmore Cir Ste 127 Phoenix AZ 85016 602-381-1185 381-1093
Web: www.aadgp.org

American Academy of Dermatology (AAD)
930 E Woodfield Rd Schaumburg IL 60173 847-330-0230 330-0050
TF: 800-868-2472 ■ *Web:* www.aad.org

American Academy of Disability Evaluating Physicians (AADEP)
223 W Jackson Blvd Ste 1104 Chicago IL 60606 312-663-1171 663-1175
TF: 800-456-6095 ■ *Web:* www.aadep.org

American Academy of Facial Plastic & Reconstructive Surgery (AAFPRS)
310 S Henry St Alexandria VA 22314 703-299-9291 299-8898
Web: aafprs.org

American Academy of Family Physicians (AAFP)
11400 Tomahawk Creek Pkwy. Leawood KS 66211 913-906-6000 906-6075
TF: 800-274-2237 ■ *Web:* www.aafp.org

American Academy of Home Care Physicians (AAHCP)
PO Box 1037 Edgewood MD 21040 410-676-7966 676-7980
Web: aahcm.org

American Academy of Hospice & Palliative Medicine (AAHPM)
4700 W Lk Ave Glenview IL 60025 847-375-4712 734-8671*
**Fax Area Code:* 877 ■ *Web:* www.aahpm.org

American Academy of Neurology (AAN)
1080 Montreal Ave Saint Paul MN 55116 651-695-1940 695-2791
TF: 800-879-1960 ■ *Web:* www.aan.com

American Academy of Nurse Practitioners (AANP)
PO Box 12846 Austin TX 78711 512-442-4262 442-6469
Web: www.aanp.org

American Academy of Ophthalmology
655 Beach St San Francisco CA 94109 415-561-8500 561-8575
TF: 866-561-8558 ■ *Web:* www.aao.org

American Academy of Optometry (AAO)
6110 Executive Blvd Ste 506 Rockville MD 20852 301-984-1441 984-4737
TF: 800-368-6263 ■ *Web:* www.aaopt.org

American Academy of Orthopaedic Surgeons (AAOS)
6300 N River Rd Rosemont IL 60018 847-823-7186 823-8125
TF: 800-346-2267 ■ *Web:* www.aaos.org

American Academy of Orthotists & Prosthetists (AAOP)
526 King St Ste 201 Alexandria VA 22314 703-836-0788 836-0737
TF: 800-669-6024 ■ *Web:* www.oandp.org

American Academy of Otolaryngology-Head & Neck Surgery (AAO-HNS)
1650 Diagonal Rd Alexandria VA 22314 703-836-4444 683-5100
TF: 877-722-6467 ■ *Web:* www.entnet.org

American Academy of Pain Management (AAPM)
13947 Mono Way Ste A Sonora CA 95370 209-533-9744 533-9750
TF: 888-519-9901 ■ *Web:* www.aapainmanage.org

American Academy of Pediatric Dentistry (AAPD)
211 E Chicago Ave Ste 1700 Chicago IL 60611 312-337-2169 337-6329
TF: 800-974-3084 ■ *Web:* www.aapd.org

American Academy of Pediatrics (AAP)
141 NW Pt Blvd Elk Grove Village IL 60007 847-434-4000 434-8000
TF: 800-433-9016 ■ *Web:* www.aap.org

American Academy of Periodontology (AAP)
737 N Michigan Ave Ste 800 Chicago IL 60611 312-787-5518 787-3670
TF: 800-282-4867 ■ *Web:* www.perio.org

American Academy of Physical Medicine & Rehabilitation (AAPM&R)
9700 W Bryn Mawr Ave Ste 200 Rosemont IL 60018 847-737-6000 737-6001
Web: www.aapmr.org

American Assn for Cancer Research (AACR)
615 Chestnut St 17th Fl Philadelphia PA 19106 215-440-9300 440-7228
TF: 866-423-3965 ■ *Web:* www.aacr.org

American Assn for Homecare
2011 Crystal Dr Ste 725 Arlington VA 22202 703-836-6263 836-6730
Web: www.aahomecare.org

American Assn for Respiratory Care (AARC)
9425 N MacArthur Blvd Ste 100 Irving TX 75063 972-243-2272 484-2720
Web: www.aarc.org

American Assn for the Study of Liver Diseases (AASLD)
1001 N Fairfax St Ste 400 Alexandria VA 22314 703-299-9766 299-9622
Web: www.aasld.org

American Assn for Thoracic Surgery (AATS)
900 Cummings Ctr Ste 221-U Beverly MA 01915 978-927-8330 524-8890
TF: 800-424-5249 ■ *Web:* www.aats.org

American Assn of Bioanalysts (AAB)
906 Olive St Ste 1200 Saint Louis MO 63101 314-241-1445 241-1449
TF: 800-457-3332 ■ *Web:* www.aab.org

American Assn of Clinical Endocrinologists (AACE)
245 Riverside Ave Ste 2000 Jacksonville FL 32202 904-353-7878 353-8185
TF: 800-435-7352 ■ *Web:* www.aace.com

American Assn of Colleges of Osteopathic Medicine (AACOM)
5550 Friendship Blvd Ste 310 Chevy Chase MD 20815 301-968-4100 968-4101
TF: 800-356-7836 ■ *Web:* www.aacom.org

American Assn of Colleges of Podiatric Medicine (AACPM)
15850 Crabbs Branch Way Ste 320 Rockville MD 20855 301-948-9760 948-1928
TF: 800-922-9266 ■ *Web:* www.aacpm.org

American Assn of Critical-Care Nurses (AACN)
101 Columbia Aliso Viejo CA 92656 949-362-2000 362-2020
TF: 800-809-2273 ■ *Web:* www.aacn.org

American Assn of Endodontists (AAE)
211 E Chicago Ave Ste 1100 Chicago IL 60611 312-266-7255 266-9867
TF: 800-872-3636 ■ *Web:* www.aae.org

American Assn of Gynecological Laparoscopists (AAGL)
6757 Katella Ave Cypress CA 90630 714-503-6200 503-6201
TF: 800-554-2245 ■ *Web:* www.aagl.org

American Assn of Immunologists (AAI)
9650 Rockville Pike Bethesda MD 20814 301-634-7178 634-7887
TF: 888-503-1050 ■ *Web:* www.aai.org

Phone Fax

American Assn of Integrated Healthcare Delivery Systems Inc (AAIHDS)
4435 Waterfront Dr Ste 101 Glen Allen VA 23060 804-747-5823 747-5316
Web: www.aaihds.org

American Assn of Medical Assistants (AAMA)
20 N Wacker Dr Ste 1575 Chicago IL 60606 312-899-1500 899-1259
TF: 800-228-2262 ■ *Web:* www.aama-ntl.org

American Assn of Medical Review Officers (AAMRO)
PO Box 12873 Research Triangle Park NC 27709 919-489-5407 490-1010
TF: 800-489-1839 ■ *Web:* www.aamro.com

American Assn of Medical Society Executives (AAMSE)
555 E Wells St Ste 1100 Milwaukee WI 53202 414-221-9275 276-3349
Web: www.aamse.org

American Assn of Neurological Surgeons (AANS)
5550 Meadowbrook Dr Rolling Meadows IL 60008 847-378-0500 378-0600
TF: 888-566-2267 ■ *Web:* www.aans.org

American Assn of Neuromuscular & Electrodiagnostic Medicine (AANEM)
2621 Superior Dr NW Rochester MN 55901 507-288-0100 288-1225
TF: 844-347-3277 ■ *Web:* www.aanem.org

American Assn of Neuroscience Nurses (AANN)
4700 W Lk Ave Glenview IL 60025 847-375-4733 375-6430
TF: 888-557-2266 ■ *Web:* www.aann.org

American Assn of Nurse Anesthetists (AANA)
222 S Prospect Ave. Park Ridge IL 60068 847-692-7050 692-6968
Web: www.aana.com

American Assn of Oral & Maxillofacial Surgeons (AAOMS)
9700 W Bryn Mawr Ave Rosemont IL 60018 847-678-6200 678-6286
TF: 800-822-6637 ■ *Web:* www.aaoms.org

American Assn of Orthodontists (AAO)
401 N Lindbergh Blvd. Saint Louis MO 63141 314-993-1700 977-8617
TF: 800-522-1899 ■ *Web:* www.mylifemysmile.org

American Assn of Physician Specialists Inc (AAPS)
5550 W Executive Dr Ste 400 Tampa FL 33609 813-433-2277 830-6599
Web: www.aapsus.org

American Assn of Poison Control Centers (AAPCC)
3201 New Mexico Ave Suite 310 Washington DC 20016 800-222-1222
TF: 800-222-1222 ■ *Web:* www.aapcc.org

American Assn of Preferred Provider Organizations (AAPPO)
222 S First St Ste 162 Louisville KY 40202 502-403-1122 403-1129
Web: nasho.org

American Assn of Tissue Banks (AATB)
1320 Old Chain Bridge Rd Ste 450 McLean VA 22101 703-827-9582 356-2198
TF: 800-635-2282 ■ *Web:* www.aatb.org

American Autoimmune Related Disease Assn (AARDA)
22100 Gratiot Ave Eastpointe MI 48021 586-776-3900 776-3903
TF: 800-598-4668 ■ *Web:* www.aarda.org

American Burn Assn (ABA)
625 N Michigan Ave Ste 2550 Chicago IL 60611 312-642-9260 642-9130
Web: www.ameriburn.org

American Cancer Society (ACS)
250 William St NW Ste 6001 Atlanta GA 30303 404-320-3333
TF: 800-227-2345 ■ *Web:* www.cancer.org

American Chiropractic Assn (ACA)
1701 Clarendon Blvd Second Fl Arlington VA 22209 703-276-8800 243-2593
TF: 800-986-4636 ■ *Web:* www.acatoday.org

American Cleft Palate-Craniofacial Assn
1504 E Franklin St Ste 102 Chapel Hill NC 27514 919-933-9044 933-9604
Web: www.acpa-cpf.org

American College Health Assn (ACHA)
PO Box 28937 Baltimore MD 21240 410-859-1500 859-1510
Web: www.acha.org

American College of Allergy Asthma & Immunology (ACAAI)
85 W Algonquin Rd Ste 550 Arlington Heights IL 60005 847-427-1200 427-1294
TF: 800-466-3649 ■ *Web:* www.acaai.org

American College of Cardiology (ACC)
2400 N St NW Washington DC 20037 202-375-6000 375-7000
TF Cust Svc: 800-253-4636 ■ *Web:* www.cardiosource.org/acc

American College of Chest Physicians (ACCP)
3300 Dundee Rd Northbrook IL 60062 847-498-1400 498-5460
TF: 800-343-2227 ■ *Web:* www.chestnet.org

American College of Clinical Pharmacy (ACCP)
13000 W 87th St Pkwy Lenexa KS 66215 913-492-3311 492-0088
Web: www.accp.com

American College of Dentists (ACD)
839 Quince Orchard Blvd Ste J Gaithersburg MD 20878 301-977-3223 977-3330
Web: www.acd.org

American College of Emergency Physicians (ACEP)
1125 Executive Cir PO Box 619911 Dallas TX 75261 972-550-0911 580-2816
TF: 800-798-1822 ■ *Web:* www.acep.org

American College of Eye Surgeons/American Board of Eye Surgery (ACES)
334 E Lake Rd Ste 135 Palm Harbor FL 34685 727-366-1487 836-9783
Web: www.aces-abes.org

American College of Foot & Ankle Surgeons (ACFAS)
8725 W Higgins Rd Ste 555 Chicago IL 60631 773-693-9300 693-9304
TF: 800-421-2237 ■ *Web:* www.acfas.org

American College of Forensic Examiners International (ACFEI)
2750 E Sunshine St Springfield MO 65804 417-881-3818 881-4702
TF: 800-423-9737 ■ *Web:* www.acfei.com

American College of Gastroenterology (ACG)
6400 Goldsboro Rd Ste 450 Bethesda MD 20817 301-263-9000 263-9025
Web: gi.org

American College of Healthcare Executives (ACHE)
One N Franklin St Ste 1700 Chicago IL 60606 312-424-2800 424-0023
Web: www.ache.org

American College of Managed Care Medicine (ACMCM)
4435 Waterfront Dr Ste 101 Glen Allen VA 23060 804-527-1905 747-5316
Web: www.acmcm.org

American College of Nurse-Midwives (ACNM)
8403 Colesville Rd Ste 1550 Silver Spring MD 20910 240-485-1800 485-1818
Web: www.midwife.org

American College of Nutrition
300 S Duncan Ave Ste 225 Clearwater FL 33755 727-446-6086 446-6202
Web: americancollegeofnutrition.org

Organization	City	State	Zip	Phone	Fax
American College of Obstetricians & Gynecologists (ACOG) 409 12th St SW PO Box 96920 *Web:* acog.org	Washington	DC	20090	202-638-5577	
American College of Occupational & Environmental Medicine (ACOEM) 25 NW Pt Blvd Ste 700 *Web:* www.acoem.org	Elk Grove Village	IL	60007	847-818-1800	818-9266
American College of Osteopathic Family Physicians (ACOFP) 330 E Algonquin Rd Ste 1 *TF:* 800-323-0794 ■ *Web:* www.acofp.org	Arlington Heights	IL	60005	847-952-5100	228-9755
American College of Physician Executives (ACPE) 400 N Ashley Dr Ste 4001 *TF:* 800-562-8088 ■ *Web:* www.acpe.org	Tampa	FL	33602	813-287-2000	287-8993
American College of Physicians (ACP) 190 N Independence Mall W *TF:* 800-523-1546 ■ *Web:* www.acponline.org	Philadelphia	PA	19106	215-351-2400	351-2594
American College of Preventive Medicine (ACPM) 455 Massachusetts Ave NW *Web:* www.acpm.org	Washington	DC	20001	202-466-2044	466-2662
American College of Radiology (ACR) 1892 Preston White Dr *TF:* 800-227-5463 ■ *Web:* www.acr.org	Reston	VA	20191	703-648-8900	
American College of Rheumatology (ACR) 2200 Lake Blvd NE *Web:* www.rheumatology.org	Atlanta	GA	30319	404-633-3777	633-1870
American College of Sports Medicine (ACSM) 401 W Michigan St PO Box 1440 *Web:* www.acsm.org	Indianapolis	IN	46202	317-637-9200	634-7817
American College of Surgeons (ACS) 633 N St Clair St *TF:* 800-621-4111 ■ *Web:* www.facs.org	Chicago	IL	60611	312-202-5000	202-5001
American Dental Assistants Assn (ADAA) 35 E Wacker Dr Ste 1730 *TF:* 877-874-3785 ■ *Web:* www.dentalassistant.org	Chicago	IL	60601	312-541-1550	541-1496
American Dental Assn (ADA) 211 E Chicago Ave **Fax:* Hum Res ■ *Web:* www.ada.org	Chicago	IL	60611	312-440-2500	440-2395*
American Dental Hygienists' Assn (ADHA) 444 N Michigan Ave Ste 3400 *TF:* 800-243-2342 ■ *Web:* www.adha.org	Chicago	IL	60611	312-440-8900	467-1806
American Diabetes Assn (ADA) 1701 N Beauregard St *TF:* 800-232-3472 ■ *Web:* www.diabetes.org	Alexandria	VA	22311	703-549-1500	836-2464
American Dietetic Assn (ADA) 120 S Riverside Plz Ste 2000 *TF:* 800-877-1600 ■ *Web:* www.eatright.org	Chicago	IL	60606	312-899-0040	899-4899
American Embryo Transfer Assn (AETA) 1111 N Dunlap Ave *Web:* secure.fass.org	Savoy	IL	61874	217-356-3182	398-4119
American Endodontic Society 265 N Main St **Fax Area Code:* 630 ■ *Web:* www.aesoc.com	Glen Ellyn	IL	60137	773-519-4879	858-0525*
American Epilepsy Society (AES) 342 N Main St *TF:* 888-233-2334 ■ *Web:* www.aesnet.org	West Hartford	CT	06117	860-586-7505	586-7550
American Federation for Aging Research (AFAR) 55 W 39th St 16th Fl *TF:* 888-582-2327 ■ *Web:* www.afar.org	New York	NY	10018	212-703-9977	997-0330
American Federation for Medical Research (AFMR) 900 Cummings Ctr Ste 221-U *TF:* 888-737-9477 ■ *Web:* www.afmr.org	Beverly	MA	01915	978-927-8330	524-8890
American Gastroenterological Assn (AGA) 4930 Del Ray Ave *TF:* 800-228-9290 ■ *Web:* www.gastro.org	Bethesda	MD	20814	301-654-2055	654-5920
American Headache Society (AHS) 19 Mantua Rd *Web:* www.americanheadachesociety.org	Mount Royal	NJ	08061	856-423-0043	423-0082
American Health Care Assn (AHCA) 1201 L St NW *TF:* 800-321-0343 ■ *Web:* www.ahcancal.org	Washington	DC	20005	202-842-4444	842-3860
American Health Information Management Assn (AHIMA) 233 N Michigan Ave Ste 2100 *TF:* 800-335-5535 ■ *Web:* www.ahima.org	Chicago	IL	60601	312-233-1100	233-1090
American Health Quality Assn (AHQA) 1725 I St NW Ste 300 *Web:* www.ahqa.org	Washington	DC	20006	202-331-5790	
American Healthcare Radiology Administrators (AHRA) 490-B Boston Post Rd Ste 200 *TF:* 800-334-2472 ■ *Web:* www.ahraonline.org	Sudbury	MA	01776	978-443-7591	443-8046
American Herbal Products Assn (AHPA) 8630 Fenton St Ste 918 *Web:* www.ahpa.org	Silver Spring	MD	20910	301-588-1171	588-1174
American Hospital Assn (AHA) 155 N Wacker Dr *TF:* 800-424-4301 ■ *Web:* www.aha.org	Chicago	IL	60606	312-422-3000	422-4796
American Institute of Ultrasound in Medicine (AIUM) 14750 Sweitzer Ln Ste 100 *TF:* 800-638-5352 ■ *Web:* www.aium.org	Laurel	MD	20707	301-498-4100	498-4450
American Lung Assn (ALA) 14 Wall St *TF:* 800-586-4872 ■ *Web:* www.lung.org	New York	NY	10005	212-315-8700	
American Medical Assn (AMA) 515 N State St *TF:* 800-621-8335 ■ *Web:* www.ama-assn.org	Chicago	IL	60610	312-464-5000	464-4184
American Medical Directors Assn (AMDA) 11000 Broken Land Pkwy Ste 400 *TF:* 800-876-2632 ■ *Web:* www.amda.com	Columbia	MD	21044	410-740-9743	740-4572
American Medical Group Assn (AMGA) 1422 Duke St *Web:* www.amga.org	Alexandria	VA	22314	703-838-0033	548-1890
American Medical Informatics Assn (AMIA) 4720 Montgomery Ln Ste 500 *Web:* www.amia.org	Bethesda	MD	20814	301-657-1291	657-1296
American Medical Rehabilitation Providers Assn (AMRPA) 1710 N St NW *TF:* 888-346-4624 ■ *Web:* www.amrpa.org	Washington	DC	20036	202-223-1920	223-1925
American Medical Technologists (AMT) 10700 W Higgins Rd Ste 150 *TF:* 800-275-1268 ■ *Web:* www.americanmedtech.org	Rosemont	IL	60018	847-823-5169	823-0458
American Nephrology Nurses Assn (ANNA) 200 E Holly Ave *TF:* 888-600-2662 ■ *Web:* www.annanurse.org	Sewell	NJ	08080	856-256-2320	589-7463
American Neurological Assn (ANA) 5841 Cedar Lk Rd Ste 204 *Web:* www.aneuroa.org	Minneapolis	MN	55416	952-545-6284	545-6073
American Nurses Assn (ANA) 8515 Georgia Ave Ste 400 *TF:* 800-274-4262 ■ *Web:* nursingworld.org	Silver Spring	MD	20910	301-628-5000	628-5001
American Occupational Therapy Assn Inc (AOTA) 4720 Montgomery Ln PO Box 31220 *TF:* 800-877-1383 ■ *Web:* www.aota.org	Bethesda	MD	20824	301-652-2682	652-7711
American Organization of Nurse Executives (AONE) 155 N Wacker Dr Ste 400 *Web:* www.aone.org	Chicago	IL	60606	312-422-2800	422-4503
American Orthopaedic Assn (AOA) 6300 N River Rd Ste 505 *Web:* www.aoassn.org	Rosemont	IL	60018	847-318-7330	318-7339
American Orthopaedic Society for Sports Medicine (AOSSM) 6300 N River Rd Ste 500 *TF:* 877-321-3500 ■ *Web:* www.sportsmed.org	Rosemont	IL	60018	847-292-4900	292-4905
American Osteopathic Assn (AOA) 142 E Ontario St *TF:* 800-621-1773 ■ *Web:* www.osteopathic.org	Chicago	IL	60611	312-202-8000	202-8200
American Pain Society (APS) 4700 W Lake Ave *TF:* 877-752-4754 ■ *Web:* www.americanpainsociety.org	Glenview	IL	60025	847-375-4715	375-6479
American Physical Therapy Assn (APTA) 1111 N Fairfax St *TF:* 800-999-2782 ■ *Web:* www.apta.org	Alexandria	VA	22314	703-684-2782	706-8536
American Physiological Society (APS) 9650 Rockville Pk *Web:* www.the-aps.org	Bethesda	MD	20814	301-634-7164	634-7241
American Podiatric Medical Assn (APMA) 9312 Old Georgetown Rd *TF:* 800-275-2762 ■ *Web:* www.apma.org	Bethesda	MD	20814	301-581-9200	530-2752
American Psychiatric Nurses Assn (APNA) 1555 Wilson Blvd Ste 530 *TF:* 866-243-2443 ■ *Web:* www.apna.org	Arlington	VA	22209	703-243-2443	243-3390
American Public Health Assn (APHA) 800 'I' St NW *Web:* www.apha.org	Washington	DC	20001	202-777-2742	777-2533
American Registry of Diagnostic Medical Sonographers (ARDMS) 51 Monroe St Plz E 1 *TF:* 800-541-9754 ■ *Web:* www.ardms.org	Rockville	MD	20850	301-738-8401	738-0312
American Roentgen Ray Society (ARRS) 44211 Slatestone Ct *TF:* 800-438-2777 ■ *Web:* www.arrs.org	Leesburg	VA	20176	703-729-3353	729-4839
American Society for Aesthetic Plastic Surgery, The (ASAPS) 11262 Monarch St *TF:* 800-364-2147 ■ *Web:* www.surgery.org	Garden Grove	CA	92841	562-799-2356	799-1098
American Society for Bone & Mineral Research (ASBMR) 2025 M St NW Ste 800 *Web:* www.asbmr.org	Washington	DC	20036	202-367-1161	367-2161
American Society for Clinical Pathology (ASCP) 33 W Monroe St Ste 1600 *TF Cust Svc:* 800-621-4142 ■ *Web:* www.ascp.org	Chicago	IL	60603	312-541-4999	541-4998
American Society for Colposcopy & Cervical Pathology (ASCCP) 152 W Washington St *TF:* 800-787-7227 ■ *Web:* www.asccp.org	Hagerstown	MD	21740	301-733-3640	733-5775
American Society for Dermatologic Surgery (ASDS) 5550 Meadowbrook Dr Ste 120 *Web:* www.asds.net	Rolling Meadows	IL	60008	847-956-0900	956-0999
American Society for Gastrointestinal Endoscopy (ASGE) 1520 Kensington Rd Ste 202 *TF:* 866-353-2743 ■ *Web:* www.asge.org	Oak Brook	IL	60523	630-573-0600	573-0691
American Society for Histocompatibility & Immunogenetics (ASHI) 15000 Commerce Pkwy Ste C *Web:* www.ashi-hla.org	Mount Laurel	NJ	08054	856-638-0428	439-0525
American Society for Laser Medicine & Surgery Inc (ASLMS) 2100 Stewart Ave Ste 240 *TF:* 877-258-6028 ■ *Web:* www.aslms.org	Wausau	WI	54401	715-845-9283	848-2493
American Society for Microbiology (ASM) 1752 N St NW *Web:* www.asm.org	Washington	DC	20036	202-737-3600	
American Society for Parenteral & Enteral Nutrition (ASPEN) 8630 Fenton St Ste 412 *TF:* 800-727-4567 ■ *Web:* www.nutritioncare.org	Silver Spring	MD	20910	301-587-6315	587-2365
American Society for Pharmacology & Experimental Therapeutics (ASPET) 9650 Rockville Pk *Web:* www.aspet.org	Bethesda	MD	20814	301-634-7060	634-7061
American Society for Reproductive Medicine (ASRM) 1209 Montgomery Hwy *Web:* www.asrm.org	Birmingham	AL	35216	205-978-5000	978-5005
American Society for Surgery of the Hand (ASSH) 822 W. Washington Blvd. **Fax Area Code:* 847 ■ *TF:* 888-343-6337 ■ *Web:* www.assh.org	Chicago	IL	60607	312-880-1900	384-1435*
American Society for Therapeutic Radiology & Oncology (ASTRO) 8280 Willow Oaks Corporate Dr Ste 500 *TF:* 800-962-7876 ■ *Web:* www.astro.org	Fairfax	VA	22031	703-502-1550	502-7852
American Society of Abdominal Surgeons (ASAS) 824 Main St Second Fl Ste 1 *Web:* www.abdominalsurg.org	Melrose	MA	02176	781-665-6102	665-4127
American Society of Addiction Medicine (ASAM) 4601 N Pk Ave Upper Arcade Ste 101 *Web:* www.asam.org	Chevy Chase	MD	20815	301-656-3920	656-3815
American Society of Andrology (ASA) 1100 E Woodfield St Ste 350 *Web:* www.andrologysociety.org	Schaumburg	IL	60173	847-619-4909	517-7229
American Society of Anesthesiologists (ASA) 520 N NW Hwy *TF:* 800-331-1600 ■ *Web:* www.asahq.org	Park Ridge	IL	60068	847-825-5586	825-1692
American Society of Bariatric Physicians (ASBP) 2821 S Parker Rd Ste 625 *Web:* www.asbp.org	Aurora	CO	80014	303-770-2526	779-4834

Phone | Fax

American Society of Cataract & Refractive Surgery (ASCRS)
4000 Legato Rd Ste 700 .... Fairfax VA 22033 703-591-2220 591-0614
TF: 800-451-1339 ■ *Web:* www.ascrs.org

American Society of Clinical Hypnosis (ASCH)
140 N Bloomingdale Rd .... Bloomingdale IL 60108 630-980-4740 351-8490
TF: 866-986-8779 ■ *Web:* www.asch.net

American Society of Clinical Oncology (ASCO)
2318 Mill Rd Ste 800 .... Alexandria VA 22314 571-483-1300 299-0255*
**Fax Area Code:* 703 ■ *TF:* 888-282-2552 ■ *Web:* www.asco.org

American Society of Consultant Pharmacists (ASCP)
1321 Duke St .... Alexandria VA 22314 703-739-1300 739-1321
TF: 800-355-2727 ■ *Web:* www.ascp.com

American Society of Dermatopathology, The
111 Deer Lake Rd Ste 100 .... ÿDeerfield IL 60015 847-400-5820 480-9282
TF: 800-445-8667 ■ *Web:* www.asdp.org

American Society of Echocardiography (ASE)
2100 Gateway Centre Blvd Ste 310 .... Morrisville NC 27560 919-861-5574 882-9900
Web: www.asecho.org

American Society of Health-System Pharmacists (ASHP)
7272 Wisconsin Ave .... Bethesda MD 20814 301-664-8700 664-8877
TF: 866-279-0681 ■ *Web:* www.ashp.org

American Society of Hematology (ASH)
1900 M St NW Ste 200 .... Washington DC 20036 202-776-0544 776-0545
Web: www.hematology.org

American Society of Hypertension (ASH)
148 Madison Ave Fifth Fl .... New York NY 10016 212-696-9099 696-0711
Web: www.ash-us.org

American Society of Neuroradiology (ASNR)
2210 Midwest Rd Ste 207 .... Oak Brook IL 60523 630-574-0220 574-0661
Web: www.asnr.org

American Society of Nuclear Cardiology (ASNC)
4550 Montgomery Ave Ste 780-N .... Bethesda MD 20814 301-215-7575 215-7113
Web: www.asnc.org

American Society of PeriAnesthesia Nurses (ASPAN)
90 Frontage Rd .... Cherry Hill NJ 08034 856-616-9600 616-9601
TF: 877-737-9696 ■ *Web:* www.aspan.org

American Society of Plastic Surgeons (ASPS)
444 E Algonquin Rd .... Arlington Heights IL 60005 847-228-9900 228-9131
TF: 888-475-2784 ■ *Web:* www.plasticsurgery.org

American Society of Radiologic Technologists (ASRT)
15000 Central Ave SE .... Albuquerque NM 87123 505-298-4500 298-5063
TF: 800-444-2778 ■ *Web:* www.asrt.org

American Society of Regional Anesthesia & Pain Medicine (ASRA)
239 Fourth Ave Ste 1714 .... Pittsburgh PA 15222 412-471-2718 471-7503
TF: 855-795-2772 ■ *Web:* www.asra.com

American Society of Tropical Medicine & Hygiene
111 Deer Lk Rd Ste 100 .... Deerfield IL 60015 847-480-9592 480-9282
Web: www.astmh.org

American Speech-Language-Hearing Assn (ASHA)
2200 Research Blvd .... Rockville MD 20850 301-296-5700 296-8580
TF: 800-498-2071 ■ *Web:* www.asha.org

American Thoracic Society (ATS)
61 Broadway 4th Fl .... New York NY 10006 212-315-8600 315-6498
TF: 866-316-2673 ■ *Web:* www.thoracic.org

American Urological Assn (AUA)
1000 Corporate Blvd .... Linthicum MD 21090 410-689-3700 689-3800
TF: 866-746-4282 ■ *Web:* www.auanet.org

American Veterinary Medical Assn (AVMA)
1931 N Meacham Rd Ste 100 .... Schaumburg IL 60173 847-925-8070 925-1329
TF: 800-248-2862 ■ *Web:* www.avma.org

AORN Inc 2170 S Parker Rd Ste 300 .... Denver CO 80231 303-755-6300 750-3212*
**Fax:* Cust Svc ■ *TF:* 800-755-2676 ■ *Web:* www.aorn.org

Arthroscopy Assn of North America (AANA)
6300 N River Rd Ste 104 .... Rosemont IL 60018 847-292-2262 292-2268
TF: 877-924-0305 ■ *Web:* www.aana.org

Assisted Living Federation of America (ALFA)
1650 King St Ste 602 .... Alexandria VA 22314 703-894-1805 894-1831
Web: www.alfa.org

Association for Applied Psychophysiology & Biofeedback (AAPB)
10200 W 44th Ave Ste 304 .... Wheat Ridge CO 80033 303-422-8436 422-8894
TF: 800-477-8892 ■ *Web:* www.aapb.org

Association for Death Education & Counseling (ADEC)
111 Deer Lk Rd Ste 100 .... Deerfield IL 60015 847-509-0403 480-9282
Web: www.adec.org

Association for Healthcare Documentation Integrity (AHDI)
4230 Kiernan Ave Ste 130 .... Modesto CA 95356 209-527-9620 527-9633
TF: 800-982-2182 ■ *Web:* www.ahdionline.org

Association for Healthcare Philanthropy (AHP)
313 Pk Ave Ste 400 .... Falls Church VA 22046 703-532-6243 532-7170
Web: www.ahp.org

Association for Professionals in Infection Control & Epidemiology Inc (APIC)
1275 K St NW Ste 1000 .... Washington DC 20005 202-789-1890 789-1899
Web: www.apic.org

Association for Research in Vision & Ophthalmology (ARVO)
12300 Twinbrook Pkwy Ste 250 .... Rockville MD 20852 240-221-2900 221-0370
Web: www.arvo.org

Association for the Advancement of Medical Instrumentation (AAMI)
4301 N Fairfax Dr Ste 301 .... Arlington VA 22203 703-525-4890 276-0793
TF: 800-332-2264 ■ *Web:* www.aami.org

Association for Vascular Access (AVA)
5526 West 13400 South Ste 229 .... Herriman UT 84096 801-792-9079 601-8012
TF: 888-576-2826 ■ *Web:* www.avainfo.org

Association of Academic Health Centers (AHC)
1400 16th St NW Ste 720 .... Washington DC 20036 202-265-9600 265-7514
Web: www.aahcdc.org

Association of American Indian Physicians (AAIP)
1225 Sovereign Row Ste 103 .... Oklahoma City OK 73108 405-946-7072 946-7651
Web: www.aaip.org

Association of Clinical Research Professionals (ACRP)
500 Montgomery St Ste 800 .... Alexandria VA 22314 703-254-8100 254-8101
TF: 888-508-5731 ■ *Web:* www.acrpnet.org

Association of Community Cancer Centers (ACCC)
11600 Nebel St Ste 201 .... Rockville MD 20852 301-984-9496 770-1949
Web: www.accc-cancer.org

Phone | Fax

Association of Emergency Physicians (AEP)
911 Whitewater Dr .... Mars PA 16046 724-772-1818 422-7794*
**Fax Area Code:* 866

Association of Military Surgeons of the United States (AMSUS)
9320 Old Georgetown Rd .... Bethesda MD 20814 301-897-8800 530-5446
TF: 800-761-9320 ■ *Web:* www.amsus.org

Association of Nurses in AIDS Care (ANAC)
3538 Ridgewood Rd .... Akron OH 44333 330-670-0101 670-0109
TF: 800-260-6780 ■ *Web:* www.nursesinaidscare.org

Association of Osteopathic Directors & Medical Educators (AODME)
142 E Ontario St .... Chicago IL 60611 312-202-8211 202-8224
TF: 800-621-1773 ■ *Web:* www.aodme.org

Association of Rehabilitation Nurses (ARN)
4700 W Lk Ave .... Glenview IL 60025 847-375-4710 375-6481
TF: 800-229-7530 ■ *Web:* www.rehabnurse.org

Association of Reproductive Health Professionals (ARHP)
1901 L St NW Ste 300 .... Washington DC 20036 202-466-3825 466-3826
TF: 877-311-8972 ■ *Web:* www.arhp.org

Association of Schools & Colleges of Optometry (ASCO)
6110 Executive Blvd Ste 420 .... Rockville MD 20852 301-231-5944 770-1828
TF: 888- 26-8377 ■ *Web:* www.opted.org

Association of Schools of Allied Health Professions (ASAHP)
4400 Jenifer St NW Ste 333 .... Washington DC 20015 202-237-6481 237-6485
Web: www.asahp.org

Association of Staff Physician Recruiters (ASPR)
1000 Westgate Dr Ste 252 .... Saint Paul MN 55114 800-830-2777
TF: 800-830-2777 ■ *Web:* www.aspr.org

Association of Surgical Technologists (AST)
Six W Dry Creek Cir Ste 200 .... Littleton CO 80120 303-694-9130 694-9169
TF: 800-637-7433 ■ *Web:* www.ast.org

Association of University Programs in Health Administration (AUPHA)
2000 N 14th St Ste 780 .... Arlington VA 22201 703-894-0941 894-0941
TF: 877-275-6462 ■ *Web:* www.aupha.org

Association of Women's Health Obstetric & Neonatal Nurses (AWHONN)
2000 L St NW Ste 740 .... Washington DC 20036 202-261-2400 728-0575
TF: 800-673-8499 ■ *Web:* www.awhonn.org

Asthma & Allergy Foundation of America (AAFA)
8201 Corporate Dr Ste 1000 .... Landover MD 20785 202-466-7643 466-8940
TF: 800-727-8462 ■ *Web:* www.aafa.org

Canada's Research-Based Pharmaceutical Cos (Rx&D)
55 Metcalfe St Ste 1220 .... Ottawa ON K1P6L5 613-236-0455 236-6756
TF: 800-363-0203 ■ *Web:* www.canadapharma.org

Canadian Academy of Sport Medicine (CASM)
180 Elgin St Ste 1400 .... Ottawa ON K2P2K3 613-748-5851 912-0128
TF: 877-585-2394 ■ *Web:* casem-acmse.org

Canadian Assn of Emergency Physicians (CAEP)
1785 Alta Vista Dr Ste 104 .... Ottawa ON K1G3Y6 613-523-3343 523-0190
TF: 800-463-1158 ■ *Web:* www.caep.ca

Canadian Medical Assn (CMA) 1867 Alta Vista Dr .... Ottawa ON K1G5W8 613-731-9331 731-7314
TF: 800-663-7336 ■ *Web:* www.cma.ca

Canadian Veterinary Medical Assn (CVMA)
339 Booth St .... Ottawa ON K1R7K1 613-236-1162 236-9681
Web: canadianveterinarians.net

Case Management Society of America (CMSA)
6301 Ranch Dr .... Little Rock AR 72223 501-225-2229 221-9068
TF: 800-216-2672 ■ *Web:* www.cmsa.org

Catholic Health Assn of the US (CHA)
4455 Woodson Rd .... Saint Louis MO 63134 314-427-2500 427-0029
Web: www.chausa.org

Children's Hospice International (CHI)
1101 King St Ste 360 .... Alexandria VA 22314 703-684-0330 684-0226
Web: www.chionline.org

Christian Medical & Dental Assn (CMDA)
2604 Hwy 421 PO Box 7500 .... Bristol TN 37620 423-844-1000 844-1005
TF: 888-231-2637 ■ *Web:* www.cmda.org

Clinical & Laboratory Standards Institute (CLSI)
940 W Valley Rd Ste 1400 .... Wayne PA 19087 610-688-0100 688-0700

Clinical Immunology Society (CIS)
555 E Wells St Ste 1100 .... Milwaukee WI 53202 414-224-8095 272-6070
Web: www.clinimmsoc.org

COLA 9881 Broken Land Pkwy Ste 200 .... Columbia MD 21046 410-381-6581 381-8611*
**Fax:* Hum Res ■ *TF:* 800-981-9883 ■ *Web:* www.cola.org

College of American Pathologists (CAP)
325 Waukegan Rd .... Northfield IL 60093 847-832-7000 832-8168
TF: 800-323-4040 ■ *Web:* www.cap.org

Emergency Nurses Assn (ENA) 915 Lee St .... Des Plaines IL 60016 847-460-4000 460-4001
TF: 800-900-9659 ■ *Web:* www.ena.org

Endocrine Society
8401 Connecticut Ave Ste 900 .... Chevy Chase MD 20815 301-941-0200 941-0259
TF: 888-363-6274 ■ *Web:* www.endocrine.org

Eye Bank Assn of America (EBAA)
1015 18th St NW Ste 1010 .... Washington DC 20036 202-775-4999 429-6036
TF: 888-491-8833 ■ *Web:* www.restoresight.org

Federation of American Hospitals
750 Ninth St NW Ste 600 .... Washington DC 20004 202-624-1500 624-1500
Web: www.fah.org

Federation of State Medical Boards of the US Inc (FSMB)
400 Fuller Wiser Rd Ste 300 .... Euless TX 76039 817-868-4000 868-4098
TF: 800-793-7939 ■ *Web:* www.fsmb.org

Gerontological Society of America, The
1220 L St NW Ste 901 .... Washington DC 20005 202-842-1275 842-1150
TF: 800-677-1116 ■ *Web:* www.geron.org

Gynecologic Oncology Group (GOG)
1600 JFK Blvd Ste 1020 .... Philadelphia PA 19103 215-854-0770 854-0716
TF: 800-225-3053 ■ *Web:* www.gog.org

Health Industry Business Communications Council (HIBCC)
2525 E Arizona Biltmore Cir Ste 127 .... Phoenix AZ 85016 602-381-1091 381-1093
TF: 800-755-5505 ■ *Web:* www.hibcc.org

Healthcare Financial Management Assn (HFMA)
Two Westbrook Corporate Ctr Ste 700 .... Westchester IL 60154 708-531-9600 531-0032
TF: 800-252-4362 ■ *Web:* www.hfma.org

Healthcare Information & Management Systems Society (HIMSS)
230 E Ohio St Ste 500 .... Chicago IL 60611 312-664-4467 664-6143
Web: www.himss.org

Phone Fax

Heart Rhythm Society 1400 K St NW Ste 500 Washington DC 20005 202-464-3400 464-3401
Web: www.hrsonline.org

Hospice & Palliative Nurses Assn (HPNA)
One Penn Ctr W # 229 Pittsburgh PA 15276 412-787-9301 787-9305
Web: www.hpna.org

Hospice Foundation of America (HFA)
1710 Rhode Island Ave NW Ste 400 Washington DC 20036 202-457-5811 457-5815
TF: 800-854-3402 ■ *Web:* www.hospicefoundation.org

Infectious Diseases Society of America (IDSA)
1300 Wilson Blvd Ste 300 Arlington VA 22209 703-299-0200 299-0204
TF: 888-844-4372 ■ *Web:* www.idsociety.org

Infusion Nurses Society (INS) 315 Norwood Pk S Norwood MA 02062 781-440-9408 440-9409
TF: 800-694-0298 ■ *Web:* www.ins1.org

Institute for Healthcare Improvement (IHI)
20 University Rd Seventh Fl Cambridge MA 02138 617-301-4800 301-4848
TF: 866-787-0831 ■ *Web:* www.ihi.org

Institute for the Advancement of Human Behavior (IAHB)
PO BOX 5527 Santa Rosa CA 95402 650-851-8411 755-3133*
*Fax Area Code: 707 ■ *TF:* 800-258-8411 ■ *Web:* www.iahb.org

Institute of Medicine 500 Fifth St NW Washington DC 20001 202-334-2352 334-1412
Web: www.iom.edu

Interamerican College of Physicians & Surgeons
233 Broadway New York NY 10279 212-777-3642
Web: icps.org

International Academy of Compounding Pharmacists (IACP)
4638 Riverstone Blvd Missouri City TX 77459 281-933-8400 495-0602
TF: 800-927-4227 ■ *Web:* www.iacprx.org

International Assn for Dental Research (IADR)
1619 Duke St Alexandria VA 22314 703-548-0066 548-1883
Web: www.iadr.com

International Chiropractors Assn (ICA)
6400 Arlington Blvd Ste 800 Falls Church VA 22042 703-528-5000 528-5023
TF: 800-423-4690 ■ *Web:* www.chiropractic.org

International College of Dentists (ICD)
51 Monroe St Ste 1400 Rockville MD 20850 301-251-8861 738-9143
TF: 800-533-6825 ■ *Web:* www.icd.org

International College of Surgeons (ICS)
1516 N Lk Shore Dr Chicago IL 60610 312-642-3555 787-1624
Web: www.icsglobal.org

International Congress of Oral Implantologists (ICOI)
248 Lorraine Ave Third Fl Upper Montclair NJ 07043 973-783-6300 295-8509*
*Fax Area Code: 267 ■ *TF:* 800-442-0525 ■ *Web:* www.icoi.org

International Society for Heart & Lung Transplantation (ISHLT)
14673 Midway Rd Ste 200 Addison TX 75001 972-490-9495 490-9499
TF: 888-722-2220 ■ *Web:* www.ishlt.org

International Society for Magnetic Resonance in Medicine (ISMRM)
2030 Addison St Ste 700 Berkeley CA 94704 510-841-1899 841-2340
TF: 877-837-4400 ■ *Web:* www.ismrm.org

International Society for Peritoneal Dialysis (ISPD)
66 Martin St Milton ON L9T2R2 905-875-2456 875-2864
Web: www.ispd.org

International Society for Pharmacoeconomics & Outcomes Research (ISPOR)
3100 Princeton Pk Bldg 3 Ste E Lawrenceville NJ 08648 609-219-0773 219-0774
TF: 800-992-0643 ■ *Web:* www.ispor.org

International Society for Pharmacoepidemiology (ISPE)
5272 River Rd Ste 630 Bethesda MD 20816 301-718-6500 656-0989
TF: 888-887-7955 ■ *Web:* www.pharmacoepi.org

International Society of Refractive Surgery (ISRS)
655 Beach St PO Box 7424 San Francisco CA 94109 415-561-8581 561-8575
TF: 866-561-8558 ■ *Web:* www.aao.org

International Society of Travel Medicine (ISTM)
315 W Ponce de Leon Ave Ste 245 Decatur GA 30030 404-373-8282 373-8283
Web: www.istm.org

International Transplant Nurses Society (ITNS)
1739 E Carson St PO Box 351 Pittsburgh PA 15203 412-343-4867 343-3959
TF: 800-776-8636 ■ *Web:* www.itns.org

Islamic Medical Assn of North America (IMANA)
101 W 22nd St Ste 106 Lombard IL 60148 630-932-0000 932-0005
Web: www.imana.org

Journal of Clinical Investigation (JCI)
15 Research Dr Ann Arbor MI 48103 734-222-6050 222-6058
Web: www.jci.org

Lamaze International 2025 M St NW Ste 800 Washington DC 20036 202-367-1128 367-2128
TF: 800-368-4404 ■ *Web:* www.lamaze.org

Medical Group Management Assn (MGMA)
104 Inverness Terr E Englewood CO 80112 303-799-1111 784-6105
TF: 877-275-6462 ■ *Web:* www.mgma.com

NA for Home Care & Hospice (NAHC)
228 Seventh St SE Washington DC 20003 202-547-7424 547-3540
Web: www.nahc.org

NA of Neonatal Nurses (NANN) 4700 W Lk Ave Glenview IL 60025 847-375-3660 375-6491
TF: 800-451-3795 ■ *Web:* www.nann.org

NA of Nurse Practitioners in Women's Health
505 C St NE Washington DC 20002 202-543-9693 543-9858
Web: www.npwh.org

National Abortion Federation (NAF)
1755 Massachusetts Ave NW Washington DC 20036 202-667-5881 667-5890
TF: 800-772-9100 ■ *Web:* www.prochoice.org

National Board of Medical Examiners (NBME)
3750 Market St Philadelphia PA 19104 215-590-9500
Web: www.nbme.org

National Community Pharmacists Assn (NCPA)
100 Daingerfield Rd Alexandria VA 22314 703-683-8200 683-3619
TF: 800-544-7447 ■ *Web:* www.ncpanet.org

National Council of State Boards of Nursing (NCSBN)
111 E Wacker Dr Ste 2900 Chicago IL 60601 312-525-3600 279-1032
TF: 866-293-9600 ■ *Web:* www.ncsbn.org

National Council on Problem Gambling Inc
730 11th St NW Ste 601 Washington DC 20001 202-547-9204 547-9206
TF: 800-522-4700 ■ *Web:* www.ncpgambling.org

National Foundation for Infectious Diseases (NFID)
4733 Bethesda Ave Ste 750 Bethesda MD 20814 301-656-0003 907-0878
Web: www.nfid.org

National Home Infusion Assn (NHIA)
100 Daingerfield Rd Alexandria VA 22314 703-549-3740 683-1484
Web: www.nhia.org

National Hospice & Palliative Care Organization (NHPCO)
1700 Diagonal Rd Ste 625 Alexandria VA 22314 703-837-1500 837-1233
TF Help Line: 800-658-8898 ■ *Web:* www.nhpco.org

National League for Nursing (NLN)
61 Broadway 33rd Fl New York NY 10006 212-363-5555 812-0391
TF: 800-669-1656 ■ *Web:* www.nln.org

National Medical Assn (NMA)
8403 Colesville Rd Ste 920 Silver Spring MD 20910 202-347-1895 347-0722
TF: 800-662-0554 ■ *Web:* www.nmanet.org

National Nursing Staff Development Organization (NNSDO)
330 N Wabash Ave Ste 2000 Chicago IL 60611 312-321-5135 673-6835
TF: 800-489-1995 ■ *Web:* www.anpd.org

National Organization for Rare Disorders (NORD)
55 Kenosia Ave PO Box 1968 Danbury CT 06813 203-744-0100 798-2291
TF: 800-999-6673 ■ *Web:* www.rarediseases.org

National Pharmaceutical Council (NPC)
1894 Preston White Dr Reston VA 20191 703-620-6390 476-0904
Web: www.npcnow.org

National Renal Administrators Assn (NRAA)
100 N 20th St Philadelphia PA 19103 215-320-4655 564-2175
Web: www.nraa.org

National Student Nurses Assn (NSNA)
45 Main St Ste 606 Brooklyn NY 11201 718-210-0705 210-0710
Web: www.nsna.org

North American Menopause Society, The (NAMS)
5900 Landerbrook Dr Ste 390 Mayfield Heights OH 44124 440-442-7550 442-2660
Web: www.menopause.org

North American Spine Society (NASS)
7075 Veterans Blvd Burr Ridge IL 60527 630-230-3600
TF: 877-774-6337 ■ *Web:* www.spine.org

Oncology Nursing Society (ONS)
125 Enterprise Dr Pittsburgh PA 15275 412-859-6100 369-5497*
*Fax Area Code: 877 ■ *TF:* 866-257-4667 ■ *Web:* www.ons.org

Optical Laboratories Assn (OLA)
225 Reinekers Ln Ste 700 Alexandria VA 22314 703-548-6619 548-4580
TF: 800-477-5652 ■ *Web:* www.ola-labs.org

Optical Society of America (OSA)
2010 Massachusetts Ave NW Washington DC 20036 202-223-8130 223-1096
TF: 800-843-6664 ■ *Web:* www.osa.org

Opticians Assn of America (OAA) 3740 Canada Rd Lakeland TN 38002 901-388-2423 388-2348
Web: www.oaa.org

Parental Drug Assn (PDA) 4350 East-West Hwy Bethesda MD 20814 301-656-5900 986-1093
Web: www.pda.org

Pharmaceutical Care Management Assn (PCMA)
601 Pennsylvania Ave NW Washington DC 20004 202-756-7210 207-3623
Web: www.pcmanet.org

Pharmaceutical Research & Manufacturers of America (PhRMA)
950 F St NW Ste 300 Washington DC 20004 202-835-3400 835-3414
Web: www.phrma.org

Physicians Committee for Responsible Medicine (PCRM)
5100 Wisconsin Ave NW Ste 400 Washington DC 20016 202-686-2210 686-2216
TF: 866-416-7276 ■ *Web:* www.pcrm.org

Physicians for Social Responsibility (PSR)
1875 Connecticut Ave NW Ste 1012 Washington DC 20009 202-667-4260 667-4201
TF: 800-459-1887 ■ *Web:* www.psr.org

Plasma Protein Therapeutics Assn (PPTA)
147 Old Solomon's Island Rd Ste 100 Annapolis MD 21401 410-266-8493
Web: usplaces.com

Radiological Society of North America (RSNA)
820 Jorie Blvd Oak Brook IL 60523 630-571-2670 571-7837
TF: 800-381-6660 ■ *Web:* www.rsna.org

Radiology Business Management Assn (RBMA)
10300 Eaton Pl Ste 460 Fairfax VA 22030 703-621-3355 621-3356
TF: 888-224-7262 ■ *Web:* www.rbma.org

Regulatory Affairs Professionals Society (RAPS)
5635 Fishers Ln Ste 550 Rockville MD 20852 301-770-2920 770-2924
Web: www.raps.org

Renal Physicians Assn (RPA)
1700 Rockville Pk Ste 220 Rockville MD 20852 301-468-3515 468-3511
Web: www.renalmd.org

Society for Academic Emergency Medicine (SAEM)
2340 S River Rd Ste 200 Des Plaines IL 60018 847-813-9823 813-5450
Web: www.saem.org

Society for Healthcare Epidemiology of America
1300 Wilson Blvd Ste 300 Arlington VA 22209 703-684-1006 684-1009
TF: 877-734-2726 ■ *Web:* www.shea-online.org

Society for Healthcare Strategy & Market Development (SHSMD)
155 N Wacker Dr Ste 400 Chicago IL 60606 312-422-3888 278-0883
TF: 800-242-2626 ■ *Web:* www.shsmd.org

Society for Investigative Dermatology Inc (SID)
526 Superior Ave E Ste 540 Cleveland OH 44114 216-579-9300 579-9333
Web: www.sidnet.org

Society for Medical Decision Making
390 Amwell Rd Ste 402 Hillsborough NJ 08844 908-359-1184 450-1119
Web: www.smdm.org

Society for Neuroscience (SFN)
1121 14th St NW Ste 1010 Washington DC 20005 202-962-4000 962-4941
Web: sfn.org

Society for Surgery of the Alimentary Tract (SSAT)
900 Cummings Ctr Ste 221-U Beverly MA 01915 978-927-8330 524-8890
TF: 866-849-5866 ■ *Web:* www.ssat.com

Society for Vascular Surgery (SVS)
633 N St Clair St 22nd Fl Chicago IL 60611 312-334-2300 334-2320
TF: 800-258-7188 ■ *Web:* www.vascularweb.org

Society of American Gastrointestinal & Endoscopic Surgeons (SAGES)
11300 W Olympic Blvd Ste 600 Los Angeles CA 90064 310-437-0544 437-0585
Web: www.sages.org

Society of Cardiovascular Anesthesiologists (SCA)
2209 Dickens Rd Richmond VA 23230 804-282-0084 282-0090
Web: www.scahq.org

				Phone	Fax
Society of Critical Care Medicine (SCCM) 500 Midway Dr Ste 200 *Web:* www.sccm.org	Mount Prospect	IL	60056	847-827-6869	827-6886
Society of Diagnostic Medical Sonography (SDMS) 2745 Dallas Pkwy *TF:* 800-229-9506 ■ *Web:* www.sdms.org	Plano	TX	75093	214-473-8057	473-8563
Society of Gastroenterology Nurses & Assoc Inc (SGNA) 401 N Michigan Ave *TF:* 800-245-7462 ■ *Web:* www.sgna.org	Chicago	IL	60611	312-321-5165	673-6694
Society of Interventional Radiology (SIR) 3975 Fair Rdige Dr Ste 400 N *TF:* 800-488-7284 ■ *Web:* www.sirweb.org	Fairfax	VA	22033	703-691-1805	691-1855
Society of Laparoendoscopic Surgeons (SLS) 7330 SW 62nd Pl Ste 410 *Web:* www.sls.org	MIAMI	FL	33143	305-665-9959	667-4123
Society of Nuclear Medicine (SNM) 1850 Samuel Morse Dr *TF:* 888-633-5343 ■ *Web:* snmmi.org/	Reston	VA	20190	703-708-9000	708-9015
Society of Teachers of Family Medicine (STFM) 11400 Tomahawk Creek Pkwy Ste 540 *TF:* 800-274-7928 ■ *Web:* www.stfm.org	Leawood	KS	66211	913-906-6000	906-6096
Society of Thoracic Surgeons (STS) 633 N St Clair St Ste 2320 *TF:* 877-865-5321 ■ *Web:* www.sts.org	Chicago	IL	60611	312-202-5800	202-5801
Society of Toxicology (SOT) 1767 Business Ctr Dr *TF:* 800-826-6762 ■ *Web:* www.toxicology.org	Reston	VA	20190	703-438-3115	438-3113
Southern Medical Assn (SMA) 35 W Lakeshore Dr *TF:* 800-423-4992	Birmingham	AL	35209	205-945-1840	945-1548
Special Care Dentistry Assn 401 N Michigan Ave Ste 2200 *Web:* www.scdaonline.org	Chicago	IL	60611	312-527-6764	673-6805
Sports Cardiovascular & Wellness Nutritionists (SCAN) 4500 Rockside Rd Ste 400 *TF General:* 800-249-2875 ■ *Web:* www.scandpg.org	Cleveland	OH	44131	216-503-0053	503-0041
Therapeutic Communities of America (TCA) 1776 I St NW Rm 937 *Web:* www.treatmentcommunitiesofamerica.org/	Washington	DC	20009	202-296-3503	
US Pharmacopeia (USP) 12601 Twinbrook Pkwy **Fax:* Hum Res ■ *TF:* 800-227-8772 ■ *Web:* www.usp.org	Rockville	MD	20852	301-881-0666	816-8525*
Visiting Nurse Assns of America (VNAA) 900 19th St NW Ste 200 *TF:* 888-866-8773 ■ *Web:* www.vnaa.org	Washington	DC	20006	202-384-1420	384-1444
World Allergy Organization (WAO) 555 E Wells St Ste 1100 *Web:* www.worldallergy.org	Milwaukee	WI	53202	414-276-1791	276-3349
Wound Ostomy & Continence Nurses Society (WOCN) 15000 Commerce Pkwy Ste C *TF:* 888-224-9626 ■ *Web:* www.wocn.org	Mount Laurel	NJ	08054	888-224-9626	

49-9 Insurance Industry Associations

				Phone	Fax
America's Health Insurance Plans (AHIP) 601 Pennsylvania Ave NW Ste 500 *TF Cust Svc:* 877-291-2247 ■ *Web:* www.ahip.org	Washington	DC	20004	202-778-3200	331-7487
American Academy of Actuaries 1100 17th St NW 7th Fl *TF:* 888-888-1778 ■ *Web:* www.actuary.org	Washington	DC	20036	202-223-8196	872-1948
American Assn of Crop Insurers (AACI) One Massachusetts Ave NW Ste 800 *Web:* www.cropinsurers.com	Washington	DC	20001	202-789-4100	408-7763
American Assn of Insurance Services (AAIS) 1745 S Naperville Rd *TF:* 800-564-2247 ■ *Web:* www.aaisonline.com	Wheaton	IL	60189	630-681-8347	681-8356
American Assn of Managing General Agents (AAMGA) 150 S Warner Rd Ste 156 *TF:* 800-467-8725 ■ *Web:* www.aamga.org	King of Prussia	PA	19406	610-225-1999	225-1996
American Council of Life Insurers (ACLI) 101 Constitution Ave NW Ste 700 W *Web:* www.acli.com	Washington	DC	20001	202-624-2000	624-2319
American Institute for CPCU & Insurance Institute of America (AICPCU/IIA) 720 Providence Rd Ste 100 *TF:* 800-644-2101 ■ *Web:* www.theinstitutes.org	Malvern	PA	19355	610-644-2100	640-9576
American Institute of Marine Underwriters (AIMU) 14 Wall St Eighth Fl *Web:* www.aimu.org	New York	NY	10005	212-233-0550	227-5102
American Insurance Assn (AIA) 2101 L St *Web:* www.aiadc.org	Washington	DC	20037	202-828-7100	293-1219
American Nuclear Insurers (ANI) 95 Glastonbury Blvd Ste 300 *TF:* 866-301-1301 ■ *Web:* www.amnucins.com	Glastonbury	CT	06033	860-682-1301	659-0002
Associated Risk Managers (ARM) 2 Pierce Pl *TF:* 800-735-5441 ■ *Web:* www.armiweb.com	Itasca	IL	60143	630-285-4324	285-3590
Association for Advanced Life Underwriting (AALU) 11921 Freedom Dr Ste 1100 *TF:* 888-275-0092 ■ *Web:* www.aalu.org	Reston	VA	20190	703-641-9400	641-9885
Association for Co-op Operations Research & Development (ACORD) One Blue Hill Plz PO Box 1529 *TF:* 800-444-3341 ■ *Web:* www.acord.org	Pearl River	NY	10965	845-620-1700	620-3600
Blue Cross & Blue Shield Assn 225 N Michigan Ave *TF:* 800-810-2583 ■ *Web:* www.bcbs.com	Chicago	IL	60601	312-297-6000	
Casualty Actuarial Society (CAS) 4350 Fairfax Dr # 250 *Web:* www.casact.org	Arlington	VA	22203	703-276-3100	276-3108
Coalition Against Insurance Fraud 1012 14th St NW Ste 200 *TF:* 800-835-6422 ■ *Web:* www.insurancefraud.org	Washington	DC	20005	202-393-7330	318-9189
Consumer Credit Industry Assn (CCIA) 6300 Powers Ferry Rd Ste 600-286 **Fax Area Code:* 312 ■ *Web:* www.cciaonline.com	Atlanta	GA	30339	678-858-4001	939-8287*
Council for Affordable Health Insurance (CAHI) 127 S Peyton St Ste 210 *Web:* www.cahi.org	Alexandria	VA	22314	703-836-6200	836-6550
Council of Insurance Agents & Brokers 701 Pennsylvania Ave NW Ste 750 *TF:* 877-267-9855 ■ *Web:* www.ciab.com	Washington	DC	20004	202-783-4400	783-4410
CPCU Society 720 Providence Rd **Fax Area Code:* 610 ■ *TF:* 800-932-2728 ■ *Web:* www.cpcusociety.org	Malvern	PA	19355	800-932-2728	251-2780*
GAMA International 2901 Telestar Ct **Fax Area Code:* 703 ■ *TF Cust Svc:* 800-345-2687 ■ *Web:* gamaweb.com	Falls Church	VA	22042	800-345-2687	770-8182*
Independent Insurance Agents & Brokers of America Inc (IIABA) 127 S Peyton St *TF:* 800-221-7917 ■ *Web:* www.independentagent.com	Alexandria	VA	22314	703-683-4422	683-7556
Institute for Business & Home Safety (IBHS) 4775 E Fowler Ave *TF:* 866-657-4247 ■ *Web:* www.disastersafety.org	Tampa	FL	33617	813-286-3400	286-9960
Insurance Information Institute Inc (III) 110 William St *TF:* 877-263-7995 ■ *Web:* www.iii.org	New York	NY	10038	212-346-5500	732-1916
Insurance Institute for Highway Safety 1005 N Glebe Rd Ste 800 *TF:* 888-327-4236 ■ *Web:* www.iihs.org	Arlington	VA	22201	703-247-1500	247-1588
Insurance Marketing Communications Assn (IMCA) 4248 Park Glen Rd *Web:* www.imcanet.com	Minneapolis	MN	55416	952-928-4644	929-1318
Insurance Research Council (IRC) 720 Providence Rd *TF:* 800-644-2101 ■ *Web:* www.insurance-research.org	Malvern	PA	19355	610-644-2212	644-5388
LIMRA International Inc 300 Day Hill Rd *TF:* 866-540-4505 ■ *Web:* www.limra.com	Windsor	CT	06095	860-688-3358	298-9555
LOMA 2300 Windy Ridge Pkwy Ste 600 *TF:* 800-275-5662 ■ *Web:* www.loma.org	Atlanta	GA	30339	770-951-1770	984-0441
Million Dollar Round Table (MDRT) 325 W Touhy Ave *TF General:* 877-883-4865 ■ *Web:* www.mdrt.org	Park Ridge	IL	60068	847-692-6378	518-8921
Mortgage Insurance Cos of America (MICA) 1425 K St NW Ste 210 *Web:* usmi.org	Washington	DC	20005	202-682-2683	
NA of Dental Plans (NADP) 12700 Pk Central Dr *Web:* www.nadp.org	Dallas	TX	75251	972-458-6998	458-2258
NA of Insurance & Financial Advisors (NAIFA) 2901 Telestar Ct *TF Sales:* 877-866-2432 ■ *Web:* www.naifa.org	Falls Church	VA	22042	703-770-8100	
NA of Surety Bond Producers (NASBP) 1140 19th St NW Ste 800 *Web:* www.nasbp.org	Washington	DC	20036	202-686-3700	686-3656
National Council for Prescription Drug Programs (NCPDP) 9240 E Raintree Dr *TF:* 888-665-2600 ■ *Web:* www.ncpdp.org	Scottsdale	AZ	85260	480-477-1000	767-1042
National Crop Insurance Services (NCIS) 8900 Indian Creek Pkwy Ste 600 *TF:* 800-951-6247 ■ *Web:* www.ag-risk.org	Overland Park	KS	66210	913-685-2767	685-3080
National Insurance Crime Bureau (NICB) 1111 E Touhy Ave Ste 400 **Fax:* Hum Res ■ *TF:* 800-447-6282 ■ *Web:* www.nicb.org	Des Plaines	IL	60018	847-544-7002	544-7102*
National Organization of Life & Health Insurance Guaranty Assn (NOLHGA) 13873 Pk Ctr Rd Ste 329 *Web:* www.nolhga.com	Herndon	VA	20171	703-481-5206	481-5209
Physician Insurers Assn of America (PIAA) 2275 Research Blvd Ste 250 *Web:* www.piaa.us	Rockville	MD	20850	301-947-9000	947-9090
Professional Insurance Marketing Assn (PIMA) 35 E Wacker Dr Ste 850 *Web:* www.pima-assn.org	Chicago	IL	60601	817-569-7462	569-7461
Professional Liability Underwriting Society 5353 Wayzata Blvd Ste 600 *TF:* 800-845-0778 ■ *Web:* www.plusweb.org	Minneapolis	MN	55416	952-746-2580	746-2599
Property Casualty Insurers Assn of America 8700 W Bryn Mawr Ave *Web:* www.pciaa.net	Des Plaines	IL	60018	847-297-7800	297-5064
Property Loss Research Bureau (PLRB) 3025 Highland Pkwy Ste 800 *TF:* 888-711-7572 ■ *Web:* www.plrb.org	Downers Grove	IL	60515	630-724-2200	724-2260
Risk & Insurance Management Society Inc (RIMS) 1065 Ave of the Americas 13th Fl *Web:* www.rims.org	New York	NY	10018	212-286-9292	986-9716
Society of Actuaries (SOA) 475 N Martingale Rd Ste 600 *Web:* www.soa.org	Schaumburg	IL	60173	847-706-3500	706-3599
Society of Financial Service Professionals (SFSP) 19 Campus Blvd Ste 100 *TF:* 800-392-6900 ■ *Web:* www.financialpro.org	Newtown Square	PA	19073	610-526-2500	527-4010
Surety & Fidelity Assn of America (SFAA) 1101 Connecticut Ave NW Ste 800 *Web:* www.surety.org	Washington	DC	20036	202-463-0600	463-0606
Workmen's Circle/Arbeter Ring Inc 247 W 37th St Fifth Fl *TF:* 800-922-2558 ■ *Web:* www.circle.org	New York	NY	10018	212-889-6800	532-7518

49-10 Legal Professionals Associations

				Phone	Fax
ABA Commission on Domestic Violence 321 N Clark St Ninth Fl **Fax Area Code:* 202 ■ *TF:* 800-799-7233 ■ *Web:* www.americanbar.org/groups/domestic_violence.html	Chicago	IL	60654	312-988-5000	662-1594*
ABA Commission on Law & Aging (COLA) 740 15th St NW 8th Fl *Web:* www.americanbar.org/groups/law_aging.html	Washington	DC	20005	202-662-1000	662-8698
American Academy of Psychiatry & the Law (AAPL) One Regency Dr PO Box 30 *TF:* 800-331-1389 ■ *Web:* www.aapl.org	Bloomfield	CT	06002	860-242-5450	286-0787

Organization	City	State	Zip	Phone	Fax
American Arbitration Assn Inc (AAA) 1633 Broadway 10th Fl. *TF:* 800-778-7879 ■ *Web:* www.adr.org	New York	NY	10019	212-716-5800	716-5905
American Assn for Justice (AAJ) 777 Sixth St NW Ste 200 *TF:* 800-424-2725 ■ *Web:* www.justice.org	Washington	DC	20001	202-965-3500	625-7313
American Bankruptcy Institute (ABI) 66 Canal Ctr Plz Ste 600 *Web:* www.abiworld.org	Alexandria	VA	22314	703-739-0800	739-1060
American Bar Assn (ABA) 321 N Clark St *TF:* 800-285-2221 ■ *Web:* www.americanbar.org	Chicago	IL	60610	312-988-5000	
American College of Trust & Estate Counsel (ACTEC) 901 15th St NW Ste 525 *Web:* www.actec.org	Washington	DC	20005	202-684-8460	684-8459
American Health Lawyers Assn (AHLA) 1620 Eye St NW *Web:* www.healthlawyers.org	Washington	DC	20006	202-833-1100	833-1105
American Immigration Lawyers Assn (AILA) 918 F St NW *Web:* www.aila.org	Washington	DC	20004	202-216-2400	783-7853
American Intellectual Property Law Assn (AIPLA) 241 18th St S Ste 700 *Web:* www.aipla.org	Arlington	VA	22202	703-415-0780	415-0786
American Judicature Society (AJS) 2700 University Ave *TF:* 800-626-4089 ■ *Web:* www.ajs.org	Des Moines	IA	50311	515-271-2281	279-3090
American Land Title Assn (ALTA) 1828 L St NW Ste 705 *TF:* 800-787-2582 ■ *Web:* www.alta.org	Washington	DC	20036	202-296-3671	223-5843
American Law Institute (ALI) 4025 Chestnut St *TF:* 800-253-6397 ■ *Web:* www.ali.org	Philadelphia	PA	19104	215-243-1600	243-1636
American Society of International Law, The (ASIL) 2223 Massachusetts Ave NW *Web:* www.asil.org	Washington	DC	20008	202-939-6000	797-7133
American Tort Reform Assn (ATRA) 1101 Connecticut Ave NW Ste 400 *TF:* 877-333-2227 ■ *Web:* www.atra.org	Washington	DC	20036	202-682-1163	682-1022
Association for Conflict Resolution (ACR) 12100 Sunset Hills Rd Ste 130 *TF:* 800-880-7303 ■ *Web:* imis100us2.com/acr/acr/default.aspx	Reston	VA	20190	703-234-4141	435-4390
Association of American Law Schools (AALS) 1201 Connecticut Ave NW Ste 800 *Web:* www.aals.org	Washington	DC	20036	202-296-8851	296-8869
Association of Corporate Counsel (ACC) 1025 Connecticut Ave NW Ste 200 *TF:* 877-647-3411 ■ *Web:* www.acc.com	Washington	DC	20036	202-293-4103	293-4701
Association of Legal Administrators (ALA) 75 Tri-State International Ste 222 *TF:* 877-675-5571 ■ *Web:* www.alanet.org	Lincolnshire	IL	60069	847-267-1252	267-1329
Battered Women's Justice Project 1801 Nicollet Ave S Ste 102 *TF:* 800-903-0111 ■ *Web:* www.bwjp.org	Minneapolis	MN	55403	612-824-8768	824-8965
Christian Legal Society (CLS) 8001 Braddock Rd Ste 300 *Web:* www.clsnet.org	Springfield	VA	22151	703-642-1070	642-1075
Commercial Law League of America (CLLA) 70 E Lake St Ste 630 *TF:* 800-978-2552 ■ *Web:* www.clla.org	Chicago	IL	60601	312-781-2000	781-2010
Defense Research Institute (DRI) 55 W Monroe St Ste 20 *TF:* 866-525-6466 ■ *Web:* www.dri.org	Chicago	IL	60603	312-795-1101	795-0749
Environmental Law Institute (ELI) 2000 L St NW Ste 620 *TF:* 800-433-5120 ■ *Web:* www.eli.org	Washington	DC	20036	202-939-3800	939-3868
Federalist Society for Law & Public Policy Studies 1015 18th St NW Ste 425 *Web:* www.fed-soc.org	Washington	DC	20036	202-822-8138	296-8061
Food & Drug Law Institute (FDLI) 1155 15th St NW Ste 800 *TF:* 800-956-6293 ■ *Web:* www.fdli.org	Washington	DC	20005	202-371-1420	371-0649
Institute for Professionals in Taxation (IPT) 600 Northpark Town Ctr 1200 Abernathy Rd Ste L-2 *Web:* www.ipt.org	Atlanta	GA	30328	404-240-2300	240-2315
International Assn of Defense Counsel (IADC) 303 W Madison St Ste 925 *Web:* www.iadclaw.org	Chicago	IL	60606	312-368-1494	368-1854
International Law Institute (ILI) 1055 Thomas Jefferson St NW Ste M-100 *Web:* www.ili.org	Washington	DC	20007	202-247-6006	247-6010
International Municipal Lawyers Assn (IMLA) 7910 Woodmont Ave Ste 1440 *TF:* 800-942-7732 ■ *Web:* www.imla.org	Bethesda	MD	20814	202-466-5424	785-0152
Justice in Aging (NSCLC) 1444 'I' St Ste 1100 *Web:* nsclc.org	Washington	DC	20005	202-289-6976	289-7224
Justice Research & Statistics Assn (JRSA) 777 N Capitol St NE Ste 801 *Web:* www.jrsainfo.org	Washington	DC	20002	202-842-9330	842-9329
Lawyers for Civil Justice (LCJ) 1140 Connecticut Ave NW Ste 503 *Web:* www.lfcj.com	Washington	DC	20036	202-429-0045	429-6982
Lawyers' Committee for Civil Rights Under Law 1401 New York Ave NW Ste 400 *TF:* 888-299-5227 ■ *Web:* www.lawyerscommittee.org	Washington	DC	20005	202-662-8600	783-0857
Media Law Resource Ctr (MLRC) 266 W 37th St Ste 20 *Web:* www.medialaw.org	New York	NY	10018	212-337-0200	
NALS - Assn for Legal Professionals 8159 E 41st St *Web:* www.nals.org	Tulsa	OK	74145	918-582-5188	582-5907
National Bar Assn (NBA) 1225 11th St NW *Web:* www.nationalbar.org	Washington	DC	20001	202-842-3900	289-6170
National Council of Juvenile & Family Court Judges (NCJFCJ) Univ of Nevada PO Box 8970 *TF:* 800-527-3223 ■ *Web:* www.ncjfcj.org	Reno	NV	89507	775-784-6012	784-6628
National Court Reporters Assn (NCRA) 8224 Old Courthouse Rd *TF:* 800-272-6272 ■ *Web:* www.ncra.org	Vienna	VA	22182	703-556-6272	556-6291
National Employment Lawyers Assn (NELA) 417 Montgomery St Fourth Fl. *Web:* www.nela.org	San Francisco	CA	94104	415-296-7629	677-9445
National Federation of Paralegal Assn (NFPA) 23607 Hwy 99 Ste 2-C *TF:* 888-525-3675 ■ *Web:* www.paralegals.org	Edmonds	WA	98020	425-967-0045	771-9588
National Legal Aid & Defender Assn (NLADA) 1140 Connecticut Ave NW Ste 900 *TF:* 800-725-4513 ■ *Web:* www.nlada.org	Washington	DC	20036	202-452-0620	872-1031
National Partnership for Women & Families 1875 Connecticut Ave NW Ste 650 *Web:* www.nationalpartnership.org	Washington	DC	20009	202-986-2600	986-2539
Native American Rights Fund (NARF) 1506 Broadway *TF:* 888-280-0726 ■ *Web:* www.narf.org	Boulder	CO	80302	303-447-8760	443-7776
Pension Rights Ctr 1350 Connecticut Ave NW Ste 206 *TF:* 866-735-7737 ■ *Web:* www.pensionrights.org	Washington	DC	20036	202-296-3776	833-2472
Practising Law Institute (PLI) 810 Seventh Ave 26th Fl *TF:* 800-260-4754 ■ *Web:* www.pli.edu	New York	NY	10019	212-824-5700	
Taxpayers Against Fraud Education Fund (TAF) 1220 19th St NW Ste 501 *TF General:* 800-873-2573 ■ *Web:* www.taf.org	Washington	DC	20036	202-296-4826	296-4838
Vera Institute of Justice 233 Broadway 12th Fl. *Web:* www.vera.org	New York	NY	10279	212-334-1300	941-9407
World Jurist Assn (WJA) 7910 Woodmont Ave Ste 1440 *Web:* www.worldjurist.org	Bethesda	MD	20814	202-466-5428	452-8540

49-11 Library & Information Science Associations

Organization	City	State	Zip	Phone	Fax
American Assn of Law Libraries (AALL) 53 W Jackson Blvd Ste 940 *Web:* www.aallnet.org	Chicago	IL	60604	312-939-4764	431-1097
American Assn of School Librarians (AASL) 50 E Huron St *TF:* 800-545-2433 ■ *Web:* www.ala.org/aasl	Chicago	IL	60611	312-280-4386	664-7459
American Library Assn (ALA) 50 E Huron St *TF:* 800-545-2433 ■ *Web:* www.ala.org	Chicago	IL	60611	312-944-6780	944-2641
American Theological Library Assn (ATLA) 300 S Wacker Dr Ste 2100 *TF:* 888-665-2852 ■ *Web:* www.atla.com	Chicago	IL	60606	312-454-5100	454-5505
Association for Library & Information Science Education (ALISE) 65 E Wacker Pl Ste 1900 *TF:* 800-522-0772 ■ *Web:* www.alise.org	Chicago	IL	60601	312-795-0996	419-8950
Association for Library Collections & Technical Services (ALCTS) 50 E Huron St *TF:* 800-545-2433 ■ *Web:* www.ala.org/alcts	Chicago	IL	60611	312-280-5038	280-5033
Association for Library Service to Children (ALSC) 50 E Huron St *TF:* 800-545-2433 ■ *Web:* www.ala.org/alsc	Chicago	IL	60611	312-280-2163	944-7671
Association for Library Trustees, Advocates, Friends & Foundations (ALTAFF) 50 E Huron St *TF:* 800-545-2433 ■ *Web:* ala.org	Chicago	IL	60611	800-545-2433	
Association of College & Research Libraries (ACRL) 50 E Huron St *TF:* 800-545-2433 ■ *Web:* www.ala.org/acrl/aboutacrl	Chicago	IL	60611	312-280-2519	280-2520
Association of Jewish Libraries PO Box 1118 *Web:* www.jewishlibraries.org	Teaneck	NJ	07666	201-371-3255	
Association of Specialized & Co-op Library Agencies (ASCLA) 50 E Huron St *TF:* 800-545-2433 ■ *Web:* www.ala.org/ascla	Chicago	IL	60611	312-280-4395	944-8085
Cal Poly Pomona Foundation Inc 3801 W Temple Ave Bldg 55 *Web:* www.foundation.csupomona.edu	Pomona	CA	91768	909-869-2950	869-3716
Canadian Assn of Law Libraries (CALL) 4 Cataraqui St Ste 310 PO Box 1570 **Fax Area Code:* 866 ■ *Web:* www.callacbd.ca	Kingston	ON	K7L5C8	613-531-9338	303-0626*
Canadian Assn of Special Libraries & Information Services (CASLIS) 1150 Morrison Dr Ste 400 *Web:* www.cla.ca/caslis/index.htm	Ottawa	ON	K2H8S9	613-232-9625	563-9895
Canadian Health Libraries Assn (CHLA) 39 River St *Web:* www.chla-absc.ca	Toronto	ON	M5A3P1	416-646-1600	646-9460
Canadian Library Assn (CLA) 328 Frank St *Web:* www.cla.ca	Ottawa	ON	K2P0X8	613-232-9625	563-9895
Library & Information Technology Assn (LITA) 50 E Huron St *TF:* 800-545-2433 ■ *Web:* www.ala.org	Chicago	IL	60611	312-280-4270	280-3257
Library Leadership & Management Assn (LLAMA) 50 E Huron St *TF:* 800-545-2433 ■ *Web:* www.ala.org/llama	Chicago	IL	60611	800-545-2433	
Medical Library Assn (MLA) 65 E Wacker Pl Ste 1900 *TF:* 800-523-1850 ■ *Web:* www.mlanet.org	Chicago	IL	60601	312-419-9094	419-8950
Music Library Assn (MLA) 8551 Research Way Ste 180 *Web:* www.musiclibraryassoc.org	Middleton	WI	53562	608-836-5825	831-8200
Online Computer Library Ctr Inc (OCLC) 6565 Kilgour Pl **Fax Area Code:* 614 ■ *TF:* 800-848-5878 ■ *Web:* www.oclc.org	Dublin	OH	43017	800-848-5878	764-6096*
Public Library Assn (PLA) 50 E Huron St *TF:* 800-545-2433 ■ *Web:* www.ala.org	Chicago	IL	60611	312-280-5752	280-5029

	City	State	Zip	Phone	Fax
Reference & User Services Assn (RUSA) 50 E Huron St *TF:* 800-545-2433 ■ *Web:* www.ala.org/rusa	Chicago	IL	60611	312-280-4398	944-8085
Special Libraries Assn (SLA) 331 S Patrick St *TF:* 866-446-6069 ■ *Web:* www.sla.org	Alexandria	VA	22314	703-647-4900	647-4901
Urban Libraries Council (ULC) 125 S Wacker Dr Ste 1050 *Web:* www.urbanlibraries.org	Chicago	IL	60606	847-866-9999	866-9989
Young Adult Library Services Assn (YALSA) 50 E Huron St *TF:* 800-545-2433 ■ *Web:* www.ala.org/yalsa	Chicago	IL	60611	312-280-4390	664-7459

49-12 Management & Business Professional Associations

	City	State	Zip	Phone	Fax
Academy of Management (AOM) 235 Elm Rd PO Box 3020 *TF:* 800-633-4931 ■ *Web:* aom.org	Briarcliff Manor	NY	10510	914-923-2607	923-2615
AMC Institute 100 N 20th St Fourth Fl *Web:* amcinstitute.org	Philadelphia	PA	19103	215-564-3484	963-9785
American Business Conference (ABC) 1828 L St NW Ste 908 *Web:* www.americanbusinessconference.org	Washington	DC	20036	202-822-9300	467-4070
American Business Women's Assn (ABWA) 11050 Roe Ave Ste 200 **Fax Area Code:* 913 ■ *TF:* 800-228-0007 ■ *Web:* www.abwa.org	Overland Park	KS	66211	800-228-0007	660-0101*
American Businesspersons Assn (ABA) 350 Fairway Dr Ste 200 *TF:* 800-221-2168 ■ *Web:* www.aba-assn.com	Deerfield Beach	FL	33441	954-571-1877	
American Chamber of Commerce Executives (ACCE) 4875 Eisenhower Ave Ste 250 *TF:* 800-394-2223 ■ *Web:* www.acce.org	Alexandria	VA	22304	703-998-0072	212-9512
American Payroll Assn (APA) 660 N Main Ave Ste 100 *Web:* americanpayroll.org	San Antonio	TX	78205	210-226-4600	226-4027
American Seminar Leaders Assn (ASLA) 2405 E Washington Blvd *TF:* 800-801-1886 ■ *Web:* www.asla.com	Pasadena	CA	91104	626-791-1211	791-0701
American Society of Assn Executives (ASAE) 1575 'I' St NW *TF:* 888-950-2723 ■ *Web:* www.asaecenter.org	Washington	DC	20005	202-626-2723	371-8825
American Society of Notaries (ASN) PO Box 5707 *Web:* www.notaries.org	Tallahassee	FL	32314	850-671-5164	671-5165
American Society of Pension Professionals & Actuaries (ASPPA) 4245 N Fairfax Dr Ste 750 *Web:* www.asppa.org	Arlington	VA	22203	703-516-9300	516-9308
American Staffing Assn (ASA) 277 S Washington St Ste 200 *TF:* 800-456-4324 ■ *Web:* www.americanstaffing.net	Alexandria	VA	22314	703-253-2020	253-2053
Appraisers Assn of America (AAA) 386 Pk Ave S Ste 2000 *Web:* appraisersassociation.org	New York	NY	10016	212-889-5404	889-5503
APQC 123 N Post Oak Ln Ste 300 *TF:* 800-776-9676 ■ *Web:* www.apqc.org	Houston	TX	77024	713-681-4020	681-8578
ARMA International 11880 College Blvd Ste 450 *TF:* 800-422-2762 ■ *Web:* www.arma.org	Overland Park	KS	66210	913-341-3808	341-3742
ASIS International 1625 Prince St *Web:* www.asisonline.org	Alexandria	VA	22314	703-519-6200	519-6299
Association for Business Communication 181 Turner St NW **Fax Area Code:* 936 ■ *Web:* www.businesscommunication.org	Blacksburg	VA	24061	540-231-1939	468-6281*
Association for Corporate Growth (ACG) 71 S Wacker Dr Ste 2760 *TF:* 877-358-2220 ■ *Web:* www.acg.org	Chicago	IL	60606	312-957-4260	
Association for Mfg Excellence (AME) 3701 W Algonquin Rd Ste G *Web:* www.ame.org	Rolling Meadows	IL	60008	224-232-5980	232-5981
Association for Mfg Technology (AMT) 7901 Westpark Dr *TF:* 800-524-0475 ■ *Web:* www.amtonline.org	McLean	VA	22102	703-893-2900	893-1151
Association of Fundraising Professionals (AFP) 4300 Wilson Blvd Ste 300 *TF:* 800-666-3863 ■ *Web:* www.afpnet.org	Arlington	VA	22203	703-684-0410	684-0540
Association of Proposal Management Professionals (APMP) PO Box 668 *Web:* www.apmp.org	Dana Point	CA	92629	949-493-9398	
Business Council for International Understanding (BCIU) 1212 Ave of the Americas 10th Fl *Web:* www.bciu.org	New York	NY	10036	212-490-0460	697-8526
Business Executives for National Security (BENS) 1030 15th St NW Ste 200 *Web:* www.bens.org	Washington	DC	20005	202-296-2125	296-2490
Business Forms Management Assn (BFMA) 3800 Old Cheney Rd Ste 101-285 **Fax Area Code:* 877 ■ *TF:* 888-367-3078 ■ *Web:* www.bfma.org	Lincoln	NE	68516	402-216-0479	204-5979*
Business Roundtable (BR) 1717 Rhode Island Ave NW Ste 800 *Web:* businessroundtable.org	Washington	DC	20036	202-872-1260	466-3509
Chief Executives Organization 7920 Norfolk Ave Ste 400 *Web:* www.ceo.org	Bethesda	MD	20814	301-656-9220	656-9221
Christian Leadership Alliance (CLA) 635 Camino De Los Mares Ste 216 *TF:* 800-263-6317 ■ *Web:* www.christianleadershipalliance.org	San Clemente	CA	92673	949-487-0900	487-0927
Club Managers Assn of America (CMAA) 1733 King St *TF:* 800-777-3529 ■ *Web:* www.cmaa.org	Alexandria	VA	22314	703-739-9500	739-0124
Conference Board Inc 845 Third Ave *Web:* www.conference-board.org	New York	NY	10022	212-759-0900	980-7014
Council for Community & Economic Research (C2ER) 1700 N Moore St Ste 2225 PO Box 100127 **Fax Area Code:* 480 ■ *Web:* www.c2er.org	Arlington	VA	22209	703-522-4980	393-5098*
Council on State Taxation (COST) 122 C St NW Ste 330 *Web:* www.cost.org	Washington	DC	20001	202-484-5222	484-5229
Employee Assistance Professionals Assn Inc (EAPA) 4350 N Fairfax Dr Ste 740 *Web:* www.eapassn.org	Arlington	VA	22203	703-387-1000	522-4585
Employee Involvement Assn 11 W Monument Ave	Dayton	OH	45402	937-586-3724	
Employers Council on Flexible Compensation (ECFC) 927 15th St NW Ste 700 *Web:* www.ecfc.org	Washington	DC	20005	202-659-4300	216-9646
ESOP Assn 1726 M St NW Ste 501 *TF:* 866-366-3832 ■ *Web:* www.esopassociation.org	Washington	DC	20036	202-293-2971	293-7568
Executive Women International (EWI) 7414 S State St *TF:* 877-439-4669 ■ *Web:* ewiconnect.com	Midvale	UT	84047	801-355-2800	355-2852
Family Firm Institute (FFI) 200 Lincoln St Ste 201 *Web:* www.ffi.org	Boston	MA	02111	617-482-3045	482-3049
Foundation on Economic Trends 4520 E W Hwy Ste 600 *Web:* www.foet.org	Bethesda	MD	20814	301-656-6272	654-0208
HR People & Strategy (HRPS) 401 N Michigan Ave Ste 2200 *Web:* www.hrps.org	Chicago	IL	60611	312-321-6805	673-6944
Institute for a Drug-Free Workplace (IDFW) 10701 Parkridge Blvd Ste 300 *TF:* 877-696-6775 ■ *Web:* www.drugfreeworkplace.org	Reston	VA	20191	703-391-7222	391-7223
Institute for Alternative Futures (IAF) 100 N Pitt St Ste 235 *Web:* www.altfutures.com	Alexandria	VA	22314	703-684-5880	684-0640
Institute for Supply Management (ISM) 2055 Centennial Cir *TF Cust Svc:* 800-888-6276 ■ *Web:* www.ism.ws	Tempe	AZ	85284	480-752-6276	752-7890
Institute of Business Appraisers (IBA) 1111 BrickyaRd Rd Ste 200 **Fax Area Code:* 866 ■ *TF:* 800-299-4130 ■ *Web:* www.go-iba.org	Salt Lake City	UT	84106	800-299-4130	353-5406*
Institute of Certified Professional Managers (ICPM) James Madison University MSC 5504 *TF:* 800-460-8013 ■ *Web:* www.icpm.biz	Harrisonburg	VA	22807	540-568-3247	
Institute of Management Consultants USA Inc (IMC USA) 2025 M St NW Ste 800 *TF:* 800-221-2557 ■ *Web:* www.imcusa.org	Washington	DC	20036	202-367-1134	367-2134
International Assn for Human Resource Information Management Inc (IHRIM) PO Box 1086 **Fax Area Code:* 781 ■ *TF:* 800-804-3983 ■ *Web:* www.ihrim.org	Burlington	MA	01803	800-804-3983	998-8011*
International Assn for Impact Assessment (IAIA) 1330 23rd St S Ste C *Web:* www.iaia.org	Fargo	ND	58103	701-297-7908	297-7917
International Assn of Administrative Professionals (IAAP) 10502 NW Ambassador Dr PO Box 20404 *Web:* www.iaap-hq.org	Kansas City	MO	64153	816-891-6600	891-9118
International Assn of Business Communicators (IABC) 601 Montgomery St Ste 1900 *TF:* 800-766-4222 ■ *Web:* www.iabc.com	San Francisco	CA	94111	415-544-4700	544-4747
International Assn of Conference Centers (IACC) 35 East Wacker Dr Ste 850 *Web:* www.iacconline.org	Chicago	IL	60601	312-224-2580	644-8557
International Assn of Venue Managers Inc (IAVM) 635 Fritz Dr Ste 100 *TF:* 800-935-4226 ■ *Web:* www.iavm.org	Coppell	TX	75019	972-906-7441	906-7418
International Assn of Workforce Professionals (IAPES) 1801 Louisville Rd *TF:* 888-898-9960 ■ *Web:* www.iawponline.org	Frankfort	KY	40601	502-223-4459	223-4127
International Council of Shopping Centers (ICSC) 1221 Ave of the Americas 41st Fl **Fax Area Code:* 212 ■ *Web:* www.icsc.org	New York	NY	10020	646-728-3800	589-5555*
International Economic Development Council (IEDC) 734 15th St NW Ste 900 *Web:* www.iedconline.org	Washington	DC	20005	202-223-7800	223-4745
International Facility Management Assn (IFMA) 800 Gessner Rd Ste 900 *Web:* www.ifma.org	Houston	TX	77024	713-623-4362	623-6124
International Graphoanalysis Society (IGAS) 842 Fifth Ave **Fax Area Code:* 509 ■ *Web:* www.igas.com	New Kensington	PA	15068	724-472-9701	271-1149*
International Public Management Assn for Hum Res (IPMA-HR) 1617 Duke St *TF:* 800-381-8378 ■ *Web:* www.ipma-hr.org	Alexandria	VA	22314	703-549-7100	684-0948
International Society for Performance Improvement (ISPI) 1400 Spring St Ste 260 *TF:* 800-825-7550 ■ *Web:* www.ispi.org	Silver Spring	MD	20910	301-587-8570	587-8573
International Society of Certified Employee Benefit Specialists (ISCEBS) 18700 W Bluemond Rd PO Box 209 *TF:* 888-334-3327 ■ *Web:* www.iscebs.org	Brookfield	WI	53008	262-786-8771	786-8650
International Trademark Assn (INTA) 655 Third Ave 10th Fl *TF:* 800-995-3579 ■ *Web:* www.inta.org	New York	NY	10017	212-768-9887	768-7796
Latin Business Assn (LBA) 120 S San Pedro St Ste 530 *TF:* 877-551-7778 ■ *Web:* lbausa.com	Los Angeles	CA	90012	213-628-8510	628-8519
Manufacturers Alliance/MAPI Inc 1600 Wilson Blvd Ste 1100 *Web:* www.mapi.net	Arlington	VA	22209	703-841-9000	841-9514
Meeting Professionals International (MPI) 3030 LBJ Fwy Ste 1700 *TF:* 866-748-9561 ■ *Web:* www.mpiweb.org	Dallas	TX	75234	972-702-3000	702-3070
NA of Parliamentarians (NAP) 213 S Main St *TF:* 888-627-2929 ■ *Web:* www.parliamentarians.org	Independence	MO	64050	816-833-3892	833-3893
NA of Professional Employer Organizations (NAPEO) 707 N St Asaph St *Web:* www.napeo.org	Alexandria	VA	22314	703-836-0466	836-0976

Phone Fax

National Black MBA Assn (NBMBAA)
180 N Michigan Ave Ste 1400 ... Chicago IL 60601 312-236-2622 236-0390
Web: www.nbmbaa.org

National Business Assn (NBA)
5151 Beltline Rd Ste 1150 ... Dallas TX 75254 972-458-0900 960-9149
TF: 800-456-0440 ■ *Web:* www.nationalbusiness.org

National Business Coalition on Health (NBCH)
1015 18th St NW Ste 730 ... Washington DC 20036 202-775-9300 775-1569
TF: 800-223-4139 ■ *Web:* www.nbch.org

National Business Incubation Assn (NBIA)
40 W St Ste 25 ... Athens OH 45701 740-593-4331 593-1996
TF: 800-766-3782 ■ *Web:* www.nbia.org

National Co-op Business Assn (NCBA)
1401 New York Ave NW Ste 1100 ... Washington DC 20005 202-638-6222 638-1374
TF: 800-356-9655 ■ *Web:* www.ncba.coop

National Coalition of Black Meeting Planners (NCBMP)
700 N. Fairfax St Suite 510 ... Alexandria VA 22314 571-527-3110 588-0011*
**Fax Area Code:* 301 ■ *TF:* 800-551-9369 ■ *Web:* www.ncbmp.com

National Contract Management Assn (NCMA)
21740 Beaumeade Cir Ste 125 ... Ashburn VA 20147 571-382-0082 448-0939*
**Fax Area Code:* 703 ■ *TF:* 800-344-8096 ■ *Web:* www.ncmahq.org

National Council for Advanced Mfg (NACFAM)
2025 M St NW Ste 800 ... Washington DC 20036 202-429-2220 429-2422
Web: www.nacfam.org

National Institute for Work & Learning (NIWL)
1825 Connecticut Ave NW Seventh Fl ... Washington DC 20009 202-884-8186 884-8422

National Management Assn (NMA) 2210 Arbor Blvd ... Dayton OH 45439 937-294-0421 294-2374
Web: www.nma1.org

National Notary Assn (NNA) 9350 DeSoto Ave ... Chatsworth CA 91313 818-739-4000 700-1830
TF: 800-876-6827 ■ *Web:* www.nationalnotary.org

National Right to Work Committee (NRTWC)
8001 Braddock Rd Ste 500 ... Springfield VA 22160 703-321-8510 321-9319
TF: 800-325-7892 ■ *Web:* nrtw.org

National Small Business Assn (NSBA)
1156 15th St NW Ste 1100 ... Washington DC 20005 202-293-8830 872-8543
TF: 800-345-6728 ■ *Web:* www.nsba.biz

National Society of Compliance Professionals (NSCP)
22 Kent Rd ... Cornwall Bridge CT 06754 860-672-0843 672-3005
Web: www.nscp.org

New York Celebrity Assistants (NYCA)
459 Columbus Ave Ste 216 ... New York NY 10024 212-803-5444
Web: www.nycelebrityassistants.com

Organization for International Investment (OFII)
1225 19th St NW Ste 501 ... Washington DC 20036 202-659-1903 659-2293
Web: www.ofii.org

Product Development & Management Assn (PDMA)
330 N Wabash Ave Ste 2000 ... Chicago IL 60611 312-321-5145 439-0525*
**Fax Area Code:* 856 ■ *TF:* 800-232-5241 ■ *Web:* www.pdma.org

Professional Convention Management Assn (PCMA)
35 E Wacker Dr Ste 500 ... Chicago IL 60601 312-423-7262 423-7222
TF: 877-827-7262 ■ *Web:* www.pcma.org

Professional Services Council (PSC)
4401 Wilson Blvd Ste 1110 ... Arlington VA 22203 703-875-8059 875-8922
TF: 800-353-9118 ■ *Web:* www.pscouncil.org

Profit Sharing/401(k) Council of America (PSCA)
20 N Wacker Dr Ste 3700 ... Chicago IL 60606 312-419-1863 419-1864
TF: 866-614-8407 ■ *Web:* www.psca.org

Project Management Institute (PMI)
14 Campus Blvd ... Newtown Square PA 19073 610-356-4600 356-4647
TF: 866-276-4764 ■ *Web:* www.pmi.org

Religious Conference Management Assn Inc (RCMA)
7702 Woodland Dr Ste 120 ... Indianapolis IN 46278 317-632-1888 632-7909
TF: 800-221-8235 ■ *Web:* www.rcmaweb.org

SCORE Assn 1175 Herndon Pkwy Ste 900 ... Herndon VA 20170 800-634-0245 487-3066*
**Fax Area Code:* 703 ■ *TF:* 800-634-0245 ■ *Web:* www.score.org

Service Industry Assn (SIA)
2164 Historic Decatur Rd Villa 19 ... San Diego CA 92106 619-221-9200 221-8201
Web: www.servicenetwork.org

Small Business & Entrepreneurship Council
301 Maple Ave W Ste 690 ... Vienna VA 22180 703-242-5840 242-5841
Web: www.sbecouncil.org

Small Business Legislative Council (SBLC)
1010 Mass Ave NW Ste 400 ... Washington DC 20001 202-639-8500
Web: www.sblc.org

Society for Human Resource Management (SHRM)
1800 Duke St ... Alexandria VA 22314 703-548-3440 836-0367
TF: 800-283-7476 ■ *Web:* www.shrm.org

Society of Competitive Intelligence Professionals (SCIP)
1700 Diagonal Rd Ste 600 ... Alexandria VA 22314 703-739-0696 739-2524
TF: 877-463-7678 ■ *Web:* www.scip.org

Society of Corporate Secretaries & Governance Professionals Inc
240 W 35th St Ste 400 ... New York NY 10001 212-681-2000 681-2005
Web: main.governanceprofessionals.org

Society of Professional Benefit Administrators (SPBA)
2 Wisconsin Cir Ste 670 ... Chevy Chase MD 20815 301-718-7722 718-9440
Web: www.spbatpa.org

US Council for International Business (USCIB)
1212 Ave of the Americas 18th Fl ... New York NY 10036 212-354-4480 575-0327
TF: 866-768-5925 ■ *Web:* www.uscib.org

US-ASEAN Business Council
1101 17th St NW Ste 411 ... Washington DC 20036 202-289-1911 289-0519
Web: usasean.org/

US-China Business Council, The
1818 N St NW Ste 200 ... Washington DC 20036 202-429-0340 775-2476
Web: www.uschina.org

US-Japan Business Council 1615 H St NW ... Washington DC 20062 202-463-5772
Web: www.usjbc.org

US-Russia Business Council
1110 Vermont Ave NW Ste 330 ... Washington DC 20005 202-739-9180 659-5920
Web: www.usrbc.org

World Trade Centers Assn (WTCA)
120 Broadway Suite 3350 ... New York NY 10271 212-432-2626 418-4801*
**Fax Area Code:* 479

Phone Fax

WorldatWork 14040 N Northsight Blvd ... Scottsdale AZ 85260 202-315-5500 315-5550
TF: 877-951-9191 ■ *Web:* www.worldatwork.org

Worldwide Employee Benefits Network Inc (WEB)
1700 Pennsylvania Ave Ste 400 ... Washington DC 20006 202-349-2049 318-8778
Web: www.webnetwork.org

Young Presidents' Organization (YPO)
600 E Las Colinas Blvd Ste 1000 ... Irving TX 75039 972-587-1500 587-1611
TF: 800-773-7976 ■ *Web:* www.ypo.org

YPO-WPO 600 E Las Colinas Blvd Ste 1000 ... Irving TX 75039 972-587-1500 587-1600
TF: 800-773-7976 ■ *Web:* www.wpo.org

49-13 Manufacturing Industry Professional & Trade Associations

Phone Fax

Adhesive & Sealant Council Inc (ASC)
7101 Wisconsin Ave # 990 ... Bethesda MD 20814 301-986-9700 986-9795
Web: www.ascouncil.org

Aluminum Assn Inc 1525 Wilson Blvd Ste 600 ... Arlington VA 22209 703-358-2960 358-2961
Web: www.aluminum.org

Aluminum Extruders Council (AEC)
1000 N Rand Rd Ste 214 ... Wauconda IL 60084 847-526-2010 526-3993
TF: 800-354-5892 ■ *Web:* www.aec.org

American Assn of Textile Chemists & Colorists (AATCC)
One Davis Dr PO Box 12215 ... Research Triangle Park NC 27709 919-549-8141 549-8933
Web: www.aatcc.org

American Boiler Manufacturers Assn (ABMA)
8221 Old Courthouse Rd Ste 207 ... Vienna VA 22182 703-356-7172 356-4543
TF: 800-227-1966 ■ *Web:* www.abma.com

American Composites Manufacturers Assn (ACMA)
3033 Wilson Blvd Ste 420 ... Arlington VA 22201 703-525-0743 525-0743
Web: www.acmanet.org

American Fiber Manufacturers Assn Inc (AFMA)
1530 Wilson Blvd Ste 690 ... Arlington VA 22209 703-875-0432 875-0907
Web: www.afma.org

American Foundry Society (AFS)
1695 N Penny Ln ... Schaumburg IL 60173 847-824-0181 824-2174
TF: 800-537-4237 ■ *Web:* www.afsinc.org

American Galvanizers Assn (AGA)
6881 S Holly Cir Ste 108 ... Centennial CO 80112 720-554-0900 554-0909
TF: 800-468-7732 ■ *Web:* www.galvanizeit.org

American Gear Manufacturers Assn (AGMA)
500 Montgomery St Ste 350 ... Alexandria VA 22314 703-684-0211 684-0242
Web: www.agma.org

American Industrial Hygiene Assn (AIHA)
2700 Prosperity Ave Ste 250 ... Fairfax VA 22031 703-849-8888 207-3561
Web: www.aiha.org

American Iron & Steel Institute (AISI)
1101 17th St NW ... Washington DC 20036 202-452-7100 463-6573
Web: www.steel.org

American Society for Quality (ASQ)
600 N Plankinton Ave ... Milwaukee WI 53203 414-272-8575 272-1734
TF: 800-248-1946 ■ *Web:* www.asq.org

American Textile Machinery Assn (ATMA)
201 Pk Washington Ct ... Falls Church VA 22046 703-538-1789 241-5603
Web: www.atmanet.org

American Wire Producers Assn (AWPA)
801 N Fairfax St Ste 211 ... Alexandria VA 22314 703-299-4434 299-9233
Web: www.awpa.org

Asia America MultiTechnology Assn (AAMA)
1270 Oakmead Pkwy ... Sunnyvale CA 94085 408-736-2554
Web: www.aamasv.com

ASM International 9639 Kinsman Rd ... Materials Park OH 44073 440-338-5151 338-4634
TF: 800-336-5152 ■ *Web:* www.asminternational.org

Association for Facilities Engineering (AFE)
12801 Worldgate Dr Ste 500 ... Herndon VA 20170 571-203-7171 766-2142
Web: www.afe.org

Association for Iron & Steel Technology (AIST)
186 Thorn Hill Rd ... Warrendale PA 15086 724-814-3000 814-3001
TF: 800-732-0999 ■ *Web:* www.aist.org

Association of Equipment Manufacturers (AEM)
6737 W Washington St Ste 2400 ... Milwaukee WI 53214 414-272-0943 272-1170
TF: 866-236-0442 ■ *Web:* www.aem.org

Association of Industrial Metallizers Coaters & Laminators (AIMCAL)
201 Springs St ... Fort Mill SC 29715 803-802-7820 802-7821
Web: www.aimcal.org

Association of Rotational Molders International (ARM)
800 Roosevelt Rd Ste C-312 ... Glen Ellyn IL 60137 630-942-6589 790-3095
Web: www.rotomolding.org

Association of Vacuum Equipment Manufacturers (AVEM)
201 Pk Washington Ct ... Falls Church VA 22046 703-538-3543 241-5603
Web: www.avem.org

Building Service Contractors Assn International (BSCAI)
401 N Michigan Ave Ste 2200 ... Chicago IL 60611 312-321-5167 673-6735
TF: 800-368-3414 ■ *Web:* www.bscai.org

Business & Institutional Furniture Manufacturers Assn (BIFMA)
678 Front Ave NW Ste 150 ... Grand Rapids MI 49504 616-285-3963 285-3765

Can Manufacturers Institute (CMI)
1730 Rhode Island Ave NW Ste 1000 ... Washington DC 20036 202-232-4677 232-5756
TF: 800-363-2726 ■ *Web:* www.cancentral.com

Chlorine Institute Inc 1300 Wilson Blvd ... Arlington VA 22209 703-894-4140 894-4130
Web: www.chlorineinstitute.org

Color Pigments Manufacturers Assn Inc
300 N Washington St Ste 105 ... Alexandria VA 22314 703-684-4044 684-1795
Web: www.pigments.org

Composite Can & Tube Institute (CCTI)
50 S Pickett St ... Alexandria VA 22304 703-823-7234 823-7237
Web: www.cctiwdc.org

Compressed Gas Assn (CGA)
4221 Walney Rd Fifth Fl ... Chantilly VA 20151 703-788-2700 961-1831
Web: www.cganet.com

Organization	City	State	ZIP	Phone	Fax
Consortium for Advanced Mfg International (CAM-I) 6836 Bee Cave Ste 256 *Web:* www.cam-i.org	Austin	TX	78746	512-296-6872	347-1672
Consumer Specialty Products Assn (CSPA) 900 17th St NW Ste 300 *Web:* www.cspa.org	Washington	DC	20006	202-872-8110	872-8114
Copper Development Assn Inc 260 Madison Ave 16th Fl *TF:* 800-232-3282 ■ *Web:* www.copper.org	New York	NY	10016	212-251-7200	251-7234
Cordage Institute 994 Old Eagle School Rd Ste 1019 *Web:* www.ropecord.com	Wayne	PA	19087	610-971-4854	971-4859
Council of Industrial Boiler Owners (CIBO) 6035 Burke Ctr Pkwy Ste 360 *TF:* 800-542-6096 ■ *Web:* www.cibo.org	Burke	VA	22015	703-250-9042	239-9042
Crane Manufacturers Assn of America (CMAA) 8720 Red Oak Blvd Ste 201 *TF:* 800-345-1815 ■ *Web:* www.mhi.org	Charlotte	NC	28217	704-676-1190	676-1199
Edison Welding Institute (EWI) 1250 Arthur E Adams Dr *Web:* www.ewi.org	Columbus	OH	43221	614-688-5000	688-5001
Engine Manufacturers Assn (EMA) 333 W Wacker Dr Ste 810 *Web:* www.truckandenginemanufacturers.org	Chicago	IL	60606	312-929-1970	929-1975
Equipment & Tool Institute (ETI) 134 W University Dr Ste 205 **Fax Area Code:* 603 ■ *Web:* etools.org	Rochester	MI	48307	248-656-5080	971-2375*
Fabricators & Manufacturers Assn International (FMA) 833 Featherstone Rd *TF:* 888-394-4362 ■ *Web:* www.fmanet.org	Rockford	IL	61107	815-399-8700	484-7700
Fibre Box Assn (FBA) 25 NW Pt Blvd Ste 510 *Web:* www.fibrebox.org	Elk Grove Village	IL	60007	847-364-9600	364-9639
Flexible Packaging Assn (FPA) 971 Corporate Blvd Ste 403 *Web:* www.flexpack.org	Linthicum	MD	21090	410-694-0800	694-0900
Fluid Controls Institute (FCI) 1300 Sumner Ave *Web:* www.fluidcontrolsinstitute.org	Cleveland	OH	44115	216-241-7333	241-0105
Fluid Power Distributors Assn (FPDA) PO Box 1420 *Web:* www.fpda.org	Cherry Hill	NJ	08034	856-424-8998	424-9248
Food Processing Suppliers Assn (FPSA) 1451 Dolley Madison Blvd Ste 101 *TF:* 800-772-9247 ■ *Web:* www.fpsa.org	McLean	VA	22101	703-761-2600	761-4334
Foodservice & Packaging Institute (FPI) 7700 Leesburg Pk *Web:* www.fpi.org	Falls Church	VA	22046	703-538-3551	241-5603
Forging Industry Assn (FIA) 1111 Superior Ave Ste 615 *Web:* www.forging.org	Cleveland	OH	44114	216-781-6260	781-0102
Glass Assn of North America (GANA) 800 SW Jackson St Ste 1500 *TF:* 877-275-2421 ■ *Web:* www.glasswebsite.com	Topeka	KS	66612	785-271-0208	271-0166
Glass Packaging Institute (GPI) 700 N Fairfax St Ste 510 *Web:* www.gpi.org	Alexandria	VA	22314	703-684-6359	299-1543
Gypsum Assn 6525 Belcrest Rd Ste 480 *Web:* www.gypsum.org	Hyattsville	MD	20782	301-277-8686	277-8747
Illuminating Engineering Society of North America (IESNA) 120 Wall St 17th Fl *Web:* www.ies.org	New York	NY	10005	212-248-5000	248-5017
INDA: Assn of the Nonwoven Fabrics Industry 1100 Crescent Green Ste 115 *Web:* www.inda.org	Cary	NC	27518	919-233-1210	233-1282
Independent Lubricant Manufacturers Assn (ILMA) 400 N Columbus St Ste 201 *Web:* www.ilma.org	Alexandria	VA	22314	703-684-5574	836-8503
Industrial Designers Society of America (IDSA) 45195 Business Ct Ste 250 *Web:* www.idsa.org	Dulles	VA	20166	703-707-6000	787-8501
Industrial Diamond Assn of America (IDA) 6081 Central Pk Dr *Web:* www.superabrasives.org	Columbus	OH	43231	614-797-2265	797-2264
Industrial Fabrics Assn International (IFAI) 1801 County Rd 'B' W *TF:* 800-225-4324 ■ *Web:* www.ifai.com	Roseville	MN	55113	651-222-2508	631-9334
Institute of Caster & Wheel Manufacturers (ICWM) 8720 Red Oak Blvd Ste 201 *TF:* 877-522-5431 ■ *Web:* www.mhi.org	Charlotte	NC	28217	704-676-1190	676-1199
Institute of Industrial Engineers (IIE) 3577 PkwyLn Ste 200 *TF Cust Svc:* 800-494-0460 ■ *Web:* www.iienet2.org	Norcross	GA	30092	770-449-0460	441-3295
Institute of Makers of Explosives (IME) 1120 19th St NW Ste 310 *TF:* 800-461-8841 ■ *Web:* www.ime.org	Washington	DC	20036	202-429-9280	293-2420
Institute of Packaging Professionals (IoPP) 1833 Centre Point Cir Ste 123 *TF:* 800-432-4085 ■ *Web:* www.iopp.org	Naperville	IL	60563	630-544-5050	544-5055
Institute of Paper Science & Technology (IPST) 500 Tenth St NW *TF:* 800-558-6611 ■ *Web:* www.ipst.gatech.edu	Atlanta	GA	30332	404-894-5700	894-4778
International AntiCounterfeiting Coalition (IACC) 1730 M St NW Ste 1020 *Web:* www.iacc.org	Washington	DC	20006	202-223-6667	223-6668
International Copper Assn 260 Madison Ave 16th Fl *Web:* copperalliance.org	New York	NY	10016	212-251-7240	251-7245
International Ground Source Heat Pump Assn (IGSHPA) Oklahoma State University 374 Cordell S *TF:* 800-626-4747 ■ *Web:* www.igshpa.okstate.edu	Stillwater	OK	74078	405-744-5175	744-5283
International Institute of Synthetic Rubber Producers Inc (IISRP) 3535 Briarpark Dr Ste 250 *Web:* www.iisrp.com	Houston	TX	77042	713-783-7511	783-7253

Organization	City	State	ZIP	Phone	Fax
International Magnesium Assn (IMA) 1000 N Rand Rd Ste 214 *Web:* www.intlmag.org	Wauconda	IL	60084	847-526-2010	526-3993
Investment Casting Institute (ICI) 136 Summit Ave *Web:* www.investmentcasting.org	Montvale	NJ	07645	201-573-9770	573-9771
Material Handling Equipment Distributors Assn (MHEDA) 201 US Hwy 45 *Web:* www.mheda.org	Vernon Hills	IL	60061	847-680-3500	362-6989
Material Handling Industry of America (MHIA) 8720 Red Oak Blvd Ste 201 *TF:* 800-345-1815 ■ *Web:* www.mhi.org	Charlotte	NC	28217	704-676-1190	676-1199
Metal Powder Industries Federation (MPIF) 105 College Rd E *TF:* 800-443-4862 ■ *Web:* www.mpif.org	Princeton	NJ	08540	609-452-7700	987-8523
Metals Service Ctr Institute (MSCI) 4201 Euclid Ave *Web:* www.msci.org	Rolling Meadows	IL	60008	847-485-3000	485-3001
Minerals Metals & Materials Society (TMS) 184 Thorn Hill Rd *TF:* 800-759-4867 ■ *Web:* www.tms.org	Warrendale	PA	15086	724-776-9000	776-3770
NACE International: Corrosion Society 1440 S Creek Dr *TF:* 800-797-6223 ■ *Web:* www.nace.org	Houston	TX	77084	281-228-6200	228-6300
National Coil Coating Assn (NCCA) 1300 Sumner Ave *TF:* 800-532-0500 ■ *Web:* www.coilcoating.org	Cleveland	OH	44115	216-241-7333	241-0105
National Council of Textile Organizations (NCTO) 910 17th St NW Ste 1020 *TF:* 800-238-7192 ■ *Web:* www.ncto.org	Washington	DC	20006	202-822-8028	822-8029
National Electrical Manufacturers Assn (NEMA) 1300 N 17th St Ste 1752 *TF:* 888-236-2427 ■ *Web:* www.nema.org	Rosslyn	VA	22209	703-841-3200	841-5900
National Fluid Power Assn (NFPA) 3333 N Mayfair Rd Ste 211 *Web:* www.nfpa.com	Milwaukee	WI	53222	414-778-3344	778-3361
National Glass Assn (NGA) 8200 Greensboro Dr Ste 302 *TF:* 866-342-5642 ■ *Web:* www.glass.org	McLean	VA	22102	703-442-4890	442-0630
National Marine Electronics Assn (NMEA) Seven Riggs Ave *TF:* 800-808-6632 ■ *Web:* www.nmea.org	Severna Park	MD	21146	410-975-9425	975-9450
National Paint & Coatings Assn (NPCA) 1500 Rhode Island Ave NW *TF:* 800-431-7900 ■ *Web:* www.paint.org	Washington	DC	20005	202-462-6272	462-8549
National Textile Assn (NTA) Six Beacon St Ste 1125 *Web:* www.nationaltextile.org	Boston	MA	02108	617-542-8220	542-2199
National Tooling & Machining Assn (NTMA) 6363 Oak Tree Blvd **Fax Area Code:* 301 ■ *TF:* 800-248-6862 ■ *Web:* www.ntma.org	Independence	OH	44131	800-248-6862	248-7104*
National Wooden Pallet & Container Assn (NWPCA) 1421 Prince St Ste 340 *Web:* www.palletcentral.com	Alexandria	VA	22314	703-519-6104	519-4720
North American Assn of Food Equipment Manufacturers (NAFEM) 161 N Clark St Ste 2020 *TF:* 888-493-5961 ■ *Web:* www.nafem.org	Chicago	IL	60601	312-821-0201	821-0202
North American Die Casting Assn (NADCA) 241 Holbrook Dr *TF:* 800-275-8373 ■ *Web:* www.diecasting.org	Wheeling	IL	60090	847-279-0001	279-0002
Open Applications Group Inc (OAGI) PO Box 4897 **Fax Area Code:* 801 ■ *TF:* 800-236-4600 ■ *Web:* www.oagi.org	Marietta	GA	30061	404-402-1962	740-0100*
Packaging Machinery Manufacturers Institute (PMMI) 4350 N Fairfax Dr Ste 600 *TF:* 888-275-7664 ■ *Web:* www.pmmi.org	Arlington	VA	22203	703-243-8555	243-8556
Polyurethane Manufacturers Assn (PMA) 6737 W Washington St Ste 1420 *Web:* www.pmahome.org	Milwaukee	WI	53214	414-431-3094	
Portable Rechargeable Battery Assn (PRBA) 1776 K St Fourth Fl *Web:* www.prba.org	Washington	DC	20006	202-719-4978	
Precision Machined Products Assn (PMPA) 6700 W Snowville Rd *TF:* 800-233-1234 ■ *Web:* www.pmpa.org	Brecksville	OH	44141	440-526-0300	526-5803
Recycled Paperboard Technical Assn PO Box 5774 *Web:* www.rpta.org	Elgin	IL	60121	847-622-2544	622-2546
Reusable Industrial Packaging Assn (RIPA) 8401 Corporate Dr Ste 450 *TF:* 800-441-8780 ■ *Web:* www.reusablepackaging.org	Landover	MD	20785	301-577-3786	577-6476
Rubber Manufacturers Assn (RMA) 1400 K St NW Ste 900 *TF:* 800-220-7622 ■ *Web:* www.rma.org	Washington	DC	20005	202-682-4800	682-4854
Sewn Products Equipment Suppliers Assn (SPESA) 9650 Strickland Rd Ste 103-324 *Web:* www.spesa.org	Raleigh	NC	27615	919-872-8909	872-1915
Society for Mining Metallurgy & Exploration Inc (SME) 8307 Shaffer Pkwy *TF:* 800-763-3132 ■ *Web:* www.smenet.org	Littleton	CO	80127	303-973-9550	973-3845
Society for Protective Coatings (SSPC) 40 24th St Sixth Fl *TF:* 877-281-7772 ■ *Web:* www.sspc.org	Pittsburgh	PA	15222	412-281-2331	281-9995
Society of Mfg Engineers (SME) One SME Dr *TF Cust Svc:* 800-733-4763 ■ *Web:* www.sme.org	Dearborn	MI	48128	313-425-3000	425-3400
Society of Plastics Engineers (SPE) 13 Church Hill Rd *Web:* www.4spe.org	Newtown	CT	06470	203-775-0471	775-8490
Society of Tribologists & Lubrication Engineers (STLE) 840 Busse Hwy *Web:* www.stle.org	Park Ridge	IL	60068	847-825-5536	825-1456
Society of Vacuum Coaters (SVC) 71 Pinon Hill Pl NE *TF:* 800-777-4643 ■ *Web:* www.svc.org	Albuquerque	NM	87122	505-856-7188	856-6716

Organization	City	State	ZIP	Phone	Fax
Spring Manufacturers Institute (SMI) 2001 Midwest Rd Ste 106 — *TF:* 866-482-5569 ■ *Web:* www.smihq.org	Oak Brook	IL	60523	630-495-8588	495-8595
Steel Founders' Society of America (SFSA) 780 McArdle Dr Ste G — *Web:* www.sfsa.org	Crystal Lake	IL	60014	815-455-8240	455-8241
Steel Manufacturers Assn (SMA) 1150 Connecticut Ave NW Ste 715 — *Web:* www.steelnet.org	Washington	DC	20036	202-296-1515	296-2506
Steel Plate Fabricators Assn (SPFA) 944 Donata Ct — *Web:* www.steeltank.com	Lake Zurich	IL	60047	847-438-8265	438-8766
Steel Tank Institute (STI) 944 Donata Ct — *Web:* www.steeltank.com	Lake Zurich	IL	60047	847-438-8265	438-8766
Sulphur Institute (TSI) 1140 Connecticut Ave NW Ste 612 — *Web:* www.sulphurinstitute.org	Washington	DC	20036	202-331-9660	293-2940
Technical Assn of the Pulp & Paper Industry (TAPPI) 15 Technology Pkwy S — *TF Sales:* 800-332-8686 ■ *Web:* www.tappi.org	Norcross	GA	30092	770-446-1400	446-6947
TRI/Princeton 601 Prospect Ave PO Box 625 — *Web:* www.triprinceton.org	Princeton	NJ	08540	609-430-4820	
Valve Manufacturers Assn of America (VMA) 1050 17th St NW Ste 280 — *TF:* 800-468-3571 ■ *Web:* www.vma.org	Washington	DC	20036	202-331-8105	296-0378
Vinyl Siding Institute (VSI) 1201 15th St NW Ste 220 — *Web:* www.vinylsiding.org	Washington	DC	20005	202-587-5100	
Wire Assn International Inc (WAI) 1570 Boston Post Rd PO Box 578 — *Web:* www.wirenet.org	Guilford	CT	06437	203-453-2777	453-8384
Wiring Harness Manufacturers Assn (WHMA) 15490 101st Ave N Ste 100 — **Fax Area Code:* 952 ■ *Web:* www.whma.org	Maple Grove	MN	55369	763-235-6461	835-4774*
Wood Machinery Manufacturers of America (WMMA) 2105 Laurel Bush Rd Ste 201 — **Fax Area Code:* 323 ■ *Web:* www.wmma.org	Bel Air	MD	21015	443-640-1052	215-0331*

49-14 Media Professionals Associations

Organization	City	State	ZIP	Phone	Fax
Academy of Television Arts & Sciences 5220 Lankershim Blvd — *Web:* emmys.com/	North Hollywood	CA	91601	818-754-2800	761-2827
Accuracy in Media Inc (AIM) 4455 Connecticut Ave NW Ste 330 — *TF:* 800-787-4567 ■ *Web:* www.aim.org	Washington	DC	20008	202-364-4401	364-4098
American Medical Writers Assn (AMWA) 30 W Gude Dr Ste 525 — *Web:* www.amwa.org	Rockville	MD	20850	301-294-5303	294-9006
American Radio Relay League (ARRL) 225 Main St — *TF:* 888-277-5289 ■ *Web:* www.arrl.org	Newington	CT	06111	860-594-0200	594-0259
American Society of Media Photographers (ASMP) 150 N Second St — *Web:* www.asmp.org	Philadelphia	PA	19106	215-451-2767	451-0880
American Society of News Editors (ASNE) 11690-B Sunrise Vly Dr — *Web:* www.asne.org	Reston	VA	20191	703-453-1122	453-1133
American Women in Radio & Television (AWRT) 8405 Greensboro Dr Ste 800 — *Web:* www.womensorganizations.org	McLean	VA	22102	703-506-3290	506-3266
Association for Maximum Service Television (MSTV) 4100 Wisconsin Ave NW First Fl — *Web:* www.mstv.org	Washington	DC	20016	202-966-1956	
Association for Women in Communications (AWC) 3337 Duke St — *Web:* www.womcom.org	Alexandria	VA	22314	703-370-7436	370-7437
Association of Alternative Newsweeklies (AAN) 115615th St NW — *TF:* 866-415-0704 ■ *Web:* www.altweeklies.com	Washington	DC	20005	202-289-8484	289-2004
Association of Independents in Radio (AIR) 42 Charles St 2nd Fl — *Web:* www.airmedia.org	Dorchester	MA	02122	617-825-4400	
Association of Public Television Stations (APTS) 2100 Crystal Dr Ste 700 — *TF:* 855-948-5853 ■ *Web:* www.apts.org	Arlington	VA	22202	202-654-4200	654-4236
Cable Television Laboratories Inc 858 Coal Creek Cir — *Web:* www.cablelabs.com	Louisville	CO	80027	303-661-9100	661-9199
Catholic Press Assn (CPA) 205 W Monroe St Ste 470 — *TF:* 800-777-7432 ■ *Web:* www.catholicpress.org	Chicago	IL	60606	312-380-6789	361-0256
Center for Media Literacy 23852 Pacific Coast Hwy Ste 472 — *Web:* www.medialit.org	Malibu	CA	90265	310-456-1225	
Content Delivery & Storage Assn (CDSA) 39 N Bayles Ave — *Web:* www.cdsaonline.org	Port Washington	NY	11050	516-767-6720	883-5793
Country Radio Broadcasters Inc (CRB) 819 18th Ave S — *Web:* countryradioseminar.com	Nashville	TN	37203	615-327-4487	329-4492
Foundation for American Communications (FACS) 85 S Grand Ave	Pasadena	CA	91105	626-584-0010	
Inter American Press Assn (IAPA) 1801 SW Third Ave Eighth Fl — *Web:* sipiapa.org/index.php	Miami	FL	33129	305-634-2465	635-2272
International Communication Assn (ICA) 1500 21st St NW — *Web:* www.icahdq.org	Washington	DC	20036	202-955-1444	955-1448
International Radio & Television Society Foundation Inc (IRTS) 1697 Broadway 10th Fl — *Web:* www.irtsfoundation.org	New York	NY	10019	212-867-6650	
Media Coalition Inc 275 Seventh Ave Ste 1504 — *TF:* 866-512-1600 ■ *Web:* www.mediacoalition.org	New York	NY	10001	212-587-4025	587-2436
Media Financial Management Assn (MFM) 550 W Frontage Rd Ste 3600 — *Web:* www.bcfm.com	Northfield	IL	60093	847-716-7000	716-7004
NA of Broadcasters (NAB) 1771 N St NW — *Web:* www.nab.org	Washington	DC	20036	202-429-5300	
NA of Television Program Executives (NATPE) 5757 Wilshire Blvd PH-10 — *Web:* www.natpe.com	Los Angeles	CA	90036	310-453-4440	453-5258
National Cable & Telecommunications Assn (NCTA) 25 Massachusetts Ave NW Ste 100 — *Web:* www.ncta.com	Washington	DC	20001	202-222-2300	
National Cable Television Co-op Inc (NCTC) 11200 Corporate Ave — **Fax Area Code:* 202 ■ *TF:* 800-720-5850 ■ *Web:* www.ncta.com	Lenexa	KS	66219	913-599-5900	222-2311*
National Federation of Community Broadcasters (NFCB) 1970 Broadway Ste 1000 — *Web:* www.nfcb.org	Oakland	CA	94612	510-451-8200	451-8208
National Newspaper Assn (NNA) PO Box 7540 — *TF:* 800-829-4662 ■ *Web:* nnaweb.org	Columbia	MO	65205	573-777-4980	777-4985
National Press Club (NPC) 529 14th St NW — *Web:* www.press.org	Washington	DC	20045	202-662-7500	662-7569
National Press Photographers Assn (NPPA) 3200 Croasdaile Dr Ste 306 — *Web:* www.nppa.org	Durham	NC	27705	919-383-7246	383-7261
National Religious Broadcasters (NRB) 9510 Technology Dr — *Web:* www.nrb.org	Manassas	VA	20110	703-330-7000	330-7100
Newspaper Assn of America (NAA) 4401 Wilson Blvd Ste 900 — *Web:* www.naa.org	Arlington	VA	22203	571-366-1000	366-1195
Overseas Press Club of America (OPC) 40 W 45th St — *Web:* www.opcofamerica.org	New York	NY	10036	212-626-9220	626-9210
Parents Television Council (PTC) 707 Wilshire Blvd Ste 2075 — *Web:* w2.parentstv.org	Los Angeles	CA	90017	213-629-9255	629-9254
Radio-Television News Directors Assn (RTNDA) 1600 K St NW Ste 700 — *Web:* www.rtdna.org	Washington	DC	20006	202-659-6510	223-4007
Satellite Broadcasting & Communications Assn (SBCA) 1730 M St NW Ste 600 — *TF:* 800-541-5981 ■ *Web:* www.sbca.com	Washington	DC	20036	202-349-3620	349-3621
Society for News Design (SND) 424 E Central Blvd Ste 406 — *Web:* www.snd.org	Orlando	FL	32801	407-420-7748	420-7697
Society for Technical Communication (STC) 9401 Lee Hwy Ste 300 — *Web:* www.stc.org	Fairfax	VA	22031	703-522-4114	522-2075
Society of Broadcast Engineers Inc (SBE) 9102 N Meridian St Ste 150 — *TF:* 800-237-1776 ■ *Web:* www.sbe.org	Indianapolis	IN	46260	317-846-9000	846-9120
Society of Environmental Journalists (SEJ) 115 W Ave — *TF:* 866-208-3372 ■ *Web:* www.sej.org	Jenkintown	PA	19046	215-884-8174	884-8175
Society of Professional Journalists (SPJ) 3909 N Meridian St — *TF:* 800-331-1212 ■ *Web:* www.spj.org	Indianapolis	IN	46208	317-927-8000	920-4789
Specialized Information Publishers Assn (SIPA) 8229 Boone Blvd Ste 260 — *TF:* 800-356-9302 ■ *Web:* www.siia.net	Vienna	VA	22182	703-992-9339	992-7512
Women in Cable Telecommunications (WICT) 2000 K St Ste 350 — *Web:* www.wict.org	Washington	DC	20006	202-827-4794	450-5596

49-15 Mental Health Professionals Associations

Organization	City	State	ZIP	Phone	Fax
American Academy of Addiction Psychiatry (AAAP) 400 Massasoit Ave Second Fl Ste 307 — *Web:* www.aaap.org	East Providence	RI	02914	401-524-3076	272-0922
American Academy of Child & Adolescent Psychiatry (AACAP) 3615 Wisconsin Ave NW — *TF:* 800-333-7636 ■ *Web:* www.aacap.org	Washington	DC	20016	202-966-7300	966-2891
American Academy of Psychiatry & the Law (AAPL) One Regency Dr PO Box 30 — *TF:* 800-331-1389 ■ *Web:* www.aapl.org	Bloomfield	CT	06002	860-242-5450	286-0787
American Assn for Geriatric Psychiatry (AAGP) 7910 Woodmont Ave Ste 1050 — *Web:* www.aagponline.org	Bethesda	MD	20814	301-654-7850	654-4137
American College of Psychiatrists 122 S Michigan Ave # 1360 — *Web:* www.acpsych.org	Chicago	IL	60603	312-662-1020	662-1025
American Council of Hypnotist Examiners 700 S Central Ave — **Fax Area Code:* 818 ■ *Web:* www.hypnotistexaminers.org	Glendale	CA	91204	619-280-7200	247-9379*
American Counseling Assn (ACA) 5999 Stevenson Ave — *TF:* 800-347-6647 ■ *Web:* www.counseling.org	Alexandria	VA	22304	703-823-9800	823-0252
American Group Psychotherapy Assn (AGPA) 25 E 21st St Sixth Fl — *TF:* 877-668-2472 ■ *Web:* www.agpa.org	New York	NY	10010	212-477-2677	979-6627
American Mental Health Counselors Assn (AMHCA) 801 N Fairfax St Ste 304 — *TF:* 800-326-2642 ■ *Web:* www.amhca.org	Alexandria	VA	22314	703-548-6002	548-4775
American Psychiatric Assn (APA) 1000 Wilson Blvd Ste 1825 — *TF:* 888-357-7924 ■ *Web:* www.psych.org	Arlington	VA	22209	703-907-7300	907-1085

Organization / Address	City	State	Zip	Phone	Fax
American Psychiatric Nurses Assn (APNA) 1555 Wilson Blvd Ste 530 *TF:* 866-243-2443 ■ *Web:* www.apna.org	Arlington	VA	22209	703-243-2443	243-3390
American Psychoanalytic Assn (APsaA) 309 E 49th St *Web:* www.apsa.org	New York	NY	10017	212-752-0450	593-0571
American Psychological Assn (APA) 750 First St NE *TF:* 800-374-2721 ■ *Web:* www.apa.org	Washington	DC	20002	202-336-5500	336-5962
American Society for Adolescent Psychiatry (ASAP) 1737 Omar Dr *Web:* adolescent-psychiatry.org	Mesquite	TX	75150	972-613-0985	613-5532
Arc Baltimore, The 7215 York Rd *Web:* www.arcofbaltimore.org	Baltimore	MD	21212	410-296-2272	296-2394
Arc of Stanly County, The 350 Pee Dee Ave Ste A *Web:* www.monarchnc.org	Albemarle	NC	28001	704-986-1500	
Association for Behavioral & Cognitive Therapies (ABCT) 305 Seventh Ave 16th Fl *TF:* 800-685-2228 ■ *Web:* www.abct.org/home	New York	NY	10001	212-647-1890	647-1865
Association for Play Therapy (APT) 3198 Willow Ave Ste 110 *Web:* www.a4pt.org	Clovis	CA	93612	559-294-2128	294-2129
Association for Psychological Type International (APTI) 2415 Westwood Ave Ste B **Fax Area Code:* 804 ■ *Web:* www.aptinternational.org	Richmond	VA	23230	518-320-7416	288-3551*
Catholic Charities of Buffalo New York Inc 741 Delaware Ave *Web:* www.ccwny.org	Buffalo	NY	14209	716-218-1400	856-2005
Depression & Related Affective Disorders Assn (DRADA) 8201 Greensboro Dr Ste 300 *Web:* www.drada.org	McLean	VA	22102	703-610-9026	
Edinburg Ctr Inc, The 1040 Waltham St *Web:* www.edinburgcenter.org	Lexington	MA	02421	781-862-3600	863-5903
Federation of Families for Children's Mental Health (FFCMH) 9605 Medical Ctr Dr Ste 280 *Web:* www.ffcmh.org	Rockville	MD	20850	240-403-1901	403-1909
International Assn of Marriage & Family Counselors (IAMFC) 5999 Stevenson Ave *TF:* 800-347-6647 ■ *Web:* www.counseling.org	Alexandria	VA	22304	800-347-6647	473-2329
International Neuropsychological Society (INS) 700 Ackerman Rd Ste 625 *Web:* www.the-ins.org	Columbus	OH	43202	614-263-4200	263-4366
International Society for Traumatic Stress Studies (ISTSS) 111 Deer Lk Rd Ste 100 *Web:* www.istss.org	Deerfield	IL	60015	847-480-9028	480-9282
Lifespring Inc 460 Spring St *TF:* 800-456-2117 ■ *Web:* lifespringhealthsystems.org	Jeffersonville	IN	47130	812-280-2080	
National Council for Therapeutic Recreation Certification Inc (NCTRC) Seven Elmwood Dr *Web:* www.nctrc.org	New City	NY	10956	845-639-1439	639-1471
National Psychological Assn for Psychoanalysis (NPAP) 40 W 13th St Ste 1 *TF:* 800-365-7006 ■ *Web:* www.npap.org	New York	NY	10011	212-924-7440	989-7543
New Ctr Community Mental Health Services 2051 W Grand Blvd *Web:* www.newcentercmhs.org	Detroit	MI	48208	313-961-3200	
Northern Arizona Regional Behavioral Health Authority Inc (NARBHA) 1300 S Yale St *TF:* 877-923-1400 ■ *Web:* www.narbha.org	Flagstaff	AZ	86001	928-774-7128	774-5665
Northwestern Counseling Support & Services Inc 107 Fisher Pond Rd *TF:* 800-834-7793 ■ *Web:* www.ncssinc.org	Saint Albans	VT	05478	802-524-6554	527-7801
SAVE - Suicide Awareness Voices of Education 8120 Penn Ave S Ste 470 *TF:* 888-511-7283 ■ *Web:* www.save.org	Bloomington	MN	55431	952-946-7998	829-0841
Scranton Counseling Ctr Inc 326 Adams Ave *Web:* www.scrantonscc.org	Scranton	PA	18503	570-348-6100	
Society for Social Work Leadership in Health Care 100 N 20th St Fourth Fl *TF:* 866-237-9542 ■ *Web:* www.sswlhc.org	Philadelphia	PA	19103	215-599-6134	564-2175
Society of Behavioral Medicine (SBM) 555 E Wells St Ste 1100 *TF:* 800-784-8669 ■ *Web:* www.sbm.org	Milwaukee	WI	53202	414-918-3156	276-3349
Suncoast Ctr Inc PO Box 10970 *Web:* www.suncoastcenter.com	Saint Petersburg	FL	33733	727-327-7656	323-8978
Valeo Behavioral Health Care Inc 5401 SW Seventh St *Web:* www.valeotopeka.org	Topeka	KS	66606	785-233-1730	
West Oakland Health Council Inc (WOHC) 700 Adeline St *Web:* www.wohc.org	Oakland	CA	94607	510-835-9610	272-0209
Yakima Neighborhood Health Services (YNHS) 12 S Eigth St PO Box 2605 *Web:* www.ynhs.org	Yakima	WA	98907	509-454-4143	454-3651

49-16 Publishing & Printing Professional Associations

Organization / Address	City	State	Zip	Phone	Fax
American Business Media (ABM) 675 Third Ave *Web:* www.abmassociation.com	New York	NY	10017	212-661-6360	370-0736
American Society of Business Publication Editors (ASBPE) 214 N Hale St *Web:* www.asbpe.org	Wheaton	IL	60187	630-510-4588	510-4501
American Society of Indexers (ASI) 1628 E Southern Ave Ste 9-223 **Fax Area Code:* 303 ■ *Web:* www.asindexing.org	Tempe	AZ	85282	480-245-6750	422-8894*
Associated Church Press (ACP) PO Box 621001 *Web:* www.theacp.org	Oviedo	FL	32762	407-341-6615	386-3236
Association of American Publishers Inc (AAP) 71 Fifth Ave *TF:* 866-271-4968 ■ *Web:* www.publishers.org	New York	NY	10003	212-255-0200	255-7007
Association of American University Presses 28 W 36th St Ste 602 *Web:* www.aaupnet.org	New York	NY	10018	212-989-1010	989-0975
Association of Directory Publishers (ADP) 116 Cass St *TF:* 800-267-9002 ■ *Web:* www.adp.org	Traverse City	MI	49684	231-486-2182	486-2182
Book Industry Study Group Inc (BISG) 370 Lexington Ave Ste 900 *Web:* www.bisg.org	New York	NY	10017	646-336-7141	336-6214
Book Manufacturers Institute Inc (BMI) Two Armand Beach Dr Ste 1-B *Web:* www.bmibook.org	Palm Coast	FL	32137	386-986-4552	986-4553
Canadian Newspaper Assn 890 Yonge St Ste 200 *TF:* 877-305-2262 ■ *Web:* www.newspaperscanada.ca	Toronto	ON	M4W3P4	416-923-3567	923-7206
Children's Book Council (CBC) 54 W 39th St 14th Fl *Web:* www.cbcbooks.org	New York	NY	10018	212-966-1990	
Copyright Clearance Ctr Inc (CCC) 222 Rosewood Dr *TF:* 855-239-3415 ■ *Web:* www.copyright.com	Danvers	MA	01923	978-750-8400	646-8600
Copyright Society of the USA One E 53rd St *Web:* www.csusa.org	New York	NY	10022	212-354-6401	354-2847
Editorial Freelancers Assn (EFA) 71 W 23rd St 4th Fl *TF:* 866-929-5400 ■ *Web:* www.the-efa.org	New York	NY	10010	212-929-5400	929-5439
Epicomm (NAPL) 1 Meadowlands Plaza Ste 1511 *TF:* 800-642-6275 ■ *Web:* www.napl.org	East Rutherford	NJ	07073	201-634-9600	634-0324
Evangelical Christian Publishers Assn (ECPA) 9633 S 48th St Ste 140 *Web:* www.ecpa.org	Phoenix	AZ	85044	480-966-3998	966-1944
Flexographic Technical Assn (FTA) 3920 Veterans Memorial Hwy Ste 9 *Web:* www.flexography.org	Bohemia	NY	11716	631-737-6020	737-6813
Greeting Card Assn (GCA) 1133 Westchester Ave Ste N136 *TF:* 866-799-5384 ■ *Web:* www.greetingcard.org	White Plains	NY	10604	914-421-3331	948-1484
Idealliance 7200 France Ave S Ste 223 *TF:* 800-255-8141 ■ *Web:* idealliance.org	Edina	MN	55435	952-896-1908	
Independent Book Publishers Assn, The (IBPA) 1020 Manhattan Beach Blvd Ste 204 *Web:* www.ibpa-online.org	Manhattan Beach	CA	90266	310-546-1818	546-3939
International Digital Enterprise Alliance 1421 Prince St Ste 230 *Web:* www.idealliance.org	Alexandria	VA	22314	703-837-1070	837-1072
International Reprographic Assn (IRgA) 401 N Michigan Ave Ste 2200 *TF:* 800-833-4742 ■ *Web:* www.irga.com	Chicago	IL	60611	312-245-1026	673-6724
Magazine Publishers of America (MPA) 810 Seventh Ave 24th Fl *TF:* 800-234-3368 ■ *Web:* www.magazine.org	New York	NY	10019	212-872-3700	888-4217
National Information Standards Organization (NISO) 3600 Clipper Mill Road Suite 302 **Fax Area Code:* 410 ■ *TF:* 877-375-2160 ■ *Web:* www.niso.org	Baltimore	MD	21211	301-654-2512	685-5278*
National Press Foundation (NPF) 1211 Connecticut Ave NW Ste 310 *TF:* 877-472-3779 ■ *Web:* www.nationalpress.org	Washington	DC	20036	202-663-7280	530-2855
NPES: Assn for Suppliers of Printing Publishing & Converting Technologies 1899 Preston White Dr *TF:* 866-381-9839 ■ *Web:* www.npes.org	Reston	VA	20191	703-264-7200	620-0994
Printing Industries of America/Graphic Arts Technical Foundation (PIA/GATF) 200 Deer Run Rd *TF:* 800-910-4283 ■ *Web:* www.printing.org	Sewickley	PA	15143	412-741-6860	741-2311
Society for Imaging Science & Technology (IS&T) 7003 Kilworth Ln *Web:* www.imaging.org	Springfield	VA	22151	703-642-9090	642-9094
Society for Scholarly Publishing (SSP) 10200 W 44th Ave Ste 304 *Web:* www.sspnet.org	Wheat Ridge	CO	80033	303-422-3914	422-8894
Specialty Graphic Imaging Assn (SGIA) 10015 Main St *TF:* 888-385-3588 ■ *Web:* www.sgia.org	Fairfax	VA	22031	703-385-1335	273-0456

49-17 Real Estate Professionals Associations

Organization / Address	City	State	Zip	Phone	Fax
American Homeowners Foundation (AHF) 6776 Little Falls Rd *Web:* www.americanhomeowners.org	Arlington	VA	22213	703-536-7776	536-7079
American Planning Assn (APA) 1030 15th St NW *Web:* www.planning.org	Washington	DC	20005	202-872-0611	872-0643
American Resort Development Assn (ARDA) 1201 15th St NW Ste 400 *Web:* www.arda.org	Washington	DC	20005	202-371-6700	289-8544
American Society of Appraisers (ASA) 555 Herndon Pkwy Ste 125 *TF:* 800-272-8258 ■ *Web:* www.appraisers.org	Herndon	VA	20170	703-478-2228	742-8471
Appraisal Institute 550 W Van Buren St Ste 1000 *TF:* 888-756-4624 ■ *Web:* www.appraisalinstitute.org	Chicago	IL	60607	312-335-4100	335-4400
Building Owners & Managers Assn International (BOMA) 1101 15th St NW Ste 800 *TF:* 800-426-6292 ■ *Web:* www.boma.org	Washington	DC	20005	202-408-2662	326-6377
CCIM Institute 430 N Michigan Ave Ste 800 *TF:* 800-621-7027 ■ *Web:* www.ccim.com	Chicago	IL	60611	312-321-4460	321-4530
CoreNet Global Inc 260 Peachtree St NW Ste 1500 *TF:* 800-726-8111 ■ *Web:* www.corenetglobal.org	Atlanta	GA	30303	404-589-3200	589-3201
Council of Real Estate Brokerage Managers (CRB) 430 N Michigan Ave Ste 300 **Fax Area Code:* 312 ■ *TF:* 800-621-8738 ■ *Web:* www.crb.com	Chicago	IL	60611	800-621-8738	329-8882*

Phone | Fax

Council of Residential Specialists
430 N Michigan Ave Ste 300 ... Chicago IL 60611 312-321-4400 329-8882
TF: 800-462-8841 ■ *Web:* www.crs.com

Counselors of Real Estate (CRE)
430 N Michigan Ave Second Fl ... Chicago IL 60611 312-329-8427 329-8881
Web: www.cre.org

Institute of Business Appraisers (IBA)
1111 BrickyaRd Rd Ste 200 ... Salt Lake City UT 84106 800-299-4130 353-5406*
**Fax Area Code:* 866 ■ *TF:* 800-299-4130 ■ *Web:* www.go-iba.org

Institute of Real Estate Management (IREM)
430 N Michigan Ave ... Chicago IL 60611 312-329-6000 338-4736*
**Fax Area Code:* 800 ■ *TF:* 800-837-0706 ■ *Web:* www.irem.org

International Downtown Assn (IDA)
1025 Thomas Jefferson St NW Ste 500 W ... Washington DC 20007 202-393-6801 393-6869
Web: www.ida-downtown.org/eweb

NA of Master 303 W Cypress St ... San Antonio TX 78212 210-271-0781
Web: faqs.org

NA of REALTORS 430 N Michigan Ave. ... Chicago IL 60611 312-329-8200 329-8390*
**Fax:* Mktg ■ *TF:* 800-874-6500 ■ *Web:* www.realtor.org

National Apartment Assn (NAA)
4300 Wilson Blvd Ste 400 ... Arlington VA 22203 703-518-6141 248-9440
TF: 800-632-3007 ■ *Web:* www.naahq.org

National Housing & Rehabilitation Assn (NH&RA)
1400 16th St NW Ste 420 ... Washington DC 20036 202-939-1750 265-4435
Web: www.housingonline.com

National Multi Housing Council (NMHC)
1850 M St NW Ste 540 ... Washington DC 20036 202-974-2300 775-0112
Web: www.nmhc.org

New Venture Communications
28 E Third Ave Ste 201 ... San Mateo CA 94401 650-343-2735 343-8492
TF: 800-307-0762 ■ *Web:* www.igreenbuild.com

Real Estate Buyer's Agent Council (REBAC)
430 N Michigan Ave ... Chicago IL 60611 800-648-6224 329-8632*
**Fax Area Code:* 312 ■ *TF:* 800-648-6224 ■ *Web:* www.rebac.net

Real Estate Roundtable
801 Pennsylvania Ave NW Ste 720 ... Washington DC 20004 202-639-8400 639-8442
Web: www.rer.org

Society of Industrial & Office Realtors (SIOR)
1201 New York Ave NW Ste 350 ... Washington DC 20005 202-449-8200 216-9325
Web: www.sior.com

Vacation Rental Managers Assn (VRMA)
9100 PuRdue Rd Ste 200 ... Indianapolis IN 46268 317-454-8315 458-3637*
**Fax Area Code:* 831 ■ *Web:* www.vrma.com

Women's Council of REALTORS (WCR)
430 N Michigan Ave ... Chicago IL 60611 800-245-8512 329-3290*
**Fax Area Code:* 312 ■ *TF:* 800-245-8512 ■ *Web:* www.wcr.org

49-18 Sales & Marketing Professional Associations

Phone | Fax

Advertising Council Inc 815 Second Ave Fl 9 ... New York NY 10016 212-922-1500 922-1676
TF: 888-200-4005 ■ *Web:* www.adcouncil.org

Advertising Research Foundation (ARF)
432 Pk Ave S Sixth Fl ... New York NY 10016 212-751-5656 319-5265
Web: thearf.org

American Adv Federation (AAF)
1101 Vermont Ave NW Ste 500 ... Washington DC 20005 202-898-0089 898-0159
TF: 800-999-2231 ■ *Web:* www.aaf.org

American Assn of Adv Agencies (AAAA)
1065 Ave of the Americas 16th Fl ... New York NY 10018 212-682-2500 682-8391
Web: www.aaaa.org

American Assn of Exporters & Importers (AAEI)
1050 17th St NW Ste 810 ... Washington DC 20036 202-857-8009 857-7843
Web: www.aaei.org

American Assn of Franchisees & Dealers (AAFD)
PO Box 10158 ... Palm Desert CA 92255 619-209-3775 855-1988*
**Fax Area Code:* 866 ■ *TF:* 800-733-9858 ■ *Web:* www.aafd.org

American Booksellers Assn (ABA)
200 White Plains Rd Ste 600 ... Tarrytown NY 10591 914-591-2665 591-2720
TF: 800-637-0037 ■ *Web:* www.bookweb.org

American Hardwood Export Council (AHEC)
1111 19th St NW Ste 800 ... Washington DC 20036 202-463-2720 463-2787
Web: www.ahec.org

American International Automobile Dealers Assn (AIADA)
500 Montgomery St Ste 800 ... Alexandria VA 22314 703-519-7800 519-7810
TF: 800-462-4232 ■ *Web:* www.aiada.org

American Machine Tool Distributors' Assn (AMTDA)
1445 Research Blvd Ste 450 ... Rockville MD 20850 301-738-1200
Web: www.amtonline.org

American Marketing Assn (AMA)
311 S Wacker Dr Ste 5800 ... Chicago IL 60606 312-542-9000 542-9001
TF: 800-262-1150 ■ *Web:* www.ama.org

American Wholesale Marketers Assn (AWMA)
2750 Prosperity Ave Ste 530 ... Fairfax VA 22031 703-208-3358 573-5738
TF: 800-482-2962 ■ *Web:* www.awmanet.org

Associated Equipment Distributors (AED)
600 22nd St Ste 220 ... Oak Brook IL 60523 630-574-0650 574-0132
TF: 800-388-0650 ■ *Web:* www.aednet.org

Association for Postal Commerce
1901 Ft Myer Dr ... Arlington VA 22209 703-524-0096 524-1871
Web: www.postcom.org

Association of National Advertisers (ANA)
708 Third Ave 33rd Fl ... New York NY 10017 212-697-5950 687-7310
Web: www.ana.net

Association of Progressive Rental Organizations (APRO)
1504 Robin Hood Trl ... Austin TX 78703 512-794-0095 794-0097
TF: 800-204-2776 ■ *Web:* www.rtohq.org

Audit Bureau of Circulations (ABC)
48 W Seegers Road ... Arlington Heights IL 60005 224-366-6939 605-0483*
**Fax Area Code:* 847 ■ *TF:* 800-759-6397 ■ *Web:* www.auditedmedia.com

Phone | Fax

Automotive Distribution Network
3085 Fountainside Dr Ste 210 ... Germantown TN 38138 901-682-9090 937-8775
TF: 800-727-8112 ■ *Web:* www.networkhq.org

BPA Worldwide 100 BeaRd Sawmill Rd Sixth Fl ... Shelton CT 06484 203-447-2800 447-2900
Web: www.bpaww.com

Brick Industry Assn (BIA)
1850 Centennial Pk Dr Ste 301 ... Reston VA 20191 703-620-0010 620-3928
TF: 866-644-1293 ■ *Web:* www.gobrick.com

Business Marketing Assn (BMA)
708 Third Ave 33rd Fl ... New York NY 10017 212-697-5950 687-7310
TF: 800-664-4262 ■ *Web:* www.marketing.org

Business Technology Assn (BTA)
12411 Wornall Rd Ste 200 ... Kansas City MO 64145 816-941-3100 941-2829
TF: 800-325-7219 ■ *Web:* www.bta.org

Center for Exhibition Industry Research (CEIR)
8111 LBJ Fwy Ste 750 ... Dallas TX 75251 972-687-9242 692-6020
Web: www.ceir.org

Chain Drug Marketing Assn (CDMA)
43157 W Nine-Mile Rd PO Box 995 ... Novi MI 48376 248-449-9300 449-9396
TF: 800-935-2362 ■ *Web:* www.chaindrug.com

Clio Awards Inc 770 Broadway Sixth Fl ... New York NY 10003 212-683-4300 683-4796
Web: www.clioawards.com

Coalition for Employment Through Exports (CEE)
1625 K St NW Ste 200 ... Washington DC 20006 202-296-6107 296-9709
Web: www.usaexport.org

Coalition for Government Procurement
1990 M St NW Ste 450 ... Washington DC 20036 202-331-0975 822-9788
Web: thecgp.org

Color Marketing Group (CMG)
1908 Mount Vernon Ave ... Alexandria VA 22301 703-329-8500 535-3190
Web: www.colormarketing.org

Council of Supply Chain Management Professionals
333 E Butterfield Rd Ste 140 ... Lombard IL 60148 630-574-0985 574-0989
Web: www.cscmp.org

Dairyamerica Inc 7815 N Palm Ave Ste 250 ... Fresno CA 93711 559-251-0992 251-1078
TF: 800-722-3110 ■ *Web:* www.dairyamerica.com

Direct Marketing Assn Inc (DMA)
1120 Ave of the Americas ... New York NY 10036 212-768-7277 302-6714
TF: 855-422-0749 ■ *Web:* thedma.org

Direct Selling Assn (DSA)
1667 K St NW Ste 1100 ... Washington DC 20006 202-452-8866 452-9010
Web: www.dsa.org

Electronics Representatives Assn (ERA)
300 W Adams St Ste 617 ... Chicago IL 60606 312-527-3050 527-3783
TF: 800-776-7377 ■ *Web:* www.era.org

Entertainment Merchants Assn
16530 Ventura Blvd Ste 400 ... Encino CA 91436 818-385-1500 933-0910
Web: www.entmerch.org

Equipment Leasing & Finance Assn (ELFA)
1825 K St NW Ste 900 ... Washington DC 20006 202-238-3400 238-3401
Web: www.elfaonline.org

Exhibit Designers & Producers Assn (EDPA)
10 Norden Pl ... Norwalk CT 06855 203-852-5698 854-6735
Web: www.edpa.com

Food Marketing Institute (FMI)
2345 Crystal Dr Ste 800 ... Arlington VA 22202 202-220-0600 429-4519
TF: 800-732-2639 ■ *Web:* www.fmi.org

Global Market Development Ctr (GMDC)
1275 Lk Plz Dr ... Colorado Springs CO 80906 719-576-4260 576-2661
Web: www.gmdc.org

Global Offset & Countertrade Assn (GOCA)
818 Connecticut Ave NW 12th Fl ... Washington DC 20006 202-887-9011 872-8324
TF: 800-343-6074 ■ *Web:* www.globaloffset.org

HARDI Hydronic Heating & Cooling Council
3455 Mill Run Dr Ste 820 ... Hilliard OH 43026 614-345-4328
TF: 888-253-2128 ■ *Web:* www.hardinet.org

Health Industry Distributors Assn (HIDA)
310 Montgomery St ... Alexandria VA 22314 703-549-4432 549-6495
TF: 800-549-4432 ■ *Web:* www.hida.org

Healthcare Convention & Exhibitors Assn (HCEA)
1100 Johnson Ferry Rd Ste 300 ... Atlanta GA 30342 404-252-3663 252-0774
TF: 800-236-1592 ■ *Web:* www.hcea.org

Healthcare Distribution Management Assn (HDMA)
901 N Glebe Rd Ste 1000 ... Arlington VA 22203 703-787-0000 935-3200
Web: www.healthcaredistribution.org

Hospitality Sales & Marketing Assn International (HSMAI)
1760 Old Meadow Rd Ste 500 ... McLean VA 22102 703-506-3280 610-9005
Web: www.hsmai.org

International Assn of Exhibitions & Events (IAEE)
12700 Park Central Dr Ste 308 ... Dallas TX 75251 972-458-8002 458-8119
Web: www.iaee.com

International Assn of Plastics Distribution (IAPD)
6734 W 121 St ... Overland Park KS 66209 913-345-1005 345-1006
Web: www.iapd.org

International Federation of Pharmaceutical Wholesalers (IFPW)
10569 Crestwood Dr ... Manassas VA 20109 703-331-3714 331-3715
Web: www.ifpw.com

International Foodservice Distributors Assn (IFDA)
1410 Spring Hill Rd Ste 210 ... McLean VA 22102 703-532-9400 538-4673
Web: www.ifdaonline.org

International Franchise Assn (IFA)
1501 K St NW Ste 350 ... Washington DC 20005 202-628-8000 628-0812
TF: 800-543-1038 ■ *Web:* www.franchise.org

International Home Furnishings Representatives Assn (IHFRA)
209 S Main St PO Box 670 ... High Point NC 27261 336-889-3920 802-1959
TF: 800-667-9506 ■ *Web:* www.ihfra.org

International Sanitary Supply Assn (ISSA)
3300 Dundee Rd ... Northbrook IL 60062 847-982-0800 982-1012
TF: 800-225-4772 ■ *Web:* global.issa.com

Licensing Executives Society (LES)
1800 Diagonal Rd Ste 280 ... Alexandria VA 22314 703-836-3106 836-3107
Web: www.lesi.org

Machinery Dealers NA (MDNA) 315 S Patrick St ... Alexandria VA 22314 703-836-9300 836-9303
TF: 800-872-7807 ■ *Web:* www.mdna.org

				Phone	Fax
Marketing Research Assn Inc (MRA) 110 National Dr *Fax Area Code:* 888 ■ *Web:* www.marketingresearch.org	Glastonbury	CT	06033	860-682-1000	512-1050*
Metals Service Ctr Institute (MSCI) 4201 Euclid Ave *Web:* www.msci.org	Rolling Meadows	IL	60008	847-485-3000	485-3001
Multi-Level Marketing International Assn (MLMIA) 119 Stanford Ct *Web:* www.mlmia.com	Irvine	CA	92612	949-854-0484	854-7687
NA of Chain Drug Stores (NACDS) 413 N Lee St *TF:* 800-678-6223 ■ *Web:* www.nacds.org	Alexandria	VA	22314	703-549-3001	836-4869
NA of College Stores (NACS) 500 E Lorain St *TF:* 800-622-7498 ■ *Web:* www.nacs.org	Oberlin	OH	44074	440-775-7777	775-4769
NA of Convenience Stores (NACS) 1600 Duke St *TF Cust Svc:* 800-966-6227 ■ *Web:* www.nacsonline.com	Alexandria	VA	22314	703-684-3600	836-4564
NA of Electrical Distributors Inc (NAED) 1181 Corporate Lk Dr *TF:* 888-791-2512 ■ *Web:* www.naed.org	Saint Louis	MO	63132	314-991-9000	991-3060
NA of Wholesaler-Distributors (NAWD) 1325 G St NW Ste 1000 *Web:* www.naw.org	Washington	DC	20005	202-872-0885	785-0586
NAMM - International Music Products Assn 5790 Armada Dr *TF:* 800-767-6266 ■ *Web:* www.namm.org	Carlsbad	CA	92008	760-438-8001	438-7327
National Agri-Marketing Assn (NAMA) 11020 King St Ste 205 *TF:* 800-530-5646 ■ *Web:* www.nama.org	Overland Park	KS	66210	913-491-6500	491-6502
National Art Materials Trade Assn 15806 Brookway Dr Ste 300 *TF:* 877-970-0832 ■ *Web:* www.namta.org	Huntersville	NC	28078	704-892-6244	892-6247
National Auctioneers Assn (NAA) 8880 Ballentine St *TF:* 877-657-1990 ■ *Web:* www.auctioneers.org	Overland Park	KS	66214	913-541-8084	894-5281
National Auto Auction Assn (NAAA) 5320 Spectrum Dr Ste D *TF:* 800-232-5411 ■ *Web:* www.naaa.com	Frederick	MD	21703	301-696-0400	631-1359
National Automatic Merchandising Assn (NAMA) 20 N Wacker Dr Ste 3500 *Web:* www.vending.org	Chicago	IL	60606	312-346-0370	704-4140
National Automobile Dealers Assn (NADA) 8400 Westpark Dr *TF:* 800-252-6232 ■ *Web:* www.nada.org	McLean	VA	22102	703-821-7000	821-7075
National Cotton Council of America 7193 Goodlett Farms Pkwy *TF:* 888-232-1738 ■ *Web:* www.cotton.org	Memphis	TN	38016	901-274-9030	725-0510
National Electrical Manufacturers Representatives Assn (NEMRA) 28 Deer St Ste 302 *Fax Area Code:* 603 ■ *TF:* 800-446-3672 ■ *Web:* www.nemra.org	Portsmouth	NH	03801	914-524-8650	319-1667*
National Electronic Distributors Assn (NEDA) 1111 Alderman Dr Ste 400 *Web:* www.eciaonline.org	Alpharetta	GA	30005	678-393-9990	393-9998
National Electronics Service Dealers Assn (NESDA) 3608 Pershing Ave *TF:* 800-946-0201 ■ *Web:* www.nesda.com	Fort Worth	TX	76107	817-921-9061	921-3741
National Foreign Trade Council (NFTC) 1625 K St NW Ste 200 *Web:* www.nftc.org	Washington	DC	20006	202-887-0278	452-8160
National Independent Automobile Dealers Assn (NIADA) 2521 Brown Blvd *TF:* 800-682-3837 ■ *Web:* www.niada.com	Arlington	TX	76006	817-640-3838	649-5866
National Independent Flag Dealers Assn (NIFDA) 7984 S Chicago Ave *Web:* www.nifda.net	Chicago	IL	60617	773-768-8076	768-3138
National Luggage Dealers Assn (NLDA) 1817 Elmdale Ave *Web:* www.nlda.com	Glenview	IL	60026	847-998-6869	998-6884
National Lumber & Bldg Material Dealers Assn (NLBMDA) 2025 M St NW *Web:* www.dealer.org	Washington	DC	20036	202-367-1169	367-2169
National Mail Order Assn LLC (NMOA) 2807 Polk St NE *TF:* 800-992-1377 ■ *Web:* www.nmoa.org	Minneapolis	MN	55418	612-788-1673	788-1147
National Marine Representatives Assn (NMRA) PO Box 360 *TF:* 800-890-3819 ■ *Web:* www.nmraonline.org	Gurnee	IL	60031	847-662-3167	336-7126
National Minority Supplier Development Council (NMSDC) 1359 Broadway 10th Fl *Web:* www.nmsdc.org	New York	NY	10018	212-944-2430	719-9611
National Retail Federation (NRF) 325 Seventh St NW Ste 1100 *TF:* 800-673-4692 ■ *Web:* www.nrf.com	Washington	DC	20004	202-783-7971	737-2849
National Retail Hardware Assn (NRHA) 5822 W 74th St *TF Cust Svc:* 800-772-4424 ■ *Web:* www.nrha.org	Indianapolis	IN	46278	317-290-0338	328-4354
National School Supply & Equipment Assn (NSSEA) 8380 Colesville Rd Ste 250 *TF:* 800-395-5550 ■ *Web:* edmarket.org	Silver Spring	MD	20910	301-495-0240	495-3330
National Shoe Retailers Assn (NSRA) 7386 N La Cholla Blvd *TF:* 800-673-8446 ■ *Web:* www.nsra.org	Tucson	AZ	85741	520-209-1710	
North American Bldg Material Distribution Assn (NBMDA) 330 N Wabash Ave Ste 2000 *TF:* 888-747-7862 ■ *Web:* www.nbmda.org	Chicago	IL	60611	312-321-6845	644-0310
North American Equipment Dealers Assn (NAEDA) 1195 Smizer Mill Rd *TF:* 866-532-7653 ■ *Web:* www.naeda.com	Fenton	MO	63026	636-349-5000	349-5443
NPTA Alliance 330 N Wabash Ave Ste 2000 *TF:* 800-355-6782 ■ *Web:* www.gonpta.com	Chicago	IL	60611	312-321-4092	673-6736
Paint & Decorating Retailers Assn (PDRA) 1401 Triad Ctr Dr *TF:* 800-737-0107 ■ *Web:* www.pdra.org	Saint Peters	MO	63376	636-326-2636	
Pet Industry Distributors Assn (PIDA) 2105 Laurel Bush Rd Ste 200 *Web:* www.pida.org	Bel Air	MD	21015	443-640-1060	640-1031
Petroleum Marketers Assn of America (PMAA) 1901 N Ft Myer Dr Ste 500 *Web:* www.pmaa.org	Arlington	VA	22209	703-351-8000	351-9160
Photo Marketing Assn International (PMA) 3000 Picture Pl *TF:* 800-762-9287 ■ *Web:* www.pmai.org	Jackson	MI	49201	517-788-8100	788-8371
Power Transmission Distributors Assn (PTDA) 230 W Monroe St Ste 1410 *Web:* www.ptda.org	Chicago	IL	60606	312-516-2100	516-2101
Private Label Manufacturers Assn (PLMA) 630 Third Ave Fourth Fl *Web:* plma.com	New York	NY	10017	212-972-3131	212-1382
Professional Beauty Assn (PBA) 15825 N 71st St Ste 100 *TF:* 800-468-2274 ■ *Web:* www.probeauty.org	Scottsdale	AZ	85254	480-281-0424	905-0708
Promotion Marketing Assn Inc (PMA) 650 First Ave Ste 2-SW *Web:* www.baalink.org	New York	NY	10016	212-420-1100	533-7622
Promotional Products Assn International (PPAI) 3125 Skyway Cir N *TF:* 888-426-7724 ■ *Web:* www.ppai.org	Irving	TX	75038	972-252-0404	258-3004
Public Relations Society of America (PRSA) 33 Maiden Ln 11th Fl *TF:* 800-350-0111 ■ *Web:* www.prsa.org	New York	NY	10038	212-460-1400	995-0757
Radio Adv Bureau (RAB) 125 W 55th St 21st Fl *TF:* 800-252-7234 ■ *Web:* www.rab.com	New York	NY	10019	212-681-7200	681-7223
Recreation Vehicle Dealers Assn (RVDA) 3930 University Dr Third Fl *TF:* 800-336 0355 ■ *Web:* www.rvda.org	Fairfax	VA	22030	703-591-7130	591-0734
Retail Adv & Marketing Assn (RAMA) 325 Seventh St NW Ste 1100 *TF:* 800-673-4692 ■ *Web:* nrf.com/who-we-are/retail-communities/marketing	Washington	DC	20004	202-783-7971	737-2849
Retail Industry Leaders Assn (RILA) 1700 N Moore St Ste 2250 *Web:* www.rila.org	Arlington	VA	22209	703-841-2300	841-1184
Retail Solutions Providers Assn (RSPA) 10130 Perimeter Pkwy Ste 420 *TF:* 800-782-2693 ■ *Web:* www.gorspa.org	Charlotte	NC	28216	704-357-3124	357-3127
Society for Marketing Professional Services (SMPS) 99 Canal Ctr Plz *TF:* 800-292-7677 ■ *Web:* www.smps.org	Alexandria	VA	22314	703-549-6117	549-2498
Society of Independent Gasoline Marketers of America (SIGMA) 3930 Pender Dr Ste 340 *Web:* www.sigma.org	Fairfax	VA	22030	703-709-7000	709-7007
Souvenirs Gifts & Novelties Trade Assn 588 Sutter St Ste 140 *TF:* 800-284-5451 ■ *Web:* pipl.com	San Francisco	CA	19003	610-645-6940	645-6943
Specialty Tools & Fasteners Distributors Assn (STAFDA) 500 Elm Grove Rd Ste 210 PO Box 44 *TF:* 800-352-2981 ■ *Web:* www.stafda.org	Elm Grove	WI	53122	262-784-4774	784-5059
Television Bureau of Adv (TVB) Three E 54th St 10th Fl *Web:* www.tvb.org	New York	NY	10022	212-486-1111	935-5631
Traffic Audit Bureau for Media Measurement (TAB) 271 Madison Ave Ste 1504 *Web:* www.tabonline.com	New York	NY	10016	212-972-8075	
Video Advertising Bureau (CAB) 830 Third Ave 2nd Fl *Web:* www.thecab.tv	New York	NY	10022	212-508-1200	832-3268

49-19 Technology, Science, Engineering Professionals Associations

				Phone	Fax
ABET Inc 111 Market Pl Ste 1050 *Web:* www.abet.org	Baltimore	MD	21202	410-347-7700	625-2238
Acoustical Society of America (ASA) Two Huntington Quadrangle Ste 1N01 *Web:* www.acousticalsociety.org	Melville	NY	11747	516-576-2360	576-2377
AES Electrophoresis Society 1202 Ann St *TF:* 800-242-4363 ■ *Web:* www.aesociety.org	Madison	WI	53713	608-258-1565	258-1569
AIM Global - Assn for Automatic Identification & Mobility 125 Warrendale-Bayne Rd Ste 100 *Web:* www.aimglobal.org	Warrendale	PA	15086	724-934-4470	934-4495
American Assn for Clinical Chemistry Inc (AACC) 1850 K St NW Ste 625 *TF Cust Svc:* 800-892-1400 ■ *Web:* www.aacc.org	Washington	DC	20006	202-857-0717	887-5093
American Assn for Laboratory Accreditation (A2LA) 5301 Buckeystown Pike Ste 350 *TF:* 888-627-8318 ■ *Web:* www.a2la.org	Frederick	MD	21704	301-644-3248	662-2974
American Assn for Laboratory Animal Science (AALAS) 9190 Crestwyn Hills Dr *Web:* www.aalas.org	Memphis	TN	38125	901-754-8620	753-0046
American Assn for the Advancement of Science (AAAS) 1200 New York Ave NW *TF:* 800-669-6820 ■ *Web:* www.aaas.org	Washington	DC	20005	202-326-6400	682-0816
American Assn of Engineering Societies (AAES) 1620 'I' St NW Ste 210 *TF Orders:* 888-400-2237 ■ *Web:* www.aaes.org	Washington	DC	20006	202-296-2237	296-1151
American Assn of Pharmaceutical Scientists (AAPS) 2107 Wilson Blvd Ste 700 *TF:* 877-998-2277 ■ *Web:* www.aaps.org	Arlington	VA	22201	703-243-2800	243-9650
American Assn of Variable Star Observers (AAVSO) 49 Bay State Rd *TF:* 888-802-7827 ■ *Web:* www.aavso.org	Cambridge	MA	02138	617-354-0484	354-0665
American Astronomical Society (AAS) 2000 Florida Ave NW Ste 400 *Web:* www.aas.org	Washington	DC	20009	202-328-2010	234-2560

	Phone	Fax

American Chemical Society (ACS)
1155 16th St NW Washington DC 20036 202-872-4600 872-4615
TF: 800-227-5558 ■ *Web:* www.acs.org

American Council of Engineering Cos (ACEC)
1015 15th St NW Eighth Fl Washington DC 20005 202-347-7474 898-0068
Web: www.acec.org

American Council of Independent Laboratories (ACIL)
1875 I St NW Ste 500 Washington DC 20006 202-887-5872 887-0021
TF: 800-368-1131 ■ *Web:* www.acil.org

American Council on Science & Health (ACSH)
1995 Broadway Second Fl New York NY 10023 212-362-7044 362-4919
TF: 866-905-2694 ■ *Web:* www.acsh.org

American Geological Institute (AGI)
4220 King St Alexandria VA 22302 703-379-2480 379-7563
TF: 800-334-2564 ■ *Web:* www.agiweb.org

American Geophysical Union (AGU)
2000 Florida Ave NW Washington DC 20009 202-462-6900 328-0566
TF: 800-966-2481 ■ *Web:* www.agu.org

American Indian Science & Engineering Society (AISES)
2305 Renard SE Ste 200 Albuquerque NM 87106 505-765-1052 765-5608
TF: 800-759-5219 ■ *Web:* www.aises.org/

American Institute of Aeronautics & Astronautics Inc (AIAA)
1801 Alexander Bell Dr Ste 500 Reston VA 20191 703-264-7500 264-7551
TF: 800-639-2422 ■ *Web:* www.aiaa.org

American Institute of Biological Sciences (AIBS)
1444 'I' St NW Ste 200 Washington DC 20005 202-628-1500 628-1509
TF: 800-992-2427 ■ *Web:* www.aibs.org

American Institute of Chemical Engineers (AIChE)
120 Wall St Fl 23 New York NY 10005 203-702-7660 775-5177
TF Cust Svc: 800-242-4363 ■ *Web:* www.aiche.org

American Institute of Chemists (AIC)
315 Chestnut St Philadelphia PA 19106 215-873-8224 925-1954
TF: 800-829-0115 ■ *Web:* www.theaic.org

American Institute of Physics
One Physics Ellipse College Park MD 20740 301-209-3100 209-0843
Web: www.aip.org

American Institute of Professional Geologists (AIPG)
1400 W 122nd Ave Ste 250 Westminster CO 80234 303-412-6205 253-9220
TF: 800-772-3773 ■ *Web:* www.aipg.org

American Mathematical Society (AMS)
201 Charles St Providence RI 02904 401-455-4000 331-3842
TF Cust Svc: 800-321-4267 ■ *Web:* www.ams.org

American Meteorological Society (AMS)
45 Beacon St Boston MA 02108 617-227-2425 742-8718
TF: 800-824-0405 ■ *Web:* www.ametsoc.org

American Nuclear Society (ANS)
555 N Kensington Ave La Grange Park IL 60526 708-352-6611 352-0499
TF: 800-323-3044 ■ *Web:* www.ans.org

American Physical Society (APS)
1 Physics Ellipse College Park MD 20740 301-209-3200 209-0865
TF: 888-221-9425 ■ *Web:* www.aps.org

American Phytopathological Society, The (APS)
3340 Pilot Knob Rd Saint Paul MN 55121 651-454-7250 454-0766
Web: www.apsnet.org/pages/default.aspx

American Rock Mechanics Assn (ARMA)
600 Woodland Terr Alexandria VA 22302 703-683-1808 683-1815
Web: www.armarocks.org

American Society for Biochemistry & Molecular Biology (ASBMB)
9650 Rockville Pk Bethesda MD 20814 301-634-7145 634-7126
Web: www.asbmb.org

American Society for Cell Biology (ASCB)
8120 Woodmont Ave Ste 750 Bethesda MD 20814 301-347-9300 347-9310
Web: www.ascb.org

American Society for Engineering Education (ASEE)
1818 N St NW Ste 600 Washington DC 20036 202-331-3500 265-8504
Web: www.asee.org

American Society for Nondestructive Testing Inc (ASNT)
1711 Arlingate Ln PO Box 28518 Columbus OH 43228 614-274-6003 274-6899
TF Orders: 800-222-2768 ■ *Web:* www.asnt.org

American Society for Photobiology (ASP)
PO Box 1897 Lawrence KS 66044 785-843-1234 843-1274
TF: 800-627-0326 ■ *Web:* www.photobiology.org

American Society for Photogrammetry & Remote Sensing, The (ASPRS)
5410 Grosvenor Ln Ste 210 Bethesda MD 20814 301-493-0290 493-0208
Web: www.asprs.org

American Society of Human Genetics (ASHG)
9650 Rockville Pike Bethesda MD 20814 301-634-7300 634-7079
TF: 866-486-4363 ■ *Web:* www.ashg.org

American Society of Ichthyologists & Herpetologists
Florida International Univ Biology Dept
11200 SW Eighth St Miami FL 33199 305-348-1235 348-1986
Web: www.asih.org

American Society of Limnology & Oceanography (ASLO)
5400 Bosque Blvd Ste 680 Waco TX 76710 254-399-9635 776-3767
TF: 800-929-2756 ■ *Web:* www.aslo.org

American Society of Plant Biologists (ASPB)
15501 Monona Dr Rockville MD 20855 301-251-0560 279-2996
Web: my.aspb.org

American Society of Safety Engineers (ASSE)
1800 E Oakton St Des Plaines IL 60018 847-699-2929 768-3434
Web: www.asse.org

American Statistical Assn (ASA)
732 N Washington St Alexandria VA 22314 703-684-1221 684-2037
TF: 888-231-3473 ■ *Web:* www.amstat.org

AOAC International
481 N Frederick Ave Ste 500 Gaithersburg MD 20877 301-924-7077 924-7089
TF: 800-379-2622 ■ *Web:* www.aoac.org

ASME International Gas Turbine Institute (IGTI)
6525 the Corners Pkwy Norcross GA 30092 404-847-0072 847-0151
Web: www.asme.org

Association for Women in Science Inc (AWIS)
1321 Duke St Ste 210 Alexandria VA 22314 703-894-4490 894-4489
TF: 800-303-0129 ■ *Web:* www.awis.org

Association of American Geographers (AAG)
1710 16th St NW Washington DC 20009 202-234-1450 234-2744
TF: 800-696-7353 ■ *Web:* www.aag.org

Association of Consulting Chemists & Chemical Engineers (ACC&CE)
PO Box 297 Sparta NJ 07871 973-729-6671 729-7088
Web: www.chemconsult.org

Association of Science-Technology Centers Inc (ASTC)
1025 Vermont Ave NW Ste 500 Washington DC 20005 202-783-7200 783-7207
Web: www.astc.org

Association of University Technology Managers (AUTM)
111 Deer Lk Rd Ste 100 Deerfield IL 60015 847-559-0846 480-9282
Web: www.autm.net

ASTM International
100 Barr Harbor Dr PO Box C700 West Conshohocken PA 19428 610-832-9500 832-9555
TF: 800-814-1017 ■ *Web:* www.astm.org

Audio Engineering Society
60 E 42nd St Rm 2520 New York NY 10165 212-661-8528 682-0477
TF: 800-541-7299 ■ *Web:* www.aes.org

AVS Science & Technology Society
120 Wall St 32nd Fl New York NY 10005 212-248-0200 248-0245
TF: 800-547-1406 ■ *Web:* www.avs.org

Biophysical Society (BPS) 9650 Rockville Pk Bethesda MD 20814 301-634-7114 634-7133
Web: www.biophysics.org

Biotechnology Industry Organization
1201 Maryland Ave SW Ste 900 Washington DC 20024 202-962-9200 488-6301
TF: 866-356-5155 ■ *Web:* www.bio.org

Center for Chemical Process Safety (CCPS)
120 Wall St New York NY 10005 646-495-1371 495-1504
TF: 800-242-4363 ■ *Web:* www.aiche.org/CCPS

Center for Science in the Public Interest (CSPI)
1875 Connecticut Ave NW Ste 300 Washington DC 20009 202-332-9110 265-4954
Web: www.cspinet.org

Clinical Laboratory Management Assn (CLMA)
401 N Michigan Ave Ste 2000 Chicago IL 60611 312-321-5111 673-6927
Web: www.clma.org

Commission on Professionals in Science & Technology (CPST)
1200 New York Ave NW Ste 113 Washington DC 20005 202-326-7080

Coordinating Research Council Inc (CRC)
3650 Mansell Rd Ste 140 Alpharetta GA 30022 678-795-0506 795-0509
TF: 800-445-8667 ■ *Web:* www.crcao.com

Council for Chemical Research Inc (CCR)
1730 Rhode Island Ave NW Ste 302 Washington DC 20036 202-429-3971 429-3976
Web: www.ccrhq.org

Council for Responsible Genetics (CRG)
5 Upland Rd Ste 3 Cambridge MA 02140 617-868-0870 491-5344
TF: 888-591-3911 ■ *Web:* www.councilforresponsiblegenetics.org

Cryogenic Society of America Inc (CSA)
218 Lake St Oak Park IL 60302 708-383-6220 383-9337
Web: www.cryogenicsociety.org

Custom Electronic Design & Installation Assn (CEDIA)
7150 Winton Dr Ste 300 Indianapolis IN 46268 317-328-4336 735-4012
TF: 800-669-5329 ■ *Web:* www.cedia.net

Drug Chemical & Associated Technologies Assn (DCAT)
One Washington Blvd Ste 7 Robbinsville NJ 08691 609-448-1000 448-1944
TF: 800-640-3228 ■ *Web:* www.dcat.org

Earthquake Engineering Research Institute (EERI)
499 14th St Ste 320 Oakland CA 94612 510-451-0905 451-5411
Web: www.eeri.org

Ecological Society of America (ESA)
1990 M St Ste 700 Washington DC 20036 202-833-8773 833-8775
Web: www.esa.org

Electrical Apparatus Service Assn (EASA)
1331 Baur Blvd Saint Louis MO 63132 314-993-2220 993-1269
Web: www.easa.com

Electrochemical Society
65 S Main St Bldg D Pennington NJ 08534 609-737-1902 737-2743
Web: www.electrochem.org

Electronics Technicians Assn International (ETA)
Five Depot St Greencastle IN 46135 765-653-8262 653-4287
TF: 800-288-3824 ■ *Web:* www.eta-i.org

Engineering Contractors' Assn (ECA)
2190 S Towne Centre Pl Anaheim CA 92806 714-937-5000 937-5030
Web: www.ecaonline.net

Entomological Society of America
10001 Derekwood Ln Ste 100 Lanham MD 20706 301-731-4535 731-4538
TF: 800-523-8635 ■ *Web:* www.entsoc.org

Federation of American Scientists (FAS)
1725 DeSales St NW Sixth Fl Washington DC 20036 202-546-3300 315-5847
Web: www.fas.org

Federation of American Societies for Experimental Biology (FASEB)
9650 Rockville Pk Bethesda MD 20814 301-634-7000 634-7001
TF: 800-433-2732 ■ *Web:* www.faseb.org

Foundation for Advanced Education in the Sciences (FAES)
One Cloister Ct Ste 230 Bethesda MD 20814 301-496-7976 402-0174
Web: www.faes.org

Generic Pharmaceutical Assn (GPhA)
2300 Clarendon Blvd Ste 400 Arlington VA 22201 703-647-2480 647-2481
TF: 800-859-8003 ■ *Web:* www.gphaonline.org

Genetics Society of America (GSA)
9650 Rockville Pk Bethesda MD 20814 301-634-7300 634-7079
TF: 866-486-4363 ■ *Web:* www.genetics-gsa.org

Geological Society of America, The (GSA)
3300 Penrose Pl PO Box 9140 Boulder CO 80301 303-357-1000 357-1070
TF: 800-472-1988 ■ *Web:* www.geosociety.org

Geoprofessional Business Association
8811 Colesville Rd Ste G106 Silver Spring MD 20910 301-565-2733 589-2017
Web: www.asfe.org

Geospatial Information & Technology Assn (GITA)
14456 E Evans Ave Aurora CO 80014 303-337-0513 337-1001
Web: www.gita.org

IEEE Broadcast Technology Society (BTS)
445 Hoes Ln Piscataway NJ 08854 732-562-5407 981-1769
TF: 800-678-4333 ■ *Web:* bts.ieee.org

Organization / Address	City	State	ZIP	Phone	Fax
IEEE Computational Intelligence Society (CIS)					
IEEE CIS / IEEE PELS 445 Hoes Ln	Piscataway	NJ	08855	732-465-5892	455-1560*
**Fax Area Code:* 858 ■ *Web:* cis.ieee.org					
IEEE Computer Society 2001 L St NW Ste 700	Washington	DC	20036	202-371-0101	728-9614
TF: 800-272-6657 ■ *Web:* www.computer.org					
IEEE Consumer Electronics Society (CES)					
445 Hoes Ln	Piscataway	NJ	08854	732-981-0060	562-6380
TF: 800-678-4333 ■ *Web:* cesoc.ieee.org					
IEEE Education Society (ES)					
IEEE Operations Ctr 445 Hoes Ln	Piscataway	NJ	08854	732-981-0060	562-6380
TF: 800-678-4333 ■ *Web:* www.ewh.ieee.org/soc/es					
IEEE Electromagnetic Compatibility Society (EMC)					
IEEE Operations Ctr 445 Hoes Ln	Piscataway	NJ	08854	732-981-0060	562-6380
TF: 800-678-4333 ■ *Web:* www.ewh.ieee.org/soc/emcs					
IEEE Electron Devices Society (EDS)					
IEEE Operations Ctr 445 Hoes Ln	Piscataway	NJ	08854	732-981-0060	562-6380
TF: 800-678-4333 ■ *Web:* eds.ieee.org					
IEEE Engineering Management Society (EMS)					
IEEE Operations Ctr 445 Hoes Ln	Piscataway	NJ	08854	732-981-0060	562-6380
TF: 800-678-4333 ■ *Web:* www.ewh.ieee.org/soc/ems					
IEEE Geoscience & Remote Sensing Society (GRSS)					
IEEE Operations Ctr 445 Hoes Ln	Piscataway	NJ	08854	732-562-5550	
TF: 800-678-4333 ■ *Web:* www.ewh.ieee.org					
IEEE Industrial Electronics Society (IES)					
IEEE Operations Ctr 445 Hoes Ln	Piscataway	NJ	08854	732-981-0060	562-6380
TF: 800-678-4333 ■ *Web:* www.ewh.ieee.org/soc/ies					
IEEE Industry Applications Society					
445 Hoes Ln	Piscataway	NJ	08854	732-465-5804	
Web: ias.ieee.org					
IEEE Instrumentation & Measurement Society (IM)					
445 Hoes Ln	Piscataway	NJ	08854	732-562-3844	981-9019
TF: 800-327-6677 ■ *Web:* www.ieee-ims.org					
IEEE Magnetics Society					
445 Hoes Ln PO Box 459	Piscataway	NJ	08855	908-981-0060	981-0225
TF: 800-678-4333 ■ *Web:* www.ieeemagnetics.org					
IEEE Microwave Theory & Techniques Society (MTT-S)					
IEEE Operations Ctr 445 Hoes Ln	Piscataway	NJ	08555	732-562-5400	981-1721
TF: 800-678-4333 ■ *Web:* www.mtt.org					
IEEE Nuclear & Plasma Sciences Society (NPSS)					
445 Hoes Ln	Piscataway	NJ	08854	732-981-0060	562-6380
TF: 800-678-4333 ■ *Web:* www.ewh.ieee.org/soc/nps					
IEEE Power Engineering Society (PES)					
IEEE Operations Ctr 445 Hoes Ln	Piscataway	NJ	08854	732-562-3883	562-3881
TF: 800-678-4333 ■ *Web:* www.ieee-pes.org					
IEEE Product Safety Engineering Society					
IEEE Operations Ctr 445 Hoes Ln	Piscataway	NJ	08854	732-981-0060	562-6380
TF: 800-678-4333 ■ *Web:* www.ewh.ieee.org/soc/pses					
IEEE Reliability Society (RS)					
IEEE Operations Ctr 445 Hoes Ln	Piscataway	NJ	08854	732-981-0060	562-6380
TF: 800-678-4333 ■ *Web:* ieee.org					
IEEE Signal Processing Society					
IEEE Operations Ctr 445 Hoes Ln	Piscataway	NJ	08854	732-981-0060	562-6380
TF: 800-678-4333 ■ *Web:* www.signalprocessingsociety.org					
IEEE Society on Social Implications of Technology (SSIT)					
IEEE Operations Ctr 445 Hoes Ln	Piscataway	NJ	08854	732-981-0060	562-6380
TF: 800-678-4333 ■ *Web:* standards.ieee.org/					
IEEE Solid State Circuits Society (SSCS)					
445 Hoes Ln	Piscataway	NJ	08854	732-981-3400	
TF: 800-678-4333 ■ *Web:* sscs.ieee.org					
IEEE Ultrasonics Ferroelectrics & Frequency Control Society					
IEEE Operations Ctr 445 Hoes Ln	Piscataway	NJ	08854	732-981-0060	562-6380
TF: 800-678-4333 ■ *Web:* www.ieee-uffc.org					
Industrial Research Institute Inc (IRI)					
2200 Clarendon Blvd Ste 1102	Arlington	VA	22201	703-647-2580	647-2581
Web: www.iriweb.org					
Institute for Operations Research & the Management Sciences (INFORMS)					
7240 Pkwy Dr Ste 300	Hanover	MD	21076	443-757-3500	757-3515
TF: 800-446-3676 ■ *Web:* www.informs.org					
Institute of Environmental Sciences & Technology (IEST)					
2340 S Arlington Heights Rd Ste 100	Arlington Heights	IL	60005	847-981-0100	981-4130
Web: www.iest.org					
International Biometric Society (IBS)					
1444 'I' St NW Ste 700	Washington	DC	20005	202-712-9049	216-9646
TF: 800-262-1171 ■ *Web:* www.biometricsociety.org					
International Ctr for Technology Assessment (ICTA)					
660 Pennsylvania Ave SE Ste 302	Washington	DC	20003	415-826-2770	
Web: www.icta.org					
International Microelectronics & Packaging Society (IMAPS)					
611 Second St NE	Washington	DC	20002	202-548-4001	548-6115
Web: www.imaps.org					
International Society for Pharmaceutical Engineering (ISPE)					
3109 W Dr ML King Jr Blvd Ste 250	Tampa	FL	33607	813-960-2105	264-2816
Web: www.ispe.org					
International Society of Automation, The					
67 Alexander Dr PO Box 12277	Research Triangle Park	NC	27709	919-549-8411	549-8288
Web: www.isa.org					
International Society of Certified Electronics Technicians (ISCET)					
3608 Pershing Ave	Fort Worth	TX	76107	817-921-9101	921-3741
TF: 800-946-0201 ■ *Web:* www.iscet.org					
International Titanium Assn (ITA)					
2655 W Midway Blvd Ste 300	Broomfield	CO	80020	303-404-2221	404-9111
Web: www.titanium.org					
Laser Institute of America (LIA)					
13501 Ingenuity Dr Ste 128	Orlando	FL	32826	407-380-1553	380-5588
TF: 800-345-2737 ■ *Web:* www.lia.org					
Materials Properties Council (MPC)					
PO Box 201547	Shaker Heights	OH	44122	216-658-3847	658-3854
Web: www.forengineers.org/mpc					
Materials Research Society (MRS)					
506 Keystone Dr	Warrendale	PA	15086	724-779-3003	779-8313
Web: www.mrs.org					
Mathematical Assn of America (MAA)					
1529 18th St NW	Washington	DC	20036	202-387-5200	265-2384
TF: 800-331-1622 ■ *Web:* www.maa.org					
MTM Assn for Standards & Research					
1111 E Touhy Ave Ste 280	Des Plaines	IL	60018	847-299-1111	299-3509
Web: www.mtm.org					
National Academies 500 Fifth St NW	Washington	DC	20001	202-334-2138	334-2158
TF: 800-624-6242 ■ *Web:* www.nas.edu					
National Academy of Engineering					
500 Fifth Ave	Washington	DC	20001	202-334-2431	334-2290
Web: www.nae.edu					
National Council on Radiation Protection & Measurements (NCRP)					
7910 Woodmont Ave Ste 400	Bethesda	MD	20814	301-657-2652	907-8768
TF: 800-462-3683 ■ *Web:* www.ncrponline.org					
National Environmental Balancing Bureau (NEBB)					
8575 Grovemont Cir	Gaithersburg	MD	20877	301-977-3698	977-9589
TF: 866-497-4447 ■ *Web:* www.nebb.org					
National Geographic Society					
1145 17th St NW	Washington	DC	20036	202-857-7000	
TF: 800-647-5463 ■ *Web:* www.nationalgeographic.com					
National Institute for Women in Trades Technology & Science (IWITTS)					
1150 Ballena Blvd Ste 102	Alameda	CA	94501	510-749-0200	749-0500
Web: www.iwitts.org					
National Society of Black Physicists (NSBP)					
1100 N Glebe Rd Ste 1010	Arlington	VA	22201	703-536-4207	536-4203
Web: www.nsbp.org					
National Society of Professional Engineers (NSPE)					
1420 King St	Alexandria	VA	22314	703-684-2800	836-4875
TF: 888-285-6773 ■ *Web:* www.nspe.org					
National Space Society (NSS)					
1620 'I' St NW Ste 615	Washington	DC	20006	202-429-1600	463-8497
TF: 888-624-8373 ■ *Web:* www.nss.org					
New York Academy of Medicine (NYAM)					
1216 Fifth Ave	New York	NY	10029	212-822-7200	423-0275
Web: www.nyam.org					
New York Academy of Sciences					
250 Greenwich St 40th Fl	New York	NY	10007	212-298-8600	298-3650
TF: 800-843-6927 ■ *Web:* www.nyas.org					
Plasma Protein Therapeutics Assn (PPTA)					
147 Old Solomon's Island Rd Ste 100	Annapolis	MD	21401	410-266-8493	
Web: usplaces.com					
Robotic Industries Assn (RIA)					
900 Victors Way Ste 140	Ann Arbor	MI	48108	734-994-6088	994-3338
Web: www.robotics.org					
Scientific Equipment & Furniture Assn (SEFA)					
65 Hilton Avenue	Garden City	NY	11530	516-294-5424	294-2758
TF: 877-294-5424 ■ *Web:* www.sefalabs.com					
Semiconductor Environmental Safety & Health Assn (SESHA)					
1313 Dolley Madison Blvd Ste 402	McLean	VA	22101	703-790-1745	790-2672
TF: 800-433-1790 ■ *Web:* www.seshaonline.org					
Semiconductor Equipment & Materials International					
3081 Zenker Rd	San Jose	CA	95134	408-943-6900	428-9600
TF: 877-746-7788 ■ *Web:* www.semi.org					
Silver Research Consortium (SRC)					
2525 Meridian Pkwy Ste 100	Durham	NC	27713	919-361-4647	361-1957
Web: www.ilzro.org					
Society for Biomaterials					
15000 Commerce Pkwy Ste C	Mount Laurel	NJ	08054	856-439-0826	439-0525
TF: 800-337-9255 ■ *Web:* www.biomaterials.org					
Society for Experimental Mechanics Inc (SEM)					
7 School St	Bethel	CT	06801	203-790-6373	790-4472
TF: 800-627-8258 ■ *Web:* www.sem.org					
Society for Industrial & Applied Mathematics (SIAM)					
3600 Market St 6th Fl	Philadelphia	PA	19104	215-382-9800	386-7999
TF: 800-447-7426 ■ *Web:* www.siam.org					
Society for Integrative & Comparative Biology (SICB)					
1313 Dolley Madison Blvd Ste 402	McLean	VA	22101	703-790-1745	790-2672
TF: 800-955-1236 ■ *Web:* www.sicb.org					
Society for Risk Analysis (SRA)					
1313 Dolley Madison Blvd Ste 402	McLean	VA	22101	703-790-1745	790-2672
TF: 800-364-5800 ■ *Web:* www.sra.org					
Society for Sedimentary Geology (SEPM)					
4111 S Darlington Ste 100	Tulsa	OK	74135	918-610-3361	621-1685
TF: 800-865-9765 ■ *Web:* www.sepm.org					
Society for the Advancement of Material & Process Engineering (SAMPE)					
1161 Pk View Dr Ste 200	Covina	CA	91724	626-331-0616	262-1431*
**Fax Area Code:* 801 ■ *TF:* 800-562-7360 ■ *Web:* www.sampe.org					
Society of Cable Telecommunications Engineers (SCTE)					
140 Philips Rd	Exton	PA	19341	610-363-6888	363-5898
TF: 800-542-5040 ■ *Web:* www.scte.org					
Society of Cosmetic Chemists (SCC)					
120 Wall St Ste 2400	New York	NY	10005	212-668-1500	668-1504
Web: www.scconline.org					
Society of Environmental Toxicology & Chemistry (SETAC)					
1010 N 12th Ave	Pensacola	FL	32501	850-469-1500	469-9778
Web: www.setac.org					
Society of Women Engineers (SWE)					
120 S La Salle St Ste 1515	Chicago	IL	60603	312-596-5223	596-5252
TF: 877-793-4636 ■ *Web:* societyofwomenengineers.swe.org					
SPIE - International Society for Optical Engineering					
1000 20th St	Bellingham	WA	98225	360-676-3290	647-1445
Web: www.spie.org					
Synthetic Organic Chemical Manufacturers Assn (SOCMA)					
1850 M St NW Ste 700	Washington	DC	20036	202-721-4100	296-8120
Web: www.socma.com					
Universities Research Assn Inc (URA)					
1111 19th St NW Ste 400	Washington	DC	20036	202-293-1382	293-5012
Web: www.ura-hq.org					
Universities Space Research Assn (USRA)					
10211 Wincopin Cir Ste 500	Columbia	MD	21044	410-730-2656	730-3496
Web: www.usra.edu					
Vibration Institute					
6262 Kingery Hwy # 212	Willowbrook	IL	60527	630-654-2254	654-2271
Web: www.vi-institute.org					

Phone Fax

Women in Technology International (WITI)
13351-D Riverside Dr Ste 441 .... Sherman Oaks CA 91423 818-788-9484 788-9410
TF: 800-334-9484 ■ *Web:* www.witi.com

World Future Society
7910 Woodmont Ave Ste 450 .... Bethesda MD 20814 301-656-8274 951-0394
TF: 800-989-8274 ■ *Web:* www.wfs.org

49-20 Telecommunications Professionals Associations

Phone Fax

Alliance for Telecommunications Industry Solutions (ATIS)
1200 G St NW Ste 500 .... Washington DC 20005 202-628-6380 393-5453
TF: 800-649-1202 ■ *Web:* www.atis.org

American Public Communications Council Inc (APCC)
625 Slaters Ln Ste 104 .... Alexandria VA 22314 703-739-1322 739-1324
TF: 800-868-2722 ■ *Web:* www.apcc.net

Communications Supply Service Assn (CSSA)
5700 Murray St. .... Little Rock AR 72209 501-562-7666 562-7616
TF: 800-252-2772 ■ *Web:* www.cssa.net

COMPTEL 900 17th St NW Ste 400 .... Washington DC 20006 202-296-6650 296-7585
Web: www.comptel.org

Computer & Communications Industry Assn (CCIA)
666 11th St NW .... Washington DC 20001 202-783-0070 783-0534
Web: www.ccianet.org

Enterprise Wireless Alliance (EWA)
8484 Westpark Dr Ste 630 .... McLean VA 22102 703-528-5115 524-1074
TF: 800-482-8282 ■ *Web:* www.enterprisewireless.org

Forest Industries Telecommunications (FIT)
1565 Oak St .... Eugene OR 97401 541-485-8441 485-7556
Web: www.landmobile.com

International Communications Industries Assn (ICIA)
11242 Waples Mill Rd Ste 200 .... Fairfax VA 22030 703-273-7200 278-8082
TF: 800-659-7469 ■ *Web:* www.infocomm.org

National Telecommunications Co-op Assn (NTCA)
4121 Wilson Blvd 10th Fl .... Arlington VA 22203 703-351-2000 351-2001
Web: www.ntca.org

Society of Telecommunications Consultants (STC)
13275 California 89 .... Old Station CA 96071 530-335-7313 335-7360
TF: 800-782-7670 ■ *Web:* sctcconsultants.org/?

Telecommunications Industry Assn (TIA)
2500 Wilson Blvd Ste 300 .... Arlington VA 22201 703-907-7700 907-7727
Web: www.tiaonline.org

US Telecom Assn (USTA) 607-14th St NW Ste 400 .... Washington DC 20005 202-326-7300 315-3603
TF: 877-869-6903 ■ *Web:* ustelecom.org

Utilities Telecom Council (UTC)
1129 20th St NW Ste 350 .... Washington DC 20036 202-872-0030 872-1331
Web: www.utc.org

Wireless Communications Assn International (WCA)
1333 H St NW Ste 700W .... Washington DC 20005 202-452-7823
Web: wcai.com

49-21 Transportation Industry Associations

Phone Fax

Aerospace Industries Assn of America (AIA)
1000 Wilson Blvd Ste 1700 .... Arlington VA 22209 703-358-1000 358-1011
TF: 866-923-7797 ■ *Web:* www.aia-aerospace.org

Air Traffic Control Assn (ATCA)
1101 King St Ste 300 .... Alexandria VA 22314 703-299-2430 299-2437
TF: 866-953-2189 ■ *Web:* www.atca.org

Aircraft Owners & Pilots Assn (AOPA)
421 Aviation Way .... Frederick MD 21701 301-695-2000 695-2375
TF: 800-872-2672 ■ *Web:* www.aopa.org

Airlines for America (ATA)
1301 Pennsylvania Ave NW Ste 1100 .... Washington DC 20004 202-626-4000
Web: airlines.org

Airports Council International of North America (ACI-NA)
1775 K St NW Ste 500 .... Washington DC 20006 202-293-8500 331-1362
Web: www.aci-na.org

American Ambulance Assn (AAA)
8201 Greensboro Dr Ste 300 .... McLean VA 22102 703-610-9018 610-9005
TF: 800-523-4447 ■ *Web:* www.the-aaa.org

American Assn of Airport Executives (AAAE)
601 Madison St Ste 400 .... Alexandria VA 22314 703-824-0500 820-1395
TF: 800-609-7374 ■ *Web:* www.aaae.org

American Assn of Port Authorities (AAPA)
1010 Duke St .... Alexandria VA 22314 703-684-5700 684-6321
Web: www.aapa-ports.org

American Assn of State Highway & Transportation Officials (AASHTO)
444 N Capitol St NW Ste 249 .... Washington DC 20001 202-624-5800 624-5806
TF: 800-880-4117 ■ *Web:* www.transportation.org

American Boat & Yacht Council Inc (ABYC)
613 Third St Ste 10 .... Annapolis MD 21403 410-990-4460 990-4466
Web: www.abycinc.org

American Bureau of Shipping (ABS)
16855 Northchase Dr .... Houston TX 77060 281-877-5800 877-5803
Web: www.eagle.org

American Helicopter Society International (AHS)
217 N Washington St .... Alexandria VA 22314 703-684-6777 739-9279
TF: 855-247-4685 ■ *Web:* www.vtol.org

American Highway Users Alliance
1101 14th St NW Ste 750 .... Washington DC 20005 202-857-1200 857-1220
Web: www.highways.org

American International Automobile Dealers Assn (AIADA)
500 Montgomery St Ste 800 .... Alexandria VA 22314 703-519-7800 519-7810
TF: 800-462-4232 ■ *Web:* www.aiada.org

American Moving & Storage Assn (AMSA)
1611 Duke St .... Alexandria VA 22314 703-683-7410 683-7527
TF: 888-849-2672 ■ *Web:* www.promover.org

American Pilots' Assn
499 S Capitol St SW Ste 409 .... Washington DC 20003 202-484-0700 484-9320
Web: www.americanpilots.org

American Public Transportation Assn (APTA)
1666 K St NW Ste 1100 .... Washington DC 20006 202-496-4800 496-4321
Web: www.apta.com

American Railway Engineering & Maintenance-of-Way Assn (AREMA)
10003 Derekwood Ln Ste 210 .... Lanham MD 20706 301-459-3200 459-8077
Web: www.arema.org

American Short Line & Regional Railroad Assn (ASLRRA)
50 F St NW Ste 7020 .... Washington DC 20001 202-628-4500 628-6430
Web: www.aslrra.org

American Society of Naval Engineers (ASNE)
1452 Duke St .... Alexandria VA 22314 703-836-6727 836-7491
TF: 800-995-3579 ■ *Web:* www.navalengineers.org

American Society of Transportation & Logistics (ASTL)
8430 W Bryn Mawr Ave Ste 1000 .... Chicago IL 60631 773-355-4900 962-3939*
**Fax Area Code:* 202 ■ *Web:* www.astl.org

American Traffic Safety Services Assn (ATSSA)
15 Riverside Pkwy Ste 100 .... Fredericksburg VA 22406 540-368-1701 368-1717
TF: 800-272-8772 ■ *Web:* www.atssa.com

American Trucking Assn (ATA)
950 N Glebe Rd Ste 210 .... Arlington VA 22203 703-838-1700
TF: 800-282-5463 ■ *Web:* www.trucking.org

American Waterways Operators (AWO)
801 N Quincy St Ste 200 .... Arlington VA 22203 703-841-9300 841-0389
Web: www.americanwaterways.com

Association of American Railroads (AAR)
425 Third St SW .... Washington DC 20024 202-639-2100 639-2286
Web: www.aar.org

Automatic Transmission Rebuilders Assn (ATRA)
2400 Latigo Ave .... Oxnard CA 93030 805-604-2000 604-2003
TF: 866-464-2872 ■ *Web:* www.atra.com

Automotive Aftermarket Industry Assn (AAIA)
7101 Wisconsin Ave .... Bethesda MD 20814 301-654-6664 654-3299
TF: 800-936-8906 ■ *Web:* autocare.org

Automotive Engine Rebuilders Assn (AERA)
500 Coventry Ln Ste 180 .... Crystal Lake IL 60014 847-541-6550 541-5808
TF: 888-326-2372 ■ *Web:* www.aera.org

Automotive Industry Action Group (AIAG)
26200 Lahser Rd Ste 200 .... Southfield MI 48033 248-358-3570 358-3253
TF: 877-275-2424 ■ *Web:* www.aiag.org

Automotive Oil Change Assn (AOCA)
330 N. Wabash Ave Ste 2000 .... Chicago IL 60611 312-321-5132 673-6832
TF: 800-230-0702 ■ *Web:* www.aoca.org

Automotive Parts Remanufacturers Assn (APRA)
4215 Lafayette Ctr Dr Ste 3 .... Chantilly VA 20151 703-968-2772 968-2878
TF: 877-734-4827 ■ *Web:* www.apra.org

Automotive Recyclers Assn (ARA)
3975 Fair Ridge Dr Ste 20N .... Fairfax VA 22033 703-385-1001 385-1494
TF: 888-385-1005 ■ *Web:* www.a-r-a.org

Automotive Service Assn (ASA) 1901 Airport Fwy .... Bedford TX 76021 800-272-7467 685-0225*
**Fax Area Code:* 817 ■ *TF Cust Svc:* 800-272-7467 ■ *Web:* www.asashop.org

Brotherhood of Railroad Signalmen
917 Shenandoah Shores Rd .... Front Royal VA 22630 540-622-6522 622-6532
Web: www.brs.org

Car Care Council 7101 Wisconsin Ave .... Bethesda MD 20814 240-333-1088 654-3299*
**Fax Area Code:* 301 ■ *Web:* www.carcare.org

Cargo Airline Assn 1620 L St NW Ste 610 .... Washington DC 20036 202-293-1030 293-4377
Web: cargoair.org

Center for Auto Safety (CAS)
1825 Connecticut Ave NW Ste 330 .... Washington DC 20009 202-328-7700 387-0140
TF: 800-424-9393 ■ *Web:* www.autosafety.org

Coalition Against Bigger Trucks (CABT)
1001 N Fairfax St Ste 515 .... Alexandria VA 22314 703-535-3131 535-3322
Web: www.cabt.org

Coalition for Auto Repair Equality (CARE)
105 Oronoco St Ste 115 .... Alexandria VA 22314 703-519-7555 519-7747
TF: 800-229-5380 ■ *Web:* www.careauto.org

Community Transportation Assn of America (CTAA)
1341 G St NW 10th Fl .... Washington DC 20005 202-628-1480 737-9197
TF: 800-891-0590 ■ *Web:* www.ctaa.org

Dangerous Goods Advisory Council (DGAC)
1100 H St NW Ste 740 .... Washington DC 20005 202-289-4550 289-4074
TF: 800-923-9123 ■ *Web:* www.dgac.org

Flight Safety Foundation
801 N Fairfax St Ste 400 .... Alexandria VA 22314 703-739-6700 739-6708
Web: www.flightsafety.org

General Aviation Manufacturers Assn (GAMA)
1400 K St NW Ste 801 .... Washington DC 20005 202-393-1500 842-4063
TF: 800-728-9607 ■ *Web:* www.gama.aero

Helicopter Assn International (HAI)
1635 Prince St .... Alexandria VA 22314 703-683-4646 683-4745
TF: 800-435-4976 ■ *Web:* www.rotor.com

Independent Liquid Terminals Assn (ILTA)
1444 'I' St NW Ste 400 .... Washington DC 20005 202-842-9200 326-8660
Web: www.ilta.org

Institute of International Container Lessors (IICL)
1990 M St NW Ste 650 .... Washington DC 20036 202-223-9800 223-9810
Web: www.iicl.org

Institute of Navigation Inc (ION)
8551 Rixlew Ln Ste 360 .... Manassas VA 20109 703-366-2723 366-2724
TF: 800-696-7353 ■ *Web:* www.ion.org

Institute of Transportation Engineers (ITE)
1099 14th St NW Ste 300W .... Washington DC 20005 202-289-0222 289-7722
Web: www.ite.org

Insurance Institute for Highway Safety
1005 N Glebe Rd Ste 800 .... Arlington VA 22201 703-247-1500 247-1588
TF: 888-327-4236 ■ *Web:* www.iihs.org

Intelligent Transportation Society of America (ITS)
1100 17th St NW Ste 1200 .... Washington DC 20036 202-484-4847 484-3483
TF: 800-374-8472 ■ *Web:* www.itsa.org

Phone Fax

Intermodal Assn of North America (IANA)
11785 Beltsville Dr Ste 1100 . . . Calverton MD 20705 301-982-3400 982-4815
TF: 877-438-8442 ■ *Web:* www.intermodal.org

International Air Cargo Assn (TIACA)
5600 NW 36th St Ste 620 . . . Miami FL 33266 786-265-7011 265-7012
Web: www.tiaca.org

International Air Transport Assn
800 Pl Victoria PO Box 113 . . . Montreal QC H4Z1M1 514-874-0202 874-9632
Web: www.iata.org

International Airlines Travel Agent Network (IATAN)
800 Pl Victoria P.O. Box 113 . . . Montreal QC H4Z1A1 514-868-8800 868-8858
TF: 877-734-2826 ■ *Web:* www.iatan.org

International Assn of Refrigerated Warehouses (IARW)
1500 King St Ste 201 . . . Alexandria VA 22314 703-373-4300 373-4301
TF: 800-488-2900 ■ *Web:* www.gcca.org

International Carwash Assn
230 East Ohio Street . . . Chicago IL 60611 888-422-8422 245-1085*
**Fax Area Code:* 312 ■ *TF:* 888-422-8422 ■ *Web:* www.carwash.org

International Motor Coach Group Inc (IMG)
8695 College Blvd Ste 260 . . . Overland Park KS 66210 913-906-0111 906-0115
TF: 888-447-3466 ■ *Web:* www.imgcoach.com

International Parking Institute (IPI)
701 Kenmore Ave Ste 200 . . . Fredericksburg VA 22401 540-371-7535 371-8022
Web: www.parking.org

International Safe Transit Assn (ISTA)
1400 Abbott Rd Ste 160 . . . East Lansing MI 48823 517-333-3437 333-3813
TF: 888-299-2208 ■ *Web:* www.ista.org

International Warehouse Logistics Assn (IWLA)
2800 S River Rd Ste 260 . . . Des Plaines IL 60018 847-813-4699 813-0115
Web: www.iwla.com

Interstate Natural Gas Assn of America (INGAA)
10 G St NE Ste 700 . . . Washington DC 20002 202-216-5900 216-0870
Web: www.ingaa.org

Japan Automobile Manufacturers Assn (JAMA)
1050 17th St NW Ste 410 . . . Washington DC 20036 202-296-8537 872-1212
Web: www.jama.org

Jewelers Shipping Assn (JSA) 125 Carlsbad St . . . Cranston RI 02920 401-943-6020 943-1490
TF: 800-688-4572 ■ *Web:* www.jewelersshipping.com

Mid-West Truckers Assn Inc
2727 N Dirksen Pkwy . . . Springfield IL 62702 217-525-0310 525-0342
Web: mid-westtruckers.com

Mobile Air Conditioning Society Worldwide (MACS)
225 S Broad St . . . Lansdale PA 19446 215-631-7020 631-7017
TF: 800-641-1133 ■ *Web:* www.macsw.org

Motor & Equipment Manufacturers Assn (MEMA)
10 Laboratory Dr . . . Research Triangle Park NC 27709 919-549-4800 406-1465

Motorcycle Industry Council (MIC)
Two Jenner St Ste 150 . . . Irvine CA 92618 949-727-4211 727-3313
Web: www.mic.org

National Air Carrier Assn (NACA)
1000 Wilson Blvd Ste 1700 . . . Arlington VA 22209 703-358-8060 358-8070
Web: www.naca.cc

National Air Transportation Assn (NATA)
4226 King St . . . Alexandria VA 22302 703-845-9000 845-8176
TF: 800-808-6282 ■ *Web:* www.nata.aero

National Automobile Dealers Assn (NADA)
8400 Westpark Dr . . . McLean VA 22102 703-821-7000 821-7075
TF: 800-252-6232 ■ *Web:* www.nada.org

National Automotive Radiator Service Assn (NARSA)
3000 Village Run Rd Ste 103 221 . . . Wexford PA 15090 724-799-8415 799-8416
TF: 800-551-3232 ■ *Web:* www.narsa.org

National Business Aviation Assn (NBAA)
1200 18th St NW Ste 400 . . . Washington DC 20036 202-783-9000 331-8364
TF: 800-394-6222 ■ *Web:* www.nbaa.org

National Cargo Bureau Inc (NCB)
17 Battery Pl Ste 1232 . . . New York NY 10004 212-785-8300 785-8333
Web: www.natcargo.org

National Customs Brokers & Forwarders Assn of America Inc (NCBFAA)
1200 18th St NW Ste 901 . . . Washington DC 20036 202-466-0222 466-0226
Web: www.ncbfaa.org

National Industrial Transportation League (NITL)
1700 N Moore St Ste 1900 . . . Arlington VA 22209 703-524-5011 524-5017
Web: www.nitl.org

National Marine Manufacturers Assn (NMMA)
200 E Randolph Dr Ste 5100 . . . Chicago IL 60601 312-946-6200 946-0388
Web: www.nmma.org

National Motor Freight Traffic Assn (NMFTA)
1001 N Fairfax St Ste 600 . . . Alexandria VA 22314 703-838-1810 683-6296
Web: www.nmfta.org

National Motorists Assn (NMA) 402 W Second St . . . Waunakee WI 53597 608-849-6000 849-8697
TF: 800-882-2785 ■ *Web:* www.motorists.org

National Private Truck Council (NPTC)
950 N Glebe Rd Ste 2330 . . . Arlington VA 22203 703-683-1300 683-1217
Web: www.nptc.org

National Tank Truck Carriers Inc
950 N Glebe Rd Ste 520 . . . Arlington VA 22203 703-838-1960
Web: www.tanktruck.org

National Truck Equipment Assn (NTEA)
37400 Hills Tech Dr . . . Farmington Hills MI 48331 248-489-7090 489-8590
TF: 800-441-6832 ■ *Web:* www.ntea.com

National Waterways Conference Inc (NWC)
4650 Washington Blvd Ste 608 . . . Arlington VA 22201 703-243-4090 243-4155
TF: 866-371-1390 ■ *Web:* www.waterways.org

NATSO Inc 1737 King St Ste 200 . . . Alexandria VA 22314 703-549-2100 684-4525
TF: 800-956-9160 ■ *Web:* www.natso.com

Owner-Operator Independent Drivers Assn Inc (OOIDA)
One NW OOIDA Dr . . . Grain Valley MO 64029 816-229-5791 229-0518
TF: 800-444-5791 ■ *Web:* www.ooida.com

Passenger Vessel Assn (PVA)
103 Oronoco St Ste 200 . . . Alexandria VA 22314 703-518-5005 518-5151
TF: 800-807-8360 ■ *Web:* www.passengervessel.com

Propeller Club of the US
3927 Old Lee Hwy Ste 101-A . . . Fairfax VA 22030 703-691-2777 691-4173
Web: www.propellerclubhq.com

Phone Fax

Railway Supply Institute Inc (RSI)
425 Third St Ste 920 . . . Washington DC 20024 202-347-4664 347-0047
TF: 800-995-3579 ■ *Web:* www.rsiweb.org

Recreation Vehicle Dealers Assn (RVDA)
3930 University Dr Third Fl . . . Fairfax VA 22030 703-591-7130 591-0734
TF: 800-336-0355 ■ *Web:* www.rvda.org

Recreation Vehicle Industry Assn (RVIA)
1896 Preston White Dr . . . Reston VA 20191 703-620-6003 620-5071
TF: 800-336-0154 ■ *Web:* www.rvia.org

Regional Airline Assn (RAA)
2025 M St NW Ste 800 . . . Washington DC 20036 202-367-1170 367-2170
Web: www.raa.org

Self Storage Assn (SSA)
1900 N Beauregard St Ste 450 . . . Alexandria VA 22311 703-575-8000 575-8901
TF: 888-735-3784 ■ *Web:* www.selfstorage.org

Shipbuilders Council of America (SCA)
655 Fifteenth St NW Ste 225 . . . Washington DC 20005 202-347-5462 347-5464
Web: www.shipbuilders.org

Shipowners Claims Bureau (SCB)
1 Battery Pk Plaza 31st Fl . . . New York NY 10004 212-847-4500 847-4599
TF: 800-774-8724 ■ *Web:* www.american-club.com

Society of Automotive Engineers Inc (SAE)
400 Commonwealth Dr . . . Warrendale PA 15096 724-776-4841 776-0790
TF: 877-606-7323 ■ *Web:* www.sae.org

Society of Naval Architects & Marine Engineers (SNAME)
601 Pavonia Ave Ste 400 . . . Jersey City NJ 07306 201-798-4800 798-4975
Web: www.sname.org

Specialized Carriers & Rigging Assn (SC&RA)
2750 Prosperity Ave Ste 620 . . . Fairfax VA 22031 703-698-0291 698-0297
Web: www.scranet.org

Specialty Equipment Market Assn (SEMA)
1575 S Vly Vista Dr . . . Diamond Bar CA 91765 909-396-0289 860-0184
Web: www.sema.org

Specialty Vehicle Institute of America (SVIA)
Two Jenner St Ste 150 . . . Irvine CA 92618 949-727-3727 727-4216
TF: 800-887-2887 ■ *Web:* www.atvsafety.org

Technology & Maintenance Council (TMC)
American Trucking Assn
950 N Glebe Rd Ste 210 . . . Arlington VA 22203 703-838-1763
Web: www.trucking.org

Transport Workers Union of America
501 Third St NW 9th Fl . . . Washington DC 20001 202-719-3900 347-0454
TF: 888-565-6898 ■ *Web:* www.twu.org

Transportation Institute 5201 Auth Way . . . Camp Springs MD 20746 301-423-3335 423-0634
Web: www.trans-inst.org

Transportation Intermediaries Assn (TIA)
1625 Prince St Ste 200 . . . Alexandria VA 22314 703-299-5700 836-0123
TF: 800-435-1791 ■ *Web:* www.tianet.org

Transportation Research Board (TRB)
500 Fifth St NW . . . Washington DC 20001 202-334-2934 334-2519
TF: 866-233-4642 ■ *Web:* www.trb.org

Truck Renting & Leasing Assn (TRALA)
675 N Washington St Ste 410 . . . Alexandria VA 22314 703-299-9120 299-9115
Web: www.trala.org

Truckload Carriers Assn (TCA)
555 E Braddock Rd . . . Alexandria VA 22314 703-838-1950 836-6610
TF: 800-666-2770 ■ *Web:* www.truckload.org

United Motorcoach Assn (UMA)
113 SW St Fourth Fl . . . Alexandria VA 22314 703-838-2929 838-2950
TF: 800-424-8262 ■ *Web:* www.uma.org

Warehousing Education & Research Council (WERC)
1100 Jorie Blvd Ste 170 . . . Oak Brook IL 60523 630-990-0001 990-0256
Web: www.werc.org

50 ATTRACTIONS

SEE ALSO Cemeteries - National p. 1908; Amusement Parks p. 1742; Aquariums - Public p. 1746; Art Dealers & Galleries p. 1750; Presidential Libraries p. 2643; Special Collections Libraries p. 2660; Museums p. 2778; Museums - Children's p. 2801; Museums & Halls of Fame - Sports p. 2803; Parks - National - Canada p. 2858; Parks - National - US p. 2859; Parks - State p. 2865; Performing Arts Facilities p. 2900; Planetariums p. 2930; Zoos & Wildlife Parks p. 3302; Botanical Gardens & Arboreta p. 1880

50-1 Churches, Cathedrals, Synagogues, Temples

Phone Fax

Antioch Baptist Church 1057 Texas Ave . . . Shreveport LA 71101 318-222-7090 222-5738

Arch Street Meeting House 320 Arch St . . . Philadelphia PA 19106 215-627-2667
Web: www.archstreetfriends.org

Basilica of Saint Mary of the Immaculate Conception, The
232 Chapel St . . . Norfolk VA 23504 757-622-4487 625-7969
Web: www.basilicaofsaintmary.org

Basilica of the Assumption
409 Cathedral St . . . Baltimore MD 21201 410-727-3565 539-0407
Web: www.baltimorebasilica.org

Black Madonna Shrine
100 St Joseph Hill Rd PO Box 181 . . . Pacific MO 63069 636-938-5361
Web: www.franciscancaring.org/blackmadonnashri.html

Boardman Park 375 BoaRdman-Poland Rd . . . Boardman OH 44512 330-726-8107 726-4562
TF: 888-795-2707 ■ *Web:* www.boardmanpark.com

Carmel Mission 3080 Rio Rd . . . Carmel CA 93923 831-624-1271 624-8050
Web: www.carmelmission.org

Cathedral Basilica of Saint Joseph
80 S Market St . . . San Jose CA 95113 408-283-8100 283-8110
Web: www.stjosephcathedral.org

Cathedral Basilica of Saint Louis (New Cathedral)
4431 Lindell Blvd . . . Saint Louis MO 63108 314-373-8200 373-8290
Web: www.cathedralstl.org

Name / Address	City	State	ZIP	Phone	Fax
Cathedral Basilica of the Sacred Heart 89 Ridge St *Web:* www.cathedralbasilica.org	Newark	NJ	07104	973-484-4600	483-8253
Cathedral Church of All Saints Martello St & University Ave *Web:* www.cathedralchurchofallsaints.com	Halifax	NS	B3H4Z1	902-423-6002	423-1437
Cathedral Church of Saint John the Divine 1047 Amsterdam Ave *Web:* www.stjohndivine.org	New York	NY	10025	212-316-7490	932-7347
Cathedral Church of Saint Mark 231 East 100 South *Web:* stmarkscathedralut.org	Salt Lake City	UT	84111	801-322-3400	322-3410
Cathedral of Christ the King 299 Colony Blvd *Web:* cathedralctk.org	Lexington	KY	40502	859-268-2861	268-8061
Cathedral of Our Lady of the Angels 555 W Temple St *TF:* 800-838-1356 ■ *Web:* www.olacathedral.org	Los Angeles	CA	90012	213-680-5200	620-1982
Cathedral of Saint Paul 239 Selby Ave *Web:* www.cathedralsaintpaul.org	Saint Paul	MN	55102	651-228-1766	228-9942
Cathedral of Saints Peter & Paul 30 Fenner St	Providence	RI	02903	401-331-2434	273-0687
Cathedral of the Blessed Sacrament 1017 11th St *Web:* www.blessedsaccathedral.org	Sacramento	CA	95814	916-444-3071	443-2749
Cathedral of the Immaculate Conception Two S Claiborne St *Web:* www.mobilecathedral.org	Mobile	AL	36602	251-434-1565	434-1588
Cathedral of the Madeleine 331 E S Temple St *Web:* www.utcotm.org	Salt Lake City	UT	84111	801-328-8941	364-6504
Catholic Diocese of Peoria, The 607 NE Madison Ave *TF:* 800-340-5630 ■ *Web:* www.cdop.org	Peoria	IL	61603	309-682-5823	682-6030
Center Church 60 Gold St *Web:* www.centerchurchhartford.org	Hartford	CT	06103	860-249-5631	246-3915
Christ Church Cathedral 45 Church St *Web:* www.cccathedral.org	Hartford	CT	06103	860-527-7231	527-5313
Christ Church in Philadelphia 20 N American St *Web:* www.christchurchphila.org	Philadelphia	PA	19106	215-922-1695	922-3578
Christ Episcopal Church 10 N Church St *Web:* www.ccgsc.org	Greenville	SC	29601	864-271-8773	242-0879
Church of the Transfiguration One E 29th St *Web:* www.littlechurch.org	New York	NY	10016	212-684-6770	684-1662
Circular Congregational Church 150 Meeting St *Web:* www.circularchurch.org	Charleston	SC	29401	843-577-6400	958-0594
Congregation Beth Elohim 90 Hasell St *Web:* www.kkbe.org	Charleston	SC	29401	843-723-1090	723-0537
Congregation Mikveh Israel 44 N Fourth St *Web:* www.mikvehisrael.org	Philadelphia	PA	19106	215-922-5446	922-1550
Crystal Cathedral 12921 S Lewis St *Fax: Hum Res ■ *Web:* www.crystalcathedral.org	Garden Grove	CA	92840	714-971-4000	971-4906*
Dagom Gaden Tensung-Ling Monastery 2150 E Dolan Rd *Web:* www.ganden.org	Bloomington	IN	47404	812-334-3456	
Dexter Avenue King Memorial Baptist Church 454 Dexter Ave *Web:* www.dexterkingmemorial.org	Montgomery	AL	36104	334-263-3970	
Duke Memorial United Methodist Church 504 W Chapel Hill St *Web:* www.dukememorial.org	Durham	NC	27701	919-683-3467	682-3349
Ebenezer Baptist Church 407 Auburn Ave NE *Web:* www.historicebenezer.org	Atlanta	GA	30312	404-688-7300	521-1129
Emanuel African Methodist Episcopal Church 110 Calhoun St *Web:* www.emanuelamechurch.org	Charleston	SC	29401	843-722-2561	722-1869
First Congregational Church 62 Centre St *Web:* nantucketfcc.org	Nantucket	MA	02554	508-228-0950	
First Unitarian Church of Philadelphia 2125 Chestnut St *Web:* www.philauu.org	Philadelphia	PA	19103	215-563-3980	563-4209
Franciscan Monastery of the Holly Land 1400 Quincy St NE *Web:* www.myfranciscan.org	Washington	DC	20017	202-526-6800	529-9889
Historic Trinity Lutheran Church 1345 Gratiot Ave *TF:* 800-268-3058 ■ *Web:* www.historictrinity.org	Detroit	MI	48207	313-567-3100	567-3209
Holy Trinity Catholic Church 315 Marshall St *Web:* www.holytrinity-shreveport.com	Shreveport	LA	71101	318-221-5990	221-3545
King's Chapel 58 Tremont St *Web:* kings-chapel.org	Boston	MA	02108	617-227-2155	227-4101
Landmark on the Park 160 Central Pk W *Web:* www.landmarkonthepark.org	New York	NY	10023	212-595-1658	
Ling Shen Ching Tze Temple 17012 NE 40th Ct *Web:* tbsseattle.org	Redmond	WA	98052	425-882-0916	
Martha's Vineyard Preservation Trust 99 Main St PO Box 5277 *Web:* www.mvpreservation.org	Edgartown	MA	02539	508-627-4440	627-8088
Mesa Arizona Temple 101 S LeSueur *TF:* 855-537-4357 ■ *Web:* www.lds.org/church/temples	Mesa	AZ	85204	480-833-1211	827-2828
Mission Dolores 3321 16th St *Web:* www.missiondolores.org	San Francisco	CA	94114	415-621-8203	621-2294
Mission of Nombre de Dios & Shrine of Our Lady of La Leche 27 Ocean Ave *TF:* 800-342-6529 ■ *Web:* www.missionandshrine.org	Saint Augustine	FL	32084	904-824-2809	829-0819
Mission San Fernando Rey De Espana 15151 San Fernando Mission Blvd *Web:* missiontour.org	Mission Hills	CA	91345	818-361-0186	
Mission San Jose 701 E Pyron Ave *Web:* www.nps.gov	San Antonio	TX	78214	210-922-0543	932-2271
Mission San Luis Rey de Francia 4050 Mission Ave *Web:* www.sanluisrey.org	Oceanside	CA	92057	760-757-3651	757-4613
Mother Bethel AME Church 419 S Sixth St *Web:* www.motherbethel.org	Philadelphia	PA	19147	215-925-0616	925-1402
National Shrine of Our Lady of Lebanon, The 2759 N Lipkey Rd *Web:* www.ourladyoflebanonshrine.com	North Jackson	OH	44451	330-538-3351	538-0455
National Shrine of Our Lady of the Snows 442 S De Mazenod Dr *TF:* 800-682-2879 ■ *Web:* www.snows.org	Belleville	IL	62223	618-397-6700	398-6549
New England Peace Pagoda, The 100 Cave Hill Rd *Web:* newenglandpeacepagoda.org/	Leverett	MA	01054	413-367-2202	
Oakland Mormon Temple 4770 Lincoln Ave *Web:* www.ldschurchtemples.com	Oakland	CA	94602	510-531-3200	531-2646
Old First Reformed Church of Christ 151 N Fourth St *Web:* www.oldfirstucc.org	Philadelphia	PA	19106	215-922-4566	922-6366
Old Mission San Jose 43300 Mission Blvd *Web:* www.saintjosephmsj.org	Fremont	CA	94539	510-657-1797	651-8332
Old North Church 193 Salem St *Web:* www.oldnorth.com	Boston	MA	02113	617-523-6676	725-0559
Old Pine Street Presbyterian Church 412 Pine St *Web:* www.oldpine.org	Philadelphia	PA	19106	215-925-8051	922-7120
Old Saint Ferdinand's Shrine One Rue St Francois *Web:* oldstferdinandshrine.com	Florissant	MO	63031	314-837-2110	
Old Saint Joseph's Church 321 Willings Alley *Web:* www.oldstjoseph.org	Philadelphia	PA	19106	215-923-1733	574-8529
Old Saint Mary's Church 123 E 13th St *Web:* www.oldstmarys.org	Cincinnati	OH	45202	513-721-2988	721-0436
Old Saint Patrick's Church 700 W Adams St *Web:* www.oldstpats.org	Chicago	IL	60661	312-648-1021	648-9025
Our Lady Queen of the Most Holy Rosary Cathedral 2535 Collingwood Blvd *Web:* www.rosarycathedral.org	Toledo	OH	43610	419-244-9575	242-1901
Queen of Angels Monastery 840 S Main St *Web:* www.benedictine-srs.org	Mount Angel	OR	97362	503-845-6141	845-6585
Saint George's Anglican Church 1101 Stanley St *Web:* www.st-georges.org	Montreal	QC	H3B2S6	514-866-7113	866-6096
Saint George's Church 2222 Brunswick St *Web:* www.roundchurch.ca	Halifax	NS	B3K2Z3	902-423-1059	423-0897
Saint Joseph Cathedral 521 N Duluth Ave *Web:* stjosephcathedral.net	Sioux Falls	SD	57104	605-336-7390	
Saint Louis Cathedral 615 Pere Antoine Alley *Web:* www.stlouiscathedral.org/	New Orleans	LA	70116	504-525-9585	525-9583
Saint Mary's Cathedral 203 E Tenth St *Web:* www.smcaustin.org	Austin	TX	78701	512-476-6182	476-8799
Saint Mary's Catholic Church 155 Market St	Memphis	TN	38105	901-522-9420	522-8314
Saint Paul's Episcopal Church 1430 J St *Web:* www.stpaulssacramento.org	Sacramento	CA	95814	916-446-2620	
Saint Photios Greek Orthodox National Shrine 41 St George St PO Box 1960 *Web:* www.stphotios.com	Saint Augustine	FL	32085	904-829-8205	829-8707
Salt Lake Temple 50 W N Temple St *TF:* 800-453-3860 ■ *Web:* www.lds.org	Salt Lake City	UT	84150	801-240-2640	240-1550
San Gabriel Mission 428 S Mission Dr *Web:* www.sangabrielmissionchurch.org	San Gabriel	CA	91776	626-457-3035	282-5308
San Miguel Mission 401 Old Santa Fe Trl	Santa Fe	NM	87501	505-983-3974	
San Xavier Del Bac Mission 1950 W San Xavier Rd *Web:* www.sanxaviermission.org	Tucson	AZ	85746	520-294-2624	
Scottish Rite Cathedral 160 S Scott Ave *Web:* tucsonscottishrite.org	Tucson	AZ	85701	520-622-8364	
Shrine of Saint John Neumann 1019 N Fifth St *Web:* www.stjohnneumann.org	Philadelphia	PA	19123	215-627-3080	627-3296
Sixteenth Street Baptist Church 1530 Sixth Ave N	Birmingham	AL	35203	205-251-9402	251-9811
Southern Union Conference Assn of The Seventh Day Adventist Church 302 Research Dr NW PO Box 849 *Web:* www.southernunion.com	Norcross	GA	30092	404-299-1832	299-9726
Touro Synagogue National Historic Site 85 Touro St *Web:* www.tourosynagogue.org	Newport	RI	02840	401-847-4794	
Trinity Cathedral 2230 Euclid Ave *Web:* www.trinitycleveland.org	Cleveland	OH	44115	216-771-3630	771-3657
Union Chapel 55 Narragansett Ave *Web:* www.mvpreservation.org	Edgartown	MA	02539	508-627-4440	
Union Church of Pocantico Hills 555 Bedford Rd *TF:* 800-638-7646 ■ *Web:* www.hudsonvalley.org	Sleepy Hollow	NY	10591	914-631-8200	631-0089
Wayfarers Chapel 5755 Palos Verdes Dr *Web:* www.wayfarerschapel.org	Rancho Palos Verdes	CA	90275	310-377-1650	541-1435
White Church Christian Church 2200 N 85th St *Web:* wcchristianchurch.com	Kansas City	KS	66109	913-299-4056	
Ysleta Mission 131 S Zaragosa Rd *Web:* www.ysletamission.org	El Paso	TX	79907	915-859-9848	860-9340

50-2 Cultural & Arts Centers

Arizona

Name / Address	City	State	ZIP	Phone	Fax
Deer Valley Rock Art Ctr 3711 W Deer Vly Rd *Web:* www.asu.edu	Glendale	AZ	85308	623-582-8007	582-8831
Mesa Arts Ctr 1 E Main St PO Box 1466 *TF:* 800-647-5463 ■ *Web:* www.mesaartscenter.com	Mesa	AZ	85201	480-644-6501	644-6503

Arkansas

Name / Address	City	State	ZIP	Phone	Fax
Arkansas Arts Ctr 501 E Ninth St *TF:* 800-264-2787 ■ *Web:* www.arkarts.com	Little Rock	AR	72202	501-372-4000	375-8053
Center for Art & Education 104 N 13th St *Web:* www.art-ed.org	Van Buren	AR	72956	479-474-7767	474-4411

California

Name / Address	City	State	ZIP	Phone	Fax
Aerie Art Garden 71-225 Aerie Rd *Web:* www.aerieartgarden.com	Palm Desert	CA	92260	760-568-6366	
African American Art & Culture Complex 762 Fulton St Ste 300 *Web:* www.aaacc.org	San Francisco	CA	94102	415-922-2049	922-5130
Huntington Beach Arts Ctr 538 Main St *Web:* huntingtonbeachartcenter.org	Huntington Beach	CA	92648	714-374-1650	374-5304
Jurupa Mountains Discovery Ctr 7621 Granite Hill Dr *Web:* www.jmdc.org	Riverside	CA	92509	951-685-5818	685-1240
Mission Cultural Ctr for Latino Arts 2868 Mission St *Web:* www.missionculturalcenter.org	San Francisco	CA	94110	415-821-1155	648-0933
Oakland Asian Cultural Ctr 388 Ninth St Ste 290 *Web:* www.oacc.cc	Oakland	CA	94607	510-637-0455	637-0459
Roy & Edna Disney/CALARTS Theater (REDCAT) (REDCAT) 631 W Second St *Web:* www.redcat.org	Los Angeles	CA	90012	213-237-2800	237-2811
Skirball Cultural Ctr 2701 N Sepulveda Blvd *Web:* www.skirball.org	Los Angeles	CA	90049	310-440-4500	440-4595

Colorado

Name / Address	City	State	ZIP	Phone	Fax
Anasazi Heritage Ctr 27501 Hwy 184 *Web:* www.blm.gov	Dolores	CO	81323	970-882-5600	882-7035
Anderson Ranch Arts Ctr 5263 Owl Creek Rd PO Box 5598 *TF:* 800-525-6363 ■ *Web:* www.andersonranch.org	Snowmass Village	CO	81615	970-923-3181	923-3871
Dairy Ctr for the Arts 2590 Walnut St *Web:* www.thedairy.org	Boulder	CO	80302	303-440-7826	440-7104
Durango Arts Ctr 802 E Second Ave *TF:* 800-838-3006 ■ *Web:* durangoarts.org	Durango	CO	81301	970-259-2606	259-6571
Southern Ute Cultural Ctr & Museum PO Box 737 *Web:* www.succm.org	Ignacio	CO	81137	970-563-9583	563-4641

Connecticut

Name / Address	City	State	ZIP	Phone	Fax
Charter Oak Cultural Ctr 21 Charter Oak Ave *Web:* www.charteroakcenter.org	Hartford	CT	06106	860-249-1207	524-8014
Rowayton Arts Ctr 145 Rowayton Ave *Web:* www.rowaytonartscenter.org	Rowayton	CT	06853	203-866-2744	866-1123
Silvermine Arts Ctr 1037 Silvermine Rd *Web:* www.silvermineart.org	New Canaan	CT	06840	203-966-9700	966-2763
Westport Arts Ctr 51 Riverside Ave *Web:* www.westportartscenter.org	Westport	CT	06880	203-222-7070	222-7999

Delaware

Name / Address	City	State	ZIP	Phone	Fax
Delaware Ctr for the Contemporary Arts 200 S Madison St *Web:* www.thedcca.org	Wilmington	DE	19801	302-656-6466	656-6944

Florida

Name / Address	City	State	ZIP	Phone	Fax
African-American Research Library & Cultural Ctr 2650 Sistrunk Blvd	Fort Lauderdale	FL	33311	954-625-2800	
Armory Art Ctr 1700 Parker Ave *Web:* www.armoryart.org	West Palm Beach	FL	33401	561-832-1776	832-0191
ArtSouth 240 N Krome Ave *Web:* www.artsouthhomestead.org	Homestead	FL	33030	305-247-9406	247-7308
Lighthouse Ctr for the Arts 373 Tequesta Dr Gallery Sq N *Web:* www.lighthousearts.org	Tequesta	FL	33469	561-746-3101	746-3241
Maitland Art Ctr 231 W Packwood Ave **Fax Area Code: 888* ■ *TF:* 800-435-7352 ■ *Web:* www.artandhistory.org	Maitland	FL	32751	407-539-2181	316-5729*

Georgia

Name / Address	City	State	ZIP	Phone	Fax
Atlanta Contemporary Art Ctr 535 Means St NW *Web:* www.thecontemporary.org	Atlanta	GA	30318	404-688-1970	577-5856
Callanwolde Fine Arts Ctr 980 Briarcliff Rd NE *Web:* www.callanwolde.org	Atlanta	GA	30306	404-872-5338	872-5175
Center for Puppetry Arts 1404 Spring St NW *TF:* 800-642-3629 ■ *Web:* www.puppet.org	Atlanta	GA	30309	404-873-3089	873-9907
City Market Art Ctr 219 W Bryan St Ste 207 *Web:* www.savannahcitymarket.com/art.html	Savannah	GA	31401	912-232-4903	232-2142

Idaho

Name / Address	City	State	ZIP	Phone	Fax
Pocatello Art Ctr (PAC) 444 N Main St *Web:* www.pocatelloartctr.org	Pocatello	ID	83204	208-232-0970	

Illinois

Name / Address	City	State	ZIP	Phone	Fax
City of Chicago 121 N LaSalle St *Web:* www.cityofchicago.org	Chicago	IL	60602	312-744-5000	
Irish American Heritage Ctr 4626 N Knox Ave *Web:* www.irish-american.org	Chicago	IL	60630	773-282-7035	282-0380
South Shore Cultural Ctr 7059 S Shore Dr *Web:* www.chicagoparkdistrict.com	Chicago	IL	60649	773-256-0149	256-1163

Indiana

Name / Address	City	State	ZIP	Phone	Fax
Indianapolis Art Ctr 820 E 67th St *Web:* indplsartcenter.org	Indianapolis	IN	46220	317-255-2464	

Kentucky

Name / Address	City	State	ZIP	Phone	Fax
Capital Gallery of Contemporary Art 314 Lewis St *Web:* ellenglasgow.com	Frankfort	KY	40601	502-223-2649	
Kentucky Ctr for African American Heritage 1701 W Muhammad Ali Blvd *Web:* www.kcaah.org	Louisville	KY	40203	502-583-4100	
Kentucky Museum of Art & Craft 715 W Main St *Web:* www.kentuckyarts.org	Louisville	KY	40202	502-589-0102	589-0154

Louisiana

Name / Address	City	State	ZIP	Phone	Fax
Acadiana Ctr for the Arts 101 W Vermilion St *Web:* www.acadianacenterforthearts.org	Lafayette	LA	70501	337-233-7060	233-7062
Barnwell Garden & Art Ctr 601 Clyde Fant Pkwy	Shreveport	LA	71101	318-673-7703	

Maine

Name / Address	City	State	ZIP	Phone	Fax
Maine Folklife Ctr 5773 S Stevens Hall University of Maine *Web:* www.umaine.edu/folklife	Orono	ME	04469	207-581-1891	581-1823

Manitoba

Name / Address	City	State	ZIP	Phone	Fax
Jewish Heritage Ctr of Western Canada C116-123 Doncaster St *Web:* www.jhcwc.org	Winnipeg	MB	R3N2B2	204-477-7460	477-7465
Saint Norbert Arts & Cultural Centre (SNAC) 100 Rue des Ruines du Monastere PO Box 1752 *Web:* www.snac.mb.ca	Winnipeg	MB	R3V1L6	204-269-0564	261-1927

Maryland

Name / Address	City	State	ZIP	Phone	Fax
Elizabeth Myers Mitchell Art Gallery 60 College Ave	Annapolis	MD	21401	410-626-2556	
Maryland Art Place (MAP) Eight Market Pl Ste 100 *Web:* www.mdartplace.org	Baltimore	MD	21202	410-962-8565	244-8017
Maryland Federation of Art Cir Gallery (MFA) 18 State Cir *Web:* www.mdfedart.com	Annapolis	MD	21401	410-268-4566	268-4570

Massachusetts

Name / Address	City	State	ZIP	Phone	Fax
Worcester Ctr for Crafts 25 Sagamore Rd *Web:* www.worcester.edu	Worcester	MA	01605	508-753-8183	797-5626

Michigan

Name / Address	City	State	ZIP	Phone	Fax
Ann Arbor Art Ctr 117 W Liberty St *Web:* www.annarborartcenter.org	Ann Arbor	MI	48104	734-994-8004	994-3610

				Phone	Fax
Detroit Gallery-Contemporary 104 Fisher Rd Ste 104	Grosse Pte Farms	MI	48230	313-873-7888	
Flint Cultural Ctr Corp 1310 E Kearsley St *TF:* 888-823-6837 ■ *Web:* www.flintculturalcenter.com	Flint	MI	48503	810-237-7333	237-7340
Lansing Art Gallery 119 N Washington Sq *Web:* www.lansingartgallery.org	Lansing	MI	48933	517-374-6400	374-6385
Nokomis Learning Ctr 5153 Marsh Rd *Web:* www.nokomis.org	Okemos	MI	48864	517-349-5777	349-8560
Oakland University Art Gallery Oakland University 208 Wilson Hall *Web:* www.ouartgallery.org	Rochester	MI	48309	248-370-3005	370-4208

Minnesota

				Phone	Fax
Rochester Art Ctr 40 Civic Ctr Dr SE *Web:* www.rochesterartcenter.org	Rochester	MN	55904	507-282-8629	282-7737

Mississippi

				Phone	Fax
Mississippi Arts Ctr 201 E Pascagoula St Ste 102 *Web:* www.arts.state.ms.us	Jackson	MS	39201	601-960-1500	960-1352
Municipal Art Gallery 839 N State St	Jackson	MS	39202	601-960-1582	960-2066

Missouri

				Phone	Fax
Center of Contemporary Arts 524 Trinity Ave *Web:* www.cocastl.org	Saint Louis	MO	63130	314-725-6555	725-6222
Portfolio Gallery & Educational Ctr 3514 Delmar Blvd *Web:* www.portfoliogallerystl.org	Saint Louis	MO	63103	314-533-3323	

Nebraska

				Phone	Fax
Bemis Ctr for Contemporary Arts 724 S 12th St *Web:* www.bemiscenter.org	Omaha	NE	68102	402-341-7130	341-9791
Gerald R Ford Conservation Ctr 1326 S 32nd St *TF:* 800-634-6932 ■ *Web:* www.nebraskahistory.org	Omaha	NE	68105	402-595-1180	595-1178

New Jersey

				Phone	Fax
Great Falls Historic District Cultural Ctr 65 McBride Ave Ext *Web:* www.patersonnj.gov	Paterson	NJ	07501	973-279-9587	279-0587

New Mexico

				Phone	Fax
Branigan Cultural Ctr 501 N Main St PO Box 20000 *Web:* www.las-cruces.org	Las Cruces	NM	88004	575-541-2154	541-2152
National Hispanic Cultural Ctr 1701 Fourth St SW *Web:* www.nhccnm.org	Albuquerque	NM	87102	505-246-2261	246-2613
South Broadway Cultural Ctr 1025 Broadway Blvd SE *TF:* 866-441-6075 ■ *Web:* cabq.gov	Albuquerque	NM	87102	505-848-1320	848-1329

New York

				Phone	Fax
African American Cultural Ctr of Buffalo Inc 350 Masten Ave *Web:* aaccbuffalo.org/	Buffalo	NY	14209	716-884-2013	885-2590
Burchfield-Penney Art Ctr *Buffalo State College* 1300 Elmwood Ave *Web:* www.burchfieldpenney.org	Buffalo	NY	14222	716-878-6011	878-6003
Hallwalls Contemporary Arts Ctr 341 Delaware Ave *Web:* www.hallwalls.org	Buffalo	NY	14202	716-854-1694	854-1696
Rochester Contemporary Art Ctr 137 E Ave *Web:* www.rochestercontemporary.org	Rochester	NY	14604	585-461-2222	461-2223

North Carolina

				Phone	Fax
Afro-American Cultural Ctr 551 S Tryon St *Web:* www.ganttcenter.org	Charlotte	NC	28202	704-547-3700	
Center for Visual Arts - Greensboro 200 N Davie St PO Box 13 *Web:* www.greensboroart.org	Greensboro	NC	27401	336-333-7475	333-7477
Delta Fine Arts Inc 2611 New Walkertown Rd *Web:* deltaartscenter.org	Winston-Salem	NC	27101	336-722-2625	722-9449
Pack Place Two S Pack Sq *Web:* www.packplace.org	Asheville	NC	28801	828-257-4500	251-5652
Page-Walker Arts & History Ctr 119 Ambassador Loop *Web:* www.townofcary.org	Cary	NC	27513	919-460-4963	388-1141
Southeastern Ctr for Contemporary Art 750 Marguerite Dr *Web:* www.secca.org	Winston-Salem	NC	27106	336-725-1904	722-6059

Ohio

				Phone	Fax
City of Dayton 40 S Edwin C Moses Blvd *Web:* www.daytonrecreationandyou.com	Dayton	OH	45402	937-333-2489	
Dayton Visual Arts Ctr 118 N Jefferson St *Web:* www.daytonvisualarts.org	Dayton	OH	45402	937-224-3822	
King Arts Complex, The 867 Mt Vernon Ave *Web:* kingartscomplex.com	Columbus	OH	43203	614-645-5464	645-0672

Oklahoma

				Phone	Fax
Greenwood Cultural Ctr 322 N Greenwood Ave *Web:* www.greenwoodculturalcenter.com	Tulsa	OK	74120	918-596-1020	596-1029

Oregon

				Phone	Fax
Bush Barn Art Ctr 600 Mission St SE *Web:* www.salemart.org	Salem	OR	97302	503-581-2228	371-3342
Maude Kerns Art Ctr 1910 E 15th Ave *Web:* www.mkartcenter.org	Eugene	OR	97403	541-345-1571	345-6248
Portland Institute for Contemporary Art 224 NW 13th Ave Ste 305 *Web:* www.pica.org	Portland	OR	97209	503-242-1419	243-1167

Pennsylvania

				Phone	Fax
Painted Bride Art Ctr 230 Vine St *Web:* www.paintedbride.org	Philadelphia	PA	19106	215-925-9914	925-7402
Pittsburgh Ctr for the Arts (PCA) 6300 Fifth Ave *Web:* www.pittsburgharts.org	Pittsburgh	PA	15232	412-361-0873	361-8338
Silver Eye Ctr for Photography 1015 E Carson St *Web:* www.silvereye.org	Pittsburgh	PA	15203	412-431-1810	431-5777

South Dakota

				Phone	Fax
Dahl Arts Ctr 713 Seventh St *Web:* www.thedahl.org	Rapid City	SD	57701	605-394-4101	394-6121
Multi-Cultural Ctr of Sioux Falls 515 N Main Ave *Web:* www.sfmcc.org	Sioux Falls	SD	57104	605-367-7401	367-7404

Tennessee

				Phone	Fax
Beck Cultural Exchange Ctr Inc 1927 Dandridge Ave *Web:* beckcenter.net	Knoxville	TN	37915	865-524-8461	524-8462

Texas

				Phone	Fax
Art Ctr of Corpus Christi 100 N Shoreline Blvd *Web:* www.artcentercc.org	Corpus Christi	TX	78401	361-884-6406	884-8836
ArtCentre of Plano, The 901 18th St *Web:* www.artcentreofplano.org	Plano	TX	75074	972-423-7809	424-0745
Bath House Cultural Ctr (BHCC) 521 E Lawther Dr *Web:* www.dallasculture.org/bathhouseculturecenter	Dallas	TX	75218	214-670-8749	670-8751
Blue Star Contemporary Arts Ctr 116 Blue Star Rd *Web:* www.bluestarart.org	San Antonio	TX	78204	210-227-6960	229-9412
Carver Community Cultural Ctr 226 N Hackberry St *Web:* www.thecarver.org	San Antonio	TX	78202	210-207-7211	207-4412
Center for Contemporary Arts, The 220 Cypress St *Web:* www.center-arts.com	Abilene	TX	79601	325-677-8389	677-1171
Dallas Ctr for Contemporary Art 161 Glass St *Web:* www.thecontemporary.net	Dallas	TX	75207	214-821-2522	821-9103
Dougherty Arts Ctr, The (DAC) 1110 Barton Springs Rd *TF:* 855-787-2227	Austin	TX	78704	512-974-4000	974-1226
Guadalupe Cultural Arts Ctr 1300 Guadalupe St *Web:* www.guadalupeculturalarts.org	San Antonio	TX	78207	210-271-3151	271-3480
Ice House Cultural Ctr 1925 Elm St Ste 500 *Web:* www.dallasculture.org	Dallas	TX	75201	214-670-7524	
La Villita Historic Arts Village 418 Villita St *Web:* www.lavillita.com	San Antonio	TX	78205	210-207-8610	207-4390
Latino Cultural Ctr 2600 Live Oak St *Web:* www.dallasculture.org	Dallas	TX	75204	214-671-0045	670-0633
Louise Hopkins Underwood Ctr for the Arts (LHUCA) 511 Ave K *Web:* www.lhuca.org	Lubbock	TX	79401	806-762-8606	762-8622
McKinney Avenue Contemporary (The MAC) 3120 McKinney Ave *Web:* www.the-mac.org	Dallas	TX	75204	214-953-1212	953-1873
Nasher Sculpture Ctr 2001 Flora St *Web:* www.nashersculpturecenter.org	Dallas	TX	75201	214-242-5100	242-5155

Utah

Name / Address	City	State	Zip	Phone	Fax
Eccles Community Art Ctr 2580 Jefferson Ave *Web:* www.ogden4arts.org	Ogden	UT	84401	801-392-6935	392-5295

Virginia

Name / Address	City	State	Zip	Phone	Fax
Arlington Arts Ctr (AAC) 3550 Wilson Blvd *Web:* www.arlingtonartscenter.org	Arlington	VA	22201	703-248-6800	248-6849
Contemporary Art Ctr of Virginia (CAC) 2200 Parks Ave *Web:* www.cacv.org	Virginia Beach	VA	23451	757-425-0000	425-8186
Ellipse Arts Ctr 3700 S Four Mile Run Dr *Web:* www.arlingtonarts.org	Arlington	VA	22206	703-228-7710	
Peninsula Fine Arts Ctr 101 Museum Dr *TF:* 800-227-2788 ■ *Web:* www.pfac-va.org	Newport News	VA	23606	757-596-8175	596-0807

Washington

Name / Address	City	State	Zip	Phone	Fax
City of Spokane 507 W Seventh Ave *Web:* beta.spokanecity.org/parksrec/	Spokane	WA	99204	509-625-6677	
Daybreak Star Ctr 3801 W Government Way PO Box 99100 *TF:* 800-321-4321 ■ *Web:* www.unitedindians.org	Seattle	WA	98199	206-285-4425	282-3640

West Virginia

Name / Address	City	State	Zip	Phone	Fax
Artworks Around Town Gallery & Art Ctr 2200 Market St *Web:* www.artworksaroundtown.org	Wheeling	WV	26003	304-233-7540	
Monongalia Arts Ctr (MAC) 107 High St PO Box 239 *Web:* www.monartscenter.com	Morgantown	WV	26507	304-292-3325	292-3326
Oglebay Institute's Stifel Fine Arts Ctr 1330 National Rd *TF:* 800-624-6988 ■ *Web:* www.oionline.com	Wheeling	WV	26003	304-242-7700	242-7747

Wisconsin

Name / Address	City	State	Zip	Phone	Fax
Irish Cultural & Heritage Ctr of Wisconsin 2133 W Wisconsin Ave *Web:* www.ichc.net	Milwaukee	WI	53233	414-345-8800	345-8805

50-3 Historic Homes & Buildings

Alabama

Name / Address	City	State	Zip	Phone	Fax
Battle-Friedman House & Gardens 1010 Greensboro Ave *Web:* www.historictuscaloosa.org	Tuscaloosa	AL	35401	205-758-6138	
Conde-Charlotte Museum House 104 Theatre St	Mobile	AL	36602	251-432-4722	
Fort Gaines Historic Site 51 Bienville Blvd *Web:* www.dauphinisland.org/fort.htm	Dauphin Island	AL	36528	251-861-6992	861-6993
Old Alabama Town 301 Columbus St *TF:* 888-240-1850 ■ *Web:* www.oldalabamatown.com	Montgomery	AL	36104	334-240-4500	240-4519
Tannehill Ironworks Historical State Park 12632 Confederate Pkwy *Web:* www.tannehill.org	McCalla	AL	35111	205-477-5711	477-9400

Arizona

Name / Address	City	State	Zip	Phone	Fax
Cosanti Originals Inc 6433 Doubletree Ranch Rd *TF:* 800-752-3187 ■ *Web:* www.cosanti.com	Paradise Valley	AZ	85253	480-948-6145	998-4312
Goldfield Ghost Town & Mine 4650 N Mammouth Rd *Web:* www.goldfieldghosttown.com	Goldfield	AZ	85119	480-983-0333	834-7947
Historic Heritage Square 115 N Sixth St *Web:* www.phoenix.gov	Phoenix	AZ	85004	602-261-8063	732-2624
OK Corral 326 E Allen St *Web:* www.ok-corral.com	Tombstone	AZ	85638	520-457-3456	457-3456
Wrigley Mansion 2501 E Telawa Trl *Web:* www.wrigleymansionclub.com	Phoenix	AZ	85016	602-955-4079	956-8439

Arkansas

Name / Address	City	State	Zip	Phone	Fax
Belle Grove Historic District 623 Garrison Ave Rm 331 *Web:* www.fortsmithar.gov	Fort Smith	AR	72902	479-784-2266	784-2462
Quapaw Quarter Curran Hall 615 E Capitol Ave *Web:* www.quapaw.com	Little Rock	AR	72202	501-371-0075	374-8142

California

Name / Address	City	State	Zip	Phone	Fax
Camron-Stanford House 1418 Lakeside Dr *Web:* www.cshouse.org	Oakland	CA	94612	510-874-7802	874-7803
Casa del Herrero 1387 E Valley Rd *Web:* www.casadelherrero.com	Santa Barbara	CA	93108	805-565-5653	969-2371
Dunsmuir Hellman Historic Estate 2960 Peralta Oaks Ct *Web:* dunsmuir-hellman.com	Oakland	CA	94605	510-615-5555	562-8294
Kimberly Crest House & Gardens 1325 Prospect Dr PO Box 206 *Web:* www.kimberlycrest.org	Redlands	CA	92373	909-792-2111	798-1716
Marston House Museum & Gardens 3525 Seventh Ave *Web:* www.sohosandiego.org/	San Diego	CA	92103	619-297-9327	
Old Sacramento Business Assn Inc 980 9th St Ste 400 *Web:* www.oldsacramento.com	Sacramento	CA	95814	916-442-8575	442-2053
Old Sacramento Schoolhouse 1200 Front St *Web:* www.scoe.net/oldsacschoolhouse	Sacramento	CA	95814	916-483-8818	
Robinson Jeffers Tor House Foundation 26304 Ocean View Ave *Web:* www.torhouse.org	Carmel	CA	93923	831-624-1813	624-3696
Village Green Heritage Ctr 221 S Palm Canyon Dr *Web:* www.pshistoricalsociety.org	Palm Springs	CA	92262	760-323-8297	320-2561
WebHost4Life 1440 29th Ave *Web:* www.cohenbrayhouse.info	Oakland	CA	94601	510-536-1703	
Winchester Mystery House 525 S Winchester Blvd *Web:* www.winchestermysteryhouse.com	San Jose	CA	95128	408-247-2000	247-2090

Connecticut

Name / Address	City	State	Zip	Phone	Fax
Bates-Scofield Homestead 45 Old King's Hwy N *Web:* darienhistorical.org	Darien	CT	06820	203-655-9233	656-3892
Bush-Holley House 39 Strickland Rd *Web:* www.hstg.org	Cos Cob	CT	06807	203-869-6899	861-9720
Hoyt-Barnum House, The 713 Bedford St *Web:* www.stamfordhistory.org/hbh.htm	Stamford	CT	06903	203-329-1183	322-1607
Isham-Terry House 211 High St *Web:* www.ctlandmarks.org	Hartford	CT	06103	860-247-8996	
Mill Hill Historic Park & Museum 2 East Wall St *Web:* www.norwalkhistoricalsociety.org	Norwalk	CT	06851	203-846-0525	
Ogden House & Gardens 1520 Bronson Rd *Web:* www.fairfieldhistoricalsociety.org	Fairfield	CT	06824	203-259-1598	255-2716
Old State House 800 Main St *Web:* www.ctosh.org	Hartford	CT	06103	860-522-6766	522-2812
Pardee-Morris House 325 Lighthouse Rd *Web:* newhavenmuseum.org	New Haven	CT	06512	203-562-4183	562-2002
Wheeler House 510 Gilmer Ferry Rd **Fax Area Code: 203* ■ *Web:* www.thewheelerhouse.net/	Ball Ground	GA	30107	770-402-1686	221-0981*

Delaware

Name / Address	City	State	Zip	Phone	Fax
Amstel House 30 Market St *Web:* www.newcastlehistory.org	New Castle	DE	19720	302-322-2794	322-8923
Greenbank Mill 500 Greenbank Rd *Web:* www.greenbankmill.org	Wilmington	DE	19808	302-999-9001	
John Dickinson Plantation 340 Kitts Hummock Rd *Web:* history.delaware.gov	Dover	DE	19901	302-739-3277	
Preservation Delaware Inc 1405 Greenhill Ave *Web:* www.preservationde.org	Wilmington	DE	19806	302-651-9617	651-9603
Read House & Gardens 42 The Strand *Web:* www.hsd.org/read.htm	New Castle	DE	19720	302-322-8411	322-8557

District of Columbia

Name / Address	City	State	Zip	Phone	Fax
Dumbarton House 2715 Q St NW *Web:* www.dumbartonhouse.org	Washington	DC	20007	202-337-2288	337-0348
Old Stone House 3051 M St NW *Web:* www.nps.gov	Washington	DC	20007	202-426-6851	
Tudor Place Historic House & Garden 1644 31st St NW *Web:* www.tudorplace.org	Washington	DC	20007	202-965-0400	965-0164

Florida

Name / Address	City	State	Zip	Phone	Fax
Ann Norton Sculpture Gardens 253 Barcelona Rd *Web:* www.ansg.org	West Palm Beach	FL	33401	561-832-5328	835-9305
Ernest Hemingway Home & Museum 907 Whitehead St *Web:* www.hemingwayhome.com	Key West	FL	33040	305-294-1136	294-2755
Historic Pensacola Village 120 Church St PO Box 12866 *Web:* www.historicpensacola.org	Pensacola	FL	32502	850-595-5985	595-5989
Merrick House 907 Coral Way *Web:* coralgables.com	Coral Gables	FL	33134	305-460-5361	
Mission San Luis Apalachee 2100 W Tennessee St *Web:* www.missionsanluis.org	Tallahassee	FL	32304	850-245-6406	488-6186
Pablo Historical Park 381 Beach Blvd *Web:* www.beachesmuseum.org	Jacksonville Beach	FL	32250	904-241-5657	
Ponce de Leon's Fountain of Youth 11 Magnolia Ave *TF:* 800-356-8222 ■ *Web:* www.fountainofyouthflorida.com	Saint Augustine	FL	32084	904-829-3168	829-1528
Sugar Mill Ruins 600 Mission Rd *Web:* www.volusia.org	New Smyrna Beach	FL	32168	386-427-2284	

Georgia

				Phone	Fax
1797 Ezekiel Harris House 560 Reynolds St *Web:* www.augustamuseum.org/harrishouse.php	Augusta	GA	30904	706-722-8454	
Andrew Low House, The 329 Abercorn St *Web:* www.andrewlowhouse.com	Savannah	GA	31401	912-233-6854	233-9239
Boyhood Home of President Woodrow Wilson 419 Seventh St *Web:* www.wilsonboyhoodhome.org	Augusta	GA	30901	706-722-9828	724-3083
Georgia Trust, The 1516 Peachtree St NW *Web:* www.georgiatrust.org	Atlanta	GA	30309	404-881-9980	875-2205
Gordon-Lee Mansion 217 Cove Rd *Web:* leeandgordonsmills.com/	Chickamauga	GA	30707	706-375-4728	357-9499
Hammonds House 503 Peeples St SW *Web:* www.hammondshouse.org	Atlanta	GA	30310	404-612-0500	752-8733
Herndon Home 587 University Pl NW *Web:* theherndonhome.org	Atlanta	GA	30314	404-581-9813	
Historic Roswell District 617 Atlanta St *Web:* www.visitroswellga.com	Roswell	GA	30075	800-776-7935	
Juliette Gordon Low Girl Scout National Ctr 10 E Oglethorpe Ave *Web:* www.juliettegordonlowbirthplace.org	Savannah	GA	31401	912-233-4501	233-4659
Margaret Mitchell House 990 Peachtree St NE *Web:* atlantahistorycenter.com/mmh	Atlanta	GA	30309	404-249-7015	249-7118
Pebble Hill Plantation Hwy 319 *Web:* pebblehill.com	Thomasville	GA	31792	229-226-2344	226-0780
Sidney Lanier Cottage 935 High St *Web:* historicmacon.org	Macon	GA	31201	478-743-3851	
Smith Plantation Home 935 Alpharetta St *Web:* www.archibaldsmithplantation.org	Roswell	GA	30075	770-641-3978	641-3974
Stately Oaks Plantation 100 Carriage Ln *Web:* historicaljonesboro.org/	Jonesboro	GA	30236	770-473-0197	473-9855
Swan House Atlanta History Ctr 130 W Paces Ferry Rd *Web:* www.atlantahistorycenter.com	Atlanta	GA	30305	404-814-4000	814-2041

Hawaii

				Phone	Fax
Queen Emma Summer Palace 2913 Pali Hwy *Web:* daughtersofhawaii.org	Honolulu	HI	96817	808-595-3167	595-4395

Idaho

				Phone	Fax
Old Idaho Penitentiary State Historic Site 2445 Old Penitentiary Rd *TF:* 877-653-4367 ■ *Web:* history.idaho.gov	Boise	ID	83712	208-334-2844	334-3225

Illinois

				Phone	Fax
Dana-Thomas House (DTH) 301 E Lawrence Ave *Web:* www.dana-thomas.org	Springfield	IL	62703	217-782-6776	
Jane Addams Hull-House Museum 800 S Halsted St *TF:* 800-625-2013 ■ *Web:* www.uic.edu	Chicago	IL	60607	312-413-5353	413-2092
John C Flanagan House 942 NE Glen Oak Ave	Peoria	IL	61603	309-674-1921	
Lewis & Clark State Historic Site One Lewis & Clark Trl *Web:* www.campdubois.com	Hartford	IL	62048	618-251-5811	
Lincoln-Herndon Law Offices State Historic Site Sixth & Adams *Web:* illinois.gov/ihpa	Springfield	IL	62701	217-785-7289	
Sears Tower 233 S Wacker Dr *TF:* 877-759-3325 ■ *Web:* www.theskydeck.com	Chicago	IL	60606	312-875-9447	906-8193
Stephen Mack Home & Whitman Trading Post 2221 Freeport Rd *Web:* www.macktownlivinghistory.com	Rockton	IL	61072	815-624-4200	

Indiana

				Phone	Fax
Morris-Butler House Museum 1204 N Pk Ave *Web:* indianalandmarks.org	Indianapolis	IN	46202	317-636-5409	
President Benjamin Harrison Home 1230 N Delaware St *Web:* www.presidentbenjaminharrison.org	Indianapolis	IN	46202	317-631-1888	632-5488
Swinney Homestead 1424 W Jefferson Blvd *Web:* www.settlersinc.org	Fort Wayne	IN	46802	260-424-7212	

Iowa

				Phone	Fax
Brucemore 2160 Linden Dr SE *Web:* www.brucemore.org	Cedar Rapids	IA	52403	319-362-7375	362-9481
Mathias Ham House Historic Site 2241 Lincoln Ave *TF:* 800-226-3369 ■ *Web:* www.mississippirivermuseum.com/features_historicsites_ham.cfm	Dubuque	IA	52001	563-557-9545	583-1241
Seminole Valley Farm 1400 Seminole Vly Rd NE *Web:* seminolevalleyfarmmuseum.net	Cedar Rapids	IA	52411	319-378-9240	
Sherman Hill National Historic District 1620 Pleasant Ste 204 *Web:* www.historicshermanhill.com	Des Moines	IA	50314	515-284-5717	
Wallace House 756 16th St *Web:* www.wallace.org	Des Moines	IA	50314	515-243-7063	243-8927

Kentucky

				Phone	Fax
Ashland-The Henry Clay Estate 120 Sycamore Rd *TF:* 800-735-5251 ■ *Web:* www.henryclay.org	Lexington	KY	40502	859-266-8581	268-7266
Berry Hill Mansion 700 Louisville Rd *Web:* www.historicproperties.ky.gov	Frankfort	KY	40601	502-564-3000	564-6505
Brennan House Historic Home 631 S Fifth St *Web:* www.thebrennanhouse.org	Louisville	KY	40202	502-540-5145	540-5165
Hunt-Morgan House (BGT) 201 N Mill St *Web:* www.bluegrasstrust.org/huntmorgantours.html	Lexington	KY	40507	859-253-0362	259-9210
Liberty Hall Historic Site 202 Wilkinson St *Web:* www.libertyhall.org	Frankfort	KY	40601	502-227-2560	227-3348
Locust Grove Historic Home 561 Blankenbaker Ln *Web:* www.locustgrove.org	Louisville	KY	40207	502-897-9845	897-0103
Loudoun House 209 Castlewood Dr *Fax Area Code: 209 ■ *TF:* 866-945-7920 ■ *Web:* nps.gov	Lexington	KY	40505	859-254-7024	372-0739*
Mary Todd Lincoln House 578 W Main St *Web:* www.mtlhouse.org	Lexington	KY	40507	859-233-9999	252-2269
Old Louisville Historic Preservation District 1340 S Fourth St *Web:* www.oldlouisville.com	Louisville	KY	40208	502-635-5244	635-5245
Riverside Farnsley-Moremen Landing 7410 Moorman Rd *Web:* riverside-landing.org	Louisville	KY	40272	502-935-6809	935-6821

Louisiana

				Phone	Fax
Beauregard-Keyes House 1113 Chartres St *Web:* bkhouse.org	New Orleans	LA	70116	504-523-7257	523-7257
Destrehan Plantation 13034 River Rd *TF:* 877-453-2095 ■ *Web:* www.destrehanplantation.org	Destrehan	LA	70047	985-764-9315	725-1929
Elms Mansion & Gardens 3029 St Charles Ave *Web:* www.elmsmansion.com	New Orleans	LA	70115	504-895-9200	
Greenwood Plantation 6838 Highland Rd *TF:* 800-259-4475 ■ *Web:* www.greenwoodplantation.com	Saint Francisville	LA	70775	225-655-4475	655-3292
Houmas House Plantation & Gardens 40136 Hwy 942 *TF:* 800-979-3370 ■ *Web:* www.houmashouse.com	Darrow	LA	70725	225-473-7841	473-7891
Rosedown Plantation State Historic Site 12501 Hwy 10 *TF:* 888-376-1867 ■ *Web:* crt.state.la.us	Saint Francisville	LA	70775	225-635-3332	784-1382

Maine

				Phone	Fax
Isaac Farrar Mansion 17 Second St *Web:* bangory.org	Bangor	ME	04401	207-941-2808	941-2812
Portland Head Light 1000 Shore Rd *Web:* www.portlandheadlight.com	Cape Elizabeth	ME	04107	207-799-2661	799-2800
Victoria Mansion 109 Danforth St *Web:* www.victoriamansion.org	Portland	ME	04101	207-772-4841	772-6290
Wadsworth-Longfellow House 489 Congress St *Web:* www.mainehistory.org/house_overview.shtml	Portland	ME	04101	207-774-1822	775-4301

Maryland

				Phone	Fax
Barracks, The 43 Pinkney St *TF:* 800-603-4020 ■ *Web:* www.annapolis.org	Annapolis	MD	21401	410-267-7619	267-6189
Chase-Lloyd House 22 Maryland Ave	Annapolis	MD	21401	410-263-2723	
Historic Annapolis Foundation 18 Pinkney St *Web:* www.annapolis.org	Annapolis	MD	21401	410-267-7619	
Waterfront Warehouse Four Pinkney St *TF:* 800-603-4020 ■ *Web:* www.annapolis.org	Annapolis	MD	21401	410-267-7619	

Massachusetts

				Phone	Fax
Captain Bangs Hallett House 11 Strawberry Ln PO Box 11 *Web:* www.hsoy.org	Yarmouth Port	MA	02675	508-362-3021	
Freedom Trail 99 Chauncy St Ste 401 *Web:* www.thefreedomtrail.org	Boston	MA	02111	617-357-8300	357-8303
Grange Hall 1067 State Rd *Web:* www.mvpreservation.org	Vineyard Haven	MA	02568	508-627-4440	627-8088
Hadwen House 96 Main St *Web:* www.nha.org	Nantucket	MA	02554	508-228-1894	228-5618
Historic Mitchell House Four Vestal St *Web:* www.mmo.org	Nantucket	MA	02554	508-228-9198	228-1031
House of the Seven Gables 115 Derby St *Web:* www.7gables.org	Salem	MA	01970	978-744-0991	741-4350
Hoxie House 18 Water St	Sandwich	MA	02563	508-888-1173	
Salisbury Mansion 40 Highland St *Web:* www.worcesterhistory.org	Worcester	MA	01609	508-753-8278	753-9070
Wistariahurst Museum 238 Cabot St *Web:* www.wistariahurst.org	Holyoke	MA	01040	413-322-5660	534-2344

Michigan

Phone | Fax

Applewood the CS Mott Estate
1400 E Kearsley St .... Flint MI 48503 810-233-0170 233-7022
Web: www.ruthmottfoundation.org

Edsel & Eleanor Ford House
1100 Lk Shore Rd .... Grosse Pointe Shores MI 48236 313-884-4222 884-5977
Web: www.fordhouse.org

Heritage Hill Historic District
126 College Ave SE .... Grand Rapids MI 49503 616-459-8950 459-2409
Web: www.heritagehillweb.org

Meyer May House 450 Madison Ave SE .... Grand Rapids MI 49503 616-246-4821
Web: meyermayhouse.steelcase.com

Turner-Dodge House & Heritage Ctr 100 E N St .... Lansing MI 48906 517-483-4220 483-6081

Minnesota

Phone | Fax

Alexander Ramsey House (ARH)
265 S Exchange St .... Saint Paul MN 55102 651-296-8760 296-0100
Web: mnhs.org/visit

Comstock Historic House 506 Eigth St S .... Moorhead MN 56560 218-291-4211
Web: mnhs.org/visit

Glensheen Mansion 3300 London Rd .... Duluth MN 55804 218-726-8910 726-8911
TF: 888-454-4536 ■ *Web:* www.d.umn.edu

Historic Fort Snelling
200 Tower Ave Ft Snelling History Ctr .... Saint Paul MN 55111 612-726-1171
Web: mnhs.org/visit

History Ctr of Olmsted County
1195 W Cir Dr SW .... Rochester MN 55902 507-282-9447 289-5481
Web: olmstedhistory.com

James J Hill House 240 Summit Ave .... Saint Paul MN 55102 651-297-2555 297-5655
TF: 888-727-8386 ■ *Web:* www.mnhs.org

Plummer House 1091 SW Plummer Ln .... Rochester MN 55902 507-328-2525
Web: rochestermn.com

Missouri

Phone | Fax

1859 Jail Marshal's Home & Museum
217 N Main St .... Independence MO 64050 816-252-1892 252-1510
Web: www.jchs.org/jail/museum.html

Frank Lloyd Wright House in Ebbsworth Park
120 N Ballas Rd .... Kirkwood MO 63122 314-822-8359
Web: www.ebsworthpark.org

General Daniel Bissell House
10225 Bellefontaine Rd .... Saint Louis MO 63137 314-544-5714 638-5009
Web: stlouisco.com

Hanley House 7600 Westmoreland St .... Clayton MO 63105 314-862-1247 290-8517
Web: hanleyhouse.blogspot.com

Harris-Kearney House 4000 Baltimore St .... Kansas City MO 64111 816-561-1821
Web: www.westporthistorical.com

Hawken House, The 1155 S Rock Hill Rd .... Saint Louis MO 63119 314-968-1857 968-1857
Web: thehotelnexus.com

Historic Samuel Cupples House
3673 W Pine Mall .... Saint Louis MO 63108 314-977-3575
Web: www.slu.edu

Oakland House 7801 Genesta St .... Saint Louis MO 63123 314-352-5654
Web: www.afftonoaklandhouse.com

Vaile Mansion 1500 N Liberty St .... Independence MO 64050 816-325-7430
Web: www.vailemansion.org

Montana

Phone | Fax

Moss Mansion 914 Div St .... Billings MT 59101 406-256-5100 252-0091
Web: www.mossmansion.com

Nebraska

Phone | Fax

General Crook House Museum
5730 N 30th St Bldg 11B .... Omaha NE 68111 402-455-9990 453-9448
TF: 800-393-6198 ■ *Web:* www.omahahistory.org/museum.htm

Joslyn Castle 3902 Davenport St .... Omaha NE 68131 402-595-2199
Web: www.joslyncastle.com

Thomas P Kennard House PO Box 82554 .... Lincoln NE 68501 402-471-4764
Web: www.nebraskahistory.org

New Hampshire

Phone | Fax

Kimball-Jenkins Estate 266 N Main St .... Concord NH 03301 603-225-3932 225-9288
Web: www.kimballjenkins.com

New Jersey

Phone | Fax

Absecon Lighthouse
31 S Rhode Island Ave .... Atlantic City NJ 08401 609-449-1360 449-1919
Web: www.abseconlighthouse.org

Ballantine House 49 Washington St .... Newark NJ 07102 973-596-6550 642-0459
Web: www.newarkmuseum.org

Batsto Historic Village
4110 Nesco Rd Wharton State Forest .... Hammonton NJ 08037 609-561-0024 567-8116
Web: www.batstovillage.org

Dey Mansion 199 Totowa Rd .... Wayne NJ 07470 973-696-1776 696-1365

Durand Hedden House & Garden Assn
523 Ridgewood Rd .... Maplewood NJ 07040 973-763-7712
Web: durandhedden.org

Wayne Van Riper Hopper Museum 533 Berdan Ave .... Wayne NJ 07470 973-694-7192 694-9100
Web: waynetownship.com

William Trent House 15 Market St .... Trenton NJ 08611 609-989-3027
Web: www.williamtrenthouse.org

New Mexico

Phone | Fax

Coronado State Monument 485 Kuaua Rd .... Bernalillo NM 87004 505-867-5351 867-1733
Web: www.nmmonuments.org

Taos Pueblo PO Box 1846 .... Taos NM 87571 575-758-1028 758-4604*
**Fax Area Code:* 505 ■ *Web:* www.taospueblo.com

New York

Phone | Fax

Camillus Octagon House 5420 W Genesee St .... Camillus NY 13031 315-488-7800
Web: octagonhouseofcamillus.org

Frank Lloyd Wright's Martin House Complex
125 Jewett Pkwy .... Buffalo NY 14214 716-856-3858 856-4009
TF: 877-377-3858 ■ *Web:* www.darwinmartinhouse.org

Friend's of Pruyn House
207 Old Niskayuna Rd PO Box 1254 .... Latham NY 12110 518-783-1435 783-1437
Web: www.pruynhouse.org

George Eastman House & Gardens 900 E Ave .... Rochester NY 14607 585-271-3361 271-3970
Web: www.eastmanhouse.org

Glenview Mansion
511 Warburton Ave Hudson River Museum .... Yonkers NY 10701 914-963-4550
Web: www.hrm.org

Gracie Mansion 88th St & E End Ave .... New York NY 10128 212-570-4751
Web: www.nyc.gov/html/om/html/gracie.html

High Falls Museum 60 Browns Race .... Rochester NY 14614 585-325-2030
Web: www.cityofrochester.gov/highfallsmuseum/

Lyndhurst 635 S Broadway .... Tarrytown NY 10591 914-631-4481
Web: www.lyndhurst.org

Sleepy Hollow Cemetery 540 N Broadway .... Sleepy Hollow NY 10591 914-631-0081 631-0085
Web: www.sleepyhollowcemetery.org

Washington Irving's Sunnyside
W Sunnyside Ln .... Tarrytown NY 10591 914-591-8763 591-4436
Web: www.hudsonvalley.org

Washington's Heaquarters/Miller House
140 Virginia Rd .... White Plains NY 10603 914-949-1236
Web: westchestergov.com

North Carolina

Phone | Fax

Blandwood Mansion 447 W Washington St .... Greensboro NC 27401 336-272-5003 272-8049
Web: www.blandwood.org

Castle McCulloch 3925 Kivett Dr .... Jamestown NC 27282 336-887-5413 887-5429
Web: www.castlemcculloch.com

Haywood Hall House & Gardens 211 New Bern Pl .... Raleigh NC 27601 919-832-8357
Web: haywoodhall.org

Historic Latta Plantation
5225 Sample Rd .... Huntersville NC 28078 704-875-2312 875-1724
Web: www.lattaplantation.org

James K Polk Memorial State Historic Site
12031 Lancaster Hwy PO Box 475 .... Pineville NC 28134 704-889-7145 889-3057
Web: www.nchistoricsites.org

Mendenhall Plantation
603 W Main St PO Box 512 .... Jamestown NC 27282 336-454-3819
Web: www.mendenhallplantation.org

Mordecai Historic Park One Mimosa St .... Raleigh NC 27604 919-857-4364
Web: www.raleighnc.gov/mordecai

Reed Gold Mine State Historic Site
9621 Reed Mine Rd .... Midland NC 28107 704-721-4653 721-4657
TF: 877-628-6386 ■ *Web:* www.nchistoricsites.org

Tannenbaum Historic Park
2200 New Garden Rd .... Greensboro NC 27410 336-545-5315 545-5314
Web: www.greensboro-nc.gov

Thomas Wolfe Memorial 52 N Market St .... Asheville NC 28801 828-253-8304 252-8171
Web: www.wolfememorial.com

Vance Birthplace State Historic Site
911 Reems Creek Rd .... Weaverville NC 28787 828-645-6706 645-0936
TF: 800-767-1560 ■ *Web:* www.nchistoricsites.org/vance/vance.htm

Ohio

Phone | Fax

Fort Meigs State Memorial
29100 W River Rd .... Perrysburg OH 43551 419-874-4121 874-9446
TF: 800-283-8916 ■ *Web:* www.fortmeigs.org

German Village 588 S Third St .... Columbus OH 43215 614-221-8888 222-4747
Web: germanvillage.com

Loghurst Western Reserve
3967 BoaRdman-Canfield Rd .... Canfield OH 44406 330-533-4330

Paul Laurence Dunbar House
219 N Paul Laurence Dunbar St .... Dayton OH 45402 937-224-7061 224-4256
TF: 800-860-0148 ■ *Web:* ohiohistory.org

Perkins Stone Mansion 550 Copley Rd .... Akron OH 44320 330-535-1120 535-0250
Web: summithistory.org

SunWatch Indian Village/Archaeological Park
2301 W River Rd .... Dayton OH 45417 937-268-8199
Web: www.sunwatch.org

Oregon

	City	State	Zip	Phone	Fax
Brunk House 5705 Salem-Dallas Hwy NW	Salem	OR	97304	503-371-8586	
Deepwood Estate 1116 Mission St SE *Web:* oregonlink.com/sorry_notfound.html	Salem	OR	97302	503-363-1825	363-3586
Mission Mill Museum 1313 Mill St SE *TF:* 800-782-6724 ■ *Web:* willametteheritage.org	Salem	OR	97301	503-585-7012	588-9902
Shelton-McMurphey-Johnson House 303 Willamette St *Web:* www.smjhouse.org	Eugene	OR	97401	541-484-0808	984-1413

Pennsylvania

	City	State	Zip	Phone	Fax
Besty Ross House 239 Arch St *Web:* historicphiladelphia.org	Philadelphia	PA	19106	215-686-1252	686-1256
Carpenters' Hall 320 Chestnut St *Web:* www.ushistory.org/carpentershall	Philadelphia	PA	19106	215-925-0167	925-3880
Cashier's House 417 State St *Web:* www.eriecountyhistory.org	Erie	PA	16501	814-454-1813	454-6890
Declaration House 599 S 7th St *Web:* www.nps.gov	Philadelphia	PA	19106	215-965-7676	
Eastern State Penitentiary Historic Site 22nd St & Fairmount Ave *Web:* www.easternstate.org	Philadelphia	PA	19130	215-236-3300	236-5289
Fallingwater 1491 Mill Run Rd *Web:* waterlandlife.org/	Mill Run	PA	15464	724-329-8501	329-0553
Fort Hunter Mansion & Park 5300 N Front St *Web:* www.forthunter.org	Harrisburg	PA	17110	717-599-5751	599-5838
Glen Foerd on the Delaware 5001 Grant Ave *Web:* www.glenfoerd.org	Philadelphia	PA	19114	215-632-5330	632-2312
Hans Herr House & Museum 1849 Hans Herr Dr *Web:* www.hansherr.org	Willow Street	PA	17584	717-464-4438	
Hartwood Mansion 200 Hartwood Acres *Web:* alleghenycounty.us	Pittsburgh	PA	15238	412-767-9200	767-0171
Historic Rock Ford Plantation 881 Rockford Rd *TF:* 800-732-0999 ■ *Web:* www.rockfordplantation.org	Lancaster	PA	17602	717-392-7223	392-7283
Independence Hall & Congress Hall Chestnut St-between Fifth & Sixth Sts *Web:* www.nps.gov/inde	Philadelphia	PA	19106	215-597-8787	597-8976
John Chadds House 1736 N Creek Rd PO Box 27 *Web:* www.chaddsfordhistory.org	Chadds Ford	PA	19317	610-388-7376	388-7480
John Harris-Simon Cameron Mansion, The 219 S Front St *Web:* www.dauphincountyhistory.org	Harrisburg	PA	17104	717-233-3462	233-6059
Lancaster County's Historical Society & President James Buchanan's Wheatland 230 N President Ave *Web:* www.lancasterhistory.org	Lancaster	PA	17603	717-392-4633	293-2739
Physick House 321 S Fourth St *Web:* www.philalandmarks.org	Philadelphia	PA	19106	215-925-2251	925-7909
Powel House 244 S Third St *TF:* 877-426-8056 ■ *Web:* www.philalandmarks.org	Philadelphia	PA	19106	215-627-0364	925-7909

Quebec

	City	State	Zip	Phone	Fax
Artillery Park Heritage Site Two D'Auteuil St PO Box 10 Stn B *TF:* 888-773-8888 ■ *Web:* www.pc.gc.ca	Quebec	QC	G1K7A1	418-648-7016	648-2506

Rhode Island

	City	State	Zip	Phone	Fax
Belcourt Castle 657 Bellevue Ave *Web:* www.belcourtcastle.com	Newport	RI	02840	401-846-0669	846-5345
Chateau-Sur-Mer 474 Bellevue Ave *Web:* www.newportmansions.org	Newport	RI	02840	401-847-1000	847-1361
Edward King House 35 King St *Web:* www.edwardkinghouse.org	Newport	RI	02840	401-846-7426	846-8310
Hunter House 54 Washington St *Web:* www.newportmansions.org	Newport	RI	02840	401-847-1000	847-1361
John Brown House Museum 52 Power St *Web:* www.rihs.org	Providence	RI	02906	401-273-7507	751-2307
Marble House 596 Bellevue Ave *Web:* www.newportmansions.org	Newport	RI	02840	401-847-1000	847-1361
Rose Island Lighthouse Foundation 365 Thames St Second Fl PO Box 1419 *Web:* www.roseislandlighthouse.org	Newport	RI	02840	401-847-4242	847-7262
Samuel Whitehorne House 416 Thames St *Web:* www.newportrestoration.org	Newport	RI	02840	401-849-7300	

South Carolina

	City	State	Zip	Phone	Fax
Aiken-Rhett House 48 Elizabeth St *Web:* www.historiccharleston.org	Charleston	SC	29401	843-723-1159	
Boone Hall Plantation & Gardens 1235 Long Pt Rd *Web:* boonehallplantation.com	Mount Pleasant	SC	29464	843-884-4371	884-0475
Fort Hill The John C Calhoun House Clemson University Ft Hill St *Web:* clemson.edu	Clemson	SC	29634	864-656-2475	656-1026
Gassaway Mansion 106 Dupont Dr *Web:* www.gassawaymansion.com	Greenville	SC	29607	864-271-0188	242-9935
Hampton-Preston Mansion & Garden 1615 Blanding St *Web:* www.historiccolumbia.org	Columbia	SC	29201	803-252-1770	929-7695
Heyward-Washington House 87 Church St *Web:* charlestonmuseum.org	Charleston	SC	29403	843-722-0354	
Kilgore-Lewis House, The 560 N Academy St PO Box 681 *Web:* www.kilgore-lewis.org	Greenville	SC	29602	864-232-3020	
Mann Simons Cottage 1403 Richland St *Web:* www.historiccolumbia.org	Columbia	SC	29201	803-252-7742	929-7695
Nathaniel Russell House 51 Meeting St *Web:* www.historiccharleston.org	Charleston	SC	29401	843-724-8481	805-6732
Old Exchange & Provost Dungeon 122 E Bay St *TF:* 888-763-0448 ■ *Web:* oldexchange.org	Charleston	SC	29401	843-727-2165	
Robert Mills House & Gardens 1616 Blanding St *Web:* www.historiccolumbia.org	Columbia	SC	29201	803-252-7742	929-7695
Seibels House & Garden 1616 Blanding St *Web:* historiccolumbia.org/site/rentals/seibels-house-garden	Columbia	SC	29201	803-252-1770	929-7695
Woodrow Wilson Family Home 1705 Hampton St *Web:* www.historiccolumbia.org	Columbia	SC	29201	803-252-7742	

South Dakota

	City	State	Zip	Phone	Fax
Corn Palace 604 N Main St *TF:* 800-289-7469 ■ *Web:* www.cornpalace.org	Mitchell	SD	57301	605-996-5031	996-8273

Tennessee

	City	State	Zip	Phone	Fax
Belmont Mansion 1900 Belmont Blvd *Web:* www.belmontmansion.com	Nashville	TN	37212	615-460-5459	460-5688
Blount Mansion 200 W Hill Ave *Web:* www.blountmansion.org	Knoxville	TN	37901	865-525-2375	546-5315
Carnton Plantation 1345 Carnton Ln *Web:* www.carnton.org	Franklin	TN	37064	615-794-0903	794-6563
Carter House 1140 Columbia Ave *Web:* battleoffranklintrust.org	Franklin	TN	37064	615-791-1861	
Confederate Memorial Hall 3148 Kingston Pk *Web:* www.knoxvillecmh.org	Knoxville	TN	37919	865-522-2371	
Davies Manor House 9336 Davies Plantation Rd *Web:* www.daviesmanorplantation.org	Memphis	TN	38133	901-386-0715	388-4677
Ramsey House 2614 Thorngrove Pk *Web:* www.ramseyhouse.org	Knoxville	TN	37914	865-546-0745	546-1851
Tipton-Haynes State Historic Site 2620 S Roan St *Web:* www.tipton-haynes.org	Johnson City	TN	37601	423-926-3631	
Travellers Rest Plantation & Museum 636 Farrell Pkwy *Web:* www.travellersrestplantation.org	Nashville	TN	37220	615-832-8197	832-8169
Woodruff-Fontaine House 680 Adams Ave *Web:* www.woodruff-fontaine.com	Memphis	TN	38105	901-526-1469	755-6075

Texas

	City	State	Zip	Phone	Fax
Fulton Mansion 317 N Fulton Beach Rd *TF:* 800-792-1112 ■ *Web:* www.tpwd.state.tx.us	Rockport	TX	78382	361-729-0386	
Guenther House 205 E Guenther St *TF:* 800-235-8186 ■ *Web:* www.guentherhouse.com	San Antonio	TX	78204	210-227-1061	351-6372
King William Historic District 1032 S Alamo St *Web:* kwfair.org	San Antonio	TX	78210	210-271-3247	227-8030
Neill-Cochran House Museum 2310 San Gabriel St *Web:* www.nchmuseum.org	Austin	TX	78705	512-478-2335	
Sidbury House 1609 N Chaparral St	Corpus Christi	TX	78401	361-883-9352	

Utah

	City	State	Zip	Phone	Fax
This is the Place Heritage Park 2601 E Sunnyside Ave *Web:* www.thisistheplace.org	Salt Lake City	UT	84108	801-582-1847	583-1869

Vermont

	City	State	Zip	Phone	Fax
Ethan Allen Homestead One Ethan Allen Homestead *Web:* www.ethanallenhomestead.org	Burlington	VT	05408	802-865-4556	

Virginia

	City	State	Zip	Phone	Fax
Adam Thoroughgood House 1636 Parish Rd	Virginia Beach	VA	23455	757-460-7588	460-7644
Athenaeum, The 201 Prince St *Web:* www.nvfaa.org	Alexandria	VA	22314	703-548-0035	
Francis Land House 3131 Virginia Beach Blvd *Web:* museumsvb.org	Virginia Beach	VA	23452	757-385-5100	
Frank Lloyd Wright's Pope-Leighey House 9000 Richmond Hwy PO Box 15097 *Web:* www.popeleighey1940.org	Alexandria	VA	22309	703-780-4000	780-8509

				Phone	Fax
George Washington's Mount Vernon Estate & Gardens George Washington Memorial Pkwy PO Box 110	Mount Vernon	VA	22121	703-780-2000	
Web: www.mountvernon.org					
James Madison's Montpelier 11407 Constitution Hwy	Montpelier Station	VA	22957	540-672-2728	672-0411
Web: www.montpelier.org					
John Marshall House, The 818 E Marshall St	Richmond	VA	23219	804-648-7998	648-5880
Web: preservationvirginia.org					
Lynnhaven House 2040 Potters Rd	Virginia Beach	VA	23454	757-491-3490	
Web: www.virginiabeachhistory.org					
Monticello 931 Thomas Jefferson Pkwy PO Box 316	Charlottesville	VA	22902	434-984-9822	977-7757
TF: 800-243-1743 ■ *Web:* www.monticello.org					
Old Cape Henry Lighthouse 583 Atlantic Ave	Fort Story	VA	23459	757-422-9421	
Pope-Leighey House 9000 Richmond Hwy	Alexandria	VA	22309	703-780-4000	780-8509
Web: www.popeleighey1940.org					
Shirley Plantation 501 Shirley Plantation Rd	Charles City	VA	23030	804-829-5121	829-6322
TF: 800-232-1613 ■ *Web:* www.shirleyplantation.com					
Sully Historic Site 3650 Historic Sully Way	Chantilly	VA	20151	703-437-1794	787-3314
Web: www.fairfaxcounty.gov/parks/sully					
Virginia House 4301 Sulgrave Rd	Richmond	VA	23221	804-353-4251	355-2399
Web: www.vahistorical.org					
Willoughby-Baylor House 601 E Freemason St	Norfolk	VA	23510	757-333-1087	333-1089
Web: www.chrysler.org/about-the-museum/historic-houses/willoughby-baylor-house					

Washington

				Phone	Fax
Covington House 4201 Main St	Vancouver	WA	98663	360-695-6750	
Web: www.co.clark.wa.us					

West Virginia

				Phone	Fax
Pearl S Buck Birthplace US 219 PO Box 126	Hillsboro	WV	24946	304-653-4430	
Web: www.pearlsbuckbirthplace.com					
TH Eckhart House 810 Main St	Wheeling	WV	26003	304-232-5439	
Web: www.eckharthouse.com					

Wisconsin

				Phone	Fax
Pabst Mansion 2000 W Wisconsin Ave	Milwaukee	WI	53233	414-931-0808	931-1005
Web: www.pabstmansion.com					
Taliesin 5607 County Hwy C	Spring Green	WI	53588	608-588-7090	588-7514
Web: www.taliesinpreservation.org					

50-4 Monuments, Memorials, Landmarks

				Phone	Fax
African-American Civil War Memorial & Museum 1200 U St NW	Washington	DC	20001	202-667-2667	667-6771
Web: www.afroamcivilwar.org					
Arkansas Post National Memorial 1741 Old Post Rd	Gillett	AR	72055	870-548-2207	548-2431
Web: www.nps.gov					
Buffalo & Erie County Naval & Military Park One Naval Pk Cove	Buffalo	NY	14202	716-847-1773	847-6405
Web: www.buffalonavalpark.org					
Bunker Hill Monument Monument Sq	Charlestown	MA	02129	617-242-5641	242-6006
Web: www.nps.gov					
Chamizal National Memorial 800 S San Marcial St	El Paso	TX	79905	915-532-7273	532-7240
TF: 877-642-4743 ■ *Web:* www.nps.gov					
Crazy Horse Memorial Ave of the Chiefs	Crazy Horse	SD	57730	605-673-4681	673-2185
Web: www.crazyhorsememorial.org					
De Soto National Memorial 8300 Desoto Memorial Hwy	Bradenton	FL	34209	941-792-0458	792-5094
TF: 888-831-7526 ■ *Web:* www.nps.gov					
Empire State Bldg 350 Fifth Ave Ste 100	New York	NY	10118	212-736-3100	
TF: 877-692-8439 ■ *Web:* www.esbnyc.com					
First Church of Christ in New Haven, The *Center Church on-the-Green* 311 Temple St	New Haven	CT	06511	203-787-0121	787-2187
Web: www.newhavencenterchurch.org					
Flight 93 National Memorial *National Park Service* PO Box 911	Shanksville	PA	15560	814-893-6322	443-2180
Web: www.nps.gov/flni/index.htm					
Fort Caroline National Memorial 12713 Ft Caroline Rd	Jacksonville	FL	32225	904-641-7155	641-3798
Web: www.nps.gov/foca					
Franklin Delano Roosevelt Memorial 900 Ohio Dr SW	Washington	DC	20024	202-426-6841	
Web: www.nps.gov/fdrm					
Gateway Arch 11 N Fourth St	Saint Louis	MO	63102	314-655-1700	655-1641
Web: www.gatewayarch.com					
General Grant National Memorial Riverside Dr & W 122nd St	New York	NY	10027	212-666-1640	932-9631
Web: www.nps.gov/gegr					
George Washington Masonic National Memorial 101 Callahan Dr	Alexandria	VA	22301	703-683-2007	519-9270
TF: 800-435-7352 ■ *Web:* www.gwmemorial.org					
Golden Gate Bridge Golden Gate Bridge Toll Plz Presidio Stn PO Box 9000	San Francisco	CA	94129	415-921-5858	956-1663
TF: 877-229-8655 ■ *Web:* www.goldengate.org					
Holocaust Memorial of the Greater Miami Jewish Federation 1933-1945 Meridian Ave	Miami Beach	FL	33139	305-538-1663	538-2423
Web: www.holocaustmmb.org					
Idaho Human Rights Education Ctr 777 S Eigth St	Boise	ID	83702	208-345-0304	433-1221
Web: idaho-humanrights.org					
Illinois Vietnam Veterans Memorial Oak Ridge Cemetery	Springfield	IL	62702	217-782-2717	524-3738
Web: www.illinois.gov					
Jefferson Memorial 13 E Basin Dr SW	Washington	DC	20242	202-426-6841	673-7747*
**Fax Area Code:* 912 ■ *Web:* www.nps.gov/thje					
Kansas City Kansas Convention & Visitors Bureau 755 Minnesota Ave	Kansas City	KS	66101	913-321-5800	
Web: visitkansascityks.com					
Korean War Veterans Memorial c/o National Capital Parks - Central 900 Ohio Dr SW	Washington	DC	20004	202-426-6841	
Web: www.nps.gov/kowa					
Liberty Bell Ctr Sixth & Market Sts	Philadelphia	PA	19106	215-965-2305	861-4950
Web: www.nps.gov					
Lincoln Boyhood National Memorial 2916 E S St PO Box 1816	Lincoln City	IN	47552	812-937-4541	937-9929
Web: www.nps.gov/libo					
Lincoln Memorial Shrine 125 W Vine St	Redlands	CA	92373	909-798-7632	798-7566
Web: www.lincolnshrine.org					
Lincoln Tomb Oak Ridge Cemetery 1500 Monument Ave	Springfield	IL	62702	217-782-2717	524-3738
Web: illinois.gov/ihpa					
Littleton Coin Company LLC 1309 Mt Eustis Rd	Littleton	NH	03561	603-444-5386	444-0121
TF: 800-645-3122 ■ *Web:* www.littletoncoin.com					
Lyndon Baines Johnson Memorial Grove on the Potomac Turkey Run Pk George Washington Memorial Pkwy	McLean	VA	22101	703-289-2500	289-2598
Web: www.nps.gov/lyba					
Mason-Dixon Historical Park 79 Buckeye Rd	Core	WV	26541	304-879-4101	
Mormon Battalion Visitors Ctr 2510 Juan St	San Diego	CA	92110	619-298-3317	
Web: lds.org					
Mormon Trail Ctr at Historic Winter Quarter 3215 State St	Omaha	NE	68112	402-453-9372	453-1538
Web: lds.org					
New Mexico Veterans Memorial 1100 Louisiana Blvd SE	Albuquerque	NM	87108	505-256-2042	
Web: nmvetsmemorial.org					
Perry's Victory & International Peace Memorial 93 Delaware Ave PO Box 549	Put-in-Bay	OH	43456	419-285-2184	285-2516
Web: www.nps.gov/pevi					
Philadelphia Vietnam Veterans Memorial 4720 Mercer St	Philadelphia	PA	19137	215-535-0643	
Web: pvvms646.org					
Pilgrim Monument & Provincetown Museum One High Pole Hill Rd	Provincetown	MA	02657	508-487-1310	487-4702
Web: www.pilgrim-monument.org					
Potomac Assn, The 540 Water St Jack London Sq	Oakland	CA	94607	510-627-1215	839-4729
Web: www.usspotomac.org					
Roger Williams National Memorial 282 N Main St	Providence	RI	02903	401-521-7266	521-7239
Web: www.nps.gov/rowi					
Rosedale Memorial Arch 1403 Southwest Blvd	Kansas City	KS	66103	913-677-5097	
Space Needle LLC 203 Sixth Ave N	Seattle	WA	98109	206-905-2200	905-2107
TF: 800-937-9582 ■ *Web:* www.spaceneedle.com					
Statue of Liberty National Monument & Ellis Island Liberty Island	New York	NY	10004	212-363-3200	
Web: www.nps.gov/stli					
Texas State Cemetery 909 Navasota St	Austin	TX	78702	512-463-0605	463-8811
TF: 877-673-6839 ■ *Web:* www.cemetery.state.tx.us					
Theodore Roosevelt Island Park c/o Turkey Run Pk George Washington Memorial Pkwy	McLean	VA	22101	703-289-2500	289-2598
Web: www.nps.gov/this					
Trenton Battle Monument 348 N Warren St	Trenton	NJ	08625	609-737-0623	
Web: www.njparksandforests.org					
US Navy Memorial & Naval Heritage Ctr 701 Pennsylvania Ave NW Ste 123	Washington	DC	20004	202-737-2300	
Web: www.navylog.org					
USS Alabama Battleship Memorial Park 2703 Battleship Pkwy PO Box 65	Mobile	AL	36602	251-433-2703	433-2777
TF: 888-414-4448 ■ *Web:* www.ussalabama.com					
USS Arizona Memorial One Arizona Memorial Pl	Honolulu	HI	96818	808-422-0561	483-8608
Web: www.nps.gov/usar					
USS Kidd Veterans Memorial & Museum 305 S River Rd	Baton Rouge	LA	70802	225-342-1942	342-2039
TF: 800-638-0594 ■ *Web:* www.usskidd.com					
USS Missouri Memorial Assn Inc 63 Cowpens St	Honolulu	HI	96818	808-455-1600	455-1598
TF: 877-644-4896 ■ *Web:* ussmissouri.org/					
Vietnam Veterans of America 3027 Walnut St	Kansas City	MO	64108	816-561-8387	
Web: vva.org					
Vietnam Women's Memorial Foundation Inc 1735 Connecticut Ave NW Third Fl	Washington	DC	20009	866-822-8963	
TF: 866-822-8963 ■ *Web:* www.vietnamwomensmemorial.org					

50-5 Nature Centers, Parks, Other Natural Areas

				Phone	Fax
Anita Purves Nature Ctr 1505 N Broadway	Urbana	IL	61801	217-384-4062	384-1052
Web: www.urbanaparks.org					
Anne Kolb Nature Ctr 751 Sheridan St	Hollywood	FL	33019	954-357-5161	926-2491
Web: www.floridanaturepictures.com/dadebrow/annkolb/ann.htm					

	City	State	Zip	Phone	Fax
Ansonia Nature & Recreation Ctr 10 Deerfield Rd *Web:* www.ansonianaturecenter.org	Ansonia	CT	06401	203-736-1053	
Aurora Reservoir 5800 S Powhaton Rd *Web:* www.auroragov.org	Aurora	CO	80016	303-690-1286	
Balboa Park 1549 El Prado Ste 1 *Web:* www.balboapark.org	San Diego	CA	92101	619-239-0512	525-2254
Bear Creek Nature Ctr 245 Bear Creek Rd *Web:* adm.elpasoco.com/parks	Colorado Springs	CO	80906	719-520-6387	636-8968
Beaver Lake Nature Ctr 8477 E Mud Lk Rd *Web:* www.onondagacountyparks.com	Baldwinsville	NY	13027	315-638-2519	638-7488
Biscayne Nature Ctr 6767 Crandon Blvd *Web:* www.biscaynenaturecenter.org	Key Biscayne	FL	33149	305-361-6767	365-8434
Black Hills Caverns 2600 Cavern Rd *TF:* 800-837-9358 ■ *Web:* www.blackhillscaverns.com	Rapid City	SD	57702	605-343-0542	
Blandford Nature Ctr 1715 Hillburn Ave NW *Web:* blandfordnaturecenter.org	Grand Rapids	MI	49504	616-735-6240	735-6255
Boulder Reservoir 5100 N 51st St *Web:* www.bouldercolorado.gov	Boulder	CO	80301	303-441-3461	441-1807
Boyden Caverns 74101 E Kings Canyon Rd *TF:* 866-762-2837 ■ *Web:* www.caverntours.com	Kings Canyon National Park	CA	93633	209-736-2708	736-0330
Butterfly House 11455 Obee Rd *Web:* butterfly-house.com	Whitehouse	OH	43571	419-877-2733	
Butterfly House - Faust Park, The 15193 Olive Blvd *TF:* 800-642-8842 ■ *Web:* www.missouribotanicalgarden.org	Chesterfield	MO	63017	636-530-0076	530-1516
Butterfly World 3600 W Sample Rd Tradewinds Pk S *Web:* www.butterflyworld.com	Coconut Creek	FL	33073	954-977-4400	977-4501
Capen Hill Nature Sanctuary 56 Capen Rd PO Box 218 *Web:* www.capenhill.org	Charlton City	MA	01508	508-248-5516	248-5516
Carson Hot Springs 1500 Hot Springs Rd *TF:* 888-917-3711 ■ *Web:* www.carsonhotspringsresort.com	Carson City	NV	89706	775-885-8844	
Cascade Caverns Park 226 Cascade Caverns Rd *Web:* www.cascadecaverns.com	Boerne	TX	78006	830-755-8080	755-2422
Cave of the Mounds 2975 CAve of the Mounds Rd PO Box 148 *Web:* www.caveofthemounds.com	Blue Mounds	WI	53517	608-437-3038	437-4181
Cave of the Winds 100 Cave of the Winds Rd PO Box 826 *Web:* www.caveofthewinds.com	Manitou Springs	CO	80829	719-685-5444	685-1712
Centennial Olympic Park 265 Pk Ave W NW *Web:* www.centennialpark.com	Atlanta	GA	30313	404-223-4412	223-4499
Central Park 830 Fifth Ave *Web:* www.centralparknyc.org	New York	NY	10065	212-360-1461	360-1329
Chattahoochee Nature Ctr 9135 Willeo Rd *Web:* chattnaturecenter.org/	Roswell	GA	30075	770-992-2055	552-0926
Connecticut Audubon Society Nature Ctr 2325 Burr St *Web:* www.ctaudubon.org	Fairfield	CT	06824	203-259-6305	254-7365
Cypress Gardens 3030 Cypress Gardens Rd *Web:* www.cypressgardens.info	Moncks Corner	SC	29461	843-553-0515	569-0644
Darien Nature Ctr Inc 120 Brookside Rd PO Box 1603 *Web:* www.dariennaturecenter.org	Darien	CT	06820	203-655-7459	655-3185
DeGraaf Nature Ctr 600 Graafschap Rd *TF:* 888-535-5792 ■ *Web:* cityofholland.com	Holland	MI	49423	616-355-1057	355-1069
Devil's Den Preserve 33 Pent Rd *Web:* www.nature.org	Weston	CT	06883	203-226-4991	226-4807
Dodge Nature Ctr 365 Marie Ave W *Web:* www.dodgenaturecenter.org	West Saint Paul	MN	55118	651-455-4531	455-2575
Domaine Maizerets 2000 Montmorency Blvd *Web:* domainemaizerets.com	Quebec	QC	G1J5E7	418-641-6335	660-6295
Eagle River Nature Ctr 32750 Eagle River Rd *Web:* ernc.org	Eagle River	AK	99577	907-694-2108	694-2119
Earthplace 10 Woodside Ln PO Box 165 *Web:* www.earthplace.org	Westport	CT	06881	203-227-7253	227-8909
El Dorado Nature Ctr 7550 E Spring St *TF:* 800-662-8887 ■ *Web:* longbeach.gov	Long Beach	CA	90815	562-570-1745	570-8530
Everglades Holiday Park 21940 Griffin Rd *Web:* www.evergladesholidaypark.com	Fort Lauderdale	FL	33332	954-434-8111	434-4252
Falls Park on the Reedy 601 S Main St *Web:* www.fallspark.com	Greenville	SC	29601	864-467-4350	
Fern Forest Nature Ctr 201 Lyons Rd S *Web:* www.broward.org/parks	Coconut Creek	FL	33063	954-970-0150	
Forest Park Nature Ctr 5809 Forest Pk Dr *Web:* peoriaparks.org	Peoria Heights	IL	61616	309-686-3360	
Genesee County Parks & Recreation 5045 Stanley Rd *TF:* 800-648-7275 ■ *Web:* 'www.geneseecountyparks.org	Flint	MI	48506	810-736-7100	736-7220
Golden Gate Park 970 47th Ave *Web:* goldengateparkgolf.com	San Francisco	CA	94121	415-751-8987	
Great Plains Nature Ctr 6232 E 29th St N *TF:* 800-222-1222 ■ *Web:* www.gpnc.org	Wichita	KS	67220	316-683-5499	688-9555
Gulf Branch Nature Ctr & Park Grounds 3608 N Military Rd *Web:* arlingtonva.us	Arlington	VA	22207	703-228-3403	228-4401
Gumbo Limbo Nature Ctr 1801 N Ocean Blvd *Web:* www.gumbolimbo.org	Boca Raton	FL	33432	561-544-8605	338-1483
Hanauma Bay Nature Preserve 100 Hanauma Bay Rd *TF:* 800-690-6200 ■ *Web:* www.honolulu.gov	Honolulu	HI	96825	808-396-4229	395-0468
Hemlock Bluffs Nature Preserve 2616 Kildaire Farm Rd *Web:* townofcary.org	Cary	NC	27518	919-387-5980	
Houston Arboretum & Nature Ctr 4501 Woodway Dr *TF:* 866-510-7219 ■ *Web:* www.houstonarboretum.org	Houston	TX	77024	713-681-8433	681-1191
Ijams Nature Ctr 2915 Island Home Ave *Web:* www.ijams.org	Knoxville	TN	37920	865-577-4717	577-1683
Indian Creek Nature Ctr 6665 Otis Rd SE *Web:* www.indiancreeknaturecenter.org	Cedar Rapids	IA	52403	319-362-0664	362-2876
Jefferson Barracks County Park 345 N Dr *TF:* 800-735-2966	Saint Louis	MO	63125	314-544-5714	615-4567
Katharine Ordway Preserve 4245 N Fairfax Dr Ste 100 *TF:* 800-628-6860 ■ *Web:* www.nature.org	Arlington	VA	22203	203-226-4991	226-4807
Lava Hot Springs State Foundation 430 E Main St PO Box 669 *TF:* 800-423-8597 ■ *Web:* www.lavahotsprings.com	Lava Hot Springs	ID	83246	208-776-5221	776-5273
Lewis & Clark National Historic Trail Interpretive Ctr 4201 Giant Springs Rd *Web:* www.fs.usda.gov/lcnf	Great Falls	MT	59405	406-727-8733	453-6157
Lincoln Memorial Garden & Nature Ctr 2301 E Lake Dr *Web:* www.lincolnmemorialgarden.org	Springfield	IL	62712	217-529-1111	529-0134
Linville Caverns Inc 19929 US 221 N **Fax Area Code:* 828 ■ *TF:* 800-419-0540 ■ *Web:* www.linvillecaverns.com	Marion	NC	28752	800-419-0540	756-4171*
Long Branch Nature Ctr 625 S Carlin Springs Rd *Web:* arlingtonva.us	Arlington	VA	22204	703-228-6535	
Lost River Caverns 726 Durham St PO Box M *TF:* 888-529-1907 ■ *Web:* www.lostcave.com	Hellertown	PA	18055	610-838-8767	838-2961
Martin Park Nature Ctr 5000 W Memorial Rd *Web:* okc.gov/parks/martin%5fpark/	Oklahoma City	OK	73142	405-755-0676	749-3072
Mississippi Petrified Forest 124 Forest Pk Rd *Web:* www.mspetrifiedforest.com	Flora	MS	39071	601-879-8189	879-8165
Morikami Museum & Japanese Gardens 4000 Morikami Pk Rd *Web:* www.morikami.org	Delray Beach	FL	33446	561-495-0233	499-2557
Morrison-Knudsen Nature Ctr 600 S Walnut St	Boise	ID	83712	208-334-2225	287-2905
Mount Saint Helens National Volcanic Monument 42218 NE Yale Bridge Rd *Web:* www.fs.fed.us	Amboy	WA	98601	360-449-7800	449-7801
Natural Bridge Caverns 26495 Natural Bridge Caverns Rd *Web:* www.naturalbridgecaverns.com	Natural Bridge Caverns	TX	78266	210-651-6101	651-6144
New Canaan Nature Ctr 144 Oenoke Ridge *Web:* www.newcanaannature.org	New Canaan	CT	06840	203-966-9577	966-6536
New York State Office of Parks Recreation & Historic Preservation Empire State Plaza Agency Bldg 1 **Fax Area Code:* 518 ■ *TF:* 800-456-2267 ■ *Web:* nysparks.com	Albany	NY	12238	716-354-9101	486-1899*
Nisqually Reach Nature Ctr (NRNC) 4949 D'Milluhr Rd NE *Web:* www.nisquallyestuary.org	Olympia	WA	98516	360-459-0387	
Ogden Nature Ctr 966 W 12th St *Web:* www.ogdennaturecenter.org	Ogden	UT	84404	801-621-7595	621-1867
Olentangy Indian Caverns 1779 Home Rd *Web:* www.olentangyindiancaverns.com	Delaware	OH	43015	740-548-7917	
Oxbow Meadows Environmental Learning Ctr 3535 S Lumpkin Rd *TF:* 866-264-2035 ■ *Web:* oxbow.columbusstate.edu	Columbus	GA	31903	706-507-8550	507-8549
Parkersville Landing Historical Park 24 S A St *Web:* portcw.com	Washougal	WA	98671	360-835-2196	835-2197
Pike National Forest 601 S Weber St *Web:* www.fs.fed.us	Colorado Springs	CO	80903	719-636-1602	477-4233
Pine Jog Environmental Education Ctr 6301 Summit Blvd *Web:* www.pinejog.fau.edu	West Palm Beach	FL	33415	561-686-6600	687-4968
Plains Conservation Ctr 21901 E Hampden Ave *Web:* www.plainscenter.org	Aurora	CO	80013	303-693-3621	693-3379
Powder Valley Conservation Nature Ctr 11715 Cragwold Rd *Web:* mdc.mo.gov	Saint Louis	MO	63122	314-301-1500	301-1501
Prairie Wetlands Learning Ctr 602 State Hwy 210 E *Web:* www.fws.gov	Fergus Falls	MN	56537	218-998-4480	
Quarry Hill Nature Ctr 701 Silver Creek Rd NE *Web:* www.qhnc.org	Rochester	MN	55906	507-328-3950	287-1345
Raccoon Mountain Caverns 319 W Hills Dr *TF:* 800-823-2267 ■ *Web:* www.raccoonmountain.com	Chattanooga	TN	37419	423-821-9403	825-1289
Randall Davey Audubon Ctr 1800 Upper Canyon Rd PO Box 9314 *Web:* www.audubon.org/chapter/nm/nm/rdac	Santa Fe	NM	87504	505-983-4609	983-2355
Red Rock Canyon National Conservation Area 4701 N Torrey Pines Dr *Web:* www.blm.gov	Las Vegas	NV	89130	702-515-5350	363-6779
Riveredge Nature Ctr 4458 W Hawthorne Dr PO Box 26 *TF:* 800-287-8098 ■ *Web:* www.riveredgenaturecenter.org	Newburg	WI	53060	262-375-2715	375-2714
Rock City Gardens 1400 Patten Rd *TF:* 800-854-0675 ■ *Web:* www.seerockcity.com	Lookout Mountain	GA	30750	706-820-2531	820-2533
Ruby Falls 1720 S Scenic Hwy *TF:* 800-755-7105 ■ *Web:* www.rubyfalls.com	Chattanooga	TN	37409	423-821-2544	821-6705
Runge Conservation Nature Ctr 2901 W Truman Blvd *TF:* 800-392-1111 ■ *Web:* www.mdc.mo.gov	Jefferson City	MO	65109	573-751-4115	751-4467
Rushmore Cave 13622 Hwy 40 *Web:* www.rushmorecave.com	Keystone	SD	57751	605-255-4384	

Name / Address	City	State	Zip	Phone	Fax
Santa Catalina Ranger District 5700 N Sabino Canyon Rd *Web:* www.fs.fed.us	Tucson	AZ	85750	520-749-8700	749-7723
Saw Mill River Audubon Inc 275 Millwood Rd *Web:* www.sawmillriveraudubon.org/pruyn.html	Chappaqua	NY	10514	914-666-6503	666-7430
Schilling Wildlife Management Area 17614 Schilling Refuge Rd *Web:* www.outdoornebraska.ne.gov	Plattsmouth	NE	68048	402-296-0041	
Schlitz Audubon Nature Ctr 1111 E Brown Deer Rd *Web:* www.sanc.org	Bayside	WI	53217	414-352-2880	352-6091
Sea Lion Caves 91560 Hwy 101 *Web:* www.sealioncaves.com	Florence	OR	97439	541-547-3111	547-3545
Seven Falls Co 2850 S Cheyenne Canyon Rd *TF:* 855-923-7272 ■ *Web:* www.sevenfalls.com	Colorado Springs	CO	80906	719-632-0765	632-0781
Severson Dells Nature Ctr 8786 Montague Rd *Web:* www.seversondells.com	Rockford	IL	61102	815-335-2915	335-2471
Sitting Bull Crystal Caverns 13745 S Hwy 16 *Web:* www.sittingbullcrystalcave.com	Rapid City	SD	57702	605-342-2777	
Snake River Birds of Prey National Conservation Area PO Box 84 *Web:* www.snakeriverbirdsofpreyfestival.com	Kuna	ID	83634	208-861-9131	384-3326
Springfield Conservation Nature Ctr 4600 S Chrisman Ave *TF:* 800-392-1111 ■ *Web:* www.mdc.mo.gov	Springfield	MO	65804	417-888-4237	888-4241
T.O. Fuller State Park 1500 W Mitchell Rd *Web:* www.tennessee.gov	Memphis	TN	38109	901-543-7581	785-8485
Tacoma Nature Ctr 1919 S Tyler St *Web:* metroparkstacoma.org	Tacoma	WA	98405	253-591-6439	593-4152
Tree Hill Nature Ctr 7152 Lone Star Rd *Web:* www.treehill.org	Jacksonville	FL	32211	904-724-4646	724-9132
Vista House 40700 E Historic Columbia River Hwy *Web:* www.vistahouse.com	Corbett	OR	97019	503-695-2230	695-2250
Weedon Island Preserve Cultural & Natural History Ctr 1800 Weedon Dr NE *Web:* www.weedonislandcenter.org	Saint Petersburg	FL	33702	727-453-6500	
Wehr Nature Ctr 9701 W College Ave *Web:* county.milwaukee.gov	Franklin	WI	53132	414-425-8550	425-6992
Western North Carolina Nature Ctr 75 Gashes Creek Rd *Web:* www.wildwnc.org	Asheville	NC	28805	828-298-5600	298-2644
Westwood Hills Nature Ctr 8300 W Franklin Ave *Web:* stlouispark.org	Saint Louis Park	MN	55426	952-924-2544	797-9691
Woldumar Nature Ctr 5739 Old Lansing Rd *Web:* www.woldumar.org	Lansing	MI	48917	517-322-0030	322-9394
Woodcock Nature Ctr 54 Deer Run Rd *Web:* www.woodcocknaturecenter.org	Wilton	CT	06897	203-762-7280	834-0062
World Bird Sanctuary 125 Bald Eagle Ridge Rd *Web:* www.worldbirdsanctuary.org	Valley Park	MO	63088	636-861-3225	861-3240

50-6 Shopping/Dining/Entertainment Districts

Name / Address	City	State	Zip	Phone	Fax
Bannister's Wharf 1 Bannister's Wharf *TF:* 800-395-1343 ■ *Web:* www.bannistersnewport.com	Newport	RI	02840	401-846-4500	849-8750
Barefoot Landing 4898 Hwy 17 S *TF:* 800-217-1511 ■ *Web:* www.bflanding.com	North Myrtle Beach	SC	29582	843-272-8349	272-1052
Bayside Marketplace 401 Biscayne Blvd *Web:* www.baysidemarketplace.com	Miami	FL	33132	305-577-3344	
Bazaar del Mundo 4133 Taylor St *Web:* www.bazaardelmundo.com	San Diego	CA	92110	619-296-3161	
Beale Street Historic District 203 Beale St Ste 300 *Web:* www.bealestreet.com	Memphis	TN	38103	901-526-0115	526-0125
Belmar 464 S Teller St *Web:* www.belmarcolorado.com	Lakewood	CO	80226	303-742-1520	987-7693
BOB the (Big Old Bldg) 20 Monroe Ave NW *Web:* www.thebob.com	Grand Rapids	MI	49503	616-356-2000	493-2011
Bricktown Two S Mickey Mantle Dr *Web:* welcometobricktown.com	Oklahoma City	OK	73104	405-236-8666	
Brightleaf Square Gregson & Main Sts 905 W Main St *Web:* www.historicbrightleaf.com	Durham	NC	27701	919-682-9229	688-1953
Broadway at the Beach 1325 Celebrity Cir *Web:* www.broadwayatthebeach.com	Myrtle Beach	SC	29577	843-444-3200	
Cannery at Del Monte Square 2801 Leavenworth St Mezzanine Level *Web:* www.delmontesquare.com	San Francisco	CA	94133	415-771-3112	771-2424
Celebration Town Hall 851 Celebration Ave *Web:* www.celebration.fl.us	Kissimmee	FL	34747	407-566-1200	
Center in the Square One Market Sq SE Fifth Fl *Web:* www.centerinthesquare.org	Roanoke	VA	24011	540-342-5700	224-1238
Centro Ybor 1600 E Eigth Ave *Web:* www.centroybor.com	Tampa	FL	33605	813-242-4660	242-4664
CityPlace 700 S Rosemary Ave *Web:* www.cityplace.com	West Palm Beach	FL	33401	561-366-1000	366-1001
CocoWalk 3015 Grand Ave *Web:* www.cocowalk.net	Coconut Grove	FL	33133	305-444-0777	441-8936
Cooper Young Business Assn 2120 Young Ave *Web:* lamplighter.cooperyoung.org	Memphis	TN	38104	901-276-7222	
Crocker Park 189 Crocker Pk Blvd *Web:* www.crockerpark.com	Westlake	OH	44145	440-871-6880	871-6889
Desert Ridge Marketplace 21001 N Tatum Blvd *Web:* www.shopdesertridge.com	Phoenix	AZ	85050	480-513-7586	563-1829
District, The 11 S Tenth St *Web:* www.discoverthedistrict.com	Columbia	MO	65201	573-442-6816	
Downtown at the Gardens 11701 Lk Victoria Gardens Ave Ste 2203 *Web:* downtownatthegardens.com	Palm Beach Gardens	FL	33410	561-340-1600	
Downtown Disney S Disneyland Dr *Web:* disneyland.disney.go.com	Anaheim	CA	92802	714-781-4565	
East Town 770 N Jefferson St *Web:* www.easttown.com	Milwaukee	WI	53202	414-271-1416	271-6401
Faneuil Hall Marketplace Four S Market Bldg Fifth Fl *Web:* www.faneuilhallmarketplace.com	Boston	MA	02109	617-523-1300	523-1779
Fifth Street Public Market 296 E Fifth Ave *Web:* www.5stmarket.com	Eugene	OR	97401	541-484-0383	686-1220
Findlay Market PO Box 14727 *Web:* www.findlaymarket.org	Cincinnati	OH	45250	513-665-4839	665-3480
FlatIron Crossing 1 W FlatIron Crossing Dr *Web:* www.flatironcrossing.com	Broomfield	CO	80021	720-887-0888	887-0707
Fort Worth Stockyards National Historic District PO Box 64203 *Web:* www.fortworthstockyards.org	Fort Worth	TX	76164	817-626-7921	740-8635
Fourth Avenue 434 E Ninth St *Web:* www.fourthavenue.org	Tucson	AZ	85705	520-624-5004	
Gaslamp Quarter Assn 614 Fifth Ave Ste E *Web:* www.gaslamp.org	San Diego	CA	92101	619-233-5227	233-4693
Gateway, The 18 Rio Grande St *Web:* www.shopthegateway.com	Salt Lake City	UT	84101	801-456-0000	456-0005
Ghirardelli Square 900 N Pt St Ste E-100 *Web:* www.ghirardellisq.com	San Francisco	CA	94109	415-775-5500	775-0912
Great Lakes Crossing Outlets 4000 Baldwin Rd *TF:* 877-746-7452 ■ *Web:* www.greatlakescrossingoutlets.com	Auburn Hills	MI	48326	248-454-5000	
Harborplace & the Gallery 201 E Pratt St *TF:* 800-722-8614 ■ *Web:* www.harborplace.com	Baltimore	MD	21202	410-332-4191	547-7317
Hillcrest Historic District Markham & Kavanaugh *Web:* www.arkansas.com	Little Rock	AR	72216	501-371-0075	374-8142
Hollywood & Highland 6801 Hollywood Blvd **Fax Area Code:* 323 ■ *Web:* www.hollywoodandhighland.com	Hollywood	CA	90028	310-562-4182	460-6003*
Hyde Park Village 1621 W Snow Cir *Web:* www.hydeparkvillage.com	Tampa	FL	33606	813-251-3500	251-4158
International Plaza & Bay Street 2223 NW Shore Blvd *Web:* www.shopinternationalplaza.com	Tampa	FL	33607	813-342-3790	342-3788
John's Pass Village & Boardwalk 150 John's Pass Boardwalk Pl *TF:* 800-755-0677 ■ *Web:* www.johnspass.com	Madeira Beach	FL	33708	727-398-6577	397-6818
Laclede's Landing 710 N Second St *Web:* lacledeslanding.com	Saint Louis	MO	63102	314-241-5875	
Larimer Square 1430 Larimer St Ste 200 *Web:* www.larimersquare.com	Denver	CO	80202	303-534-2367	
Mellwood Arts & Entertainment Ctr 1860 Mellwood Ave *Web:* www.mellwoodartcenter.com	Louisville	KY	40206	502-895-3650	895-3680
Metreon 865 Market St *Web:* www.westfield.com	San Francisco	CA	94103	415-495-5656	369-6025
Miracle Mile Shops at Planet Hollywood 3663 Las Vegas Blvd S *TF:* 888-800-8284 ■ *Web:* www.miraclemileshopslv.com	Las Vegas	NV	89109	702-866-0703	866-0717
New Roc City 19 LeCount Pl *Web:* www.funfuziononline.com	New Rochelle	NY	10801	914-637-7575	637-1048
Newport on the Levee One Levee Way Ste 1113 *TF:* 866-538-3359 ■ *Web:* www.newportonthelevee.com	Newport	KY	41071	859-291-0550	291-7020
Ocean Walk Shoppes at the Village 250 N Atlantic Ave Ste 201 *Web:* www.oceanwalkshoppes.com	Daytona Beach	FL	32118	386-258-9544	238-3864
Peabody Place 100 Peabody Pl Ste 1400 *Web:* www.belz.com	Memphis	TN	38103	901-260-7348	
Penn's Landing 301 S Columbus Blvd *Web:* www.delawareriverwaterfront.com	Philadelphia	PA	19106	215-922-2386	923-2801
Pike Outlets, The 95 S Pine Ave *Web:* www.thepikeatlongbeach.com	Long Beach	CA	90802	562-432-8325	
Pike Place Market (PPM PDN) 85 Pike St Rm 500 *Web:* www.pikeplacemarket.org	Seattle	WA	98101	206-682-7453	625-0646
Pioneer Square 310 First Ave S *Web:* www.pioneersquare.org	Seattle	WA	98104	206-667-0687	667-9739
Ports O'Call Village Berth 75-79 *Web:* www.sanpedro.com/sp_point/portcall.htm	San Pedro	CA	90731	310-548-8076	
Power Plant Live! 34 Market St *Web:* www.powerplantlive.com	Baltimore	MD	21202	410-752-5444	659-9491
Renaissance Ctr Detroit River *Web:* marriott.com/hotels/propertypage/dtwdt	Detroit	MI	48243	313-568-8000	568-5606
River Walk 110 Broadway Ste 500 *TF:* 800-417-4139 ■ *Web:* www.thesanantonioriverwalk.com	San Antonio	TX	78204	210-227-4262	212-7602
Santana Row 3055 Olin Ave Ste 2100 *Web:* www.santanarow.com	San Jose	CA	95128	408-551-4611	551-4616
Seaport Village 849 W Harbor Dr Ste D *Web:* www.seaportvillage.com	San Diego	CA	92101	619-235-4014	696-0025
Shops at Columbus Circle, The 10 Columbus Cir *Web:* www.shopsatcolumbuscircle.com	New York	NY	10019	212-823-6300	
Shoreline Village 429 Shoreline Village Dr # 100 *Web:* www.shorelinevillage.com	Long Beach	CA	90802	562-435-2668	435-6445
South Street Seaport 19 Fulton St Pier 17 *Web:* www.southstreetseaport.com	New York	NY	10038	212-732-8257	964-8056
Stockyards Station 130 E Exchange Ave *Web:* www.stockyardsstation.com	Fort Worth	TX	76164	817-625-9715	

	City	State	Zip	Phone	Fax
Streets at Southpoint & Main Street 6910 Fayetteville Rd *Web:* www.streetsatsouthpoint.com	Durham	NC	27713	919-572-8800	572-8818
Sundance Square 201 Main St Ste 700 *Web:* www.sundancesquare.com	Fort Worth	TX	76102	817-255-5700	390-8709
Underground Atlanta 50 Central Ave SW Ste 007 *Web:* www.underground-atlanta.com	Atlanta	GA	30303	404-523-2311	523-0507
Universal Studios CityWalk Hollywood Universal City Plz *Web:* www.citywalkhollywood.com	Los Angeles	CA	91608	818-622-4455	
Water Tower Place 835 N Michigan Ave *Web:* www.shopwatertower.com	Chicago	IL	60611	312-440-3166	440-1259
Waterside Festival Marketplace 333 Waterside Dr *Web:* www.watersidemarketplace.com	Norfolk	VA	23510	757-627-3300	
West Port Plaza 111 W Port Plz Ste 550 *Web:* www.westportstl.com	Saint Louis	MO	63146	314-576-7100	
Westport Historical Society 4000 Baltimore St *Web:* www.westporthistorical.com	Kansas City	MO	64111	816-561-1821	

50-7 Wineries

The wineries listed in this category feature wine-tasting as an attraction.

	City	State	Zip	Phone	Fax
A Nonini Winery Inc 2640 N Dickenson *Web:* www.noniniwinery.com	Fresno	CA	93723	559-275-1936	
Adams County Winery 251 Peach Tree Rd *Web:* www.adamscountywinery.com	Orrtanna	PA	17353	717-334-4631	334-4026
Alaska Denali Winery 1301 E Dowling Rd Ste 107 *Web:* denaliwinery.com	Anchorage	AK	99518	907-563-9434	563-9501
Arbor Crest Wine Cellars 4705 N Fruithill Rd *Web:* www.arborcrest.com	Spokane	WA	99217	509-927-9463	927-0574
Bogle Vineyards & Winery 37783 County Rd 144 *Web:* www.boglewinery.com	Clarksburg	CA	95612	916-744-1139	744-1187
Butler Winery 1022 N College Ave *Web:* www.butlerwinery.com	Bloomington	IN	47404	812-339-7233	
Cap*Rock Winery 408 E Woodrow Rd *Web:* www.caprockwinery.com	Lubbock	TX	79423	806-686-4452	
Casa Rondena Winery 733 Chavez Rd NW *Web:* www.casarondena.com	Albuquerque	NM	87107	505-344-5911	343-1823
Caterina Winery 905 N Washington St *Web:* caterina.com	Spokane	WA	99201	509-328-5069	328-9694
Chaddsford Winery 632 Baltimore Pk *Web:* www.chaddsford.com	Chadds Ford	PA	19317	610-388-6221	388-0360
Chateau Elan Winery 100 Tour de France *TF:* 800-233-9463 ■ *Web:* www.chateauelan.com	Braselton	GA	30517	678-425-0900	425-6000
Chateau Julien Wine Estate 8940 Carmel Valley Rd *Web:* www.chateaujulien.com	Carmel	CA	93923	831-624-2600	624-6138
Chateau Morrisette Winery 287 Winery Rd SW *TF:* 866-695-2001 ■ *Web:* thedogs.com	Floyd	VA	24091	540-593-2865	593-2868
Chateau Saint Jean 8555 Sonoma Hwy PO Box 293 *Web:* www.chateaustjean.com	Kenwood	CA	95452	707-833-4134	833-4200
Chateau Ste Michelle Winery 14111 NE 145th St *TF:* 800-267-6793 ■ *Web:* www.ste-michelle.com	Woodinville	WA	98072	425-415-3300	415-3657
Cherry Hill Winery 7867 Crowley Rd PO Box 66 *Web:* www.cherryhillwinery.com	Rickreall	OR	97371	503-623-7867	623-7878
Columbia Winery 14030 NE 145th St PO Box 1248 *TF:* 800-488-2347 ■ *Web:* www.columbiawinery.com	Woodinville	WA	98072	425-488-2776	488-3460
Countryside Vineyards Winery 658 Henry Harr Rd *Web:* cvwineryandsupply.com	Blountville	TN	37617	423-323-1660	323-1660
Easley Winery 205 N College Ave *Web:* www.easleywinery.com	Indianapolis	IN	46202	317-636-4516	974-0128
Eola Hills Wine Cellars 501 S Pacific Hwy 99 W *TF:* 800-291-6730 ■ *Web:* www.eolahillswinery.com	Rickreall	OR	97371	503-623-2405	623-0350
Forks of Cheat Winery 2811 Stewart Town Rd *TF:* 877-989-4637 ■ *Web:* www.wvwines.com	Morgantown	WV	26508	304-598-2019	
Georgia Winery, The 6469 Battlefield Pkwy *Web:* www.georgiawines.com	Ringgold	GA	30736	706-937-9463	937-9860
Gruet Winery 8400 Pan American Fwy NE *TF:* 888-857-9463 ■ *Web:* www.gruetwinery.com	Albuquerque	NM	87113	505-821-0055	857-0066
Honeywood Winery 1350 Hines St SE *TF:* 800-726-4101 ■ *Web:* www.honeywoodwinery.com	Salem	OR	97302	503-362-4111	362-4112
Huber's Orchard & Winery 19816 Huber Rd *Web:* huberwinery.com	Borden	IN	47106	812-923-9463	923-3013
J Lohr Vineyards & Wines 1000 Lenzen Ave *Web:* www.jlohr.com	San Jose	CA	95126	408-288-5057	993-2276
James Arthur Vineyards & Winery 2001 W Raymond Rd *Web:* www.jamesarthurvineyards.com	Raymond	NE	68428	402-783-5255	783-5256
King Estate Winery 80854 Territorial Rd *TF:* 800-884-4441 ■ *Web:* www.kingestate.com	Eugene	OR	97405	541-942-9874	942-9867
La Vina Winery 4201 S Hwy 28 *Web:* www.lavinawinery.com	La Union	NM	88021	575-882-7632	
Latah Creek Winery 13030 E Indiana Ave *TF:* 800-528-2427 ■ *Web:* www.latahcreek.com	Spokane	WA	99216	509-926-0164	
LaVelle Vineyards 89697 Sheffler Rd *Web:* www.lavellevineyards.com	Elmira	OR	97437	541-935-9406	935-7202
Llano Estacado Winery 3426 E FM 1585 PO Box 3487 *TF:* 800-634-3854 ■ *Web:* www.llanowine.com	Lubbock	TX	79404	806-745-2258	748-1674
Mazza Vineyards 11815 E Lake Rd *TF:* 800-796-9463 ■ *Web:* www.mazzawines.com	North East	PA	16428	814-725-8695	725-3948
Michael-David Winery 4580 W Hwy 12 *Web:* www.michaeldavidwinery.com	Lodi	CA	95242	209-368-7384	368-5801
Mountain Dome Winery 16315 E Temple Rd *Web:* www.mountaindome.com	Spokane	WA	99217	509-928-2788	
Nassau Valley Vineyards 32165 Winery Way *TF:* 800-425-2355 ■ *Web:* www.nassauvalley.com	Lewes	DE	19958	302-645-9463	645-6666
Oak Ridge Winery 6100 E Victor Rd *Web:* www.oakridgewinery.com	Lodi	CA	95240	209-369-4758	369-0202
Oliver Winery 8024 N SR-37 *TF:* 800-258-2783 ■ *Web:* www.oliverwinery.com	Bloomington	IN	47404	812-876-5800	876-9309
Orfila Vineyards & Winery 13455 San Pasqual Rd *TF:* 800-868-9463 ■ *Web:* www.orfila.com	Escondido	CA	92025	760-738-6500	745-3773
Penn Shore Vineyards & Winery 10225 Lake Rd *Web:* www.pennshore.com	North East	PA	16428	814-725-8688	725-8689
Redhawk Vineyard & Winery 2995 Michigan City Ave NW *Web:* www.redhawkwine.com	Salem	OR	97304	503-362-1596	589-9189
Saint Innocent Winery 5657 Zena Rd NW *Web:* www.stinnocentwine.com	Salem	OR	97304	503-378-1526	378-1041
Sakonnet Vineyards 162 W Main Rd *TF:* 800-919-4637 ■ *Web:* www.sakonnetwine.com	Little Compton	RI	02837	401-635-8486	635-2101
San Sebastian Winery 157 King St *TF:* 888-352-9463 ■ *Web:* www.sansebastianwinery.com	Saint Augustine	FL	32084	904-826-1594	826-1595
Silvan Ridge/Hinman Vineyards 27012 Briggs Hill Rd *Web:* www.silvanridge.com	Eugene	OR	97405	541-345-1945	345-6174
Talon Winery & Vineyards 7086 Tates Creek Rd *Web:* www.talonwine.com	Lexington	KY	40515	859-971-3214	971-8787
Westbend Vineyards 5394 Williams Rd *Web:* www.westbendvineyards.com	Lewisville	NC	27023	336-945-5032	945-5294
Williamsburg Winery Ltd 5800 Wessex Hundred *Web:* www.williamsburgwinery.com	Williamsburg	VA	23185	757-229-0999	229-0911
Winery at Wolf Creek 2637 Cleveland Massillon Rd *TF:* 800-436-0426 ■ *Web:* www.wineryatwolfcreek.com	Norton	OH	44203	330-666-9285	665-1445

51 AUCTIONS

	City	State	Zip	Phone	Fax
Abidon Leasing 5301 E State St Ste 215	Rockford	IL	61108	815-226-8700	226-8769
ADESA Inc 13085 Hamilton Crossing Blvd *TF:* 800-923-3725 ■ *Web:* www.adesa.com	Carmel	IN	46032	317-815-1100	249-4600
Akron Auto Auction Inc 2471 Ley Dr *TF:* 800-773-0033 ■ *Web:* www.akronautoauction.com	Akron	OH	44319	330-773-8245	773-1641
American Auction Co 951 W Watkins *TF:* 800-801-8880 ■ *Web:* www.auctionandappraise.com	Phoenix	AZ	85007	602-252-4842	
Bonhams & Butterfields 220 San Bruno Ave *TF:* 800-223-2854 ■ *Web:* www.bonhams.com	San Francisco	CA	94103	415-861-7500	861-8951
Collectors Universe Inc PO Box 6280 *NASDAQ: CLCT* ■ *TF:* 800-325-1121 ■ *Web:* www.collectors.com	Newport Beach	CA	92658	949-567-1234	833-7955
Doyle New York 175 E 87th St *Web:* www.doylenewyork.com	New York	NY	10128	212-427-2730	369-0892
Earl's Auction Co 5199 Lafayette Rd *Web:* www.earlsauction.com	Indianapolis	IN	46254	317-291-5843	291-5844
eBay Inc 2065 Hamilton Ave *NASDAQ: EBAY* ■ *TF:* 800-322-9266 ■ *Web:* www.ebay.com	San Jose	CA	95125	408-376-7400	376-7401
Fasig-Tipton Co Inc 2400 Newtown Pike *TF:* 877-945-2020 ■ *Web:* www.fasigtipton.com	Lexington	KY	40511	859-255-1555	254-0794
Freeman/Fine Arts of Philadelphia 1808 Chestnut St *Web:* www.freemansauction.com	Philadelphia	PA	19103	215-563-9275	563-8236
Gallery of History Inc 3601 W Sahara Ave Ste Promenade *TF:* 800-425-5379 ■ *Web:* www.galleryofhistory.com	Las Vegas	NV	89102	702-364-1000	364-1285
Gordon Bros Group LLC 101 Huntington Ave 10th Fl **Fax Area Code:* 617 ■ *TF:* 888-424-1903 ■ *Web:* www.gordonbrothers.com	Boston	MA	02199	888-424-1903	422-6222*
Greater Rockford Auto Auction Inc (GRAA) 5937 Sandy Hollow Rd *TF:* 800-830-4722 ■ *Web:* www.graa.net	Rockford	IL	61109	815-874-7800	874-1325
Harry Davis & Co 1725 Blvd of Allies *TF:* 800-775-2289 ■ *Web:* www.harrydavis.com	Pittsburgh	PA	15219	412-765-1170	765-1170
Henderson Auctions 13340 Florida Blvd PO Box 336 *TF:* 800-334-7443 ■ *Web:* www.hendersonauctions.com	Livingston	LA	70754	225-686-2252	686-0647
Heritage Place Inc 2829 S MacArthur *TF:* 888-343-9831 ■ *Web:* www.heritageplace.com	Oklahoma City	OK	73128	405-682-4551	686-1267
iCollector Technologies Inc 1750 Coast Meridian Rd Ste 114 *TF:* 866-313-0123 ■ *Web:* www.icollector.com	Port Coquitlam	BC	V3C6R8	604-941-2221	
Insurance Auto Auctions Inc Two Westbrook Corporate Ctr Ste 500 *TF:* 800-872-1501 ■ *Web:* www.iaai.com	Westchester	IL	60154	708-492-7000	
Ironplanet Inc 3825 Hopyard Rd Ste 250 **Fax:* Cust Svc ■ *TF Cust Svc:* 888-433-5426 ■ *Web:* www.ironplanet.com.au	Pleasanton	CA	94588	925-225-8600	225-8610*
Kennedy-Wilson Inc 9701 Wilshire Blvd Ste 700 *TF:* 800-522-6664 ■ *Web:* kennedywilson.com	Beverly Hills	CA	90212	310-887-6400	887-6414
Liquidity Services Inc 1920 L St NW Sixth Fl *NASDAQ: LQDT* ■ *TF:* 800-310-4604 ■ *Web:* www.liquidityservicesinc.com	Washington	DC	20036	202-467-6868	467-5475
NexTag.com Inc 2955 Campus Dr Third Fl *Web:* www.nextag.com	San Mateo	CA	94403	650-645-4700	341-3779

				Phone	Fax
Priceline.com LLC 800 Connecticut Ave	Norwalk	CT	06854	800-774-2354	299-8955*
NASDAQ: PCLN ■ *Fax Area Code: 203 ■ *Fax: Mktg ■ TF: 800-774-2354 ■ Web: www.priceline.com					
Rene Bates Auctioneers Inc 4660 County Rd 1006	McKinney	TX	75071	972-548-9636	542-5495
Web: www.renebates.com					
Sotheby's Inc 1334 York Ave	New York	NY	10021	212-606-7000	894-1141
Web: www.sothebys.com					
Swann Galleries Inc 104 E 25th St	New York	NY	10010	212-254-4710	979-1017
Web: www.swanngalleries.com					
Theriault's PO Box 151	Annapolis	MD	21404	410-224-3655	224-2515
TF: 800-966-3655 ■ Web: www.theriaults.com					
uBid Inc 740 Hilltop Dr	Itasca	IL	60143	866-946-8243	
TF: 866-946-8243 ■ Web: www.ubid.com					
Yahoo! Auctions 701 First Ave	Sunnyvale	CA	94089	408-349-3300	616-3702
Web: info.yahoo.com					

52 AUDIO & VIDEO EQUIPMENT

				Phone	Fax
Alfred Williams & Co 410 S Salisbury St	Raleigh	NC	27601	919-832-9570	
Web: alfredwilliams.com					
Alpine Electronics of America 19145 Gramercy Pl	Torrance	CA	90501	310-326-8000	320-5089*
*Fax: Hum Res ■ TF: 800-257-4631 ■ Web: www.alpine-usa.com					
Amplifier Technologies Inc 1749 Chapin Rd	Montebello	CA	90640	323-278-0001	278-0083
Web: www.bgw.com					
AmpliVox Sound Systems LLC 3995 Commercial Ave	Northbrook	IL	60062	847-498-9000	498-6691
TF: 800-267-5486 ■ Web: www.ampli.com					
Amx LLC 3000 Reseach Dr	Richardson	TX	75082	469-624-8000	
Web: amx.com					
Applied Research & Technology 215 Tremont St	Rochester	NY	14608	585-436-2720	436-3942
TF: 800-775-2427 ■ Web: artproaudio.com					
Atlas Sound 1601 Jack McKay Blvd	Ennis	TX	75119	972-875-8413	765-3435*
*Fax Area Code: 800 ■ TF: 800-876-3333 ■ Web: www.atlassound.com					
Audio America Inc 15132 Park Of Commerce Blvd Ste 100	Jupiter	FL	33478	561-863-7704	
Web: www.audioamerica.com					
Audio Command Systems 694 Main St	Westbury	NY	11590	516-997-5800	997-2195
TF: 800-382-2939 ■ Web: www.audiocommand.com					
Audio Research Corp 3900 Annapolis Ln N	Plymouth	MN	55447	763-577-9700	577-0323
Web: www.audioresearch.com					
Audio-Video Corp 213 Broadway	Albany	NY	12204	518-449-7213	449-1205
Web: www.audiovideocorp.com					
Audiosears Corp Two S St	Stamford	NY	12167	607-652-7305	652-3653
TF: 800-533-7863 ■ Web: www.audiosears.com					
Audiovox Corp 180 Marcus Blvd	Hauppauge	NY	11788	631-231-7750	
NASDAQ: VOXX ■ TF: 800-645-4994 ■ Web: www.voxxintl.com					
Automated Voice Systems Inc (AVSI) 17059 El Cajon Ave	Yorba Linda	CA	92886	714-524-4488	996-1127
Avidex Industries LLC 13555 Bel-Red Rd Ste 226	Bellevue	WA	98005	425-643-0330	
Web: www.avidexav.com					
Biamp Systems Inc 9300 SW Gemini Dr	Beaverton	OR	97008	800-826-1457	626-0281*
*Fax Area Code: 503 ■ TF: 800-826-1457 ■ Web: www.biamp.com					
Bogen Communications International Inc 50 Spring St	Ramsey	NJ	07446	201-934-8500	934-6532
OTC: BOGN ■ TF: 800-999-2809 ■ Web: www.bogen.com					
Bose Corp The Mountain	Framingham	MA	01701	508-766-1099	820-3465
TF Sales: 800-379-2073 ■ Web: global.bose.com					
Car Toys Inc 20 W Galer St	Seattle	WA	98119	206-443-0980	443-2525
TF: 800-997-3644 ■ Web: www.cartoys.com					
Cerwin-Vega Inc 3000 SW 42nd St	Hollywood	FL	33312	954-316-1501	316-1590
Web: www.cerwinvega.com					
Chemguard Inc 204 S Sixth Ave	Mansfield	TX	76063	817-473-9964	
Web: www.chemguard.com					
City of Chula Vista 276 Fourth Ave	Chula Vista	CA	91910	619-691-5047	
TF: 877-478-5478 ■ Web: chulavistaca.gov					
Clarion Corp of America 6200 Gateway Dr	Cypress	CA	90630	310-327-9100	327-1999
TF: 800-347-8667 ■ Web: www.clarion.com					
Community Professional Loudspeakers 333 E Fifth St	Chester	PA	19013	610-876-3400	874-0190
TF: 800-523-4934 ■ Web: www.communitypro.com					
Cornet Technology Inc 6800 Versar Ctr Ste 216	Springfield	VA	22151	703-658-3400	658-3440
Web: www.cornet.com					
Creative Labs Inc 1901 McCarthy Blvd	Milpitas	CA	95035	408-428-6600	428-6611
TF Cust Svc: 800-998-1000 ■ Web: www.us.creative.com					
Crescendo Designs 641 County Rd 39A	Southampton	NY	11968	631-283-2133	
Web: crescendodesigns.com					
Crest Electronics Inc 3706 Alliance Dr	Greensboro	NC	27407	336-855-6422	855-6676
TF: 888-502-7378 ■ Web: www.crestelectronics.com					
Crown Audio Inc 1718 W Mishawaka Rd	Elkhart	IN	46517	574-294-8000	294-8301
Web: www.crownaudio.com					
Dana Innovations 212 Avenida Fabricante	San Clemente	CA	92672	949-492-7777	
TF: 800-582-7777 ■ Web: www.sonance.com					
Dangerous Music Inc 231 Stevens Rd	Edmeston	NY	13335	607-965-8011	
Web: www.dangerousmusic.com					
DEI Holdings Inc One Viper Way	Vista	CA	92081	760-598-6200	598-6400
OTC: DEIX ■ TF: 800-876-0800 ■ Web: deiholdings.com					
Digit Professional Inc 5050 Seymour Rd	Jackson	MI	49201	734-677-0840	
Web: prodvx.com					
Digital Innovations 3436 N Kennicott Ste 200	Arlington Heights	IL	60004	847-463-9000	463-9001
TF: 888-762-7858 ■ Web: digitalinnovations.com					
Digital Video Systems Inc (DVS) 357 Castro St Ste 5	Mountain View	CA	94041	650-938-8815	938-8829
Web: www.dvsystems.com					
Dolby Laboratories Inc 100 Potrero Ave	San Francisco	CA	94103	415-558-0200	645-4000
NYSE: DLB ■ Web: dolby.co.in/index.html					

				Phone	Fax
Dreamgear LLC 20001 S Western Ave	Torrance	CA	90501	310-222-5522	222-5577
Web: www.dreamgear.com					
DTS Inc 5220 Las Virgenes Rd	Calabasas	CA	91302	818-436-1000	706-1868
NASDAQ: DTSI ■ Web: www.dts.com					
Dynamic Instruments Inc 3860 Calle Fortunada	San Diego	CA	92123	858-278-4900	278-6700
TF: 800-793-3358 ■ Web: www.dynamicinst.com					
Echo Digital Audio Corp 6450 Via Real Ste 1	Carpinteria	CA	93013	805-684-4593	
Web: www.echoaudio.com					
Educational Technology Inc 300 Bedford Ave Ste 202	Bellmore	NY	11710	516-221-8440	
TF Cust Svc: 800-942-2136 ■ Web: www.educationaltechnology.com					
Eminence Speaker LLC 838 Mulberry Pike PO Box 360	Eminence	KY	40019	502-845-5622	845-5622
TF: 800-897-8373 ■ Web: www.eminence.com					
Encore Productions Inc 5150 S Decatur Blvd	Las Vegas	NV	89118	702-739-8803	739-8831
Web: encore-us.com					
Extron Electronics 1230 S Lewis St	Anaheim	CA	92805	714-491-1500	491-1517
TF Tech Supp: 800-633-9876 ■ Web: www.extron.com					
FlexHead Industries Inc 56 Lowland St	Holliston	MA	01746	508-893-9596	
Web: www.flexhead.com					
Ford Audio-Video Systems Inc 4800 W I- 40	Oklahoma City	OK	73128	405-946-9966	946-9991
TF: 800-654-6744 ■ Web: www.fordav.com					
Foster Electric America 1000 E State Pkwy Ste G	Schaumburg	IL	60173	847-310-8200	310-8212
Web: www.fosterelectric.com/					
Fujitsu Ten Corp of America 19600 S Vermont Ave	Torrance	CA	90502	310-327-2151	767-4355
TF: 800-233-2216 ■ Web: www.eclipse-web.com					
Funai Corp 201 Rt 17 N Ste 903	Rutherford	NJ	07070	201-727-4560	288-8019
Web: www.funai.us					
Furman Sound LLC 1690 Corporate Cir	Petaluma	CA	94954	707-763-1010	763-1310
TF: 877-486-4738 ■ Web: www.furmansound.com					
GlobalMedia Group LLC 15020 N 74th St	Scottsdale	AZ	85260	480-922-0044	922-1090
Web: www.globalmed.com					
Grass Valley Inc 3499 Douglas-B.-Floreani	Montreal	QC	H4S2C6	514-333-1772	333-9828
Web: www.grassvalley.com					
Harman International Industries Inc 400 Atlantic St 15th Fl	Stamford	CT	06901	203-328-3500	328-3964
NYSE: HAR ■ TF: 800-473-0602 ■ Web: www.harman.com					
Harman Kardon Inc 250 Crossways Pk Dr	Woodbury	NY	11797	516-496-3400	682-3520
Web: www.harmankardon.com					
Harman Music Group 8760 S Sandy Pkwy	Sandy	UT	84070	801-566-8800	566-7005
Web: www.dbxpro.com					
Harman/Becker Automotive Systems 39001 W 12 Mile Rd	Farmington Hills	MI	48331	248-994-2100	994-2900
Web: www.harman.com					
Interactive Digital Solutions Inc 14701 Cumberland Rd Ste 400	Noblesville	IN	46060	317-770-3521	
Web: www.e-idsolutions.com					
JBL Professional 8500 Balboa Blvd	Northridge	CA	91329	818-894-8850	830-1220
TF: 800-852-5776 ■ Web: www.jblpro.com					
Jeopardy Productions Inc 10202 Washington Blvd	Culver City	CA	90232	310-244-8855	
Web: www.jeopardy.com					
JVC Professional Products Co 1700 Valley Rd	Wayne	NJ	07470	973-317-5000	317-5030
TF: 800-252-5722 ■ Web: www.pro.jvc.com/prof					
Kaleidescape 440 Potrero Ave	Sunnyvale	CA	94085	650-625-6100	
Web: kaleidescape.com					
Kenwood USA Corp 2201 E Dominguez St	Long Beach	CA	90810	310-639-9000	
TF: 800-536-9663 ■ Web: www.kenwoodusa.com					
KK Audio Inc 12620 Raymer St	North Hollywood	CA	91605	818-765-2921	
KLH Audio Systems 11131 Dora St	Sun Valley	CA	91352	818-767-2843	
Web: www.klhaudio.com					
Klipsch LLC 137 Hempstead 278	Hope	AR	71801	888-250-8561	777-6753*
*Fax Area Code: 870 ■ TF: 888-250-8561 ■ Web: www.klipsch.com					
Koss Corp 4129 N Port Washington Ave	Milwaukee	WI	53212	414-964-5000	964-8615
NASDAQ: KOSS ■ TF: 800-872-5677 ■ Web: www.koss.com					
Krell Industries Inc 45 Connair Rd	Orange	CT	06477	203-799-9954	799-9796
Web: www.krellonline.com					
KSC Industries Inc 881 Kuhn Dr Ste 200	Chula Vista	CA	91914	619-671-0110	671-0330
Web: www.kscind.com					
Law Enforcement Assoc Corp (LEA) 120 Penmarc Dr Ste 125	Raleigh	NC	27616	919-872-6210	872-6431
OTC: LAWEQ ■ TF: 800-354-9669 ■ Web: www.leacorp.com					
Lectrosonics Inc PO Box 15900	Rio Rancho	NM	87174	505-892-4501	892-6243
TF: 800-821-1121 ■ Web: www.lectrosonics.com					
LifeSize Communications Inc 1601 S Mopac Expwy Ste 100	Austin	TX	78746	512-347-9300	347-9301
TF: 877-543-3749 ■ Web: www.lifesize.com					
Line 6 26580 Agoura Rd	Calabasas	CA	91302	818-575-3600	575-3601
Web: www.line6.com					
LKG Industries Inc 3660 Publisher's Dr	Rockford	IL	61109	815-874-2301	874-2896
Web: www.crankinpower.com					
Logitech Inc 6505 Kaiser Dr	Fremont	CA	94555	510-795-8500	792-8901
TF Sales: 800-231-7717 ■ Web: www.logitech.com					
LOUD Technologies Inc 16220 Wood Red Rd NE	Woodinville	WA	98072	425-892-6500	487-4337
OTC: LTEC ■ TF: 866-858-5832 ■ Web: www.loudtechinc.com					
Loudspeaker Components Corp 7596 US Hwy 61 S	Lancaster	WI	53813	608-723-2127	723-7775
Web: loudspeakercomponents.com					
Lowell Manufacturing Co 100 Integram Dr	Pacific	MO	63069	636-257-3400	257-6606
TF: 800-325-9660 ■ Web: www.lowellmfg.com					
Marantz America Inc 100 Corporate Dr	Mahwah	NJ	07430	201-762-6500	762-6670
Web: www.marantz.com					
MartinLogan Ltd 2101 Delaware St	Lawrence	KS	66046	785-749-0133	749-5320
Web: www.martinlogan.com					
McIntosh Laboratory Inc Two Chambers St	Binghamton	NY	13903	607-723-3512	724-0549
TF: 800-538-6576 ■ Web: mcintoshlabs.com					

Company	City	State	Zip	Phone	Fax
Metra Electronics Corp 460 Walker St. *TF Sales:* 800-221-0932 ■ *Web:* www.metraonline.com	Holly Hill	FL	32117	386-257-1186	255-3965
Meyer Sound Laboratories Inc 2832 San Pablo Ave *Web:* www.meyersound.com	Berkeley	CA	94702	510-486-1166	486-8356
Microsearch 3903 Stoney Brook Dr *Web:* www.microsearch.com	Houston	TX	77063	713-988-2818	
Mitsubishi Digital Electronics America Inc 9351 Jeronimo Rd *TF:* 800-332-2119 ■ *Web:* www.mitsubishi-tv.com	Irvine	CA	92618	949-465-6000	
Mitsubishi Electric & Electronics USA Inc *Elevator & Escalator Div* 5665 Plz Dr *Web:* www.mitsubishielectric.com/elevator	Cypress	CA	90630	714-220-4700	220-4812
Monster Cable Products Inc 455 Valley Dr *TF:* 877-800-8989 ■ *Web:* www.monsterproducts.com	Brisbane	CA	94005	415-840-2000	
Mustek Inc 15271 Barranca Pkwy *TF:* 800-308-7226 ■ *Web:* www.mustek.com	Irvine	CA	92618	949-790-3800	247-8960
Nady Systems Inc 6701 Shellmound St *Web:* www.nady.com	Emeryville	CA	94608	510-652-2411	652-5075
Norcon Communications Inc 510 Burnside Ave *Web:* norconcomm.com	Inwood	NY	11096	516-239-0300	
Omnitronics LLC 6573 Cochran Rd *TF:* 800-762-9266 ■ *Web:* www.cadaudio.com	Solon	OH	44139	440-349-4900	349-4900
OSRAM Sylvania Inc 100 Endicott St *Web:* www.sylvania.com	Danvers	MA	01923	978-777-1900	750-2152
Panasonic Three Panasonic Way **Fax Area Code:* 888 ■ *Web:* panasonic.com	Secaucus	NJ	07094	201-348-7000	553-0723*
Panasonic Avionics Corp 26200 Enterprise Way *TF:* 877-627-2300 ■ *Web:* panasonic.aero	Lake Forest	CA	92630	949-672-2000	462-7100
Panasonic Consumer Electronics Co 1 Panasonic Way *NYSE:* PC ■ **Fax Area Code:* 201 ■ *TF:* 800-103-1333 ■ *Web:* www.panasonic.com	Secaucus	NJ	07094	888-762-2097	392-6168*
Panasonic Corp of North America 1 Panasonic Way **Fax Area Code:* 201 ■ **Fax:* Hum Res ■ *TF Cust Svc:* 800-211-7262 ■ *Web:* www.panasonic.com	Secaucus	NJ	07094	888-762-2097	348-7016*
Peavey Electronics Corp 5022 Hartley Peavey Dr *TF:* 877-732-8391 ■ *Web:* www.peavey.com	Meridian	MS	39305	601-483-5365	486-1278
Phase Technology 6400 Youngerman Cir *TF:* 888-742-7385 ■ *Web:* www.phasetech.com	Jacksonville	FL	32244	904-777-0700	
Pioneer Electronics (USA) Inc 1925 E Dominguez St *TF:* 800-421-1404 ■ *Web:* www.pioneerelectronics.com	Long Beach	CA	90810	310-952-2000	952-2402
Polk Audio Inc 5601 Metro Dr *TF:* 800-377-7655 ■ *Web:* www.polkaudio.com	Baltimore	MD	21215	410-358-3600	764-5266
Precision Econowind Inc 8940 N Fork Dr *Web:* www.precisioneconowind.com	North Fort Myers	FL	33903	239-997-3860	
Primo Microphones Inc 1805 Couch Dr *TF:* 800-767-7463 ■ *Web:* www.primomic.com	McKinney	TX	75069	972-548-9807	548-1351
QSC Audio Products LLC 1675 MacArthur Blvd **Fax:* Mktg ■ *TF:* 800-854-4079 ■ *Web:* www.qscaudio.com	Costa Mesa	CA	92626	714-754-6175	754-6174*
Quam-Nichols Company Inc 234 E Marquette Rd *TF:* 800-633-3669 ■ *Web:* www.quamspeakers.com	Chicago	IL	60637	773-488-5800	488-6944
Rane Corp 10802 47th Ave W *TF:* 877-764-0093 ■ *Web:* www.rane.com	Mukilteo	WA	98275	425-355-6000	347-7757
Record Play Tek Inc 110 E Vistula St *TF:* 800-809-5233 ■ *Web:* www.recordplaytek.com	Bristol	IN	46507	574-848-5233	848-5333
Remote Technologies Inc 5775 12th Ave E Ste 180 *Web:* www.rticorp.com	Shakopee	MN	55379	952-253-3100	
Renkus-heinz Inc 19201 Cook St *TF:* 855-411-2364 ■ *Web:* www.renkus-heinz.com	Foothill Ranch	CA	92610	949-588-9997	588-9514
ReQuest Inc 100 Saratoga Village Blvd Ste 45 **Fax:* Sales ■ *TF Sales:* 800-236-2812 ■ *Web:* www.request.com	Ballston Spa	NY	12020	518-899-1254	899-1251*
Roanwell Corp 2564 Pk Ave *Web:* www.roanwell.com	Bronx	NY	10451	718-401-0288	401-0663
Rockford Corp 600 S Rockford Dr *OTC:* ROFO ■ *TF:* 800-903-2897 ■ *Web:* www.rockfordcorp.com	Tempe	AZ	85281	480-967-3565	966-3983
Sanyo Fisher Co 21605 Plummer St *Web:* us.sanyo.com	Chatsworth	CA	91311	818-998-7322	
Sanyo Mfg Corp 3333 Sanyo Rd *TF:* 800-100-3003 ■ *Web:* us.sanyo.com	Forrest City	AR	72335	870-633-5030	
SDI Technologies Inc 1299 Main St *TF:* 800-333-3092 ■ *Web:* www.sditechnologies.com	Rahway	NJ	07065	800-333-3092	
Sharp Electronics Corp One Sharp Plz *TF:* 800-237-4277 ■ *Web:* www.sharpusa.com	Mahwah	NJ	07430	201-529-8200	529-8413
Sherwood America 6120 Valley View Buena Pk *Web:* www.sherwoodamerica.com	Buena Park	CA	90620	714-739-2000	739-2009
Shure Inc 5800 W Touhy Ave *TF:* 800-257-4873 ■ *Web:* www.shure.com	Niles	IL	60714	847-866-2200	600-1212
Sima Products Corp 120 Pennsylvania Ave *TF:* 800-345-7462 ■ *Web:* simaproducts.com	Oakmont	PA	15139	412-828-3700	828-3775
Skymicro Inc 2060 E Avenida De Los Arboles Ste D344 *Web:* www.skymicro.com	Thousand Oaks	CA	91362	805-491-8995	
Snell Acoustics 300 Jubilee Dr *Web:* www.snellacoustics.com	Peabody	MA	01960	978-538-6262	
Sony Corp of America 550 Madison Ave *TF:* 800-282-2848 ■ *Web:* www.sony.com	New York	NY	10022	212-833-6800	
Sony Electronics Inc One Sony Dr **Fax:* Hum Res ■ *TF Cust Svc:* 800-222-7669 ■ *Web:* www.sony.com	Park Ridge	NJ	07656	201-930-1000	358-4058*
Sony of Canada Ltd 115 Gordon Baker Rd *Web:* store.sony.ca	Toronto	ON	M2H3R6	416-499-1414	497-1774
Sound Com Corp 227 Depot St *TF:* 800-628-8739 ■ *Web:* www.soundcom.net	Berea	OH	44017	440-234-2604	234-2614
Southern Audio Services 14763 Florida Blvd *TF Cust Svc:* 800-843-8823 ■ *Web:* www.bazooka.com	Baton Rouge	LA	70819	225-272-7135	272-9844
Stancil Corp 2644 S Croddy Way *TF:* 800-290-4103 ■ *Web:* www.stancilcorp.com	Santa Ana	CA	92704	714-546-2002	546-2092
Sunfire Corp 1969 Kellogg Ave *Web:* www.sunfire.com	Carlsbad	CA	92008	760-710-0993	
TDK USA Corp 525 RXR Plaza PO Box 9302 **Fax:* Sales ■ *TF General:* 800-285-2783 ■ *Web:* www.tdk.com	Uniondale	NY	11556	516-535-2600	294-8318*
TEAC America Inc 7733 Telegraph Rd *Web:* www.teac.com	Montebello	CA	90640	323-726-0303	727-7656
Telex Communications Inc 12000 Portland Ave S *TF:* 877-863-4169 ■ *Web:* www.telex.com	Burnsville	MN	55337	952-884-4051	884-0043
Toshiba America Inc 1251 Ave of the Americas Ste 4100 *TF:* 800-457-7777 ■ *Web:* www.toshiba.com	New York	NY	10020	212-596-0600	593-3875
Universal Audio Inc 1700 Green Hills Rd *TF:* 877-698-2834 ■ *Web:* www.uaudio.com	Scotts Valley	CA	95066	831-440-1176	461-1550
Universal Electronics Inc 201 E. Sandpointe Ave Ste 200 *NASDAQ:* UEIC ■ *Web:* www.uei.com	Santa Ana	CA	92707	714-918-9500	918-4100
Verrex Corp 1130 Rt 22 W *Web:* www.verrex.com	Mountainside	NJ	07092	908-232-7000	232-7991
Vialta Inc 48461 Fremont Blvd *Web:* www.vialta.com	Fremont	CA	94538	510-870-3088	
Washington Professional Systems (WPS) 109GaitherDr Ste 301 *Web:* www.wpsworld.com	Mount Laurel	NJ	08054	856-273-8688	273-8558
Wisdom Audio Corp 1572 College Pkwy Ste 164 *Web:* www.wisdomaudio.com	Carson City	NV	89706	775-887-8850	887-8820
Xantech Corp 1969 Kellogg Ave **Fax Area Code:* 800 ■ *TF Sales:* 800-843-5465 ■ *Web:* www.xantech.com	Carlsbad	CA	92008	818-362-0353	492-6832*
Yamaha Electronics Corp 6660 Orangethorpe Ave **Fax Area Code:* 800 ■ *TF:* 800-292-2982 ■ *Web:* usa.yamaha.com	Buena Park	CA	90620	714-522-9888	634-0355*
Z Systems 3724 Oregon Ave S *Web:* www.zsyst.com	Minneapolis	MN	55426	952-974-3140	
Zenith Electronics Corp 2000 Millbrook Dr *Web:* www.zenith.com	Lincolnshire	IL	60069	847-941-8000	

53 AUTO CLUBS

Company	City	State	Zip	Phone	Fax
AAA Akron 111 W Ctr St *Web:* www.aaa.com	Akron	OH	44308	330-762-0631	762-5965
AAA Allied Group Inc 15 W Central Pkwy *TF:* 800-543-2345 ■ *Web:* ohiovalley.aaa.com	Cincinnati	OH	45202	513-762-3100	762-3282
AAA Carolinas 6600 AAA Dr *TF:* 800-477-4222 ■ *Web:* carolinas.aaa.com	Charlotte	NC	28212	704-569-3600	285-6176
AAA Chicago Motor Club 975 Meridian Lake Dr **Fax Area Code:* 630 ■ *TF:* 866-968-7222 ■ *Web:* www.aaa.com	Aurora	IL	60504	866-968-7222	499-8200*
AAA Colorado 4100 E Arkansas Ave *TF:* 866-625-3601 ■ *Web:* www.colorado.aaa.com	Denver	CO	80222	303-753-8800	300-7710
AAA East Central 5900 Baum Blvd *Web:* www.aaa.com	Pittsburgh	PA	15206	412-363-5100	362-8943
AAA East Penn 1020 W Hamilton St *TF:* 800-222-4357 ■ *Web:* www.aaa.com	Allentown	PA	18101	800-222-4357	
AAA Hawaii 1130 N Nimitz Hwy Ste A-170 *TF:* 800-736-2886 ■ *Web:* hawaii.aaa.com/home.html	Honolulu	HI	96817	808-593-2221	591-9359
AAA Hoosier Motor Club 3750 Guion Rd **Fax:* Cust Svc ■ *Web:* www.aaa.com	Indianapolis	IN	46222	317-923-1500	923-5991*
AAA Hudson Valley 618 Delaware Ave *Web:* www.aaa.com	Albany	NY	12209	518-426-1000	426-1595
AAA Massillon Auto Club 1972 Wales Rd NE *TF:* 800-222-4357 ■ *Web:* www.aaa.com	Massillon	OH	44646	330-833-1084	833-5542
AAA Merrimack Valley 49 OrchaRd Hill Rd *Web:* www.aaa.com	North Andover	MA	01845	978-681-9200	688-4891
AAA Michigan 1 Auto Club Dr *TF:* 800-222-6424 ■ *Web:* www.aaa.com	Dearborn	MI	48126	313-336-1920	
AAA Minneapolis 5400 Auto Club Way *Web:* www.aaa.com	Minneapolis	MN	55416	952-927-2600	927-2559
AAA Minnesota/Iowa 600 W Travelers Trl *TF:* 800-222-1333 ■ *Web:* www.aaa.com/ppinternational/international.html	Burnsville	MN	55337	952-707-4500	707-4220
AAA Missouri 12901 N Forty Dr *TF:* 800-222-4357 ■ *Web:* aaa.com	Saint Louis	MO	63141	314-523-7350	523-7427
AAA MountainWest 2100 11th Ave *TF:* 800-332-6119 ■ *Web:* www.aaa.com	Helena	MT	59601	406-447-8100	442-5671
AAA Nebraska 910 N 96th St *TF:* 800-222-6327 ■ *Web:* www.aaa.com/ppinternational/international.html	Omaha	NE	68114	402-390-1000	
AAA North Penn 1035 N Washington Ave *TF:* 800-222-4357 ■ *Web:* www.aaa.com	Scranton	PA	18509	570-348-2511	348-2563
AAA Northampton County 3914 Hecktown Rd *Web:* www.aaa.com	Easton	PA	18045	610-258-2371	258-5256
AAA Northern New England 68 Marginal Way *TF:* 800-222-4357 ■ *Web:* www.northernnewengland.aaa.com	Portland	ME	04104	207-780-6800	780-6986
AAA Northway 112 Railroad St *TF:* 866-222-7283 ■ *Web:* aaa.com	Schenectady	NY	12305	518-374-4696	374-3140
AAA Northwest Ohio 7150 W Central Ave *TF:* 800-428-0060 ■ *Web:* www.nwohio.aaa.com	Toledo	OH	43617	419-843-1200	843-1249
AAA Ohio Auto Club 90 E Wilson Bridge Rd *TF:* 888-222-6446 ■ *Web:* ohio.aaa.com	Worthington	OH	43085	614-431-7901	431-7918
AAA Oklahoma 2121 E 15th St *TF:* 800-222-2582 ■ *Web:* www.ok.aaa.com	Tulsa	OK	74104	918-748-1000	748-1111
AAA Reading-Berks 920 Van Reed Rd *Web:* www.aaa.com	Wyomissing	PA	19610	610-374-4531	374-1325
AAA Schuylkill County 340 S Centre St *Web:* www.aaa.com	Pottsville	PA	17901	570-622-4991	622-8179
AAA Shelby County 920 Wapakoneta Ave *Web:* www.aaa.com	Sidney	OH	45365	937-492-3167	492-7297

				Phone	Fax
AAA South Jersey 700 Laurel Oak Rd *Web:* www.aaa.com	Voorhees	NJ	08043	856-783-4222	627-9100
AAA Southern New England 110 Royal Little Dr *TF:* 800-222-7448 ■ *Web:* www.aaa.com	Providence	RI	02904	401-868-2000	868-2085
AAA Southern Pennsylvania 2840 Eastern Blvd *TF:* 800-222-1469 ■ *Web:* www.aaa.com	York	PA	17402	717-600-8700	755-2142
AAA Susquehanna Valley 1001 Market St *Web:* www.aaa.com	Sunbury	PA	17801	570-286-4507	286-1130
AAA Tidewater Virginia 5366 Virginia Beach Blvd *Web:* www.aaa.com	Virginia Beach	VA	23462	757-233-3800	233-3896
AAA Utica & Central New York 409 Ct St *Web:* www.aaa.com	Utica	NY	13502	315-797-5000	797-5005
AAA Washington-Inland 1745 114th Ave SE *TF:* 800-222-4357 ■ *Web:* newsroom.aaa.com	Bellevue	WA	98004	425-646-2058	467-7729
AAA Western & Central New York 100 International Dr *TF:* 800-836-2582 ■ *Web:* westerncentralny.aaa.com	Williamsville	NY	14221	716-633-9860	633-4439
AAA Wisconsin 8401 Excelsior Dr *TF:* 800-236-1300 ■ *Web:* newsroom.aaa.com	Madison	WI	53717	608-836-6555	
AARP Motoring Plan 601 E Street N.W *TF:* 800-555-1121 ■ *Web:* www.aarproadside.com/aarp/forwardto.do?pagename=contact_us	Washington	DC	20049	800-555-1121	
American Automobile Association, Inc. 435 E Broadway *TF:* 800-727-2552 ■ *Web:* www.aaa.com	Louisville	KY	40202	502-582-3311	584-1455
Auto Club Ltd PO Box 162526 *TF:* 866-247-3728 ■ *Web:* www.paragonmotorclub.com	Austin	TX	78716	866-247-3728	
Auto Club of America Corp (ACA) 9411 N Georgia St *TF:* 800-411-2007 ■ *Web:* www.autoclubofamerica.com	Oklahoma City	OK	73120	405-751-4430	751-4462
Auto Club of New York Inc 1415 Kellum Pl *Web:* www.aaa.com/PPInternational/Benefits_Intl_to_US.html	Garden City	NY	11530	516-746-7730	873-2320
Automobile Club of Southern California 2601 S Figueroa St *TF:* 800-400-4222 ■ *Web:* www.aaa.com	Los Angeles	CA	90007	213-741-3686	741-4890
BP MotorClub PO Box 4441 *TF:* 800-334-3300 ■ *Web:* www.bpmotorclub.com	Carol Stream	IL	60197	800-334-3300	
Brickell Financial Services Motor Club Inc 7300 Corporate Ctr Dr Ste 601 *TF:* 800-262-7262 ■ *Web:* www.road-america.com	Miami	FL	33126	305-392-4300	392-4301
British Columbia Automobile Assn (BCAA) 4567 Canada Way *TF:* 800-222-4357 ■ *Web:* www.bcaa.com	Burnaby	BC	V5G4T1	604-268-5000	268-5569
CAA Central Ontario 60 Commerce Vly Dr E *TF:* 800-268-3750 ■ *Web:* www.caasco.com	Thornhill	ON	L3T7P9	905-771-3000	771-3101
CAA Manitoba 870 Empress St *TF:* 800-222-4357 ■ *Web:* www.caamanitoba.com	Winnipeg	MB	R3C2Z3	204-262-6166	774-9961
CAA Maritimes Ltd 378 Westmorland Rd *TF:* 800-471-1611 ■ *Web:* ww2.aaa.com	Saint John	NB	E2J2G4	506-634-1400	653-9500
CAA North & East Ontario PO Box 8350 *TF:* 800-267-8713 ■ *Web:* caaneo.ca	Ottawa	ON	K1G3T2	613-820-1890	820-4646
CAA Quebec 444 Bouvier St *TF:* 800-222-4357 ■ *Web:* www.caaquebec.com	Quebec	QC	G2J1E3	418-624-8222	623-7331
CAA Stoney Creek 163 Centennial Pkwy N *TF:* 800-992-8143 ■ *Web:* www.caasco.com	Hamilton	ON	L8E1H8	905-664-8000	664-8080
California State Automobile Assn 150 Van Ness Ave *TF Cust Svc:* 800-922-8228 ■ *Web:* calstate.aaa.com	San Francisco	CA	94102	800-922-8228	
Canadian Automobile Assn (CAA) 2151 Thurston Dr Ste 200 *TF:* 800-267-8713 ■ *Web:* www.caa.ca	Ottawa	ON	K1G6C9	613-820-1890	247-0118
Cross Country Automotive Services (CCAS) one Cabot Rd *Web:* www.crosscountry-auto.com	Medford	MA	02155	781-393-9300	395-6706
Dallas Model A Ford Club PO Box 1028 *Web:* www.dmafc.com	Addison	TX	75001	972-279-4786	
Findlay Automobile Club 1550 Tiffin Ave *TF:* 800-222-4357 ■ *Web:* www.aaa.com	Findlay	OH	45840	419-422-4961	422-5620
National Automobile Club (NAC) 373 Vintage Park Dr Ste E *Web:* www.nationalautoclub.com	Foster City	CA	94404	650-294-7000	294-7040
National Motor Club of America Inc (NMC) 130 E John Carpenter Fwy *TF:* 800-523-4582 ■ *Web:* www.nmc.com	Irving	TX	75062	972-999-1099	
Pennsylvania AAA Federation 600 N Third St *Web:* www.aaapa.org	Harrisburg	PA	17101	717-238-7192	238-6574
Pinnacle Motor Club 130 E John Carpenter Fwy *TF:* 800-446-1289 ■ *Web:* www.pinnaclemotorclub.com	Irving	TX	75062	800-446-1289	
Travelers Motor Club 720 NW 50th St *TF:* 800-654-9208 ■ *Web:* www.travelersmotorclub.com	Oklahoma City	OK	73154	405-848-1711	
Zipcar Inc 25 First St Fl 4 *NASDAQ: ZIP* ■ *Web:* www.zipcar.com	Cambridge	MA	02141	617-995-4231	995-4300

54 AUTO SUPPLY STORES

				Phone	Fax
A 1 Auto Recyclers 7804 S Hwy 79 *TF:* 800-456-0715 ■ *Web:* www.a1autorecyclers.com	Rapid City	SD	57701	605-348-8442	
Advance Auto Parts Inc 5008 Airport Rd *NYSE: AAP* ■ *TF:* 877-238-2623 ■ *Web:* advanceautoparts.com	Roanoke	VA	24012	540-561-8452	
Aeromotive Inc 7805 Barton St *Web:* www.aeromotiveinc.com	Lenexa	KS	66214	913-647-7300	
Air Lift Co 2727 Snow Rd *Web:* www.airliftcompany.com	Lansing	MI	48917	517-322-2144	
Air Specialists Inc 27 Hollenberg Ct *Web:* airspec.com	Bridgeton	MO	63044	314-298-7400	
American Crane & Tractor Parts Inc 2200 State Line Rd *Web:* www.actparts.com	Kansas City	KS	66103	913-371-8585	
American Glass Distributors 3901 Airline Dr *Web:* www.allamericanglass.com	Houston	TX	77022	713-692-8522	692-9002
Amex World Trade Corp 18765 Sw 78th Ct *Web:* www.amexworldtrade.com	Cutler Bay	FL	33157	305-238-3010	
Anatech Ltd 771 Crosspoint Dr *Web:* www.anatechltd.com	Denver	NC	28037	704-489-1488	
Anthony Liftgates Inc 1037 W Howard St *Web:* www.anthonyliftgates.com	Pontiac	IL	61764	815-842-3383	
Atlanta Commercial Tire Inc 146 Forest Pkwy *Web:* www.actire.com	Forest Park	GA	30297	404-675-9998	
Ats All Tire Supply Co 6600 Long Point Rd Ste 101 *TF:* 888-339-6665 ■ *Web:* www.alltiresupply.com	Houston	TX	77055	888-339-6665	
Auto Barn 13 Harbor Pk Dr *Web:* www.autobarn.com	Port Washington	NY	11050	516-484-9500	484-4341
AutoZone Inc 123 S Front St *NYSE: AZO* ■ *TF:* 800-288-6966 ■ *Web:* www.autozone.com	Memphis	TN	38103	901-495-6500	495-8300
B & b Selectcom Inc 1109 S Fremont Ave *Web:* bbselectcom.com	Tucson	AZ	85719	520-882-0911	
Bap Geon LLC 3310 Austin Bluffs Pkwy *Web:* www.bapgeon.com	Colorado Springs	CO	80918	719-637-9600	
Bavarian Autosport Inc 275 Constitution Ave *Web:* www.bavauto.com	Portsmouth	NH	03801	603-427-2002	
Bennett Auto Supply Inc 3141 SW Tenth St **Fax Area Code:* 899 ■ **Fax:* Hum Res ■ *TF:* 800-766-5913 ■ *Web:* www.bennettauto.com	Pompano Beach	FL	33069	954-335-8700	924-0003*
Benny's Inc 340 Waterman Ave *Web:* www.hellobennys.com	Smithfield	RI	02917	401-231-1000	231-1080
Bill Smith Auto Parts 400 Ash St *Web:* www.billsmithauto.com	Danville	IL	61832	217-442-0156	
Black's Tire Service Inc 30 Bitmore Rd *Web:* www.blackstire.com	Whiteville	NC	28472	910-642-4123	
Blue Star Automobile Stores Inc 2001 S State St	Chicago	IL	60616	312-225-7174	
BMW of Manhattan Inc 555 W 57th St *Web:* www.bmwnyc.com	New York	NY	10019	212-586-2269	
Bond Auto Parts 45 Summer St *TF:* 800-639-1982 ■ *Web:* www.bondauto.com	Barre	VT	05641	802-476-3108	
Bowditch Ford Inc 11076 Warwick Blvd *Web:* bowditchford.com	Newport News	VA	23601	757-595-2211	
Bridgestone Retail Operations LLC 333 E Lake St Ste 300 *Web:* www.bsro.com	Bloomingdale	IL	60108	630-259-9000	
Briggs Auto Group Inc 2312 Stagg Hill Rd *Web:* www.briggsauto.com	Manhattan	KS	66502	785-537-8330	
Burien Toyota Collision Center 15025 First Ave S *Web:* www.burientoyota.com	Burien	WA	98148	206-243-0700	
C & R Racing Inc 6950 Guion Rd *Web:* www.crracing.com	Indianapolis	IN	46268	317-293-4100	
Cape Electronics 19 Dupont Ave *Web:* capeelectronics.com	South Yarmouth	MA	02664	508-394-2405	
Carquest Corp 2635 E Millbrook Rd **Fax:* Mktg ■ *TF:* 800-876-1291 ■ *Web:* www.carquest.com	Raleigh	NC	27604	919-573-3000	573-3558*
CEC Industries Ltd 599 Bond St *Web:* cecindustries.com	Lincolnshire	IL	60069	847-821-1199	
Chet Nichols Inc 315 E Main St *Web:* www.chetnichols.com	Benton Harbor	MI	49022	269-925-2136	
Chris Alston Chassisworks Inc 8661 Younger Creek Dr *Web:* www.cachassisworks.com	Sacramento	CA	95828	916-388-0288	
Clark Brothers Instrument Company Inc 56680 Mound Rd *Web:* www.clarkbrothers.net	Shelby Township	MI	48316	586-781-7000	
Coan Engineering LLC 1602 E Havens St *Web:* www.coanracing.com	Kokomo	IN	46901	765-456-3957	
Coastal Automotive Service Garage 2006 Cottonwood Ave *Web:* www.awesomenet.net	Bay City	TX	77414	979-245-8361	
CRP 4X4 Truck OutFitters 2102 Ninth St Ste A *Web:* crptruck.com	Greeley	CO	80631	970-351-8603	
Cumberland Truck Parts 15 Sylmar Rd *Web:* www.cumberlandtruck.com	Nottingham	PA	19362	610-932-1152	
Custom Truck Accessories Inc 13408 Hwy 65 Ne *TF:* 800-333-1282 ■ *Web:* www.customtruckaccess.com	Ham Lake	MN	55304	763-757-5326	757-5994
Day Motor Sports LLC 6100 Hwy 69 N *Web:* www.daymotorsports.com	Tyler	TX	75706	903-593-9815	
Delco Diesel Services Inc 1100 S Agnew Ave *Web:* www.delcodiesel.com	Oklahoma City	OK	73108	405-232-3595	
Delta World Tire Co 203 Guilbeau Rd *Web:* www.deltaworldtire.com	Lafayette	LA	70506	337-984-3098	
Des-Case Corp 675 N Main St *Web:* www.des-case.com	Goodlettsville	TN	37072	615-672-8800	
Doug Richert Pontiac Cadillac 1900 Sw Topeka Blvd *Web:* www.dougrichert.com	Topeka	KS	66612	785-233-1361	
Fabrication Technologies Industries Inc 2200 Haffley Ave *Web:* www.ftisd.com	National City	CA	91950	619-477-4141	
Fluke Electronics Canada LP 400 Britannia Rd E Unit 1 *Web:* www.flukecanada.ca	Mississauga	ON	L4Z1X9	905-890-7600	
Frank Millman Distributors Inc Eight Progress St *Web:* www.millmans.com	Edison	NJ	08820	908-561-7300	

Phone Fax

Gallo Equipment Company Inc 11835 S Ave O .... Chicago IL 60617 773-374-5515
Web: www.galloequipment.com

Go Industries Inc 420 N Grove Rd .... Richardson TX 75081 972-783-7444 437-3425
Web: goindustries.com

Green Oak Tire Inc 7480 Kensington Rd .... Brighton MI 48116 248-437-1753
Web: www.greenoaktire.com

Hedahls Inc 100 East Broadway .... Bismarck ND 58502 701-223-8393 221-4251
TF: 800-433-2457 ■ *Web:* www.hedahls.com

Index Engines Inc
960 Holmdel Rd Bldg One First Fl .... Holmdel NJ 07733 732-817-1060
Web: www.indexengines.com

Inflexxion Inc 320 Needham St Ste 100 .... Newton MA 02464 617-332-6028
Web: www.inflexxion.com

Jack's Tire & Oil Management Company Inc
1795 N Main St .... North Logan UT 84341 435-752-7811
Web: www.jackstireandoil.com

JE Adams Industries Ltd
1025 63rd Ave Sw .... Cedar Rapids IA 52404 319-363-0237
Web: www.jeadams.com

JohnDow Industries Inc 151 Snyder Ave .... Barberton OH 44203 330-753-6895
Web: johndow.com

Johnson Power Ltd 2530 Braga Dr .... Broadview IL 60155 708-345-4300
Web: www.johnsonpower.com

Knecht's Auto Parts 3400 Main St .... Springfield OR 97478 541-746-4446 746-0884
Web: www.knechts.com

KOI Warehouse Inc 2701 Spring Grove Ave .... Cincinnati OH 45225 513-357-2400 723-9204
TF: 800-354-0408 ■ *Web:* www.koiautoparts.com

Kuhn Honda 3900 W Kennedy Blvd .... Tampa FL 33609 813-872-4841
Web: www.kuhnhondavw.com

Mar-K Quality Parts LLC
6625 W Wilshire Blvd Ste 2 .... Oklahoma City OK 73132 405-721-7945
Web: mar-k.com

Matsuo Industries USA Inc
408 Municipal Dr .... Jefferson City TN 37760 865-475-9085
Web: www.matsuousa.com

Max Auto Supply Co 1101 Monroe St .... Toledo OH 43604 419-243-7281 243-1626

Meridian Auto Parts
10211 Pacific Mesa Blvd Ste 404 .... San Diego CA 92121 800-874-1974
Web: www.meridianautoparts.com

Merle's Automotive Supply Inc
33 W University Blvd .... Tucson AZ 85705 520-622-3526 622-2760
TF: 800-546-6040 ■ *Web:* www.merlesauto.com

Midway Auto Supply Inc 1101 S Hampton Rd .... Dallas TX 75208 214-943-4341
Web: www.midwayautosupply.com

Midwest Automotive Inc 1065 Lee St .... Des Plaines IL 60016 847-827-8452
Web: www.firestonetire.com

Mike Gatto Inc 15 W Hibiscus Blvd .... Melbourne FL 32901 321-676-2710 952-1302
Web: www.gattos.com

Millennium Line X & Truck Accessories
905 N Raceway Rd .... Indianapolis IN 46234 317-209-8000
Web: www.millenniumlinings.com

Minor Tire & Wheel Company Inc
3512 Sixth Ave Se .... Decatur AL 35603 256-353-4957
Web: www.visionwheel.com

Momo Automotive Accessories Inc
20512 Crescent Bay Ste 104 .... Lake Forest CA 92630 949-380-7556
Web: www.momo.com

Motor State Distributing 8300 Lane Dr .... Watervliet MI 49098 269-463-4113
Web: www.motorstate.com

Motorad of America 6292 Walmore Rd .... Niagara Falls NY 14304 716-731-6442
Web: www.motoradusa.com

Myers Brothers of Kansas City Inc
1210 W 28th St .... Kansas City MO 64108 816-931-5501
Web: www.myersbrotherskc.com

Nitto Denko Automotive Ohio Inc 1620 S Main St .... Piqua OH 45356 937-773-4820
Web: www.piquatechnologies.com

NORD Drivesystems 800 Nord Dr .... Waunakee WI 53597 888-314-6673
TF: 888-314-6673 ■ *Web:* www.nord.com

Northland Auto & Truck Accessories
1106 S 29th St W .... Billings MT 59102 406-245-0595
Web: www.northlandautomotive.com

Nu-Star Inc 1425 Stagecoach Rd .... Shakopee MN 55379 952-445-8295
Web: www.nustarinc.com

O'Reilly Automotive Inc 233 S Patterson .... Springfield MO 65802 417-862-6708 863-2242
NASDAQ: ORLY ■ *TF:* 888-327-7153 ■ *Web:* www.oreillyauto.com

OC Seacrets Inc 117 49th St .... Ocean City MD 21842 410-524-4900
Web: www.seacrets.com

Original Parts Group Inc (OPGI)
1770 Saturn Way .... Seal Beach CA 90740 562-594-1000 594-1050
TF: 800-243-8355 ■ *Web:* www.opgi.com

Palm Beach Motoring Accessories Inc
7744 Sw Jack James Dr .... Stuart FL 34997 772-286-2701
Web: www.autogeek.net

Parkhouse Tire Service Inc
5960 Shull St .... Bell Gardens CA 90201 562-928-0421
Web: www.parkhousetire.com

Parks Auto Parts Professionals
2320 Savannah Hwy .... Charleston SC 29414 843-556-4703
Web: parksautoparts.com

PDQ of The Rockies Inc
8214 Park Meadows Dr .... Lone Tree CO 80124 303-662-9100
Web: www.pdqoftherockies.com

Peerless Tire Co 5000 Kingston St .... Denver CO 80239 303-371-4300
TF: 800-999-7810 ■ *Web:* www.peerlesstyreco.com

Phoenix USA Inc 51 E Borden St .... Cookeville TN 38501 931-526-6128
Web: www.phoenixusa.com

PJS Used Cars & Auto Parts Inc
2708 Caledonia Leroy Rd .... Caledonia NY 14423 585-538-2391
Web: www.pjs4lkq.com

Power Station Inc 7360 Reseda Blvd Ste D .... Reseda CA 91335 818-344-8148
Web: www.mauriss.com

Phone Fax

Precision Engine Controls Corp
11661 Sorrento Vly Rd .... San Diego CA 92121 858-792-3217
Web: www.precisioneng.com

R Cushman & Associates Inc
32840 W 8 Mile Rd .... Farmington MI 48336 248-477-9900
Web: www.rcushman.com

Rent A Tire Inc 2466 Jacksboro Hwy Ste 400 .... Fort Worth TX 76114 817-626-4294
Web: www.rentatire.com

Rent A Wheel 2500 Firestone Blvd Ste G .... South Gate CA 90280 818-786-7906
Web: mobile.rentawheel.com

Roadster Factory, The 328 Killen Rd .... Armagh PA 15920 814-446-4444
Web: www.the-roadster-factory.com

Robertson Tire Company Inc PO Box 472287 .... Tulsa OK 74147 918-664-2211 622-7221
Web: www.robertson-tire.com

Runway Tire Service Inc 4115 19th Ave .... Astoria NY 11105 718-545-5200
Web: www.runwaytireservice.com

S & S Tire & Auto Service Center
1475 Jingle Bell Ln .... Lexington KY 40509 800-685-6794
TF: 800-685-6794 ■ *Web:* www.sstire.com

S&R Truck Tire Center Inc
1402 Truckers Blvd .... Jeffersonville IN 47130 812-282-4799
Web: www.srtrucktire.com

Sales Automation Support Inc
17025 W Rogers Dr .... New Berlin WI 53151 262-754-8712
Web: www.docsspot.com

SAP USA Truck & Auto Parts Inc
5301 NW 74 Ave Ste 200 .... Miami FL 33166 305-594-2844
Web: www.sapcorp.net

Spal-Usa Inc 1731 SE Oralabor Rd .... Ankeny IA 50021 515-289-7000
Web: www.spalusa.com

Specmo Auto Sound & Speed G3189 S Dort Hwy .... Burton MI 48529 800-545-7910
TF: 800-545-7910 ■ *Web:* www.specmo.com

Standard Auto Parts Corp
2020 Hollins Ferry Rd .... Baltimore MD 21230 410-659-5400
Web: www.standardautoparts.com

Suburban Wheel Cover Co
1420 Landmeier Rd .... Elk Grove Village IL 60007 847-758-0388
Web: www.suburbanwheelcover.com

Terry-haggerty Tire Company Inc 980 Broadway ..... Menands NY 12204 518-449-5185
Web: www.terry-haggerty.com

Thieman Tailgates Inc 600 E Wayne St .... Celina OH 45822 419-586-7727
Web: www.thieman.com

Tire Warehouse 200 Holleder Pkwy .... Rochester NY 14615 800-876-6676
TF: 800-876-6676 ■ *Web:* www.tirewarehouse.net

Tireman Auto Service Centers Ltd PO Box 3456 .... Toledo OH 43607 419-724-8473 724-8474
Web: www.thetireman.com

TNT Parts Inc
3000 S Corporate Pkwy Ste 400 .... Forest Park GA 30297 678-244-8532
Web: www.tntpartsinc.com

Total Quality Inc 229 Washington Ave .... Grand Haven MI 49417 616-846-4529
Web: www.shiptqi.com

Town Fair Tire Company Inc 460 Coe Ave .... East Haven CT 06512 800-972-2245 467-1630*
**Fax Area Code: 203* ■ *TF:* 800-972-2245 ■ *Web:* www.townfairtire.com

Tradesman Truck Accessories LLC
305 N Frisco St .... Winters TX 79567 325-754-4561
Web: www.tradesmantruck.com

Transdiesel 1310 George Jenkins Blvd .... Lakeland FL 33815 863-688-5881
Web: www.heavydutytransmissions.com

Trew Industrial Wheels Inc 310 Wilhagan Rd .... Nashville TN 37217 615-360-9100
Web: www.trew-wheels.com

Turbo Parts LLC 767 Pierce Rd Ste 2 .... Clifton Park NY 12065 518-885-3199
Web: www.mdaturbines.com

United Auto Supply 625 Third St .... La Crosse WI 54601 608-784-9198
Web: www.uasparts.com

US Axle Inc 275 Shoemaker Rd .... Pottstown PA 19464 610-323-3800
Web: www.usaxle.com

Utilimaster Holding Co 603 Earthway Blvd .... Bristol IN 46507 800-237-7806
TF: 800-237-7806 ■ *Web:* www.utilimaster.com

Vanguard Trucks Centers 700 Ruskin Dr .... Forest Park GA 30297 866-216-7925 363-4659*
**Fax Area Code: 404* ■ *TF:* 866-216-7925 ■ *Web:* www.vanguardtrucks.com

Weathers Auto Supply Inc 23308 Airpark Dr .... Petersburg VA 23803 804-861-1076
Web: www.weathers.com

Wellers Utility Trailers 16889 N Main St .... Bridgeville DE 19933 302-337-8228
Web: www.pacetrailers.com

West Coast Differentials
2429 Mercantile Dr Ste A .... Rancho Cordova CA 95742 916-635-0950
Web: www.differentials.com

Westbay Auto Parts Inc
2610 SE Mile Hill Dr .... Port Orchard WA 98366 360-876-8008 876-7999
Web: www.westbayautoparts.com

XKS Unlimited Inc 850 Fiero Ln .... San Luis Obispo CA 93401 805-544-7864
Web: www.xks.com

55 AUTOMATIC MERCHANDISING EQUIPMENT & SYSTEMS

SEE ALSO Food Service p. 2320

Phone Fax

Affiliated Control Equipment Inc
640 Wheat Ln .... Wood Dale IL 60191 630-595-4680 595-6151
Web: www.affiliatedcontrol.com

AIR-serv Group LLC
1370 Mendota Heights Rd .... Mendota Heights MN 55120 651-454-0465 454-9542
TF: 800-247-8363 ■ *Web:* www.air-serv.com

American Coin Merchandising Inc
325 Interlocken Pkwy .... Broomfield CO 80021 303-444-2559 247-1728

American Vending Sales Inc
750 Morse Ave .... Elk Grove Village IL 60007 847-439-9400 439-9405
TF: 800-441-0009 ■ *Web:* www.americanvending.com

Automatic Products International Ltd
165 Bridgepoint Dr .... Saint Paul MN 55075 800-523-8363
TF: 800-523-8363 ■ *Web:* www.automaticproducts.com

	City	State	Zip	Phone	Fax
Bastian Material Handling LLC (BMH) 10585 N Meridian St Third Fl *TF:* 800-772-0464 ■ *Web:* www.bastiansolutions.com	Indianapolis	IN	46290	317-575-9992	575-8596
Betson Enterprises Inc 303 Patterson Plank Rd *TF:* 800-524-2343 ■ *Web:* www.betson.com	Carlstadt	NJ	07072	201-438-1300	438-4837
Birmingham Vending Co 540 Second Ave N *TF:* 800-288-7635 ■ *Web:* www.bhmvending.com	Birmingham	AL	35204	205-324-7526	322-6639
Coin Acceptors Inc 300 Hunter Ave *TF:* 800-325-2646 ■ *Web:* www.coinco.com	Saint Louis	MO	63124	314-725-0100	725-2896
Coinstar Inc 1800 114th Ave SE *TF:* 800-928-2274 ■ *Web:* www.coinstar.com	Bellevue	WA	98004	425-943-8000	
Dixie-Narco Inc 3330 Dixie-Narco Blvd *TF:* 800-688-9090 ■ *Web:* www.dixie-narco.com	Williston	SC	29853	803-266-5000	266-5000
Glacier Water Services Inc 1385 Pk Ctr Dr *OTC: GWSV* ■ *TF:* 800-452-2437 ■ *Web:* www.glacierwater.com	Vista	CA	92081	760-560-1111	560-3333
Harcourt Outlines Inc 7765 S 175 W PO Box 128 *TF:* 800-428-6584 ■ *Web:* www.harcourtoutlines.com	Milroy	IN	46156	800-428-6584	278-5165
Melo-Tone Vending Inc 130 Broadway *Web:* melo-tone-vending-inc.placestars.com	Somerville	MA	02145	617-666-4900	666-4906
Northwestern Corp PO Box 490 *TF:* 800-942-1316 ■ *Web:* www.nwcorp.com	Morris	IL	60450	815-942-1300	942-4417

56 AUTOMATIC TELLER MACHINES (ATMS)

	City	State	Zip	Phone	Fax
Accu-time Systems Inc 420 Somers Rd *TF:* 000-355-4640 ■ *Web:* www.accu-time.com	Ellington	CT	06029	860-870-5000	872-1511
Diebold Inc 5995 Mayfair Rd *NYSE: DBD* ■ *TF:* 800-999-3600 ■ *Web:* www.diebold.com	North Canton	OH	44720	330-490-4000	
Electronic Cash Systems Inc (ECS) 30352 Esperanza Ste 110 *TF:* 888-327-2860 ■ *Web:* www.ecspayments.com	Rancho Santa Margarita	CA	92688	949-888-8580	888-8024
Everi Holdings Inc (GCA) 7250 S Tenaya Way Ste 100 *NYSE: EVRI* ■ *TF:* 800-833-7110 ■ *Web:* www.everi.com	Las Vegas	NV	89113	702-855-3000	
Tidel Engineering Inc 2025 W Belt Line Rd Ste 114 *TF:* 800-678-7577 ■ *Web:* www.tidel.com	Carrollton	TX	75006	972-484-3358	484-1014

57 AUTOMOBILE DEALERS & GROUPS

SEE ALSO Automobile Sales & Related Services - Online p. 1838

	City	State	Zip	Phone	Fax
#1 Cochran of Monroeville 4520 William Penn Hwy *Web:* cochran.com	Monroeville	PA	15146	412-373-3333	
15625 Ft Bend Ltd 15625 SW Fwy	Sugar Land	TX	77478	281-207-1500	
32 Ford Mercury Inc 610 W Main St	Batavia	OH	45103	513-732-2124	
A & T Chevrolet Inc 801 Bethlehem Pk	Sellersville	PA	18960	215-257-8022	
A C Nelson Rv World 11818 L St *TF:* 888-655-2332 ■ *Web:* www.acnrv.com	Omaha	NE	68137	402-333-1122	333-1054
AAA Aircraft Supply LLC 68 Shaker Rd *Web:* aaa-aircraft.com	Enfield	CT	06082	860-749-5192	
Aberdeen Chrysler Center Inc 901 Auto Plz Dr *Web:* www.aberdeenchrysler.com	Aberdeen	SD	57401	605-225-1656	
ACK Controls Inc 2600 Happy Vly Rd	Glasgow	KY	42141	270-678-6200	
Action Tire 2405 Weaver Way *Web:* www.actiontireco.com	Doraville	GA	30340	770-263-9695	448-3888
Acura 101 West 24650 Calabasas Rd *TF:* 800-472-3173 ■ *Web:* www.acura101west.com	Calabasas	CA	91302	818-222-5555	222-6495
Acura Medical Systems Inc 8990 Cotter St *Web:* acuramed.com	Lewis Center	OH	43035	614-781-0600	
Acura Neon 1801 N Willow Ave *Web:* www.anisigns.com	Broken Arrow	OK	74012	918-252-2258	
Acura of Bellevue 13424 NE 20th St *Web:* www.acuraofbellevue.com	Bellevue	WA	98005	425-644-3000	
Adams Auto Corp 501 NE Colbern Rd	Lee'S Summit	MO	64086	816-358-7600	
Adamson Motors Inc 4800 Hwy 52 N *Web:* adamsonmotors.com	Rochester	MN	55901	507-289-4004	
Advanced Auto Service & Tire Centers 1947 N Higley Rd *Web:* advancedauto.com	Mesa	AZ	85205	480-985-5400	
Aeroman 139 SW 51st Ter	Cape Coral	FL	33914	239-540-0040	
Alberic Colon Auto Sales Inc Ave John F Kennedy Carr Ste 2 KM 3.4 *TF:* 877-292-4610 ■ *Web:* albericgm.com	San Juan	PR	00920	877-292-4610	
Alden Buick Gmc Truck Inc Six Whalers Way *Web:* aldengmc.com	Fairhaven	MA	02719	508-999-3300	
Alford Motors Inc Hwy 171 *Web:* www.alfordmotors.com	Leesville	LA	71461	337-397-4144	
All American Ford Inc 520 River St *Web:* www.allamericanfordinhackensack.com	Hackensack	NJ	07601	201-487-6700	
Allen Turner Hyundai Inc 6000 Pensacola Blvd *Web:* www.allenturnerauto.com	Pensacola	FL	32505	850-479-9667	
Allgeier Auto Parts Inc 7650 Harrison Ave *Web:* allgeierautoparts.com	Cincinnati	OH	45247	513-353-3377	
Allied Toyotalift 1640 Island Home Ave *TF:* 866-538-0667 ■ *Web:* www.alliedtoyotalift.com	Knoxville	TN	37920	865-573-0995	
America's Car-Mart Inc 802 SE Plz Ave Ste 200 *NASDAQ: CRMT* ■ *Web:* www.car-mart.com	Bentonville	AR	72712	479-464-9944	273-7556
American Augers Inc 135 US Rt 42 *TF:* 800-324-4930 ■ *Web:* www.americanaugers.com	West Salem	OH	44287	419-869-7107	869-7727
Anchor Subaru LLC 949 Eddie Dowling Hwy *Web:* anchorsubaru.com	North Smithfield	RI	02896	401-769-1199	
Ancira Winton Chevrolet 6111 Bandera Rd *TF General:* 800-299-5286 ■ *Web:* chevroletancira.com	San Antonio	TX	78238	210-390-6255	
Anthony Underwood Inc 4006 Bessemer Hwy *Web:* anthonyunderwood.com	Bessemer	AL	35020	205-424-4033	
Apple Tree Enterprises Inc 195 Underwood Rd *Web:* www.appletreeautos.com	Fletcher	NC	28732	828-684-4400	
Arizona Bus Sales Corp 3615 S 28th St *Web:* www.arizonabussales.com	Phoenix	AZ	85040	602-437-2255	
Arlington Toyota Inc 10939 Atlantic Blvd *Web:* www.arlingtontoyota.com	Jacksonville	FL	32225	904-721-3000	
Arrow Truck Sales Inc 3200 Manchester Trfy *TF:* 800-311-7144 ■ *Web:* www.arrowtruck.com	Kansas City	MO	64129	816-923-5000	923-4005
Art Morrison Enterprises Inc 5301 Eighth St E *TF:* 888-640-0516 ■ *Web:* www.artmorrison.com	Fife	WA	98424	253-922-7188	
Asbury Automotive Group Inc 2905 Premiere Pkwy Ste 300 *NYSE: ABG* ■ **Fax Area Code:* 678 ■ *Web:* www.asburyauto.com	Duluth	GA	30097	770-418-8200	542-2701*
Asheville Chevrolet Inc 205 Smokey Pk Hwy *TF:* 866-921-1073 ■ *Web:* www.ashevillechevrolet.com	Asheville	NC	28806	828-665-4444	665-9848
Associated Aircraft Mfg & Sales Inc 2735 NW 63rd Ct *Web:* www.aamsi.com	Fort Lauderdale	FL	33309	954-772-6606	
Astoria Ford 710 W Marine Dr *TF:* 888-760-9303 ■ *Web:* www.astoriaford.net	Astoria	OR	97103	503-325-6411	
Astro Spar Inc 1121 Fullerton Rd *Web:* www.astrospar.com	City Of Industry	CA	91748	626-965-1511	
Astron Wireless Technologies Inc 22560 Glenn Dr Ste 114 *Web:* www.astronwireless.com	Sterling	VA	20164	703-450-5517	
Atlanta Toyota Inc 2345 Pleasant Hill Rd *Web:* www.atlantatoyota.com	Duluth	GA	30096	770-476-8282	
Atlantic Automotive Corp 23 Walker Ave *Web:* www.mileonecorporate.com	Baltimore	MD	21208	410-602-6177	
Atlantic British Ltd Halfmoon Light Industrial Pk 6 Enterprise Ave *TF:* 800-533-2210 ■ *Web:* www.roverparts.com	Clifton Park	NY	12065	518-664-6169	
Atlantic Tire & Supply Company Inc 1430 Saint Georges Ave *Web:* www.emcar.com	Avenel	NJ	07001	732-381-0100	
Atlantic Tractor LLC 31415 John Deere Dr *Web:* atlantictractor.net	Salisbury	MD	21804	410-860-0676	
Auto Credit Express Inc 3271 Five Points Dr Ste 200 *Web:* www.autocreditexpress.net	Auburn Hills	MI	48326	248-370-6600	
Auto Lenders Liquidation Center 104 Rt 73 *Web:* www.autolenders.com	Voorhees	NJ	08043	856-768-0053	
Auto Mall, The 800 Pytney Rd *Web:* www.brattautomall.com	Brattleboro	VT	05301	802-275-4510	257-9327
Auto Supply Company Inc 1032 Winston St *Web:* www.ascodc.com	Greensboro	NC	27405	336-275-6193	
Auto Toy Store, The 727 N Federal Hwy *Web:* www.thenewautotoystore.com	Fort Lauderdale	FL	33304	754-551-7900	
AutoFair Automotive Group 200 Keller St *Web:* www.autofair.com	Manchester	NH	03103	603-634-1000	622-4079
Autoland 170 Rt 22 E *TF Sales:* 877-813-7239 ■ *Web:* www.1800autoland.com	Springfield	NJ	07081	973-467-2900	467-1824
Automann Inc 850 Randolph Rd *Web:* www.automann.com	Somerset	NJ	08873	201-529-4996	
Automobile Racing Club of America 8117 Lewis Ave *TF:* 800-385-2503 ■ *Web:* www.arcaracing.com	Temperance	MI	48182	734-847-6726	
AutoNation Inc 200 SW First Ave Ste 1600 *NYSE: AN* ■ **Fax:* PR ■ *Web:* www.autonation.com/	Fort Lauderdale	FL	33301	954-769-7000	769-6537*
Autoquotes Florida Inc 4425 Merrimac Ave Ste 3 *Web:* aqnet.com	Jacksonville	FL	32210	904-384-2279	
Autorama Inc 5389 Poplar Ave *Web:* www.mbofmemphis.com	Memphis	TN	38119	901-345-6211	
AutoRevo LTD 7920 Belt Line Rd Ste 450 *TF:* 888-311-7386 ■ *Web:* www.autorevo.com	Dallas	TX	75254	972-715-8600	
Aviation Devices & Electronic Components LLC 1810 Mony St *Web:* www.avdec.com	Fort Worth	TX	76102	817-738-9161	
Aviation Ground Equipment Corp 53 Hanse Ave *Web:* www.aviationgroundequip.com	Freeport	NY	11520	516-546-0003	
B & b Automotive Inc 301 W Market St *Web:* www.bbauto.org	Aberdeen	WA	98520	360-533-4113	
Badger Truck Ctr Inc 2326 W St Paul Ave *Web:* www.badgertruck.com	Milwaukee	WI	53233	414-344-9500	344-4323
Badger Utility Inc 4334 Daentl Rd *Web:* www.badger-utility.com	Deforest	WI	53532	608-249-5301	
Bain & Holden Tire Company Inc 100 N Amhurst Pl	Englewood	TN	37329	423-887-7932	
Baker & Sons Equipment Co 45381 SR- 145 *Web:* www.bakerandsons.com	Lewisville	OH	43754	740-567-3317	
Baker Motor Company Inc 1511 Savannah Hwy *Web:* www.bakermotorcompany.com	Charleston	SC	29407	843-852-4000	
Bale Chevrolet Co 13101 Chenal Pkwy *Web:* balechevrolet.com	Little Rock	AR	72211	501-221-9191	221-9484
Ball Automotive Group 1935 National City Blvd *Web:* www.ballauto.com	National City	CA	91950	619-474-6431	
Banner Equipment Company Inc 1370 Bungalow Rd *Web:* www.bannerbeer.com	Morris	IL	60450	815-941-9600	
Barry Bunker Chevrolet Inc 1307 N Wabash Ave *TF Sales:* 866-603-8625 ■ *Web:* barrybunker.com	Marion	IN	46952	765-664-1275	651-4238
Bartow Ford Co 2800 Us Hwy 98 N *Web:* bartowford.com	Bartow	FL	33830	863-533-0425	

				Phone	Fax
Baskin Auto Truck & Tractor Inc 1844 Hwy 51 S *TF:* 877-476-2626 ■ *Web:* www.baskintrandtr.com	Covington	TN	38019	901-476-2626	476-2658
Bates Ford 1673 W Main St *Web:* tonybatesford.com	Lebanon	TN	37087	615-444-8221	
Batterycorp Inc Three Speen St Ste 210 *Web:* www.batterycorp.com	Framingham	MA	01701	508-270-8402	
Baxter Chrysler Jeep Inc 17950 Burt St *Web:* baxterchryslerjeepdodge.net	Omaha	NE	68118	402-493-7800	
Bayway Lincoln-mercury Inc 12333 Gulf Fwy *Web:* clickmotive.com	Houston	TX	77034	888-262-9275	
Beach Ford Inc 2717 Virginia Beach Blvd *Web:* beachfordvirginiabeach.com	Virginia Beach	VA	23452	757-486-2717	
Becker Avionics Inc 10376 Usa Today Way *Web:* www.becker-avionics.com	Miramar	FL	33025	954-450-3137	
Bed Wood & Parts LLC 8345 Madisonville Rd *Web:* bedwoodandparts.com	Hopkinsville	KY	42240	270-424-3000	
Bell Aviation Inc 2404 Edmund Hwy *Web:* www.bellaviation.com	West Columbia	SC	29170	803-822-4114	822-8970
Bell Ford Inc 2401 W Bell Rd *Web:* www.bellford.com	Phoenix	AZ	85023	602-866-1776	
Bellamy Automotive Group Inc 145 Industrial Blvd *Web:* bellamystrickland.com	Mcdonough	GA	30253	770-954-3000	
Ben Davis Chevrolet 931 W Seventh St *Web:* bendavischevrolet.net	Auburn	IN	46706	260-925-3715	
Berge Ford 460 E Auto Ctr Dr *Web:* www.bergefordfleet.com	Mesa	AZ	85204	480-497-1111	
Bergstrom Automotive One Neenah Ctr *Web:* www.bergstromauto.com	Neenah	WI	54956	920-725-4444	729-5145
Bergstrom of Kaukauna 2929 Lawe St *TF:* 866-939-0130 ■ *Web:* www.bergstromchryslerjeep.com/contact-form.htm	Kaukauna	WI	54130	866-939-0130	
Best Chevrolet Inc 128 Derby St *Fax Area Code: 781 ■ *TF:* 866-208-7873 ■ *Web:* www.bestchevyusa.com	Hingham	MA	02043	866-208-7873	749-8153*
Big Country Autoland 4004 Spur Business 84 *Web:* bigcountryautoland.com	Snyder	TX	79549	325-573-5456	573-8391
Biggers Chevrolet 1385 E Chicago St *TF:* 866-431-1555 ■ *Web:* www.biggerschevy.com	Elgin	IL	60120	847-742-9000	742-0061
Bill Abbott Inc 500 W Ctr *Web:* billabbottinc.com	Monticello	IL	61856	217-762-2576	762-9932
Bill Black Chevrolet Cadillac Inc 601 E Bessemer Ave *Web:* billblackauto.com	Greensboro	NC	27405	336-275-9641	
Bill Collins 4220 BaRdstown Rd *TF:* 888-327-9095 ■ *Web:* billcollinsford.net	Louisville	KY	40218	502-459-9550	459-1966
Bill Currie Ford Inc 5815 N Dale Mabry Hwy *Web:* billcurrieford.com/	Tampa	FL	33614	813-872-5555	
Bill Penney Toyota 4808 University Dr NW *Web:* www.billpenneytoyota.com	Huntsville	AL	35816	256-837-1111	837-2077
Bill Snethkamp Lansing Dodge Inc 6131 S Pennsylvania Ave *TF:* 800-863-6343 ■ *Web:* www.billsnethkamp.com	Lansing	MI	48911	517-394-1200	394-1205
Bill Stasek Chevrolet Inc 700 W Dundee Rd *Web:* www.stasekchevrolet.com	Wheeling	IL	60090	847-537-7000	
Billings Nissan 2100 King Ave W *Web:* billingsnissan.com	Billings	MT	59102	406-655-1111	
Birchwood Automotive Group Ltd 35D-3965 Portage Ave *Web:* birchwood.ca	Winnipeg	MB	R3K2H7	204-832-1676	
Blaise Alexander Chevrolet Inc 933 Broad St *TF:* 877-575-4256 ■ *Web:* blaisealexander.com	Montoursville	PA	17754	570-368-8677	368-1010
Blossom Chevrolet Inc 1850 N Shadeland Ave *Web:* blossomchevy.com	Indianapolis	IN	46219	317-357-1121	
BMW of Darien 140 Ledge Rd *Web:* www.bmwdarien.com	Darien	CT	06820	203-656-1804	
BMW Toronto 11 Sunlight Park Rd *Web:* bmwtoronto.ca	Toronto	ON	M4M1B5	416-623-4269	
Bob Allen Ford 9239 Metcalf Ave *TF:* 888-573-6364 ■ *Web:* www.boballenford.com	Overland Park	KS	66212	913-381-3000	
Bob Brown Chevrolet Inc 3600 111th St *Web:* bobbrownchevy.com	Urbandale	IA	50322	515-278-7800	
Bob Davidson Ford Lincoln 1845 E Joppa Rd *TF:* 888-643-0263 ■ *Web:* www.bobdavidsonford.com	Baltimore	MD	21234	410-661-6400	668-4306
Bob Fisher Chevrolet Inc 4111 Pottsville Pike *Web:* www.bobfisherchev.com	Reading	PA	19605	610-370-6683	921-2202
Bob Montgomery Chevrolet Honda Inc 5340 Dixie Hwy *Web:* www.bobmontgomery.com	Louisville	KY	40216	502-448-2820	449-8553
Bob Sight Ford Inc 610 NW Blue Pkwy *Web:* bobsightford.com	Lees Summit	MO	64063	816-524-6550	
Bob Stall Chevrolet 7601 Alvarado Rd *TF:* 800-295-2695 ■ *Web:* www.bobstall.com	La Mesa	CA	91942	619-460-1311	
Bobby Murray Chevrolet Inc 1820 Capital Blvd *Web:* bobbymurray.com	Raleigh	NC	27604	919-834-6441	
Bohnert Equipment Company Inc 1010 S Ninth St *Web:* www.bohnert.com	Louisville	KY	40203	502-584-3391	
Bommarito Automotive Group 15736 Manchester Rd *TF:* 800-367-2289 ■ *Web:* www.bommarito.com	Ellisville	MO	63011	636-391-7200	394-3241
Bonner Chevrolet Company Inc 694 Wyoming Ave *Web:* www.bonnerchevrolet.com	Kingston	PA	18704	570-763-4799	288-0853
Bosserman Aviation Equipment Inc 2327 SR- 568 *Web:* www.bossermanaviationequip.com	Carey	OH	43316	419-396-6256	
Boucher Group Inc 4141 S 108th St *Web:* www.boucher.com	Greenfield	WI	53228	414-427-4141	427-4140
Bozard Ford Co 540 Outlet Mall Blvd *Web:* bozardford.com	St Augustine	FL	32084	904-824-1641	
Brasher Motor Company of Weimar Inc 1700 I- 10 *TF:* 800-783-1746 ■ *Web:* www.brashermotors.com	Weimar	TX	78962	979-725-8515	725-8118
Braxton Automotive Group Inc 1604 Howell Mill Rd NW Ste 3 *Web:* www.braxtonautogroup.com	Atlanta	GA	30318	404-367-4767	
Brickner Motors Inc 16450 County Rd A *Web:* bricknermotors.net	Marathon	WI	54448	715-842-5611	
Brighton Chrysler Plymouth Dodge Inc 9827 E Grand River	Brighton	MI	48116	810-229-4100	
Brighton Ford Inc 8240 W Grand River *Web:* brightonford.com	Brighton	MI	48114	810-227-1171	
Brogan Cadillac Co 112 Rt 46 E *Web:* brogancadillac.com	Totowa	NJ	07512	973-785-4300	
Brown & Miller Racing Solutions LLC 4005 Dearborn Pl NW *Web:* www.bmrs.net	Concord	NC	28027	704-793-4319	
Brown Automotive Group LP 4300 S Georgia *Web:* smallerprofit.com	Amarillo	TX	79110	806-353-7211	
Brumos Motor Cars Inc 10231 Atlantic Blvd *Web:* brumosmercedesjax.com	Jacksonville	FL	32225	866-955-5902	
BTECH Inc 10 Astro Pl *Web:* www.btechinc.com	Rockaway	NJ	07866	973-983-1120	
Buchanan Automotive Group 50 Central Ave Ste 900 *TF:* 888-292-4883 ■ *Web:* www.buchananautogroup.com	Sarasota	FL	34236	941-364-9500	
Buckeye Nissan Inc 3820 Pkwy Ln *Web:* buckeyenissan.com	Hilliard	OH	43026	614-771-2345	771-2363
Bud Weiser Motors Inc 2676 Milwaukee Rd *Web:* budweisermotors.com	Beloit	WI	53511	608-364-6340	
Burr Truck & Trailer Sales Inc 2901 Vestal Rd *TF:* 866-230-2383 ■ *Web:* www.burrtruck.com	Vestal	NY	13850	607-729-2211	729-4375
Bus Andrews Truck Equipment Inc 2828 N E Ave *TF:* 800-273-0733 ■ *Web:* busandrews.com	Springfield	MO	65803	417-869-1541	869-1656
Bush Inc 2581 Hickory Blvd SE *Web:* www.roosterbush.com	Lenoir	NC	28645	828-728-4222	728-7075
Butler County Ford 400 S Main St *Web:* www.butlercountyford.net	Butler	PA	16001	724-287-2766	283-0372
Byerly Ford 4041 Dixie Hwy *TF:* 888-436-0819 ■ *Web:* www.byerlyford.com	Louisville	KY	40216	502-448-1661	448-0819
Cable-Dahmer Chevrolet Inc 1834 S Noland Rd *TF:* 888-738-5260 ■ *Web:* www.cabledahmer.com	Independence	MO	64055	816-521-7508	521-7542
Cadillac Jack Inc 2450 Satellite Blvd *Web:* cadillacjack.com	Duluth	GA	30096	770-908-2094	
Cal Tech Precision Inc 1830 N Lemon St *Web:* www.caltechprecision.com	Anaheim	CA	92801	714-992-4130	
Callaway Cars Inc Three High St *Web:* www.callawaycars.com	Old Lyme	CT	06371	860-434-9002	
Camar Aircraft Parts Co 743 Flynn Rd *Web:* www.camarac.com	Camarillo	CA	93012	805-389-8944	
Canfield Equipment Service 21533 Mound Rd *Web:* www.canfieldequipment.com	Warren	MI	48091	586-757-2020	
Capistrano Scion 33395 Camino Capistrano *TF:* 888-493-0040 ■ *Web:* www.capistranoscion.com	San Juan Capistrano	CA	92675	949-493-4100	240-2445
Capital Automobile Co 2210 Cobb Pkwy SE *Web:* www.capitalcadillac.com	Smyrna	GA	30080	770-952-2277	989-8439
Capital Ford Inc 4900 Capital Blvd *TF:* 877-659-2496 ■ *Web:* www.capitalford.com	Raleigh	NC	27616	919-790-4600	871-6900
Capitol Chevrolet Montgomery 711 Eastern Blvd *TF Sales:* 800-410-1137 ■ *Web:* www.capitolchevrolet.com	Montgomery	AL	36117	334-272-8700	260-7179
Capitol Mitsubishi 750 Capitol Expy Automall *TF:* 888-479-0842 ■ *Web:* capitolmitsubishi.com	San Jose	CA	95136	408-264-9999	
Car City Motor Company Inc 3100 S US Hwy 169 *TF:* 800-525-7008 ■ *Web:* www.carcitymotors.com	Saint Joseph	MO	64503	816-233-9149	279-0639
Cardinal Honda 531 Rt 12 *Web:* www.cardinalhonda.com	Groton	CT	06340	860-449-0411	
CarMax Inc 12800 Tuckahoe Creek Pkwy *NYSE:* KMX ■ *TF:* 888-722-7629 ■ *Web:* www.carmax.com	Richmond	VA	23238	804-747-0422	217-6819
Carolina International Trucks Inc 1619 Bluff Rd *TF:* 800-868-4923 ■ *Web:* www.carolinainternational.com	Columbia	SC	29201	803-799-4923	
Carr Auto Group 11635 SW Canyon Rd *Web:* www.carrauto.com	Beaverton	OR	97005	503-644-2161	
Cars & Trucks r Us 7676 Happy Vly Rd *Web:* ucarsandtrucks.com	Cave City	KY	42127	270-773-2886	
Carter Motor Co 400 S Railroad St *Web:* www.cartermotor.com	Warren	IL	61087	815-745-2100	
Cascade Autocenter 148 Easy St *Web:* www.cascadeautocenter.com	Wenatchee	WA	98801	509-663-0011	
Cascadia International LLC 2312 Milwaukee Way *Web:* www.cascadiaint.com	Tacoma	WA	98421	520-622-6767	
Cavender Cadillac Co 801 Broadway St *Web:* www.cavendercadillac.com	San Antonio	TX	78215	210-226-7221	
Centric Parts Inc 14528 Bonelli St *Web:* centricparts.com	City Of Industry	CA	91746	626-961-5775	
CFI Tire Service 1520 E S Omaha Bridge Rd *Web:* cfitirecb.com	Council Bluffs	IA	51503	712-388-9744	
Champion Chevrolet Cadillac of Johnson City LLC 3606 Bristol Hwy *Web:* www.championjc.com/	Johnson City	TN	37601	423-282-2121	
Champion Preferred Automotive 2020 Lexington Rd *Web:* www.championpreferredautos.com	Nicholasville	KY	40356	859-269-4141	

				Phone	Fax
Chaplins Bellevue Subaru-volkswagen 15000 SE Eastgate Way	Bellevue	WA	98007	425-641-2002	
Web: www.chaplins.com					
Charles Gabus Ford Inc 4545 Merle Hay Rd	Des Moines	IA	50310	515-270-0707	270-2162
TF Sales: 800-934-2287 ■ *Web:* charlesgabusford.com/					
Checkered Flag Motor Car Corp 5225 Virginia Beach Blvd	Virginia Beach	VA	23462	757-687-3486	
TF: 866-414-7820 ■ *Web:* www.checkeredflag.com					
Chenoweth Ford Inc Rt 50 E	Clarksburg	WV	26301	304-623-6501	
Cherry Creek Dodge 2727 S Havana St	Denver	CO	80014	303-751-1104	
TF Sales: 888-891-7522 ■ *Web:* www.cherrycreekdodge.com					
Chino Hills Ford 4480 Chino Hills Pkwy	Chino	CA	91710	909-393-4617	
Web: chinohillsford.com					
Chrysler at Drivers Village 5885 E Cir Dr Ste 135	Cicero	NY	13039	315-452-1556	
Web: burdickdodgechryslerjeep.com					
Chuck Patterson Inc 200 E Ave	Chico	CA	95926	530-895-1771	230-2371
Web: www.chuckpattersontoyota.net					
Circle Buick Gmc Inc 2440 45th St	Highland	IN	46322	219-865-4400	
Web: circleautomotive.com					
City Auto Sales 4932 Elmore Rd	Memphis	TN	38128	901-377-9502	
Web: www.cityauto.com					
City Motors of Cartersville 352 N Tennessee St	Cartersville	GA	30120	770-382-5780	
Cityside Subaru 790 Pleasant St	Belmont	MA	02478	617-826-5000	
Web: citysidesubaru.com					
Cliff Findlay Auto Ctr Inc 3730 Stockton Hill Rd	Kingman	AZ	86409	928-757-4041	757-9701
Clinton Family Ford Lincoln Mercury of Rock Hill Inc 1884 Canterbury Glen Ln	Rock Hill	SC	29730	803-366-3181	
Web: clintonfamilyford.com					
Coastal Tractor Inc 10 Harris Pl	Salinas	CA	93901	831-757-4101	
Web: www.coastaltractor.com					
Coastline Equipment 1930 Lockwood St	Oxnard	CA	93036	805-485-2106	
Web: www.coastlineequipment.com					
Cobalt Truck Equipment 4620 E Trent Ave	Spokane	WA	99212	509-534-0446	
Web: www.critzer.com					
Coffman Truck Sales 1149 W Lake S PO Box 151	Aurora	IL	60507	630-892-7093	892-1080
TF: 800-255-7641 ■ *Web:* www.coffmantrucks.com					
College Station Ford 1351 Earl Rudder Fwy S	College Station	TX	77845	979-694-2022	
TF: 888-508-0241 ■ *Web:* varsityfordtexas.com					
Colussy Chevrolet 3073 Washington Pike	Bridgeville	PA	15017	412-564-4132	221-1607
Web: colussy.com					
Component Repair Technologies Inc 8507 Tyler Blvd	Mentor	OH	44060	440-255-1793	
Web: componentrepair.com					
Composite Solutions Corp 1820 W Vly Hwy N	Auburn	WA	98001	253-833-1878	
Web: www.compositesolutions.com					
Conant Auto Retail Group 18900 Studebaker Rd	Cerritos	CA	90703	888-318-5001	402-0442*
**Fax Area Code:* 562 ■ *TF:* 888-318-5001 ■ *Web:* www.thecargroup.com					
Concord Road Equipment Manufacturing Inc 348 Chester St	Painesville	OH	44077	440-357-5344	
Web: www.concordroadequipment.com					
Concours Motors Inc 1400 W Silver Spring Dr	Milwaukee	WI	53209	414-290-1400	
Web: concoursmotors.com					
Consumer Safety Technology Inc 10520 Hickman Rd Ste F	Des Moines	IA	50325	515-331-7643	
Web: www.intoxalock.com					
Control Logistics Inc 1213 Pope Ln	Lake Worth	FL	33460	561-641-2031	
Web: www.aerowindows.com					
Cook Gm Super Store 1193 W Saginaw Rd	Vassar	MI	48768	989-882-4074	823-7321
Web: cookgm.com					
Cook Truck Equipment & Tools 3701 Harlee Ave	Charlotte	NC	28208	704-392-4138	
Web: www.cooktruck.com					
Cooley Motors Corp 401 N Greenbush Rd	Rensselaer	NY	12144	518-283-2902	283-0258
TF: 866-308-0724 ■ *Web:* www.cooleyvw.com					
Cooper Motors Inc 985 York St	Hanover	PA	17331	717-632-4225	
Web: coopermotorsinc.com					
Coral Springs Auto Mall 9400 W Atlantic Blvd	Coral Springs	FL	33071	954-796-4525	
TF: 800-353-8660 ■ *Web:* www.coralspringsautomall.com					
Corning Ford Inc 2280 Short Dr	Corning	CA	96021	530-824-5434	
Web: www.corningford.com					
Costa Mesa Nissan 2850 Harbor Blvd	Costa Mesa	CA	92626	714-444-4220	
Web: www.connellnissan.com					
Coulter Cadillac Inc 1188 E Camelback Rd	Phoenix	AZ	85014	602-264-1188	532-4676
TF: 800-843-4237 ■ *Web:* coulteroncamelback.com					
Country Club Nissan 55 Oneida St	Oneonta	NY	13820	607-432-2800	
Web: otsegomitsubishi.com					
Court Street Ford Inc 558 William Latham Dr	Bourbonnais	IL	60914	815-939-9600	
Web: courtstreetford.com					
Courtesy Chevrolet 1233 E Camelback Rd	Phoenix	AZ	85014	602-235-0255	230-8072
TF: 877-295-4648 ■ *Web:* www.houseofcourtesy.com					
Courtesy Chrysler Jeep Dodge 9207 Adamo Dr E	Tampa	FL	33619	813-620-4300	
Web: www.courtesychryslerjeepdodge.com					
Courtney Honda 767 Bridgeport Ave	Milford	CT	06460	203-877-2888	
Web: courtneyhonda.com					
Crescent Ford Truck Sales 6121 Jefferson Hwy	Harahan	LA	70123	504-818-1818	818-0997
TF: 800-575-8785 ■ *Web:* crescenttrucks.com					
Criswell Automotive 503 Quince Orchard Rd	Gaithersburg	MD	20878	301-948-0880	
Web: www.criswellauto.com					
Crivelli Chevrolet Buick Inc 600 N Church St	Mt Pleasant	PA	15666	724-547-2200	
Crivelli Ford Inc 2085 Brodhead Rd	Aliquippa	PA	15001	724-857-0400	
Web: crivelliford.com					
Crown Auto Dealerships Inc 5237 34th St N	St Petersburg	FL	33714	727-527-7151	
Web: crowncars.com					
Crown Motors Ltd 196 Regent Blvd	Holland	MI	49423	616-396-5268	396-4850
TF: 800-466-7000 ■ *Web:* www.crownmotors.com					
Cumberland Chrysler Ctr 1550 Interstate Dr	Cookeville	TN	38501	888-277-4902	528-5851*
**Fax Area Code:* 931 ■ *TF:* 888-277-4902 ■ *Web:* www.cumberlandchryslercenter.com					
D-Patrick Inc 200 N Green River Rd	Evansville	IN	47716	812-473-6500	
TF: 800-831-6870 ■ *Web:* www.dpat.com					
Daewoo Motor America Inc 159 W Orangethorpe Ave Ste A	Placentia	CA	90870	714-961-7493	
Web: daewoous.com					
Dale Willey Automotive 2840 Iowa St PO Box 803	Lawrence	KS	66046	785-727-1124	843-4903
Web: dalewilleyauto.com					
Dan Wolf Chevrolet of Naperville 1515 W Ogden Ave	Naperville	IL	60540	630-596-1189	
TF: 800-243-8872 ■ *Web:* www.chevroletofnaperville.com					
DarCars Ltd 12210 Cherry Hill Rd	Silver Spring	MD	20904	301-622-0300	622-4915
Web: www.darcars.com					
Dave Sinclair Ford Inc 7466 S Lindbergh Blvd	Saint Louis	MO	63125	314-892-2600	
Web: www.davesinclairford.com					
Dave Walter 447 W Exchange St	Akron	OH	44302	330-434-8989	
Web: www.davewaltervw.com					
Dave White Chevrolet Inc 5880 Monroe St	Sylvania	OH	43560	419-517-6111	
Web: www.davewhitechevy.com					
David Taylor Cadillac Company Inc 10422 SW Fwy Bldg B	Houston	TX	77074	713-777-7151	
Web: www.davidtaylor.com					
Davis Automotive Group Inc 6135 Kruse Dr	Solon	OH	44139	440-542-0600	542-0700
Web: www.davisautomotive.com					
Day Automotive Group 1600 Golden Mile Hwy	Monroeville	PA	15146	724-327-0900	327-0765*
**Fax:* Acctg ■ *Web:* dayauto.com					
DCH Honda of Nanuet 10 Rt 304	Nanuet	NY	10954	845-623-1200	
TF: 888-495-8660 ■ *Web:* www.hondaofnanuet.com					
Dean Team Automotive Group Inc 15121 Manchester Rd	Ballwin	MO	63011	636-227-0100	227-0776
Web: www.deanteam.com					
Dearth Motors Inc 520 Eigth St	Monroe	WI	53566	608-325-3181	325-1262
TF: 877-495-5321 ■ *Web:* www.dearthmotorsinc.com					
Delaney Automotive Group 626 Water St	Indiana	PA	15701	724-349-3000	349-1188
Web: www.delaneyauto.com					
Dellenbach Motors 3111 S College Ave	Fort Collins	CO	80525	866-963-5689	226-0233*
**Fax Area Code:* 970 ■ *TF:* 866-963-5689 ■ *Web:* www.dellenbach.com					
DeMontrond 888 I- 45 S	Conroe	TX	77304	281-443-2500	442-7370*
**Fax Area Code:* 936 ■ *TF Sales:* 888-843-6583 ■ *Web:* www.demontrond.com					
Dempewolf Ford Inc 2530 Us 41 N	Henderson	KY	42420	270-827-3566	
Web: dempewolfford.com					
Denooyer Chevrolet Inc 127 Wolf Rd	Albany	NY	12205	518-458-7700	
Web: denooyerchevrolet.com					
Desert European Motorcars Ltd 71387 Hwy 111	Rancho Mirage	CA	92270	760-773-5000	773-4406
TF: 877-839-3035 ■ *Web:* www.indigoautogroupsocal.com					
Desert Sun Motors Inc 2600 N White Sands Blvd	Alamogordo	NM	88310	575-437-7530	
Web: www.desertsunmotors.com					
Designer Auto Sales 1304 10th Dr SE	Austin	MN	55912	507-434-0123	
Diamond Motors/Mazda 10968 Airline Hwy	Baton Rouge	LA	70816	225-295-3900	
Web: diamondmazda.com					
Diamond Truck Body Manufacturing Inc 1908 E Fremont St	Stockton	CA	95205	209-943-1655	
Web: www.diamondtruckbody.com					
Dick Brantmeier Ford Inc 3624 Kohler Memorial Dr	Sheboygan	WI	53081	920-458-6111	
Web: dickbrantmeier.com					
Dick Masheter Ford Inc 1090 S Hamilton Rd	Columbus	OH	43227	614-861-7150	861-7303
Web: masheterford.net					
Diehl Automotive Group Inc 258 Pittsburgh Rd	Butler	PA	16002	724-282-8898	
TF: 866-543-4523 ■ *Web:* www.diehlauto.com					
Dillon Dennis Auto Park & Truck Ctr Inc 2777 S Orchard St	Boise	ID	83705	208-336-6000	
Web: www.dennisdillon.com					
Direct Tire & Auto Service 126 Galen St	Watertown	MA	02472	617-923-1800	
Web: directtire.com					
Don Beyer Motors Inc 1231 W Broad St	Falls Church	VA	22046	703-237-5000	
Web: www.donbeyervolvo.com					
Don Chalmers Ford Inc 2500 Rio Rancho Blvd	Rio Rancho	NM	87124	505-897-2500	
Web: www.donchalmersford.com					
Don Herring Enterprises Ltd 4225 W Plano Pkwy	Plano	TX	75093	972-387-8600	
Web: www.donherring.com					
Don Hewlett Chevrolet Buick Inc 7601 S Interstate 35	Georgetown	TX	78626	512-681-3000	
Web: www.donhewlett.com					
Don McGill Toyota Inc 11800 Katy Fwy	Houston	TX	77079	281-496-2000	977-3097
TF: 877-259-6888 ■ *Web:* www.donmcgilltoyota.com					
Don Rasmussen Co 720 NE Grand Ave	Portland	OR	97232	503-230-7700	
Web: www.landroverportland.com					
Dossett Big 4 Buick Pontiac Cadillac Gmc Inc 628 S Gloster St	Tupelo	MS	38801	662-842-4162	
Web: dossettbig4.com					
Dothan Chrysler-Dodge Inc 4074 Ross Clark Cir NW	Dothan	AL	36303	877-674-9574	794-2600*
**Fax Area Code:* 334 ■ *TF:* 877-674-9574 ■ *Web:* www.dothanchryslerdodge.net					
DriveTime Corp 4020 E Indian School Rd	Phoenix	AZ	85018	888-418-1212	852-6696*
**Fax Area Code:* 602 ■ *TF:* 888-418-1212 ■ *Web:* www.drivetime.com					
Dueck Auto Group 12100 Featherstone Way	Richmond	BC	V6W1K9	604-273-1311	
TF: 877-993-8325 ■ *Web:* www.dueckgm.com					
Dunning Motors Inc 3745 Jackson Rd	Ann Arbor	MI	48103	734-997-7600	
Web: www.dunningtoyota.com					

Name / Address	City	State	Zip	Phone	Fax
Durand Chevrolet Inc 223 Washington St. *Web:* durandchevrolet.com	Hudson	MA	01749	978-562-7915	
Durocher Auto Sales Inc 4651 Rt 9 *TF:* 877-215-8954 ■ *Web:* www.durocherauto.com	Plattsburgh	NY	12901	877-215-8954	
Dyna-Empire Inc 1075 Stewart Ave *Web:* www.dyna-empire.com	Garden City	NY	11530	516-222-2700	
Earnhardt Auto Centers 7300 W Orchid Ln **Fax:* Sales ■ *TF:* 888-378-7711 ■ *Web:* www.earnhardt.com	Chandler	AZ	85226	480-926-4000	558-4050*
East Bay Ford Truck Sales Inc 70 Hegenberger Loop *TF:* 888-219-8551 ■ *Web:* www.eastbaytruckcenter.com	Oakland	CA	94621	510-272-4400	746-4486
Eastern Carolina Nissan 3315 Hwy 70 E *TF:* 888-944-7822 ■ *Web:* ecnissan.com	New Bern	NC	28564	252-636-1000	
Eau Claire Ford Lincoln Mercury 2909 Lorch Ave. *Web:* www.eauclaireford.com	Eau Claire	WI	54701	715-852-1000	
Eckenrod Ford Lincoln Mercury of Cullman Inc 5255 Alabama Hwy 157 *Web:* eckenrodford.com	Cullman	AL	35058	256-734-3361	
Ed Bozarth Chevrolet Inc 3731 S Topeka Ave. *Web:* www.edbozarthchevrolet.com	Topeka	KS	66609	785-266-5151	
Ed Martin Inc 3800 E 96th St *Web:* edmartinacura.com	Indianapolis	IN	46240	317-846-3800	
Ed Schmidt Automotive Group Inc 26875 Dixie Hwy *Web:* edschmidt.com	Perrysburg	OH	43551	419-874-4331	
El Cajon Motors D/B/A El Cajon Ford 1595 E Main St. *Web:* elcajonford.com	El Cajon	CA	92021	619-579-8888	
El Camino Store, The 420 Athena Dr. *TF:* 888-685-5987 ■ *Web:* www.elcaminostore.com	Athens	GA	30601	706-546-9217	
ELCO Chevrolet Cadillac 15110 Manchester Rd. *Web:* www.elcochevrolet.com	Ballwin	MO	63011	636-227-5333	
Electro Enterprises Inc 3601 N I-35 Service Rd *TF:* 800-324-6591 ■ *Web:* www.electroenterprises.com	Oklahoma City	OK	73111	405-427-6591	
Elk Grove Toyota 9640 W Stockton Blvd *Web:* www.elkgrovetoyota.com	Elk Grove	CA	95757	916-405-8000	
Elm Chevrolet Co Inc 301 E Church St *TF:* 877-265-6708 ■ *Web:* elmchevrolet.com	Elmira	NY	14901	607-734-4141	734-7649
Erhard Bmw Of Bloomfield Hills 4065 W Maple Rd *TF:* 888-481-4058 ■ *Web:* erhardbmw.com	Bloomfield Hills	MI	48301	248-642-6565	
Ernie Von Schledorn Country Inc N88 W14167 Main St *Web:* evsauto.com	Menomonee Falls	WI	53051	262-255-6000	
Ernst Auto Ctr Inc 615 E 23rd St *Web:* www.ernstauto.com	Columbus	NE	68601	402-835-4221	564-4566
F C Kerbeck & Sons 100 Rt 73 N *TF General:* 855-846-1500 ■ *Web:* www.fckerbeck.com	Palmyra	NJ	08065	856-829-8200	829-7036
Fair Oaks Ford Inc 2055 Wodgen Ave *Web:* fairoaksford.com	Naperville	IL	60540	630-355-8140	
Fairway Lincoln-Mercury Inc 10101 Abercorn St *Web:* www.fairwaylincolnmercury.com	Savannah	GA	31419	912-927-1000	
Feduke Ford 2200 Vestal Pkwy E *Web:* fedukeford.com	Vestal	NY	13850	607-754-5533	
Ferguson Buick Gmc 1015 N I- Dr *Web:* fergusonchallenge.com	Norman	OK	73069	405-253-0918	360-8854
Ferman Automotive Group 1306 W Kennedy Blvd. *Web:* www.fermanauto.com	Tampa	FL	33606	813-251-2765	254-4798
Ferrotherm Corp 4758 Warner Rd. *Web:* www.ferrotherm.com	Cleveland	OH	44125	216-883-9350	
Feussner'S Ford Inc 470 S St. *Web:* feussnersford.com	Freeland	PA	18224	570-636-3920	
Finchey Corp of California Dba Pacific Bmw 800 S Brand Blvd	Glendale	CA	91204	818-246-5600	
Findlay Automotive Group 310 N Gibson Rd. *Web:* www.findlayauto.com	Henderson	NV	89014	702-558-8888	
Finish Line Ford Inc 2211 W Pioneer Pkwy *TF:* 888-841-4002 ■ *Web:* www.finishlineford.net	Peoria	IL	61615	309-693-2525	
First Truck Centre Inc 11313 170 St *TF:* 888-882-8530 ■ *Web:* www.firsttruck.ca	Edmonton	AB	T5M3P5	780-413-8800	
Fitzgerald Auto Mall 10915 Georgia Ave *Web:* www.fitzmall.com	Wheaton	MD	20902	855-776-0552	
Fitzgerald Auto Mall Inc 114 Baughmans Ln *Web:* www.fitzmall.com	Frederick	MD	21702	301-696-9200	
Five Star Dodge 3068 Riverside Dr *TF:* 877-748-9845 ■ *Web:* www.fivestaronline.com	Macon	GA	31210	478-474-3700	757-4000
Five Star International LLC 6100 Wattsburg Rd *Web:* fivestarinternational.com	Erie	PA	16509	814-825-6150	
Fletch's Inc 825 Charlevoix Ave PO Box 265 *TF:* 877-238-0816 ■ *Web:* www.fletchs.com	Petoskey	MI	49770	231-347-9651	487-9665
Fletcher Jones Imports 7300 W Sahara Ave *TF:* 888-350-8850 ■ *Web:* www.fjimports.com	Las Vegas	NV	89117	702-364-2700	795-7154
Folsom Buick Gmc 12640 Auto Mall Cir *Web:* folsombuickgmc.com/	Folsom	CA	95630	916-358-8963	355-1230
Folsom Lake Ford 12755 Folsom Blvd *TF:* 800-730-0457 ■ *Web:* www.folsomlakeford.com	Folsom	CA	95630	916-353-2000	
Ford 504 N Main St. *Web:* galstererford.com	Frankenmuth	MI	48734	989-652-6157	
Ford of Montebello Inc 2747 Via Campo *TF:* 888-313-2305 ■ *Web:* www.fordofmontebello.com	Montebello	CA	90640	323-838-6920	
FordDirect 1740 Us Hwy 60 PO Box 700 *TF:* 888-865-2576 ■ *Web:* republicford-lincoln.com/	Republic	MO	65738	888-865-2576	
Fordham Auto Sales Inc 236 W Fordham Rd. **Fax Area Code:* 718 ■ *TF:* 800-407-1153 ■ *Web:* www.fordhamtoyota.com	Bronx	NY	10468	800-407-1153	367-0773*
Formula Ford Inc 265 River St. *Web:* formulatruckland.com	Montpelier	VT	05602	802-223-5201	
Fowler Holding Company Inc 2721 NW 36th Ave *Web:* fowlerholding.com	Norman	OK	73072	405-573-9909	
Francis Coppola Winery LLC 620 Airpark Rd *Web:* franciscoppolawinery.com	Napa	CA	94558	707-251-3200	
Frank Kent Cadillac Inc 3800 SW Blvd *Web:* frankkentcad.com	Fort Worth	TX	76116	817-763-5000	
Frank W Diver Inc 2101 Pennsylvania Ave *Web:* www.diverchev.com	Wilmington	DE	19806	302-575-0161	658-4599
Franklin Truck Parts Inc 6925 Bandini Blvd *Web:* www.franklintruckparts.com	Commerce	CA	90040	323-726-1034	
Frederick Motor Co, The One Waverley Dr	Frederick	MD	21702	301-663-6111	
FreeFlight Systems Inc 8150 Springwood Dr Ste 100 *Web:* www.freeflightsystems.com	Irving	TX	75063	254-662-0000	
Freightliner of Hartford Inc 222 Roberts St *TF:* 800-453-6967 ■ *Web:* freightlinerofhartford.com	East Hartford	CT	06108	860-289-0201	610-6242
Friendship Automotive Inc 1855 Volunteer Pkwy *Web:* friendshipford.com	Bristol	TN	37620	423-652-6200	652-6207
Frontier Ford 3701 Stevens Creek Blvd *Web:* frontierford.com	Santa Clara	CA	95051	408-241-1800	
Gabrielli Truck Sales Ltd 153-20 S Conduit Ave *Web:* www.gabriellitruck.com	Jamaica	NY	11434	718-977-7348	
Galpin Motors Inc 15505 Roscoe Blvd **Fax:* Acctg ■ *TF:* 800-256-7137 ■ *Web:* www.galpin.com	North Hills	CA	91343	818-787-3800	778-2210*
Gateway Industrial Power Inc 921 Fournie Ln *TF:* 888-865-8675 ■ *Web:* gipower.com	Collinsville	IL	62234	618-345-0123	
Gatorland Toyota-scion 2985 N Main St *Web:* gatorlandtoyota.com	Gainesville	FL	32609	352-376-3262	
Gene Langley Ford Inc 3500 E End Dr *Web:* genelangleyford.com	Humboldt	TN	38343	731-784-9311	
Germain Motor Co *Stevegermain* 4300 Morse Crossing *Web:* www.germain.com	Columbus	OH	43219	614-759-3033	
Gettel Automotive Group 3500 Bee Ridge Rd *Web:* www.gettel.com	Sarasota	FL	34239	941-921-2655	
Gillman Cos 10595 W Sam Houston Pkwy S **Fax:* Acctg ■ *TF:* 888-532-8956 ■ *Web:* www.gillmanauto.com	Houston	TX	77099	713-776-7000	*
Gilroy Chevrolet Cadillac Inc 6720 Bear Cat Ct *TF:* 800-201-7241 ■ *Web:* gilroychevy.com	Gilroy	CA	95020	408-842-9301	846-0649
GKN Armstrong Wheels Inc 801 E Skinner St	Wichita	KS	67211	316-943-3571	
Gladstone Dodge 5610 N Oak Trafficway **Fax Area Code:* 816 ■ *TF:* 866-695-2043 ■ *Web:* www.gladstonedodgekansascity.com	Gladstone	MO	64118	866-695-2043	414-3546*
Glendale Infiniti 812 S Brand Blvd *TF:* 800-449-9375 ■ *Web:* www.glendaleinfiniti.com	Glendale	CA	91204	818-543-5000	
Global Filtration Inc 9207 Emmott St *TF:* 888-717-0888 ■ *Web:* www.globalfiltration.com	Houston	TX	77040	713-856-9800	
GlobalPartsaero 901 Industrial Rd *Web:* www.globalparts.aero	Augusta	KS	67010	316-733-9240	
Globe Motor Car Co 1230 Bloomfield Ave *Web:* www.mbofcaldwell.com	Fairfield	NJ	07004	973-227-3600	575-7835
Globe Motors Inc 2275 Stanley Ave *TF:* 800-433-5700 ■ *Web:* www.globe-motors.com	Dayton	OH	45404	937-228-3171	
Godfrey Chevrolet-Buick Inc 1701 N Mitchell St *Web:* www.godfreychevroletbuick.com	Cadillac	MI	49601	231-775-4661	775-5120
Gore Design Completions Ltd 607 N Frank Luke Dr *Web:* www.goredesign.com	San Antonio	TX	78226	210-496-5614	
Gorges Motor Company Inc 2660 S Oliver St	Wichita	KS	67210	316-685-2201	
Graff Truck Centers Inc 1401 S Saginaw St *TF:* 888-870-4203 ■ *Web:* www.grafftruckcenter.com	Flint	MI	48503	810-239-8300	239-8561
Gray Chevrolet Cadillac 1245 N Ninth St *Web:* graychevrolet.com	Stroudsburg	PA	18360	570-517-5500	
Gregory Logistics Inc 2844 Fair St *Web:* www.gregorylogistics.com	Poplar Bluff	MO	63901	573-785-1088	
Gregs Japanese Auto Parts & Service 1506 S 348th St *Web:* www.gregs.com	Federal Way	WA	98003	253-815-1500	
Gridley Country Ford-mercury 1709 State Hwy 99 *Web:* www.gridleycountryford.com	Gridley	CA	95948	530-846-4724	
Grossinger Motorcorp Inc 6900 N McCormick Blvd *Web:* grossinger.com	Lincolnwood	IL	60712	847-674-9000	
Grossinger Motors 1430 Fort Jesse Rd *Web:* www.sudsmotorcars.com	Normal	IL	61761	888-719-0095	
Group 1 Automotive Inc 800 Gessner Ste 500 *NYSE:* GPI ■ **Fax:* Hum Res ■ *TF:* 888-707-4094 ■ *Web:* www.group1auto.com	Houston	TX	77024	713-647-5700	647-5858*
Grubbs Infiniti Ltd 1661 Airport Fwy *TF:* 800-685-1111 ■ *Web:* infiniti.grubbs.com	Euless	TX	76040	817-318-1200	359-4100
Gryphon Mobile Electronics LLC 489 Yorbita Rd Ste B *Web:* gryphonmobile.com	La Puente	CA	91744	626-810-7770	
Guardian Jet LLC 1445 Boston Post Rd Ste 1 *Web:* www.guardianjet.com	Guilford	CT	06437	203-453-0800	
Gulf Coast Autoplex Inc 407 Shankland Ave *Web:* gulfcoastautoplex.net	Jennings	LA	70546	337-824-4486	
Gunn Automotive Group 227 Broadway *Web:* www.gunnauto.com	San Antonio	TX	78205	210-472-2501	472-2514
Gurley Leep Automotive Group 5302 Grape Rd *Web:* www.gurleyleep.com	Mishawaka	IN	46545	574-272-0990	256-5427
Gurley Motor Co 701 W Coal *Web:* gurleymotor.com	Gallup	NM	87301	505-722-6621	
Gustman Chevrolet Sales Inc 1450 Delanglade St *Web:* www.gustman.com	Kaukauna	WI	54130	920-766-3581	766-0520
H & H Chevrolet LLC 4645 S 84 St *Web:* hhchevy.com	Omaha	NE	68127	402-339-2222	

Phone Fax

H&R Construction Parts & Equipment Inc
20 Milburn St .... Buffalo NY 14212 716-891-4311
Web: www.hrparts.com

Hainen Ford Inc 800 Hwy 5 S .... Tipton MO 65081 888-526-6979
TF: 888-526-6979 ■ *Web:* hainenford.com

Hall Automotive LLC 441 Viking Dr .... Virginia Beach VA 23452 757-431-9944
Web: www.hallauto.com

Hamilton Chevrolet 5800 E 14 Mile Rd .... Warren MI 48092 586-264-1400 276-1531
TF: 888-466-7827 ■ *Web:* hamiltonchevy.com/

Harte Nissan Inc 165 W Service Rd .... Hartford CT 06120 860-549-2800
TF: 866-687-8971 ■ *Web:* www.hartenissan.com

Harvey Cadillac Co 2600 28th St SE .... Grand Rapids MI 49512 616-949-1140 954-1201
Web: harveycadillac.com

Hastings Automotive Inc 3625 Vermillion St .... Hastings MN 55033 651-437-4030
Web: hastingsautos.com

Headquarter Toyota 5895 NW 167th St .... Miami FL 33015 305-364-9800 824-1298
TF: 800-549-0947 ■ *Web:* www.headquartertoyota.com

Hendrick Automotive Group
6000 Monroe Rd Ste 100 .... Charlotte NC 28212 704-568-5550 566-3295
Web: www.hendrickauto.com

Hendrick Buick GMC Cadillac
1151 W 104th St .... Kansas City MO 64114 816-942-7100
TF: 888-255-9362 ■ *Web:* www.hendrickcadillackansascity.com

Henna Chevrolet Inc 8805 N Ih 35 .... Austin TX 78753 512-832-1888
Web: henna.com

Hennessy River View Ford 2200 US Hwy 30 .... Oswego IL 60543 630-897-8900 897-3366
Web: www.riverviewford.com

Herb Chambers 259 McGrath Hwy .... Somerville MA 02145 617-666-8333 666-8448
Web: www.herbchambers.com

Herb Chambers I 95 Inc 107 Andover St .... Danvers MA 01923 877-907-1965 774-5116*
*Fax Area Code: 978 ■ *TF:* 877-907-1965 ■ *Web:* www.herbchamberschevrolet.com

Herb Easley Motors Inc
1125 Central Fwy .... Wichita Falls TX 76306 940-723-6631 767-3655
TF: 866-232-8859 ■ *Web:* www.herbeasley.com

Herb Gordon Nissan
3131 Automobile Blvd .... Silver Spring MD 20904 866-399-7502
TF: 855-414-4810 ■ *Web:* www.herbgordonnissan.com

Heritage Ford Inc 2100 Sisk Rd .... Modesto CA 95350 209-529-5110
Web: www.heritagefordmodesto.com

Herson's Inc 15525 Frederick Rd .... Rockville MD 20855 888-203-8318 517-8369*
*Fax Area Code: 301 ■ *TF:* 888-203-8318 ■ *Web:* www.hersonsauto.com

Hertrich Family of Automobile Dealerships
26905 Sussex Hwy .... Seaford DE 19973 302-629-4553 629-8428
Web: www.hertrichs.com

Hesser Toyota Scion 1811 Humes Rd .... Janesville WI 53545 608-754-7754 756-8894
Web: www.hessertoyota.com

High Country Performance 4x4 Inc
1695 W Hamilton Pl .... Englewood CO 80110 303-761-7379
Web: hcp4x4.com

Hiland Toyota 5500 45th Ave Dr .... Moline IL 61265 309-764-2481 764-3141
Web: www.hilandtoyota.com

Hines Park Lincoln Inc 40601 Ann Arbor Rd .... Plymouth MI 48170 734-453-2424 453-8333
Web: www.hinesparklincolnplymouth.com/

Hinshaws Acura/Honda 5955 20th St E .... Fife WA 98424 253-922-8830
Web: hinshawsacura.com

Holler Automotive Group 1011 N Wymore Rd .... Winter Park FL 32789 407-645-4969
Web: www.hollerclassic.com

Holman Cadillac Co 1200 Rt 73 S .... Mount Laurel NJ 08054 856-778-1000 222-9136
TF: 866-865-6973 ■ *Web:* holmancadillac.com

Holz Motors Inc 5961 S 108th Pl .... Hales Corners WI 53130 414-425-2400
Web: www.holzmotors.com

HomeRunAutoSales 301 Green Ave N .... Stevens Point WI 54481 715-341-2440 341-5424
Web: www.homerunautosales.com

Honda Carland 11085 Alpharetta Hwy .... Roswell GA 30076 770-993-2805
Web: hondacarland.com

Honda of Santa Monica
1726 Santa Monica Blvd .... Santa Monica CA 90404 310-264-4900 829-7289*
*Fax: Sales ■ *TF:* 800-269-2031 ■ *Web:* www.hondaofsantamonica.com

Honda World 10645 Studebaker Rd .... Downey CA 90241 562-929-7000
TF: 888-458-9404 ■ *Web:* www.lahondaworld.com

Honolulu Ford Lincoln & Mercury
1370 N King St .... Honolulu HI 96817 808-532-1700
Web: www.honoluluford.com

Hoover Toyota 2686 Hwy 150 .... Hoover AL 35244 205-978-2600 978-2594
TF: 866-980-8082 ■ *Web:* www.hoovertoyota.com

Horwith Trucks Inc PO Box 7 .... NorthHampton PA 18067 610-261-2220 261-2916
TF: 800-220-8807 ■ *Web:* www.horwithfreightliner.com

Hoselton Chevrolet Inc
909 Fairport Rd .... East Rochester NY 14445 585-586-7373
Web: hoselton.com

House Chevrolet Co 410 Main St S .... Stewartville MN 55976 507-533-4255
Web: housechevrolet.com

Hunt Ford Inc 6825 Crain Hwy .... La Plata MD 20646 301-934-8186
Web: huntfordinc.com

Ididit Inc 610 S Maumee St .... Tecumseh MI 49286 517-424-0577
Web: www.ididitinc.com

Igarashi Motor Sales USA LLC
710 Colomba Ct .... Saint Charles IL 60174 630-587-1177
Web: www.igusa.com

Imlay City Ford Inc 1788 S Cedar St .... Imlay City MI 48444 810-724-5900
Web: imlaycityford.com

Import Auto World 21571 Mission Blvd .... Hayward CA 94541 510-581-1200 581-1228
Web: importautoworldinc.com

Indy Honda 8455 US 31 S .... Indianapolis IN 46227 317-887-0800 885-5723
TF: 888-752-4589 ■ *Web:* www.indyhonda.com

Injen Technology Company Ltd 244 Pioneer Pl .... Pomona CA 91768 909-839-0706
Web: www.injen.com

Island Lincoln-Mercury Inc
1850 E Merritt Island Cswy .... Merritt Island FL 32952 321-452-9220
TF: 800-392-3673

Jack Giambalvo Motor Co 1390 Eden Rd .... York PA 17402 717-781-2154 854-5509
Web: jackgiambalvo.com

Phone Fax

Jack Powell Ford-Mercury Inc
1418 Se 1 St .... Mineral Wells TX 76067 940-325-1331
Web: jackpowellford.com

James Wood Motors Inc 2111 Us Hwy 287 S .... Decatur TX 76234 940-627-2177 627-8542
TF: 888-833-7230 ■ *Web:* www.jameswood.com

Jay Wolfe Automotive Group
1011 W 103rd St .... Kansas City MO 64114 816-943-6060 942-5399
Web: www.jaywolfe.com

Jedco Inc 1615 Broadway NW .... Grand Rapids MI 49504 616-459-5161
Web: jedco.us

Jenkins & Wynne Inc 328 College St .... Clarksville TN 37040 931-647-3353 245-5288
Web: www.jenkinsandwynne.com

Jerry Haag Motors Inc 1475 N High St .... Hillsboro OH 45133 937-402-2090 393-4860
Web: www.jerryhaagmotors.com

Jet X Aerospace 400 N York Rd .... Bensenville IL 60106 847-750-8888
Web: www.jetxaerospace.com

Jim Ellis Auto Dealerships
5901 Peachtree Industrial Blvd S .... Atlanta GA 30341 770-458-6811
Web: www.jimellis.com

Jim McKay Chevrolet Inc 3509 University Dr .... Fairfax VA 22030 703-591-4800 591-8021
Web: jimmckaychevrolet.com

JM Family Enterprises Inc
100 Jim Moran Blvd .... Deerfield Beach FL 33442 954-429-2000 429-2244
Web: www.jmfamily.com

Joe Holland Chevrolet Inc
210 Maccorkle Ave SW .... South Charleston WV 25303 304-744-1561
Web: www.joeholland.com

Joe Van Horn Chevrolet Inc PO Box 238 .... Plymouth WI 53073 920-893-6361 893-0953
TF: 800-236-1415 ■ *Web:* www.vanhornchev.com

John Hine Mazda Inc 1545 Camino Del Rio S .... San Diego CA 92108 619-297-4251 682-3713
Web: www.johnhine.com

John Lance Ford Inc 23775 Ctr Ridge Rd .... Westlake OH 44145 440-871-8600
Web: autonationfordwestlake.com

John Mcclaren Chevrolet Inc
1015 E Mcgregor Dr .... Mcgregor TX 76657 254-840-3261
Web: johnmcclarenchevrolet.com

John Watson Chevrolet 3535 Wall Ave .... Ogden UT 84401 801-394-2611 393-5002
TF: 866-647-9930 ■ *Web:* www.johnwatsonchevrolet.com

Johnny Londoff Chevrolet Inc 1375 Dunn Rd .... Florissant MO 63031 314-837-1800 837-0105

Johnson Lexus of Raleigh 5839 Capital Blvd .... Raleigh NC 27616 919-877-1800
Web: johnsonlexusraleigh.com

Johnson Motors Inc 1891 Blinker Pkwy .... Du Bois PA 15801 814-371-4444 371-1272
TF: 800-537-1768 ■ *Web:* www.johnsonauto.com

Jon Lancaster Inc 3501 Lancaster Dr .... Madison WI 53718 608-243-5500
Web: eastmadisontoyota.com/

Joyce Motors Corp 3166 SR- 10 .... Denville NJ 07834 973-361-3000
TF: 844-332-5955 ■ *Web:* www.joycehonda.com

Karl Tyler Chevrolet Inc 3663 N Reserve .... Missoula MT 59808 406-721-2438
Web: gmofmontana.com

Keeler Motor Car Co 1111 Troy Schenectady Rd .... Latham NY 12110 518-785-4197
TF: 800-474-4197 ■ *Web:* www.keeler.com

Ken Fowler Motors 1265 Airport Pk Blvd .... Ukiah CA 95482 707-468-0101 462-2475
TF: 800-287-0107 ■ *Web:* www.fowlerautocenter.com

Ken Garff Automotive Group
405 S Main St .... Salt Lake City UT 84111 801-257-3400
TF: 888-630-6838 ■ *Web:* www.kengarff.com

Ken Grody Ford 6211 Beach Blvd .... Buena Park CA 90621 714-521-3110
Web: www.kengrody.com

Ken Wilson Ford Inc 769 Champion Dr .... Canton NC 28716 828-648-2313
Web: www.kenwilsonford.net

Kendall Imports LLC 10943 S Dixie Hwy .... Miami FL 33156 305-665-6581
Web: www.kendalltoyota.com

Kenworth Northwest Inc
20220 International Blvd S PO Box 98967 .... SeaTac WA 98198 206-433-5911 878-7676
TF: 800-562-0060 ■ *Web:* www.kenworthnorthwest.com

Kenworth of Indianapolis Inc
2929 S Holt Rd .... Indianapolis IN 46241 317-247-8421 241-5742
TF: 800-827-8421 ■ *Web:* www.palmertrucks.com

Key Cadillac Inc 6825 York Ave S .... Edina MN 55435 952-920-4300 920-4821
Web: keycadillac.com

Keyes Toyota 5855 Van Nuys Blvd .... Van Nuys CA 91401 818-782-0122 907-4128
Web: www.keyestoyota.com

Keyser & Miller Ford Inc
Eight E Main St .... Collegeville PA 19426 610-489-9366 489-4590
Web: www.keysermillerford.com

Keyser Bros Cadillac Inc
4130 Sheridan Dr .... Williamsville NY 14221 716-634-4100 634-4326

Kightlinger Motors Inc 358 Rt 6 W .... Coudersport PA 16915 814-274-9660
Web: kightlingermotor.com

King-o'rourke Cadillac Inc
756 Smithtown Byp .... Smithtown NY 11787 631-724-4700 724-4784
Web: kingorourkeautogroup.com

Klick-lewis Inc 720 E Main St .... Palmyra PA 17078 717-838-1353
Web: www.klicklewis.com

Knippelmier Chevrolet Inc 1811 E Hwy 62 E .... Blanchard OK 73010 405-485-3333
Web: knippelmier.com

Koerner Ford of Syracuse Inc
805 W Genesee St .... Syracuse NY 13204 315-474-4275
Web: koernerford.com

Kolosso Toyota 3000 W Wisconsin Ave .... Appleton WI 54914 920-738-3666 738-3661
TF: 888-565-6776 ■ *Web:* www.kolossotoyota.com

Koons Ford of Annapolis Inc 2540 Riva Rd .... Annapolis MD 21401 410-224-2100
TF: 888-313-5524 ■ *Web:* www.koonsford.com

Kuni Automotive Group
17800 SE Mill Plain Blvd Ste 190 .... Vancouver WA 98683 503-372-7457
Web: www.kuniauto.com

L & S Truck Ctr of Appleton Inc
330 N Bluemound Dr PO Box 1255 .... Appleton WI 54914 920-749-1700 749-0818
TF: 888-617-3140 ■ *Web:* www.lstruck.com

La Beau Bros Inc
295 N Harrison Ave PO Box 246 .... Kankakee IL 60901 815-933-5519 933-4366
TF: 800-747-9519 ■ *Web:* www.labeautrucks.com

				Phone	*Fax*
La Belle Dodge Chrysler Jeep Inc 501 S Main St	Labelle	FL	33935	863-675-2701	379-6125*
**Fax Area Code:* 941 ■ *TF:* 800-226-1193 ■ *Web:* www.labelledodgechryslerjeep.com					
La Mesa Rv Ctr Inc 7430 Copley Pk Pl	San Diego	CA	92111	858-874-8000	874-8021
TF Sales: 888-509-4199 ■ *Web:* www.lamesarv.com					
Lafferty Chevrolet 829 W St Rd	Warminster	PA	18974	215-259-5817	672-3594
Web: www.laffertychevy.com					
Lafontaine Honda 2245 S Telegraph Rd	Dearborn	MI	48124	866-567-5088	
TF: 866-567-5088 ■ *Web:* lafontainehonda.com					
Lakeside International LLC 11000 W Silver Spring Rd	Milwaukee	WI	53225	414-353-4800	353-2743
TF: 800-236-0444 ■ *Web:* www.lakesidetrucks.com					
Lakeside Toyota 3701 N Cswy Blvd	Metairie	LA	70002	504-833-3311	831-7310
TF Sales: 877-512-8274 ■ *Web:* www.lakesidetoyota.com					
Lambert Buick Pontiac-Gmc Truck Inc 2409 Front St	Cuyahoga Falls	OH	44221	330-923-9771	
Web: lambertgm.com					
Lancaster Toyota Inc 5270 Manheim Pk	East Petersburg	PA	17520	888-424-1295	569-6713*
**Fax Area Code:* 717 ■ *TF:* 888-424-1295 ■ *Web:* www.lancastertoyota.com					
Land Rover of Calgary 175 Glendeer Cir SE	Calgary	AB	T2H2S8	403-255-1994	
Web: landrovercalgary.com					
Landers Ford Inc 2082 W Poplar Ave	Collierville	TN	38017	888-281-5266	
TF: 888-281-5266 ■ *Web:* www.landersfordmemphis.com					
Landmark Lincoln-Mercury Inc 5000 S Broadway	Englewood	CO	80113	303-761-1560	761-0405
TF: 866-971-7207 ■ *Web:* landmarklincoln.com					
Lankota Inc 270 Wpark Ave	Huron	SD	57350	605-352-4550	
Web: www.lankota.com					
Larry Green Chevrolet Oldsmobile & Geo Inc 2050 Rodeo Dr	Cottonwood	AZ	86326	928-634-2227	
Web: larrygreenchevrolet.com					
Larry H Miller Automotive Group 9350 S 150 E Ste 1000	Sandy	UT	84070	801-563-4100	563-4198
Web: www.lhmauto.com					
Larry Hopkins Honda 1048 W El Camino Real	Sunnyvale	CA	94087	408-720-1888	
Web: www.larryhopkinshonda.com					
Larry Roesch Chrysler-jeep-dodge LLC 200 W Grand Ave	Elmhurst	IL	60126	630-834-8000	
Web: www.larryroesch.com					
Lavery Chevrolet-Buick Inc 1096 W State St	Alliance	OH	44601	330-823-1100	823-8754
Web: laveryauto.com					
Lawrence Hall Chevrolet Inc 1385 S Danville Dr	Abilene	TX	79605	325-695-8800	692-1657
TF: 800-568-7158 ■ *Web:* www.lawrencehall.com					
Leach Enterprises 4304 Il Rt 176	Crystal Lake	IL	60014	815-459-6917	
Web: www.leach-ent.com					
Lee Air Company Inc 7545 Wheatland Ave	Sun Valley	CA	91352	818-767-0777	
Web: www.leeairinc.com					
LEKTRO Inc 1190 SE Flightline Dr	Warrenton	OR	97146	503-861-2288	
TF: 800-535-8767 ■ *Web:* www.lektro.com					
Lemay Auto Group 8220-75th St	Kenosha	WI	53142	262-694-2000	764-2687
TF: 866-689-1492 ■ *Web:* www.lemayautogroup.com					
Les Stanford Chevrolet Inc 21730 Michigan Ave	Dearborn	MI	48124	313-457-0364	
TF: 800-836-0972 ■ *Web:* lesstanfordchevrolet.com					
Levin Tire Center 5713 Broadway	Merrillville	IN	46410	219-887-0531	
Web: www.levintirecenter.com					
Lewis Ford Sales Inc 3373 N College Ave PO Box 8430	Fayetteville	AR	72703	479-442-5301	443-7293
Web: lewiscars.com/					
Lexus of Memphis Inc 2600 Ridgeway Rd	Memphis	TN	38119	901-362-8833	
TF Sales: 877-876-9996 ■ *Web:* lexusofmemphis.com					
Lia Auto Group, The 1258 Central Ave PO Box 5789	Albany	NY	12205	518-489-2111	489-2112
Web: www.liacars.com					
Liccardi Ford Inc 1615 Rt 22 W	Watchung	NJ	07069	908-561-7500	
Web: liccardifordlincoln.com					
Lindsay Cadillac Co 1525 Kenwood Ave	Alexandria	VA	22302	703-998-6600	
Web: lindsaycars.com/					
Lithia Motors Inc 360 E Jackson St	Medford	OR	97501	866-318-9660	774-7617*
NYSE: LAD ■ **Fax Area Code:* 541 ■ *TF:* 866-318-9660 ■ *Web:* www.lithia.com					
Lockhart Cadillac Inc 5550 N Keystone Ave	Indianapolis	IN	46220	317-644-2817	
Web: www.lockhartcadillac.com					
Loeber Motors Inc 4255 W Touhy Ave	Lincolnwood	IL	60712	847-675-1000	
TF: 888-211-4485 ■ *Web:* www.loebermotors.com					
Lordco Parts Ltd 22866 Dewdney Trunk Rd	Maple Ridge	BC	V2X3K6	604-467-1581	463-7557
TF: 877-591-1581 ■ *Web:* www.lordco.com					
Lou Bachrodt Auto Group 7070 Cherryvale N Blvd	Rockford	IL	61112	815-332-3000	
TF: 866-635-2349 ■ *Web:* www.bachrodt.com					
Lujack's Northpark Auto Plaza 3700 N Harrison St	Davenport	IA	52806	855-383-1590	
Web: www.lujack.com					
Lupient Automotive Group (LAG) 750 Pennsylvania Ave S	Minneapolis	MN	55426	763-544-6666	513-5517
Web: www.lupient.com					
Lynch Ford - Mt Vernon Inc 410 Hwy 30 SW	Mount Vernon	IA	52314	319-895-8500	895-8100
Web: www.lynchfordchevrolet.com					
Lynch Management Co 2165 River Blvd	Jacksonville	FL	32204	904-387-1537	
Lynn Layton Chevrolet Inc 2416 Hwy 31 S	Decatur	AL	35601	256-274-4665	
Web: www.lynnlaytonchevrolet.com					
Mac Haik Auto Group 11711 Katy Fwy	Houston	TX	77079	281-596-6261	
TF: 888-877-1748 ■ *Web:* www.machaik.com					
Mac Haik Ford Inc 10333 Katy Fwy	Houston	TX	77024	713-932-5000	932-5027
Web: www.machaikford.com					
Maclean Assoc LLC Dba Land Rover Guilford 1700 Boston Post Rd	Guilford	CT	06437	203-453-7060	
Magnussen Dealership Group 401 Burgess Dr Ste A	Menlo Park	CA	94025	650-327-4100	
Main Line Tire & Service 102 Robbins Rd	Downingtown	PA	19335	610-514-3600	
Web: unitedtire.com					
Maple Hill Auto Group 5622 W Main St	Kalamazoo	MI	49009	269-342-6600	327-9883
Web: www.maplehillauto.com					
Mark Chevrolet Inc 33200 Michigan Ave	Wayne	MI	48184	734-629-4964	
Web: www.markchevrolet.com					
Mark Thomas Motors Inc 2315 Santiam Hwy PO Box 188	Albany	OR	97321	541-967-9105	
Web: www.markthomasmotors.com					
Markley Motors 3325 S College Ave	Fort Collins	CO	80525	970-226-2214	226-2237
TF: 888-480-5167 ■ *Web:* www.markleymotors.com					
Marquette Public Service Garage 919 W Baraga Ave	Marquette	MI	49855	906-662-4395	
Web: www.publicservicegarage.com					
Marshal Mize Ford Inc 5348 Hwy 153	Chattanooga	TN	37343	888-633-5038	
Web: marshalmizeford.net/					
Martin Automotive Group 12101 W Olympic Blvd	Los Angeles	CA	90064	310-622-9334	622-9334
Web: martinautogroup.com					
Martin Automotive Group Inc 1065 Ashley St Ste 100	Bowling Green	KY	42103	270-783-8080	781-4792
Web: www.martingp.com					
Marty Franich Ford Lincoln 550 Auto Ctr Dr	Watsonville	CA	95076	831-722-4181	724-6897
Marvin K. Brown Auto Ctr Inc 1441 Camino Del Rio S	San Diego	CA	92108	619-291-2040	
Web: www.mkb.com					
Massive Audio 2261 S Atlantic Blvd	Commerce	CA	90040	323-262-2262	
Web: www.massiveaudio.com					
Matt Blatt Inc 501 Delsea Dr N	Glassboro	NJ	08028	856-881-0444	
Web: www.mattblatt.com					
Matthews Currie Ford Company Inc 130 N Tamiami Trl	Nokomis	FL	34275	941-488-6787	
Web: matthewscurrie.net/					
Mazda Knoxville 8814 Kingston Pk	Knoxville	TN	37923	865-690-9395	690-0619
Web: www.mazdaknoxville.com					
Mazda of Roswell 11185 Alpharetta Hwy	Roswell	GA	30076	770-993-6999	
Web: mazdaofroswell.com					
McCloskey Motors Inc 6710 N Academy Blvd	Colorado Springs	CO	80918	719-594-9400	535-8036
TF: 877-389-6671 ■ *Web:* www.bigjoeauto.com					
McDevitt Trucks Inc One Mack Ave PO Box 4640	Manchester	NH	03108	603-668-1700	668-1865
TF: 800-370-6225 ■ *Web:* www.mctrucks.com					
McGrath Auto Group 4610 Ctr Pt Rd NE	Cedar Rapids	IA	52402	888-902-8414	294-3025*
**Fax Area Code:* 319 ■ *TF:* 888-902-8414 ■ *Web:* www.mcgrathauto.com					
Mclean Implement Inc 793 Illinois Rte 130	Albion	IL	62806	618-445-3676	445-2846
TF: 888-720-4440 ■ *Web:* www.mcleanimp.com					
Meade Auto Group 45001 Northpointe Blvd	Utica	MI	48315	586-803-6250	
Web: www.meadeauto.com					
Medved Autoplex 11001 N I 70 Service Rd	Wheat Ridge	CO	80033	303-421-0100	
Web: www.medved.com					
Medved Chevrolet Inc 11001 W I-70 Frontage Rd N	Wheat Ridge	CO	80033	303-421-0100	
Web: medved.com					
Meiji Corp 660 Fargo Ave	Elk Grove Village	IL	60007	847-364-9333	
Web: www.meijicorp.com					
Melloy Nissan 7707 Lomas Blvd NE	Albuquerque	NM	87110	505-265-8721	268-0124
Web: www.melloynissan.com					
Memering Motorplex Inc 1949 Hart St	Vincennes	IN	47591	812-882-5367	886-4605
Web: www.memeringmotorplex.com					
Mercedes-Benz Canada Inc 98 Vanderhoof Ave	Toronto	ON	M4G4C9	416-425-3550	
Web: www.mercedes-benz.ca					
Mercedes-Benz of San Francisco 500 Eigth St	San Francisco	CA	94103	415-673-2000	673-6100
TF: 877-554-6016 ■ *Web:* www.sfbenz.com					
Mercedes-Benz USA LLC 4500 Stevens Creek Blvd	San Jose	CA	95129	408-641-4610	615-4335
Web: mbofstevenscreek.com/					
Merchants Automotive Group Inc 1278 Hooksett Rd	Hooksett	NH	03106	603-669-4100	
Web: www.merchantsauto.com					
Merollis Chevrolet Sales & Service Inc 21800 Gratiot Ave	Eastpointe	MI	48021	586-775-8300	
Web: www.merollischevy.com					
Metro Ford Inc 9000 NW Seventh Ave	Miami	FL	33150	877-811-9402	
TF: 877-811-9402 ■ *Web:* www.metroford.com					
Michael Roberts Auto Sales 9051 SR- 2830	Maceo	KY	42355	270-264-7100	
Mid-City Motor World 4800 N Hwy 101	Eureka	CA	95503	707-443-4871	
Web: midcitymotorworld.com					
Mike Calvert Toyota Inc 2333 S Loop W	Houston	TX	77054	713-558-8100	
Web: mikecalverttoyota.com					
Mike Reed Chevrolet 1559 E Oglethorpe	Hinesville	GA	31313	877-228-3943	368-2336*
**Fax Area Code:* 912 ■ *TF:* 877-228-3943 ■ *Web:* mikereedchevy.com					
Mike Savoie Chevrolet Inc PO Box 520	Troy	MI	48084	248-643-8000	649-3007
Web: www.mikesavoie.com					
Miller Motorcars Inc 342 W Putnam Ave	Greenwich	CT	06830	203-629-3890	
Web: www.millermotorcars.com					
Milton Martin Toyota 2350 Browns Bridge Rd	Gainesville	GA	30504	770-532-4355	536-1385
Web: www.miltonmartintoyota.com					
Minato Auto LLC Dba Toyota of Portsmouth 150 Greenleaf Ave	Portsmouth	NH	03801	603-431-6100	
Mission Golf Cars 18865 Redland Rd	San Antonio	TX	78259	210-545-7868	402-0576
Web: www.missiongolfcars.com					
Mission Valley Ford Truck Sales Inc 780 E Brokaw Rd PO Box 611150	San Jose	CA	95112	408-933-2300	436-0313
TF: 888-284-7471 ■ *Web:* missionvalleykubota.com					
Modern Chevrolet of Winston-Salem 5955 University Pkwy	Winston Salem	NC	27105	336-722-4191	785-8455
TF General: 888-306-0825 ■ *Web:* www.modernchevy.com					
Molle Toyota Inc 601 W 103rd St	Kansas City	MO	64114	816-942-5200	942-4796
TF: 888-510-7705 ■ *Web:* www.molletoyota.com					
Montesi Motors Inc 444 State St	North Haven	CT	06473	203-281-0481	287-3734
TF: 866-598-2263 ■ *Web:* www.montesivolkswagen.com					

				Phone	Fax
Morganton Honda 1600 Burkemont Ave *Web:* morgantonhonda.com	Morganton	NC	28655	828-437-3181	
Morrison Industrial Equipment Co 1825 Monroe NW PO Box 1803 *Web:* www.morrison-ind.com	Grand Rapids	MI	49505	616-447-3800	361-0885
Mossy Motors Inc 1331 S Broad St *Web:* www.mossymotors.com	New Orleans	LA	70125	504-822-2050	826-5614
Motor Inn of Knoxville LLC 114 S Sixth St *Web:* motorinnautogroup.com	Estherville	IA	51334	712-362-5834	
Motorcars International 3015 E Cairo St *TF:* 866-970-6800 ■ *Web:* www.motorcars-intl.com	Springfield	MO	65802	417-831-9999	831-9995
Motors Management Inc D/B/Atroy Honda 1835 Maplelawn	Troy	MI	48084	248-649-0202	
Murray Motor Imports Co 4300 E Kentucky Ave *Web:* murraymotors.com	Glendale	CO	80246	303-759-3400	
Muzi Motors Inc 557 Highland Ave *Web:* www.muzimotors.com	Needham Heights	MA	02494	781-444-5300	
Nalley Lexus Smyrna 2750 Cobb Pkwy SE *TF:* 877-454-4206 ■ *Web:* www.nalleylexussmyrna.com	Smyrna	GA	30080	877-454-4206	
National Auto Stores Inc 2512 Quakertown Rd *Web:* www.nationalautostores.com	Pennsburg	PA	18073	215-679-2300	
National Car Mart Inc 9255 Brookpark Rd *Web:* www.nationalcarmart.com	Cleveland	OH	44129	216-505-1750	
National Standard Parts Assoc Inc 4400 Mobile Hwy *TF:* 800-874-6813 ■ *Web:* www.nspa.com	Pensacola	FL	32506	850-456-5771	
National Tire & Wheel Five Garden Ct *TF:* 800-847-3287 ■ *Web:* www.ntwonline.com	Wheeling	WV	26003	304-233-7917	
National Tool Warehouse 221 W Fourth St Ste 4 *Web:* nationaltoolwarehouse.com	Carthage	MO	64836	417-358-1919	
Nationwide Lift Trucks Inc 3900 N 28th Terr *TF:* 800-327-4431 ■ *Web:* www.toyotanlt.com	Hollywood	FL	33020	954-922-4645	922-8770
Nevada Auto Mall Inc 2501 E Austin Blvd *Web:* nevadaautomall.net	Nevada	MO	64772	417-667-3385	
New Country Motor Car Group 358 Broadway Ste 403 *Web:* www.newcountry.com	Saratoga Springs	NY	12866	518-584-7700	584-8611
New Country Volkswagen of Greenwich 200 W Putnam Ave **Fax Area Code:* 203 ■ *TF:* 866-584-6747 ■ *Web:* newcountry.com	Greenwich	CT	06830	866-584-6747	622-1001*
Newins Bay Shore Ford Inc 219 W Main St *Web:* www.newinsbayshoreford.com	Bay Shore	NY	11706	631-665-1300	665-1311
Nextran Corp 1986 W Beaver St *TF:* 800-347-6225 ■ *Web:* www.nextrancorp.com	Jacksonville	FL	32209	904-354-3721	
NFI Inc Dba Harrisonburg Honda Mitsubishi Hyundai 2885 S Main St	Harrisonburg	VA	22801	540-433-1467	
Nick Alexander Imports Inc 6333 S Alameda St *Web:* alexanderbmw.com	Los Angeles	CA	90001	323-583-1901	
Nick Crivelli Chevrolet Inc 294 State Ave *Web:* nickcrivelli.com	Beaver	PA	15009	724-987-5000	728-9730
Nielsen Dodge Chrysler Jeep Ram 175 Rt 10 E *Web:* nielsendodgechryslerjeepram	East Hanover	NJ	07936	973-884-2100	884-2737
Nissan of Atlantic City 6021 Black Horse Pike *Web:* www.admiralnissan.com	Egg Hbr Twp	NJ	08234	609-646-1104	646-0730
Nitrous Express Inc 5411 Seymour Hwy *TF:* 888-463-2781 ■ *Web:* www.nitrousexpress.com	Wichita Falls	TX	76310	940-767-7694	767-7697
Noarus Auto Group 6701 Ctr Dr W Ste 925 *Web:* www.noarus.com	Los Angeles	CA	90045	310-258-0920	337-4860
Norauto Inc 23 111 Rte O *Web:* norautoamos.com	Amos	QC	J9T2X6	819-732-5352	
Norduyn Inc 6200 Henri-Bourassa W *Web:* www.norduyn.com	Montreal	QC	H4R1C3	514-334-3210	334-2989
Norman Frede Chevrolet Co 16801 Feather Craft Ln *TF:* 888-307-1703 ■ *Web:* www.fredechevrolet.com	Houston	TX	77058	281-486-2200	486-2201
Norris Ford 901 Merritt Blvd *TF Sales:* 866-460-5275 ■ *Web:* www.norrisford.com	Baltimore	MD	21222	410-285-0200	285-0872
North Bay Nissan Inc 1250 Auto Ctr Dr *TF:* 877-818-6866 ■ *Web:* www.northbaynissan.com	Petaluma	CA	94952	707-769-7700	
North Park Lincoln 9207 San Pedro St *TF:* 888-696-5480 ■ *Web:* nplincoln.com	San Antonio	TX	78216	210-341-8841	
Northtown Automotive Cos Inc 1135 Millersport Hwy *Web:* www.northtownauto.com	Amherst	NY	14226	716-614-7000	
Northway Toyota 727 New Loudon Rd *TF:* 877-525-3488 ■ *Web:* www.northwaytoyota.net	Latham	NY	12110	518-783-1951	785-4957
O Neill's Chevrolet & Buick Inc Five W Main St PO Box A *Web:* www.oneillschevybuick.com	Avon	CT	06001	860-269-3279	
O'Gara Coach Company LLC 8833 W Olympic Blvd **Fax Area Code:* 310 ■ *TF:* 888-291-5533 ■ *Web:* www.ogaracoach.com	Beverly Hills	CA	90211	888-291-5533	652-9656*
O'rielly Chevrolet Inc 6100 E Broadway Blvd *Web:* www.orielly.com	Tucson	AZ	85711	520-829-4400	790-7356
Orange Coast Chrysler Jeep Dodge 2929 Harbor Blvd *Web:* www.ocauto.com	Costa Mesa	CA	92626	714-549-8023	549-2558
Orange Motors Company Inc 799 Central Ave *Web:* www.orangemotors.com	Albany	NY	12206	518-489-5414	489-5501
Orlando Dodge Chrysler Jeep 4101 W Colonial Dr *Web:* orlandododge.com	Orlando	FL	32808	407-299-1120	
Otics USA Inc 5555 Interstate View Dr *Web:* oticsusa.com	Morristown	TN	37813	423-581-9933	
Otto Instrument Service Inc 1441 Valencia Pl *Web:* www.ottoinstrument.com	Ontario	CA	91761	909-930-5800	

				Phone	Fax
Outten Chevrolet Inc 1701 W Tilghman St *Web:* outtenchevyallentown.com	Allentown	PA	18104	610-628-3600	820-5774
Overseas Military Sales Corp 175 Crossways Park Dr W *Web:* www.encs.com	Woodbury	NY	11797	516-921-2800	
Paddock Chevrolet Inc 3232 Delaware Ave *Web:* www.paddockchevrolet.com	Kenmore	NY	14217	716-876-0945	876-4016
Palm Automotive Group 1801 Tamiami Trail PO Box 512049 *TF General:* 800-643-2112 ■ *Web:* www.palmautomall.com	Punta Gorda	FL	33950	941-639-1155	
Palm Beach Motor Cars Ltd Inc 915 S Dixie Hwy *Web:* palmbeachmotorcars.com	West Palm Beach	FL	33401	561-659-6206	
Palmetto Chevrolet Company Inc 1122 Fourth Ave *Web:* palmettochevy.com	Conway	SC	29526	843-248-4283	
Papastavros Assoc Medical Imaging Inc 1701 Augustine Cut Off Bldg 4 *Web:* www.papastavros.com	Wilmington	DE	19803	302-652-3016	652-2534
Paradise Chevrolet 6350 Leland St *Web:* www.paradisechevrolet.com	Ventura	CA	93003	805-642-0111	
Park Place Volvo 3515 Inwood Rd *Web:* parkplace.com/	Dallas	TX	75209	214-956-5500	
Parktown Imports Inc 10230 Manchester Rd *Web:* parktownimports.com	Kirkwood	MO	63122	314-965-7711	
Parsons Buick Co, The 151 E St *TF:* 877-274-2613 ■ *Web:* www.parsonsbuick.com	Plainville	CT	06062	860-747-1693	747-5734
Partschannel Inc 119 Regal Row Rd Ste B *TF:* 800-562-2126 ■ *Web:* www.partschannel.com	Dallas	TX	75247	214-688-0018	
Pat Milliken Ford Inc 9600 Telegraph Rd *Web:* www.patmillikenford.com	Redford	MI	48239	313-255-3100	
Paul Heuring Motors Inc 720 N Hobart Rd *TF:* 888-851-9702 ■ *Web:* www.paulheuring.com	Hobart	IN	46342	219-942-3673	942-9637
Paul Moak Automotive Inc 740 Larson St **Fax Area Code:* 800 ■ *TF:* 888-804-2108 ■ *Web:* www.paulmoak.com	Jackson	MS	39202	601-352-2700	331-3333*
PDQ Auto Supply of Manville Inc 240 N First Ave	Manville	NJ	08835	908-526-0888	
Pearman Motor Company Ltd 240 N Marcus *Web:* pearmanmotor.com	Alto	TX	75925	936-858-4188	
Pepe Motors group/Mercedes-Benz of White Plains 50 Bank St *Web:* www.mbwhiteplains.com	White Plains	NY	10606	914-949-4000	
Perth Amboy Spring Works 185 Sheridan St	Perth Amboy	NJ	08861	732-442-4420	
Pertronix Inc 440 E Arrow Hwy *Web:* www.pertronix.com	San Dimas	CA	91773	909-599-5955	
Pete Baur Buick GMC Inc 14000 Pearl Rd *Web:* petebaur.com	Cleveland	OH	44136	440-580-4256	572-8639
Peters of Nashua 300 Amherst St *Web:* www.petersauto.com	Nashua	NH	03063	603-889-1166	
Phil Long Dealerships 1212 Motor City Dr *TF:* 866-644-1378 ■ *Web:* phillong.com	Colorado Springs	CO	80905	866-644-1378	
Phil Smart Inc 600 E Pike St *TF:* 877-241-4528 ■ *Web:* www.mbseattle.com	Seattle	WA	98122	206-324-5959	328-4478
Phil Smith Automotive Group 4250 N Federal Hwy *Web:* www.philsmithauto.com	Lighthouse Point	FL	33064	954-867-1234	316-9469
Phillips Automotive Inc 4949 Virginia Beach Blvd *Web:* mercedesbenzofvirginiabeach.com/	Virginia Beach	VA	23462	757-499-3771	
Phillips Buick-Pontiac-Gmc Truck Inc 2160 US Hwy 441 *TF:* 888-664-7454 ■ *Web:* www.phillips-buick.com	Fruitland Park	FL	34731	352-728-1212	728-1444
Piercey Automotive Group 16901 Millikan Ave *TF:* 877-280-1044 ■ *Web:* www.pierceyautogroup.com	Irvine	CA	92606	949-396-6000	
Pignataro Volkswagon 10633 Evergreen Way *Web:* pignataro.com	Everett	WA	98204	425-348-3141	
Pitts Toyota Inc 210 N Jeffreson St PO Box 4013 *TF:* 888-561-8030 ■ *Web:* www.pittstoyota.com	Dublin	GA	31021	478-272-3244	272-1524
Planet Honda 2285 Us Hwy 22 W *Web:* www.planethondanj.com	Union	NJ	07083	908-964-1600	
Pollard Friendly Ford Company 3301 S Loop 289 *Web:* pollardfriendlyford.com/	Lubbock	TX	79423	806-797-3441	
Porsche of Maplewood 2780 Maplewood Dr *TF:* 888-693-6579 ■ *Web:* www.porscheofstpaul.com	Maplewood	MN	55109	888-679-1698	
Potamkin Automotive Group Inc 6200 NW 167th Ste B *Web:* www.potamkinautomotive.com	Miami Lakes	FL	33137	305-728-5000	774-7697
Potter-webster Co 41 NE Walker St *Web:* www.potterwebster.com	Portland	OR	97211	503-283-4792	
Premier Subaru LLC 150 N Main St PO Box 3366 *TF:* 800-411-4551 ■ *Web:* www.premiersubaru.com	Branford	CT	06405	203-481-0687	481-1861
Premier Truck Parts Inc 5800 W Canal Rd *Web:* www.premiertruckparts.com	Cleveland	OH	44125	216-642-5000	
Prestige Chrysler Dodge Inc 200 Alpine St *TF:* 866-439-1926 ■ *Web:* www.prestigechryslerdodge.com	Longmont	CO	80501	303-651-3000	
Price Ford of Turlock 5200 N Golden State Blvd *Web:* www.pricefordofturlock.com	Turlock	CA	95382	209-669-5200	669-5235
Priority Chevrolet of Chesapeake 1495 S Military Hwy *TF:* 855-315-0212 ■ *Web:* www.priorityauto.com	Chesapeake	VA	23320	757-424-1811	
Pro-system Inc 121 Oakpark Dr *Web:* www.prosystems.com	Mooresville	NC	28115	704-799-8100	
Production Automation Co 6200 Bury Dr *Web:* www.gotopac.com	Eden Prairie	MN	55346	952-903-0333	
Prostrollo Motor Sales Inc PO Box 1415 **Fax Area Code:* 605 ■ *TF:* 866-466-4515 ■ *Web:* www.prostrollo.com	Huron	SD	57350	866-466-4515	352-9286*
Puklich Chevrolet Inc 3701 State St *Web:* puklichchevrolet.com	Bismarck	ND	58502	701-223-5800	

Phone | Fax

Purvis Ford Inc
3660 Jefferson Davis Hwy Ste 1 Ste 1 .... Fredericksburg VA 22408 540-898-3000 710-1432
Web: purvisford.net

Putnam Lexus 390 Convention Way............ Redwood City CA 94063 650-363-8500
Web: www.putnamlexus.com

Quality Tower Erectors & Service Inc
2280 10th St SE ....Largo FL 33771 727-585-6176
Web: www.qualitytower.com

RAPCO Inc 445 Cardinal Ln.........................Hartland WI 53029 262-367-2292
Web: rapcoinc.com

Ray Catena Motor Car Corp 910 US Hiwy Rt 1 ....Edison NJ 08817 732-549-6600 549-6983
Web: www.raycatena.com

Ray Seraphin Ford Inc
100 Windsor Ave ....Vernon Rockville CT 06066 860-875-3369
Web: rayseraphinfordinc.com

RC Olsen Cadillac Inc 201 Cambridge Rd.............Woburn MA 01801 781-336-4814
Web: olsencadillac.com

Real Don Johnson Brownsville, The
2101 Central Blvd.............................Brownsville TX 78520 956-546-2288
Web: www.realdonjohnson.com

Reed Motors Inc 3776 W Colonial Dr ....Orlando FL 32808 407-297-7333 581-1968
Web: www.reednissan.com

Reichard Buick GMC 161 Salem Ave ....Dayton OH 45406 937-401-2034 220-6746
Web: www.reichardbuick.com

Reliable Chevrolet Inc 800 N Central Expy .... Richardson TX 75080 972-952-1500 897-6000*
**Fax Area Code:* 505 ■ *Web:* www.reliablechev.com

Renntech Inc 1369 N Killian Dr....................Lake Park FL 33403 561-845-7888
Web: www.renntechmercedes.com

RF Inc T/A Frankel Acura 10400 York Rd......... Cockeysville MD 21030 410-666-5300

Rhoden Auto Ctr Inc 3400 S Expy St .... Council Bluffs IA 51501 712-309-4000 309-4001
TF: 866-562-6248 ■ *Web:* www.rhodenloancity.com

Ricart Automotive Group 4255 S Hamilton Rd .... Columbus OH 43125 888-631-9726 836-6286*
**Fax Area Code:* 614 ■ *TF:* 888-225-6783 ■ *Web:* www.ricart.com

Rick Case Automotive Group
875 N SR 7.................................Fort Lauderdale FL 33317 888-502-8130 587-6381*
**Fax Area Code:* 954 ■ *Web:* www.rickcase.com

Rickenbaugh Cadillac Co 777 Broadway ....Denver CO 80203 303-573-7773 573-5808
Web: rickenbaughvolvo.com

Rippy Cadillac LLC 4951 New Centre Dr........... Wilmington NC 28403 910-799-2421

River States Truck & Trailer
3959 N Kinney Coulee Rd........................ La Crosse WI 54601 608-784-1149
Web: www.riverstates.com

Riverside Ford 1419 Ludington St..................Escanaba MI 49829 906-786-1130 786-7788
TF: 877-326-5326 ■ *Web:* www.riversidefordescanaba.com

Riverside Ford Inc 2089 Riverside Dr PO Box 225.......Macon GA 31204 478-464-2900 752-7850
TF Sales: 800-395-6210 ■ *Web:* www.riversideford.net

Rnr Custom Wheels & Tires
8030 Florida Blvd............................ Baton Rouge LA 70806 225-926-7466
Web: rnrwheels.com

RnR RV Ctr 23203 E Knox Ave....................Liberty Lake WA 99019 866-386-4875
TF: 866-386-4875 ■ *Web:* www.rnrrv.com

Robberson Ford Lincoln Mercury Mazda
2289 NE Third St...............................Prineville OR 97754 541-447-6820
Web: www.robberson.com

Roberson Motors Inc 3100 Ryan Dr SE .... Salem OR 97301 503-363-4117
TF: 888-281-6220 ■ *Web:* www.robersonmotorschryslerjeep.com

Roger Dean Chevrolet Inc
2235 Okeechobee Blvd.....................West Palm Beach FL 33409 561-683-8100 683-7332
TF: 877-827-4705 ■ *Web:* www.rogerdeanchevrolet.com

Roland D Kelly Infiniti Inc
155 Andover St Rt 114.............................Danvers MA 01923 978-774-1000 774-8788
Web: www.kellyauto.com

Romero Mazda 1307 Kettering Dr .... Ontario CA 91761 909-390-8484 390-4595
TF: 888-317-2233 ■ *Web:* www.romeromazda.com

Ron Carter Automotive Group 3205 FM 528............ Alvin TX 77511 281-331-3111 358-3253*
**Fax Area Code:* 248 ■ *TF:* 800-531-8285 ■ *Web:* www.roncarter.com

Ron Tonkin Dealerships 122 NE 122nd Ave...........Portland OR 97230 503-255-4100 252-4899
Web: tonkinchevrolet.com

Rosen Aviation LLC 1020 Owen Loop S .... Eugene OR 97402 541-342-3802
Web: www.rosenaviation.com

Rosenthal Automotive Organization
1902 Association Dr...............................Reston VA 20191 703-553-4300 553-8435
Web: www.rosenthalauto.com

Rosewell Toyota 2211 W Second St................. Roswell NM 88201 575-622-5860
Web: www.roswelltoyota.com

Rosner Auto Group
3507 Jefferson Davis Hwy .... Fredericksburg VA 22408 855-265-5075 710-8580*
**Fax Area Code:* 540 ■ *TF Sales:* 855-271-7618 ■ *Web:* www.rosnerauto.com

Rowleys Tires & Automotive Services
3596 Wilder Rd..................................Bay City MI 48706 989-686-1144
Web: www.rowleystires.com

Roy Nichols Motors Ltd 2728 Courtice Rd ....Courtice ON L1E2M7 905-436-2222
Web: roynicholsmotors.com

Ruggeri-Jensen-Azar & Assoc
4690 Chabot Dr.................................Pleasanton CA 94588 925-227-9100
Web: rja-gps.com

Rush Truck Center - Whittier 2450 Kella Ave .... Whittier CA 90601 562-551-5000 695-1737
TF: 877-605-7623 ■ *Web:* rushtruckcenters.com

Russ Darrow Group Inc
W133 N8569 Executive Pkwy .... Menomonee Falls WI 53051 262-250-9600
Web: russdarrow.com

Russell Karting Specialties Inc PO Box 1220........ Raymore MO 64083 816-322-3330 322-2860
TF: 800-821-3359 ■ *Web:* russellkarting.com

Russo & Steele LLC 5230 S 39th St ....Phoenix AZ 85040 602-252-2697
Web: russoandsteele.com

RV World Inc of Nokomis 2110 Tamiami Trl N .... Nokomis FL 34275 941-966-2182 966-4356
TF: 800-262-2182 ■ *Web:* www.rvworldinc.com

Ryan Automotive LLC 200 Carter Dr...................Edison NJ 08817 732-650-1550

Rye Ford Inc 1151 Boston Post Rd .... Rye NY 10580 914-967-6300
Web: ryeford.com

Saccucci Honda 1350 W Main Rd................ Middletown RI 02842 401-847-4737
Web: saccucci.com

Salisbury Motor Company Inc
700 W Innes St PO Box 4137.......................Salisbury NC 28144 704-636-1341
Web: www.salisburymotorcompany.com

Sam Swope Auto Group LLC
I-64 Hurstbourne Pkwy Ste I........................Louisville KY 40201 502-499-5020
Web: www.samswope.com

Sam Swope Volkswagen of Clarksville
125 W Lewis & Clark Pkw .... Clarksville IN 47129 812-948-1541 948-1240
TF: 866-308-0592 ■ *Web:* samswopevolkswagen.com

Sandy Sansing Chevrolet
6200 N Pensacola Blvd.......................... Pensacola FL 32505 850-476-2480 476-1163
TF Sales: 888-885-1844 ■ *Web:* www.sandysansingchevrolet.com

Santa Maria Ford Lincoln
1035 E Battles Rd ....Santa Maria CA 93454 805-925-2445 925-7165
Web: santamariaford.com

Santa Maria Tire Inc 249 Montgomery Ave ....Oxnard CA 93036 805-642-0174
Web: www.smtire.com

Saratoga Honda
3402 S Broadway PO Box 797 ....Saratoga Springs NY 12866 518-587-9300 587-0846
Web: www.saratogahonda.com

Scap Auto Group 421 Tunxis Hill Rd ....Fairfield CT 06825 203-384-9300
Web: www.scapauto.com

Scat Enterprises Inc
1400 Kingsdale Ave .... Redondo Beach CA 90278 310-370-5501
Web: www.procarbyscat.com

Schmit Ford-Mercury Corp
121 N Main St PO Box 8.........................Thiensville WI 53092 262-242-1100 242-7028
Web: schmitfordmerc.net/?lang=en

Schukei Chevrolet Inc
721 S Monroe PO Box 1525..................... Mason City IA 50401 641-423-5402
TF: 866-918-6497 ■ *Web:* schukei.com

Schumacher European Ltd
18530 N Scottsdale Rd.............................Phoenix AZ 85054 480-991-1155
Web: mbofnorthscottsdale.com/

Scott Family of Dealerships 3333 Lehigh St......... Allentown PA 18103 800-274-1039 966-3742*
**Fax Area Code:* 610 ■ *TF:* 800-274-1039 ■ *Web:* www.scottcars.com

Scott-Mc Rae Advertising
701 Riverside Pk Pl ....Jacksonville FL 32204 904-354-4000
Web: scottmcraejobs.com

Scranton Motors Inc 777 Talcottville Rd...............Vernon CT 06066 860-872-9145
Web: scrantonmotors.com

Sears Imported Autos Inc
13500 Wayzata Blvd ....Minnetonka MN 55305 952-546-5301 546-2899
TF Sales: 800-493-1720 ■ *Web:* sears.mercedesdealer.com

Seekins Ford Lincoln Inc
1625 Seekins Ford Dr.............................Fairbanks AK 99701 907-459-4000
Web: seekins.com

Seneca Tank Inc 5585 NE 16th St................Des Moines IA 50313 515-262-5900
TF: 800-362-2910 ■ *Web:* www.senecatank.com

Serra Automotive 3118 E Hill Rd................Grand Blanc MI 48439 810-694-1720
Web: serrausa.com

Servco Pacific Inc 2850 Pukoloa Ste 300............Honolulu HI 96819 808-564-1300 523-3937
Web: www.servco.com

Shamaley Buick GMC 955 Crockett Way .... El Paso TX 79922 915-317-5958 581-9203
Web: www.shamaleygm.com

Sheehy Auto Stores 12701 Fair Lakes Cir.............. Fairfax VA 22033 703-802-3480
Web: www.sheehy.com

Shelly Automotive Group
Irvine BMW 9881 Research Dr....................Irvine CA 92618 888-853-7429
TF: 888-853-7429 ■ *Web:* www.shellygroup.com

Sheppard Motors 2300 W Seventh Ave............... Eugene OR 97402 541-343-8811
TF Sales: 877-362-1865 ■ *Web:* www.sheppardmotors.com

Shock Tech Inc 360 Rt 59 Ste 3..................... Airmont NY 10952 845-368-8600
Web: www.shocktech.com

Showcase Honda 1333 E Camelback Rd..............Phoenix AZ 85014 866-956-6481
TF: 855-788-5798 ■ *Web:* www.showcasehonda.com

Shults Management Group Inc
181 E Fairmount Ave........................... Lakewood NY 14750 716-763-1551

Sierra Volkswagen Inc
510 E Norris Dr PO Box 456........................Ottawa IL 61350 866-308-5670 431-2519*
**Fax Area Code:* 815 ■ *TF:* 866-308-5670 ■ *Web:* www.sierravw.com

Silver Star Automotive Group
Lotus of Thousand Oaks
3601 Auto Mall Dr....................... Thousand Oaks CA 91362 800-472-5450
TF: 800-472-5450 ■ *Web:* www.silverstarauto.com

Simmons-rockwell Inc 784 County Rd 64 .... Elmira NY 14903 607-796-5555
Web: www.simmons-rockwell.com

Simplex Manufacturing Co
13340 NE Whitaker Way...........................Portland OR 97230 503-257-3511
Web: simplex.aero/

Simpsons on The Spot Auto Detailing
2953 Pleasant Grove Rd..........................Lansing MI 48910 517-393-7910

Sisbarro Dealerships 425 W Boutz Rd .... Las Cruces NM 88005 575-524-7707
TF: 888-241-1007 ■ *Web:* www.sisbarro.com

Sitton Buick GMC 2640 Laurens Rd .... Greenville SC 29607 864-288-5600
TF: 888-484-8009 ■ *Web:* sittongm.net

Sky Mart Sales Corp
9475 NW 13th St PO Box 522007 ....Miami FL 33172 305-592-0263 592-8359
Web: www.skymartsales.com

Skybooks Inc 1310 Tradeport Dr ....Jacksonville FL 32218 904-741-8700
TF: 866-929-8700 ■ *Web:* www.skybooks.com

Skycom Avionics Inc 2441 Aviation Rd .... Waukesha WI 53188 262-521-8180
Web: www.skycomavionics.com

Smith Motors Inc of Hammond
6405 Indianapolis Blvd.......................... Hammond IN 46320 219-845-4000 989-7233
TF: 877-392-2689 ■ *Web:* www.smithchevyusa.com

Smoky Mountain Truck Ctr LLC
841 Eastern Star Rd PO Box 5729 ....Kingsport TN 37663 423-349-3000 349-0431
TF: 800-451-1508 ■ *Web:* www.smtruckcenter.com

Smythe Volvo Inc 326 Morris Ave.................. Summit NJ 07901 908-273-4200
Web: smythevolvo.com

Snell MotorsInc 1900 Madison Ave................... Mankato MN 56001 507-345-4626
Web: snellmotors.com

Phone Fax

Snowfire 100 Us Rt 2 Waterbury VT 05676 802-244-5606
Web: snowfireauto.com

Snyder Chevrolet 524 N Perry St. Napoleon OH 43545 419-599-1015 599-5232
TF: 800-569-3957 ■ *Web:* www.snyderchevrolet.com

Sommer's Automotive 7211 W Meq PO Box 37 Mequon WI 53092 262-242-0100
TF: 888-494-4193 ■ *Web:* www.sommerscars.com

Sonic Automotive Inc 4401 Colwick Rd Charlotte NC 28211 704-566-2400
NYSE: SAH ■ *Web:* www.sonicautomotive.com

South Charlotte Nissan 9215 S Blvd Charlotte NC 28273 704-552-9191 236-2502*
**Fax Area Code:* 256 ■ *TF:* 888-411-1423 ■ *Web:* www.scottclarknissan.com

South Motors Infiniti 16915 S Dixie Hwy Miami FL 33157 305-256-2000 256-2018
Web: www.southinfiniti.com

South Tacoma Honda 7802 S Tacoma Way Tacoma WA 98409 253-472-2300 472-2390
TF: 888-497-2416 ■ *Web:* www.southtacomahonda.com

Southfield Dodge Chrysler Jeep Ram
28100 Telegraph Rd Southfield MI 48034 248-354-2950 352-3776
TF Sales: 888-388-0451 ■ *Web:* www.southfieldchrysler.com

Southwick Inc 2400 Shattuck Ave Berkeley CA 94704 510-845-2530
TF: 888-686-0046 ■ *Web:* www.toyotaofberkeley.com

Sparta Chevrolet 8955 Sparta Ave NW Sparta MI 49345 616-887-1791
Web: spartachevy.com

Specialty Hearse & Ambulance Sale Corp
60 Engineers Ln E. Farmingdale NY 11735 516-349-7700 349-0482
TF General: 800-349-6102 ■ *Web:* www.specialtyhearse.com

Sport Chevrolet 3101 Automobile Blvd Silver Spring MD 20904 301-890-6000 890-5650
Web: sportautomotive.com

St Charles Nissan Inc
5625 Veterans Memorial Pkwy Saint Peters MO 63376 636-441-4481
Web: stcharlesauto.com

Stadium International Trucks Inc
105 Seventh N St Liverpool NY 13088 315-475-8471
Web: www.stadiumtrucks.com

Stadium Toyota 5088 N Dale Mabry Hwy Tampa FL 33614 813-872-4881
Web: www.stadiumtoyota.com

Staluppi Auto Group 133 US Hwy 1 Palm Beach FL 33408 561-844-7148

Standard Auto Parts 2930 Texas Ave Texas City TX 77590 409-945-3333

Standard Motors Ltd 44 Second Ave NW Swift Current SK S9H3V6 306-773-3131
TF: 800-268-3131 ■ *Web:* www.standardmotors.ca

Star Ford Lincoln 1100 S Brand Blvd. Glendale CA 91204 818-956-0977
TF: 800-239-0755 ■ *Web:* www.starford.com

Steele Truck Ctr Inc 2150 Rockfill Rd. Fort Myers FL 33916 239-334-7300 334-4676
TF: 888-806-4839 ■ *Web:* www.steeletruck.com

Steve Barry Buick Inc 16000 Detroit Ave Lakewood OH 44107 216-920-0866 221-7001
TF: 866-327-5818 ■ *Web:* www.stevebarrybuick.com

Steve Millen Sportparts Inc
3176 Airway Ave. Costa Mesa CA 92626 714-540-5566
TF: 866-250-5542 ■ *Web:* www.stillen.com

Stew Hansen Dodge Ram Chrysler Jeep
12103 Hickman Rd Urbandale IA 50323 515-331-2900
Web: www.stewhansens.com

Stillwater Motor Co
5900 Stillwater Blvd N Stillwater MN 55082 651-323-2245 439-4425
Web: www.stillwatermotors.com

Stokes Automotive Inc
8650 Rivers Ave North Charleston SC 29406 843-572-4700
Web: www.stokeshondanorth.com

Stoops Freightliner- Quality Trailer Inc
1851 W Thompson Rd Indianapolis IN 46217 317-788-1533
Web: www.stoops.com

Suburban Collection 1810 Maplelawn Dr. Troy MI 48084 877-471-7100 519-9793*
**Fax Area Code:* 248 ■ *TF:* 877-471-7100 ■ *Web:* www.suburbancollection.com

Sullivan Automotive Group 2406 N Section St Sullivan IN 47882 812-268-4321 268-4323
Web: www.shopsullivanauto.com

Sulphur Springs Ford Lincoln Inc
1040 Gilmer St Sulphur Springs TX 75482 903-885-0502 438-4166
Web: www.toliverford.com

Sunland Tire Co of Upland Inc
461 E Foothill Blvd Upland CA 91750 909-982-1396
Web: sunlandtire.com

Sunnyside Motor Co Inc 944 Main St Holden MA 01520 508-829-4333 829-5362
Web: www.sunnysideford.com

Sunset Logistics Inc 710 Fm 1620 Seguin TX 78155 830-560-1032 557-5829
Web: sunsetlogistics.com

Superior Hyundai 110 S Quintard Ave Anniston AL 36201 256-403-4991
Web: www.superiorhyundaial.com

Surf City Garage Inc
5872 Engineer Dr Huntington Beach CA 92649 714-894-1707
Web: www.surfcitygarage.com

Surrey Honda 15291 Fraser Hwy Surrey BC V3R3P3 604-583-7421
Web: surreyhonda.com

Susan Schein Automotive
3171 Pelham Pkwy PO Box 215 Pelham AL 35124 205-664-1491 620-2935
TF: 800-845-1578 ■ *Web:* www.susanschein.com

Sutton Ford Inc 21315 S Central Ave. Matteson IL 60443 708-720-8115
TF: 866-232-2966 ■ *Web:* www.suttonford.com

Szott Ford 8800 E Holly Rd Holly MI 48442 248-634-4411
Web: szottford.com

T G H Aviation 2389 Rickenbacker Way. Auburn CA 95602 530-823-6204
TF: 800-843-4976 ■ *Web:* www.tghaviation.com

Tallman Truck Centre Ltd 750 Dalton Ave Kingston ON K7M8N8 613-546-3336
Web: ttctruck.ca

Taylor Ford Inc 13500 Telegraph Taylor MI 48180 313-291-0300
Web: shoptaylorford.com

Taylor's Auto Max 4100 10th Ave S. Great Falls MT 59405 406-727-0380
Web: www.taylorsautomax.com

Team Volkswagen of Hayward Corp
25115 Mission Blvd Hayward CA 94544 866-308-2825
TF: 866-308-2825 ■ *Web:* www.vwhayward.com

Tennessee Tractor LLC 15 S Bells St Ste. Alamo TN 38001 731-696-5598 696-4458
Web: www.tennesseetractor.com

Terry Thompson Chevrolet Olds 1402 Us Hwy 98 Daphne AL 36526 251-626-0631
Web: terry-thompson.com

Phone Fax

Terrys Ford Lincoln 363 N Harlem Ave Peotone IL 60468 708-258-9200
Web: www.terrys.com

Texas Direct Auto 12053 SW Fwy (Hwy 59) Stafford TX 77477 281-499-8200
Web: www.texasdirectauto.com

Thompson Lexus 50 W Swamp Rd Doylestown PA 18901 215-345-1110
Web: www.1800thompson.com

Thoroughbred Ford Inc
I-29 At Barry Rd 8501 N Boardwalk Ave Kansas City MO 64154 816-505-1818
Web: www.thoroughbredford.com

Tidewater Fleet Supply LLC
1324 Lindale Dr Chesapeake VA 23320 757-436-7679
Web: www.tidewaterfleetsupply.com

Tipotex Chevrolet Inc 1600 N Expy # 77 Brownsville TX 78521 956-541-3131 983-1890
Web: www.tipotexchevrolet.com

Titus Will Ford 3606 S Sprague Tacoma WA 98409 253-475-4151
Web: tituswillford.com

Tom Bensen Chevrolet Co Inc
9400 San Pedro San Antonio TX 78216 210-341-3311
TF: 866-635-6971

Tom Gibbs Chevrolet Inc 5850 E Hwy 100 Palm Coast FL 32164 386-437-3314
Web: tomgibbschevy.com

Tom Hesser Chevrolet Inc
1001 N Washington Ave Scranton PA 18509 570-343-1221
Web: tomhesserbmw.com

Tom Holzer Ford Inc
39300 W Ten Mile. Farmington Hills MI 48335 248-474-1234
Web: tholzerford.com

Tom Naquin Chevrolet Inc
2500 W Lexington Ave Elkhart IN 46514 574-293-8621 294-3095
Web: www.tomnaquin.com

Toms Truck Ctr Inc
1008 E Fourth St PO Box 88. Santa Ana CA 92701 714-338-6060 836-6039
TF: 800-638-1015 ■ *Web:* www.ttruck.com

Toyota of Greenwich 75 E Putnam Ave. Cos Cob CT 06807 203-661-5055
Web: www.toyotaofgreenwich.com

Toyota of Watertown Inc 149 Arsenal St Watertown MA 02472 617-926-5200
Web: toyotaofwatertown.com

Toyota Sunnyvale 898 W El Camino Real Sunnyvale CA 94087 408-245-6640
Web: toyotasunnyvale.com

Transource Inc 8700 Triad Dr Colfax NC 27235 336-996-6060
Web: www.transourcetrucks.com

Transwest 20770 I-76 Frontage Rd. Brighton CO 80603 303-289-3161 288-2310
TF: 800-289-3161 ■ *Web:* www.transwest.com

Trebol Motors Corp PO Box 11204 San Juan PR 00910 787-793-2828
Web: www.trebolmotors.com

Trend Motors Ltd 221 Us Hwy 46 Rockaway NJ 07866 973-625-0100
Web: trendmotorsvw.com

Tri County Ford Mercury Inc
5101 W Hwy 146 PO Box 425 Buckner KY 40010 502-241-7333
TF: 800-945-2520 ■ *Web:* www.tricountyford.com

Tri-State Motors 298 S Main St Cedar City UT 84720 435-586-6563
Web: tristatemotors.com

Triad Automation Group Inc
4994 Indiana Ave Ste F. Winston Salem NC 27106 336-767-1379
Web: www.triadautomationgroup.com

Trident Auto Sales 550 Hollis Rd Hollis Center ME 04042 207-929-5858

Tropical Ford 9900 S Orange Blossom Trial. Orlando FL 32837 407-851-3800 240-6116
TF Sales: 800-790-7137 ■ *Web:* www.tropicalford.com

Truck Enterprises Inc 3440 S Main St Harrisonburg VA 22801 540-564-6900
Web: www.truckenterprises.com

Truck Sales & Service Inc PO Box 262 Midvale OH 44653 740-922-3412 922-7239
TF: 800-282-6100 ■ *Web:* www.trksls.com

Truck Tire Sales Inc 426 W Pershing Rd Chicago IL 60609 773-285-3000
Web: trucktiresalesil.com

Truck Works Inc 3220 W Sherman St Phoenix AZ 85009 602-233-3713
TF: 877-894-8757 ■ *Web:* truckworksinc.com

Truckwell of Alaska Inc 5801 Silverado Way Anchorage AK 99518 907-349-8845
Web: truckwell.com

Tuffy Security Products Inc 25733 Rd H. Cortez CO 81321 970-564-1762
Web: www.tuffyproducts.com

Tustin Nissan 30 Auto Ctr Dr Tustin CA 92782 714-669-8282
TF Sales: 888-468-1391 ■ *Web:* www.tustinnissan.com

Ultimate Linings Ltd 6630 Roxburgh Dr Ste 175 Houston TX 77041 713-466-0302 937-0052
Web: www.ultimatelinings.com

Usem Inc 703 17th Ave NW. Austin MN 55912 507-396-4720 433-1876
Web: useminc.com

Utility Trailor Manufacturing Co
2921 Hwy 49 N. Paragould AR 72450 870-236-9195
Web: www.utm.com

Utility/Keystone Trailer Sales Inc
1976 Auction Rd. Manheim PA 17545 717-653-9444 653-9443
TF: 888-327-4236 ■ *Web:* www.utilitykeystone.com

V&H Inc 1505 S Central Ave. Marshfield WI 54449 715-486-8800
TF: 800-826-2308 ■ *Web:* www.vhtrucks.com

Valley Freightliner Inc 277 Stewart Rd SW Pacific WA 98047 800-523-8014 863-6473*
**Fax Area Code:* 253 ■ *TF:* 800-523-8014 ■ *Web:* www.valleyfreightliner.com

Van Bortel Subaru 6327 SR- 96. Victor NY 14564 585-924-5230 924-5500
TF: 800-724-8872 ■ *Web:* www.vanbortelsubaru.net

Van Boxtel Rv & Auto LLC 1956 Bond St Green Bay WI 54303 920-497-3072
Web: vanboxtelrv.com

Vendetti Motors Inc 411 W Central St Franklin MA 02038 508-528-3450
Web: vendettimotors.com

Vic Canever Chevrolet Inc 3000 Owen Rd. Fenton MI 48430 810-519-5634 750-1307
Web: www.viccaneverchevy.com

Village Motors Inc 75 N Beacon St. Boston MA 02134 330-674-2055 674-5364
Web: www.villageautomotive.com

Vin Devers Inc 5570 Monroe St Sylvania OH 43560 419-885-5111 824-2595
TF: 888-847-9535 ■ *Web:* www.vindevers.com

Vip Auto Group 2006 Hwy 161 North Little Rock AR 72117 501-955-5556

VIP Motor Cars Ltd
4095 E Palm Canyon Dr Palm Springs CA 92264 760-328-6525

				Phone	Fax
Virginia Truck Center Inc 3243 Lee Hwy *Web:* www.virginiatruckcenter.com	Weyers Cave	VA	24486	540-234-0999	
Vision Ford Lincoln 1500 S White Sands Blvd *Fax Area Code: 575 ■ *TF:* 888-811-2921 ■ *Web:* www.visionfordlm.com	Alamogordo	NM	88310	888-285-7516	434-4809*
Visionaire Inc 502 Jesse St *TF:* 866-838-2810 ■ *Web:* www.visionaire-inc.com	Grand Prairie	TX	th St	972-647-1056	
Vista Auto 21501 Ventura Blvd *TF:* 888-887-6530 ■ *Web:* vistaford.net	Woodland Hills	CA	91364	888-313-4252	
Vogler Motor Co Inc 1170 E Main *Web:* voglermotorcompany.com	Carbondale	IL	62901	618-457-8135	529-3010
Volvo of Tucson 831 W Wetmore Rd *Web:* www.volvooftucson.com	Tucson	AZ	85705	520-792-1070	
VT Inc 8500 Shawnee Mission Pkwy *TF:* 800-747-4400 ■ *Web:* dmv.com	Shawnee Mission	KS	66202	913-895-0200	789-1039
Walker Ford Company Inc 17556 Us Hwy 19 N *Web:* walkerford.com	Clearwater	FL	33764	727-535-3673	
Walker Honda 1616 Macarthur Dr *Web:* www.walkerhonda.com	Alexandria	LA	71301	318-445-6421	
Wallingford Buick GMC 1122 Old N Colony Rd *TF Cust Svc:* 888-765-9107 ■ *Web:* www.wallingfordbuickgmc.com	Wallingford	CT	06492	203-269-8741	284-8275
Wareham Ford Inc 2628 Cranberry Hwy *Web:* warehamford.com	Wareham	MA	02571	508-295-3643	
Watson Quality Ford 6130 I-55 N *Web:* watsonquality.com	Jackson	MS	39211	601-956-7000	
Watson'S Manistee Chrysler Inc 208 Parkdale Ave *Web:* watsonsmanisteechrysler.com	Manistee	MI	49660	231-723-6528	
Wellesley Volkswagen Buick Inc 231 Linden St *Web:* buywellesleyvw.com	Wellesley	MA	02482	781-237-3553	
West-Herr Automotive Group Inc 3448 McKinley Pkwy *TF:* 800-643-2112 ■ *Web:* www.westherr.com	Blasdell	NY	14219	716-649-5640	
Westchester Toyota Service 75 Vredenburgh Ave *TF:* 866-232-7662 ■ *Web:* www.westchestertoyota.com	Yonkers	NY	10704	914-968-6500	
Western Automation Inc 23011 Moulton Pkwy Ste F1 *Web:* www.waisales.com	Laguna Hills	CA	92653	949-859-6988	
Western Bus Sales Inc 30355 SE Hwy 212 *TF:* 800-258-2473 ■ *Web:* www.westernbus.com	Boring	OR	97009	503-905-0002	905-0003
Western Slope Auto Co 2264 Hwy 6 & 50 *TF:* 888-461-3493 ■ *Web:* www.westernslopeauto.com	Grand Junction	CO	81505	970-243-0843	
Westland Ford 3450 Wall Ave *Web:* westlandford.com	Ogden	UT	84401	801-394-8803	
Westman Freightliner Inc 2200 Fourth Ave Mankato PO Box 699 *TF:* 866-576-6914 ■ *Web:* www.westmanfreightliner.com	Mankato	MN	56001	507-625-4118	625-4127
Westside Lexus 12000 Katy Fwy *Web:* www.westsidelexus.com	Houston	TX	77079	281-558-3030	558-7859
Westway Ford 801 W Airport Fwy *Web:* westwayford.com	Irving	TX	75062	972-000-1111	659-2256
Whatever It Takes Transmission Parts Inc 4282 E Blue Lick Rd *Web:* www.wittrans.com	Louisville	KY	40229	502-955-6035	
Whitaker Buick Co 131 19th St SW *TF:* 877-324-8885 ■ *Web:* whitakerauto.com	Forest Lake	MN	55025	651-674-3931	
White Allen Chevrolet Inc 442 N Main St *Web:* www.whiteallen.com	Dayton	OH	45405	937-222-3701	
White Plains Honda 344 Central Ave *TF:* 877-553-9292 ■ *Web:* www.whiteplainshonda.com	White Plains	NY	10606	914-948-3305	428-0990
Whited Ford 207 Perry Rd *Web:* www.whitedford.com	Bangor	ME	04401	207-947-3673	
Wiers International Trucks Inc 2111 Jim Neu Dr *Web:* wiers.com	Plymouth	IN	46563	574-936-4076	
Wilcor Autos Inc Dba Toyota Vallejo 201 Auto Mall Pkwy	Vallejo	CA	94591	707-552-4545	
Wilde Automotive Management of Wisc Onsin Inc 1710 A Hwy 164 *TF:* 888-379-5817 ■ *Web:* wildeauto.com	Waukesha	WI	53186	262-513-2770	
Wilkie Lexus 568 W Lancaster Ave *Web:* wilkielexus.com	Haverford	PA	19041	610-525-0900	
Willey Honda 2215 S 500 W *Fax Area Code: 801 ■ *Web:* performancehondautah.com	Bountiful	UT	84010	888-431-4490	295-6831*
Williams Nationalease Ltd 400 W Northtown Rd *Web:* wnlgroup.com	Normal	IL	61761	309-452-1110	
Wilson Automotive Group 1400 N Tustin St *Web:* www.davidwilsonautogroup.com	Orange	CA	92867	714-516-3111	997-9200
Winner Chevrolet Inc PO Box 1867 *Web:* www.winnerchevy.com	Colfax	CA	95713	530-349-4151	346-8258
Winslow BMW 730 N Cir Dr *TF:* 866-635-2349 ■ *Web:* www.winslowbmw.com	Colorado Springs	CO	80909	719-473-1373	
Wisconsin Kenworth 5100 E Pk Ave *Web:* www.wisconsinkenworth.com	Madison	WI	53718	608-241-5616	
Witt Lincoln 588 Camino Del Rio N *TF:* 877-245-6856 ■ *Web:* wittlincoln.com	San Diego	CA	92108	619-358-5000	358-5008
WMK Inc 810 Moe Dr *TF:* 877-275-4912 ■ *Web:* www.mobilityworks.com	Akron	OH	44310	330-633-1118	
Woodbine Chrysler Ltd 8280 Woodbine Ave *Web:* www.woodbinechrysler.ca	Markham	ON	L3R2N8	905-415-2260	
World Auto Group 3057 New Jersey *Web:* www.denvillenissan.com	Denville	NJ	07834	973-442-0500	
World Class Automotive Group 4730 Wistar Rd *Web:* www.worldclassag.com	Richmond	VA	23228	804-308-1877	
Wray Ford Inc 2851 Benton Rd *Web:* wrayford.net	Bossier City	LA	71111	318-686-7300	
Yonkers Motors Corp 2000 Central Pk Ave *Web:* www.yonkershonda.com	Yonkers	NY	10710	914-961-8180	
York Ford Inc 1481 Bwy *TF:* 888-874-0636 ■ *Web:* www.yorkford.com	Saugus	MA	01906	781-231-1945	941-2212
Zeigler Chevrolet Inc 13153 Dunnings Hwy *Web:* zeiglerchevy.com	Claysburg	PA	16625	814-239-2125	
Ziems Ford Corners Inc 5700 E Main St *Web:* ziemsfordcorners.com	Farmington	NM	87402	505-325-1961	325-6592
Zimmerman Auto Center 4001 First Ave *TF:* 855-877-4223 ■ *Web:* www.gozimmerman.com	Cedar Rapids	IA	52402	855-877-4223	
Zimmerman Ford Inc 2525 E Main St *Web:* www.zimmermanford.com	Saint Charles	IL	60174	630-584-1800	584-3753

AUTOMOBILE LEASING

SEE Fleet Leasing & Management p. 2291; Credit & Financing - Commercial p. 2177; Credit & Financing - Consumer p. 2178

58 AUTOMOBILE SALES & RELATED SERVICES - ONLINE

SEE ALSO Automobile Dealers & Groups p. 1829

				Phone	Fax
Autobytel Inc 18872 MacArthur Blvd *NASDAQ: ABTL* ■ *TF:* 888-422-8999 ■ *Web:* www.autobytel.com	Irvine	CA	92612	949-225-4500	225-4541
Autofusion Corp 6215 Ferris Sq Ste 200 *TF:* 800-410-7354 ■ *Web:* www.autofusion.com	San Diego	CA	92121	858-270-9444	270-6116
Automobile Consumer Services Inc 6249 Stewart Rd *TF:* 800-223-4882 ■ *Web:* www.acscorp.com	Cincinnati	OH	45227	513-527-7700	527-7705
Automotive Information Ctr 18872 MacArthur Blvd *Fax Area Code: 949 ■ *TF:* 888-422-8999 ■ *Web:* www.autobytel.com	Irvine	CA	92612	888-422-8999	757-8920*
AutoVIN Inc 50 Mansell Ct *Web:* www.autovin.com	Roswell	GA	30076	678-585-8000	
Carfax Inc 10304 Eaton Pl Ste 500 *TF:* 800-274-2277 ■ *Web:* www.carfax.com	Fairfax	VA	10304	703-934-2664	218-2853
Cars.com 175 W Jackson Blvd Ste 800 *TF:* 888-246-6298 ■ *Web:* www.cars.com	Chicago	IL	60604	312-601-5000	601-5755
CarsDirect.com Inc 909 N Sepulveda Blvd 11th Fl *TF Cust Svc:* 888-227-7347 ■ *Web:* www.carsdirect.com	El Segundo	CA	90245	888-227-7347	
CarSmart 18872 MacArthur Blvd Ste 200 *Web:* www.autobytel.com	Irvine	CA	92612	949-225-4500	
Kelley Blue Book Company Inc 195 Technology Dr *TF:* 800-258-3266 ■ *Web:* www.kbb.com	Irvine	CA	92623	949-770-7704	837-1904
Williamson Cadillac Co 7815 SW 104th St *TF:* 877-228-6093 ■ *Web:* williamsonautomotivegroup.com	Miami	FL	33156	305-670-7100	670-7136

59 AUTOMOBILES - MFR

SEE ALSO All-Terrain Vehicles p. 1740; Motor Vehicles - Commercial & Special Purpose p. 2773; Motorcycles & Motorcycle Parts & Accessories p. 2776; Snowmobiles p. 3176

				Phone	Fax
4 Guys Inc 230 Industrial Pk Rd *Web:* www.4guysfire.com	Meyersdale	PA	15552	814-634-8373	634-0076
AM General LLC 105 N Niles Ave PO Box 7025 *Web:* www.amgeneral.com	South Bend	IN	46617	574-237-6222	
American Honda Motor Company Inc 1919 Torrance Blvd *TF:* 800-999-1009 ■ *Web:* www.honda.com	Torrance	CA	90501	310-783-3170	
American Suzuki Motor Corp 3251 Imperial Hwy *Web:* www.suzuki.com	Brea	CA	92821	714-996-7040	524-2512
Audi of America 3800 Hamlin Rd *TF:* 888-237-2834 ■ *Web:* www.audiusa.com	Auburn Hills	MI	48326	888-237-2834	
Bentley Motors Inc 2200 Ferdinand Porsche Dr Ste 3701 *Web:* www.bentleymotors.com	Herndon	VA	20171	703-364-7990	
BMW Manufacturing Co 1400 Hwy 101 S *Web:* www.bmwusfactory.com	Greer	SC	29651	864-989-6000	
BMW of North America LLC 300 Chestnut Ridge Rd *TF:* 800-831-1117 ■ *Web:* www.bmwusa.com	Woodcliff Lake	NJ	07677	201-307-4000	307-4095
Braun Industries Inc 1170 Production Dr *Web:* www.braunambulances.com	Van Wert	OH	45891	419-232-7020	
Chrysler Canada Inc One Riverside Dr W *Web:* www.chryslercanada.ca	Windsor	ON	N9A5K3	519-973-2000	
Chrysler Group LLC 1000 Chrysler Dr *TF Cust Svc:* 800-423-6343 ■ *Web:* www.dodge.com	Auburn Hills	MI	48326	800-423-6343	
Collins Bus Corp PO Box 2946 *TF:* 800-533-1850 ■ *Web:* www.collinsbuscorp.com	Hutchinson	KS	67504	620-662-9000	662-3838
DaimlerChrysler Corp Jeep Div PO Box 21-8004 *TF Cust Svc:* 800-992-1997 ■ *Web:* www.jeep.com	Auburn Hills	MI	48321	800-992-1997	
Eldorado National Inc 9670 Galena St *TF:* 800-338-3211 ■ *Web:* www.enconline.com	Riverside	CA	92509	909-591-9557	591-5285
Ferrara Fire Apparatus Inc PO Box 249 *TF:* 800-443-9006 ■ *Web:* www.ferrarafire.com	Holden	LA	70744	225-567-7100	567-5260
Ferrari North America Inc 250 Sylvan Ave *Web:* www.ferrari.com	Englewood Cliffs	NJ	07632	201-816-2600	816-2626
Ford Motor Co PO Box 6248 *NYSE: F* ■ *TF:* 800-392-3673 ■ *Web:* www.ford.com	Dearborn	MI	48126	313-845-8540	
Freightliner Specialty Vehicles Inc 2300 S 13th St *TF:* 800-358-7624 ■ *Web:* www.sportchassis.com	Clinton	OK	73601	580-323-4100	323-4111
General Motors Corp (GMC) 100 Renaissance Ctr *NYSE: GM* ■ *Web:* www.gm.com	Detroit	MI	48265	313-556-5000	
General Motors Corp Buick Motor Div 300 Renaissance Ctr PO Box 33136 *TF Cust Svc:* 800-521-7300 ■ *Web:* www.buick.com	Detroit	MI	48265	800-521-7300	

Phone Fax

Glaval Bus 914 County Rd 1 ... Elkhart IN 46514 574-262-2212 264-9036
TF: 800-445-2825 ■ *Web:* www.glavalbus.com

Honda Mfg of Alabama LLC 1800 Honda Dr ... Lincoln AL 35096 205-355-5000 355-5020
Web: www.hondaalabama.com

Horton Emergency Vehicles
3800 McDowell Rd ... Grove City OH 43123 614-539-8181 539-8165
Web: www.hortonambulance.com

Hyundai Motor America
10550 Talbert Ave ... Fountain Valley CA 92708 714-965-3000 594-3561*
**Fax:* Mktg ■ *TF Cust Svc:* 800-633-5151 ■ *Web:* www.hyundaiusa.com

International Armoring Corp 80 N 1400 W ... Centerville UT 84014 801-393-1075 298-0858
Web: www.armormax.com

Jefferson Industries Corp
6670 Ohio 29 ... West Jefferson OH 43162 614-879-5300

Land Rover North America Inc
555 MacArthur Blvd ... Mahwah NJ 07430 800-637-6837
TF: 800-637-6837 ■ *Web:* www.landrover.com

Lincoln-Mercury Co PO Box 6128 ... Dearborn MI 48121 800-521-4140
TF: 800-521-4140 ■ *Web:* www.mercuryvehicles.com

Lotus Cars USA Inc
2402 Tech Ctr Pkwy NE ... Lawrenceville GA 30043 770-476-6540 476-6541
TF Cust Svc: 800-245-6887 ■ *Web:* www.lotuscars.com

Mazda North American Operations
7755 Irvine Ctr Dr PO Box 19734 ... Irvine CA 92618 949-727-1990 727-6101
TF Cust Svc: 800-222-5500 ■ *Web:* www.mazdausa.com

Medix Specialty Vehicles Inc 3008 Mobile Dr ... Elkhart IN 46514 574-266-0911
Web: www.medixambulance.com

Mercedes-Benz U.S. International Inc
One Mercedes Dr ... Vance AL 35490 205-507-2252
Web: www.mbusi.com

Mitsubishi Canada Ltd
2800-200 Granville St Ste 2800 ... Vancouver BC V6C1G6 604-654-8000 654-8222
Web: www.mitsubishicorp.com

Mobile Concepts by Scotty Inc
480 Bessemer Rd ... Mount Pleasant PA 15666 724-542-7640
Web: www.mobileconcepts.com

Nissan Canada Inc (NCI) 5290 Orbitor Dr ... Mississauga ON L4W4Z5 800-387-0122 629-6553*
**Fax Area Code:* 905 ■ *TF:* 800-387-0122 ■ *Web:* www.nissan.ca

Nissan Motor Corp USA Infiniti Div
One Nissan Way PO Box 685003 ... Franklin TN 37067 800-662-6200
TF: 800-662-6200 ■ *Web:* www.infinitiusa.com

Nissan North America Inc 25 Vantage way ... Nashville TN 37228 800-647-7261 629-9742*
**Fax Area Code:* 905 ■ *TF:* 800-647-7261 ■ *Web:* www.nissanusa.com

Peugeot Motors of America Inc
150 Clove Rd Ste 3 ... Little Falls NJ 07424 973-812-4444 812-2280
TF: 800-223-0587 ■ *Web:* www.peugeot.com

Porsche Cars North America Inc
980 Hammond Dr Ste 1000 ... Atlanta GA 30328 770-290-3500 290-3708
TF: 800-505-1041 ■ *Web:* www.porsche.com

Saleen Automotive Inc 2735 Wardlow Rd ... Corona CA 92882 800-888-8945
TF: 800-888-8945 ■ *Web:* www.saleen.com

Subaru of America Inc
2235 Marlton Pike W ... Cherry Hill NJ 08002 856-488-8500 488-0485
TF: 800-782-2783 ■ *Web:* www.subaru.com

T3 Motion Inc 2990 Airway Ave Ste A ... Costa Mesa CA 92626 714-619-3600
Web: www.t3motion.com

Terrafugia Inc 23 Rainin Rd ... Woburn MA 01801 781-491-0812
Web: www.terrafugia.com

Tesla Motors Inc 3500 Deer Creek Rd ... Palo Alto CA 94304 650-681-5000
TF: 888-518-3752 ■ *Web:* www.teslamotors.com

Toyota Canada Inc One Toyota Pl ... Scarborough ON M1H1H9 416-438-6320
TF Cust Svc: 888-869-6828 ■ *Web:* www.toyota.ca

Toyota Motor Manufacturing Kentucky Inc
1001 Cherry Blossom Way ... Georgetown KY 40324 502-868-2000
Web: www.toyotageorgetown.com

Toyota Motor Sales USA Inc
19001 S Western Ave ... Torrance CA 90501 310-468-4000 468-7814
TF Cust Svc: 800-331-4331 ■ *Web:* www.toyota.com

Toyota Motor Sales USA Inc Lexus Div
19001 S Western Ave ... Torrance CA 90501 800-255-3987 468-7800*
**Fax Area Code:* 310 ■ *TF Cust Svc:* 800-255-3987 ■ *Web:* www.lexus.com

Trikon Design Inc 2295 N Opdyke Rd Ste F ... Auburn Hills MI 48326 248-340-0460
Web: www.trikoncorp.com

Verspeeten Cartage Ltd 274129 Wallace Line ... Ingersoll ON N5C3J7 519-425-7881
Web: www.verspeeten.com

Volkswagen Canada Inc 777 Bayly St W ... Ajax ON L1S7G7 905-428-6700 428-5898
TF: 800-822-8987 ■ *Web:* www.vw.ca

Volkswagen Group of America Inc
2200 Ferdinand Porsche Dr ... Herndon VA 20171 248-754-5000
Web: www.volkswagengroupamerica.com

Volkswagen of America Inc
3800 Hamlin Rd ... Auburn Hills MI 48326 800-822-8987
TF: 800-822-8987 ■ *Web:* www.vw.com

Volvo Cars of North America One Volvo Dr ... Rockleigh NJ 07647 201-768-7300
TF Cust Svc: 800-458-1552 ■ *Web:* www.volvocars.com

60 AUTOMOTIVE PARTS & SUPPLIES - MFR

SEE ALSO Carburetors, Pistons, Piston Rings, Valves p. 1902; Electrical Equipment for Internal Combustion Engines p. 2228; Engines & Turbines p. 2276; Gaskets, Packing, Sealing Devices p. 2355; Hose & Belting - Rubber or Plastics p. 2479; Motors (Electric) & Generators p. 2776

Phone Fax

Acadia Polymers Inc 5251 Concourse Dr ... Roanoke VA 24019 540-265-2700
Web: roanoke.gopickle.com

Accuride Corp 7140 Office Cir ... Evansville IN 47715 812-962-5000 962-5400
NYSE: ACW ■ *TF Cust Svc:* 800-823-8332 ■ *Web:* www.accuridecorp.com

Aer Mfg Inc PO Box 979 ... Carrollton TX 75011 972-417-2582 341-9743*
**Fax Area Code:* 402 ■ *TF:* 800-753-5237 ■ *Web:* www.aermanufacturing.com

Affinia Group Inc 1101 Technology Dr ... Ann Arbor MI 48108 734-827-5400 827-5407
Web: www.affiniagroup.com

Airtex Products 407 W Main St ... Fairfield IL 62837 618-842-2111 842-5019
TF: 800-880-3056 ■ *Web:* www.airtexproducts.com

Aisin Holdings of America Inc
1665 E Fourth St ... Seymour IN 47274 812-524-8144 524-8146
Web: www.aisinworld.com

Aisin USA Mfg Inc 1700 E Fourth St ... Seymour IN 47274 812-523-1969 523-1984
Web: www.aisinusa.com

Alma Products Co 2000 Michigan Ave ... Alma MI 48801 989-463-1151 457-2719*
**Fax Area Code:* 800 ■ *TF:* 877-427-2624 ■ *Web:* almaproducts.sharepoint.com

AMBAC International Inc 910 Spears Creek Ct ... Elgin SC 29045 803-735-1400 735-2163
TF: 800-628-6894 ■ *Web:* ambacdiesel.com

American Auto Accessories Inc
35-06 Leavitt St Unit C ... Flushing NY 11354 718-886-6600 625-8600*
**Fax Area Code:* 347 ■ *Web:* www.3aracing.com

AMSTED Industries Inc
180 N Stetson St Ste 1800 ... Chicago IL 60601 312-645-1700 819-8494*
**Fax:* Hum Res ■ *Web:* www.amsted.com

Angstrom Precision Metals Inc 8229 Tyler Blvd ... Mentor OH 44060 440-255-6700 255-4263

AP Exhaust Technologies Inc
300 Dixie Trial ... Goldsboro NC 27530 919-580-2000 580-2025
TF: 800-277-2787 ■ *Web:* www.apexhaust.com

ARC Automotive Inc 1729 Midpark Rd Ste D ... Knoxville TN 37921 865-583-7800
Web: www.arcautomotive.com

ArvinMeritor Inc 2135 W Maple Rd ... Troy MI 48084 248-435-1000 435-1393
NYSE: MTOR ■ *Web:* www.meritor.com

Atwood Mobile Products 1120 N Main St ... Elkhart IN 46514 574-264-2131 262-2194
TF: 800-546-8759 ■ *Web:* www.atwoodmobile.com

Autocam Corp 4070 E Paris Ave ... Kentwood MI 49512 616-698-0707 698-6876
TF: 800-747-6978 ■ *Web:* www.autocam.com

Avis Industrial Corp 1909 S Main St ... Upland IN 46989 765-998-8100 998-8111
Web: www.avisindustrial.com

Aw Transmission Engineering USA Inc
14920 Keel St ... Plymouth MI 48170 734-454-1710 454-1091
Web: www.awtec.com

Baldwin Filters 4400 Hwy 30 ... Kearney NE 68847 800-822-5394 828-4453
TF: 800-822-5394 ■ *Web:* www.baldwinfilter.com

Beach Manufacturing Co PO Box 129 ... Donnelsville OH 45319 937-882-6372 882-6153
TF: 800-543-5942 ■ *Web:* www.beachmfgco.com

Black River Manufacturing Inc
2625 20th St ... Port Huron MI 48060 810-982-9812 982-2074
Web: www.blackrivermfg.biz

Bode North America Inc 660 John Dodd Rd ... Spartanburg SC 29303 864-578-9683
Web: www.bodecorpusa.com

BorgWarner Automatic Transmission Systems
3800 Automation Ave ... Auburn Hills MI 48326 248-754-9600
Web: www.borgwarner.com

BorgWarner Inc 3850 Hamlin Rd ... Auburn Hills MI 48326 248-754-9200
NYSE: BWA ■ *Web:* www.borgwarner.com

BorgWarner Morse TEC 800 Warren Rd ... Ithaca NY 14850 607-257-6700 257-3359
Web: www.borgwarner.com

BorgWarner TorqTransfer Systems
3800 Automation Ave ... Auburn Hills MI 48326 248-754-9600 754-9356
Web: www.borgwarner.com

Borla Performance Industries Inc
500 Borla Dr ... Johnson City TN 37604 423-979-4000 979-4099
TF: 877-462-6752 ■ *Web:* www.borla.com

Bowles Fluidics Corp 6625 Dobbin Rd ... Columbia MD 21045 410-381-0400 381-2718
OTC: BOWE ■ *Web:* www.bowlesfluidics.com

Bushwacker Inc 6710 N Catlin Ave ... Portland OR 97203 503-283-4335 283-3007
TF: 800-234-8920 ■ *Web:* www.bushwacker.com

Car Parts Warehouse Inc 5200 W 130th St ... Akron OH 44311 216-676-5100 676-5516
Web: www.carpartswarehouse.net

Cardone Industries Inc
5501 Whitaker Ave ... Philadelphia PA 19124 215-912-3000 912-3700
TF Cust Svc: 800-777-4780 ■ *Web:* www.cardone.com

Carlisle Cos Inc
13925 Ballantyne Corporate Pl Ste 400 ... Charlotte NC 28277 704-501-1100 501-1190
NYSE: CSL ■ *TF:* 800-248-5995 ■ *Web:* www.carlisle.com

Carlisle Industrial Brake
1031 E Hillside Dr ... Bloomington IN 47401 812-336-3811 334-8775
TF: 800-873-6361 ■ *Web:* www.carlislebrake.com

Champion Laboratories Inc 200 S Fourth St ... Albion IL 62806 618-445-6011 445-4040
Web: www.champlabs.com

Clarcor Inc 840 Crescent Ctr Dr Ste 600 ... Franklin TN 37067 615-771-3100 771-5616
NYSE: CLC ■ *TF:* 800-252-7267 ■ *Web:* www.clarcor.com

Commercial Vehicle Group Inc
7800 Walton Pkwy ... New Albany OH 43054 614-289-5360 289-5361
NASDAQ: CVGI ■ *Web:* www.cvgrp.com

Competition Cams Inc 3406 Democrat Rd ... Memphis TN 38118 901-795-2400 366-1807
TF: 800-999-0853 ■ *Web:* www.compcams.com

Consolidated Metco Inc
13940 N Rivergate Blvd ... Portland OR 97203 800-547-9473 240-5488*
**Fax Area Code:* 503 ■ **Fax:* Sales ■ *TF Sales:* 800-547-9473 ■ *Web:* www.conmet.com

Cooper-Standard Automotive Fluid Systems Div
2110 Executive Hills Ct ... Auburn Hills MI 48326 248-836-9400 836-9116
Web: www.cooperstandard.com

Cooper-Standard Automotive Inc
39550 Orchard Hill Pl Dr ... Novi MI 48375 248-596-5900 596-6540*
**Fax:* Hum Res ■ *Web:* www.cooperstandard.com

Crower Cams & Equipment
6180 Business Ctr Ct ... San Diego CA 92154 619-661-6477 661-6466
Web: www.crower.com

Cummins Filtration 2931 Elm Hill Pike ... Nashville TN 37214 615-367-0040 999-8664*
**Fax Area Code:* 800 ■ *TF:* 800-777-7064 ■ *Web:* www.cumminsfiltration.com

Cummins Inc 500 Jackson St PO Box 3005 ... Columbus IN 47201 812-377-5000 377-3334
NYSE: CMI ■ *TF:* 800-343-7357 ■ *Web:* www.cummins.com

CWC Textron 1085 W Sherman Blvd ... Muskegon MI 49441 231-733-1331 739-2649
Web: www.cwctextron.com

DACCO Transmission Parts
741 Dacco Dr PO Box 2789 ... Cookeville TN 38502 931-528-7581
TF Cust Svc: 866-645-1452 ■ *Web:* www.daccoatparts.com

				Phone	Fax
Danaher Corp					
2200 Pennsylvania Ave NW Ste 800	Washington	DC	20037	202-828-0850	828-0860
NYSE: DHR ■ *TF:* 800-833-9200 ■ *Web:* www.danaher.com					
Davco Technology LLC					
1600 Woodland Dr PO Box 487	Saline	MI	48176	734-429-5665	429-0741
TF: 800-328-2611 ■ *Web:* www.davcotec.com					
Dayton Parts LLC					
3500 Industrial Rd PO Box 5795	Harrisburg	PA	17110	717-255-8500	255-8500
TF Cust Svc: 800-225-2159 ■ *Web:* daytonparts.com					
Decoma International Inc					
Magna Exteriors & Interiors 50 Casmir Ct	Concord	ON	L4K4J5	905-669-2888	528-6450*
**Fax Area Code:* 248 ■ *TF:* 888-348-2398 ■ *Web:* www.magna.com					
Delphi Corp 5725 Delphi Dr	Troy	MI	48098	248-813-2334	813-6866
Web: www.delphi.com					
Delphi Energy & Chassis Systems 5725 Delphi Dr	Troy	MI	48098	248-813-2334	813-6866
Web: www.delphi.com					
Denso International America Inc					
24777 Denso Dr	Southfield	MI	48033	248-350-7500	213-2337
TF: 800-321-6021 ■ *Web:* www.densocorp-na.com					
Dexter Axle 2900 Industrial Pkwy	Elkhart	IN	46516	574-295-7888	295-8666
TF: 800-522-7291 ■ *Web:* www.dexteraxle.com					
Dorman Products Inc 3400 E Walnut St	Colmar	PA	18915	215-997-1800	
NASDAQ: DORM ■ *TF:* 800-523-2492 ■ *Web:* www.rbinc.com					
Douglas Autotech Corp 300 Albers Rd	Bronson	MI	49028	517-369-2315	369-7217
Web: www.douglasautotech.com					
Dreison International Inc 4540 W 160th St	Cleveland	OH	44135	216-265-8006	265-0130
Web: www.dreison.com					
DST Industries Inc 34364 Goddard Rd	Romulus	MI	48174	734-941-0300	
Web: www.dstindustries.com					
Dura Automotive Systems Inc					
1780 Pond Run	Auburn Hills	MI	48326	248-299-7500	211-7544*
**Fax Area Code:* 442 ■ *TF:* 800-362-3872 ■ *Web:* www.duraauto.com					
Eagle Wings Industries Inc (EWI)					
400 Shellhouse Dr	Rantoul	IL	61866	217-892-4322	
Web: www.ewiusa.com					
East Penn Mfg Co Inc PO Box 147	Lyon Station	PA	19536	610-682-6361	682-6361
Web: eastpennmanufacturing.com/					
Eaton Corp 1111 Superior Ave Eaton Ctr	Cleveland	OH	44114	216-523-5000	
Web: www.eaton.com					
Edelbrock Corp 2700 California St	Torrance	CA	90503	310-781-2222	320-1187
TF: 800-739-3737 ■ *Web:* www.edelbrock.com					
Engine Power Components Inc PO Box 837	Grand Haven	MI	49417	616-846-0110	847-0500
Web: www.engpwr.com					
EnPro Industries Inc					
5605 Carnegie Blvd Ste 500	Charlotte	NC	28209	704-731-1500	731-1511
NYSE: NPO ■ *TF:* 800-356-6955 ■ *Web:* www.enproindustries.com					
Evercoat 6600 Cornell Rd	Cincinnati	OH	45242	513-489-7600	489-9229
TF: 800-729-7600 ■ *Web:* www.evercoat.com					
Faurecia Exhaust Systems Inc 543 Matzinger Rd	Toledo	OH	43612	419-727-5000	727-5025
Web: www.faurecia.com					
Federal-Mogul Corp 27300 W 11 Mile Rd	Southfield	MI	48034	248-354-7700	354-7700
NASDAQ: FDML ■ *TF Cust Svc:* 800-325-8886 ■ *Web:* www.federalmogul.com					
Firestone Industrial Products Co					
250 W 96th St	Indianapolis	IN	46260	317-818-8600	818-8645
TF: 800-888-0650 ■ *Web:* www.firestoneip.com					
Flex-N-Gate Corp 1306 E University Ave	Urbana	IL	61802	217-278-2600	278-2616
TF: 800-398-1496 ■ *Web:* www.flex-n-gate.com					
Fontaine Fifth Wheel 7574 Commerce Cir	Trussville	AL	35173	205-661-4900	655-9982
TF: 800-874-9780 ■ *Web:* www.fifthwheel.com					
Fontaine Truck Equipment Co					
7574 Commerce Cir	Trussville	AL	35173	205-661-4900	655-9982
TF: 800-874-9780 ■ *Web:* www.fontaine.com					
Franklin Precision Industry Inc (FPI)					
3220 Bowling Green Rd	Franklin	KY	42134	270-598-4300	586-0180
Web: www.fpik.com					
Freudenberg-NOK General Partnership					
47690 E Anchor Ct	Plymouth	MI	48170	734-451-0020	451-0043
Web: www.fst.com					
Griffin Thermal Products					
100 Hurricane Creek Rd	Piedmont	SC	29673	864-845-5000	845-5001
TF: 800-722-3723 ■ *Web:* www.griffinrad.com					
Grote Industries Inc 2600 Lanier Dr	Madison	IN	47250	812-273-2121	265-8440
TF: 800-628-0809 ■ *Web:* www.grote.com					
Gunite Corp 302 Peoples Ave	Rockford	IL	61104	815-964-3301	964-0775
TF: 800-677-3786 ■ *Web:* www.accuridewheelendsolutions.com					
Hastings Manufacturing Co 325 N Hanover St	Hastings	MI	49058	269-945-2491	945-4667
TF: 800-776-1088 ■ *Web:* www.hastingsmfg.com					
Hayden Automotive 1801 Waters Ridge Dr	Lewisville	TX	75057	888-505-4567	
TF: 888-505-4567 ■ *Web:* www.haydenauto.com					
Heckethorn Manfacturing Cos Inc					
2005 Forrest St	Dyersburg	TN	38024	731-285-3310	286-2739
Web: www.hecomfg.com					
Hendrickson International					
800 S Frontage Rd	Woodridge	IL	60517	630-910-2800	910-2899
TF: 855-743-3733 ■ *Web:* www.hendrickson-intl.com					
Hennessy Industries Inc					
1601 JP Hennesey Dr	La Vergne	TN	37086	615-641-7533	641-6069*
**Fax:* Mktg ■ *TF:* 800-688-6359 ■ *Web:* www.ammcoats.com					
Holley Performance Products Inc					
1801 Russellville Rd	Bowling Green	KY	42101	270-782-2900	781-9940*
**Fax:* Cust Svc ■ *TF Sales:* 800-638-0032 ■ *Web:* www.holley.com					
Hopkins Manufacturing Corp 428 Peyton St	Emporia	KS	66801	620-342-7320	340-8590
TF: 800-524-1458 ■ *Web:* www.hopkinsmfg.com					
Hutchens Industries Inc					
215 N Patterson Ave	Springfield	MO	65802	417-862-5012	862-2317*
**Fax:* Cust Svc ■ *TF:* 800-654-8824 ■ *Web:* hutchensindustries.com					
HWH Corp 2096 Moscow Rd	Moscow	IA	52760	563-724-3396	724-3408
TF: 800-321-3494 ■ *Web:* www.hwhcorp.com					
Ilmor Engineering Inc					
43939 Plymouth Oaks Blvd	Plymouth	MI	48170	734-456-3600	
Web: www.ilmor.com					
Indian Head Industries Inc					
8530 Cliff Cameron Dr	Charlotte	NC	28269	704-547-7411	547-9367
TF: 800-527-1534 ■ *Web:* www.indianheadindustries.com					
Indian Head Industries Inc MGM Brakes Div					
8530 Cliff Cameron Dr	Charlotte	NC	28269	704-547-7411	547-9367
TF: 800-527-1534 ■ *Web:* www.mgmbrakes.com					
Injex Industries Inc 30559 San Antonio St	Hayward	CA	94544	510-487-4960	487-8886
Web: injexindustries.com					
Insight USA Inc					
23330 Cottonwood Pkwy Ste 333	California	MD	20619	301-866-1990	
Web: www.mds-inc.com					
Interparts International Inc					
190 Express St	Plainview	NY	11803	516-576-2000	
Web: www.interparts.com					
Irvin Automotive Products Inc					
2600 Centerpoint Pkwy	Pontiac	MI	48341	248-451-4100	451-4101
Web: www.irvinautomotive.com					
J B Poindexter & Company Inc					
600 Travis St Ste 200	Houston	TX	77002	713-655-9800	951-9038
Web: www.jbpoindexter.com					
Jacobs Vehicle Systems Inc					
22 E Dudley Town Rd	Bloomfield	CT	06002	860-243-1441	243-7632
Web: www.jacobsvehiclesystems.com					
Jason Inc 411 E Wisconsin Ave Ste 2120	Milwaukee	WI	53202	414-277-9300	
Web: www.jasoninc.com					
JASPER Engines & Transmissions					
815 Wernsing Rd PO Box 650	Jasper	IN	47547	812-482-1041	634-1820
TF: 800-827-7455 ■ *Web:* www.jasperengines.com					
John Bean Co 309 Exchange Ave	Conway	AR	72032	501-450-1500	450-1585
TF: 800-225-5786 ■ *Web:* www.johnbean.com					
Johnson Controls Inc Automotive Systems Group					
49200 Halyard Dr	Plymouth	MI	48170	734-254-5000	254-5843*
**Fax:* Hum Res ■ *Web:* www.johnsoncontrols.com					
JSJ Corp 700 Robbins Rd	Grand Haven	MI	49417	616-842-6350	847-3112
Web: www.jsjcorp.com					
KONI North America 1961-A International Way	Hebron	KY	41048	859-586-4100	334-3340
Web: www.koni-na.com					
Linamar Corp 287 Speedvale Ave W	Guelph	ON	N1H1C5	519-836-7550	824-8479
TSE: LNR ■ *Web:* www.linamar.com					
Lorain County Automotive Systems Inc					
7470 Industrial Pkwy Dr	Lorain	OH	44053	440-960-7470	960-1878
Web: www.camacollc.com					
LuK USA LLC 3401 Old Airport Rd	Wooster	OH	44691	330-264-4383	264-4333
Web: www.schaeffler.us					
Lund International Holdings Inc					
4325 Hamilton Mill Rd Ste 400	Buford	GA	30518	678-804-3912	
TF: 800-241-7219 ■ *Web:* www.lundinternational.com					
Luverne Truck Equipment Inc 1200 Birch St	Brandon	SD	57005	605-582-7200	582-3486
Web: www.luvernetruck.com					
MacLean-Fogg Co 1000 Allanson Rd	Mundelein	IL	60060	847-566-0010	949-0285
TF: 800-323-4536 ■ *Web:* www.macleanfogg.com					
Magna International Inc 337 Magna Dr	Aurora	ON	L4G7K1	905-726-2462	726-7164
TSE: MG ■ *Web:* www.magna.com					
Magna International of America 750 Tower Dr	Troy	MI	48098	248-631-1100	729-2410
Web: www.magna.com					
MAGNA Powertrain AG 1870 Technology Dr	Troy	MI	48083	248-680-4900	680-4924
Web: www.magnapowertrain.com					
Magneti Marelli Powertrain USA Inc					
2101 Nash St	Sanford	NC	27330	919-776-4111	775-6337*
**Fax:* Mktg ■ *Web:* www.magnetimarelli.com					
MAHLE Industries Inc 2020 Sanford St	Muskegon	MI	49444	231-722-1300	724-1941
TF: 888-255-1942 ■ *Web:* www.us.mahle.com					
Manley Performance Engineering					
1960 Swarthmore Ave	Lakewood	NJ	08701	732-905-3366	
Web: manleyperformance.com					
Marmon-Herrington Co 13001 Magisterial Dr	Louisville	KY	40223	502-253-0277	253-0317
TF: 800-227-0727 ■ *Web:* marmon-herrington.com					
Mayco International LLC					
42400 Merrill Rd	Sterling Heights	MI	48314	586-803-6000	
Web: maycointernational.com					
Melling Tool Co 2620 Saradan St PO Box 1188	Jackson	MI	49204	517-787-8172	787-5304
Web: www.melling.com					
Metaldyne Corp 47603 Halyard Dr	Plymouth	MI	48170	734-207-6200	207-6500
Web: www.metaldyne.com					
Mikuni American Corp 8910 Mikuni Ave	Northridge	CA	91324	818-885-1242	993-6877
Web: www.mikuni.com					
Mitsuba Bardstown Inc 901 Withrow Ct	Bardstown	KY	40004	502-348-3100	
Web: www.americanmitsuba.com					
Neapco Inc 740 Queen St PO Box 399	Pottstown	PA	19464	610-323-6000	327-2551
TF: 800-821-2374 ■ *Web:* www.neapco.com					
Omni Gear 7502 Mesa Rd	Houston	TX	77028	713-635-6331	635-6360
Web: www.omnigear.com					
P. T. M. Corp 6560 Bethuy Rd	Fair Haven	MI	48023	586-725-2211	725-6753
TF: 800-486-2212 ■ *Web:* www.ptmcorporation.com					
Penda Corp PO Box 449	Portage	WI	53901	800-356-7704	
TF: 800-356-7704 ■ *Web:* pendaform.com/markets_automotive.php					
Penntecq Inc 106 Kuder Dr	Greenville	PA	16125	724-646-4250	646-4261
Web: www.penntecq.com					
Perfection Clutch Co 100 Perfection Way	Timmonsville	SC	29161	843-326-5544	
TF: 800-258-8312 ■ *Web:* www.perfectionclutch.com					
Phillips & Temro Industries					
9700 W 74th St	Eden Prairie	MN	55344	952-941-9700	941-2285
TF: 800-328-6108 ■ *Web:* www.phillipsandtemro.com					
Prime Wheel Corp 17705 S Main St	Gardena	CA	90248	310-516-9126	516-9676
Web: www.primewheel.com					
Raybestos Powertrain LLC 711 Tech Dr	Crawfordsville	IN	47933	800-729-7763	
TF: 800-729-7763 ■ *Web:* www.raybestospowertrain.com					
Remy International Inc 600 Corp Dr	Pendleton	IN	46064	765-778-6499	
NYSE: REMY ■ *TF:* 800-372-3555 ■ *Web:* www.remyinc.com					
Ridewell Corp PO Box 4586	Springfield	MO	65808	417-833-4565	
TF: 877-434-8088 ■ *Web:* www.ridewellcorp.com					

Phone Fax

Rieter Automotive North America Inc
38555 Hills Tech Dr ... Farmington Hills MI 48331 248-848-0100 848-0130
Web: www.rieter.com

Robert Bosch LLC 2800 S 25th Ave ... Broadview IL 60155 708-865-5200 865-6430
Web: www.bosch.us

Roush Manufacturing Inc 12068 Market St ... Livonia MI 48150 734-779-7028
TF: 800-215-9658 ■ *Web:* www.roush.com

Ryobi Die Casting Inc 800 W Mausoleum Rd ... Shelbyville IN 46176 317-398-3398 421-3725
Web: www.ryobidiecasting.com

SAF-Holland USA 1950 Industrial Blvd ... Muskegon MI 49442 231-773-3271
Web: corporate.safholland.com

Sealco Commercial Vehicle Products Inc
215 E Watkins St ... Phoenix AZ 85004 602-253-1007 222-2334*
**Fax Area Code:* 800 ■ *Web:* www.sealcocvp.com

Simpson Performance Products Inc
328 FM 306 ... New Braunfels TX 78130 830-625-1774
Web: www.simpsonraceproducts.com

SmarTire Systems Inc 13151 Vanier Pl Ste 150 ... Richmond BC V5V2J1 604-276-9884 276-2350
TF: 800-247-2725 ■ *Web:* www.smartire.com

Spalding Automotive Inc 4529 Adams Cir ... Bensalem PA 19020 215-826-4000 550-9035*
**Fax Area Code:* 267 ■ *Web:* www.spaldingautomotive.com

Stanadyne Corp 92 Deerfield Rd ... Windsor CT 06095 860-525-0821 687-4235
TF: 888-336-3473 ■ *Web:* www.stanadyne.com

Standard Motor Products Inc
37-18 Northern Blvd ... Long Island City NY 11101 718-392-0200 729-4549
NYSE: SMP ■ *Web:* www.smpcorp.com

Stemco LP 300 Industrial Blvd PO Box 1989 ... Longview TX 75606 903-758-9981 232-3508*
**Fax:* Sales ■ *TF:* 800-527-8492 ■ *Web:* www.stemco.com

Stoneridge Inc 9400 E Market St ... Warren OH 44484 330-856-2443 856-3618
NYSE: SRI ■ *Web:* www.stoneridge.com

Strattec Security Corp 3333 W Good Hope Rd ... Milwaukee WI 53209 414-247-3333 247-3329
NASDAQ: STRT ■ *TF General:* 877-251-8799 ■ *Web:* www.strattec.com

Summit Polymers Inc 6717 S Sprinkle Rd ... Portage MI 49002 269-324-9330 324-9311
Web: www.summitpolymers.com

Superior Industries International Inc
7800 Woodley Ave ... Van Nuys CA 91406 818-781-4973 780-3500
NYSE: SUP ■ *Web:* www.supind.com

Systrand Manufacturing Corp
19050 Allen Rd ... Brownstown MI 48183 734-479-8100 479-8107
Web: www.systrand.com

TAG Holdings LLC 2075 W Big Beaver Rd Ste 500 ... Troy MI 48084 248-822-8056 822-8012
Web: www.taghold.com

Taylor Devices Inc
90 Taylor Dr PO Box 748 ... North Tonawanda NY 14120 716-694-0800 695-6015
NASDAQ: TAYD ■ *Web:* www.taylordevices.com

TBDN Tennessee Co 1410 Hwy 70 Bypass ... Jackson TN 38301 731-421-4800 421-4879
Web: www.tbdn.com

Teleflex Medical
2917 Weck Dr PO Box 12600 ... Research Triangle Park NC 27709 919-544-8000 361-3914
TF: 866-246-6990 ■ *Web:* www.teleflex.com

TeleflexGFI Control Systems LP
100 Hollinger Crescent ... Kitchener ON N2K2Z3 519-576-4270 576-7045
TF: 800-667-4275 ■ *Web:* www.gficontrolsystems.com

Tenneco Inc 500 N Field Dr ... Lake Forest IL 60045 847-482-5000 482-5940
NYSE: TEN ■ *TF:* 866-839-3259 ■ *Web:* www.tenneco.com

Thermacore Inc 780 Eden Rd ... Lancaster PA 17601 717-569-6551
Web: www.thermacore.com

Titan International Inc 2701 Spruce St ... Quincy IL 62301 217-228-6011 228-9331*
NYSE: TWI ■ **Fax:* Cust Svc ■ *TF:* 800-872-2327 ■ *Web:* www.titan-intl.com

Titan Wheel Corp 2701 Spruce St ... Quincy IL 62301 217-228-6011 228-9331*
**Fax:* Cust Svc ■ *TF:* 800-872-2327 ■ *Web:* www.titan-intl.com

Transform Automotive LLC
7026 Sterling Ponds Ct ... Sterling Heights MI 48312 586-826-8500 826-3656
Web: www.transformauto.com

Trelleborg Automotive Americas
400 Aylworth Ave ... South Haven MI 49090 269-637-2116 394-5005*
**Fax Area Code:* 828 ■ *TF:* 800-635-9331 ■ *Web:* www.trelleborg.com

Triangle Suspension Systems Inc
47 E Maloney Rd ... Du Bois PA 15801 814-375-7211 237-2396*
**Fax Area Code:* 800 ■ *TF:* 800-458-6077 ■ *Web:* www.triangleusa.com

Trico Products Corp 3255 W Hamlin Rd ... Rochester Hills MI 48309 248-371-1700 371-8300
Web: www.tricoproducts.com

TRW Automotive 12025 Tech Ctr Dr ... Livonia MI 48150 734-855-2600
Web: www.trwauto.com

TS Trim Industries Inc 59 Gender Rd ... Canal Winchester OH 43110 614-837-4114 837-4127
Web: www.tstrim.com

Universal Manufacturing Co
405 Diagonal St PO Box 190 ... Algona IA 50511 515-295-3557 295-5537
OTC: UFMG ■ *TF:* 800-651-7445 ■ *Web:* www.universalmanf.com

US Chemical & Plastics
600 Nova Dr SE PO Box 709 ... Massillon OH 44646 330-830-6000 830-6005
TF: 800-321-0672 ■ *Web:* www.uschem.com

US Manufacturing Corp 28201 Van Dyke Ave ... Warren MI 48093 586-467-1600 467-1630
Web: www.usmfg.com

Valeo Inc 3000 University Dr ... Auburn Hills MI 48326 248-209-8253 209-8280*
**Fax:* Hum Res ■ *Web:* www.valeo.com

Velvac Inc 2405 S Calhoun Rd ... New Berlin WI 53151 262-786-0700 786-7323
TF: 800-783-8871 ■ *Web:* www.velvac.com

Visteon Corp 1 Village Ctr Dr ... Van Buren Township MI 48111 734-710-5000
NYSE: VC ■ *TF:* 866-967-0260 ■ *Web:* www.visteon.com

Voith Turbo Inc 25 Winship Rd ... York PA 17406 717-767-3200 767-3210
Web: www.usa.voithturbo.com

Webasto Roof Systems Inc
1757 Northfield Dr ... Rochester Hills MI 48309 248-997-5100 997-5581
Web: www.webasto.com

Webb Automotive Group Inc 3911 E Main St ... Farmington NM 87402 505-325-1911 325-1911
Web: webbauto.com

Webb Wheel Products Inc
2310 Industrial Dr SW ... Cullman AL 35055 256-739-6660 739-6246*
**Fax:* Sales ■ *TF:* 800-633-3256 ■ *Web:* www.webbwheel.com

Wescast Industries Inc
150 Savannah Oaks Dr ... Brantford ON N3T5V7 519-750-0000 427-9895*
TSE: WCS.A ■ **Fax Area Code:* 570 ■ *TF:* 800-564-6253 ■ *Web:* www.wecast.com

Westport Innovations Inc
1750 W 75th Ave Ste 101 ... Vancouver BC V6P6G2 604-718-2000 718-2001
TSE: WPT ■ *Web:* www.westport.com

Wix Filtration Products
1 Wix Way PO Box 1967 ... Gastonia NC 28053 704-864-6711 864-9277*
**Fax:* Cust Svc ■ *Web:* www.wixfilters.com

61 AUTOMOTIVE PARTS & SUPPLIES - WHOL

Phone Fax

AA Wheel & Truck Supply Inc
717 E 16th Ave ... Kansas City MO 64116 816-221-9556 221-9558
TF: 800-486-4335 ■ *Web:* www.aawheel.com

Aapco Automotive Warehouse
2997 E La Palma Ave ... Anaheim CA 92806 714-630-5600 666-2913

ABM Equipment & Supply LLC 333 Second St NE ... Hopkins MN 55343 952-938-5451 938-0159
Web: www.abm-highway.com

Ace Tool Co 7337 Bryan Dairy Rd ... Largo FL 33777 727-544-4331 544-6211
TF: 800-777-5910 ■ *Web:* www.acetoolco.com

Acterra Group Inc
Corporate Centre 200 200 35th St ... Marion IA 52302 319-377-6357
Web: www.acterragroup.com

Advantage Truck Accessories Inc
5400 S State Rd PO Box 1747 ... Ann Arbor MI 48108 800-773-3110 227-8899*
**Fax Area Code:* 877 ■ *TF:* 800-773-3110 ■ *Web:* www.advantagetruckaccessories.com

Advantech International Inc PO Box 6739 ... Somerset NJ 08875 732-805-1900 805-0122
TF: 800-322-6150 ■ *Web:* www.advantechinternational.com

AFX Industries LLC 522 Michigan St Ste B ... Port Huron MI 48060 810-966-4650 966-9522
Web: www.afxindustries.com

All Products Automotive Inc
4701 W Cortland St ... Chicago IL 60639 773-889-4500
Web: locations.autovalue.com

Allomatic Products Co
102 Jericho Tpke Ste 104 Floral Pk ... Floral Park NY 11001 516-775-0330
TF: 800-568-0330 ■ *Web:* www.allomatic.com

Alto Products Corp One Alto Way ... Atmore AL 36502 251-368-7777
Web: www.altousa.com

Arnold Motor Supply & The Merrill Co
601 First Ave S W ... Spencer IA 51301 712-262-1141
Web: www.arnoldmotorsupply.com

Atsco ReMfg Inc 4525 N 43rd Ave ... Phoenix AZ 85031 623-842-4047 842-0485
TF: 800-470-2387 ■ *Web:* www.atscoreman.com

Auto Parts Warehouse Inc 1073 E Artesia Blvd ... Carson CA 90746 310-884-5000 604-5088
Web: www.apwks.com

Automotive Distributors Company Inc
2981 Morse Rd ... Columbus OH 43231 800-421-5556 476-9469*
**Fax Area Code:* 614 ■ *TF:* 800-421-5556 ■ *Web:* www.adw1.com

Automotive Mfg & Supply Co
90 Plant Ave Ste 1 ... Hauppauge NY 11788 631-435-1400
Web: www.amscovf.com

Automotive Parts Headquarters
2959 Clearwater Rd ... Saint Cloud MN 56301 320-252-5411 252-4256
TF: 800-247-0339 ■ *Web:* www.autopartshq.com

Balkamp Inc 2601 S Holt Rd ... Indianapolis IN 46241 317-244-7241 227-1100
Web: www.balkamp.com

Barron Motor Inc
1850 McCloud Pl NE PO Box 1327 ... Cedar Rapids IA 52402 800-332-7953 393-4864*
**Fax Area Code:* 319 ■ *TF:* 800-332-7953 ■ *Web:* www.barronmotorsupply.com

Battery Systems Inc 12322 Monarch St ... Garden Grove CA 92841 310-667-9320
Web: www.batterysystems.net

Bell Industries Inc Recreational Products Group
580 Yankee Doodle Rd ... Eagan MN 55121 651-450-9020
TF: 800-866-5017

Bendix Commercial Vehicle Systems LLC
901 Cleveland St ... Elyria OH 44035 440-329-9000 329-9557
TF: 800-247-2725 ■ *Web:* www.bendix.com

Brake & Wheel Parts Industries Inc (BWP)
2415 W 21st St PO Box 08375 ... Chicago IL 60608 773-847-7000 847-5149
Web: www.bwpindustries.com

Bucyrus 1232 Whetstone St ... Bucyrus OH 44820 419-562-7987 562-8577

CAM International LLC 503 Space Park S ... Nashville TN 37211 615-331-1550
Web: www.caminternational.com

Carolina Rim & Wheel Co
1308 Upper Asbury Ave ... Charlotte NC 28206 704-334-7276 334-7270
TF: 800-247-4337 ■ *Web:* www.truckpro.com

Carolinas Auto Supply House Inc
2135 Tipton Dr ... Charlotte NC 28206 704-334-4646 377-7016*
**Fax Area Code:* 800 ■ *TF:* 800-438-4070 ■ *Web:* www.autosupplyhouse.com

Carquest Corp 2635 E Millbrook Rd ... Raleigh NC 27604 919-573-3000 573-3558*
**Fax:* Mktg ■ *TF:* 800-876-1291 ■ *Web:* www.carquest.com

Celltron Inc 1110 W Seventh St ... Galena KS 66739 620-783-1333
Web: www.celltron.com

Chalmers Group 6400 Northam Dr ... Mississauga ON L4V1J1 905-362-6400
Web: www.chalmersgroup.com

Champion Power Equipment Inc
10006 Santa Fe Springs Rd ... Santa Fe Springs CA 90670 562-236-9422
TF: 877-338-0999 ■ *Web:* www.championpowerequipment.com

Charleston Auto Parts Inc
3108 Losee Rd ... North Las Vegas NV 89030 800-879-7901 642-9174*
**Fax Area Code:* 702 ■ *TF:* 800-879-7901 ■ *Web:* cap-carquest.com

Coast Distribution System
350 Woodview Ave ... Morgan Hill CA 95037 408-782-6686 782-7790
NYSE: CRV ■ *TF:* 800-495-5858 ■ *Web:* www.coastdistribution.com

Cold Air Distributors Warehouse of Florida Inc
3053 Industrial 31st St ... Fort Pierce FL 34946 772-466-3036
Web: www.coldairdistributors.com

Colonial Garage & Distributors Ltd
59 Majors Path ... St John'S NL A1A4Z9 709-579-4015
Web: www.colonialautoparts.ca

Crw Parts Inc 1211 68th St ... Baltimore MD 21237 410-866-3300
Web: www.crwparts.com

				Phone	Fax
Custom Chrome Inc 155 E Main Ave Ste 150	Morgan Hill	CA	95037	408-778-0500	359-5700
TF: 800-729-3332 ■ *Web:* www.customchrome.com					
DAA Draexlmaier Automotive of America LLC					
1751 E Main St	Duncan	SC	29334	864-433-8910	
Delcoline Inc 4919 Lawrence St	Hyattsville	MD	20781	301-864-4455	
Web: www.delcoline.com					
Dero Bike Racks Inc					
504 Malcolm Ave SE Ste 100	Minneapolis	MN	55414	612-359-0689	
TF: 888-337-6729 ■ *Web:* www.dero.com					
Distributors Warehouse Inc 1900 Tenth St	Paducah	KY	42001	270-442-8201	442-4914
Web: btbauto.com					
Dorian Drake International Inc					
Two Gannett Dr	White Plains	NY	10604	914-697-9800	697-9683
Web: www.doriandrake.com					
Dreyco Inc 263 Veterans Blvd	Carlstadt	NJ	07072	201-896-9000	896-1378
Web: www.dreycoinc.com					
Drive Products Income Fund					
1665 Shawson Dr	Mississauga	ON	L4W1T7	905-564-5800	
Web: www.driveproducts.com					
Drive Train Industries Inc 5555 Joliet St	Denver	CO	80239	303-292-5176	297-0473
TF: 800-525-6177 ■ *Web:* www.drivetrainindustries.com					
Eagle Parts & Products Inc					
1411 Marvin Griffin Rd	Augusta	GA	30906	706-790-6687	790-6066
TF: 888-972-9911 ■ *Web:* www.eagleproducts.us					
Enginetech Inc 1205 W Crosby Rd	Carrollton	TX	75006	972-245-0110	245-2093
TF: 800-869-8711 ■ *Web:* www.enginetech.com					
Fast Undercar Inc 4277 Transport St	Ventura	CA	93003	805-676-3410	
Web: www.fastundercar.com					
Fisher Auto Parts					
512 Greenville Ave PO Box 2248	Staunton	VA	24401	540-885-8901	
Web: www.fisherautoparts.com					
Fleet Brake Parts & Service Ltd					
7707 54 St SE	Calgary	AB	T2C4R7	403-279-8661	
Web: www.fleetbrake.com					
Fleet Products LLC 6510 Golden Groves Ln	Tampa	FL	33610	813-621-1734	
Web: www.fleetproductsfl.com					
Fleetilla LLC 1745 Fritz Dr	Trenton	MI	48183	734-676-5100	
Web: www.fleetilla.com					
Flowers Auto Parts Co 935 Hwy 70 SE	Hickory	NC	28602	828-322-5414	322-9070
TF Cust Svc: 800-538-6272 ■ *Web:* napaonline.com					
Frank Edwards Co 3626 Pkwy Blvd	West Valley City	UT	84120	801-736-8000	736-8051
TF: 800-366-8851 ■ *Web:* feco.net					
General Truck Parts & Equipment Co					
3835 W 42nd St	Chicago	IL	60632	773-247-6900	247-2632
TF: 800-621-3914 ■ *Web:* www.generaltruckparts.com					
Genuine Parts Co 2999 Cir 75 Pkwy	Atlanta	GA	30339	770-953-1700	
NYSE: GPC ■ *Web:* www.genpt.com					
GK Industries Ltd 50 Precidio Ct	Brampton	ON	L6S6E3	905-799-1972	799-0852
TF: 800-463-8889 ■ *Web:* www.gkindustries.com					
Global Parts Distributors LLC					
3279 Avondale Mill Rd	Macon	GA	31216	478-781-9854	
Web: www.globalpartsdist.com					
Greddy Performance Products Inc Mnmt					
Nine Vanderbilt	Irvine	CA	92618	949-588-8300	588-6318
Web: www.greddy.com					
Grinstead Group Inc					
13289 O'Bannon Stn Way	Louisville	KY	40223	800-860-9028	
Web: www.grinsteadgroup.com					
Grupo Antolin Kentucky Inc					
208 Commerce Ct	Hopkinsville	KY	42240	270-885-2703	
Web: www.grupoantolin.com					
Hahn Automotive Warehouse Inc					
415 W Main St	Rochester	NY	14608	585-235-1595	
Web: www.hahnauto.com					
Hanson Distributing Company Inc					
10802 Rush St	South El Monte	CA	91733	626-448-4683	
Harada Industry of America Inc 22925 Venture Dr	Novi	MI	48375	248-374-9000	374-9100
Web: www.harada.com					
Harmonic Drive LLC 247 Lynnfield St	Peabody	MA	01960	978-532-1800	
TF: 800-921-3332 ■ *Web:* www.harmonicdrive.net					
Hedahls Inc 100 East Broadway	Bismarck	ND	58502	701-223-8393	221-4251
TF: 800-433-2457 ■ *Web:* www.hedahls.com					
Henderson Wheel & Warehouse Supply					
1825 South 300 West	Salt Lake City	UT	84115	801-486-2073	486-0353
TF: 800-748-5111 ■ *Web:* www.hendersonwheel.com					
Hilite International Inc 250 Kay Industrial Dr	Orion	MI	48359	248-475-4580	475-4581
Web: www.hilite.com					
IEA Inc 9625 55th St	Kenosha	WI	53144	262-942-1414	
Web: www.iearad.com					
IGD Industries Inc 4150 C St SW	Cedar Rapids	IA	52404	319-396-2222	
Web: www.igdindustries.com					
Indiana Heat Transfer Corp					
500 W Harrison St	Plymouth	IN	46563	574-936-3171	
Web: www.ihtc.net					
Instrument Sales & Service Inc					
16427 NE Airport Way	Portland	OR	97230	503-239-0754	333-4678*
**Fax Area Code:* 800 ■ *TF:* 800-333-7976 ■ *Web:* www.instrumentsales.com					
InterAmerican Motor Corp (IMC)					
8901 Canoga Ave	Canoga Park	CA	91304	818-678-1200	775-5152*
**Fax:* Sales ■ *TF:* 800-874-8925 ■ *Web:* www.imcparts.net					
Interstate Batteries 12770 Merit Dr Ste 400	Dallas	TX	75251	972-991-1444	392-1453
TF: 800-541-8419 ■ *Web:* www.interstatebatteries.com					
Intraco Corp 530 Stephenson Hwy	Troy	MI	48083	248-585-6900	585-6920
Web: www.intracousa.com					
Jead Auto Supply Corp 1810 E Tremont Ave	Bronx	NY	10460	718-792-7113	824-2898
Web: www.jeadauto.com					
JEGS Performance Auto Parts 101 Jeg'S Pl	Delaware	OH	43015	614-294-5050	
TF: 800-345-4545 ■ *Web:* www.jegs.com					
Jobbers Automotive Warehouse Inc					
801 E Zimmerly St	Wichita	KS	67211	316-267-4393	
Web: www.jawinc.com					
Johnson Industries 5944 Peachtree Corners E	Norcross	GA	30071	770-441-1128	248-2896
TF Orders: 800-922-8111 ■ *Web:* www.teamji.com					
Kansas City Peterbilt Inc					
8915 Woodend Rd	Kansas City	KS	66111	913-441-2888	422-5029
TF: 800-489-1122 ■ *Web:* www.kcpete.com					
Kenmar Corp 17515 W 9 Mile Rd Eighth Fl	Southfield	MI	48075	248-424-8200	
Web: www.ekenmar.com					
Keystone Automotive Operations Inc					
44 Tunkhannock Ave	Exeter	PA	18643	570-655-4514	603-2003
TF: 800-521-9999 ■ *Web:* www.keystoneautomotive.com					
Knopf Automotive 93 Shrewsbury Ave	Red Bank	NJ	07701	732-212-0444	212-0443
Web: www.mmknopf.com					
KYB America LLC 140 N Mitchell Ct	Addison	IL	60101	630-620-5555	
Web: www.kyb.com					
L & M Radiator Inc 1414 E 37th St	Hibbing	MN	55746	218-263-8993	
TF: 800-346-3500 ■ *Web:* www.mesabi.com					
Lakeshirts Inc 750 Randolph Rd	Detroit Lakes	MN	56501	218-847-2171	
TF: 800-627-2780 ■ *Web:* www.lakeshirts.com					
LKQ Corp 120 N LaSalle St Ste 3300	Chicago	IL	60602	312-621-1950	621-1969
NASDAQ: LKQX ■ *TF:* 877-557-2677 ■ *Web:* www.lkqcorp.com					
London Machinery Inc 15790 Robin's Hill Rd	London	ON	N5V0A4	519-963-2500	
Web: www.lmi.ca					
Lumbee Enterprises Inc 356 W Phillips Rd	Greer	SC	29650	864-989-0149	
Web: www.lumbeena.com					
Lynco Flange & Fitting Inc 5114 Steadmont Dr	Houston	TX	77040	713-690-0040	690-5095*
**Fax Area Code:* 903 ■ *Web:* www.lyncoflange.com					
Maxzone Vehicle Lighting Corp					
15889 Slover Ave Ste A	Fontana	CA	92337	909-822-3288	822-3399
Web: www.maxzone.com					
McGard LLC 3875 California Rd	Orchard Park	NY	14127	716-662-8980	662-8985
TF: 800-444-5847 ■ *Web:* www.mcgard.com					
Mico Industries Inc					
1425 Burlingame Ave SW	Grand Rapids	MI	49509	616-245-6426	
Web: www.micoindustries.com					
Mid America Motorworks					
17082 N Us Hwy 45 PO Box 1368	Effingham	IL	62401	217-540-4200	540-4800
TF: 866-350-4543 ■ *Web:* www.mamotorworks.com					
Midwest Action Cycle Inc 251 Host Dr	Lake Geneva	WI	53147	262-249-0600	249-0608
Web: www.midwestactioncycle.com					
Midwest Truck & Auto Parts Inc					
1001 W Exchange	Chicago	IL	60609	773-247-3400	579-3788
TF: 800-934-2727 ■ *Web:* www.midwesttruck.com					
Mighty Distributing System of America Inc					
650 Engineering Dr	Norcross	GA	30092	770-448-3900	446-8627
TF: 800-829-3900 ■ *Web:* www.mightyautoparts.com					
Mile Marker International Inc					
2121 BLOUNT Rd	Pompano Beach	FL	33069	800-886-8647	
TF: 800-886-8647 ■ *Web:* milemarker.com					
Minnpar LLC 5273 Program Ave	Mounds View	MN	55112	612-379-0606	
Web: www.minnpar.com					
Mutual Wheel Co Inc 2345 Fourth Ave	Moline	IL	61265	309-757-1200	757-1241
TF: 800-798-6926 ■ *Web:* www.mutualwheel.com					
N.b.c. Truck Equipment Inc					
28130 Groesbeck Hwy	Roseville	MI	48066	586-774-4900	772-1280
TF: 800-778-8207 ■ *Web:* www.nbctruckequip.com					
National Automotive Parts Assn (NAPA)					
2999 Circle 75 Pkwy	Atlanta	GA	30339	770-953-1700	
TF: 800-538-6272 ■ *Web:* genpt.com					
Newstream Enterprises LLC					
1925 E Chestnut Expy	Springfield	MO	65802	417-831-3112	
Web: www.newstreaming.com					
Northeast Battery & Alternator Inc					
240 Washington St	Auburn	MA	01501	508-832-2700	832-2706
TF: 800-441-8824 ■ *Web:* www.northeastbattery.com					
Northern Factory Sales Inc PO Box 660	Willmar	MN	56201	320-235-2288	235-2297
TF: 800-328-8900 ■ *Web:* www.northernfactory.com					
NTP Distribution Inc 27150 SW Kinsman Rd	Wilsonville	OR	97070	503-570-0171	
TF: 800-242-6987 ■ *Web:* www.ntpdistribution.com					
O.E.M. Systems LLC PO Box 473	Okarche	OK	73762	405-263-7488	
Web: www.oemsystems.net					
PACCAR Parts 750 Houser Way N	Renton	WA	98055	425-254-4400	
Web: www.paccar.com					
Parts Authority Inc 495 Merrick Rd	Rockville Centre	NY	11570	516-678-3900	
Web: www.partsauthority.com					
Parts Central Inc 3243 Whitfield St	Macon	GA	31204	478-745-0878	746-1177
TF: 800-226-9396 ■ *Web:* www.partscentral.net					
PBE Warehouse Inc 12171 Pangborn Ave	Downey	CA	90241	562-803-4691	
Web: www.pbewarehouse.com					
Pioneer Inc 5184 Pioneer Rd	Meridian	MS	39301	601-482-6068	
Web: www.pioneerautoind.com					
Plaza Fleet Parts Inc 1520 S Broadway	Saint Louis	MO	63104	314-231-5047	231-5109
TF: 800-325-7618 ■ *Web:* plazafleetparts.com					
Pneumercator Inc 120 Finn Ct	Farmingdale	NY	11735	631-293-8450	
Web: www.pneumercator.com					
Racer Parts Wholesale 411 Dorman	Indianapolis	IN	46202	317-639-0725	
Web: www.racerpartswholesale.com					
Rebuilders Automotive Supply Company Inc					
1650 Flat River Rd	Coventry	RI	02816	401-822-3030	
Web: www.coresupply.com					
Regional International Corp					
1007 Lehigh Stn Rd	Henrietta	NY	14467	585-359-2011	359-2418
TF: 800-836-0409 ■ *Web:* www.regionalinternational.com					
Service Champ Inc 180 New Britain Blvd	Chalfont	PA	18914	215-822-8500	
Web: www.servicechamp.com					
Six Robblees' Inc					
11010 Tukwila International Blvd	Tukwila	WA	98168	206-767-7970	763-7416
TF: 800-275-7499 ■ *Web:* www.sixrobblees.com					
Six States Distributors Inc					
247 West 1700 South	Salt Lake City	UT	84115	801-488-4666	488-4676
TF Cust Svc: 800-453-5703 ■ *Web:* www.sixstates.com					
Space Electronics LLC 81 Fuller Way	Berlin	CT	06037	860-829-0001	
Web: space-electronics.com					
Stewart Title Insurance Co					
300 E 42nd St 10th Fl	New York	NY	10017	212-922-0050	
TF: 800-913-4170 ■ *Web:* www.stewartnewyork.com					

Company	City	State	Zip	Phone	Fax
TCG International Inc 8658 Commerce Ct *Web:* www.tcgi.com	Burnaby	BC	V5A4N6	604-438-1000	
Trade Union International Inc 4651 State St *Web:* tradeunion.com	Montclair	CA	91763	909-628-7500	
Tri-City Glass & Door Inc 100 W Northland Ave *Web:* www.tricityglass-door.com	Appleton	WI	54911	920-731-8176	
Tucker Rocky Distributing Inc 4900 Alliance Gateway Fwy **Fax:* Cust Svc ■ *Web:* www.tuckerrocky.com	Fort Worth	TX	76177	817-258-9000	258-9095*
Twinco Romax 4635 Willow Dr *TF Cust Svc:* 800-682-3800 ■ *Web:* www.twincoromax.com	Hamel	MN	55340	763-478-2360	478-3411
U S Auto Parts Network Inc 16941 Keegan Ave *NASDAQ: PRTS* ■ *Web:* www.usautoparts.net	Carson	CA	90746	310-735-0085	
UAP Inc 7025 Rue Ontario E. *Web:* www.napacanada.com	Montreal	QC	H1N2B3	514-256-5031	256-8469
Uriman Inc 650 N Puente St *Web:* www.uriman.com	Brea	CA	92821	714-257-2080	
Vander Haag's Inc 3809 Fourth Ave W *TF:* 888-940-5030 ■ *Web:* www.vanderhaags.com	Spencer	IA	51301	712-262-7000	262-7421
W. W. Tire Service Inc 204 Main St PO Box 22 *Web:* www.wwtireservice.com	Bryant	SD	57221	605-628-2501	628-2018
WAIglobal 411 Eagleview Blvd Ste 100 **Fax Area Code:* 800 ■ *TF:* 800-877-3340 ■ *Web:* waiglobal.com	Exton	PA	19341	484-875-6600	948-6121*
Warn Industries Inc 12900 SE Capps Rd *Web:* www.warn.com	Clackamas	OR	97015	503-722-1200	
Weddle Industries 7200 Hollister Ave Ste C *Web:* www.weddleindustries.com	Goleta	CA	93117	805-562-8600	
Western Truck Parts & Equip Co 3801 Airport Way S. *TF:* 800-255-7383 ■ *Web:* www.wtpe.com	Seattle	WA	98108	206-624-5099	
Westin Automotive Products Inc 5200 N Irwindale Ave Ste 220 *TF:* 800-345-8476 ■ *Web:* www.westinautomotive.com	Irwindale	CA	91706	626-960-6762	
WM Automotive Inc 208 Penland St *Web:* www.wmautomotive.com	Fort Worth	TX	76111	817-834-5559	
WORLDPAC Inc 37137 Hickory St *TF:* 800-888-9982 ■ *Web:* www.worldpac.com	Newark	CA	94560	510-742-8900	
Wurth USA Inc 93 Grant St *TF:* 800-987-8487 ■ *Web:* www.wurthusa.com	Ramsey	NJ	07446	201-825-2710	825-3706

62 AUTOMOTIVE SERVICES

SEE ALSO Gas Stations p. 2354

Company	City	State	Zip	Phone	Fax
7 Stars Test Only 7905 Balboa Ave Ste D *Web:* 7starstestonly.com	San Diego	CA	92111	858-278-8737	
Adaptive Driving Access Inc 3430 E Sam Houston Pkwy S *Web:* www.adaptivedriving.com	Pasadena	TX	77505	281-487-1969	
Boyd Group Inc, The 3570 Portage Ave. *Web:* www.boydgroup.com	Winnipeg	MB	R3K0Z8	204-895-1244	
Canopies Party Rental 7234 N 60th St *Web:* canopiesevents.com	Milwaukee	WI	53223	414-760-0770	
Charles Agapiou Ltd 9017 Santa Monica Blvd. *Web:* www.rollsandbentley.com	West Hollywood	CA	90069	310-274-6201	
Jeeps Unlimited 10 Ambrose St. *Web:* jeepsunlimited.net	Providence	RI	02908	401-273-1860	
Kele Inc PO Box 34817 *Web:* www.kele.com	Memphis	TN	38184	901-382-4300	592-5756
Speedemissions Inc 220 1015 Tyrone Rd *Web:* www.speedemissions.com	Tyrone	GA	30290	770-306-7667	

62-1 Appearance Care - Automotive

Company	City	State	Zip	Phone	Fax
Autobell Car Wash Inc 1521 E Third St *TF:* 800-582-8096 ■ *Web:* www.autobell.com	Charlotte	NC	28204	704-527-9274	333-0526
Blue Beacon International Inc 500 Graves Blvd. *Web:* www.bluebeacon.com	Salina	KS	67401	785-825-2221	825-0801
Color-Glo International 7111 Ohms Ln *TF:* 800-333-8523 ■ *Web:* colorglo.com	Minneapolis	MN	55439	952-835-1338	835-1395
Creative Colors International Inc 19015 S Jodi Rd Ste E *TF:* 800-933-2656 ■ *Web:* www.wecanfixthat.com	Mokena	IL	60448	708-478-1437	478-1636
Dr Vinyl & Assoc Ltd 1350 SE Hamblen Rd *TF General:* 800-531-6600 ■ *Web:* www.drvinyl.com	Lees Summit	MO	64081	816-525-6060	
Flagstop Corp 11031 Ironbridge Rd *Web:* www.flagstopcarwash.com	Chester	VA	23831	804-768-0090	768-0094
Fleetwash Inc PO Box 1577 **Fax Area Code:* 973 ■ *TF:* 800-847-3735 ■ *Web:* www.fleetwash.com	West Caldwell	NJ	07007	800-847-3735	882-0585*
Hoffman Car Wash 1757 Central Ave *Web:* www.hoffmancarwash.com	Albany	NY	12205	518-869-3218	869-3574
Kaady Car Washes 7400 SW Barbur Blvd *Web:* www.kaady.com	Portland	OR	97219	503-246-7735	245-0851
Mister Car Wash 3561 E Sunrise Dr Ste 125 *TF Cust Svc:* 866-254-3229 ■ *Web:* www.mistercarwash.com	Tucson	AZ	85718	520-615-4000	615-4001
Mr.Clean Car Wash 2567 EW Conn SW *Web:* www.mrcleancarwash.com	Austell	GA	30106	770-222-5811	
Oasis Carwash LLC 3425 E Flamingo Rd *Web:* oasishandcarwash.com	Las Vegas	NV	89121	702-433-3680	
Precision Auto Care Inc 748 Miller Dr SE *OTC: PACI* ■ *TF:* 800-438-8863 ■ *Web:* www.precisiontune.com	Leesburg	VA	20175	703-777-9095	771-7108
ScrubaDub Auto Wash Centers Inc 172 Worcester Rd *Web:* www.scrubadub.com	Natick	MA	01760	508-650-1155	655-9261
Simoniz Car Wash 435 Eastern Ave **Fax Area Code:* 800 ■ *Web:* www.washdepot.com	Malden	MA	02148	781-321-1900	339-2760*
Vizza Wash Services LLC 2208 NW Loop 410 *TF Cust Svc:* 866-493-8822 ■ *Web:* washtub.com	San Antonio	TX	78230	210-493-8822	
Wash Depot Holdings Inc 14 Summer St. *TF:* 800-339-3949 ■ *Web:* www.washdepot.com	Malden	MA	02148	781-324-2000	321-5483
Ziebart International Corp 1290 E Maple Rd **Fax:* Orders ■ *TF:* 800-877-1312 ■ *Web:* www.ziebart.com	Troy	MI	48083	248-588-4100	588-0431*

62-2 Glass Replacement - Automotive

Company	City	State	Zip	Phone	Fax
All Star Glass Co Inc 1845 Morena Blvd *TF:* 800-225-4184 ■ *Web:* www.allstarglass.net	San Diego	CA	92110	619-275-3343	275-6367
City Auto Glass Inc 116 S Concord Exchange **Fax Area Code:* 612 ■ *TF:* 888-552-4272 ■ *Web:* www.cityautoglass.com	South Saint Paul	MN	55075	651-552-1000	552-1080*
Martin Glass Co 25 Ctr Plz. **Fax Area Code:* 800 ■ *TF:* 800-325-1946 ■ *Web:* www.martinglass.net	Belleville	IL	62220	618-277-1946	551-4592*
NOVUS Auto Glass 12800 Hwy 13 S Ste 500 *TF:* 800-776-6887 ■ *Web:* www.novusglass.com	Savage	MN	55378	952-736-7843	
Safelite Group Inc 2400 Farmers Dr *TF:* 877-664-8931 ■ *Web:* www.safelite.com	Columbus	OH	43235	877-664-8931	
Speedy Auto & Glass Inc 2422 Arctic Blvd	Anchorage	AK	99503	907-272-1435	
SuperGlass Windshield Repair Inc 6101 Chancellor Dr Ste 200 *TF:* 866-557-7497 ■ *Web:* www.superglass.com	Orlando	FL	32809	407-240-1920	240-3266

62-3 Mufflers & Exhaust Systems Repair - Automotive

Company	City	State	Zip	Phone	Fax
Car-X Assoc Corp 1375 E Woodfield Rd Ste 500 *TF:* 800-359-2359 ■ *Web:* www.carx.com	Schaumburg	IL	60173	847-273-8920	619-3310
Midas International Corp 1300 Arlington Heights Rd *TF:* 800-621-8545 ■ *Web:* www.midas.com	Itasca	IL	60143	630-438-3000	438-3700
Monro Muffler Brake Inc 200 Holleder Pkwy. *NASDAQ: MNRO* ■ *TF:* 800-876-6676 ■ *Web:* www.monro.com	Rochester	NY	14615	585-647-6400	647-0945

62-4 Paint & Body Work - Automotive

Company	City	State	Zip	Phone	Fax
CARSTAR Quality Collision Service 8400 W 110th St Ste 200 *TF Cust Svc:* 800-227-7827 ■ *Web:* www.carstar.com	Overland Park	KS	66210	913-451-1294	451-4436
CK Technologies LLC 1701 Magda Dr *Web:* www.cktech.biz	Montpelier	OH	43543	419-485-1110	485-1405
Colors on Parade 125 Daytona St PO Box 50940 *TF Cust Svc:* 866-756-4207 ■ *Web:* www.colorsonparade.com	Conway	SC	29526	843-347-8818	
Dent Clinic 711 48th Ave SE *TF:* 888-722-3368 ■ *Web:* www.dentclinic.com	Calgary	AB	T2G2A7	403-255-3111	258-3555
Dent Wizard International 4710 Earth City Expway *TF:* 800-267-9369 ■ *Web:* www.dentwizard.com	Bridgeton	MO	63044	314-592-1800	592-1951
Gerber Auto Collision & Glass Centers Inc 8250 Skokie Blvd *TF:* 877-743-7237 ■ *Web:* www.gerbercollision.com	Skokie	IL	60077	847-679-0510	679-0549
Gerber Collision & Glass 44700 Enterprise Dr *TF General:* 877-743-7237 ■ *Web:* www.gerbercollision.com	Clinton Township	MI	48038	586-954-3850	954-0912
Holmes Body Shop Inc 1095 E Colorado Blvd	Pasadena	CA	91106	626-795-6447	795-9653
Maaco LLC 440 S Church St Ste 700 **Fax Area Code:* 866 ■ *TF:* 800-523-1180 ■ *Web:* www.maaco.com	Charlotte	NC	28202	704-377-8855	702-4602*
Mike Rose's Auto Body Inc 2260 Via de Marcardos. *TF:* 855-340-1739 ■ *Web:* mikesautobody.com	Concord	CA	94520	925-689-1739	689-0991
Service King Collision Repair Centers 808 S Central Expy *TF:* 866-730-5464 ■ *Web:* www.serviceking.com	Richardson	TX	75080	972-960-7595	980-4266

62-5 Repair Service (General) - Automotive

Company	City	State	Zip	Phone	Fax
All Tune & Lube Brakes & More Inc 8334 Veteran's Hwy. *TF:* 877-978-1758 ■ *Web:* www.alltuneandlube.com	Millersville	MD	21108	410-987-1011	987-7273
All Tune & Lube International Inc *ATL International Inc* 8334 Veterans Hwy *TF Cust Svc:* 877-978-1758 ■ *Web:* www.alltuneandlube.com	Millersville	MD	21108	410-987-1011	987-7273
Basin Tire & Auto Inc 2700 E Main St **Fax Area Code:* 970 ■ *TF:* 800-832-9832 ■ *Web:* directoryplus.com	Farmington	NM	87402	505-326-2231	385-2460*
Belle Tire Inc 1000 Enterprise Dr *TF:* 888-462-3553 ■ *Web:* www.belletire.com	Allen Park	MI	48101	313-271-9400	271-6793
Bergey's Inc 462 Harleysville Pike *TF:* 800-237-4397 ■ *Web:* www.bergeys.com	Souderton	PA	18964	215-723-6071	721-3479
Bridgestone Americas Holding Inc 535 Marriott Dr. *TF Cust Svc:* 877-201-2373 ■ *Web:* www.bridgestone-firestone.com	Nashville	TN	37214	615-937-1000	937-3621
Clark Tire & Auto Supply Co Inc 220 S Ctr St *TF:* 800-968-3092 ■ *Web:* www.clarktire.com	Hickory	NC	28602	828-322-2303	324-2906
Cross-Midwest Tire Co 401 S 42nd St *Web:* www.crossmidwest.com	Kansas City	KS	66106	913-321-3003	
Evans Tire & Service Centers Inc 510 N Broadway **Fax Area Code:* 760 ■ *TF:* 877-338-2678 ■ *Web:* www.evanstire.com	Escondido	CA	92025	877-338-2678	480-1089*
Express Oil Change 1880 S Pk Dr. *TF:* 888-945-1771 ■ *Web:* www.expressoil.com	Hoover	AL	35244	205-945-1771	413-8732

Phone Fax

Express Tire 1148 Industrial Ave .... Escondido CA 92029 760-741-4044 741-5942
Web: www.expresstire.com

Fyda Freightliner Youngstown Inc
5260 76th Dr .... Youngstown OH 44515 330-797-0224 797-0230
TF: 800-837-3932 ■ *Web:* www.fydafreightliner.com

Grease Monkey International
7450 E Progress Pl. .... Greenwood Village CO 80111 303-308-1660 308-5908
TF: 800-822-7706 ■ *Web:* www.greasemonkeyintl.com

Hunter Engineering Co 11250 Hunter Dr .... Bridgeton MO 63044 314-731-3020 731-1776
TF: 800-448-6848 ■ *Web:* www.hunter.com

Jack Williams Tire Co Inc PO Box 3655 .... Scranton PA 18505 800-833-5051
TF: 800-833-5051 ■ *Web:* www.jackwilliams.com

Jensen Tire & Auto 10609 I St .... Omaha NE 68127 402-339-2917 339-8815
Web: www.jensentireandauto.com

Jiffy Lube PO Box 4427............................ Houston TX 77210 800-344-6933
TF: 800-344-6933 ■ *Web:* www.jiffylube.com

Jubitz Corp 33 NE Middlefield Rd..................... Portland OR 97211 503-283-1111 240-5834
TF: 800-523-0600 ■ *Web:* www.jubitz.com

Kansas City Peterbilt Inc
8915 Woodend Rd .... Kansas City KS 66111 913-441-2888 422-5029
TF: 800-489-1122 ■ *Web:* www.kcpete.com

Kolstad Company Inc 8501 Naples St NE.......... Minneapolis MN 55449 763-792-1033
Web: www.kolstadco.com

Lamb's Tire & Automotive 2100 Kramer Ln. .... Austin TX 78758 512-257-2350 257-1895
Web: www.lambstire.com

Lucor Inc 790 Pershing Rd .... Raleigh NC 27608 919-828-9511 828-4847

Merlin Corp 3815 E Main St Ste D .... Saint Charles IL 60174 630-513-8200 513-1388
TF: 800-652-9910 ■ *Web:* www.merlins.com

Mr Tire Auto Service Centers Inc
200 Holleder Pkwy .... Rochester NY 14615 800-876-6676 647-0945*
**Fax Area Code:* 585 ■ *TF:* 800-876-6676 ■ *Web:* www.mrtire.com

NDI Group Inc 310 Simmons Rd .... Knoxville TN 37922 865-777-1250
Web: ndigroup.com

Oil Butler International Corp 1599 US 22............. Union NJ 07083 908-687-3453 687-7617

Parrish Tire Company Inc
5130 Indiana Ave .... Winston-Salem NC 27106 336-767-0202 744-2716
TF: 800-849-8473 ■ *Web:* www.parrishtire.com

Payne Trucking Co
10411 Hall Industrial Dr .... Fredericksburg VA 22408 540-898-1346
Web: www.paynetrucking.com

Perry Bros Tire Service Inc 610 Wicker St .... Sanford NC 27330 919-775-7225 774-4853
Web: www.perrybros.com

Plaza Tire Service 2075 Corporate Cr........... Cape Girardeau MO 63702 877-787-1691 334-0322*
**Fax Area Code:* 573 ■ *TF:* 877-787-1691 ■ *Web:* plazatireservice.com

Precision Auto Care Inc 748 Miller Dr SE............ Leesburg VA 20175 703-777-9095 771-7108
OTC: PACI ■ *TF:* 800-438-8863 ■ *Web:* www.precisiontune.com

Raben Tire Company Inc
2100 N New York Ave............................ Evansville IN 47711 812-465-5565
Web: www.rabentire.com

Schmidt's Auto Inc 1621 Beld St .... Madison WI 53715 608-257-0505
Web: www.schmidtsauto.com

Somerset Tire Services Inc PO Box 5936.......... Bridgewater NJ 08807 732-356-8500 356-8821
TF: 800-445-1434 ■ *Web:* www.ststire.com

Sullivan Tire Co Inc PO Box 370..................... Rockland MA 02370 781-871-2299 871-7212
TF: 877-855-4826 ■ *Web:* www.sullivantire.com

Sun Devil Auto Inc 1824 E Elliot Rd.................... Tempe AZ 85284 480-831-2831 491-4204
Web: www.sunautoservice.com

Techni-Car Inc 450 Commerce Blvd .... Oldsmar FL 34677 813-855-0022 855-2101
TF: 800-886-0022 ■ *Web:* www.techni-car.com

Tire-Rama Inc
1401 Industrial Ave PO Box 23509.................... Billings MT 59104 406-245-4006 245-0257
TF: 800-828-1642 ■ *Web:* www.tirerama.com

Tires Plus Total Car Care
2021 Sunnydale Blvd .... Clearwater FL 33765 727-441-3727 443-2401
TF: 800-440-4167 ■ *Web:* www.tiresplus.com

Tom Stinnett Rv's 520 Marriott Dr................. Clarksville IN 47129 812-282-7718 285-7578
Web: www.stinnettrv.com

Tri-State Trailer Sales Inc PO Box 9322........... Pittsburgh PA 15225 412-747-7777 777-4010
Web: www.tristatetrailer.com

Tuffy Assoc Corp 7150 Granite Cir.................... Toledo OH 43617 419-865-6900 865-7343
TF: 800-228-8339 ■ *Web:* www.tuffy.com

VIP Tires & Service 12 Lexington St................. Lewiston ME 04240 207-784-5423 784-9178
Web: www.vipauto.com

Warren Tire Service Ctr Inc
Four Highland Ave .... Queensbury NY 12804 518-792-0316
Web: www.warrentiresvc.com

Wingfoot Commercial Tire Systems LLC
1000 S 21st St .... Fort Smith AR 72901 479-788-6400 788-6486
TF: 800-643-7330 ■ *Web:* goodyearctsc.com

62-6 Transmission Repair - Automotive

Phone Fax

All Tune Transmissions
8334 Veteran's Hwy........................... Millersville MD 21108 410-987-1011 987-7273
TF: 877-978-1758 ■ *Web:* www.alltuneandlube.com

Certified Transmission Rebuilders Inc
1801 S 54th St .... Omaha NE 68106 402-558-2117 558-2202
Web: www.certifiedtransmission.com

Lee Myles Auto Group 847 Fern Ave.................. Reading PA 19607 201-262-0555 262-5177
TF: 800-533-6953 ■ *Web:* www.leemyles.com

Mr Transmission 9675 Yonge St Second Fl .... Richmond Hill ON L4C1V7 905-884-1511 884-4727
TF: 800-373-8432 ■ *Web:* www.mistertransmission.com

62-7 Van Conversions

Phone Fax

Clock Mobility 6700 Clay Ave .... Grand Rapids MI 49548 616-698-9400 698-9495
TF: 800-732-5625 ■ *Web:* www.clockmobility.com

Foley Inc 855 Centennial Ave .... Piscataway NJ 08854 732-885-5555 885-6612
TF: 888-417-6464 ■ *Web:* www.foleyinc.com

Land Rover Carolinas 1450 Laurens Rd .... Greenville SC 29607 864-232-7493 232-3380
Web: www.landrovercarolinas.com

Marathon Coach 91333 Coburg Industrial Way .... Coburg OR 97408 541-343-9991 343-2401
TF: 800-234-9991 ■ *Web:* www.marathoncoach.com

Monaco Coach Corp 91320 Coburg Industrial Way ...... Coburg OR 97408 877-466-6226 724-5238*
**Fax Area Code:* 260 ■ **Fax:* Hum Res ■ *TF:* 888-327-4236 ■ *Web:* monacocoach.com

Rollx Vans 6591 Hwy 13 W........................... Savage MN 55378 952-890-7851 890-1903
TF: 800-956-6668 ■ *Web:* www.rollxvans.com

Sherrod Vans Inc 3151 Industrial Blvd .... Waycross GA 31503 800-824-6333 490-1212*
**Fax Area Code:* 912 ■ *TF:* 800-824-6333 ■ *Web:* www.sherrodvans.com

Sidewinder Conversions 44658 Yale Rd W.......... Chilliwack BC V2R0G5 604-792-2082 792-8920
TF: 888-266-2299 ■ *Web:* www.sidewinder-conversions.com

Unique Conversions Inc 1502 Hwy 157 N Ste D ...... Mansfield TX 76063 817-477-5251 477-2711
Web: laredoconversions.com

Van Conversions Inc 925 S Trooper Rd............. Norristown PA 19403 610-666-9100 666-9102
TF Cust Svc: 800-884-8267 ■ *Web:* www.vanconinc.com

Vantage Mobility International (VMI)
5202 S 28th Pl .... Phoenix AZ 85040 602-243-2700 304-3290
TF: 800-348-8267 ■ *Web:* www.vantagemobility.com

Waldoch Crafts Inc 13821 Lake Dr NE .... Forest Lake MN 55025 651-464-3215 464-1117
TF: 800-328-9259 ■ *Web:* www.waldoch.com

63 AVIATION - FIXED-BASE OPERATIONS

SEE ALSO Air Cargo Carriers p. 1725; Air Charter Services p. 1726; Aircraft Rental p. 1735; Aircraft Service & Repair p. 1736

Phone Fax

A & M Aviation Inc
130 S Clow International Pkwy Ste B .... Bolingbrook IL 60490 630-759-1555 759-2281
Web: www.aandmaviation.com

A&D Environmental Services Inc
2718 Uwharrie Rd................................ Archdale NC 27261 336-434-7750
Web: www.adenviro.com

Abilene Aero 2850 Airport Blvd .... Abilene TX 79602 325-677-2601 671-8018
Web: www.abileneaero.com

Aerodynamics Inc
25700 Science Park Dr Ste 210 .... Beachwood OH 30152 404-410-7612 666-2307*
**Fax Area Code:* 248 ■ *Web:* www.flyadi.com

Aerosmith Aviation 321 Corporate Rd .... Longview TX 75603 903-643-0898
Web: www.aerosmithaviation.com

Aircraft Specialists Inc
6005 Propeller Ln............................. Sellersburg IN 47172 812-246-4696 246-4365
Web: www.800projets.com

Airline Services International Inc
5160 Explorer Dr Ste 4......................... Mississauga ON L4W4T7 905-629-4522
Web: www.airlineservices.com

American Aviation 2495 Broad St. .... Brooksville FL 34604 352-796-5173 799-4681
Web: www.americanaviation.com

Atlantic Aviation 17725 John F Kennedy Blvd .... Houston TX 77032 281-443-3434 821-9149
Web: www.atlanticaviation.com

Atlantic Aviation Services
19711 Campus Dr Ste 100 John Wayne Airport........ Santa Ana CA 92707 949-851-5061 851-1450
Web: www.atlanticaviation.com

Aurora Aviation 22785 Airport Rd NE .... Aurora OR 97002 503-678-1217 678-1219
Web: www.auroraaviation.com

Banyan Air Service 5360 NW 20th Terr......... Fort Lauderdale FL 33309 954-491-3170 771-0281
TF: 800-200-2031 ■ *Web:* www.banyanair.com

Basler Flight Service
Wittman Regional Airport PO Box 2464 .... Oshkosh WI 54903 920-236-7827 236-7833
Web: www.baslerflightservice.com

Bayview Environmental Services Inc
6925 San Leandro St .... Oakland CA 94621 510-562-6181
Web: www.bayviewenvironmental.com

Belshire Environmental Services Inc
25971 Towne Centre Dr .... Foothill Ranch CA 92610 949-460-5200
Web: www.belshire.com

BMG Aviation Inc 984 S Kirby Rd .... Bloomington IN 47403 812-825-7979 825-7978
TF: 888-457-3787 ■ *Web:* www.bmgaviation.com

Central Flying Service Inc 1501 Bond St .... Little Rock AR 72202 501-375-3245 375-7355
TF: 800-888-5387 ■ *Web:* www.flycfs.com

Channel Islands Aviation
305 Durley Ave Camarillo Airport.................... Camarillo CA 93010 805-987-1301 987-8301
Web: www.flycia.com

Chicago Executive Airport 1020 Plant Rd........... Wheeling IL 60090 847-537-2580
Web: chiexec.com

Co-Mar Aviation 1020 Woodhurst St............ Bowling Green KY 42103 270-781-9797 793-0525
Web: www.comaraviation.com

Colonial Air 1605 Airport Rd .... New Bedford MA 02746 508-997-0620 990-2582
Web: www.colonial-air.com

Columbia Air Services
175 Tower Ave Groton-New London Airport .... Groton CT 06340 860-449-1400 405-7269
TF: 800-787-5001 ■ *Web:* columbiaaironline.com/

Cook Aviation Inc 970 S Kirby Rd .... Bloomington IN 47403 812-825-2392 825-3701
TF: 800-880-3499 ■ *Web:* www.cookaviation.com

Corporate Air LLC
15 Allegheny County Airport...................... West Mifflin PA 15122 412-469-6800 466-1162
TF: 888-429-5377 ■ *Web:* www.travelredefined.com

Crow Executive Air Inc
28331 Lemoyne Rd Toledo Metcalf Airport............. Millbury OH 43447 419-838-6921 838-6911
TF: 800-972-2769 ■ *Web:* www.crowair.com

DB Aviation Inc 3550 N McAree Rd .... Waukegan IL 60087 847-336-9220
TF: 888-362-6738 ■ *Web:* www.landmarkaviation.com

Deer Horn Aviation Ltd Co PO Box 60248 .... Midland TX 79711 432-563-2033

Dodgen Aircraft 740 Grand St......................... Allegan MI 49010 269-673-4157 673-4157
Web: www.dodgenaircraft.com

Dolphin Aviation Inc 8191 N Tamiami Tr .... Sarasota FL 34243 941-355-2902 *
**Fax:* Cust Svc ■ *Web:* dolphinaviation.com/

				Phone	Fax
Dulles Aviation Inc					
10501 Observation Rd Manassas Regl Airport	Manassas	VA	20110	703-361-2171	361-4478
TF: 888-835-9324 ■ *Web:* www.dullesaviation.com					
Dunkirk Aviation Sales & Service Inc					
3389 Middle Rd	Dunkirk	NY	14048	716-366-6938	366-6986
Web: www.dkk.com					
Dyersburg Avionics of Caruthersville					
2204 Airport Dr.	Caruthersville	MO	63830	573-333-4296	
Eaa Environmental Abatement Associates Inc					
143 W Main St	Plymouth	PA	18651	570-779-4242	
Web: environmental-abatement.com					
Eagle Aviation					
2861 Aviation Way					
Columbia Metropolitan Airport	West Columbia	SC	29170	803-822-5555	822-5529
TF: 800-849-3245 ■ *Web:* www.eagle-aviation.com					
Edwards Jet Ctr 1691 Aviation Pl	Billings	MT	59105	406-252-0508	245-9491
TF: 866-353-8245 ■ *Web:* www.edwardsjetcenter.com					
Epps Aviation Inc					
One Aviation Way DeKalb Peachtree Airport	Atlanta	GA	30341	770-458-9851	458-0320
TF: 800-241-6807 ■ *Web:* www.eppsaviation.com					
Executive Air					
2131 Airport Dr					
Austin Straubel International Airport	Green Bay	WI	54313	920-498-4880	498-4890
Web: www.executiveair.com					
Fargo Jet Center Inc 3802 20th St N	Fargo	ND	58102	701-235-3600	
Web: www.fargojet.com					
Felts Field Aviation Inc 5829 E Rutter Ave.	Spokane	WA	99212	509-535-9011	535-9014
TF: 800-676-5538 ■ *Web:* www.feltsfield.com					
Flight Light Inc 2708 47th Ave.	Sacramento	CA	95822	916-394-2800	
Web: www.flightlight.com					
Flightline Group Inc 3256 Capital Cir SW	Tallahassee	FL	32310	850-574-4444	576-4210
Web: www.flightlinegroup.com					
Galvin Flying Services 7149 Perimeter Rd	Seattle	WA	98108	206-763-9706	
TF: 800-341-4102 ■ *Web:* www.galvinflying.com					
Gibbs Flying Service Inc					
3717 John J Montgomery Dr	San Diego	CA	92123	858-277-0310	277-0678
Web: gibbsflyingservice.com					
Grand Aire Express Inc					
11777 W Airport Service Rd	Swanton	OH	43558	800-704-7263	865-2965*
**Fax Area Code:* 419 ■ *TF:* 800-704-7263 ■ *Web:* www.grandaire.com					
Grand Strand Airport					
2800 Terminal St.	North Myrtle Beach	SC	29582	843-272-5337	
Greater Toronto Airports Authority					
Toronto Pearson International Airport 3111 Convair Dr					
PO Box 6031	Toronto	ON	L5P1B2	416-776-3000	
Web: www.torontopearson.com					
Holman Aviation Co 1940 Airport Ct.	Great Falls	MT	59404	406-453-7613	453-7204
Web: www.holmanaviation.com					
Hunt Pan Am Aviation Inc					
505 Amelia Earhart Dr.	Brownsville	TX	78521	956-542-9111	542-9133
TF: 800-888-7524 ■ *Web:* www.huntpanam.com					
Inter-State Aviation					
4800 Airport Complex N Airport Rd	Pullman	WA	99163	509-332-6596	334-1751
Web: inter-stateaviation.com					
Interstate Aviation 62 Johnson Ave.	Plainville	CT	06062	860-747-5519	589-1853
TF: 800-573-5519 ■ *Web:* www.interstateaviation.com					
Jet Harbor Inc 2860 NW 59th St.	Fort Lauderdale	FL	33309	954-772-2863	772-6510
Web: www.jetharbor.com					
Kansas City Aviation Ctr Inc					
15325 S Pflumm Rd	Olathe	KS	66062	913-782-0530	782-9462
TF: 800-720-5222 ■ *Web:* www.kcac.com					
Keystone Aviation Services Inc					
288 Christian St	Oxford	CT	06478	203-264-6525	264-0295
TF: 866-436-2177 ■ *Web:* keystoneav.com					
Landmark Aviation 3501 Aviation Ave	Sioux Falls	SD	57104	605-336-7791	336-8009
TF General: 800-888-1646 ■ *Web:* www.landmarkaviation.com					
Lane Aviation Corp					
4389 International Gateway	Columbus	OH	43219	614-237-3747	231-4741*
**Fax:* Cust Svc ■ *TF:* 800-848-6263 ■ *Web:* www.laneaviation.com					
Loyd's Aviation Services Inc					
1601 Skyway Dr Ste 100 PO Box 80958	Bakersfield	CA	93308	661-393-1334	393-0824
TF: 800-284-1334 ■ *Web:* www.bakersfieldjetcenter.com					
Maine Instrument Flight Inc PO Box 2	Augusta	ME	04332	207-622-1211	622-7858
TF: 888-643-3597 ■ *Web:* www.maineinstrumentflight.com					
Malloy Air East Inc Avenue B	WestHampton Beach	NY	11978	631-288-5410	
McCall Aviation 300 Deinhard Ln	McCall	ID	83638	208-634-7137	634-3917
TF: 800-992-6559 ■ *Web:* www.mccallaviation.com					
Mid-Ohio Aviation 6250 N Honeytown Rd.	Smithville	OH	44677	330-669-2671	669-2402
TF: 800-669-4243 ■ *Web:* www.midohioaviation.com					
Midwest Corporate Aviation 3512 N Webb Rd	Wichita	KS	67226	316-636-9700	636-9747
TF: 800-435-9622 ■ *Web:* www.midwestaviation.com					
Millenium Aviation					
2365 Bernville Rd Reading Regional Airport	Reading	PA	19605	610-372-4728	374-7580
TF: 800-366-9419 ■ *Web:* www.majets.com					
Miller Environmental Services Inc					
401 Navigation Blvd	Corpus Christi	TX	78408	361-289-9800	
Web: www.millerenviro.com					
Million Air 4300 Westgrove Dr	Addison	TX	75001	972-248-1600	733-5803
TF: 800-248-1602 ■ *Web:* www.millionair.com					
Minuteman Aviation Inc (MAI)					
5225 HWY 10 W PO Box 16	Missoula	MT	59808	406-728-9363	728-6981
Web: www.minutemanaviation.com					
Monterey Jet Center LLC 300 Skypark Dr	Monterey	CA	93940	831-373-0100	
Web: www.montereyjetcenter.com					
Montgomery Aviation Corp 4525 Selma Hwy	Montgomery	AL	36108	334-288-7334	288-7337
TF: 800-392-8044 ■ *Web:* www.montgomeryaviation.com					
National Jets					
3495 SW Ninth Ave PO Box 22460	Fort Lauderdale	FL	33315	954-359-9900	359-0064
TF: 800-327-3710 ■ *Web:* www.nationaljets.com/natjet/jet					
Neuber Environmental Services Inc					
42 Ridge Rd	Phoenixville	PA	19460	610-933-4332	
Web: www.neuberenv.com					
North Coast Air 4645 W 12th St	Erie	PA	16505	814-836-9220	836-9901
Web: www.ncair.com					
Northeast Airmotive Inc 1011 Westbrook St.	Portland	ME	04102	207-774-6318	874-4714
TF: 877-354-7881 ■ *Web:* www.northeastair.com					
Ocean Aire PO Box 1245	Toms River	NJ	08754	732-797-1077	797-1076
Web: www.oceanaire.net					
Paul Fournet Air Service Inc PO Box 53448	Lafayette	LA	70505	337-237-0520	232-1188
Web: www.fournet.com					
Pelican Aviation 1314 Hangar Dr	New Iberia	LA	70560	337-367-1401	
Pensacola Aviation Ctr Inc					
4145 Jerry L MayGarden Rd	Pensacola	FL	32504	850-434-0636	434-3984
TF: 800-874-6580 ■ *Web:* www.pensacolaaviation.com					
Perfect Sweep Inc 1202 S Expressway Dr	Toledo	OH	43608	419-726-1801	
Web: www.perfectsweep.com					
Premier Jet Ctr 3301 NE Cornell Rd Ste A	Hillsboro	OR	97124	503-693-1096	930-0124*
**Fax Area Code:* 760					
Prior Aviation Service Inc 50 N Airport Dr	Buffalo	NY	14225	716-633-1000	633-1432
TF: 800-621-2923 ■ *Web:* www.prioraviation.com					
Pro-Tec Fire Services Ltd 2129 S Oneida St	Green Bay	WI	54304	920-494-8851	
Web: www.protecfire.com					
PS Air Inc 3411 Beech Way SW	Cedar Rapids	IA	52404	319-846-3600	846-3605
Web: www.psair.com					
Regional Jet Ctr 12344 Tower Dr	Bentonville	AR	72712	479-205-1100	205-1101
TF: 866-962-3835 ■ *Web:* www.regionaljetcenter.com					
Richmor Aviation Inc					
1142 Rt 9 H Columbia County Airport	Hudson	NY	12534	518-828-9461	828-1303
TF: 800-331-6101 ■ *Web:* www.richmor.com					
Robinson Aviation 50 Thompson Ave.	East Haven	CT	06512	203-467-9555	467-6346
Web: www.robinsonaviation.com					
Rose Aircraft Interiors Inc 2786 Hwy 8 E	Mena	AR	71953	479-394-2551	
Web: www.roseaircraft.com					
Safegate Airport Systems					
7101 Northland Cir N Ste 110	Minneapolis	MN	55428	763-535-9299	
Web: www.safegate.com					
Saker Aviation Services Inc					
20 South St Pier 6 E River	New York	NY	10004	212-776-4046	
Web: www.sakeraviation.com					
Sanford Aircraft Services Inc					
701 Rod Sullivan Rd	Sanford	NC	27330	919-708-5549	774-9627
TF: 888-871-1947 ■ *Web:* www.sanford-aircraft.com					
Santa Fe Air Ctr Inc					
121 Aviation Dr Bldg 3005	Santa Fe	NM	87507	505-471-2525	362-6738*
**Fax Area Code:* 888 ■ *Web:* www.santafejet.biz					
Shannon Airport					
3380 Shannon Airport Cir.	Fredericksburg	VA	22408	540-373-4431	373-0035
SheltAir Aviation Services Fort Lauderdale					
4860 NE 12th Ave	Fort Lauderdale	FL	33334	954-771-2210	771-3745
TF: 800-700-2210 ■ *Web:* www.sheltairaviation.com					
Showalter Flying Service					
600 Herndon Ave PO Box 140753	Orlando	FL	32803	407-326-6062	894-5094
TF: 800-894-7331 ■ *Web:* www.showalter.com					
Signature Flight Support					
201 S Orange Ave Ste 1100-S	Orlando	FL	32801	407-648-7200	206-8428*
**Fax:* Hum Res ■ *Web:* www.signatureflight.com					
Silverhawk Aviation Inc 1751 W Kearney Ave.	Lincoln	NE	68524	402-475-8600	
Web: www.silverhawkaviation.com					
Sky Bright 65 Aviation Dr	Gilford	NH	03249	603-528-6818	528-1814
TF: 800-639-6012 ■ *Web:* www.skybright.com					
Skyservice Airlines Inc 9785 Ryan Ave.	Dorval	QC	H9P1A2	514-636-3300	636-4855
TF: 888-985-1402 ■ *Web:* skyservice.com					
SkyTech Inc 550 Airport Rd	Rock Hill	SC	29732	803-366-5108	366-1519
TF: 888-386-3596 ■ *Web:* www.skytechinc.com					
Smyrna Air Ctr 300 Doug Warpoole Rd	Smyrna	TN	37167	888-863-9996	
Web: www.smyrnaaircenter.com					
Snohomish Flying Service Inc					
9900 Airport Way	Snohomish	WA	98296	360-568-1541	568-6034
TF: 800-827-1000 ■ *Web:* www.snohomishflying.com					
Southwest Airport Services Inc					
11811 N Brantly Ave Ste 500	Houston	TX	77034	281-484-6551	996-8826*
**Fax Area Code:* 713 ■ *TF:* 888-362-6738 ■ *Web:* www.swjetops.com					
Space Coast Jet Ctr 7003 Challenger Ave	Titusville	FL	32780	321-267-8355	267-0129
TF: 800-559-5473 ■ *Web:* www.spacecoastjetcenter.com					
Spanaflight 16705 103rd Ave Ct E	Puyallup	WA	98374	253-848-2020	840-5843
Web: www.spanaflight.com					
St Paul Flight Ctr 270 Airport Rd	Saint Paul	MN	55107	651-227-8108	227-6195
TF: 800-368-0107 ■ *Web:* www.stpaulflight.com					
Statesville Flying Service					
238 Airport Rd	Statesville	NC	28677	704-873-1111	
Web: statesvilleregion.com					
Stevens Aviation Inc					
600 Delaware St Donaldson Industrial Pk	Greenville	SC	29605	864-678-6000	879-6215
TF: 800-359-7838 ■ *Web:* www.stevensaviation.com					
Stuart Jet Ctr LLC 2501 Aviation Way	Stuart	FL	34996	772-288-6700	288-3782
TF: 877-735-9538 ■ *Web:* www.stuartjet.com					
Sundance Aviation Inc					
Sundance Airpark NW 122nd & Sara Rd	Oklahoma City	OK	73099	405-373-3886	373-3893
Web: sundanceairport.com					
Swift Aviation 2710 E Old Tower Rd.	Phoenix	AZ	85034	602-273-3770	273-3773
Web: www.swiftaviation.com					
Texas Jet Management LLC					
200 Texas Way Hngr 23n	Fort Worth	TX	76106	817-624-8438	
Web: www.texasjet.com					
Top Gun Aviation Inc 405 Industrial Pk Rd	Hammond	LA	70401	985-542-0719	542-2077
Web: www.airnav.com/airport/KHDC/TOP_GUN					
Truman Arnold Cos 701 S Robison Rd	Texarkana	TX	75501	903-794-3835	335-2612*
**Fax Area Code:* 806 ■ *Web:* www.tacair.com					
TWC Aviation 1162 Aviation Ave.	San Jose	CA	95110	408-286-3832	
TF: 800-359-7060 ■ *Web:* www.twcaviation.com					
Unipak Aviation 2049 Ninth Ave	Ronkonkoma	NY	11779	631-471-9801	
Web: www.unipakaviation.net					
United States Aviation 4141 N Memorial Dr	Tulsa	OK	74115	918-836-7345	
TF: 800-897-5387 ■ *Web:* www.unitedstatesaviation.com					

Phone *Fax*

Vail Valley Jet Center LLC
871 Cooley Mesa Rd Eagle County Regional Airport
.... Gypsum CO 81637 970-524-7700
Web: vvjc.com

Valley International Airport
3002 Heritage Way .... Harlingen TX 78550 956-430-8605
Web: www.flythevalley.com

Vantage Airport Group Ltd
West 73rd Ave Ste 1410 - 1200 .... Vancouver BC V6P6G5 604-269-0080
Web: www.vantageairportgroup.com

Vee Neal Aviation Inc 148 Aviation Ln Ste 109 .... Latrobe PA 15650 724-539-4533 539-5501
TF: 800-278-2710 ■ *Web:* www.veeneal.com

West Valley Flying Club
1901 Embarcadero Rd .... Palo Alto CA 94303 650-856-2030
Web: www.wvfc.org

Western Aircraft Inc 4300 S Kennedy St .... Boise ID 83705 208-338-1800 338-1887
TF: 800-333-3442 ■ *Web:* www.westair.com

Western Cardinal Inc 205 Durley Ave .... Camarillo CA 93010 805-482-2586 484-2713
TF: 800-882-3018 ■ *Web:* www.westerncardinal.com

Wilson Air Ctr
2930 Winchester Rd
Memphis International Airport .... Memphis TN 38118 901-345-2992 345-1088
TF: 800-464-2992 ■ *Web:* www.wilsonair.com

Wings Air Charter
236 Airport Hanger Dr .... Wisconsin Rapids WI 54494 715-424-3737 424-3737
Web: www.wingsaircharter.com

Wisconsin Aviation Inc 1741 River Dr............. Watertown WI 53094 920-261-4567 206-6386
TF: 800-657-0761 ■ *Web:* www.wisconsinaviation.com

Woodland Aviation Inc 25170 Aviation Ave............. Davis CA 95616 530-759-6037
TF: 800-442-1333 ■ *Web:* www.woodlandaviation.com

64 BABY PRODUCTS

SEE ALSO Children's & Infants' Clothing p. 1953; Household Furniture p. 2345; Paper Products - Sanitary p. 2856; Toys, Games, Hobbies p. 3246

Phone *Fax*

Baby Jogger Co 8575 Magellan Pkwy Ste 1000........ Richmond VA 23227 800-241-1848 262-6277*
**Fax Area Code:* 804 ■ *TF:* 800-241-1848 ■ *Web:* www.babyjogger.com

Baby Trend Inc 1567 S Campus Ave .... Ontario CA 91761 800-328-7363 773-0108*
**Fax Area Code:* 909 ■ *TF Cust Svc:* 800-328-7363 ■ *Web:* www.babytrend.com

Baby's Dream Furniture Inc
411 Industrial Blvd PO Box 579 .... Buena Vista GA 31803 229-649-4404 649-2007
TF: 800-835-2742 ■ *Web:* www.babysdream.com

Ball Bounce & Sport Inc/Hedstrom Plastics
One Hedstrom Dr .... Ashland OH 44805 419-289-9310 281-3371
TF: 800-765-9665 ■ *Web:* www.hedstrom.com

Britax Child Safety Inc 13501 S Ridge Dr .... Charlotte NC 28273 704-409-1700 409-1665*
**Fax:* Cust Svc ■ *TF:* 888-427-4829 ■ *Web:* www.britaxusa.com

Cardinal Gates 79 Amlajack Way..................... Newnan GA 30265 770-252-4200 252-4122
TF: 800-318-3380 ■ *Web:* www.cardinalgates.com

Central Specialties Ltd 220 Exchange Dr ....Crystal Lake IL 60014 815-459-6000 459-6562
TF: 800-873-4370 ■ *Web:* www.csltd.com

Crown Crafts Infant Products Inc
711 W Walnut St.................................. Compton CA 90220 310-763-8100 295-1954*
**Fax Area Code:* 562 ■ **Fax:* Cust Svc ■ *TF:* 800-421-0526 ■ *Web:* www.ccipinc.com

Delta Enterprises 114 W 26th St Eighth Fl ....New York NY 10001 212-736-7000 627-0352
TF: 800-377-3777 ■ *Web:* www.deltachildren.com

Dolly Packaging 320 N Fourth St......................... Tipp City OH 45371 937-667-5414

Dorel Juvenile Group USA 2525 State St .... Columbus IN 47201 812-372-0141 372-0911
TF: 800-544-1108 ■ *Web:* www.djgusa.com

Evenflo Company Inc 1801 Commerce Dr ....Piqua OH 45356 800-233-5921 415-3112*
**Fax Area Code:* 937 ■ **Fax:* Hum Res ■ *TF:* 800-233-5921 ■ *Web:* www.evenflo.com

Fisher-Price Inc 636 Girard Ave................... East Aurora NY 14052 716-687-3000 687-3476
TF: 800-432-5437 ■ *Web:* www.fisher-price.com

Gerber Products Co 445 State St.......................Fremont MI 49413 800-284-9488 928-2723*
**Fax Area Code:* 231 ■ *TF:* 800-284-9488 ■ *Web:* www.gerber.com

Infantino LLC
4920 Carroll Canyon Rd Ste 200 .... San Diego CA 92121 800-840-4916 457-0181*
**Fax Area Code:* 858 ■ *TF:* 800-840-4916 ■ *Web:* www.infantino.com

Kelty 6235 Lookout Rd.............................. Boulder CO 80301 800-535-3589 504-2745
TF: 800-423-2320 ■ *Web:* www.kelty.com

KidCo Inc 1013 Technology Way...................Libertyville IL 60048 847-549-8600 549-8660
TF: 800-553-5529 ■ *Web:* www.kidco.com

Kids II 555 N Pt Ctr E Ste 600 .... Alpharetta GA 30022 770-751-0442 751-0543
TF: 877-325-7056 ■ *Web:* www.kidsii.com

Kolcraft Enterprises Inc 10832 NC Hwy 211 E.........Aberdeen NC 28315 910-944-9345
TF Cust Svc: 800-453-7673 ■ *Web:* www.kolcraft.com

Little Tikes Co, The 2180 Barlow Rd .... Hudson OH 44236 800-321-0183
TF Cust Svc: 800-321-0183 ■ *Web:* www.littletikes.com

Manhattan Toy 300 First Ave N Suite 200.......... Minneapolis MN 55401 612-337-9600 341-4457
TF: 800-541-1345 ■ *Web:* www.manhattantoy.com

Peg-Perego USA Inc 3625 Independence Dr .... Fort Wayne IN 46808 260-482-8191 484-2940
TF Cust Svc: 800-671-1701 ■ *Web:* global.pegperego.com

Prince Lionheart Inc 2421 Westgate Rd.............Santa Maria CA 93455 805-922-2250 922-9442
TF: 800-544-1132 ■ *Web:* www.princelionheart.com

REI 1700 45th St E................................... Sumner WA 98352 253-891-2500 891-2523
TF: 800-426-4840 ■ *Web:* www.rei.com

Sassy Inc 2305 Breton Industrial Pk Dr............. Kentwood MI 49508 616-243-0767 243-1042
TF: 800-323-6336 ■ *Web:* www.sassybaby.com

Step2 Co 10010 Aurora-Hudson Rd................. Streetsboro OH 44241 330-656-0440 655-9685
TF Cust Svc: 800-347-8372 ■ *Web:* www.step2.com

Tough Traveler Ltd 1012 State St................. Schenectady NY 12307 518-377-8526 377-5434
TF Cust Svc: 800-468-6844 ■ *Web:* www.toughtraveler.com

Triboro Quilt Mfg Inc 172 S Broadway .... White Plains NY 10605 914-428-7551 428-0130
TF: 800-227-2077 ■ *Web:* www.cuddletime.com

Triple Play Products LLC 904 Main St Ste 330 ....Hopkins MN 55343 952-938-0531 935-4835
TF: 800-829-1625 ■ *Web:* www.lillygold.com

65 BAGS - PAPER

Phone *Fax*

AJM Packaging Corp
E-4111 Andover Rd ....Bloomfield Hills MI 48302 248-901-0040 901-0061
Web: www.ajmpack.com

Bancroft Bag Inc 425 Bancroft Blvd ....West Monroe LA 71292 318-387-2550 324-2316*
**Fax:* Cust Svc ■ *TF:* 800-551-4950 ■ *Web:* www.bancroftbag.com

Bemis Company Inc
One Neenah Ctr Fourth Fl PO Box 669................ Neenah WI 54957 920-727-4100
NYSE: BMS ■ *Web:* www.bemis.com

Bemis Company Inc Paper Packaging Div
2445 Deer Pk Blvd ....Omaha NE 68105 800-541-4303 938-2609*
**Fax Area Code:* 402 ■ *TF:* 800-541-4303 ■ *Web:* www.bemispaper.com

Bonita Pioneer Packaging Products Inc
7333 SW Bonita Rd ....Portland OR 97224 800-677-7725 323-6027
TF: 800-677-7725 ■ *Web:* www.bonitapioneer.com

Colonial Bag Co
One Ocean Pond Ave PO Box 929 ....Lake Park GA 31636 229-559-8484 559-0085
TF: 800-392-4875 ■ *Web:* colonial-bag.com

El Dorado Paper Bag Mfg Company Inc
204 Prescolite Dr .... El Dorado AR 71730 870-862-4977 862-8520
Web: eldoradopaperbag.com

Hood Packaging Corp 25 Woodgreen Pl............. Madison MS 39110 601-853-7260 853-7299
TF: 800-321-8115 ■ *Web:* www.hoodpkg.com

KapStone Paper and Packaging Corp
300 Fibre Way PO Box 639.........................Longview WA 98632 360-425-1550 230-5135
Web: www.longviewfibre.com

KYD Inc 2949 Koapaka St..........................Honolulu HI 96819 808-836-3221 833-8995
Web: www.kydinc.com

Master Design Co 789 State Rt 94 E.................. Fulton KY 42041 270-838-7060 838-7060
Web: www.masterdesign.org

Pacific Bag Inc
15300 Woodinville Redmond Rd NE Ste A..........Woodinville WA 98072 425-455-1128 990-8582
TF: 800-562-2247 ■ *Web:* www.pacificbag.com

Roses Southwest Papers Inc
1701 Second St SW.......................... Albuquerque NM 87102 505-842-0134 242-0342
Web: www.rosessouthwest.com

Ross & Wallace Paper Products Inc
204 Old Covington Hwy .... Hammond LA 70403 800-854-2300 345-1370*
**Fax Area Code:* 985 ■ *TF:* 800-854-2300 ■ *Web:* www.rossandwallace.com

Stewart Sutherland Inc 5411 E 'V' Ave............. Vicksburg MI 49097 269-649-0530 649-3961
TF: 800-253-1034 ■ *Web:* www.ssbags.com

Werthan Packaging Inc 605 HWY 76 .... White House TN 37188 615-672-3336 242-2801
TF: 800-467-0348 ■ *Web:* www.werthan.com

Weyerhaeuser Co 33663 Weyerhaeuser Way S ......Federal Way WA 98003 253-924-2345 924-2685
NYSE: WY ■ *TF:* 800-525-5440 ■ *Web:* www.weyerhaeuser.com

Zenith Specialty Bag Company Inc
17625 E Railroad St PO Box 8445 ....City of Industry CA 91748 800-962-2247 284-8493
TF: 800-962-2247 ■ *Web:* www.zsb.com

66 BAGS - PLASTICS

Phone *Fax*

Aabaco Plastics Inc
9520 Midwest Ave ....Garfield Heights OH 44125 216-663-9494 663-9475*
**Fax:* Sales ■ *Web:* www.aabacoplastics.com

Admiral Packaging Inc 10 Admiral St .... Providence RI 02908 401-274-7000 331-1910
TF: 800-556-6454 ■ *Web:* www.admiralpkg.com

Ampac Packaging LLC 12025 Tricon Rd............ Cincinnati OH 45246 513-671-1777 671-2920*
**Fax:* Cust Svc ■ *TF:* 800-543-7030 ■ *Web:* www.ampaconline.com

Apco Extruders Inc 180 National Rd.................Edison NJ 08817 732-287-3000 287-1421
TF Orders: 800-942-8725

Armand Manufacturing Inc
2399 Silver Wolf Dr ....Henderson NV 89011 702-565-7500 565-3838
TF: 800-669-9811 ■ *Web:* www.armandmfg.com

Associated Bag Co 400 W Boden St................Milwaukee WI 53207 800-926-6100 926-4610
TF: 800-926-6100 ■ *Web:* www.associatedbag.com

Bag Makers Inc 6606 S Union Rd .... Union IL 60180 800-458-9031 458-9023
TF: 800-458-9031 ■ *Web:* www.bagmakersinc.com

Bema Incorporated 744 N Oaklawn Ave .... Elmhurst IL 60126 630-279-7800 279-0284
TF: 800-833-6657 ■ *Web:* bemaprint.com

Bemis Company Inc
One Neenah Ctr Fourth Fl PO Box 669................ Neenah WI 54957 920-727-4100
NYSE: BMS ■ *Web:* www.bemis.com

Buckeye Boxes Inc 601 N Hague Ave.............. Columbus OH 43204 614-274-8484 274-7381
Web: www.buckeyeboxes.com

Clear View Bag Co 5 Burdick Dr......................Albany NY 12205 518-458-7153 458-1401
TF: 800-458-7153 ■ *Web:* www.clearviewbag.com

Clorox Co 1221 Broadway...........................Oakland CA 94612 510-271-7000 832-1463
NYSE: CLX ■ *TF Cust Svc:* 800-424-9300 ■ *Web:* www.thecloroxcompany.com

Colonial Bag Corp 205 E Fullerton Ave............ Carol Stream IL 60188 630-690-3999 690-1571
TF: 800-445-7496 ■ *Web:* www.colonialbag.com

Crown Poly Inc 5700 Bickett St .... Huntington Park CA 90255 323-585-5522
Web: www.crownpoly.com

Enviro-Tote Inc 4 Cote Ln.......................... Bedford NH 03110 603-647-7171 647-0116
TF: 800-868-3224 ■ *Web:* www.enviro-tote.com

Fortune Plastics Inc One Williams Ln ....Old Saybrook CT 06475 860-388-3426 388-9930
TF: 800-243-0306 ■ *Web:* www.fortuneplastics.com

Heritage Bags 1648 Diplomat Dr.................... Carrollton TX 75006 800-527-2247 241-5543*
**Fax Area Code:* 972 ■ *TF:* 800-527-2247 ■ *Web:* www.heritage-bag.com

Home Care Industries Inc 1 Lisbon St................Clifton NJ 07013 973-365-1600 365-1770
TF: 888-382-1222 ■ *Web:* www.homecareind.com

International Poly Bag Inc 990 Pk Ctr Dr Ste F .... Vista CA 92081 760-598-2468 598-2469
TF: 800-976-5922 ■ *Web:* www.intlpolybag.com

KYD Inc 2949 Koapaka St..........................Honolulu HI 96819 808-836-3221 833-8995
Web: www.kydinc.com

Mexico Plastics Company (Inc) 2000 W Blvd .... Mexico MO 65265 800-325-0216
TF: 800-325-0216 ■ *Web:* www.continentalproducts.com

				Phone	Fax
Pacific Bag Inc 15300 Woodinville Redmond Rd NE Ste A *TF:* 800-562-2247 ■ *Web:* www.pacificbag.com	Woodinville	WA	98072	425-455-1128	990-8582
Pactiv Corp 1900 W Field Ct *TF:* 888-828-2850 ■ *Web:* www.pactiv.com	Lake Forest	IL	60045	847-482-2000	482-4738
Pitt Plastics Inc 1400 Atkinson Ave. *TF:* 800-835-0366 ■ *Web:* www.pittplastics.com	Pittsburg	KS	66762	800-835-0366	314-8449
Plastic Packaging Inc 1246 Main Ave SE **Fax:* Sales ■ *TF:* 800-333-2466 ■ *Web:* www.ppi-hky.com	Hickory	NC	28602	828-328-2466	322-1830*
Poly-America Inc 2000 W Marshall Dr. *TF:* 800-527-3322 ■ *Web:* www.poly-america.com	Grand Prairie	TX	75051	972-337-7100	647-8061
Poly-Pak Industries Inc 125 Spagnoli Rd **Fax Area Code:* 631 ■ *TF:* 800-969-1993 ■ *Web:* www.poly-pak.com	Melville	NY	11747	800-969-1993	454-6366*
Presto Products Co 670 N Perkins St PO Box 2399 *TF:* 800-558-3525 ■ *Web:* www.prestoproducts.com	Appleton	WI	54912	920-739-9471	738-1432
Ronpak Inc 4301 New Brunswick Ave. *Web:* www.ronpak.com	South Plainfield	NJ	07080	732-968-8000	968-1357
Roplast Industries Inc 3155 S Fifth Ave. *TF:* 800-767-5278 ■ *Web:* www.roplast.com	Oroville	CA	95965	530-532-9500	532-9576
Shields Bag & Printing Co 1009 Rock Ave *TF:* 800-541-8630 ■ *Web:* shieldsbag.com	Yakima	WA	98902	509-248-7500	248-6304
Star Packaging Corp 453 85th Cir *Web:* www.interflexgroup.com/	Atlanta	GA	30349	404-763-2800	763-1914
Superbag Corp 9291 Baythrone Dr *TF:* 888-842-1177 ■ *Web:* www.superbag.com	Houston	TX	77041	713-462-1173	462-8145
Tara Plastics Corp 175 Lk Mirror Rd. *Web:* www.taraplastics.com	Forest Park	GA	30297	404-366-4464	366-3816
Waverly Plastics Company Inc PO Box 801 *TF:* 800-454-6377 ■ *Web:* www.waverlyplastics.com	Waverly	IA	50677	319 352 3333	352-3338
Webster Industries Inc 95 Chestnut Ridge Rd, **Fax Area Code:* 570 ■ *TF:* 800-955-2374 ■ *Web:* www.aepinc.com	Montvale	NJ	07645	800-999-2374	474-9578*
Western Summit Manufacturing Corp 13290 Daum Dr	City of Industry	CA	91746	626-333-3333	961-2247
White Bag Co Inc 8027 Hwy 161 N PO Box 15357 *TF:* 800-527-1733 ■ *Web:* www.whitebag.com	North Little Rock	AR	72117	501-835-1444	835-2226
Wisconsin Film & Bag Inc 3100 E Richmond St. *TF:* 800-765-9224 ■ *Web:* www.wifb.com	Shawano	WI	54166	715-524-2565	524-3527

67 BAGS - TEXTILE

SEE ALSO Handbags, Totes, Backpacks p. 2444; Luggage, Bags, Cases p. 2680

				Phone	Fax
A Rifkin Co 1400 Sans Souci Pkwy *TF Cust Svc:* 800-458-7300 ■ *Web:* www.arifkin.com	Wilkes-Barre	PA	18706	570-825-9551	825-5282
Bearse Manufacturing Co 3815 W Cortland St. *Web:* www.bearseusa.com	Chicago	IL	60647	773-235-8710	235-8716
Bulk Lift International Inc (BLI) 1013 Tamarac Dr. *TF:* 800-879-2247 ■ *Web:* www.bulklift.com	Carpentersville	IL	60110	847-428-6059	428-7180
Corman Bag Co 32 Arlington St PO Box 505649 *Web:* www.cormanbag.com	Chelsea	MA	02150	617-884-7600	437-7917
Fox Packaging Co 2200 Fox Dr. *Web:* www.foxbag.com	McAllen	TX	78504	956-682-6176	682-5768
Fulton-Denver Co 3500 Wynkoop St *Web:* fultonpacific.com	Denver	CO	80216	303-294-9292	
GEM Group Nine International Way *TF:* 800-800-3200 ■ *Web:* gemline.com	Lawrence	MA	01843	978-691-2000	691-2085
Halsted Corp 78 Halladay St. *TF:* 800-843-5184 ■ *Web:* www.halstedbag.com	Jersey City	NJ	07304	201-433-3323	333-0670
HBD Inc 3901 Riverdale Rd. *TF:* 800-403-2247 ■ *Web:* www.hbdinc.com	Greensboro	NC	27406	336-275-4800	
Indian Valley Industries Inc PO Box 810 *TF:* 800-659-5111 ■ *Web:* www.iviindustries.com	Johnson City	NY	13790	607-729-5111	729-5158
J & M Industries Inc 300 Ponchatoula Pkwy *TF:* 800-989-1002 ■ *Web:* www.jm-ind.com	Ponchatoula	LA	70454	985-386-6000	386-9066
Langston Cos Inc 1760 S Third St. *Web:* langstonbag.com	Memphis	TN	38109	901-774-4440	
LBU Inc 217 Brook Ave. *TF:* 800-678-4528 ■ *Web:* www.lbuinc.com	Passaic	NJ	07055	973-773-4800	773-6005
Menardi One Maxwell Dr. *TF:* 800-321-3218 ■ *Web:* menardi-filtex.com	Trenton	SC	29847	803-663-6551	663-4029
NYP Corp 805 E Grand St. *TF:* 800-524-1052 ■ *Web:* www.nyp-corp.com	Elizabeth	NJ	07201	908-351-6550	351-0108
Sacramento Bag Manufacturing Co 440 N Pioneer Ave Ste 300 *TF:* 800-287-2247 ■ *Web:* www.sacbag.com	Woodland	CA	95776	530-662-6130	662-6381
Super Sack Manufacturing Corp 11510 Data Dr *TF:* 800-331-9200 ■ *Web:* www.bagcorp.com	Dallas	TX	75218	214-340-7060	340-4598

68 BAKERIES

				Phone	Fax
Ace Endico Corp 80 International Blvd. *Web:* www.aceendico.com	Brewster	NY	10509	845-940-1501	940-1516
Alvarado Street Bakery 2225 S Mcdowell Blvd Ext *Web:* www.alvaradostreetbakery.com	Petaluma	CA	94954	707-283-0300	
American Harvest Baking Company Inc 823 Est Gate Dr Ste 3 *Web:* www.ahbfoods.com	Mt Laurel	NJ	08054	856-642-9955	
Andre-Boudin Bakeries 221 Main St Ste 1230 *Web:* www.boudinbakery.com	San Francisco	CA	94105	415-882-1849	
Atlanta Bread Co 1200 Wilson Way Ste 100 **Fax Area Code:* 678 ■ *TF:* 800-398-3728 ■ *Web:* www.atlantabread.com	Smyrna	GA	30082	770-432-0933	366-3361*
Au Bon Pain 19 Fid Kennedy Ave *TF:* 800-825-5227 ■ *Web:* www.aubonpain.com	Boston	MA	02210	617-423-2100	423-7879
Awrey Bakeries Inc 12301 Farmington Rd *TF:* 800-950-2253 ■ *Web:* www.awrey.com	Livonia	MI	48150	734-522-1100	522-1453
Benson's Bakery Inc 134 Elder St *Web:* www.bensonsbakery.com	Bogart	GA	30622	770-725-5711	
Big Apple Bagels 500 Lk Cook Rd Ste 475 *TF:* 800-251-6101 ■ *Web:* www.babcorp.com	Deerfield	IL	60015	847-948-7520	405-8140
Bimbo Bakery USA 5662 Eastgate Dr. *Web:* bimbobakeriesusa.com	San Diego	CA	92121	858-457-9860	
Bruegger's Enterprises 159 Bank St *Web:* www.brueggers.com	Burlington	VT	05401	802-660-4020	652-9293
Busken Bakery Inc 2675 Madison Rd. *Web:* www.busken.com	Cincinnati	OH	45208	513-871-5330	871-2662
Butterkrust Bakery Inc 3355 W Memorial Blvd *Web:* flowersfoods.com	Lakeland	FL	33815	863-682-1155	
Certified Oil Corp 949 King Ave *Web:* certifiedoil.com	Columbus	OH	43212	614-421-7500	
Cheryl & Co 646 McCorkle Blvd **Fax Area Code:* 614 ■ *TF:* 800-443-8124 ■ *Web:* www.cheryls.com	Westerville	OH	43082	800-443-8124	891-8699*
Coles Quality Foods Inc 25 Ottawa SW Fourth Fl *Web:* www.coles.com	Grand Rapids	MI	49503	616-975-0081	
Collin Street Bakery Inc 401 W Seventh Ave. *TF Sales:* 800-504-1896 ■ *Web:* www.collinstreet.com	Corsicana	TX	75151	903-872-8111	872-6879
Cookies By Design Inc 1865 Summit Ave Ste 605 *TF:* 800-945-2665 ■ *Web:* www.cookiesbydesign.com	Plano	TX	75074	972-398-9536	398-9542
Cookies From Home Inc 1605 W University Dr Ste 106 *Web:* www.cookiesfromhome.com	Tempe	AZ	85281	480-894-1944	
Cookies in Bloom Inc 7208 La Casa Rd *Web:* www.cookiesinbloom.com	Dallas	TX	75248	972-490-8644	
Corner Bakery Cafe 12700 Pk Central Dr Ste 1300 *TF General:* 800-309-4642 ■ *Web:* www.cornerbakerycafe.com	Dallas	TX	75251	972-619-4100	
Crest Foods Inc 101 W Renner Rd Ste 240 *Web:* www.nestlecafe.com	Richardson	TX	75082	214-495-9533	853-5347
Damascus Bakery Inc 56 Gold St **Fax Area Code:* 718 ■ *TF:* 800-367-7482 ■ *Web:* www.damascusbakery.com	Brooklyn	NY	11201	800-367-7482	403-0948*
Dancing Deer Baking Company Inc 65 Sprague St W A *Web:* www.dancingdeer.com	Boston	MA	02136	617-442-7300	
Dare Foods Ltd 2481 Kingsway Dr *Web:* www.darefoods.com	Kitchener	ON	N2C1A6	519-893-5500	
Daylight Donut Flour Company LLC 11707 E 11th St *TF:* 800-331-2245 ■ *Web:* www.daylightdonuts.com	Tulsa	OK	74128	918-438-0800	438-0804
Dunkin' Donuts 130 Royall St *TF Cust Svc:* 800-859-5339 ■ *Web:* www.dunkindonuts.com	Canton	MA	02021	781-737-3000	737-4000
East Balt Inc 1801 W 31st Pl *TF:* 800-621-8555 ■ *Web:* www.eastbalt.com	Chicago	IL	60608	773-376-4444	376-8137
Eleni's 75 Ninth Ave. **Fax Area Code:* 718 ■ *TF:* 888-435-3647 ■ *Web:* www.elenis.com	New York	NY	10011	888-435-3647	361-8272*
Fiera Foods Co 50 Marmora St. *Web:* www.fierafoods.com	Toronto	ON	M9M2X5	416-746-1010	
Freed's Bakery LLC 299 Pepsi Rd. *Web:* www.freedsbakery.org	Manchester	NH	03109	603-627-7746	
Galasso's Inc 10820 San Sevaine Way. *Web:* www.galassos.com	Mira Loma	CA	91752	951-360-1211	
Gold Medal Bakery Inc 1397 Bay St. *TF:* 800-642-7568 ■ *Web:* www.goldmedalbakery.com	Fall River	MA	02724	508-674-5766	674-6090
Gonnella Baking Co 1001 W Chicago Ave *TF:* 800-262-3442 ■ *Web:* www.gonnella.com	Chicago	IL	60642	312-733-2020	733-7056
Great American Cookie Company Inc 1346 Oakbrook Dr Ste 170 *TF:* 877-639-2361 ■ *Web:* www.greatamericancookies.com	Norcross	GA	30093	877-639-2361	
Great Harvest Bread Co 28 S Montana St *TF:* 800-442-0424 ■ *Web:* www.greatharvest.com	Dillon	MT	59725	406-683-6842	683-5537
Harbar LLC 320 Turnpike St. *Web:* www.harber.com	Canton	MA	02021	781-828-0848	
Hill & Valley Inc 3915 9th St *Web:* www.hillandvalley.net	Rock Island	IL	61201	309-793-0161	
Holsum Bakery Inc 2322 W Lincoln St *TF:* 888-246-5786 ■ *Web:* www.holsumaz.com	Phoenix	AZ	85009	602-252-2351	
Honey Dew Assoc Inc Two Taunton St *TF:* 800-946-6393 ■ *Web:* www.honeydewdonuts.com	Plainville	MA	02762	508-699-3900	699-3949
Horizon Snack Foods Inc 7066 Las Positas Rd Ste G	Livermore	CA	94551	925-373-7700	
Hot Stuff Pizza 2930 W Maple St *TF:* 800-336-1320 ■ *Web:* www.hotstuffpizza.com	Sioux Falls	SD	57107	605-336-6961	336-0141
Interbake Foods LLC 3951 Werre Pkwy *Web:* www.interbake.com	Richmond	VA	23233	804-755-7107	
Jessie Lord Bakery LLC 21100 S Western Ave *Web:* www.jessielordpies.com	Torrance	CA	90501	310-533-6010	328-2608
Joseph Campione Garlic Bread 2201 W S Branch Blvd *Web:* www.josephcampione.com	Oak Creek	WI	53154	414-761-8944	761-2005
Just Desserts Inc 550 85th Ave *Web:* www.justdesserts.com	Oakland	CA	94621	510-567-2900	
King Arthur Flour Co Inc, The 135 Rt 5 S *Web:* www.kingarthurflour.com	Norwich	VT	05055	802-649-3881	649-3365
Krispy Kreme Doughnuts Corp 370 Knollwood St Ste 500 *NYSE: KKD* ■ *TF:* 800-457-4779 ■ *Web:* www.krispykreme.com	Winston-Salem	NC	27103	336-725-2981	733-3796
Le Boulanger Inc 305 N Mathilda. *Web:* www.leboulanger.com	Sunnyvale	CA	94085	408-774-9000	
Manhattan Bagel Co Inc 555 Zang St Ste 300 *TF:* 800-224-3563 ■ *Web:* www.manhattanbagel.com	Lakewood	CO	80228	303-568-8000	
Maple Donuts Inc 3455 E Market St *TF:* 800-627-5348 ■ *Web:* www.mapledonutsinc.com	York	PA	17402	717-757-7826	755-8725
New Horizons Baking Co Inc 211 Woodlawn Ave *Web:* www.genesisbaking.com	Norwalk	OH	44857	419-663-6432	

Company	City	State	Zip	Phone	Fax
Olde Tyme Pastries 2225 Geer Rd *Web:* www.otpastries.com	Turlock	CA	95382	209-668-0928	668-2741
Orange Bakery Inc 17751 Cowan Ave *Web:* www.orangebakery.com	Irvine	CA	92614	949-863-1377	
Panera Bread Co 3630 S Geyer Rd *NASDAQ: PNRA* ■ *TF:* 800-301-5566 ■ *Web:* www.panerabread.com	Saint Louis	MO	63127	314-984-1000	909-3300
PARTNERS A Tasteful Choice Co 20232 72nd Ave *TF:* 800-632-7477 ■ *Web:* www.partnerscrackers.com	South Kent	WA	98032	253-867-1580	
Pioneer Frozen Foods Inc 627 Big Stone Gap *Web:* www.chguenther.com	Duncanville	TX	75137	972-298-4281	
Puritan Bakery Inc 1624 E Carson St *Web:* www.puritanbakery.com	Carson	CA	90745	310-830-5451	
Quality Naturally Foods 18830 E San Jose Ave *Web:* www.qnfoods.com	City of Industry	CA	91748	626-854-6363	965-0978
Rotella's Italian Bakery Inc 6949 S 108th St *Web:* www.rotellasbakery.com	La Vista	NE	68128	402-592-6600	592-2989
Schulze & Burch Biscuit Co 1133 W 35th St *Web:* schulzeburch.com/brands/pastries.asp	Chicago	IL	60609	773-927-6622	
Southern Maid Donut Flour Co 3615 Cavalier Dr *Web:* www.southernmaiddonuts.com	Garland	TX	75042	972-272-6425	276-3549
Sprinkles Cupcakes Inc 9635 S Santa Monica Blvd *Web:* www.sprinkles.com	Beverly Hills	CA	90210	310-274-8765	
Sterling Foods LLC 1075 Arion Pkwy *Web:* www.sterlingfoodsusa.com	San Antonio	TX	78216	210-490-1669	490-7964
Sunrise Bakery Inc 4564 Second Ave 47th St *Web:* www.sunrisebakery.org	Brooklyn	NY	11232	718-788-7884	
SuperMom's LLC 625 Second St	Saint Paul Park	MN	55071	651-459-2253	
Sweet Street Desserts Inc 722 Hiesters Ln *Web:* www.sweetstreet.com	Reading	PA	19605	610-921-8113	
Treats International Franchise Corp 1550-A Laperriere Ave Ste 201 *TF:* 800-461-4003 ■ *Web:* www.treats.com	Ottawa	ON	K1Z7T2	613-563-4073	563-1982
Van's Natural Foods 3285 E Vernon Ave *Web:* www.vansfoods.com	Vernon	CA	90058	323-585-5581	
Vie de France Yamazaki Inc 2070 Chain Bridge Rd Ste 500 *TF General:* 800-446-4404 ■ *Web:* www.vdfy.com	Vienna	VA	22182	703-442-9205	821-2695
Wetzel's Pretzels LLC 35 Hugus Alley Ste 300 *Web:* www.wetzels.com	Pasadena	CA	91103	626-432-6900	432-6904
Wicks Pies Inc 217 Greenville Ave *Web:* www.wickspies.com	Winchester	IN	47394	765-584-8401	

69 BANKING-RELATED SERVICES

Company	City	State	Zip	Phone	Fax
Atm Merchant Systems 1667 Helm Dr *Web:* www.atmms.com	Las Vegas	NV	89119	702-837-8787	
Austin Trust Co 336 S Congress Ave Ste 100 *Web:* www.austintrust.com	Austin	TX	78704	512-478-2121	478-2616
Automatic Funds Transfer Services 151 S Landers St Ste C *TF:* 800-275-2033 ■ *Web:* www.afts.com	Seattle	WA	98134	206-254-0975	254-0968
Blackhawk Bank PO Box 719 *TF:* 888-769-2600 ■ *Web:* www.blackhawkbank.com	Beloit	WI	53511	608-364-4534	364-8946
Bremer Financial Corp 2100 Bremer Tower 445 Minnesota St *TF:* 800-908-2265 ■ *Web:* www.bremer.com	Saint Paul	MN	55101	651-227-7621	312-3675
Capital Farm Credit Aca 7000 Woodway Dr PO Box 20097 *TF:* 877-944-5500 ■ *Web:* www.capitalfarmcredit.com	Waco	TX	76702	254-776-7506	776-8112
Citizens Federal Savings & Loan Assn 110 N Main St PO Box 9 *TF:* 800-436-5177 ■ *Web:* www.citizensfederalsl.com	Bellefontaine	OH	43311	937-593-0015	593-6577
Civista Bank 100 E Water St *TF:* 888-645-4121 ■ *Web:* www.citizensbankco.com	Sandusky	OH	44870	419-625-4121	627-3359
Comdata Corp 5301 Maryland Way *TF:* 800-266-3282 ■ *Web:* www.comdata.com	Brentwood	TN	37027	615-370-7000	370-7828
Community Bank 790 E Colorado Blvd *TF:* 800-788-9999 ■ *Web:* www.cbank.com	Pasadena	CA	91101	800-788-9999	
Directcash Payments Inc 1420 28 St NE Bay 6 *Web:* www.directcash.net	Calgary	AB	T2A7W6	403-387-2103	
eCivis Inc 418 N Fair Oaks Ave Ste 301 *TF:* 877-232-4847 ■ *Web:* www.ecivis.com	Pasadena	CA	91103	877-232-4847	
Emida Corp 27442 Portola Pkwy Ste 150 *Web:* www.emida.net	Foothill Ranch	CA	92610	949-699-1401	699-1420
Emprise Financial Corp 257 N Broadway St PO Box 2970 *TF Cust Svc:* 800-201-7118 ■ *Web:* www.emprisebank.com	Wichita	KS	67202	316-383-4301	383-4433
Eureka Homestead 1922 Veterans Memorial Blvd *Web:* www.eurekahomestead.com	Metairie	LA	70005	504-834-0242	834-6909
Fiserv Inc 255 Fiserv Dr PO Box 979 *NASDAQ: FISV* ■ *TF Sales:* 800-872-7882 ■ *Web:* www.fiserv.com	Brookfield	WI	53008	262-879-5000	
Hawaii National Bank 45 N King St *TF:* 800-528-2273 ■ *Web:* www.hawaiinational.com	Honolulu	HI	96817	808-528-7711	528-7728
HomEquity Bank 1881 Yonge St Ste 300 *Web:* www.homequitybank.ca	Toronto	ON	M4S3C4	416-925-4757	
Lockwood Advisors Inc 760 Moore Rd *TF:* 800-200-3033 ■ *Web:* www.lockwoodadvisors.com	King Of Prussia	PA	19406	800-200-3033	
Moelis & Co LLC 399 Pk Ave 5th Fl *Web:* www.moelis.com	New York	NY	10022	212-883-3800	880-4260
MoneyGram International Inc 2828 N Harwood Fl 15 *NASDAQ: MGI* ■ *TF:* 800-666-3947 ■ *Web:* www.moneygram.com	Dallas	TX	75201	800-666-3947	
Moneytree Inc 6720 Ft Dent Way *TF:* 877-613-6669 ■ *Web:* www.moneytreeinc.com	Seattle	WA	98188	206-246-3500	248-3400
NYCE Corp 400 Plaza Dr **Fax Area Code:* 201 ■ *TF:* 888-323-0310 ■ *Web:* www.nyce.net	Secaucus	NJ	07094	904-438-6000	330-3374*
Oak Ridge Financial 701 Xenia Ave S Ste 100 *TF:* 800-231-8364 ■ *Web:* www.oakridgefinancial.com	Minneapolis	MN	55416	763-923-2200	923-2283
OANDA Corp 140 Broadway 46th Fl *TF:* 800-826-8164 ■ *Web:* www.oanda.com	New York	NY	10005	416-593-9436	593-0185
Orchard First Source (OFS) 10 S Wacker Dr Ste 2500 *Web:* www.ofscapital.com	Chicago	IL	60606	847-734-2000	734-7910
Philadelphia Trust Co, The 1760 Market St Second Fl *Web:* philadelphiatrust.com	Philadelphia	PA	19103	215-979-3434	
PULSE 1301 McKinney St Ste 2500 *TF:* 800-420-2122 ■ *Web:* www.pulsenetwork.com	Houston	TX	77010	713-223-1400	223-1204
Rock Springs National Bank 200 Second St PO Box 880 *TF:* 800-469-8801 ■ *Web:* www.rsnb.com	Rock Springs	WY	82902	307-362-8801	362-9432
Sherman Financial Group LLC 335 Madison Ave *Web:* sfg.com	New York	NY	10017	212-922-1616	
Travelex Worldwide Money 29 Broadway *Web:* www.travelex.com	New York	NY	10006	212-363-6206	
United Bank & Trust 205 E Chicago Blvd 2nd Fl **Fax Area Code:* 517 ■ *Web:* www.ubat.com	Tecumseh	MI	49286	800-731-2265	423-5041*
Universal Money Centers Inc 6800 Squibb Rd *Web:* www.universalmoney.com	Shawnee Mission	KS	66202	913-831-2055	831-0248
Western Union Holdings Inc 12500 E Belford Ave *NYSE: WU* ■ *TF Cust Svc:* 800-325-6000 ■ *Web:* westernunion.com	Englewood	CO	80112	720-332-1000	332-4753
Your Community Bank 2323 Ring Rd *TF:* 800-314-2265 ■ *Web:* www.ffsbky.com	Elizabethtown	KY	42701	270-765-2131	765-2135

70 BANKS - COMMERCIAL & SAVINGS

SEE ALSO Credit & Financing - Commercial p. 2177; Credit & Financing - Consumer p. 2178; Credit Unions p. 2179; Bank Holding Companies p. 2459

Company	City	State	Zip	Phone	Fax
1st Bank 120 Second St NW	Sidney	MT	59270	406-433-3212	
1st Bank & Trust of Broken Bow 710 S Park Dr *Web:* 1stbankandtrust.com	Broken Bow	OK	74728	580-584-9123	
1st Colonial Bancorp Inc 1040 Haddon Ave *OTC: FCOB* ■ *TF:* 800-500-1044 ■ *Web:* www.1stcolonial.com	Collingswood	NJ	08108	856-858-1100	858-9255
1st Community Bank 2911 N Westwood Blvd *TF:* 888-785-1772 ■ *Web:* www.1stcombank.com	Poplar Bluff	MO	63901	573-778-0101	778-9138
1st Source Bank 100 N Michigan St **Fax:* Mktg ■ *TF:* 800-513-2360 ■ *Web:* www.1stsource.com	South Bend	IN	46601	574-235-2254	235-2948*
1st Summit Bancorp 125 Donald Ln *Web:* 1stsummit.com	Johnstown	PA	15904	814-262-4000	
3rd Federal Bank 3 Penns Trail *TF:* 800-822-3321 ■ *Web:* www.3rdfedbank.com	Newtown	PA	18940	215-579-4600	579-2381
Alaska Pacific Bank 2094 Jordan Ave *Web:* www.alaskapacificbank.com	Juneau	AK	99801	907-789-4844	
Albany Bank & Trust Company NA 3400 W Lawrence Ave *Web:* www.albanybank.com	Chicago	IL	60625	773-267-7300	267-7337
Alderwood Capital LLC 505 Montgomery St 11th Fl *Web:* www.alderwoodcapital.com	San Francisco	CA	94111	415-874-3388	
Alerus Financial 2300 S Columbia Rd *Web:* alerusfinancial.com	Grand Forks	ND	58201	701-795-3200	
Allegiance Capital Corp 5429 Lbj Fwy Ste 750 *Web:* www.allcapcorp.com	Dallas	TX	75240	214-217-7750	217-7751
Alliance Bank 541 Lawrence Rd *NASDAQ: ALLB* ■ *TF:* 800-472-3272 ■ *Web:* www.allianceanytime.com	Broomall	PA	19008	610-353-2900	359-6908
Alliance Bank of Arizona One E Washington St *Web:* www.alliancebankofarizona.com	Phoenix	AZ	85004	602-629-1776	850-7390
Allied Irish Banks 405 Pk Ave *Web:* www.aib.ie	New York	NY	10022	212-339-8080	339-3007
Alma Exchange Bank 501 W 12th St PO Box 1988 *Web:* www.aebalma.com	Alma	GA	31510	912-632-8631	
Alostar Bank 3680 Grandview Pkwy Ste 200 **Fax Area Code:* 866 ■ *TF:* 877-738-6391 ■ *Web:* www.alostarbank.com	Birmingham	AL	35243	205-298-6391	715-6601*
Alpine Capital Bank 680 Fifth Ave *Web:* www.alpinecapitalbank.com	New York	NY	10019	212-328-2555	
AltaCorp Capital Inc 1100 888-3rd St SW *Web:* www.altacorpcapital.com	Calgary	AB	T2P5C5	403-539-8600	
Amalgamated Bank of Chicago 1 W Monroe PO Box 800 *Web:* secureforms.c3vault1.com	Chicago	IL	60603	312-822-3000	267-8767
Amalgamated Bank of New York 275 Seventh Ave *TF:* 800-662-0860 ■ *Web:* www.amalgamatedbank.com	New York	NY	10001	800-662-0860	
Amarillo National Bank 410 S Taylor St Plaza 1 **Fax:* Cust Svc ■ *TF:* 800-253-1031 ■ *Web:* www.anb.com	Amarillo	TX	79101	806-378-8000	378-8066*
Amboy National Bank 3590 US Hwy 9 S *TF:* 800-942-6269 ■ *Web:* www.amboybank.com	Old Bridge	NJ	08857	732-591-8700	591-0705
Amegy Bank of Texas 4400 Post Oak Pkwy *TF:* 800-287-0301 ■ *Web:* www.amegybank.com	Houston	TX	77027	713-235-8800	235-8816
American Bank 4029 W Tilghman St *Web:* ambk.com	Allentown	PA	18104	610-366-1800	
American Bank of Commerce 610 W Fifth St *Web:* www.theabcbank.com	Austin	TX	78701	512-391-5500	391-5599

Name / Address	City	State	ZIP	Phone	Fax
American Bank of Texas NA 200 N Austin St	Seguin	TX	78155	830-379-5236	
TF: 800-567-1817 ■ *Web:* www.abtexas.com					
American Exchange Bank (AEB) 510 W Main St PO Box 818	Henryetta	OK	74437	918-652-3321	652-7057
TF: 888-652-3321 ■ *Web:* www.aebbank.net					
American Express Centurion Bank 4315 South 2700 West	Salt Lake City	UT	84184	801-945-3000	
Web: www.americanexpress.com					
American First National Bank 9999 Bellaire Blvd	Houston	TX	77036	713-596-2888	596-2555
Web: www.afnb.com					
American Heritage Bank 2 S Main PO Box 1408	Sapulpa	OK	74067	918-224-3210	224-7689
TF: 866-669-2427 ■ *Web:* www.ahb-ok.com					
American Metro Bank 4878 N Broadway	Chicago	IL	60640	773-769-6868	769-6288
Web: www.americanmetrobank.com					
American National Bank PO Box 2139	Omaha	NE	68103	402-399-5000	391-8546
TF Cust Svc: 800-279-0007 ■ *Web:* www.anbank.com					
American Savings Bank FSB 1001 Bishop St PO Box 2300	Honolulu	HI	96813	808-539-7843	536-3141
TF: 800-272-2566 ■ *Web:* www.asbhawaii.com					
AmericanWest Bank 2237 NW 57th St	Seattle	WA	98107	206-784-2200	784-6650
Web: www.awbank.net					
Ameriserv Financial 216 Franklin St PO Box 520	Johnstown	PA	15907	814-533-5300	
NASDAQ: ASRV ■ *TF:* 800-837-2265 ■ *Web:* www.ameriserv.com					
Amfirst Bank NA Mccook 602 W B St	Mccook	NE	69001	308-345-1555	
Web: amfirstbank.com					
AmTrust Bank 1801 E Ninth St	Cleveland	OH	44114	216-736-3480	987-8732
TF: 888-696-4444 ■ *Web:* www.mynycb.com					
Anadarko Bank & Trust Co 110 W Oklahoma Ave	Anadarko	OK	73005	405-247-3311	
Web: abandt.biz					
Anchor Bank 1055 Wayzata Blvd E	Wayzata	MN	55391	952-473-4606	476-5219
TF: 800-425-5150 ■ *Web:* www.anchorlink.com					
Anchor Commercial Bank 13951 Us Hwy One	Juno Beach	FL	33408	561-383-3150	
Web: www.anchorcommercialbank.com					
AnchorBank 25 W Main St PO Box 7933	Madison	WI	53703	608-252-8827	252-8783
TF: 800-252-6246 ■ *Web:* www.anchorbank.com					
ANZ Securities Inc 1177 Ave of the Americas 6th Fl	New York	NY	10036	212-801-9160	801-9163
Web: www.anz.com					
Apple Bank for Savings 122 E 42nd St Ninth Fl	New York	NY	10168	914-902-2775	
TF: 800-824-0710 ■ *Web:* www.applebank.com					
Apple Creek Banc Corp Three W Main St PO Box 237	Apple Creek	OH	44606	330-698-2631	698-4770
Web: www.applecreekbank.com					
Arthur State Bank 100 E Main St PO Box 769	Union	SC	29379	864-427-1213	429-8537
TF: 877-226-5246 ■ *Web:* www.arthurstatebank.com					
Artisan's Bank 2961 Centerville Rd	Wilmington	DE	19808	302-658-6881	654-0559
TF: 800-282-8255 ■ *Web:* www.artisansbank.com					
Arundel FSB 333 E Patapsco Ave	Baltimore	MD	21225	410-355-9300	355-0335
Web: arundelfederal.com					
Asheville Savings Bank S S B PO Box 652	Asheville	NC	28802	828-254-7411	252-1512
Web: www.ashevillesavings.com					
Ashir Capital Inc 40 Wall St 59th Fl	New York	NY	10005	212-269-2300	
Asia Bank NA 135-34 Roosevelt Ave	Flushing	NY	11354	718-961-9700	
Web: asiabank-na.com					
Associated Bank 2870 Holmgren Way	Green Bay	WI	54304	262-879-0133	
TF: 800-728-3501 ■ *Web:* www.associatedbank.com					
Associated Bank Green Bay NA 200 N Adams St	Green Bay	WI	54301	920-433-3200	433-3028
TF: 800-728-3501 ■ *Web:* www.associatedbank.com					
Associated Bank Illinois NA 612 N Main St	Rockford	IL	61103	815-987-3500	
TF: 800-236-8866 ■ *Web:* www.associatedbank.com					
Associated Bank Milwaukee 401 E Kilbourn Ave	Milwaukee	WI	53202	414-271-1786	283-2204
TF: 800-236-8866 ■ *Web:* www.associatedbank.com					
Associated Bank North 303 S First Ave	Wausau	WI	54401	715-848-4793	
TF: 800-236-8866 ■ *Web:* www.associatedbank.com					
Athens State Bank 6530 N State Rt 29	Springfield	IL	62707	217-487-7766	487-7733
TF: 800-367-7576 ■ *Web:* athensstatebank.com					
Baldwin & Clarke Corporate Finance Inc Coldstream Park 116B S River Rd	Bedford	NH	03110	603-668-4353	
Web: www.bcfinance.com					
Banc Statements Inc 4700 Birmingham St	Birmingham	AL	35217	205-956-5004	
Web: www.bsisite.com					
Bancorp Bank 409 Silverside Rd Ste 105	Wilmington	DE	19809	302-385-5000	385-5099
NASDAQ: TBBK ■ *TF Cust Svc:* 800-545-0289 ■ *Web:* thebancorp.com					
Bangor Savings Bank Three State St	Bangor	ME	04401	207-942-5211	941-2752
TF: 877-226-4671 ■ *Web:* www.bangor.com					
Bank Financial 6415 W 95th St	Chicago Ridge	IL	60415	800-894-6900	675-6421*
**Fax Area Code:* 708 ■ *TF:* 800-894-6900 ■ *Web:* www.bankfinancial.com					
Bank First National PO Box 10	Manitowoc	WI	54221	920-684-6611	652-3180
Web: www.bankfirstnational.com					
Bank Leumi USA 579 Fifth Ave	New York	NY	10017	917-542-2343	542-2254
TF: 800-892-5430 ■ *Web:* www.leumiusa.com					
Bank Midwest NA 1111 Main St Ste 1600	Kansas City	MO	64105	816-471-9800	472-5668
Web: www.bankmw.com					
Bank of Albuquerque NA 201 3rd St NW Ste 1400	Albuquerque	NM	87102	505-855-0855	222-8481
Web: www.bankofalbuquerque.com					
Bank of Bartlett Inc 6281 Stage Rd	Bartlett	TN	38134	901-382-6600	
Web: bankofbartlett.com					
Bank of Bennington (Bennington NE) 12212 N 156th St	Bennington	NE	68007	402-238-2245	
Web: www.bankbenn.com					
Bank of Bennington, The 155 N St	Bennington	VT	05201	802-442-8121	
Web: www.thebankofbennington.com					
Bank of Blue Valley PO Box 26128	Overland Park	KS	66225	913-338-1000	338-2801
Web: www.bankbv.com					
Bank of Cashton 723 Main St	Cashton	WI	54619	608-654-5121	
Web: bankofcashton.com					
Bank of Delmar Inc 2245 Northwood Dr	Salisbury	MD	21801	410-548-1100	
Web: www.bankofdelmarvahb.com					
Bank of Denver 810 E 17th Ave	Denver	CO	80218	303-572-3600	
Web: thebankofdenver.com					
Bank of Erath 105 W Edwards	Erath	LA	70533	337-937-5816	
Web: bankoferath.com					
Bank of Georgia, The 100 Westpark Dr	Peachtree City	GA	30269	770-631-9488	487-4368
TF: 866-645-1139 ■ *Web:* www.bankofgeorgia.com					
Bank of Gleason 203 Main St PO Box 231	Gleason	TN	38229	731-648-5506	648-5090
Web: www.gleasononline.com					
Bank of Glen Burnie, The 101 Crain Hwy SE	Glen Burnie	MD	21061	410-766-3300	787-8886
Web: www.thebankofglenburnie.com					
Bank of Gravett 211 Se Main St	Gravette	AR	72736	479-787-5251	
Web: bankofgravett.net					
Bank of Hazlehurst PO Box 628	Hazlehurst	GA	31539	912-375-4228	375-4210
Web: www.bankofhazlehurst.com					
Bank of Herrin, The 101 S Park Ave	Herrin	IL	62948	618-942-6666	
Bank of Holly Springs PO Box 250	Holly Springs	MS	38635	662-252-2511	252-1816
Web: www.bankofhollysprings.com					
Bank of Kirksville 214 S Franklin	Kirksville	MO	63501	660-665-7766	
Web: bankofkirksville.com					
Bank of Landisburg, The 100 N Carlisle St PO Box 179	Landisburg	PA	17040	717-789-3213	789-4702
Web: www.bankoflandisburg.com					
Bank of Louisiana 300 St Charles Ave	New Orleans	LA	70130	504-592-0600	592-0606
TF: 866-392-9952 ■ *Web:* www.bankoflouisiana.com					
Bank of Marin 504 Tamalpais Dr	Corte Madera	CA	94925	415-927-2265	927-8920
NASDAQ: BMRC ■ *TF:* 800-654-5111 ■ *Web:* www.bankofmarin.com					
Bank of Mauston, The 503 State Rd 82 E PO Box 226	Mauston	WI	53948	608-847-6200	847-5372
Web: www.bankofmauston.com					
Bank of McKenney 20718 First St	McKenney	VA	23872	804-478-4434	478-4704
OTC: BOMK ■ *TF:* 800-528-2273 ■ *Web:* www.bankofmckenney.com					
Bank of Montreal (BMO) 100 King St W 1 First Canadian Pl 19th Fl	Toronto	ON	M5X1A1	416-867-6785	867-6793
NYSE: BMO ■ *Web:* www.bmo.com					
Bank of Morton 366 S Fourth St PO Box 229	Morton	MS	39117	601-732-8944	732-8599
Web: www.bankofmorton.com					
Bank of Napa Na 2007 Redwood Rd Ste 101	Napa	CA	94558	707-257-7777	
Web: www.thebankofnapa.com					
Bank of Nevada 2700 W Sahara Ave	Las Vegas	NV	89102	702-248-4200	248-8661
TF: 877-750-0010 ■ *Web:* www.bankofnevada.com					
Bank of New Glarus 501 First St	New Glarus	WI	53574	608-527-5205	
Web: bankofnewglarus.com					
Bank of North Dakota 1200 Memorial Hwy	Bismarck	ND	58504	701-328-5600	328-5632
TF: 800-472-2166 ■ *Web:* www.banknd.nd.gov					
Bank of Nova Scotia 1 Liberty Plaza 26th Fl	New York	NY	10006	212-225-5011	225-5480
TSE: BNS ■ *TF:* 800-472-6842 ■ *Web:* www.scotiabank.com					
Bank of Oak Ridge 2211 Oak Ridge Rd	Oak Ridge	NC	27310	336-644-9944	644-6644
OTC: BKOR ■ *Web:* www.bankofoakridge.com					
Bank of Oklahoma NA PO Box 2300	Tulsa	OK	74192	918-588-6010	
TF: 800-234-6181 ■ *Web:* www.bankofoklahoma.com					
Bank of Springfield 2600 Adlai Stevenson Dr	Springfield	IL	62703	217-529-5555	529-5080
Web: www.bankwithbos.com					
Bank of Stanly PO Box 338	Albemarle	NC	28002	704-983-6181	983-5548
TF: 800-438-6864 ■ *Web:* www.uwharrie.com					
Bank of Stockton PO Box 1110	Stockton	CA	95201	209-929-1600	929-1434
TF: 800-941-1494 ■ *Web:* www.bankofstockton.com					
Bank of Sunset & Trust Co 863 Napoleon Ave	Sunset	LA	70584	337-662-5222	662-5705
TF: 800-264-5578 ■ *Web:* www.bankofsunset.com					
Bank of Tampa, The 601 Bayshore Blvd	Tampa	FL	33606	813-872-1220	
Web: bankoftampa.com					
Bank of Tescott, The 600 S Santa Fe	Salina	KS	67401	785-825-1621	
Bank of the Carolinas 135 Boxwood Village Dr	Mocksville	NC	27028	336-751-5755	751-4222
OTC: BCAR ■ *TF:* 877-751-5755 ■ *Web:* www.bankofthecarolinas.com					
Bank of the Cascades 121 N Ninth St	Boise	ID	83702	208-343-7848	343-7979
Web: botc.com					
Bank of the Ozarks 4328 Old Spanish Trail	Houston	TX	77021	713-747-9000	912-4201*
**Fax Area Code:* 817 ■ *TF:* 800-274-4482 ■ *Web:* www.omnibank.com					
Bank of the Sierra PO Box 1930	Porterville	CA	93258	559-782-4900	782-4994
TF Cust Svc: 888-454-2265 ■ *Web:* www.bankofthesierra.com					
Bank of Tokyo-Mitsubishi Ltd 1251 Ave of the Americas	New York	NY	10020	212-782-4000	782-6570*
**Fax:* Hum Res ■ *Web:* www.bk.mufg.jp					
Bank of Tuscaloosa 2200 Jack Warner Pkwy	Tuscaloosa	AL	35401	205-345-6200	
Web: bankoftuscaloosa.synovus.com					
Bank Of Utica 222 Genesee St	Utica	NY	13502	315-797-2700	797-2707
OTC: BKUT ■ *TF:* 800-442-1028 ■ *Web:* www.bankofutica.com					
Bank of Virginia 11730 Hull St Rd	Midlothian	VA	23112	804-744-7576	744-2306
NASDAQ: BOVA ■ *TF:* 800-500-1044 ■ *Web:* bankofva.com					
Bank of Walterboro 1100 N Jeffries Blvd	Walterboro	SC	29488	843-549-2265	
Web: bankofwalterboro.com					
Bank Street Group LLC, The Four Landmark Sq Third Fl	Stamford	CT	06901	203-252-2800	
Web: www.bankstreet.com					
Bank2 909 S Meridian	Oklahoma City	OK	73108	405-946-2265	
Web: bank2online.com					
BankAtlantic 200 W Second St	Winston-Salem	NC	27101	888-628-3926	
TF: 800-226-5228 ■ *Web:* www.bbt.com					
Bankeast 607 Market St PO Box 24	Knoxville	TN	37902	865-540-5800	
Web: usbank.com					
Bankers' Bank 7700 Mineral Point Rd	Madison	WI	53717	608-833-5550	829-5590
TF: 800-388-5550 ■ *Web:* www.bankersbankusa.com					
Bankwest Corporation 2050 N California Blvd	Walnut Creek	CA	94597	925-933-7810	
TF: 888-389-8668 ■ *Web:* www.bankofthewest.com					
Bankwest Inc 420 S Pierre St PO Box 998	Pierre	SD	57501	605-224-7391	224-7393
TF: 800-253-0362 ■ *Web:* www.bankwest-sd.com					

				Phone	Fax
Banner Bank 10 S First Ave PO Box 907 *Fax: Hum Res ■ TF: 800-272-9933 ■ Web: www.bannerbank.com	Walla Walla	WA	99362	509-527-3636	526-8898*
Banterra Corp 1404 US Rt 45 S TF: 877-541-2265 ■ Web: www.banterrabank.com	Eldorado	IL	62930	618-273-9346	273-5617
Baraboo BanCorp Inc, The 101 Third Ave	Baraboo	WI	53913	608-356-7703	
Barrington Bank & Trust Company Na 201 S Hough St Web: www.barringtonbank.com	Barrington	IL	60010	847-842-4500	304-6697
Bay Banks of Virginia Inc 100 S Main St PO Box 1869 OTC: BAYK ■ Web: www.bankoflancaster.com	Kilmarnock	VA	22482	804-435-1171	
Bay Business Credit 1460 Maria Ln Ste 300 Web: baybizcr.com	Walnut Creek	CA	94596	925-256-9003	
Baybank Corp 104 S 10th St Web: baybank.us	Gladstone	MI	49837	906-428-4040	
Baylake Bank 217 N Fourth Ave. TF: 800-267-3610 ■ Web: www.baylake.com	Sturgeon Bay	WI	54235	920-743-5551	746-3984
BB & T Corp 200 W Second St. NYSE: BBT ■ TF: 800-226-5228 ■ Web: www.bbt.com	Winston-Salem	NC	27101	336-733-2500	
BDO Capital Advisors LLC 1888 Century Park E. Web: www.bdocap.com	Los Angeles	CA	90067	310-557-0300	
Beal Bank SSB 6000 Legacy Dr *Fax Area Code: 972 ■ Web: www.bealbank.com	Plano	TX	75024	469-467-5000	309-3800*
Bear State Bank 600 Hwy 71 S Web: www.fnbweb.biz	Mena	AR	71953	479-394-3552	
Beneficial Mutual Savings Bank 530 Walnut St. TF: 800-784-8490 ■ Web: www.thebeneficial.com	Philadelphia	PA	19106	215-864-6000	864-6198
Berkshire Bank PO Box 1308 TF: 800-773-5601 ■ Web: www.berkshirebank.com	Pittsfield	MA	01202	413-443-5601	443-3587
Better Banks 10225 N Knoxville Ave Web: betterbanks.com	Peoria	IL	61615	309-243-1000	
Blackbridge Partners LLC 800 W Cummings Pk Ste 2000. Web: www.blackbridgepartners.com	Woburn	MA	01801	617-273-2404	
Blue Ridge Bank & Trust Co 4240 Blue Ridge Blvd Ste 100 TF: 800-569-4287 ■ Web: www.blueridgebank.net	Kansas City	MO	64133	816-358-5000	252-2630
Blueharbor Bank 106 Corporate Park Dr. TF: 877-322-8228 ■ Web: www.blueharborbank.com	Mooresville	NC	28117	704-662-7700	
BMO Harris Bank 111 W Monroe St. TF: 888-340-2265 ■ Web: www.bmoharris.com	Chicago	IL	60603	847-238-2265	
BNA Bank 133 E Bankhead. Web: bnabank.com	New Albany	MS	38652	662-534-8171	
BNC National Bank 322 E Main Ave PO Box 4050. TF: 800-262-2265 ■ Web: www.bncbank.com	Bismarck	ND	58501	701-250-3000	250-3028
Boiling Springs Savings Bank (BSSB) 25 Orient Way. TF: 888-388-7459 ■ Web: www.bssbank.com	Rutherford	NJ	07070	201-939-5000	939-3957
Boone County National Bank 720 E Broadway PO Box 678 TF: 800-842-2262 ■ Web: www.boonebank.com	Columbia	MO	65201	573-874-8535	874-8432
Borel Private Bank & Trust Co 160 Bovet Rd Web: www.bostonprivatebank.com	San Mateo	CA	94402	650-378-3700	378-3774
Bowen Advisors Inc 25 Recreation Park Dr Ste 210 Web: www.bowenadvisors.com	Hingham	MA	02043	617-245-1660	
Branch Banking & Trust Company of South Carolina 301 College St *Fax Area Code: 864 ■ TF: 800-226-5228 ■ Web: www.bbt.com	Greenville	SC	29601	800-226-5228	242-9500*
BroadSpan Capital 1450 Brickell Ave Ste 2620 Web: www.brocap.com	Miami	FL	33131	305-424-3400	
Broadway Bank 1177 NE Loop 410. Web: www.broadwaybank.com	San Antonio	TX	78209	210-283-6500	
Brotherhood Bank & Trust 756 Minnesota Ave. Web: www.brotherhoodbank.com	Kansas City	MO	66101	913-321-4242	371-5392
Brown Bros Harriman & Co 140 Broadway *Fax: Hum Res ■ Web: www.bbh.com	New York	NY	10005	212-483-1818	493-7287*
Burke & Herbert Bank & Trust Co 100 S Fairfax St TF: 877-440-0800 ■ Web: www.burkeandherbertbank.com	Alexandria	VA	22314	703-751-7701	548-5759
Byline Bank 3639 N Broadway St. TF: 866-957-7700 ■ Web: www.northcommunitybank.com	Chicago	IL	60613	773-244-7000	
C1 Bank 2025 Lakewood Ranch Blvd Web: www.c1bank.com	Lakewood Ranch	FL	34211	941-750-0700	
Cabool State Bank 600 Main PO Box 800 Web: caboolstatebank.com	Cabool	MO	65689	417-962-3168	
Cabrillo Advisors LLC 4330 La Jolla Village Dr Ste 270 Web: www.cabrilloadvisors.com	San Diego	CA	92122	858-452-9500	
California Bank & Trust 11622 El Camino Real Ste 200. TF: 800-400-6080 ■ Web: www.calbanktrust.com	San Diego	CA	92130	858-793-7400	793-7438
Cambridge Savings Bank 1374 Massachusetts Ave *Fax: Cust Svc ■ TF: 800-540-6322 ■ Web: cambridgesavings.com	Cambridge	MA	02138	617-441-4155	520-5306*
Cambridge Trust Co 1336 Massachusetts Ave Web: cambridgetrust.com	Cambridge	MA	02138	617-876-5500	
Canadian Imperial Bank of Commerce (CIBC) 199 Bay St Commerce Ct W NYSE: CM ■ TF: 800-465-2422 ■ Web: www.cibc.com	Toronto	ON	M5L1A2	800-465-2422	
Canadian Western Bank 10303 Jasper Ave Ste 3000 TSE: CWB ■ TF: 866-317-0356 ■ Web: www.cwbank.com	Edmonton	AB	T5J3X6	780-423-8888	423-8897
Canandaigua National Corp 72 S Main St OTC: CNND ■ Web: www.cnbank.com	Canandaigua	NY	14424	585-394-4260	394-4001
Cape Bank 225 N Main St Web: www.capebanknj.com	Cape May Court House	NJ	08210	609-465-5600	
Cape Cod Five Cents Savings Bank 19 W Rd PO Box 20 *Fax: Mktg ■ TF: 800-678-1855 ■ Web: www.capecodfive.com	Orleans	MA	02653	508-240-0555	240-1895*
Capital Alliance Corp 2777 N Stemmons Fwy Ste 1220 Web: www.cadallas.com	Dallas	TX	75207	214-638-8280	638-8009
Capital City Bank 2111 N Monroe St PO Box 900 TF: 888-671-0400 ■ Web: www.ccbg.com	Tallahassee	FL	32302	850-402-7500	
Capital One Auto Finance Inc PO Box 60511 TF: 800-946-0332 ■ Web: www.capitalone.com	City of Industry	CA	91716	800-946-0332	
Capital One FSB Capital One Bank 15000 Capital One Dr Web: www.capitalone.com	Richmond	VA	23238	804-273-1144	
Capitol FSB 700 S Kansas Ave TF: 800-432-2926 ■ Web: www.capfed.com	Topeka	KS	66603	785-235-1341	231-6329
Carolina Premier Bank 6225 Blakeney Park Dr Web: www.carolinapremierbank.com	Charlotte	NC	28277	704-752-9292	
Carolina Trust Bank 901 E Main St. NASDAQ: CART ■ TF: 877-983-5537 ■ Web: www.carolinatrust.com	Lincolnton	NC	28092	704-735-1104	735-1104
Carter Bank & Trust 1300 Kings Mtn Rd. Web: carterbankandtrust.com	Martinsville	VA	24112	276-656-1776	
Carver FSB 75 W 125th St. Web: www.carverbank.com	New York	NY	10027	718-230-2900	
Cascade Credit Services Inc 1635 Se Malden St Ste D Web: cascadecredit.com	Portland	OR	97202	503-722-2009	
Casey State Bank 305-307 N Central Ave TF: 866-666-2754 ■ Web: www.caseystatebank.com	Casey	IL	62420	217-932-2136	932-4370
CBC National Bank 1891 S 14th St Web: cbcnationalbank.com	Fernandina Beach	FL	32034	904-321-0400	277-0167
CCB Community Bank 225 E Three Notch St. Web: bankccb.com	Andalusia	AL	36420	334-222-2561	
CCC Investment Banking 150 King St W Ste 2020. Web: www.cccinvestmentbanking.com	Toronto	ON	M5H1J9	416-599-4206	
CedarStone Bank 900 W Main St. Web: www.cedarstonebank.com	Lebanon	TN	37087	615-443-1411	
Centerstate Banks Inc 42725 Us Hwy 27 Web: centerstatebank.com	Davenport	FL	33837	855-863-2265	
Central BanCo 238 Madison St Web: www.centralbancompany.com	Jefferson City	MO	65101	573-634-1155	634-1100
Central Bank of Kansas City 2301 Independence Ave Web: www.centralbankkc.com	Kansas City	MO	64124	816-483-1210	483-2586
Central National Bank 800 Se Quincy St. Web: centralnational.com	Topeka	KS	66612	785-234-2265	234-9660
Central Pacific Bank PO Box 3590 NYSE: CPF ■ TF Cust Svc: 800-342-8422 ■ Web: www.centralpacificbank.com	Honolulu	HI	96811	808-544-0500	
Central Valley Bank 537 W Second Ave. TF General: 800-422-1566 ■ Web: www.cvbankwa.com	Toppenish	WA	98948	509-865-2511	865-2086
Centreville Savings Bank 1218 Main St. Web: www.centrevillebank.com	West Warwick	RI	02893	401-821-9100	
Century National Bank 14 S Fifth St TF Cust Svc: 800-548-3557 ■ Web: www.centurynationalbank.com	Zanesville	OH	43701	740-454-2521	455-7201
CFG Community Bank 1422 Clarkview Rd. TF: 866-619-1417 ■ Web: www.cfgcommunitybank.com	Baltimore	MD	21209	410-823-0500	823-6685
CharterBank 1233 OG Skinner Dr. TF: 800-763-4444 ■ Web: www.charterbk.com	West Point	GA	31833	706-645-1391	645-1370
Chase Bank One Chase Manhattan Plz TF: 800-935-9935 ■ Web: www.chase.com	New York	NY	10081	800-935-9935	
Cherokee Bank 1275 Riverstone Pkwy PO Box 4250 OTC: CHKJ ■ Web: www.cherokeebank.com	Canton	GA	30114	770-479-3400	720-6923
Chesapeake Bank of Maryland 2001 E Joppa Rd Web: chesapeakebank.com	Baltimore	MD	21234	410-661-1141	665-8604
Chiba Bank Ltd 1133 Ave of the Americas 15th Fl Web: chibabank.co.jp	New York	NY	10036	212-354-7777	354-8575
Chinatrust Bank USA 801 S Figueroa St Ste 2300 TF: 888-839-9000 ■ Web: www.chinatrustusa.com	Los Angeles	CA	90017	310-791-2828	791-2880
Choice Financial Group 645 Hill Ave. Web: choicefinancialgroup.com	Grafton	ND	58237	701-352-0242	
Citibank (Delaware) 4500 New Linden Hill Rd TF: 800-374-9700 ■ Web: online.citi.com/US/Welcome.c	Wilmington	DE	19808	302-323-3600	
Citibank NA 399 Pk Ave *Fax Area Code: 212 ■ TF: 800-627-3999 ■ Web: citigroup.com	New York	NY	10022	800-627-3999	559-7373*
Citibank (South Dakota) NA 701 E 60th St N TF: 800-627-3999 ■ Web: citibank.com	Sioux Falls	SD	57104	605-370-6261	331-7518
Citizen National Bank Of Bluffton, The 102 S Main St PO Box 88. Web: www.cnbohio.com	Bluffton	OH	45817	419-358-8040	358-5227
Citizens Bank of Clovis 420 Wheeler TF: 844-657-3553 ■ Web: www.citizensbankofclovis.com	Texico	NM	88135	575-482-3381	762-7259
Citizens Bank of Las Cruces 505 S Main St. *Fax Area Code: 505 ■ Web: www.citizenslc.com	Las Cruces	NM	88004	575-647-4100	526-3409*
Citizens Bank of Massachusetts 28 State St. TF: 800-610-7300 ■ Web: www.citizensbank.com	Boston	MA	02109	800-610-7300	
Citizens Bank of Mukwonago 301 N Rochester St PO Box 223. TF: 877-546-5868 ■ Web: www.citizenbank.com	Mukwonago	WI	53149	262-363-6500	363-6515
Citizens Bank of Rhode Island One Citizens Plz TF Cust Svc: 800-922-9999 ■ Web: www.citizensbank.com	Providence	RI	02903	401-456-7000	455-5715
Citizens Business Bank (CBB) 701 N Haven Ave TF Cust Svc: 888-222-5432 ■ Web: www.cbbank.com	Ontario	CA	91764	909-980-4030	481-2130
Citizens Financial Services 707 Ridge Rd *Fax Area Code: 317 ■ TF: 866-622-1370 ■ Web: www.firstmerchants.com	Munster	IN	46321	219-836-5500	770-7572*

Phone | Fax

Citizens State Bank
1300 W Hildebrand Ave PO Box 5970 San Antonio TX 78201 210-785-2300 785-2301
TF: 800-870-2472 ■ *Web:* Www.csbsa.com

Citizens Trust Bank 1700 3rd Ave N Birmingham AL 35203 205-328-2041 214-3048
TF: 888-214-3099 ■ *Web:* www.ctbconnect.com

City National Bank 400 N Roxbury Dr Beverly Hills CA 90210 310-888-6000 888-6045*
**Fax:* Mktg ■ *TF Cust Svc:* 800-773-7100 ■ *Web:* www.cnb.com

City National Bank of Florida
450 E Las Olas Blvd Ste 160 Fort Lauderdale FL 33301 954-467-6667 524-8247
TF: 800-762-2489 ■ *Web:* www.citynationalcm.com

City National Bank of New Jersey (CNB)
900 Broad St Newark NJ 07102 973-624-0865 624-5754
TF: 877-350-3524 ■ *Web:* www.citynatbank.com

City National Bank of Sulphur Springs, The
201 Connally Sulphur Springs TX 75482 903-885-7523

City National Bank of West Virginia
3601 McCorckle Ave Charleston WV 25304 304-926-3324 925-8073
TF: 888-816-8064 ■ *Web:* www.bankatcity.com

City Savings Bank & Trust 301 N Pine St Deridder LA 70634 337-463-8661
Web: citysavingsbank.com

Clay County Savings Bank
1178 W Kansas St PO Box 277 Liberty MO 64069 816-781-4500 781-1668
Web: www.claycountysavings.com

Clearfield Bank & Trust Co
11 N Second St PO Box 171 Clearfield PA 16830 814-765-7551 765-2943
TF: 888-765-7551 ■ *Web:* www.cbtfinancial.com

Cnlbank 450 S Orange Ave Ste 400 Orlando FL 32801 407-244-3100 244-3180
TF: 800-910-2187 ■ *Web:* www.cnlbank.com

Coast Capital Savings 645 Tyee Rd Ste 400 Victoria BC V9A6X5 250-483-7000
TF: 888-517-7000 ■ *Web:* www.coastcapitalsavings.com

College Savings Bank Five Vaughn Dr Ste 100 Princeton NJ 08540 800-888-2723 987-3760*
**Fax Area Code:* 609 ■ *TF:* 800-888-2723 ■ *Web:* www.collegesavings.com

Colorado East Bank & Trust Inc 100 W Pearl St Lamar CO 81052 719-336-5200 336-5944
Web: www.coloeast.com

Colorado Fsb
8400 E Prentice Ave Ste 545 Greenwood Village CO 80111 303-793-3555 793-3560
TF: 877-484-2372 ■ *Web:* www.coloradofederalbank.com

Colorado State Bank & Trust NA PO Box 2300 Tulsa OK 74192 303-861-2111
Web: www.csbt.com

Columbia Bank, The 7168 Columbia Gateway Dr Columbia MD 21046 888-822-2265
TF: 888-822-2265 ■ *Web:* www.thecolumbiabank.com

Columbia Savings Bank 19-01 Rt 208 Fair Lawn NJ 07410 800-522-4167 281-6331*
**Fax Area Code:* 513 ■ *TF Cust Svc:* 800-747-4428 ■ *Web:* www.columbiabankonline.com

Columbia State Bank PO Box 2156 Tacoma WA 98401 253-305-1900 396-6960*
**Fax:* Hum Res ■ *TF:* 800-305-1905 ■ *Web:* www.columbiabank.com

Columbus Bank & Trust Co 1148 Broadway Columbus GA 31901 706-649-4900
TF: 800-334-9007 ■ *Web:* columbusbankandtrust.synovus.com

Comerica Bank 411 W Lafayette Detroit MI 48226 313-222-3344
TF: 800-643-4418 ■ *Web:* www.comerica.com

Comerica Bank-California
333 W Santa Clara St San Jose CA 95113 408-556-5300 298-6449*
**Fax:* Hum Res ■ *TF:* 800-522-2265 ■ *Web:* www.comerica.com

Comerica Bank-Texas 1717 Main St Dallas TX 75201 800-925-2160
TF: 800-925-2160 ■ *Web:* www.comerica.com

Comerica Inc 1717 Main St Comerica Bank Tower Dallas TX 75201 800-266-3742 969-6450*
NYSE: CMA ■ **Fax Area Code:* 214 ■ *TF:* 800-266-3742 ■ *Web:* www.comerica.com

Commerce Bank & Trust Co 386 Main St Worcester MA 01608 508-797-6842 797-6836
TF: 800-698-2265 ■ *Web:* www.bankatcommerce.com

Commercewest Bank NA 2111 Business Ctr Dr Irvine CA 92612 949-251-6959 251-6957
OTC: CWBK ■ *Web:* www.cwbk.com

Commercial Bank 301 N State St PO Box 638 Alma MI 48801 989-463-2185 463-5996
OTC: CEFC ■ *TF:* 800-547-8531 ■ *Web:* www.commercial-bank.com

Commerzbank AG Two World Financial Ctr New York NY 10281 212-266-7200 266-7235
Web: www.corporate-clients.commerzbank.com

Commonwealth Bank of Australia
599 Lexington Ave 17th Fl New York NY 10022 212-848-9200
Web: www.commbank.com.au

Commonwealth National Bank
2214 St Stephens Rd Mobile AL 36617 251-476-5938 476-5946
Web: ecommonwealthbank.com

Community Bank of Florida
28801 SW 157th Ave Homestead FL 33033 305-245-2211 242-4639
TF: 866-820-1533 ■ *Web:* www.communitybankfl.com

Community Bank of Midwest
2220 Broadway Ave Great Bend KS 67530 620-792-5111 792-5168
Web: www.communitybankmidwest.com

Community Bank of Raymore PO Box 200 Raymore MO 64083 816-322-2100 322-5915
TF: 800-322-6772 ■ *Web:* www.cbronline.net

Community First Bank 925 Wisconsin Ave Boscobel WI 53805 608-375-4117 375-4119
Web: www.cfbank.com

Community National Bank PO Box 259 Derby VT 05829 802-334-7915 334-3148
Web: www.communitynationalbank.com

Community State Bank 814 Walnut St Coffeyville KS 67337 620-251-5500
Web: condonnationalbank.com

Community Trust Bank NA
346 N Mayo Trl PO Box 2947 Pikeville KY 41501 606-432-1414
TF: 800-422-1090 ■ *Web:* www.ctbi.com

Confluence Advisors LLC 200 Wallace Rd Wexford PA 15090 724-940-1900
Web: www.confluenceadvisorsllc.com

Conneaut Savings Bank 305 Main St PO Box 740 Conneaut OH 44030 440-599-8121 593-6446
TF: 888-453-2311 ■ *Web:* www.conneautsavings.com

Continental Bank
620 W Germantown Pike Ste 350 Plymouth Meeting PA 19462 800-705-5500
Web: www.thecontinentalbank.com

Cooper State Bank An Ohio Corp
5811 Sawmill Rd Dublin OH 43017 614-408-0235
Web: csbank.com

Cornhusker Bank 1101 Cornhusker Hwy Lincoln NE 68521 402-434-2265 434-2262
Web: www.cornhuskerbank.com

Coronado First Bank 801 Orange Ave Ste 101 Coronado CA 92118 619-437-1000
Web: www.coronadofirst.com

CorTrust Bank 1801 S Marion Rd Sioux Falls SD 57106 605-361-8356 361-9237
Web: www.cortrustbank.com

Country Bank for Savings 75 Main St Ware MA 01082 413-967-6221 967-3289
TF: 800-322-8233 ■ *Web:* www.countrybank.com

Creative Health Capital LLC
351 Hubbard St Ste 312 Chicago IL 60654 312-574-3740
Web: www.chcapital.com

Credit Union of Denver 9305 W Alameda Ave Lakewood CO 80226 303-234-1700 239-1108
TF: 800-951-9014 ■ *Web:* www.cudenver.com

Crescent Bank & Trust
1100 Poydras St Ste 100 New Orleans LA 70163 504-556-5950 552-4458
Web: cbtno.com

CRT Investment Banking LLC
262 Harbor Dr Third Fl Stamford CT 06902 203-569-6800
Web: www.mmdillon.com

CSB Bancshares Inc 203 N Douglas Ellsworth KS 67439 785-472-3141
Web: csbanc.com

CTS Capital Advisors LLC
4520 E W Hwy Ste 610 Bethesda MD 20814 240-482-3240
Web: www.ctsca.com

D L Evans Bank 397 N Overland PO Box 1188 Burley ID 83318 208-678-9076 678-9093
TF: 888-873-9777 ■ *Web:* www.dlevans.com

Dailey Partners LLC 1610 Wynkoop St Ste 150 Denver CO 80202 303-545-9500
Web: www.daileypartners.com

Dakota Community Bank & Trust 1727 State St Bismarck ND 58501 701-255-9000
Web: dakotacommunitybank.com

Daroth Capital Advisors LLC
130 E 59th St 12th Fl New York NY 10022 212-687-2500
Web: www.daroth.com

Davis Capital Corp 200 S Wacker Dr 31st Fl Chicago IL 60606 312-623-4500
Web: www.daviscapital.com

DBS Bank Ltd 725 N Figueroa St Los Angeles CA 90017 213-627-0222 636-6366*
**Fax Area Code:* 662 ■ *TF:* 800-232-5901 ■ *Web:* www.dbs.com

Dedham Institution For Savings
55 Elm St PO Box 9107 Dedham MA 02026 781-329-6700 326-9893
TF: 888-289-0342 ■ *Web:* www.dedhamsavings.com

Delta National Bank 2711 Mchenry Ave Modesto CA 95350 209-527-3700 527-0820
Web: www.deltabank.com

Deutsche Bank Canada (DB)
199 Bay St Ste 4700 Commerce Ct W Toronto ON M5L1E9 416-682-8000 682-8383
Web: www.db.com

Devon Bank 6445 N Western Ave Chicago IL 60645 866-683-3866 973-5647*
**Fax Area Code:* 773 ■ *TF:* 866-683-3866 ■ *Web:* www.devonbank.com

Dexia Bank 445 Pk Ave 7th Fl New York NY 10022 212-515-7000
Web: www.dexia.com

Dime Bank, The 820 Church St PO Box 509 Honesdale PA 18431 570-253-1902 253-5845
TF: 888-469-3463 ■ *Web:* www.thedimebank.com

Discover Bank PO Box 30416 Salt Lake City UT 84130 302-323-7810
TF: 800-347-7000 ■ *Web:* www.discover.com

Dollar Bank FSB 225 Forbes Ave Pittsburgh PA 15222 412-261-2343
TF: 800-828-5527 ■ *Web:* www.dollarbank.com

Durant Bancorp / First United Bank
1400 W Main Durant OK 74701 580-924-2211
Web: firstunitedbank.com

E*Trade Bank 671 N Glebe Rd Arlington VA 22203 877-800-1208 624-8502*
**Fax Area Code:* 678 ■ *TF:* 800-387-2331 ■ *Web:* us.etrade.com

Eagle Bancorp Montana Inc 1400 Prospect Ave Helena MT 59601 406-442-3080 457-4035
NASDAQ: EBMT ■ *Web:* www.americanfederalsavingsbank.com

East Boston Savings Bank 10 Meridian St Boston MA 02128 617-567-1500 569-5681
TF: 800-657-3272 ■ *Web:* www.ebsb.com

Eastern Bank One Eastern Pl Lynn MA 01901 781-599-2100 598-7697
TF: 800-327-8376 ■ *Web:* www.easternbank.com

El Dorado Savings Bank 4040 El Dorado Rd Placerville CA 95667 530-622-1492 621-1659
TF: 800-874-9779 ■ *Web:* www.eldoradosavingsbank.com

Elmira Savings Bank 333 E Water St Elmira NY 14901 607-734-3374 732-4007
NASDAQ: ESBK ■ *TF:* 888-372-9299 ■ *Web:* www.elmirasavingsbank.com

Empire Bank PO Box 3397 Springfield MO 65808 417-881-3100
TF: 888-231-4637 ■ *Web:* www.empirebank.com

Empire State Bank 68 N Plank Rd Newburgh NY 12550 845-561-0003
Web: esbna.com

Encore Bank 3003 Tamiami Trail N Ste 100 Naples FL 34103 239-919-5888 261-0578
TF: 800-472-3272 ■ *Web:* www.encorebank.com

Energy Capital Solutions LP
2651 N Harwood Ste 410 Dallas TX 75201 214-219-8200
Web: www.nrgcap.com

Ennis State Bank 815 W Ennis Ave Ennis TX 75119 972-875-9676 875-1574
Web: ennisstatebank.com

Enterprise Bank of SC
13497 Broxton Bridge Rd PO Box 8 Ehrhardt SC 29081 803-267-3191 267-2316
TF: 800-554-8969 ■ *Web:* www.ebanksc.com

Envoy Advisors 268 Summer St Sixth Fl Boston MA 02210 617-292-7676
Web: www.envoyadvisors.com

Equitable Bank 113 N Locust St Grand Island NE 68802 308-382-3136
Web: equitableonline.com

Essex Savings Bank PO Box 950 Essex CT 06426 860-767-4414 767-4411
TF: 877-377-3922 ■ *Web:* www.essexsavings.com

Euro Pacific Capital Inc
88 Post Rd W Third Fl Westport CT 06880 203-662-9700
TF: 800-727-7922 ■ *Web:* www.europac.net

Evangeline Bank & Trust Co, The
497 W Main St Ville Platte LA 70586 337-363-5541 363-0678
Web: www.therealbank.com

Exchange State Bank
3992 Chandler St PO Box 68 Carsonville MI 48419 810-657-9333 657-9810
TF: 888-488-9300 ■ *Web:* www.exchangestatebank.com

F & M Bank & Trust Co 1330 S Harvard Tulsa OK 74112 918-748-4000 743-0104
Web: fmbanktulsa.com

F&M Bank PO Box 1130 Clarksville TN 37041 931-645-2400 553-2020
TF: 800-645-4199 ■ *Web:* www.myfmbank.com

Farm Bureau Bank 2165 Green Vista Dr Ste 204 Sparks NV 89431 775-673-4566 913-5087*
**Fax Area Code:* 866 ■ *TF:* 800-492-3276 ■ *Web:* farmbureaubank.com

Farmers Bank & Savings Company Inc
211 W Second St Pomeroy OH 45769 740-992-2136 667-3162
Web: www.fbsc.com

Phone | Fax

Farmers Bank, The 9 E Clinton St PO Box 129 .... Frankfort IN 46041 765-654-8731 654-8738
TF: 800-883-0131 ■ *Web:* www.thefarmersbank.com

Farmers Building & Savings Bank
290 W Park St .... Rochester PA 15074 724-774-4970

Farmers Merchants Bank & Trust Co
100 S Main St PO Box 910 .... Breaux Bridge LA 70517 337-332-2115 332-5089
Web: www.fmbanking.com

Farmers National Bank of Buhl
914 Main St PO Box 392 .... Buhl ID 83316 208-543-4351 543-8323
Web: www.farmersnatlbank.com

Farmers National Bank of Prophetstown, The
114 W Third St .... Prophetstown IL 61277 815-772-3700
Web: www.fnbptown.com

Farmers State Bancshares Inc
100 W Main St PO Box 9 .... Mountain City TN 37683 423-727-8121 727-5382
Web: www.fsbankmctn.com

Farmers State Bank & Trust Co, The
200 W State St .... Jacksonville IL 62650 217-479-4000 479-4125
Web: www.fsbtco.com

Fauquier Bank, The (TFB)
10 Courthouse Sq PO Box 561 .... Warrenton VA 20186 540-347-2700
TF: 800-638-3798 ■ *Web:* www.fauquierbank.com

Fidelity Bancshares Nc Inc PO Box 8 .... Fuquay Varina NC 27526 919-552-2242 557-4563
TF: 800-816-9608 ■ *Web:* www.fidelitybanknc.com

Fidelity Bank 100 E English St .... Wichita KS 67201 800-658-1637 268-7383*
**Fax Area Code:* 316 ■ *TF:* 800-658-1637 ■ *Web:* www.fidelitybank.com

Fidelity Bank & Trust
9400 Old Hammond Hwy .... Baton Rouge LA 70809 225-923-0232 326-3000*
**Fax Area Code:* 242

Fidelity State Bank & Trust Co
600 S Kansas Ave .... Topeka KS 66603 785-295-2100 233-7571
Web: www.fidelitytopeka.com

Fife Commercial Bank Inc 5209 Pacific Hwy E .... Fife WA 98424 253-922-5100
Web: fifebank.com

Fifth Third Bank Central Ohio 21 E State St .... Columbus OH 43215 800-972-3030 744-7516*
**Fax Area Code:* 614 ■ *TF:* 800-972-3030 ■ *Web:* www.53.com

First Alliance Bank 51 Germantown Ct Ste 100 .... Cordova TN 38018 901-753-8339
Web: fabtn.com

First American Bank
261 S Western Ave .... Carpentersville IL 60110 847-426-6300 426-6300
Web: www.firstambank.com

First American Bank & Trust
2785 Hwy 20 W PO Box 550 .... Vacherie LA 70090 225-265-2265 265-7339
TF: 800-738-2265 ■ *Web:* www.fabt.com

First Arkansas Bank & Trust
600 W Main St .... Jacksonville AR 72076 501-982-4511
Web: firstarkansasbank.com

First Bank Financial Centre (FBFC)
155 W Wisconsin Ave PO Box 1004 .... Oconomowoc WI 53066 262-569-9900
TF: 888-569-9909 ■ *Web:* www.fbfcwi.com

First Bank Muleshoe 202 S 1st PO Box 565 .... Muleshoe TX 79347 806-272-4515 272-4436
Web: fbmuleshoe.com

First Bank of Georgia 3527 Wheeler Rd .... Augusta GA 30909 706-731-6600 731-6601
Web: www.firstbankofga.com

First Bankers Trust Company NA
1201 Broadway PO Box 3566 .... Quincy IL 62305 217-228-8000 228-8091
Web: www.firstbankers.com

First Bethany Bank & Trust 6500 NW 39th Expy .... Bethany OK 73008 405-789-1110
Web: firstbethany.com

First Business Financial Services Inc
401 Charmany Dr .... Madison WI 53719 608-238-8008 232-5994
NASDAQ: FBIZ ■ *TF:* 888-455-2263 ■ *Web:* www.firstbusiness.com

First Calgary Savings 510 16th Ave NE .... Calgary AB T2E1K4 866-923-4778 276-5299*
**Fax Area Code:* 403 ■ *TF:* 866-923-4778 ■ *Web:* www.firstcalgary.com

First Century Bank NA 500 Federal St .... Bluefield WV 24701 304-325-8181 325-3727
TF: 877-214-9426 ■ *Web:* www.firstcentury.com

First Citizens Bank & Trust Co Inc
1230 Main St .... Columbia SC 29201 803-733-2025 733-2031
TF: 888-612-4444 ■ *Web:* www.firstcitizensonline.com

First City Bank 1885 Northwest Blvd .... Columbus OH 43212 614-487-1010 481-7294
Web: bankcolumbusoh.com

First Clover Leaf Bank
6814 Goshen Rd PO Box 540 .... Edwardsville IL 62025 618-656-6122 656-1712
Web: www.firstcloverleafbank.com

First County Bank Inc, The 117 Prospect St .... Stamford CT 06901 203-462-4200 462-4442
Web: www.firstcountybank.com

First Federal Bank Fsb
6900 N Executive Dr .... Kansas City MO 64120 816-241-7800 245-4348
Web: www.ffbkc.com

First Federal Bank Of Ohio
140 N Columbus St PO Box 957 .... Galion OH 44833 419-468-1518 468-2973
Web: www.firstfederalbankofohio.com

First Federal Lakewood 14806 Detroit Ave .... Lakewood OH 44107 216-529-2700 226-0622
TF: 800-966-7300 ■ *Web:* www.ffl.net

First Financial Bankshares
212 E Third St PO Box 272 .... Hereford TX 79045 806-363-8200 363-8295
NASDAQ: FFIN ■ *Web:* www.hsbhereford.com

First Foundation Bank
18101 Von Karman Ave Ste 750 .... Irvine CA 92612 949-202-4100
TF: 800-224-7931 ■ *Web:* www.ff-inc.com

First General Bank 1744 S Nogales St .... Rowland Heights CA 91748 626-820-1234
Web: www.fgbusa.com

First Hawaiian Bank 999 Bishop St .... Honolulu HI 96813 808-525-6340 525-8708*
**Fax:* Mktg ■ *TF:* 888-844-4444 ■ *Web:* www.fhb.com

First Intercontinental Bank, The
5593 Buford Hwy .... Doraville GA 30340 770-451-7200
Web: firsticbank.com

First Interstate Bank
401 N 31st St PO Box 30918 .... Billings MT 59101 406-255-5000
TF: 888-752-3341 ■ *Web:* www.firstinterstatebank.com

First Jackson Bank 43243 Us Hwy 72 .... Stevenson AL 35772 256-437-2107
Web: firstjacksonbank.com

First Mercantile Trust Co
57 Germantown Ct Fourth Fl .... Cordova TN 38018 901-753-9080
TF: 800-753-3682 ■ *Web:* www.firstmerc.com

First Metro Bank 406 Avalon Ave .... Muscle Shoals AL 35661 256-386-0600 386-0651
Web: www.firstmetro.com

First Mid-Illinois Bank & Trust
1515 Charleston Ave .... Mattoon IL 61938 217-258-0653 258-0426
OTC: FMBH ■ *Web:* www.firstmid.com

First National Bank
316 E Bremer Ave PO Box 837 .... Waverly IA 50677 319-352-1340 352-6323
Web: www.fnbwaverly.com

First National Bank Alaska
101 W 36 Ave PO Box 100720 .... Anchorage AK 99510 907-777-4362 777-3828
OTC: FBAK ■ *TF:* 800-856-4362 ■ *Web:* www.fnbalaska.com

First National Bank Creston PO Box 445 .... Creston IA 50801 641-782-2195 843-2485*
**Fax Area Code:* 816 ■ *TF:* 877-782-2195 ■ *Web:* www.fnbcreston.com

First National Bank In Alamogordo
414 Tenth St PO Box 9 .... Alamogordo NM 88311 575-437-4880 437-1631
Web: fnbalamo.com

First National Bank In Tremont
134 S Sampson St PO Box 23 .... Tremont IL 61568 309-925-2121 925-5448
Web: www.tremontbank.com

First National Bank of Illinois Inc
3256 Ridge Rd .... Lansing IL 60438 708-474-1300 474-1331
Web: www.fnbiweb.com

First National Bank Of Jasper 200 W 18th St .... Jasper AL 35501 205-221-3121
Web: firstbankofjasper.synovus.com

First National Bank of Muscatine
300 E Second St .... Muscatine IA 52761 563-263-4221 262-4213
TF: 800-722-2678 ■ *Web:* www.fnbmusc.com

First National Bank of Omaha 1620 Dodge St .... Omaha NE 68197 402-341-0500 342-4332
TF: 800-228-4411 ■ *Web:* www.fnbomaha.com

First National Bank of Oneida, The
18418 Alberta St PO Box 4699 .... Oneida TN 37841 423-569-8586 569-9826
TF: 866-546-8273 ■ *Web:* www.fnboneida.com

First National Bank of Paragould
200 W Ct St .... Paragould AR 72450 870-239-8521
Web: www.fnbank.net

First National Bank of Santa Fe PO Box 609 .... Santa Fe NM 87504 505-992-2000 992-2188
TF: 888-912-2265 ■ *Web:* www.firstnationalsantafe.com

First National Bank of South Miami
5750 Sunset Dr 877-823-6276 .... Miami FL 33143 305-667-5511 662-5440
Web: fnbsm.com

First National Bankers Bankshares Inc (FNBB)
7813 Office Pk Blvd .... Baton Rouge LA 70809 225-924-8015 952-0899
TF: 800-421-6182 ■ *Web:* www.bankers-bank.com

First NBC (CPB) 29092 Kretel Rd .... Lacombe LA 70445 985-819-1200
TF: 800-423-7503 ■ *Web:* www.firstnbcbank.com

First Newton National Bank 100 N Second Ave W .... Newton IA 50208 641-792-3010
Web: firstnnb.com

First Niagara Financial Group
726 Exchange St Ste 618 .... Buffalo NY 14210 716-625-7500 434-0160
TF: 800-421-0004 ■ *Web:* www.firstniagara.com

First Palmetto Savings Bank Fsb PO Box 430 .... Camden SC 29021 803-432-2265
TF: 800-922-7411 ■ *Web:* www.firstpalmetto.com

First Personal Bank 14701 Ravinia Ave .... Orland Park IL 60462 708-226-2727
Web: firstpersonalbank.net

First Pryority Bank 310 E Graham .... Pryor OK 74361 918-825-2121
Web: www.firstpryoritybank.com

First Reliance Bank 2170 W Palmetto St .... Florence SC 29501 843-656-5000
Web: firstreliance.com

First Republic Bank
111 Pine St Third Fl .... San Francisco CA 94111 415-392-1400 392-1413
NYSE: FRC ■ *TF:* 800-392-1400 ■ *Web:* www.firstrepublic.com

First Savings Bank 2804 N Telshor Blvd .... Las Cruces NM 88011 575-521-7931 521-7906
TF: 800-555-6895 ■ *Web:* www.firstsavingsbanks.com

First Security Bank of Missoula
1704 Dearborn PO Box 4506 .... Missoula MT 59801 406-728-3115
Web: www.fsbmsla.com

First Security Bank of Sleepy Eye
100 E Main PO Box 469 .... Sleepy MN 56085 507-794-3911 794-5140
Web: www.firstsecuritybanks.com

First Sentinel Bank 315 Railroad Ave .... Richlands VA 24641 276-963-0836
Web: firstsentinelbank.com

First State Bank & Trust Co 1005 E 23rd St .... Fremont NE 68025 402-721-2500 727-0208
TF: 888-674-4344 ■ *Web:* www.firststatebankandtrust.com

First State Bank of Kansas City
650 Kansas Ave .... Kansas City KS 66105 913-371-1242 371-7516
TF: 800-883-1242 ■ *Web:* www.cfbkc.com

First Tennessee Bank 165 Madison Ave .... Memphis TN 38103 901-523-4883 523-4145*
**Fax:* Mktg ■ *TF:* 800-382-5465 ■ *Web:* www.firsttennessee.com

First Texas Bank 501 E Third St PO Box 671 .... Lampasas TX 76550 512-556-3691 556-6104
TF: 866-220-1598 ■ *Web:* www.firstexbank.com

First Utah BanCorp
3826 South 2300 East .... Salt Lake City UT 84109 801-272-9454
Web: firstutahbank.com

First Western Bank & Trust PO Box 1090 .... Minot ND 58702 701-852-3711 857-7195
TF: 800-688-2584 ■ *Web:* bankfirstwestern.com

First Whitney Bank & Trust
223 Chestnut St PO Box 271 .... Atlantic IA 50022 712-243-3195
Web: firstwhitneybank.com

First-Knox National Bank One S Main St .... Mount Vernon OH 43050 740-399-5500
TF: 800-837-5266 ■ *Web:* www.firstknox.com

FirsTier Bank (Kimball NE) 115 S Walnut .... Kimball NE 69145 308-235-4633
Web: www.firstierbanks.com/

Firstrust Savings Bank
15 E Ridge Pike 4th Fl .... Conshohocken PA 19428 610-941-9898 941-5544
TF: 800-220-2265 ■ *Web:* www.firstrust.com

Flagstar Bank FSB 5151 Corporate Dr .... Troy MI 48098 248-312-2000 312-6834*
**Fax:* Hum Res ■ *TF:* 800-945-7700 ■ *Web:* www.flagstar.com

Florence Savings Bank
85 Main St PO Box 60700 .... Florence MA 01062 413-586-1300 582-9947
Web: www.florencesavings.com

Phone Fax

Floridian Financial Group
175 Timacuan Blvd Lake Mary FL 32746 407-321-3233
Web: floridianfinancialgroup.com

Flushing Savings Bank FSB
144-51 Northern Blvd Flushing NY 11354 718-512-2929
Web: www.flushingbank.com

Foresight Financial Group Inc
3106 N Rockton Ave Rockford IL 61103 815-847-7500
Web: foresightfg.com

Foster Bank 5005 Newport Dr Rolling Meadows IL 60008 773-588-7700
Web: fosterbank.com

Founders Community Bank
237 Higuera St San Luis Obispo CA 93401 805-543-6500
Web: founderscommunitybank.com

Four Oaks Bank & Trust Co PO Box 309 Four Oaks NC 27524 919-963-2177 963-2768
TF: 877-963-6257 ■ *Web:* www.fouroaksbank.com

Fowler State Bank 300 E Fifth St PO Box 511 Fowler IN 47944 765-884-1200 884-3239
TF: 800-439-3951 ■ *Web:* www.fowlerstatebank.com

Fox Chase Bank 4390 Davisville Rd Hatboro PA 19040 215-682-7400
Web: foxchasebank.com

Franchise Capital Advisors Inc
9903 E Bell Rd Ste 130 Scottsdale AZ 85260 480-355-4390
Web: www.franchisecapitaladvisors.com

Fremont Bank PO Box 5101 Fremont CA 94538 510-792-2300 795-5760
TF: 800-359-2265 ■ *Web:* www.fremontbank.com

Frontenac Bank 3330 Rider Trl S Earth City MO 63045 314-298-8200
TF: 877-205-5777 ■ *Web:* www.frontenacbank.com

Galway Group LP 3050 Post Oak Blvd Ste 1300 Houston TX 77056 713-952-0186
Web: www.galwaylp.com

Garden State Community Bank (GSCB) 36 Ferry St Newark NJ 07105 973-589-8616 589-1141
NYSE: NYB ■ *TF:* 877-786-6560

Garnett State Savings Bank
106 E Fifth St PO Box 329 Garnett KS 66032 785-448-3111 448-6613
Web: www.gssb.us.com

Gebsco Inc 245 S Eau Claire St Mondovi WI 54755 715-926-4234

Genesis Capital LLC
3414 Peachtree Rd Ne Ste 700 Atlanta GA 30326 404-816-7540
TF: 800-998-8479 ■ *Web:* www.genesis-capital.com

Giantbank.com 6300 NE First Ave Fort Lauderdale FL 33334 954-958-0001 958-0190
TF: 877-446-4200 ■ *Web:* www.giantbank.com

Gibraltar Savings Bank 1039 S Orange Ave Newark NJ 07106 973-372-1221
Web: gibraltarbanknj.com/

Glenview State Bank 800 Waukegan Rd Glenview IL 60025 847-729-1900
Web: gsb.com

Glenwood State Bank
5 E Minnesota Ave PO Box 197 Glenwood MN 56334 320-634-5111 634-5114
TF: 800-207-7333 ■ *Web:* www.glenwoodstate.com

Golden Valley Bank Community Foundation
190 Cohasset Rd Ste 170 Chico CA 95926 530-894-1000
TF: 800-808-2070 ■ *Web:* www.goldenvalleybank.com

Gorham Savings Bank 64 Main St Gorham ME 04038 207-839-4450 839-4790
Web: www.gorhamsavingsbank.com

Grabill Bank 10403 Leo Rd Fort Wayne IN 46825 260-482-7079 484-9959
Web: iabfinancial.com

Grants State Bank
824 W Santa Fe Ave PO Box 1088 Grants NM 87020 505-285-6611 287-2260
TF: 877-285-6611 ■ *Web:* www.grantsbank.com

Grayson National Bank (GNB) 113 W Main St Independence VA 24348 276-773-2811 773-3890
Web: www.graysonnationalbank.com

Great Western Bank 6015 NW Radial Hwy Omaha NE 68104 402-952-6000 223-6057*
**Fax Area Code:* 515 ■ *TF:* 800-952-2043 ■ *Web:* www.greatwesternbank.com

Greenfield Savings Bank
400 Main St PO Box 1537 Greenfield MA 01302 413-774-3191 774-6755
Web: www.greenfieldsavings.com

Greensburg State Bank 240 S Main St Greensburg KS 67054 620-723-2131
Web: bestbank.us

GreensLedge Group LLC, The
520 Madison Ave 37th Fl New York NY 10022 212-792-5270
Web: www.greensledge.com

Greenville First Bank
100 Verdae Blvd Ste 100 Greenville SC 29072 864-679-9000 679-9099
TF: 877-679-9646 ■ *Web:* www.southernfirst.com

Guaranty Bank 4000 W Brown Deer Rd Brown Deer WI 53209 414-362-4000 290-6433
TF: 800-235-4636 ■ *Web:* www.guarantybank.com

Guaranty Bank & Trust Co PO Box 1807 Cedar Rapids IA 52406 319-286-6200 362-7894
TF: 888-777-4590 ■ *Web:* www.guaranty-bank.com

Guaranty State Bank & Trust Company Beloit Kansas, The
201 S Mill St Beloit KS 67420 785-738-3501
Web: guarantystate.com

Guilford Savings Bank (GSB) PO Box 369 Guilford CT 06437 203-453-2015 458-3927
TF: 866-878-1480 ■ *Web:* www.gsb-yourbank.com

Gulf Coast Bank 4310 Johnston St Lafayette LA 70503 337-989-1133 989-2172
TF: 800-722-5363 ■ *Web:* www.gcbank.com

Habib American Bank 99 Madison Ave New York NY 10016 212-532-4444 532-7136
Web: www.habbank.com/

Hamler State Bank 210 Randolph St PO Box 358 Hamler OH 43524 419-274-3955
TF: 888-508-3955 ■ *Web:* www.hamlerstatebank.com

Hampden Bank PO Box 2048 Springfield MA 01202 413-736-1812
Web: www.hampdenbank.com

Hampton Roads Bankshares Inc
999 Waterside Dr Norfolk VA 23510 757-217-1000
NASDAQ: HMPR ■ *Web:* www.gatewaybankandtrust.com

Hardin County Bank, The (HCB)
235 Wayne Rd PO Box 940 Savannah TN 38372 731-925-9001 925-8106
Web: www.hardincountybank.com

Harvard Savings Bank 58 N Ayer St Harvard IL 60033 815-943-5261
Web: harvardsavingsbank.com

Hastings City Bank 150 W Court St Hastings MI 49058 269-945-2401
Web: hastingscitybank.com

Hatboro Federal Savings 221 S York Rd Hatboro PA 19040 215-675-4000 672-6684
Web: www.hatborofed.com

Havana National Bank, The 112 S Orange St Havana IL 62644 309-543-3361

Phone Fax

Hebron Savings Bank (HSB) 101 N Main St PO Box 59 Hebron MD 21830 410-749-1185 543-0703
Web: www.hebronsavingsbank.com

Hemet Bancorp 3715 Sunnyside Dr Riverside CA 92506 951-784-5771

Heritage Group Inc 1101 12th St Aurora NE 68818 402-694-3136
TF: 888-463-6611 ■ *Web:* www.bankonheritage.com

Hibernia Bancorp Inc 325 Carondelet St New Orleans LA 70130 504-522-3203
Web: hibbank.com

Hickory Point Bank & Trust FSB PO Box 2548 Decatur IL 62525 217-875-3131
TF Cust Svc: 800-872-0081 ■ *Web:* www.hickorypointbank.com

Highland Community Bank
307 Thacker Ave PO Box 1059 Covington VA 24426 540-962-2265 962-1203
Web: www.highlandscommunitybank.com

Hills Bank & Trust Co 131 Main St PO Box 70 Hills IA 52235 319-679-2291 679-2180
TF: 800-445-5725 ■ *Web:* www.hillsbank.com

Hingham Institution for Savings 55 Main St Hingham MA 02043 781-749-2200 740-4889
NASDAQ: HIFS ■ *TF:* 877-447-2265 ■ *Web:* www.hinghamsavings.com

Hocking Valley Bank
7 W Stimson Ave PO Box 4847 Athens OH 45701 740-592-4441 594-3147
Web: www.hvbonline.com

Home Savings & Loan Company of Youngstown
275 W Federal St Youngstown OH 44503 330-742-0500 742-0615
TF: 888-822-4751 ■ *Web:* www.homesavings.com

HomeStreet Bank
601 Union St 2 Union Sq Ste 2000 Seattle WA 98101 206-623-3050 389-4458
TF: 800-654-1075 ■ *Web:* homestreet.com

Hometown Bank 245 N Peters Ave Fond du Lac WI 54935 920-907-2220
TF: 877-261-2220 ■ *Web:* www.hometownbancorp.com

Hometrust Bank, The PO Box 10 Asheville NC 28802 828-259-3939 258-8503
Web: www.hometrustbanking.com

Homewood FSB 3228-30 Eastern Ave Baltimore MD 21224 410-327-5220 558-1719
TF: 800-554-8969 ■ *Web:* www.homewoodfsb.com

Hopewell Valley Community Bank
Four Rt 31 S Pennington NJ 08534 609-466-2900 731-9144
OTC: HWDY ■ *Web:* www.hvcbonline.com

Hopkins Financial Corp 100 E Havens Mitchell SD 57301 605-996-7775
Web: cortrustbank.com

Houlihan Valuation Advisors Inc
28662 W Northwest Hwy Ste 3 Lake Barrington IL 60010 847-381-3616
Web: www.houlihan-hva.com

Hudson City Savings Bank W 80 Century Rd Paramus NJ 07652 201-967-1900
TF: 800-222-0194 ■ *Web:* www.hudsoncitysavingsbank.com

Hudson Valley Bank 21 Scarsdale Rd Yonkers NY 10707 914-961-6100
Web: www.hudsonvalleybank.com

Huntington National Bank
41 S High St Huntington Ctr Columbus OH 43287 614-480-8300 480-4973
TF: 800-480-2265 ■ *Web:* www.huntington.com

Huron Community Bank 301 Newman St East Tawas MI 48730 989-362-6700
Web: bankhcb.com

Hyden Citizens Bank 22023 Main St PO Box 948 Hyden KY 41749 606-672-2344 672-3627
Web: www.hydencitizensbank.com

Iberville Bank 23405 Eden St Plaquemine LA 70764 225-687-2091 687-0539
Web: ibervillebank.com

Illinois National Bank 322 E Capitol Springfield IL 62701 217-747-5500 747-5530
Web: www.illinoisnationalbank.com

Illinois Service Federal S & L
4619 S King Dr Chicago IL 60653 773-624-2000 624-5340
Web: www.isfbank.com

Independence FSB 1301 Ninth St NW Washington DC 20001 202-628-5500 626-7106
Web: www.ifsb.com

Indiana Bankers Assn 6925 Parkdale Pl Indianapolis IN 46254 317-387-9380
Web: www.indianabankers.org

Industrial Bank NA 4812 Georgia Ave NW Washington DC 20011 202-722-2000 461-5056*
**Fax Area Code:* 800 ■ *Web:* www.industrial-bank.com

Inova Federal Credit Union 358 S Elkhart Ave Elkhart IN 46516 574-294-6553
Web: inovafcu.org

InsurBanc 10 Executive Dr Farmington CT 06032 860-677-9701 677-9793
TF: 866-467-2262 ■ *Web:* www.insurbanc.com

Integra Technologies LLC
3450 N Rock Rd Bldg 100 Ste 111 Wichita KS 67226 316-630-6800
Web: integra-tech.com

Inter-County Bakers Inc
1095 Long Island Ave Ste 1 Deer Park NY 11729 631-957-1350 957-1013
TF: 800-696-1350 ■ *Web:* www.icbakers.com

InterBank 4921 N May Ave Oklahoma City OK 73112 405-782-4200
Web: www.interbankus.com

International Bank of Commerce (IBC)
1200 San Bernardo Ave Laredo TX 78042 956-726-6651 726-6618
Web: www.ibc.com

Investors Savings Bank 101 Wood Ave S Iselin NJ 08830 973-924-5100 376-5357
NASDAQ: ISBC ■ *TF:* 855-422-6548 ■ *Web:* www.myinvestorsbank.com

Inwood National Bank 7621 Inwood Rd Dallas TX 75209 214-358-5281 351-7381
Web: www.inwoodbank.com

Iowa State Savings Bank 401 W Adams St Creston IA 50801 641-782-1000
Web: issbbank.com

Ireland Bank 33 Bannock St Malad City ID 83252 208-766-2254
Web: ireland-bank.com

Israel Discount Bank of New York (IDBB)
511 Fifth Ave New York NY 10017 212-551-8500 551-8540
Web: www.idbny.com

Jeff Davis Bancshares Inc
507 N Main St PO Box 730 Jennings LA 70546 337-824-3424 824-7283
OTC: JDVB ■ *TF:* 866-889-8176 ■ *Web:* www.jdbank.com

Jersey Shore State Bank
300 Market St PO Box 967 Williamsport PA 17701 570-322-1111 398-2280
TF: 888-412-5772 ■ *Web:* www.jssb.com

Jersey State Bank 1000 S State St Jerseyville IL 62052 618-498-6466
Web: jerseystatebank.com

Johnson Bank 4001 N Main St Racine WI 53402 262-639-6010 681-4627
Web: johnsonbank.com

JP Morgan Chase & Co 270 Pk Ave New York NY 10017 212-270-6000
Web: www.jpmorganchase.com

Phone | Fax

JumpStart Partners Inc
3616 Far W Blvd Ste 117-294 . . . . . Austin TX 78731 512-576-9000
Web: www.jumpstartpartners.com

Kearny FSB 120 Passaic Ave. . . . . . Fairfield NJ 07004 973-244-4500 991-6713*
**Fax Area Code:* 201 ■ *TF:* 800-273-3406 ■ *Web:* www.kearnyfederalsavings.com

Kennebec Savings Bank 150 State St PO Box 50 . . . . . Augusta ME 04332 207-622-5801 626-2858
TF: 888-303-7788 ■ *Web:* www.kennebecsavings.com

Kentucky Bank PO Box 157 . . . . . Paris KY 40362 859-987-1795 987-5829
TF: 877-322-8228 ■ *Web:* www.kybank.com

Key Bank 65 Dutch Hill Rd. . . . . . Orangeburg NY 10962 800-539-2968 365-5890*
**Fax Area Code:* 845 ■ *TF Cust Svc:* 800-539-2968 ■ *Web:* www.key.com

Kingston National Bank
Two N Main St PO Box 613 . . . . . Kingston OH 45644 740-642-2191 642-2195
TF: 866-642-2191 ■ *Web:* www.kingstonnationalbank.com

Kirkwood Bank & Trust Co 2911 N 14th St. . . . . . Bismarck ND 58503 701-258-6550
Web: kirkwoodbank.com

Kish Bancorp Inc 4255 E Main St PO Box 917 . . . . . Belleville PA 17004 717-935-2191 935-5511
OTC: KISB ■ *TF:* 888-554-4748 ■ *Web:* www.kishbank.com

Klein Financial Inc 1550 Audubon Rd . . . . . Chaska MN 55318 952-448-2484
Web: kleinbank.com

KPMG Corporate Finance LLC 345 Park Ave. . . . . . New York NY 10154 212-758-9700
Web: www.kpmgcorporatefinance.com

Labette Bank Fourth & Huston PO Box 497. . . . . . Altamont KS 67330 620-784-5311 784-5323
TF: 800-711-5311 ■ *Web:* www.labettebank.com

Lake Bank Shares Inc 437 Bridge Ave . . . . . Albert Lea MN 56007 507-373-1481

Lakeside Bank 55 W Wacker Dr. . . . . . Chicago IL 60601 312-435-5100
TF: 866-892-1572 ■ *Web:* www.lakesidebank.com

Lamesa National Bank, The 602 S First St. . . . . . Lamesa TX 79331 806-872-5457

Landmark Bank 801 E Broadway. . . . . . Columbia MO 65201 573-499-7333
Web: landmarkbank.com

LaPorte Savings Bank, The 710 Indiana Ave. . . . . . LaPorte IN 46350 219-362-7511 324-2269
TF: 866-362-7511 ■ *Web:* www.laportesavingsbank.com

Laurentian Bank of Canada
1981 McGill College Ave . . . . . Montreal QC H3A3K3 514-284-4500 284-3988
TSE: LB ■ *TF:* 800-252-1846 ■ *Web:* www.laurentianbank.ca

LCNB National Bank 3209 W Galbraith Rd . . . . . Cincinnati OH 45239 513-932-1414 741-0019
TF: 800-344-2265 ■ *Web:* www.lcnb.com

Leaders Bank, The 2001 York Rd Ste 150 . . . . . Oak Brook IL 60523 630-572-5323
Web: leadersbank.com

Ledyard National Bank 320 Main St . . . . . Norwich VT 05055 802-649-2050 649-2060
Web: www.ledyardbank.com

Legacy Bank
1580 E Cheyenne Mtn Blvd . . . . . Colorado Springs CO 80906 719-579-9150 226-6694
TF: 866-627-0800 ■ *Web:* legacyib.com

Liberty Bank 315 Main St. . . . . . Middletown CT 06457 800-354-8950
TF: 800-622-6732 ■ *Web:* www.liberty-bank.com

Liberty Bank & Trust Co PO Box 60131. . . . . . New Orleans LA 70160 504-240-5100 240-5153
TF: 800-883-3943 ■ *Web:* www.libertybank.net

Liberty Savings Bank FSB 2251 Rombach Ave . . . . . Wilmington OH 45177 800-436-6300
TF: 800-627-7890 ■ *Web:* www.libertysavingsbank.com

Libertyville Bank & Trust Co
507 N Milwaukee Ave. . . . . . Libertyville IL 60048 847-367-6800 468-0952*
**Fax Area Code:* 866 ■ *Web:* www.libertyvillebank.com

Litchfield National Bank 316 N State St . . . . . Litchfield IL 62056 217-324-6161 324-3817
Web: www.litchfieldnationalbank.com

Little Bank Inc, The 804 Carey Rd . . . . . Kinston NC 28501 252-939-9990 317-2837
OTC: LTLB ■ *TF:* 855-449-0975 ■ *Web:* www.thelittlebank.com

Llano National Bank 1001 Ford St. . . . . . Llano TX 78643 325-247-5701 247-3765
Web: www.llanonationalbank.com

Lone Star National Bank Shares Neveda
520 E Nolana Ave Ste 110 . . . . . Mcallen TX 78504 956-682-1722
Web: www.lonestarnationalbank.com

Lowell Five Cent Savings Bank, The
One Merrimack Plz . . . . . Lowell MA 01852 978-452-1300 441-6534
Web: www.lowellfive.com

Lubbock National Bank
4811 50th St PO Box 6100. . . . . . Lubbock TX 79493 806-792-1000 792-0976
Web: lubbocknational.com

Luther Burbank Savings 804 Fourth St . . . . . Santa Rosa CA 95404 707-578-9216 526-7844
TF: 888-407-9904 ■ *Web:* www.lutherburbanksavings.com

M & I Bank Northeast 310 W Walnut St . . . . . Green Bay WI 54303 920-436-1800
Web: www.bmoharris.com

M&T Bank One M & T Plz 13th Fl. . . . . . Buffalo NY 14203 716-842-4470 848-3709
NYSE: MTB ■ *TF:* 800-724-2440 ■ *Web:* www.mtb.com

Machias Savings Bank 4 Ctr St PO Box 318 . . . . . Machias ME 04654 207-255-3347 255-3170
TF: 800-982-7179 ■ *Web:* www.machiassavings.com

Mackinac Savings Bank FSB
2901-A N Military Trl . . . . . West Palm Beach FL 33409 561-686-2352 638-2616
Web: mackinacbank.com

Macquarie Infrastructure Company Inc
125 W 55th St. . . . . . New York NY 10019 212-231-1000 231-1010
NYSE: MIC ■ *Web:* www.macquarie.com

Magyar Bancorp Inc 400 Somerset St . . . . . New Brunswick NJ 08901 732-342-7600 342-7611
NASDAQ: MGYR ■ *Web:* www.magbank.com/home/home

Magyar Bank 400 Somerset St. . . . . . New Brunswick NJ 08901 732-342-7600
TF: 800-472-3272 ■ *Web:* www.magbank.com

Main Banc Inc 2424 Louisiana Blvd Ne. . . . . . Albuquerque NM 87110 505-880-1700
Web: mainbank.com

Main Source Bank 201 N Broadway . . . . . Greensburg IN 47240 812-663-0133 663-4904
Web: www.mainsourcebank.com

Malvern FSB Inc 42 E Lancaster Ave . . . . . Paoli PA 19301 610-644-9400 644-1943
Web: www.malvernfederal.com

Maren Group LLC 11th Fl 400 Madison Ave. . . . . . New York NY 10017 212-584-2340
Web: marengroup.us

Marine Bank of Champaign-Urbana
2434 Village Green Pl. . . . . . Champaign IL 61822 217-239-0100
Web: www.ibankmarine.com

Marquette Bank 10000 W 151st St. . . . . . Orland Park IL 60462 708-226-8026
TF: 888-254-9500 ■ *Web:* www.emarquettebank.com

Marquette Savings Bank 920 Peach St. . . . . . Erie PA 16501 814-455-4481 453-5345
TF: 866-672-3743 ■ *Web:* www.marquettesavings.com

Phone | Fax

Maspeth Federal Savings 56-18 69th St. . . . . . Maspeth NY 11378 718-335-1300 446-3671
TF: 888-558-1300 ■ *Web:* www.maspethfederal.com

Max Credit Union 400 Eastdale Cir . . . . . Montgomery AL 36117 334-260-2600
TF: 800-776-6776 ■ *Web:* www.mymax.com

Mayflower Co-op Bank
30 S Main St PO Box 311. . . . . . Middleboro MA 02346 508-947-4343 923-0864
NASDAQ: MFLR

Mayville Savings Bank 200 S Main St. . . . . . Mayville WI 53050 920-387-2310
Web: mayvillesavings.com

Mc Kenzie Banking Co (MBC) 676 N Main St . . . . . McKenzie TN 38201 731-352-2262 352-7778
TF: 866-321-7063 ■ *Web:* www.foundationbank.org

McHenry Savings Bank 353 Bank Dr. . . . . . McHenry IL 60050 815-385-3000 385-4433
Web: www.mchenrysavings.com

MCNB Bank & Trust Co PO Box 549. . . . . . Welch WV 24801 304-436-4112
TF: 800-532-9553 ■ *Web:* www.mcnbbanks.com

MEA Advisors LLC
Graybar Bldg Ste 300 420 Lexington Ave . . . . . New York NY 10170 212-249-2239
Web: www.meaadvisorsllc.com

Mechanics Savings Bank
100 Minot Ave PO Box 400 . . . . . Auburn ME 04210 207-786-5700 786-5709
TF: 877-886-1020 ■ *Web:* www.mechanicssavings.com/home/home

Members Trust Co 14025 Riveredge Dr Ste 280. . . . . . Tampa FL 33637 813-631-9191
TF: 888-727-9191 ■ *Web:* www.memberstrust.com

Meramec Valley Bank 199 Clarkson Rd . . . . . Ellisville MO 63011 636-230-3500 230-3191
Web: www.meramecvalleybank.com

Mercana Growth Partners 390 Bay St Ste 1706 . . . . . Toronto ON M5H2Y2 416-947-1300
Web: www.mercanagrowth.com

Mercantil Commercebank NA
220 Alhambra Cir. . . . . . Coral Gables FL 33134 305-460-8701 460-4010
TF: 888-629-0810 ■ *Web:* www.mercantilcb.com

Merchants National Bank of Bangor Inc
25 Broadway PO Box 227. . . . . . Bangor PA 18013 610-588-0981 588-6886
Web: www.merchantsbangor.com

Meredith Village Savings Bank (MVSB)
24 State Rt 25 PO Box 177. . . . . . Meredith NH 03253 603-279-7986 279-5710
TF: 800-922-6872 ■ *Web:* www.mvsb.com

Meridian Bank NA PO Box 6630. . . . . . Peoria AZ 85385 602-636-4939 274-7200
Web: www.meridianbank.com

Mesa 85 Fifth Ave Sixth Fl. . . . . . New York NY 10003 212-792-3950
Web: www.mesaglobal.com

Metairie Bank & Trust Co 3344 Metairie Rd. . . . . . Metairie LA 70001 504-834-6330
Web: www.metairiebank.com

Metropolitan National Bank 501 Main St . . . . . Pine Bluff AR 71601 870-541-1000
Web: simmonsfirst.com/

Midamerica National Bancshares 100 W Elm St . . . . . Canton IL 61520 309-647-5000 647-8551
TF: 877-647-5050 ■ *Web:* www.midnatbank.com

Middlebury National Corp PO Box 189. . . . . . Middlebury VT 05753 802-388-4982
OTC: MDVT ■ *Web:* nbmvt.com

Middlesex Savings Bank 120 Flanders Rd . . . . . Westborough MA 01581 508-653-0300 389-9367
TF: 877-463-6287 ■ *Web:* www.middlesexbank.com

MidFirst Bank PO Box 76149 . . . . . Oklahoma City OK 73147 405-943-8002 840-0862*
**Fax:* Cust Svc ■ *TF:* 888-643-3477 ■ *Web:* www.midfirst.com

Midland National Bank 527 N Main. . . . . . Newton KS 67114 316-283-1700 283-3813
TF: 800-810-9457 ■ *Web:* www.midlandnb.com

Midstate Financial Corp
One E Main St PO Box 230. . . . . . Brownsburg IN 46112 317-852-2268

Midwest Bank 105 E Soo St PO Box 40 . . . . . Parkers Prairie MN 56361 218-338-6054 338-5070
TF: 877-365-5155 ■ *Web:* www.midwestbank.net

Midwest Federal Savings & Loan Assn of St Joseph
1901 Frederick Ave. . . . . . St Joseph MO 64501 816-233-5148

Mifflinburg Bank & Trust Co (MBTC)
250 E Chestnut St PO Box 186. . . . . . Mifflinburg PA 17844 570-966-1041 966-7432
TF: 888-966-3131 ■ *Web:* www.mbtc.com

Milford Bank 33 Broad St. . . . . . Milford CT 06460 203-783-5700 783-5755
TF: 800-340-4862 ■ *Web:* www.milfordbank.com

Milford National Bank & Trust Co, The
300 E Main St. . . . . . Milford MA 01757 508-634-4100 634-4107
Web: www.milfordnational.com

Minier Financial Inc 101 S Main PO Box 800 . . . . . Minier IL 61759 309-392-2623
Web: firstfarmers.com

Minster Bank 95 W Fourth St. . . . . . Minster OH 45865 419-628-2351
Web: www.minsterbank.com

Missouri Bank & Trust Co 1044 Main St. . . . . . Kansas City MO 64105 816-881-8200 881-8236
Web: www.mobank.com

Mitchell Bank 1039 W Mitchell St. . . . . . Milwaukee WI 53204 414-645-0600 645-4020
Web: www.mitchellbank.com

Monarch Financial Holdings Inc
1034 S Battlefield Blvd Ste 301 . . . . . Chesapeake VA 23322 757-482-2727 389-5100
NASDAQ: MNRK ■ *Web:* www.monarchbank.com

Monroe Bank & Trust 102 E Front St . . . . . Monroe MI 48161 734-241-3431 384-8101*
**Fax:* Hum Res ■ *TF:* 800-321-0032 ■ *Web:* www.mbandt.com

Montecito Bank & Trust 1000 State St . . . . . Santa Barbara CA 93101 805-963-7511
Web: www.montecito.com

Montgomery Bank
1 Montgomery Bank Plaza PO Box 948 . . . . . Sikeston MO 63801 573-471-2275 472-5595
Web: www.montgomerybank.com

Morton Community Bank 721 W Jackson St . . . . . Morton IL 61550 309-266-5337
Web: hometownbanks.com

Mountain Valley Bank 317 DAVIS Ave. . . . . . Elkins WV 26241 304-637-2265 637-2270
TF: 800-555-3503 ■ *Web:* www.mountainvalleybank.com

Mountain West Bank of Helena 1225 Cedar St. . . . . . Helena MT 59604 406-449-2265
TF: 888-752-3341 ■ *Web:* www.mtnwestbank.com

MSB Financial Corp (MSBF) 1902 Long Hill Rd . . . . . Millington NJ 07946 908-647-4000 647-6196
NASDAQ: MSBF ■ *TF:* 844-265-9680 ■ *Web:* www.millingtonsb.com

MT Mckinley Bank 500 Fourth Ave . . . . . Fairbanks AK 99701 907-452-1751
Web: mtmckinleybank.com

Murray Bank, The 405 S 12th St. . . . . . Murray KY 42071 270-753-5626
TF: 877-965-1122 ■ *Web:* www.themurraybank.com

Mutual Bank 570 Washington St . . . . . Whitman MA 02382 781-447-4488
Web: www.mymutualbank.com

Mutual of Omaha Bank 3333 Farnam St . . . . . Omaha NE 68131 877-471-7896
TF: 866-351-5646 ■ *Web:* www.mutualofomahabank.com

				Phone	Fax
Nantucket Bank 104 Pleasant St *TF:* 800-533-9313 ■ *Web:* www.nantucketbank.com	Nantucket	MA	02554	508-228-0580	
National Australia Bank Americas 245 Pk Ave Ste 2800 *TF:* 866-706-0509 ■ *Web:* www.nab.com.au	New York	NY	10167	212-916-9500	
National Bank & Trust Co, The 48 N S St PO Box 711 *Web:* www.nbtdirect.com	Wilmington	OH	45177	937-382-1441	382-4385
National Bank & Trust Company of Sycamore, The 230 W State St *Web:* www.banknbt.com	Sycamore	IL	60178	815-895-2125	895-8961
National Bank of Arizona 335 N Wilmot Rd Ste 100 *TF:* 800-497-8168 ■ *Web:* www.nbarizona.com	Tucson	AZ	85711	520-571-1500	513-0134
National Bank of Blacksburg PO Box 90002 *TF:* 800-552-4123 ■ *Web:* www.nbbank.com	Blacksburg	VA	24062	540-552-2011	951-6337
National Bank of Gatesville PO Box 779 *Web:* www.natlbank.com	Gatesville	TX	76528	254-865-2211	865-8916
National Bank of Kansas City (NBOFKC) 3510 W 95th St *TF:* 888-431-0097 ■ *Web:* www.bankofkc.com	Leawood	KS	66206	913-341-1144	383-5632
National Bank, The 852 Middle Rd *TF:* 877-321-4347 ■ *Web:* www.bankwithtriumph.com	Bettendorf	IA	52722	563-344-3935	823-3350
National Exchange Bank & Trust 130 S Main St PO Box 988 *Web:* www.nebat.com	Fond Du Lac	WI	54936	920-921-7700	923-7021
Naugatuck Valley Financial Corp 333 Church St *NASDAQ: NVSL* ■ *TF:* 800-251-2161 ■ *Web:* www.nvsl.com	Naugatuck	CT	06770	203-720-5000	720-5016
NBT Bank NA PO Box 351 *TF:* 800-628-2265 ■ *Web:* www.nbtbank.com	Norwich	NY	13815	607-337-2265	336-8670
NCAL Bancorp 12121 Wilshire Blvd *OTC: NCAL* ■ *TF:* 866-453-4042 ■ *Web:* www.nbcal.com	Los Angeles	CA	90025	310-882-4800	882-4890
Neffs Bancorp Inc 5629 Rt 873 PO Box 10 *OTC: NEFB* ■ *Web:* www.neffsnatl.com	Neffs	PA	18065	610-767-3875	767-1890
Neighborhood National Bank 3511 National Ave. *Web:* mynnb.com	San Diego	CA	92113	619-239-3360	
Nevada State Bank PO Box 990 *TF:* 800-727-4743 ■ *Web:* www.nsbank.com	Las Vegas	NV	89125	702-383-0009	
New Century Bank 700 W Cumberland St *Web:* www.selectbank.com/	Dunn	NC	28334	910-892-7080	
New Omni Bank NA 1235 S Garfield Ave *Web:* newomnibank.com	Alhambra	CA	91801	626-284-5555	
New Washington State Bank 402 E Main St PO Box 10 *TF:* 800-883-0131 ■ *Web:* www.newwashbank.com	New Washington	IN	47162	812-293-3321	293-3072
New West Banks of Colorado Inc 55 S Elm Ave *Web:* bankofcolorado.com	Eaton	CO	80615	970-454-1800	454-1802
New York Community Bank 615 Merrick Ave *Web:* www.mynycb.com	Westbury	NY	11590	877-786-6560	
New York Private Bank & Trust FSB 200 Bellevue Pkwy Ste 150 *Web:* www.nypbt.com	Wilmington	DE	19809	302-798-2160	
NewBridge Bancorp 1501 Highwoods Blvd Ste 400 *NASDAQ: NBBC* ■ **Fax Area Code:* 910 ■ *Web:* www.newbridgebank.com	Greensboro	NC	27410	336-369-0900	509-0406*
Newburyport Five Cents Savings Bank Inc, The 63 State St PO Box 350 *TF:* 877-462-3136 ■ *Web:* www.newburyportbank.com	Newburyport	MA	01950	978-462-3136	462-9672
Newfield National Bank 18 SW Blvd *Web:* www.newfieldbank.com	Newfield	NJ	08344	856-692-3440	697-3114
Newtown Savings Bank Foundation Inc 39 Main St PO Box 497 *TF:* 800-461-0672 ■ *Web:* www.nsbonline.com	Newtown	CT	06470	203-426-2563	
Noble Bank & Trust NA 1509 Quintard Ave *Web:* noblebank.com	Anniston	AL	36202	256-741-1800	
North American Development Bank 203 S St Mary'S Ste 300 *TF:* 800-499-6232 ■ *Web:* www.nadb.org	San Antonio	TX	78205	210-231-8000	
North American Savings Bank (NASB) 12520 S 71 Hwy **Fax:* Cust Svc ■ *TF:* 800-677-6272 ■ *Web:* www.nasb.com	Grandview	MO	64030	816-765-2200	316-4503*
North Middlesex Savings Bank Inc Seven Main St PO Box 469 *TF:* 800-762-3306 ■ *Web:* www.nmsb.com	Ayer	MA	01432	978-772-3306	772-9131
North Milwaukee State Bank (NMS) 5630 W Fond Du Lac Ave *Web:* www.nmsbank.com	Milwaukee	WI	53216	414-466-2344	466-6248
North Shore Bank FSB 15700 W Bluemound Rd **Fax:* Cust Svc ■ *TF:* 800-236-4672 ■ *Web:* www.northshorebank.com	Brookfield	WI	53005	262-797-3858	797-3376*
North Shore Trust & Savings 700 S Lewis Ave PO Box 980 *Web:* www.northshoretrust.com	Waukegan	IL	60085	847-336-4430	336-4438
North Side Bank & Trust Co, The 4125 Hamilton Ave PO Box 23128 *Web:* www.northsidebankandtrust.com	Cincinnati	OH	45223	513-542-7800	541-6941
Northeast Bank 77 Broadway St Ne *Web:* www.northeastbank-mn.com	Minneapolis	MN	55413	612-379-8811	362-3262
Northern Trust Co 50 S LaSalle St *NASDAQ: NTRS* ■ *TF:* 888-289-6542 ■ *Web:* www.northerntrust.com	Chicago	IL	60603	312-630-6000	
Northfield Savings Bank (NSB) PO Box 347 **Fax Area Code:* 718 ■ *TF:* 800-672-2274 ■ *Web:* www.nsbvt.com	Northfield	VT	05663	802-485-5871	981-1572*
Northrim BanCorp Inc 3111 C St *NASDAQ: NRIM* ■ **Fax:* Mktg ■ *TF:* 800-478-3311 ■ *Web:* www.northrim.com	Anchorage	AK	99503	907-562-0062	261-3594*
Northstar Bank of Texas 400 N Carroll Blvd *Web:* www.nstarbank.com	Denton	TX	76201	940-591-1200	384-1947
Northstar Global Partners LLC The Prudential Tower 800 Boylston St	Boston	MA	02199	617-375-5800	
Northwest Community Bank 86 Main St PO Box 1019 *TF:* 800-455-6668 ■ *Web:* www.nwcommunitybank.com	Winsted	CT	06098	860-379-7561	379-9717

				Phone	Fax
Northwest Georgia Bank 5063 Alabama Hwy PO Box 789 *TF:* 800-528-2273 ■ *Web:* www.northwestgabankonline.com	Ringgold	GA	30736	706-965-3000	
Northwest Savings Bank 100 Liberty St PO Box 128 **Fax:* Mktg ■ *TF:* 800-822-2009 ■ *Web:* www.northwestsavingsbank.com	Warren	PA	16365	814-726-2140	728-7716*
Northwestern Bank 202 N Bridge St PO Box 49 *Web:* www.northwesternbank.com	Chippewa Falls	WI	54729	715-723-4461	723-0586
Norway Savings Bank 261 Main St *Web:* norwaysavingsbank.com	Norway	ME	04268	207-743-7986	
NovaFund Advisors 140 Rowayton Ave *Web:* www.novafundadvisors.com	Norwalk	CT	06853	203-831-0111	
Oak Bank 1000 N Rush St Ste 1	Chicago	IL	60611	312-440-4000	
OBA Financial Services Inc 20300 Seneca Meadows Pkwy *NASDAQ: OBAF*	Germantown	MD	20876	301-916-6400	
Ocean Bank 780 NW 42nd Ave *TF:* 877-688-2265 ■ *Web:* www.oceanbank.com	Miami	FL	33126	305-442-2660	
Ocean City Home Savings & Loan Inc 1001 Asbury Ave *Web:* www.ochome.com	Ocean City	NJ	08226	609-927-7722	399-3614
OceanFirst Bank 975 Hooper Ave PO Box 2009 *TF:* 888-623-2633 ■ *Web:* www.oceanfirstonline.com	Toms River	NJ	08753	732-240-4500	349-5070
Ocwen Federal Bank FSB 1661 Worthington Rd Ste 100 **Fax:* Hum Res ■ *TF:* 800-280-3863 ■ *Web:* www.ocwen.com	West Palm Beach	FL	33409	561-682-8000	682-8166*
Old Line Bank 1525 Pointer Ridge Pl *NASDAQ: WSB* ■ *TF:* 800-416-6373 ■ *Web:* Www.oldlinebank.com	Bowie	MD	20716	301-430-2500	430-8723
Old National Bancorp One Main St *Web:* www.oldnational.com	Evansville	IN	47708	812-464-1294	522-9561
Old National Bank 1 Main St PO Box 718 **Fax Area Code:* 812 ■ **Fax:* Cust Svc ■ *TF:* 800-731-2265 ■ *Web:* www.oldnational.com	Evansville	IN	47705	800-731-2265	464-1551*
Onebanc 300 W Capitol Ave *Web:* www.onebanc.com	Little Rock	AR	72201	501-370-4400	370-4505
OneUnited Bank 3683 Crenshaw Blvd *Web:* www.oneunited.com	Los Angeles	CA	90016	323-290-4848	389-0548
Oostburg State Bank 905 Center Ave *Web:* oostburgbank.com	Oostburg	WI	53070	920-564-2336	
Orange County Trust Co PO Box 790 *TF:* 888-341-5100 ■ *Web:* www.orangecountytrust.com	Middletown	NY	10940	845-341-5000	
Oritani Financial Corp 370 Pascack Rd PO Box 1329 *NASDAQ: ORIT* ■ *TF:* 888-674-8264 ■ *Web:* www.oritani.com	Washington Township	NJ	07676	201-664-5400	497-1223
Ossian State Bank 102 N Jefferson St *Web:* ossianstatebank.com	Ossian	IN	46777	260-622-4141	
Oversea-Chinese Banking Corp Ltd 1700 Broadway 18th Fl *Web:* www.ocbc.com	New York	NY	10019	212-586-6222	586-0636
Oxford Bank PO Box 129 *TF:* 800-236-2442 ■ *Web:* www.oxford-bank.com	Addison	IL	60101	630-629-5000	628-1575
Pacific City Financial Corp 3701 Wilshire Blvd Ste 402 *OTC: PFCF* ■ *Web:* www.paccity.net	Los Angeles	CA	90010	213-210-2000	210-2032
Pacific Continental Corp 111 W Seventh Ave PO Box 10727 *NASDAQ: PCBK* ■ *TF:* 877-231-2265 ■ *Web:* www.therightbank.com	Eugene	OR	97440	541-686-8685	344-2807
Palmetto State Bank 601 First St W *Web:* www.palmettostatebank.com	Hampton	SC	29924	803-943-2671	943-5634
Panhandle State Bank 414 Church St PO Box 967 *Web:* www.panhandlebank.com	Sandpoint	ID	83864	208-263-0505	265-5295
Paragon Advising Group LP 3200 SW Fwy Ste 2350	Houston	TX	77027	713-599-0111	
Paragon National Bank 5400 Poplar Ave Ste 350 *Web:* bankparagon.com	Memphis	TN	38119	901-273-2900	
Paris National Bank 118 N Main St *Web:* parisnational.com	Paris	MO	65275	660-327-4181	
Parkway Bancorp Inc 4800 N Harlem Ave *Web:* www.parkwaybank.com	Harwood Heights	IL	60706	708-867-6600	867-1119
Pasadera Capital LLC 115 W El Prado Ste 1 *Web:* www.pasaderacapital.com	San Antonio	TX	78212	210-804-4240	
Pathway Bank 306 S High St *Web:* pathwaybank.com	Cairo	NE	68824	308-485-4232	
PBK Bank Inc 120 Frontier Blvd *Web:* pbkbank.com	Stanford	KY	40484	606-365-7098	
Penn Liberty Bank 724 W Lancaster Ave Ste 210 *Web:* www.pennlibertybank.com	Wayne	PA	19087	610-535-4500	
Penseco Financial Services Corp 150 N Washington Ave *NASDAQ: PFIS* ■ *Web:* psbt.com/index.php	Scranton	PA	18503	570-346-7741	
Pentucket Bank One Merrimack St *Web:* www.pentucketbank.com	Haverhill	MA	01830	978-372-7731	372-4499
People Bank 201 N Bardstown Rd PO Box 95 *Web:* www.peoplesbankmtw.com	Mount Washington	KY	40047	502-538-7301	538-6606
People's United Bank 850 Main St Bridgeport Ctr. *TF:* 800-772-1090 ■ *Web:* www.peoples.com	Bridgeport	CT	06604	203-338-7171	338-2310
Peoples Bank of Bullitt County 1612 Hwy 44 E *Web:* www.pbofbc.com	Shepherdsville	KY	40165	502-543-2226	543-3517
Peoples Financial Services Corp 82 Franklin Ave *NASDAQ: PFIS* ■ *TF:* 888-868-3858 ■ *Web:* psbt.com/index.php	Hallstead	PA	18822	570-879-2175	
Peoples National Bank 5175 N Academy Blvd *TF:* 800-862-6696 ■ *Web:* www.epeoples.com	Colorado Springs	CO	80918	719-528-4000	260-2256
Peoples Savings Bank (PSB) 414 N Adams PO Box 248 *TF:* 877-493-3799 ■ *Web:* www.bankpsb.com	Wellsburg	IA	50680	641-869-3721	869-3855

Name / Address	City	State	Zip	Phone	Fax
Peoples State Bank 445 S Lewis Ave *Web:* peoplesbanktulsa.com	Tulsa	OK	74104	918-583-9800	587-9307
Periculum Capital Company LLC Four Ctr Green Ste 200 *Web:* www.periculumcapital.com	Carmel	IN	46032	317-636-1800	
Perrin Holden & Davenport Capital Corp Five Hanover Sq	New York	NY	10004	212-269-3500	
Petsky Prunier LLC 60 Broad St 38th Fl *Web:* www.petskyprunier.com	New York	NY	10004	212-842-6020	
Piedmont FSB (PFSB) 16 W Third St PO Box 215 *Web:* www.piedmontfederal.com	Winston-Salem	NC	27101	336-770-1000	770-1055
Pilgrim BanCorp 2401 S Jefferson Ave *Web:* pilgrimbank.com	Mount Pleasant	TX	75455	903-575-2150	575-1550
Pine Country Bank 412 N Hwy 10 PO Box 25 *Web:* www.pinecountrybank.com	Royalton	MN	56373	320-584-5522	584-8385
Pineries Bank, The 3601 Main St *Web:* pineries.com	Stevens Point	WI	54481	715-341-5600	
Pinnacle Trust Partners LLC 540 Hopmeadow St *Web:* www.pinnacletrustpartners.com	Simsbury	CT	06070	860-264-1595	
Pintoresco Advisors LLC 466 Foothill Blvd Ste 333 *TF:* 866-217-1140 ■ *Web:* www.pintorescoadvisors.com	La Canada Flintridge	CA	91011	213-223-2070	
Piqua State Bank 1356 Xylan Rd *Web:* piquastatebank.com	Piqua	KS	66761	620-468-2555	
Platte Valley Bank of Missouri 2400 Prairie View Rd PO Box 1250 *Web:* www.plattevalleybank.com	Platte City	MO	64079	816-858-5400	858-5300
Plaza Bank 7460 W Irving Pk Rd **Fax Area Code:* 760 ■ *TF General:* 877-714-9599 ■ *Web:* plazabank.com/contactus/	Norridge	IL	60706	708-456-3440	452-2214*
Plums Bank 35 S Lindan Ave *NASDAQ: PLBC* ■ *Web:* www.plumasbank.com	Quincy	CA	95971	530-283-7305	283-3557
PNC Bank 600 Grant St *NYSE: PNC-L* ■ *TF:* 888-762-2265 ■ *Web:* www.pnc.com	Pittsburgh	PA	15219	888-762-2265	
PNC Bank Delaware 300 Delaware Ave *TF:* 888-762-2265 ■ *Web:* www.pnc.com	Wilmington	DE	19899	302-429-1361	429-2872
PNC Bank NA 249 Fifth Ave 1 PNC Plaza *TF:* 888-762-2265 ■ *Web:* www.pnc.com	Pittsburgh	PA	15222	412-762-2000	705-3584
Potter State Bank of Potter, The 301 Chestnut St *Web:* potterstatebank.com	Potter	NE	69156	308-879-4451	
Prairie State Bank & Trust 1361 Toronto Rd *Web:* www.psbank.net	Springfield	IL	62712	217-786-2509	786-2512
Preferred Bank Los Angeles 601 S Figueroa St 29th Fl *NASDAQ: PFBC* ■ *TF:* 888-673-1808 ■ *Web:* www.preferredbank.com	Los Angeles	CA	90017	213-891-1188	622-0369
Premier Bank & Trust 600 S Main St Ste C *TF:* 855-728-6010 ■ *Web:* www.mypremierbankandtrust.com	North Canton	OH	44720	330-499-1900	
Premier Valley Bank 255 E River Pk Cir Ste 180 *TF:* 877-438-2002 ■ *Web:* www.premiervalleybank.com	Fresno	CA	93720	559-438-2002	432-0572
Presidential Online Bank 4520 East-West Hwy *TF:* 800-383-6266 ■ *Web:* www.presidential.com	Bethesda	MD	20814	301-652-0700	951-3582
Primebank 37 First Ave NW *Web:* primebank.com	Le Mars	IA	51031	712-546-4175	
Profile Bank 45 Wakefield St PO Box 1808 *TF:* 800-554-8969 ■ *Web:* www.profilebank.com	Rochester	NH	03866	603-332-2610	332-2519
Progressive Bank NA 1090 E Bethlehem Blvd *TF:* 866-235-1923 ■ *Web:* www.progbank.com	Wheeling	WV	26003	304-238-0040	238-0045
Provident Savings Bank FSB 3756 Central Ave *TF:* 800-442-5201 ■ *Web:* www.myprovident.com	Riverside	CA	92506	951-686-6060	786-4725
Prudential Savings Bank 1834 W Oregon Ave *TF:* 800-554-8969 ■ *Web:* www.prudentialsavingsbank.com	Philadelphia	PA	19145	215-755-1500	336-7122
Pueblo Bank & Trust Co 301 W Fifth St PO Box 639 *Web:* www.pbandt.com	Pueblo	CO	81003	719-545-1834	
Putnam Bank 40 Main St PO Box 151 *Web:* www.putnambank.com	Putnam	CT	06260	860-928-6501	
Pyramax Bank Fsb 7001 W Edgerton Ave	Greenfield	WI	53220	414-421-8200	
QNB Corp 15 N Third St PO Box 9005 *OTC: QNBC* ■ *TF:* 800-491-9070 ■ *Web:* qnbbank.com/2690/mirror/redirect.htm	Quakertown	PA	18951	215-538-5600	538-5765
Quarton Partners LLC 300 Park St Ste 480 *Web:* www.quartonpartners.com	Birmingham	MI	48009	248-594-0400	
Queens County Savings Bank 13665 Roosevelt Ave *Web:* www.mynycb.com	Flushing	NY	11354	718-460-4800	
Queenstown Bank of Maryland 7101 Main St PO Box 120 *TF:* 888-827-4300 ■ *Web:* www.queenstown-bank.com	Queenstown	MD	21658	410-827-8881	827-8190
Quontic Bank Three Grace Ave *Web:* www.quonticbank.com	Great Neck	NY	11021	516-686-0707	
Rabo Bank 1026 E Grand Ave *TF:* 800-942-6222 ■ *Web:* www.rabobankamerica.com	Arroyo Grande	CA	93420	805-473-7710	
Randolph Savings Bank 129 N Main St PO Box 354 *TF:* 877-963-2100 ■ *Web:* www.randolphsavings.com	Randolph	MA	02368	781-963-2100	961-7916
RBC Royal Bank PO Box 6001 Ste A **Fax Area Code:* 514 ■ *TF:* 800-769-2599 ■ *Web:* www.rbcroyalbank.com	Montreal	QC	H3C3A9	800-769-2599	874-3055*
RBC Trust Company (Delaware) Ltd 4550 New Linden Hill Rd Ste 200 *TF:* 800-441-7698 ■ *Web:* www.rbctrust.com	Wilmington	DE	19808	302-892-6976	
Reelfoot Bank 1491 S First St *Web:* reelfootbank.com	Union City	TN	38261	731-885-1010	
Regents Bank NA PO Box 9137 *TF:* 866-395-5800 ■ *Web:* www.regentsbank.com	La Jolla	CA	92038	858-729-7700	454-9052
Regions Bank 1900 Fifth Ave N *TF:* 800-734-4667 ■ *Web:* www.regions.com	Birmingham	AL	35203	800-734-4667	
Reliance Bancshares Inc 10401 Clayton Rd *OTC: RLBS* ■ *Web:* www.reliancebankstl.com	St. Louis	MO	63131	314-569-7200	
Renasant Bank 209 Troy St PO Box 709 *TF:* 800-680-1601 ■ *Web:* www.renasantbank.com	Tupelo	MS	38802	662-680-1001	680-1518
Republic Bank & Trust Co 601 W Market St *TF:* 888-584-3600 ■ *Web:* www.republicbank.com	Louisville	KY	40202	502-584-3600	584-3753
Ridgewood Savings Bank 71-02 Forest Ave *TF:* 800-250-4832 ■ *Web:* www.ridgewoodbank.com	Ridgewood	NY	11385	718-240-4800	240-4877
Rio Bank 1655 N 23rd *Web:* riobk.com	Mcallen	TX	78501	956-631-7890	972-1574
River City Bank PO Box 15247 *OTC: RCBC* ■ *TF Cust Svc:* 800-564-7144 ■ *Web:* www.rivercitybank.com	Sacramento	CA	95851	916-567-2899	567-2784
Riverview Community Bank 900 Washington St Ste 100 *TF:* 800-822-2076 ■ *Web:* www.riverviewbank.com	Vancouver	WA	98660	360-693-6650	
Rockland Trust 435 Market St *NASDAQ: PEOP* ■ *Web:* www.pfsb.com	Brighton	MA	02135	617-254-0707	
Rockport National Bank 16 Main St *Web:* rockportnational.com	Rockport	MA	01966	978-546-3411	
Roselle Savings Bank Inc 235 Chestnut St PO Box 349 *Web:* www.rosellesavings.com	Roselle	NJ	07203	908-245-1885	245-2256
Royal Bank America 732 Montgomery Ave *Web:* www.royalbankamerica.com	Narberth	PA	19072	610-668-4700	668-3670
Royal Bank of Canada 200 Bay St Ninth Fl S Twr *TSE: RY* ■ *TF:* 800-769-2599 ■ *Web:* www.rbc.com	Toronto	ON	M5J2J5	416-955-7806	974-3535
Royal Savings Bank 9226 S Commercial Ave *Web:* www.royalbankweb.com	Chicago	IL	60617	773-768-4800	
S&T Bank 800 Philadelphia St PO Box 190 *TF Cust Svc:* 800-325-2265 ■ *Web:* www.stbank.com	Indiana	PA	15701	724-349-1800	465-6874
Safra National Bank of New York 546 Fifth Ave *Web:* www.safra.com	New York	NY	10036	212-704-5500	704-9397
Salem Five & Savings Bank 210 Essex St *TF Cust Svc:* 800-850-5000 ■ *Web:* www.salemfive.com	Salem	MA	01970	978-745-5555	745-1073
Sandhills Bank 300 King St E *Web:* www.sandhillsbank.com	Bethune	SC	29009	843-334-2265	334-6013
Sandy Spring National Bank of Maryland 17801 Georgia Ave *TF:* 800-399-5919 ■ *Web:* www.sandyspringbank.com	Olney	MD	20832	301-774-6400	483-6701
SCB Bancorp Inc 1501 E Eldorado St *TF:* 888-769-2265 ■ *Web:* www.soybank.com	Decatur	IL	62521	217-428-7781	
Scottdale Bank & Trust 125 S Arch St *Web:* sbtbank.com	Connellsville	PA	15425	724-628-3200	
Seamen's Bank 221 Commercial St PO Box 659 *TF:* 855-227-5347 ■ *Web:* www.seamensbank.com	Provincetown	MA	02657	508-487-0035	487-8421
Seaway Bank & Trust Co 645 E 87th St *Web:* www.seawaybank.us	Chicago	IL	60619	773-487-4800	487-0452
Security Bank of Pulaski County 110 Lynn St PO Box S *TF:* 800-264-4274 ■ *Web:* www.sbpc.com	Waynesville	MO	65583	573-774-6417	774-6465
Security National Bank 40 S Limestone St *Web:* www.securitynationalbank.com	Springfield	OH	45502	937-324-6800	324-6861
Security National Bank of Enid 201 W Maine Ave *Web:* www.snbenid.com	Enid	OK	73701	580-234-5151	249-9199
Security National Bank of Omaha (Inc) 1120 S 101st St PO Box 31400 *Web:* www.snbconnect.com	Omaha	NE	68124	402-344-7300	
Security National Bank of Sioux City Iowa PO Box 147 *Web:* www.snbonline.com	Sioux City	IA	51101	712-277-6666	
Security State Bank & Trust (Inc) 201 W Main St PO Box 471 *Web:* www.ssbtexas.com	Fredericksburg	TX	78624	830-997-7575	997-7994
Severn Bancorp Inc 200 Westgate Cir Ste 200 *NASDAQ: SVBI* ■ *TF:* 800-752-5854 ■ *Web:* www.severnbank.com	Annapolis	MD	21401	410-260-2000	841-6296
Shelby State Bank 242 N Michigan Ave *Web:* shelbybank.com	Shelby	MI	49455	231-861-2123	
Signature Bank 565 Fifth Ave 12th Fl *NASDAQ: SBNY* ■ *TF:* 866-744-5463 ■ *Web:* www.signatureny.com	New York	NY	10017	646-822-1500	822-1447
Silicon Valley Bank (SVB) 3003 Tasman Dr **Fax:* Mktg ■ *Web:* www.svb.com	Santa Clara	CA	95054	408-654-7400	654-6209*
Silvergate Bank 4275 Executive Sq Ste 800 *TF:* 800-595-5856 ■ *Web:* www.silvergatebank.com	La Jolla	CA	92037	858-362-6300	362-6333
Siuslaw Bank 777 Hwy 101 PO Box 280 *OTC: SFGP* ■ *Web:* www.siuslawbank.com	Florence	OR	97439	541-997-3486	
Societe Generale USA 245 Park Ave *Web:* www.sgcib.com	New York	NY	10167	212-278-6000	278-6789
Solvay Bank 628 S Main St *Web:* www.solvaybank.com	North Syracuse	NY	13212	315-458-7492	458-7669
Somerset Trust Co 151 W Main St PO Box 777 *TF:* 800-972-1651 ■ *Web:* www.somersettrust.com	Somerset	PA	15501	814-443-9200	
Sooner Southwest Bankshares Inc 1751 E 71st St	Tulsa	OK	74136	918-496-4242	
South Coastal Bank 279 Union St *Web:* mobile.mountainone.com/	Rockland	MA	02370	781-878-5252	
South Louisiana Bank (SLB) 1362 W Tunnel Blvd PO Box 1718 *TF:* 877-275-3342 ■ *Web:* ayeee.com	Houma	LA	70361	985-851-3434	879-3095
Southbridge Savings Bank Inc 253-257 Main St PO Box 370 *TF:* 800-939-9103 ■ *Web:* www.southbridgesavingsbank.com	Southbridge	MA	01550	508-765-9103	765-1187
Southern Commercial Bank 5515 S Grand Blvd *Web:* www.southerncommercial.net	Saint Louis	MO	63111	314-481-6800	633-6025
Southern Michigan Bank & Trust 51 W Pearl St PO Box 309 *TF:* 800-379-7628 ■ *Web:* www.smb-t.com	Coldwater	MI	49036	517-279-5500	278-7358
SouthWest Capital Bank 622 Douglas Ave *TF:* 800-748-2406 ■ *Web:* www.southwestcapital.com	Las Vegas	NM	87701	505-425-7565	425-8501
Southwest Missouri Bank 2417 S Grand Ave *TF:* 800-943-8488 ■ *Web:* www.smbonline.com	Carthage	MO	64836	417-358-1770	358-4081
Sovereign Bank FSB PO Box 12646 *TF Cust Svc:* 877-768-2265 ■ *Web:* www.santanderbank.com	Reading	PA	19612	877-768-2265	

Phone | Fax

Spencer Savings Bank PO Box 912 .... Spencer MA 01562 508-885-5313 885-6505
TF: 800-547-2885 ■ *Web:* www.spencerbankonline.com

Spencer Savings Bank SLA 611 River Dr. .... Elmwood Park NJ 07407 973-772-6700
TF: 800-363-8115 ■ *Web:* www.spencersavings.com

St Martin Bank & Trust Co
301 S Main St. .... Saint Martinville LA 70582 337-394-7800 394-7831
Web: www.stmartinbank.com

Standard Bank & Trust Co
7800 W 95th St. .... Hickory Hills IL 60457 708-598-7400
TF: 866-499-2265 ■ *Web:* www.standardbanks.com

Standard Chartered Bank 1 Madison Ave .... New York NY 10010 212-667-0700 667-0380
Web: www.sc.com/

Star Bank 201 Second Ave NW PO Box 188 .... Bertha MN 56437 218-924-4055 924-2265
Web: www.starbank.net

STAR Financial Group Inc PO Box 11409 .... Fort Wayne IN 46858 260-467-5507
OTC: SFIGA ■ *Web:* www.starfinancial.com

State Bank 175 N Leroy St .... Fenton MI 48430 810-629-2263 629-3892
TF: 800-535-0517 ■ *Web:* www.thestatebank.com

State Bank & Trust 3100 13th Ave S. .... Fargo ND 58103 701-298-1500
Web: statebanks.com

State Bank & Trust Co 1025 Sixth St PO Box 327 .... Nevada IA 50201 515-382-2191 382-3826
Web: www.banksbt.com

State Bank of Countryside Inc (SBC)
6734 Joliet Rd .... Countryside IL 60525 708-485-3100 485-3106
Web: www.statebankofcountryside.com

State Bank of Cross Plains
1205 Main St PO Box 218 .... Cross Plains WI 53528 608-798-3961 798-3591
Web: www.crossplainsbank.com

State Bank of Toledo 100 E High St PO Box 309 .... Toledo IA 52342 641-484-2980 484-2333
Web: www.banktoledo.com

State Bank of Waterloo PO Box 148 .... Waterloo IL 62298 618-939-7194 939-4140
TF: 800-367-7576 ■ *Web:* www.statebankofwaterloo.com

State Farm Financial Services FSB
PO Box 2316 .... Bloomington IL 61702 877-734-2265
TF: 877-734-2265 ■ *Web:* www.statefarm.com/bank/bank.htm

State National Bank & Trust Co
122 Main St PO Box 130 .... Wayne NE 68787 402-375-1130 375-1822
Web: www.state-national-bank.com

State Street Corp One Lincoln St. .... Boston MA 02111 617-786-3000 664-6316*
NYSE: STT ■ **Fax:* Mktg ■ *Web:* www.statestreet.com

Stephenson National Bank & Trust, The
1820 Hall Ave PO Box 137 .... Marinette WI 54143 715-732-1732 732-5478
Web: www.snbt.com

Sterling Bank & Trust FSB
1 Town Sq 19th Fl. .... Southfield MI 48076 248-351-3442 359-6660
TF: 866-619-2265 ■ *Web:* www.sterlingbank.com

Sterling Savings Bank 105 W Simpson Ave. .... Mccleary WA 98557 800-650-7141 *
**Fax:* Hum Res ■ *TF:* 800-650-7141 ■ *Web:* www.bankwithsterling.com

Steuben Trust Co One Steuben Sq. .... Hornell NY 14843 607-324-5010
Web: steubentrust.com

Stillman Banccorp NA PO Box 150 .... Stillman Valle IL 61084 815-645-2000 645-2341
TF: 877-275-3342 ■ *Web:* www.stillmanbank.com

Stock Exchange Bank 103 S Main PO Box 273 .... Caldwell KS 67022 620-845-6431
Web: stockxbank.com

Stockmans Bank 100 Kennedy .... Gould OK 73544 580-676-3921
Web: stockmansbankok.com

Stonegate Bank 1430 N Federal Hwy .... Fort Lauderdale FL 33304 954-315-5500
Web: stonegatebank.com

Stoneham Savings Bank
359 Main St PO Box 80071 .... Stoneham MA 02180 781-438-9400 438-8596
Web: www.stonesav.com

Sturgis Bank & Trust Co
113-125 E Chicago Rd PO Box 600 .... Sturgis MI 49091 269-651-9345 651-5512*
OTC: STBI ■ **Fax Area Code:* 616 ■ *Web:* www.sturgisbank.com

Sumitomo Mitsui Banking Corp (SMBC) 277 Pk Ave . . New York NY 10172 212-224-4000 593-9522
Web: www.smbcgroup.com

Sumitomo Mitsui Trust Bank (USA) (SMTBUSA)
111 River St .... Hoboken NJ 07030 201-420-9470 983-3730*
**Fax Area Code:* 718 ■ *Web:* logon.sumitomotrustusa.com/

Summit Bank 2969 Broadway. .... Oakland CA 94611 510-839-8800 839-8853
TF: 800-380-9333 ■ *Web:* www.summitbanking.com

Sun National Bank
350 Fellowship Road Ste. 101 .... Mount Laurel NJ 08054 800-786-9066
TF: 800-786-9066 ■ *Web:* www.sunnationalbank.com

Suntrust Bank PO Box 4418 .... Atlanta GA 30302 800-786-8787
NYSE: STI ■ *TF:* 800-786-8787 ■ *Web:* www.suntrust.com

Susquehanna Bank
1570 Manheim Pk PO Box 3300. .... Lancaster PA 17604 717-735-8730
Web: www.susquehanna.net

Svenska Handelsbanken
875 Third Ave Fourth Fl .... New York NY 10022 212-326-5100 326-2705
Web: www.handelsbanken.se

Swedbank One Penn Plz 15th Fl. .... New York NY 10119 212-486-8400 486-3220
Web: www.swedbank.com

Swineford National Bank
1255 N Susquehanna Trial PO Box 241 .... Hummels Wharf PA 17831 570-743-7786 743-8562
TF: 866-762-1903 ■ *Web:* www.swineford.com

Tallahassee State Bank
2720 W Tennessee St .... Tallahassee FL 32304 850-576-1182 893-7192
Web: talstatebank.synovus.com

Talmer Bancorp Inc 2301 W Big Beaver Rd Ste 525. .... Troy MI 48084 248-649-2301
Web: talmerbank.com

TAP Advisors LLC 152 W 57th St 34th Fl .... New York NY 10019 212-909-9010
Web: www.tapadvisors.com

TCF National Bank 801 Marquette Ave .... Minneapolis MN 55402 612-661-6500 745-2773
Web: www.tcfbank.com

TD Bank NA 1701 Rt 70 E .... Cherry Hill NJ 08034 856-751-2739 761-8536*
**Fax Area Code:* 207 ■ *TF:* 888-751-9000 ■ *Web:* www.tdbank.com

TD Banknorth Massachusetts 295 Pk Ave .... Worcester MA 01609 508-752-2584 751-8090
TF Cust Svc: 800-747-7000 ■ *Web:* www.tdbank.com

Tempo Bank 28 W Broadway. .... Trenton IL 62293 618-224-9228
Web: tempobank.com

Phone | Fax

Tennessee Commerce Bank
381 Mallory Stn Rd Ste 207 .... Franklin TN 37067 877-275-3342 599-2275*
**Fax Area Code:* 615 ■ *Web:* fdic.gov

Texas Bank & Trust Co
300 E Whaley PO Box 3188 .... Longview TX 75606 903-237-5500 237-1890
Web: www.texasbankandtrust.com

Texas Capital Bank 2000 McKinney Ave Ste 700 .... Dallas TX 75201 214-932-6600 932-6604
TF: 877-839-2265 ■ *Web:* www.texascapitalbank.com

Texas Star Bank
177 E Jefferson PO Box 608. .... Van Alstyne TX 75495 903-482-5234 482-5239
TF: 866-546-8273 ■ *Web:* www.texasstarbank.com

Third Federal Savings & Loan Assn of Cleveland
7007 Broadway Ave .... Cleveland OH 44105 216-429-5228 906-0857*
**Fax Area Code:* 877 ■ *TF:* 888-844-7333 ■ *Web:* www.thirdfederal.com

Thomas Capital Group Inc
4221 Harborview Dr Ste 200. .... Gig Harbor WA 98332 253-777-4477
Web: www.thomascapital.com

Thomaston Savings Bank
203 Main St PO Box 907 .... Thomaston CT 06787 860-283-1874 283-6621
TF General: 855-344-1874 ■ *Web:* www.thomastonsavingsbank.com

Thumb National Bank & Trust Co
7254 Michigan Ave. .... Pigeon MI 48755 989-453-3113
Web: thumbnational.com

Tompkins Trust Co PO Box 460. .... Ithaca NY 14851 607-273-3210 277-6874
NYSE: TMP ■ *TF:* 888-273-3210 ■ *Web:* www.tompkinstrust.com

Town Bank 850 W N Shore Dr. .... Hartland WI 53029 262-367-1900
TF: 800-433-3076 ■ *Web:* www.townbank.us

TowneBank 4501 Cox Rd PO Box 5310. .... Glen Allen VA 23060 804-967-7000 967-7050
TF: 800-372-4445 ■ *Web:* www.franklinfederal.com

Traditional Bank
49 W Main St PO Box 326 .... Mount Sterling KY 40353 859-498-0414 498-0643
TF: 800-498-0414 ■ *Web:* www.traditionalbank.com

Transportation Alliance Bank Inc
4185 Harrison Blvd Ste 200 .... Ogden UT 84403 801-624-4800
Web: www.tabbank.com

Tri City Bankshares Corp 6400 S 27th St. .... Oak Creek WI 53154 414-761-1610 761-2019
OTC: TRCY ■ *Web:* www.tcnb.com

Tri-State 1St Banc Inc 16924 St Clair .... East Liverpool OH 43920 330-385-9200
Web: 1stncb.com

Tri-State Bank & Trust 4321 Youree Dr .... Shreveport LA 71105 318-861-6184 861-9046

Tristar Bank 719 E College St. .... Dickson TN 37055 615-446-7100
Web: tristarbank.com

Triumph Savings Bank SSB
5220 Spring Valley Rd Ste 160. .... Dallas TX 75254 214-237-3170
Web: www.triumphssb.com

Trust Bank 600 E Main St PO Box 158 .... Olney IL 62450 618-395-4311 395-4312
TF: 800-766-3451 ■ *Web:* www.trustbank.net

Trust Company of Virginia, The
9030 Stony Point Pkwy Ste 300 .... Richmond VA 23235 804-272-9044

TSG Partners
The Promenade Ii 1230 Peachtree St 24th Fl .... Atlanta GA 30309 630-818-7302
Web: www.tsg-partners.com

Twin River National Bank 1507 G St .... Lewiston ID 83501 208-746-4848 746-4949
TF: 877-743-4948 ■ *Web:* www.twinriverbank.com

UBS AG 1285 Ave of the Americas .... New York NY 10019 212-713-2000
Web: www.ubs.com

Ulster Savings Bank
180 Schwenk Dr PO Box 3337 .... Kingston NY 12401 845-338-6322 339-9008
Web: www.ulstersavings.com/home/home

UMB Bank NA 1010 Grand Blvd .... Kansas City MO 64106 816-860-7000 860-4642
TF: 800-821-2171 ■ *Web:* www.umb.com

Umpqua Bank PO Box 1820. .... Roseburg OR 97470 503-973-5945 973-5943
TF: 866-486-7782 ■ *Web:* www.umpquabank.com

Unibank For Savings 49 Church St. .... Whitinsville MA 01588 508-234-8112 234-4648
TF: 800-578-4270 ■ *Web:* www.unibank.com

Union Bank & Trust Inc
312 Central Ave SE. .... Minneapolis MN 55414 612-379-3222 379-8837
Web: www.ubtmn.com

Union Bank of California NA
400 California St First Fl. .... San Francisco CA 94104 415-765-3434
TF: 800-238-4486 ■ *Web:* www.unionbank.com

Union FSB 1565 Mineral Spring Ave .... North Providence RI 02904 401-353-8900 353-8938
TF: 888-226-0819 ■ *Web:* www.unionfsb.com

Union Savings Bank
223 W Stephenson St PO Box 540. .... Freeport IL 61032 815-235-0800
Web: www.unionsavingsbank.com

Union SQUARE Advisors LLC
Two Embarcadero Ctr Ste 1330. .... San Francisco CA 94111 415-501-8000
Web: www.usadvisors.com

Union State Bank
127 S Summit St PO Box 928. .... Arkansas City KS 67005 620-442-5200 442-8081
Web: www.myunionstate.com

United American Bank 101 S Ellsworth Ave. .... San Mateo CA 94401 650-579-1500 579-1501
OTC: UABK ■ *TF:* 877-275-3342 ■ *Web:* www.unitedamericanbank.com

United Americas Bank NA 3789 Roswell Rd .... Atlanta GA 30342 404-240-0101 240-0101

United Bank 11185 Fairfax Blvd .... Fairfax VA 22030 703-219-4850 352-8730
TF: 800-327-9862 ■ *Web:* www.bankwithunited.com

United Bank of Philadelphia
30 S 15th St Ste 1200. .... Philadelphia PA 19102 215-351-4600
Web: www.ubphila.com

United Central Bank 4555 W Walnut St .... Garland TX 75042 972-487-1505 276-3972
TF: 855-773-8778 ■ *Web:* www.ucbtx.com

United Financial Bancorp Inc
95 Elm St PO Box 9020 .... West Springfield MA 01090 413-787-1700 737-7879
NASDAQ: UBNK ■ *TF:* 866-959-2265 ■ *Web:* www.bankatunited.com

United Overseas Bank Ltd (UOB)
592 Fifth Ave 10th Fl 48th St .... New York NY 10036 212-382-0088 382-1881
Web: www.uob.com.sg

United Security Bancshares
2126 Inyo St Dept 98 .... Fresno CA 93721 559-248-4943 320-1220
NASDAQ: UBFO ■ *TF:* 888-683-6030 ■ *Web:* www.unitedsecuritybank.com

Phone | Fax

UPS Capital Business Credit
35 Glenlake Pkwy NE … Atlanta GA 30328 877-263-8772
TF: 877-263-8772 ■ *Web:* www.upscapital.com

US Bank NA 1900 N University Dr … Fargo ND 58102 701-280-3547 280-3532
Web: www.usbank.com

USAA FSB (USAAFSB) 10750 McDermott Fwy … San Antonio TX 78288 800-531-8722 531-5717
TF: 800-531-8722 ■ *Web:* www.usaa.com

Vakifbank 399 Park Ave … New York NY 10022 212-319-4630

Valley National Bank 615 Main Ave … Passaic NJ 07055 973-777-6768 777-7963
TF: 800-522-4100 ■ *Web:* valleynationalbank.com

Valley Republic Bank
5000 California Ave Ste 110 … Bakersfield CA 93309 661-371-2000
Web: valleyrepublicbank.com

Vectra Bank Colorado NA
2000 S Colorado Blvd Ste 2-1200 … Denver CO 80222 720-947-7700 947-7760
TF: 800-232-8948 ■ *Web:* www.vectrabank.com

Velocity Credit Union 610 E 11th St … Austin TX 78701 512-469-7000 469-7024
Web: www.velocitycu.com

Vibra Bank 530 Broadway … Chula Vista CA 91910 619-422-5300
Web: www.vibrabank.com

Village Bank & Trust 234 W NW Hwy … Arlington Heights IL 60004 847-670-1000 670-7744
Web: www.bankatvillage.com

VirtualBank
3801 PGA Blvd Ste 700
PO Box 109638 … Palm Beach Gardens FL 33410 877-998-2265 776-6378*
**Fax Area Code:* 561 ■ *TF:* 877-998-2265 ■ *Web:* www.virtualbank.com

Wachovia Bank 11601 Wilshire Blvd … Los Angeles CA 90025 310-477-8004 796-8722*
**Fax Area Code:* 336 ■ *TF:* 800-225-5935 ■ *Web:* www.wellsfargo.com

Wachovia Bank NA 301 S College St … Charlotte NC 28202 704-335-5878
Web: www.wellsfargo.com

Wallace H Coulter Foundation, The
790 NW 107th Ave … Miami FL 33172 305-559-2991
Web: www.whcf.org

Wallkill Valley Federal Savings & Loan Assn
23 Wallkill Ave … Wallkill NY 12589 845-895-2051
Web: www.wallkill.com

Walpole Co-op Bank Inc 982 Main St PO Box 350 … Walpole MA 02081 508-668-1080 660-2690
TF: 877-322-8228 ■ *Web:* www.walpolecoop.com

Waterman State Bank
248 W Lincoln Hwy PO Box 209 … Waterman IL 60556 815-264-3201
Web: watermanbank.com

Waterstone Bank 7500 W State St … Wauwatosa WI 53213 414-258-5880
Web: www.wsbonline.com

Waukesha State Bank
151 E St Paul Ave PO Box 648 … Waukesha WI 53187 262-549-8500 549-8593
Web: www.waukeshabank.com

Weatherbank Inc 1015 Waterwood Pkwy Ste J … Edmond OK 73034 405-359-0773 341-0115
TF: 800-687-3562 ■ *Web:* www.weatherbank.com

Wellesley Bank 40 Central St … Wellesley MA 02482 781-235-2550
Web: wellesleybank.com

Wells Fargo Bank 5622 Third St … Katy TX 77493 281-391-2101 391-1338
TF: 800-869-3557 ■ *Web:* www.wellsfargo.com

Wells Fargo Bank Indiana NA
111 E Wayne St … Fort Wayne IN 46802 260-461-6430
TF: 800-869-3557 ■ *Web:* www.wellsfargo.com

Wells Fargo Bank Iowa NA
666 Walnut St PO Box 837 … Des Moines IA 50309 515-245-3304
Web: www.wellsfargo.com

Wells Fargo Bank Minnesota South NA
21 First St SW … Rochester MN 55902 507-285-2800
Web: www.wellsfargo.com

Wells Fargo Bank Montana NA 175 N 27th St … Billings MT 59101 406-657-3503
Web: www.wellsfargo.com

Wells Fargo Bank NA 420 Montgomery St … San Francisco CA 94104 415-396-2619 477-9075
TF: 800-869-3557 ■ *Web:* www.wellsfargo.com

Wells Fargo Bank Nebraska NA 1919 Douglas St … Omaha NE 68102 402-536-2022
Web: www.wellsfargo.com

Wells Fargo Bank South Dakota NA
101 N Phillips Ave … Sioux Falls SD 57104 605-575-6900
Web: www.wellsfargo.com

Wells Fargo Bank Texas NA
707 Castroville Rd … San Antonio TX 78237 210-856-6224 856-5038
TF: 800-869-3557 ■ *Web:* www.wellsfargo.com

WesBanco Inc One Bank Plz … Wheeling WV 26003 304-234-9000 234-9298
NASDAQ: WSBC ■ *TF:* 800-328-3369 ■ *Web:* www.wesbanco.com

West Alabama Bank & Trust
509 First Ave W PO Box 310 … Reform AL 35481 205-375-6261 375-2289
Web: www.wabt.com

West Coast Bank 506 SW Coast Hwy … Newport OR 97365 877-272-3678
TF Cust Svc: 800-895-3345 ■ *Web:* www.wcb.com

West Milton State Bank 940 High St … West Milton PA 17886 570-568-6851
Web: westmiltonstatebank.com

West Suburban Bank 711 Westmore Meyers Rd … Lombard IL 60148 630-652-2000 629-0278
TF: 800-258-4009 ■ *Web:* www.westsuburbanbank.com

Westamerica Bancorp 1108 Fifth Ave … San Rafael CA 94901 415-257-8000
NASDAQ: WABC ■ *TF:* 800-848-1088 ■ *Web:* www.westamerica.com

Western Commerce Bank
1910 Wyoming Blvd Ne … Albuquerque NM 87112 505-271-9964 271-9879
Web: www.wcb.net

Western Security Bank 2812 First Ave N … Billings MT 59101 406-371-8200 371-8225
TF: 800-983-5537 ■ *Web:* www.westernsecuritybank.com

Western State Bank 110 Fourth St S … Devils Lake ND 58301 701-662-4936
Web: www.westernbanks.com

Westfield Bank 140 Portage Trail … Cuyahoga Falls OH 44221 330-923-0454
Web: www.valleysavingsbank.com

Westpac Banking Corp Americas Div
575 Fifth Ave 39th Fl … New York NY 10017 212-551-1800 551-1999
TF: 888-269-2377 ■ *Web:* www.westpac.com.au

White Sands Federal Credit Union
2190 E Lohman Ave … Las Cruces NM 88001 575-647-4500 647-4540
TF: 800-658-9933 ■ *Web:* www.wsfcu.org

Whitney National Bank 228 St Charles Ave … New Orleans LA 70130 504-586-7456 586-7383
TF: 800-844-4450 ■ *Web:* www.whitneybank.com

Phone | Fax

Wilcox | Swartzwelder & Company LLC
Waterway Tower 433 E Las Colinas Blvd
Ste 1200 … Irving TX 75039 972-831-1300
Web: www.ws-ibank.com

Wilmington Trust Co 1100 N Market St … Wilmington DE 19890 302-651-1000 651-8937*
**Fax:* Hum Res ■ *TF:* 800-441-7120 ■ *Web:* www.wilmingtontrust.com

Wilshire State Bank
3200 Wilshire Blvd Ste 1400 … Los Angeles CA 90010 213-368-7700 427-6562*
**Fax:* Cust Svc ■ *TF:* 866-886-2265 ■ *Web:* www.wilshirebank.com

Wilson Bank Holding Co 623 W Main St … Lebanon TN 37087 615-444-2265 443-7117
OTC: WBHC ■ *Web:* www.wilsonbank.com

Winnsboro State Bank & Trust Co
3875 Front St … Winnsboro LA 71295 318-435-7535
Web: winnsborobank.com

Winter Hill Bank 342 Broadway … Somerville MA 02145 617-666-8600 629-3327
TF: 800-444-4300 ■ *Web:* www.winterhillbank.com/Default.asp

Woodforest Financial Group Inc PO Box 7889 … Spring TX 77387 832-375-2000 375-3001
TF: 877-968-7962 ■ *Web:* www.woodforest.com

Woodsville Guaranty Savings Bank
10 Pleasant St PO Box 266 … Woodsville NH 03785 603-747-2735 747-3267
TF: 800-564-2735 ■ *Web:* www.theguarantybank.com

WoodTrust Financial Corp
181 Second St S … Wisconsin Rapids WI 54494 715-423-7600 422-0300
TF: 800-716-3742 ■ *Web:* www.woodtrust.com

Yadkin Bank 1318 N Bridge St … Elkin NC 28621 336-526-6371
NASDAQ: YDKN ■ *TF:* 866-867-9979 ■ *Web:* www.yadkinbank.com

Yakima Federal Savings & Loan Assn
118 E Yakima Ave … Yakima WA 98901 509-248-2634
TF: 800-331-3225 ■ *Web:* www.yakimafed.com

Ynb 401 Elm St PO Box 851700 … Yukon OK 73099 405-354-5281
Web: ynbok.com

Yoakum National Bank 301 W Grand Ave … Yoakum TX 77995 361-293-5225 293-7322
Web: yoakumnationalbank.com

York State Bank & Trust Co 700 N Lincoln AvE … York NE 68467 402-362-4411 362-4192
TF: 888-295-5540 ■ *Web:* www.yorkstatebank.com

Zions First National Bank 1 S Main St … Salt Lake City UT 84111 801-974-8800 524-2277
TF: 800-974-8800 ■ *Web:* www.zionsbank.com

71 BANKS - FEDERAL RESERVE

Phone | Fax

Bank of Sacramento 1750 Howe Ave Ste 100 … Sacramento CA 95825 916-648-2100 648-0548
Web: www.bankofsacramento.com

Eli Lilly Federal Credit Union
225 SE St Ste 300 … Indianapolis IN 46202 317-276-2105 276-7773
TF: 800-621-2105 ■ *Web:* www.elfcu.org

Federal Reserve Bank of Atlanta
1000 Peachtree St NE … Atlanta GA 30309 404-498-8353
TF: 888-500-7390 ■ *Web:* www.frbatlanta.org
Birmingham Branch 524 Liberty Pkwy … Birmingham AL 35242 205-968-6700 968-6175
TF: 800-257-7013 ■ *Web:* www.frbatlanta.org
Jacksonville Branch 800 Water St … Jacksonville FL 32204 904-632-1000
Web: federalreserve.gov
Miami Branch 9100 NW 36th St … Miami FL 33178 305-591-2065 471-6240
Web: frbatlanta.org
Nashville Branch 301 Rosa L Parks … Nashville TN 37203 615-251-7100
Web: www.frbatlanta.org
New Orleans Branch 525 St Charles Ave … New Orleans LA 70130 504-593-3200 593-3213
Web: www.frbatlanta.org

Federal Reserve Bank of Boston
600 Atlantic Ave … Boston MA 02210 617-973-3000 619-8501
Web: www.bostonfed.org

Federal Reserve Bank of Chicago
230 S LaSalle St … Chicago IL 60604 312-322-5322 322-5515
Web: www.chicagofed.org
Detroit Branch 1600 E Warren Ave … Detroit MI 48207 313-961-6880
Web: chicagofed.org

Federal Reserve Bank of Cleveland
1455 E Sixth St PO Box 6387 … Cleveland OH 44101 216-579-2000
Web: www.clevelandfed.org
Cincinnati Branch 150 E Fourth St … Cincinnati OH 45202 513-721-4787 455-4583
TF: 877-372-2457 ■ *Web:* www.clevelandfed.org

Federal Reserve Bank of Dallas
2200 N Pearl St PO Box 655906 … Dallas TX 75201 214-922-6000 922-5268
TF: 800-333-4460 ■ *Web:* www.dallasfed.org
El Paso Branch 301 E Main St … El Paso TX 79901 915-521-5200 521-8284
Web: www.dallasfed.org
Houston Branch 1801 Allen Pkwy … Houston TX 77019 713-483-3000
Web: www.dallasfed.org
San Antonio Branch 402 Dwyer Ave … San Antonio TX 78204 210-978-1200
TF: 800-333-4460 ■ *Web:* www.dallasfed.org

Federal Reserve Bank of Kansas City
1 Memorial Dr PO Box 1200 … Kansas City MO 64198 816-881-2000 881-2704
TF: 800-333-1010 ■ *Web:* www.kc.frb.org
Denver Branch 1 Memorial Dr … Kansas City MO 64198 888-851-1920 881-2704*
**Fax Area Code:* 816 ■ *TF:* 888-851-1920 ■ *Web:* kansascityfed.org
Oklahoma City Branch
226 Dean A McGee Ave … Oklahoma City OK 73102 405-270-8400 270-8676
TF: 800-333-1030 ■ *Web:* www.kc.frb.org
Omaha Branch 2201 Farnam St … Omaha NE 68102 402-221-5500 221-5715
TF: 800-333-1040 ■ *Web:* www.kansascityfed.org

Federal Reserve Bank of Minneapolis
90 Hennepin Ave … Minneapolis MN 55401 612-204-5000 204-5905
TF: 800-553-9656 ■ *Web:* www.minneapolisfed.org
Helena Branch 100 Neill Ave … Helena MT 59601 406-447-3800 447-3808
Web: federalreserve.gov

Federal Reserve Bank of Philadelphia
10 Independence Mall … Philadelphia PA 19106 215-574-6000
TF: 877-574-1776 ■ *Web:* www.phil.frb.org

Federal Reserve Bank of Richmond
701 E Byrd St … Richmond VA 23219 804-697-8000
Web: www.richmondfed.org

Phone Fax

Baltimore Branch 502 S Sharp St Baltimore MD 21201 410-576-3300
Web: www.richmondfed.org

Federal Reserve Bank of Saint Louis
411 Locust St Saint Louis MO 63102 314-444-8444
TF: 800-333-0810 ■ *Web:* www.stlouisfed.org

Little Rock Branch
111 Ctr St Ste 1000 Stephens Bldg Little Rock AR 72201 501-324-8300 324-8201
TF: 877-372-2457 ■ *Web:* frbservices.org

Louisville Branch 101 S Fifth St Ste 1920 Louisville KY 40202 502-568-9200 568-9247
Web: frbservices.org

Federal Reserve Bank of San Francisco (FRBSF)
101 Market St San Francisco CA 94105 415-974-2000 974-2855
TF: 800-227-4133 ■ *Web:* www.frbsf.org

Los Angeles Branch 950 S Grand Ave Los Angeles CA 90015 213-683-2300 683-2488
Web: www.frbsf.org

Portland Branch 1500 SW First Ave Ste 100 Portland OR 97201 503-276-3000 276-3002
TF: 800-227-4133 ■ *Web:* www.frbsf.org

Salt Lake City Branch 101 Market St San Francisco CA 94105 415-974-2000 974-2168
TF: 800-227-4133 ■ *Web:* www.frbsf.org

First Federal of Northern Michigan
100 S Second Ave. Alpena MI 49707 989-356-9041 354-8671
NASDAQ: FFNM ■ *TF:* 800-916-8800 ■ *Web:* www.first-federal.com

First FSB 633 La Salle St Ottawa IL 61350 815-434-3500 434-1775
TF: 800-443-8780 ■ *Web:* www.ffsbweb.com

First Shore Federal
106-108 S Div St PO Box 4248 Salisbury MD 21803 410-546-1101 546-9590
TF: 800-634-6309 ■ *Web:* www.firstshorefederal.com

Frandsen Bank & Trust
501 Chestnut St W PO Box 1147 Virginia MN 55792 218-741-2040
Web: www.qcfb.com

Lake Shore Bancorp Inc 128 E Fourth St Dunkirk NY 14048 716-366-4070 366-2965
NASDAQ: LSBK ■ *Web:* www.lakeshoresavings.com

Lincoln FSB 1101 N St 68508 PO Box 80038 Lincoln NE 68501 402-474-1400 474-1585
TF: 800-333-2158 ■ *Web:* www.lincolnfed.com

Martha's Vineyard Savings Bank
78 Main St PO Box 1069 Edgartown MA 02539 508-627-4266 627-7588
Web: mvbank.com

Milford Federal Savings & Loan Assn
PO Box 210 Milford MA 01757 508-634-2500 634-2500
TF: 800-478-6990 ■ *Web:* www.milfordfederal.com

Naugatuck Savings Bank
251 Church St PO Box 370 Naugatuck CT 06770 203-729-5291
TF: 877-729-4442 ■ *Web:* www.naugatucksavingsbank.com

Pioneer Bank 21 Second St PO Box 1048 Troy NY 12181 518-274-4800
TF: 866-873-9573 ■ *Web:* www.pioneersb.com

Ponce De Leon Fsb 2244 Westchester Ave Bronx NY 10462 718-931-9000 542-9733
Web: www.poncedeleonbank.com

Putnam County Savings Bank (PCSB)
2477 Rt 6 PO Box 417 Brewster NY 10509 845-279-7101 279-9321
Web: www.pcsb.com

Security Federal Bank (SFB) 238 Richland Ave W Aiken SC 29801 803-641-3000
TF: 866-851-3000 ■ *Web:* www.securityfederalbank.com

Sterling Federal Bank
110 E Fourth St PO Box 617 Sterling IL 61081 815-626-0614 626-6921
Web: www.sterlingfederal.com

Summit State Bank
500 Bicentennial Way PO Box 6188 Santa Rosa CA 95406 707-568-6000 568-7090
NASDAQ: SSBI ■ *TF:* 800-428-5008 ■ *Web:* www.summitstatebank.com

Thomas County Federal Savings & Loan Assn Inc
131 S Dawson St PO Box 1197 Thomasville GA 31799 229-226-3221 226-3459
Web: www.tcfederal.com

Webster First Federal Credit Union
271 Greenwood St Worcester MA 01607 508-671-5000
TF: 800-962-4452 ■ *Web:* www.websterfirst.com

72 BAR ASSOCIATIONS - STATE

SEE ALSO Legal Professionals Associations p. 1801

Phone Fax

Alabama State Bar 415 Dexter Ave Montgomery AL 36104 334-269-1515 261-6310
TF: 800-392-5660 ■ *Web:* www.alabar.org

Alaska Bar Assn
550 W Seventh Ave Ste 1900 PO Box 100279 Anchorage AK 99501 907-272-7469 272-2932
TF: 800-478-4372 ■ *Web:* www.alaskabar.org

Arkansas Bar Assn 2224 Cottondale Ln Little Rock AR 72202 501-375-4606 375-4901
Web: arkbar.com

Colorado Bar Assn 1900 Grant St Ste 900 Denver CO 80203 303-860-1115 894-0821
Web: www.cobar.org

Connecticut Bar Assn
30 Bank St PO Box 350 New Britain CT 06050 860-223-4400 223-4400
Web: www.ctbar.org

Delaware State Bar Assn 405 N King St Wilmington DE 19801 302-658-5279
TF: 855-872-5911

District of Columbia Bar, The
1101 K St NW Ste 200 Washington DC 20005 202-737-4700 626-3453
TF: 877-333-2227 ■ *Web:* www.dcbar.org

Florida Bar 651 E Jefferson St Tallahassee FL 32399 850-561-5600 561-1141
TF: 800-342-8060 ■ *Web:* www.floridabar.org

Hawaii State Bar Assn (HSBA)
1100 Alakea St Ste 1000 Honolulu HI 96813 808-537-1868 521-7936
Web: www.hsba.org

Idaho State Bar 525 W Jefferson St Boise ID 83702 208-334-4500 334-4515
TF: 800-221-3295 ■ *Web:* www.isb.idaho.gov

Illinois State Bar Assn 424 S Second St Springfield IL 62701 217-525-1760 525-0712
TF: 800-252-8908 ■ *Web:* www.isba.org

Indiana State Bar Assn
One Indiana Sq Ste 530 Indianapolis IN 46204 317-639-5465 266-2588
Web: www.inbar.org

Iowa State Bar Assn 625 E Ct Ave Des Moines IA 50309 515-243-3179 243-2511
Web: www.iowabar.org

Kansas Bar Assn 1200 SW Harrison St Topeka KS 66612 785-234-5696 234-3813
TF: 800-928-3111 ■ *Web:* www.ksbar.org

Phone Fax

Kentucky Bar Assn 514 W Main St Frankfort KY 40601 502-564-3795 564-3225
Web: www.kybar.org

Louisiana State Bar Assn (LSBA)
601 St Charles Ave New Orleans LA 70130 504-566-1600 566-0930
TF: 800-421-5722 ■ *Web:* www.lsba.org

Maine State Bar Assn 124 State St Augusta ME 04330 207-622-7523 623-0083
TF: 800-475-7523 ■ *Web:* www.mainebar.org

Maryland State Bar Assn Inc
520 W Fayette St Baltimore MD 21201 410-685-7878 685-1016
TF: 800-492-1964 ■ *Web:* www.msba.org

Massachusetts Bar Assn 20 W St Boston MA 02111 617-338-0500 338-0650
Web: mass.gov

Minnesota State Bar Assn
600 Nicollet Mall Ste 380 Minneapolis MN 55402 612-333-1183 333-4927
TF: 800-882-6722 ■ *Web:* www.mnbar.org

Mississippi Bar 643 N State St Jackson MS 39202 601-948-4471 355-8635
Web: www.msbar.org

Missouri Bar, The
326 Monroe St PO Box 119 Jefferson City MO 65102 573-635-4128 635-2811
Web: www.mobar.org

Nebraska State Bar Assn 635 S 14th St Ste 200 Lincoln NE 68501 402-475-7091 475-7098
TF: 800-927-0117 ■ *Web:* www.nebar.com

New Hampshire Bar Assn
Two Pillsbury St Ste 300 Concord NH 03301 603-224-6942 224-2910
Web: www.nhbar.org

New Jersey State Bar Assn
One Constitution Sq New Jersey Law Ctr New Brunswick NJ 08901 732-249-5000 249-2815
Web: www.njsba.com

New York State Bar Assn 1 Elk St Albany NY 12207 518-463-3200 487-5517
TF: 800-342-3661 ■ *Web:* www.nysba.org

North Carolina State Bar
217 E Edenton St PO Box 25996 Raleigh NC 27601 919-828-4620 821-9168
TF: 800-662-7407 ■ *Web:* ncbar.gov

Ohio State Bar Assn (OSBA) 1700 Lk Shore Dr Columbus OH 43204 614-487-2050 487-1008
TF: 800-282-6556 ■ *Web:* www.ohiobar.org

Oklahoma Bar Assn
1901 N Lincoln Blvd PO Box 53036 Oklahoma City OK 73105 405-416-7000 416-7001
TF: 800-522-8065 ■ *Web:* www.okbar.org

Oregon State Bar Assn
16037 SW Upper Boones Ferry Rd Tigard OR 97224 503-620-0222 684-1366
TF: 800-452-8260 ■ *Web:* www.osbar.org

Pennsylvania Bar Assn 100 S St Harrisburg PA 17101 717-238-6715 238-1204
TF: 800-932-0311 ■ *Web:* www.pabar.org

Rhode Island Bar Assn 115 Cedar St Providence RI 02903 401-421-5740 421-2703
TF: 877-659-0801 ■ *Web:* www.ribar.com

South Carolina Bar 950 Taylor St Columbia SC 29201 803-799-6653 799-4118
TF: 877-797-2227 ■ *Web:* www.scbar.org

State Bar Assn of North Dakota
504 N Washington St PO Box 2136 Bismarck ND 58502 701-255-1404 224-1621
TF: 800-472-2685 ■ *Web:* www.sband.org

State Bar of Arizona 4201 N 24th St Ste 200 Phoenix AZ 85016 602-252-4804 271-4930
TF: 866-482-9227 ■ *Web:* www.azbar.org

State Bar of California 180 Howard St San Francisco CA 94105 415-538-2000 538-2304
Web: www.calbar.ca.gov

State Bar of Georgia
104 Marietta St NW Ste 100 Atlanta GA 30303 404-527-8700 527-8717
TF: 800-334-6865 ■ *Web:* www.gabar.org

State Bar of Michigan 306 Townsend St Lansing MI 48933 517-346-6300 482-6248
TF: 800-968-1442 ■ *Web:* www.michbar.org

State Bar of Montana PO Box 577 Helena MT 59624 406-442-7660 442-7763
Web: www.montanabar.org

State Bar of Nevada 600 E Charleston Blvd Las Vegas NV 89104 702-382-2200 385-2878
TF: 800-254-2797 ■ *Web:* www.nvbar.org

State Bar of New Mexico
5121 Masthead St NE PO Box 92860 Albuquerque NM 87109 505-797-6000 828-3765
TF: 800-876-6227 ■ *Web:* www.nmbar.org

State Bar of South Dakota
222 E Capitol Ave Ste 3 Pierre SD 57501 605-224-7554 224-0282
Web: www.sdbar.org

State Bar of Texas 1414 Colorado St Austin TX 78701 512-427-1463 427-4100
TF: 800-204-2222 ■ *Web:* www.texasbar.com

State Bar of Wisconsin 5302 Eastpark Blvd Madison WI 53718 608-257-3838 257-5502
TF: 800-728-7788 ■ *Web:* www.wisbar.org

Tennessee Bar Assn 221 Fourth Ave N Ste 400 Nashville TN 37219 615-383-7421 297-8058
TF: 800-899-6993 ■ *Web:* tba.org

Utah State Bar 645 S 200 E Salt Lake City UT 84111 801-531-9077 531-0660
TF: 877-752-2611 ■ *Web:* www.utahbar.org

Vermont Bar Assn (VBA) 35-37 Ct St PO Box 100 Montpelier VT 05601 802-223-2020 223-1573
Web: www.vtbar.org

Virginia State Bar 707 E Main St Ste 1500 Richmond VA 23219 804-775-0500 775-0544
TF: 800-552-7977 ■ *Web:* www.vsb.org

Washington State Bar Assn
1325 Fourth Ave Ste 600 Seattle WA 98101 206-727-8200 727-8320
TF: 800-945-9722 ■ *Web:* www.wsba.org

West Virginia State Bar
2000 Deitrick Blvd Charleston WV 25311 304-553-7220 558-2467
TF: 866-989-8227 ■ *Web:* www.wvbar.org

Wyoming State Bar 4124 Laramie St Cheyenne WY 82001 307-632-9061 632-3737
Web: www.wyomingbar.org

73 BASKETS, CAGES, RACKS, ETC - WIRE

SEE ALSO Pet Products p. 2916

Phone Fax

Adrian Fabricators Inc 545 Industrial Dr Adrian MI 49221 517-266-5700
Web: adrian.cylex-usa.com

Apco Products Inc PO Box 236 Essex CT 06426 860-767-2108 767-7259
Web: www.apco-products.com

Archer Wire International Corp
7300 S Narragansett Ave. Bedford Park IL 60638 708-563-1700 563-1740
Web: www.archerwire.com

Company	City	State	Zip	Phone	Fax
Bright Co-op Inc 803 W Seale St *TF:* 800-562-0730 ■ *Web:* www.brightcoop.com	Nacogdoches	TX	75964	936-564-8378	564-3281
Equipment Fabricating Corp 729 45th Ave *Web:* www.equipmentfabricating.com	Oakland	CA	94601	510-261-0343	261-0715
Glamos Wire Products Company Inc 5561 N 152nd St *TF:* 800-328-5062 ■ *Web:* www.glamoswire.com	Hugo	MN	55038	651-429-5386	429-7733
InterMetro Industries Corp 651 N Washington St **Fax:* Hum Res ■ *TF Cust Svc:* 800-992-1776 ■ *Web:* www.metro.com	Wilkes-Barre	PA	18705	570-825-2741	823-2852*
Kaspar Wire Works Inc PO Box 667 *TF:* 800-337-0610 ■ *Web:* www.kwire.com/wirewrk.htm	Shiner	TX	77984	361-594-3327	594-3311
Kewanna Metal Specialties Inc (KMS) 419 W Main St *Web:* www.kmswire.com	Kewanna	IN	46939	574-653-2554	653-2556
Lab Products Inc 742 Sussex Ave PO Box 639 *TF:* 800-526-0469 ■ *Web:* www.labproductsinc.com	Seaford	DE	19973	302-628-4300	628-4309
Marlboro Wire 2403 N 24th St *Web:* www.marlborowire.com	Quincy	IL	62305	217-224-7989	224-7990
Midwest Wire Products Inc 800 Woodward Heights *TF:* 800-989-9881 ■ *Web:* www.midwestwire.com	Ferndale	MI	48220	248-399-5100	542-7104
Nashville Wire Products Manufacturing Co 199 Polk Ave *TF:* 800-448-2125 ■ *Web:* www.nashvillewire.com	Nashville	TN	37210	615-743-2500	242-4225
Progress Wire Products Inc 3535 W 140th St *Web:* www.progresswire.com	Cleveland	OH	44111	216-251-2181	251-2699
Riverdale Mills Corp 130 Riverdale St PO Box 200 *TF:* 800-762-6374 ■ *Web:* www.riverdale.com	Northbridge	MA	01534	508-234-8715	234-9593
Stevens Wire Products Inc 351 NW 'F' St PO Box 1146 *Web:* www.stevenswire.com	Richmond	IN	47374	765-966-5534	962-3586
Technibilt Ltd 700 E P St PO Box 310 **Fax Area Code:* 800 ■ *Web:* www.technibilt.com	Newton	NC	28658	828-464-7388	968-8934*
Wirefab Inc 75 Blackstone River Rd *Web:* www.wirefab.com	Worcester	MA	01607	508-754-5359	797-3620

74 BATTERIES

Company	City	State	Zip	Phone	Fax
A123 Systems Inc 200 W St *TF:* 800-224-7654 ■ *Web:* www.a123systems.com	Waltham	MA	02451	617-778-5700	924-8910
Applied Energy Solutions LLC One Technology Pl **Fax:* Sales ■ *TF:* 800-836-2132 ■ *Web:* www.appliedenergysol.com	Caledonia	NY	14423	585-538-4421	538-6345*
Atlantic Battery Company Inc 309 Main St *Web:* www.atlanticbatterycompany.com/	Watertown	MA	02472	617-924-2868	
Battery Handling Systems Inc 1488 Page Industrial Ct *Web:* www.bhs1.com	Saint Louis	MO	63132	314-423-7091	
Bren-Tronics Inc 10 Brayton Ct *Web:* www.bren-tronics.com	Commack	NY	11725	631-499-5155	499-5504
C & D Technologies Inc 1400 Union Meeting Rd PO Box 3053 *TF:* 800-543-8630 ■ *Web:* www.cdtechno.com	Blue Bell	PA	19422	215-619-2700	619-7899
Cell-con Inc 305 Commerce Dr Ste 300 *TF:* 800-771-7139 ■ *Web:* www.cell-con.com	Exton	PA	19341	610-280-7630	280-7685
Continental Battery Corp 4919 Woodall St *TF:* 800-442-0081 ■ *Web:* www.continentalbattery.com	Dallas	TX	75247	214-631-5701	634-7846
Crown Battery Manufacturing Co 1445 Majestic Dr *TF:* 800-487-2879 ■ *Web:* www.crownbattery.com	Fremont	OH	43420	419-334-7181	334-7416
Douglas Battery Manufacturing Co 500 Battery Dr **Fax Area Code:* 336 ■ **Fax:* Hum Res ■ *TF:* 800-368-4527 ■ *Web:* www.douglasbattery.com	Winston-Salem	NC	27107	800-368-4527	650-7002*
Duracell 14 Research Dr **Fax Area Code:* 866 ■ *TF:* 800-551-2355 ■ *Web:* www.duracell.com	Bethel	CT	06801	203-791-3014	889-7911*
EaglePicher Technologies LLC C & Porter St *Web:* www.eaglepicher.com	Joplin	MO	64801	417-623-8000	
Ener1 Inc 3023 Distribution Wy **Fax Area Code:* 954 ■ *Web:* www.ener1.com	Greenfield	IN	46140	317-703-1800	556-4031*
EnerSys 2366 Bernville Rd *NYSE: ENS* ■ *TF:* 800-538-3627 ■ *Web:* enersys.com	Reading	PA	19605	610-208-1991	372-8457
EnerSys Inc 617 N Ridgeview Dr *Web:* www.enersysreservepower.com	Warrensburg	MO	64093	660-429-2165	429-1758
Exide Technologies 13000 Deerfield Pkwy Bldg 200 *NASDAQ: XIDE* ■ *TF:* 800-782-7848 ■ *Web:* www.exideworld.com	Milton	GA	30004	678-566-9000	566-9188
Hawker Powersource Inc 9404 Ooltewah Industrial Dr PO Box 808 *TF:* 800-238-8658 ■ *Web:* www.hawkerpowersource.com	Ooltewah	TN	37363	423-238-5700	238-6060
Industrial Battery & Charger Inc 5831 Orr Rd *TF:* 800-833-8412 ■ *Web:* www.ibcipower.com	Charlotte	NC	28213	704-597-7330	597-0855
MarathonNorco Aerospace Inc 8301 Imperial Dr *Web:* www.mnaerospace.com	Waco	TX	76712	254-776-0650	776-6558
Mathews Assoc Inc 220 Power Ct *TF:* 800-871-5262 ■ *Web:* www.maifl.com	Sanford	FL	32771	407-323-3390	323-3115
Micro Power Electronics Inc 13955 SW Millikan Way *TF:* 866-233-4553 ■ *Web:* oregonlive.com	Beaverton	OR	97005	503-693-7600	648-9625
Power Battery Co Inc 25 McLean Blvd *TF:* 800-455-0054 ■ *Web:* powerbatteryco.com	Paterson	NJ	07514	973-523-8630	523-3023
PulseTech Products Corp 1100 S Kimball Ave *Web:* www.pulsetech.net	Southlake	TX	76092	817-329-6099	
R & D Batteries Inc 3300 Corporate Ctr Dr PO Box 5007 *TF:* 800-950-1945 ■ *Web:* www.rdbatteries.com	Burnsville	MN	55306	952-890-0629	890-7912
Staab Battery Manufacturing Co 931 S 11th St *Web:* www.staabbattery.com	Springfield	IL	62703	217-528-0421	
Surefire LLC 18300 Mt Baldy Cir *TF:* 800-828-8809 ■ *Web:* www.surefire.com	Fountain Valley	CA	92708	714-545-9444	545-9537
Tadiran Batteries 2001 Marcus Ave Ste 125E *TF:* 800-537-1368 ■ *Web:* www.tadiranbat.com	New Hyde Park	NY	11042	516-621-4980	621-4517
TNR Technical Inc 301 Central Pk Dr *OTC: TNRK* ■ *TF:* 800-346-0601 ■ *Web:* www.batterystore.com	Sanford	FL	32771	407-321-3011	321-3208
Trojan Battery Co 12380 Clark St *TF Cust Svc:* 800-423-6569 ■ *Web:* www.trojanbattery.com	Santa Fe Springs	CA	90670	562-236-3000	236-3282
Ultralife Batteries Inc 2000 Technology Pkwy *NASDAQ: ULBI* ■ *TF:* 800-332-5000 ■ *Web:* www.ultralifecorporation.com	Newark	NY	14513	315-332-7100	331-7800
Valence Technology Inc 12303 Technology Blvd Ste 950 *TF:* 888-825-3623 ■ *Web:* www.valence.com	Austin	TX	78727	512-527-2900	527-2910
Yardney Technical Products Inc 82 Mechanic St *Web:* www.yardney.com	Pawcatuck	CT	06379	860-599-1100	599-3903

75 BEARINGS - BALL & ROLLER

Company	City	State	Zip	Phone	Fax
Accurate Bushing Company Inc 443 N Ave *TF Sales:* 800-932-0076 ■ *Web:* www.smithbearing.com	Garwood	NJ	07027	908-789-1121	789-9429
ACL Distribution Inc 4722 Danvers Dr *Web:* www.aclperformance.com.au	Grand Rapids	MI	49512	616-956-1300	
Advanced Green Components LLC 4005 Corporate Dr *Web:* www.advgreen.com	Winchester	KY	40391	859-737-6000	
Aetna Bearing Co 1081 Sesame St *Web:* www.aetnabearing.com	Franklin Park	IL	60131	630-694-0024	
Alinabal Inc 28 Woodmont Rd *Web:* www.alinabal.com	Milford	CT	06460	203-877-3241	874-5063
American Roller Bearing Co 400 Second Ave NW *Web:* www.amroll.com	Hickory	NC	28601	828-624-1460	
AST Bearings 115 Main Rd *TF:* 800-526-1250 ■ *Web:* www.astbearings.com	Montville	NJ	07045	973-335-2230	335-6987
Aurora Bearing Co 901 Aucutt Rd *Web:* www.aurorabearing.com	Montgomery	IL	60538	630-859-2030	
Avon Bearings Inc 1500 Nagle Rd *Web:* www.kaydonbearings.com	Avon	OH	44011	440-871-2500	
Bearing Inspection Inc 4500 Mount Pleasant NW **Fax Area Code:* 714 ■ *TF Cust Svc:* 800-416-8881 ■ *Web:* www.timken.com	North Canton	OH	44720	234-262-3000	484-2428*
Bearing Service Co of Pennsylvania 630 Alpha Dr RIDC Park *TF:* 800-783-2327 ■ *Web:* www.bearing-service.com	Pittsburgh	PA	15238	412-963-7710	963-8005
Berliss Bearing Co 644 Rt 10 Po Box 45 *Web:* www.berliss.com	Livingston	NJ	07039	973-992-4242	992-6669
C & S Engineering Corp 956 Old Colony Rd *Web:* www.cscos.com	Meriden	CT	06451	203-235-5727	
Cooper Split Roller Bearing Corp, The 5365 Robin Hood Rd Ste B *Web:* www.cooperbearings.com	Norfolk	VA	23513	757-460-0925	
Del-tron Precision Inc Five Trowbridge Dr *Web:* deltron.com	Bethel	CT	06801	203-778-2727	
EDT Corp 1006-J NE 146th St *Web:* www.edtcorp.com	Vancouver	WA	98685	360-574-7294	
Flexible Concepts 1620 Middlebury St *Web:* www.flexibleconcepts.com	Elkhart	IN	46516	574-296-0941	
Freeway Corp 9301 Allen Dr **Fax:* Sales ■ *Web:* www.freewaycorp.com	Cleveland	OH	44125	216-524-9700	524-7396*
General Bearing Corp 44 High St *TF Sales:* 800-431-1766 ■ *Web:* www.generalbearing.com	West Nyack	NY	10994	845-358-6000	358-6277
Hartford Technologies 1022 Elm St *Web:* www.hartfordtechnologies.com	Rocky Hill	CT	06067	860-571-3602	571-3604
JTEKT Corporation 29570 Clemens Rd *TF Cust Svc:* 800-263-5163 ■ *Web:* www.koyousa.com	Westlake	OH	44145	440-835-1000	835-9347
LSB Industries Inc 16 S Pennsylvania Ave *NYSE: LXU* ■ *Web:* www.lsbindustries.com	Oklahoma City	OK	73107	405-235-4546	235-5067
Lutco Bearings Inc 130 Higgins St *Web:* www.lutco.com	Worcester	MA	01606	508-853-2114	853-1105
Lutco Inc 677 Cambridge St *Web:* www.lutco.com	Worcester	MA	01610	508-756-6296	799-6848
Mechatronics Inc 8152 304th Ave SE PO Box 5012 *Web:* www.mechatronicsinc.com	Preston	WA	98050	425-222-5900	
Nachi America Inc 715 Pushville Rd *TF:* 888-340-2747 ■ *Web:* www.nachiamerica.com	Greenwood	IN	46143	317-530-1001	530-1011
National Bearing Co 1596 Manheim Pk *Web:* www.nationalbearings.com	Lancaster	PA	17604	717-569-0485	569-1605
New Hampshire Ball Bearings Inc 175 Jaffrey Rd **Fax:* Cust Svc ■ *Web:* www.nhbb.com	Peterborough	NH	03458	603-924-3311	924-4419*
NSK-AKS Precision Ball Co 1100A N First St *Web:* www.aksball-us.com	Clarinda	IA	51632	712-542-6515	
Ntn Bower 2086 Military St S *Web:* ntnbower.com	Hamilton	AL	35570	205-952-9355	
Peer Bearing Co 2200 Norman Dr S **Fax:* Orders ■ *TF:* 800-433-7337 ■ *Web:* www.peerbearing.com	Waukegan	IL	60085	847-578-1000	578-1200*
Professional Instruments Co 7800 Powell Rd *Web:* www.airbearings.com	Hopkins	MN	55343	952-933-1222	933-3315
Roller Bearing Company of America 400 Sullivan Way *Web:* www.rbcbearings.com	West Trenton	NJ	08628	609-882-5050	882-5533
Rotek Inc 1400 S Chillicothe Rd PO Box 312 **Fax:* Sales ■ *TF:* 800-221-8043 ■ *Web:* www.rotek-inc.com	Aurora	OH	44202	330-562-4000	562-4620*
S/n Precision Enterprises Inc 145 Jordan Rd *Web:* www.pacamor.com	Troy	NY	12180	518-283-8002	283-8032

Company / Address	City	State	ZIP	Phone	Fax
Schaeffler Group USA Inc 308 Springhill Farm Rd *TF:* 800-361-5841 ■ *Web:* www.schaeffler.us	Fort Mill	SC	29715	803-548-8500	548-8599
Schatz Bearing Corp 10 Fairview Ave *TF:* 800-554-1406 ■ *Web:* www.schatzbearing.com	Poughkeepsie	NY	12601	845-452-6000	452-1660
SKF USA Inc Roller Bearing Div 20 Industrial Dr *Web:* skf.com	Hanover	PA	17331	717-637-8981	
Timken Co 1835 Dueber Ave SW *NYSE: TKR* ■ *TF:* 800-223-1954 ■ *Web:* www.timken.com	Canton	OH	44706	330-438-3000	458-6006
Universal Bearings Inc 431 N Birkey St *Web:* www.univbrg.com	Bremen	IN	46506	574-546-2261	546-5085
Virginia Industries Inc 1022 Elm St *Web:* www.virginia.gov	Rocky Hill	CT	06067	860-571-3600	571-3604
Wecsys LLC 8825 Xylon Ave N *Web:* www.wecsysllc.com	Minneapolis	MN	55445	763-504-1069	
Wieland Metals Inc 567 Northgate Pkwy *Web:* www.wielandus.com	Wheeling	IL	60090	847-537-3990	537-4085
Winsted Precision Ball Corp 159 Colebrook River Rd *TF:* 800-462-3075 ■ *Web:* www.winball.com	Winsted	CT	06098	860-379-2788	379-9650

76 BEAUTY SALON EQUIPMENT & SUPPLIES

Company / Address	City	State	ZIP	Phone	Fax
Arbonne International 9400 Jeronimo Rd *Web:* arbonne.com	Irvine	CA	92618	949-770-2610	
Beaute Craft Supply Co 600 W Maple Rd	Troy	MI	48084	248-362-0400	362-7996*
Belvedere USA Corp 1 Belvedere Blvd **Fax Area Code:* 800 ■ *TF:* 800-435-5491 ■ *Web:* www.belvedere.com	Belvidere	IL	61008	815-544-3131	626-9750*
Betty Dain Creations Inc 9701 NW 112 Ave Ste 10 *TF General:* 800-327-5256 ■ *Web:* www.bettydain.com	Miami	FL	33178	305-769-3451	
Brad-Pak Enterprises Inc 124 S Ave *Web:* brad-pak.com	Garwood	NJ	07027	908-233-1234	
Burmax Co 28 Barretts Ave **Fax Area Code:* 631 ■ *TF:* 800-645-5118 ■ *Web:* www.burmax.com	Holtsville	NY	11742	800-645-5118	289-7590*
Cedar Bay Inc 1224 Whitestone Dr	Murphy	TX	75094	972-384-0410	
Collins Manufacturing Co 2000 Bowser Rd *TF:* 800-292-6450 ■ *Web:* www.collinsmfgco.com	Cookeville	TN	38506	931-528-5151	528-5472
Dr Kern USA Inc 221 S Franklin Rd *TF:* 800-908-9885 ■ *Web:* www.drkern.com	Indianapolis	IN	46219	317-472-0873	472-0873
European Touch Ltd II 8301 W Parkland Ct	Milwaukee	WI	53223	414-357-7016	
IdeaVillage Products Corp 155 Rt 46 W 4th Fl *Web:* www.ideavillage.com	Wayne	NJ	07470	973-826-8418	
Jerdon Style LLC 1820 N Glenville Dr Ste 124 *Web:* www.jerdonstyle.com	Richardson	TX	75081	972-690-4286	
Jeunesse Global LLC 650 Douglas Ave *TF:* 800-400-2676 ■ *Web:* www.jeunesseglobal.com	Altamonte Springs	FL	32714	407-215-7414	
Living Earth Crafts 3210 Executive Ridge Dr *TF:* 800-358-8292 ■ *Web:* www.livingearthcrafts.com	Vista	CA	92081	760-597-2155	599-7374
Middlebridge Mktg Inc 1525 Old Louisquisset Pk	Lincoln	RI	02865	401-728-0040	
National Salon Resources Inc 3109 Louisiana Ave N **Fax Area Code:* 800 ■ *TF:* 800-622-0003 ■ *Web:* www.nationalsalon.com	Minneapolis	MN	55427	763-541-1000	577-2512*
Pibbs Industries 133-15 32nd Ave *TF:* 800-551-5020 ■ *Web:* www.pibbs.com	Flushing	NY	11354	718-445-8046	461-3910
Sally Beauty Company Inc 3001 Colorado Blvd *TF:* 800-777-5706 ■ *Web:* www.sallybeauty.com	Denton	TX	76210	940-898-7500	297-2110
T3 Micro Inc 228 Main St Ste 12	Venice	CA	90291	310-452-2888	
Takara Belmont USA Inc 101 Belmont Dr **Fax Area Code:* 732 ■ *TF:* 877-283-1289 ■ *Web:* www.takarabelmont.com	Somerset	NJ	08873	877-283-1289	283-1687*
TouchAmerica 1403 S Third Street Ext *TF:* 800-678-6824 ■ *Web:* www.touchamerica.com	Hillsborough	NC	27278	919-732-6968	732-1173
Valley Barber & Beauty Supply 413 W Harrison St	Harlingen	TX	78550	956-423-0727	423-0757
William Marvy Company Inc 1540 St Clair Ave *TF:* 800-874-2651 ■ *Web:* www.wmmarvyco.com	Saint Paul	MN	55105	651-698-0726	698-4048

77 BEAUTY SALONS

Company / Address	City	State	ZIP	Phone	Fax
A-tech Security Inc 10001 Wilshire Ave Ne *Web:* www.atechsecurity.com	Albuquerque	NM	87122	505-821-5777	
Adam Broderick Salon & Spa 89 Danbury Rd *Web:* www.adambroderick.com	Ridgefield	CT	06877	203-431-3994	
Aedes De Venustas Inc Nine Christopher St Frnt B *Web:* aedes.com	New York	NY	10014	212-206-8674	
Alejandra Hair Salon 14208 Palm Dr *Web:* www.alejandrahair.com	Desert Hot Springs	CA	92240	760-329-6465	
Alexandre de Paris Inc 12751 Federal Systems Park Dr *Web:* www.alexandredeparis.com	Fairfax	VA	22033	703-222-7661	
Aloe Up Suncare 9700 W 76th St Ste H *Web:* www.aloeup.com	Eden Prairie	MN	55344	952-933-7724	
Amber Waves Inc 11 S Ave W *Web:* www.amberwavesinc.com	Richardton	ND	58652	701-974-4230	
Ambiance Day Spa & Salon 1777 Monte Vista Ave *Web:* www.claremontclub.com	Claremont	CA	91711	909-625-5535	
Aromaland Inc 1326 Rufina Cir *Web:* www.aromaland.com	Santa Fe	NM	87507	505-438-0402	
Ascent Biomedical Ventures 142 W 57th St Ste 4A *Web:* www.ankarcapital.com	New York	NY	10019	212-303-1680	
Balance Day Spa LLC 2138 Lawndale Dr *Web:* www.balancedayspa.com	Greensboro	NC	27408	336-574-2556	
Ball Beauty Supplies 416 N Fairfax Ave *Web:* www.ballbeauty.com	Los Angeles	CA	90036	323-655-2330	
Beauty Bar LLC 2919 W Central Ave *Web:* www.beauty-bar.com	Toledo	OH	43606	419-537-5400	
Beauty Brands Inc 4600 Madison St Ste 400 *TF:* 877-640-2248 ■ *Web:* www.beautybrands.com	Kansas City	MO	64112	816-531-2266	
Beauty Collection Inc 7862 Burnet Ave *Web:* beautycollection.com	Van Nuys	CA	91405	818-785-7447	
Beauty Craft Supply & Equipment Co 11110 Bren Rd W *Web:* www.beautycraft.com	Hopkins	MN	55343	952-935-4420	
Beauty Management Inc 270 Beavercreek Rd *Web:* www.perfectlooksalons.com	Oregon City	OR	97045	503-723-3200	
Beauty Schools of America 1176 Southwest 67 Ave *Web:* www.bsa.edu	Miami	FL	33144	305-824-2070	
Bellapelle Skin Studio 166 Geary St Fl 6th *Web:* bellapelle.com	San Francisco	CA	94108	415-362-6384	
Belpointe Capital 125 Greenwich Ave *Web:* www.belpointe.com	Greenwich	CT	06830	203-629-3300	
Beyer Barber Co 1136 Hamilton St Ste 103 *Web:* www.beyerbarber.com	Allentown	PA	18101	610-435-9577	
Borealis Compounds LLC 176 Thomas Rd *Web:* www.borealisgroup.com	Port Murray	NJ	07865	908-850-6200	
Boyd Brothers Inc 425 E 15th St *Web:* www.boyd-printing.com	Panama City	FL	32405	850-763-1741	
Bullhead City Bee 1905 Lakeside Dr *Web:* www.bullheadcitybee.com	Bullhead City	AZ	86442	928-763-9339	
Buy Me Beauty 4221 NE 12th Terrace *Web:* www.buymebeauty.com	Oakland Park	FL	33334	954-568-7150	
Cain's Barber College Inc 365 E 51st St *Web:* www.cbcon51st.org	Chicago	IL	60615	773-536-4441	
Capitol Towers 1500 Seventh St Ste 1c *Web:* fftrinity.com	Sacramento	CA	95814	916-447-3288	
Cartoon Cuts LP 927 N University Dr Ste 410 *Web:* www.cartooncuts.com	Coral Springs	FL	33071	954-341-4221	
Celadon Spa 1180 F St Nw Frnt 1 *Web:* www.celadonspa.com	Washington	DC	20004	202-347-3333	
Changes Salon & Day Spa Inc 1475 N Broadway *Web:* changessalon.com	Walnut Creek	CA	94596	925-947-1814	
Charles Penzone Inc 1480 Manning Pkwy *Web:* www.charlespenzone.com	Powell	OH	43065	614-898-1200	898-1194
Chella Professional Skin Care 507 Calle San Pablo *Web:* www.chella.com	Camarillo	CA	93012	805-383-7711	
Cinta Salon 23 Grant Ave *Web:* cinta.com	San Francisco	CA	94108	415-989-1000	
Colourbox Hairdressing 305 Cordova St W *Web:* colourboxhair.com	Vancouver	BC	V6B1E5	604-669-6354	
Daired's Salon & Spa Pangea 2400 W Interstate 20 *Web:* daireds.com	Arlington	TX	76017	817-465-9797	
Denver Dermatology Consultants Pc 1551 Milky Way *Web:* www.denverderm.com	Thornton	CO	80260	303-426-4525	
Dermatology Associates of Tyler 1367 Dominion Plz *Web:* www.dermatologytyler.com	Tyler	TX	75703	903-534-6200	
Desiccare Inc 3400 Pomona Blvd *Web:* www.desiccare.com	Pomona	CA	91768	909-444-8272	
Dipietro Todd Salon 177 Post St Fl 2 *Web:* www.dipietrotodd.com	San Francisco	CA	94108	415-397-0177	
Dosha Salon & Spa 3490 Se Hawthorne Blvd *Web:* www.dosha.org	Portland	OR	97214	503-231-4993	
Dunwoody Village 3500 W Chester Pk *Web:* www.dunwoody.org	Newtown Square	PA	19073	610-359-4400	
Durham Christian Homes Hair Styling 200 Glen Hill Dr *Web:* durhamchristianhomes.salonpages.ca	Whitby	ON	L1N7J7	905-668-3840	
EG Capital Group LLC 39 W 54th St *Web:* www.egcapitalgroup.com	New York	NY	10019	212-956-2600	
Fantastic Sams Inc 50 Dunham Rd 3rd Fl **Fax Area Code:* 978 ■ *Web:* www.fantasticsams.com	Beverly	MA	01915	651-770-1449	232-5601*
Farmington Center Salem an Oregon LP 960 Boone Rd SE *Web:* www.farmingtonsquare-salem.com	Salem	OR	97306	503-715-0727	
Fintronx LLC 130 Iowa Ln Ste 204 *Web:* www.fintronx.com	Cary	NC	27511	919-467-5800	
Floral Plant Growers LLC North 781 Curran Rd *Web:* www.naturalbeautygrowers.com	Denmark	WI	54208	920-863-2107	
Fountain, The 1100 State Rt 17 *Web:* www.fountain.com	Ramsey	NJ	07446	201-327-5155	
Fuga 3853 N Southport Ave *Web:* www.salonfuga.com	Chicago	IL	60613	773-880-1280	
Gadabout Inc 6393 E Grant Near Grant and Tanque Verde Near Costco *Web:* www.gadabout.com	Tucson	AZ	85715	520-885-0000	
Genesis Biosystems Inc 1500 Eagle Ct # 75057 *Web:* www.genesisbiosystems.com	Lewisville	TX	75057	972-315-7888	
Geralds of Northville Inc 41012 Five Mile Rd *Web:* www.geraldssalon.com	Plymouth	MI	48170	734-420-0111	

Name / Address	City	State	Zip	Phone	Fax
Ginger Bay Salon Group Ltd 439 S Kirkwood Rd	Saint Louis	MO	63122	314-966-0655	
Web: www.gingerbay.com					
Gino Morena Enterprises LLC 111 Starlite St	South San Francisco	CA	94080	800-227-6905	
TF: 800-227-6905 ■ *Web:* www.ginomorena.com					
Gould's Styling Salons 2760 N Germantown Pkwy Ste 197	Memphis	TN	38133	901-386-5101	
Web: www.gouldsalons.com					
Great Clips Inc 7700 France Ave S Ste 425	Minneapolis	MN	55435	952-893-9088	844-3444
TF: 800-999-5959 ■ *Web:* www.greatclips.com					
Green Tangerine Spa & Salon 238 Patriot Pl	Foxborough	MA	02035	508-203-9414	
Web: www.greentangerinespa.com					
Hair Club for Men LTD Inc 1515 S Federal Hwy Ste 401	Boca Raton	FL	33432	561-361-7600	
Web: www.hairclub.com					
Hair It Is 977 Perry Hwy Ste 4	Pittsburgh	PA	15237	412-366-5511	
Web: www.hairitis.biz					
Hair Loss Control Clinic Four Avis Dr Ste 10	Latham	NY	12110	518-220-1500	
Web: www.hlcconline.com					
Hairart International Inc 4630 Van Nuys Blvd Second Fl	Sherman Oaks	CA	91403	818-905-7730	
Web: hairartinc.com					
Hairboutique 651 N Plano Rd Ste 401	Richardson	TX	75081	972-231-5225	
Web: www.hairboutique.com					
HK Enterprises Inc 3190-B Coronado Dr	Santa Clara	CA	95054	408-988-5880	
Holiday Hair 7201 Metro Blvd	Minneapolis	MN	55439	800-345-7811	
TF: 800-345-7811 ■ *Web:* www.holidayhair.com					
Holtzman Enterprises Inc 8501 Turnpike Dr Ste 103	Westminster	CO	80031	303-428-3364	
Web: greatclips.com					
Ideal Image Development Inc One Urban Ctr 4830 W Kennedy Blvd Ste 440	Tampa	FL	33609	813-286-8100	
Web: www.idealimage.com					
Imperial Salon & Spa Inc Three Suntree Pl Ste 101	Melbourne	FL	32940	321-254-4432	
Web: www.imperialsalonandspa.com					
In Stock Retail 128 Holiday Ct Ste 105	Franklin	TN	37067	615-790-2934	
Web: instockrs.com					
Instyle Hair Designs Inc 175 Littleton Rd	Westford	MA	01886	978-692-7851	
Web: www.instylehd.com					
J D Beauty 5 Adams Ave	Hauppauge	NY	11788	631-273-2800	
Web: www.jdbeauty.com					
Jai Transforme Salon 12730 Olive Blvd	Saint Louis	MO	63141	314-439-5542	
Web: www.jaitransformesalon.com					
John Masters Organic Hair Care Inc 77 Sullivan St	New York	NY	10012	212-343-9590	
Web: www.johnmasters.com					
Just Hair 1845 Eastwest Pkwy	Fleming Island	FL	32003	904-215-2995	
Web: www.justhairinc.com					
Kenneth Shuler School of Cosmetology & Hair Design Inc 449 Saint Andrews Rd	Columbia	SC	29210	803-772-6042	
Web: www.kennethshuler.com					
L Salon & Color Group 223 S San Mateo Dr	San Mateo	CA	94401	650-342-6668	
Web: www.lsalon.com					
La Camarilla Racquet Fitness & Swim Club 5320 E Shea Blvd Ste A	Scottsdale	AZ	85254	480-998-3388	
Web: www.lacamarilla.com					
Las Olas Beauty 1503 E Las Olas Blvd	Fort Lauderdale	FL	33301	954-779-2616	832-0165
Web: www.lasolasbeauty.com					
Los Angeles School of Make-up Inc 129 S San Fernando Blvd	Burbank	CA	91502	818-729-9420	
Web: www.makeupschool.com					
Maka Beauty Systems 3959 E Speedway Blvd Ste 308	Tucson	AZ	85712	520-322-6252	
Web: www.maka.com					
Mane Street Manor Hair Salon & Day Spa 1108 S Main St	Hampstead	MD	21074	410-239-1425	
Web: manestreetmanorspa.com					
Mango Hair Salon 123 Libbie Ave	Richmond	VA	23226	804-285-2800	
Web: mangosalon.com					
Mark Anthony Inc 1105 Walnut St Ste F-160	Cary	NC	27511	919-467-9641	
Web: www.mitchellspas.com					
Meriwether Godsey Inc 4944 Old Boonsboro Rd	Lynchburg	VA	24503	434-384-3663	
Web: www.merig.com					
Mi Pueblito Beauty Salon 4534 E Tropicana Ave	Las Vegas	NV	89121	702-433-6435	
Web: local.yahoo.com					
Miracell Botanicals 921 North 1430 West	Orem	UT	84057	801-434-8165	
Web: www.miracell.com					
Mitchells Salon & Day Spa 5901 E Galbraith Rd	Cincinnati	OH	45236	513-793-0900	
Web: www.mitchellssalon.com					
Mohegan Tribal Gaming Authority One Mohegan Sun Blvd	Uncasville	CT	06382	888-226-7711	
TF: 888-226-7711 ■ *Web:* www.mtga.com					
Moxie Hair Salon 2649 Lyndale Ave S	Minneapolis	MN	55408	612-813-0330	
Web: moxiesalon.com					
Naimies Beauty Center Inc 12640 Riverside Dr	Valley Village	CA	91607	818-655-9933	
Web: www.naimies.com					
Navii Salon Spa 316 E Us Hwy 30	Schererville	IN	46375	219-865-6515	
Web: www.navii.com					
Nexia Holdings Inc 59 West 100 South Second Fl	Salt Lake City	UT	84101	801-575-8073	
Web: www.nexiaholdings.com					
Noelle Spa-beauty & Wellness 1100 High Ridge Rd Ste 202	Stamford	CT	06905	203-322-3445	
Web: www.noelle.com					
OC Jones & Sons Inc 1520 Fourth St	Berkeley	CA	94710	510-526-3424	
Web: www.ocjones.com					
One Step Logic 17615 Mayall St	Northridge	CA	91325	818-700-7837	
Web: www.onesteplogic.com					
Ovation Hair Design 18 Davenport St	Somerville	NJ	08876	908-526-5110	
Web: ovationhairdesign.com					
Over The Rainbow Children & Adult Hair Styling Salon 8300 Tampa Ave Ste C	Northridge	CA	91324	818-886-9325	
Web: overtherainbowshop.com					
Panzer Dermatology Association 537 Stanton Christiana Rd Ste 207	Newark	DE	19713	302-633-7550	
Web: www.premierdermde.com					
Paragon Salons Inc 6775 Harrison Ave	Cincinnati	OH	45247	513-574-7610	
Web: paragonsalon.com					
Perry Anthony Design Group 5331 Limestone Rd	Wilmington	DE	19808	302-239-6161	
Web: www.perryanthony.com					
Pino's Salon & Spa 70 Victoria St N	Kitchener	ON	N2H5C2	519-578-8898	
Web: www.pinosalon.com					
Pizzazz Hair Design at Abacoa Inc 771 Village Blvd Ste 208	West Palm Bch	FL	33409	561-689-1177	
Web: www.wellingtoncomputer.com					
Planet 21 8040 Providence Rd Ste 300	Charlotte	NC	28277	704-543-1083	
Web: www.planet21salon.com					
Planet Beauty Inc 3199 Red Hill Ave Ste A	Costa Mesa	CA	92626	949-752-1885	
Web: www.planet-beauty.com					
Premier Salons Inc 8341 Tenth Ave N Golden Vly	Golden Valley	MN	55427	800-542-4247	470-8174*
**Fax Area Code:* 905 ■ *TF:* 800-542-4247 ■ *Web:* www.halcyondayspa.com					
Preston Wynne Spa Inc 14567 Big Basin Way	Saratoga	CA	95070	408-741-5525	
Web: www.prestonwynne.com					
Pro-Link Inc 510 Chapman St	Canton	MA	02021	781-828-9550	
Web: www.prolinkhq.com					
Quinn Medical Day Spa 6920 W 121st St Ste 102	Leawood	KS	66209	913-663-5483	
Web: www.quinnplasticsurgery.com					
Rasmussen John 730 Sand Lk Rd	Orlando	FL	32809	407-859-5255	
Web: www.rasmussen-usa.com					
Ratner co 1577 Spring Hill Rd Ste 500	Vienna	VA	22182	703-269-5400	
Web: www.ratnerco.com					
Redex Industries Inc 1176 Salem Pkwy	Salem	OH	44460	330-332-9800	
Web: www.uddercream.com					
Regis Corp 7201 Metro Blvd	Minneapolis	MN	55439	952-947-7777	
NYSE: RGS ■ *TF:* 888-888-7778 ■ *Web:* www.regiscorp.com					
Regis Corp MasterCuts Div 7201 Metro Blvd	Minneapolis	MN	55439	952-947-7777	947-7801
TF: 877-857-2070 ■ *Web:* www.mastercuts.com					
Regis Corp Pro-Cuts Div 7201 Metro Blvd	Minneapolis	MN	55439	952-947-7777	
TF: 877-857-2070 ■ *Web:* www.procuts.com					
Regis Corp Regis Hairstylists Div 7201 Metro Blvd	Minneapolis	MN	55439	952-947-7777	
TF: 877-857-2070 ■ *Web:* www.regissalons.com					
Regis Corp SmartStyle Div 7201 Metro Blvd	Minneapolis	MN	55439	952-947-7777	
TF: 877-857-2070 ■ *Web:* www.smartstyle.com					
Regis Corp Trade Secret Div 7201 Metro Blvd	Minneapolis	MN	55439	952-947-7777	
TF: 888-888-7778 ■ *Web:* www.regiscorp.com					
Regis Group Inc, The 102 N King St	Leesburg	VA	20176	703-777-2233	
Web: www.regisgroup.com					
Retreat Spa & Salon LLC 4246 Washington Rd	Evans	GA	30809	706-364-8292	
Web: retreatspaandsalon.com					
Rick Engineering Co 5620 Friars Rd	San Diego	CA	92110	619-291-0707	
Web: www.rickengineering.com					
Rios Golden Cut Inc 121 N Pk Blvd	San Antonio	TX	78204	210-227-4996	
Rip Curl Inc 3030 Airway Ave	Costa Mesa	CA	92626	714-422-3642	
Web: www.ripcurl.com					
Rita Hazan Salon 720 Fifth Ave Fl 11	New York	NY	10019	212-586-4343	
Web: www.ritahazan.com					
River City Engineering 1011 W County Line Rd	New Braunfels	TX	78130	830-626-3588	626-3601
Web: www.rcetx.com					
Robert Jeffrey Hair Studio 3434 N Halsted St	Chicago	IL	60657	773-525-8800	
Web: robertjeffrey.com					
Rocco Altobelli Inc 14301 Burnsville Pkwy W	Burnsville	MN	55306	952-707-1900	
Web: www.roccoaltobelli.com					
RZ & Company Inc 6602 Odana Rd	Madison	WI	53719	608-827-7979	
Web: rzco.com					
Sagittarius Hair Designs Ltd 1136 Conrad Ct	Hagerstown	MD	21740	301-797-8008	
Web: www.sagittariussalon.com					
Salon Service Group Inc 1859 W Arbor Ct	Springfield	MO	65807	800-933-5733	
Web: www.salonservicegroup.com					
Salon Services & Supplies Inc 740 SW 34th St	Renton	WA	98057	425-251-8840	
Web: www.salonservicesnw.com					
Scentisphere LLC 97 Old Rt 6	Carmel	NY	10512	845-225-3600	
Web: www.oscom.net					
Shelter Mortgage Company LLC 4000 W Brown Deer Rd	Milwaukee	WI	53209	414-362-4000	
Web: www.shelter-mortgage.com					
Sport Clips Inc 110 Briarwood Dr	Georgetown	TX	78628	512-869-1201	
TF: 800-872-4247 ■ *Web:* www.sportclips.com					
Steiner Leisure Ltd 770 S Dixie Hwy Ste 200	Coral Gables	FL	33146	305-358-9002	372-9310
NASDAQ: STNR ■ *Web:* www.steinerleisure.com					
Stewart School of Cosmetology 604 NW Ave	Sioux Falls	SD	57104	605-336-2775	357-0288
TF: 800-537-2625 ■ *Web:* www.stewartschool.com					
Studio 10 Hair Design 7015 W Tidwell Rd Ste G103	Houston	TX	77092	713-895-8070	
Web: www.wilcrest.com					
Studio Booth LLC 6343 Penn Ave	Pittsburgh	PA	15206	412-362-6684	
Web: studio-booth.com					
Sue Kolve'S Salon & Day Spa 230 Main St	Onalaska	WI	54650	608-784-2363	
Web: suekolves.com					

	City	State	Zip	Phone	Fax
Sugar House Day Spa & Salon 111 N Alfred St *Web:* sugarhousedayspa.com	Alexandria	VA	22314	703-549-9940	
Supercuts 7201 Metro Blvd **Fax Area Code:* 952 ■ *TF:* 877-857-2070 ■ *Web:* www.supercuts.com	Minneapolis	MN	55439	877-857-2070	947-7300*
Theraderm and Therapon Skin Health Inc 2081 Dime Dr *Web:* www.therapon.com	Springdale	AR	72764	479-751-7345	
Toni & Guy USA Inc 2311 Midway Rd **Fax Area Code:* 972 ■ *TF:* 800-256-9391 ■ *Web:* www.toniguy.com	Carrollton	TX	75006	800-256-9391	931-1999*
Total Beauty Media Inc 3420 Ocean Park Blvd Ste 3050 *Web:* www.totalbeautymedia.com	Santa Monica	CA	90405	310-399-7400	
Tutta Bella Hair Salon 17400 Monterey St Ste 1e *Web:* tuttabellasalon.com	Morgan Hill	CA	95037	408-778-6949	
Twizzle Hair Studio 2670 Fourth Ave W *Web:* twizzle.ca	Vancouver	BC	V6K1P7	604-738-1733	
Ultraderm Medspa 3311 Mission Dr *Web:* www.garnermd.com	Santa Cruz	CA	95065	831-475-4315	
Universal Companies Inc 18260 Oak Park Dr *Web:* www.universalcompanies.com	Abingdon	VA	24210	276-466-9110	
Victoria & Albert Hair Studio 10715 Charter Dr Ste 160 *Web:* www.victoriaandalberthair.com	Columbia	MD	21044	410-992-3000	
Vidal Sassoon Salons 399 Boylston St *Web:* www.sassoon.com	Boston	MA	02116	617-536-5496	
Visible Changes Inc 1303 Campbell Rd *Web:* www.visiblechanges.com	Houston	TX	77055	713-984-8800	984-2632
Xanadu Salon & Spa 3745 Park Ave W *Web:* xanadusalonspa.com	Ontario	OH	44903	419-529-6173	
Xpres Spa 3 East 54th St 9th Fl *Web:* www.xpresspa.com	New York	NY	10022	212-750-9595	
Z Salon & Spa Inc 9407 Shelbyville Rd *Web:* www.zsalon.com	Louisville	KY	40222	502-426-2226	
Ziba Beauty Center Inc 17832 Pioneer Blvd *Web:* zibabeauty.com	Artesia	CA	90701	562-402-5131	

78 BETTER BUSINESS BUREAUS - CANADA

	City	Prov	Postal	Phone	Fax
Canadian Council of Better Business Bureaus Two St Clair Ave E *Web:* www.bbb.org	Toronto	ON	M4T2T5	416-644-4936	644-4945
Better Business Bureau of Eastern Ontario & the Outaouais Inc 700 Industrial Ave Unit 505	Ottawa	ON	K1G0Y9	613-237-4856	237-4878
Better Business Bureau of Quebec 1565 Boul de l'Avenir Ste 206 **Fax Area Code:* 450 ■ *Web:* www.occq-qcco.com	Laval	QC	H7S2N5	514-905-3893	663-6316*
Better Business Bureau of Saskatchewan 980 Albert St Ste 201 *Web:* bbb.org/saskatchewan	Regina	SK	S4R2P7	306-352-7601	565-6236
Better Business Bureau of Southern Alberta 7330 Fisher St SE Ste 350 *Web:* calgary.bbb.org	Calgary	AB	T2H2H8	403-531-8784	640-2514
Better Business Bureau of the Maritime Provinces 1888 Brunswick St Ste 805 *Web:* bbb.org/atlantic-provinces	Halifax	NS	B3J3J8	902-422-6581	429-6457
Better Business Bureau of Vancouver Island 220-1175 Cook St Ste 220 *TF:* 877-826-4222 ■ *Web:* bbb.org/vancouver-island	Victoria	BC	V8V4A1	250-386-6348	386-2367
Better Business Bureau Serving Central & Northern Alberta 16102 100 Ave NW *Web:* edmonton.bbb.org	Edmonton	AB	T5P0L3	780-482-2341	482-1150
Better Business Bureau Serving Mainland British Columbia 788 Beatty St Ste 404 *TF:* 888-803-1222 ■ *Web:* mbc.bbb.org	Vancouver	BC	V6B2M1	604-682-2711	681-1544
Better Business Bureau Serving Western Ontario 200 Queens Ave Ste 308 PO Box 2153 *TF:* 877-283-9222 ■ *Web:* bbb.org/western-ontario	London	ON	N6A3M8	519-673-3222	673-5966
Better Business Bureau Serving Windsor & Southwestern Ontario 880 Ouellette Ave Ste 302 *Web:* westernontario.bbb.org	Windsor	ON	N9A1C7	519-258-7222	
Better Business Bureau Serving Winnipeg & Manitoba 1030B Empress St *TF:* 800-385-3074 ■ *Web:* www.manitoba.bbb.org	Winnipeg	MB	R3G3H4	204-989-9010	989-9016

79 BETTER BUSINESS BUREAUS - US

SEE ALSO Consumer Interest Organizations p. 1768

	City	State	Zip	Phone	Fax
Better Business Bureau Online *Council of Better Business Bureaus, The* 4200 Wilson Blvd Ste 800 *TF:* 800-459-8875 ■ *Web:* www.bbb.org	Arlington	VA	22203	703-276-0100	525-8277
Better Business Bureau Heartland 11811 P St *TF:* 800-649-6814 ■ *Web:* bbb.org/nebraska	Omaha	NE	68137	402-391-7612	391-7535
Better Business Bureau In Alaska Oregon & Western Washington 341 W Tudor Rd Ste 209 *Web:* bbb.org/alaskaoregonwesternwashington	Anchorage	AK	99503	907-562-0704	644-5222
Better Business Bureau Inc 1000 Broadway Ste 625 *TF:* 866-411-2221 ■ *Web:* bbb.org/greater-san-francisco	Oakland	CA	94607	510-844-2000	844-2100
Better Business Bureau of Acadiana 4007 W Congress St Ste B *Web:* bbb.org/acadiana	Lafayette	LA	70506	337-981-3497	981-7559
Better Business Bureau of Alaska Oregon & Western Washington 1000 Stn Dr Ste 222 *Web:* bbb.org/alaskaoregonwesternwashington	Dupont	WA	98327	206-431-2222	431-2200
Better Business Bureau of Ark-La-Tex 401 Edwards St Ste 135 *TF:* 800-372-4222 ■ *Web:* bbb.org/shreveport	Shreveport	LA	71101	318-222-7575	222-7576
Better Business Bureau of Arkansas 12521 Kanis Rd *Web:* bbb.org/	Little Rock	AR	72211	501-664-7274	664-0024
Better Business Bureau of Asheville/Western North Carolina 112 Executive Pk *Web:* bbb.org/asheville	Asheville	NC	28801	828-253-2392	252-5039
Better Business Bureau of Brazos Valley & Deep East Texas 418 Tarrow *Web:* bbb.org/bryan	College Station	TX	77840	979-260-2222	846-0276
Better Business Bureau of Canton Region/West Virginia 1434 Cleveland Ave NW *TF:* 800-362-0494 ■ *Web:* bbb.org/canton	Canton	OH	44703	330-454-9401	456-8957
Better Business Bureau of Central & Eastern Kentucky 1460 Newtown Pk *TF:* 800-866-6668 ■ *Web:* bbb.org/lexington	Lexington	KY	40511	859-259-1008	259-1639
Better Business Bureau of Central & South Central Texas 1005 La Posada Dr *Web:* bbb.org/central-texas	Austin	TX	78752	512-445-2096	445-2096
Better Business Bureau of Central Alabama & the Wiregrass Area 4750 Woodmere Blvd Ste D *Web:* bbb.org/csal	Montgomery	AL	36106	334-273-5530	
Better Business Bureau of Central Alabama & the Wiregrass Area Dothan Branch 1971 S Brannon Stand Rd *Web:* bbb.org/csal	Dothan	AL	36305	334-794-0492	794-0659
Better Business Bureau of Central East Texas 3600 Old Bullard Rd Bldg 1 *TF:* 800-443-0131 ■ *Web:* bbb.org/east-texas	Tyler	TX	75701	903-581-5704	534-8644
Better Business Bureau of Central East Texas Longview Branch 102 Commander Ste 7 *TF:* 800-443-0131 ■ *Web:* bbb.org/east-texas	Longview	TX	75605	903-758-3222	534-8644
Better Business Bureau of Central Florida 1600 S Grant St *Web:* bbb.org/central-florida	Longwood	FL	32750	407-621-3300	786-2625
Better Business Bureau of Central Georgia 277 ML King Jr Blvd Ste 102 *Web:* bbb.org/central-georgia	Macon	GA	31201	478-742-7999	742-8191
Better Business Bureau of Central Illinois 112 Harrison St *TF:* 800-763-4222 ■ *Web:* bbb.org/central-illinois	Peoria	IL	61602	309-688-3741	681-7290
Better Business Bureau of Central Indiana 151 N Delaware St *TF:* 866-463-9222 ■ *Web:* bbb.org/indy	Indianapolis	IN	46204	317-488-2222	488-2224
Better Business Bureau of Central Louisiana & Ark-La-Tex 5220-C Rue Verdun *TF General:* 800-372-4222 ■ *Web:* bbb.org/shreveport	Alexandria	LA	71303	318-473-4494	473-8906
Better Business Bureau of Central New England & Northeast Connecticut 340 Main St Ste 802 *Web:* bbb.org/central-western-massachusetts	Worcester	MA	01608	508-755-3340	754-4158
Better Business Bureau of Central North Carolina 3608 W Friendly Ave *Web:* bbb.org/greensboro	Greensboro	NC	27410	336-852-4240	852-7540
Better Business Bureau of Central Northeast Northwest & Southwest Arizona 4428 N 12th St *TF:* 877-291-6222 ■ *Web:* bbb.org/phoenix	Phoenix	AZ	85014	602-264-1721	263-0997
Better Business Bureau of Central Ohio 1169 Dublin Rd *TF:* 800-759-2400 ■ *Web:* bbb.org/centralohio	Columbus	OH	43215	614-486-6336	486-6631
Better Business Bureau of Central Oklahoma 17 S Dewey Ave *Web:* bbb.org/oklahoma-city	Oklahoma City	OK	73102	405-239-6081	235-5891
Better Business Bureau of Central Texas 445 Central TX Expy Ste 1 *Web:* bbb.org/central-texas	Harker Heights	TX	76548	512-445-2911	445-2096
Better Business Bureau of Central Virginia 720 Moorefield Pk Dr Ste 300 *Web:* bbb.org/richmond	Richmond	VA	23236	804-648-0016	320-0248
Better Business Bureau of Chicago & Northern Illinois 330 N Wabash Ave Ste 2006 *Web:* bbb.org/chicago	Chicago	IL	60611	312-832-0500	832-9985
Better Business Bureau of Cincinnati 7 W Seventh St Ste 1600 *Web:* bbb.org/cincinnati	Cincinnati	OH	45202	513-421-3015	621-0907
Better Business Bureau of Coastal North & South Carolina 314 Laurel St Ste 203 *Web:* bbb.org/myrtle-beach	Conway	SC	29526	843-488-0238	488-0998
Better Business Bureau of Connecticut 94 S Tpke Rd *Web:* bbb.org/connecticut	Wallingford	CT	06492	203-269-2700	294-3694
Better Business Bureau of Dayton/Miami Valley 15 W Fourth St Ste 300 *Web:* bbb.org/dayton	Dayton	OH	45402	937-222-5825	222-3338
Better Business Bureau of Delaware 60 Reads Way *Web:* bbb.org/delaware	New Castle	DE	19720	302-221-5255	221-5265
Better Business Bureau of Detroit & Eastern Michigan 26777 Central Pk Blvd Ste 100 *Web:* bbb.org/detroit	Southfield	MI	48076	248-223-9400	356-5135
Better Business Bureau of Eastern Massachusetts Maine Rhode Island & Vermont 290 Donald Lynch Blvd Ste 102 *TF:* 800-422-2811 ■ *Web:* bbb.org/boston	Marlborough	MA	01752	508-652-4800	652-4820
Better Business Bureau of Eastern Missouri & Southern Illinois 211 N Broadway Ste 2060 *Web:* bbb.org/stlouis	Saint Louis	MO	63102	314-645-3300	645-2666
Better Business Bureau of Eastern North Carolina 5540 Munford Rd Ste 130 *Web:* bbb.org/raleigh-durham	Raleigh	NC	27612	919-277-4222	277-4221
Better Business Bureau of Eastern Oklahoma 1722 S Carson Ave Ste 3200 *Web:* bbb.org/tulsa	Tulsa	OK	74119	918-492-1266	492-1276

				Phone	Fax

Better Business Bureau of Eastern Pennsylvania
1880 JFK Blvd Ste 1330 .... Philadelphia PA 19103 215-985-9313 563-4907
Web: bbb.org/washington-dc-eastern-pa

Better Business Bureau of El Paso
720 Arizona Ave .... El Paso TX 79902 915-577-0191 577-0209
Web: bbb.org/elpaso

Better Business Bureau of Four Corners & Grand Junction Colorado
308 N Locke Ave .... Farmington NM 87401 505-326-6501

Better Business Bureau of Greater East Tennessee
255 N Peters Rd Ste A PO Box 31377 .... Knoxville TN 37923 865-692-1600 692-1590
Web: bbb.org/knoxville

Better Business Bureau of Greater Iowa Quad Cities & Sioux Land Region
505 Fifth Ave Ste 950 .... Des Moines IA 50309 515-243-8137 243-2227
Web: www.iowa.bbb.org

Better Business Bureau of Greater Kansas City
8080 Ward Pkwy Ste 401 .... Kansas City MO 64114 816-421-7800 472-5442
TF: 877-606-0695 ■ *Web:* bbb.org/kansas-city

Better Business Bureau of Greater Maryland
502 S Sharp St Ste 1200 .... Baltimore MD 21201 410-347-3990 347-3936
Web: bbb.org/greater-maryland

Better Business Bureau of Greater New Orleans
710 Baronne St Ste C .... New Orleans LA 70113 504-581-6222 524-9110
Web: bbb.org/new-orleans

Better Business Bureau of Hampton Roads
586 Virginian Dr .... Norfolk VA 23505 757-531-1300 531-1388
Web: bbb.org/norfolk

Better Business Bureau of Hawaii
1132 Bishop St Ste 615 .... Honolulu HI 96813 808-536-6956 628-3970
TF: 877-222-6551 ■ *Web:* bbb.org/hawaii

Better Business Bureau of Kansas Inc
345 N Riverview St Ste 720 .... Wichita KS 67203 316-263-3146 263-3063
TF: 800-856-2417 ■ *Web:* bbb.org/nebraska

Better Business Bureau of Louisville Southern Indiana & Western Kentucky
844 S Fourth St .... Louisville KY 40203 502-583-6546 589-9940
TF: 800-388-2222 ■ *Web:* bbb.org/louisville

Better Business Bureau of Maine
290 Donald Lynch Blvd Ste 102 .... Marlborough MA 01752 508-652-4800 652-4820
TF: 800-422-2811 ■ *Web:* boston.bbb.org

Better Business Bureau of Metro Washington DC & Eastern Pennsylvania
1411 K St NW Ste 1000 .... Washington DC 20005 202-393-8000 393-1198
Web: bbb.org/washington-dc-eastern-pa

Better Business Bureau of Metropolitan Atlanta
503 Oak Pl Ste 590 .... Atlanta GA 30349 404-766-0875 768-1085
Web: bbb.org/atlanta

Better Business Bureau of Metropolitan Dallas & Northeast Texas
1601 Elm St Ste 3838 .... Dallas TX 75201 214-220-2000 740-0321
Web: bbb.org/dallas

Better Business Bureau of Metropolitan Houston
1333 W Loop S Ste 1200 .... Houston TX 77027 713-868-9500 867-4947
Web: bbb.org/houston

Better Business Bureau of Metropolitan New York
257 Pk Ave S .... New York NY 10010 212-533-6200 477-4912
Web: bbb.org/new-york-city

Better Business Bureau of Middle Tennessee Inc
201 Fourth Ave N Ste 100 .... Nashville TN 37219 615-242-4222 250-4245
Web: bbb.org/nashville

Better Business Bureau of Minnesota & North Dakota
2706 Gannon Rd .... Saint Paul MN 55116 651-699-1111 695-2488
Web: bbb.org/minnesota

Better Business Bureau of New Jersey
1700 Whitehorse-Hamilton Sq Rd Ste D-5 .... Trenton NJ 08690 609-588-0808 588-0546
TF: 888-494-4009 ■ *Web:* bbb.org/new-jersey

Better Business Bureau of North Central Texas
4245 Kemp Blvd Ste 900 .... Wichita Falls TX 76308 940-691-1172 691-1175
Web: bbb.org/wichita-falls

Better Business Bureau of Northeast California
3075 Beacon Blvd .... West Sacramento CA 95691 916-443-6843 443-0376
Web: bbb.org/northeast-california

Better Business Bureau of Northeast Florida & The Southeast Atlantic
4417 Beach Blvd Ste 202 .... Jacksonville FL 32207 904-721-2288 428-6249*
**Fax Area Code:* 818 ■ *TF:* 800-713-6661 ■ *Web:* bbb.org/north-east-florida

Better Business Bureau of Northeast Kansas
345 N. Riverview St Ste 720 .... Wichita KS 67203 316-263-3146

Better Business Bureau of Northeast Louisiana
1900 N 18th St Ste 411 .... Monroe LA 71201 318-387-4600
TF: 800-960-7756 ■ *Web:* bbb.org/north-east-louisiana

Better Business Bureau of Northeast Ohio
2800 Euclid Ave Fourth Fl .... Cleveland OH 44115 216-241-7678 861-6365
TF: 800-233-0361 ■ *Web:* bbb.org/cleveland

Better Business Bureau of Northeastern & Central Pennsylvania
1054 Oak St .... Scranton PA 18508 570-342-5100 342-1282
Web: bbb.org/washington-dc-eastern-pa

Better Business Bureau of Northern Alabama
107 Lincoln St .... Huntsville AL 35804 256-533-1640 533-1177
Web: bbb.org/northern-alabama

Better Business Bureau of Northern Colorado & East Central Wyoming
8020 S County Rd 5 Ste 100 .... Fort Collins CO 80528 970-484-1348 221-1239
TF: 800-564-0371 ■ *Web:* bbb.org/wyoming-and-northern-colorado

Better Business Bureau of Northern Indiana
4011 Parnell Ave .... Fort Wayne IN 46805 260-423-4433 423-3301
Web: bbb.org/northernindiana

Better Business Bureau of Northern Nevada
4834 Sparks Blvd Ste 102 .... Sparks NV 89436 775-322-0657 322-8163
Web: bbb.org/reno

Better Business Bureau of Northwest Florida
912 E Gadsden St .... Pensacola FL 32501 850-429-0002 429-0006
Web: bbb.org/northwest-florida

Better Business Bureau of Northwest Indiana
7863 Broadway Ste 124 .... Merrillville IN 46410 260-423-4433 884-2123*
**Fax Area Code:* 219 ■ *Web:* bbb.org/northernindiana

Better Business Bureau of Northwest North Carolina
500 W Fifth St Ste 202 .... Winston-Salem NC 27101 336-725-8348 777-3727
TF: 800-777-8348 ■ *Web:* bbb.org/northwestern-north-carolina

Better Business Bureau of Northwest Ohio & Southeast Michigan
7668 King's Pt Rd .... Toledo OH 43617 419-531-3116 578-6001
TF: 800-743-4222 ■ *Web:* bbb.org/toledo

Better Business Bureau of Rockford
330 North Wabash Ave Ste 3120 .... Chicago IL 60611 312-832-0500 832-9985
TF: 800-955-5100 ■ *Web:* www.bbb.org/chicago

Better Business Bureau of San Diego & Imperial Counties
5050 Murphy Canyon Rd Ste 110 .... San Diego CA 92123 858-637-6199 496-2141
Web: bbb.org/sdoc

Better Business Bureau of South Alabama
960 S Schillinger Rd Ste I .... Mobile AL 36695 251-433-5494 438-3191
Web: bbb.org/csal

Better Business Bureau of South Central Louisiana
748 Main St .... Baton Rouge LA 70802 225-346-5222 346-1029
Web: bbb.org/baton-rouge

Better Business Bureau of South Texas
1333 W Loop S Ste 1200 .... Houston TX 77027 713-868-9500 867-4947
Web: bbb.org/houston

Better Business Bureau of Southeast Florida & the Caribbean
4411 Beacon Cir Ste 4 .... West Palm Beach FL 33407 561-842-1918 845-7234
TF: 866-966-7226 ■ *Web:* bbb.org/south-east-florida

Better Business Bureau of Southeast Tennessee & Northwest Georgia
508 N Market St .... Chattanooga TN 37405 423-266-6144 267-1924
TF: 800-548-4456 ■ *Web:* bbb.org/chattanooga

Better Business Bureau of Southeast Texas
550 Fannin St Ste 100 .... Beaumont TX 77701 409-835-5348 838-6858
TF: 800-685-7650 ■ *Web:* bbb.org/southeast-texas

Better Business Bureau of Southern Arizona
434 S Williams Blvd Ste 102 .... Tucson AZ 85711 520-888-5353 888-6262
Web: bbb.org/tucson

Better Business Bureau of Southern Colorado
25 N Wahsatch Ave .... Colorado Springs CO 80903 719-636-1155 636-5078
Web: bbb.org/southern-colorado

Better Business Bureau of Southern Nebraska
3633 'O' St Ste 1 .... Lincoln NE 68510 402-436-2345 476-8221
Web: bbb.org/nebraska

Better Business Bureau of Southern Nevada
6040 S Jones Blvd .... Las Vegas NV 89118 702-320-4500 320-4560
Web: bbb.org/southern-nevada

Better Business Bureau of Southern Piedmont Carolinas
13860 Ballantyne Corporate Pl Ste 225 .... Charlotte NC 28277 704-927-8611 927-8615
Web: bbb.org/charlotte

Better Business Bureau of Southwest Georgia
PO Box 2587 .... Columbus GA 31902 706-324-0712 324-2181
TF: 800-768-4222 ■ *Web:* bbb.org/columbus-georgia

Better Business Bureau of Southwest Idaho & Eastern Oregon
1200 N Curtis Rd PO Box 9817 .... Boise ID 83706 208-342-4649 342-5116
TF: 800-218-1001 ■ *Web:* bbb.org/snakeriver

Better Business Bureau of Southwest Louisiana Inc
2309 E Prien Lk Rd .... Lake Charles LA 70601 337-478-6253 474-8981
TF: 800-542-7085 ■ *Web:* bbb.org/lakecharles

Better Business Bureau of Southwest Missouri
430 S Glenstone Ave .... Springfield MO 65802 417-862-4222 869-5544
Web: bbb.org/southwestern-missouri

Better Business Bureau of the Abilene Area
3300 S 14th St Ste 307 .... Abilene TX 79605 325-691-1533 691-0309
Web: bbb.org/abilene

Better Business Bureau of the Akron Inc
222 W Market St .... Akron OH 44303 330-253-4590 253-6249
TF: 800-825-8887 ■ *Web:* bbb.org/akron

Better Business Bureau of the Bakersfield Area
1601 H St Ste 101 .... Bakersfield CA 93301 661-322-2074 322-8318
TF: 800-675-8118 ■ *Web:* bbb.org/central-california-inland-empire

Better Business Bureau of the Denver-Boulder Metro Area
1020 Cherokee St .... Denver CO 80204 303-758-2100 758-8321
TF: 800-356-6333 ■ *Web:* bbb.org/denver

Better Business Bureau of the Mid-Hudson
150 White Plains Rd Ste 107 .... Tarrytown NY 10591 914-333-0550 333-7519
Web: bbb.org/new-york-city

Better Business Bureau of the Mid-South
3693 Tyndale Dr .... Memphis TN 38125 901-759-1300 757-2997
TF: 800-222-8754 ■ *Web:* bbb.org/memphis

Better Business Bureau of the Permian Basin Area of West Texas
1005 La Posada Dr .... Austin TX 78752 432-563-1880 445-2096*
**Fax Area Code:* 512 ■ *Web:* www.bbb.org

Better Business Bureau of the San Angelo Area
3134 Executive Dr .... San Angelo TX 76904 325-949-2989 949-3514
Web: bbb.org/san-angelo

Better Business Bureau of the Santa Clara Valley San Benito Santa Cruz & Monterey Inc
1112 S Bascom Ave .... San Jose CA 95128 408-278-7400 278-7444
Web: bbb.org/losangelessiliconvalley

Better Business Bureau of the South Central Area
1800 NE Loop 410 Ste 400 .... San Antonio TX 78217 210-828-9441 828-3101
Web: bbb.org/central-texas

Better Business Bureau of the South Plains of Texas
3333 66th St .... Lubbock TX 79413 806-763-0459 744-9748
Web: bbb.org/south-plains-texas

Better Business Bureau of the Southeast Atlantic
6555 Abercorn St Ste 120 .... Savannah GA 31405 912-354-7521 354-5068
Web: bbb.org/north-east-florida

Better Business Bureau of the Southland Inc
315 N La Cadena Dr .... Colton CA 92324 909-825-7280 503-1890

Better Business Bureau of the Southwest
2625 Pennsylvania St NE Ste 2050 .... Albuquerque NM 87110 505-326-6501 346-0696
Web: bbb.org/new-mexico-southwest-colorado

Better Business Bureau of the Texas Panhandle
720 S Tyler St Ste B112 PO Box 1905 .... Amarillo TX 79101 806-379-6222 379-8206
Web: bbb.org/amarillo

Better Business Bureau of the Tri-Counties
PO Box 129 .... Santa Barbara CA 93102 805-963-8657 962-8557
Web: bbb.org/santa-barbara

Better Business Bureau of the Tri-Parish Area
801 Barrow St Ste 400 .... Houma LA 70360 985-868-3456
Web: bbb.org/new-orleans

Phone Fax

Better Business Bureau of Upstate New York
100 Bryant Woods S . . . . Amherst NY 14228 716-881-5222 883-5349
Web: bbb.org/upstate-new-york

Better Business Bureau of Utah
5673 S Redwood Rd Ste 22 . . . . Salt Lake City UT 84123 801-892-6009 892-6002
TF: 800-456-3907 ■ *Web:* bbb.org/utah

Better Business Bureau of West Central Ohio
219 N McDonel St . . . . Lima OH 45801 419-223-7010
Web: www.bbb.org/phoenix/businessreviews/betterbusinessbureaus/thebbbservingwestcentralohioinli-maoh97003194

Better Business Bureau of West Florida
2655 McCormick Dr . . . . Clearwater FL 33759 727-535-5522 539-6301
TF: 800-525-1447 ■ *Web:* bbb.org/west-florida

Better Business Bureau of West Georgia & East Alabama
PO Box 2587 . . . . Columbus GA 31902 706-324-0712 324-2181
TF: 800-768-4222 ■ *Web:* bbb.org/columbus-georgia

Better Business Bureau of Western Massachusetts
35 Ctr St Ste 203 . . . . Chicopee MA 01013 866-566-9222 594-2167*
**Fax Area Code:* 413 ■ *TF:* 866-566-9222 ■ *Web:* bbb.org/central-western-massachusetts

Better Business Bureau of Western Michigan
40 Pearl St NW Ste 354 . . . . Grand Rapids MI 49503 616-774-8236 774-2014
Web: bbb.org/western-michigan

Better Business Bureau of Western Pennsylvania
400 Holiday Dr Ste 220 . . . . Pittsburgh PA 15220 412-456-2700 922-8656
Web: bbb.org/pittsburgh

Better Business Bureau of Wisconsin
10101 W Greenfield Ave Ste 125 . . . . Milwaukee WI 53214 414-847-6000 302-0355
Web: bbb.org/wisconsin

Better Business Bureau Serving Central California
4201 W Shaw Ave Ste 107 . . . . Fresno CA 93722 559-222-8111 228-6518
TF: 800-675-8118 ■ *Web:* bbb.org/central-california-inland-empire

Better Business Bureau Serving Eastern Washington North Idaho & Montana Inc
152 S Jefferson St Ste 200 . . . . Spokane WA 99201 509-455-4200 838-1079
Web: www.bbb.org

Better Business Bureau Upstate South Carolina
408 N Church St Ste C . . . . Greenville SC 29601 864-242-5052 271-9802
Web: bbb.org/upstatesc

Tri-State Better Business Bureau
5401 Vogel Rd Ste 410 . . . . Evansville IN 47715 812-473-0202 473-3080
TF: 800-359-0979 ■ *Web:* bbb.org/evansville

80 BEVERAGES - MFR

SEE ALSO Breweries p. 1887; Water - Bottled p. 3294

80-1 Liquor - Mfr

Phone Fax

A. Smith Bowman Distillery
One Bowman Dr . . . . Fredericksburg VA 22408 540-373-4555 371-2236
Web: www.asmithbowman.com

Anheuser-Busch Cos Inc 1200 Lynch St . . . . Saint Louis MO 63118 314-577-3559 525-0810
TF: 800-379-2739 ■ *Web:* www.anheuser-busch.com

Bacardi USA Inc
2701 S Le Jeune Rd Ste 400 . . . . Coral Gables FL 33134 305-573-8511 573-7507*
**Fax:* Hum Res ■ *TF:* 800-222-2734 ■ *Web:* www.bacardi.com

Beam Inc 510 Lk Cook Rd . . . . Deerfield IL 60015 847-948-8888
Web: www.jimbeam.com

Black Prince Distillery Inc 691 Clifton Ave . . . . Clifton NJ 07011 973-365-2050 365-0746
Web: www.blackprincedistillery.com

City Brewing Company LLC 925 S Third St . . . . La Crosse WI 54601 608-785-4200 785-4300
Web: www.citybrewery.com

Diageo North America 801 Main Ave . . . . Norwalk CT 06851 203-229-2100
Web: www.diageo.com

Dickel George A Co 1950 Cascade Hollow Rd . . . . Tullahoma TN 37388 931-857-4110
Web: www.dickel.com

Four Roses Distillery LLC
1224 Bonds Mill Rd . . . . Lawrenceburg KY 40342 502-839-3436 839-8338
Web: www.fourrosesbourbon.com

Gekkeikan Sake USA Inc 1136 Sibley St . . . . Folsom CA 95630 916-985-3111 985-2221
Web: www.gekkeikan-sake.com

Heavenhill Distilleries Inc
1064 Loretto Rd . . . . Bardstown KY 40004 502-348-3921 348-0162
Web: heavenhill.com

Jack Daniel Distillery 182 Lynchburg Hwy . . . . Lynchburg TN 37352 931-759-6357
Web: www.jackdaniels.com

Jacquin Charles et Cie Inc
2633 Trenton Ave . . . . Philadelphia PA 19125 215-425-9300

Laird & Co One LaiRd Rd . . . . Scobeyville NJ 07724 732-542-0312 542-2244
TF: 877-438-5247 ■ *Web:* www.lairdandcompany.com

Maker's Mark Distillery Inc
3350 Burke Spring Rd . . . . Loretto KY 40037 270-865-2881 865-2196
Web: www.makersmark.com

McCormick Distilling Co Inc 1 McCormick Ln . . . . Weston MO 64098 816-640-2276 640-3082
Web: www.mccormickdistilling.com

Montebello Brands Inc
1919 Willow Spring Rd . . . . Baltimore MD 21222 410-282-8800 282-8809

Pernod Ricard USA 100 Manhattanville Rd . . . . Purchase NY 10577 914-848-4800 539-4550
TF: 800-847-5949 ■ *Web:* www.pernod-ricard-usa.com

Sunrich LLC 3824 SW 93rd St PO Box 128 . . . . Hope MN 56046 507-451-6030 451-8201
TF: 800-297-5997 ■ *Web:* www.sunrich.com

Takara Sake USA Inc 708 Addison St . . . . Berkeley CA 94710 510-540-8250 486-8758
Web: takarasake.com

Walker MS Inc 20 Third Ave . . . . Somerville MA 02143 617-776-6700 776-5808
TF: 800-528-2787 ■ *Web:* www.mswalker.com

80-2 Soft Drinks - Mfr

Phone Fax

Adirondack Beverages Inc 701 Corporations Pk . . . . Scotia NY 12302 518-370-3621 370-3762
Web: www.adirondackbeverages.com

American Beverage Corp 1 Daily Way . . . . Verona PA 15147 412-828-9020 828-3462
Web: www.ambev.com

Classic Distributing & Beverage Group Inc
120 N Puente Ave . . . . City Of Industry CA 91746 626-934-3700
Web: www.cdbginc.com

Coca-Cola Co One Coca-Cola Plz PO Box 1734 . . . . Atlanta GA 30313 404-676-2121 676-6792
NYSE: KO ■ *TF:* 800-438-2653 ■ *Web:* us.coca-cola.com

Cosco International Inc
1633 Sands Pl SE Cumberland Business Pk . . . . Marietta GA 30067 770-303-0797 303-0795
Web: www.coscous.com

Cott Corp 6525 Viscount Rd . . . . Mississauga ON L4V1H6 905-672-1900 881-1926*
NYSE: COT ■ **Fax Area Code:* 813 ■ *TF:* 888-378-4361 ■ *Web:* www.cott.com

Crystal Rock Holdings Inc
1050 Buckingham St . . . . Watertown CT 06795 860-945-0661 274-0397
NYSE: AMEX ■ *TF:* 800-525-0070 ■ *Web:* www.crystalrock.com

Davis Beverage Group 1530-A Bobali Dr . . . . Harrisburg PA 17104 717-914-1295

Double Cola Company USA
537 Market St Ste 100 . . . . Chattanooga TN 37402 423-267-5691 267-0793
Web: double-cola.com

Dr Pepper/Seven-Up Inc 5301 Legacy Dr . . . . Plano TX 75024 972-673-7000 673-7000*
**Fax:* Hum Res ■ *TF:* 800-696-5891 ■ *Web:* www.drpeppersnapplegroup.com

Faygo Beverages Inc 3579 Gratiot Ave . . . . Detroit MI 48207 313-925-1600
Web: www.faygo.com

Fiji Water Company LLC
11444 W Olympic Blvd Second Fl . . . . Los Angeles CA 90064 310-312-2850 312-2828
TF: 888-426-3454 ■ *Web:* www.fijiwater.com

Great Plains Coca-Cola Bottling Company Inc
600 N May Ave . . . . Oklahoma City OK 73107 405-280-2000 946-5739
TF: 800-753-2653 ■ *Web:* www.greatplainscocacola.com

Jones Soda Co 234 Ninth Ave N . . . . Seattle WA 98109 206-624-3357 624-6857
OTC: JSDA ■ *TF:* 800-690-6903 ■ *Web:* www.jonessoda.com

Middlesboro Coca-Cola Bottling Works Inc
1324 Cumberland Ave PO Box 1485 . . . . Middlesboro KY 40965 877-692-4679 248-1382*
**Fax Area Code:* 606 ■ *TF:* 800-442-0102 ■ *Web:* www.mccbw.com

Monarch Beverage Co
1123 Zonolite Rd NE Ste 10 . . . . Atlanta GA 30306 404-262-4040 612-3389*
**Fax Area Code:* 317 ■ *TF:* 800-408-3590 ■ *Web:* pageinsider.com

Oneta Co 1401 S Padre Island Dr . . . . Corpus Christi TX 78416 361-853-0123 853-5327
Web: www.onetacc.com

Pepsi-Cola Bottling Company of Yuba City Inc
750 Sutter St . . . . Yuba City CA 95991 530-673-9205
Web: pepsico.com

Polar Beverages Inc 1001 Southbridge St . . . . Worcester MA 01610 508-753-4300 793-0813
TF Cust Svc: 800-734-9800 ■ *Web:* www.polarbev.com

Primal Essence Inc 1351 Maulhardt Ave . . . . Oxnard CA 93030 805-981-2409
Web: www.primalessence.com

Procesadora Campo Fresco Inc PO Box 755 . . . . Santa Isabel PR 00757 787-845-4747 845-3490
Web: www.campofresco.com

Shasta Beverages Inc 26901 Industrial Blvd . . . . Hayward CA 94545 510-783-3200 783-8681*
**Fax:* Sales ■ *TF:* 800-834-9980 ■ *Web:* www.shastapop.com

Wallingford Coffee Mills Inc
11401 Rockfield Ct . . . . Cincinnati OH 45241 513-771-4570 771-3138
TF: 800-533-3690 ■ *Web:* www.wallingfordcoffee.com

White Rock Products Corp
141-07 20th Ave Ste 403 . . . . Whitestone NY 11357 718-746-3400 767-0413
TF: 800-969-7625 ■ *Web:* www.whiterockbeverages.com

80-3 Wines - Mfr

Phone Fax

A Bommarito Wines Inc
2827 S Brentwood Blvd . . . . Saint Louis MO 63144 314-961-8996
Web: www.abommaritowines.com

Ambiente Wine Importing Company Inc
2314 Rutland Dr Ste 205 . . . . Austin TX 78758 512-835-2299
Web: www.ambientewine.com

Barton Brescome Inc 69 Defco Park Rd . . . . North Haven CT 06473 203-239-4901
Web: www.brescomebarton.com

Beaulieu Vineyard 1960 St Helena Hwy . . . . Rutherford CA 94573 707-967-5233 963-5920
TF: 800-373-5896 ■ *Web:* www.bvwines.com

Benziger Family Winery
1883 London Ranch Rd . . . . Glen Ellen CA 95442 707-935-3000 935-3016
Web: www.benziger.com

Bronco Wine Co 6342 Bystrum Rd . . . . Ceres CA 95307 209-538-3131 538-2178
TF: 855-874-2394 ■ *Web:* classicwinesofcalifornia.com

Brotherhood Winery
100 Brotherhood Plz Dr PO Box 190 . . . . Washingtonville NY 10992 845-496-3661
Web: www.brotherhood-winery.com

Bully Hill Vineyards
8843 Greyton H Taylor Memorial Dr . . . . Hammondsport NY 14840 607-868-3610 868-3205
Web: www.bullyhill.com

Canandaigua Wine Company Inc
235 N Bloomfield Rd . . . . Canandaigua NY 14424 585-396-7600
TF: 888-659-7900 ■ *Web:* www.cbrands.com

Chateau Montelena Winery 1429 Tubbs Ln . . . . Calistoga CA 94515 707-942-5105 942-4221
Web: www.montelena.com

Chatham Imports Inc 245 Fifth Ave . . . . New York NY 10016 212-473-1100
Web: www.chathamimports.com

Classic Wines LLC 6489 E 39th Ave . . . . Denver CO 80207 303-825-1360
Web: www.classicwines.net

Clos du Bois 19410 Geyserville Ave . . . . Geyserville CA 95441 707-857-1651
TF Sales: 800-222-3189 ■ *Web:* www.closdubois.com

Columbia Crest Winery
Hwy 221 Columbia Crest Dr PO Box 231 . . . . Paterson WA 99345 509-875-4227 415-3657*
**Fax Area Code:* 425 ■ *TF:* 888-309-9463 ■ *Web:* www.columbiacrest.com

Crossroad Vintners 4045 Vincennes Rd . . . . Indianapolis IN 46268 317-471-1038
Web: crossroadvintners.com

Diageo Chateau & Estate Wines Co
240 Gateway Rd W . . . . Napa CA 94558 707-299-2600 299-2777
Web: www.diageowines.com

	City	State	Zip	Phone	Fax
Dolce Winery Inc PO Box 327	Oakville	CA	94562	707-944-8868	944-2312
Web: www.dolcewine.com					
Domaine Chandon Inc One California Dr	Yountville	CA	94599	888-242-6366	944-1123*
**Fax Area Code:* 707 ■ *TF:* 888-242-6366 ■ *Web:* www.chandon.com					
Domaine Select Wine Estates LLC 555 Eighth Ave Ste 2302	New York	NY	10018	212-279-0799	
Web: www.domaineselect.com					
Dreyfus Ashby & Co 630 Third Ave 15th Fl	New York	NY	10017	212-818-0770	
Web: www.dreyfusashby.com					
F Korbel & Bros Inc 13250 River Rd	Guerneville	CA	95446	707-824-7000	869-2506
Web: www.korbel.com					
Franciscan Estates 1178 Galleron Rd	Saint Helena	CA	94574	707-967-3830	396-7831*
**Fax Area Code:* 585 ■ *TF:* 800-529-9463 ■ *Web:* www.franciscan.com					
Freixenet USA 967 Broadway	Sonoma	CA	95476	707-996-4981	996-0720
Web: www.freixenetusa.com					
Garvey Wholesale Beverage Inc 2542 San Gabriel Blvd	Rosemead	CA	91770	626-280-5244	
Web: garveywholesalebeverage.com					
Giumarra Vineyards Corp 1601 E Olympic Blvd Bldg 400	Los Angeles	CA	93220	213-627-2900	628-4878
Web: giumarra.com					
Hogue Cellars 2800 Lee Rd	Prosser	WA	99350	800-565-9779	786-4580*
**Fax Area Code:* 509 ■ *TF:* 800-565-9779 ■ *Web:* www.hoguecellars.com					
i2c Inc 1300 Island Dr Ste 105	Redwood City	CA	94065	650-593-5400	
Web: www.i2cinc.com					
Imperial Brands Inc 11505 Fairchild Gardens Ave Ste 204	Palm Beach Gardens	FL	33410	561-624-5662	
Web: www.ibrandsinc.com					
Jarboe Sales Co 6833 E Reading Pl	Tulsa	OK	74115	918-836-2511	
Web: www.jarboesales.com					
Jefferson Vineyards LP 1353 Thmas Jefferson Pkwy	Charlottesville	VA	22902	434-977-3042	
Web: www.jeffersonvineyards.com					
Jwsieg Wines 1180 Seminole Trl Ste 290	Charlottesville	VA	22901	434-244-5300	
Web: www.jwsiegwines.com					
Kendall-Jackson Wine Estates Ltd 425 Aviation Blvd	Santa Rosa	CA	95403	707-544-4000	544-4013
TF: 800-769-3649 ■ *Web:* www.kj.com					
Kysela Pere Et Fils Ltd 331 Victory Rd	Winchester	VA	22602	540-722-9228	
TF: 877-492-7917 ■ *Web:* www.kysela.com					
Laetitia Vineyards & Winery Inc 453 Laetitia Vineyard Dr	Arroyo Grande	CA	93420	805-481-1772	481-6920
TF: 888-809-8463 ■ *Web:* www.laetitiawine.com					
Louis M Martini Winery 254 S St Helena Hwy	Saint Helena	CA	94574	866-549-2582	963-8750*
**Fax Area Code:* 707 ■ *TF:* 866-549-2582 ■ *Web:* www.louismartini.com					
Magnotta Winery Corp 271 Chrislea Rd	Vaughan	ON	L4L8N6	905-738-9463	738-5551
TF: 800-461-9463 ■ *Web:* www.magnotta.com					
Major Brands Inc 6701 SW Ave	St Louis	MO	63143	314-645-1843	
Web: www.majorbrands.com					
Meier's Wine Cellars Inc 6955 Plainfield Rd	Cincinnati	OH	45236	513-891-2900	891-6370
Web: www.meierswinecellars.com					
Mendocino Wine Co 501 PaRducci Rd	Ukiah	CA	95482	707-463-5350	462-7260
TF: 800-362-9463 ■ *Web:* www.mendocinowineco.com					
MHW Ltd 1129 Northern Blvd Ste 312	Manhasset	NY	11030	516-869-9170	
Web: www.mhwltd.com					
Michel-schlumberger Partners LP 4155 Wine Creek Rd	Healdsburg	CA	95448	707-433-7427	433-0444
TF: 800-447-3060 ■ *Web:* www.michelschlumberger.com					
Monsieur Touton Selections of Massachusetts Ltd 25 Industrial Way Ste 6	Wilmington	MA	01887	978-657-0405	
Web: www.mtouton.com					
Newlands Systems Inc 602-30731 Simpson Rd	Abbotsford	BC	V2T6Y7	604-855-4890	855-8826
Web: nsibrew.com					
Noble Wines Ltd 9860 40th Ave S	Seattle	WA	98118	206-326-5274	
Web: www.noblewinesltd.com					
Old Mill Winery 403 S Broadway	Geneva	OH	44041	800-227-6972	466-4417*
**Fax Area Code:* 440 ■ *TF:* 800-227-6972 ■ *Web:* www.ohiowines.org					
Opici Import Co 25 Deboer Dr	Glen Rock	NJ	07452	201-689-1200	
Web: www.opici.com					
Ozeki Sake (USA) Inc 249 Hillcrest Rd	Hollister	CA	95023	831-637-9217	637-0953
Web: www.ozekisake.com					
Pine Ridge Winery LLC 5901 Silverado Trail	Napa	CA	94558	800-575-9777	
TF: 800-575-9777 ■ *Web:* www.pineridgevineyards.com					
Ravenswood Winery Inc 18701 Gehricke Rd	Sonoma	CA	95476	888-669-4679	
TF: 888-669-4679 ■ *Web:* www.ravenswoodwinery.com					
Raymond Vineyard 849 Zinfandel Ln	Saint Helena	CA	94574	707-963-6941	
TF: 800-525-2659 ■ *Web:* www.raymondvineyards.com					
Renault Winery Resort 72 N Bremen Ave	Egg Harbor City	NJ	08215	609-965-2111	
Web: www.renaultwinery.com					
Roanoke Valley Wine Co 1250 Intervale	Salem	VA	24153	540-444-4440	
Web: rvwc.com					
Robert Mondavi Co 7801 St Helena Hwy	Oakville	CA	94562	707-226-1395	
TF: 888-766-6328 ■ *Web:* www.robertmondaviwinery.com					
Rodney Strong Vineyards 11455 Old Redwood Hwy	Healdsburg	CA	95448	707-431-1533	
TF: 800-678-4763 ■ *Web:* www.rodneystrong.com					
Royal Wine Corp 63 Le Fante Ln	Bayonne	NJ	07002	201-437-9131	388-8444*
**Fax Area Code:* 718 ■ *Web:* www.royalwine.com					
Sebastiani Vineyards Inc 389 Fourth St E	Sonoma	CA	95476	707-933-3230	933-3370
TF: 855-232-2338 ■ *Web:* www.sebastiani.com					
Trefethen Vineyards Winery Inc 1160 Oak Knoll Ave	Napa	CA	94558	707-255-7700	255-0793
TF: 866-895-7696 ■ *Web:* www.trefethen.com					
Tryon Distributing Company LLC 4701 Stockholm Ct	Charlotte	NC	28273	704-334-0849	
Web: www.tryondist.com					
Vie-Del Co 11903 S Chestnut	Fresno	CA	93725	559-834-2525	834-1348
Warner Vineyards Inc 706 S Kalamazoo St	Paw Paw	MI	49079	269-657-3165	
TF: 800-756-5357 ■ *Web:* warnerwines.com					
Weatherford Laboratories Inc 8845 Fallbrook Dr	Houston	TX	77064	832-237-4000	
Web: www.weatherfordlabs.com					
Weibel Vineyards One Winemaster Way	Lodi	CA	95240	209-365-9463	365-9469
TF: 800-932-9463 ■ *Web:* www.weibel.com					
Willamette Valley Vineyards Inc 8800 Enchanted Way SE	Turner	OR	97392	503-588-9463	588-8894
NASDAQ: WVVI ■ *TF Sales:* 800-344-9463 ■ *Web:* www.wvv.com					
Wilson Daniels Ltd 1201 Dowdell Ln	St Helena	CA	94574	707-963-9661	
Web: www.wilsondaniels.com					
WineCommune LLC 7305 Edgewater Dr Ste D	Oakland	CA	94621	510-632-5300	
Web: www.winecommune.com					

81 BEVERAGES - WHOL

81-1 Beer & Ale - Whol

	City	State	Zip	Phone	Fax
All State Beverage Co 130 Sixth St	Montgomery	AL	36104	334-265-0507	263-2367
Web: www.allstatebeverage.com					
Allentown Beverage Company Inc 1249 N Quebec St	Allentown	PA	18109	610-432-4581	821-8311
Web: allentownbeverage.com					
Anheuser-Busch, Inc., 900 John St	West Henrietta	NY	14586	585-427-0090	
Web: www.lakebeverage.com					
Arkansas Distributing Company LLC 800 E Barton Ave	West Memphis	AR	72301	870-735-3506	735-0052
TF: 877-735-3506					
Associated Distributors LLC 401 Woodlake Dr	Chesapeake	VA	23320	757-424-6300	424-4616
TF: 800-308-2600					
Atlas Distributing Corp 44 Southbridge St	Auburn	MA	01501	508-791-6221	791-0812
TF: 800-649-6221 ■ *Web:* www.atlasdistributing.com					
Banko Beverage Co 5001 Crackersport Rd	Allentown	PA	18104	610-434-0147	
TF General: 800-322-9295					
Beauchamp Distributing Co 1911 S Santa Fe Ave	Compton	CA	90221	310-639-5320	537-8641
TF: 800-734-5102 ■ *Web:* www.beauchampdist.com					
Bergseth Bros Co 501 23rd St N	Fargo	ND	58102	701-232-8818	232-8684
Web: bergsethbeer.com					
Birmingham Beverage Company Inc 211 Citation Ct	Birmingham	AL	35219	205-942-9403	
Web: alabev.com					
Blach Distributing Co 131 W Main St	Elko	NV	89801	775-738-7111	650-4321*
**Fax Area Code:* 631 ■ *TF:* 800-310-5099 ■ *Web:* www.abwholesaler.com					
Blue Ridge Beverage Company Inc 44-46 Barley Dr	Salem	VA	24153	540-380-2000	
Web: www.blueridgebeverage.com					
Bonanza Beverage Co 6333 Ensworth St	Las Vegas	NV	89119	702-361-4166	361-6408
TF Cust Svc: 800-677-4166 ■ *Web:* www.bonanzabev.com					
Buck Distributing Company Inc 15827 Commerce Ct	Upper Marlboro	MD	20774	301-952-0400	627-5380
TF Cust Svc: 800-750-2825 ■ *Web:* www.buckdistributing.com					
Burke Beverages Inc 4900 S Vernon Ave	McCook	IL	60525	708-688-2000	688-2050
Web: www.burkebev.com					
Carenbauer Distributing Corp 1900 Jacob St	Wheeling	WV	26003	304-232-3000	232-3630
Web: www.abwholesaler.com					
Central Distributors Inc 15 Foss Rd	Lewiston	ME	04240	207-784-4026	784-7869
TF Cust Svc: 800-427-5757 ■ *Web:* www.centraldistributors.com					
Central European Distribution Corp (CEDC) 3000 Atrium Way Ste 265	Mount Laurel	NJ	08054	856-273-6980	
NASDAQ: CEDC ■ *Web:* www.cedc.com/					
Cherokee Distributing Company Inc 200 Miller Main Cir	Knoxville	TN	37919	865-588-7641	558-8941
Web: cherokeedistributing.com					
Chicago Beverage Systems LLC 4239 W Ferdinand St	Chicago	IL	60624	773-826-4100	826-8023
Web: reyesholdings.com					
City Beverages of Orlando 10928 Florida Crown Dr	Orlando	FL	32824	407-251-4049	851-7100
Web: www.abwholesaler.com					
Clare Rose Inc 255 Pinelawn Rd	Melville	NY	11747	631-475-1840	650-4331
Web: www.abwholesaler.com/group03/clarerose/home					
Classic City Beverages LLC 530 Calhoun Dr	Athens	GA	30601	706-353-1650	353-1655
Web: jandlventuresllc.com					
Coastal Beverage Co Inc 301 Harley Rd	Wilmington	NC	28405	910-799-3011	392-3674
Web: www.coastalbev.com					
Columbia Distributing Co 6840 N Cutter Cir	Portland	OR	97217	503-289-9600	240-8389
TF: 888-417-5001 ■ *Web:* www.columbia-dist.com					
Commercial Distributing Co Inc 46 S Broad St	Westfield	MA	01085	413-562-9691	562-7302
TF Cust Svc: 800-332-8999 ■ *Web:* commercialdist.com					
Consolidated Beverages Inc 12 St Mark St	Auburn	MA	01501	508-832-5311	832-9831
TF: 800-922-8128 ■ *Web:* consolidatedbeverages.com					
Coors Distributing Co (CBC) 5400 N Pecos St	Denver	CO	80221	303-433-6541	964-5577
Web: www.coors.com					
Couch Distributing Company Inc 104 Lee Rd	Watsonville	CA	95076	831-724-0649	724-4293
Web: www.couchdistributing.com					
Crescent Crown Distributing 5900 Almonaster Ave	New Orleans	LA	70126	504-240-5900	240-5500
Web: crescentcrown.com					
Crest Beverage Co 8870 Liquid Ct	San Diego	CA	92121	858-452-2300	
Web: www.crestbeverage.com					
D Canale Beverages Inc 45 W EH Crump Blvd	Memphis	TN	38106	901-948-4543	
Web: www.abwholesaler.com/dcanalebeverages					
DBI Beverage 245 S Spruce Ave Ste 900	San Francisco	CA	94080	415-643-9900	
Web: www.dbibeverage.com					

				Phone	Fax
DET Distributing Co 301 Great Cir Rd *Fax Area Code: 617 ■ Web: www.detdist.com	Nashville	TN	37228	615-244-4113	255-0122*
Dutchess Beer Distributors Inc 5 Laurel St TF Cust Svc: 800-427-6308 ■ Web: dutchessbeer.com	Poughkeepsie	NY	12601	845-452-0940	452-0958
Eagle Distributing Co Inc 1100 S Bud Blvd *Fax Area Code: 865	Fremont	NE	68025	402-721-9723	525-9530*
Eagle Distributing Company Inc 310 Radford Pl Web: eagledistributing.com	Knoxville	TN	37917	865-637-3311	525-9530
Eastown Distributors Co 14400 Oakland Ave Web: www.eastown.com	Highland Park	MI	48203	313-867-6900	
Fahr Beverage Inc PO Box 358 Web: www.fahrbeverage.com	Waterloo	IA	50704	319-234-2605	234-5644
Five Star Distributing Inc 4055 E Parl 30 Dr Web: www.fivestardistributing.net	Columbia City	IN	46725	260-244-3775	
Frank B Fuhrer Wholesale Co 3100 E Carson St TF: 800-837-2212 ■ Web: www.fuhrerwholesale.com	Pittsburgh	PA	15203	412-488-8844	488-0195
Gambrinus Co, The 14800 San Pedro Ave Third Fl TF: 800-596-6486 ■ Web: www.gambrinusco.com	San Antonio	TX	78232	210-490-9128	490-9984
General Distributing Co 5350 Amelia Earhart Dr Web: generaldistributing.weebly.com	Salt Lake City	UT	84116	801-531-7895	363-4924
Georgia Crown Distributing Co 100 Georgia Crown Dr TF: 800-342-2350 ■ Web: www.georgiacrown.com	McDonough	GA	30253	770-302-3000	302-3080
Girardi Distributors LLC Five Railroad Pl Web: businessfinder.masslive.com	Athol	MA	01331	978-249-3581	
Golden Eagle Distributors Inc 705 E Ajo Way Web: www.gedaz.com	Tucson	AZ	85713	520-884-5999	884-1804
Golden Eagle of Arkansas Inc 1900 E 15th St	Little Rock	AR	72202	501-372-2800	376-2404
Grantham Distributing Co Inc 2685 Hansrob Rd	Orlando	FL	32804	407-299-6446	295-7104
Great Bay Distributors Inc 2310 Starkey Rd Web: www.greatbaybud.com	Largo	FL	33771	727-584-8626	585-9425
Gretz Beer Co 710 E Main St *Fax Area Code: 631 ■ TF General: 800-310-5099 ■ Web: www.abwholesaler.com	Norristown	PA	19401	610-275-0285	650-4321*
Guiffre Distributing Co 6839 Industrial Rd Web: guiffredistributing.com	Springfield	VA	22151	703-642-1700	642-2855
Gusto Brands Inc 707 Douglas St Web: gustobrands.com	LaGrange	GA	30240	706-882-2573	882-2412
Heineken USA 360 Hamilton Ave Ste 1103 Web: www.heineken.com	White Plains	NY	10601	914-681-4100	681-1900
Henry A Fox Sales Co 4494 36th St SE Web: www.fox-sales.com	Grand Rapids	MI	49512	616-949-1210	
Hensley & Co 4201 N 45th Ave *Fax Area Code: 623 ■ Web: www.abwholesaler.com	Phoenix	AZ	85031	602-264-1635	247-7094*
High Grade Beverage Inc 891 Georges Rd Web: www.highgradebeverage.com	Monmouth Junction	NJ	08852	732-821-7600	821-2898
Hill Distributing Co 2555 Harrison Rd	Columbus	OH	43204	614-276-6533	
House of Schwan Inc 3636 Comotara St Web: wichitabeer.com	Wichita	KS	67226	316-636-9100	636-6210
Hubert Distributors Inc 1200 Auburn Rd Web: www.abwholesaler.com	Pontiac	MI	48342	248-858-2340	858-7777
Iron City Distributing Co 2670 Commercial Ave TF Cust Svc: 800-759-2671 ■ Web: www.ironcitydist.com	Mingo Junction	OH	43938	740-598-4171	598-4677
JJ Taylor Cos Inc 655 N AIA Web: www.jjtaylor.com	Jupiter	FL	33477	561-354-2900	
Koerner Distributors Inc 1305 W Wabash St PO Box 67 Web: www.koernerdistributor.com	Effingham	IL	62401	217-347-7113	347-8736
Labatt Breweries of Canada 207 Queen's Quay W Ste 299 TF Cust Svc: 800-268-2337 ■ Web: www.labatt.com	Toronto	ON	M5J1A7	416-361-5050	
Leon Farmer & Co 100 Rail Ridge Rd Web: www.leonfarmer.com	Athens	GA	30607	706-353-1166	
Lion Brewery Inc 700 N Pennsylvania Ave TF: 888-295-2337 ■ Web: www.lionbrewery.com	Wilkes-Barre	PA	18705	570-823-8801	823-6686
Louis Glunz Beer Inc 7100 N Capitol Dr Web: www.glunzbeers.com	Lincolnwood	IL	60712	847-676-9500	675-5678
Maple City Ice Co Inc 371 Cleveland Rd *Fax Area Code: 614 ■ TF Cust Svc: 877-762-9119 ■ Web: norwalkreflector.com	Norwalk	OH	44857	419-668-2531	644-0720*
Markstein Beverage Co 505 S Pacific St Web: abwholesaler.com/group08/markstein	San Marcos	CA	92078	760-744-9100	
Mautino Distributing Co 500 N Richards St TF Cust Svc: 800-851-2756	Spring Valley	IL	61362	815-664-4311	664-2224
McLaughlin & Moran Inc 40 Slater Rd TF: 800-423-0156	Cranston	RI	02920	401-463-5454	
Merrimack Valley Distributing Co 50 Prince St TF: 800-698-0250 ■ Web: mvdc.com	Danvers	MA	01923	978-777-2213	774-7487
Metz Beverage Company Inc 302 N Custer St	Sheridan	WY	82801	307-674-4818	
Mission Beverage Co 550 S Mission Rd	Los Angeles	CA	90033	323-266-6238	266-6559
Moon Distributors Inc 2800 Vance St Web: moondist.com	Little Rock	AR	72206	501-375-8291	
Muller Inc 2800 Grant Ave Web: mullerbev.com	Philadelphia	PA	19114	215-676-7575	698-0414
New Hampshire Distributors Inc 65 Regional Dr TF: 800-852-3781 ■ Web: nhdist.com	Concord	NH	03301	603-224-9991	224-0415
NKS Distributors Inc 399 Churchmans Rd TF: 800-310-5099 ■ Web: www.abwholesaler.com	New Castle	DE	19720	302-322-1811	324-4024
Pacific Beverage Co 5305 Ekwill St Web: www.pacificbeveragecompany.com	Santa Barbara	CA	93111	805-964-3574	

				Phone	Fax
Paradise Beverages Inc 94-1450 Moaniani St *Fax: Sales ■ Web: www.paradisebeverages.com	Waipahu	HI	96797	808-678-4000	677-8280*
Pepin Distributing Co 4121 N 50th St Web: www.pepindistributing.com	Tampa	FL	33610	813-626-6176	626-5800
Pike Distributors Inc 401 E John St PO Box 465 Web: pikedistributors.com	Newberry	MI	49868	906-293-8611	
Pine State Trading Co 8 Ellis Ave TF: 800-873-3825 ■ Web: www.pinestatetrading.com	Augusta	ME	04330	207-622-3741	626-5844
Powers Distributing Company Inc 3700 Giddings Rd Web: powersdistributing.com	Orion	MI	48359	248-393-3700	
Premium Distributors 3500 Fort Lincoln Dr NE TF: 800-827-4020 ■ Web: reyesholdings.com	Washington	DC	20018	202-526-3900	
Premium Distributors of Maryland LLC 530 Monocacy Blvd Web: www.reyesholdings.com	Frederick	MD	21701	301-662-0372	663-9488
Premium Distributors of VA LLC 15001 Northridge Dr Web: reyesholdings.com	Chantilly	VA	20151	703-227-1200	227-1202
Quality Beverage Inc 525 Miles Standish Blvd	Taunton	MA	02780	508-822-6200	823-9092
Richland Beverage Assoc 2415 Midway Rd Ste 115	Carrollton	TX	75006	214-357-0248	357-9581
Saccani Distributing Co 2600 Fifth St PO Box 1764 Web: www.saccanidist.com	Sacramento	CA	95818	916-441-0213	441-0806
Saratoga Eagle Sales & Service Inc 45 Duplainville Rd TF: 800-310-5099 ■ Web: www.abwholesaler.com	Saratoga Springs	NY	12866	518-581-7377	581-7777
Savannah Distributing Co Inc 2425 W Gwinnett St PO Box 1388 TF General: 800-551-0777 ■ Web: www.savdist.com	Savannah	GA	31415	912-233-1167	233-1557
Silver Eagle Distributors LP 7777 Washington Ave TF: 855-332-2110 ■ Web: silvereagle.com	Houston	TX	77007	713-869-4361	867-8112
Skokie Valley Beverage Co 199 Shepard Ave Web: www.svbco.com	Wheeling	IL	60090	847-541-1500	541-2059
Southern Wine & Spirits of Colorado 5270 Fox St PO Box 5603 TF: 800-332-9956 ■ Web: www.southernwine.com	Denver	CO	80216	303-292-1711	297-9967
Standard Beverage Corp 2416 E 37th St N Web: www.standardbeverage.com	Wichita	KS	67219	316-838-7707	838-1396
Standard Sales Co Inc 4800 E 42nd St Ste 400 TF: 800-331-5453 ■ Web: standardsalescompanylp.com	Odessa	TX	79762	432-367-7662	367-9526
Star Distributors Inc 460 Frontage Rd TF: 877-922-3501	West Haven	CT	06516	203-932-3636	932-5977
Stoudt Co 1618 Judson Rd PO Box 4147	Longview	TX	75601	903-753-7239	
Three Lakes Distributing Co 111 Overton St	Hot Springs	AR	71901	501-623-8201	624-4499
Town & Country Distributors Inc 1050 W Ardmore Ave Web: tcbeer.com	Itasca	IL	60143	630-250-0590	250-8946
Treu House of Munch Inc 8000 Arbor Dr Web: www.abwholesaler.com	Northwood	OH	43619	419-666-7770	666-5712
Tri-County Beverage Co 2651 E 10 Mile Rd Web: www.tricountybeverage.com	Warren	MI	48091	586-757-4900	
United Distributors Inc 5500 United Dr SE Web: udiga.com	Smyrna	GA	30082	678-305-2080	
Watson Kunda & Sons Inc 349 S Henderson Rd Web: www.kundabev.com	King of Prussia	PA	19406	610-265-3113	265-3190
Western Beverages Inc 4545 E 51st Ave Web: western-beverage-distributing-company.placestars.com	Denver	CO	80216	303-388-5755	336-3336
Western Wyoming Beverages Inc 100 Reliance Rd TF: 800-551-8244 ■ Web: www.westernwyomingbeverages.com	Rock Springs	WY	82901	307-362-6332	362-6335
Williams Distributing Corp 880 Burnett Rd TF: 800-332-9634 ■ Web: williamsdistributing.com	Chicopee	MA	01020	413-594-4900	594-4911
Wirtz Beverage Nevada 1849 W Cheyenne Ave Web: www.wirtzbev.com	North Las Vegas	NV	89032	702-735-9141	
Wright Wisner Distributing Corp 3165 Brighton-Henrietta Town Line Rd *Fax Area Code: 716 ■ Web: wrightbev.com	Rochester	NY	14623	585-427-2880	272-1216*

81-2 Soft Drinks - Whol

				Phone	Fax
Admiral Beverage Corp PO Box 726 Web: www.admiralbeverage.com	Worland	WY	82401	307-347-4201	
All State Beverage Co 130 Sixth St Web: www.allstatebeverage.com	Montgomery	AL	36104	334-265-0507	263-2367
Atlas Distributing Corp 44 Southbridge St TF: 800-649-6221 ■ Web: www.atlasdistributing.com	Auburn	MA	01501	508-791-6221	791-0812
Buffalo Rock Co 111 Oxmoor Rd TF: 800-822-9799 ■ Web: www.buffalorock.com	Birmingham	AL	35209	205-942-3435	942-2601
Carolina Canners Inc PO Box 1628 Web: carolinacanners.com	Cheraw	SC	29520	843-537-5281	537-6743
Coca-Cola Bottling Co 725 E Erie Ave	Philadelphia	PA	19134	215-427-4500	423-5557
Coca-Cola Bottling Co Consolidated 4100 Coca-Cola Plaza NASDAQ: COKE ■ TF: 800-777-2653 ■ Web: www.cokeconsolidated.com	Charlotte	NC	28211	704-557-4000	557-4646
Coca-Cola Enterprises Inc 2500 Windy Ridge Pkwy NYSE: CCE ■ Web: www.cokecce.com	Atlanta	GA	30339	770-989-3000	989-3597
Gusto Brands Inc 707 Douglas St Web: gustobrands.com	LaGrange	GA	30240	706-882-2573	882-2412
Made-Rite Co PO Box 3283 Web: www.themade-ritecompany.com	Longview	TX	75606	903-753-8604	236-9743

Phone / Fax

Malolo Beverages & Supplies Ltd
120 Sand Island Access Rd .... Honolulu HI 96819 808-845-4830 845-4835
Web: malolobeverages.com

Markstein Beverage Co 505 S Pacific St........ San Marcos CA 92078 760-744-9100
Web: abwholesaler.com/group08/markstein

Metz Beverage Company Inc 302 N Custer St .... Sheridan WY 82801 307-674-4818

Nor-Cal Beverage Company Inc
2286 Stone Blvd........ West Sacramento CA 95691 916-372-0600 374-2602
Web: www.ncbev.com

Swire Coca-Cola USA 12634 S 265 W .... Draper UT 84020 801-816-5300 816-5423
TF: 800-497-2653 ■ *Web:* swirecc.com

Temple Bottling Company Ltd
3510 Pkwy Dr PO Box 308........ Temple TX 76501 254-773-3376 778-5414
Web: www.templebot.com

Vital Pharmaceuticals Inc 1600 N Pk Dr .... Weston FL 33326 954-641-0570 641-4960
TF: 800-954-7904 ■ *Web:* www.vpxsports.com

Western Wyoming Beverages Inc
100 Reliance Rd........ Rock Springs WY 82901 307-362-6332 362-6335
TF: 800-551-8244 ■ *Web:* www.westernwyomingbeverages.com

Wis-Pak Inc 860 W St PO Box 496........ Watertown WI 53094 920-262-6300 262-9273
Web: wis-pak.com

81-3 Wine & Liquor - Whol

Phone / Fax

Alabama Crown Distributing
421 Industrial Ln .... Birmingham AL 35211 205-941-1155 942-3767
TF: 800-548-1869 ■ *Web:* georgiacrown.com

Bacardi Bottling Corp 12200 N Main St........ Jacksonville FL 32218 904-757-1290 751-1397

Badger Liquor Company Inc
850 S Morris St .... Fond du Lac WI 54936 920-923-8160 923-8169
TF: 800-242-9708 ■ *Web:* www.badgerliquor.com

Badger West Wine & Spirits LLC
5400 Old Town Hall Rd PO Box 869........ Eau Claire WI 54701 715-836-8600 836-8609
TF: 800-472-6674 ■ *Web:* www.badgerliquor.com

Ben Arnold Beverage Company LP
101 Beverage Blvd .... Ridgeway SC 29130 803-337-3500 337-5310*
**Fax:* Cust Svc ■ *TF Acctg:* 888-262-9787 ■ *Web:* www.charmer-sunbelt.com

Beverage Distributors Co 14200 E Moncrieff Pl........ Aurora CO 80011 303-371-3421 270-5983*
**Fax Area Code:* 334 ■ *TF General:* 800-772-2096 ■
Web: www.charmer-sunbelt.com/beveragedistr/Pages/Welcome.aspx

Blue Ridge Beverage Company Inc
44-46 Barley Dr .... Salem VA 24153 540-380-2000
Web: www.blueridgebeverage.com

Capitol-Husting Company Inc
12001 W Carmen Ave........ Milwaukee WI 53225 414-353-1000 353-0768
Web: www.capitol-husting.com

Cardinal Distributing Company LLC
269 Jackrabbit Ln........ Bozeman MT 59718 406-586-0241 587-1156
Web: www.cardinaldistributing.com

Castle Brands Inc 122 E 42nd St Ste 4700........ New York NY 10168 646-356-0200 356-0222
NYSE: ROX ■ *TF:* 800-882-8140 ■ *Web:* www.castlebrandsinc.com

Central Distributors Inc 15 Foss Rd .... Lewiston ME 04240 207-784-4026 784-7869
TF Cust Svc: 800-427-5757 ■ *Web:* www.centraldistributors.com

Charmer Sunbelt Group, The
60 E 42nd St Ste 1915 .... New York NY 10165 212-699-7000 699-7099
TF: 800-772-2096 ■ *Web:* www.charmer-sunbelt.com

Columbia Distributing Co 6840 N Cutter Cir........ Portland OR 97217 503-289-9600 240-8389
TF: 888-417-5001 ■ *Web:* www.columbia-dist.com

Constellation Brands Inc
207 High Pt Dr Bldg 100 .... Victor NY 14564 888-724-2169 678-7103*
NYSE: STZ ■ **Fax Area Code:* 585 ■ *TF:* 888-724-2169 ■ *Web:* www.cbrands.com

Diageo Chateau & Estate Wines Co
240 Gateway Rd W .... Napa CA 94558 707-299-2600 299-2777
Web: www.diageowines.com

Dichello Distributors Inc
55 Marsh Hill Rd PO Box 562........ Orange CT 06477 203-891-2100
Web: www.dichello.com

Fedway Assoc Inc 505 Westgate Dr .... Basking Ridge NJ 07920 973-624-6444 589-3556
TF: 800-447-4736 ■ *Web:* www.fedway.com

Frederick Wildman & Sons Ltd 307 E 53rd St........ New York NY 10022 212-355-0700 355-4719
TF General: 800-733-9463 ■ *Web:* www.frederickwildman.com

General Beer Distributors
6169 McKee Rd PO Box 44326 .... Fitchburg WI 53719 608-271-1237
Web: visitmadison.com

General Wine & Liquor Co
373 Victor Ave .... Highland Park MI 48203 313-867-0521 867-4039
Web: www.gwlc.com

Georgia Crown Distributing Co
100 Georgia Crown Dr .... McDonough GA 30253 770-302-3000 302-3080
TF: 800-342-2350 ■ *Web:* www.georgiacrown.com

Glazer's Wholesale Drug Company Inc
14911 Quorum Dr Ste 400........ Dallas TX 75254 972-392-8200 702-8508
TF: 800-275-2854 ■ *Web:* www.glazers.com

Goldring Gulf Distributing Co
675 S Pace Blvd........ Pensacola FL 32501 850-432-9883 432-5509
Web: www.goldringgulf.com

Grantham Distributing Co Inc 2685 Hansrob Rd .... Orlando FL 32804 407-299-6446 295-7104

Hammer Company Inc 9450 Rosemont Dr .... Streetsboro OH 44241 330-422-1471

Henry A Fox Sales Co 4494 36th St SE........ Grand Rapids MI 49512 616-949-1210
Web: www.fox-sales.com

Horizon Wine & Spirits Nashville
3851 Industrial Pkwy .... Nashville TN 37218 615-320-7292 321-4173
Web: www.hwas.com

Johnson Bros Wholesale Liquor Co
1999 ShepaRd Rd........ Saint Paul MN 55116 651-649-5800 649-5894
TF: 800-723-2424 ■ *Web:* www.johnsonbrothers.com

Kings Liquor Inc 2810 W Berry St .... Fort Worth TX 76109 817-923-3737
Web: www.kingsliquor.com

Luxco 5050 Kemper Ave........ Saint Louis MO 63139 314-772-2626 772-6021
Web: www.luxco.com

Phone / Fax

Maisons Marques & Domaines USA Inc
383 Fourth St Ste 400........ Oakland CA 94607 510-286-2000 286-2010
Web: www.mmdusa.net

Merrimack Valley Distributing Co
50 Prince St .... Danvers MA 01923 978-777-2213 774-7487
TF: 800-698-0250 ■ *Web:* mvdc.com

Moet Hennessy USA 85 Tenth Ave........ New York NY 10011 212-251-8200 251-8388
Web: www.mhusa.com

Moon Distributors Inc 2800 Vance St........ Little Rock AR 72206 501-375-8291
Web: moondist.com

National Wine & Spirits Inc PO Box 2187 .... Indianapolis IN 46206 317-602-6644 602-6720
Web: www.nwscorp.com

NKS Distributors Inc 399 Churchmans Rd .... New Castle DE 19720 302-322-1811 324-4024
TF: 800-310-5099 ■ *Web:* www.abwholesaler.com

Paradise Beverages Inc 94-1450 Moaniani St .... Waipahu HI 96797 808-678-4000 677-8280*
**Fax:* Sales ■ *Web:* www.paradisebeverages.com

Paterno Wines International 900 Armour Dr .... Lake Bluff IL 60044 847-604-8900 604-5828
Web: www.terlatowines.com

Pernod Ricard USA 100 Manhattanville Rd........ Purchase NY 10577 914-848-4800 539-4550
TF: 800-847-5949 ■ *Web:* www.pernod-ricard-usa.com

Phillips Distributing Corp 3010 Nob Hill Rd........ Madison WI 53713 608-222-9177 222-0558
TF: 800-236-7269 ■ *Web:* www.phillipsdistributing.com

Premier Beverage Company of Florida
9801 Premier Pkwy........ Miramar FL 33025 954-436-9200 436-9039
TF: 800-432-2002 ■ *Web:* www.charmer-sunbelt.com

Quality Beverage Inc 525 Miles Standish Blvd .... Taunton MA 02780 508-822-6200 823-9092

R & R Marketing LLC 10 Patton Dr .... West Caldwell NJ 07006 973-228-5100 403-8679
TF: 800-772-2096 ■ *Web:* www.charmer-sunbelt.com

Remy Cointreau USA Inc
1290 Ave of the Americas........ New York NY 10104 212-399-4200 424-2259
TF General: 800-858-9898 ■ *Web:* www.remy-cointreau.com

Republic National Distributing Co (RNDC)
6511 Tri County Pkwy........ Schertz TX 78154 210-224-7531 274-1809*
**Fax Area Code:* 301 ■ *Web:* www.rndc-usa.com

Savannah Distributing Co Inc
2425 W Gwinnett St PO Box 1388 .... Savannah GA 31415 912-233-1167 233-1557
TF General: 800-551-0777 ■ *Web:* www.savdist.com

Southern Wine & Spirits of America Inc
1600 NW 163rd St .... Miami FL 33169 305-625-4171
TF: 800-776-0180 ■ *Web:* www.southernwine.com

Southern Wine & Spirits of Colorado
5270 Fox St PO Box 5603 .... Denver CO 80216 303-292-1711 297-9967
TF: 800-332-9956 ■ *Web:* www.southernwine.com

Southern Wine & Spirits of Illinois
300 E Crossroads Pkwy
Bolingbrook Corp Ctr........ Bolingbrook IL 60440 630-685-3000 685-3700
TF: 800-776-0180 ■ *Web:* www.southernwine.com

Southern Wine & Spirits of New York
313 Underhill Blvd PO Box 9034 .... Syosset NY 11791 516-921-9005 921-8526
Web: www.southernwine.com

Standard Beverage Corp 2416 E 37th St N .... Wichita KS 67219 316-838-7707 838-1396
Web: www.standardbeverage.com

Sterling Distributing Co 4433 S 96th St .... Omaha NE 68127 402-339-2300 339-3772
Web: sterlingdistributing.com

Terlato Wine Group, The (TWG) 900 Armour Dr .... Lake Bluff IL 60044 847-604-8900
TF: 800-950-7676 ■ *Web:* terlatowines.com/

William Grant & Sons Inc 130 Fieldcrest Ave .... Edison NJ 08837 732-225-9000
Web: www.grantusa.com

Winebow Inc 75 Chestnut Ridge Rd........ Montvale NJ 07645 201-445-0620
TF: 800-859-0689 ■ *Web:* www.winebow.com

Wirtz Beverage Illinois LLC (WBI)
3333 S Laramie Ave 11th Fl .... Cicero IL 60804 708-298-3333
TF: 800-344-2838 ■ *Web:* www.wirtzbev.com

Wirtz Beverage Nevada
1849 W Cheyenne Ave .... North Las Vegas NV 89032 702-735-9141
Web: www.wirtzbev.com

Wisconsin Distributors Inc
900 Progress Way........ Sun Prairie WI 53590 608-834-2337 834-2300
Web: www.wisconsindistributors.com

Young's Market Company LLC
500 S Central Ave........ Los Angeles CA 90013 213-612-1248 612-1238*
**Fax:* Hum Res ■ *TF:* 800-627-2777 ■ *Web:* www.youngsmarket.com

82 BICYCLES & BICYCLE PARTS & ACCESSORIES

SEE ALSO Sporting Goods p. 3182; Toys, Games, Hobbies p. 3246

Phone / Fax

Cane Creek Cycling Components
355 Cane Creek Rd........ Fletcher NC 28732 828-684-3551 684-1057
TF: 800-234-2725 ■ *Web:* www.canecreek.com

Giant Bicycle USA 3587 Old Conejo Rd .... Newbury Park CA 91320 805-267-4600 637-9704*
**Fax Area Code:* 800 ■ *Web:* www.giant-bicycles.com

Haro Bicycles 1230 Avenida Chelsea........ Vista CA 92081 760-599-0544 599-1237
Web: www.harobikes.com

Huffy Bicycle Co
6551 Centerville Business Pkwy........ Centerville OH 45459 937-865-2800 865-5470
TF: 800-872-2453 ■ *Web:* www.huffybikes.com

K2 Bike 1600 Calebs Path Ext Ste 203........ Hauppauge NY 11788 631-780-5360 780-5358
Web: www.ecycylesupply.com

Pacific Cycle Inc 4902 Hammersley Rd .... Madison WI 53711 800-666-8813
Web: www.pacificcycle.com

Quality Bicycle Products Inc
6400 W 105th St........ Bloomington MN 55438 952-941-9391
Web: peopleforbikes.org

Raleigh America Inc 6004 S 190th St Ste 101........ Kent WA 98032 800-222-5527 872-0257*
**Fax Area Code:* 253 ■ *TF:* 800-222-5527 ■ *Web:* www.diamondback.com

Raleigh USA 6004 S 190th St Ste 101 .... Kent WA 98032 253-395-1100 872-0257
TF: 800-222-5527 ■ *Web:* www.raleighusa.com

Shimano American Corp 1 Holland Dr........ Irvine CA 92618 949-951-5003 768-0920
Web: www.shimano.com

				Phone	Fax
SMITH Mfg Company Inc 1610 S Dixie Hwy *TF:* 800-653-9311 ■ *Web:* www.smithmfg.com	Pompano Beach	FL	33060	954-941-9744	545-0348
Specialized Bicycle Components 15130 Concord Cir *TF:* 877-808-8154 ■ *Web:* www.specialized.com	Morgan Hill	CA	95037	408-779-6229	779-1631
SRAM Corp 1333 N Kingsbury St 4th Fl *TF:* 800-346-2928 ■ *Web:* www.sram.com	Chicago	IL	60622	312-664-8800	664-8826
Terry Precision Bicycles for Women Inc 47 Maple St **Fax Area Code:* 802 ■ *TF:* 800-289-8379 ■ *Web:* www.terrybicycles.com	Burlington	VT	05401	800-289-8379	861-2956*
Trek Bicycle Corp 801 W Madison St *Web:* www.trekbikes.com	Waterloo	WI	53594	920-478-2191	478-2774
Wald LLC 800 E Fifth St **Fax:* Sales ■ *Web:* www.waldllc.com	Maysville	KY	41056	606-564-4077	564-5248*
Worksman Trading Corp 94-15 100th St *TF:* 800-962-2453 ■ *Web:* www.worksman.com	Ozone Park	NY	11416	718-322-2000	529-4803

83 BIO-RECOVERY SERVICES

Companies listed here provide services for managing and eliminating biohazard dangers that may be present after a death or injury. These services include cleaning, disinfecting, and deodorizing biohazard scenes resulting from accidents, homicides, suicides, natural deaths, and similar events.

				Phone	Fax
Advanced Ozone Engineering Inc 6038 Oakwood Ave	Cincinnati	OH	45224	513-681-3871	681-3991
Allied Services 3001 1/2 Gill St Ste E	Bloomington	IL	61704	309-662-0008	
Bio-Recovery Corp 1863 Pond Rd Ste 4 *TF:* 800-556-0621 ■ *Web:* www.biorecovery.com	Ronkonkoma	NY	11779	631-676-2600	
Bio-Scene Recovery 13191 Meadow St NE *TF:* 877-380-5500 ■ *Web:* www.bioscene.com	Alliance	OH	44601	330-823-5500	823-4405
Biocare Inc 122 Clair Dr	Piedmont	SC	29673	864-295-9000	
Grangeville Environmental Services (GES) *GES Property Pros LLC* 585 McAllister St *TF:* 866-437-5151 ■ *Web:* www.gespropertypros.com	Hanover	PA	17331	717-637-6152	630-2713
JP Maguire Assoc Inc 266 Brookside Rd *TF:* 877-576-2484 ■ *Web:* www.fixmydamage.com	Waterbury	CT	06708	203-755-2297	573-8547
Peerless Cleaners Inc 519 N Monroe St *TF:* 800-879-7056 ■ *Web:* www.peerlessrestoration.com	Decatur	IL	62522	217-423-7703	
Richey Restoration Inc 9574 Lebanon Rd *Web:* www.richeyrestoration.com	Mount Juliet	TN	37122	615-533-3760	
RMRC Services Inc 5870 S Walden Ct **Fax Area Code:* 720 ■ *Web:* www.rockymountainmold.com	Centennial	CO	80015	303-667-0400	870-2696*

84 BIOMETRIC IDENTIFICATION EQUIPMENT & SOFTWARE

				Phone	Fax
AcSys Biometrics Corp 1100 Burloak Dr Ste 703 *Web:* www.acsysbiometrics.com	Burlington	ON	L7L6B2	905-331-7337	634-1101
Aspect Business Solutions 7550 IH-10 W 14th Fl	San Antonio	TX	78229	210-298-5000	298-5001
AuthenTec Inc 100 Rialto Pl # 100	Melbourne	FL	32901	321-308-1300	308-1430
Bio Medic Data Systems Inc One Silas Rd *TF:* 800-526-2637 ■ *Web:* www.bmds.com	Seaford	DE	19973	302-628-4100	628-4110
BIO-key International Inc 300 Nickerson Rd *Web:* www.bio-key.com	Marlborough	MA	01752	508-460-4000	
Communication Intelligence Corp (CIC) 275 Shoreline Dr Ste 500 *OTC: CICI* ■ *Web:* www.cic.com	Redwood Shores	CA	94065	650-802-7888	802-7777
Count Me In LLC 1530 E Dundee Ste 150 **Fax Area Code:* 702 ■ *TF:* 866-514-5888 ■ *Web:* www.countmeinllc.com	Palatine	IL	60074	866-514-5888	515-7473*
Cross Match Technologies 3950 RCA Blvd Ste 5001 *Web:* www.crossmatch.com	Palm Beach Gardens	FL	33410	561-622-1650	622-9938
Crossmatch 720 Bay Rd Ste 100 *TF:* 866-463-7792 ■ *Web:* www.digitalpersona.com	Redwood City	CA	94063	650-474-4000	298-8313
Datastrip Inc 211 Welsh Pool Rd Ste 100	Exton	PA	19341	610-594-6130	594-6065
International Biometric Group LLC One Battery Pk Plz Ste 2901 *Web:* www.ibgweb.com	New York	NY	10004	212-809-9491	809-6197
Lightning Powder Company Inc 13386 International Pkwy *Web:* www.redwop.com	Jacksonville	FL	32218	904-485-1836	741-5407
MorphoTrak Inc 113 S Columbus St 4th Fl *TF:* 800-601-6790 ■ *Web:* www.morphotrak.com	Alexandria	VA	22314	703-797-2600	706-9549
NEC Corp of America 10850 Gold Ctr Dr Ste 200 *TF:* 800-632-4636 ■ *Web:* www.necam.com	Rancho Cordova	CA	95670	916-463-7000	
SecuGen Corp 2065 Martin Ave Ste 108 *Web:* www.secugen.com	Santa Clara	CA	95050	408-727-7787	834-7762
Security First Corp 29811 Santa Margarita Pkwy Ste 600 *Web:* securityfirstcorp.com	Rancho Santa Margarita	CA	92688	949-858-7525	858-7092
SIRCHIE Finger Print Laboratories Inc 100 Hunter Pl *TF:* 800-356-7311 ■ *Web:* www.sirchie.com	Youngsville	NC	27596	919-554-2244	554-2266
Ultra-Scan Corp 4240 Ridge Lea Rd Ste 10 *Web:* www.ultra-scan.com	Amherst	NY	14226	716-832-6269	832-2810

85 BIOTECHNOLOGY COMPANIES

SEE ALSO Diagnostic Products p. 2198; Medicinal Chemicals & Botanical Products p. 2736; Pharmaceutical Companies p. 2921; Pharmaceutical Companies - Generic Drugs p. 2924

				Phone	Fax
ACADIA Pharmaceuticals Inc 3911 Sorrento Vly Blvd *NASDAQ: ACAD* ■ *Web:* www.acadia-pharm.com	San Diego	CA	92121	858-558-2871	558-2872
Acorda Therapeutics Inc 420 Saw Mill River RD *NASDAQ: ACOR* ■ *Web:* www.acorda.com	Ardsley	NY	10502	914-347-4300	347-4560
Acusphere Inc 99 Hayden Ave Ste 385 *OTC: ACUS* ■ **Fax Area Code:* 978 ■ *Web:* www.acusphere.com	Lexington	MA	02421	617-648-8800	863-9993*
Adherex Technologies Inc 68 TW Alexander Dr PO Box 13628 *TSE: AHX* ■ *Web:* www.adherex.com	Research Triangle Park	NC	27709	919-636-4530	890-0490
Aeolus Pharmaceuticals Inc 26361 Crown Vly Pkwy Ste 150 *Web:* www.aeoluspharma.com	Mission Viejo	CA	92691	949-481-9825	
AEterna Zentaris Inc 1405 Parc Technologique Blvd *TSE: AEZ* ■ *Web:* www.aezsinc.com/en/index.php	Quebec	QC	G1P4P5	418-652-8525	652-0881
Affymax Inc 4001 Miranda Ave *OTC: AFFY* ■ *Web:* www.affymax.com	Palo Alto	CA	94304	650-812-8700	
Alexion Pharmaceuticals Inc 352 Knotter Dr *NASDAQ: ALXN* ■ *Web:* www.alxn.com	Cheshire	CT	06410	203-272-2596	271-8198
Alexza Pharmaceuticals Inc 2091 Stierlin Ct *NASDAQ: ALXA* ■ *Web:* www.alexza.com	Mountain View	CA	94043	650-944-7000	944-7999
Alkermes Inc 852 Winter St *NASDAQ: ALKS* ■ *TF:* 800-848-4876 ■ *Web:* www.alkermes.com	Waltham	MA	02451	781-609-6000	
Allos Therapeutics Inc 11080 Cir Pt Rd Ste 200 *NASDAQ: ALTH*	Westminster	CO	80020	303-426-6262	
Alnylam Pharmaceuticals Inc 300 Third St 3rd Fl *NASDAQ: ALNY* ■ *TF:* 866-330-0326 ■ *Web:* www.alnylam.com	Cambridge	MA	02142	617-551-8200	551-8101
Amarillo Biosciences Inc 4134 Business Pk Dr *Web:* www.amarbio.com	Amarillo	TX	79110	806-376-1741	376-9301
American Bio Medica Corp (ABMC) 122 Smith Rd *OTC: ABMC* ■ *TF General:* 800-227-1243 ■ *Web:* www.abmc.com	Kinderhook	NY	12106	518-758-8158	758-8172
Amgen Canada Inc 6775 Financial Dr Ste 100 *TF:* 800-665-4273 ■ *Web:* www.amgen.ca	Mississauga	ON	L5N0A4	905-285-3000	285-3100
Amgen Inc One Amgen Ctr Dr *TF:* 800-563-9798 ■ *Web:* www.amgen.com	Thousand Oaks	CA	91320	805-447-1000	
AmpliPhi Biosciences Corp 4870 Sadler Rd Ste 300 *OTC: APHB* ■ *TF:* 877-795-3647 ■ *Web:* www.ampliphibio.com	Glen Allen	VA	23060	804-205-5069	
Antibodies Inc PO Box 1560 **Fax Area Code:* 530 ■ *TF:* 800-824-8540 ■ *Web:* www.antibodiesinc.com	Davis	CA	95617	800-824-8540	758-6307*
Applied Molecular Evolution Inc (AME) 10300 Campus Pt Dr Ste 200	San Diego	CA	92121	858-597-4990	597-4950
Apricus Biosciences 11975 El Camino Real Ste 300 *NASDAQ: APRI* ■ *Web:* www.apricusbio.com	San Diego	CA	92130	858-222-8041	866-0482
Ardea Biosciences Inc 4939 Directors Pl *Web:* ardeabio.com	San Diego	CA	92121	858-652-6500	625-0760
Arena Pharmaceuticals Inc 6166 Nancy Ridge Dr *NASDAQ: ARNA* ■ *Web:* www.arenapharm.com	San Diego	CA	92121	858-453-7200	453-7210
ARIAD Pharmaceuticals Inc 26 Landsdowne St *NASDAQ: ARIA* ■ *Web:* www.ariad.com	Cambridge	MA	02139	617-494-0400	494-8144
Aridis Pharmaceuticals LLC 5941 Optical Ct *Web:* www.aridispharma.com	San Jose	CA	95138	408-385-1742	
ArQule Inc 19 Presidential Way *NASDAQ: ARQL* ■ *TF:* 800-373-7827 ■ *Web:* www.arqule.com	Woburn	MA	01801	781-994-0300	376-6019
Array BioPharma Inc 3200 Walnut St *NASDAQ: ARRY* ■ *TF:* 877-633-2436 ■ *Web:* www.arraybiopharma.com	Boulder	CO	80301	303-381-6600	449-5376
Astellas Pharma US Inc One Astellas Way **Fax Area Code:* 877 ■ *TF:* 800-695-4321 ■ *Web:* www.astellas.us	Northbrook	IL	60062	800-695-4321	829-7942*
Astex Pharmaceuticals 4140 Dublin Blvd Ste 200 *TF:* 877-534-2590 ■ *Web:* astx.com	Dublin	CA	94568	925-560-0100	560-0101
AtriCure Inc 6217 Centre Pk Dr *NASDAQ: ATRC* ■ *TF:* 888-347-6403 ■ *Web:* www.atricure.com	West Chester	OH	45069	513-755-4100	755-4567
Autoimmune Technologies LLC 1010 Common St Ste 1705 *Web:* www.autoimmune.com	New Orleans	LA	70112	504-529-9944	529-8982
AVANIR Pharmaceuticals 30 Enterprise Ste 400 *NASDAQ: AVNR* ■ *Web:* www.avanir.com	Aliso Viejo	CA	92656	949-389-6700	643-6800
AVAX Technologies Inc 2000 Hamilton St Ste 204 *Web:* avax-tech.com	Philadelphia	PA	19130	215-241-9760	241-9684
Bayer CropScience Two TW Alexander Dr *Web:* www.bayercropscience.us	Research Triangle Park	NC	27709	919-549-2000	
BD Biosciences PharMingen 10975 Torreyana Rd **Fax Area Code:* 619 ■ *TF:* 800-848-6227 ■ *Web:* www.bdbiosciences.com	San Diego	CA	92121	858-812-8800	812-8888*
Bellus Health Inc 275 Armand Frappier Blvd *TSE: BLU* ■ *TF:* 877-680-4500 ■ *Web:* www.bellushealth.com	Laval	QC	H7V4A7	450-680-4500	680-4501
BioCryst Pharmaceuticals Inc 2190 Pkwy Lk Dr *NASDAQ: BCRX* ■ *Web:* www.biocryst.com	Birmingham	AL	35244	205-444-4600	444-4640
BioDelivery Sciences International Inc (BDSI) 801 Corporate Ctr Dr Ste 210 *NASDAQ: BDSI* ■ *Web:* www.bdsi.com	Raleigh	NC	27607	919-582-9050	582-9051
Biogen Idec Inc 133 Boston Post Rd *NASDAQ: BIIB* ■ **Fax Area Code:* 617 ■ *TF:* 877-750-8536 ■ *Web:* www.biogenidec.com	Weston	MA	02493	781-464-2000	679-2617*
BioLife Solutions Inc 3303 Monte Villa Pkwy Ste 310 *Web:* biolifesolutions.com	Bothell	WA	98021	425-402-1400	
BioMarin Pharmaceutical Inc 105 Digital Dr *NASDAQ: BMRN* ■ *Web:* www.bmrn.com	Novato	CA	94949	415-506-6700	382-7889

Phone | Fax

BioNumerik Pharmaceuticals Inc
8122 Datapoint Dr Ste 1250 .... San Antonio TX 78229 210-614-1701 615-8030
Web: www.bionumerik.com

Bioo Scientific Corp 3913 Todd Ln Ste 312 .... Austin TX 78744 512-707-8993
Web: www.biooscientific.com

Bioqual Corp 9600 Medical Ctr Dr Ste 200 .... Rockville MD 20850 301-251-2801 251-1260
Web: www.bioqual.com

BioReliance Corp 14920 Broschart Rd .... Rockville MD 20850 301-738-1000 610-2590
TF: 800-553-5372 ■ *Web:* www.bioreliance.com

BioTechLogic Inc 717 Indian Rd .... Glenview IL 60025 847-730-3475
Web: www.biotechlogic.com

BioTime Inc 1301 Harbor Bay Pkwy .... Alameda CA 94502 510-521-3390 521-3389
Web: www.biotimeinc.com

Callisto Pharmaceuticals Inc
420 Lexington Ave Ste 2012 .... New York NY 10170 212-297-0010 297-0019
AMEX: KAL ■ *Web:* www.synergypharma.com/

Cangene Corp 155 Innovation Dr .... Winnipeg MB R3T5Y3 204-275-4200
TSE: CNJ ■ *TF:* 800-768-2304 ■ *Web:* www.cangene.com

Cardiome Pharma Corp
6190 Agronomy Rd 6th Fl .... Vancouver BC V6T1Z3 604-677-6905 677-6915
NASDAQ: CRME ■ *TF:* 800-330-9928 ■ *Web:* www.cardiome.com

CEL-SCI Corp 8229 Boone Blvd Ste 802 .... Vienna VA 22182 703-506-9460 506-9471
NYSE: CVM ■ *TF:* 800-422-6237 ■ *Web:* www.cel-sci.com

Celera Genomics Group 1401 Harbor Bay Pkwy .... Alameda CA 94502 510-749-4200
Web: www.celera.com

Celgene Corp 86 Morris Ave .... Summit NJ 07901 908-673-9000 673-9001
NASDAQ: CELG ■ *TF:* 888-771-0141 ■ *Web:* www.celgene.com

Cell Therapeutics Inc (CTI)
501 Elliott Ave W Ste 400 .... Seattle WA 98119 206-282-7100 284-6206
NASDAQ: CTIC ■ *TF:* 800-215-2355 ■ *Web:* ctibiopharma.com/

Cerus Corp 2550 Stanwell Dr .... Concord CA 94520 925-288-6000 288-6001
NASDAQ: CERS ■ *TF:* 800-401-1957 ■ *Web:* www.cerus.com

Cima Labs Inc 7325 Aspen Ln .... Brooklyn Park MN 55428 763-488-4700 488-4800
Web: www.cimalabs.com

CMC Biologics 22021 20th Ave SE .... Bothell WA 98021 425-485-1900 486-0300
Web: www.cmcbio.com

Colorado Serum Co 4950 York St PO Box 16428 .... Denver CO 80216 303-295-7527 295-1923
TF Orders: 800-525-2065 ■ *Web:* www.colorado-serum.com

CombiMatrix Corp 300 Goddard Ste 100 .... Irvine CA 92618 949-753-0624 753-1504
NASDAQ: CBMX ■ *TF:* 800-710-0624 ■ *Web:* www.combimatrix.com

Cook Biotech Inc 1425 Innovation Pl .... West Lafayette IN 47906 765-497-3355 497-2361
TF: 888-299-4224 ■ *Web:* www.cookbiotech.com

Corcept Therapeutics Inc
149 Commonwealth Dr .... Menlo Park CA 94025 650-327-3270 327-3218
NASDAQ: CORT ■ *Web:* www.corcept.com

Covance Inc 210 Carnegie Ctr .... Princeton NJ 08540 609-419-2240
NYSE: CVD ■ *TF:* 888-268-2623 ■ *Web:* www.covance.com

Cryolife Inc 1655 Roberts Blvd NW .... Kennesaw GA 30144 770-419-3355 426-0031
NYSE: CRY ■ *TF:* 800-438-8285 ■ *Web:* www.cryolife.com

Cubist Pharmaceuticals Inc 65 Hayden Ave .... Lexington MA 02421 781-860-8660 861-0566
NASDAQ: CBST ■ *TF:* 877-282-4786 ■ *Web:* www.cubist.com

Curis Inc Four Maguire Rd .... Lexington MA 02421 617-503-6500 503-6501
NASDAQ: CRIS ■ *Web:* www.curis.com

Cytokinetics Inc 280 E Grand Ave .... South San Francisco CA 94080 650-624-3000 624-3010
NASDAQ: CYTK ■ *TF:* 800-546-5141 ■ *Web:* www.cytokinetics.com

Cytori Therapeutics Inc 3020 Callan Rd .... San Diego CA 92121 858-458-0900 458-0994
NASDAQ: CYTX ■ *Web:* www.cytori.com

CytRx Corp 11726 San Vicente Blvd Ste 650 .... Los Angeles CA 90049 310-826-5648 826-6139
NASDAQ: CYTR ■ *Web:* www.cytrx.com

Danisco US Inc Genencor Div
925 Page Mill Rd .... Palo Alto CA 94304 650-846-7500 845-6500
Web: biosciences.dupont.com

Dendreon Corp 3005 First Ave .... Seattle WA 98121 206-256-4545 256-0571
OTC: DNDNQ ■ *TF:* 877-256-4545 ■ *Web:* www.dendreon.com

DepoMed Inc 7999 Gateway Blvd Ste 300 .... Newark CA 94560 510-744-8000
NASDAQ: DEPO ■ *Web:* depomed.com

DexCom Inc 6340 Sequence Dr .... San Diego CA 92121 858-200-0200 200-0201
NASDAQ: DXCM ■ *TF:* 888-738-3646 ■ *Web:* www.dexcom.com

diaDexus Inc 349 Oyster Pt Blvd .... South San Francisco CA 94080 650-246-6400 246-6499
OTC: DDXS ■ *Web:* www.diadexus.com

Discovery Laboratories Inc
2600 Kelly Rd Ste 100 .... Warrington PA 18976 215-488-9300 488-9301
NASDAQ: DSCO ■ *Web:* www.discoverylabs.com

Dow AgroSciences LLC 9330 Zionsville Rd .... Indianapolis IN 46268 317-337-3000 905-7326*
**Fax Area Code:* 800 ■ *TF:* 800-258-1470 ■ *Web:* www.dowagro.com

DURECT Corp Two Results Way .... Cupertino CA 95014 408-777-1417 777-3577
NASDAQ: DRRX ■ *Web:* www.durect.com

DUSA Pharmaceuticals Inc 25 Upton Dr .... Wilmington MA 01887 978-657-7500 657-9193
NASDAQ: DUSA ■ *TF:* 877-533-3872 ■ *Web:* www.dusapharma.com

Dyadic International Inc
140 Intracoastal Pointe Dr Ste 404 .... Jupiter FL 33477 561-743-8333 743-8343
OTC: DYAI ■ *Web:* www.dyadic.com

Dyax Corp 55 Network Dr .... Burlington MA 01803 617-225-2500 225-2501
NASDAQ: DYAX ■ *Web:* www.dyax.com

Elite Pharmaceuticals Inc 165 Ludlow Ave .... Northvale NJ 07647 201-750-2646 750-2755
OTC: ELTP ■ *Web:* www.elitepharma.com

Elusys Therapeutics Inc 25 Riverside Dr .... Pine Brook NJ 07058 973-808-0222
Web: www.elusys.com

EMD Serono Inc 1 Technology Pl .... Rockland MA 02370 781-982-9000 871-6754
TF: 800-283-8088 ■ *Web:* www.emdserono.com

Emergent Biosolutions Inc
2273 Research Blvd Ste 400 .... Rockville MD 20850 301-795-1800 795-1899
Web: www.emergentbiosolutions.com

Emisphere Technologies Inc
240 Cedar Knolls Rd Ste 200 .... Cedar Knolls NJ 07927 973-532-8000 532-8115
Web: www.emisphere.com

Encore Medical Corp 9800 Metric Blvd .... Austin TX 78758 512-832-9500 834-6300
TF: 800-456-8696 ■ *Web:* www.djoglobal.com

Enzo Biochem Inc 527 Madison Ave .... New York NY 10022 212-583-0100 583-0150
NYSE: ENZ ■ *TF:* 800-522-5052 ■ *Web:* www.enzo.com

Phone | Fax

Enzon Pharmaceuticals Inc
20 Kingsbridge Rd .... Piscataway NJ 08854 732-980-4500
NASDAQ: ENZN ■ *Web:* www.enzon.com

Exelixis Inc
210 E Grand Ave PO Box 511 .... South San Francisco CA 94080 650-837-7000 837-8300
NASDAQ: EXEL ■ *Web:* www.exelixis.com

Fate Therapeutics Inc
3535 General Atomics Ct Ste 200 .... San Diego CA 92121 858-875-1800
Web: www.fatetherapeutics.com

Galectin Therapeutics Seven Wells Ave Ste 34 .... Newton MA 02459 617-559-0033 928-3450
TF: 888-286-8010 ■ *Web:* www.galectintherapeutics.com

Genaera Corp 5110 Campus Dr .... Plymouth Meeting PA 19462 610-941-4020
TF: 800-299-9156 ■ *Web:* www.genaera.com

Generex Biotechnology Corp
555 Richmond St W Ste 202 .... Toronto ON M5J2G2 416-364-2551 364-9363
OTC: GNBT ■ *TF:* 800-391-6755 ■ *Web:* www.generex.com

GeneThera Inc 7577 W 103rd Ave Ste 212 .... Westminster CO 80021 303-439-2085
Web: www.genethera.net

Genomic Health Inc 101 Galveston Dr .... Redwood City CA 94063 650-556-9300 556-1132
NASDAQ: GHDX ■ *TF:* 866-662-6897 ■ *Web:* www.genomichealth.com

GenVec Inc 65 W Watkins Mill Rd .... Gaithersburg MD 20878 240-632-0740 632-0735
NASDAQ: GNVC ■ *Web:* www.genvec.com

Genzyme Corp 500 Kendall St .... Cambridge MA 02142 617-252-7500
TF: 800-745-4447 ■ *Web:* www.genzyme.com

Geron Corp 149 Commonwealth Dr .... Menlo Park CA 94025 650-473-7700 473-7750
NASDAQ: GERN ■ *Web:* www.geron.com

Gilead 5045 Orbitor Dr .... Mississauga ON L4W4Y4 905-629-9761
TSE: GILD ■ *Web:* www.gilead.com

Gilead Sciences Inc 333 Lakeside Dr .... Foster City CA 94404 650-574-3000 578-9264
NASDAQ: GILD ■ *TF:* 800-445-3235 ■ *Web:* www.gilead.com

Grifols USA LLC 2410 Lillyvale Ave .... Los Angeles CA 90032 888-474-3657
TF: 888-474-3657 ■ *Web:* www.grifolsusa.com

GTC Biotherapeutics Inc 175 Crossing Blvd .... Framingham MA 01702 508-620-9700 370-3797
Web: revobiologics.com/

GTx Inc 175 Toyota Plz Seventh Fl .... Memphis TN 38103 901-523-9700 844-8075
NASDAQ: GTXI ■ *Web:* www.gtxinc.com

Helix Biopharma Corp
305 Industrial Pkwy S Unit 3 .... Aurora ON L4G6X7 905-841-2300 841-2244
TSE: HBP ■ *Web:* www.helixbiopharma.com

Hemispherx Biopharma Inc
1617 JFK Blvd Ste 500 .... Philadelphia PA 19103 215-988-0080 988-1730
NYSE: HEB ■ *Web:* www.hemispherx.net

Idenix Pharmaceuticals Inc
One Merck Dr P.O. Box 100 .... Whitehouse Station NJ 08889 908-423-1000 631-5996*
NYSE: MRK ■ **Fax Area Code:* 215 ■ *TF:* 800-770-4674 ■ *Web:* www.merck.com/contact/home.html

Idera Pharmaceuticals Inc 167 Sidney St .... Cambridge MA 02139 617-679-5500 679-5592
NASDAQ: IDRA ■ *Web:* www.iderapharma.com

Illumina Inc 9885 Towne Centre Dr .... San Diego CA 92121 858-202-4500 202-4545
NASDAQ: ILMN ■ *TF:* 800-809-4566 ■ *Web:* www.illumina.com

ImmunoGen Inc 830 Winter St .... Waltham MA 02451 781-895-0600 895-0611
NASDAQ: IMGN ■ *Web:* www.immunogen.com

Immunomedics Inc 300 American Rd .... Morris Plains NJ 07950 973-605-8200 605-8282
NASDAQ: IMMU ■ *TF:* 800-327-7211 ■ *Web:* www.immunomedics.com

Incyte Corp 1801 Augustine Cut-Off .... Wilmington DE 19803 302-498-6700 425-2750
NASDAQ: INCY ■ *Web:* www.incyte.com

Innovus Pharmaceuticals, Inc.
1981 Murray Holladay R .... Salt Lake City UT 84117 801-272-9294
Web: innovuspharma.com/

INSMED Inc 4851 Lk Brook Dr Ste 200 .... Glen Allen VA 23060 804-565-3000
NASDAQ: INSM ■ *Web:* www.insmed.com

Intarcia Therapeutics Inc
24650 Industrial Blvd .... Hayward CA 94545 510-782-7800 782-7801
Web: www.intarcia.com

Integra LifeSciences Holdings Corp
311 Enterprise Dr .... Plainsboro NJ 08536 609-275-0500 799-3297
NASDAQ: IART ■ *TF:* 800-654-2873 ■ *Web:* www.integra-ls.com

ioGenetics LLC 3591 Anderson St Ste 218 .... Madison WI 53704 608-310-9540
Web: www.iogenetics.com

Irvine Scientific 2511 Daimler St .... Santa Ana CA 92705 949-261-7800 261-6522
TF: 800-577-6097 ■ *Web:* www.irvinesci.com

Isis Pharmaceuticals Inc 2855 Gazelle Ct .... Carlsbad CA 92008 760-931-9200 603-2700
NASDAQ: ISIS ■ *TF:* 800-679-4747 ■ *Web:* www.isispharm.com

Ivers-Lee Inc 31 Hansen S .... Brampton ON L6W3H7 905-451-5535
TF: 800-265-1009 ■ *Web:* jonespackaging.com

La Jolla Pharmaceutical Co
4660 La Jolla Village Dr Ste 400 .... San Diego CA 92122 858-207-4264
Web: lajollapharmaceutical.com

Leo Pharma Inc
123 Commerce Vly Dr E Ste 400 .... Thornhill ON L3T7W8 905-886-9822 886-6622
TF General: 800-668-7234 ■ *Web:* www.leo-pharma.com

Lescarden Inc 420 Lexington Ave Ste 212 .... New York NY 10170 212-687-1050 687-1051
Web: www.lescarden.com

Lexicon Pharmaceuticals Inc
8800 Technology Forest Pl .... The Woodlands TX 77381 281-863-3000 863-8088
NASDAQ: LXRX ■ *TF:* 855-828-4651 ■ *Web:* www.lexicon-genetics.com

LifeCore Biomedical LLC 3515 Lyman Blvd .... Chaska MN 55318 952-368-4300 368-3411
TF Cust Svc: 800-752-2663 ■ *Web:* www.lifecore.com

LiphaTech Inc 3600 W Elm St .... Milwaukee WI 53209 888-331-7900 247-8166*
**Fax Area Code:* 414 ■ *TF:* 888-331-7900 ■ *Web:* www.liphatech.com

Lorus Therapeutics Inc Two Meridian Rd .... Toronto ON M9W4Z7 416-798-1200 798-2200
NYSE: LOR ■ *Web:* www.lorusthera.com

Lundbeck Canada Inc
1000 de la GauchetiFre W Ste 500 .... Montreal QC H3B4W5 514-844-8515 844-5495
Web: www.lundbeck.com

MannKind Corp 28903 N Ave Paine .... Valencia CA 91355 661-775-5300 775-2081
NASDAQ: MNKD ■ *Web:* www.mannkindcorp.com

Martek Biosciences Corp 6480 Dobbin Rd .... Columbia MD 21045 410-740-0081 740-2985
Web: www.lifesdha.com

Medicines Co Eight Sylvan Way .... Parsippany NJ 07054 973-290-6000 656-9898
NASDAQ: MDCO ■ *TF:* 800-388-1183 ■ *Web:* www.themedicinescompany.com

MediGene Inc
10650 Scripps Ranch Blvd Ste 206 .... San Diego CA 92131 858-586-2240
Web: www.medigene.com

	Phone	Fax
Mera Pharmaceuticals Inc 73-4460 Queen Kaahumanu Hwy Ste 110 . . . . Kailua-Kona HI 96740 *TF:* 800-480-6515 ■ *Web:* www.merapharma.com	808-326-9301	326-9401
Millennium Pharmaceuticals Inc 40 Lansdowne St . . . . Cambridge MA 02139 *Web:* www.millennium.com	617-679-7000	374-7788
Momenta Pharmaceuticals Inc 675 W Kendall St . . . . Cambridge MA 02142 *NASDAQ: MNTA* ■ *Web:* www.momentapharma.com	617-491-9700	621-0431
Myriad Genetics Inc 320 Wakara Way . . . . Salt Lake City UT 84108 *NASDAQ: MYGN* ■ *TF:* 800-469-7423 ■ *Web:* www.myriad.com	801-584-3600	584-3640
N.E.T. Inc 5651 Palmer Way Ste C . . . . Carlsbad CA 92010 *TF:* 800-888-4638 ■ *Web:* www.netmindbody.com	760-929-5980	929-5981
Natural Industries Inc 12320 Cutten Rd. . . . . Houston TX 77066 *Web:* www.naturalindustries.com	281-580-1643	
Nektar Therapeutics 455 Mission Bay Blvd S . . . . San Francisco CA 94158 *NASDAQ: NKTR* ■ *Web:* www.nektar.com	415-482-5300	
Neuralstem Inc 9700 Great Seneca Hwy . . . . Rockville MD 20850 *Web:* investor.neuralstem.com	301-366-4841	
Neurocrine Biosciences Inc 12790 El Camino Rl . . . . San Diego CA 92130 *NASDAQ: NBIX* ■ *Web:* www.neurocrine.com	858-617-7600	617-7602
Nordion 447 March Rd. . . . . Ottawa ON K2K1X8 *NYSE: NDZ* ■ *TF:* 800-465-3666 ■ *Web:* www.nordion.com	613-592-2790	592-6937
Novartis Vaccines & Diagnostics One Health Plz Bldg 122. . . . . East Hanover NJ 07936 *NYSE: NVS* ■ *TF:* 888-644-8585 ■ *Web:* www.novartis-vaccines.com	862-778-8300	
Novavax Inc 9920 Belward Campus Dr. . . . . Rockville MD 20850 *NASDAQ: NVAX* ■ *TF:* 800-642-1687 ■ *Web:* www.novavax.com	240-268-2000	268-2100
NPS Pharmaceuticals Inc 550 Hills Dr Third Fl. . . . . Bedminster NJ 07921 *NASDAQ: NPSP* ■ *Web:* www.npsp.com	908-450-5300	450-5351
Nucro-Technics 2000 Ellesmere Rd Unit 16. . . . . Scarborough ON M1H2W4 *Web:* www.nucro-technics.com	416-438-6727	438-3463
Nuo Therapeutics Inc 207A Perry Pkwy Ste 1 . . . . Gaithersburg MD 20877 *OTC: NUOT* ■ *TF:* 866-298-6633 ■ *Web:* www.cytomedix.com	866-298-6633	
Nuvo Research Inc 7560 Airport Rd Unit 10 . . . . Mississauga ON L4T4H4 *TSE: NRI* ■ *TF:* 888-398-3463 ■ *Web:* www.nuvoresearch.com	905-673-6980	673-1842
Oakwood Laboratories LLC 7670 First Pl Ste A . . . . Oakwood Village OH 44146 *TF:* 888-625-9352 ■ *Web:* www.oakwoodlabs.com	440-359-0000	359-0001
Oncolytics Biotech Inc 1167 Kensington Crescent NW Ste 210 . . . . Calgary AB T2N1X7 *TSE: ONC* ■ *TF:* 800-731-5319 ■ *Web:* www.oncolyticsbiotech.com	403-670-7377	283-0858
Oncothyreon Inc 2601 Fourth Ave Ste 500. . . . . Seattle WA 98121 *Web:* www.oncothyreon.com	206-801-2100	801-2101
Onyx Pharmaceuticals Inc 249 E Grand Av. . . . . South San Francisco CA 94080 *NASDAQ: ONXX* ■ *TF:* 877-669-9121 ■ *Web:* www.onyx.com	650-266-0000	266-0100
Organogenesis Inc 150 Dan Rd . . . . Canton MA 02021 *Web:* www.organogenesis.com	781-575-0775	575-0440
Osiris Therapeutics Inc 7015 Albert Einstein Dr. . . . . Columbia MD 21046 *NASDAQ: OSIR* ■ *Web:* www.osiristx.com	443-545-1800	545-1701
Osteotech Inc 710 Medtronic Pkwy. . . . . Minneapolis MN 55432 **Fax Area Code:* 732 ■ **Fax:* Hum Res ■ *TF:* 800-633-8766 ■ *Web:* www.medtronic.com	763-514-4000	542-9312*
OXiGENE Inc 701 Gateway Blvd Ste 210 . . . . South San Francisco CA 94080 *NASDAQ: OXGN* ■ *Web:* www.oxigene.com	650-635-7000	635-7001
Oxis International Inc 468 N Camden Dr Second Fl . . . . Beverly Hills CA 90210 *OTC: OXIS* ■ *Web:* www.oxis.com	310-860-5184	
Pacira Inc 10450 Science Ctr Dr. . . . . San Diego CA 92121 *Web:* www.pacira.com	858-625-2424	625-2439
Paladin Labs Inc 100 Blvd Alexis Nihon Ste 600. . . . . St-Laurent QC H4M2P2 *TSE: PLB* ■ *TF:* 888-376-7830 ■ *Web:* www.paladin-labs.com	514-340-1112	344-4675
Palatin Technologies Inc 4-C Cedar Brook Dr . . . . Cranbury NJ 08512 *NYSE: PTN* ■ *Web:* www.palatin.com	609-495-2200	495-2201
Paratek Pharmaceuticals Inc 75 Kneeland St . . . . Boston MA 02111 *Web:* www.paratekpharm.com	617-275-0040	275-0039
Peregrine Pharmaceuticals Inc 14282 Franklin Ave Ste 100 . . . . Tustin CA 92780 *NASDAQ: PPHM* ■ *TF:* 800-987-8256 ■ *Web:* www.peregrineinc.com	714-508-6000	838-5817
Pharmacyclics Inc 995 E Arques Ave . . . . Sunnyvale CA 94085 *NASDAQ: PCYC* ■ *TF:* 800-458-0330 ■ *Web:* www.pharmacyclics.com	408-774-0330	774-0340
Poniard Pharmaceuticals Inc 750B Attery St Ste 330 . . . . South San Francisco CA 94111 *OTC: PARD*	650-583-3774	
Pozen Inc 1414 Raleigh Rd Ste 400 . . . . Chapel Hill NC 27517 *NASDAQ: POZN* ■ *Web:* www.pozen.com	919-913-1030	913-1039
PRA International *PRA* 4130 Parklake Ave Ste 400. . . . . Raleigh NC 27612 *Web:* prahs.com	919-786-8200	786-8201
Pressure BioSciences Inc 14 Norfolk Ave. . . . . South Easton MA 02375 *OTC: PBIO* ■ *Web:* pressurebiosciences.com	508-230-1828	230-1829
Primorigen Biosciences Inc 510 Charmany Dr . . . . Madison WI 53719 *TF:* 866-372-7442 ■ *Web:* www.primorigen.com	608-441-8332	
Progenics Pharmaceuticals Inc 777 Old Saw Mill River Rd . . . . Tarrytown NY 10591 *NASDAQ: PGNX* ■ *TF:* 866-644-7188 ■ *Web:* www.progenics.com	914-789-2800	789-2817
Protein Sciences Corp 1000 Research Pkwy . . . . Meriden CT 06450 *TF:* 800-488-7099 ■ *Web:* www.proteinsciences.com	203-686-0800	686-0268
pSivida Inc 400 Pleasant St . . . . Watertown MA 02472 *NASDAQ: PSDV* ■ *Web:* www.psivida.com	617-926-5000	926-5050
Psychemedics Corp 125 Nagog Pk Ste 200. . . . . Acton MA 01720 *NASDAQ: PMD* ■ *TF:* 800-628-8073 ■ *Web:* www.psychemedics.com	978-206-8220	264-9236
QLT Inc 887 Great Northern Way Ste 101 . . . . Vancouver BC V5T4T5 *NASDAQ: QLT* ■ *TF:* 800-663-5486 ■ *Web:* www.qltinc.com	604-707-7000	707-7001
Questcor Pharmaceuticals Inc 1300 N Kellogg Ste D. . . . . Anaheim Hills CA 92807 *NASDAQ: QCOR* ■ *TF:* 888-435-2284 ■ *Web:* mallinckrodt.com/questcor	714-786-4200	
Regeneron Pharmaceuticals Inc 777 Old Saw Mill River Rd . . . . Tarrytown NY 10591 *NASDAQ: REGN* ■ *TF:* 800-637-8322 ■ *Web:* www.regeneron.com	914-847-7000	
Repligen Corp 41 Seyon St . . . . Waltham MA 02453 *NASDAQ: RGEN* ■ *TF Sales:* 800-622-2259 ■ *Web:* www.repligen.com	781-250-0111	250-0115
Repros Therapeutics Inc 2408 Timberloch Pl Ste B-7 . . . . The Woodlands TX 77380 *NASDAQ: RPRX* ■ *Web:* www.reprosrx.com	281-719-3400	719-3446
Research Triangle Park Laboratories 7201 Acc Blvd # 104 . . . . Raleigh NC 27617 *Web:* www.rtp-labs.com	919-510-0228	510-0141
Revivicor Inc 1700 Kraft Dr Ste 2400. . . . . Blacksburg VA 24060 *Web:* www.revivicor.com	540-961-5559	961-7958
Rigel Pharmaceuticals Inc 1180 Veterans Blvd. . . . . South San Francisco CA 94080 *NASDAQ: RIGL* ■ *Web:* www.rigel.com	650-624-1100	624-1101
Roche Palo Alto LLC 4300 Hacienda Dr . . . . Pleasanton CA 94588 *TF:* 866-796-1569 ■ *Web:* www.roche.com	925-730-8000	730-8388
Royalty Pharma 110 E 59th St 33rd Fl. . . . . New York NY 10022 *Web:* www.royaltypharma.com	212-883-0200	883-2260
RTI Biologics Inc 11621 Research Cir . . . . Alachua FL 32615 *NASDAQ: RTIX* ■ *TF:* 877-343-6832 ■ *Web:* www.rtix.com	386-418-8888	418-0342
Samaritan Pharmaceuticals Inc 101 Convention Ctr Dr Ste 310. . . . . Las Vegas NV 89109 *OTC: SPHC*	702-735-7001	
Sangamo BioSciences Inc 501 Canal Blvd Ste A100 . . . . Richmond CA 94804 *NASDAQ: SGMO* ■ *Web:* www.sangamo.com	510-970-6000	236-8951
Sanofi Pasteur Inc Discovery Dr. . . . . Swiftwater PA 18370 **Fax:* Hum Res ■ *TF Orders:* 800-822-2463 ■ *Web:* www.sanofipasteur.us	570-839-7187	839-7187*
Sanofi-Aventis Canada 2150 St Elzear Blvd W . . . . Laval QC H7L4A8 *TF:* 800-363-6364 ■ *Web:* sanofi-aventis.ca/index.html	514-331-9220	334-8016
Santarus Inc 3721 Vly Centre Dr Ste 400 Fourth Fl. . . . . San Diego CA 92130 *NASDAQ: SNTS* ■ *TF Cust Svc:* 888-778-0887 ■ *Web:* salix.com/	858-314-5700	314-5701
Seattle Genetics Inc 21823 30th Dr SE . . . . Bothell WA 98021 *NASDAQ: SGEN* ■ *Web:* www.seattlegenetics.com	425-527-4000	527-4001
Selexys Pharmaceuticals Corp 840 Research Pkwy Ste 516 . . . . Oklahoma City OK 73104 *Web:* www.selexys.com	405-319-8195	
Sequenom Inc 3595 John Hopkins Ct . . . . San Diego CA 92121 *NASDAQ: SQNM* ■ *TF:* 877-821-7266 ■ *Web:* www.sequenom.com	858-202-9000	202-9001
Soligenix Inc 29 Emmons Dr Ste C-10 . . . . Princeton NJ 08540 *OTC: SNGX* ■ *TF:* 877-407-3974 ■ *Web:* soligenix.com	609-538-8200	452-6467
Spectrum Pharmaceuticals Inc 11500 S Eastern Ave Ste 240 . . . . Henderson NV 89052 *NASDAQ: SPPI* ■ *TF:* 800-332-1088 ■ *Web:* www.spectrumpharm.com	702-835-6300	260-7405
SRP Environmental LLC 348 Aero Dr . . . . Shreveport LA 71107 *Web:* www.srpenvironmental.com	318-222-2364	
Supernus Pharmaceuticals Inc 1550 E Gude Dr . . . . Rockville MD 20850 *NASDAQ: SUPN* ■ *Web:* www.supernus.com	301-838-2500	
Synthetech Inc 1290 Industrial Way . . . . Albany OR 97322 *Web:* grace.com/pharma-and-biotech/en-us	541-967-6575	967-9424
Takeda Canada Inc 435 N Service Rd W Ste 101 . . . . Oakville ON L6M4X8 *TF:* 888-367-3331 ■ *Web:* www.takedacanada.com	905-469-9333	469-4883
Tamir Biotechnology Inc 12625 High Bluff Dr Ste 113. . . . . San Diego CA 92130 *OTC: ACEL* ■ *Web:* www.alfacell.com	732-823-1003	652-4575
Tekmira Pharmaceuticals Corp 100 - 8900 Glenlyon Pkwy . . . . Burnaby BC V5J5J8 *TSE: TKM* ■ *Web:* tekmira.com	604-419-3200	419-3201
Telesta Therapeutics Inc 275 Labrosse Ave . . . . Pointe-Claire QC H9R1A3 *TSE: TST* ■ *TF:* 800-387-0825 ■ *Web:* www.telestatherapeutics.com	514-697-6636	697-7966
Theratechnologies Inc 2310 Alfred Nobel Blvd. . . . . Montreal QC H4S2B4 *TSE: TH* ■ *Web:* www.theratech.com	514-336-7800	336-7242
Theravance Inc 901 Gateway Blvd . . . . South San Francisco CA 94080 *NASDAQ: THRX* ■ *Web:* www.theravance.com	650-808-6000	
Threshold Pharmaceuticals Inc 170 Harbor Way Suite 300 . . . . South San Francisco CA 94080 *NASDAQ: THLD* ■ *TF:* 866-276-9886 ■ *Web:* www.thresholdpharm.com	650-474-8200	474-2529
Titan Pharmaceuticals Inc 400 Oyster Pt Blvd Ste 505. . . . . South San Francisco CA 94080 *OTC: TTNP* ■ *TF:* 888-417-8516 ■ *Web:* www.titanpharm.com	650-244-4990	244-4956
Unigene Laboratories Inc 81 Fulton St . . . . Boonton NJ 07005 *Web:* www.unigene.com/	973-265-1100	
United Biomedical Inc 25 Davids Dr . . . . Hauppauge NY 11788 *Web:* www.unitedbiomedical.com	631-273-2828	273-1717
Urigen Pharmaceuticals Inc 501 Silverside Rd PO Box 95 . . . . Wilmington DE 19809 *Web:* www.urigen.com	925-280-2861	280-2861
Verdezyne Inc 2715 Loker Ave W . . . . Carlsbad CA 92010 *Web:* www.verdezyne.com	760-707-5200	
Vericel Corp 24 Frank Lloyd Wright Dr Domino's Farms Lobby K . . . . Ann Arbor MI 48105 *NASDAQ: ASTM* ■ *Web:* www.aastrom.com	734-418-4400	665-0485
Vical Inc 10390 Pacific Ctr Ct . . . . San Diego CA 92121 *NASDAQ: VICL* ■ *Web:* www.vical.com	858-646-1100	646-1150
ViroPharma Inc 730 Stockton Dr. . . . . Exton PA 19341 *NASDAQ: VPHM* ■ *TF:* 877-841-4559 ■ *Web:* shire.com/shireplc/en/home	610-458-7300	458-7380
Viventia Biotechnologies Inc 147 Hamelin St Ste 204 . . . . Winnipeg MB R3T3Z1 **Fax Area Code:* 905 ■ *Web:* www.viventia.com	204-478-1023	362-2973*
XenoPort Inc 3410 Central Expy . . . . Santa Clara CA 95051 *NASDAQ: XNPT* ■ *Web:* www.xenoport.com	408-616-7200	616-7210
XOMA (US) LLC 2910 Seventh St. . . . . Berkeley CA 94710 *NASDAQ: XOMA* ■ *TF:* 800-468-9716 ■ *Web:* www.xoma.com	510-204-7200	644-2011

Phone Fax

ZymoGenetics Inc 1201 Eastlake Ave E .... Seattle WA 98102 206-442-6600 442-6608
TF: 800-332-2056 ■ *Web:* www.bms.com

86 BLANKBOOKS & BINDERS

SEE ALSO Checks - Personal & Business p. 1943

Phone Fax

Abco Inc 1621 Wall St .... Dallas TX 75215 214-565-1191 428-8996
TF: 800-969-2226 ■ *Web:* abcodigital.com

Acme Sample Books Inc 2410 Schirra Pl .... High Point NC 27263 336-883-4187 883-4565
Web: www.acmesample.com

Advanced Looseleaf Technologies Inc
1424 Somerset Ave .... Dighton MA 02715 508-669-6354 669-6143
TF: 800-339-6354 ■ *Web:* www.binder.com

Allison Payment Systems LLC
2200 Production Dr .... Indianapolis IN 46241 800-755-2440 808-2477*
**Fax Area Code:* 317 ■ *TF:* 800-755-2440 ■ *Web:* www.apsllc.com

American Thermoplastic Co (ATC) 106 Gamma Dr ... Pittsburgh PA 15238 800-245-6600
TF: 800-245-6600 ■ *Web:* www.binders.com

Blackbourn 200 Fourth Ave N .... Edgerton MN 56128 800-842-7550 442-4313*
**Fax Area Code:* 507 ■ *TF:* 800-842-7550 ■ *Web:* www.blackbourn.com

Blair Packaging Inc
1515 Independence St .... Cape Girardeau MO 63703 573-334-2146
TF: 800-624-3150

Colad Group 801 Exchange St .... Buffalo NY 14210 716-961-1776 961-1753
TF: 800-950-1755 ■ *Web:* www.colad.com

Colwell Industries Inc 123 N Third St .... Minneapolis MN 55401 612-340-0365
Web: www.colwellindustries.com

Continental Binder & Specialty Corp
407 W Compton Blvd .... Gardena CA 90248 310-324-8227 715-6740
TF: 800-872-2897 ■ *Web:* www.continentalbinder.com

Continental Loose Leaf Inc 1122 16th Ave .... Minneapolis MN 55414 612-378-4800 378-7680
TF: 888-719-5013 ■ *Web:* www.continentallooseleaf.com

Daret Inc 287 Margaret King Ave .... Ringwood NJ 07456 973-962-6001
Web: daret.com

Data Management Inc 537 New Britain Ave .... Farmington CT 06034 860-677-8586 428-1951*
**Fax Area Code:* 800 ■ *TF Orders:* 800-243-1969 ■ *Web:* www.datamanage.com

Dilley Manufacturing Co 215 E Third St .... Des Moines IA 50309 515-288-7289 288-4210
TF: 800-247-5087 ■ *Web:* www.dilleymfg.com

EBSCO Industries Inc Vulcan Information Packaging Div
PO Box 29 .... Vincent AL 35178 800-633-4526 344-8939
TF: 800-633-4526 ■ *Web:* www.vulcan-online.com

Eckhart & Company Inc 4011 W 54th St .... Indianapolis IN 46254 317-347-2665 347-2666
TF: 800-443-3791 ■ *Web:* www.eckhartandco.com

Federal Business Products Inc 95 Main Ave .... Clifton NJ 07014 973-667-9800
TF: 800-927-5123 ■ *Web:* www.feddirect.com

Fey Industries Inc 200 Fourth Ave N .... Edgerton MN 56128 507-442-4311 442-3686
TF: 800-533-5340 ■ *Web:* fey-line.com

Formflex Inc PO Box 218 .... Bloomingdale IN 47832 800-255-7659 498-5200*
**Fax Area Code:* 765 ■ *TF:* 800-255-7659 ■ *Web:* www.formflexproducts.com

General Loose Leaf Bindery Co
3811 Hawthorn Ct .... Waukegan IL 60087 847-244-9700 244-9741
TF: 800-621-0493 ■ *Web:* www.looseleaf.com

General Products 4045 N Rockwell St .... Chicago IL 60618 773-463-2424 463-3028
Web: www.gpalbums.com

HALO Branded Solutions Inc
1980 Industrial Dr .... Sterling IL 61081 815-632-6800 632-6900
Web: www.halo.com

HC Miller Co 3030 Lowell Dr .... Green Bay WI 54311 920-465-3030 465-3035
Web: hcmillerpress.com

Holum & Sons Company Inc 740 Burr Oak Dr .... Westmont IL 60559 630-654-8222 654-2929
TF: 800-447-4479 ■ *Web:* www.holumandsons.com

Kurtz Bros Company Inc
400 Reed St PO Box 392 .... Clearfield PA 16830 814-765-6561 765-8690
TF: 800-252-3811 ■ *Web:* www.kurtzbros.com

Leed Selling Tools Corp 9700 Hwy 57 .... Evansville IN 47725 812-867-4340 867-4353
Web: leedsamples.com

Michael Lewis Co 8900 W 50th St .... McCook IL 60525 708-688-2200 688-2880
TF: 800-323-8808 ■ *Web:* www.mlco.com

NAPCO Inc 120 Trojan Ave .... Sparta NC 28675 336-372-5228 372-8602
TF: 800-854-8621 ■ *Web:* www.napcousa.com

Northeast Data Services 1316 College Ave .... Elmira NY 14901 607-733-5541
TF Cust Svc: 800-699-5636 ■ *Web:* the-leader.com

Pioneer Photo Albums Inc 9801 Deering Ave .... Chatsworth CA 91311 818-882-2161 882-6239
Web: www.pioneerphotoalbums.com

Roaring Spring Blank Book Co
740 Spang St .... Roaring Spring PA 16673 814-224-5141 224-5429
TF: 800-441-1653 ■ *Web:* www.rspaperproducts.com

Samsill Corp 5740 Hartman Rd .... Fort Worth TX 76119 817-536-1906 535-6900
TF: 800-255-1100 ■ *Web:* www.samsill.com

Southwest Plastic Binding Co
109 Millwell Ct .... Maryland Heights MO 63043 314-739-4400 942-2010*
**Fax Area Code:* 800 ■ *TF:* 800-325-3628 ■ *Web:* www.swplastic.com

Spiral Binding Company Inc One Maltese Dr .... Totowa NJ 07511 973-256-0666 256-5981*
**Fax:* Cust Svc ■ *TF:* 800-631-3572 ■ *Web:* www.spiralbinding.com

Superior Press Inc 11930 Hamden Pl .... Santa Fe Springs CA 90670 562-948-1866 948-4966
TF Cust Svc: 888-590-7998 ■ *Web:* www.superior-press.com

Trendex Inc 240 E Maryland Ave .... Saint Paul MN 55117 651-489-4655 489-4423
TF: 800-328-9200 ■ *Web:* www.trendex.com

Unified Packaging Inc 1187 E 68th Ave .... Denver CO 80229 303-733-1000 733-6789
Web: www.unifiedbinders.com

Union Group 649 Alden St .... Fall River MA 02722 508-675-4545 677-0130
TF: 800-289-3523 ■ *Web:* www.theuniongroup.com

US Ring Binder 6800 Arsenal St .... Saint Louis MO 63139 314-645-7880 645-7239
TF: 800-888-8772 ■ *Web:* www.usring.com

ViaTech Publishing Solutions
1440 Fifth Ave .... Bay Shore NY 11706 631-968-8500 968-0830
TF: 800-645-8558 ■ *Web:* www.viatechpub.com

West Coast Samples Inc 14450 Central Ave .... Chino CA 91710 909-464-1616 465-9982

87 BLINDS & SHADES

Phone Fax

Aeroshade Inc 433 Oakland Ave .... Waukesha WI 53186 262-547-2101 547-0546
TF: 800-331-7179

Beauti-Vue Products Inc
8555 194th Ave Bristol Industrial Pk .... Bristol WI 53104 262-857-2306 329-9431*
**Fax Area Code:* 800 ■ *TF:* 800-558-9431 ■ *Web:* www.beautivue.com

Budget Blinds Inc 1927 N Glassell St .... Orange CA 92865 714-637-2100 637-1400
TF: 800-800-9250 ■ *Web:* www.budgetblinds.com

Carnegie Fabrics Inc
110 N Centre Ave .... Rockville Centre NY 11570 516-678-6770 678-6875
Web: www.carnegiefabrics.com

Comfortex Window Fashions Inc 21 Elm St .... Maplewood NY 12189 518-273-3333 336-4580*
**Fax Area Code:* 800 ■ *TF Cust Svc:* 800-843-4151 ■ *Web:* www.comfortex.com

Delaine James Inc 10508C Boyer Blvd Ste 400 .... Austin TX 78758 512-835-5333 999-5555*
**Fax Area Code:* 800 ■ *TF Claims:* 800-999-5333 ■ *Web:* www.delainejames.com

Dixon Blind & Awning Service
1800 Sunset Ave .... Rocky Mount NC 27804 252-442-2145

Hunter Douglas Inc 1 Hunter Douglas Dr .... Cumberland MD 21502 301-722-7700 950-3399*
**Fax Area Code:* 800 ■ *TF:* 800-365-3399 ■ *Web:* www.hdfab.com

Kenney Mfg Co 1000 Jefferson Blvd .... Warwick RI 02886 401-739-2200 736-1822
TF Cust Svc: 800-753-6639 ■ *Web:* www.kenney.com

Lafayette Venetian Blind Inc
3000 Klondike Rd. P.O. Box 2838 .... West Lafayette IN 47996 800-342-5523 423-2402*
**Fax Area Code:* 765 ■ *TF:* 800-342-5523 ■ *Web:* www.lafvb.com

Levolor Kirsch Window Fashions
4110 Premier Dr .... High Point NC 27265 336-812-8181
TF: 800-752-9677 ■ *Web:* www.levolor.com

Mill Supply Div 266 Morse St .... Hamden CT 06517 203-777-7668 777-4515
TF General: 888-585-9354 ■ *Web:* www.millsupplydiv.com

Ralph Friedland & Bros 17 Industrial Dr .... Keyport NJ 07735 732-290-9800
Web: friedlandshades.com

Sun Control Products Window Shades
1908 Second St SW .... Rochester MN 55902 507-282-2620
TF: 800-533-0010 ■ *Web:* suncontrolwindowshades.com

Superior Shade & Blind Company Inc
1571 N Powerline Rd .... Pompano Beach FL 33069 954-975-8122 975-2938
Web: www.superiorshade.com

Warm Co 5529 186th Pl SW .... Lynnwood WA 98037 425-248-2424 248-2422
TF: 800-234-9276 ■ *Web:* www.warmcompany.com

88 BLISTER PACKAGING

Phone Fax

A-1 Creative Packaging Corp
400 Industrial Blvd .... Palmyra WI 53156 262-495-2151
Web: creativeplastics.com

Aaron Thomas Company Inc
7421 Chapman Ave .... Garden Grove CA 92841 714-894-4468
Web: www.packaging.com

Accu-Tec Inc 1735 W Burnett St .... Louisville KY 40210 502-339-7511
Web: www.accu-tec.com

Adec Industries 2700 Industrial Pkwy .... Elkhart IN 46516 574-295-3167
Web: www.adecinc.com

Aero Fulfillment Services Corp 3900 Aero Dr .... Mason OH 45040 513-459-3900
Web: www.aerofulfillment.com

Andex Industries Inc 1911 Fourth Ave N .... Escanaba MI 49829 800-338-9882 786-3133*
**Fax Area Code:* 906 ■ *TF:* 800-338-9882 ■ *Web:* www.andex.net

Andpak Inc 400 Jarvis Dr .... Morgan Hill CA 95037 408-782-2500
Web: www.andpak.com

AQL Decorating Company Inc 215 Bergen Blvd .... Fairview NJ 07022 201-941-1610
Web: www.aqldecorating.com

Axiom Label 1360 W Walnut Pkwy .... Compton CA 90220 310-603-8910
Web: www.axiomlabel.com

Bms Management Inc 1200 W Commerce Way .... Lincoln NE 68521 402-474-4014
Web: bmswarehouse.com

Brisar Industries Inc 150 E Seventh St .... Paterson NJ 07524 973-278-2500
Web: www.brisar.com

Card Pak Inc 29601 Solon Rd .... Solon OH 44139 440-542-3100 542-3399
TF: 800-824-3342 ■ *Web:* www.cardpak.com

Chrysalis Packaging & Assembly Corp
130 W Edgerton Ave Ste 130 .... Milwaukee WI 53207 414-744-8550
Web: www.chryspac.com

CS Packaging Inc 1620 Fullerton Ct .... Glendale Heights IL 60137 630-534-4500
Web: www.cspackaging.com

Display Pack 1340 Monroe Ave NW .... Grand Rapids MI 49505 616-451-3061 451-8907
Web: www.displaypack.com

DIY Group Inc 2401 W 26th .... Muncie IN 47302 765-284-9000
Web: www.diygroup.com

EPC Industries Ltd 12 Tupper Blvd .... Amherst NS B4H4S7 902-667-7241
Web: www.polycello.com

Genesee Packaging Inc 2010 Dort Hwy .... Flint MI 48506 810-235-6120
Web: www.genpackaging.com

Genie Manufacturing Corp
999 Rush Henrietta Townli .... Rush NY 14543 585-359-4100
Web: www.geniemfg.com

GSC Packaging Inc 575 Wharton Dr .... Atlanta GA 30336 404-505-9925
Web: www.gscpackaging.com

Guernsey Industries 60772 Southgate Rd .... Byesville OH 43723 740-439-5017
Web: guernseycountydd.org

Guy Chemical Company Inc 150 Dominion Dr .... Somerset PA 15501 814-443-9455
Web: www.guychemical.com

Hmc Products Inc 5196 27th Ave .... Rockford IL 61109 815-397-9145
Web: www.hmcproducts.com

Hy-Test Packaging Corp 515 E 41st St .... Paterson NJ 07504 973-754-7000
Web: www.hy-testpackaging.com

Imperial Dax Company Inc 120 New Dutch Ln .... Fairfield NJ 07004 973-227-6105
Web: www.imperialdax.com

Phone | Fax

Innovated Packaging Company Inc
38505 Cherry St . . . Newark CA 94560 510-745-8180
Web: www.innovpak.com

James Alexander Corp 845 Route 94 . . . Blairstown NJ 07825 908-362-9266
Web: www.james-alexander.com

Jay Packaging Group (JPG)
100 Warwick Industrial Dr . . . Warwick RI 02886 401-739-7200 738-0137*
**Fax:* Cust Svc ■ *Web:* www.jaypack.com

Jenco Productions Inc 401 South J St . . . San Bernardino CA 92410 909-381-9453
Web: www.jencoproductions.com

Kent Sussex Industries Inc
301 N Rehoboth Blvd . . . Milford DE 19963 302-422-4014
Web: www.ksiinc.org

Metro Label Group Inc 999 Progress Ave . . . Toronto ON M1B6J1 416-292-6600
Web: www.metrolabel.com

Nelson Packaging Company Inc 1801 Reservoir Rd . . . Lima OH 45804 419-229-3471
Web: www.nelsonpackagingco.com

Nk Parts Industry Inc Main Facility
777 S Kuther Rd . . . Sidney OH 45365 937-498-4651
Web: www.nkparts.com

PackageX Inc 17100 Ventura Blvd Ste 223 . . . Encino CA 91316 818-789-6910
Web: www.packagex.com

Pak-Rite Ltd 2395 S Burrell St . . . Milwaukee WI 53207 414-489-0450
Web: www.pak-rite.com

Placon Corp 6096 McKee Rd . . . Madison WI 53719 608-271-5634 271-3162
TF: 800-541-1535 ■ *Web:* www.placon.com

Pri-Pak Inc 2000 Schenley Pl . . . Greendale IN 47025 812-537-7300
Web: www.pripak.com

Primary Packaging Inc
10810 Industrial Pkwy NW . . . Bolivar OH 44612 330-874-3131 874-3811
TF: 800-774-2247 ■ *Web:* www.primarypackaging.com

Pro-Tech Design & Manufacturing Inc
14561 Marquardt Ave . . . Santa Fe Springs CA 90670 562-207-1680
Web: www.protechdesign.net

Quetico LLC 5521 Schaefer Ave . . . Chino CA 91710 909-628-6200
Web: www.queticollc.com

Rand Direct
21 Gateway Commerce Ctr Dr W . . . Edwardsville IL 62025 618-931-7805
Web: randdirect.com

Remar Inc 6200 E Division St . . . Lebanon TN 37090 615-449-0231
Web: www.remarinc.com

Sealed Air Corp 200 Riverfront Blvd . . . Elmwood Park NJ 07407 201-791-7600
NYSE: SEE ■ *Web:* www.sealedair.com

Software Partners Inc
447 Old Boston Rd Rt 1 . . . Topsfield MA 01983 978-887-6409
Web: www.softwarepartners.com

Sourcentra Inc 150 Speen St . . . Framingham MA 01701 508-405-2605
Web: www.sourcentra.com

Sun Packing Inc 10077 Wallisville Rd . . . Houston TX 77013 713-673-4600
Web: www.sunpacking.com

Tailored Label Products Inc
W165 N5731 Ridgewood Dr . . . Menomonee Falls WI 53051 262-703-5000
Web: www.tailoredlabel.com

Tpgtex Label Solutions Inc 5830 Ludington Dr . . . Houston TX 77035 713-726-9636
Web: www.tpgtex.com

Unified Solutions Inc 9801 80th Ave . . . Pleasant Prairie WI 53158 262-942-5200
Web: usipackaging.com

Valley Packaging Industries Inc
110 N Kensington Dr . . . Appleton WI 54915 920-749-5840
Web: www.vpind.com

Virtual Images 1177 Idaho St Ste 100 . . . Redlands CA 92374 909-388-1000
Web: www.viu.com

Visual Pak Co 1909 Waukegan Rd . . . Waukegan IL 60085 847-689-1000
Web: www.visualpak.com

Vulsay Industries Ltd 35 Regan Rd . . . Brampton ON L7A1B2 905-846-2200
Web: www.vulsay.com

WePackItAll Inc 2745 Huntington Dr . . . Duarte CA 91010 626-301-9214
Web: www.wepackitall.com

Westpak Inc 10326 Roselle St Ste 101 . . . San Diego CA 92121 858-623-8100
Web: www.westpak.com

Wynalda Packaging 8221 Graphic Dr NE . . . Belmont MI 49306 616-866-1561 866-4316
TF General: 800-952-8668 ■ *Web:* www.wynalda.com

Xela Pack Inc 8300 Boettner Rd . . . Saline MI 48176 734-944-1300
Web: www.xelapack.com

89 BLOOD CENTERS

SEE ALSO Laboratories - Drug-Testing p. 2616; Laboratories - Genetic Testing p. 2616; Laboratories - Medical p. 2616

The centers listed here are members of America's Blood Centers (ABC), the national network of non-profit, independent community blood centers. ABC members are licensed and regulated by the US Food & Drug Administration.

Phone | Fax

Belle Bonfils Memorial Blood Ctr
717 Yosemite St . . . Denver CO 80230 303-341-4000 363-2239
TF: 800-365-0006 ■ *Web:* www.bonfils.org

Blood & Tissue Ctr of Central Texas
4300 N Lamar Blvd . . . Austin TX 78756 512-206-1266 458-3859
Web: www.bloodandtissue.org

Blood Assurance Inc 705 E Fourth St . . . Chattanooga TN 37403 423-756-0966 752-8460
TF: 800-962-0628 ■ *Web:* www.bloodassurance.org

Blood Bank of Alaska 4000 Laurel St . . . Anchorage AK 99508 907-222-5600 563-1371
Web: www.bloodbankofalaska.org

Blood Bank of Delmarva 100 Hygeia Dr . . . Newark DE 19713 302-737-8405 737-8233
TF: 800-548-4009 ■ *Web:* www.delmarvablood.org

Blood Bank of Hawaii 2043 Dillingham Blvd . . . Honolulu HI 96819 808-845-9966 848-4737
TF: 800-372-9966 ■ *Web:* www.bbh.org

Blood Bank of the Redwoods
2324 Bethards Dr . . . Santa Rosa CA 95405 707-545-1222 575-8178
TF: 888-393-4483 ■ *Web:* www.bloodcenters.org

Phone | Fax

Blood Centers of the Pacific
250 Bush St . . . San Francisco CA 94104 415-567-6400 749-6620
TF: 888-393-4483 ■ *Web:* www.bloodcenters.org

Blood Ctr of New Jersey 45 S Grove St . . . East Orange NJ 07018 973-676-4700 573-4626*
**Fax Area Code:* 201 ■ *TF:* 866-228-1500 ■ *Web:* www.bloodnj.org

Blood Ctr of Northcentral Wisconsin
211 Forest St . . . Wausau WI 54403 715-842-0761 845-6429

Blood Ctr, The 2609 Canal St . . . New Orleans LA 70112 504-524-1322 592-1580
TF: 800-862-5663 ■ *Web:* www.thebloodcenter.org

BloodCenter of Wisconsin 638 N 18th St . . . Milwaukee WI 53233 414-933-5000 937-6332
TF: 877-232-4376 ■ *Web:* www.bcw.edu

BloodSource 1608 Q St . . . Sacramento CA 95811 916-456-1500
TF: 800-995-4420 ■ *Web:* www.bloodsource.org

Carter BloodCare 2205 Hwy 121 . . . Bedford TX 76021 817-412-5000 412-5992
TF: 800-366-2834 ■ *Web:* www.carterbloodcare.org

Cascade Regional Blood Services 220 S 'I' St . . . Tacoma WA 98405 253-383-2553 572-3698
TF: 877-242-5663 ■ *Web:* www.crbs.net

Central California Blood Ctr
4343 W Herndon Ave . . . Fresno CA 93722 559-389-5433 225-1602
Web: donateblood.org

Central Illinois Community Blood Ctr
1134 S Seventh St . . . Springfield IL 62703 217-753-1530 753-8116
TF Help Line: 800-448-3253 ■ *Web:* bloodcenter.org/home.aspx?region=104&sap=1

Central Jersey Blood Ctr 494 Sycamore Ave . . . Shrewsbury NJ 07702 732-842-5750
TF: 888-712-5663 ■ *Web:* www.cjbcblood.org

Central Kentucky Blood Ctr
3121 Beaumont Centre Cir . . . Lexington KY 40513 859-276-2534 233-4166
TF: 800-775-2522 ■ *Web:* www.ckbc.org

Central Pennsylvania Blood Bank
8167 Adams Dr . . . Hummelstown PA 17036 717-566-6161 566-7850
TF: 800-771-0059 ■ *Web:* www.cpbb.org

Coastal Bend Blood Ctr
209 N Padre Island Dr . . . Corpus Christi TX 78406 361-855-4943 855-2641
TF: 800-299-4943 ■ *Web:* www.coastalbendbloodcenter.org

Coffee Memorial Blood Ctr 7500 Wallace Dr . . . Amarillo TX 79124 806-358-4563 358-2982
Web: www.thegiftoflife.org

Community Blood Bank of Northwest Pennsylvania
2646 Peach St . . . Erie PA 16508 814-456-4206 452-3966
TF: 877-842-0631 ■ *Web:* www.fourhearts.org

Community Blood Ctr 349 S Main St . . . Dayton OH 45402 937-461-3450 461-9217
TF: 800-388-4483 ■ *Web:* www.cbccts.org
Blue Springs Ctr 4040 Main St . . . Kansas City MO 64111 816-753-4040 968-4047
TF: 888-647-4040 ■ *Web:* www.savealifenow.org
Gladstone Ctr 7265 N Oak Trafficway . . . Gladstone MO 64118 816-468-9813
Web: www.savealifenow.org
Olathe Ctr 1463 E 151st St . . . Olathe KS 66062 913-829-3724
Web: www.savealifenow.org

Community Blood Ctr Inc 4406 W Spencer St . . . Appleton WI 54914 920-738-3131 738-3139
TF: 800-280-4102 ■ *Web:* www.communityblood.org

Community Blood Ctr of the Ozarks
220 W Plainview Rd . . . Springfield MO 65810 417-227-5000 227-5400
TF: 800-280-5337 ■ *Web:* www.cbco.org

Community Blood Services
970 Linwood Ave W PO Box 39 . . . Paramus NJ 07653 201-444-3900 670-6174
Web: www.communitybloodservices.org

Community Blood Services of Illinois
1408 W University Ave . . . Urbana IL 61801 217-367-2202 367-6403
TF: 800-217-4483 ■ *Web:* bloodcenter.org/home.aspx?region=134&sap=2

Delta Blood Bank 65 N Commerce St . . . Stockton CA 95201 209-943-3830 462-0221
TF: 888-942-5663 ■ *Web:* www.deltabloodbank.org

Gulf Coast Regional Blood Ctr
1400 La Concha Ln . . . Houston TX 77054 713-790-1200 791-6644
TF: 888-482-5663 ■ *Web:* www.giveblood.org

Heartland Blood Centers 1200 N Highland Ave . . . Aurora IL 60506 630-892-7055 892-4590
TF: 800-786-4483 ■ *Web:* www.heartlandbc.org

Hemacare Corp 15350 Sherman Way Ste 350 . . . Van Nuys CA 91406 818-226-1968 251-5300
TF: 877-310-0717 ■ *Web:* www.hemacare.com

Houchin Community Blood Bank
5901 Truxtun Ave . . . Bakersfield CA 93309 661-327-8541
Web: www.hcbb.com

Hoxworth Blood Ctr University of Cincinnati Medical Ctr
3130 Highland Ave ML0055 . . . Cincinnati OH 45267 513-558-1200 558-1209
TF: 800-265-1515 ■ *Web:* www.hoxworth.org

Inland Northwest Blood Ctr 210 W Cataldo Ave . . . Spokane WA 99201 509-624-0151 232-4523
TF: 800-423-0151 ■ *Web:* www.inbcsaves.org

Lane Memorial Blood Bank 2211 Willamette St . . . Eugene OR 97405 541-484-9111 484-6976
Web: lanebloodcenter.org

Lifeblood Mid-South Regional Blood Ctr
DeSoto Ctr 577 Goodman Rd Ste 5 . . . Southaven MS 38671 901-271-1260 349-2427*
**Fax Area Code:* 662 ■ *Web:* www.lifeblood.org

LifeServe Blood Ctr 431 E Locust St . . . Des Moines IA 50309 800-287-4903 288-0833*
**Fax Area Code:* 515 ■ *TF:* 800-287-4903 ■ *Web:* www.lifeservebloodcenter.org

LifeShare Blood Centers 8910 Linwood Ave . . . Shreveport LA 71106 318-222-7770 222-8886
TF: 800-256-4483 ■ *Web:* www.lifeshare.org

LifeShare Community Blood Services
105 Cleveland St . . . Elyria OH 44035 440-322-5700 322-6240
TF: 800-317-5412 ■ *Web:* www.lifeshare.cc

LifeSource Blood Services 2764 Aurora Ave . . . Naperville IL 60540 877-543-3768 298-4473*
**Fax Area Code:* 847 ■ *TF:* 877-543-3768 ■ *Web:* lifesource.org

LifeSouth Community Blood Centers
4039 Newberry Rd . . . Gainesville FL 32607 888-795-2707 224-1650*
**Fax Area Code:* 352 ■ *TF:* 888-795-2707 ■ *Web:* events.gainesville.com

LifeSouth Community Blood Centers Atlanta
4891 Ashford Dunwoody Rd . . . Atlanta GA 30338 404-329-1994 329-1707
TF: 888-795-2707 ■ *Web:* lifesouth.org

Memorial Blood Centers (MBC) 737 Pelham Blvd . . . Saint Paul MN 55114 651-332-7000 332-7001
TF Cust Svc: 888-448-3253 ■ *Web:* www.mbc.org

Michigan Community Blood Centers
1036 Fuller Ave NE . . . Grand Rapids MI 49503 616-774-2300 233-8567
TF: 866-642-5663 ■ *Web:* www.miblood.org

Michigan Community Blood Centers Northwest
2575 Aero Pk Dr . . . Traverse City MI 49686 231-935-3030
TF General: 866-642-5663 ■ *Web:* www.miblood.org

Phone *Fax*

Miller-Keystone Blood Ctr
1465 Vly Ctr Pkwy .... Bethlehem PA 18017 610-691-5850 691-5423
Web: www.hcsc.org

Mississippi Blood Services 115 Tree St .... Flowood MS 39232 601-981-3232
TF: 888-902-5663 ■ *Web:* www.msblood.com

Mississippi Valley Regional Blood Ctr
5500 Lakeview Pkwy .... Davenport IA 52807 563-359-5401 359-8603
TF: 800-747-5401 ■ *Web:* www.bloodcenter.org

MVRBC 5500 Lakeview Pkwy .... Davenport IA 52501 641-682-8149
TF: 800-747-5401 ■ *Web:* bloodcenter.org

Nebraska Community Blood Bank 100 N 84th St .... Lincoln NE 68505 402-486-9414 486-9429
TF: 877-486-9414 ■ *Web:* www.ncbb.org

New York Blood Ctr 310 E 67th St .... New York NY 10065 212-570-3242
Web: www.nybloodcenter.org

Northern California Community Blood Bank
2524 Harrison Ave .... Eureka CA 95501 707-443-8004 443-8007
Web: www.nccbb.org

Northwest Florida Blood Ctr
2209 N Ninth Ave .... Pensacola FL 32503 850-434-2535 432-8941
Web: www.oneblood.org

Oklahoma Blood Institute (OBI)
1001 N Lincoln Blvd .... Oklahoma City OK 73104 405-278-3100 477-0446*
**Fax Area Code:* 918 ■ *TF:* 866-708-4995 ■ *Web:* www.obi.org

Puget Sound Blood Ctr 921 Terry Ave .... Seattle WA 98104 206-292-6500 292-8030
TF: 800-366-2831 ■ *Web:* www.psbc.org

Rhode Island Blood Ctr 405 Promenade St .... Providence RI 02908 401-453-8360 453-8557
TF: 800-283-8385 ■ *Web:* www.ribc.org

Rock River Valley Blood Ctr
3065 N Perryville Rd Ste 105 .... Rockford IL 61114 815-965-8751 965-8756
TF General: 877-778-2299 ■ *Web:* www.rrvbc.org

San Diego Blood Bank 440 Upas St .... San Diego CA 92103 619-296-6393 296-0126
TF: 800-479-3902 ■ *Web:* www.sandiegobloodbank.org

SeraCare Life Sciences Inc 37 Birch St .... Milford MA 01757 508-244-6400 634-3394
NASDAQ: SRLS ■ *TF:* 800-676-1881 ■ *Web:* www.seracare.com

Shepeard Community Blood Ctr
1533 Wrightsboro Rd .... Augusta GA 30904 706-737-4551 733-5214
Web: www.shepeardblood.org

South Texas Blood & Tissue Ctr
6211 IH-10 W .... San Antonio TX 78201 210-731-5555 731-5501
TF: 800-292-5534 ■ *Web:* southtexasblood.org

Suncoast Communities Blood Bank
1760 Mound St .... Sarasota FL 34236 941-954-1600 951-2629
Web: www.scbb.org

Texoma Regional Blood Ctr 3911 N Texoma Pkwy .... Sherman TX 75090 903-893-4314 893-8628
Web: texomablood.org

United Blood Services
united blood services 4119 Broad St .... San luis obispo CA 93401 805-543-4290 751-1985*
**Fax Area Code:* 831 ■ *Web:* www.unitedbloodservices.org

United Blood Services of Arizona
Chandler 6220 E Oak St Ste 33 .... Scottsdale AZ 85252 877-827-4376 732-9009*
**Fax Area Code:* 480 ■ *TF:* 877-827-4376 ■ *Web:* www.unitedbloodservices.org
San Luis Obispo 4119 Broad St Ste 100 .... San Luis Obispo CA 93401 805-543-4290 543-4926
TF: 877-827-4376 ■ *Web:* www.unitedbloodservices.org

United Blood Services of Colorado
146 Sawyer Dr .... Durango CO 81303 970-385-4601
TF: 800-288-2199 ■ *Web:* www.unitedbloodservices.org
Baton Rouge 8234 1 Calais Ave .... Baton Rouge LA 70809 225-769-7233
Web: www.unitedbloodservices.org/louisiana

United Blood Services of Louisiana
Lafayette 1503 Bertrand Dr .... Lafayette LA 70506 337-235-5433
Web: www.unitedbloodservices.org
Morgan City 1234 David Dr Ste 102 .... Morgan City LA 70380 985-384-5671
Web: www.unitedbloodservices.org/louisiana

United Blood Services of Mississippi
Hattiesburg 805 S 28th Ave .... Hattiesburg MS 39402 601-264-0743
Web: www.unitedbloodservices.org
Meridian 1115 25th Ave .... Meridian MS 39301 601-482-2482 483-4204
TF: 877-827-4376 ■ *Web:* www.unitedbloodservices.org
Tupelo 4326 S Eason Blvd .... Tupelo MS 38801 662-842-8871
Web: www.unitedbloodservices.org/nt

United Blood Services of Montana
Billings 1444 Grand Ave .... Billings MT 59102 406-248-9168 248-1025
TF: 800-365-4450 ■ *Web:* www.unitedbloodservices.org
Butte 3745 Harrison Ave .... Butte MT 59701 406-723-3264
Web: www.unitedbloodservices.org
Carson City 256 E Winnie Ln .... Carson City NV 89706 775-887-9111
Web: www.unitedbloodservices.org
Green Valley 1125 Terminal Way Bldg D Ste 20 .... Reno NV 89502 775-324-6454
Web: www.unitedbloodservices.org

United Blood Services of Nevada
Las Vegas 4950 W Craig Rd .... Las Vegas NV 89130 702-645-3600
Web: www.unitedbloodservices.org
Las Vegas 6930 W Charleston Blvd .... Las Vegas NV 89117 702-228-4483
Web: www.unitedbloodservices.org
Albuquerque 1515 University Blvd NE .... Albuquerque NM 87102 800-333-8037
TF: 800-333-8037 ■ *Web:* www.unitedbloodservices.org/nm

United Blood Services of New Mexico
Farmington 475 E 20th St .... Farmington NM 87401 888-804-9913
TF: 888-804-9913 ■ *Web:* www.unitedbloodservices.org
Las Cruces 1200 Commerce Dr .... Las Cruces NM 88011 575-527-1322
TF General: 800-582-3146 ■ *Web:* www.unitedbloodservices.org

United Blood Services of North Dakota
Bismarck 517 S Seventh St .... Bismarck ND 58504 800-456-6159
TF: 800-456-6159 ■ *Web:* www.unitedbloodservices.org/nd
Fargo 3231 S 11th St .... Fargo ND 58104 701-293-9453
TF General: 800-288-2199 ■ *Web:* www.unitedbloodservices.org/nd

United Blood Services of South Dakota
Rapid City 2209 W Omaha St .... Rapid City SD 57702 605-342-8585
Web: www.unitedbloodservices.org
El Paso 424 S Mesa Hills .... El Paso TX 79912 915-544-5422 675-5767*
**Fax Area Code:* 480 ■ *TF:* 877-827-4376 ■ *Web:* www.unitedbloodservices.org

United Blood Services of Texas
Lubbock 2523 48th St .... Lubbock TX 79413 806-797-6804 797-1824
Web: www.unitedbloodservices.org
McAllen 1400 S Sixth St .... McAllen TX 78501 956-213-7500
TF General: 888-827-4376 ■ *Web:* www.unitedbloodservices.org/RG
San Angelo 2020 W Beauregard Ave .... San Angelo TX 76901 325-223-7500
TF General: 800-756-0024 ■ *Web:* www.unitedbloodservices.org
Casper 112 E. 8th Ave Ste 102 .... Cheyenne WY 82001 307-638-3326
Web: www.unitedbloodservices.org

United Blood Services of Wyoming
Cheyenne 112 E Eigth Ave .... Cheyenne WY 82001 307-638-3326
Web: www.unitedbloodservices.org

90 BOATS - RECREATIONAL

Phone *Fax*

Action Craft Inc 830 NE 24th Ln .... Cape Coral FL 33909 239-574-7800 574-7805
Web: www.actioncraft.com

Albemarle Sportfishing Boats Inc
140 Midway Dr .... Edenton NC 27932 252-482-7600 482-8289
Web: www.albemarleboats.com

Albin Marine Inc 143 River Rd PO Box 228 .... Cos Cob CT 06807 203-661-4341 661-6040
Web: www.albinmarine.com

Albury Bros Boats 1401 Broadway .... Riviera Beach FL 33404 561-863-7006 863-7746
Web: www.alburybrothers.com

Alpin Haus Ski Shop 4850 State Hwy 30 .... Amsterdam NY 12010 518-843-4400 843-5159
Web: www.alpinhaus.com

Alumacraft Boat Co 315 St Julien St .... Saint Peter MN 56082 507-931-1050 931-9056
Web: www.alumacraft.com

Alumaweld Boats Inc 1601 Ave F .... White City OR 97503 541-826-7171 830-6907
TF: 800-401-2628 ■ *Web:* www.alumaweldboats.com

Arima Boats 7510 Bree Dr .... Bremerton WA 98312 360-813-3600 813-3513
Web: www.arimaboats.com

Avalon Pontoon Boats 903 Michigan Ave PO Box 698 .... Alma MI 48801 989-463-2112 463-8226
Web: boatersbook.com

B & B Boats Inc 3568 Old Winter Garden Rd .... Orlando FL 32805 407-299-2190

Baja Marine Corp
1653 Whichards Beach Rd PO Box 151 .... Washington NC 27889 252-975-2000 975-6793
Web: www.bajamarine.com

Bay Craft Inc 1785 Langley Ave .... DeLand FL 32724 386-943-8877 943-8617
Web: www.baycraftinc.com

Beneteau America Inc 1313 Hwy 76 W .... Marion SC 29571 843-629-5320
Web: www.beneteauamerica.com

Bertram Yacht Inc 3663 NW 21st St .... Miami FL 33142 305-633-8011 633-2868
TF: 800-256-4646 ■ *Web:* www.bertram.com

Boston Whaler Inc 100 Whaler Way .... Edgewater FL 32141 877-294-5645 423-8589*
**Fax Area Code:* 386 ■ *TF:* 877-294-5645 ■ *Web:* www.bostonwhaler.com

Briggs Boat Works Inc 370 Harbor Rd .... Wanchese NC 27981 252-473-2393 473-2392
Web: www.briggsboatworks.com

Brunswick Boat Group 800 S Gay St 17th Fl .... Knoxville TN 37929 865-582-2200 582-2301
Web: brunswick.com

Brunswick Corp One N Field Ct .... Lake Forest IL 60045 847-735-4700 735-4765
NYSE: BC ■ *Web:* www.brunswick.com

Brunswick Corp Sea Ray Group
2600 Sea Ray Blvd .... Knoxville TN 37914 865-522-4181
Web: global.searay.com

Cape Cod Shipbuilding Co Seven Narrows Rd .... Wareham MA 02571 508-295-3550 295-3551
Web: www.capecodshipbuilding.com

Carolina Classic Boats Inc
109 Anchors Way Dr PO Box 968 .... Edenton NC 27932 252-482-3699
Web: www.carolinaclassicboats.com

Carolina Skiff Inc 3231 Fulford Rd .... Waycross GA 31503 912-287-0547 287-0533
TF: 800-422-7282 ■ *Web:* www.carolinaskiff.com

Carver Boat Corp LLC
790 Markham Dr PO Box 1010 .... Pulaski WI 54162 920-822-3214
Web: www.carveryachts.com

Catalina Yachts Inc
21200 Victory Blvd .... Woodland Hills CA 91367 818-884-7700 884-3810
Web: www.catalinayachts.com

Chaparral Boats Inc
300 Industrial park Blvd .... Nashville GA 31639 229-686-7481 686-3660
Web: www.chaparralboats.com

Chris-Craft Boats 8161 15th St E .... Sarasota FL 34243 941-351-4900 358-3717
TF: 800-845-5255 ■ *Web:* chriscraft.com

Cigarette Racing Team LLC 4355 NW 128th St .... Opa Locka FL 33054 305-931-4564 769-4355
Web: www.cigaretteracing.com

Cobalt Boats LLC 1715 N Eigth St .... Neodesha KS 66757 620-325-2653 325-2361
TF: 800-468-5764 ■ *Web:* www.cobaltboats.com

Concept Boats Corp 2410 NW 147th St .... Opa Locka FL 33054 305-635-8712 635-9543
TF: 888-635-8712 ■ *Web:* www.conceptboats.com

Correct Craft Inc 14700 Aerospace Pkwy .... Orlando FL 32809 407-855-4141 855-4141
TF: 800-346-2092 ■ *Web:* www.nautique.com

Crestliner Inc 9040 Quaday Ave NE .... Ostego MN 55330 320-632-6686 256-4676
Web: www.crestliner.com

Crownline Boats Inc
11884 Country Club Rd .... West Frankfort IL 62896 618-937-6426
Web: www.crownline.com

Defiant Marine Inc 228 Redbud Ln .... Bostic NC 28018 828-245-2059 245-2079
Web: defiantmarine.net

Donzi Marine
1653 WhichaRds Beach Rd PO Box 457 .... Washington NC 27889 800-624-3304
TF: 800-624-3304 ■ *Web:* www.donzimarine.com

Ebbtide Corp 2545 Jones Creek Rd .... White Bluff TN 37187 615-797-3193 797-4889
TF: 866-467-4010 ■ *Web:* www.ebbtideboats.com

EdgeWater Power Boats 211 Dale St .... Edgewater FL 32132 386-426-5457 427-9783
Web: www.ewboats.com

Egg Harbor Yachts Inc
801 Philadelphia Ave PO Box 702 .... Egg Harbor City NJ 08215 609-965-2300 965-3517
TF: 800-960-6764 ■ *Web:* www.eggharboryachts.com

Everglades Boats 544 Air Pk Rd .... Edgewater FL 32132 386-409-2202 409-7939
TF: 800-368-5647 ■ *Web:* www.evergladesboats.com

Company	City	State	ZIP	Phone	Fax
Fishing Holdings, LLC PO Box 179 *Fax: Hum Res ■ Web: www.rangerboats.com	Flippin	AR	72634	870-453-2222	*
Flats Cat Boats 1565 Patton Rd Web: www.flatscat.com	Rosenberg	TX	77471	281-342-3940	
Four Winns Inc 925 Frisbie St Web: www.fourwinns.com	Cadillac	MI	49601	231-775-1343	779-2345
Garlington Landeweer Marine Inc 3370 SE Slater St Web: www.garlingtonyachts.com	Stuart	FL	34997	772-283-7124	220-1049
Gibson Boats Inc 130 Davis St Web: www.gibsonboats.com	Portland	TN	37148	615-325-9320	325-9321
Glacier Bay Catamarans 1090 W Saint James St TF: 855-662-4855 ■ Web: www.glacierbaycats.com	Tarboro	NC	27886	855-662-4855	
Glastron Boats 710 Co Rd 75 TF: 855-272-2709 ■ Web: www.glastron.com	St Joseph	MN	56374	320-433-2141	
Grady-White Boats Inc 5121 Martin Luther King Jr Hwy Web: www.gradywhite.com	Greenville	NC	27834	252-752-2111	752-4217
Grand Banks Yachts Ltd 2288 W Commodore Way Ste 200 Web: www.grandbanks.com	Seattle	WA	98199	206-352-0116	352-1711
Hatteras Yachts Inc 110 N Glenburnie Rd Web: www.hatterasyachts.com	New Bern	NC	28560	252-633-3101	634-4813
Hinckley Co, The One Little Harbor Landing TF: 866-446-2553 ■ Web: www.hinckleyyachts.com	Portsmouth	RI	02871	401-683-7005	
Hobie Cat Co 4925 Oceanside Blvd TF: 800-462-4349 ■ Web: www.hobiecat.com	Oceanside	CA	92056	760-758-9100	758-1841
Intrepid Powerboats 11700 S Belcher Rd Web: www.intrepidboats.com	Largo	FL	33773	727-548-1260	544-1796
Island Runner Boats PO Box 530098 TF: 800-749-4322 ■ Web: www.islandrunner.com	Lake Park	FL	33403	954-829-3252	563-2511
Jefferson Yachts Inc 700 E Market St Web: stores.kyyachtsales.com	Jeffersonville	IN	47130	812-282-8111	
Jersey Cape Yachts Inc 2143 River Rd Web: www.jerseycapeyachts.com	Lower Bank	NJ	08215	609-965-8650	965-7480
Johnson Outdoors Inc 555 Main St NASDAQ: JOUT ■ TF: 800-468-9716 ■ Web: www.johnsonoutdoors.com	Racine	WI	53403	262-631-6600	631-6601
KenCraft Manufacturing Inc 4155 Dixie Inn Rd Web: www.kencraftboats.com	Wilson	NC	27893	252-291-0271	291-0815
Key West Boats Inc 593 Ridgeville Rd PO Box 399 Web: www.keywestboatsinc.com	Ridgeville	SC	29472	843-873-0112	821-6334
Klamath Boat Co 5199 Fulton Dr Ste I Web: www.klamathboats.com	Fairfield	CA	94534	707-643-0447	643-0483
Knight & Carver Yachtcenter Inc 1313 Bay Marina Dr	National City	CA	91950	619-336-4141	336-4050
L & H Boats Inc 3350 SE Slater St Web: www.lhboats.com	Stuart	FL	34997	772-288-2291	288-9878
Larson Boats 700 Paul Larson Memorial Dr TF General: 800-336-2628 ■ Web: www.larsonboats.com	Little Falls	MN	56345	320-632-5481	
Lowe Boats 2900 Industrial Dr TF: 800-641-4372 ■ Web: www.loweboats.com	Lebanon	MO	65536	417-532-9101	532-8991
Mainship Corp 255 Diesel Rd TF: 800-771-5556 ■ Web: www.mainship.com	St Augustine	FL	32084	904-827-2007	
Marine Safety Corp PO Box 465 Web: marinesafetycorporation.com	Farmingdale	NJ	07727	732-938-5668	938-4839
MasterCraft Boat Co 100 Cherokee Cove Dr TF: 800-443-8774 ■ Web: mastercraft.com	Vonore	TN	37885	423-884-2221	884-2295
Maverick Boat Company Inc 3207 Industrial 29th St Web: www.maverickboats.com	Fort Pierce	FL	34946	772-465-0631	489-2168
Melges Boatworks Inc PO Box 1 Web: www.melges.com	Zenda	WI	53195	262-275-1110	275-8012
Merritt's Boat & Engine Works Inc 2931 NE 16th St Web: www.merrittboat.com	Pompano Beach	FL	33062	954-943-6250	942-1531
Monterey Boats 1579 SW 18th St Web: www.montereyboats.com	Williston	FL	32696	352-528-2628	529-2628
Pacific Seacraft PO Box 189 Web: www.pacificseacraft.com	Washington	NC	27889	252-948-1421	948-1422
Palmer Johnson Boats Inc 128 Kentucky St Web: palmerjohnson.com	Sturgeon Bay	WI	54235	920-743-1043	
Parker Marine Enterprises Inc 2570 N Carolina 101 Web: www.parkerboats.net	Beaufort	NC	28516	252-728-5621	728-2770
Port Harbor Marine Inc One Spring Pt Dr PO Box 2350 Web: www.portharbormarine.com	South Portland	ME	04106	207-767-3254	767-5940
Porta-Bote International 1074 Independence Ave TF: 800-227-8882 ■ Web: www.porta-bote.com	Mountain View	CA	94043	650-961-5334	961-3800
Porter Inc 2200 W Monroe St TF: 800-736-7685 ■ Web: www.formulaboats.com	Decatur	IN	46733	260-724-9111	
Pursuit Boats 3901 St Lucie Blvd TF: 800-947-8778 ■ Web: www.pursuitboats.com	Fort Pierce	FL	34946	772-465-6006	465-6177
Regal Marine Industries Inc 2300 Jetport Dr *Fax: Sales ■ TF: 800-877-3425 ■ Web: www.regalboats.com	Orlando	FL	32809	407-851-4360	857-1256*
Riverside Marine Inc 11051 Pulaski Hwy TF: 800-448-6872 ■ Web: www.riversideboats.com	White Marsh	MD	21162	410-335-1500	335-1569
Rybovich Spencer Group 4200 N Flagler Dr Web: www.rybovich.com	West Palm Beach	FL	33407	561-844-1800	844-8393
Sabre Corp PO Box 134 Web: www.sabreyachts.com	South Casco	ME	04077	207-655-3831	655-5050
Scout Boats Inc 2531 US 78 Web: www.scoutboats.com	Summerville	SC	29483	843-821-0068	821-4786
Sea Cat Boats Inc 1005 Marina Rd Web: www.seacatboats.com	Titusville	FL	32796	321-268-2628	269-8483
Sea Fox Boat Company Inc 2550 Hwy 52 Web: www.seafoxboats.com	Moncks Corner	SC	29461	843-761-6090	761-6139
SeaArk Boats 728 W Patton St Web: www.seaarkboats.net	Monticello	AR	71655	870-367-5317	
Seminole Marine 2501 Milestone Industrial Pk Web: www.sailfishboats.com	Cairo	GA	39828	229-377-2125	377-1855
Silverton Marine Corp 301 Riverside Dr *Fax: Mktg ■ TF: 800-524-2804 ■ Web: www.silverton.com	Millville	NJ	08332	856-825-4117	825-2064*
Skeeter Products Inc One Skeeter Rd Web: www.skeeterboats.com	Kilgore	TX	75662	903-984-0541	984-7856
Skier's Choice Inc 1717 Henry G Ln St Web: www.supraboats.com	Maryville	TN	37801	865-856-3035	
Smoker Craft PO Box 65 TF: 866-719-7873 ■ Web: www.smokercraft.com	New Paris	IN	46553	866-719-7873	
Sonic power boats 309 Angle Rd Web: www.sonic-boats.com	Fort Pierce	FL	34947	772-429-8888	
Stamas Yacht Inc 300 Pampas Ave TF Sales: 800-782-6271 ■ Web: www.stamas.com	Tarpon Springs	FL	34689	727-937-4118	934-1339
Starcraft Marine LLC 68143 Clunette St PO Box 65 TF: 800-535-5722 ■ Web: www.starcraftmarine.com	New Paris	IN	46553	574-831-2103	831-7332
Stevens Marine Inc 9180 SW Burnham St TF: 800-225-7023 ■ Web: www.stevensmarine.com	Tigard	OR	97223	503-620-7023	684-8952
Stoltzfus RV's & Marine 1335 Wilmington Pike Web: stoltzfus-rec.com	West Chester	PA	19382	866-755-8858	
Sundance Boats Inc 6131 Sundance Rd Web: www.sundanceboats.com	Blackshear	GA	31516	912-449-0033	449-0038
Tartan Yachts 1920 Fairport Nursery Rd Web: www.tartanyachts.com	Fairport Harbor	OH	44077	440-332-0578	354-6162
Tiara Yachts Inc 725 E 40th St Web: www.tiarayachts.com	Holland	MI	49423	616-392-7163	394-7466
Tracker Marine Group LLC 2500 E Kearney St *Fax: Mktg ■ Web: www.trackermarine.com	Springfield	MO	65803	417-873-5900	873-5068*
Valiant Yachts Inc 500 Harbour View Rd Web: www.valiantsailboats.com	Gordonville	TX	76245	903-523-4899	523-4077
Viking Yacht Company Inc PO Box 308 Web: www.vikingyachts.com	New Gretna	NJ	08224	609-296-6000	296-3956
Willard Marine Inc 1250 N Grove St Web: www.willardmarine.com	Anaheim	CA	92806	714-666-2150	632-8136
Wooldridge Boats Inc 1303 S 96th St Web: www.wooldridgeboats.com	Seattle	WA	98108	206-722-8998	
World Cat 1090 W St James St TF: 866-485-8899 ■ Web: www.worldcat.com	Tarboro	NC	27886	252-641-8000	641-9866
Xpress Boats 199 Extrusion Pl Web: www.xpressboats.com	Hot Springs	AR	71901	501-262-5300	262-5053
Zodiac of North America Inc 540 Thompson Creek Rd Web: www.zodiacmilpro.com	Stevensville	MD	21666	410-643-8123	643-4491

91 BOILER SHOPS

Company	City	State	ZIP	Phone	Fax
A & A Industries Inc 320 Jubilee Dr Web: www.aandaindustries.com	Peabody	MA	01960	978-977-9660	
Adamson Global Technology Corp 13101 N Enon Church Rd *Fax Area Code: 804 ■ TF: 800-525-7703 ■ Web: www.adamsontank.com	Chester	VA	23836	800-525-7703	796-2037*
Aerofin Corp 4621 Murray Pl PO Box 10819 *Fax: Sales ■ TF: 800-237-6346 ■ Web: www.aerofin.com	Lynchburg	VA	24506	434-845-7081	528-6242*
Aesys Technologies LLC 693 N Hills Rd Web: www.aesystech.com	York	PA	17402	717-755-1081	755-0020
AlfaLaval Inc 5400 International Trade Dr Web: www.alfalaval.com	Richmond	VA	23231	804-222-5300	236-3276
American Welding & Tank Co 4718 Old Gettysburg Rd Ste 300 TF: 800-345-2495 ■ Web: www.propanetank.com	Mechanicsburg	PA	17055	717-763-5080	763-5081
Amtrol Inc 1400 Div Rd Web: www.amtrol.com	West Warwick	RI	02893	401-884-6300	885-2567
API Heat Transfer Inc 2777 Walden Ave TF: 877-274-4328 ■ Web: www.apiheattransfer.com	Buffalo	NY	14225	716-684-6700	684-2129
Armstrong Engineering Assoc Inc PO Box 566 Web: www.rmarmstrong.com	West Chester	PA	19381	610-436-6080	436-0374
Arrow Tank & Engineering Co 650 N Emerson St TF: 888-892-7769 ■ Web: www.arrowtank.com	Cambridge	MN	55008	763-689-3360	689-1263
AustinMohawk & Company Inc 2175 Beechgrove Pl TF: 800-765-3110 ■ Web: www.austinmohawk.com	Utica	NY	13501	315-793-3000	793-9370
Babcock & Wilcox Co 20 S Van Buren Ave TF: 800-222-2625 ■ Web: www.babcock.com	Barberton	OH	44203	330-753-4511	860-1886
Babcock Power Inc One Corporate Place 55 Ferncroft Road Ste 210 TF: 800-523-0480 ■ Web: www.babcockpower.com	Danvers	MA	01923	978-646-3300	646-3301
Benicia Fabrication & Machine Inc 101 E Ch Rd Web: www.beniciafab.com	Benicia	CA	94510	707-745-8111	745-8102
Bristol Metals LP 390 Bristol Metals Rd Web: www.brismet.com	Bristol	TN	37620	423-989-4700	
Bryan Steam LLC 783 Chili Ave Web: www.bryanboilers.com	Peru	IN	46970	765-473-6651	473-3074
C Burgett & Assoc Inc 1462 N FM 2199 Rd	Scottsville	TX	75688	903-938-6638	938-6638
Caldwell Tanks Inc 4000 Tower Rd Web: www.caldwelltanks.com	Louisville	KY	40219	502-964-3361	966-8732
Chart Industries Inc one Infinity Corporate Centre Dr Ste 300 Web: www.chartindustries.com	Garfield Heights	OH	44125	440-753-1490	753-1491
Chicago Boiler Co 1300 NW Ave TF Cust Svc: 800-522-7343 ■ Web: cbmills.com	Gurnee	IL	60031	847-662-4000	662-4003

	City	State	Zip	Phone	Fax
Chicago Boiler Co CB Mills Div 1300 NW Ave *TF:* 800-522-7343 ■ *Web:* www.cbmills.com	Gurnee	IL	60031	847-662-4000	662-4003
Clawson Tank Co 4545 Clawson Tank Dr *TF:* 800-272-1367 ■ *Web:* www.clawsontank.com	Clarkston	MI	48346	248-625-8700	625-3066
Cleaver Brooks 11950 W Lk Pk Dr *Web:* cleaver-brooks.com	Milwaukee	WI	53224	414-359-0600	577-3171
Cleaver Brooks Thomasville 221 Law St *Web:* www.cleaver-brooks.com	Thomasville	GA	31792	229-226-3024	226-3027
Coen Co Inc 11920 East Apache St *Web:* www.coen.com	Tulsa	CA	74116	918-234-1800	
Columbia Boiler Co 390 Old Reading Pk PO Box 1070 *Web:* www.columbiaboiler.com	Pottstown	PA	19464	610-323-2700	323-7292
Columbian Tectank 2101 S 21st St PO Box 996 *TF:* 800-555-8265 ■ *Web:* www.cstindustries.com	Parsons	KS	67357	620-421-0200	421-9122
Connell LP One International Pl 31st Fl *Web:* www.connell-lp.com	Boston	MA	02110	617-391-5577	737-1617
CP Industries Inc (CPI) 2214 Walnut St **Fax:* Sales ■ *Web:* www.cp-industries.com	McKeesport	PA	15132	412-664-6604	664-6653*
DCI Inc 600 N 54th Ave *Web:* www.dciinc.com	Saint Cloud	MN	56303	320-252-8200	252-0866
Delta Industries 39 Bradley Pk Rd *Web:* mbaerospace.com	East Granby	CT	06026	860-653-5041	653-5792
Dynasteel Corp PO Box 27640 *Web:* www.dynasteel.net	Memphis	TN	38167	901-358-6231	358-4401
Eaton Metal Products Co 4803 York St *TF:* 800-208-2657 ■ *Web:* www.eatonsalesservice.com	Denver	CO	80216	303-296-4800	296-4800
Ecodyne MRM 8203 Market St *Web:* www.ecodynehx.com	Houston	TX	77029	713-675-3511	675-7922
Enerfab Inc 4955 Spring Grove Ave *TF:* 800-772-5066 ■ *Web:* www.enerfab.com	Cincinnati	OH	45232	513-641-0500	242-6833
Energy Exchanger Co 1844 N Garnett Rd *TF:* 800-760-6700 ■ *Web:* www.energyexchanger.com	Tulsa	OK	74116	918-437-3000	437-7144
Engineered Storage Products Co 345 Harvestore Dr *TF:* 800-880-3663 ■ *Web:* www.cstindustries.com	DeKalb	IL	60115	815-756-1551	756-7821
Essick Air Products Inc 5800 Murray St *TF:* 800-643-8341 ■ *Web:* www.essickair.com	Little Rock	AR	72209	501-562-1094	562-9485
Exothermics Inc 5040 Enterprise Blvd *Web:* www.eclipsenet.com	Toledo	OH	43612	419-729-9726	729-9705
Fafco Inc 435 Otterson Dr *TF:* 800-994-7652 ■ *Web:* www.fafco.com	Chico	CA	95928	530-332-2100	332-2109
Fisher Tank Co 3131 W Fourth St *Web:* www.fishertank.com	Chester	PA	19013	610-494-7200	485-0157
GEA Rainey Corp 5202 W Ch Rd *Web:* www.gearainey.com	Catoosa	OK	74015	918-266-3060	266-2464
Geiger & Peters Inc 761 S Sherman Dr PO Box 33807 *Web:* www.gpsteel.com	Indianapolis	IN	46203	317-359-9521	359-9525
General Welding Works Inc 2060 N Loop W Ste 200 PO Box 925749 *Web:* www.generalwelding.com	Houston	TX	77018	713-869-6401	869-5405
Goodhart Sons Inc 2515 Horseshoe Rd *Web:* www.goodhartsons.com	Lancaster	PA	17605	717-656-2404	656-3301
Hammersmith Mfg & Sales Inc 401 Central Ave *TF:* 800-375-8245 ■ *Web:* www.vailproducts.com	Horton	KS	66439	785-486-2121	486-2454
Harsco Industrial Air-X-Changers 5215 Arkansas Rd PO Box 1804 *TF:* 800-404-3904 ■ *Web:* www.harscoaxc.com	Catoosa	OK	74015	918-619-8000	384-5000
HB Smith Company Inc 47 Westfield Industrial Pk Rd *Web:* hbsmith.com	Westfield	MA	01085	413-568-3148	568-0525
Highland Tank & Manufacturing Co One Highland Rd *Web:* www.highlandtank.com	Stoystown	PA	15563	814-893-5701	893-6126
Hughes-Anderson Heat Exchangers Inc 1001 N Fulton Ave *Web:* www.hughesanderson.com	Tulsa	OK	74115	918-836-1681	836-5967
Hurst Boiler & Welding Company Inc PO Box 530 *TF:* 877-994-8778 ■ *Web:* www.hurstboiler.com	Coolidge	GA	31738	229-346-3545	346-3874
Indeck Energy Services Inc 600 N Buffalo Grove Rd Ste 300 *Web:* indeckenergy.com	Buffalo Grove	IL	60089	847-520-3212	520-9883
ITT Standard 175 Standard Pkwy **Fax Area Code:* 716 ■ *TF:* 800-447-7700 ■ *Web:* www.ittstandard.com	Cheektowaga	NY	14227	800-281-4111	897-1777*
Joseph Oat Corp 2500 Broadway *Web:* www.josephoat.com	Camden	NJ	08104	856-541-2900	541-0864
Koch Heat Transfer Company LP 12602 FM 529 *Web:* www.kochheattransfer.com	Houston	TX	77041	713-466-3535	466-3701
Krueger Engineering & Manufacturing Co 12001 Hirsch Rd PO Box 11308 *Web:* www.kemco.net	Houston	TX	77293	281-442-2537	442-6668
McAbee Construction Inc 5724 21st St PO Box 1460 *Web:* www.mcabeeconstruction.com	Tuscaloosa	AL	35403	205-349-2212	758-0762
Metalforms Manufacturing Inc PO Box 20118 *Web:* www.metalformsltd.com	Beaumont	TX	77720	409-842-1626	842-1503
Mgs Inc 178 Muddy Creek Church Rd *TF:* 800-952-4228 ■ *Web:* www.mgsincorporated.com	Denver	PA	17517	717-336-7528	336-0514
Mississippi Tank & Manufacturing Co 3000 W Seventh St *Web:* www.mstank.com	Hattiesburg	MS	39403	601-264-1800	264-0769
MiTek Industries Inc 14515 N Outer 40 Rd Ste 300 *TF:* 800-325-8075 ■ *Web:* mii.com	Chesterfield	MO	63017	314-434-1200	434-5343
Mitternight Boiler Works Inc 5301 Hwy 43 N PO Box 489 *Web:* www.mitternight.com	Satsuma	AL	36572	251-675-2550	675-2671
Modern Welding Company Inc 2880 New Hartford Rd *TF:* 800-922-1932 ■ *Web:* www.modweldco.com	Owensboro	KY	42303	270-685-4400	684-6972
Ohmstede 895 N Main St *TF:* 800-568-2328 ■ *Web:* www.ohmstede.com	Beaumont	TX	77704	409-833-6375	839-4948
Ottenweller Company Inc 3011 Congressional Pkwy *Web:* www.ottenweller.com	Fort Wayne	IN	46808	260-484-3166	484-9798
Pasadena Tank Corp 15915 Jacintoport Blvd *Web:* www.ptctanks.com	Houston	TX	77015	281-457-3996	
Pentair Residential Filtration LLC 20580 Enterprise Ave *TF:* 888-784-9065 ■ *Web:* www.pentairwatertreatment.com	Brookfield	WI	53008	262-784-4490	785-6535
Plant Maintenance Service Corp 3000 Fite Rd *TF:* 800-459-9131 ■ *Web:* www.pmscmphs.com	Memphis	TN	38168	901-353-9880	353-0882
Precision Custom Components 500 Lincoln St **Fax:* Mktg ■ *Web:* www.pcc-york.com	York	PA	17401	717-848-1126	843-5733*
PVI Industries LLC 3209 Galvez Ave PO Box 7124 *TF:* 800-784-8326 ■ *Web:* www.pvi.com	Fort Worth	TX	76111	817-335-9531	332-6742
R. W. Fernstrum & Co 1716 11th Ave PO Box 97 *Web:* www.fernstrum.com	Menominee	MI	49858	906-863-5553	863-5634
Reco Constructors Inc 710 Hospital St *Web:* www.recoconstructors.com	Richmond	VA	23219	804-644-2611	643-3561
Redman Equipment & Mfg Co 19800 Normandie Ave *TF:* 888-733-2602 ■ *Web:* www.redmaneq.com	Torrance	CA	90502	310-329-1134	324-5656
Rocky Mountain Fabrication Inc PO Box 16409 *TF:* 888-763-5307 ■ *Web:* www.rmf-slc.com	Salt Lake City	UT	84116	801-596-2400	322-2702
Ross Technology Corp 104 N Maple Ave *TF:* 800-345-8170 ■ *Web:* www.rosstechnology.com	Leola	PA	17540	717-656-2200	656-3281
Roy E Hanson Jr Mfg 1600 E Washington Blvd *TF:* 800-421-9395 ■ *Web:* www.hansontank.com	Los Angeles	CA	90021	213-747-7514	747-7724
Sen-Dure Products Inc 6785 NW 17th Ave *TF:* 800-394-5112 ■ *Web:* www.sen-dure.com	Fort Lauderdale	FL	33309	954-973-1260	968-7213
Sivalls Inc 2200 E Second St *Web:* www.sivalls.com	Odessa	TX	79761	432-337-3571	337-2624
Smithco Engineering Inc 6312 S 39th W Ave *Web:* www.smithco-eng.com	Tulsa	OK	74132	918-446-4406	445-2857
Snap-Tite Autoclave Engineers Div 8325 Hessinger Dr *TF:* 800-458-0409 ■ *Web:* snap-tite.com	Erie	PA	16509	814-838-5700	833-0145
SPX Cooling Technologies 7401 W 129th St *TF:* 800-462-7539 ■ *Web:* www.spxcooling.com	Overland Park	KS	66213	913-664-7400	664-7439
Super Steel Products Corp 7900 W Tower Ave *Web:* www.supersteel.com	Milwaukee	WI	53223	414-355-4800	355-0372
Superior Boiler Works Inc 3524 E Fourth St PO Box 1527 *TF:* 800-444-6693 ■ *Web:* www.superiorboiler.com	Hutchinson	KS	67504	620-662-6693	662-7586
Superior Die Set Corp 900 W Drexel Ave **Fax Area Code:* 800 ■ *TF:* 800-558-6040 ■ *Web:* www.supdie.com	Oak Creek	WI	53154	414-764-4900	657-0855*
Sussman Automatic Corp 43-20 34th St *TF:* 800-727-8326 ■ *Web:* www.mrsteam.com	Long Island City	NY	11101	718-937-4500	786-4051
Tampa Tank Inc 2710 E Fifth Ave *Web:* www.tampatank.com	Tampa	FL	33605	813-623-2675	622-7514
Taylor Forge Engineered Systems Inc 208 N Iron St *Web:* www.tfes.com	Paola	KS	66071	913-294-5331	294-5337
Taylor-Wharton 4718 Gettysburg Rd Ste 300 *Web:* www.taylorwharton.com	Mechanicsburg	PA	17055	717-763-5060	731-7988
Thermal Engineering International Inc 10375 Slusher Dr *Web:* www.babcockpower.com	Santa Fe Springs	CA	90670	323-726-0641	726-9592
Thermal Transfer Corp 50 N Linden St *Web:* www.hamonusa.com	Duquesne	PA	15110	412-460-4004	466-2899
ThermaSys Corp 2776 Gunter Pk Dr E Ste RS *TF:* 877-274-4328 ■ *Web:* www.thermasys.com	Montgomery	AL	36109	334-244-9240	244-9248
Thermodynetics Inc 651 Day Hill Rd *OTC:* TDYT ■ *TF:* 800-394-1633 ■ *Web:* www.thermodynetics.com	Windsor	CT	06095	860-683-2005	285-0139
Titanium Fabrication Corp 110 Lehigh Dr *Web:* www.tifab.com	Fairfield	NJ	07004	973-227-5300	227-6541
Tranter Inc 1900 Old Burk Hwy *TF:* 800-414-6908 ■ *Web:* www.tranter.com	Wichita Falls	TX	76306	940-723-7125	723-5131
Ultraflote Corp 3640 W 12th St *Web:* www.ultraflote.com	Houston	TX	77008	713-461-2100	461-2213
Weil-McLain Co 500 Blaine St *Web:* www.weil-mclain.com	Michigan City	IN	46360	219-879-6561	879-4025
Winbco Tank Co 1200 E Main St PO Box 618 **Fax Area Code:* 641 ■ *TF:* 800-822-1855 ■ *Web:* www.winbco.com	Ottumwa	IA	52501	800-822-1855	683-8265*
Worthington Industries 200 Old E Wilson Bridge Rd *TF:* 866-928-2657 ■ *Web:* www.worthingtoncylinders.com	Columbus	OH	43085	614-438-3013	438-3083
Zak Inc One Tibbits Ave *Web:* www.zakinc.com	Green Island	NY	12183	518-273-3912	273-2744

92 BOOK BINDING & RELATED WORK

SEE ALSO Printing Companies - Book Printers p. 2964

	City	State	Zip	Phone	Fax
Area Trade Bindery Co 157 W Providencia Ave	Burbank	CA	91502	818-846-6041	
Bindagraphics Inc 2701 Wilmarco Ave *TF:* 800-326-0300 ■ *Web:* www.bindagraphics.com	Baltimore	MD	21223	410-362-7200	362-7233
Bindtech Inc 1232 Antioch Pk *Web:* www.bindtechinc.com	Nashville	TN	37211	615-834-0404	
Booksource Inc 1230 Macklind Ave **Fax Area Code:* 800 ■ *TF:* 800-444-0435 ■ *Web:* www.booksource.com	Saint Louis	MO	63110	314-647-0600	647-1923*

Phone Fax

Bound to Stay Bound Books Inc (BTSB)
1880 W Morton Ave ... Jacksonville IL 62650 217-245-5191 747-2872*
*Fax Area Code: 800 ■ TF: 800-637-6586 ■ Web: www.btsb.com

Continental Bindery Corp
700 Fargo Ave ... Elk Grove Village IL 60007 847-439-6811 439-6847

Contract Converting LLC PO Box 247 ... Greenville WI 54942 920-757-4000 757-4004*
*Fax Area Code: 902 ■ Web: www.contractconverting.com

Dekker Bookbinding 2941 Clydon Ave SW ... Grand Rapids MI 49519 616-538-5160 538-0720
Web: www.dekkerbook.com

Finishing Plus Inc 4546 W 47th St ... Chicago IL 60632 773-523-5510 523-9155
Web: finishingplus.com

Form House, The 4640 S Kolmar ... Chicago IL 60632 773-577-8500 523-9155
Web: theformhouse.com

HF Group, The 8844 Mayfield Rd Ste A ... Chesterland OH 44026 440-729-2445 729-3909
Web: hfgroup.com/index.php/

Kater-Crafts Bookbinders Inc
4860 Gregg Rd ... Pico Rivera CA 90660 562-692-0665 692-7920
Web: www.katercrafts.com

Kolbus America Inc 812 Huron Rd Ste 750 ... Cleveland OH 44115 216-931-5100 931-5101
Web: www.kolbusweb.de

Lake Book Manufacturing Inc
2085 N Cornell Ave ... Melrose Park IL 60160 708-345-7000 345-1544
Web: www.lakebook.com

Library Binding Service (LBS)
1801 Thompson Ave ... Des Moines IA 50316 515-262-3191 262-4091*
*Fax Area Code: 800 ■ TF: 800-247-5323 ■ Web: www.lbsbind.com

Marshall & Bruce Printing Co
689 Davidson St ... Nashville TN 37213 615-256-3661 256-6803
Web: www.marbruco.com

National Library Bindery Co
100 Hembree Pk Dr ... Roswell GA 30076 770-442-5490 442-0183

Parker Powis Inc 775 Heinz Ave ... Berkeley CA 94710 510-848-2463 848-2462
TF: 800-321-2463 ■ Web: www.powis.com

Perma-Bound 617 E Vandalia Rd ... Jacksonville IL 62650 217-243-5451 551-1169*
*Fax Area Code: 800 ■ TF: 800-637-6581 ■ Web: www.perma-bound.com

Reindl Bindery Company Inc
W194 N11381 McCormick Dr ... Germantown WI 53022 262-293-1444 293-1445
TF: 800-878-1121 ■ Web: www.reindlbindery.com

Rickard Circular Folding Co
325 N Ashland Ave ... Chicago IL 60607 312-243-6300 243-6323
TF: 800-747-1389 ■ Web: www.rickardbindery.com

Riverside Group 655 Driving Pk Ave ... Rochester NY 14613 585-458-2090 458-2123
TF: 800-777-2463 ■ Web: www.riversidegroup.com

Roswell Bookbinding Co 2614 N 29th Ave ... Phoenix AZ 85009 602-272-9338 272-9786
TF: 888-803-8883 ■ Web: www.roswellbookbinding.com

Talas Inc 330 Morgan Ave 5th Fl ... Brooklyn NY 11211 212-219-0770 219-0735
Web: www.talas-nyc.com

United Bindery Service Inc
1845 W Carroll Ave ... Chicago IL 60612 312-243-0240 243-3080

Wert Bookbinding Inc 9975 Allentown Blvd ... Grantville PA 17028 717-469-0629 469-0629
TF Cust Svc: 800-344-9378 ■ Web: www.wertbookbinding.com

93 BOOK, MUSIC, VIDEO CLUBS

Phone Fax

Booksfree.com 8453 Tyco Rd # P ... Vienna VA 22182 703-748-2390
Web: www.booksfree.com

Crossings Book Club PO Box 916400 ... Rantoul IL 61866 717-918-2665
Web: www.crossings.com

Direct Brands Inc 1225 S Market St ... Mechanicsburg PA 17055 717-697-0311

eMusic.com Inc 511 Avenue of the Americas ... New York NY 10011 212-201-9240
Web: www.emusic.com

GameFly Inc 3000 Ocean Pk Blvd ... Santa Monica CA 90405 310-664-6400
Web: www.gamefly.com

NetFlix Inc 100 Winchester Cir ... Los Gatos CA 95032 408-540-3700 540-3737
NASDAQ: NFLX ■ TF: 800-290-8191 ■ Web: netflix.com/

Quality Paperback Book Club (QPBC)
PO Box 916400 ... Rantoul IL 61866 866-284-3202
Web: www.qpb.com

Rhapsody Book Club PO Box 916400 ... Rantoul IL 61866 866-250-3166
Web: www.rhapsodybookclub.com

Scholastic Arrow Book Club 555 Broadway ... New York NY 10012 212-343-6100 223-4011*
*Fax Area Code: 800 ■ TF Orders: 800-724-6527 ■ Web: clubs2.scholastic.com

Science Fiction Book Club PO Box 916400 ... Rantoul IL 61866 717-918-2665
Web: www.sfbc.com

Writer's Digest Book Club
4700 E Galbraith Rd ... Cincinnati OH 45236 513-531-2690 445-4087*
*Fax Area Code: 715 ■ TF Cust Svc: 800-759-0963 ■ Web: www.writersdigestshop.com

94 BOOK PRODUCERS

Book producers, or book packagers, work with authors, editors, printers, publishers, and others to provide all publication services except sales and order fulfillment. These publication services include editing of manuscripts, formatting of computer disks, producing books as a finished product, and helping the book publisher to develop marketing plans. Book producers listed here are members of the American Book Producers Association.

Phone Fax

Agincourt Press 25 Main St ... Chatham NY 12037 518-392-2898

AGS BookWorks PO Box 460313 ... San Francisco CA 94146 415-285-8799
Web: www.agsbookworks.com

Ardent Media Inc 522 E 82nd St ... New York NY 10028 212-861-1501 861-0998

Becker & Mayer! Ltd 11120 NE 33rd Pl # 101 ... Bellevue WA 98004 425-827-7120 828-9659
Web: www.beckermayer.com

Current Medical Directions Inc 230 Pk Ave S ... New York NY 10003 212-614-6218 598-6909
Web: www.cmdny.com

Emprise Publishing Inc 1104 Murrayhill Rd ... Vestal NY 13850 607-772-0559

Evanston Publishing Inc
4824 Brownsboro Ctr ... Louisville KY 40207 502-899-1919 896-0246
Web: www.evanstonpublishing.com

Phone Fax

Focus Strategic Communications Inc
2474 Waterford St ... Oakville ON L6L5E6 905-825-8757
TF: 866-263-6287 ■ Web: www.focussc.com

GGP Publishing Inc 105 Calvert St Ste 201 ... Harrison NY 10528 914-834-8896 834-7566
Web: ggppublishing.com

Gonzalez Defino Seven E 14th St Ste 20s ... New York NY 10003 212-414-1058
Web: www.gonzalezdefino.com

Guru Labs 801 North 500 West Ste 202 ... Bountiful UT 84010 801-298-5227
Web: www.gurulabs.com

Innovative USA Inc 50 Washington St ... Norwalk CT 06854 203-838-6400 855-5582
Web: www.innovativekids.com

Learning Source Ltd 644 Tenth St ... Brooklyn NY 11215 718-768-0231 369-3467
Web: www.learningsourceltd.com

MetriTech Inc 4106 Fieldstone Rd ... Champaign IL 61826 217-398-4868
Web: www.metritech.com

Mountain Lion Inc Nine Voorhees Ct ... Hopewell NJ 08525 609-730-1665
Web: www.mtlioninc.com

MTM Publishing Inc 435 W 23rd St Ste 8C ... New York NY 10011 212-242-6930 242-6906
Web: www.mtmpublishing.com

Palace Printing & Design 80 Mark Dr ... San Rafael CA 94903 415-526-1378
Web: www.palacepress.com

Philip Lief Group Inc (PLG) 130 Wall St ... Princeton NJ 08540 609-430-1000 430-0300
Web: www.philipliefgroup.com

Rosa + Wesley Inc 400 S Knoll St Ste B ... Wheaton IL 60187 630-588-9801 588-9804
Web: www.rosawesley.com

Schlager Group Inc 325 N Saint Paul Ste 3425 ... Dallas TX 75201 888-416-5727 347-9469*
*Fax Area Code: 214 ■ TF: 888-416-5727 ■ Web: www.schlagergroup.com

Shackleton Group Inc 1410 Vance St Ste 205 ... Lakewood CO 80214 303-482-2370
Web: shkgrp.com

Shoreline Publishing Group
125 Santa Rosa Pl ... Santa Barbara CA 93109 805-564-1004 840-6713*
*Fax Area Code: 800 ■ Web: www.shorelinepublishing.com

Sideshow Media 611 Broadway Ste 734 ... New York NY 10012 212-674-5335 367-0006*
*Fax Area Code: 646 ■ Web: www.sideshowbooks.com

Smallwood & Stewart Inc Five E 20th St ... New York NY 10003 212-505-3268
Web: www.smallwoodandstewart.com

Stonesong Press LLC 270 W 39th St Ste 201 ... New York NY 10018 212-929-4600 486-9123
Web: www.stonesong.com

Training to Inc 2200 N Central Ave Ste 100 ... Phoenix AZ 85004 602-266-1500
Web: www.trainingtoyou.com

Victory Productions Inc 55 Linden St ... Worcester MA 01609 508-755-0051 755-0025
Web: victoryprd.com

Welcome Enterprises Inc
Six W 18th St Third Fl ... New York NY 10011 212-989-3200 989-3205
Web: www.welcomebooks.com

95 BOOK STORES

Phone Fax

710 Book Store 819 S Illinois Ave ... Carbondale IL 62901 618-549-7304
Web: www.seventen.com

Alibris Inc 1250 45th St Ste 100 ... Emeryville CA 94608 510-594-4500 550-6052
Web: www.alibris.com

Amazon.com Inc 1200 12th Ave S Ste 1200 ... Seattle WA 98144 206-266-1000 266-7601*
NASDAQ: AMZN ■ *Fax: Hum Res ■ TF Cust Svc: 800-201-7575 ■ Web: www.amazon.com

Antigone Books 411 N Fourth Ave ... Tucson AZ 85705 520-792-3715 882-8802
Web: www.antigonebooks.com

Artisan Books & Bindery
509 Pendleton Point Rd ... Islesboro ME 04848 207-734-6852
Web: www.artisanbooksandbindery.com

Associated Students Ucla
308 Westwood Plz ... Los Angeles CA 90095 310-825-7711
Web: www.asucla.ucla.edu

Bakersfield Magazine Inc
1601 New Stine Rd Ste 200 ... Bakersfield CA 93309 661-834-4126
Web: www.bakersfieldmagazine.net

Barbour Publishing Inc
1810 Barbour Dr PO Box 719 ... Uhrichsville OH 44683 740-922-6045
Web: www.barbourbooks.com

Barnes & Noble College Bookstores Inc
120 Mtn View Blvd ... Basking Ridge NJ 07920 908-991-2665
Web: www.bncollege.com

Barnes & Noble Inc 122 Fifth Ave ... New York NY 10011 212-633-3300 727-4827*
NYSE: BKS ■ *Fax: Cust Svc ■ Web: www.barnesandnoble.com

barnesandnoble.com Inc 76 Ninth Ave Fl 9 ... New York NY 10011 212-414-6000
TF: 800-843-2665 ■ Web: www.barnesandnoble.com

BarristerBooks Inc 615 Florida St ... Lawrence KS 66044 785-856-2772
Web: www.barristerbooks.com

Bauman Rare Books 535 Madison Ave Frnt 1 ... New York NY 10022 212-751-0011
Web: www.baumanrarebooks.com

Bear Pond Books 77 Main St ... Montpelier VT 05602 802-229-0774 229-1069
Web: www.bearpondbooks.com

Becks Bookstores Inc 4520 N Broadway ... Chicago IL 60640 773-784-7963 784-0066
Web: www.becksbooks.com

Better World Books Inc 55740 Currant Rd ... Mishawaka IN 46545 574-252-5303
Web: www.betterworldbooks.com

Bon Venture Services Inc 34 Ironia Rd ... Flanders NJ 07836 973-584-5699
Web: www.bonventure.net

Book Exchange Inc 152 Willey St ... Morgantown WV 26505 304-292-7354
Web: www.bookexchangewv.com

Book House Inc, The 208 W Chicago St ... Jonesville MI 49250 800-248-1146
TF: 800-248-1146 ■ Web: www.thebookhouse.com

Book Loft 631 S Third St ... Columbus OH 43206 614-464-1774 464-3443
Web: www.bookloft.com

Book Passage 51 Tamal Vista Blvd ... Corte Madera CA 94925 415-927-0960 927-3069
TF: 800-999-7909 ■ Web: www.bookpassage.com

Book Revue 313 New York Ave ... Huntington NY 11743 631-271-1442 271-5890
Web: www.bookrevue.com

Book Soup 8818 Sunset Blvd ... West Hollywood CA 90069 310-659-3110 659-3410
TF: 888-527-8238 ■ Web: www.booksoup.com

Phone | Fax

BookBuyers 317 Castro St ... Mountain View CA 94041 650-968-7323
Web: www.bookbuyers.com

Bookmans Entertainment Exchange
8034 N 19th Ave ... Phoenix AZ 85021 602-433-0255
Web: www.bookmans.com

BookPal LLC 18101 Von Karman Ave Ste 1240 ... Irvine CA 92612 866-522-6657
TF: 866-522-6657 ■ *Web:* book-pal.com

BookPeople 603 N Lamar ... Austin TX 78703 512-472-5050 482-8495
TF: 800-853-9757 ■ *Web:* www.bookpeople.com

Books & Books 265 Aragon Ave ... Coral Gables FL 33134 305-442-4408 444-9751
Web: www.booksandbooks.com

Books Inc 2251 Chestnut St ... San Francisco CA 94123 415-931-3633
Web: www.booksinc.net

Books of Discovery 5660 Valmont Rd Ste C ... Boulder CO 80301 303-443-1794
Web: www.booksofdiscovery.com

Books on the Square 471 Angell St ... Providence RI 02906 401-331-9097 331-2845
TF: 888-669-9660 ■ *Web:* www.booksq.com

Books-A-Million Inc 402 Industrial Ln ... Birmingham AL 35211 205-942-3737
NASDAQ: BAMM ■ *TF:* 800-201-3550 ■ *Web:* www.booksamillion.com

BookSense.com 200 White Plains Rd ... Tarrytown NY 10591 914-631-2415 591-2720
TF: 800-637-0037 ■ *Web:* www.indiebound.org

Boston Consumers Checkbook 185 Franklin St ... Boston MA 02110 617-951-9995
Web: www.checkbook.org

Boulder Book Store 1107 Pearl St ... Boulder CO 80302 303-447-2074 447-3946
TF: 800-244-4651 ■ *Web:* www.boulderbookstore.com

BPDI Corp 1000 S Lynndale Dr Apt O ... Appleton WI 54914 920-830-7897
Web: www.bookworldstores.com

Brazos Bookstore 2421 Bissonnet ... Houston TX 77005 713-523-0701
Web: www.brazosbookstore.com

Brookline Booksmith 279 Harvard St ... Brookline MA 02446 617-566-6660 734-9125
Web: www.brooklinebooksmith.com

Changing Hands Bookstore 6428 S McClintock Dr ... Tempe AZ 85283 480-730-0205 730-1196
Web: www.changinghands.com

Chaucer's Books 3321 State St ... Santa Barbara CA 93105 805-682-6787 682-1129
Web: www.chaucersbooks.com

Chicago Architecture Foundation
224 S Michigan Ave Ste 116 ... Chicago IL 60604 312-922-3432
Web: www.architecture.org

Childrens Plus Inc 1387 Dutch American Way ... Beecher IL 60401 800-230-1279
TF: 800-230-1279 ■ *Web:* www.childrensplusinc.com

Chinaberry Inc
2780 Via Orange Way Ste B ... Spring Valley CA 91978 619-670-5200
Web: www.chinaberryinc.com

Chinati Foundation PO Box 1135 ... Marfa TX 79843 432-729-4362 729-4597
Web: www.chinati.org

City Lights Booksellers
261 Columbus Ave ... San Francisco CA 94133 415-362-8193 362-4921
Web: www.citylights.com

Collector Books 5801 Kentucky Dam Rd ... Paducah KY 42003 270-898-6211
Web: www.collectorbooks.com

Comic Strip Live 1568 Second Ave Frnt ... New York NY 10028 212-861-9386
Web: www.comicstriplive.com

Curious George Goes to WordsWorth
One John F Kennedy St ... Cambridge MA 02138 617-547-4500
Web: thecuriousgeorgestore.com

Curtis Circulation Company LLC
730 River Rd ... New Milford NJ 07646 201-634-7400
Web: www.curtiscirc.com

Daedalus Books Inc 9645 Gerwig Ln ... Columbia MD 21046 410-309-2706
Web: www.daedalusbooks.com

Dallas Bar Association 2101 Ross Ave ... Dallas TX 75201 214-220-7400
Web: www.dallasbar.org

Deseret Book Co 57 W S Temple ... Salt Lake City UT 84111 801-534-1515
TF: 800-453-4532 ■ *Web:* www.deseretbook.com

Dickens Books Ltd
219 N Milwaukee St Third Fl ... Milwaukee WI 53202 800-236-7323 274-8690*
**Fax Area Code: 414* ■ *TF:* 800-236-7323 ■ *Web:* 800ceoread.com

Digital Manga Inc 1487 W 178th St Ste 300 ... Gardena CA 90248 310-817-8010
Web: www.digitalmanga.com

Dillard University 2601 Gentilly Blvd ... New Orleans LA 70122 504-283-8822
Web: www.dillard.edu

Doodles Campus Store 935 Main St ... Montevallo AL 35115 205-665-1719
Web: www.doodlesbooks.com

Drama Book Shop Inc 250 E 40th St Frnt 2 ... New York NY 10018 212-944-0595 730-8739
TF: 800-322-0595 ■ *Web:* www.dramabookshop.com

Dunn & Company Inc 75 Green St ... Clinton MA 01510 978-368-8505
Web: booktrauma.com

East West Bookshop of Palo Alto
324 Castro St ... Mountain View CA 94041 650-988-9800
Web: www.eastwest.com

Eastern National
470 Maryland Dr Ste 1 ... Fort Washington PA 19034 215-283-6900
Web: www.easternnational.org

EC Council University Inc
6330 Riverside Plz Ln Nw Ste 210 ... Albuquerque NM 87120 505-341-3228
Web: www.eccouncil.org

Elliott Bay Book Co 101 S Main St ... Seattle WA 98104 206-624-6600 903-1601
TF: 800-962-5311 ■ *Web:* www.elliottbaybook.com

Elmendorf Strategies LLC
900 Seventh St Nw Ste 750 ... Washington DC 20001 202-737-1010
Web: www.elmendorfryan.com

Emmanuel Books 702 Delaware St ... New Castle DE 19720 302-325-9515
Web: www.emmanuelbooks.com

EOIR Technologies Inc
10300 Spotsylvania Ave Ste 420 ... Fredericksburg VA 22408 540-834-4888
Web: www.eoir.com

Evangel Cathedral 13901 Central Ave ... Upper Marlboro MD 20774 301-249-9400
Web: www.evangelcathedral.net

Family Christian Stores Inc
5300 Patterson Ave ... Grand Rapids MI 49530 616-554-8700 554-8608
Web: www.familychristian.com

Phone | Fax

Fanfare Sports & Entertainment
4415 S Westnedge Ave ... Kalamazoo MI 49008 269-349-8866
Web: www.fanfare-se.com

FJH Music Company Inc, The
2525 Davie Rd Ste 360 ... Davie FL 33317 954-382-6061
Web: www.fjhmusic.com

Florida Instructional Materials Center
5002 N Lois Ave ... Tampa FL 33614 813-872-5281
Web: www.fimcvi.org

Follett Corp
3 Westbrook Corporate Center Ste 200 ... Westchester IL 60154 800-365-5388 452-0169*
**Fax Area Code: 708* ■ *TF:* 800-365-5388 ■ *Web:* www.follett.com

Follett Higher Education Group
Three Westbrook Corporate Ctr Ste 200 ... Westchester IL 60154 800-323-4506 279-2569*
**Fax Area Code: 630* ■ *TF:* 800-323-4506 ■ *Web:* www.fheg.follett.com

Full Cir Bookstore 1900 NW Expy ... Oklahoma City OK 73118 405-842-2900 842-2894
TF: 800-683-7323 ■ *Web:* www.fullcirclebooks.com

Half Price Books Records & Magazines Inc
5803 E Northwest Hwy ... Dallas TX 75231 214-360-0833 379-8010
Web: www.hpb.com

Harvard Book Store Inc
1256 Massachusetts Ave ... Cambridge MA 02138 617-661-1515
Web: harvard.com

Harvard Square Co-op Society
1400 Massachusetts Ave ... Cambridge MA 02238 617-499-2000 547-2768
Web: www.harvardsquare.com

Hastings Entertainment Inc 3601 Plains Blvd ... Amarillo TX 79102 877-427-8464 351-2424*
NASDAQ: HAST ■ **Fax Area Code: 806* ■ *TF Cust Svc:* 877-427-8464 ■ *Web:* www.gohastings.com

Horizon Books 243 E Front St ... Traverse City MI 49684 231-946-7290
Web: www.horizonbooks.com

Hosanna 2421 Aztec Rd Ne ... Albuquerque NM 87107 505-881-3321
Web: www.faithcomesbyhearing.com

I See Me! Inc 4305 Chimo E St ... Wayzata MN 55391 952-473-3939
Web: www.myveryownname.com

In The Line of Duty
10727 Indian Head Industrial Blvd ... Saint Louis MO 63132 314-890-8733
Web: www.lineofduty.com

Indigo Books & Music Inc
468 King St W Ste 500 ... Toronto ON M5V1L8 416-364-4499 364-0355
NYSE: IDG ■ *TF Cust Svc:* 800-832-7569 ■ *Web:* www.chapters.indigo.ca

Jessica's Biscuit Mobile Book Fair
82 Needham St ... Newton MA 02461 617-965-0530

Jimmy Bs Audiobooks 324 Ave I ... Redondo Beach CA 90277 310-375-3134
Web: www.audiobooks.com

Kalkomey Enterprises Inc 14086 Proton Rd ... Dallas TX 75244 214-351-0461
Web: www.kalkomey.com

Karrass Seminars
8370 Wilshire Blvd Fl 3 ... Beverly Hills CA 90211 323-951-7500
Web: www.karrass.com

Keyano College 8115 Franklin Ave ... Fort Mcmurray AB T9H2H7 780-791-4800
Web: www.keyano.ca

Kinetic Books Company Inc
2003 Western Ave Ste 100 ... Seattle WA 98121 206-448-1141
Web: www.kineticbooks.com

Kinokuniya Book Stores of America Company Ltd
1581 Webster St ... San Francisco CA 94115 415-673-7431
Web: www.kinokuniya.com

Kinokuniya Bookstores
1073 Ave of the Americas ... New York NY 10018 212-869-1700 869-1703
Web: www.kinokuniya.co.jp

Lee & Low Books Inc 95 Madison Ave Ste 1205 ... New York NY 10016 212-779-4400
Web: www.leeandlow.com

Left Bank Books 399 N Euclid Ave ... Saint Louis MO 63108 314-367-6731 367-3256
Web: www.left-bank.com

LibertyTree 100 Swan Way ... Oakland CA 94621 510-632-1366 568-6040
TF: 800-927-8733 ■ *Web:* www.independent.org

Mastermind LP 2134 Queen St E ... Toronto ON M4E1E3 416-699-3797
Web: www.mastermindtoys.com

Matthews Book Co
11559 Rock Island Ct ... Maryland Heights MO 63043 314-432-1400 432-7044
TF: 800-633-2665 ■ *Web:* www.matthewsbooks.com

MCE Technologies LLC 30 Hughes Ste 203 ... Irvine CA 92618 949-458-0800
Web: www.mcetech.com

McNally Robinson Booksellers Inc
1120 Grant Ave ... Winnipeg MB R3M2A6 204-475-0483
Web: www.mcnallyrobinson.com

Merchant One Payment Systems Inc
524 Arthur Godfrey Rd 3rd Fl ... Miami Beach FL 33140 305-534-1666
TF: 888-854-0347 ■ *Web:* www.merchantone.com

Millman Search Group Inc
11419 Cronridge Dr Ste 17 ... Owings Mills MD 21117 410-902-6600
Web: www.millmansearch.com

Moe's Books 2476 Telegraph Ave ... Berkeley CA 94704 510-849-2087 849-9938
Web: www.moesbooks.com

Mountaineers Books
1001 Sw Klickitat Way Ste 201 ... Seattle WA 98134 206-223-6303
Web: www.mountaineersbooks.org

MovieStop Inc 1300 Cobb International Blvd ... Kennesaw GA 30152 770-590-1765
Web: www.moviestop.com

Mrs Nelsons Library Service
1650 W Orange Grove Ave ... Pomona CA 91768 909-397-7820
Web: www.mrsnelsons.com

National Book Network Inc
4501 Forbes Blvd Ste 200 ... Lanham MD 20706 301-459-3366
Web: www.nbnbooks.com

Newbury Comics Inc 5 Guest St ... Brighton MA 02135 617-254-1666 254-1085
Web: www.newbury.com

Newslink Group LLC 6910 NW 12th St ... Miami FL 33126 305-594-5754
Web: newslinkgroup.net

Northshire Information Inc
4869 Main St ... Manchester Center VT 05255 802-362-2200 362-1233
TF: 800-437-3700 ■ *Web:* www.northshire.com

	City	State	Zip	Phone	Fax
On Demand Books 584 Broadway Rm 1100 *Web:* www.ondemandbooks.com	New York	NY	10012	212-966-2222	
Page One Bookstore 11018 Montgomery Blvd NE *TF:* 800-521-4122 ■ *Web:* www.page1book.com	Albuquerque	NM	87111	505-294-2026	294-5576
Parable Christian Stores 3563 Empleo St *Web:* www.parable.com	San Luis Obispo	CA	93401	805-248-7395	201-9026
Paragraph Book Store Inc 2220 McGill College Ave *Web:* www.paragraphbooks.com	Montreal	QC	H3A3P9	514-845-5811	
Park Place Mobile Homes 731 E Arrow Hwy Ste A *Web:* www.reasons.org	Glendora	CA	91740	626-914-2992	
Pentecostals of Alexandria, The 2817 Rapides Ave *Web:* www.thepentecostals.org	Alexandria	LA	71301	318-487-8976	
Poetry Pals Inc 295 SW Brushy Mound Rd *Web:* www.poetrypals.com	Burleson	TX	76028	817-295-6680	
Poisoned Pen Bookstore 4014 N Goldwater Blvd *TF:* 888-560-9919 ■ *Web:* www.poisonedpen.com	Scottsdale	AZ	85251	480-947-2974	945-1023
Politics & Prose Bookstore 5015 Connecticut Ave NW *TF:* 800-722-0790 ■ *Web:* www.politics-prose.com	Washington	DC	20008	202-364-1919	966-7532
Powell's Books Inc Seven NW Ninth Ave *TF:* 800-878-7323 ■ *Web:* www.powells.com	Portland	OR	97209	503-228-0540	228-1142
Powell's City of Books 40 NW Tenth Ave *TF:* 800 878 7323 ■ *Web:* www.powells.com	Portland	OR	97209	503-228-4651	228-4631
Prairie Lights Bookstore 15 S Dubuque St *Web:* www.prairielights.com	Iowa City	IA	52240	319-337-2681	887-3084
Printed Matter Inc 195 Tenth Ave Frnt 1 *Web:* www.printedmatter.org	New York	NY	10011	212-925-0325	
R J Julia Booksellers LLC 768 Boston Post Rd *Web:* booksasgifts.com	Madison	CT	06443	203-245-3959	
Regulator Bookshop 720 Ninth St *Web:* regulatorbookshop.com	Durham	NC	27705	919-286-2700	286-6063
Remuda Ranch Co One E Apache St *Web:* www.remudaranch.com	Wickenburg	AZ	85390	928-684-3913	
Safari Books Online LLC 1003 Gravenstein Hwy N *Web:* my.safaribooksonline.com	Sebastopol	CA	95472	707-827-4100	
Samuel French Inc 45 W 25th St *Web:* www.samuelfrench.com	New York	NY	10010	212-206-8990	
Schuler Books & Music Inc 2660 28th St SE *Web:* www.schulerbooks.com	Grand Rapids	MI	49512	616-942-2561	
SciTech Publishing Inc 911 Paverstone Dr Ste B *Web:* www.scitechpub.com	Raleigh	NC	27615	919-847-2434	
Seagull Book & Tape Inc 1720 S Redwood Rd *TF:* 800-999-6257 ■ *Web:* www.seagullbook.com	Salt Lake City	UT	84104	800-999-6257	
Seminary Co-op Bookstore 5757 S University Ave *Web:* www.semcoop.com	Chicago	IL	60637	773-752-4381	752-8507
Skylight Books 1818 N Vermont Ave *Web:* www.skylightbooks.com	Los Angeles	CA	90027	323-660-1175	660-0232
Social Studies School Service 10200 Jefferson Blvd PO Box 802 **Fax Area Code:* 800 ■ *TF:* 800-421-4246 ■ *Web:* www.socialstudies.com	Culver City	CA	90232	310-839-2436	944-5432*
Square Books 160 Courthouse Sq *TF:* 800-648-4001 ■ *Web:* www.squarebooks.com	Oxford	MS	38655	662-236-2262	234-9630
Strand Book Store Inc 828 Broadway *Web:* www.strandbooks.com	New York	NY	10003	212-473-1452	
Student Book Store 421 E Grand River Ave *Web:* www.sbsmsu.com	East Lansing	MI	48823	517-351-4210	
Sunshine Books Inc 49 River St Ste 3 *Web:* www.clickertraining.com	Waltham	MA	02453	781-398-0754	
Tatnuck Bookseller 18 Lyman St *Web:* www.tatnuck.com	Westborough	MA	01581	508-366-4959	366-7929
Tattered Cover Book Store Inc 1628 16th St *TF:* 800-833-9327 ■ *Web:* www.tatteredcover.com	Denver	CO	80202	303-436-1070	629-1704
That Bookstore in Blytheville 316 W Main St *Web:* thatbookstoreinblytheville.com	Blytheville	AR	72315	870-763-3333	763-1125
Title Wave Inc 1360 W Northern Lights Blvd *Web:* www.wavebooks.com	Anchorage	AK	99503	907-278-9283	
Travis Avenue Baptist Church 800 E Berry St *Web:* www.travis.org	Fort Worth	TX	76110	817-924-4266	921-9620
Unicor Medical Inc 4160 Carmichael Rd *TF:* 800-825-7421 ■ *Web:* www.unicormed.com	Montgomery	AL	36106	800-825-7421	
University Book Store, The 711 State St *Web:* www.uwbookstore.com	Madison	WI	53703	608-257-3784	
University of Oregon Bookstore Inc PO Box 3176 *TF:* 800-352-1733 ■ *Web:* www.uoduckstore.com	Eugene	OR	97403	541-346-4331	346-3645
University Press Books (UPB) 2430 Bancroft Way *TF:* 800-676-8722 ■ *Web:* www.universitypressbooks.com	Berkeley	CA	94704	510-548-0585	849-9214
Valley Books PO Box 2127 *Web:* www.valleybooks.com	Amherst	MA	01004	413-256-1508	
Viewpoint Books 548 Washington St *Web:* www.viewpointbooks.com	Columbus	IN	47201	812-376-0778	376-1089
Vroman's Bookstore 695 E Colorado Blvd *Web:* www.vromansbookstore.com	Pasadena	CA	91101	626-449-5320	
Western Continental Book Co 6425 Washington St *Web:* www.continentalbook.com	Denver	CO	80229	303-289-1761	
Wild Onion Books 3441 N Ashland Ave *Web:* www.loyolapress.com	Chicago	IL	60657	773-281-1818	
Word Among Us Inc 9639 Doctor Perry Rd *Web:* wau.org	Ijamsville	MD	21754	301-874-1700	

96 BOOKS, PERIODICALS, NEWSPAPERS - WHOL

	City	State	Zip	Phone	Fax
21st Century Christian Inc PO Box 40526 *TF:* 800-251-2477 ■ *Web:* www.21stcc.com	Nashville	TN	37204	615-383-3842	
Advantage Mktg Inc 14 W Main St *TF:* 800-670-7479 ■ *Web:* www.advantagemkt.com	Ashland	OH	44805	419-281-4762	
Alexander City Outlook 548 Cherokee Rd *Web:* www.alexcityoutlook.com	Alexander City	AL	35010	256-234-4281	
Alliance Paper & Food Service Inc 11058 W Addison St *Web:* www.allpfs.com	Franklin Park	IL	60131	847-349-1500	
American Book Co 11130 Kingston Pk Ste 1-183 *Web:* www.americanbookco.com	Knoxville	TN	37934	865-966-7454	675-0557
American Overseas Book Company Inc 550 Walnut St *Web:* www.aobc.com	Norwood	NJ	07648	201-767-7600	
ATA Retail Services Inc 30773 Wiegman Rd *Web:* www.ataretail.com	Hayward	CA	94544	510-401-5300	
Auto Export Shipping Inc One Slater Dr *Web:* aesshipping.com	Elizabeth	NJ	07206	908-436-2150	
Baker & Taylor Inc 2550 W Tyvola Rd Ste 300 **Fax Area Code:* 704 ■ *TF:* 800-775-1800 ■ *Web:* www.btol.com	Charlotte	NC	28217	800-775-1800	998-3316*
BMI Educational Services PO Box 800 **Fax Area Code:* 800 ■ *TF:* 800-222-8100 ■ *Web:* www.bmionline.com	Dayton	NJ	08810	732-329-6991	986-9393*
Book Depot Inc 67 Front St N *Web:* www.bookdepot.com	Thorold	ON	L2V1X3	905-680-7230	
Bookazine Company Inc 75 Hook Rd *TF:* 800-221-8112 ■ *Web:* www.bookazine.com	Bayonne	NJ	07002	201-339-7777	339-7778
Booksource Inc 1230 Macklind Ave **Fax Area Code:* 800 ■ *TF:* 800-444-0435 ■ *Web:* www.booksource.com	Saint Louis	MO	63110	314-647-0600	647-1923*
Brodart Company Book Services Div 500 Arch St *TF:* 800-474-9816 ■ *Web:* www.brodartbooks.com	Williamsport	PA	17701	570-326-2461	
C2F Inc 6600 SW 111th Ave *TF:* 800-544-8825 ■ *Web:* www.c2f.com	Beaverton	OR	97008	503-643-9050	
Campus Text Inc 107 Forrest Ave *Web:* campustext.com	Narberth	PA	19072	610-664-6900	
Canadian Industrial Distributors Inc 175 Sun Pac Blvd Ste 2A *TF:* 877-280-0243 ■ *Web:* www.cid.ca	Brampton	ON	L6S5Z6	905-595-0411	
Capitol Fiber Inc 6610 Electronics Dr *Web:* capitolfiber.com	Springfield	VA	22151	703-658-0200	658-0212
Choice Books LLC 2387 Grace Chapel Rd *TF:* 800-224-5006 ■ *Web:* www.choicebooks.org	Harrisonburg	VA	22801	540-434-1827	434-9894
Comag Marketing Group LLC 155 Village Blvd 3rd Fl *TF:* 866-790-9353 ■ *Web:* www.i-cmg.com	Princeton	NJ	08540	609-524-1800	524-1629
Comint Apparel Group LLC 463 Seventh Ave 11th Fl *Web:* www.comintapparel.com	New York	NY	10018	212-947-7474	
Command Spanish Inc P.O. Box 1091 *Web:* www.commandspanish.com	Petal	MS	39465	601-582-8378	582-5177
Consortium Book Sales & Distribution Inc The Keg House 34 Thirteenth Ave NE Ste 101 *Web:* www.cbsd.com	Minneapolis	MN	55413	612-746-2600	
Coppel Corp 503 Scaroni Rd *Web:* www.coppel.com	Calexico	CA	92231	760-357-3707	
Cousin Corp of America 12333 Enterprise Blvd *Web:* www.cousin.com	Largo	FL	33773	727-536-3568	
Csubs 155 Chestnut Ridge Rd *Web:* www.csubs.com	Montvale	NJ	07645	201-307-9900	
Davidson Titles Inc 2345 Dr F E Wright Dr *Web:* www.davidsontitles.com	Jackson	TN	38305	731-988-5333	
Direct Holdings Americas Inc 8280 Willow Oaks Corporate Dr *Web:* www.timelife.com	Fairfax	VA	22031	800-950-7887	
Directory Distributing Assoc (DDA) 1602 Pk 370 Ct *TF General:* 800-325-1964 ■ *Web:* www.ddai.com	Hazelwood	MO	63042	314-592-8600	592-8790
EBSCO Subscription Services 110 Olmsted St Ste 100 *TF:* 800-653-2726 ■ *Web:* www.ebsco.com/home/about/ess.asp	Birmingham	AL	35242	205-995-1596	995-1518
Educational Development Corp 10302 E 55th Pl *NASDAQ: EDUC* ■ *TF:* 800-475-4522 ■ *Web:* www.edcpub.com	Tulsa	OK	74146	918-622-4522	665-7919
Emery-pratt Co 1966 W M 21 *Web:* www.emery-pratt.com	Owosso	MI	48867	989-723-5291	
ePromos Promotional Products Inc 120 Broadway Ste 1360 *TF:* 877-377-6667 ■ *Web:* www.epromos.com	New York	NY	10271	212-286-8008	
Fall River News Co 25 Westwood Ave	New London	CT	06320	860-442-4394	
Flexpak Inc 1894 West 2425 South *Web:* www.flexpak.net	Woods Cross	UT	84087	801-956-0696	
Follett Corp 3 Westbrook Corporate Center Ste 200 **Fax Area Code:* 708 ■ *TF:* 800-365-5388 ■ *Web:* www.follett.com	Westchester	IL	60154	800-365-5388	452-0169*
Follett Educational Services 1433 International Pkwy **Fax Area Code:* 800 ■ *TF:* 800-621-4272 ■ *Web:* www.fes.follett.com	Woodridge	IL	60517	630-972-5600	638-4424*
General Pet Supply Inc 7711 N 81st St *TF:* 800-433-9786 ■ *Web:* www.generalpet.com	Milwaukee	WI	53223	414-365-3400	
Harlequin Enterprises Ltd Distribution Ctr 3010 Walden Ave *TF:* 888-432-4879 ■ *Web:* www.harlequin.com	Depew	NY	14043	716-684-1800	

				Phone	Fax
Independent Publishers Group 814 N Franklin St	Chicago	IL	60610	312-337-0747	337-5985
TF Orders: 800-888-4741 ■ *Web:* www.ipgbook.com					
InfraRed Imaging Systems Inc 22718 Holycross Epps Rd	Marysville	OH	43040	888-987-5768	
Web: www.irimagesys.com					
Ingram Book Group 1 Ingram Blvd	La Vergne	TN	37086	615-793-5000	213-5710
TF: 800-937-8000 ■ *Web:* www.ingrambookgroup.com					
Kable News Company Inc 14 Wall St # 4C	New York	NY	10005	212-705-4600	705-4666
Web: www.kable.com					
Kirk Co 201 St Helens Ave	Tacoma	WA	98402	253-627-2133	
Web: www.kirktrees.com					
MacKellar Assoc Inc 1729 Northfield Dr	Rochester Hills	MI	48309	248-335-4440	
Web: www.mackellar.com					
MBS Textbook Exchange Inc 2711 W Ash St	Columbia	MO	65203	573-445-2243	446-5254
TF Cust Svc: 800-325-0530 ■ *Web:* www.mbsbooks.com					
Midwest Library Service Inc 11443 St Charles Rock Rd	Bridgeton	MO	63044	314-739-3100	739-1326
TF: 800-325-8833 ■ *Web:* www.midwestls.com					
Milligan News Co Inc 150 N Autumn St	San Jose	CA	95110	408-286-7604	
Web: www.milligannews.com					
Nebraska Book Co 4700 S 19th St	Lincoln	NE	68512	402-421-7300	421-0001
TF: 800-869-0366 ■ *Web:* www.nebook.com					
Network Paper & Packaging Ltd 1391 Kebet Way	Port Coquitlam	BC	V3C6G1	604-941-2999	
Web: www.netpak.net					
Neway Packaging Corp 1973 E Via Arado	Rancho Dominguez	CA	90220	310-898-3400	
Web: www.newaypackaging.com					
Newsways Distributors Inc 1324 Cypress Ave	Los Angeles	CA	90065	323-258-6000	256-9999
Web: www.newsways.com/					
Packaging Progressions Inc 102 G P Clement Dr	Collegeville	PA	19426	610-489-8601	
Web: www.pacproinc.com					
Product Development Corp 20 Ragsdale Dr Ste 100	Monterey	CA	93940	831-333-1100	333-0110
Web: teampdc.com					
Publishers Group West (PGW) 1700 Fourth St	Berkeley	CA	94710	510-809-3700	809-3777
Web: www.pgw.com					
Publishers' Warehouse 2700 Crestwood Blvd	Irondale	AL	35210	205-956-2078	
TF: 800-653-2726 ■ *Web:* ebscoind.com					
Quality Books Inc 1003 W Pines Rd	Oregon	IL	61061	815-732-4450	732-4499
TF Cust Svc: 800-323-4241 ■ *Web:* www.quality-books.com					
Readerlink Distribution Services LLC 1420 Kensington Rd Ste 300	Oak Brook	IL	60523	708-547-4400	
TF: 800-549-5389 ■ *Web:* www.levybooks.com					
Rittenhouse Book Distributors Inc 511 Feheley Dr	King of Prussia	PA	19406	800-345-6425	223-7488*
**Fax:* Orders ■ *TF Cust Svc:* 800-345-6425 ■ *Web:* www.rittenhouse.com					
Saddleback Educational Publishing Inc Three Watson	Irvine	CA	92618	949-860-2500	
Web: www.sdlback.com					
SCB Distributors 15608 New Century Dr	Gardena	CA	90248	310-532-9400	
Web: scbdistributors.com					
Scholastic Book Fairs Inc 1080 Greenwood Blvd	Lake Mary	FL	32746	407-829-7300	
TF: 800-874-4809 ■ *Web:* www.scholastic.com/bookfairs					
Seda France Inc 8301 Springdale Rd Ste 800	Austin	TX	78724	512-206-0105	
TF: 800-474-0854 ■ *Web:* www.sedafrance.com					
Selamat Designs 231 S Maple Ave	South San Francisco	CA	94080	650-243-4840	
Web: www.selamatdesigns.com					
Send The Light Distribution LLC 100 Biblica Way	Elizabethton	TN	37643	423-547-5100	
Service Paper Co 4501 W Vly Hwy E Ste A	Sumner	WA	98390	253-321-3300	
Web: bunzldistribution.com					
Smith Mountain Industries Inc 1000 Dillard Dr	Forest	VA	24551	434-385-1305	
Snack Factory LLC 11 Tamarack Cir	Skillman	NJ	08558	609-683-5400	
Web: www.snackfactory.com					
Source Interlink Cos Inc 27500 Riverview Ctr Blvd	Bonita Springs	FL	34134	239-949-4450	949-7623
Southwestern/Great American 2451 Atrium Way	Nashville	TN	37214	888-602-7867	391-2503*
**Fax Area Code:* 615 ■ **Fax:* Cust Svc ■ *TF Cust Svc:* 888-602-7867 ■ *Web:* www.southwestern.com					
Spring Arbor Distributors One Ingram Blvd	La Vergne	TN	37086	615-793-5000	213-7140*
**Fax:* Sales ■ *TF:* 800-395-4340 ■ *Web:* www.ingramcontent.com					
Tarps & Tie-Downs Inc 24967 Huntwood Ave	Hayward	CA	94544	510-782-8772	
Web: tarpstiedowns.com					
Texas Book Co 8501 Technology Cir	Greenville	TX	75402	903-455-6937	454-2442
Web: www.texasbook.com					
Vulcan Service 5724 Hwy 280 E	Birmingham	AL	35242	800-841-9600	980-3891*
**Fax Area Code:* 205 ■ *TF:* 800-841-9600 ■ *Web:* www.vulcanservice.com					
YBP Library Services 999 Maple St	Contoocook	NH	03229	603-746-3102	746-5628
TF: 800-258-3774 ■ *Web:* www.ybp.com					

97 BOTANICAL GARDENS & ARBORETA

SEE ALSO Zoos & Wildlife Parks p. 3302

				Phone	Fax
Adkins Arboretum 12610 Eveland Rd PO Box 100	Ridgely	MD	21660	410-634-2847	634-2878
Web: www.adkinsarboretum.org					
Airlie Gardens 300 Airlie Rd	Wilmington	NC	28403	910-798-7700	256-5083
Web: airliegardens.org					
Alaska Botanical Garden 4601 Campbell Airstrip Rd	Anchorage	AK	99520	907-770-3692	770-0555
Web: www.alaskabg.org					
Aldridge Botanical Gardens 3530 Lorna Rd	Hoover	AL	35216	205-682-8019	
Web: www.aldridgegardens.com					
Alexandra Botanic Gardens Wellesley College 106 Central St	Wellesley	MA	02481	781-283-1000	
Web: www.wellesley.edu					
Alfred B Maclay State Gardens 3540 Thomasville Rd	Tallahassee	FL	32309	850-487-4556	487-8808
Web: www.floridastateparks.org/maclaygardens					
Alta Vista Gardens 200 Civic Ctr Dr PO Box 1988	Vista	CA	92084	760-945-3954	
Web: www.altavistagardens.org					
Amarillo Botanical Gardens 1400 Streit Dr	Amarillo	TX	79106	806-352-6513	352-6227
Web: www.amarillobotanicalgardens.org					
Anderson Japanese Gardens 318 Spring Creek Rd	Rockford	IL	61107	815-229-9390	
Web: andersongardens.org					
Annmarie Garden 13480 Dowell Rd PO Box 99	Dowell	MD	20629	410-326-4640	326-4887
Web: www.annmariegarden.org					
Applewood the CS Mott Estate 1400 E Kearsley St	Flint	MI	48503	810-233-0170	233-7022
Web: www.ruthmottfoundation.org					
Arboretum at California State University Fresno 2351 E Barstow Ave	Fresno	CA	93740	559-278-7422	278-7698
Web: www.fresnostate.edu					
Arboretum at Flagstaff 4001 S Woody Mtn Rd	Flagstaff	AZ	86001	928-774-1442	774-1441
Web: www.thearb.org					
Arboretum at Penn State 336 Forest Resources Bldg	University Park	PA	16802	814-865-9118	865-3725
Web: www.arboretum.psu.edu					
Arboretum at Penn State Behrend 4701 College Dr Glenhill Farmhouse	Erie	PA	16563	814-898-6160	898-6461
Web: www.psbehrend.psu.edu					
Arboretum at the University of California Santa Cruz 1156 High St Ste 500	Santa Cruz	CA	95064	831-427-2998	427-1524
Web: arboretum.ucsc.edu					
Arboretum of the Barnes Foundation 300 N Latch's Ln	Merion	PA	19066	610-667-0290	664-4026
Web: www.barnesfoundation.org					
Arboretum, The Arboretum Rd University of Guelph	Guelph	ON	N1G2W1	519-824-4120	763-9598
Web: www.uoguelph.ca/arboretum					
Arizona Arboretums (ASU) Facilities Management Dept	Tempe	AZ	85287	480-965-3633	965-9470
Web: www.azarboretum.org					
Arnold Arboretum of Harvard University 125 Arborway	Jamaica Plain	MA	02130	617-524-1718	524-1418
Web: arboretum.harvard.edu					
Atlanta Botanical Garden 1345 Piedmont Ave NE	Atlanta	GA	30309	404-876-5859	876-7472
Web: www.atlantabotanicalgarden.org					
Awbury Arboretum & Historic Estate 1 Awbury Rd Francis Cope House	Philadelphia	PA	19138	215-849-2855	849-0213
Web: www.awbury.org					
Bartlett Arboretum & Gardens 151 Brookdale Rd	Stamford	CT	06903	203-322-6971	595-9168
Web: www.bartlettarboretum.org					
Bartram's Garden 54th St & Lindbergh Blvd	Philadelphia	PA	19143	215-729-5281	729-1047
Web: www.bartramsgarden.org					
Beardsley Zoo 1875 Noble Ave	Bridgeport	CT	06610	203-394-6565	394-6566
Web: www.beardsleyzoo.org					
Bellagio Conservatory & Botanical Gardens 3600 S Las Vegas Blvd	Las Vegas	NV	89109	702-693-7111	693-8508
TF: 888-987-6667 ■ *Web:* bellagio.com					
Bellevue Botanical Garden 12001 Main St	Bellevue	WA	98005	425-452-2750	452-2748
Web: www.bellevuebotanical.org					
Bellingrath Gardens & Home 12401 Bellingrath Garden Rd	Theodore	AL	36582	251-973-2217	973-0540
TF: 800-247-8420 ■ *Web:* bellingrath.org					
Berkshire Botanical Garden 5 W Stockbridge Rd PO Box 826	Stockbridge	MA	01262	413-298-3926	298-4897
Web: www.berkshirebotanical.org					
Bernheim Arboretum & Research Forest 2499 Clermont Rd PO Box 130	Clermont	KY	40110	502-955-8512	955-4039
Web: bernheim.org					
Better Homes & Gardens Test Garden 1716 Locust St	Des Moines	IA	50309	515-284-3994	
TF: 800-374-4244 ■ *Web:* www.bhg.com					
Betty Ford Alpine Gardens 183 Gore Creek Dr	Vail	CO	81657	970-476-0103	476-1685
Web: bettyfordalpinegardens.org					
Bicentennial Gardens 1105 Hobbs Rd	Greensboro	NC	27410	336-297-4162	373-7941
Web: greensborobeautiful.org					
Bickelhaupt Arboretum 340 S 14th St	Clinton	IA	52732	563-242-4771	
Web: bick-arb.org					
Birmingham Botanical Gardens 2612 Ln Pk Rd	Birmingham	AL	35223	205-414-3900	414-3906
Web: www.bbgardens.org					
Blithewold Mansion Gardens & Arboretum 101 Ferry Rd Rt 114	Bristol	RI	02809	401-253-2707	253-0412
Web: www.blithewold.org					
Bloedel Reserve, The 7571 NE Dolphin Dr	Bainbridge Island	WA	98110	206-842-7631	842-3295
Web: bloedelreserve.org					
Boerner Botanical Gardens 9400 Boerner Dr	Hales Corners	WI	53130	414-525-5601	525-5610
Web: www.boernerbotanicalgardens.org					
Botanic Garden of Smith College Smith College	NorthHampton	MA	01063	413-585-2740	585-2744
Web: www.smith.edu/garden					
Botanica the Wichita Gardens 701 N Amidon Ave	Wichita	KS	67203	316-264-0448	264-0587
Web: www.botanica.org					
Botanical Garden of the Ozarks 4703 N Crossover Rd PO Box 10407	Fayetteville	AR	72764	479-750-2620	756-1920
Web: www.bgozarks.org					

Name / Address	City	State	ZIP	Phone	Fax
Botanical Gardens at Asheville 151 WT Weaver Blvd. *TF:* 888-823-4622 ■ *Web:* www.ashevillebotanicalgardens.org	Asheville	NC	28804	828-252-5190	252-1211
Botanical Research Institute of Texas 1700 University Dr *Web:* www.brit.org	Fort Worth	TX	76102	817-332-4441	332-4112
Bowman's Hill Wildflower Preserve 1635 River Rd PO Box 685 *Web:* www.bhwp.org	New Hope	PA	18938	215-862-2924	862-1846
Boxerwood Nature Ctr & Woodland Garden 963 Ross Rd *Web:* www.boxerwood.org	Lexington	VA	24450	540-463-2697	
Boyce Thompson Arboretum 37615 US Hwy 60 *TF:* 877-763-5315 ■ *Web:* cals.arizona.edu	Superior	AZ	85273	520-689-2723	689-5858
Brenton Arboretum 25141 260th St *Web:* www.thebrentonarboretum.org	Dallas Center	IA	50063	515-992-4211	992-3303
Brookgreen Gardens 1931 Brookgreen Dr *TF:* 800-849-1931 ■ *Web:* www.brookgreen.org	Murrells Inlet	SC	29576	843-235-6000	235-6039
Brooklyn Botanic Garden 1000 Washington Ave *Web:* www.bbg.org	Brooklyn	NY	11225	718-623-7200	857-2430
Brookside Gardens 1800 Glenallan Ave *TF:* 800-366-2012 ■ *Web:* www.montgomeryparks.org	Wheaton	MD	20902	301-962-1400	962-7878
Buffalo & Erie County Botanical Gardens 2655 S Pk Ave *Web:* www.buffalogardens.com	Buffalo	NY	14218	716-827-1584	828-0091
Butchart Gardens, The 800 Benvenuto Ave *TF:* 866-652-4422 ■ *Web:* www.butchartgardens.com	Brentwood Bay	BC	V8M1J8	250-652-4422	652-7751
Calgary Zoo Botanical Garden & Prehistoric Park 1300 Zoo Rd NE *TF:* 800-588-9993 ■ *Web:* www.calgaryzoo.com	Calgary	AB	T2E7V6	403-232-9300	237-7582
Callaway Gardens 17800 Hwy 27 *TF:* 800-225-5292 ■ *Web:* www.callawaygardens.com	Pine Mountain	GA	31822	706-663-2281	663-5122
Camden Children's Garden Three Riverside Dr *Web:* www.camdenchildrensgarden.org	Camden	NJ	08103	856-365-8733	365-8733
Cape Fear Botanical Garden 536 N Eastern Blvd PO Box 53485 *Web:* capefearbg.org	Fayetteville	NC	28301	910-486-0221	486-4209
Carleen Bright Arboretum 9001 Bosque Blvd *Web:* www.woodway-texas.com	Woodway	TX	76712	254-399-9204	
Casa del Herrero 1387 E Valley Rd *Web:* www.casadelherrero.com	Santa Barbara	CA	93108	805-565-5653	969-2371
Cathedral Church of Saint Peter & Saint Paul 3101 Wisconsin Ave NW *TF:* 800-622-6304 ■ *Web:* www.nationalcathedral.org	Washington	DC	20016	202-537-6200	364-6600
Cave Hill Cemetery & Arboretum 701 Baxter Ave *Web:* www.cavehillcemetery.com	Louisville	KY	40204	502-451-5630	451-5655
Cedar Crest College 100 College Dr *Fax: Admissions ■ *TF Admissions:* 800-360-1222 ■ *Web:* www.cedarcrest.edu	Allentown	PA	18104	610-437-4471	606-4647*
Cedar Valley Arboretum & Botanic Gardens 1927 E Orange Rd *Web:* www.cedarvalleyarboretum.org	Waterloo	IA	50701	319-226-4966	226-4966
Chanticleer Garden 786 Church Rd *Web:* www.chanticleergarden.org	Wayne	PA	19087	610-687-4163	293-0149
Cheekwood Museum of Art & Botanical Garden 1200 Forrest Pk Dr *TF:* 877-356-8150 ■ *Web:* www.cheekwood.org	Nashville	TN	37205	615-356-8000	353-0919
Chesapeake Arboretum 624 Oak Grove Rd *Web:* chesarbor.org	Chesapeake	VA	23328	757-382-7060	
Cheyenne Botanic Gardens 710 S Lions Pk Dr *Web:* www.botanic.org	Cheyenne	WY	82001	307-637-6458	637-6453
Chicago Botanic Garden 1000 Lake Cook Rd *TF:* 877-829-5500 ■ *Web:* www.chicagobotanic.org	Glencoe	IL	60022	847-835-5440	835-4484
Chihuahuan Desert Research Institute (CDRI) 43869 State Hwy 118 PO Box 905 *Web:* cdri.org	Fort Davis	TX	79734	432-364-2499	364-2686
Chimney Rock Park 431 Main St *TF:* 800-277-9611 ■ *Web:* www.chimneyrockpark.com	Chimney Rock	NC	28720	828-625-9611	625-9610
Cincinnati Zoo & Botanical Garden 3400 Vine St *TF:* 800-944-4776 ■ *Web:* www.cincinnatizoo.org	Cincinnati	OH	45220	513-281-4700	559-7790
Clark County Museum 1830 S Boulder Hwy *Web:* clarkcountynv.gov	Henderson	NV	89002	702-455-7955	455-7948
Cleveland Botanical Garden 11030 E Blvd *Web:* www.cbgarden.org	Cleveland	OH	44106	216-721-1600	721-2056
Cleveland Metroparks Zoo 3900 Wildlife Way *Web:* clevelandmetroparks.com/zoo/zoo.aspx	Cleveland	OH	44109	216-661-6500	
Clovis Botanical Garden 945 N Clovis Ave *Web:* clovisbotanicalgarden.org/	Clovis	CA	93611	559-298-3091	
Coastal Maine Botanical Gardens PO Box 234 *Web:* www.mainegardens.org	Boothbay	ME	04537	207-633-4333	633-2366
Como Zoo & Conservatory 1225 Estabrook Dr *Web:* comozooconservatory.org	Saint Paul	MN	55103	651-487-8200	487-8254
Connecticut College Arboretum 270 Mohegan Ave PO Box 5201 *Web:* www.conncoll.edu	New London	CT	06320	860-439-5020	439-5482
Conservatory Garden 14 E 60th St Central Pk *Web:* www.centralparknyc.org	New York	NY	10022	212-310-6600	860-1388
Conservatory of Flowers San Francisco Recreation & Pk Dept 100 John F Kennedy Dr *Web:* www.conservatoryofflowers.org	San Francisco	CA	94118	415-846-0538	666-7257
Cooley Gardens PO Box 14164 *Web:* www.cooleygardens.org	Lansing	MI	48901	517-483-4277	
Cornell Plantations 1 Plantations Rd *TF:* 800-269-8368 ■ *Web:* www.cornellplantations.org	Ithaca	NY	14850	607-255-2400	255-2404
Cox Arboretum MetroPark 6733 Springboro Pike *TF:* 877-359-3291 ■ *Web:* www.metroparks.org/Parks/CoxArboretum	Dayton	OH	45449	937-434-9005	438-1221
Crosby Arboretum 370 Ridge Rd *Web:* www.msstate.edu	Picayune	MS	39466	601-799-2311	799-2372
CW Post Community Arboretum *Long Island University* 720 Northern Blvd *Web:* www.liu.edu	Brookville	NY	11548	516-299-2000	299-3223
Dallas Arboretum & Botanical Garden 8525 Garland Rd *Web:* www.dallasarboretum.org	Dallas	TX	75218	214-515-6500	515-6522
Daniel Stowe Botanical Garden 6500 S New Hope Rd *Web:* www.dsbg.org	Belmont	NC	28012	704-825-4490	829-1240
Dawes Arboretum 7770 Jacksontown Rd SE *TF:* 800-443-2937 ■ *Web:* www.dawesarb.org	Newark	OH	43056	740-323-2355	323-4058
Delaware Ctr for Horticulture 1810 N DuPont St *Web:* www.thedch.org	Wilmington	DE	19806	302-658-6262	658-6267
Denver Botanic Gardens 1005 York St *Web:* www.botanicgardens.org	Denver	CO	80206	720-865-3500	
Des Moines Botanical Ctr 909 Robert D Ray Dr *Web:* www.dmbotanicalgarden.com	Des Moines	IA	50316	515-323-6290	309-2484
Descanso Gardens 1418 Descanso Dr *Web:* www.descansogardens.org	La Canada	CA	91011	818-949-4200	790-3291
Desert Botanical Garden 1201 N Galvin Pkwy *Web:* www.dbg.org	Phoenix	AZ	85008	480-941-1225	481-8124
Devonian Botanic Garden University of Alberta *Web:* www.ales.ualberta.ca	Edmonton	AB	T6G2M7	780-987-3054	987-4141
Dixon Gallery & Gardens 4339 Pk Ave *Web:* www.dixon.org	Memphis	TN	38117	901-761-5250	682-0943
Dothan Area Botanical Gardens 5130 Headland Ave *Web:* www.dabg.com	Dothan	AL	36303	334-793-3224	793-5275
Dow Gardens 1809 Eastman Ave *Web:* www.dowgardens.org	Midland	MI	48640	989-631-2677	
Dr Sun Yat-Sen Classical Chinese Garden 578 Carrall St *Web:* www.vancouverchinesegarden.com	Vancouver	BC	V6B5K2	604-662-3207	682-4008
Dubuque Arboretum & Botanical Gardens 3800 Arboretum Dr *Web:* www.dubuquearboretum.com	Dubuque	IA	52001	563-556-2100	556-2443
Duke Farms 80 Rt 206 S *Web:* www.dukefarms.org	Hillsborough	NJ	08844	908-722-3700	
Dyck Arboretum of the Plains 177 W Hickory St *Web:* www.dyckarboretum.org	Hesston	KS	67062	620-327-8127	327-3151
Earl Burns Miller Japanese Garden 1250 Bellflower Blvd *TF:* 800-985-8880 ■ *Web:* www.csulb.edu/~jgarden	Long Beach	CA	90840	562-985-8885	985-5362
East Texas Arboretum (ETABS) 1601 Patterson Rd PO Box 2231 *Web:* www.eastexasarboretum.org	Athens	TX	75751	903-675-5630	675-1618
Edith J Carrier Arboretum & Botanical Gardens at James Madison University 780 University Blvd MSC 3705 *TF:* 888-568-2586 ■ *Web:* www.jmu.edu	Harrisonburg	VA	22807	540-568-3194	568-5115
Elizabeth Gamble Garden 1431 Waverley St *Web:* www.gamblegarden.org	Palo Alto	CA	94301	650-329-1356	329-1688
Elizabeth Park Rose Gardens 1561 Asylum Ave	West Hartford	CT	06117	860-231-9443	
Elizabethan Gardens 1411 National Pk Dr *Web:* www.elizabethangardens.org	Manteo	NC	27954	252-473-3234	473-3244
Enid A Haupt Glass Garden 400 E 34th St NYU Medical Ctr Rusk Inst of Rehabilitative Medicine *Web:* www.med.nyu.edu	New York	NY	10016	212-263-6058	263-2091
Erie Zoo 423 W 38th St *TF:* 877-371-5422 ■ *Web:* www.eriezoo.org	Erie	PA	16508	814-864-4091	864-1140
Fairchild Tropical Botanic Garden 10901 Old Cutler Rd *Web:* www.fairchildgarden.org	Coral Gables	FL	33156	305-667-1651	661-8953
Fernwood Botanical Gardens & Nature Preserve 13988 Range Line Rd *Web:* www.fernwoodbotanical.org	Niles	MI	49120	269-695-6491	
Filoli 86 Canada Rd *TF:* 866-691-9080 ■ *Web:* www.filoli.org	Woodside	CA	94062	650-364-8300	366-7836
Flamingo Gardens 3750 S Flamingo Rd *TF:* 800-435-7352 ■ *Web:* www.flamingogardens.org	Davie	FL	33330	954-473-2955	473-1738
Florida Botanical Gardens 12520 Ulmerton Rd *Web:* www.flbg.org	Largo	FL	33774	727-582-2100	582-2149
Foellinger-Freimann Botanical Conservatory 1100 S Calhoun St *TF:* 866-220-8842 ■ *Web:* www.botanicalconservatory.org	Fort Wayne	IN	46802	260-427-6440	427-6450
For-Mar Nature Preserve & Arboretum 2142 N Genesee Rd *Web:* www.geneseecountyparks.org	Burton	MI	48509	810-789-8567	
Forestiere Underground Gardens 5021 W Shaw Ave *Web:* www.undergroundgardens.com	Fresno	CA	93722	559-271-0734	
Fort Worth Botanic Garden 3220 Botanic Garden Blvd *Web:* www.fwbg.org	Fort Worth	TX	76107	817-871-7686	871-7638
Foster Botanical Garden 50 N Vineyard Blvd *Web:* www.honolulu.gov/parks/hbg/fbg.htm	Honolulu	HI	96817	808-522-7066	522-7050
Founders Memorial Garden 2450 Milledge Ave *Web:* gardenclub.uga.edu	Athens	GA	30602	706-227-5369	227-5370
Franklin Park Conservatory & Botanical Gardens 1777 E Broad St *TF:* 800-241-7275 ■ *Web:* www.fpconservatory.org	Columbus	OH	43203	614-715-8000	715-8199
Frederik Meijer Gardens & Sculpture Park 1000 E Beltline Ave NE *TF:* 877-975-3171 ■ *Web:* www.meijergardens.org	Grand Rapids	MI	49525	616-957-1580	957-5792
Friends of the Topiary Park 480 E Town St *Web:* www.topiarygarden.org	Columbus	OH	43215	614-645-0197	645-0172
Fruit & Spice Park 24801 SW 187th Ave *Web:* www.floridaplants.com/fruit&spice	Homestead	FL	33031	305-247-5727	245-3369

Name / Address	City	State	Zip	Phone	Fax

Fullerton Arboretum 1900 Associated Rd. Fullerton CA 92831 657-278-3407 278-7066
Web: www.fullertonarboretum.org

Ganna Walska Lotusland 695 Ashley Rd Santa Barbara CA 93108 805-969-3767 969-4423
Web: www.lotusland.org

Garden of the Coastal Plain at Georgia Southern University
1505 Bland Ave PO Box 8039 Statesboro GA 30460 912-871-1149 871-1777
Web: academics.georgiasouthern.edu

Gardens of the American Rose Ctr
8877 Jefferson-Paige Rd Shreveport LA 71119 318-938-5402 938-5402
TF: 800-637-6534 ■ *Web:* rose.org/arc/gardens.htm

Gardens on Spring Creek 2145 Centre Ave Fort Collins CO 80526 970-416-2486 416-2280
Web: www.fcgov.com

Garfield Park Conservatory
300 N Central Pk Ave Chicago IL 60624 312-746-5100 638-1777*
**Fax Area Code: 773* ■ *Web:* www.garfield-conservatory.org

Gari Melchers Home and Studio
224 Washington St Fredericksburg VA 22405 540-654-1015 654-1785
Web: garimelchers.org

Garvan Woodland Gardens
550 Arkridge Rd PO Box 22240 Hot Springs AR 71903 501-262-9300 262-9301
TF: 800-366-4664 ■ *Web:* www.garvangardens.org

George Eastman House & Gardens 900 E Ave Rochester NY 14607 585-271-3361 271-3970
Web: www.eastmanhouse.org

George L Luthy Memorial Botanical Gardens
2520 N Prospect Peoria IL 61603 309-686-3362
Web: www.peoriaparks.org

Georgeson Botanical Garden
University of Alaska Fairbanks Campus
117 W Tanana Dr PO Box 757200 Fairbanks AK 99775 907-474-7222 474-1841
Web: www.georgesonbg.org

Gifford Arboretum
1301 Memorial Dr University of Miami Coral Gables FL 33146 305-284-5364 284-3039
Web: www.bio.miami.edu/arboretum

Gilroy Gardens Family Theme Park
3050 Hecker Pass Hwy Gilroy CA 95020 408-840-7100
Web: www.gilroygardens.org

Glacier Gardens Rainforest Adventure
7600 Old Glacier Hwy Juneau AK 99801 907-790-3377 790-3907
Web: www.glaciergardens.com

Goodstay Gardens
26002800 Pennsylvania Ave Wilmington DE 19806 302-573-4450
Web: www.udel.edu

Goodwood Museum & Gardens
1600 Miccosukee Rd Tallahassee FL 32308 850-877-4202 877-3090
Web: www.goodwoodmuseum.org

Green Bay Botanical Garden 2600 Larsen Rd Green Bay WI 54303 920-490-9457 490-9461
TF: 877-355-4224 ■ *Web:* www.gbbg.org

Green Spring Gardens Park
4603 Green Spring Rd Alexandria VA 22312 703-642-5173 642-8095
Web: www.fairfaxcounty.gov/parks/gsgp

Grotto, The 8840 NE Skidmore St Portland OR 97220 503-254-7371 254-7948
Web: www.thegrotto.org

Guadalupe River Park & Gardens
438 Coleman Ave San Jose CA 95110 408-298-7657 288-9048
Web: www.grpg.org

Harry P Leu Gardens 1920 N Forest Ave Orlando FL 32803 407-246-2620 246-2849
Web: www.leugardens.org

Haverford College Arboretum
370 Lancaster Ave Haverford PA 19041 610-896-1101 896-1095
Web: haverford.edu

Hawaii Tropical Botanical Garden
27-717 Old Mamalahoa Hwy PO Box 80 Papaikou HI 96781 808-964-5233 964-1338
Web: www.hawaiigarden.com

Heathcote Botanical Gardens
210 Savannah Rd Fort Pierce FL 34982 772-464-4672 489-2748
Web: www.heathcotebotanicalgardens.org

Hendricks Park & Gardens 1800 Skyline Blvd Eugene OR 97403 541-682-4812
Web: www.eugene-or.gov

Henry Schmieder Arboretum
Delaware Valley College 700 E Butler Ave Doylestown PA 18901 215-489-2283 489-2404
Web: www.delval.edu

Hershey Gardens 170 Hotel Rd Hershey PA 17033 717-534-3492 533-5095
Web: www.hersheygardens.org

Hidden Lake Gardens 6214 Monroe Rd Tipton MI 49287 517-431-2060 431-9148
Web: www.hiddenlakegardens.msu.edu

Highline SeaTac Botanical Gardens
13735 24th Ave S PO Box 69384 SeaTac WA 98168 206-391-4003
Web: www.highlinegarden.org

Highstead Arboretum
127 Lonetown Rd PO Box 1097 Redding CT 06875 203-938-8809 938-0343
Web: highsteadarboretum.org

Hilltop Arboretum 11855 Highland Rd Baton Rouge LA 70810 225-767-6916 768-7740
Web: hilltop.lsu.edu

Hilltop Garden & Nature Ctr
Indiana University Campus
2367 E Tenth St Bloomington IN 47408 812-855-8808

Hillwood Estate Museum & Gardens
4155 Linnean Ave NW Washington DC 20008 202-686-5807 966-7846
Web: www.hillwoodmuseum.org

Holden Arboretum 9500 Sperry Rd Kirtland OH 44094 440-946-4400 602-3857
Web: www.holdenarb.org

Honolulu Botanical Gardens
50 N Vineyard Blvd Honolulu HI 96817 808-768-3003 768-3053
Web: www.honolulu.gov/parks/hbg

Hoyt Arboretum 4000 SW Fairview Blvd Portland OR 97221 503-865-8733 823-5213
Web: www.hoytarboretum.org

Hudson Gardens & Event Ctr
6115 S Santa Fe Dr Littleton CO 80120 303-797-8565 797-8647
Web: www.hudsongardens.org

Humber Arboretum 205 Humber College Blvd Toronto ON M9W5L7 416-675-6622 675-2755
Web: www.humberarboretum.on.ca

Humboldt Botanical Gardens
402 E St PO Box 6117 Eureka CA 95501 707-442-5139 442-6634
Web: www.hbgf.org

Huntington Library Art Collections & Botanical Gardens, The
1151 Oxford Rd San Marino CA 91108 626-405-2100 405-0225
Web: www.huntington.org

Huntington Museum of Art Inc
2033 McCoy Rd Huntington WV 25701 304-529-2701 529-7447
Web: www.hmoa.org

Huntsville Botanical Garden
4747 Bob Wallace Ave Huntsville AL 35805 256-830-4447 830-5314
TF: 800-300-4916 ■ *Web:* www.hsvbg.org

Idaho Botanical Garden 2355 N Penitentiary Rd Boise ID 83712 208-343-8649 343-3601
TF: 877-527-8233 ■ *Web:* www.idahobotanicalgarden.org

Inniswood Metro Gardens
940 S Hempstead Rd Westerville OH 43081 614-895-6216 895-6352
Web: www.inniswood.org

Iowa Arboretum 1875 Peach Ave Madrid IA 50156 515-795-3216 795-2619
Web: www.iowaarboretum.org

J Paul Getty Museum 1200 Getty Ctr Dr Los Angeles CA 90049 310-440-7300 440-7720*
**Fax: Hum Res* ■ *Web:* www.getty.edu

James Madison's Montpelier
11407 Constitution Hwy Montpelier Station VA 22957 540-672-2728 672-0411
Web: www.montpelier.org

Japanese Garden 611 SW Kingston Ave Portland OR 97205 503-223-1321 223-8303
Web: www.japanesegarden.com

JC Raulston Arboretum
North Carolina State University PO Box 7522 Raleigh NC 27695 919-513-7457 515-5361
TF: 888-842-2442 ■ *Web:* www.ncsu.edu/jcraulstonarboretum

Jenkins Arboretum (JA) 631 Berwyn Baptist Rd Devon PA 19333 610-647-8870 647-6664
Web: www.jenkinsarboretum.org

JJ Neilson Arboretum
Ridgetown College
University of Guelph 120 Main St E Ridgetown ON N0P2C0 519-674-1500 674-1515
Web: www.ridgetownc.uoguelph.ca/aboutus/arboretum.cfm

Journey Museum 222 New York St Rapid City SD 57701 605-394-6923 394-6940
TF: 877-343-8220 ■ *Web:* www.journeymuseum.org

Jungle Gardens Hwy 329 Avery Island LA 70513 337-369-6243 369-6254
Web: www.junglegardens.org

Jungle Island 1111 Parrot Jungle Trl Miami FL 33132 305-400-7000 400-7290
Web: www.jungleisland.com

Kalmia Gardens of Coker College
1624 W Carolina Ave Hartsville SC 29550 843-383-8145 383-8149
Web: www.coker.edu

Kenilworth Aquatic Gardens
1550 Anacostia Ave NE Washington DC 20019 202-426-6905 426-5991
TF: 877-642-4743 ■ *Web:* www.nps.gov/keaq/

Key West Botanical Garden 5210 College Rd Key West FL 33040 305-296-1504 296-2242
Web: www.keywestbotanicalgarden.org

Kingwood Ctr 900 Pk Ave W Mansfield OH 44906 419-522-0211
Web: www.kingwoodcenter.org

Klehm Arboretum & Botanic Garden
2715 S Main St Rockford IL 61102 815-965-8146 965-5914
Web: www.klehm.org

Kruckeberg Botanic Garden
20312 15th Ave NW Shoreline WA 98177 206-546-1281
Web: www.kruckeberg.org

Ladew Topiary Gardens 3535 Jarettsville Pk Monkton MD 21111 410-557-9466 557-7763
Web: www.ladewgardens.com

Lady Bird Johnson Wildflower Ctr
4801 LaCrosse Ave Austin TX 78739 512-292-4200 232-0156
TF: 877-945-3357 ■ *Web:* www.wildflower.org

Lake Wilderness Arboretum
22520 SE 248th St PO Box 72 Maple Valley WA 98038 425-413-2572
Web: www.lakewildernessarboretum.org

Lakewold Gardens 12317 Gravelly Lk Dr SW Lakewood WA 98499 253-584-4106 584-3021
TF: 888-858-4106 ■ *Web:* lakewoldgardens.org

Landis Arboretum 174 Lape Rd PO Box 186 Esperance NY 12066 518-875-6935 875-6394
Web: www.landisarboretum.org

Lauritzen Gardens Omaha's Botanical Ctr
100 Bancroft St Omaha NE 68108 402-346-4002 346-8948
Web: www.lauritzengardens.org

Leach Botanical Garden
6704 SE 122 Ave PO Box 90667 Portland OR 97236 503-823-9503 823-9504
Web: www.leachgarden.org

Leila Arboretum Society
928 W Michigan Ave Battle Creek MI 49037 269-969-0270 969-0616
Web: www.leilaarboretumsociety.org

Lewis Ginter Botanical Garden
1800 Lakeside Ave Richmond VA 23228 804-262-9887 262-6329
Web: www.lewisginter.org

Lincoln Botanical Garden & Arboretum (BGA)
University of Nebraska 1309 N 17th St Lincoln NE 68588 402-472-2679 472-9615
TF: 800-742-8800 ■ *Web:* www.unl.edu/bga

Living Desert Zoo & Gardens
47900 Portola Ave Palm Desert CA 92260 760-346-5694 568-9685
Web: www.livingdesert.org

Lockerly Arboretum 1534 Irwinton Rd Milledgeville GA 31061 478-452-2112 452-1020
Web: www.lockerly.org

Long House Reserve 133 Hands Creek Rd East Hampton NY 11937 631-329-3568 329-4299
Web: longhouse.org

Longue Vue House & Gardens
Seven Bamboo Rd New Orleans LA 70124 504-488-5488 486-7015
Web: www.longuevue.com

Longwood Gardens PO Box 501 Kennett Square PA 19348 610-388-1000 388-5488
TF: 800-737-5500 ■ *Web:* longwoodgardens.org

Los Angeles County Arboretum & Botanic Garden
301 N Baldwin Ave Arcadia CA 91007 626-821-3222 445-1217
Web: www.arboretum.org

Los Angeles Zoo & Botanical Gardens
5333 Zoo Dr Los Angeles CA 90027 323-644-4200 662-9786
Web: www.lazoo.org

Phone Fax

Lubbock Memorial Arboretum
4111 University Ave ... Lubbock TX 79413 806-797-4520
Web: www.lubbockarboretum.org

Luther Burbank Home & Gardens
204 Santa Rosa Ave ... Santa Rosa CA 95404 707-524-5445 524-5827
Web: www.lburbank.users.sonic.net

Magnolia Plantation & Gardens
3550 Ashley River Rd ... Charleston SC 29414 843-571-1266 571-5346
TF: 800-367-3517 ■ *Web:* www.magnoliaplantation.com

Marie Selby Botanical Gardens
811 S Palm Ave ... Sarasota FL 34236 941-366-5731 366-9807
Web: www.selby.org

Marjorie McNeely Conservatory at Como Park
1225 Estabrook Dr ... Saint Paul MN 55103 651-487-8201 487-8203
Web: www.comozooconservatory.org

Markham Regional Arboretum 1202 La Vista Ave ... Concord CA 94521 925-681-2968
Web: www.markhamarboretum.org

Marywood University Arboretum
2300 Adams Ave ... Scranton PA 18509 570-348-6218
Web: www.marywood.edu

Matthaei Botanical Gardens
1800 N Dixboro Rd ... Ann Arbor MI 48105 734-647-7600 998-6205
TF: 800-666-8693 ■ *Web:* www.lsa.umich.edu/mbg

McKee Botanical Garden 350 US 1 ... Vero Beach FL 32962 772-794-0601 794-0602
Web: www.mckeegarden.org

Meadowlark Botanical Gardens
9750 Meadowlark Gardens Ct ... Vienna VA 22182 703-255-3631 255-2392
Web: www.nvrpa.org/park/meadowlark_botanical_gardens

Memphis Botanic Garden 750 Cherry Rd ... Memphis TN 38117 901-576-4100 682-1561
TF: 877-829-5500 ■ *Web:* www.memphisbotanicgarden.com

Mendocino Coast Botanical Gardens
18220 N Hwy 1 ... Fort Bragg CA 95437 707-964-4352 964-3114
Web: www.gardenbythesea.org

Mepkin Abbey Botanical Garden
1098 Mepkin Abbey Rd ... Moncks Corner SC 29461 843-761-8509 761-6719
Web: www.mepkinabbey.org

Mercer Arboretum & Botanic Gardens
22306 Aldine Westfield Rd ... Humble TX 77338 281-443-8731 209-9767
TF: 877-321-2652 ■ *Web:* www.hcp4.net/mercer

Miami Beach Botanical Garden
2000 Convention Ctr Dr ... Miami Beach FL 33139 305-673-7256
Web: www.mbgarden.org

Minnesota Landscape Arboretum
3675 Arboretum Dr ... Chaska MN 55318 952-443-1400 443-2521
Web: www.arboretum.umn.edu

Missouri Botanical Garden 4344 Shaw Blvd ... Saint Louis MO 63110 314-577-5100
TF: 800-642-8842 ■ *Web:* www.missouribotanicalgarden.org

Mobile Botanical Gardens 5151 Museum Dr ... Mobile AL 36608 251-342-0555 342-3149
Web: www.mobilebotanicalgardens.org

Montgomery Botanical Ctr 11901 Old Cutler Rd ... Miami FL 33156 305-667-3800 661-5984
TF: 800-435-7352 ■ *Web:* www.montgomerybotanical.org

Monticello
931 Thomas Jefferson Pkwy PO Box 316 ... Charlottesville VA 22902 434-984-9822 977-7757
TF: 800-243-1743 ■ *Web:* www.monticello.org

Montreal Botanical Garden
4101 Sherbrooke St E ... Montreal QC H1X2B2 514-872-1400 872-1455
Web: ville.montreal.qc.ca

Morris Arboretum of the University of Pennsylvania
100 E NW Ave ... Philadelphia PA 19118 215-247-5777 247-7862
Web: www.business-services.upenn.edu/arboretum

Morton Arboretum 4100 Illinois Rt 53 ... Lisle IL 60532 630-968-0074 719-2433
Web: www.mortonarb.org

Morven Museum & Gardens 55 Stockton St ... Princeton NJ 08540 609-924-8144 924-8331
Web: morven.org

Mount Holyoke College Botanic Garden
50 College St ... South Hadley MA 01075 413-538-2116
Web: www.mtholyoke.edu

Mount Pisgah Arboretum 34901 Frank Parrish Rd ... Eugene OR 97405 541-747-1504 741-4904
Web: mountpisgaharboretum.org

Mountain Top Arboretum
Rt 23C Maude Adams Rd PO Box 379 ... Tannersville NY 12485 518-589-3903
Web: www.mtarboretum.org

Mounts Botanical Garden
531 N Military Trl ... West Palm Beach FL 33415 561-233-1757 233-1782
Web: www.mounts.org

Muttart Conservatory 9626 96A St ... Edmonton AB T6C4L8 780-496-8755 496-8747
Web: www.edmonton.ca

Mynelle Gardens 4736 Clinton Blvd ... Jackson MS 39209 601-960-1894 960-1576
TF: 800-354-7695 ■ *Web:* city.jackson.ms.us

Myriad Botanical Gardens/Crystal Bridge Tropical Conservatory
301 W Reno Ave ... Oklahoma City OK 73102 405-445-7080 297-3620
Web: www.myriadgardens.com

Naples Botanical Garden 4820 Bayshore Dr ... Naples FL 34112 239-643-7275 649-7306
Web: www.naplesgarden.org

National Garden 100 Maryland Ave ... Washington DC 20001 202-225-8333 225-7910
Web: www.usbg.gov

Native Plant Ctr at Westchester Community College
75 Grasslands Rd ... Valhalla NY 10595 914-606-7870 606-6143
Web: www.sunywcc.edu

Nebraska Statewide Arboretum
University of Nebraska 206 Biochemistry Hall ... Lincoln NE 68583 402-472-2971 472-8095
Web: www.arboretum.unl.edu

New England Tropical Conservatory (NETC)
413 US Rt 7S PO Box 4715 ... Bennington VT 05201 802-447-7419
Web: oneworldconservationcenter.org

New England Wild Flower Society
180 Hemenway Rd ... Framingham MA 01701 508-877-7630 877-3658
TF: 888-636-0033 ■ *Web:* www.newfs.org

Niagara Parks Botanical Gardens
2565 Niagara Pkwy N PO Box 150 ... Niagara Falls ON L2E6T2 905-356-8554 356-5488
TF: 877-642-7275 ■
Web: niagaraparks.com/garden-trail/botanical-gardens.html

Phone Fax

Nichols Arboretum
University of Michigan
1600 Washington Heights ... Ann Arbor MI 48104 734-647-7600
Web: www.lsa.umich.edu

Nikka Yuko Japanese Garden PO Box 751 ... Lethbridge AB T1J3Z6 403-328-3511 328-0511
Web: www.nikkayuko.com

Norfolk Botanical Garden
6700 Azalea Garden Rd ... Norfolk VA 23518 757-441-5830 441-5837
Web: norfolkbotanicalgarden.org/

Normandale Community College Japanese Garden
9700 France Ave S ... Bloomington MN 55431 952-358-8200
Web: normandale.edu

North Carolina Arboretum
100 Frederick Law Olmsted Way ... Asheville NC 28806 828-665-2492 665-2371
Web: www.ncarboretum.org

North Carolina Botanical Garden
University of North Carolina, The
CB 3375 Totten Ctr ... Chapel Hill NC 27599 919-962-0522 962-3531
Web: www.ncbg.unc.edu

Oklahoma Botanical Garden & Arboretum
Oklahoma State University
Dept of Horticulture 358 Ag Hall ... Stillwater OK 74078 405-744-4531 744-9709
Web: botanicgarden.okstate.edu/

Olbrich Botanical Gardens 3330 Atwood Ave ... Madison WI 53704 608-246-4550 246-4719
Web: www.olbrich.org

Old City Cemetery Museums & Arboretum
401 Taylor St ... Lynchburg VA 24501 434-847-1465 856-2004
Web: www.gravegarden.org

Oldfields - Lilly House & Gardens
4000 Michigan Rd ... Indianapolis IN 46208 317-923-1331 931-1978
Web: www.imamuseum.org

Oregon Garden, The 879 W Main St PO Box 155 ... Silverton OR 97381 503-874-8100 339-2996
TF: 877-674-2733 ■ *Web:* www.oregongarden.org

Overfelt Gardens 368 Educational Pk Dr ... San Jose CA 95133 408-251-3323
Web: www.sanjoseca.gov

Philbrook Museum of Art & Gardens
2727 S Rockford Rd ... Tulsa OK 74114 918-749-7941 743-4230
Web: www.philbrook.org

Phipps Conservatory & Botanical Gardens
One Schenley Pk ... Pittsburgh PA 15213 412-622-6914 622-7363
Web: www.phipps.conservatory.org

Pine Tree State Arboretum 153 Hospital St ... Augusta ME 04330 207-626-7989
Web: www.vilesarboretum.org

Pinecrest Gardens 11000 Red Rd ... Pinecrest FL 33156 305-669-6990 669-6944
Web: www.pinecrest-fl.gov

Polly Hill Arboretum
809 State Rd PO Box 561 ... West Tisbury MA 02575 508-693-9426
Web: www.pollyhillarboretum.org

Polynesian Cultural Ctr 55-370 Kamehameha Hwy ... Laie HI 96762 808-293-3005 293-3027
TF: 800-367-7060 ■ *Web:* www.polynesia.com

Powell Gardens 1609 NW US Hwy 50 ... Kingsville MO 64061 816-697-2600 697-2619
Web: www.powellgardens.org

Preservation Delaware Inc
1405 Greenhill Ave ... Wilmington DE 19806 302-651-9617 651-9603
Web: www.preservationde.org

Quad City Botanical Ctr 2525 Fourth Ave ... Rock Island IL 61201 309-794-0991 794-1572
Web: www.qcgardens.com

Quarryhill Botanical Garden
12841 Sonoma Hwy PO Box 232 ... Glen Ellen CA 95442 707-996-3166 996-3198
Web: www.quarryhillbg.org

Queens Botanical Garden 43-50 Main St ... Flushing NY 11355 718-886-3800 463-0263
Web: www.queensbotanical.org

Rancho Santa Ana Botanic Garden
1500 N College Ave ... Claremont CA 91711 909-625-8767 626-7670
Web: www.rsabg.org

Red Butte Garden & Arboretum
300 Wakara Way University of Utah ... Salt Lake City UT 84108 801-581-4747 585-6491
Web: www.redbuttegarden.org

Reeves-Reed Arboretum 165 Hobart Ave ... Summit NJ 07901 908-273-8787 273-6869
Web: www.reeves-reedarboretum.org

Reflection Riding Arboretum & Botanical Garden
400 Garden Rd ... Chattanooga TN 37419 423-821-1160
Web: www.reflectionriding.org

Reiman Gardens
Iowa State University 1407 University Blvd ... Ames IA 50011 515-294-2710 294-4817
Web: www.reimangardens.com

Reynolda Gardens of Wake Forest University
100 Reynolda Village ... Winston-Salem NC 27106 336-758-5593 758-4132
Web: www.reynoldagardens.org

Rhododendron Species Botanical Garden
2525 S 336th St PO Box 3798 ... Federal Way WA 98063 253-838-4646 838-4686
TF: 877-242-2528 ■ *Web:* www.rhodygarden.org

Riverbanks Zoo & Botanical Garden
500 Wildlife Pkwy ... Columbia SC 29210 803-779-8717 253-6381
Web: www.riverbanks.org

Robert Allerton Park & Conference Ctr
515 Old Timber Rd ... Monticello IL 61856 217-333-3287 762-3742
Web: www.allerton.illinois.edu

Rotary Botanical Gardens 1455 Palmer Dr ... Janesville WI 53545 608-752-3885 752-3853
Web: rotarybotanicalgardens.org

Royal Botanical Gardens (RBG)
680 Plains Rd W ... Burlington ON L7T4H4 905-527-1158 577-0375
TF: 800-694-4769 ■ *Web:* www.rbg.ca

Royal Roads University Botanical Garden
2005 Sooke Rd ... Victoria BC V9B5Y2 250-391-2511 391-2500
TF: 800-788-8028 ■ *Web:* www.royalroads.ca

Rutgers Gardens
112 Ryders Ln
Cook College/Rutgers University ... New Brunswick NJ 08901 732-932-8451 932-7060
Web: www.rutgersgardens.rutgers.edu

Ruth Bancroft Garden 1552 Bancroft Rd ... Walnut Creek CA 94598 925-210-9663 256-1889
Web: www.ruthbancroftgarden.org

Phone Fax

San Antonio Botanical Garden & Lucile Halsell Conservatory
555 Funston Pl ... San Antonio TX 78209 210-207-3250 207-3274
Web: www.sabot.org

San Diego Botanic Garden
230 Quail Gardens Dr PO Box 230005 ... Encinitas CA 92023 760-436-3036 632-0917
Web: www.sdbgarden.org

San Francisco Botanical Garden
9th Ave & Lincoln Way ... San Francisco CA 94122 415-661-1316 331-1316
Web: www.sfbotanicalgarden.org

San Jose Heritage Rose Garden (SJHRG)
438 Coleman Ave ... San Jose CA 95110 408-298-7657
Web: www.grpg.org

San Luis Obispo Botanical Garden
3450 Dairy Creek Rd ... San Luis Obispo CA 93405 805-541-1400 541-1466
Web: www.slobg.org

Sandhills Horticultural Gardens
3395 Airport Rd ... Pinehurst NC 28374 910-695-3883
Web: sandhillshorticulturalgardens.com

Santa Barbara Botanic Garden
1212 Mission Canyon Rd ... Santa Barbara CA 93105 805-682-4726 563-0352
Web: www.sbbg.org

Sarah P Duke Gardens 420 Anderson St ... Durham NC 27708 919-684-3698 668-3610
Web: gardens.duke.edu

Sawtooth Botanical Garden (SBG)
11 Gimlet Rd PO Box 928 ... Ketchum ID 83340 208-726-9358 726-5435
Web: www.sbgarden.org

Schedel Arboretum & Gardens
19255 W Portage River S Rd ... Elmore OH 43416 419-862-3182
Web: www.schedel-gardens.org

Schoepfle Garden 12882 Diagonal Rd ... La Grange OH 44050 440-458-5121 458-8924
TF: 800-526-7275 ■
Web: www.metroparks.cc/reservation-schoepfle-garden.php

Schreiner's Iris Gardens 3625 Quinaby Rd NE ... Salem OR 97303 503-393-3232 393-5590
TF: 800-525-2367 ■ *Web:* www.schreinersgardens.com

Scott Arboretum of Swarthmore College
500 College Ave ... Swarthmore PA 19081 610-328-8025
Web: www.scottarboretum.org

Secrest Arboretum 1680 Madison Ave ... Wooster OH 44691 330-464-2148 263-3886
Web: secrest.osu.edu

Shambhala Mountain Ctr
151 Shambhala Wy ... Red Feather Lakes CO 80545 970-881-2184 881-2909
TF: 888-788-7221 ■ *Web:* www.shambhalamountain.org

Shangri La Botanical Gardens & Nature Ctr
2111 W Pk Ave ... Orange TX 77630 409-670-9113 670-9341
Web: starkculturalvenues.org

Sherman Library & Gardens
2647 E Coast Hwy ... Corona del Mar CA 92625 949-673-2261 675-5458
Web: www.slgardens.org

Sherwood Fox Arboretum
University of Western Ontario
1151 Richmond St ... London ON N6A5B7 519-850-2542 661-3935
Web: uwo.ca//biology/research/biology_facilities/arboretum.html

Skylands PO Box 302 ... Ringwood NJ 07456 973-962-9534 962-1553
Web: www.njbg.org

Slayton Arboretum of Hilsdale College
33 E College St ... Hillsdale MI 49242 517-607-2241
Web: hillsdale.edu/home

Sonnenberg Gardens 151 Charlotte St ... Canandaigua NY 14424 585-394-4922 394-2192
Web: www.sonnenberg.org

South Carolina Botanical Garden
150 Discovery Ln Clemson University ... Clemson SC 29634 864-656-3405 656-6230
Web: www.clemson.edu/public/scbg

South Coast Botanic Garden
26300 Crenshaw Blvd ... Palos Verdes Peninsula CA 90274 310-544-6815 544-6820
Web: www.southcoastbotanicgarden.org

South Texas Botanical Gardens & Nature Ctr
8545 S Staples St ... Corpus Christi TX 78413 361-852-2100 852-7875
Web: www.stxbot.org

Stan Hywet Hall & Gardens 714 N Portage Path ... Akron OH 44303 330-836-5533
TF: 888-836-5533 ■ *Web:* www.stanhywet.org

State Arboretum of Virginia 400 Blandy Farm Ln ... Boyce VA 22620 540-837-1758 837-1523
Web: www.virginia.edu

State Botanical Garden of Georgia
2450 S Milledge Ave ... Athens GA 30605 706-542-1244 542-3091
Web: botgarden.uga.edu

Stonecrop Gardens 81 Stonecrop Ln ... Cold Spring NY 10516 845-265-2000 265-2405
Web: www.stonecrop.org

Stranahan Arboretum 4131 Tantara Dr ... Toledo OH 43623 419-841-1007 530-4421
Web: www.utoledo.edu

Texas Discovery Gardens
3601 Martin Luther King Junior Blvd ... Dallas TX 75210 214-428-7476 428-5338
Web: www.texasdiscoverygardens.org

Tofino Botanical Gardens Foundation
1084 Pacific Rim Hwy PO Box 886 ... Tofino BC V0R2Z0 250-725-1220 725-2435
Web: www.tbgf.org

Tohono Chul Park 7366 N Paseo del Norte ... Tucson AZ 85704 520-742-6455 797-1213
Web: www.tohonochulpark.org

Toledo Botanical Garden 5403 Elmer Dr ... Toledo OH 43615 419-536-5566 536-5574
Web: www.toledogarden.org

Tower Hill Botanic Garden
11 French Dr PO Box 598 ... Boylston MA 01505 508-869-6111 869-0314
Web: www.towerhillbg.org

Tucson Botanical Gardens 2150 N Alvernon Way ... Tucson AZ 85712 520-326-9686 324-0166
Web: www.tucsonbotanical.org

Tulsa Garden Ctr 2435 S Peoria Ave ... Tulsa OK 74114 918-746-5125 746-5128
Web: www.tulsagardencenter.com

Tyler Arboretum 515 Painter Rd ... Media PA 19063 610-566-9134 891-1490
Web: www.tylerarboretum.org

UC Davis Arboretum
University of California La Ru Rd ... Davis CA 95616 530-752-4880 752-5796
Web: arboretum.ucdavis.edu

University of Alabama Arboretum
PO Box 870344 ... Tuscaloosa AL 35487 205-553-3278 553-3728
Web: www.arboretum.ua.edu

University of British Columbia Botanical Garden & Centre for Plant Research
6804 SW Marine Dr ... Vancouver BC V6T1Z4 604-822-4208 822-2016
Web: www.botanicalgarden.ubc.ca

University of California Botanical Garden at Berkeley
200 Centennial Dr ... Berkeley CA 94720 510-643-2755 642-5045
Web: www.botanicalgarden.berkeley.edu

University of California Riverside Botanic Gardens
900 University Ave ... Riverside CA 92521 951-784-6962 784-6962
Web: gardens.ucr.edu

University of Chicago Botanic Garden
5555 S Ellis Ave ... Chicago IL 60637 773-702-1700 702-5814
Web: www.uchicago.edu

University of Delaware Botanic Garden
University of Delaware
Plant & Soil Science Dept 152 Townsend Hall ... Newark DE 19716 302-831-0153 831-0605
Web: www.ag.udel.edu/udbg

University of Idaho Arboretum & Botanical Garden
875 Perimeter Dr PO Box 442281 ... Moscow ID 83844 208-885-5978 885-5748
Web: www.uidaho.edu/arboretum

University of Kentucky Lexington-Fayette Urban County Government Arboretum
500 Alumni Dr ... Lexington KY 40503 859-257-6955
Web: www.ca.uky.edu/arboretum

University of Missouri Botanic Garden
General Services Bldg ... Columbia MO 65211 573-882-4240 884-3032
TF: 800-856-2181 ■ *Web:* gardens.missouri.edu/about/index.php

University of Rochester Arboretum
612 Wilson Blvd ... Rochester NY 14627 585-273-5627 461-3055
Web: www.facilities.rochester.edu/arboretum

University of South Florida Botanical Gardens
4202 E Fowler Ave ... Tampa FL 33620 813-974-2329 974-4808
Web: gardens.usf.edu

University of Southern Maine Arboretum
PO Box 9300 ... Portland ME 04104 800-800-4876 780-5143*
**Fax Area Code: 207* ■ *TF:* 800-800-4876 ■ *Web:* www.usm.maine.edu/arboretum

University of Tennessee Arboretum
901 S Illinois Ave ... Oak Ridge TN 37830 865-483-3571 483-3572
Web: forestry.tennessee.edu

University of Tennessee Gardens
2431 Joe Johnson Dr ... Knoxville TN 37996 865-974-7324 974-1947
Web: utgardens.tennessee.edu

University of Wisconsin Arboretum
1207 Seminole Hwy ... Madison WI 53711 608-263-7888 262-5209
Web: www.uwarboretum.org

US Botanic Garden 100 Maryland Ave ... Washington DC 20001 202-225-8333 225-1561
Web: www.aoc.gov

US National Arboretum
3501 New York Ave NE ... Washington DC 20002 202-245-2726 245-4575
Web: www.usna.usda.gov

Utah Botanical Ctr
920 South 50 West PO Box 265 ... Kaysville UT 84037 801-593-8969 593-5330
Web: usubotanicalcenter.org

Van Vleck House & Gardens 21 Van Vleck St ... Montclair NJ 07042 973-744-4752 746-1082
Web: www.vanvleck.org

Vander Veer Botanical Park
215 W Central Pk Ave ... Davenport IA 52803 563-326-7818 326-7955
Web: www.cityofdavenportiowa.com

Vanderbilt University 2201 W End Ave ... Nashville TN 37240 615-322-7311 343-7765
TF: 800-288-0432 ■ *Web:* www.vanderbilt.edu

Vermont Garden Park 1100 Dorset St ... South Burlington VT 05403 802-863-5251 864-6889
TF: 800-538-7476 ■ *Web:* www.garden.org

Virginia Tech Horticulture Garden (VTHG)
Virginia Tech 301 Saunders Hall ... Blacksburg VA 24061 540-231-5451
Web: www.hort.vt.edu/vthg

Waddell Barnes Botanical Gardens
100 College Stn Dr Macon State College ... Macon GA 31206 478-471-2780
Web: www.mga.edu

Washington Park Arboretum
2300 Arboretum Dr E ... Seattle WA 98112 206-543-8800 616-2871
Web: www.depts.washington.edu

Washington Park Botanical Garden
1740 W Fayette Ave ... Springfield IL 62704 217-753-6228 546-0257
Web: www.springfieldparks.org

Wave Hill W 249th St & Independence Ave ... Bronx NY 10471 718-549-3200 884-8952
Web: www.wavehill.org

Wegerzyn Gardens MetroPark
1301 E Siebenthaler Ave ... Dayton OH 45414 937-275-7275 277-6546
Web: www.metroparks.org

Welkinweir 1368 Prizer Rd ... Pottstown PA 19465 610-469-7543 469-2218
Web: www.welkinweir.org

West Virginia Botanic Garden
714 Venture Dr ... Morgantown WV 26508 304-376-2717
Web: www.wvbg.org

White River Gardens
1200 W Washington St PO Box 22309 ... Indianapolis IN 46222 317-630-2001 630-5153
Web: www.indianapoliszoo.com

Wing Haven Gardens & Bird Sanctuary
248 Ridgewood Ave ... Charlotte NC 28209 704-331-0664 331-9368
Web: www.winghavengardens.com

Winterthur Museum & Country Estate
5105 Kennett Pk ... Winterthur DE 19735 302-888-4600 888-4880
TF: 800-448-3883 ■ *Web:* www.winterthur.org

WJ Beal Botanical Garden
Michigan State University 412 Olds Hall ... East Lansing MI 48824 517-355-9582 432-1090
Web: www.cpa.msu.edu

Woodland Cemetery & Arboretum Foundation
118 Woodland Ave ... Dayton OH 45409 937-228-3221 222-7259
Web: www.woodlandcemetery.org

Wrigley Memorial & Botanical Garden
125 Claressa Ave ... Avalon CA 90704 310-510-2897 510-2325
Web: catalina.com/the-wrigley-memorial-botanical-gardens/

	City	State	Zip	Phone	Fax
WW Seymour Botanical Conservatory 316 S 'G' St. *Web:* metroparkstacoma.org	Tacoma	WA	98405	253-591-5330	627-2192
Yale University Marsh Botanical Gardens Yale University Corner of Prospect & Hillside St. *Web:* marshbotanicalgarden.yale.edu	New Haven	CT	06511	203-432-6320	
Yew Dell Gardens 6220 Old LaGrange Rd PO Box 1334 *Web:* www.yewdellgardens.org	Crestwood	KY	40014	502-241-4788	241-8338
Zilker Botanical Garden 2220 Barton Springs Rd *Web:* www.zilkergarden.org	Austin	TX	78746	512-477-8672	481-8254
ZooMontana & Botanical Gardens 2100 S Shiloh Rd *Web:* www.zoomontana.org	Billings	MT	59106	406-652-8100	652-9281

BOTTLES - GLASS

SEE Glass Jars & Bottles p. 2358

98 BOTTLES - PLASTICS

	City	State	Zip	Phone	Fax
Alpha Packaging 1555 Page Industrial Blvd. *TF:* 800-421-4772 ■ *Web:* www.alphap.com	Saint Louis	MO	63132	314-427-4300	427-5445
Amcor Packaging 935 Technology Dr Ste 100 **Fax Area Code:* 714 ■ *Web:* www.amcor.com/petpackaging	Ann Arbor	MI	48108	734 428 0741	562 6059*
CCW Products Inc 5861 Tennyson St *Web:* www.ccwproducts.com	Arvada	CO	80003	303-427-9663	
Colt's Plastics Co 969 N Main St PO Box 429 *TF:* 800-222-2658 ■ *Web:* www.coltsplastics.com	Dayville	CT	06241	860-774-2301	774-2301
Comar LLC 141 N Fifth St *TF:* 800-962-6627 ■ *Web:* www.paradigmpackaging.com	Saddle Brook	NJ	07663	201-909-3400	
Cortland Plastics International LLC 211 Main St *Web:* www.cortlandplastics.com	Cortland	NY	13045	607-662-0120	
Drug Plastics & Glass Company Inc One Bottle Dr *Web:* www.drugplastics.com	Boyertown	PA	19512	610-367-5000	367-9800
Graham Packaging Company Inc 2401 Pleasant Vly Rd *Web:* www.grahampackaging.com	York	PA	17402	717-849-8500	854-4269
In Zone Brands 2859 Paces Ferry Rd SE Ste 2100	Atlanta	GA	30339	678-718-2000	
Midland Mfg Company Inc 101 E County Line Rd PO Box 899 *Web:* www.midlandmfgco.com	Monroe	IA	50170	641-259-2625	259-3216
NEW Plastics Corp 112 Fourth St *TF:* 800-666-5207 ■ *Web:* www.newplasticscorp.com	Luxemburg	WI	54217	920-845-2326	845-2439
Nutrifaster Inc 209 S Bennett St *TF:* 800-800-2641 ■ *Web:* www.nutrifaster.com	Seattle	WA	98108	206-767-5054	762-2209
Ozarks Coca-Cola Dr Pepper Bottling Co 1777 N Packer Rd *TF:* 866-223-4498 ■ *Web:* www.cocacolaozarks.com	Springfield	MO	65803	417-865-9900	865-7967
Plastipak Packaging Inc 41605 Ann Arbor Rd PO Box 2500C *Web:* www.plastipak.com	Plymouth	MI	48170	734-455-3600	354-7391
Pluto Corp PO Box 391 *Web:* www.plutocorp.com	French Lick	IN	47432	812-936-9988	936-2828
Poly-Tainer Inc 450 W Los Angeles Ave *Web:* www.polytainer.com	Simi Valley	CA	93065	805-526-3424	526-3430
Progressive Plastics Inc 14801 Emery Ave *TF:* 800-252-0053 ■ *Web:* www.progressive-plastics.com	Cleveland	OH	44135	216-252-5595	252-6327
Quality Containers of New England 247 Portland St Ste 300 *TF:* 800-639-1550 ■ *Web:* www.qualitycontainersne.com	Yarmouth	ME	04096	207-846-5420	846-3755
Redi Bag USA 135 Fulton Ave *Web:* www.redibagusa.com	New Hyde Park	NY	11040	516-746-0600	
RN Fink Mfg Company Inc 1530 Noble Rd PO Box 245 *Web:* www.rnfink.com	Williamston	MI	48895	517-655-4351	655-5119
Silgan Plastics Corp 14515 N Outer Forty Ste 210 **Fax Area Code:* 314 ■ *TF:* 800-274-5426 ■ *Web:* www.silganplastics.com	Chesterfield	MO	63017	800-274-5426	469-5387*
Weber International Packing Company LLC 318 Cornelia St. *Web:* www.weberintl.com	Plattsburgh	NY	12901	518-561-8282	561-4509
Western Container Corp 1600 First Ave *Web:* westerncontainercoke.com	Big Spring	TX	79720	432-263-8361	263-8075

99 BOWLING CENTERS

	City	State	Zip	Phone	Fax
Allen's Crosley Lanes 2400 E Evergreen Blvd *Web:* www.crosleylanes.com	Vancouver	WA	98661	360-693-4789	
AMF Bowling Worldwide Inc 7313 Bell Creek Rd. *TF:* 800-342-5263 ■ *Web:* www.amf.com	Mechanicsville	VA	23111	800-342-5263	
Bowl America Inc 6446 Edsall Rd *NYSE: BWL.A* ■ *Web:* www.bowl-america.com	Alexandria	VA	22312	703-941-6300	256-2430
Bowl-a-roll Lanes 1560 Jefferson Rd *Web:* www.bowl-a-roll.com	Rochester	NY	14623	585-427-7250	
Collins Bowling Centers Inc 750 E New Cir Rd *Web:* www.collinsbowling.com	Lexington	KY	40505	859-252-3429	
Fourth Street Bowl 1441 N Fourth St *Web:* www.4thstreetbowl.com	San Jose	CA	95112	408-453-5555	
Freeway Lanes Bowling Group 7300 Palisades Pkwy *Web:* freewaylanes.com	Mentor	OH	44060	440-946-5131	
George Pappas' Liberty Lanes 2501 S York Rd *Web:* www.gpllbowling.com	Gastonia	NC	28052	704-868-2695	
Holiday Lanes 3316 Old Minden Rd. *Web:* www.bowlholidaylanes.com	Bossier City	LA	71112	318-746-7331	
Lucky Strike Lanes Orange 20 City Blvd W Ste G2 *Web:* www.bowlluckystrike.com	Orange	CA	92868	714-937-5263	
Moolah Lanes 3821 Lindell Blvd Ste 2. *Web:* moolahlanes.com	Saint Louis	MO	63108	314-446-6866	
Oakwood Lanes Inc 234 State Route 31 N *Web:* www.oakwoodlanes.com	Washington	NJ	07882	908-689-0310	
Plano Super Bowl Inc 2521 K Ave *Web:* planosuperbowl.com	Plano	TX	75074	972-881-0242	
Rowlett Bowl-A-Rama 5021 Lakeview Pkwy *Web:* www.rowlettbowlarama.com	Rowlett	TX	75088	972-475-7080	
Southern Bowl 1010 Us Hwy 31 S. *Web:* www.royalpin.com	Greenwood	IN	46143	317-881-8686	

100 BOXES - CORRUGATED & SOLID FIBER

	City	State	Zip	Phone	Fax
Accurate Box Company Inc 86 Fifth Ave. *Web:* www.accuratebox.com	Paterson	NJ	07524	973-345-2000	
Action Box Co Inc 6207 N Houston Rosslyn Rd *Web:* www.actionboxinc.com	Houston	TX	77091	713-869-7701	869-2086
Action Packaging 6995 Southbelt Dr Se. *Web:* www.actionpackaging.com	Caledonia	MI	49316	616-871-5200	
Advance Packaging Corp 4459 40th St SE PO Box 888311 *Web:* www.advancepkg.com	Grand Rapids	MI	49588	616-949-6610	954-7373
Advanced Design 5090 McDougall Dr SW *Web:* www.stronghaven.com	Atlanta	GA	30336	404-699-1952	
Age Industries Ltd 3601 County Rd 316c *Web:* www.ageindustries.com	Cleburne	TX	76031	817-641-8178	641-2509
Akers Packaging Service Inc 2820 Lefferson Rd *Web:* www.akers-pkg.com	Middletown	OH	45044	513-422-6312	422-2829
Alma Container Corp 1000 Charles Ave *Web:* www.almacontainer.com	Alma	MI	48801	989-463-2106	
American Corrugated Products Inc 4700 Alkire Rd *Web:* www.americancorrugated.com	Columbus	OH	43228	614-870-2000	
American Environmental Container Corp 2302 Lasso Ln *Web:* www.sanjuanpools.com	Lakeland	FL	33801	863-666-3020	
Anchor Bay Packaging Corp 30905 23 Mile Rd. *Web:* www.anchorbaypackaging.com	New Baltimore	MI	48047	586-949-4040	949-9998
Arrowhead Containers Inc 4330 Clary Blvd *Web:* www.smcpackaging.com	Kansas City	MO	64130	816-861-8050	
Artistic Carton Co 1975 Big Timber Rd. *TF:* 800-735-7225 ■ *Web:* www.artisticcarton.com	Elgin	IL	60123	847-741-0247	741-8529
Arvco Container Corp 845 Gibson St *TF:* 800-968-9127 ■ *Web:* www.arvco.com	Kalamazoo	MI	49001	269-381-0900	381-2919
Atlas Container Corp 8140 Telegraph Rd *TF:* 800-394-4894 ■ *Web:* www.atlascontainer.com	Severn	MD	21144	410-551-6300	551-2703
Bates Container 6433 Davis Blvd *TF:* 800-792-8736 ■ *Web:* www.batescontainer.com	North Richland Hills	TX	76182	817-498-3200	581-8802
Bay Corrugated Container Inc 1655 W Seventh St. *Web:* www.baycorrugated.com	Monroe	MI	48161	734-243-5400	
Beacon Container Corp 700 W First St *TF:* 800-422-8383 ■ *Web:* www.beaconcontainer.com	Birdsboro	PA	19508	610-582-2222	582-3992
Bell Container Corp 615 Ferry St *Web:* www.bellcontainer.com	Newark	NJ	07105	973-344-4400	344-0817
Boxes of St Louis Inc 1833 Knox Ave. *Web:* www.boxesinc.com	Saint Louis	MO	63139	314-781-2600	
Brandt Box & Paper Company Inc Six W Crisman Rd *Web:* www.brandtboxnj.com	Columbia	NJ	07832	908-496-4500	
Buckeye Container Inc 3350 Long Rd. *TF:* 800-968-6894 ■ *Web:* www.buckeyecorrugated.com	Wooster	OH	44691	330-264-6336	264-0127
Buckeye Corrugated Inc 275 Springside Dr *Web:* www.buckeyecorrugated.com	Akron	OH	44333	330-576-0590	576-0600
Bulk-pack Inc 1025 N Ninth St *TF:* 800-498-4215 ■ *Web:* www.bulk-pack.com	Monroe	LA	71201	318-387-3260	387-6362
Cano Container Corp 3920 Enterprise Ct *Web:* www.canocontainer.com	Aurora	IL	60504	630-585-7500	
Capitol City Container Corp 8240 Zionsville Rd *Web:* www.capcitycont.com	Indianapolis	IN	46268	317-875-0290	
Carolina Container Co 909 Prospect St *TF:* 800-627-0825 ■ *Web:* www.carolinacontainer.com	High Point	NC	27260	336-883-7146	883-7576
Central Florida Box Corp 2950 Lk Emma Rd *Web:* www.centralfloridabox.com	Lake Mary	FL	32746	407-936-1277	
Central Graphics & Container Group Ltd 5526 Timberlea Blvd. *Web:* www.centralgraphics.ca	Mississauga	ON	L4W2T7	905-238-8400	238-8127
Colorado Container Corp 4221 Monaco St *Web:* www.packagingcorp.com	Denver	CO	80216	303-331-0400	331-9455
Columbus Container Inc 3460 Commerce Dr *Web:* www.columbuscontainer.com	Columbus	IN	47201	812-376-9301	
Cornell Paper & Box Co 162 Van Dyke St *Web:* cornellpaper.com	Brooklyn	NY	11231	718-875-3202	875-3281
Corrugated Container Corp 6405 Commonwealth Dr SW *Web:* www.cccbox.com	Roanoke	VA	24018	540-774-0500	

Company / Address	City	State	Zip	Phone	Fax
DanHil Containers II Ltd 3715 Lucius McCelvey Dr *Web:* www.danhilcontainers.com	Temple	TX	76503	254-773-0704	
DeLine Box & Display 3700 Lima St *Web:* www.delinebox.com	Denver	CO	80239	303-373-1430	373-2325
Delta Corrugated Paper Products Corp W Ruby Ave *Web:* www.deltacorrugated.com	Palisades Park	NJ	07650	201-941-1910	941-9399
EMT International Inc 780 Centerline Dr *Web:* www.emtinternational.com	Hobart	WI	54155	920-468-5475	
Ferguson Supply & Box Manufacturing Co 10820 Quality Dr *TF:* 800-821-1023 ■ *Web:* www.fergusonbox.com	Charlotte	NC	28278	704-597-0310	597-5623
Flutes Inc 8252 Zionsville Rd *Web:* www.flutesllc.com	Indianapolis	IN	46268	317-870-6010	
Great Lakes Packaging Corp W 190 N 11393 Carnegie Dr *TF:* 800-261-4572 ■ *Web:* www.glpc.com	Germantown	WI	53022	262-255-2100	255-7290
Great Northern Corp 395 Stroebe Rd *TF:* 800-236-3671 ■ *Web:* www.greatnortherncorp.com	Appleton	WI	54914	920-739-3671	739-7096
Green Bay Packaging Inc 1700 Webster Ct *TF:* 800-236-8400 ■ *Web:* www.gbp.com	Green Bay	WI	54302	920-433-5111	
Island Container Group 44 Island Container Plz *Web:* www.islandcontainer.com	Wyandanch	NY	11798	631-253-4400	
KapStone Paper and Packaging Corp 300 Fibre Way PO Box 639 *Web:* www.longviewfibre.com	Longview	WA	98632	360-425-1550	230-5135
Kearny Steel Container Corp 401 S St *Web:* www.kearnysteel.com	Newark	NJ	07105	973-589-2070	
Kelly Box & Packaging Corp 2801 Covington Rd *Web:* www.kellybox.com	Fort Wayne	IN	46802	260-432-4570	
Key Container Corp 21 Campbell St *TF:* 800-343-8811 ■ *Web:* www.keycontainercorp.com	Pawtucket	RI	02861	401-723-2000	725-5980
Lakeway Container Inc 5715 Superior Dr *Web:* www.lakewaycontainer.com	Morristown	TN	37814	423-581-2164	
Landaal Packaging Systems Inc 3256 B Iron St *Web:* www.landaal.com	Burton	MI	48529	810-742-2730	
Lawrence Paper Co 2801 Lakeview Rd *TF:* 800-535-4553 ■ *Web:* www.lpco.net	Lawrence	KS	66049	785-843-8111	749-3904
Lone Star Container Corp 700 N Wildwood Dr **Fax Area Code:* 972 ■ *TF:* 800-552-6937 ■ *Web:* www.lonestarcontainer.com	Irving	TX	75061	800-552-6937	554-6081*
Menasha Corp 1645 Bergstrom Rd *TF:* 800-558-5073 ■ *Web:* www.menasha.com	Neenah	WI	54956	920-751-1000	751-1236
Menasha Packaging Co 1645 Bergstrom Rd *TF:* 800-558-5073 ■ *Web:* www.menashapackaging.com	Neenah	WI	54956	920-751-1000	751-1075
Midland Packaging & Display Inc 3545 Nicholson Rd *Web:* midlandpkg.com	Franksville	WI	53126	262-886-8851	
Miller Container Corp 3402 78th Ave W *Web:* www.millercontainer.com	Rock Island	IL	61201	309-787-6161	
Montebello Container Corp 13220 Molette St *Web:* www.montcc.com	Santa Fe Springs	CA	90670	562-404-6221	
New England Wooden Ware Corp 205 School St Ste 201 *TF:* 800-252-9214 ■ *Web:* www.newoodenware.com	Gardner	MA	01440	978-632-3600	630-1513
North American Container Corp 1811 W Oak Pkwy Ste D *TF:* 800-929-0610 ■ *Web:* www.nacontainer.com	Marietta	GA	30062	770-431-4858	431-6957
Packaging Corp of America 1955 W Field Ct *NYSE: PKG* ■ **Fax Area Code:* 847 ■ *TF:* 800-456-4725 ■ *Web:* www.packagingcorp.com	Lake Forest	IL	60045	800-456-4725	615-6379*
Packaging Services Incorporated of Tennessee 120 T Elmer Cox Rd *Web:* www.psipack.com	Greeneville	TN	37743	423-787-7711	
Pactiv Corp 1900 W Field Ct *TF:* 888-828-2850 ■ *Web:* www.pactiv.com	Lake Forest	IL	60045	847-482-2000	482-4738
Paragon Packaging Products Inc 625 Beaver Rd *Web:* www.parapack.com	Girard	PA	16417	814-774-9621	
Planet Paper Box Inc 2841 Langstaff Rd *Web:* www.planetpaper.com	Concord	ON	L4K4W7	416-798-7641	
President Container Inc 200 W Commercial Ave *Web:* www.presidentcontainer.com	Moonachie	NJ	07074	201-933-7500	
Progress Container Corp 635 Patrick Mill Rd SW *Web:* www.progresscontainer.com	Winder	GA	30680	678-425-2000	
R & R Corrugated Container Inc 360 Minor Rd *Web:* www.randrcorrugated.com	Bristol	CT	06010	860-584-1194	
R D A Container Corp 70 Cherry Rd *Web:* www.rdacontainer.com	Gates	NY	14624	585-247-2323	
Reliable Container Corp 9206 Santa Fe Springs Rd *Web:* www.reliablecontainer.com	Santa Fe Springs	CA	90670	562-861-6226	
Rock TENN 1415 W 44th St *TF:* 877-643-5414 ■ *Web:* www.rocktenn.com	Chicago	IL	60609	773-254-1030	
Rock-Tenn Co 504 Thrasher St *NYSE: RKT* ■ *TF:* 877-643-5414 ■ *Web:* www.rocktenn.com	Norcross	GA	30071	770-448-2193	
Romanow Inc 346 University Ave *Web:* www.romanowcontainer.com	Westwood	MA	02090	781-320-9200	
Royal Group 1301 S 47th Ave *Web:* royalbox.com	Cicero	IL	60804	708-656-2020	
Sacramento Container Corp 4841 Urbani Ave *Web:* www.saccontainer.biz	Mcclellan	CA	95652	916-614-0580	
Sharpsville Container Corp 600 Main St *Web:* sharpsvillecontainer.com	Sharpsville	PA	16150	724-962-1100	
Shoreline Container Inc 4450 N 136th Ave PO Box 1993 *TF:* 800-968-2088 ■ *Web:* www.shorelinecontainer.com	Holland	MI	49422	616-399-2088	399-7240
Smurfit-Stone Container Corp 222 N LaSalle St *Web:* www.smurfit.com	Chicago	IL	60601	312-346-6600	
Southern Container Ltd 10410 Papalote St Ste 130 *Web:* www.southerncontainer.com	Houston	TX	77041	713-466-5661	466-4223
Specialty Container Corp 1608 Plantation Rd *Web:* www.specialtycontainer.com	Dallas	TX	75235	214-637-0160	
Stephen Gould Corp 35 S Jefferson Rd *TF:* 800-456-7896 ■ *Web:* www.stephengould.com	Whippany	NJ	07981	973-428-1500	428-5274
Strathcona Paper LP 77 County Rd 16 RR #7 *Web:* www.strathconapaper.com	Napanee	ON	K7R3L2	613-378-6672	
Stronghaven Inc 5090 McDougall Dr SW *TF:* 866-374-9148 ■ *Web:* www.stronghaven.com	Atlanta	GA	30336	404-699-1952	699-1825
Technology Container Corp 207 Greenwood St *Web:* www.techcontainer.com	Worcester	MA	01607	508-752-8000	
Tharco Inc 2222 Grant Ave *TF:* 800-772-2332 ■ *Web:* packagingcorp.com/pages/splash_page/145.php	San Lorenzo	CA	94580	800-772-2332	322-4862
TimBar Packaging & Display 148 N Penn St PO Box 449 *TF:* 800-572-6061 ■ *Web:* www.timbar.com	Hanover	PA	17331	717-632-4727	632-1243
Tri-lakes Container 533 S First St *Web:* www.tri-lakes.com	Pierceton	IN	46562	574-594-2217	594-2501
Valiant Enterprise LLC 2300 Mcdermott Rd Ste 200-385 *Web:* www.valiantdesigners.com	Plano	TX	75025	972-390-7410	447-9156
Victory Packaging LP 3555 Timmons Ln Ste 1440 *Web:* www.victorypackaging.com	Houston	TX	77027	713-961-3299	
Welch Packaging Group 1020 Herman St *TF:* 800-246-2475 ■ *Web:* www.welchpkg.com	Elkhart	IN	46516	574-295-2460	295-1527
York Container 138 Mt Scion Rd PO Box 3008 *Web:* www.yorkcontainer.com	York	PA	17402	717-757-7611	755-8090

101 BOXES - PAPERBOARD

Products made by these companies include setup, folding, and nonfolding boxes.

Company / Address	City	State	Zip	Phone	Fax
Advance Paper Box Co 6100 S Gramercy Pl *Web:* www.advancepaperbox.com	Los Angeles	CA	90047	323-750-2550	752-8133
Apex Paper Box Co 5601 Walworth Ave **Fax:* Sales ■ *TF Cust Svc:* 800-438-2269 ■ *Web:* boxit.com	Cleveland	OH	44102	216-416-9475	*
Arkay Packaging Corp 350 E Pk Dr *Web:* www.arkay.com	Roanoke	VA	24019	540-977-3031	977-2503
Astronics Corp 130 Commerce Way *NASDAQ: ATRO* ■ *Web:* www.astronics.com	East Aurora	NY	14052	716-805-1599	655-0309
Boelter Industries Inc 202 Galewski Dr Airport Industrial Pk *Web:* www.wspackaging.com	Winona	MN	55987	507-452-2315	452-2649
Boutwell Owens & Co Inc 251 Authority Dr *Web:* www.boutwellowens.com	Fitchburg	MA	01420	978-343-3067	343-9132
Burd & Fletcher 3000 W Geospace Dr *TF:* 800-821-2776 ■ *Web:* www.burdfletcher.com	Independence	MO	64056	816-257-0291	257-9928
Calpine Containers Inc 9499 N Ford Wahington Rd Ste 103 *Web:* www.calpinecontainers.com	Fresno	CA	93730	559-519-7199	
Caraustar Industries Inc 5000 Austell-Powder Springs Rd Ste 300 *TF:* 800-223-1373 ■ *Web:* www.caraustar.com	Austell	GA	30106	770-948-3100	
Carton Service Inc First Quality Dr PO Box 702 *TF General:* 800-533-7744 ■ *Web:* www.cartonservice.com	Shelby	OH	44875	419-342-5010	342-4804
Climax Packaging Inc 4515 Easton Rd **Fax Area Code:* 315 ■ *TF:* 800-225-4629	Saint Joseph	MO	64503	816-233-3181	376-2034*
Colbert Packaging Corp 28355 N Bradley Rd *Web:* www.colbertpkg.com	Lake Forest	IL	60045	847-367-5990	367-4403
Complemar Partners 500 Lee Rd Ste 200 *TF:* 800-388-7254 ■ *Web:* www.complemar.com	Rochester	NY	14606	585-647-5800	647-5800
Cornell Paper & Box Co 162 Van Dyke St *Web:* cornellpaper.com	Brooklyn	NY	11231	718-875-3202	875-3281
Curtis Packaging Corp 44 Berkshire Rd *Web:* www.curtispackaging.com	Sandy Hook	CT	06482	203-426-5861	426-2684
Dee Paper Box Company Inc 100 Broomall St *TF:* 800-359-0041 ■ *Web:* deepaperbox.com	Chester	PA	19013	610-876-9285	876-7040
Diamond Packaging Company Inc 111 Commerce Dr PO Box 23620 *TF:* 800-333-4079 ■ *Web:* www.diamondpackaging.com	Rochester	NY	14692	585-334-8030	334-9141
Fuller Box Co 150 Chestnut St *Web:* www.fullerbox.com	North Attleboro	MA	02760	508-695-2525	695-2187
Graphic Packaging International 1500 Riveredge Parkway NW *NYSE: GPK* ■ *TF:* 888-548-8395 ■ *Web:* www.graphicpkg.com	Atlanta	GA	30328	770-240-7200	
House of Packaging Inc 2225 Via Cerro Ste B *Web:* www.hopbox.com	Riverside	CA	92509	626-369-3371	
Hub Folding Box Co Inc 774 Norfolk St *TF:* 800-334-1113 ■ *Web:* www.hubfoldingbox.com	Mansfield	MA	02048	508-339-0005	339-0102
Knight Paper Box Company Inc 4651 W 72nd St *Web:* knightpack.com	Chicago	IL	60629	773-585-2035	585-3824
Mafcote Industries Inc 108 Main St *TF Cust Svc:* 800-221-3056 ■ *Web:* www.mafcote.com	Norwalk	CT	06851	203-847-8500	849-9177
Malnove Inc 13434 F St *TF:* 800-228-9877 ■ *Web:* www.malnove.com	Omaha	NE	68137	402-330-1100	330-2941
Menasha Corp 1645 Bergstrom Rd *TF:* 800-558-5073 ■ *Web:* www.menasha.com	Neenah	WI	54956	920-751-1000	751-1236
MOD-PAC Corp 1801 Elmwood Ave *NASDAQ: MPAC* ■ *TF Cust Svc:* 866-216-6193 ■ *Web:* www.modpac.com	Buffalo	NY	14207	716-873-0640	873-6008
Pactiv Corp 1900 W Field Ct *TF:* 888-828-2850 ■ *Web:* www.pactiv.com	Lake Forest	IL	60045	847-482-2000	482-4738
Panoramic Inc 1500 N Parker Dr *TF:* 800-333-1394 ■ *Web:* www.panoramicinc.com	Janesville	WI	53545	608-754-8850	754-5703
Paragon Packaging Inc 7700 Centerville Rd *TF:* 888-615-0065 ■ *Web:* www.paragonpackaging.com	Ferndale	CA	95536	707-786-4004	786-4014

Phone | Fax

Rice Packaging Inc 356 Somers Rd . . . . Ellington CT 06029 860-872-8341 871-6834
TF: 800-367-6725 ■ *Web:* www.ricepackaging.com
Rose City Printing & Packaging Inc
900 SE Tech Crt Dr . . . . Vancouver WA 98683 800-704-8693
TF: 800-704-8693 ■ *Web:* www.rcpp.com
Royal Paper Box Company of California Inc
PO Box 458 . . . . Montebello CA 90640 323-728-7041 722-2646
Web: www.royalpaperbox.com
RTS Packaging LLC 504 Thrasher St . . . . Norcross GA 30071 800-558-6984 449-0261*
**Fax Area Code:* 770 ■ *TF:* 800-558-6984 ■ *Web:* www.rtspackaging.com
Rusken Packaging Inc PO Box 2100 . . . . Cullman AL 35056 256-734-0092 734-3008
TF: 800-232-8108 ■ *Web:* www.rusken.com
Seaboard Folding Box Co Inc 35 Daniels St . . . . Fitchburg MA 01420 978-342-8921 342-1105
TF: 800-225-6313 ■ *Web:* seaboardfoldingbox.com
Sheboygan Paper Box Co
716 Clara Ave PO Box 326 . . . . Sheboygan WI 53082 920-458-8373 458-2901
Web: www.spbox.com
Southern Standard Cartons Inc
2415 Plantside Dr . . . . Louisville KY 40299 502-491-2760 491-2767
Web: thestandardgroup.com
Stephen Gould Corp 35 S Jefferson Rd . . . . Whippany NJ 07981 973-428-1500 428-5274
TF: 800-456-7896 ■ *Web:* www.stephengould.com
Sterling Paper Co 2155 E Castor Ave . . . . Philadelphia PA 19134 215-744-5350 546-1180
TF: 800-745-5350 ■ *Web:* fieldnotesphilly.wordpress.com
Tetra Pak Inc 101 Corporate Woods Pkwy . . . . Vernon Hills IL 60061 847-955-6000 955-6500
Web: www.tetrapak.com
Thoro-Packaging Inc 1467 Davril Cir . . . . Corona CA 92880 951-278-2100
Web: www.thoropkg.com
Triumph Packaging Group
515 W Crossroads Pkwy . . . . Bolingbrook IL 60440 630-771-0900
Web: www.triumphpackaging.com
Utah Paper Box Company Inc
920 South 700 West . . . . Salt Lake City UT 84104 801-363-0093 363-9212
Web: www.upbslc.com

102 BREWERIES

SEE ALSO Malting Products p. 2703

Phone | Fax

Abita Brewing Co 21084 Hwy 36 . . . . Covington LA 70433 985-893-3143 898-3546
TF: 800-737-2311 ■ *Web:* www.abita.com
Alaskan Brewing Co 5429 Shaune Dr . . . . Juneau AK 99801 907-780-5866 780-4514
Web: www.alaskanbeer.com
Anchor Brewing Co 1705 Mariposa St . . . . San Francisco CA 94107 415-863-8350 552-7094
TF: 800-478-2227 ■ *Web:* www.anchorbrewing.com
Anheuser-Busch InBev 250 Pk Ave . . . . New York NY 10177 212-573-8800
Web: www.ab-inbev.com
Asahi Beer USA Inc 3625 Del Amo Blvd Ste 250 . . . . Torrance CA 90503 310-214-9051 542-5108
Web: www.asahibeerusa.com
Boston Beer Co One Design Ctr Pl Ste 850 . . . . Boston MA 02210 617-368-5000 368-5500
NYSE: SAM ■ *TF:* 888-661-2337 ■ *Web:* www.bostonbeer.com
Boulder Beer Co 2880 Wilderness Pl . . . . Boulder CO 80301 303-444-8448 444-4796
Web: www.boulderbeer.com
Boulevard Brewing Co 2501 SW Blvd . . . . Kansas City MO 64108 816-474-7095 474-1722
Web: www.boulevard.com
BridgePort Brewing Co 1318 NW Northrup St . . . . Portland OR 97209 503-241-7179 241-0625
TF: 888-834-7546 ■ *Web:* www.bridgeportbrew.com
Brooklyn Brewery, The 79 N 11th St . . . . Brooklyn NY 11211 718-486-7422 486-7440
Web: www.brooklynbrewery.com
Capital Brewery 7734 Terr Ave . . . . Middleton WI 53562 608-836-7100
Web: www.capital-brewery.com
Cold Spring Brewing Co
219 Red River Ave N PO Box 476 . . . . Cold Spring MN 56320 320-685-8686 685-8318
Web: www.coldspringbrewery.com
Craft Brew Alliance 929 N Russell St . . . . Portland OR 97227 503-331-7270
NASDAQ: BREW ■ *Web:* craftbrew.com
DG Yuengling & Son Inc
5th & Mahantongo St . . . . Pottsville PA 17901 570-622-4141 622-4011
Web: www.yuengling.com
DL Geary Brewing Company Inc
38 Evergreen Dr . . . . Portland ME 04103 207-878-2337 878-2388
Web: www.gearybrewing.com
Flying Dog Brewery LLC 4607 Wedgewood Blvd . . . . Frederick MD 21703 301-694-7899 694-2971
Web: www.flyingdogales.com
Fresh Ale Pubs LLC
1317 W Northern Lights Blvd Ste 8 . . . . Anchorage AK 99503 907-222-1560
Web: freshalepubs.com
Harpoon Brewery 306 Northern Ave . . . . Boston MA 02210 617-574-9551 482-9361
Web: www.harpoonbrewery.com
Heineken USA 360 Hamilton Ave Ste 1103 . . . . White Plains NY 10601 914-681-4100 681-1900
Web: www.heineken.com
Humboldt Brews 856 Tenth St . . . . Arcata CA 95521 707-826-2739 826-2045
Web: www.humbrews.com
Jacob Leinenkugel Brewing Co
124 E Elm St . . . . Chippewa Falls WI 54729 715-723-5558 723-7158
TF General: 888-534-6437 ■ *Web:* www.leinie.com
Keurig Inc 55 Walkers Brook Dr . . . . Reading MA 01867 866-901-2739
TF: 866-901-2739 ■ *Web:* www.keurig.com
Labatt Breweries of Canada
207 Queen's Quay W Ste 299 . . . . Toronto ON M5J1A7 416-361-5050
TF Cust Svc: 800-268-2337 ■ *Web:* www.labatt.com
Latrobe Brewing Co 119 Jefferson St . . . . Latrobe PA 15650 724-537-5545 537-4035
Web: www.rollingrock.com
Lion Brewery Inc 700 N Pennsylvania Ave . . . . Wilkes-Barre PA 18705 570-823-8801 823-6686
TF: 888-295-2337 ■ *Web:* www.lionbrewery.com
Long Trail Brewing Co 5520 Rt 4 . . . . Bridgewater Corners VT 05035 802-672-5011 672-5012
Web: www.longtrail.com
Malt Products Corp 88 Market St . . . . Saddle Brook NJ 07663 201-845-4420 845-0028
TF: 800-526-0180 ■ *Web:* www.maltproducts.com
Matt Brewing Co 811 Edward St . . . . Utica NY 13502 315-624-2400 624-2452
Web: www.saranac.com

Phone | Fax

McMenamins 430 N Killingsworth . . . . Portland OR 97217 503-223-0109 294-0837
TF: 800-669-8610 ■ *Web:* www.mcmenamins.com
Mendocino Brewing Co 455 Kunzler Ranch Rd . . . . Ukiah CA 95482 707-462-1697 462-1699
Web: www.mendobrew.com
Minhas Craft Brewery 1208 14th Ave . . . . Monroe WI 53566 608-325-3191 325-3198
Web: www.minhasbrewery.com
Molson Coors Brewing Co 1225 17th St Ste 3200 . . . . Denver CO 80202 303-927-2337 655-5049*
NYSE: TAP ■ **Fax Area Code:* 302 ■ *TF:* 800-645-5376 ■ *Web:* www.molsoncoors.com
New Belgium Brewing Co 500 Linden St . . . . Fort Collins CO 80524 970-221-0524 221-0535
Web: www.newbelgium.com
North Coast Brewing Company Inc
455 N Main St . . . . Fort Bragg CA 95437 707-964-2739 964-8768
TF: 866-955-4190 ■ *Web:* www.northcoastbrewing.com
Odell Brewing Co 800 E Lincoln Ave . . . . Fort Collins CO 80524 970-498-9070 498-0706
TF: 888-887-2797 ■ *Web:* www.odells.com
Pabst Brewing Co, The
10635 Santa Monica Blvd Ste 350 . . . . Los Angeles CA 90025 800-947-2278
TF: 800-947-2278 ■ *Web:* www.pabstbrewingco.com
Pittsburgh Brewing Co 3340 Liberty Ave . . . . Pittsburgh PA 15201 412-682-7400
Web: ironcitybrewingcompany.com
Pyramid Brewing Co 91 S Royal Brougham Way . . . . Seattle WA 98134 206-682-8322 682-8420
Web: www.pyramidbrew.com
Rogue Ales Co 2320 OSU Dr . . . . Newport OR 97365 541-867-3660 867-3260
Web: www.rogue.com
Sierra Nevada Brewing Co 1075 E 20th St . . . . Chico CA 95928 530-893-3520 893-1275
Web: www.sierranevada.com
Summit Brewing Co 910 Montreal Cir . . . . Saint Paul MN 55102 651-265-7800 265-7801
Web: www.summitbrewing.com
Widmer Bros Brewing Co 929 N Russell St . . . . Portland OR 97227 503-281-2437 281-1496
Web: www.widmerbrothers.com

BROKERS

SEE Real Estate Agents & Brokers p. 3030; Securities Brokers & Dealers p. 3151; Insurance Agents, Brokers, Services p. 2566; Electronic Communications Networks (ECNs) p. 2232; Commodity Contracts Brokers & Dealers p. 2010; Mortgage Lenders & Loan Brokers p. 2766

103 BRUSHES & BROOMS

SEE ALSO Art Materials & Supplies - Mfr p. 1752

Phone | Fax

A & B Brush Manufacturing Corp
1150 Three Ranch Rd . . . . Duarte CA 91010 626-303-8856 303-1207
Web: abbrush.com
Abco Cleaning Products 6800 NW 36th Ave . . . . Miami FL 33147 305-694-2226 694-0451
TF: 888-694-2226 ■ *Web:* www.abcoproducts.com
American Brush Company Inc
300 Industrial Blvd . . . . Claremont NH 03743 603-542-9951
Web: www.americanbrush.com
Brush Research Mfg Company Inc
4642 Floral Dr . . . . Los Angeles CA 90022 323-261-2193 268-6587
Web: www.brushresearch.com
Brushes Corp 5400 Smith Rd . . . . Cleveland OH 44142 216-267-8084 267-9077
Web: www.brushescorp.com
Brushtech Inc Four Matt Ave . . . . Plattsburgh NY 12901 518-563-8420 563-0581
Web: brushtechbrushes.com
Carlisle Sanitary Maintenance Products
402 S Black River St . . . . Sparta WI 54656 608-269-2151 872-4701*
**Fax Area Code:* 800 ■ *TF:* 800-654-8210 ■ *Web:* www.carlislefsp.com
Corona Brushes Inc 5065 Savarese Cir . . . . Tampa FL 33634 813-885-2525 882-9810
TF: 800-458-3483 ■ *Web:* www.coronabrushes.com
Crystal Lake Manufacturing Inc
2225 Alabama 14 PO Box 159 . . . . Autaugaville AL 36003 334-365-3342 365-3332
TF: 800-633-8720 ■ *Web:* www.crystallakemfg.com
Detroit Quality Brush Mfg
32165 Schoolcraft Rd . . . . Livonia MI 48150 734-525-5660 525-0437
TF: 800-722-3037 ■ *Web:* dqb.com
Felton Brush Inc Seven Burton Dr . . . . Londonderry NH 03053 603-425-0200 425-0200
TF: 800-258-9702 ■ *Web:* www.feltoninc.com
Fuller Brush Co, The
P.O. Box 729 1 Fuller Way . . . . Great Bend KS 67530 620-792-1711 793-4523
TF Cust Svc: 800-522-0499 ■ *Web:* www.fuller.com
Gordon Brush Mfg Company Inc
6247 Randolph St . . . . Commerce CA 90040 323-724-7777 724-1111
TF: 800-950-7950 ■ *Web:* www.gordonbrush.com
Greenwood Mop & Broom Inc 312 Palmer St . . . . Greenwood SC 29646 864-227-8411 227-3200
TF: 800-635-6849 ■ *Web:* www.greenwoodmopandbroom.com
Hamburg Industries Inc 218 Pine St . . . . Hamburg PA 19526 610-562-3031 562-0209
Web: www.hamburgindustries.com
Harper Brush Works Inc 400 N Second St . . . . Fairfield IA 52556 641-472-5186 472-3187
TF: 800-223-7894 ■ *Web:* www.harperbrush.com
Industrial Brush Company Inc
105 Clinton Rd . . . . Fairfield NJ 07004 973-575-0455 575-6169
TF: 800-241-9860 ■ *Web:* www.indbrush.com
Industries for the Blind 445 S Curtis Rd . . . . West Allis WI 53214 414-778-3040 778-3041
TF: 800-642-8778 ■ *Web:* www.ibmilw.com
Industries of the Blind Inc 920 W Lee St . . . . Greensboro NC 27403 336-274-1591
Web: www.industriesoftheblind.com
Kline Hawkes & Co
11726 San Vicente Blvd Ste 300 . . . . Los Angeles CA 90049 310-442-4700 826-2299
Laitner Brush Co 1561 Laitner Dr . . . . Traverse City MI 49686 231-929-3300 929-7219
TF Cust Svc: 800-423-6805 ■ *Web:* www.laitner.com
Libman Co 220 N Sheldon St . . . . Arcola IL 61910 800-646-6262 268-4168*
**Fax Area Code:* 217 ■ *TF:* 800-646-6262 ■ *Web:* www.libman.com
Linzer Products Corp 248 Wyandanch Ave . . . . West Babylon NY 11704 631-253-3333 253-9750
Web: www.linzerproducts.com
Magnolia Brush Mfg Ltd
1000 N Cedar PO Box 932 . . . . Clarksville TX 75426 903-427-2261 427-5231*
**Fax Area Code:* 800 ■ *TF:* 800-248-2261 ■ *Web:* www.magnoliabrush.com

Company	City	State	ZIP	Phone	Fax
Mill-Rose Co 7995 Tyler Blvd TF: 800-321-3533 ■ Web: www.millrose.com	Mentor	OH	44060	440-255-9171	255-5039
Osborn International 5401 Hamilton Ave TF Cust Svc: 800-720-3358 ■ Web: www.osborn.com	Cleveland	OH	44114	216-361-1900	361-1913
Padco Inc 2220 Elm St SE TF: 800-328-5513 ■ Web: www.padco.com	Minneapolis	MN	55414	612-378-7270	378-9388
PFERD Milwaukee Brush Company Inc 30 Jytek Dr TF: 800-342-9015 ■ Web: www.pferdusa.com	Leominster	MA	01453	978-840-6420	840-6421
Rubberset Co 101 W Prospect Ave TF: 800-345-4939 ■ Web: www.rubberset.com	Cleveland	OH	44115	800-345-4939	
Sanderson-MacLeod Inc 1199 S Main St PO Box 50 TF: 866-522-3481 ■ Web: www.sandersonmacleod.com	Palmer	MA	01069	413-283-3481	289-1919
SM Arnold Inc 7901 Michigan Ave TF Cust Svc: 800-325-7865 ■ Web: www.smarnold.com	Saint Louis	MO	63111	314-544-4103	544-3159
Super Brush Co 800 Worcester St Web: www.superbrush.com	Springfield	MA	01151	413-543-1442	543-1523
Sweepster Inc 2800 N Zeeb Rd TF: 800-456-7100 ■ Web: www.paladinlightconstructiongroup.com	Dexter	MI	48130	734-996-9116	996-9014
Universal Brush Manufacturing Co 16200 Dixie Hwy TF: 800-323-3474 ■ Web: www.universalbrush.com	Markham	IL	60428	708-331-1700	331-4923
Weiler Corp 1 Wildwood Dr TF Cust Svc: 800-835-9999 ■ Web: www.weilercorp.com	Cresco	PA	18326	570-595-7495	595-2002
Wooster Brush Co 604 Madison Ave TF: 800-392-7246 ■ Web: www.woosterbrush.com	Wooster	OH	44691	330-264-4440	263-0495

104 BUILDING MAINTENANCE SERVICES

SEE ALSO Cleaning Services p. 1951

Company	City	State	ZIP	Phone	Fax
Ability Janitorial Services Ltd 884 Churchill Ave S	Ottawa	ON	K1Z5H2	613-722-3566	
Able Service Contractors Inc 13505 Dulles Technology Dr Ste 2 Web: www.ableservice.com	Herndon	VA	20171	571-323-2990	
Advance Building Maintenance 9601 Wilshire Blvd Ste Gl25 Web: www.advancemaintenance.com	Beverly Hills	CA	90210	310-247-0077	
AHI Facility Services Inc 625 Yuma Ct Web: www.ahifs.com	Dallas	TX	75208	214-741-3714	
Aid Maintenance Co 300 Roosevelt Ave PO Box 476 Web: www.aidmaintenance.com	Pawtucket	RI	02860	401-722-6627	723-6860
Allied Building Service Company of Detroit Inc 1801 Howard St Web: www.teamallied.com	Detroit	MI	48216	313-230-0800	
AM Facility Services 8481 Bash St Ste 1700 Web: www.amincorporated.com	Indianapolis	IN	46250	317-578-2290	
Ambius Inc 485 E Half Day Rd Ste 450 Web: www.ambius.com	Buffalo Grove	IL	60089	847-634-4258	
AME Services Inc 23 Barreca St Web: www.ameservicesinc.com	Norco	LA	70079	504-712-3220	
Anka Behavioral Health Inc 1850 Gateway Blvd Ste 900 Web: www.ankabhi.org	Concord	CA	94520	925-825-4700	
Associated Building Maintenance Company Inc 2140 Priest Bridge Ct Web: www.abmcoinc.com	Crofton	MD	21114	410-721-1818	
Aztec Landscaping Inc 7980 Lemon Grove Way Web: www.azteclandscaping.com	Lemon Grove	CA	91945	619-464-3303	
Broadway Services Inc 3709 E Monument St Web: www.broadwayservices.com	Baltimore	MD	21205	410-563-6900	563-6960
Building Maintenance Services LLC 1541 S Beretania St Ste 204 Web: www.bmsnationwide.com	Honolulu	HI	96826	808-983-1250	
Building Restoration Inc 2423 Ravine Rd Web: www.gobri.com	Kalamazoo	MI	49004	269-345-0567	
Burns Janitor Service 1631 W Hill St Web: www.burnsjanitor.com	Louisville	KY	40210	502-585-4548	
Busy Bee Cleaning Company Inc 18 Wilson Ave Web: busybeecleaningcompany.com	West Chester	PA	19382	610-430-6888	
Calico Building Services Inc 15550-C Rockfield Blvd Web: www.calicoweb.com	Irvine	CA	92618	800-576-7313	
Castle Keepers of Charleston Inc 2030 Harley St Web: www.castle-keepers.com	North Charleston	SC	29406	843-572-4757	
CBM Systems Inc 13515 Sw Millikan Way	Beaverton	OR	97005	503-520-1660	
CCS of South Carolina Inc 2325 Prosperity Way Ste 8 Web: www.cleanworldusa.com	Florence	SC	29501	843-669-2273	
Coastal Building Maintenance 15405 Nw Seventh Ave Web: www.cbmflorida.com	Miami	FL	33169	305-681-6100	
Courtesy Building Services Inc 2154 W Northwest Hwy Ste 214 Web: www.courtesybldgservices.com	Dallas	TX	75220	972-831-1444	
Cristi Cleaning Service Corp 77 Trinity Pl Web: www.cristicleaning.com	Hackensack	NJ	07601	201-883-1717	
Cummins Facility Services 5202 Marion Waldo Rd Web: www.cumminsfs.com	Prospect	OH	43342	740-726-9800	
Customized Performance Inc 1342 Ridder Park Dr Web: www.custgroup.com	San Jose	CA	95131	408-437-1720	
Data Clean Corp 1033 Graceland Ave Web: www.dataclean.com	Des Plaines	IL	60016	847-296-3100	
Davis Professional Services Inc 820 Greenbrier Cir Ste 18 Web: www.davisproserv.com	Chesapeake	VA	23320	757-431-1344	
Defender Services Inc 9031 Garners Ferry Rd Web: www.defenderservices.com	Columbia	SC	29209	803-776-4220	
DMS Facility Services Inc 417 East Huntington Dr TF: 800-443-8677 ■ Web: www.dmsfacilityservices.com	Monrovia	CA	91016	626-305-8500	
Dominion Due Diligence Group 4121 Cox Rd Ste 200 Web: www.d3g.biz	Glen Allen	VA	23060	804-358-2020	
Drayton Group 2295 N Opdyke Rd Ste D TF: 888-655-4442 ■ Web: www.draytongroupinc.com	Auburn Hills	MI	48326	888-655-4442	
E- Konomy Pool Service Inc 4912 E 22nd St Web: www.e-konomy.com	Tucson	AZ	85711	520-325-6427	
Eagle Cleaning Service Inc 525 Belview St Web: www.eaglecleaningservice.com	Bessemer	AL	35020	205-424-5252	
Ecolo Odor Control Technologies Inc 59 Penn Dr Web: www.ecolo.com	Toronto	ON	M9L2A6	416-740-3900	740-3800
Epic Industries Inc 1007 Jersey Ave Web: www.epicindustries.com	New Brunswick	NJ	08901	732-249-6867	
FBG Service Corp 407 S 27th Ave TF: 800-777-8326 ■ Web: www.fbgservices.com	Omaha	NE	68131	402-346-4422	595-5044
Flagship Facility Services Inc 1050 N Fifth St Web: www.flagshipinc.com	San Jose	CA	95112	408-977-0155	
Fresh Start Janitorial & Property Services Inc 806 E Ninth St Web: www.freshstartjanitorial.com	South Sioux City	NE	68776	402-494-9980	
Gerrus Maintenance Inc 95 Northfield Ave Web: www.gerrus.com	Edison	NJ	08837	732-225-0662	
GFS Building Maintenance Inc 20 Blaine St Ste 1 Web: www.gfsservices.com	Manchester	NH	03102	603-668-6612	
Goodwill Ind of Fort Worth PO Box 15520 Web: www.goodwillfortworth.org	Fort Worth	TX	76119	817-332-7866	
Griesbach Diamond Water N1022 Quality Dr Web: www.diamondh2o.com	Greenville	WI	54942	920-757-5440	
Hastings Water Works Inc 10331 Brecksville Rd Web: hastingswaterworks.com	Brecksville	OH	44141	440-832-7700	
Horizon Services Co 250 Governor St Web: www.horizonsvcs.com	East Hartford	CT	06108	860-291-9111	
Interstate Contract Cleaning Services Inc 509 Blairhill Rd Web: www.interstateccs.com	Charlotte	NC	28217	704-522-7773	
ISS Facilities Services Inc 1019 Central Pkwy N Ste 100 Web: www.us.issworld.com	San Antonio	TX	78232	210-495-6021	
James L Maher Center 120 Hillside Ave Web: www.mahercenter.org	Newport	RI	02840	401-846-0340	
Janitronics Bldg Services 29 Sawyer Rd Web: www.janitronics.com	Waltham	MA	02453	781-647-5570	893-5878
Kleen Air Research Inc 4510 Helton Dr Web: www.filterpro.com	Florence	AL	35630	256-767-5122	
Landmark Building Maintenance Inc 1725 W 17th St Web: www.landmarkcleaning.com	Tempe	AZ	85281	480-303-0244	
M&I Professional Services Inc 7667 N Ave Web: www.mlproclean.com	Lemon Grove	CA	91945	619-469-1604	
Man-maid Cleaning Services Inc 574 Montauk Hwy Web: www.ammi.biz	Shirley	NY	11967	631-281-5308	
Master Klean Janitorial Inc 2149 S Clermont St Web: www.masterklean.com	Denver	CO	80222	303-753-6084	
Master-Lee Energy Services Corp 5631 Route 981 Web: www.masterlee.com	Latrobe	PA	15650	724-539-8060	
Merex Inc 853 Via Alondra Web: www.merexinc.com	Camarillo	CA	93012	805-446-2700	
Metroclean Commercial Building Services Inc 9000 Southwest Fwy Ste 412 Web: www.metrocleanonline.com	Houston	TX	77074	713-255-0100	
Meyer Brothers Building Company Inc 800 E 101st Ter Ste 120 Web: www.meyerbro.com	Kansas City	MO	64131	816-246-4800	
Midwest Janitorial Service 2831 Falls Ave Web: www.midwestjanitorial.com	Waterloo	IA	50701	319-233-6787	
Mister Kleen Maintenance Company Inc 7302 Beulah St Web: www.misterkleen.com	Alexandria	VA	22315	703-719-6900	
My Cleaning Service Inc 2701 Cresmont Ave Web: www.mycleaningservice.com	Baltimore	MD	21211	410-889-0505	
Pacific Building Maintenance Inc 2646 Palma Dr Ste 320 Web: www.pacificbuildingmaintenance.com	Ventura	CA	93003	805-642-0214	
Peerless Maintenance Service 1100 S Euclid St Web: www.peerlesssvc.com	Fullerton	CA	92832	714-871-3380	
Peninsula Cleaning Service Inc 12610 Patrick Henry Dr Ste A Web: www.peninsulacleaning.com	Newport News	VA	23602	757-833-1603	
Powerlink Facilities Management Services 3031 W Grand Blvd Ste 640 Web: www.powerlinkonline.com	Detroit	MI	48202	313-309-2020	
Powerplant Maintenance Specialists Inc (PMSI) 2900 Bristol St Ste H202 Web: www.pmsipower.com	Costa Mesa	CA	92626	714-427-6900	427-6906
Professional Maintenance Care 4912 Naples St Web: www.pmsjanitorial.com	San Diego	CA	92110	619-276-1150	

	City	State	Zip	Phone	Fax
Rembrandt Commercial Cleaning 20900 Swenson Dr Ste 250 *Web:* www.rembrandtcleaning.com	Waukesha	WI	53186	262-798-1038	
Rooftodeck Restoration Inc 1410 Energy Park Dr Ste 6 *Web:* www.rooftodeckdecoration.com	Saint Paul	MN	55108	651-699-3504	
Sealco Data Center Services Ltd 1761 International Pkwy Ste 127 *Web:* www.sealco.net	Richardson	TX	75081	972-234-5567	
Shamrock Acquisition Corp 10901 Danka Cir N Ste B *Web:* www.shamrockclean.com	Saint Petersburg	FL	33716	727-585-6007	
Shannon Diversified Inc 1190 N Del Rio Pl *TF:* 800-794-2345 ■ *Web:* www.shannoncompany.com	Ontario	CA	91764	800-794-2345	
Sonitec-Vortisand Inc 1400 Tees St *Web:* www.sonitec.com	St-laurent	QC	H4R2B6	514-335-2200	
Style Crest Inc 2450 Enterprise St *TF:* 800-925-4440 ■ *Web:* www.stylecrestinc.com	Fremont	OH	43420	419-332-7369	332-8763
Temco Service Industries Inc 417 Fifth Ave Ninth Fl *Web:* temcoservices.com	New York	NY	10016	212-889-6353	213-9854
Toledo Building Services 2121 Adams St *Web:* www.toledobuildingservices.com	Toledo	OH	43604	419-241-3101	
Treco Service Inc 904 N Zarzamora St *Web:* www.trecoservices.com	San Antonio	TX	78207	210-432-4100	
Unichem Inc Eight N Kings Rd *Web:* www.unichem.com	Greenville	SC	29605	864-422-0191	
United Building Maintenance Inc 165 Easy St *Web:* www.ubm-usa.com	Carol Stream	IL	60188	630 653 4848	
UV Pure Technologies Inc 60 Venture Dr Unit 19 *Web:* www.uvpure.com	Toronto	ON	M1B3S4	416-208-9884	
Vanguard Resources Inc 17300 Henderson Pass Ste 200 *Web:* www.vanguardresources.com	San Antonio	TX	78232	210-495-1950	
Whitehall Associates Inc 416 Southview Ave *Web:* www.whitehallassociates.com	Silver Spring	MD	20905	301-879-1421	
Xpicor Inc 4411 W Market St Ste 100 *Web:* www.xpicor.com	Greensboro	NC	27407	336-510-0333	
Zazula Process Equipment Ltd 4609 Manitoba Rd Se *Web:* www.zazula.com	Calgary	AB	T2G4B9	403-244-0751	

105 BUILDINGS - PREFABRICATED - METAL

	City	State	Zip	Phone	Fax
American Buildings Co 1150 State Docks Rd *TF:* 888-307-4338 ■ *Web:* www.americanbuildings.com	Eufaula	AL	36027	334-687-2032	688-2261
American Modular Technologies (AMT) 6306 Old 421 Rd PO Box 1069 *Web:* www.americanmodulartechnologies.com	Liberty	NC	27298	336-622-6200	622-6473
Behlen Manufacturing Co 4025 E 23rd St *TF:* 800-553-5520 ■ *Web:* www.behlenmfg.com	Columbus	NE	68601	402-564-3111	563-7405
Butler Manufacturing Co 1540 Genessee St **Fax:* Hum Res ■ *Web:* www.butlermfg.com	Kansas City	MO	64102	816-968-3000	968-6506*
Canatal Industries Inc 2885 Boul Frontenac E *Web:* www.canatal.com	Thetford Mines	QC	G6G6P6	418-338-6044	338-6829
Ceco Bldg Systems 2400 Hwy 45 N *Web:* www.cecobuildings.com	Columbus	MS	39705	662-328-6722	243-2781
CEMCO 263 N Covina Ln **Fax Area Code:* 626 ■ *TF:* 800-775-2362 ■ *Web:* www.cemcosteel.com	City Of Industry	CA	91744	800-775-2362	330-7598*
Clearspan Components Inc 6110 Old Hwy 80 W *Web:* merchantcircle.com	Meridian	MS	39307	601-483-3941	483-3941
Dean Steel Buildings Inc 2929 Industrial Ave *Web:* www.deanintl.com	Fort Myers	FL	33901	239-334-1051	334-2432
DeRaffele Mfg Company Inc 2525 Palmer Ave	New Rochelle	NY	10801	914-636-6850	636-6596
Dura-Bilt Products Inc PO Box 188 *Web:* www.durabilt.com	Wellsburg	NY	14894	570-596-2000	596-3296
Empire Iron Works Ltd 21104 - 107 Ave *Web:* www.empireiron.com	Edmonton	AB	T5S1X2	780-447-4650	447-4005
Erect-A-Tube Inc 701 W Pk St PO Box 100 *TF:* 800-624-9219 ■ *Web:* www.erect-a-tube.com	Harvard	IL	60033	815-943-4091	943-4095
Four Seasons Solar Products LLC 5005 Veterans Memorial Hwy *TF:* 800-368-7732 ■ *Web:* www.fourseasonssunrooms.com	Holbrook	NY	11741	631-563-4000	563-4010
Garco Bldg Systems 2714 S Garfield Rd *TF:* 800-941-2291 ■ *Web:* www.garcobuildings.com	Airway Heights	WA	99001	509-244-5611	244-2850
Gichner Systems Group Inc 490 E Locust St *Web:* www.gichner.us	Dallastown	PA	17313	717-244-7611	246-5496
Gulf States Manufacturers 101 Airport Rd PO Box 1128 *Web:* gsmnucor.com	Starkville	MS	39760	662-323-8021	324-2984
Imperial Industries Inc 505 Industrial Pk Ave *TF:* 800-558-2945 ■ *Web:* www.imperialind.com	Rothschild	WI	54474	715-359-0200	355-5349
Kirby Bldg Systems Inc 124 Kirby Dr *TF:* 800-348-7799 ■ *Web:* www.kirbybuildingsystems.com	Portland	TN	37148	615-325-4165	325-4700
Lark Builders Inc 409 Dixon St *Web:* www.larkbuilders.com	Vidalia	GA	30474	912-538-1888	
Ludwig Buildings Inc 521 Timesaver Ave *Web:* ludwigbuildings.com	Harahan	LA	70123	504-733-6260	733-7458
Madison Industries Inc of Georgia 1035 Iris Dr *Web:* www.madisonind.com	Conyers	GA	30094	770-483-4401	785-7967
Mesco Bldg Solutions 5244 Bear Creek Ct *TF:* 800-556-3726 ■ *Web:* www.mescobldg.com	Irving	TX	75061	214-687-9999	687-9736
Metl-Span LLC 1720 Lakepointe Dr Ste 101 *TF:* 877-585-9969 ■ *Web:* www.metlspan.com	Lewisville	TX	75057	972-221-6656	420-9382
Mid-West Steel Bldg Co 7301 Fairview *TF:* 800-777-9378 ■ *Web:* www.mid-weststeel.com	Houston	TX	77041	713-466-7788	466-3194
Morton Buildings Inc 252 W Adams St PO Box 399 *TF:* 800-447-7436 ■ *Web:* www.mortonbuildings.com	Morton	IL	61550	309-263-7474	266-5123
Mueller Inc 1913 Hutchins Ave *TF:* 877-268-3553 ■ *Web:* www.muellerinc.com	Ballinger	TX	76821	325-365-3555	365-8181
NCI Bldg Systems Inc 10943 N Sam Houston PkwyWest *NYSE: NCS* ■ *Web:* www.ncibuildingsystems.com	Houston	TX	77064	281-897-7788	477-9674
Pacific Building Systems (PBS) 2100 N Pacific Hwy *TF General:* 800-727-7844 ■ *Web:* www.pbsbuildings.com	Woodburn	OR	97071	503-981-9581	981-9584
Package Industries Inc 15 Harback Rd *TF:* 800-225-7242 ■ *Web:* www.packagesteel.com	Sutton	MA	01590	508-865-5871	865-9130
Parkline Inc PO Box 65 *TF:* 800-786-4855 ■ *Web:* www.parkline.com	Winfield	WV	25213	304-586-2113	586-3842
Porta-Fab Corp 18080 Chesterfield Airport Rd *TF:* 800-325-3781 ■ *Web:* www.portafab.com	Chesterfield	MO	63005	636-537-5555	537-2955
PorterCorp 4240 136th Ave *TF:* 800-354-7721 ■ *Web:* www.portercorp.com	Holland	MI	49424	616-399-1963	399-9123
Protect Controls Inc (PCI) 303 Little York Rd *Web:* www.protectcontrols.com	Houston	TX	77076	713-691-5183	691-0159
Red Dot Corp 1209 W Corsicana St **Fax Area Code:* 903 ■ *TF Cust Svc:* 800-657-2234 ■ *Web:* www.reddotbuildings.com	Athens	TX	75751	800-657-2234	675-9180*
Rigid Bldg Systems Ltd 18933 Aldine Westfield Rd *TF:* 888-467-4443 ■ *Web:* www.rigidbuilding.com	Houston	TX	77073	281-443-9065	443-9064
Ruffin Bldg Systems Inc 6914 Louisiana 2 *TF:* 800-421-4232 ■ *Web:* www.ruffinbuildingsystems.com	Oak Grove	LA	71263	318-428-2305	428-2231
ShelterLogic Corp 150 Callendar Rd *TF:* 800-932-9344 ■ *Web:* www.shelterlogic.com	Watertown	CT	06795	860-945-6442	
Star Bldg Systems 8600 S I-35 **Fax Area Code:* 405 ■ *TF:* 800-879-7827 ■ *Web:* www.starbuildings.com	Oklahoma City	OK	73149	800-879-7827	636-2419*
Tampa Tank Inc 2710 E Fifth Ave *Web:* www.tampatank.com	Tampa	FL	33605	813-623-2675	622-7514
Temo Sunrooms Inc 20400 Hall Rd **Fax Area Code:* 586 ■ *TF:* 800-344-8366 ■ *Web:* www.temosunrooms.com	Clinton Township	MI	48038	800-344-8366	226-1706*
Trachte Bldg Systems Inc 314 Wilburn Rd *TF:* 800-356-5824 ■ *Web:* www.trachte.com	Sun Prairie	WI	53590	800-356-5824	981-9014
Tyler Bldg Systems LP 3535 Shiloh Rd	Tyler	TX	75701	903-561-3000	
United Structures of America Inc 1912 Buschong *Web:* www.usabldg.com	Houston	TX	77039	281-442-8247	442-2125
Varco Pruden Buildings 3200 Players Club Cir *Web:* www.vp.com	Memphis	TN	38125	901-748-8000	748-9323
Whirlwind Steel 8234 Hansen Rd **Fax Area Code:* 832 ■ *TF:* 800-324-9992 ■ *Web:* www.whirlwindsteel.com	Houston	TX	77075	713-946-7140	553-4992*
Winandy Greenhouse Co 2211 Peacock Rd *Web:* winandygreenhouse.com	Richmond	IN	47374	765-935-2111	935-2110
Worldwide Steel Buildings PO Box 588 *TF:* 800-825-0316 ■ *Web:* www.worldwidesteelbuildings.com	Peculiar	MO	64078	800-825-0316	
XS Smith Inc 932 Page Rd *TF:* 800-631-2226 ■ *Web:* www.xssmith.com	Washington	NC	27889	252-940-5060	946-0724

106 BUILDINGS - PREFABRICATED - WOOD

	City	State	Zip	Phone	Fax
A & S Building Systems LP 1880 Hwy 116 *Web:* www.a-s.com	Caryville	TN	37714	865-426-2141	
Acorn Deck House Co 852 Main St *TF:* 800-727-3325 ■ *Web:* www.deckhouse.com	Acton	MA	01720	978-263-6800	263-4159
Alenco Inc 16201 W 110th St *Web:* www.alenconline.com	Lenexa	KS	66219	913-438-1902	
Alfresco Grills Inc 7039 E Slauson Ave *Web:* www.alfrescogrills.com	Commerce	CA	90040	323-722-7900	
Algeco Scotsman Inc 901 S Bond St Ste 600 *Web:* www.algecoscotsman.com	Baltimore	MD	21231	410-931-6000	
Barden & Robeson Corp 103 Kelly Ave *TF:* 800-724-0141 ■ *Web:* www.bardenhomes.com	Middleport	NY	14105	716-735-3732	735-3752
Bebco Industries Inc 4725 Lawndale *Web:* www.okbebco.com	La Marque	TX	77568	409-935-5743	
Bellcomb Inc 5001 Boone Ave N *Web:* www.bellcomb.com	Minneapolis	MN	55428	763-746-0000	
Blazer Industries Inc PO Box 489 *TF:* 877-211-3437 ■ *Web:* www.blazerind.com	Aumsville	OR	97325	503-749-1900	749-3969
BOXX Modular Inc 555 Jubilee Ln Ste A *Web:* www.boxxmodularus.com	Lewisville	TX	75056	972-492-4040	
Cardinal Homes Inc 525 Barnesville Hwy PO Box 10 *Web:* www.cardinalhomes.com	Wylliesburg	VA	23976	434-735-8111	735-8824
Cedarstore.com 5410 Rt 8 *Web:* www.cedarstore.com	Gibsonia	PA	15044	724-444-5300	
Dacro Industries Inc 9325-51 Ave *Web:* www.dacro.com	Edmonton	AB	T6E4W8	780-434-8900	433-3138
Deluxe Bldg Systems Inc 499 W Third St *TF:* 800-843-7372 ■ *Web:* deluxecrm.com/crm/	Berwick	PA	18603	570-752-5914	752-1525
Demtec Inc 50, Blvd Industriel *TF:* 800-560-2043 ■ *Web:* www.demtec.com	Princeville	QC	G6L4P2	819-364-2043	364-3448
Design Homes Inc 600 N Marquette Rd *TF:* 800-627-9443 ■ *Web:* www.designhomes.com	Prairie du Chien	WI	53821	608-326-6041	326-4233
Dickinson Homes Inc 404 N Stephenson Ave Hwy US-2 PO Box 2245 *TF:* 800-438-4687 ■ *Web:* www.dickinsonhomes.com	Iron Mountain	MI	49801	906-774-2186	774-5207
Dynamic Homes LLC 525 Roosevelt Ave **Fax:* Orders ■ *TF:* 800-492-4833 ■ *Web:* www.dynamichomes.com	Detroit Lakes	MN	56501	218-847-2611	847-2617*

Phone Fax

Fleetwood Homes of California Inc
7007 Jurupa Ave. Riverside CA 92504 951-351-2494 351-0378
Web: www.fleetwoodhomes.com

Flexospan Steel Buildings Inc
253 Railroad St. Sandy Lake PA 16145 724-376-7221
TF: 800-245-0396 ■ Web: www.flexospan.com

Foremost Industries Inc
2375 Buchanan Trl W Greencastle PA 17225 717-597-7166 597-5579
TF: 877-284-5334 ■ Web: www.foremosthomes.com

Gary Doupnik Manufacturing Inc
3237 Rippey Rd PO Box 527 Loomis CA 95650 916-652-9291 652-9021

General Shelters of Texas Ltd
1639 State Hwy 87 N Center TX 75935 936-598-3389 598-1432
Web: www.generalshelters.com

Global Precast Inc 2101 Teston Rd. Maple ON L6A1R3 905-832-4307 832-4388
Web: www.globalprecast.com

Gold Capital LLC 3566 Olivet Church Rd Paducah KY 42001 270-408-4653
Web: www.goldcapitalky.com

Harbor Technologies LLC
Eight Business Pkwy. Brunswick ME 04011 207-725-4878
Web: www.harbortech.us

Haven Homes Inc 554 Eagle Vly Rd. Beech Creek PA 16822 570-962-2111
Web: lockhaven.com

Heckaman Homes Inc 2676 E Market St Nappanee IN 46550 574-773-4167 773-2546
Web: www.heckamanhomes.com

Heritage Log Homes Inc 119 W Dumplin Vly Rd. Kodak TN 37764 865-932-0202 429-4434
Web: thegreatsmokeymountainsparkway.com

Homes by Keystone Inc
13338 Midvale Rd PO Box 69. Waynesboro PA 17268 800-890-7926
TF: 800-890-7926 ■ Web: www.homesbykeystone.com

Imperial Manufacturing Inc 2271 NE 194th. Portland OR 97230 503-665-5539
Web: www.imperialmfg.com

Indaco Metal Three American Way. Shawnee OK 74804 877-300-7334
TF: 877-300-7334 ■ Web: www.indacometals.com

Industries Bonneville Ltee
601 rue de l'Industrie Beloeil QC J3G4S5 450-464-1001
Web: www.maisonsbonneville.com

International Homes of Cedar Inc (IHC)
PO Box 886 Woodinville WA 98072 360-668-8511 668-5562
TF: 800-767-7674 ■ Web: www.ihoc.com

Keiser Homes 56 Mechanic Falls Rd PO Box 9000 Oxford ME 04270 888-333-1748 539-0944*
*Fax Area Code: 207 ■ TF: 888-333-1748 ■ Web: www.keisermaine.com

Kerkstra Precast Inc 3373 Busch Dr. Grandville MI 49418 616-224-6176
Web: www.kerkstra.com

KIT HomeBuilders West LLC 1124 Garber St. Caldwell ID 83605 208-454-5000 455-2995
TF: 800-859-0347 ■ Web: www.kitwest.com

Kontek Industries Inc 1200 Dawson Rd. New Madrid MO 63869 573-748-5561
Web: www.kontekindustries.com

Lester Bldg Systems LLC
1111 Second Ave S. Lester Prairie MN 55354 320-395-2531 395-5393
TF: 800-826-4439 ■ Web: www.lesterbuildings.com

Lindal Cedar Homes Inc 4300 S 104th Pl Seattle WA 98178 206-725-0900 725-1615
TF Prod Info: 800-426-0536 ■ Web: www.lindal.com

Log Cabin Homes Ltd 410 N Pearl St. Rocky Mount NC 27804 252-454-1500
Web: www.logcabinhomes.com

Manufactured Structures Corp (MSC)
3089 E Fort Wayne Rd PO Box 350 Rochester IN 46975 574-223-4794
TF: 800-662-5344 ■ Web: www.mscoffice.com

Mod-U-Kraf Homes LLC
260 Weaver St PO Box 573. Rocky Mount VA 24151 540-483-0291 483-2228
TF: 888-663-5723 ■ Web: www.mod-u-kraf.com

Modtech Holdings Inc
1660 Chicago Ave Ste M-21. Riverside CA 92507 951-686-3633
Web: www.modtech.com

Montana Idaho Log & Timber 1069 Us Hwy 93 N Victor MT 59875 406-961-3092
Web: www.mtidlog.com

Morgan Bldg Systems Inc 2800 McCree Rd Garland TX 75041 972-864-7300 864-7307
TF: 800-935-0321 ■ Web: www.morganusa.com

Nassal Co, The 415 W Kaley St Orlando FL 32806 407-648-0400 648-0841
Web: www.nassal.com

National Barn Company 818 N Broadway Portland TN 37148 615-325-2700
Web: www.nationalbarn.com

Nationwide Custom Homes 1100 Rives Rd. Martinsville VA 24115 800-216-7001 632-1181*
*Fax Area Code: 276 ■ TF: 800-216-7001 ■ Web: www.nationwide-homes.com

Natural Structures 2005 Tenth St Baker City OR 97814 541-523-0224
Web: www.naturalstructures.com

New Acton Mobile Industries LLC
809 Gleneagles Ct Baltimore MD 21286 800-251-1600
TF: 800-251-1600 ■ Web: www.actonmobile.com

New England Homes 270 Ocean Rd. Greenland NH 03840 603-436-8830 431-8540
TF: 800-800-8831 ■ Web: www.newenglandhomes.net

Nexus Corp 10983 Leroy Dr Northglenn CO 80233 303-457-9199
TF: 800-228-9639 ■ Web: www.nexuscorp.com

Northeastern Log Homes Inc 10 Ames Rd Kenduskeag ME 04450 207-884-7000 884-3000
TF: 800-624-2797 ■ Web: www.northeasternlog.com

Original Lincoln Logs Ltd
Five Riverside Dr PO Box 135. Chestertown NY 12817 800-833-2461 494-3008*
*Fax Area Code: 518 ■ TF: 800-833-2461 ■ Web: www.lincolnlogs.com

Pacific Modern Homes Inc (PMHI)
9723 Railroad St. Elk Grove CA 95624 916-685-9514 685-1306
TF: 800-395-1011 ■ Web: www.pmhi.com

Pan Abode Cedar Homes Inc 1100 Maple Ave SW Renton WA 98057 425-255-8260 255-8630
TF: 800-782-2633 ■ Web: www.panabodehomes.com

Pittsville Homes Inc
5094 Second Ave PO Box C Pittsville WI 54466 715-884-2511 884-2136

Rocky Mountain Log Homes 1883 Hwy 93 S Hamilton MT 59840 406-363-5680 363-2109
Web: www.rockymountainloghomes.com

Sand Creek Post & Beam 116 W First St. Wayne NE 68787 402-833-5600
Web: www.sandcreekpostandbeam.com

Satellite Shelters Inc 2530 Xenium Ln N Plymouth MN 55441 763-553-1900
Web: www.satelliteco.com

Schulte Building Systems Inc 17600 Badtke Rd. Hockley TX 77447 281-304-6111
TF: 877-257-2534 ■ Web: www.sbslp.com

Phone Fax

Simplex Homes 1 Simplex Dr. Scranton PA 18504 570-346-5113 346-3732
TF: 800-233-4233 ■ Web: www.simplexind.com

Southern Bleacher Company Inc 801 Fifth St Graham TX 76450 940-549-0733
Web: www.southernbleacher.com

Starrco Company Inc
11700 Fairgrove Industrial Blvd Maryland Heights MO 63043 314-567-5533
Web: www.starrco.com

Sterling Bldg Systems PO Box 1967 Wausau WI 54402 800-455-0545
Web: sterlingbldg.com/contact-us

Stratford Homes LP 402 S Weber Ave. Stratford WI 54484 715-687-3133 687-3453
TF: 800-448-1524 ■ Web: www.stratfordhomes.com

Suntec Concrete Inc 2221 W Shangri-La Rd Phoenix AZ 85029 602-997-0937
Web: www.suntecconcrete.com

Timberland Homes Inc 1201 37th St NW. Auburn WA 98001 253-735-3435 939-8803
TF: 800-488-5036 ■ Web: www.timberland-homes.com

Trading Post Homes 490 Sparrow Dre Shepherdsville KY 40165 502-955-5622
Web: www.tradingposthomes.com

Unibilt Industries Inc
8005 Johnson Stn Rd PO Box 373. Vandalia OH 45377 800-777-9942 890-8303*
*Fax Area Code: 937 ■ TF: 800-777-9942 ■ Web: www.unibiltcustomhomes.com

Ward Cedar Log Homes 37 Bangor St PO Box 72. Houlton ME 04730 800-341-1566 532-7806*
*Fax Area Code: 207 ■ TF Cust Svc: 800-341-1566 ■ Web: www.wardcedarloghomes.com

Wausau Homes Inc PO Box 8005 Wausau WI 54402 715-359-7272
Web: www.wausauhomes.com

Weatherhaven Global Resources Ltd
8355 Riverbend Ct Burnaby BC V3N5E7 604-451-8900
Web: www.weatherhaven.com

Westchester Modular Homes Inc
30 Reagans Mill Rd Wingdale NY 12594 845-832-9400
Web: www.westchestermodular.com

Whitley Manufacturing Inc
201 W First St PO Box 496. South Whitley IN 46787 260-723-5131 723-6949
Web: www.whitleyman.com

Wisconsin Homes Inc 425 W McMillan St. Marshfield WI 54449 715-384-2161 387-3627
Web: www.wisconsinhomesinc.com

Yankee Barn Homes 131 Yankee Barn Rd. Grantham NH 03753 800-258-9786
Web: www.yankeebarnhomes.com

107 BUS SERVICES - CHARTER

Phone Fax

A Yankee Line 370 W First St Boston MA 02127 617-268-8890 268-6960
TF: 800-942-8890 ■ Web: www.yankeeline.us

Agape Tours & Charter 2730 Commerce St. Wichita Falls TX 76301 940-767-4935 692-8477
Web: www.agapetoursinc.com

All West Coach Lines 7701 Wilbur Way Sacramento CA 95828 916-423-4000 689-5926
TF: 800-843-2121 ■ Web: coachusa.com

Anderson Coach & Travel One Anderson Plz. Greenville PA 16125 724-588-8310 588-0257
TF: 800-345-3435 ■ Web: www.goanderson.com

Arrow Stage Lines 720 E Norfolk Ave Norfolk NE 68701 402-371-3850 371-3267
TF: 800-672-8302 ■ Web: www.arrowstagelines.com

B & C Transportation Inc
427 Continental Dr. Maryville TN 37804 865-983-4653 983-5354
TF: 877-812-2287 ■ Web: bctransportation.net/

Badger Bus 5501 Femrite Dr. Madison WI 53718 608-255-1511 258-3484
TF: 800-442-8259 ■ Web: www.badgerbus.com

Blue Lakes Charters & Tours 12154 N Saginaw Rd Clio MI 48420 810-686-4287 686-9772
TF: 800-282-4287 ■ Web: www.bluelakes.com

Boise-Winnemucca Stage Lines Inc
1105 S La Pt St. Boise ID 83706 208-336-3300 336-3303
TF: 800-448-5692 ■ Web: www.boise-winnemuccastages.com

Brown Coach Inc 50 Venner Rd. Amsterdam NY 12010 518-843-4700 843-3600
TF: 800-424-4700 ■ Web: www.browntours.com

Butler Motor Transit Company Inc
210 S Monroe St PO Box 1602. Butler PA 16003 724-282-1000 282-3080
Web: www.coachusa.com/butler

C & H Bus Lines Inc 448 Pine St Macon GA 31201 478-746-6441 743-5597

Carl R Bieber Tourways Inc
320 Fair St PO Box 180 Kutztown PA 19530 610-683-7333
TF: 800-243-2374 ■ Web: www.biebertourways.com

Central States Coach Repairs
3426 Gilbert Rd Grand Prairie TX 75050 972-399-1059 986-7262
TF: 800-533-1939 ■ Web: www.bus-charter.com

Chippewa Trails 510 E S Ave. Chippewa Falls WI 54729 715-726-2457 726-2455
TF: 866-777-1399 ■ Web: www.chippewatrailstours.com

Citizen Auto Stage Co 67 E Baffert Dr. Nogales AZ 85621 520-281-0400
TF: 800-276-1528 ■ Web: graylinearizona.com

Coach Tours Ltd 475 Federal Rd Brookfield CT 06804 203-740-1118 775-6851
TF: 800-822-6224 ■ Web: www.coachtour.com

Colorado Charter Lines 4960 Locust St. Commerce City CO 80022 303-287-0239 287-2819
TF: 800-821-7491 ■ Web: www.bus-charter.com/coloradocharter.htm

Conestoga Tours Inc 1530 Commerce Dr Ste A. Lancaster PA 17601 717-569-1111
Web: pagraphics.com

Covered Wagon Tours LLC 158 Thacher St Hornell NY 14843 607-324-3900
Web: www.coveredwagontours.net

Cowtown Bus Charters Inc
5504 Forest Hill Dr. Fort Worth TX 76119 817-531-3287
Web: www.cowtowncharters.com

Croswell Bus Lines Inc 975 W Main St Williamsburg OH 45176 513-724-2206 724-3261
TF: 800-782-8747 ■ Web: gocroswell.com

CYR Bus Lines 153 Gilman Falls Ave Old Town ME 04468 207-827-2335 827-6763
TF: 800-244-2335 ■ Web: www.cyrbustours.com

DATTCO Inc 583 S St. New Britain CT 06051 860-229-4878 826-1115
TF: 800-229-4879 ■ Web: dattco.com

Delta Bus Lines Inc 3107 Hwy 82E Greenville MS 38701 662-335-2633 335-2634
Web: deltabuslines.net

Discovery Care Centre Corp 601 N Tenth St. Hamilton MT 59840 406-363-2273
Web: www.discoverycare.com

Easton Coach Co 1200 Conroy Pl Easton PA 18040 610-253-4055
Web: eastoncoach.com

	City	State	Zip	Phone	Fax
Elite Coach 1685 W Main St. TF: 800-722-6206 ■ Web: www.elitecoach.com	Ephrata	PA	17522	717-733-7710	733-7133
Escot Bus Lines Inc 6890 142nd Ave Web: www.escotbuslines.com	Largo	FL	33771	727-545-2088	
Eyre Bus Service Inc 13600 Triadelphia Rd PO Box 239 TF: 800-321-3973 ■ Web: www.eyre.com	Glenelg	MD	21737	410-442-1330	442-0010
Gold Coast Tours 105 Gemini Ave Web: www.goldcoasttours.com	Brea	CA	92821	714-449-6888	
Good Time Tours 455 Corday St. TF: 800-446-0886 ■ Web: www.goodtimetours.com	Pensacola	FL	32503	850-476-0046	476-7637
Gray Line Worldwide 1835 Gaylord St Web: www.grayline.com	Denver	CO	80206	303-394-6920	394-6950
Great Southern Coaches 900 Burke Ave Web: yellowpagesgoesgreen.org	Jonesboro	AR	72401	870-935-5569	
Greyhound Canada Transportation Corp 1111 International Blvd Ste 700 TF: 800-661-8747 ■ Web: www.greyhound.ca	Burlington	ON	L7L6W1	800-661-8747	
Hampton Jitney Inc (HJ) 395 County Rd 39A Ste 6 Web: www.hamptonjitney.com	SouthHampton	NY	11968	631-283-4600	287-4759
Harms Charters 532 S Vly View Rd TF: 800-678-6543 ■ Web: www.foremanchartersandtours.com	Sioux Falls	SD	57106	605-336-3339	
Hawkeye Stages Inc 703 Dudley St TF: 877-464-2954 ■ Web: www.hawkeyestages.com	Decorah	IA	52101	563-382-3639	
Indian Trails Inc 109 E Comstock St TF: 800-292-3831 ■ Web: www.indiantrails.com	Owosso	MI	48867	989-725-5105	725-9584
Kerrville Bus Co One S Main St. TF: 800-474-3352 ■ Web: www.iridekbc.com	Del Rio	TX	78840	830-775-7515	
Lamers Bus Lines Inc 2407 S Pt Rd TF: 800-236-1240 ■ Web: www.golamers.com	Green Bay	WI	54313	920-496-3600	496-3611
Marin Charter & Tours Eight Lovell Ave Web: www.marinairporter.com	San Rafael	CA	94901	415-256-8830	256-8839
Martz First Class Coach Company Inc 4783 37th St N TF: 800-282-8020 ■ Web: www.martzfirstclass.com	Saint Petersburg	FL	33714	727-526-9086	522-5548
Mid-America Charter Lines 2513 E Higgins Rd TF: 800-323-0312 ■ Web: bus-charter.com	Elk Grove Village	IL	60007	847-437-3779	437-4978
MV Transportation Inc 5910 N Central Expy Ste 1145 *Fax Area Code: 707 ■ Web: www.mvtransit.com	Dallas	TX	75206	972-391-4600	863-8944*
Northfield Lines Inc 32611 Northfield Blvd. TF: 888-670-8068 ■ Web: www.northfieldlines.com	Northfield	MN	55057	507-645-5267	645-5635
Onondaga Coach Corp PO Box 277 TF: 800-451-1570 ■ Web: www.onondagacoach.com	Auburn	NY	13021	315-255-2216	255-0925
Pacific Western Transportation Ltd 6999 ordan Dr TF: 800-387-6787 ■ Web: www.pacificwesterntoronto.com	Mississauga	ON	L5T1K6	905-564-3232	564-5959
Peter Pan Bus Lines PO Box 1776 TF: 800-343-9999 ■ Web: www.peterpanbus.com	Springfield	MA	01102	800-343-9999	
Peter Pan Bus Lines Inc 1776 Main St TF: 800-237-8747 ■ Web: www.peterpanbus.com	Springfield	MA	01103	413-786-9300	747-7626
Premier Coach Company Inc 946 Rte 7 S TF: 800-532-1811 ■ Web: www.premiercoach.net	Milton	VT	05468	802-655-4456	655-4213
Punchbowl Inc 50 Speen St Ste 202 TF: 877-570-4340 ■ Web: punchbowl.com	Framingham	MA	01701	508-589-4486	270-4541
Red Carpet Charters 4820 SW 20th TF: 888-878-5100 ■ Web: www.redcarpetcharters.com	Oklahoma City	OK	73128	405-672-5100	672-9613
Rimrock Stages Inc 1660 W Broadway St. TF: 800-255-7655 ■ Web: webstore.trailways.com	Missoula	MT	59808	406-549-2339	
Riteway Bus Service Inc Motorcoach Div W201 N13900 Fond du Lac Ave TF: 800-776-7026 ■ Web: goriteway.com/	Richfield	WI	53076	262-677-3282	677-3121
Rockland Coaches Inc 180 Old Hook Rd. Web: www.coachusa.com/rockland	Westwood	NJ	07675	201-263-1254	664-8036
Salter Bus Lines Inc 212 Hudson Ave. TF: 800-223-8056 ■ Web: www.salter.us	Jonesboro	LA	71251	318-259-2522	259-2522
SBS Transit Inc 3747 Colorado Ave Web: loraincounty.com	Sheffield Village	OH	44054	440-949-8121	
Shafer's Tour & Charter 500 N St TF: 800-287-8986 ■ Web: www.shaferbus.com	Endicott	NY	13760	607-797-2006	797-1183
Sharp Bus Lines Ltd 567 Oak Park Rd. Web: www.sharpbus.com	Brantford	ON	N3T5L8	519-426-0050	
Silver Fox Tours & Motorcoaches Three Silver Fox Dr. TF: 800-342-5998 ■ Web: www.silverfoxcoach.com	Millbury	MA	01527	508-865-6000	865-4660
Southeastern Stages Inc 260 University Ave SW Web: www.southeasternstages.com	Atlanta	GA	30315	404-591-2780	591-2745
Starr Bus Charter & Tours 2531 E State St. TF: 800-782-7703 ■ Web: www.starrtours.com	Trenton	NJ	08619	609-587-0626	587-3052
Storer Coachways 3519 McDonald Ave TF: 800-621-3383 ■ Web: www.storercoachways.com	Modesto	CA	95358	209-521-8250	578-4888
Swarthout Coaches Inc 115 Graham Rd TF: 800-772-7267 ■ Web: www.goswarthout.com	Ithaca	NY	14850	607-257-2277	257-0218
Trailways Transportation System Inc 3554 Chain Bridge Rd Ste 301 TF: 877-467-3346 ■ Web: www.trailways.com	Fairfax	VA	22030	703-691-3052	691-9047
Triple J Tours Inc 4455 S Cameron St. Web: www.lasvegasbus.com	Las Vegas	NV	89103	702-261-0131	736-5103
Van Galder Bus Co 715 S Pearl St TF: 800-747-0994 ■ Web: www.coachusa.com	Janesville	WI	53548	608-752-5407	752-7120
VIP Tour & Charter Bus Co 129-137 Fox St. TF General: 800-231-2222 ■ Web: www.vipchartercoaches.com	Portland	ME	04101	207-772-4457	772-7020
Voyageur Transportation Services 573 Admiral Ct Web: www.voyageurtransportation.ca	London	ON	N5V4L3	519-455-4580	
White Hat Management LLC 159 S Main St Ste 600 Web: www.whitehatmgmt.com	Akron	OH	44308	330-535-6868	
Wilson Bus Lines Inc 203 Patriots Rd PO Box 415 TF: 800-253-5235 ■ Web: www.wilsonbus.com	East Templeton	MA	01438	978-632-3894	632-9005
Winn Transportation 1831 Westwood Ave TF: 800-296-9466 ■ Web: www.winnbus.com	Richmond	VA	23227	804-358-9466	353-2606
Wisconsin Coach Lines Inc 1520 Arcadian Ave TF: 877-324-7767 ■ Web: www.coachusa.com	Waukesha	WI	53186	262-542-8861	542-2036
Young Transportation & Tours 843 Riverside Dr. TF: 800-622-5444 ■ Web: www.youngtransportation.com	Asheville	NC	28804	828-258-0084	252-3342

108 BUS SERVICES - INTERCITY & RURAL

SEE ALSO Bus Services - School p. 1892; Mass Transportation (Local & Suburban) p. 2719

	City	State	Zip	Phone	Fax
A. J. Edmond Co 1530 W 16th St. Web: ajedmondco.com	Long Beach	CA	90813	562-437-1802	
Adirondack Trailways 499 Hurley Ave. TF: 800-858-8555 ■ Web: www.trailwaysny.com	Hurley	NY	12443	845-339-4230	225-6815
Autobus Girardin Inc 4000 Girardin St. Web: www.girardinbluebird.com	Drummondville	QC	J2E0A1	819-477-3222	
C & L Bus Company Inc 12200 W Broward Blvd. Web: www.ahschool.com	Plantation	FL	33325	954-472-7800	
Calgary Handi-bus Assn 231 37 Ave Ne. Web: www.calgaryhandibus.com	Calgary	AB	T2E8J2	403-276-8028	
Colorado Valley Transit Inc 108 Cardinal Ln PO Box 940 TF: 800-548-1068 ■ Web: www.gotransit.org	Columbus	TX	78934	979-732-6281	732-6283
Elgie Bus Lines Ltd 400 Sovereign Rd. Web: www.elgiebuslines.com	London	ON	N6M1A5	519-451-4440	
Everything Parking Inc 1415 S Church St Ste T Web: www.parkinc.com	Charlotte	NC	28203	704-377-1755	
Gary Public Transportation Corp 2101 W 35th Ave Web: www.gptcbus.com	Gary	IN	46408	219-884-6100	
GATRA 2 Oak St Web: www.gatra.org	Taunton	MA	02780	508-823-8828	
Geauga County Transit 12555 Merritt Rd. TF Cust Svc: 888-287-7190 ■ Web: www.geaugatransit.org	Chardon	OH	44024	440-279-2150	285-9476
Girardin Minibus Inc 3000 rue Girardin Web: www.girardin.com	Drummondville	QC	J2E0A1	819-477-2012	
Greyhound Canada Transportation Corp 1111 International Blvd Ste 700 TF: 800-661-8747 ■ Web: www.greyhound.ca	Burlington	ON	L7L6W1	800-661-8747	
Indianapolis Public Transportation Corporation ÿ1501 W Washington St Web: www.indygo.net	Indianapolis	IN	46204	317-635-3344	
Jefferson Lines 2100 E 26th St TF Cust Svc: 800-767-5333 ■ Web: www.jeffersonlines.com	Minneapolis	MN	55404	612-359-3400	359-3437
Jefferson Partners LP 2100 E 26th St TF Cust Svc: 800-767-5333 ■ Web: www.jeffersonlines.com	Minneapolis	MN	55404	612-359-3400	359-3437
Long Beach Transit 1963 E Anaheim St Web: www.lbtransit.com	Long Beach	CA	90813	562-591-2301	
M & L Transit Systems Inc 60 Olympia Ave Ste 1 Web: www.mlts.com	Woburn	MA	01801	781-938-8646	
Martha's Vineyard Regional Transit Authority 11 A St MV Business Pk RR 1 PO Box 10. Web: www.vineyardtransit.com	Edgartown	MA	02539	508-693-9440	693-9953
Martz Trailways 239 Old River Rd Web: www.martztrailways.com	Wilkes-Barre	PA	18702	570-821-3838	821-3835
Merced Transportation Co 300 Grogan Ave	Merced	CA	95341	209-384-2575	
Mid-City Transit Corp 518 State Rt 17M. Web: www.midcitytransit.com	Middletown	NY	10940	845-343-4702	
Ozark Regional Transit 2423 E Robinson Ave TF: 800-865-5901 ■ Web: www.ozark.org	Springdale	AR	72764	479-756-5901	
Pacific Transit System 216 N Second St TF: 800-833-6388 ■ Web: www.pacifictransit.org	Raymond	WA	98577	360-875-9418	942-3193
Pelivan Transit 333 S Oak St PO Box B. TF: 800-482-4594 ■ Web: okladot.state.ok.us	Big Cabin	OK	74332	918-783-5793	783-5786
Peter Pan Bus Lines Inc 1776 Main St TF: 800-237-8747 ■ Web: www.peterpanbus.com	Springfield	MA	01103	413-786-9300	747-7626
Pima County Dept of Transportation Transportation Systems Div 201 N Stone Ave Fourth Fl Web: www.dot.pima.gov	Tucson	AZ	85701	520-740-6410	740-6341
Powder River Transportation 1700 U S 14. TF: 888-970-7233 ■ Web: www.coachusa.com	Gillette	WY	82716	307-682-0960	
Rail Transit Consultants Inc 901 S Railroad St. Web: www.railtransit.com	Penn	PA	15675	724-527-2386	
RailCrew Xpress LLC 15729 College Blvd Web: www.railcrewxpress.com	Lenexa	KS	66219	913-928-5000	
Ramblin Express Transportation 3465 Astrozon Pl Web: www.ramblinexpress.com	Colorado Springs	CO	80910	719-590-8687	
Rimrock Stages Inc 1660 W Broadway St. TF: 800-255-7655 ■ Web: webstore.trailways.com	Missoula	MT	59808	406-549-2339	
Rural Community Transportation Inc (RCT) 1161 Portland St. Web: sites.google.com/a/rctvt.org/riderct	Saint Johnsbury	VT	05819	802-748-8170	748-5275
Rural Transit Enterprises Coordinated Inc (RTEC) 100 E Main St. TF: 800-321-7832 ■ Web: www.4rtec.com	Mount Vernon	KY	40456	606-256-9835	256-2181
Southeastern Stages Inc 260 University Ave SW Web: www.southeasternstages.com	Atlanta	GA	30315	404-591-2780	591-2745
Spokane Transit Authority Route & Schedule Information 328 Ride 701 W Riverside Ave. Web: www.spokanetransit.com	Spokane	WA	99201	509-456-7277	

Phone *Fax*

Star Shuttle & Charter 1343 Hallmark Dr San Antonio TX 78216 210-341-6000
Web: www.starshuttle.com

Suburban Transit Corp 750 Somerset St New Brunswick NJ 08901 732-249-1100 545-7015
TF: 800-222-0492 ■ *Web:* www.coachusa.com

Thunderbird Rural Public Transportation System
2801 W Loop 306 Ste A PO Box 60050 San Angelo TX 76904 325-944-9666 947-8286
TF: 877-947-8729 ■ *Web:* www.cvcog.org/cvcog/trans_rural.html

Tornado Bus Company Inc 535 E Jefferson Blvd Dallas TX 75203 214-941-7399
Web: www.tornadobus.com

Training Advantage, The PO Box 800 Ignacio CO 81137 970-563-4517
Web: www.sucap.org

Trans-Bridge Lines Inc 2012 Industrial Dr Bethlehem PA 18017 610-868-6001 868-9057
TF: 800-962-9135 ■ *Web:* www.transbridgelines.com

Veolia Transport Quebec Inc
720 rue Trotter Saint-jean-sur-richelieu QC J3B8T2 450-348-5599
Web: www.veoliatransport.qc.ca

Viking Trailways 201 Glendale Rd Joplin MO 64804 417-781-2779 781-2778
TF: 800-400-2779 ■ *Web:* trailways.com

109 BUS SERVICES - SCHOOL

Phone *Fax*

Birnie Bus Service Inc 248 Otis St Rome NY 13441 315-336-3950 339-5957
TF: 800-734-3950 ■ *Web:* birniebus.com

Brown Bus Co 2111 E Sherman Ave Nampa ID 83686 208-466-4181 466-2861
Web: www.brownbuscompany.com

Cook-Illinois Corp 4845 167th St Ste 300 Oak Forest IL 60452 708-560-9840 560-0661
Web: cookillinois.com

Davidsmeyer Bus Service Inc
2513 E Higgins Rd Elk Grove Village IL 60007 847-437-3767 437-4978
TF: 800-323-0312 ■ *Web:* www.bus-charter.com/aboutus-dsm.htm

Dean Transportation Inc 4812 Aurelius Rd Lansing MI 48910 517-319-8300 319-8384
TF: 800-282-3326 ■ *Web:* deantransportation.com

First Student Inc 600 Vine St Cincinnati OH 45202 513-241-2200
Web: www.firststudentinc.com

Hastings Bus Co 425 31st St E Hastings MN 55033 651-437-1888 438-3319
TF: 800-210-6362 ■ *Web:* www.minnesotacoaches.com

Independent Coach Corp 25 Wanser Ave Inwood NY 11096 516-239-1100 239-8641
Web: independentcoach.com

John T Cyr & Sons Inc 153 Gilman Falls Ave Old Town ME 04468 207-827-2335 827-6763
TF: 800-244-2335 ■ *Web:* www.cyrbustours.com

Johnson School Bus Services Inc
2151 W Washington St PO Box 285 West Bend WI 53095 262-334-3146 334-8019
Web: www.johnsonschoolbus.com

Kobussen Buses Ltd W914 County Rd CE Kaukauna WI 54130 920-766-0606 766-0797
TF: 800-447-0116 ■ *Web:* www.kobussen.com

Krapf Bus Cos 1030 Andrew Dr West Chester PA 19380 610-594-2664 594-5011
Web: www.krapfbus.com

Krise Bus Service Inc 119 Bus Ln Punxsutawney PA 15767 814-938-5250

Michael's Transportation Service Inc
140 Yolano Dr Vallejo CA 94589 707-643-2099 643-1906
TF Cust Svc: 800-295-2448 ■ *Web:* bustransportation.com

Mid-Columbia Bus Co 73458 Bus Barn Ln Pendleton OR 97801 541-278-1444 276-5205
Web: www.midcobus.com

Monroe School Transportation
970 Emerson St Rochester NY 14606 585-458-3230 458-9159
Web: monroeschooltrans.com

Pioneer Transportation Corp
2890 Arthur Kill Rd Staten Island NY 10309 718-984-8077 984-6588
Web: pioneerbus.com

Riteway Bus Service Inc Motorcoach Div
W201 N13900 Fond du Lac Ave Richfield WI 53076 262-677-3282 677-3121
TF: 800-776-7026 ■ *Web:* goriteway.com/

Rocky Mountain Transportation Inc
1410 E Edgewood Whitefish MT 59937 406-863-1200 863-1213
Web: www.rockymountaintrans.com

Royal Coach Lines Inc 924 Broadway Thornwood NY 10594 914-747-9494 747-9497
Web: royalcoachlines.com

Safe-Way Bus Co 6030 Carmen Ave Inver Grove Heights MN 55076 651-451-1375 451-3525

Stock Transportation Ltd
128 Wellington St W Ste 201 Barrie ON L4N1K9 888-952-0878
TF: 888-952-0878 ■ *Web:* www.stocktransportation.com

Student Transportation of America Inc (STA)
3349 Hwy 138 Bldg B Ste D Wall NJ 07719 732-280-4200 280-4214
TF: 888-942-2250 ■ *Web:* www.ridestbus.com

Suffolk Transportation Service Inc
10 Moffitt Blvd Bay Shore NY 11706 631-665-3245 665-3186
Web: www.suffolkbus.com

WE Transport Inc 75 Commercial St Plainview NY 11803 516-349-8200 349-8275
Web: www.wetransport.com

Williams Bus Lines Inc PO Box 1272 Springfield VA 22151 703-560-5355 560-7851
Web: www.williamsbus.com

110 BUSINESS FORMS

SEE ALSO Printing Companies - Commercial Printers p. 2965

Phone *Fax*

Ace Forms of Kansas Inc 2900 N Rotary Terr Pittsburg KS 66762 800-223-9287 232-1111*
**Fax Area Code:* 620 ■ *TF:* 800-223-9287 ■ *Web:* www.aceforms.com

Allison Payment Systems LLC
2200 Production Dr Indianapolis IN 46241 800-755-2440 808-2477*
**Fax Area Code:* 317 ■ *TF:* 800-755-2440 ■ *Web:* www.apsllc.com

Amsterdam Printing & Litho Corp
166 Wallins Corners Rd Amsterdam NY 12010 518-842-6000 843-5204
TF Cust Svc: 800-833-6231 ■ *Web:* www.amsterdamprinting.com

Apex Color 200 N Lee St Jacksonville FL 32204 800-367-6790 358-8811*
**Fax Area Code:* 904 ■ *TF:* 800-367-6790 ■ *Web:* www.apexcolor.net

Bestforms Inc 1135 Avenida Acaso Camarillo CA 93012 805-383-6993 987-5280
TF: 800-350-0618 ■ *Web:* www.bestforms.com

Phone *Fax*

Central States Business Forms Inc
2500 Industrial Pkwy Dewey OK 74029 800-331-0920 534-3470*
**Fax Area Code:* 918 ■ *TF:* 800-331-0920 ■ *Web:* www.centralstates.net

Champion Industries Inc
PO Box 2968 PO Box 2968 Huntington WV 25728 304-528-2791 528-2746
OTC: CHMP ■ *TF:* 800-624-3431 ■ *Web:* champion-industries.com

Curtis 1000 Inc 1725 Breckinridge Pkwy Ste 500 Duluth GA 30096 678-380-9095 944-8817*
**Fax Area Code:* 800 ■ *TF:* 877-287-8715 ■ *Web:* www.curtis1000.com

Custom Business Forms Inc 210 Edge Pl Minneapolis MN 55418 612-789-0002 789-6321
TF General: 800-234-1221 ■ *Web:* www.cbfnet.com

DATA Group (DBF) 9195 Torbram Rd Brampton ON L6S6H2 905-791-3151 791-3277
Web: ca.kompass.com

Data Papers Inc 468 Industrial Pk Rd Muncy PA 17756 800-233-3032 546-2366*
**Fax Area Code:* 888 ■ *TF:* 800-233-3032 ■ *Web:* www.datapapers.com

Data Source Inc 1400 Universal Ave Kansas City MO 64120 816-483-3282 483-3284
TF: 877-846-9120 ■ *Web:* www.data-source.com

Datatel Resources Corp 1729 Pennsylvania Ave Monaca PA 15061 724-775-5300 775-0688
TF: 800-245-2688 ■ *Web:* www.datatelcorp.com

DFS Group 500 Main St Groton MA 01471 800-225-9528 876-6337
TF General: 800-225-9528 ■ *Web:* www.dfsbusiness.com

Dupli-Systems Inc 8260 Dow Cir Strongsville OH 44136 440-234-9415 234-2350
TF: 800-321-1610 ■ *Web:* www.dupli-systems.com

Eagle Graphics Inc 150 N Moyer St Annville PA 17003 717-867-5576 867-5579
Web: www.eaglegraphic.com

Eastern Business Forms Inc PO Box 10 Mauldin SC 29662 800-387-2648
TF: 800-387-2648 ■ *Web:* www.ebf-inc.com

Falcon Business Forms Inc 45 Industrial Pk Corsicana TX 75110 903-874-6583
Web: www.ennis.com

Federal Business Products Inc 95 Main Ave Clifton NJ 07014 973-667-9800
TF: 800-927-5123 ■ *Web:* www.feddirect.com

FedEx 450 W First Ave Roselle NJ 07203 908-245-4400
TF: 800-463-3339 ■ *Web:* www.howardpress.com

Flesh Co 2118 59th St Saint Louis MO 63110 314-781-4400 781-5546*
**Fax:* Sales ■ *TF:* 800-869-3330 ■ *Web:* www.fleshco.com

Forms Manufacturers Inc 312 E Forest Ave Girard KS 66743 620-724-8225 724-8188
TF: 800-835-0614 ■ *Web:* www.formsmanufacturers.com

Freedom Graphic Systems Inc (FGS)
1101 S Janesville St Milton WI 53563 800-334-3540
TF: 800-334-3540 ■ *Web:* fgs.com

General Credit Forms Inc (GCF)
3595 Rider Trl S Earth City MO 63045 314-216-8600 216-8570
TF: 888-423-6397 ■ *Web:* www.gcfinc.com

Genoa Business Forms Inc 445 Pk Ave Sycamore IL 60178 800-383-2801 895-8206*
**Fax Area Code:* 815 ■ *TF:* 800-383-2801 ■ *Web:* www.genoabusforms.com

Gulf Business Forms Inc
2460 S IH-35 PO Box 1073 San Marcos TX 78667 512-353-8313 353-8866
TF: 800-433-4853 ■ *Web:* www.gulfforms.com

Highland Computer Forms Inc 1025 W Main St Hillsboro OH 45133 937-393-4215 842-6485*
**Fax Area Code:* 800 ■ **Fax:* Sales ■ *TF:* 800-669-5213 ■ *Web:* www.hcf.com

Hospital Forms & Systems Corp
8900 Ambassador Row Dallas TX 75247 214-634-8900 905-3819
TF: 800-527-5081 ■ *Web:* www.hforms.com

IBS Direct 431 Yerkes Rd King of Prussia PA 19406 610-265-8210 265-7997
TF: 800-220-1255 ■ *Web:* www.ibsdm.com

Imperial Graphics Inc
3100 Walkent Dr NW Grand Rapids MI 49544 800-777-2591 784-8256*
**Fax Area Code:* 616 ■ *TF:* 800-777-2591 ■ *Web:* www.imperialcrs.com

Integrated Print & Graphics (IPG)
645 Stevenson Rd South Elgin IL 60177 847-695-6777 741-4090
Web: www.ipandginc.com

Kaye-Smith 4101 Oakesdale Ave SW Renton WA 98057 425-228-8600 271-0203
TF: 800-822-9987 ■ *Web:* www.kayesmith.com

Liberty-Pittsburgh Systems Inc
3498 Grand Ave Pittsburgh PA 15225 412-771-9900 577-3456*
**Fax Area Code:* 877

NCP Solutions 5200 E Lake Blvd Birmingham AL 35217 205-849-5200 421-7387
Web: www.ncpsolutions.com

New Jersey Business Forms Manufacturing Co
55 W Sheffield Ave Englewood NJ 07631 201-569-4500 569-1137
TF: 800-466-6523 ■ *Web:* www.njbf.com

Paris Business Products 800 Highland Dr Westampton NJ 08060 609-265-9200 261-4853
TF Cust Svc: 800-523-6454 ■ *Web:* www.pariscorp.com

Patterson Office Supplies 3310 N Duncan Rd Champaign IL 61822 217-351-5400
TF: 800-637-1140 ■ *Web:* www.pattersonofficesupplies.com

Performance Office Papers
21565 Hamburg Ave Lakeville MN 55044 800-458-7189 488-5058
TF: 800-458-7189 ■ *Web:* www.perfpapers.com

PrintEdd Products of North America
2641 N Forum Dr Grand Prairie TX 75052 972-660-3800 641-2564
TF: 800-367-6728 ■ *Web:* www.printedd.com

Quality Forms 4317 W US Rt 36 Piqua OH 45356 937-773-4595 550-3937*
**Fax Area Code:* 888 ■ *Web:* www.qualforms.com

Rotary Forms Press Inc 835 S High St Hillsboro OH 45133 937-393-3426 393-8473
TF: 800-654-2876 ■ *Web:* www.rotaryformspress.com

Royal Business Forms Inc 3301 Ave E E Arlington TX 76011 817-640-5248 633-2164
TF: 800-255-9303 ■ *Web:* royalbf.com

Socrates Media LLC 111 S Wacker Dr Chicago IL 60606 877-860-4649
TF: 877-860-4649 ■ *Web:* www.tops-products.com

Source4 3944 S Morgan Chicago IL 60609 773-247-4141 247-1313
Web: www.source4.com

Specialized Printed Forms Inc 352 Ctr St Caledonia NY 14423 585-538-2381 538-4922
TF: 800-688-2381 ■ *Web:* www.spforms.com

Standard Register Co 600 Albany St Dayton OH 45417 937-221-1825 221-1205*
OTC: SRCTQ ■ **Fax:* Sales ■ *TF:* 800-755-6405 ■ *Web:* www.stdreg.com

Sterling Business Forms PO Box 2486 White City OR 97503 800-759-3676 234-2409
TF Cust Svc: 800-759-3676 ■ *Web:* www.sbfnet.com

Stry-Lenkoff Co Inc 1100 W Broadway Louisville KY 40232 502-587-6804 587-6822
TF: 800-626-8247 ■ *Web:* www.strylenkoff.com

United Business Forms Inc
8482 W Allens Bridge Rd Greeneville TN 37743 423-639-5551
Web: greenevillesun.com/

Victor Printing Inc One Victor Way Sharon PA 16146 724-342-2106 342-6147
TF: 800-443-2845 ■ *Web:* www.victorptg.com

Phone Fax

Ward-Kraft Inc 2401 Cooper St .... Fort Scott KS 66701 620-223-5500 223-6953
TF: 800-821-4021 ■ *Web:* www.wardkraft.com

Wilmer Service Line 515 W Sycamore St .... Coldwater OH 45828 800-494-5637 553-4849
TF: 800-494-5637 ■ *Web:* www.4wilmer.com

Wise Business Forms Inc
555 McFarland 400 Dr .... Alpharetta GA 30004 770-442-1060 442-9849
TF: 888-815-9473 ■ *Web:* www.wbf.com

Witt Printing Company Inc
301 Oak St .... El Dorado Springs MO 64744 417-876-4721 876-4794
TF: 800-641-4342 ■ *Web:* www.wittprinting.com

Wright Business Forms Inc
645 Stevenson Rd .... South Elgin IL 60177 708-865-7600

Wright Business Graphics (WBG)
18440 NE San Rafael St PO Box 20489 .... Portland OR 97230 800-547-8397 661-0515*
**Fax Area Code:* 503 ■ *TF:* 800-547-8397 ■ *Web:* www.wrightbg.com

111 BUSINESS MACHINES - MFR

SEE ALSO Business Machines - Whol p. 1894; Calculators - Electronic p. 1899; Computer Equipment p. 2011; Photocopying Equipment & Supplies p. 2926

Phone Fax

Aaxon Laundry Systems
6100 N Powerline Rd .... Ft. Lauderdale FL 33309 954-772-7100
Web: www.aaxon.com

Abbott Vascular 26531 Ynez Rd .... Temecula CA 92591 800-227-9902
TF: 800-227-9902 ■ *Web:* www.abbottvascular.com

ACR Supply Company Inc 4040 S Alston Ave .... Durham NC 27713 919-765-8081
Web: www.acrsupply.com

Action Industrial Group LLC
1623 Cedar Line Dr .... Rock Hill SC 29730 803-324-2658
Web: www.actionindgroup.com

Agissar Corp 526 Benton St .... Stratford CT 06615 203-375-8662 375-5345
TF: 800-627-8256 ■ *Web:* www.agissar.com

Amano Cincinnati Inc 140 Harrison Ave .... Roseland NJ 07068 973-403-1900 364-1086
TF: 800-526-2559 ■ *Web:* www.amano.com

Atlantic Zeiser Inc 15 Patton Dr .... West Caldwell NJ 07006 973-228-0800 228-9064
Web: www.atlanticzeiser.com

Atlas Companies, The
5101 Commerce Crossing Dr .... Louisville KY 40259 502-779-2100
Web: www.atlas-co.com

Autometrix Precision Cutting Systems Inc
12098 Charles Dr .... Grass Valley CA 95945 530-477-5065
Web: www.autometrix.com

Better Packages Inc 255 Canal St PO Box 711 .... Shelton CT 06484 203-926-3722 926-3706
TF: 800-237-9151 ■ *Web:* www.betterpackages.com

Bidwell Industrial Group Inc
2055 S Main St .... Middletown CT 06457 860-346-9283 347-8775
Web: www.bidwellinc.com

Biosafe Engineering LLC
485 Southpoint Cir Ste 200 .... Brownsburg IN 46112 317-858-8099
Web: www.biosafelifesciences.com

Borin Manufacturing Inc
5741 Buckingham Pkwy Unit B .... Culver City CA 90230 310-822-1000
Web: borin.com

Brandt Tractor Ltd Hwy 1 E PO Box 3856 .... Regina SK S4P3R8 306-791-7777
Web: www.brandt.ca

Brother International Corp
100 Somerset Corporate Blvd .... Bridgewater NJ 08807 908-704-1700 704-8235
TF Cust Svc: 877-552-6255 ■ *Web:* www.brother-usa.com

Broudy Precision Equipment Co
Nine Union Hill Rd .... West Conshohocken PA 19428 610-825-7200
Web: www.broudyprecision.com

CCTF Corp 5407 - 53 Ave NW .... Edmonton AB T6B3G2 780-463-8700
Web: www.cctf.com

CCX Corp 1399 Horizon Ave .... Lafayette CO 80026 303-666-5206
Web: www.ccxcorp.com

CMD Corp 2901-3005 E Pershing St PO Box 1279 .... Appleton WI 54912 920-730-6888
Web: www.cmd-corp.com

CNC Industries Inc 3810 Fourier Dr .... Fort Wayne IN 46818 260-490-5700
Web: www.cncind.com

Col-Met Spray Booths Inc 1635 Innovation Dr .... Rockwall TX 75032 972-772-1919
Web: www.colmetsb.com

Con-tek Machine Inc 3575 Hoffman Rd E .... Saint Paul MN 55110 651-779-6058
Web: www.con-tek.com

Coop Purdel LA 155 Rue Saint-Jean-Baptiste .... Le Bic QC G0L1B0 418-736-4363
Web: www.purdel.qc.ca

Corma Inc 10 McCleary Court Concord .... Toronto ON L4K2Z3 905-669-9397
Web: www.corma.com

CP Bourg Inc 50 Samuel Barnet Blvd .... New Bedford MA 02745 508-998-2171 998-2391
Web: www.cpbourg.com

CRANE Merchandising Systems
2043 Woodland Pkwy Ste 102 .... St. Louis MO 63146 314-298-3500
Web: www.cranems.com

Crown Lift Trucks LLC 10685 Medallion Dr .... Cincinnati OH 45241 513-874-2600
Web: www.okisys.com

Cubeit Portable Storage Canada Inc
100 Canadian Rd .... Scarborough ON M1R4Z5 647-478-7618
Web: www.cubeit.ca

Cummins-Allison Corp
852 Feehanville Dr .... Mount Prospect IL 60056 847-299-9550 299-9550
TF: 800-786-5528 ■ *Web:* www.cumminsallison.com

Danco Equipment Inc 9111-41 Ave .... Edmonton AB T6E6M5 780-468-5151
Web: www.dancoequipment.com

Data Cable Technologies Inc
1306 Enterprise Dr .... Romeoville IL 60446 630-226-5600
Web: www.datacabletech.com

Dedoes Industries Inc
1060 W West Maple Rd .... Walled Lake MI 48390 248-624-7710
Web: www.dedoes.com

Dillin Engineered Systems Corp
8030 Broadstone Rd .... Perrysburg OH 43551 419-666-6789
Web: www.dillinautomation.com

Phone Fax

Distek Inc 121 N Ctr Dr .... North Brunswick NJ 08902 732-422-7585
Web: www.distekinc.com

Dynetics Engineering Corp 515 Bond St .... Lincolnshire IL 60069 847-541-7300 541-7488
TF: 800-888-8110 ■ *Web:* www.dyneticsengineering.com

Ecco Business Systems Inc
60 W 38th St 4th Fl .... New York NY 10018 212-921-4545 921-2198
TF: 800-558-6777 ■ *Web:* www.eccobusiness.com

ECRM Inc 554 Clark Rd .... Tewksbury MA 01876 978-851-0207 851-7016
TF: 800-537-3276 ■ *Web:* www.ecrm.com

Edgewater Automation LLC
481 Renaissance Dr .... St. Joseph MI 49085 269-983-1300
Web: www.edgewaterautomation.com

Elliot Equipment Corp
1131 Country Club Rd .... Indianapolis IN 46234 317-271-3065
Web: www.elliottequipment.com

Engrenage Provincial Inc 960 rue Raoul-Jobin .... Quebec QC G1N1S9 418-683-2745
Web: www.engrenageprovincial.com

Ernest Green & Son Ltd 2395 Skymark Ave .... Mississauga ON L4W4Y6 905-629-8999
Web: www.ernestgreen.com

Essex Electro Engineering Inc
2015 Mitchell Blvd .... Schaumburg IL 60193 847-891-4444
Web: www.essexelectro.com

Exocor Inc 271 Ridley Rd .... St. Catharines ON L2R6P7 905-704-0603
Web: exocor.com

Fabgroups Technologies Inc
1100 Saint Amour .... Saint-laurent QC H4S1J2 514-331-3712
Web: www.fabgroups.com

Fargo Automation Inc 969 34th St N .... Fargo ND 58102 701-232-1780
Web: www.fargoautomation.com

FCA LLC 7601 John Deere Pkwy PO Box 758 .... Moline IL 61266 309-792-3444
Web: www.fcapackaging.com

Felins USA Inc 8306 W Parkland Ct .... Milwaukee WI 53223 414-355-7747
Web: www.felins.com

Fellowes Inc 1789 Norwood Ave .... Itasca IL 60143 630-893-1600 893-1600*
**Fax:* Cust Svc ■ *TF:* 800-945-4545 ■ *Web:* www.fellowes.com

Fireside Hearth & Home 7571 215th St W .... Lakeville MN 55044 800-669-4328
TF: 800-669-4328 ■ *Web:* m.fireside.com

Fogg Filler Co 3455 John F Donnelly Dr .... Holland MI 49424 616-786-3644
Web: www.foggfiller.com

Foremost Machine Builders Inc
23 Spielman Rd .... Fairfield NJ 07004 973-227-0700
Web: foremostmachine.com

Fountain Industries Co 922 E 14th St .... Albert Lea MN 56007 507-373-2351
Web: www.fountainindustries.com

G & O Thermal Supply Co 5435 N Northwest Hwy .... Chicago IL 60630 773-763-1300
Web: www.gothermal.com

GalFab Inc 612 W 11th St PO Box 39 .... Winamac IN 46996 574-946-7767
Web: www.galfab.com

GenServe Inc 80 Sweeneydale Ave .... Bay Shore NY 11706 631-435-0437
Web: www.genserveinc.com

Global Payment Technologies Inc
170 Wilbur Pl .... Bohemia NY 11716 631-563-2500 563-2630
OTC: GPTX

Gradco USA Inc 871 Coronado Ctr Dr Ste 200 .... Henderson NV 89052 949-595-4374 595-4367
Web: www.gradco.com

Groves Industrial Supply Inc
7301 Pinemont Dr .... Houston TX 77040 713-675-4747
Web: www.grovesindustrial.com

Hewitt Material Handling Inc 425 Millway Ave .... Concord ON L4K3V8 905-669-6590
Web: www.hewittmaterialhandling.ca

HILLS Inc 7785 Ellis Rd .... West Melbourne FL 32904 321-724-2370
Web: www.hillsinc.net

HTS Engineering Ltd 115 Norfinch Dr .... Toronto ON M3N1W8 416-661-3400
Web: www.htseng.com

Imaging Business Machines LLC
2750 Crestwood Blvd .... Birmingham AL 35210 205-439-7100 956-5309
TF: 800-627-2269 ■ *Web:* www.ibml.com

Industrial Shredders
12037 S Ave PO Box 218 .... North Lima OH 44452 330-549-9960 549-9961
Web: www.industrialshredders.com

International Business Machines Corp (IBM)
One New OrchaRd Rd .... Armonk NY 10504 914-499-1900
NYSE: IBM ■ *TF:* 800-426-4968 ■ *Web:* www.ibm.com

J C Foodservice Inc
415 S Atlantic Blvd .... Monterey Park CA 91754 626-308-1988
Web: www.actionsales.com

Lakeside Process Controls Ltd
5250 Orbitor Dr .... Mississauga ON L4W5G7 905-629-9340
Web: www.lakesidecontrols.ca

Lathem Time Corp 200 Selig Dr SW .... Atlanta GA 30336 404-691-0400 252-2208*
**Fax Area Code:* 800 ■ *TF:* 800-241-4990 ■ *Web:* www.lathem.com

Leeson Canada Inc 320 Superior Blvd .... Mississauga ON L5T2N7 905-670-4770
Web: www.leeson.ca

Lynde-Ordway Company Inc 3308 W Warner Ave .... Santa Ana CA 92704 714-957-1311 433-2166
TF: 800-762-7057 ■ *Web:* www.lynde-ordway.com

MAAC Machinery Corp 590 Tower Blvd .... Carol Stream IL 60188 630-665-1700
Web: maacmachinery.com

Magnatech International Inc
17 E Meadow Ave .... Robesonia PA 19551 610-693-8866
Web: magnatech-int.com

Manitex Liftking ULC 7135 Islington Ave .... Woodbridge ON L4L1V9 905-851-3988
Web: www.manitexliftking.com

Maple Farm Equipment Partnership Hwy 10 E .... Yorkton SK S3N2V7 306-783-9459
Web: www.maplefarm.com

Martin Yale Industries Inc 251 Wedcor Ave .... Wabash IN 46992 260-563-0641 563-4575
TF: 800-225-5644 ■ *Web:* www.martinyale.com

MBM Corp (MBM) 3134 Industry Dr .... North Charleston SC 29418 843-552-2700 552-2974
TF Cust Svc: 800-223-2508 ■ *Web:* www.mbmcorp.com

Morehouse-COWLES 13930 Magnolia Ave .... Chino CA 91710 909-627-7222
Web: www.morehousecowles.com

National Lift Truck Inc
3333 Mount Prospect Rd .... Franklin Park IL 60131 630-782-1000
Web: www.nlt.com

Phone Fax

Neopost Inc Canada 150 Steelcase Rd W............Markham ON L3R3J9 905-475-3722 475-7699
TF: 800-636-7678 ■ Web: www.neopost.ca
Newbold Corp 450 Weaver St....................Rocky Mount VA 24151 540-489-4400 489-4417
TF: 800-552-3282 ■ Web: www.addressograph.com
Nissei America Inc 1480 N Hancock St..............Anaheim CA 92807 714-693-3000
Web: www.nisseiamerica.com
Noble Trade Inc 7171 Jane St......................Concord ON L4K1A7 416-754-5533
Web: www.noble.ca
Norchem Corp 5649 Alhambra Ave................Los Angeles CA 90032 323-221-0221
Web: norchemcorp.com
Nordon Inc One Cabot Blvd E.....................Langhorne PA 19047 215-504-4700
Web: www.nordoninc.com
Norsask Farm Equipment Ltd Box 49.........North Battleford SK S9A2X6 306-445-8128
Web: www.norsaskfarmequipmentltd.com
Norwesco Industries (1983) Ltd
6908L - Sixth St SE...............................Calgary AB T2H2K4 403-258-3883
Web: www.norwesco.ab.ca
Ossur 27412 Aliso Viejo Pkwy.....................Aliso Viejo CA 92656 800-233-6263
TF: 800-233-6263 ■ Web: www.ossur.com
Outotec (Canada) Ltd 1551 Corporate Dr...........Burlington ON L7L6M3 905-335-0002
Web: www.outotec.com
Paymaster Technologies Inc
61 Garlisch Dr...........................Elk Grove Village IL 60007 847-758-1234
Web: www.paymastertech.com
Peerless Inc 79 Perry St............................Buffalo NY 14203 716-852-4784
Web: www.peerless-inc.com
Pitney Bowes Inc One Elmcroft Rd.................Stamford CT 06926 203-356-5000 460-3851
NYSE: PBI ■ TF: 800-672-6937 ■ Web: pitneybowes.com/us
Preston Phipps Inc 6400 Vanden Abeele............Montreal QC H4S1R9 514-333-5340
Web: prestonphipps.com
Process Control Corp 6875 Mimms Dr...............Atlanta GA 30340 770-449-8810
Web: www.process-control.com
Proco Machinery 1111 Brevik Pl.................Mississauga ON L4W3R7 905-602-6066
Web: procomachinery.com
Proline Concrete Tools Inc 2560 Jason Ct.........Oceanside CA 92056 760-758-7240
Web: www.prolinestamps.com
Pubco Corp 3830 Kelley Ave.......................Cleveland OH 44114 216-881-5300 881-8380
TF: 800-878-3399 ■ Web: fundinguniverse.com
Puregas LLC 226 Commerce St Unit A...............Broomfield CO 80020 303-427-3700
Web: puregas.com
Rapid Line Industries Inc 455 N Ottawa St.............Joliet IL 60432 815-727-4362
Web: rapidline.com
Red Streak Corp 1627 Main St Ste 901............Kansas City MO 64108 816-471-6979 471-1143
Reed Machinery Inc 10A New Bond St.............Worcester MA 01606 508-595-9090
Web: www.reed-machinery.com
Rimex Supply Ltd 9726 186th St......................Surrey BC V4N3N7 604-888-0025
Web: www.rimex.com
Royal Consumer Information Products Inc
379 Campus Dr 2nd Fl..........................Somerset NJ 08873 732-627-9977 232-9769*
*Fax Area Code: 800 ■ TF Sales: 888-261-4555 ■ Web: www.royalsupplies.com
Russell Forest Products Inc
719 Railroad St SW...............................Hartselle AL 35640 256-773-1607
Web: www.russellforest.com
Schaumburg Specialties Co
550 Albion Ave Unit 30........................Schaumburg IL 60193 800-834-8125
TF: 800-834-8125 ■ Web: www.shopcraftracks.com
Schold Machine Corp 7201 W 64th Pl............Bedford Park IL 60638 708-458-3788
Web: www.schold.com
Schuneman Equipment Co
15058 SD Hwy 15 PO Box 229.......................Milbank SD 57252 605-432-5523
Web: www.schunemanequipment.com
Seamless Technologies Inc 35 Airport Rd.........Morristown NJ 07960 973-326-8900
Web: www.seamlessti.com
Security Check LLC 2612 Jackson Ave W..............Oxford MS 38655 662-234-0440
Security Engineered Machinery Company Inc
Five Walkup Dr PO Box 1045...................Westborough MA 01581 508-366-1488 836-4154
TF Sales: 800-225-9293 ■ Web: www.semshred.com
Shalon Ventures 155 Island Dr.....................Palo Alto CA 94301 650-566-8200
Web: www.shalon.com
Sharp Electronics Corp One Sharp Plz...............Mahwah NJ 07430 201-529-8200 529-8413
TF: 800-237-4277 ■ Web: www.sharpusa.com
Skyjack Inc 55 Campbell Rd.........................Guelph ON N1H1B9 519-837-0888
Web: www.skyjack.com
Sonar Products Inc 609 Industrial Rd..............Carlstadt NJ 07072 201-729-1116
Web: sonarproductsinc.com
Sonoro Energy Ltd
Ste 1000 600 - Sixth Ave SW........................Calgary AB T2P0S5 403-262-3252
Web: www.sonoroenergy.com
Spartan Controls Ltd 305 - 27 St SE.................Calgary AB T2A7V2 403-207-0700
Web: www.spartancontrols.com
Staplex Co 777 Fifth Ave..........................Brooklyn NY 11232 718-768-3333 965-0750
TF Cust Svc: 800-221-0822 ■ Web: www.staplex.com
Stemmerich Inc 4728 Gravois Ave................Saint Louis MO 63116 314-832-7726
Web: www.stemmerich.com
STT Enviro Corp 8485 Parkhill Dr.....................Milton ON L9T5E9 905-693-9301
Web: www.sttsemcan.com
Sturtevant Inc 348 Circuit St.......................Hanover MA 02339 781-829-6501
Web: www.sturtevantinc.com
Supfina Machine Company Inc
181 Circuit Dr............................North Kingstown RI 02852 401-294-6600
Web: www.supfina.com
Swintec Corp 320 W Commercial Ave..............Moonachie NJ 07074 201-935-0115 933-9745
TF: 800-225-0867 ■ Web: www.swintec.com
TeraDiode Inc 30 Upton Dr......................Wilmington MA 01887 978-988-1040
Web: www.teradiode.com
Tundra Process Solutions Ltd
7523 Flint Rd SE...................................Calgary AB T2H1G3 403-255-5222
Web: www.tundrasolutions.ca
Updike Supply Inc 8241 Expansion Way..........Huber Heights OH 45424 937-482-4000
Web: www.updikesupply.com
Vincent Corp 2810 E Fifth Ave.........................Tampa FL 33605 813-248-2650
Web: www.vincentcorp.com
Westward Parts Services Ltd 6517 - 67 St..........Red Deer AB T4P1A3 403-340-1160
Web: www.westwardparts.com
William F. White International Inc
800 Islington Ave................................Toronto ON M8Z6A1 416-239-5050
Web: www.whites.com
Wolseley Canada Inc 880 Laurentian Dr...........Burlington ON L7N3V6 905-335-7373
Web: www.wolseleyinc.ca
Wright Implement Company LLC
3225 Carter Rd..................................Owensboro KY 42301 270-683-3606
Web: wrightimp.com

112 BUSINESS MACHINES - WHOL

SEE ALSO Business Machines - Mfr p. 1893; Computer Equipment & Software - Whol p. 2015; Photocopying Equipment & Supplies p. 2926

Phone Fax

Adams Remco Inc PO Box 3968..................South Bend IN 46619 574-288-2113 288-1105
TF: 800-627-2113 ■ Web: www.adamsremco.com
Blue Technologies 5885 Grant Ave.................Cleveland OH 44105 216-271-4800 271-0084*
*Fax: Sales ■ Web: www.bluetechnologiesinc.com
Canon Business Solutions-Central
425 N Martingale Rd Ste 100.....................Schaumburg IL 60173 847-706-3400 706-3419*
*Fax: Hum Res ■ TF: 800-706-3303 ■ Web: www.solutions.canon.com
Canon Business Solutions-Southeast Inc
300 Commerce Sq Blvd...........................Burlington NJ 08016 609-387-8700 *
*Fax: Mktg ■ TF: 844-443-4636 ■ Web: www.solutions.canon.com
Canon Business Solutions-West
One Canon Park.....................................Melville CA 11747 844-443-4636
TF: 844-443-4636 ■ Web: www.solutions.canon.com
Carr Business Systems Inc 130 Spagnoli Rd...........Melville NY 11747 631-249-9880 249-0740
TF: 800-244-1880 ■ Web: www.carr-global.com
Copiers Northwest Inc 601 Dexter Ave N..............Seattle WA 98109 206-282-1200 282-2010
TF: 866-692-0700 ■ Web: www.copiersnw.com
CRS Inc 4851 White Bear Pkwy.....................Saint Paul MN 55110 651-294-2700 294-2900
TF: 800-333-4949 ■ Web: www.crs-usa.com
Daisy IT Supplies Sales & Service
8575 Red Oak Ave......................Rancho Cucamonga CA 91730 909-989-5585 989-5585
TF: 800-266-5585 ■ Web: daisyit.com
Datamax Office Systems Inc
6717 Waldemar Ave...............................Saint Louis MO 63139 314-633-1400 633-1402
TF: 800-325-9299 ■ Web: www.datamaxstl.com
Dieterich-Post Co 616 Monterey Pass Rd........Monterey Park CA 91754 626-289-5021 688-3729*
*Fax Area Code: 800 ■ TF: 800-955-3729 ■ Web: www.dieterich-post.com
El Dorado Trading Group Inc
760 San Antonio Rd..............................Palo Alto CA 94303 800-227-8292 494-1995*
*Fax Area Code: 650 ■ TF: 800-227-8292 ■ Web: www.edtg.com
FP Mailing Solutions 140 N Mitchell Ct..............Addison IL 60101 630-827-5500 225-5248
TF: 800-341-6052 ■ Web: www.fp-usa.com
Global Imaging Systems Inc
3820 Northdale Blvd Ste 200A.........................Tampa FL 33624 813-960-5508 264-7877
TF: 888-628-7834 ■ Web: www.global-imaging.com
GS Precision Inc
101 John Seitz Dr 1 Industrial Pk..................Brattleboro VT 05301 802-257-5200 257-7937
Web: www.gsprecision.com
Illinois Wholesale Cash Register Inc
2790 Pinnacle Dr...................................Elgin IL 60124 847-310-4200 310-8490
TF: 800-544-5493 ■ Web: www.illinoiswholesale.com
Konica Minolta Business Solutions USA Inc
100 Williams Dr....................................Ramsey NJ 07446 201-825-4000
Web: www.kmbs.konicaminolta.us
Merchants Solutions Co 4422 Roosevelt Rd...........Hillside IL 60162 708-449-6650 449-1432
TF: 800-486-3214 ■ Web: www.merchants-solutions.com
Metro - Sales Inc 1640 E 78th St................Minneapolis MN 55423 612-861-4000 866-8069
TF: 800-862-7414 ■ Web: www.metrosales.com
Numeridex Inc 632 S Wheeling Rd.................Wheeling IL 60090 800-323-7737 541-8392*
*Fax Area Code: 847 ■ TF: 800-323-7737 ■ Web: www.numeridex.com
Pitney Bowes Inc One Elmcroft Rd.................Stamford CT 06926 203-356-5000 460-3851
NYSE: PBI ■ TF: 800-672-6937 ■ Web: pitneybowes.com/us
Ricoh Americas Corp Five Dedrick Pl............West Caldwell NJ 07006 973-882-2000 882-2100
TF: 800-727-1885 ■ Web: www.ricoh-usa.com
Secap USA Inc 10 Clipper Rd..................Conshohocken PA 19428 610-825-6205 825-6205
TF: 800-523-0320 ■ Web: www.secap.com
Standard Duplicating Machines Corp
10 Connector Rd.................................Andover MA 01810 978-470-1920 475-1900
TF: 800-526-4774 ■ Web: www.sdmc.com
Stewart Engineering Supply Inc
3221 E Pioneer Pkwy.............................Arlington TX 76010 817-640-1767 633-7231
TF: 800-533-1265 ■ Web: www.sesisupply.com
Systel Business Equipment Company Inc
3756 Sycamore Dairy Rd.......................Fayetteville NC 28303 910-483-7114 483-2846
TF: 800-849-5900 ■ Web: www.systeloa.com
Transco Business Technologies (TBT)
34 Leighton Rd...................................Augusta ME 04330 207-622-6251 621-8620
TF: 800-322-0003 ■ Web: www.transcobusiness.com

BUSINESS ORGANIZATIONS

SEE Management & Business Professional Associations p. 1803; Chambers of Commerce - Canadian p. 1909; Chambers of Commerce - International p. 1911; Chambers of Commerce - US - Local p. 1914; Chambers of Commerce - US - State p. 1942

113 BUSINESS SERVICE CENTERS

Phone Fax

A & d Technical Supply Company Inc
4320 S 89th St .... Omaha NE 68127 402-592-4950
Web: www.adtechnicalsupplyco.com

Acclaim Print & Copy Centers Inc
7106 Dublin Blvd .... Dublin CA 94568 925-829-7750
Web: www.acclaimprint.com

Accurate Printing Inc
2380 Research Court Ste 100..................... Woodbridge VA 22192 703-494-0707
Web: www.accurateprinting.com

Allegra Graphic Design Group
3983 Linden Ave SE .... Grand Rapids MI 49548 616-248-4110
Web: allegragr.com

Allegra Network LLC 47585 Galleon Dr .... Plymouth MI 48170 248-596-8600 596-8601
TF General: 800-726-9050 ■ *Web:* www.allegranetwork.com

Aloha Petroleum Ltd 1132 Bishop St Ste 1700......... Honolulu HI 96813 808-522-9700 522-9707
TF: 800-621-4654 ■ *Web:* www.alohagas.com

Alphanumeric Systems Inc 3801 Wake Forest Rd ...... Raleigh NC 27609 919-781-7575 872-1440
TF: 800-638-6556 ■ *Web:* www.alphanumeric.com

Aminian Business Services Inc 50 Tesla .... Irvine CA 92618 949-724-1155
Web: www.aminian.com

Annex Brands Inc
7580 Metropolitan Dr Ste 200 .... San Diego CA 92108 619-563-4800 563-9850
TF: 877-722-5236 ■ *Web:* www.gopackagingstore.com

Ares Corp 1440 Chapin Ave Ste 390 .... Burlingame CA 94010 650-401-7100 401-7101
Web: www.arescorporation.com

Asi System Integration Inc 48 W 37th St............. New York NY 10018 866-308-3920 629-3944*
**Fax Area Code:* 212 ■ *TF:* 866-308-3920 ■ *Web:* www.asisystem.com

Avalon Copy Centers of America Inc
901 N State St.................................. Syracuse NY 13208 315-471-3333
Web: www.teamavalon.com

B2B Workforce Inc 200 N Pt Ctr E Ste 150 .... Alpharetta GA 30022 770-667-7200 479-2423*
**Fax Area Code:* 404

Barrister Digital Solutions LLC
1700 K St Nw Ste B100 .... Washington DC 20006 202-289-7279
Web: www.barristerdigital.com

Belmark Inc 600 Heritage Rd PO Box 5310 .... De Pere WI 54115 920-336-2848 336-4577
Web: www.belmark.com

Bright Trading LLC 4850 Harrison Dr .... Las Vegas NV 89121 702-739-1393 739-1398
Web: www.stocktrading.com

C2 Reprographics Inc 3180 Pullman St .... Costa Mesa CA 92626 714-545-0112
Web: www.c2repro.com

Capitol Copy Service 116 W State St .... Trenton NJ 08608 609-989-8776
Web: capitol-copy.com

Coastal Reprographics Services
880 Via Esteban Ste B....................... San Luis Obispo CA 93401 805-543-5247
Web: coastalreprographics.com

Color Reflections 10795 Rockley Rd.................. Houston TX 77099 713-626-4045 623-6810
Web: www.colorreflections.com

Composites Horizons Inc 1471 Industrial Pk St .... Covina CA 91722 626-331-0861 339-3220
Web: aipaerospace.com/composites-home/

Concentrix Corp 3750 Monroe Ave................... Pittsford NY 14534 585-218-5300 218-5301
TF: 800-747-0583 ■ *Web:* www.concentrix.com

Copymat Digibranch 191 Battery St .... San Francisco CA 94111 415-981-1300
Web: www.copymat3.com

Core Bts Inc 3001 W Beltline Hwy .... Madison WI 53713 608-661-7700
Web: www.corebts.com

Corporation Service Co
2711 Centerville Rd Ste 400...................... Wilmington DE 19808 302-636-5400 636-5454
TF: 866-403-5272 ■ *Web:* www.cscglobal.com

Craters & Freighters 331 Corporate Cir Ste J .... Golden CO 80401 800-736-3335 399-9964*
**Fax Area Code:* 303 ■ *TF:* 800-736-3335 ■ *Web:* www.cratersandfreighters.com

Davinci Institute Inc
511 E S Boulder Rd Ste 3.......................... Louisville CO 80027 303-666-4133
Web: davinciinstitute.com

Digital Discovery Solutions LP
504 Lavaca St 800 .... Austin TX 78701 512-476-3371
Web: digitaldiscoverysolutions.com

Ditto Document Solutions
610 Smithfield St .... Pittsburgh PA 15222 412-434-6666
Web: www.dittodocument.com

Dragonfly Technologies 48 Wall St Ste 1100 .... New York NY 10005 212-713-5250 202-4625
Web: www.dragonflytech.com

Duncan-Parnell Inc 900 S McDowell St .... Charlotte NC 28204 704-372-7766 333-3845
TF: 800-849-7708 ■ *Web:* www.duncan-parnell.com

e4e Inc 10720 Gilroy Rd .... Hunt Valley MD 21031 410-568-3075
Web: www.e4e.com

Elbar Duplicator Corp
10526 Jamaica Ave........................... Richmond Hill NY 11418 718-441-1123
Web: www.reliable-mail.com

Errand Solutions LLC 118 S Clinton St Ste 250 .... Chicago IL 60661 312-475-3800
Web: www.errandsolutions.com

Evolve Discovery Inc
611 Mission St Fourth Fl .... San Francisco CA 94105 415-398-8600
Web: www.evolvediscovery.com

FedEx Kinko's Office & Print Services Inc
13155 Noel Rd Ste 1600............................. Dallas TX 75240 214-550-7000 550-7001
Web: fedex.com

Galaxie Coffee Services 110 Sea Ln............. Farmingdale NY 11735 631-694-2688
Web: galaxiecoffee.com

Group O Inc 4905 77th Ave............................ Milan IL 61264 309-736-8300 736-8301
TF Cust Svc: 800-752-0730 ■ *Web:* www.groupo.com

Hackworth Reprographics 1700 Liberty St......... Chesapeake VA 23324 757-545-7675
Web: www.hackworth.co

Himes Vending Inc 4654 Groves Rd .... Columbus OH 43232 614-868-6931
Web: himesvending.com

JAD Business Services Inc
1502 Columbia Cove Ct......................... Shady Side MD 20764 301-261-5538
Web: www.jadbsi.com

Phone Fax

Java Dave's Executive Coffee Service
6239 E 15th St .... Tulsa OK 74112 918-836-5570
Web: www.javadavescoffee.com

Juran Institute Inc 160 Main St Ste 100........... Southington CT 06489 203-267-3445 267-3446
Web: www.juran.com

Kal-blue Reprographics Inc 914 E Vine St.......... Kalamazoo MI 49001 269-349-8681
Web: www.kalblue.com

Mail Boxes Etc 6060 Cornerstone Ct W.............. San Diego CA 92121 858-455-8800 546-7493
TF: 800-789-4623 ■ *Web:* www.mbe.com

Mej Personal Business Services Inc
245 E 116th St .... New York NY 10029 212-426-6017
Web: www.mejpbs.com

Mele Printing Company LLC 619 N Tyler St.......... Covington LA 70433 985-893-9522
Web: www.meleprinting.com

Mid-West Fabricating Co 313 N Johns St............ Amanda OH 43102 740-969-4411 969-4433
Web: www.midwestfab.com

Miller Blue Print Co 501 W Sixth St .... Austin TX 78701 512-478-8793
Web: millerblueprint.com

Miller Systems Inc 175 Portland St 5th fl .... Boston MA 02114 617-266-4200
Web: www.millersystems.com

MRSCO Inc 801 N Capitol Ave..................... Indianapolis IN 46204 317-631-1000
Web: www.marbaugh.com

Ms Dallas Reprographics Inc 2300 Reagan St .... Dallas TX 75219 214-521-7000
Web: www.msdallas.com

Navis Logistics Network
6551 S Revere Pkwy Ste 250 .... Centennial CO 80111 800-344-3528 741-6653*
**Fax Area Code:* 303 ■ *TF:* 800-344-3528 ■ *Web:* www.gonavis.com

Navis Pack & Ship Centers
6551 S Revere Pkwy Ste 250 .... Centennial CO 80111 800-344-3528 741-6653*
**Fax Area Code:* 303 ■ *TF:* 800-344-3528 ■ *Web:* www.gonavis.com

New Jersey Legal Copy Inc 501 King Ave .... Cherry Hill NJ 08002 856-910-0202
Web: njlone.com

Objectwin Technology Inc
14800 St Mary's Ln Ste 100 .... Houston TX 77079 713-782-8200 782-8283
Web: www.objectwin.com

Office Depot Inc 2200 Old Germantown Rd......... Delray Beach FL 33445 561-438-4800 *
NASDAQ: ODP ■ **Fax:* Hum Res ■ *TF:* 800-937-3600 ■ *Web:* www.officedepot.com

Pacific Event Productions Inc
6989 Corte Santa Fe............................. San Diego CA 92121 858-458-9908 458-1173
Web: www.pacificevents.com

Pak Mail Centers of America Inc
7173 S Havana St Ste 600 .... Centennial CO 80112 303-957-1000 957-1015
TF Cust Svc: 800-778-6665 ■ *Web:* www.pakmail.com

Parcel Plus Inc 13121 Louetta Rd .... Cypress TX 77429 281-376-0054 376-0056
TF: 888-280-2053 ■ *Web:* www.parcelpluscypress.com

Peachtree Planning Corp 5040 Roswell Rd NE.......... Atlanta GA 30342 404-260-1600 260-1700
TF: 800-366-0839 ■ *Web:* www.peachtreeplanning.com

Postal Connections of America
6136 Frisco Sq Blvd Ste 400 .... Frisco TX 75034 800-767-8257 294-4550*
**Fax Area Code:* 619 ■ *TF:* 800-767-8257 ■ *Web:* www.postalconnections.com

PostalAnnex+ Inc
7580 Metropolitan Dr Ste 200 .... San Diego CA 92108 619-563-4800 563-9850
TF: 800-456-1525 ■ *Web:* www.postalannex.com

PostNet International Franchise Corp
1819 Wazee St .... Denver CO 80202 303-771-7100 771-7133
TF: 800-841-7171 ■ *Web:* www.postnet.com

Property One Inc
4141 Veterans Memorial Blvd Ste 300 .... Metairie LA 70002 504-681-3400 681-3438
Web: www.property-one.com

Schoeneckers Inc 7630 Bush Lake Rd............ Minneapolis MN 55439 952-835-4800 844-4033
Web: www.biworldwide.com

Sharp Decisions Inc 1040 Ave of the A............... New York NY 10018 212-481-5533 481-8751
TF: 800-742-7792 ■ *Web:* www.sharpdecisions.com

Shee Atika Inc 315 Lincoln St Ste 300.................. Sitka AK 99835 907-747-3534 747-5727
TF: 800-478-3534 ■ *Web:* www.sheeatika.com

Sir Speedy Inc 26722 Plaza Dr .... Mission Viejo CA 92691 949-348-5000 348-5066
TF: 800-854-8297 ■ *Web:* www.sirspeedy.com

Speedway Printing & Copy Center Inc
2575 N Causeway Blvd.......................... Mandeville LA 70471 985-327-7391
Web: speedwayprinting.net

Stone Rudolph & Henry PLC
124 Ctr Pointe Dr .... Clarksville TN 37040 931-648-4786 647-5445
Web: www.srhcpas.com

Target Copy 635 W Tennessee St .... Tallahassee FL 32304 850-224-3007
Web: www.targetcopy.com

Team National Inc 8210 W State Rd 84.................. Davie FL 33324 954-584-2151 584-2747
Web: www.bign.com

Technical Training Inc (TTI)
3903 W. Hamlin Rd......................... Rochester Hills MI 48309 248-853-5550 853-2411
Web: www.ttinao.com

Techno-sciences Inc
11750 Beltsville Dr Ste 300 .... Beltsville MD 20705 240-790-0600
Web: www.technosci.com

Total Energy Solutions LLC (TES)
100 International Dr Ste 260...................... Portsmouth NH 03801 877-436-9812 436-9837*
**Fax Area Code:* 603 ■ *TF:* 877-436-9812 ■ *Web:* www.totalenergyllc.com

Toth Financial Advisory Corp
608 S King St Ste 300 .... Leesburg VA 20175 703-443-8684
Web: www.tothfinancial.com

Ubics Inc 333 Technology Dr Ste 210.............. Canonsburg PA 15317 724-746-6001 743-4115
OTC: UBIX ■ *TF:* 800-441-0077 ■ *Web:* www.ubics.com

Unique Copy Center of New York
252 Greene St.................................. New York NY 10003 212-420-9198
Web: uniquecopycenter.com

UPS Store, The 6060 Cornerstone Ct W.............. San Diego CA 92121 858-455-8800 546-7492
TF: 800-789-4623 ■ *Web:* www.theupsstore.com

Zeller Corp 1000 University Ave Ste 800............ Rochester NY 14607 585-254-8840 254-0982
Web: www.zellercorp.com

Zoom Information Inc 307 Waverley Oaks Rd.......... Waltham MA 02452 781-693-7500 693-7510
TF: 800-949-7040 ■ *Web:* www.zoominfo.com

114 BUYER'S GUIDES - ONLINE

SEE ALSO Investment Guides - Online p. 2604

Phone / Fax

Ace Mart - Downtown San Antonio
1220 S St Mary's .... San Antonio TX 78210 210-224-0082 224-1629
TF: 888-898-8079 ■ *Web:* acemart.com

Epinions Inc 8000 Marina Blvd Fifth Fl .... Brisbane CA 94005 650-616-6500
Web: www.epinions.com

ePublicEye.com 1010 N Central Ave .... Glendale CA 91202 818-547-0222

InsWeb Inc 11290 Pyrites Way Ste 200 .... Gold River CA 95670 916-853-3300 853-3325
TF: 866-697-9085 ■ *Web:* www.insweb.com

Market America Inc 1302 Pleasant Ridge Rd .... Greensboro NC 27409 336-605-0040 605-0041
TF: 866-420-1709 ■ *Web:* www.marketamerica.com

Parke-Bell Ltd Inc 709 W 12th St .... Huntingburg IN 47542 812-683-3707 683-5921
TF: 800-457-7456 ■ *Web:* www.touchofclass.com

Shopping.com Inc 8000 Marina Blvd Fifth Fl .... Brisbane CA 94005 650-616-6500 616-6510
Web: www.shopping.com

115 CABINETS - WOOD

SEE ALSO Carpentry & Flooring Contractors p. 2093; Household Furniture p. 2345

Phone / Fax

Allen Lumber Company Inc 502 N Main St .... Barre VT 05641 802-476-4156
Web: www.allenlumbercompany.com

American Woodmark Corp 3102 Shawnee Dr .... Winchester VA 22601 540-665-9100 665-9176
NASDAQ: AMWD ■ *Web:* www.americanwoodmark.com

Ampco Products Inc 11400 NW 36th Ave .... Miami FL 33167 305-821-5700 642-5300*
**Fax Area Code:* 866 ■ *Web:* www.ampco.com

Anton Cabinetry 2002 W Pioneer Pkwy .... Pantego TX 76013 817-460-8681 469-6105
Web: www.antoncabinetry.com

Bertch Cabinet Manufacturing Inc
4747 Crestwood Dr .... Waterloo IA 50702 319-296-2987 296-2315
Web: www.bertch.com

Bloch Industries 140 Commerce Dr .... Rochester NY 14623 585-334-9600 334-9636
TF: 800-992-5624 ■ *Web:* www.blochindustries.com

Brandom Cabinets Co 404 Hawkins St .... Hillsboro TX 76645 512-805-0280 959-2801*
**Fax Area Code:* 800 ■ *TF Cust Svc:* 800-366-8001 ■ *Web:* www.brandom.com

Britten Woodworks 1954 N Betsie River Rd .... Interlochen MI 49643 231-275-5457
Web: www.eyewood.com

Cabinetry By Karman Inc
6000 Stratler St .... Salt Lake City UT 84107 801-281-6400
TF: 800-255-3581 ■ *Web:* www.cabinetrybykarman.com

Cabinets 2000 Inc 11100 Firestone Blvd .... Norwalk CA 90650 562-868-0909 868-4131
Web: www.cabinets2000.com

California Kitchen Cabinet Door Corp
400 Cochrane Cir .... Morgan Hill CA 95037 408-782-5700 782-9000
TF: 888-225-3667 ■ *Web:* www.caldoor.com

Cambria Inc 31496 Cambria Ave Ste 220 .... Le Sueur MN 56058 507-665-5003
Web: www.cambriausa.com

Candlelight Cabinetry Inc 24 Michigan St .... Lockport NY 14094 716-434-6543 434-6748
Web: www.candlelightcab.com

Canyon Creek Cabinet Co 16726 Tye St SE .... Monroe WA 98272 360-348-4973 348-4810
TF: 800-228-1830 ■ *Web:* www.canyoncreek.com

Capitol Granite & Marble 1700 Oak Lk Blvd .... Midlothian VA 23112 804-379-2641
Web: www.capitolgraniteandmarble.com

Cardell Cabinetry
3215 N Panam Expy PO Box 200850 .... San Antonio TX 78219 210-225-0290 212-5823
Web: www.cardellcabinetry.com

Chandlers Plywood Products Inc
3716 Waverly Rd .... Huntington WV 25704 304-429-1311 429-1331
TF: 800-414-1311 ■ *Web:* www.chandlerkitchens.com

Cole Kepro International LLC
4170-103 Distribution Cir .... North Las Vegas NV 89030 702-633-4270
Web: www.coleindustries.net

Commercial Wood Products Co 10019 Yucca Rd .... Adelanto CA 92301 760-246-4530 246-8226
Web: www.commercialwood.com

Conestoga Wood Specialties Inc
245 Reading Rd .... East Earl PA 17519 800-964-3667 638-7198
TF: 800-964-3667 ■ *Web:* www.conestogawood.com

Continental Cabinet Inc 2841 Pierce St .... Dallas TX 75233 214-467-4444 467-1132
Web: www.continentalcabinet.com

Crystal Cabinet Works Inc 1100 Crystal Dr .... Princeton MN 55371 800-347-5045 389-5846*
**Fax Area Code:* 763 ■ *TF:* 800-347-5045 ■ *Web:* www.ccworks.com

Cutting Edge Countertops Inc
1300 Flagship Dr .... Perrysburg OH 43551 419-873-9500
Web: www.cectops.com

Cygnus Inc 1701 Standish Ave .... Petoskey MI 49770 231-347-5404
Web: www.cygnusinc.net

Dalia Kitchen Design Inc
1 Design Ctr Pl Ste 643 .... Boston MA 02210 617-482-2566 482-2744
Web: www.daliakitchendesign.com

Decore-ative Specialties Inc 2772 S Peck Rd .... Monrovia CA 91016 626-254-9191 254-1515
TF: 800-729-7277 ■ *Web:* www.decore.com

Designers Choice Cabinetry Inc 100 TGK Cir .... Rockledge FL 32955 321-632-0772
Web: www.dccabinetry.com

Dewils Industries Inc 6307 NE 127th Ave .... Vancouver WA 98682 360-892-0300
Web: www.dewils.com

Doormark Inc 430 Goolsby Blvd .... Deerfield Beach FL 33442 954-418-4700
Web: www.doormark.com

Dura Supreme Inc 300 Dura Dr .... Howard Lake MN 55349 320-543-3872 543-3310
Web: www.durasupreme.com

Dutch Made Custom Cabinetry 10415 Roth Rd .... Grabill IN 46741 260-657-3311 657-5778
Web: www.dutchmade.com

EGR Inc 601 N Miller Blvd .... Oklahoma City OK 73107 405-943-0900
Web: egronline.com

Evans Cabinet Corp 1321 N Franklin St .... Dublin GA 31021 478-272-2530 272-2731
Web: www.evanscabinet.com

Phone / Fax

Fashion Cabinet Mfg Inc 5440 Axel Pk Rd .... West Jordan UT 84081 801-280-0646 280-8934
Web: www.fashioncabinet.com

Fixture Exchange Corp 3000 W Pafford St .... Fort Worth TX 76110 817-429-2496 927-8451
Web: fixturex.com

Flo-Form Industries Ltd 125 Hamelin St .... Winnipeg MB R3T3Z1 204-474-2334 453-0639
Web: www.floform.com

Fortune Brands Home & Hardware Inc
520 Lk Cook Rd .... Deerfield IL 60015 847-484-4400
Web: www.fortunebrands.com

Grabill Cabinet Company Inc 13844 Sawmill Dr .... Grabill IN 46741 877-472-2782 627-3539*
**Fax Area Code:* 260 ■ *TF:* 877-472-2782 ■ *Web:* www.grabillcabinets.com

Grandview Products Co 1601 Superior Dr .... Parsons KS 67357 620-421-6950 421-4211
TF: 800-247-9105 ■ *Web:* www.grandviewcabinets.com

Granite-Tops Inc 1480 Prairie Dr .... Cold Spring MN 56320 320-685-3005
Web: www.granite-tops.com

Haas Cabinet Company Inc 625 W Utica St .... Sellersburg IN 47172 812-246-4431 246-5420
TF: 800-457-6458 ■ *Web:* www.haascabinet.com

Halabi Inc 2100 Huntington Dr .... Fairfield CA 94533 707-402-1600
Web: www.duracite.com

Helmut Guenschel Inc 10 Emala Ave .... Baltimore MD 21220 410-686-5900
Web: www.guenschel.com

Hoff Enterprises Inc 151 Freidhoff Ln .... Johnstown PA 15902 814-535-8371
Web: www.hoffent.com

HomeCrest Cabinetry 1002 Eisenhower Dr N .... Goshen IN 46526 574-535-9300
TF: 800-960-3660 ■ *Web:* www.homecrestcabinetry.com

Huntwood Industries 23800 E Apple Way .... Liberty Lake WA 99019 509-924-5858 928-6647
TF: 800-873-7350 ■ *Web:* www.huntwood.com

Innovative Surfaces Inc 515 Spiral Blvd .... Hastings MN 55033 651-437-1004
Web: www.innovativesurfaces.com

Jim Bishop Cabinets Inc 5640 Bell Rd .... Montgomery AL 36116 800-410-2444 281-3950*
**Fax Area Code:* 334 ■ *TF:* 800-410-2444 ■ *Web:* www.bishopcabinets.com

Kabinart Corp 3650 Trousdale Dr .... Nashville TN 37204 615-833-1961 781-8026

Kitchen Craft Cabinetry 1180 Springfield Rd .... Winnipeg MB R2C2Z2 204-224-3211 222-7608
Web: www.kitchencraft.com

Kitchen Kompact Inc 911 E 11th St .... Jeffersonville IN 47130 812-282-6681 282-7880
Web: www.kitchenkompact.com

Kraftmaid Cabinetry Inc
15535 S State Ave PO Box 1055 .... Middlefield OH 44062 888-562-7744
TF: 888-562-7744 ■ *Web:* www.kraftmaid.com

Legere Group Ltd PO Box 1527 .... Avon CT 06001 860-674-0392 674-0469
Web: www.legeregroup.com

Marsh Furniture Co PO Box 870 .... High Point NC 27261 336-884-7363 884-3553
TF: 800-696-2774 ■ *Web:* www.marshfurniture.com

Martin Cabinet Inc 336 S Washington St .... Plainville CT 06062 860-747-5769 747-9595
Web: martincabinet.com

Masco Cabinetry LLC 5353 W US 223 PO Box 1946 .... Adrian MI 49221 517-263-0771 265-3325
TF: 866-850-8557 ■ *Web:* www.merillat.com

Masco Corp 21001 Van Born Rd .... Taylor MI 48180 313-274-7400 792-4177
NYSE: MAS ■ *TF:* 888-627-6397 ■ *Web:* www.masco.com

Mastercraft Industries Inc 777 S St .... Newburgh NY 12550 845-565-8850 565-9392
TF: 800-835-7812 ■ *Web:* mastercraftusa.com

Medallion Cabinetry 1 Medallion Way .... Waconia MN 55387 952-442-5171 442-4998
TF: 800-543-4074 ■ *Web:* www.medallioncabinetry.com

Mesa Fully Formed Inc 1111 S Sirrine .... Mesa AZ 85210 480-834-9331
Web: www.mesa.org

Mid-America Cabinet Inc 20980 Marion Lee Rd .... Gentry AR 72734 479-736-2671 736-8086
Web: www.midamericacabinets.com

Mouser Custom Cabinetry
2112 N Hwy 31 W .... Elizabethtown KY 42701 270-737-7477 737-7446
TF: 800-345-7537 ■ *Web:* www.mousercc.com

Norcraft cabinetry 3020 Denmark Ave .... Eagan MN 55121 651-234-3300
TF: 877-888-0002 ■ *Web:* www.norcraftcompanies.com

Northern Contours Inc
1355 Mendota Heights Rd Ste 100 .... Mendota Heights MN 55120 651-695-1698 695-1714
TF: 866-344-8132 ■ *Web:* www.northerncontours.com

Omega Cabinetry Ltd 1205 Peters Dr .... Waterloo IA 50703 319-235-5700 235-5860*
**Fax:* Cust Svc ■ *Web:* www.omegacabinetry.com

Patella Industries Inc
721 Grand Bernier N .... Saint-Jean-Sur-Richelieu QC J3B8H6 450-359-0040

Patrick Industries Inc
107 W Franklin St PO Box 638 .... Elkhart IN 46515 574-294-7511 522-5213
NASDAQ: PATK ■ *TF:* 800-331-2151 ■ *Web:* www.patrickind.com

Plato Woodwork Inc 200 Third St SW .... Plato MN 55370 320-238-2193 238-2131
TF: 800-328-5924 ■ *Web:* www.platowoodwork.com

Precision Countertops Inc
26200 SW 95th Ave Ste 303 .... Wilsonville OR 97070 503-692-6660
Web: www.precisioncountertops.com

Republic Industries Inc 1400 Warren Dr .... Marshall TX 75672 903-935-3680 935-3697
TF: 866-284-0941 ■ *Web:* republicind.com

Rosebud Mfg Co Inc 701 SE 12th St .... Madison SD 57042 605-256-4561 256-3842
TF: 800-256-4561 ■ *Web:* www.rosebudmfg.com

Roy's Wood Products Inc 329 Thrush Ln .... Lugoff SC 29078 803-438-1590
Web: www.royswoodproducts.com

Royal Cabinets 1299 E Phillips Blvd .... Pomona CA 91766 909-629-8565 629-7762
Web: www.royalcabinets.com

RSI Home Products Inc 400 E Orangethorpe Ave .... Anaheim CA 92801 714-449-2200 449-2222*
**Fax:* Cust Svc ■ *TF:* 888-774-8062 ■ *Web:* www.rsihomeproducts.com

Rutt HandCrafted Cabinetry
215 Diller Ave .... New Holland PA 17557 717-351-1700
Web: ruttcabinetry.com

Rynone Mfg Corp PO Box 128 .... Sayre PA 18840 570-888-5272 888-1175
TF: 800-839-1654 ■ *Web:* www.rynone.com

Shamrock Cabinet & Fixture Corp
10201 E 65th St .... Raytown MO 64133 816-737-2300 356-7835
Web: www.shamrockcabinet.com

Showplace Wood Products Inc
One Enterprise St .... Harrisburg SD 57032 605-743-2200
Web: www.showplacewood.com

Spectrum Cabinet Sales Inc
90 Crossways Park Dr W .... Woodbury NY 11797 516-496-9888
Web: www.spectrumkitchens.com

Phone Fax

Starmark Cabinetry 600 E 48th St N .... Sioux Falls SD 57104 800-594-9444 336-5574*
*Fax Area Code: 605 ■ TF: 800-755-7789 ■ Web: www.starmarkcabinetry.com

Thomasville Furniture Industries Inc
401 E Main St PO Box 339 .... Thomasville NC 27361 336-472-4000 472-4085
Web: www.thomasville.com

Tri-Star Cabinet & Top Co Inc 1000 S Cedar .... New Lenox IL 60451 815-485-2564 485-5747
Web: www.tristarcabinets.com

Ultracraft Co 6163 Old 421 Rd .... Liberty NC 27298 800-262-4046
TF: 800-262-4046 ■ Web: www.ultracraft.com

Valley Cabinet Inc 845 Prosper Rd .... De Pere WI 54115 920-336-3174 383-5580
TF: 800-236-8981 ■ Web: www.valleycabinetinc.com

Wellborn Forest Products Inc
2212 Airport Blvd .... Alexander City AL 35010 256-234-7900 234-2750
TF: 800-846-2562 ■ Web: www.wellbornforest.com

WM Ohs-Kitchen Showroom 115 Madison St .... Denver CO 80206 303-321-3232
Web: www.wmohs.com

Woodcase Fine Cabinetry Inc 3255 W Osborn Rd ...... Phoenix AZ 85017 480-948-0756 269-1242*
*Fax Area Code: 602 ■ Web: www.woodcaseinc.net

Woodcraft Industries Inc
525 Lincoln Ave SE .... Saint Cloud MN 56304 320-252-1503 656-2199
Web: www.woodcraftind.com

WW Wood Products Inc 10182 Old Hwy 60 .... Dudley MO 63936 573-624-7090 624-6671
Web: wwwoodproducts.com

116 CABLE & OTHER PAY TELEVISION SERVICES

Phone Fax

Aboriginal People's Television Network Inc
339 Portage Ave .... Winnipeg MB R3B2C3 204-947-9331
Web: www.aptn.ca

Access Cable Television Inc
302 Enterprise Dr .... Somerset KY 42501 606-677-2444
Web: www.accesshsd.net

Access Communications Co-operative Ltd
2250 Park St .... Regina SK S4N7K7 306-569-2225
Web: www.myaccess.ca

Aegis Film Group Inc
7510 Sunset Blvd Ste 275 .... Los Angeles CA 90046 323-848-7977
Web: www.aegisfilmgroup.com

All West Communications Inc 50 West 100 North .... Kamas UT 84036 435-783-4361
Web: www.allwest.net

Allen's TV Cable Service Inc
800 Victor II Blvd .... Morgan City LA 70380 985-384-8335
Web: www.atvc.net

Almega Cable Inc 4001 W Airport Fwy Ste 530 .... Bedford TX 76021 817-685-9588 685-6488

Alpine Communications LC 923 Humphrey St .... Elkader IA 52043 563-245-4000
Web: www.alpinecom.net

American Cable Company Inc
231 E Luzerne St .... Philadelphia PA 19124 215-456-0700
Web: www.americancableco.com

Antietam Cable Television Inc
1000 Willow Cir .... Hagerstown MD 21740 301-797-5000
Web: www.antietamcable.com

Areacall Inc 7803 Stratford Rd .... Bethesda MD 20814 301-657-2718
Web: www.areacall.com

Armstrong Group of Cos One Armstrong Pl .... Butler PA 16001 724-283-0925 283-9655
Web: www.armstrongonewire.com

Astral Media Inc 1800 McGill College Ste 600 .... Montreal QC H3A3J6 514-939-5000 939-1515
Web: www.bellmedia.ca

Azteca America Inc
1139 Grand Central Ave Ste 1000 .... Glendale CA 91201 818-241-5400
Web: us.azteca.com/

Barre y Lane LLC 9318 Drawbridge Rd .... Mechanicsville VA 23116 804-723-4035
Web: www.barreylane.com

Big Bend Telephone Company Inc 808 N Fifth St .... Alpine TX 79830 432-364-1000
TF: 800-520-0092 ■ Web: www.bigbend.net

Black Rock Cable 1512 Fairview St .... Bellingham WA 98229 360-738-3116

Broadband Solutions Inc 1886 Commerce Dr .... De Pere WI 54115 920-339-8056
Web: www.broadband-solutions.com

Broadcast Equipment Corp
1035 44th Dr .... Long Island City NY 11101 718-784-5540
Web: www.becny.com

Broadnet Teleservices LLC
1805 Shea Ctr Dr Ste 160 .... Highlands Ranch CO 80129 303-268-5500
Web: www.broadnet.us

Buckeye CableSystem 5566 Southwick Blvd .... Toledo OH 43614 419-724-9802 724-7074
Web: www.buckeyecablesystem.com

Buford Media Group LLC (BMG) 6125 Paluxy Dr .... Tyler TX 75703 903-561-4411 561-4031

Cable Center, The 2000 Buchtel Blvd .... Denver CO 80210 720-502-7500
Web: www.cablecenter.org

Cable Com Inc 12115 Roxie Dr .... Austin TX 78729 512-250-5901
Web: www.cablecominc.com

Cable Connection, The 52 Heppner Dr .... Carson City NV 89706 775-885-1443 885-2734
TF: 800-851-2961 ■ Web: www.thecableconnection.com

Cable Coop 27 E College St .... Oberlin OH 44074 440-775-4001
Web: www.oberlin.net

Cable Line Inc 311 N Seventh St Ste 2 .... Perkasie PA 18944 215-258-1380
Web: www.cable-line.com

Cable One Inc 210 E Earll Drive .... Phoenix AZ 85012 602-364-6000 364-6010
TF: 877-692-2253 ■ Web: www.cableone.net

Cable Vision Services 1701 Cogswell Ave .... Pell City AL 35125 205-884-4545
Web: www.coosahs.net

Cable-Comm Technologies Inc
800 Enterprise Ct .... Naperville IL 60563 630-717-7179
Web: www.cable-comm.com

CableAmerica Corp 350 E 10th Dr .... Mesa AZ 85210 866-871-4492
TF: 866-871-4492 ■ Web: www.cableamerica.com

Cablecom LLC 3701 W Burnham St Ste C .... Milwaukee WI 53215 414-226-2205
Web: cablecomllc.com

Cablevision Systems Corp 1111 Stewart Ave .... Bethpage NY 11714 516-803-2300 803-3134*
NYSE: CVC ■ *Fax: Hum Res ■ Web: www.cablevision.com

Phone Fax

Campus Televideo Inc 100 First Stamford Pl .... Stamford CT 06902 203-983-5400
TF: 866-615-8674 ■ Web: www.campustelevideo.com

Capital News 9 104 Watervliet Ave Ext .... Albany NY 12206 518-459-9999
Web: www.capitalnews9.com

Capitol Connection
George Mason University Television 4400 University Dr
MS 1D2 .... Fairfax VA 22030 703-993-3100 273-2417
Web: capitolconnection.org

CaptionMax Inc 2438 27th Ave South .... Minneapolis MN 55406 612-341-3566
Web: www.captionmax.com

Cass Cable Tv Inc 100 Redbud Rd .... Virginia IL 62691 217-452-7725
TF: 800-252-1799 ■ Web: www.casscomm.com

CDR Data Corp 1028 N Lake Ave Ste 105 .... Pasadena CA 91104 626-791-9700
Web: www.cdrdata.com

Charter Communications Inc
12405 Powerscourt Dr Ste 100 .... Saint Louis MO 63131 314-965-0555 965-9745
NASDAQ: CHTR ■ TF: 888-438-2427 ■ Web: www.charter.com

Chisholm Trail Broadcasting Co 316 E Willow Rd .... Enid OK 73701 580-237-1390

Citizens Telephone Company 26 S Main St .... Hammond NY 13646 315-324-5911
Web: www.cit-tele.com

Coast Communications Company Inc
349 Damon Rd .... Ocean Shores WA 98569 360-289-2252
Web: www.coastaccess.com

Cogeco Cable Inc 5 Pl Ville-Marie Ste 915 .... Montreal QC H3B2G2 514-874-2600 874-2625
TF: 800-855-0511 ■ Web: www.cogeco.ca

Comcast Cable Communications LLC
1701 John F Kennedy Blvd .... Philadelphia PA 19103 215-665-1700 981-7790
Web: www.comcast.com

Comcast Corp Cable Div 1500 Market St .... Philadelphia PA 19102 215-665-1700 981-7790
Web: www.comcast.com

Comcast SPORTSNET Bay Area LP
360 Third St Second Fl .... San Francisco CA 94107 415-296-8900
Web: www.csnbayarea.com

Comcast Wholesale 4100 East Dry Creek Rd .... Centennial CO 80122 303-486-3800
Web: www.comcastmediacenter.com

ComSouth Telecommunications Inc
99 Broad St PO Box 1298 .... Hawkinsville AK 31036 478-783-4001
Web: www.comsouth.net

Connect802 Corp 111 Deerwood Rd Ste 200 .... San Ramon CA 94583 925-552-0802
Web: www.connect802.com

Country Cablevision Inc
9449 State Hwy 197 S .... Burnsville NC 28714 828-682-4074
Web: www.ccvn.com

Cox Communications Inc 1400 Lake Hearn Dr .... Atlanta GA 30319 404-843-5000 843-5000
TF: 866-961-0027 ■ Web: cox.com

Curious Pictures Corp 440 Lafayette St .... New York NY 10003 212-674-7600
Web: www.curiouspictures.com

Custom Cable Corp 242 Butler St .... Westbury NY 11590 516-334-3600
Web: www.customwireandcable.com

Data Cell Systems Inc 250 Hwy 3201 .... Winnsboro LA 71295 318-435-5800
Web: www.data-cell.com

Datacom Inc 2517 S Santa Fe Ave .... Vista CA 92083 760-598-6000
Web: www.datacom.com

DC Connections 22650 Executive Dr Ste 125 .... Sterling VA 20166 703-471-9757
Web: www.dcconnections.com

Decibels Inc 1551 Center St .... Tacoma WA 98409 253-473-5855
Web: www.decibels.com

Defender Security Company Inc
3750 Priority Way S Dr Ste 200 .... Indianapolis IN 46240 317-810-4720
Web: www.defenderdirect.com

DIRECTV Inc 2230 E Imperial Hwy .... El Segundo CA 90245 310-535-5000 535-5315*
*Fax: Hum Res ■ TF Cust Svc: 800-531-5000 ■ Web: www.directv.com

DISH Network LLC 9601 S Meridian Blvd .... Englewood CO 80112 800-823-4929
NASDAQ: DISH ■ TF: 800-823-4929 ■ Web: www.dish.com

E-Z Form Cable Corp 285 Welton St .... Hamden CT 06517 203-785-8215
Web: www.ezform.com

Electric Cable Compounds Inc 108 Rado Dr .... Naugatuck CT 06770 203-723-2590
Web: www.electriccablecompounds.com

Engineered Environments Inc
1620 Timocuan Way Ste 130 .... Longwood FL 32750 407-831-6998
Web: www.eeigc.net

EOSPACE Inc 6222 185th AVE NE .... Redmond WA 98052 425-869-8673
Web: www.eospace.com

Everest Production Corp 300 Franklin Sq Dr .... Somerset NJ 08873 732-560-0800
Web: www.everestpro.com

Excell Communications Inc
6247 Amber Hills Rd .... Trussville AL 35173 205-956-0198
Web: www.excellcommunications.com

Fandango Inc 12200 W Olympic Blvd Ste 400 .... Los Angeles CA 90064 310-954-0278
Web: www.fandango.com

Favorite Office Automation
2011 W State St Ste B .... New Castle PA 16101 724-658-8300
Web: www.favorite1.com

Fibercomm Lc 1605 Ninth St .... Sioux City IA 51101 712-224-2020
Web: www.fibercomm.net

Fidelity Communications Company Inc
64 N Clark St .... Sullivan MO 63080 573-468-8081
Web: www.fidelitycommunications.com

Florida Cable Inc 23505 State Rd 40 .... Astor FL 32102 352-759-2788
Web: www.floridacable.com

Fluent Media Group LLC 5230 Alton Rd .... Miami Beach FL 33140 305-424-1030
Web: www.fluentmediagroup.com

Fox Latin America
2121 Ponce De Leon Blvd Ste 1020 .... Coral Gables FL 33134 305-567-9788
Web: www.mundofox.com

Giant Communications Inc 418 W Fifth St Ste C .... Holton KS 66436 785-362-2532
Web: www.giantcomm.net

GM Cable Contractors Inc 9232 Joor Rd .... Baton Rouge LA 70818 225-261-9800
Web: gmcable.com

Grace To You 28001 Harrison Pkwy .... Valencia CA 91355 661-295-5777
Web: gty.org

Phone | Fax

Greater Media Detroit Wcsx Wmg
One Radio Plz St .... Ferndale MI 48220 248-591-6800
Web: greatermediadetroit.com

Green Earth Cleaning 51 W 135th St .... Kansas City MO 64145 816-926-0895
Web: www.greenearthcleaning.com

Haefele Tv Inc 24 E Tioga St .... Spencer NY 14883 607-589-6235
Web: www.htva.net

Hamilton Telephone Co 1001 12th St .... Aurora NE 68818 402-694-5101
TF: 800-821-1831 ■ *Web:* www.hamiltontelephone.com

Harlan Community Television Inc
124 S First St .... Harlan KY 40831 606-573-2945
Web: www.harlanonline.net

Hawaii Pacific Teleport LP
91-340 Farrington Hwy .... Kapolei HI 96707 808-674-9157
Web: www.hawaiiteleport.com

Heartland Video Systems Inc 1311 Pilgrim Rd .... Plymouth WI 53073 920-893-4204
Web: hvs-inc.com

High Power Technical Services Inc (HPTS)
2230 Ampere Dr .... Louisville KY 40299 866-398-3474
TF: 866-398-3474 ■ *Web:* inc.com

Home Town Cable TV LLC
10486 SW Village Ctr Dr .... Port Saint Lucie FL 34987 772-345-6000

Horvath Communications Inc
312 W Colfax Ave .... South Bend IN 46601 574-237-0464
Web: www.horvathcommunications.com

ImOn Communications LLC 625 First St SE .... Cedar Rapids IA 52401 319-298-6484
Web: www.imon.net

Inside Edition Inc 1700 Broadway 33rd Fl .... New York NY 10019 212-817-5423
Web: www.insideedition.com

Inter Mountain Cable Inc
20 Laynesville Rd PO Box 159 .... Harold KY 41635 606-478-9406
Web: www.imctv.com

Isotropic Networks Inc W2835 Krueger Rd .... Lake Geneva WI 53147 262-248-9600
Web: www.isosat.net

ITV Studios America Inc
15303 Ventura Blvd Bldg C Ste 800 .... Los Angeles CA 91403 818-455-4600
Web: www.itvstudios.com

J P Diamond Co 25 E James St .... Falconer NY 14733 716-665-4100
Web: www.jpdiamond.com

Kable Link Communications
15273 Flight Path Dr .... Brooksville FL 34604 352-796-7639
Web: www.kablelink.com

Keene Valley Video Inc 1948 nys Rt 73 .... Keene Valley NY 12943 518-576-4510
Web: www.kvvi.net

Kelly Cable Corp 9065 Quince St .... Henderson CO 80640 303-287-1112
Web: www.sitewise.net

KenCast Inc 290 Harbor Dr .... Stamford CT 06902 203-359-6984
Web: www.kencast.com

KFDM-TV Channel 6 2955 I-10 E .... Beaumont TX 77702 409-892-6622
Web: www.kfdm.com

Kincardine Cable TV Ltd 223 Bruce Ave .... Kincardine ON N2Z2P2 519-396-8880
TF: 800-265-3064 ■ *Web:* www.tnt21.com

Kmtelecom 18 Second Ave NW .... Kasson MN 55944 507-634-2511
TF: 888-232-3796 ■ *Web:* www.kmtel.com

Knight Enterprises Inc 6056 Ulmerton Rd .... Clearwater FL 33760 727-524-6235
Web: www.knight-enterprises.com

Ksbj 1722 Treble Dr .... Humble TX 77338 281-446-5725 540-2198
TF: 877-644-5725 ■ *Web:* www.ksbj.org

Ksby-Tv 1772 Calle Joaquin .... San Luis Obispo CA 93405 805-541-6666
TF: 800-583-4135 ■ *Web:* www.ksby.com

Kytx-Tv Cbs 19 2211 Ese Loop 323 .... Tyler TX 75701 903-581-2211
Web: www.cbs19.tv

Lanshack.com 155 Meadow Rd Ste 100 .... Clark NJ 07066 732-396-3600
Web: www.lanshack.com

Lincolnville Telephone Co
133 Back Meadow Rd .... Nobleboro ME 04555 207-763-9911
Web: www.lintelco.net

Link Electronics Inc 2137 Rust Ave .... Cape Girardeau MO 63703 573-334-4433
TF: 800-776-4411 ■ *Web:* www.linkelectronics.com

Live Wire Net 4577 Pecos St .... Denver CO 80211 303-458-5667
Web: www.livewirenet.com

Louisiana Radio Network Inc
10500 Coursey Blvd Ste 104 .... Baton Rouge LA 70816 225-291-2727
Web: louisianaradionetwork.com

Main Line Equipment Inc 20917 Higgins Ct .... Torrance CA 90501 310-357-4450

Manhattan Neighborhood Network
537 W 59th St .... New York NY 10019 212-757-2670
Web: www.mnn.org

Max Media LLC 900 Laskin Rd .... Virginia Beach VA 23451 757-437-9800
Web: www.maxmediallc.com

Mediacom Communications Corp
100 Crystal Run Rd .... Middletown NY 10941 845-695-2600
TF General: 800-479-2082 ■ *Web:* mediacomcable.com

MediaOne Services LLC
901 Battery St Ste 220 .... San Francisco CA 94111 415-262-4222
Web: www.linktv.org

Metrocast Cablevision of New Hampshire LLC
Nine Apple Rd .... Belmont NH 03220 603-524-4425
Web: www.metrocast.com

Mid-coast Cablevision Lp 505 N Mechanic St .... El Campo TX 77437 979-543-6858
Web: www.warpspeed1.net

Midcontinent Communications PO Box 5010 .... Sioux Falls SD 57117 605-274-9810
TF: 800-888-1300 ■ *Web:* www.midcocomm.com

Middleburgh Telephone Co, The
103 Cliff St .... Middleburgh NY 12122 518-827-5211
Web: www.midtel.net

Multicom Inc 1076 Florida Central Pkwy .... Longwood FL 32750 407-331-7779
Web: www.multicominc.com

National Cable Television Co-op Inc (NCTC)
11200 Corporate Ave .... Lenexa KS 66219 913-599-5900 222-2311*
*Fax Area Code: 202 ■ *TF:* 800-720-5850 ■ *Web:* www.ncta.com

Newport Television LLC 460 Nichols Rd .... Kansas City MO 64112 816-751-0200

Nistica Inc 745 Rt 202-206 .... Bridgewater NJ 08807 908-707-9500
Web: www.nistica.com

No Good Entertainment Inc
9944 Santa Monica Blvd .... Beverly Hills CA 90212 310-556-8600
Web: www.ngtv.com

North Shore Communications Group Inc
85 Eastern Ave Ph Ste 306 .... Gloucester MA 01930 978-282-8222
Web: www.northshorecommunications.com

Northland Telecommunications Corp
101 Stewart St Ste 700 .... Seattle WA 98101 206-621-1351
Web: yournorthland.com

Npg of Oregon Inc 62990 O B Riley Rd .... Bend OR 97701 541-383-2121
Web: www.ktvz.com

Oceanic Time Warner Cable 200 Akamainui St .... Mililani HI 96789 808-643-2100
Web: www.oceanic.com

Oceanside Community Service Television Corp
3038 Industry St .... Oceanside CA 92054 760-722-4433
Web: www.koct.org

Omega Communications Inc
41 E Washington Ste 110 .... Indianapolis IN 46204 317-264-4000 264-4020
Web: www.omegac.com

OrbitCom Inc 1701 N Louise Dr .... Sioux Falls SD 57107 605-977-6900
Web: www.orbitcom.biz

Otter Tail Telcom 230 W Lincoln Ave .... Fergus Falls MN 56537 218-826-6161
TF: 800-247-2706 ■ *Web:* www.prtel.com

Panora Cooperative Telephone Association Inc
114 E Main St .... Panora IA 50216 641-755-2424
Web: www.panoratelco.com

Paragould Light Water & Cable (PLWC)
1901 Jones Rd .... Paragould AR 72450 870-239-7700 239-7798
TF: 800-482-8998 ■ *Web:* www.paragould.com/

Phoenix Cable Inc (PCI) 145 N Franklin Tpke .... Ramsey NJ 07446 201-825-9090

Phonoscope Ltd 6105 Wline Dr .... Houston TX 77036 713-272-4600
Web: www.phonoscope.com

Pine Telephone System Inc 104 Ctr St .... Halfway OR 97834 541-742-2201
Web: www.pinetel.com

Polar Communications 110 Fourth St E .... Park River ND 58270 701-284-7221
Web: www.polarcomm.com

Premier Communications 339 First Ave Ne .... Sioux Center IA 51250 712-722-3451
Web: www.mtcnet.net

Quality Cable & Electronics
1780 Nw 15th Ave Ste 500 .... Pompano Beach FL 33069 954-532-0165
Web: www.qualitycable.com

Quebecor Media Inc 612 Rue St Jacques .... Montreal QC H3C4M8 514-380-1999 985-8652
Web: www.quebecor.com

Quick Cable Corp 3700 Quick Dr .... Franksville WI 53126 262-824-3100
Web: www.quickcable.com

Rainbow Network Communications
620 Hicksville Rd .... Bethpage NY 11714 516-803-0300
Web: www.rncnetwork.com

Real Hip-Hop Network Inc, The
1455 Pennsylvania Ave NW Ste 400 .... Washington DC 20004 202-379-3115
Web: rhn.tv

Richard A Foreman Assoc Inc 330 Emery Dr E .... Stamford CT 06902 203-327-2800
Web: www.rafamedia.com

Rifkin & Assoc Inc 360 S Monroe St .... Denver CO 80209 303-333-1215
Web: www.rifkinco.com

River Valley Telecommunications Coop & Cable Tv
1607 Rolling St .... Ruthven IA 51358 712-837-5522
Web: www.ruthventel.com

RLTV 5525 Research Park Dr .... Catonsville MD 21228 410-402-9600
Web: www.cedarcrestvillage.com

Romanoff Group, The 1288 Research Rd .... Gahanna OH 43230 614-755-4500
Web: www.romanoffgroup.cc

Rooftop Media Inc 530 Howard St Ste 400 .... San Francisco CA 94105 800-860-0293
TF: 800-860-0293 ■ *Web:* www.rooftopmedia.net

RTM Productions Inc 130 SE Pkwy Ct .... Franklin TN 37064 615-503-9700
Web: www.horsepowertv.com

Satellite Receivers Ltd
1740 Cofrin Dr Ste 2 .... Green Bay WI 54302 920-432-5777
Web: www.cashdepotplus.com

Scio Cablevision 38982 Se Second Ave .... Scio OR 97374 503-394-2995
Web: www.smt-net.com

See World Satellites Inc 1321 Wayne Ave .... Indiana PA 15701 724-463-3200
Web: www.seeworld.biz

Service Electric Cable TV & Communications
2260 Ave A .... Bethlehem PA 18017 610-865-9100 865-7888
TF: 800-232-9100 ■ *Web:* www.sectv.com

Shaw Communications Inc 630 Third Ave SW .... Calgary AB T2P4L4 403-750-4500 750-4501*
TSE: SJR/B ■ *Fax: Mktg ■ *TF:* 888-472-2222 ■ *Web:* www.shaw.ca

Shen-Heights TV Assoc Inc 38 N Main St .... Shenandoah PA 17976 570-462-1911
Web: www.shenhgts.net

Silverado Cable Co 1840 W First Ave .... Mesa AZ 85202 480-655-8751
Web: www.silveradocable.com

Sky Radio Network Inc
5320 Laurel Canyon Blvd .... Valley Village CA 91607 818-762-6800

Soup2Nuts Inc 311 Arsenal St .... Watertown MA 02472 617-600-2222
Web: www.soup2nuts.tv

Southern Cable Communications
2101 S Fraser St .... Georgetown SC 29440 843-546-2200
Web: www.sccc.tv

Southern Vermont Cable Co PO Box 166 .... Bondville VT 05340 800-544-5931
TF: 800-544-5931 ■ *Web:* www.svcable.net

Specialty Cable Corp Two Tower Dr .... Wallingford CT 06492 203-265-7126
Web: www.specialtycable.com

Spencer Municipal Utilities 712 Grand Ave .... Spencer IA 51301 712-580-5800
Web: www.smunet.net

Suddenlink Communications 6151 Paluxy Dr .... Tyler TX 75703 877-694-9474
TF: 877-694-9474 ■ *Web:* www.suddenlink.com

Syringa Networks LLC 3795 S Development Ave .... Boise ID 83705 208-229-6100
Web: www.syringanetworks.net

TCI Tire Centers LLC 10 Mt Read Blvd Ste A .... Rochester NY 14611 585-328-1440

Phone Fax

Techni Logic Communications
959 E Collins Blvd Ste 120 .... Richardson TX 75081 972-455-5500
Web: tlcworld.com
Technical Cable Concepts Inc 350 Lear Ave .... Costa Mesa CA 92626 714-835-1081
Web: www.techcable.com
Tel Star Cablevison Inc 1295 Lourdes Rd. .... Metamora IL 61548 309-383-2677
Web: www.telstar-online.net
Tel Tech Networks Inc 810 E Hammond Ln .... Phoenix AZ 85034 602-431-9399
Web: www.teltechnetworks.com
Tele-Media Corp
804 Jacksonville Rd P.O. Box 39 .... Bellefonte PA 16823 814-353-2025 353-2072
TF: 800-704-4254 ■ *Web:* www.tele-media.com
Telecommunication Support Services Inc
720 N Dr. .... Melbourne FL 32934 321-242-0000
Web: www.tssincorp.com
Telepictures Production Inc
3500 W Olive St Ste 1000. .... Burbank CA 91505 818-972-0777
Web: www.telepicturestv.com
Telesphere Networks Ltd
9237 E Via de Ventura Ste 250 .... Scottsdale AZ 85258 480-385-7000
Web: www.telesphere.com
Terrasat Communications Inc
235 Vineyard Ct Ste 100. .... Morgan Hill CA 95037 408-782-5911
Web: www.terrasatinc.com
Titan Broadcast Management LLC
888 Third St NW Ste A. .... Atlanta GA 30318 678-904-0555
Web: www.titanbroadcast.com
TiVo Inc 2160 Gold St .... Alviso CA 95002 408-519-9100 519-5330
NASDAQ: TIVO ■ *TF:* 877-367-8486 ■ *Web:* www.tivo.com
Touch Base 1614 15th St .... Denver CO 80202 303-862-3300
Web: touchbaseglobal.com
TowerComm LLC 6017 Triangle Dr. .... Raleigh NC 27613 919-781-3496
Web: www.towercommonline.com
TV5 Quebec Canada
1755 Blvd Rene-Levesque E Bureau 101 .... Montreal QC H2K4P6 514-522-5322
Web: www.tv5.ca
TVWorks LLC Two Belvedere Pl Ste 200 .... Mill Valley CA 94941 415-380-6200
Web: www.tvworks.com
United Cable Systems Inc PO Box 1410 .... Hindman KY 41822 606-785-3450
Web: www.tvscable.com
United Telephone Mutual Aid Corp
411 Seventh Ave. .... Langdon ND 58249 701-256-5156
Web: www.utma.com
US Cable Corp 28 W Grand Ave Ste 10 .... Montvale NJ 07645 201-930-9000
Web: uscable.com
V-me Media Inc 450 W 33rd St 11th Fl .... New York NY 10001 212-273-4800
Web: www.vmetv.com
Vernon Telephone Company Inc 103 N Main St. .... Westby WI 54667 608-634-3136
Web: www.vernontel.com
Vertical Structures Inc
309 Spangler Dr Ste E .... Richmond KY 40475 859-624-8360
Web: verticalstructures.com
Viodi LLC 5255 Stevens Creek Blvd Ste 127 .... Santa Clara CA 95051 408-551-0320
Web: www.viodi.com
VISTA Satellite Communications Inc
73-104 SW 12th Ave. .... Dania Beach FL 33004 954-838-0900
Web: www.vistasat.com
Voyport LLC 8200 Greensboro Dr. .... Mc Lean VA 22102 703-462-5468
Web: www.voyport.com
W H Q r 913 Fm 254 N Front St Ste 300 .... Wilmington NC 28401 910-343-1640
Web: www.whqr.org
Wally World Satellite Local Direct Tv Dealer
524 Cemetery Rd .... Park City MT 59063 406-633-2811
Wavevision 10300 Wstffice Dr Ste 200 .... Houston TX 77042 832-495-4109
Web: www.wavevision.com
WBOY-TV Inc 904 W Pike St. .... Clarksburg WV 26301 304-623-3311
Web: www.wboy.com
Wbsd 400 Mc Canna Pkwy .... Burlington WI 53105 262-763-0195
WDMP Radio 2163 State Rd 23-151 .... Dodgeville WI 53533 608-935-2302
Web: d99point3.com
Wehco Video Inc 115 E Capitol Ave .... Little Rock AR 72201 501-378-3529 376-8594
Web: www.wehco.com/
Westar Satellite Services LP
777 Westar Ln. .... Cedar Hill TX 75104 972-291-6000
Web: www.westarsat.com
Western Broadband LLC
9666 E Riggs Rd Ste 108 .... Sun Lakes AZ 85248 480-895-8084
Web: www.westernbroadband.net
Wght Radio 1878 Lincoln Ave. .... Pompton Lakes NJ 07442 973-839-1500
Web: www.ghtradio.com
White Mountain Cable Construction LLC
2113 Dover Rd .... Epsom NH 03234 603-736-4766
Web: www.wmc1.com
Wiat-tv 2075 Golden Crest Dr .... Birmingham AL 35209 205-322-4200
Web: www.cbs42.com
Wirelesswerks USA Inc
7981 168th Ave Ne Ste 116 .... Redmond WA 98052 425-869-2356
Web: www.wirelesswerks.com
Wjac-Tv 49 Old Hickory Ln .... Johnstown PA 15905 814-255-7600
Web: www.wjactv.com
YKK AP America Inc 7680 The Bluffs Ste 100. .... Austell GA 30168 678-838-6000
Web: www.ykkap.com
Young Broadcasting of San Francisco Inc
599 Lexington Ave .... New York NY 10022 212-754-7070
Web: www.kron.com
Zero Point Zero Production Inc
875 Ave of the Americas 19th Fl. .... New York NY 10001 212-620-2730
Web: www.zeropointzero.com
Zito Media LP 102 S Main St .... Coudersport PA 16915 814-260-9570
Web: www.zitomedia.com

117 CABLE REELS

Phone Fax

American Reeling Devices Inc
15 Airpark Vista Blvd .... Dayton NV 89403 800-354-7335 246-1002*
**Fax Area Code: 775* ■ *TF Sales:* 800-354-7335 ■ *Web:* americanreeling.net/
Conductix 10102 F St. .... Omaha NE 68127 402-339-9300 339-9627
TF: 800-521-4888 ■ *Web:* www.conductix.us
Gleason Reel Corp 600 S Clark St. .... Mayville WI 53050 920-387-4120 387-4189
TF: 888-504-5151 ■ *Web:* www.hubbell-gleason.com
Hannay Reels Inc 553 SR 143 .... Westerlo NY 12193 518-797-3791 797-3259
TF: 877-467-3357 ■ *Web:* www.hannay.com

118 CALCULATORS - ELECTRONIC

Phone Fax

Calculated Industries Inc 4840 Hytech Dr .... Carson City NV 89706 775-885-4900 885-4949
TF: 800-854-8075 ■ *Web:* www.calculated.com
Sharp Electronics Corp One Sharp Plz. .... Mahwah NJ 07430 201-529-8200 529-8413
TF: 800-237-4277 ■ *Web:* www.sharpusa.com
Sweda Company LLC 17411 Vly Blvd .... City of Industry CA 91744 626-357-9999 357-6080
Web: www.swedausa.com
Texas Instruments Inc 12500 TI Blvd. .... Dallas TX 75243 972-995-3773 927-6377
NASDAQ: TXN ■ *TF Cust Svc:* 800-336-5236 ■ *Web:* www.ti.com
Victor Technology LLC
175 E Crossroads Pkwy .... Boling Brook IL 60440 630-754-4400 972-3902
TF: 800-628-2420 ■ *Web:* www.victortech.com

119 CAMERAS & RELATED SUPPLIES - RETAIL

Phone Fax

Abe's of Maine Cameras & Electronics
Five Fernwood Ave .... Edison NJ 08837 732-225-1777 228-8727*
**Fax Area Code: 718* ■ *TF:* 800-992-2237 ■ *Web:* www.abesofmaine.com
Adorama Camera Inc 42 W 18th St .... New York NY 10011 212-741-0052 463-7223
TF: 800-223-2500 ■ *Web:* www.adorama.com
B & H Photo-Video-Pro Audio Corp
420 Ninth Ave. .... New York NY 10001 212-444-6600 239-7770
TF: 800-947-9954 ■ *Web:* www.bhphotovideo.com
Beach Camera 203 Rt 22 E .... Green Brook NJ 08812 732-968-6400 968-7709
TF: 800-572-3224 ■ *Web:* www.beachcamera.com
Black Photo Corp 200 Consilium Pl Ste 1600. .... Toronto ON M1H3J3 416-279-0007 475-8814*
**Fax Area Code: 905* ■ *TF:* 800-668-3826 ■ *Web:* www.blacks.ca
CambridgeWorld 34 Franklin Ave. .... Brooklyn NY 11205 718-858-5002 858-5437
TF: 800-221-2253 ■ *Web:* www.cambridgeworld.com
Camera Corner Inc PO Box 1899 .... Burlington NC 27216 336-228-0251 222-8011
TF: 800-868-2462 ■ *Web:* www.camcor.com
Cress Photo PO Box 4262. .... Wayne NJ 07474 973-694-1280 694-6965
Web: www.flashbulbs.com
Dodd Camera 2077 E 30th St .... Cleveland OH 44115 216-361-6800 361-6819
TF: 800-507-1676 ■ *Web:* www.doddcamera.com
Dury's 701 Ewing Ave. .... Nashville TN 37203 615-255-3456 255-3506
TF: 800-824-2379 ■ *Web:* www.durys.com
F-11 Photographic Supplies 16 E Main St .... Bozeman MT 59715 406-586-3281
TF: 888-548-0203 ■ *Web:* www.f11photo.com
Focus Camera Inc 905 McDonald Ave .... Brooklyn NY 11218 718-437-8810 437-8895
TF: 800-221-0828 ■ *Web:* www.focuscamera.com
Foto Source Canada Inc
2333 Wyecroft Rd Unit 10. .... Oakville ON L6L6L4 905-465-2759 465-0470
Web: www.fotosource.com
Kenmore Camera Inc
18031 67th Ave NE PO Box 82467 .... Kenmore WA 98028 425-485-7447 489-2843
TF: 888-485-7447 ■ *Web:* www.kenmorecamera.com
Lawrence Photo & Video Inc
2550 S Campbell St .... Springfield MO 65807 417-883-8300 883-8305
Web: www.lawrencephotovideo.com
Ritz Camera & Image
2 Bergen Turnpike. .... Ridgefield Park NJ 07660 201-881-1900
TF Cust Svc: 855-622-7489 ■ *Web:* www.ritzcamera.com
Samy's Camera Inc 431 S Fairfax Ave. .... Los Angeles CA 90036 323-938-2420 692-0750
TF: 800-321-4726 ■ *Web:* www.samys.com

120 CAMPERS, TRAVEL TRAILERS, MOTOR HOMES

Phone Fax

A & N Trailer Parts 6028 S 118th E Ave. .... Tulsa OK 74146 918-461-8404
Web: www.antrailerparts.com
Aerospace Engineering & Support Inc
1307 West 2550 South .... Ogden UT 84401 801-394-9565
Web: aesut.com
Airstream Inc 419 W Pike St .... Jackson Center OH 45334 937-596-6111
Web: www.airstream.com
Alaskan Campers Inc 420 NE Alaskan Way .... Chehalis WA 98532 360-748-6494 748-1475
Web: www.alaskancamper.net
All American Group Inc 2831 Dexter Dr .... Elkhart IN 46514 574-266-2500 266-2559
Benlee Dunright 30383 Ecorse Rd. .... Romulus MI 48174 734-722-8100
Web: www.benlee.com
Cam Superline Inc 4763 Zane A Miller Dr .... Waynesboro PA 17268 717-749-3369
Web: www.camsuperline.com
Coach House Inc 3480 Technology Dr. .... Nokomis FL 34275 941-485-0984 488-4095
TF: 800-235-0984 ■ *Web:* www.coachhouserv.com
Cool Amphibious Manufacturers International LLC
714 Okeetee Rd. .... Ridgeland SC 29936 843-717-2444 717-2424
TF: 888-926-6553 ■ *Web:* www.camillc.com
Cruise America 11 W Hampton Ave. .... Mesa AZ 85210 480-464-7300 464-7321
TF: 800-671-8042 ■ *Web:* www.cruiseamerica.com

Phone *Fax*

Custom Fiberglass Mfg Corp
Snugtop 1711 Harbor Ave PO Box 121 .... Long Beach CA 90813 562-432-5454 435-2992
TF: 800-768-4867 ■ *Web:* www.snugtop.com

Davidson-kennedy Co 800 Industrial Park Dr .... Marietta GA 30062 770-427-9467
Web: www.equipmentinnovators.com

Dexter Chassis Group 501 Miller Dr .... White Pigeon MI 49099 269-483-7681
Web: dexterchassisgroup.com

Doepker Industries Ltd 300 Doepker Ave .... Annaheim SK S0K0G0 306-598-2171
Web: www.doepker.com

Dutchmen Mfg Inc 2164 Caragana Ct PO Box 2164 ...... Goshen IN 46527 574-537-0600
TF: 866-425-4369 ■ *Web:* www.dutchmen-rv.com

Exiss Aluminum Trailers Inc
900 East Trailer Blvd .... El Reno OK 73036 877-553-9477
Web: www.exiss.com

Forest River Inc 58277 SR 19 S .... Elkhart IN 46517 574-296-7700 295-8749
Web: www.forestriverinc.com

Foretravel Motorcoach Inc
1221 NW Stallings Dr .... Nacogdoches TX 75964 936-564-8367 564-0391
TF: 800-955-6226 ■ *Web:* www.foretravel.com

Four Wheel Campers 1460 Churchill Downs Ave ...... Woodland CA 95776 530-666-1442 666-1486
TF: 800-242-1442 ■ *Web:* www.fourwheelcampers.com

Gulf Stream Coach Inc
503 S Oakland Ave PO Box 1005 .... Nappanee IN 46550 574-773-7761 773-5761
TF: 800-289-8787 ■ *Web:* www.gulfstreamcoach.com

Jayco Inc 903 S Main St .... Middlebury IN 46540 574-825-5861 825-7354
TF Cust Svc: 800-283-8267 ■ *Web:* www.jayco.com

Keystone RV Co 2642 Hackberry Dr PO Box 2000 .... Goshen IN 46527 574-535-2100 535-2199
TF: 866-425-4369 ■ *Web:* www.keystonerv.com

Lance Camper Mfg Corp 43120 Venture St .... Lancaster CA 93535 661-949-3322 949-1262
TF: 800-423-7996 ■ *Web:* www.lancecampers.com

Monaco Coach Corp 91320 Coburg Industrial Way ...... Coburg OR 97408 877-466-6226 724-5238*
**Fax Area Code:* 260 ■ **Fax:* Hum Res ■ *TF:* 888-327-4236 ■ *Web:* monacocoach.com

Myco Trailers LLC 2703 29th Ave E .... Bradenton FL 34208 941-748-2397
Web: www.mycotrailers.com

New Horizons RV Corp 2401 Lacy Dr .... Junction City KS 66441 785-238-7575 238-4992
TF: 800-235-3140 ■ *Web:* www.horizonsrv.com

Newell Coach Corp 6411 S Hwy 69 PO Box 511 .... Miami OK 74354 918-542-3344 542-2028
TF: 888-363-9355 ■ *Web:* www.newellcoach.com

Newmar Corp 355 Delaware St .... Nappanee IN 46550 574-773-7791 773-2895
TF: 800-731-8300 ■ *Web:* www.newmarcorp.com

Nu-Wa Industries Inc 3701 Johnson Rd .... Chanute KS 66720 620-431-2088 431-2513
TF: 800-835-0676 ■ *Web:* www.nuwa.com

pace-edwards 2400 Commercial Rd .... Centralia WA 98531 360-736-9991 736-9992
TF: 800-338-3697 ■ *Web:* www.pace-edwards.com

Palomino RV 1047 E M86 .... Colon MI 49040 269-432-3271 432-2516
Web: www.palominorv.com

Peterson Industries Inc 616 E Hwy 36 .... Smith Center KS 66967 785-282-6825 282-3810
TF: 800-368-3759 ■ *Web:* www.petersonind.com

Renegade/Kibbi LLC 52216 State Rd 15 .... Bristol IN 46507 574-848-1126 848-1127
TF: 888-522-1126 ■ *Web:* www.renegaderv.com

Rexhall Industries Inc 46147 Seventh St W .... Lancaster CA 93534 661-726-0565
OTC: REXLQ ■ *TF:* 800-765-7500 ■ *Web:* www.rexhall.com

Skyline Corp 2520 By-Pass Rd .... Elkhart IN 46514 574-294-6521 295-8601
NYSE: SKY ■ *TF:* 800-348-7469 ■ *Web:* www.skylinecorp.com

Thor Industries Inc 419 W Pike St .... Jackson Center OH 45334 937-596-6111 596-6111*
NYSE: THO ■ **Fax Area Code:* 877 ■ *Web:* thorindustries.com

Tiffin Motor Homes Inc (TMH) 105 Second St NW ...... Red Bay AL 35582 256-356-8661 356-8219
Web: www.tiffinmotorhomes.com

Vanguard National Trailer Corp
289 E Water Tower Dr .... Monon IN 47959 219-253-2000
Web: www.vanguardtrailer.com

Viking Recreational Vehicles LLC
580 W Burr Oak St PO Box 549 .... Centreville MI 49032 269-467-6321 467-6021
Web: coachmenrv.com

Walt's Drive-A-Way Services Inc
321 N Kerth Ave .... Evansville IN 47711 812-424-8927
Web: www.waltsonline.com

Winnebago Industries Inc
605 W Crystal Lk Rd PO Box 152 .... Forest City IA 50436 641-585-3535 585-6966
NYSE: WGO ■ *TF:* 800-643-4892 ■ *Web:* www.winnebagoind.com

121 CAMPGROUND OPERATORS

Phone *Fax*

Banner Day Camp 1225 Riverwoods Rd .... Lake Forest IL 60045 847-295-4900
Web: www.bannerdaycamp.com

CanaDream Corp 2510 27 St NE .... Calgary AB T1Y7G1 403-291-1000
Web: www.canadream.com

Carson Valley Inn Inc 1627 US Hwy 395 N .... Minden NV 89423 775-782-9711
Web: www.cvinn.com

Champion Electric Inc 3950 Garner Rd .... Riverside CA 92501 951-276-9619
Web: www.championelec.com

Coan Construction Company Inc
1481 E Grand Ave .... Pomona CA 91766 909-868-6812
Web: www.coanconstruction.com

F Visions Services 500 Greenwich St Fl 3 .... New York NY 10013 212-625-1616
Web: www.visionsvcb.org

Glen Eden Corp 25999 Glen Eden Rd .... Corona CA 92883 951-277-4650
Web: www.gleneden.com

Hart Ranch Camping Resort Club
23756 Arena Dr .... Rapid City SD 57702 605-399-2582
Web: www.hartranchresort.com

Holiday Trails Resorts (Western) Inc
53730 Bridal Falls Rd .... Rosedale BC V0X1X1 604-794-7876 794-3756
TF: 800-663-2265 ■ *Web:* www.holidaytrailsresorts.com

Kampgrounds of America Inc (KOA) PO Box 30558 .... Billings MT 59114 888-562-0000 255-7402*
**Fax Area Code:* 406 ■ *TF:* 888-562-0000 ■ *Web:* www.koa.com

Leisure Systems Inc 50 W Techne Ctr Dr Ste G .... Milford OH 45150 513-831-2100 576-8670
TF: 866-928-9644 ■ *Web:* www.jellystonefranchise.com

Pismo Coast Village Inc
165 S Dolliver St .... Pismo Beach CA 93449 805-773-5649
Web: www.pismocoastvillage.com

Red River Computer Company Inc
21 Water St Ste 500 .... Claremont NH 03743 603-448-8880
Web: www.redriver.com

Swan Lake Resort & Campground
17463 County Hwy 29 .... Fergus Falls MN 56537 218-736-4626
Web: swanlkresort.com

Touch of Nature Environmental Center
1206 Touch Of Nature Rd .... Makanda IL 62958 618-453-1121
Web: www.pso.siu.edu

Vernon Edwards Constructors Inc
2045 Preisker Ln Ste A .... Santa Maria CA 93454 805-614-9909
Web: www.vedwards.com

Western Horizon Resorts (WHR)
103 W Tomichi Ave Ste 201A .... Gunnison CO 81230 970-641-5387 642-4591
TF: 800-378-3709 ■ *Web:* www.westernhorizonresorts.net

122 CANDLES

SEE ALSO Gift Shops p. 2357

Phone *Fax*

Blyth Inc One E Weaver St .... Greenwich CT 06831 203-661-1926 661-1969
NYSE: BTH ■ *Web:* www.blyth.com

Dadant & Sons Inc 51 S Second St .... Hamilton IL 62341 217-847-3324 847-3660
TF: 888-922-1293 ■ *Web:* www.dadant.com

General Wax & Candle Co
6863 Beck Ave PO Box 9398 .... North Hollywood CA 91605 818-765-5800 765-0555
TF: 800-929-7867 ■ *Web:* www.generalwax.com

Knorr Beeswax Products Inc
14906 Via De La Valle .... Del Mar CA 92014 760-431-2007 431-8977
TF: 800-807-2337 ■ *Web:* www.knorrbeeswax.com

Original Cake Candle Co, The
102 Sundale Rd PO Box 97 .... Norwich OH 43767 740-872-3248 872-3312
TF: 800-288-2340 ■ *Web:* cakecandle.com

Reed Candle Co
1531 W Poplar St PO Box 7261 .... San Antonio TX 78207 210-734-4243 734-2342
Web: reedcandlecompany.com

Root Candles Co 623 W Liberty St .... Medina OH 44256 330-725-6677 725-5624
TF: 800-289-7668 ■ *Web:* www.rootcandles.com

Swans Candles 8933 Gravelly Lk Dr SW .... Lakewood WA 98499 253-584-4666 584-2874
TF: 888-848-7926 ■ *Web:* www.swanscandles.com

123 CANDY STORES

Phone *Fax*

Adamson Associates Architects
401 Wellington St W 3rd Fl .... Toronto ON M5V1E7 416-967-1500
Web: www.adamson-associates.com

Burdette Beckmann Inc 5851 Johnson St .... Hollywood FL 33021 954-983-4360
Web: www.bbiteam.com

Candy Bouquet International Inc
510 Mclean St .... Little Rock AR 72202 501-375-9990 375-9998
TF: 877-226-3901 ■ *Web:* www.candybouquet.com

Candy Express 3320 Greencastle Rd .... Burtonsville MD 20866 301-384-5889 384-1788
Web: candyexpress.com

Gardners Candies Inc 2600 Adams Ave PO Box E .... Tyrone PA 16686 814-684-3925 684-3928
TF: 800-242-2639 ■ *Web:* www.gardnerscandies.com

Gertrude Hawk Chocolates Inc 9 Keystone Pk .... Dunmore PA 18512 800-822-2032 338-0947*
**Fax Area Code:* 570 ■ *TF:* 866-932-4295 ■ *Web:* www.gertrudehawkchocolates.com

Gorant Candies 8301 Market St .... Youngstown OH 44512 330-726-8821 726-0325
Web: gorant.com

JaCiva's Chocolate 4733 SE Hawthorne Ave .... Portland OR 97215 503-234-8115 234-6076
Web: www.jacivas.com

Kilwins Quality Confections Inc (KQC)
1050 Bay View Rd .... Petoskey MI 49770 888-454-5946
TF: 888-454-5946 ■ *Web:* www.kilwins.com

Lammes Candies Since 1885 Inc PO Box 1885 .... Austin TX 78767 512-310-2223 238-2019
TF: 800-252-1885 ■ *Web:* www.lammes.com

Provide Commerce Inc 4840 Eastgate Mall .... San Diego CA 92121 858-638-4900 909-4201
TF Cust Svc: 800-776-3569 ■ *Web:* www.providecommerce.com

Rocky Mountain Chocolate Factory Inc (RMCF)
265 Turner Dr .... Durango CO 81303 970-259-0554 382-7371
NASDAQ: RMCF ■ *TF Cust Svc:* 888-525-2462 ■ *Web:* www.rockymountainchocolatefactory.com

See's Candies Inc
210 El Camino Real .... South San Francisco CA 94080 650-761-2490
TF Cust Svc: 800-877-7337 ■ *Web:* www.sees.com

124 CANS - METAL

SEE ALSO Containers - Metal (Barrels, Drums, Kegs) p. 2146

Phone *Fax*

Allstate Can Corp One Wood Hollow Rd .... Parsippany NJ 07054 973-560-9030 560-9217
Web: www.allstatecan.com

BWAY Corp 8607 Roberts Dr Ste 250 .... Atlanta GA 30350 770-645-4800 645-4810
TF: 800-527-2267 ■ *Web:* www.bwaycorp.com

Can Corp of America Inc 326 June Ave .... Blandon PA 19510 610-926-3044 926-5041
Web: www.cancorpam.com

Carolina Fabricators Inc 3831 Hwy 321 .... West Columbia SC 29169 803-794-4906 794-8455
Web: www.carolinafab.net

CCL Container Corp One Llodio Dr .... Hermitage PA 16148 724-981-4420
Web: www.cclcontainer.com

Champion Container Corp
180 Essex Ave PO Box 90 .... Avenel NJ 07001 732-636-6700 855-8663
Web: www.championcontainer.com

Consolidated Fabricators Corp
14620 Arminta St .... Van Nuys CA 91402 818-901-1005
Web: www.con-fab.com

Company	City	State	Zip	Phone	Fax
Container Supply Company Inc 12571 Western Ave. Web: containersupplycompany.com	Garden Grove	CA	92841	714-892-8321	892-3824
Cork Supply USA Inc 531 Stone Rd. Web: corksupply.com/	Benicia	CA	94510	707-746-0353	
Crown Holdings Inc One Crown Way. NYSE: CCK ■ TF: 800-523-3644 ■ Web: www.crowncork.com	Philadelphia	PA	19154	215-698-5100	698-5201
DS Containers Inc 1789 Hubbard Ave. Web: www.dscontainers.com	Batavia	IL	60510	630-406-9600	
Eagle Mfg Company Inc 2400 Charles St. Web: www.eagle-mfg.com	Wellsburg	WV	26070	304-737-3171	737-3171
Euclid Spiral Paper Tube Corp 339 Mill St. Web: www.euclidspiral.com	Apple Creek	OH	44606	330-698-4711	
Exal Corp One Performance Pl. Web: www.exal.com	Youngstown	OH	44502	330-744-2267	
G3 Enterprises Inc 502 E Whitmore Ave. Web: www.g3enterprises.com	Modesto	CA	95358	209-341-4045	
Hupp & Assoc Inc 1690 Summit St. Web: www.huppaerospace.com	New Haven	IN	46774	260-748-8282	
Independent Can Co 1300 Brass Mill Rd. Web: www.independentcan.com	Belcamp	MD	21017	410-272-0090	273-7500
Intertape Polymer US Inc 3647 Cortez Rd W. Web: www.itape.com	Bradenton	FL	34210	941-727-5788	
JL Clark Mfg Co 923 23rd Ave. TF: 877-482-5275 ■ Web: www.jlclark.com	Rockford	IL	61104	815-962-8861	
JL Clark Mfg Company Lancaster Div 303 N Plum St. Web: www.jlclark.com	Lancaster	PA	17602	717-392-4125	392-5587
KOR Water Inc 95 Enterprise Ste 310. TF: 877-708-7567 ■ Web: www.korwater.com	Aliso Viejo	CA	92656	714-708-7567	
Liberty Bottle Co 2900 Sutherland Dr. Web: libertybottles.com	Union Gap	WA	98903	509-834-6500	494-0189
Peak International Inc 3432 Greystone Dr Ste 202. Web: www.peakf.com	Austin	TX	78731	512-339-4684	
Pochet of America Inc 415 Hamburg Tpke Ste D21	Wayne	NJ	07470	973-942-4923	
Polar Tech Industries Inc 415 E Railroad Ave. Web: www.polar-tech.com	Genoa	IL	60135	815-784-9000	
Protectoseal Co 225 W Foster Ave. TF: 800-323-2268 ■ Web: www.protectoseal.com	Bensenville	IL	60106	630-595-0800	595-8059
Rexam Beverage Can Americas 8770 W Bryn Mawr Ave. Web: rexam.com	Chicago	IL	60631	773-399-3000	399-8088
Rexam Inc 4201 Congress St Ste 340. TF: 800-944-2217 ■ Web: www.rexam.com	Charlotte	NC	28209	704-551-1500	551-1572
Ring Container Technology 65 Industrial Park Rd. *Fax Area Code: 901 ■ TF: 800-280-6333 ■ Web: www.ringcompanies.com	Oakland	TN	38060	800-280-6333	465-1179*
Silgan Containers Corp 21800 Oxnard St Ste 600. Web: www.silgancontainers.com	Woodland Hills	CA	91367	818-348-3700	593-2255
Silgan Holdings Inc Four Landmark Sq Ste 400. NASDAQ: SLGN ■ Web: www.silganholdings.com	Stamford	CT	06901	203-975-7110	975-7902
Simmons Metal Container 103 E Benge Rd. Web: simmonspetfood.simmonsglobal.com	Fort Gibson	OK	74434	918-478-2117	

125 CANS, TUBES, DRUMS - PAPER (FIBER)

Company	City	State	Zip	Phone	Fax
Acme Spirally Wound Paper Products Inc 4810 W 139th St PO Box 35320. TF: 800-274-2797 ■ Web: www.acmespiral.com	Cleveland	OH	44135	216-267-2950	267-0239
American Paper Products Company Inc 1722 Sumneytown Pk. Web: www.americanpaperproducts.com	Kulpsville	PA	19443	215-362-8582	362-8246
Armbrust Paper Tubes Inc 6255 S Harlem Ave. Web: www.tubesrus.com	Chicago	IL	60638	773-586-3232	
Callenor Company Inc N 60 W 15725 Kohler Ln. TF: 800-813-7429 ■ Web: www.callenor.com	Menomonee Falls	WI	53051	262-252-3343	252-3873
Caraustar Industries Inc 5000 Austell-Powder Springs Rd Ste 300. TF: 800-223-1373 ■ Web: www.caraustar.com	Austell	GA	30106	770-948-3100	
Chicago Mailing Tube Co 400 N Leavitt St. Web: www.mailing-tube.com	Chicago	IL	60612	312-243-6050	243-6545
Custom Paper Tubes Inc 15900 Industrial Pkwy. TF: 800-343-8823 ■ Web: www.custompapertubes.com	Cleveland	OH	44135	216-362-2964	362-2980
Fibercorp Mills Inc 670 17th St NW. Web: fibercorr.com	Massillon	OH	44647	330-837-5151	
Greif Inc 425 Winter Rd. NYSE: GEF ■ TF: 877-781-9797 ■ Web: www.greif.com	Delaware	OH	43015	740-549-6000	657-6592
Industrial Paper Tube Inc 1335 E Bay Ave. *Fax Area Code: 718 ■ TF: 800-345-0960 ■ Web: www.mailingtubes-ipt.com	Bronx	NY	10474	800-345-0960	378-0055*
LCH Paper Tube & Core Co 11930 Larc Industrial Blvd. TF: 800-472-3477 ■ Web: www.lchpackaging.com	Burnsville	MN	55337	952-358-3587	224-0087
Master Package Corp 200 Madson St. TF: 800-396-8425 ■ Web: www.masterpackage.com	Owen	WI	54460	715-229-2156	229-2689
New England Paper Tube Company Inc PO Box 186. Web: nepapertube.com	Pawtucket	RI	02862	401-725-2610	
NYSCO Products Inc 2350 Lafayette Ave. Web: www.nysco.com	Bronx	NY	10473	718-792-9000	792-7732
Ohio Paper Tube Co 3422 Navarre Rd SW. Web: www.ohiopapertube.com	Canton	OH	44706	330-478-5171	
OX Paper Tube & Core Inc 331 Maple Ave. TF: 800-414-2476 ■ Web: oxpapertube.com	Hanover	PA	17331	800-414-2476	972-8823
Pacific Paper Tube Inc 1025 98th Ave. TF: 888-377-8823 ■ Web: www.pacificpapertube.com	Oakland	CA	94603	510-562-8823	562-9002
Precision Paper Tube Company Inc 1033 S Noel Ave. Web: www.pptube.com	Wheeling	IL	60090	847-537-4250	537-5777
Precision Paper Tube Company Resinite Corp Div 1033 S Noel Ave. Web: www.pptube.com	Wheeling	IL	60090	847-537-4250	537-5777
Self-Seal Container Corp 401 E Fourth St. TF: 800-334-1428 ■ Web: www.selfsealtubes.com	Bridgeport	PA	19405	610-275-2300	275-4430
TEKPAK Inc 1410 Washington St. *Fax Area Code: 630 ■ TF: 866-901-8073 ■ Web: www.tekpakinc.com	Marion	AL	36756	334-683-6121	406-0577*
Trend-Pak of Canada 71 Railside Rd. Web: www.trendpak.com	North York	ON	M3A1B2	416-510-3129	510-8371
Yankee Containers 110 Republic Dr. Web: www.yankeecontainers.com	North Haven	CT	06473	203-288-3851	288-9936
Yazoo Mills Inc PO Box 369. TF Cust Svc: 800-242-5216 ■ Web: www.yazoomills.com	New Oxford	PA	17350	717-624-8993	624-4420

126 CAR RENTAL AGENCIES

SEE ALSO Fleet Leasing & Management p. 2291; Truck Rental & Leasing p. 3259

Company	City	State	Zip	Phone	Fax
A Betterway Rent-a-car Inc 1110 Northchase Pkwy SE. TF: 800-527-0700 ■ Web: www.budgetatl.com	Marietta	GA	30067	770-240-3305	240-3340
ACE Rent A Car 5773 W Washington St. TF: 800-242-7368 ■ Web: www.acerentacar.com	Indianapolis	IN	46241	317-248-5686	248-7251
Advantage Rent-A-Car 1288 Old Bayshore Hwy Ste 116. TF Cust Svc: 800-777-5500 ■ Web: www.advantage.com	Burlingame	CA	94010	650-343-3052	343-3858
Affiliated Car Rental 105 Hwy 36. *Fax Area Code: 732 ■ TF: 800-367-5159 ■ Web: www.affiliatedcarrental.com	Eatontown	NJ	07724	800-367-5159	380-0404*
Affordable Car Rental LC 105 Hwy 36. TF: 800-367-5159 ■ Web: www.affiliatedcarrental.com	Eatontown	NJ	07724	732-272-8736	380-0404
Aulick Leasing Corp 305 Ninth Ave PO Box 1369. Web: www.aulickleasing.com	Scottsbluff	NE	69361	308-220-4000	
Auto Europe 39 Commercial St. TF: 800-223-5555 ■ Web: www.autoeurope.com	Portland	ME	04101	207-842-2000	842-2222
Avis Rent A Car System Inc 6 Sylvan Way. *Fax: Sales ■ TF: 800-331-1212 ■ Web: www.avis.com	Parsippany	NJ	07054	973-496-3500	496-3444*
Budget Rent A Car System Inc Six Sylvan Way. TF: 800-527-0700 ■ Web: www.budget.com	Parsippany	NJ	07054	800-283-4382	
Car Rentals Inc 1570 S Washington Ave. Web: www.avisnj.com	Piscataway	NJ	08854	732-752-6800	981-1953
Communauto Inc 335 rue St-Joseph Est Ste 310. Web: www.communauto.com	Quebec	QC	G1K3B4	418-523-1788	
Dewey Ford Inc 3055 SE Delaware Ave. TF: 888-378-8516 ■ Web: www.deweyford.com	Ankeny	IA	50021	515-289-4949	289-4956
Discount Car & Truck Rentals Ltd 720 Arrow Rd. *Fax Area Code: 416 ■ TF: 866-742-5968 ■ Web: www.discountcar.com	North York	ON	M9M2M1	866-742-5968	744-8340*
Dollar Rent A Car Inc 5330 E 31st St. *Fax: Sales ■ TF: 800-800-4000 ■ Web: www.dollar.com	Tulsa	OK	74135	918-669-3000	669-3009*
Dollar Thrifty Automotive Group Inc 5330 E 31st St PO Box 35985. TF: 800-334-1705 ■ Web: www.thrifty.com	Tulsa	OK	74135	918-660-7700	
Driving Force Inc, The 170 Airport Rd Box 2568. Web: www.drivingforce.ca	Inuvik	NT	X0E0T0	867-777-2346	
Enterprise Rent-A-Car 600 Corporate Pk Dr. TF: 800-325-8007 ■ Web: www.enterprise.com	Saint Louis	MO	63105	314-512-5000	512-5940
Europe by Car 40 Exchange Pl Ste 1720. TF: 800-223-1516 ■ Web: www.europebycarblog.com	New York	NY	10005	212-581-3040	246-1458
Foss National Leasing 7200 Yonge St. Web: www.fossnational.com	Thornhill	ON	L4J1V8	905-886-4244	
Hale Trailer Brake & Wheel Inc Rt 73 & Cooper Rd. TF: 800-232-6535 ■ Web: www.haletrailer.com	Voorhees	NJ	08043	856-768-1330	
Hertz Global Holdings Inc 225 Brae Blvd. NYSE: HTZ ■ TF: 800-654-3131 ■ Web: www.hertz.com	Park Ridge	NJ	07656	201-307-2000	307-2644
Kemwel Inc 39 Commercial St. TF: 800-678-0678 ■ Web: www.kemwel.com	Portland	ME	04112	207-842-2285	842-2147
Omaha Truck Center Inc 10710 I St PO Box 27379. TF: 800-866-2204 ■ Web: truckcentercompanies.com/	Omaha	NE	68127	402-592-2440	
P V Rentals Ltd 5810 S Rice Ave. Web: www.pvrentals.com	Houston	TX	77081	713-667-0665	
Steve Foley Cadillac 100 Skokie Blvd. Web: www.stevefoley.com	Northbrook	IL	60062	847-564-4090	
Thrifty Car Rental 5330 E 31st St. TF: 888-400-8877 ■ Web: www.thrifty.com	Tulsa	OK	74135	918-665-3930	
Tnt Automotive Leasing Ltd 10124 W Broad St Ste G. Web: tntauto.com	Glen Allen	VA	23060	804-270-2912	
U-Save Auto Rental of America Inc 1052 Highland Colony Pkwy Ste 204. TF General: 800-438-2300 ■ Web: www.usave.com	Ridgeland	MS	39157	601-713-4333	

127 CARBON & GRAPHITE PRODUCTS

Company	City	State	Zip	Phone	Fax
Advance Carbon Products Inc 2036 National Ave. TF: 800-283-1249 ■ Web: store.advancecarbon.com	Hayward	CA	94545	510-293-5930	293-5939
Carbonyx International USA Inc 1255 W 15th St Ste 320. Web: www.carbonyx.com	Plano	TX	75025	972-943-3355	
Fiber Materials Inc Five Morin St. Web: www.fibermaterialsinc.com	Biddeford	ME	04005	207-282-5911	282-7529

Phone *Fax*

GrafTech International Holdings Inc
12900 Snow Rd . . . . . Parma OH 44130 216-676-2000
NYSE: GTI ■ *Web:* www.graftech.com

Graphite Machining Inc 240 N Main St. . . . . Topton PA 19562 610-682-0080
Web: www.graphitemachininginc.com

Graphite Systems Inc 1613 Danciger Dr . . . . . Fort Worth TX 76112 817-457-1851 457-2664

Helwig Carbon Products Inc
8900 W Tower Ave . . . . . Milwaukee WI 53224 414-354-2411 354-2421
TF: 800-365-3113 ■ *Web:* www.helwigcarbon.com

Hyper-therm Htc
18411 Gothard St Ste B . . . . . Huntington Beach CA 92648 714-375-4085
Web: www.htcomposites.com

Mersen USA BN Corp 400 Myrtle Ave . . . . . Boonton NJ 07005 800-526-0877 334-6394*
**Fax Area Code:* 973 ■ *TF General:* 800-526-0877 ■ *Web:* www.mersen.com

Micro Mech Inc 33 Tpke Rd. . . . . Ipswich MA 01938 978-356-2966

National Electrical Carbon
251 Forrester Dr. . . . . Greenville SC 29607 864-284-9728 280-7706*
**Fax Area Code:* 408 ■ *TF:* 800-471-7842 ■ *Web:* ndt.org

Oxbow Carbon & Minerals Inc
1601 Forum Pl Ste 1400. . . . . West Palm Beach FL 33401 561-697-4300 697-1876
Web: www.oxbow.com

Process Engineering Corp PO Box 279. . . . . Crystal Lake IL 60039 815-459-1734 459-3676
Web: www.pecfrictionfighters.com

Pyrotek Inc 9503 E Montgomery Ave. . . . . Spokane Valley WA 99206 509-926-6212 927-2408
Web: www.pyrotek-inc.com

Saint Marys Carbon Co 259 Eberl St . . . . . Saint Marys PA 15857 814-781-7333 834-9201
Web: www.stmaryscarbon.com

Saturn Industries Inc 157 Union Tpke . . . . . Hudson NY 12534 518-828-9956 828-9868
TF: 800-775-1651 ■ *Web:* www.saturnedm.com

SCHUNKÿGmbHÿ&ÿCo.ÿKG 211 Kitty Hawk Dr. . . . . Morrisville NC 27560 919-572-2705
Web: www.schunk.com

Scion Aviation LLC 3693 E County Rd 30 . . . . . Fort Collins CO 80528 970-207-1721
Web: www.scionaviation.com

SGL Carbon LLC 307 Jamestown Rd . . . . . Morganton NC 28655 828-437-3221 432-5885
TF: 800-828-6601 ■ *Web:* www.sglgroup.com

SPARTA Inc 25531 Commercentre Dr Ste 120 . . . . . Lake Forest CA 92630 949-768-8161

Superior Graphite
10 S Riverside Plaza Ste 1470 . . . . . Chicago IL 60606 312-559-2999 542-0200*
**Fax Area Code:* 800 ■ *TF Cust Svc:* 800-327-0337 ■ *Web:* www.superiorgraphite.com

TEC Industries LLC 403 14th St SE . . . . . Orange City IA 51041 712-707-9200
Web: www.quatrocomposites.com

US Graphite Inc 1620 E Holland Ave . . . . . Saginaw MI 48601 989-755-0441 755-0445
Web: www.usgraphite.net

Vector Composites Inc 3251 Mc Call St . . . . . Dayton OH 45417 937-281-1444
Web: www.vectorcomposites.com

Zoltek Cos Inc 3101 McKelvey Rd . . . . . Bridgeton MO 63044 314-291-5110 291-8536
NASDAQ: ZOLT ■ *Web:* www.zoltek.com

128 CARBURETORS, PISTONS, PISTON RINGS, VALVES

SEE ALSO Aircraft Engines & Engine Parts p. 1731; Automotive Parts & Supplies - Mfr p. 1839

Phone *Fax*

Compressor Products International
4410 Greenbriar Dr. . . . . Stafford TX 77477 281-207-4600 207-4612
TF: 800-675-6646 ■ *Web:* www.c-p-i.com

Dexter Automatic Products Co
2500 Bishop Cir E . . . . . Dexter MI 48130 734-426-8900 426-2622
Web: www.dapcoind.com

Grant Piston Rings 1360 Jefferson St. . . . . Anaheim CA 92807 714-996-0050 524-6607
TF: 800-854-3540 ■ *Web:* www.grantpistonrings.com

Grover Corp 2759 S 28th St . . . . . Milwaukee WI 53234 414-384-9472 384-0201
TF: 800-776-3602 ■ *Web:* www.grovercorp.com

Hastings Manufacturing Co 325 N Hanover St. . . . . Hastings MI 49058 269-945-2491 945-4667
TF: 800-776-1088 ■ *Web:* www.hastingsmfg.com

Helio Precision Products Inc
601 N Skokie Hwy . . . . . Lake Bluff IL 60044 847-473-1300 473-1306
Web: www.hnprecision.com

Holley Performance Products Inc
1801 Russellville Rd. . . . . Bowling Green KY 42101 270-782-2900 781-9940*
**Fax:* Cust Svc ■ *TF Sales:* 800-638-0032 ■ *Web:* www.holley.com

Hydreco 1500 County Naple Blvd . . . . . Charlotte NC 28273 704-295-7575 295-7574
Web: www.hydreco.com

IMPCO Technologies Inc 3030 S Susan St . . . . . Santa Ana CA 92704 714-656-1200 656-1400*
**Fax:* Sales ■ *Web:* www.impcotechnologies.com

LE Jones Co 1200 34th Ave. . . . . Menominee MI 49858 906-863-4411 863-4867
Web: www.lejones.com

MAHLE Industries Inc 2020 Sanford St . . . . . Muskegon MI 49444 231-722-1300 724-1941
TF: 888-255-1942 ■ *Web:* www.us.mahle.com

Martin Wells Industries PO Box 01406 . . . . . Los Angeles CA 90001 323-581-6266 589-2334
TF: 800-421-6000 ■ *Web:* martinwellsco.com

Pacific Piston Ring Co Inc
3620 Eastham Dr . . . . . Culver City CA 90232 310-836-3322
Web: www.pacificpistonring.com

Safety Seal Piston Ring Co 4000 Airport Rd. . . . . Marshall TX 75672 903-938-9241 938-9317*
**Fax:* Sales ■ *TF Sales:* 800-962-3631 ■ *Web:* www.sswesco.com

Total Seal Inc 22642 N 15th Ave . . . . . Phoenix AZ 85027 623-587-7400 587-7600
TF: 800-874-2753 ■ *Web:* www.totalseal.com

United Engine & Machine Company Inc
1040 Corbett St . . . . . Carson City NV 89706 775-882-7790 882-7773
TF: 800-648-7970 ■ *Web:* www.uempistons.com

Wiseco Piston Inc 7201 Industrial Pk Blvd. . . . . Mentor OH 44060 440-951-6600 951-6606
TF: 800-321-1364 ■ *Web:* www.wiseco.com

Zenith Fuel Systems Inc
14570 Industrial Pk Rd. . . . . Bristol VA 24202 276-669-5555 645-8696
Web: www.zenithfuelsystems.com

129 CARD SHOPS

SEE ALSO Gift Shops p. 2357

Phone *Fax*

Ad-venture Promotions LLC 2625 Regency Rd . . . . . Lexington KY 40503 859-263-4299
Web: www.ad-venturepromotions.com

American Greetings Corp Carlton Cards Div
1 American Rd . . . . . Cleveland OH 44144 216-252-7300 252-6778
TF: 800-777-4891 ■ *Web:* www.corporate.americangreetings.com

Captiv 8 57 E 11th St Fl 5 . . . . . New York NY 10003 212-473-2440
Web: www.captiv8promos.com

Coral Productions Inc 100 Bickford St. . . . . Rochester NY 14606 585-254-2580
Web: www.coralproductions.com

Design It Yourself Gift Baskets LLC
7999 Hansen Rd Ste 204 . . . . . Houston TX 77061 713-944-3440
Web: www.designityourselfgiftbaskets.com

Future of Flight Foundation
8415 Paine Field Blvd. . . . . Mukilteo WA 98275 425-438-8100
Web: www.futureofflight.org

Get Noticed Promotions Inc 152 Sonwil Dr. . . . . Buffalo NY 14225 716-688-8152
Web: getnoticedpromotions.com

Hallmark Cards Inc 2501 McGee St . . . . . Kansas City MO 64108 816-274-5111 274-5061*
**Fax:* Mail Rm ■ *TF:* 800-425-5627 ■ *Web:* www.hallmark.com

Howe Caverns Inc 255 Discovery Dr. . . . . Howes Cave NY 12092 518-296-8900
Web: www.howecaverns.com

Papyrus Franchise Corp 500 Chadbourne Rd . . . . . Fairfield CA 94533 800-789-1649 428-0641*
**Fax Area Code:* 707 ■ *TF:* 800-789-1649 ■ *Web:* www.papyrusonline.com

Party Concepts
4691 S Butterfield Dr Palo Verde . . . . . Tucson AZ 85714 520-750-0550
Web: party-concepts.com

Recycled Paper Greetings Inc
111 N Canal St Ste 700 . . . . . Chicago IL 60606 800-777-3331 929-7123*
**Fax Area Code:* 773 ■ *TF:* 800-777-3331 ■ *Web:* www.prgreetings.com

130 CARDS - GREETING - MFR

Phone *Fax*

123Greetingscom Inc 1674 Broadway Ste 403. . . . . New York NY 10019 212-246-0044
Web: www.123greetings.com

Amber Lotus Publishing PO Box 11329. . . . . Portland OR 97211 503-284-6400 284-6417
TF: 800-326-2375 ■ *Web:* www.amberlotus.com

American Artists Group Inc PO Box 49313 . . . . . Athens GA 30604 706-227-0708 637-3105*
**Fax Area Code:* 270 ■ *Web:* www.americanartistsgroup.com

American Greetings Corp 1 American Rd . . . . . Cleveland OH 44144 216-252-7300 252-6778
NYSE: AM ■ *TF Sales:* 800-777-4891 ■ *Web:* www.corporate.americangreetings.com

AtticSalt Greetings Inc PO Box 5773 . . . . . Topeka KS 66605 888-345-6005 333-0225*
**Fax Area Code:* 866 ■ *TF:* 888-345-6005 ■ *Web:* www.atticsaltgreetings.com

Avanti Press Inc 155 W Congress St Ste 200 . . . . . Detroit MI 48226 313-961-0022 875-9690*
**Fax Area Code:* 800 ■ *TF:* 800-228-2684 ■ *Web:* www.avantipress.com

B Designs Letterpress 23 Noel St Ste 2 . . . . . Amesbury MA 01913 978-388-1052
Web: www.bdesignsletterpress.com

Bayview Press 30 Knox St PO Box 153. . . . . Thomaston ME 04861 207-354-9919 354-9919
TF: 800-903-2346 ■ *Web:* www.bayviewpress.com

Birchcraft Studios Inc 10 Railroad St . . . . . Abington MA 02351 781-878-5152 678-5151*
**Fax Area Code:* 800 ■ *TF:* 800-333-0405 ■ *Web:* www.birchcraft.com

Blue Mountain Arts Inc PO Box 4549 . . . . . Boulder CO 80306 303-449-0536 417-6496*
**Fax:* Cust Svc ■ *TF Sales:* 800-545-8573 ■ *Web:* www.sps.com

Blue Turtle Studio 4884 Broiles Rd . . . . . Christiana TN 37037 615-585-5757
Web: www.blueturtlestudio.com

Bonair Daydreams PO Box 1522. . . . . Wrightsville Beach NC 28480 910-617-3887 509-4108
TF: 888-226-6247 ■ *Web:* www.bonairdaydreams.com

Carole Joy Creations Inc
1087 Federal Rd Unit 8. . . . . Brookfield CT 06804 203-740-4490 740-4495
TF Sales: 800-223-6945 ■ *Web:* www.carolejoy.com

Checkerboard Ltd 216 W Boylston St . . . . . West Boylston MA 01583 508-835-2475 835-4355
Web: checkernet.com

Colors By Design 7723 Densmore Ave. . . . . Van Nuys CA 91406 800-832-8436 824-2530
TF: 800-832-8436 ■ *Web:* www.cbdcards.com

Curiosities Greeting Cards 21 Ashwood Ct . . . . . Lancaster NY 14086 716-681-2801 685-2141
Web: www.curiosities.com

DaySpring Cards Inc 21154 Hwy 16 E . . . . . Siloam Springs AR 72761 479-524-9301 524-8813
TF: 800-944-8000 ■ *Web:* www.dayspring.com

Design Design Inc 19 La Grave SE . . . . . Grand Rapids MI 49503 616-774-2448 774-4020
TF: 800-334-3348 ■ *Web:* www.designdesign.us

Eclectik 1332 W Lake St. . . . . Chicago IL 60607 312-676-2442 751-2075*
**Fax Area Code:* 773 ■ *TF:* 866-308-1231 ■ *Web:* www.eclectik.com

Fantus Paper Products P.S. Greetings Inc
5730 N Tripp Ave . . . . . Chicago IL 60646 773-267-6069 267-6055
TF Sales: 800-621-8823 ■ *Web:* www.psg-fpp.com

Fotofolio Inc 561 Broadway. . . . . New York NY 10012 212-226-0923 226-0072
Web: www.fotofolio.com

Freedom Greeting Card Company Inc
774 American Dr. . . . . Bensalem PA 19020 215-604-0300 604-0436
TF Sales: 800-359-3301 ■ *Web:* www.freedomgreetings.com

Galison Publishing LLC 28 W 44th St Ste 1411. . . . . New York NY 10036 212-354-8840
TF: 800-670-7441 ■ *Web:* www.galison.com

Gallant Greetings Corp
4300 United Pkwy. . . . . Schiller Park IL 60176 847-671-6500 671-5900
TF: 800-621-4279 ■ *Web:* www.gallantgreetings.com

Gina B Designs Inc
12700 Industrial Pk Blvd Ste 40. . . . . Plymouth MN 55441 763-559-7595 559-3899
TF: 800-228-4856 ■ *Web:* www.ginabdesigns.com

Graphique De France Nine State St . . . . . Woburn MA 01801 781-935-3405 935-5145
TF Sales: 800-444-1464 ■ *Web:* www.graphiquedefrance.com

Great Arrow Graphics 2495 Main St Ste 457 . . . . . Buffalo NY 14214 716-836-0408 836-0702
TF: 800-835-0490 ■ *Web:* www.greatarrow.com

Hallmark Cards Inc 2501 McGee St . . . . . Kansas City MO 64108 816-274-5111 274-5061*
**Fax:* Mail Rm ■ *TF:* 800-425-5627 ■ *Web:* www.hallmark.com

Hallmark International PO Box 419034. . . . . Kansas City MO 64141 816-274-5111 545-2305
TF: 800-425-5627 ■ *Web:* www.hallmark.com

Phone Fax

JewishCard 7360 Viewpoint Rd ... Aptos CA 95003 831-469-8883 662-2746
Web: www.jewishcard.com

Laughing Elephant 3645 Interlake Ave N ... Seattle WA 98103 800-354-0400
TF: 800-354-0400 ■ *Web:* www.laughingelephant.com

Laurel Ink 911 N 145th St ... Seattle WA 98133 800-850-0081
TF Cust Svc: 800-850-0081 ■ *Web:* www.laurelink.com

Leanin' Tree Inc 6055 Longbow Dr ... Boulder CO 80301 303-530-1442 530-7283
Web: www.leanintree.com

Marian Heath Greeting Cards Inc
Nine Kendrick Rd ... Wareham MA 02571 508-291-0766 291-2976
TF Sales: 800-688-9998 ■ *Web:* www.marianheath.com

Meri Meri 63 Leonard St ... Belmont MA 02478 617-484-5571
TF: 800-638-2881 ■ *Web:* www.merimeri.com

Museum Facsimiles 117 Fourth St ... Pittsfield MA 01201 413-499-0020 442-3011
TF: 877-499-0020 ■ *Web:* www.museumfacsimiles.com

New England Art Publisher
10 Railroad St ... North Abington MA 02351 781-616-2508
TF: 800-333-0405 ■ *Web:* www.birchcraft.com

NobleWorks Inc 500 Paterson Plank Rd ... Union City NJ 07087 201-420-0095 420-0679
TF: 800-346-6253 ■ *Web:* www.nobleworkscards.com

Northern Exposure Greeting Cards
2301 Circadian Way Ste 300 ... Santa Rosa CA 95407 707-546-2153 546-0875
TF: 800-237-3524 ■ *Web:* www.necards.com

Nouvelles Images Inc 68 Morgan Ave ... Danbury CT 06810 203-730-1004
TF: 800-345-1383 ■ *Web:* www.nouvellesimages.com

Palm Press Inc 1442A Walnut St PO Box 120 ... Berkeley CA 94709 510-486-0502 486-1158
TF: 800-322-7256 ■ *Web:* www.palmpressinc.com

Paperdoll Co 4944 Encino Ave ... Encino CA 91316 818-906-8411 907-0225
TF: 866-223-1145 ■ *Web:* thepaperdollcompany.com

Peaceable Kingdom Press
950 Gilman St Ste 200 ... Berkeley CA 94710 510-558-2051 558-2052
TF: 877-444-5195 ■ *Web:* www.peaceablekingdom.com

Penny Laine Papers
2211 Century Ctr Blvd Ste 110 ... Irving TX 75062 972-812-3000 812-3004
TF: 800-456-6484 ■ *Web:* pennylainepapers.com

Perma-Greetings Inc 2470 Schuetz Rd ... Maryland Heights MO 63043 314-567-4606 567-0674
Web: permagraphics.net

Persimmon Press PO Box 297 ... Belmont CA 94002 650-802-8325 910-5095*
**Fax Area Code:* 800 ■ *TF:* 800-910-5080 ■ *Web:* www.persimmoncards.com

PostMark Press Inc 16 Spruce St ... Watertown MA 02472 617-924-3520 924-1371
Web: www.postmarkpress.com

Posty Cards 1600 Olive St ... Kansas City MO 64127 816-231-2323 577-3800*
**Fax Area Code:* 888 ■ *TF:* 800-821-7968 ■ *Web:* www.postycards.com

Potluck Press 920 S Bayview St ... Seattle WA 98134 206-268-0458 328-4633
Web: www.potluckpress.com

Quotable Cards Inc 611 Broadway Rm 810 ... New York NY 10012 212-420-7552 420-7558
Web: www.quotablecards.com

Recycled Paper Greetings Inc
111 N Canal St Ste 700 ... Chicago IL 60606 800-777-3331 929-7123*
**Fax Area Code:* 773 ■ *TF:* 800-777-3331 ■ *Web:* www.prgreetings.com

Schurman Fine Papers
500 Chadbourne Rd PO Box 6030 ... Fairfield CA 94533 800-789-1649 428-0641*
**Fax Area Code:* 707 ■ *TF Sales:* 800-789-1649 ■ *Web:* www.papyrusonline.com

Sillies Greeting Card Co 14762 Oak Run Ln ... Burnsville MN 55306 952-892-5666

StellArt 2012 Waltzer Rd ... Santa Rosa CA 95403 707-569-1378 569-1379
TF: 866-621-1987 ■ *Web:* www.stellart.com

Sunshine Business Class
150 Kingswood Rd PO Box 8465 ... Mankato MN 56001 800-873-7681 842-9371
TF: 800-873-7681 ■ *Web:* www.sunshinebusinessclass.com

Sunshine Girl Creations Inc
11111 Excelsior Blvd ... Hopkins MN 55343 952-931-2464 931-2575
Web: www.sunshinegirlcreations.net

Up With Paper 6049 Hi-Tek Ct ... Mason OH 45040 513-759-7473 293-8471*
**Fax Area Code:* 800 ■ *TF:* 800-852-7677 ■ *Web:* www.upwithpaper.com

US Allegiance Inc 63075 NE 18th St ... Bend OR 97701 800-327-1402 622-8212

Victorian Trading Co 15600 W 99th St ... Lenexa KS 66219 913-438-3995 724-7697*
**Fax Area Code:* 800 ■ *TF Cust Svc:* 800-700-2035 ■ *Web:* www.victoriantradingco.com

Viktorina Cards 89 Stonehurst Ave Ste 311 ... Ottawa ON K1Y4R6 613-422-6337
Web: www.amazzzingcards.com

Willow Creek Press Inc
9931 Hwy 70 W PO Box 147 ... Minocqua WI 54548 715-358-7010 358-2807
TF Cust Svc: 800-850-9453 ■ *Web:* www.willowcreekpress.com

ZPR International Inc
27900 Chagrin Blvd Ste 208 ... Beachwood OH 44122 216-464-2667

131 CARPETS & RUGS

SEE ALSO Flooring - Resilient p. 2292; Tile - Ceramic (Wall & Floor) p. 3236
The companies listed here include carpet finishers and makers of mats and padding.

Phone Fax

Americas Floor Source 3442 Millennium Ct ... Columbus OH 43219 614-237-3181
Web: www.americasfloorsource.com

Architectural Floor Systems Inc
595 Supreme Dr ... Bensenville IL 60106 877-437-3567
TF: 877-437-3567 ■ *Web:* www.gerflorusa.com

Art of The Knot Inc 5893 Sunset Dr ... South Miami FL 33143 305-667-2000

Artisans Inc W4146 Second St PO Box 278 ... Glen Flora WI 54526 715-322-5285
TF: 800-311-8756 ■ *Web:* www.artisanscarpet.com

Atlas Carpet Mills Inc
2200 Saybrook Ave ... City of Commerce CA 90040 323-724-9000 724-4526
TF: 800-272-8527 ■ *Web:* www.atlascarpetmills.com

Bacova Guild Ltd 1000 Commerce Ctr Dr ... Covington VA 24426 540-863-2600 863-2645
Web: www.bacova.com

Barrett Carpet Mills Inc 2216 Abutment Rd ... Dalton GA 30720 800-241-4064
Web: krausflooring.com/barrett

Beaulieu of America Inc
1502 Coronet Dr PO Box 1248 ... Dalton GA 30722 800-227-7211
TF: 800-227-7211 ■ *Web:* www.blissflooring.com

Bentley Prince Street
14641 E Don Julian Rd ... City of Industry CA 91746 800-423-4709 741-7420
TF: 800-423-4709 ■ *Web:* www.bentleyprincestreet.com

Phone Fax

Blackton Inc 1714 Alden Rd ... Orlando FL 32803 407-898-2661
Web: www.blacktoninc.com

Bloomsburg Carpet Industries Inc
4999 Columbia Blvd ... Bloomsburg PA 17815 570-784-9188
TF: 800-233-8773 ■ *Web:* www.bloomsburgcarpet.com

Brintons USA
1000 Cobb Pl Blvd Bldg 200 Ste 200 ... Kennesaw GA 30144 678-594-9300
Web: brintons.net/

Camelot Carpet Mills Inc 17111 Red Hill Ave ... Irvine CA 92614 949-474-4000 553-8238
TF: 800-854-8331 ■ *Web:* www.camelotcarpetmills.com

Capel Inc 831 N Main St ... Troy NC 27371 800-382-6574 572-7040*
**Fax Area Code:* 910 ■ *TF:* 800-334-3711 ■ *Web:* www.capelrugs.com

Carpet Cushions & Supplies Inc
1520 Pratt Blvd ... Elk Grove Village IL 60007 847-364-6760 364-6785
Web: www.carpetcushions.com

Carpet Exchange 1133 S Platte River Dr ... Denver CO 80223 303-744-3300
Web: www.carpetexchangeonline.com

Carpets Plus by Design 330 Lockwood ... Woodville WI 54028 715-698-2200
Web: carpetsplusbydesign.com

Challenger Industries Inc 205 Boring Dr ... Dalton GA 30721 706-278-7707
Web: www.challengerind.com

CMH Space Flooring Products Inc
2732 Hwy 74 W ... Wadesboro NC 28170 704-694-6213
Web: www.cmhspace.com

Compagnie Beaulieu Canada 335 Ch Roxton ... Acton Vale QC J0H1A0 450-546-5000

Consolidated Carpet Assoc LLC
45 W 25th St Fl 8 ... New York NY 10010 212-226-4600
Web: www.consolidatedcarpet.com

Continental Precision Corp
230 Saint Nicholas Ave ... South Plainfield NJ 07080 908-754-7663
Web: www.montrosemolders.com

Culver Floor Covering Company Inc
2411 Ave X ... Brooklyn NY 11235 718-332-3434
Web: www.culverfloors.org

Delaware Valley Corp 500 Broadway ... Lawrence MA 01841 978-688-6995 688-5825
Web: www.dvc500.com

Dixie Group Inc 104 Nowlin Ln Ste 101 ... Chattanooga TN 37421 423-510-7000 510-7015
NASDAQ: DXYN ■ *TF:* 800-289-4811 ■ *Web:* www.thedixiegroup.com

Dorsett Industries Inc 1304 May St PO Box 805 ... Dalton GA 30721 706-278-1961 217-1775
TF: 800-241-4035 ■ *Web:* www.dorsettind.com

Durkan Patterned Carpet Inc 405 Virgil Dr ... Dalton GA 30721 800-981-2009 428-8270*
**Fax Area Code:* 706 ■ *TF:* 800-981-2009 ■ *Web:* www.durkan.com

EMW Carpets & Furniture 2141 S Broadway ... Denver CO 80210 303-744-2754
Web: emwcarpets.com

Flex Foam 617 N 21st Ave ... Phoenix AZ 85009 602-252-5819
TF: 800-266-3626 ■ *Web:* www.flexfoam.net

Floors Are Us Inc 2275 Seminole Ln ... Charlottesville VA 22901 434-978-4454
Web: www.floorsareusinc.com

Floors by Foutch 5555 Woodland Hills Dr ... Denton TX 76208 940-383-4499

Forbo Flooring Inc
Eight Maplewood Dr Humboldt Industrial Pk
PO Box 667 ... Hazleton PA 18202 570-459-0771
Web: www.forbo-flooring.com

Fortune Contract Inc 272 Kraft Dr ... Dalton GA 30721 706-279-3669
Web: www.fortunecontract.com

Garland Sales Inc PO Box 1870 ... Dalton GA 30720 706-278-7880
TF: 800-524-0361 ■ *Web:* www.garlandrug.com

H & s Floors & Furnishings Inc
210 Russell St ... Darlington SC 29532 843-393-0456

Home Dynamix LLC One Carol Pl ... Moonachie NJ 07074 201-807-0111
TF: 800-726-9290 ■ *Web:* www.homedynamix.com

Indian Summer Carpet Mills Inc
601 Callahan Rd PO Box 3577 ... Dalton GA 30719 706-277-6277 279-1884
TF: 800-824-4010 ■ *Web:* www.southwindcarpet.com

Interface Inc 2859 Paces Ferry Rd Ste 2000 ... Atlanta GA 30339 770-437-6800
NASDAQ: TILE ■ *Web:* www.interfaceglobal.com

J & J Industries Inc 818 J & J Dr PO Box 1287 ... Dalton GA 30721 706-529-2100 275-4433
TF: 800-241-4586 ■ *Web:* www.jjindustries.com

Jaipur Rugs Inc 2775 Pacific Dr ... Norcross GA 30071 404-351-2360
TF: 888-676-7330 ■ *Web:* www.jaipurrugs.com

Johnson Wholesale Floors Inc
1874 Defoor Ave NW ... Atlanta GA 30318 404-352-2700
Web: johnsonwholesalefloors.com

Johnsonite Inc 16910 Munn Rd ... Chagrin Falls OH 44023 440-543-8916
TF: 800-899-8916 ■ *Web:* www.johnsonite.com

KAS Oriental Rugs Inc 62 Veronica Ave ... Somerset NJ 08873 732-545-1900
Web: www.kasrugs.com

Langhorne Carpet Co
201 W Lincoln Hwy PO Box 7175 ... Penndel PA 19047 215-757-5155 757-2212
Web: www.langhornecarpets.com

Lexmark Carpet Mills Inc 285 Kraft Dr ... Dalton GA 30721 800-871-3211
TF: 800-871-3211 ■ *Web:* www.lexmarkcarpet.com

Manufacturers Chemicals LLC
4325 Old Tasso Rd ... Cleveland TN 37320 423-476-6518
Web: manufacturerschemicals.com

Maples Industries Inc 2210 Moody Ridge Rd ... Scottsboro AL 35768 256-259-1327 259-2072
TF Hum Res: 800-537-5447

Marglen Industries Inc 1748 WaRd Mtn Rd ... Rome GA 30161 706-295-5621
Web: www.marglen.us

Masland Carpets Inc 716 Bill Myles Dr ... Saraland AL 36571 800-633-0468 675-5808*
**Fax Area Code:* 251 ■ *TF:* 800-633-0468 ■ *Web:* www.maslandcarpets.com

Mats Inc 37 Shuman Ave ... Stoughton MA 02072 781-344-1536
Web: www.matsinc.com

Milliken & Co 920 Milliken Rd ... Spartanburg SC 29303 864-503-2020 503-2100*
**Fax:* Hum Res ■ *Web:* www.milliken.com

Milliken & Co KEX Div
201 Lukken Industrial Dr W MS 801 ... LaGrange GA 30240 706-880-5511 880-5358*
**Fax:* Cust Svc ■ *TF:* 800-241-4826 ■ *Web:* www.millikencarpet.com

Mohawk Industries Inc 160 S Industrial Blvd ... Calhoun GA 30703 706-629-7721
NYSE: MHK ■ *TF:* 800-241-4494 ■ *Web:* www.mohawkind.com

Mohawk Industries Inc Karastan Div
508 E Morris St ... Dalton GA 30721 800-234-1120
TF: 800-234-1120 ■ *Web:* www.karastan.com

Phone Fax

Mohawk Industries Inc Lees Carpets Div
160 S Industrial Blvd Ste 300 .... Calhoun GA 30701 706-629-7721 250-3590*
*Fax Area Code: 866 ■ TF: 800-241-4494 ■ Web: mohawkind.com/content.aspx?id=1785
Natco Products Corp 155 Brookside Ave .... West Warwick RI 02893 401-828-0300 823-7670
Netchannel Inc 8310 Rio Grande Blvd NW .... Albuquerque NM 87114 505-843-8282
TF: 888-843-8282 ■ Web: www.netchannel.com
Oriental Weavers of America
3252 Lower Dug Gap Rd SW .... Dalton GA 30720 706-277-9666 277-9639
TF: 800-832-8020 ■ Web: www.orientalweavers.com
Packerland Rent-a-mat Inc 12580 W Rohr Ave .... Butler WI 53007 262-781-5321
TF: 800-472-9339 ■ Web: www.packerland.net
Quality Mat Co 6550 Tram Rd .... Beaumont TX 77713 409-722-4594
Web: www.qmat.com
Rieter Automotive North America - Carpet
480 W Fifth St .... Bloomsburg PA 17815 570-784-4100 848-0130*
*Fax Area Code: 248
Rite Rug Co 3949 Business Park Dr .... Columbus OH 43204 614-261-6060
Web: www.riterug.com
Royalty Carpet Mills Inc 17111 Red Hill Ave .... Irvine CA 92614 949-474-4000 553-8238
TF: 800-854-8331 ■ Web: www.royaltycarpetmills.com
RTY Installations Inc
13903 Ballantyne Meadows Dr .... Charlotte NC 28277 704-544-0726
S & S Mills Inc 414 C N Pk Dr .... Dalton GA 30720 706-277-3677
TF: 800-241-4013 ■ Web: www.ssmillsinc.com
Schmidt Custom Floors Inc
N8W22590 Johnson Dr .... Waukesha WI 53186 262-547-8763
Web: www.schmidtflooring.com
Scottdel Inc 400 Church St .... Swanton OH 43558 419-825-2341 825-1523
TF: 800-446-2341 ■ Web: www.scottdel.com
Shaw Industries Inc 616 E Walnut Ave .... Dalton GA 30722 800-441-7429
TF: 800-441-7429 ■ Web: www.shawfloors.com
Southwind Carpet Mills
601 Callahan Rd SE PO Box 3577 .... Dalton GA 30719 706-277-6277
Web: www.cherokeecarpet.com
Subaru of Indiana Automotive Inc
5500 State Rd 38 E .... Lafayette IN 47905 765-449-1111 449-6888
Web: www.subaru-sia.com
Syntec Industries LLC
438 Lavender Dr PO Box 1653 .... Rome GA 30162 706-235-1158 235-1768
Web: www.syntecind.com
Tandus Centiva
311 Smith Industrial Blvd PO Box 1447 .... Dalton GA 30722 706-259-9711 259-9711*
*Fax: Mktg ■ TF: 800-248-2878 ■ Web: tandus-centiva.com
Tri State Wholesale Flooring Inc
3900 W 34th St N .... Sioux Falls SD 57107 605-336-3080
Web: tsf.com
Unique Carpets Ltd 7360 Jurupa Ave .... Riverside CA 92504 951-352-8125 352-8140
TF: 800-547-8266 ■ Web: www.uniquecarpetsltd.com
Universal Rugs & Oil Paintings Inc
325 N Brand Blvd .... Glendale CA 91203 818-549-0095

132 CASINO COMPANIES

SEE ALSO Games & Gaming p. 2353

Phone Fax

7clans Paradise Casino 7500 Hwy 177 .... Red Rock OK 74651 580-723-4005
Web: www.okparadisecasino.com
Affinity Gaming LLC 3440 W Russel Rd .... Las Vegas NV 89118 702-889-7695
Web: www.affinitygaming.com
Ameristar Casinos Inc
3773 Howard Hughes Pkwy Ste 490-S .... Las Vegas NV 89169 702-567-7000 378-3011*
NASDAQ: ASCA ■ *Fax Area Code: 219 ■ TF: 888-203-1112 ■ Web: www.ameristar.com
Angel of The Winds Casino
3438 Stoluckquamish Ln .... Arlington WA 98223 360-474-9740
Web: www.angelofthewinds.com
Boomtown Inc 2100 Garson Rd .... Verdi NV 89439 775-345-6000 *
*Fax: Hum Res ■ TF: 800-648-3790 ■ Web: www.boomtownreno.com
Boyd Gaming Corp
3883 Howard Hughes Pkwy 9th Fl .... Las Vegas NV 89169 702-792-7200
NYSE: BYD ■ TF: 800-522-4700 ■ Web: boydgaming.com
Buffalo Run Casino 1000 Buffalo Run Blvd .... Miami OK 74354 918-542-7140
Web: www.buffalorun.com
Century Casinos Inc
2860 S Cir Dr Ste 350 .... Colorado Springs CO 80906 719-527-8300 527-8301
NASDAQ: CNTY ■ TF: 888-966-2257 ■ Web: www.cnty.com
Colony Palms Hotel
572 N Indian Canyon Dr .... Palm Springs CA 92262 760-969-1800
Web: www.colonypalmshotel.com
Delaware North Cos Gaming & Entertainment
40 Fountain Plz .... Buffalo NY 14202 716-858-5000 858-5926
TF: 800-828-7240 ■ Web: www.delawarenorth.com
Empire Resorts Inc 204 Rt 17B .... Monticello NY 12701 845-807-0001 791-1402
NASDAQ: NYNY ■ Web: www.empireresorts.com
Fond du Lac Band of Lake Superior Chippewa
1720 Big Lake Rd .... Cloquet MN 55720 218-879-4593 878-7169
TF: 888-888-6007 ■ Web: fdlrez.com
Fort Mojave Tribal Council 500 Merriman Ave .... Needles CA 92363 760-629-4591
Web: www.fortmojave.com
Four Winds Casino Resort 11111 Wilson Rd .... New Buffalo MI 49117 866-494-6371
TF: 866-494-6371 ■ Web: www.fourwindscasino.com
Full House Resorts Inc
4670 S Fort Apache Rd Ste 190 .... Las Vegas NV 89147 702-221-7800 221-8101
NASDAQ: FLL ■ TF: 800-240-6709 ■ Web: www.fullhouseresorts.com
Granite Gaming Group 115 N First St .... Las Vegas NV 89101 702-385-4250 385-4935
Gulph Creek Hotels Inc 333 W Lancaster Ave .... Wayne PA 19087 610-687-9283
Web: gulphcreekhotels.com
Harrah's Las Vegas 3475 Las Vegas Blvd S .... Las Vegas NV 89109 800-214-9110
TF: 800-214-9110 ■ Web: www.harrahslasvegas.com
Hilton Ponce Golf & Casino Resort
1150 Ave Caribe Ste 207 .... Ponce PR 00716 787-259-7676
Web: www.hiltonponceresort.com
Hotel Fusion 140 Ellis St .... San Francisco CA 94102 415-568-2525
Web: hotelfusionsf.com
Kerzner International Ltd
1000 S Pine Island Rd Ste 800 .... Plantation FL 33324 954-809-2000 809-2317
TF: 800-321-3000 ■ Web: www.kerzner.com
Lakes Entertainment Inc
130 Cheshire Ln Ste 101 .... Minnetonka MN 55305 952-449-9092 449-9353
TF: 800-946-9464 ■ Web: www.lakesentertainment.com
Majestic Investor Holdings LLC
One Buffington Harbor Dr .... Gary IN 46406 800-522-4700 977-7811*
*Fax Area Code: 219 ■ TF: 800-522-4700 ■ Web: www.majesticstar.com
Mille Lacs Band of Ojibwe 43408 Oodena Dr .... Onamia MN 56359 320-532-4181 532-7505
TF: 800-709-6445 ■ Web: www.millelacsband.com
Mountain High Resort 24510 State Hwy 2 .... Wrightwood CA 92397 760-316-7889
Web: www.mthigh.com
Mountaineer Park Inc Route 2 .... Chester WV 26034 304-387-8300
Web: www.moreatmountaineer.com
Nevada Gold & Casinos Inc
133 E Warm Springs Rd Ste 102 .... Las Vegas NV 89119 702-685-1000 621-6919*
NYSE: UWN ■ *Fax Area Code: 713 ■ Web: www.nevadagold.com
Nevada Property 1 LLC
3708 Las Vegas Blvd South .... Las Vegas NV 89109 702-698-7000
Web: www.cosmopolitanlasvegas.com
New York Hotel Trades 707 Eighth Ave .... New York NY 10036 212-245-8100
Web: www.hotelworkers.org
Northmere The Sro Hotel 4943 N Kenmore Ave .... Chicago IL 60640 773-561-4234
Web: chicago-hotels.tripadvisor.com
Park House Hotel Corp 1206 48th St .... Brooklyn NY 11219 718-871-8100
Web: www.parkhousehotelbrooklyn.com
Pinnacle Entertainment Inc
3980 Howard Hughes Pkwy .... Las Vegas NV 89169 702-541-7777
NYSE: PNK ■ TF: 877-764-8750 ■ Web: www.pnkinc.com
Portland Square Hotel 132 W 47th St .... New York NY 10036 212-382-0600
Web: www.sanctuaryhotelnyc.com
Proximity Hotel 704 Green Vly Rd .... Greensboro NC 27408 336-379-8200
Web: www.proximityhotel.com
Red Lake Gaming Enterprises Inc PO Box 543 .... Red Lake MN 56671 218-679-2111 679-2191
TF: 888-679-2501 ■ Web: www.sevenclanscasino.com
Savannah Suites 3421 Wrightsboro Rd .... Augusta GA 30909 706-849-3100
Web: www.savannahsuites.com
Shoalwater Bay Casino 4112 State Hwy 105 .... Tokeland WA 98590 360-267-2048
Web: www.shoalwaterbaycasino.com
Silver Reef Casino 4876 Haxton Way .... Ferndale WA 98248 360-383-0777
Web: silverreefcasino.com
Station Casinos Inc 1505 S Pavilion Ctr Dr .... Las Vegas NV 89135 702-495-3000
TF Resv: 800-634-3101 ■ Web: www.sclv.com
Tachi Palace Hotel & Casino, The
17225 Jersey Ave .... Lemoore CA 93245 559-924-7751
Web: tachipalace.com
Tivoli Hotel 936 Warren Ave .... Downers Grove IL 60515 630-968-6450
Web: www.tivolihotel.com
Trump Taj Mahal
1000 Boardwalk at Virginia Ave .... Atlantic City NJ 08401 609-449-1000 449-6586
Web: www.trumptaj.com

133 CASINOS

SEE ALSO Games & Gaming p. 2353
Listings for casinos are alphabetized by states.

Phone Fax

Birmingham Race Course
1000 John Rogers Dr .... Birmingham AL 35210 205-838-7500 838-7407
TF: 800-998-8238 ■ Web: www.birminghamracecourse.com
Baccarat Casino 10128 104th Ave .... Edmonton AB T5J4Y8 780-413-3178 413-3177
Web: www.gatewaycasinos.com
Deerfoot Inn & Casino 1000 11500 35th St SE .... Calgary AB T2Z3W4 403-236-7529 252-4767
TF: 877-236-5225 ■ Web: www.deerfootinn.com
Palace Casino
2710 8882-170th St
W Edmonton Mall .... Northwest Edmonton AB T5T4J2 780-444-2112 444-1155
Web: www.palacecasino.com
Pure Canadian Gaming Corp 7055 Argyll Rd .... Edmonton AB T6C4A5 780-465-5377
Web: www.purecanadiangaming.com
Apache Greyhound Park
2551 W Apache Trl .... Apache Junction AZ 85220 480-982-2371 983-0013
Web: phoenixgreyhoundpark.com
Casino Arizona at Salt River
524 N 92nd St .... Scottsdale AZ 85256 480-850-7777 850-7741
TF General: 866-877-9897 ■ Web: www.casinoarizona.com
Fort McDowell Casino
10424 N Ft McDowell Rd .... Fort Mcdowell AZ 85264 480-837-1424
TF: 800-843-3678 ■ Web: www.fortmcdowellcasino.com
Tucson Greyhound Park 2601 S 3rd Ave .... Tucson AZ 85713 520-884-7576 624-9389
Web: tucsongreyhound.com/
River Rock Casino Resort 8811 River Rd .... Richmond BC V6X3P8 604-247-8900 207-2641
TF: 866-748-3718 ■ Web: www.riverrock.com
Agua Caliente Casino Resort Spa
32-250 Bob Hope Dr .... Rancho Mirage CA 92270 760-321-2000
TF: 888-999-1995 ■ Web: www.hotwatercasino.com
Augustine Casino 84-001 Ave 54 .... Coachella CA 92236 760-391-9500 398-4447
TF: 888-752-9294 ■ Web: www.augustinecasino.com
Barona Resort & Casino
1932 Wildcat Canyon Rd .... Lakeside CA 92040 619-443-2300 443-2856
TF: 888-722-7662 ■ Web: www.barona.com
Cache Creek Casino Resort 14455 Hwy 16 .... Brooks CA 95606 530-796-3118
Web: cachecreek.com
Club One Casino 1033 Van Ness Ave .... Fresno CA 93721 559-497-3000 237-2582
Web: www.clubonecasino.com
Commerce Casino 6131 Telegraph Rd .... Commerce CA 90040 323-721-2100 838-3472*
*Fax: Cust Svc ■ Web: www.commercecasino.com
Eagle Mountain Casino 681 S Tule Resv Rd .... Porterville CA 93257 559-788-6220 788-6223
TF: 800-903-3353 ■ Web: www.eaglemtncasino.com

Phone Fax

Fantasy Springs Resort Casino
84-245 Indio Springs Pkwy .... Indio CA 92203 760-342-5000
TF Cust Svc: 800-827-2946 ■ *Web:* www.fantasyspringsresort.com

Golden West Casino 1001 S Union Ave .... Bakersfield CA 93307 661-324-6936 324-6977
TF: 800-267-3983 ■ *Web:* www.goldenwestcasino.net

Hawaiian Gardens Casino
11871 Carson St. .... Hawaiian Gardens CA 90716 562-860-5887 860-6762
Web: www.thegardenscasino.com

Pala Casino Resort & Spa 35008 Pala-Temecula Rd .... Pala CA 92059 760-510-5100 510-5191
TF: 877-946-7252 ■ *Web:* www.palacasino.com

Pechanga Resort & Casino
45000 Pechanga Pkwy .... Temecula CA 92592 951-693-1819 695-7410
TF: 877-711-2946 ■ *Web:* www.pechanga.com

San Manuel Indian Bingo & Casino
777 San Manuel Blvd .... Highland CA 92346 800-359-2464 425-3557*
**Fax Area Code:* 909 ■ *TF:* 800-359-2464 ■ *Web:* www.sanmanuel.com

Spa Resort Casino 401 E Amado Rd .... Palm Springs CA 92262 888-999-1995
TF: 888-999-1995 ■ *Web:* www.sparesortcasino.com

Spotlight 29 Casino 46-200 Harrison Pl. .... Coachella CA 92236 760-775-5566 775-7677
TF: 800-655-1330 ■ *Web:* www.spotlight29.com

Sycuan Casino 5485 Casino Way .... El Cajon CA 92019 619-445-6002 445-6752
Web: sycuan.com/resort/

Sycuan Casino & Resort 5469 Casino Way .... El Cajon CA 92019 619-445-6002 445-1961
TF General: 800-279-2826 ■ *Web:* www.sycuan.com

Table Mountain Casino 8184 Table Mountain Rd .... Friant CA 93626 559-822-7777 822-2081
TF: 800-541-3637 ■ *Web:* www.tmcasino.com

Thunder Valley Casino 1200 Athens Ave .... Lincoln CA 95648 916-408-7777 408-8370
TF: 877-468-8777 ■ *Web:* www.thundervalleyresort.com

Viejas Casino 5000 Willows Rd .... Alpine CA 91901 619-445-5400 644-8314
TF: 800-847-6537 ■ *Web:* www.viejas.com

Black Hawk Station Casino
141 Gregory St PO Box 417 .... Black Hawk CO 80422 303-582-5582 582-5590
Web: blackhawkcolorado.com

Bronco Billy's Casino
233 E Bennett Ave PO Box 590 .... Cripple Creek CO 80813 719-689-2142 689-2869
TF: 877-989-2142 ■ *Web:* www.broncobillyscasino.com

Canyon Casino 131 Main St PO Box 30 .... Black Hawk CO 80422 303-777-1111 582-0311
Web: www.canyoncasino.com

Dostal Alley Casino 1 Dostal Alley .... Central City CO 80427 303-582-1610 582-0143
TF: 888-949-2757 ■ *Web:* www.centralcitycolorado.com

Double Eagle Hotel & Casino
442 E Bennett Ave. .... Cripple Creek CO 80813 719-689-5000 689-5096
TF: 800-711-7234 ■ *Web:* decasino.com

Famous Bonanza Casino 107 Main St .... Central City CO 80427 303-582-5914 582-0447
Web: www.famousbonanza.com

Gilpin Hotel Casino 111 Main St .... Black Hawk CO 80422 303-582-1133
Web: thegilpincasino.com

Golden Gates Casino 300 Main St .... Black Hawk CO 80422 303-582-5600 582-5700
Web: thegoldengatescasino.com

Golden Mardi Gras 300 Main St .... Black Hawk CO 80422 303-582-5600 582-5700
Web: thegoldengatescasino.com

Grande Plateau Casino 131 Main St .... Black Hawk CO 80422 303-777-1111 582-0311
Web: www.blackhawkcolorado.com

Isle of Capri Casino 401 Main St .... Black Hawk CO 80422 303-998-7777 582-9601
TF resv: 800-843-4753 ■ *Web:* www.isleofcapricasinos.com

Lodge Casino 240 Main St PO Box 50 .... Black Hawk CO 80422 303-582-1771 582-6464
Web: www.thelodgecasino.com

Midnight Rose Hotel & Casino
256 E Bennett Ave. .... Cripple Creek CO 80813 719-689-2446 689-3413
TF: 800-635-5825 ■ *Web:* triplecrowncasinos.com

Red Dolly Casino 530 Gregory St .... Black Hawk CO 80422 303-582-1100 582-1435
Web: reddollycasino.net

Reserve Casino Hotel 321 Gregory St .... Central City CO 80427 303-582-0800 582-5860
TF: 800-924-6646 ■ *Web:* www.reservecasinohotel.com

Sky Ute Casino 14324 US Hwy 172 N .... Ignacio CO 81137 970-563-7777 563-9546
TF: 888-842-4180 ■ *Web:* www.skyutecasino.com

Ute Mountain Casino Three Weeminuche Dr. .... Towaoc CO 81334 970-565-8800 565-6553
TF: 800-258-8007 ■ *Web:* www.utemountaincasino.com

Wild Card Saloon & Casino 120 Main St .... Black Hawk CO 80422 303-582-3412 582-3508
Web: www.thewildcardsaloon.com

Mohegan Sun Resort & Casino
One Mohegan Sun Blvd .... Uncasville CT 06382 860-862-8150
TF: 888-226-7711 ■ *Web:* www.mohegansun.com

Winners Sports Haven 600 Long Wharf Dr. .... New Haven CT 06511 800-468-2260 946-3222*
**Fax Area Code:* 203 ■ *TF:* 800-468-2260 ■ *Web:* www.mywinners.com

Gulfstream Park 901 S Federal Hwy .... Hallandale FL 33009 954-454-7000 576-510*
**Fax Area Code:* 544 ■ *TF:* 866-840-8069 ■ *Web:* www.gulfstreampark.com

Seminole Casino Hollywood
4150 N State Rd 7 .... Hollywood FL 33021 954-961-3220
TF: 866-222-7466 ■ *Web:* www.seminolehollywoodcasino.com

Seminole Casino Immokalee 506 S First St .... Immokalee FL 34142 800-218-0007 658-1515*
**Fax Area Code:* 239 ■ *TF:* 800-218-0007 ■ *Web:* www.seminoleimmokaleecasino.com

Seminole Coconut Creek Casino
5550 NW 40th St .... Coconut Creek FL 33073 954-977-6700 970-7721
TF: 866-222-7466 ■ *Web:* www.seminolecoconutcreekcasino.com

Seminole Hard Rock Hotel & Casino Tampa (SHRH & C)
5223 N Orient Rd .... Tampa FL 33610 813-627-7625 983-0242*
**Fax Area Code:* 954 ■ *TF General:* 866-222-7466 ■ *Web:* www.seminolehardrocktampa.com

Argosy's Alton Belle Casino One Piasa St .... Alton IL 62002 800-711-4263
TF: 800-711-4263 ■ *Web:* www.argosyalton.com

Casino Queen 200 S Front St .... East Saint Louis IL 62201 618-874-5000 874-5081
TF: 800-777-0777 ■ *Web:* www.casinoqueen.com

Harrah's Joliet 151 N Joliet St .... Joliet IL 60432 815-740-7800 740-2223
TF: 800-522-4700 ■ *Web:* www.harrahsjoliet.com

Hollywood Casino Joliet 777 Hollywood Blvd. .... Joliet IL 60436 800-426-2537
TF: 800-426-2537 ■ *Web:* www.hollywoodcasinojoliet.com

Belterra Casino Resort 777 Belterra Dr. .... Florence IN 47020 812-427-7777 427-7823
TF: 888-235-8377 ■ *Web:* www.belterracasino.com

Blue Chip Casino Inc 777 Blue Chip Dr .... Michigan City IN 46360 219-879-7711 877-2112
TF: 888-879-7711 ■ *Web:* www.bluechipcasino.com

Casino Aztar 421 NW Riverside Dr. .... Evansville IN 47708 812-433-4000
TF: 800-342-5386 ■ *Web:* www.tropevansville.com

Horseshoe Casino 777 Casino Ctr Dr .... Hammond IN 46320 219-473-7000
TF: 800-522-4700 ■ *Web:* www.totalrewards.com

Majestic Star Casino & Hotel
One Buffington Harbor Dr .... Gary IN 46406 219-977-7777
TF: 800-522-4700 ■ *Web:* www.majesticstar.com

Rising Star Casino Resort
777 Rising Star Dr .... Rising Sun IN 47040 812-438-1234
TF: 800-472-6311 ■ *Web:* www.risingstarcasino.com

Ameristar Casino Hotel Council Bluffs
2200 River Rd .... Council Bluffs IA 51501 712-328-8888
TF: 866-667-3386 ■ *Web:* www.ameristar.com

Harrah's Council Bluffs
1 Harrahs Blvd .... Council Bluffs IA 51501 712-329-6000 329-6491
TF: 800-342-7724 ■ *Web:* www.harrahscouncilbluffs.com

Horseshoe Council Bluffs
2701 23rd Ave .... Council Bluffs IA 51501 712-323-2500
Web: www.totalrewards.com

Meskwaki Bingo Hotel Casino 1504 305th St .... Tama IA 52339 800-728-4263 484-1618*
**Fax Area Code:* 641 ■ *TF:* 800-728-4263 ■ *Web:* www.meskwaki.com

Peninsula Gaming Corp 301 Bell St .... Dubuque IA 52001 563-690-4975
Web: www.diamondjo.com

Prairie Meadows Racetrack & Casino
1 Prairie Meadows Dr PO Box 1000 .... Altoona IA 50009 515-967-1000 967-1344
TF: 800-325-9015 ■ *Web:* www.prairiemeadows.com

Rhythm City Casino 101 W River Dr .... Davenport IA 52801 563-328-8000
TF: 844-852-4386 ■ *Web:* rhythmcitycasino.co

Prairie Band Casino & Resort 12305 150th Rd .... Mayetta KS 66509 785-966-7777 966-7799
TF: 888-727-4946 ■ *Web:* www.pbpgaming.com

Sac & Fox Casino 1322 Us Hwy 75 .... Powhattan KS 66527 785-467-8000
Web: www.sacandfoxcasino.com

Belle of Baton Rouge Casino
103 France St .... Baton Rouge LA 70802 800-676-4847 344-8056*
**Fax Area Code:* 225 ■ *TF:* 800-676-4847 ■ *Web:* www.belleofbatonrouge.com

Boomtown Casino New Orleans 4132 Peters Rd .... Harvey LA 70058 504-366-7711 364-8796
TF: 800-366-7711 ■ *Web:* www.boomtownneworleans.com

Boomtown Hotel Casino 300 Riverside Dr. .... Bossier City LA 71111 318-746-0711 226-9434
Web: www.boomtownbossier.com

Coushatta Casino Resort
777 Coushatta Dr PO Box 1510 .... Kinder LA 70648 800-584-7263 738-7386*
**Fax Area Code:* 337 ■ *TF:* 800-584-7263 ■ *Web:* coushattacasinoresort.com

DiamondJacks Casino Resort
711 Diamond Jacks Blvd .... Bossier City LA 71111 318-678-7777 424-1470
TF: 866-552-9629 ■ *Web:* diamondjacks.com

Eldorado Resort Casino Shreveport
451 Clyde Fant Pkwy .... Shreveport LA 71101 318-220-0711 220-0160
TF: 877-602-0711 ■ *Web:* www.eldoradoshreveport.com

Harrah's New Orleans 8 Canal St .... New Orleans LA 70130 504-533-6000
TF: 800-427-7247 ■ *Web:* www.harrahsneworleans.com

Hollywood Casino Baton Rouge
1717 River Rd N .... Baton Rouge LA 70802 877-770-7867 709-7770*
**Fax Area Code:* 225 ■ *TF:* 800-447-6843 ■ *Web:* www.hollywoodbr.com

Horseshoe Southern Indiana Hotel & Casino
711 Horseshoe Blvd .... Bossier City LA 71111 800-895-0711
TF: 800-895-0711 ■ *Web:* horseshoebossiercity.com

Isle of Capri Casino Hotel Lake Charles
100 W Lake Ave .... Westlake LA 70669 800-843-4753
TF: 800-843-4753 ■ *Web:* www.lake-charles.isleofcapricasinos.com

Paragon Casino Resort 711 Paragon Pl. .... Marksville LA 71351 800-946-1946
TF: 800-946-1946 ■ *Web:* www.paragoncasinoresort.com

Sam's Town Hotel & Casino Shreveport
315 Clyde Fant Pkwy .... Shreveport LA 71101 877-770-7867 424-5658*
**Fax Area Code:* 318 ■ *TF:* 877-770-7867 ■ *Web:* www.samstownshreveport.com

Treasure Chest Casino 5050 Williams Blvd. .... Kenner LA 70065 504-443-8000 469-4115
TF: 800-298-0711 ■ *Web:* www.treasurechest.com

Pimlico Race Course 5201 Park Heights Ave .... Baltimore MD 21215 410-542-9400 466-2521
Web: pimlico.com

Rosecroft Raceway 6336 Rosecroft Dr. .... Fort Washington MD 20744 301-567-4500 567-1053
TF: 877-818-9467 ■ *Web:* www.rosecroft.com

Suffolk Downs 111 Waldemar Ave .... East Boston MA 02128 617-567-3900 567-7511
TF: 800-225-3460 ■ *Web:* www.suffolkdowns.com

Greektown Superholdings Inc 555 E Lafayette .... Detroit MI 48226 313-223-2999
Web: www.greektowncasino.com

MGM Grand Detroit 1777 Third St. .... Detroit MI 48226 313-465-1400
TF: 877-888-2121 ■ *Web:* www.mgmgranddetroit.com

MotorCity Casino Hotel 2901 Grand River Ave .... Detroit MI 48201 313-237-7711 961-3312
TF: 866-752-9622 ■ *Web:* www.motorcitycasino.com

Rock Gaming LLC 1086 Woodward Ave .... Detroit MI 48226 313-373-3700
Web: www.rock-gaming.com

Soaring Eagle Casino & Resort
6800 E Soaring Eagle Blvd .... Mount Pleasant MI 48858 888-732-4537 775-5383*
**Fax Area Code:* 989 ■ *TF:* 888-732-4537 ■ *Web:* www.soaringeaglecasino.com

Black Bear Casino Resort
1785 Hwy 210 PO Box 777 .... Carlton MN 55718 218-878-2327 878-2414
TF: 888-771-0777 ■ *Web:* www.blackbearcasinohotel.com

Grand Casino Hinckley 777 Lady Luck Dr .... Hinckley MN 55037 800-472-6321 384-4775*
**Fax Area Code:* 320 ■ *TF:* 800-472-6321 ■ *Web:* www.grandcasinomn.com

Grand Casino Mille Lacs
777 Grand Ave PO Box 343 .... Onamia MN 56359 800-626-5825 532-8103*
**Fax Area Code:* 320 ■ *TF:* 800-626-5825 ■ *Web:* www.grandcasinomn.com

Jackpot Junction Casino Hotel
39375 County Hwy 24 PO Box 420 .... Morton MN 56270 507-697-8000 644-2529
TF: 800-946-2274 ■ *Web:* www.jackpotjunction.com

Mystic Lake Casino Hotel
2400 Mystic Lk Blvd .... Prior Lake MN 55372 952-445-9000 403-5210
TF: 800-262-7799 ■ *Web:* www.mysticlake.com

Ameristar Casino Hotel Vicksburg
4116 Washington St .... Vicksburg MS 39180 601-638-1000
Web: www.ameristar.com

Bally's Casino Tunica
1450 Bally's Blvd .... Robinsonville MS 38664 866-422-5597
TF: 866-422-5597 ■ *Web:* www.ballystunica.com

Boomtown Casino Biloxi 676 Bayview Ave .... Biloxi MS 39530 228-435-7000 435-7964
TF: 800-627-0777 ■ *Web:* www.boomtownbiloxi.com

Phone | Fax

Fitzgeralds Casino & Hotel Tunica
711 Lucky Ln ... Robinsonville MS 38664 662-363-5825 363-3579
TF: 888-766-5825 ■ *Web:* www.fitzgeraldstunica.com

Gold Strike Casino Resort
1010 Casino Ctr Dr ... Tunica Resorts MS 38664 662-357-1111 357-1306
TF Resv: 888-245-7829 ■ *Web:* www.goldstrikemississippi.com

Golden Nugget Hotels & Casinos 151 Beach Blvd ... Biloxi MS 39530 228-435-5400 436-7834
TF: 800-777-7568 ■ *Web:* www.goldennugget.com

Hard Rock Hotel & Casino Biloxi
777 Beach Blvd ... Biloxi MS 39530 228-374-7625 276-7655
TF: 877-877-6256 ■ *Web:* www.hardrockbiloxi.com

Harrah's Tunica 1021 Casino Ctr Dr ... Robinsonville MS 38664 800-303-7463
TF: 800-946-4946 ■ *Web:* horseshoetunica.com

Hollywood Casino Bay Saint Louis
711 Hollywood Blvd ... Bay Saint Louis MS 39520 866-758-2591 467-3080*
*Fax Area Code: 228 ■ *Fax: Hum Res ■ *TF:* 866-758-2591 ■ *Web:* hollywoodgulfcoast.com

IP Casino Resort & Spa 850 Bayview Ave ... Biloxi MS 39530 228-436-3000 432-3260
TF Resv: 888-946-2847 ■ *Web:* www.ipbiloxi.com

Island View Casino Resort
3300 W Beach Blvd PO Box 1600 ... Gulfport MS 39502 228-314-2100
TF General: 888-777-9696 ■ *Web:* www.islandviewcasino.com

St Jo Frontier Casino 777 Winners Cir ... St Joseph MO 64505 816-279-5514
Web: www.stjocasino.com

Casino New Brunswick LP 21 Casino Dr ... Moncton NB E1G0R7 506-859-7770
TF: 877-859-7775 ■ *Web:* www.casinonb.ca

Horsemen's Park 6303 Q St ... Omaha NE 68117 402-731-2900 731-5122
Web: www.horsemenspark.com

Aquarius Casino Resort 1900 S Casino Dr ... Laughlin NV 89029 702-298-5111
TF: 888-662-5825 ■ *Web:* www.aquariuscasinoresort.com

Arizona Charlie's Boulder Casino & Hotel
4575 Boulder Hwy ... Las Vegas NV 89121 702-951-5800
TF: 888-236-9066 ■ *Web:* www.arizonacharliesboulder.com

Arizona Charlie's Decatur Casino & Hotel
740 S Decatur Blvd ... Las Vegas NV 89107 702-258-5200 258-5192
TF: 888-236-8645 ■ *Web:* www.arizonacharliesdecatur.com

Atlantis Casino Resort 3800 S Virginia St ... Reno NV 89502 775-825-4700 332-2211
TF: 800-723-6500 ■ *Web:* www.atlantiscasino.com

Bally's Las Vegas 3645 Las Vegas Blvd S ... Las Vegas NV 89109 702-967-4111 739-4379
TF Resv: 800-522-4700 ■ *Web:* www.ballyslasvegas.com

Best Western Carson Station Hotel & Casino
900 S Carson St ... Carson City NV 89701 775-883-0900 882-7569
TF: 800-501-2929 ■ *Web:* www.carsonstation.com

Binion's Gambling Hall & Hotel
128 E Fremont St ... Las Vegas NV 89101 702-382-1600
Web: www.binions.com

Boomtown Casino & Hotel Reno 2100 Garson Rd ... Verdi NV 89439 775-345-6000 345-8696
TF Resv: 800-648-3790 ■ *Web:* boomtownreno.com

Boulder Station Hotel & Casino
4111 Boulder Hwy ... Las Vegas NV 89121 702-432-7777 367-6138*
*Fax: Circulation Desk ■ *TF:* 800-683-7777 ■ *Web:* boulderstation.sclv.com

Buffalo Bill's Resort & Casino
31900 Las Vegas Blvd S ... Primm NV 89019 702-386-7867 679-7766
TF: 888-386-7867 ■ *Web:* primmvalleyresorts.com

Cactus Jack's Casino 420 N Carson St ... Carson City NV 89701 775-882-8770

California Hotel & Casino 12 E Ogden Ave ... Las Vegas NV 89101 702-385-1222 388-2660
TF: 800-634-6505 ■ *Web:* www.thecal.com

Carson City Nugget 507 N Carson St ... Carson City NV 89701 775-882-1626 883-1106
TF: 800-426-5239 ■ *Web:* www.ccnugget.com

Carson Horseshoe Club Casino
402 N Carson St ... Carson City NV 89701 775-883-2211 883-2262
Web: carsonhorseshoe.com

Casino Fandango 3800 S Carson St ... Carson City NV 89701 775-885-7000 885-7008
Web: www.casinofandango.com

Casino Royale Hotel 3411 Las Vegas Blvd S ... Las Vegas NV 89109 702-737-3500 650-4743
TF: 800-854-7666 ■ *Web:* www.casinoroyalehotel.com

Circus Circus Hotel & Casino Reno
500 N Sierra St ... Reno NV 89503 775-329-0711 328-9652
TF: 800-648-5010 ■ *Web:* www.circusreno.com

Circus Circus Hotel Casino & Theme Park Las Vegas
2880 Las Vegas Blvd S ... Las Vegas NV 89109 702-734-0410
TF Resv: 800-634-3450 ■ *Web:* www.circuscircus.com

Colorado Belle Hotel & Casino
2100 S Casino Dr ... Laughlin NV 89029 702-298-4000
TF Resv: 877-460-0777 ■ *Web:* www.coloradobelle.com

Don Laughlin's Riverside Resort & Casino
1650 Casino Dr ... Laughlin NV 89029 702-298-2535 298-2695
TF: 800-227-3849 ■ *Web:* www.riversideresort.com

Edgewater Hotel & Casino 2020 S Casino Dr ... Laughlin NV 89029 702-298-2453 298-5606*
*Fax: Mktg ■ *TF Resv:* 800-677-4837 ■ *Web:* www.edgewater-casino.com

El Cortez Hotel & Casino 600 E Fremont St ... Las Vegas NV 89101 702-385-5200 474-3633
TF: 800-634-6703 ■ *Web:* www.elcortezhotelcasino.com

Eldorado Hotel Casino 345 N Virginia St ... Reno NV 89501 775-786-5700 322-7124
TF Resv: 800-879-8879 ■ *Web:* www.eldoradoreno.com

Excalibur Hotel & Casino
3850 Las Vegas Blvd S PO Box 96776 ... Las Vegas NV 89109 702-597-7777 597-7009
TF: 877-750-5464 ■ *Web:* www.excalibur.com

Fiesta Rancho Casino Hotel
2400 N Rancho Dr ... Las Vegas NV 89130 702-631-7000 638-3645
TF Resv: 800-731-7333 ■ *Web:* fiestarancho.sclv.com

Fremont Hotel & Casino 200 Fremont St ... Las Vegas NV 89101 702-385-3232 385-6270
TF: 800-634-6460 ■ *Web:* www.fremontcasino.com

Gold Coast Hotel & Casino
4000 W Flamingo Rd ... Las Vegas NV 89103 702-367-7111 367-8575
TF: 800-331-5334 ■ *Web:* www.goldcoastcasino.com

Gold Dust West Carson City
2171 E William St ... Carson City NV 89701 775-885-9000 888-8018
TF: 877-519-5567 ■ *Web:* www.gdwcasino.com

Gold Ranch Casino & RV Resort
350 Gold Ranch Rd PO Box 160 ... Verdi NV 89439 775-345-6789 345-2356
TF: 877-914-6789 ■ *Web:* www.goldranchrvcasino.com

Gold Spike Hotel & Casino
217 Las Vegas Blvd N ... Las Vegas NV 89101 702-476-4923
Web: goldspike.com

Gold Strike Hotel & Gambling Hall
One Main St PO Box 19278 ... Jean NV 89019 702-477-5000 671-1665
TF: 800-634-1359 ■ *Web:* goldstrikejean.com

Golden Nugget Laughlin 2300 S Casino Dr ... Laughlin NV 89029 702-298-7111 298-3023
TF: 800-950-7700 ■ *Web:* www.goldennugget.com

Grand Sierra Resort & Casino 2500 E Second St ... Reno NV 89595 775-789-2000 789-2130
TF: 800-501-2651 ■ *Web:* www.grandsierraresort.com

Green Valley Ranch Resort Casino & Spa
2300 Paseo Verde Pkwy ... Henderson NV 89052 702-617-7777
TF Resv: 866-782-9487 ■ *Web:* greenvalleyranch.sclv.com

Harrah's Laughlin 2900 S Casino Dr ... Laughlin NV 89029 702-298-4600 298-1234
TF: 800-427-7247 ■ *Web:* www.totalrewards.com

Harveys Lake Tahoe
Hwy 50 at Stateline Ave PO Box 128 ... Lake Tahoe NV 89449 775-588-6611
TF: 800-522-4700 ■ *Web:* www.harveystahoe.com

Hooters Casino Hotel 115 E Tropicana Ave ... Las Vegas NV 89109 702-739-9000
TF: 866-584-6687 ■ *Web:* www.hooterscasinohotel.com

Hyatt Regency Lake Tahoe Resort & Casino
111 Country Club Dr ... Incline Village NV 89451 775-832-1234 831-2171
TF: 800-233-1234 ■ *Web:* www.laketahoe.hyatt.com

John Ascuaga's Nugget Hotel Casino
1100 Nugget Ave ... Sparks NV 89431 775-356-3300 356-3434*
*Fax: Resv ■ *TF:* 800-648-1177 ■ *Web:* www.janugget.com

Las Vegas Club Hotel & Casino (LVC)
18 E Fremont St ... Las Vegas NV 89101 702-385-1664
TF: 800-634-6532 ■ *Web:* www.lasvegasclubcasino.com

Laughlin River Lodge. 2700 S Casino Dr ... Laughlin NV 89029 702-298-2242 298-2117
TF: 800-835-7903 ■ *Web:* www.river-palms.com

Luxor Hotel & Casino 3900 Las Vegas Blvd S ... Las Vegas NV 89119 702-262-4000 262-4404
TF Resv: 800-288-1000 ■ *Web:* www.luxor.com

M Resort LLC, The 12300 Las Vegas Blvd S ... Henderson NV 89044 702-797-1000
Web: www.themresort.com

Mandalay Bay Resort & Casino
3950 Las Vegas Blvd S ... Las Vegas NV 89119 702-632-7777 632-7234
TF: 877-632-7800 ■ *Web:* www.mandalaybay.com

MGM Grand Hotel & Casino
3799 Las Vegas Blvd S ... Las Vegas NV 89109 702-891-1111 891-3036
TF: 877-880-0880 ■ *Web:* www.mgmgrand.com

Monte Carlo Resort & Casino
3770 Las Vegas Blvd S ... Las Vegas NV 89109 702-730-7777 730-7200
TF: 800-311-8999 ■ *Web:* www.montecarlo.com

New York New York Hotel & Casino
3790 Las Vegas Blvd S ... Las Vegas NV 89109 702-740-6969 740-6700
TF: 800-689-1797 ■ *Web:* www.newyorknewyork.com

Orleans Las Vegas Hotel & Casino
4500 W Tropicana Ave ... Las Vegas NV 89103 702-365-7111 365-7500
TF: 800-675-3267 ■ *Web:* www.orleanscasino.com

Palace Station Hotel & Casino
2411 W Sahara Ave ... Las Vegas NV 89102 702-367-2411
TF Resv: 800-634-3101 ■ *Web:* palacestation.sclv.com

Palms Casino Resort 4321 W Flamingo Rd ... Las Vegas NV 89103 702-942-7777 942-7001
TF: 866-942-7777 ■ *Web:* palms.com

Peppermill Hotel & Casino 2707 S Virginia St ... Reno NV 89502 775-826-2121 689-7041
TF: 800-648-6992 ■ *Web:* www.peppermillreno.com

Railroad Pass Hotel & Casino
2800 S Boulder Hwy ... Henderson NV 89002 702-294-5000 294-0092
TF: 800-654-0877 ■ *Web:* www.railroadpass.com

Red Rock Resort Spa & Casino
11011 W Charleston Blvd ... Las Vegas NV 89135 702-797-7777 797-7890
TF: 866-767-7773 ■ *Web:* redrock.sclv.com

Riviera Hotel & Casino
2901 Las Vegas Blvd S ... Las Vegas NV 89109 702-734-5110 232-9236*
*Fax Area Code: 800 ■ *TF Resv:* 866-275-6030 ■ *Web:* www.rivierahotel.com

Sam's Town Hotel & Gambling Hall
5111 Boulder Hwy ... Las Vegas NV 89122 702-456-7777 454-8107
TF: 800-897-8696 ■ *Web:* www.samstownlv.com

Santa Fe Station 4949 N Rancho Dr ... Las Vegas NV 89130 702-658-4900
TF Resv: 888-786-7389 ■ *Web:* santafestation.sclv.com

Silver Legacy Resort & Casino 407 N Virginia St ... Reno NV 89501 775-325-7401 325-7474
TF: 800-687-8733 ■ *Web:* www.silverlegacyreno.com

Silverton Hotel & Casino
3333 Blue Diamond Rd ... Las Vegas NV 89139 702-263-7777
TF: 866-722-4608 ■ *Web:* www.silvertoncasino.com

South Point Hotel & Casino
9777 Las Vegas Blvd S ... Las Vegas NV 89183 702-796-7111 797-8041
TF: 866-796-7111 ■ *Web:* www.southpointcasino.com

Stratosphere Tower Hotel & Casino
2000 S Las Vegas Blvd ... Las Vegas NV 89104 702-380-7777 383-4755*
*Fax: Sales ■ *TF:* 800-998-6937 ■ *Web:* www.stratospherehotel.com

Suncoast Hotel & Casino 9090 Alta Dr ... Las Vegas NV 89145 702-636-7111 636-7288
TF: 877-677-7111 ■ *Web:* www.suncoastcasino.com

Sunset Station Hotel & Casino
1301 W Sunset Rd ... Henderson NV 89014 702-547-7777
TF: 888-786-7389 ■ *Web:* sunsetstation.sclv.com

Texas Station Gambling Hall & Hotel
2101 Texas Star Ln ... North Las Vegas NV 89032 702-631-1000
TF Resv: 800-654-8888 ■ *Web:* texasstation.sclv.com

Treasure Island Hotel & Casino
3300 Las Vegas Blvd S ... Las Vegas NV 89109 702-894-7111 894-7414
TF: 800-288-7206 ■ *Web:* www.treasureisland.com

Tropicana Express 2121 S Casino Dr ... Laughlin NV 89029 702-298-4200 298-4619
TF: 800-243-6846 ■ *Web:* troplaughlin.com/

Tuscany Suites & Casino 255 E Flamingo Rd ... Las Vegas NV 89169 702-893-8933 947-5994
TF Resv: 877-887-2261 ■ *Web:* www.tuscanylv.com

Western Village Inn & Casino 815 Nichols Blvd ... Sparks NV 89434 800-648-1170 331-4912*
*Fax Area Code: 775 ■ *Fax: PR ■ *TF:* 800-648-1170 ■ *Web:* www.westernvillagesparks.com

Westin Casuarina Las Vegas Hotel Casino & Spa
160 E Flamingo Rd ... Las Vegas NV 89109 702-836-5900 836-9776
Web: www.starwoodhotels.com

Wynn Las Vegas 3131 Las Vegas Blvd S ... Las Vegas NV 89109 702-770-7000 770-1571
TF: 877-321-9966 ■ *Web:* www.wynnlasvegas.com

Phone Fax

Harrah's Resort Atlantic City
777 Harrah's Blvd ... Atlantic City NJ 08401 609-441-5000
TF: 800-342-7724 ■ *Web:* www.caesars.com/harrahsac

Resorts Casino Hotel 1133 Boardwalk ... Atlantic City NJ 08401 800-334-6378
TF: 800-334-6378 ■ *Web:* www.resortsac.com

Tropicana Entertainment 2831 Boardwalk ... Atlantic City NJ 08401 800-843-8767 340-4457*
OTC: TPCA ■ **Fax Area Code:* 609 ■ *TF:* 800-843-8767 ■ *Web:* www.tropicana.net

Trump Taj Mahal Casino Resort
1000 Boardwalk & Virginia Ave ... Atlantic City NJ 08401 609-449-1000
TF: 800-426-2537 ■ *Web:* www.trumptaj.com

Camel Rock Casino 17486A Hwy 84/285 ... Santa Fe NM 87506 505-983-2667 982-2331
TF: 800-483-1040 ■ *Web:* www.camelrockcasino.com

Cities of Gold Casino
10-B Cities of Gold Rd ... Santa Fe NM 87506 505-455-3313 455-7188
TF: 800-455-3313 ■ *Web:* www.citiesofgold.com

Route 66 Casino Hotel 14500 Central Ave ... Albuquerque NM 87121 505-352-7866 352-7880
TF: 866-352-7866 ■ *Web:* www.rt66casino.com

Sandia Resort & Casino 30 Rainbow Rd NE ... Albuquerque NM 87113 505-796-7500
TF: 800-526-9366 ■ *Web:* www.sandiacasino.com

Seneca Niagara Casino 310 Fourth St ... Niagara Falls NY 14303 716-299-1100 299-1099
TF: 877-873-6322 ■ *Web:* www.senecaniagaracasino.com

Turning Stone Resort Casino LLC
5218 Patrick Rd ... Verona NY 13478 315-361-7711
TF: 800-771-7711 ■ *Web:* turningstone.com

Harrah's Cherokee Casino & Hotel
777 Casino Dr ... Cherokee NC 28719 828-497-7777 497-5076
TF General: 877-811-0777 ■ *Web:* harrahscherokee.com

Prairie Knights Casino & Resort
7932 Hwy 24 ... Fort Yates ND 58538 701-854-7777 854-7786
TF: 800-425-8277 ■ *Web:* www.prairieknights.com

Casino Nova Scotia 1983 Upper Water St ... Halifax NS B3J3Y5 902-425-7777 425-7777
TF: 888-642-6376 ■ *Web:* www.casinonovascotia.com

Caesars License Company LLC
377 Riverside Dr E ... Windsor ON N9A7H7 519-258-7878 258-0020
TF: 800-991-7777 ■ *Web:* www.caesarswindsor.com

Casino Niagara 5705 Falls Ave ... Niagara Falls ON L2E6T3 905-374-3598 353-7039
TF: 888-325-5788 ■ *Web:* www.casinoniagara.com

Fallsview Casino Resort
6380 Fallsview Blvd ... Niagara Falls ON L2G7X5 888-325-5788 371-7952*
**Fax Area Code:* 905 ■ *TF:* 888-325-5788 ■ *Web:* www.fallsviewcasinoresort.com

Bluberi Gaming & Technologies inc
2120 Rue Letendre ... Drummondville QC J2C7E9 819-475-5155
Web: www.bluberi.com

Newport Grand Jai Alai
150 Admiral Kalbfus Rd ... Newport RI 02840 401-849-5000 846-0290
TF: 800-451-2500 ■ *Web:* www.newportgrand.com

Saskatchewan Indian Gaming Authority
250 - 103 C Packham Ave ... Saskatoon SK S7N4K4 306-477-7777
TF: 800-306-6789 ■ *Web:* www.siga.sk.ca

Speaking Rock Entertainment Centre
122 S Old Pueblo Rd ... El Paso TX 79907 915-860-7777
Web: www.speakingrockentertainment.com

Emerald Downs 2300 Emerald Downs Dr PO Box 617 ... Auburn WA 98001 253-288-7000
TF: 888-931-8400 ■ *Web:* www.emeralddowns.com

Emerald Queen Casino (EQC) 2024 E 29th St ... Tacoma WA 98404 253-594-7777
TF: 888-831-7655 ■ *Web:* www.emeraldqueen.com

Great American Casino 10117 S Tacoma Way ... Lakewood WA 98499 253-396-0500 882-1001
Web: www.greatamericancasino.com

Lucky Eagle Casino 12888 188th Ave SW ... Rochester WA 98579 360-273-2000
TF: 800-720-1788 ■ *Web:* www.luckyeagle.com

Northern Quest Casino
100 N Hayford Rd ... Airway Heights WA 99001 509-242-7000 343-2163
TF: 877-871-6772 ■ *Web:* www.northernquest.com

Red Wind Casino 12819 Yelm Hwy ... Olympia WA 98513 360-412-5000 455-0364
TF: 866-946-2444 ■ *Web:* www.redwindcasino.com

Skagit Valley Casino Resort 5984 N Darrk Ln ... Bow WA 98232 360-724-7777 724-0222
TF: 877-275-2448 ■ *Web:* www.theskagit.com

Snoqualmie Entertainment Authority
37500 SE N Bend Way ... Snoqualmie WA 98065 425-888-1234
Web: www.snocasino.com

Wheeling Island Gaming Inc One S Stone St ... Wheeling WV 26003 304-232-5050
TF: 877-943-3546 ■ *Web:* www.wheelingisland.com

Dairyland Greyhound Park 5522 104th Ave ... Kenosha WI 53144 262-657-8200 657-8231
TF: 800-233-3357 ■ *Web:* www.huckrealty.com

Ho-Chunk Casino S 3214 County Rd BD ... Baraboo WI 53913 800-746-2486
TF: 800-746-2486 ■ *Web:* www.ho-chunk.com

Lake of the Torches Resort Casino
510 Old Abe Rd ... Lac du Flambeau WI 54538 715-588-7070
TF: 800-258-6724 ■ *Web:* www.lakeofthetorches.com

Potawatomi Bingo Casino 1721 W Canal St ... Milwaukee WI 53233 414-645-6888 847-7727
TF: 800-729-7244 ■ *Web:* www.paysbig.com

134 CASKETS & VAULTS

SEE ALSO Mortuary, Crematory, Cemetery Products & Services p. 2767

Phone Fax

American Wilbert Vault Corp
7525 W 99th Pl ... Bridgeview IL 60455 708-366-3210 366-3281
Web: www.americanwilbert.com

Batesville Casket Co 1 Batesville Blvd ... Batesville IN 47006 812-934-7500 934-7613
TF Cust Svc: 800-622-8373 ■ *Web:* www.batesville.com

Brown-Wilbert Inc 2280 Hamline Ave N ... Saint Paul MN 55113 651-631-1234 631-1428
Web: www.wilbert.net

Clark Grave Vault Co, The 375 E Fifth Ave ... Columbus OH 43201 614-294-3761
Web: www.clarkvault.com

CSI Care Services Inc 432 First St PO Box 172 ... Eynon PA 18403 570-876-2642 876-5613
Web: www.casketshellsinc.com

Norwalk-Wilbert Vault Co 425 Harral Ave ... Bridgeport CT 06604 203-366-5678
Web: www.norwalkwilbert.com

Paul Casket Co 505 S Green St ... Cambridge City IN 47327 765-478-3991 962-0911
TF: 800-521-8202

Pettigrew & Sons Casket Co
6151 Power Inn Rd ... Sacramento CA 95824 916-383-0777 383-2445
Web: www.pettigrewcaskets.com

Providence Casket Co One Industrial Cir ... Lincoln RI 02865 401-726-1700 726-1700

Sound Casket Co 20350 71st Ave NE Ste G ... Arlington WA 98223 360-403-3132

York Group Inc 2 Northshore Ctr Ste 100 ... Pittsburgh PA 15212 412-995-1600 995-1690
TF: 800-223-4964 ■ *Web:* www.yorkgrp.com

Zane Casket Co 1201 Hall Ave ... Zanesville OH 43701 740-452-4680

135 CEMENT

Phone Fax

Adjustable Forms Inc One E Progress Rd ... Lombard IL 60148 630-953-8700
Web: www.adjustableforms.com

All Rite Ready Mix Inc 108 Williams Way ... Wilder KY 41076 859-572-9951
Web: www.allritereadymix.com

Ash Grove Cement Co
8900 Indian Creek Pkwy ... Overland Park KS 66210 913-451-8900 451-8324
OTC: ASHG ■ *TF:* 800-545-1882 ■ *Web:* www.ashgrove.com

California Portland Cement Co
2025 E Financial Way Ste 200 ... Glendora CA 91741 626-852-6200 691-2269
TF Cust Svc: 800-272-1891 ■ *Web:* www.calportland.com

Carriere Bernier Ltee
25 Petit Bernier CP 548 ... Saint-jean-sur-richelieu QC J3B6Z8 450-545-2000
Web: www.carrierebernier.com

Cemex USA 840 Gessner Ste 1400 ... Houston TX 77024 713-650-6200 317-6047*
NYSE: CX ■ **Fax Area Code:* 212 ■ *TF:* 888 292 0070 ■ *Web:* www.cemex.com

CGM Inc 1445 Ford Rd ... Bensalem PA 19020 215-638-4400 638-7949
TF: 800-523-6570 ■ *Web:* www.cgmbuildingproducts.com

Coastal Cement Corp 36 Drydock Ave ... Boston MA 02210 617-350-0183 350-0186
TF: 800-828-8352 ■ *Web:* dragonproducts.com

Continental Cement Company LLC
14755 N Outer 40 Ste 514 ... Chesterfield MO 63017 636-532-7440 532-7445
TF: 800-625-1144 ■ *Web:* www.continentalcement.com

Daniel G Schuster LLC 3717 Crondall Ln ... Owings Mills MD 21117 410-363-3837
Web: www.schusterconcrete.com

Dragon Products Co 960 Ocean Ave ... Portland ME 04103 207-774-6355 761-5694
TF: 800-828-8352 ■ *Web:* www.dragonproducts.com

E Z Grout Corp 405 Watertown Rd ... Waterford OH 45786 740-749-3512
Web: www.ezgrout.com

Eagle Materials Inc
3811 Turtle Creek Blvd Ste 1100 ... Dallas TX 75219 214-432-2000 432-2100
NYSE: EXP ■ *Web:* www.eaglematerials.com

ESSROC Materials Inc 3251 Bath Pike ... Nazareth PA 18064 610-837-6725 837-9614
TF: 800-437-7762 ■ *Web:* www.essroc.com

Faddis Concrete Products
2206 Horseshoe Pk ... Honey Brook PA 19344 610-269-4685
Web: www.faddis.com

Federal White Cement Ltd PO Box 1609 ... Woodstock ON N4S0A8 519-485-5410 485-5892
TF Sales: 800-265-1806 ■ *Web:* www.federalwhitecement.com

Folsom Ready Mix Inc
3401 Fitzgerald Rd ... Rancho Cordova CA 95742 916-851-8300
Web: www.folsomreadymix.com

GCC of America Inc 130 Rampart Way Ste 200 ... Denver CO 80230 303-739-5900
Web: www.gccusa.com

Grand Junction Concrete Pipe Co
2868 I-70 Business Loop ... Grand Junction CO 81501 970-243-4604
Web: www.gjpipe.com

Hawaiian Cement 99-1300 Halawa Vly St ... Aiea HI 96701 808-532-3400 532-3499
Web: www.hawaiiancement.com

Illinois Cement Co 1601 Rockwell Rd ... La Salle IL 61301 815-224-2112
Web: www.eaglematerials.com

Knife River Corp 1150 W Century Ave ... Bismarck ND 58503 701-530-1400 530-1451
Web: www.kniferiver.com

Lafarge North America Inc
12950 Worldgate Dr Ste 600 ... Herndon VA 20170 703-480-3600 480-3899
Web: www.lafarge-na.com

Lee's Ready-Mix & Trucking Inc
1100 W John F Kennedy Dr ... North Vernon IN 47265 812-346-9767

Lehigh Inland Cement Ltd 12640 Inland Way ... Edmonton AB T5V1K2 780-420-2500 420-2550
TF Orders: 800-252-9304 ■ *Web:* www.lehighhansoncanada.com

Maxxon Corp 920 Hamel Rd ... Hamel MN 55340 763-478-9600
Web: www.maxxon.com

Monarch Cement Co 449 1200 St PO Box 1000 ... Humboldt KS 66748 620-473-2222 473-2447
OTC: MCEM ■ *Web:* www.monarchcement.com

Mountain Cement Co 5 Sand Creek Rd ... Laramie WY 82070 307-745-4879 742-4534
Web: www.mountaincement.com

Nashville Ready Mix Inc 605 Cowan St ... Nashville TN 37207 615-256-2071
Web: www.nashvillereadymix.net

Ozinga Ready Mix Concrete Inc 400 Blaine St ... Gary IN 46406 219-949-9800
Web: www.ozinga.com

Permatile Concrete Products Company
100 Beacon Rd ... Bristol VA 24203 276-669-5332
Web: www.permatile.com

Phoenix Cement Co
8800 E Chaparral Rd Ste 155 ... Scottsdale AZ 85250 480-850-5757 850-5758
Web: www.srmaterials.com

Prairie Group Inc 7601 W 79th St ... Bridgeview IL 60455 708-458-0400 458-6007
TF Sales: 800-649-3690 ■ *Web:* www.prairiegroup.com

Prestressed Systems Inc
4955 Walker Rd Hwy 401 ... Windsor ON N9A6J3 519-737-1216
Web: www.psi-hci.com

RJS & Assoc Inc 1675 Sabre St ... Hayward CA 94545 510-670-9111

Texas Cement Products Inc 4000 Pinemont Dr ... Houston TX 77018 713-682-8411
Web: www.texascement.com

Titan America Inc 1151 Azalea Garden Rd ... Norfolk VA 23502 757-858-6500 855-7707
TF: 800-468-7622 ■ *Web:* www.titanamerica.com

136 CEMETERIES - NATIONAL

SEE ALSO Historic Homes & Buildings p. 1817; Parks - National - US p. 2859

Phone *Fax*

Alexandria National Cemetery
209 E Shamrock St. . . . . Pineville LA 71360 318-449-1793 449-9327
TF: 800-827-1000 ■ *Web:* www.cem.va.gov

Alton National Cemetery 600 Pearl St. . . . . Alton IL 62003 314-845-8320
TF: 800-535-1117 ■ *Web:* www.cem.va.gov

Balls Bluff National Cemetery Rt 7. . . . . Leesburg VA 22075 540-825-0027 825-6684
Web: www.cem.va.gov

Baltimore National Cemetery
5501 Frederick Ave. . . . . Baltimore MD 21228 410-644-9696 644-1563
TF: 800-535-1117 ■ *Web:* cem.va.gov

Barrancas National Cemetery
Naval Air Stn 80 Hovey Rd . . . . . Pensacola FL 32508 850-453-4108 453-4635
Web: www.cem.va.gov

Bath National Cemetery VA Medical Ctr . . . . . Bath NY 14810 607-664-4853 664-4761
Web: www.cem.va.gov

Battleground National Cemetery
6625 Georgia Ave NW. . . . . Washington DC 20012 202-829-4650
Web: www.nps.gov

Bay Pines National Cemetery
10000 Bay Pines Blvd. . . . . Saint Petersburg FL 33708 727-398-9426 398-9520
Web: www.cem.va.gov

Beaufort National Cemetery 1601 Boundary St. . . . . Beaufort SC 29902 843-524-3925 524-8538
TF: 800-273-8255 ■ *Web:* www.cem.va.gov

Beverly National Cemetery 916 Bridgeboro Rd . . . . . Beverly NJ 08010 215-504-5610 871-4691*
*Fax Area Code: 609 ■ *Web:* www.cem.va.gov/cems/nchp/beverly.asp

Biloxi National Cemetery 400 Veterans Ave . . . . . Biloxi MS 39531 228-388-6668 523-5784
Web: www.cem.va.gov

Black Hills National Cemetery
20901 Pleasant Vly Dr . . . . . Sturgis SD 57785 605-347-3830 720-7298
Web: www.cem.va.gov

Calverton National Cemetery
210 Princeton Blvd. . . . . Calverton NY 11933 631-727-5410 727-5815
TF: 800-829-1040 ■ *Web:* www.cem.va.gov

Camp Butler National Cemetery
5063 Camp Butler Rd . . . . . Springfield IL 62707 217-492-4070 492-4072
TF: 877-907-8585 ■ *Web:* www.cem.va.gov/cems/nchp/campbutler.asp

Camp Nelson National Cemetery
6980 Danville Rd . . . . . Nicholasville KY 40356 859-885-5727 887-4860
TF: 800-827-1000 ■ *Web:* www.cem.va.gov

Chattanooga National Cemetery
1200 Bailey Ave . . . . . Chattanooga TN 37404 423-855-6590 855-6597
TF: 877-907-8585 ■ *Web:* www.cem.va.gov

City Point National Cemetery
10th Ave & Davis St. . . . . Hopewell VA 23860 804-795-2031 795-1064
Web: www.cem.va.gov/cems/nchp/citypoint.asp

Corinth National Cemetery 1551 Horton St . . . . . Corinth MS 38834 901-386-8311 382-0750
TF: 800-273-8255 ■ *Web:* www.cem.va.gov

Crown Hill National Cemetery
700 W 38th St. . . . . Indianapolis IN 46208 765-674-0284
Web: www.cem.va.gov

Culpeper National Cemetery 305 US Ave. . . . . Culpeper VA 22701 540-825-0027 825-6684
TF: 800-827-1000 ■ *Web:* www.cem.va.gov/cems/nchp/culpeper.asp

Cypress Hills National Cemetery
625 Jamaica Ave. . . . . Brooklyn NY 11208 631-454-4949 694-5422
TF: 800-535-1117 ■ *Web:* www.cem.va.gov/cems/nchp/cypresshills.asp

Danville National Cemetery 721 Lee St . . . . . Danville VA 24541 704-636-2661 636-1115
Web: www.cem.va.gov/cems/nchp/danvilleva.asp

Dayton National Cemetery 4100 W Third St. . . . . Dayton OH 45428 937-262-2115 262-2187
TF: 800-273-8255 ■ *Web:* www.cem.va.gov

Eagle Point National Cemetery
2763 Riley Rd. . . . . Eagle Point OR 97524 541-826-2511 826-2888
TF: 800-535-1117 ■ *Web:* www.cem.va.gov

Fayetteville National Cemetery
700 S Government Ave. . . . . Fayetteville AR 72701 479-444-5051 444-5094
Web: www.cem.va.gov

Finn's Point National Cemetery
454 Ft. Mott Rd. . . . . Pennsville NJ 08070 215-504-5610 504-5611
TF: 800-827-1000 ■ *Web:* www.cem.va.gov/cems/nchp/finnspoint.asp

Florence National Cemetery
803 E National Cemetery Rd. . . . . Florence SC 29506 843-669-8783 662-8318
TF: 877-907-8585 ■ *Web:* www.cem.va.gov

Florida National Cemetery 6502 SW 102nd Ave. . . . . Bushnell FL 33513 352-793-7740 793-9560
TF: 877-907-8585 ■ *Web:* www.cem.va.gov

Fort Bayard National Cemetery
200 Camino De Paz PO Box 44 . . . . . Fort Bayard NM 88036 915-564-0201 564-3746
Web: www.cem.va.gov/cems/nchp/ftbayard.asp

Fort Bliss National Cemetery PO Box 6342 . . . . . El Paso TX 79906 915-564-0201 564-3746
TF: 800-273-8255 ■ *Web:* www.cem.va.gov

Fort Custer National Cemetery
15501 Dickman Rd. . . . . Augusta MI 49012 269-731-4164 731-2428
TF: 800-273-8255 ■ *Web:* www.cem.va.gov

Fort Gibson National Cemetery
1423 Cemetery Rd . . . . . Fort Gibson OK 74434 918-478-2334 478-2661
Web: www.cem.va.gov

Fort Leavenworth National Cemetery
395 Biddle Blvd . . . . . Fort Leavenworth KS 66027 913-758-4105 758-4136
Web: www.cem.va.gov

Fort Logan National Cemetery
4400 W Kenyon Ave . . . . . Denver CO 80236 303-761-0117 781-9378
Web: www.cem.va.gov

Fort Lyon National Cemetery
15700 County Rd HH . . . . . Las Animas CO 81054 303-761-0117 781-9378
Web: www.cem.va.gov

Fort Mitchell National Cemetery
553 Hwy 165 . . . . . Fort Mitchell AL 36856 334-855-4731 855-4740
Web: www.cem.va.gov

Phone *Fax*

Fort Richardson National Cemetery
Bldg 58-512 Davis Hwy PO Box 5-498. . . . . Fort Richardson AK 99505 907-384-7075 384-7111
Web: www.cem.va.gov/cems/nchp/ftrichardson.asp

Fort Rosecrans National Cemetery
PO Box 6237 . . . . . San Diego CA 92166 619-553-2084 553-6593
Web: www.cem.va.gov/cems/nchp/ftrosecrans.asp

Fort Sam Houston National Cemetery
1520 Harry Wurzbach Rd . . . . . San Antonio TX 78209 210-820-3891 820-3445
Web: cem.va.gov

Fort Scott National Cemetery
900 E National Ave . . . . . Fort Scott KS 66701 620-223-2840 223-2505
Web: www.cem.va.gov/cems

Fort Smith National Cemetery
522 Garland Ave. . . . . Fort Smith AR 72901 479-783-5345 785-4189
TF: 800-535-1117 ■ *Web:* www.cem.va.gov

Fort Snelling National Cemetery
7601 34th Ave. . . . . Minneapolis MN 55450 612-726-1127 726-9119
Web: www.cem.va.gov

Golden Gate National Cemetery
1300 Sneath Ln . . . . . San Bruno CA 94066 650-589-7737 873-6578
Web: cem.va.gov

Grafton National Cemetery 431 Walnut St . . . . . Grafton WV 26354 304-265-2044 265-4336
TF: 800-535-1117 ■ *Web:* www.cem.va.gov

Hampton National Cemetery
Cemetery Rd at Marshall Ave . . . . . Hampton VA 23669 757-723-7104 728-3144
Web: www.cem.va.gov

Houston National Cemetery
10410 Veterans Memorial Dr . . . . . Houston TX 77038 281-447-8686 447-0580
Web: www.cem.va.gov

Indiantown Gap National Cemetery
RR 2 PO Box 484 . . . . . Annville PA 17003 717-865-5254 865-5256
Web: www.cem.va.gov/cems/nchp/indiantowngap.asp

Jefferson Barracks National Cemetery
2900 Sheridan Rd. . . . . Saint Louis MO 63125 314-845-8320 221-2185*
*Fax Area Code: 703 ■ *TF:* 800-827-1000

Jefferson City National Cemetery
1024 E McCarty St . . . . . Jefferson City MO 65101 314-845-8320 845-8355
TF: 877-907-8585 ■ *Web:* www.cem.va.gov/cems/nchp/jeffersoncity.asp

Keokuk National Cemetery 1701 J St. . . . . Keokuk IA 52632 309-782-2094 524-8118*
*Fax Area Code: 319 ■ *TF:* 800-273-8255 ■ *Web:* www.cem.va.gov/cems/nchp/keokuk.asp

Kerrville National Cemetery
3600 Memorial Blvd . . . . . Kerrville TX 78028 210-820-3891 820-3445
TF: 800-273-8255 ■ *Web:* www.cem.va.gov

Knoxville National Cemetery
939 Tyson St NW . . . . . Knoxville TN 37917 423-855-6590 855-6597
Web: www.cem.va.gov/cems/nchp/knoxville.asp

Leavenworth National Cemetery
150 Muncie Rd. . . . . Leavenworth KS 66048 913-758-4105 758-4136
Web: www.cem.va.gov/cems

Lebanon National Cemetery 20 Hwy 208 . . . . . Lebanon KY 40033 270-692-3390 692-0018
Web: www.cem.va.gov

Little Rock National Cemetery
2523 Confederate Blvd . . . . . Little Rock AR 72206 501-324-6401 324-7182
Web: www.cem.va.gov

Long Island National Cemetery
2040 Wellwood Ave . . . . . Farmingdale NY 11735 631-454-4949 694-5422
Web: www.cem.va.gov/cems/nchp/longisland.asp

Los Angeles National Cemetery
950 S Sepulveda Blvd. . . . . Los Angeles CA 90049 310-268-4494 268-3257
Web: www.cem.va.gov

Loudon Park National Cemetery
3445 Frederick Rd . . . . . Baltimore MD 21228 410-644-9696 644-1563
Web: www.cem.va.gov/cems/nchp/loudonpark.asp

Marietta National Cemetery
500 Washington Ave. . . . . Marietta GA 30060 866-236-8159 479-9311*
*Fax Area Code: 770 ■ *TF:* 866-236-8159 ■ *Web:* www.cem.va.gov

Marion National Cemetery 1700 E 38th St . . . . . Marion IN 46953 765-674-0284 674-4521
Web: www.cem.va.gov

Massachusetts National Cemetery Conery Rd . . . . . Bourne MA 02532 508-563-7113 221-2185*
*Fax Area Code: 703 ■ *TF:* 800-827-1000 ■ *Web:* www.cem.va.gov

Memphis National Cemetery 3568 Townes Ave . . . . . Memphis TN 38122 901-386-8311 382-0750
Web: www.cem.va.gov

Mill Springs National Cemetery 9044 W Hwy 80 . . . . . Nancy KY 42544 859-885-5727 887-4860
Web: www.cem.va.gov/cems/nchp/millsprings.asp

Mobile National Cemetery 1202 Virginia St . . . . . Mobile AL 36604 850-453-4108 453-4635
TF: 800-827-1000 ■ *Web:* www.cem.va.gov

Mound City National Cemetery
Hwy 37 & 51 PO Box 128. . . . . Mound City IL 62963 314-845-8320 845-8355
Web: www.cem.va.gov/cems/nchp/moundcity.asp

Mountain Home National Cemetery
PO Box 8 . . . . . Mountain Home TN 37684 423-979-3535 979-3521
TF: 800-827-1000 ■ *Web:* www.cem.va.gov/cems/nchp/mountainhome.asp

Nashville National Cemetery
1420 Gallatin Rd S . . . . . Madison TN 37115 615-860-0086 860-8691
Web: www.cem.va.gov

Natchez National Cemetery 41 Cemetery Rd . . . . . Natchez MS 39120 601-445-4981 445-8815
Web: www.cem.va.gov

National Memorial Cemetery of Arizona
23029 N Cave Creek Rd . . . . . Phoenix AZ 85024 480-513-3600 513-1412
Web: www.cem.va.gov

New Albany National Cemetery
1943 Ekin Ave. . . . . New Albany IN 47150 502-893-3852 893-6612
Web: www.cem.va.gov/cems/nchp/newalbany.asp

New Bern National Cemetery
1711 National Ave. . . . . New Bern NC 28560 252-637-2912 637-7145
TF: 800-827-1000 ■ *Web:* www.cem.va.gov

Philadelphia National Cemetery
Haines St & Limekiln Pike . . . . . Philadelphia PA 19138 215-504-5610 504-5611
Web: www.cem.va.gov/cems/nchp/philadelphia.asp

Port Hudson National Cemetery
20978 Port Hickey Rd. . . . . Zachary LA 70791 225-654-3767 654-3728
Web: www.cem.va.gov

Phone Fax

Prescott National Cemetery 500 Hwy 89 N ... Prescott AZ 86301 928-717-7569 221-2185*
Fax Area Code: 703 ■ *TF:* 800-827-1000

Quantico National Cemetery 18424 Joplin Rd ... Triangle VA 22172 703-221-2183 221-2185
Web: www.cem.va.gov

Quincy National Cemetery 36th & Maine St ... Quincy IL 62301 309-782-2094 782-2097
Web: www.cem.va.gov/cems/nchp/quincy.asp

Raleigh National Cemetery 501 Rock Quarry Rd ... Raleigh NC 27610 252-637-2912 637-7145
Web: www.cem.va.gov/cems/nchp/raleigh.asp

Riverside National Cemetery
22495 Van Buren Blvd ... Riverside CA 92518 951-653-8417 653-5233
Web: www.cem.va.gov

Rock Island National Cemetery Bldg 118 ... Rock Island IL 61299 309-782-2094 782-2097
Web: www.cem.va.gov/cems/nchp/rockisland.asp

Roseburg National Cemetery
1770 Harvard Blvd ... Roseburg OR 97470 541-826-2511 826-2111
TF: 800-535-1117 ■ *Web:* www.cem.va.gov/cems/nchp/roseburg.asp

Saint Augustine National Cemetery
104 Marine St ... Saint Augustine FL 32084 352-793-7740 793-9560
TF: 800-273-8255 ■ *Web:* www.cem.va.gov/cems/nchp/staugustine.asp

Salisbury National Cemetery
501 Statesville Blvd ... Salisbury NC 28144 704-636-2661 636-1115
Web: www.cem.va.gov/cems/nchp/salisbury.asp

San Antonio National Cemetery
1520 Harry Wurzback Rd ... San Antonio TX 78209 210-820-3891 820-3445
Web: www.cem.va.gov

San Francisco National Cemetery
Presidio of San Francisco
1 Lincoln Blvd ... San Francisco CA 94129 650-589-7737 873-6578
Web: www.cem.va.gov/cems/nchp/sanfrancisco.asp

San Joaquin Valley National Cemetery
32053 W McCabe Rd ... Santa Nella CA 95322 209-854-1040 854-3944
Web: www.cem.va.gov/cems/nchp/sanjoaquinvalley.asp

Santa Fe National Cemetery
501 N Guadalupe St ... Santa Fe NM 87501 505-988-6400 988-6497
Web: www.cem.va.gov

Seven Pines National Cemetery
400 E Williamsburg Rd ... Sandston VA 23150 804-795-2031 795-1064
TF: 800-535-1117 ■ *Web:* www.cem.va.gov/cems/nchp/sevenpines.asp

Sitka National Cemetery 803 Sawmill Creek Rd ... Sitka AK 99835 907-384-7075 384-7111
TF: 800-273-8255 ■ *Web:* www.cem.va.gov

Springfield National Cemetery
1702 E Seminole St ... Springfield MO 65804 417-881-9499 881-7862
Web: www.cem.va.gov

Staunton National Cemetery 901 Richmond Ave ... Staunton VA 24401 540-825-0027 825-6684
TF: 800-273-8255 ■ *Web:* www.cem.va.gov/cems/nchp/staunton.asp

Tahoma National Cemetery 18600 SE 240th St ... Kent WA 98042 425-413-9614 413-9618
TF: 800-827-1000 ■ *Web:* www.cem.va.gov

Togus National Cemetery VA Regional Office Ctr ... Togus ME 04330 508-563-7113 564-9946
TF: 800-273-8255 ■ *Web:* www.cem.va.gov/cems/nchp/togus.asp

West Virginia National Cemetery
42 Veterans Memorial Lane ... Grafton WV 26354 304-265-2044 265-4336
TF: 800-273-8255 ■ *Web:* www.cem.va.gov/cems/nchp/westvirginia.asp

Willamette National Cemetery
11800 SE Mt Scott Blvd ... Portland OR 97086 503-273-5250 273-5330
Web: www.cem.va.gov

Wilmington National Cemetery
2011 Market St ... Wilmington NC 28403 910-815-4877 637-7145*
Fax Area Code: 252 ■ *TF:* 800-535-1117 ■ *Web:* www.cem.va.gov

Winchester National Cemetery
401 National Ave ... Winchester VA 22601 540-825-0027 825-6684
Web: www.cem.va.gov/cems/nchp/winchester.asp

Wood National Cemetery
5000 W National Ave Bldg 1301 ... Milwaukee WI 53295 414-382-5300 382-5321
TF: 888-878-3256 ■ *Web:* www.cem.va.gov

Woodlawn National Cemetery 1825 Davis St ... Elmira NY 14901 607-732-5411 732-1769
TF: 877-907-8585 ■ *Web:* www.cem.va.gov

Yorktown National Cemetery PO Box 210 ... Yorktown VA 23690 757-898-2410 898-6346
Web: www.nps.gov/york/index.htm

Zachary Taylor National Cemetery
4701 Brownsboro Rd ... Louisville KY 40207 502-893-3852 893-6612
Web: www.cem.va.gov

137 CHAMBERS OF COMMERCE - CANADIAN

Listings are organized by provinces and then are alphabetized within each province grouping according to the name of the city in which each chamber is located.

Phone Fax

Brooks & District Chamber of Commerce
403-2 Ave W Suite 6 Ste 400 ... Brooks AB T1R1B4 403-362-7641 362-6893
Web: www.brookschamber.ab.ca

Calgary Chamber of Commerce 237 8th Ave SE ... Calgary AB T2G5C3 403-750-0400 266-3413
Web: www.calgarychamber.com

Alberta Chambers of Commerce
10025 - 102A Ave Edmonton Ctr Ste 1808 ... Edmonton AB T5J2Z2 780-425-4180 429-1061
TF: 800-272-8854 ■ *Web:* www.abchamber.ca

Edmonton Chamber of Commerce
9990 Jasper Ave Ste 700 ... Edmonton AB T5J1P7 780-426-4620 424-7946
Web: www.edmontonchamber.com

Fort McMurray Chamber of Commerce
9612 Franklin Ave Ste 304 ... Fort McMurray AB T9H2J9 780-743-3100 790-9757
Web: www.fortmcmurraychamber.ca

Grande Prairie & District Chamber of Commerce
11330 106th St Ste 127 ... Grande Prairie AB T8V6T7 780-532-5340 532-2926
Web: www.grandeprairiechamber.com

Lethbridge Chamber of Commerce
529 Sixth St S Ste 200 ... Lethbridge AB T1J2E1 403-327-1586 327-1001
Web: lethbridgechamber.com

Medicine Hat & District Chamber of Commerce
413 Sixth Ave SE ... Medicine Hat AB T1A2S7 403-527-5214 527-5182
Web: www.medicinehatchamber.com

Phone Fax

Peace River Chamber of Commerce
9309-100 St PO Box 6599 ... Peace River AB T8S1S4 780-624-4166 624-4663
Web: www.peaceriverchamber.com

Red Deer Chamber of Commerce 3017 Gaetz Ave ... Red Deer AB T4N5Y6 403-347-4491 343-6188
Web: www.reddeerchamber.com

Saint Albert Chamber of Commerce
71 St Albert Rd ... Saint Albert AB T8N6L5 780-458-2833 458-6515
Web: www.stalbertchamber.com

Abbotsford Chamber of Commerce
32900 S Fraser Way Unit 207 ... Abbotsford BC V2S5A1 604-859-9651 850-6880
Web: www.abbotsfordchamber.com

Burnaby Board of Trade 4555 Kings Way Ste 201 ... Burnaby BC V5H4T8 604-412-0100 412-0102
Web: www.bbot.ca

Campbell River & District Chamber of Commerce
900 Alder St PO Box 459 ... Campbell River BC V9W2P6 250-287-4636 286-6490
Web: www.campbellriverchamber.ca

Chilliwack Chamber of Commerce
46093 Yale Rd Ste 201 ... Chilliwack BC V2P2L8 604-793-4323 793-4303
Web: www.chilliwackchamber.com

Tri-Cities Chamber of Commerce
1209 Pinetree Way ... Coquitlam BC V3B7Y3 604-464-2716 464-6796
Web: www.tricitieschamber.com

Comox Valley Chamber of Commerce
2040 Cliffe Ave ... Courtenay BC V9N2L3 250-334-3234 334-4908
TF: 888-357-4471 ■ *Web:* www.comoxvalleychamber.com

Delta Chamber of Commerce 6201 60th Ave ... Delta BC V4K4E2 604-946-4232 946-5285
Web: www.deltachamber.ca

Duncan Cowichan Chamber of Commerce
2896 Drinkwater Rd ... Duncan BC V9L2C6 250-748-1111 746-8222
Web: duncancc.bc.ca

Fort Saint John & District Chamber of Commerce
9325 100th St Ste 202 ... Fort Saint John BC V1J4N4 250-785-6037 785-6050
Web: www.fsjchamber.com

Kamloops Chamber of Commerce
1290 W Trans-Canada Hwy ... Kamloops BC V2C6R3 250-372-7722 828-9500
Web: www.kamloopschamber.ca

Kelowna Chamber of Commerce 544 Harvey Ave ... Kelowna BC V1Y6C9 250-861-3627 861-3624
Web: www.kelownachamber.org

Langley Chamber of Commerce
5761 Glover Rd Unit 1 ... Langley BC V3A8M8 604-530-6656 530-7066
Web: www.langleychamber.com

Mission Regional Chamber of Commerce
34033 Lougheed Hwy ... Mission BC V2V5X8 604-826-6914 826-5916
Web: www.missionchamber.bc.ca

Greater Nanaimo Chamber of Commerce
2133 Bowen Rd ... Nanaimo BC V9S1H8 250-756-1191 756-1584
Web: www.nanaimochamber.bc.ca

New Westminster Chamber of Commerce
601 Queens Ave ... New Westminster BC V3M1L1 604-521-7781 521-0057
Web: www.newwestchamber.com

North Vancouver Chamber of Commerce
124 W First St Ste 102 ... North Vancouver BC V7M3N3 604-987-4488 987-8272
Web: www.nvchamber.ca

Parksville Chamber of Commerce (PDCC)
PO Box 99 ... Parksville BC V9P2G3 250-248-3613 248-5210
Web: parksvillechamber.com

Penticton & Wine Country Chamber of Commerce
553 Railway St ... Penticton BC V2A8S3 250-492-4103 492-6119
TF: 800-663-5052 ■ *Web:* www.penticton.org

Alberni Valley Chamber of Commerce
2533 Port Alberni Hwy ... Port Alberni BC V9Y8P2 250-724-6535 724-6560
Web: www.albernichamber.ca

Prince George Chamber of Commerce
890 Vancouver St ... Prince George BC V2L2P5 250-562-2454 562-6510
Web: www.pgchamber.bc.ca

Richmond Chamber of Commerce
5811 Cooney Rd Ste 101 ... Richmond BC V6X3M1 604-278-2822 278-2972
Web: www.richmondchamber.ca

Saanich Peninsula Chamber of Commerce
209-2453 Beacon Ave ... Sidney BC V8L1X7 250-656-3616 656-7111
Web: www.peninsulachamber.ca

Surrey Board of Trade 14439 104th Ave Ste 101 ... Surrey BC V3R1M1 604-581-7130 588-7549
Web: www.businessinsurrey.com

British Columbia Chamber of Commerce
750 W Pender St Ste 1201 ... Vancouver BC V6C2T8 604-683-0700 683-0416
Web: www.bcchamber.org

Vancouver Board of Trade
999 Canada Pl Ste 400 ... Vancouver BC V6C3E1 604-681-2111 681-0437
Web: www.boardoftrade.com

Greater Victoria Chamber of Commerce
852 Ft St Ste 100 ... Victoria BC V8W1H8 250-383-7191 385-3552
Web: www.victoriachamber.ca

West Vancouver Chamber of Commerce
1846 Marine Dr ... West Vancouver BC V7V1J6 604-926-6614 925-7220
TF: 888-471-9996 ■ *Web:* www.westvanchamber.com

Westbank & District Chamber of Commerce
2372 Dobbin Rd ... Westbank BC V4T2H9 250-768-3378 768-3465
Web: gwboardoftrade.com/

Brandon Chamber of Commerce 1043 Rosser Ave ... Brandon MB R7A0L5 204-571-5340 571-5347
Web: www.brandonchamber.ca

Portage & District Chamber of Commerce
56 Royal Rd N ... Portage la Prairie MB R1N1V1 204-857-7778 856-5001
Web: www.portagechamber.com

Saint-Boniface Chamber of Commerce
383 boul Provencher PO Box 204 ... Saint-Boniface MB R2H3B4 204-235-1406 377-8514
Web: www.ccfsb.mb.ca

Selkirk & District Chamber of Commerce (SDCC)
200 Eaton Ave ... Selkirk MB R1A0W6 204-482-7176 482-5448
Web: www.selkirkanddistrictchamber.ca

Manitoba Chambers of Commerce
227 Portage Ave ... Winnipeg MB R3B2A6 204-948-0100 948-0110
Web: www.mbchamber.mb.ca

Name / Address	City	Prov	Postal Code	Phone	Fax
Winnipeg Chamber of Commerce, The 259 Portage Ave Ste 100 *Web:* www.winnipeg-chamber.com	Winnipeg	MB	R3B2A9	204-944-8484	944-8492
Enterprise Fredericton 10 Knowledge Pk Dr Ste 110 *TF:* 866-534-9270 ■ *Web:* enterpriserentacar.ca	Fredericton	NB	E3C2M7	506-444-4686	
Fredericton Chamber of Commerce 270 Rookwood Rd Ste 200 *Web:* www.frederictonchamber.ca	Fredericton	NB	E3B4Y9	506-458-8006	451-1119
Miramichi Chamber of Commerce 120 Newcastle Blvd Ste 2 PO Box 342 *Web:* www.miramichichamber.com	Miramichi	NB	E1N3A7	506-622-5522	622-5959
Greater Moncton Chamber of Commerce 1273 Main St Ste 200 *Web:* www.gmcc.nb.ca	Moncton	NB	E1C0P4	506-857-2883	857-9209
Saint John Board of Trade (SJBT) 40 King St PO Box 6037 *Web:* www.sjboardoftrade.com	Saint John	NB	E2L4R5	506-634-8111	632-2008
Greater Corner Brook Board of Trade 11 Confederation Dr PO Box 475 *Web:* www.gcbbt.com	Corner Brook	NL	A2H6E6	709-634-5831	639-9710
Gander & Area Chamber of Commerce 109 Trans Canada Hwy *Web:* www.ganderchamber.nf.ca	Gander	NL	A1V1P6	709-256-7110	256-4080
Northwest Territories Chamber of Commerce 4802 - 50th Ave Ste 13 *Web:* www.nwtchamber.com	Yellowknife	NT	X1A1C4	867-920-9505	873-4174
Bridgewater & Area Chamber of Commerce 373 King St *Web:* www.bridgewaterchamber.com	Bridgewater	NS	B4V1B1	902-543-4263	543-1156
Metropolitan Halifax Chamber of Commerce 656 Windmill Rd Ste 200 *Web:* www.halifaxchamber.com	Dartmouth	NS	B3B1B8	902-468-7111	468-7333
Pictou County Chamber of Commerce 980 E River Rd *Web:* www.pictouchamber.com	New Glasgow	NS	B2H3S8	902-755-3463	755-2848
Sydney & Area Chamber of Commerce 275 Charlotte St *Web:* www.sydneyareachamber.ca	Sydney	NS	B1P1C6	902-564-6453	539-7487
Truro & District Chamber of Commerce Prince PO Box 54	Truro	NS	B2N1G2	902-895-6328	897-6641
Greater Barrie Chamber of Commerce 97 Toronto St *Web:* www.barriechamber.com	Barrie	ON	L4N1V1	705-721-5000	726-0973
Belleville & District Chamber of Commerce Five Moira St E *TF:* 888-852-9992 ■ *Web:* www.bellevillechamber.ca	Belleville	ON	K8N5B3	613-962-4597	962-3911
Caledon Chamber of Commerce 12598 Hwy Ste 50 S *Web:* www.caledonchamber.com	Bolton	ON	L7E1T6	905-857-7393	857-7405
Brampton Board of Trade 33 Queen St W 2nd Fl *Web:* www.bramptonbot.com	Brampton	ON	L6V1A2	905-451-1122	450-0295
Brantford Brant Chamber of Commerce (BBCC) 77 Charlotte St *Web:* www.brantfordbrantchamber.com	Brantford	ON	N3T2W8	519-753-2617	753-0921
Burlington Chamber of Commerce 414 Locust St Ste 201 *Web:* www.burlingtonchamber.com	Burlington	ON	L7S1T7	905-639-0174	333-3956
Cambridge Chamber of Commerce 750 Hespeler Rd *TF General:* 800-749-7560 ■ *Web:* www.cambridgechamber.com	Cambridge	ON	N3H5L8	519-622-2221	622-0177
Chatham-Kent Chamber of Commerce 54 Fourth St *Web:* www.chatham-kentchamber.ca	Chatham	ON	N7M2G2	519-352-7540	352-8741
Cornwall & Area Chamber of Commerce 113 Second St E *Web:* www.chamber.cornwall.on.ca	Cornwall	ON	K6H1Y5	613-933-4004	933-8466
Dryden District Chamber of Commerce 284 Government St Hwy 17 *TF:* 877-934-6922 ■ *Web:* www.drydenchamber.ca	Dryden	ON	P8N2P3	807-223-2622	223-2626
Flamborough Chamber of Commerce 7 Innovation Dr Ste 227 *Web:* www.flamboroughchamber.ca	Flamborough	ON	L9H7H9	905-689-7650	689-1313
Halton Hills Chamber of Commerce 328 Guelph St *Web:* www.haltonhillschamber.on.ca	Georgetown	ON	L7G4B5	905-877-5117	877-5117
Guelph Chamber of Commerce 111 Farquhar St *Web:* www.guelphchamber.com	Guelph	ON	N1H3N4	519-822-8081	822-8451
Hamilton Chamber of Commerce 120 King St W Ste 770 *Web:* www.hamiltonchamber.ca	Hamilton	ON	L8P4V2	905-522-1151	522-1154
Greater Kingston Chamber of Commerce 67 Brock St *Web:* kingstonchamber.ca	Kingston	ON	K7L1R8	613-548-4453	548-4743
Chamber of Commerce of Kitchener & Waterloo 80 Queen St N PO Box 2367 *Web:* www.greaterkwchamber.com	Kitchener	ON	N2H6L4	519-576-5000	742-4760
Leamington District Chamber of Commerce 318 Erie St S *TF:* 800-393-3769 ■ *Web:* www.leamingtonchamber.com	Leamington	ON	N8H3C5	519-326-2721	326-3204
London Chamber of Commerce 244 Pall Mall St Ste 101 *Web:* www.londonchamber.com	London	ON	N6A5P6	519-432-7551	432-8063
Markham Board of Trade 80 F Centurian Dr Ste 206 *Web:* www.markhamboard.com	Markham	ON	L3R8C1	905-474-0730	474-0685
Southern Georgia Bay Chamber of Commerce 208 King St *Web:* southerngeorgianbay.ca	Midland	ON	L4R3L9	705-526-7884	526-1744
Milton Chamber of Commerce 251 Main St E Ste 104 *Web:* miltonchamber.ca	Milton	ON	L9T1P1	905-878-0581	878-4972
Mississauga Board of Trade 77 City Centre Dr Ste 701 *Web:* www.mbot.com	Mississauga	ON	L5B1M5	905-273-6151	273-4937
Newmarket Chamber of Commerce 470 Davis Dr *Web:* www.newmarketchamber.com	Newmarket	ON	L3Y2P3	905-898-5900	853-7271
Niagara Falls Canada Chamber of Commerce 4056 Dorchester Rd *Web:* www.niagarafallschamber.com	Niagara Falls	ON	L2E6M9	905-374-3666	374-2972
North Bay & District Chamber of Commerce 1375 Seymour St PO Box 747 *TF:* 888-249-8998 ■ *Web:* www.northbaychamber.com	North Bay	ON	P1B8J8	705-472-8480	472-8027
Oakville Chamber of Commerce 700 Kerr St Ste 200 *Web:* www.oakvillechamber.com	Oakville	ON	L6K3W5	905-845-6613	845-6475
Greater Dufferin Area Chamber of Commerce PO Box 101 *Web:* www.gdacc.ca	Orangeville	ON	L9W2Z5	519-941-0490	941-0492
Greater Oshawa Chamber of Commerce 44 Richmond St W Ste 100 *Web:* www.oshawachamber.com	Oshawa	ON	L1G1C7	905-728-1683	432-1259
Canadian Chamber of Commerce 350 Albert St Ste 420 *Web:* www.chamber.ca	Ottawa	ON	K1R7X7	613-238-4000	238-7643
Ottawa Chamber of Commerce 328 Somerset St W *Web:* www.ottawachamber.ca	Ottawa	ON	K2P0J9	613-236-3631	236-7498
Upper Ottawa Valley Chamber of Commerce Two International Dr *Web:* www.upperottawavalleychamber.com	Pembroke	ON	K8A6W5	613-732-1492	732-5793
Perth & District Chamber of Commerce 34 Herriott St *Web:* www.perthchamber.com	Perth	ON	K7H1T2	613-267-3200	267-6797
Greater Peterborough Chamber of Commerce 175 George St N *TF:* 877-640-4037 ■ *Web:* www.peterboroughchamber.ca	Peterborough	ON	K9J3G6	705-748-9771	743-2331
Port Colborne-Wainfleet Chamber of Commerce 76 Main St W *Web:* www.pcwchamber.com	Port Colborne	ON	L3K3V2	905-834-9765	834-1542
Richmond Hill Chamber of Commerce (RHCOC) 376 Church St S *Web:* www.rhcoc.com	Richmond Hill	ON	L4C9V8	905-884-1961	884-1962
Timmins Chamber of Commerce PO Box 985 *Web:* www.timminschamber.on.ca	Schumacher	ON	P4N7H6	705-360-1900	360-1193
Simcoe & District Chamber of Commerce 95 Queensway W *Web:* www.simcoechamber.on.ca	Simcoe	ON	N3Y2M8	519-426-5867	428-7718
Stratford & District Chamber of Commerce 55 Lorne Ave E *Web:* www.stratfordchamber.com	Stratford	ON	N5A6S4	519-273-5250	273-2229
Greater Sudbury Chamber of Commerce 40 Elm St Ste 1 *Web:* sudburychamber.ca/	Sudbury	ON	P3C1S8	705-673-7133	673-1951
Thunder Bay Chamber of Commerce 200 Syndicated Ave S Ste 102 *Web:* www.tb-chamber.on.ca	Thunder Bay	ON	P7E1C9	807-624-2626	622-7752
Canadian Chamber of Commerce Toronto Office 55 University Ave Ste 901 *Web:* www.chamber.ca	Toronto	ON	M5J2H7	416-868-6415	868-0189
Vaughan Chamber of Commerce 25 Edilcan Dr Ste 2 *TF:* 888-943-8937 ■ *Web:* vaughanchamber.ca	Vaughan	ON	L4K3S4	905-761-1366	761-1918
Welland/Pelham Chamber of Commerce 32 E Main St	Welland	ON	L3B3W3	905-732-7515	732-7175
Whitby Chamber of Commerce 128 Brock St S *Web:* www.whitbychamber.org	Whitby	ON	L1N4J8	905-668-4506	668-1894
Windsor-Essex Regional Chamber of Commerce 2575 Ouellette Pl *Web:* www.windsorchamber.org	Windsor	ON	N8X1L9	519-966-3696	966-0603
Woodstock District Chamber of Commerce 476 Peel St Ste 3 *Web:* woodstockchamber.ca	Woodstock	ON	N4S1K1	519-539-9411	456-1611
Greater Charlottetown Area Chamber of Commerce PO Box 67 *Web:* www.charlottetownchamber.com	Charlottetown	PE	C1A7K2	902-628-2000	368-3570
La Chambre de Commerce de Drummond 234 Rue St Marcel CP 188 *Web:* www.ccid.qc.ca	Drummondville	QC	J2B6V7	819-477-7822	477-2823
Chambre de Commerce Haute-Yamaska Region (CDCHY) 650 Rue Principale *Web:* cchyr.ca	Granby	QC	J2G8L4	450-372-6100	372-3161
Laval Chamber of Commerce 1555 boul Chomedey Ste 200 *Web:* www.ccilaval.qc.ca	Laval	QC	H7V3Z1	450-682-5255	682-5735
Mont-Laurier Chamber of Commerce 360 Rue Du Pont *Web:* www.ccmont-laurier.com	Mont-Laurier	QC	J9L2R4	819-623-3642	623-5220
Canadian Chamber of Commerce Montreal Office 1155 University St Ste 709 *Web:* www.chamber.ca	Montreal	QC	H3B3A7	514-866-4334	866-7296
Chambre de Commerce du Quebec 17 rue St-Louis *Web:* www.fccq.ca	Quebec	QC	G1R3Y8	418-692-3853	694-2286
Chambre de Commerce et d'Industrie du Quebec Metropolitain 17 St Louis St *Web:* www.cciquebec.ca	Quebec	QC	G1R3Y8	418-692-3853	694-2286
Sept-Iles Chamber of Commerce 700 boul Laure Bureau 237 *Web:* www.ccseptiles.com	Sept-Iles	QC	G4R1Y1	418-968-3488	968-3432
Chambre de Commerce de la Region Sherbrookoise 9 Rue Wellington S *Web:* www.ccsherbrooke.com	Sherbrooke	QC	J1H5C8	819-822-6151	822-6156
Moose Jaw & District Chamber of Commerce 88 Saskatchewan St E *Web:* www.mjchamber.com	Moose Jaw	SK	S6H0V4	306-692-6414	694-6463

Phone | Fax

Battlefords Chamber of Commerce
PO Box 1000 Jcts of Hws 16 & 40 E............North Battleford SK S9A3E6 306-445-6226 445-6633
Web: www.battlefordschamber.com

Prince Albert & District Chamber of Commerce
3700 Second Ave W..........................Prince Albert SK S6W1A2 306-764-6222 922-4727
Web: www.princealbertchamber.com

Regina Chamber of Commerce 2145 Albert St..........Regina SK S4P2V1 306-757-4658 757-4668
Web: www.reginachamber.com

Greater Saskatoon Chamber of Commerce
104-202 Fourth Ave N..........................Saskatoon SK S7K0K1 306-244-2151 244-8366
Web: www.saskatoonchamber.com

Whitehorse Chamber of Commerce
302 Steele St Ste 101..........................Whitehorse YT Y1A2C5 867-667-7545 667-4507
Web: www.whitehorsechamber.com

138 CHAMBERS OF COMMERCE - INTERNATIONAL

SEE ALSO Chambers of Commerce - Canadian p. 1909
Included here are organizations that work to promote business and trade relationships between the United States and other countries.

Phone | Fax

262 With Donna 11762 marco beach dr............Jacksonville FL 32224 904-551-0732
Web: breastcancermarathon.com

AAAA Benefits 11020 David Taylor Dr Ste 305..........Charlotte NC 28262 704-594-6270
Web: www.aaaabenefits.com

Ace Charter High School 1929 N Stone Ave............Tucson AZ 85705 520-628-8316
Web: www.acehs.org

African Chamber of Commerce Dallas/Fort Worth (ACCDFW)
2639 Walnut Hill Ln Ste 125..........................Dallas TX 75229 214-628-2569
Web: www.africanchamberdfw.org

Alaska Primary Care Association Inc
903 W Northern Lights Blvd Ste 200................Anchorage AK 99503 907-929-2722
Web: www.alaskapca.org

Alberta Association of Municipal Districts & Counties
2510 Sparrow Dr..................................Nisku AB T9E8N5 780-955-3639
Web: www.aamdc.com

Alberta Senior Citizens Housing Association
9711 47 Ave Nw..................................Edmonton AB T6E5M7 780-439-6473
Web: www.ascha.com

Alberta Soccer 9023 111 Ave Nw..................Edmonton AB T5B0C3 780-474-2200
Web: www.albertasoccer.com

Alent Technologies LLC 8201 Bondage Dr.........Gaithersburg MD 20882 301-963-0455
Web: www.alent.net

America-Israel Chamber of Commerce - Chicago
247 S State St Ste 1325............................Chicago IL 60604 312-641-2937 641-2941
Web: www.israeltrade.org

American Egyptian Cooperation Foundation
1535 W Loop S Ste 200............................Houston TX 77027 713-624-7113

American-Indonesian Chamber of Commerce
317 Madison Ave Ste 1619..........................New York NY 10017 212-687-4505 687-5844
Web: www.aiccusa.org

American-Israel Chamber of Commerce & Industry of Minnesota
13100 Wayzata Blvd............................Minnetonka MN 55305 952-593-8666
Web: www.aiccmn.org

American-Israel Chamber of Commerce Southeast Region (AICC)
400 Northridge Rd Ste 260..........................Atlanta GA 30350 404-843-9426 843-1416
Web: www.aiccse.org

American-Russian Chamber of Commerce & Industry
1101 Pennsylvania Ave NW Sixth Fl................Washington DC 20004 202-756-4943 362-4634
Web: www.arcci.org

Answer Racing 1055 Montecito Dr..................Corona CA 92879 951-736-5369
Web: answerracing.com

Aqtis 533 Rue Ontario E............................Montreal QC H2L1N8 514-844-2113
Web: www.aqtis.qc.ca

Arizona Automobile Dealers Association
4701 N 24th St Ste B3............................Phoenix AZ 85016 602-468-0888
Web: www.aada.com

Arizona Bankers Association
111 W Monroe St Ste 440..........................Phoenix AZ 85003 602-258-1200
Web: www.azbankers.org

Aski Financial Inc 419 Notre Dame Ave.............Winnipeg MB R3B1R3 204-987-7180
Web: www.askifinancial.ca

Association of American Chambers of Commerce in Latin America
1615 H St NW 3rd Fl..............................Washington DC 20062 202-463-5485 463-3126
TF: 800-638-6582 ■ *Web:* www.aaccla.org

Australian American Chamber of Commerce of Houston
604 Archer St...................................Houston TX 77009 713-527-9688 415-0545*
**Fax Area Code:* 832 ■ *Web:* www.aacc-houston.org

Australian-American Chamber of Commerce - San Francisco
PO Box 471285............................San Francisco CA 94147 415-485-6718
Web: sfaussies.com

Bc Maritime Employers Assn 349 Railway St........Vancouver BC V6A1A4 604-688-1155
Web: www.bcmea.com

Belgian-American Chamber of Commerce in the US (BACC)
1177 Ave of the Americas Eighth Fl..................New York NY 10036 212-541-0779
Web: www.belcham.org

BioNova 1721 Lower Water St.........................Halifax NS B3J1S5 902-421-5705
Web: www.bionova.ns.ca

BPI Information Systems
6055 W Snowville Rd............................Brecksville OH 44141 440-717-4112
Web: www.bpiohio.com

Brazilian-American Chamber of Commerce Inc
509 Madison Ave Ste 304..........................New York NY 10022 212-751-4691 751-7692
Web: www.brazilcham.com

Brazilian-American Chamber of Commerce of Florida
PO Box 310038...................................Miami FL 33231 305-579-9030 579-9756
Web: www.brazilchamber.org

British-American Business Council (BABC)
52 Vanderbilt Ave 20th Fl..........................New York NY 10017 212-661-4060 661-4074
Web: www.babc.org

British-American Business Council of Los Angeles
15303 Ventura Blvd Ste 1040....................Sherman Oaks CA 91403 310-312-1962 995-4124*
**Fax Area Code:* 818 ■ *Web:* www.babcla.org

British-American Chamber of Commerce Great Lakes Region (BACC)
PO Box 360707..................................Strongsville OH 44136 216-621-0222 696-2582
Web: www.baccohio.org

British-American Chamber of Commerce of Miami
501 Brickell Key Dr Ste 410..........................Miami FL 33131 305-377-0992

Buffalo Economic Renaissance Corp
920 City Hall.....................................Buffalo NY 14202 716-842-6923
Web: www.berc.org

Burns Bog Conservation Society 7953 120 St...........Delta BC V4C6P6 604-572-0373
Web: www.burnsbog.org

Canadian Advanced Technology Alliance
388 Albert St.....................................Ottawa ON K1R5B2 613-236-6550
Web: www.cata.ca

Canadian Bar Assn 845 Cambie St Ste 1000.........Vancouver BC V6B5T3 604-687-3404
Web: www.cba.org

Canadian Cancer Society 10 Alcorn Ave Ste 200.......Toronto ON M4V3B1 416-961-7223
Web: www.cancer.ca

Canadian Electricity Association 66 Slater St.........Ottawa ON K1P5H1 613-230-9263
Web: www.electricity.ca

Canadian Finance & Leasing Association
15 Toronto St.....................................Toronto ON M5C2E3 416-860-1133
Web: www.cfla-acfl.ca

Canadian Manufacturers & Exporters
One Nicholas St Ste 1500............................Ottawa BC K1N7B7 613-238-8888
Web: www.cme-mec.ca

Canadian Mental Health Association
Eight King St E Ste 810.............................Toronto ON M5C1B5 416-484-7750
Web: www.cmha.ca

Canadian Musical Reproduction Rights Agency Ltd The
56 Wellesley St W Ste 320..........................Toronto ON M5S2S3 416-926-1966
Web: www.cmrra.ca

Canadian Payroll Association 250 Bloor St E.........Toronto ON M4W1E6 416-487-3380
Web: www.payroll.ca

Canadian Seed Growers' Association
240 Catherine St...................................Ottawa ON K2P2G8 613-236-0497
Web: www.seedgrowers.ca

Canadian Society of Customs Brokers
55 Murray St Ste 320...............................Ottawa ON K1N5M3 613-562-3543
Web: cscb.ca

Cape Jourimain Nature Centre Inc
5039 Route 16....................................Bayfield NB E4M3Z8 506-538-2220
Web: www.capejourimain.ca

Carefirst Seniors & Community Services Association
3601 Victoria Park Ave..........................Scarborough ON M1W3Y3 416-502-2323
Web: www.carefirstseniors.com

Chicago Automobile Trade Association
18 W 200 Butterfield Rd.....................Oakbrook Terrace IL 60181 630-495-2282
Web: cata.info

Chile-US Chamber of Commerce
1825 Ponce de Leon Blvd Ste 96................Coral Gables FL 33134 305-403-9760 472-8799*
**Fax Area Code:* 786 ■ *Web:* www.chileus.org

Chinese Chamber of Commerce of Hawaii
Eight S King St...................................Honolulu HI 96817 808-533-3181
Web: www.chinesechamber.com

Chinese Chamber of Commerce of Los Angeles
977 N Broadway Ground Fl Ste E.................Los Angeles CA 90012 213-617-0396 617-2128
TF: 800-400-7115 ■ *Web:* www.lachinesechamber.org

Chinese Chamber of Commerce of San Francisco
730 Sacramento St..............................San Francisco CA 94108 415-982-3000 982-4720

Cic Plus Inc 7321 ridgeway ave........................Skokie IL 60076 847-677-7037
Web: www.cicplus.com

CIO Association of Canada
7270 Woodbine Ave Ste 204........................Markham ON L3R4B9 905-752-1899
Web: www.ciocan.ca

Coach Canada's Health Informatics Association
250 Consumers Rd..............................North York ON M2J4V6 416-494-9324
Web: www.coachorg.com

Colombian American Chamber of Commerce
2305 NW 107 Ave Suite 1m14 box 105.................Miami FL 33172 305-446-2542 446-2038
Web: www.colombiachamber.com

Constructors Association of Western Pennsylvania
1201 Banksville Rd..............................Pittsburgh PA 15216 412-343-8000
Web: www.cawp.org

Dairy Farmers of Ontario
6780 Campobello Rd..........................Mississauga ON L5N2L8 905-821-8970
Web: www.milk.org

Danish-American Chamber of Commerce
885 Second Ave 18th Fl...........................New York NY 10017 646-790-7169 754-1904*
**Fax Area Code:* 212 ■ *Web:* www.daccny.com

Deaf Inter-link 100 Saint Francois St...............Florissant MO 63031 314-837-7757
Web: www.deafinterlink.com

Downtown Austin Alliance
211 E Seventh St Ste 818............................Austin TX 78701 512-469-1766
Web: downtownaustin.com

Ecuadorian-American Chamber of Commerce of Greater Miami
1390 Brickell Ave Ste 220...........................Miami FL 33131 305-539-0010
Web: www.ecuachamber.com

Eden i & r Inc 570 B St............................Hayward CA 94541 510-537-2710
Web: www.edenir.org

Edmonton Folk Music Festival
10115 97a Ave Nw...............................Edmonton AB T5K2T3 780-429-1899
Web: www.edmontonfolkfest.org

Electric Cooperatives of South Carolina Inc, The
808 Knox Abbott Dr..................................Cayce SC 29033 803-796-6060
Web: www.ecsc.org

Electronic Transactions Association, The
1101 16th St NW Ste 402........................Washington DC 20036 202-828-2635
Web: www.electran.org

Organization	City	State	ZIP	Phone	Fax
Empire Building Services 1570 E Edinger Ave *Web:* www.ebuildingservices.com	Santa Ana	CA	92705	714-836-7700	
European-American Business Council 919 18th St NW Ste 220 *Web:* transatlanticbusiness.org	Washington	DC	20006	202-828-9104	828-9106
Ex-Students' Association, The 2110 San Jacinto Blvd *Web:* www.texasexes.org	Austin	TX	78712	512-471-8839	
Federal Bar Council 123 Main St Ste L100 *Web:* federalbarcouncil.org	White Plains	NY	10601	914-682-8800	
Fine Arts Association, The 38660 Mentor Ave *Web:* www.fineartsassociation.org	Willoughby	OH	44094	440-951-6637	
Finnish American Chamber of Commerce Inc 866 United Nations Plz Ste 250 *Web:* www.facc-ny.com	New York	NY	10017	212-821-0225	750-4418
Flagship Fire Inc 1500 15th Ave dr e *Web:* www.flagshipfire.com	Palmetto	FL	34221	941-723-7230	
Flashbanc LLC 185 nw spanish river blvd *Web:* www.flashbanc.com	Boca Raton	FL	33431	561-278-8888	
Florida Association of Counties 100 S Monroe St *Web:* www.fl-counties.com	Tallahassee	FL	32301	850-922-4300	
Florida Retail Federation Services Inc 227 S Adams St *Web:* www.frf.org	Tallahassee	FL	32301	850-222-4082	
Florida Venture Forum Inc, The 707 W Azeele St *Web:* www.flventure.org	Tampa	FL	33606	813-335-8116	
French-American Chamber of Commerce in New York 1350 Broadway Ste 2101 *TF:* 800-821-2241 ■ *Web:* www.faccnyc.org	New York	NY	10018	212-867-0123	867-9050
French-American Chamber of Commerce of Atlanta 3399 Peachtree Rd NE Ste 500 *Web:* www.facc-atlanta.com	Atlanta	GA	30326	404-997-6800	997-6810
French-American Chamber of Commerce of Chicago (FACC) 35 E Wacker Dr Ste 670 *Web:* www.facc-chicago.com	Chicago	IL	60601	312-578-0444	578-0445
French-American Chamber of Commerce of Florida 100 N Biscayne Blvd Ste 1105 *Web:* www.faccmiami.com	Miami	FL	33131	305-374-5000	358-8203
French-American Chamber of Commerce of Houston 777 Post Oak Blvd Ste 600	Houston	TX	77056	713-985-3280	
French-American Chamber of Commerce of Philadelphia (FACC) 1528 Walnut St Ste 2020 *Web:* www.faccphila.org	Philadelphia	PA	19102	215-545-0123	545-0144
French-American Chamber of Commerce of San Francisco 26 O'Farrell St Ste 500 *Web:* www.faccsf.com	San Francisco	CA	94108	415-442-4717	442-4621
French-American Chamber of Commerce of the Pacific Northwest (FACCPNW) 2200 Alaskan Way Ste 490 *Web:* www.faccpnw.org	Seattle	WA	98121	206-443-4703	448-4218
FSNA 1052 St Laurent Blvd *Web:* www.fsna.com	Ottawa	ON	K1K3B4	613-745-2559	
Georgia Poultry Improvement Assn 4457 Oakwood Rd *Web:* gapoultrylab.org	Oakwood	GA	30566	770-535-5996	
Georgia Society of Cpa's 3353 Peachtree Rd NE Ste 400 *Web:* www.gscpa.org	Alpharetta	GA	30326	404-231-8676	
German-American Chamber of Commerce Inc 75 Broad St 21st Fl *Web:* www.gaccny.com	New York	NY	10004	212-974-8830	974-8867
German-American Chamber of Commerce Inc - Philadelphia 1617 John F Kennedy Blvd Ste 340 1 Penn Ctr *Web:* www.gaccphiladelphia.com	Philadelphia	PA	19103	215-665-1585	665-0375
German-American Chamber of Commerce of the Midwest Inc 321 N Clark St Ste 1425 *Web:* www.gaccmidwest.org	Chicago	IL	60654	312-644-2662	644-0738
German-American Chamber of Commerce of the Southern US Inc 1170 Howell Mill Rd Ste 300 *Web:* www.gaccsouth.com	Atlanta	GA	30318	404-586-6800	586-6820
Global Hope Network Po Box 560026 *Web:* www.ghni.org	Orlando	FL	32856	407-207-3256	
Grants Manager Network 141 Homestead Ave *Web:* gmnetwork.org	Metairie	LA	70005	504-834-9656	
Graphic Arts Association 1210 Northbrook Dr Ste 250 *Web:* gaa1900.com	Feasterville Trevose	PA	19053	215-396-2300	
Hass Avocado Board 38 Discovery Ste 150 *Web:* www.hassavocadoboard.com	Irvine	CA	92618	949-341-3250	
Health Unit Brant County 194 Ter Hill St *Web:* www.bchu.org	Brantford	ON	N3R1G7	519-753-4937	
Healthshare Inc Po Box 679010 *Web:* www.healthshare-tha.com	Austin	TX	78767	512-465-1000	
Heart of Virginia Council Inc Boy Scouts of America 4015 Fitzhugh Ave *Web:* hovc.org	Richmond	VA	23230	804-355-4306	
Hellenic-American Chamber of Commerce (HACC) 370 Lexington Ave 27th Fl *Web:* www.hellenicamerican.cc	New York	NY	10017	212-629-6380	564-9281
Heritage Solar 5035 surfside dr *Web:* heritagesolar.com	San diego	CA	92154	619-200-9073	
Hive Modern Design 820 nw glisan st *Web:* hivemodern.com	Portland	OR	97209	503-242-1967	
Home Builders Association of Washtenaw County 179 Little Lk Dr *Web:* bragannarbor.com	Ann Arbor	MI	48103	734-996-0100	
Honolulu-Japanese Chamber of Commerce 2454 S Beretania St Ste 201 *Web:* hjcc.org	Honolulu	HI	96826	808-949-5531	949-3020
Houston Apartment Association Inc 4810 Westway Park Blvd *Web:* www.haaonline.org	Houston	TX	77041	713-595-0300	
Houston Area Safety Council 1301 W 13th St *Web:* hacsc.com	Deer Park	TX	77536	281-476-9900	
Iada Services Inc 1111 Office Park Rd *Web:* www.iada.com	West Des Moines	IA	50265	515-440-7621	
Ibb Design Group 5798 Genesis Ct *Web:* www.ibbdesign.com	Frisco	TX	75034	214-618-6600	
Icelandic-American Chamber of Commerce 800 Third Ave 36th Fl *Web:* www.iceland.is	New York	NY	10022	212-593-2700	593-6269
Illinois Soybean Assoc 1605 Commerce Pkwy *Web:* www.ilsoy.org	Bloomington	IL	61704	309-662-3373	
Indiana Black Expo Inc 3145 N Meridian St *Web:* www.indianablackexpo.com	Indianapolis	IN	46208	317-925-2702	
Info. Quality Healthcare 385b Highland Colony Pkwy Ste 504 *Web:* www.iqh.org	Ridgeland	MS	39157	601-957-1575	
Inland Press Association 701 Lee St Ste 925 *Web:* inlandpress.org	Des Plaines	IL	60016	847-795-0380	
Intensity Corp 12730 High Bluff Dr Ste 300 *Web:* intensity.com	San Diego	CA	92130	858-876-9101	
Iowa Soybean Association 4554 114th st *Web:* www.iasoybeans.com	Urbandale	IA	50322	515-251-8640	
Ireland Chamber of Commerce in the US 556 Central Ave *Web:* www.iccusa.org	New Providence	NJ	07974	908-286-1300	286-1200
Italian American Chamber of Commerce of Chicago (IACC) 500 N Michigan Ave Ste 506 *Web:* www.iacc-chicago.com	Chicago	IL	60611	312-553-9137	553-9142
Italy-America Chamber of Commerce Inc 730 Fifth Ave Ste 600 *Web:* www.italchamber.org	New York	NY	10019	212-459-0044	459-0090
Italy-America Chamber of Commerce of Texas Inc 1800 W Loop S Ste 1120 *Web:* www.iacctexas.com	Houston	TX	77027	713-626-9303	626-9309
Italy-America Chamber of Commerce Southeast Inc 2 S Biscayne Blvd Ste 1880 *TF:* 800-428-3003 ■ *Web:* www.iacc-miami.com	Miami	FL	33131	305-577-9868	577-3956
Italy-America Chamber of Commerce West Inc 10537 Santa Monica Blvd Ste 210 *Web:* www.iaccw.net	Los Angeles	CA	90025	310-557-3017	557-1217
Japanese Chamber of Commerce & Industry of Chicago 541 N Fairbanks Ct Ste 2050 *Web:* jccc-chi.org/ja/ai1ec_event/environmentallaw/	Chicago	IL	60611	312-245-8344	245-8355
Japanese Chamber of Commerce & Industry of Hawaii 714 Kanoelehua Ave *Web:* jccih.org	Hilo	HI	96720	808-934-0177	934-0178
Japanese Chamber of Commerce & Industry of New York Inc 145 W 57th St Sixth Fl *Web:* www.jcciny.org	New York	NY	10019	212-246-8001	246-8002
Japanese Chamber of Commerce of Northern California 1875 S Grant St Ste 760 *Web:* www.jccnc.org	San Mateo	CA	94402	650-522-8500	522-8300
JJ Kane 8008 US Hwy 130 Bldg One Ste 214 *Web:* www.jjkane.com	Delran	NJ	08075	856-764-7163	
Johnnie Appleseed Visitor Center 110 Erdman Way *Web:* www.appleseed.org	Leominster	MA	01453	978-534-2302	
Kids Help Phone 300-439 University Ave *Web:* www.kidshelpphone.ca	Toronto	ON	M5G1Y8	416-586-5437	
Kieckhafer & Co 6201 Oak Canyon Dr *Web:* www.ksandco.com	Irvine	CA	92618	949-250-3900	
Korean Chamber of Commerce 3435 Wilshire Blvd Ste 2450	Los Angeles	CA	90010	213-480-1115	
Korean Chamber of Commerce & Industry in the USA Inc 460 Pk Ave Ste 410 *Web:* www.kocham.org	New York	NY	10022	212-644-0140	644-9106
Labor Law Center Inc 12534 Vly view st. *TF:* 800-745-9970 ■ *Web:* www.laborlawcenter.com	Garden Grove	CA	92845	800-745-9970	
Latin Chamber of Commerce of the US (CAMACOL) 1417 W Flagler St *Web:* www.camacol.org	Miami	FL	33135	305-642-3870	642-0653
Lernia Training Solutions 3603 winding way *Web:* www.lernia-ts.com	Newtown Square	PA	19073	610-356-1792	
Lignite Energy Council 1016 E Owens Ave *Web:* www.lignite.com	Bismarck	ND	58502	701-258-7117	
Luxembourg-American Chamber of Commerce 17 Beekman Pl *Web:* laccny.com	New York	NY	10022	212-888-6701	935-5896
Maine Hospital Association 33 Fuller Rd *Web:* themha.org	Augusta	ME	04330	207-622-4794	
MANTEC Inc 600 N Hartley St Ste 100 *Web:* www.mantec.org	York	PA	17404	717-843-5054	
Marine Corps Reserve Association 8626 Lee Hwy Ste 201 *Web:* www.nationalmcla.org	Fairfax	VA	22031	703-207-0626	
Mavro Imaging LLC 22 maple tree dr *Web:* www.mavroimaging.com	Westampton	NJ	08060	609-265-3803	
Meclabs LLC 1300 Marsh Landing Pkwy Ste 106 *TF:* 800-517-5531 ■ *Web:* www.meclabs.com	Jacksonville Beach	FL	32250	800-517-5531	
Mercer Engineering & Research 135 Osigian Blvd *Web:* www.merc-mercer.org	Warner Robins	GA	31088	478-953-6800	
Merlino Foods po box 80069 *Web:* www.merlino.com	Seattle	WA	98108	206-723-4700	

Organization	City	State	Zip	Phone	Fax
Michigan Association of Insurance Agents 1141 Centennial Way *Web:* www.michagent.org	Lansing	MI	48917	517-323-9473	
Michigan Bankers Association 507 S Grand Ave *Web:* www.mibankers.com	Lansing	MI	48933	517-485-3600	
Michigan Manufacturers Association, The 620 S Capitol Ave *Web:* www.mma-net.org	Lansing	MI	48901	517-372-5900	
Milyli Inc 415 n sangamon st *Web:* www.milyli.com	Chicago	IL	60642	312-265-0136	
Mining Association of Canada The 1105-350 Sparks St *Web:* mining.ca	Ottawa	ON	K1R7S8	613-233-9391	
Minnesota Multi Housing Services Inc 1600 W 82nd St Ste 110 *Web:* www.mmha.com	Bloomington	MN	55431	952-854-8500	
Mobius Executive Leadership 177 worcester st *Web:* www.mobiusleadership.com	Wellesley Hills	MA	02481	781-237-1362	
Mutual Fund Dealers Association of Canada 800-6th Ave SW Ste 850 *Web:* www.mfda.ca	CALGARY	AB	T2P3G3	416-361-6332	
N.c. Center for Nonprofit Organizations Inc 1110 Navaho Dr Ste 200 *Web:* www.ncnonprofits.org	Raleigh	NC	27609	919-790-1555	
Nacm Chicago-midwest 3005 Tollview Dr *Web:* www.nacmchicago.org	Rolling Meadows	IL	60008	847-483-6400	
Naffs 3301c State Rt 66 Ste 205 *Web:* naffs.org	Neptune	NJ	07753	732-922-3218	
Namgis First Nation 49 Atli St *Web:* www.namgis.bc.ca	Alert Bay	BC	V0N1A0	250-974-5556	
National Swine Registry 2639 Yeager Rd *Web:* www.nationalswine.com	West Lafayette	IN	47906	765-463-3594	
National US-Arab Chamber of Commerce 1330 Post Oak Blvd Ste 1600 *Web:* www.nusacc.org	Houston	TX	77056	713-963-4620	963-4609
Nazcare Inc 599 White Spar Rd *Web:* www.nazcare.org	Prescott	AZ	86303	928-442-9205	
Nbcot 12 S Summit Ave Ste 100 *Web:* www.nbcot.org	Gaithersburg	MD	20877	301-990-7979	
Neal Systems Inc 122 Terry Dr *Web:* www.nealsystems.com	Newtown	PA	18940	215-968-7577	
Nebraska Bankers Association Inc 233 S 13th St Ste 700 *Web:* www.nebankers.org	Lincoln	NE	68508	402-474-1555	
Nebraska Beef Council 1319 Central Ave *Web:* www.nebeef.org	Kearney	NE	68848	308-236-7551	
Nebraska Farm Bureau Federation 5225 S 16th St *Web:* www.nefb.org	Lincoln	NE	68512	402-421-4400	
NEDMA 396 Washington St Ste 387 *Web:* www.nedma.com	Wellesley Hills	MA	02481	781-237-1366	
Netherlands Chamber of Commerce 267 Fifth Ave	New York	NY	10016	212-265-6461	
New Tech Network 1250 Main St Ste 100 *Web:* www.newtechnetwork.org	Napa	CA	94559	707-253-6951	
New York Women in Film & Television Six E 39th St Ste 1200 *Web:* www.nywift.org	New York	NY	10016	212-679-0870	
Nj Assn-osteopathic One Distribution Way *Web:* www.njosteo.com	Monmouth Junction	NJ	08852	732-940-9000	
Nofa-ny Certified Organic LLC 840 Upper Front St *Web:* www.nofany.org	Binghamton	NY	13905	607-724-9851	
Norwegian-American Chamber of Commerce Inc, The 655 Third Ave Ste 1810 *Web:* www.naccusa.org	New York	NY	10017	212-885-9737	885-9710
Norwegian-American Chamber of Commerce Southwest Chapter (NACC) 5219 Pine Arbor Dr *Web:* www.nacchouston.org	Houston	TX	77066	281-537-6879	587-9284
Ohio Contractors Association 1313 Dublin Rd *Web:* ohiocontractors.org	Columbus	OH	43215	614-488-0724	
Ohio Health Care Association, The 55 Green Meadows Dr S *Web:* www.ohca.org	Lewis Center	OH	43035	614-436-4154	
Ohio Manufacturers' Association 33 N High St *Web:* www.ohiomfg.com	Columbus	OH	43215	614-224-5111	
Ohio Motorcycle Dealers Association 655 Metro Pl S Ste 270 *Web:* oada.com	Dublin	OH	43017	614-766-9100	
Oklahoma Alliance for Manufacturing Excellence Inc 525 S Main St Ste 210 *Web:* www.okalliance.com	Tulsa	OK	74103	918-592-0722	
Oklahoma Primary Care Association 4300 N Lincoln Blvd Ste 203 *Web:* okpca.org	Oklahoma City	OK	73105	405-424-2282	
Ontario Association of Archietects 111 Moatfield Dr *Web:* www.oaa.on.ca	North York	ON	M3B3L6	416-449-5756	
Ontario Dental Nurses & Assistants Association 869 Dundas St *Web:* odaa.org	London	ON	N5W2Z8	519-679-2566	
Ontario Equestrian Federation One W Pearce St *Web:* horse.on.ca	Richmond Hill	ON	L4B3K3	905-709-6545	
Open Geospatial Consortium Inc 35 Main St Ste 5 *Web:* www.opengeospatial.org	Wayland	MA	01778	508-655-5858	

Organization	City	State	Zip	Phone	Fax
Oregon Bankers Association 777 13th St Se Ste 130 *Web:* oregonbankers.com	Salem	OR	97301	503-581-3522	
Oregon Primary Care Association 110 Sw Yamhill St Ste 300 *Web:* www.orpca.org	Portland	OR	97204	503-228-8852	
Palm Beach Chamber of Commerce 400 Royal Palm Way *Web:* www.palmbeachchamber.com	Palm Beach	FL	33480	561-655-3282	
Pathways to Independence 25 Dundas St W *Web:* www.pathwaysind.com	Belleville	ON	K8P3M7	613-962-2541	
Pce Systems 28530 orchard Lk rd *Web:* www.pcesystems.com	Farmington hills	MI	48334	248-932-4888	
Pennag Industries Association 2215 Forest Hills Dr Ste 39 *Web:* pennag.com	Harrisburg	PA	17112	717-651-5920	
Polaris Meetings Group 1215 Sixth ave *Web:* www.polarismeetings.com	San francisco	CA	94122	415-731-4648	
Portugal-US Chamber of Commerce 590 Fifth Ave Fourth Fl *Web:* www.portugal-us.com	New York	NY	10036	212-354-4627	575-4737
Poteet Strawberry Festival Association 9199 N State Hwy 16 *Web:* www.strawberryfestival.com	Poteet	TX	78065	830-742-8144	
Project Lifesaver International Headquarters 815 Battlefield Blvd S *Web:* www.projectlifesaver.org	Chesapeake	VA	23322	757-546-5502	
PromaxBDA 1522 E Cloverfield Blvd *Web:* www.promaxbda.org	Santa Monica	CA	90404	310-788-7600	
Prores Group Inc 480 w 78th st *Web:* www.proresgroup.com	Chanhassen	MN	55317	952-906-5951	
Puerto Rican Chamber of Commerce of South Florida 3550 Biscayne Blvd Ste 306 *Web:* www.puertoricanchamber.com	Miami	FL	33137	305-571-8007	571-8007
Pump It Up Party 11411 W 183rd St *Web:* www.pumpitupparty.com	Orland Park	IL	60467	708-479-2220	
Quadis Technologies Inc 5925 s 56th st *Web:* www.summitgroupsoftware.com	Lincoln	NE	68516	402-423-4660	
Regional Plan Association Inc Four Irving Place Seventh Fl *Web:* www.rpa.org	New York	NY	10003	212-253-2727	
Representative of German Industry & Trade 1776 I St NW Ste 1000 *Web:* www.rgit-usa.com	Washington	DC	20006	202-659-4777	659-4779
RJ & Makay LLC 100 S Ridge St Ste 101 *Web:* www.rjandmakay.com	Breckenridge	CO	80424	970-306-0600	
Rlj Financial Services Inc 1788 Mitchell Rd Ste 102 *Web:* www.rljfinancial.com	Ceres	CA	95307	209-538-7758	
ROC USA LLC Seven Wall St *Web:* www.rocusa.org	Concord	NH	03301	603-224-6669	
Rosewood Care Center Holding Co 100 Rosewood Village Dr *Web:* www.rosewoodnursing.com	Swansea	IL	62226	618-236-1391	
Royal Canadian Yacht Club, The 141 St George St *Web:* rcyc.ca	Toronto	ON	M5R2L8	416-967-7245	
Safety Training Seminars 598 Vermont St *Web:* www.cprcpr.com	San Francisco	CA	94107	415-437-1600	
Santie Oil Co 126 Larcel Dr *Web:* www.santiemidwest.com	Sikeston	MO	63801	314-436-3569	
Scoliosis Research Society 555 E Wells St Ste 1100 *Web:* www.srs.org	Milwaukee	WI	53202	414-289-9107	
Sierra Club of Canada Bc Chapter 304-733 Johnson St *Web:* www.sierraclub.bc.ca	Victoria	BC	V8W3C7	250-386-5255	
SMC Business Councils 600 Cranberry Woods Dr Ste 190 *Web:* www.smc.org	Cranberry Township	PA	16066	412-371-1500	
SOCAN 41 Valleybrook Dr *Web:* www.socan.ca	Toronto	ON	M3B2S6	416-445-8700	
Spain-US Chamber of Commerce 350 Fifth Ave Ste 2600 *Web:* www.spainuscc.org	New York	NY	10118	212-967-2170	564-1415
SPEECH Morphing SYSTEMS Inc 1320 White Oaks Rd *Web:* www.speechmorphing.com	Campbell	CA	95008	408-371-8014	
Speed Skating Canada 2781 Lancaster Rd *Web:* www.speedskating.ca	Ottawa	ON	K1B1A7	613-260-3660	
Sports Inc 333 Second Ave N *Web:* www.sportsinc.com	Lewistown	MT	59457	406-538-3496	
St. Louis Association of Realtors 12777 Olive Blvd *Web:* www.stlrealtors.com	St. Louis	MO	63141	314-576-0033	
Stanford Alumni Association 326 Galvez St *Web:* www.stanfordalumni.org	Stanford	CA	94305	650-723-2021	
Suzuki Association of The Americas Inc 1900 Folsom St Ste 101 *Web:* www.suzukiassociation.org	Boulder	CO	80302	303-444-0948	
Swedish-American Chamber of Commerce Atlanta Inc (SACC) 4775 Peachtree Industrial Blvd Bldg 300 Ste 300 *Web:* www.sacc-georgia.org	Norcross	GA	30092	770-670-2480	670-2578
Swedish-American Chamber of Commerce Inc New York Chapter 570 Lexington Ave 20th Fl *Web:* www.saccny.org	New York	NY	10022	212-838-5530	755-7953
Swedish-American Chamber of Commerce San Diego 4475 Mission Blvd Ste 201 *Web:* www.sacc-sandiego.org	San Diego	CA	92109	858-598-4809	598-4809

Organization	City	State	Zip	Phone	Fax
Swedish-American Chamber of Commerce Washington DC Inc 2900 K St NW *Web:* sacc-usa.org/beta/dc/	Washington	DC	20007	202-536-1570	
Swiss-American Chamber of Commerce *New York Chapter* 500 Fifth Ave Rm 1800 *Web:* www.amcham.ch	New York	NY	10110	212-246-7789	246-1366
Syncratec Solutions LLC Seven upton ln. *Web:* www.syncratec.com	Yardley	PA	19067	267-266-5596	
Tahoe Keys Property Owners Association 356 Ala Wai Blvd *Web:* www.tahoekeyspoa.org	South Lake Tahoe	CA	96150	530-542-6444	
TerraLex Inc 2050 Coral Way Ste 601 *Web:* www.terralex.org	Miami	FL	33145	305-858-8825	
Texas Oil & Gas Association Inc 304 W 13th St. *Web:* www.txoga.org	Austin	TX	78701	512-478-6631	
Theatre Historical Society of America 152 N York St Second Fl. *Web:* www.historictheatres.org	Elmhurst	IL	60126	630-782-1800	
Toronto Construction Association 70 Leek Cres. *Web:* www.tcanetworks.com	Richmond Hill	ON	L4B1H1	416-499-4000	
Toronto Law Office Management Association 43 Daniel Ct *Web:* www.tloma.on.ca	Markham	ON	L3P4B8	416-410-1979	
Tourism Industry Association of Pei 25 Queen St *Web:* www.tiapei.pe.ca	Charlottetown	PE	C1A4A2	902-566-5008	
Trackers Earth Inc 1424 se 76th ave. *Web:* trackerspdx.com	Portland	OR	97215	503-453-3038	
TransferOnline 512 SE Salmon St. *Web:* www.transferonline.com	Portland	OR	97214	503-227-2950	
Travel Goods Association Five Vaughn Dr Ste 105 *Web:* www.travel-goods.org	Princeton	NJ	08540	609-720-0620	
Travel Support Systems Inc 22410 68th Ave E *Web:* www.ossn.com	Bradenton	FL	34211	941-322-9700	
Trusted Computing Group 3855 SW 153rd Dr *Web:* www.trustedcomputinggroup.org	Beaverton	OR	97006	503-619-0562	
Tsleil-Waututh Nation, The 3075 Takaya Dr *Web:* www.twnation.ca	North Vancouver	BC	V7H3A8	604-929-3454	
Turfgrass Producers International 1855-A Hicks Rd *Web:* www.turfgrassod.org	Rolling Meadows	IL	60008	847-705-9898	
Uni-Bell PVC Pipe Association 2711 LBJ Fwy Ste 1000 *Web:* www.uni-bell.org	Dallas	TX	75234	972-243-3902	
Upstate Carolina Angel Network LLC, The NEXT Innovation Ctr 411 University Ridge Ste 211 *Web:* www.upstateangels.com	Greenville	SC	29601	864-751-4805	
US-Angola Chamber of Commerce 1100 17th St NW Ste 1000 *Web:* www.us-angola.org	Washington	DC	20036	202-857-0789	223-0551
US-Austrian Chamber of Commerce 165 W 46th St. *Web:* usaustrianchamber.org	New York	NY	10036	212-819-0117	
US-Mexico Chamber of Commerce 1300 Pennsylvania Ave NW Ste 0003 *Web:* www.usmcoc.org	Washington	DC	20004	202-312-1520	312-1530
US-Mexico Chamber of Commerce California Pacific Chapter 2450 Colorado Ave Ste 400E *TF:* 800-997-9148 ■ *Web:* www.usmcocca.org	Santa Monica	CA	90404	310-586-7901	586-7800
Vietnamese-American Chamber of Commerce of Hawaii PO Box 240352 *Web:* www.vacch.org	Honolulu	HI	96824	808-545-1889	734-2315
Volunteer Calgary 1202 Centre St Se *Web:* www.volunteercalgary.ab.ca	Calgary	AB	T2G5A5	403-265-5633	
Wireless Network Group Warehouse 220 w Pkwy *Web:* www.wnginc.com	Pompton Plains	NJ	07444	973-831-4015	
Wisconsin Hospital Association Inc 5510 Research Park Dr *Web:* www.wha.org	Fitchburg	WI	53711	608-274-1820	
Women Lawyers Association of Los Angeles 634 S Spring St Ste 617 *Web:* www.wlala.org	Los Angeles	CA	90014	213-892-8982	
Wyoming Hospital Association 2005 Warren Ave *Web:* www.wyohospitals.com	Cheyenne	WY	82001	307-632-9344	
Ymca Canada 42 Charles St E *Web:* www.ymca.ca	Toronto	ON	M4Y1T4	416-967-9622	
Young Drivers of Canada Inc One James St S Ste 300 *Web:* www.yd.com	Hamilton	ON	L8P4R5	905-529-5501	

139 CHAMBERS OF COMMERCE - US - LOCAL

SEE ALSO Civic & Political Organizations p. 1765
Chambers listed here represent areas with a population of 25,000 or more. Listings are organized by states and then are alphabetized within each state grouping according to the name of the city in which each chamber is located.

Alabama

Organization	City	State	Zip	Phone	Fax
Alexander City Chamber of Commerce 120 Tallapoosa St *Web:* www.alexandercity.org	Alexander City	AL	35010	256-234-3461	234-0094
Calhoun County Chamber of Commerce 1330 Quintard Ave *Web:* www.calhounchamber.com	Anniston	AL	36201	256-237-3536	237-0126
Greater Limestone County Chamber of Commerce 101 S Beaty St *TF:* 866-953-6565 ■ *Web:* www.tourathens.com	Athens	AL	35611	256-232-2600	232-2609
Auburn Chamber of Commerce 714 E Glenn Ave PO Box 1370 *Web:* www.auburnchamber.com	Auburn	AL	36831	334-887-7011	821-5500
North Baldwin Chamber of Commerce 301 McMeans Ave *Web:* www.northbaldwinchamber.com	Bay Minette	AL	36507	251-937-5665	937-5670
Bessemer Area Chamber of Commerce 321 N 18th St *TF:* 888-423-7736 ■ *Web:* www.bessemerchamber.com	Bessemer	AL	35020	205-425-3253	425-4979
Birmingham Business Alliance 505 N 20th St Ste 200 *Web:* birminghambusinessalliance.com	Birmingham	AL	35203	205-324-2100	324-2560
Cullman Area Chamber of Commerce 301 Second Ave SW *TF:* 800-313-5114 ■ *Web:* www.cullmanchamber.org	Cullman	AL	35055	256-734-0454	737-7443
Eastern Shore Chamber of Commerce 29750 Larry Dee Cawyer Dr PO Box 310 *Web:* www.eschamber.com	Daphne	AL	36526	251-621-8222	621-8001
Decatur-Morgan County Chamber of Commerce 515 Sixth Ave NE *Web:* www.dcc.org	Decatur	AL	35601	256-353-5312	353-2384
Dothan Area Chamber of Commerce 102 Jamestown Blvd. *TF:* 800-221-1027 ■ *Web:* www.dothan.com	Dothan	AL	36301	334-792-5138	794-4796
Eufaula/Barbour County Chamber of Commerce 333 E Broad St *Web:* eufaulachamber.com	Eufaula	AL	36027	334-687-6664	
Shoals Chamber of Commerce 20 Hightower Pl PO Box 1331 *TF:* 877-764-4661 ■ *Web:* www.shoalschamber.com	Florence	AL	35630	256-764-4661	331-5386
South Baldwin Chamber of Commerce (SBCC) 112 W Laurel Ave PO Box 1117 *TF:* 877-461-3712 ■ *Web:* www.southbaldwinchamber.com	Foley	AL	36535	251-943-3291	943-6810
Gadsden & Etowah County Chamber One Commerce Sq *TF:* 800-659-2955 ■ *Web:* www.gadsdenchamber.com	Gadsden	AL	35901	256-543-3472	543-9887
Greenville Area Chamber of Commerce 1 Depot Sq *TF:* 800-959-0717 ■ *Web:* www.greenvillealchamber.com	Greenville	AL	36037	334-382-3251	
Hoover Chamber of Commerce PO Box 36005 *Web:* www.hooverchamber.org	Hoover	AL	35236	205-988-5672	988-8383
Chamber of Commerce of Huntsville/Madison County 225 Church St *Web:* www.huntsvillealabamausa.com	Huntsville	AL	35801	256-535-2000	535-2015
Walker County Chamber of Commerce 204 19th St E Ste 101 **Fax Area Code:* 706 ■ *TF General:* 800-384-4571 ■ *Web:* www.walkerchamber.us	Jasper	AL	35501	205-384-4571	375-7797*
Greater Valley Area Chamber of Commerce 2102 S Broad Ave PO Box 205 *Web:* www.greatervalleyarea.com	Lanett	AL	36863	334-642-1411	642-1410
Mobile Area Chamber of Commerce 451 Government St. *TF:* 800-422-6951 ■ *Web:* www.mobilechamber.com	Mobile	AL	36602	251-433-6951	432-1143
Montgomery Area Chamber of Commerce 41 Commerce St PO Box 79 *Web:* www.montgomerychamber.com	Montgomery	AL	36104	334-834-5200	265-4745
Blount County-Oneonta Chamber of Commerce 225 Second Ave E. *Web:* bocc.publishpath.com/	Oneonta	AL	35121	205-274-2153	274-2099
Ozark Area Chamber of Commerce 294 Painter Ave *TF:* 800-582-8497 ■ *Web:* www.ozarkalchamber.com	Ozark	AL	36360	334-774-9321	774-8736
Greater Shelby County Chamber of Commerce 1301 County Services Dr *Web:* www.shelbychamber.org	Pelham	AL	35124	205-663-4542	663-4524
Phenix City-Russell County Chamber of Commerce 1107 Broad St. *TF:* 800-892-2248 ■ *Web:* www.pc-rcchamber.com	Phenix City	AL	36867	334-298-3639	298-3846
Greater Jackson County Chamber of Commerce PO Box 973 *TF:* 800-259-5508 ■ *Web:* www.jacksoncountychamber.com	Scottsboro	AL	35768	256-259-5500	259-4447
Selma-Dallas County Chamber of Commerce 912 Selma Ave *TF:* 800-457-3562 ■ *Web:* www.selmaalabama.com	Selma	AL	36701	334-875-7241	875-7142
Greater Talladega Area Chamber of Commerce 210 E St S PO Box A *Web:* www.talladegachamber.com	Talladega	AL	35160	256-362-9075	362-9093
Chamber of Commerce of West Alabama 2200 University Blvd *Web:* www.tuscaloosachamber.com	Tuscaloosa	AL	35401	205-758-7588	391-0565

Alaska

Organization	City	State	Zip	Phone	Fax
Anchorage Chamber of Commerce 1016 W Sixth Ave Ste 303 *Web:* www.anchoragechamber.org	Anchorage	AK	99501	907-272-2401	272-4117
Fairbanks Chamber of Commerce 100 Cushman St Ste 102 *TF:* 800-770-8255 ■ *Web:* www.fairbankschamber.org	Fairbanks	AK	99701	907-452-1105	456-6968
Juneau Chamber of Commerce 9301 Glacier Hwy Suite 110 *TF:* 888-581-2201 ■ *Web:* www.juneauchamber.com	Juneau	AK	99801	907-463-3488	463-3489

Arizona

Organization	City	State	Zip	Phone	Fax
Apache Junction Chamber of Commerce 567 W Apache Trl *Web:* www.ajchamber.com	Apache Junction	AZ	85220	480-982-3141	982-3234

Phone Fax

Bullhead Area Chamber of Commerce
1251 Hwy 95 ....Bullhead City AZ 86429 928-754-4121 754-5514
TF: 800-987-7457 ■ *Web:* bullheadareachamber.com

Chandler Chamber of Commerce
25 S Arizona Pl Ste 201 ....Chandler AZ 85225 480-963-4571 963-0188
TF: 800-963-4571 ■ *Web:* www.chandlerchamber.com

Cottonwood Chamber of Commerce
1010 S Main St...............................Cottonwood AZ 86326 928-634-7593 634-7594
Web: www.cottonwoodchamberaz.org

Flagstaff Chamber of Commerce 101 W Rt 66 ....Flagstaff AZ 86001 928-774-4505 779-1209
Web: www.flagstaffchamber.com

Gilbert Chamber of Commerce
119 N Gilbert Rd Ste 101 PO Box 527 ....Gilbert AZ 85299 480-892-0056 892-1980*
**Fax Area Code:* 602 ■ *Web:* www.gilbertaz.com

Southwest Valley Chamber of Commerce
289 N Litchfield Rd...............................Goodyear AZ 85338 623-932-2260 932-9057
Web: www.southwestvalleychamber.org

Kingman Area Chamber of Commerce
120 W Andy Devine Ave ....Kingman AZ 86401 928-753-6253 753-1049
Web: www.kingmanchamber.org

Lake Havasu Area Chamber of Commerce
314 London Bridge Rd ....Lake Havasu City AZ 86403 928-855-4115 680-0010
TF: 800-307-3610 ■ *Web:* www.havasuchamber.com

Mesa Chamber of Commerce 120 N Ctr St.............Mesa AZ 85201 480-969-1307 827-0727
Web: www.mesachamber.org

Nogales Chamber of Commerce 123 W Kino Pk ....Nogales AZ 85621 520-287-3685 287-3687
Web: thenogaleschamber.com

Rim Country Regional Chamber of Commerce
100 W Main St ....Payson AZ 85547 928-474-4515 474-0812
TF: 800-249-2678 ■ *Web:* www.rimcountrychamber.com

Greater Phoenix Chamber of Commerce
201 N Central Ave Ste 2700 ....Phoenix AZ 85004 602-495-2195 495-8913
Web: www.phoenixchamber.com

Prescott Chamber of Commerce
117 W Goodwin St ....Prescott AZ 86303 928-445-2000 445-0068
TF: 800-266-7534 ■ *Web:* www.prescott.org

Prescott Valley Chamber of Commerce
3001 N Main St Ste 2A.......................Prescott Valley AZ 86314 928-772-8857 772-4267
TF: 800-355-0843 ■ *Web:* www.pvchamber.org

Graham County Chamber of Commerce
1111 Thatcher Blvd...............................Safford AZ 85546 928-428-2511 428-0744
TF: 888-837-1841 ■ *Web:* www.graham-chamber.com

Scottsdale Area Chamber of Commerce
7501 E McCormick Pkwy Ste 202-N.................Scottsdale AZ 85258 480-355-2700 355-2710
Web: www.scottsdalechamber.com

Greater Sierra Vista Area Chamber of Commerce
21 E Wilcox Dr ....Sierra Vista AZ 85635 520-458-6940 452-0878
TF: 800-288-3861 ■ *Web:* www.sierravistachamber.org

Tempe Chamber of Commerce 909 E Apache Blvd.......Tempe AZ 85281 480-967-7891 966-5365
Web: www.tempechamber.org

Tucson Metropolitan Chamber of Commerce
465 W St Mary's Rd PO Box 991 ....Tucson AZ 85702 520-792-2250 882-5704
Web: www.tucsonchamber.org

Yuma County Chamber of Commerce
180 W First St Ste A...............................Yuma AZ 85364 928-782-2567 343-0038
TF: 877-782-0438 ■ *Web:* www.yumachamber.org

Arkansas

Phone Fax

Bentonville/Bella Vista Chamber of Commerce (BBVCC)
200 E Central St PO Box 330 ....Bentonville AR 72712 479-273-2841 273-2180
Web: www.bbvchamber.com

Berryville Chamber of Commerce
506 S Main PO Box 402...........................Berryville AR 72616 870-423-3704
Web: www.berryvillear.com

Fayetteville Chamber of Commerce
123 W Mountain St.............................Fayetteville AR 72702 479-521-1710 521-1791
TF: 866-893-5007 ■ *Web:* www.fayettevillear.com

Fort Smith Regional Chamber of Commerce
612 Garrison Ave ....Fort Smith AR 72901 479-783-3111 783-6110
Web: www.fortsmithchamber.org

Phillips County Chamber of Commerce
111 Hickory Hill Dr PO Box 447.....................Helena AR 72342 870-338-8327 338-8882
Web: www.phillipscountychamber.org

Greater Hot Springs Chamber of Commerce
659 Ouachita Ave ....Hot Springs AR 71901 501-321-1700 321-3551
Web: www.hotspringschamber.com

Jonesboro Regional Chamber of Commerce
PO Box 789 ....Jonesboro AR 72403 870-932-6691 933-5758
Web: jonesborochamber.com

Little Rock Regional Chamber of Commerce
One Chamber Plz ....Little Rock AR 72201 501-374-2001 374-6018
Web: www.littlerockchamber.com

Magnolia-Columbia County Chamber of Commerce
211 W Main St PO Box 866.........................Magnolia AR 71753 870-234-4352 234-9291
Web: www.magnoliachamber.com

Mountain Home Area Chamber of Commerce
1023 Hwy 62 ....Mountain Home AR 72653 870-425-5111 425-4446
TF: 800-822-3536 ■ *Web:* www.enjoymountainhome.com

Paragould Regional Chamber of Commerce
300 W Ct St PO Box 124 ....Paragould AR 72451 870-236-7684 236-7142
Web: www.paragould.org

Rogers-Lowell Area Chamber of Commerce
317 W Walnut St...................................Rogers AR 72756 479-636-1240 636-5485
TF: 800-364-1240 ■ *Web:* www.rogerslowell.com

Russellville Area Chamber of Commerce
708 W Main St ....Russellville AR 72801 479-968-2530 968-5894
TF: 855-678-2447 ■ *Web:* www.russellvillechamber.org

Springdale Chamber of Commerce 202 W Emma....Springdale AR 72765 479-872-2222 228-1371*
**Fax Area Code:* 202 ■ *Web:* www.springdale.com

Phone Fax

West Memphis Chamber of Commerce
108 W Broadway.............................West Memphis AR 72301 870-735-1134 735-6283
Web: www.wmcoc.com

California

Phone Fax

Alameda Chamber of Commerce
2210D S Shore Ctr ....Alameda CA 94501 510-522-0414 522-7677
Web: www.alamedachamber.com

Alhambra Chamber of Commerce 104 S First St......Alhambra CA 91801 626-282-8481 282-5596
Web: www.alhambrachamber.org

Altadena Chamber of Commerce
730 E Altadena Dr................................Altadena CA 91001 626-794-3988
Web: altadenachamber.org

Anaheim Chamber of Commerce 201 E Ctr St........ Anaheim CA 92805 714-758-0222 758-0468
Web: www.anaheimchamber.org

Antioch Chamber of Commerce 101 H St #4.......... Antioch CA 94509 925-757-1800 757-5286
Web: www.antiochchamber.com

Aptos Chamber of Commerce
7605-A Old Dominion Ct ....Aptos CA 95003 831-688-1467 688-6961
Web: www.aptoschamber.com

Arcadia Chamber of Commerce
388 W Huntington Dr ....Arcadia CA 91007 626-447-2159 445-0273
Web: arcadiacachamber.org

Atascadero Chamber of Commerce
6904 El Camino Real ....Atascadero CA 93422 805-466-2044 466-9218
TF: 877-204-9830 ■ *Web:* www.atascaderochamber.org

Atwater Chamber of Commerce 1101 Third St .... Atwater CA 95301 209-358-4251
Web: atwaterchamberofcommerce.com

Azusa Chamber of Commerce 240 W Foothill Blvd........Azusa CA 91702 626-334-1507 334-5217
Web: www.azusachamber.org

Greater Bakersfield Chamber of Commerce
1725 Eye St ....Bakersfield CA 93301 661-327-4421 327-8751
Web: www.bakersfieldchamber.org

Kern County Board of Trade 2101 Oak St ....Bakersfield CA 93301 661-868-5376 868-5376
TF General: 800-787-9920 ■ *Web:* www.visitkern.com

Bell Chamber of Commerce 4401 Gage Ave .... Bell CA 90201 323-560-8755 560-2060

Bell Gardens Chamber of Commerce
7535 Perry Rd................................Bell Gardens CA 90201 562-806-2355
Web: www.bellgardenschamber.org

Bellflower Chamber of Commerce
16730 Bellflower Blvd............................Bellflower CA 90706 562-867-1744 866-7545
Web: bellflowerchamber.com

Belmont Chamber of Commerce
1059 Alameda De Las Pulgas........................Belmont CA 94002 650-595-8696 204-6232
Web: www.belmontchamber.org

Benicia Chamber of Commerce
601 First St Ste 100 ....Benicia CA 94510 707-745-2120 745-2275
Web: www.beniciachamber.com

Berkeley Chamber of Commerce
1834 University Ave ....Berkeley CA 94703 510-549-7000 549-1789
TF: 800-847-4823 ■ *Web:* www.berkeleychamber.com

Beverly Hills Chamber of Commerce
239 S Beverly Dr.............................Beverly Hills CA 90212 310-248-1000 248-1020
TF: 800-345-2210 ■ *Web:* www.beverlyhillschamber.com

Blythe Area Chamber of Commerce
207 E Hobsonway.................................. Blythe CA 92225 760-922-8166 922-4010
Web: www.blythechamberofcommerce.com

Brea Chamber of Commerce One Civic Ctr Cir............Brea CA 92821 714-529-4938 529-6103
Web: www.breachamber.com

Burbank Chamber of Commerce
200 W Magnolia Blvd..............................Burbank CA 91502 818-846-3111 846-0109
Web: www.burbankchamber.org

Burlingame Chamber of Commerce
417 California Dr ....Burlingame CA 94010 650-344-1735 344-1763
Web: www.burlingamechamber.org

Camarillo Chamber of Commerce
2400 Ventura Blvd ....Camarillo CA 93010 805-484-4383 484-1395
Web: camarillochamber.org

Campbell Chamber of Commerce
1628 W Campbell Ave ....Campbell CA 95008 408-378-6252 378-0192
Web: www.campbellchamber.com

Canoga Park/West Hills Chamber of Commerce
7248 Owensmouth Ave.........................Canoga Park CA 91303 818-884-4222 884-4604
Web: www.cpwhchamber.org

Carmichael Chamber of Commerce
6825 Fair Oaks Blvd Ste 100 .... Carmichael CA 95608 916-481-1002 481-1003
Web: carmichaelchamber.com

Carson Chamber of Commerce 530 E Del Amo Blvd .....Carson CA 90746 310-217-4590 217-4591
Web: www.carsonchamber.com

Castro Valley Chamber of Commerce
3467 Castro Vly Blvd ....Castro Valley CA 94546 510-537-5300 537-5335
Web: www.edenareachamber.com

Cathedral City Chamber of Commerce
68950 E Palm Canyon Dr......................Cathedral City CA 92234 760-328-1213 321-0659
Web: www.cathedralcitycc.com

Ceres Chamber of Commerce 2491 Lawrence St ....Ceres CA 95307 209-537-2601 537-2699
Web: www.cereschamber.org

Cerritos Chamber of Commerce 13259 S St ....Cerritos CA 90703 562-467-0800 467-0840
Web: www.cerritos.org

Chatsworth Chamber of Commerce
10038 Old Depot Plz Rd ....Chatsworth CA 91311 818-341-2428 341-4930
Web: www.chatsworthchamber.com

Chico Chamber of Commerce 441 Main St.............Chico CA 95928 530-891-5556 891-3613
TF: 800-852-8570 ■ *Web:* www.chicochamber.com

Chino Valley Chamber of Commerce
13150 Seventh St .... Chino CA 91710 909-627-6177 627-4180
Web: chinovalleychamberofcommerce.com

Chula Vista Chamber of Commerce
233 Fourth Ave.................................Chula Vista CA 91910 619-420-6602 420-1269
Web: www.chulavistachamber.org

Entry	City	State	Zip	Phone	Fax
Citrus Heights Chamber of Commerce 7115 Greenback Ln # A *Web:* www.chchamber.com	Citrus Heights	CA	95621	916-722-4545	722-4543
Claremont Chamber of Commerce 205 Yale Ave. *Web:* www.claremontchamber.org	Claremont	CA	91711	909-624-1681	624-6629
Clovis Chamber of Commerce 325 Pollasky Ave *Web:* www.clovischamber.com	Clovis	CA	93612	559-299-7363	299-2969
Colton Chamber of Commerce 655 N La Cadena Dr. *Web:* coltonchamber.org	Colton	CA	92324	909-825-2222	824-1650
Greater Concord Chamber of Commerce 2280 Diamond Blvd Ste 200 *TF:* 800-427-8686 ■ *Web:* www.concordchamber.com	Concord	CA	94520	925-685-1181	685-5623
Corona Chamber of Commerce 904 E Sixth St *Web:* www.mychamber.org	Corona	CA	92879	951-737-3350	737-3531
Coronado Chamber of Commerce 875 Orange Ave Ste 102 *Web:* www.coronadochamber.com	Coronado	CA	92118	619-435-9260	522-6577
Costa Mesa Chamber of Commerce 1700 Adams Ave Ste 101 *Web:* www.costamesachamber.com	Costa Mesa	CA	92626	714-885-9092	885-9094
Covina Chamber of Commerce 935 W Badillo St Ste 100 *Web:* www.covina.org	Covina	CA	91722	626-967-4191	966-9660
Culver City Chamber of Commerce 6000 Sepulveda Blvd Ste 1260 *Web:* www.culvercitychamber.com	Culver City	CA	90230	310-287-3850	287-1350
Cupertino Chamber of Commerce 20455 Silverado Ave. *Web:* cupertino-chamber.org	Cupertino	CA	95014	408-252-7054	252-0638
Cypress Chamber of Commerce 5550 Cerritos Ave Ste D *Web:* www.cypresschamber.org	Cypress	CA	90630	714-827-2430	827-1229
Daly City-Colma Chamber of Commerce 355 Gellert Blvd Ste 138 *Web:* www.dalycity-colmachamber.org	Daly City	CA	94015	650-755-3900	755-5160
Dana Point Chamber of Commerce 24681 La Plz Ste 115 *Web:* www.danapoint-chamber.com	Dana Point	CA	92629	949-496-1555	496-5321
San Diego Coastal Chamber of Commerce 1104 Camino Del Mar Ste 1 *Web:* www.delmarchamber.org	Del Mar	CA	92014	858-755-4844	793-5293
Downey Chamber of Commerce 11131 Brookshire Ave. *TF:* 877-345-4633 ■ *Web:* www.downeychamber.com	Downey	CA	90241	562-923-2191	869-0461
Dublin Chamber of Commerce 7080 Donlon Way Ste 110 *Web:* www.dublinchamberofcommerce.org	Dublin	CA	94568	925-828-6200	828-4247
San Diego East County Chamber of Commerce 201 S Magnolia Ave *Web:* eastcountychamber.org	El Cajon	CA	92020	619-440-6161	440-6164
El Centro Chamber of Commerce & Visitors Bureau 1095 S Fourth St *Web:* www.elcentrochamber.org	El Centro	CA	92243	760-352-3681	352-3246
El Monte/South El Monte Chamber of Commerce 10505 Valley Blvd Ste 312 *Web:* www.emsem.com	El Monte	CA	91731	626-443-0180	443-0463
Encinitas Chamber of Commerce 527 Encinitas Blvd *TF:* 800-953-6041 ■ *Web:* www.encinitaschamber.com	Encinitas	CA	92024	760-753-6041	753-6270
Encino Chamber of Commerce 4933 Balboa Blvd *Web:* encinochamber.org	Encino	CA	91316	818-789-4711	789-2485
Escondido Chamber of Commerce 720 N Broadway *Web:* www.escondidochamber.org	Escondido	CA	92025	760-745-2125	745-1183
Greater Eureka Chamber of Commerce, The 2112 Broadway *TF:* 866-267-4255 ■ *Web:* www.eurekachamber.com	Eureka	CA	95501	707-442-3738	442-0079
Fairfield-Suisun Chamber of Commerce 1111 Webster St *Web:* www.ffsc-chamber.com	Fairfield	CA	94533	707-425-4625	425-0826
Fallbrook Chamber of Commerce 233 E Mission Rd *Web:* www.fallbrookchamberofcommerce.org	Fallbrook	CA	92028	760-728-5845	728-4031
Folsom Chamber of Commerce 200 Wool St *Web:* www.folsomchamber.com	Folsom	CA	95630	916-985-2698	985-4117
Fontana Chamber of Commerce 8491 Sierra Ave *Web:* www.fontanachamber.org	Fontana	CA	92335	909-822-4433	822-6238
Mendocino Coast Chamber of Commerce 217 S Main St PO Box 1141 *TF:* 800-382-7244 ■ *Web:* www.mendocinocoast.com	Fort Bragg	CA	95437	707-961-6300	964-2056
Foster City Chamber of Commerce 1031 E Hillsdale Blvd Ste F *Web:* www.fostercitychamber.com	Foster City	CA	94404	650-573-7600	573-5201
Fountain Valley Chamber of Commerce 10055 Slater Ave Ste 250 *Web:* www.fvchamber.com	Fountain Valley	CA	92708	714-962-3822	
Fremont Chamber of Commerce 39488 Stevenson Pl Ste 100 *Web:* www.fremontbusiness.com	Fremont	CA	94539	510-795-2244	795-2240
Fresno Chamber of Commerce 2331 Fresno St *Web:* www.fresnochamber.com	Fresno	CA	93721	559-495-4800	495-4811
Fullerton Chamber of Commerce 444 N Harbor Blvd Ste 200 *Web:* www.fullertonchamber.com	Fullerton	CA	92832	714-871-3100	871-2871
Garden Grove Chamber of Commerce 12866 Main St Ste 102 *TF:* 800-959-5560 ■ *Web:* gardengrovechamber.com	Garden Grove	CA	92840	714-638-7950	636-6672
Gardena Valley Chamber of Commerce 1204 W Gardena Blvd Ste E *Web:* www.gardenachamber.com	Gardena	CA	90247	310-532-9905	329-7307
Gilroy Chamber of Commerce 7471 Monterey St *Web:* www.gilroy.org	Gilroy	CA	95020	408-842-6437	842-6010
Glendale Chamber of Commerce 200 S Louise St *Web:* www.glendalechamber.com	Glendale	CA	91205	818-240-7870	240-2872
Glendora Chamber of Commerce 131 E Foothill Blvd *TF:* 866-987-1611 ■ *Web:* www.glendora-chamber.org	Glendora	CA	91741	626-963-4128	914-4822
Goleta Valley Chamber of Commerce 271 N Fairview Ave Ste 104 *TF:* 800-646-5382 ■ *Web:* www.goletavalley.com	Goleta	CA	93117	805-967-2500	967-4615
Granada Hills Chamber of Commerce 17723 Chatsworth St *Web:* www.granadachamber.com	Granada Hills	CA	91344	818-368-3235	366-7425
Hanford Chamber of Commerce 113 Ct St *Web:* www.hanfordchamber.com	Hanford	CA	93230	559-582-0483	582-0960
Hawthorne Chamber of Commerce 12629 Crenshaw Blvd. *TF:* 800-977-4770 ■ *Web:* www.hawthorne-chamber.com	Hawthorne	CA	90250	310-676-1163	676-7661
Hayward Chamber of Commerce 22561 Main St *Web:* www.hayward.org	Hayward	CA	94541	510-537-2424	537-2730
Hemet Jacinto Valley Chamber of Commerce 615 N San Jacinto St *Web:* hsjvc.com	Hemet	CA	92543	951-658-3211	766-5013
Hesperia Chamber of Commerce 16816 Main St Ste D *TF:* 855-574-7337 ■ *Web:* www.hesperiachamber.org	Hesperia	CA	92345	760-244-2135	244-1333
Highland Area Chamber of Commerce 27255 Messina St. *Web:* www.highlandchamber.org	Highland	CA	92346	909-864-4073	864-4583
Hollywood Chamber of Commerce 7018 Hollywood Blvd *Web:* walkoffame.com	Hollywood	CA	90028	323-469-8311	469-2805
Huntington Beach Chamber of Commerce 19891 Beach Blvd Ste 100 *Web:* hbchamber.com	Huntington Beach	CA	92648	714-536-8888	960-7654
Greater Huntington Park Area Chamber of Commerce 6330 Pacific Blvd Ste 208 *Web:* www.hpchamber1.com	Huntington Park	CA	90255	323-585-1155	585-2176
Imperial Beach Chamber of Commerce & Visitors Bureau 702 Seacoast Dr *Web:* www.ib-chamber.com	Imperial Beach	CA	91932	619-424-3151	424-3008
Indio Chamber of Commerce 82921 Indio Blvd *TF:* 800-464-7928 ■ *Web:* www.indiochamber.org	Indio	CA	92201	760-347-0676	347-6069
Inglewood Chamber of Commerce 330 E Queen St *Web:* www.inglewoodchamber.com	Inglewood	CA	90301	310-677-1121	677-1001
Irvine Chamber of Commerce 2485 McCabe Way Ste 150 *TF General:* 800-321-2211 ■ *Web:* www.irvinechamber.com	Irvine	CA	92614	949-660-9112	660-0829
Orange County Business Council 2 Pk Plz Ste 100 *Web:* www.ocbc.org	Irvine	CA	92614	949-476-2242	476-9240
Amador County Chamber of Commerce 115 Main St PO Box 596 *TF General:* 800-822-9466 ■ *Web:* www.amadorcountychamber.com	Jackson	CA	95642	209-223-0350	223-4425
Crescenta Valley Chamber of Commerce 3131 Foothill Blvd Ste D *Web:* www.crescentavalleychamber.org	La Crescenta	CA	91214	818-248-4957	248-9625
La Habra Area Chamber of Commerce 321 E La Habra Blvd *Web:* www.lahabrachamber.com	La Habra	CA	90631	562-697-1704	697-8359
La Jolla Town Council PO Box 1101 *Web:* lajollatowncouncil.org	La Jolla	CA	92038	858-454-1444	
La Verne Chamber of Commerce 2078 Bonita Ave *Web:* www.lavernechamber.org	La Verne	CA	91750	909-593-5265	596-0579
Laguna Beach Chamber of Commerce 357 Glenneyre St *Web:* www.lagunabeachchamber.org	Laguna Beach	CA	92651	949-494-1018	376-8916
Laguna Niguel Chamber of Commerce 28062 Forbes Rd Ste C *Web:* www.lnchamber.com	Laguna Niguel	CA	92677	949-363-0136	363-9026
Lake Elsinore Valley Chamber of Commerce 132 W Graham Ave *Web:* www.lakeelsinorechamber.com	Lake Elsinore	CA	92530	951-245-8848	245-9127
Lakeport Regional Chamber of Commerce 875 Lakeport Blvd PO Box 295 *TF:* 866-525-3767 ■ *Web:* www.lakeportchamber.com	Lakeport	CA	95453	707-263-5092	263-5104
Lakeside Chamber of Commerce 9924 Vine St *Web:* lakesidechamber.org	Lakeside	CA	92040	619-561-1031	561-7951
Antelope Valley Chambers of Commerce 554 W Lancaster Blvd *Web:* lancasterchamber.org	Lancaster	CA	93534	661-948-4518	949-1212
Livermore Chamber of Commerce 2157 First St *Web:* www.livermorechamber.org	Livermore	CA	94550	925-447-1606	447-1641
Lodi District Chamber of Commerce 35 S School St *Web:* www.lodichamber.com	Lodi	CA	95240	209-367-7840	369-9344
Lompoc Valley Chamber of Commerce & Visitors Bureau PO Box 626 *TF:* 800-240-0999 ■ *Web:* www.lompoc.com	Lompoc	CA	93438	805-736-4567	737-0453
Long Beach Area Chamber of Commerce One World Trade Ctr Ste 206 *Web:* www.lbchamber.com	Long Beach	CA	90831	562-436-1251	436-7099
Los Altos Chamber of Commerce 321 University Ave *Web:* www.losaltoschamber.org	Los Altos	CA	94022	650-948-1455	948-6238
Century City Chamber of Commerce 2029 Century Pk E Concourse Level *TF:* 800-462-7899 ■ *Web:* www.centurycitycc.com	Los Angeles	CA	90067	310-553-2222	553-4623
Eagle Rock Chamber of Commerce PO Box 41354 *Web:* www.eaglerockchamberofcommerce.com	Los Angeles	CA	90041	323-257-2197	257-4245

Name / Address	City	State	ZIP	Phone	Fax
East Los Angeles Chamber of Commerce 4716 E Cesar Chavez Ave; *Web:* www.eastlachamber.com	Los Angeles	CA	90022	323-263-2005	263-2006
LAX Coastal Area Chamber of Commerce 9100 S Sepulveda Blvd Ste 210; *Web:* laxcoastal.com	Los Angeles	CA	90045	310-645-5151	645-0130
Lincoln Heights Chamber of Commerce 2716 N Broadway Ste 210	Los Angeles	CA	90031	323-221-6571	221-1513
Los Angeles Area Chamber of Commerce 350 S Bixel St; *Web:* www.lachamber.com	Los Angeles	CA	90017	213-580-7500	580-7511
Los Gatos Chamber of Commerce 349 N Santa Cruz Ave; *Web:* www.losgatoschamber.com	Los Gatos	CA	95030	408-354-9300	399-1594
Madera District Chamber of Commerce 120 NE St; **Fax:* Acctg ■ *TF:* 866-382-7822 ■ *Web:* www.maderachamber.com	Madera	CA	93638	559-673-3563	673-5009*
Malibu Chamber of Commerce 23805 Stuart Ranch Rd Ste 210; *TF:* 800-442-4988 ■ *Web:* www.malibu.org	Malibu	CA	90265	310-456-9025	456-0195
Manhattan Beach Chamber of Commerce 425 15th St PO Box 3007; *Web:* manhattanbeachchamber.com	Manhattan Beach	CA	90266	310-545-5313	
Manteca Chamber of Commerce 183 W N St Ste 6; *Web:* www.manteca.org	Manteca	CA	95336	209-823-6121	239-6131
Marina Chamber of Commerce PO Box 425; *Web:* www.marinachamber.com	Marina	CA	93933	831-384-0155	
Martinez Area Chamber of Commerce 603 Marina Vista; *TF:* 877-055-5506 ■ *Web:* www.martinezchamber.com	Martinez	CA	94553	925-228-2345	228-2356
Yuba-Sutter Chamber of Commerce 429 Tenth St; *Web:* www.yubasutterchamber.com	Marysville	CA	95901	530-743-6501	741-8645
Menifee Valley Chamber of Commerce 29683 New Hub Dr Ste C; *Web:* www.menifeevalleychamber.com	Menifee	CA	92586	951-672-1991	672-4022
Menlo Park Chamber of Commerce 1100 Merrill St; *Web:* www.menloparkchamber.com	Menlo Park	CA	94025	650-325-2818	325-0920
Greater Merced Chamber of Commerce 1640 N St Ste 120; *TF:* 800-877-2345 ■ *Web:* www.merced-chamber.com	Merced	CA	95340	209-384-7092	384-8472
Merced County Chamber of Commerce 860 W 18th St; *Web:* www.mercedcountychamber.com	Merced	CA	95340	209-722-3864	722-2406
Modesto Chamber of Commerce 1114 J St PO Box 844; *Web:* www.modchamber.org	Modesto	CA	95354	209-577-5757	577-2673
Monrovia Chamber of Commerce 620 S Myrtle Ave; *Web:* www.monroviacc.com	Monrovia	CA	91016	626-358-1159	357-6036
Montclair Chamber of Commerce 5220 Benito St; *Web:* www.montclairchamber.com	Montclair	CA	91763	909-624-4569	625-2009
Montebello Chamber of Commerce 109 N 19th St; *Web:* www.montebellochamber.org	Montebello	CA	90640	323-721-1153	721-7946
Monterey Peninsula Chamber of Commerce 30 Ragsdale Dr #200; *Web:* www.montereychamber.com	Monterey	CA	93940	831-648-5360	649-3502
Monterey Park Chamber of Commerce 700 El Mercado Ave; *Web:* montereyparkchamber.org	Monterey Park	CA	91754	626-570-9429	570-9491
Moorpark Chamber of Commerce 18 E High St; *Web:* www.moorparkchamber.com	Moorpark	CA	93021	805-529-0322	529-5304
Moreno Valley Chamber of Commerce 12625 Frederick St; *Web:* www.movalchamber.org	Moreno Valley	CA	92553	951-697-4404	697-0995
Morgan Hill Chamber of Commerce 17485 Monterey St Ste 105; *Web:* www.morganhill.org	Morgan Hill	CA	95037	408-779-9444	779-5405
Chamber of Commerce Mountain View 580 Castro St; *TF:* 800-229-7728 ■ *Web:* www.chambermv.org	Mountain View	CA	94041	650-968-8378	968-5668
Murrieta Chamber of Commerce 25125 Madison Ave Ste 108; *Web:* www.murrietachamber.org	Murrieta	CA	92562	951-677-7916	677-9976
Napa Chamber of Commerce 1556 First St; *TF:* 877-807-2249 ■ *Web:* napachamber.com	Napa	CA	94559	707-226-7455	226-1171
National City Chamber of Commerce 901 National City Blvd; *Web:* www.nationalcitychamber.org	National City	CA	91950	619-477-9339	477-5018
Newark Chamber of Commerce 37101 Newark Blvd Ste 8; *Web:* www.newark-chamber.com	Newark	CA	94560	510-744-1000	744-1003
Newport Beach Chamber of Commerce 1470 Jamboree Rd; *Web:* www.newportbeach.com	Newport Beach	CA	92660	949-729-4400	729-4417
Universal City-North Hollywood Chamber of Commerce 6369 Bellingham Ave; *Web:* www.noho.org	North Hollywood	CA	91606	818-508-5155	508-5156
North Valley Regional Chamber of Commerce 9401 Reseda Blvd Ste 100; *Web:* www.nvrcc.com	Northridge	CA	91324	818-349-5676	349-4343
Norwalk Chamber of Commerce 12040 Foster Rd; *TF:* 800-427-2200 ■ *Web:* norwalkchamber.com	Norwalk	CA	90650	562-864-7785	864-8539
Novato Chamber of Commerce 807 DeLong Ave; *TF:* 800-897-1164 ■ *Web:* www.novatochamber.com	Novato	CA	94945	415-897-1164	898-9097
Oakhurst Area Chamber of Commerce 49074 Civic Cir; *Web:* www.oakhurstchamber.com	Oakhurst	CA	93644	559-683-7766	658-2942
Oakland Metropolitan Chamber of Commerce 475 14th St Ste 100; *Web:* www.oaklandchamber.com	Oakland	CA	94612	510-874-4800	839-8817
Oceanside Chamber of Commerce 928 N Coast Hwy; *Web:* www.oceansidechamber.com	Oceanside	CA	92054	760-722-1534	722-8336
Ojai Valley Chamber of Commerce 201 S Signal St; *Web:* www.ojaichamber.org	Ojai	CA	93023	805-646-8126	646-9762
Ontario Chamber of Commerce 520 N Euclid Ave Ste 200; *Web:* www.ontario.org	Ontario	CA	91762	909-984-2458	984-6439
Orange Chamber of Commerce 439 E Chapman Ave; *TF:* 866-273-9817 ■ *Web:* www.orangechamber.com	Orange	CA	92866	714-538-3581	532-1675
Orangevale Chamber of Commerce 9267 Greenback Ln Ste B-91; *Web:* www.orangevalechamber.com	Orangevale	CA	95662	916-988-0175	988-1049
Oroville Area Chamber of Commerce 1789 Montgomery St; *TF:* 800-655-4653 ■ *Web:* www.orovillechamber.net	Oroville	CA	95965	530-538-2542	538-2546
Oxnard Chamber of Commerce 400 E Esplanade Dr Ste 302; *Web:* www.oxnardchamber.org	Oxnard	CA	93036	805-983-6118	604-7331
Pacifica Chamber of Commerce 225 Rockaway Beach Ave Ste 1; *Web:* pacificachamber.com	Pacifica	CA	94044	650-355-4122	355-6949
Palm Desert Chamber of Commerce (PDCC) 72559 Hwy 111; *Web:* www.pdcc.org	Palm Desert	CA	92260	760-346-6111	346-3263
Palm Springs Chamber of Commerce 190 W Amado Rd; *TF:* 888-947-6667 ■ *Web:* www.pschamber.org	Palm Springs	CA	92262	760-325-1577	325-8549
Antelope Valley Board of Trade 41319-12th St W Ste 104; *Web:* www.avbot.org	Palmdale	CA	93551	661-947-9033	723-9279
Palmdale Chamber of Commerce 817 E Ave Q-9; *Web:* www.palmdalechamber.org	Palmdale	CA	93550	661-273-3232	273-8508
Palo Alto Chamber of Commerce 355 Alma St; *Web:* www.paloaltochamber.com	Palo Alto	CA	94301	650-324-3121	324-1215
Paradise Chamber of Commerce 5550 Sky Way Ste 1; *TF:* 800-838-3006 ■ *Web:* www.paradisechamber.com	Paradise	CA	95969	530-877-9356	877-1865
Paramount Chamber of Commerce 15357 Paramount Blvd; *Web:* paramountchamber.com	Paramount	CA	90723	562-634-3980	634-0891
Pasadena Chamber of Commerce & Civic Assn 844 E Green St Ste 208; *Web:* www.pasadena-chamber.org	Pasadena	CA	91101	626-795-3355	795-5603
Petaluma Area Chamber of Commerce Six Petaluma Blvd N Ste A-2; *Web:* www.petalumachamber.com	Petaluma	CA	94952	707-762-2785	762-4721
Pico Rivera Chamber of Commerce 5016 Passons Blvd; *Web:* www.picoriverachamber.org	Pico Rivera	CA	90660	562-949-2473	949-8320
Pittsburg Chamber of Commerce 985 Railroad Ave; *Web:* pittsburgchamber.org	Pittsburg	CA	94565	925-432-7301	427-5555
Placentia Chamber of Commerce 201 E Yorba Linda Blvd Ste C; *TF:* 844-730-0418 ■ *Web:* www.placentiachamber.com	Placentia	CA	92870	714-528-1873	528-1879
El Dorado County Chamber of Commerce 542 Main St; *TF:* 800-457-6279 ■ *Web:* www.eldoradocounty.org	Placerville	CA	95667	530-621-5885	642-1624
Pleasant Hill Chamber of Commerce 91 Gregory Ln Ste 11; *Web:* www.pleasanthillchamber.com	Pleasant Hill	CA	94523	925-687-0700	676-7422
Pleasanton Chamber of Commerce 777 Peters Ave; *TF:* 877-807-2249 ■ *Web:* www.pleasanton.org	Pleasanton	CA	94566	925-846-5858	846-9697
Pomona Chamber of Commerce 101 W Mission Blvd Ste 223; *Web:* www.pomonachamber.org	Pomona	CA	91766	909-622-8484	620-5986
Porterville Chamber of Commerce 93 N Main St Ste A; *Web:* www.portervillechamber.org	Porterville	CA	93257	559-784-7502	784-0770
Poway Chamber of Commerce 13381 Poway Rd PO Box 868; *Web:* www.poway.com	Poway	CA	92064	858-748-0016	748-1710
Ramona Chamber of Commerce 960 Main St; *TF:* 800-411-7343 ■ *Web:* www.ramonachamber.com	Ramona	CA	92065	760-789-1311	789-1317
Rancho Cordova Chamber of Commerce 2729 Prospect Pk Dr Ste 117; *Web:* www.ranchocordova.org	Rancho Cordova	CA	95670	916-273-5688	273-5727
Rancho Cucamonga Chamber of Commerce 9047 Arrow Route Suite 180; *TF:* 800-677-5434 ■ *Web:* www.ranchochamber.org	Rancho Cucamonga	CA	91730	909-987-1012	987-5917
Greater Redding Chamber of Commerce 747 Auditorium Dr; *Web:* www.reddingchamber.com	Redding	CA	96001	530-225-4433	225-4398
Redlands Chamber of Commerce 1 E Redlands Blvd; *TF:* 800-966-6428 ■ *Web:* www.redlandschamber.org	Redlands	CA	92373	909-793-2546	335-6388
Redondo Beach Chamber of Commerce & Visitors Bureau 200 N Pacific Coast Hwy; *Web:* www.redondochamber.org	Redondo Beach	CA	90277	310-376-6911	374-7373
Redwood City-San Mateo County Chamber of Commerce 1450 Veterans Blvd Ste 125; *Web:* www.redwoodcitychamber.com	Redwood City	CA	94063	650-364-1722	364-1729
Rialto Chamber of Commerce 120 N Riverside Ave; *TF:* 800-597-4955 ■ *Web:* www.rialtochamber.org	Rialto	CA	92376	909-875-5364	875-6790
Ridgecrest Chamber of Commerce 128-B E California Ave Ste B; *Web:* www.ridgecrestchamber.com	Ridgecrest	CA	93555	760-375-8331	375-0365
Greater Riverside Chambers of Commerce 3985 University Ave; *Web:* www.riverside-chamber.com	Riverside	CA	92501	951-683-7100	683-2670

Phone | Fax

Rocklin Area Chamber of Commerce
3700 Rocklin Rd ... Rocklin CA 95677 916-624-2548 624-5743
TF: 800-228-3380 ■ *Web:* www.rocklinchamber.com

Rohnert Park Chamber of Commerce
101 Golf Course Dr Ste C-7 ... Rohnert Park CA 94928 707-584-1415 584-2945
TF: 888-364-7379 ■ *Web:* www.rohnertparkchamber.org

Palos Verdes Peninsula Chamber of Commerce
707 Silver Spur Rd Ste 100 ... Rolling Hills Estates CA 90274 310-377-8111 377-0614
Web: www.palosverdeschamber.com

Rosemead Chamber of Commerce
3953 Muscatel Ave ... Rosemead CA 91770 626-288-0811 288-2514
Web: rosemeadchamber.org

Roseville Chamber of Commerce
650 Douglas Blvd ... Roseville CA 95678 916-783-8136 783-5261
Web: www.rosevillechamber.com

Sacramento Metro Chamber of Commerce
One Capital Mall Ste 300 ... Sacramento CA 95814 916-552-6800 443-2672
Web: www.metrochamber.org

Salinas Valley Chamber of Commerce
119 E Alisal St ... Salinas CA 93901 831-751-7725 424-8639
TF: 888-678-2871 ■ *Web:* www.salinaschamber.com

San Bernardino Area Chamber of Commerce
PO Box 658 ... San Bernardino CA 92402 909-885-7515 384-9979
TF: 800-928-5091 ■ *Web:* www.sbachamber.org

San Bruno Chamber of Commerce
618 San Mateo Ave ... San Bruno CA 94066 650-588-0180 588-6473
Web: www.sanbrunochamber.com

San Carlos Chamber of Commerce
1500 Laurel St Ste B ... San Carlos CA 94070 650-593-1068 593-9108
Web: www.sancarloschamber.org

San Clemente Chamber of Commerce
1100 N El Camino Real ... San Clemente CA 92672 949-492-1131 492-3764
TF: 877-411-3662 ■ *Web:* www.scchamber.com

Peninsula Chamber of Commerce PO Box 6015 ... San Diego CA 92166 619-223-1629 225-1294
Web: www.peninsulachamber.com

San Diego Regional Chamber of Commerce
402 W Broadway Ste 1000 ... San Diego CA 92101 619-544-1300
Web: www.sdchamber.org

San Dimas Chamber of Commerce
246 E Bonita Ave ... San Dimas CA 91773 909-592-3818 592-8178
Web: www.sandimaschamber.com

San Francisco Chamber of Commerce
235 Montgomery St 12th Fl ... San Francisco CA 94104 415-392-4520 392-0485
TF: 888-834-3040 ■ *Web:* www.sfchamber.com

San Gabriel Chamber of Commerce
620 W Santa Anita St ... San Gabriel CA 91776 626-576-2525 289-2901
Web: sangabrielchamber.org

San Jose Silicon Valley Chamber of Commerce (SJSVCC)
101 W Santa Clara St ... San Jose CA 95113 408-291-5250 286-5019
Web: www.sjchamber.com

San Juan Capistrano Chamber of Commerce
31421 La Matanza St ... San Juan Capistrano CA 92675 949-493-4700 489-2695
Web: www.sanjuanchamber.com

San Leandro Chamber of Commerce
15555 E 14th St Ste 100 ... San Leandro CA 94578 510-317-1400 317-1404
Web: www.sanleandrochamber.com

San Luis Obispo Chamber of Commerce
1039 Chorro St ... San Luis Obispo CA 93401 805-781-2777 543-1255
Web: www.slochamber.org

San Marcos Chamber of Commerce
939 Grand Ave ... San Marcos CA 92078 760-744-1270 744-5230
TF: 800-814-7241 ■ *Web:* www.sanmarcoschamber.com

San Mateo Area Chamber of Commerce
1700 S El Camino Real Ste 108 ... San Mateo CA 94402 650-401-2440 401-2446
Web: www.sanmateoca.org

San Pablo Chamber of Commerce
13925 San Pablo Ave ... San Pablo CA 94806 510-234-2067 234-0604
Web: ci.san-pablo.ca.us

San Pedro Peninsula Chamber of Commerce
390 W Seventh St ... San Pedro CA 90731 310-832-7272 832-0685
Web: www.sanpedrochamber.com

San Rafael Chamber of Commerce
817 Mission Ave ... San Rafael CA 94901 415-454-4163 454-7039
TF: 888-378-0777 ■ *Web:* srchamber.com

San Ramon Chamber of Commerce
2410 Camino Ramon #125 ... San Ramon CA 94583 925-242-0600 242-0603
Web: www.sanramon.org

San Ysidro Chamber of Commerce
663 E San Ysidro Blvd ... San Ysidro CA 92173 619-428-1281 428-1294
Web: www.sanysidrochamber.org

Santa Ana Chamber of Commerce
1631 W Sunflower Ave Ste C35 ... Santa Ana CA 92704 714-541-5353 541-2238
Web: www.santaanachamber.com

Santa Barbara Region Chamber of Commerce
924 Anacapa St Ste 1 ... Santa Barbara CA 93101 805-965-3023 966-5954
Web: www.sbchamber.org

Santa Clara Chamber of Commerce
1850 Warburton Ave ... Santa Clara CA 95050 408-244-8244 244-7830
Web: www.santaclarachamber.com

Santa Clarita Valley Chamber of Commerce
27451 Tourney Rd Ste 160 ... Santa Clarita CA 91355 661-702-6977 702-6980
Web: www.scvchamber.com

Santa Cruz Chamber of Commerce
611 Ocean St Ste 1 ... Santa Cruz CA 95060 831-457-3713 423-1847
TF: 866-282-5900 ■ *Web:* www.santacruzchamber.org

Santa Maria Valley Chamber of Commerce
614 S Broadway ... Santa Maria CA 93454 805-925-2403 925-0840
TF: 800-331-3779 ■ *Web:* www.santamaria.com

Santa Monica Chamber of Commerce
1234 Sixth St Ste 100 ... Santa Monica CA 90401 310-393-9825 394-1868
Web: www.smchamber.com

Santa Paula Chamber of Commerce
200 N Tenth St ... Santa Paula CA 93060 805-525-5561 546-0770*
**Fax Area Code:* 858 ■ *Web:* www.santapaulachamber.com

Santa Rosa Chamber of Commerce
637 First St ... Santa Rosa CA 95404 707-545-1414 545-6914
Web: www.santarosachamber.com

Santee Chamber of Commerce
10315 Mission Gorge Rd ... Santee CA 92071 619-449-6572 562-7906
Web: santeechamber.com

Saratoga Chamber of Commerce
14485 Big Basin Way ... Saratoga CA 95070 408-867-0753 867-5213
Web: www.saratogachamber.org

Seal Beach Chamber & Business Assn
201 Eigth St Ste 120 ... Seal Beach CA 90740 562-799-0179 795-5637
Web: www.sealbeachchamber.org

Sebastopol Area Chamber of Commerce
265 S Main St ... Sebastopol CA 95472 707-823-3032 823-8439
Web: www.sebastopol.org

Greater Sherman Oaks Chamber of Commerce
14827 Ventura Blvd Ste 207 ... Sherman Oaks CA 91403 818-906-1951 783-3100
Web: www.shermanoakschamber.org

Simi Valley Chamber of Commerce
40 W Cochran St Ste 100 ... Simi Valley CA 93065 805-526-3900 526-6234
Web: www.simivalleychamber.org

Sonoma Valley Chamber of Commerce
651A Broadway ... Sonoma CA 95476 707-996-1033 996-9402
Web: www.sonomachamber.org

Tuolumne County Chamber of Commerce
222 S Shepherd St ... Sonora CA 95370 209-532-4212 532-8068
TF: 877-532-4212 ■ *Web:* www.tcchamber.com

South Gate Chamber of Commerce
3350 Tweedy Blvd ... South Gate CA 90280 323-567-1203
Web: sgchamber.org

South San Francisco Chamber of Commerce
213 Linden Ave ... South San Francisco CA 94080 650-588-1911 588-2534
Web: www.ssfchamber.com

Spring Valley Chamber of Commerce
3322 Sweetwater Springs Blvd Ste 202 ... Spring Valley CA 91977 619-670-9902 670-9924
Web: www.springvalleychamber.org

Stanton Chamber of Commerce
8381 Katella Ave Ste H ... Stanton CA 90680 714-995-1485 995-1184
Web: www.stantonchamber.org

Greater Stockton Chamber of Commerce
445 W Weber Ave Ste 220 ... Stockton CA 95203 209-547-2770 466-5271
Web: www.stocktonchamber.org

Studio City Chamber of Commerce
4024 Radford Ave Edit 2 Ste F ... Studio City CA 91604 818-655-5916 655-8392
TF: 877-227-0088 ■ *Web:* www.studiocitychamber.com

Sun Valley Area Chamber of Commerce
11501 Strathern St PO Box 308 ... Sun Valley CA 91352 818-768-2014 767-1947
TF: 877-834-7064 ■ *Web:* www.svacc.com

Sunland-Tujunga Chamber of Commerce
8250 Foothill Blvd Ste A ... Sunland CA 91040 818-352-4433 353-7551
Web: www.stchamber.com

Sunnyvale Chamber of Commerce
260 S Sunnyvale Ave Ste 4 ... Sunnyvale CA 94086 408-736-4971 736-1919
Web: www.svcoc.org

Lassen County Chamber of Commerce
75 N Weatherlow St ... Susanville CA 96130 530-257-4323 251-2561
TF: 877-686-7878 ■ *Web:* www.lassencountychamber.org

Greater Tehachapi Chamber of Commerce
209 E Tehachapi Blvd PO Box 401 ... Tehachapi CA 93581 661-822-4180 822-9036
Web: www.tehachapi.com

Temecula Valley Chamber of Commerce (TVCC)
26790 Ynez Ct Ste A ... Temecula CA 92591 951-676-5090 694-0201
TF: 866-676-5090 ■ *Web:* www.temecula.org

Temple City Chamber of Commerce
9050 Las Tunas Dr ... Temple City CA 91780 626-286-3101 286-2590
Web: www.templecitychamber.org

Harbor City-Harbor Gateway Chamber of Commerce
19401 S Vermont Ave Ste H-112 ... Torrance CA 90502 310-534-3143 516-7734
Web: www.hchgchamber.com

Torrance Area Chamber of Commerce
3400 Torrance Blvd Ste 100 ... Torrance CA 90503 310-540-5858 540-7662
Web: www.torrancechamber.com

Tracy Chamber of Commerce 223 E Tenth St ... Tracy CA 95376 209-835-2131 833-9526
Web: www.tracychamber.org

Greater Tulare Chamber of Commerce
220 E Tulare Ave ... Tulare CA 93274 559-686-1547 686-4915
Web: www.tularechamber.org

Turlock Chamber of Commerce
115 S Golden State Blvd ... Turlock CA 95380 209-632-2221 632-5289
TF: 800-834-0401 ■ *Web:* turlockchamber.com

Tustin Chamber of Commerce
700 W First St Ste 7 ... Tustin CA 92780 714-544-5341 544-2083
Web: www.tustinchamber.org

Twentynine Palms Chamber of Commerce
73484 Twentynine Palms Hwy ... Twentynine Palms CA 92277 760-367-3445 367-3366
Web: www.29chamber.org

Ukiah Chamber of Commerce 200 S School St ... Ukiah CA 95482 707-462-4705 462-2088
Web: www.ukiahchamber.com

Union City Chamber of Commerce
3939 Smith St ... Union City CA 94587 510-952-9637 952-9647
Web: www.unioncitychamber.com

Upland Chamber of Commerce
215 N Second Ave Ste D ... Upland CA 91786 909-204-4465 204-4464
Web: www.uplandchamber.org

Vacaville Chamber of Commerce 300 Main St ... Vacaville CA 95688 707-448-6424 448-0424
Web: www.vacavillechamber.com

Vallejo Chamber of Commerce 427 York St ... Vallejo CA 94590 707-644-5551 644-5590
TF: 877-397-7936 ■ *Web:* www.vallejochamber.com

Mid Valley Chamber of Commerce
7120 Hayvenhurst Ave Ste 114 ... Van Nuys CA 91406 818-989-0300 989-3836
Web: www.sanfernandovalleychamber.com

Venice Chamber of Commerce
327 Washington Blvd PO Box 202 ... Venice CA 90294 310-822-5425 664-7938
Web: www.venicechamber.net

Phone Fax

Ventura Chamber of Commerce
505 Poli St 2nf Fl . . . Ventura CA 93001 805-643-7222 653-8015
Web: venturachamber.com

Victorville Chamber of Commerce
14174 Green Tree Blvd . . . Victorville CA 92395 760-245-6506 245-6505
Web: vvchamber.com

Visalia Chamber of Commerce
220 N Santa Fe St. . . . Visalia CA 93292 559-734-5876 734-7479
Web: www.visaliachamber.org

Regional Chamber of Commerce San Gabriel Valley
19720 E Walnut Dr 1170 . . . Walnut CA 91789 909-869-0701 869-0761
Web: www.regionalchambersgv.com

Walnut Creek Chamber of Commerce
1777 Botelho Dr Ste 103 . . . Walnut Creek CA 94596 925-934-2007 934-2404
Web: www.walnut-creek.com

Pajaro Valley Chamber of Commerce
44 Brennan St PO Box 1748. . . . Watsonville CA 95076 831-724-3900 724-5821
Web: www.pajarovalleychamber.com

West Hollywood Chamber of Commerce
8272 Santa Monica Blvd. . . . West Hollywood CA 90046 323-650-2688 650-2689
Web: www.wehochamber.com

West Sacramento Chamber of Commerce
1414 Merkley Ave Ste 1 . . . West Sacramento CA 95691 916-371-7042 371-7007
Web: www.westsacramentochamber.com

Westminster Chamber of Commerce
1025 Westminster Mall. . . . Westminster CA 92683 714-898-2559 373-1499
TF: 800-929-3556 ■ *Web:* www.westminsterchamber.org

Whittier Area Chamber of Commerce
8158 Painter Ave. . . . Whittier CA 90602 562-698-9554 693-2700
Web: www.whittierchamber.com

Willows Chamber of Commerce 118 W Sycamore. . . . Willows CA 95988 530-934-8150
TF: 855-233-6362 ■ *Web:* willowschamber.com

Wilmington Chamber of Commerce
544 N Avalon Blvd Ste 104. . . . Wilmington CA 90744 310-834-8586 834-8887
Web: www.wilmington-chamber.com

Woodland Chamber of Commerce 307 First St. . . . Woodland CA 95695 530-662-7327 662-4086
TF: 888-843-2636 ■ *Web:* www.woodlandchamber.org

Woodland Hills Chamber of Commerce
20121 Ventura Blvd Ste 309. . . . Woodland Hills CA 91364 818-347-4737 347-3321
TF: 877-527-3247 ■ *Web:* www.woodlandhillscc.net

Yorba Linda Chamber of Commerce
17670 Yorba Linda Blvd . . . Yorba Linda CA 92886 714-993-9537 993-7764
Web: www.yorbalindachamber.org

Yucaipa Valley Chamber of Commerce
35139 Yucaipa Blvd . . . Yucaipa CA 92399 909-790-1841 363-7373
Web: yucaipachamber.org

Yucca Valley Chamber of Commerce
56711 29 Palms Hwy . . . Yucca Valley CA 92284 760-365-6323 365-0763
TF: 855-568-5348 ■ *Web:* www.yuccavalley.org

Colorado

Phone Fax

Arvada Chamber of Commerce 7305 Grandview Ave . . . Arvada CO 80002 303-424-0313 424-5370
Web: www.arvadachamber.org

Aspen Chamber Resort Assn 425 Rio Grande Pl. . . . Aspen CO 81611 970-925-1940 920-1173
TF: 800-670-0792 ■ *Web:* www.aspenchamber.org

Aurora Chamber of Commerce
14305 E Alameda Ave Ste 300 . . . Aurora CO 80012 303-344-1500 344-1564
TF: 877-770-4438 ■ *Web:* www.aurorachamber.org

Vail Valley Chamber of Commerce
101 Fawcett Rd Ste 240 . . . Avon CO 81620 970-476-1000 476-6008
TF: 800-525-3875 ■ *Web:* www.visitvailvalley.com

Boulder Chamber of Commerce 2440 Pearl St. . . . Boulder CO 80302 303-442-1044 938-8837
Web: www.boulderchamber.com

Broomfield Chamber of Commerce
350 Interlocken Blvd Ste 250 . . . Broomfield CO 80021 303-466-1775 466-4481
Web: www.broomfieldchamber.com

Canon City Chamber of Commerce
403 Royal Gorge Blvd. . . . Canon City CO 81212 719-275-2331 275-2332
TF: 800-876-7922 ■ *Web:* www.canoncity.com

South Metro Denver Chamber of Commerce
6840 S University Blvd. . . . Centennial CO 80122 303-795-0142 795-7520
Web: www.bestchamber.com

Colorado Springs Chamber of Commerce
Six S Tejon St Ste 700 . . . Colorado Springs CO 80903 719-635-1551 635-1571
Web: www.coloradospringsbusinessalliance.com

Delta Area Chamber of Commerce 301 Main St . . . Delta CO 81416 970-874-8616 874-8618
Web: www.deltacolorado.org

Denver Metro Chamber of Commerce
1445 Market St. . . . Denver CO 80202 303-534-8500 534-3200
Web: www.denverchamber.org

Durango Area Chamber of Commerce
111 S Camino del Rio. . . . Durango CO 81303 970-247-0312 385-7884
TF: 888-414-0835 ■ *Web:* www.durangobusiness.org

Fort Collins Area Chamber of Commerce
225 S Meldrum St . . . Fort Collins CO 80521 970-482-3746 482-3774
TF: 877-652-8607 ■ *Web:* www.fortcollinschamber.com

Fort Morgan Area Chamber of Commerce
300 Main St . . . Fort Morgan CO 80701 970-867-6702 867-6121
TF: 800-354-8660 ■ *Web:* www.fortmorganchamber.org

Greater Golden Chamber of Commerce
1010 Washington Ave. . . . Golden CO 80402 303-279-3113 279-0332
Web: www.goldencochamber.org

West Chamber of Commerce
1667 Cole Blvd Bldg 19 Ste 400. . . . Golden CO 80401 303-233-5555 237-7633
Web: www.westchamber.org

Grand Junction Area Chamber of Commerce
360 Grand Ave . . . Grand Junction CO 81501 970-242-3214 242-3694
TF: 800-352-5286 ■ *Web:* www.gjchamber.org

Greeley-Weld Chamber of Commerce
902 Seventh Ave. . . . Greeley CO 80631 970-352-3566 352-3572
TF: 800-449-3866 ■ *Web:* www.greeleychamber.com

Phone Fax

La Veta/Cuchara Chamber of Commerce
132 W Ryus Ave . . . La Veta CO 81055 719-742-3676
TF: 866-277-5550 ■ *Web:* www.lavetacucharachamber.com

Longmont Area Chamber of Commerce
528 Main St . . . Longmont CO 80501 303-776-5295 776-5657
Web: www.longmontchamber.org

Loveland Chamber of Commerce
5400 Stone Creek Cir Ste 200 . . . Loveland CO 80538 970-667-6311 667-5211
Web: www.loveland.org

Montrose Chamber of Commerce 1519 E Main St . . . Montrose CO 81401 970-249-5000 249-2907
TF: 800-923-5515 ■ *Web:* montrosechamber.com

Parker Chamber of Commerce
19590 E Main St Ste 100 . . . Parker CO 80138 303-841-4268 841-8061
Web: www.parkerchamber.com

Greater Pueblo Chamber of Commerce
302 N Santa Fe Ave. . . . Pueblo CO 81003 719-542-1704 542-1624
TF: 800-233-3446 ■ *Web:* www.pueblochamber.org

Metro North Chamber of Commerce
14583 Orchard Pkwy Ste 300 . . . Westminster CO 80023 303-288-1000 227-1050
TF: 877-888-8811 ■ *Web:* www.metronorthchamber.com

Connecticut

Phone Fax

Shoreline Chamber Of Commercey
764 E Main St. . . . Branford CT 06405 203-488-5500 488-5046
Web: shorelinechamberct.com

Bridgeport Regional Business Council
10 Middle St 14th Fl. . . . Bridgeport CT 06604 203-335-3800 366-0105
Web: www.brbc.org

Greater Bristol Chamber of Commerce
200 Main St . . . Bristol CT 06010 860-584-4718 584-4722
TF: 855-344-1874 ■ *Web:* www.centralctchambers.org

Cheshire Chamber of Commerce 195 S Main St . . . Cheshire CT 06410 203-272-2345 271-3044
Web: www.cheshirechamber.org

Greater Danbury Chamber of Commerce 39 W St . . . Danbury CT 06810 203-743-5565 794-1439
Web: www.danburychamber.com

Northeastern Connecticut Chamber of Commerce
Three Central St . . . Danielson CT 06239 860-774-8001 774-4299
Web: www.newenglanditgroup.com/nectcc

East Hartford Chamber of Commerce
1137 Main St . . . East Hartford CT 06108 860-289-0239 289-0230
Web: www.easthartfordchamber.com

East Haven Chamber of Commerce
200 Kimberly Ave PO Box 120055 . . . East Haven CT 06512 203-467-4305
Web: www.easthavenchamber.com

Fairfield Chamber of Commerce 1597 Post Rd . . . Fairfield CT 06824 203-255-1011 256-9990
Web: www.fairfieldctchamber.com

Chamber of Commerce of Eastern Connecticut Inc
39 Kings Hwy PO Box 726 . . . Gales Ferry CT 06335 860-464-7373 464-7374
Web: www.chamberect.com

Glastonbury Chamber of Commerce
2400 Main St Ste 2. . . . Glastonbury CT 06033 860-659-3587 659-0102
Web: www.glastonburychamber.net

Greenwich Chamber of Commerce
45 E Putnam Ave Ste 121 . . . Greenwich CT 06830 203-869-3500 869-3502
Web: www.greenwichchamber.com

Hamden Chamber of Commerce 2969 Whitney Ave. . . . Hamden CT 06518 203-288-6431 288-4499
Web: www.hamdenchamber.com

MetroHartford Alliance 31 Pratt St 5th Fl. . . . Hartford CT 06103 860-525-4451 293-2592
Web: www.metrohartford.com

Greater Manchester Chamber of Commerce
20 Hartford Rd . . . Manchester CT 06040 860-646-2223 646-5871
Web: www.manchesterchamber.com

Greater Meriden Chamber of Commerce
3 Colony St Ste 301 . . . Meriden CT 06451 203-235-7901 686-0172
TF: 877-283-8158 ■ *Web:* www.midstatechamber.com/default.asp

Middlesex County Chamber of Commerce
393 Main St . . . Middletown CT 06457 860-347-6924 346-1043
Web: www.middlesexchamber.com

Milford Chamber of Commerce Five Broad St . . . Milford CT 06460 203-878-0681 876-8517
Web: www.milfordct.com

Mystic Chamber of Commerce
12 Roosevelt Ave,2nd Fl PO Box 143 . . . Mystic CT 06355 860-572-9578 572-9273
TF: 866-572-9578 ■ *Web:* www.mysticchamber.org

Chamber of Commerce 195 Water St. . . . Naugatuck CT 06770 203-729-4511 729-4512
Web: www.waterburychamber.com

Greater New Britain Chamber of Commerce
1 Ct St 4th Fl . . . New Britain CT 06051 860-229-1665 223-8341
Web: www.newbritainchamber.com

Greater New Haven Chamber of Commerce
900 Chapel St 10th Fl. . . . New Haven CT 06510 203-787-6735 782-4329
Web: www.gnhcc.com

Greater New Milford Chamber of Commerce
11 Railroad St. . . . New Milford CT 06776 860-354-6080 354-8526
Web: www.newmilford-chamber.com

Greater Norwalk Chamber of Commerce
101 E Ave . . . Norwalk CT 06851 203-866-2521 852-0583
Web: www.norwalkchamberofcommerce.com

Old Saybrook Chamber of Commerce
One Main St . . . Old Saybrook CT 06475 860-388-3266 388-9433
Web: www.oldsaybrookchamber.com

Greater Valley Chamber of Commerce
900 Bridgeport Ave Second Fl . . . Shelton CT 06484 203-925-4981 925-4984
Web: www.greatervalleychamber.com

Greater Southington Chamber of Commerce
One Factory Sq Ste 202 . . . Southington CT 06489 860-628-8036 276-9696
Web: www.southingtoncoc.com

Business Council of Fairfield County (SACIA)
One Landmark Sq Ste 300 . . . Stamford CT 06901 203-359-3220 967-8294
Web: www.businessfairfield.com

Name / Address	City	State	Zip	Phone	Fax
Stamford Chamber of Commerce 733 Summer St Ste 104	Stamford	CT	06901	203-359-4761	363-5069
TF: 866-262-4548 ■ *Web:* www.stamfordchamber.com					
Chamber of Commerce of Northwest Connecticut 333 Kennedy Dr Ste R101 PO Box 59	Torrington	CT	06790	860-482-6586	489-8851
Web: www.nwctchamberofcommerce.org					
Tolland County Chamber of Commerce 30 Lafayette Sq	Vernon	CT	06066	860-872-0587	872-0588
TF: 800-243-3174 ■ *Web:* www.tollandcountychamber.org					
Quinnipiac Chamber of Commerce 50 N Main St	Wallingford	CT	06492	203-269-9891	269-1358
Web: www.quinncham.com					
Greater Waterbury Chamber of Commerce 83 Bank St	Waterbury	CT	06702	203-757-0701	
Web: www.waterburychamber.com					
West Hartford Chamber of Commerce 948 Farmington Ave	West Hartford	CT	06107	860-521-2300	521-1996
Web: www.whchamber.com					
West Haven Chamber of Commerce 355 Main St Ground Fl	West Haven	CT	06516	203-933-1500	931-1940
Web: www.westhavenchamber.com					
Windham Region Chamber of Commerce 1010 Main St	Willimantic	CT	06226	860-423-6389	423-8235
TF: 800-635-9161 ■ *Web:* www.windhamchamber.com					
Windsor Chamber of Commerce 261 Broad St	Windsor	CT	06095	860-688-5165	688-0809
Web: www.windsorcc.org					

Delaware

Name / Address	City	State	Zip	Phone	Fax
Rehoboth Beach-Dewey Beach Chamber of Commerce 501 Rehoboth Ave	Rehoboth Beach	DE	19971	302-227-2233	227-8351
TF: 800-441-1329 ■ *Web:* www.beach-fun.com					

Florida

Name / Address	City	State	Zip	Phone	Fax
Amelia Island-Fernandina Beach-Yulee Chamber of Commerce 961687 Gateway Blvd Ste 101-G	Amelia Island	FL	32034	904-261-3248	261-6997
Web: www.islandchamber.com					
Apalachicola Bay Chamber of Commerce 122 Commerce St	Apalachicola	FL	32320	850-653-9419	653-8219
TF: 866-269-3022 ■ *Web:* www.apalachicolabay.org					
SouthShore Chamber of Commerce 137 Harbor Village Ln	Apollo Beach	FL	33570	813-645-1366	645-2099
Web: www.southshorechamberofcommerce.org					
DeSoto County Chamber of Commerce 16 S Volusia Ave	Arcadia	FL	34266	863-494-4033	494-3312
Web: www.desotochamberfl.com					
Belleview-South Marion Chamber of Commerce 5301 SE Abshier Blvd	Belleview	FL	34420	352-245-2178	245-7673
Web: belleviewsouthmarionchamber.org					
Lower Keys Chamber of Commerce 31020 Overseas Hwy	Big Pine Key	FL	33043	305-872-2411	872-0752
TF: 800-872-3722 ■ *Web:* www.lowerkeyschamber.com					
Greater Boca Raton Chamber of Commerce 1800 N Dixie Hwy	Boca Raton	FL	33432	561-395-4433	392-3780
TF: 800-435-7352 ■ *Web:* www.bocaratonchamber.com					
Bonita Springs Area Chamber of Commerce 25071 Chamber of Commerce Dr	Bonita Springs	FL	34135	239-992-2943	992-5011
TF: 800-226-2943 ■ *Web:* www.bonitaspringschamber.com					
Greater Boynton Beach Chamber of Commerce 1880 N Congress Ave Ste 106	Boynton Beach	FL	33426	561-732-9501	734-4304
Web: www.boyntonbeach.org					
Manatee Chamber of Commerce 222 Tenth St W	Bradenton	FL	34205	941-748-3411	745-1877
Web: www.manateechamber.com					
Greater Brandon Chamber of Commerce 330 Pauls Dr Ste 100	Brandon	FL	33511	813-689-1221	689-9440
Web: www.brandonchamber.com					
Greater Hernando County Chamber of Commerce 15588 Aviation Loop Dr	Brooksville	FL	34604	352-796-0697	796-3704
Web: www.hernandochamber.com					
Clearwater Regional Chamber of Commerce 401 Cleveland St	Clearwater	FL	33755	727-461-0011	449-2889
TF: 877-447-7356 ■ *Web:* www.clearwaterflorida.org					
Coral Gables Chamber of Commerce 224 Catalonia	Coral Gables	FL	33134	305-446-1657	446-9900
Web: coralgableschamber.org					
Coral Springs Chamber of Commerce 11805 Heron Bay Blvd	Coral Springs	FL	33076	954-752-4242	827-0543
Web: www.cschamber.com					
Crestview Area Chamber of Commerce 1447 Commerce Dr	Crestview	FL	32539	850-682-3212	682-7413
Web: www.crestviewchamber.com					
Citrus County Chamber of Commerce 28 NW Us Hwy 19	Crystal River	FL	34428	352-795-3149	
Web: www.citruscountychamber.com					
Davie-Cooper City Chamber of Commerce 4185 Davie Rd	Davie	FL	33314	954-581-0790	581-9684
Web: www.davie-coopercity.org					
Greater Deerfield Beach Chamber of Commerce 1601 E Hillsboro Blvd	Deerfield Beach	FL	33441	954-427-1050	427-1056
Web: www.deerfieldchamber.com					
DeLand Area Chamber of Commerce 336 N Woodland Blvd	DeLand	FL	32720	386-734-4331	734-4333
TF: 800-611-5207 ■ *Web:* delandchamber.com					
Greater Delray Beach Chamber of Commerce 140 NE 1st St	Delray Beach	FL	33444	561-278-0424	278-6012
Web: www.delraybeach.com					
Destin Area Chamber of Commerce 4484 Legendary Dr Ste A	Destin	FL	32541	850-837-6241	654-5612
TF: 877-487-2671 ■ *Web:* www.destinchamber.com					
Dunedin Chamber of Commerce 301 Main St	Dunedin	FL	34698	727-733-3197	734-8942
Web: www.dunedin-fl.com					
Dunnellon Area Chamber of Commerce 20500 E Pennsylvania Ave	Dunnellon	FL	34432	352-489-2320	489-6846
Web: www.dunnellonchamber.org					
Englewood-Cape Haze Area Chamber of Commerce 601 S Indiana Ave	Englewood	FL	34223	941-474-5511	475-9257
TF: 800-603-7198 ■ *Web:* www.englewoodchamber.com					
Broward County Chamber of Commerce 2425 E Commercial Blvd #103	Fort Lauderdale	FL	33308	954-565-5750	566-3398
Web: www.browardbiz.com					
Greater Fort Lauderdale Chamber of Commerce 512 NE Third Ave	Fort Lauderdale	FL	33301	954-462-6000	527-8766
TF: 800-683-8338 ■ *Web:* www.ftlchamber.com					
Chamber of Southwest Florida 5237 Summerlin Commons Blvd Ste 114	Fort Myers	FL	33907	239-278-4001	275-2103
Web: www.chamber-swflorida.com					
Greater Fort Myers Chamber of Commerce 2310 Edwards Dr	Fort Myers	FL	33901	239-332-3624	332-7276
TF: 800-366-3622 ■ *Web:* www.fortmyers.org					
Fort Myers Beach Chamber of Commerce 17200 San Carlos Blvd	Fort Myers Beach	FL	33931	239-454-7500	454-7910
TF: 866-998-9250 ■ *Web:* www.fortmyersbeach.org					
Greater Fort Walton Beach Chamber of Commerce 34 Miracle Strip Pkwy SE	Fort Walton Beach	FL	32548	850-244-8191	244-1935
Web: www.fwbchamber.org					
Gainesville Area Chamber of Commerce 300 E University Ave Ste 100	Gainesville	FL	32601	352-334-7100	334-7141
TF: 888-795-2707 ■ *Web:* www.gainesvillechamber.com					
Goldenrod Area Chamber of Commerce 4755 Palmetto Ave PO Box 61	Goldenrod	FL	32733	407-677-5980	677-4928
Web: www.goldenrodchamber.com					
Hallandale Beach Chamber of Commerce 400 S Federal Hwy Ste 192	Hallandale Beach	FL	33009	954-454-0541	454-0930
Web: www.hallandalebeachchamber.com					
Hialeah Chamber of Commerce & Industries 240 E First Ave Ste 217	Hialeah	FL	33010	305-888-7780	888-7804
Web: hialeahchamber.org					
Greater Hollywood Chamber of Commerce 330 N Federal Hwy	Hollywood	FL	33020	954-923-4000	923-8737
Web: www.hollywoodchamber.org					
Greater Homestead/Florida City Chamber of Commerce 455 N Flagler Ave	Homestead	FL	33030	305-247-2332	224-9101
TF: 888-247-5012 ■ *Web:* www.chamberinaction.com					
Islamorada Chamber of Commerce PO Box 915	Islamorada	FL	33036	305-664-4503	664-4289
TF: 800-322-5397 ■ *Web:* www.islamoradachamber.com					
Jacksonville Chamber of Commerce Three Independent Dr	Jacksonville	FL	32202	904-366-6600	
Web: www.myjaxchamber.com					
Jacksonville Chamber of Commerce Beaches Div Three Independent Dr	Jacksonville	FL	32202	904-366-6600	
Web: www.myjaxchamber.com					
North Palm Beach County Chamber of Commerce 800 N US Hwy 1	Jupiter	FL	33477	561-746-7111	745-7519
Web: www.npbchamber.com					
Northern Palm Beach County Chamber of Commerce 800 N US Hwy 1	Jupiter	FL	33477	561-746-7111	745-7519
TF: 800-482-8293 ■ *Web:* www.npbchamber.com					
Key Largo Chamber of Commerce 106000 Overseas Hwy	Key Largo	FL	33037	305-451-1414	451-4726
TF: 866-820-1533 ■ *Web:* keylargochamber.org					
Kissimmee/Osceola County Chamber of Commerce 1425 E Vine St	Kissimmee	FL	34744	407-847-3174	870-8607
Web: www.kissimmeechamber.com					
Lake City/Columbia County Chamber of Commerce 162 S Marion Ave	Lake City	FL	32025	386-752-3690	755-7744
Web: www.lakecitychamber.com					
Greater Lake Placid Chamber of Commerce 18 N Oak Ave	Lake Placid	FL	33852	863-465-4331	465-2588
Web: www.lpfla.com					
Lake Wales Area Chamber of Commerce 340 W Central Ave	Lake Wales	FL	33859	863-676-3445	676-3446
Web: www.lakewaleschamber.com					
Greater Lake Worth Chamber of Commerce 501 Lake Ave	Lake Worth	FL	33460	561-582-4401	547-8300
Web: www.cpbchamber.com					
Lakeland Area Chamber of Commerce 35 Lk Morton Dr	Lakeland	FL	33801	863-688-8551	683-7454
Web: www.lakelandchamber.com					
Central Pasco Chamber of Commerce 2810 Land O' Lakes Blvd	Land O' Lakes	FL	34639	813-909-2722	909-0827
Web: www.centralpascochamber.com					
Central Pinellas Chamber of Commerce 151 Third St NW	Largo	FL	33770	727-584-2321	586-3112
Web: www.centralchamber.biz					
Lehigh Acres Chamber of Commerce 25 Homestead Rd N	Lehigh Acres	FL	33936	239-369-3322	368-0500
Web: www.lehighacreschamber.org					
Suwannee County Chamber of Commerce 212 N Ohio Ave	Live Oak	FL	32064	386-362-3071	362-4758
Web: www.suwanneechamber.com					
Palms West Chamber of Commerce 13901 Southern Blvd	Loxahatchee	FL	33470	561-790-6200	791-2069
TF: 800-790-2364 ■ *Web:* www.cpbchamber.com					
Maitland Area Chamber of Commerce 110 N Maitland Ave	Maitland	FL	32751	407-644-0741	539-2529
Web: www.maitlandchamber.com					
Greater Marathon Chamber of Commerce 12222 Overseas Hwy	Marathon	FL	33050	305-743-5417	289-0183
TF: 800-262-7284 ■ *Web:* www.floridakeysmarathon.com					
Marco Island Chamber of Commerce 1102 N Collier Blvd	Marco Island	FL	34145	239-394-7549	394-3061
TF: 800-788-6272 ■ *Web:* www.marcoislandchamber.org					

Organization	City	State	ZIP	Phone	Fax
Cocoa Beach Area Chamber of Commerce 400 Fortenberry Rd *TF:* 888-874-2674 ■ *Web:* www.cocoabeachchamber.com	Merritt Island	FL	32952	321-459-2200	459-2232
Greater Miami Chamber of Commerce 1601 Biscayne Blvd *TF:* 888-660-5955 ■ *Web:* www.miamichamber.com	Miami	FL	33132	305-350-7700	374-6902
Miami-Dade Chamber of Commerce 11380 NW 27th Ave Ste 1328 *Web:* www.m-dcc.org	Miami	FL	33167	305-751-8648	758-3839
North Dade Regional Chamber of Commerce 1300 NW 167th St Ste 2 *Web:* www.thechamber.cc	Miami	FL	33169	305-690-9123	690-9124
Miami Beach Chamber of Commerce 1920 Meridian Ave 3rd Fl *TF:* 800-501-0401 ■ *Web:* www.miamibeachchamber.com	Miami Beach	FL	33139	305-672-1270	538-4336
Santa Rosa County Chamber of Commerce 5247 Stewart St *TF:* 800-239-8732 ■ *Web:* www.srcchamber.com	Milton	FL	32570	850-623-2339	623-4413
Greater Naples Chamber of Commerce, The 2390 Tamiami Trl N Ste 210 *Web:* www.napleschamber.org	Naples	FL	34103	239-262-6376	262-8374
West Pasco Chamber of Commerce 5443 Main St *Web:* www.westpasco.com	New Port Richey	FL	34652	727-842-7651	848-0202
Southeast Volusia Chamber of Commerce 115 Canal St *Web:* www.sevchamber.com	New Smyrna Beach	FL	32168	386-428-2449	423-3512
Niceville-Valparaiso Chamber of Commerce 1055 E John Sims Pkwy *Web:* www.nicevillechamber.com	Niceville	FL	32578	850-678-2323	678-2602
North Fort Myers Chamber of Commerce 2787 N Tamiami Trl Unit 10 *Web:* www.nfmchamber.com	North Fort Myers	FL	33903	239-997-9111	997-4026
Greater North Miami Chamber of Commerce 13100 W Dixie Hwy *Web:* www.northmiamichamber.com	North Miami	FL	33161	305-891-7811	893-8522
North Miami Beach Chamber of Commerce 1870 NE 171st St *Web:* www.nmbchamber.com	North Miami Beach	FL	33162	305-944-8500	944-8191
Ocala-Marion County Chamber of Commerce 310 SE Third St *TF:* 800-466-5055 ■ *Web:* ocalacep.com	Ocala	FL	34471	352-629-8051	629-7651
Okeechobee Chamber of Commerce 55 S Parrott Ave *Web:* www.okeechobeebusiness.com	Okeechobee	FL	34972	863-467-6246	
Upper Tampa Bay Regional Chamber of Commerce 101 State St W *Web:* www.utbchamber.com	Oldsmar	FL	34677	813-855-4233	854-1237
Clay County Chamber of Commerce 1734 Kingsley Ave *TF:* 800-435-7352 ■ *Web:* www.claychamber.com	Orange Park	FL	32073	904-264-2651	264-0070
Orlando Regional Chamber of Commerce 75 S Ivanhoe Blvd *Web:* www.orlando.org	Orlando	FL	32804	407-425-1234	835-2500
Ormond Beach Chamber of Commerce 165 W Granada Blvd *Web:* www.ormondchamber.com	Ormond Beach	FL	32174	386-677-3454	677-4363
Putnam County Chamber of Commerce 1100 Reid St *Web:* www.putnamcountychamber.com	Palatka	FL	32177	386-328-1503	328-7076
Flagler County Chamber of Commerce 20 Airport Rd Ste C *Web:* www.flaglerchamber.org	Palm Coast	FL	32164	386-437-0106	437-5700
Greater Palm Harbor Area Chamber of Commerce 1151 Nebraska Ave *Web:* www.palmharborcc.org	Palm Harbor	FL	34683	727-784-4287	786-2336
Bay County Chamber of Commerce 235 W Fifth St *Web:* www.panamacity.org	Panama City	FL	32401	850-785-5206	763-6229
Panama City Beaches Chamber of Commerce 309 Richard Jackson Blvd *Web:* www.pcbeach.org	Panama City Beach	FL	32407	850-235-1159	235-2301
Miramar-Pembroke Pines Regional Chamber of Commerce 10100 Pines Blvd Fourth Fl *Web:* www.miramarpembrokepines.org	Pembroke Pines	FL	33026	954-432-9808	432-9193
Pensacola Area Chamber of Commerce 117 W Garden St *Web:* www.pensacolachamber.com	Pensacola	FL	32502	850-438-4081	438-6369
Pinellas Park Mid-County Chamber of Commerce 5851 Pk Blvd *Web:* www.pinellasparkchamber.com	Pinellas Park	FL	33781	727-544-4777	209-0837
Greater Plant City Chamber of Commerce 106 N Evers St *TF:* 800-760-2315 ■ *Web:* www.plantcity.org	Plant City	FL	33563	813-754-3707	752-8793
Greater Plantation Chamber of Commerce 7401 NW Fourth St *Web:* www.plantationchamber.org	Plantation	FL	33317	954-587-1410	587-1886
Greater Pompano Beach Chamber of Commerce 2200 E Atlantic Blvd *Web:* www.pompanobeachchamber.com	Pompano Beach	FL	33062	954-941-2940	785-8358
Port Orange-South Daytona Chamber of Commerce 3431 S Ridgewood Ave *Web:* www.pschamber.com	Port Orange	FL	32129	386-761-1601	788-9165
Charlotte County Chamber of Commerce 311 W Retta Esplanade *Web:* www.charlottecountychamber.org	Punta Gorda	FL	33950	941-639-6330	639-6330
Gadsden County Chamber of Commerce 208 N Adams St *TF:* 800-627-9231 ■ *Web:* www.gadsdencc.com	Quincy	FL	32351	850-627-9231	875-3299
Greater Riverview Chamber of Commerce 10011 Water Works Ln *Web:* www.riverviewchamber.com	Riverview	FL	33578	813-234-5944	234-5945
Saint Johns County Chamber of Commerce One Riberia St *Web:* www.stjohnscountychamber.com	Saint Augustine	FL	32084	904-829-5681	829-6477
Saint Cloud/Greater Osceola Chamber of Commerce 1200 New York Ave *Web:* www.stcloudflchamber.com	Saint Cloud	FL	34769	407-892-3671	892-5289
Tampa Bay Beaches Chamber of Commerce 6990 Gulf Blvd *TF:* 855-344-5999 ■ *Web:* www.tampabaybeaches.com	Saint Pete Beach	FL	33706	727-360-6957	360-2233
Sanford Chamber of Commerce 400 E First St *Web:* www.sanfordchamber.com	Sanford	FL	32771	407-322-2212	322-8160
Sanibel & Captiva Islands Chamber of Commerce 1159 Cswy Rd *Web:* www.sanibel-captiva.org	Sanibel	FL	33957	239-472-1080	472-1070
Walton Area Chamber of Commerce 63 S Centry Trl *Web:* waltonareachamber.com	Santa Rosa Beach	FL	32459	850-267-0683	267-0603
Greater Sarasota Chamber of Commerce 1945 Fruitville Rd *Web:* www.sarasotachamber.com	Sarasota	FL	34236	941-955-8187	366-5621
Sebastian River Area Chamber of Commerce 700 Main St *Web:* www.sebastianchamber.com	Sebastian	FL	32958	772-589-5969	589-5993
Greater Sebring Chamber of Commerce 227 US 27 N *Web:* sebring.org	Sebring	FL	33870	863-385-8448	385-8810
Greater Seminole Area Chamber of Commerce 7995 113th St N *Web:* www.seminolechamber.net	Seminole	FL	33772	727-392-3245	397-7753
Chamber South 6410 SW 80th St *TF:* 800-206-3715 ■ *Web:* www.chambersouth.com	South Miami	FL	33143	305-661-1621	666-0508
Stuart-Martin County Chamber of Commerce 1650 S Kanner Hwy *TF:* 800-962-2873 ■ *Web:* www.stuartmartinchamber.org	Stuart	FL	34994	772-287-1088	220-3437
Sumter County Chamber of Commerce PO Box 100 *Web:* www.sumterchamber.org	Sumterville	FL	33535	352-793-3099	793-2120
Sunny Isles Beach Tourism & Marketing Council 18070 Collins Ave *Web:* www.sunnyislesbeachmiami.com	Sunny Isles Beach	FL	33160	305-792-1952	792-1672
Sunrise Chamber of Commerce 10297 NW 53rd St Ste 318 *Web:* www.sunrisechamber.org	Sunrise	FL	33351	954-835-2428	561-9685
Greater Tallahassee Chamber of Commerce 115 N Calhoun St *TF:* 866-566-6106 ■ *Web:* www.talchamber.com	Tallahassee	FL	32301	850-224-8116	561-3860
Tamarac Chamber of Commerce 7525 NW 88th Ave # 103 *Web:* www.tamaracchamber.org	Tamarac	FL	33321	954-722-1520	721-2725
Greater Tampa Chamber of Commerce 201 N Franklin St Ste 201 *TF:* 877-693-5236 ■ *Web:* www.tampachamber.com	Tampa	FL	33602	813-228-7777	223-7899
North Tampa Chamber of Commerce PO Box 82043 *Web:* www.northtampachamber.com	Tampa	FL	33682	813-961-2420	961-2903
Ybor City Chamber of Commerce 1800 E Ninth Ave *Web:* www.ybor.org	Tampa	FL	33605	813-248-3712	247-1764
Tarpon Springs Chamber of Commerce 111 E Tarpon Ave *Web:* tarponspringschamber.com	Tarpon Springs	FL	34689	727-937-6109	937-2879
Titusville Area Chamber of Commerce 2000 S Washington Ave *TF:* 800-435-7352 ■ *Web:* www.titusville.org	Titusville	FL	32780	321-267-3036	264-0127
Venice Area Chamber of Commerce 597 Tamiami Trl S *Web:* www.venicechamber.com	Venice	FL	34285	941-488-2236	484-5903
Indian River County Chamber of Commerce 1216 21st St *TF:* 888-703-8130 ■ *Web:* www.indianriverchamber.com	Vero Beach	FL	32960	772-567-3491	778-3181
Chamber of Commerce of the Palm Beaches 401 N Flagler Dr *Web:* www.palmbeaches.org	West Palm Beach	FL	33401	561-833-3711	833-5582
West Orange Chamber of Commerce 12184 W Colonial Dr *TF:* 877-999-9981 ■ *Web:* www.wochamber.com	Winter Garden	FL	34787	407-656-1304	656-0221
Greater Winter Haven Area Chamber of Commerce 401 Ave 'B' NW *Web:* winterhavenchamber.com	Winter Haven	FL	33881	863-293-2138	297-5818
Winter Park Chamber of Commerce 151 W Lyman Ave *TF Help Line:* 877-972-4262 ■ *Web:* www.winterpark.org	Winter Park	FL	32789	407-644-8281	644-7826
Zephyrhills Chamber of Commerce 38550 Fifth Ave *TF:* 800-851-8754 ■ *Web:* www.zephyrhillschamber.org	Zephyrhills	FL	33542	813-782-1913	783-6060

Georgia

Organization	City	State	ZIP	Phone	Fax
Greater North Fulton Chamber of Commerce (GNFCC) 11605 Haynes Bridge Rd Ste 100 *TF:* 866-840-5770 ■ *Web:* www.gnfcc.com	Alpharetta	GA	30009	770-993-8806	594-1059
Americus-Sumter County Chamber of Commerce 409 Elm Ave PO Box 724 *Web:* www.sumtercountychamber.com	Americus	GA	31709	229-924-2646	924-8784
Cobb Chamber of Commerce 240 I- N Pkwy *TF:* 800-228-2545 ■ *Web:* www.cobbchamber.org	Atlanta	GA	30339	770-980-2000	980-9510
Metro Atlanta Chamber of Commerce 235 International Blvd NW *Web:* www.metroatlantachamber.com	Atlanta	GA	30303	404-880-9000	
Augusta Metro Chamber of Commerce 701 Greene St PO Box 1837 *Web:* augustametrochamber.com/	Augusta	GA	30901	706-821-1300	821-1330

				Phone	Fax

Bainbridge-Decatur County Chamber of Commerce
100 Earl May Boat Basin Cir — Bainbridge GA 39819 — 229-246-4774 — 243-7633
Web: www.bainbridgega.com

Brunswick-Golden Isles Chamber of Commerce
4 Glynn Ave — Brunswick GA 31520 — 912-265-0620 — 265-0629
Web: www.brunswickgoldenisleschamber.com

Gordon County Chamber of Commerce
300 S Wall St — Calhoun GA 30701 — 706-625-3200 — 625-5062
TF: 800-887-3811 ■ *Web:* www.gordonchamber.org

Cherokee County Chamber of Commerce
3605 Marietta Hwy — Canton GA 30114 — 770-345-0400 — 345-0030
Web: www.cherokee-chamber.com

Carroll County Chamber of Commerce
200 Northside Dr — Carrollton GA 30117 — 770-832-2446 — 832-1300
Web: www.carroll-ga.org

Cartersville-Bartow County Chamber of Commerce
122 W Main St PO Box 307 — Cartersville GA 30120 — 770-382-1466 — 382-2704
Web: www.cartersvillechamber.com

Chatsworth-Murray County Chamber of Commerce
PO Box 516 — Chatsworth GA 30705 — 706-695-2834 — 517-1623
TF: 800-969-9490 ■ *Web:* www.murraycountychamber.org

White County Chamber of Commerce
122 N Main St — Cleveland GA 30528 — 706-865-5356 — 865-0758
TF: 800-392-8279 ■ *Web:* www.whitecountychamber.org

Greater Columbus Chamber of Commerce
1200 Sixth Ave PO Box 1200 — Columbus GA 31902 — 706-327-1566 — 327-7512
TF: 800-360-8552 ■ *Web:* www.columbusgachamber.com

Conyers-Rockdale Chamber of Commerce
1186 Scott St — Conyers GA 30012 — 770-483-7049 — 922-8415
Web: www.conyers-rockdale.com

Habersham County Chamber of Commerce
668 Clarkesville St — Cornelia GA 30531 — 706-778-4654 — 776-1416
TF: 800-835-2559 ■ *Web:* www.habershamchamber.com

Newton County Chamber of Commerce
2101 Clark St — Covington GA 30014 — 770-786-7510 — 786-1294
TF: 866-462-6873 ■ *Web:* www.newtonchamber.com

Cumming-Forsyth County Chamber of Commerce
212 Kelly Mill Rd — Cumming GA 30040 — 770-887-6461 — 781-8800
Web: www.cummingforsythchamber.org

Paulding County Chamber of Commerce
455 Jimmy Campbell Pkwy — Dallas GA 30132 — 770-445-6016 — 445-3050
Web: www.pauldingchamber.org

Dalton-Whitfield Chamber of Commerce
890 College Dr — Dalton GA 30720 — 706-278-7373 — 226-8739
Web: www.daltonchamber.org

Douglas-Coffee County Chamber of Commerce
211 S Gaskin Ave — Douglas GA 31533 — 912-384-1873 — 383-6304
TF: 888-426-3334 ■ *Web:* www.douglasga.org

Douglas County Chamber of Commerce
6658 Church St — Douglasville GA 30134 — 770-942-5022 — 942-5876
Web: www.douglascountygeorgia.com

Dublin-Laurens County Chamber of Commerce
1200 Bellvue — Dublin GA 31021 — 478-272-5546 — 275-0811
TF: 800-829-4933 ■ *Web:* www.dublin-georgia.com

Gwinnett Chamber of Commerce
6500 Sugarloaf Pkwy — Duluth GA 30097 — 770-232-3000 — 232-8807
Web: www.gwinnettchamber.org

Fayette County Chamber of Commerce
200 Courthouse Sq — Fayetteville GA 30214 — 770-461-9983 — 461-9622
TF: 877-527-3712 ■ *Web:* www.fayettechamber.org

Greater Hall Chamber of Commerce
230 EE Butler Pkwy — Gainesville GA 30501 — 770-532-6206 — 535-8419
Web: www.ghcc.com

Griffin-Spalding Chamber of Commerce
143 N Hill St — Griffin GA 30223 — 770-228-8200 — 228-8031
Web: www.griffinchamber.com

Liberty County Chamber of Commerce
425 W Oglethorpe Hwy — Hinesville GA 31313 — 912-368-4445 — 368-4677
TF: 855-766-2466 ■ *Web:* www.libertycounty.org

Jackson County Area Chamber of Commerce
270 Athens St PO Box 629 — Jefferson GA 30549 — 706-387-0300 — 387-0304
TF: 800-243-6921 ■ *Web:* www.jacksoncountyga.com

Clayton County Chamber of Commerce
2270 Mt Zion Rd — Jonesboro GA 30236 — 678-610-4021 — 610-4025
TF: 877-790-1831 ■ *Web:* www.claytonchamber.org

LaGrange-Troup County Chamber of Commerce
111 Bull St — LaGrange GA 30240 — 706-884-8671 — 882-8012
Web: www.lagrangechamber.com

Greater Macon Chamber of Commerce
305 Coliseum Dr — Macon GA 31217 — 478-621-2000 — 621-2021
Web: www.maconchamber.com

Henry County Chamber of Commerce
1709 Hwy 20 W W Rdg Business Ctr — McDonough GA 30253 — 770-957-5786 — 957-8030
Web: www.henrycounty.com

Milledgeville-Baldwin County Chamber of Commerce
130 S Jefferson St — Milledgeville GA 31061 — 478-453-9311 — 453-0051
Web: milledgevillega.com

Walton County Chamber of Commerce
132 E Spring St — Monroe GA 30655 — 770-267-6594 — 267-0961
Web: www.waltonchamber.org

Moultrie-Colquitt County Chamber of Commerce
116 First Ave SE — Moultrie GA 31768 — 229-985-2131
TF: 888-408-4748 ■ *Web:* www.moultriechamber.com

Newnan-Coweta Chamber of Commerce
23 Bullsboro Dr — Newnan GA 30263 — 770-253-2270 — 253-2271
Web: www.newnancowetachamber.org

Catoosa County Area Chamber of Commerce
264 Catoosa Cir — Ringgold GA 30736 — 706-965-5201 — 965-8224
Web: www.catoosachamberofcommerce.com

Polk County Chamber of Commerce/Development Authority
133 S Marble St — Rockmart GA 30153 — 770-684-8760 — 825-9002
Web: www.polkgeorgia.com

Greater Rome Chamber of Commerce
One Riverside Pkwy — Rome GA 30161 — 706-291-7663 — 232-5755
TF: 800-234-3154 ■ *Web:* www.romega.com

Camden County Chamber of Commerce
2603 Osborne Rd Ste R — Saint Marys GA 31558 — 912-729-5840 — 576-7924
TF: 888-837-4002 ■ *Web:* www.camdenchamber.com

Savannah Area Chamber of Commerce
101 E Bay St — Savannah GA 31401 — 912-644-6400 — 644-6499
TF: 877-728-2662 ■ *Web:* www.savannahchamber.com

Effingham County Chamber of Commerce
520 W Third St PO Box 1078 — Springfield GA 31329 — 912-754-3301 — 754-1236
TF: 800-241-3333 ■ *Web:* www.effinghamcounty.com

Statesboro-Bulloch Chamber of Commerce
102 S Main St — Statesboro GA 30458 — 912-764-6111 — 489-3108
TF: 855-478-5551 ■ *Web:* www.statesboro-chamber.org

Thomaston-Upson Chamber of Commerce
110 W Main St — Thomaston GA 30286 — 706-647-9686 — 647-1703
Web: www.thomastonchamber.com

Tifton-Tift County Chamber of Commerce
100 Central Ave — Tifton GA 31794 — 229-382-6200 — 386-2232
TF: 800-550-8438 ■ *Web:* www.tiftonison.com

Toccoa-Stephens County Chamber of Commerce
160 N Alexander St — Toccoa GA 30577 — 706-886-2132 — 886-2133
Web: www.toccoagachamber.com

DeKalb Chamber of Commerce
125 Clairemont Ave Ste 235 — Tucker GA 30084 — 404-378-8000 — 378-3397
TF: 800-428-7337 ■ *Web:* www.dekalbchamber.org

Valdosta-Lowndes County Chamber of Commerce
416 N Ashley St — Valdosta GA 31601 — 229-247-8100 — 245-0071
Web: www.valdostachamber.com

Warner Robins Area Chamber of Commerce
1228 Watson Blvd — Warner Robins GA 31093 — 478-922-8585 — 328-7745
Web: www.warner-robins.com

Waycross-Ware County Chamber of Commerce
315 Plant Ave Ste B — Waycross GA 31501 — 912-283-3742 — 283-0121
Web: www.waycrosschamber.org

Barrow County Chamber of Commerce PO Box 456 — Winder GA 30680 — 770-867-9444 — 867-6366
Web: www.barrowchamber.com

Hawaii

				Phone	Fax

Hawaii Island Chamber of Commerce 117 Keawe St — Hilo HI 96720 — 808-935-7178 — 961-4435
TF: 877-482-4411 ■ *Web:* hicc.biz

Kailua Chamber of Commerce
600 Kailua Rd Ste 107 — Kailua HI 96734 — 808-261-2727
TF: 888-261-7997 ■ *Web:* www.kailuachamber.com

Kona-Kohala Chamber of Commerce
75-5737 Kuakini Hwy Ste 208 — Kailua-Kona HI 96740 — 808-329-1758 — 329-8564
Web: www.kona-kohala.com

Kaua'i Chamber of Commerce 2970 Kele St # 112 — Lihue HI 96766 — 808-245-7363 — 245-8815
Web: www.kauaichamber.org

Idaho

				Phone	Fax

Boise Metro Chamber of Commerce PO Box 2368 — Boise ID 83701 — 208-472-5205 — 472-5201
Web: www.boisechamber.org

Caldwell Chamber of Commerce 704 Blaine St — Caldwell ID 83605 — 208-459-7493 — 454-1284
TF: 877-375-7382 ■ *Web:* www.cityofcaldwell.com

Coeur d'Alene Area Chamber of Commerce
105 N First St Ste 100 — Coeur d'Alene ID 83814 — 208-664-3194 — 667-9338
TF: 877-782-9232 ■ *Web:* www.cdachamber.com

Mini-Cassia Chamber of Commerce (MCC)
1177 Seventh St — Heyburn ID 83336 — 208-679-4793 — 679-4794
Web: www.minicassiachamber.com

Sun Valley/Ketchum Chamber & Visitors Bureau
491 Sun Vly Rd — Ketchum ID 83340 — 208-726-3423 — 726-4533
TF: 800-634-3347 ■ *Web:* www.visitsunvalley.com

Meridian Chamber of Commerce
215 E Franklin Rd — Meridian ID 83642 — 208-888-2817 — 888-2682
TF: 866-833-3330 ■ *Web:* www.meridianchamber.org

Moscow Chamber of Commerce 411 S Main St — Moscow ID 83843 — 208-882-1800 — 882-6186
TF: 855-202-0973 ■ *Web:* www.moscowchamber.com

Nampa Chamber of Commerce 315 11th Ave S — Nampa ID 83651 — 208-466-4641 — 466-4677
Web: www.nampa.com

Greater Pocatello Chamber of Commerce
324 S Main St — Pocatello ID 83204 — 208-233-1525 — 233-1527
Web: www.pocatelloidaho.com

Twin Falls Area Chamber of Commerce
858 Blue Lakes Blvd N — Twin Falls ID 83301 — 208-733-3974 — 733-9216
TF: 866-734-3838 ■ *Web:* www.twinfallschamber.com

Illinois

				Phone	Fax

Addison Chamber of Commerce & Industry
777 W Army Trl Blvd Ste D — Addison IL 60101 — 630-543-4300 — 543-4355
Web: www.addisonchamber.org

Arlington Heights Chamber of Commerce
311 S Arlington Heights Rd Ste 20 — Arlington Heights IL 60005 — 847-253-1703 — 253-9133
Web: www.arlingtonhtschamber.com

Barrington Area Chamber of Commerce
325 N Hough St — Barrington IL 60010 — 847-381-2525 — 381-2540
Web: www.barringtonchamber.com

Bartlett Chamber of Commerce 138 S Oak Ave — Bartlett IL 60103 — 630-830-0324 — 830-9724
Web: www.bartlettchamber.com

Belvidere Area Chamber of Commerce
130 S State St Ste 300 — Belvidere IL 61008 — 815-544-4357 — 547-7654
Web: www.belviderechamber.com

Organization	City	State	ZIP	Phone	Fax
Berwyn Development Corp 3322 S Oak Pk Ave 2nd Fl *TF:* 877-247-7792 ■ *Web:* www.berwyn.net	Berwyn	IL	60402	708-788-8100	788-0966
McLean County Chamber of Commerce 210 SE St *Web:* www.mcleancochamber.org	Bloomington	IL	61701	309-829-6344	827-3940
Bolingbrook Area Chamber of Commerce & Industry 201 Canterbury Ln Unit B *Web:* bolingbrook.org	Bolingbrook	IL	60440	630-226-8420	226-8426
Kankakee Regional Chamber of Commerce 1137 E 5000 N Rd *Web:* kankakee.org	Bourbonnais	IL	60914	815-933-7721	933-7675
Buffalo Grove Area Chamber of Commerce 50 1/2 Raupp Blvd PO Box 7124 *Web:* www.bgacc.org	Buffalo Grove	IL	60089	847-541-7799	541-7819
Calumet City Chamber of Commerce 80 River Oaks Ctr Westwood Bldg ARC 6 *Web:* www.calumetcitychamber.com	Calumet City	IL	60409	708-891-5888	891-8877
Carbondale Chamber of Commerce 131 S Illinois Ave *Web:* www.carbondalechamber.com	Carbondale	IL	62901	618-549-2146	529-5063
Northern Kane County Chamber of Commerce 20 S Grove St Ste 101 *Web:* www.nkcchamber.com	Carpentersville	IL	60110	847-426-8565	
Charleston Area Chamber of Commerce 501 Jackson Ave *Web:* www.charlestonchamber.com	Charleston	IL	61920	217-345-7041	345-7042
Albany Park Chamber of Commerce 3403 W Lauren Ave Ste 201 *Web:* www.albanyparkchamber.org	Chicago	IL	60625	773-478-0202	478-0282
Business Partners the Chamber for Uptown 4753 N Broadway St Ste 822 *Web:* www.uptownbusinesspartners.com	Chicago	IL	60640	773-878-1184	878-3678
Chicagoland Chamber of Commerce 200 E Randolph St Ste 2200 *Web:* www.chicagolandchamber.org	Chicago	IL	60601	312-494-6700	861-0660
Cosmopolitan Chamber of Commerce 30 E Adams St Ste 1050 *Web:* www.cosmococ.org	Chicago	IL	60603	312-499-0611	701-0095
East Side Chamber of Commerce 3501 E 106th St Ste 200 *Web:* www.eastsidechamber.com	Chicago	IL	60617	773-721-7948	
Lincoln Park Chamber of Commerce 1925 N Clybourn Ave Ste 301 *Web:* www.lincolnparkchamber.com	Chicago	IL	60614	773-880-5200	880-0266
Portage Park Chamber of Commerce 5829 W Irving Pk Rd	Chicago	IL	60634	773-777-2020	777-0202
Collinsville Chamber of Commerce 221 W Main St *Web:* www.discovercollinsville.com	Collinsville	IL	62234	618-344-2884	344-7499
Crete Area Chamber of Commerce 1182 Main St PO Box 263 *Web:* www.cretechamber.com	Crete	IL	60417	708-672-9216	672-7640
Crystal Lake Chamber of Commerce 427 W Virginia St *TF:* 800-946-2248 ■ *Web:* www.clchamber.com	Crystal Lake	IL	60014	815-459-1300	459-0243
Vermillion Advantage 28 W N St *Web:* ebertfest425.h.media.illinois.edu/	Danville	IL	61832	217-442-1887	442-6228
Greater Decatur Chamber of Commerce 101 S Main St Ste 102 *Web:* www.decaturchamber.com	Decatur	IL	62523	217-422-2200	422-4576
Deerfield Bannockburn & Riverwoods Chamber of Commerce 601 Deerfield Rd Ste 200 *Web:* www.dbrchamber.com	Deerfield	IL	60015	847-945-4660	940-0381
Des Plaines Chamber of Commerce & Industry 1401 E Oakton St *Web:* www.dpchamber.com	Des Plaines	IL	60018	847-824-4200	824-7932
Downers Grove Area Chamber of Commerce & Industry 2001 Butterfield Rd Ste 105 *TF:* 800-922-3565 ■ *Web:* www.downersgrove.org	Downers Grove	IL	60515	630-968-4050	968-8368
Elgin Area Chamber of Commerce 31 S Grove Ave *TF:* 800-621-3362 ■ *Web:* www.elginchamber.com	Elgin	IL	60120	847-741-5660	741-5677
Greater O'Hare Assn of Industry & Commerce PO Box 1516 *TF:* 877-355-4768 ■ *Web:* thegoa.com	Elk Grove Village	IL	60009	630-773-2944	350-2979
Elmhurst Chamber of Commerce & Industry 300 A W Lk St Ste 201 *Web:* www.elmhurstchamber.org	Elmhurst	IL	60126	630-834-6060	834-6002
Mont Clare-Elmwood Park Chamber of Commerce 11 Conti Pkwy *Web:* grandchamber.org/	Elmwood Park	IL	60707	708-456-8000	456-8680
Evanston Chamber of Commerce 1840 Oak Ave *Web:* evchamber.com	Evanston	IL	60201	847-328-1500	328-1510
Evergreen Park Chamber of Commerce 9233 S Homan Ave Third Fl *Web:* www.evergreenparkchamber.org	Evergreen Park	IL	60805	708-423-1118	423-1859
Freeport Area Chamber of Commerce 27 W Stephenson St *TF:* 877-881-7339 ■ *Web:* www.freeportilchamber.com	Freeport	IL	61032	815-233-1350	235-4038
Galesburg Area Chamber of Commerce 185 S Kellogg St *Web:* www.galesburg.org	Galesburg	IL	61401	309-343-1194	343-1195
Glen Ellyn Chamber of Commerce 800 Roosevelt Rd Bldg D Ste 108 *TF:* 800-622-9000 ■ *Web:* www.glenellynchamber.com	Glen Ellyn	IL	60137	630-469-0907	469-0426
Glenview Chamber of Commerce 2320 Glenview Rd *Web:* www.glenviewchamber.com	Glenview	IL	60025	847-724-0900	724-0202
Growth Assn of Southwestern Illinois 5800 Godfrey Rd Alden Hall *TF:* 855-852-9460 ■ *Web:* www.growthassociation.com	Godfrey	IL	62035	618-467-2280	466-8289
Chamber of Commerce of Southwestern Madison County 3600 Nameoki Rd Ste 202 *Web:* www.chamberswmadisoncounty.com	Granite City	IL	62040	618-876-6400	876-6448
Lake County Chamber of Commerce 5221 Grand Ave *Web:* www.lakecountychamber.com	Gurnee	IL	60031	847-249-3800	249-3892
Highland Park Chamber of Commerce 508 Central Ave Ste 206 *Web:* www.chamberhp.com	Highland Park	IL	60035	847-432-0284	432-2802
West Suburban Chamber of Commerce 9440 Joliet Rd Ste B *TF:* 800-796-9696 ■ *Web:* www.wscci.org	Hodgkins	IL	60525	708-387-7550	387-7556
Hoffman Estates Chamber of Commerce 2200 W Higgins Rd Ste 201 *Web:* www.hechamber.com	Hoffman Estates	IL	60169	847-781-9100	781-9172
Chicago Southland Chamber of Commerce 920 W 175th St *Web:* www.chicagosouthlandchamber.com	Homewood	IL	60430	708-957-6950	957-6968
Jacksonville Area Chamber of Commerce 310 E State St *Web:* www.jacksonvilleil.org	Jacksonville	IL	62650	217-243-5678	245-0661
Joliet Region Chamber of Commerce & Industry 63 N Chicago St *TF:* 877-499-9669 ■ *Web:* www.jolietchamber.com	Joliet	IL	60432	815-727-5371	727-5374
Illinois Valley Area Chamber of Commerce & Economic Development 300 Bucklin St *Web:* www.ivaced.org	La Salle	IL	61301	815-223-0227	223-4827
Algonquin/Lake in the Hills Chamber of Commerce 2114 W Algonquin Rd *Web:* www.alchamber.com	Lake In the Hills	IL	60156	847-658-5300	658-6546
Lake Zurich Area Chamber of Commerce First Bank Plz Ste 308 *Web:* www.lzacc.com	Lake Zurich	IL	60047	847-438-5572	438-5574
Lansing Chamber of Commerce 3330 181st Pl Ste 103 *Web:* www.chamberoflansing.com	Lansing	IL	60438	708-474-4170	474-7393
GLMV Chamber of Commerce 1123 S Milwaukee Ave *Web:* www.glmvchamber.org	Libertyville	IL	60048	847-680-0750	680-0760
Lincoln/Logan County Chamber of Commerce 1555 Fifth St *Web:* www.lincolnillinois.com	Lincoln	IL	62656	217-735-2385	735-9205
Lombard Area Chamber of Commerce 10 Lilac Ln *Web:* www.lombardchamber.com	Lombard	IL	60148	630-627-5040	627-5519
Parks Chamber of Commerce 100 Heart Blvd *Web:* www.parkschamber.com	Loves Park	IL	61111	815-633-3999	633-4057
Macomb Area Chamber of Commerce & Downtown Development Corp 214 N Lafayette St *TF:* 800-232-0270 ■ *Web:* www.macombareachamber.com	Macomb	IL	61455	309-837-4855	837-4857
Greater Marion Area Chamber of Commerce 2305 W Main St *TF:* 800-699-1760 ■ *Web:* www.marionillinois.com	Marion	IL	62959	618-997-6311	233-8765
McHenry Area Chamber of Commerce 1257 N Green St *Web:* www.mchenrychamber.com	McHenry	IL	60050	815-385-4300	385-9142
Illinois Quad City Chamber of Commerce 622 19th St *Web:* www.quadcitieschamber.com	Moline	IL	61265	309-757-5416	757-5435
Grundy County Chamber of Commerce & Industry 909 Liberty St *TF:* 800-825-1785 ■ *Web:* www.grundychamber.com	Morris	IL	60450	815-942-0113	942-0117
Mount Prospect Chamber of Commerce 107 S Main St *TF:* 800-584-4452 ■ *Web:* www.mountprospectchamber.org	Mount Prospect	IL	60056	847-398-6616	398-6780
Naperville Area Chamber of Commerce 55 S Main St Ste 351 *Web:* www.naperville.net	Naperville	IL	60540	630-355-4141	355-8335
Niles Chamber of Commerce 8060 Oakton St *Web:* www.nileschamber.com	Niles	IL	60714	847-268-8180	268-8186
Northbrook Chamber of Commerce & Industry 2002 Walters Ave *TF:* 855-354-3337 ■ *Web:* www.northbrookchamber.org	Northbrook	IL	60062	847-498-5555	498-5510
Oak Forest - Crestwood Area Chamber of Commerce 15440 S Central Ave *TF:* 800-526-7879 ■ *Web:* www.oakforestchamber.org	Oak Forest	IL	60452	708-687-4600	396-2699
Oak Lawn Chamber of Commerce 5120 Museum Dr *Web:* www.oaklawnchamber.com	Oak Lawn	IL	60453	708-424-8300	229-2236
Oak Park-River Forest Chamber of Commerce PO Box 4554 *Web:* www.oprfchamber.org	Oak Park	IL	60304	708-613-0550	
Orland Park Area Chamber of Commerce 8799 W 151 St *Web:* www.orlandparkchamber.org	Orland Park	IL	60462	708-349-2972	349-7454
Palatine Area Chamber of Commerce 579 First Bank Dr #205 *Web:* www.palatinechamber.com	Palatine	IL	60067	847-359-7200	359-7246
Pekin Area Chamber of Commerce 402 Ct St *Web:* www.pekinchamber.com	Pekin	IL	61554	309-346-2106	346-2104
Peoria Area Chamber of Commerce 100 SW Water St *Web:* www.peoriachamber.org	Peoria	IL	61602	309-676-0755	676-7534
Quincy Area Chamber of Commerce 300 Civic Ctr Plz Ste 245 *Web:* www.quincychamber.org	Quincy	IL	62301	217-222-7980	222-3033
Rockford Chamber of Commerce 308 W State St Ste 190 *TF:* 888-375-3000 ■ *Web:* www.rockfordchamber.com	Rockford	IL	61101	815-987-8100	987-8122
Rolling Meadows Chamber of Commerce 2775 Algonquin Rd Ste 310 *Web:* www.rmchamber.com	Rolling Meadows	IL	60008	847-398-3730	398-3745
Round Lake Area Chamber of Commerce & Industry 2007 Civic Ctr Way *TF:* 800-334-7661 ■ *Web:* www.rlchamber.org	Round Lake Beach	IL	60073	847-546-2002	546-2254
Skokie Chamber of Commerce 5002 Oakton St PO Box 106 *Web:* www.skokiechamber.org	Skokie	IL	60077	847-673-0240	673-0249

				Phone	Fax
Greater Springfield Chamber of Commerce, The 1011 S Second St *Web:* www.gscc.org	Springfield	IL	62701	217-525-1173	525-8768
Illinois Assn of Chamber of Commerce Executives 215 E Adams St *Web:* www.iacce.org	Springfield	IL	62701	217-522-5512	522-5518
Streamwood Chamber of Commerce 22 W Streamwood Blvd PO Box 545 *Web:* www.streamwoodchamber.com	Streamwood	IL	60107	630-837-5200	837-5251
Streator Area Chamber of Commerce & Industry 320 E Main St PO Box 360 *Web:* www.streatorchamber.com	Streator	IL	61364	815-672-2921	672-1768
Tinley Park Chamber of Commerce 17316 Oak Pk Ave *Web:* www.tinleychamber.org	Tinley Park	IL	60477	708-532-5700	532-1475
Wheaton Chamber of Commerce 108 E Wesley St *Web:* www.wheatonchamber.com	Wheaton	IL	60187	630-668-6464	668-2744
Wheeling/Prospect Heights Area Chamber of Commerce & Industry Two Community Blvd Ste 203 *Web:* www.wphchamber.com	Wheeling	IL	60090	847-541-0170	541-0296
Wilmette Chamber of Commerce (WCC) 1150 Wilmette Ave Ste 19 A *Web:* www.wilmettechamber.org	Wilmette	IL	60091	847-251-3800	251-6321
Woodridge Area Chamber of Commerce 6440 Main St Ste 330 *Web:* chamber630.com	Woodridge	IL	60517	630-960-7080	852-2316
Woodstock Chamber of Commerce & Industry 136 Cass St *Web:* www.woodstockilchamber.com	Woodstock	IL	60098	815-338-2436	338-2927

Indiana

				Phone	Fax
Madison County Chamber of Commerce, The 2701 Enterprise Dr Ste 109 *Web:* www.getlinkedmadison.com	Anderson	IN	46013	765-642-0264	642-0266
Greater Bloomington Chamber of Commerce 400 W Seventh St Ste 102 *Web:* www.chamberbloomington.org	Bloomington	IN	47404	812-336-6381	336-0651
Warrick County Chamber of Commerce 224 W Main St Ste 203 *Web:* warrickchamber.org	Boonville	IN	47601	812-897-2340	897-2360
Carmel-Clay Chamber of Commerce 21 S Rangeline Rd Ste 300A *Web:* www.carmelchamber.com	Carmel	IN	46032	317-846-1049	844-6843
Columbus Area Chamber of Commerce 500 Franklin St *Web:* www.columbusareachamber.com	Columbus	IN	47201	812-379-4457	378-7308
Connersville Chamber-Commerce 504 N Central Ave *Web:* connersvillechamber.com	Connersville	IN	47331	765-825-2561	825-4613
Chamber of Commerce of Harrison County 111 W Walnut St *TF:* 800-666-0255 ■ *Web:* www.harrisonchamber.org	Corydon	IN	47112	812-738-0120	738-0500
Crawfordsville-Montgomery County Chamber of Commerce 309 N Green St *Web:* www.crawfordsvillechamber.com	Crawfordsville	IN	47933	765-362-6800	362-6900
Greater Elkhart Chamber of Commerce 418 S Main St *Web:* www.elkhart.org	Elkhart	IN	46516	574-293-1531	294-1859
Chamber of Commerce of Southwest Indiana 318 Main St Ste 401 *Web:* swinchamber.com	Evansville	IN	47708	812-425-8147	421-5883
Greater Fort Wayne Chamber of Commerce 826 Ewing St *TF:* 888-259-9175 ■ *Web:* greaterfortwayneinc.com	Fort Wayne	IN	46802	260-424-1435	426-7232
Clinton County Chamber of Commerce 259 E Walnut St *Web:* www.ccinchamber.org	Frankfort	IN	46041	765-654-5507	654-9592
Gary Chamber of Commerce 839 Broadway Ste S103 *Web:* www.garychamber.com	Gary	IN	46402	219-885-7407	885-7408
Goshen Chamber of Commerce 232 S Main St *TF:* 800-307-4204 ■ *Web:* www.goshen.org	Goshen	IN	46526	574-533-2102	533-2103
Greencastle Chamber of Commerce 16 S Jackson St *Web:* www.gogreencastle.com	Greencastle	IN	46135	765-653-4517	653-6385
Greater Greenwood Chamber of Commerce 65 Airport Pkwy *TF:* 800-462-7585 ■ *Web:* www.greenwoodchamber.com	Greenwood	IN	46143	317-888-4856	865-2609
Lakeshore Chamber of Commerce 5246 Hohman Ave Ste 100 *TF:* 855-464-6368 ■ *Web:* www.lakeshorechamber.com	Hammond	IN	46320	219-931-1000	937-8778
Greater Indianapolis Chamber of Commerce 111 Monument Cir Ste 1950 *Web:* www.indychamber.com	Indianapolis	IN	46204	317-464-2200	464-2217
Greater Lawrence Township Chamber of Commerce 9120 Otis Ave Ste 100 *TF:* 800-473-2328 ■ *Web:* www.lawrencechamberofcommerce.org	Indianapolis	IN	46216	317-541-9876	541-9875
Kokomo/Howard County Chamber of Commerce 325 N Main St *Web:* greaterkokomo.com	Kokomo	IN	46901	765-457-5301	452-4564
Lafayette-West Lafayette Chamber of Commerce 337 Columbia St *Web:* www.lafayettechamber.com	Lafayette	IN	47901	765-742-4041	742-6276
LaGrange County Chamber of Commerce 901 S Detroit St Ste A *TF:* 877-735-0340 ■ *Web:* www.lagrangechamber.org	LaGrange	IN	46761	260-463-2443	463-2683
Dearborn County Chamber of Commerce 320 Walnut St *TF:* 800-322-8198 ■ *Web:* www.dearborncountychamber.org	Lawrenceburg	IN	47025	812-537-0814	537-0845
Boone County Chamber of Commerce 221 N Lebanon St *Web:* www.boonechamber.org	Lebanon	IN	46052	765-482-1320	482-3114
Logansport/Cass County Chamber of Commerce 300 E Broadway Ste 103 *Web:* www.logan-casschamber.com	Logansport	IN	46947	574-753-6388	735-0909
Madison Area Chamber of Commerce 301 E Main St *Web:* www.madisonchamber.org	Madison	IN	47250	812-265-3135	265-9784
Marion-Grant County Chamber of Commerce 215 S Adams St *Web:* www.marionchamber.org	Marion	IN	46952	765-664-5107	668-5443
Michigan City Area Chamber of Commerce 200 E Michigan Blvd *Web:* www.michigancitychamber.com	Michigan City	IN	46360	219-874-6221	873-1204
Greater Monticello Chamber of Commerce 116 N Main St *TF:* 800-541-7906 ■ *Web:* www.monticelloin.com	Monticello	IN	47960	574-583-7220	583-3399
Muncie-Delaware County Chamber of Commerce 401 S High St *TF:* 800-336-1373 ■ *Web:* www.muncie.com	Muncie	IN	47305	765-288-6681	751-9151
One Southern Indiana 4100 Charlestown Rd *TF:* 800-521-2232 ■ *Web:* www.1si.org	New Albany	IN	47150	812-945-0266	948-4664
Noblesville Chamber of Commerce 601 Conner St *Web:* www.noblesvillechamber.com	Noblesville	IN	46060	317-773-0086	773-1966
Jennings County Chamber of Commerce 203 N State St PO Box 340 *Web:* www.jenningscountychamber.com	North Vernon	IN	47265	812-346-2339	
Miami County Chamber of Commerce 13 E Main St *TF:* 800-521-9945 ■ *Web:* www.miamicochamber.com	Peru	IN	46970	765-472-1923	472-7099
Greater Portage Chamber of Commerce 2642 Eleanor St *Web:* www.portageinchamber.com	Portage	IN	46368	219-762-3300	763-2450
Wayne County Area Chamber of Commerce 33 S Seventh St Ste 2 *Web:* www.wcareachamber.org	Richmond	IN	47374	765-962-1511	966-0882
Schererville Chamber of Commerce 149 E Joliet St *Web:* www.46375.org	Schererville	IN	46375	219-322-5412	322-0598
Shelby County Chamber of Commerce 501 N Harrison St *TF:* 800-318-4083 ■ *Web:* www.shelbychamber.net	Shelbyville	IN	46176	317-398-6647	392-3901
Chamber of Commerce of Saint Joseph County 401 E Colfax Ave Ste 310 *Web:* www.sjchamber.org	South Bend	IN	46617	574-234-0051	289-0358
Winchester Area Chamber of Commerce 211 S Main St *Web:* www.winchesterareachamber.org	Winchester	IN	47394	765-584-3731	584-5544

Iowa

				Phone	Fax
Ames Chamber of Commerce 1601 Golden Aspen Dr Ste 110 *Web:* www.ameschamber.com	Ames	IA	50010	515-232-2310	232-6716
Burlington/West Burlington Area Chamber of Commerce 610 N Fourth St Ste 200 *TF:* 800-827-4837 ■ *Web:* www.greaterburlington.com	Burlington	IA	52601	319-752-6365	752-6454
Greater Cedar Falls Chamber of Commerce 312 W 1st St *Web:* cedarvalleyalliance.com	Cedar Falls	IA	50613	319-266-3593	277-4325
Cedar Rapids Area Chamber of Commerce 424 First Ave NE *Web:* www.cedarrapids.org	Cedar Rapids	IA	52401	319-398-5317	398-5228
Clinton Area Chamber of Commerce 721 S Second St *Web:* www.clintonia.com	Clinton	IA	52732	563-242-5702	242-5803
Council Bluffs Area Chamber of Commerce 149 W Bdwy *TF:* 800-228-6878 ■ *Web:* www.councilbluffsiowa.com	Council Bluffs	IA	51503	712-325-1000	322-5698
Greater Des Moines Partnership 700 Locust St Ste 100 *TF:* 800-376-9059 ■ *Web:* www.desmoinesmetro.com	Des Moines	IA	50309	515-286-4950	286-4974
Dubuque Area Chamber of Commerce 300 Main St Ste 200 *TF:* 800-798-4748 ■ *Web:* www.dubuquechamber.com	Dubuque	IA	52001	563-557-9200	557-1591
Fort Dodge Chamber of Commerce 24 N 9th St Ste A *Web:* www.greaterfortdodge.com	Fort Dodge	IA	50501	515-955-5500	955-3245
Iowa City Area Chamber of Commerce 325 E Washington St Ste 100 *TF:* 800-283-6592 ■ *Web:* www.iowacityarea.com	Iowa City	IA	52240	319-337-9637	338-9958
Keokuk Area Chamber of Commerce 329 Main St *Web:* www.keokukchamber.wildapricot.org	Keokuk	IA	52632	319-524-5055	524-5016
Marion Chamber of Commerce 1225 Sixth Ave Ste 100 *Web:* www.cedarrapids.org	Marion	IA	52302	319-377-6316	377-1576
Marshalltown Area Chamber of Commerce 709 S Ctr St PO Box 1000 *TF:* 800-725-5301 ■ *Web:* www.marshalltown.org	Marshalltown	IA	50158	641-753-6645	752-8373
Mason City Area Chamber of Commerce 25 W State St *Web:* www.masoncityia.com	Mason City	IA	50401	641-423-5724	423-5725
Ottumwa Area Chamber of Commerce 217 E Main St *Web:* www.ottumwaiowa.com	Ottumwa	IA	52501	641-682-3465	682-3466
Siouxland Chamber of Commerce 101 Pierce St *Web:* www.siouxlandchamber.com	Sioux City	IA	51101	712-255-7903	258-7578
Urbandale Chamber of Commerce 3600 NW 86th St *Web:* uniquelyurbandale.com	Urbandale	IA	50322	515-331-6855	331-2987
Greater Cedar Valley Chamber of Commerce 10 W 4th St Ste 310 *TF:* 800-288-1047 ■ *Web:* cedarvalleyalliance.com	Waterloo	IA	50703	319-232-1156	233-4580

Name / Address	City	State	Zip	Phone	Fax
West Des Moines Chamber of Commerce 4200 Mills Civic Pkwy Ste E-200 *Web:* www.wdmchamber.org	West Des Moines	IA	50265	515-225-6009	225-7129

Kansas

Name / Address	City	State	Zip	Phone	Fax
Arkansas City Area Chamber of Commerce PO Box 795 *Web:* www.arkcity.org	Arkansas City	KS	67005	620-442-0230	441-0048
Dodge City Area Chamber of Commerce 311 W Spruce St *Web:* www.dodgechamber.com	Dodge City	KS	67801	620-227-3119	227-2957
Emporia Area Chamber of Commerce 719 Commercial St *TF:* 800-279-3730 ■ *Web:* www.emporiakschamber.org	Emporia	KS	66801	620-342-1600	342-3223
Garden City Area Chamber of Commerce 1511 E Fulton Terr *Web:* www.gardencity.net	Garden City	KS	67846	620-275-1900	276-3290
Hutchinson/Reno County Chamber of Commerce 117 N Walnut St *TF:* 800-691-4262 ■ *Web:* www.hutchchamber.com	Hutchinson	KS	67501	620-662-3391	662-2168
Junction City Area Chamber of Commerce 222 W Sixth St PO Box 26 *Web:* www.junctioncitychamber.org	Junction City	KS	66441	785-762-2632	762-3353
Kansas City Kansas Area Chamber of Commerce 727 Minnesota Ave *Web:* www.kckchamber.com	Kansas City	KS	66117	913-371-3070	371-3732
Women's Chamber of Commerce PO Box 171337 *Web:* www.womenschamberkck.org	Kansas City	KS	66117	913-371-6153	
Leavenworth-Lansing Area Chamber of Commerce 518 Shawnee St *Web:* www.llchamber.com	Leavenworth	KS	66048	913-682-4112	682-8170
Lenexa Chamber of Commerce 11180 Lackman Rd *TF:* 800-679-0177 ■ *Web:* www.lenexa.org	Lenexa	KS	66219	913-888-1414	888-3770
Liberal Area Chamber of Commerce PO Box 676 *Web:* www.liberalkschamber.com	Liberal	KS	67905	620-624-3855	624-8851
Manhattan Area Chamber of Commerce 501 Poyntz Ave *TF:* 800-759-0134 ■ *Web:* www.manhattan.org	Manhattan	KS	66502	785-776-8829	776-0679
Olathe Chamber of Commerce 18001 W 106th St Ste 160 *Web:* www.olathe.org	Olathe	KS	66061	913-764-1050	782-4636
Overland Park Chamber of Commerce 9001 W 110th St Ste 150 *Web:* www.opks.org	Overland Park	KS	66210	913-491-3600	491-0393
Pittsburg Area Chamber of Commerce 117 W Fourth St *TF:* 800-794-4780 ■ *Web:* www.pittsburgareachamber.com	Pittsburg	KS	66762	620-231-1000	231-3178
Salina Area Chamber of Commerce 120 W Ash St *Web:* www.salinakansas.org	Salina	KS	67401	785-827-9301	827-9758
Shawnee Chamber of Commerce 15100 W 67th St Ste 202 *Web:* www.shawneekschamber.com	Shawnee	KS	66217	913-631-6545	631-9628
Greater Topeka Chamber of Commerce 120 SE Sixth St Ste 110 *Web:* www.topekachamber.org	Topeka	KS	66603	785-234-2644	234-8656
Wichita Area Chamber of Commerce 350 W Douglas Ave *Web:* www.wichitachamber.org	Wichita	KS	67202	316-265-7771	265-7502

Kentucky

Name / Address	City	State	Zip	Phone	Fax
Ashland Alliance Chamber of Commerce 1733 Winchester Ave *TF:* 800-233-3826 ■ *Web:* www.ashlandalliance.com	Ashland	KY	41101	606-324-5111	325-4607
Bowling Green Area Chamber of Commerce 710 College St *TF:* 866-330-2422 ■ *Web:* www.bgchamber.com	Bowling Green	KY	42101	270-781-3200	843-0458
Danville-Boyle County Chamber of Commerce 105 East Walnut St *Web:* www.betterindanville.com	Danville	KY	40422	859-236-2805	236-3197
Elizabethtown-Hardin County Chamber of Commerce (HCCC) 111 W Dixie Ave *Web:* hardinchamber.com	Elizabethtown	KY	42701	270-765-4334	737-0690
Northern Kentucky Chamber of Commerce 300 Buttermilk Pk Ste 330 *Web:* www.nkychamber.com	Fort Mitchell	KY	41017	859-578-8800	578-8802
Frankfort Area Chamber of Commerce 100 Capitol Ave *Web:* www.frankfortky.info	Frankfort	KY	40601	502-223-8261	223-5942
Georgetown-Scott County Chamber of Commerce 160 E Main St *Web:* www.gtown.org	Georgetown	KY	40324	502-863-5424	863-5756
Glasgow-Barren County Chamber of Commerce 118 E Public Sq *TF:* 800-264-3161 ■ *Web:* www.glasgowbarrenchamber.com	Glasgow	KY	42141	270-651-3161	651-3122
Greenville-Muhlenberg Chamber of Commerce 100 E Main Cross PO Box 313 *TF:* 866-227-4812 ■ *Web:* www.greatermuhlenbergchamber.com	Greenville	KY	42345	270-338-5422	338-5440
Harlan County Chamber of Commerce PO Box 268 *Web:* www.harlancountychamber.com	Harlan	KY	40831	606-573-4717	
Hopkinsville-Christian County Chamber of Commerce 2800 Port Campbell Blvd *TF:* 800-842-9959 ■ *Web:* www.christiancountychamber.com	Hopkinsville	KY	42240	270-885-9096	881-9366
Jeffersontown Chamber of Commerce 10434 Watterson Tr *Web:* www.jtownchamber.com	Jeffersontown	KY	40299	502-267-1674	267-6874
Oldham County Chamber of Commerce 412 E Main St *Web:* www.oldhamcountychamber.com	LaGrange	KY	40031	502-222-1635	222-3159
Greater Lexington Chamber of Commerce Inc 330 E Main St Ste 100 *Web:* www.commercelexington.com	Lexington	KY	40507	859-254-4447	233-3304
Greater Louisville Inc 614 W Main St *Web:* www.greaterlouisville.com	Louisville	KY	40202	502-625-0000	625-0010
Madisonville-Hopkins County Chamber of Commerce 15 E Ctr St *Web:* www.madisonville-hopkinschamber.com	Madisonville	KY	42431	270-821-3435	821-9190
Mayfield-Graves County Chamber of Commerce 201 E College St *Web:* www.mayfieldchamber.com	Mayfield	KY	42066	270-247-6101	247-6110
Bell County Chamber of Commerce PO Box 788 *Web:* www.bellcountychamber.net	Middlesboro	KY	40965	606-248-1075	248-8851
Chamber of Commerce - Murray-Calloway County, The 805 N 12th St *Web:* www.mymurray.com	Murray	KY	42071	270-753-5171	
Greater Owensboro Chamber of Commerce 200 E Third St PO Box 825 *Web:* www.owensboro.com	Owensboro	KY	42302	270-926-1860	926-3364
Paducah Area Chamber of Commerce 300 S Third St *Web:* www.paducahchamber.org	Paducah	KY	42003	270-443-1746	442-9152
Radcliff Hardin County Chamber of Commerce 306 N Wilson Rd *Web:* www.hardinchamber.com	Radcliff	KY	40160	270-351-4450	352-4449
Bullitt County Chamber of Commerce 279 S Buckman PO Box 1656 *Web:* www.bullittchamber.org	Shepherdsville	KY	40165	502-955-9641	955-9641
Somerset-Pulaski County Chamber of Commerce 445 S Hwy 27 Ste 101 *TF:* 877-629-9722 ■ *Web:* somersetpulaskichamber.com	Somerset	KY	42501	606-679-7323	679-1744
Winchester-Clark County Chamber of Commerce Two S Maple St *Web:* www.winchesterkychamber.com	Winchester	KY	40391	859-744-6420	744-9229

Louisiana

Name / Address	City	State	Zip	Phone	Fax
Central Louisiana Chamber of Commerce 1118 Third St PO Box 992 *Web:* www.cenlachamber.org	Alexandria	LA	71309	318-442-6671	442-6734
Bastrop-Morehouse Parish Chamber of Commerce 110 N Franklin St *Web:* bastroplacoc.org	Bastrop	LA	71220	318-281-3794	
Greater Baton Rouge Chamber of Commerce 564 Laurel St *Web:* www.brac.org	Baton Rouge	LA	70801	225-381-7125	336-4306
Bossier Chamber of Commerce 710 Benton Rd *TF:* 888-414-2695 ■ *Web:* www.bossierchamber.com	Bossier City	LA	71111	318-746-0252	746-0357
Saint Tammany West Chamber of Commerce 610 Hollycrest Blvd *Web:* www.sttammanychamber.org	Covington	LA	70433	985-892-3216	893-4244
Livingston Parish Chamber of Commerce PO Box 591 *Web:* cm.livingstonparishchamber.org	Denham Springs	LA	70726	225-665-8155	665-2411
Greater Beauregard Chamber of Commerce 111 N Washington St PO Box 309 *Web:* www.beauchamber.org	DeRidder	LA	70634	337-463-5533	463-2244
Ascension Chamber of Commerce 1006 W Hwy 30 *Web:* www.ascensionchamber.com	Gonzales	LA	70737	225-647-7487	647-5124
Houma-Terrebonne Chamber of Commerce 6133 Louisiana 311 *Web:* www.houmachamber.com	Houma	LA	70360	985-876-5600	876-5611
Jeff Davis Parish Business Alliance 246 N Main St PO Box 1209 *Web:* jdba.us/	Jennings	LA	70546	337-824-0933	824-0934
One Acadiana 804 E St Mary Blvd *Web:* www.lafchamber.org	Lafayette	LA	70503	337-233-2705	234-8671
Chamber/Southwest Louisiana 120 W Pujo St *Web:* allianceswla.org	Lake Charles	LA	70601	337-433-3632	436-3727
Chamber of Lafourche & the Bayou Region 107 W 26th St *Web:* www.lafourchechamber.com	Larose	LA	70373	985-693-6700	693-6702
Greater Vernon Chamber of Commerce PO Box 1228 *Web:* www.chambervernonparish.com	Leesville	LA	71496	337-238-0349	238-0340
DeSoto Parish Chamber of Commerce 115 N Washington Ave *Web:* www.desotoparishchamber.net	Mansfield	LA	71052	318-872-1310	871-1875
Jefferson Chamber of Commerce 3421 N Cswy Blvd Ste 203 *Web:* jeffersonchamber.org	Metairie	LA	70002	504-835-3880	835-3828
Monroe Chamber of Commerce 212 Walnut St Ste 100 *TF:* 888-677-5200 ■ *Web:* www.monroe.org	Monroe	LA	71201	318-323-3461	322-7594
Natchitoches Area Chamber of Commerce 550 Second St *TF:* 877-646-6689 ■ *Web:* www.natchitocheschamber.com	Natchitoches	LA	71457	318-352-6894	352-5385
Greater Iberia Chamber of Commerce 111 W Main St *Web:* iberiachamber.org	New Iberia	LA	70560	337-364-1836	367-7405
New Orleans Chamber of Commerce 1515 Poydras St Ste 1010 *Web:* www.neworleanschamber.org	New Orleans	LA	70112	504-799-4260	799-4259
Iberville Parish Chamber of Commerce 23675 Church St *TF:* 800-266-2692 ■ *Web:* www.ibervillechamber.com	Plaquemine	LA	70764	225-687-3560	687-3575
Ruston/Lincoln Chamber of Commerce 211 N Trenton *TF:* 800-392-9032 ■ *Web:* www.rustonlincoln.org	Ruston	LA	71270	318-255-2031	255-3481

Phone Fax

Greater Shreveport Chamber of Commerce
400 Edwards St. .... Shreveport LA 71101 318-677-2500 677-2541
TF: 800-448-5432 ■ *Web:* www.shreveportchamber.org

East St Tammany Chamber of Commerce
118 W Hall Ave. .... Slidell LA 70460 985-643-5678 649-2460
TF: 800-870-3673 ■ *Web:* estchamber.com

Thibodaux Chamber of Commerce
318 E Bayou Rd PO Box 467 .... Thibodaux LA 70302 985-446-1187 446-1191
Web: thibodauxchamber.com

Maine

Phone Fax

Kennebec Valley Chamber of Commerce
21 University Dr .... Augusta ME 04330 207-623-4559 626-9342
Web: www.augustamaine.com

Bangor Region Chamber of Commerce
208 Maine Ave .... Bangor ME 04401 207-947-0307 990-1427
Web: www.bangorregion.com

Bar Harbor Chamber of Commerce
Two Cottage St .... Bar Harbor ME 04609 207-288-5103 667-9080
TF: 888-540-9990 ■ *Web:* www.barharborinfo.com

Belfast Area Chamber of Commerce 14 Main St .... Belfast ME 04915 207-338-5900 338-3808
TF: 877-338-9015 ■ *Web:* www.belfastmaine.org

Saint Croix Valley Chamber of Commerce
39 Union St .... Calais ME 04619 207-454-2308 454-2308
Web: www.visitcalais.com

Ellsworth Area Chamber of Commerce
163 High St .... Ellsworth ME 04605 207-667-5584 667-2617
TF: 855-635-6278 ■ *Web:* www.ellsworthchamber.org

Androscoggin County Chamber of Commerce
PO Box 59 .... Lewiston ME 04243 207-783-2249 783-4481
Web: www.androscoggincounty.com

Greater Lincoln Lakes Region Chamber of Commerce
256 W Broadway. .... Lincoln ME 04457 207-794-8065
Web: www.lincolnmechamber.org

Portland Regional Chamber 443 Congress St .... Portland ME 04101 207-772-2811 772-1179
Web: www.portlandregion.com

Biddeford-Saco Chamber of Commerce & Industry
138 Main St Ste 101. .... Saco ME 04072 207-282-1567 282-3149
Web: www.biddefordsacochamber.org

Sanford-Springvale Chamber of Commerce & Economic Development
917 Main St Ste B. .... Sanford ME 04073 207-324-4280 324-8290
Web: www.sanfordchamber.org

Oxford Hills Chamber of Commerce
Four Western Ave .... South Paris ME 04281 207-743-2281 743-0687
Web: www.oxfordhillsmaine.com

Southern Midcoast Maine Chamber
Two Main St Border Trust Business Ctr .... Topsham ME 04086 207-725-8797 725-9787
TF: 877-725-8797 ■ *Web:* www.midcoastmaine.com

Mid-Maine Chamber of Commerce 50 Elm St .... Waterville ME 04901 207-873-3315 877-0087
Web: www.midmainechamber.com

Maryland

Phone Fax

Annapolis & Anne Arundel County Chamber of Commerce
49 Old Solomons Island Rd Ste 204. .... Annapolis MD 21401 410-266-3960 266-8270
Web: www.annapolischamber.com

Harford County Chamber of Commerce
108 S Bond St .... Bel Air MD 21014 410-838-2020 893-4715
TF: 800-682-8536 ■ *Web:* www.harfordchamber.org

Greater Bethesda-Chevy Chase Chamber of Commerce
7910 Woodmont Ave Ste 1204. .... Bethesda MD 20814 301-652-4900 657-1973
TF: 800-333-6778 ■ *Web:* www.bccchamber.org

Greater Bowie Chamber of Commerce
1525 Pointer Ridge Pl Ste 206 .... Bowie MD 20715 301-262-0920 262-0921
Web: www.bowiechamber.org

Dorchester Chamber of Commerce
528 Poplar St .... Cambridge MD 21613 410-228-3575 228-6848
Web: www.dorchesterchamber.org

Queen Anne's County Chamber of Commerce
1561 Postal Rd .... Chester MD 21619 410-643-8530 643-8477
Web: www.qacchamber.com

Howard County Chamber of Commerce
5560 Sterrett Pl Ste 105 .... Columbia MD 21044 410-730-4111 730-4584
Web: www.howardchamber.com

Greater Crofton Chamber of Commerce
PO Box 4146 .... Crofton MD 21114 410-721-9131 274-6060*
**Fax Area Code:* 443 ■ *TF:* 866-852-4237 ■
Web: www.greatercroftonchamberofcommerce.wildapricot.org

Allegany County Chamber of Commerce
24 Frederick St .... Cumberland MD 21502 301-722-2820 722-5995
Web: www.alleganycountychamber.com

Caroline County Chamber of Commerce
24820 Meeting House Rd Ste 1 .... Denton MD 21629 410-479-4638 479-4862
Web: www.carolinechamber.org

Talbot County Chamber of Commerce
101 Marlboro Ave Ste 53 .... Easton MD 21601 410-822-4606 822-7922
Web: www.talbotchamber.org

Cecil County Chamber of Commerce
106 E Main St Ste 101 .... Elkton MD 21921 410-392-3833 392-6225
Web: www.cecilchamber.com

Frederick County Chamber of Commerce
8420 Gas House Pk Ste B. .... Frederick MD 21701 301-662-4164 846-4427
Web: www.frederickchamber.org

Gaithersburg-Germantown Chamber of Commerce
Four Professional Dr Ste 132 .... Gaithersburg MD 20879 301-840-1400 963-3918
Web: www.ggchamber.org

Hagerstown-Washington County Chamber of Commerce
28 W Washington St. .... Hagerstown MD 21740 301-739-2015 739-1278
Web: www.hagerstown.org

Phone Fax

Charles County Chamber of Commerce
101 Centennial St Ste A .... La Plata MD 20646 301-932-6500 932-3945
TF: 800-992-3194 ■ *Web:* www.charlescountychamber.org

Prince George's Chamber of Commerce
4640 Forbes Blvd Ste 130 .... Lanham MD 20706 301-731-5000 731-5013
Web: www.pgcoc.org

Baltimore/Washington Corridor Chamber of Commerce
312 Marshall Ave Ste 104. .... Laurel MD 20707 301-725-4000 725-0776
Web: www.baltwashchamber.org

Garrett County Chamber of Commerce
15 Visitors Ctr Dr .... McHenry MD 21541 301-387-4386 387-2080
TF: 888-387-5237 ■ *Web:* www.visitdeepcreek.com

Essex-Middle River-White Marsh Chamber of Commerce
405 Williams Ct Ste 108. .... Middle River MD 21220 443-317-8763 317-8772
Web: www.chesapeakechamber.org

Greater Ocean City Chamber of Commerce
12320 Ocean Gateway .... Ocean City MD 21842 410-213-0144 213-7521
TF: 888-626-3386 ■ *Web:* www.oceancity.org

West Anne Arundel County Chamber of Commerce
8385 Piney Orchard Pkwy. .... Odenton MD 21113 410-672-3422 672-3475
Web: www.westcountychamber.org

Olney Chamber of Commerce
3460 Olney-Laytonsville Rd Ste 211. .... Olney MD 20832 301-774-7117 774-4944
Web: www.olneymd.org

Pikesville Chamber of Commerce
Seven Church Ln Ste 14. .... Pikesville MD 21208 410-484-2337 484-4151
Web: www.pikesvillechamber.org

Calvert County Chamber of Commerce
PO Box 9 .... Prince Frederick MD 20678 410-535-2577 295-7213*
**Fax Area Code:* 443 ■ *Web:* www.calvertchamber.org

Montgomery County Chamber of Commerce
51 Monroe St Ste 1800. .... Rockville MD 20850 301-738-0015 738-8792
Web: www.montgomerycountychamber.com

Rockville Chamber of Commerce
One Research Ct # 450 .... Rockville MD 20850 301-424-9300 762-7599
Web: www.rockvillechamber.org

Salisbury Area Chamber of Commerce
144 E Main St. .... Salisbury MD 21801 410-749-0144 860-9925
Web: www.salisburyarea.com

Greater Severna Park Chamber of Commerce
1 Holly Ave .... Severna Park MD 21146 410-647-3900 647-3999
Web: www.severnaparkchamber.com

Greater Silver Spring Chamber of Commerce
8601 Georgia Ave Ste 203 .... Silver Spring MD 20910 301-565-3777 565-3377
Web: www.silverspringchamber.com

Snow Hill Chamber of Commerce 100 Pearl St .... Snow Hill MD 21863 410-632-2080 632-3158
Web: www.snowhillmd.com

Baltimore County Chamber of Commerce
102 W Pennsylvania Ave Ste 101 .... Towson MD 21204 410-825-6200 821-9901
Web: www.baltcountycc.com

Eastern Baltimore Area Chamber of Commerce
102 W Pennsylvania Ave Ste 101 .... Towson MD 21204 410-825-6200 821-9901
TF: 888-224-9740 ■ *Web:* www.baltcountycc.com

Wheaton-Kensington Chamber of Commerce
2401 Blueridge Ave Ste 101 .... Wheaton MD 20902 301-949-0080 949-0081
TF: 800-927-9061 ■ *Web:* www.wkchamber.org

Massachusetts

Phone Fax

Middlesex West Chamber of Commerce
179 Great Road Suite 104B. .... Acton MA 01720 978-263-0010 264-0303
TF: 800-439-0183 ■ *Web:* www.mwcoc.com

Amherst Area Chamber of Commerce 28 Amity St. .... Amherst MA 01002 413-253-0700 256-0771
Web: www.amherstarea.com

North Quabbin Chamber of Commerce
251 Exchange St. .... Athol MA 01331 978-249-3849 249-7151
Web: www.northquabbinchamber.com

United Regional Chamber of Commerce
42 Union St .... Attleboro MA 02703 508-222-0801 222-1498
TF: 800-333-6624 ■ *Web:* www.unitedregionalchamber.org

Beverly Chamber of Commerce
100 Cummings Ctr Ste 107K .... Beverly MA 01915 978-232-9559 232-9372
Web: www.greaterbeverlychamber.com/

Greater Boston Chamber of Commerce
265 Franklin St. .... Boston MA 02110 617-227-4500 227-7505
Web: www.bostonchamber.com

Metro South Chamber of Commerce
60 School St. .... Brockton MA 02301 508-586-0500 587-1340
TF: 877-777-4414 ■ *Web:* www.metrosouthchamber.com

Brookline Chamber of Commerce
251 Harvard St Ste 1. .... Brookline MA 02446 617-739-1330 739-1200
Web: www.brooklinechamber.com

Cape Cod Canal Regional Chamber of Commerce
70 Main St .... Buzzards Bay MA 02532 508-759-6000 759-6965
TF: 888-332-2732 ■ *Web:* www.capecodcanalchamber.org

Cape Cod Chamber of Commerce
Five Shoot Flying Hill Rd .... Centerville MA 02632 508-362-3225 362-3698
TF: 888-332-2732 ■ *Web:* www.capecodchamber.org

Chicopee Chamber of Commerce
264 Exchange St. .... Chicopee MA 01013 413-594-2101 594-2103
Web: www.chicopeechamber.org

Wachusett Chamber of Commerce 167 Church St. .... Clinton MA 01510 978-368-7687
Web: wachusettchamber.com

North Shore Chamber of Commerce
Five Cherry Hill Dr Ste 100. .... Danvers MA 01923 978-774-8565 774-3418
Web: www.northshorechamber.org

Nashoba Valley Chamber of Commerce
100 Sherman Ave .... Devens MA 01434 978-772-6976 772-3503
TF: 877-322-8228 ■ *Web:* www.nvcoc.com

Everett Chamber of Commerce 467 Broadway. .... Everett MA 02149 617-387-9100 389-6655
Web: www.everettmachamber.com

Phone Fax

Fall River Area Chamber of Commerce & Industry
200 Pocasset St . . . . Fall River MA 02721 508-676-8226 675-5932
TF: 800-647-2824 ■ *Web:* www.fallriverchamber.com

Falmouth Chamber of Commerce 20 Academy Ln . . . . Falmouth MA 02540 508-548-8500 548-8521
TF: 800-526-8532 ■ *Web:* www.falmouthchamber.com

North Central Massachusetts Chamber of Commerce
860 S St . . . . Fitchburg MA 01420 978-353-7600 353-4896
Web: www.northcentralmass.com

Metro West Chamber of Commerce
1671 Worcester Rd Ste 201 . . . . Framingham MA 01701 508-879-5600 875-9325
TF: 866-709-9401 ■ *Web:* www.metrowest.org

Greater Gardner Chamber of Commerce
29 Parker St PO Box 1381 . . . . Gardner MA 01440 978-632-1780 630-1767
Web: www.gardnerma.com

Cape Ann Chamber of Commerce
33 Commercial St . . . . Gloucester MA 01930 978-283-1601 283-4740
Web: capeannchamber.com

Greater Haverhill Chamber of Commerce
80 Merrimack St . . . . Haverhill MA 01830 978-373-5663 373-8060
Web: www.haverhillchamber.com

Greater Holyoke Chamber of Commerce
177 High St . . . . Holyoke MA 01040 413-534-3376 534-3385
Web: www.holycham.com

Assabet Valley Chamber of Commerce
18 Church St PO Box 578 . . . . Hudson MA 01749 978-568-0360 562-4118
Web: www.assabetvalleychamber.org

Hyannis Area Chamber of Commerce 397 Main St . . . . Hyannis MA 02601 508-775-2201
Web: www.hyannis.com

Merrimack Valley Chamber of Commerce
264 Essex St . . . . Lawrence MA 01840 978-686-0900 794-9953
TF: 800-966-3375 ■ *Web:* www.merrimackvalleychamber.com

Lexington Chamber of Commerce
1875 Massachusetts Ave . . . . Lexington MA 02420 781-862-2480
Web: www.lexingtonchamber.org

Greater Lowell Chamber of Commerce
131 Merrimack St . . . . Lowell MA 01852 978-459-8154 452-4145
TF: 800-338-0221 ■ *Web:* greaterlowellcc.org

Lynn Area Chamber of Commerce
583 Chestnut St Unit 8 . . . . Lynn MA 01901 781-592-2900 592-2903
Web: www.lynnareachamber.com

Malden Chamber of Commerce
200 Pleasant St Ste 416 . . . . Malden MA 02148 781-322-4500 322-4866
Web: www.maldenchamber.org

Marlborough Regional Chamber of Commerce
11 Florence St . . . . Marlborough MA 01752 508-485-7746 481-1819
Web: www.marlboroughchamber.org

Medford Chamber of Commerce
1 Shipyard Way Ste 302 . . . . Medford MA 02155 781-396-1277 396-1278
Web: medfordchambermass.com

Melrose Chamber of Commerce One W Foster St . . . . Melrose MA 02176 781-665-3033 665-5595
Web: www.melrosechamber.org

Cranberry Country Chamber of Commerce
40 N Main St . . . . Middleboro MA 02346 508-947-1499 947-1446
Web: www.cranberrycountry.org

Milford Area Chamber of Commerce
258 Main St PO Box 621 . . . . Milford MA 01757 508-473-6700 473-8467
Web: www.milfordchamber.org

New Bedford Area Chamber of Commerce
794 Purchase St . . . . New Bedford MA 02740 508-999-5231 999-5237
Web: www.newbedfordchamber.com

Newton-Needham Chamber of Commerce
281 Needham St . . . . Newton MA 02464 617-244-5300 244-5302
Web: www.nnchamber.com

Greater Northampton Chamber of Commerce
99 Pleasant St . . . . NorthAmpton MA 01060 413-584-1900 584-1934
TF: 800-392-6090 ■ *Web:* www.explorenorthampton.com

Neposet Valley Chamber of Commerce
190 Vanderbilt Ave . . . . Norwood MA 02062 781-769-1126 769-0808
Web: www.nvcc.com

Quaboag Valley Chamber of Commerce
Three Converse St Ste 103 . . . . Palmer MA 01069 413-283-2418 289-1355
Web: qhma.com/

Peabody Chamber of Commerce (PACC)
24 Main St Ste 28 . . . . Peabody MA 01960 978-531-0384 532-7227
Web: www.peabodychamber.com

Berkshire Chamber of Commerce
66 Allen St Ste 360 . . . . Pittsfield MA 01201 413-499-4000 447-9641
Web: www.berkshirechamber.com

Plymouth Area Chamber of Commerce
10 Cordage Pk Cir Ste 231 . . . . Plymouth MA 02360 508-830-1620 830-1621
Web: www.plymouthchamber.com

Reading-North Reading Chamber of Commerce
PO Box 771 . . . . Reading MA 01867 978-664-5060 944-6125*
**Fax Area Code:* 781 ■ *Web:* www.readingnreadingchamber.org

South Shore Chamber of Commerce
1050 Hingham St . . . . Rockland MA 02370 781-421-3900 479-9274*
**Fax Area Code:* 617 ■ *Web:* www.southshorechamber.org

Salem Chamber of Commerce 265 Essex St . . . . Salem MA 01970 978-744-0004 745-3855
Web: www.salem-chamber.org

Somerville Chamber of Commerce
Two Alpine St PO Box 44034 . . . . Somerville MA 02144 617-776-4100
Web: www.somervillechamber.org

Affiliated Chamber of Commerce of Greater Springfield
1441 Main St . . . . Springfield MA 01103 413-787-1555 731-8530
TF: 888-283-3757 ■ *Web:* www.myonlinechamber.com

West Springfield Chamber of Commerce
1441 Main St . . . . Springfield MA 01103 413-787-1555 731-8530
Web: www.myonlinechamber.com

Taunton Area Chamber of Commerce
12 Taunton Green Ste 201 . . . . Taunton MA 02780 508-824-4068 884-8222
TF: 800-225-0394 ■ *Web:* www.tauntonareachamber.org

Wakefield Chamber of Commerce 467 Main St . . . . Wakefield MA 01880 781-245-0741
Web: wakefieldchamber.org/

Phone Fax

Waltham/West Suburban Chamber of Commerce
84 S St . . . . Waltham MA 02453 781-894-4700 894-1708
Web: www.walthamchamber.com

Watertown-Belmont Chamber of Commerce
182 Main St PO Box 45 . . . . Watertown MA 02471 617-926-1017 926-2322
Web: www.wbcc.org

Wellesley Chamber of Commerce
One Hollis St Ste 232 . . . . Wellesley MA 02482 781-235-2446 235-7326
Web: www.wellesleychamber.org

Greater Westfield Chamber of Commerce
16 N Elm St . . . . Westfield MA 01085 413-568-1618
Web: www.westfieldbiz.org/contact-us.html

Blackstone Valley Chamber of Commerce
110 Church St . . . . Whitinsville MA 01588 508-234-9090 234-5152
TF: 800-841-0919 ■ *Web:* www.blackstonevalley.org

North Suburban Chamber of Commerce
76-R Winn St Ste 3D . . . . Woburn MA 01801 781-933-3499 933-1071
Web: www.northsuburbanchamber.com

Worcester Regional Chamber of Commerce
446 Main St Ste 200 . . . . Worcester MA 01608 508-753-2924 754-8560
Web: www.worcesterchamber.org

Michigan

Phone Fax

Lenawee Economic Development Corp
5285 W US Hwy 223 Ste A . . . . Adrian MI 49221 517-265-5141 263-6065
Web: www.lenaweenow.org

Allen Park Chamber of Commerce
6543 Allen Rd . . . . Allen Park MI 48101 313-382-7303 382-4409
Web: www.allenparkchamber.org

Gratiot Area Chamber of Commerce
110 W Superior St PO Box 516 . . . . Alma MI 48801 989-463-5525 463-6588
Web: www.gratiot.org

Alpena Area Chamber of Commerce
235 W Chisholm St . . . . Alpena MI 49707 989-354-4181 356-3999
TF: 800-425-7362 ■ *Web:* www.alpenachamber.com

Battle Creek Area Chamber of Commerce
One Riverwalk Ctr ste 3A
34 W Jackson St . . . . Battle Creek MI 49017 269-962-4076 962-6309
Web: www.battlecreek.org

Bay Area Chamber of Commerce 901 Saginaw St . . . . Bay City MI 48708 989-893-4567 895-5594
Web: www.baycityarea.com

Belleville Area Chamber of Commerce
248 Main St . . . . Belleville MI 48111 734-697-7151 697-1415
Web: www.belleville areachamber.org

Cornerstone Alliance Chamber Services
38 W Wall St . . . . Benton Harbor MI 49022 269-925-6100 925-4471
Web: www.cstonealliance.org

Mecosta County Area Chamber of Commerce
246 N State St . . . . Big Rapids MI 49307 231-796-7649 796-1625
Web: www.mecostacounty.com

Birmingham-Bloomfield Chamber of Commerce
725 S Adams Rd Ste 130 . . . . Birmingham MI 48009 248-644-1700 644-0286
Web: www.bbcc.com

Greater Brighton Area Chamber of Commerce
218 E Grand Riv . . . . Brighton MI 48116 810-227-5086 227-5940
Web: www.brightoncoc.org

Brooklyn-Irish Hills Chamber of Commerce
131 N Main St PO Box 805 . . . . Brooklyn MI 49230 517-592-8907
Web: irishhills.com

Cadillac Area Chamber of Commerce
222 N Lake St . . . . Cadillac MI 49601 231-775-9776 775-1440
Web: www.cadillac.org

Canton Chamber of Commerce 45525 Hanford Rd . . . . Canton MI 48187 734-453-4040 453-4503
Web: www.cantonchamber.com

Clarkston Area Chamber of Commerce
5856 S Main St . . . . Clarkston MI 48346 248-625-8055 625-8041
Web: www.clarkston.org

Cold Water Area Chamber of Commerce
20 Div St . . . . Coldwater MI 49036 517-278-5985 278-8369
Web: www.branchareachamber.com

Dearborn Chamber of Commerce
22100 Michigan Ave . . . . Dearborn MI 48124 313-584-6100 584-9818
TF: 800-844-5440 ■ *Web:* dearbornareachamber.org

Dearborn Heights Chamber of Commerce
24951 W Warren St Ste 2 . . . . Dearborn Heights MI 48127 313-274-7480 724-0757
Web: www.dearbornareachamber.org

Detroit Regional Chamber
One Woodward Ave Ste 1900 . . . . Detroit MI 48226 313-964-4000 964-0183
Web: detroitchamber.com

Delta County Area Chamber of Commerce
230 Ludington St . . . . Escanaba MI 49829 906-786-2192 786-8830
TF: 888-335-8264 ■ *Web:* www.deltami.org

Ferndale Chamber of Commerce
407 E 9-Mile Rd . . . . Ferndale MI 48220 248-542-2160 542-8979
Web: www.ferndalechamber.com

Genesee Regional Chamber of Commerce
519 S Saginaw St Ste 200 . . . . Flint MI 48502 810-600-1404 600-1461
TF: 888-823-6837 ■ *Web:* www.flintandgenesee.org

Grand Blanc Chamber of Commerce
512 E Grand Blanc Rd . . . . Grand Blanc MI 48439 810-695-4222 695-0053
Web: www.grandblancchamber.com

Chamber of Commerce - Grand Haven-Spring Lake-Ferrysburg
One S Harbor Dr . . . . Grand Haven MI 49417 616-842-4910 842-0379
Web: www.grandhavenchamber.org

Grand Rapids Area Chamber of Commerce
111 Pearl St NW . . . . Grand Rapids MI 49503 616-771-0300 771-0318
Web: www.grandrapids.org

Holland Area Chamber of Commerce
272 E Eigth St . . . . Holland MI 49423 616-392-2389 392-7379
TF: 800-421-3512 ■ *Web:* www.westcoastchamber.org

				Phone	Fax
Keweenaw Peninsula Chamber of Commerce 902 College Ave PO Box 336 *TF:* 800-796-0004 ■ *Web:* www.keweenaw.org	Houghton	MI	49931	906-482-5240	482-5241
Howell Area Chamber of Commerce (HACC) 123 E Washington St *Web:* www.howell.org	Howell	MI	48843	517-546-3920	546-4115
Dickinson Area Partnership 600 S Stephenson Ave *TF:* 888-543-2139 ■ *Web:* www.dickinsonchamber.com	Iron Mountain	MI	49801	906-774-2002	774-2004
Greater Jackson Chamber of Commerce 141 S Jackson St *TF:* 800-366-3699 ■ *Web:* www.jacksonchamber.org	Jackson	MI	49201	517-782-8221	780-3688
Orion Area Chamber of Commerce PO Box 484 Ste 112 *Web:* orionlibrary.org/	Lake Orion	MI	48361	248-693-6300	
Lansing Regional Chamber of Commerce 500 E Michigan Ave Ste 200 *Web:* www.lansingchamber.org	Lansing	MI	48912	517-487-6340	484-6910
Lapeer Area Chamber of Commerce 108 W Pk St *Web:* www.lapeerareachamber.org	Lapeer	MI	48446	810-664-6641	664-4349
Livonia Chamber of Commerce 33233 5 Mile Rd *Web:* www.livonia.org	Livonia	MI	48154	734-427-2122	427-6055
Madison Heights-Hazel Park Chamber of Commerce (MHP) 939 E 12 Mile Rd *Web:* www.madisonheightschamber.com	Madison Heights	MI	48071	248-542-5010	542-6821
Midland Area Chamber of Commerce 300 Rodd St Ste 101 *TF:* 800-715-0074 ■ *Web:* www.macc.org	Midland	MI	48640	989-839-9901	835-3701
Huron Valley Chamber of Commerce 317 Union St *Web:* www.huronvcc.com	Milford	MI	48381	248-685-7129	685-9047
Monroe County Chamber of Commerce 1645 N Dixie Hwy Ste 20 *TF:* 855-386-1280 ■ *Web:* monroecountychamber.com	Monroe	MI	48162	734-384-3366	384-3367
Macomb County Chamber 28 First St Ste B *TF:* 800-564-3136 ■ *Web:* macombcountychamber.com	Mount Clemens	MI	48043	586-493-7600	493-7602
Macomb County Chamber of Commerce 28 First St *Web:* macombcountychamber.com	Mount Clemens	MI	48043	586-493-7600	493-7602
Muskegon Area Chamber of Commerce 380 W Western Ste 202 *TF:* 800-659-2955 ■ *Web:* www.muskegon.org	Muskegon	MI	49440	231-722-3751	728-7251
Anchor Bay Chamber of Commerce (ABCC) 36341 Front St Ste 2 *Web:* www.suscc.com	New Baltimore	MI	48047	586-725-5148	725-5369
Four Flags Area Chamber of Commerce 321 E Main St *Web:* www.nilesmi.com	Niles	MI	49120	269-683-3720	683-3722
Novi Chamber of Commerce, The 41875 W 11 Mile Rd Ste 201 *TF:* 888-440-7325 ■ *Web:* www.novichamber.com	Novi	MI	48375	248-349-3743	349-9719
Petoskey Regional Chamber of Commerce 401 E Mitchell St *Web:* www.petoskey.com	Petoskey	MI	49770	231-347-4150	348-1810
Plymouth Community Chamber of Commerce 850 W Ann Arbor Trl *Web:* www.plymouthchamber.org	Plymouth	MI	48170	734-453-1540	453-1724
Pontiac Regional Chamber of Commerce 402 N Telegraph Rd *Web:* www.pontiacchamber.com	Pontiac	MI	48341	248-335-9600	335-9601
Blue Water Area Chamber of Commerce 512 McMorran Blvd *TF:* 800-361-0526 ■ *Web:* www.bluewaterchamber.com	Port Huron	MI	48060	810-985-7101	985-7311
Redford Township Chamber of Commerce 26050 5-Mile Rd *Web:* www.redfordchamber.com	Redford	MI	48239	313-535-0960	535-6356
Rockford Area Chamber of Commerce 598 Byrne Industrial Dr *Web:* www.rockfordmichamber.com	Rockford	MI	49341	616-866-2000	866-2141
Romeo-Washington Chamber of Commerce 228 N Main St PO Box 175 *Web:* www.rwchamber.com	Romeo	MI	48065	586-752-4436	752-2835
Saginaw County Chamber of Commerce 515 N Washington Ave 2nd Fl *TF:* 888-609-8342 ■ *Web:* www.saginawchamber.org	Saginaw	MI	48607	989-752-7161	752-9055
Sault Area Chamber of Commerce 2581 I-75 Business Spur *Web:* www.saultstemarie.org	Sault Sainte Marie	MI	49783	906-632-3301	632-2331
South Lyon Area Chamber of Commerce 125 N Lafayette St *Web:* www.southlyonchamber.com	South Lyon	MI	48178	248-760-6308	437-4116
Southfield Chamber of Commerce 24300 Southfield Rd Ste 101 *Web:* www.southfieldchamber.com	Southfield	MI	48075	248-557-6661	557-3931
Sterling Heights Area Chamber of Commerce 12900 Hall Rd Ste 190 *Web:* www.suscc.com	Sterling Heights	MI	48313	586-731-5400	731-3521
Southern Wayne County Chamber of Commerce 20904 Northline Rd *Web:* swcrc.com	Taylor	MI	48180	734-284-6000	284-0198
Traverse City Area Chamber of Commerce 202 E Grandview Pkwy *TF:* 800-942-5322 ■ *Web:* www.tcchamber.org	Traverse City	MI	49684	231-947-5075	946-2565
Troy Chamber of Commerce 4555 Investment Dr Ste 300 *Web:* www.troychamber.com	Troy	MI	48098	248-641-8151	641-0545
Lakes Area Chamber of Commerce 305 N Pontiac Trl Ste B *Web:* www.lakesareachamber.com	Walled Lake	MI	48390	248-624-2826	624-2892
West Bloomfield Chamber of Commerce 5745 W Maple Rd Ste 206 *Web:* www.westbloomfieldchamber.com	West Bloomfield	MI	48322	248-626-3636	626-4218
Westland Chamber of Commerce 36900 Ford Rd *TF:* 800-737-4859 ■ *Web:* www.westlandchamber.com	Westland	MI	48185	734-326-7222	326-6040
Wyoming-Kentwood Area Chamber of Commerce 590 32nd St SE *Web:* www.southkent.org	Wyoming	MI	49548	616-531-5990	531-0252

Minnesota

				Phone	Fax
Albert Lea-Freeborn County Chamber of Commerce 2580 Bridge Ave *Web:* www.albertlea.org	Albert Lea	MN	56007	507-373-3938	373-0344
Alexandria Lakes Area Chamber of Commerce 206 Broadway *TF:* 800-235-9441 ■ *Web:* www.alexandriamn.org	Alexandria	MN	56308	320-763-3161	763-6857
Anoka Area Chamber of Commerce 12 Bridge Sq *Web:* www.anokaareachamber.com	Anoka	MN	55303	763-421-7130	421-0577
Apple Valley Chamber of Commerce 14800 Galaxie Ave Ste 101 *TF:* 800-301-9435 ■ *Web:* www.applevalleychamber.com	Apple Valley	MN	55124	952-432-8422	432-7964
Bemidji Area Chamber of Commerce 300 Bemidji Ave *TF:* 800-458-2223 ■ *Web:* www.bemidji.org	Bemidji	MN	56601	218-444-3541	444-4276
Brainerd Lakes Area Chamber of Commerce 124 N Sixth St PO Box 356 *TF:* 800-450-2838 ■ *Web:* www.explorebrainerdlakes.com	Brainerd	MN	56401	218-829-2838	829-8199
Burnsville Chamber of Commerce 101 W Burnsville Pkwy Ste 101 *Web:* www.burnsvillechamber.com	Burnsville	MN	55337	952-435-6000	435-6972
Cloquet Area Chamber of Commerce 225 Sunnyside Dr *TF:* 800-554-4350 ■ *Web:* www.cloquet.com	Cloquet	MN	55720	218-879-1551	878-0223
Cottage Grove Area Chamber of Commerce 7516 80th St S Ste 205 PO Box 16 *Web:* www.cottagegrovechamber.org	Cottage Grove	MN	55016	651-458-8334	458-8383
Detroit Lakes Regional Chamber of Commerce 700 Summit Ave *TF:* 800-542-3992 ■ *Web:* www.visitdetroitlakes.com	Detroit Lakes	MN	56501	218-847-9202	847-9082
Duluth Area Chamber of Commerce 5 W First St Ste 101 *TF:* 800-385-8842 ■ *Web:* www.duluthchamber.com	Duluth	MN	55802	218-722-5501	722-3223
Dakota County Regional Chamber of Commerce 1121 Town Ctr Dr Ste 102 *Web:* www.dcrchamber.com	Eagan	MN	55123	651-452-9872	452-8978
Eden Prairie Chamber of Commerce 11455 Viking Dr Ste 270 *Web:* www.epchamber.org	Eden Prairie	MN	55344	952-944-2830	944-0229
Forest Lake Area Chamber of Commerce 56 E Broadway Ave *Web:* www.flacc.org	Forest Lake	MN	55025	651-464-3200	464-3201
Hastings Area Chamber of Commerce & Tourism Bureau 111 E Third St *TF:* 888-612-6122 ■ *Web:* www.hastingsmn.org	Hastings	MN	55033	651-437-6775	437-2697
River Heights Chamber of Commerce 5782 Blackshire Path *Web:* www.riverheights.com	Inver Grove Heights	MN	55076	651-451-2266	451-0846
Lakeville Area Chamber of Commerce & Convention & Visitors Bureau 19950 Dodd Blvd Ste 101 *TF:* 888-525-3845 ■ *Web:* www.lakevillechamber.org	Lakeville	MN	55044	952-469-2020	469-2028
Minneapolis Regional Chamber of Commerce 81 S Ninth St Ste 200 *Web:* www.minneapolischamber.org	Minneapolis	MN	55402	612-370-9100	370-9195
Richfield Chamber of Commerce 6601 Lyndale Ave S Ste 106 *Web:* richfieldmnchamber.org	Minneapolis	MN	55423	612-866-5100	861-8302
Chamber of Commerce of Fargo Moorhead 202 First Ave N *Web:* www.fmchamber.com	Moorhead	MN	56560	218-233-1100	233-1200
Twin Cities North Chamber of Commerce 525 Main St Ste 200 *Web:* www.twincitiesnorth.org	New Brighton	MN	55112	763-571-9781	572-7950
North Hennepin Chamber of Commerce 229 First Ave NE *Web:* www.nhachamber.com	Osseo	MN	55369	763-424-6744	424-6927
Owatonna Area Chamber of Commerce & Tourism 320 Hoffman Dr *TF:* 800-423-6466 ■ *Web:* www.owatonna.org	Owatonna	MN	55060	507-451-7970	451-7972
TwinWest Chamber of Commerce 10700 Old County Rd 15 *Web:* www.twinwest.com	Plymouth	MN	55441	763-450-2220	450-2221
Rochester Area Chamber of Commerce 220 S Broadway Ste 100 *Web:* www.rochestermnchamber.com	Rochester	MN	55904	507-288-1122	282-8960
Saint Paul Area Chamber of Commerce 401 N Robert St Ste 150 *Web:* www.saintpaulchamber.com	Saint Paul	MN	55101	651-223-5000	223-5119
Greater Stillwater Chamber of Commerce 200 Chestnut St E Ste 204 *Web:* www.ilovestillwater.com	Stillwater	MN	55082	651-439-4001	439-4035
Leech Lake Area Chamber of Commerce 205 Minnesota Ave E *TF:* 800-833-1118 ■ *Web:* www.leech-lake.com	Walker	MN	56484	218-547-1313	547-1338
White Bear Lake Area Chamber of Commerce 4751 Hwy 61 *Web:* www.whitebearchamber.com	White Bearlake	MN	55110	651-429-8593	429-8592
Willmar Lakes Area Chamber of Commerce 2104 Hwy 12 E *Web:* www.willmarareachamber.com	Willmar	MN	56201	320-235-0300	231-1948

Mississippi

				Phone	Fax
Panola Partnership Inc 150-A Public Sq *TF:* 888-872-6652 ■ *Web:* www.panolacounty.com	Batesville	MS	38606	662-563-3126	563-0704

	City	State	Zip	Phone	Fax
Rankin County Chamber of Commerce 101 Service Dr *TF:* 800-987-8280 ■ *Web:* www.rankinchamber.com	Brandon	MS	39043	601-825-2268	825-1977
Brookhaven-Lincoln County Chamber of Commerce 230 S Whitworth Ave *TF:* 800-613-4667 ■ *Web:* brookhavenchamber.org	Brookhaven	MS	39601	601-833-1411	833-1412
Clarksdale-Coahoma County Chamber of Commerce & Industrial Foundation 1540 DeSoto Ave *TF:* 800-626-3764 ■ *Web:* www.clarksdale.com	Clarksdale	MS	38614	662-627-7337	627-1313
Cleveland-Bolivar County Chamber of Commerce 600 Third St *Web:* clevelandmschamber.com	Cleveland	MS	38732	662-843-2712	843-2718
Marion County Development Partnership (MCDP) 412 Courthouse Sq PO Box 272 *Web:* www.mcdp.info	Columbia	MS	39429	601-736-6385	736-6392
Alliance, The 810 Tate St *TF:* 877-347-0545 ■ *Web:* www.corinthalliance.com	Corinth	MS	38834	662-287-5269	
Greenwood-Leflore County Chamber of Commerce 402 Hwy 82 *Web:* www.greenwoodms.com	Greenwood	MS	38930	662-453-4152	453-8003
Gulfport Chamber of Commerce 11975-E Seaway Rd *Web:* mscoastchamber.com	Gulfport	MS	39503	228-604-0014	604-0105
Mississippi Gulf Coast Chamber of Commerce 11975-E Seaway Rd *Web:* www.mscoastchamber.com	Gulfport	MS	39503	228-604-0014	604-0105
Area Development Partnership One Convention Ctr Plz *TF:* 800-238-4288 ■ *Web:* www.theadp.com	Hattiesburg	MS	39401	601-296-7500	296-7505
Greater Jackson Chamber Partnership PO Box 22548 *Web:* www.greaterjacksonpartnership.com	Jackson	MS	39225	601-948-7575	352-5539
Jones County Chamber of Commerce PO Box 527 *TF General:* 800-392-9629 ■ *Web:* jonescounty.com	Laurel	MS	39441	601-649-3031	428-2047
Pike County Chamber of Commerce & Economic Development District 112 N Railroad Blvd *TF:* 800-844-2653 ■ *Web:* www.pikeinfo.com	McComb	MS	39648	601-684-2291	684-4899
East Mississippi Business Development Corp 1901 Front St P.O Box 790 *Web:* www.embdc.org	Meridian	MS	39302	601-693-1306	693-5638
Natchez-Adams County Chamber of Commerce 108 S Commerce St *Web:* www.natchezchamber.com	Natchez	MS	39120	601-445-4611	445-9361
Olive Branch Chamber of Commerce 9123 Pigeon Roost PO Box 608 *Web:* www.olivebranchms.com	Olive Branch	MS	38654	662-895-2600	895-2625
Oxford-Lafayette County Chamber of Commerce 299 W Jackson Ave *TF:* 800-880-6967 ■ *Web:* www.oxfordms.com	Oxford	MS	38655	662-234-4651	234-4655
Community Development Partnership 410 Poplar Ave 256 W Beacon *TF:* 877-752-2643 ■ *Web:* www.neshoba.org	Philadelphia	MS	39350	601-656-1000	656-1066
Madison County Chamber of Commerce 618 Crescent Blvd Ste 101 *Web:* www.madisoncountychamber.com	Ridgeland	MS	39157	601-605-2554	605-2260
Southaven Chamber of Commerce 8700 NW Dr Ste 100 *Web:* www.southavenchamber.com	Southaven	MS	38671	662-342-6114	342-6365
Greater Starkville Development Partnership 200 E Main St *TF:* 800-649-8687 ■ *Web:* www.starkville.org	Starkville	MS	39759	662-323-3322	323-5815
Vicksburg-Warren County Chamber of Commerce 2020 Mission 66 *Web:* www.vicksburgchamber.org	Vicksburg	MS	39180	601-636-1012	636-4422
Yazoo County Chamber of Commerce 212 E Broadway Ste 7 *TF:* 800-638-6582 ■ *Web:* uschamber.com	Yazoo City	MS	39194	662-746-1273	746-7238

Missouri

	City	State	Zip	Phone	Fax
Affton Chamber of Commerce 10203 Gravois Rd *Web:* www.递afftonchamber.com	Affton	MO	63123	314-631-3100	849-6399
Blue Springs Chamber of Commerce 1000 W Main St *Web:* bluespringschamber.com	Blue Springs	MO	64015	816-229-8558	229-1244
Branson/Lakes Area Chamber of Commerce PO Box 1897 *TF:* 800-214-3661 ■ *Web:* www.bransonchamber.com	Branson	MO	65615	417-334-4084	334-4139
Northwest Chamber of Commerce 11965 St Charles Rock Rd Ste 203 *Web:* www.northwestchamber.com	Bridgeton	MO	63044	314-291-2131	291-2153
Cape Girardeau Area Chamber of Commerce 1267 N Mt Auburn Rd *Web:* www.capechamber.com	Cape Girardeau	MO	63701	573-335-3312	335-4686
Cassville Area Chamber of Commerce 504 Main St *Web:* www.cassville.com	Cassville	MO	65625	417-847-2814	847-0804
Chesterfield Chamber of Commerce 101 Chesterfield Business Pkwy *TF:* 888-242-4262 ■ *Web:* www.chesterfieldmochamber.com	Chesterfield	MO	63005	636-532-3399	532-7446
Columbia Chamber of Commerce 300 S Providence Rd *Web:* www.columbiamochamber.com	Columbia	MO	65203	573-874-1132	443-3986
West Saint Louis County Chamber of Commerce 15965 Manchester Rd Ste 102 *Web:* www.westcountychamber.com	Ellisville	MO	63011	636-230-9900	230-9912
Twin City Area Chamber of Commerce 114 Main St *Web:* www.twincity.org	Festus	MO	63028	636-931-7697	937-0925
Greater North County Chamber of Commerce 420 W Washington St *Web:* greaternorthcountychamber.com	Florissant	MO	63031	314-831-3500	831-9682
Kingdom of Callaway Chamber of Commerce 409 Ct St *TF:* 800-257-3554 ■ *Web:* fultonmochamber.com/	Fulton	MO	65251	573-642-3055	642-5182
Gladstone Area Chamber of Commerce 6913 N Cherry *Web:* gladstonechamber.com	Gladstone	MO	64118	816-436-4523	436-4352
Independence Chamber of Commerce 210 W Truman Rd *Web:* ichamber.biz	Independence	MO	64050	816-252-4745	252-4917
Jefferson City Area Chamber of Commerce 213 Adams St *TF:* 866-223-6535 ■ *Web:* www.jcchamber.org	Jefferson City	MO	65101	573-634-3616	634-3805
Joplin Area Chamber of Commerce 320 E Fourth St *Web:* www.joplincc.com	Joplin	MO	64801	417-624-4150	624-4303
Greater Kansas City Chamber of Commerce 911 Main St Ste 2600 *TF:* 800-767-7700 ■ *Web:* www.kcchamber.com	Kansas City	MO	64105	816-221-2424	221-7440
Northland Regional Chamber of Commerce 634 NW Englewood Rd *Web:* www.northlandchamber.com	Kansas City	MO	64118	816-455-9911	455-9933
South Kansas City Chamber of Commerce 406 E Bannister Rd Ste F *Web:* southkcchamber.com	Kansas City	MO	64131	816-761-7660	761-7340
Lebanon Area Chamber of Commerce 186 N Adams St *TF:* 888-588-5710 ■ *Web:* www.lebanonmissouri.com	Lebanon	MO	65536	417-588-3256	588-3251
Lee's Summit Chamber of Commerce 220 SE Main St *TF:* 888-816-5757 ■ *Web:* lschamber.com	Lee's Summit	MO	64063	816-524-2424	524-5246
Kirkwood-Des Peres Area Chamber of Commerce 108 W Adams Ave *Web:* www.kirkwooddesperes.com	Louis	MO	63122	314-821-4161	821-5229
Neosho Area Chamber of Commerce 216 W Spring St *Web:* www.neoshocc.com	Neosho	MO	64850	417-451-1925	451-8097
O'Fallon Chamber of Commerce 2145 Bryan Vly Commercial Dr *Web:* www.ofallonchamber.org	O'Fallon	MO	63366	636-240-1818	
Park Hills Leadington Chamber of Commerce (PHLCOC) 12 Municipal Dr *Web:* www.phlcoc.net	Park Hills	MO	63601	573-431-1051	431-2327
Raytown Area Chamber of Commerce 5909 Raytown Trafficway *Web:* www.raytownchamber.com	Raytown	MO	64133	816-353-8500	353-8525
Rolla Area Chamber of Commerce 1311 KingsHwy *TF:* 888-809-3817 ■ *Web:* www.rollachamber.org	Rolla	MO	65401	573-364-3577	364-5222
Saint Charles Chamber of Commerce 2201 First Capitol Dr *Web:* www.gstccc.com	Saint Charles	MO	63301	636-946-0633	946-0301
Saint Joseph Area Chamber of Commerce 3003 Frederick Ave *TF:* 800-748-7856 ■ *Web:* www.saintjoseph.com	Saint Joseph	MO	64506	816-232-4461	364-4873
Maryland Heights Chamber of Commerce 547 W Port Plz *Web:* www.mhcc.com	Saint Louis	MO	63146	314-576-6603	576-6855
South County Chamber of Commerce 4179 Crescent Dr Ste A *Web:* southcountychamber.org	Saint Louis	MO	63129	314-894-6800	
Waynesville-Saint Robert Area Chamber of Commerce 137 St Robert Blvd Ste B *Web:* www.waynesville-strobertchamber.com	Saint Robert	MO	65584	573-336-5121	336-5472
Sedalia Area Chamber of Commerce 600 E Third St *Web:* www.sedaliachamber.com	Sedalia	MO	65301	660-826-2222	826-2223
Springfield Area Chamber of Commerce 202 S John Q Hammons Pkwy *Web:* www.springfieldchamber.com	Springfield	MO	65806	417-862-5567	862-1611
Washington Area Chamber of Commerce 323 W Main St *Web:* www.washmo.org	Washington	MO	63090	636-239-2715	239-1381

Montana

	City	State	Zip	Phone	Fax
Billings Area Chamber of Commerce 815 S 27th St *TF:* 855-328-9116 ■ *Web:* www.billingschamber.com	Billings	MT	59101	406-245-4111	245-7333
Bozeman Area Chamber of Commerce 2000 Commerce Way *Web:* www.bozemanchamber.com	Bozeman	MT	59715	406-586-5421	586-8286
Butte-Silver Bow Chamber of Commerce 1000 George St *TF:* 800-735-6814 ■ *Web:* www.buttechamber.org	Butte	MT	59701	406-723-3177	723-1215
Great Falls Area Chamber of Commerce 100 First Ave N *TF:* 800-735-8535 ■ *Web:* www.greatfallschamber.org	Great Falls	MT	59401	406-761-4434	761-6129
Bitterroot Valley Chamber of Commerce 105 E Main St *Web:* bitterrootchamber.com	Hamilton	MT	59840	406-363-2400	363-2402
Helena Area Chamber of Commerce 225 Cruse Ave *TF:* 800-743-5362 ■ *Web:* www.helenachamber.com	Helena	MT	59601	406-442-4120	447-1532
Kalispell Area Chamber of Commerce 15 Depot Pk *Web:* www.kalispellchamber.com	Kalispell	MT	59901	406-758-2800	758-2805
Missoula Area Chamber of Commerce 825 E Front St *TF:* 800-814-2342 ■ *Web:* www.missoulachamber.com	Missoula	MT	59802	406-543-6623	543-6625

Nebraska

Phone *Fax*

Bellevue Chamber of Commerce
1102 Galvin Rd S .... Bellevue NE 68005 402-898-3000 291-8729
Web: www.bellevuenebraska.com

Grand Island Area Chamber of Commerce
309 W Second St .... Grand Island NE 68802 308-382-9210 382-1154
Web: gichamber.com

Kearney Area Chamber of Commerce
1007 Second Ave PO Box 607 .... Kearney NE 68848 308-237-3101 237-3103
TF: 800-227-8340 ■ *Web:* www.kearneycoc.org

Lincoln Chamber of Commerce
1135 M St PO Box 83006 .... Lincoln NE 68508 402-436-2350 436-2360
Web: www.lcoc.com

North Platte Area Chamber & Development
502 S Dewey St .... North Platte NE 69101 308-532-4966 532-4827
Web: www.nparea.com

Greater Omaha Chamber of Commerce
1301 Harney St .... Omaha NE 68102 402-346-5000 346-7050
Web: www.omahachamber.org

Sarpy County Chamber of Commerce
7775 Olson Dr Ste 207 .... Papillion NE 68046 402-339-3050 339-9968
Web: www.sarpychamber.org

Nevada

Phone *Fax*

Carson City Area Chamber of Commerce
1900 S Carson St Ste 200 .... Carson City NV 89701 775-882-1565 882-4179
Web: www.carsoncitychamber.com

Elko Area Chamber of Commerce 1405 Idaho St .... Elko NV 89801 775-738-7135 738-7136
Web: www.elkonevada.com

Fallon Chamber of Commerce 85 N Taylor St .... Fallon NV 89406 775-423-2544 423-0540
Web: www.fallonchamber.com

Carson Valley Chamber of Commerce & Visitors Authority
1477 Hwy 395 N Ste A .... Gardnerville NV 89410 775-782-8144 782-1025
TF: 800-727-7677 ■ *Web:* www.carsonvalleynv.org

Henderson Chamber of Commerce
590 S Boulder Hwy .... Henderson NV 89015 702-565-8951 565-3115
Web: www.hendersonchamber.com

Las Vegas Chamber of Commerce
575 Symphony Park Ave Ste 100 .... Las Vegas NV 89105 702-641-5822 735-0406
TF: 888-635-7272 ■ *Web:* www.lvchamber.com

Latin Chamber of Commerce 300 N 13th St .... Las Vegas NV 89101 702-385-7367 385-2614
Web: www.lvlcc.com

North Las Vegas Chamber of Commerce
3365 W Craig Rd Ste 25 .... North Las Vegas NV 89032 702-642-9595 642-0439
Web: www.nlvchamber.org

Lake Tahoe Chamber of Commerce 169 Hwy 50 .... Stateline NV 89449 775-588-1728 588-1941
Web: www.tahoechamber.org

Tonopah Chamber of Commerce 301 Brougher Ave .... Tonopah NV 89049 775-482-3859
Web: www.tonopahnevada.com

New Hampshire

Phone *Fax*

Souhegan Valley Chamber of Commerce
69 New Hampshire 101A .... Amherst NH 03031 603-673-4360 673-5018
Web: www.souhegan.net

Greater Derry Chamber of Commerce
29 W Broadway .... Derry NH 03038 603-432-8205 432-7938
Web: www.gdlchamber.org

Greater Dover Chamber of Commerce
550 Central Ave .... Dover NH 03820 603-742-2218 749-6317
Web: www.dovernh.org

Hampton Area Chamber of Commerce
One Layfayette Rd .... Hampton NH 03842 603-926-8718 926-9977
Web: www.hamptonchamber.com

Greater Keene Chamber of Commerce
48 Central Sq .... Keene NH 03431 603-352-1303 358-5341
Web: www.keenechamber.com

Lakes Region Chamber 383 S Main St .... Laconia NH 03246 603-524-5531
Web: lakesregionchamber.org

Greater Nashua Chamber of Commerce
142 Main St .... Nashua NH 03060 603-881-8333 881-7323
Web: www.nashuachamber.com

Greater Portsmouth Chamber of Commerce
500 Market St PO Box 239 .... Portsmouth NH 03802 603-610-5510 436-5118
Web: www.portsmouthchamber.org

Greater Rochester Chamber of Commerce
18 S Main St .... Rochester NH 03867 603-332-5080 332-5216
Web: www.rochesternh.org

Greater Salem Chamber of Commerce 81 Main St .... Salem NH 03079 603-893-3177 894-5158
Web: www.gschamber.com

New Jersey

Phone *Fax*

Asbury Park Chamber of Commerce
1201 Springwood Ave .... Asbury Park NJ 07712 732-775-7676 775-7675
Web: www.asburyparkchamber.com

Greater Atlantic City Chamber
12 S Virginia Ave .... Atlantic City NJ 08401 609-345-4524 345-1666
TF: 800-123-4567 ■ *Web:* acchamber.com

Bayonne Chamber of Commerce 621 Ave C .... Bayonne NJ 07002 201-436-4333 436-8546
Web: www.bayonnenj.org

Brick Township Chamber of Commerce
270 Chambers Bridge Rd .... Brick NJ 08723 732-477-4949 477-5788
TF: 877-539-2020 ■ *Web:* brickchamber.com

Phone *Fax*

Bridgeton Area Chamber of Commerce
76 Magnolia Ave PO Box 1063 .... Bridgeton NJ 08302 856-455-1312 453-9795
Web: www.baccnj.com

Somerset County Business Partnership
360 Grove St .... Bridgewater NJ 08807 908-218-4300 722-7823
Web: www.scbp.org

Cape May County Chamber of Commerce
13 Crest Haven Rd PO Box 74 .... Cape May Court House NJ 08210 609-465-7181 465-5017
Web: www.capemaycountychamber.com

Cherry Hill Regional Chamber of Commerce
1060 Kings Hwy N Ste 200 .... Cherry Hill NJ 08034 856-667-1600 667-1464
TF: 800-669-6801 ■ *Web:* camdencountychamber.com

North Jersey Regional Chamber of Commerce
1033 Rt. 46 E Ste A103 .... Clifton NJ 07013 973-470-9300 470-9245
Web: northjerseychamber.org/

Edison Chamber of Commerce
336 Raritan Ctr Pkwy .... Edison NJ 08837 732-738-9482 738-9485
Web: www.edisonchamber.com

Gateway Regional Chamber of Commerce
135 Jefferson Ave PO Box 300 .... Elizabeth NJ 07207 908-352-0900 352-0865
Web: www.gatewaychamber.com

Englewood Chamber of Commerce
2-10 N Van Brunt St .... Englewood NJ 07631 201-567-2381
Web: www.englewood-chamber.com

Fair Lawn Chamber of Commerce
12-45 River Rd .... Fair Lawn NJ 07410 201-796-7050 475-0619
Web: www.fairlawnchamber.org

Hunterdon County Chamber of Commerce
14 Mine St .... Flemington NJ 08822 908-782-7115 782-7283
Web: www.hunterdon-chamber.org

Greater Fort Lee Chamber of Commerce (GFLCOC)
210 Whiteman St .... Fort Lee NJ 07024 201-944-7575 944-5168
Web: www.fortleechamber.com

Greater Monmouth Chamber of Commerce
57 Schanck Rd Ste C-3 .... Freehold NJ 07728 732-462-3030 462-2123
TF: 800-700-6400 ■ *Web:* www.greatermonmouthchamber.com

Greater Hackensack Chamber of Commerce
Five University Plz Dr .... Hackensack NJ 07601 201-489-3700 489-1741
Web: www.hackensackchamber.org

MIDJersey Chamber of Commerce
1A Quakerbridge Plaza Dr Ste 2 .... Hamilton NJ 08619 609-689-9960
Web: www.midjerseychamber.org

Greater Hammonton Chamber of Commerce
PO Box 554 .... Hammonton NJ 08037 609-561-9080 561-9411
Web: www.hammontonnj.us

Northern Monmouth Chamber of Commerce
1340 State Hwy 36 Ste 22 Ste 22 .... Hazlet NJ 07730 732-203-0340 676-7778
Web: www.monmouthcountychamber.com

Howell Chamber of Commerce
103 W Second St PO Box 196 .... Howell NJ 07731 732-363-4114 363-8747
Web: www.howellchamber.com

Hudson County Chamber of Commerce
857 Bergen Ave Third Fl .... Jersey City NJ 07306 201-386-0699 386-8480
Web: www.hudsonchamber.org

Parsippany Area Chamber of Commerce
14 N Beverwyck Rd .... Lake Hiawatha NJ 07034 973-402-6400
Web: www.parsippanychamber.org

Greater Long Branch Chamber of Commerce
228 Broadway PO Box 628 .... Long Branch NJ 07740 732-222-0400 571-3385
Web: www.longbranchchamber.org

Matawan-Aberdeen Chamber of Commerce
201 Broad St PO Box 522 .... Matawan NJ 07747 732-290-1125 290-1125
Web: macocnj.com

Millville Chamber of Commerce
Four City Pk Dr .... Millville NJ 08332 856-825-2600 825-5333
Web: www.millville-nj.com

North Essex Chamber of Commerce
26 Park St Ste 2062 .... Montclair NJ 07042 973-226-5500 783-4407
Web: www.northessexchamber.com

Morris County Chamber of Commerce
25 Lindsley Dr Ste 105 .... Morristown NJ 07960 973-539-3882 539-3960
Web: www.morrischamber.org

Randolph Area Chamber of Commerce
PO Box 391 .... Mount Freedom NJ 07970 973-361-3462 895-3297
Web: www.randolphchamber.org

Burlington County Regional Chamber of Commerce
100 Technology Way Ste 110 .... Mount Laurel NJ 08054 856-439-2520 439-2523
Web: www.bccoc.com

Middlesex County Regional Chamber of Commerce
109 Church St .... New Brunswick NJ 08901 732-745-8090 745-8098
Web: www.mcrcc.org

Newark Regional Business Partnership
744 Broad St 26th Fl .... Newark NJ 07102 973-522-0099 824-6587
TF: 800-662-6878 ■ *Web:* www.newarkrbp.org

Sussex County Chamber of Commerce
120 Hampton House Rd .... Newton NJ 07860 973-579-1811 579-3031
TF: 844-256-7328 ■ *Web:* www.sussexcountychamber.org

Nutley Chamber of Commerce 172 Chestnut St .... Nutley NJ 07110 973-667-5300
Web: www.nutleychamber.com

Commerce & Industry Assn of New Jersey (CIANJ)
61 S Paramus Rd .... Paramus NJ 07652 201-368-2100 368-3438
Web: www.cianj.org

Greater Paramus Chamber of Commerce
58 E Midland Ave .... Paramus NJ 07652 201-261-3344 261-3346
Web: paramuschamber.org

Greater Paterson Chamber of Commerce
100 Hamilton Plaza Ste 1201 .... Paterson NJ 07505 973-881-7300 881-8233
TF: 800-220-2892 ■ *Web:* www.greaterpatersoncc.org

Piscataway/Middlesex/South Plainfield Chamber of Commerce
275 Old New Brunswick Rd Ste 105 .... Piscataway NJ 08854 732-394-0220 394-0223

Point Pleasant Beach Chamber of Commerce
517-A Arnold Ave .... Point Pleasant Beach NJ 08742 732-899-2424 899-0103
Web: pointpleasantbeachchamber.com

Phone Fax

Princeton Regional Chamber of Commerce
9 Vandeventer Ave ... Princeton NJ 08542 609-924-1776 924-5776
Web: www.princetonchamber.org

Meadowlands Regional Chamber of Commerce
201 Rt 17 ... Rutherford NJ 07070 201-939-0707 939-0522
Web: www.meadowlands.org

Southern Ocean County Chamber of Commerce
265 W Ninth St ... Ship Bottom NJ 08008 609-494-7211 494-5807
TF: 800-292-6372 ■ *Web:* www.visitlbiregion.com

Franklin Township Chamber of Commerce
675 Franklin Blvd ... Somerset NJ 08873 732-545-7044 545-7043
Web: www.franklinchamber.com

Suburban Chambers of Commerce 71 Summit Ave ... Summit NJ 07901 908-522-1700 522-9252
Web: www.suburbanchambers.org

Toms River-Ocean County Chamber of Commerce
1200 Hooper Ave ... Toms River NJ 08753 732-349-0220 349-1252
Web: www.oc-chamber.com

Union Township Chamber of Commerce
355 Chestnut St Second Fl ... Union NJ 07083 908-688-2777 688-0338
Web: www.unionchamber.com

Greater Vineland Chamber of Commerce
2115 S Delsea Dr ... Vineland NJ 08360 856-691-7400 691-2113
TF: 800-922-1766 ■ *Web:* www.vinelandchamber.org

Chamber of Commerce of Southern New Jersey
4015 Main St ... Voorhees NJ 08043 856-424-7776 424-8180
Web: www.chambersnj.com

Jersey Shore Chamber of Commerce
2510 Belmar Blvd Ste I-20 ... Wall NJ 07719 732-280-8800 280-8505
Web: www.southernmonmouthchamber.com

Tri-County Chamber of Commerce
2055 Hamburg Tpke ... Wayne NJ 07470 973-831-7788 831-9112
Web: www.tricounty.org

Westfield Area Chamber of Commerce (WACC)
173 Elm St Third Fl ... Westfield NJ 07090 908-233-3021 654-8183
Web: www.westfieldareachamber.com

New Mexico

Phone Fax

Alamogordo Chamber of Commerce
1301 N White Sands Blvd ... Alamogordo NM 88310 575-437-6120 437-6334
TF: 800-826-0294 ■ *Web:* www.alamogordo.com

Greater Albuquerque Chamber of Commerce
115 Gold Ave SW # 201 ... Albuquerque NM 87102 505-764-3700 764-3714
Web: www.abqchamber.com

Carlsbad Chamber of Commerce
302 S Canal St PO Box 910 ... Carlsbad NM 88220 575-887-6516 885-1455
TF: 866-822-9226 ■ *Web:* www.carlsbadchamber.com

Clovis/Curry County Chamber of Commerce
105 E Third St ... Clovis NM 88101 575-763-3435 763-7266
TF: 800-261-7656 ■ *Web:* www.clovisnm.org

Espanola Valley Chamber of Commerce
One Calle de las Espanolas Ste F & G ... Espanola NM 87532 505-753-2831 753-1252
Web: www.espanolanmchamber.com

Farmington Chamber of Commerce
100 W Broadway ... Farmington NM 87401 505-325-0279 327-7556
Web: www.gofarmington.com

Grants/Cibola County Chamber of Commerce
100 N Iron Ave ... Grants NM 87020 505-287-4802 287-8224
TF: 866-270-5110 ■ *Web:* www.grants.org

Hobbs Chamber of Commerce 400 N Marland Blvd ... Hobbs NM 88240 575-397-3202 397-1689
TF: 800-658-6291 ■ *Web:* www.hobbschamber.org

Greater Las Cruces Chamber of Commerce
760 W Picacho Ave ... Las Cruces NM 88005 575-524-1968 527-5546
Web: www.lascruces.org

Rio Rancho Chamber of Commerce
4001 Southern Blvd SE ... Rio Rancho NM 87124 505-892-1533 892-6157
Web: www.rrchamber.org

Roswell Chamber of Commerce 131 W Second St ... Roswell NM 88202 575-623-5695 624-6870
TF: 877-849-7679 ■ *Web:* www.roswellnm.org

Santa Fe Chamber of Commerce
1644 St Michael's Dr Ste 302 ... Santa Fe NM 87507 505-988-3279 984-2205
Web: www.santafechamber.com

Silver City-Grant County Chamber of Commerce
201 N Hudson St ... Silver City NM 88061 575-538-3785 538-3786
TF: 800-548-9378 ■ *Web:* www.silvercity.org

New York

Phone Fax

Albany-Colonie Regional Chamber of Commerce
5 Computer Dr S ... Albany NY 12205 518-431-1400 431-1402
Web: www.acchamber.org

Orleans County Chamber of Commerce
102 N Main St Ste 1 ... Albion NY 14411 585-589-7727 589-7326
Web: www.orleanschamber.com

Cayuga County Chamber of Commerce
Two State St ... Auburn NY 13021 315-252-7291 255-3077
Web: www.cayugacountychamber.com

Genesee County Chamber of Commerce
210 E Main St ... Batavia NY 14020 585-343-7440 343-7487
TF: 800-622-2686 ■ *Web:* www.geneseeny.com

Steuben County Chamber of Commerce
110 Liberty St PO Box 488 ... Bath NY 14810 607-776-7122 776-7122
Web: www.centralsteubenchamber.com

Bay Shore Chamber of Commerce
77 E Main St PO Box 5110 ... Bay Shore NY 11706 631-665-7003 665-5204
Web: www.bayshorecommerce.com

Greater Binghamton Chamber of Commerce
49 Ct St ... Binghamton NY 13901 607-772-8860 722-4513
Web: www.greaterbinghamtonchamber.com

Phone Fax

Bronx Chamber of Commerce
1200 Waters Pl Ste 106 ... Bronx NY 10461 718-828-3900
Web: www.bronxmall.com

Brooklyn Chamber of Commerce
25 Elm Pl Ste 200 ... Brooklyn NY 11201 718-875-1000 237-4274
Web: www.ibrooklyn.com

Buffalo Niagara Partnership
665 Main St Ste 200 ... Buffalo NY 14203 716-852-7100 852-2761
TF: 800-241-0474 ■ *Web:* www.thepartnership.org

St Lawrence County Chamber of Commerce
101 Main St ... Canton NY 13617 315-386-4000 379-0134
TF: 877-228-7810 ■ *Web:* www.northcountryguide.com

Greene County Chamber of Commerce
327 Main St PO Box 248 ... Catskill NY 12414 518-943-4222 943-1700
Web: greenecountychamberny.com

Cheektowaga Chamber of Commerce
2875 Union Rd Ste 50 ... Cheektowaga NY 14227 716-684-5838 684-5571
Web: www.cheektowaga.org

Chamber of Southern Saratoga County
15 Pk Ave Ste 7-B ... Clifton Park NY 12065 518-371-7748 371-5025
Web: www.southernsaratoga.org

Corning Area Chamber of Commerce
One W Market St Ste 302 ... Corning NY 14830 607-936-4686 936-4685
TF: 866-463-6264 ■ *Web:* www.corningny.com

Bethlehem Chamber of Commerce
318 Delaware Ave Ste 11 ... Delmar NY 12054 518-439-0512 475-0910
Web: www.bethlehemchamber.com

Chautauqua County Chamber of Commerce
10785 Bennett Rd ... Dunkirk NY 14048 716-366-6200 366-4276
Web: www.chautauquachamber.org

Greater East Aurora Chamber of Commerce
652 Main St ... East Aurora NY 14052 716-652-8444 652-8384
Web: www.eanycc.com

Chemung County Chamber of Commerce
400 E Church St ... Elmira NY 14901 607-734-5137 734-4490
TF General: 800-627-5892 ■ *Web:* www.chemungchamber.org

Livingston County Chamber of Commerce
4635 Millennium Dr ... Geneseo NY 14454 585-243-2222 243-4824
TF: 800-538-7365 ■ *Web:* www.fingerlakeswest.com

Adirondack Regional Chambers of Commerce
136 Glen St Ste 3 ... Glens Falls NY 12801 518-798-1761 792-4147
TF: 888-516-7247 ■ *Web:* www.adirondackchamber.org

Guilderland Chamber of Commerce
2050 Western Ave Ste 109 ... Guilderland NY 12084 518-456-6611 456-6690
Web: www.guilderlandchamber.com

Hicksville Chamber of Commerce
10 W Marie St ... Hicksville NY 11801 516-931-7170 931-8546
Web: www.hicksvillechamber.com

Southern Ulster County Chamber of Commerce
3553 Rt 9W PO Box 320 ... Highland NY 12528 845-691-6070 691-9194
Web: www.southernulsterchamber.org

Schoharie County Chamber of Commerce
143 Caverns Rd ... Howes Cave NY 12092 518-296-8820 296-8825
Web: www.schohariechamber.com

Columbia County Chamber of Commerce
507 Warren St ... Hudson NY 12534 518-828-4417 822-9539
Web: columbiachamber-ny.com

Huntington Township Chamber of Commerce
164 Main St ... Huntington NY 11743 631-423-6100 351-8276
TF: 888-962-9932 ■ *Web:* www.huntingtonchamber.com

Hyde Park Chamber of Commerce PO Box 17 ... Hyde Park NY 12538 845-229-8612 229-8638
Web: www.hydeparkchamber.org

Tompkins County Chamber of Commerce
904 E Shore Dr ... Ithaca NY 14850 607-273-7080 272-7617
Web: www.tompkinschamber.org

Queens Chamber of Commerce
75-20 Astoria Blvd Ste 140 ... Jackson Heights NY 11370 718-898-8500 898-8599
TF: 877-256-5556 ■ *Web:* www.queenschamber.org

Jamaica Chamber of Commerce
15711 Rockaway Blvd ... Jamaica NY 11434 718-877-7704
Web: jamaicachambernyc.com

Kenmore-Town of Tonawanda Chamber of Commerce
3411 Delaware Ave ... Kenmore NY 14217 716-874-1202 874-3151
TF: 888-710-6626 ■ *Web:* www.ken-ton.org

Chamber of Commerce of Ulster County
55 Albany Ave ... Kingston NY 12401 845-338-5100 338-0968
Web: www.ulsterchamber.org

Lake Placid/Essex County Visitors Bureau
49 Parkside Dr ... Lake Placid NY 12946 518-523-2445 523-2605
TF: 800-447-5224 ■ *Web:* www.lakeplacid.com

Greater Liverpool Chamber of Commerce
314 Second St ... Liverpool NY 13088 315-457-3895 234-3226
Web: www.liverpoolchamber.com

Long Beach Chamber of Commerce
350 National Blvd ... Long Beach NY 11561 516-432-6000 432-0273
Web: www.thelongbeachchamber.com

Lewis County Chamber of Commerce
7576 S State St ... Lowville NY 13367 315-376-2213 376-0326
TF: 800-724-0242 ■ *Web:* www.lewiscountychamber.org

Greater Mahopacs-Carmel Chamber of Commerce
953 S Lake Blvd PO Box 160 ... Mahopac NY 10541 845-628-5553 628-5962
Web: www.mahopaccarmelonline.com

Chamber of Commerce of the Massapequas Inc
674 Broadway ... Massapequa NY 11758 516-541-1443 541-8625
Web: massapequachamber.org/

Long Island Assn
300 Broadhollow Rd Ste 110-W ... Melville NY 11747 631-499-4400 499-2194
Web: longislandassociation.org

Herkimer County Chamber of Commerce
28 W Main St ... Mohawk NY 13407 315-866-7820 866-7833
TF: 877-984-4636 ■ *Web:* www.herkimercountychamber.com

Orange County Chamber of Commerce
30 Scott's Corners Dr ... Montgomery NY 12549 845-457-9700 457-8799
Web: www.orangeny.com

Phone *Fax*

Sullivan County Chamber of Commerce
457 W Broadway Ste 1 .... Monticello NY 12701 845-791-4200 791-4220
Web: www.catskills.com

Mount Vernon Chamber of Commerce
65 Haven Ave .... Mount Vernon NY 10553 914-667-7500 699-0139
Web: www.mtvernonchamber.org

Chamber of Commerce of New Rochelle
459 Main St .... New Rochelle NY 10801 914-632-5700 632-0708
Web: www.newrochellechamber.org

Greater New York Chamber of Commerce
20 W 44th St Fourth Fl .... New York NY 10036 212-686-7220 686-7232
Web: www.ny-chamber.com

Manhattan Chamber of Commerce
1375 Broadway 3rd F .... New York NY 10018 212-479-7772 473-8074
TF: 855-868-7692 ■ *Web:* www.manhattancc.org

New York City Partnership & Chamber of Commerce Inc
One Battery Pk Plz Fifth Fl .... New York NY 10004 212-493-7400 344-3344
Web: www.pfnyc.org

Chamber of Commerce of the Tonawandas
15 Webster St .... North Tonawanda NY 14120 716-692-5120 692-1867
Web: www.the-tonawandas.com

Commerce Chenango 15 S Broad St .... Norwich NY 13815 607-334-1400 336-6963
Web: www.chenangony.org

Greater Olean Area Chamber of Commerce
120 N Union St .... Olean NY 14760 716-372-4433 372-7912
Web: www.oleanny.com

Otsego County Chamber 189 Main St Ste 201 .... Oneonta NY 13820 607-432-4500 432-4506
Web: otsegocc.com

Orchard Park Chamber of Commerce
4211 N Buffalo St Ste 14 .... Orchard Park NY 14127 716-662-3366 662-5946
Web: orchardparkchamber.org

Greater Oswego-Fulton Chamber of Commerce (GOFCC)
44 E Bridge St .... Oswego NY 13126 315-343-7681 342-0831
Web: www.oswegofultonchamber.com

Tioga County Chamber of Commerce 80 N Ave .... Owego NY 13827 607-687-2020 687-9028
Web: www.tiogachamber.com

Hudson Valley Gateway Chamber of Commerce
One S Div St .... Peekskill NY 10566 914-737-3600 737-0541
Web: www.hvgatewaychamber.com

Plattsburgh North Country Chamber of Commerce
7061 Rt 9 .... Plattsburgh NY 12901 518-563-1000 563-1028
Web: www.northcountrychamber.com

Tri-State Chamber of Commerce
5 S Broome St .... Port Jervis NY 12771 845-856-6694 856-6695
TF: 800-707-6925 ■ *Web:* tristatechamber.org

Port Washington Chamber of Commerce
329 Main St .... Port Washington NY 11050 516-883-6566 883-6591
Web: www.pwguide.com

Dutchess County Regional Chamber of Commerce
1 Civic Ctr Plaza Ste 400 .... Poughkeepsie NY 12601 845-454-1700 454-1702
TF: 800-817-2918 ■ *Web:* www.dcrcoc.org

Rochester Business Alliance 150 State St .... Rochester NY 14614 585-244-1800 263-3679
Web: www.rochesterbusinessalliance.com

Rome Area Chamber of Commerce 139 W Dominick St ... Rome NY 13440 315-337-1700 337-1715
Web: www.romechamber.com

Niagara USA Chamber of Commerce
6311 Inducon Corporate Dr Ste 2 .... Sanborn NY 14132 716-285-9141 285-0941
Web: niagarachamber.org

Saratoga County Chamber of Commerce
28 Clinton St .... Saratoga Springs NY 12866 518-584-3255 798-0163
TF: 855-765-7873 ■ *Web:* www.saratoga.org

Chamber of Schenectady County
306 State St .... Schenectady NY 12305 518-372-5656 370-3217
TF: 800-962-8007 ■ *Web:* www.schenectadychamber.org

Seneca County Chamber of Commerce
2020 Rt 5 & 20 W .... Seneca Falls NY 13148 315-568-2906 568-1730
Web: fingerlakescentral.com

Smithtown Chamber of Commerce
79 E Main St Ste E .... Smithtown NY 11787 631-979-8069 979-2206
Web: www.smithtownchamber.org

Southampton Chamber of Commerce
76 Main St .... SoutHampton NY 11968 631-283-0402 283-8707
Web: www.southamptonchamber.com

Staten Island Chamber of Commerce
130 Bay St .... Staten Island NY 10301 718-727-1900 727-2295
Web: www.sichamber.com

Rensselaer County Regional Chamber of Commerce
255 River St .... Troy NY 12180 518-274-7020 272-7729
TF: 800-822-2400 ■ *Web:* www.renscochamber.com

Mohawk Valley Chamber of Commerce
200 Genesee St .... Utica NY 13502 315-724-3151 724-3177
Web: greateruticachamber.org/

Warwick Valley Chamber of Commerce (WVCC)
PO Box 202 .... Warwick NY 10990 845-986-2720 986-6982
Web: www.warwickcc.org

Greater Watertown-North Country Chamber of Commerce
1241 Coffeen St .... Watertown NY 13601 315-788-4400 788-3369
TF: 800-642-4272 ■ *Web:* www.watertownny.com

Webster Chamber of Commerce
1110 Crosspointe Ln Ste C .... Webster NY 14580 585-265-3960 265-3702
Web: www.websterchamber.com

Business Council of Westchester
108 Corporate Pk Dr Ste 101 .... White Plains NY 10604 914-948-2110 948-0122
Web: www.westchesterny.org

Amherst Chamber of Commerce
350 Essjay Rd Ste 200 .... Williamsville NY 14221 716-632-6905 632-0548
Web: www.amherst.org

Yonkers Chamber of Commerce
55 Main St Second Fl .... Yonkers NY 10701 914-963-0332 963-0455
Web: www.yonkerschamber.com

North Carolina

Phone *Fax*

Ahoskie Chamber of Commerce
310 Catherine Creek Rd .... Ahoskie NC 27910 252-332-2042 332-8617
Web: ahoskiechamber.net

Stanly County Chamber of Commerce
116 E N St .... Albemarle NC 28001 704-982-8116 983-5000
Web: www.stanlychamber.org

Archdale-Trinity Chamber of Commerce
213 Balfour Dr .... Archdale NC 27263 336-434-2073 431-5845
Web: www.archdaletrinitychamber.com

Asheville Area Chamber of Commerce
36 Montford Ave .... Asheville NC 28802 828-258-6101 251-0926
TF: 888-314-1041 ■ *Web:* www.ashevillechamber.org

Black Mountain-Swannanoa Chamber of Commerce
201 E State St .... Black Mountain NC 28711 828-669-2300 669-1407
TF: 800-669-2301 ■ *Web:* www.blackmountain.org

Blowing Rock Chamber of Commerce
7738 Vly Blvd .... Blowing Rock NC 28605 828-295-7851 295-4643
TF: 800-295-7851 ■ *Web:* www.blowingrock.com

Brevard-Transylvania Chamber of Commerce
175 E Main St .... Brevard NC 28712 828-883-3700 883-8550
TF: 800-648-4523 ■ *Web:* www.brevardncchamber.org

Alamance County Area Chamber of Commerce
610 S Lexington Ave .... Burlington NC 27215 336-228-1338 228-1330
Web: www.alamancechamber.com

Cary Chamber of Commerce 307 N Academy St .... Cary NC 27513 919-467-1016 469-2375
Web: www.carychamber.com

Chapel Hill-Carrboro Chamber of Commerce
104 S Estes Dr .... Chapel Hill NC 27515 919-967-7075 968-6874
Web: www.carolinachamber.org

Charlotte Chamber of Commerce
330 S Tryon St PO Box 32785 .... Charlotte NC 28202 704-378-1300 374-1903
Web: www.charlottechamber.com

Lake Norman Chamber of Commerce
19900 W Catawba Ave Ste 101 .... Cornelius NC 28031 704-892-1922 892-5313
TF: 800-305-2508 ■ *Web:* www.lakenormanchamber.org

Greater Durham Chamber of Commerce
300 W Morgan St Ste 1400 PO Box 3829 .... Durham NC 27702 919-328-8700 688-8351
Web: www.durhamchamber.org

Elizabeth City Area Chamber of Commerce
502 E Ehringhaus St .... Elizabeth City NC 27909 252-335-4365 335-5732
Web: www.elizabethcitychamber.org

Yadkin Valley Chamber of Commerce
116 E Market St PO Box 496 .... Elkin NC 28621 336-526-1111 526-1879
Web: www.yadkinvalley.org

Cumberland County Business Council
1019 Hay St .... Fayetteville NC 28305 910-483-8133 483-0263
Web: fayettevillencchamber.org

Fuquay-Varina Area Chamber of Commerce
121 N Main St .... Fuquay-Varina NC 27526 919-552-4947 552-1029
Web: www.fuquay-varina.com

Gaston Chamber of Commerce
601 W Franklin Blvd .... Gastonia NC 28052 704-864-2621 854-8723
TF: 800-933-3909 ■ *Web:* www.gastonchamber.com

Wayne County Chamber of Commerce
308 N Williams St .... Goldsboro NC 27530 919-734-2241 734-2247
Web: www.waynecountychamber.com

Greensboro Area Chamber of Commerce
342 N Elm St .... Greensboro NC 27401 336-387-8300 275-9299
Web: www.greensborochamber.com

Greenville-Pitt County Chamber of Commerce
302 S Greene St .... Greenville NC 27834 252-752-4101 752-5934
Web: www.greenvillenc.org

Henderson-Vance County Chamber of Commerce
414 S Garnett St .... Henderson NC 27536 252-438-8414 492-8989
Web: www.hendersonvance.org

Hendersonville County Chamber of Commerce
204 Kanuga Rd .... Hendersonville NC 28739 828-692-1413 693-8802
Web: www.hendersoncountychamber.org

Catawba County Chamber of Commerce
1055 Southgate Pk SW PO Box 1828 .... Hickory NC 28603 828-328-6111 328-1175
Web: www.catawbachamber.org

High Point Chamber of Commerce
1634 N Main St .... High Point NC 27262 336-882-5000 889-9499
TF: 877-852-9462 ■ *Web:* www.highpointchamber.org

Jacksonville/Onslow Chamber of Commerce
1099 Gum Branch Rd .... Jacksonville NC 28541 910-347-3141 347-4705
TF: 800-877-8339 ■ *Web:* www.jacksonvilleonline.org

Cabarrus Regional Chamber of Commerce
3003 Dale Earnhardt Blvd .... Kannapolis NC 28083 704-782-4000 782-4050
Web: www.cabarrus.biz

Outer Banks Chamber of Commerce
101 Town Hall Dr PO Box 1757 .... Kill Devil Hills NC 27948 252-441-8144
Web: www.outerbankschamber.com

Kinston-Lenoir County Chamber of Commerce
301 N Queen St .... Kinston NC 28501 252-527-1131 527-1914
Web: www.kinstonchamber.com

Laurinburg/Scotland County Area Chamber of Commerce
606 Atkinson St .... Laurinburg NC 28352 910-276-7420 277-8785
Web: www.laurinburgchamber.com

Caldwell County Chamber of Commerce
1909 Hickory Blvd SE .... Lenoir NC 28645 828-726-0616 726-0385
Web: www.caldwellcochamber.org

Lincolnton-Lincoln County Chamber of Commerce
101 E Main St .... Lincolnton NC 28092 704-735-3096 735-5449
Web: www.lincolnchambernc.org

Greater Franklin County Chamber of Commerce
112 E Nash St PO Box 62 .... Louisburg NC 27549 919-496-3056 496-0422
Web: www.franklin-chamber.org

Phone Fax

Lumberton Area Chamber of Commerce
800 N Chestnut St .... Lumberton NC 28358 910-739-4750 671-9722
Web: www.lumbertonchamber.com

Western Rockingham Chamber of Commerce
112 W Murphy St .... Madison NC 27025 336-548-6248 548-4466
Web: www.westernrockinghamchamber.com

McDowell County Chamber of Commerce
1170 W Tate St .... Marion NC 28752 828-652-4240 659-9620
Web: www.mcdowellchamber.com

Davie County Chamber of Commerce
135 S Salisbury St .... Mocksville NC 27028 336-751-3304 751-5697
Web: www.daviechamber.com

Mooresville-South Iredell Chamber of Commerce
149 E Iredell Ave .... Mooresville NC 28115 704-664-3898 664-2549
Web: www.mooresvillenc.org

Carteret County Chamber of Commerce
801 Arendell St Ste 1 .... Morehead City NC 28557 252-726-6350 726-3505
TF: 800-622-6278 ■ *Web:* www.nccoastchamber.com

Burke County Chamber of Commerce
110 E Meeting St .... Morganton NC 28655 828-437-3021 437-1613
Web: burkecountychamber.org

Greater Mount Airy Chamber of Commerce
200 N Main St .... Mount Airy NC 27030 336-786-6116 786-1488
TF: 800-948-0949 ■ *Web:* www.mtairyncchamber.org

Mount Olive Area Chamber of Commerce
123 N Ctr St .... Mount Olive NC 28365 919-658-3113 658-3125
Web: www.moachamber.com

New Bern Area Chamber of Commerce
316 S Front St .... New Bern NC 28560 252-637-3111 637-7541
TF: 877-811-1776 ■ *Web:* www.newbernchamber.com

Wilkes Chamber of Commerce
717 Main St .... North Wilkesboro NC 28659 336-838-8662 838-3728
Web: wilkeschamber.com

Granville County Chamber of Commerce
124 Hillsboro St .... Oxford NC 27565 919-693-6125 693-6126
Web: www.granville-chamber.com

Raeford-Hoke Chamber of Commerce
101 N Main St .... Raeford NC 28376 910-875-5929 875-1010
Web: www.raefordhokechamber.com

Greater Raleigh Chamber of Commerce
PO Box 2978 .... Raleigh NC 27602 919-664-7000 664-7097
TF: 866-291-0854 ■ *Web:* www.raleighchamber.org

Roanoke Valley Chamber of Commerce
260 Premier Blvd .... Roanoke Rapids NC 27870 252-537-3513 535-5767
Web: www.rvchamber.com

Richmond County Chamber of Commerce
101 W Broad Ave PO Box 86 .... Rockingham NC 28380 910-895-9058 895-9056
Web: www.richmondcountychamber.com

Rocky Mount Area Chamber of Commerce
100 Coastline St Ste 200 .... Rocky Mount NC 27804 252-446-0323 446-5103
TF: 800-682-6746 ■ *Web:* www.rockymountchamber.org

Roxboro Area Chamber of Commerce
211 N Main St .... Roxboro NC 27573 336-599-8333 599-8335
Web: www.roxboronc.com

Rowan County Chamber of Commerce
204 E Innes St Ste 110 .... Salisbury NC 28144 704-633-4221 639-1200
Web: www.rowanchamber.com

Sanford Area Chamber of Commerce
143 Charlotte Ave Ste 101 .... Sanford NC 27330 919-775-7341 884-2547*
**Fax Area Code:* 855 ■ *Web:* www.sanford-nc.com

Brunswick County Chamber of Commerce
4948 Main St .... Shallotte NC 28459 910-754-6644 754-6539
TF: 800-426-6644 ■ *Web:* www.brunswickcountychamber.org

Cleveland County Chamber of Commerce
200 S Lafayette St .... Shelby NC 28150 704-487-8521 487-7458
Web: www.clevelandchamber.org

Chatham Chamber of Commerce
531 E Third St .... Siler City NC 27344 919-742-3333 742-1333
Web: www.ccucc.net

Greater Smithfield-Selma Area Chamber of Commerce
1115 Industrial Pk Dr .... Smithfield NC 27577 919-934-9166 934-1337
Web: www.smithfieldselma.com

Moore County Chamber of Commerce
10677 Hwy 15-501 .... Southern Pines NC 28387 910-692-3926 692-0619
Web: www.moorecountychamber.com

Jackson County Chamber of Commerce
773 W Main St .... Sylva NC 28779 828-586-2155 586-4887
TF: 800-962-1911 ■ *Web:* www.mountainlovers.com

Tarboro Edgecombe Chamber of Commerce
509 Trade St .... Tarboro NC 27886 252-823-7241 823-1499
TF: 888-404-3424 ■ *Web:* www.tarborochamber.com

Thomasville Area Chamber of Commerce
PO Box 1400 .... Thomasville NC 27361 336-475-6134 475-4802
Web: www.thomasvillechamber.net

Carolina Foothills Chamber of Commerce
2753 Lynn Rd Ste A .... Tryon NC 28782 828-859-6236 859-2301
Web: www.carolinafoothillschamber.com

Washington-Beaufort County Chamber of Commerce
102 Stewart Pkwy PO Box 665 .... Washington NC 27889 252-946-9168 946-9169
Web: www.wbcchamber.com

Haywood County Chamber of Commerce
28 Walnut Street .... Waynesville NC 28786 828-456-3021 452-7265
TF: 877-456-3073 ■ *Web:* www.haywood-nc.com

Martin County Chamber of Commerce
415 E Blvd .... Williamston NC 27892 252-792-4131 792-1013
Web: martincountync.com

Greater Wilmington Chamber of Commerce
1 Estell Lee Pl .... Wilmington NC 28401 910-762-2611 762-9765
TF: 800-829-4477 ■ *Web:* www.wilmingtonchamber.org

Wilson Chamber of Commerce 200 Nash St NE .... Wilson NC 27893 252-237-0165 243-7931
TF: 855-905-0604 ■ *Web:* www.wilsonncchamber.com

Windsor-Bertie Area Chamber of Commerce
121 Granville St PO Box 572 .... Windsor NC 27983 252-794-4277 794-5070
TF: 800-334-5010 ■ *Web:* www.windsorbertiechamber.com

Greater Winston-Salem Chamber of Commerce
411 W Fourth St Ste 211 .... Winston-Salem NC 27101 336-728-9200 721-2209
Web: www.winstonsalem.com

Yadkin County Chamber of Commerce
205 S Jackson St PO Box 1840 .... Yadkinville NC 27055 336-679-2200 679-3034
Web: www.yadkinchamber.org

North Dakota

Phone Fax

Bismarck Mandan Chamber of Commerce
1640 Burnt Boat Dr .... Bismarck ND 58502 701-223-5660 255-6125
Web: www.bismarckmandan.com

Grand Forks Chamber of Commerce
202 N Third St .... Grand Forks ND 58203 701-772-7271 772-9238
TF: 855-233-6362 ■ *Web:* www.gochamber.org

Jamestown Area Chamber of Commerce
120 Second St SE PO Box 1530 .... Jamestown ND 58401 701-252-4830 952-4837
Web: www.jamestownchamber.com

Minot Area Chamber of Commerce
1020 20th Ave SW .... Minot ND 58701 701-852-6000 838-2488
Web: www.minotchamber.org

Ohio

Phone Fax

Greater Akron Chamber One Cascade Plz 17th Fl .... Akron OH 44308 330-376-5550 379-3164
Web: www.greaterakronchamber.org

Alliance Area Chamber of Commerce
210 E Main St .... Alliance OH 44601 330-823-6260 823-4434
Web: www.allianceohiochamber.org

Ashtabula Area Chamber of Commerce
4536 Main Ave .... Ashtabula OH 44004 440-998-6998 992-8216
Web: www.ashtabulachamber.net

Athens Area Chamber of Commerce
449 E State St Ste 1 .... Athens OH 45701 740-594-2251 594-2252
TF: 877-360-3608 ■ *Web:* www.athenschamber.com

Barberton South Summitt Chamber of Commerce
503 W Pk Ave .... Barberton OH 44203 330-745-3141 777-0597
Web: www.southsummitchamber.org

Beavercreek Chamber of Commerce
3210 Beaver-Vu Dr .... Beavercreek OH 45431 937-426-2202 426-2204
Web: www.beavercreekchamber.org

Logan County Chamber of Commerce
100 S Main St .... Bellefontaine OH 43311 937-599-5121 599-2411
TF: 877-360-3608 ■ *Web:* www.logancountyohio.com

Muskingum Valley Area Chamber of Commerce
PO Box 837 .... Beverly OH 45715 740-984-8259
Web: www.mvacc.com

Bowling Green Chamber of Commerce (BGCC)
163 N Main St PO Box 31 .... Bowling Green OH 43402 419-353-7945 353-3693
Web: www.bgchamber.net

Brunswick Area Chamber of Commerce
3511 Ctr Rd Ste A-B .... Brunswick OH 44212 330-225-8411 273-8172
Web: www.brunswickareachamber.org

Cambridge Area Chamber of Commerce
918 Wheeling Ave .... Cambridge OH 43725 740-439-6688 439-6689
Web: www.cambridgeohiochamber.com

Canton Regional Chamber of Commerce
222 Market Ave N .... Canton OH 44702 330-456-7253 452-7786
TF: 800-533-4302 ■ *Web:* www.cantonchamber.org

Carroll County Chamber of Commerce & Economic Development
61 N Lisbon St PO Box 277 .... Carrollton OH 44615 330-627-4811 627-3647
TF: 800-956-4684 ■ *Web:* www.carrollohchamber.com

Celina-Mercer County Chamber of Commerce
226 N Main St .... Celina OH 45822 419-586-2219 586-8645
Web: www.celinamercer.com

Chagrin Valley Chamber of Commerce
83 N Main St .... Chagrin Falls OH 44022 440-247-6607
Web: www.cvcc.org

Chillicothe-Ross Chamber of Commerce
45 E Main St .... Chillicothe OH 45601 740-702-2722 702-2727
Web: www.chillicotheohio.com

Cincinnati USA Regional Chamber
441 Vine St Ste 300 .... Cincinnati OH 45202 513-579-3100 579-3102
Web: www.cincinnatichamber.com

Clermont Chamber of Commerce
4355 Ferguson Dr Ste 150 .... Cincinnati OH 45245 513-576-5000 576-5001
Web: www.clermontchamber.com

Pickaway County Chamber of Commerce
PO Box 841 .... Circleville OH 43113 740-474-4923 477-6800
Web: www.pickaway.com

Greater Cleveland Partnership
50 Public Sq Ste 200 .... Cleveland OH 44113 216-621-3300 621-6013
TF: 888-304-4769 ■ *Web:* www.gcpartnership.com

Columbus Chamber of Commerce
150 S Front St Ste 200 .... Columbus OH 43215 614-221-1321 221-1408
TF: 888-382-1574 ■ *Web:* www.columbus.org

Coshocton County Chamber of Commerce
401 Main St .... Coshocton OH 43812 740-622-5411 622-9902
Web: www.coshoctoncounty.net

Cuyahoga Falls Chamber of Commerce (CFCC)
151 Portage Trl Ste 1 .... Cuyahoga Falls OH 44221 330-929-6756 929-4278
Web: cfchamber.com

Dayton Area Chamber of Commerce
1 Chamber Plaza Ste 200 .... Dayton OH 45402 937-226-1444 226-8254
TF: 800-621-9131 ■ *Web:* www.daytonchamber.org

South Metro Regional Chamber of Commerce
7887 Washington Village Dr Ste 210 .... Dayton OH 45459 937-433-2032 433-6881
Web: www.smrcoc.org

Defiance Area Chamber of Commerce
325 Clinton St .... Defiance OH 43512 419-782-7946 782-0111
Web: www.defiancechamber.com

Organization	Address	City	State	ZIP	Phone	Fax	Toll-free / Web
Southern Columbiana County Regional Chamber of Commerce	529 Market St PO Box 94	East Liverpool	OH	43920	330-385-0845	385-0581	*Web:* www.sccregionalchamber.org
Eaton-Preble County Chamber of Commerce	122 W Decatur St PO Box 303	Eaton	OH	45320	937-456-4949	456-4949	*Web:* www.preblecountyohio.com
Lorain County Chamber of Commerce	226 Middle Ave.	Elyria	OH	44035	440-328-2550	328-2557	*Web:* www.loraincountychamber.com
Englewood-Northmont Chamber of Commerce	PO Box 62	Englewood	OH	45322	937-836-2550	836-2485	*Web:* www.northmontchamber.com
Euclid Chamber of Commerce	22639 Euclid Ave PO Box 32611	Euclid	OH	44117	216-731-9322	865-4925	*Web:* www.euclidchamber.com
Fairborn Area Chamber of Commerce	12 N Central Ave.	Fairborn	OH	45324	937-878-3191	878-3197	*Web:* www.fairborn.com
Findlay-Hancock County Chamber of Commerce	123 E Main Cross St.	Findlay	OH	45840	419-422-3313	422-9508	*Web:* www.findlayhancockalliance.com
Fostoria Area Chamber of Commerce (FACC)	121 N Main St	Fostoria	OH	44830	419-435-7789	435-0936	*Web:* www.fostoriaohio.org
Chamber of Commerce of Sandusky County	101 S Front St	Fremont	OH	43420	419-332-1591	332-8666	*Web:* www.scchamber.org
Gahanna Area Chamber of Commerce	181 Granville St Ste 200	Gahanna	OH	43230	614-471-0451	471-5122	*Web:* www.gahannaareachamber.com
Gallia County Chamber of Commerce	16 State St PO Box 465	Gallipolis	OH	45631	740-446-0596	446-7031	*Web:* www.galliacounty.org
Garfield Heights Chamber of Commerce	5522 Turney Rd.	Garfield Heights	OH	44125	216-475-7775	475-2237	*Web:* www.garfieldchamber.com
Geneva Area Chamber of Commerce	866 E Main St.	Geneva	OH	44041	440-466-8694	466-0823	*Web:* www.genevachamber.org
Brown County Chamber of Commerce	PO Box 21606	Georgetown	OH	45121	937-378-4784	378-1634	*Web:* www.browncountyohiochamber.com
Darke County Chamber of Commerce	622 S Broadway	Greenville	OH	45331	937-548-2102	548-5608	*Web:* www.darkecountyohio.com
Greater Hamilton Chamber of Commerce	201 Dayton St.	Hamilton	OH	45011	513-844-1500	844-1999	*Web:* www.hamilton-ohio.com
Highland County Chamber of Commerce	PO Box 183	Hillsboro	OH	45133	937-393-1111	393-9604	*Web:* www.highlandcountychamber.com
Huber Heights Chamber of Commerce	4756 Fishburg Rd.	Huber Heights	OH	45424	937-233-5700		*Web:* huberheightschamber.com
Jackson-Beldon Chamber of Commerce	5735 Wales Ave NW	Jackson Township	OH	44646	330-833-4400	833-4456	*Web:* www.jbcc.org
Kent Area Chamber of Commerce	138 E Main St Ste 102	Kent	OH	44240	330-673-9855	673-9860	*Web:* www.kentbiz.com
Hardin County Chamber of Commerce (HCCBA)	225 S Detroit St	Kenton	OH	43326	419-673-4131	674-4876	*TF:* 888-642-7346 ■ *Web:* www.hardinohio.org
Kettering-Moraine-Oakwood Area Chamber of Commerce	2977 Far Hills Ave	Kettering	OH	45419	937-299-3852	299-3851	*Web:* www.kmo-coc.org
Lancaster-Fairfield County Chamber of Commerce	109 N Broad St Ste 100	Lancaster	OH	43130	740-653-8251	653-7074	*Web:* www.lancoc.org
Lima/Allen County Chamber of Commerce	144 S Main St Ste 100	Lima	OH	45801	419-222-6045	229-0266	*Web:* www.limachamber.com
Logan-Hocking Chamber of Commerce	Four E Hunter St.	Logan	OH	43138	740-385-6836	385-7259	*Web:* www.logan-hockingchamber.com
Madison-Perry Area Chamber of Commerce	5965 N Ridge Rd	Madison	OH	44057	440-428-3760	428-6668	*Web:* www.mpacc.org
Richland Area Chamber of Commerce	55 N Mulberry St	Mansfield	OH	44902	419-522-3211	526-6853	*Web:* www.mrachamber.com
Marietta Area Chamber of Commerce	100 Front St Ste 200.	Marietta	OH	45750	740-373-5176	373-7808	*Web:* www.mariettachamber.com
Marion Area Chamber of Commerce	267 W Ctr St Ste 100	Marion	OH	43302	740-382-2181	387-7722	*Web:* www.marionareachamber.org
Massillon Area Chamber of Commerce	137 Lincoln Way E	Massillon	OH	44646	330-833-3146	833-8944	*Web:* www.massillonohchamber.com
Mentor Chamber of Commerce	6972 Spinach Dr.	Mentor	OH	44060	440-255-1616	255-1717	*TF:* 800-825-6755 ■ *Web:* www.mentorchamber.org
Chamber of Commerce serving Middletown Monroe & Trenton	1500 Central Ave	Middletown	OH	45044	513-422-4551	422-6831	*TF:* 800-837-3200 ■ *Web:* thechamberofcommerce.org
Milford-Miami Township Chamber of Commerce	983 Lila Ave	Milford	OH	45150	513-831-2411	831-3547	*TF:* 877-723-0513 ■ *Web:* www.milfordmiamitownship.com
Holmes County Chamber of Commerce	35 N Monroe St	Millersburg	OH	44654	330-674-3975	674-3976	*Web:* www.holmescountychamber.com
Morrow County Chamber of Commerce	17 1/2 W High St PO Box 174	Mount Gilead	OH	43338	419-946-2821	946-3861	*Web:* www.morrowchamber.org
Mount Vernon-Knox County Chamber of Commerce	400 S Gay St.	Mount Vernon	OH	43050	740-393-1111	393-1590	*Web:* www.knoxchamber.com
Napoleon/Henry County Chamber of Commerce	611 N Perry St	Napoleon	OH	43545	419-592-1786	592-4945	*TF:* 800-322-6849 ■ *Web:* henrycountychamber.org
Tuscarawas County Chamber of Commerce	1323 Fourth St NW	New Philadelphia	OH	44663	330-343-4474	343-6526	*Web:* www.tuschamber.com
Licking County Chamber of Commerce	50 W Locust St	Newark	OH	43055	740-345-9757	345-5141	*Web:* www.lickingcountychamber.com
North Canton Area Chamber of Commerce	121 S Main St.	North Canton	OH	44720	330-499-5100	499-7181	*TF:* 888-263-3423 ■ *Web:* www.northcantonchamber.org
North Olmsted Chamber of Commerce	28938 Lorain Rd Ste 204	North Olmsted	OH	44070	440-777-3368	777-9361	*Web:* www.nolmstedchamber.org
North Royalton Chamber of Commerce	13737 State Rd.	North Royalton	OH	44133	440-237-6180	237-6181	*Web:* www.nroyaltonchamber.com
Eastern Maumee Bay Chamber of Commerce	2460 Navaree Ave.	Oregon	OH	43616	419-693-5580	693-9990	*Web:* www.embchamber.org
Painesville Area Chamber of Commerce	One Victoria Pl Ste 265-A.	Painesville	OH	44077	440-357-7572	357-8752	*Web:* www.painesvilleohchamber.org
Parma Area Chamber of Commerce	7908 Day Dr.	Parma	OH	44129	440-886-1700	886-1770	*Web:* www.parmaareachamber.org
Perrysburg Area Chamber of Commerce	105 W Indiana Ave	Perrysburg	OH	43551	419-874-9147	872-9347	*Web:* www.perrysburgchamber.com
Portsmouth Area Chamber of Commerce	342 Second St PO Box 509	Portsmouth	OH	45662	740-353-7647	353-5824	*TF:* 800-648-2574 ■ *Web:* www.portsmouth.org
Reynoldsburg Area Chamber of Commerce	1580 Brice Rd.	Reynoldsburg	OH	43068	614-866-4753	866-7313	*Web:* www.reynoldsburgchamber.com
Erie County Chamber of Commerce	225 W Washington Row	Sandusky	OH	44870	419-625-6421	625-7914	*Web:* eriecountychamber.com
Sidney-Shelby County Chamber of Commerce	101 S Ohio Ave Second Fl	Sidney	OH	45365	937-492-9122	498-2472	*Web:* www.sidneyshelbychamber.com
Greater Lawrence County Area Chamber of Commerce	216 Collins Ave	South Point	OH	45680	740-377-4550	377-2091	*TF:* 800-408-1334 ■ *Web:* www.lawrencecountyohio.org
Stow-Munroe Falls Chamber of Commerce	4381 Hudson Dr Ste 2450	Stow	OH	44224	330-688-1579	688-6234	*Web:* www.smfcc.com
Strongsville Chamber of Commerce	18829 Royalton Rd	Strongsville	OH	44136	440-238-3366	238-7010	*Web:* www.strongsvillechamber.com
Sylvania Area Chamber of Commerce	5632 Main St	Sylvania	OH	43560	419-882-2135	885-7740	*Web:* www.sylvaniachamber.org
Tiffin Area Chamber of Commerce	62 S Washington St	Tiffin	OH	44883	419-447-4141	447-5141	*Web:* www.tiffinchamber.com
Toledo Regional Chamber of Commerce	300 Madison Ave Ste 200.	Toledo	OH	43604	419-243-8191	241-8302	*Web:* www.toledochamber.com
Trotwood Chamber of Commerce	5790 Denlinger Rd	Trotwood	OH	45426	937-837-1484	837-1508	*Web:* www.trotwoodchamber.org
Upper Arlington Area Chamber of Commerce	2152 Tremont Ctr	Upper Arlington	OH	43221	614-481-5710	481-5711	*Web:* www.uachamber.org
Champaign County Chamber of Commerce	113 Miami St	Urbana	OH	43078	937-653-5764	652-1599	*TF:* 877-873-5764 ■ *Web:* www.champaignohio.com
Vandalia-Butler Chamber of Commerce	544 W National Rd	Vandalia	OH	45377	937-898-5351	898-5491	*Web:* www.vandaliabutlerchamber.org
West Chester Chamber Alliance	7617 Voice of America Centre Dr	West Chester	OH	45069	513-777-3600	777-0188	*Web:* www.thechamberalliance.com
Adams County Travel & Visitors Bureau	509 E Main St.	West Union	OH	45693	937-544-5639		*TF:* 877-232-6764 ■ *Web:* www.adamscountytravel.org
Westerville Area Chamber of Commerce	99 Commerce Pk Dr # A	Westerville	OH	43082	614-882-8917	882-2085	*Web:* www.westervillechamber.com
Willougby Area Chamber of Commerce	28 Public Sq.	Willoughby	OH	44094	440-942-1632	942-0586	*TF:* 877-229-4361 ■ *Web:* www.wwlcchamber.com
Wilmington Clinton County Chamber of Commerce (WCCC)	100 W Main St	Wilmington	OH	45177	937-382-2737		*Web:* www.wcchamber.com
Wooster Area Chamber of Commerce	377 W Liberty St.	Wooster	OH	44691	330-262-5735	262-5745	*Web:* www.woosterchamber.com
Worthington Area Chamber of Commerce	25 W New England Ave Ste 100	Worthington	OH	43085	614-888-3040	841-4842	*Web:* www.worthingtonchamber.org
Xenia Area Chamber of Commerce	334 W Market St	Xenia	OH	45385	937-372-3591	372-2192	*Web:* xacc.com
Youngstown Warren Regional Chamber	11 Central Sq Ste 1600.	Youngstown	OH	44503	330-744-2131	746-0330	*TF:* 877-807-2249 ■ *Web:* www.regionalchamber.com
Zanesville-Muskingum County Chamber of Commerce	205 N Fifth St.	Zanesville	OH	43701	740-455-8282	454-2963	*TF:* 800-743-2303 ■ *Web:* www.zmchamber.com

Oklahoma

Chamber	City	State	Zip	Phone	Fax
Ada Area Chamber of Commerce 209 W Main St *Web:* www.adachamber.com	Ada	OK	74820	580-332-2506	332-3265
Bartlesville Area Chamber of Commerce 201 S Keeler Ave *Web:* www.bartlesville.com	Bartlesville	OK	74003	918-336-8708	337-0216
Broken Arrow Chamber of Commerce 210 N Main Ste C *Web:* www.brokenarrow.org	Broken Arrow	OK	74012	918-251-1518	251-1777
Del City Chamber of Commerce PO Box 15643 *Web:* www.delcitychamber.com	Del City	OK	73155	405-677-1910	
Durant Area Chamber of Commerce 215 N Fourth St *Web:* www.durantchamber.org	Durant	OK	74701	580-924-0848	924-0348
Edmond Area Chamber of Commerce 825 E Second St *Web:* www.edmondchamber.com	Edmond	OK	73034	405-341-2808	340-5512
Greater Enid Chamber of Commerce PO Box 907 *TF:* 877-233-4232 ■ *Web:* www.enidchamber.com	Enid	OK	73702	580-237-2494	237-2497
Midwest City Chamber of Commerce 5905 Trosper Rd *Web:* www.midwestcityok.com	Midwest City	OK	73110	405-733-3801	
Moore Chamber of Commerce 305 W Main St *Web:* www.moorechamber.com	Moore	OK	73160	405-794-3400	794-8555
Greater Muskogee Area Chamber of Commerce PO Box 797 *Web:* www.visitmuskogee.com	Muskogee	OK	74402	918-682-2401	682-2403
Greater Oklahoma City Chamber of Commerce 123 Pk Ave *Web:* www.okcchamber.com	Oklahoma City	OK	73102	405-297-8900	297-8916
South Oklahoma City Chamber of Commerce 701 SW 74 St *TF:* 877-309-2070 ■ *Web:* www.southokc.com	Oklahoma City	OK	73139	405-634-1436	634-1462
Owasso Chamber of Commerce 315 S Cedar St *Web:* www.owassochamber.com	Owasso	OK	74055	918-272-2141	272-8564
Ponca City Area Chamber of Commerce 420 E Grand Ave *Web:* www.poncacitychamber.com	Ponca City	OK	74601	580-765-4400	765-2798
Poteau Chamber of Commerce 201 S Broadway *Web:* poteauchamber.com	Poteau	OK	74953	918-647-9178	647-4099
Sallisaw Chamber of Commerce 301 E Cherokee Ave *Web:* sallisawchamber.com	Sallisaw	OK	74955	918-775-2558	775-4021
Greater Shawnee Area Chamber of Commerce 131 N Bell Ave *TF:* 800-762-7695 ■ *Web:* www.shawneechamber.com	Shawnee	OK	74801	405-273-6092	275-9851
Stillwater Chamber of Commerce 409 S Main St *TF:* 800-593-5573 ■ *Web:* www.stillwaterchamber.org	Stillwater	OK	74075	405-372-5573	372-4316
Tulsa Metro Chamber One West Third St Ste 100 **Fax:* Hum Res ■ *TF:* 888-424-9411 ■ *Web:* www.tulsachamber.com	Tulsa	OK	74103	918-585-1201	599-6173*
Yukon Chamber of Commerce 510 Elm St *Web:* www.yukoncc.com	Yukon	OK	73099	405-354-3567	350-0724

Oregon

Chamber	City	State	Zip	Phone	Fax
Albany Area Chamber of Commerce 435 W First Ave W *Web:* www.albanychamber.com	Albany	OR	97321	541-926-1517	926-7064
Beaverton Area Chamber of Commerce 12655 SW Ctr St Ste 140 *Web:* www.beaverton.org	Beaverton	OR	97005	503-644-0123	526-0349
Bend Chamber of Commerce 777 NW Wall St Ste 200 *TF:* 800-905-2363 ■ *Web:* www.bendchamber.org	Bend	OR	97701	541-382-3221	385-9929
Corvallis Area Chamber of Commerce 420 NW Second St *Web:* www.corvallischamber.com	Corvallis	OR	97330	541-757-1505	766-2996
Eugene Chamber of Commerce 1401 Willamette St *Web:* www.eugenechamber.com	Eugene	OR	97401	541-484-1314	484-4942
Florence Area Chamber of Commerce 290 Hwy 101 *TF:* 800-585-3737 ■ *Web:* www.florencechamber.com	Florence	OR	97439	541-997-3128	997-4101
Grants Pass Chamber of Commerce 1995 NW Vine St PO Box 970 *TF:* 800-547-5927 ■ *Web:* www.grantspasschamber.org	Grants Pass	OR	97526	541-476-7717	476-9574
Gresham Area Chamber of Commerce 701 NE Hood Ave *Web:* www.greshamchamber.org	Gresham	OR	97030	503-665-1131	666-1041
Hermiston Chamber of Commerce 415 S Hwy 395 PO Box 185 *Web:* www.hermistonchamber.com	Hermiston	OR	97838	541-567-6151	564-9109
Hillsboro Chamber of Commerce 5193 NE Elam Young Pkwy Ste A *Web:* hillsborochamberor.com	Hillsboro	OR	97124	503-648-1102	681-0535
Keizer Chamber of Commerce 980 Chemawa Rd NE *Web:* www.keizerchamber.com	Keizer	OR	97303	503-393-9111	393-1003
Klamath County Chamber of Commerce 205 Riverside Dr *Web:* www.klamath.org	Klamath Falls	OR	97601	541-884-5193	884-5195
La Grande-Union County Chamber of Commerce 102 Elm St *TF:* 800-848-9969 ■ *Web:* www.unioncountychamber.org	La Grande	OR	97850	541-963-8588	963-3936
Lake Oswego Chamber of Commerce 242 B Ave *Web:* www.lake-oswego.com	Lake Oswego	OR	97034	503-636-3634	636-7427
Chamber of Medford/Jackson County 101 E Eigth St *Web:* www.medfordchamber.com	Medford	OR	97501	541-779-4847	776-4808
North Clackamas County Chamber of Commerce 7740 SE Harmony Rd *Web:* www.yourchamber.com	Milwaukie	OR	97222	503-654-7777	653-9515
Greater Newport Chamber of Commerce 555 SW Coast Hwy *TF:* 800-262-7844 ■ *Web:* www.newportchamber.org	Newport	OR	97365	541-265-8801	265-5589
Oregon City Chamber of Commerce 1201 Washington St *Web:* www.oregoncity.org	Oregon City	OR	97045	503-656-1619	656-2274
Portland Business Alliance 200 SW Market St Ste 150 *TF:* 800-224-1180 ■ *Web:* www.portlandalliance.com	Portland	OR	97201	503-224-8684	323-9186
Salem Area Chamber of Commerce 1110 Commercial St NE *Web:* www.salemchamber.org	Salem	OR	97301	503-581-1466	581-0972
Springfield Chamber of Commerce 101 S 'A' St *TF:* 866-346-1651 ■ *Web:* www.springfield-chamber.org	Springfield	OR	97477	541-746-1651	726-4727
Tigard Area Chamber of Commerce (TACC) 12345 SW Main St *Web:* www.tigardareachamber.org	Tigard	OR	97223	503-639-1656	639-6302

Pennsylvania

Chamber	City	State	Zip	Phone	Fax
Greater Lehigh Valley Chamber of Commerce 840 Hamilton St Ste 205 *TF:* 800-845-7941 ■ *Web:* www.lehighvalleychamber.org	Allentown	PA	18101	610-841-5800	437-4907
Two Rivers Area Chamber of Commerce 840 Hamilton St Ste 205 *Web:* www.lehighvalleychamber.org	Allentown	PA	18101	610-841-5800	437-4907
Altoona-Blair County Chamber of Commerce 3900 Industrial Pk Dr Ste 12 *Web:* www.blairchamber.com	Altoona	PA	16602	814-943-8151	943-5239
Beaver County Chamber of Commerce 798 Turnpike St Ste 202 *Web:* beavercountychamber.com	Beaver	PA	15009	724-775-3944	728-9737
Bedford County Chamber of Commerce 137 E Pitt St *TF:* 800-732-0999 ■ *Web:* bedfordcountychamber.com	Bedford	PA	15522	814-623-2233	623-6089
Bellefonte Intervalley Chamber of Commerce 320 W High St *Web:* www.bellefonte.com	Bellefonte	PA	16823	814-355-2917	355-2761
Lehigh Valley Chamber of Commerce 561 Main St Ste 200 *Web:* www.lehighvalleychamber.org	Bethlehem	PA	18018	610-841-5862	758-9533
Bloomsburg Area Chamber of Commerce 238 Market St *Web:* www.bloomsburg.org	Bloomsburg	PA	17815	570-784-2522	784-2661
Columbia Montour chamber of Commerce, The 238 Market St *Web:* www.columbiamontourchamber.com	Bloomsburg	PA	17815	570-784-2522	784-2661
Butler County Chamber of Commerce 101 E Diamond St Ste 116 *Web:* www.butlercountychamber.com	Butler	PA	16001	724-283-2222	283-0224
West Shore Chamber of Commerce 4211 E Trindle Rd *Web:* www.wschamber.org	Camp Hill	PA	17011	717-761-0702	761-4315
Greater Chambersburg Chamber of Commerce 100 Lincoln Way E Ste A *Web:* www.chambersburg.org	Chambersburg	PA	17201	717-264-7101	267-0399
Clarion Area Chamber of Business & Industry 21 N Sixth Ave *Web:* www.clarionpa.com	Clarion	PA	16214	814-226-9161	226-4903
Perkiomen Valley Chamber of Commerce 351 E Main St *TF:* 800-349-7623 ■ *Web:* perkiomenvalleychamber.org	Collegeville	PA	19426	610-489-6660	454-1270
Central Bucks Chamber of Commerce 252 W Swamp Rd Ste 23 *Web:* www.centralbuckschamber.com	Doylestown	PA	18901	215-348-3913	348-7154
Erie Regional Chamber & Growth Partnership 208 E Bayfront Pkwy *TF:* 888-300-3743 ■ *Web:* www.eriepa.com	Erie	PA	16507	814-454-7191	459-0241
Exton Region Chamber of Commerce 967 E Swedesford Rd Ste 409 *Web:* www.ercc.net	Exton	PA	19341	610-644-4985	
Lower Bucks County Chamber of Commerce 409 Hood Blvd *TF:* 800-786-2234 ■ *Web:* www.lbccc.org	Fairless Hills	PA	19030	215-943-7400	943-7404
Franklin Area Chamber of Commerce (FACC) 1259 Liberty St *TF:* 888-547-2377 ■ *Web:* www.franklinareachamber.org	Franklin	PA	16323	814-432-5823	437-2453
Gettysburg-Adams County Area Chamber of Commerce 18 Carlisle St Ste 203 *TF:* 800-699-1176 ■ *Web:* www.gettysburg-chamber.org	Gettysburg	PA	17325	717-334-8151	334-3368
Westmoreland Chamber of Commerce 241 Tollgate Hill Rd *TF:* 866-468-1231 ■ *Web:* www.westmorelandchamber.com	Greensburg	PA	15601	724-834-2900	837-7635
Hanover Area Chamber of Commerce 146 Carlisle St *Web:* www.hanoverchamber.com	Hanover	PA	17331	717-637-6130	637-9127
Harrisburg Regional Chamber 3211 N Front St Ste 201 *TF:* 877-883-8339 ■ *Web:* www.harrisburgregionalchamber.org	Harrisburg	PA	17110	717-232-4099	232-5184
Huntingdon County Business & Industry 9136 William Penn Hwy *Web:* www.hcbi.com	Huntingdon	PA	16652	814-506-8287	
Indiana County Chamber of Commerce 1019 Philadelphia St *Web:* www.indianapa.com	Indiana	PA	15701	724-465-2511	465-3706
Norwin Chamber of Commerce 321 Main St *TF:* 800-480-2265 ■ *Web:* www.norwinchamber.com	Irwin	PA	15642	724-863-0888	863-5133

				Phone	Fax
Greater Johnstown/Cambria County Chamber of Commerce					
245 Market St Ste 100	Johnstown	PA	15901	814-536-5107	539-5800
TF: 800-790-4522 ■ *Web:* www.johnstownchamber.com					
Southern Chester County Chamber of Commerce					
217 W State St	Kennett Square	PA	19348	610-444-0774	444-5105
TF: 800-343-6583 ■ *Web:* www.scccc.com					
Armstrong County Chamber of Commerce					
124 Market St	Kittanning	PA	16201	724-543-1305	548-2951
Web: allekiskistrong.com					
Lancaster Chamber of Commerce & Industry					
PO Box 1558	Lancaster	PA	17608	717-397-3531	293-3159
Web: lancasterchamber.com					
PennSuburban Chamber of Commerce					
34 Susquehanna Ave	Lansdale	PA	19446	215-362-9200	362-0393
TF: 800-847-9772 ■ *Web:* pennsuburban.org					
Latrobe Area Chamber of Commerce PO Box 463	Latrobe	PA	15650	724-537-2671	537-2690
Web: www.latrobearea.com					
Lebanon Valley Chamber of Commerce					
604 Cumberland St	Lebanon	PA	17042	717-273-3727	273-7940
Web: www.lvchamber.org					
Juniata Valley Area Chamber of Commerce					
1 W Market St	Lewistown	PA	17044	717-248-6713	248-6714
TF: 866-377-1234 ■ *Web:* www.juniatarivervalley.org					
Clinton County Economic Partnership					
212 N Jay St	Lock Haven	PA	17745	570-748-5782	893-0433
TF: 888-388-6991 ■ *Web:* www.clintoncountyinfo.com					
Meadville-Western Crawford County Chamber of Commerce					
908 Diamond Pk	Meadville	PA	16335	814-337-8030	337-8022
TF: 800-332-2338 ■ *Web:* www.meadvillechamber.com					
Delaware County Chamber of Commerce					
602 E Baltimore Pk	Media	PA	19063	610-565-3677	565-1606
Web: www.delcochamber.org					
Pike County Chamber of Commerce					
209 E Hartford St	Milford	PA	18337	570-296-8700	296-3921
Web: www.pikechamber.com					
Monroeville Area Chamber of Commerce					
4268 Northern Pike	Monroeville	PA	15146	412-856-0622	856-1030
TF: 800-527-8941 ■ *Web:* www.monroevillechamber.com					
Pittsburgh Airport Area Chamber of Commerce					
850 Beaver Grade Rd	Moon Township	PA	15108	412-264-6270	264-1575
Web: www.paacc.com					
Laurel Highlands Chamber of Commerce					
537 W Main St	Mount Pleasant	PA	15666	724-547-7521	547-5530
Web: www.westmorelandchamber.com					
Nazareth Area Chamber of Commerce					
201 N Main St PO Box 173	Nazareth	PA	18064	610-759-9188	759-5262
TF: 866-776-8240 ■ *Web:* www.nazarethchamber.com					
Pennridge Chamber of Commerce					
538 W Market St	Perkasie	PA	18944	215-257-5390	257-6840
Web: www.pennridge.com					
Greater Northeast Philadelphia Chamber of Commerce					
8601 E Roosevelt Blvd	Philadelphia	PA	19152	215-332-3400	332-6050
Web: www.gnpcc.org					
Greater Philadelphia Chamber of Commerce					
200 S Broad St Ste 700	Philadelphia	PA	19102	215-545-1234	790-3600
Web: www.greaterphilachamber.com					
Moshannon Valley Economic Development Partnership					
200 Shady Ln	Philipsburg	PA	16866	814-342-2260	342-2878
Web: www.mvedp.org					
Phoenixville Regional Chamber of Commerce					
171 Bridge St	Phoenixville	PA	19460	610-933-3070	917-0503
Web: www.phoenixvillechamber.org					
East Liberty Quarter Chamber of Commerce					
5907 Penn Ave Ste 305	Pittsburgh	PA	15206	412-661-9660	661-9661
Web: www.eastlibertychamber.org					
Greater Pittsburgh Chamber of Commerce					
425 Sixth Ave Ste 1100	Pittsburgh	PA	15219	412-392-4500	392-1040
Web: www.alleghenyconference.org					
North Side Chamber of Commerce					
809 Middle St	Pittsburgh	PA	15212	412-231-6500	321-6760
Web: www.northsidechamberofcommerce.com					
Penn Hills Chamber of Commerce					
12013 Frankstown Rd	Pittsburgh	PA	15235	412-795-8741	795-7993
Web: www.pennhillschamber.org					
South Hills Chamber of Commerce					
1910 Cochran Rd Ste 140	Pittsburgh	PA	15220	412-306-8090	306-8093
Web: www.shchamber.org					
South Side Chamber of Commerce					
1100 E Carson St PO Box 42380	Pittsburgh	PA	15203	412-431-3360	481-2624
Web: www.southsidechamber.org					
Tri County Area Chamber of Commerce					
152 E High St Ste 360	Pottstown	PA	19464	610-326-2900	970-9705
TF: 800-869-5566 ■ *Web:* www.tricountyareachamber.com					
Schuylkill Chamber of Commerce					
91 S Progress Ave	Pottsville	PA	17901	570-622-1942	622-1638
TF: 800-755-1942 ■ *Web:* www.schuylkillchamber.com					
Upper Bucks Chamber of Commerce					
2170 Portzer Rd	Quakertown	PA	18951	215-536-3211	536-7767
TF: 888-942-8257 ■ *Web:* www.ubcc.org					
Greater Reading Chamber of Commerce & Industry					
201 Penn St	Reading	PA	19601	610-376-6766	376-4135
TF: 877-438-4338 ■ *Web:* www.greaterreadingchamber.org					
Greater Scranton Chamber of Commerce					
222 Mulberry St	Scranton	PA	18503	570-342-7711	347-6262
Web: www.scrantonchamber.com					
Greater Susquehanna Valley Chamber of Commerce					
2859 N Susquehanna Trl PO Box 10	Shamokin Dam	PA	17876	570-743-4100	743-1221
TF: 800-410-2880 ■ *Web:* www.gsvcc.org					
Shenango Valley Chamber of Commerce					
41 Chestnut St	Sharon	PA	16146	724-981-5880	981-5480
TF: 800-732-0993 ■ *Web:* www.svchamber.com					
Shippensburg Area Chamber of Commerce					
53 W King St	Shippensburg	PA	17257	717-532-5509	532-7501
Web: www.shippensburg.org					
Somerset County Chamber of Commerce					
601 N Ctr Ave	Somerset	PA	15501	814-445-6431	443-4313
Web: www.somersetcountychamber.com					
Chamber of Business & Industry of Centre County					
200 Innovation Blvd Ste 150	State College	PA	16803	814-234-1829	234-5869
TF: 877-234-5050 ■ *Web:* www.cbicc.org					
Indian Valley Chamber of Commerce					
100 Penn Ave	Telford	PA	18969	215-723-9472	723-2490
Web: www.indianvalleychamber.com					
Fayette Chamber of Commerce 65 W Main St	Uniontown	PA	15401	724-437-4571	438-3304
TF: 800-916-9365 ■ *Web:* www.fayettechamber.com					
StrongLand Chamber of Commerce					
1129 Industrial Pk Rd Ste 108 PO Box 10	Vandergrift	PA	15690	724-845-5426	
Web: allekiskistrong.com/					
Warren County Chamber of Commerce (WCCBI)					
308 Market St	Warren	PA	16365	814-723-3050	723-6024
Web: www.wccbi.org					
Main Line Chamber of Commerce					
175 Strafford Ave Ste 130	Wayne	PA	19087	610-687-6232	687-8085
Web: www.mlcc.org					
Greater Waynesboro Chamber of Commerce					
Five Roadside Ave	Waynesboro	PA	17268	717-762-7123	762-7124
Web: www.waynesboro.org					
Greater West Chester Chamber of Commerce					
119 N High St	West Chester	PA	19380	610-696-4046	696-9110
Web: www.greaterwestchester.com					
Greater Wilkes-Barre Chamber of Business & Industry					
2 Public Sq PO Box 5340	Wilkes-Barre	PA	18710	570-823-2101	822-5951
TF: 800-701-8449 ■ *Web:* www.wilkes-barre.org					
Williamsport/Lycoming Chamber of Commerce					
100 W Third St	Williamsport	PA	17701	570-326-1971	321-1208
TF: 800-732-2258 ■ *Web:* www.williamsport.org					
York County Chamber of Commerce					
96 S George St Ste 300	York	PA	17401	717-848-4000	843-6737
Web: www.ycea-pa.org					

Rhode Island

				Phone	Fax
East Providence Chamber of Commerce					
1011 Waterman Ave	East Providence	RI	02914	401-438-1212	435-4581
Web: www.eastprovchamber.com					
North Central Chamber of Commerce					
255 Greenville Ave	Johnston	RI	02919	401-349-4674	349-4676
Web: www.ncrichamber.com					
Northern Rhode Island Chamber of Commerce					
Six Blackstone Vly Pl Ste 301	Lincoln	RI	02865	401-334-1000	334-1009
Web: www.nrichamber.com					
Newport County Chamber of Commerce					
35 Valley Rd	Middletown	RI	02842	401-847-1600	849-5848
Web: www.newportchamber.com					
North Kingstown Chamber of Commerce					
8045 Post Rd	North Kingstown	RI	02852	401-295-5566	295-5582
Web: www.northkingstown.com					
Greater Providence Chamber of Commerce					
30 Exchange Terr	Providence	RI	02903	401-521-5000	621-6109
Web: www.providencechamber.com					
Southern Rhode Island Chamber of Commerce					
230 Old Tower Hill Rd	Wakefield	RI	02879	401-783-2801	789-3120
Web: www.skchamber.com					
East Bay Chamber of Commerce					
16 Cutler St Ste 102	Warren	RI	02885	401-245-0750	245-0110
TF: 877-797-9790 ■ *Web:* www.eastbaychamberri.org					
Central Rhode Island Chamber of Commerce					
3288 Post Rd	Warwick	RI	02886	401-732-1100	732-1107
Web: www.centralrichamber.com					

South Carolina

				Phone	Fax
Abbeville Chamber of Commerce 107 Ct Sq	Abbeville	SC	29620	864-366-4600	366-4068
Web: www.visitabbevillesc.com					
Greater Aiken Chamber of Commerce					
121 Richland Ave E PO Box 892	Aiken	SC	29802	803-641-1111	641-4174
Web: www.aikenchamber.net					
Anderson Area Chamber of Commerce					
907 N Main St Ste 200	Anderson	SC	29621	864-226-3454	226-3300
TF: 800-922-1150 ■ *Web:* www.andersonscchamber.com					
Kershaw County Chamber of Commerce					
607 S Broad St	Camden	SC	29020	803-432-2525	432-4181
TF: 800-968-4037 ■ *Web:* www.kershawcountychamber.org					
West Metro Chamber of Commerce 1006 12th St	Cayce	SC	29033	803-794-6504	794-6505
TF: 866-720-5400 ■ *Web:* wmvc.publishpath.com/					
Chester County Chamber of Commerce					
109 Gadsden St	Chester	SC	29706	803-581-4142	581-2431
Web: www.chesterchamber.com					
Laurens County Chamber of Commerce					
291 Professional Pk Rd	Clinton	SC	29325	864-833-2716	833-6935
TF: 866-548-9674 ■ *Web:* www.laurenscounty.org					
Greater Columbia Chamber of Commerce					
930 Richland St	Columbia	SC	29201	803-733-1110	733-1149
Web: www.columbiachamber.com					
Conway Area Chamber of Commerce 203 Main St	Conway	SC	29526	843-248-2273	248-0003
TF: 888-272-8700 ■ *Web:* www.conwayscchamber.com					
Greater Darlington Chamber of Commerce					
38 Public Sq	Darlington	SC	29532	843-393-2641	393-8059
Web: hstanle3.wix.com/darlingtonchamber					
Dillon County Chamber of Commerce					
100 N MacArthur Ave	Dillon	SC	29536	843-774-8551	774-0114
Web: www.cityofdillonsc.us					
Greater Easley Chamber of Commerce					
2001 E Main St PO Box 241	Easley	SC	29641	864-859-2693	859-1941
Web: www.easleychamber.net					

Phone | Fax

Georgetown County Chamber of Commerce
531 Front St ... Georgetown SC 29440 843-546-8436 520-4876
TF: 800-777-7705 ■ *Web:* www.visitgeorge.com

Greater Greenville Chamber of Commerce
24 Cleveland St ... Greenville SC 29601 864-242-1050 282-8509*
**Fax:* PR ■ *TF:* 866-485-5262 ■ *Web:* www.greenvillechamber.org

Greenwood Chamber of Commerce
110 Phoenix St ... Greenwood SC 29646 864-223-8431 229-9785
Web: www.greenwoodscchamber.org

Greater Hartsville Chamber of Commerce
PO Box 578 ... Hartsville SC 29551 843-332-6401 332-8017
TF: 866-747-0060 ■ *Web:* www.hartsvillechamber.org

Hilton Head Island-Bluffton Chamber of Commerce
One Chamber Dr ... Hilton Head Island SC 29928 843-785-3673 785-7110
TF: 800-523-3373 ■ *Web:* www.hiltonheadisland.org

Williamsburg Hometown Chamber of Commerce
136 N Academy St PO Box 696 ... Kingstree SC 29556 843-355-6431 355-3343
Web: www.williamsburgsc.org

Lancaster County Chamber of Commerce
PO Box 430 ... Lancaster SC 29721 803-283-4105 286-4360
Web: www.lancasterchambersc.org

Clarendon County Chamber of Commerce
19 N Brooks St ... Manning SC 29102 803-435-4405 435-2653
TF: 800-731-5253 ■ *Web:* www.clarendoncounty.com

Berkeley County Chamber of Commerce
PO Box 968 ... Moncks Corner SC 29461 843-761-8238 899-6491
TF: 800-882-0337 ■ *Web:* www.berkeleysc.org

Myrtle Beach Area Chamber of Commerce
1200 N Oak St ... Myrtle Beach SC 29577 843-626-7444 626-0009
TF: 800-356-3016 ■ *Web:* www.visitmyrtlebeach.com

Newberry County Chamber of Commerce
1209 Caldwell St PO Box 396 ... Newberry SC 29108 803-276-4274 276-4373
Web: newberrycountychamber.com/

North Augusta Chamber of Commerce
406 W Ave ... North Augusta SC 29841 803-279-2323 279-0003
Web: www.northaugustachamber.org

Charleston Metro Chamber of Commerce
4500 Leeds Ave Ste 100 ... North Charleston SC 29405 843-577-2510 723-4853
Web: www.charlestonchamber.net

Orangeburg County Chamber of Commerce
155 Riverside Dr SW PO Box 328 ... Orangeburg SC 29116 803-534-6821 531-9435
TF: 800-545-6153 ■ *Web:* www.orangeburgchamber.com

York County Regional Chamber of Commerce
116 E Main St ... Rock Hill SC 29731 803-324-7500 324-1889
Web: www.yorkcountychamber.com

Spartanburg Area Chamber of Commerce
105 N Pine St ... Spartanburg SC 29302 864-594-5000 594-5055
Web: www.spartanburgchamber.com

Greater Summerville-Dorchester County Chamber of Commerce
402 N Main St ... Summerville SC 29483 843-873-2931 875-4464
Web: greatersummerville.org

Greater Sumter Chamber of Commerce
32 E Calhoun St ... Sumter SC 29150 803-775-1231 775-0915
TF: 888-868-0737 ■ *Web:* www.sumterchamber.com

Union County Chamber of Commerce 135 W Main St ... Union SC 29379 864-427-9039 427-9030
TF: 877-202-8755 ■ *Web:* www.unionsc.info

Walterboro-Colleton Chamber of Commerce
109 Benson St ... Walterboro SC 29488 843-549-9595 549-5775
Web: walterboro.org

South Dakota

Phone | Fax

Aberdeen Area Chamber of Commerce
516 S Main St ... Aberdeen SD 57401 605-225-2860 225-2437
TF: 800-874-9038 ■ *Web:* www.aberdeen-chamber.com

Pierre Area Chamber of Commerce
800 W Dakota Ave ... Pierre SD 57501 605-224-7361 224-6485
TF: 800-962-2034 ■ *Web:* www.pierre.org

Rapid City Area Chamber of Commerce
444 Mt Rushmore Rd N ... Rapid City SD 57701 605-343-1744 343-6550
Web: www.rapidcitychamber.com

Sioux Falls Area Chamber of Commerce
200 N Phillips Ave Ste 102 ... Sioux Falls SD 57104 605-336-1620 336-6499
Web: www.siouxfalls.com

Tennessee

Phone | Fax

Cheatham County Chamber of Commerce
108 N Main St PO Box 354 ... Ashland City TN 37015 615-792-6722 792-5001
Web: www.cheathamchamber.org

Bartlett Area Chamber of Commerce
2969 Elmore Pk Rd ... Bartlett TN 38134 901-372-9457 372-9488
Web: www.bartlettchamber.org

Bristol Chamber of Commerce
20 Volunteer Pkwy ... Bristol TN 37620 423-989-4850 989-4867
Web: www.bristolchamber.org

Chattanooga Area Chamber of Commerce
811 Broad St ... Chattanooga TN 37402 423-756-2121 267-7242
TF: 877-756-7684 ■ *Web:* www.chattanoogachamber.com

Clarksville Area Chamber of Commerce
25 Jefferson St Ste 300 ... Clarksville TN 37040 931-647-2331 645-1574
TF: 800-530-2487 ■ *Web:* www.clarksvillechamber.com

Cleveland/Bradley Chamber of Commerce
225 Keith St ... Cleveland TN 37311 423-472-6587 472-2019
TF: 800-533-9930 ■ *Web:* www.clevelandchamber.com

Anderson County Chamber of Commerce
245 N Main St Ste 200 ... Clinton TN 37716 865-457-2559 463-7480
Web: www.andersoncountychamber.org

Collierville Chamber of Commerce
485 Halle Pk Dr ... Collierville TN 38017 901-853-1949 853-2399
Web: www.colliervillechamber.com

Phone | Fax

Maury Alliance 106 W Sixth St ... Columbia TN 38401 931-388-2155 380-0335
Web: www.mauryalliance.com

Cookeville Area-Putnam County Chamber of Commerce
One W First St ... Cookeville TN 38501 931-526-2211 526-4023
TF: 800-264-5541 ■ *Web:* www.cookevillechamber.com

Covington-Tipton County Chamber of Commerce
PO Box 683 ... Covington TN 38019 901-476-9727 476-0056
Web: www.covington-tiptoncochamber.com

Crossville Cumberland County Chamber of Commerce
34 S Main St ... Crossville TN 38555 931-484-8444 484-7511
TF: 877-465-3861 ■ *Web:* www.crossville-chamber.com

Jefferson County Chamber of Commerce
532 Patriot Dr ... Dandridge TN 37725 865-397-9642 397-0164
TF: 877-237-3847 ■ *Web:* www.jefferson-tn-chamber.org

Dickson County Chamber of Commerce
119 Hwy 70 E ... Dickson TN 37055 615-446-2349 441-3112
TF: 877-718-4967 ■ *Web:* www.dicksoncountychamber.com

Weakley County Chamber of Commerce
114 W Maple St PO Box 67 ... Dresden TN 38225 731-364-3787 364-2099
Web: www.weakleycountychamber.com

Dyersburg/Dyer County Chamber of Commerce
2000 Commerce Ave ... Dyersburg TN 38024 731-285-3433 286-4926
Web: dyerchamber.com

Elizabethton/Carter County Chamber of Commerce
Hwy 19 E ... Elizabethton TN 37644 423-547-3850 547-3854
Web: www.elizabethtonchamber.com

Fayetteville-Lincoln County Chamber of Commerce
208 S Elk Ave ... Fayetteville TN 37334 931-433-1234 433-9087
TF: 888-433-1238 ■ *Web:* www.fayettevillelincolncountychamber.com

Williamson County-Franklin Chamber of Commerce
5005 Meridian Blvd Ste 150 ... Franklin TN 37067 615-771-1912 790-5337
TF: 800-356-3445 ■ *Web:* williamsonchamber.com

Germantown Area Chamber of Commerce
2195 S Germantown Rd ... Germantown TN 38138 901-755-1200 755-9168
Web: www.germantownchamber.com

Greene County Partnership & Chamber of Commerce
115 Academy St ... Greeneville TN 37743 423-638-4111 638-5345
Web: www.greenecountypartnership.com

Hendersonville Area Chamber of Commerce
100 Country Dr Ste 104 ... Hendersonville TN 37075 615-824-2818 250-3637
Web: www.hendersonvillechamber.com

Jackson Area Chamber of Commerce
197 Auditorium St ... Jackson TN 38301 731-423-2200 424-4860
TF: 866-262-8867 ■ *Web:* www.jacksontn.com

Johnson City/Jonesborough/Washington County Chamber of Commerce
603 E Market St ... Johnson City TN 37601 423-461-8000 461-8047
TF: 800-852-3392 ■ *Web:* www.johnsoncitytnchamber.com

Kingsport Area Chamber of Commerce
151 E Main St ... Kingsport TN 37660 423-392-8800
Web: www.kingsportchamber.org

Roane County Chamber of Commerce
1209 N Kentucky St ... Kingston TN 37763 865-376-5572 376-4978
Web: www.roanealliance.org

Knoxville Area Chamber Partnership
17 Market Sq Ste 201 ... Knoxville TN 37902 865-637-4550 523-2071
Web: www.knoxvillechamber.com

Lawrence County Chamber of Commerce
1609 N Locust Ave PO Box 86 ... Lawrenceburg TN 38464 931-762-4911 762-3153
TF: 877-388-4911 ■ *Web:* www.selectlawrence.com

Lebanon-Wilson County Chamber of Commerce
149 Public Sq ... Lebanon TN 37087 615-444-5503 443-0596
Web: www.lebanonwilsontnchamber.org

Loudon County Chamber of Commerce (LCCC)
318 Angel Row ... Loudon TN 37774 865-458-2067 458-1206
Web: www.loudoncountychamberofcommerce.com

Madison Rivergate Area Chamber of Commerce
301 Madison St ... Madison TN 37115 615-865-5400 865-0448
Web: www.madisonrivergatechamber.com

Blount County Chamber of Commerce
201 S Washington St ... Maryville TN 37804 865-983-2241 984-1386
Web: www.blountchamber.com

McMinnville-Warren County Chamber of Commerce
110 S Ct Sq ... McMinnville TN 37110 931-473-6611 473-4741
Web: www.warrentn.com

Memphis Regional Chamber of Commerce
22 N Front St Ste 200 ... Memphis TN 38103 901-543-3500 543-3510
Web: www.memphischamber.com

Morristown Area Chamber of Commerce
825 W First N St ... Morristown TN 37814 423-586-6382 586-6576
Web: www.morristownchamber.com

Mount Juliet/West Wilson County Chamber of Commerce
46 W Caldwell St ... Mount Juliet TN 37122 615-758-3478 754-8595
Web: www.mtjulietchamber.com

Rutherford County Chamber of Commerce
501 Memorial Blvd ... Murfreesboro TN 37129 615-893-6565 890-7600
TF: 800-716-7560 ■ *Web:* www.rutherfordchamber.org

Donelson-Hermitage Chamber of Commerce
125 Donelson Pike PO Box 140200 ... Nashville TN 37214 615-883-7896 391-4880
TF: 800-688-9889 ■ *Web:* www.d-hchamber.com

Nashville Chamber of Commerce
211 Commerce St Ste 100 ... Nashville TN 37201 615-743-3000 743-3004
Web: www.nashvillechamber.com

Newport/Cocke County Chamber of Commerce
433-B Prospect Ave ... Newport TN 37821 423-623-7201
Web: www.cockecounty.org

Oak Ridge Chamber of Commerce
1400 Oak Ridge Tpke ... Oak Ridge TN 37830 865-483-1321 483-1678
Web: www.orcc.org

Paris-Henry County Chamber of Commerce
2508 Eastwood St ... Paris TN 38242 731-642-3431 642-3454
TF: 800-345-1103 ■ *Web:* www.paristnchamber.com

Giles County Chamber of Commerce
110 N Second St ... Pulaski TN 38478 931-363-3789 363-7279
Web: www.gilescountychamber.com

	City	State	Zip	Phone	Fax
Rogersville/Hawkins County Chamber of Commerce 107 E Main St Ste 100 *Web:* www.rogersvillechamber.us	Rogersville	TN	37857	423-272-2186	272-2186
Shelbyville-Bedford County Chamber of Commerce 100 N Cannon Blvd *TF:* 888-662-2525 ■ *Web:* www.shelbyvilletn.com	Shelbyville	TN	37160	931-684-3482	684-3483
Robertson County Chamber ofCommerce 503 W Ct Sq *Web:* robertsonchamber.org	Springfield	TN	37172	615-384-3800	384-1260
Claiborne County Chamber of Commerce 1732 Main St PO Box 649 *TF:* 800-332-8164 ■ *Web:* www.claibornecounty.com	Tazewell	TN	37879	423-626-4149	626-1611
Greater Gibson County Area Chamber of Commerce 200 E Eaton St *Web:* www.gibsoncountytn.com	Trenton	TN	38382	731-855-0973	855-0979
Franklin County Chamber of Commerce 44 Chamber Way PO Box 280 *TF:* 866-462-5991 ■ *Web:* www.franklincountychamber.com	Winchester	TN	37398	931-967-6788	967-9418

Texas

	City	State	Zip	Phone	Fax
Abilene Chamber of Commerce 174 Cypress St Ste 200 *Web:* www.abilenechamber.com	Abilene	TX	79601	325-677-7241	677-0622
Alice Chamber of Commerce (ACC) 612 E Main St PO Box 1609 *Web:* www.alicetxchamber.org	Alice	TX	78333	361-664-3454	664-2291
Allen Chamber of Commerce 210 W McDermott Dr *Web:* www.allenchamber.com	Allen	TX	75013	972-727-5585	727-9000
Alvin-Manvel Area Chamber of Commerce 105 W Willis St *TF:* 888-755-6864 ■ *Web:* www.alvinmanvelchamber.org	Alvin	TX	77511	281-331-3944	585-8662
Amarillo Chamber of Commerce 1000 S Polk St *Web:* www.amarillo-chamber.org	Amarillo	TX	79101	806-373-7800	373-3909
Arlington Chamber of Commerce 505 E Border St *Web:* www.arlingtontx.com	Arlington	TX	76010	817-275-2613	701-0893
Atlanta Area Chamber of Commerce 101 NE St *Web:* www.atlantatexas.org	Atlanta	TX	75551	903-796-3296	796-5711
Greater Austin Chamber of Commerce 535 E 5th St *TF:* 888-409-5380 ■ *Web:* www.austinchamber.com	Austin	TX	78701	512-478-9383	478-9615
Bastrop Chamber of Commerce 927 Main St *Web:* www.bastropchamber.com	Bastrop	TX	78602	512-321-2419	303-0305
Baytown Chamber of Commerce 1300 Rolling Brook Ste 400 *Web:* www.baytownchamber.com	Baytown	TX	77521	281-422-8359	428-1758
Beaumont Chamber of Commerce 1110 Pk St *Web:* www.bmtcoc.org	Beaumont	TX	77701	409-838-6581	833-6718
Hurst-Euless-Bedford Chamber of Commerce 2109 Martin Dr *Web:* www.heb.org	Bedford	TX	76021	817-283-1521	267-5111
Bee County Chamber of Commerce 1705 N St Mary *Web:* www.beecountychamber.org	Beeville	TX	78102	361-358-3267	
Bonham Area Chamber of Commerce 327 N. Main *Web:* www.fannincountytexas.com/	Bonham	TX	75418	903-583-4811	583-7972
Washington County Chamber of Commerce 314 S Austin St *TF:* 888-273-6426 ■ *Web:* www.brenhamtexas.com	Brenham	TX	77833	979-836-3695	836-2540
Brownsville Chamber of Commerce 1600 University Blvd *Web:* www.brownsvillechamber.com	Brownsville	TX	78520	956-542-4341	504-3348
Brownwood Area Chamber of Commerce 600 E Depot St *Web:* www.brownwoodchamber.org	Brownwood	TX	76801	325-646-9535	643-6686
Bryan-College Station Chamber of Commerce 4001 E 29th St Ste 175 *TF:* 800-777-8292 ■ *Web:* www.bcschamber.org	Bryan	TX	77802	979-260-5200	164-9791
Burleson Area Chamber of Commerce 1044 SW Wilshire Blvd *Web:* burlesonchamber.com/	Burleson	TX	76028	817-295-6121	295-6192
Canyon Chamber of Commerce 1518 Fifth Ave *TF:* 800-999-9481 ■ *Web:* www.canyonchamber.org	Canyon	TX	79015	806-655-7815	655-4608
Panola County Chamber of Commerce 300 W Panola St *Web:* www.carthagetexas.com	Carthage	TX	75633	903-693-6634	693-8578
Cleburne Chamber of Commerce 1511 W Henderson St *TF:* 888-253-2876 ■ *Web:* www.cleburnechamber.com	Cleburne	TX	76033	817-645-2455	641-3069
Greater Conroe-Lake Conroe Area Chamber of Commerce 505 W Davis St *Web:* www.conroe.org	Conroe	TX	77301	936-756-6644	756-6462
Greater Conroe/Lake Conroe Area Chamber of Commerce PO Box 2347 *Web:* www.conroe.org	Conroe	TX	77305	936-756-6644	756-6462
Coppell Chamber of Commerce 509 W Bethel Rd Ste 200 *Web:* www.coppellchamber.org	Coppell	TX	75019	972-393-2829	393-0659
Copperas Cove Chamber of Commerce 204 E Robertson Ave *Web:* www.copperascove.com	Copperas Cove	TX	76522	254-547-7571	547-5015
Corsicana Area Chamber of Commerce 120 N 12th St *TF:* 866-222-7100 ■ *Web:* www.corsicana.org	Corsicana	TX	75110	903-874-4731	874-4187
Cy-Fair Houston Chamber of Commerce 11734 Barker Cypress Ste 105 *Web:* www.cyfairchamber.com	Cypress	TX	77433	281-373-1390	373-1394
Dallas Northeast Chamber of Commerce 9543 Losa Dr Ste 118 *Web:* www.eastdallaschamber.com	Dallas	TX	75218	214-328-4100	
Greater Dallas Chamber of Commerce 700 N Pearl St Ste 1200 *Web:* www.dallaschamber.org	Dallas	TX	75201	214-746-6600	746-6799
Metrocrest Chamber of Commerce 5100 Belt Line Rd Ste 430 *Web:* www.metrocrestchamber.com	Dallas	TX	75254	469-587-0420	587-0428
North Dallas Chamber of Commerce 10707 Preston Rd *Web:* www.ndcc.org	Dallas	TX	75230	214-368-6485	691-5584
Oak Cliff Chamber of Commerce 400 S Zang Blvd Ste 110 *Web:* www.oakcliffchamber.org	Dallas	TX	75208	214-943-4567	943-4582
Southeast Dallas Chamber of Commerce 802 S Buckner Blvd *Web:* www.sedallaschamber.org	Dallas	TX	75217	214-398-9590	398-9591
Deer Park Chamber of Commerce 110 Ctr St *Web:* www.deerpark.org	Deer Park	TX	77536	281-479-1559	476-4041
Del Rio Chamber of Commerce (DRCoC) 1915 Veterans Blvd *TF General:* 800-889-8149 ■ *Web:* www.drchamber.com	Del Rio	TX	78840	830-775-3551	774-1813
Denton Chamber of Commerce 414 W Pkwy St *TF:* 800-747-2316 ■ *Web:* www.denton-chamber.org	Denton	TX	76201	940-382-9693	382-0040
DeSoto Chamber of Commerce 2010 N Hampton Rd Ste 200 *Web:* www.desotochamber.org	DeSoto	TX	75115	972-224-3565	354-1022
North Galveston County Chamber of Commerce 218 FM 517 W *Web:* www.northgalvestoncountychamber.com	Dickinson	TX	77539	281-534-4380	534-4389
Duncanville Chamber of Commerce 300 E Wheatland Rd *Web:* www.duncanvillechamber.org	Duncanville	TX	75116	972-780-4990	298-9370
Eagle Pass Chamber of Commerce 400 E Garrison St *TF:* 888-355-3224 ■ *Web:* eaglepasstexas.com	Eagle Pass	TX	78852	830-773-3224	773-8844
Edinburg Chamber of Commerce 602 W University Dr *TF:* 800-800-7214 ■ *Web:* www.edinburg.com	Edinburg	TX	78540	956-383-4974	383-6942
Greater El Paso Chamber of Commerce 10 Civic Ctr Plz *Web:* www.elpaso.org	El Paso	TX	79901	915-534-0500	534-0510
Farmers Branch Chamber of Commerce 12875 Josey Ln Ste 150 *Web:* www.fbchamber.com	Farmers Branch	TX	75234	972-243-8966	243-8968
Flower Mound Chamber of Commerce 700 Parker Sq Ste 100 *Web:* www.flowermoundchamber.com	Flower Mound	TX	75028	972-539-0500	539-4307
Fort Worth Chamber of Commerce 777 Taylor St Ste 900 *Web:* www.fortworthchamber.com	Fort Worth	TX	76102	817-336-2491	877-4034
Friendswood Chamber of Commerce 1100 S Friendswood Dr *Web:* www.friendswood-chamber.com	Friendswood	TX	77546	281-482-3329	482-3911
Garland Chamber of Commerce 520 N Glenbrook Dr *Web:* www.garlandchamber.com	Garland	TX	75040	972-272-7551	276-9261
Georgetown Chamber of Commerce 100 Stadium Dr *Web:* www.georgetownchamber.org	Georgetown	TX	78626	512-930-3535	930-3587
Gilmer Area Chamber of Commerce 106 Buffalo St *Web:* www.gilmerareachamber.com	Gilmer	TX	75644	903-843-2413	843-3759
Lake Granbury Area Chamber of Commerce 3408 E Hwy 377 *Web:* www.granburychamber.com	Granbury	TX	76049	817-573-1622	573-0805
Grapevine Chamber of Commerce 200 Vine St *TF:* 866-322-8667 ■ *Web:* www.grapevinechamber.org	Grapevine	TX	76051	817-481-1522	424-5208
Northeast Tarrant Chamber of Commerce 5001 Denton Hwy *Web:* www.netarrant.org	Haltom City	TX	76117	817-281-9376	281-9379
Harlingen Area Chamber of Commerce 311 E Tyler St *Web:* www.harlingen.com	Harlingen	TX	78550	956-423-5440	425-3870
Henderson Area Chamber of Commerce 201 N Main St *Web:* www.hendersontx.com	Henderson	TX	75652	903-657-5528	657-9454
Clear Lake Area Chamber of Commerce 1201 NASA Pkwy *TF:* 800-877-8339 ■ *Web:* www.clearlakearea.com	Houston	TX	77058	281-488-7676	488-8981
Galleria Area Chamber of Commerce 10370 Richmond Ave Ste 125 *Web:* www.hwcoc.org	Houston	TX	77042	713-785-4922	785-4944
Greater Heights Area Chamber of Commerce 545 W 19th St Second Fl *Web:* www.heightschamber.com	Houston	TX	77008	713-861-6735	861-9310
Greater Houston Partnership 1200 Smith St Ste 700 *Web:* www.houston.org	Houston	TX	77002	713-844-3600	844-0200
Houston Intercontinental Chamber of Commerce 250 N Sam Houston Pkwy E Ste 200 *Web:* www.nhgcc.org	Houston	TX	77060	281-260-3163	
Houston Northwest Chamber of Commerce (HNW) 3920 Cypress Creek Pkwy *Web:* www.houstonnwchamber.org	Houston	TX	77068	281-440-4160	440-5302
Houston West Chamber of Commerce 10370 Richmond Ave Ste 125 *Web:* www.hwcoc.org	Houston	TX	77042	713-785-4922	785-4944
North Ch Area Chamber of Commerce 13301 E Fwy # 100 *Web:* www.northchannelarea.com	Houston	TX	77015	713-450-3600	450-0700
South Belt-Ellington Chamber of Commerce 10500 Scarsdale Blvd *Web:* www.southbeltchamber.com	Houston	TX	77089	281-481-5516	922-7045

Chamber / Address	City	State	ZIP	Phone	Fax
Lake Houston Area Chamber of Commerce, The 110 W Main St *Web:* www.humbleareachamber.org	Humble	TX	77338	281-446-2128	446-7483
Huntsville-Walker County Chamber of Commerce 1327 11th St *TF:* 800-289-0389 ■ *Web:* www.chamber.huntsville.tx.us	Huntsville	TX	77340	936-295-8113	295-0571
Kerrville Area Chamber of Commerce 1700 Sidney Baker St Ste 100 *Web:* www.kerrvilletx.com	Kerrville	TX	78028	830-896-1155	896-1175
Greater Killeen Chamber of Commerce One Santa Fe Plz *TF:* 866-790-4769 ■ *Web:* www.killeenchamber.com	Killeen	TX	76540	254-526-9551	526-6090
Kingsville Chamber of Commerce 635 E King Ave # 124 *Web:* www.kingsville.org	Kingsville	TX	78363	361-592-6438	592-0866
La Porte-Bayshore Chamber of Commerce 712 W Fairmont Pkwy *Web:* www.laportechamber.org	La Porte	TX	77571	281-471-1123	471-1710
Brazosport Area Chamber of Commerce 300 Abner Jackson Pkwy *Web:* www.brazosport.org	Lake Jackson	TX	77566	979-285-2501	285-2505
Laredo-Webb County Chamber of Commerce 2310 San Bernardo Ave *TF:* 800-292-2122 ■ *Web:* www.laredochamber.com	Laredo	TX	78042	956-722-9895	791-4503
Lewisville Chamber of Commerce 551 N Valley Pkwy *Web:* www.lewisvillechamber.org	Lewisville	TX	75067	972-436-9571	436-5949
Liberty-Dayton Area Chamber of Commerce 1801 Trinity St *Web:* www.libertydaytonchamber.com	Liberty	TX	77575	936-336-5736	336-1159
Longview Partnership 410 N Ctr St *TF:* 800-338-7232 ■ *Web:* www.longviewchamber.com	Longview	TX	75601	903-237-4000	237-4049
Lubbock Chamber of Commerce 1500 Broadway Ste 101 *Web:* www.lubbockchamber.com	Lubbock	TX	79401	806-761-7000	761-7013
Lufkin/Angelina County Chamber of Commerce 1615 S Chestnut St *TF:* 800-409-5659 ■ *Web:* www.lufkintexas.org	Lufkin	TX	75901	936-634-6644	634-8726
Greater Cedar Creek Lake Area Chamber of Commerce 604 S Third St Ste E *TF:* 800-331-6844 ■ *Web:* www.cclake.net	Mabank	TX	75147	903-887-3152	887-3695
Greater Marshall Chamber of Commerce 213 W Austin St *TF:* 800-953-7868 ■ *Web:* www.marshall-chamber.com	Marshall	TX	75670	903-935-7868	935-9982
McAllen Chamber of Commerce 1200 Ash Ave *Web:* www.mcallenchamber.com	McAllen	TX	78501	956-682-2871	687-2917
McKinney Chamber of Commerce 2150 S Central Expy # 150 *Web:* www.mckinneychamber.com	McKinney	TX	75070	972-542-0163	548-0876
Mesquite Chamber of Commerce 617 N Ebrite St *TF:* 800-541-2355 ■ *Web:* www.mesquitechamber.com	Mesquite	TX	75149	972-285-0211	285-3535
Midland Chamber of Commerce 109 N Main St *TF:* 800-624-6435 ■ *Web:* www.midlandtxchamber.com	Midland	TX	79701	432-683-3381	686-3556
Mineral Wells Area Chamber of Commerce 511 E Hubbard St *TF:* 800-252-6989 ■ *Web:* www.mineralwellstx.com	Mineral Wells	TX	76067	940-325-2557	328-0850
Mission Chamber of Commerce 202 W Tom Landry St *Web:* www.missionchamber.com	Mission	TX	78572	956-585-2727	585-3044
Mount Pleasant-Titus County Chamber of Commerce 1604 N Jefferson Ave *Web:* www.mtpleasanttx.com	Mount Pleasant	TX	75455	903-572-8567	572-0613
Nacogdoches County Chamber of Commerce 2516 N St *Web:* www.nacogdoches.org	Nacogdoches	TX	75965	936-560-5533	560-3920
New Braunfels Chamber of Commerce 390 S Seguin St *TF:* 800-572-2626 ■ *Web:* innewbraunfels.com	New Braunfels	TX	78130	830-625-2385	625-7918
Odessa Chamber of Commerce 700 N Grant St Ste 200 *TF:* 800-780-4678 ■ *Web:* www.odessachamber.com	Odessa	TX	79761	432-332-9111	333-7858
Greater Orange Area Chamber of Commerce 1012 Green Ave *Web:* www.orangetexaschamber.org	Orange	TX	77630	409-883-3536	886-3247
Lamar County Chamber of Commerce 1125 Bonham St *TF:* 800-727-4789 ■ *Web:* www.paristexas.com	Paris	TX	75460	903-784-2501	784-2503
Pasadena Chamber of Commerce 4334 Fairmont Pkwy *Web:* www.pasadenachamber.org	Pasadena	TX	77504	281-487-7871	487-5530
Pearland Area Chamber of Commerce 6117 Broadway St *TF:* 888-604-5888 ■ *Web:* www.pearlandchamber.com	Pearland	TX	77581	281-485-3634	485-2420
Greater Pflugerville Chamber of Commerce 101 S Third St PO Box 483 *Web:* www.pfchamber.com	Pflugerville	TX	78691	512-251-7799	251-7802
Pharr Chamber of Commerce 308 W Pk St **Fax Area Code:* 512 ■ *Web:* www.pharrchamber.com	Pharr	TX	78577	956-787-1481	477-0836*
Plainview Chamber of Commerce 1906 W Fifth St *Web:* www.plainviewtexaschamber.com	Plainview	TX	79072	806-296-7431	296-0819
Plano Chamber of Commerce 1200 E 15th St *Web:* www.planochamber.org	Plano	TX	75074	972-424-7547	422-5182
Greater Port Arthur Chamber of Commerce 4749 Twin City Hwy Ste 300 *Web:* www.portarthurtexas.com	Port Arthur	TX	77642	409-963-1107	962-1997
Richardson Chamber of Commerce 411 Belle Grove Dr *Web:* www.richardsonchamber.com	Richardson	TX	75080	972-792-2800	792-2825
Rockwall County Chamber of Commerce 697 E IH- 30 *Web:* www.rockwallchamber.org	Rockwall	TX	75087	972-771-5733	772-3642
Rosenberg-Richmond Area Chamber of Commerce 4120 Ave H *TF:* 877-382-7414 ■ *Web:* www.cfbca.org	Rosenberg	TX	77471	281-342-5464	342-2990
Round Rock Chamber of Commerce 212 E Main St *TF:* 800-227-7776 ■ *Web:* www.roundrockchamber.org	Round Rock	TX	78664	512-255-5805	255-3345
Rowlett Chamber of Commerce 3910 Main St *Web:* www.rowlettchamber.com	Rowlett	TX	75088	972-475-3200	463-1699
Greater San Antonio Chamber of Commerce 602 E Commerce St *TF:* 888-828-8680 ■ *Web:* www.sachamber.org	San Antonio	TX	78205	210-229-2100	229-1600
North San Antonio Chamber of Commerce 12930 Country Pkwy *TF:* 877-495-5888 ■ *Web:* www.northsachamber.com	San Antonio	TX	78216	210-344-4848	525-8207
South San Antonio Chamber of Commerce 7902 Challenger Dr *Web:* www.southsachamber.org	San Antonio	TX	78235	210-533-1600	533-1611
San Marcos Area Chamber of Commerce 202 N CM Allen Pkwy *TF:* 888-200-5620 ■ *Web:* www.sanmarcostexas.com	San Marcos	TX	78666	512-393-5900	393-5912
Seguin Area Chamber of Commerce 116 N Camp St *TF:* 888-674-7224 ■ *Web:* www.seguinchamber.com	Seguin	TX	78155	830-379-6382	379-6971
Randolph Metrocom Chamber of Commerce 9374 Valhalla *Web:* metrocomchamber.org	Selma	TX	78154	210-658-8322	654-1606
Springtown Chamber of Commerce 112 S Main St *Web:* www.springtowntexas.com	Springtown	TX	76082	817-220-7828	523-3268
Fort Bend Chamber of Commerce 445 Commerce Green Blvd *Web:* www.fortbendchamber.com	Sugar Land	TX	77478	281-491-0800	491-0112
Hopkins County Chamber of Commerce 300 Connally St *Web:* www.sulphursprings-tx.com	Sulphur Springs	TX	75482	903-885-6515	885-6516
Temple Chamber of Commerce Two N Fifth St PO Box 158 *Web:* www.templetx.org	Temple	TX	76501	254-773-2105	773-0661
Texarkana Chamber of Commerce 819 N State Line Ave *Web:* www.texarkanachamber.com	Texarkana	TX	75501	903-792-7191	793-4304
Texas City-La Marque Chamber of Commerce 9702 Emmett F Lowry Expy *TF General:* 877-986-8719 ■ *Web:* www.texascitychamber.com	Texas City	TX	77591	409-935-1408	316-0901
South Montgomery County Woodlands Chamber of Commerce 1400 Woodloch Forest Dr Ste 300 *Web:* www.woodlandschamber.org	The Woodlands	TX	77380	281-367-5777	292-1655
Tyler Area Chamber of Commerce 315 N Broadway Ave *TF:* 800-235-5712 ■ *Web:* www.tylertexas.com	Tyler	TX	75702	903-592-1661	593-2746
Victoria Chamber of Commerce 3404 N Ben Wilson St *Web:* www.victoriachamber.org	Victoria	TX	77901	361-573-5277	573-5911
Greater Waco Chamber of Commerce 101 S Third St *Web:* www.wacochamber.com	Waco	TX	76701	254-752-6551	752-6618
Weatherford Chamber of Commerce 401 Ft Worth St *TF:* 888-594-3801 ■ *Web:* www.weatherford-chamber.com	Weatherford	TX	76086	817-596-3801	613-9216
Rio Grande Valley Chamber of Commerce 322 S Missouri St *TF:* 800-628-5115 ■ *Web:* www.valleychamber.com	Weslaco	TX	78596	956-968-3141	968-0210
Weslaco Area Chamber of Commerce 301 W Railroad *TF:* 800-700-2443 ■ *Web:* www.weslaco.com	Weslaco	TX	78596	956-968-2102	968-6451
Lake Tawakoni Regional Chamber of Commerce 100 Hwy 276 W PO Box 1149 *Web:* www.laketawakonichamber.org	West Tawakoni	TX	75474	903-447-3020	231-1120
Wichita Falls Board of Commerce & Industry 900 Eigth St Ste 218 *Web:* wichitafallschamber.com/	Wichita Falls	TX	76301	940-723-2741	723-8773

Utah

Chamber / Address	City	State	ZIP	Phone	Fax
Davis Chamber of Commerce 450 Simmons Way # 220 *Web:* www.davischamberofcommerce.com	Kaysville	UT	84037	801-593-2200	593-2212
Cache Chamber of Commerce 160 N Main St *Web:* www.cachechamber.com	Logan	UT	84321	435-752-2161	753-5825
Murray Area Chamber of Commerce (MACC) 5250 S Commerce Dr Ste 180 *TF:* 877-209-0068 ■ *Web:* www.murraychamber.org	Murray	UT	84107	801-263-2632	263-8262
Commission for Economic Development in Orem 56 N State St Rm 101 *Web:* econdev.orem.org	Orem	UT	84058	801-229-7172	226-2678
Provo/Orem Chamber of Commerce 111 S University Ave Ste 215 *Web:* thechamber.org	Provo	UT	84601	801-851-2555	851-2557
St George Area Chamber of Commerce 97 E St George Blvd *Web:* www.stgeorgechamber.com	Saint George	UT	84770	435-628-1658	673-1587
Salt Lake City Chamber of Commerce 175 East University Blvd 400 S Ste 600 *Web:* www.slchamber.com	Salt Lake City	UT	84111	801-364-3631	328-5098
Sandy Area Chamber of Commerce 8807 South 700 East *Web:* www.sandychamber.com	Sandy	UT	84070	801-566-0344	566-0346
South Salt Lake Chamber of Commerce 220 E Morris Ave Ste 150 *Web:* www.sslchamber.com	South Salt Lake	UT	84115	801-466-3377	467-3322
Tooele County Chamber of Commerce 154 S Main *TF:* 800-378-0690 ■ *Web:* www.tooelechamber.com	Tooele	UT	84074	435-882-0690	833-0946

Name / Address	City	State	ZIP	Phone	Fax
West Jordan Chamber of Commerce 8000 Redwood Rd *Web:* www.westjordanchamber.com	West Jordan	UT	84088	801-569-5151	569-5153
ChamberWest 1241 W Village Main Dr Ste B *Web:* www.chamberwest.org	West Valley City	UT	84119	801-977-8755	977-8329

Vermont

Name / Address	City	State	ZIP	Phone	Fax
Great Falls Region Chamber of Commerce Five Westminster St *Web:* www.gfrcc.org	Bellows Falls	VT	05101	802-463-4280	
Bennington Area Chamber of Commerce 100 Veterans Memorial Dr *TF:* 800-229-0252 ■ *Web:* www.bennington.com	Bennington	VT	05201	802-447-3311	447-1163
Central Vermont Chamber of Commerce 33 Stewart Rd *TF:* 877-887-3678 ■ *Web:* www.central-vt.com	Berlin	VT	05602	802-229-5711	229-5713
Brattleboro Area Chamber of Commerce 180 Main St *TF:* 877-254-4565 ■ *Web:* www.brattleborochamber.org	Brattleboro	VT	05301	802-254-4565	254-5675
Lake Champlain Regional Chamber of Commerce 60 Main St Ste 100 *TF:* 877-686-5253 ■ *Web:* www.vermont.org	Burlington	VT	05401	802-863-3489	863-1538
Addison County Chamber of Commerce 93 Ct St *Web:* www.addisoncounty.com	Middlebury	VT	05753	802-388-7951	388-8066
Vermont's North Country Chamber of Commerce 246 Cswy St *TF:* 800-635-4643 ■ *Web:* www.vtnorthcountry.org	Newport	VT	05855	802-334-7782	334-7238
Franklin County Regional Chamber of Commerce Two N Main St Ste 101 *Web:* www.visitfranklincountyvt.com	Saint Albans	VT	05478	802-524-2444	527-2256

Virginia

Name / Address	City	State	ZIP	Phone	Fax
Alexandria Chamber of Commerce 801 N Fairfax St Ste 402 *Web:* www.alexchamber.com	Alexandria	VA	22314	703-549-1000	739-3805
Mount Vernon-Lee Chamber of Commerce 6911 Richmond Hwy Ste 320 *Web:* www.mtvernon-leechamber.org	Alexandria	VA	22306	703-360-6925	360-6928
Amherst County Chamber of Commerce 154 S Main St *Web:* www.amherstvachamber.com	Amherst	VA	24521	434-946-0990	946-0879
Annandale Chamber of Commerce 7263 Maple Pl Ste 207 *Web:* www.annandalechamber.com	Annandale	VA	22003	703-256-7232	256-7233
Bedford Area Chamber of Commerce 305 E Main St *Web:* www.bedfordareachamber.com	Bedford	VA	24523	540-586-9401	587-6650
Danville Pittsylvania County Chamber of Commerce 8653 US Hwy 29 PO Box 99 *Web:* www.dpchamber.org	Blairs	VA	24527	434-836-6990	836-6955
Charlottesville Regional Chamber of Commerce 209 Fifth St NE *Web:* www.cvillechamber.com	Charlottesville	VA	22902	434-295-3141	295-3144
Pulaski County Chamber of Commerce 4440 Cleburne Blvd Ste B *Web:* www.pulaskichamber.info	Dublin	VA	24084	540-674-1991	674-4163
Central Fairfax Chamber of Commerce 11166 Fairfax Blvd Ste 407 *Web:* www.cfcc.org	Fairfax	VA	22030	703-591-2450	591-2820
Botetourt County Chamber of Commerce 13 W Main St *Web:* www.bot-co-chamber.com	Fincastle	VA	24090	540-473-8280	473-8365
Greater Augusta Regional Chamber of Commerce 30 Ladd Rd PO Box 1107 *Web:* augustava.com	Fishersville	VA	22939	540-324-1133	324-1136
Franklin-Southampton Area Chamber of Commerce 108 W Third Ave PO Box 531 *Web:* fsachamber.com	Franklin	VA	23851	757-562-4900	562-6138
Fredericksburg Regional Chamber of Commerce 2300 Fall Hill Ave Ste 240 *TF:* 888-338-0252 ■ *Web:* www.fredericksburgchamber.org	Fredericksburg	VA	22401	540-373-9400	373-9570
Front Royal-Warren County Chamber of Commerce 106 Chester St *Web:* www.frontroyalchamber.com	Front Royal	VA	22630	540-635-3185	635-9758
Galax-Carroll-Grayson Chamber of Commerce 405 N Main St *Web:* twincountychamber.com/	Galax	VA	24333	276-236-2184	236-1338
Virginia Peninsula Chamber of Commerce 21 Enterprise Pkwy Ste 100 *TF:* 800-462-3204 ■ *Web:* www.virginiapeninsulachamber.com	Hampton	VA	23666	757-262-2000	262-2009
Harrisonburg-Rockingham Chamber of Commerce 800 Country Club Rd *Web:* www.hrchamber.org	Harrisonburg	VA	22802	540-434-3862	434-4508
Hopewell-Prince George Chamber of Commerce 210 N Second Ave *Web:* hpgchamber.org	Hopewell	VA	23860	804-458-5536	458-0041
Loudoun County Chamber of Commerce 19301 Winmeade Dr Ste 210 *Web:* www.loudounchamber.org	Lansdowne	VA	20176	703-777-2176	777-1392
Lexington-Rockbridge County Chamber of Commerce 100 E Washington St *Web:* www.lexrockchamber.com	Lexington	VA	24450	540-463-5375	463-3567
Lynchburg Regional Chamber of Commerce 2015 Memorial Ave *Web:* www.lynchburgchamber.org	Lynchburg	VA	24501	434-845-5966	522-9592
Prince William County-Greater Manassas Chamber of Commerce 9720 Capital Ct Ste 203 *TF:* 877-867-3853 ■ *Web:* www.pwchamber.org	Manassas	VA	20110	703-368-6600	368-4733
Prince William Regional Chamber of Commerce 9720 Capital Ct Suite 203 *TF:* 877-867-3853 ■ *Web:* pwchamber.org/	Manassas	VA	20110	703-368-6600	368-4733
Chamber of Commerce of Smyth County 214 W Main St *Web:* www.smythchamber.org	Marion	VA	24354	276-783-3161	783-8003
Martinsville-Henry County Chamber of Commerce 115 Broad St *TF:* 800-811-6302 ■ *Web:* www.martinsville.com	Martinsville	VA	24112	276-632-6401	632-5059
Eastern Shore of Virginia Chamber of Commerce 19056 Pkwy Rd *Web:* www.esvachamber.org	Melfa	VA	23410	757-787-2460	787-8687
Hampton Roads Chamber of Commerce 500 E Main St Ste 700 *Web:* www.hamptonroadschamber.com	Norfolk	VA	23510	757-622-2312	622-5563
Hampton Roads Chamber of Commerce-Suffolk 500 E Main St Ste 700 *Web:* www.hamptonroadschamber.com	Norfolk	VA	23510	757-622-2312	622-5563
Wise County Chamber of Commerce 765 Pk Ave PO Box 226 *Web:* www.wisecountychamber.org	Norton	VA	24273	276-679-0961	679-2655
Petersburg Chamber of Commerce 325 E Washington St PO Box 928 *Web:* www.petersburgvachamber.com	Petersburg	VA	23804	804-733-8131	733-9891
Greater Reston Chamber of Commerce 1763 Fountain Dr *TF:* 844-430-7073 ■ *Web:* www.restonchamber.org	Reston	VA	20190	703-707-9045	707-9049
Greater Richmond Chamber of Commerce 600 E Main St Seventh Fl *Web:* www.grcc.com	Richmond	VA	23219	804-648-1234	783-9366
Roanoke Regional Chamber of Commerce 210 S Jefferson St *TF:* 800-506-0489 ■ *Web:* www.roanokechamber.org	Roanoke	VA	24011	540-983-0700	983-0723
Salem/Roanoke County Chamber of Commerce 611 E Main St *Web:* www.s-rcchamber.org	Salem	VA	24153	540-387-0267	387-4110
Halifax County Chamber of Commerce 515 Broad St *Web:* www.halifaxchamber.net	South Boston	VA	24592	434-572-3085	572-1733
Greater Springfield Chamber of Commerce 6434 Brandon Ave Ste 208 *Web:* www.springfieldchamber.org	Springfield	VA	22150	703-866-3500	866-3501
Tazewell Area Chamber of Commerce Tazewell Mall PO Box 6 *TF:* 855-233-6362 ■ *Web:* www.tazewellchamber.com	Tazewell	VA	24651	276-988-5091	988-5093
Fairfax County Chamber of Commerce (FCCC) 8230 Old Courthouse Rd Ste 350 *Web:* www.fairfaxchamber.org	Vienna	VA	22182	703-749-0400	749-9075
Vienna-Tysons Regional Chamber of Commerce 513 Maple Ave W Second Fl *Web:* www.tysonschamber.org	Vienna	VA	22180	703-281-1333	242-1482
Fauquier County Chamber of Commerce 205-1 Keith St *Web:* www.fauquierchamber.org	Warrenton	VA	20186	540-347-4414	347-7510
Williamsburg Area Chamber of Commerce 421 N Boundary St PO Box 3495 *TF:* 800-368-6511 ■ *Web:* www.williamsburgcc.com	Williamsburg	VA	23187	757-229-6511	253-1397
Top of Virginia Regional Chamber 407 S Loudoun St *Web:* www.regionalchamber.biz	Winchester	VA	22601	540-662-4118	722-6365
Wytheville-Wythe-Bland Chamber of Commerce Inc 150 E Monroe St PO Box 563 *Web:* www.wwbchamber.com	Wytheville	VA	24382	276-223-3365	223-3412

Washington

Name / Address	City	State	ZIP	Phone	Fax
Grays Harbor Chamber of Commerce 506 Duffy St *TF:* 800-321-1924 ■ *Web:* www.graysharbor.org	Aberdeen	WA	98520	360-532-1924	533-7945
Auburn Area Chamber of Commerce 25 2nd St NW Ste B *Web:* www.auburnareawa.org	Auburn	WA	98001	253-833-0700	735-4091
Bellingham/Whatcom Chamber of Commerce & Industry 119 N Commercial St Ste 110 *Web:* bellingham.com	Bellingham	WA	98225	360-734-1330	734-1332
Bremerton Area Chamber of Commerce 286 Fourth St *Web:* www.bremertonchamber.org	Bremerton	WA	98337	360-479-3579	479-1033
Camas-Washougal Chamber of Commerce 422 NE Fourth Ave *TF:* 800-468-5865 ■ *Web:* www.cwchamber.com	Camas	WA	98607	360-834-2472	834-9171
Centralia-Chehalis Chamber of Commerce 500 NW Chamber of Commerce Way *TF:* 800-525-3323 ■ *Web:* www.chamberway.com	Chehalis	WA	98532	360-748-8885	748-8763
Greater Edmonds Chamber of Commerce 121 Fifth Ave N *Web:* www.edmondswa.com	Edmonds	WA	98020	425-670-1496	712-1808
Enumclaw Area Chamber of Commerce 1421 Cole St *Web:* www.enumclawchamber.com	Enumclaw	WA	98022	360-825-7666	825-8369
Greater Federal Way Chamber of Commerce 31919 First Ave S Ste 202 *Web:* www.federalwaychamber.com	Federal Way	WA	98003	253-838-2605	661-9050
Gig Harbor/Peninsula Area Chamber of Commerce 3311 Harborview Dr Ste 101 *Web:* www.gigharborchamber.net	Gig Harbor	WA	98332	253-851-6865	851-6881
Greater Issaquah Chamber of Commerce 155 NW Gilman Blvd *TF:* 800-668-3030 ■ *Web:* www.issaquahchamber.com	Issaquah	WA	98027	425-392-7024	392-8101

	City	State	ZIP	Phone	Fax
Tri-City Area Chamber of Commerce 7130 W Grandridge Blvd *Web:* www.tricityregionalchamber.com	Kennewick	WA	99336	509-736-0510	783-1733
Kent Chamber of Commerce 524 W Meeker St Ste 1 *TF:* 800-321-2808 ■ *Web:* www.kentchamber.com	Kent	WA	98032	253-854-1770	854-8567
Greater Kirkland Chamber of Commerce 401 Pk Pl Ste 102 *Web:* www.kirklandchamber.org	Kirkland	WA	98033	425-822-7066	827-4878
Lacey-Thurston County Chamber of Commerce 8300 Quinault Dr NE # A *Web:* www.laceychamber.com	Lacey	WA	98516	360-491-4141	491-9403
Lakewood Chamber of Commerce 4650 Steilacoom Blvd SW Ste 109 *Web:* lakewood-chamber.com	Lakewood	WA	98499	253-582-9400	581-5241
Kelso Longview Chamber of Commerce 1563 Olympia Way *Web:* www.kelsolongviewchamber.org	Longview	WA	98632	360-423-8400	423-0432
Greater Maple Valley-Black Diamond Chamber of Commerce 23745 225th Way SE Ste 205 *Web:* www.maplevalleychamber.org	Maple Valley	WA	98038	425-432-0222	413-8017
Moses Lake Area Chamber of Commerce 324 S Pioneer Way *TF:* 800-992-6234 ■ *Web:* www.moseslake.com	Moses Lake	WA	98837	509-765-7888	
Greater Oak Harbor Chamber of Commerce 32630 SR 20 PO Box 883 *Web:* www.oakharborchamber.com	Oak Harbor	WA	98277	360-675-3755	679-1624
Olympia/Thurston County Chamber of Commerce 809 Legion Way *Web:* www.thurstonchamber.com	Olympia	WA	98501	360-357-3362	357-3376
Port Orchard Chamber of Commerce 1014 Bay St Ste 3 *Web:* www.portorchard.com	Port Orchard	WA	98366	360-876-3505	895-1920
Pullman Chamber of Commerce 415 N Grand Ave *TF:* 800-365-6948 ■ *Web:* www.pullmanchamber.com	Pullman	WA	99163	509-334-3565	332-3232
Eastern Pierce County Chamber of Commerce 323 N Meridian PO Box 1298 *Web:* www.puyallupsumnerchamber.com	Puyallup	WA	98371	253-845-6755	
Redmond Chamber of Commerce 8383 158th Ave NE Ste 225 *Web:* www.oneredmond.org	Redmond	WA	98052	425-885-4014	882-0996
Greater Renton Chamber of Commerce 625 S Fourth St *TF:* 877-467-3686 ■ *Web:* www.gorenton.com	Renton	WA	98057	425-226-4560	226-4287
Ballard Chamber of Commerce 2208 NW Market St Ste 100 *Web:* www.ballardchamber.com	Seattle	WA	98107	206-784-9705	783-8154
Greater Seattle Chamber of Commerce 1301 Fifth Ave Ste 1500 *TF:* 866-978-2997 ■ *Web:* www.seattlechamber.com	Seattle	WA	98101	206-389-7200	389-7288
Greater University Chamber of Commerce 4710 University Way NE Ste 114 *Web:* udistrictpartnership.org/	Seattle	WA	98105	206-547-4417	547-5266
Lake City Chamber of Commerce 12345 30th Ave NE Ste FG *Web:* www.lakecitychamber.org	Seattle	WA	98125	206-363-3287	363-6456
Shelton-Mason County Chamber of Commerce 215 W Railroad Ave PO Box 2389 *TF:* 800-576-2021 ■ *Web:* www.sheltonchamber.org	Shelton	WA	98584	360-426-2021	426-8678
Shoreline Chamber of Commerce 18560 First Ave NE *Web:* www.shorelinechamber.com	Shoreline	WA	98155	206-361-2260	361-2268
Greater Spokane Inc 801 W Riverside Ave Ste 100 *TF:* 800-776-5263 ■ *Web:* www.greaterspokane.org	Spokane	WA	99201	509-624-1393	747-0077
Spokane Valley Chamber of Commerce 9507 E Sprague Ave *Web:* www.spokanevalleychamber.org	Spokane Valley	WA	99206	509-924-4994	924-4992
Tacoma-Pierce County Chamber of Commerce 950 Pacific Ave Ste 300 *Web:* www.tacomachamber.org	Tacoma	WA	98402	253-627-2175	597-7305
Southwest King County Chamber of Commerce 14220 Interurban Ave S Ste 134 *TF:* 800-638-8613 ■ *Web:* www.swkcc.org	Tukwila	WA	98168	206-575-1633	575-2007
Greater Vancouver Chamber of Commerce 1101 Broadway Ste 100 *Web:* www.vancouverusa.com	Vancouver	WA	98660	360-694-2588	693-8279
Walla Walla Valley Chamber of Commerce 29 E Sumach St *TF:* 866-826-9422 ■ *Web:* www.wwvchamber.com	Walla Walla	WA	99362	509-525-0850	522-2038
Wenatchee Valley Chamber of Commerce 2 S Mission St *TF:* 800-572-7753 ■ *Web:* www.wenatchee.org	Wenatchee	WA	98801	509-662-2116	663-2022
Greater Yakima Chamber of Commerce 10 N 9th St PO Box 1490 *Web:* www.yakima.org	Yakima	WA	98901	509-248-2021	248-0601

West Virginia

	City	State	ZIP	Phone	Fax
Beckley-Raleigh County Chamber of Commerce 245 N Kanawha St *TF:* 877-987-3847 ■ *Web:* www.brccc.com	Beckley	WV	25801	304-252-7328	252-7373
Buckhannon-Upshur Chamber of Commerce 14 E Main St *Web:* www.buchamber.com	Buckhannon	WV	26201	304-472-1722	472-4938
Charleston Regional Chamber of Commerce 1116 Smith St *TF:* 800-792-4326 ■ *Web:* www.charlestonareaalliance.org	Charleston	WV	25301	304-340-4253	340-4275
Harrison County Chamber of Commerce 520 W Main St *Web:* www.harrisoncountychamber.com	Clarksburg	WV	26301	304-624-6331	624-5190
Elkins-Randolph County Chamber of Commerce (ERCCC) 200 Executive Plz *Web:* www.erccc.com	Elkins	WV	26241	304-636-2717	636-8046
Marion County Chamber of Commerce 110 Adams St *TF:* 800-975-8379 ■ *Web:* www.marionchamber.com	Fairmont	WV	26554	304-363-0442	363-0480
Huntington Regional Chamber of Commerce 720 Fourth Ave *Web:* www.huntingtonchamber.org	Huntington	WV	25701	304-525-5131	525-5158
Mineral County Chamber of Commerce 40« Main St *Web:* www.mineralchamber.com	Keyser	WV	26726	304-788-2513	
Preston County Chamber of Commerce 200 W Main St Ste A *Web:* www.prestonchamber.com	Kingwood	WV	26537	304-329-0576	329-1407
Greater Greenbrier Chamber of Commerce 200 W Washington St Ste C *TF:* 800-833-2068 ■ *Web:* www.greenbrierwvchamber.org	Lewisburg	WV	24901	304-645-2818	497-3001
Martinsburg-Berkeley County Chamber of Commerce 198 Viking Way *TF:* 800-332-9007 ■ *Web:* www.berkeleycounty.org	Martinsburg	WV	25401	304-267-4841	263-4695
Morgantown Area Chamber of Commerce 1029 University Ave Ste 101 *TF General:* 800-618-2525 ■ *Web:* www.morgantownchamber.org	Morgantown	WV	26505	304-292-3311	296-6619
Marshall County Chamber of Commerce 609 Jefferson Ave *Web:* www.marshallcountychamber.com	Moundsville	WV	26041	304-845-2773	845-2773
Wetzel County Chamber of Commerce 201 Main St PO Box 271 *Web:* www.wetzelcountychamber.com	New Martinsville	WV	26155	304-455-3825	455-3637
Mason County Area Chamber of Commerce 305 Main St *Web:* www.masoncountychamber.org	Point Pleasant	WV	25550	304-675-1050	675-1601
Frontier Communications 1522 N Walker St **Fax Area Code:* 716 ■ *TF:* 877-378-9289 ■ *Web:* frontier.my.yahoo.com/	Princeton	WV	24740	304-487-1502	551-3346*
Wheeling Area Chamber of Commerce 1310 Market St *Web:* www.wheelingchamber.com	Wheeling	WV	26003	304-233-2575	233-1320

Wisconsin

	City	State	ZIP	Phone	Fax
Fox Cities Chamber of Commerce & Industry 125 N Superior St *TF:* 800-456-0152 ■ *Web:* www.foxcitieschamber.com	Appleton	WI	54911	920-734-7101	734-7161
Greater Beloit Chamber of Commerce 500 Public Ave *TF:* 866-981-5969 ■ *Web:* greaterbeloitchamber.org	Beloit	WI	53511	608-365-8835	365-6850
Greater Brookfield Chamber of Commerce 17100 W Bluemound Rd Ste 202 *Web:* www.brookfieldchamber.com	Brookfield	WI	53005	262-786-1886	786-1959
Chippewa Falls Area Chamber of Commerce 10 S Bridge St *TF:* 888-723-0024 ■ *Web:* www.chippewachamber.org	Chippewa Falls	WI	54729	715-723-0331	723-0332
Eau Claire Area Chamber of Commerce 101 N Farwell St Ste 101 *Web:* www.eauclairechamber.org	Eau Claire	WI	54703	715-834-1204	834-1956
Fond du Lac Area Assn of Commerce 207 N Main St *TF:* 800-279-8811 ■ *Web:* www.fdlac.com	Fond du Lac	WI	54935	920-921-9500	921-9559
Green Bay Area Chamber of Commerce PO Box 1660 *Web:* www.titletown.org	Green Bay	WI	54305	920-437-8704	437-1024
Greenfield Chamber of Commerce 4818 S 76th St Ste 129 **Fax Area Code:* 877 ■ *Web:* www.thegreenfieldchamber.com	Greenfield	WI	53220	414-327-8500	327-0084*
Heart of the Valley Chamber of Commerce 101 E Wisconsin Ave *Web:* www.heartofthevalleychamber.com	Kaukauna	WI	54130	920-766-1616	766-5504
Kenosha Area Chamber of Commerce 600 52nd St Ste 130 *Web:* www.kenoshaareachamber.com	Kenosha	WI	53140	262-654-1234	654-4655
Greater Madison Chamber of Commerce PO Box 71 *Web:* www.greatermadisonchamber.com	Madison	WI	53701	608-256-8348	256-0333
Manitowoc-Two Rivers Area Chamber of Commerce 1515 Memorial Dr *TF:* 866-727-5575 ■ *Web:* chambermanitowoccounty.org	Manitowoc	WI	54220	920-684-5575	684-1915
Menomonee Falls Chamber of Commerce N 88 W 16621 Appleton Ave *Web:* www.fallschamber.com	Menomonee Falls	WI	53051	262-251-2430	
Greater Menomonie Area Chamber of Commerce 342 E Main St *TF:* 800-283-1862 ■ *Web:* www.menomoniechamber.org	Menomonie	WI	54751	715-235-9087	235-2824
Merrill Area Chamber of Commerce 705 N Ctr Ave *TF:* 877-907-2757 ■ *Web:* www.merrillchamber.org	Merrill	WI	54452	715-536-9474	539-2043
Metropolitan Milwaukee Assn of Commerce 756 N Milwaukee St *TF:* 800-362-9472 ■ *Web:* www.mmac.org	Milwaukee	WI	53202	414-287-4100	271-7753
Monroe Chamber of Commerce & Industry 1505 Ninth St *Web:* www.monroechamber.org	Monroe	WI	53566	608-325-7648	328-2241
Oconomowoc Area Chamber of Commerce 175 E Wisconsin Ave *Web:* www.oconomowoc.org	Oconomowoc	WI	53066	262-567-2666	567-3477
Oshkosh Chamber of Commerce 120 Jackson St *Web:* www.oshkoshchamber.com	Oshkosh	WI	54901	920-303-2266	303-2263
Racine Area Mfg & Commerce 300 Fifth St *Web:* www.racinechamber.com	Racine	WI	53403	262-634-1931	634-7422
Ripon Area Chamber of Commerce 127 Jefferson St *Web:* www.ripon-wi.com	Ripon	WI	54971	920-748-6764	748-6784

Phone *Fax*

Shawano Country Chamber of Commerce
1263 S Main St. Shawano WI 54166 715-524-2139 524-3127
TF: 800-235-8528 ■ *Web:* www.shawanocountry.com

Sheboygan County Chamber of Commerce
621 S Eigth St. Sheboygan WI 53081 920-457-9491 457-6269
TF: 800-457-9497 ■ *Web:* www.sheboygan.org

Portage County Business Council
5501 Vern Holmes Dr. Stevens Point WI 54481 715-344-1940 344-4473
Web: www.portagecountybiz.com

Superior-Douglas County Chamber of Commerce
205 Belknap St. Superior WI 54880 715-394-7716 394-3810
TF: 800-942-5313 ■ *Web:* www.superiorchamber.org

Waukesha County Chamber of Commerce
2717 N Grandview Blvd Ste 204. Waukesha WI 53188 262-542-4249 542-8068
TF: 800-937-2965 ■ *Web:* www.waukesha.org

Wausau Area Chamber of Commerce
200 Washington St Ste 120 Wausau WI 54403 715-845-6231 845-6235
Web: www.wausauchamber.com

Wauwatosa Chamber of Commerce
10437 Innovation Dr. Wauwatosa WI 53226 414-453-2330
Web: tosachamber.org

West Allis-West Milwaukee Chamber of Commerce
6737 W Washington St Ste 2141 West Allis WI 53214 414-302-9901 302-9918
TF: 800-554-1448 ■ *Web:* www.wawmchamber.com

West Bend Area Chamber of Commerce
304 S Main St. West Bend WI 53095 262-338-2666 338-1771
TF: 888-338-8666 ■ *Web:* www.wbachamber.org

Heart of Wisconsin Business & Economic Alliance
1120 Lincoln St Wisconsin Rapids WI 54494 715-423-1830 423-1865
Web: www.wisconsinrapidschamber.com

Wyoming

Phone *Fax*

Casper Area Chamber of Commerce 500 N Ctr St Casper WY 82601 307-234-5311 265-2643
TF: 866-234-5311 ■ *Web:* www.casperwyoming.org

Greater Cheyenne Chamber of Commerce
121 W 15th St Ste 204 Cheyenne WY 82001 307-638-3388 778-1407
Web: www.cheyennechamber.org

Campbell County Chamber of Commerce
314 S Gillette Ave Gillette WY 82716 307-682-3673 682-0538
TF: 877-682-3481 ■ *Web:* www.gillettechamber.com

Jackson Hole Chamber of Commerce 112 Ctr St Jackson WY 83001 307-733-3316 733-5585
Web: www.jacksonholechamber.com

Laramie Area Chamber of Commerce
800 S Third St Laramie WY 82070 307-745-7339 745-4624
TF: 866-876-1012 ■ *Web:* www.laramie.org

Rock Springs Chamber of Commerce
1897 Dewar Dr Rock Springs WY 82901 307-362-3771 362-3838
TF: 800-463-8637 ■ *Web:* www.rockspringswyoming.net

Sheridan County Chamber of Commerce
1517 E Fifth St Sheridan WY 82801 307-672-2485 672-7321
TF: 800-453-3650 ■ *Web:* www.sheridanwyomingchamber.org

140 CHAMBERS OF COMMERCE - US - STATE

Phone *Fax*

US Chamber of Commerce 1615 H St NW Washington DC 20062 202-659-6000 463-5836
TF: 800-638-6582 ■ *Web:* www.uschamber.com

Alaska State Chamber of Commerce
471 W 36th Ave Anchorage AK 99503 907-586-2010
Web: www.alaskachamber.com

Arizona Chamber of Commerce & Industry
3200 N Central Ave Ste 1125 Phoenix AZ 85012 602-248-9172 265-1262
TF: 800-498-6973 ■ *Web:* www.azchamber.com

Arkansas State Chamber of Commerce
1200 W Capitol Ave PO Box 3645 Little Rock AR 72203 501-372-2222 372-2722
TF: 800-482-1127 ■ *Web:* www.arkansasstatechamber.com

Association of Washington Business
PO Box 658 Olympia WA 98507 360-943-1600 943-5811
TF: 800-521-9325 ■ *Web:* www.awb.org

Business Council of Alabama
Two N Jackson St PO Box 76 Montgomery AL 36101 334-834-6000
TF: 800-665-9647 ■ *Web:* www.bcatoday.org

Business Council of New York State Inc
152 Washington Ave. Albany NY 12210 518-465-7511 465-4389
TF: 800-358-1202 ■ *Web:* www.bcnys.org

California Chamber of Commerce
1215 K St Ste 1400 PO Box 1736 Sacramento CA 95812 916-444-6670 325-1272
Web: www.calchamber.com

Colorado Assn of Commerce & Industry
1600 Broadway Ste 1000 Denver CO 80202 303-831-7411 860-1439
Web: www.cochamber.com

Connecticut Business & Industry Assn
350 Church St Hartford CT 06103 860-244-1900 278-8562
Web: www.cbia.com

Delaware State Chamber of Commerce
1201 N Orange St Ste 200 PO Box 671 Wilmington DE 19899 302-655-7221 654-0691
TF: 800-292-9507 ■ *Web:* www.dscc.com

District of Columbia Chamber of Commerce
506 Ninth St NW. Washington DC 20004 202-347-7201 638-6762
Web: www.dcchamber.org

Florida Chamber of Commerce
136 S Bronough St PO Box 11309 Tallahassee FL 32302 850-521-1200 521-1219
TF: 877-521-1230 ■ *Web:* www.flchamber.com

Georgia Chamber of Commerce
233 Peachtree St NE Ste 2000 Atlanta GA 30303 404-223-2264 223-2290
TF: 800-241-2286 ■ *Web:* www.gachamber.com

Idaho Assn of Commerce & Industry
816 W Bannock St Boise ID 83701 208-343-1849 338-5623
Web: www.iaci.org

Phone *Fax*

Illinois State Chamber of Commerce
300 S Wacker Dr Ste 1600 Chicago IL 60606 312-983-7100 983-7101
Web: www.ilchamber.org

Indiana State Chamber of Commerce
115 W Washington St Ste 850-S Indianapolis IN 46204 317-264-3110 264-6855
Web: www.indianachamber.com

Iowa Assn of Business & Industry
400 E Ct Ave Ste 100 Des Moines IA 50309 515-280-8000 244-8907
TF: 800-383-4224 ■ *Web:* www.iowaabi.org

Kansas Chamber of Commerce & Industry
835 SW Topeka Blvd. Topeka KS 66612 785-357-6321 357-4732
Web: www.kansaschamber.org

Kentucky Chamber of Commerce
464 Chenault Rd. Frankfort KY 40601 502-695-4700 695-6824
TF: 800-533-0127 ■ *Web:* www.kychamber.com

Louisiana Assn of Business & Industry
3113 Vly Creek Dr PO Box 80258. Baton Rouge LA 70898 225-928-5388 929-6054
TF: 888-816-5224 ■ *Web:* www.labi.org

Maine State Chamber of Commerce
125 Community Dr Ste 101 Augusta ME 04330 207-623-4568 622-7723
Web: www.mainechamber.org

Maryland Chamber of Commerce
60 W St Ste 100 Annapolis MD 21401 410-269-0642 269-5247
Web: www.mdchamber.org

Michigan Chamber of Commerce 600 S Walnut St Lansing MI 48933 517-371-2100 371-7224
TF: 800-748-0266 ■ *Web:* www.michamber.com

Minnesota Chamber of Commerce
400 Robert St N Ste 1500. Saint Paul MN 55101 651-292-4650 292-4656
TF: 800-821-2230 ■ *Web:* www.mnchamber.com

Mississippi Economic Council PO Box 23276. Jackson MS 39225 601-969-0022 353-0247
TF: 800-748-7626 ■ *Web:* www.msmec.com

Missouri Chamber of Commerce
428 E Capitol Ave PO Box 149 Jefferson City MO 65102 573-634-3511 634-8855
Web: www.mochamber.com

Montana Chamber of Commerce
900 Gibbon St PO 1730 Helena MT 59624 406-442-2405 442-2409
TF: 888-442-6668 ■ *Web:* www.montanachamber.com

Nebraska Chamber of Commerce & Industry
1320 Lincoln Mall # 201A Lincoln NE 68508 402-474-4422 474-5681
Web: www.nechamber.net

New England Council Inc
98 N Washington St Ste 201 Boston MA 02114 617-723-4009 723-3943
Web: www.newenglandcouncil.com

New Jersey State Chamber of Commerce
216 W State St Trenton NJ 08608 609-989-7888 989-9696
Web: www.njchamber.com

New Mexico Assn of Commerce & Industry (ACI)
2201 Buena Vista Dr SE Ste 410
PO Box 9706 Albuquerque NM 87106 505-842-0644 842-0734
Web: aci-nm.org/

North Carolina Chamber
701 Corporate Ctr Dr Ste 400 Raleigh NC 27607 919-836-1400 836-1425
Web: www.ncchamber.net/mx/hm.asp?id=home

North Dakota Chamber of Commerce
2000 Schafer St PO Box 2639 Bismarck ND 58502 701-222-0929 222-1611
TF: 800-382-1405 ■ *Web:* www.ndchamber.com

Ohio Chamber of Commerce
230 E Town St PO Box 15159 Columbus OH 43215 614-228-4201 228-6403
TF: 800-622-1893 ■ *Web:* www.ohiochamber.com

Oklahoma State Chamber 330 NE Tenth St Oklahoma City OK 73104 405-235-3669 235-3670
Web: www.okstatechamber.com

Pennsylvania Chamber of Business & Industry
417 Walnut St. Harrisburg PA 17101 717-255-3252 255-3298
TF: 800-225-7224 ■ *Web:* www.pachamber.org

Puerto Rico Chamber of Commerce
PO Box 9024033 San Juan PR 00902 787-721-6060 723-1891
Web: www.camarapr.org

South Carolina Chamber of Commerce
1201 Main St Ste1100 Columbia SC 29201 803-799-4601 779-6043
TF: 800-799-4601 ■ *Web:* www.scchamber.net

South Dakota Chamber of Commerce & Industry
108 N Euclid Ave Pierre SD 57501 605-224-6161 224-7198
TF: 800-742-8112 ■ *Web:* www.sdchamber.biz

Tennessee Chamber of Commerce & Industry
611 Commerce St Ste 3030 Nashville TN 37203 615-256-5141 256-6726
Web: www.tnchamber.org

Texas Assn of Business 1209 Nueces St Austin TX 78701 512-477-6721 477-0836
Web: www.txbiz.org

Vermont Chamber of Commerce PO Box 37 Montpelier VT 05601 802-223-3443 223-4257
TF: 800-451-4279 ■ *Web:* www.vtchamber.com

Virginia Chamber of Commerce 919 E Main St Richmond VA 23219 804-644-1607 783-6112
TF: 800-847-4882 ■ *Web:* www.vachamber.com

West Virginia Chamber of Commerce
1624 Kanawha Blvd E Charleston WV 25311 304-342-1115 342-1130
Web: www.wvchamber.com

Wisconsin Manufacturers & Commerce
PO Box 352 Madison WI 53701 608-258-3400 258-3413
Web: www.wmc.org

141 CHECK CASHING SERVICES

Phone *Fax*

ACE Cash Express 1231 Greenway Dr Ste 600 Irving TX 75038 972-550-5000 550-5150
TF: 800-817-5106 ■ *Web:* www.acecashexpress.com

Advance America Cash Advance Centers Inc
135 N Church St. Spartanburg SC 29306 864-342-5600 342-5612
NYSE: AEA ■ *TF:* 800-538-1579 ■ *Web:* www.advanceamerica.net

Cash Plus Inc 3002 Dow Ave Ste 120 Tustin CA 92780 714-731-2274 731-2099
TF: 888-707-2274 ■ *Web:* www.cashplusinc.com

Check Cashing Store (CCS)
6340 NW Fifth Way. Fort Lauderdale FL 33309 954-938-3550 938-3565
Web: www.thecheckcashingstore.com

Phone Fax

Check Cashing USA Inc 899 NW 37th Ave.............. Miami FL 33125 305-644-1840
Web: www.checkcashingusa.com

Dollar Financial Corp
1436 Lancaster Ave Ste 300......................... Berwyn PA 19312 610-296-3400 296-7844
Web: www.dfcglobalcorp.com

eCommLink Inc 319 E Warm Springs Rd Ste 100...... Las Vegas NV 89119 702-588-5100
Web: www.ecommlink.com

Enviro-Pro-Tech Inc Eight E Quintet Rd............ Cantonment FL 32533 850-587-5588
Web: www.eptpensacola.com

Extra Help Inc 3911 W Ernestine Dr.................... Marion IL 62959 618-993-9675
Web: www.extrahelpinc.com

First Cash Financial Services Inc
690 E Lamar Blvd Ste 400......................... Arlington TX 76011 817-460-3947 461-7019
NASDAQ: FCFS ■ *Web:* ww2.firstcash.com

First Fidelity Funding & Mortgage Corp
6100 Lk Forrest Dr Ste 245........................... Atlanta GA 30328 404-943-1533
Web: firstfidelityfunding.com

Mister Money Investment 2057 Vermont Dr........ Fort Collins CO 80525 970-493-0574 490-2099
TF: 888-336-0403 ■ *Web:* ww2.firstcash.com

NIX Neighborhood Lending
1440 Rosecrans Ave........................ Manhattan Beach CA 90266 310-603-5889
Web: nixlending.com

Pay-O-Matic Corp 160 Oak Dr...................... Syosset NY 11791 516-496-4900
TF: 888-545-6311 ■ *Web:* www.payomatic.com

Policy Research Associates Inc
345 Delaware Ave................................. Delmar NY 12054 518-439-7415
Web: www.prainc.com

QC Holdings Inc
9401 Indian Creek Pkwy Ste 1500............... Overland Park KS 66210 866-660-2243
NASDAQ: QCCO ■ *TF:* 866-660-2243 ■ *Web:* www.qcholdings.com

Service General Corp 13 E Laurel St.............. Georgetown DE 19947 302-856-3500
Web: www.servicegeneral.net

United Financial Services Group
325 Chestnut St Ste 3000....................... Philadelphia PA 19106 215-238-0300 238-9056
Web: www.unitedfsg.com

Waterfield Technologies Inc
One W Third St Ste 1115............................. Tulsa OK 74103 918-858-6400
Web: www.waterfieldtechnologies.com

Widearea Systems Inc 201A Broadway St............ Frederick MD 21701 301-418-6180
Web: wideareasystems.com

142 CHECKS - PERSONAL & BUSINESS

Phone Fax

4checks.com 8245 N Union Blvd........... Colorado Springs CO 80920 866-923-0451
TF: 866-923-0451 ■ *Web:* www.4checks.com

Artistic Checks Inc
PO Box 40003 PO Box 1000................ Colorado Springs CO 80935 800-243-2577 567-5560*
**Fax Area Code:* 866 ■ *TF:* 800-243-2577 ■ *Web:* www.artisticchecks.com

Check Printers Inc 1530 Antioch Pike................ Antioch TN 37013 800-766-1217 324-3323*
**Fax Area Code:* 615 ■ *TF:* 800-766-1217 ■ *Web:* www.check-printers.com

Checks In The Mail Inc 2435 Goodwin Ln........ New Braunfels TX 78135 830-609-5500 609-6522
TF: 800-733-4443 ■ *Web:* www.secure.checksinthemail.com

Checks Unlimited
8245 N Union Blvd PO Box 35630........... Colorado Springs CO 80920 800-634-2563 231-7024*
**Fax Area Code:* 866 ■ *TF:* 800-634-2563 ■ *Web:* www.checksunlimited.com

Deluxe Business Forms 3680 Victoria St N.......... Shoreview MN 55126 651-483-7111 447-1407*
**Fax Area Code:* 800 ■ **Fax:* Sales ■ *TF Cust Svc:* 800-328-7205 ■ *Web:* ww.deluxe.com

Safeguard Business Systems Inc
8585 N Stemmons Fwy Ste 600 N........................ Dallas TX 75247 800-523-2422 439-3423
TF: 800-523-2422 ■ *Web:* www.gosafeguard.com/

CHEMICALS - AGRICULTURAL

SEE Fertilizers & Pesticides p. 2287

143 CHEMICALS - INDUSTRIAL (INORGANIC)

Phone Fax

Advance Research Chemicals Inc
1110 Keystone Ave............................... Catoosa OK 74015 918-266-6789 266-6796
Web: www.fluoridearc.com

Air Liquide America LP
2700 Post Oak Blvd Ste 1800....................... Houston TX 77056 877-855-9533 624-8793*
**Fax Area Code:* 713 ■ **Fax:* Mktg ■ *TF:* 877-855-9533 ■ *Web:* www.airliquide.com

Air Products & Chemicals Inc
7201 Hamilton Blvd............................ Allentown PA 18195 610-481-4911 706-8161*
NYSE: APD ■ **Fax:* Sales ■ *TF Prod Info:* 800-345-3148 ■ *Web:* www.airproducts.com

AkzoNobel Surface Chemistry LLC
525 W Van Buren St.............................. Chicago IL 60607 312-544-7000 544-7410
TF Cust Svc: 877-565-8432 ■ *Web:* www.akzonobel.com

Almatis Inc 501 W Pk Rd.......................... Leetsdale PA 15056 412-630-2800 630-2900
TF: 800-643-8771 ■ *Web:* www.almatis.com

American Chemet Corp 740 Waukegan Rd........... Deerfield IL 60015 847-948-0800 948-0811
Web: www.chemet.com

Americhem Inc 2000 Americhem Way.......... Cuyahoga Falls OH 44221 330-929-4213 929-4144
TF: 800-228-3476 ■ *Web:* www.americhem.com

Ampacet Corp 660 White Plains Rd.................. Tarrytown NY 10591 914-631-6600 631-7197
TF Cust Svc: 800-888-4267 ■ *Web:* www.ampacet.com

Ashta Chemicals Inc 3509 Middle Rd................ Ashtabula OH 44004 440-997-5221 992-0151
TF Cust Svc: 800-492-5082 ■ *Web:* www.ashtachemicals.com

Baerlocher production USA LLC
5890 Highland Ridge Dr......................... Cincinnati OH 45232 513-482-6300 242-9213
Web: www.baerlocher.com

BASF Canada 100 Milverton Dr Fifth Fl............ Mississauga ON L5R4H1 289-360-1300 360-6000
TF Cust Svc: 866-485-2273 ■ *Web:* www2.basf.us/basf-canada

BASF Corp 100 Campus Dr...................... Florham Park NJ 07932 973-245-6000 895-8002
TF: 800-526-1072 ■ *Web:* www.basf.com

Phone Fax

Bio-Lab Inc
1725 N Brown Rd PO Box 30000................ Lawrenceville GA 30043 678-502-4000
TF: 800-859-7946 ■ *Web:* www.biolabinc.com

BWX Technologies Inc
13024 Ballantyne Corporate Pl Ste 700.............. Lynchburg VA 28277 434-522-6000 522-5922
Web: www.babcock.com

Cabot Corp 2 Seaport Ln Ste 1300...................... Boston MA 02210 617-345-0100 342-6103
NYSE: CBT ■ *TF:* 800-322-1236 ■ *Web:* www.cabot-corp.com

Calgon Carbon Corp 500 Calgon Carbon Dr.......... Pittsburgh PA 15205 412-787-6700 787-6676
NYSE: CCC ■ *TF Cust Svc:* 800-422-7266 ■ *Web:* www.calgoncarbon.com

Carus Corp 315 Fifth St.................................. Peru IL 61354 815-223-1500 224-6697
TF: 800-435-6856 ■ *Web:* www.caruscorporation.com

Centrus Energy Corp
6903 Rockledge Dr Ste 400......................... Bethesda MD 20817 301-564-3200 564-3201
NYSE: USU ■ *TF:* 800-273-7754 ■ *Web:* www.usec.com

Chemical Products Corp 102 Old Mill Rd......... Cartersville GA 30120 770-382-2144
TF Cust Svc: 877-210-9814 ■ *Web:* www.chemicalproductscorp.com

Circle-Prosco Inc 401 N Gates Dr............... Bloomington IN 47404 812-339-3653 331-2566
Web: www.circleprosco.com

Cormetech Inc 5000 International Dr.................. Durham NC 27712 919-620-3000 620-3001
Web: www.cormetech.com

Criterion Catalysts & Technologies
16825 Northchase Dr Ste 1000....................... Houston TX 77060 281-874-2600 874-2641
Web: www.criterioncatalysts.com

Dow Chemical Co 2030 Dow Ctr........................ Midland MI 48674 989-636-1463 636-1830
NYSE: DOW ■ *TF Cust Svc:* 800-422-8193 ■ *Web:* www.dow.com

DuPont Titanium Technologies
1007 Market St............................... Wilmington DE 19898 302-774-1000 774-7321
TF: 800-441-7515 ■ *Web:* www.dupont.com

Elementis Specialties Inc
469 Old Trenton Rd........................... East Windsor NJ 08512 800-866-6800 443-2422*
**Fax Area Code:* 609 ■ *TF:* 800-866-6800 ■ *Web:* www.elementis.com

Energy Research & Generation Inc
900 Stanford Ave................................ Oakland CA 94608 510-658-9785 658-7428
Web: www.ergaerospace.com

Ensersul LP 7210 Blackfood Terr SE.................... Calgary AB T2H1M5 403-253-5969 259-2771
Web: www.enersul.com

ExxonMobil Chemical Co 13501 Katy Fwy............ Houston TX 77079 281-870-6000
Web: www.exxonmobilchemical.com

Ferro Corp Electronic Materials Div
4150 E 56th St................................ Cleveland OH 44105 216-641-8580
Web: ferro.com

FMC Corp 1735 Market St...................... Philadelphia PA 19103 215-299-6000 299-5998
NYSE: FMC ■ *TF:* 888-548-4486 ■ *Web:* www.fmc.com

FMC Corp Industrial Chemicals Group
1735 Market St............................... Philadelphia PA 19103 215-299-6000 299-6728
TF: 800-323-7107 ■ *Web:* www.fmcchemicals.com

Front Range Energy LLC
31375 Great Western Dr............................ Windsor CO 80550 970-674-2910
Web: www.frontrangeenergy.com

General Chemical Group Inc 90 E Halsey Rd....... Parsippany NJ 07054 973-515-0900 496-9414*
**Fax Area Code:* 416 ■ *TF:* 800-244-6224 ■ *Web:* www.generalchemical.com

Georgia Gulf Corp
115 Perimeter Ctr Pl Ste 460.......................... Atlanta GA 30346 770-395-4500 395-4529
Web: www.axiall.com

Giles Chemical Corp 102 Commerce St............ Waynesville NC 28786 828-452-4784 452-4786
Web: www.gileschemical.com

Green Plains Renewable Energy Inc
450 Regency Pkwy Ste 400............................ Omaha NE 68114 402-884-8700 884-8776
NASDAQ: GPRE ■ *TF:* 877-886-2288 ■ *Web:* www.gpreinc.com

Hawkins Inc 3100 E Hennepin Ave................ Minneapolis MN 55413 612-331-6910 331-5304
NASDAQ: HWKN ■ *TF:* 800-328-5460 ■ *Web:* www.hawkinschemical.com

Heucotech Ltd 99 Newbold Rd.................. Fairless Hills PA 19030 800-483-2224 736-2249*
**Fax Area Code:* 215 ■ *TF:* 800-483-2224 ■ *Web:* www.heubachcolor.de

Horsehead Corp
4955 Steubenville Pk Ste 405...................... Pittsburgh PA 15205 724-774-1020
TF: 800-648-8897 ■ *Web:* www.horsehead.net

Interstate Chemical Co Inc
2797 Freedland Rd............................... Hermitage PA 16148 724-981-3771 981-8383
TF: 800-422-2436 ■ *Web:* www.interstatechemical.com

Johnson Matthey Inc Catalysts & Chemicals Div
2001 Nolte Dr................................ West Deptford NJ 08066 856-384-7001 384-7276
Web: www.chemicals.matthey.com

Jones Hamilton Co 30354 Tracy Rd................. Walbridge OH 43465 419-666-9838 666-1817
TF: 888-858-4425 ■ *Web:* www.jones-hamilton.com

Kanto Corp 13424 N Woodrush Way.................. Portland OR 97203 503-283-0405 240-0409
TF: 866-609-5571 ■ *Web:* www.kantocorp.com

Keystone Aniline Corp 2501 W Fulton St.............. Chicago IL 60612 312-666-2015 666-8530
TF: 800-522-4393 ■ *Web:* www.dyes.com

LSB Industries Inc
16 S Pennsylvania Ave....................... Oklahoma City OK 73107 405-235-4546 235-5067
NYSE: LXU ■ *Web:* www.lsbindustries.com

Martin Marietta Magnesia Specialties Inc
8140 Corporate Dr Ste 220......................... Nottingham MD 21236 410-780-5500 780-5777
TF: 800-648-7400 ■ *Web:* www.magnesiaspecialties.com

Matheson Tri-Gas Inc 959 Rt 46 E................ Parsippany NJ 07054 973-257-1100
Web: www.mathesongas.com

Moravek Biochemicals Inc 577 Mercury Ln.............. Brea CA 92821 714-990-2018 990-1824
Web: www.moravek.com

NL Industries 16801 Greenspoint Pk Dr.............. Houston TX 77060 281-423-3300 423-3236
NYSE: NL ■ *TF:* 800-866-5600 ■ *Web:* www.nl-ind.com

Noah Technologies Corp of Texas
One Noah Pk.................................. San Antonio TX 78249 210-691-2000 691-2600
Web: www.noahtech.com

Nuclear Fuel Services Inc 1205 Banner Hill Rd.......... Erwin TN 37650 423-743-9141 743-9025
Web: www.nuclearfuelservices.com

Occidental Chemical Corp 5005 LBJ Fwy............ Dallas TX 75244 972-404-3800
Web: www.oxy.com

Old Bridge Chemicals Inc PO Box 175............. Old Bridge NJ 08857 732-727-2225 727-2653
TF: 800-275-3924 ■ *Web:* www.oldbridgechem.com

Olin Corp Olin Chlor Alkali Products Div
490 Stuart Rd NE................................ Cleveland TN 37312 423-336-4850 336-4876
Web: www.chloralkali.com

Company	City	State	Zip	Phone	Fax
OMYA Inc 39 Main St. TF: 800-451-4468 ■ Web: www.omya-na.com	Proctor	VT	05765	802-459-3311	459-6327
Phibro Animal Health Corp 300 Frank W Burr Blvd Ste 21 TF: 800-223-0434 ■ Web: www.phibrochem.com	Teaneck	NJ	07660	201-329-7300	329-7399
Plasticolors Inc 2600 Michigan Ave PO Box 816 TF: 888-661-7675 ■ Web: www.chromaflo.com	Ashtabula	OH	44005	440-997-5137	992-3613
Potash Corp 1101 Skokie Blvd TF: 800-667-0403 ■ Web: www.potashcorp.com	Northbrook	IL	60062	847-849-4200	849-4695
Praxair Inc 39 Old Ridgebury Rd NYSE: PX ■ TF: 800-772-9247 ■ Web: www.praxair.com	Danbury	CT	06810	203-837-2000	837-2731
Rutgers Organics Corp (ROC) 201 Struble Rd TF: 888-469-2188 ■ Web: federalregister.gov	State College	PA	16801	814-238-2424	
Shepherd Chemical Co 4900 Beech St. Web: www.shepchem.com	Cincinnati	OH	45212	513-731-1110	731-1532
Silberline Mfg Company Inc 130 Lincoln Dr PO Box B TF: 800-348-4824 ■ Web: www.silberline.com	Tamaqua	PA	18252	570-668-6050	668-0197
Solvay America Inc 3333 Richmond Ave TF General: 800-365-6565 ■ Web: www.solvay.com	Houston	TX	77098	713-525-6000	525-7887
Southern Ionics Inc 201 Commerce St. TF: 800-953-3585 ■ Web: www.southernionics.com	West Point	MS	39773	662-494-3055	495-2590
Synalloy Corp 775 Spartan Blvd Ste 102 PO Box 5627 NASDAQ: SYNL ■ TF Orders: 800-937-5449 ■ Web: www.synalloy.com	Spartanburg	SC	29304	864-585-3605	596-1501
Tanner Systems Inc 625 19th Ave NE TF: 800-461-6454 ■ Web: www.tannersystems.com	Saint Joseph	MN	56374	320-363-1800	
TETRA Technologies Inc 25025 I-45 N NYSE: TTI ■ TF: 800-327-7817 ■ Web: www.tetratec.com	The Woodlands	TX	77380	281-367-1983	364-4306
Texas United Corp 4800 San Felipe TF: 800-554-8658 ■ Web: www.unitedsalt.com	Houston	TX	77056	713-877-2600	877-2664
TOR Minerals International Inc 722 Burleson St NASDAQ: TORM ■ Web: www.torminerals.com	Corpus Christi	TX	78402	361-883-5591	883-7619
Tronox Inc 3301 NW 150th St TF: 866-775-5009 ■ Web: www.tronox.com	Oklahoma City	OK	73134	405-775-5000	775-5155
UOP LLC 25 E Algonquin Rd TF: 800-877-6184 ■ Web: www.uop.com	Des Plaines	IL	60017	847-391-2000	391-2253
Vulcan Materials Co 1200 Urban Ctr Dr PO Box 385014 NYSE: VMC ■ TF: 800-615-4331 ■ Web: www.vulcanmaterials.com	Birmingham	AL	35238	205-298-3000	298-2942
Westlake Chemical Corp 2801 Post Oak Blvd Ste 600 NYSE: WLK ■ TF: 888-953-3623 ■ Web: www.westlakechemical.com	Houston	TX	77056	713-960-9111	963-1562

144 CHEMICALS - INDUSTRIAL (ORGANIC)

Company	City	State	Zip	Phone	Fax
Abengoa Bioenergy Corp 16150 Main Cir Dr Ste 300 Web: www.abengoabioenergy.com	Chesterfield	MO	63017	636-728-0508	728-1148
AF Rx Inc 751 S Rose Ave Web: www.agrx.com	Oxnard	CA	93030	805-487-0696	483-6146
Altair Nanotechnologies Inc 204 Edison Way NASDAQ: ALTI ■ Web: www.altairnano.com	Reno	NV	89502	775-856-2500	856-1619
American Natural Soda Ash Corp 15 Riverside Ave Web: www.ansac.com	Westport	CT	06880	203-226-9056	227-1484
Ampacet Corp 660 White Plains Rd TF Cust Svc: 800-888-4267 ■ Web: www.ampacet.com	Tarrytown	NY	10591	914-631-6600	631-7197
Arizona Chemical Co Inc 4600 Touchton Rd E Ste 1200 Web: www.arizonachemical.com	Jacksonville	FL	32246	904-928-8700	928-8779
Badger State Ethanol LLC 820 W 17th St PO Box 317 Web: www.badgerstateethanol.com	Monroe	WI	53566	608-329-3900	329-3866
Bayer Inc 77 Belfield Rd *Fax: Hum Res ■ TF: 800-622-2937 ■ Web: www.bayer.ca	Toronto	ON	M9W1G6	416-248-0771	248-6762*
BP PLC 28100 Torch Pkwy NYSE: BP ■ TF: 877-638-5672 ■ Web: www.bp.com	Warrenville	IL	60555	630-420-5111	
Cambrex Corp 1 Meadowlands Plaza 15th Fl NYSE: CBM ■ TF: 866-286-9133 ■ Web: www.cambrex.com	East Rutherford	NJ	07073	201-804-3000	804-9852
Cardolite Corp 500 Doremus Ave *Fax Area Code: 973 ■ TF: 800-322-7365 ■ Web: www.cardolite.com	Newark	NJ	07105	800-322-7365	344-1197*
Celanese Corp 1601 W LBJ Fwy NYSE: CE ■ Web: www.celanese.com	Dallas	TX	75234	972-443-4000	
Chemical Exchange Industries Inc 900 Clinton Dr PO Box 67 Web: www.cxi.com	Galena Park	TX	77547	713-455-1206	455-8959
Chemstar Products Co 3915 Hiawatha Ave TF: 800-328-5037 ■ Web: www.chemstar.com	Minneapolis	MN	55406	612-722-0079	722-2473
Chevron Phillips Chemical Company LP 10001 Six Pines Dr TF: 800-231-1212 ■ Web: www.cpchem.com	The Woodlands	TX	77380	832-813-4100	
Colorcon Inc 415 Moyer Blvd Web: www.colorcon.com	West Point	PA	19486	215-699-7733	661-2605
CorsiTech 3200 SW Fwy Ste 2700 PO Box 27727 *Fax Area Code: 713 ■ Web: www.corsicanatech.com	Houston	TX	77027	281-431-3628	623-4652*
Dow Chemical Canada Inc (DCCI) 450 First St SW Ste 2100 TF: 800-447-4369 ■ Web: www.dow.com	Calgary	AB	T2P5H1	403-267-3500	267-3597
Dow Chemical Co 2030 Dow Ctr NYSE: DOW ■ TF Cust Svc: 800-422-8193 ■ Web: www.dow.com	Midland	MI	48674	989-636-1463	636-1830
Dow Corning Corp PO Box 994 *Fax: Hum Res ■ TF Cust Svc: 800-248-2481 ■ Web: www.dowcorning.com	Midland	MI	48686	989-496-4000	496-1886*
DSM Chemicals North America Inc 1 Columbia Nitrogen Rd *Fax: Cust Svc ■ TF: 800-526-0189 ■ Web: www.dsm.com	Augusta	GA	30901	706-849-6600	849-6999*
Eastman Chemical Co 200 S Wilcox Dr NYSE: EMN ■ *Fax: Mktg ■ TF Cust Svc: 800-327-8626 ■ Web: www.eastman.com	Kingsport	TN	37660	423-229-2000	229-1194*
Elan Chemical Co 268 Doremus Ave Web: www.elan-chemical.com	Newark	NJ	07105	973-344-8014	344-8014
First Chemical Corp 1001 Industrial Rd TF: 877-243-6178 ■ Web: dupont.com	Pascagoula	MS	39581	228-762-0870	762-5213
Heucotech Ltd 99 Newbold Rd *Fax Area Code: 215 ■ TF: 800-483-2224 ■ Web: www.heubachcolor.de	Fairless Hills	PA	19030	800-483-2224	736-2249*
Huntsman Corp 500 Huntsman Way NYSE: HUN ■ TF: 888-490-8484 ■ Web: www.huntsman.com	Salt Lake City	UT	84108	801-584-5700	584-5781
ICC Industries Inc 460 Pk Ave TF: 800-422-1720 ■ Web: www.iccchem.com	New York	NY	10022	212-521-1700	521-1970
Innospec Inc 8375 S Willow St NASDAQ: IOSP ■ *Fax Area Code: 302 ■ Web: www.innospecinc.com	Littleton	CO	80124	303-792-5554	451-1380*
Inolex Chemical Co 2101 S Swanson St *Fax: Cust Svc ■ TF Cust Svc: 800-521-9891 ■ Web: www.inolex.com	Philadelphia	PA	19148	215-271-0800	271-6282*
International Flavors & Fragrances Inc (IFF) 521 W 57th St NYSE: IFF ■ Web: www.iff.com	New York	NY	10019	212-765-5500	708-7132
International Specialty Products Inc (ISP) 1361 Alps Rd TF: 800-622-4423 ■ Web: www.ashland.com	Wayne	NJ	07470	973-628-4000	
Lifeline Foods LLC 2811 S 11th St Rd Web: www.lifeline-foods.com	Saint Joseph	MO	64503	816-279-1651	279-1652
Light Fabrications Inc 40 Hytec Cir TF: 800-836-6920 ■ Web: www.lightfab.com	Rochester	NY	14606	585-426-5330	426-5239
Methanex Corp 1800 Waterfront Centre 200 Burrard St TSE: MX ■ TF: 800-661-8851 ■ Web: www.methanex.com	Vancouver	BC	V6C3M1	604-661-2600	661-2676
Mitsui Chemicals America Inc 800 Westchester Ave *Fax: PR ■ TF: 800-972-7252 ■ Web: www.mitsuichemicals.com	Rye Brook	NY	10573	914-701-5245	253-0790*
National Enzyme Co Inc 15366 US Hwy 160 TF: 800-825-8545 ■ Web: www.nationalenzyme.com	Forsyth	MO	65653	417-546-4796	546-6433
Niacet Corp 400 47th St TF: 800-828-1207 ■ Web: www.niacet.com	Niagara Falls	NY	14304	716-285-1474	285-1497
Norquay Technology Inc 800 W Front St PO Box 468 Web: www.norquaytech.com	Chester	PA	19013	610-874-4330	874-3575
Oakwood Products Inc 1741 Old Dunbar Rd TF: 800-467-3386 ■ Web: www.oakwoodchemical.com	West Columbia	SC	29172	803-739-8800	739-6957
Pencco Inc 831 Bartlett Rd PO Box 600 TF: 800-864-1742 ■ Web: www.pencco.com	San Felipe	TX	77473	979-885-0005	885-3208
Perstorp Polyols Inc 600 Matzinger Rd TF Cust Svc: 800-537-0280 ■ Web: www.perstorp.com	Toledo	OH	43612	419-729-5448	729-3291
PMC Specialties Group Inc 501 Murray Rd TF: 800-543-2466 ■ Web: www.pmcsg.com	Cincinnati	OH	45217	513-242-3300	482-7315
RT Vanderbilt Company Inc 30 Winfield St TF Cust Svc: 800-243-6064 ■ Web: www.rtvanderbilt.com	Norwalk	CT	06855	203-853-1400	853-1452
Sachem Inc 821 Woodward St Web: www.sacheminc.com	Austin	TX	78704	512-444-3626	445-5066
Sasol North America Inc 900 Threadneedle St Ste 100 Web: www.sasolnorthamerica.com	Houston	TX	77079	281-588-3000	588-3144
Selee Corp 700 Shepherd St TF: 800-842-3818 ■ Web: www.selee.com	Hendersonville	NC	28792	828-697-2411	693-1868
Shell Chemical Co 910 Louisiana St Web: www.shell.com	Houston	TX	77002	713-241-6161	241-4044
Shin-Etsu Silicones of America 1150 Damar Dr TF: 800-544-1745 ■ Web: www.shinetsusilicones.com	Akron	OH	44305	330-630-9860	630-9855
Struktol Company of America Inc PO Box 1649 TF: 800-327-8649 ■ Web: www.struktol.com	Stow	OH	44224	330-928-5188	928-8726
Sun Chemical Corp 35 Waterview Blvd TF: 800-543-2323 ■ Web: www.sunchemical.com	Parsippany	NJ	07054	973-404-6000	404-6001
Sunoco Chemicals 1735 Market St Ste LL TF: 800-786-6261	Philadelphia	PA	19103	215-977-3000	977-3470
Sunoco Inc 1735 Market St Ste LL NYSE: SUN ■ TF: 800-786-6261 ■ Web: www.sunocoinc.com	Philadelphia	PA	19103	215-977-3000	977-3409
Synalloy Corp 775 Spartan Blvd Ste 102 PO Box 5627 NASDAQ: SYNL ■ TF Orders: 800-937-5449 ■ Web: www.synalloy.com	Spartanburg	SC	29304	864-585-3605	596-1501
Tedia Company Inc 1000 Tedia Way TF: 800-787-4891 ■ Web: www.tedia.com	Fairfield	OH	45014	513-874-5340	874-5346
Velsicol Chemical Corp 10400 W Higgins Rd Ste 700 TF Cust Svc: 877-847-8351 ■ Web: www.velsicol.com	Rosemont	IL	60018	847-813-7888	768-3227
Vulcan Materials Co 1200 Urban Ctr Dr PO Box 385014 NYSE: VMC ■ TF: 800-615-4331 ■ Web: www.vulcanmaterials.com	Birmingham	AL	35238	205-298-3000	298-2942
Wacker Chemical Corp 3301 Sutton Rd TF: 888-922-5374 ■ Web: www.wacker.com	Adrian	MI	49221	517-264-8500	264-8246
Waterworks America Inc 5005 Rockside Rd Crown Ctr Sixth Fl Web: www.1water.com	Independence	OH	44131	440-526-4815	
Wausau Chemical Corp 2001 N River Dr TF: 800-950-6656 ■ Web: www.wausauchemical.com	Wausau	WI	54403	715-842-2285	842-9059
Western Polymer Corp 32 Rd 'R' SE Web: www.westernpolymer.com	Moses Lake	WA	98837	509-765-1803	765-0327
Wyoming Ethanol LLC 1919 E A St	Torrington	WY	82240	307-532-2449	

CHEMICALS - MEDICINAL

145 CHEMICALS - SPECIALTY

Company	City	State	Zip	Phone	Fax
ADA-ES Inc 8100 Southpark Way Ste B NASDAQ: ADES ■ TF: 888-822-8617 ■ Web: www.adaes.com	Littleton	CO	80120	303-734-1727	734-0330
Afton Chemical Corp 500 Spring St Web: www.aftonchemical.com	Richmond	VA	23219	804-788-5800	788-5184

	Phone	Fax
Airosol Company Inc 1206 Illinois St . . . . . Neodesha KS 66757 *TF:* 800-633-9576 ■ *Web:* www.airosol.com	620-325-2666	325-2602
Akzo Nobel Chemicals Inc 10 Finderne Ave. . . . . Bridgewater NJ 08807 **Fax Area Code:* 908 ■ *TF:* 888-331-6212 ■ *Web:* www.akzonobel.com	888-331-6212	707-3664*
Alex C Fergusson LLC (AFCO) 5000 Letterkenny Rd. . . . . Chambersburg PA 17201 **Fax Area Code:* 717 ■ *TF:* 800-345-1329 ■ *Web:* www.afcocare.us	800-345-1329	264-9182*
Alfa Aesar Co 26 Parkridge Rd Second Fl. . . . . Ward Hill MA 01835 **Fax Area Code:* 800 ■ *TF:* 800-343-0660 ■ *Web:* www.alfa.com	978-521-6300	322-4757*
AM Todd Co 1717 Douglas Ave . . . . . Kalamazoo MI 49007 *Web:* www.wildflavors.com	269-343-2603	343-3399
American Pacific Corp (AMPAC) 3883 Howard Hughes Pkwy Ste 700. . . . . Las Vegas NV 89169 *NASDAQ: APFC* ■ *Web:* www.apfc.com	702-735-2200	735-4876
American Polywater Corp 11222 60th St N . . . . . Stillwater MN 55082 *TF:* 800-328-9384 ■ *Web:* www.polywater.com	651-430-2270	430-3634
American Radiolabeled Chemicals Inc (ARC) 101 ARC Dr . . . . . Saint Louis MO 63146 *TF:* 800-331-6661 ■ *Web:* www.arc-inc.com	314-991-4545	991-4692
American Vanguard Corp 4695 MacArthur Ct. . . . . Newport Beach CA 92660 *NYSE: AVD* ■ *Web:* www.american-vanguard.com	949-260-1200	260-1201
Ameron International Corp 245 S Los Robles Ave. . . . . Pasadena CA 91101 *Web:* www.nov.com	626-683-4000	683-4060
AMPAC Fine Chemicals (AFC) MS 1007 PO Box 1718. . . . . Rancho Cordova CA 95741 *TF:* 800-311-9668 ■ *Web:* www.ampacfinechemicals.com	916-357-6880	353-3523
AMREP Inc 990 Industrial Pk Dr. . . . . Marietta GA 30062 *TF Cust Svc:* 800-241-7766 ■ *Web:* www.amrep.com	770-422-2071	422-1737
Anderson Chemical Co 325 S Davis . . . . . Litchfield MN 55355 *TF:* 800-366-2477 ■ *Web:* www.accomn.com	320-693-2477	693-8238
Anderson Development Co 1415 E Michigan St. . . . . Adrian MI 49221 *Web:* www.andersondevelopment.com	517-263-2121	263-1000
Andersons, Inc., The 908 N Vine St PO Box 110. . . . . Mount Pulaski IL 62548 *Web:* www.mtpulaski.com	217-792-3211	
Angstrom Technologies Inc 7880 Foundation Dr. . . . . Florence KY 41042 *TF Cust Svc:* 800-543-7358 ■ *Web:* www.angstromtechnologies.com	859-282-0020	282-8577
Apollo Chemical Company LLC 1105 Southerland St. . . . . Graham NC 27253 *Web:* www.apollochemical.com	336-226-1161	226-7494
Arch Chemicals Inc 1200 Old Lower River Rd PO Box 800 . . . . . Charleston TN 37310 *NYSE: ARJ* ■ *TF:* 800-638-8174 ■ *Web:* lonza.com/	423-780-2724	780-2330
Ashland Specialty Chemical Co 1745 Cottage St . . . . . Ashland OH 44805 *Web:* www.ashland.com	419-289-9588	
Athea Laboratories Inc 1900 W Cornell St . . . . . Milwaukee WI 53209 **Fax Area Code:* 414 ■ *TF:* 800-743-6417 ■ *Web:* www.athea.com	800-743-6417	354-9219*
Atlas Refinery Inc 142 Lockwood St. . . . . Newark NJ 07105 *Web:* www.atlasrefinery.com	973-589-2002	589-7377
Baker Hughes Inc Baker Petrolite Div 12645 W Airport Blvd. . . . . Sugar Land TX 77478 **Fax:* Hum Res ■ *TF:* 800-231-3606 ■ *Web:* www.bakerhughes.com	281-276-5400	275-7392*
Barclay Water Management Inc 55 Chapel St. . . . . Newton MA 02458 *Web:* www.barclaywm.com	617-926-3400	924-5467
Bedoukian Research Inc 21 Finance Dr . . . . . Danbury CT 06810 *Web:* www.bedoukian.com	203-830-4000	830-4010
Berje Inc 700 Blair Rd. . . . . Bloomfield NJ 07003 *Web:* www.berjeinc.com	973-748-8980	680-9618
Birchwood Laboratories Inc 7900 Fuller Rd . . . . . Eden Prairie MN 55344 *TF:* 800-328-6156 ■ *Web:* www.birchwoodcasey.com	952-937-7900	937-7979
Blue Grass Chemical Specialties LP 895 Industrial Blvd. . . . . New Albany IN 47150 *Web:* newalbanymetalworks.com	812-948-1115	948-1561
Brulin & Company Inc 2920 Dr AJ Brown Ave . . . . . Indianapolis IN 46205 *TF:* 800-776-7149 ■ *Web:* www.brulin.com	317-923-3211	925-4596
Buckman Laboratories Inc 1256 N McLean Blvd . . . . . Memphis TN 38108 *TF:* 800-282-5626 ■ *Web:* www.buckman.com	901-278-0330	
Bullen Midwest 900 E 103rd St. . . . . Chicago IL 60628 *TF:* 800-621-8553 ■ *Web:* www.nuancesol.com	773-785-2300	
Cabot Corp 2 Seaport Ln Ste 1300 . . . . . Boston MA 02210 *NYSE: CBT* ■ *TF:* 800-322-1236 ■ *Web:* www.cabot-corp.com	617-345-0100	342-6103
Cabot Microelectronics Corp 870 N Commons Dr. . . . . Aurora IL 60504 *NASDAQ: CCMP* ■ *TF:* 800-811-2756 ■ *Web:* www.cabotcmp.com	630-375-6631	375-5539
Cabot Specialty Fluids Inc Waterway Plaza Two 10001 Woodlock Forest Dr Ste 275. . . . . The Woodlands TX 77380 *TF:* 800-322-1236 ■ *Web:* www.formatebrines.com	281-298-9955	298-6190
Cal-Pac Chemical Company Inc 6231 Maywood Ave . . . . . Huntington Park CA 90255 *Web:* cal-pac-chemicals.com	323-585-2178	585-3087
Cambridge Isotope Laboratories Inc 50 Frontage Rd. . . . . Andover MA 01810 *TF:* 800-322-1174 ■ *Web:* www.isotope.com	978-749-8000	749-2768
Champion Technologies Inc 3200 SW Fwy Ste 2700 . . . . . Houston TX 77027 *Web:* nalcochampion.com/	713-627-3303	627-7603
Chemtool Inc 8200 Ridgefield Rd . . . . . Crystal Lake IL 60039 *Web:* www.chemtool.com	815-459-1250	459-1955
Chemtronics Inc 8125 Cobb Centre Dr. . . . . Kennesaw GA 30152 *TF:* 800-645-5244 ■ *Web:* www.chemtronics.com	770-424-4888	423-0748
Chippewa Valley Ethanol Company LLC 270 20th St NW . . . . . Benson MN 56215 *Web:* www.cvec.com	320-843-4813	843-4800
CHT R Beitlich Corp 5046 Old Pineville Rd. . . . . Charlotte NC 28217	704-523-4242	
Citrus & Allied Essences Ltd 3000 Marcus Ave Ste 3E11. . . . . Lake Success NY 11042 *Web:* www.citrusandallied.com	516-354-1200	354-1262

	Phone	Fax
Claire Manufacturing Co 1005 S Westgate Ave. . . . . Addison IL 60101 *TF Sales:* 800-252-4731 ■ *Web:* www.clairemfg.com	630-543-7600	543-4310
Columbian Chemicals Co 1800 W Oak Commons Ct . . . . . Marietta GA 30062 *TF:* 800-235-4003 ■ *Web:* www.birlacarbon.com	770-792-9400	
Coral Chemical Co 1915 Industrial Ave. . . . . Zion IL 60099 *TF:* 800-228-4646 ■ *Web:* www.coral.com	847-246-6666	246-6667
Cortec Corp 4119 White Bear Pkwy . . . . . Saint Paul MN 55110 *TF:* 800-426-7832 ■ *Web:* www.cortecvci.com	651-429-1100	429-1122
CPC Aeroscience Inc 2700 SW 14th St . . . . . Pompano Beach FL 33069 **Fax Area Code:* 954 ■ *TF Cust Svc:* 800-327-1835 ■ *Web:* cpcaeroscience.com/	800-327-1835	977-7513*
CRC Industries Inc 885 Louis Dr. . . . . Warminster PA 18974 *TF Cust Svc:* 800-556-5074 ■ *Web:* www.crcindustries.com	215-674-4300	674-2196
Croda Inc 300 Columbus Cir Ste A. . . . . Edison NJ 08837 *TF:* 888-842-7632 ■ *Web:* www.croda.com	732-417-0800	417-0804
Cytec Industries Inc Five Garret Mtn Plz. . . . . West Paterson NJ 07424 *NYSE: CYT* ■ *TF:* 800-652-6013 ■ *Web:* www.cytec.com	973-357-3100	357-3060
Delta Chemical Corp 2601 Cannery Ave. . . . . Baltimore MD 21226 *TF:* 800-282-5322 ■ *Web:* www.usalco.com	410-354-0100	354-1021
Detrex Corp 24901 NW Hwy Ste 410 . . . . . Southfield MI 48075 *Web:* www.detrex.com	248-358-5800	799-7192
Diversified Chemical Technologies Inc (DCT) 15477 Woodrow Wilson St. . . . . Detroit MI 48238 *TF:* 800-243-1424 ■ *Web:* www.dchem.com	313-867-5444	867-3831
Dober Chemical Group 11230 Katherine Crossing Ste 100. . . . . Woodridge IL 60517 *TF:* 800-323-4983 ■ *Web:* www.dobergroup.com	630-410-7300	410-7444
Dover Chemical Corp 3676 Davis Rd NW. . . . . Dover OH 44622 *TF General:* 800-321-8805 ■ *Web:* www.doverchem.com	330-343-7711	365-3927
Dow Chemical Co, The 100 Independence Mall W . . . . . Philadelphia PA 19106 *Web:* www.dow.com	215-592-3000	
DSM Desotech Inc 1122 St Charles St. . . . . Elgin IL 60120 **Fax:* Sales ■ *TF:* 800-222-7189 ■ *Web:* www.dsm.com	847-697-0400	468-7785*
DuPont Chemical Solutions 1007 Market St. . . . . Wilmington DE 19898 *TF:* 800-441-7515 ■ *Web:* www.dupont.com	302-774-1000	355-4013
Dynaloy LLC 6445 Olivia Ln . . . . . Indianapolis IN 46226 *TF:* 800-669-5709 ■ *Web:* www.dynaloy.com	317-788-5694	788-5690
Elantas PDG Inc 5200 N Second St. . . . . Saint Louis MO 63147 *TF:* 800-325-7492 ■ *Web:* www.elantas.com	314-621-5700	436-1030
Enthone Inc 350 Frontage Rd. . . . . West Haven CT 06516 *TF:* 800-431-2200 ■ *Web:* www.enthone.com	203-934-8611	799-1513
Excelda Manufacturing Co 12785 Emerson Dr. . . . . Brighton MI 48116 *TF:* 877-486-3801 ■ *Web:* www.excelda.com	248-486-3800	486-3810
FMC Corp Specialty Chemicals Group 1735 Market St. . . . . Philadelphia PA 19103 *Web:* www.fmc.com	215-299-6000	299-5998
Foseco Metallurgical Inc 20200 Sheldon Rd . . . . . Cleveland OH 44142 *TF:* 800-321-3132 ■ *Web:* www.foseco.com	440-826-4548	243-7658
Frac Tech Services LLC 301 E 18th St. . . . . Cisco TX 76437 *TF:* 866-877-1008 ■ *Web:* www.ftsi.com	817-850-1008	850-1026
Freezetone Products Inc 7986 NW 14th St. . . . . Doral FL 33126 *Web:* www.freezetone-usa.com	305-640-0414	640-0454
Fremont Industries Inc 4400 Vly Industrial Blvd N PO Box 67 . . . . . Shakopee MN 55379 *TF:* 800-436-1238 ■ *Web:* www.fremontind.com	952-445-4121	496-3027
GE Betz 4636 Somerton Rd. . . . . Trevose PA 19053 *TF Cust Svc:* 866-439-2837 ■ *Web:* www.gewater.com	215-355-3300	
Genieco Inc 200 N Laflin St . . . . . Chicago IL 60607 *TF:* 800-223-8217 ■ *Web:* gonesh.com	312-421-2383	421-3042
GEO Specialty Chemicals Inc 401 S Earl Ave . . . . . Lafayette IN 47904 *Web:* www.geosc.com	765-448-9412	
Gold Eagle Co 4400 S Kildare Ave . . . . . Chicago IL 60632 **Fax Area Code:* 773 ■ *TF:* 800-367-3245 ■ *Web:* www.goldeagle.com	800-367-3245	376-5749*
Goulston Technologies Inc 700 N Johnson St . . . . . Monroe NC 28110 *Web:* www.goulston.com	704-289-6464	296-6400
Grace Construction Products 62 Whittemore Ave . . . . . Cambridge MA 02140 *Web:* grace.com/construction/en-us	617-876-1400	498-4311
Grace Davison 7500 Grace Dr . . . . . Columbia MD 21044 *TF:* 800-638-6014 ■ *Web:* www.grace.com	410-531-4000	531-4197
H Krevit & Company Inc 73 Welton St . . . . . New Haven CT 06511 *Web:* www.hkrevit.com	203-772-3350	776-0730
Harcros Chemicals Inc 5200 Speaker Rd. . . . . Kansas City KS 66106 *TF:* 800-504-8071 ■ *Web:* www.harcroschem.com	913-321-3131	621-7718
Hexion Specialty Chemicals Inc 180 E Broad St . . . . . Columbus OH 43215 *Web:* www.momentive.com	614-225-4000	
Hitachi Chemical Company America Ltd 10080 N Wolfe Rd Ste SW3-200 . . . . . Cupertino CA 95014 *Web:* www.hitachi-chemical.com	408-873-2200	873-2284
Honeywell 101 Columbia Rd . . . . . Morristown NJ 07960 *TF:* 800-822-7673 ■ *Web:* www.honeywellprocess.com	973-455-2000	455-4807
Honeywell Fluorine Products 101 Columbia Rd . . . . . Morristown NJ 07962 *TF:* 800-951-1527 ■ *Web:* honeywell.com/pages/redirect.aspx?redirectid=179	973-455-2000	455-6394
Houghton Chemical Corp 52 Cambridge St. . . . . Allston MA 02134 *TF:* 800-777-2466 ■ *Web:* www.houghton.com	617-254-1010	
Hybrid Plastics 55 WL Runnels Industrial Dr. . . . . Hattiesburg MS 39401 *Web:* www.hybridplastics.com	601-544-3466	545-3103
I-K-I Mfg Company Inc 116 Swift St. . . . . Edgerton WI 53534 *Web:* www.ikimfg.com	608-884-3411	884-4712
ICC Chemicals 4660 Spring Grove Ave. . . . . Cincinnati OH 45232 *Web:* www.icc-chemicals.com	513-541-7100	541-6880
International Chemical Co 2628 N Mascher St. . . . . Philadelphia PA 19133 *TF:* 888-225-5422 ■ *Web:* www.e-icc.com	215-739-2313	423-7171
JM Huber Corp 499 Thornall St 8th Fl . . . . . Edison NJ 08837 **Fax:* Hum Res ■ *TF:* 877-418-0038 ■ *Web:* www.huber.com	732-549-8600	549-2239*

Phone Fax

Kao Specialties Americas LLC
243 Woodbine St PO Box 2316 High Point NC 27261 336-884-2214 884-8786
TF: 800-727-2214 ■ *Web:* chemical.kao.com

Kester Inc 800 W Thorndale Ave Itasca IL 60143 630-616-4000 616-4044
TF: 800-253-7837 ■ *Web:* www.kester.com

KIK Custom Products 2730 Middlebury St Elkhart IN 46516 574-295-0000 296-1700
TF: 800-479-6603 ■ *Web:* www.kikcorp.com

KIK Pool Additives Inc 5160 E Airport Dr Ontario CA 91761 909-390-9912 390-9911
TF: 800-745-4536 ■ *Web:* www.kem-tek.com

King Industries Inc One Science Rd Norwalk CT 06852 203-866-5551 866-1268
TF: 800-431-7900 ■ *Web:* www.kingindustries.com

KMCO LP 16503 Ramsey Rd Crosby TX 77532 281-272-4100 328-9528
Web: www.kmcoinc.com

Kolene Corp 12890 Westwood Ave Detroit MI 48223 313-273-9220 273-5207
TF: 800-521-4182 ■ *Web:* www.kolene.com

Koppers Inc 436 Seventh Ave Pittsburgh PA 15219 412-227-2001 227-2333
NYSE: KOP ■ *TF:* 800-321-9876 ■ *Web:* www.koppers.com

Kronos Worldwide Inc
14950 Heathrow Forest Prkwy Ste 230 Houston TX 77060 281-423-3300 423-3258
NYSE: KRO ■ *TF:* 800-866-5600 ■ *Web:* www.kronostio2.com

Leadership Performance Sustainability Laboratories
4647 Hugh Howell Rd Tucker GA 30084 800-241-8334 243-8899*
**Fax Area Code:* 770 ■ *TF:* 800-241-8334 ■ *Web:* www.lpslabs.com

Lloyd Laboratories Inc 24 Fitch Ct Wakefield MA 01880 781-224-0083
TF: 800-361-6766

Lubrizol Corp 29400 Lakeland Blvd Wickliffe OH 44092 440-943-4200 943-5337
NYSE: LZ ■ *TF:* 800-380-5397 ■ *Web:* www.lubrizol.com

MacDermid Inc 245 Freight St Waterbury CT 06702 203-575-5700
Web: www.macdermid.com

Master Builders Solutions by BASF
23700 Chagrin Blvd Cleveland OH 44122 216-839-7500 839-8821
TF: 800-628-9990 ■ *Web:* www.basf-admixtures.com

McGean-Rohco Inc 2910 Harvard Ave Cleveland OH 44105 216-441-4900 441-1377
TF Orders: 800-932-7006 ■ *Web:* www.mcgean.com

Micro Powders Inc 580 White Plains Rd Tarrytown NY 10591 914-793-4058 472-7098
Web: www.micropowders.com

Microchem Corp 90 Oak St Newton MA 02464 617-965-5511 965-5818
Web: www.microchem.com

Milacron Inc 3010 Disney St Cincinnati OH 45209 513-487-5000 487-5086
Web: www.milacron.com

Miller-Stephenson Chemical Co 55 Backus Ave Danbury CT 06810 203-743-4447 791-8702
TF Tech Supp: 800-992-2424 ■ *Web:* www.miller-stephenson.com

Momar Inc 1830 Ellsworth Industrial Dr Atlanta GA 30318 404-355-4580 849-5684*
**Fax Area Code:* 800 ■ *TF:* 800-556-3967 ■ *Web:* www.momar.com

Monroe Fluid Technology Inc
36 Draffin Rd PO Box 810 Hilton NY 14468 585-392-3434 392-2691
TF: 800-828-6351 ■ *Web:* www.monroefluid.com

Montana Sulphur & Chemical Co PO Box 31118 Billings MT 59107 406-252-9324 252-8250
Web: www.montanasulphur.com

Montello Inc 6106 E 32nd Pl Ste 100 Tulsa OK 74135 800-331-4628 665-1480*
**Fax Area Code:* 918 ■ *TF:* 800-331-4628 ■ *Web:* www.montelloinc.com

Moses Lake Industries Inc
8248 Randolph Rd NE Moses Lake WA 98837 509-762-5336 762-5981
Web: www.mlindustries.com

Multisorb Technologies Inc 325 Harlem Rd Buffalo NY 14224 716-824-8900 824-4128
Web: www.multisorb.com

Nalco Co 1601 W Diehl Rd Naperville IL 60563 630-305-1000 305-2900
TF: 800-288-0879 ■ *Web:* www.nalco.com

Nanophase Technologies Corp
1319 Marquette Dr Romeoville IL 60446 630-771-6700 771-0825
OTC: NANX ■ *Web:* www.nanophase.com

National Starch & Chemical Co
10 Finderne Ave Bridgewater NJ 08807 866-961-6285 685-5005*
**Fax Area Code:* 908 ■ *TF:* 866-961-6285 ■ *Web:* www.nationalstarch.com

Northern Technologies International Corp (NTIC)
4201 Woodland Rd Circle Pines MN 55014 763-225-6600 225-6645
NASDAQ: NTIC ■ *Web:* natur-tec.com

Nox-Crete Inc 1444 S 20th St Omaha NE 68108 402-341-2080 341-9752
TF: 800-669-2738 ■ *Web:* www.nox-crete.com

OM Group Inc 811 Sharon Dr Westlake OH 44145 440-899-2950 808-7114
NYSE: OMG ■ *TF:* 800-519-0083 ■ *Web:* www.omgi.com

OMNOVA Solutions Inc 175 Ghent Rd Fairlawn OH 44333 330-869-4200 869-4288
NYSE: OMN ■ *Web:* www.omnova.com

OMNOVA Solutions Inc Performance Chemicals Div
165 S Cleveland Ave Mogadore OH 44260 330-628-6536 628-6500
TF: 888-253-5454 ■ *Web:* www.omnova.com

Ortec Inc 505 Gentry Memorial Hwy PO Box 1469 Easley SC 29641 864-859-1471 859-8580
Web: www.ortecinc.com

Pacific Ethanol Corp
400 Capitol Mall Ste 2060 Sacramento CA 95814 916-403-2123 446-3937
NASDAQ: PEIX ■ *TF:* 866-508-4969 ■ *Web:* www.pacificethanol.net

Pavco Inc 1935 John Crosland Jr Dr Charlotte NC 28208 704-496-6800 496-6810
TF Orders: 800-321-7735 ■ *Web:* www.pavco.com

Peach State Labs Inc (PSL)
180 Burlington Rd PO Box 1087 Rome GA 30162 706-291-8743 921-4888
TF: 800-634-1653 ■ *Web:* www.peachstatelabs.com

Penford Corp 7094 S Revere Pkwy Centennial CO 80112 303-649-1900 649-1700
NASDAQ: PENX ■ *Web:* penford.com/

Peninsula Copper Industries Inc (PCI)
220 Calumet St Lake Linden MI 49945 906-296-9918 296-9484
Web: www.pencopper.com

Penray Cos Inc 440 Denniston Ct Wheeling IL 60090 847-459-5000 459-5043
TF: 800-373-6729 ■ *Web:* www.penray.com

PMC Global Inc 12243 Branford St Sun Valley CA 91352 818-896-1101 686-2531
Web: www.pmcglobalinc.com

Precision Laboratories Inc
1429 S Shields Dr Waukegan IL 60085 847-596-3001 596-3017
TF: 800-323-6280 ■ *Web:* www.precisionlab.com

Premier Colors Inc 100 Industrial Dr Union SC 29379 864-427-0338 427-5824
TF: 800-245-6944 ■ *Web:* www.premiercolorsinc.com

PVS Chemicals Inc 10900 Harper Ave Detroit MI 48213 313-921-1200 921-1378
TF: 800-932-8860 ■ *Web:* www.pvschemicals.com

Phone Fax

Quaker Chemical Corp 901 Hector St Conshohocken PA 19428 610-832-4000 832-8682
NYSE: KWR ■ *TF:* 800-523-7010 ■ *Web:* quakerchem.com

Qualitek International Inc 315 Fairbank St Addison IL 60101 630-628-8083 628-6543
Web: www.qualitek.com

Radiator Specialty Co 1900 Wilkinson Blvd Charlotte NC 28208 704-688-2405
TF: 877-464-4865 ■ *Web:* www.gunk.com

Rentech Inc 10877 Wilshire Blvd 10th Fl Los Angeles CA 90024 310-571-9800 571-9799
NASDAQ: RTK ■ *Web:* www.rentechinc.com

Rochester Midland Corp 333 Hollenbeck St Rochester NY 14621 585-336-2200 467-4406
TF: 800-836-1627 ■ *Web:* www.rochestermidland.com

Roebic Laboratories Inc
25 Connair Rd PO Box 927 Orange CT 06477 203-795-1283 795-5227
Web: www.roebic.com

Royal Chemical Co
1755 Enterprise Pkwy Ste 600 Twinsburg OH 44087 330-467-1300 405-0975
TF: 800-468-2975 ■ *Web:* www.royalchemical.com

SA Day Mfg Co Inc 1489 Niagara St Buffalo NY 14213 716-881-3030 881-4353
TF: 800-747-0030 ■ *Web:* www.saday.com

Senomyx Inc 4767 Nexus Centre Dr San Diego CA 92121 858-646-8300 404-0752
NASDAQ: SNMX ■ *Web:* www.senomyx.com

Sid Richardson Carbon & Energy Cos
201 Main St Fort Worth TX 76102 817-390-8600
Web: www.sidrich.com

Sigma-Aldrich Corp 3050 Spruce St Saint Louis MO 63103 314-771-5765 325-5052*
NASDAQ: SIAL ■ **Fax Area Code:* 800 ■ *TF:* 800-325-3010 ■ *Web:* www.sigmaaldrich.com

Sika Corp 201 Polito Ave Lyndhurst NJ 07071 201-933-8800
TF: 800-933-7452 ■ *Web:* www.usa.sika.com

Solutek Corp 94 Shirley St Boston MA 02119 617-445-5335 445-9623
TF: 800-403-0770 ■ *Web:* www.solutekcorporation.com

Spartan Chemical Company Inc 1110 Spartan Dr Maumee OH 43537 419-531-5551 536-8423
TF: 800-537-8990 ■ *Web:* www.spartanchemical.com

Specco Industries Inc 13087 Main St Lemont IL 60439 630-257-5060 257-9006
TF: 800-441-6646 ■ *Web:* www.specco.com

Spectra Gases Inc One Greenwich St Stewartsville NJ 08886 908-329-9700 329-9740
Web: www.lindepremiumproducts.com

Sprayway Inc 500 S Vista Ave Addison IL 60101 630-628-3000 543-7797
TF: 800-332-9000 ■ *Web:* www.spraywayinc.com

Stapleton Technologies Inc 1350 W 12th St Long Beach CA 90813 562-437-0541 437-8632
TF: 800-266-0541 ■ *Web:* www.stapletontech.com

Stepan Co 22 W Frontage Rd Northfield IL 60093 847-446-7500 501-2100
TF Cust Svc: 800-745-7837 ■ *Web:* www.stepan.com

Sunland Chemical & Research Corp
5447 San Fernando Rd W Los Angeles CA 90039 818-244-9600 246-0478
Web: www.sunlandchemical.com

Symrise Inc 300 N St Teterboro NJ 07608 201-288-3200 462-2200
TF General: 800-422-1559 ■ *Web:* www.symrise.com

Technic Inc 47 Molter St Cranston RI 02910 401-781-6100 781-2890
Web: www.technic.com

Technical Chemical Co 3327 Pipeline Rd Cleburne TX 76033 817-645-6088 556-0694
TF: 800-527-0885 ■ *Web:* www.technicalchemical.com

United Color Manufacturing Inc (UCM) PO Box 480 Newtown PA 18940 215-860-2165 860-8560
TF: 800-852-5942 ■ *Web:* www.unitedcolor.com

United Laboratories Inc 320 37th Ave Saint Charles IL 60174 800-323-2594 443-2087*
**Fax Area Code:* 630 ■ *TF:* 800-323-2594 ■ *Web:* www.unitedlabsinc.com

United Salt Corp 4800 San Felipe St Houston TX 77056 713-877-2600 877-2609
TF: 800-554-8658 ■ *Web:* www.unitedsalt.com

Univertical Corp 203 Weatherhead St Angola IN 46703 260-665-1500 665-1400
Web: www.univertical.com

Vertellus Specialties Inc
201 N Illinois St Ste 1800 Indianapolis IN 46204 317-247-8141 248-6402
Web: www.vertellus.com

Watcon Inc 2215 S Main St South Bend IN 46613 574-287-3397 287-2427
Web: www.watcon-inc.com

WestRock Company 5255 Virginia Ave North Charleston SC 29406 843-740-2300 740-2147
Web: meadwestvaco.com

WR Grace & Co 7500 Grace Dr Columbia MD 21044 410-531-4000 531-4367
NYSE: GRA ■ *TF:* 800-638-6014 ■ *Web:* www.grace.com

XL Brands 198 Nexus Dr Dalton GA 30721 706-272-5800 272-5801
TF: 800-367-4583 ■ *Web:* www.xlbrands.com

Zinkan Enterprises Inc 1919 Case Pkwy N Twinsburg OH 44087 800-229-6801 425-8202*
**Fax Area Code:* 330 ■ *TF:* 800-229-6801 ■ *Web:* www.zinkan.com

146 CHEMICALS & RELATED PRODUCTS - WHOL

Phone Fax

Advanced Polymers Inc
400 Paterson Plank Rd Carlstadt NJ 07072 201-933-0600
Web: www.advpolymer.com

Airgas Inc 259 N Radnor-Chester Rd Ste 100 Radnor PA 19087 610-687-5253 687-1052
NYSE: ARG ■ *TF:* 800-255-2165 ■ *Web:* www.airgas.com

Airgas Refrigerants Inc
2530 Sever Rd Ste 300 Lawrenceville GA 30043 770-717-2210
Web: www.airgasrefrigerants.com

Americas Styrenics LLC
24 Waterway Ave Ste 1200 Woodlands TX 77380 281-203-5451
Web: www.amstyrenics.com

Amfine Chemical Corp
10 Montnview Rd Ste 215N Upper Saddle River NJ 07458 201-818-0159 818-0259
Web: www.amfine.com

Anitox Corp 1055 Progress Cir Lawrenceville GA 30043 678-376-1055
Web: www.anitox.co.uk

Aquatic Informatics Inc
570 Granville St Ste 1100 Vancouver BC V6C3P1 604-873-2782
Web: aquaticinformatics.com

Aramsco Inc 1480 Grandview Ave Paulsboro NJ 08086 856-686-7700
TF: 800-767-6933 ■ *Web:* www.aramsco.com

Ashland Distribution Co
5200 Blazer Pkwy PO Box 2219 Columbus OH 43216 614-790-3333
Web: www.ashland.com

Astro Chemicals Inc 126 Memorial Dr Springfield MA 01104 413-781-7240 781-7246
TF: 800-223-0776 ■ *Web:* www.astrochemicals.com

Company / Address	City	State	Zip	Phone	Fax
Austin Chemical Company Inc 1565 Barclay Blvd. *Web:* www.austinchemical.com	Buffalo Grove	IL	60089	847-520-9600	520-9160
Avchem Inc 5757 Phantom Dr Ste 300 *Web:* www.avchem.com	Hazelwood	MO	63042	314-880-2700	
B & b Medical Services Inc 5401 S Sheridan Rd Ste 204 *Web:* www.bandbmedical.com	Tulsa	OK	74145	918-743-9400	
B&P Process Equipment & Systems LLC 1000 Hess Ave *Web:* www.bpprocess.com	Saginaw	MI	48601	989-757-1300	
Barton Solvents Inc 1920 NE Broadway Ave *TF:* 800-728-6488 ■ *Web:* www.barsol.com	Des Moines	IA	50313	515-265-7998	265-0259
Berryman Products Inc 3800 E Randol Mill Rd *TF:* 800-433-1704 ■ *Web:* www.berrymanproducts.com	Arlington	TX	76011	817-640-2376	640-4850
Birko Corp 9152 Yosemite St. *Web:* www.birkocorp.com	Henderson	CO	80640	303-289-1090	
Blendco Systems LLC One Pearl Buck Ct *Web:* www.blendco.com	Bristol	PA	19007	215-781-3600	
Boral Material Technologies Inc 45 NE Loop 410 Ste 700 *Web:* www.boralmti.com	San Antonio	TX	78216	210-349-4069	
Brandt Technologies Inc 231 W Grand Ave *Web:* www.brandttech.com	Bensenville	IL	60106	630-787-1800	787-1801
Brenntag Canada Inc 35 Vulcan St *TF:* 866-516-9707 ■ *Web:* www.brenntag.ca/en	Rexdale	ON	M9W1L3	416-243-9615	243-9731
Brenntag Great Lakes LLC PO Box 444 **Fax:* Sales ■ *TF:* 800 558-8501 ■ *Web:* www.brenntaggreatlakes.com	Butler	WI	53007	262-252-3550	252-5250*
Brenntag Mid-South Inc 1405 Hwy 136 W **Fax:* Hum Res ■ *TF:* 800-950-1727 ■ *Web:* www.brenntagmid-south.com	Henderson	KY	42419	270-830-1200	827-3990*
Brenntag North America Inc 5083 Pottsville Pk PO Box 13786 *Web:* www.brenntag.com	Reading	PA	19605	610-926-6100	
Brenntag Northeast Inc 81 W Huller Ln *Web:* www.brenntagnortheast.com	Reading	PA	19605	610-926-4151	926-4160
Brenntag Pacific 4545 Ardine St. *TF:* 800-732-0562 ■ *Web:* brenntagpacific.com	South Gate	CA	90280	323-832-5000	773-0909
Brenntag Southeast Inc 2000 E Pedigree St **Fax Area Code:* 270 ■ *TF:* 800-849-7000 ■ *Web:* www.brenntagmid-south.com	Durham	NC	27703	919-596-0681	827-3990*
Brenntag Southwest Inc 610 Fisher Rd. *TF:* 800-945-4528 ■ *Web:* www.brenntagsouthwest.com	Longview	TX	75604	903-759-7151	759-3145
Brown Machine LLC 330 N Ross St. *TF:* 877-702-4142 ■ *Web:* www.brown-machine.com	Beaverton	MI	48612	989-435-7741	
Bulk Chemicals Inc 1074 Stinson Dr *Web:* www.bulkchemicals.com	Reading	PA	19605	610-926-4128	
Cal-chlor Corp 627 Jefferson St. *Web:* www.cal-chlor.com	Lafayette	LA	70501	337-264-1449	264-9359
Callahan Chemical Co 200 Industrial Ave. *TF:* 800-526-7000 ■ *Web:* www.calchem.com	Ridgefield Park	NJ	07660	201-440-9000	440-5441
Canada Colors & Chemicals Ltd 175 Bloor St E Ste 1300 N Twr *Web:* www.ccc-group.com	Toronto	ON	M4W3R8	416-443-5500	449-9039
Canpotex Ltd 111 Second Ave S Ste 400 PO Box 1600 *Web:* www.canpotex.com	Saskatoon	SK	S7K3R7	306-931-2200	653-5505
Cardinal Color Inc 50 First Ave *Web:* www.cardinalcolor.com	Paterson	NJ	07524	973-684-1919	684-0865
Centerchem Inc 20 Glover Ave Merritt On The River *Web:* www.centerchem.com	Norwalk	CT	06850	203-822-9800	
Charkit Chemical Corp 32 Haviland St Unit 1 *Web:* www.charkit.com	Norwalk	CT	06854	203-299-3220	299-1355
Chempacific Corp 6200 Freeport Ctr *Web:* www.chempacific.com	Baltimore	MD	21224	410-633-5771	
Chemroy Canada Inc 106 Summerlea Rd *Web:* www.chemroy.com	Brampton	ON	L6T4X3	905-789-0701	789-7170
Chemsolv Inc 1140 Industry Ave SE *TF:* 800-523-3099 ■ *Web:* www.chemsolv.com	Roanoke	VA	24013	540-427-4000	427-3207
Chemtura USA Corp 199 Benson Rd *Web:* chemtura.com	Middlebury	CT	06749	203-573-2000	
ClearTech Industries Inc 2302 Hanselman Ave *Web:* www.cleartech.ca	Saskatoon	SK	S7L5Z3	306-664-2522	
Cole Chemical & Distributing Inc 1500 S Dairy Ashford St Ste 450 *Web:* www.colechem.com	Houston	TX	77077	713-465-2653	461-3462
Connell Bros Co Ltd 345 California St 27th Fl. *TF:* 800-210-9839 ■ *Web:* www.connellbrothers.com	San Francisco	CA	94104	415-772-4000	772-4100
Coolant Control Inc 5353 Spring Grove Ave *TF:* 800-535-3885 ■ *Web:* www.coolantcontrol.com	Cincinnati	OH	45217	513-471-8770	
Dar-tech Inc 16485 Rockside Rd *TF:* 800-228-7347 ■ *Web:* www.dar-tech.com	Cleveland	OH	44137	216-663-7600	663-8007
DB Becker Company Inc 46 Leigh St *TF:* 800-394-3991 ■ *Web:* www.dbbecker.com	Clinton	NJ	08809	908-730-6010	730-9118
Denso North America Inc 9747 Whithorn Dr *TF:* 888-821-2300 ■ *Web:* www.densona.com	Houston	TX	77095	281-821-3355	
DM Figley Company Inc 10 Kelly Ct *TF:* 800-292-9919 ■ *Web:* www.dmfigley.com	Menlo Park	CA	94025	650-329-8700	329-0601
Dorsett & Jackson Inc 3800 Noakes St *TF:* 800-871-8365 ■ *Web:* www.dorsettandjackson.com	Los Angeles	CA	90023	323-268-1815	268-9082
Durr Marketing Assoc Inc PO Box 17600 **Fax Area Code:* 412 ■ *TF:* 800-937-3877 ■ *Web:* www.durrmarketing.com	Pittsburgh	PA	15235	800-937-3877	829-7680*
Ellsworth Corp PO Box 1002 *TF:* 877-454-9224 ■ *Web:* www.ellsworth.com	Germantown	WI	53022	262-253-8600	253-8619
EMCO Chemical Distributors Inc 2100 Commonwealth Ave *Web:* www.emcochem.com	North Chicago	IL	60064	847-689-2200	689-8470
ET Horn Co 16050 Canary Ave *TF:* 800-442-4676 ■ *Web:* www.ethorn.com	La Mirada	CA	90638	714-523-8050	670-6851
Evonik Corp 299 Jefferson Rd *Web:* north-america.evonik.com	Parsippany	NJ	07054	973-929-8000	
Evonik Oil Additives USA Inc 723 Electronic Dr *Web:* www.rohmax.com	Horsham	PA	19044	215-706-5800	
EW Kaufmann Co 140 Wharton Rd *TF:* 800-635-5358 ■ *Web:* www.ewkaufmann.com	Bristol	PA	19007	215-364-0240	364-4397
Expo Chemical Company Inc 6807 Theall Rd Ste A *Web:* expochem.com	Houston	TX	77066	281-895-9200	
Expro Americas LLC 738 Hwy 6 S Ste 1000 *Web:* www.kinley.com	Houston	TX	77079	281-994-1158	
Fitz Chem Corp 450 E Devon Ave Ste 175 *Web:* www.fitzchem.com	Itasca	IL	60143	630-467-8383	467-1183
Francis Drilling Fluids Ltd 240 Jasmine Rd *Web:* www.fdfltd.com	Crowley	LA	70526	337-783-8685	
FutureFuel Corp 8235 Forsyth Blvd Fourth Fl. *NYSE:* FF ■ *Web:* www.futurefuelcorporation.com	Clayton	MO	63105	805-565-9800	565-0800
Gallade Chemical Inc 1230 E St Gertrude Pl *TF:* 888-830-9092 ■ *Web:* www.galladechem.com	Santa Ana	CA	92707	714-546-9901	546-2501
General Air Service & Supply Company Inc 1105 Zuni St. *TF:* 877-782-8434 ■ *Web:* www.generalair.com	Denver	CO	80204	303-892-7003	595-9036
George S Coyne Chemical Co 3015 State Rd *TF:* 800-523-1230 ■ *Web:* www.coynechemical.com	Croydon	PA	19021	215-785-3000	785-1585
GJ Chemical Co 370-376 Adams St. *Web:* www.gjchemical.com	Newark	NJ	07105	973-589-1450	589-5786
Grignard Company LLC 505 Capobianco Plz *Web:* www.grignard.com	Rahway	NJ	07065	732-340-1111	
GTC Technology Inc 1001 S Dairy Ashford Ste 500 *Web:* gtctech.com	Houston	TX	77077	281-597-4800	
Hand Industries/Dirilyte Line 315 S Hand Ave *Web:* www.handindustries.com	Warsaw	IN	46580	574-267-3525	267-7349
Harcros Chemicals Inc 5200 Speaker Rd *TF:* 800-504-8071 ■ *Web:* www.harcroschem.com	Kansas City	KS	66106	913-321-3131	621-7718
Hardide Coatings Inc 440 Louisiana St *Web:* www.hardide.com	Houston	TX	77002	713-221-9020	
Haviland Enterprises Inc 421 Ann St NW *TF:* 800-456-1134 ■ *Web:* www.havilandusa.com	Grand Rapids	MI	49504	616-361-6691	361-9772
Helm US Chemical Corp 1110 Centennial Ave *Web:* www.helmus.com	Piscataway	NJ	08854	732-981-1116	981-0528
Hill Bros Chemical Co 1675 N Main St *TF:* 800-994-8801 ■ *Web:* www.hillbrothers.com	Orange	CA	92867	714-998-8800	998-6310
HM Royal Inc 689 Pennington Ave *TF:* 800-257-9452 ■ *Web:* www.hmroyal.com	Trenton	NJ	08618	609-396-9176	396-3185
Homax Products Inc 1835 Barkley Blvd *Web:* www.homaxproducts.com	Bellingham	WA	98226	360-733-9029	
Hubbard-Hall Inc 563 S Leonard St *TF:* 800-331-6871 ■ *Web:* www.hubbardhall.com	Waterbury	CT	06708	203-756-5521	756-9017
Hydrite Chemical Co 300 N Patrick Blvd *TF:* 800-543-4560 ■ *Web:* www.hydrite.com	Brookfield	WI	53045	262-792-1450	792-8721
ICC Chemical Corp 460 Pk Ave *TF:* 800-422-1720 ■ *Web:* www.iccchem.com	New York	NY	10022	212-521-1700	521-1970
Ideal Chemical & Supply Co 4025 Air Pk St *TF:* 800-232-6776 ■ *Web:* www.idealchemical.com	Memphis	TN	38118	901-363-7720	366-0864
Independent Chemical Corp 79-51 Cooper Ave *TF:* 800-892-2578 ■ *Web:* www.independentchemical.com	Glendale	NY	11385	718-894-0700	894-9224
Industrial Chemicals Inc 2042 Montreat Dr *TF Cust Svc:* 800-476-2042 ■ *Web:* www.industrialchem.com	Vestavia	AL	35216	205-823-7330	978-0485
Innophos Holdings Inc 259 Prospect Plains Rd *NASDAQ:* IPHS ■ *Web:* www.innophos.com	Cranbury	NJ	08512	609-495-2495	560-0138
InnoVactiv Inc Two St-Germain St E Ste 200 *Web:* www.innovactiv.com	Rimouski	QC	G5L8T7	418-721-2308	
INTERCAT Inc 2399 Hwy 34 Ramshorn Executive Ctr Ste C-1	Manasquan	NJ	08736	732-223-4644	
John R Hess & Company Inc 400 Stn St PO Box 3615 *TF:* 800-828-4377 ■ *Web:* www.jrhessco.com	Cranston	RI	02910	401-785-9300	785-2510
John R White Company Inc PO Box 10043 *TF:* 800-245-1183 ■ *Web:* www.johnrwhite.com	Birmingham	AL	35202	205-595-8381	595-8386
KA Steel Chemicals Inc 15185 Main St PO Box 729 *TF:* 800-677-8335 ■ *Web:* www.kasteelchemicals.com	Lemont	IL	60439	630-257-3900	257-3922
KB International LLC 735 Broad St Ste 209 *Web:* www.kbtech.com	Chattanooga	TN	37402	423-266-6964	
KMG-Bernuth Inc 9555 W Sam Houston Pkwy S Ste 600 *Web:* kmgchemicals.com	Houston	TX	77099	713-600-3800	
Kraft Chemical Co 1975 N Hawthorne Ave *TF:* 800-345-5200 ■ *Web:* www.kraftchemical.com	Melrose Park	IL	60160	708-345-5200	345-4005
Kroff Inc One N Shore Ctr Ste 450 12 Federal St. *Web:* www.kroff.com	Pittsburgh	PA	15212	412-321-9800	
Lambent Technologies Corp 3938 Porett Dr *Web:* www.lambentcorp.com	Gurnee	IL	60031	847-244-3410	
LidoChem Inc 20 Village Ct *Web:* www.lidochem.com	Hazlet	NJ	07730	732-888-8000	264-2751
Lipo Chemicals Inc 207 19th Ave *Web:* www.lipochemicals.com	Paterson	NJ	07504	973-345-8600	345-8365
LV Lomas Ltd 99 Summerlea Rd *TF:* 800-575-3382 ■ *Web:* www.lvlomas.com	Brampton	ON	L6T4V2	905-458-1555	458-0722
Maroon Inc 1390 Jaycox Rd *TF General:* 877-627-6661 ■ *Web:* maroongroupllc.com//	Avon	OH	44011	440-937-1000	937-1001
Mays Chemical Company Inc 5611 E 71st St *Web:* www.mayschem.com	Indianapolis	IN	46220	317-842-8722	
McCullough & Assoc 1746 NE Expy PO Box 29803 *TF:* 800-969-1606 ■ *Web:* www.mccanda.com	Atlanta	GA	30329	404-325-1606	329-0208
MF Cachat Co 14725 Detroit Ave Ste 300 *TF:* 800-729-8900 ■ *Web:* www.mfcachat.com	Lakewood	OH	44107	216-228-8900	228-9916

Company	City	State	ZIP	Phone	Fax
Miles Chemical Co 12801 Rangoon St *Web:* www.mileschemical.com	Arleta	CA	91321	818-504-3355	
Milport Enterprises Inc 2829 S Fifth Ct *Web:* www.milport.com	Milwaukee	WI	53207	414-769-7350	769-0167
Mitsubishi International Corp 655 Third Ave *Web:* www.mitsubishicorp.com	New York	NY	10017	212-605-2000	
Mutchler Inc 20 Elm St *Web:* mutchler.net	Harrington Park	NJ	07640	201-768-1100	
Nagase America Holdings Inc 546 Fifth Ave 16th Fl *Web:* nagaseamerica.com	New York	NY	10036	212-703-1340	398-0687
Neutron Products Inc 22301 Mount Ephraim Rd *Web:* neutronprod.com	Dickerson	MD	20842	301-349-5001	
Nexeo Solutions LLC Three Waterway Sq Pl Ste 1000 *Web:* nexeosolutions.com	The Woodlands	TX	77380	281-297-0700	
Nisseki Chemical Texas Inc 10500 Bay Area Blvd	Pasadena	TX	77507	713-754-1000	
NuCo2 Inc 2800 SE Marketplace *TF:* 800-472-2855 ■ *Web:* www.nuco2.com	Stuart	FL	34997	772-221-1754	781-3500
Optima Chemical Group LLC 200 Willacoochee Hwy *Web:* www.optimachem.com	Douglas	GA	31535	912-384-5101	
Pain Enterprises Inc 101 Daniels Way *Fax Area Code: 812 ■ *Web:* www.painenterprises.com	Bloomington	IN	47404	800-245-8583	330-1544*
Palmer Holland Inc 25000 Country Club Blvd Ste 444 *Fax Area Code: 440 ■ *TF:* 800-635-4822 ■ *Web:* www.palmerholland.com	North Olmsted	OH	44070	800-635-4822	686-2180*
Pidilite USA Inc 902 South US Highway 1 Ste 18 *TF:* 800-843-7813 ■ *Web:* www.cyclo.com	Jupiter	FL	33477	561-775-9600	622-1055
Plaza Group Inc 10375 Richmond Ave Ste 1620 *TF:* 800-876-3738 ■ *Web:* www.theplazagrp.com	Houston	TX	77042	713-266-0707	266-8660
Pride Solvents & Chemical Co of New York Inc 6 Long Island Ave *TF:* 800-424-8802 ■ *Web:* www.pridesol.com	Holtsville	NY	11742	631-758-0200	758-0290
Purity Cylinder Gases Inc PO Box 9390 *Web:* www.puritygas.com	Grand Rapids	MI	49509	616-532-2375	532-5626
Quadra Chemicals Ltd 3901 Fixtessier *Fax: Hum Res ■ *TF:* 800-665-6553 ■ *Web:* www.quadra.ca	Vaudreuil-Dorion	QC	J7V5V5	450-424-0161	424-9458*
Reagent Chemical & Research Inc 115 Rt 202 *TF:* 800-231-1807 ■ *Web:* www.reagentchemical.com	Ringoes	NJ	08551	908-284-2800	284-6090
Ribelin Sales Inc 3857 Miller Pk Dr *Fax Area Code: 877 ■ *TF:* 800-374-1594 ■ *Web:* www.ribelin.com	Garland	TX	75042	972-272-1594	474-2354*
Rowell Chemical Corp 15 Salt Creek Ln Ste 205 *TF:* 888-261-7963 ■ *Web:* www.rowellchemical.com	Hinsdale	IL	60521	630-920-8833	920-8994
SARCOM Inc AEP Colloids Div 6299 Rt 9N *TF:* 800-848-0658 ■ *Web:* www.aepcolloids.com	Hadley	NY	12835	518-696-9900	696-9997
Sasol Wax North America Corp 21325-B Cabot Blvd *Web:* www.sasolwax.com	Hayward	CA	94545	510-783-9295	670-8659
Sessions Specialty Co 5090 Styers Ferry Rd *Fax Area Code: 800 ■ *Web:* www.sessionsusa.com	Lewisville	NC	27023	336-766-2880	723-0055*
Shamrock Technologies Inc Foot Of Pacific St *TF:* 800-349-1822 ■ *Web:* www.shamrocktechnologies.com	Newark	NJ	07114	973-242-2999	
Solmax International Inc 2801 Marie-Victorin Blvd *Web:* www.solmax.com	Varennes	QC	J3X1P7	450-929-1234	
Solvents & Chemicals Inc 4704 Shank Rd PO Box 490 *TF:* 800-622-3990 ■ *Web:* www.solvchem.com	Pearland	TX	77581	281-485-5377	485-6129
Special Materials Co 70 W 40th St Second Fl *Web:* www.smc-global.com	New York	NY	10018	646-366-0400	
Specified Technologies Inc 200 Evans Way Ste 2 *TF:* 800-992-1180 ■ *Web:* www.stifirestop.com	Somerville	NJ	08876	908-526-8000	526-9623
Spectra Colors Corp 25 Rizzolo Rd *TF:* 800-527-8588 ■ *Web:* www.spectracolors.com	Kearny	NJ	07032	201-997-0606	997-0504
Strem Chemicals Inc Seven Mulliken Way *TF:* 800-647-8736 ■ *Web:* www.strem.com	Newburyport	MA	01950	978-499-1600	
Sumitomo Chemical America Inc 335 Madison Ave Ste 830 *Web:* www.sumitomo-chem.co.jp	New York	NY	10017	212-572-8200	572-8234
Sunbelt Chemicals Corp 71 Hargrove Grade *Web:* www.sunbeltchemicals.com	Palm Coast	FL	32137	386-446-4595	446-4627
Sweetlake Chemical Ltd 7402 Neuhaus St	Houston	TX	77061	713-827-8707	
Tanner Industries Inc 735 Davisville Rd Third Fl *Fax: Sales ■ *TF:* 800-643-6226 ■ *Web:* www.tannerind.com	SouthHampton	PA	18966	215-322-1238	322-7791*
Tarr LLC 2429 N Borthwick St *Fax Area Code: 503 ■ *TF:* 800-422-5069 ■ *Web:* www.tarrllc.com	Portland	OR	97227	800-422-5069	288-0421*
TCR Industries 26 Centerpointe Dr Ste 120 *Web:* www.tcrindustries.com	La Palma	CA	90623	714-521-5222	521-1636
Tilley Chemical Company Inc 501 Chesapeake Pk Plz *TF:* 800-638-6968 ■ *Web:* tilleychem.com	Baltimore	MD	21220	410-574-4500	391-6665
Tm Deer Park Services LP 2525 Battleground Rd PO Box 1914 *TF:* 800-488-0648 ■ *Web:* www.texasmolecular.com	Deer Park	TX	77536	281-930-2525	930-2535
TR International Trading Company Inc 1218 Third Ave Ste 2100 *Web:* www.tritrading.com	Seattle	WA	98101	206-505-3500	505-3501
TransChemical Inc 419 De Soto Ave *TF:* 888-873-6481 ■ *Web:* www.transchemical.com	Saint Louis	MO	63147	314-231-6905	231-5851
Tulstar Products Inc 5510 S Lewis Ave *Web:* www.tulstar.com	Tulsa	OK	74105	918-749-9060	747-1444
Ultra Clean Technologies Corp 746 Shiloh Pk *Web:* ultracleantech.com	Bridgeton	NJ	08302	856-451-2176	
Union Carbide Corp 1254 Enclave Pkwy *Web:* www.unioncarbide.com	Houston	TX	77077	281-966-2016	966-2394
Univar Canada Ltd 9800 Van Horne Way *Web:* www.univar.com	Richmond	BC	V6X1W5	604-273-1441	273-2046
Univar USA Inc 17425 NE Union Hill Rd *TF:* 855-888-8648 ■ *Web:* www.univar.com	Redmond	WA	98052	425-889-3400	889-4100
Van Horn Metz & Company Inc 201 E Elm St *Web:* www.vanhornmetz.com	Conshohocken	PA	19428	610-828-4500	
VanDeMark Chemical Inc One N Transit Rd *Web:* www.vandemarkinc.com	Lockport	NY	14094	716-433-6764	
Victory Petroleum Inc 2200 S Dixie Hwy Ste 601 *Web:* www.victorypetroleum.com	Miami	FL	33133	305-255-4145	
Webb Chemical Service Corp 2708 Jarman St *Web:* www.webbchemical.com	Muskegon	MI	49444	231-733-2181	739-5454
Wego Chemical & Mineral Corp 239 Great Neck Rd *Web:* www.wegochem.com	Great Neck	NY	11021	516-487-3510	487-3794
Whitaker Oil Co 1557 Marietta Rd NW *TF:* 888-895-3506 ■ *Web:* www.whitakeroil.com	Atlanta	GA	30318	404-355-8220	355-8217
Wilshire Technologies Inc 145 Witherspoon St *Web:* www.wilshiretechnologies.com	Princeton	NJ	08542	609-683-1117	
Wilson Industrial Sales Company Inc 201 S Wilson *TF:* 800-633-5427 ■ *Web:* www.wilsonindustrial.com	Brook	IN	47922	219-275-7333	275-9622

147 CHILD CARE MONITORING SYSTEMS - INTERNET

Company	City	State	ZIP	Phone	Fax
Jewish Child Care Assn of New York 120 Wall St Fl 12 *Web:* www.jccany.org	New York	NY	10005	212-425-3333	425-9397
Mississippi Action For Progress Inc (MAP) 1751 Morson Rd *TF:* 800-924-4615 ■ *Web:* www.mapheadstart.org	Jackson	MS	39209	601-923-4100	923-4114

148 CHILDREN'S LEARNING CENTERS

Company	City	State	ZIP	Phone	Fax
Abrakadoodle Inc 46030 Manekin Pl Ste 110 *Web:* www.abrakadoodle.com	Sterling	VA	20166	703-860-6570	860-6574
Abundant Life Christian Academy 1494 Banks Rd *Web:* www.alcapro.com	Margate	FL	33063	954-979-2665	
Alabama Christian Academy 4700 Wares Ferry Rd *Web:* www.alabamachristian.com	Montgomery	AL	36109	334-277-1985	
Alexandra Park Neighbourhood Learning Centre 707 Dundas St W *Web:* www.apnlc.org	Toronto	ON	M5T2W6	416-591-7384	
Autistic Treatment Center Inc 10503 Metric Dr *Web:* www.atcoftexas.org	Dallas	TX	75243	972-644-2076	
Bright Horizons Family Solutions LLC 200 Talcott Ave S *TF:* 800-324-4386 ■ *Web:* www.brighthorizons.com	Watertown	MA	02472	617-673-8000	673-8001
Bristow Academy Inc 365 Golden Knights Blvd *Web:* www.heli.com	Titusville	FL	32780	321-385-2919	
Cape Christian Academy 10 Oyster Rd *Web:* capechristianacademy.com	Cape May Court House	NJ	08210	609-465-4132	
Chase Collegiate School 565 Chase Pkwy *Web:* www.smmct.org	Waterbury	CT	06708	203-236-9500	
Child Care Links 6601 Owens Dr Ste 100 *Web:* www.childcarelinks.org	Pleasanton	CA	94588	925-417-8733	730-4942
Child Development Assoc Inc 678 Third Ave Ste 201 *TF:* 888-755-2445 ■ *Web:* www.cdasandiego.com	Chula Vista	CA	91910	619-427-4411	205-6294
Childcare Network Inc 1501 13th St Ste D *TF:* 866-521-5437 ■ *Web:* www.childcarenetwork.com	Columbus	GA	31901	706-562-8600	
Children's Home + Aid 125 S Wacker Dr Fl 14 *Web:* www.childrenshomeandaid.org	Chicago	IL	60606	312-424-0200	
Churchill School & Center, The 301 E 29th St *Web:* www.churchillschool.com	New York	NY	10016	212-722-0610	
College Internship Program Inc 18 Park St *Web:* www.cipworldwide.org	Lee	MA	01238	413-243-0710	
Collinsville Community 240 Regency Ctr *Web:* kahoks.org	Collinsville	IL	62234	618-343-2878	
Colonial Intermediate Unit 20 Six Danforth Rd *Web:* www.ciu20.org	Easton	PA	18045	610-252-5550	252-5740
Competency & Credentialing Institute 2170 S Parker Rd Ste 295 *Web:* www.cc-institute.org	Denver	CO	80231	303-369-9566	
Computer Explorers 12715 Telge Rd *Fax Area Code: 281 ■ *TF:* 800-531-5053 ■ *Web:* www.computerexplorers.com	Cypress	TX	77429	800-531-5053	373-4450*
Council for Secular Humanism & Csicop 3965 Rensch Rd *Web:* www.centerforinquiry.net	Amherst	NY	14228	716-636-4869	
Da Vinci Academy 37w080 Hopps Rd *Web:* www.dvacademy.org	Elgin	IL	60124	224-856-5013	
DePelchin Children's Ctr 4950 Memorial Dr *TF:* 888-730-2335 ■ *Web:* www.depelchin.org	Houston	TX	77007	713-730-2335	802-3801
Derby Academy 56 Burditt Ave *Web:* derbyacademy.org	Hingham	MA	02043	781-749-0746	
Education Inc Two Main St Ste 2A *Web:* www.educationinc.us	Plymouth	MA	02360	508-732-9101	
Elgin Academy 350 Park St *Web:* www.elginacademy.org	Elgin	IL	60120	847-695-0300	

				Phone	Fax
Erskine Academy 309 Windsor Rd *Web:* erskineacademy.org	South China	ME	04358	207-445-2962	
FasTracKids International Ltd 6900 E Belleview Ave Ste 100 *TF:* 888-576-6888 ■ *Web:* fastrackids.com	Greenwood Village	CO	80111	303-224-0200	224-0222
Goddard Systems Inc 1016 W Ninth Ave *TF:* 800-463-3273 ■ *Web:* www.goddardschool.com	King of Prussia	PA	19406	610-265-8510	265-8867
Golflogix Inc 15685 N Greenway-Hayden Loop Ste 100A *TF:* 877-977-0162 ■ *Web:* www.golflogix.com	Scottsdale	AZ	85260	877-977-0162	
Greater Holy Temple Christian Academy 5575 N 76th St *Web:* greaterholy.org	Milwaukee	WI	53218	414-265-4131	
Gymboree Corp Play & Music Program 500 Howard St *TF Cust Svc:* 877-449-6932 ■ *Web:* www.gymboree.com	San Francisco	CA	94105	415-278-7000	278-7100
Hansa Language Centre of Toronto Inc 51 Eglinton Ave E *Web:* www.hansacanada.com	Toronto	ON	M4P1G7	416-487-8643	
Head Start of Greater Dallas Inc 3954 Gannon Ln *Web:* www.hsgd.org	Dallas	TX	75237	972-283-6400	
Hill Country Christian School of Austin 12124 Ranch Rd 620 N *Web:* www.hillcountrychristianschool.org	Austin	TX	78750	512-331-7036	
Huntington Learning Centers Inc 496 Kinderkamack Rd *TF:* 800-653-8400 ■ *Web:* huntingtonhelps.com	Oradell	NJ	07649	201-261-8400	
KinderCare Learning Centers Inc 650 NE Holladay St Ste 1400 PO Box 6760 **Fax Area Code:* 503 ■ *TF:* 800-633-1488 ■ *Web:* www.kindercare.com	Portland	OR	97232	800-633-1488	872-1427*
Knowledge Universe 650 NE Holladay St Ste 1400 *Web:* www.kueducation.com/us	Portland	OR	97232	503-872-1300	
Kumon North America Inc 300 Frank W Burr Blvd Glenpointe Ctr E Ste 6 *TF:* 800-222-6284 ■ *Web:* www.kumon.com	Teaneck	NJ	07666	201-928-0444	928-0044
Lad Lake Inc W350s1401 Waterville Rd *Web:* www.ladlake.org	Dousman	WI	53118	262-965-2131	
Learning Care Group Inc 21333 Haggerty Rd Ste 300 *TF:* 877-817-3883 ■ *Web:* learningcaregroup.com	Novi	MI	48375	248-697-9000	697-9002
Literacy Kansas City 211 W Armour Blvd Fl 3 *Web:* literacykc.org	Kansas City	MO	64111	816-960-7144	
Marburn Academy 1860 Walden Dr *Web:* marburnacademy.org	Columbus	OH	43229	614-433-0822	
Marin Christian Academy 1370 S Novato Blvd *Web:* visitmca.org	Novato	CA	94947	415-892-5713	
Matt Swanson's School of Golf 12000 Almeda Rd *Web:* swingpure.com	Houston	TX	77045	713-413-4484	
Miami Valley Child Development Centers 215 Horace St *Web:* www.mvcdc.org	Dayton	OH	45402	937-226-5664	
Missionary Oblates 327 Oblate Dr *Web:* www.oblatemissions.com	San Antonio	TX	78216	210-349-1475	
Morgan Park Academy 2153 W 111th St *Web:* www.morganparkacademy.org	Chicago	IL	60643	773-881-6722	
Nacel Open Door Inc 380 Jackson St Ste 200 *Web:* www.nacelopendoor.org	St. Paul	MN	55101	651-686-0080	
Nardin Academy 135 Cleveland Ave *Web:* www.frcdb.org	Buffalo	NY	14222	716-881-6262	
Naturebridge 28 Geary St Ste 650 *Web:* www.naturebridge.org	San Francisco	CA	94108	415-992-4700	
New Horizon Kids Quest Inc 3405 Annapolis Ln N Ste 100 **Fax Area Code:* 763 ■ *TF:* 800-941-1007 ■ *Web:* www.kidsquest.com	Plymouth	MN	55447	800-941-1007	383-6101*
Our Cooperative 525 Old Bellefonte Rd *Web:* www.oursc.k12.ar.us	Harrison	AR	72601	870-743-9100	
Pingree School 537 Highland St *Web:* pingree.org	South Hamilton	MA	01982	978-468-6232	
Pioneer Clubs 27w130 Saint Charles Rd *Web:* www.pioneerclubs.org	Carol Stream	IL	60188	630-293-1600	
Planet Granite 815 Stewart Dr *Web:* planetgranite.com	Sunnyvale	CA	94085	408-991-9090	
Porter & Chester Institute Inc, The 670 Lordship Blvd *Web:* www.porterchester.com	Stratford	CT	06615	203-375-4463	
Potomac Appalachian Trail Club Inc, The 118 Park St Se *Web:* patc.net	Vienna	VA	22180	703-242-0965	
Primrose School Franchising Co 3660 Cedarcrest Rd *TF:* 800-745-0677 ■ *Web:* www.primroseschools.com	Acworth	GA	30101	770-529-4100	529-1551
Rejoice Church 13413 E 106th St N *Web:* www.rejoicechurch.com	Owasso	OK	74055	918-272-5291	
Rosedale Technical Institute 215 Beecham Dr Ste 2 *Web:* www.rosedaletech.org	Pittsburgh	PA	15205	412-521-6200	
Rural Resources Community Action 956 S Main St Ste A *TF:* 800-538-7659 ■ *Web:* www.ruralresources.org	Colville	WA	99114	509-684-8421	684-4740
Sivananda Yoga Vedanta Center 1200 Arguello Blvd *Web:* www.sivananda.org	San Francisco	CA	94122	415-681-2731	
Sky Ranch 24657 CR 448 *Web:* www.skyranch.org	Van	TX	75790	903-266-3300	
Spirit Rock Meditation Center 5000 Sir Francis Drake Blvd *Web:* www.spiritrock.org	Woodacre	CA	94973	415-488-0164	
St Raphael Academy 123 Walcott St *Web:* www.saintraphaelacademy.org	Pawtucket	RI	02860	401-723-8100	
Strake Jesuit College Preparatory Inc 8900 Bellaire Blvd *Web:* www.strakejesuit.org	Houston	TX	77036	713-774-7651	
Stride Learning Center 326 Parsley Blvd *Web:* www.stridekids.com	Cheyenne	WY	82007	307-632-2991	
Syracuse Academy of Science 1001 Park Ave *Web:* sascs.org	Syracuse	NY	13204	315-428-8997	
Talladega Clay Randolph Child Care Corp 925 N St E	Talladega	AL	35160	256-362-3852	
Tri Rivers Career Center 2222 Marion Mount Gilead Rd *Web:* www.tririvers.com	Marion	OH	43302	740-389-4681	
Vertical Endeavors 28141 Diehl Rd *Web:* verticalendeavors.com	Warrenville	IL	60555	630-836-0122	
Voyager Academy 101 Hock Parc *Web:* www.voyageracademy.net	Durham	NC	27704	919-433-3301	
West Highland Christian Academy 1116 S Hickory Ridge Rd *Web:* www.whca-k12.org	Milford	MI	48380	248-887-6698	
Woodstock Academy 57 Academy Rd *Web:* www.woodstockacademy.org	Woodstock	CT	06281	860-928-6575	
World Wide Group LLC 717 S Pines Rd *Web:* worldwidegrouptravel.com	Spokane	WA	99206	509-924-0955	
Yeled V'yalda Early Childhood Ctr Inc 1312 38th St *Web:* www.yeled.org	Brooklyn	NY	11218	718-686-3700	
Zenya Yoga & Message Studio 101 Herman Melville Ave *Web:* www.zenyayoga.com	Newport News	VA	23606	757-643-6900	

149 CIRCUS, CARNIVAL, FESTIVAL OPERATORS

				Phone	Fax
Accent on Arrangements Inc 615 Baronne St Ste 303 *Web:* www.accent-dmc.com	New Orleans	LA	70113	504-524-1227	
Big Apple Circus One Metrotech Ctr Third Fl *TF:* 800-922-3772 ■ *Web:* www.bigapplecircus.org	Brooklyn	NY	11201	212-268-2500	268-3163
Chippendales USA LLC 95 E Bethpage Rd *Web:* www.chippendales.com	Plainview	NY	11803	516-454-0981	
Cirque du Soleil Inc 8400 Second Ave *TF:* 800-678-2119 ■ *Web:* www.cirquedusoleil.com	Montreal	QC	H1Z4M6	514-722-2324	722-3692
Crazy Horse Gentlemen's Club 980 Market St *Web:* crazyhorse.com	San Francisco	CA	94102	415-771-6259	
Culpepper & Merriweather Circus PO Box 813 *Web:* www.cmcircus.com	Hugo	OK	74743	580-326-8833	326-8866
Encore Creative Inc 410 S Madison Dr *Web:* www.encorecreative.com	Tempe	AZ	85281	480-736-2800	
Extraordinary Events 13425 Ventura Blvd Ste 300 *Web:* www.extraordinaryevents.net	Sherman Oaks	CA	91423	818-783-6112	
Feld Entertainment Inc 8607 Westwood Ctr Dr *Web:* www.feldentertainment.com	Vienna	VA	22182	703-448-4000	448-4100
Green Tree Event Consultants 35 Storer St *Web:* www.nemadeshows.com	Saco	ME	04072	207-781-2982	
Maryland Renaissance Festival PO Box 315 *TF:* 800-296-7304 ■ *Web:* www.rennfest.com	Crownsville	MD	21032	410-266-7304	573-1508
Palace Cafe, The 139 S Murphy Ave *Web:* m.palacecafe.net	Sunnyvale	CA	94086	408-774-6111	
Ringling Bros & Barnum & Bailey Circus 8607 Westwood Ctr Dr *Web:* www.ringling.com	Vienna	VA	22182	703-448-4000	448-4100
Starkey International Institute for Household Management Inc, The 1350 Logan St *Web:* www.starkeyintl.com	Denver	CO	80203	303-832-5510	
Taikoproject 244 S San Pedro St Ste 505 *Web:* www.jaccc.org	Los Angeles	CA	90012	213-268-4011	
Wonder World Enterprises Inc 411 Porter St Apt 3 *Web:* www.wonderworldonline.com	Glendale	CA	91205	818-546-2254	

150 CLAY PRODUCTS - STRUCTURAL

SEE ALSO Brick, Stone, Related Materials p. 2106

				Phone	Fax
Acme Brick Co 3024 Acme Brick Plaza **Fax Area Code:* 423 ■ *TF:* 866-430-2263 ■ *Web:* www.acmebrick.com	Fort Worth	TX	76109	817-332-4101	821-3550*
Belden Brick Company Inc 700 Tuscarawas St W *Web:* www.beldenbrick.com	Canton	OH	44702	330-456-0031	456-2694
Boral Bricks Inc 9143 Bob Williams Pkwy *TF:* 800-526-7255 ■ *Web:* boralamerica.com	Covington	GA	30014	678-625-4051	
Bowerston Shale Co, The PO Box 199 *Web:* www.bowerstonshale.com	Bowerston	OH	44695	740-269-2921	269-5456
Brampton Brick Ltd 225 Wanless Dr *TSE:* BBLA ■ *Web:* www.bramptonbrick.com	Brampton	ON	L7A1E9	905-840-1011	840-1535
Cherokee Brick & Tile Co Inc 3250 Waterville Rd *TF:* 800-277-2745 ■ *Web:* www.cherokeebrick.com	Macon	GA	31206	478-781-6800	781-8964
Colloid Environmental Technologies Co (CETCO) 2870 Forbs Ave **Fax Area Code:* 800 ■ *TF:* 800-527-9948 ■ *Web:* www.cetco.com	Hoffman Estates	IL	60192	847-851-1899	527-9948*
Cunningham Brick Co Inc 701 N Main St *TF:* 800-672-6181 ■ *Web:* www.cunninghambrick.com	Lexington	NC	27292	336-248-8541	472-2404
Elgin-Butler Brick Co 2601 McHale Crt *Web:* www.elginbutler.com	Austin	TX	78758	512-453-7366	281-3003
Endicott Clay Products Co 57120 707 Rd *Web:* www.endicott.com	Endicott	NE	68350	402-729-3315	729-5804
Endicott Tile LLC 57120 707 Rd *Web:* www.endicott.com	Endicott	NE	68350	402-729-3315	729-5804

Phone Fax

General Shale Products LLC
3015 Bristol Hwy .... Johnson City TN 37601 423-282-4661 952-4104
TF: 800-414-4661 ■ *Web:* www.generalshale.com

Glen-Gery Corp 1166 Spring St PO Box 7001 .... Wyomissing PA 19610 610-374-4011 374-1622
Web: www.glengerybrick.com

Henry Brick Co Inc 3409 Water Ave .... Selma AL 36703 334-875-2600
TF: 800-218-3906 ■ *Web:* www.henrybrick.com

I-XL Industries Ltd
612 Porcelain Ave SE .... Medicine Hat AB T1A8S4 403-504-5901
Web: www.ixlbrick.com

International Chimney Corp
55 S Long St .... Williamsville NY 14221 800-828-1446 634-3983*
*Fax Area Code: 716 ■ *TF:* 800-828-1446 ■ *Web:* www.internationalchimney.com

Kansas Brick & Tile Inc 767 N US Hwy 281 .... Hoisington KS 67544 620-653-2157 653-7609
Web: www.kansasbrick.com

Kinney Brick Co
100 Prosperity Rd PO Box 1804 .... Albuquerque NM 87103 505-877-4550 877-4557
TF: 800-464-4605 ■ *Web:* kinneybrickco.com

Lee Brick & Tile Co
3704 Hawkins Ave PO Box 1027 .... Sanford NC 27330 919-774-4800 774-7557
TF: 800-672-7559 ■ *Web:* www.leebrickonline.com

Logan Clay Products Co 201 S Walnut St .... Logan OH 43138 800-848-2141 385-9336*
*Fax Area Code: 740 ■ *TF:* 800-848-2141 ■ *Web:* www.loganclaypipe.com

Ludowici Roof Tile Inc
4757 Tile Plant Rd PO Box 69 .... New Lexington OH 43764 740-342-1995 342-0025
TF Cust Svc: 800-945-8453 ■ *Web:* www.ludowici.com

Marion Ceramics Inc PO Box 1134 .... Marion SC 29571 843-423-1311 423-1515
TF: 800-845-4010 ■ *Web:* www.marionceramics.com

McNear Brick & Block
One McNear BrickyaRd Rd PO Box 151380 .... San Rafael CA 94901 415-453-7702 453-3141
TF: 888-442-6811 ■ *Web:* www.mcnear.com

MCP Industries Inc Mission Clay Products Div
708 S Temescal St Ste 101 .... Corona CA 92879 951-736-1881 549-8280
Web: www.mcpind.com

Morin Brick Co 130 Morin Brick Rd PO Box 1510 .... Auburn ME 04210 207-784-9375 784-2013
Web: www.morinbrick.com

Mutual Materials Co 605 119th Ave NE .... Bellevue WA 98005 425-452-2300 454-7732
TF: 800-477-3008 ■ *Web:* www.mutualmaterials.com

Old Virginia Brick Co 2500 W Main St .... Salem VA 24153 540-389-2357 929-6411*
*Fax Area Code: 434 ■ *TF:* 800-879-8227

Pacific Clay Products Inc
14741 Lake St .... Lake Elsinore CA 92530 951-674-2131 674-4909
Web: www.pacificclay.com

Palmetto Brick Co 3501 BrickyaRd Rd .... Wallace SC 29596 843-537-7861 537-4802
TF: 800-922-4423 ■ *Web:* www.palmettobrick.com

Pine Hall Brick Co 2701 Shorefair Dr .... Winston-Salem NC 27116 800-334-8689 725-3940*
*Fax Area Code: 336 ■ *TF:* 800-334-8689 ■ *Web:* www.pinehallbrick.com

Potomac Valley Brick & Supply Co
15810 Indianola Dr Ste 100 .... Rockville MD 20855 301-309-9600 309-0929
Web: www.pvbrick.com

Redland Brick Inc 15718 Clear Spring Rd .... Williamsport MD 21795 301-223-7700
TF: 800-366-2742 ■ *Web:* redlandbrick.com/

Richards Brick Co 234 Springer Ave .... Edwardsville IL 62025 618-656-0230 656-0944
Web: www.richardsbrick.com

Sioux City Brick & Tile Co
310 S Floyd Blvd .... Sioux City IA 51101 712-258-6571 252-3215
Web: www.siouxcitybrick.com

Statesville Brick Co 391 BrickyaRd Rd .... Statesville NC 28677 704-872-4123 872-4125
TF: 800-522-4716 ■ *Web:* www.statesvillebrick.com

Summitville Tiles Inc 15364 Ohio 644 .... Summitville OH 43962 330-223-1511 223-1414
Web: www.summitville.com

Superior Clay Corp 6566 Superior Rd SE .... Uhrichsville OH 44683 740-922-4122 922-6626
TF: 800-848-6166 ■ *Web:* www.superiorclay.com

Taylor Clay Products Co
185 Peeler Rd PO Box 2128 .... Salisbury NC 28145 704-636-2411 636-2413
Web: taylorclaybrick.com/wp/index.php

Triangle Brick Co 6523 NC Hwy 55 .... Durham NC 27713 919-544-1796 544-3904
TF: 800-672-8547 ■ *Web:* www.trianglebrick.com

Whitacre Greer Fireproofing Inc
1400 S Mahoning Ave .... Alliance OH 44601 330-823-1610 823-5502
TF Cust Svc: 800-947-2837 ■ *Web:* www.wgpaver.com

Yankee Hill Brick & Tile
3705 S Coddington Ave .... Lincoln NE 68522 402-477-6663 477-2832
Web: www.yankeehillbrick.com

151 CLEANING PRODUCTS

SEE ALSO Brushes & Brooms p. 1887; Mops, Sponges, Wiping Cloths p. 2766

Phone Fax

ABC Compounding Company Inc & Acme Wholesale
6970 Jonesboro Rd .... Morrow GA 30260 770-968-9222 968-7281
TF: 800-795-9222 ■ *Web:* www.abccompounding.com

Abso-Clean Industries Inc 199 Wales Ave .... Tonawanda NY 14150 716-693-2111 693-2155

Adco Inc 1909 W Oakridge .... Albany GA 31707 800-821-7556
TF: 800-821-7556 ■ *Web:* www.adco-inc.com

AJ Funk & Co 1471 Timber Dr .... Elgin IL 60123 847-741-6760 741-6767
Web: www.glasscleaner.com

American Cleaning Solutions
39-30 Review Ave .... Long Island City NY 11101 718-392-8080 482-9366
TF: 888-929-7587 ■ *Web:* www.cleaning-solutions.com

Arrow-Magnolia International 2646 Rodney Ln .... Dallas TX 75229 972-247-7111 484-2896
TF: 800-527-2101 ■ *Web:* www.arrowmagnolia.com

Aztec International Inc 3010 Henson Rd .... Knoxville TN 37921 865-588-5357 538-2062*
*Fax Area Code: 615 ■ *TF:* 800-369-5357 ■ *Web:* www.candlemaking.com

BAF Industries Inc 1451 Edinger Ave .... Tustin CA 92780 714-258-8055
TF: 800-437-9893 ■ *Web:* www.prowax.com

Buckeye International Inc
2700 Wagner Pl .... Maryland Heights MO 63043 314-291-1900 298-2850
TF: 800-321-2583 ■ *Web:* www.buckeyeinternational.com

Phone Fax

Bullen Cos 1640 Delmar Dr PO Box 37 .... Folcroft PA 19032 610-534-8900 534-8912
TF: 800-444-8900 ■ *Web:* bullenonline.com

C & H Chemical Inc
13505 Industrial Park Blvd .... Plymouth MN 55441 763-582-1140 746-9235
TF: 800-966-2909 ■ *Web:* seacole.com

Camco Chemical Co 8145 Holton Dr .... Florence KY 41042 859-727-3200 727-1508
TF Cust Svc: 800-354-1001 ■ *Web:* www.camco-chem.com

Canberra Corp 3610 Holland Sylvania Rd .... Toledo OH 43615 419-841-6616 841-7597
TF: 800-832-8992 ■ *Web:* www.canberracorp.com

Car-Freshner Corp
21205 Little Tree Dr PO Box 719 .... Watertown NY 13601 315-788-6250 788-7467
TF: 800-545-5454 ■ *Web:* www.car-freshner.com

Carroll Co 2900 W Kingsley Rd .... Garland TX 75041 972-278-1304 840-0678
TF: 800-527-5722 ■ *Web:* www.carrollco.com

Cello Professional Products
1354 Old Post Rd .... Havre de Grace MD 21078 410-939-1234 939-3028
TF: 800-638-4850 ■ *Web:* www.cello-online.com

Champion Chemical Co 8319 S Greenleaf Ave .... Whittier CA 90602 800-424-9300 898-8064
TF: 800-424-9300 ■ *Web:* www.championchemical.com

Chemical Specialties Manufacturing Corp
901 N Newkirk St .... Baltimore MD 21205 410-675-4800 675-0038
TF Sales: 800-638-7370 ■ *Web:* www.chemspecworld.com

Church & Dwight Company Inc
469 N Harrison St .... Princeton NJ 08543 609-683-5900
NYSE: CHD ■ *Web:* www.churchdwight.com

Clorox Co 1221 Broadway .... Oakland CA 94612 510-271-7000 832-1463
NYSE: CLX ■ *TF Cust Svc:* 800-424-9300 ■ *Web:* www.thecloroxcompany.com

Copper Brite Inc
1482 E Valley Rd Ste 29 Ste 29 .... Santa Barbara CA 93108 805-565-1566 565-1394
Web: www.copperbrite.com

Correlated Products Inc
5616 Progress Rd .... Indianapolis IN 46242 317-243-3248 244-8461
TF: 800-428-3266 ■ *Web:* www.cpicorrelated.com

Crain Chemical Co 2624 Andjon Dr .... Dallas TX 75220 214-358-3301 358-3304

Damon Industries Inc 12435 Rockhill Ave NE .... Alliance OH 44601 330-821-5310 821-6355
TF: 800-362-9850 ■ *Web:* www.damonq.com

Delta Carbona LP 376 Hollywood Ave Ste 208 .... Fairfield NJ 07004 973-808-6260 808-5661
TF: 888-746-5599 ■ *Web:* www.carbona.com

DeSoto LLC 900 Washington St PO Box 609 .... Joliet IL 60433 815-727-4931 727-4333

Diamond Chemical Company Inc
Union Ave & Dubois St .... East Rutherford NJ 07073 201-935-4300 935-6997
TF: 800-654-7627 ■ *Web:* www.diamondchem.com

Dreumex USA 3445 BoaRd Rd .... York PA 17406 717-767-6881 767-6888
TF: 800-233-9382 ■ *Web:* www.gentlkleen.com

Dubois Chemicals 3630 E Kemper Rd .... Cincinnati OH 45241 800-438-2647 543-1720
TF: 800-438-2647 ■ *Web:* www.duboischemicals.com

Dura Wax Co 4101 W Albany St .... McHenry IL 60050 815-385-5000 344-8056
TF: 800-435-5705 ■ *Web:* www.durawax.com

Elco Laboratories Inc
2545 Palmer Ave .... University Park IL 60484 708-534-3000 534-0445
Web: elcolabs.com

Empire Cleaning Supply
12821 S Figueroa St .... Los Angeles CA 90061 310-527-0132
TF: 888-868-7336 ■ *Web:* www.empirecleaningsupply.com

Emulso Corp 2750 Kenmore Ave .... Tonawanda NY 14150 716-854-2889 854-2809
Web: www.emulso.com

Falcon Safety Products Inc 25 Chubb Way .... Somerville NJ 08876 908-707-4900 707-8855
TF: 800-332-5266 ■ *Web:* www.falconsafety.com

Fine Organics Corp 420 Kuller Rd PO Box 2277 .... Clifton NJ 07015 973-478-1000 478-6120*
*Fax: Sales ■ *TF:* 800-526-7480 ■ *Web:* www.fineorganicscorp.com

Frank B Ross Co 970-H New Brunswick Ave .... Rahway NJ 07065 732-669-0810 669-0814
Web: www.frankbross.com

Glissen Chemical Company Inc 1321 58th St .... Brooklyn NY 11219 718-436-4200

Goodwin Company Inc, The
12102 Industry St .... Garden Grove CA 92841 714-894-0531 894-6293
Web: www.goodwininc.com

Granitize Products Inc 11022 Vulcan St .... South Gate CA 90280 562-923-5438 861-3475
Web: www.granitize.com

Heritage-Crystal Clean Inc 2175 Pt Blvd Ste 375 .... Elgin IL 60123 847-836-5670 836-5677
TF: 877-938-7948 ■ *Web:* www.crystal-clean.com

Hill Mfg Company Inc 1500 Jonesboro Rd SE .... Atlanta GA 30315 404-522-8364 522-9694
TF: 800-445-5123 ■ *Web:* www.hillmfg.com

Hillyard Chemical Company Inc
302 N Fourth St .... Saint Joseph MO 64501 816-233-1321 861-0256*
*Fax Area Code: 800 ■ *TF:* 800-365-1555 ■ *Web:* www.hillyard.com

Impact Products LLC 2840 Centennial Rd .... Toledo OH 43617 419-841-2891 841-7861
TF Cust Svc: 800-333-1541 ■ *Web:* www.impact-products.com

ITW Dymon 805 E Old 56 Hwy .... Olathe KS 66061 913-829-6296 397-8707
TF: 800-443-9536 ■ *Web:* itwprofessionalbrands.com

James Austin Co 115 Downieville Rd PO Box 827 .... Mars PA 16046 724-625-1535 625-3288
TF: 800-245-1942 ■ *Web:* www.jamesaustin.com

JohnsonDiversey Inc
8310 16th St PO Box 902 .... Sturtevant WI 53177 262-631-4001 631-4282
Web: www.diversey.com

Kay Chemical Co 8300 Capital Dr .... Greensboro NC 27409 336-668-7290 225-3098*
*Fax Area Code: 651 ■ *TF:* 877-315-1115 ■ *Web:* www.ecolab.com

Koger/Air Corp PO Box 2098 .... Martinsville VA 24113 276-638-8821 638-4305
TF: 800-368-2096 ■ *Web:* www.kogerair.com

Leadership Performance Sustainability Laboratories
4647 Hugh Howell Rd .... Tucker GA 30084 800-241-8334 243-8899*
*Fax Area Code: 770 ■ *TF:* 800-241-8334 ■ *Web:* www.lpslabs.com

Lincoln Shoe Polish Co 172 Commercial St .... Sunnyvale CA 94086 408-732-5120 732-0659
Web: www.lincolnshoepolish.com

Lonn Mfg Co Inc 5450 W 84th St .... Indianapolis IN 46268 317-897-1440 898-4561
Web: www.lonn.net

Luseaux Laboratories Inc 16816 S Gramercy Pl .... Gardena CA 90247 310-324-1555
Web: luseaux.com

Madison Chemical Company Inc 3141 Clifty Dr .... Madison IN 47250 812-273-6000 273-6002
TF: 800-345-1915 ■ *Web:* madchem.com

Magic American Corp
26901 Cannon Rd Ste 190 .... Bedford Heights OH 44146 800-729-9029 786-3102*
*Fax Area Code: 440 ■ *TF Cust Svc:* 800-729-9029 ■ *Web:* www.magicamerican.com

Phone Fax

Matchless Metal Polish Co 840 W 49th Pl. Chicago IL 60609 773-924-1515 924-5513
Web: www.matchlessmetal.com

Maxim Technologies Inc 1607 Derwent Way. Delta BC V3M6K8 800-663-9925 526-1618*
**Fax Area Code:* 604 ■ *TF:* 800-663-9925 ■ *Web:* www.maxim-technologies.com

Meguiar's Inc 17991 Mitchell S. Irvine CA 92614 949-752-8000 752-5784
TF Cust Svc: 800-347-5700 ■ *Web:* www.meguiars.com

Micro Care Corp 595 John Downey Dr New Britain CT 06051 860-827-0626 827-8105
TF: 800-638-0125 ■ *Web:* www.microcare.com

Mission Laboratories 2433 Birkdale St Los Angeles CA 90031 323-223-1405 223-9968
Web: www.missionlabs.net

Morga-Gallacher Inc
8707 Millergrove Dr Santa Fe Springs CA 90670 562-695-1232 699-8953
Web: www.morgan-gallacher.com

Mother's Polishes Waxes & Cleaners
5456 Industrial Dr. Huntington Beach CA 92649 714-891-3364 893-1827
TF: 800-221-8257 ■ *Web:* www.mothers.com

National Chemical Laboratories Inc
401 N Tenth St Philadelphia PA 19123 215-922-1200 922-5517
TF: 800-628-2436 ■ *Web:* www.nclonline.com

National Chemicals Inc
105 Liberty St PO Box 32 Winona MN 55987 507-454-5640 858-4141*
**Fax Area Code:* 877 ■ *TF Cust Svc:* 800-533-0027 ■ *Web:* www.nationalchemicals.com

NCH Corp 2727 Chemsearch Blvd Irving TX 75062 972-438-0211 438-0186
TF: 800-527-9919 ■ *Web:* www.nch.com

New Pig Corp One Pork Ave Tipton PA 16684 814-684-0101 621-7447*
**Fax Area Code:* 800 ■ *TF:* 800-468-4647 ■ *Web:* www.newpig.com

Northern Labs Inc 5800 W Dr PO Box 850 Manitowoc WI 54220 920-684-7137 684-4957
TF: 800-558-7621 ■ *Web:* www.northernlabs.com

Nuvite Chemical Compounds Corp
213 Freeman St Brooklyn NY 11222 718-383-8351 383-0008
TF: 800-394-8351 ■ *Web:* www.nuvitechemical.com

Ocean Bio-Chem Inc (OBCI)
4041 SW 47th Ave Fort Lauderdale FL 33314 954-587-6280 587-2813
NASDAQ: OBCI ■ *TF:* 800-327-8583 ■ *Web:* www.oceanbiochem.com

Paramount Chemical Specialties Inc
14750 NE 95th St Redmond WA 98052 425-882-2673
TF: 877-846-7826 ■ *Web:* www.kidsnpetsbrand.com

Prestige Brands International Inc
660 White Plains Rd Ste 250 Tarrytown NY 10591 914-524-6800 524-6815
Web: www.prestigebrandsinc.com

Prosoco Inc 3741 Greenway Cir Lawrence KS 66046 800-255-4255 830-9797*
**Fax Area Code:* 785 ■ *TF:* 800-255-4255 ■ *Web:* www.prosoco.com

Reckitt Benckiser Inc
399 Interpace Pkwy PO Box 225 Parsippany NJ 07054 973-404-2600 404-5700
TF Cust Svc: 800-333-3899 ■ *Web:* www.rb.com

Safeguard Chemical Corp 411 Wales Ave. Bronx NY 10454 718-585-3170 585-3657
TF: 800-536-3170 ■ *Web:* www.safeguardchemical.com

Safetec of America Inc 887 Kensington Ave Buffalo NY 14215 716-895-1822 895-2969
TF: 800-456-7077 ■ *Web:* www.safetec.com

SC Johnson & Son Inc 1525 Howe St Racine WI 53403 262-260-2154 260-6004
TF: 800-494-4855 ■ *Web:* www.scjohnson.com

Scott Fetzer Company Scot Laboratories Div
16841 Pk Cir Dr Chagrin Falls OH 44023 440-543-3033 543-1825
TF: 800-486-7268 ■ *Web:* scotstuffdirect.com

Scott's Liquid Gold Inc 4880 Havana St. Denver CO 80239 303-373-4860
OTC: SLGD ■ *TF:* 800-447-1919 ■ *Web:* www.scottsliquidgold.com

Seventh Generation Inc 60 Lake St Burlington VT 05401 802-658-3773 658-1771
TF: 800-456-1191 ■ *Web:* www.seventhgeneration.com

Share Corp 7821 N Faulkner Rd Milwaukee WI 53224 414-355-4000 355-0516
TF: 800-776-7192 ■ *Web:* www.sharecorp.com

Simoniz USA 201 Boston Tpke Bolton CT 06043 860-646-0172 645-6070
TF: 800-227-5536 ■ *Web:* www.simoniz.com

Snyder Manufacturing Corp
1541 W Cowles St Long Beach CA 90813 562-432-2038 432-1603
Web: www.snydermanufacturing.com

State Industrial Products
3100 Hamilton Ave Cleveland OH 44114 216-861-7114
TF: 877-747-6986 ■ *Web:* www.stateindustrial.com

Stearns Packaging Corp 4200 Sycamore Ave Madison WI 53714 608-246-5150 246-5149
TF: 800-655-5008 ■ *Web:* www.stearnspkg.com

Summit Industries Inc PO Box 7329 Marietta GA 30065 800-241-6996
TF: 800-241-6996 ■ *Web:* www.summitinds.com

Sunshine Makers Inc
15922 Pacific Coast Hwy Huntington Harbour CA 92649 562-795-6000 592-3034
TF: 800-228-0709 ■ *Web:* www.simplegreen.com

Unit Chemical Corp 7360 Commercial Way Henderson NV 89015 702-564-6454 564-6629
TF: 800-879-8648 ■ *Web:* www.unitchemical.com

UNX Inc 707 E Arlington Blvd PO Box 7206 Greenville NC 27835 252-756-8616 756-2764
Web: www.unxinc.com

Warsaw Chemical Company Inc
Argonne Rd PO Box 858 Warsaw IN 46580 574-267-3251 267-3884
TF: 800-548-3396 ■ *Web:* www.warsaw-chem.com

WD-40 Co 1061 Cudahy Pl San Diego CA 92110 619-275-1400 275-5823
NASDAQ: WDFC ■ *TF:* 800-448-9340 ■ *Web:* www.wd40company.com

Webco Chemical Corp 420 W Main St Dudley MA 01571 508-943-9500 987-0366
Web: www.webco-chemical.com

West Penetone Corp 700 Gotham Pkwy Carlstadt NJ 07072 201-567-3000 510-3973
TF: 800-631-1652 ■ *Web:* www.west-penetone.com

Willert Home Products Inc 4044 Pk Ave. Saint Louis MO 63110 314-772-2822 772-1409
TF: 877-373-4858 ■ *Web:* www.willert.com

ZEP Inc 1310 Seaboard Industrial Blvd NW Atlanta GA 30318 404-352-1680 603-7958
NYSE: ZEP ■ *TF:* 877-428-9937 ■ *Web:* www.zepinc.com

152 CLEANING SERVICES

SEE ALSO Building Maintenance Services p. 1888; Bio-Recovery Services p. 1869

Phone Fax

1-800-Water Damage 1167 Mercer St Seattle WA 98109 206-381-3041 381-3052
TF: 800-928-3732 ■ *Web:* www.1800waterdamage.com

ABM Industries 600 Harrison St Ste 600 San Francisco CA 94107 415-351-4428
Web: locations.abm.com

BearCom Bldg Services 7022 S 400 W Midvale UT 84047 801-569-9500 569-8400
Web: bearcomservices.com

Boston's Best Chimney Sweep 76 Bacon St. Waltham MA 02451 781-893-6611 893-1132
TF Cust Svc: 800-660-6708 ■ *Web:* www.bestchimney.com

Braco Window Cleaning Service Inc
One Braco International Blvd Wilder KY 41076 859-442-6000 442-6001
Web: www.bracowindowcleaning.com

Clean Power LLC 124 N 121st St Milwaukee WI 53226 414-302-3000 302-3015
TF: 888-566-1717 ■ *Web:* www.cleanpower1.com

Clean-Tech Co 211 S Jefferson Ave. Saint Louis MO 63103 314-652-2388
Web: www.cleantechcompany.com

Cleaning Authority
7230 Lee DeForest Dr Ste 200 Columbia MD 21046 410-740-1900 740-1906
TF: 888-658-0659 ■ *Web:* www.thecleaningauthority.com

CleanNet USA 9861 Brokenland Pkwy Ste 208 Columbia MD 21046 410-720-6444 720-5307
TF: 800-735-8838 ■ *Web:* www.cleannetusa.com

Coverall Cleaning Concepts
5201 Congress Ave Ste 275 Boca Raton FL 33487 866-296-8944 922-2423*
**Fax Area Code:* 561 ■ *TF:* 800-537-3371 ■ *Web:* www.coverall.com

Diversified Maintenance Systems Inc
5110 Eisenhower Blvd Ste250 Tampa FL 33634 813-383-0238
TF: 800-351-1557 ■ *Web:* www.diveinc.com

Duraclean International Inc
220 W Campus Dr Arlington Heights IL 60004 847-704-7100 704-7101
TF: 800-862-5326 ■ *Web:* www.duraclean.com

Federal Bldg Services Inc
1641 Barclay Blvd. Buffalo Grove IL 60089 847-279-7360 215-7600
TF: 800-982-9234 ■ *Web:* www.federalbuildingservice.com

Fish Window Cleaning Services Inc
200 Enchanted Pkwy. Manchester MO 63021 636-779-1500 530-7856
TF: 877-707-3474 ■ *Web:* www.fishwindowcleaning.com

GCA Services Group 1350 Euclid Ave Ste 1500 Cleveland OH 44115 800-422-8760 583-0481*
**Fax Area Code:* 216 ■ *TF:* 800-422-8760 ■ *Web:* www.gcaservices.com

Healthcare Services Group Inc (HCSG)
3220 Tillman Dr Ste 300 Bensalem PA 19020 215-639-4274
TF: 800-486-3289 ■ *Web:* www.hcsgcorp.com

Heaven's Best Carpet & Upholstery Cleaning
PO Box 607 Rexburg ID 83440 208-359-1106 359-1236
TF: 800-359-2095 ■ *Web:* www.heavensbest.com

Ih Services Inc PO Box 5033 Greenville SC 29606 864-297-3748 297-9219
TF: 800-340-9088 ■ *Web:* www.ihservices.com

Jan-Pro International Inc (JPI)
2520 Northwinds Pkwy Ste 375 Alpharetta GA 30009 678-336-1780 336-1781
TF: 866-355-1064 ■ *Web:* www.jan-pro.com

Jani-King International Inc
16885 Dallas Pkwy Addison TX 75001 972-991-0900 991-5723
TF: 800-526-4546 ■ *Web:* www.janiking.com

Linc Services Mid-Atlantic LLC
3701 Saunders Ave. Richmond VA 23227 804-254-5790
Web: www.lincservice.com

Maid Brigade USA/Minimaid Canada
Four Concourse Pkwy Ste 200 Atlanta GA 30328 770-551-9630 391-9092
TF: 800-722-6243 ■ *Web:* www.maidbrigade.com

MaidPro Corp 180 Canal St Boston MA 02114 617-742-8787 720-0700
TF: 888-624-3776 ■ *Web:* www.maidpro.com

Maids International 9394 W Dodge Rd Ste 140 Omaha NE 68114 402-558-8600 558-4112
TF: 800-843-6243 ■ *Web:* www.maids.com

Merry Maids 3839 Forrest Hill-Irene Rd Memphis TN 38125 800-776-4663 597-8140*
**Fax Area Code:* 901 ■ *TF:* 866-212-5846 ■ *Web:* www.merrymaids.com

MPW Industrial Services Group Inc
9711 Lancaster Rd SE PO Box 10 Hebron OH 43025 740-927-8790 928-8140
TF: 800-827-8790 ■ *Web:* mpwservices.com

Neighbors Stores Inc 1314 Old Hwy 601 S Mount Airy NC 27030 336-789-5561 789-7067

OctoClean Franchising Systems
3357 Chicago Ave. Riverside CA 92507 951-683-5859 779-0270
Web: www.octoclean.com

Platinum Maintenance Services Corp
120 Broadway 36th Fl New York NY 10271 212-535-9700 480-2699
Web: www.platinummaintenance.com

Professional Contract Services Inc
718 W FM 1626 Austin TX 78748 512-358-8887 358-8890
Web: www.pcsi.org/

Professional Janitorial Service of Houston Inc
2303 Nance St Houston TX 77020 713-850-0287 963-9420
Web: www.pjs.com

Rainbow International 1010 N University Pk Dr Waco TX 76707 254-756-5463 745-2592
TF: 855-724-6269 ■ *Web:* www.rainbowintl.com

Serv-U-Clean 207 Edgeley Blvd Unit 5 Concord ON L4K4B5 416-667-0696 660-0550*
**Fax Area Code:* 905 ■ *Web:* www.servuclean.com

Service Management Systems
7135 Charlotte Pike Ste 100 Nashville TN 37209 615-399-1839 399-1438
Web: www.smsclean.com

ServiceMaster Clean
3839 Forrest Hill Irene Rd. Memphis TN 38125 800-245-4622 597-7600*
**Fax Area Code:* 901 ■ *TF General:* 800-255-9687 ■ *Web:* www.servicemaster.com

Servpro Industries Inc 801 Industrial Blvd. Gallatin TN 37066 615-451-0600 451-0291
TF: 800-826-9586 ■ *Web:* www.servpro.com

Sharian Inc 368 W Ponce de Leon Ave Decatur GA 30030 404-373-2274 370-1812
Web: sharian.com

St Moritz Bldg Services Inc
4616 Clairton Blvd Pittsburgh PA 15236 412-885-2100 885-3953
Web: www.bsinc.com

Steam Bros Inc 2400 Vermont Ave. Bismarck ND 58504 701-222-1263 222-1372
TF: 800-767-5064 ■ *Web:* www.steambrothers.com

Steamatic Inc 3333 Quorum Dr Ste 280 Fort Worth TX 76137 817-332-1575 796-1231
TF General: 888-783-2628 ■ *Web:* www.steamatic.com

Support Services of America Inc
12440 Firestone Blvd Ste 312 Norwalk CA 90650 562-868-3550 868-7811
TF: 888-564-0005 ■ *Web:* www.supportservicesamerica.com

Swisher Hygiene Co 4725 Piedmont Row Dr Charlotte NC 28210 704-364-7707 444-4565*
**Fax Area Code:* 800 ■ *TF:* 800-444-4138 ■ *Web:* www.swsh.com

Phone | Fax

T.u.c.s. Cleaning Service Inc 166 Central Ave..........Orange NJ 07050 973-673-0700
TF: 800-992-5998 ■ *Web:* www.tucscleaning.com

Vanguard Cleaning Systems Inc
655 Mariners Island Blvd Ste 303...................San Mateo CA 94404 650-287-2400 717-2082*
*Fax Area Code: 479 ■ *TF:* 800-564-6422 ■ *Web:* www.vanguardcleaning.com

Venoco Inc 370 17th St Ste 3900......................Denver CO 80202 303-626-8300 626-8315
NYSE: VQ ■ *TF:* 877-777-4778 ■ *Web:* www.venocoinc.com

Window Gang 405 Arendell St....................Morehead City NC 28557 252-726-1463 726-2837
TF: 877-946-4264 ■ *Web:* www.windowgang.com

153 CLOCKS, WATCHES, RELATED DEVICES, PARTS

Phone | Fax

Borg Indak Inc 701 Enterprise Dr.....................Delavan WI 53115 262-728-5531 728-3788
Web: www.borgindak.com

Bulova Corp 1 Bulova Ave.........................Woodside NY 11377 718-204-3300 204-3546
TF: 800-228-5682 ■ *Web:* www.bulova.com

Canterbury International
5632 W Washington Blvd.......................Los Angeles CA 90016 323-936-7111 936-7115
TF: 800-935-7111 ■ *Web:* www.canterburyintl.com

Citizen Watch Co of America Inc
1000 W 190th St................................. Torrance CA 90502 800-321-1023
TF: 800-321-1023 ■ *Web:* www.citizenwatch.com

E Gluck Corp 60-15 Little Neck Pkwy ....Little Neck NY 11362 718-784-0700 482-2702
TF: 800-840-2933 ■ *Web:* www.armitron.com

Hamilton Watch Company Inc
1200 Harbor Blvd.............................Weehawken NJ 07086 201-271-4680 271-4633
Web: www.hamiltonwatch.com

Howard Miller Clock Co 860 E Main Ave..............Zeeland MI 49464 616-772-7277 772-1670
Web: www.howardmiller.com

Movado Group Inc 650 From Rd Ste 375 ....Paramus NJ 07652 201-267-8000 267-8428
NYSE: MOV ■ *TF Cust Svc:* 800-810-2311 ■ *Web:* www.movadogroupinc.com

Pyramid Technologies Inc 45 Gracey Ave...............Meriden CT 06451 203-238-0550 634-1696
TF: 888-479-7264 ■ *Web:* www.pyramidtechnologies.com

Seiko Corp of America 1111 MacArthur Blvd...........Mahwah NJ 07430 201-529-5730 *
Fax: Cust Svc ■ *TF Cust Svc:* 800-545-2783 ■ *Web:* www.seikousa.com

Seiko Instruments USA Inc
21221 S Western Ave Ste 250...................... Torrance CA 90501 310-517-7700 517-7709
TF Sales: 800-688-0817 ■ *Web:* www.seikoinstruments.com

Swatch Group 1200 Harbor Blvd 7th Fl ....Weehawken NJ 07086 201-271-1400 981-8589*
*Fax Area Code: 431 ■ *TF:* 800-456-5354 ■ *Web:* www.swatchgroup.com

Timex Group USA Inc
555 Christian Rd PO Box 310....................Middlebury CT 06762 203-346-5000 573-5143
TF: 800-448-4639 ■ *Web:* www.timex.com

Verdin Co, The 444 Reading Rd.....................Cincinnati OH 45202 800-543-0488 241-1855*
*Fax Area Code: 513 ■ *TF:* 800-543-0488 ■ *Web:* www.verdin.com

Vulcan Inc 410 E Berry Ave............................Foley AL 36535 888-846-2728 943-9270*
*Fax Area Code: 251 ■ *TF:* 888-846-2728 ■ *Web:* www.vulcaninc.com

World of Watches 101 S State Rd 7 Ste 201...........Hollywood FL 33023 954-983-2181
TF: 866-961-8463 ■ *Web:* www.worldofwatches.com

154 CLOSURES - METAL OR PLASTICS

Phone | Fax

AptarGroup Inc
475 W Terra Cotta Ave Ste E.................... Crystal Lake IL 60014 815-477-0424 477-0481
NYSE: ATR ■ *Web:* www.aptar.com

Caplugs LLC 2150 Elmwood Ave.......................Buffalo NY 14207 716-876-9855 874-1680
TF Cust Svc: 888-227-5847 ■ *Web:* www.caplugs.com

Carpin Manufacturing Inc 411 Austin Rd ....Waterbury CT 06705 203-574-2556 753-8771
Web: www.carpin.com

Champion Container Corp
180 Essex Ave PO Box 90...........................Avenel NJ 07001 732-636-6700 855-8663
Web: www.championcontainer.com

Essentra PLC 3123 Stn Rd............................. Erie PA 16510 814-899-9263
TF: 800-847-0486 ■ *Web:* us.essentracomponents.com

Magenta Corp 3800 N Milwaukee Ave................Chicago IL 60641 773-777-5050 777-4055
Web: www.magentallc.com

Phoenix Closures Inc 1899 High Grove Ln...........Naperville IL 60540 630-420-4750 420-4769
Web: www.phoenixclosures.com

Polytop Corp 110 Graham Dr.....................Slatersville RI 02876 401-767-2400 765-2694

Rexam Closures & Containers
3245 Kansas Rd................................. Evansville IN 47725 812-867-6671
Web: www.rexamcatalogue.com

Silgan Holdings Inc Four Landmark Sq Ste 400 ....Stamford CT 06901 203-975-7110 975-7902
NASDAQ: SLGN ■ *Web:* www.silganholdings.com

StockCap 123 Manufacturers Dr.....................Arnold MO 63010 636-282-6800 282-6888
TF: 800-827-2277 ■ *Web:* www.stockcap.com

Stull Technologies Inc 17 Veronica Ave..............Somerset NJ 08873 732-873-5000 873-7131
Web: www.stulltech.com

Tipper Tie Inc 2000 Lufkin Rd .... Apex NC 27502 919-362-8811 362-7058
TF: 800-331-2905 ■ *Web:* www.tippertie.com

Van Blarcom Closures Inc 156 Sandford St...........Brooklyn NY 11205 718-855-3810 935-9855
Web: www.vbcpkg.com

Weatherchem Corp 2222 Highland Rd..............Twinsburg OH 44087 330-425-4206 425-1385
TF: 800-316-0072 ■ *Web:* www.weatherchem.com

155 CLOTHING & ACCESSORIES - MFR

SEE ALSO Clothing & Accessories - Whol p. 1956; Fashion Design Houses p. 2286; Footwear p. 2321; Leather Goods - Personal p. 2640; Personal Protective Equipment & Clothing p. 2914; Baby Products p. 1846

155-1 Athletic Apparel

Phone | Fax

Bristol Products Corp 700 Shelby St..................Bristol TN 37620 423-968-4140 968-2084
TF Orders: 800-336-8775 ■ *Web:* www.bristolproducts.com

Champion Athletic Wear
1000 E Hanes Mill Rd.......................Winston-Salem NC 27105 800-315-0563
TF: 800-315-0563 ■ *Web:* www.championusa.com

Choi Bros Inc 3401 W Div St ....Chicago IL 60651 773-489-2800 489-3030
TF: 800-524-2464 ■ *Web:* www.choibrothers.com

Columbia Sportswear Co
14375 NW Science Pk Dr..........................Portland OR 97229 503-985-4000 985-5800
NASDAQ: COLM ■ *TF:* 800-622-6953 ■ *Web:* www.columbia.com

Cutter & Buck Inc 701 N 34th St Ste 400..............Seattle WA 98103 888-338-9944 448-0589*
*Fax Area Code: 206 ■ *TF:* 800-713-7810 ■ *Web:* www.cutterbuck.com

Dodger Industries
2075 Stultz Rd PO Box 711 ....Martinsville VA 24112 800-247-7879 638-7161*
*Fax Area Code: 276 ■ *TF Cust Svc:* 800-247-7879 ■ *Web:* www.dodgerindustries.com

Elite Sportswear LP 2136 N 13th St.................Reading PA 19604 610-921-1469 921-0208
TF Cust Svc: 800-345-4087 ■ *Web:* www.gkelite.com

Gear for Sports Inc 9700 Commerce Pkwy.............Lenexa KS 66219 913-693-3200 689-1692
TF: 800-255-1065 ■ *Web:* www.gearforsports.com

MJ Soffe Co 1 Soffe Dr .... Fayetteville NC 28312 888-257-8673 486-9030*
*Fax Area Code: 910 ■ *TF:* 888-257-8673 ■ *Web:* www.soffe.com

No Fear Plaza Camino Real
2525 El Camino Real Ste 2525..................... Carlsbad CA 92008 760-720-0189
Web: www.nofear.com

Powers Manufacturing Co
1340 Sycamore St PO Box 2157.................... Waterloo IA 50704 319-233-6118 234-8048
Web: www.powersathletic.com

Race Face Components Inc
100 Braid St Unit 100.....................New Westminster BC V3L3P4 604-527-9996 527-9959
TF: 800-527-9244 ■ *Web:* www.raceface.com

Royal Textile Mills Inc 929 Firetower Rd.......... Yanceyville NC 27379 800-334-9361 934-9360
TF: 800-334-9361 ■ *Web:* www.dukeathletic-tactical.com

Russell Corp 755 Lee St......................Alexander City AL 35010 256-500-4000

Scotty's Fashions Inc 636 Pen Argyl St..............Pen Argyl PA 18072 610-863-6454
Web: www.scottysfashions.com

Southland Athletic Manufacturing Co
PO Box 280 .... Terrell TX 75160 972-563-3321 563-0943
Web: www.southland-athletic.com

Volcom Inc 1740 Monrovia Ave ....Costa Mesa CA 92627 949-646-2175 646-5247
Web: www.volcom.com

155-2 Belts (Leather, Plastics, Fabric)

Phone | Fax

Circa Corp 1330 Fitzgerald Ave.................San Francisco CA 94124 415-822-1600
Web: circacorp.com

Gem Dandy Inc 200 W Academy St................... Madison NC 27025 336-548-9624 427-7105
TF: 800-334-5101 ■ *Web:* www.gem-dandy.com

Max Leather Group Inc 1415 Redfern Ave .... Far Rockaway NY 11691 718-471-3300 471-3707

Tandy Brands Accessories Inc
3631 W Davis St Ste A............................. Dallas TX 75211 214-519-5200
NASDAQ: TBAC

155-3 Casual Wear (Men's & Women's)

Phone | Fax

Alps Sportswear Manufacturing Co
15 Union St ....Lawrence MA 01840 978-683-2438 686-8051

Attraction Inc 672 Rue du Parc.......................Lac-Drolet QC G0Y1C0 819-549-2477 549-2734
TF: 800-567-6095 ■ *Web:* www.attraction.com

Badger Sportswear Inc 111 Badger Ln .... Statesville NC 28625 704-871-0990
TF: 888-871-0990 ■ *Web:* www.badgersport.com

Big Dogs 519 Lincoln County Pkwy.................Lincolnton NC 28092 800-244-3647
TF: 800-244-3647 ■ *Web:* www.bigdogs.com

Bobby Jones Retail Corp
2093 Old Route 15 PO Box 214 ....New Columbia PA 17856 855-785-1930
TF Cust Svc: 855-437-5537 ■ *Web:* www.bobbyjones.com

California Manufacturing Co
2270 Weldon Pkwy............................. Saint Louis MO 63146 314-567-4404 567-5062
Web: www.cmcbrands.com

Cherokee Inc 5990 Sepulveda Blvd Ste 600 ....Sherman Oaks CA 91411 818-908-9868
NASDAQ: CHKE ■ *Web:* www.thecherokeegroup.com

Columbia Sportswear Co
14375 NW Science Pk Dr..........................Portland OR 97229 503-985-4000 985-5800
NASDAQ: COLM ■ *TF:* 800-622-6953 ■ *Web:* www.columbia.com

Crazy Shirts Inc 99-969 Iwaena St.......................Aiea HI 96701 808-487-9919 486-1276
TF: 800-771-2720 ■ *Web:* www.crazyshirts.com

Deckers Outdoor Corp 495-A S Fairview Ave........... Goleta CA 93117 805-967-7611 967-9722
NYSE: DECK ■ *TF:* 877-337-8333 ■ *Web:* www.deckers.com

Delta Apparel Inc 2750 Premier Pkwy Ste 100 .... Duluth GA 30097 678-775-6900 775-6992
NYSE: DLA ■ *TF:* 800-285-4456 ■ *Web:* www.deltaapparel.com

Fruit of the Loom Inc
One Fruit of the Loom Dr PO Box 90015 ....Bowling Green KY 42102 270-781-6400 781-1754
TF: 888-378-4829 ■ *Web:* www.fruitactivewear.com

Fun-Tees 4735 Corporate Dr Ste 100 .... Concord NC 28027 704-788-3003 795-9300
Web: www.funtees.com

Hamrick Inc 742 Peachoid Rd .... Gaffney SC 29341 864-489-6095 489-9514
TF: 800-487-5411 ■ *Web:* www.hamricks.com

L & L Manufacturing Co 815 N Nash St........... El Segundo CA 90245 310-615-0000 615-4549

Ms. Bubbles Inc 2731 S Alameda St ....Los Angeles CA 90058 323-544-0300 239-9709*
*Fax Area Code: 213 ■ *Web:* www.msbubbles.com

Quiksilver Inc 15202 Graham St .... Huntington Beach CA 92649 714-893-5187
NYSE: ZQK ■ *Web:* quiksilver.in/#?intcmp=qs_us_redirection:qs_in

Rothschild & Company Inc 500 Seventh Ave ....New York NY 10018 212-354-8550 382-1187

	City	State	Zip	Phone	Fax
Sherry Mfg 3287 NW 65th St *TF:* 800-741-4750 ■ *Web:* www.sherrymfg.com	Miami	FL	33147	305-693-7000	691-6132
Sport-Haley Inc 200 Union Blvd Ste 400 *TF:* 800-627-9211 ■ *Web:* www.sporthaley.com	Denver	CO	80228	303-320-8800	320-8822
Stussy Inc 17426 Daimler St *Web:* www.stussy.com	Irvine	CA	92614	949-474-9255	474-8229
Surf Line Hawaii Ltd 1451 Kalani St *Web:* www.jamsworld.com	Honolulu	HI	96817	808-847-5985	841-5254
Tonix Corp 40910 Encyclopedia Cir *TF:* 800-227-2072 ■ *Web:* www.tonixteams.com	Fremont	CA	94538	510-651-8050	651-8052
VF Corp 105 Corporate Ctr Blvd *NYSE:* VFC ■ *Web:* www.vfc.com	Greensboro	NC	27408	336-424-6000	424-7634
Whisper Knits Inc 175 E New Hampshire *Web:* www.whisperknits.com	Southern Pines	NC	28387	910-246-0450	246-0550
Wolf Manufacturing Co 1801 W Waco Dr PO Box 3100 **Fax Area Code:* 257 ■ *TF:* 800-437-0940 ■ *Web:* www.wolfmfg.com	Waco	TX	76707	254-753-7301	753-8919*

155-4 Children's & Infants' Clothing

	City	State	Zip	Phone	Fax
Byer California 66 Potrero Ave **Fax Area Code:* 925 ■ *TF:* 844-628-4498 ■ *Web:* byerca.com/	San Francisco	CA	94103	415-626-7844	245-0183*
Candlesticks Inc 112 W 34th St Ste 901	New York	NY	10120	212-947-8900	643-9653
Devil Dog Mfg Company Inc 400 E Gannon Ave	Zebulon	NC	27597	919-269-7485	269-5962
Donegal Industries Inc 860 Anderson Ferry Rd	Mount Joy	PA	17552	717-653-4818	
Florence Eiseman company LLC 1966 S Fourth St *TF:* 800-558-9013 ■ *Web:* www.florenceeiseman.com	Milwaukee	WI	53204	800-558-9013	
Gerber Childrenswear Inc 7005 Pelham Rd Ste D *TF:* 800-642-4452 ■ *Web:* www.gerberchildrenswear.com	Greenville	SC	29602	864-987-5200	987-5264
Good Lad Apparel 431 E Tioga St *Web:* goodlad.com	Philadelphia	PA	19134	215-739-0200	
Happy Kids Inc 100 W 33rd St *Web:* happykidspersonalized.com	New York	NY	10001	212-239-4563	736-0397
IFG Corp 1372 Broadway	New York	NY	10018	212-239-8615	
Irwin Manufacturing Corp 398 Fitzgerald Hwy	Ocilla	GA	31774	229-468-9481	468-9484
Kahn Lucas Lancaster Inc 112 W 34th St Ste 600 *Web:* www.kahnlucas.com	New York	NY	10120	212-244-4500	643-1345
LT Apparel Group 100 W 33rd St Ste 1012 *Web:* www.lollytogs.com	New York	NY	10001	212-502-6000	268-5160
Mayfair Infants Group 100 W 33rd St Ste 813 *Web:* tawil.com	New York	NY	10001	212-279-3211	
New ICM LP PO Box 1060 *TF:* 800-987-9008 ■ *Web:* www.newicm.com	El Campo	TX	77437	979-578-0543	578-0503
Rare Editions for Girls 1250 Broadway *Web:* www.rareeditions.com	New York	NY	10001	212-244-1390	967-4915
Royal Park Uniforms Co 14139 Hwy 86 S	Prospect Hill	NC	27314	336-562-3345	562-3832
S Schwab Co Inc 12101 Upper Potomac Industrial Pk St *TF:* 800-638-2937 ■ *Web:* times-news.com	Cumberland	MD	21502	301-729-4488	722-4870

155-5 Coats (Overcoats, Jackets, Raincoats, etc)

	City	State	Zip	Phone	Fax
Alpha Industries Inc 14200 Pk Meadow Dr Ste 110S *TF General:* 866-631-0719 ■ *Web:* www.alphaindustries.com	Chantilly	VA	20151	703-378-1420	378-4910
Essex Mfg Inc 350 Fifth Ave Ste 501 *TF:* 800-648-6010 ■ *Web:* www.baum-essex.com	New York	NY	10118	212-239-0080	714-2958
G-III Apparel Group Ltd 512 Seventh Ave *NASDAQ:* GIII ■ *Web:* www.g-iii.com	New York	NY	10018	212-403-0500	403-0551
Helly Hansen US Inc 4104 C St NE Ste 200 *TF:* 800-435-5901 ■ *Web:* www.hellyhansen.com	Auburn	WA	98002	800-435-5901	
Holloway Sportswear Inc 2633 Campbell Rd **Fax Area Code:* 937 ■ **Fax:* Cust Svc ■ *TF:* 800-331-5156 ■ *Web:* www.hollowayusa.com	Sidney	OH	45365	800-331-5156	497-7337*
Item House Inc 2920 S Steele St *Web:* itemhouseinc.com	Tacoma	WA	98409	253-627-7168	627-1070
London Fog 1615 Kellogg Dr *TF:* 877-588-8189 ■ *Web:* www.londonfog.com	Douglas	GA	31535	912-384-8189	
MECA Sportswear 1120 Townline Rd *TF:* 800-729-6322 ■ *Web:* www.mecasportswear.com	Tomah	WI	54660	608-374-6450	374-6405
Pendleton Woolen Mills Inc 220 NW Broadway *TF:* 800-760-4844 ■ *Web:* www.pendleton-usa.com	Portland	OR	97209	503-226-4801	535-5502
RefrigiWear Inc 54 Breakstone Dr *TF Cust Svc:* 800-645-3744 ■ *Web:* www.refrigiwear.com	Dahlonega	GA	30533	706-864-5757	864-5898
Rennoc Corp 645 Pine St *TF:* 800-372-7100 ■ *Web:* www.rennoc.com	Greenville	OH	45331	800-372-7100	675-1727
Sport Obermeyer Ltd USA Inc 115 AABC *TF:* 800-525-4203 ■ *Web:* www.obermeyer.com	Aspen	CO	81611	970-925-5060	925-9203
Sport-Haley Inc 200 Union Blvd Ste 400 *TF:* 800-627-9211 ■ *Web:* www.sporthaley.com	Denver	CO	80228	303-320-8800	320-8822
Standard Mfg Company Inc 750 Second Ave *TF Cust Svc:* 800-227-1056 ■ *Web:* www.sportsmaster.com	Troy	NY	12182	518-235-2200	235-2668
Woolrich Inc 2 Mill St *TF:* 800-995-1299 ■ *Web:* www.woolrich.com	Woolrich	PA	17779	570-769-6464	769-6234

155-6 Costumes

	City	State	Zip	Phone	Fax
Cleveland Costume & Display 18489 Pearl Rd *Web:* clevelandcostume.com	Strongsville	OH	44136	440-846-9292	846-9294
Costume Gallery 4451 Rt 130 *TF:* 800-222-8125 ■ *Web:* www.costumegallery.net	Burlington	NJ	08016	609-386-6501	386-0677
Costume Specialists Inc 211 N Fifth St *TF:* 800-596-9357 ■ *Web:* www.costumespecialists.com	Columbus	OH	43215	614-464-2115	464-2114
Curtain Call Costumes 333 E Seventh Ave **Fax Area Code:* 800 ■ *TF:* 888-808-0801 ■ *Web:* www.curtaincallcostumes.com	York	PA	17404	717-852-6910	839-1039*
Disguise 12120 Kear Pl *TF:* 877-875-2557 ■ *Web:* www.disguise.com	Poway	CA	92064	858-391-3600	391-3601
Morris Costumes Inc 4300 Monroe Rd *Web:* morriscostumes.com	Charlotte	NC	28205	704-333-4653	348-3032
Sew Biz Industries 174 Cross St	Central Falls	RI	02863	401-724-8410	726-9845
Stagecraft Costuming Inc 3950 Spring Grove Ave *Web:* www.stagecraft.on-rev.com/stagecraft,_inc./contact_information.html	Cincinnati	OH	45223	513-541-7150	541-7159

155-7 Fur Goods

	City	State	Zip	Phone	Fax
American Legend Co-op PO Box 58308 *TF:* 800-266-3314 ■ *Web:* www.americanlegend.com	Seattle	WA	98138	425-251-3200	251-3222
Blum & Fink Inc 333 Seventh Ave	New York	NY	10001	212-695-2606	
Corniche Furs Inc 345 Seventh Ave 20th Fl *Web:* www.corniche furs.com	New York	NY	10001	212-239-8655	239-1811
Goodman Couture 130 W 30th St	New York	NY	10001	212-244-7422	
Jerry Sorbara Furs Inc 39 W 32nd St Ste 1400 *Web:* sorbarafur.com	New York	NY	10001	212-594-3897	643-9098
Kaitery Furs Ltd 25-29 49th St *Web:* kaiterydenafurs.com	Long Island City	NY	11103	718-204-0696	204-0721
LA Rockler Fur Co 16 N Fourth St *Web:* rocklerfur.com	Minneapolis	MN	55401	612-332-8643	332-2926
Mohl Fur Company Inc 345 Seventh Ave Third Fl	New York	NY	10001	212-736-7676	629-4832
Sekas International Ltd 345 Seventh Ave 19th Fl *Web:* www.sekasinternational.com	New York	NY	10001	212-629-6095	629-6097
Steve's Original Furs Inc 150 W 30th St Eighth Fl *Web:* stevesoriginalfurs.com	New York	NY	10001	212-967-8007	967-3871

155-8 Gloves & Mittens

	City	State	Zip	Phone	Fax
Carolina Glove Co 116 Mclin Creek Rd PO Box 999 *TF:* 800-335-1918 ■ *Web:* www.carolinaglove.com	Conover	NC	28613	828-464-1132	485-2416
Fownes Bros & Company Inc 16 E 34th St *TF All:* 800-345-6837 ■ *Web:* urpowered.com	New York	NY	10016	212-683-0150	683-2832
Gloves Inc 1950 Collins Boulevard *TF:* 800-476-4568 ■ *Web:* www.glovesinc.com/contacts	Austell	MA	30106	770-944-9186	944-0012
Guard-Line Inc 215 S Louise St PO Box 1030 **Fax:* Orders ■ *TF:* 800-527-8822 ■ *Web:* www.guardline.com	Atlanta	TX	75551	903-796-4111	796-7262*
Illinois Glove Co 3701 Commercial Ave *TF:* 800-342-5458 ■ *Web:* www.illinoisglove.com	Northbrook	IL	60062	847-291-1700	291-7722
Kinco International 4286 NE 185th Dr *TF General:* 800-547-8410 ■ *Web:* www.kinco.com	Portland	OR	97230	800-547-8410	536-4905
Magid Glove & Safety Manufacturing Co 2060 N Kolmar Ave *TF:* 800-444-8010 ■ *Web:* www.magidglove.com	Chicago	IL	60639	773-384-2070	384-6677
MCR Safety 5321 E Shelby Dr **Fax Area Code:* 800 ■ **Fax:* Sales ■ *TF:* 800-955-6887 ■ *Web:* www.mcrsafety.com	Memphis	TN	38118	901-795-5810	999-3908*
Midwest Quality Gloves Inc 835 Industrial Rd *TF:* 800-821-3028 ■ *Web:* www.midwestglove.com	Chillicothe	MO	64601	660-646-2165	646-6933
Montpelier Glove Co Inc 129 N Main St *TF:* 800-645-3931 ■ *Web:* www.montpeliergsp.com	Montpelier	IN	47359	765-728-2481	
Nationwide Glove Co 925 Bauman Ln	Harrisburg	IL	62946	618-252-6303	
North Star Glove Co 2916 S Steele St *TF:* 800-423-1616 ■ *Web:* www.northstarglove.com	Tacoma	WA	98409	253-627-7107	627-0597
Saranac Glove Co 999 LOmbardi Ave *TF:* 800-727-2622 ■ *Web:* www.saranacglove.com	Green Bay	WI	54304	920-435-3737	435-7618
Slate Springs Glove Co 148 Vance St	Calhoun City	MS	38916	662-637-2222	637-2515
Southern Glove Mfg Company Inc 749 AC Little Dr *TF Cust Svc:* 800-222-1113 ■ *Web:* www.southernglove.com	Newton	NC	28658	828-464-4884	464-7968
Swany America Corp 115 Corp Dr *TF:* 800-237-9269 ■ *Web:* www.swanyamerica.com	Johnstown	NY	12095	518-725-3333	725-2026
Totes Isotoner Corp 9655 International Blvd *TF:* 800-762-8712 ■ *Web:* www.totes-isotoner.com	Cincinnati	OH	45246	513-682-8200	682-8606
Wells Lamont Corp 6640 W Touhy Ave *TF:* 800-323-2830 ■ *Web:* www.wellslamont.com	Niles	IL	60714	847-647-8200	647-6943
Wells Lamont Industry Group 6640 W Touhy Ave *TF:* 800-247-3295 ■ *Web:* wellslamontindustrial.com	Niles	IL	60714	800-247-3295	

155-9 Hats & Caps

	City	State	Zip	Phone	Fax
180s Inc 700 S Caroline St *TF:* 877-725-4386 ■ *Web:* www.180s.com	Baltimore	MD	21231	410-534-6320	534-6321
Ahead LLC 270 Samuel Barnet Blvd **Fax:* Cust Svc ■ *TF:* 800-282-2246 ■ *Web:* www.aheadweb.com	New Bedford	MA	02745	508-985-9898	985-2371*
American Needle Inc 1275 Busch Pkwy *Web:* www.shop.americanneedle.com	Buffalo Grove	IL	60089	847-215-0011	
Arlington Hat Co Inc 4725 34th St	Long Island City	NY	11101	718-361-3000	361-8713
Bollman Hat Co 110 E Main St PO Box 517 *TF:* 800-959-4287 ■ *Web:* www.bollmanhats.com	Adamstown	PA	19501	717-484-4361	484-2139
F & M Hat Co Inc 103 Walnut St PO Box 40 *TF:* 800-953-4287 ■ *Web:* www.fmhat.com	Denver	PA	17517	717-336-5505	336-0501
Greg Norman Collection 134 W 37th St Ste 4 *Web:* gregnormancollection.com	New York	NY	10018	646-840-5200	

	City	State	Zip	Phone	Fax
Julie Hat Co 5948 Industrial Blvd	Patterson	GA	31557	912-647-2031	
Korber Hats Inc 394 Kilburn St *TF Cust Svc:* 800-428-9911 ■ *Web:* korberhats.com	Fall River	MA	02724	508-672-7033	673-0762
Kraft Hat Manufacturers Inc Seven Veterans Pkwy *Web:* www.krafthat.com	Pearl River	NY	10965	845-735-6200	735-2299
MPC Promotions 4300 Produce Rd PO Box 34336 **Fax Area Code:* 888 ■ *TF:* 800-331-0989 ■ *Web:* www.mpcpromotions.com	Louisville	KY	40232	502-451-4900	451-8475*
New Era Cap Company Inc 160 Delaware Ave *TF General:* 877-632-5950 ■ *Web:* www.neweracap.com	Buffalo	NY	14202	716-604-9000	
Paramount Apparel International Inc One Paramount Dr *TF:* 800-255-4287 ■ *Web:* www.paramountapparel.com	Bourbon	MO	65441	573-732-4411	
Stratton Hats Inc 3200 Randolph St *TF:* 877-453-3777 ■ *Web:* www.strattonhats.com	Bellwood	IL	60104	708-544-5220	544-5243
Town Talk Inc 6310 Cane Run Rd PO Box 58157 *TF:* 800-626-2220 ■ *Web:* www.ttcaps.com	Louisville	KY	40258	502-933-7575	

155-10 Hosiery & Socks

	City	State	Zip	Phone	Fax
Acme-McCrary Corp 159 N St *Web:* www.acme-mccrary.com	Asheboro	NC	27203	336-625-2161	629-2263
Americal Corp 389 Americal Rd	Henderson	NC	27537	252-762-2000	762-0176
Berkshire General Store, The 25 Edison Dr *Web:* www.berkshiregeneralstore.com	Wayne	NJ	07470	973-696-6204	
Bossong Hosiery Mills Inc 840 W Salisbury St	Asheboro	NC	27203	336-625-2175	626-6607
Carolina Hosiery Mills Inc 710 Plantation Dr	Burlington	NC	27215	336-226-5581	
Commonwealth Hosiery Mills Inc 4964 Island Ford Rd *Web:* commonwealthhosiery.com/	Randleman	NC	27317	336-498-2621	498-5560
Cooper Hosiery Mills Inc 4005 Gault Ave N	Fort Payne	AL	35967	256-845-1491	845-3554
Crescent Inc PO Box 669 *Web:* www.crescenthosiery.com	Niota	TN	37826	423-568-2101	568-2104
Fox River Mills Inc 227 Poplar Stq PO Box 298 *TF:* 800-247-1815 ■ *Web:* www.foxsox.com	Osage	IA	50461	641-732-3798	732-5128
Harriss & Covington Hosiery Mills Inc 1250 Hickory Chapel Rd *Web:* www.harrissandcov.com	High Point	NC	27260	336-882-6811	889-2412
Highland Mills Inc 340 E 16th St *Web:* www.highlandmills.com	Charlotte	NC	28206	704-375-3333	342-0391
Holt Hosiery Mills Inc 733 Koury Dr *Web:* holthosiery.com	Burlington	NC	27215	336-227-1431	227-8614
Jefferies Socks 2203 Tucker St **Fax Area Code:* 800 ■ *TF:* 800-334-6831 ■ *Web:* www.jefferiessocks.com	Burlington	NC	27215	336-226-7315	727-5502*
Jockey International Inc 2300 60th St PO Box 1417 **Fax Area Code:* 262 ■ *TF:* 800-562-5391 ■ *Web:* www.jockey.com	Kenosha	WI	53140	800-562-5391	658-1812*
Keepers International Inc 9420 Eton Ave *TF:* 800-797-6257 ■ *Web:* www.keepers.com	Chatsworth	CA	91311	800-797-6257	
Lea-wayne Knitting Mills Inc 5937 Commerce Blvd	Morristown	TN	37814	423-586-7513	586-6437
Lemco Mills Inc 766 Koury Dr	Burlington	NC	27215	336-226-5548	
Mayo Knitting Mills Inc 2204 Austin St PO Box 160 *Web:* mayoknitting.com	Tarboro	NC	27886	252-823-3101	823-0368
Moretz Inc 514 W 21st St *TF:* 866-714-8486 ■ *Web:* www.goldtoe.com	Newton	NC	28658	828-464-0751	
Renfro Corp 661 Linville Rd *TF:* 800-334-9091 ■ *Web:* www.renfro.com	Mount Airy	NC	27030	336-719-8000	719-8215
Slane Hosiery Mills Inc 313 S Centennial St *Web:* www.slanehosiery.com	High Point	NC	27261	336-883-4136	886-4543
Tefron USA Inc 201 St Germain Ave SW *Web:* www.tefron.com	Valdese	NC	28690	828-879-6500	
Thor-Lo Inc 2210 Newton Dr *TF:* 888-846-7567 ■ *Web:* www.thorlo.com	Statesville	NC	28677	704-872-6522	838-7010
Trimfit Inc 1900 Frost Rd Ste 111 *TF:* 800-347-7697 ■ *Web:* trimfit.myshopify.com/	Bristol	PA	19007	215-781-0600	781-1803
Twin City Knitting Company Inc (TCK) 104 Rock Barn Rd NE *TF:* 800-438-6884 ■ *Web:* www.tcksports.com	Conover	NC	28613	828-464-4830	
Wigwam Mills Inc 3402 Crocker Ave *TF:* 800-558-7760 ■ *Web:* www.wigwam.com	Sheboygan	WI	53082	920-457-5551	457-0311

155-11 Jeans

	City	State	Zip	Phone	Fax
Aalfs Mfg Co 1005 Fourth St *TF:* 888-412-2537 ■ *Web:* aalfs.com	Sioux City	IA	51101	712-252-1877	252-5205
Ditto Apparel of California Inc 229 Webb Smith Dr	Colfax	LA	71417	318-627-3264	
Elk Brand Manufacturing Co 1601 County Hospital Rd PO Box 281287 *Web:* www.elkbrand.com	Nashville	TN	37228	615-254-4300	
Flynn Enterprises Inc 2203 Walnut St	Hopkinsville	KY	42240	270-886-0223	
Jordache Enterprises 1400 Broadway *TF:* 888-295-3267 ■ *Web:* www.jordache.com	New York	NY	10018	212-944-1330	768-5736
Lee Jeans 9001 W 67th St *TF Cust Svc:* 800-453-3348 ■ *Web:* www.lee.com	Merriam	KS	66202	913-384-4000	384-0190
Levi Strauss & Co 1155 Battery St *TF:* 866-290-6064 ■ *Web:* www.levistrauss.com	San Francisco	CA	94111	415-501-6000	501-7112
Miller International Inc Rocky Mountain Clothing Company Div 8500 Zuni St *Web:* www.rockymountainclothing.com	Denver	CO	80260	303-428-5696	

	City	State	Zip	Phone	Fax
Reed Mfg Co Inc 1321 S Veterans Blvd **Fax Area Code:* 800 ■ *TF:* 800-466-1154 ■ *Web:* www.reedmanufacturing.com	Tupelo	MS	38804	662-842-4472	237-5898*
VF Corporation PO Box 21488 **Fax Area Code:* 800 ■ *Web:* www.vfc.com	Greensboro	NC	27420	336-424-6000	283-3113*

155-12 Men's Clothing

	City	State	Zip	Phone	Fax
After Six 118 W 20th St *TF:* 800-444-8304 ■ *Web:* www.aftersix.com	New York	NY	10011	646-638-9600	
American Apparel LLC 747 Warehouse St *TF:* 888-747-0070 ■ *Web:* www.americanapparel.net	Los Angeles	CA	90021	213-488-0226	488-0334
Anniston Sportswear Corp P.O. Box 189 *TF:* 866-814-9253 ■ *Web:* www.annistonstar.com	Anniston	AL	36201	256-236-1551	831-9414
Antigua Sportswear Inc 16651 N 84 Ave *TF:* 800-528-3133 ■ *Web:* www.antigua.com	Peoria	AZ	85382	623-523-6000	523-6001
Barry Better Menswear 125 John W Morrow Pkwy Ste 242B *Web:* barrysmenswear.com	Gainesville	GA	30501	770-534-7685	
Capital Mercury Apparel 1359 Broadway 19th Fl	New York	NY	10018	212-704-4800	
David Peyser Sportswear Inc 90 Spence St	Bay Shore	NY	11706	631-231-7788	435-8018
English American Tailoring Co 411 N Cranberry Rd *Web:* www.englishamericanco.com	Westminster	MD	21157	410-857-5774	386-0417
Fishman & Tobin Inc 4000 Chemical Rd Ste 500 Metroplex Corp Ctr-1 *Web:* www.fishmantobin.com	Plymouth Meeting	PA	19462	610-828-8400	
Franklin Clothing Company Inc 208 Lurgan Ave	Shippensburg	PA	17257	717-532-4146	
Gitman & Co 2309 Chestnut St *TF:* 800-526-3929 ■ *Web:* www.gitman.com/	Ashland	PA	17921	570-875-3100	875-1066
Gitman Bros Shirt Company Inc 641 Lexington Ave 19th Fl *TF General:* 800-526-3929 ■ *Web:* www.gitman.com	New York	NY	10019	212-581-6968	581-6960
Granite Knitwear Inc 805 S Salberry Ave Hwy 52S *TF Cust Svc:* 800-476-9944 ■ *Web:* www.calcru.com	Granite Quarry	NC	28072	704-279-5526	279-8205
Greg Norman Collection 134 W 37th St Ste 4 *Web:* gregnormancollection.com	New York	NY	10018	646-840-5200	
H Freeman & Son Inc 411 N Cranberry Rd *TF:* 800-876-7700 ■ *Web:* www.hfreemanco.com	Westminster	MD	21157	410-857-5774	857-1560
Haggar Clothing Co 11511 Luna Rd 2 Colinas Crossing *TF:* 877-841-2219 ■ *Web:* www.haggar.com	Dallas	TX	75234	214-352-8481	956-4367
Hardwick Clothes Inc 3800 Old Tasso Rd *TF:* 800-251-6392 ■ *Web:* hardwick.com/	Cleveland	TN	37312	800-251-6392	442-7394
Hart Schaffner Marx (HSM) 1680 E Touhy Ave *TF:* 800-327-4466 ■ *Web:* www.hartschaffnermarx.com	Des Plaines	IL	60018	800-327-4466	
Hickey Freeman 1155 N Clinton Ave *TF Cust Svc:* 844-755-7344 ■ *Web:* www.hickeyfreeman.com	Rochester	NY	14621	585-467-7021	
Hugo Boss Fashions Inc 601 W 26th St Ste 845 *Web:* www.fragrances.hugoboss.com	New York	NY	10001	212-940-0600	940-0616
Indiana Knitwear Corp 230 E Osage St	Greenfield	IN	46140	317-462-4413	462-0994
Individualized Shirts Co 581 Cortland St *Web:* individualizedshirts.com	Perth Amboy	NJ	08861	732-826-8400	
Jos A Bank Clothiers 500 Hanover Pk *TF Cust Svc:* 800-999-7472 ■ *Web:* www.josbank.com	Hampstead	MD	21074	410-239-2700	239-5700
Nautica Retail USA Inc 40 W 57th St 3rd Fl *Web:* www.nautica.com	New York	NY	10019	212-541-5757	
Oxford Industries Inc 999 Peachtree St NE Ste 688 *NYSE: OXM* ■ *Web:* www.oxfordinc.com	Atlanta	GA	30309	404-659-2424	653-1545
Oxxford Clothes Inc 1220 W Van Buren St *Web:* www.oxxfordclothes.com	Chicago	IL	60607	312-829-3600	829-6075
Phillips-Van Heusen Corp 200 Madison Ave *NYSE: PVH* ■ *TF:* 866-214-6694 ■ *Web:* www.pvh.com	New York	NY	10016	212-381-3500	
Scotty's Fashions Inc 636 Pen Argyl St *Web:* www.scottysfashions.com	Pen Argyl	PA	18072	610-863-6454	
Smart Apparel US Inc 1400 Broadway 10th Fl *Web:* smartapparelus.com	New York	NY	10018	212-329-3400	329-3486
Southwick Clothing LLC 20 Computer Dr *Web:* www.southwick.com	Haverhill	MA	01832	978-686-3833	
Tom James Co 263 Seaboard Ln *TF:* 800-236-9023 ■ *Web:* www.tomjames.com	Franklin	TN	37067	615-771-0795	
Weatherproof Garment Co 1071 Ave of the Americas *TF:* 800-645-7788 ■ *Web:* weatherproofgarment.com	New York	NY	10018	212-695-7716	

155-13 Neckwear

	City	State	Zip	Phone	Fax
Burma Bibas Inc 597 Fifth Ave 10th Fl *Web:* www.burmabibas.com	New York	NY	10017	212-750-2500	
Carolina Mfg 7025 Augusta Rd *TF:* 800-845-2744 ■ *Web:* thebandannacompany.com	Greenville	SC	29605	864-299-0600	299-0603
Carter & Holmes N1510 Geneva Ave *TF:* 800-621-4646 ■ *Web:* www.carterholmes.com	Lake Geneva	WI	53147	262-215-5494	248-1425
Echo Design Group 10 E 40th St 16th Fl *TF General:* 800-331-3246 ■ *Web:* www.echodesign.com	New York	NY	10016	212-686-8771	686-5017
Mallory & Church LLC 676 S Industrial Way	Seattle	WA	98108	206-587-2100	587-2971
MMG Corp 1717 Olive St	Saint Louis	MO	63103	314-421-2182	421-4912
PVH Neckwear Inc 1735 S Santa Fe Ave *Web:* www.pvh.com	Los Angeles	CA	90021	213-688-7970	623-3226
Ralph Marlin & Co 1701 Pearl St Ste 4	Waukesha	WI	53186	262-549-5100	549-5122
Robert Talbott Inc 2901 Monterey-Salinas Hwy *Web:* www.roberttalbott.com	Camel Valley	CA	93940	831-649-6000	

155-14 Robes (Ceremonial)

Company	City	State	Zip	Phone	Fax
Academic Apparel 20644 Superior St *TF:* 800-626-5000 ■ *Web:* www.academicapparel.com	Chatsworth	CA	91311	818-886-8697	886-8743
CM Almy Inc One Ruth Rd *TF:* 800-225-2569 ■ *Web:* www.almy.com	Pittsfield	ME	04967	207-487-3232	487-3240
Gaspard Inc 200 N Janacek Rd *TF:* 800-784-6868 ■ *Web:* www.gaspardinc.com	Brookfield	WI	53045	262-784-6800	784-7567
Jostens Inc 3601 Minnesota Ave Ste 400 **Fax:* Hum Res ■ *TF:* 800-235-4774 ■ *Web:* www.jostens.com	Minneapolis	MN	55435	952-830-3300	830-3293*
Oak Hall Industries 840 Union St *TF:* 800-223-0429 ■ *Web:* www.oakhalli.com	Salem	VA	24153	540-387-0000	387-2034
Thomas Creative Apparel Inc One Harmony Pl *TF:* 800-537-2575 ■ *Web:* www.thomasrobes.com	New London	OH	44851	419-929-1506	929-0122
Willsie Cap & Gown Co 1220 S 13th St *TF:* 800-234-4696 ■ *Web:* www.willsieco.com	Omaha	NE	68108	402-341-6536	

155-15 Sleepwear

Company	City	State	Zip	Phone	Fax
Isaco International Corp 5980 Miami Lakes Dr *Web:* www.isaco.com	Miami	FL	33014	305-594-4455	594-4496
Milco Industries Inc 550 E Fifth St *Web:* millcolnd.com	Bloomsburg	PA	17815	570-784-0400	387-8433
Miss Elaine Inc 8430 Valcour Ave *TF:* 800-458-1422 ■ *Web:* www.misselaine.com	Saint Louis	MO	63123	314-631-1900	
Roytex Inc 16 E 34th St 17th Fl *Web:* www.roytex.com	New York	NY	10016	212-686-3500	686-4336
Wormser Corp 150 Coolidge Ave *TF:* 800-546-4040 ■ *Web:* www.wormsercorp.com	Englewood	NJ	07631	800-546-4040	

155-16 Sweaters (Knit)

Company	City	State	Zip	Phone	Fax
Binghamton Knitting Co Inc 11 Alice St *TF:* 877-746-3368 ■ *Web:* www.brimwick.com	Binghamton	NY	13904	607-722-6941	722-4621
Mamiye Bros Inc Group 112 W 34th St Ste 1000 *Web:* mamiye.com	New York	NY	10120	212-279-4150	695-2659

155-17 Swimwear

Company	City	State	Zip	Phone	Fax
A & H Sportswear Company Inc 500 William St	Pen Argyl	PA	18072	610-863-4176	
AH Schreiber Co 460 W 34th St Ste 1002	New York	NY	10001	212-564-2700	
Blue Sky Swimwear 729 E International Speedway Blvd *TF Orders:* 800-799-6445 ■ *Web:* www.blueskyswimwear.com	Daytona Beach	FL	32118	386-255-2590	253-5938
Quiksilver Inc 15202 Graham St *NYSE: ZQK* ■ *Web:* quiksilver.in/#?intcmp=qs_us_redirection:qs_in	Huntington Beach	CA	92649	714-893-5187	
TYR Sport 1790 Apollo Ct *TF:* 800-252-7878 ■ *Web:* tyr.com	Seal Beach	CA	90740	714-897-0799	
Venus Swimwear 11711 Marco Beach Dr 1 Venus Plz **Fax Area Code:* 800 ■ *TF:* 800-366-7946 ■ *Web:* www.venus.com	Jacksonville	FL	32224	904-645-6000	648-0411*

155-18 Undergarments

Company	City	State	Zip	Phone	Fax
Alpha Mills Corp 122 S Margaretta St *Web:* alphamillscorporation.com	Schuylkill Haven	PA	17972	570-385-0511	385-0467
Biflex Intimates Group 180 Madison Ave Sixth Fl *Web:* biflex.com	New York	NY	10016	212-532-8340	
Champion Athletic Wear 1000 E Hanes Mill Rd *TF:* 800-315-0563 ■ *Web:* www.championusa.com	Winston-Salem	NC	27105	800-315-0563	
Cupid Foundations Inc 475 Pk Ave S 17th Fl *Web:* cupidintimates.com	New York	NY	10016	212-686-6224	481-9357
Delta Galil USA One Harmon Plz Fifth Fl *Web:* www.deltagalil.com	Secaucus	NJ	07094	201-902-0055	902-0070
Gelmart Industries Inc 136 Madison Ave 4th Fl *TF General:* 800-746-0014 ■ *Web:* www.gelmart.com	New York	NY	10016	212-743-6900	725-7248
Glamorise Foundations Inc 135 Madison Ave *Web:* glamorise.com	New York	NY	10016	212-684-5025	689-7793
Indera Mills Co 350 W Maple St PO Box 309 *TF:* 800-334-8605 ■ *Web:* www.inderamills.com	Yadkinville	NC	27055	336-679-4440	679-4475
Jockey International Inc 2300 60th St PO Box 1417 **Fax Area Code:* 262 ■ *TF:* 800-562-5391 ■ *Web:* www.jockey.com	Kenosha	WI	53140	800-562-5391	658-1812*
Leading Lady 24050 Commerce Pk *TF Cust Svc:* 800-321-4804 ■ *Web:* www.leadinglady.com	Beachwood	OH	44122	216-464-5490	464-9365
Reliable of Milwaukee Inc 6737 W Washington Ste 3200 *TF:* 800-336-6876 ■ *Web:* www.reliableofmilwaukee.com	Milwaukee	WI	53214	414-272-5084	272-6443
Robinson Mfg Company Inc 798 Market St PO Box 338 *TF:* 800-251-7286 ■ *Web:* www.robinsonmfg.com	Dayton	TN	37321	423-775-2212	
Spencers Inc 290 Quarry Rd	Mount Airy	NC	27030	336-789-9111	
Spirite Industries Inc 150 S Dean St *TF:* 800-272-6897 ■ *Web:* www.spirite.com	Englewood	NJ	07631	201-871-4910	

Company	City	State	Zip	Phone	Fax
VF Corp 105 Corporate Ctr Blvd *NYSE: VFC* ■ *Web:* www.vfc.com	Greensboro	NC	27408	336-424-6000	424-7634
Wacoal America 50 Polito Ave *TF:* 800-922-6250 ■ *Web:* www.wacoal-america.com	Lyndhurst	NJ	07071	212-743-9600	696-5608
Wacoal Europe 65 Sprague St *TF:* 800-733-8964 ■ *Web:* www.eveden.com	Hyde Park	MA	02136	617-361-7559	361-7527

155-19 Uniforms & Work Clothes

Company	City	State	Zip	Phone	Fax
A+ School Apparel 401 Knoss Ave **Fax Area Code:* 888 ■ *TF:* 800-227-3215 ■ *Web:* www.schoolapparel.com	Star City	AR	71667	800-227-3215	628-9020*
Action Sports Systems Inc 617 Carbon City Rd PO Box 1442 *TF:* 800-631-1091 ■ *Web:* www.actionsportsuniforms.com	Morganton	NC	28655	828-584-8000	
Algy Team Collection 440 NE First Ave **Fax Area Code:* 888 ■ *TF:* 800-458-2549 ■ *Web:* www.algyteam.com	Hallandale	FL	33009	954-457-8100	928-2282*
American Uniform Co 4363 Ocoee St N Ste 3	Cleveland	TN	37312	423-476-6561	479-6241
Anson Shirt Co Cloud Ave	Wadesboro	NC	28170	704-694-5148	
Barco Uniforms Inc 350 W Rosecrans Ave **Fax:* Cust Svc ■ *TF:* 800-421-1874 ■ *Web:* www.barcouniforms.com	Gardena	CA	90248	310-323-7315	324-5274*
Berne Apparel Co 2210 Summit St *TF:* 800-843-7657 ■ *Web:* www.berneapparel.com	New Haven	IN	46774	260-469-3136	
Blauer Mfg Co Inc 20 Aberdeen St *TF:* 800-225-6715 ■ *Web:* www.blauer.com	Boston	MA	02215	617-536-6606	536-6948
Blue Generation Div of M Rubin & Sons Inc 34-01 38th Ave *TF:* 888-336-4687 ■ *Web:* www.bluegeneration.com	Long Island City	NY	11101	718-361-2800	361-2680
Carhartt Inc 5750 Mercury Dr *TF:* 800-833-3118 ■ *Web:* www.carhartt.com	Dearborn	MI	48126	313-271-8460	271-3455
Choi Bros Inc 3401 W Div St *TF:* 800-524-2464 ■ *Web:* www.choibrothers.com	Chicago	IL	60651	773-489-2800	489-3030
City Shirt Company Inc 10 City Shirt Rd	Frackville	PA	17931	570-874-4251	
DeMoulin Bros & Company Inc 1025 S Fourth St *TF:* 800-228-8134 ■ *Web:* www.demoulin.com	Greenville	IL	62246	618-664-2000	664-1712
Dennis Uniform Mfg Company Inc 135 SE Hawthorne Blvd *TF:* 800-544-7123 ■ *Web:* www.dennisuniform.com	Portland	OR	97214	503-234-7431	238-2529
Dickson Industries Inc 2425 Dean Ave *Web:* www.dicksonindustries.com	Des Moines	IA	50317	515-262-8061	262-1844
Earl's Apparel Inc 908 S Fourth St PO Box 939 *TF:* 800-527-3148 ■ *Web:* www.stanray.us	Crockett	TX	75835	936-544-5521	544-7973
Elbeco Inc 4418 Pottsville Pk *TF:* 800-468-4654 ■ *Web:* www.elbeco.com	Reading	PA	19605	610-921-0651	921-8651
Encompass Group LLC 615 Macon Rd *TF:* 800-284-4540 ■ *Web:* www.encompassgroup.net	McDonough	GA	30253	770-957-1211	957-1888
Euclid Garment Manufacturing Co 333 Martinel Dr PO Box 550 *Web:* www.euclidgarment.com	Kent	OH	44240	330-673-7413	673-0228
Fechheimer Bros Company Inc 4545 Malsbary Rd *TF:* 800-543-1939 ■ *Web:* www.fechheimer.com	Cincinnati	OH	45242	513-793-5400	793-7819
Gibson & Barnes 1900 Weld Blvd Ste 140 **Fax Area Code:* 800 ■ *TF Sales:* 800-748-6693 ■ *Web:* www.gibson-barnes.com	El Cajon	CA	92020	619-440-6977	748-6694*
Golden Mfg Company Inc 125 Hwy 366 PO Box 390	Golden	MS	38847	662-454-3428	454-9240
Howard Uniform Co 1915 Annapolis Rd *TF:* 800-628-8299 ■ *Web:* www.howarduniform.com	Baltimore	MD	21230	410-727-3086	727-3142
I Spiewak & Sons Inc 463 Seventh Ave *TF:* 800-223-6850 ■ *Web:* www.spiewak.com	New York	NY	10018	212-695-1620	629-4803
Integrated Textile Solutions Inc 865 Cleveland Ave *Web:* www.intextile.com	Salem	VA	24153	540-389-8113	387-5855
Key Industries Inc 400 Marble Rd *TF:* 800-835-0365 ■ *Web:* www.keyapparel.com	Fort Scott	KS	66701	620-223-2000	223-5882
Landau Uniforms Inc 8410 W Sandidge Rd *TF General:* 800-387-0641 ■ *Web:* www.landau.com	Olive Branch	MS	38654	662-895-7200	
LC King Mfg Company Inc 24 Seventh St PO Box 367 *TF:* 800-826-2510 ■ *Web:* www.pointerbrand.com	Bristol	TN	37620	423-764-5188	764-6809
Leventhal Ltd PO Box 564 *TF General:* 800-847-4095 ■ *Web:* www.leventhalltd.com	Fayetteville	NC	28302	800-847-4095	352-6635
Lion Apparel Inc 7200 Poe Ave Ste 400 **Fax:* Hum Res ■ *TF:* 800-548-6614 ■ *Web:* www.lionprotects.com	Dayton	OH	45414	937-898-1949	898-2848*
Nationwide Uniform Corp 235 Shepherdsville Rd	Hodgenville	KY	42748	270-358-4173	358-8255
Riverside Manufacturing Co 301 Riverside Dr *TF:* 800-841-8677 ■ *Web:* www.riversideuniforms.com	Moultrie	GA	31768	229-985-5210	890-2932
Royal Park Uniforms Co 14139 Hwy 86 S	Prospect Hill	NC	27314	336-562-3345	562-3832
Rubin Bros Inc 2241 S Halsted St *Web:* www.rubinbrothers.com	Chicago	IL	60608	312-942-1111	
SCORE American Soccer Company Inc 726 E Anaheim St *TF:* 800-626-7774 ■ *Web:* www.scoresports.com	Wilmington	CA	90744	800-626-7774	426-1222
Scotty's Fashions Inc 636 Pen Argyl St *Web:* www.scottysfashions.com	Pen Argyl	PA	18072	610-863-6454	
Stanbury Uniforms Inc 108 Stanbury Industrial Dr PO Box 100 *TF:* 800-826-2246 ■ *Web:* www.stanbury.com	Brookfield	MO	64628	660-258-2246	258-5781
Standard Textile Company Inc One Knollcrest Dr *TF:* 800-999-0400 ■ *Web:* www.standardtextile.com	Cincinnati	OH	45237	513-761-9255	761-0467
Superior Uniform Group Inc 10055Seminole Blvd *NASDAQ: SGC* ■ *TF Cust Svc:* 800-727-8643 ■ *Web:* superioruniformgroup.com	Seminole	FL	33772	727-397-9611	
Topps Safety Apparel Inc 2516 E State Rd 14 *TF:* 800-348-2990 ■ *Web:* www.toppssafetyapparel.com	Rochester	IN	46975	574-223-4311	223-8622
Universal Overall Co 1060 W Van Buren St *TF Cust Svc:* 800-621-3344 ■ *Web:* www.universaloverall.com	Chicago	IL	60607	312-226-3336	226-1986

Phone *Fax*

Wenaas AGS Inc
12211 Parc Crest Dr Bldg Ste 100 .... Stafford TX 77477 281-931-4300 931-4328
TF: 888-576-2668 ■ *Web:* www.wenaasusa.com

Williamson-Dickie Mfg Co
509 W Vickery Blvd .... Fort Worth TX 76104 866-411-1501 336-5183*
**Fax Area Code:* 817 ■ *TF:* 866-411-1501 ■ *Web:* www.dickies.com

155-20 Western Wear (Except Hats & Boots)

Phone *Fax*

Darwood Manufacturing Co
620 W Railroad St S PO Box 625 .... Pelham GA 31779 229-294-4932 294-9323
Web: www.darwoodmfg.com

Miller International Inc Rocky Mountain Clothing Company Div
8500 Zuni St...................................... Denver CO 80260 303-428-5696
Web: www.rockymountainclothing.com

Niver Western Wear Inc PO Box 101224 .... Fort Worth TX 76185 817-924-4299 924-4296
TF Orders: 800-433-5752 ■ *Web:* www.niverww.com

Rockmount Ranch Wear Manufacturing Co
1626 Wazee St .... Denver CO 80202 303-629-7777 629-5836
TF: 800-776-2566 ■ *Web:* www.rockmount.com

Sidran Inc 1050 Venture Ct Ste 100 .... Carrollton TX 75006 214-352-7979 352-0439
TF: 800-969-5015 ■ *Web:* www.sidraninc.com

155-21 Women's Clothing

Phone *Fax*

Adrianna Papell 512 Seventh Ave 10th Fl............. New York NY 10018 212-695-5244
Web: www.adriannapapell.com

Alfred Angelo Inc 1301 Virginia Dr............ Fort Washington PA 19034 215-659-5300 659-1532
TF: 888-218-0044 ■ *Web:* www.alfredangelo.com

Bari-Jay Fashions Inc
225 W 37th St Seventh Fl........................... New York NY 10018 212-921-1551 391-0165
Web: www.barijay.com

Basham Industries 10325 SR 56 .... Coalmont TN 37313 931-692-3218 692-3481
Web: www.bashamindustries.com/contact.htm

bebe stores Inc 400 Valley Dr .... Brisbane CA 94005 415-715-3900 715-3939
NASDAQ: BEBE ■ *TF:* 877-232-3777 ■ *Web:* www.bebe.com

Bernard Chaus Inc 530 Seventh Ave 18th Fl........... New York NY 10018 212-354-1280
Web: www.chausnewyork.com

Byer California 66 Potrero Ave.................. San Francisco CA 94103 415-626-7844 245-0183*
**Fax Area Code:* 925 ■ *TF:* 844-628-4498 ■ *Web:* byerca.com/

Carole Wren Inc 30-30 47th Ave .... Long Island City NY 11101 718-552-3800
Web: www.carolewren.com

Christine Alexander Inc
34210 Ninth Ave S Ste 101...................... Federal Way WA 98003 253-874-5570 927-4516
TF General: 800-554-2539 ■ *Web:* www.christinealexander.com

Darue of California Inc 14102 S Broadway .... Los Angeles CA 90061 310-323-1350
TF: 877-693-2783 ■ *Web:* www.darue.com

Donna Karan International Inc
550 Seventh Ave 15th Fl.......................... New York NY 10018 212-789-1500 789-1820
TF General: 888-737-5743 ■ *Web:* www.donnakaran.com

Gator of Florida Inc 5002 N Howard Ave .... Tampa FL 33603 813-877-8267
Web: gatorofflorida.com

Graff Californiawear 1515 E 15th St.............. Los Angeles CA 90021 213-751-7507 746-5754

JLM Couture Inc 525 Seventh Ave Ste 1703 .... New York NY 10018 212-221-8203 921-7608
TF: 800-924-6475 ■ *Web:* www.jlmcouture.com

Jones Apparel Group Inc Jones New York Collection Div
1411 Broadway.................................. New York NY 10018 212-355-4449
TF: 800-999-1877 ■ *Web:* ninewest.com/financial-information

Kellwood Co 600 Kellwood Pkwy................. Chesterfield MO 63017 314-576-3100 576-3434
Web: www.kellwood.com

Leon Max Inc 3100 New York Dr.................... Pasadena CA 91107 626-797-9991 797-8555
TF: 888-334-4629 ■ *Web:* www.maxstudio.com

Scotty's Fashions Inc 636 Pen Argyl St.............. Pen Argyl PA 18072 610-863-6454
Web: www.scottysfashions.com

Sunrise Brands 801 S Figueroa St Ste 2500 .... Los Angeles CA 90017 323-780-8250 881-0369
Web: www.sunrisebrands.com

Tama Mfg Company Inc 100 Cascade Dr .... Allentown PA 18109 610-231-3100 231-3180
Web: www.tamamfg.com

Tanner Cos LLC 581Rock Rd .... Rutherfordton NC 28139 828-287-4205 287-6196
TF: 877-872-4578 ■ *Web:* rutherfordcoc.org

Ursula of Switzerland Inc 31 Mohawk Ave .... Waterford NY 12188 800-826-4041 237-3038*
**Fax Area Code:* 518 ■ *TF:* 800-826-4041 ■ *Web:* www.ursula.com

156 CLOTHING & ACCESSORIES - WHOL

Phone *Fax*

Alternative Apparel Inc 700 Lake Ave................. Atlanta GA 30307 404-522-2665 460-1260
Web: www.iceboxcoolstuff.com

Crew Outfitters Inc 1001 Virginia Ave.................. Atlanta GA 30354 888-345-5353
TF: 888-345-5353 ■ *Web:* www.crewoutfitters.com

Elastic Therapy Inc 718 Industrial Park Ave........... Asheboro NC 27205 336-625-0529
Web: www.elastictherapy.com

Foria International Inc
18689 Arenth Ave........................... City of Industry CA 91748 626-912-6100 964-9933
Web: www.foria.com

Herman's Inc 2820 Blackhawk Rd .... Rock Island IL 61201 309-788-9568 786-8296
TF: 800-447-1295 ■ *Web:* hermansinc.com

Jacob Ash Company Inc 301 Munson Ave........ McKees Rocks PA 15136 412-331-6660 331-6347
TF: 800-245-6111 ■ *Web:* www.jacobash.com

Marmaxx Group 770 Cochituate Rd.............. Framingham MA 01701 508-390-1000 390-3132
Web: www.tjx.com

Noamex Inc 625 Wortman Ave .... Brooklyn NY 11208 718-342-5330 342-2258
Web: www.noamex.com

Smokin Joes Cigars LLC
2293 Saunders Settlement Rd........................ Sanborn NY 14132 716-261-9327 754-4184
Web: www.smokinjoes.com

Phone *Fax*

Soex West USA LLC 3294 E 26th St................ Los Angeles CA 90058 323-264-8300 227-6845
Web: www.soexgroup.com

Topwin Corp 1808 Abalone Ave .... Torrance CA 90501 310-325-2255 325-1877
Web: www.topwin.co.jp

TSC Apparel LLC 12080 Mosteller Rd................ Cincinnati OH 45241 513-771-1138 248-1069*
**Fax Area Code:* 800 ■ *TF:* 800-543-7230 ■ *Web:* www.tscapparel.com

Tucker Rocky Distributing Inc
4900 Alliance Gateway Fwy .... Fort Worth TX 76177 817-258-9000 258-9095*
**Fax:* Cust Svc ■ *Web:* www.tuckerrocky.com

William B Coleman Company Inc
4001 Earhart Blvd................................ New Orleans LA 70125 504-822-1000 822-3152

World Wide Dreams LLC 4 W 33rd St................ New York NY 10016 212-244-4034

WS Emerson Co Inc 15 Acme Rd........................ Brewer ME 04412 800-789-6120 989-8540*
**Fax Area Code:* 207 ■ *TF:* 800-789-6120 ■ *Web:* www.wsemerson.com

157 CLOTHING STORES

SEE ALSO Department Stores p. 2197

157-1 Children's Clothing Stores

Phone *Fax*

Base Camp Franchising 170 S 1000 E........... Salt Lake City UT 84102 801-359-0071
Web: basecampfranchising.com

Children's Place Retail Stores Inc
500 Plz Dr... Secaucus NJ 07094 201-558-2400 558-2819*
NASDAQ: PLCE ■ **Fax:* Cust Svc ■ *TF:* 877-752-2387 ■ *Web:* www.childrensplace.com

Goldbug Inc 18245 E 40th Ave .... Aurora CO 80011 303-371-2535
Web: goldbuginc.com

Gymboree Corp 500 Howard St .... San Francisco CA 94105 415-278-7000 278-7100
NASDAQ: GYMB ■ *TF:* 877-449-6932 ■ *Web:* www.gymboree.com

Kid to Kid 1244 Township Line Rd.................. Drexel Hill PA 19026 610-446-2544
Web: www.kidtokid.com

Stretch-O-Rama Inc Five Paddock St .... Avenel NJ 07001 732-855-1400
Web: longstreet.com

Tween Brands Inc 8323 Walton Pkwy .... New Albany OH 43054 614-775-3500
Web: www.tooinc.com

Valor Brands LLC 3159 Royal Dr Ste 360............. Alpharetta GA 30022 770-346-9250
TF: 866-949-9098 ■ *Web:* www.valorbrands.com

Winmark Corp 605Hwy 169 N Ste 400............ Minneapolis MN 55441 763-520-8500 520-8410
NASDAQ: WINA ■ *TF:* 800-433-2540 ■ *Web:* www.winmarkcorporation.com

157-2 Family Clothing Stores

Phone *Fax*

Belvest USA Inc Five E 57th St .... New York NY 10022 212-317-0460
Web: www.belvest.com

Blue Canoe Inc 390 Lk Benbow Dr................. Garberville CA 95542 707-923-1373
Web: www.bluecanoe.com

Bob's Stores Inc 160 Corporate Ct................... Meriden CT 06450 203-235-5775 235-1898
TF: 866-333-2627 ■ *Web:* www.bobstores.com

Citi Trends Inc 104 Coleman Blvd .... Savannah GA 31408 912-236-1561 443-3085
NASDAQ: CTRN ■ *TF:* 800-605-8174 ■ *Web:* www.cititrends.com

Dawahares Inc 1845 Alexandria Dr.................. Lexington KY 40504 859-278-0422 514-3299
TF: 800-677-9108 ■ *Web:* www.dawahares.com

De Byle's Inc 20 N Brown St...................... Rhinelander WI 54501 715-362-4406

Forman Mills
1070 Thomas Busch Memorial Hwy............... Pennsauken NJ 08110 856-486-1447
Web: formanmills.com

Foursome Inc 3570 Vicksveurg Ln N Ste 100 .... Plymouth MN 55447 763-473-4667 504-5555
TF: 888-368-7766 ■ *Web:* www.thefoursome.com

Genetic Denim LLC
1013 S Los Angeles St Ninth Fl .... Los Angeles CA 90015 213-747-3344
Web: geneticlosangeles.com/

Halston LLC 59 Greene St Ste 2 .... New York NY 10012 646-396-5418
Web: www.halston.com

Hammer's Store 1415 W Dinah Shore Blvd.......... Winchester TN 37398 931-967-2886
Web: hammersstore.com

Kittery Trading Post 301 US 1 .... Kittery ME 03904 603-334-1157 439-8001*
**Fax Area Code:* 207 ■ *TF:* 888-587-6246 ■ *Web:* www.kitterytradingpost.com

Madewell Inc 486 Broadway .... New York NY 10013 212-226-6954
Web: www.madewell.com

Marshalls Inc 770 Cochituate Rd................. Framingham MA 01701 800-627-7425 390-3147*
**Fax Area Code:* 508 ■ **Fax:* Hum Res ■ *Web:* www.marshallsonline.com

Name Brands Inc 7215 S Memorial Dr .... Tulsa OK 74133 918-307-0289
Web: www.halfofhalf.com

National Stores Inc 15001 S Figueroa St.............. Gardena CA 90248 310-324-9962 856-0162
Web: www.factory2-u.com

Palais Royal 10201 S Main St .... Houston TX 77025 713-346-2430 838-4494
TF: 800-743-8730 ■ *Web:* stagestores.com/store?brand=palaisroyal

Puritan of Cape Cod 408 Main St.................... Hyannis MA 02601 508-775-2400 771-3277
TF: 800-924-0606 ■ *Web:* www.puritancapecod.com

SDG, Inc 200 N Broadway St .... Checotah OK 74426 918-473-2233
Web: www.sharpeclothing.com

Thom Browne Inc 100 Hudson St .... New York NY 10013 212-633-1197
Web: www.thombrowne.com

TJ Maxx 770 Cochituate Rd .... Framingham MA 01701 508-390-1000
TF Cust Svc: 800-926-6299 ■ *Web:* tjmaxx.tjx.com

United Fashions of Texas LLC
4629 Macro Dr .... San Antonio TX 78218 210-662-7140 666-3211
Web: melrosestore.com

Victor Talbots Inc 47 Glen Cove Rd .... Greenvale NY 11548 516-625-1787
Web: victortalbots.com

Wakefield's Inc 1212 Quintard Ave PO Box 400........ Anniston AL 36201 256-237-9521
TF: 800-333-1552 ■ *Web:* www.wakefields.com

Zumiez Inc 6300 Merrill Creek Pkwy Ste B.............. Everett WA 98203 425-551-1500 551-1555
NASDAQ: ZUMZ ■ *TF:* 877-828-6929 ■ *Web:* www.zumiez.com

157-3 Men's Clothing Stores

Company / Address	City	State	ZIP	Phone	Fax
Boyds Philadelphia 1818 Chestnut St *Web:* www.boydsphila.com	Philadelphia	PA	19103	215-564-9000	564-2876
Caplan's Mens Shops Inc 916 Third St *Web:* www.shopcaplans.com	Alexandria	LA	71301	318-427-7700	
Carroll & Co 425 N Canon Dr *TF:* 800-238-9400 ■ *Web:* www.carrollandco.com	Beverly Hills	CA	90210	310-273-9060	273-7974
Casual Male Retail Group Inc 555 Tpke St *NASDAQ: DXLG* ■ *Web:* casual-male-big-and-tall.destinationxl.com	Canton	MA	02021	781-828-9300	
Culwell & Son Inc 6319 Hillcrest Ave *Web:* www.culwell.com	Dallas	TX	75205	214-522-7000	521-7329
Dr. Denim Inc 1136 Market St *TF:* 888-761-6520 ■ *Web:* www.drdenim.com	Philadelphia	PA	19107	215-564-2767	564-2984
JA Apparel Corp 650 Fifth Ave *Web:* www.josephabboud.com	New York	NY	10019	212-586-9140	397-9360
Jack O'Reilly Tuxedos LLC 2701 Fifth St Hwy *Web:* jackoreillytuxedos.com	Reading	PA	19605	610-929-9409	
Jos A Bank Clothiers 500 Hanover Pk *TF Cust Svc:* 800-999-7472 ■ *Web:* www.josbank.com	Hampstead	MD	21074	410-239-2700	239-5700
Kizan International Inc 100 W Hill Dr *Web:* www.louisraphael.com	Brisbane	CA	94005	415-468-7360	468-0444
Louis Boston 60 Northern Ave *TF:* 800-225-5135 ■ *Web:* www.louisboston.com	Boston	MA	02210	617-262-6100	
Men's Wearhouse Inc 6380 Rogerdale Rd *NYSE: MW* ■ *TF:* 877-986-9669 ■ *Web:* www.menswearhouse.com	Houston	TX	77072	281-776-7000	776-7038
Miltons Inc 250 Granite St *TF:* 800-645-8673 ■ *Web:* www.miltons.com	Braintree	MA	02184	781-848-1880	848-1090
Mitchells Family of Stores 270 Main St *Web:* mitchellstores.com	Huntington	NY	11743	631-423-1660	
Norton Ditto Company Inc 2425 W Alabama St *Web:* www.nortonditto.com	Houston	TX	77098	713-688-9800	621-3875
Patrick James Inc 780 W Shaw Ave *TF:* 888-427-6003 ■ *Web:* www.patrickjames.com	Fresno	CA	93704	559-224-5500	448-0601
Paul Fredrick Menstyle 223 W Poplar St *TF:* 800-247-1417 ■ *Web:* www.paulfredrick.com	Fleetwood	PA	19522	610-944-0909	944-6452
Rochester Big & Tall 700 Mission St *Web:* rochester-big-and-tall.destinationxl.com	San Francisco	CA	94103	415-982-6455	
Rubenstein Bros Inc 102 St Charles Ave *TF:* 800-102-7862 ■ *Web:* rubensteinsneworleans.com/	New Orleans	LA	70130	504-581-6666	581-3305
Shaws Menswear Inc 1061 Village Park Dr Ste 204	Greensboro	GA	30642	706-454-5041	

157-4 Men's & Women's Clothing Stores

Company / Address	City	State	ZIP	Phone	Fax
Abercrombie & Fitch Co 6301 Fitch Pass *NYSE: ANF* ■ *Web:* www.abercrombie.com	New Albany	OH	43054	614-283-6500	283-6565
American Eagle Outfitters Inc 77 Hot Metal St *NYSE: AEO* ■ **Fax Area Code: 724* ■ *TF Cust Svc:* 888-232-4535 ■ *Web:* www.ae.com	Pittsburgh	PA	15203	412-432-3300	776-6160*
Barneys New York Inc 575 Fifth Ave **Fax:* Hum Res ■ *Web:* www.barneys.com	New York	NY	10017	212-450-8700	450-8489*
Bergdorf Goodman Inc 754 Fifth Ave *TF Cust Svc:* 800-558-1855 ■ *Web:* www.bergdorfgoodman.com	New York	NY	10019	212-753-7300	872-8886
Buckle Inc 2407 W 24th St *NYSE: BKE* ■ *TF:* 800-626-1255 ■ *Web:* www.buckle.com	Kearney	NE	68845	308-236-8491	236-4493
Burberry Ltd (New York) Nine E 57th St *Web:* www.burberry.com	New York	NY	10022	212-407-7100	
Cohoes Fashions Inc 156 Hillside Rd Garden City Ctr *Web:* www.cohoesfashions.com	Cranston	NY	02920	908-354-6775	
Eddie Bauer LLC PO Box 7001 *TF Orders:* 800-426-8020 ■ *Web:* www.eddiebauer.com	Groveport	OH	43125	800-426-8020	
Gap Inc Two Folsom St *NYSE: GPS* ■ *TF:* 800-333-7899 ■ *Web:* www.gapinc.com	San Francisco	CA	94105	650-952-4400	
J Crew Group Inc 770 Broadway *TF:* 800-562-0258 ■ *Web:* www.jcrew.com	New York	NY	10003	212-209-2500	209-2666
J McLaughlin 1008 Lexington Ave *Web:* jmclaughlin.com	New York	NY	10021	212-879-9565	879-0066
Jack Henry Clothing Company Inc 612 W 47th St *Web:* kcclothiers.com	Kansas City	MO	64112	816-753-3800	753-0284
James Davis 400 S Grove Pk Rd *Web:* jamesdavisstore.com	Memphis	TN	38117	901-767-4640	682-3338
Joe's Jeans Inc 2340 S Eastern Ave *NASDAQ: JOEZ* ■ *TF:* 877-528-5637 ■ *Web:* www.joesjeans.com	Commerce	CA	90040	323-837-3700	837-3790
John B Malouf Inc 8201 Quaker Ave Ste 106 *Web:* www.maloufs.com	Lubbock	TX	79424	806-794-9500	798-3428
L Brands Inc 3 Limited Pkwy *NYSE: LTD* ■ *Web:* lb.com/	Columbus	OH	43230	614-415-7000	
Maurices Inc 105 W Superior St *TF:* 866-977-1542 ■ *Web:* www.maurices.com	Duluth	MN	55802	218-727-8431	720-2102
Oak Hall Inc 6150 Poplar Ave Ste 146 *Web:* www.oakhall.com	Memphis	TN	38119	901-761-3580	761-5731
Pacific Sunwear of California Inc 3450 E Miraloma Ave *NASDAQ: PSUN* ■ *TF:* 800-444-6770 ■ *Web:* shop.pacsun.com	Anaheim	CA	92806	714-414-4000	414-4251
Patagonia Inc 259 W Santa Clara St PO Box 150 *TF Cust Svc:* 800-638-6464 ■ *Web:* www.patagonia.com	Ventura	CA	93001	805-643-8616	648-8020
Paul Stuart Inc Madison Ave & 45th St *TF Orders:* 800-678-8278 ■ *Web:* www.paulstuart.com	New York	NY	10017	212-682-0320	
Plato's Closet 23021 Outer Dr *TF:* 800-592-8049 ■ *Web:* www.platoscloset.com	Allen Park	MI	48101	313-278-2300	
South Pole 222 Bridge Plz S *Web:* www.southpole-usa.com	Fort Lee	NJ	07024	201-242-5900	242-8466
Specialty Retailers Inc 10201 S Main St **Fax Area Code: 713* ■ *TF:* 800-579-2302 ■ *Web:* www.stagestoresinc.com	Houston	TX	77025	800-579-2302	669-2709*
Stanley Korshak 500 Crescent Ct Ste 100 *TF:* 855-749-9539 ■ *Web:* www.stanleykorshak.com	Dallas	TX	75201	214-871-3600	871-3617
TJX Cos Inc 770 Cochituate Rd *NYSE: TJX* ■ *TF:* 800-926-6299 ■ *Web:* www.tjx.com	Framingham	MA	01701	508-390-1000	390-2091
Town & County 2660 S Glenstone Ave *Web:* townandcountyclothing.com	Springfield	MO	65804	417-883-6131	
Urban Outfitters Inc 30 Industrial Pk Blvd *TF:* 800-282-2200 ■ *Web:* www.urbanoutfitters.com	Trenton	SC	29847	800-282-2200	959-8795
Watch LA 1138 Wall St *Web:* www.watchla.com	Los Angeles	CA	90015	213-747-1838	747-2888

157-5 Specialty Clothing Stores

Specialty clothing stores are those which sell a specific type of clothing, such as Western wear, uniforms, etc.

Company / Address	City	State	ZIP	Phone	Fax
5.11 Inc 4300 Spyres Way *TF:* 866-451-1726 ■ *Web:* www.511tactical.com	Modesto	CA	95356	209-527-4511	527-1511
Aeropostale Inc 112 W 34th St Ste 22 *NYSE: ARO* ■ *Web:* www.aeropostale.com	New York	NY	10120	646-485-5410	485-5440
Alvin's Stores Inc 11400 NW 34rd St *Web:* www.alvinsisland.com	Panama City	FL	33178	305-471-9394	
Carlen Enterprises Inc 1760 Apollo Ct *Web:* www.carlen.com	Seal Beach	CA	90740	562-296-1055	296-1052
Cavender's 2025 SW Loop 323 *Web:* www.cavenders.com	Tyler	TX	75701	903-561-2510	561-6758
Country Curtains PO Box 955 *TF:* 800-937-1237 ■ *Web:* www.countrycurtains.com	Stockbridge	MA	01262	413-243-1474	243-1067
Dunham's Sports 5000 Dixie Hwy *Web:* www.dunhamssports.com	Waterford	MI	48329	248-674-4991	674-1407
Hat World Corp 7555 Woodland Dr *TF:* 888-564-4287 ■ *Web:* www.lids.com	Indianapolis	IN	46278	888-564-4287	
Hilo Hattie 700 N Nimitz Hwy **Fax Area Code: 808* ■ *TF:* 800-233-8912 ■ *Web:* www.hilohattie.com	Honolulu	HI	96817	800-233-8912	356-1510*
HorseLoverZ com 254 N Cedar St *TF:* 877-804-7810 ■ *Web:* www.horseloverz.com	Hazleton	PA	18201	570-579-0054	
Hot Topic Inc 18305 E San Jose Ave *NASDAQ: HOTT* ■ *Web:* www.hottopic.com	City of Industry	CA	91748	626-839-4681	839-4686
Mark's Work Warehouse 30-1035 64th Ave SE *TF:* 800-663-6275 ■ *Web:* marks.com	Calgary	AB	T2H2J7	403-255-9220	255-6005
Mobile Nations 3151 E Thomas St *TF:* 888-599-8998 ■ *Web:* www.smartphoneexperts.com	Inverness	FL	34453	352-400-4400	
Modell's Sporting Goods 498 Seventh Ave 20th Fl *TF:* 888-645-8667 ■ *Web:* www.modells.com	New York	NY	10018	800-275-6633	
Niver Western Wear Inc PO Box 101224 *TF Orders:* 800-433-5752 ■ *Web:* www.niverww.com	Fort Worth	TX	76185	817-924-4299	924-4296
Northwest Designs Ink Inc 13456 SE 27th Pl Ste 200 **Fax Area Code: 877* ■ *TF:* 800-925-9327 ■ *Web:* www.northwestdesigns.com	Bellevue	WA	98005	800-925-9327	925-9327*
Overland Sheepskin Company Inc 2096 Nutmeg Ave *TF:* 800-683-7526 ■ *Web:* www.overland.com	Fairfield	IA	52556	641-472-8434	472-8474
Post & Nickel 144 N 14th St *Web:* www.postandnickel.com	Lincoln	NE	68508	402-476-3432	476-3454
Pro Image Sports 233 N 1250 W Ste 200 *Web:* www.proimagesports.com	Centerville	UT	84014	801-296-9999	296-1319
Sheplers Inc 6501 W Kellogg Dr *TF:* 888-835-4004 ■ *Web:* www.sheplers.com	Wichita	KS	67209	888-835-4004	
U S Cavalry Inc 2855 Centennial Ave *TF:* 800-777-7172 ■ *Web:* www.uscav.com	Radcliff	KY	40160	270-351-1164	352-0266
Watumull Bros Ltd 307 Lewers St Ste 600	Honolulu	HI	96815	808-971-8800	971-8824
Wilsons Leather Inc 7401 Boone Ave N *TF:* 800-967-6270 ■ *Web:* www.wilsonsleather.com	Brooklyn Park	MN	55428	763-391-4000	
Work 'n Gear Stores 2300 Crown Colony Dr Ste 300 **Fax Area Code: 781* ■ *TF:* 800-987-0218 ■ *Web:* www.workngear.com	Quincy	MA	02169	800-987-0218	746-0180*

157-6 Women's Clothing Stores

Company / Address	City	State	ZIP	Phone	Fax
A & E Stores Inc 1000 Huyler St *Web:* www.aestores.com	Teterboro	NJ	07608	201-393-0600	393-0233
A Nose For Clothes 14271 SW 120th St Ste 102 *Web:* www.anoseforclothes.com	Miami	FL	33186	305-253-8631	235-4370
A'Gaci LLC 12460 Network Blvd Ste 106 **Fax Area Code: 702* ■ *TF:* 866-265-3036 ■ *Web:* www.agacistore.com	San Antonio	TX	78249	210-377-3393	258-8634*
ABS by Allan Schwartz 1231 Long Beach Ave **Fax:* Hum Res ■ *Web:* www.absstyle.com	Los Angeles	CA	90021	213-895-4400	891-2812*
Altru Apparel 718 Gladys Ave Ste 2 *Web:* altruapparel.com	Los Angeles	CA	90021	213-622-0588	
Ann Inc Seven Times Sq *NYSE: ANN* ■ *TF:* 800-677-6788 ■ *Web:* www.anninc.com	New York	NY	10036	212-541-3300	541-3299
AnnTaylor Inc Seven Times Sq *TF:* 800-677-6788 ■ *Web:* www.anntaylor.com	New York	NY	10036	212-541-3300	
Avenue Stores Inc 365 W Passaic St **Fax:* Mktg ■ *TF:* 888-843-2836 ■ *Web:* www.avenue.com	Rochelle Park	NJ	07662	201-845-0880	*
Barbara Katz Sportswear Co 2240 SW 19th St Ste 601 *Web:* barbarakatz.com	Boca Raton	FL	33431	561-391-1066	391-5284
Big Girls Bras Etcetera Inc 3540 NW 56th St Ste 207 *Web:* www.biggerbras.com	Lauderdale	FL	33309	954-484-2701	
Big M Inc 12 Vreeland Ave *Web:* mandee.com	Totowa	NJ	07512	973-890-0021	
Bluefly Inc 42 W 39th St Ninth Fl *NASDAQ: BFLY* ■ *TF Cust Svc:* 877-258-3359 ■ *Web:* www.bluefly.com	New York	NY	10018	212-944-8000	354-3400

Phone Fax

Born Into It Inc 185 New Boston St ... Woburn MA 01801 781-491-0707
TF: 800-560-2840 ■ *Web:* www.chowdaheadz.com

Brioni Roman Style USA Corp
610 Fifth Ave Ste 404 ... New York NY 10020 212-332-6900
Web: brioni.com

C28 1180 Galleria At Tyler ... Riverside CA 92503 951-354-9777

Canada Sportswear Corp 230 Barmac Dr ... North York ON M9L2Z3 416-740-8020 740-7106
Web: www.canadasportswear.com

Capsmith Inc 2240 Old Lk Mary Rd ... Sanford FL 32771 407-328-7660
TF: 800-228-3889 ■ *Web:* capsmith.com

Cato Corp, The 8100 Denmark Rd ... Charlotte NC 28273 704-554-8510
TF: 800-526-9169 ■ *Web:* www.catofashions.com

Ceri Linden LLC 180 Linden St ... Wellesley MA 02482 781-416-0900
Web: ceriboutique.com

Charlotte Russe Inc
5910 Pacific Center Blvd ... San Diego CA 92121 888-211-7271
TF: 888-211-7271 ■ *Web:* www.charlotterusse.com

Charming Shoppes Inc 933 MacArthur Blvd ... Mahwah NJ 07430 551-777-6700
NASDAQ: ASNA ■ *Web:* www.ascenaretail.com

Chico's FAS Inc 11215 Metro Pkwy ... Fort Myers FL 33966 888-855-4986 277-5237*
NYSE: CHS ■ **Fax Area Code:* 239 ■ *TF:* 800-690-6903 ■ *Web:* www.chicosfas.com

Christopher & Banks Corp 2400 Xenium Ln N ... Plymouth MN 55441 763-551-5000 551-5198
NYSE: CBK ■ *Web:* www.christopherandbanks.com

Citizens of Humanity Inc
5715 Bickett St ... Huntington Park CA 90255 323-923-1240
Web: www.citizensofhumanity.com

Claire's Accessories
2400 W Central Rd ... Hoffman Estates IL 60192 847-765-1100 765-4676
TF: 800-252-4737 ■ *Web:* www.claires.co.uk

Close To My Heart 1199 West 700 South ... Pleasant Grove UT 84062 801-763-8395
Web: www.closetomyheart.com

Clothes Minded Inc 1160 Sandhill Ave ... Carson CA 90746 310-638-9931
Web: www.clothesminded.com

Clothing Cove, The 414 N Main St ... Milford MI 48381 248-685-2500

Cosabella 12186 SW 128th St ... Miami FL 33186 305-253-9904

Daffodil 163 Pearl St ... Essex Junction VT 05452 802-879-0212 872-3221

David's Bridal Inc 1001 Washington St ... Conshohocken PA 19428 610-943-5000 642-7642*
**Fax:* Cust Svc ■ *TF:* 800-823-2403 ■ *Web:* www.davidsbridal.com

Destination Maternity Corp
456 N Fifth St ... Philadelphia PA 19123 215-873-2200 625-3843*
NASDAQ: DEST ■ **Fax:* Cust Svc ■ *TF:* 800-466-6223 ■ *Web:* destinationmaternitycorp.com/home.asp

DND Fashion Inc 10434 Rush St ... South El Monte CA 91733 626-442-1423

Drapers & Damons Nine Pasteur Ste 200 ... Irvine CA 92618 800-843-1174
TF: 800-843-1174 ■ *Web:* drapers.blair.com

Edwards Lowell 8712 Wilshire Blvd ... Beverly Hills CA 90211 310-360-0466

El Ad US Holding Inc 575 Madison Ave 22nd Fl ... New York NY 10022 212-213-8833
Web: www.eladgroup.com

Embry's 3361 Tates Creek Rd ... Lexington KY 40502 859-269-3390
Web: embrys.com

Express One Limited Pkwy ... Columbus OH 43230 888-397-1980
NYSE: EXPR ■ *TF:* 888-397-1980 ■ *Web:* www.express.com

Flemington Fur Co Eight Spring St ... Flemington NJ 08822 908-782-2212 782-2773
Web: www.flemingtonfurs.com

Forever 21 Inc 2001 S Alameda St ... Los Angeles CA 90058 213-741-5100
TF Cust Svc: 800-966-1355 ■ *Web:* www.forever21.com

Fox's 80 Main St ... Mineola NY 11501 516-294-8321 294-2682
Web: www.foxs.com

Frederick's of Hollywood Inc PO Box 2949 ... Phoenix AZ 85062 800-323-9525
TF: 800-323-9525 ■ *Web:* www.fredericks.com

Gartenhaus Furs 7101 Wisconsin Ave ... Bethesda MD 20814 301-656-2800
Web: www.fursbygartenhaus.com

GWK Enterprises 123 S Ctr St ... Geneseo IL 61254 309-944-6516
Web: fourseasonsdirect.com

Hemingway Apparel Manufacturing Inc
60 Apparel Dr ... Hemingway SC 29554 843-558-2525
Web: www.hemingwayapparel.com

Henig Inc 4135 Carmichael Rd ... Montgomery AL 36106 334-277-7610 272-3562
Web: www.henigfurs.com

Henri Bendel Inc 712 Fifth Ave ... New York NY 10019 212-247-1100
TF: 866-875-7975 ■ *Web:* lb.com/

Indice Mode 5401 Boul Des Galeries ... Quebec QC G2K1N4 418-624-9330
Web: lindicemode.com

Irresistibles Seven Hawkes St ... Marblehead MA 01945 781-631-1248 631-8965
TF: 800-555-9865 ■ *Web:* www.irresistibles.com

J Brand Holdings LLC 1214 E 18th St ... Los Angeles CA 90021 213-749-3500
Web: www.jbrandjeans.com

Jeans Warehouse Inc 2612 Waiwai Loop ... Honolulu HI 96819 808-839-2421
Web: jeanswarehousehawaii.com

Joyce Leslie Inc 170 W Commercial Ave ... Moonachie NJ 07074 201-804-7800 804-8841
Web: www.joyceleslie.com

Just For Wraps 5815 Smithway St ... Commerce CA 90040 213-239-0503
Web: www.wrapper.com

L & L Wings Inc 666 Broadway Second Fl ... New York NY 10012 212-481-8299 481-8218
Web: www.wingsbeachwear.com

L Brands Inc 3 Limited Pkwy ... Columbus OH 43230 614-415-7000
NYSE: LTD ■ *Web:* lb.com/

Lady Grace Stores Inc
Five Commonwealth Ave Ste 1 ... Woburn MA 01801 781-569-0727 437-9123*
**Fax Area Code:* 800 ■ *TF:* 800-922-0504 ■ *Web:* www.ladygrace.com

Lane Bryant Inc 3344 Morse Crossing ... Columbus OH 43215 954-970-2205
TF Cust Svc: 866-886-4731 ■ *Web:* www.lanebryant.com

Lingerie Outlet Store 3720 S Santa Fe Ave ... Vernon CA 90058 323-588-6917

Louis Vuitton NA Inc One E 57th St ... New York NY 10022 212-758-8877
TF Cust Svc: 866-884-8866 ■ *Web:* louisvuitton.com

Lovers Lane & Co 46750 Port St ... Plymouth MI 48170 734-414-0010
Web: www.loverslane.com

Maison Weiss 4500 I-55 at Highland Village ... Jackson MS 39211 601-981-4621 981-4671
Web: maisonweiss.com

Mandee Shop 12 Vreeland Ave ... Totowa NJ 07512 973-890-0021
TF Cust Svc: 877-756-1958 ■ *Web:* www.mandee.com

Marla Junes Clothing Company Inc
207 Se Ct Ave ... Pendleton OR 97801 541-276-0778
Web: marlajunes.com

Marshall Retail Group 5385 Wynn Rd ... Las Vegas NV 89118 702-385-5233 385-4285
Web: www.marshallretailgroup.com

Miken Sales Inc 539 S Mission Rd ... Los Angeles CA 90033 323-266-2560 266-2580
Web: mikenusa.com

Motherhood Maternity 456 N Fifth St ... Philadelphia PA 19123 215-873-2200 625-3843*
**Fax:* Cust Svc ■ *TF:* 800-291-7800 ■ *Web:* www.motherhood.com

New York & Co 330 W 34th St 5th Fl ... New York NY 10001 800-961-9906
TF: 800-961-9906 ■ *Web:* www.nyandcompany.com

NYDJ Apparel LLC 5401 S Soto St ... Vernon CA 90058 323-581-9040
TF: 800-407-6001 ■ *Web:* www.nydj.com

Paul's Boutique Inc 99 Rivington St ... New York NY 10002 646-805-0384

Revolve Clothing Exchange 1620 E Seventh Ave ... Tampa FL 33605 813-242-5970
Web: revolve.cx

rue21 Inc 800 Commonwealth Dr Ste 100 ... Warrendale PA 15086 724-776-9780 741-9020
NASDAQ: RUE ■ *TF:* 888-871-2744 ■ *Web:* www.rue21.com

Saks Jandel 5510 Wisconsin Ave ... Chevy Chase MD 20815 301-652-2250 652-2044
Web: thebridalsalonatsaksjandel.com

Schweser's Stores Inc PO Box 1469 ... Fremont NE 68026 402-721-1700 727-4925
Web: www.schwesersstores.com

Sherpa Adventure Gear Inc 7857 S 180th St ... Kent WA 98032 425-251-0760
Web: www.sherpaadventuregear.com

Sister Sam LLC 2150 E 10th St ... Los Angeles CA 90021 213-228-1930
Web: www.bailey44.com

Soft Surroundings
33 The Blvd Saint Louis ... Saint Louis MO 63117 314-262-4949
Web: softsurroundings.com

Stylexchange 1220 Belk Dr ... Mount Pleasant SC 29464 843-884-2244

Swim 'n Sport Retail Inc 2396 NW 96th Ave ... Miami FL 33172 800-497-2111 593-2669*
**Fax Area Code:* 305 ■ *TF:* 800-497-2111 ■ *Web:* www.swimnsport.com

Sydneys Closet 11840 Dorsett Rd ... Maryland Heights MO 63043 314-344-5066
TF: 888-479-3639 ■ *Web:* www.sydneyscloset.com

Ulla Popken Ltd 12201 Long Green Pk ... Glen Arm MD 21057 410-592-9190
Web: www.ullapopken.com

Vanity Shop of Grand Forks Inc
2410 Great Northern Dr ... Fargo ND 58102 701-237-3330 237-4692
TF: 866-247-7920 ■ *Web:* www.vanity.com

Victoria's Secret Stores 4 Limited Pkwy ... Reynoldsburg OH 43068 800-411-5116 577-7844*
**Fax Area Code:* 614 ■ *TF:* 800-411-5116 ■ *Web:* www.victoriassecret.com

Wedding Shoppe Inc, The 1196 Grand Ave ... Saint Paul MN 55105 651-298-1144
TF: 877-294-4991 ■ *Web:* www.weddingshoppeinc.com

Western Glove Works Ltd 555 Logan Ave ... Winnipeg MB R3A0S4 204-788-4249
Web: westerngloveworks.ca

Wet Seal Inc 26972 Burbank Ave ... Foothill Ranch CA 92610 949-699-3900
NASDAQ: WTSLA ■ *TF:* 866-746-7938 ■ *Web:* www.wetseal.com

White House/Black Market (WHBM)
11215 Metro Pkwy ... Fort Myers FL 33966 239-277-6200
TF: 877-948-2525 ■ *Web:* www.whitehouseblackmarket.com

Windsor Inc 4533 Pacific Blvd ... Vernon CA 90058 323-282-9000 973-4224
TF: 888-494-6376 ■ *Web:* www.windsorstore.com

158 COAST GUARD INSTALLATIONS

Phone Fax

Barbers Point Coast Guard Air Station
One Coral Sea Rd ... Kapolei HI 96707 808-682-2771
Web: www.uscg.mil

Borinquen Coast Guard Air Station
260 GuaRd Rd ... Aguadilla PR 00603 787-890-8400 890-8407
Web: www.uscg.mil/d7/airstaborinquen

Cape Cod Coast Guard Air Station
2300 Wilson Blvd Ste 500 ... Arlington VA 20598 202-372-4620
TF: 877-669-8724 ■ *Web:* uscg.mil/d1/airstacapecod

Charleston Coast Guard Base 196 Tradd St ... Charleston SC 29401 843-724-7600 724-7633
Web: www.uscg.mil

Coast Guard Sector Detroit
110 Mt Elliott Ave ... Detroit MI 48207 206-220-7000 568-9469*
**Fax Area Code:* 313 ■ *Web:* www.uscg.mil

Coast Guard Sector Sault Sainte Marie
337 Water St ... Sault Sainte Marie MI 49783 906-635-3217
Web: www.uscg.mil/d9/sectSaultSteMarie

Corpus Christi Coast Guard Air Station
8930 Ocean Dr Hgr 41 ... Corpus Christi TX 78419 361-939-6393
Web: www.uscg.mil/history/stations/airsta_corpuschristi.asp

Elizabeth City Coast Guard Air Station
1461 N Rd St ... Elizabeth City NC 27909 252-335-4365 335-5732
Web: business.elizabethcitychamber.org

Houston Coast Guard Air Station
1178 Ellington Field ... Houston TX 77034 713-578-3000
Web: www.uscg.mil/d8/airstahouston

Integrated Support Command Miami Beach
100 MacArthur Cswy ... Miami Beach FL 33139 305-535-4300 535-4491
TF: 866-772-8724 ■ *Web:* www.uscg.mil/d7/sectmiami

Ketchikan Integrated Support Command
1300 Stedman St ... Ketchikan AK 99901 907-228-0340
Web: www.uscg.mil

Mayport Coast Guard Base
4200 Ocean St ... Atlantic Beach FL 32233 904-564-7521
Web: www.uscg.mil

Miami Coast Guard Air Station
Opa Locka Airport 14750 NW 44th Ct ... Opa Locka FL 33054 305-953-2130
Web: www.uscg.mil

Milwaukee Coast Guard Base
2420 S Lincoln Memorial Dr ... Milwaukee WI 53207 414-747-7100 747-7108
TF: 866-772-8724 ■ *Web:* www.uscg.mil

Port Angeles Coast Guard Air Station
Ediz Hook Rd ... Port Angeles WA 98362 360-417-5840 457-5849
Web: www.uscg.mil

Phone | Fax

Sacramento Coast Guard Air Station
6037 Price Ave .... McClellan CA 95652 916-643-7659 643-7700
Web: www.uscg.mil

United States Coast Guard/Personnel Services & Support Unit
400 Sand Island Pkwy .... Honolulu HI 96819 808-842-2062 842-2026
Web: www.uscg.mil

US Coast Guard Air Station Detroit
1461 N Perimeter Rd Selfridge ANGB .... Selfridge MI 48045 800-424-8802 307-6705*
**Fax Area Code:* 586 ■ *TF:* 800-424-8802 ■ *Web:* www.uscg.mil/d9/airstadetroit

US Coast Guard Air Station New Orleans
400 Russell Ave .... New Orleans LA 70143 504-393-6005 393-6016
Web: uscg.mil

US Coast Guard Air Station Savannah
1297 N Lightning Rd Hunter AAF .... Savannah GA 31409 912-652-4646
Web: www.uscg.mil/d7/airstasavannah

159 COFFEE & TEA STORES

Phone | Fax

Bad Ass Coffee Co of Hawaii Inc
3530 S State St .... Salt Lake City UT 84115 801-265-1182 463-2606
Web: www.badasscoffee.com

Caribou Coffee Company Inc
3900 Lakebreeze Ave N .... Minneapolis MN 55429 763-592-2200 592-2300
NASDAQ: CBOU ■ *TF Cust Svc:* 888-227-4268 ■ *Web:* www.cariboucoffee.com

Coffee Beanery Ltd, The 3429 Pierson Pl .... Flushing MI 48433 800-441-2255 733-1536*
**Fax Area Code:* 810 ■ *TF:* 800-441-2255 ■ *Web:* www.coffeebeanery.com

Coffee People Inc 33 Coffee Ln .... Waterbury VT 05676 888-879-4627
TF: 888-879-4627 ■ *Web:* www.greenmountaincoffee.com

Dunkin' Donuts 130 Royall St .... Canton MA 02021 781-737-3000 737-4000
TF Cust Svc: 800-859-5339 ■ *Web:* www.dunkindonuts.com

Hawaii Coffee Company Inc 1555 Kalani St .... Honolulu HI 96817 808-847-3600 972-0777*
**Fax Area Code:* 800 ■ *TF:* 800-338-8353 ■ *Web:* hawaiicoffeecompany.com

International Coffee & Tea Inc
1945 S La Cienega Blvd .... Los Angeles CA 90034 310-237-2326 484-0105*
**Fax Area Code:* 805 ■ *TF:* 877-653-1963 ■ *Web:* www.coffeebean.com

McNulty's Tea & Coffee Company Inc
109 Christopher St .... New York NY 10014 212-242-5351
TF: 800-356-5200 ■ *Web:* www.mcnultys.com

Montana Coffee Traders Inc 5810 Hwy 93 S .... Whitefish MT 59937 406-862-7633 862-7680
TF: 800-345-5282 ■ *Web:* www.coffeetraders.com

Moxie Java International LLC
4990 W Chinden Blvd .... Boise ID 83714 208-322-7773 321-0279
Web: moxiejava.com

Peet's Coffee & Tea Inc 1400 Pk Ave .... Emeryville CA 94608 510-594-2100 *
NASDAQ: GMCR ■ **Fax:* Orders ■ *TF Orders:* 800-999-2132 ■ *Web:* www.peets.com

Seattle's Best Coffee Co PO Box 3717 .... Seattle WA 98124 800-611-7793
TF: 800-611-7793 ■ *Web:* www.seattlesbest.com

Second Cup Ltd 6303 Airport Rd .... Mississauga ON L4V1R8 877-212-1818
TF: 877-212-1818 ■ *Web:* www.secondcup.com

Shefield Group 2265 W Railway St .... Abbotsford BC V2S2E3 604-859-1014 859-1711
Web: www.shefield.com

Starbucks Coffee Co 2401 Utah Ave S .... Seattle WA 98134 206-447-1575 318-3432
TF: 800-782-7282 ■ *Web:* www.starbucks.com

Tully's Coffee Corp 3100 Airport Way .... Seattle WA 98134 206-233-2070 233-2077
Web: tullyscoffeeshops.com

VKI Technologies Inc 3200 2e rue .... Saint-hubert QC J3Y8Y7 450-676-0504
Web: www.vkitech.com

160 COLLECTION AGENCIES

Phone | Fax

A.R.M. Solutions Inc PO Box 2929 .... Camarillo CA 93011 888-772-6468
TF: 888-772-6468 ■ *Web:* www.armsolutions.net

AAA Collections Inc 3500 S First Ave Cir .... Sioux Falls SD 57105 605-339-1333
Web: www.aaa-coll.com

ABC-Amega Inc 1100 Main St .... Buffalo NY 14209 716-885-4444 878-2872
Web: www.abc-amega.com

Access Credit Management Inc
11225 Huron Ln Ste 222 .... Little Rock AR 72211 501-664-2922
Web: www.arcollectors.com

Accounts Management Center Inc
1976 E Grand Ave .... Hot Springs AR 71901 501-623-5594

ACE Recovery Inc 450 Blackbrook Rd .... Painesville OH 44077 440-856-7000
Web: www.acerecovery.com

Afni Inc 404 Brock Dr .... Bloomington IL 61702 309-828-5226
Web: www.afnicareers.com

AllianceOne Inc 4850 E St Rd Ste 300 .... Trevose PA 19053 215-354-5511 396-7255
TF: 866-405-7241 ■ *Web:* www.allianceoneinc.com

Allied International Credit Corp
16635 Young St Unit 26 .... Newmarket ON L3X1V6 877-451-2594 470-8155*
**Fax Area Code:* 905 ■ *TF:* 877-451-2594 ■ *Web:* www.aiccorp.com

American Accounts & Advisors
PO Box 250 .... Cottage Grove MN 55016 651-287-6100 287-6190
TF: 866-714-0489 ■ *Web:* www.amaccts.com

American Agencies Company Inc
21 E Ogden Ave Ste 201 .... Westmont IL 60559 630-493-1776 493-1781

Amsher Collection Services Inc
600 Beacon Pkwy W Ste 300 .... Birmingham AL 35209 205-322-4110
Web: www.amsher.com

Arthur p Jones & Associates Inc
98 Cottage St .... Easthampton MA 01027 413-527-2388
Web: www.apjones.com

Asset Acceptance Capital Corp (AACC)
28405 Van Dyke Ave .... Warren MI 48093 586-939-9600 446-7837
NASDAQ: AACC ■ *TF:* 800-545-9931 ■ *Web:* www.assetacceptance.com

Atlantic Credit & Finance Inc
2727 Franklin Rd .... Roanoke VA 24014 540-772-7800 772-7895
TF: 800-888-9419 ■ *Web:* www.atlanticcreditfinance.com

Phone | Fax

Berlin-Wheeler Inc 711 W McCarty St .... Jefferson City MO 65101 573-634-3030
Web: www.berlinwheeler.com

Bonneville Billing & Collection Inc
1186 East 4600 South Ste 100 .... Ogden UT 84403 801-621-7880 393-5808
TF: 888-621-7880 ■ *Web:* www.bonncoll.com

Brennan & Clark LLC 721 E Madison Ste 200 .... Villa Park IL 60181 630-279-7600
Web: brennanclark.com

Carter Business Service Inc 150A Andover St .... Danvers MA 01923 781-246-4300
Web: carterbusiness.com

CBV Collections 1200-100 Sheppard Ave E .... North York ON M2N6N5 416-482-9323
Web: www.cbvcollections.com

CBY Systems Inc 33 S Duke St .... York PA 17401 717-843-8685
Web: www.cby.com

Cc Columbia Collectors Inc
1104 Main St Ste 311 .... Vancouver WA 98660 360-694-7585
Web: columbiacollectors.com

Cedars Business Services LLC
24009 Ventura Blvd .... Calabasas CA 91302 818-224-3800
Web: www.cedarfinancial.com

Client Services Inc
3451 Harry S Truman Blvd .... St Charles MO 63301 636-947-2321

CMI Credit Mediators Inc 414 Sansom St .... Upper Darby PA 19082 610-352-5151
Web: www.cmiweb.com

Coast Professional Inc 214 Expo Cir Ste 7 .... West Monroe LA 71292 318-807-4500
Web: www.coastprofessional.net

Coldebt Collection Systems
Eight S Michigan Ave Ste 618 .... Chicago IL 60603 312-759-3804
Web: www.coldebtcollections.com

Collectcents Inc
1450 Meyerside Dr Second Fl .... Mississauga ON L5T2N5 905-670-7575
Web: www.collectcents.com

Collectcorp Corp 400 E Van Buren St Ste 700 .... Phoenix AZ 85004 602-443-2920 432-2923*
**Fax Area Code:* 888

Communications Credit & Recovery (CCR)
200 Garden City Plz Ste 200 .... Garden City NY 11530 516-294-6800 294-5682
Web: www.ccrcollect.com

Computer Credit Inc 640 W Fourth St .... Winston-Salem NC 27101 336-761-1524 761-8852
TF: 800-942-2995

Conrad Acceptance Corp 476 W Vermont Ave .... Escondido CA 92025 760-735-5000
Web: www.payconrad.com

Continental Service Group Inc
200 Cross Keys Office Pk .... Fairport NY 14450 585-421-1000
TF: 800-724-7500 ■ *Web:* www.conserve-arm.com

Credit Consulting Services Inc
201 John St Ste E .... Salinas CA 93901 831-424-0606
Web: www.creditconsultingservices.com

Credit Control Services Inc (CCS)
2 Wells Ave Ste 1 .... Newton MA 02459 617-965-2000 762-3035
TF: 800-526-0532 ■ *Web:* gsaadvantage.gov

Credit Management LP
4200 International Pkwy .... Carrollton TX 75007 800-377-7713 862-4440*
**Fax Area Code:* 972 ■ *TF:* 800-377-7713 ■ *Web:* www.thecmigroup.com

Creditors Adjustment Bureau-LC Financial (CABLCF)
14226 Ventura Blvd .... Sherman Oaks CA 91423 818-990-4800 780-3112
TF: 800-800-4523 ■ *Web:* www.lcf.net

Creditors Financial Group LLC
3131 S Vaughn Way Ste 110 .... Aurora CO 80014 303-369-2345
Web: www.creditorsfinancialgroup.com

Creditors Service Bureau Inc
3410 Sw Van Buren St Ste 101 .... Topeka KS 66611 785-266-3223
Web: tbcsoftware.com

Delmarva Collections Inc 820 E Main St .... Salisbury MD 21804 410-546-3742
Web: delmarvacollections.com

Denovus Corporation Ltd 480 Johnson Rd .... Washington PA 15301 724-250-1970
Web: www.denovus.com

Diversified Collection Services Inc
1080 S Harlan Rd .... Lathrop CA 95330 209-858-3500

Dun & Bradstreet Receivable Management Services
103 JFK Pkwy .... Short Hills NJ 07078 973-921-5500
Web: www.dnbasia.com

Dynamic Recovery Services Inc
4101 McEwen Rd Ste 150 .... Farmers Branch TX 75244 972-241-5611 484-3718
TF: 800-886-8088 ■ *Web:* www.drsinc.us

Encore Capital Group Inc
8875 Aero Dr Ste 200 .... San Diego CA 92123 858-560-2600 306-4443*
NASDAQ: ECPG ■ **Fax Area Code:* 800 ■ *TF:* 877-445-4581 ■ *Web:* www.encorecapital.com

Expert Global Solutions, Inc
507 Prudential Rd .... Horsham PA 19044 215-441-3000 441-3923
TF: 800-220-2274 ■ *Web:* www.ncogroup.com

Federated Adjustment Company Inc
7929 N Port Washington Rd .... Milwaukee WI 53217 414-228-0900
Web: facpaid.com

Fidelity Creditor Service Inc
216 S Louise St .... Glendale CA 91205 818-502-1981
Web: fcscollect.com

FMA Alliance Ltd 12339 Cutten Rd .... Houston TX 77066 281-931-5050
Web: www.fmaalliance.com

Focus Receivables Management LLC
1130 Northchase Pkwy Ste 150 .... Marietta GA 30067 678-305-9606 228-0019
TF: 877-362-8766 ■ *Web:* www.focusrm.com

GB Collects LLC 145 Bradford Dr .... West Berlin NJ 08091 856-768-9995
Web: www.gbcollects.com

GC Services LP 6330 Gulfton St .... Houston TX 77081 713-777-4441 776-6641
TF: 800-756-6524 ■ *Web:* www.gcserv.com

General Collection Inc
310 N Walnut PO Box 1423 .... Grand Island NE 68802 308-381-1423
Web: www.generalcollection.com

General Revenue Corp 4660 Duke Dr Ste 300 .... Mason OH 45040 800-234-6258 469-7428*
**Fax Area Code:* 513 ■ *TF:* 800-234-6258 ■ *Web:* www.generalrevenue.com

General Service Bureau Inc 8429 Blondo St .... Omaha NE 68134 402-255-5025
Web: www.gsbcollect.com

				Phone	Fax
Gulf Coast Collection Bureau Inc 5630 Marquesas Cir *TF:* 877-827-4820 ■ *Web:* www.gulfcoastcollection.com	Sarasota	FL	34233	941-927-6999	926-8872
Harvard Collection Services Inc 4839 N Elston Ave *Web:* www.harvardcollect.com	Chicago	IL	60630	773-283-7500	
Hill Top Collections Inc 38 W 32nd St Ste 1510 *TF:* 800-361-6871 ■ *Web:* businessfinder.silive.com	New York	NY	10001	212-564-2322	
Hospital Billing & Collection Service Ltd 118 Lukens Dr *TF:* 877-254-9580 ■ *Web:* www.hbcs.org	New Castle	DE	19720	302-552-8000	254-3750
I.C. System Inc 444 Hwy 96 E *Web:* www.icsystem.com	St. Paul	MN	55127	651-481-6333	
James, Stevens & Daniels Inc 1283 College Park Dr *Web:* www.jsdinc.net	Dover	DE	19904	302-735-4628	
Keybridge Medical Revenue Management 2348 Baton Rouge Ave *Web:* www.keybridgemed.com	Lima	OH	45805	419-879-4114	
Kings Credit Services 510 N Douty St *Web:* www.kingscredit.com	Hanford	CA	93230	559-587-4200	
Lamont, Hanley & Associates Inc 1138 Elm St *Web:* www.lhainc.com	Manchester	NH	03105	603-625-5547	
M G Credit Inc 5115 San Juan Ave *Web:* www.mgcredit.com	Jacksonville	FL	32210	904-387-6503	
Matthews Pierce & Lloyd Inc 830 Walker Rd Ste 12 *Web:* mpli.net	Dover	DE	19904	302-678-5500	
Med Shield Inc 2424 E 55th St *Web:* www.medshield.com	Indianapolis	IN	46220	317-613-3700	
Merchants & Medical Credit Corporation Inc 6324 Taylor Dr *Web:* www.mermed.com	Flint	MI	48507	810-239-3030	
MJ Altman Cos Inc 112 Se Ft King St *Web:* mjaltman.com	Ocala	FL	34471	352-732-1112	
Monarch Recovery Management Inc 10965 Decatur Rd *Web:* monarchrm.com	Philadelphia	PA	19154	215-281-7500	
Nationwide Credit Inc (NCI) 2002 Summit Blvd Ste 600 **Fax Area Code:* 770 ■ *TF:* 800-456-4729 ■ *Web:* www.ncirm.com	Atlanta	GA	30319	800-456-4729	612-7340*
Nationwide Recovery Systems Inc (NRS) 4635 McEwen Rd *TF:* 800-458-6357 ■ *Web:* www.nrs.us	Dallas	TX	75244	972-798-1000	798-1020
Northland Group Inc 7831 Glenroy Rd Ste 250 *Web:* www.northlandgroup.com	Edina	MN	55439	952-831-4005	
Payment America Systems Inc 450 10th Cir N *Web:* www.paymentamerica.com	Nashville	TN	37203	615-255-9200	
Penncro Associates Inc 95 James Way Ste 113 *Web:* www.penncro.com	Southampton	PA	18966	215-322-2438	
Pentagroup Financial LLC 5959 Corp Dr Ste 1400 *TF:* 800-385-9060 ■ *Web:* www.pentagroup.us	Houston	TX	77036	832-615-2100	
Pioneer Credit Recovery Inc 26 Edward St *Web:* www.pioneer-credit.com	Arcade	NY	14009	585-492-1234	
Portfolio Recovery Assoc LLC 120 Corporate Blvd Ste 100 Reverside Commerce Ctr *NASDAQ:* PRAA ■ **Fax Area Code:* 757 ■ *TF:* 888-772-7326 ■ *Web:* www.portfoliorecovery.com	Norfolk	VA	23502	888-772-7326	518-0901*
Quality Asset Recovery Seven Foster Ave *Web:* www.qarcollect.com	Gibbsboro	NJ	08026	856-925-1010	
Radius Global Solutions LLC 50 W Skippack Pk *Web:* www.radiusgs.com	Ambler	PA	19002	267-419-1111	
Receivable Management Inc 107 W Randol Mill Rd *Web:* receivablemanagement.net	Arlington	TX	76011	817-261-7534	
Recovery Partners LLC 4151 N Marshall Way Ste 12 *Web:* www.recoverypartners.com	Scottsdale	AZ	85251	480-747-9888	
Richmond North Assoc Inc 4232 Ridge Lea Rd Ste 12 *Web:* www.rnacollects.com	Amherst	NY	14226	716-832-5668	832-4236
Roquemore & Roquemore Inc 329 Oaks Trl Ste 212 *Web:* www.roquemore.com	Garland	TX	75043	972-226-9266	
Rose, Snyder & Jacobs LLP 15821 Ventura Blvd Ste 490 *Web:* rsjcpa.com	Encino	CA	91436	818-461-0600	
Sierra Receivables Management Inc 2500 Goodwater Ave *Web:* www.sierrareceivables.com	Redding	CA	96002	530-224-1360	
Stanislaus Credit Control Service Inc 914-14th St *Web:* www.sccscollects.com	Modesto	CA	95354	209-523-1813	
States Recovery Systems Inc 2951 Surrise Blvd Ste 100 *Web:* www.statesrecovery.com	Rancho Cordova	CA	95742	916-631-7085	
Stevens Business Service Inc 92 Bolt St Ste 1 *Web:* www.sbs4money.com	Lowell	MA	01852	978-458-2500	
Szabo Assoc Inc 3355 Lenox Rd NE Ste 945 *Web:* www.szabo.com	Atlanta	GA	30326	404-266-2464	
Todd, Bremer & Lawson Inc 560 S Herlong Ave *Web:* www.tbandl.com	Rock Hill	SC	29732	803-323-5200	
Total Credit Recovery Ltd 225 Yorkland Blvd *Web:* www.totalcrediting.com	Toronto	ON	M2J4Y7	416-774-4000	
Transmodus Corp 500 Esplanade Dr Ste 700 *Web:* www.transmodus.net	Oxnard	CA	93036	805-604-4472	
Transworld Systems Inc 2235 Mercury Way Ste 275 *TF:* 888-446-4733 ■ *Web:* www.transworldsystems.com	Santa Rosa	CA	95407	707-236-3800	
Tri-state Adjustments Inc 3439 East Ave S *Web:* www.wecollectmore.com	La Crosse	WI	54601	608-788-8683	
Tucker Albin & Assoc Inc 1702 N Collins Blvd *Web:* tuckeralbin.com	Richardson	TX	75080	469-424-3033	
Twenty-First Century Assoc 266 Summit Ave *TF:* 888-760-5052 ■ *Web:* www.tfc-associates.com	Hackensack	NJ	07601	201-678-1144	678-9088
Union Adjustment Company Inc 3214 W Burbank Blvd *Web:* www.unionadjustment.com	Burbank	CA	91505	818-566-8330	
Unique Management Services Inc 119 E Maple St *Web:* www.unique-mgmt.com	Jeffersonville	IN	47130	812-285-0886	
United Collection Bureau Inc 5620 Southwyck Blvd *Web:* ucbinc.com	Toledo	OH	43614	419-866-6227	
United Recovery Systems LP 5800 N Course Dr *TF:* 800-568-0399 ■ *Web:* www.unitedrecoverysystems.com	Houston	TX	77072	713-977-1234	977-0119
USCB Inc 3333 Wilshire Blvd *Web:* www.uscbinc.com	Los Angeles	CA	90010	213-387-6181	
Van Ru Credit Corp 1350 E Touhy Ave Ste 300E **Fax Area Code:* 847 ■ *TF:* 800-468-2678 ■ *Web:* www.vanru.com	Des Plaines	IL	60018	800-468-2678	673-5360*
Vengroff Williams & Assoc Inc (VWA) 2099 S State College Bvld *TF:* 800-238-9655 ■ *Web:* www.vwinc.com	Anaheim	CA	92806	866-737-4344	
Williams & Fudge Inc 300 Chatham Ave *Web:* wfcorp.com	Rock Hill	SC	29730	803-329-9791	
Williams, Charles & Scott Ltd 2171 Jericho Tpke LL1 *Web:* www.wcscollects.com	Commack	NY	11725	631-462-1553	

161 COLLEGES - BIBLE

SEE ALSO Colleges & Universities - Christian p. 1979

				Phone	Fax
Alaska Bible College 248 E Elmwood Ave *TF:* 800-478-7884 ■ *Web:* www.akbible.edu	Palmer	AK	99645	907-822-3201	822-5027
Allegheny Wesleyan College 2161 Woodsdale Rd *TF:* 800-292-3153 ■ *Web:* www.awc.edu	Salem	OH	44460	330-337-6403	337-6255
American Baptist College 1800 Baptist World Ctr Dr *Web:* www.abcnash.edu	Nashville	TN	37207	615-256-1463	226-7855
Baptist Bible College 538 VenaRd Rd *TF General:* 800-451-7664 ■ *Web:* www.bbc.edu	Clarks Summit	PA	18411	570-586-2400	585-9400
Baptist University of the Americas 8019 S Pan Am Expy *TF:* 800-721-1396 ■ *Web:* www.bua.edu	San Antonio	TX	78224	210-924-4338	924-2701
Barclay College 607 N Kingman St *TF:* 800-862-0226 ■ *Web:* www.barclaycollege.edu	Haviland	KS	67059	620-862-5252	862-5403
Bethesda Christian University 730 N Euclid *Web:* buc.edu	Anaheim	CA	92801	714-517-1945	
Beulah Heights Bible College 892 Berne St SE PO Box 18145 **Fax:* Admissions ■ *TF:* 888-777-2422 ■ *Web:* www.beulah.org	Atlanta	GA	30316	404-627-2681	627-0702*
Boise Bible College 8695 W Marigold St *TF:* 800-893-7755 ■ *Web:* www.boisebible.edu	Boise	ID	83714	208-376-7731	376-7743
Calvary Bible College & Theological Seminary 15800 Calvary Rd **Fax:* Admissions ■ *TF:* 800-326-3960 ■ *Web:* www.calvary.edu	Kansas City	MO	64147	816-322-3960	331-4474*
Central Christian College of the Bible 911 E Urbandale Dr *TF:* 888-263-3900 ■ *Web:* www.cccb.edu	Moberly	MO	65270	660-263-3900	263-3936
Cincinnati Christian University 2700 Glenway Ave *TF:* 800-949-4228 ■ *Web:* www.ccuniversity.edu	Cincinnati	OH	45204	513-244-8100	244-8140
Clear Creek Baptist Bible College 300 Clear Creek Rd *Web:* www.ccbbc.edu	Pineville	KY	40977	606-337-3196	337-2372
College of Biblical Studies-Houston 7000 Regency Sq Blvd Ste 110 *Web:* www.cbshouston.edu	Houston	TX	77036	713-785-5995	532-8150
Columbia International University 7435 Monticello Rd *TF:* 800-777-2227 ■ *Web:* www.ciu.edu	Columbia	SC	29203	803-754-4100	786-4209
Crossroads Bible College 601 N Shortridge Rd *TF:* 800-822-3119 ■ *Web:* www.crossroads.edu	Indianapolis	IN	46219	317-352-8736	352-9145
Crossroads College 920 Mayowood Rd SW *TF:* 800-456-7651 ■ *Web:* www.crossroadscollege.edu	Rochester	MN	55902	507-288-4563	288-9046
Crown College 8700 College View Dr *TF:* 800-682-7696 ■ *Web:* www.crown.edu	Saint Bonifacius	MN	55375	952-446-4100	446-4149
Dallas Christian College 2700 Christian Pkwy *TF:* 800-688-1029 ■ *Web:* www.dallas.edu	Dallas	TX	75234	972-241-3371	241-8021
Ecclesia College 9653 Nations Dr *TF:* 800-735-9926 ■ *Web:* ecollege.edu	Springdale	AR	72762	479-248-7236	248-1455
Emmaus Bible College 2570 Asbury Rd *TF:* 800-397-2425 ■ *Web:* www.emmaus.edu	Dubuque	IA	52001	563-588-8000	588-1216
Faith Baptist Bible College 1900 NW Fourth St *TF:* 800-409-3305 ■ *Web:* www.faith.edu	Ankeny	IA	50023	515-964-0601	964-1638
Florida Christian College 1011 Bill Beck Blvd **Fax Area Code:* 321 ■ *TF:* 888-468-6322 ■ *Web:* johnsonu.edu/florida	Kissimmee	FL	34744	407-847-8966	206-2007*
Free Will Baptist Bible College 3606 W End Ave *TF:* 800-763-9222 ■ *Web:* welch.edu	Nashville	TN	37205	615-844-5000	269-6028
God's Bible School & College 1810 Young St *TF:* 800-486-4637 ■ *Web:* www.gbs.edu	Cincinnati	OH	45202	513-721-7944	721-1357

				Phone	Fax
Grace Bible College 1011 Aldon St SW PO Box 910 *TF:* 800-968-1887 ■ *Web:* www.gbcol.edu	Grand Rapids	MI	49509	616-538-2330	538-0599
Grace University 1311 S Ninth St *TF:* 800-383-1422 ■ *Web:* www.graceuniversity.edu	Omaha	NE	68108	402-449-2800	341-9587
Great Lakes Christian College 6211 W Willow Hwy *TF Admissions:* 800-937-4522 ■ *Web:* www.glcc.edu	Lansing	MI	48917	517-321-0242	321-5902
Heritage Christian University 3625 Helton Dr PO Box HCU *TF:* 800-367-3565 ■ *Web:* www.hcu.edu	Florence	AL	35630	256-766-6610	760-0981
Hobe Sound Bible College PO Box 1065 *TF:* 800-881-5534 ■ *Web:* www.hsbc.edu	Hobe Sound	FL	33475	772-546-5534	545-1422
Johnson University 7900 Johnson Dr *TF:* 800-827-2122 ■ *Web:* www.johnsonu.edu	Knoxville	TN	37998	865-573-4517	251-2337
Kentucky Mountain Bible College 855 Hwy 541 PO Box 10 *TF:* 800-879-5622 ■ *Web:* www.kmbc.edu	Vancleve	KY	41385	606-693-5000	693-4884
King's College & Seminary 14800 Sherman Way *Web:* www.tku.edu	Van Nuys	CA	91405	818-779-8500	
Kuyper College 3333 E Beltline Ave NE *TF:* 800-511-3749 ■ *Web:* www.kuyper.edu	Grand Rapids	MI	49525	616-222-3000	222-3045
Lancaster Bible College 901 Eden Rd PO Box 83403 *TF:* 800-544-7335 ■ *Web:* www.lbc.edu	Lancaster	PA	17608	717-569-7071	560-8213
Laurel University 1215 Eastchester Dr *TF:* 855-528-7358 ■ *Web:* www.laureluniversity.edu	High Point	NC	27265	336-887-3000	889-2261
Life Pacific College 1100 W Covina Blvd *TF:* 877-886-5433 ■ *Web:* www.lifepacific.edu	San Dimas	CA	91773	909-599-5433	599-6690
Lincoln Christian College Seminary 100 Campus View Dr *TF:* 888-522-5228 ■ *Web:* lincolnchristian.edu	Lincoln	IL	62656	217-732-3168	732-4078
Manhattan Christian College 1415 Anderson Ave. *TF:* 877-246-4622 ■ *Web:* www.mccks.edu	Manhattan	KS	66502	785-539-3571	776-9251
Mid-Atlantic Christian Universit 715 N Poindexter St *TF:* 866-996-6228 ■ *Web:* www.macuniversity.edu/	Elizabeth City	NC	27909	252-334-2070	334-2071
Moody Bible Institute 820 N La Salle St **Fax:* Admissions ■ *TF:* 800-967-4624 ■ *Web:* www.moody.edu	Chicago	IL	60610	312-329-4400	329-8955*
Multnomah Bible College & Biblical Seminary 8435 NE Glisan St *TF:* 800-275-4672 ■ *Web:* www.multnomah.edu	Portland	OR	97220	503-255-0332	254-1268
Oak Hills Christian College 1600 Oak Hills Rd SW *TF:* 888-751-8670 ■ *Web:* www.oakhills.edu	Bemidji	MN	56601	218-751-8670	751-8825
Ozark Christian College 1111 N Main St *TF:* 800-299-4622 ■ *Web:* www.occ.edu	Joplin	MO	64801	417-624-2518	624-0090
Rosedale Bible College 2270 Rosedale Rd **Fax Area Code:* 877 ■ *Web:* www.rosedale.edu	Irwin	OH	43029	740-857-1311	857-1312*
Saint Louis Christian College 1360 Grandview Dr *TF Admissions:* 800-887-7522 ■ *Web:* www.slcconline.edu	Florissant	MO	63033	314-837-6777	837-8291
Southeastern Baptist College 4229 Hwy 15 N *Web:* www.southeasternbaptist.edu	Laurel	MS	39440	601-426-6346	426-6347
Toccoa Falls College 107 Kincaid Dr *TF General:* 800-868-3257 ■ *Web:* www.tfc.edu	Toccoa Falls	GA	30598	706-886-6831	282-6012
Tri-State Bible College 506 Margaret St *TF:* 800-333-3243 ■ *Web:* www.tsbc.edu	South Point	OH	45680	740-377-2520	377-0001
Trinity Bible College 50 Sixth Ave N *TF:* 800-523-1603 ■ *Web:* www.trinitybiblecollege.edu	Ellendale	ND	58436	701-349-3621	349-5786
Trinity College of Florida 2430 Welbilt Blvd *TF:* 800-388-0869 ■ *Web:* www.trinitycollege.edu	Trinity	FL	34655	727-376-6911	569-1410
Washington Bible College/Capital Bible Seminary 6511 Princess Garden Pkwy *TF:* 877-793-7227 ■ *Web:* www.bible.edu	Lanham	MD	20706	301-552-1400	552-2775
Zion Bible College 27 Middle Hwy *TF:* 800-356-4014 ■ *Web:* northpoint.edu	Barrington	RI	02806	401-246-0900	246-0906

162 COLLEGES - COMMUNITY & JUNIOR

SEE ALSO Colleges - Fine Arts p. 1977; Colleges - Tribal p. 1978; Colleges & Universities - Four-Year p. 1980; Vocational & Technical Schools p. 3287

Institutions that offer academic degrees that can be transferred to a four-year college or university.

				Phone	Fax
Morris Brown College 643 Martin Luther King Jr Dr *Web:* www.morrisbrown.edu	Atlanta	GA	30314	404-739-1010	
Mediatech Institute of Austin 4719 s congress ave. *Web:* mediatech.edu	Austin	TX	78745	512-447-2002	
Delta College of Arts & Technology 7380 Exchange Pl *Web:* www.deltacollege.com	Baton Rouge	LA	70806	225-928-7770	
Loyalist College Wallbridge-Loyalist Rd *Web:* www.loyalistc.on.ca	Belleville	ON	K8N5B9	613-969-1913	
Manatee Technical Institute East Campus 5520 lakewood ranch blvd *Web:* www.manateetechnicalinstitute.org	Bradenton	FL	34211	941-752-8100	
Southern Alberta Institute of Technology 1301 16th Ave NW Ste 107 *Web:* www.sait.ca	Calgary	AB	T2M0L4	403-284-7248	
Kaskaskia College 27210 College Rd *Web:* kaskaskia.edu	Centralia	IL	62801	618-545-3090	
Holland College 140 Weymouth St *Web:* www.hollandc.pe.ca	Charlottetown	PE	C1A4Z1	902-566-9510	
Universidad Popular 2801 S Hamlin Ave *Web:* www.universidadpopular.us	Chicago	IL	60623	773-733-5055	
Us Health Connect Inc 500 Office Ctr Dr *TF:* 800-889-4944 ■ *Web:* www.omniaeducation.com	Fort Washington	PA	19034	800-889-4944	
County Regional Vocational Sch 147 Pond St *Web:* www.tri-county.tc	Franklin	MA	02038	508-528-5400	
State Center Community College District 1525 e weldon ave *Web:* www.scccd.edu	Fresno	CA	93704	559-226-0720	
Mohawk College of Applied Arts & Technology 135 Fennell Ave W West Fifth St *Web:* www.mohawkcollege.ca	Hamilton	ON	L8C1E9	905-575-1212	
Chabot College 25555 Hesperian Blvd *Web:* www.chabotcollege.edu	Hayward	CA	94545	925-485-5215	
Okanagan College 1000 KLO Rd *Web:* www.okanagan.bc.ca	Kelowna	BC	V1Y4X8	250-762-5445	
Queen's School of Business Queen's University 143 Union St *Web:* business.queensu.ca	Kingston	ON	K7L3N6	613-533-2330	
A.T. Still University of Health Sciences 800 W Jefferson St *Web:* www.atsu.edu	Kirksville	MO	63501	660-626-2121	
Fleming College 200 Albert St S *Web:* flemingcollege.ca	Lindsay	ON	K9V5E6	705-324-9144	
Ata Career Education 10180 Linn Sta Rd Ste A200 *Web:* www.ata.edu	Louisville	KY	40223	502-371-8330	
Manhattan Area Technical College 3136 Dickens *Web:* manhattantech.edu	Manhattan	KS	66503	785-587-2800	
College De Rosemont 6400 16e Ave *Web:* www.crosemont.qc.ca	Montreal	QC	H1X2S9	514-376-1620	
Ecole des Hautes Etudes Commerciales de Montreal 3000 chemin de la Cote-Sainte-Catherine *Web:* www.hec.ca	Montreal	QC	H3T2A7	514-340-6000	
Ecole Polytechnique de Montreal 2900 Boul Edouard-Montpetit *Web:* www.polymtl.ca	Montreal	QC	H3T1J4	514-340-4711	
Buckeye Career Center 545 University Dr Ne *Web:* www.buckeyecareercenter.org	New Philadelphia	OH	44663	330-339-2288	
Justice Institute of British Columbia 715 McBride Blvd *Web:* www.jibc.bc.ca	New Westminster	BC	V3L5T4	604-525-5422	
Swedish Institute Inc 226 W 26th St Fl 5 *Web:* www.swedishinstitute.edu	New York	NY	10001	212-924-5900	
Olds College 4500-50 St *Web:* www.oldscollege.ab.ca	Olds	AB	T4H1R6	403-556-8281	
Willis College of Business & Technology 85 O'Connor St *Web:* williscollege.com	Ottawa	ON	K1P5M6	613-233-1128	
William Carey International University 1539 e howard st *Web:* www.global-prayer-digest.com	Pasadena	CA	91104	626-797-1200	
Western University of Health Sciences 309 E Second St *Web:* www.westernu.edu	Pomona	CA	91766	909-623-6116	
Eastwick Colleges Inc 10 S Franklin Tpke *Web:* www.eastwickcollege.edu	Ramsey	NJ	07446	201-327-8877	
Cegep De Sainte-Foy 2410 Ch Sainte-Foy *Web:* www.cegep-ste-foy.qc.ca	Sainte-foy	QC	G1V1T2	418-659-6600	
St. Mary's University San Antonio One Camino Santa Maria *Web:* www.rattlerbooks.com	San Antonio	TX	78228	210-436-3011	
Lambton College of Applied Arts & Technology, The 1457 London Rd *Web:* www.lambton.on.ca	Sarnia	ON	N7S6K4	519-542-7751	
Saskatoon Business College Ltd 221 Third Ave N *Web:* www.sbccollege.ca	Saskatoon	SK	S7K2H7	306-244-6333	
Sault College of Applied Arts & Technology, The 443 Northern Ave *Web:* www.saultcollege.ca	Sault Ste. Marie	ON	P6A5L3	705-759-6700	
Rio Salado College 2323 W 14Th St *Web:* www.riosalado.edu	Tempe	AZ	85281	480-517-8000	
Cegep De Thetford 671 Boul Frontenac O *Web:* www.cegepth.qc.ca	Thetford Mines	QC	G6G1N1	418-338-8591	
College of Nurses of Ontario 101 Davenport Rd *Web:* www.cno.org	Toronto	ON	M5R3P1	416-928-0900	
Herzing College Toronto 220 Yonge St Eaton Centre Galleria Offices Ste 202 *Web:* www.herzing.ca	Toronto	ON	M5B2H1	416-599-6996	
Ashton College 1190 Melville St *Web:* www.ashtoncollege.com	Vancouver	BC	V6E3W1	604-899-0803	
Faculty of Education University of British Columbia 2125 Main Mall *Web:* educ.ubc.ca	Vancouver	BC	V6T1Z4	604-822-5242	
Langara College 100 W 49th Ave *Web:* www.langara.bc.ca	Vancouver	BC	V5Y2Z6	604-323-5511	
Vancouver Community College 1155 E Broadway *Web:* www.vcc.ca	Vancouver	BC	V5T4V5	604-871-7000	
Camosun College 3100 Foul Bay Rd *Web:* camosun.ca	Victoria	BC	V8P4X8	250-370-3018	
Niagara College of Applied Arts & Technology 300 Woodlawn Rd *Web:* www.niagaracollege.ca	Welland	ON	L3C7L3	905-641-2252	
St. Clair College of Applied Arts & Technology, The 2000 Talbot Rd W *Web:* www.stclairc.on.ca	Windsor	ON	N9A6S4	519-966-1656	

Phone Fax

Perry Technical Institute
2011 W Washington Ave. . . . Yakima WA 98903 509-453-0374
Web: www.perrytech.edu

Alabama

Phone Fax

Central Alabama Community College
1675 Cherokee Rd . . . . Alexander City AL 35010 256-234-6346 215-4244
TF: 800-643-2657 ■ *Web:* www.cacc.edu

Lurleen B Wallace Community College
Andalusia 1000 Dannelly Blvd PO Box 1418 . . . . Andalusia AL 36420 334-222-6591 881-2201*
**Fax:* Admissions ■ *TF:* 877-382-4357 ■ *Web:* www.lbwcc.edu
Atmore 6574 Hwy 21 N . . . . Atmore AL 36504 251-368-7610 368-7667
Web: www.jdcc.edu

Faulkner State Community College
Bay Minette 1900 Hwy 31 S. . . . Bay Minette AL 36507 251-580-2111 580-2134
TF: 800-381-3722 ■ *Web:* www.faulknerstate.edu

Jefferson State Community College
2601 Carson Rd . . . . Birmingham AL 35215 205-853-1200 856-6070*
**Fax:* Admissions ■ *TF:* 800-239-5900 ■ *Web:* www.jeffstateonline.com

Snead State Community College
220 N Walnut St PO Box 734 . . . . Boaz AL 35957 256-593-5120 593-7180*
**Fax:* Admissions ■ *Web:* www.snead.edu

Jefferson Davis Community College
Brewton 220 Alco Dr . . . . Brewton AL 36426 251-867-4832 809-1596
Web: www.jdcc.edu
Childersburg 34091 US Hwy 280 . . . . Childersburg AL 35044 256-378-5576 378-2027
Web: www.cacc.edu

Wallace Community College 1141 Wallace Dr . . . . Dothan AL 36303 334-983-3521 983-6066*
**Fax:* Admissions ■ *TF:* 800-543-2426 ■ *Web:* www.wallace.edu

Enterprise State Community College (ESCC)
600 Plz Dr. . . . . Enterprise AL 36330 334-347-2623 393-6223
Web: www.escc.edu
Fairhope 440 Fairhope Ave . . . . Fairhope AL 36532 251-990-0420 580-2285*
**Fax:* Admissions ■ *TF:* 800-231-3752 ■ *Web:* www.faulknerstate.edu

Gadsden State Community College
1001 George Wallace Dr PO Box 227 . . . . Gadsden AL 35902 256-549-8200 549-8205*
**Fax:* Admissions ■ *TF:* 800-226-5563 ■ *Web:* www.gadsdenstate.edu
Gulf Shores 3301 Gulf Shores Pkwy . . . . Gulf Shores AL 36542 251-968-3101 968-3120
TF: 800-231-3752 ■ *Web:* www.faulknerstate.edu

Wallace State Community College
801 Main St . . . . Hanceville AL 35077 256-352-8000 352-8129
TF: 866-350-9722 ■ *Web:* www.wallacestate.edu
Huntsville 102B Wynn Dr. . . . . Huntsville AL 35805 256-890-4701 890-4775*
**Fax:* Admissions ■ *TF:* 800-626-3628 ■ *Web:* www.calhoun.edu

Bevill State Community College
Jasper 1411 Indiana Ave . . . . Jasper AL 35501 205-387-0511 387-5191*
**Fax:* Admissions ■ *TF:* 800-648-3271 ■ *Web:* www.bscc.edu

Marion Military Institute 1101 Washington St . . . . Marion AL 36756 334-683-2306 683-2383
TF: 800-664-1842 ■ *Web:* www.marionmilitary.edu
Baker-Gaines Central 1365 Dr ML King Jr Ave . . . . Mobile AL 36603 251-662-5400 405-4427
Web: bishop.edu

Bishop State Community College
Southwest 925 Dauphin Island Pkwy. . . . . Mobile AL 36605 251-665-4100
Web: bishop.edu

Northwest-Shoals Community College
Muscle Shoals 800 George Wallace Blvd. . . . . Muscle Shoals AL 35661 256-331-5200 331-5366*
**Fax:* Admissions ■ *Web:* www.nwscc.edu

Southern Union State Community College
Opelika 1701 Lafayette Pkwy . . . . Opelika AL 36801 334-745-6437 742-9418*
**Fax:* Admissions ■ *TF:* 800-707-0057 ■ *Web:* www.suscc.edu

Chattahoochee Valley Community College
2602 College Dr . . . . Phenix City AL 36869 334-291-4900 291-4994*
**Fax:* Admissions ■ *Web:* www.cv.edu
Phil Campbell 2080 College Rd. . . . . Phil Campbell AL 35581 256-331-6200 331-6272*
**Fax:* Admissions ■ *TF:* 800-645-8967 ■ *Web:* www.nwscc.edu

Northeast Alabama Community College
PO Box 159 . . . . Rainsville AL 35986 256-228-6001 228-6861
TF: 866-572-5433 ■ *Web:* www.nacc.edu

Calhoun Community College
Redstone Arsenal 6250 Hwy 31 N . . . . Tanner AL 35671 256-306-2500 306-2941
TF: 800-626-3628 ■ *Web:* www.calhoun.edu

Alabama Southern Community College
30755 Hwy 43 . . . . Thomasville AL 36784 334-636-9642 636-1380
TF: 866-901-1117 ■ *Web:* www.ascc.edu

Shelton State Community College
9500 Old Greensboro Rd . . . . Tuscaloosa AL 35405 205-391-2211 391-3910*
**Fax:* Admissions ■ *Web:* www.sheltonstate.edu
Valley 321 Fob James Dr. . . . . Valley AL 36854 334-756-4151 756-5183*
**Fax:* Admissions ■ *TF:* 800-707-0057 ■ *Web:* www.suscc.edu

Alaska

Phone Fax

University of Alaska Southeast Ketchikan
2600 Seventh Ave. . . . . Ketchikan AK 99901 907-225-6177 225-3624
TF: 877-465-6400 ■ *Web:* www.ketch.alaska.edu

University of Alaska Anchorage Kodiak College
117 Benny Benson Dr. . . . . Kodiak AK 99615 907-486-4161 486-1264
TF: 800-486-7660 ■ *Web:* www.koc.alaska.edu
Northwest 400 E Front St PO Box 400 . . . . Nome AK 99762 907-443-2201 443-5602
TF: 800-478-2202 ■ *Web:* www.nwc.uaf.edu

University of Alaska Southeast Sitka
1332 Seward Ave . . . . Sitka AK 99835 907-747-6653 747-7768
TF: 800-478-6653 ■ *Web:* www.uas.alaska.edu

University of Alaska Anchorage Kenai Peninsula College
156 College Rd. . . . . Soldotna AK 99669 877-262-0330 262-0322*
**Fax Area Code:* 907 ■ *TF:* 877-262-0330 ■ *Web:* www.kpc.alaska.edu

Arizona

Phone Fax

Estrella Mountain Community College
3000 N Dysart Rd . . . . Avondale AZ 85323 623-935-8000 935-8870*
**Fax:* Admissions ■ *Web:* www.emc.maricopa.edu
Bullhead City 3400 Hwy 95 . . . . Bullhead City AZ 86442 928-758-3926 704-9460
TF: 866-664-2832 ■ *Web:* www.mohave.edu

Chandler-Gilbert Community College
Pecos 2626 E Pecos Rd . . . . Chandler AZ 85225 480-732-7000 732-7099*
**Fax:* Admissions ■ *Web:* www.cgc.maricopa.edu
Verde Valley 601 Black Hills Dr . . . . Clarkdale AZ 86324 928-634-7501 634-6549*
**Fax:* Admissions ■ *TF:* 800-922-6787 ■ *Web:* www.yc.edu

Mohave Community College
North Mohave PO Box 980 . . . . Colorado City AZ 86021 928-875-2799 875-2831*
**Fax:* Admissions ■ *TF:* 800-678-3992 ■ *Web:* www.mohave.edu

Central Arizona College 8470 N Overfield Rd . . . . Coolidge AZ 85228 520-494-5444 494-5083*
**Fax:* Admissions ■ *TF:* 800-237-9814 ■ *Web:* www.centralaz.edu

Cochise College 4190 W Hwy 80 . . . . Douglas AZ 85607 520-364-7943 417-4006*
**Fax:* Admissions ■ *TF:* 800-966-7943 ■ *Web:* cochise.edu

Coconino Community College
Lonetree 2800 S Lone Tree Rd . . . . Flagstaff AZ 86001 928-527-1222 226-4110*
**Fax:* Admissions ■ *TF:* 800-350-7122 ■ *Web:* www.coconino.edu

Glendale Community College 6000 W Olive Ave . . . . Glendale AZ 85302 623-845-3000 845-3303*
**Fax:* Admissions ■ *Web:* www2.gccaz.edu
North 5727 W Happy Vly Rd . . . . Glendale AZ 85310 623-845-4000 845-4010
Web: www.gc.maricopa.edu/gccnorth

Northland Pioneer College PO Box 610 . . . . Holbrook AZ 86025 928-532-6111 536-3382*
**Fax:* Admissions ■ *TF:* 800-266-7845 ■ *Web:* www.npc.edu
Lake Havasu 1977 W Acoma Blvd . . . . Lake Havasu City AZ 86403 928-855-7812 680-5955*
**Fax:* Admissions ■ *TF:* 866-664-2832 ■ *Web:* www.mohave.edu
Williams 7360 E Tahoe Ave . . . . Mesa AZ 85212 480-988-8000 988-8993
Web: www.cgc.maricopa.edu

Mesa Community College 1833 W Southern Ave. . . . . Mesa AZ 85202 480-461-7000 461-7321*
**Fax:* Admissions ■ *TF:* 866-532-4983 ■ *Web:* mesacc.edu/
Red Mountain 7110 E McKellips Rd . . . . Mesa AZ 85207 480-654-7200 654-7379
Web: mesacc.edu/

GateWay Community College 108 N 40th St . . . . Phoenix AZ 85034 602-286-8000 286-8072
TF: 888-994-4433 ■ *Web:* www.gatewaycc.edu

Paradise Valley Community College
18401 N 32nd St . . . . Phoenix AZ 85032 602-787-6500 787-7025*
**Fax:* Admissions ■ *Web:* paradisevalley.edu

Phoenix College 1202 W Thomas Rd . . . . Phoenix AZ 85013 602-285-7800 285-7700
Web: www.phoenixcollege.edu

South Mountain Community College
7050 S 24th St . . . . Phoenix AZ 85042 602-243-8000 243-8199*
**Fax:* Admissions ■ *TF:* 855-622-2332 ■ *Web:* www.southmountaincc.edu

Yavapai College 1100 E Sheldon St . . . . Prescott AZ 86301 928-445-7300 776-2151*
**Fax:* Admissions ■ *TF:* 800-922-6787 ■ *Web:* www.yc.edu

Scottsdale Community College
9000 E Chaparral Rd. . . . . Scottsdale AZ 85256 480-423-6000 423-6200*
**Fax:* Admissions ■ *TF:* 800-784-2433 ■ *Web:* www.scottsdalecc.edu
Sierra Vista 901 N Colombo Ave . . . . Sierra Vista AZ 85635 520-515-0500 515-5452*
**Fax:* Admissions ■ *TF:* 800-966-7943 ■ *Web:* cochise.edu

Eastern Arizona College 615 N Stadium Ave. . . . . Thatcher AZ 85552 928-428-8472 428-2578
TF: 800-678-3808 ■ *Web:* www.eac.edu
Desert Vista 5901 S Calle Santa Cruz . . . . Tucson AZ 85709 520-206-5030 206-5050*
**Fax:* Admissions ■ *Web:* pima.edu
East 8181 E Irvington Rd . . . . Tucson AZ 85709 520-206-7000 206-7875*
**Fax:* Admissions ■ *Web:* ecc.pima.edu

Pima Community College
West 2202 W Anklam Rd . . . . Tucson AZ 85709 520-206-6600 206-6728*
**Fax:* Admissions ■ *TF:* 800-860-7462 ■ *Web:* www.pima.edu

Arizona Western College 2020 S Ave 8 E . . . . Yuma AZ 85366 928-317-6000 344-7543
TF: 888-293-0392 ■ *Web:* www.azwestern.edu

Arkansas

Phone Fax

NorthWest Arkansas Community College
One College Dr. . . . . Bentonville AR 72712 479-636-9222 619-2229*
**Fax:* Admissions ■ *TF:* 800-995-6922 ■ *Web:* www.nwacc.edu

Arkansas Northeastern College
2501 S Div St PO Box 1109 . . . . Blytheville AR 72316 870-762-1020 763-1654*
**Fax:* Admissions ■ *Web:* www.anc.edu

South Arkansas Community College
PO Box 7010 . . . . El Dorado AR 71731 870-862-8131 864-7134*
**Fax:* Admissions ■ *TF:* 800-955-2289 ■ *Web:* www.southark.edu

East Arkansas Community College
1700 Newcastle Rd. . . . . Forrest City AR 72335 870-633-4480 633-3840*
**Fax:* Admissions ■ *Web:* www.eacc.edu

North Arkansas College 1515 Pioneer Dr . . . . Harrison AR 72601 870-743-3000 391-3339
TF: 800-679-6622 ■ *Web:* www.northark.edu

Phillips Community College PO Box 785 . . . . Helena AR 72342 870-338-6474 338-7542
Web: www.pccua.edu

National Park Community College
101 College Dr. . . . . Hot Springs AR 71913 501-760-4222 760-4236*
**Fax:* Admissions ■ *TF:* 800-760-1825 ■ *Web:* www.npcc.edu

Ouachita Technical College 1 College Cir . . . . Malvern AR 72104 501-337-5000 337-9382
Web: coto.edu

Ozarka College 218 College Dr . . . . Melbourne AR 72556 870-368-7371 368-2091
TF: 800-821-4335 ■ *Web:* www.ozarka.edu

Rich Mountain Community College 1100 College Dr . . . . Mena AR 71953 479-394-7622 394-2760*
**Fax:* Admissions ■ *Web:* www.rmcc.edu

Arkansas State University Mountain Home
1600 S College St. . . . . Mountain Home AR 72653 870-508-6100 508-6287
Web: www.asumh.edu

Arkansas State University Newport
7648 Victory Blvd . . . . Newport AR 72112 870-512-7800 512-7825*
**Fax:* Admissions ■ *TF:* 800-976-1676 ■ *Web:* www.asun.edu

Phone Fax

Pulaski Technical College
3000 W Scenic Dr. .... North Little Rock AR 72118 501-812-2200 771-2844
Web: www.pulaskitech.edu

Shorter College 604 N Locust St .... North Little Rock AR 72114 501-374-6305 374-9333*

Crowley's Ridge College 100 College Dr. .... Paragould AR 72450 870-236-6901 236-7748*
**Fax:* Admissions ■ *TF:* 800-264-1096 ■ *Web:* www.crc.edu

Southeast Arkansas College 1900 Hazel St .... Pine Bluff AR 71603 870-543-5915
TF: 888-732-7582

Black River Technical College
1410 Hwy 304 E .... Pocahontas AR 72455 870-248-4000 248-4100
TF: 866-890-6933 ■ *Web:* www.blackrivertech.org

Mid-South Community College
2000 W Broadway .... West Memphis AR 72301 870-733-6722 733-6719*
**Fax:* Admissions ■ *Web:* www.midsouthcc.edu

California

Phone Fax

College of Alameda
555 Ralph Appezzato Meml Pkwy .... Alameda CA 94501 510-522-7221 769-6019
Web: www.alameda.peralta.edu

Cabrillo College 6500 Soquel Dr. .... Aptos CA 95003 831-479-6100 479-5782*
**Fax:* Admitting ■ *TF:* 800-218-0013 ■ *Web:* www.cabrillo.edu

Bakersfield College 1801 Panorama Dr. .... Bakersfield CA 93305 661-395-4011 395-4500*
**Fax:* Admissions ■ *Web:* www.bakersfieldcollege.edu

Barstow College 2700 Barstow Rd .... Barstow CA 92311 760-252-2411 252-1875
TF: 877-823-2378 ■ *Web:* barstow.edu

Berkeley City College 2050 Ctr St .... Berkeley CA 94704 510-981-2800 841-7333
Web: berkeleycitycollege.edu

Cerro Coso Community College
Bishop 4090 W Line St .... Bishop CA 93514 760-872-1565 872-5319*
**Fax:* Admissions ■ *TF:* 888-537-6932 ■ *Web:* www.cerrocoso.edu

Palo Verde College One College Dr .... Blythe CA 92225 760-921-5500 921-3608*
**Fax:* Admissions ■ *Web:* www.paloverde.edu

MiraCosta College
San Elijo 3333 Manchester Ave .... Cardiff CA 92007 760-944-4449 634-7875
TF: 888-201-8480 ■ *Web:* www.miracosta.cc.ca.us

Southwestern College 900 Otay Lakes Rd. .... Chula Vista CA 91910 619-421-6700 482-6489*
**Fax:* Admissions ■ *TF:* 866-262-9881 ■ *Web:* swccd.edu
Coalinga 300 Cherry Ln. .... Coalinga CA 93210 559-934-2000 935-3788*
**Fax:* Admissions ■ *TF:* 800-266-1114 ■ *Web:* www.westhillscollege.com

El Camino College
Compton Ctr 1111 E Artesia Blvd .... Compton CA 90221 310-900-1600
Web: www.compton.edu

Orange Coast College
2701 Fairview Rd PO Box 5005 .... Costa Mesa CA 92628 714-432-0202 432-5957*
**Fax:* Admissions ■ *Web:* orangecoastcollege.edu
Del Norte 883 W Washington Blvd. .... Crescent City CA 95531 707-465-2300 464-6867*
**Fax:* Admissions ■ *TF:* 800-641-0400 ■ *Web:* www.redwoods.edu

West Los Angeles College
9000 Overland Ave .... Culver City CA 90230 310-287-4200 287-4327*
**Fax:* Admissions ■ *Web:* www.wlac.edu

DeAnza College 21250 Stevens Creek Blvd .... Cupertino CA 95014 408-864-5678 864-8329*
**Fax:* Admissions ■ *Web:* www.deanza.edu

Cypress College 9200 Vly View St .... Cypress CA 90630 714-484-7000 484-7446*
**Fax:* Admissions ■ *Web:* www.cypresscollege.edu
South Kern 140 Methusa Ave. .... Edwards AFB CA 93524 661-258-8644 258-0651*
**Fax:* Admissions ■ *Web:* www.cerrocoso.edu/sk

Cuyamaca College 900 Rancho San Diego Pkwy .... El Cajon CA 92019 619-660-4000 660-4575*
**Fax:* Admissions ■ *TF:* 800-234-1597 ■ *Web:* www.cuyamaca.net

Grossmont College 8800 Grossmont College Dr .... El Cajon CA 92020 619-644-7000 644-7933*
**Fax:* Admissions ■ *Web:* www.grossmont.edu

College of the Redwoods 7351 Tompkins Hill Rd .... Eureka CA 95501 707-476-4100 476-4406*
**Fax:* Admissions ■ *TF:* 800-641-0400 ■ *Web:* www.redwoods.edu

Solano Community College
4000 Suisun Vly Rd .... Fairfield CA 94534 707-864-7171 864-7175*
**Fax:* Admissions ■ *Web:* www.solano.edu
Mendocino Coast 440 Alger St .... Fort Bragg CA 95437 707-962-2600 961-0943
TF: 800-641-0400 ■ *Web:* www.redwoods.edu

Coastline Community College
11460 Warner Ave .... Fountain Valley CA 92708 714-546-7600 241-6288*
**Fax:* Admissions ■ *TF:* 866-422-2645 ■ *Web:* www.coastline.edu

Ohlone College 43600 Mission Blvd .... Fremont CA 94539 510-659-6000 659-7321*
**Fax:* Admissions ■ *Web:* www.ohlone.edu

Queen of the Holy Rosary College
43326 Mission Blvd .... Fremont CA 94539 510-657-2468 657-1734*
**Fax:* Admissions ■ *Web:* www.msjdominicans.org

Fresno City College 1101 E University Ave. .... Fresno CA 93741 559-442-4600 237-4232*
**Fax:* Admissions ■ *TF:* 866-245-3276 ■ *Web:* www.fresnocitycollege.edu

Fullerton College 321 E Chapman Ave .... Fullerton CA 92832 714-992-7000 870-7751*
**Fax:* Admissions ■ *Web:* www.fullcoll.edu

Gavilan College 5055 Santa Teresa Blvd .... Gilroy CA 95020 408-847-1400 846-4940*
**Fax:* Admissions ■ *Web:* www.gavilan.edu

Citrus College 1000 W Foothill Blvd .... Glendora CA 91741 626-963-0323 914-8613*
**Fax:* Admissions ■ *Web:* www.citruscollege.edu

Sierra College
Nevada County 250 Sierra College Dr .... Grass Valley CA 95945 530-274-5300 274-5324*
**Fax:* Admissions ■ *TF:* 800-242-4004 ■ *Web:* www.sierracollege.edu

Golden West College
15744 Golden W St PO Box 2748 .... Huntington Beach CA 92647 714-892-7711 895-8960*
**Fax:* Admissions ■ *Web:* www.goldenwestcollege.edu

Imperial Valley College
380 E Atten Rd PO Box 158 .... Imperial CA 92251 760-352-8320 355-2663*
**Fax:* Admissions ■ *Web:* www.imperial.edu

Irvine Valley College 5500 Irvine Ctr Dr .... Irvine CA 92618 949-451-5100 451-5443*
**Fax:* Admissions ■ *Web:* www.ivc.edu

Copper Mountain College 6162 Rotary Way .... Joshua Tree CA 92252 760-366-3791 366-5255
Web: www.cmccd.edu

College of Marin 835 College Ave. .... Kentfield CA 94904 415-457-8811 460-0773*
**Fax:* Admissions ■ *Web:* www.marin.edu

Phone Fax

Kern River Valley
5520 Lk Isabella Blvd. .... Lake Isabella CA 93240 760-379-5501 379-5547*
**Fax:* Admissions ■ *TF:* 888-537-6932 ■ *Web:* www.cerrocoso.edu

Antelope Valley College 3041 W Ave K .... Lancaster CA 93536 661-722-6300 722-6531*
**Fax:* Admissions ■ *Web:* www.avc.edu

West Hills College
Lemoore 555 College Ave .... Lemoore CA 93245 559-925-3000 924-1539
Web: www.westhillscollege.com

Las Positas College 3033 Collier Canyon Rd .... Livermore CA 94551 925-424-1000 443-0742
Web: www.laspositascollege.edu

Allan Hancock College
Lompoc Valley One Hancock Dr. .... Lompoc CA 93436 805-735-3366
Web: hancockcollege.edu

Long Beach City College 4901 E Carson St .... Long Beach CA 90808 562-938-4111 938-4858*
**Fax:* Admissions ■ *TF:* 888-442-4551 ■ *Web:* www.lbcc.edu

Foothill College 12345 El Monte Rd .... Los Altos Hills CA 94022 650-949-7777 949-7048*
**Fax:* Admissions ■ *TF:* 800-234-1597 ■ *Web:* www.foothill.edu

Los Angeles City College
855 N Vermont Ave. .... Los Angeles CA 90029 323-953-4000 953-4013*
**Fax:* Admissions ■ *TF:* 800-266-6883 ■ *Web:* www.lacitycollege.edu

Los Angeles Southwest College
1600 W Imperial Hwy .... Los Angeles CA 90047 323-241-5225
Web: www.lasc.edu

Los Angeles Trade Technical College
400 W Washington Blvd .... Los Angeles CA 90015 213-763-7000 763-5386*
**Fax:* Admissions ■ *Web:* college.lattc.edu

Mount Saint Mary's University Doheny
10 Chester Pl .... Los Angeles CA 90007 213-477-2500 477-2569*
**Fax:* Admissions ■ *TF Admissions:* 800 999 9893 ■ *Web:* www.msmc.la.edu
Mammoth 101 College Pkwy PO Box 1865 .. Mammoth Lakes CA 93546 760-934-2875 924-1613*
**Fax:* Admissions ■ *TF:* 888-537-6932 ■ *Web:* www.cerrocoso.edu

Merced College 3600 M St .... Merced CA 95348 209-384-6000 384-6339*
**Fax:* Admissions ■ *TF:* 800-784-2433 ■ *Web:* www.mccd.edu

Saddleback College
28000 Marguerite Pkwy .... Mission Viejo CA 92692 949-582-4500 347-8315*
**Fax:* Admissions ■ *Web:* www.saddleback.edu

Modesto Junior College 435 College Ave .... Modesto CA 95350 209-575-6550 575-6859*
**Fax:* Admissions ■ *Web:* www.mjc.edu

Monterey Peninsula College 980 Fremont St. .... Monterey CA 93940 831-646-4000 646-4015*
**Fax:* Admissions ■ *TF:* 877-663-5433 ■ *Web:* www.mpc.edu

East Los Angeles College
1301 Avenida Cesar Chavez .... Monterey Park CA 91754 323-265-8650 265-8688*
**Fax:* Admissions ■ *Web:* www.elac.edu

Moorpark College 7075 Campus Rd. .... Moorpark CA 93021 805-378-1400 378-1583*
**Fax:* Admissions ■ *Web:* moorparkcollege.edu
Moreno Valley 16130 Lasselle St. .... Moreno Valley CA 92551 951-571-6100 571-6188*
**Fax:* Admissions ■ *Web:* www.rcc.edu

Napa Valley College 2277 Napa-Vallejo Hwy .... Napa CA 94558 707-256-7000 253-3064
TF: 800-826-1077 ■ *Web:* www.napavalley.edu
Norco 2001 Third St .... Norco CA 92860 951-372-7000 372-7054*
**Fax:* Admissions ■ *Web:* www.rcc.edu

Cerritos College 11110 Alondra Blvd .... Norwalk CA 90650 562-860-2451 467-5068*
**Fax:* Admitting ■ *Web:* www.cerritos.edu
Indian Valley 1800 Ignacio Blvd. .... Novato CA 94949 415-883-2211 884-0429*
**Fax:* Admissions ■ *Web:* www.marin.edu

Laney College 900 Fallon St. .... Oakland CA 94607 510-834-5740 466-7394*
**Fax:* Admissions ■ *Web:* laney.edu

Merritt College 12500 Campus Dr .... Oakland CA 94619 510-531-4911 436-2405*
**Fax:* Admissions ■ *Web:* www.merritt.edu
Oceanside One Barnard Dr Ste 7 .... Oceanside CA 92056 760-757-2121 795-6626*
**Fax:* Admissions ■ *TF:* 888-201-8480 ■ *Web:* www.miracosta.edu

Santiago Canyon College 8045 E Chapman Ave .... Orange CA 92869 714-628-4900 628-4723*
**Fax:* Admissions ■ *Web:* www.sccollege.edu

Butte College 3536 Butte Campus Dr. .... Oroville CA 95965 530-895-2511 879-4313*
**Fax:* Admissions ■ *TF Hum Res:* 800-933-8322 ■ *Web:* www.butte.edu

Oxnard College 4000 S Rose Ave. .... Oxnard CA 93033 805-986-5800 986-5943*
**Fax:* Admissions ■ *Web:* www.oxnardcollege.edu

College of the Desert
43-500 Monterey Ave .... Palm Desert CA 92260 760-346-8041 862-1379*
**Fax:* Admissions ■ *Web:* www.collegeofthedesert.edu

Pasadena City College 1570 E Colorado Blvd. .... Pasadena CA 91106 626-585-7123 585-7915*
**Fax:* Admissions ■ *Web:* www.pasadena.edu

Cuesta College
North County 2800 Buena Vista Dr .... Paso Robles CA 93446 805-591-6200 591-6370
Web: academic.cuesta.edu

Los Medanos College 2700 E Leland Rd. .... Pittsburg CA 94565 925-439-2181 427-1599
TF: 800-677-6337 ■ *Web:* www.losmedanos.edu

Diablo Valley College 312 Golf Club Rd. .... Pleasant Hill CA 94523 925-685-1230 609-8085
TF: 800-227-1060 ■ *Web:* www.dvc.edu

Porterville College 100 E College Ave .... Porterville CA 93257 559-791-2200 791-2349*
**Fax:* Admissions ■ *Web:* portervillecollege.edu/

Feather River College 570 Golden Eagle Ave. .... Quincy CA 95971 530-283-0202 283-9961*
**Fax:* Admissions ■ *TF:* 800-442-9799 ■ *Web:* www.frc.edu

Chaffey College 5885 Haven Ave .... Rancho Cucamonga CA 91737 909-987-1737 466-2875*
**Fax:* Admissions ■ *Web:* www.chaffey.edu

Canada College 4200 Farm Hill Blvd. .... Redwood City CA 94061 650-306-3100 306-3113*
**Fax:* Admissions ■ *Web:* www.canadacollege.edu

Reedley College 995 N Reed Ave .... Reedley CA 93654 559-638-3641 638-5040
TF: 866-245-3276 ■ *Web:* reedleycollege.edu
Indian Wells Valley
3000 College Heights Blvd .... Ridgecrest CA 93555 760-384-6100 384-6377*
**Fax:* Admissions ■ *TF:* 888-537-6932 ■ *Web:* www.cerrocoso.edu

Riverside Community College
Riverside 4800 Magnolia Ave. .... Riverside CA 92506 951-222-8000 328-3503*
**Fax:* Admissions ■ *Web:* www.rcc.edu

Sierra Community College 5000 Rocklin Rd .... Rocklin CA 95677 916-624-3333
Web: www.sierracollege.edu

American River College
4700 College Oak Dr .... Sacramento CA 95841 916-484-8011 484-8864*
**Fax:* Admissions ■ *Web:* www.arc.losrios.edu

Cosumnes River College 8401 Ctr Pkwy .... Sacramento CA 95823 916-691-7410 691-7467*
**Fax:* Admissions ■ *Web:* www.crc.losrios.edu

Phone Fax

Sacramento City College
3835 Freeport Blvd . . . . Sacramento CA 95822 916-558-2351 558-2190*
*Fax: Admissions ■ Web: www.scc.losrios.edu

Hartnell College 156 Homestead Ave . . . . Salinas CA 93901 831-755-6700 759-6014*
*Fax: Admissions ■ TF: 888-678-2871 ■ Web: www.hartnell.edu

San Bernardino Valley College
701 S Mt Vernon Ave . . . . San Bernardino CA 92410 909-384-4400 889-4988
Web: www.valleycollege.edu

Skyline College 3300 College Dr . . . . San Bruno CA 94066 650-738-4100 738-4222*
*Fax: Admissions ■ Web: www.skylinecollege.edu

San Diego City College 1313 Pk Blvd . . . . San Diego CA 92101 619-388-3400 388-3241*
*Fax: Admissions ■ Web: www.sdcity.edu

San Diego Mesa College
7250 Mesa College Dr . . . . San Diego CA 92111 619-388-2600 388-2960
Web: sdmesa.edu

San Diego Miramar College
10440 Black Mtn Rd . . . . San Diego CA 92126 619-388-7844 388-7915*
*Fax: Admissions ■ Web: www.sdmiramar.edu

City College of San Francisco
50 Phelan Ave . . . . San Francisco CA 94112 415-239-3000 239-3936*
*Fax: Admissions ■ TF: 800-433-3243 ■ Web: www.ccsf.edu

Mount San Jacinto College
1499 N State St . . . . San Jacinto CA 92583 951-487-6752 654-6738*
*Fax: Admissions ■ TF: 800-624-5561 ■ Web: www.msjc.edu

Evergreen Valley College
3095 Yerba Buena Rd . . . . San Jose CA 95135 408-274-7900 223-9351*
*Fax: Admissions ■ Web: www.evc.edu

San Jose City College 2100 Moorpark Ave . . . . San Jose CA 95128 408-298-2181 298-1935*
*Fax: Admissions ■ Web: www.sjcc.edu

Palomar College 1140 W Mission Rd . . . . San Marcos CA 92069 760-744-1150 744-8123*
*Fax: Admissions ■ Web: www.palomar.edu

College of San Mateo 1700 W Hillsdale Blvd . . . . San Mateo CA 94402 650-574-6161 574-6506*
*Fax: Admissions ■ Web: www.collegeofsanmateo.edu

Contra Costa College 2600 Mission Bell . . . . San Pablo CA 94806 510-235-7800 412-0769
Web: coast.contracosta.edu

Santa Ana College 1530 W 17th St . . . . Santa Ana CA 92706 714-564-6000 564-6455*
*Fax: Admissions ■ Web: www.sac.edu

Santa Barbara City College
721 Cliff Dr . . . . Santa Barbara CA 93109 805-965-0581 963-7222*
*Fax: Admissions ■ Web: www.sbcc.edu

Mission College
3000 Mission College Blvd . . . . Santa Clara CA 95054 408-988-2200 980-8980*
*Fax: Admissions ■ Web: www.missioncollege.org

College of the Canyons
26455 Rockwell Canyon Rd . . . . Santa Clarita CA 91355 661-259-7800 362-5566*
*Fax: Admissions ■ Web: www.canyons.edu

Santa Monica College 1900 Pico Blvd . . . . Santa Monica CA 90405 310-434-4000 434-3645*
*Fax: Admissions ■ Web: www.smc.edu

Santa Rosa Junior College
1501 Mendocino Ave . . . . Santa Rosa CA 95401 707-527-4011 527-4798
TF: 800-564-7752 ■ Web: www.santarosa.edu

West Valley College 14000 Fruitvale Ave . . . . Saratoga CA 95070 408-867-2200 867-5033*
*Fax: Admissions ■ Web: www.westvalley.edu

Lake Tahoe Community College
One College Dr . . . . South Lake Tahoe CA 96150 530-541-4660 542-1781*
*Fax: Admissions ■ Web: www.ltcc.edu

San Joaquin Delta College 5151 Pacific Ave . . . . Stockton CA 95207 209-954-5151 954-5769*
*Fax: Admissions ■ Web: www.deltacollege.edu

Lassen Community College
478-200 Hwy 139 PO Box 3000 . . . . Susanville CA 96130 530-257-6181 257-8964*
*Fax: Admissions ■ Web: www.lassencollege.edu

Los Angeles Mission College
13356 Eldridge Ave . . . . Sylmar CA 91342 818-364-7600 364-7806*
*Fax: Admissions ■ Web: www.lamission.edu

Taft College 29 Emmons Pk Dr . . . . Taft CA 93268 661-763-7700 763-7758*
*Fax: Admissions ■ TF: 800-379-6784 ■ Web: www.taftcollege.edu

Mendocino College 1000 Hensley Creek Rd . . . . Ukiah CA 95482 707-468-3000 468-3430*
*Fax: Admissions ■ Web: www.mendocino.edu

Los Angeles Valley College
5800 Fulton Ave . . . . Valley Glen CA 91401 818-947-2600 947-2501*
*Fax: Admissions ■ Web: www.lavc.cc.ca.us

Ventura College 4667 Telegraph Rd . . . . Ventura CA 93003 805-654-6400 654-6357*
*Fax: Admissions ■ Web: www.venturacollege.edu

Victor Valley Community College
18422 Bear Valley Rd . . . . Victorville CA 92392 760-245-4271 245-9745
TF: 877-741-8532 ■ Web: www.vvc.edu

College of the Sequoias 915 S Mooney Blvd . . . . Visalia CA 93277 559-730-3700 737-4820*
*Fax: Admissions ■ Web: www.cos.edu

Mount San Antonio College 1100 N Grand Ave . . . . Walnut CA 91789 909-594-5611
Web: www.mtsac.edu

College of the Siskiyous 800 College Ave . . . . Weed CA 96094 530-938-4461 938-5367*
*Fax: Admissions ■ TF: 888-397-4339 ■ Web: www.siskiyous.edu

Rio Hondo College 3600 Workman Mill Rd . . . . Whittier CA 90601 562-692-0921 699-7386
Web: www.riohondo.edu

Los Angeles Harbor College
1111 Figueroa Pl . . . . Wilmington CA 90744 310-233-4000 233-4223
Web: www.lahc.cc.ca.us

Crafton Hills College 11711 Sand Canyon Rd . . . . Yucaipa CA 92399 909-794-2161 389-9141*
*Fax: Admissions ■ Web: www.craftonhills.edu

Colorado

Phone Fax

Aspen 0255 Sage Way . . . . Aspen CO 81611 970-925-7740 925-6045
TF: 800-621-8559 ■ Web: www.coloradomtn.edu

Community College of Aurora
16000 E Centretech Pkwy . . . . Aurora CO 80011 303-360-4700 361-7432*
*Fax: Admissions ■ TF: 844-493-8255 ■ Web: www.ccaurora.edu

Pikes Peak Community College
Centennial 5675 S Academy Blvd . . . . Colorado Springs CO 80906 719-502-2000
TF: 800-456-6847 ■ Web: www.ppcc.edu

Downtown Studio
100 W Pikes Peak Ave . . . . Colorado Springs CO 80903 719-502-2000
TF: 800-456-6847 ■ Web: www.ppcc.edu

Rampart Range 11195 Hwy 83 . . . . Colorado Springs CO 80921 719-502-2000
TF: 800-456-6847 ■ Web: www.ppcc.edu

Craig 50 College Dr . . . . Craig CO 81625 800-562-1105 824-1134*
*Fax Area Code: 970 ■ *Fax: Admissions ■ TF: 800-562-1105 ■ Web: www.cncc.edu

Community College of Denver 1111 E Colfax Ave . . . . Denver CO 80204 303-556-2600 556-2431
Web: www.ccd.edu

Larimer 4616 S Shields St . . . . Fort Collins CO 80526 970-226-2500 204-8484
TF: 888-800-9198 ■ Web: www.frontrange.edu

Aims Community College
Fort Lupton 260 County Rd 29 1/2 . . . . Fort Lupton CO 80621 303-857-4022 352-5443*
*Fax Area Code: 970 ■ Web: www.aims.edu

Morgan Community College 920 Barlow Rd . . . . Fort Morgan CO 80701 970-542-3100 867-6608
TF: 800-622-0216 ■ Web: www.morgancc.edu

Colorado Mountain College
Roaring Fork-Spring Valley
3000 County Rd 114 . . . . Glenwood Springs CO 81601 970-945-7481 928-9668
TF: 800-621-8559 ■ Web: www.coloradomtn.edu

Otero Junior College 1802 Colorado Ave . . . . La Junta CO 81050 719-384-6831 384-6933*
*Fax: Admissions ■ Web: www.ojc.edu

Red Rocks Community College
13300 W Sixth Ave . . . . Lakewood CO 80228 303-914-6600 914-6666
Web: www.rrcc.edu

Lamar Community College 2401 S Main St . . . . Lamar CO 81052 719-336-2248 336-2400*
*Fax: Admissions ■ TF: 800-968-6920 ■ Web: lamarcc.edu/

Timberline 901 US Hwy 24 . . . . Leadville CO 80461 719-486-2015 486-3212
Web: www.coloradomtn.edu

Arapahoe Community College
5900 S Santa Fe Dr . . . . Littleton CO 80160 303-797-0100 797-5970*
*Fax: Admissions ■ TF: 888-800-9198 ■ Web: www.arapahoe.edu

Boulder County 2190 Miller Dr . . . . Longmont CO 80501 303-678-3722 678-3699*
*Fax: Admissions ■ TF: 888-800-9198 ■ Web: www.frontrange.edu

Pueblo Community College 900 W Orman Ave . . . . Pueblo CO 81004 719-549-3200 543-7566*
*Fax: Admissions ■ TF: 888-642-6017 ■ Web: www.pueblocc.edu

Colorado Northwestern Community College
500 Kennedy Dr . . . . Rangely CO 81648 970-675-3335 675-3343*
*Fax: Admissions ■ TF: 800-562-1105 ■ Web: www.cncc.edu

Alpine 1330 Bob Adams Dr . . . . Steamboat Springs CO 80487 970-870-4444 870-4535*
*Fax: Admissions ■ TF: 800-621-8559 ■ Web: www.coloradomtn.edu

Northeastern Junior College 100 College Ave . . . . Sterling CO 80751 970-521-6600 522-4664
TF: 800-626-4637 ■ Web: www.njc.edu

Trinidad State Junior College
600 Prospect St . . . . Trinidad CO 81082 719-846-5011 846-5620*
*Fax: Admissions ■ TF: 800-621-8752 ■ Web: www.trinidadstate.edu

Front Range Community College
Westminster 3645 W 112th Ave . . . . Westminster CO 80031 303-404-5000 466-1623*
*Fax: Admissions ■ Web: www.frontrange.edu

Connecticut

Phone Fax

Housatonic Community College
900 Lafayette Blvd . . . . Bridgeport CT 06604 203-332-5000 332-5123*
*Fax: Admissions ■ TF: 866-733-2463 ■ Web: www.hctc.commnet.edu

Quinebaug Valley Community College
742 Upper Maple St . . . . Danielson CT 06239 860-774-1160 779-2998*
*Fax: Admissions ■ Web: www.qvctc.commnet.edu

Asnuntuck Community College 170 Elm St . . . . Enfield CT 06082 860-253-3000 253-3014*
*Fax: Admissions ■ TF: 800-501-3967 ■ Web: www.asnuntuck.edu

Tunxis Community College
271 Scott Swamp Rd . . . . Farmington CT 06032 860-773-1300
Web: tunxis.edu

Avery Point 1084 Shennecossett Rd . . . . Groton CT 06340 860-405-9019 405-9018
TF: 888-247-5556 ■ Web: www.averypoint.uconn.edu

Capital Community College 950 Main St . . . . Hartford CT 06103 860-906-5000 906-5129
TF: 800-894-6126 ■ Web: www.ccc.commnet.edu

Manchester Community College PO Box 1046 . . . . Manchester CT 06045 860-512-2800 512-3221*
*Fax: Admissions ■ TF: 888-999-5545 ■ Web: www.mcc.commnet.edu

Norwalk Community College 188 Richards Ave . . . . Norwalk CT 06854 203-857-7060 857-3335*
*Fax: Admissions ■ TF: 800-565-3036 ■ Web: www.ncc.commnet.edu

Three Rivers Community College Mohegan
Seven Mahan Dr . . . . Norwich CT 06360 860-886-0177 885-1684*
*Fax: Admissions ■ Web: www.trcc.commnet.edu

Three Rivers Community College Thames Valley
Seven Mahan Dr . . . . Norwich CT 06360 860-886-0177 892-5753*
*Fax: Admissions ■ Web: www.trcc.commnet.edu

Torrington 855 University Dr . . . . Torrington CT 06790 860-626-6800 626-6847
Web: www.torrington.uconn.edu

Naugatuck Valley Community College
750 Chase Pkwy . . . . Waterbury CT 06708 203-575-8040 596-8766*
*Fax: Admissions ■ Web: www.nv.edu

Waterbury 99 E Main St . . . . Waterbury CT 06702 203-236-9800 236-9805
Web: www.waterbury.uconn.edu

Greater Hartford 85 Lawler Rd . . . . West Hartford CT 06117 860-570-9214
Web: www.hartford.uconn.edu

Northwestern Connecticut Community College
Park Pl E . . . . Winsted CT 06098 860-738-6300 738-6437*
*Fax: Admissions ■ Web: www.nwctc.commnet.edu

Florida

Phone Fax

South Florida Community College
600 W College Dr . . . . Avon Park FL 33825 863-453-6661 453-2365*
*Fax: Admissions ■ Web: www.southflorida.edu

Belle Glade 1977 College Dr . . . . Belle Glade FL 33430 561-996-7222
Web: www.palmbeachstate.edu

Boca Raton 3000 St Lucie Ave . . . . Boca Raton FL 33431 561-862-4340 862-4350
Web: palmbeachstate.edu

Phone | Fax

State College of Florida 5840 26th St W Bradenton FL 34207 941-752-5000 727-6380
Web: www.scf.edu

Pasco-Hernando Community College
North 11415 Ponce de Leon Blvd Brooksville FL 34601 352-796-6726 797-5133
TF: 877-879-7422 ■ *Web:* phsc.edu
Levy County 114 Rodgers Blvd Chiefland FL 32626 352-493-9533 493-9994
Web: www.cf.edu

Lake-Sumter State College
South Lake 1250 N Hancock Rd Clermont FL 34711 352-243-5722 243-0117
Web: lssc.edu

Brevard Community College (BCC)
Cocoa 1519 Clearlake Rd Cocoa FL 32922 321-632-1111 433-7357*
**Fax:* Admissions ■ *TF:* 888-747-2802 ■ *Web:* www.easternflorida.edu
North 1000 Coconut Creek Blvd Coconut Creek FL 33066 954-201-2240 201-2242*
**Fax:* Admissions ■ *TF:* 888-654-6482 ■ *Web:* www.broward.edu
Central 3501 SW Davie Rd Davie FL 33314 954-201-6500 201-6954
Web: www.broward.edu

Daytona Beach Community College
1200 W International Speedway Blvd Daytona Beach FL 32114 386-506-3000 506-3940
TF: 800-352-2583 ■ *Web:* www.daytonastate.edu
Downtown Ctr 111 E Las Olas Blvd Fort Lauderdale FL 33301 954-201-7350 201-7466*
**Fax:* Admissions ■ *TF:* 888-654-6482 ■ *Web:* www.broward.edu

Edison College
Lee County 8099 College Pkwy SW Fort Myers FL 33919 239-489-9054 489-9372*
**Fax:* Admissions ■ *TF:* 800-749-2322 ■ *Web:* fsw.edu/lee

Indian River State College (IRSC)
3209 Virginia Ave Fort Pierce FL 34981 772-462-4772 462-4699
TF: 866-792-4772 ■ *Web:* www.irsc.edu

Miami Dade College
North-Hialeah Ctr 1780 W 49th St Hialeah FL 33012 305-237-8700
Web: www.mdc.edu
Homestead 500 College Terr Rm A230 Homestead FL 33030 305-237-5555 237-5019*
**Fax:* Admissions ■ *Web:* www.mdc.edu/homestead

Florida Community College at Jacksonville
Downtown 101 State St W Jacksonville FL 32202 904-633-8100
TF: 877-633-5950 ■ *Web:* www.fscj.edu
Kent 3939 Roosevelt Blvd Jacksonville FL 32205 904-381-3400 381-3771*
**Fax:* Admissions ■ *Web:* www.fccj.org
South 11901 Beach Blvd Jacksonville FL 32246 904-646-2111 646-2124*
**Fax:* Admissions ■ *Web:* www.fccj.org

Florida State College at Jacksonville
North 4501 Capper Rd Jacksonville FL 32218 904-766-6500 713-6002
Web: www.fccj.org

Florida Keys Community College
5901 College Rd Key West FL 33040 305-296-9081 292-5155*
**Fax:* Admissions ■ *TF:* 866-567-2665 ■ *Web:* www.fkcc.edu
Osceola 1800 Denn John Ln PO Box 3028 Kissimmee FL 32802 407-299-5000
Web: valenciacollege.edu

Florida Gateway College 149 SE College Pl Lake City FL 32025 386-752-1822 754-4594*
**Fax:* Admissions ■ *Web:* www.fgc.edu
Lake Worth 4200 Congress Ave Lake Worth FL 33461 561-868-3350 868-3584*
**Fax:* Admissions ■ *TF:* 866-576-7222 ■ *Web:* palmbeachstate.edu
Citrus County 3800 S Lecanto Hwy Lecanto FL 34461 352-746-6721 249-1218
Web: www.cf.edu

North Florida Community College
325 NW Turner Davis Dr Madison FL 32340 850-973-2288 973-1696
TF: 877-501-0956 ■ *Web:* www.nfcc.edu
Melbourne 3865 N Wickham Rd Melbourne FL 32935 321-632-1111 433-5770*
**Fax:* Admissions ■ *TF:* 888-747-2802 ■ *Web:* www.easternflorida.edu
Kendall 11011 SW 104th St Miami FL 33176 305-237-2000 237-2964*
**Fax:* Admissions ■ *Web:* www.mdc.edu/kendall
Medical Ctr 950 NW 20th St Miami FL 33127 305-237-4100 237-4339
Web: www.mdc.edu/medical
North 11380 NW 27th Ave Miami FL 33167 305-237-1000 237-8070*
**Fax:* Admissions ■ *Web:* www.mdc.edu/north
Wolfson 300 NE Second Ave Miami FL 33132 305-237-3000 237-3669*
**Fax:* Admissions ■ *Web:* www.mdc.edu/wolfson
Collier County 7007 Lely Cultural Pkwy Naples FL 34113 239-732-3701 732-3761*
**Fax:* Admissions ■ *TF:* 800-749-2322 ■ *Web:* fsw.edu/

Northwest Florida State College
100 College Blvd Niceville FL 32578 850-729-5397 729-5273

Central Florida Community College
Ocala 3001 SW College Rd Ocala FL 34474 352-237-2111 291-4450
Web: cf.edu

Valencia Community College
East 701 N Econlockhatchee Trl Orlando FL 32825 407-299-5000 582-2621
Web: valenciacollege.edu

Seminole Community College
Oviedo 2505 Lockwood Blvd Oviedo FL 32765 407-971-5000 971-5012
Web: seminolestate.edu
Palm Bay 250 Community College Pkwy Palm Bay FL 32909 321-632-1111 433-5325*
**Fax:* Admissions ■ *TF:* 888-747-2802 ■ *Web:* www.easternflorida.edu

Palm Beach Community College
Palm Beach Gardens 3160 PGA Blvd Palm Beach Gardens FL 33410 561-207-5340
TF: 866-576-7222 ■ *Web:* www.palmbeachstate.edu

Gulf Coast Community College
5230 W Hwy 98 Panama City FL 32401 850-769-1551 913-3308*
**Fax:* Admissions ■ *TF:* 800-311-3685 ■ *Web:* www.gulfcoast.edu

Broward Community College
Pines 16957 Sheridan St Pembroke Pines FL 33331 954-201-3601 201-3614
Web: www.broward.edu/locations/pines
South 7200 Hollywood/Pines Blvd Pembroke Pines FL 33024 954-201-8835 201-8060*
**Fax:* Admissions ■ *Web:* www.broward.edu

Pensacola Junior College 1000 College Blvd Pensacola FL 32504 850-484-1000 484-1829*
**Fax:* Admissions ■ *Web:* pensacolastate.edu
Warrington 5555 W Hwy 98 Pensacola FL 32507 850-484-2200 484-2375
TF: 888-897-3605 ■ *Web:* pensacolastate.edu
Plant City 1206 N Pk Rd Plant City FL 33566 813-757-2102 757-2187
Web: www.hccfl.edu
Charlotte 26300 Airport Rd Punta Gorda FL 33950 941-637-5629 637-3538*
**Fax:* Admissions ■ *TF:* 800-749-2322 ■ *Web:* fsw.edu/

Saint Johns River Community College
Saint Augustine 2990 College Dr Saint Augustine FL 32084 904-808-7400 808-7420*
**Fax:* Admissions ■ *Web:* sjrstate.edu

Saint Petersburg College (SPC)
PO Box 13489 Saint Petersburg FL 33710 727-341-4772
Web: www.spcollege.edu

Seminole State College
2701 Boren Blvd PO Box 351 Sanford FL 32773 405-382-9950
TF: 877-738-6365 ■ *Web:* sscok.edu
Seminole 9200 113th St N Seminole FL 33772 727-394-6000 394-6132
Web: www.spcollege.edu/se/campus
Sumter 1405 CR 526A Sumterville FL 33585 352-568-0001 568-7515
Web: lssc.edu

Tallahassee Community College
444 Appleyard Dr Tallahassee FL 32304 850-201-6200 201-8474*
**Fax:* Admissions ■ *Web:* www.tcc.fl.edu

Hillsborough Community College (HCC)
Brandon 10414 E Columbus Dr Tampa FL 33619 813-253-7801
Web: www.hccfl.edu/campus/br
Dale Mabry 4001 Tampa Bay Blvd Tampa FL 33614 813-253-7000 253-7400*
**Fax:* Admissions ■ *Web:* www.hccfl.edu
Ybor City 2112 N 15th St PO Box 5096 Tampa FL 33675 813-253-7602
Web: www.hccfl.edu
Titusville 1311 N US 1 Titusville FL 32796 321-632-1111 433-5115
TF: 888-747-2802 ■ *Web:* www.easternflorida.edu

Manatee Community College
South 8000 S Tamiami Tr Venice FL 34293 941-408-1300
Web: www.scf.edu

Polk State College 999 Ave H NE Winter Haven FL 33881 863-297-1000 297-1060*
**Fax:* Admissions ■ *Web:* www.polk.edu

Georgia

Phone | Fax

Darton College 2400 Gillionville Rd Albany GA 31707 229-430-6742 317-6607*
**Fax:* Admissions ■ *TF:* 866-775-1214 ■ *Web:* www.darton.edu

Atlanta Metropolitan College
1630 Metropolitan Pkwy SW Atlanta GA 30310 404-756-4000 756-4407*
**Fax:* Admissions ■ *Web:* www.atlm.edu

Emory University Oxford College
201 Dowman Dr PO Box 1418 Atlanta GA 30322 404-727-6069 784-8359*
**Fax Area Code:* 770 ■ *TF:* 800-723-8328 ■ *Web:* www.emory.edu
Cartersville 5441 Hwy 20 NE Cartersville GA 30121 678-872-8000 872-8013
TF: 800-332-2406 ■ *Web:* www.highlands.edu
Clarkston 555 N Indian Creek Dr Clarkston GA 30021 678-891-3200
Web: www.gpc.edu

Middle Georgia College 1100 Second St SE Cochran GA 31014 478-934-6221 934-3403*
**Fax:* Admissions ■ *Web:* www.mga.edu

Andrew College 501 College St Cuthbert GA 39840 800-664-9250 732-2176*
**Fax Area Code:* 229 ■ *TF:* 800-664-9250 ■ *Web:* www.andrewcollege.edu

Georgia Perimeter College
Decatur Campus 3251 Panthersville Rd Decatur GA 30034 678-891-2300
Web: www.gpc.edu
Dunwoody 2101 Womack Rd Dunwoody GA 30338 770-274-5000
Web: www.gpc.edu

Georgia Military College
201 E Green St Milledgeville GA 31061 478-387-4900 445-6520*
**Fax:* Admissions ■ *TF:* 800-342-0413 ■ *Web:* www.gmc.edu

Gainesville State College
University of N Georgia Gainesville Campus
3820 Mundy Mill Rd Oakwood GA 30566 678-717-3639
Web: ung.edu/visitors/campuses/gainesville/

Georgia Highlands College
Floyd 3175 Cedartown Hwy Rome GA 30161 706-802-5000 295-6341
TF: 800-332-2406 ■ *Web:* www.highlands.edu

East Georgia College 131 College Cir Swainsboro GA 30401 478-289-2000 289-2140*
**Fax:* Admissions ■ *TF:* 800-715-4255 ■ *Web:* www.ega.edu

Abraham Baldwin Agricultural College
2802 Moore Hwy ABAC 3 Tifton GA 31793 229-391-5001 391-4931*
**Fax:* Admissions ■ *TF:* 800-733-3653 ■ *Web:* www.abac.edu

Valdosta Technical College 4089 Val Tech Rd Valdosta GA 31602 229-333-2100
Web: valdostatech.org

Waycross College 2001 S Georgia Pkwy Waycross GA 31503 912-449-7600 285-6158*
**Fax:* Admissions ■ *Web:* sgsc.edu

Young Harris College PO Box 116 Young Harris GA 30582 706-379-3111 379-3108*
**Fax:* Admissions ■ *TF:* 800-241-3754 ■ *Web:* www.yhc.edu

Hawaii

Phone | Fax

Hawaii Community College 200 W Kawili St Hilo HI 96720 808-934-2500 974-7692*
**Fax:* Admissions ■ *Web:* www.hawcc.hawaii.edu

University of Hawaii
Hilo 200 W Kawili St Hilo HI 96720 808-974-7414 933-0861*
**Fax:* Admissions ■ *TF Admissions:* 800-897-4456 ■ *Web:* hilo.hawaii.edu
Honolulu Community College
874 Dillingham Blvd Honolulu HI 96817 808-845-9129 847-9829*
**Fax:* Admissions ■ *Web:* www.honolulu.hawaii.edu
Kapiolani Community College
4303 Diamond Head Rd Honolulu HI 96816 808-734-9000 734-9896
Web: www.kcc.hawaii.edu

Maui Community College 310 W Kaahumanu Ave Kahului HI 96732 808-984-3267 242-9618*
**Fax:* Admissions ■ *TF:* 800-479-6692 ■ *Web:* www.maui.hawaii.edu
Windward Community College
45-720 Keaahala Rd Kaneohe HI 96744 808-235-7400 247-5362*
**Fax:* Admissions ■ *Web:* www.wcc.hawaii.edu

Kauai Community College 3-1901 Kaumualii Hwy Lihue HI 96766 808-245-8311 245-8220
TF: 800-776-4816 ■ *Web:* www.kauai.hawaii.edu

Leeward Community College 96-045 Ala Ike Pearl City HI 96782 808-455-0011 454-8804*
**Fax:* Admissions ■ *TF:* 888-442-4551 ■ *Web:* www.leeward.hawaii.edu

Phone Fax

Leeward Community College
96-045 Ala Ike St. Pearl City HI 96782 808-455-0011 454-8804*
*Fax: Admissions ■ Web: www.leeward.hawaii.edu

Idaho

Phone Fax

North Idaho College 1000 W Garden Ave Coeur d'Alene ID 83814 208-769-3300 769-3399*
*Fax: Library ■ TF: 877-404-4536 ■ Web: www.nic.edu
College of Southern Idaho PO Box 1238 Twin Falls ID 83303 208-733-9554 736-3014*
*Fax: Admissions ■ Web: www.csi.edu

Illinois

Phone Fax

Southwestern Illinois College
2500 Carlyle Ave. Belleville IL 62221 618-235-2700 222-9768*
*Fax: Admissions ■ TF: 800-222-5131 ■ Web: www.swic.edu
Spoon River College (SRC) 23235 N County Hwy 22 Canton IL 61520 309-647-4645 649-6393*
*Fax: Admissions ■ TF: 800-334-7337 ■ Web: www.src.edu
John A Logan College
700 Logan College Rd Carterville IL 62918 618-985-2828 985-4433*
Parkland College 2400 W Bradley Ave Champaign IL 61821 217-351-2200 353-2640*
*Fax: Admissions ■ TF: 888-467-6065 ■ Web: www.parkland.edu
City Colleges of Chicago 226 W Jackson Chicago IL 60606 312-553-2500 553-3075*
*Fax: Admissions ■ TF: 866-908-7582 ■ Web: www.ccc.edu
Harry S Truman College 1145 W Wilson Ave Chicago IL 60640 773-878-1700 907-4464*
*Fax: Admissions ■ TF: 877-863-6339 ■ Web: www.ccc.edu
Kennedy-King College 6301 S Halsted St. Chicago IL 60621 773-602-5000 602-5247*
*Fax: Admissions ■ Web: www.ccc.edu/colleges/kennedy/pages/default.aspx
Malcolm X College 1900 W Van Buren St. Chicago IL 60612 312-850-7000 850-7092
TF: 877-542-0285 ■
Web: www.ccc.edu/colleges/malcolm-x/Pages/default.aspx
Olive-Harvey College 10001 S Woodlawn Ave. Chicago IL 60628 773-291-6100 291-6185
Web: www.ccc.edu/colleges/olive-harvey/pages/default.aspx
Richard J Daley College 226 W Jackson Chicago IL 60606 312-553-2500
Web: www.ccc.edu
Saint Augustine College 1345 W Argyle St Chicago IL 60640 773-878-8756 878-0937*
*Fax: Admissions ■ Web: www.staugustine.edu
Wilbur Wright College
4300 N Narragansett Ave Chicago IL 60634 773-777-7900 481-8185
Web: www.ccc.edu/colleges/wright/pages/default.aspx
Prairie State College
202 S Halsted St. Chicago Heights IL 60411 708-709-3500 709-3951*
*Fax: Admissions ■ TF: 866-255-5437 ■ Web: www.prairiestate.edu
Morton College 3801 S Central Ave. Cicero IL 60804 708-656-8000 656-9592*
*Fax: Admitting ■ Web: www.morton.edu
McHenry County College 8900 US Hwy 14 Crystal Lake IL 60012 815-455-3700 455-3766
TF: 888-977-4847 ■ Web: www.mchenry.edu
Danville Area Community College
2000 E Main St. Danville IL 61832 217-443-3222 443-8560*
*Fax: Hum Res ■ TF: 877-342-3042 ■ Web: dacc.edu
Richland Community College 1 College Pk Decatur IL 62521 217-875-7200 875-6965*
*Fax: Hum Res ■ Web: www.richland.edu
Sauk Valley Community College
173 Illinois Rt 2 Dixon IL 61021 815-288-5511 288-3190*
*Fax: Admissions ■ Web: www.svcc.edu
Elgin Community College 1700 Spartan Dr Elgin IL 60123 847-697-1000 608-5458*
*Fax: Admissions ■ TF: 855-850-2525 ■ Web: www.elgin.edu
Highland Community College
2998 W Pearl City Rd Freeport IL 61032 815-235-6121 235-6130*
*Fax: Admissions ■ Web: www.highland.cc.il.us
Carl Sandburg College
2400 Tom L Wilson Blvd. Galesburg IL 61401 309-344-2518 344-3291
TF: 877-236-1862 ■ Web: www.sandburg.edu
College of DuPage 425 Fawell Blvd Glen Ellyn IL 60137 630-858-2800 790-2686*
*Fax: Admissions ■ Web: www.cod.edu
Granite City 4950 Maryville Rd Granite City IL 62040 618-931-0600 931-1598
Web: www.swic.edu
Grayslake 19351 W Washington St Grayslake IL 60030 847-223-6601 543-3061*
*Fax: Admissions ■ Web: www.clcillinois.edu
Southeastern Illinois College
3575 College Rd. Harrisburg IL 62946 618-252-6376 252-3062*
*Fax: Admissions ■ TF: 866-338-2742 ■ Web: www.sic.edu
Rend Lake College 468 N Ken Gray Pkwy Ina IL 62846 618-437-5321 437-5677*
*Fax: Admitting ■ TF: 800-369-5321 ■ Web: rlc.edu
Joliet Junior College 1215 Houbolt Rd Joliet IL 60431 815-729-9020 280-2493*
*Fax: Admissions ■ Web: www.jjc.edu
North 1215 Houbolt Rd Joliet IL 60431 815-729-9020 886-4331
TF: 800-899-4722 ■ Web: www.jjc.edu
Kankakee Community College 100 College Dr Kankakee IL 60901 815-802-8100 802-8101*
*Fax: Admissions ■ TF: 800-526-0844 ■ Web: www.kcc.edu
Black Hawk College
East 1501 State Hwy 78 Kewanee IL 61443 309-852-5671 856-6005*
*Fax: Admissions ■ TF: 800-233-5671 ■ Web: www.bhc.edu
Lincoln College 300 Keokuk St Lincoln IL 62656 217-732-3155 732-8859
TF: 800-569-0556 ■ Web: www.lincolncollege.edu
Kishwaukee College 21193 Malta Rd Malta IL 60150 815-825-2086 825-2306
TF: 888-656-7329 ■ Web: www.kishwaukeecollege.edu
Lake Land College 5001 Lk Land Blvd Mattoon IL 61938 217-234-5253 234-5390*
*Fax: Admissions ■ Web: www.lakeland.cc.il.us
Quad Cities 6600 34th Ave. Moline IL 61265 309-796-5000 796-5209*
*Fax: Admissions ■ TF: 800-334-1311 ■ Web: www.bhc.edu
Heartland Community College 1500 W Raab Rd Normal IL 61761 309-268-8000 268-7992
Web: www.hcc.cc.il.us
Illinois Valley Community College
815 N Orlando Smith Ave Oglesby IL 61348 815-224-2720 224-3033*
*Fax: Admissions ■ Web: ivcc.edu
Olney Central College 305 NW St Olney IL 62450 618-395-7777 395-1261*
*Fax: Admissions ■ TF: 866-622-4322
Harper College 1200 W Algonquin Rd Palatine IL 60067 847-925-6000 925-6044*
*Fax: Admissions ■ Web: www.harpercollege.edu

Phone Fax

Moraine Valley Community College
9000 W College Pkwy. Palos Hills IL 60465 708-974-4300 974-0169
Web: www.morainevalley.edu
Pittsfield 1308 W Washington St Pittsfield IL 62363 217-285-5319 641-4192
Web: www.jwcc.edu
John Wood Community College 1301 S 48th St Quincy IL 62305 217-224-6500 641-4192*
*Fax: Admissions ■ Web: www.jwcc.edu
Red Bud 500 W S Fourth St Red Bud IL 62278 618-282-6682
Web: www.swic.edu
Triton College 2000 N Fifth Ave River Grove IL 60171 708-456-0300 583-3147*
*Fax: Admissions ■ Web: www.triton.edu
Lincoln Trail College 11220 State Hwy 1 Robinson IL 62454 618-544-8657 *
*Fax: Admissions ■ TF: 866-582-4322 ■ Web: www.iecc.edu
Rock Valley College 3301 N Mulford Rd Rockford IL 61114 815-921-7821 921-4269*
*Fax: Admissions ■ TF: 800-973-7821 ■ Web: www.rockvalleycollege.edu
Oakton Community College
Skokie Campus 7701 N Lincoln Ave Skokie IL 60077 847-635-1600 635-1497
TF: 877-823-2378 ■ Web: www.oakton.edu
South Suburban College
15800 S State St. South Holland IL 60473 708-596-2000 225-5806*
*Fax: Admissions ■ Web: ssc.edu
Lincoln Land Community College
5250 Shepherd Rd PO Box 19256 Springfield IL 62794 217-786-2200 786-2468
TF: 800-727-4161 ■ Web: www.llcc.edu
Springfield College in Illinois - Benedictine University
1500 N Fifth St Springfield IL 62702 217-525-1420 525-1497
TF: 800-635-7289 ■ Web: ben.edu
Waubonsee Community College
Rt 47 At Waubonsee Dr. Sugar Grove IL 60554 630-466-7900
Web: waubonsee.edu
Shawnee Community College
8364 Shawnee College Rd Ullin IL 62992 618-634-3200 634-3300*
*Fax: Admitting ■ Web: www.shawneecc.edu
College of Lake County
Lakeshore 33 N Genessee St Waukegan IL 60085 847-623-8686 543-2170*
*Fax: Admissions ■ Web: www.clcillinois.edu

Indiana

Phone Fax

Jasper 850 College Ave Jasper IN 47546 812-482-3030 481-5960*
*Fax: Admissions ■ TF: 800-809-8852 ■ Web: vujc.vinu.edu/
Vincennes University 1002 N First St Vincennes IN 47591 812-888-4313 888-5707*
*Fax: Admissions ■ TF: 800-742-9198 ■ Web: www.vinu.edu

Iowa

Phone Fax

Des Moines Area Community College
Ankeny 2006 S Ankeny Blvd Ankeny IA 50021 515-964-6200 964-6391*
*Fax: Admissions ■ TF: 800-362-2127 ■ Web: go.dmacc.edu
Scott Community College 500 Belmont Rd Bettendorf IA 52722 563-441-4001 441-4131*
*Fax: Admissions ■ TF: 888-336-3907 ■ Web: www.eicc.edu
Boone 1125 Hancock Dr Boone IA 50036 515-432-7203 433-5033*
*Fax: Admissions ■ TF: 800-362-2127 ■ Web: go.dmacc.edu
Northeast Iowa Community College
Calmar 1625 Hwy 150 S PO Box 400 Calmar IA 52132 563-562-3263 562-4369*
*Fax: Admissions ■ TF: 800-728-2256 ■ Web: www.nicc.edu
Carroll 906 N Grant Rd Carroll IA 51401 712-792-1755 792-6358
TF: 800-622-3334 ■ Web: go.dmacc.edu
Kirkwood Community College
6301 Kirkwood Blvd SW. Cedar Rapids IA 52404 319-398-5411 398-1244*
*Fax: Admissions ■ TF: 800-332-2055 ■ Web: www.kirkwood.edu
Iowa Western Community College
Clarinda 923 E Washington St Clarinda IA 51632 712-542-5117 542-4608*
*Fax: Admissions ■ TF: 800-521-2073 ■ Web: www.iwcc.cc.ia.us
Clinton Community College 1000 Lincoln Blvd Clinton IA 52732 563-244-7001 244-7107*
*Fax: Library ■ TF: 877-495-3320 ■ Web: www.eicc.edu
Southwestern Community College
1501 W Townline St Creston IA 50801 641-782-7081 782-3312*
*Fax: Admissions ■ TF: 800-247-4023 ■ Web: www.swcciowa.edu
Urban/Des Moines 1100 Seventh St Des Moines IA 50314 515-244-4226 248-7253
TF: 800-622-3334 ■ Web: go.dmacc.edu
Iowa Lakes Community College
300 S 18th St Estherville IA 51334 712-362-2604 362-8363*
*Fax: Admissions ■ TF: 800-242-5106 ■ Web: www.iowalakes.edu
Iowa Central Community College
2031 Quail Ave. Fort Dodge IA 50501 515-576-7201 576-7724*
*Fax: Admissions ■ TF: 800-362-2793 ■ Web: www.iccc.cc.ia.us
Ellsworth Community College
1100 College Ave. Iowa Falls IA 50126 641-648-4611 648-3128*
*Fax: Admissions ■ TF: 800-322-9235 ■ Web: www.iavalley.cc.ia.us
Southeastern Community College South
335 Messenger Rd Keokuk IA 52632 319-524-3221 524-8621*
*Fax: Admissions ■ TF: 866-722-4692 ■ Web: scciowa.edu
Marshalltown Community College
3700 S Ctr St Marshalltown IA 50158 641-752-7106 752-8149
TF: 866-622-4748 ■ Web: www.iavalley.cc.ia.us
North Iowa Area Community College
500 College Dr Mason City IA 50401 641-423-1264 422-4385*
*Fax: Admissions ■ TF: 888-466-4222 ■ Web: niacc.edu/
Muscatine Community College
152 Colorado St. Muscatine IA 52761 563-288-6001 288-6104*
*Fax: Admissions ■ TF: 888-336-3907 ■ Web: www.eicc.edu
Indian Hills Community College
525 Grandview Ave. Ottumwa IA 52501 641-683-5111 683-5741
TF: 800-726-2585 ■ Web: www.indianhills.edu
Peosta 10250 Sundown Rd Peosta IA 52068 563-556-5110 557-0347*
*Fax: Admissions ■ TF: 800-728-7367 ■ Web: www.nicc.edu
Northwest Iowa Community College 603 W Pk St Sheldon IA 51201 712-324-5061 324-4136
TF: 800-352-4907 ■ Web: www.nwicc.edu

	City	State	Zip	Phone	Fax
Hawkeye Community College 1501 E Orange Rd	Waterloo	IA	50704	319-296-2320	296-2874*
**Fax:* Admissions ■ *TF:* 800-670-4769 ■ *Web:* www.hawkeyecollege.edu					
Southeastern Community College North 1500 W Agency Rd	West Burlington	IA	52655	319-752-2731	524-8621*
**Fax:* Admissions ■ *TF:* 866-722-4692					

Kansas

	City	State	Zip	Phone	Fax
Cowley County Community College & Area Vocational-Technical School PO Box 1147	Arkansas City	KS	67005	620-442-0430	441-5350
TF: 800-593-2222 ■ *Web:* www.cowley.edu					
Neosho County Community College 800 W 14th St	Chanute	KS	66720	620-431-2820	431-0082*
**Fax:* Admissions ■ *Web:* www.neosho.edu					
Coffeyville Community College 400 W 11th St	Coffeyville	KS	67337	620-251-7700	252-7010*
**Fax:* Admissions ■ *TF:* 877-517-2836 ■ *Web:* coffeyville.edu					
Colby Community College 1255 S Range Ave	Colby	KS	67701	785-462-3984	460-4691*
**Fax:* Admissions ■ *TF:* 888-634-9350 ■ *Web:* www.colbycc.edu					
Cloud County Community College 2221 Campus Dr	Concordia	KS	66901	785-243-1435	243-1040*
**Fax:* Admissions ■ *TF:* 800-729-5101 ■ *Web:* www.cloud.edu					
Dodge City Community College 2501 N 14th Ave	Dodge City	KS	67801	620-225-1321	227-9277*
**Fax:* Admissions ■ *TF:* 800-367-3222 ■ *Web:* www.dc3.edu					
Butler Community College 901 S Haverhill Rd	El Dorado	KS	67042	316-321-2222	322-3316*
**Fax:* Admissions ■ *Web:* www.butlercc.edu					
Fort Scott Community College 2108 S Horton St	Fort Scott	KS	66701	620-223-2700	223-6530*
**Fax:* Admissions ■ *TF:* 800-874-3722 ■ *Web:* www.fortscott.edu					
Garden City Community College 801 N Campus Dr	Garden City	KS	67846	620-276-7611	276-9573
TF: 800-658-1696 ■ *Web:* www.gcccks.edu					
Barton County Community College 245 NE 30th Rd	Great Bend	KS	67530	620-792-2701	786-1160*
**Fax:* Admissions ■ *TF:* 800-722-6842 ■ *Web:* www.bartonccc.edu					
Hesston College 325 S College Dr PO Box 3000	Hesston	KS	67062	620-327-4221	327-8300
TF: 800-995-2757 ■ *Web:* www.hesston.edu					
Hutchinson Community College & Area Vocational School 1300 N Plum St	Hutchinson	KS	67501	620-665-3500	728-8199*
**Fax:* Admissions ■ *TF:* 800-289-3501 ■ *Web:* www.hutchcc.edu					
Independence Community College 1057 W College Ave PO Box 708	Independence	KS	67301	620-331-4100	331-0946*
**Fax:* Admissions ■ *TF:* 800-842-6063 ■ *Web:* indycc.squarespace.com					
Allen County Community College 1801 N Cottonwood St	Iola	KS	66749	620-365-5116	365-7406*
**Fax:* Admissions ■ *TF:* 800-444-0535 ■ *Web:* www.allencc.edu					
Donnelly College 608 N 18th St	Kansas City	KS	66102	913-621-6070	621-8734*
**Fax:* Admissions ■ *TF:* 800-908-9946 ■ *Web:* www.donnelly.edu					
Kansas City Kansas Community College 7250 State Ave	Kansas City	KS	66112	913-334-1100	288-7648*
**Fax:* Admissions ■ *Web:* www.kckcc.edu					
Seward County Community College 1801 N Campus Ave PO Box 1137	Liberal	KS	67905	620-624-1951	629-2725
TF: 800-373-9951 ■ *Web:* www.sccc.edu					
Ottawa 226 S Beech St	Ottawa	KS	66067	785-242-2067	242-2068*
**Fax:* Admissions ■ *Web:* www.neosho.edu					
Johnson County Community College 12345 College Blvd	Overland Park	KS	66210	913-469-8500	469-2524
TF: 866-896-5893 ■ *Web:* www.jccc.edu					
Labette Community College 200 S 14th St	Parsons	KS	67357	620-421-6700	421-0180*
**Fax:* Admissions ■ *TF:* 888-522-3883 ■ *Web:* www.labette.cc.ks.us					
Pratt Community College 348 NE SR-61	Pratt	KS	67124	620-672-5641	
Web: www.prattcc.edu					

Kentucky

	City	State	Zip	Phone	Fax
Ashland Community & Technical College 1400 College Dr	Ashland	KY	41101	606-326-2000	326-2192*
**Fax:* Admissions ■ *TF:* 800-928-4256 ■ *Web:* www.ashland.kctcs.edu					
Southeast Kentucky Community & Technical College *Cumberland* 700 College Rd	Cumberland	KY	40823	606-589-2145	589-3175*
**Fax:* Admissions ■ *TF:* 888-274-7322 ■ *Web:* southeast.kctcs.edu					
Elizabethtown Community & Technical College 600 College St Rd	Elizabethtown	KY	42701	270-769-2371	769-0736
TF: 877-246-2322 ■ *Web:* www.elizabethtown.kctcs.edu					
Hazard Community & Technical College One Community College Dr	Hazard	KY	41701	606-436-5721	439-2988
TF: 800-246-7521 ■ *Web:* www.hazcc.kctcs.edu					
Hazard Campus 101 Vo Tech Dr	Hazard	KY	41701	606-435-6101	487-8417
TF: 800-246-7521 ■ *Web:* www.hazcc.kctcs.edu					
Henderson Community College 2660 S Green St	Henderson	KY	42420	270-827-1867	831-9612*
**Fax:* Admissions ■ *TF:* 800-696-9958 ■ *Web:* henderson.kctcs.edu					
Hopkinsville Community College 720 N Dr	Hopkinsville	KY	42240	270-886-3921	886-0237*
**Fax:* Admissions ■ *TF:* 866-534-2224 ■ *Web:* www.hopkinsville.kctcs.edu					
Lees Campus 601 Jefferson Ave	Jackson	KY	41339	606-666-7521	
TF: 800-246-7521 ■ *Web:* www.hazard.kctcs.edu					
Bluegrass Community & Technical College *Cooper Campus* 470 Cooper Dr	Lexington	KY	40506	859-246-6200	246-4666
TF: 866-774-4872 ■ *Web:* www.bluegrass.kctcs.edu					
Jefferson Community & Technical College 109 E Broadway	Louisville	KY	40202	502-584-0181	213-2540*
**Fax:* Admissions ■ *TF:* 855-246-5282 ■ *Web:* www.jefferson.kctcs.edu					
Madisonville Community College 2000 College Dr	Madisonville	KY	42431	270-821-2250	824-1864*
**Fax:* Admissions ■ *TF:* 866-227-4812 ■ *Web:* www.madisonville.kctcs.edu					
Maysville Community & Technical College 1755 US 68	Maysville	KY	41056	606-759-7141	759-5818
TF: 888-452-7322 ■ *Web:* www.maysville.kctcs.edu					
Middlesboro 1300 Chichester Ave	Middlesboro	KY	40965	606-242-2145	248-3233
TF: 888-274-7322 ■ *Web:* southeast.kctcs.edu					
West Kentucky Community & Technical College 4810 Alben Barkley Dr PO Box 7380	Paducah	KY	42001	270-554-9200	554-6203*
**Fax:* Admissions ■ *TF:* 855-469-5282 ■ *Web:* www.westkentucky.kctcs.edu					
Mayo 513 Third St	Paintsville	KY	41240	606-789-5321	789-9753
Web: www.kctcs.net					
Big Sandy Community & Technical College One Bert T Combs Dr	Prestonsburg	KY	41653	606-886-3863	886-6943*
**Fax:* Admissions ■ *TF:* 888-641-4132 ■ *Web:* www.bigsandy.kctcs.edu					
Saint Catharine College 2735 BaRdstown Rd	Saint Catharine	KY	40061	859-336-5082	336-5031*
**Fax:* Admissions ■ *Web:* www.sccky.edu					
Somerset Community College 808 Monticello St	Somerset	KY	42501	606-679-8501	676-9065
TF: 877-629-9722 ■ *Web:* www.somerset.kctcs.edu					
Whitesburg Two Long Ave	Whitesburg	KY	41858	606-633-0279	589-3377
TF: 888-274-7322 ■ *Web:* southeast.kctcs.edu					

Louisiana

	City	State	Zip	Phone	Fax
Louisiana State University *Alexandria* 8100 US Hwy 71 S	Alexandria	LA	71302	318-445-3672	473-6418*
**Fax:* Admissions ■ *TF Admissions:* 888-473-6417 ■ *Web:* www.lsua.edu					
Baton Rouge Community College (BRCC) 201 Community College Dr	Baton Rouge	LA	70806	225-216-8000	216-8010
TF: 866-217-9823 ■ *Web:* www.mybrcc.edu					
Bossier Parish Community College 6220 E Texas St	Bossier City	LA	71111	318-678-6000	678-6390
Web: www.bpcc.edu					
Elaine P Nunez Community College 3710 Paris Rd	Chalmette	LA	70043	504-278-7497	278-7480
TF: 866-825-1954 ■ *Web:* www.nunez.edu					
Eunice PO Box 1129	Eunice	LA	70535	337-457-7311	550-1306*
**Fax:* Admissions ■ *TF:* 888-367-5783 ■ *Web:* www.lsue.edu					
Louisiana Delta Community College 7500 Millhaven Rd	Monroe	LA	71203	318-345-9000	
TF: 866-500-5322 ■ *Web:* www.ladelta.edu					

Maine

	City	State	Zip	Phone	Fax
Washington County Community College One College Dr	Calais	ME	04619	207-454-1000	454-1092
Web: www.wccc.me.edu					
Kennebec Valley Community College 92 Western Ave	Fairfield	ME	04937	207-453-5000	453-5010
TF: 800-528-5882 ■ *Web:* www.kvcc.me.edu					
York County Community College 112 College Dr	Wells	ME	04090	207-646-9282	641-0837
TF: 800-580-3820 ■ *Web:* www.yccc.edu					

Maryland

	City	State	Zip	Phone	Fax
Baltimore City Community College 2901 Liberty Heights Ave	Baltimore	MD	21215	410-462-8000	462-8345*
**Fax:* Admissions ■ *TF:* 888-203-1261 ■ *Web:* www.bccc.edu					
Community College of Baltimore County *Dundalk* 7200 Sollers Pt Rd	Baltimore	MD	21222	410-282-6700	285-9903
Web: www.ccbcmd.edu					
Essex 7201 Rossville Blvd	Baltimore	MD	21237	410-682-6000	840-2824*
**Fax Area Code:* 443 ■ **Fax:* Admissions ■ *TF:* 877-557-2575 ■ *Web:* ccbcmd.edu					
Harford Community College 401 Thomas Run Rd	Bel Air	MD	21015	410-879-8920	836-4169*
**Fax:* Admissions ■ *Web:* www.harford.edu					
Catonsville 800 S Rolling Rd	Catonsville	MD	21228	410-455-6050	719-6546*
**Fax:* Admissions ■ *Web:* www.ccbcmd.edu					
Howard Community College 10901 Little Patuxent Pkwy	Columbia	MD	21044	410-772-4800	876-8855*
**Fax:* Admissions ■ *TF:* 888-442-4551 ■ *Web:* www.howardcc.edu					
Allegany College of Maryland 12401 Willowbrook Rd SE	Cumberland	MD	21502	301-784-5000	784-5027*
**Fax:* Admissions ■ *TF:* 800-974-0203 ■ *Web:* www.allegany.edu					
Frederick Community College 7932 Opossumtown Pk	Frederick	MD	21702	301-846-2400	846-2498
Web: www.frederick.edu					
Hagerstown Community College 11400 Robinwood Dr	Hagerstown	MD	21742	301-790-2800	791-9165*
**Fax:* Admissions ■ *Web:* www.hagerstowncc.edu					
Hunt Valley 11101 McCormick Rd	Hunt Valley	MD	21031	410-771-6835	
Web: www.ccbcmd.edu					
La Plata 8730 Mitchell Rd PO Box 910	La Plata	MD	20646	301-934-2251	870-3008
Web: www.csmd.edu					
Prince George's Community College 301 Largo Rd	Largo	MD	20774	301-336-6000	322-0119*
**Fax:* Admissions ■ *Web:* www.pgcc.edu					
College of Southern Maryland *Leonardtown* 22950 Hollywood Rd	Leonardtown	MD	20650	240-725-5300	725-5400*
**Fax:* Admissions ■ *TF:* 800-933-9177 ■ *Web:* www.csmd.edu					
Garrett College 687 Mosser Rd	McHenry	MD	21541	301-387-3000	387-3038*
**Fax:* Admissions ■ *TF:* 866-554-2773 ■ *Web:* www.garrettcollege.edu					
Cecil Community College One Seahawk Dr	North East	MD	21901	410-287-6060	287-1001*
**Fax:* Admissions ■ *Web:* www.cecil.edu					
Owings Mills 110 Painters Mill Rd	Owings Mills	MD	21117	410-363-4111	363-6575
TF: 877-557-2575 ■ *Web:* www.ccbcmd.edu					
Prince Frederick 115 J W Williams Rd	Prince Frederick	MD	20678	443-550-6000	550-6100
TF: 800-933-9177 ■ *Web:* www.csmd.edu					

				Phone	Fax
Montgomery College Rockville 51 Mannakee St	Rockville	MD	20850	301-279-5000	
Web: cms.montgomerycollege.edu					
Wor-Wic Community College 32000 Campus Dr	Salisbury	MD	21804	410-334-2800	334-2954*
**Fax:* Admissions ■ *TF:* 800-735-2258 ■ *Web:* www.worwic.edu					
Carroll Community College 1601 Washington Rd	Westminster	MD	21157	410-386-8000	386-8431*
**Fax:* Admissions ■ *Web:* www.carrollcc.edu					
Chesapeake College PO Box 8	Wye Mills	MD	21679	410-758-1537	827-5878*
**Fax:* Admissions ■ *Web:* www.chesapeake.edu					

Massachusetts

				Phone	Fax
Attleboro 11 Field St	Attleboro	MA	02703	508-226-2484	222-7638
Web: bristolcc.edu					
Middlesex Community College 590 Springs Rd	Bedford	MA	01730	978-656-3370	280-3603*
**Fax Area Code:* 781 ■ *Web:* www.middlesex.mass.edu					
Charlestown 250 New Rutherford Ave	Boston	MA	02129	617-228-2000	228-2082*
**Fax:* Admissions ■ *TF:* 877-218-8829 ■ *Web:* www.bhcc.mass.edu					
Fisher College 118 Beacon St	Boston	MA	02116	617-236-8800	236-5473*
**Fax:* Admissions ■ *TF:* 866-266-6007 ■ *Web:* www.fisher.edu					
Massasoit Community College One Massasoit Blvd	Brockton	MA	02302	508-588-9100	427-1255*
**Fax:* Admissions ■ *Web:* www.massasoit.mass.edu					
Bunker Hill Community College *Chelsea* 175 Hawthorne St Bellingham Sq	Chelsea	MA	02150	617-228-2101	228-2106
Web: www.bhcc.mass.edu					
North Shore Community College One Ferncroft Rd	Danvers	MA	01923	978-762-4000	762-4015*
**Fax:* Admissions ■ *Web:* www.northshore.edu					
Bristol Community College 777 Elsbree St	Fall River	MA	02720	508-678-2811	730-3255*
**Fax:* Admissions ■ *Web:* www.bristol.mass.edu					
New Bedford 777 Elsbree St.	Fall River	MA	02720	508-678-2811	
Web: www.bristolcc.edu					
Framingham 19 Flagg Dr	Framingham	MA	01702	508-270-4000	872-4067
Web: www.massbay.edu					
Dean College 99 Main St	Franklin	MA	02038	508-541-1508	541-8726*
**Fax:* Admissions ■ *TF:* 877-879-3326 ■ *Web:* www.dean.edu					
Mount Wachusett Community College 444 Green St.	Gardner	MA	01440	978-632-6600	630-9554*
**Fax:* Admissions ■ *Web:* mwcc.edu					
Greenfield Community College One College Dr	Greenfield	MA	01301	413-775-1837	775-1827*
**Fax:* Admissions ■ *Web:* gcc.mass.edu/					
Northern Essex Community College 100 Elliott St.	Haverhill	MA	01830	978-556-3000	556-3729*
**Fax:* Admissions ■ *TF:* 800-422-4453 ■ *Web:* www.necc.mass.edu					
Holyoke Community College 303 Homestead Ave	Holyoke	MA	01040	413-538-7000	552-2192*
**Fax:* Admissions ■ *TF:* 877-442-6222 ■ *Web:* www.hcc.edu					
Berkshire Community College 1350 W St	Pittsfield	MA	01201	413-499-4660	447-7840
Web: www.berkshirecc.edu					
Quincy College *Plymouth* 36 Cordage Pk Cir	Plymouth	MA	02360	508-747-0400	
Web: www.quincycollege.edu					
Roxbury Community College 1234 Columbus Ave	Roxbury Crossing	MA	02120	617-541-5310	427-5316*
**Fax:* Admitting ■ *Web:* www.rcc.mass.edu					
Springfield Technical Community College 1 Armory Sq PO Box 900	Springfield	MA	01102	413-781-7822	746-0344*
**Fax:* Admissions ■ *TF:* 800-326-6142 ■ *Web:* www.stcc.edu					
Marian Court College 35 Littles Pt Rd	Swampscott	MA	01907	781-595-6768	595-3560*
**Fax:* Admissions ■ *Web:* www.mariancourt.edu					
Massachusetts Bay Community College *Wellesley Hills* 50 Oakland St	Wellesley Hills	MA	02481	781-239-3000	239-1047
TF: 800-233-3182 ■ *Web:* www.massbay.edu					
Cape Cod Community College 2240 Iyanough Rd	West Barnstable	MA	02668	508-362-2131	375-4089*
**Fax:* Admissions ■ *TF:* 877-846-3672 ■ *Web:* www.capecod.edu					
Wall Street Horizon Inc 400 W Cummings Park Ste 513	Woburn	MA	01801	781-994-3500	
Web: www.wallstreethorizon.com					
Quinsigamond Community College 670 W Boylston St	Worcester	MA	01606	508-853-2300	854-4357*
**Fax:* Admissions ■ *Web:* www.qcc.edu					

Michigan

				Phone	Fax
Alpena Community College (ACC) 665 Johnson St	Alpena	MI	49707	989-356-9021	
TF: 888-468-6222 ■ *Web:* discover.alpenacc.edu					
Washtenaw Community College 4800 E Huron River Dr PO Box 1610	Ann Arbor	MI	48106	734-973-3300	677-5408*
**Fax:* Admissions ■ *Web:* www.wccnet.edu					
Auburn Hills 2900 Featherstone Rd	Auburn Hills	MI	48326	248-232-4100	
Web: www.oaklandcc.edu					
Keweenaw Bay Ojibwa Community College 111 Beartown Rd	Baraga	MI	49908	906-353-4600	353-8107
Web: www.kbocc.org					
Kellogg Community College 450 N Ave	Battle Creek	MI	49017	269-965-3931	966-4089*
**Fax:* Admissions ■ *Web:* kellogg.edu					
Western Campus 9555 Haggerty Rd	Belleville	MI	48111	734-699-7008	699-7152
Web: www.wcccd.edu					
Oakland Community College 2480 Opdyke Rd	Bloomfield Hills	MI	48304	248-341-2000	341-2199
TF: 800-829-1040 ■ *Web:* www.oaklandcc.edu					
Southfield 2480 Opdyke Rd	Bloomfield Hills	MI	48304	248-341-2000	233-2828*
**Fax:* Library ■ *TF:* 800-829-1040 ■ *Web:* www.oaklandcc.edu					
Bay Mills Community College 12214 W Lakeshore Dr	Brimley	MI	49715	906-248-3354	248-3351
TF: 800-844-2622 ■ *Web:* www.bmcc.edu					
Glen Oaks Community College 62249 Shimmel Rd	Centreville	MI	49032	269-467-9945	467-9068*
**Fax:* Admissions ■ *TF:* 888-994-7818 ■ *Web:* www.glenoaks.edu					
Macomb Community College *Center* 44575 Garfield Rd	Clinton Township	MI	48038	586-445-7999	286-4787*
**Fax:* Admissions ■ *TF:* 866-622-6621 ■ *Web:* www.macomb.edu					
Henry Ford Community College 5101 Evergreen Rd	Dearborn	MI	48128	313-845-9600	845-9891*
**Fax:* Admissions ■ *TF:* 800-585-4322 ■ *Web:* www.hfcc.edu					
Downtown 1001 W Ft St	Detroit	MI	48226	313-496-2758	961-9648
Web: www.wcccd.edu					
Wayne County Community College *Eastern Campus* 5901 Conner	Detroit	MI	48213	313-922-3311	922-1104
Web: www.wcccd.edu					
Northwest 8200 W Outer Dr	Detroit	MI	48219	313-943-4000	
Web: www.wcccd.edu					
Southwestern Michigan College (SMC) 58900 Cherry Grove Rd	Dowagiac	MI	49047	269-782-1000	782-1331
TF: 800-456-8675 ■ *Web:* www.swmich.edu					
Bay de Noc Community College 2001 N Lincoln Rd	Escanaba	MI	49829	906-786-5802	786-8515*
**Fax:* Admissions ■ *TF:* 800-221-2001 ■ *Web:* mybay.baycollege.edu					
Orchard Ridge 27055 OrchaRd Lake Rd	Farmington Hills	MI	48334	248-522-3400	341-2126*
**Fax:* Library ■ *Web:* www.oaklandcc.edu					
Charles Stewart Mott Community College 1401 E Ct St	Flint	MI	48503	810-762-0200	762-5611
Web: www.mcc.edu					
Grand Rapids Community College 143 Bostwick Ave NE	Grand Rapids	MI	49503	616-234-4000	234-4107*
**Fax:* Admissions ■ *Web:* www.grcc.edu					
Mid Michigan Community College (MMCC) 1375 S Clare Ave	Harrison	MI	48625	989-386-6622	386-6613
Web: www.midmich.edu					
Hillsdale 3120 W Carleton Rd PO Box 712	Hillsdale	MI	49242	517-437-3343	437-0232
TF: 888-522-7344 ■ *Web:* www.jccmi.edu					
Gogebic Community College E 4946 Jackson Rd	Ironwood	MI	49938	906-932-4231	932-0868*
**Fax:* Admissions ■ *TF:* 800-682-5910 ■ *Web:* www.gogebic.cc.mi.us					
Jackson Community College 2111 Emmons Rd	Jackson	MI	49201	517-787-0800	796-8631*
**Fax:* Admissions ■ *TF:* 888-522-7344 ■ *Web:* www.jccmi.edu					
Arcadia Commons 202 N Rose St	Kalamazoo	MI	49007	269-373-7800	373-7892
Web: kvcc.edu					
Kalamazoo Valley Community College *Texas Township* 6767 W 'O' Ave	Kalamazoo	MI	49003	269-488-4400	488-4161*
**Fax:* Admissions ■ *Web:* www.kvcc.edu					
Lansing Community College 419 N Washington Sq	Lansing	MI	48933	517-483-1957	483-9668
TF: 800-644-4522 ■ *Web:* www.lansing.cc.mi.us					
Schoolcraft College 18600 Haggerty Rd	Livonia	MI	48152	734-462-4400	462-4553*
**Fax:* Admissions ■ *TF:* 844-727-6763 ■ *Web:* www.schoolcraft.edu					
Monroe County Community College 1555 S Raisinville Rd	Monroe	MI	48161	734-242-7300	242-9711*
**Fax:* Admissions ■ *TF:* 877-937-6222 ■ *Web:* www.monroeccc.edu					
Saginaw Chippewa Tribal College 2274 Enterprise Dr	Mount Pleasant	MI	48858	989-775-4123	775-4528
TF: 800-225-8172 ■ *Web:* www.sagchip.org					
Muskegon Community College 221 S Quarterline Rd	Muskegon	MI	49442	231-773-9131	777-0255*
**Fax:* Admissions ■ *TF:* 866-711-4622					
Bertrand Crossing 1905 Foundation Dr	Niles	MI	49120	269-695-1391	695-2999
TF: 800-252-1562 ■ *Web:* www.lakemichigancollege.edu					
Niles Area 2229 US 12	Niles	MI	49120	269-782-1233	
TF: 800-456-8675 ■ *Web:* www.swmich.edu					
North Central Michigan College 1515 Howard St	Petoskey	MI	49770	231-348-6605	348-6672*
**Fax:* Admissions ■ *TF:* 888-298-6605 ■ *Web:* www.ncmich.edu					
Kirtland Community College 10775 N St Helen Rd	Roscommon	MI	48653	989-275-5000	275-6789
TF: 866-632-9992 ■ *Web:* www.kirtland.edu					
Royal Oak 739 S Washington Ave	Royal Oak	MI	48067	248-246-2400	246-2520*
**Fax:* Library ■ *Web:* www.oaklandcc.edu					
West Shore Community College PO Box 277	Scottville	MI	49454	231-845-6211	845-3944*
**Fax:* Admissions ■ *TF:* 800-848-9722 ■ *Web:* www.westshore.edu					
Montcalm Community College 2800 College Dr	Sidney	MI	48885	989-328-2111	328-2950*
**Fax:* Admissions ■ *Web:* www.montcalm.edu					
Lake Michigan College *South Haven* 125 Veterans Blvd	South Haven	MI	49090	269-639-8442	637-7515
TF: 800-252-1562 ■ *Web:* www.lakemichigancollege.edu					
Downriver 21000 Northline Rd	Taylor	MI	48180	734-946-3500	374-0240
Web: www.wcccd.edu					
Northwestern Michigan College 1701 E Front St	Traverse City	MI	49686	231-995-1000	995-1339*
**Fax:* Admissions ■ *TF:* 800-748-0566 ■ *Web:* www.nmc.edu					
Delta College 1961 Delta Rd	University Center	MI	48710	989-686-9000	667-2202*
**Fax:* Admissions ■ *TF:* 888-636-4211 ■ *Web:* www.delta.edu					
South 14500 E 12-Mile Rd	Warren	MI	48088	586-445-7000	445-7140*
**Fax:* Admissions ■ *TF:* 866-622-6621 ■ *Web:* www.macomb.edu					
Highland Lakes 7350 Cooley Lake Rd	Waterford	MI	48327	248-942-3100	942-3113
TF: 800-829-1040 ■ *Web:* www.oaklandcc.edu					

Minnesota

				Phone	Fax
Riverland Community College 1900 Eigth Ave NW	Austin	MN	55912	507-433-0600	433-0515
TF: 800-247-5039 ■ *Web:* www.riverland.edu					
Normandale Community College 9700 France Ave S	Bloomington	MN	55431	952-487-8200	487-8230*
**Fax:* Admissions ■ *TF:* 866-880-8740 ■ *Web:* www.normandale.edu					
Brainerd 501 W College Dr	Brainerd	MN	56401	218-855-8199	855-8057*
**Fax:* Admissions ■ *TF:* 800-933-0346 ■ *Web:* www.clcmn.edu					
North Hennepin Community College 7411 85th Ave N	Brooklyn Park	MN	55445	763-424-0702	424-0929*
**Fax:* Admissions ■ *TF:* 800-818-0395 ■ *Web:* www.nhcc.edu					

	City	State	Zip	Phone	Fax
Cambridge 300 Polk St S	Cambridge	MN	55008	763-433-1100	433-1841*
**Fax:* Admissions ■ *Web:* www.anokaramsey.edu					
Leech Lake Tribal College					
6945 Little Wolf Rd PO Box 180	Cass Lake	MN	56633	218-335-4200	335-4209
TF: 800-627-3529 ■ *Web:* www.lltc.edu					
Fond du Lac Tribal & Community College					
2101 14th St	Cloquet	MN	55720	218-879-0800	879-0814
TF: 800-657-3712 ■ *Web:* www.fdltcc.edu					
Anoka-Ramsey Community College					
11200 Mississippi Blvd NW	Coon Rapids	MN	55433	763-433-1100	433-1521
Web: www.anokaramsey.edu					
Detroit Lakes 900 Hwy 34E	Detroit Lakes	MN	56501	218-846-3700	846-3794
TF: 800-492-4836 ■ *Web:* www.minnesota.edu					
Lake Superior College 2101 Trinity Rd	Duluth	MN	55811	218-733-7600	733-5945*
**Fax:* Admissions ■ *TF:* 800-432-2884 ■ *Web:* lsc.edu					
East Grand Forks					
2022 Central Ave NE	East Grand Forks	MN	56721	218-773-3441	793-2842
TF: 800-451-3441 ■ *Web:* www.northlandcollege.edu					
Vermilion Community College 1900 E Camp St	Ely	MN	55731	218-365-7200	365-7218
TF: 800-657-3608 ■ *Web:* www.vcc.edu					
Mesabi Range Community & Technical College					
1100 Industrial Pk Dr PO Box 648	Eveleth	MN	55734	218-741-3095	744-7466
TF: 800-657-3860 ■ *Web:* www.mr.mnscu.edu					
Faribault 1225 Third St	Faribault	MN	55021	507-332-5800	332-5888
TF: 800-422-0391 ■ *Web:* www.southcentral.edu					
Minnesota State Community & Technical College					
Fergus Falls 1414 College Way	Fergus Falls	MN	56537	218-736-1500	736-1510*
**Fax:* Admissions ■ *TF:* 877-450-3322 ■ *Web:* www.minnesota.edu					
Itasca Community College					
1851 E Us Hwy 169	Grand Rapids	MN	55744	218-327-4460	327-4350
TF: 800-996-6422 ■ *Web:* www.itascacc.edu					
Hibbing Community College 1515 E 25th St	Hibbing	MN	55746	218-262-6700	262-6717*
**Fax:* Admissions ■ *TF:* 800-224-4422 ■ *Web:* www.hcc.mnscu.edu					
Rainy River Community College					
1501 Hwy 71	International Falls	MN	56649	218-285-7722	285-2239*
**Fax:* Admissions ■ *TF:* 800-456-3996 ■ *Web:* www.rrcc.mnscu.edu					
Inver Hills Community College					
2500 80th St E	Inver Grove Heights	MN	55076	651-450-8500	450-8677*
**Fax:* Admissions ■ *TF:* 866-576-0689 ■ *Web:* www.inverhills.edu					
Minneapolis Community & Technical College					
1501 Hennepin Ave	Minneapolis	MN	55403	612-659-6200	659-6210*
**Fax:* Admissions ■ *TF:* 800-247-0911 ■ *Web:* www.minneapolis.edu					
Moorhead 1900 28th Ave S	Moorhead	MN	56560	218-299-6500	299-6584*
**Fax:* Admissions ■ *TF:* 800-426-5603 ■ *Web:* www.minnesota.edu					
South Central College					
Mankato 1920 Lee Blvd	North Mankato	MN	56003	507-389-7200	388-9951
TF: 800-722-9359 ■ *Web:* www.southcentral.edu					
Rochester Community & Technical College					
851 30th Ave SE	Rochester	MN	55904	507-285-7210	280-3529*
**Fax:* Admissions ■ *TF:* 800-247-1296 ■ *Web:* www.rctc.edu					
Central Lakes College					
Staples 1830 Airport Rd	Staples	MN	56479	218-894-5100	894-5185
TF: 800-247-6836 ■ *Web:* www.clcmn.edu					
Northland Community & Technical College					
1101 US Hwy 1 E	Thief River Falls	MN	56701	218-681-0701	681-0774*
**Fax:* Admissions ■ *TF:* 800-959-6282 ■ *Web:* www.northlandcollege.edu					
Century College 3300 Century Ave N	White Bear Lake	MN	55115	651-779-3300	773-1796*
**Fax:* Admissions ■ *TF:* 800-228-1978 ■ *Web:* www.century.edu					
Minnesota West Community & Technical College					
1450 Collegeway	Worthington	MN	56187	507-372-3400	372-5803*
**Fax:* Admissions ■ *TF:* 800-657-3966 ■ *Web:* www.mnwest.edu					

Mississippi

	City	State	Zip	Phone	Fax
Northeast Mississippi Community College					
101 Cunningham Blvd	Booneville	MS	38829	662-728-7751	720-7405*
**Fax:* Admissions ■ *TF:* 800-555-2154 ■ *Web:* www.nemcc.edu					
East Central Community College PO Box 129	Decatur	MS	39327	601-635-2111	635-4060*
**Fax:* Admissions ■ *TF:* 877-462-3222 ■ *Web:* www.eccc.edu/transcripts.html					
Jones County Junior College 900 S Ct St	Ellisville	MS	39437	601-477-4000	477-4258*
**Fax:* Admissions ■ *Web:* jcjc.edu					
Fulton 602 W Hill St	Fulton	MS	38843	662-862-8000	862-8234*
**Fax:* Admissions ■ *TF:* 800-433-3243 ■ *Web:* www.iccms.edu					
Jackson County 2300 Hwy 90 PO Box 100	Gautier	MS	39553	228-497-9602	497-7873
TF: 866-735-1122 ■ *Web:* www.mgccc.edu					
Holmes Community College PO Box 399	Goodman	MS	39079	662-472-2312	
TF: 800-465-6374 ■ *Web:* holmescc.edu					
Mississippi Gulf Coast Community College					
Jefferson Davis 2226 Switzer Rd	Gulfport	MS	39507	228-896-3355	896-2520*
**Fax:* Admissions ■ *TF:* 866-735-1122 ■ *Web:* www.mgccc.edu					
Meridian Community College 910 Hwy 19 N	Meridian	MS	39307	601-483-8241	481-1305*
**Fax:* Admissions ■ *TF:* 800-622-8431 ■ *Web:* www.mcc.cc.ms.us					
Mississippi Delta Community College					
PO Box 668	Moorhead	MS	38761	662-246-6322	246-6288
Web: www.msdelta.edu					
Natchez 11 Co-Lin Cir	Natchez	MS	39120	601-442-9111	446-1225*
**Fax:* Admissions ■ *TF:* 866-296-6522 ■ *Web:* www.colin.edu					
Rankin 3805 Hwy 80 E	Pearl	MS	39208	601-932-5237	936-1833*
**Fax:* Admissions ■ *Web:* www.hindscc.edu					
Pearl River Community College					
101 Hwy 11 N	Poplarville	MS	39470	601-403-1000	403-1339*
**Fax:* Admissions ■ *TF:* 877-772-2338 ■ *Web:* www.prcc.edu					
Hinds Community College					
501 E Main St PO Box 1100	Raymond	MS	39154	601-857-5261	857-3539*
**Fax:* Admissions ■ *TF:* 800-446-3722 ■ *Web:* www.hindscc.edu					
East Mississippi Community College (EMCC)					
1512 Kemper St	Scooba	MS	39358	662-476-8442	
Web: www2.eastms.edu					
Northwest Mississippi Community College					
4975 Hwy 51 N	Senatobia	MS	38668	662-562-3200	562-3221
Web: www.northwestms.edu					
Southwest Mississippi Community College					
1156 College Dr	Summit	MS	39666	601-276-2000	276-3888
Web: www.smcc.edu					
Itawamba Community College					
Tupelo 2176 S Eason Blvd	Tupelo	MS	38804	662-620-5000	620-5315*
**Fax:* Admissions ■ *Web:* www.iccms.edu					
Copiah-Lincoln Community College PO Box 649	Wesson	MS	39191	601-643-8488	643-8225*
**Fax:* Admissions ■ *TF:* 866-296-6522 ■ *Web:* www.colin.edu					

Missouri

	City	State	Zip	Phone	Fax
Watley Ctr 4020 N Main St	Cassville	MO	65625	417-847-1706	847-1367
Web: www.crowder.edu					
Jefferson College 1000 Viking Dr	Hillsboro	MO	63050	636-789-3951	789-5103*
**Fax:* Admissions ■ *Web:* www.jeffco.edu					
Metropolitan Community College Blue River					
20301 E 78 Hwy	Independence	MO	64057	816-220-6500	220-6577*
**Fax:* Admissions ■ *Web:* www.mcckc.edu					
Maple Woods Community College					
2601 NE Barry Rd	Kansas City	MO	64156	816-437-3000	437-3351*
**Fax:* Admissions ■ *Web:* www.mcckc.edu					
Metropolitan Community College Penn Valley					
3201 SW Trafficway	Kansas City	MO	64111	816-759-4000	759-4161
TF: 866-676-6224 ■ *Web:* www.mcckc.edu					
Metropolitan Community College Longview					
500 SW Longview Rd	Lee's Summit	MO	64081	816-672-2000	672-2378*
**Fax:* Admissions ■ *Web:* www.mcckc.edu					
Moberly Area Community College					
101 College Ave	Moberly	MO	65270	660-263-4110	263-2406
TF: 800-622-2070 ■ *Web:* www.macc.edu					
Crowder College 601 Laclede Ave	Neosho	MO	64850	417-451-3223	455-5731*
**Fax:* Admissions ■ *TF:* 866-238-7788 ■ *Web:* www.crowder.edu					
Cottey College 1000 W Austin Blvd	Nevada	MO	64772	417-667-8181	667-8103*
**Fax:* Admissions ■ *TF:* 888-526-8839 ■ *Web:* www.cottey.edu					
Mineral Area College					
5270 Frat River Rd PO Box 1000	Park Hills	MO	63601	573-431-4593	518-2166*
**Fax:* Admissions ■ *Web:* www.mineralarea.edu					
Three Rivers Community College					
2080 Three Rivers Blvd	Poplar Bluff	MO	63901	573-840-9600	840-9058*
**Fax:* Admissions ■ *TF:* 877-879-8722 ■ *Web:* www.trcc.edu					
Saint Louis Community College (STLCC)					
300 S Broadway	Saint Louis	MO	63102	314-539-5000	539-5170*
**Fax:* Admissions ■ *Web:* www.stlcc.edu					
Forest Park 5600 Oakland Ave	Saint Louis	MO	63110	314-644-9100	644-9375*
**Fax:* Admissions ■ *Web:* www.stlcc.edu/fp					
State Fair Community College 3201 W 16th St	Sedalia	MO	65301	660-530-5800	596-5820
TF: 877-311-7322 ■ *Web:* www.sfccmo.edu					
Ozarks Technical Community College					
1001 E Chestnut Expy	Springfield	MO	65802	417-447-7500	447-6906*
**Fax:* Admissions ■ *Web:* www.otc.edu					
North Central Missouri College 1301 Main St	Trenton	MO	64683	660-359-3948	359-2211*
**Fax:* Admissions ■ *TF:* 800-880-6180 ■ *Web:* www.ncmissouri.edu					
East Central College 1964 Prairie Dell Rd	Union	MO	63084	636-583-5193	583-1897*
**Fax:* Admissions ■ *TF:* 800-273-8255 ■ *Web:* www.eastcentral.edu					

Montana

	City	State	Zip	Phone	Fax
Dawson Community College 300 College Dr	Glendive	MT	59330	800-821-8320	*
**Fax:* Admissions ■ *TF:* 800-821-8320 ■ *Web:* dawsonbucs.com					
Chief Dull Knife College PO Box 98	Lame Deer	MT	59043	406-477-6215	477-6219
Web: www.cdkc.edu					
Flathead Valley Community College					
Libby 225 Commerce Way	Libby	MT	59923	406-293-2721	293-5112*
**Fax:* Admissions ■ *Web:* www.fvcc.edu					
Miles Community College 2715 Dickinson St	Miles City	MT	59301	406-874-6100	874-6283*
**Fax:* Admissions ■ *TF:* 800-541-9281 ■ *Web:* www.milescc.edu					
Salish Kootenai College PO Box 70	Pablo	MT	59855	406-275-4800	275-4801*
**Fax:* Admissions ■ *TF:* 877-752-6553 ■ *Web:* www.skc.edu					
Fort Peck Community College PO Box 398	Poplar	MT	59255	406-768-6300	768-6301
Web: www.fpcc.edu					

Nebraska

	City	State	Zip	Phone	Fax
Beatrice 4771 W Scott Rd	Beatrice	NE	68310	402-228-3468	228-2218*
**Fax:* Admissions ■ *TF:* 800-233-5027 ■ *Web:* www.southeast.edu					
Columbus 4500 63rd St PO Box 1027	Columbus	NE	68602	402-564-7132	562-1201*
**Fax:* Admissions ■ *Web:* www.cccneb.edu					
Metropolitan Community College					
Elkhorn Valley 829 N 204th	Elkhorn	NE	68022	402-289-1200	
Web: www.mccneb.edu					
Grand Island 3134 W Hwy 34 PO Box 4903	Grand Island	NE	68802	308-398-4222	398-7399*
**Fax:* Admissions ■ *Web:* www.cccneb.edu					
Central Community College					
Hastings 550 Technical Blvd	Hastings	NE	68901	402-463-9811	461-2454
Web: www.cccneb.edu					
Southeast Community College					
Lincoln 8800 'O' St	Lincoln	NE	68520	402-471-3333	437-2404*
**Fax:* Admissions ■ *TF:* 800-642-4075 ■ *Web:* www.southeast.edu					
Nebraska Indian Community College PO Box 428	Macy	NE	68039	402-837-5078	837-4183*
**Fax:* Admissions ■ *TF:* 844-440-6422 ■ *Web:* www.thenicc.edu					
McCook Community College 1205 E Third St	McCook	NE	69001	308-345-8100	345-8180*
**Fax:* Admissions ■ *TF:* 800-658-4348 ■ *Web:* www.mpcc.edu					
Northeast Community College					
801 E Benjamin Ave PO Box 469	Norfolk	NE	68702	402-371-2020	844-7396*
**Fax:* Admissions ■ *Web:* www.northeast.edu					
North Platte Community College					
North 1101 Halligan Dr	North Platte	NE	69101	308-535-3601	534-5767*
**Fax:* Admissions ■ *TF:* 800-658-4308 ■ *Web:* www.mpcc.edu					

Phone Fax

South 601 W State Farm Rd ... North Platte NE 69101 800-658-4348 535-3794*
**Fax Area Code:* 308 ■ *TF:* 800-658-4348 ■ *Web:* www.mpcc.edu

Western Nebraska Community College
1601 E 27th St ... Scottsbluff NE 69361 308-635-3606 635-6732
TF: 800-348-4435 ■ *Web:* www.wncc.net

Little Priest Tribal College
601 E College Dr PO Box 270 ... Winnebago NE 68071 402-878-2380 878-2355
Web: www.littlepriest.edu

Nevada

Phone Fax

Western Nevada Community College
Fallon 160 Campus Way ... Fallon NV 89406 775-423-7565 423-8029
Web: www.wnc.edu/location/fallon
Henderson 700 College Dr ... Henderson NV 89002 702-651-3000 651-3509*
**Fax:* Admissions ■ *Web:* csn.edu

Community College of Southern Nevada
West Charleston 6375 W Charleston Blvd ... Las Vegas NV 89146 702-651-5610
Web: www.csn.edu
Douglas 1680 Bently Pkwy S ... Minden NV 89423 775-782-2413 782-2415
TF: 877-838-2778 ■ *Web:* www.wnc.edu

College of Southern Nevada
Cheyenne 3200 E Cheyenne Ave ... North Las Vegas NV 89030 702-651-4000
Web: www.csn.edu

Truckee Meadows Community College
7000 Dandini Blvd Red Mtn Bldg Rm 319 ... Reno NV 89512 775-673-7000 673-7028*
**Fax:* Admissions ■ *Web:* www.tmcc.edu

New Hampshire

Phone Fax

White Mountains Community College (WMCC)
2020 Riverside Dr ... Berlin NH 03570 603-752-1113 752-6335
TF: 800-445-4525 ■ *Web:* www.wmcc.edu

Community College System of New Hampshire (CCSNH)
26 College Dr ... Concord NH 03301 603-271-2722 271-2725
Web: www.ccsnh.edu

NHTI Concord's Community College
31 College Dr ... Concord NH 03301 603-271-6484 271-7139
TF: 800-247-0179 ■ *Web:* www.nhti.edu

Lakes Region Community College (LRCC)
379 Belmont Rd ... Laconia NH 03246 603-524-3207 524-8084
TF: 800-357-2992 ■ *Web:* www.lrcc.edu

New Jersey

Phone Fax

Camden County College 200 College Dr ... Blackwood NJ 08012 856-227-7200 374-4917
TF: 888-228-2466 ■ *Web:* www.camdencc.edu
Camden City 200 N Broadway Ste 1 ... Camden NJ 08102 856-338-1817
Web: www.camdencc.edu

Salem Community College
460 Hollywood Ave ... Carneys Point NJ 08069 856-299-2100 351-2763*
**Fax:* Admissions ■ *Web:* www.salemcc.edu

Union County College 1033 Springfield Ave ... Cranford NJ 07016 908-709-7000 709-7125*
**Fax:* Admissions ■ *TF:* 877-468-3229 ■ *Web:* www.ucc.edu

Middlesex County College
2600 Woodbridge Ave PO Box 3050 ... Edison NJ 08818 732-548-6000 906-7728*
**Fax:* Admissions ■ *TF:* 888-442-4551 ■ *Web:* middlesexcc.edu

Hudson County Community College
162 Sip Ave ... Jersey City NJ 07306 201-714-7200 714-2136*
**Fax:* Admissions ■ *Web:* www.hccc.edu

Brookdale Community College
765 Newman Springs Rd ... Lincroft NJ 07738 732-842-1900 224-2271*
**Fax:* Admissions ■ *TF:* 866-767-9512 ■ *Web:* www.brookdalecc.edu

Assumption College for Sisters
350 BernaRdsville Rd ... Mendham NJ 07945 973-543-6528 543-1738
Web: www.acs350.org

Essex County College 303 University Ave ... Newark NJ 07102 973-877-3000 877-3446*
**Fax:* Admissions ■ *Web:* www.essex.edu

Sussex County Community College
One College Hill Rd ... Newton NJ 07860 973-300-2100 579-5226*
**Fax:* Admissions ■ *Web:* www.sussex.edu

Bergen Community College 400 Paramus Rd ... Paramus NJ 07652 201-447-7200 670-7973*
**Fax:* Admissions ■ *TF:* 877-612-5381 ■ *Web:* www.bergen.edu

Passaic County Community College
One College Blvd ... Paterson NJ 07505 973-684-6800 684-6778*
**Fax:* Admissions ■ *Web:* www.pccc.cc.nj.us

Burlington County College
601 Pemberton Browns Mills Rd ... Pemberton NJ 08068 609-894-9311 726-0401*
**Fax:* Admissions ■ *Web:* bcc.edu

County College of Morris 214 Ctr Grove Rd ... Randolph NJ 07869 973-328-5000 328-5199*
**Fax:* Admissions ■ *TF:* 888-726-3260 ■ *Web:* www.ccm.edu

Gloucester County College 1400 TanyaRd Rd ... Sewell NJ 08080 856-468-5000 468-8498*
**Fax:* Admissions ■ *Web:* www.gccnj.edu

Raritan Valley Community College
PO Box 3300 ... Somerville NJ 08876 908-526-1200 704-3442*
**Fax:* Admissions ■ *TF:* 888-326-4058 ■ *Web:* www.raritanval.edu

Ocean County College
College Dr PO Box 2001 ... Toms River NJ 08754 732-255-0400 255-0444
Web: www.ocean.edu

Mercer County Community College PO Box B ... Trenton NJ 08690 609-586-4800 586-6944
TF: 800-982-9491 ■ *Web:* www.mccc.edu
Kerney Ctr N Broad & Academy St ... Trenton NJ 08608 609-586-4800 570-3106
TF: 800-982-9491 ■ *Web:* www.mccc.edu

Cumberland County College 3322 College Dr ... Vineland NJ 08360 856-691-8600 691-3002*
**Fax:* Admissions ■ *TF:* 800-433-3243 ■ *Web:* www.cccnj.net

Warren County Community College
475 Rt 57 W ... Washington NJ 07882 908-835-9222 689-5824*
**Fax:* Admissions ■ *Web:* www.warren.edu

Phone Fax

West Essex 730 Bloomfield Ave ... West Caldwell NJ 07006 973-877-3175
Web: www.essex.edu
West Windsor 1200 Old Trenton Rd ... West Windsor NJ 08550 609-586-4800 570-3861*
**Fax:* Admissions ■ *TF:* 800-982-9491 ■ *Web:* www.mccc.edu

New Mexico

Phone Fax

Alamogordo (NMSU-A) 2400 N Scenic Dr ... Alamogordo NM 88310 575-439-3600 439-3760
Web: www.nmsua.edu

University of New Mexico (UNM)
One University of New Mexico ... Albuquerque NM 87131 505-277-0111 277-6686
TF: 800-225-5866 ■ *Web:* www.unm.edu
Carlsbad 1500 University Dr ... Carlsbad NM 88220 505-234-9200
TF: 888-888-2199 ■ *Web:* carlsbad.nmsu.edu

Clovis Community College (CCC) 417 Schepps Blvd ... Clovis NM 88101 575-769-2811 769-4190*
**Fax:* Admissions ■ *TF:* 800-769-1409 ■ *Web:* www.clovis.edu

Northern New Mexico College
921 Paseo de Onate ... Espanola NM 87532 505-747-2100 747-5449
TF: 800-477-3632 ■ *Web:* www.nnmc.edu

San Juan College 4601 College Blvd ... Farmington NM 87402 505-326-3311 566-3500*
**Fax:* Admissions ■ *TF:* 866-426-1233 ■ *Web:* www.sanjuancollege.edu
Grants 1500 Third St ... Grants NM 87020 505-287-6678 287-2329*
**Fax:* Admissions ■ *Web:* www.grants.nmsu.edu

New Mexico Junior College One Thunderbird Cir ... Hobbs NM 88240 505-392-4510 392-0322
TF: 800-657-6260 ■ *Web:* www.nmjc.edu

Dona Ana Branch Community College (DACC)
2800 N Sonoma Ranch Blvd PO Box 30001 ... Las Cruces NM 88011 575-528-7000 528-7300*
**Fax:* Admissions ■ *TF:* 800-903-7503 ■ *Web:* dabcc.nmsu.edu

New Mexico State University (NMSU)
MSC-3A PO Box 30001 ... Las Cruces NM 88003 575-646-3121 646-6330*
**Fax:* Admissions ■ *TF Admissions:* 800-662-6678 ■ *Web:* www.nmsu.edu

Luna Community College 366 Luna Dr ... Las Vegas NM 87701 505-454-2500 454-2519
TF: 800-588-7232 ■ *Web:* luna.edu
Los Alamos 4000 University Dr ... Los Alamos NM 87544 505-662-5919 661-4698*
**Fax:* Admissions ■ *Web:* losalamos.unm.edu
Valencia 280 La Entrada ... Los Lunas NM 87031 505-925-8580 925-8563*
**Fax:* Admissions ■ *TF:* 800-225-5866 ■ *Web:* www.unm.edu

Eastern New Mexico University Roswell
52 University Blvd PO Box 6000 ... Roswell NM 88202 800-243-6687 624-7144*
**Fax Area Code:* 505 ■ **Fax:* Admissions ■ *TF:* 800-243-6687 ■ *Web:* www.roswell.enmu.edu

Santa Fe Community College
6401 Richards Ave ... Santa Fe NM 87508 505-428-1000
Web: www.sfcc.edu

Mesalands Community College 911 S Tenth St ... Tucumcari NM 88401 575-461-4413 461-1901*
**Fax Area Code:* 505 ■ *Web:* www.mesalands.edu

New York

Phone Fax

Maria College 700 New Scotland Ave ... Albany NY 12208 518-438-3111 453-1366
Web: mariacollege.edu

College of Technology at Alfred
10 Upper College Dr ... Alfred NY 14802 607-587-4215 587-4299*
**Fax:* Admissions ■ *TF:* 800-425-3733 ■ *Web:* www.alfredstate.edu

Cayuga Community College 197 Franklin St ... Auburn NY 13021 315-255-1743 255-2117
TF: 866-598-8883 ■ *Web:* www.cayuga-cc.edu

Genesee Community College 1 College Rd ... Batavia NY 14020 585-343-0068 345-6810
TF: 866-225-5422 ■ *Web:* www.genesee.edu

Queensborough Community College
222-05 56th Ave ... Bayside NY 11364 718-631-6262 281-5189*
**Fax:* Admissions ■ *TF:* 877-253-7122 ■ *Web:* www.qcc.cuny.edu

Broome Community College 901 Front St ... Binghamton NY 13905 607-778-5000 778-5442*
**Fax:* Admissions ■ *TF:* 800-836-0689 ■ *Web:* www.sunybroome.edu

Suffolk County Community College
Grant 1001 Crooked Hill Rd ... Brentwood NY 11717 631-851-6700 851-6819*
**Fax:* Admissions ■ *TF:* 800-621-3362 ■ *Web:* www.sunysuffolk.edu
Brockport 350 New Campus Dr ... Brockport NY 14420 585-395-2751 395-5452
TF: 888-800-0029 ■ *Web:* www.brockport.edu

Bronx Community College 2155 University Ave ... Bronx NY 10453 718-289-5100 289-6003*
**Fax:* Admissions ■ *TF:* 866-888-8777 ■ *Web:* www.bcc.cuny.edu

Hostos Community College 500 Grand Concourse ... Bronx NY 10451 718-518-4444 518-4256*
**Fax:* Admissions ■ *TF:* 888-993-7650 ■ *Web:* www.hostos.cuny.edu

Kingsborough Community College
2001 Oriental Blvd ... Brooklyn NY 11235 718-368-5000 368-5356*
**Fax:* Admissions ■ *Web:* www.kbcc.cuny.edu

Trocaire College 360 Choate Ave ... Buffalo NY 14220 716-826-1200 828-6107*
**Fax:* Admissions ■ *Web:* www.trocaire.edu

Villa Maria College 240 Pine Ridge Rd ... Buffalo NY 14225 716-896-0700 896-0705
Web: www.villa.edu

Finger Lakes Community College
4340 Lakeshore Dr ... Canandaigua NY 14424 585-394-3500 394-5005
Web: www.fingerlakes.edu
Canton 34 Cornell Dr ... Canton NY 13617 315-386-7011 386-7929
TF: 800-388-7123 ■ *Web:* www.canton.edu

Corning Community College One Academic Dr ... Corning NY 14830 607-962-9251 962-9582*
**Fax:* Admissions ■ *Web:* www.corning-cc.edu
Delhi Two Main St ... Delhi NY 13753 607-746-4000 746-4104
TF: 800-963-3544 ■ *Web:* www.delhi.edu

Tompkins Cortland Community College 170 N St ... Dryden NY 13053 607-844-8211 844-6541*
**Fax:* Admissions ■ *TF:* 888-567-8211 ■ *Web:* www.tc3.edu

Nassau Community College
One Education Dr ... Garden City NY 11530 516-572-7500 572-9743
Web: www.ncc.edu

Herkimer County Community College
100 Reservoir Rd ... Herkimer NY 13350 315-866-0300 866-0062*
**Fax:* Admissions ■ *TF:* 844-464-4375 ■ *Web:* www.herkimer.edu

Columbia-Greene Community College 4400 Rt 23 ... Hudson NY 12534 518-828-4181 822-2015
TF: 888-668-4293 ■ *Web:* www.sunycgcc.edu

Jamestown Community College
525 Faulkner St PO Box 20 ... Jamestown NY 14702 716-338-1000
TF: 800-388-8557 ■ *Web:* www.sunyjcc.edu

Phone Fax

Fulton-Montgomery Community College
2805 New York 67 ... Johnstown NY 12095 518-762-4651 762-4334
Web: www.fmcc.edu

Sullivan County Community College
112 College Rd ... Loch Sheldrake NY 12759 845-434-5750 434-0923*
*Fax: Admissions ■ *Web:* www.sullivan.suny.edu

LaGuardia Community College
31-10 Thomson Ave ... Long Island City NY 11101 718-482-5000 609-2033*
*Fax: Admissions ■ *Web:* www.lagcc.cuny.edu/home/

Orange County Community College 115 S St ... Middletown NY 10940 845-344-6222 342-8662
Web: www.sunyorange.edu

Bank Street College Library 610 W 112th St ... New York NY 10025 212-875-4595 875-4594
Web: www.bankstreet.edu

Borough of Manhattan Community College
199 Chambers St Rm S-300 ... New York NY 10007 212-220-1265 220-2366
TF: 877-222-8387 ■ *Web:* www.bmcc.cuny.edu

Three of Us Corp 39 W 19th St ... New York NY 10011 212-645-0030
Web: sft.edu

Cattaraugus County 260 N Union St PO Box 5901 ... Olean NY 14760 716-376-7500 376-7020*
*Fax: Admissions ■ *TF:* 800-388-9776 ■ *Web:* www.sunyjcc.edu

Erie Community College
South 4041 Southwestern Blvd ... Orchard Park NY 14127 716-851-1003 851-1687*
*Fax: Admissions ■ *Web:* www.ecc.edu

Dutchess Community College
53 Pendell Rd ... Poughkeepsie NY 12601 845-431-8010 431-8605
Web: www.sunydutchess.edu

Adirondack Community College 640 Bay Rd ... Queensbury NY 12804 518-743-2200 745-1433
Web: www.sunyacc.edu

Eastern 121 Speonk-Riverhead Rd ... Riverhead NY 11901 631-548-2500 548-2504*
*Fax: Admissions ■ *Web:* www.sunysuffolk.edu

Monroe Community College
1000 E Henrietta Rd ... Rochester NY 14623 585-292-2000 292-3860
Web: www.monroecc.edu

Niagara County Community College
3111 Saunders Settlement Rd ... Sanborn NY 14132 716-614-6222 614-6820*
*Fax: Admissions ■ *TF:* 800-875-6269 ■ *Web:* www.niagaracc.suny.edu

North Country Community College
23 Santanoni Ave ... Saranac Lake NY 12983 518-891-2915 891-2915
TF: 888-879-6222 ■ *Web:* www.nccc.edu

Schenectady County Community College
78 Washington Ave ... Schenectady NY 12305 518-381-1200 381-1477
Web: www.sunysccc.edu

Ammerman 533 College Rd ... Selden NY 11784 631-451-4110 451-4094
Web: www.sunysuffolk.edu

Ulster County Community College
Cottekill Rd ... Stone Ridge NY 12484 845-687-5000 687-5090
TF: 800-724-0833 ■ *Web:* www.sunyulster.edu

Rockland Community College 145 College Rd ... Suffern NY 10901 845-574-4000 574-4433
TF: 800-722-7666 ■ *Web:* www.sunyrockland.edu

Onondaga Community College 4941 Onondaga Rd ... Syracuse NY 13215 315-498-2622 498-2107
TF: 800-827-1000 ■ *Web:* www.sunyocc.edu

Hudson Valley Community College
80 Vandenburgh Ave ... Troy NY 12180 518-629-4822 629-4576*
*Fax: Admissions ■ *TF:* 877-325-4822 ■ *Web:* www.hvcc.edu

Mohawk Valley Community College
1101 Sherman Dr ... Utica NY 13501 315-792-5400 792-5527
Web: www.mvcc.edu

Westchester Community College
75 Grasslands Rd ... Valhalla NY 10595 914-606-6600 606-6880*
*Fax: Admissions ■ *TF:* 800-235-7267 ■ *Web:* www.sunywcc.edu

Jefferson Community College
1220 Coffeen St ... Watertown NY 13601 315-786-2200 786-2459
TF: 888-435-6522 ■ *Web:* www.sunyjefferson.edu

North 6205 Main St ... Williamsville NY 14221 716-634-0800 851-1429
Web: www.ecc.edu

North Carolina

Phone Fax

Roanoke-Chowan Community College
109 Community College Rd ... Ahoskie NC 27910 252-862-1200 862-1355*
*Fax: Admissions ■ *Web:* www.roanoke.cc.nc.us

Randolph Community College
629 Industrial Pk Ave ... Asheboro NC 27205 336-633-0200 629-4695
TF: 800-433-3243 ■ *Web:* www.randolph.edu

Asheville-Buncombe Technical Community College
340 Victoria Rd ... Asheville NC 28801 828-254-1921 251-6718*
*Fax: Admissions ■ *Web:* www.abtech.edu

Brunswick Community College 50 College Rd ... Bolivia NC 28422 910-755-7300
TF: 800-754-1050 ■ *Web:* www.brunswickcc.edu

Transylvania 45 Oak Pk Dr ... Brevard NC 28712 828-883-2520 884-5725
Web: www.blueridge.edu

Central Piedmont Community College
1201 Elizabeth Ave ... Charlotte NC 28204 704-330-2722 330-6136*
*Fax: Admissions ■ *TF:* 877-530-8815 ■ *Web:* www.cpcc.edu

Cato 8120 Grier Rd PO Box 35009 ... Charlotte NC 28235 704-330-4801 330-4884*
*Fax: Admissions ■ *Web:* www.cpcc.edu

Harper 315 W Hebron St ... Charlotte NC 28273 704-330-4400 330-4444
Web: www.cpcc.edu

Sampson Community College PO Box 318 ... Clinton NC 28329 910-592-8081 592-8048*
*Fax: Admissions ■ *Web:* sampsoncc.edu

Haywood Community College 185 Freedlander Dr ... Clyde NC 28721 828-627-2821 627-4513*
*Fax: Admissions ■ *TF:* 866-468-6422 ■ *Web:* www.haywood.edu

South 1531 Trinity Church Rd ... Concord NC 28027 704-216-7222 788-2168*
*Fax: Admissions ■ *Web:* rccc.edu

South PO Box 39 ... Creedmoor NC 27522 919-528-4737 528-1201*
*Fax: Admissions ■ *TF:* 877-823-2378 ■ *Web:* www.vgcc.edu

Gaston College 201 Hwy 321-S ... Dallas NC 28034 704-922-6200 922-2344*
*Fax: Admissions ■ *TF:* 800-634-7854 ■ *Web:* gaston.edu

Surry Community College 630 S Main St ... Dobson NC 27017 336-386-8121
Web: surry.edu

Phone Fax

Bladen Community College PO Box 266 ... Dublin NC 28332 910-879-5556 879-5513
Web: www.bladencc.edu

Durham Technical Community College
1637 E Lawson St ... Durham NC 27703 919-686-3300 686-3669*
*Fax: Admissions ■ *Web:* www.durhamtech.edu

College of the Albemarle PO Box 2327 ... Elizabeth City NC 27906 252-335-0821 335-2011*
*Fax: Admissions ■ *Web:* www.albemarle.edu

Fayetteville Technical Community College
2201 Hull Rd ... Fayetteville NC 28303 910-678-8400 678-8407
TF: 877-245-5520 ■ *Web:* www.faytechcc.edu

Wayne Community College
3000 Wayne Memorial Dr PO Box 8002 ... Goldsboro NC 27533 919-735-5151 736-9425*
*Fax: Admissions ■ *TF:* 866-414-5064 ■ *Web:* www.waynecc.edu

Alamance Community College PO Box 8000 ... Graham NC 27253 336-578-2002 578-3964
TF: 877-667-7533 ■ *Web:* alamancecc.edu

Pamlico Community College PO Box 185 ... Grantsboro NC 28529 252-249-1851 249-2377*
*Fax: Library ■ *Web:* www.pamlico.cc.nc.us

Richmond Community College PO Box 1189 ... Hamlet NC 28345 910-410-1700 582-7102*
*Fax: Admissions ■ *TF:* 800-908-9946 ■ *Web:* www.richmondcc.edu

Vance-Granville Community College
200 Community College Rd ... Henderson NC 27537 252-492-2061 430-0460
Web: www.vgcc.edu

Catawba Valley Community College
2550 US Hwy 70 SE ... Hickory NC 28602 828-327-7000 327-7276
TF: 800-433-3243 ■ *Web:* www.cvcc.edu

Caldwell Community College & Technical Institute
2855 Hickory Blvd ... Hudson NC 28638 828-726-2200 726-2216*
*Fax: Admissions ■ *Web:* www.caldwell.cc.nc.us

North 11930 Verhoeff Dr ... Huntersville NC 28078 704-330-4100 330-4113*
*Fax: Admissions ■ *Web:* www.cpcc.edu/campuses/north

Coastal Carolina Community College
444 Western Blvd ... Jacksonville NC 28546 910-455-1221 455-7027*
*Fax: Admissions ■ *Web:* coastalcarolina.edu

Guilford Technical Community College
601 Highpoint Rd PO Box 309 ... Jamestown NC 27282 336-334-4822 819-2022*
*Fax: Admissions ■ *Web:* www.gtcc.edu

James Sprunt Community College
133 James Sprunt Dr ... Kenansville NC 28349 910-296-2400 296-1636*
*Fax: Admissions ■ *Web:* jamessprunt.edu

Lenoir Community College PO Box 188 ... Kinston NC 28502 252-527-6223 233-6879
TF: 800-848-5497 ■ *Web:* www.lenoircc.edu

Davidson County Community College
PO Box 1287 ... Lexington NC 27293 336-249-8186 224-0240*
*Fax: Admissions ■ *TF:* 800-233-4050 ■ *Web:* www.davidsonccc.edu

Louisburg College 501 N Main St ... Louisburg NC 27549 919-496-2521 496-1788*
*Fax: Admissions ■ *TF:* 800-775-0208 ■ *Web:* www.louisburg.edu

Franklin 8100 Nc 56 Hwy ... Louisburg NC 27549 919-496-1567 496-6604
Web: www.vgcc.edu

Robeson Community College
5160 Fayetteville Rd PO Box 1420 ... Lumberton NC 28360 910-272-3700 272-3328
Web: robeson.edu

McDowell Technical Community College
54 College Dr ... Marion NC 28752 828-652-6021 652-1014*
*Fax: Admissions ■ *Web:* mcdowelltech.edu

Madison 4646 US Hwy 25-70 ... Marshall NC 28753 828-649-2947 281-9859
Web: www.abtech.edu

Levine 2800 Campus Ridge Rd ... Matthews NC 28105 704-330-4200 330-4210
Web: cpcc.edu

Carteret Community College
3505 Arendell St ... Morehead City NC 28557 252-222-6000 222-6265
Web: www.carteret.edu

Western Piedmont Community College
1001 Burkemont Ave ... Morganton NC 28655 828-438-6000
Web: www.wpcc.edu

Tri-County Community College 21 Campus Cir ... Murphy NC 28906 828-837-6810 837-3266
Web: www.tricountycc.edu

Craven Community College 800 College Ct ... New Bern NC 28562 252-638-4131 638-4649*
*Fax: Admissions ■ *Web:* www.cravencc.edu

Sandhills Community College
3395 Airport Rd ... Pinehurst NC 28374 910-692-6185 695-3981*
*Fax: Admissions ■ *TF:* 800-338-3944 ■ *Web:* www.sandhills.edu

South Piedmont Community College 680 Hwy 74 ... Polkton NC 28135 704-272-5300 272-5303*
*Fax: Admissions ■ *TF:* 800-766-0319 ■ *Web:* www.spcc.edu

Wake Technical Community College
9101 Fayetteville Rd ... Raleigh NC 27603 919-662-3500 661-0117*
*Fax: Admissions ■ *Web:* www.waketech.edu

Nash Community College PO Box 7488 ... Rocky Mount NC 27804 252-443-4011 443-0828*
*Fax: Admissions ■ *Web:* www.nashcc.edu

Piedmont Community College
1715 College Dr PO Box 1197 ... Roxboro NC 27573 336-599-1181 597-3817*
*Fax: Admissions ■ *Web:* www.piedmont.cc.nc.us

Rowan-Cabarrus Community College
North
1333 Jake Alexander Blvd S PO Box 1595 ... Salisbury NC 28146 704-216-7222 633-6804*
*Fax: Admissions ■ *Web:* www.rccc.edu/

Central Carolina Community College
1105 Kelly Dr ... Sanford NC 27330 919-775-5401 718-7380*
*Fax: Admissions ■ *Web:* www.cccc.edu

Cleveland Community College 137 S Post Rd ... Shelby NC 28152 704-484-4000
Web: clevelandcc.edu

Johnston Community College 245 College Rd ... Smithfield NC 27577 919-934-3051 989-7862*
*Fax: Admissions ■ *Web:* johnstoncc.edu

Isothermal Community College
286 ICC Loop Rd PO Box 804 ... Spindale NC 28160 828-286-3636 286-4014
Web: www.isothermal.edu

Mayland Community College
200 Mayland Dr PO Box 547 ... Spruce Pine NC 28777 828-765-7351 765-0728*
*Fax: Admissions ■ *TF:* 800-462-9526 ■ *Web:* www.mayland.edu

Mitchell Community College
500 W Broad St ... Statesville NC 28677 704-878-3200 878-0872
Web: www.mitchellcc.edu

Edgecombe Community College 2009 W Wilson St ... Tarboro NC 27886 252-823-5166 823-6817*
*Fax: Admissions ■ *TF:* 877-823-2378 ■ *Web:* www.edgecombe.cc.nc.us

	City	State	Zip	Phone	Fax
Warren County PO Box 207	Warrenton	NC	27536	252-257-1900	257-3612*
**Fax:* Admissions ■ *TF:* 877-823-2378 ■ *Web:* www.vgcc.edu					
Beaufort County Community College					
5337 Hwy 264 E	Washington	NC	27889	252-946-6194	940-6393*
**Fax:* Admissions ■ *Web:* beaufortccc.edu					
Halifax Community College 100 College Dr	Weldon	NC	27890	252-536-2551	536-4144
Web: www.halifaxcc.edu					
Rockingham Community College					
215 Wrenn Memorial Rd	Wentworth	NC	27375	336-342-4261	342-1809
Web: www.rockinghamcc.edu					
Southeastern Community College PO Box 151	Whiteville	NC	28472	910-642-7141	642-1267*
**Fax:* Admissions ■ *Web:* www.sccnc.edu					
Wilkes Community College					
1328 S Collegiate Dr PO Box 120	Wilkesboro	NC	28697	336-838-6100	838-6277
Web: www.wilkescc.edu					
Martin Community College					
1161 Kehukee Pk Rd	Williamston	NC	27892	252-792-1521	792-0826
Web: www.martin.cc.nc.us					
Cape Fear Community College					
411 N Front St	Wilmington	NC	28401	910-362-7000	362-7080*
**Fax:* Admissions ■ *TF:* 877-498-8868 ■ *Web:* www.cfcc.edu					
Pitt Community College					
1986 Pitt Tech Rd PO Box 7007	Winterville	NC	28590	252-493-7200	321-4401
Web: www.pittcc.edu					
Caswell County					
331 Piedmont Dr PO Box 1150	Yanceyville	NC	27379	336-694-5707	694-7086
Web: www.piedmont.cc.nc.us					

North Dakota

	City	State	Zip	Phone	Fax
Turtle Mountain Community College					
10145 BIA Rd 7	Belcourt	ND	58316	701-477-7862	477-7892
TF: 800-827-1100 ■ *Web:* www.tm.edu					
Bismarck State College 1500 Edwards Ave	Bismarck	ND	58501	701-224-5400	224-5643*
**Fax:* Admissions ■ *TF:* 800-445-5073 ■ *Web:* www.bismarckstate.edu					
Minot State University Bottineau					
105 Simrall Blvd	Bottineau	ND	58318	701-228-5451	228-5499*
**Fax:* Admissions ■ *TF:* 800-542-6866 ■ *Web:* dakotacollege.edu					
Lake Region State College					
1801 College Dr N	Devils Lake	ND	58301	701-662-1514	662-1581*
**Fax:* Admissions ■ *TF:* 800-443-1313 ■ *Web:* www.lrsc.nodak.edu					
Cankdeska Cikana Community College					
PO Box 269	Fort Totten	ND	58335	701-766-4415	766-4077
TF: 888-783-1463 ■ *Web:* www.littlehoop.edu					
Fort Berthold Community College PO Box 490	New Town	ND	58763	701-627-4738	627-3609*
**Fax:* Admissions ■ *Web:* fortbertholdcc.edu					
North Dakota State College of Science					
800 Sixth St N	Wahpeton	ND	58076	701-671-2401	671-2201*
**Fax:* Admissions ■ *TF:* 800-342-4325 ■ *Web:* www.ndscs.edu					
Williston State College					
1410 University Ave PO Box 1326	Williston	ND	58802	701-774-4200	774-4211*
**Fax:* Admissions ■ *TF:* 888-863-9455 ■ *Web:* willistonstate.edu					

Ohio

	City	State	Zip	Phone	Fax
Ashtabula 3300 Lake Rd W	Ashtabula	OH	44004	440-964-3322	964-4269*
**Fax:* Admissions ■ *TF:* 800-988-5368 ■ *Web:* www.ashtabula.kent.edu					
University of Cincinnati Clermont College					
4200 Clermont College Dr	Batavia	OH	45103	513-732-5200	732-5303*
**Fax:* Admissions ■ *TF:* 866-446-2822 ■ *Web:* www.ucclermont.edu					
Geauga 14111 Claridon-Troy Rd	Burton	OH	44021	440-834-4187	834-8846*
**Fax:* Admissions ■ *Web:* www.geauga.kent.edu					
Wright State University Lake					
7600 Lk Campus Dr	Celina	OH	45822	419-586-0300	586-0358*
**Fax:* Admissions ■ *TF:* 800-237-1477 ■ *Web:* lake.wright.edu/					
Cincinnati State Technical & Community College					
3520 Central Pkwy	Cincinnati	OH	45223	513-569-1500	569-1562*
**Fax:* Admissions ■ *TF:* 877-569-0115 ■ *Web:* www.cincinnatistate.edu					
Cuyahoga Community College					
Metropolitan 2900 Community College Ave	Cleveland	OH	44115	216-987-4200	696-2567*
**Fax:* Admitting ■ *TF:* 800-954-8742 ■ *Web:* www.tri-c.edu					
Columbus State Community College					
550 E Spring St	Columbus	OH	43215	614-287-2400	287-6019*
**Fax:* Admissions ■ *TF:* 800-621-6407 ■ *Web:* www.cscc.edu					
Sinclair Community College 444 W Third St	Dayton	OH	45402	937-512-3000	512-2393*
**Fax:* Admissions ■ *Web:* www.sinclair.edu					
Lorain County Community College					
1005 N Abbe Rd	Elyria	OH	44035	440-365-5222	366-4167
TF: 800-995-5222 ■ *Web:* www.lorainccc.edu					
Findlay 3200 Bright Rd	Findlay	OH	45840	800-466-9367	424-5194*
**Fax Area Code:* 419 ■ *TF:* 800-466-9367 ■ *Web:* www.owens.edu					
Terra Community College 2830 Napoleon Rd	Fremont	OH	43420	419-334-8400	334-9035
TF: 800-334-3886 ■ *Web:* www.terra.edu					
Hamilton 1601 University Blvd	Hamilton	OH	45011	513-785-3000	785-3148*
**Fax:* Admissions ■ *Web:* www.ham.miamioh.edu					
Eastern 4250 Richmond Rd	Highland Hills	OH	44122	216-987-2024	987-2214*
**Fax:* Admissions ■ *TF:* 800-954-8742 ■ *Web:* www.tri-c.edu					
Bowling Green State University Firelands					
One University Dr	Huron	OH	44839	419-433-5560	433-9696*
**Fax:* Admissions ■ *Web:* www.firelands.bgsu.edu					
Lakeland Community College					
7700 Clocktower Dr	Kirtland	OH	44094	440-525-7000	525-7651*
**Fax:* Admissions ■ *TF:* 800-589-8520 ■ *Web:* lakelandcc.edu					
Washington State Community College					
710 Colegate Dr	Marietta	OH	45750	740-374-8716	376-0257
Web: www.wscc.edu					
University of Akron Wayne College					
1901 Smucker Rd	Orrville	OH	44667	330-683-2010	684-8989
TF: 800-221-8308 ■ *Web:* www.wayne.uakron.edu					
Miami University 501 E High St	Oxford	OH	45056	513-529-1809	529-1550*
**Fax:* Admissions ■ *TF:* 866-426-4643 ■ *Web:* miamioh.edu					
Western 11000 Pleasant Valley Rd	Parma	OH	44130	216-987-2800	987-5071*
**Fax:* Admissions ■ *TF:* 800-954-8742 ■ *Web:* www.tri-c.edu					
Owens Community College					
Toledo 30335 Oregon Rd	Perrysburg	OH	43551	419-661-7000	661-7734*
**Fax:* Admissions ■ *TF:* 800-466-9367 ■ *Web:* www.owens.edu					
Edison Community College 1973 Edison Dr	Piqua	OH	45356	937-778-8600	778-1920
TF: 800-922-3722 ■ *Web:* www.edisonohio.edu					
University of Rio Grande Rio Grande Community College					
218 N College Ave	Rio Grande	OH	45674	740-245-5353	*
**Fax:* Admissions ■ *TF:* 800-282-7201 ■ *Web:* www.rio.edu					
South 12681 US Rt 62	Sardinia	OH	45171	937-695-0307	695-8093*
**Fax:* Admissions ■ *TF:* 877-644-6562 ■ *Web:* www.sscc.edu					
Clark State Community College					
570 E Leffel Ln	Springfield	OH	45506	937-325-0691	328-6097
Web: www.clarkstate.edu					
Southern State Community College					
North 1850 Davids Dr	Wilmington	OH	45177	937-382-6645	383-1206*
**Fax:* Admissions ■ *TF:* 877-644-6562 ■ *Web:* www.sscc.edu					

Oklahoma

	City	State	Zip	Phone	Fax
Western Oklahoma State College 2801 N Main St	Altus	OK	73521	580-477-2000	477-7723
TF: 800-662-1113 ■ *Web:* www.wosc.edu					
Rogers State University Bartlesville					
1701 W Will Rogers Blvd	Claremore	OK	74107	918-343-7777	343-7681*
**Fax:* Admissions ■ *TF:* 800-256-7511 ■ *Web:* www.rsu.edu					
Redlands Community College					
1300 S Country Club Rd	El Reno	OK	73036	405-262-2552	422-1200*
**Fax:* Admissions ■ *TF:* 866-415-6367 ■ *Web:* www.redlandscc.edu					
Comanche Nation College 1608 SW Ninth St	Lawton	OK	73501	580-591-0203	353-7075
TF: 877-591-0203 ■ *Web:* www.cnc.cc.ok.us					
Northeastern Oklahoma A&M College 200 I St NE	Miami	OK	74354	918-542-8441	540-6946*
**Fax:* Admissions ■ *Web:* neo.edu					
Rose State College 6420 SE 15th St	Midwest City	OK	73110	405-733-7372	736-0309*
**Fax:* Admissions ■ *Web:* www.rose.edu					
Oklahoma City Community College					
7777 S May Ave	Oklahoma City	OK	73159	405-682-1611	682-7521*
**Fax:* Admissions ■ *Web:* www.occc.edu					
Oklahoma City 900 N Portland Ave	Oklahoma City	OK	73107	405-947-4421	945-9120*
**Fax:* Admissions ■ *TF:* 800-560-4099 ■ *Web:* www.osuokc.edu					
Carl Albert State College 1507 S McKenna St	Poteau	OK	74953	918-647-1300	647-1306
Web: www.carlalbert.edu					
Rogers State University Pryor 421 S Elliott St	Pryor	OK	74361	918-825-6117	825-6135*
**Fax:* Admissions ■ *TF:* 800-256-7511 ■ *Web:* www.rsu.edu					
Southwestern Oklahoma State University Sayre					
409 E Mississippi St	Sayre	OK	73662	580-928-5533	928-1140*
**Fax:* Admissions ■ *Web:* www.swosu.edu/sayre					
Oklahoma State University					
219 Student Union Bldg	Stillwater	OK	74078	405-744-5000	744-7092
TF: 800-852-1255 ■ *Web:* www.okstate.edu					
Murray State College One Murray Campus	Tishomingo	OK	73460	580-371-2371	371-9844*
**Fax:* Admissions ■ *TF:* 800-342-0698 ■ *Web:* www.mscok.edu					
Northern Oklahoma College					
1220 E Grand St PO Box 310	Tonkawa	OK	74653	580-628-6200	628-6371*
**Fax:* Admissions ■ *TF:* 866-278-7134 ■ *Web:* noc.edu					
Metro 909 S Boston Ave	Tulsa	OK	74119	918-595-7000	595-7347*
**Fax:* Admissions ■ *TF:* 866-970-0233 ■ *Web:* www.tulsacc.edu					
Tulsa Community College					
Northeast 3727 E Apache St	Tulsa	OK	74115	918-595-7000	595-7594
Web: www.tulsacc.edu					
Southeast 10300 E 81st St	Tulsa	OK	74133	918-595-7000	595-7748
Web: www.tulsacc.edu					
West 7505 W 41st St	Tulsa	OK	74107	918-595-7000	595-8130
Web: www.tulsacc.edu					
Connors State College 1000 College Rd	Warner	OK	74469	918-463-2931	463-6324
TF: 888-594-5171 ■ *Web:* connorsstate.edu					
Eastern Oklahoma State College					
1301 W Main St	Wilburton	OK	74578	918-465-2361	465-4417
Web: www.eosc.edu					

Ontario

	City	State	Zip	Phone	Fax
Institute of Corporate Directors					
602 - 40 University Ave	Toronto	ON	M5J1T1	416-593-7741	
Web: www.icd.ca					

Oregon

	City	State	Zip	Phone	Fax
Linn-Benton Community College					
6500 Pacific Blvd SW	Albany	OR	97321	541-917-4999	917-4838*
**Fax:* Admissions ■ *Web:* www.linnbenton.edu					
Clatsop Community College 1653 Jerome Ave	Astoria	OR	97103	503-325-0910	325-5738
TF: 855-252-8767 ■ *Web:* www.clatsopcc.edu					
Central Oregon Community College					
2600 NW College Way	Bend	OR	97701	541-383-7700	383-7506*
**Fax:* Admissions ■ *Web:* www.cocc.edu					
Southwestern Oregon Community College					
1988 Newmark Ave	Coos Bay	OR	97420	541-888-2525	888-1513
TF: 800-962-2838 ■ *Web:* www.socc.edu					
Cottage Grove 1275 S River Rd PO Box 96	Cottage Grove	OR	97424	541-463-4202	942-5186
Web: www.lanecc.edu					
Lane Community College 4000 E 30th Ave	Eugene	OR	97405	541-463-3000	463-3995*
**Fax:* Admissions ■ *TF:* 800-321-2211 ■ *Web:* www.lanecc.edu					
Florence 3149 Oak St	Florence	OR	97439	541-997-8444	997-8448
TF: 800-222-3290 ■ *Web:* www.lanecc.edu					

	City	State	Zip	Phone	Fax
Mount Hood Community College					
26000 SE Stark St.	Gresham	OR	97030	503-491-6422	491-7388*
*Fax: Admissions ■ Web: www.mhcc.edu					
Klamath Community College					
7390 S Sixth St.	Klamath Falls	OR	97603	541-882-3521	885-7758
Web: www.kcc.cc.or.us					
Rogue Community College					
Riverside 117 S Central	Medford	OR	97501	541-245-7500	245-7648
Web: www.roguecc.edu					
Treasure Valley Community College					
650 College Blvd	Ontario	OR	97914	541-881-8822	881-2721*
*Fax: Admissions ■ TF: 888-292-5247 ■ Web: www.tvcc.cc.or.us					
Blue Mountain Community College					
2411 NW Carden Ave PO Box 100	Pendleton	OR	97801	541-276-1260	278-5871*
*Fax: Admissions ■ Web: www.bluecc.edu					
Portland Community College					
Sylvania 12000 SW 49th Ave.	Portland	OR	97219	503-244-6111	977-4740*
*Fax: Admissions ■ Web: www.pcc.edu					
Umpqua Community College					
1140 Umpqva College Rd PO Box 967	Roseburg	OR	97470	541-440-4600	440-4612
TF: 800-820-5161 ■ Web: www.umpqua.edu					
Chemeketa Community College					
4000 Lancaster Dr NE PO Box 14007	Salem	OR	97309	503-399-5006	399-3918*
*Fax: Admissions ■ Web: www.chemeketa.edu					
Tillamook Bay Community College					
4301 Third St	Tillamook	OR	97141	503-842-8222	
TF: 888-306-8222 ■ Web: www.tbcc.cc.or.us					

Pennsylvania

	City	State	Zip	Phone	Fax
NanoHorizons Inc					
270 Rolling Ridge Dr Ste 100	Bellefonte	PA	16823	814-355-4700	
TF: 866-584-6235 ■ Web: www.nanohorizons.com					
Northampton Community College					
3835 Green Pond Rd	Bethlehem	PA	18020	610-861-5300	861-4560*
*Fax: Admissions ■ TF: 877-543-0998 ■ Web: www.northampton.edu					
Central 340 DeKalb Pk.	Blue Bell	PA	19422	215-641-6300	619-7188*
*Fax: Admitting ■ Web: mc3.edu					
Bristol 1280 New Rodgers Rd	Bristol	PA	19007	215-781-3939	781-3928
Web: www.bucks.edu					
Harcum College 750 Montgomery Ave	Bryn Mawr	PA	19010	610-525-4100	526-6147*
*Fax: Admissions ■ TF: 800-650-0035 ■ Web: www.harcum.edu					
Butler County Community College					
107 College Dr	Butler	PA	16002	724-287-8711	285-6047
TF: 888-826-2829 ■ Web: www.bc3.edu					
Downingtown 100 Bond Dr	Downingtown	PA	19335	484-237-6200	237-6305
Web: dccc.edu					
DuBois One College Pl	Du Bois	PA	15801	814-375-4700	375-4784*
*Fax: Admissions ■ TF: 800-346-7627 ■ Web: www.ds.psu.edu					
Worthington Scranton 120 Ridge View Dr	Dunmore	PA	18512	570-963-2500	963-2524*
*Fax: Admissions ■ Web: www.sn.psu.edu					
Pennsylvania Highlands Community College					
881 Hills Plz Dr Ste 450	Ebensburg	PA	15931	814-262-6446	262-6420
Web: www.pennhighlands.edu					
Lehigh Valley 8380 Mohr Ln PO Box 549	Fogelsville	PA	18051	610-285-5000	285-5220*
*Fax: Admissions ■ Web: www.lv.psu.edu					
Harrisburg Area Community College					
Gettysburg 731 Old Harrisburg Rd.	Gettysburg	PA	17325	717-337-3855	337-3015*
*Fax: Admissions ■ TF: 800-222-4222 ■ Web: www.hacc.edu					
Hazleton 76 University Dr	Hazleton	PA	18202	570-450-3000	450-3182*
*Fax: Admissions ■ TF: 800-279-8495 ■ Web: www.hn.psu.edu					
Manor College 700 Fox Chase Rd	Jenkintown	PA	19046	215-885-2360	576-6564*
*Fax: Admissions ■ Web: www.manor.edu					
Lebanon 735 Cumberland St	Lebanon	PA	17042	717-270-4222	270-6385
TF: 800-222-4222 ■ Web: www.hacc.edu					
Wilkes-Barre Old Rt 115 PO Box PSU	Lehman	PA	18627	570-675-2171	675-9113*
*Fax: Admissions ■ Web: www.wb.psu.edu					
Fayette 2201 University Dr.	Lemont Furnace	PA	15456	724-430-4100	430-4175*
*Fax: Admissions ■ TF: 877-568-4130 ■ Web: www.fe.psu.edu					
Delaware County Community College					
901 Media Line Rd	Media	PA	19063	610-359-5000	359-5343
TF: 800-908-9946 ■ Web: www.dccc.edu					
Community College of Beaver County					
One Campus Dr	Monaca	PA	15061	724-775-8561	728-7599*
*Fax: Admissions ■ TF: 800-335-0222 ■ Web: www.ccbc.edu					
Beaver 100 University Dr	Monaca	PA	15061	724-773-3500	773-3578*
*Fax: Admissions ■ TF: 877-564-6778 ■ Web: www.br.psu.edu					
Boyce 595 Beatty Rd	Monroeville	PA	15146	724-325-6614	325-6859*
*Fax: Admissions ■ Web: www.ccac.edu					
Mont Alto One Campus Dr.	Mont Alto	PA	17237	717-749-6000	749-6132*
*Fax: Admissions ■ TF: 800-392-6173 ■ Web: www.ma.psu.edu					
Luzerne County Community College					
1333 S Prospect St.	Nanticoke	PA	18634	800-377-5222	740-0238*
*Fax Area Code: 570 ■ *Fax: Admissions ■ TF: 800-377-5222 ■ Web: www.luzerne.edu					
New Kensington					
3550 Seventh St Rd Rt 780	New Kensington	PA	15068	724-334-5466	334-6111
Web: www.nk.psu.edu					
Bucks County Community College 275 Swamp Rd	Newtown	PA	18940	215-968-8000	968-8110*
*Fax: Admissions ■ Web: www.bucks.edu					
Upper County One Hillendale Dr	Perkasie	PA	18944	215-258-7700	258-7749
Web: www.bucks.edu					
Community College of Philadelphia					
1700 Spring Garden St.	Philadelphia	PA	19130	215-751-8000	751-8001*
*Fax: Admissions ■ Web: www.ccp.edu					
Community College of Allegheny County					
Allegheny 808 Ridge Ave	Pittsburgh	PA	15212	412-237-2525	237-4581*
*Fax: Admissions ■ Web: www.ccac.edu					
North 8701 Perry Hwy	Pittsburgh	PA	15237	412-366-7000	369-3635*
*Fax: Admissions ■ Web: www.ccac.edu					
Montgomery County Community College					
Pottstown 101 College Dr	Pottstown	PA	19464	610-718-1800	718-1999
Web: mc3.edu					
Berks PO Box 7009	Reading	PA	19610	610-396-6000	396-6077
Web: www.bk.psu.edu					
Reading Area Community College					
10 S Second St PO Box 1706	Reading	PA	19603	610-372-4721	607-6290*
*Fax: Admissions ■ TF: 800-626-1665 ■ Web: www.racc.edu					
Lehigh Carbon Community College					
4525 Education Pk Dr.	Schnecksville	PA	18078	610-799-2121	799-1527
TF General: 800-414-3975 ■ Web: www.lccc.edu					
Schuylkill 200 University Dr	Schuylkill Haven	PA	17972	570-385-6000	385-6272*
*Fax: Admissions ■ TF: 800-243-2374 ■ Web: www.sl.psu.edu					
Lackawanna College 501 Vine St	Scranton	PA	18509	570-961-7810	961-7843*
*Fax: Admissions ■ TF: 877-346-3552 ■ Web: facebook.com/lackawanna					
Shenango 147 Shenango Ave	Sharon	PA	16146	724-983-2803	983-2820*
*Fax: Admissions ■ TF: 800-275-7009 ■ Web: www.shenango.psu.edu					
Southeast 2000 Elmwood Ave	Sharon Hill	PA	19079	610-957-5700	957-5787
Web: www.dccc.edu					
Morgan Ctr 234 High St.	Tamaqua	PA	18252	570-668-6880	668-7296
TF: 800-424-2460 ■ Web: www.lccc.edu					
Monroe Three Old Mill Rd PO Box 530	Tannersville	PA	18372	570-620-9221	620-9317
TF: 877-543-0998 ■ Web: www.northampton.edu					
University of Pittsburgh					
Titusville 504 E Main St.	Titusville	PA	16354	888-878-0462	827-4519*
*Fax Area Code: 814 ■ *Fax: Admissions ■ TF: 888-878-0462 ■ Web: www.upt.pitt.edu					
Pennsylvania State University					
201 Shields Bldg Ofc of Admissions	University Park	PA	16802	814-865-4700	863-7590
Web: www.psu.edu					
McKeesport 201 Old Main	University Park	PA	16802	412-675-9000	
Web: www.psu.edu					
Valley Forge Military Academy & College					
1001 Eagle Rd	Wayne	PA	19087	610-989-1300	688-1545*
*Fax: Admissions ■ TF: 800-234-8362 ■ Web: www.vfmac.edu					
South 1750 Clairton Rd Rt 885	West Mifflin	PA	15122	412-469-1100	469-6291*
*Fax: Admissions ■ Web: www.ccac.edu					
York 1031 Edgecomb Ave	York	PA	17403	717-771-4000	771-4005*
*Fax: Admissions ■ TF: 800-778-6227 ■ Web: www.yk.psu.edu					
Westmoreland County Community College					
145 Pavilion Ln	Youngwood	PA	15697	724-925-4000	
TF: 800-262-2103 ■ Web: wccc.edu					

Quebec

	City	State	Zip	Phone	Fax
College Merici 755 Ch St-Louis	Quebec City	QC	G1S1C1	418-683-1591	682-8938
TF: 800-208-1463 ■ Web: www.merici.ca					

Rhode Island

	City	State	Zip	Phone	Fax
Community College of Rhode Island					
Flanagan 1762 Louisquisset Pk	Lincoln	RI	02865	401-333-7000	333-7122*
*Fax: Admissions ■ Web: www.ccri.edu					
Liston One Hilton St.	Providence	RI	02905	401-455-6000	455-6014
Web: www.ccri.edu					
Knight 400 E Ave	Warwick	RI	02886	401-825-1000	825-2394*
*Fax: Admissions ■ Web: www.ccri.edu					

South Carolina

	City	State	Zip	Phone	Fax
Northeastern Technical College					
1201 Chesterfield Hwy	Cheraw	SC	29520	843-921-6900	537-6148
TF: 800-921-7399 ■ Web: www.netc.edu					
Midlands Technical College PO Box 2408	Columbia	SC	29202	803-738-1400	790-7524*
*Fax: Admissions ■ TF: 800-922-8038 ■ Web: www.midlandstech.edu					
University of South Carolina					
1600 Hampton St	Columbia	SC	29208	803-777-7000	777-0101*
*Fax: Admissions ■ TF: 800-868-5872 ■ Web: www.sc.edu					
Aiken Technical College					
2276 Jefferson Davis Pkwy PO Box 696	Graniteville	SC	29829	803-593-9231	593-6526*
*Fax: Admissions ■ Web: www.atc.edu					
Greenville Technical College					
Barton 506 S Pleasantburg Dr	Greenville	SC	29607	864-250-8111	
TF All: 800-723-0673 ■ Web: www.gvltec.edu					
Brashier PO Box 5616	Greenville	SC	29606	864-250-8000	228-5009
Web: www.greenvilletech.com					
Williamsburg Technical College					
601 MLK Jr Ave	Kingstree	SC	29556	843-355-4110	355-4289*
*Fax: Admissions ■ TF: 800-768-2021 ■ Web: www.williamsburgtech.com					
Orangeburg-Calhoun Technical College					
3250 St Matthews Rd	Orangeburg	SC	29118	803-536-0311	
Web: www.octech.edu					
Clinton Junior College 1029 Crawford Rd	Rock Hill	SC	29730	803-327-7402	328-6318*
*Fax: Admissions ■ TF: 877-837-9645					
York Technical College 452 S Anderson Rd.	Rock Hill	SC	29730	803-327-8000	327-8059
TF: 800-922-8324 ■ Web: www.yorktech.com					
Spartanburg Methodist College					
1000 Powell Mill Rd.	Spartanburg	SC	29301	864-587-4000	587-4355*
*Fax: Admissions ■ TF: 800-772-7286 ■ Web: smcsc.edu					
Greer 2522 Locust Hill Rd	Taylors	SC	29687	800-723-0673	
TF: 800-723-0673 ■ Web: www.gvltec.edu/greer					
North Greenville University					
7801 N Tigerville Rd PO Box 1892	Tigerville	SC	29688	864-977-7000	977-7177*
*Fax: Admissions ■ TF: 800-468-6642 ■ Web: www.ngu.edu					
Union 401 E Main St	Union	SC	29379	864-429-8728	427-3682
TF: 800-768-5566 ■ Web: uscunion.sc.edu					

South Dakota

Phone Fax

Mitchell Technical Institute
821 N Capital St Mitchell SD 57301 800-675-1969 995-3083*
**Fax Area Code:* 605 ■ *TF:* 800-952-0042 ■ *Web:* www.mitchelltech.edu
Kilian Community College 300 E Sixth St Sioux Falls SD 57103 605-221-3100 336-2606*
**Fax:* Admissions ■ *TF:* 800-888-1147 ■ *Web:* www.kilian.edu
Sisseton Wahpeton College 12572 BIA Hwy 700 Sisseton SD 57262 605-698-3966 742-0394
Web: www.swc.tc
Lake Area Technical Institute
230 11th St NE PO Box 730 Watertown SD 57201 605-882-5284 882-6299
TF: 800-657-4344 ■ *Web:* lakeareatech.edu

Tennessee

Phone Fax

Chattanooga State Technical Community College
4501 Amnicola Hwy Chattanooga TN 37406 423-697-4400 697-4709*
**Fax:* Admissions ■ *TF:* 866-547-3733 ■ *Web:* www.chattanoogastate.edu
Cleveland State Community College
3535 Adkisson Dr Cleveland TN 37312 423-472-7141 478-6255
Web: clevelandstatecc.edu
Clifton 795 Main St Clifton TN 38425 931-676-6966 676-6941
Web: columbiastate.edu
Columbia State Community College
1665 Hampshire Pk Columbia TN 38401 931-540-2722 540-2830*
**Fax:* Admissions ■ *Web:* www.columbiastate.edu
Dyersburg State Community College
1510 Lake Rd Dyersburg TN 38024 731-286-3200 286-3325*
**Fax:* Admissions ■ *Web:* www.dscc.edu
Volunteer State Community College
1480 Nashville Pk Gallatin TN 37066 615-452-8600 230-4875*
**Fax:* Admissions ■ *TF:* 888-335-8722 ■ *Web:* www.volstate.edu
Roane State Community College 276 Patton Ln Harriman TN 37748 865-354-3000 882-4562*
**Fax:* Admitting ■ *TF:* 800-343-9104 ■ *Web:* www.roanestate.edu
Jackson State Community College 2046 N Pkwy Jackson TN 38301 731-424-3520 425-9559*
**Fax:* Admissions ■ *Web:* www.jscc.edu
Pellissippi State Technical Community College
10915 HaRdin Vly Rd Knoxville TN 37933 865-694-6400 539-7217*
**Fax:* Admissions ■ *Web:* www.pstcc.edu
Lexington-Henderson County 932 E Church St Lexington TN 38351 731-968-5722 968-1539
Web: www.jscc.edu
Motlow State Community College PO Box 8500 Lynchburg TN 37352 931-393-1500
TF: 800-654-4877 ■ *Web:* www.mscc.edu
Hiwassee College
225 Hiwassee College Dr Madisonville TN 37354 423-442-2001 442-8521*
**Fax:* Admissions ■ *TF:* 800-356-2187 ■ *Web:* www.hiwassee.edu
Southwest Tennessee Community College
PO Box 780 Memphis TN 38101 901-333-5000 333-4473
TF: 877-717-7822 ■ *Web:* www.southwest.tn.edu
Walters State Community College
500 S Davy Crockett Pkwy Morristown TN 37813 423-585-2600 585-6786*
**Fax:* Admissions ■ *TF:* 800-225-4770 ■ *Web:* www.ws.edu

Texas

Phone Fax

Cisco Junior College
Abilene 717 E Industrial Blvd Abilene TX 79602 325-794-4400 442-5100*
**Fax Area Code:* 254 ■ *Web:* cisco.edu
Abilene 650 E Hwy 80 Abilene TX 79601 325-672-7091 643-5987
TF: 800-852-8784 ■ *Web:* www.tstc.edu
Amarillo College 2201 S Washington St Amarillo TX 79109 806-371-5000 371-5066
Web: www.actx.edu
Smith System Driver Improvement Institute Inc
2201 Brookhollow Plz Dr Ste 200 Arlington TX 76006 817-652-6969
TF: 800-777-7648 ■ *Web:* www.smith-system.com
Southeast 2100 SE Pkwy Arlington TX 76018 817-515-3100 515-3182*
**Fax:* Admissions ■ *Web:* www.tccd.edu
Athens 100 Cardinal Dr Athens TX 75751 903-675-6200 675-6209*
**Fax:* Admissions ■ *TF:* 866-882-2937 ■ *Web:* www.tvcc.edu
Austin Community College (ACC)
5930 Middle Fiskville Rd Austin TX 78752 512-223-7000 223-7665*
**Fax:* Admissions ■ *TF:* 877-442-3522 ■ *Web:* www.austincc.edu
Cypress Creek 5930 Middle Fiskville Rd Austin TX 78752 512-223-4222 223-2048
Web: www.austincc.edu
Eastview 3401 Webberville Rd Austin TX 78702 512-223-5100 223-5900*
**Fax:* Admissions ■ *TF:* 888-626-1697 ■
Web: austincc.edu/locations/campuses/eastview-campus
Northridge 11928 Stonehollow Dr Austin TX 78758 512-223-4000 223-4651*
**Fax:* Admissions ■ *TF:* 877-990-0462 ■
Web: austincc.edu/locations/campuses/northridge-campus
Pinnacle 7748 Hwy 290 W Austin TX 78736 512-223-8001 223-8122
TF: 888-626-1697 ■
Web: austincc.edu/locations/campuses/pinnacle-campus
Rio Grande 1212 Rio Grande St Austin TX 78701 512-223-3000 223-3444*
**Fax:* Admissions ■ *TF:* 877-990-0462 ■
Web: austincc.edu/locations/campuses/rio-grande-campus
Riverside 1020 Grove Blvd Austin TX 78741 512-223-6000 223-6767*
**Fax:* Admissions ■ *TF:* 877-990-0462 ■
Web: austincc.edu/locations/campuses/riverside-campus
Lee College 200 Lee Dr Baytown TX 77520 281-427-5611 425-6555
Web: www.lee.edu
Coastal Bend College
Beeville 3800 Charco Rd Beeville TX 78102 361-358-2838 354-2254*
**Fax:* Admissions ■ *TF:* 866-722-2838 ■ *Web:* coastalbend.edu
Howard College 1001 Birdwell Ln Big Spring TX 79720 432-264-5000 264-5082*
**Fax:* Admissions ■ *TF:* 877-898-3833 ■ *Web:* www.howardcollege.edu
Southwest Collegiate Institute for the Deaf
3200 Ave C Big Spring TX 79720 432-264-3700 264-3707*
**Fax:* Admissions ■ *Web:* www.howardcollege.edu

Phone Fax

Frank Phillips College (FPC) PO Box 5118 Borger TX 79008 806-457-4200 274-6835
Web: www.fpctx.edu
North Central Texas College
Bowie 810 S Mill St Bowie TX 76230 940-872-4002 872-3065
Web: www.nctc.edu
Blinn College 902 College Ave Brenham TX 77833 979-830-4000 830-4110*
**Fax:* Admissions ■ *Web:* www.blinn.edu
Texas Southmost College 80 Fort Brown St Brownsville TX 78520 956-882-8200 882-8811
TF: 800-850-0160 ■ *Web:* www.utb.edu
Panola College 1109 W Panola St Carthage TX 75633 903-693-2000 693-2031*
**Fax:* Admissions ■ *Web:* www.panola.edu
Clarendon College
1122 College Dr PO Box 968 Clarendon TX 79226 806-874-3571 874-5080*
**Fax:* Admissions ■ *TF:* 800-687-9737 ■ *Web:* www.clarendoncollege.edu
Texas A&M Transportation Institute
3135 Tamu College Station TX 77843 979-845-1713
Web: tti.tamu.edu
Montgomery College 3200 College Pk Dr Conroe TX 77384 936-273-7000
Web: www.lonestar.edu
Del Mar College
East 101 Baldwin Blvd Corpus Christi TX 78404 361-698-1200 698-1595*
**Fax:* Admissions ■ *TF:* 800-652-3357 ■ *Web:* www.delmar.edu
Navarro College 3200 W Seventh Ave Corsicana TX 75110 903-874-6501 875-7353*
**Fax:* Admissions ■ *TF:* 800-628-2776 ■ *Web:* www.navarrocollege.edu
El Centro College 801 Main St Dallas TX 75202 214-860-2037 860-2233*
**Fax:* Admissions ■ *Web:* elcentrocollege.edu
Mountain View College 4849 W Illinois Ave Dallas TX 75211 214-860-8680 860-8570*
**Fax:* Admissions ■ *Web:* www.mvc.dcccd.edu
Richland College 12800 Abrams Rd Dallas TX 75243 972-238-6100 238-6346*
**Fax:* Admissions ■ *Web:* www.rlc.dcccd.edu
Grayson County College 6101 Grayson Dr Denison TX 75020 903-465-6030 463-5284*
**Fax:* Admissions ■ *Web:* www.grayson.edu
Mission Del Paso 10700 Gateway E El Paso TX 79927 915-831-7017
Web: www.epcc.edu
Northwest 6701 S Desert Blvd El Paso TX 79932 915-831-8848 831-8926
Web: www.epcc.edu
El Paso Community College
Valle Verde 919 Hunter Dr El Paso TX 79915 915-831-2000 831-2161*
**Fax:* Admissions ■ *TF:* 800-531-8292 ■ *Web:* www.epcc.edu
Brookhaven College 3939 Vly View Ln Farmers Branch TX 75244 972-860-4700 860-4886*
**Fax:* Admitting ■ *Web:* www.brookhavencollege.edu
Tarrant County College
Northwest 4801 Marine Creek Pkwy Fort Worth TX 76179 817-515-7100 515-7732*
**Fax:* Admissions ■ *TF:* 800-799-7233 ■ *Web:* www.tccd.edu
South 5301 Campus Dr Fort Worth TX 76119 817-515-4100 515-4110*
**Fax:* Admissions ■ *Web:* www.tccd.edu
Preston Ridge 9700 Wade Blvd Frisco TX 75035 972-377-1582 377-1723*
**Fax:* Admissions ■ *Web:* collin.edu
Galveston College 4015 Ave Q Galveston TX 77550 409-763-6551 944-1501*
**Fax:* Admissions ■ *TF:* 866-483-4242 ■ *Web:* www.gc.edu
Harlingen 1902 N Loop 499 Harlingen TX 78550 956-364-4000 364-5117
TF: 800-852-8784 ■ *Web:* www.tstc.edu
Hill College 112 Lamar Dr PO Box 619 Hillsboro TX 76645 254-659-7500 582-7591*
**Fax:* Admissions ■ *Web:* www.hillcollege.edu
Houston Community College
Central College 1300 Holman Houston TX 77004 713-718-6000 718-7745
Web: central.hccs.edu
NortheastCollege 4638 Airline Dr Houston TX 77022 713-718-8100 718-7500
Web: www.hccs.edu
North Harris College 2700 WW Thorne Rd Houston TX 77073 281-618-5400 618-7141*
**Fax:* Admissions ■ *Web:* www.lonestar.edu
North 5800 Uvalde Rd Houston TX 77049 281-458-4050 459-7688*
**Fax:* Admissions ■ *Web:* www.sanjac.edu
South 13735 Beamer Rd Houston TX 77089 281-998-6150 922-3485
Web: www.sanjac.edu
Northeast 828 W Harwood Rd Hurst TX 76054 817-515-8223 515-6988*
**Fax:* Admissions ■ *TF:* 800-799-7233 ■
Web: www.tccd.edu/Campuses_and_Centers/Northeast_Campus.html
North Lake College 5001 N MacArthur Blvd Irving TX 75038 972-273-3000 273-3112*
**Fax:* Admissions ■ *Web:* www.northlakecollege.edu
Jacksonville College
105 BJ Albritton Dr Jacksonville TX 75766 903-586-2518 586-0743*
**Fax:* Admissions ■ *Web:* www.jacksonville-college.edu
Kilgore College 1100 Broadway Kilgore TX 75662 903-984-8531 988-7531*
**Fax:* Admissions ■ *Web:* www.kilgore.edu
Central Texas College PO Box 1800 Killeen TX 76540 254-526-7161 526-1481
TF: 800-792-3348 ■ *Web:* www.online.ctcd.edu
Kingwood College 20000 Kingwood Dr Kingwood TX 77339 281-312-1600 312-1456
TF: 800-883-7939 ■ *Web:* www.lonestar.edu/kingwood.htm
Brazosport College 500 College Dr Lake Jackson TX 77566 979-230-3000 230-3443*
**Fax:* Admissions ■ *TF:* 877-717-7873 ■ *Web:* www.brazosport.edu
Cedar Valley College 3030 N Dallas Ave Lancaster TX 75134 972-860-8201 860-2910*
**Fax:* Admissions ■ *Web:* www.dcccd.edu
Laredo Community College (LCC)
W End Washington St Laredo TX 78040 956-722-0521 721-5493
Web: www.laredo.edu
South Plains College 1401 S College Ave Levelland TX 79336 806-894-9611 897-3167*
**Fax:* Admissions ■ *Web:* www.southplainscollege.edu
Collin County Community College
Central Park 2200 W University Dr McKinney TX 75070 972-548-6790 548-6702*
**Fax:* Admissions ■ *Web:* collin.edu
Eastfield College 3737 Motley Dr Mesquite TX 75150 972-860-7100 860-8306
TF: 800-260-8000 ■ *Web:* eastfieldcollege.edu
Midland College 3600 N Garfield St Midland TX 79705 432-685-4500 685-6480*
**Fax:* Admissions ■ *Web:* www.midland.edu
Northeast Texas Community College
1735 Chapel Hill Rd Mount Pleasant TX 75455 903-572-1911 572-6712*
**Fax:* Admissions ■ *TF:* 800-870-0142 ■ *Web:* www.ntcc.edu
Odessa College 201 W University Blvd Odessa TX 79764 432-335-6400 335-6824
TF: 866-968-2862 ■ *Web:* www.odessa.edu
Lamar State College
Orange 410 Front St Orange TX 77630 409-883-7750 882-3055*
**Fax:* Admissions ■ *Web:* www.lsco.edu

Phone Fax

Trinity Valley Community College
Palestine PO Box 2530 Palestine TX 75802 903-729-0256 729-2325
Web: www.tvcc.edu

Paris Junior College 2400 Clarksville St. Paris TX 75460 903-785-7661 782-0427*
**Fax:* Admissions ■ *TF:* 800-232-5804 ■ *Web:* www.parisjc.edu

San Jacinto College
Central 8060 Spencer Hwy. Pasadena TX 77505 281-476-1501 476-1892
Web: www.sanjac.edu

Spring Creek 2800 E Spring Creek Pkwy Plano TX 75074 972-881-5790 881-5174*
**Fax:* Admissions ■ *Web:* collin.edu

Port Arthur PO Box 310 Port Arthur TX 77641 409-983-4921 984-6025*
**Fax:* Admissions ■ *TF:* 800-477-5872 ■ *Web:* lamarpa.edu

Ranger College 1100 College Cir Ranger TX 76470 254-647-3234 647-3739*
**Fax:* Admissions ■ *TF:* 800-772-1213 ■ *Web:* www.rangercollege.edu

Western Texas College 6200 College Ave Snyder TX 79549 325-573-8511 573-9321*
**Fax:* Admissions ■ *TF:* 888-468-6982 ■ *Web:* www.wtc.edu

Southwest College 9910 Cash Rd Stafford TX 77477 713-718-2000 718-7793
Web: southwest.hccs.edu

Sugar Land 14004 University Blvd. Sugar Land TX 77479 281-243-8447 243-8583
TF: 800-561-9252 ■ *Web:* www.wcjc.edu

Texas State Technical College
Sweetwater 300 Homer K Taylor Dr Sweetwater TX 79556 325-235-7300 235-7443
TF: 877-450-3595 ■ *Web:* www.tstc.edu

Temple College 2600 S First St Temple TX 76504 254-298-8300 298-8288*
**Fax:* Admissions ■ *TF Admissions:* 800-460-4636 ■ *Web:* www.templejc.edu

Texarkana College 2500 N Robison Rd Texarkana TX 75599 903-838-4541 832-5030*
**Fax:* Admissions ■ *TF:* 877-275-4377 ■ *Web:* www.texarkanacollege.edu

College of the Mainland 1200 N Amburn Rd Texas City TX 77591 409-938-1211 933-8010
Web: www.com.edu

Tomball College 30555 Tomball Pkwy. Tomball TX 77375 281-351-3300 351-3384*
**Fax:* Admissions ■ *Web:* www.lonestar.edu

Tyler Junior College PO Box 9020 Tyler TX 75711 903-510-2523 510-2161*
**Fax:* Admissions ■ *TF:* 800-687-5680 ■ *Web:* www.tjc.edu

Southwest Texas Junior College
2401 Garner Field Rd Uvalde TX 78801 830-278-4401 591-7396*
**Fax:* Admissions ■ *TF:* 888-886-8490 ■ *Web:* www.swtjc.net

Vernon College 4400 College Dr Vernon TX 76384 940-552-6291 553-1753
TF: 866-336-9371 ■ *Web:* www.vernoncollege.edu

Victoria College 2200 E Red River St Victoria TX 77901 361-573-3291 582-2525
Web: www.vc.cc.tx.us

McLennan Community College 1400 College Dr. Waco TX 76708 254-299-8000 299-8694*
**Fax:* Admissions ■ *TF:* 866-339-5555 ■ *Web:* www.mclennan.edu

Waco 3801 Campus Dr Waco TX 76705 254-799-3611 867-3044
TF: 800-792-8784 ■ *Web:* www.waco.tstc.edu

Weatherford College 225 College Pk Dr Weatherford TX 76086 817-594-5471 598-6205*
**Fax:* Admissions ■ *TF:* 800-287-5471 ■ *Web:* www.wc.edu

Wharton County Junior College 911 Boling Hwy. Wharton TX 77488 979-532-4560 532-6494*
**Fax:* Admissions ■ *TF:* 800-561-9252 ■ *Web:* www.wcjc.edu

Utah

Phone Fax

San Juan 639 West 100 South Blanding UT 84511 435-678-2201 678-2220*
**Fax:* Admissions ■ *TF:* 800-395-2969 ■ *Web:* sjc.usu.edu

Snow College 150 College Ave PO Box 1028 Ephraim UT 84627 435-283-7000 283-7157*
**Fax:* Admissions ■ *TF:* 800-848-3399 ■ *Web:* www.snow.edu

Stevens Henager College 1890 South 1350 West Ogden UT 84401 800-622-2640 621-0853*
**Fax Area Code:* 801 ■ *TF:* 800-622-2640 ■ *Web:* www.stevenshenager.edu

Utah Valley State College 800 W University Pkwy Orem UT 84058 801-863-4636 *
**Fax:* Admissions ■ *TF:* 800-952-8220 ■ *Web:* www.uvu.edu

College of Eastern Utah 451 E 400 N Price UT 84501 435-797-1000 613-5814*
**Fax:* Admissions ■ *TF:* 800-336-2381 ■ *Web:* eastern.usu.edu

Salt Lake Community College
Redwood 4600 S Redwood Rd. Salt Lake City UT 84130 801-957-4111 957-4444
Web: www.slcc.edu

South City 1575 S State St. Salt Lake City UT 84115 801-957-4111
Web: www.slcc.edu

Vermont

Phone Fax

Community College of Vermont
Bennington 324 Main St Bennington VT 05201 802-447-2361 447-3246*
**Fax:* Admissions ■ *TF:* 800-431-0025 ■
Web: ccv.edu/event/bennington-center-2014-graduation-celebration/

Brattleboro 70 Landmark Hill Ste 101 Brattleboro VT 05301 802-254-6370 257-2593
TF: 800-431-0025 ■
Web: ccv.edu/documents/2014/07/brattleboro-parking.pdf

Middlebury 10 Merchants Row Ste 223 Middlebury VT 05753 802-388-3032 388-4686*
**Fax:* Admissions ■ *TF:* 800-431-0025 ■ *Web:* www.ccv.edu

Montpelier PO Box 489 Montpelier VT 05602 802-828-4060 828-2801*
**Fax:* Admissions ■ *TF:* 800-228-6686 ■ *Web:* www.ccv.edu

Morrisville 197 Harrell St Ste 2 Morrisville VT 05661 802-888-4258 888-2554*
**Fax:* Admissions ■ *TF:* 800-431-0025 ■ *Web:* www.ccv.edu

Newport 100 Main St Ste 150 Newport VT 05855 802-334-3387 334-5373*
**Fax:* Admissions ■ *TF:* 800-431-0025 ■ *Web:* ccv.edu/event/newport-open-house/

Landmark College One River Rd S Putney VT 05346 802-387-6718
Web: landmark.edu

Rutland 60 W St Rutland VT 05701 802-786-6996 786-4980*
**Fax:* Admissions ■ *TF:* 800-228-6686 ■ *Web:* www.ccv.edu

Saint Albans 142 S Main St Ste 2 Saint Albans VT 05478 802-524-6541 524-5216*
**Fax:* Admissions ■ *Web:* www.ccv.edu

Saint Johnsbury 1197 Main St Ste 3 Saint Johnsbury VT 05819 802-748-6673 748-5014*
**Fax:* Admissions ■ *Web:* www.ccv.edu

Springfield 307 S St. Springfield VT 05156 802-885-8360 885-8373
Web: www.ccv.edu

Phone Fax

Upper Valley
145 Billings Farm Rd White River Junction VT 05001 802-295-8822 295-8862*
**Fax:* Admissions ■ *TF:* 800-431-0025 ■ *Web:* www.ccv.edu

Virginia

Phone Fax

Virginia Highlands Community College
100 VHCC Dr PO Box 828 Abingdon VA 24212 276-739-2400 739-2590*
**Fax:* Admissions ■ *Web:* www.vhcc.edu

Southside Virginia Community College
109 Campus Dr Alberta VA 23821 434-949-1000 949-7863
TF: 888-220-7822 ■ *Web:* www.southside.edu

Alexandria 3001 N Beauregard St Alexandria VA 22311 703-845-6200 845-6046*
**Fax:* Admissions ■ *TF:* 855-259-1019 ■ *Web:* www.nvcc.edu

Northern Virginia Community College
Annandale 8333 Little River Tpke. Annandale VA 22003 703-323-3000
TF: 877-408-2028 ■ *Web:* www.nvcc.edu

Mountain Empire Community College
3441 Mtn Empire Rd. Big Stone Gap VA 24219 276-523-2400 523-8297*
**Fax:* Admissions ■ *Web:* www.me.cc.va.us

Southwest Virginia Community College
724 Community College Rd Cedar Bluff VA 24609 276-964-2555 964-7716*
**Fax:* Admissions ■ *TF:* 855-877-3944 ■ *Web:* www.sw.edu

Piedmont Virginia Community College
501 College Dr Charlottesville VA 22902 434-977-3900 961-5425*
**Fax:* Admissions ■ *Web:* www.pvcc.edu

Chesapeake 1428 Cedar Rd Chesapeake VA 23322 757-822-5100 822-5122
TF: 800-371-0898 ■ *Web:* www.tcc.edu

John Tyler Community College
13101 Jefferson Davis Hwy Chester VA 23831 804-796-4000 796-4362*
**Fax:* Admissions ■ *Web:* www.jtcc.edu

Dabney S Lancaster Community College
1000 Dabney Dr PO Box 1000 Clifton Forge VA 24422 540-863-2800 863-2915
Web: dslcc.edu

Danville Community College 1008 S Main St. Danville VA 24541 434-797-2222 797-8541*
**Fax:* Admissions ■ *TF:* 800-560-4291 ■ *Web:* www.dcc.vccs.edu

New River Community College
5251 College PO Box 1127 Dublin VA 24084 540-674-3600 674-3644*
**Fax:* Admissions ■ *TF:* 866-462-6722 ■ *Web:* www.nr.edu

Paul D Camp Community College
100 N College Dr PO Box 737 Franklin VA 23851 757-569-6700 569-6795*
**Fax:* Admissions ■ *TF:* 866-933-0508 ■ *Web:* www.pdc.edu

Fredericksburg 10000 Germanna Pt Dr Fredericksburg VA 22408 540-891-3000 710-2092*
**Fax:* Admissions ■ *Web:* www.germanna.edu

Rappahannock Community College
Glenns 12745 College Dr. Glenns VA 23149 804-758-6700 758-6830*
**Fax:* Admissions ■ *TF:* 800-836-9381 ■ *Web:* www.rappahannock.edu

Thomas Nelson Community College
99 Thomas Nelson Dr. Hampton VA 23666 757-825-2700 825-2763*
**Fax:* Admissions ■ *Web:* newport-news-virginia.apartmenthomeliving.com

Blue Ridge Community College Harrisonburg
160 N Mason St Harrisonburg VA 22802 540-432-3690
Web: www.brcc.edu

Germanna Community College
Locust Grove 2130 Germanna Hwy Locust Grove VA 22508 540-423-9030 727-3207
Web: www.germanna.edu

Central Virginia Community College
3506 WaRds Rd Lynchburg VA 24502 434-832-7600 832-7793*
**Fax:* Admissions ■ *Web:* cvcc.vccs.edu

Manassas 6901 Sudley Rd. Manassas VA 20109 703-257-6600 257-6565*
**Fax:* Admitting ■ *TF:* 855-259-1019 ■ *Web:* www.nvcc.edu

Patrick Henry Community College
645 Patriot Ave PO Box 5311 Martinsville VA 24112 276-638-8777 656-0352*
**Fax:* Admissions ■ *TF:* 855-874-6692 ■ *Web:* www.ph.vccs.edu

Eastern Shore Community College
29300 Lankford Hwy. Melfa VA 23410 757-789-1789 789-1737*
**Fax:* Admissions ■ *Web:* www.es.vccs.edu

Middletown 173 Skirmisher Ln Middletown VA 22645 540-868-7000 868-7005*
**Fax:* Admissions ■ *TF:* 800-906-5322 ■ *Web:* www.lfcc.edu

Norfolk 315 Granby St Norfolk VA 23510 757-822-1110 822-1154
TF: 800-371-0898 ■ *Web:* www.tcc.edu/welcome/locations/norfolk

Richard Bland College 11301 Johnson Rd Petersburg VA 23805 804-862-6100 862-6490*
**Fax:* Admissions ■ *Web:* www.rbc.edu

Tidewater Community College
Portsmouth 7000 College Dr Portsmouth VA 23703 757-822-2124 822-2002*
**Fax:* Admissions ■ *TF:* 800-371-0898 ■ *Web:* www.tcc.edu

J Sargeant Reynolds Community College
PO Box 85622 Richmond VA 23285 804-371-3000 371-3650*
**Fax:* Admissions ■ *Web:* www.reynolds.edu

Downtown 700 E Jackson St Richmond VA 23219 804-523-5455 371-3650
Web: www.jsr.vccs.edu

Virginia Western Community College
3094 Colonial Ave PO Box 14007 Roanoke VA 24038 540-857-8922 857-6102*
**Fax:* Admissions ■ *TF:* 855-874-6690 ■ *Web:* www.virginiawestern.edu

Hobbs Suffolk 271 Kenyon Rd Suffolk VA 23434 757-925-6300 925-6370*
**Fax:* Admissions ■ *TF:* 855-877-3918 ■ *Web:* pdc.edu/about/hobbs-suffolk-campus/

Virginia Beach 1700 College Crescent Virginia Beach VA 23453 757-822-7100 822-7350
TF: 800-371-0898 ■ *Web:* www.tcc.edu

Lord Fairfax Community College
Fauquier 6480 College St Warrenton VA 20187 540-351-1505 351-1530*
**Fax:* Admissions ■ *Web:* www.lfcc.edu

Warsaw 52 Campus Dr Warsaw VA 22572 804-333-6700 333-0106*
**Fax:* Admissions ■ *TF:* 800-836-9381 ■ *Web:* www.rappahannock.edu

Blue Ridge Community College
1 College Ln PO Box 80 Weyers Cave VA 24486 540-234-9261 453-2437*
**Fax:* Admissions ■ *TF:* 888-750-2722 ■ *Web:* www.brcc.edu

Phone | Fax

Wytheville Community College
1000 E Main St ... Wytheville VA 24382 276-223-4700 223-4860*
*Fax: Admissions ■ Web: www.wcc.vccs.edu

Washington

Phone | Fax

Grays Harbor College 1620 Edward P Smith Dr ... Aberdeen WA 98520 360-532-9020 538-4293*
*Fax: Admissions ■ TF: 800-562-4830 ■ Web: www.ghc.edu
Green River Community College
12401 SE 320th St ... Auburn WA 98092 253-833-9111 288-3454*
*Fax: Admissions ■ Web: www.greenriver.edu
Bellevue Community College
3000 Landerholm Cir SE ... Bellevue WA 98007 425-564-1000 564-4065*
*Fax: Admissions ■ Web: www.bellevuecollege.edu
Northwest Indian College 2522 Kwina Rd ... Bellingham WA 98226 360-676-2772 392-4333*
*Fax: Admissions ■ TF: 866-676-2772 ■ Web: www.nwic.edu
Whatcom Community College
237 W Kellogg Rd ... Bellingham WA 98226 360-676-2170 676-2171
TF: 855-767-9003 ■ Web: www.whatcom.ctc.edu
Olympic College 1600 Chester Ave ... Bremerton WA 98337 360-792-6050 475-7202*
*Fax: Admissions ■ TF: 800-259-6718 ■ Web: www.olympic.edu
Centralia College 600 W Locust St ... Centralia WA 98531 360-736-9391 330-7503*
*Fax: Admissions ■ Web: www.centralia.edu
Everett Community College 2000 Tower St ... Everett WA 98201 425-388-9100 388-9129*
*Fax: Admissions ■ TF: 866-575-9027 ■ Web: www.everettcc.edu
Grandview 500 W Main St ... Grandview WA 98930 509-882-7000 882-7012
Web: www.yvcc.edu
Clover Park Technical College
4500 Steilacoom Blvd SW ... Lakewood WA 98499 253-589-5800 589-5750
Web: www.cptc.edu
Pierce College 9401 Farwest Dr SW ... Lakewood WA 98498 253-964-6500 964-6427*
*Fax: Admissions ■ Web: www.pierce.ctc.edu
Lower Columbia College
1600 Maple St PO Box 3010 ... Longview WA 98632 360-442-2301 442-2379*
*Fax: Admissions ■ TF: 866-900-2311 ■ Web: www.lowercolumbia.edu
Edmonds Community College 20000 68th Ave W ... Lynnwood WA 98036 425-640-1500 640-1159
TF: 866-886-4854 ■ Web: www.edcc.edu
Big Bend Community College
7662 Chanute St ... Moses Lake WA 98837 509-793-2222 762-6243*
*Fax: Admissions ■ Web: www.bigbend.edu
Skagit Valley College
2405 E College Way ... Mount Vernon WA 98273 360-416-7600 416-7890*
*Fax: Admissions ■ TF: 877-385-5360 ■ Web: www.skagit.edu
South Puget Sound Community College
2011 Mottman Rd SW ... Olympia WA 98512 360-754-7711 596-5709*
*Fax: Admissions ■ Web: www.spscc.ctc.edu
Omak 116 W Apple Ave PO Box 2058 ... Omak WA 98841 509-422-7803 422-7801*
*Fax: Admissions ■ Web: www.wvc.edu
Columbia Basin College 2600 N 20th Ave ... Pasco WA 99301 509-547-0511 546-0401
Web: www.columbiabasin.edu
Peninsula College 1502 E Lauridsen Blvd ... Port Angeles WA 98362 360-452-9277 417-6581*
*Fax: Admissions ■ Web: www.pc.ctc.edu
Puyallup 1601 39th Ave SE ... Puyallup WA 98374 253-840-8400 840-8449*
*Fax: Admissions ■ TF: 877-353-6763 ■ Web: www.pierce.ctc.edu
Renton Technical College 3000 NE Fourth St ... Renton WA 98056 425-235-2352 235-7832
Web: www.rtc.edu
North Seattle Community College
9600 College Way N ... Seattle WA 98103 206-527-3600 527-3671
TF: 877-299-3593 ■ Web: www.northseattle.edu
South Seattle Community College
6000 16th Ave SW ... Seattle WA 98106 206-764-5300 764-7947
Web: www.southseattle.edu
Shelton 937 W Alpine Way ... Shelton WA 98584 360-427-2119 432-5412*
*Fax: Admissions ■ TF: 800-259-6718 ■ Web: www.olympic.edu
Shoreline Community College
16101 Greenwood Ave N ... Shoreline WA 98133 206-546-4101 546-5835
TF: 866-427-4747 ■ Web: www.shoreline.edu
Spokane Community College 1810 N Greene St ... Spokane WA 99217 509-533-7000 533-8181
TF: 800-248-5644 ■ Web: www.scc.spokane.edu
Spokane Falls Community College
3410 W Ft George Wright Dr ... Spokane WA 99224 509-533-3500 533-3237*
*Fax: Admissions ■ TF: 888-509-7944 ■ Web: www.spokanefalls.edu
Bates Technical College 1101 S Yakima Ave ... Tacoma WA 98405 253-680-7000 680-7001*
*Fax: Admissions ■ Web: www.bates.ctc.edu
Tacoma Community College 6501 S 19th St ... Tacoma WA 98466 253-566-5000 566-6011*
*Fax: Admissions ■ Web: www.tacomacc.edu
Clark College 1800 E McLoughlin Blvd ... Vancouver WA 98663 360-992-2000 992-2876*
*Fax: Admissions ■ Web: www.clark.edu
Walla Walla Community College
500 Tausick Way ... Walla Walla WA 99362 509-522-2500 527-3661*
*Fax: Admissions ■ TF: 877-992-9922 ■ Web: www.wwcc.edu
Wenatchee Valley College 1300 Fifth St ... Wenatchee WA 98801 509-682-6800 682-6801*
*Fax: Admissions ■ TF: 877-982-4968 ■ Web: www.wvc.edu
Yakima Valley Community College
South 16th Ave & Nob Hill Blvd ... Yakima WA 98902 509-574-4600 574-4649
Web: www.yvcc.edu

West Virginia

Phone | Fax

Potomac State College 101 Ft Ave ... Keyser WV 26726 304-788-6800 788-6939*
*Fax: Admissions ■ TF: 800-262-7332 ■ Web: www.potomacstatecollege.edu
Eastern West Virginia Community & Technical College
316 Eastern Dr ... Moorefield WV 26836 304-434-8000 434-7000
TF: 877-982-2322 ■ Web: www.easternwv.edu
West Virginia University PO Box 6009 ... Morgantown WV 26506 304-293-2121 293-3080
TF: 800-344-9881 ■ Web: www.wvu.edu
Southern West Virginia Community & Technical College
Logan 2900 Dempsey Branch Rd PO Box 2900 ... Mount Gay WV 25637 304-792-7098 792-7028*
*Fax: Admissions ■ Web: www.southernwv.edu
Parkersburg 300 Campus Dr ... Parkersburg WV 26104 304-424-8000 424-8315
TF: 800-982-9887 ■ Web: www.wvup.edu
West Virginia Northern Community College
1704 Market St ... Wheeling WV 26003 304-233-5900 232-8187
Web: wvncc.edu

Wisconsin

Phone | Fax

Baraboo/Sauk County 1006 Connie Rd ... Baraboo WI 53913 608-355-5200 355-5291*
*Fax: Admissions ■ TF: 800-621-7440 ■ Web: www.baraboo.uwc.edu
Fond du Lac 400 University Dr ... Fond du Lac WI 54935 920-929-3600
Web: www.fdl.uwc.edu
Lac Courte Oreilles Ojibwa Community College
13466 W Trepania Rd ... Hayward WI 54843 715-634-4790 634-5049*
*Fax: Admissions ■ TF: 888-526-6221 ■ Web: www.lco.edu
Rock County 2909 Kellogg Ave ... Janesville WI 53546 608-758-6523 758-6579
Web: www.rock.uwc.edu
College of Menominee Nation PO Box 1179 ... Keshena WI 54135 715-799-5600 799-4392*
*Fax: Admissions ■ TF: 800-567-2344 ■ Web: www.menominee.edu
Manitowoc 705 Viebahn St ... Manitowoc WI 54220 920-683-4700 683-4776
TF: 800-657-3866 ■ Web: www.manitowoc.uwc.edu
Marinette 750 W Bay Shore St ... Marinette WI 54143 715-735-4300 735-4304*
*Fax: Admissions ■ Web: www.marinette.uwc.edu
Marshfield/Wood County 2000 W Fifth St ... Marshfield WI 54449 715-389-6530 384-1718
TF: 800-273-8255 ■ Web: www.marshfield.uwc.edu
Fox Valley 1478 Midway Rd ... Menasha WI 54952 920-832-2600 832-2674
TF: 800-273-8255 ■ Web: www.uwfox.uwc.edu
Barron County 1800 College Dr ... Rice Lake WI 54868 715-234-8176 234-1975
TF: 800-608-4578 ■ Web: www.barron.uwc.edu
Richland 1200 Hwy 14 W ... Richland Center WI 53581 608-647-6186 647-2275*
*Fax: Admissions ■ TF: 800-947-3529 ■ Web: richland.uwc.edu
Sheboygan One University Dr ... Sheboygan WI 53081 920-459-6600 459-6602*
*Fax: Admissions ■ Web: sheboygan.uwc.edu
Waukesha 1500 N University Dr ... Waukesha WI 53188 262-521-5200 521-5491*
*Fax: Admissions ■ Web: waukesha.uwc.edu
Marathon County 518 S Seventh Ave ... Wausau WI 54401 715-261-6100 261-6331
TF: 888-367-8962 ■ Web: www.uwmc.uwc.edu
Washington County 400 S University Dr ... West Bend WI 53095 262-335-5200 335-5220
TF: 800-240-0276 ■ Web: washington.uwc.edu

Wyoming

Phone | Fax

Casper College 125 College Dr ... Casper WY 82601 307-268-2110 268-2611*
*Fax: Admissions ■ TF: 800-442-2963 ■ Web: www.caspercollege.edu
Laramie County Community College
1400 E College Dr ... Cheyenne WY 82007 307-778-5222 778-1350*
*Fax: Admissions ■ TF: 800-522-2993 ■ Web: www.lccc.cc.wy.us
Sheridan College
Gillette 300 W Sinclair St ... Gillette WY 82718 307-686-0254 686-0339*
*Fax: Admissions ■ TF: 800-913-9139 ■ Web: www.sheridan.edu
Albany County 1125 Boulder Dr ... Laramie WY 82070 307-721-5138 772-4266
TF: 800-522-2993 ■ Web: www.lccc.wy.edu
Northwest College 231 W Sixth St ... Powell WY 82435 307-754-6000 754-6249*
*Fax: Admissions ■ TF: 800-560-4692 ■ Web: www.northwestcollege.edu
Central Wyoming College 2660 Peck Ave ... Riverton WY 82501 307-855-2000 855-2092
TF: 800-735-8418 ■ Web: www.cwc.edu
Western Wyoming Community College
2500 College Dr ... Rock Springs WY 82901 307-382-1600 382-1636*
*Fax: Admissions ■ TF: 800-226-1181 ■ Web: www.wwcc.wy.edu
Eastern Wyoming College 3200 W 'C' St ... Torrington WY 82240 307-532-8200 532-8222*
*Fax: Admissions ■ TF: 800-658-3195 ■ Web: new.ewc.wy.edu

163 COLLEGES - CULINARY ARTS

Phone | Fax

Arizona Culinary Institute
10585 N 114th St Ste 401 ... Scottsdale AZ 85259 480-603-1066 603-1067
TF: 866-294-2433 ■ Web: www.azculinary.edu
Baltimore International College
17 Commerce St ... Baltimore MD 21202 410-752-4710 752-3730*
*Fax: Admissions ■ TF: 800-624-9926 ■ Web: www.stratford.edu
Cambridge School of Culinary Arts
2020 Massachusetts Ave ... Cambridge MA 02140 617-354-2020 576-1963
Web: www.cambridgeculinary.com
Capital Culinary Institute of Keiser College
Melbourne 900 S Babcock St ... Melbourne FL 32901 321-409-4800 725-3766
TF: 877-636-3618 ■ Web: keiseruniversity.edu/not-found/
Cascade Culinary Institute 2600 NW College Way ... Bend OR 97701 541-383-7700
Web: www.cocc.edu
Center for Culinary Arts 106 Sebethe Dr ... Cromwell CT 06416 800-780-2091
Web: www.lincolnedu.com
Chef John Folse Culinary Institute
PO Box 2099 ... Thibodaux LA 70310 985-449-7100 449-7089
Web: www.nicholls.edu
Cook Street School of Fine Cooking
1937 Market St ... Denver CO 80202 303-308-9300 308-9400
Web: www.cookstreet.com
Cooking & Hospitality Institute of Chicago
361 W Chestnut St ... Chicago IL 60610 312-944-0882 944-8557
TF Admissions: 877-828-7772 ■ Web: www.chefs.edu
Culinard-the Culinary Institute of Virginia College
436 Palisades Blvd ... Birmingham AL 35209 205-802-1200 943-3940
Web: www.culinard.com
Culinary Academy of Long Island
Manhattan 154 W 14th St ... New York NY 10011 212-675-6655
Web: www.starcareeracademy.com
Culinary Institute Alain & Marie LeNotre
7070 Allensby ... Houston TX 77022 713-692-0077 692-7399
TF: 888-536-6873 ■ Web: www.culinaryinstitute.edu

				Phone	Fax
Culinary Institute of America 1946 Campus Dr	Hyde Park	NY	12538	845-452-9430	451-1068
TF Admissions: 800-285-4627 ■ *Web:* www.ciachef.edu					
Culinary Institute of America at Greystone 2555 Main St	Saint Helena	CA	94574	707-967-1100	
Web: www.ciachef.edu					
Culinary Institute of Charleston 7000 Rivers Ave	Charleston	SC	29406	843-574-6111	820-5060
TF: 877-349-7184 ■ *Web:* www.tridenttech.edu					
Florida Culinary Institute 2410 Metro Centre Blvd	West Palm Beach	FL	33407	561-842-8324	245-3238*
**Fax Area Code:* 850 ■ *TF:* 800-254-0547 ■ *Web:* www.lincolnedu.com					
French Culinary Institute 462 Broadway	New York	NY	10013	888-324-2433	431-3065*
**Fax Area Code:* 212 ■ **Fax:* Admissions ■ *TF:* 888-324-2433 ■ *Web:* www.internationalculinarycenter.com					
Institute of Culinary Education 50 W 23rd St	New York	NY	10010	212-847-0700	847-0723
TF: 800-522-4610 ■ *Web:* www.ice.edu					
JNA Institute of Culinary Arts 1212 S Broad St	Philadelphia	PA	19146	215-468-8800	468-8838
Web: www.culinaryarts.com					
Kendall College 900 N North Branch St	Chicago	IL	60622	312-752-2000	*
**Fax:* Admissions ■ *TF:* 866-667-3344 ■ *Web:* www.kendall.edu					
Kitchen Academy 6370 W Sunset Blvd	Hollywood	CA	90028	866-548-2223	
TF: 866-548-2223 ■ *Web:* www.chefs.edu					
L'Academie de Cuisine Inc 16006 Industrial Dr	Gaithersburg	MD	20877	301-670-8670	670-0450
TF: 800-664-2433 ■ *Web:* www.lacademie.com					
Atlanta 1927 Lakeside Pkwy	Tucker	GA	30084	770-938-4711	
TF: 888-549-8222 ■ *Web:* www.chefs.edu					
Le Cordon Bleu College of Culinary Arts *Las Vegas* 1451 Ctr Crossing Rd	Las Vegas	NV	89144	702-365-7690	365-7911
Web: www.chefs.edu					
LINCOLN EDUCATIONAL SERVICES 85 Sigourney St	Hartford	CT	06105	800-254-0547	895-6101*
**Fax Area Code:* 860 ■ *TF:* 800-762-4337 ■ *Web:* www.lincolnedu.com					
Suffield 8 PROGRESS DR	Shelton	CT	06484	203-929-0592	
TF: 800-254-0547 ■ *Web:* www.lincolnedu.com					
Louisiana Culinary Institute 10550 Airline Hwy	Baton Rouge	LA	70816	877-533-3198	769-8792*
**Fax Area Code:* 225 ■ *TF:* 877-533-3198 ■ *Web:* www.lci.edu/site.php					
New England Culinary Institute 56 College St	Montpelier	VT	05602	802-223-6324	225-3280
TF: 877-223-6324 ■ *Web:* www.neci.edu					
Restaurant School at Walnut Hill College 4207 Walnut St	Philadelphia	PA	19104	215-222-4200	222-2811*
**Fax:* Admissions ■ *Web:* www.walnuthillcollege.edu					
Robert Morris University Institute of Culinary Arts 401 S State St	Chicago	IL	60605	312-935-4100	935-4182*
**Fax:* Admissions ■ *TF:* 800-762-5960 ■ *Web:* www.robertmorris.edu/culinary					
Dupage 905 Meridian Lk Dr	Aurora	IL	60504	800-762-5960	375-8020*
**Fax Area Code:* 630 ■ *TF:* 800-762-5960 ■ *Web:* www.robertmorris.edu					
San Diego Culinary Institute (SDCI) 8024 La Mesa Blvd	La Mesa	CA	91941	619-644-2100	644-2106
Web: sandiegoculinary.edu					
Sclafani's Cooking School Inc 107 Gennaro Pl	Metairie	LA	70001	504-833-7861	833-7872
TF: 800-583-1282 ■ *Web:* www.sclafanicookingschool.com					
Scottsdale Culinary Institute 8100 E Camelback Rd Ste 1001	Scottsdale	AZ	85251	480-990-3773	990-0351
TF: 888-557-4222 ■ *Web:* www.chefs.edu					
Star Career Academy 125 Michael Dr	Syosset	NY	11791	516-364-4344	275-0549*
**Fax Area Code:* 202 ■ *Web:* starcareeracademy.com					
Stratford University School of Culinary Arts 7777 Leesburg Pk	Falls Church	VA	22043	703-821-8570	734-5339
TF: 800-444-0804 ■ *Web:* www.stratford.edu/?page=home_culinary					
Tante Marie's Cooking School 271 Francisco St	San Francisco	CA	94133	415-788-6699	788-8924
Web: www.tantemarie.com					

164 COLLEGES - FINE ARTS

SEE ALSO Colleges & Universities - Four-Year p. 1980; Vocational & Technical Schools p. 3287

				Phone	Fax
American Academy of Art 332 S Michigan Ave 3rd Fl	Chicago	IL	60604	312-461-0600	294-9570
TF: 888-461-0600 ■ *Web:* www.aaart.edu					
American Academy of Dramatic Arts 120 Madison Ave	New York	NY	10016	212-686-9244	545-7934
TF: 800-463-8990 ■ *Web:* aada.edu/					
Antonelli Institute 300 Montgomery Ave	Erdenheim	PA	19038	215-836-2222	836-2794
TF: 800-722-7871 ■ *Web:* www.antonelli.edu					
Art Academy of Cincinnati 1212 Jackson St	Cincinnati	OH	45202	513-562-6262	562-8778
TF: 800-323-5692 ■ *Web:* www.artacademy.edu					
Art Ctr College of Design 1700 Lida St	Pasadena	CA	91103	626-396-2200	795-0578
Web: www.artcenter.edu					
Art Institute of Atlanta 6600 Peachtree Dunwoody Rd NE 100 Embassy Row	Atlanta	GA	30328	770-394-8300	394-0008
TF: 800-275-4242 ■ *Web:* new.artinstitutes.edu					
Art Institute of Boston at Lesley (AIB) 700 Beacon St Ste 202	Boston	MA	02215	617-585-6600	349-8855
TF: 800-773-0494 ■ *Web:* www.lesley.edu					
Inland Empire 674 E Brier Dr	San Bernardino	CA	92408	909-915-2100	
TF: 800-353-0812 ■ *Web:* new.artinstitutes.edu					
Los Angeles 2900 31st St	Santa Monica	CA	90405	310-752-4700	752-4708
TF: 888-646-4610 ■ *Web:* new.artinstitutes.edu					
Orange County 3601 W Sunflower Ave	Santa Ana	CA	92704	714-830-0200	556-1923
Web: new.artinstitutes.edu					
Art Institute of California *San Diego* 7650 Mission Valley Rd	San Diego	CA	92108	858-598-1200	291-3206*
**Fax Area Code:* 619 ■ *TF:* 888-624-0300 ■ *Web:* new.artinstitutes.edu					
San Francisco 1170 Market St	San Francisco	CA	94102	415-865-0198	863-6344
TF: 888-493-3261 ■ *Web:* new.artinstitutes.edu					
Art Institute of Charlotte 2110 Water Ridge Pkwy 3 LakePointe Plz	Charlotte	NC	28217	704-357-8020	357-1133
TF: 800-872-4417 ■ *Web:* new.artinstitutes.edu					
Art Institute of Colorado 1200 Lincoln St	Denver	CO	80203	303-837-0825	
TF: 800-275-2420 ■ *Web:* new.artinstitutes.edu					
Art Institute of Dallas 8080 Pk Ln Ste 100	Dallas	TX	75231	214-692-8080	275-4243*
**Fax Area Code:* 800 ■ *TF:* 800-275-4243 ■ *Web:* new.artinstitutes.edu					
Art Institute of Fort Lauderdale 1799 SE 17th St	Fort Lauderdale	FL	33316	954-463-3000	728-8637
TF: 800-275-7603 ■ *Web:* new.artinstitutes.edu					
Art Institute of Houston 1900 Yorktown St	Houston	TX	77056	713-623-2040	966-2700
TF: 800-275-4244 ■ *Web:* new.artinstitutes.edu					
Art Institute of Indianapolis 3500 Depauw Blvd	Indianapolis	IN	46268	317-613-4800	613-4808
TF: 866-441-9031 ■ *Web:* new.artinstitutes.edu					
Art Institute of Las Vegas 2350 Corporate Cir	Henderson	NV	89074	702-369-9944	992-8458
TF: 800-833-2678 ■ *Web:* new.artinstitutes.edu					
Art Institute of New York City 218-232 W 40th St	New York	NY	10018	212-226-5500	625-6065
Web: new.artinstitutes.edu					
Art Institute of Ohio *Cincinnati* 8845 Governor's Hill Dr Ste 100	Cincinnati	OH	45249	513-833-2400	833-2411
TF: 866-613-5184 ■ *Web:* new.artinstitutes.edu					
Art Institute of Philadelphia 1622 Chestnut St	Philadelphia	PA	19103	215-567-7080	405-6398
TF: 800-275-2474 ■ *Web:* new.artinstitutes.edu					
Art Institute of Pittsburgh 420 Blvd of the Allies	Pittsburgh	PA	15219	412-263-6600	263-6667
TF: 800-275-2470 ■ *Web:* new.artinstitutes.edu					
Art Institute of Portland 1122 NW Davis St	Portland	OR	97209	503-228-6528	227-1945*
**Fax:* Admissions ■ *TF:* 888-228-6528 ■ *Web:* new.artinstitutes.edu					
Art Institute of Seattle 2323 Elliott Ave	Seattle	WA	98121	206-448-0900	448-2501
TF: 800-275-2471 ■ *Web:* new.artinstitutes.edu					
Art Institute of Tampa 4401 N Himes Ave Ste 150	Tampa	FL	33614	813-873-2112	873-2171
TF: 866-703-3277 ■ *Web:* new.artinstitutes.edu					
Art Institute of Washington 1820 N Ft Myer Dr	Arlington	VA	22209	703-358-9550	358-9759
TF: 877-303-3771 ■ *Web:* www.artinstitutes.edu/arlington					
Art Institutes International Minnesota 15 S Ninth St	Minneapolis	MN	55402	612-332-3361	332-3934
TF: 800-777-3643 ■ *Web:* new.artinstitutes.edu					
Bradley Academy for the Visual Arts 1409 Williams Rd	York	PA	17402	717-755-2300	840-1951
TF: 800-864-7725 ■ *Web:* new.artinstitutes.edu					
California College of the Arts *Oakland* 5212 Broadway	Oakland	CA	94618	510-594-3600	594-3601
TF: 800-447-1278 ■ *Web:* www.cca.edu					
San Francisco 1111 Eigth St	San Francisco	CA	94107	415-703-9500	703-9539
TF: 800-447-1278 ■ *Web:* www.cca.edu					
California Design College 3440 Wilshire Blvd 10th Fl	Los Angeles	CA	90010	213-251-3636	
TF: 877-468-6232 ■ *Web:* new.artinstitutes.edu					
California Institute of the Arts 24700 McBean Pkwy	Valencia	CA	91355	661-255-1050	253-7710
TF: 800-545-2787 ■ *Web:* www.calarts.edu					
Cleveland Institute of Art 11141 E Blvd	Cleveland	OH	44106	800-223-4700	754-3634*
**Fax Area Code:* 216 ■ *TF:* 800-223-4700 ■ *Web:* www.cia.edu					
Columbus College of Art & Design 60 Cleveland Ave	Columbus	OH	43215	614-224-9101	222-4040
TF: 877-997-2223 ■ *Web:* www.ccad.edu					
Corcoran School of the Arts & Design 500 17th St NW	Washington	DC	20006	202-639-1800	639-1802
Web: corcoran.gwu.edu					
Cornish College of the Arts 710 E Roy St	Seattle	WA	98121	206-323-1400	720-1011
TF: 800-726-2787 ■ *Web:* www.cornish.edu					
Fashion Institute of Design & Merchandising *Los Angeles* 919 S Grand Ave	Los Angeles	CA	90015	213-624-1200	624-4799
TF Admissions: 800-624-1200 ■ *Web:* fidm.edu					
Orange County 17590 Gillette Ave	Irvine	CA	92614	949-851-6200	851-6808
TF: 888-974-3436 ■ *Web:* fidm.edu					
San Diego 350 Tenth Ave	San Diego	CA	92101	619-235-2049	232-4322
TF: 800-243-3436 ■ *Web:* fidm.edu					
San Francisco 55 Stockton St	San Francisco	CA	94108	415-675-5200	296-7299
TF: 800-422-3436 ■ *Web:* fidm.edu					
Fashion Institute of Technology 227 W 27th St	New York	NY	10001	212-217-7999	
Web: www.fitnyc.edu					
Florida School of the Arts 5001 St Johns Ave	Palatka	FL	32177	386-312-4300	312-4306
Web: floarts.org					
Hussian School of Art 111 S Independence Mall E	Philadelphia	PA	19106	215-574-9600	574-9800
Web: www.hussianart.edu					
Chicago 350 N Orleans St Ste 136-L	Chicago	IL	60654	312-280-3500	280-8562
TF: 800-351-3450 ■ *Web:* www.artinstitutes.edu					
Illinois Institute of Art *Schaumburg* 1000 N Plz Dr	Schaumburg	IL	60173	847-619-3450	619-3064
TF: 800-314-3450 ■ *Web:* new.artinstitutes.edu					
Institute of American Indian Arts (IAIA) 83 Avan Nu Po Rd	Santa Fe	NM	87508	505-424-2300	424-0505
TF: 800-804-6422 ■ *Web:* www.iaia.edu					
Chicago One N State St Ste 500	Chicago	IL	60602	312-386-7681	
TF: 888-318-6111 ■ *Web:* www.iadt.edu					
Las Vegas 2495 Village View Dr	Henderson	NV	89074	702-990-0150	990-0161
TF: 866-400-4238 ■ *Web:* www.iadt.edu					
International Academy of Design & Technology *Tampa* 5104 Eisenhower Blvd	Tampa	FL	33634	813-881-0007	888-4006*
**Fax Area Code:* 407 ■ *TF General:* 866-302-4238 ■ *Web:* www.iadt.edu					

Phone Fax

Kansas City Art Institute
4415 Warwick Blvd .... Kansas City MO 64111 816-474-5224 802-3309
TF: 800-522-5224 ■ *Web:* www.kcai.edu

Maine College of Art 97 Spring St .... Portland ME 04101 207-775-3052 772-5069
TF: 800-639-4808 ■ *Web:* www.meca.edu

Maryland Institute College of Art
1300 W Mt Royal Ave .... Baltimore MD 21217 410-669-9200 225-2337
Web: www.mica.edu

Memphis College of Art 1930 Poplar Ave .... Memphis TN 38104 901-272-5100 272-5158
TF: 800-727-1088 ■ *Web:* www.mca.edu

Miami International University of Art & Design
1501 Biscayne Blvd .... Miami FL 33132 305-428-5700 374-5933
TF: 800-225-9023 ■ *Web:* www.artinstitutes.edu/miami

Minneapolis College of Art & Design
2501 Stevens Ave .... Minneapolis MN 55404 612-874-3760 874-3701
TF: 800-874-6223 ■ *Web:* www.mcad.edu

Montclair Kimberley Academy, The
201 Valley Rd .... Montclair NJ 07042 973-746-9800
Web: www.montclairkimberley.org

Moore College of Art & Design
20th St & the Pkwy .... Philadelphia PA 19103 215-965-4000 568-8017
TF: 800-523-2025 ■ *Web:* www.moore.edu

New England Institute of Art
10 Brookline Pl W .... Brookline MA 02445 617-739-1700 582-4500
TF: 800-903-4425 ■ *Web:* new.artinstitutes.edu

New Hampshire Institute of Art
148 Concord St .... Manchester NH 03104 603-623-0313 647-0658
TF: 866-241-4918 ■ *Web:* www.nhia.edu

North Carolina School of the Arts
1533 S Main St .... Winston-Salem NC 27127 336-770-3399 770-3370
Web: uncsa.edu

Otis College of Art & Design
9045 Lincoln Blvd .... Los Angeles CA 90045 310-665-6820 665-6821
TF: 800-527-6847 ■ *Web:* www.otis.edu

Pennsylvania Academy of the Fine Arts
School of Fine Arts 118 N Broad St .... Philadelphia PA 19102 215-972-7600 569-0153
TF: 800-799-7233 ■ *Web:* www.pafa.org

Pennsylvania College of Art & Design
204 N Prince St PO Box 59 .... Lancaster PA 17608 717-396-7833 396-1339
Web: www.pcad.edu

Rhode Island School of Design
Two College St .... Providence RI 02903 401-454-6100 454-6309
TF: 800-364-7473 ■ *Web:* www.risd.edu

Ringling College of Art & Design
2700 N Tamiami Trl .... Sarasota FL 34234 941-351-5100 359-7517
TF: 800-255-7695 ■ *Web:* www.ringling.edu

San Francisco Art Institute
800 Chestnut St .... San Francisco CA 94133 415-771-7020 749-4590
TF: 800-345-7324 ■ *Web:* www.sfai.edu

Savannah College of Art & Design
Atlanta 1600 Peachtree St PO Box 77300 .... Atlanta GA 30357 404-253-2700 253-3466
TF: 877-722-3285 ■ *Web:* www.scad.edu

School of Visual Arts 209 E 23rd St .... New York NY 10010 212-592-2000 592-2116
TF: 800-436-4204 ■ *Web:* www.sva.edu

University of the Arts 320 S Broad St .... Philadelphia PA 19102 215-717-6049 717-6000
TF: 800-616-2787 ■ *Web:* www.uarts.edu

Virginia Marti College of Art & Design
11724 Detroit Ave .... Lakewood OH 44107 216-221-8584 221-2311
TF: 800-473-4350 ■ *Web:* vmcad.edu

Watkins College of Art & Design
2298 Rose Parks Blvd .... Nashville TN 37228 615-383-4848 383-4849
TF: 866-877-6395 ■ *Web:* watkins.edu

165 COLLEGES - TRIBAL

SEE ALSO Colleges - Community & Junior p. 1961
Tribal Colleges generally serve geographically isolated American Indian populations that have no other means of accessing education beyond the high school level. They are unique institutions that combine personal attention with cultural relevance.

Phone Fax

Aaniiih Nakoda College
269 Blackfeet Ave - Agency .... Harlem MT 59523 406-353-2607 353-2898*
**Fax:* Admissions ■ *Web:* ancollege.edu

Anaheim University
1240 S State College Blvd Ste 110 .... Anaheim CA 92806 714-772-3330
Web: www.anaheim.edu

Ashland County West Holmes Career Center Jvs
1783 State Rt 60 .... Ashland OH 44805 419-289-3313
Web: www.acwhcc-jvs.k12.oh.us

Baker University 618 E Eighth St .... Baldwin City KS 66006 785-594-6451
Web: www.bakeru.edu

Bay Mills Community College
12214 W Lakeshore Dr .... Brimley MI 49715 906-248-3354 248-3351
TF: 800-844-2622 ■ *Web:* www.bmcc.edu

Briarcliffe College 1055 Stewart Ave .... Bethpage NY 11714 516-918-3600
Web: www.briarcliffe.edu

Buffalo Seminary 205 Bidwell Pkwy .... Buffalo NY 14222 716-885-6780
Web: buffaloseminary.org

Cankdeska Cikana Community College
PO Box 269 .... Fort Totten ND 58335 701-766-4415 766-4077
TF: 888-783-1463 ■ *Web:* www.littlehoop.edu

Career Point Institute 485 Spencer Ln .... San Antonio TX 78201 210-732-3000
Web: www.careerpointcollege.edu

Cegep Andre Laurendeau 1111 Rue Lapierre .... Lasalle QC H8N2J4 514-364-3320
Web: www.claurendeau.qc.ca

Cegep De L'outaouais
333 Boul De La Cite-des-jeunes .... Gatineau QC J8Y6M4 819-770-4012
Web: www.cegepoutaouais.qc.ca

Cegep Marie-Victorin
7000 rue Marie-Victorin .... Montreal QC H1G2J6 514-325-0150
Web: www.collegemv.qc.ca

Phone Fax

Central Bible College 3000 N Grant Ave .... Springfield MO 65803 417-833-2551
Web: www.cbcag.edu

Chief Dull Knife College PO Box 98 .... Lame Deer MT 59043 406-477-6215 477-6219
Web: www.cdkc.edu

College De Maisonneuve
3800 Rue Sherbrooke E .... Montreal QC H1X2A2 514-251-1444
Web: www.cmaisonneuve.qc.ca

College De Valleyfield (cegep)
169 Rue Champlain .... Salaberry-de-valleyfield QC J6T1X6 450-373-9441
Web: www.colval.qc.ca

College of Menominee Nation PO Box 1179 .... Keshena WI 54135 715-799-5600 799-4392*
**Fax:* Admissions ■ *TF:* 800-567-2344 ■ *Web:* www.menominee.edu

College of Registered Nurses of Manitoba
890 Pembina Hwy .... Winnipeg MB R3M2M8 204-774-3477
Web: www.crnm.mb.ca

Comanche Nation College 1608 SW Ninth St .... Lawton OK 73501 580-591-0203 353-7075
TF: 877-591-0203 ■ *Web:* www.cnc.cc.ok.us

Earth & Ocean Sciences 6339 Stores Rd .... Vancouver BC V6T1Z4 604-822-1697
Web: www.eos.ubc.ca

Econcordia 1250 Guy .... Montreal QC H3G1M8 514-848-8770
Web: www.econcordia.com

Edp College of Pr Inc 560 Ave Ponce De Leon .... San Juan PR 00918 787-765-3560
Web: www.edpcollege.edu

Fanshawe College 1460 Oxford St E .... London ON N5Y5R6 519-452-4430
Web: www.fanshawec.on.ca

Fond du Lac Tribal & Community College
2101 14th St .... Cloquet MN 55720 218-879-0800 879-0814
TF: 800-657-3712 ■ *Web:* www.fdltcc.edu

Fort Berthold Community College PO Box 490 .... New Town ND 58763 701-627-4738 627-3609*
**Fax:* Admissions ■ *Web:* fortbertholdcc.edu

Fort Peck Community College PO Box 398 .... Poplar MT 59255 406-768-6300 768-6301
Web: www.fpcc.edu

Grande Prairie Regional College
10726 106 Ave .... Grande Prairie AB T8V4C4 780-539-2911
Web: www.gprc.ab.ca

Haskell Indian Nations University
155 Indian Ave PO Box 5031 .... Lawrence KS 66046 785-749-8454 749-8429*
**Fax:* Admissions ■ *Web:* www.haskell.edu

Hebrew Theological College 7135 Carpenter Rd .... Skokie IL 60077 847-674-7750
Web: www.htcnet.edu

Institute of American Indian Arts (IAIA)
83 Avan Nu Po Rd .... Santa Fe NM 87508 505-424-2300 424-0505
TF: 800-804-6422 ■ *Web:* www.iaia.edu

Keweenaw Bay Ojibwa Community College
111 Beartown Rd .... Baraga MI 49908 906-353-4600 353-8107
Web: www.kbocc.org

La Cite collegiale
801 promenade de l'Aviation .... Ottawa ON K1K4R3 613-742-2483
Web: www.collegelacite.ca

Lac Courte Oreilles Ojibwa Community College
13466 W Trepania Rd .... Hayward WI 54843 715-634-4790 634-5049*
**Fax:* Admissions ■ *TF:* 888-526-6221 ■ *Web:* www.lco.edu

Leech Lake Tribal College
6945 Little Wolf Rd PO Box 180 .... Cass Lake MN 56633 218-335-4200 335-4209
TF: 800-627-3529 ■ *Web:* www.lltc.edu

Little Big Horn College
8645 South Weaver Dr PO Box 370 .... Crow Agency MT 59022 406-638-3100 638-3169
Web: www.lbhc.edu

Little Priest Tribal College
601 E College Dr PO Box 270 .... Winnebago NE 68071 402-878-2380 878-2355
Web: www.littlepriest.edu

Milwaukee Academy of Science
2000 W Kilbourn Ave .... Milwaukee WI 53233 414-933-1335
Web: milwaukeeacademyofscience.org

Navajo Technical College PO Box 849 .... Crownpoint NM 87313 505-786-4100 786-5644
Web: www.navajotech.edu

Nebraska Indian Community College PO Box 428 .... Macy NE 68039 402-837-5078 837-4183*
**Fax:* Admissions ■ *TF:* 844-440-6422 ■ *Web:* www.thenicc.edu

Nicola Valley Institute of Technology
4355 Mathissi Pl .... Burnaby BC V5G4S8 604-602-9555
Web: www.nvit.bc.ca

Northeast Lakeview College
1201 Kitty Hawk Rd .... Universal City TX 78148 210-486-5484
Web: alamo.edu

Northwest Indian College 2522 Kwina Rd .... Bellingham WA 98226 360-676-2772 392-4333*
**Fax:* Admissions ■ *TF:* 866-676-2772 ■ *Web:* www.nwic.edu

O s u Center for Health Sciences
1111 W 17th St .... Tulsa OK 74107 918-582-1972
Web: www.healthsciences.okstate.edu

Oglala Lakota College PO Box 629 .... Martin SD 57551 605-455-6000 455-2787
Web: www.olc.edu

Ontario Universities Application Centre
170 Research Ln .... Guelph ON N1G5E2 519-823-1940
Web: www.ouac.on.ca

Palmer College-chiropractic
4705 S Clyde Morris Blvd .... Port Orange FL 32129 386-763-2709
Web: palmer.edu

Polaris Career Center 7285 Old Oak Blvd .... Cleveland OH 44130 440-891-7600
Web: www.polaris.edu

Robertson College 3-265 Notre Dame Ave .... Winnipeg MB R3B1N9 204-943-5661
Web: m.robertsoncollege.com

Royal College of Dental Surgeons of Ontario
Six Crescent Rd .... Toronto ON M4W1T1 416-961-6555
Web: rcdso.org

Saginaw Chippewa Tribal College
2274 Enterprise Dr .... Mount Pleasant MI 48858 989-775-4123 775-4528
TF: 800-225-8172 ■ *Web:* www.sagchip.org

Salish Kootenai College PO Box 70 .... Pablo MT 59855 406-275-4800 275-4801*
**Fax:* Admissions ■ *TF:* 877-752-6553 ■ *Web:* www.skc.edu

Seneca College 1750 Finch Ave E .... Toronto ON M2J2X5 416-491-5050
Web: www.senecac.on.ca

				Phone	Fax
Sinte Gleska University 101 Antelope Lk Cir Dr PO Box 105	Mission	SD	57555	605-856-8100	856-4194
Web: www.sintegleska.edu					
Sisseton Wahpeton College 12572 BIA Hwy 700	Sisseton	SD	57262	605-698-3966	742-0394
Web: www.swc.tc					
Sitting Bull College 9299 Hwy 24	Fort Yates	ND	58538	701-854-8000	854-3403*
**Fax:* Admissions ■ *Web:* www.sittingbull.edu					
Southwestern Indian Polytechnic Institute 9169 Coors Blvd NW PO Box 10146	Albuquerque	NM	87120	505-346-2306	346-2311
TF: 800-586-7474 ■ *Web:* www.sipi.edu					
Stone Child College 8294 Upper Box Elder Rd	Box Elder	MT	59521	406-395-4875	395-4836*
**Fax:* Admissions ■ *Web:* www.stonechild.edu					
Turtle Mountain Community College 10145 BIA Rd 7	Belcourt	ND	58316	701-477-7862	477-7892
TF: 800-827-1100 ■ *Web:* www.tm.edu					
United Tribes Technical College 3315 University Dr	Bismarck	ND	58504	701-255-3285	530-0640
Web: www.uttc.edu					
Van Hoose Associates Inc 714 E Monument St	Dayton	OH	45402	937-531-6680	
Web: www.vhainc.com					

166 COLLEGES - WOMEN'S (FOUR-YEAR)

				Phone	Fax
Agnes Scott College 141 E College Ave	Decatur	GA	30030	404-471-6000	471-6414*
**Fax:* Admissions ■ *TF:* 800-868-8602 ■ *Web:* www.agnesscott.edu					
Alverno College PO Box 343922	Milwaukee	WI	53234	414-382-6100	382-6055
TF: 800-933-3401 ■ *Web:* www.alverno.edu					
Barnard College Columbia University 3009 Broadway	New York	NY	10027	212-854-2014	854-6220*
**Fax:* Admissions ■ *Web:* www.barnard.edu					
Bay Path College 588 Longmeadow St	Longmeadow	MA	01106	800-782-7284	565-1105*
**Fax Area Code:* 413 ■ *TF:* 800-782-7284 ■ *Web:* www.baypath.edu					
Bennett College 900 E Washington St	Greensboro	NC	27401	336-370-8624	517-2166*
**Fax:* Admissions ■ *TF Admissions:* 800-413-5323 ■ *Web:* www.bennett.edu					
Blue Mountain College PO Box 160	Blue Mountain	MS	38610	662-685-4771	685-4776*
**Fax:* Admissions ■ *TF:* 800-235-0136 ■ *Web:* www.bmc.edu					
Brenau University 500 Washington St	Gainesville	GA	30501	770-534-6299	538-4701*
**Fax:* Admissions ■ *TF:* 800-252-5119 ■ *Web:* www.brenau.edu					
Bryn Mawr College 101 N Merion Ave	Bryn Mawr	PA	19010	610-526-5000	526-7471*
**Fax:* Admissions ■ *TF Admissions:* 800-262-2586 ■ *Web:* www.brynmawr.edu					
Carlow University 3333 Fifth Ave	Pittsburgh	PA	15213	412-578-6000	578-6689
TF: 800-333-2275 ■ *Web:* www.carlow.edu					
Cedar Crest College 100 College Dr	Allentown	PA	18104	610-437-4471	606-4647*
**Fax:* Admissions ■ *TF Admissions:* 800-360-1222 ■ *Web:* www.cedarcrest.edu					
Chatham University 1 Woodland Rd	Pittsburgh	PA	15232	412-365-1100	365-1609
TF: 800-837-1290 ■ *Web:* www.chatham.edu					
College of New Rochelle 29 Castle Pl	New Rochelle	NY	10805	914-654-5000	654-5464
TF: 800-933-5923 ■ *Web:* www.cnr.edu					
College of Notre Dame of Maryland 4701 N Charles St	Baltimore	MD	21210	410-435-0100	532-6287*
**Fax:* Admissions ■ *TF Admissions:* 800-753-3757 ■ *Web:* www.ndm.edu					
College of Saint Catherine 2004 Randolph Ave	Saint Paul	MN	55105	651-690-6000	690-6024*
**Fax:* Admissions ■ *TF:* 800-945-4599 ■ *Web:* www.stkate.edu					
Minneapolis 601 25th Ave S	Minneapolis	MN	55454	651-690-7700	690-7849*
**Fax:* Admissions ■ *TF:* 800-945-4599 ■ *Web:* www.stkate.edu					
College of Saint Elizabeth 2 Convent Rd	Morristown	NJ	07960	973-290-4700	290-4710*
**Fax:* Admissions ■ *TF Admissions:* 800-210-7900 ■ *Web:* www.cse.edu					
College of Saint Mary 7000 Mercy Rd	Omaha	NE	68106	402-399-2400	399-2412*
**Fax:* Admissions ■ *TF:* 800-926-5534 ■ *Web:* www.csm.edu					
Converse College 580 E Main St	Spartanburg	SC	29302	864-596-9000	596-9225*
**Fax:* Admissions ■ *TF Admissions:* 800-766-1125 ■ *Web:* www.converse.edu					
Fordham University *Westchester* 400 Westchester Ave	West Harrison	NY	10604	914-332-8295	817-3921*
**Fax Area Code:* 718 ■ *TF:* 800-606-6090 ■ *Web:* www.fordham.edu					
Georgian Court University 900 Lakewood Ave	Lakewood	NJ	08701	800-458-8422	987-2000*
**Fax Area Code:* 732 ■ **Fax:* Admissions ■ *TF:* 800-458-8422 ■ *Web:* www.georgian.edu					
Hollins University PO BOX 9707	Roanoke	VA	24020	540-362-6401	362-6218*
**Fax:* Admissions ■ *TF Admissions:* 800-456-9595 ■ *Web:* www.hollins.edu					
Judson College 302 Bibb St	Marion	AL	36756	334-683-5110	683-5282*
**Fax:* Admissions ■ *TF Admissions:* 800-447-9472 ■ *Web:* www.judson.edu					
Mary Baldwin College 318 Prospect St	Staunton	VA	24401	540-887-7019	887-7292*
**Fax:* Admissions ■ *TF Admissions:* 800-468-2262 ■ *Web:* www.mbc.edu					
Meredith College 3800 Hillsborough St	Raleigh	NC	27607	919-760-8581	760-2348*
**Fax:* Admissions ■ *TF All:* 800-637-3348 ■ *Web:* www.meredith.edu					
Midway College 512 E Stephens St	Midway	KY	40347	859-846-5346	846-5787*
**Fax:* Admissions ■ *TF:* 800-755-0031 ■ *Web:* midway.edu					
Mills College 5000 MacArthur Blvd	Oakland	CA	94613	510-430-2135	430-3314*
**Fax:* Admissions ■ *TF Admissions:* 877-746-4557 ■ *Web:* www.mills.edu					
Moore College of Art & Design 20th St & the Pkwy	Philadelphia	PA	19103	215-965-4000	568-8017
TF: 800-523-2025 ■ *Web:* www.moore.edu					
Mount Holyoke College 50 College St	South Hadley	MA	01075	413-538-2000	538-2409
TF: 800-642-4483 ■ *Web:* www.mtholyoke.edu					
Mount Mary College 2900 N Menomonee River Pkwy	Milwaukee	WI	53222	414-256-1219	256-0180*
**Fax:* Admissions ■ *TF Admissions:* 800-321-6265 ■ *Web:* www.mtmary.edu					
Mount Saint Mary' s University 12001 Chalon Rd	Los Angeles	CA	90049	310-954-4250	954-4259*
**Fax:* Admissions ■ *TF Admissions:* 800-999-9893 ■ *Web:* www.msmc.la.edu					
Newcomb College Institute for Women 43 Newcomb Pl	New Orleans	LA	70118	504-865-5422	862-8589
TF: 888-327-0009 ■ *Web:* tulane.edu					
Pine Manor College 400 Heath St	Chestnut Hill	MA	02467	617-731-7104	731-7102
TF: 800-762-1357 ■ *Web:* www.pmc.edu					
Randolph College 2500 Rivermont Ave	Lynchburg	VA	24503	434-947-8000	947-8996*
**Fax:* Admissions ■ *TF Admissions:* 800-745-7692 ■ *Web:* www.randolphcollege.edu					
Rosemont College 1400 Montgomery Ave	Rosemont	PA	19010	610-527-0200	526-2971*
**Fax:* Admissions ■ *TF Admissions:* 800-331-0708 ■ *Web:* www.rosemont.edu					
Russell Sage College 45 Ferry St	Troy	NY	12180	518-244-2217	244-6880*
**Fax:* Admissions ■ *TF Admissions:* 888-837-9724 ■ *Web:* www.sage.edu					
Saint Mary's College Le Mans Hall Rm 122	Notre Dame	IN	46556	574-284-4587	284-4841*
**Fax:* Admissions ■ *TF Admissions:* 800-551-7621 ■ *Web:* www.saintmarys.edu					
Saint Mary-of-the-Woods College 3301 St Mary Rd	Saint Mary Of The Woods	IN	47876	812-535-5106	535-5010*
**Fax:* Admissions ■ *TF:* 800-926-7692 ■ *Web:* www.smwc.edu					
Salem College 601 S Church St	Winston-Salem	NC	27101	336-721-2600	917-5572*
**Fax:* Admissions ■ *TF Admissions:* 800-327-2536 ■ *Web:* www.salem.edu					
Scripps College 1030 Columbia Ave	Claremont	CA	91711	909-621-8149	607-7508*
**Fax:* Admissions ■ *TF:* 800-770-1333 ■ *Web:* scrippscollege.edu/					
Simmons College 300 The Fenway	Boston	MA	02115	617-521-2000	521-3190*
**Fax:* Admissions ■ *TF:* 800-345-8468 ■ *Web:* www.simmons.edu					
Smith College Seven College Ln	NorthHampton	MA	01063	413-584-2700	585-2527
TF: 800-383-3232 ■ *Web:* www.smith.edu					
Spelman College 350 Spelman Ln SW	Atlanta	GA	30314	404-681-3643	270-5201*
**Fax:* Admissions ■ *TF Admissions:* 800-982-2411 ■ *Web:* www.spelman.edu					
Stephens College 1200 E Broadway	Columbia	MO	65215	573-442-2211	*
**Fax:* Admissions ■ *Web:* collegeapps.about.com					
Sweet Briar College 134 Chappel Rd	Sweet Briar	VA	24595	434-381-6100	381-6152*
**Fax:* Admissions ■ *TF Admissions:* 800-381-6142 ■ *Web:* www.sbc.edu					
Texas Woman's University 304 Admin Dr PO Box 425589	Denton	TX	76204	940-898-3188	898-3081*
**Fax:* Admissions ■ *TF:* 866-809-6130 ■ *Web:* www.twu.edu					
University of Saint Joseph 1678 Asylum Ave	West Hartford	CT	06117	860-232-4571	*
**Fax:* Admissions ■ *Web:* www.sjc.edu					
Ursuline College 2550 Lander Rd	Pepper Pike	OH	44124	440-449-4200	684-6138*
**Fax:* Admissions ■ *TF:* 888-778-5463 ■ *Web:* www.ursuline.edu					
Wellesley College 106 Central St	Wellesley	MA	02481	781-283-1000	283-3678*
**Fax:* Admissions ■ *Web:* www.wellesley.edu					
Wesleyan College 4760 Forsyth Rd	Macon	GA	31210	478-477-1110	757-4030*
**Fax:* Admissions ■ *TF:* 800-447-6610 ■ *Web:* www.wesleyancollege.edu					
William Peace University 15 E Peace St	Raleigh	NC	27604	919-508-2000	508-2326*
**Fax:* Admissions ■ *TF:* 800-732-2347 ■ *Web:* www.peace.edu					
Wilson College 1015 Philadelphia Ave	Chambersburg	PA	17201	717-264-4141	264-1578*
**Fax:* Admissions ■ *TF Admissions:* 800-421-8402 ■ *Web:* www.wilson.edu					
Women's College of the University of Denver 1901 E Asbury Ave	Denver	CO	80208	303-871-6848	871-6897
Web: www.womenscollege.du.edu					

167 COLLEGES & UNIVERSITIES - CHRISTIAN

SEE ALSO Colleges - Bible p. 1960; Colleges & Universities - Jesuit p. 2009
The institutions listed here are members of the Council for Christian Colleges & Universities (CCCU). Although many other colleges and universities describe themselves as "religiously affiliated," members of CCCU are intentionally Christ-centered. Among the criteria for membership in CCCU, schools must have curricular and extra-curricular programs that reflect the integration of scholarship, biblical faith, and service.

				Phone	Fax
Anderson University 1100 E Fifth St	Anderson	IN	46012	765-649-9071	641-4091*
**Fax:* Admissions ■ *TF Admissions:* 800-428-6414 ■ *Web:* www.anderson.edu					
Asbury College One Macklem Dr	Wilmore	KY	40390	859-858-3511	858-3921*
**Fax:* Admissions ■ *TF Admissions:* 800-888-1818 ■ *Web:* www.asbury.edu					
Azusa Pacific University 901 E Alosta Ave PO Box 7000	Azusa	CA	91702	626-969-3434	812-3096
TF: 800-825-5278 ■ *Web:* www.apu.edu					
Belhaven College 1500 Peachtree St PO Box 153	Jackson	MS	39202	601-968-5940	968-8946*
**Fax:* Admissions ■ *TF:* 800-960-5940 ■ *Web:* www.belhaven.edu					
Bethel College 1001 W McKinley Ave	Mishawaka	IN	46545	574-807-7000	807-7000*
**Fax:* Admissions ■ *TF Admissions:* 800-422-4101 ■ *Web:* www.bethelcollege.edu					
Biola University 13800 Biola Ave	La Mirada	CA	90639	562-903-6000	903-4709*
**Fax:* Admissions ■ *TF Admissions:* 800-652-4652 ■ *Web:* www.biola.edu					
Bluffton University 1 University Dr	Bluffton	OH	45817	419-358-3000	358-3081*
**Fax:* Admissions ■ *TF:* 800-488-3257 ■ *Web:* www.bluffton.edu					
Bryan College 721 Bryan Dr PO Box 7000	Dayton	TN	37321	423-775-2041	775-7199
TF: 800-277-9522 ■ *Web:* www.bryan.edu					
California Baptist University 8432 Magnolia Ave	Riverside	CA	92504	951-689-5771	343-4525*
**Fax:* Admissions ■ *TF:* 877-228-8866 ■ *Web:* www.calbaptist.edu					
Calvin College 3201 Burton St SE	Grand Rapids	MI	49546	616-526-6000	526-6777*
**Fax:* Admissions ■ *TF:* 800-688-0122 ■ *Web:* www.calvin.edu					
Campbellsville University One University Dr	Campbellsville	KY	42718	270-789-5000	789-5071*
**Fax:* Admissions ■ *TF Admissions:* 800-264-6014 ■ *Web:* www.campbellsville.edu					
Carson-Newman College 1646 Russell Ave	Jefferson City	TN	37760	865-471-2000	471-3502*
**Fax:* Admissions ■ *TF:* 800-678-9061 ■ *Web:* www.cn.edu					
Cedarville University 251 N Main St	Cedarville	OH	45314	937-766-7700	766-7575*
**Fax:* Admissions ■ *TF:* 800-233-2784 ■ *Web:* www.cedarville.edu					
College of the Ozarks 1 Industrial Dr PO Box 17	Point Lookout	MO	65726	417-334-6411	335-2618*
**Fax:* Admissions ■ *TF Admissions:* 800-222-0525 ■ *Web:* www.cofo.edu					
Colorado Christian University 8787 W Alameda Ave	Lakewood	CO	80226	303-963-3200	963-3201
TF: 800-443-2484 ■ *Web:* www.ccu.edu					
Corban College 5000 Deer Pk Dr SE	Salem	OR	97317	503-581-8600	585-4316
TF: 800-845-3005 ■ *Web:* www.corban.edu					
Cornerstone University 1001 E Beltline Ave NE	Grand Rapids	MI	49525	616-222-1426	222-1418*
**Fax:* Admissions ■ *TF Admissions:* 800-787-9778 ■ *Web:* www.cornerstone.edu					
Covenant College 14049 Scenic Hwy	Lookout Mountain	GA	30750	706-820-1560	820-0893*
**Fax:* Admissions ■ *TF:* 888-451-2683 ■ *Web:* www.covenant.edu					
Crown College 8700 College View Dr	Saint Bonifacius	MN	55375	952-446-4100	446-4149
TF: 800-682-7696 ■ *Web:* www.crown.edu					
Dallas Baptist University 3000 Mtn Creek Pkwy	Dallas	TX	75211	214-333-7100	333-5447*
**Fax:* Admissions ■ *TF:* 800-460-1328 ■ *Web:* www.dbu.edu					
Dordt College 498 Fourth Ave NE	Sioux Center	IA	51250	712-722-6080	722-1198
TF: 800-343-6738 ■ *Web:* www.dordt.edu					

	City	State	Zip	Phone	Fax
East Texas Baptist University 1209 N Grove St *Fax: Admissions ■ TF: 800-804-3828 ■ Web: www.etbu.edu	Marshall	TX	75670	903-935-7963	923-2001*
Eastern Mennonite University 1200 Pk Rd *Fax: Admissions ■ TF Admissions: 800-368-2665 ■ Web: www.emu.edu	Harrisonburg	VA	22802	540-432-4118	432-4444*
Eastern Nazarene College 23 E Elm Ave TF: 800-883-6288 ■ Web: www.enc.edu	Quincy	MA	02170	617-745-3000	745-3929
Eastern University 1300 Eagle Rd *Fax: Admissions ■ TF Admissions: 800-452-0996 ■ Web: www.eastern.edu	Wayne	PA	19087	610-341-5800	341-1723*
Erskine College Two Washington St *Fax: Admissions ■ TF Admissions: 800-241-8721 ■ Web: www.erskine.edu	Due West	SC	29639	864-379-2131	379-3048*
Evangel University 1111 N Glenstone Ave TF: 800-382-6435 ■ Web: evangel.edu	Springfield	MO	65802	417-865-2815	865-9599
Fresno Pacific University 1717 S Chestnut Ave PO Box 2005 *Fax: Admissions ■ TF: 800-660-6089 ■ Web: www.fresno.edu	Fresno	CA	93702	559-453-2039	453-7151*
Geneva College 3200 College Ave *Fax: Admissions ■ TF: 800-847-8255 ■ Web: www.geneva.edu	Beaver Falls	PA	15010	724-847-6500	847-6776*
George Fox University 414 N Meridian St *Fax: Admissions ■ TF: 800-765-4369 ■ Web: www.georgefox.edu	Newberg	OR	97132	503-538-8383	554-3110*
Gordon College 255 Grapevine Rd *Fax: Admissions ■ TF: 800-343-1379 ■ Web: www.gordon.edu	Wenham	MA	01984	978-927-2300	867-4682*
Goshen College 1700 S Main St *Fax: Admissions ■ TF: 800-348-7422 ■ Web: www.goshen.edu	Goshen	IN	46526	574-535-7000	535-7609*
Grace College 200 Seminary Dr *Fax: Admissions ■ TF: 800-544-7223 ■ Web: www.grace.edu	Winona Lake	IN	46590	574-372-5100	372-5120*
Greenville College 315 E College Ave *Fax: Admissions ■ TF: 800-345-4440 ■ Web: www.greenville.edu	Greenville	IL	62246	618-664-7100	664-9841*
Hardin-Simmons University 2200 Hickory St *Fax: Admissions ■ TF: 877-464-7889 ■ Web: www.hsutx.edu	Abilene	TX	79698	325-670-1206	671-2115*
Hope International University 2500 E Nutwood Ave *Fax: Admissions ■ TF: 866-722-4673 ■ Web: www.hiu.edu	Fullerton	CA	92831	714-879-3901	526-0231*
Houghton College One Willard Ave PO Box 128 *Fax: Admissions ■ TF: 800-777-2556 ■ Web: www.houghton.edu	Houghton	NY	14744	585-567-9200	567-9522*
Houston Baptist University 7502 Fondren Rd *Fax: Admissions ■ TF Admissions: 800-969-3210 ■ Web: www.hbu.edu	Houston	TX	77074	281-649-3000	649-3217*
Howard Payne University 1000 Fisk Ave TF: 800-950-8465 ■ Web: www.hputx.edu	Brownwood	TX	76801	325-646-2502	649-8900
Huntington University 2303 College Ave *Fax: Admissions ■ TF Admissions: 800-642-6493 ■ Web: www.huntington.edu	Huntington	IN	46750	260-356-6000	358-3699*
Indiana Wesleyan University 4201 S Washington St *Fax: Admissions ■ TF: 800-332-6901 ■ Web: www.indwes.edu	Marion	IN	46953	765-677-2138	677-2333*
John Brown University 2000 W University St *Fax: Admissions ■ TF Admissions: 877-528-4636 ■ Web: www.jbu.edu	Siloam Springs	AR	72761	479-524-9500	524-4196*
Judson College 302 Bibb St *Fax: Admissions ■ TF Admissions: 800-447-9472 ■ Web: www.judson.edu	Marion	AL	36756	334-683-5110	683-5282*
Judson University 1151 N State St *Fax: Admissions ■ TF Admissions: 800-879-5376 ■ Web: www.judsonu.edu	Elgin	IL	60123	847-628-2500	628-2526*
Kentucky Christian University 100 Academic Pkwy *Fax: Admissions ■ TF Admissions: 800-522-3181 ■ Web: www.kcu.edu	Grayson	KY	41143	606-474-3000	474-3155*
King College 1350 King College Rd TF Admissions: 800-362-0014 ■ Web: www.king.edu	Bristol	TN	37620	423-652-4861	968-4456
King's University College 9125 50th St TF: 800-661-8582 ■ Web: kingsu.ca	Edmonton	AB	T6B2H3	780-465-3500	465-3534
Lee University 1120 N Ocoee St *Fax: Admissions ■ TF: 800-533-9930 ■ Web: www.leeuniversity.edu	Cleveland	TN	37311	423-614-8000	614-8533*
LeTourneau University 2100 S Mobberly Ave *Fax: Admissions ■ TF: 800-759-8811 ■ Web: www.letu.edu	Longview	TX	75602	903-233-3000	233-4301*
Lipscomb University 3901 Granny White Pk *Fax: Admissions ■ TF: 800-333-4358 ■ Web: www.lipscomb.edu	Nashville	TN	37204	615-966-1000	966-1804*
Louisiana College 1140 College Dr *Fax: Admissions ■ TF: 800-487-1906 ■ Web: www.lacollege.edu	Pineville	LA	71359	318-487-7011	487-7550*
Malone College 515 25th St NW *Fax: Admissions ■ TF: 800-521-1146 ■ Web: www.malone.edu	Canton	OH	44709	330-471-8100	471-8149*
Master's College 21726 Placerita Canyon Rd *Fax: Admissions ■ TF: 800-568-6248 ■ Web: www.masters.edu	Santa Clarita	CA	91321	661-259-3540	288-1037*
Messiah College PO Box 3005 *Fax: Admissions ■ TF: 800-233-4220 ■ Web: www.messiah.edu	Grantham	PA	17027	717-691-6000	796-5374*
MidAmerica Nazarene University 2030 E College Way *Fax: Admissions ■ TF: 800-800-8887 ■ Web: www.mnu.edu	Olathe	KS	66062	913-782-3750	971-3481*
Milligan College PO Box 500 *Fax: Admissions ■ TF: 800-262-8337 ■ Web: www.milligan.edu	Milligan College	TN	37682	423-461-8730	461-8982*
Mississippi College 200 S Capitol St PO Box 4026 *Fax: Admissions ■ TF: 800-738-1236 ■ Web: www.mc.edu	Clinton	MS	39058	601-925-3000	925-3950*
Missouri Baptist University One College Pk Dr TF: 877-434-1115 ■ Web: www.mobap.edu	Saint Louis	MO	63141	314-434-1115	434-7596
Montreat College 310 Gaither Cir PO Box 1267 TF: 800-622-6968 ■ Web: www.montreat.edu	Montreat	NC	28757	828-669-8011	669-0120
Mount Vernon Nazarene University 800 Martinsburg Rd TF Admissions: 800-766-8206 ■ Web: www.mvnu.edu	Mount Vernon	OH	43050	740-392-6868	
North Greenville University 7801 N Tigerville Rd PO Box 1892 *Fax: Admissions ■ TF: 800-468-6642 ■ Web: www.ngu.edu	Tigerville	SC	29688	864-977-7000	977-7177*
North Park University 3225 W Foster Ave TF: 800-888-6728 ■ Web: www.northpark.edu	Chicago	IL	60625	773-244-5500	244-4953
Northwest Christian College 828 E 11th Ave TF: 877-463-6622 ■ Web: www.nwcu.edu	Eugene	OR	97401	541-343-1641	684-7317
Northwest Nazarene University 623 Holly St *Fax: Admissions ■ TF Admissions: 877-668-4968 ■ Web: www.nnu.edu	Nampa	ID	83686	208-467-8000	467-8645*
Northwest University 5520 108th Ave NE *Fax: Admissions ■ TF Admissions: 800-669-3781 ■ Web: www.northwestu.edu	Kirkland	WA	98033	425-822-8266	889-5224*
Northwestern College 101 Seventh St SW *Fax: Admissions ■ TF: 800-747-4757 ■ Web: www.nwciowa.edu	Orange City	IA	51041	712-707-7000	707-7164*
Nyack College One S Blvd *Fax: Admissions ■ TF Admissions: 800-336-9225 ■ Web: www.nyack.edu	Nyack	NY	10960	845-358-1710	358-3047*
Oklahoma Baptist University 500 W University St *Fax: Admissions ■ TF: 800-654-3285 ■ Web: www.okbu.edu	Shawnee	OK	74804	405-275-2850	878-2068*
Oklahoma Christian University PO Box 11000 *Fax: Admissions ■ TF: 800-877-5010 ■ Web: www.oc.edu	Oklahoma City	OK	73136	405-425-5000	425-5069*
Olivet Nazarene University One University Ave *Fax: Admissions ■ TF: 800-648-1463 ■ Web: www.olivet.edu	Bourbonnais	IL	60914	815-939-5011	935-4998*
Oral Roberts University 7777 S Lewis Ave *Fax: Admissions ■ TF: 800-678-8876 ■ Web: www.oru.edu	Tulsa	OK	74171	918-495-6161	495-6222*
Palm Beach Atlantic University PO Box 24708 *Fax: Admissions ■ TF: 888-468-6722 ■ Web: www.pba.edu	West Palm Beach	FL	33416	561-803-2000	803-2115*
Point Loma Nazarene University 3900 Lomaland Dr *Fax: Admissions ■ TF Admissions: 800-733-7770 ■ Web: www.pointloma.edu	San Diego	CA	92106	619-849-2200	849-2601*
Redeemer University College 777 Garner Rd E TF: 877-779-0913 ■ Web: www.redeemer.ca	Ancaster	ON	L9K1J4	905-648-2131	648-2134
Roberts Wesleyan College 2301 Westside Dr *Fax: Admissions ■ TF Admissions: 800-777-4792 ■ Web: www.roberts.edu	Rochester	NY	14624	585-594-6000	594-6371*
Seattle Pacific University 3307 Third Ave W *Fax: Admissions ■ TF: 800-366-3344 ■ Web: www.spu.edu	Seattle	WA	98119	206-281-2000	281-2544*
Simpson University 2211 College View Dr *Fax: Admissions ■ TF: 888-974-6776 ■ Web: www.simpsonu.edu	Redding	CA	96003	530-226-4606	226-4861*
Southeastern University 1000 Longfellow Blvd TF: 800-500-8760 ■ Web: seu.edu	Lakeland	FL	33801	863-667-5000	667-5200
Southern Nazarene University 6729 NW 39th Expy *Fax: Admissions ■ TF: 800-648-9899 ■ Web: www.snu.edu	Bethany	OK	73008	405-789-6400	491-6320*
Southern Wesleyan University 907 Wesleyan Dr *Fax: Admissions ■ TF: 800-282-8798 ■ Web: www.swu.edu	Central	SC	29630	864-644-5000	644-5972*
Southwest Baptist University 1600 University Ave *Fax Area Code: 417 ■ *Fax: Admissions ■ TF: 800-526-5859 ■ Web: www.sbuniv.edu	Bolivar	MO	65613	800-526-5859	328-1808*
Spring Arbor University 106 E Main St *Fax: Admissions ■ TF Admissions: 800-968-9103 ■ Web: saucougars.com	Spring Arbor	MI	49283	517-750-1200	750-2745*
Tabor College 400 S Jefferson St *Fax: Admissions ■ TF Admissions: 800-822-6799 ■ Web: www.tabor.edu	Hillsboro	KS	67063	620-947-3121	947-6276*
Taylor University 236 W Reade Ave *Fax: Admissions ■ TF: 800-882-3456 ■ Web: www.taylor.edu	Upland	IN	46989	765-998-2751	998-4925*
Trevecca Nazarene University 333 Murfreesboro Rd *Fax: Admissions ■ TF: 888-210-4868 ■ Web: www.trevecca.edu	Nashville	TN	37210	615-248-1200	248-7406*
Trinity Christian College 6601 W College Dr Web: www.trnty.edu	Palos Heights	IL	60463	708-597-3000	239-4826
Trinity International University 2065 Half Day Rd TF: 800-822-3225 ■ Web: www.tiu.edu	Deerfield	IL	60015	847-945-8800	317-8097
Trinity Western University 7600 Glover Rd *Fax: Admissions ■ TF: 888-468-6898 ■ Web: www.twu.ca	Langley	BC	V2Y1Y1	604-888-7511	513-2064*
Union University 1050 Union University Dr *Fax: Admissions ■ TF: 800-338-6466 ■ Web: www.uu.edu	Jackson	TN	38305	731-661-5210	661-5589*
University of Sioux Falls 1101 W 22nd St TF: 800-888-1047 ■ Web: www.usiouxfalls.edu	Sioux Falls	SD	57105	605-331-6600	331-6615
Vanguard University of Southern California 55 Fair Dr *Fax: Admissions ■ TF Admissions: 800-722-6279 ■ Web: www.vanguard.edu	Costa Mesa	CA	92626	714-556-3610	966-5471*
Warner Pacific College 2219 SE 68th Ave TF: 800-804-1510 ■ Web: www.warnerpacific.edu	Portland	OR	97215	503-517-1020	517-1352
Warner Southern College 13895 Hwy 27 *Fax: Admissions ■ TF: 800-309-9563 ■ Web: warner.edu	Lake Wales	FL	33859	800-309-9563	949-7248*
Wayland Baptist University 1900 W Seventh St *Fax: Admissions ■ TF: 800-588-1928 ■ Web: www.wbu.edu	Plainview	TX	79072	806-291-1000	291-1973*
Waynesburg College 51 W College St *Fax: Admissions ■ TF Admissions: 800-225-7393 ■ Web: www.waynesburg.edu	Waynesburg	PA	15370	724-627-8191	627-8124*
Westmont College 955 La Paz Rd *Fax: Admissions ■ TF Admissions: 800-777-9011 ■ Web: www.westmont.edu	Santa Barbara	CA	93108	805-565-6000	565-6234*
Whitworth College 300 W Hawthorne Rd *Fax: Admissions ■ TF Admissions: 800-533-4668 ■ Web: www.whitworth.edu	Spokane	WA	99251	509-777-1000	777-3758*
Williams Baptist College 60 W Fulbright St *Fax: Admissions ■ TF: 800-722-4434 ■ Web: www.wbcoll.edu	Walnut Ridge	AR	72476	870-886-6741	886-3924*

168 COLLEGES & UNIVERSITIES - FOUR-YEAR

SEE ALSO Colleges - Community & Junior p. 1961; Colleges - Fine Arts p. 1977; Colleges - Women's (Four-Year) p. 1979; Colleges & Universities - Christian p. 1979; Colleges & Universities - Graduate & Professional Schools p. 2001; Colleges & Universities - Historically Black p. 2008; Colleges & Universities - Jesuit p. 2009; Military Service Academies p. 2760; Universities - Canadian p. 3268; Vocational & Technical Schools p. 3287

Alabama

	City	State	Zip	Phone	Fax
Alabama Agricultural & Mechanical University 4900 Meridian St PO Box 1087 TF: 800-553-0816 ■ Web: www.aamu.edu	Huntsville	AL	35810	256-372-5000	372-5906
Alabama State University 915 S Jackson St *Fax: Admissions ■ TF Admissions: 800-253-5037 ■ Web: www.alasu.edu	Montgomery	AL	36104	334-229-4100	229-4984*
Amridge University 1200 Taylor Rd TF: 888-790-8080 ■ Web: www.amridgeuniversity.edu	Montgomery	AL	36117	334-387-3877	387-3878
Montgomery 7440 E Dr TF: 800-227-2649 ■ Web: www.aum.edu	Montgomery	AL	36117	334-244-3000	244-3795

	City	State	Zip	Phone	Fax
Birmingham-Southern College 900 Arkadelphia Rd	Birmingham	AL	35254	205-226-4600	226-3074*
**Fax:* Admissions ■ *TF:* 800-523-5793 ■ *Web:* www.bsc.edu					
Concordia College Selma 1712 Broad St	Selma	AL	36701	334-874-5700	874-5755
Faulkner University 5345 Atlanta Hwy	Montgomery	AL	36109	334-272-5820	386-7511*
**Fax:* Admissions ■ *TF:* 800-879-9816 ■ *Web:* www.faulkner.edu					
Huntingdon College 1500 E Fairview Ave	Montgomery	AL	36106	334-833-4497	833-4497*
**Fax:* Admissions ■ *TF Admissions:* 800-763-0313 ■ *Web:* www.huntingdon.edu					
Jacksonville State University 700 Pelham Rd N	Jacksonville	AL	36265	256-782-5781	782-5953*
**Fax:* Admissions ■ *TF:* 800-231-5291 ■ *Web:* www.jsu.edu					
Judson College 302 Bibb St	Marion	AL	36756	334-683-5110	683-5282*
**Fax:* Admissions ■ *TF Admissions:* 800-447-9472 ■ *Web:* www.judson.edu					
Ludwig Von Mises Institute 518 W Magnolia Ave	Auburn	AL	36832	334-321-2100	
Web: www.mises.org					
Miles College 5500 Myron Massey Blvd	Fairfield	AL	35064	205-929-1000	929-1627*
**Fax:* Admissions ■ *TF Admissions:* 800-445-0708 ■ *Web:* www.miles.edu					
Oakwood College 7000 Adventist Blvd	Huntsville	AL	35896	256-726-7356	726-7154*
**Fax:* Admissions ■ *TF:* 800-824-5312 ■ *Web:* www.oakwood.edu					
Samford University 800 Lakeshore Dr	Birmingham	AL	35229	205-726-3673	726-2171*
**Fax:* Admissions ■ *TF Admissions:* 800-888-7218 ■ *Web:* www.samford.edu					
Selma University 1501 Lapsley St	Selma	AL	36701	334-872-2533	872-7746
Web: selmauniversity.org					
South University *Montgomery* 5355 Vaughn Rd	Montgomery	AL	36116	334-395-8800	395-8859*
**Fax:* Admissions ■ *TF:* 866-629-2962 ■ *Web:* www.southuniversity.edu					
Spring Hill College 4000 Dauphin St	Mobile	AL	36608	251-380-4000	460-2186*
**Fax:* Admissions ■ *TF Admissions:* 800-742-6704 ■ *Web:* badgerweb.shc.edu					
Stillman College 3601 Stillman Blvd	Tuscaloosa	AL	35401	205-349-4240	366-8941
TF: 800-841-5722 ■ *Web:* www.stillman.edu					
Talladega College 627 W Battle St	Talladega	AL	35160	256-362-0206	362-0274*
**Fax:* Admissions ■ *TF:* 866-540-3956 ■ *Web:* talladega.brinkster.net					
Troy University 600 University Ave	Troy	AL	36082	334-670-3100	670-3733*
**Fax:* Admissions ■ *TF:* 800-551-9716 ■ *Web:* www.troy.edu					
Montgomery 231 Montgomery St PO Box 4419	Montgomery	AL	36104	888-357-8843	241-5448*
**Fax Area Code:* 334 ■ **Fax:* Admissions ■ *TF:* 888-357-8843 ■ *Web:* troy.edu					
Phenix City One University Pl	Phenix City	AL	36869	334-297-1007	448-5229*
**Fax:* Admissions ■ *Web:* troy.edu					
Tuskegee University 1200 W Montgomery Rd	Tuskegee	AL	36088	334-727-8011	727-5750*
**Fax:* Admissions ■ *TF Admissions:* 800-622-6531 ■ *Web:* www.tuskegee.edu					
United States Sports Academy, The One Academy Dr	Daphne	AL	36526	251-626-3303	
Web: www.ussa.edu					
University of Alabama PO Box 870132	Tuscaloosa	AL	35487	205-348-6010	348-9046*
**Fax:* Admissions ■ *TF Admissions:* 800-933-2262 ■ *Web:* www.ua.edu					
Birmingham 1530 Third Ave S THT 647	Birmingham	AL	35294	205-996-6670	975-7114*
**Fax:* Admissions ■ *TF:* 800-421-8743 ■ *Web:* www.uab.edu					
Huntsville 301 Sparkman Dr	Huntsville	AL	35899	256-824-1000	824-7780*
**Fax:* Admissions ■ *TF:* 800-824-2255 ■ *Web:* www.uah.edu					
University of Mobile 5735 College Pkwy	Mobile	AL	36613	251-675-5990	442-2498*
**Fax:* Admissions ■ *TF:* 800-946-7267 ■ *Web:* www.umobile.edu					
University of North Alabama 1 Harrison Plaza	Florence	AL	35632	256-765-4608	*
**Fax:* Admissions ■ *TF:* 800-825-5862 ■ *Web:* www.una.edu					
University of South Alabama 2500 Meisler Hall	Mobile	AL	36688	251-460-6141	460-7876
TF: 800-872-5247 ■ *Web:* www.usouthal.edu					
University of West Alabama Stn 200 UWA	Livingston	AL	35470	205-652-3400	652-3522*
**Fax:* Admissions ■ *TF Admissions:* 800-621-8044 ■ *Web:* www.uwa.edu					

Alaska

	City	State	Zip	Phone	Fax
Alaska Pacific University 4101 University Dr	Anchorage	AK	99508	907-564-8248	
TF: 800-252-7528 ■ *Web:* www.alaskapacific.edu					
University of Alaska Anchorage 3211 Providence Dr	Anchorage	AK	99508	907-786-1800	786-4888*
**Fax:* Admissions ■ *TF:* 888-822-8973 ■ *Web:* www.uaa.alaska.edu					
University of Alaska Fairbanks *Bristol Bay* 527 Seward St PO Box 1070	Dillingham	AK	99576	907-842-5109	842-5692*
**Fax:* Admissions ■ *TF:* 800-478-5109 ■ *Web:* www.uaf.edu					
University of Alaska Southeast 11120 Glacier Hwy	Juneau	AK	99801	907-296-6000	
TF: 877-465-4827 ■ *Web:* opportunityequation.org					
Wayland Baptist University Anchorage 7801 E 32 Ave	Anchorage	AK	99504	907-333-2277	337-8122
Web: www.wbu.edu					

Arizona

	City	State	Zip	Phone	Fax
American Indian College of the Assemblies of God 10020 N 15th Ave	Phoenix	AZ	85021	602-944-3335	943-8299
TF: 800-621-7440 ■ *Web:* www.aicag.edu					
Arizona State University 1151 S Forest Ave PO Box 870312	Tempe	AZ	85281	480-965-9011	727-6453
Web: www.asu.edu					
East 7001 E Williams Field Rd	Mesa	AZ	85212	480-727-9911	965-3610
Web: campus.asu.edu/polytechnic					
West PO Box 37100	Phoenix	AZ	85069	602-543-5500	543-8312*
**Fax:* Admissions ■ *TF:* 855-278-5080 ■ *Web:* campus.asu.edu					
Conservatory of Recording Arts & Sciences 2300 E Broadway Rd	Tempe	AZ	85282	480-858-9400	
Web: www.audiorecordingschool.com					
Embry-Riddle Aeronautical University Prescott 3700 Willow Creek Rd	Prescott	AZ	86301	928-777-3728	777-6606*
**Fax:* Admissions ■ *TF:* 800-888-3728 ■ *Web:* www.erau.edu					
Grand Canyon University 3300 W Camelback Rd	Phoenix	AZ	85017	602-639-7500	639-7835*
**Fax:* Library ■ *TF:* 800-800-9776 ■ *Web:* www.gcu.edu					
Indian Bible College 2918 N Aris Ave	Flagstaff	AZ	86004	928-774-3890	774-2655
TF: 866-503-7789 ■ *Web:* www.indianbible.org					
International Baptist College 2211 W Germann Rd	Chandler	AZ	85286	480-245-7900	505-3299
Web: www.tricityministries.org					
Northern Arizona University PO Box 4084	Flagstaff	AZ	86011	928-523-5511	523-6023*
**Fax:* Admissions ■ *TF Admissions:* 888-628-2968 ■ *Web:* www.nau.edu					
Ottawa University Phoenix 10020 N 25th Ave	Phoenix	AZ	85021	602-371-1188	371-0035
TF: 800-235-9586 ■ *Web:* www.ottawa.edu					
Prescott College 220 Grove Ave	Prescott	AZ	86301	877-350-2100	776-5242*
**Fax Area Code:* 928 ■ **Fax:* Admissions ■ *TF:* 877-350-2100 ■ *Web:* www.prescott.edu					
University of Arizona PO Box 210300	Tucson	AZ	85721	520-621-2211	621-9799*
**Fax:* Admissions ■ *Web:* www.arizona.edu					
Western International University 9215 N Black Canyon Hwy	Phoenix	AZ	85021	602-943-2311	
TF: 866-948-4636 ■ *Web:* west.edu					

Arkansas

	City	State	Zip	Phone	Fax
Arkansas State University PO Box 1630	State University	AR	72467	870-972-3024	972-3406
TF: 800-382-3030 ■ *Web:* www.astate.edu					
Central Baptist College 1501 College Ave	Conway	AR	72034	501-329-6872	
Web: www.cbc.edu					
Harding University 900 E Ctr Ave	Searcy	AR	72149	501-279-4000	279-4129
TF: 800-477-4407 ■ *Web:* www.harding.edu					
Henderson State University 1100 Henderson St	Arkadelphia	AR	71999	870-230-5000	230-5066*
**Fax:* Admissions ■ *TF:* 800-228-7333 ■ *Web:* www.hsu.edu					
Hendrix College 1600 Washington Ave	Conway	AR	72032	501-329-6811	450-3843*
**Fax:* Admissions ■ *TF:* 800-277-9017 ■ *Web:* www.hendrix.edu					
John Brown University 2000 W University St	Siloam Springs	AR	72761	479-524-9500	524-4196*
**Fax:* Admissions ■ *TF Admissions:* 877-528-4636 ■ *Web:* www.jbu.edu					
Lyon College 2300 Highland Rd	Batesville	AR	72501	870-793-9813	
Web: www.lyon.edu					
Ouachita Baptist University 410 Ouachita St	Arkadelphia	AR	71998	870-245-5000	245-5500*
**Fax:* Admissions ■ *TF Admissions:* 800-342-5628 ■ *Web:* www.obu.edu					
Philander Smith College 900 Daisy Bates Dr	Little Rock	AR	72202	501-370-5221	370-5225*
**Fax:* Admissions ■ *TF:* 800-446-6772 ■ *Web:* www.philander.edu					
Southern Arkansas University 100 E University St	Magnolia	AR	71753	870-235-4000	235-5005*
**Fax:* Admissions ■ *TF:* 800-332-7286 ■ *Web:* web.saumag.edu					
University of Arkansas 232 Silas Hunt Hall	Fayetteville	AR	72701	479-575-5346	575-7515*
**Fax:* Admissions ■ *TF Admissions:* 800-377-8632 ■ *Web:* www.uark.edu					
Little Rock 2801 S University Ave	Little Rock	AR	72204	501-569-3000	569-8956
Web: www.ualr.edu					
Monticello PO Box 3600	Monticello	AR	71656	870-460-1026	460-1926*
**Fax:* Admissions ■ *TF:* 800-844-1826 ■ *Web:* www.uamont.edu					
Pine Bluff 1200 N University Dr	Pine Bluff	AR	71601	870-575-8000	575-4608*
**Fax:* Admissions ■ *TF Admissions:* 800-264-6585 ■ *Web:* www.uapb.edu					
University of Central Arkansas 201 Donaghey Ave	Conway	AR	72035	501-450-5000	450-5228*
**Fax:* Admissions ■ *TF Admissions:* 888-407-4747 ■ *Web:* www.uca.edu					
University of the Ozarks 415 N College Ave	Clarksville	AR	72830	479-979-1227	979-1417*
**Fax:* Admissions ■ *TF Admissions:* 800-264-8636 ■ *Web:* www.ozarks.edu					
Williams Baptist College 60 W Fulbright St	Walnut Ridge	AR	72476	870-886-6741	886-3924*
**Fax:* Admissions ■ *TF:* 800-722-4434 ■ *Web:* www.wbcoll.edu					

British Columbia

	City	State	Zip	Phone	Fax
North Island College 2300 Ryan Rd	Courtenay	BC	V9N8N6	250-334-5000	
Web: www.nic.bc.ca					
Northern Lights College 11401 - Eigth St	Dawson Creek	BC	V1G4G2	250-782-5251	784-7549
Web: www.nlc.bc.ca					
Pearson College 650 Pearson College Dr	Victoria	BC	V9C4H7	250-391-2411	
Web: www.pearsoncollege.ca					
Selkirk College 301 Frank Beinder Way	Castlegar	BC	V1N4L3	250-365-7292	365-6568
Web: www.selkirk.ca					

California

	City	State	Zip	Phone	Fax
Academy of Art University 79 New Montgomery St	San Francisco	CA	94105	415-274-2200	618-6287
TF: 800-544-2787 ■ *Web:* www.academyart.edu					
Alliant International University 10455 Pomerado Rd	San Diego	CA	92131	858-635-4772	635-4555*
**Fax:* Admissions ■ *TF:* 866-825-5426 ■ *Web:* www.alliant.edu					
American Career College Inc 151 Innovation Dr	Irvine	CA	92617	949-783-4800	
Web: americancareercollege.edu					
Azusa Pacific University 901 E Alosta Ave PO Box 7000	Azusa	CA	91702	626-969-3434	812-3096
TF: 800-825-5278 ■ *Web:* www.apu.edu					
Biola University 13800 Biola Ave	La Mirada	CA	90639	562-903-6000	903-4709*
**Fax:* Admissions ■ *TF Admissions:* 800-652-4652 ■ *Web:* www.biola.edu					
California Baptist University 8432 Magnolia Ave	Riverside	CA	92504	951-689-5771	343-4525*
**Fax:* Admissions ■ *TF:* 877-228-8866 ■ *Web:* www.calbaptist.edu					
California Christian College 4881 E University Ave	Fresno	CA	93703	559-251-4215	251-4231
Web: www.calchristiancollege.edu					
California Institute of Technology 1200 E California Blvd	Pasadena	CA	91125	626-395-6811	683-3026*
**Fax:* Admissions ■ *TF:* 800-568-8324 ■ *Web:* www.caltech.edu					

	City	State	Zip	Phone	Fax
California International University 3130 Wilshire Blvd. *Fax: Admissions ■ Web: www.ciula.edu	Los Angeles	CA	90010	213-381-3710	381-6990*
California Lutheran University 60 W Olsen Rd TF: 877-258-3678 ■ Web: www.callutheran.edu	Thousand Oaks	CA	91360	805-493-3135	493-3114
California Maritime Academy 200 Maritime Academy Dr *Fax: Admissions ■ TF: 800-561-1945 ■ Web: www.csum.edu	Vallejo	CA	94590	707-654-1330	654-1336*
California Pacific University 1017 E Grand Ave Web: www.cpu.edu	Escondido	CA	92025	760-739-7730	
California Polytechnic State University 1 Grand Ave TF: 800-424-6723 ■ Web: www.calpoly.edu	San Luis Obispo	CA	93407	805-756-1111	756-5400
California State Polytechnic University Pomona 3801 W Temple Ave *Fax: Admissions ■ Web: www.csupomona.edu	Pomona	CA	91768	909-869-7659	869-4555*
California State University 401 Golden Shore TF: 800-325-4000 ■ Web: www.calstate.edu	Long Beach	CA	90802	562-951-4000	951-4899
Bakersfield 9001 Stockdale Hwy *Fax: Admissions ■ Web: auxiliary.calstate.edu	Bakersfield	CA	93311	661-654-2011	654-3389*
Channel Islands One University Dr *Fax: Admissions ■ Web: www.csuci.edu	Camarillo	CA	93012	805-437-8400	437-8509*
Chico CSU Chico *Fax: Admissions ■ TF Admissions: 800-542-4426 ■ Web: www.csuchico.edu	Chico	CA	95929	530-898-6321	898-6456*
Dominguez Hills 1000 E Victoria St *Fax: Admissions ■ TF: 888-545-6512 ■ Web: www.csudh.edu	Carson	CA	90747	310-243-3300	516-4573*
East Bay 25800 Carlos Bee Blvd TF: 877-829-5500 ■ Web: www.csueastbay.edu	Hayward	CA	94542	510-885-3000	885-4059
Fresno 5241 N Maple Ave *Fax: Admissions ■ TF: 800-700-2320 ■ Web: www.fresnostate.edu	Fresno	CA	93740	559-278-4240	278-4812*
Fullerton 800 N State College Blvd TF: 888-433-9406 ■ Web: www.fullerton.edu	Fullerton	CA	92834	714-278-2011	278-2300
Long Beach 1250 Bellflower Blvd *Fax: Admissions ■ TF: 800-663-1144 ■ Web: www.csulb.edu	Long Beach	CA	90840	562-985-4111	985-4973*
Los Angeles 5151 State University Dr *Fax: Admissions ■ Web: www.calstatela.edu	Los Angeles	CA	90032	323-343-3000	343-6306*
Monterey Bay 100 Campus Ctr *Fax: Admissions ■ Web: www.csumb.edu	Seaside	CA	93955	831-582-3518	582-3738*
Northridge 18111 Nordhoff St TF: 800-399-4529 ■ Web: www.csun.edu	Northridge	CA	91330	818-677-1200	677-3766
Sacramento 6000 J St Web: www.csus.edu	Sacramento	CA	95819	916-278-3901	278-7473
San Bernardino 5500 University Pkwy TF: 866-275-3772 ■ Web: www.csusb.edu	San Bernardino	CA	92407	909-537-5188	537-7034
San Marcos 333 S Twin Oaks Valley Rd *Fax: Admissions ■ TF: 888-225-5427 ■ Web: www.csusm.edu	San Marcos	CA	92096	760-750-4000	750-3248*
Stanislaus 1 University Cir TF: 800-235-9292 ■ Web: www.csustan.edu	Turlock	CA	95382	209-667-3152	667-3788
California State University Stanislaus					
Library One University Cir Web: ivy.csustan.edu	Turlock	CA	95382	209-667-3234	667-3164
Stockton Ctr 612 E Magnolia St Web: www.csustan.edu	Stockton	CA	95202	209-467-5300	467-5333
Chapman University One University Dr *Fax: Admissions ■ TF: 888-282-7759 ■ Web: www.chapman.edu	Orange	CA	92866	714-997-6815	997-6713*
Charles R Drew University of Medicine & Science 1731 E 120th St *Fax: Admissions ■ Web: www.cdrewu.edu	Los Angeles	CA	90059	323-563-4800	563-4957*
Claremont McKenna College 500 E Ninth St Web: www.claremontmckenna.edu	Claremont	CA	91711	909-621-8088	621-8516
Cleveland Chiropractic College of Los Angeles Inc 590 N Vermont Ave Web: www.cleveland.edu	Los Angeles	CA	90004	323-660-6166	
CODAN US Corp 3511 W Sunflower Ave Web: www.codanuscorp.com	Santa Ana	CA	92704	714-545-2111	
Cogswell Polytechnical College 1175 Bordeaux Dr *Fax: Admissions ■ TF: 800-264-7955 ■ Web: www.cogswell.edu	Sunnyvale	CA	94089	408-541-0100	747-0764*
Coleman College 8888 Balboa Ave Web: www.coleman.edu	San Diego	CA	92123	858-499-0202	499-0233
Columbia College Hollywood 18618 Oxnard St TF: 800-785-0585 ■ Web: www.columbiacollege.edu	Tarzana	CA	91356	818-345-8414	345-9053
Concordia University Irvine 1530 Concordia W TF: 800-229-1200 ■ Web: www.cui.edu	Irvine	CA	92612	949-854-8002	854-6894
Continuing Education of The Bar Sute 410 300 Frank H Ogawa Plz Ste 410 Web: www.ceb.com	Oakland	CA	94612	510-302-2000	
Design Institute of San Diego 8555 Commerce Ave Web: www.disd.edu	San Diego	CA	92121	858-566-1200	566-2711
Dominican University of California 50 Acacia Ave *Fax: Admissions ■ TF Admissions: 888-323-6763 ■ Web: www.dominican.edu	San Rafael	CA	94901	415-457-4440	485-3214*
Ex'pression College for Digital Arts 6601 Shellmound St Web: www.expression.edu	Emeryville	CA	94608	510-654-2934	
Fresno Pacific University 1717 S Chestnut Ave PO Box 2005 *Fax: Admissions ■ TF: 800-660-6089 ■ Web: www.fresno.edu	Fresno	CA	93702	559-453-2039	453-7151*
Harvey Mudd College 301 Platt Blvd Kingston Hall *Fax: Admissions ■ TF: 877-827-5462 ■ Web: www.hmc.edu	Claremont	CA	91711	909-621-8011	607-7046*
Hebrew Union College Los Angeles 3077 University Ave *Fax: Admissions ■ TF: 800-899-0925 ■ Web: www.huc.edu	Los Angeles	CA	90007	213-749-3424	747-6128*
Holy Names University 3500 Mountain Blvd *Fax: Admissions ■ TF: 800-430-1321 ■ Web: www.hnu.edu	Oakland	CA	94619	510-436-1000	436-1325*
Hope International University 2500 E Nutwood Ave *Fax: Admissions ■ TF: 866-722-4673 ■ Web: www.hiu.edu	Fullerton	CA	92831	714-879-3901	526-0231*
Humboldt State University One Harpst St *Fax: Admissions ■ TF: 866-850-9556 ■ Web: www.humboldt.edu	Arcata	CA	95521	707-826-3011	826-6190*
Humphreys College 6650 Inglewood Ave TF: 800-433-3243 ■ Web: www.humphreys.edu	Stockton	CA	95207	209-478-0800	478-8721
John F Kennedy University 100 Ellinwood Way *Fax: Admissions ■ TF: 800-696-5358 ■ Web: www.jfku.edu	Pleasant Hill	CA	94523	925-969-3300	969-3101*
La Sierra University 4500 Riverwalk Pkwy TF: 800-874-5587 ■ Web: www.lasierra.edu	Riverside	CA	92515	951-785-2000	785-2901
Laguna College of Art & Design 2222 Laguna Canyon Rd TF: 800-255-0762 ■ Web: www.lcad.edu	Laguna Beach	CA	92651	949-376-6000	376-6009
Lee Strasberg Theatre Institute, The 7936 Santa Monica Blvd Web: www.strasberg.com	West Hollywood	CA	90046	323-650-7777	
Loma Linda University 11234 Anderson St Web: www.llu.edu	Loma Linda	CA	92354	909-558-1000	
Loyola Marymount University One LMU Dr TF: 800-568-4636 ■ Web: www.lmu.edu	Los Angeles	CA	90045	310-338-2700	338-2797
Master's College 21726 Placerita Canyon Rd *Fax: Admissions ■ TF: 800-568-6248 ■ Web: www.masters.edu	Santa Clarita	CA	91321	661-259-3540	288-1037*
Menlo College 1000 El Camino Real TF: 800-556-3656 ■ Web: www.menlo.edu	Atherton	CA	94027	650-543-3753	543-4496
Mills College 5000 MacArthur Blvd *Fax: Admissions ■ TF Admissions: 877-746-4557 ■ Web: www.mills.edu	Oakland	CA	94613	510-430-2135	430-3314*
Mount Saint Mary's University 12001 Chalon Rd *Fax: Admissions ■ TF Admissions: 800-999-9893 ■ Web: www.msmc.la.edu	Los Angeles	CA	90049	310-954-4250	954-4259*
National Hispanic University 14271 Story Rd *Fax: Admissions ■ TF: 877-762-9801 ■ Web: www.nhu.edu	San Jose	CA	95127	408-254-6900	254-1369*
National University 11255 N Torrey Pines Rd TF: 800-628-8648 ■ Web: www.nu.edu	La Jolla	CA	92037	858-642-8000	642-8709
Northwestern Polytechnic University 47671 Westinghouse Dr TF: 877-878-8883 ■ Web: www.npu.edu	Fremont	CA	94539	510-657-5913	657-8975
Notre Dame de Namur University 1500 Ralston Ave *Fax: Admissions ■ TF: 800-263-0545 ■ Web: www.ndnu.edu	Belmont	CA	94002	650-508-3600	508-3426*
Occidental College 1600 Campus Rd *Fax: Admissions ■ TF Admissions: 800-825-5262 ■ Web: www.oxy.edu	Los Angeles	CA	90041	323-259-2700	341-4875*
Pacific College Oriental Med Inc 7445 Mission Vly Rd Ste 105 Web: www.pacificcollege.edu	San Diego	CA	92108	619-574-6909	
Pacific Oaks College 5 Westmoreland Pl Web: www.pacificoaks.edu	Pasadena	CA	91103	877-314-2380	
Pacific States University 1516 S Western Ave Web: www.psuca.edu	Los Angeles	CA	90006	323-731-2383	
Pacific Union College One Angwin Ave *Fax: Admissions ■ TF: 800-862-7080 ■ Web: www.puc.edu	Angwin	CA	94508	707-965-6336	965-6432*
Pacifica Graduate Institute 249 Lambert Rd Web: www.pacifica.edu	Carpinteria	CA	93013	805-969-3626	
Patten University 2433 Coolidge Ave *Fax: Admissions ■ TF: 877-472-8836 ■ Web: www.patten.edu	Oakland	CA	94601	510-261-8500	534-4344*
Pepperdine University 24255 Pacific Coast Hwy *Fax: Admissions ■ Web: www.pepperdine.edu	Malibu	CA	90263	310-506-4000	506-4861*
Phillips Graduate Institute 5445 Balboa Blvd Web: pgi.edu	Encino	CA	91316	818-654-1721	
Pitzer College 1050 N Mills Ave *Fax: Admissions ■ TF: 800-748-9371 ■ Web: www.pitzer.edu	Claremont	CA	91711	909-621-8129	621-8770*
Point Loma Nazarene University 3900 Lomaland Dr *Fax: Admissions ■ TF Admissions: 800-733-7770 ■ Web: www.pointloma.edu	San Diego	CA	92106	619-849-2200	849-2601*
Pomona College 333 N College Way *Fax: Admissions ■ Web: www.pomona.edu	Claremont	CA	91711	909-621-8134	621-8952*
Rudolf Steiner College 9200 Fair Oaks Blvd Web: www.steinercollege.edu	Fair Oaks	CA	95628	916-961-8729	
Ryokan College 11965 Venice Blvd Ste 304 *Fax: Admissions ■ TF: 866-796-5261 ■ Web: www.ryokan.edu	Los Angeles	CA	90066	310-390-7560	391-9756*
Sage College 12125 Day St Ste L Web: www.sagecollege.edu	Moreno Valley	CA	92557	951-781-2727	
Saint Mary's College of California 1928 St Mary's Rd *Fax: Admissions ■ TF Admissions: 800-800-4762 ■ Web: www.stmarys-ca.edu	Moraga	CA	94556	925-631-4000	376-7193*
Samuel Merritt College 370 Hawthorne Ave *Fax: Admissions ■ TF Admissions: 800-607-6377 ■ Web: www.samuelmerritt.edu	Oakland	CA	94609	510-869-6576	869-6525*
San Diego Christian College 2100 Greenfield Dr *Fax: Admissions ■ TF: 800-676-2242 ■ Web: www.sdcc.edu	El Cajon	CA	92019	619-441-2200	590-1739*
San Diego State University 5500 Campanile Dr *Fax: Admissions ■ Web: www.sdsu.edu	San Diego	CA	92182	619-594-5200	594-1250*
Imperial Valley 720 Heber Ave *Fax: Admissions ■ Web: www.ivcampus.sdsu.edu	Calexico	CA	92231	760-768-5520	768-5589*
San Francisco Conservatory of Music 50 Oak St TF: 800-999-8219 ■ Web: www.sfcm.edu	San Francisco	CA	94102	415-864-7326	503-6299
San Francisco State University 1600 Holloway Ave *Fax: Admissions ■ Web: www.sfsu.edu	San Francisco	CA	94132	415-338-1111	338-7196*
San Joaquin College of Law 901 Fifth St Web: www.sjcl.edu	Clovis	CA	93612	559-323-2100	
San Jose State University 1 Washington Sq TF: 800-273-8255 ■ Web: www.sjsu.edu	San Jose	CA	95192	408-924-1000	924-2050
Santa Clara University 500 El Camino Real Web: www.scu.edu	Santa Clara	CA	95053	408-554-4000	554-5255
Scripps College 1030 Columbia Ave *Fax: Admissions ■ TF: 800-770-1333 ■ Web: scrippscollege.edu/	Claremont	CA	91711	909-621-8149	607-7508*

Phone Fax

Silicon Valley University
2160 Lundy Ave Ste 110 .... San Jose CA 95131 408-435-8989
Web: www.svuca.edu

Simpson University 2211 College View Dr .... Redding CA 96003 530-226-4606 226-4861*
**Fax:* Admissions ■ *TF:* 888-974-6776 ■ *Web:* www.simpsonu.edu

Sonoma State University
1801 E Cotati Ave .... Rohnert Park CA 94928 707-664-2880 664-2060*
**Fax:* Admissions ■ *Web:* www.sonoma.edu

South Baylo University 1126 N Brookhurst St .... Anaheim CA 92801 714-533-1495 533-6040
TF: 888-642-2956 ■ *Web:* www.southbaylo.edu

Southern California Institute of Architecture
960 E Third St .... Los Angeles CA 90013 213-613-2200 613-2260*
**Fax:* Admissions ■ *Web:* www.sciarc.edu

Southern California Seminary
2075 E Madison Ave .... El Cajon CA 92019 888-389-7244 442-4510*
**Fax Area Code:* 619 ■ *Web:* www.socalsem.edu

St Mary Med Tech School 1050 Linden Ave .... Long Beach CA 90813 562-491-9000
Web: stmarymed.com

Stanford University 450 Serra Mall .... Stanford CA 94305 650-723-2091 725-2846
TF: 877-407-9529 ■ *Web:* www.stanford.edu

Thomas Aquinas College 10000 Ojai Rd .... Santa Paula CA 93060 805-525-4417 525-9342
TF: 800-634-9797 ■ *Web:* www.thomasaquinas.edu

Trinity Life Bible College
5225 Hillsdale Blvd .... Sacramento CA 95842 916-348-4689 334-2315*
**Fax:* Admissions ■ *Web:* epic.edu

University of California (UCLA)
Berkeley 110 Sproul Hall MC Ste 5800 .... Berkeley CA 94720 510-642-6000 643-7333
TF: 866-740-1260 ■ *Web:* berkeley.edu
Davis One Shields Ave .... Davis CA 95616 530-752-1011 752-1280
Web: www.ucdavis.edu
Irvine 510 Aldrich Hall .... Irvine CA 92697 949-824-5011 824-2711
Web: www.uci.edu
Los Angeles 405 Hilgard Ave .... Los Angeles CA 90095 310-825-4321 206-1206*
**Fax:* Admissions ■ *Web:* www.ucla.edu
Merced PO Box 2039 .... Merced CA 95344 209-724-4400 724-4244*
**Fax:* Admissions ■ *TF:* 866-270-7301 ■ *Web:* www.ucmerced.edu
Riverside
900 University Ave 1120 Hinderaker Hall .... Riverside CA 92521 951-827-3411 827-6344
TF: 800-426-2586 ■ *Web:* www.ucr.edu
San Diego 9500 Gilman Dr .... La Jolla CA 92093 858-534-2230 534-4831*
**Fax:* Admissions ■ *Web:* www.ucsd.edu
San Francisco 505 Parnassus Ave .... San Francisco CA 94122 415-476-9000 353-3925
Web: www.ucsf.edu
Santa Barbara 1210 Cheadle Hall .... Santa Barbara CA 93106 805-893-8000 893-2676
TF: 888-488-8272 ■ *Web:* www.ucsb.edu
Santa Cruz 1156 High St Hahn Bldg Rm 150 .... Santa Cruz CA 95064 831-459-2131 459-4163
TF: 800-933-7584 ■ *Web:* www.ucsc.edu

University of California Irvine College of Health Sciences
1001 Health Science Rd .... Irvine CA 92697 949-824-9267 824-2118
Web: www.cohs.uci.edu

University of Judaism
15600 Mulholland Dr .... Los Angeles CA 90077 310-476-9777 471-3657*
**Fax:* Admissions ■ *TF:* 888-853-6763 ■ *Web:* www.aju.edu

University of La Verne 1950 Third St .... La Verne CA 91750 909-593-3511 392-2714*
**Fax:* Admissions ■ *TF Admissions:* 800-876-4858 ■ *Web:* laverne.edu

University of Redlands
1200 E Colton Ave PO Box 3080 .... Redlands CA 92373 909-793-2121 335-4089*
**Fax:* Admissions ■ *TF:* 800-455-5064 ■ *Web:* www.redlands.edu

University of San Diego 5998 Alcala Pk .... San Diego CA 92110 619-260-4506 260-6836
TF: 800-248-4873 ■ *Web:* www.sandiego.edu

University of San Francisco
2130 Fulton St .... San Francisco CA 94117 415-422-5555 422-2217*
**Fax:* Admissions ■ *TF Admissions:* 800-225-5873 ■ *Web:* www.usfca.edu

University of Southern California
University Pk Campus .... Los Angeles CA 90089 213-740-2311 740-5229*
**Fax:* Admissions ■ *Web:* www.usc.edu

University of the Pacific 3601 Pacific Ave .... Stockton CA 95211 209-946-2211 946-2413
TF: 800-959-2867 ■ *Web:* www.pacific.edu

Vanguard University of Southern California
55 Fair Dr .... Costa Mesa CA 92626 714-556-3610 966-5471*
**Fax:* Admissions ■ *TF Admissions:* 800-722-6279 ■ *Web:* www.vanguard.edu

Weimar College 20601 W Paoli Ln PO Box 486 .... Weimar CA 95736 530-637-4111 422-7949
Web: weimar.edu

Westmont College 955 La Paz Rd .... Santa Barbara CA 93108 805-565-6000 565-6234*
**Fax:* Admissions ■ *TF Admissions:* 800-777-9011 ■ *Web:* www.westmont.edu

Whittier College 13406 E Philadelphia St .... Whittier CA 90608 562-907-4200 907-4870*
**Fax:* Admissions ■ *Web:* www.whittier.edu

William Jessup University 333 Sunset Blvd .... Rocklin CA 95765 916-577-2200 577-2220*
**Fax:* Admissions ■ *TF:* 800-355-7522 ■ *Web:* www.jessup.edu

Woodbury University 7500 Glenoaks Blvd .... Burbank CA 91510 818-767-0888 767-7520
TF: 800-784-9663 ■ *Web:* www.woodbury.edu

World University 107 N Ventura St PO Box 1567 .... Ojai CA 93024 805-646-1444 646-1217
TF: 888-370-7589 ■ *Web:* www.worldu.edu

Colorado

Phone Fax

Adams State College 208 Edgemont Blvd .... Alamosa CO 81102 719-587-7712 587-7522
TF: 800-824-6494 ■ *Web:* www.adams.edu

Auraria Higher Education Ctr
1068 Ninth St Park .... Denver CO 80204 303-556-2400
Web: www.ahec.edu

Beth-El College of Nursing & Health Sciences
1420 Austin Bluffs Pkwy .... Colorado Springs CO 80918 719-255-8227 262-4416
TF: 800-990-8227 ■ *Web:* uccs.edu/~bethel

Colorado Christian University
8787 W Alameda Ave .... Lakewood CO 80226 303-963-3200 963-3201
TF: 800-443-2484 ■ *Web:* www.ccu.edu
Loveland 3553 Clydesdale Pkwy Ste 300 .... Loveland CO 80538 970-669-8700 669-8701*
**Fax:* Admissions ■ *TF:* 800-443-2484 ■ *Web:* www.ccu.edu

Colorado College
14 E Cache La Poudre St .... Colorado Springs CO 80903 719-389-6344 389-6816*
**Fax:* Admissions ■ *TF:* 800-542-7214 ■ *Web:* www.coloradocollege.edu

Colorado School of Mines 1600 Maple St .... Golden CO 80401 303-273-3000 273-3509
TF: 800-446-9488 ■ *Web:* www.mines.edu

Colorado State University 200 W Lake St .... Fort Collins CO 80523 970-491-1101 491-7799*
**Fax:* Admissions ■ *Web:* www.colostate.edu
Pueblo 2200 Bonforte Blvd .... Pueblo CO 81001 719-549-2100 269-7500*
**Fax Area Code:* 814 ■ *TF:* 877-307-5678

Colorado Technical University
4435 N Chestnut St .... Colorado Springs CO 80907 719-598-0200
TF: 855-230-0555 ■ *Web:* www.coloradotech.edu

Fort Lewis College 1000 Rim Dr .... Durango CO 81301 970-247-7010 247-7179*
**Fax:* Admissions ■ *TF:* 877-352-2656 ■ *Web:* www.fortlewis.edu

Johnson & Wales University Denver
7150 E Montview Blvd .... Denver CO 80220 303-256-9300 256-9333
TF: 877-598-3368 ■ *Web:* www.jwu.edu

Mesa State College 1100 N Ave .... Grand Junction CO 81501 970-248-1020 248-1973*
**Fax:* Admissions ■ *TF:* 800-982-6372 ■ *Web:* coloradomesa.edu

Metropolitan State College of Denver
CB 9 PO Box 173362 .... Denver CO 80217 303-556-3440 556-2720*
**Fax:* Admissions ■ *Web:* roadrunnersathletics.com

Naropa University 2130 Arapahoe Ave .... Boulder CO 80302 303-444-0202 546-3536
TF: 800-772-6951 ■ *Web:* www.naropa.edu

National American University Colorado Springs
1915 Jamboree Dr Ste 185 .... Colorado Springs CO 80920 316-448-5400 590-8305*
**Fax Area Code:* 719 ■ *TF:* 855-448-2318 ■ *Web:* www.national.edu

National American University Denver
1325 S Colorado Blvd Ste 100 .... Denver CO 80222 303-876-7100 876-7105*
**Fax:* Admissions ■ *Web:* www.national.edu

Regis University
Colorado Springs
7450 Campus Dr Ste 100 .... Colorado Springs CO 80920 800-568-8932 264-7095*
**Fax Area Code:* 719 ■ **Fax:* Admissions ■ *TF:* 800-568-8932 ■ *Web:* www.regis.edu

Springs Baptist Academy
3500 N Nevada Ave .... Colorado Springs CO 80907 719-593-7887 593-1798

University of Colorado
Boulder CB 552 .... Boulder CO 80309 303-492-1411 492-7115*
**Fax:* Admissions ■ *Web:* www.colorado.edu
Colorado Springs PO Box 7150 .... Colorado Springs CO 80933 719-262-3000 262-3116*
**Fax:* Admissions ■ *TF:* 800-990-8227 ■ *Web:* www.uccs.edu

University of Colorado at Denver 1250 14th St .... Denver CO 80217 303-556-2400 556-4838
Web: www.ucdenver.edu/pages/ucdwelcomepage.aspx

University of Denver 2199 S University Blvd .... Denver CO 80210 303-871-2036 871-3301
TF: 800-525-9495 ■ *Web:* www.du.edu

University of Northern Colorado
501 20th St CB 92 .... Greeley CO 80639 970-351-2881 351-2984*
**Fax:* Admissions ■ *TF Admissions:* 888-700-4862 ■ *Web:* www.unco.edu

US Air Force Academy (USAFA)
2304 Cadet Dr Ste 2300 .... Air Force Academy CO 80840 719-333-1110 333-3644
TF: 800-443-9266 ■ *Web:* www.usafa.af.mil

Western State College of Colorado
600 N Adams St .... Gunnison CO 81231 970-943-2119 943-2363*
**Fax:* Admissions ■ *TF Admissions:* 800-876-5309 ■ *Web:* www.western.edu

Women's College of the University of Denver
1901 E Asbury Ave .... Denver CO 80208 303-871-6848 871-6897
Web: www.womenscollege.du.edu

Yeshiva Toras Chaim Talmudical Seminary
1555 Stuart St .... Denver CO 80204 303-629-8200
Web: ytcdenver.org

Connecticut

Phone Fax

Albertus Magnus College 700 Prospect St .... New Haven CT 06511 203-773-8550 773-5248*
**Fax:* Admissions ■ *TF Admissions:* 800-578-9160 ■ *Web:* www.albertus.edu

Briarwood College 2279 Mt Vernon Rd .... Southington CT 06489 860-628-4751 628-6444*
**Fax:* Admissions ■ *TF:* 800-952-2444 ■ *Web:* www.lincolncollegene.edu

Central Connecticut State University
1615 Stanley St .... New Britain CT 06050 860-832-3200 832-2295
Web: www.ccsu.edu

Charter Oak State College
55 Paul J Manafort Dr .... New Britain CT 06053 860-832-3800
Web: www.charteroak.edu

Connecticut College 270 Mohegan Ave .... New London CT 06320 860-439-2000 439-4301*
**Fax:* Admissions ■ *TF:* 800-892-3363 ■ *Web:* www.conncoll.edu

Eastern Connecticut State University
83 Windham St .... Willimantic CT 06226 860-465-5000 465-5544*
**Fax:* Admissions ■ *TF Admissions:* 877-353-3278 ■ *Web:* www.easternct.edu

Fairfield University 1073 N Benson Rd .... Fairfield CT 06824 203-254-4000 254-4199*
**Fax:* Admissions ■ *Web:* www.fairfield.edu

Hartford Seminary 77 Sherman St .... Hartford CT 06105 860-509-9500 509-9509*
**Fax:* Admissions ■ *TF:* 877-860-2255 ■ *Web:* www.hartsem.edu

Holy Apostles College & Seminary
33 Prospect Hill Rd .... Cromwell CT 06416 860-632-3077
Web: www.holyapostles.edu

Lyme Academy College of Fine Arts
84 Lyme St .... Old Lyme CT 06371 860-434-5232
Web: www.lymeacademy.edu

Mitchell College 437 Pequot Ave .... New London CT 06320 860-701-5000 444-1209*
**Fax:* Admissions ■ *TF Admitting:* 800-443-2811 ■ *Web:* www.mitchell.edu

Paier College of Art Inc 20 Gorham Ave .... Hamden CT 06514 203-287-3031 287-3021
Web: www.paiercollegeofart.edu

Post University 800 Country Club Rd .... Waterbury CT 06723 203-596-4500 756-5810*
**Fax:* Admissions ■ *TF:* 800-345-2562 ■ *Web:* www.post.edu

Quinnipiac University 275 Mt Carmel Ave .... Hamden CT 06518 203-582-8600 582-8906*
**Fax:* Admissions ■ *TF Admissions:* 800-462-1944 ■ *Web:* www.quinnipiac.edu

Sacred Heart University 5151 Pk Ave .... Fairfield CT 06825 203-371-7999 365-7609
Web: www.sacredheart.edu

Southern Connecticut State University
501 Crescent St .... New Haven CT 06515 203-392-5200 392-5727
TF: 888-500-7278 ■ *Web:* www.southernct.edu

	City	State	ZIP	Phone	Fax
St Vincent's College 2800 Main St *Web:* www.stvincentscollege.edu	Bridgeport	CT	06606	203-576-5235	
Trinity College 300 Summit St **Fax:* Admissions ■ *Web:* www.trincoll.edu	Hartford	CT	06106	860-297-2529	297-2287*
University of Bridgeport 126 Pk Ave **Fax:* Admissions ■ *TF:* 800-392-3582 ■ *Web:* www.bridgeport.edu	Bridgeport	CT	06604	203-576-4000	576-4941*
Stamford One University Pl *Web:* www.stamford.uconn.edu	Stamford	CT	06901	203-251-8400	251-8556
University of Hartford 200 Bloomfield Ave *TF:* 800-947-4303 ■ *Web:* www.hartford.edu	West Hartford	CT	06117	860-768-4296	768-4961
University of New Haven 300 Boston Post Rd **Fax:* Admissions ■ *TF:* 800-342-5864 ■ *Web:* www.newhaven.edu	West Haven	CT	06516	203-932-7319	931-6093*
University of Saint Joseph 1678 Asylum Ave **Fax:* Admissions ■ *Web:* www.sjc.edu	West Hartford	CT	06117	860-232-4571	*
US Coast Guard Academy 15 Mohegan Ave *TF:* 800-883-8724 ■ *Web:* www.cga.edu	New London	CT	06320	860-444-8500	701-6700
Wesleyan University 70 Wyllys Ave **Fax:* Admissions ■ *Web:* www.wesleyan.edu	Middletown	CT	06459	860-685-3000	685-3001*
Western Connecticut State University 181 White St *Web:* wcsu.edu	Danbury	CT	06810	203-837-8200	837-8234
Yale University 38 Hill House Ave **Fax:* Admissions ■ *Web:* www.yale.edu	New Haven	CT	06520	203-432-4771	432-9392*

Delaware

	City	State	ZIP	Phone	Fax
Delaware State University 1200 N DuPont Hwy **Fax:* Admissions ■ *TF Admissions:* 800-845-2544 ■ *Web:* www.desu.edu	Dover	DE	19901	302-857-6351	857-6352*
Goldey Beacom College 4701 Limestone Rd **Fax:* Admissions ■ *TF:* 800-833-4877 ■ *Web:* gbc.edu	Wilmington	DE	19808	302-998-8814	996-5408*
University of Delaware Hullihen Hall Rm 209 **Fax:* Admissions ■ *Web:* www.udel.edu	Newark	DE	19716	302-831-2792	831-6905*
Wilmington University 320 N DuPont Hwy **Fax:* Admissions ■ *TF Admissions:* 877-967-5464 ■ *Web:* www.wilmu.edu	New Castle	DE	19720	302-356-6739	328-5902*

District of Columbia

	City	State	ZIP	Phone	Fax
American University 4400 Massachusetts Ave NW *TF:* 800-829-1040 ■ *Web:* www.american.edu	Washington	DC	20016	202-885-1000	885-2558
Catholic University of America 620 Michigan Ave NE *Web:* www.cua.edu	Washington	DC	20064	202-319-5000	319-6533
Gallaudet University 800 Florida Ave NE *TF:* 800-995-0550 ■ *Web:* www.gallaudet.edu	Washington	DC	20002	202-651-5000	651-5744
George Washington University *Mount Vernon College* 2100 Foxhall Rd NW **Fax:* Admissions ■ *TF:* 800-447-3765 ■ *Web:* www.gwu.edu	Washington	DC	20007	202-994-1000	994-0325*
Georgetown University 37th & 'O' Sts NW *Web:* www.georgetown.edu	Washington	DC	20057	202-687-3600	687-5084
Howard University 2400 Sixth St NW **Fax:* Admissions ■ *TF:* 800-822-6363 ■ *Web:* www.howard.edu	Washington	DC	20059	202-806-6100	806-4465*
Potomac College 4000 Chesapeake St NW *Web:* potomac.edu	Washington	DC	20016	202-686-0876	
Strayer University *Takoma Park* 6830 Laurel St NW **Fax:* Admissions ■ *TF:* 888-311-0355 ■ *Web:* www.strayer.edu	Washington	DC	20012	202-722-8100	722-8108*
University of the District of Columbia 4200 Connecticut Ave NW *Web:* www.udc.edu	Washington	DC	20008	202-274-5000	274-5552

Florida

	City	State	ZIP	Phone	Fax
American Intercontinental University South Florida 2250 N Commerce Pkwy *TF:* 855-377-1888 ■ *Web:* www.aiuniv.edu	Weston	FL	33326	954-446-6100	
Ave Maria University 5050 Ave Maria Blvd **Fax:* Admissions ■ *TF:* 877-283-8648 ■ *Web:* avemaria.edu	Naples	FL	34119	239-280-2500	280-2556*
Baptist College of Florida 5400 College Dr **Fax:* Admissions ■ *TF:* 800-328-2660 ■ *Web:* www.baptistcollege.edu	Graceville	FL	32440	850-263-3261	263-7506*
Orlando 1650 Sandlake Rd Ste 390 **Fax:* Admissions ■ *TF:* 800-756-6000 ■ *Web:* barry.edu	Orlando	FL	32809	407-438-4150	438-9774*
Tallahassee 325 John Knox Rd Bldg A **Fax:* Admissions ■ *TF:* 800-756-6000 ■ *Web:* barry.edu	Tallahassee	FL	32303	850-385-2279	385-7576*
Bethune-Cookman College 640 Dr Mary McLeod Bethune Blvd **Fax:* Admissions ■ *TF Admissions:* 800-448-0228 ■ *Web:* www.cookman.edu	Daytona Beach	FL	32114	386-481-2900	481-2601*
Chipola College 3094 Indian Cir **Fax:* Admissions ■ *Web:* www.chipola.edu	Marianna	FL	32446	850-526-2761	718-2287*
Clearwater Christian College 3400 Gulf to Bay Blvd **Fax:* Admissions ■ *TF Admissions:* 800-348-4463 ■ *Web:* www.clearwater.edu	Clearwater	FL	33759	727-726-1153	726-8597*
Columbia College Orlando 2600 Technology Dr Ste 100 **Fax:* Admissions ■ *TF:* 800-231-2391 ■ *Web:* www.ccis.edu	Orlando	FL	32804	407-293-9911	293-8530*
Dade Medical College 3401 NW Seventh St *Web:* www.dademedical.edu	Miami	FL	33125	305-644-1171	
Eckerd College 4200 54th Ave S **Fax:* Admissions ■ *TF Admissions:* 800-456-9009 ■ *Web:* www.eckerd.edu	Saint Petersburg	FL	33711	727-867-1166	866-2304*
Embry-Riddle Aeronautical University *Daytona Beach* 600 S Clyde Morris Blvd **Fax:* Admissions ■ *TF:* 800-862-2416 ■ *Web:* www.erau.edu	Daytona Beach	FL	32114	386-226-6000	226-7070*
Flagler College 74 King St **Fax:* Admissions ■ *TF Admissions:* 800-304-4208 ■ *Web:* www.flagler.edu	Saint Augustine	FL	32084	904-829-6481	819-6466*
Florida Atlantic University (FAU) 777 Glades Rd **Fax:* Admissions ■ *TF Admissions:* 800-299-4328 ■ *Web:* www.fau.edu	Boca Raton	FL	33431	561-297-3000	297-2758*
Davie 3200 College Ave *TF:* 800-764-2222 ■ *Web:* www.fau.edu/broward/davie	Davie	FL	33314	954-236-1000	
Fort Lauderdale 111 E Las Olas Blvd *TF:* 800-764-2222 ■ *Web:* www.fau.edu/broward/fortlauderdale	Fort Lauderdale	FL	33301	954-236-1000	
MacArthur 5353 Parkside Dr **Fax:* Admissions ■ *TF:* 888-328-2586 ■ *Web:* www.fau.edu/jupiter	Jupiter	FL	33458	561-799-8500	799-8721*
Treasure Coast 500 NW California Blvd **Fax:* Admissions ■ *Web:* www.fau.edu	Port Saint Lucie	FL	34986	772-873-3300	873-3304*
Florida College 119 N Glen Arven Ave **Fax:* Admissions ■ *TF:* 800-326-7655 ■ *Web:* www.floridacollege.edu	Temple Terrace	FL	33617	813-988-5131	899-6772*
Florida College of Emergency Physicians 3717 S Conway Rd *Web:* www.fcep.org	Orlando	FL	32812	407-281-7396	
Florida College of Integrative Medicine 7100 Lk Ellenor Dr *Web:* www.fcim.edu	Orlando	FL	32809	407-888-8689	
Florida Institute of Technology 150 W University Blvd **Fax:* Admissions ■ *TF:* 800-888-4348 ■ *Web:* www.fit.edu	Melbourne	FL	32901	321-674-8000	674-8004*
Florida International University 11200 SW Eigth St *TF:* 800-677-6337 ■ *Web:* www.fiu.edu	Miami	FL	33199	305-348-2000	348-3648
Florida Memorial University 15800 NW 42nd Ave *TF:* 800-822-1362 ■ *Web:* www.fmuniv.edu	Miami Gardens	FL	33054	305-626-3600	
Florida Southern College 111 Lk Hollingsworth Dr **Fax:* Admissions ■ *TF Admissions:* 800-274-4131 ■ *Web:* www.flsouthern.edu	Lakeland	FL	33801	863-680-4131	680-4120*
Florida State University, The 600 W College Ave *Web:* www.fsu.edu	Tallahassee	FL	32306	850-644-4357	
Hodges University 2655 Northbrooke Dr **Fax:* Admissions ■ *TF:* 800-466-8017 ■ *Web:* www.hodges.edu	Naples	FL	34119	239-513-1122	598-6254*
Fort Myers 4501 Colonial Blvd *TF:* 800-466-0019 ■ *Web:* myhugo.hodges.edu	Fort Myers	FL	33966	239-482-0019	
Jacksonville University 2800 University Blvd N **Fax:* Admissions ■ *TF:* 800-225-2027 ■ *Web:* www.ju.edu	Jacksonville	FL	32211	904-256-8000	256-7012*
Johnson & Wales University North Miami 1701 NE 127th St *TF:* 866-598-3567 ■ *Web:* www.jwu.edu	North Miami	FL	33181	305-892-7551	892-7020
Jones College 5353 Arlington Expy **Fax:* Admissions ■ *TF:* 800-331-0176 ■ *Web:* www.jones.edu	Jacksonville	FL	32211	904-743-1122	371-1182*
Logos Christian College 9000 Regency Sq Blvd **Fax:* Admissions ■ *TF:* 800-252-4253 ■ *Web:* www.logos.edu	Jacksonville	FL	32211	904-745-3311	743-8866*
Lynn University 3601 N Military Trl **Fax:* Admissions ■ *TF Admissions:* 800-888-5966 ■ *Web:* www.lynn.edu	Boca Raton	FL	33431	561-237-7900	237-7100*
New College of Florida 5800 Bay Shore Rd **Fax:* Admissions ■ *TF:* 800-435-7352 ■ *Web:* www.ncf.edu	Sarasota	FL	34243	941-487-5000	487-5010*
Northwood University Florida 2600 N Military Trl **Fax:* Admissions ■ *TF Admissions:* 800-458-8325 ■ *Web:* www.northwood.edu	West Palm Beach	FL	33409	561-478-5500	681-7901*
Nova Southeastern University 3301 College Ave **Fax:* Admissions ■ *TF:* 800-541-6682 ■ *Web:* www.nova.edu	Fort Lauderdale	FL	33314	954-262-8000	262-3811*
Palm Beach Atlantic University PO Box 24708 **Fax:* Admissions ■ *TF:* 888-468-6722 ■ *Web:* www.pba.edu	West Palm Beach	FL	33416	561-803-2000	803-2115*
Pensacola Christian College 250 Brent Ln **Fax Area Code:* 800 ■ *TF:* 800-722-4636 ■ *Web:* www.pcci.edu	Pensacola	FL	32503	850-478-8496	722-3355*
Rollins College 1000 Holt Ave **Fax:* Admissions ■ *TF:* 800-799-2586 ■ *Web:* www.rollins.edu	Winter Park	FL	32789	407-646-2000	646-1502*
Rosenstiel School of Marine & Atmospheric Science University of Miami 4600 Rickenbacker Causeway Rosenstiel School *Web:* www.rsmas.miami.edu	Miami	FL	33149	305-421-4000	
Saint Leo University 33701 State Rd 52 **Fax:* Admissions ■ *TF:* 800-334-5532 ■ *Web:* www.saintleo.edu	Saint Leo	FL	33574	352-588-8200	588-8257*
Palatka Ctr 33701 State Rd 52 PO Box 6665 *TF:* 800-334-5532 ■ *Web:* www.saintleo.edu	Saint Leo	FL	33574	352-588-8200	
Saint Thomas University 16401 NW 37th Ave *TF:* 800-367-9010 ■ *Web:* www.stu.edu	Miami Gardens	FL	33054	305-628-6546	628-6591
South University West Palm Beach 9801 Belvedere Rd University Ctr **Fax:* Admissions ■ *TF:* 800-688-0932 ■ *Web:* www.southuniversity.edu	West Palm Beach	FL	33411	561-273-6500	697-9944*
Southeastern University 1000 Longfellow Blvd *TF:* 800-500-8760 ■ *Web:* seu.edu	Lakeland	FL	33801	863-667-5000	667-5200
Stetson University 421 N Woodland Blvd Unit 8378 **Fax:* Admissions ■ *TF Admissions:* 800-688-0101 ■ *Web:* www.stetson.edu	DeLand	FL	32723	386-822-7100	822-7112*
Trinity International University South Florida 8190 W SR 84 *TF:* 800-822-3225 ■ *Web:* www.tiu.edu	Davie	FL	33324	954-382-6400	382-6420
University of Central Florida 4000 Central Florida Blvd PO Box 160000 **Fax:* Admissions ■ *Web:* www.ucf.edu	Orlando	FL	32816	407-823-2000	823-5625*
University of Florida 219 Grinter Hall PO Box 115500 **Fax:* Admissions ■ *TF:* 866-876-4472 ■ *Web:* www.ufl.edu	Gainesville	FL	32611	352-392-3261	392-2115*
University of Miami 1252 Memorial Dr *Web:* www.miami.edu	Coral Gables	FL	33146	305-284-4323	284-2507
University of North Florida 4567 St Johns Bluff Rd S *TF:* 866-697-7150 ■ *Web:* www.unf.edu	Jacksonville	FL	32224	904-620-1000	620-2414
Saint Petersburg 140 Seventh Ave S *Web:* www.usfsp.edu	Saint Petersburg	FL	33701	727-873-4135	873-4525

Phone | Fax

Sarasota-Manatee 8350 N Tamiami Trail Sarasota FL 34243 941-359-4200 359-4236*
*Fax: Admissions ■ TF: 866-974-1222 ■ Web: usfsm.edu/

Tampa 4202 E Fowler Ave Tampa FL 33620 813-974-2011 974-4346
TF: 877-873-2855 ■ Web: www.usf.edu

University of South Florida Polytechnic
Lakeland 3433 Winter Lake Rd. Lakeland FL 33803 863-667-7017 667-7096*
*Fax: Admissions ■ TF: 800-873-5636 ■ Web: poly.usf.edu

University of Tampa 401 W Kennedy Blvd Tampa FL 33606 813-253-3333 258-7398
Web: www.ut.edu

Warner Southern College 13895 Hwy 27 Lake Wales FL 33859 800-309-9563 949-7248*
*Fax: Admissions ■ TF: 800-309-9563 ■ Web: warner.edu

Webber International University
1201 N Scenic Hwy Babson Park FL 33827 863-638-2910 638-1591*
*Fax: Admissions ■ TF: 800-741-1844 ■ Web: www.webber.edu

Georgia

Phone | Fax

Agnes Scott College 141 E College Ave Decatur GA 30030 404-471-6000 471-6414*
*Fax: Admissions ■ TF: 800-868-8602 ■ Web: www.agnesscott.edu

Albany State University 504 College Dr Rd Albany GA 31705 229-430-4600 430-1614*

American InterContinental University
Atlanta
6600 Peachtree Dunwoody Rd
500 Embassy Row NE Atlanta GA 30328 404-965-6500
TF: 800-491-0182 ■ Web: www.aiuniv.edu
Dunwoody
6600 Peachtree-Dunwoody Rd 500 Embassy Row Atlanta GA 30328 404-965-6500 695-4538*
*Fax Area Code: 866 ■ *Fax: Admissions ■ TF: 855-377-1888 ■ Web: www.aiuniv.edu

Armstrong Atlantic State University
11935 Abercorn St Savannah GA 31419 800-633-2349 344-3470*
*Fax Area Code: 912 ■ TF: 800-633-2349 ■ Web: www.armstrong.edu

Atlanta Christian College
2605 Ben Hill Rd East Point GA 30344 404-761-8861 214-0648*
*Fax: Admissions ■ TF: 855-377-6468 ■ Web: point.edu

Augusta State University 2500 Walton Way Augusta GA 30904 706-737-1632 667-4355
TF: 800-341-4373 ■ Web: www.gru.edu

Berry College
2277 Martha Berry Hwy PO Box 490159 Mount Berry GA 30149 706-232-5374 290-2178*
*Fax: Admissions ■ TF: 800-237-7942 ■ Web: www.berry.edu

Brenau University 500 Washington St. Gainesville GA 30501 770-534-6299 538-4701*
*Fax: Admissions ■ TF: 800-252-5119 ■ Web: www.brenau.edu

Brewton-Parker College
201 David-Eliza Fountain Cir Hwy 280
PO Box 197 Mount Vernon GA 30445 912-583-2241 583-3598*
*Fax: Admissions ■ TF: 800-342-1087 ■ Web: www.bpc.edu

Carver Bible College 3870 Cascade Rd Atlanta GA 30331 404-527-4520 527-4524
Web: www.carver.edu

Clark Atlanta University
223 James P Brawley Dr SW Atlanta GA 30314 404-880-8000 880-6174*
*Fax: Admissions ■ TF Admissions: 800-688-3228 ■ Web: www.cau.edu

Clayton State University
2000 Clayton State Blvd Morrow GA 30260 678-466-4000 466-4149*
*Fax: Admissions ■ Web: www.clayton.edu

Columbus State University
4225 University Ave Columbus GA 31907 706-507-8800 326-1479*
*Fax Area Code: 570 ■ TF: 866-264-2035 ■ Web: columbusstate.edu

Covenant College 14049 Scenic Hwy Lookout Mountain GA 30750 706-820-1560 820-0893*
*Fax: Admissions ■ TF: 888-451-2683 ■ Web: www.covenant.edu

Dalton State College 650 N College Dr Dalton GA 30720 706-272-4436 529-9266*
*Fax: Admissions ■ TF: 800-829-4436 ■ Web: www.daltonstate.edu

Emory University 201 Dowman Dr. Atlanta GA 30322 404-727-6036 727-4303
TF Admissions: 800-727-6036 ■ Web: www.emory.edu

Fort Valley State University
1005 State University Dr. Fort Valley GA 31030 478-825-6211 825-6169*
*Fax: Admissions ■ TF: 877-462-3878 ■ Web: www.fvsu.edu

Georgia College & State University
Macon 433 Cherry St. Macon GA 31206 478-752-4278 752-1064
TF: 800-342-0471 ■ Web: graduate.gcsu.edu

Georgia Institute of Technology 225 N Ave NW Atlanta GA 30332 404-894-2000 894-9511*
*Fax: Admissions ■ Web: www.gatech.edu

Georgia Southern University PO Box 8024 Statesboro GA 30460 912-478-5391 478-7240
Web: www.georgiasouthern.edu

Georgia Southwestern State University
800 Gsw State University Dr Americus GA 31709 229-928-1273 931-2983
TF Admissions: 800-338-0082 ■ Web: www.gsw.edu

Georgia State University
33 Gilmer St SE Ste 200 Atlanta GA 30303 404-413-2000 413-2002
Web: www.gsu.edu

Gwinnett College of Business
4230 Lawrenceville Hwy Nw Ste 11 Lilburn GA 30047 770-381-7200
Web: www.gwinnettcollege.edu

Kennesaw State University 1000 Chastain Rd Kennesaw GA 30144 770-423-6000 420-4435*
*Fax: Admissions ■ TF: 800-542-2233 ■ Web: www.kennesaw.edu

LaGrange College 601 Broad St LaGrange GA 30240 706-880-8005 880-8010*
*Fax: Admissions ■ TF Admissions: 800-593-2885

Life University 1269 Barclay Cir. Marietta GA 30060 770-426-2884
Web: www.life.edu

Luther Rice College & Seminary
3038 Evans Mill Rd Lithonia GA 30038 770-484-1204
Web: www.lru.edu

Macon State College
Warner Robins 100 University Blvd Warner Robins GA 31093 478-929-6700 929-6726
Web: www.mga.edu

Medical College of Georgia 1120 15th St Augusta GA 30912 706-721-0211 721-7028
TF: 800-736-2273 ■ Web: gru.edu

Mercer University 1400 Coleman Ave. Macon GA 31207 478-301-2650 301-2828*
*Fax: Admissions ■ TF: 800-637-2378 ■ Web: www.mercer.edu
Cecil B Day 3001 Mercer University Dr Atlanta GA 30341 678-547-6089 547-6367
TF: 800-840-8577 ■ Web: www.mercer.edu

Morehouse College 830 Westview Dr SW Atlanta GA 30314 404-681-2800 572-3668*
*Fax: Admissions ■ Web: www.morehouse.edu

Phone | Fax

Oglethorpe University 3000 Woodrow Way NE Atlanta GA 30319 404-364-8307 364-8491
TF: 800-428-4484 ■ Web: www.oglethorpe.edu

Paine College 1235 15th St Augusta GA 30901 706-821-8200 821-8293*
*Fax: Admissions ■ TF: 800-476-7703 ■ Web: www.paine.edu

Piedmont College 165 Central Ave Demorest GA 30535 706-776-0103 776-6635*
*Fax: Admissions ■ TF: 800-277-7020 ■ Web: www.piedmont.edu

Reinhardt College 7300 Reinhardt College Cir. Waleska GA 30183 770-720-5526 720-5899*
*Fax: Admissions ■ TF: 877-346-4273 ■ Web: www.reinhardt.edu

Shorter University 315 Shorter Ave. Rome GA 30165 706-233-7319 233-7224*
*Fax: Admissions ■ TF: 800-868-6980 ■ Web: www.shorter.edu

South University Savannah 709 Mall Blvd Savannah GA 31406 912-201-8000 201-8117*
*Fax: Admissions ■ TF: 800-688-0932 ■ Web: www.southuniversity.edu

Southern Polytechnic State University
1100 S Marietta Pkwy Marietta GA 30060 678-915-4188 915-7292*
*Fax: Admissions ■ TF Admissions: 800-635-3204 ■ Web: www.spsu.edu

Spelman College 350 Spelman Ln SW Atlanta GA 30314 404-681-3643 270-5201*
*Fax: Admissions ■ TF Admissions: 800-982-2411 ■ Web: www.spelman.edu

Thomas University 1501 Millpond Rd. Thomasville GA 31792 229-226-1621
TF: 800-538-9784 ■ Web: www.thomasu.edu

Truett-McConnell College 100 Alumni Dr Cleveland GA 30528 706-865-2134 865-7615*
*Fax: Admissions ■ TF: 800-226-8621 ■ Web: www.truett.edu

University of West Georgia 1600 Maple St. Carrollton GA 30117 678-839-5000 839-4747
Web: www.westga.edu

Valdosta State University
1500 N Patterson St Valdosta GA 31698 229-333-5800 333-5482*
*Fax: Admissions ■ TF: 800-618-1878 ■ Web: www.valdosta.edu

Wesleyan College 4760 Forsyth Rd Macon GA 31210 478-477-1110 757-4030*
*Fax: Admissions ■ TF: 800-447-6610 ■ Web: www.wesleyancollege.edu

Guam

Phone | Fax

University of Guam
University Dr 303 University Sta Mangialo GU 96929 671-735-2910
Web: www.uog.edu

Hawaii

Phone | Fax

Atlantic International University
900 Ft St Mall Honolulu HI 96813 808-924-9567
Web: www.aiu.edu

Brigham Young University Hawaii
55-220 Kulanui St Laie HI 96762 808-293-3211 293-3741*
*Fax: Admissions ■ Web: www.byuh.edu

Chaminade University 3140 Waialae Ave. Honolulu HI 96816 808-735-4711 735-4735*
*Fax: Admissions ■ TF: 800-735-3733 ■ Web: www.chaminade.edu

Hawaii Pacific University
Windward Hawaii Loa 1164 Bishop St Honolulu HI 96813 808-544-0200
TF Admissions: 866-225-5478 ■ Web: www.hpu.edu

University of Hawaii
Hilo 200 W Kawili St Hilo HI 96720 808-974-7414 933-0861*
*Fax: Admissions ■ TF Admissions: 800-897-4456 ■ Web: hilo.hawaii.edu
Manoa 2600 Campus Rd Rm 001 Honolulu HI 96822 808-956-8975 956-4148*
*Fax: Admissions ■ TF Admissions: 800-823-9771 ■ Web: www.manoa.hawaii.edu
West Oahu 96-129 Ala Ike Pearl City HI 96782 808-454-4700 453-6075
TF: 866-299-8656 ■ Web: www.uhwo.hawaii.edu

Idaho

Phone | Fax

Boise State University 1910 University Dr. Boise ID 83725 208-426-1156 426-3765
TF: 800-824-7017 ■ Web: my.boisestate.edu

Brigham Young University Idaho 525 S Ctr Rexburg ID 83460 866-672-2984 496-1220*
*Fax Area Code: 208 ■ *Fax: Admissions ■ Web: www.byui.edu

College of Idaho 2112 Cleveland Blvd Caldwell ID 83605 208-459-5011 459-5757*
*Fax: Admissions ■ TF Admissions: 800-224-3246 ■ Web: www.collegeofidaho.edu

Idaho State University 921 S Eigth Ave Pocatello ID 83209 208-282-2475 282-4511*
*Fax: Admissions ■ Web: www.isu.edu

Lewis-Clark State College 500 Eigth Ave. Lewiston ID 83501 208-792-5272 792-2210*
*Fax: Admissions ■ TF: 800-933-5272 ■ Web: www.lcsc.edu

Northwest Nazarene University 623 Holly St. Nampa ID 83686 208-467-8000 467-8645*
*Fax: Admissions ■ TF Admissions: 877-668-4968 ■ Web: www.nnu.edu

University of Idaho
Boise 322 E Front St Ste 190 Boise ID 83702 208-334-2999 364-4035
TF: 866-264-7384 ■ Web: www.uidaho.edu

Illinois

Phone | Fax

Adler School of Professional Psychology
65 E Wacker Pl Ste 2100 Chicago IL 60601 312-201-5900
Web: www.adler.edu

American InterContinental University Los Angeles
231 N Martingale Rd Sixth Fl Schaumburg IL 60173 877-701-3800
TF: 877-701-3800 ■ Web: www.aiuniv.edu

American Islamic College 640 W Irving Pk Rd. Chicago IL 60613 773-281-4700 281-8552*
*Fax: Admissions ■ Web: www.aicusa.edu

Augustana College 639 38th St Rock Island IL 61201 309-794-7000 794-7174*
*Fax: Admissions ■ TF: 800-798-8100 ■ Web: www.augustana.edu

Aurora University 347 S Gladstone Ave. Aurora IL 60506 630-844-5533 844-5535
TF: 800-742-5281 ■ Web: www.aurora.edu

Benedictine University 5700 College Rd Lisle IL 60532 630-829-6300 829-6301
TF: 888-829-6363 ■ Web: www.ben.edu

Blackburn College 700 College Ave. Carlinville IL 62626 217-854-3231 854-3713*
*Fax: Admissions ■ TF: 800-233-3550 ■ Web: www.blackburn.edu

Bradley University 1501 W Bradley Ave Peoria IL 61625 309-676-7611 677-2797
TF Admissions: 800-447-6460 ■ Web: www.bradley.edu

Chicago State University 9501 S King Dr. Chicago IL 60628 773-995-2513 995-3820*
*Fax: Admissions ■ Web: www.csu.edu

	City	State	Zip	Phone	Fax
Columbia College 600 S Michigan Ave 3rd Fl	Chicago	IL	60605	312-663-1600	344-8024*
*Fax: Admissions ■ TF: 866-705-0200 ■ Web: www.colum.edu					
Concordia University Chicago					
7400 Augusta St	River Forest	IL	60305	708-771-8300	263-7462*
*Fax Area Code: 312 ■ TF: 888-258-6773 ■ Web: www.cuchicago.edu					
DePaul University One E Jackson Blvd Ste 9100	Chicago	IL	60614	312-362-8300	362-5749
Web: www.depaul.edu					
Dominican University 7900 W Div St	River Forest	IL	60305	708-366-2490	524-5990*
*Fax: Admissions ■ TF: 800-828-8475 ■ Web: www.dom.edu					
East-West University					
816 S Michigan Ave Ste 800	Chicago	IL	60605	312-939-0111	939-0083
TF: 877-398-9376 ■ Web: www.eastwest.edu					
Eastern Illinois University					
600 Lincoln Ave	Charleston	IL	61920	217-581-2223	581-7060*
*Fax: Admissions ■ TF Admissions: 800-252-5711 ■ Web: www.eiu.edu					
Elmhurst College 190 Prospect Ave	Elmhurst	IL	60126	630-617-3400	617-5501
TF: 800-697-1871 ■ Web: public.elmhurst.edu					
Eureka College 300 E College Ave	Eureka	IL	61530	309-467-6350	467-6576*
*Fax: Admissions ■ TF Admissions: 888-438-7352 ■ Web: www.eureka.edu					
Governors State University					
1 University Pkwy	University Park	IL	6048	708-534-5000	534-1640*
*Fax: Admissions ■ TF: 800-478-8478 ■ Web: www.govst.edu					
Greenville College 315 E College Ave	Greenville	IL	62246	618-664-7100	664-9841*
*Fax: Admissions ■ TF: 800-345-4440 ■ Web: www.greenville.edu					
Harrington College of Design					
200 W Madison St	Chicago	IL	60606	866-590-4423	
TF: 866-590-4423 ■ Web: www.harrington.edu					
Illinois College 1101 W College Ave	Jacksonville	IL	62650	217-245-3030	245-3034*
*Fax: Admissions ■ TF Admissions: 866-464-5265 ■ Web: www.ic.edu					
Rice 201 E Loop Rd	Wheaton	IL	60189	630-682-6000	682-6010*
*Fax: Admissions ■ Web: www.iit.edu/rice					
Illinois State University					
North and School Streets Hovey Hall 201	Normal	IL	61790	309-438-2111	438-3932*
*Fax: Admissions ■ TF Admissions: 800-366-2478 ■ Web: illinoisstate.edu					
Illinois Wesleyan University 1312 Pk St	Bloomington	IL	61701	309-556-3031	556-3820*
*Fax: Admissions ■ TF Admissions: 800-332-2498 ■ Web: www.iwu.edu					
Judson University 1151 N State St	Elgin	IL	60123	847-628-2500	628-2526*
*Fax: Admissions ■ TF Admissions: 800-879-5376 ■ Web: www.judsonu.edu					
Lake Forest College 555 N Sheridan Rd	Lake Forest	IL	60045	847-234-3100	735-6271
TF: 800-828-4751 ■ Web: www.lakeforest.edu					
Lakeview College of Nursing 903 N Logan Ave	Danville	IL	61832	217-443-5238	
Web: www.lakeviewcol.edu					
Lewis University					
One University Pkwy Unit 297	Romeoville	IL	60446	815-836-5250	836-5002
TF: 800-897-9000 ■ Web: www.lewisu.edu					
Cudahy Library 1032 W Sheridan Rd	Chicago	IL	60660	773-508-2632	
Web: libraries.luc.edu/cudahy					
Lake Shore 6525 N Sheridan Rd	Chicago	IL	60626	773-508-3075	508-8926
Web: www.luc.edu					
Loyola University Chicago					
Water Tower 820 N Michigan Ave	Chicago	IL	60611	312-915-6500	915-7216*
*Fax: Admissions ■ TF Admissions: 800-262-2373 ■ Web: www.luc.edu					
MacMurray College 447 E College Ave	Jacksonville	IL	62650	217-479-7056	291-0702*
*Fax: Admissions ■ TF: 800-252-7485 ■ Web: www.mac.edu					
McKendree College 701 College Rd	Lebanon	IL	62254	618-537-4481	537-6496*
*Fax: Admissions ■ TF: 800-232-7228 ■ Web: www.mckendree.edu					
Millikin University 1184 W Main St	Decatur	IL	62522	217-424-6211	425-4669*
*Fax: Admissions ■ TF: 800-373-7733 ■ Web: www.millikin.edu					
Monmouth College 700 E Broadway Ave	Monmouth	IL	61462	309-457-2311	457-2141
TF: 888-827-8268 ■ Web: www.monmouthcollege.edu					
National University of Health Sciences					
200 E Roosevelt Rd	Lombard	IL	60148	630-629-2000	889-6554
TF: 800-826-6285 ■ Web: www.nuhs.edu					
National-Louis University 1000 Capitol Dr	Wheeling	IL	60090	847-947-5718	465-5730*
*Fax: Admissions ■ TF: 800-443-5522 ■ Web: www.nl.edu					
Chicago 122 S Michigan Ave	Chicago	IL	60603	888-658-8632	465-5730*
*Fax Area Code: 847 ■ *Fax: Admissions ■ TF: 800-443-5522 ■ Web: www.nl.edu					
North Central College 30 N Brainard St	Naperville	IL	60540	630-637-5800	637-5819*
*Fax: Admissions ■ TF: 800-411-1861 ■ Web: northcentralcollege.edu					
North Park University 3225 W Foster Ave	Chicago	IL	60625	773-244-5500	244-4953
TF: 800-888-6728 ■ Web: www.northpark.edu					
Northeastern Illinois University					
5500 N St Louis Ave	Chicago	IL	60625	773-442-4050	442-4020*
*Fax: Admissions ■ TF: 800-393-0865 ■ Web: www.neiu.edu					
Northern Illinois University					
1425 W Lincoln Hwy	DeKalb	IL	60115	815-753-1000	753-8312*
*Fax: Admissions ■ TF: 800-892-3050 ■ Web: www.niu.edu					
Northwestern University 1801 Hinman Ave	Evanston	IL	60208	847-491-7271	467-2331*
*Fax: Admissions ■ TF: 800-227-7368 ■ Web: www.northwestern.edu					
Olivet Nazarene University					
One University Ave	Bourbonnais	IL	60914	815-939-5011	935-4998*
*Fax: Admissions ■ TF: 800-648-1463 ■ Web: www.olivet.edu					
Principia College One Maybeck Pl	Elsah	IL	62028	618-374-2131	374-4000*
*Fax: Admissions ■ TF: 800-277-4648 ■ Web: www.principia.edu					
Quincy University 1800 College Ave	Quincy	IL	62301	217-222-8020	228-5257*
*Fax: Admissions ■ TF: 866-703-4004 ■ Web: quhawks.com/index.aspx					
Chicago 401 S State St	Chicago	IL	60605	312-935-6800	935-4182
TF: 800-762-5960 ■ Web: www.robertmorris.edu					
DuPage 905 Meridian Lk Dr	Aurora	IL	60504	630-375-8100	375-8020*
*Fax: Admissions ■ TF Admissions: 800-762-5960 ■ Web: www.robertmorris.edu					
Robert Morris College					
Orland Park 43 Orland Sq Dr	Orland Park	IL	60462	708-226-3800	226-5350
TF: 800-225-1520 ■ Web: www.robertmorris.edu					
Springfield 3101 Montvale Dr	Springfield	IL	62704	217-793-2500	793-4210*
*Fax: Admitting ■ TF: 800-762-5960 ■ Web: www.robertmorris.edu					
Rockford College 5050 E State St	Rockford	IL	61108	815-226-4000	226-2822*
*Fax: Admissions ■ TF: 800-892-2984 ■ Web: www.rockford.edu					
Roosevelt University 430 S Michigan Ave	Chicago	IL	60605	312-341-3500	341-3827*
*Fax: Admissions ■ TF Admissions: 877-277-5978 ■ Web: www.roosevelt.edu					
Albert A Robin 1400 N Roosevelt Blvd	Schaumburg	IL	60173	847-619-8600	619-8636*
*Fax: Admissions ■ TF Admissions: 877-277-5978 ■ Web: www.roosevelt.edu					
Rush University 600 S Paulina St Rm 440	Chicago	IL	60612	312-942-7100	942-2219*
*Fax: Admissions ■ Web: www.rushu.rush.edu					
Saint Anthony College of Nursing					
5658 E State St	Rockford	IL	61108	815-395-5091	
Web: sacn.edu					
Saint Xavier University 3700 W 103rd St	Chicago	IL	60655	773-298-3000	298-3076*
*Fax: Admissions ■ TF: 800-462-9288 ■ Web: www.sxu.edu					
School of the Art Institute of Chicago					
36 S Wabash Ave	Chicago	IL	60603	312-629-6100	629-6101*
*Fax: Admissions ■ TF Admissions: 800-232-7242 ■ Web: www.artic.edu					
Shimer College 3424 S State St	Chicago	IL	60616	312-235-3506	
TF: 800-215-7173 ■ Web: www.shimer.edu					
Southern Illinois University					
Edwardsville SR 157	Edwardsville	IL	62026	618-650-2000	650-5013*
*Fax: Admissions ■ TF: 888-328-5168 ■ Web: www.siue.edu					
Southern Illinois University Carbondale					
900 S Normal Ave Woody Hall MC 4716	Carbondale	IL	62901	618-536-7791	453-3250*
*Fax: Admissions ■ Web: gradschool.siu.edu					
Trinity Christian College					
6601 W College Dr	Palos Heights	IL	60463	708-597-3000	239-4826
Web: www.trnty.edu					
Trinity International University					
2065 Half Day Rd	Deerfield	IL	60015	847-945-8800	317-8097
TF: 800-822-3225 ■ Web: www.tiu.edu					
University of Chicago 5801 S Ellis Ave	Chicago	IL	60637	773-702-1234	702-4199*
*Fax: Admissions ■ Web: www.uchicago.edu					
Chicago 601 S Morgan	Chicago	IL	60607	312-996-7000	413-7628
Web: www.uic.edu					
University of Illinois					
Springfield					
One University Plz MS UHB 1080	Springfield	IL	62703	217-206-4847	206-6620*
*Fax: Admissions ■ TF: 888-977-4847 ■ Web: www.uis.edu					
Urbana-Champaign 901 W Illinois St	Urbana	IL	61801	217-333-0302	244-4614
Web: illinois.edu					
University of St Francis 500 Wilcox St	Joliet	IL	60435	800-735-7500	
TF: 800-735-7500 ■ Web: www.stfrancis.edu					
VanderCook College of Music					
3140 S Federal St	Chicago	IL	60616	312-225-6288	225-5211*
*Fax: Admissions ■ Web: www.vandercook.edu					
Quad Cities 3561 60th St	Moline	IL	61265	309-762-9481	764-7172*
*Fax: Admissions ■ TF: 877-742-5948 ■ Web: www.wiu.edu					

Indiana

	City	State	Zip	Phone	Fax
American Conservatory of Music					
252 Wildwood Rd	Hammond	IN	46324	219-931-6000	931-6089*
*Fax: Admissions ■ Web: www.americanconservatory.edu					
Anderson University 1100 E Fifth St	Anderson	IN	46012	765-649-9071	641-4091*
*Fax: Admissions ■ TF Admissions: 800-428-6414 ■ Web: www.anderson.edu					
Ball State University 2000 W University Ave	Muncie	IN	47306	765-289-1241	285-1632*
*Fax: Admissions ■ TF: 800-382-8540 ■ Web: cms.bsu.edu					
Bethel College 1001 W McKinley Ave	Mishawaka	IN	46545	574-807-7000	807-7000*
*Fax: Admissions ■ TF Admissions: 800-422-4101 ■ Web: www.bethelcollege.edu					
Butler University 4600 Sunset Ave	Indianapolis	IN	46208	317-940-8100	940-8150*
*Fax: Admissions ■ TF: 800-368-6852 ■ Web: www.butler.edu					
Calumet College of Saint Joseph					
2400 New York Ave	Whiting	IN	46394	219-473-4215	473-4336*
*Fax: Admissions ■ TF: 877-700-9100 ■ Web: www.ccsj.edu					
DePauw University 101 E Seminary St	Greencastle	IN	46135	765-658-4006	658-4007*
*Fax: Admissions ■ TF: 800-447-2495 ■ Web: www.depauw.edu					
Earlham College 801 National Rd W	Richmond	IN	47374	765-983-1600	983-1560*
*Fax: Admissions ■ TF: 800-327-5426 ■ Web: www.earlham.edu					
Franklin College 101 Branigin Blvd	Franklin	IN	46131	317-738-8000	738-8274*
*Fax: Admissions ■ TF: 800-852-0232 ■ Web: www.franklincollege.edu					
Goshen College 1700 S Main St	Goshen	IN	46526	574-535-7000	535-7609*
*Fax: Admissions ■ TF: 800-348-7422 ■ Web: www.goshen.edu					
Grace College 200 Seminary Dr	Winona Lake	IN	46590	574-372-5100	372-5120*
*Fax: Admissions ■ TF: 800-544-7223 ■ Web: www.grace.edu					
Hanover College 484 Ball Dr	Hanover	IN	47243	812-866-7000	866-7098
TF: 800-213-2178 ■ Web: www.hanover.edu					
Holy Cross College 54515 SR 933 N	Notre Dame	IN	46556	574-239-8400	239-8323*
*Fax: Admissions ■ Web: www.hcc-nd.edu					
Huntington University 2303 College Ave	Huntington	IN	46750	260-356-6000	358-3699*
*Fax: Admissions ■ TF Admissions: 800-642-6493 ■ Web: www.huntington.edu					
Indiana State University					
200 N Seventh St	Terre Haute	IN	47809	800-468-6478	237-8023*
*Fax Area Code: 812 ■ TF: 800-468-6478 ■ Web: cms.indstate.edu					
Indiana Tech 1600 E Washington Blvd	Fort Wayne	IN	46803	260-422-5561	422-7696
TF: 800-937-2448 ■ Web: www.indianatech.edu					
East 2325 Chester Blvd	Richmond	IN	47374	765-973-8208	973-8288*
*Fax: Admissions ■ TF: 800-959-3278 ■ Web: www.iue.edu					
Kokomo 2300 S Washington St PO Box 9003	Kokomo	IN	46904	765-455-9217	455-9537*
*Fax: Admissions ■ TF: 888-875-4485 ■ Web: www.iuk.edu					
Northwest 3400 Broadway	Gary	IN	46408	219-980-6500	981-4219*
*Fax: Admissions ■ TF: 888-968-7486 ■ Web: www.iun.edu					
South Bend 1700 Mishawaka Ave PO Box 7111	South Bend	IN	46634	574-520-4870	523-4834*
*Fax: Admissions ■ TF: 877-462-4872 ■ Web: www.iusb.edu					
Indiana University					
Southeast 4201 Grant Line Rd	New Albany	IN	47150	812-941-2212	941-2595
Web: www.ius.edu					
Indiana University-Purdue University					
Columbus 4601 Central Ave	Columbus	IN	47203	812-348-7271	348-7257
Web: iupuc.edu					
Fort Wayne 2101 E Coliseum Blvd	Fort Wayne	IN	46805	260-481-6100	481-6880*
*Fax: Hum Res ■ TF: 800-324-4739 ■ Web: www.ipfw.edu					
Indianapolis 425 University Blvd	Indianapolis	IN	46202	317-274-5555	278-1862
Web: www.iupui.edu					
Indiana Wesleyan University					
4201 S Washington St	Marion	IN	46953	765-677-2138	677-2333*
*Fax: Admissions ■ TF: 800-332-6901 ■ Web: www.indwes.edu					
Manchester College					
604 E College Ave	North Manchester	IN	46962	260-982-5000	982-5239*
*Fax: Admissions ■ TF Admissions: 800-852-3648 ■ Web: www.manchester.edu					

Phone | Fax

Marian University 3200 Cold Spring Rd .... Indianapolis IN 46222 317-955-6038 955-6401*
Fax: Admissions ■ *TF Admissions:* 800-772-7264 ■ *Web:* www.marian.edu
Martin University 2171 Avondale Pl .... Indianapolis IN 46218 317-543-3235 543-4790
Web: www.martin.edu
Oakland City University
138 N Lucretia St .... Oakland City IN 47660 812-749-4781 749-1433
TF: 800-737-5125 ■ *Web:* www.oak.edu
Purdue University
Schleman Hall 475 Stadium Mall Dr .... West Lafayette IN 47907 765-494-1776 494-0544*
Fax: Admissions ■ *Web:* www.purdue.edu
Calumet 2200 169th St .... Hammond IN 46323 219-989-2400 989-2775*
Fax: Admissions ■ *TF:* 800-447-8738 ■ *Web:* webs.purduecal.edu
North Central 1401 S US Hwy 421 .... Westville IN 46391 219-785-5200 785-5538*
Fax: Admissions ■ *Web:* www.pnc.edu
Rose-Hulman Institute of Technology
5500 Wabash Ave .... Terre Haute IN 47803 812-877-1511 877-8941
TF Admissions: 800-248-7448 ■ *Web:* www.rose-hulman.edu
Saint Mary's College Le Mans Hall Rm 122 .... Notre Dame IN 46556 574-284-4587 284-4841*
Fax: Admissions ■ *TF Admissions:* 800-551-7621 ■ *Web:* www.saintmarys.edu
Saint Mary-of-the-Woods College
3301 St Mary Rd .... Saint Mary Of The Woods IN 47876 812-535-5106 535-5010*
Fax: Admissions ■ *TF:* 800-926-7692 ■ *Web:* www.smwc.edu
Taylor University 236 W Reade Ave .... Upland IN 46989 765-998-2751 998-4925*
Fax: Admissions ■ *TF:* 800-882-3456 ■ *Web:* www.taylor.edu
Fort Wayne 915 W Rudisill Blvd .... Fort Wayne IN 46807 260-744-8790 745-4974
TF General: 800-882-3456 ■ *Web:* fw.taylor.edu
Tri-State University 1 University Blvd .... Angola IN 46703 781-800-5000 665-4578*
Fax Area Code: 260 ■ *Fax:* Admissions ■ *Web:* tripadvisor.com
Trine University
4101 Edison Lakes Pkwy Ste 250 .... Mishawaka IN 46545 574-243-0500
Web: www.trine.edu
Trinity College of The Bible & Trinity Theological Seminary
4233 Medwel Dr .... Newburgh IN 47630 812-853-0611
Web: www.trinitysem.edu
University of Evansville 1800 Lincoln Ave .... Evansville IN 47722 812-488-2000 488-4076*
Fax: Admissions ■ *TF:* 800-423-8633 ■ *Web:* www.evansville.edu
University of Indianapolis
1400 E Hanna Ave .... Indianapolis IN 46227 317-788-3368 788-3300*
Fax: Admissions ■ *TF:* 800-232-8634 ■ *Web:* www.uindy.edu
University of Notre Dame 220 Main Bldg .... Notre Dame IN 46556 574-631-7505 631-8665*
Fax: Admissions ■ *Web:* www.nd.edu
University of Saint Francis-ft Wayne
2701 Spring St .... Fort Wayne IN 46808 260-399-7700
Web: www.sf.edu
University of Southern Indiana
8600 University Blvd .... Evansville IN 47712 812-464-1765 465-7154
TF: 800-467-1965 ■ *Web:* www.usi.edu
Valparaiso University 1700 Chapel Dr .... Valparaiso IN 46383 219-464-5011 464-6898*
Fax: Admissions ■ *TF:* 888-468-2576 ■ *Web:* www.valpo.edu
Wabash College
410 W Wabash Ave PO Box 352 .... Crawfordsville IN 47933 765-361-6225 361-6437*
Fax: Admissions ■ *TF:* 800-345-5385 ■ *Web:* www.wabash.edu

Iowa

Phone | Fax

Ashford University 400 N Bluff Blvd .... Clinton IA 52732 563-242-4023 243-6102*
Fax: Admissions ■ *TF:* 800-242-4153 ■ *Web:* www.ashford.edu
Briar Cliff University 3303 Rebecca St .... Sioux City IA 51104 712-279-5321 279-1632*
Fax: Admissions ■ *TF:* 800-662-3303 ■ *Web:* www.briarcliff.edu
Buena Vista University 610 W Fourth St .... Storm Lake IA 50588 712-749-2253 749-2035
TF: 800-383-9600 ■ *Web:* www.bvu.edu
Central College 812 University St .... Pella IA 50219 641-628-5285 628-5983*
Fax: Admissions ■ *TF:* 877-462-3687 ■ *Web:* www.central.edu
Clarke College 1550 Clarke Dr .... Dubuque IA 52001 563-588-6300 588-6789*
Fax: Admissions ■ *TF:* 888-825-2753 ■ *Web:* www.clarke.edu
Coe College 1220 First Ave NE .... Cedar Rapids IA 52402 319-399-8500 399-8816
TF: 877-225-5263 ■ *Web:* www.coe.edu
Cornell College 600 First St SW .... Mount Vernon IA 52314 319-895-4215 895-4451*
Fax: Admissions ■ *TF Admissions:* 800-747-1112 ■ *Web:* www.cornellcollege.edu
Divine Word College 102 Jacoby Dr SW .... Epworth IA 52045 563-876-3353 876-3407*
Fax: Admissions ■ *TF:* 800-553-3321 ■ *Web:* www.dwci.edu
Dordt College 498 Fourth Ave NE .... Sioux Center IA 51250 712-722-6080 722-1198
TF: 800-343-6738 ■ *Web:* www.dordt.edu
Drake University 2507 University Ave .... Des Moines IA 50311 515-271-3181 271-2831
TF: 800-443-7253 ■ *Web:* www.drake.edu
Graceland University 1 University Pl .... Lamoni IA 50140 641-784-5000 784-5480*
Fax: Admissions ■ *TF:* 800-859-1215 ■ *Web:* www.graceland.edu
Grand View College 1200 Grandview Ave .... Des Moines IA 50316 515-263-2800 263-2974*
Fax: Admissions ■ *TF:* 800-444-6083 ■ *Web:* www.gvc.edu
Grinnell College 1115 8th Ave .... Grinnell IA 50112 641-269-3600 269-4800
TF: 800-247-0113 ■ *Web:* www.grinnell.edu
Iowa Braille & Sight Saving School 1002 G Ave .... Vinton IA 52349 319-472-5221
Web: www.iowa-braille.k12.ia.us
Iowa State Innovation System
2501 N Loop Dr Ste 1000 .... Ames IA 50010 515-296-7275
Web: www.isupark.org
Iowa State University 100 Alumni Hall .... Ames IA 50011 515-294-4111 294-2592*
Fax: Admissions ■ *TF Admissions:* 800-262-3810 ■ *Web:* www.iastate.edu
Iowa Wesleyan College 601 N Main St .... Mount Pleasant IA 52641 800-582-2383 385-6240*
Fax Area Code: 319 ■ *Fax:* Admissions ■ *TF:* 800-582-2383 ■ *Web:* www.iwc.edu
Loras College 1450 Alta Vista St .... Dubuque IA 52001 563-588-7100 588-7119*
Fax: Admissions ■ *TF:* 800-245-6727 ■ *Web:* www.loras.edu
Luther College 700 College Dr .... Decorah IA 52101 563-387-2000 387-2159*
Fax: Admissions ■ *TF:* 800-458-8437 ■ *Web:* www.luther.edu
Maharishi University of Management
1000 N Fourth St .... Fairfield IA 52557 641-472-1110 472-1179
TF: 800-369-6480 ■ *Web:* www.mum.edu
Midwest Associates of Colleges Empl
100 E Grand Ave Ste 330 .... Des Moines IA 50309 515-243-2360
Web: www.nalmco.org

Phone | Fax

Morningside College 1501 Morningside Ave .... Sioux City IA 51106 712-274-5000 274-5101*
Fax: Admissions ■ *TF:* 800-831-0806 ■ *Web:* www.morningside.edu
Mount Mercy College 1330 Elmhurst Dr NE .... Cedar Rapids IA 52402 319-368-6460 861-2390
TF: 800-248-4504 ■ *Web:* www.mtmercy.edu
Northwestern College 101 Seventh St SW .... Orange City IA 51041 712-707-7000 707-7164*
Fax: Admissions ■ *TF:* 800-747-4757 ■ *Web:* www.nwciowa.edu
Saint Ambrose University 518 W Locust St .... Davenport IA 52803 563-333-6000 333-6243*
Fax: Admissions ■ *TF Admissions:* 800-383-2627 ■ *Web:* www.sau.edu
Simpson College 701 N 'C' St .... Indianola IA 50125 515-961-6251 961-1870*
Fax: Admissions ■ *TF:* 800-362-2454 ■ *Web:* www.simpson.edu
University of Dubuque 2000 University Ave .... Dubuque IA 52001 563-589-3000 589-3690*
Fax: Admissions ■ *TF:* 800-722-5583 ■ *Web:* www.dbq.edu
University of Iowa 107 Calvin Hall .... Iowa City IA 52242 319-335-3847 335-1535
TF: 800-553-4692 ■ *Web:* www.uiowa.edu
University of Northern Iowa
1222 W 27th St .... Cedar Falls IA 50614 319-273-2281 273-2885*
Fax: Admissions ■ *TF Admissions:* 800-772-2037 ■ *Web:* www.uni.edu
Upper Iowa University
605 Washington St PO Box 1857 .... Fayette IA 52142 563-425-5200 425-5323*
Fax: Admissions ■ *TF Admissions:* 800-553-4150 ■ *Web:* www.uiu.edu
Waldorf College 106 S Sixth St .... Forest City IA 50436 641-585-2450 585-8184*
Fax: Admissions ■ *TF:* 800-292-1903 ■ *Web:* www.waldorf.edu
Wartburg College 100 Wartburg Blvd .... Waverly IA 50677 319-352-8264 352-8579*
Fax: Admissions ■ *TF:* 800-772-2085 ■ *Web:* www.wartburg.edu
William Penn University 201 Trueblood Ave .... Oskaloosa IA 52577 800-779-7366 673-2113*
Fax Area Code: 641 ■ *Fax:* Admissions ■ *TF:* 800-779-7366 ■ *Web:* www.wmpenn.edu

Kansas

Phone | Fax

Benedictine College 1020 N Second St .... Atchison KS 66002 913-367-5340 367-5462*
Fax: Admissions ■ *TF:* 800-467-5340 ■ *Web:* www.benedictine.edu
Central Christian College PO Box 1403 .... McPherson KS 67460 620-241-0723 241-6032*
Fax: Admissions ■ *TF:* 800-835-0078 ■ *Web:* www.centralchristian.edu
Emporia State University
1200 Commercial St CB 4023 .... Emporia KS 66801 620-341-1200 341-5599
TF: 877-468-6378 ■ *Web:* www.emporia.edu
Fort Hays State University 600 Pk St .... Hays KS 67601 785-628-4000 628-4187*
Fax: Admissions ■ *TF Admissions:* 800-628-3478 ■ *Web:* www.fhsu.edu
Friends University 2100 University St .... Wichita KS 67213 316-295-5000
TF: 800-794-6945 ■ *Web:* www.friends.edu
Haskell Indian Nations University
155 Indian Ave PO Box 5031 .... Lawrence KS 66046 785-749-8454 749-8429*
Fax: Admissions ■ *Web:* www.haskell.edu
Kansas State University 119 Anderson Hall .... Manhattan KS 66506 785-532-6250 532-6393*
Fax: Admissions ■ *TF Admissions:* 800-432-8270 ■ *Web:* www.k-state.edu
Kansas State University-Salina
College of Technology & Aviation
2310 Centennial Rd .... Salina KS 67401 785-826-2640 532-7494*
Fax: Admissions ■ *Web:* www.sal.ksu.edu
Kansas University
Edwards 12600 Quivira Rd .... Overland Park KS 66213 913-897-8400 897-8490*
Fax: Admissions ■ *Web:* www.edwardscampus.ku.edu
Kansas Wesleyan University 100 E Claflin Ave .... Salina KS 67401 785-827-5541 827-0927*
Fax: Admissions ■ *TF:* 800-874-1154 ■ *Web:* www.kwu.edu
McPherson College PO Box 1402 .... McPherson KS 67460 620-241-0731 241-8443*
Fax: Admissions ■ *TF:* 800-365-7402 ■ *Web:* www.mcpherson.edu
MidAmerica Nazarene University
2030 E College Way .... Olathe KS 66062 913-782-3750 971-3481*
Fax: Admissions ■ *TF:* 800-800-8887 ■ *Web:* www.mnu.edu
Newman University 3100 McCormick Ave .... Wichita KS 67213 316-942-4291 942-4483*
Fax: Admissions ■ *TF:* 877-639-6268 ■ *Web:* www.newmanu.edu
Ottawa University 1001 S Cedar St .... Ottawa KS 66067 785-242-5200 229-1008*
Fax: Admissions ■ *TF Admissions:* 800-755-5200 ■ *Web:* www.ottawa.edu
Pittsburg State University
1701 S Broadway St .... Pittsburg KS 66762 620-235-4251 235-6003*
Fax: Admissions ■ *TF:* 800-854-7488 ■ *Web:* www.pittstate.edu
Tabor College 400 S Jefferson St .... Hillsboro KS 67063 620-947-3121 947-6276*
Fax: Admissions ■ *TF Admissions:* 800-822-6799 ■ *Web:* www.tabor.edu
University of Kansas 1502 Iowa St .... Lawrence KS 66045 785-864-2700 864-5017
Web: www.ku.edu
University of Saint Mary
4100 S Fourth St .... Leavenworth KS 66048 913-682-5151 758-6140*
Fax: Admissions ■ *TF:* 800-752-7043 ■ *Web:* www.stmary.edu
Washburn University 1700 SW College Ave .... Topeka KS 66621 785-670-1010 670-1079
TF: 800-736-9060 ■ *Web:* www.washburn.edu
Wichita State University 1845 Fairmount St .... Wichita KS 67260 316-978-3456 978-3174*
Fax: Admissions ■ *TF Admissions:* 800-362-2594 ■ *Web:* www.wichita.edu

Kentucky

Phone | Fax

Alice Lloyd College 100 Purpose Rd .... Pippa Passes KY 41844 606-368-6000 368-6215*
Fax: Admissions ■ *TF Admissions:* 888-280-4252 ■ *Web:* www.alc.edu
Asbury College One Macklem Dr .... Wilmore KY 40390 859-858-3511 858-3921*
Fax: Admissions ■ *TF Admissions:* 800-888-1818 ■ *Web:* www.asbury.edu
Bellarmine University 2001 Newburg Rd .... Louisville KY 40205 502-272-8000 452-8002
TF: 800-274-4723 ■ *Web:* www.bellarmine.edu
Berea College 101 Chestnut St .... Berea KY 40403 859-985-3500 985-3512*
Fax: Admissions ■ *TF:* 800-326-5948 ■ *Web:* www.berea.edu
Brescia University 717 Frederica St .... Owensboro KY 42301 270-685-3131 686-4314*
Fax: Admissions ■ *TF Admissions:* 877-273-7242 ■ *Web:* brescia.edu
Campbellsville University
One University Dr .... Campbellsville KY 42718 270-789-5000 789-5071*
Fax: Admissions ■ *TF Admissions:* 800-264-6014 ■ *Web:* www.campbellsville.edu
Centre College 600 W Walnut St .... Danville KY 40422 859-238-5350 238-5373
TF: 800-423-6236 ■ *Web:* www.centre.edu
Eastern Kentucky University
521 Lancaster Ave .... Richmond KY 40475 859-622-2106 622-8024
TF: 800-465-9191 ■ *Web:* www.eku.edu
Georgetown College 400 E College St .... Georgetown KY 40324 502-863-8000 868-7733*
Fax: Admissions ■ *TF Admissions:* 800-788-9985 ■ *Web:* www.georgetowncollege.edu

	Phone	Fax
Kentucky Christian University 100 Academic Pkwy .... Grayson KY 41143 *Fax: Admissions ■ TF Admissions: 800-522-3181 ■ Web: www.kcu.edu	606-474-3000	474-3155*
Kentucky State University 400 E Main St .... Frankfort KY 40601 *Fax: Admissions ■ TF Admissions: 800-325-1716 ■ Web: www.kysu.edu	502-597-6000	597-5814*
Kentucky Wesleyan College 3000 Frederica St .... Owensboro KY 42301 *Fax: Admissions ■ TF Admissions: 800-999-0592 ■ Web: www.kwc.edu	270-852-3120	852-3133*
Lindsey Wilson College 210 Lindsey Wilson St .... Columbia KY 42728 *Fax: Admissions ■ TF: 800-264-0138 ■ Web: www.lindsey.edu	270-384-2126	384-8591*
Louisville Bible College PO Box 91046 .... Louisville KY 40291 TF: 888-676-7458 ■ Web: www.louisvillebiblecollege.org	502-231-5221	231-5222
Mid-Continent University 99 Powell Rd E .... Mayfield KY 42066 *Fax: Admissions ■ TF: 888-628-4723 ■ Web: www.midcontinent.edu	270-247-8521	247-3115*
Midway College 512 E Stephens St .... Midway KY 40347 *Fax: Admissions ■ TF: 800-755-0031 ■ Web: midway.edu	859-846-5346	846-5787*
Morehead State University 100 Admissions Ctr .... Morehead KY 40351 *Fax: Admissions ■ TF: 800-585-6781 ■ Web: www.moreheadstate.edu	606-783-2000	783-5038*
Murray State University 102 Curris Ctr .... Murray KY 42071 *Fax: Admissions ■ TF: 800-272-4678 ■ Web: www.murraystate.edu	270-809-3741	809-3780*
Hopkinsville 5305 Ft Campbell Blvd .... Hopkinsville KY 42240 *Fax: Admissions ■ Web: murraystate.edu	270-707-1525	707-1535*
Northern Kentucky University Nunn Dr .... Highland Heights KY 41099 *Fax: Admissions ■ TF Admissions: 800-637-9948 ■ Web: www.nku.edu	859-572-5220	572-6665*
Pikeville College 147 Sycamore St .... Pikeville KY 41501 *Fax: Admissions ■ TF: 866-232-7700 ■ Web: upike.edu	606-218-5250	218-5255*
Spalding University 851 S Fourth St .... Louisville KY 40203 TF: 800-896-8941 ■ Web: www.spalding.edu	502-585-9911	585-7158
Sullivan University 3101 BaRdstown Rd .... Louisville KY 40205 TF: 800-844-1354 ■ Web: www.sullivan.edu	502-456-6505	456-0040
Thomas More College 333 Thomas More Pkwy .... Crestview Hills KY 41017 TF: 800-825-4557 ■ Web: www.thomasmore.edu	859-344-3332	344-3444
Transylvania University 300 N Broadway .... Lexington KY 40508 TF: 800-872-6798 ■ Web: www.transy.edu	859-233-8242	233-8797
University of Kentucky 800 Rose St .... Lexington KY 40536 TF: 866-900-4685 ■ Web: www.uky.edu	859-257-9000	257-3823
University of Louisville 2301 S Third St .... Louisville KY 40292 TF: 800-334-8635 ■ Web: louisville.edu	502-852-5555	852-6526
University of the Cumberlands 6191 College Stn Dr .... Williamsburg KY 40769 TF: 800-343-1609 ■ Web: www.ucumberlands.edu	606-539-4201	
Western Kentucky University 1906 College Heights Blvd .... Bowling Green KY 42101 *Fax: Admissions ■ TF Admissions: 800-495-8463 ■ Web: www.wku.edu	270-745-0111	745-6133*

Louisiana

	Phone	Fax
Centenary College of Louisiana 2911 Centenary Blvd .... Shreveport LA 71104 *Fax: Admissions ■ TF Admissions: 800-234-4448 ■ Web: www.centenary.edu	318-869-5131	869-5005*
Grambling State University 403 Main St .... Grambling LA 71245 TF: 800-569-4714 ■ Web: www.gram.edu	318-247-3811	
Louisiana College 1140 College Dr .... Pineville LA 71359 *Fax: Admissions ■ TF: 800-487-1906 ■ Web: www.lacollege.edu	318-487-7011	487-7550*
Louisiana State University		
Alexandria 8100 US Hwy 71 S .... Alexandria LA 71302 *Fax: Admissions ■ TF Admissions: 888-473-6417 ■ Web: www.lsua.edu	318-445-3672	473-6418*
Baton Rouge 110 Thomas Boyd Hall .... Baton Rouge LA 70803 *Fax: Admissions ■ TF: 888-846-6810 ■ Web: www.lsu.edu	225-578-3202	578-4433*
Shreveport One University Pl .... Shreveport LA 71115 *Fax: Admissions ■ Web: www.lsus.edu	318-797-5000	797-5286*
Louisiana Tech University 305 Wisteria St .... Ruston LA 71272 *Fax: Admissions ■ TF Admissions: 800-528-3241 ■ Web: www.latech.edu	318-257-2000	257-2499*
Monroe Library 6363 St Charles Ave .... New Orleans LA 70118 Web: library.loyno.edu	504-864-7111	864-7247
Loyola University		
New Orleans 6363 St Charles Ave CB 18 .... New Orleans LA 70118 *Fax: Admissions ■ TF Admissions: 800-456-9652 ■ Web: www.loyno.edu	504-865-3240	865-3383*
McNeese State University 4205 Ryan St .... Lake Charles LA 70609 *Fax: Admissions ■ TF: 800-622-3352 ■ Web: www.mcneese.edu	337-475-5000	475-5151*
Newcomb College Institute for Women 43 Newcomb Pl .... New Orleans LA 70118 TF: 888-327-0009 ■ Web: tulane.edu	504-865-5422	862-8589
Nicholls State University 906 E First St .... Thibodaux LA 70310 *Fax: Admissions ■ TF Admissions: 877-446-0561 ■ Web: www.nicholls.edu	985-448-4507	448-4929*
Northwestern State University 200 Central Ave .... Natchitoches LA 71497 TF: 800-767-8115 ■ Web: www.nsula.edu	318-357-6361	357-4660
Our Lady of Holy Cross College 4123 Woodland Dr .... New Orleans LA 70131 TF: 800-259-7744 ■ Web: www.olhcc.edu	504-394-7744	394-1182
Our Lady of the Lake College 7434 Perkins Rd .... Baton Rouge LA 70808 *Fax: Admissions ■ TF Admissions: 877-242-3509 ■ Web: www.ololcollege.edu	225-768-1700	768-1726*
Southeastern Louisiana University 500 Western Ave .... Hammond LA 70402 *Fax: Admissions ■ TF: 800-222-7358 ■ Web: www.southeastern.edu	985-549-2062	549-5632*
Southern University & A & M College 156 Elton C Harrison Dr PO Box 9757 .... Baton Rouge LA 70813 *Fax: Admissions ■ TF Admissions: 800-256-1531 ■ Web: www.subr.edu	225-771-5180	771-4762*
Tulane University 6823 St Charles Ave .... New Orleans LA 70118 *Fax: Admissions ■ TF Admissions: 800-873-9283 ■ Web: www.tulane.edu	504-865-5000	862-8715*
Unitech Training Academy-houma 1227 Grand Caillou Rd .... Houma LA 70363 Web: www.unitechtrainingacademy.com	985-223-1755	
Lafayette 611 McKinley St .... Lafayette LA 70504 TF: 800-752-6553 ■ Web: www.louisiana.edu	337-482-1000	482-1317
University of Louisiana		
Monroe 700 University Ave .... Monroe LA 71209 TF Admissions: 800-372-5127 ■ Web: www.ulm.edu	318-342-5430	
University of New Orleans Administrative Bldg Rm 103 Lakefront .... New Orleans LA 70148 TF Admissions: 800-256-5866 ■ Web: www.uno.edu	504-280-6000	280-5522
Xavier University of Louisiana 1 Drexel Dr .... New Orleans LA 70125 TF: 877-520-7388 ■ Web: www.xula.edu	504-486-7411	520-7922

Maine

	Phone	Fax
Bates College 2 Andrews Rd Ln Hall .... Lewiston ME 04240 *Fax: Admissions ■ TF: 888-522-8371 ■ Web: www.bates.edu	207-786-6255	786-6025*
Bowdoin College 5000 College Stn .... Brunswick ME 04011 *Fax: Admissions ■ TF: 800-829-1040 ■ Web: www.bowdoin.edu	207-725-3000	725-3101*
Colby College 4800 Mayflower Hill .... Waterville ME 04901 *Fax: Admissions ■ TF Admissions: 800-723-3032 ■ Web: www.colby.edu	207-859-4800	859-4828*
College of the Atlantic 105 Eden St .... Bar Harbor ME 04609 *Fax: Admissions ■ TF Admissions: 800-528-0025 ■ Web: www.coa.edu	207-288-5015	288-4126*
Husson College One College Cir .... Bangor ME 04401 *Fax: Admissions ■ TF: 800-448-7766 ■ Web: www.husson.edu	207-941-7000	941-7935*
Maine Maritime Academy 66 Pleasant St .... Castine ME 04420 *Fax: Admissions ■ TF Admissions: 800-227-8465 ■ Web: www.mainemaritime.edu	207-326-4311	326-2515*
New England Bible College 879 Sawyer St PO Box 2886 .... South Portland ME 04116 *Fax: Admissions ■ TF: 800-286-1859 ■ Web: www.nebc.edu	207-799-5979	799-6586*
Saint Joseph's College of Maine 278 Whites Bridge Rd .... Standish ME 04084 *Fax: Admissions ■ TF Admissions: 800-338-7057 ■ Web: www.sjcme.edu	207-893-7746	893-7862*
Thomas College 180 W River Rd .... Waterville ME 04901 *Fax: Admissions ■ TF Admissions: 800-339-7001 ■ Web: www.thomas.edu	207-859-1111	859-1114*
Unity College 90 Quaker Hill Rd .... Unity ME 04988 TF: 800-624-1024 ■ Web: www.unity.edu	207-948-3131	
Augusta 46 University Dr .... Augusta ME 04330 *Fax: Admissions ■ Web: www.uma.edu	207-621-3000	621-3333*
University of Maine		
Farmington 111 S St .... Farmington ME 04938 *Fax: Admissions ■ Web: www.umf.maine.edu	207-778-7000	778-8182*
Fort Kent 23 University Dr .... Fort Kent ME 04743 *Fax: Admissions ■ TF Admissions: 888-879-8635 ■ Web: www.umfk.edu	207-834-7500	834-7609*
Machias Nine O'Brien Ave .... Machias ME 04654 *Fax: Admissions ■ TF Admissions: 888-468-6866 ■ Web: machias.edu	207-255-1200	255-1363*
Presque Isle 181 Main St .... Presque Isle ME 04769 *Fax: Admissions ■ Web: www.umpi.maine.edu	207-768-9400	768-9777*
University of New England 11 Hills Beach Rd .... Biddeford ME 04005 *Fax: Admissions ■ TF Admissions: 800-477-4863 ■ Web: www.une.edu	207-283-0171	602-5900*
Westbrook College 716 Stevens Ave .... Portland ME 04103 TF Admissions: 800-477-4863 ■ Web: www.une.edu	207-797-7261	
University of Southern Maine 96 Falmouth St .... Portland ME 04103 TF: 800-800-4876 ■ Web: www.usm.maine.edu	207-780-4141	780-5640
Gorham 37 College Ave .... Gorham ME 04038 *Fax: Admissions ■ TF: 800-800-4876 ■ Web: www.usm.maine.edu	207-780-5670	780-5640*
Lewiston-Auburn College 51 Westminster St .... Lewiston ME 04240 *Fax: Admissions ■ TF: 800-800-4876 ■ Web: www.usm.maine.edu	207-753-6500	753-6555*

Maryland

	Phone	Fax
Bowie State University 14000 Jericho Pk Rd .... Bowie MD 20715 TF: 877-772-6943 ■ Web: www.bowiestate.edu	301-860-4000	860-3518
Capitol Technology University 11301 Springfield Rd .... Laurel MD 20708 *Fax: Admissions ■ TF: 800-950-1992 ■ Web: www.capitol-college.edu	301-369-2800	953-1442*
College of Notre Dame of Maryland 4701 N Charles St .... Baltimore MD 21210 *Fax: Admissions ■ TF Admissions: 800-753-3757 ■ Web: www.ndm.edu	410-435-0100	532-6287*
Coppin State University 2500 W N Ave .... Baltimore MD 21216 *Fax: Admissions ■ TF Admissions: 800-635-3674 ■ Web: www.coppin.edu	410-951-3600	523-7351*
Frostburg State University 101 Braddock Rd .... Frostburg MD 21532 *Fax: Admissions ■ Web: www.frostburg.edu	301-687-4000	687-7074*
Goucher College 1021 Dulaney Vly Rd .... Towson MD 21204 *Fax: Admissions ■ TF: 800-468-2437 ■ Web: www.goucher.edu	410-337-6000	337-6354*
Hood College 401 Rosemont Ave .... Frederick MD 21701 *Fax: Admissions ■ TF: 800-922-1599 ■ Web: www.hood.edu	301-696-3400	696-3819*
Johns Hopkins University 3400 N Charles St .... Baltimore MD 21218 Web: www.jhu.edu	410-516-8000	516-6025
Loyola College 4501 N Charles St .... Baltimore MD 21210 *Fax: Admissions ■ TF: 800-221-9107 ■ Web: www.loyola.edu	410-617-5012	617-2176*
McDaniel College 2 College Hill .... Westminster MD 21157 *Fax: Admissions ■ TF Admissions: 800-638-5005 ■ Web: www.mcdaniel.edu	410-857-2230	857-2757*
Morgan State University 1700 E Cold Spring Ln .... Baltimore MD 21251 *Fax: Admissions ■ TF: 800-319-4678 ■ Web: www.morgan.edu	443-885-3333	885-8260*
Mount Saint Mary's University 16300 Old Emmitsburg Rd .... Emmitsburg MD 21727 *Fax: Admissions ■ TF Admissions: 800-448-4347 ■ Web: www.msmary.edu	301-447-5214	447-5860*
Peabody Institute of the Johns Hopkins University		
Peabody Conservatory of Music One E Mt Vernon Pl .... Baltimore MD 21202 TF: 800-368-2521 ■ Web: www.peabody.jhu.edu	410-659-8110	659-8102
Saint Mary's College of Maryland 18952 E Fisher Rd .... Saint Marys City MD 20686 *Fax: Admissions ■ TF Admissions: 800-492-7181 ■ Web: www.smcm.edu	240-895-2000	895-5001*
Salisbury University 1200 Camden Ave .... Salisbury MD 21801 *Fax: Admissions ■ TF: 888-543-0148 ■ Web: www.salisbury.edu	410-543-6000	546-6016*
Sojourner-Douglass College 200 N Central Ave .... Baltimore MD 21202 TF: 800-732-2630 ■ Web: www.sdc.edu	410-276-0306	675-1810

Phone Fax

Strayer University Prince George's
4710 Auth Pl Ste 100 ..... Suitland MD 20746 888-311-0355 423-3999*
Fax Area Code: 301 ■ **Fax:* Admissions ■ *TF:* 866-344-3297 ■ *Web:* www.strayer.edu

Towson University 8000 York Rd. ..... Towson MD 21252 410-704-2113 704-3030
TF: 866-301-3375 ■ *Web:* www.towson.edu

University of Baltimore 1420 N Charles St ..... Baltimore MD 21201 410-837-4200 837-4793
TF Admitting: 877-277-5982 ■ *Web:* www.ubalt.edu

University of Maryland
Baltimore County 1000 Hilltop Cir ..... Baltimore MD 21250 410-455-1000 455-1094
TF: 800-810-0271 ■ *Web:* www.umbc.edu
Eastern Shore
30665 Student Services Ctr Ln ..... Princess Anne MD 21853 410-651-2200 651-7922
Web: www.umes.edu

US Naval Academy 121 Blake Rd ..... Annapolis MD 21402 410-293-1000 293-4348*
**Fax:* Admissions ■ *TF Admissions:* 888-249-7707 ■ *Web:* www.usna.edu

Villa Julie College
1525 Green Spring Valley Rd ..... Stevenson MD 21153 410-486-7001 352-4440*
**Fax Area Code:* 443 ■ *TF:* 877-468-6852 ■ *Web:* stevenson.edu

Washington Adventist University
7600 Flower Ave ..... Takoma Park MD 20912 301-891-4000 891-4167
TF: 800-835-4212 ■ *Web:* www.wau.edu

Washington College 300 Washington Ave ..... Chestertown MD 21620 410-778-2800 778-7287
TF: 800-422-1782 ■ *Web:* www.washcoll.edu

Massachusetts

Phone Fax

American International College
1000 State St ..... Springfield MA 01109 413-205-3201 205-3051*
**Fax:* Admissions ■ *TF Admissions:* 800-242-3142 ■ *Web:* www.aic.edu

Amherst College 220 S Pleasant St ..... Amherst MA 01002 413-542-2000 542-2040*
**Fax:* Admissions ■ *TF:* 866-542-4438 ■ *Web:* www.amherst.edu

Anna Maria College 50 Sunset Ln ..... Paxton MA 01612 800-344-4586
TF: 800-344-4586 ■ *Web:* www.annamaria.edu

Asian University for Women
1100 Massachusetts Ave Ste 3 ..... Cambridge MA 02138 617-914-0500
Web: asian-university.org

Assumption College 500 Salisbury St ..... Worcester MA 01609 508-767-7000 799-4412
TF: 888-882-7786 ■ *Web:* www.assumption.edu

Atlantic Union College 338 Main St ..... South Lancaster MA 01561 978-368-2000 368-2517
TF: 800-282-2030 ■ *Web:* www.auc.edu

Babson College 231 Forest St ..... Babson Park MA 02457 781-235-1200 239-4006*
**Fax:* Admissions ■ *TF Admissions:* 800-488-3696 ■ *Web:* www.babson.edu

Bay Path College 588 Longmeadow St ..... Longmeadow MA 01106 800-782-7284 565-1105*
**Fax Area Code:* 413 ■ *TF:* 800-782-7284 ■ *Web:* www.baypath.edu

Becker College 61 Sever St ..... Worcester MA 01609 508-791-9241 890-1500*
**Fax:* Admissions ■ *TF:* 877-523-2537 ■ *Web:* www.becker.edu

Bentley College 175 Forest St ..... Waltham MA 02452 781-891-2244 891-3414*
**Fax:* Admissions ■ *TF Admissions:* 800-642-7131 ■ *Web:* www.bentley.edu

Berklee College of Music 1140 Boylston St ..... Boston MA 02215 617-747-2221 747-2047*
**Fax:* Admissions ■ *TF:* 800-421-0084 ■ *Web:* www.berklee.edu

Boston Baptist College
950 Metropolitan Ave ..... Hyde Park MA 02136 617-364-3510
Web: boston.edu

Boston College 140 Commonwealth Ave ..... Chestnut Hill MA 02467 617-552-3100 552-0798
TF: 800-360-2522 ■ *Web:* www.bc.edu

Boston Conservatory of Music Dance & Theater
Eight Fenway ..... Boston MA 02215 617-536-6340 247-3159*
**Fax:* Admissions ■ *Web:* www.bostonconservatory.edu

Brandeis University 415 S St ..... Waltham MA 02454 781-736-3500 736-3536
TF: 800-622-0622 ■ *Web:* www.brandeis.edu

Bridgewater State College 131 Summer St ..... Bridgewater MA 02325 508-531-1000 531-1746*
**Fax:* Admissions ■ *Web:* www.bridgew.edu

Clark University 950 Main St ..... Worcester MA 01610 508-793-7711 793-8821
TF: 800-462-5275 ■ *Web:* www.clarku.edu

College of the Holy Cross 1 College St ..... Worcester MA 01610 508-793-2011 793-3888
TF: 800-442-2421 ■ *Web:* www.holycross.edu

Curry College 1071 Blue Hill Ave ..... Milton MA 02186 617-333-2210 333-2114
TF: 800-669-0686 ■ *Web:* www.curry.edu

Eastern Nazarene College 23 E Elm Ave ..... Quincy MA 02170 617-745-3000 745-3929
TF: 800-883-6288 ■ *Web:* www.enc.edu

ELMS College 291 Springfield St ..... Chicopee MA 01013 413-592-3189 594-2781*
**Fax:* Admissions ■ *TF Admissions:* 800-255-3567 ■ *Web:* www.elms.edu

Emerson College 10 Boylston Pl ..... Boston MA 02116 617-824-8500 824-8609
TF: 888-627-7115 ■ *Web:* www.emerson.edu

Emmanuel College 400 Fenway ..... Boston MA 02115 617-735-9715 735-9801
Web: www.emmanuel.edu

Endicott College 376 Hale St ..... Beverly MA 01915 978-232-2021 232-2520*
**Fax:* Admissions ■ *TF Admissions:* 800-325-1114 ■ *Web:* www.endicott.edu

Framingham State College
100 State St PO Box 9101 ..... Framingham MA 01701 508-620-1220 626-4017*
**Fax:* Admissions ■ *TF:* 866-361-8970 ■ *Web:* www.framingham.edu

Franklin W Olin College of Engineering
1000 Olin Way ..... Needham MA 02492 781-292-2300 292-2210*
**Fax:* Admissions ■ *Web:* www.olin.edu

Gordon College 255 Grapevine Rd ..... Wenham MA 01984 978-927-2300 867-4682*
**Fax:* Admissions ■ *TF:* 800-343-1379 ■ *Web:* www.gordon.edu

Hampshire College 893 W St ..... Amherst MA 01002 413-549-4600 559-5631*
**Fax:* Admissions ■ *Web:* www.hampshire.edu

Harvard University 12 Holyoke St ..... Cambridge MA 02138 617-495-1000 495-8821
Web: www.harvard.edu

Hellenic College-Holy Cross School of Theology
50 Goddard Ave ..... Brookline MA 02445 617-731-3500 850-1460*
**Fax:* Admissions ■ *Web:* www.hchc.edu

Lasell College 1844 Commonwealth Ave ..... Newton MA 02466 617-243-2225 243-2380*
**Fax:* Admissions ■ *TF Admissions:* 888-527-3554 ■ *Web:* www.lasell.edu

Lesley University 29 Everett St ..... Cambridge MA 02138 617-868-9600 349-8313
TF: 800-999-1959 ■ *Web:* www.lesley.edu

Massachusetts College of Art
621 Huntington Ave ..... Boston MA 02115 617-879-7222 879-7250
TF: 800-834-3242 ■ *Web:* www.massart.edu

Phone Fax

Massachusetts College of Liberal Arts
375 Church St ..... North Adams MA 01247 413-662-5000 662-5179
Web: www.mcla.edu

Massachusetts College of Pharmacy & Health Sciences
179 Longwood Ave ..... Boston MA 02115 617-732-2850 732-2118
TF: 800-225-5506 ■ *Web:* www.mcphs.edu

Massachusetts Institute of Technology
77 Massachusetts Ave ..... Cambridge MA 02139 617-253-1000 258-8304
Web: www.web.mit.edu

Massachusetts Maritime Academy
101 Academy Dr ..... Buzzards Bay MA 02532 508-830-5000 830-5077*
**Fax:* Admissions ■ *TF Admissions:* 800-544-3411 ■ *Web:* www.maritime.edu

Merrimack College 315 Tpke St ..... North Andover MA 01845 978-837-5000 837-5133*
**Fax:* Admissions ■ *Web:* www.merrimack.edu

MGH Institute of Health Professions Inc
Charlestown Navy Yard 36 First Ave ..... Boston MA 02129 617-726-2947
Web: www.mghihp.edu

Montserrat College of Art
23 Essex St PO Box 26 ..... Beverly MA 01915 978-921-4242 921-4241*
**Fax:* Admissions ■ *TF:* 800-836-0487 ■ *Web:* www.montserrat.edu

Mount Holyoke College 50 College St ..... South Hadley MA 01075 413-538-2000 538-2409
TF: 800-642-4483 ■ *Web:* www.mtholyoke.edu

Mount Ida College 777 Dedham St ..... Newton Center MA 02459 617-928-4500 928-4507*
**Fax:* Admissions ■ *Web:* www.mountida.edu

National Graduate School of Quality Management Inc, The
186 Jones Rd ..... Falmouth MA 02540 508-457-1313
Web: www.ngs.edu

New England Conservatory 290 Huntington Ave ..... Boston MA 02115 617-585-1100 585-1115*
**Fax:* Admissions ■ *Web:* necmusic.edu

Newbury College 129 Fisher Ave ..... Brookline MA 02445 617-730-7000 731-9618*
**Fax:* Admitting ■ *TF:* 800-755-7071 ■ *Web:* www.newbury.edu

Nichols College 124 Ctr Rd ..... Dudley MA 01571 508-213-1560 943-9885
TF: 800-470-3379 ■ *Web:* www.nichols.edu

Northeastern University 360 Huntington Ave ..... Boston MA 02115 617-373-2000 373-8780*
**Fax:* Admissions ■ *TF:* 855-476-3391 ■ *Web:* www.northeastern.edu

Pine Manor College 400 Heath St ..... Chestnut Hill MA 02467 617-731-7104 731-7102
TF: 800-762-1357 ■ *Web:* www.pmc.edu

Salem State College 352 Lafayette St ..... Salem MA 01970 978-542-6000 542-6893
Web: www.salemstate.edu

School of the Museum of Fine Arts
230 The Fenway ..... Boston MA 02115 617-369-3626 369-4264*
**Fax:* Admissions ■ *TF Admissions:* 800-643-6078 ■ *Web:* www.smfa.edu

Simmons College 300 The Fenway ..... Boston MA 02115 617-521-2000 521-3190*
**Fax:* Admissions ■ *TF:* 800-345-8468 ■ *Web:* www.simmons.edu

Simon's Rock College of Bard
84 Alford Rd ..... Great Barrington MA 01230 413-644-4400 528-7380*
**Fax:* Admissions ■ *Web:* www.simons-rock.edu

Smith College Seven College Ln ..... NorthHampton MA 01063 413-584-2700 585-2527
TF: 800-383-3232 ■ *Web:* www.smith.edu

South Shore Educational Collaborative
75 Abington St ..... Hingham MA 02043 781-749-7518
Web: www.ssec.org

Springfield College 263 Alden St ..... Springfield MA 01109 413-748-3136 748-3694*
**Fax:* Admissions ■ *TF Admissions:* 800-343-1257 ■ *Web:* springfieldcollege.edu/

Stonehill College 320 Washington St ..... Easton MA 02357 508-565-1000 565-1545*
**Fax:* Admissions ■ *Web:* www.stonehill.edu

Suffolk University Eight Ashburton Pl ..... Boston MA 02108 617-573-8460 557-1574
TF: 800-678-3365 ■ *Web:* www.suffolk.edu

Tufts University 4 Colby St ..... Medford MA 02155 617-628-5000 627-4079
TF: 800-326-4001 ■ *Web:* www.tufts.edu

University of Massachusetts
Amherst 181 Presidents Dr ..... Amherst MA 01003 413-545-0111 545-4312*
**Fax:* Admissions ■ *Web:* www.umass.edu
Boston 100 Morrissey Blvd Campus Ctr ..... Boston MA 02125 617-287-6100 287-5999*
**Fax:* Admitting ■ *Web:* www.umb.edu
Dartmouth 285 Old Westport Rd ..... North Dartmouth MA 02747 508-999-8000 999-8755*
**Fax:* Admissions ■ *Web:* www.umassd.edu
Lowell One University Ave ..... Lowell MA 01854 978-934-4000 934-3086*
**Fax:* Admissions ■ *Web:* www.uml.edu

Wellesley College 106 Central St ..... Wellesley MA 02481 781-283-1000 283-3678*
**Fax:* Admissions ■ *Web:* www.wellesley.edu

Wentworth Institute of Technology
550 Huntington Ave ..... Boston MA 02115 617-989-4590 989-4010*
**Fax:* Admissions ■ *TF:* 800-556-0610 ■ *Web:* www.wit.edu

Western New England College
1215 Wilbraham Rd ..... Springfield MA 01119 413-782-3111 782-1777*
**Fax:* Admissions ■ *Web:* wne.edu

Westfield State University 577 Western Ave ..... Westfield MA 01086 413-572-5300 572-0520*
**Fax:* Admissions ■ *Web:* www.westfield.ma.edu

Wheaton College 26 E Main St ..... Norton MA 02766 508-286-8200 286-8271
TF Admissions: 800-394-6003 ■ *Web:* wheatoncollege.edu

Wheelock College 200 The Riverway ..... Boston MA 02215 617-879-2206 879-2449
TF: 800-734-5212 ■ *Web:* www.wheelock.edu

Williams College 880 Main St ..... Williamstown MA 01267 413-597-3131 597-4052*
**Fax:* Admissions ■ *TF:* 877-374-7526 ■ *Web:* www.williams.edu

Worcester Polytechnic Institute
100 Institute Rd ..... Worcester MA 01609 508-831-5000 831-5875*
**Fax:* Admissions ■ *Web:* www.wpi.edu

Michigan

Phone Fax

Adrian College 110 S Madison St ..... Adrian MI 49221 517-265-5161 264-3331*
**Fax:* Admissions ■ *TF Admissions:* 800-877-2246 ■ *Web:* www.adrian.edu

Albion College 611 E Porter St ..... Albion MI 49224 517-629-1000 629-0569
TF: 800-858-6770 ■ *Web:* www.albion.edu

Alma College 614 W Superior St ..... Alma MI 48801 989-463-7139 463-7057
TF: 800-321-2562 ■ *Web:* www.alma.edu

Andrews University 3976 Rose Dr ..... Berrien Springs MI 49103 269-471-7771 471-2670
TF: 800-253-2874 ■ *Web:* www.andrews.edu
Auburn Hills 1500 University Dr ..... Auburn Hills MI 48326 248-340-0600 340-0608*
**Fax:* Admissions ■ *TF:* 888-429-0410 ■ *Web:* www.baker.edu

	Phone	Fax
Cadillac 9600 E 13th St........Cadillac MI 49601	231-876-3100	876-3440
TF: 888-313-3463 ■ *Web:* www.baker.edu		
Clinton Township		
34950 Little Mack Ave........Clinton Township MI 48035	586-791-6610	791-5790*
**Fax:* Admissions ■ *TF:* 888-272-2842 ■ *Web:* www.baker.edu		
Flint 1050 W Bristol Rd........Flint MI 48507	810-767-7600	766-4255*
**Fax:* Admissions ■ *TF:* 800-964-4299 ■ *Web:* www.baker.edu		
Baker College		
Jackson 2800 Springport Rd........Jackson MI 49202	517-788-7800	788-6187
TF: 888-343-3683 ■ *Web:* www.baker.edu		
Owosso 1020 S Washington St........Owosso MI 48867	989-729-3350	729-3359*
**Fax:* Admissions ■ *TF:* 800-879-3797 ■ *Web:* www.baker.edu		
Port Huron 3403 Lapeer Rd........Port Huron MI 48060	810-985-7000	985-7066
TF: 888-262-2442 ■ *Web:* www.baker.edu		
Calvin College 3201 Burton St SE........Grand Rapids MI 49546	616-526-6000	526-6777*
**Fax:* Admissions ■ *TF:* 800-688-0122 ■ *Web:* www.calvin.edu		
Central Michigan University		
102 Warriner Hall........Mount Pleasant MI 48859	989-774-4000	774-7267*
**Fax:* Admissions ■ *TF Admissions:* 888-292-5366 ■ *Web:* www.cmich.edu		
Chime Education Foundation		
3300 Washtenaw Ave Ste 225........Ann Arbor MI 48104	734-665-0000	
Web: www.cio-chime.org		
Concordia University Ann Arbor		
4090 Geddes Rd........Ann Arbor MI 48105	734-995-7322	995-4610
TF: 888-282-2338 ■ *Web:* www.cuaa.edu		
Cornerstone University		
1001 E Beltline Ave NE........Grand Rapids MI 49525	616-222-1426	222-1418*
**Fax:* Admissions ■ *TF Admissions:* 800-787-9778 ■ *Web:* www.cornerstone.edu		
Dearborn 4801 Oakman Blvd........Dearborn MI 48126	313-581-4400	581-4480
TF: 800-585-1479 ■ *Web:* www.davenport.edu		
Flint 4318 Miller Rd Ste A........Flint MI 48507	810-732-9977	732-9128*
**Fax:* Admissions ■ *TF:* 800-727-1443 ■ *Web:* www.davenport.edu		
Lansing 220 E Kalamazoo St........Lansing MI 48933	517-484-2600	484-1132*
**Fax:* Admissions ■ *TF:* 800-686-1600 ■ *Web:* www.davenport.edu		
Davenport University		
Lettinga Campus 6191 Kraft Ave SE........Grand Rapids MI 49512	616-698-7111	554-5214
TF: 866-925-3884 ■ *Web:* www.davenport.edu		
Saginaw 5300 Bay Rd........Saginaw MI 48604	989-799-7800	799-9696*
**Fax:* Admissions ■ *TF:* 800-968-8133 ■ *Web:* www.davenport.edu		
Warren 27650 Dequindre Rd........Warren MI 48092	586-558-8700	558-7868*
**Fax:* Admissions ■ *TF:* 800-724-7708 ■ *Web:* www.davenport.edu		
De La Salle Collegiate 14600 Common Rd........Warren MI 48093	586-778-2207	
Web: www.delasallehs.com		
Eastern Michigan University		
1000 College Pl........Ypsilanti MI 48197	734-487-1849	487-6559*
**Fax:* Admissions ■ *TF:* 800-468-6368 ■ *Web:* www.emich.edu		
Traverse City		
2200 Dendrinos Dr Ste 200H........Traverse City MI 49684	231-995-1734	995-1736*
**Fax:* Admissions ■ *TF:* 866-857-1954 ■ *Web:* www.ferris.edu		
Finlandia University 601 Quincy St........Hancock MI 49930	906-482-5300	487-7383*
**Fax:* Admissions ■ *TF:* 800-682-7604 ■ *Web:* www.finlandia.edu		
Grand Valley State University 1 Campus Dr........Allendale MI 49401	616-331-5000	331-2000
TF: 800-748-0246 ■ *Web:* www.gvsu.edu		
Hillsdale College 33 E College St........Hillsdale MI 49242	517-437-7341	437-3923*
**Fax:* Admissions ■ *TF:* 888-886-1174 ■ *Web:* www.hillsdale.edu		
Hope College 69 E Tenth St PO Box 9000........Holland MI 49422	616-395-7850	395-7130*
**Fax:* Admissions ■ *TF Admissions:* 800-968-7850 ■ *Web:* www.hope.edu		
Kalamazoo College 1200 Academy St........Kalamazoo MI 49006	269-337-7166	337-7390*
**Fax:* Admissions ■ *TF Admissions:* 800-253-3602 ■ *Web:* www.kzoo.edu		
Kendall College of Art & Design of Ferris State University		
17 Fountain St NW........Grand Rapids MI 49503	616-451-2787	831-9689
TF: 800-676-2787 ■ *Web:* www.kcad.edu		
Kettering University 1700 University Ave........Flint MI 48504	810-762-9500	762-9837
TF: 800-955-4464 ■ *Web:* www.kettering.edu		
Lake Superior State University		
650 W Easterday Ave........Sault Sainte Marie MI 49783	906-632-6841	635-6696*
**Fax:* Admissions ■ *TF Admissions:* 888-800-5778 ■ *Web:* www.lssu.edu		
Lawrence Technological University		
21000 W 10-Mile Rd........Southfield MI 48075	248-204-3160	204-3188*
**Fax:* Admissions ■ *TF:* 800-225-5588 ■ *Web:* www.ltu.edu		
Madonna University 36600 Schoolcraft Rd........Livonia MI 48150	734-432-5339	432-5424
TF: 800-852-4951 ■ *Web:* www.madonna.edu		
Marygrove College 8425 W McNichols Rd........Detroit MI 48221	313-927-1200	927-1399*
**Fax:* Admissions ■ *TF Admissions:* 866-313-1927 ■ *Web:* www.marygrove.edu		
Michigan Jewish Institute		
25401 Coolidge Hwy........Oak Park MI 48237	248-414-6900	
Web: www.mji.edu		
Michigan State University		
250 Hannah Admin Bldg........East Lansing MI 48824	517-355-1855	353-1647
Web: www.msu.edu		
Michigan Technological University		
1400 Townsend Dr........Houghton MI 49931	906-487-2335	487-2125*
**Fax:* Admissions ■ *TF:* 888-688-1885 ■ *Web:* www.mtu.edu		
Northern Michigan University		
1401 Presque Isle Ave........Marquette MI 49855	906-227-2650	227-1747*
**Fax:* Admissions ■ *TF:* 800-682-9797 ■ *Web:* www.nmu.edu		
Northwood University Michigan		
4000 Whiting Dr........Midland MI 48640	989-837-4200	837-4490*
**Fax:* Admissions ■ *TF:* 800-622-9000 ■ *Web:* www.northwood.edu		
Oakland University 2200 Squirrel Rd........Rochester MI 48309	248-370-2100	370-4462*
**Fax:* Admissions ■ *TF Admissions:* 800-625-8648 ■ *Web:* www.oakland.edu		
Olivet College 320 S Main St........Olivet MI 49076	269-749-7000	749-6617*
**Fax:* Admissions ■ *TF:* 800-456-7189 ■ *Web:* www.olivetcollege.edu		
Rochester College 800 W Avon Rd........Rochester Hills MI 48307	248-218-2011	218-2025*
**Fax:* Admissions ■ *TF:* 800-521-6010 ■ *Web:* www.rc.edu		
Saginaw Valley State University		
7400 Bay Rd........University Center MI 48710	989-964-4200	790-0180
TF: 800-968-9500 ■ *Web:* www.svsu.edu		
Siena Heights University		
1247 E Siena Heights Dr........Adrian MI 49221	517-263-0731	264-7745
TF: 800-521-0009 ■ *Web:* www.sienaheights.edu		
Spring Arbor University 106 E Main St........Spring Arbor MI 49283	517-750-1200	750-2745*
**Fax:* Admissions ■ *TF Admissions:* 800-968-9103 ■ *Web:* saucougars.com		
University of Detroit Mercy		
4001 W McNichols Rd........Detroit MI 48221	313-993-1000	993-3326*
**Fax:* Admissions ■ *TF Admissions:* 800-635-5020 ■ *Web:* www.udmercy.edu		
University of Detroit Mercy School of Dentistry		
Corktown Campus 2700 MLK Dr........Detroit MI 48219	313-494-6611	
Web: www.udmercy.edu		
University of Michigan 515 E Jefferson St........Ann Arbor MI 48109	734-764-1817	
Web: www.umich.edu		
Dearborn 4901 Evergreen Rd........Dearborn MI 48128	313-593-5100	436-9167*
**Fax:* Admissions ■ *Web:* umdearborn.edu/		
Flint 303 E Kearsley St........Flint MI 48502	810-762-3000	762-3272
TF: 800-942-5636 ■ *Web:* www.flint.umich.edu		
Wayne State University 42 W Warren........Detroit MI 48202	313-577-3577	577-7536*
**Fax:* Admissions ■ *TF:* 877-978-4636 ■ *Web:* www.wayne.edu		
Western Michigan University		
1903 W Michigan Ave........Kalamazoo MI 49008	269-387-1000	387-2096*
**Fax:* Admissions ■ *Web:* www.wmich.edu		

Minnesota

	Phone	Fax
Apostolic Bible Institute Inc		
6944 Hudson Blvd N........Saint Paul MN 55128	651-739-7686	730-8669*
**Fax:* Admissions ■ *Web:* www.apostolic.org		
Argosy University 1515 Central Pkwy........Eagan MN 55121	651-846-2882	994-7956*
**Fax:* Admissions ■ *TF:* 888-844-2004 ■ *Web:* argosy.edu		
Augsburg College 2211 Riverside Ave........Minneapolis MN 55454	612-330-1000	330-1590
TF: 800-788-5678 ■ *Web:* www.augsburg.edu		
Bemidji State University		
1500 Birchmont Dr NE........Bemidji MN 56601	218-755-2001	755-4048
TF Admissions: 800-475-2001 ■ *Web:* www.bemidjistate.edu		
Bethany Lutheran College 700 Luther Dr........Mankato MN 56001	507-344-7000	344-7376*
**Fax:* Admissions ■ *TF:* 800-944-3066 ■ *Web:* www.blc.edu		
Carleton College 100 S College St........Northfield MN 55057	507-646-4000	646-4526*
**Fax:* Admissions ■ *TF Admissions:* 800-995-2275 ■ *Web:* www.carleton.edu		
College of Saint Catherine		
2004 Randolph Ave........Saint Paul MN 55105	651-690-6000	690-6024*
**Fax:* Admissions ■ *TF:* 800-945-4599 ■ *Web:* www.stkate.edu		
Minneapolis 601 25th Ave S........Minneapolis MN 55454	651-690-7700	690-7849*
**Fax:* Admissions ■ *TF:* 800-945-4599 ■ *Web:* www.stkate.edu		
College of Saint Scholastica 1200 Kenwood Ave........Duluth MN 55811	218-723-6046	723-5991*
**Fax:* Admissions ■ *TF:* 800-447-5444 ■ *Web:* www.css.edu		
Concordia College 901 Eigth St S........Moorhead MN 56562	218-299-4000	299-4720
TF: 800-699-9897 ■ *Web:* www.concordiacollege.edu		
Gustavus Adolphus College		
800 W College Ave........Saint Peter MN 56082	507-933-8000	933-7474
TF: 800-487-8288 ■ *Web:* www.gustavus.edu		
Hamline University 1536 Hewitt Ave........Saint Paul MN 55104	651-523-2207	523-2458
TF: 800-753-9753 ■ *Web:* www.hamline.edu		
Hospitality Institute of Technology & Management Inc		
670 Transfer Rd Ste 21a........Saint Paul MN 55114	651-646-7077	
Web: www.hi-tm.com		
Macalester College 1600 Grand Ave........Saint Paul MN 55105	651-696-6357	696-6724*
**Fax:* Admissions ■ *TF Admissions:* 800-231-7974 ■ *Web:* www.macalester.edu		
Martin Luther College 1995 Luther Ct........New Ulm MN 56073	507-354-8221	354-8225*
**Fax:* Admissions ■ *TF:* 877-652-1995 ■ *Web:* www.mlc-wels.edu		
McNally Smith College of Music Foundation		
19 Exchange St E........Saint Paul MN 55101	651-361-3320	
Web: www.mcnallysmith.edu		
Metropolitan State University		
700 E Seventh St........Saint Paul MN 55106	651-793-1300	793-1310*
**Fax:* Admissions ■ *TF:* 888-234-2690 ■ *Web:* www.metrostate.edu		
Mankato 122 Taylor Ctr........Mankato MN 56001	507-389-1822	389-1511
TF Admissions: 800-722-0544 ■ *Web:* www.mnsu.edu		
Minnesota State University		
Moorhead 1104 Seventh Ave S........Moorhead MN 56563	218-477-2161	477-4374*
**Fax:* Admissions ■ *TF:* 800-593-7246 ■ *Web:* www.mnstate.edu		
North Central University		
910 Elliot Ave S........Minneapolis MN 55404	612-343-4460	343-4146*
**Fax:* Admissions ■ *TF Admissions:* 800-289-6222 ■ *Web:* www.northcentral.edu		
Rasmussen College Inc		
4400 W 78th St Sixth Fl........Bloomington MN 55345	952-545-2000	
Web: www.rasmussen.edu		
Saint John's University PO Box 2000........Collegeville MN 56321	320-363-2196	363-3206*
**Fax:* Admissions ■ *TF Admissions:* 800-544-1489 ■ *Web:* www.csbsju.edu		
Saint Mary's University of Minnesota		
700 Terr Heights........Winona MN 55987	507-452-4430	457-1722*
**Fax:* Admissions ■ *TF:* 800-635-5987 ■ *Web:* www.smumn.edu		
Southwest Minnesota State University		
1501 State St........Marshall MN 56258	800-642-0684	537-7145*
**Fax Area Code:* 507 ■ **Fax:* Admissions ■ *TF:* 800-642-0684 ■ *Web:* smsumustangs.com		
Crookston 2900 University Ave 170 Owen Hall....Crookston MN 56716	218-281-8569	281-8575*
**Fax:* Admissions ■ *TF:* 800-862-6466 ■ *Web:* www.crk.umn.edu		
Duluth 1049 University Dr........Duluth MN 55812	218-726-8000	726-6394*
**Fax:* Admissions ■ *TF:* 800-232-1339 ■ *Web:* www.d.umn.edu		
Morris 600 E Fourth St........Morris MN 56267	320-589-6035	589-1673*
**Fax:* Admissions ■ *TF:* 800-992-8863 ■ *Web:* www.morris.umn.edu		
University of Minnesota		
Twin Cities		
240 Williamson Hall 231 Pillsbury Dr SE........Minneapolis MN 55455	612-625-2008	626-1693
TF: 800-752-1000 ■ *Web:* www.umn.edu		
Winona State University 175 W Mark St........Winona MN 55987	507-457-5000	457-5620*
**Fax:* Admissions ■ *TF:* 800-342-5978 ■ *Web:* www.winona.edu		

Mississippi

	Phone	Fax
Belhaven College 1500 Peachtree St PO Box 153........Jackson MS 39202	601-968-5940	968-8946*
**Fax:* Admissions ■ *TF:* 800-960-5940 ■ *Web:* www.belhaven.edu		
Blue Mountain College PO Box 160........Blue Mountain MS 38610	662-685-4771	685-4776*
**Fax:* Admissions ■ *TF:* 800-235-0136 ■ *Web:* www.bmc.edu		

Phone Fax

Delta State University 1003 W Sunflower Rd......... Cleveland MS 38733 662-846-4020 846-4684*
Fax: Admissions ■ *TF:* 800-468-6378 ■ *Web:* www.deltastate.edu

Jackson State University
1400 John R Lynch St.............................Jackson MS 39217 601-979-2121 979-3445*
Fax: Admissions ■ *TF:* 800-848-6817 ■ *Web:* www.jsums.edu

Millsaps College 1701 N State St....................Jackson MS 39210 601-974-1000 974-1059*
Fax: Admissions ■ *TF Admissions:* 800-352-1050 ■ *Web:* www.millsaps.edu

Mississippi College
200 S Capitol St PO Box 4026...................... Clinton MS 39058 601-925-3000 925-3950*
Fax: Admissions ■ *TF:* 800-738-1236 ■ *Web:* www.mc.edu

Mississippi State University
PO Box 6305 ....Mississippi State MS 39762 662-325-2224 325-7360*
Fax: Admissions ■ *Web:* www.msstate.edu

Mississippi University for Women
1100 College St MUW-1613 .... Columbus MS 39701 662-329-4750 241-7481*
Fax: Admissions ■ *TF:* 877-462-8439 ■ *Web:* web3.muw.edu

Mississippi Valley State University
14000 Hwy 82 .... Itta Bena MS 38941 662-254-9041 254-3759
TF: 800-844-6885 ■ *Web:* www.mvsu.edu

Rust College 150 Rust Ave..................... Holly Springs MS 38635 662-252-8000 252-2258*
Fax: Admissions ■ *TF:* 888-886-8492 ■ *Web:* www.rustcollege.edu

Tougaloo College 500 W County Line Rd............ Tougaloo MS 39174 601-977-7700 977-4501*
Fax: Admissions ■ *TF Admissions:* 888-424-2566 ■ *Web:* www.tougaloo.edu

University of Mississippi PO Box 1848............ University MS 38677 662-915-7211 915-5869*
Fax: Admissions ■ *Web:* www.olemiss.edu
Tupelo 1918 Briar Ridge Rd......................Tupelo MS 38804 662-844-5622 844-5625*
Fax: Admissions ■ *TF:* 888-846-5622 ■ *Web:* www.outreach.olemiss.edu

University of Southern Mississippi
Gulf Park 730 E Beach Blvd..................Long Beach MS 39560 228-865-4500 865-4587*
Fax: Admissions ■ *Web:* www.usm.edu

William Carey University 498 Tuscan Ave.......... Hattiesburg MS 39401 601-318-6051 318-6454*
Fax: Admissions ■ *TF:* 800-962-5991 ■ *Web:* www.wmcarey.edu

Missouri

Phone Fax

Avila University 11901 Wornall Rd ....Kansas City MO 64145 816-501-2400 501-2453
TF: 800-862-3678 ■ *Web:* www.avila.edu

Central Methodist University
411 Central Methodist Sq............................Fayette MO 65248 660-248-3391 248-1872*
Fax: Admissions ■ *TF:* 877-268-1854 ■ *Web:* www.centralmethodist.edu

Chamberlain College of Nursing
11830 Westline Industrial Ste 106 .... Saint Louis MO 63146 314-991-6200 768-5673
TF: 888-556-8226 ■ *Web:* www.chamberlain.edu

College of the Ozarks
1 Industrial Dr PO Box 17...................... Point Lookout MO 65726 417-334-6411 335-2618*
Fax: Admissions ■ *TF Admissions:* 800-222-0525 ■ *Web:* www.cofo.edu

Columbia College Jefferson City
3314 Emerald Ln .... Jefferson City MO 65109 573-634-3250 634-8507
TF: 800-231-2391 ■ *Web:* ccis.edu/jeffcity

Columbia College Lake of the Ozarks
900 College Blvd .... Osage Beach MO 65065 573-348-6463 348-1791
TF: 800-231-2391 ■ *Web:* www.ccis.edu

Drury University 900 N Benton Ave.................Springfield MO 65802 417-873-7879 866-3873
TF: 800-922-2274 ■ *Web:* www.drury.edu

Evangel University 1111 N Glenstone Ave ....Springfield MO 65802 417-865-2815 865-9599
TF: 800-382-6435 ■ *Web:* evangel.edu

Graceland University Independence
1401 W Truman Rd.............................. Independence MO 64050 816-833-0524 833-2990*
Fax: Admissions ■ *TF:* 800-833-0524 ■ *Web:* www.graceland.edu

Grantham University Inc 7200 NW 86th St.........Kansas City MO 64153 816-595-5759
Web: www.grantham.edu

Hannibal-LaGrange College 2800 Palmyra Rd .... Hannibal MO 63401 573-221-3675 221-6594
TF Admissions: 800-454-1119 ■ *Web:* www.hlg.edu

Harris-Stowe State University
3026 Laclede Ave............................. Saint Louis MO 63103 314-340-3366 340-3555
Web: www.hssu.edu

Lincoln University
820 Chestnut St B-7 Young Hall.................Jefferson City MO 65102 573-681-5599 681-5889*
Fax: Admissions ■ *TF Admissions:* 800-521-5052 ■ *Web:* www.lincolnu.edu

Lindenwood University
209 S Kingshighway..........................Saint Charles MO 63301 636-949-2000 949-4989*
Fax: Admissions ■ *TF:* 877-615-8212 ■ *Web:* www.lindenwood.edu

Missouri Baptist University
One College Pk Dr .... Saint Louis MO 63141 314-434-1115 434-7596
TF: 877-434-1115 ■ *Web:* www.mobap.edu
Troy/Wentzville Extension
75 College Campus Dr.................... Moscow Mills MO 63362 636-366-4363 356-4119*
Fax: Admissions ■ *Web:* www.mobap.edu

Missouri Southern State University
3950 Newman Rd................................... Joplin MO 64801 417-625-9300 659-4429
TF: 866-818-6778 ■ *Web:* www.mssu.edu

Missouri State University (MSU)
901 S National Ave..............................Springfield MO 65897 417-836-5000 836-6334
TF: 800-492-7900 ■ *Web:* www.missouristate.edu

Missouri University of Science & Technology
Rolla 1870 Miner Cir G2 Parker Hall .... Rolla MO 65409 573-341-4111 341-4082*
Fax: Admissions ■ *TF:* 800-522-0938 ■ *Web:* www.mst.edu

Missouri Valley College 500 E College St.......... Marshall MO 65340 660-831-4000 831-4233*
Fax: Admissions ■ *TF:* 800-999-8219 ■ *Web:* www.moval.edu

Missouri Western State University
4525 Downs Dr.............................. Saint Joseph MO 64507 816-271-4266 271-5833
TF: 800-662-7041 ■ *Web:* www.missouriwestern.edu

National American University Independence
3620 Arrowhead Ave......................... Independence MO 64057 816-412-7700 412-7705
TF: 866-628-1288 ■ *Web:* www.national.edu

Northwest Missouri State University
800 University Dr................................Maryville MO 64468 660-562-1148 562-1821*
Fax: Admissions ■ *TF:* 800-633-1175 ■ *Web:* www.nwmissouri.edu

Ozark Bible Institute & College
906 Summit St PO Box 398 .... Neosho MO 64850 417-451-2057 451-2059*
Fax: Admissions ■ *Web:* obicollege.com

Phone Fax

Park University 8700 NW River Pk Dr .... Parkville MO 64152 816-741-2000 741-9668
TF: 800-745-7275 ■ *Web:* www.park.edu

Rockhurst University 1100 Rockhurst Rd ....Kansas City MO 64110 816-501-4000 501-4241*
Fax: Admissions ■ *TF:* 800-842-6776 ■ *Web:* www.rockhurst.edu

Saint Louis College of Pharmacy
4588 Parkview Pl .... Saint Louis MO 63110 314-367-8700 446-8304*
Fax: Admissions ■ *TF:* 800-278-5267 ■ *Web:* www.stlcop.edu

Saint Louis University 221 N Grand Blvd........... Saint Louis MO 63103 314-977-7288 977-7136*
Fax: Admissions ■ *TF:* 800-758-3678 ■ *Web:* www.slu.edu
Parks College of Engineering Aviation & Technology
3450 Lindell Blvd........................... Saint Louis MO 63103 314-977-8203 977-8403
Web: parks.slu.edu

Southeast Missouri State University
1 University Plaza......................... Cape Girardeau MO 63701 573-651-2000 651-5936*
Fax: Admissions ■ *TF:* 866-562-6801 ■ *Web:* www.semo.edu

Southwest Baptist University
1600 University Ave..............................Bolivar MO 65613 800-526-5859 328-1808*
Fax Area Code: 417 ■ *Fax:* Admissions ■ *TF:* 800-526-5859 ■ *Web:* www.sbuniv.edu

Stephens College 1200 E Broadway.................Columbia MO 65215 573-442-2211 *
Fax: Admissions ■ *Web:* collegeapps.about.com

Truman State University 100 E Normal St...........Kirksville MO 63501 660-785-4000 785-7456*
Fax: Admissions ■ *TF:* 800-892-7792 ■ *Web:* www.truman.edu
Columbia 104 Jesse Hall..................... Columbia MO 65211 573-882-6333 882-7887*
Fax: Admissions ■ *TF:* 800-856-2181 ■ *Web:* www.missouri.edu
Kansas City 5100 Rockhill Rd ....Kansas City MO 64110 816-235-1000 235-5544
TF: 800-775-8652 ■ *Web:* www.umkc.edu
Saint Louis One University Blvd.............. Saint Louis MO 63121 314-516-5000 516-5310*
Fax: Admissions ■ *TF Admissions:* 888-462-8675 ■ *Web:* www.umsl.edu

Washington University in Saint Louis
One Brookings Dr............................. Saint Louis MO 63130 314-935-5000 935-4290
TF: 800-638-0700 ■ *Web:* www.wustl.edu

Westminster College 501 Westminster Ave............ Fulton MO 65251 573-592-5251 592-5255
TF Admissions: 800-475-3361 ■ *Web:* www.wcmo.edu

William Jewell College
500 College Hill WJC PO Box 1002.....................Liberty MO 64068 816-781-7700 415-5040
TF: 888-253-9355 ■ *Web:* www.jewell.edu

William Woods University One University Ave.......... Fulton MO 65251 573-592-4221 592-1146*
Fax: Admissions ■ *TF Admissions:* 800-995-3159 ■ *Web:* www.williamwoods.edu

Montana

Phone Fax

Academy of Nail Skin & Hair Inc
928 Broadwater Ave Ste C .... Billings MT 59101 406-252-3232
Web: academyofnailandskin.com

Carroll College 1601 N Benton Ave...................Helena MT 59625 406-447-4300 447-4533
TF: 800-992-3648 ■ *Web:* www.carroll.edu
Billings 1500 University Dr ....Billings MT 59101 406-657-2011 657-2302*
Fax: Admissions ■ *Web:* www.msubillings.edu

Montana State University
Bozeman PO Box 172190 ....Bozeman MT 59717 406-994-2452 994-7360*
Fax: Admissions ■ *TF Admissions:* 888-678-2287 ■ *Web:* www.montana.edu
Northern PO Box 7751............................ Havre MT 59501 406-265-3700 265-3792*
Fax: Admissions ■ *TF:* 800-662-6132 ■ *Web:* www.montana.edu

Montana Tech of the University of Montana
1300 W Pk St.. Butte MT 59701 406-496-4101 496-4710*
Fax: Admissions ■ *TF Admissions:* 800-445-8324 ■ *Web:* www.mtech.edu

Rocky Mountain College 1511 Poly Dr.............. Billings MT 59102 406-657-1000 657-1189*
Fax: Admissions ■ *TF:* 800-877-6259 ■ *Web:* www.rocky.edu

Student Assistance Foundation of Montana
2500 E Broadway St ....Helena MT 59601 406-495-7800
Web: www.trustudent.com

University of Great Falls 1301 20th St S............Great Falls MT 59405 800-856-9544 791-5209*
Fax Area Code: 406 ■ *Fax:* Admissions ■ *TF Admissions:* 800-856-9544 ■ *Web:* www.ugf.edu
Western 710 S Atlantic St......................... Dillon MT 59725 406-683-7011 683-7493*
Fax: Admissions ■ *TF Admissions:* 877-683-7331 ■ *Web:* www.umwestern.edu

Yellowstone Baptist College
1515 S Shiloh Rd .... Billings MT 59106 406-656-9950 656-3737*
Fax: Admissions ■ *TF:* 800-487-9950 ■ *Web:* yellowstonechristian.edu

Nebraska

Phone Fax

Bellevue University 1000 Galvin Rd S ....Bellevue NE 68005 402-293-2000 557-5438*
Fax: Admissions ■ *TF:* 800-756-7920 ■ *Web:* www.bellevue.edu

Chadron State College 1000 Main St................ Chadron NE 69337 308-432-6263 432-6229
TF: 800-242-3766 ■ *Web:* www.csc.edu

Clarkson College 101 S 42nd St.....................Omaha NE 68131 402-552-3100 552-6057*
Fax: Admissions ■ *TF:* 800-647-5500 ■ *Web:* www.clarksoncollege.edu

College of Saint Mary 7000 Mercy Rd................Omaha NE 68106 402-399-2400 399-2412*
Fax: Admissions ■ *TF:* 800-926-5534 ■ *Web:* www.csm.edu

Concordia University Nebraska
800 N Columbia Ave.............................. Seward NE 68434 402-643-3651 643-4073*
Fax: Admissions ■ *TF:* 800-535-5494 ■ *Web:* www.cune.edu

Creighton University 2500 California Plz..............Omaha NE 68178 402-280-2700 280-2685*
Fax: Admissions ■ *TF:* 800-282-5835 ■ *Web:* www.creighton.edu

Doane College 1014 Boswell Ave........................ Crete NE 68333 402-826-2161 826-8600
TF: 800-333-6263 ■ *Web:* www.doane.edu
Grand Island 3180 W US Hwy 34............Grand Island NE 68801 308-398-0800 398-1726
TF: 800-333-6263 ■ *Web:* www.doane.edu
Lincoln 303 N 52nd St........................... Lincoln NE 68504 402-466-4774 466-4228
TF: 888-803-6263 ■ *Web:* www.doane.edu

Hastings College 710 N Turner Ave.................. Hastings NE 68901 402-463-2402 461-7490*
Fax: Admissions ■ *TF:* 800-532-7642 ■ *Web:* www.hastings.edu

Midland University 900 N Clarkson St ....Fremont NE 68025 402-941-6270 941-6513*
Fax: Admissions ■ *TF:* 800-642-8382 ■ *Web:* my.midlandu.edu

Nebraska Wesleyan University
5000 St Paul Ave .... Lincoln NE 68504 402-466-2371 465-2177*
Fax: Admissions ■ *TF:* 800-541-3818 ■ *Web:* www.nebrwesleyan.edu

Peru State College 600 Hoyt St PO Box 10................Peru NE 68421 402-872-3815 872-2296*
Fax: Admissions ■ *TF:* 800-742-4412 ■ *Web:* www.peru.edu

Phone Fax

Summit Christian College 2025 21st St .... Gering NE 69341 308-632-6933 632-8599
TF: 888-305-8083 ■ *Web:* www.summitcc.net

Union College 3800 S 48th St .... Lincoln NE 68506 402-486-2504 486-2566*
**Fax:* Admissions ■ *TF Admissions:* 800-228-4600 ■ *Web:* www.ucollege.edu

University of Nebraska
Kearney 905 W 25th St .... Kearney NE 68849 308-865-8441 865-8987*
**Fax:* Admissions ■ *TF:* 800-532-7639 ■ *Web:* www.unk.edu
Lincoln 1410 Q St .... Lincoln NE 68588 402-472-2023 472-0670*
**Fax:* Admissions ■ *TF:* 800-742-8800 ■ *Web:* www.unl.edu
Omaha 6001 Dodge St........................... Omaha NE 68182 402-554-2800 554-3472*
**Fax:* Admissions ■ *TF:* 800-858-8648 ■ *Web:* www.unomaha.edu

Wayne State College 1111 Main St .... Wayne NE 68787 402-375-7000 375-7180*
**Fax:* Admissions ■ *TF:* 800-228-9972 ■ *Web:* www.wsc.edu

York College 1125 E Eigth St .... York NE 68467 402-363-5600 363-5623*
**Fax:* Admissions ■ *TF:* 800-950-9675 ■ *Web:* www.york.edu

Nevada

Phone Fax

Career College of Northern Nevada
1421 Pullman Dr .... Sparks NV 89434 775-856-2266
Web: www.ccnn.edu

Great Basin College 1500 College Pkwy.................. Elko NV 89801 775-738-8493 753-2311*
**Fax:* Admissions ■ *TF:* 888-590-6726 ■ *Web:* www.gbcnv.edu

Morrison University
10315 Professional Cir Ste 201 .... Reno NV 89521 775-850-0700 850-0711
Web: www.anthem.edu

Sierra Nevada College 999 Tahoe Blvd .... Incline Village NV 89451 775-831-1314 831-1347*
**Fax:* Admissions ■ *TF:* 866-412-4636 ■ *Web:* www.sierranevada.edu
Las Vegas 4505 S Maryland Pkwy.............. Las Vegas NV 89154 702-895-3011 895-1118*
**Fax:* Admissions ■ *Web:* www.unlv.edu

University of Nevada
Reno 1664 N Virginia St .... Reno NV 89557 775-784-1110 784-4283*
**Fax:* Admissions ■ *TF:* 866-263-8232 ■ *Web:* www.unr.edu

New Hampshire

Phone Fax

Colby-Sawyer College 541 Main St.............. New London NH 03257 603-526-3700 526-3452*
**Fax:* Admissions ■ *TF Admissions:* 800-272-1015 ■ *Web:* www.colby-sawyer.edu

Daniel Webster College 20 University Dr.............. Nashua NH 03063 603-577-6000 577-6001
TF: 800-325-6876 ■ *Web:* www.dwc.edu

Dartmouth College 6016 McNutt Hall................. Hanover NH 03755 603-646-1110 646-1216
Web: www.dartmouth.edu
Concord Five Chenell Dr .... Concord NH 03301 603-228-1155
TF: 800-437-0048 ■ *Web:* www.franklinpierce.edu

Franklin Pierce University
Keene 17 Bradco St .... Keene NH 03431 603-357-0079 899-1062*
**Fax:* Admissions ■ *TF:* 800-325-1090 ■ *Web:* www.franklinpierce.edu
Lebanon 24 Airport Rd Ste 19 .... West Lebanon NH 03784 603-298-5549 899-1065*
**Fax:* Admissions ■ *TF:* 800-325-1090 ■ *Web:* www.franklinpierce.edu
Manchester 670 N Commercial St............. Manchester NH 03101 603-626-4972 626-4815
TF Admissions: 800-437-0048 ■ *Web:* www.franklinpierce.edu
Portsmouth 73 Corporate Dr .... Portsmouth NH 03801 603-433-2000 899-1067*
**Fax:* Admissions ■ *TF:* 800-325-1090 ■ *Web:* www.franklinpierce.edu
Rindge 40 University Dr......................... Rindge NH 03461 603-899-4000 899-4394*
**Fax:* Admissions ■ *TF Admissions:* 800-437-0048 ■ *Web:* www.franklinpierce.edu
Berlin 2020 Riverside Dr Rm 144.................. Berlin NH 03570 603-447-3970 752-6335
Web: www.granite.edu

Granite State College
Portsmouth 51 International Dr .... Portsmouth NH 03801 603-332-8335 334-6313
Web: www.granite.edu

Hesser College 3 Sundial Ave .... Manchester NH 03103 603-668-6660 621-8994*
**Fax:* Admissions ■ *TF:* 888-971-2190 ■ *Web:* www.mountwashington.edu

Keene State College 229 Main St...................... Keene NH 03435 603-352-1909 358-2767*
**Fax:* Admissions ■ *TF:* 800-572-1909 ■ *Web:* www.keene.edu

New England College 98 Bridge St.................. Henniker NH 03242 603-428-2223 428-3155*
**Fax:* Admissions ■ *TF Admissions:* 800-521-7642 ■ *Web:* www.nec.edu

Plymouth State University 17 High St .... Plymouth NH 03264 603-535-2237 535-2714*
**Fax:* Admissions ■ *TF:* 800-842-6900 ■ *Web:* www.plymouth.edu

Rivier College 420 S Main St........................ Nashua NH 03060 603-888-1311 891-1799*
**Fax:* Admissions ■ *TF:* 800-447-4843 ■ *Web:* www.rivier.edu

Saint Anselm College 100 St Anselm Dr .... Manchester NH 03102 603-641-7500 641-7550
TF: 888-426-7356 ■ *Web:* www.anselm.edu

Southern New Hampshire University
2500 N River Rd.............................. Manchester NH 03106 603-668-2211 655-0236*
**Fax Area Code:* 802 ■ *TF:* 800-668-1249 ■ *Web:* www.snhu.edu

University of New Hampshire
Three Garrison Ave Grant House...................... Durham NH 03824 603-862-1234 862-0077*
**Fax:* Admissions ■ *Web:* www.unh.edu
Manchester 400 Commercial St.............. Manchester NH 03101 603-641-4321 641-4305
TF: 800-287-9793 ■ *Web:* manchester.unh.edu

New Jersey

Phone Fax

Bloomfield College 467 Franklin St .... Bloomfield NJ 07003 973-748-9000 748-0916
TF: 800-848-4555 ■ *Web:* www.bloomfield.edu

Caldwell College Nine Ryerson Ave .... Caldwell NJ 07006 973-618-3500 618-3600*
**Fax:* Admissions ■ *TF Admissions:* 888-864-9516 ■ *Web:* www.caldwell.edu

Centenary College 400 Jefferson St.............. Hackettstown NJ 07840 908-852-1400 852-3454*
**Fax:* Admissions ■ *TF Admissions:* 800-236-8679 ■ *Web:* www.centenarycollege.edu

College of New Jersey
2000 Pennington Rd PO Box 7718.......................... Ewing NJ 08628 609-771-1855 637-5174*
**Fax:* Admissions ■ *TF:* 800-644-3562 ■ *Web:* tcnj.pages.tcnj.edu

College of Saint Elizabeth 2 Convent Rd .... Morristown NJ 07960 973-290-4700 290-4710*
**Fax:* Admissions ■ *TF Admissions:* 800-210-7900 ■ *Web:* www.cse.edu

Douglass College 100 George St.............. New Brunswick NJ 08901 848-932-9500 932-8877*
**Fax Area Code:* 732 ■ *Web:* douglass.rutgers.edu

Phone Fax

Drake College of Business
125 Broad St Fl 2 .... Elizabeth NJ 07201 908-352-5509
Web: www.drakecollege.com

Drew University 36 Madison Ave.................... Madison NJ 07940 973-408-3000 408-3068*
**Fax:* Admissions ■ *Web:* www.drew.edu

Fairleigh Dickinson University
285 Madison Ave .... Madison NJ 07940 973-443-8500 443-8088*
**Fax:* Admissions ■ *TF:* 800-338-8803 ■ *Web:* www.fdu.edu
Metropolitan 1000 River Rd..................... Teaneck NJ 07666 201-692-2000 692-2560
TF: 800-338-8803 ■ *Web:* www.fdu.edu

Felician College
Rutherford 223 Montross Ave .... Rutherford NJ 07070 201-559-6000 559-3578
TF: 888-442-4551 ■ *Web:* www.felician.edu

Georgian Court University 900 Lakewood Ave .... Lakewood NJ 08701 800-458-8422 987-2000*
**Fax Area Code:* 732 ■ **Fax:* Admissions ■ *TF:* 800-458-8422 ■ *Web:* www.georgian.edu

Kean University 1000 Morris Ave Kean Hall .... Union NJ 07083 908-737-7100 737-7105*
**Fax:* Admissions ■ *TF:* 800-882-1037 ■ *Web:* www.kean.edu

Monmouth University 400 Cedar Ave......... West Long Branch NJ 07764 732-571-3456 263-5166*
**Fax:* Admissions ■ *TF:* 800-543-9671 ■ *Web:* www.monmouth.edu

Montclair State University 1 Normal Ave............ Montclair NJ 07043 973-655-4000 655-7700*
**Fax:* Admissions ■ *TF Admissions:* 800-331-9205 ■ *Web:* www.montclair.edu

New Jersey City University 2039 JFK Blvd .... Jersey City NJ 07305 201-200-2000 200-2044
TF: 888-441-6528 ■ *Web:* www.njcu.edu

New Jersey Institute of Technology
University Heights .... Newark NJ 07102 973-596-3000 596-3461
TF: 800-925-6548 ■ *Web:* www.njit.edu

Princeton University 33 Washington Rd .... Princeton NJ 08544 609-258-3000 258-6743*
**Fax:* Admissions ■ *TF:* 877-609-2273 ■ *Web:* www.princeton.edu

Ramapo College of New Jersey
505 Ramapo Vly Rd .... Mahwah NJ 07430 201-684-7500 684-7964*
**Fax:* Admissions ■ *Web:* www.ramapo.edu

Richard Stockton College of New Jersey
PO Box 195 .... Pomona NJ 08240 609-652-1776 748-5541*
**Fax:* Admissions ■ *Web:* www.stockton.edu

Rider University
Westminster Choir College 101 Walnut Ln .... Princeton NJ 08540 609-921-7100 921-2538*
**Fax:* Admissions ■ *TF:* 800-962-4647 ■ *Web:* www.rider.edu

Rowan University 201 Mullica Hill Rd.............. Glassboro NJ 08028 856-256-4200 256-4430*
**Fax:* Admissions ■ *TF Admissions:* 877-787-6926 ■ *Web:* www.rowan.edu
Camden 406 Penn St.......................... Camden NJ 08102 856-225-6104 225-6498*
**Fax:* Admissions ■ *Web:* www.camden.rutgers.edu

Rutgers The State University of New Jersey
Newark 249 University Ave Rm 100............... Newark NJ 07102 973-353-5205 353-1440*
**Fax:* Admissions ■ *Web:* www.newark.rutgers.edu

Rutgers University Foundation
Seven College Ave Winants Hall................ New Brunswick NJ 08901 732-932-7777
Web: www.rutgers.edu

Seton Hall University 400 S Orange Ave.......... South Orange NJ 07079 973-761-9332 275-2321*
**Fax:* Admissions ■ *TF:* 800-992-4723 ■ *Web:* www.shu.edu

Stevens Institute of Technology
Castle Pt on the Hudson........................... Hoboken NJ 07030 201-216-5194 216-8348*
**Fax:* Admissions ■ *TF:* 800-458-5323 ■ *Web:* www.stevens.edu

Thomas Edison State College 101 W State St .... Trenton NJ 08608 888-442-8372 984-8447*
**Fax Area Code:* 609 ■ **Fax:* Admissions ■ *TF:* 888-442-8372 ■ *Web:* tesc.edu

William Paterson University 300 Pompton Rd.......... Wayne NJ 07470 973-720-2000 720-2910
TF: 877-978-3923 ■ *Web:* www.wpunj.edu

New Mexico

Phone Fax

College of Santa Fe 1600 St Michaels Dr............ Santa Fe NM 87505 505-473-6011
TF: 800-862-7759 ■ *Web:* mycollegeoptions.org

College of the Southwest 6610 N Lovington Hwy........ Hobbs NM 88240 575-392-6561 392-6006*
**Fax Area Code:* 505 ■ **Fax:* Admissions ■ *TF:* 800-530-4400 ■ *Web:* www.usw.edu

Eastern New Mexico University
1500 S Ave K Stn 7.................................. Portales NM 88130 575-562-1011 562-2118*
**Fax Area Code:* 505 ■ **Fax:* Admissions ■ *TF:* 800-367-3668 ■ *Web:* www.enmu.edu

Eastern New Mexico University-ruidoso
709 Mechem Dr .... Ruidoso NM 88345 575-257-2120
Web: www.ruidoso.enmu.edu

New Mexico Highlands University
901 University Ave .... Las Vegas NM 87701 505-425-7511 454-3552
TF: 877-850-9064 ■ *Web:* www.nmhu.edu

New Mexico Institute of Mining & Technology (NMT)
801 Leroy Pl .... Socorro NM 87801 505-835-5434 835-5989*
**Fax:* Admissions ■ *TF Admissions:* 800-428-8324 ■ *Web:* www.nmt.edu

New Mexico State University (NMSU)
MSC-3A PO Box 30001 .... Las Cruces NM 88003 575-646-3121 646-6330*
**Fax:* Admissions ■ *TF Admissions:* 800-662-6678 ■ *Web:* www.nmsu.edu

Santa Fe University of Art & Design
1600 St Michaels Dr.............................. Santa Fe NM 87505 800-456-2673 473-6011*
**Fax Area Code:* 505 ■ **Fax:* Admissions ■ *TF:* 800-456-2673 ■ *Web:* www.santafeuniversity.edu

University of New Mexico (UNM)
One University of New Mexico .... Albuquerque NM 87131 505-277-0111 277-6686
TF: 800-225-5866 ■ *Web:* www.unm.edu
Gallup 200 College Rd............................ Gallup NM 87301 505-863-7500 863-7610
TF: 800-225-5866 ■ *Web:* www.gallup.unm.edu

Western New Mexico University
1000 W College St PO Box 680 .... Silver City NM 88061 505-538-6011 538-6278*
**Fax Area Code:* 575 ■ *TF Admissions:* 800-872-9668 ■ *Web:* www.wnmu.edu

New York

Phone Fax

Adelphi University PO Box 701.................. Garden City NY 11530 516-877-3050 877-3039*
**Fax:* Admissions ■ *TF:* 800-233-5744 ■ *Web:* www.adelphi.edu
Manhattan Ctr 75 Varick St Second Fl........... New York NY 10013 212-965-8340 431-5161
TF: 800-233-5744 ■ *Web:* www.adelphi.edu

Albany College of Pharmacy (ACPHS)
106 New Scotland Ave .... Albany NY 12208 518-694-7221 694-7322*
**Fax:* Admissions ■ *TF General:* 888-203-8010 ■ *Web:* www.acphs.edu

Phone Fax

Albert A List College of Jewish Studies
3080 Broadway New York NY 10027 212-678-8832 280-6022*
*Fax: Admissions ■ *Web:* www.jtsa.edu/x670.xml

Bard College PO Box 5000 Annandale-on-Hudson NY 12504 845-758-7472 758-5208
TF: 800-872-7423 ■ *Web:* www.bard.edu

Barnard College Columbia University
3009 Broadway New York NY 10027 212-854-2014 854-6220*
*Fax: Admissions ■ *Web:* www.barnard.edu

Baruch College 55 Lexington Ave at 24th St New York NY 10010 646-312-1000 312-1362
TF: 800-273-8255 ■ *Web:* www.baruch.cuny.edu

Binghamton University 4400 Vestal Pkwy E Binghamton NY 13902 607-777-2000 777-4445*
*Fax: Admissions ■ *TF:* 800-782-0289 ■ *Web:* www.binghamton.edu

Boricua College 3755 Broadway New York NY 10032 212-694-1000 694-1015*
*Fax: Admissions ■ *Web:* www.boricuacollege.edu

Brooklyn College 2900 Bedford Ave Brooklyn NY 11210 718-951-5000 951-4506*
*Fax: Admissions ■ *Web:* www.brooklyn.cuny.edu

Buffalo State College 1300 Elmwood Ave Buffalo NY 14222 716-878-4000 878-6100*
*Fax: Admissions ■ *Web:* www.buffalostate.edu

Canisius College 2001 Main St Buffalo NY 14208 716-888-2200 888-3230*
*Fax: Admissions ■ *TF:* 800-843-1517 ■ *Web:* www.canisius.edu

Cazenovia College Eight Sullivan St Cazenovia NY 13035 315-655-7208 655-4860
TF: 800-654-3210 ■ *Web:* cazenovia.edu

City College of New York
138th St & Convent Ave New York NY 10031 212-650-6448 650-6417*
*Fax: Admissions ■ *TF Admissions:* 800-286-9937 ■ *Web:* www.ccny.cuny.edu

Clarkson University 10 Clarkson Ave Potsdam NY 13699 315-268-6480 268-7647*
*Fax: Admissions ■ *TF Admissions:* 800-527-6577 ■ *Web:* www.clarkson.edu

Colgate University 13 Oak Dr Hamilton NY 13346 315-228-1000 228-7544*
*Fax: Admissions ■ *Web:* www.colgate.edu

College of Mount Saint Vincent
6301 Riverdale Ave Riverdale NY 10471 718-405-3304 405-3490*
*Fax: Admissions ■ *TF:* 877-392-6844 ■ *Web:* www.mountsaintvincent.edu

College of New Rochelle 29 Castle Pl New Rochelle NY 10805 914-654-5000 654-5464
TF: 800-933-5923 ■ *Web:* www.cnr.edu

College of Saint Rose 432 Western Ave Albany NY 12203 518-454-5150 454-2013*
*Fax: Admissions ■ *TF:* 800-637-8556 ■ *Web:* www.strose.edu

College of Staten Island
2800 Victory Blvd Staten Island NY 10314 718-982-2000 982-2500
TF: 888-442-4551 ■ *Web:* www.csi.cuny.edu

Columbia University 2960 Broadway New York NY 10027 212-854-1754
Web: www.columbia.edu

Concordia College New York
171 White Plains Rd Bronxville NY 10708 914-337-9300 395-4636*
*Fax: Admissions ■ *TF Admissions:* 800-937-2655 ■ *Web:* www.concordia-ny.edu

Cooper Union for the Advancement of Science & Art
30 Cooper Sq New York NY 10003 212-353-4100 353-4327*
*Fax: Admissions ■ *TF:* 800-872-2777 ■ *Web:* www.cooper.edu

Cornell University 410 Thurston Ave Ithaca NY 14850 607-255-5241 254-5175*
*Fax: Admissions ■ *Web:* www.cornell.edu

D'Youville College 320 Porter Ave Buffalo NY 14201 716-829-7600 829-7900*
*Fax: Admissions ■ *TF:* 800-777-3921 ■ *Web:* www.dyc.edu

Daemen College 4380 Main St Amherst NY 14226 716-839-8225 839-8229*
*Fax: Admissions ■ *TF:* 800-462-7652 ■ *Web:* www.daemen.edu

Dominican College 470 Western Hwy Orangeburg NY 10962 845-359-7800 365-3150*
*Fax: Admissions ■ *TF:* 866-432-4636 ■ *Web:* www.dc.edu

Dowling College 150 Idle Hour Blvd Oakdale NY 11769 631-244-3000 244-1059*
*Fax: Admissions ■ *TF:* 800-369-5464 ■ *Web:* www.dowling.edu

Elmira Business Institute-elmira Campus
303 N Main St Ste 7 Elmira NY 14901 607-733-7177
Web: www.ebi-college.com

Elmira College 1 Pk Pl Elmira NY 14901 607-735-1724 735-1718*
*Fax: Admissions ■ *TF Admissions:* 800-935-6472 ■ *Web:* www.elmira.edu

Eugene Lang College 65 W 11th St New York NY 10011 212-229-5600 229-5355*
*Fax: Admissions ■ *Web:* www.newschool.edu/lang

Excelsior College Seven Columbia Cir Albany NY 12203 518-464-8500 464-8833*
*Fax: Admissions ■ *TF:* 888-647-2388 ■ *Web:* www.excelsior.edu

Farmingdale State University of New York
2350 Broadhollow Rd Farmingdale NY 11735 631-420-2000 420-2633
Web: www.farmingdale.edu

Five Towns College 305 N Service Rd Dix Hills NY 11746 631-424-7000
Web: www.ftc.edu

College at Lincoln Ctr 113 W 60th St New York NY 10023 212-636-6710 636-7002
TF: 800-367-3426 ■ *Web:* www.fordham.edu

Fordham University
Westchester 400 Westchester Ave West Harrison NY 10604 914-332-8295 817-3921*
*Fax Area Code: 718 ■ *TF:* 800-606-6090 ■ *Web:* www.fordham.edu

Fredonia State University of New York
Fredonia 280 Central Ave Fredonia NY 14063 716-673-3111 *
*Fax: Admissions ■ *Web:* www.fredonia.edu

Hamilton College 198 College Hill Rd Clinton NY 13323 315-859-4421 859-4457*
*Fax: Admissions ■ *TF Admissions:* 800-843-2655 ■ *Web:* www.hamilton.edu

Hartwick College One Hartwick Dr Oneonta NY 13820 607-431-4150 431-4154*
*Fax: Admissions ■ *TF:* 888-427-8942 ■ *Web:* www.hartwick.edu

Hilbert College 5200 S Pk Ave Hamburg NY 14075 716-649-7900 649-1152
TF: 800-649-8003 ■ *Web:* www.hilbert.edu

Hobart & William Smith Colleges
300 Pulteney St Geneva NY 14456 315-781-3000 781-3914*
*Fax: Admissions ■ *TF Admissions:* 800-852-2256 ■ *Web:* www.hws.edu

Hofstra University 1000 Fulton Ave Hempstead NY 11549 516-463-6600 463-5100*
*Fax: Admissions ■ *TF:* 800-463-7872 ■ *Web:* www.hofstra.edu/home

Houghton College One Willard Ave PO Box 128 Houghton NY 14744 585-567-9200 567-9522*
*Fax: Admissions ■ *TF:* 800-777-2556 ■ *Web:* www.houghton.edu

Hunter College 695 Pk Ave Rm 1212W New York NY 10065 212-772-4490 650-3472
Web: www.hunter.cuny.edu

Iona College 715 N Ave New Rochelle NY 10801 914-633-2502 633-2486
TF: 800-264-6350 ■ *Web:* www.iona.edu

Ithaca College 953 Danby Rd Ithaca NY 14850 607-274-3124 274-1900*
*Fax: Admissions ■ *TF Admissions:* 800-429-4274 ■ *Web:* www.ithaca.edu

Jewish Theological Seminary 3080 Broadway New York NY 10027 212-678-8832 678-6022
Web: www.jtsa.edu

Keuka College 141 Central Ave Keuka Park NY 14478 315-279-5254 536-5386*
*Fax: Admissions ■ *TF Admissions:* 800-335-3852 ■ *Web:* www.keuka.edu

Phone Fax

Laboratory Institute of Merchandising
12 E 53rd St New York NY 10022 212-752-1530 421-4341*
*Fax: Admissions ■ *TF:* 800-677-1323 ■ *Web:* www.limcollege.edu

Le Moyne College 1419 Salt Springs Rd Syracuse NY 13214 315-445-4100 445-4711*
*Fax: Admissions ■ *TF Admissions:* 800-333-4733 ■ *Web:* www.lemoyne.edu

Lehman College 250 Bedford Pk Blvd W Bronx NY 10468 718-960-8000 960-8712*
*Fax: Admissions ■ *TF:* 800-311-5656 ■ *Web:* www.lehman.cuny.edu

Long Island University
Brentwood 100 Second Ave Brentwood NY 11717 631-273-5112 273-3155
Web: www.liunet.edu
Brooklyn One University Plz Brooklyn NY 11201 718-488-1011 797-2399*
*Fax: Admissions ■ *TF:* 800-548-7526 ■ *Web:* www.liu.edu

Manhattan College 4513 Manhattan College Pkwy Bronx NY 10471 718-862-8000 862-8019*
*Fax: Admissions ■ *TF:* 800-622-9235 ■ *Web:* www.manhattan.edu

Manhattan School of Music 120 Claremont Ave New York NY 10027 212-749-2802 749-3025*
*Fax: Admissions ■ *Web:* www.msmnyc.edu

Manhattanville College 2900 Purchase St Purchase NY 10577 914-323-5464 694-1732
TF: 800-328-4553 ■ *Web:* www.mville.edu

Mannes College of Music 150 W 85th St New York NY 10024 212-580-0210 580-1738*
*Fax: Admissions ■ *Web:* www.newschool.edu

Marist College 3399 N Rd Poughkeepsie NY 12601 845-575-3000 575-3215
TF: 800-436-5483 ■ *Web:* www.marist.edu

Marymount Manhattan College 221 E 71st St New York NY 10021 212-517-0400 517-0448
TF: 866-667-6572 ■ *Web:* www.mmm.edu

Medaille College 18 Agassiz Cir Buffalo NY 14214 716-880-2200 880-2007*
*Fax: Admissions ■ *TF:* 800-292-1582 ■ *Web:* www.medaille.edu

Medgar Evers College 1650 Bedford Ave Brooklyn NY 11225 718-270-4900 270-6411*
*Fax: Admissions ■ *TF:* 866-277-5719 ■ *Web:* www.mec.cuny.edu

Mercy College 555 Broadway Dobbs Ferry NY 10522 914-693-4500 674-7382*
*Fax: Admissions ■ *TF:* 800-637-2969 ■ *Web:* www.mercy.edu
Manhattan 66 W 35th St New York NY 10001 212-615-3313
TF: 800-637-2969 ■ *Web:* www.mercy.edu
White Plains 277 Martine Ave White Plains NY 10601 914-948-3666 948-6732
TF: 888-464-6737 ■ *Web:* www.mercy.edu
Yorktown Heights 2651 Strang Blvd Yorktown Heights NY 10598 914-245-6100 962-0931*
*Fax: Admissions ■ *TF:* 877-637-2946 ■ *Web:* www.mercy.edu

Metropolitan College of New York
431 Canal St New York NY 10013 212-343-1234 625-2072*
*Fax: Admissions ■ *TF:* 800-338-4465 ■ *Web:* www.metropolitan.edu

Molloy College
1000 Hempstead Ave PO Box 5002 Rockville Centre NY 11571 516-678-5000
TF Admissions: 888-466-5569 ■ *Web:* www.molloy.edu

Morrisville State College
80 Eaton St PO Box 901 Morrisville NY 13408 315-684-6000 684-6427*
*Fax: Admissions ■ *TF Admissions:* 800-258-0111 ■ *Web:* www.morrisville.edu

Mount Saint Mary College 330 Powell Ave Newburgh NY 12550 845-569-3248 562-6762
TF: 888-937-6762 ■ *Web:* www.msmc.edu

Nazareth College of Rochester 4245 E Ave Rochester NY 14618 585-389-2525 389-2817
TF: 800-860-6942 ■ *Web:* www.naz.edu

New School 66 W 12th St New York NY 10011 212-229-5600 989-3887*
*Fax: Admissions ■ *Web:* www.newschool.edu

New York City College of Technology
300 Jay St Brooklyn NY 11201 718-260-5000 260-5504*
*Fax: Admissions ■ *TF:* 855-492-3633 ■ *Web:* www.citytech.cuny.edu

New York Institute of Technology
New York Institute of Technology Northern Blvd
PO Box 8000 Old Westbury NY 11568 516-686-1000 686-7613*
*Fax: Admissions ■ *TF:* 800-345-6948 ■ *Web:* www.nyit.edu
Islip PO Box 9029 Central Islip NY 11722 516-686-1000
TF: 800-345-6948 ■ *Web:* www.nyit.edu
Manhattan 1855 Broadway New York NY 10023 212-261-1500 261-1505*
*Fax: Admissions ■ *TF:* 800-345-6948 ■ *Web:* www.nyit.edu

New York School of Interior Design
170 E 70th St New York NY 10021 212-472-1500 472-1867*
*Fax: Admissions ■ *TF:* 800-336-9743 ■ *Web:* www.nysid.edu

New York University 22 Washington Sq N New York NY 10011 212-998-4500 995-4902*
*Fax: Admissions ■ *TF:* 888-243-2358 ■ *Web:* www.nyu.edu

Niagara University
5795 Lewiston Rd PO Box 2011 Niagara University NY 14109 716-286-8700 286-8710*
*Fax: Admissions ■ *TF:* 800-462-2111 ■ *Web:* www.niagara.edu

Northeastern Seminary at Roberts Wesleyan College
2265 Westside Dr Rochester NY 14624 585-594-6800
Web: www.nes.edu

Nyack College One S Blvd Nyack NY 10960 845-358-1710 358-3047*
*Fax: Admissions ■ *TF Admissions:* 800-336-9225 ■ *Web:* www.nyack.edu
Pleasantville/Briarcliff
861 Bedford Rd Pleasantville NY 10570 914-773-3200 773-3851*
*Fax: Admissions ■ *TF:* 866-722-3338 ■ *Web:* www.pace.edu

Parsons New School for Design
65 Fifth Ave Rm 103 New York NY 10003 212-229-8989 229-8975*
*Fax: Admissions ■ *TF Admissions:* 800-252-0852 ■ *Web:* www.newschool.edu

Paul Smith's College
Rt 30 & 86 PO Box 265 Paul Smiths NY 12970 518-327-6227 327-6016*
*Fax: Admissions ■ *TF Admissions:* 800-421-2605 ■ *Web:* www.paulsmiths.edu

Polytechnic University
Long Island 105 Maxess Rd Melville NY 11747 631-755-4300 755-4404*
*Fax: Admissions ■ *TF Admissions:* 877-503-7659 ■ *Web:* engineering.nyu.edu/

Pratt Institute 200 Willoughby Ave Brooklyn NY 11205 718-636-3669 636-3670
TF: 800-331-0834 ■ *Web:* www.pratt.edu

Purchase College 735 Anderson Hill Rd Purchase NY 10577 914-251-6000 251-6314*
*Fax: Admissions ■ *TF:* 800-553-8118 ■ *Web:* www.purchase.edu

Queens College 65-30 Kissena Blvd Flushing NY 11367 718-997-5000 997-5617
TF: 888-888-0606 ■ *Web:* www.qc.cuny.edu

Rensselaer Polytechnic Institute 110 Eigth St Troy NY 12180 518-276-6216 276-4072*
*Fax: Admissions ■ *Web:* www.rpi.edu

Roberts Wesleyan College 2301 Westside Dr Rochester NY 14624 585-594-6000 594-6371*
*Fax: Admissions ■ *TF Admissions:* 800-777-4792 ■ *Web:* www.roberts.edu

Rochester Institute of Technology
One Lomb Memorial Dr Rochester NY 14623 585-475-2411 475-7424*
*Fax: Admissions ■ *Web:* www.rit.edu

Russell Sage College 45 Ferry St Troy NY 12180 518-244-2217 244-6880*
*Fax: Admissions ■ *TF Admissions:* 888-837-9724 ■ *Web:* www.sage.edu

Phone / Fax

Sage College of Albany 140 New Scotland Ave .... Albany NY 12208 518-292-1730 292-1912*
*Fax: Admissions ■ *TF Admissions:* 888-837-9724 ■ *Web:* www.sage.edu

Saint Francis College 180 Remsen St .... Brooklyn Heights NY 11201 718-522-2300
Staten Island 300 Howard Ave .... Staten Island NY 10301 718-390-4500 390-4298*
*Fax: Admissions ■ *Web:* www.stjohns.edu

Saint Joseph's College
Brooklyn 245 Clinton Ave .... Brooklyn NY 11205 718-940-5300 636-8303*
*Fax: Admissions ■ *Web:* www.sjcny.edu

Saint Joseph's College NY
Suffolk 155 W Roe Blvd .... Patchogue NY 11772 631-687-5100
Web: www.sjcny.edu

Saint Lawrence University 23 Romoda Dr .... Canton NY 13617 315-229-5261 229-5818*
*Fax: Admissions ■ *TF Admissions:* 800-285-1856 ■ *Web:* www.stlawu.edu

Saint Thomas Aquinas College 125 Rt 340 .... Sparkill NY 10976 845-398-4000 398-4114
Web: www.stac.edu

Sarah Lawrence College One Meadway .... Bronxville NY 10708 800-888-2858 395-2515*
*Fax Area Code: 914 ■ *Fax: Admissions ■ *TF:* 800-888-2858 ■ *Web:* www.slc.edu

Siena College 515 Loudon Rd .... Loudonville NY 12211 518-783-2300 783-2436*
*Fax: Admissions ■ *TF Admissions:* 888-287-4362 ■ *Web:* www.siena.edu

Skidmore College 815 N Broadway .... Saratoga Springs NY 12866 518-580-5000 580-5584*
*Fax: Admissions ■ *TF:* 800-867-6007 ■ *Web:* www.skidmore.edu
Brockport 350 New Campus Dr .... Brockport NY 14420 585-395-2751 395-5452
TF: 888-800-0029 ■ *Web:* www.brockport.edu
College at Old Westbury, The
PO Box 210 .... Old Westbury NY 11568 516-876-3073 876-3307*
*Fax: Admissions ■ *Web:* www.oldwestbury.edu
College at Oneonta Ravine Pkwy .... Oneonta NY 13820 607-436-3500 436-3074*
*Fax: Admissions ■ *Web:* www.oneonta.edu
College of Agriculture & Technology at Cobleskill
Rt 7 .... Cobleskill NY 12043 518-255-5525 255-6769*
*Fax: Admissions ■ *TF:* 800-295-8988 ■ *Web:* www.cobleskill.edu
College of Environmental Science & Forestry
One Forestry Dr .... Syracuse NY 13210 315-470-6500 470-6933*
*Fax: Admissions ■ *TF Admissions:* 800-777-7373 ■ *Web:* www.esf.edu

State University of New York
Cortland PO Box 2000 .... Cortland NY 13045 607-753-2011 753-5998*
*Fax: Admissions ■ *Web:* www.cortland.edu
Empire State College One Union Ave .... Saratoga Springs NY 12866 518-587-2100 587-9759*
*Fax: Admissions ■ *TF:* 800-847-3000 ■ *Web:* www.esc.edu
Geneseo 1 College Cir .... Geneseo NY 14454 585-245-5571 245-5550*
*Fax: Admitting ■ *TF Admitting:* 866-245-5211 ■ *Web:* www.geneseo.edu
Institute of Technology PO Box 3050 .... Utica NY 13504 315-792-7500 792-7837*
*Fax: Admissions ■ *TF:* 866-278-6948 ■ *Web:* www.sunyit.edu
Maritime College 6 Pennyfield Ave Fort Schuyler .... Bronx NY 10465 718-409-7200 409-7465
TF: 888-800-0029 ■ *Web:* www.sunymaritime.edu
New Paltz One Hawk Dr .... New Paltz NY 12561 845-257-3212 257-3209*
*Fax: Admissions ■ *TF:* 877-696-7411 ■ *Web:* www.newpaltz.edu
Oswego 7060 SR 104 .... Oswego NY 13126 315-312-2500 312-3260*
*Fax: Admissions ■ *Web:* www.oswego.edu
Plattsburgh 101 Broad St .... Plattsburgh NY 12901 518-564-2040 564-2045*
*Fax: Admissions ■ *TF Admissions:* 888-673-0012 ■ *Web:* www.plattsburgh.edu
Potsdam 44 Pierrpont Ave .... Potsdam NY 13676 315-267-2180 267-2163*
*Fax: Admissions ■ *TF Admissions:* 877-768-7326 ■ *Web:* www.potsdam.edu
University at Buffalo 12 Capen Hall .... Buffalo NY 14260 716-645-2450 645-6411*
*Fax: Admissions ■ *TF:* 888-822-3648 ■ *Web:* www.buffalo.edu

Stern College for Women of Yeshiva University
245 Lexington Ave .... New York NY 10016 212-340-7701 340-7788*
*Fax: Admissions ■ *Web:* www.yu.edu/stern

Stony Brook University 100 Nicolls Rd .... Stony Brook NY 11794 631-689-6000 632-9898
Web: www.stonybrook.edu

Syracuse University 900 S Crouse Ave .... Syracuse NY 13244 315-443-3611 443-4226*
*Fax: Admissions ■ *TF:* 800-782-5867 ■ *Web:* www.syr.edu

Touro College 27-33 W 23rd St .... New York NY 10010 212-463-0400 627-9144
TF: 888-247-1387 ■ *Web:* www.touro.edu
Lander College for Men
75-31 150th St .... Kew Gardens Hills NY 11367 718-820-4884 820-4838
Web: www.touro.edu

Tri-State College of Acupuncture
80 Eigth Ave Ste 400 .... New York NY 10011 212-242-2255
Web: www.tsca.edu

University at Albany 1400 Washington Ave .... Albany NY 12222 518-442-3300 442-5383*
*Fax: Admissions ■ *TF:* 800-293-7869 ■ *Web:* www.albany.edu

University of Rochester
Wallace Hall PO Box 270251 .... Rochester NY 14627 585-275-2121 461-4595*
*Fax: Admissions ■ *TF Admissions:* 888-822-2256 ■ *Web:* www.rochester.edu

University of Saint Francis
180 Remsen St .... Brooklyn Heights NY 11201 718-522-2300
TF: 800-356-8329 ■ *Web:* www.sfc.edu

US Merchant Marine Academy
300 Steamboat Rd .... Kings Point NY 11024 516-726-5800 773-5390*
*Fax: Admissions ■ *TF:* 866-546-4778 ■ *Web:* www.usmma.edu

US Military Academy
Admissions Bldg 606 Third Fl .... West Point NY 10996 845-938-4041 938-8121
Web: www.usma.edu

Utica College 1600 Burrstone Rd .... Utica NY 13502 315-792-3111 792-3003*
*Fax: Admissions ■ *TF Admissions:* 800-782-8884 ■ *Web:* www.utica.edu

Vassar College 124 Raymond Ave .... Poughkeepsie NY 12604 845-437-7000 437-7063
TF: 800-827-7270 ■ *Web:* www.vassar.edu

Vaughn College of Aeronautics & Technology
86-01 23rd Ave .... East Elmhurst NY 11369 718-429-6600
TF: 800-695-3317 ■ *Web:* vaughn.edu

Wagner College 1 Campus Rd .... Staten Island NY 10301 718-390-3400 390-3105
TF Admissions: 800-221-1010 ■ *Web:* www.wagner.edu

Webb Institute 298 Crescent Beach Rd .... Glen Cove NY 11542 516-671-2213 674-9838*
*Fax: Admissions ■ *TF:* 866-708-9322 ■ *Web:* webb.edu

Wells College 170 Main St PO Box 500 .... Aurora NY 13026 315-364-3266 364-3227*
*Fax: Admissions ■ *TF Admissions:* 800-952-9355 ■ *Web:* www.wells.edu

Yeshiva University 500 W 185th St .... New York NY 10033 212-960-5400 960-0086*
*Fax: Admissions ■ *Web:* www.yu.edu

North Carolina

Phone / Fax

Barton College PO Box 5000 .... Wilson NC 27893 252-399-6300 399-6572
TF: 800-345-4973 ■ *Web:* www.barton.edu

Belmont Abbey College
100 Belmont-Mt Holly Rd .... Belmont NC 28012 704-461-6748 825-6220*
*Fax: Admissions ■ *TF:* 888-222-0110 ■ *Web:* www.belmontabbeycollege.edu

Bennett College 900 E Washington St .... Greensboro NC 27401 336-370-8624 517-2166*
*Fax: Admissions ■ *TF Admissions:* 800-413-5323 ■ *Web:* www.bennett.edu

Brevard College One Brevard College Dr .... Brevard NC 28712 828-883-8292 884-3790*
*Fax: Admissions ■ *TF Admissions:* 800-527-9090 ■ *Web:* www.brevard.edu

Campbell University
450 Leslie Campbell Ave PO Box 546 .... Buies Creek NC 27506 910-893-1290 893-1288*
*Fax: Admissions ■ *TF:* 800-334-4111 ■ *Web:* www.campbell.edu

Catawba College 2300 W Innes St .... Salisbury NC 28144 704-637-4111 637-4222*
*Fax: Admissions ■ *TF:* 800-228-2922 ■ *Web:* www.catawba.edu

Chowan University 1 University Pl .... Murfreesboro NC 27855 252-398-6439 398-1190*
*Fax: Admissions ■ *TF Admissions:* 888-424-6926 ■ *Web:* www.chowan.edu

Davidson College PO Box 7156 .... Davidson NC 28035 704-894-2000 894-2016*
*Fax: Admissions ■ *TF:* 800-768-0380 ■ *Web:* www.davidson.edu

Duke University 2138 Campus Dr PO Box 90586 .... Durham NC 27708 919-684-3214 681-8941*
*Fax: Admissions ■ *Web:* www.duke.edu

East Carolina University E Fifth St .... Greenville NC 27858 252-328-6131 328-6640
Web: www.ecu.edu

Elizabeth City State University
1704 Weeksville Rd .... Elizabeth City NC 27909 252-335-3400 335-3537*
*Fax: Admissions ■ *TF Admissions:* 800-347-3278 ■ *Web:* www.ecsu.edu

Elon University 314 E Haggard Ave .... Elon NC 27244 336-278-2000 278-7699
TF: 800-334-8448 ■ *Web:* www.elon.edu

Fayetteville State University
1200 Murchison Rd .... Fayetteville NC 28301 910-672-1371 672-1414*
*Fax: Admissions ■ *TF Admissions:* 800-222-2594 ■ *Web:* www.uncfsu.edu

Gardner-Webb University PO Box 817 .... Boiling Springs NC 28017 704-406-4498 406-4488*
*Fax: Admissions ■ *TF:* 800-253-6472 ■ *Web:* www.gardner-webb.edu

Greensboro College 815 W Market St .... Greensboro NC 27401 336-272-7102 378-0154*
*Fax: Admissions ■ *TF:* 800-346-8226 ■ *Web:* greensboro.edu

Guilford College 5800 W Friendly Ave .... Greensboro NC 27410 336-316-2000 316-2954*
*Fax: Admissions ■ *TF Admissions:* 800-992-7759 ■ *Web:* www.guilford.edu

Heritage Bible College
1747 Bud Hawkins Rd PO Box 1628 .... Dunn NC 28334 910-892-3178 892-1809
TF: 800-297-6351 ■ *Web:* www.heritagebiblecollege.edu

High Point University 833 Montlieu Ave .... High Point NC 27262 336-841-9216 888-6382*
*Fax: Admissions ■ *TF:* 800-345-6993 ■ *Web:* www.highpoint.edu

Johnson & Wales University Charlotte
801 W Trade St .... Charlotte NC 28202 980-598-1100 598-1111*
*Fax: Admissions ■ *TF:* 866-598-2427 ■ *Web:* www.jwu.edu

Johnson C Smith University
100 Beatties Ford Rd .... Charlotte NC 28216 704-378-1000 378-1242*
*Fax: Admissions ■ *TF Admissions:* 800-782-7303 ■ *Web:* www.jcsu.edu

King's College Library 322 Lamar Ave .... Charlotte NC 28204 704-372-0266
Web: www.kingscollegecharlotte.edu

Lees-McRae College 191 Main St W .... Banner Elk NC 28604 828-898-5241 898-8707
TF: 800-280-4562 ■ *Web:* www.lmc.edu

Lenoir-Rhyne University 625 Seventh Ave NE .... Hickory NC 28601 828-328-7300 328-7378
TF: 800-277-5721 ■ *Web:* www.lr.edu

Livingstone College 701 W Monroe St .... Salisbury NC 28144 704-216-6963 216-6215
TF: 800-835-3435 ■ *Web:* www.livingstone.edu

Mars Hill College 100 Athletics St .... Mars Hill NC 28754 828-689-1219 465-4696*
*Fax Area Code: 860 ■ *Fax: Admissions ■ *Web:* marshilllions.com

Meredith College 3800 Hillsborough St .... Raleigh NC 27607 919-760-8581 760-2348*
*Fax: Admissions ■ *TF All:* 800-637-3348 ■ *Web:* www.meredith.edu

Methodist University 5400 Ramsey St .... Fayetteville NC 28311 910-630-7000 630-7285*
*Fax: Admissions ■ *TF:* 800-488-7110 ■ *Web:* www.methodist.edu

Montreat College 310 Gaither Cir PO Box 1267 .... Montreat NC 28757 828-669-8011 669-0120
TF: 800-622-6968 ■ *Web:* www.montreat.edu

Mount Olive College 634 Henderson St .... Mount Olive NC 28365 919-658-2502 658-9816*
*Fax: Admissions ■ *TF:* 800-653-0854 ■ *Web:* umo.edu/

North Carolina A & T State University
1601 E Market St .... Greensboro NC 27411 336-334-7946 334-7478*
*Fax: Admissions ■ *TF Admissions:* 800-443-8964 ■ *Web:* www.ncat.edu

North Carolina Central University
1801 Fayetteville St .... Durham NC 27707 919-530-6100 530-7625*
*Fax: Admissions ■ *TF Admissions:* 877-667-7533 ■ *Web:* www.nccu.edu

North Carolina State University
2200 Hillsborough St .... Raleigh NC 27695 919-515-2011 515-5039*
*Fax: Admissions ■ *TF:* 800-662-7301 ■ *Web:* www.ncsu.edu

North Carolina Wesleyan College
3400 N Wesleyan Blvd .... Rocky Mount NC 27804 252-985-5100 985-5295*
*Fax: Admissions ■ *TF Admissions:* 800-488-6292 ■ *Web:* www.ncwc.edu

Pfeiffer University 48380 Hwy 52 N .... Misenheimer NC 28109 704-463-1360 463-1363*
*Fax: Admissions ■ *TF:* 800-338-2060 ■ *Web:* www.pfeiffer.edu

Piedmont Baptist College
420 S Broad St .... Winston-Salem NC 27101 336-725-8344 725-5522*
*Fax: Admissions ■ *TF Admissions:* 800-937-5097 ■ *Web:* www.piedmontu.edu

Queens University of Charlotte
1900 Selwyn Ave .... Charlotte NC 28274 704-337-2212 337-2403*
*Fax: Admissions ■ *TF:* 800-849-0202 ■ *Web:* www.queens.edu

Saint Andrews Presbyterian College
1700 Dogwood Mile .... Laurinburg NC 28352 910-277-5555 277-5020*
*Fax: Admissions ■ *TF:* 800-763-0198 ■ *Web:* www.sa.edu

Saint Augustine's College 1315 Oakwood Ave .... Raleigh NC 27610 919-516-4016 516-5805*
*Fax: Admissions ■ *TF Admissions:* 800-948-1126 ■ *Web:* www.st-aug.edu

Salem College 601 S Church St .... Winston-Salem NC 27101 336-721-2600 917-5572*
*Fax: Admissions ■ *TF Admissions:* 800-327-2536 ■ *Web:* www.salem.edu

Shaw University 118 E S St .... Raleigh NC 27601 919-546-8275 546-8271*
*Fax: Admissions ■ *TF Admissions:* 800-214-6683 ■ *Web:* www.shawu.edu

University of North Carolina
Asheville One University Heights CPO 1320 .... Asheville NC 28804 828-251-6481 251-6482*
*Fax: Admissions ■ *TF:* 800-531-9842 ■ *Web:* www.unca.edu
Chapel Hill Jackson Hall CB 2200 .... Chapel Hill NC 27599 919-966-3621 962-3045*
*Fax: Admissions ■ *Web:* www.unc.edu

				Phone	Fax
Charlotte 9201 University City Blvd *Web:* www.uncc.edu	Charlotte	NC	28223	704-687-2000	687-6483
Greensboro 1400 Spring Garden St *TF:* 877-862-4123 ■ *Web:* www.uncg.edu	Greensboro	NC	27412	336-334-5000	334-4180
Pembroke PO Box 1510 **Fax:* Admissions ■ *TF:* 800-949-8627 ■ *Web:* www.uncp.edu	Pembroke	NC	28372	910-521-6000	521-6497*
Wilmington 601 S College Rd **Fax:* Admissions ■ *TF:* 800-596-2880 ■ *Web:* uncw.edu	Wilmington	NC	28403	910-962-3000	962-3038*
Wake Forest University 1834 Wake Forest Rd **Fax:* Admissions ■ *Web:* www.wfu.edu	Winston-Salem	NC	27106	336-758-5255	758-4324*
Warren Wilson College 701 Warren Wilson Rd **Fax:* Admissions ■ *TF Admissions:* 800-934-3536 ■ *Web:* www.warren-wilson.edu	Swannanoa	NC	28778	828-298-3325	298-1440*
Western Carolina University (WCU) One University Dr *TF:* 877-928-4968 ■ *Web:* www.wcu.edu	Cullowhee	NC	28723	828-227-7211	227-7319
William Peace University 15 E Peace St **Fax:* Admissions ■ *TF:* 800-732-2347 ■ *Web:* www.peace.edu	Raleigh	NC	27604	919-508-2000	508-2326*
Wingate University 315 E Wilson St *TF:* 800-755-5550 ■ *Web:* www.wingate.edu	Wingate	NC	28174	704-233-8000	233-8110
Winston-Salem State University 601 S ML King Jr Dr 206 Thompson Ctr **Fax:* Admissions ■ *TF Admissions:* 800-257-4052 ■ *Web:* www.wssu.edu	Winston-Salem	NC	27110	336-750-2000	750-2079*

North Dakota

				Phone	Fax
Dickinson State University 291 Campus Dr **Fax:* Admissions ■ *TF:* 800-279-4295 ■ *Web:* www.dickinsonstate.edu	Dickinson	ND	58601	701-483-2507	483-9959*
Jamestown College 6000 College Ln *TF:* 800-336-2554 ■ *Web:* www.uj.edu	Jamestown	ND	58405	701-252-3467	253-4318
Mayville State University 330 Third St NE **Fax Area Code:* 701 ■ **Fax:* Admissions ■ *TF:* 800-437-4104 ■ *Web:* leightoninteractive.com	Mayville	ND	58257	800-437-4104	788-4748*
Minot State University 500 University Ave W *TF:* 800-777-0750 ■ *Web:* www.minotstateu.edu	Minot	ND	58707	701-858-3000	858-3888
North Dakota State University 1301 12th Ave N **Fax:* Admissions ■ *TF:* 800-488-6378 ■ *Web:* www.ndsu.edu	Fargo	ND	58105	701-231-8643	231-8802*
University of Mary 7500 University Dr **Fax:* Admissions ■ *TF Admissions:* 800-288-6279 ■ *Web:* www.umary.edu	Bismarck	ND	58504	701-255-7500	255-7687*
University of North Dakota PO Box 8357 *TF:* 800-225-5863 ■ *Web:* und.edu	Grand Forks	ND	58202	701-777-3000	
Valley City State University 101 College St SW *TF:* 800-532-8641 ■ *Web:* www.vcsu.edu	Valley City	ND	58072	701-845-7990	845-7299

Ohio

				Phone	Fax
Ashland University 401 College Ave *TF:* 800-882-1548 ■ *Web:* www.ashland.edu	Ashland	OH	44805	419-289-4142	289-5999
Baldwin-Wallace College 275 Eastland Rd **Fax:* Admissions ■ *TF:* 877-292-7759 ■ *Web:* www.bw.edu	Berea	OH	44017	440-826-2222	826-3830*
Bluffton University 1 University Dr **Fax:* Admissions ■ *TF:* 800-488-3257 ■ *Web:* www.bluffton.edu	Bluffton	OH	45817	419-358-3000	358-3081*
Bowling Green State University 1001 E Wooster St *TF:* 866-246-6732 ■ *Web:* www.bgsu.edu	Bowling Green	OH	43403	419-372-2531	372-6955
Capital University College & Main St **Fax:* Admissions ■ *TF:* 866-544-6175 ■ *Web:* www.capital.edu	Columbus	OH	43209	614-236-6101	236-6926*
Case Western Reserve University 2061 Cornell Rd *TF:* 800-967-8898 ■ *Web:* www.case.edu	Cleveland	OH	44106	216-368-2000	368-5111
Cedarville University 251 N Main St **Fax:* Admissions ■ *TF:* 800-233-2784 ■ *Web:* www.cedarville.edu	Cedarville	OH	45314	937-766-7700	766-7575*
Central State University 1400 Brush Row Rd PO Box 1004 **Fax:* Admissions ■ *TF:* 800-388-2781 ■ *Web:* www.centralstate.edu	Wilberforce	OH	45384	937-376-6011	376-6648*
Cleveland Institute of Music 11021 E Blvd *Web:* www.cim.edu	Cleveland	OH	44106	216-791-5000	791-3063
Cleveland State University 2121 Euclid Ave **Fax:* Admissions ■ *TF:* 888-278-6446 ■ *Web:* www.csuohio.edu	Cleveland	OH	44115	216-687-2000	687-9210*
College of Mount Saint Joseph 5701 Delhi Rd *TF:* 800-654-9314 ■ *Web:* www.msj.edu	Cincinnati	OH	45233	513-244-4200	244-4601
College of Wooster 1189 Beall Ave *TF:* 800-877-9905 ■ *Web:* www.wooster.edu	Wooster	OH	44691	330-263-2000	263-2621
Defiance College 701 N Clinton St **Fax:* Admissions ■ *TF:* 800-520-4632 ■ *Web:* www.defiance.edu	Defiance	OH	43512	419-784-4010	783-2468*
Denison University 100 W College St **Fax:* Admissions ■ *TF:* 800-336-4766 ■ *Web:* www.denison.edu	Granville	OH	43023	740-587-6394	587-8321*
Franklin University 201 S Grant Ave *TF:* 877-341-6300 ■ *Web:* www.franklin.edu	Columbus	OH	43215	614-797-4700	221-4449
Hebrew Union College Cincinnati 3101 Clifton Ave **Fax:* Admissions ■ *Web:* www.huc.edu	Cincinnati	OH	45220	513-221-1875	221-0321*
Heidelberg University 310 E Market St *TF:* 800-434-3352 ■ *Web:* www.heidelberg.edu	Tiffin	OH	44883	419-448-2000	448-2334
Hiram College PO Box 67 **Fax:* Admissions ■ *TF Admissions:* 800-362-5280 ■ *Web:* www.hiram.edu	Hiram	OH	44234	330-569-5169	569-5944*
Hondros College 4140 Executive Pkwy *TF:* 888-466-3767 ■ *Web:* www.hondros.edu	Westerville	OH	43081	888-466-3767	
John Carroll University 20700 N Pk Blvd **Fax:* Admissions ■ *TF:* 888-335-6800 ■ *Web:* www.jcu.edu	Cleveland	OH	44118	216-397-1886	397-4981*
Ashtabula 3300 Lake Rd W **Fax:* Admissions ■ *TF:* 800-988-5368 ■ *Web:* www.ashtabula.kent.edu	Ashtabula	OH	44004	440-964-3322	964-4269*
East Liverpool 400 E Fourth St *Web:* www.kent.edu	East Liverpool	OH	43920	330-385-3805	
Salem 2491 SR-45 S **Fax:* Admissions ■ *Web:* www.salem.kent.edu	Salem	OH	44460	330-332-0361	337-4122*
Stark 6000 Frank Ave NW **Fax:* Admissions ■ *TF:* 800-988-5368 ■ *Web:* www.stark.kent.edu	North Canton	OH	44720	330-499-9600	499-0301*
Trumbull Campus 4314 Mahoning Ave NW **Fax:* Admissions ■ *TF:* 800-988-5368 ■ *Web:* www.trumbull.kent.edu	Warren	OH	44483	330-847-0571	675-8888*
Tuscarawas 330 University Dr NE **Fax:* Admissions ■ *TF:* 800-988-5368 ■ *Web:* www.tusc.kent.edu	New Philadelphia	OH	44663	330-339-3391	339-3321*
Kenyon College 103 College Dr *TF:* 800-848-2468 ■ *Web:* www.kenyon.edu	Gambier	OH	43022	740-427-5000	427-5770
Lake Erie College 391 W Washington St **Fax:* Admissions ■ *TF:* 800-533-4996 ■ *Web:* www.lec.edu	Painesville	OH	44077	440-375-7050	375-7005*
Lourdes College 6832 Convent Blvd **Fax:* Admissions ■ *TF:* 800-878-3210 ■ *Web:* www.lourdes.edu	Sylvania	OH	43560	419-885-5291	882-3987*
Malone College 515 25th St NW **Fax:* Admissions ■ *TF:* 800-521-1146 ■ *Web:* www.malone.edu	Canton	OH	44709	330-471-8100	471-8149*
Marietta College 215 Fifth St **Fax:* Admissions ■ *TF Admissions:* 800-331-7896 ■ *Web:* www.marietta.edu	Marietta	OH	45750	740-376-4000	376-8888*
Miami University 501 E High St **Fax:* Admissions ■ *TF:* 866-426-4643 ■ *Web:* miamioh.edu	Oxford	OH	45056	513-529-1809	529-1550*
Middletown 4200 E University Blvd *TF:* 877-898-4656 ■ *Web:* www.mid.muohio.edu	Middletown	OH	45042	513-727-3200	727-3223
Mount Union College 1972 Clark Ave **Fax:* Admissions ■ *TF Admissions:* 800-334-6682 ■ *Web:* mountunion.edu	Alliance	OH	44601	330-823-2590	823-5097*
Mount Vernon Nazarene University 800 Martinsburg Rd *TF Admissions:* 800-766-8206 ■ *Web:* www.mvnu.edu	Mount Vernon	OH	43050	740-392-6868	
Muskingum College 163 Stormont St **Fax:* Admissions ■ *TF Admissions:* 800-752-6082 ■ *Web:* www.muskingum.edu	New Concord	OH	43762	740-826-8211	826-8100*
Notre Dame College of Ohio 4545 College Rd **Fax:* Admissions ■ *Web:* www.ndc.edu	South Euclid	OH	44121	216-381-1680	916-4999*
Oberlin College 101 N Professor St *Web:* home.oberlin.edu	Oberlin	OH	44074	440-775-8121	775-6905
Ohio Business College 5202 Timber Commons Dr *Web:* www.ohiobusinesscollege.edu	Sandusky	OH	44870	419-627-8345	
Ohio Dominican University 1216 Sunbury Rd **Fax:* Admissions ■ *TF:* 800-955-6446 ■ *Web:* www.ohiodominican.edu	Columbus	OH	43219	614-251-4500	251-0156*
Ohio Northern University 525 S Main St **Fax:* Admissions ■ *TF Admissions:* 888-408-4668 ■ *Web:* www.onu.edu	Ada	OH	45810	419-772-2000	772-2313*
Ohio State University 154 W 12th Ave **Fax:* Admissions ■ *TF:* 800-426-5046 ■ *Web:* www.osu.edu	Columbus	OH	43210	614-292-3980	292-4818*
Lima 4240 Campus Dr *TF:* 800-228-1102 ■ *Web:* www.lima.osu.edu	Lima	OH	45804	419-995-8391	995-8483
Mansfield 1760 University Dr *Web:* mansfield.osu.edu	Mansfield	OH	44906	419-755-4011	
Newark 1179 University Dr **Fax:* Admissions ■ *TF:* 800-963-9275 ■ *Web:* newark.osu.edu	Newark	OH	43055	740-366-3321	364-9645*
Ohio University					
Chillicothe 101 University Dr *TF:* 877-462-6824 ■ *Web:* chillicothe.ohiou.edu	Chillicothe	OH	45601	740-774-7200	
Eastern 45425 National Rd **Fax:* Admissions ■ *TF:* 800-648-3331 ■ *Web:* www.ohio.edu	Saint Clairsville	OH	43950	740-695-1720	695-7079*
Lancaster 1570 Granville Pike **Fax:* Admissions ■ *TF:* 800-444-2910 ■ *Web:* www.ohio.edu	Lancaster	OH	43130	740-654-6711	687-9497*
Southern 1804 Liberty Ave **Fax:* Admissions ■ *TF:* 800-626-0513 ■ *Web:* ohio.edu/southern/	Ironton	OH	45638	740-533-4600	533-4632*
Zanesville 1425 Newark Rd *Web:* www.ohio.edu	Zanesville	OH	43701	740-453-0762	453-6161
Ohio Wesleyan University 61 S Sandusky St Slocum Hall **Fax:* Admissions ■ *Web:* www.owu.edu	Delaware	OH	43015	740-368-2000	368-3314*
Otterbein College One S Grove St **Fax:* Admissions ■ *TF Admissions:* 800-488-8144 ■ *Web:* www.otterbein.edu	Westerville	OH	43081	614-823-1500	823-1200*
Shawnee State University 940 Second St *TF:* 800-959-2778 ■ *Web:* www.shawnee.edu	Portsmouth	OH	45662	740-351-3221	351-3111
Tiffin University 155 Miami St *TF:* 800-968-6446 ■ *Web:* www.tiffin.edu	Tiffin	OH	44883	419-447-6442	443-5006
Union Institute & University 440 E McMillan St **Fax:* Admissions ■ *TF:* 800-486-3116 ■ *Web:* myunion.edu	Cincinnati	OH	45206	513-861-6400	861-0779*
University of Akron 277 E Buchtel Ave *TF Admissions:* 800-655-4884 ■ *Web:* www.uakron.edu	Akron	OH	44325	330-972-7100	972-7022
University of Dayton 300 College Pk **Fax:* Admissions ■ *TF:* 800-837-7433 ■ *Web:* www.udayton.edu	Dayton	OH	45469	937-229-4411	229-4729*
University of Findlay 1000 N Main St *TF:* 800-472-9502 ■ *Web:* www.findlay.edu	Findlay	OH	45840	419-422-8313	434-4822
University of Rio Grande 218 N College Ave **Fax:* Admissions ■ *TF:* 800-282-7201 ■ *Web:* www.rio.edu	Rio Grande	OH	45674	740-245-5353	245-7260*
University of Toledo 2801 W Bancroft St **Fax:* Admissions ■ *TF:* 800-586-5336 ■ *Web:* www.utoledo.edu	Toledo	OH	43606	419-530-4636	530-5745*
Ursuline College 2550 Lander Rd **Fax:* Admissions ■ *TF:* 888-778-5463 ■ *Web:* www.ursuline.edu	Pepper Pike	OH	44124	440-449-4200	684-6138*
Walsh University 2020 E Maple St **Fax:* Admissions ■ *TF Admissions:* 800-362-9846 ■ *Web:* www.walsh.edu	North Canton	OH	44720	330-499-7090	490-7165*
Wilberforce University 1055 N Bickett Rd PO Box 1001 **Fax:* Admissions ■ *TF Admissions:* 800-367-8568 ■ *Web:* www.wilberforce.edu	Wilberforce	OH	45384	937-376-2911	376-4751*
Wilmington College of Ohio 1870 Quaker Way **Fax:* Admissions ■ *TF:* 800-341-9318 ■ *Web:* www.wilmington.edu	Wilmington	OH	45177	937-382-6661	383-8542*
Wittenberg University 200 W Ward St PO Box 720 **Fax:* Admissions ■ *TF:* 800-677-7558 ■ *Web:* www.wittenberg.edu	Springfield	OH	45501	937-327-6314	327-6379*
Wright State University 3640 Colonel Glenn Hwy **Fax:* Admissions ■ *TF Admissions:* 800-247-1770 ■ *Web:* www.wright.edu	Dayton	OH	45435	937-775-5740	775-5795*
Xavier University 3800 Victory Pkwy **Fax:* Admissions ■ *TF:* 800-344-4698 ■ *Web:* www.xavier.edu	Cincinnati	OH	45207	513-745-3000	745-4319*
Youngstown State University One University Plz *TF Admissions:* 877-468-6978 ■ *Web:* www.ysu.edu	Youngstown	OH	44555	330-941-3000	

Oklahoma

Phone | Fax

Bacone College 2299 Old Bacone Rd .... Muskogee OK 74403 918-683-4581 781-7416*
*Fax: Admissions ■ *TF Admissions:* 888-682-5514 ■ *Web:* www.bacone.edu
Cameron University 2800 W Gore Blvd ....Lawton OK 73505 580-581-2289 581-5514*
*Fax: Admissions ■ *TF Admissions:* 888-454-7600 ■ *Web:* www.cameron.edu
East Central University 1100 E 14th St .... Ada OK 74820 580-332-8000 310-5432*
*Fax: Admissions ■ *Web:* www.ecok.edu
Hillsdale Free Will Baptist College
PO Box 7208 .... Moore OK 73153 405-912-9000 912-9050*
*Fax: Admissions ■ *TF:* 800-460-6328 ■ *Web:* www.hc.edu
Langston University
2013 Langston University PO Box 1500..............Langston OK 73050 405-466-3237 466-3271
Web: www.lunet.edu
Mid-America Christian University
3500 SW 119th St ....Oklahoma City OK 73170 405-691-3800 692-3165*
*Fax: Admissions ■ *Web:* www.macu.edu
Broken Arrow 3100 E New Orleans .... Broken Arrow OK 74014 918-449-6000 449-6190*
*Fax: Admissions ■ *Web:* www.nsuba.edu
Muskogee 2400 W Shawnee ....Muskogee OK 74401 918-683-0040 458-2106
TF: 800-722-9614 ■ *Web:* www.nsuok.edu
Northeastern State University
Tahlequah 600 N Grand Ave..................Tahlequah OK 74464 918-456-5511 458-2342
TF: 800-722-9614 ■ *Web:* www.nsuok.edu
Northwestern Oklahoma State University
709 Oklahoma Blvd ....Alva OK 73717 580-327-1700 327-8699
Web: nwosu.edu
Oklahoma Baptist University
500 W University St .... Shawnee OK 74804 405-275-2850 878-2068*
*Fax: Admissions ■ *TF:* 800-654-3285 ■ *Web:* www.okbu.edu
Oklahoma Christian University
PO Box 11000 ....Oklahoma City OK 73136 405-425-5000 425-5069*
*Fax: Admissions ■ *TF:* 800-877-5010 ■ *Web:* www.oc.edu
Oklahoma City University
2501 N Blackwelder Ave......................Oklahoma City OK 73106 405-208-5050 208-5916*
*Fax: Admissions ■ *TF Admissions:* 800-633-7242 ■ *Web:* www.okcu.edu
Oklahoma Panhandle State University
323 Eagle Blvd ....Goodwell OK 73939 580-349-2611 349-2302*
*Fax: Admitting ■ *TF:* 800-664-6778 ■ *Web:* www.opsu.edu
Oklahoma State University
219 Student Union Bldg.............................Stillwater OK 74078 405-744-5000 744-7092
TF: 800-852-1255 ■ *Web:* www.okstate.edu
Tulsa 700 N Greenwood Ave ....Tulsa OK 74106 918-594-8000 594-8202
TF: 800-522-4002 ■ *Web:* www.osu-tulsa.okstate.edu
Oral Roberts University 7777 S Lewis Ave.............. Tulsa OK 74171 918-495-6161 495-6222*
*Fax: Admissions ■ *TF:* 800-678-8876 ■ *Web:* www.oru.edu
Rogers State University
1701 W Will Rogers Blvd........................Claremore OK 74017 918-343-7546 343-7595*
*Fax: Admissions ■ *TF:* 800-256-7511 ■ *Web:* www.rsu.edu
Saint Gregory's University
1900 W MacArthur St........................... Shawnee OK 74804 405-878-5100 878-5198
TF Admissions: 888-784-7347 ■ *Web:* www.stgregorys.edu
Southeastern Oklahoma State University
1405 N Fourth St ....Durant OK 74701 580-745-2000 745-7502*
*Fax: Admissions ■ *TF:* 800-435-1327 ■ *Web:* www.se.edu
Southern Nazarene University
6729 NW 39th Expy ....Bethany OK 73008 405-789-6400 491-6320*
*Fax: Admissions ■ *TF:* 800-648-9899 ■ *Web:* www.snu.edu
Southwestern Christian University
7210 NW 39th Expy PO Box 340 ....Bethany OK 73008 405-789-7661 495-0078*
*Fax: Admissions ■ *TF:* 888-418-9272 ■ *Web:* swcu.publishpath.com/
University of Central Oklahoma
100 N University Dr ....Edmond OK 73034 405-974-2000
Web: www.uco.edu
University of Oklahoma 1000 Asp Ave ....Norman OK 73019 405-325-0311 325-7124
TF: 800-234-6868 ■ *Web:* www.ou.edu
University of Oklahoma Health Sciences Center
1100 N Lindsay ....Oklahoma City OK 73104 405-271-4000
Web: www.ouhsc.edu
University of Sciences & Arts of Oklahoma
1727 W Alabama Ave ....Chickasha OK 73018 405-224-3140 574-1220*
*Fax: Admissions ■ *TF:* 800-933-8726 ■ *Web:* www.usao.edu
University of Tulsa 800 S Tucker Rd.................... Tulsa OK 74104 918-631-2307 631-5003*
*Fax: Admissions ■ *TF:* 800-331-3050 ■ *Web:* www.utulsa.edu

Ontario

Phone | Fax

Foundation for Montessori Education
291B Jane St .... Toronto ON M6S3Z3 416-769-7457
Web: www.montessori-ami.ca

Oregon

Phone | Fax

Concordia University Portland
2811 NE Holman St ....Portland OR 97211 503-288-9371 280-8531*
*Fax: Admissions ■ *TF:* 800-321-9371 ■ *Web:* www.cu-portland.edu
Corban College 5000 Deer Pk Dr SE................... Salem OR 97317 503-581-8600 585-4316
TF: 800-845-3005 ■ *Web:* www.corban.edu
Eastern Oregon University
One University Blvd .... La Grande OR 97850 541-962-3393 962-3418*
*Fax: Admissions ■ *TF:* 800-452-8639 ■ *Web:* www.eou.edu
George Fox University 414 N Meridian St .... Newberg OR 97132 503-538-8383 554-3110*
*Fax: Admissions ■ *TF:* 800-765-4369 ■ *Web:* www.georgefox.edu
Gutenberg College 1883 University St................ Eugene OR 97403 541-683-5141 683-6997
Web: www.gutenberg.edu
Lewis & Clark College
0615 SW Palatine Hill Rd ....Portland OR 97219 503-768-7040 768-7055*
*Fax: Admissions ■ *TF Admissions:* 800-444-4111 ■ *Web:* www.lclark.edu
Linfield College 900 SE Baker St................. McMinnville OR 97128 503-883-2213 883-2472*
*Fax: Admissions ■ *TF Admissions:* 800-640-2287 ■ *Web:* www.linfield.edu
Marylhurst University
17600 Pacific Hwy 43 PO Box 261.................Marylhurst OR 97036 503-636-8141 635-6585*
*Fax: Admissions ■ *TF:* 800-634-9982 ■ *Web:* www.marylhurst.edu
Northwest Christian College 828 E 11th Ave.......... Eugene OR 97401 541-343-1641 684-7317
TF: 877-463-6622 ■ *Web:* www.nwcu.edu
Oregon College of Art & Craft
8245 Sw Barnes Rd ....Portland OR 97225 503-297-5544
Web: www.ocac.edu
Oregon Health & Science University Hospital
3181 SW Sam Jackson Pk Rd.......................Portland OR 97239 503-494-8311 494-3400
TF: 800-292-4466 ■ *Web:* www.ohsu.edu
Oregon Institute of Technology
3201 Campus Dr ....Klamath Falls OR 97601 541-885-1150 885-1024*
*Fax: Admissions ■ *TF:* 800-422-2017 ■ *Web:* www.oit.edu
Oregon State University
104 Kerr Admin Bldg .... Corvallis OR 97331 541-737-4411 737-2482
TF: 800-291-4192 ■ *Web:* www.oregonstate.edu
Pacific Northwest College of Art
1241 NW Johnson St ....Portland OR 97209 503-226-4391 821-8978
TF: 888-390-7499 ■ *Web:* www.pnca.edu
Pacific University 2043 College Way .... Forest Grove OR 97116 503-352-2007 352-2975*
*Fax: Admissions ■ *TF Admissions:* 800-677-6712 ■ *Web:* www.pacificu.edu
Pioneer Pacific College
27501 Sw Pkwy Ave .... Wilsonville OR 97070 503-682-3903
Web: pioneerpacific.edu
Portland State University 1825 SW Broadway ....Portland OR 97201 503-725-3000 725-5525
TF: 800-547-8887 ■ *Web:* www.pdx.edu
Reed College 3203 SE Woodstock Blvd..............Portland OR 97202 503-777-7511 777-7553
TF Admissions: 800-547-4750 ■ *Web:* www.reed.edu
Southern Oregon University
1250 Siskiyou Blvd Britt Hall ....Ashland OR 97520 541-552-6411 552-8403*
*Fax: Admissions ■ *TF:* 800-482-7672 ■ *Web:* www.sou.edu
University of Oregon 1585 E 13th Ave .... Eugene OR 97403 541-346-1000 346-5815*
*Fax: Admissions ■ *TF Admissions:* 800-232-3825 ■ *Web:* www.uoregon.edu
University of Portland
5000 N Willamette Blvd ....Portland OR 97203 503-943-7147 943-7315*
*Fax: Admissions ■ *TF:* 888-627-5601 ■ *Web:* www.up.edu
Warner Pacific College 2219 SE 68th Ave.............Portland OR 97215 503-517-1020 517-1352
TF: 800-804-1510 ■ *Web:* www.warnerpacific.edu
Western Oregon University
345 Monmouth Ave N.............................Monmouth OR 97361 503-838-8000 838-8067
TF Admissions: 877-877-1593 ■ *Web:* www.wou.edu
Willamette University 900 State St.................. Salem OR 97301 503-370-6303 375-5363*
*Fax: Admissions ■ *TF:* 877-542-2787 ■ *Web:* www.willamette.edu

Pennsylvania

Phone | Fax

Albright College 1621 N 13th St.....................Reading PA 19604 610-921-2381 921-7294
TF: 800-252-1856 ■ *Web:* www.albright.edu
Allegheny College 520 N Main St.................Meadville PA 16335 814-332-4351 337-0431
TF: 800-521-5293 ■ *Web:* www.allegheny.edu
Alvernia College 540 Upland Ave ....Reading PA 19611 610-796-8200 790-2873
TF: 888-258-3764 ■ *Web:* www.alvernia.edu
Arcadia University 450 S Easton Rd................ Glenside PA 19038 215-572-2900 881-8767*
*Fax: Admissions ■ *TF:* 888-232-8373 ■ *Web:* www.arcadia.edu
Automotive Training Center-warminster pa Campus
114 Pickering Way ....Exton PA 19341 610-363-6716
Web: www.autotraining.edu
Bloomsburg University 400 E Second St...........Bloomsburg PA 17815 570-389-3900 389-4795*
*Fax: Admissions ■ *TF:* 888-651-6117 ■ *Web:* www.bloomu.edu
Bryn Mawr College 101 N Merion Ave ....Bryn Mawr PA 19010 610-526-5000 526-7471*
*Fax: Admissions ■ *TF Admissions:* 800-262-2586 ■ *Web:* www.brynmawr.edu
Bucknell University 701 Moore Ave.............. Lewisburg PA 17837 570-577-2000 577-1345*
*Fax: Admissions ■ *Web:* www.bucknell.edu
Cabrini College 610 King of Prussia Rd................Radnor PA 19087 610-902-8552 902-8508*
*Fax: Acctg ■ *TF:* 800-848-1003 ■ *Web:* www.cabrini.edu
California University of Pennsylvania
250 University Ave ....California PA 15419 724-938-4000 938-4564
TF: 888-412-0479 ■ *Web:* calu.edu
Carlow University 3333 Fifth Ave .... Pittsburgh PA 15213 412-578-6000 578-6689
TF: 800-333-2275 ■ *Web:* www.carlow.edu
Carnegie Mellon University
5000 Forbes Ave.................................Pittsburgh PA 15213 412-268-2000 268-7838*
*Fax: Admissions ■ *TF:* 844-625-4600 ■ *Web:* www.cmu.edu
Cedar Crest College 100 College Dr................ Allentown PA 18104 610-437-4471 606-4647*
*Fax: Admissions ■ *TF Admissions:* 800-360-1222 ■ *Web:* www.cedarcrest.edu
Chatham University 1 Woodland Rd............... Pittsburgh PA 15232 412-365-1100 365-1609
TF: 800-837-1290 ■ *Web:* www.chatham.edu
Chestnut Hill College
9601 Germantown Ave .... Philadelphia PA 19118 215-248-7001 248-7082*
*Fax: Admissions ■ *TF:* 800-248-0052 ■ *Web:* www.chc.edu
Cheyney University of Pennsylvania
1837 University Cir PO Box 200..................... Cheyney PA 19319 610-399-2275 399-2099*
*Fax: Admissions ■ *TF:* 800-243-9639 ■ *Web:* www.cheyney.edu
Clarion University of Pennsylvania
840 Wood St... Clarion PA 16214 814-393-2306 393-2030*
*Fax: Admissions ■ *TF:* 800-672-7171 ■ *Web:* www.clarion.edu
Venango 1801 W First St............................ Oil City PA 16301 814-676-6591 676-1348
TF: 800-672-7171 ■ *Web:* www.clarion.edu
Curtis Institute of Music
1726 Locust St................................ Philadelphia PA 19103 215-893-5252 893-9065
TF: 800-640-4155 ■ *Web:* www.curtis.edu
Delaware Valley College 700 E Butler Ave .... Doylestown PA 18901 215-489-2211
TF: 800-233-5825 ■ *Web:* www.delval.edu/
DeSales University 2755 Stn Ave .... Center Valley PA 18034 610-282-1100 282-0131
TF: 877-433-7253 ■ *Web:* www.desales.edu
Dickinson College PO Box 1773..................... Carlisle PA 17013 717-243-5121 245-1442*
*Fax: Admissions ■ *TF:* 800-644-1773 ■ *Web:* www.dickinson.edu

Phone Fax

Drexel University 3141 Chestnut St. . . . . Philadelphia PA 19104 215-895-2000 895-5939*
*Fax: Admissions ■ *TF Admissions:* 866-358-1010 ■ *Web:* www.drexel.edu

Duquesne University 600 Forbes Ave. . . . . Pittsburgh PA 15282 412-396-6000 396-5779*
*Fax: Admissions ■ *TF:* 800-456-0590 ■ *Web:* www.duq.edu

East Stroudsburg University
200 Prospect St . . . . East Stroudsburg PA 18301 570-422-3542 422-3933*
*Fax: Admissions ■ *TF Admissions:* 877-230-5547 ■ *Web:* www.esu.edu

Eastern University 1300 Eagle Rd. Wayne PA 19087 610-341-5800 341-1723*
*Fax: Admissions ■ *TF Admissions:* 800-452-0996 ■ *Web:* www.eastern.edu

Edinboro University of Pennsylvania
200 E Normal St . . . . Edinboro PA 16444 814-732-2761 732-2420*
*Fax: Admissions ■ *TF:* 888-846-2676 ■ *Web:* www.edinboro.edu

Elizabethtown College One Alpha Dr . . . . Elizabethtown PA 17022 717-361-1000 361-1365*
*Fax: Admissions ■ *Web:* www.etown.edu

Franklin & Marshall College PO Box 3003 . . . . Lancaster PA 17604 717-291-3951 291-4389*
*Fax: Admissions ■ *TF:* 877-678-9111 ■ *Web:* www.fandm.edu

Gannon University 109 University Sq . . . . Erie PA 16541 814-871-7000 871-5803
TF Admissions: 800-426-6668 ■ *Web:* www.gannon.edu

Geneva College 3200 College Ave. . . . . Beaver Falls PA 15010 724-847-6500 847-6776*
*Fax: Admissions ■ *TF:* 800-847-8255 ■ *Web:* www.geneva.edu

Gettysburg College 300 N Washington St . . . . Gettysburg PA 17325 717-337-6000 337-6145*
*Fax: Admissions ■ *TF:* 800-431-0803 ■ *Web:* www.gettysburg.edu

Gratz College 7605 Old York Rd. . . . . Melrose Park PA 19027 215-635-7300 635-7320*
*Fax: Admissions ■ *TF:* 800-475-4635 ■ *Web:* www.gratz.edu

Great Lakes Institute of Technology Toni & Guy Hairdressing Academy
5100 Peach St . . . . Erie PA 16509 814-864-6666
Web: www.glit.edu

Grove City College 100 Campus Dr. . . . . Grove City PA 16127 724-458-2000 458-3395*
*Fax: Admissions ■ *Web:* www.gcc.edu

Gwynedd-Mercy College
1325 Sunneytown Pk PO Box 901 . . . . Gwynedd Valley PA 19437 215-646-7300 641-5556*
*Fax: Admissions ■ *TF Admissions:* 800-342-5462 ■ *Web:* gmercyu.edu/

Harrisburg University of Science & Technology
215 Market St. . . . . Harrisburg PA 17101 717-901-5100
Web: www.harrisburgu.net

Haverford College 370 Lancaster Ave. . . . . Haverford PA 19041 610-896-1000 896-1338
Web: www.haverford.edu

Holy Family University
9801 Frankford Ave. . . . . Philadelphia PA 19114 215-637-7700 281-1022*
*Fax: Admissions ■ *TF:* 800-422-0010 ■ *Web:* holyfamily.edu/

Immaculata University 1145 King Rd . . . . Immaculata PA 19345 610-647-4400 640-0836*
*Fax: Admissions ■ *TF:* 877-428-6329 ■ *Web:* www.immaculata.edu

Indiana University of Pennsylvania
1011 S Dr Sutton Hall Ste 117 . . . . Indiana PA 15705 724-357-2230 357-6281*
*Fax: Admissions ■ *TF:* 800-442-6830 ■ *Web:* www.iup.edu

Juniata College 1700 Moore St. . . . . Huntingdon PA 16652 814-641-3000 641-3100*
*Fax: Admissions ■ *TF:* 877-586-4282 ■ *Web:* www.juniata.edu

Keystone College One College Green . . . . La Plume PA 18440 570-945-5141 945-7916*
*Fax: Admissions ■ *TF:* 800-824-2764 ■ *Web:* keystone.edu

King's College 133 N River St . . . . Wilkes-Barre PA 18711 570-208-5858 208-5971*
*Fax: Admissions ■ *TF:* 800-955-5777 ■ *Web:* www.kings.edu

Kutztown University 15200 Kutztown Rd . . . . Kutztown PA 19530 610-683-4000 683-1375
TF: 877-628-1915 ■ *Web:* www.kutztown.edu

La Roche College 9000 Babcock Blvd . . . . Pittsburgh PA 15237 412-367-9300 536-1048*
*Fax: Admissions ■ *TF Admissions:* 800-838-4572 ■ *Web:* www.laroche.edu

La Salle University 1900 W Olney Ave. . . . . Philadelphia PA 19141 215-951-1500 951-1656*
*Fax: Admissions ■ *TF:* 800-328-1910 ■ *Web:* www.lasalle.edu

Lafayette College 730 High St . . . . Easton PA 18042 610-330-5000 330-5355*
*Fax: Admissions ■ *Web:* www.lafayette.edu

Lebanon Valley College 101 N College Ave. . . . . Annville PA 17003 717-867-6181 867-6026*
*Fax: Admissions ■ *TF:* 866-582-4236 ■ *Web:* www.lvc.edu

Lock Haven University 401 N Fairview St. . . . . Lock Haven PA 17745 570-484-2011 484-2201*
*Fax: Admissions ■ *TF:* 800-233-8978 ■ *Web:* www.lhup.edu

Lycoming College 700 College Pl. . . . . Williamsport PA 17701 570-321-4000 321-4317*
*Fax: Admissions ■ *TF:* 800-345-3920 ■ *Web:* www.lycoming.edu

Mansfield University Alumni Hall . . . . Mansfield PA 16933 570-662-4000 662-4121
TF Admissions: 800-577-6826 ■ *Web:* www.mansfield.edu

Marywood University 2300 Adams Ave . . . . Scranton PA 18509 570-348-6234 961-4763*
*Fax: Admissions ■ *TF:* 866-279-9663 ■ *Web:* www.marywood.edu

Mercyhurst College 501 E 38th St . . . . Erie PA 16546 814-824-2202 824-3634*
*Fax: Admissions ■ *TF:* 800-825-1926 ■ *Web:* www.mercyhurst.edu

Messiah College PO Box 3005 . . . . Grantham PA 17027 717-691-6000 796-5374*
*Fax: Admissions ■ *TF:* 800-233-4220 ■ *Web:* www.messiah.edu

Millersville University of Pennsylvania
One S George St PO Box 1002 . . . . Millersville PA 17551 717-872-3011 871-2147
TF: 800-682-3648 ■ *Web:* www.millersville.edu

Misericordia University 301 Lake St. . . . . Dallas PA 18612 570-674-6400 675-2441*
*Fax: Admissions ■ *TF:* 866-262-6363 ■ *Web:* www.misericordia.edu

Moravian College 1200 Main St . . . . Bethlehem PA 18018 610-861-1300 625-7930*
*Fax: Admissions ■ *Web:* www.moravian.edu

Mount Aloysius College
7373 Admiral Perry Hwy. . . . . Cresson PA 16630 814-886-6383 886-6441
TF: 888-823-2220 ■ *Web:* www.mtaloy.edu

Muhlenberg College 2400 Chew St . . . . Allentown PA 18104 484-664-3100 664-3234
Web: muhlenberg.edu

Neumann College 1 Neumann Dr . . . . Aston PA 19014 610-459-0905 361-5265*
*Fax: Admissions ■ *TF:* 855-563-8626 ■ *Web:* www.neumann.edu

Peirce College 1420 Pine St . . . . Philadelphia PA 19102 215-545-6400 670-9366*
*Fax: Admissions ■ *TF:* 888-467-3472 ■ *Web:* www.peirce.edu

Pennsylvania State University
201 Shields Bldg Ofc of Admissions . . . . University Park PA 16802 814-865-4700 863-7590
Web: www.psu.edu
Abington College 1600 Woodland Rd . . . . Abington PA 19001 215-881-7300 881-7412*
*Fax: Admissions ■ *Web:* www.abington.psu.edu
Altoona 3000 Ivyside Pk . . . . Altoona PA 16601 814-949-5466 949-5564*
*Fax: Admissions ■ *TF:* 800-848-9843 ■ *Web:* www.altoona.psu.edu
Brandywine 25 Yearsley Mill Rd. Media PA 19063 610-892-1200 892-1357*
*Fax: Admissions ■ *Web:* www.brandywine.psu.edu
Harrisburg 777 W Harrisburg Pk . . . . Middletown PA 17057 717-948-6250 948-6325*
*Fax: Admissions ■ *TF:* 800-222-2056 ■ *Web:* www.hbg.psu.edu

Phone Fax

Pennsylvania State University at Erie
Behrend College 4701 College Dr . . . . Erie PA 16563 814-898-6000 898-6044
TF: 866-374-3378 ■ *Web:* psbehrend.psu.edu

Philadelphia University 4201 Henry Ave . . . . Philadelphia PA 19144 215-951-2800 951-2907*
*Fax: Admissions ■ *TF Admissions:* 800-951-7287 ■ *Web:* www.philau.edu

Point Park University 201 Wood St . . . . Pittsburgh PA 15222 412-391-4100 392-3902*
*Fax: Admissions ■ *TF Admissions:* 800-321-0129 ■ *Web:* www.pointpark.edu

Robert Morris University
6001 University Blvd . . . . Moon Township PA 15108 412-262-8200 397-2425
TF: 800-762-0097 ■ *Web:* www.rmu.edu

Rosemont College 1400 Montgomery Ave . . . . Rosemont PA 19010 610-527-0200 526-2971*
*Fax: Admissions ■ *TF Admissions:* 800-331-0708 ■ *Web:* www.rosemont.edu

Saint Francis University 117 Evergreen Dr . . . . Loretto PA 15940 814-472-3000
Web: www.francis.edu

Saint Joseph's University 5600 City Ave . . . . Philadelphia PA 19131 610-660-1000 660-1314*
*Fax: Admissions ■ *TF:* 888-232-4295 ■ *Web:* www.sju.edu

Saint Vincent College 300 Fraser Purchase Rd . . . . Latrobe PA 15650 724-532-6600 805-2953*
*Fax: Admissions ■ *TF:* 800-782-5549 ■ *Web:* www.stvincent.edu

Seton Hill University One Seton Hill Dr . . . . Greensburg PA 15601 724-838-4255 830-1294*
*Fax: Admissions ■ *TF:* 800-826-6234 ■ *Web:* www.setonhill.edu

Shippensburg University
1871 Old Main Dr. . . . . Shippensburg PA 17257 717-477-1231 477-4016*
*Fax: Admissions ■ *TF:* 800-822-8028 ■ *Web:* www.ship.edu

Slippery Rock University
One Morrow Way . . . . Slippery Rock PA 16057 724-738-9000 738-2913*
*Fax: Admissions ■ *TF:* 800-929-4778 ■ *Web:* www.sru.edu

South Hills School of Business & Technology
480 Waupelani Dr. . . . . State College PA 16801 814-234-7755
Web: www.southhills.edu

Susquehanna University
514 University Ave . . . . Selinsgrove PA 17870 570-374-0101 372-2722
TF: 800-326-9672 ■ *Web:* www.susqu.edu

Swarthmore College 500 College Ave . . . . Swarthmore PA 19081 610-328-8300 328-8580*
*Fax: Admissions ■ *TF Admissions:* 800-667-3110 ■ *Web:* www.swarthmore.edu

Temple University 1801 N Broad St . . . . Philadelphia PA 19122 215-204-7000 204-5694
Web: www.temple.edu

Thiel College 75 College Ave . . . . Greenville PA 16125 724-589-2000 589-2013*
*Fax: Admissions ■ *TF:* 800-248-4435 ■ *Web:* www.thiel.edu

Thomas Jefferson University
1020 Walnut St . . . . Philadelphia PA 19107 215-955-6000 955-5151
TF: 866-594-4722 ■ *Web:* www.jefferson.edu
Bradford 300 Campus Dr . . . . Bradford PA 16701 814-362-7555 362-5150
TF: 800-872-1787 ■ *Web:* www.upb.pitt.edu
Greensburg 150 Finoli Dr . . . . Greensburg PA 15601 724-837-7040 836-7160*
*Fax: Admissions ■ *TF:* 888-843-4563 ■ *Web:* www.greensburg.pitt.edu
Johnstown 157 Blackington Hall . . . . Johnstown PA 15904 814-269-7050 269-7044
TF: 800-765-4875 ■ *Web:* www.upj.pitt.edu

University of Scranton
800 Linden St St Thomas Hall . . . . Scranton PA 18510 570-941-7400 941-5928*
*Fax: Admissions ■ *TF:* 888-727-2686 ■ *Web:* scranton.edu

University of the Sciences in Philadelphia
600 S 43rd St . . . . Philadelphia PA 19104 215-596-8800 596-8821*
*Fax: Admissions ■ *TF:* 888-857-6264 ■ *Web:* www.usciences.edu

Ursinus College
601 E Main St PO Box 1000. . . . . Collegeville PA 19426 610-409-3200 409-3662*
*Fax: Admissions ■ *TF:* 877-448-3282 ■ *Web:* www.ursinus.edu

Valley Forge Christian College
1401 Charlestown Rd . . . . Phoenixville PA 19460 610-935-0450 917-2069*
*Fax: Admissions ■ *TF:* 800-432-8322 ■ *Web:* www.vfcc.edu

Villanova University 800 Lancaster Ave . . . . Villanova PA 19085 610-519-4500 519-6450
Web: www.villanova.edu

Washington & Jefferson College
60 S Lincoln St . . . . Washington PA 15301 724-222-4400 223-6534*
*Fax: Admissions ■ *TF:* 888-926-3529 ■ *Web:* www.washjeff.edu

Waynesburg College 51 W College St . . . . Waynesburg PA 15370 724-627-8191 627-8124*
*Fax: Admissions ■ *TF Admissions:* 800-225-7393 ■ *Web:* www.waynesburg.edu

West Chester University 700 S High St . . . . West Chester PA 19383 610-436-1000 436-2907
TF: 877-315-2165 ■ *Web:* www.wcupa.edu

Widener University One University Pl. . . . . Chester PA 19013 610-499-4000 499-4676*
*Fax: Admissions ■ *TF Admissions:* 888-943-3637 ■ *Web:* www.widener.edu

Wilkes University 84 W S St . . . . Wilkes-Barre PA 18766 800-945-5378 408-4904*
*Fax Area Code: 570 ■ *Fax: Admissions ■ *TF:* 800-945-5378 ■ *Web:* www.wilkes.edu

Wilson College 1015 Philadelphia Ave . . . . Chambersburg PA 17201 717-264-4141 264-1578*
*Fax: Admissions ■ *TF Admissions:* 800-421-8402 ■ *Web:* www.wilson.edu

York College of Pennsylvania
441 Country Club Rd . . . . York PA 17403 717-846-7788 815-6862*
*Fax: Hum Res ■ *Web:* www.ycp.edu

Puerto Rico

Phone Fax

EDIC College Inc
Ave Rafael Cordero Calle Gnova Urb Caguas Norte
. . . . Caguas PR 00726 787-744-8519
Web: www.ediccollege.com

Quebec

Phone Fax

John Abbott College
21275 Ch Lakeshore Bureau 2000
. . . . Sainte-anne-de-bellevue QC H9X3L9 514-457-6610 457-4730
Web: www.johnabbott.qc.ca

Marianopolis College 4873 Av Westmount . . . . Westmount QC H3Y1X9 514-931-8792
Web: www.marianopolis.edu

Rhode Island

Phone Fax

Brown University 45 Prospect St. . . . . Providence RI 02912 401-863-2378 863-9300*
*Fax: Admissions ■ *Web:* www.brown.edu

Phone Fax

Bryant University 1150 Douglas Pk. . . . . Smithfield RI 02917 401-232-6000 232-6741*
**Fax:* Admissions ■ *TF Admissions:* 800-622-7001 ■ *Web:* www.bryant.edu
Emma Pendleton Bradley Hospital
1011 Veterans Memorial Pkwy . . . . East Providence RI 02915 401-432-1000
Web: lifespan.org
Johnson & Wales University
Providence Eight Abbott Pk Pl . . . . Providence RI 02903 401-598-1000 598-4641
TF: 800-342-5598 ■ *Web:* www.jwu.edu
Providence College One Cunningham Sq . . . . Providence RI 02918 401-865-1000 865-2826*
**Fax:* Admissions ■ *TF Admissions:* 800-721-6444 ■ *Web:* www.providence.edu
Rhode Island College 600 Mt Pleasant Ave . . . . Providence RI 02908 401-456-8000 456-8817
TF: 800-669-5760 ■ *Web:* www.ric.edu
Roger Williams University One Old Ferry Rd. . . . . Bristol RI 02809 401-254-3500 254-3557*
**Fax:* Admissions ■ *TF:* 800-458-7144 ■ *Web:* www.rwu.edu
Salve Regina University 100 Ochre Pt Ave. . . . . Newport RI 02840 401-847-6650 848-2823*
**Fax:* Admissions ■ *TF:* 888-467-2583 ■ *Web:* www.salve.edu
University of Rhode Island (URI)
45 Upper College Rd . . . . Kingston RI 02881 401-874-1000 874-5523
Web: ww2.uri.edu
Feinstein Providence 80 Washington St. . . . . Providence RI 02903 401-277-5000
Web: ww2.uri.edu

South Carolina

Phone Fax

Allen University 1530 Harden St . . . . Columbia SC 29204 803-376-5700 376-5733*
**Fax:* Mail Rm ■ *TF:* 877-625-5368 ■ *Web:* www.allenuniversity.edu
Benedict College 1600 Harden St. Columbia SC 29204 803-253-5000
TF: 800-868-6598 ■ *Web:* www.benedict.edu
Bob Jones University
1700 Wade Hampton Blvd . . . . Greenville SC 29614 864-242-5100 232-9258*
**Fax Area Code:* 800 ■ **Fax:* Admissions ■ *TF Admissions:* 800-252-6363 ■ *Web:* www.bju.edu
Charleston Southern University
9200 University Blvd . . . . Charleston SC 29423 843-863-7050 863-7070
TF: 800-947-7474 ■ *Web:* www.csuniv.edu
Citadel, The 171 Moultrie St . . . . Charleston SC 29409 843-953-5230 953-7036
TF: 800-868-1842 ■ *Web:* www.citadel.edu
Claflin University 400 Magnolia St . . . . Orangeburg SC 29115 803-535-5000 535-5385
TF: 800-922-1276 ■ *Web:* www.claflin.edu
Clemson University 105 Sikes Hall. . . . . Clemson SC 29634 864-656-3311 656-2464*
**Fax:* Admissions ■ *TF:* 800-640-2657 ■ *Web:* www.clemson.edu
Coastal Carolina University PO Box 261954 . . . . Conway SC 29528 843-349-2170 349-2127
TF: 800-277-7000 ■ *Web:* www.coastal.edu
Coker College 300 E College Ave. Hartsville SC 29550 843-383-8000 383-8056*
**Fax:* Admissions ■ *TF:* 800-950-1908 ■ *Web:* www.coker.edu
College of Charleston 66 George St. . . . . Charleston SC 29424 843-805-5507 953-6322
TF: 800-355-9983 ■ *Web:* www.cofc.edu
Converse College 580 E Main St. . . . . Spartanburg SC 29302 864-596-9000 596-9225*
**Fax:* Admissions ■ *TF Admissions:* 800-766-1125 ■ *Web:* www.converse.edu
Erskine College Two Washington St . . . . Due West SC 29639 864-379-2131 379-3048*
**Fax:* Admissions ■ *TF Admissions:* 800-241-8721 ■ *Web:* www.erskine.edu
Francis Marion University PO Box 100547. . . . . Florence SC 29501 843-661-1231 661-4635*
**Fax:* Admissions ■ *TF:* 800-368-7551 ■ *Web:* www.fmarion.edu
Furman University 3300 Poinsett Hwy . . . . Greenville SC 29613 864-294-2000 294-2018*
**Fax:* Admissions ■ *Web:* www.furman.edu
Lander University 320 Stanley Ave . . . . Greenwood SC 29649 864-388-8307 388-8125*
**Fax:* Admissions ■ *TF Admissions:* 800-922-1117 ■ *Web:* www.lander.edu
Limestone College 1115 College Dr. . . . . Gaffney SC 29340 864-489-7151 488-8206*
**Fax:* Admissions ■ *TF:* 800-795-7151 ■ *Web:* www.limestone.edu
Medical University of South Carolina
41 Bee St MSC 203 . . . . Charleston SC 29425 843-792-3281 792-3764*
**Fax:* Admissions ■ *TF:* 800-424-6872 ■ *Web:* www.musc.edu
Morris College 100 W College St. Sumter SC 29150 803-934-3200 773-8241*
**Fax:* Admissions ■ *TF Admissions:* 866-853-1345 ■ *Web:* www.morris.edu
Newberry College 2100 College St. Newberry SC 29108 803-276-5010 321-5138*
**Fax:* Admissions ■ *TF:* 800-845-4955 ■ *Web:* www.newberry.edu
Presbyterian College 503 S Broad St . . . . Clinton SC 29325 864-833-2820 833-8481*
**Fax:* Admissions ■ *TF:* 800-476-7272 ■ *Web:* www.presby.edu
South Carolina State University
300 College St NE PO Box 7127. Orangeburg SC 29117 803-536-7000 536-8990
TF Admissions: 800-260-5956 ■ *Web:* www.scsu.edu
South University Columbia Nine Science Ct . . . . Columbia SC 29203 803-799-9082 935-4382*
**Fax:* Admissions ■ *TF:* 800-688-0932 ■ *Web:* www.southuniversity.edu
Southern Wesleyan University 907 Wesleyan Dr. . . . . Central SC 29630 864-644-5000 644-5972*
**Fax:* Admissions ■ *TF:* 800-282-8798 ■ *Web:* www.swu.edu
Technical College of the Lowcountry
921 Ribaut Rd. . . . . Beaufort SC 29902 843-525-8211
Web: www.tcl.edu
University of South Carolina
1600 Hampton St . . . . Columbia SC 29208 803-777-7000 777-0101*
**Fax:* Admissions ■ *TF:* 800-868-5872 ■ *Web:* www.sc.edu
Aiken 471 University Pkwy. . . . . Aiken SC 29801 803-648-6851 641-3727*
**Fax:* Admissions ■ *TF:* 800-937-0762 ■ *Web:* www.usca.edu
Beaufort 801 Carteret St. . . . . Beaufort SC 29902 843-521-4100 521-4198*
**Fax:* Admissions ■ *TF:* 866-455-4753 ■ *Web:* www.sc.edu
Sumter 200 Miller Rd. . . . . Sumter SC 29150 803-775-8727 775-2180*
**Fax:* Admissions ■ *TF:* 888-872-7868 ■ *Web:* www.uscsumter.edu
Upstate 800 University Way . . . . Spartanburg SC 29303 864-503-5246 503-5727*
**Fax:* Admissions ■ *TF:* 800-277-8727 ■ *Web:* www.uscupstate.edu
Voorhees College 213 Wiggins Dr PO Box 678 . . . . Denmark SC 29042 803-780-1234 753-9077
TF Admissions: 800-446-6250 ■ *Web:* www.voorhees.edu
Winthrop University 701 Oakland Ave . . . . Rock Hill SC 29733 803-323-2211 323-2137*
**Fax:* Admissions ■ *Web:* www.winthrop.edu
Wofford College 429 N Church St. . . . . Spartanburg SC 29303 864-597-4000 597-4149*
**Fax:* Admissions ■ *Web:* www.wofford.edu

South Dakota

Phone Fax

Black Hills State University
1200 University St Unit 9502 . . . . Spearfish SD 57799 605-642-6343 642-6254
TF: 800-255-2478 ■ *Web:* www.bhsu.edu
Dakota State University 820 N Washington Ave . . . . Madison SD 57042 605-256-5139 256-5020
TF: 888-378-9988 ■ *Web:* www.dsu.edu
Dakota Wesleyan University
1200 W University Ave . . . . Mitchell SD 57301 605-995-2600 995-2699
TF: 800-333-8506 ■ *Web:* www.dwu.edu
Globe University 5101 S Broadband Ln. . . . . Sioux Falls SD 57108 605-977-0705
Web: globeuniversity.edu
Mount Marty College 1105 W Eigth St. . . . . Yankton SD 57078 605-668-1545 668-1508*
**Fax:* Admissions ■ *TF Admissions:* 800-658-4552 ■ *Web:* www.mtmc.edu
National American University
321 Kansas City St . . . . Rapid City SD 57701 605-394-4800 394-4871*
**Fax:* Admissions ■ *TF:* 800-843-8892 ■ *Web:* www.national.edu
Sioux Falls 5801 S Kiwanis Ave. . . . . Sioux Falls SD 57108 605-336-4600 336-4605*
**Fax:* Admissions ■ *TF:* 800-388-5430 ■ *Web:* www.national.edu
Northern State University 1200 S Jay St. . . . . Aberdeen SD 57401 605-626-3011 626-2587*
**Fax:* Admissions ■ *TF:* 800-678-5330 ■ *Web:* www.northern.edu
Oglala Lakota College PO Box 629 . . . . Martin SD 57551 605-455-6000 455-2787
Web: www.olc.edu
Presentation College 1500 N Main St. . . . . Aberdeen SD 57401 605-225-1634 229-8425
TF: 800-437-6060 ■ *Web:* www.presentation.edu
South Dakota School of Mines & Technology
501 E St Joseph St . . . . Rapid City SD 57701 605-394-2414 394-1268
TF: 800-544-8162 ■ *Web:* www.sdsmt.edu/
South Dakota State University PO Box 2201 . . . . Brookings SD 57007 605-688-4121 688-6891
TF: 800-952-3541 ■ *Web:* www.sdstate.edu
University of Sioux Falls 1101 W 22nd St. . . . . Sioux Falls SD 57105 605-331-6600 331-6615
TF: 800-888-1047 ■ *Web:* www.usiouxfalls.edu
University of South Dakota 414 E Clark St. . . . . Vermillion SD 57069 605-677-5341 677-6323*
**Fax:* Admissions ■ *TF:* 877-269-6837 ■ *Web:* www.usd.edu

Tennessee

Phone Fax

Aquinas College 4210 HaRding Rd . . . . Nashville TN 37205 615-297-7545
TF Admissions: 800-649-9956 ■ *Web:* aquinascollege.edu
Austin Peay State University
601 College St . . . . Clarksville TN 37044 931-221-7661 221-6168*
**Fax:* Admissions ■ *TF Admissions:* 800-844-2778 ■ *Web:* www.apsu.edu
Belmont University 1900 Belmont Blvd . . . . Nashville TN 37212 615-460-6000 460-5434*
**Fax:* Admissions ■ *TF:* 800-563-6765 ■ *Web:* www.belmont.edu
Bethel University 325 Cherry Ave. . . . . McKenzie TN 38201 731-352-4000 352-4241*
**Fax:* Admissions ■ *Web:* www.bethelu.edu
Bryan College 721 Bryan Dr PO Box 7000. . . . . Dayton TN 37321 423-775-2041 775-7199
TF: 800-277-9522 ■ *Web:* www.bryan.edu
Carson-Newman College
1646 Russell Ave . . . . Jefferson City TN 37760 865-471-2000 471-3502*
**Fax:* Admissions ■ *TF:* 800-678-9061 ■ *Web:* www.cn.edu
Christian Bros University 650 E Pkwy S . . . . Memphis TN 38104 901-321-3000 321-3494*
**Fax:* Admissions ■ *TF Admissions:* 800-288-7576 ■ *Web:* www.cbu.edu
Cumberland University One Cumberland Sq. . . . . Lebanon TN 37087 615-444-2562 444-2569
TF: 800-467-0562 ■ *Web:* www.cumberland.edu
East Tennessee State University
PO Box 70731 . . . . Johnson City TN 37614 423-439-4213 439-4630
TF: 800-462-3878 ■ *Web:* www.etsu.edu
Fisk University 1000 17th Ave N . . . . Nashville TN 37208 615-329-8500 329-8774
TF: 888-702-0022 ■ *Web:* www.fisk.edu
Freed-Hardeman University 158 E Main St . . . . Henderson TN 38340 731-989-6651 989-6047
TF: 800-348-3481 ■ *Web:* www.fhu.edu
King College 1350 King College Rd . . . . Bristol TN 37620 423-652-4861 968-4456
TF Admissions: 800-362-0014 ■ *Web:* www.king.edu
Lambuth University 705 Lambuth Blvd. . . . . Jackson TN 38301 731-427-4725 422-2169*
**Fax:* Admissions ■ *TF:* 800-526-2305 ■ *Web:* memphis.edu
Lane College 545 Ln Ave . . . . Jackson TN 38301 731-426-7500 426-7559*
**Fax:* Admissions ■ *TF Admissions:* 800-960-7533 ■ *Web:* www.lanecollege.edu
Lee University 1120 N Ocoee St. Cleveland TN 37311 423-614-8000 614-8533*
**Fax:* Admissions ■ *TF:* 800-533-9930 ■ *Web:* www.leeuniversity.edu
Lincoln Memorial University
6965 Cumberland Gap Pkwy . . . . Harrogate TN 37752 423-869-3611 869-6444
TF: 800-325-0900 ■ *Web:* www.lmunet.edu
Lipscomb University 3901 Granny White Pk . . . . Nashville TN 37204 615-966-1000 966-1804*
**Fax:* Admissions ■ *TF:* 800-333-4358 ■ *Web:* www.lipscomb.edu
Martin Methodist College 433 W Madison St. . . . . Pulaski TN 38478 931-363-9804 363-9803*
**Fax:* Admissions ■ *TF:* 800-467-1273 ■ *Web:* www.martinmethodist.edu
Maryville College
502 E Lamar Alexander Pkwy . . . . Maryville TN 37804 865-981-8000 981-8005*
**Fax:* Admissions ■ *TF:* 800-597-2687 ■ *Web:* www.maryvillecollege.edu
Middle Tennessee State University
1301 E Main St. . . . . Murfreesboro TN 37132 615-898-2111 898-5478*
**Fax:* Admissions ■ *TF Admissions:* 800-433-6878 ■ *Web:* www.mtsu.edu
Milligan College PO Box 500 . . . . Milligan College TN 37682 423-461-8730 461-8982*
**Fax:* Admissions ■ *TF:* 800-262-8337 ■ *Web:* www.milligan.edu
Nossi College of Art 590 Cheron Rd. . . . . Madison TN 37115 615-514-2787
Web: www.nossi.edu
O'More College of Design 423 S Margin St. . . . . Franklin TN 37064 615-794-4254 790-1662
TF: 888-662-1970 ■ *Web:* www.omorecollege.edu
Oxford Graduate School Inc 500 Oxford Dr. . . . . Dayton TN 37321 423-775-6596
Web: www.ogs.edu
Rhodes College 2000 N Pkwy . . . . Memphis TN 38112 901-843-3700 843-3631*
**Fax:* Admissions ■ *TF:* 800-844-5969 ■ *Web:* www.rhodes.edu
Southern Adventist University
4881 Taylor Cir. . . . . Collegedale TN 37315 423-236-2000 236-1000
TF: 800-768-8437 ■ *Web:* www.southern.edu
Tennessee State University
3500 John A Merritt Blvd PO Box 9609 . . . . Nashville TN 37209 615-963-5000 963-5108
TF Admissions: 888-463-6878 ■ *Web:* www.tnstate.edu
Tennessee Technological University
One William L Jones Dr . . . . Cookeville TN 38505 931-372-3888 372-6250
TF: 800-255-8881 ■ *Web:* www.tntech.edu
Tennessee Temple University
1815 Union Ave . . . . Chattanooga TN 37404 423-493-4100 493-4497*
**Fax:* Admissions ■ *TF:* 800-553-4050 ■ *Web:* www.tntemple.edu

Phone Fax

Tennessee Wesleyan College
204 E College St PO Box 40 . . . Athens TN 37371 423-745-7504 744-9968
TF: 800-742-5892 ■ Web: www.twcnet.edu

Trevecca Nazarene University
333 Murfreesboro Rd . . . Nashville TN 37210 615-248-1200 248-7406*
*Fax: Admissions ■ TF: 888-210-4868 ■ Web: www.trevecca.edu

Tusculum College 60 Shiloh Rd Hwy 107 . . . Greeneville TN 37743 423-636-7300 798-1622*
*Fax: Admissions ■ TF: 800-729-0256 ■ Web: www.tusculum.edu

Union University 1050 Union University Dr . . . Jackson TN 38305 731-661-5210 661-5589*
*Fax: Admissions ■ TF: 800-338-6466 ■ Web: www.uu.edu

University of Tennessee (UTHSC)
1331 Cir Pk Dr 320 Student Services Bldg . . . Knoxville TN 37996 865-974-1000 974-3851*
*Fax: Admissions ■ Web: www.utk.edu
Chattanooga 615 McCallie Ave . . . Chattanooga TN 37403 423-425-4111 425-4157*
*Fax: Admissions ■ TF: 800-882-6627 ■ Web: www.utc.edu
Health Science Ctr 920 Madison Ave . . . Memphis TN 38163 901-448-5500
Web: www.uthsc.edu
Martin 544 University St . . . Martin TN 38238 731-881-7020 881-7029
TF: 800-829-8861 ■ Web: www.utm.edu

University of the South 735 University Ave . . . Sewanee TN 37383 931-598-1238 598-3248*
*Fax: Admissions ■ TF: 800-522-2234 ■ Web: www.sewanee.edu

Vanderbilt University 2201 W End Ave . . . Nashville TN 37240 615-322-7311 343-7765
TF: 800-288-0432 ■ Web: www.vanderbilt.edu

Texas

Phone Fax

Amberton University 1700 Eastgate Dr . . . Garland TX 75041 972-279-6511 279-9773
Web: www.amberton.edu

Angelina County Junior College District Texas
3500 S First St . . . Lufkin TX 75904 936-639-1301
Web: www.angelina.edu

Angelo State University
2601 W Ave N ASU Stn 11014 . . . San Angelo TX 76909 325-942-2041 942-2078*
*Fax: Admissions ■ TF: 800-946-8627 ■ Web: www.angelo.edu

Arlington Baptist College 3001 W Div St . . . Arlington TX 76012 817-461-8741 274-1138*
*Fax: Admissions ■ Web: arlingtonbaptistcollege.edu

Austin College 900 N Grand Ave . . . Sherman TX 75090 903-813-3000 813-3197*
*Fax: Admissions ■ TF: 866-776-0056 ■ Web: www.austincollege.edu

Austin Graduate School of Theology
7640 Guadalupe St . . . Austin TX 78752 512-476-2772 476-3919
TF: 866-287-4723 ■ Web: www.austingrad.edu

Baylor University
1311 S Fifth St 1 Bear Pl 98013 . . . Waco TX 76798 254-710-3718 710-1066
TF: 800-229-5678 ■ Web: www.baylor.edu

Concordia University Austin 3400 IH-35 N . . . Austin TX 78705 512-486-2000 486-1350
TF: 800-865-4282 ■ Web: www.concordia.edu

Criswell College 4010 Gaston Ave . . . Dallas TX 75246 214-821-5433 818-1310*
*Fax: Admissions ■ TF: 800-899-0012 ■ Web: www.criswell.edu

Dallas Baptist University 3000 Mtn Creek Pkwy . . . Dallas TX 75211 214-333-7100 333-5447*
*Fax: Admissions ■ TF: 800-460-1328 ■ Web: www.dbu.edu

East Texas Baptist University
1209 N Grove St . . . Marshall TX 75670 903-935-7963 923-2001*
*Fax: Admissions ■ TF: 800-804-3828 ■ Web: www.etbu.edu

Graduate Institute of Applied Linguistics Inc
7500 W Camp Wisdom Rd . . . Dallas TX 75236 972-708-7340
Web: www.gial.edu

Hardin-Simmons University 2200 Hickory St . . . Abilene TX 79698 325-670-1206 671-2115*
*Fax: Admissions ■ TF: 877-464-7889 ■ Web: www.hsutx.edu

Houston Baptist University 7502 Fondren Rd . . . Houston TX 77074 281-649-3000 649-3217*
*Fax: Admissions ■ TF Admissions: 800-969-3210 ■ Web: www.hbu.edu

Howard Payne University 1000 Fisk Ave . . . Brownwood TX 76801 325-646-2502 649-8900
TF: 800-950-8465 ■ Web: www.hputx.edu

Huston-Tillotson University 900 Chicon St . . . Austin TX 78702 512-505-3000 505-3192*
*Fax: Admissions ■ TF: 877-487-8702 ■ Web: www.htu.edu

Jarvis Christian College PO Box 1470 . . . Hawkins TX 75765 903-769-5700 769-1282*
*Fax: Admissions ■ Web: www.jarvis.edu

Lamar University 4400 ML King Jr Pkwy . . . Beaumont TX 77710 409-880-7011 880-8463
Web: www.lamar.edu

LeTourneau University 2100 S Mobberly Ave . . . Longview TX 75602 903-233-3000 233-4301*
*Fax: Admissions ■ TF: 800-759-8811 ■ Web: www.letu.edu

Lubbock Christian University 5601 19th St . . . Lubbock TX 79407 806-720-7151 720-7162*
*Fax: Admissions ■ TF: 800-933-7601 ■ Web: www.lcu.edu

McMurry University
1 McMurry University 1400 Sayles Blvd . . . Abilene TX 79697 325-793-4700
TF: 800-460-2392 ■ Web: www.mcm.edu

Midwestern State University
3410 Taft Blvd . . . Wichita Falls TX 76308 940-397-4000 397-4672*
*Fax: Admissions ■ TF Admissions: 800-842-1922 ■ Web: www.mwsu.edu

Northwood University
Texas 1114 W FM 1382 . . . Cedar Hill TX 75104 972-291-1541 291-3824
TF: 800-927-9663 ■ Web: www.northwood.edu

Our Lady of the Lake University
411 SW 24th St . . . San Antonio TX 78207 210-434-6711 431-4036*
*Fax: Admissions ■ TF: 800-436-6558 ■ Web: www.ollusa.edu

Paul Quinn College 3837 Simpson Stuart Rd . . . Dallas TX 75241 214-376-1000 *
*Fax: Admissions ■ TF: 800-433-3243 ■ Web: www.pqc.edu

Prairie View A & M University
PO Box 519 . . . Prairie View TX 77446 936-857-2626 261-1079*
*Fax: Admissions ■ TF: 800-787-7826 ■ Web: www.pvamu.edu

Rice University 6100 Main St . . . Houston TX 77005 713-348-0000 348-5323*
*Fax: Admissions ■ TF: 800-527-6957 ■ Web: www.rice.edu

Sam Houston State University
1903 University Ave . . . Huntsville TX 77340 936-294-1111 294-3758*
*Fax: Admissions ■ TF: 866-232-7528 ■ Web: www.shsu.edu

Schreiner University 2100 Memorial Blvd . . . Kerrville TX 78028 830-792-7217 792-7226*
*Fax: Admissions ■ TF: 800-343-4919 ■ Web: www.schreiner.edu

Southern Methodist University 6425 Boaz Ln . . . Dallas TX 75205 214-768-2000 768-0202*
*Fax: Admissions ■ TF: 800-323-0672 ■ Web: www.smu.edu

Southwestern Adventist University
100 W Hillcrest Dr PO Box 567 . . . Keene TX 76059 817-645-3921 556-4753
TF Admissions: 888-732-7928 ■ Web: www.swau.edu

Phone Fax

Southwestern Assemblies of God University
1200 Sycamore St . . . Waxahachie TX 75165 972-937-4010 923-0006*
*Fax: Admissions ■ TF: 888-937-7248 ■ Web: www.sagu.edu

Southwestern Christian College PO Box 10 . . . Terrell TX 75160 972-524-3341 563-7133
TF: 800-925-9357 ■ Web: www.swcc.edu

Southwestern University PO Box 770 . . . Georgetown TX 78627 512-863-1200 863-9601*
*Fax: Admissions ■ TF: 800-252-3166 ■ Web: www.southwestern.edu

Stephen F Austin State University
1936 N St PO Box 13051 . . . Nacogdoches TX 75962 936-468-2504 468-3149*
*Fax: Admissions ■ Web: www.sfasu.edu

Sul Ross State University E Hwy 90 . . . Alpine TX 79832 432-837-8011 837-8431*
*Fax: Admissions ■ TF: 888-722-7778 ■ Web: www.sulross.edu

Tarleton State University
1333 W Washington PO Box T-0030 . . . Stephenville TX 76402 254-968-9000 968-9951*
*Fax: Admissions ■ TF: 800-687-8236 ■ Web: www.tarleton.edu

Texas A & M International University
5201 University Blvd . . . Laredo TX 78041 956-326-2001 326-2199
TF: 888-489-2648 ■ Web: www.tamiu.edu
Corpus Christi 6300 Ocean Dr . . . Corpus Christi TX 78412 361-825-7024 825-5887*
*Fax: Admissions ■ Web: www.tamucc.edu
Galveston 200 Seawolf Pkwy Bldg 3026 . . . Galveston TX 77553 409-740-4428 740-4731
TF: 877-322-4443 ■ Web: www.tamug.edu
Kingsville 700 University Blvd MSC 128 . . . Kingsville TX 78363 361-593-2111 593-2195*
*Fax: Admissions ■ TF: 800-726-8192 ■ Web: www.tamuk.edu
Texarkana 7101 University Ave . . . Texarkana TX 75503 903-223-3000 223-3140
TF: 866-791-9120 ■ Web: www.tamut.edu

Texas Christian University
TCU PO Box 297043 . . . Fort Worth TX 76129 817-257-7490 257-7268
TF: 800-828-3764 ■ Web: www.tcu.edu

Texas College 2404 N Grand Ave . . . Tyler TX 75702 903-593-8311 593-0588*
*Fax: Admissions ■ TF: 800-306-6299 ■ Web: www.texascollege.edu

Texas Lutheran University 1000 W Ct St . . . Seguin TX 78155 830-372-8000 372-8096
TF: 800-771-8521 ■ Web: www.tlu.edu

Texas Southern University 3100 Cleburne St . . . Houston TX 77004 713-313-7011 313-1859
TF: 800-252-5400 ■ Web: www.tsu.edu

Texas State University
San Marcos 601 University Dr . . . San Marcos TX 78666 512-245-2340 245-8044*
*Fax: Admissions ■ TF Admissions: 866-294-0987 ■ Web: www.txstate.edu

Texas Tech University PO Box 45005 . . . Lubbock TX 79409 806-742-1480 742-0062*
*Fax: Admissions ■ TF: 888-270-3369 ■ Web: www.ttu.edu

Texas Wesleyan University
1201 Wesleyan St . . . Fort Worth TX 76105 817-531-4444 212-4141*
*Fax: Admissions ■ TF: 800-580-8980 ■ Web: txwes.edu

Texas Woman's University
304 Admin Dr PO Box 425589 . . . Denton TX 76204 940-898-3188 898-3081*
*Fax: Admissions ■ TF: 866-809-6130 ■ Web: www.twu.edu

Trinity University One Trinity Pl . . . San Antonio TX 78212 210-999-7011 999-8164*
*Fax: Admissions ■ TF: 800-874-6489 ■ Web: www.trinity.edu

University of Dallas 1845 E Northgate Dr . . . Irving TX 75062 972-721-5266 721-5017*
*Fax: Admissions ■ TF Admissions: 800-628-6999 ■ Web: www.udallas.edu

University of Houston 4800 Calhoun Rd . . . Houston TX 77004 713-743-1000 743-9665
Web: www.uh.edu
Clear Lake 2700 Bay Area Blvd . . . Houston TX 77058 281-283-7600 283-2522*
*Fax: Admissions ■ Web: uhcl.edu
Victoria 3007 N Ben Wilson St . . . Victoria TX 77901 361-570-4848 570-4114*
*Fax: Admissions ■ TF: 877-970-4848 ■ Web: www.uhv.edu

University of Mary Hardin-Baylor
900 College St PO Box 8004 . . . Belton TX 76513 254-295-8642 295-5049*
*Fax: Admissions ■ TF: 800-727-8642 ■ Web: www.umhb.edu

University of North Texas PO Box 311277 . . . Denton TX 76203 940-565-2681 565-2408*
*Fax: Admissions ■ TF: 800-868-8211 ■ Web: www.unt.edu

University of Saint Thomas
3800 Montrose Blvd . . . Houston TX 77006 713-522-7911 525-3558*
*Fax: Admissions ■ TF: 800-856-8565 ■ Web: www.stthom.edu
Allied Health Sciences School
5323 Harry Hines Blvd . . . Dallas TX 75390 214-648-3111 475-7641*
*Fax Area Code: 512
Austin 2400 Inner Campus Dr Mail Bldg Rm 7 . . . Austin TX 78712 512-475-7399 475-7399*
*Fax: Admissions ■ Web: www.utexas.edu
Brownsville 80 Fort Brown St . . . Brownsville TX 78520 956-882-8200 477-4859*
*Fax Area Code: 423 ■ *Fax: Admissions ■ TF: 800-892-3348 ■ Web: opportunityequation.org
Dallas 800 W Campbell Rd Ste Be3204 . . . Richardson TX 75080 972-883-2111 883-2599
TF: 800-889-2443 ■ Web: www.utdallas.edu
El Paso 500 W University Ave . . . El Paso TX 79968 915-747-5000 747-8893*
*Fax: Admissions ■ TF Admissions: 800-551-0294 ■ Web: www.utep.edu
Pan American 1201 W University Dr . . . Edinburg TX 78539 956-381-8872 381-2212
TF: 866-441-8872 ■ Web: www.utpa.edu
Permian Basin 4901 E University Blvd . . . Odessa TX 79762 432-552-2020 552-3605*
*Fax: Admissions ■ TF Admissions: 866-552-8872 ■ Web: www.utpb.edu

University of Texas
San Antonio 6900 N Loop 1604 W . . . San Antonio TX 78249 210-458-4011 458-7716*
*Fax: Admissions ■ TF: 800-669-0919 ■ Web: www.utsa.edu
Tyler 3900 University Blvd . . . Tyler TX 75799 903-566-7000 566-7068*
*Fax: Admissions ■ TF: 800-888-9537 ■ Web: www.uttyler.edu

University of Texas Investment Management Co
401 Congress Ave Ste 2800 . . . Austin TX 78701 512-225-1600
Web: www.utimco.org

University of the Incarnate Word
4301 Broadway St . . . San Antonio TX 78209 210-829-6000 829-3921*
*Fax: Admissions ■ TF Admissions: 800-749-9673 ■ Web: www.uiw.edu

Wayland Baptist University
1900 W Seventh St . . . Plainview TX 79072 806-291-1000 291-1973*
*Fax: Admissions ■ TF: 800-588-1928 ■ Web: www.wbu.edu

West Texas A & M University 2501 Fourth Ave . . . Canyon TX 79016 806-651-2020 651-5285*
*Fax: Admissions ■ TF: 877-656-2065 ■ Web: www.wtamu.edu

Wiley College 711 Wiley Ave . . . Marshall TX 75670 903-927-3300 927-3366*
*Fax: Admissions ■ TF Admissions: 800-658-6889 ■ Web: www.wileyc.edu

Utah

Phone Fax

Brigham Young University 770 E University Pkwy . . . Provo UT 84602 801-422-4636

Phone Fax

Dixie State College of Utah 225 S 700 E. . . . . Saint George UT 84770 435-652-7500 656-4005*
*Fax: Admissions ■ TF: 855-628-8140 ■ Web: dixie.edu

Southern Utah University 351 W Ctr St. . . . . Cedar City UT 84720 435-586-7700 865-8223*
*Fax: Admissions ■ Web: www.suu.edu

Uintah Basin Applied Technology College
1100 E Lagoon St. . . . . .Roosevelt UT 84066 435-722-4523
Web: ubatc.edu

University of Utah
201 South 1460 East Rm 250 S . . . . Salt Lake City UT 84112 801-581-7281
Web: www.utah.edu

Utah State University 1600 Old Main Hill. . . . . Logan UT 84322 435-797-1116 797-1110
TF: 800-488-8108 ■ Web: www.usu.edu
Davis 2750 N University Pk Blvd . . . . .Layton UT 84041 801-395-3473 395-3538*
*Fax: Admissions ■ TF: 800-848-7770 ■ Web: www.weber.edu

Vermont

Phone Fax

Bennington College One College Dr . . . . Bennington VT 05201 802-442-5401 447-4269
TF: 800-833-6845 ■ Web: www.bennington.edu

Burlington College 351 N Ave . . . . Burlington VT 05401 800-862-9616 660-4331*
*Fax Area Code: 802 ■ TF: 800-862-9616 ■ Web: www.burlington.edu

Castleton State College 86 Seminary St. . . . . .Castleton VT 05735 802-468-5611 468-1476*
*Fax: Admissions ■ TF: 800-639-8521 ■ Web: www.csc.vsc.edu

Champlain College 163 S Willard St . . . . Burlington VT 05401 802-860-2700 860-2767
TF: 800-570-5858 ■ Web: www.champlain.edu

College of Saint Joseph in Vermont
71 Clement Rd . . . . Rutland VT 05701 802-773-5900 776-5258*
*Fax: Admissions ■ TF Admissions: 877-270-9998 ■ Web: www.csj.edu

Goddard College 123 Pitkin Rd . . . . Plainfield VT 05667 802-454-8311 454-1029*
*Fax: Admissions ■ TF: 800-468-4888 ■ Web: goddard.edu

Green Mountain College One Brennan Cir. . . . . Poultney VT 05764 802-287-8000 287-8099
TF Admissions: 800-776-6675 ■ Web: www.greenmtn.edu

Johnson State College 337 College Hill . . . . Johnson VT 05656 802-635-2356 635-1230
TF: 800-635-2356 ■ Web: www.jsc.edu

Lyndon State College
1001 College Rd PO Box 919. . . . . Lyndonville VT 05851 802-626-6413 626-6335
TF: 800-225-1998 ■ Web: www.lyndonstate.edu

Marlboro College 2582 S Rd PO Box A . . . . Marlboro VT 05344 802-257-4333 451-7555
TF: 800-343-0049 ■ Web: www.marlboro.edu

Marlboro College Graduate Center
28 Vernon St Ste 120 . . . . .Brattleboro VT 05301 802-258-9200
Web: gradcenter.marlboro.edu

Middlebury College 131 S Main St . . . . Middlebury VT 05753 802-443-3000 443-2056*
*Fax: Admissions ■ TF: 877-214-3330 ■ Web: www.middlebury.edu

Norwich University 158 Harmon Dr . . . . Northfield VT 05663 802-485-2001 485-2032
TF: 800-468-6679 ■ Web: www.norwich.edu

Saint Michael's College One Winooski Pk. . . . . .Colchester VT 05439 802-654-2000 654-2906
TF: 800-762-8000 ■ Web: www.smcvt.edu

School for International Training
One Kipling Rd . . . . .Brattleboro VT 05302 802-257-7751
Web: www.sit.edu

Southern Vermont College 982 Manison Dr. . . . . Bennington VT 05201 802-442-5427 447-4695*
*Fax: Admissions ■ TF: 800-378-2782 ■ Web: www.svc.edu

University of Vermont 85 S Prospect St. . . . . .Burlington VT 05405 802-656-3131 656-8611
TF: 800-499-0113 ■ Web: www.uvm.edu

Virginia

Phone Fax

Bluefield College 3000 College Dr . . . . Bluefield VA 24605 276-326-3682 326-4395*
*Fax: Admissions ■ TF: 800-872-0175 ■ Web: www.bluefield.edu

Bridgewater College 402 E College St. . . . . .Bridgewater VA 22812 540-828-5375 828-5481
TF: 800-759-8328 ■ Web: www.bridgewater.edu

Christendom College 134 Christendom Dr . . . . Front Royal VA 22630 540-636-2900 636-1655*
*Fax: Admissions ■ TF: 800-877-5456 ■ Web: www.christendom.edu

Christopher Newport University
One University Pl . . . . .Newport News VA 23606 757-594-7015 594-7333*
*Fax: Admissions ■ TF Admissions: 800-333-4268 ■ Web: www.cnu.edu

College of William & Mary PO Box 8795 . . . . .Williamsburg VA 23187 757-221-4000 221-1242*
*Fax: Admissions ■ Web: www.wm.edu

Eastern Mennonite University 1200 Pk Rd . . . . . . .Harrisonburg VA 22802 540-432-4118 432-4444*
*Fax: Admissions ■ TF Admissions: 800-368-2665 ■ Web: www.emu.edu

Emory & Henry College PO Box 10 . . . . Emory VA 24327 276-944-4121 944-6935*
*Fax: Admissions ■ TF Admissions: 800-848-5493 ■ Web: www.ehc.edu

Ferrum College 215 Ferrum Mtn Rd . . . . .Ferrum VA 24088 540-365-2121 365-4266
TF: 800-868-9797 ■ Web: www.ferrum.edu

George Mason University
Prince William 10900 University Blvd . . . . Manassas VA 20110 703-993-8350 993-8378
Web: www.princewilliam.gmu.edu

Hampden-Sydney College PO Box 667 . . . . . . Hampden Sydney VA 23943 434-223-6120 223-6120*
*Fax: Admissions ■ TF Admissions: 800-755-0733 ■ Web: www.hsc.edu

Hampton University 100 E Queen St. . . . . Hampton VA 23668 757-727-5000
TF: 800-624-3341 ■ Web: www.hamptonu.edu

Hollins University PO BOX 9707. Roanoke VA 24020 540-362-6401 362-6218*
*Fax: Admissions ■ TF Admissions: 800-456-9595 ■ Web: www.hollins.edu

James Madison University 800 S Main St. . . . . .Harrisonburg VA 22807 540-568-6211 568-3332*
*Fax: Admissions ■ Web: www.jmu.edu

Liberty University 1971 University Blvd . . . . Lynchburg VA 24502 434-582-2000 542-2311*
*Fax Area Code: 800 ■ *Fax: Admissions ■ TF: 800-543-5317 ■ Web: www.liberty.edu

Longwood University 201 High St . . . . Farmville VA 23909 434-395-2060 395-2332*
*Fax: Admissions ■ TF: 800-281-4677 ■ Web: www.longwood.edu

Lynchburg College 1501 Lakeside Dr. . . . . .Lynchburg VA 24501 434-544-8100 544-8653*
*Fax: Admissions ■ TF: 800-426-8101 ■ Web: www.lynchburg.edu

Mary Baldwin College 318 Prospect St . . . . Staunton VA 24401 540-887-7019 887-7292*
*Fax: Admissions ■ TF Admissions: 800-468-2262 ■ Web: www.mbc.edu

Marymount University 2807 N Glebe Rd. . . . . .Arlington VA 22207 703-522-5600 522-0349
TF: 800-548-7638 ■ Web: www.marymount.edu

Norfolk State University 700 Pk Ave . . . . Norfolk VA 23504 757-823-8600 823-2078*
*Fax: Admissions ■ TF: 800-274-1821 ■ Web: www.nsu.edu

Phone Fax

Old Dominion University Rollins Hall . . . . Norfolk VA 23529 757-683-3685 683-3255*
*Fax: Admissions ■ TF: 800-348-7926 ■ Web: www.odu.edu

Peace Operations Training Institute Inc
1309 Jamestown Rd Ste 202 .Williamsburg VA 23185 757-253-6933
Web: peaceopstraining.org

Radford University 801 E Main St. Radford VA 24142 540-831-5371 831-5038*
*Fax: Admissions ■ TF Admissions: 800-890-4265 ■ Web: www.radford.edu

Randolph College 2500 Rivermont Ave. . . . . .Lynchburg VA 24503 434-947-8000 947-8996*
*Fax: Admissions ■ TF Admissions: 800-745-7692 ■ Web: www.randolphcollege.edu

Randolph-Macon College PO Box 5005. . . . . Ashland VA 23005 804-752-7200 752-4707*
*Fax: Admissions ■ TF: 800-888-1762 ■ Web: www.rmc.edu

Roanoke College 221 College Ln . . . . Salem VA 24153 540-375-2270 375-2267*
*Fax: Admissions ■ TF Admissions: 800-388-2276 ■ Web: www.roanoke.edu

Saint Paul's College 115 College Dr. . . . . .Lawrenceville VA 23868 434-848-3111 848-6407*
*Fax: Admissions ■ Web: www.saintpauls.edu

Shenandoah University 1460 University Dr. . . . . Winchester VA 22601 540-665-4581 *
*Fax: Admissions ■ TF: 800-432-2266 ■ Web: www.su.edu

Southern Virginia University
One University Hill Dr. . . . . .Buena Vista VA 24416 540-261-8400 261-8559
TF: 800-229-8420 ■ Web: www.svu.edu

Strayer University Alexandria
2730 Eisenhower Ave. . . . . .Alexandria VA 22314 888-311-0355 329-9602*
*Fax Area Code: 703 ■ *Fax: Admissions ■ TF: 888-311-0355 ■ Web: www.strayer.edu

Strayer University Arlington
2121 15th St N . . . . .Arlington VA 22201 703-892-5100 769-2677*
*Fax: Admissions ■ TF: 888-478-7293 ■ Web: www.strayer.edu

Strayer University Fredericksburg
150 Riverside Pkwy Ste 100 . . . . Fredericksburg VA 22406 540-374-4300 301-1711*
*Fax: Admissions ■ TF: 888-311-0355 ■ Web: www.strayer.edu

Strayer University Loudoun
45150 Russell Branch Pkwy Ste 200 . . . . .Ashburn VA 20147 703-729-8800 729-8820
Web: www.strayer.edu

Strayer University Manassas
9990 Battleview Pkwy. . . . . Manassas VA 20109 703-330-8400 330-8135*
*Fax: Admissions ■ Web: www.strayer.edu

Strayer University Woodbridge
13385 Minnieville Rd . . . . .Woodbridge VA 22192 703-878-2800
Web: www.strayer.edu

Sweet Briar College 134 Chappel Rd . . . . Sweet Briar VA 24595 434-381-6100 381-6152*
*Fax: Admissions ■ TF Admissions: 800-381-6142 ■ Web: www.sbc.edu

Swvhec PO Box 1987 . . . . .Abingdon VA 24212 276-619-4302
Web: www.swcenter.edu

Tabernacle Baptist Bible College & Theological Seminary
717 N Whitehurst Landing Rd. . . . . .Virginia Beach VA 23464 757-424-4673 424-3014*
*Fax: Admissions ■ Web: www.tbbcts.org

University of Mary Washington
1301 College Ave . . . . Fredericksburg VA 22401 540-654-2000 654-1857*
*Fax: Admissions ■ TF Admissions: 800-468-5614 ■ Web: www.umw.edu

University of Richmond
Westhampton College
28 Westhampton Way . . . . .University Of Richmond VA 23173 804-289-8000
TF: 800-700-1662 ■ Web: wc.richmond.edu

University of Virginia
Peabody Hall PO Box 400160. . . . . .Charlottesville VA 22903 434-982-3200 924-3587*
*Fax: Admissions ■ Web: www.virginia.edu

University of Virginia's College at Wise
One College Ave . . . . Wise VA 24293 276-328-0102 328-0251*
*Fax: Admissions ■ TF Admissions: 888-282-9324 ■ Web: www.uvawise.edu

Virginia Commonwealth University
910 W Franklin St. . . . . Richmond VA 23284 804-828-0100 828-1899
TF: 800-841-3638 ■ Web: www.vcu.edu

Virginia Intermont College 1013 Moore St. . . . . Bristol VA 24201 276-669-6101 466-7855*
*Fax: Admissions ■ Web: www.vic.edu

Virginia Military Institute
319 Letcher Ave . . . . Lexington VA 24450 540-464-7211 464-7746*
*Fax: Admissions ■ TF: 800-767-4207 ■ Web: www.vmi.edu

Virginia Polytechnic Institute & State University
112 Burruss Hall. . . . . Blacksburg VA 24061 540-231-6000 231-3242*
*Fax: Admissions ■ TF: 800-555-9292 ■ Web: www.vt.edu

Virginia State University One Hayden Dr . . . . .Petersburg VA 23806 804-524-5000 524-5055
TF Admissions: 800-871-7611 ■ Web: www.vsu.edu

Virginia Union University
1500 N Lombardy St. . . . . Richmond VA 23220 804-342-3570 342-3511*
*Fax: Admissions ■ TF: 800-368-3227 ■ Web: www.vuu.edu

Virginia University of Lynchburg - Community Development Corp
2058 Garfield Ave . . . . .Lynchburg VA 24501 434-528-5276
Web: vul.edu

Virginia Wesleyan College 1584 Wesleyan Dr . . . . Norfolk VA 23502 757-455-3200 461-5238*
*Fax: Admissions ■ TF: 800-737-8684 ■ Web: www.vwc.edu

Washington & Lee University
204 W Washington St. . . . . Lexington VA 24450 540-458-8710 458-8062*
*Fax: Admissions ■ TF: 800-221-3943 ■ Web: www.wlu.edu

Weldon Cooper Ctr-Public Service
2400 Old Ivy Rd . . . . .Charlottesville VA 22903 434-982-5522
Web: www.coopercenter.org

Zamorano 9300 Lee Hwy Ste G130. .Fairfax VA 22031 202-737-5580
Web: www.zamorano.edu

Washington

Phone Fax

Antioch University 2326 Sixth Ave . . . . Seattle WA 98121 206-441-5352 268-4242
TF: 888-268-4477 ■ Web: www.antiochsea.edu

Central Washington University
400 E University Way . . . . .Ellensburg WA 98926 509-963-1111 963-3022*
*Fax: Admissions ■ TF Admissions: 866-298-4968 ■ Web: www.cwu.edu

City University 11900 NE First St. .Bellevue WA 98005 425-637-1010
TF Admissions: 800-426-5596 ■ Web: www.cityu.edu

Digipen Institute of Technology
5001 150th Ave Ne. . . . . .Redmond WA 98052 425-558-0299
Web: www.digipen.edu

Eastern Washington University 526 Fifth St . . . . Cheney WA 99004 509-359-6200 359-6692*
*Fax: Admissions ■ Web: www.ewu.edu

Phone | Fax

Evergreen State College 2700 Evergreen Pkwy ....Olympia WA 98505 360-867-6000 867-5114
TF: 888-492-9480 ■ Web: www.evergreen.edu

Gonzaga University 502 E Boone Ave................Spokane WA 99258 509-323-6572 323-5780*
*Fax: Admissions ■ TF: 800-986-9585 ■ Web: www.gonzaga.edu

Heritage University 3240 Ft Rd ....Toppenish WA 98948 509-865-8500 865-8659*
*Fax: Admissions ■ TF: 888-272-6190 ■ Web: www.heritage.edu

Northwest University 5520 108th Ave NE ....Kirkland WA 98033 425-822-8266 889-5224*
*Fax: Admissions ■ TF Admissions: 800-669-3781 ■ Web: www.northwestu.edu

Pacific Lutheran University 1010 122nd St S..........Tacoma WA 98444 253-531-6900 536-5136*
*Fax: Admissions ■ TF: 800-274-6758 ■ Web: www.plu.edu

Saint Martin's University 5300 Pacific Ave SE...........Lacey WA 98503 360-438-4311 412-6189*
*Fax: Admissions ■ TF Admissions: 800-368-8803 ■ Web: www.stmartin.edu

Seattle Pacific University 3307 Third Ave W ....Seattle WA 98119 206-281-2000 281-2544*
*Fax: Admissions ■ TF: 800-366-3344 ■ Web: www.spu.edu

Seattle University 901 12th Ave ....Seattle WA 98122 206-296-6000 296-5656*
*Fax: Admissions ■ TF: 800-426-7123 ■ Web: www.seattleu.edu

University of Puget Sound 1500 N Warner St..........Tacoma WA 98416 253-879-3100
TF: 800-396-7191 ■ Web: www.pugetsound.edu

University of Washington 1410 NE Campus Pkwy ....Seattle WA 98195 206-543-2100 685-3655*
*Fax: Admissions ■ Web: www.washington.edu

Walla Walla University
204 S College Ave ....College Place WA 99324 509-527-2327 527-2397
TF: 800-541-8900 ■ Web: www.wallawalla.edu

Washington State University PO Box 641040.........Pullman WA 99164 509-335-3564 335-4902
TF: 888-468-6978 ■ Web: www.wsu.edu
Spokane 310 N Riverpoint Blvd PO Box 1495......Spokane WA 99210 509-358-7978 358-7538
TF: 800-233-3247 ■ Web: spokane.wsu.edu
Vancouver 14204 NE Salmon Creek Ave ....Vancouver WA 98686 360-546-9788
Web: www.vancouver.wsu.edu

Western Washington University 516 High St.......Bellingham WA 98225 360-650-3000 650-7369
Web: www.wwu.edu

Whitman College 345 Boyer Ave..................Walla Walla WA 99362 509-527-5111 527-4967*
*Fax: Admissions ■ TF Admissions: 877-462-9448 ■ Web: www.whitman.edu

Whitworth College 300 W Hawthorne Rd..........Spokane WA 99251 509-777-1000 777-3758*
*Fax: Admissions ■ TF Admissions: 800-533-4668 ■ Web: www.whitworth.edu

West Virginia

Phone | Fax

Alderson-Broaddus College
101 College Hill Rd CB 2003........................Philippi WV 26416 304-457-1700 457-6239*
*Fax: Admissions ■ TF Admissions: 800-263-1549 ■ Web: www.ab.edu

Bethany College One Main St......................Bethany WV 26032 304-829-7000 829-7142*
*Fax: Admissions ■ TF: 800-922-7611 ■ Web: www.bethanywv.edu

Bluefield State College 219 Rock St................Bluefield WV 24701 304-327-4000 325-7747*
*Fax: Admissions ■ TF: 800-654-7798 ■ Web: bluefieldstate.edu

Concord University PO Box 1000.....................Athens WV 24712 304-384-3115 384-3218*
*Fax: Admissions ■ TF: 800-344-6679 ■ Web: www.concord.edu

Davis & Elkins College 100 Campus Dr................Elkins WV 26241 304-637-1900 637-1800*
*Fax: Admissions ■ TF: 800-624-3157 ■ Web: dewv.edu

Fairmont State University 1201 Locust Ave..........Fairmont WV 26554 304-367-4892 367-4789*
*Fax: Admissions ■ TF Admissions: 800-641-5678 ■ Web: www.fairmontstate.edu

Glenville State College 200 High St ....Glenville WV 26351 304-462-7361 462-8619*
*Fax: Admissions ■ TF Admissions: 800-924-2010 ■ Web: www.glenville.edu

Marshall University One John Marshall Dr..........Huntington WV 25755 304-696-3170 696-3135*
*Fax: Admissions ■ TF: 800-642-3463 ■ Web: www.marshall.edu

Ohio Valley University One Campus View Dr ....Vienna WV 26105 304-865-6000 865-6175*
*Fax: Admissions ■ TF Admissions: 877-446-8668 ■ Web: www.ovu.edu

Salem International University 223 W Main St ....Salem WV 26426 304-326-1109
TF: 800-283-4562 ■ Web: www.salemu.edu

Shepherd University 301 N King St ....Shepherdstown WV 25443 304-876-5000 876-5165*
*Fax: Admissions ■ TF: 800-344-5231 ■ Web: www.shepherd.edu

University of Charleston
2300 MacCorkle Ave SE.........................Charleston WV 25304 304-357-4800 357-4715*
*Fax: Admissions ■ TF Admissions: 800-995-4682 ■ Web: www.ucwv.edu

West Virginia State University
Barron Dr Rt 25 E PO Box 1000.....................Institute WV 25112 304-766-3000 766-5182*
*Fax: Admissions ■ TF: 800-987-2112 ■ Web: www.wvstateu.edu

West Virginia University PO Box 6009 ....Morgantown WV 26506 304-293-2121 293-3080
TF: 800-344-9881 ■ Web: www.wvu.edu
Institute of Technology 405 Fayette Pk.........Montgomery WV 25136 304-442-1000
TF: 888-554-8324 ■ Web: www.wvutech.edu

West Virginia Wesleyan College
59 College Ave..............................Buckhannon WV 26201 304-473-8000 473-8108*
*Fax: Admissions ■ TF Admitting: 800-722-9933 ■ Web: www.wvwc.edu

Wheeling Jesuit University
316 Washington Ave.............................Wheeling WV 26003 304-243-2000 243-2397*
*Fax: Admissions ■ TF: 800-624-6992 ■ Web: www.wju.edu

Wisconsin

Phone | Fax

Alverno College PO Box 343922..................Milwaukee WI 53234 414-382-6100 382-6055
TF: 800-933-3401 ■ Web: www.alverno.edu

Bellin College of Nursing 3201 Eaton Rd...........Green Bay WI 54311 920-433-6699 433-1922
TF: 800-236-8707 ■ Web: www.bellincollege.edu

Beloit College 700 College St........................Beloit WI 53511 608-363-2500 363-2075*
*Fax: Admissions ■ TF Admissions: 800-331-4943 ■ Web: www.beloit.edu

Cardinal Stritch University
6801 N Yates Rd..............................Milwaukee WI 53217 414-410-4000
TF: 800-347-8822 ■ Web: www.stritch.edu

Carroll University 100 NE Ave.....................Waukesha WI 53186 262-547-1211 951-3037*
*Fax: Admissions ■ TF: 800-227-7655 ■ Web: www.carrollu.edu

Carthage College 2001 Alford Pk Dr................Kenosha WI 53140 262-551-8500 551-5762*
*Fax: Admissions ■ TF Admissions: 800-351-4058 ■ Web: www.carthage.edu

Columbia College of Nursing (CCON)
4425 N Port Washington Rd........................Glendale WI 53212 414-326-2330 326-2331
TF: 800-221-5573 ■ Web: www.ccon.edu

Concordia University Wisconsin
12800 N Lake Shore Dr ....Mequon WI 53097 262-243-5700 243-4545*
*Fax: Admissions ■ TF Admissions: 888-628-9472 ■ Web: www.cuw.edu

Phone | Fax

Edgewood College 1000 Edgewood College Dr........Madison WI 53711 608-663-2294 663-2214
TF: 800-444-4861 ■ Web: www.edgewood.edu

Immanuel Lutheran College Inc
501 Grover Rd ....Eau Claire WI 54701 715-836-6636
Web: ilc.edu

Lakeland College PO Box 359 ....Sheboygan WI 53082 920-565-2111 565-1215*
*Fax: Admissions ■ TF: 800-569-2166 ■ Web: www.lakeland.edu

Lawrence University 115 S Drew St.................Appleton WI 54911 920-832-7000 832-6782
TF: 888-959-2016 ■ Web: www.lawrence.edu

Maranatha Baptist Bible College
745 W Main St.................................Watertown WI 53094 920-206-2330 261-9109*
*Fax: Admissions ■ TF: 800-622-2947 ■ Web: mbu.edu/

Marquette University 1217 W Wisconsin Ave........Milwaukee WI 53233 414-288-7302 288-3764*
*Fax: Admissions ■ TF Admissions: 800-222-6544 ■ Web: www.marquette.edu

Milwaukee Institute of Art & Design
273 E Erie St..................................Milwaukee WI 53202 414-276-7889 291-8077*
*Fax: Admissions ■ TF: 888-749-6423 ■ Web: www.miad.edu

Milwaukee School of Engineering
1025 N Broadway St.............................Milwaukee WI 53202 414-277-6763 277-7475*
*Fax: Admissions ■ TF: 800-332-6763 ■ Web: www.msoe.edu

Mount Mary College
2900 N Menomonee River Pkwy....................Milwaukee WI 53222 414-256-1219 256-0180*
*Fax: Admissions ■ TF Admissions: 800-321-6265 ■ Web: www.mtmary.edu

Northland Baptist Bible College (NBBC)
W10085 Pike Plains Rd ....Dunbar WI 54119 715-324-6900 324-6133
TF: 800-425-9385 ■ Web: www.ni.edu

Northland College 1411 Ellis Ave...................Ashland WI 54806 715-682-1224 682-1258*
*Fax: Admissions ■ TF: 800-753-1840 ■ Web: www.northland.edu

Ripon College 300 Seward St PO Box 248...............Ripon WI 54971 800-947-4766 748-8335*
*Fax Area Code: 920 ■ *Fax: Admissions ■ TF Admissions: 800-947-4766 ■ Web: www.ripon.edu

Saint Norbert College 100 Grant St ....De Pere WI 54115 920-403-3005 403-4072*
*Fax: Admissions ■ TF Admissions: 800-236-4878 ■ Web: www.snc.edu

Silver Lake College 2406 S Alverno Rd ....Manitowoc WI 54220 920-686-6175 684-7082*
*Fax: Admissions ■ TF: 800-236-4752 ■ Web: www.sl.edu
Baraboo/Sauk County 1006 Connie Rd ....Baraboo WI 53913 608-355-5200 355-5291*
*Fax: Admissions ■ TF: 800-621-7440 ■ Web: www.baraboo.uwc.edu

University of Wisconsin
Eau Claire 105 Garfield Ave PO Box 4004........Eau Claire WI 54701 715-836-2637 836-2409*
*Fax: Admissions ■ TF: 800-473-2255 ■ Web: www.uwec.edu
Green Bay 2420 Nicolet Dr....................Green Bay WI 54311 920-465-2000 465-5754*
*Fax: Admissions ■ TF: 800-465-4329 ■ Web: www.uwgb.edu
La Crosse 1725 State St 115 Graff Main Hall......La Crosse WI 54601 608-785-8000 785-6695
TF: 800-382-2150 ■ Web: www.uwlax.edu
Madison 702 W Johnson St Ste 1101 ....Madison WI 53715 608-262-3961 262-7706*
*Fax: Admissions ■ Web: www.wisc.edu
Milwaukee PO Box 413 ....Milwaukee WI 53201 414-229-1122 229-6940*
*Fax: Admissions ■ Web: www.uwm.edu
Oshkosh 800 Algoma Blvd PO Box 2423.........Oshkosh WI 54903 920-424-0202 424-1207*
*Fax: Admissions ■ Web: www.uwosh.edu
Parkside 900 Wood Rd........................Kenosha WI 53141 262-595-2345 595-2008*
*Fax: Admissions ■ Web: www.uwp.edu
Platteville One University Plz ....Platteville WI 53818 608-342-1125 342-1122*
*Fax: Admissions ■ TF: 800-362-5515 ■ Web: www.uwplatt.edu
River Falls
410 S Third St B3 E Hathorn Hall ....River Falls WI 54022 715-425-3911 425-0698
TF: 800-852-5711 ■ Web: www.uwrf.edu
Stevens Point 2100 Main St...............Stevens Point WI 54481 715-346-0123 346-3296*
*Fax: Admissions ■ Web: www.uwsp.edu
Stout 802 S Broadway ....Menomonie WI 54751 715-232-1232 232-1667*
*Fax: Admissions ■ TF Admissions: 800-447-8688 ■ Web: www.uwstout.edu
Superior Belknap & Catlin PO Box 2000..........Superior WI 54880 715-394-8101 394-8407
TF: 877-345-3494 ■ Web: www.uwsuper.edu
Whitewater 800 W Main St..................Whitewater WI 53190 262-472-1440 472-1515*
*Fax: Admissions ■ Web: www.uww.edu

Viterbo University 900 Viterbo Dr.................La Crosse WI 54601 608-796-3000 796-3020*
*Fax: Admissions ■ TF: 800-848-3726 ■ Web: www.viterbo.edu

Wisconsin Lutheran College
8800 W Bluemound Rd............................Milwaukee WI 53226 414-443-8800 443-8514*
*Fax: Admissions ■ TF: 800-765-4977 ■ Web: www.wlc.edu

Wyoming

Phone | Fax

University of Wyoming
1000 E University Ave Dept 3435....................Laramie WY 82071 307-766-5160 766-4042*
*Fax: Admissions ■ TF Admissions: 800-342-5996 ■ Web: www.uwyo.edu

169 COLLEGES & UNIVERSITIES - GRADUATE & PROFESSIONAL SCHOOLS

Phone | Fax

American Public University System (AMU)
111 W Congress St...........................Charles Town WV 25414 304-724-3700
TF: 877-777-9081 ■ Web: www.amu.apus.edu

Kern Community College District
2100 Chester Ave..............................Bakersfield CA 93301 661-336-5100
Web: www.kccd.edu

169-1 Law Schools

Law schools listed here are approved by the American Bar Association.

Phone | Fax

Albany Law School of Union University (ALS)
80 New Scotland Ave ....Albany NY 12208 518-445-2311 445-2369
TF: 800-448-3500 ■ Web: www.albanylaw.edu

American University Washington College of Law
4801 Massachusetts Ave NW ....Washington DC 20016 202-274-4101 274-4107
TF: 800-995-6423 ■ Web: www.wcl.american.edu

	City	State	Zip	Phone	Fax
Appalachian School of Law 1169 Edgewater Dr.	Grundy	VA	24614	276-935-4349	935-8261
TF: 800-895-7411 ■ *Web:* www.asl.edu					
Arizona State University					
1151 S Forest Ave PO Box 870312	Tempe	AZ	85281	480-965-9011	727-6453
Web: www.asu.edu					
Sandra Day O'Connor College of Law					
PO Box 877906	Tempe	AZ	85287	480-965-6181	727-7930
TF: 855-278-5080 ■ *Web:* www.law.asu.edu					
Ave Maria University School of Law					
1025 Commons Cir	Naples	FL	34119	239-687-5300	
Web: www.avemarialaw.edu					
Barry University Dwayne O Andreas School of Law					
6441 E Colonial Dr	Orlando	FL	32807	321-206-5600	206-5662
Web: www.barry.edu					
Baylor University School of Law					
1114 S University Parks Dr 1 Bear Pl 97288	Waco	TX	76798	254-710-1911	710-2316
TF: 800-229-5678 ■ *Web:* baylor.edu					
Benjamin N Cardozo School of Law Yeshiva University					
55 Fifth Ave Brookdale Ctr	New York	NY	10003	212-790-0200	790-0256
TF: 800-232-5463 ■ *Web:* www.cardozo.yu.edu					
Boston College Law School 885 Centre St	Newton	MA	02459	617-552-8550	552-2615
TF: 800-321-2211 ■ *Web:* www.bc.edu					
Boston University School of Law					
765 Commonwealth Ave	Boston	MA	02215	617-353-3100	353-0578
TF: 800-321-2211 ■ *Web:* www.bu.edu/law					
Brooklyn Law School 250 Joralemon St	Brooklyn	NY	11201	718-780-7906	780-0395*
**Fax:* Admissions ■ *Web:* www.brooklaw.edu					
California Western School of Law					
225 Cedar St	San Diego	CA	92101	619-525-1401	615-1401
TF: 800-255-4252 ■ *Web:* www.cwsl.edu					
Campbell University Norman Adrian Wiggins School of Law					
113 Main St	Buies Creek	NC	27506	919-865-5991	893-1780*
**Fax Area Code:* 910 ■ *TF:* 800-334-4111 ■ *Web:* www.law.campbell.edu					
Capital University Law School					
303 E Broad St	Columbus	OH	43215	614-236-6500	236-6972
TF: 800-362-2779 ■ *Web:* www.law.capital.edu					
Case Western Reserve University School of Law					
11075 E Blvd	Cleveland	OH	44106	216-368-3600	368-1042*
**Fax:* Admissions ■ *TF:* 800-756-0036 ■ *Web:* law.case.edu					
Catholic University of America Columbus School of Law					
3600 John McCormack Rd NE	Washington	DC	20064	202-319-5140	319-4459
Web: www.law.edu					
Chapman University School of Law					
One University Dr Kennedy Hall	Orange	CA	92866	714-628-2500	628-2501*
**Fax:* Admissions ■ *Web:* www.chapman.edu					
Chicago-Kent College of Law Illinois Institute of Technology					
565 W Adams St	Chicago	IL	60661	312-906-5000	906-5280
Web: www.kentlaw.iit.edu					
City University of New York School of Law					
65-21 Main St	Flushing	NY	11367	718-340-4200	340-4435*
**Fax:* Admissions ■ *Web:* www.law.cuny.edu					
Cleveland State University Cleveland-Marshall College of Law					
1801 Euclid Ave LB 138	Cleveland	OH	44115	216-687-2344	687-6881
TF: 866-687-2304 ■ *Web:* www.law.csuohio.edu					
Columbia University School of Law					
435 W 116th St	New York	NY	10027	212-854-2640	854-1109
Web: www.law.columbia.edu					
Cornell Law School 226 Myron Taylor Hall	Ithaca	NY	14853	607-255-5141	255-7193
Web: www.lawschool.cornell.edu					
Creighton University School of Law					
2500 California Plz	Omaha	NE	68178	402-280-2872	280-3161
Web: law.creighton.edu					
DePaul University College of Law					
25 E Jackson Blvd	Chicago	IL	60604	312-362-8701	362-5280*
**Fax:* Admissions ■ *TF:* 800-445-8667 ■ *Web:* www.law.depaul.edu					
Drake University School of Law					
2507 University Ave	Des Moines	IA	50311	515-271-2824	271-1958
TF: 800-443-7253 ■ *Web:* www.law.drake.edu					
Duke University School of Law					
201 Science Dr PO Box 90362	Durham	NC	27708	919-613-7006	
TF: 888-529-2586 ■ *Web:* www.law.duke.edu					
Duquesne University School of Law					
600 Forbes Ave	Pittsburgh	PA	15282	412-396-6300	396-1073
TF: 800-732-8353 ■ *Web:* www.duq.edu					
Emory University School of Law					
1301 Clifton Rd	Atlanta	GA	30322	404-727-6816	727-6802*
**Fax:* Admissions ■ *Web:* www.law.emory.edu					
Florida Coastal School of Law					
8787 Bay Pine Rd	Jacksonville	FL	32256	904-680-7700	680-7692*
**Fax:* Admissions ■ *TF:* 877-210-2591 ■ *Web:* www.fcsl.edu					
Florida State University College of Law					
425 W Jefferson St	Tallahassee	FL	32306	850-644-3400	644-5487
Web: www.law.fsu.edu					
Fordham University School of Law					
140 W 62nd St	New York	NY	10023	212-636-6810	636-7984*
**Fax:* Admissions ■ *Web:* www.law.fordham.edu					
George Mason University School of Law					
3301 N Fairfax Dr New Bldg A01	Arlington	VA	22201	703-993-8000	993-8088
Web: www.law.gmu.edu					
George Washington University Law School					
2000 H St NW	Washington	DC	20052	202-994-6261	994-7230*
**Fax:* Admissions ■ *Web:* www.law.gwu.edu					
Georgetown University Law Ctr					
600 New Jersey Ave NW	Washington	DC	20001	202-662-9000	662-9439*
**Fax:* Admissions ■ *Web:* www.law.georgetown.edu					
Georgia State University College of Law					
140 Decatur St	Atlanta	GA	30303	404-651-2048	651-1244*
**Fax:* Admissions ■ *Web:* www.law.gsu.edu					
Golden Gate University School of Law					
536 Mission St	San Francisco	CA	94105	415-442-6600	442-6609
TF: 800-448-4968 ■ *Web:* law.ggu.edu					
Gonzaga University School of Law					
721 N Cincinnati St PO Box 3528	Spokane	WA	99220	509-313-3700	
TF Admissions: 800-793-1710 ■ *Web:* www.law.gonzaga.edu					
Hamline University School of Law					
1536 Hewitt Ave	Saint Paul	MN	55104	651-523-2800	523-3064*
**Fax:* Admissions ■ *TF:* 800-388-3688 ■ *Web:* hamline.edu/law/home					
Harvard Law School 1515 Massachusetts Ave	Cambridge	MA	02138	617-495-3109	
Web: www.law.harvard.edu					
Hofstra University School of Law					
121 Hofstra University	Hempstead	NY	11549	516-463-5916	463-5100*
**Fax:* Admissions ■ *TF:* 800-463-7872 ■ *Web:* law.hofstra.edu					
Howard University School of Law					
2900 Van Ness St NW	Washington	DC	20008	202-806-8000	806-8162*
**Fax:* Admissions ■ *TF:* 800-829-9019 ■ *Web:* www.law.howard.edu					
Indiana University School of Law Bloomington					
211 S Indiana Ave	Bloomington	IN	47405	812-855-7995	855-0555
Web: www.law.indiana.edu					
Indiana University School of Law Indianapolis					
Lawrence W Inlow Hall 530 W New York St	Indianapolis	IN	46202	317-274-8523	274-3955
Web: mckinneylaw.iu.edu					
John Marshall Law School 315 S Plymouth Ct	Chicago	IL	60604	312-427-2737	427-5136*
**Fax:* Admissions ■ *TF:* 800-285-2221 ■ *Web:* www.jmls.edu					
Lewis & Clark Law School					
10015 SW Terwilliger Blvd	Portland	OR	97219	503-768-6600	768-6793*
**Fax:* Admissions ■ *Web:* www.lclark.edu					
Louis D Brandeis School of Law at the Univeristy of Louisville					
2301 S Third St	Louisville	KY	40208	502-852-6358	852-0862
Web: www.law.louisville.edu					
Louisiana State University Paul M Hebert Law Ctr					
Paul M Hebert Law Ctr	Baton Rouge	LA	70803	225-578-8646	578-8647
Web: www.law.lsu.edu					
Loyola Marymount Law School					
919 Albany St	Los Angeles	CA	90015	213-736-1000	736-6523
Web: www.lls.edu					
Cudahy Library 1032 W Sheridan Rd	Chicago	IL	60660	773-508-2632	
Web: libraries.luc.edu/cudahy					
School of Law 25 E Pearson St	Chicago	IL	60611	312-915-7120	915-7201
TF: 866-596-7890 ■ *Web:* www.luc.edu					
Loyola University New Orleans College of Law					
7214 St Charles Ave PO Box 901	New Orleans	LA	70118	504-861-5550	
Web: www.law.loyno.edu					
Marquette University Law School					
1215 W Michigan St	Milwaukee	WI	53233	414-288-7090	288-6403
Web: www.law.marquette.edu					
Michigan State University College of Law					
368 Law College Bldg	East Lansing	MI	48824	517-432-6810	432-0098*
**Fax:* Admissions ■ *TF:* 800-844-9352 ■ *Web:* www.law.msu.edu					
Mississippi College School of Law					
151 E Griffith St	Jackson	MS	39201	601-925-7100	925-7166*
**Fax:* Admissions ■ *Web:* www.law.mc.edu					
New England School of Law 154 Stuart St	Boston	MA	02116	617-451-0010	457-3033*
**Fax:* Admissions ■ *Web:* www.nesl.edu					
New York Law School 185 W Broadway	New York	NY	10013	212-431-2100	966-1522
Web: www.nyls.edu					
New York University School of Law					
110 W Third St	New York	NY	10012	212-998-6100	995-4527*
**Fax:* Admissions ■ *TF:* 800-522-0925 ■ *Web:* www.law.nyu.edu					
North Carolina Central University School of Law					
1801 Fayetteville St	Durham	NC	27707	919-530-6333	530-6339
Web: www.nccu.edu					
Northeastern University School of Law					
400 Huntington Ave	Boston	MA	02115	617-373-2395	373-8865
TF: 800-732-3400 ■ *Web:* www.northeastern.edu/law					
Northern Illinois University College of Law					
Swen Parson Hall	DeKalb	IL	60115	815-753-9655	753-4501
TF: 800-892-3050 ■ *Web:* law.niu.edu/law					
Northwestern University School of Law					
357 E Chicago Ave	Chicago	IL	60611	312-503-3100	503-0178*
**Fax:* Admissions ■ *TF:* 800-229-2032 ■ *Web:* www.law.northwestern.edu					
Notre Dame Law School					
University of Notre Dame 103 Law School	Notre Dame	IN	46556	574-631-6627	631-4197
Web: www.law.nd.edu					
Nova Southeastern University Shepard Broad Law Ctr					
3305 College Ave	Fort Lauderdale	FL	33314	954-262-6100	262-3844*
**Fax:* Admissions ■ *TF:* 800-986-6529 ■ *Web:* www.nsulaw.nova.edu					
Ohio Northern University Claude W Pettit College of Law					
525 S Main St	Ada	OH	45810	419-772-2211	772-3042
TF: 877-452-9668 ■ *Web:* www.law.onu.edu					
Ohio State University Moritz College of Law					
55 W 12th Ave	Columbus	OH	43210	614-292-2631	292-1492
Web: www.moritzlaw.osu.edu					
Oklahoma City University School of Law					
2501 N Blackwelder Ave	Oklahoma City	OK	73106	405-208-5000	
TF: 800-230-3012 ■ *Web:* www.okcu.edu					
Pace University School of Law					
78 N Broadway	White Plains	NY	10603	914-422-4210	989-8714*
**Fax:* Admissions ■ *Web:* www.law.pace.edu					
Pennsylvania State University Dickinson School of Law					
150 S College St	Carlisle	PA	17013	717-240-5000	241-3503*
**Fax:* Admissions ■ *TF:* 800-840-1122 ■ *Web:* law.psu.edu/					
Pepperdine University School of Law					
24255 Pacific Coast Hwy	Malibu	CA	90263	310-506-4631	506-7668*
**Fax:* Admissions ■ *Web:* www.law.pepperdine.edu					
Quinnipiac University School of Law					
275 Mt Carmel Ave	Hamden	CT	06518	203-582-3400	582-3339
TF: 800-462-1944 ■ *Web:* www.quinnipiac.edu					
Roger Williams University Ralph R Papitto School of Law					
10 Metacom Ave	Bristol	RI	02809	401-254-4500	254-4516*
**Fax:* Admissions ■ *TF:* 800-633-2727 ■ *Web:* www.law.rwu.edu					
Camden 406 Penn St	Camden	NJ	08102	856-225-6104	225-6498*
**Fax:* Admissions ■ *Web:* www.camden.rutgers.edu					
School of Law Camden 217 N Fifth St	Camden	NJ	08102	856-225-6375	
TF: 800-466-7561 ■ *Web:* www.camlaw.rutgers.edu					
Saint Louis University School of Law					
3700 Lindell Blvd	Saint Louis	MO	63108	314-977-2766	977-3333
TF: 800-758-3678 ■ *Web:* www.slu.edu					

Phone | Fax

Saint Thomas University School of Law
16401 NW 37th Ave . . . Miami Gardens FL 33054 305-623-2310 623-2357*
Fax: Admissions ■ *TF:* 800-245-4569 ■ *Web:* stu.edu/law

Samford University Cumberland School of Law
800 Lakeshore Dr . . . Birmingham AL 35229 205-726-2400 726-2057
Web: cumberland.samford.edu/

Santa Clara University School of Law
500 El Camino Real . . . Santa Clara CA 95053 408-554-4361 554-5095*
Fax: Admissions ■ *Web:* www.scu.edu

Seattle University School of Law
901 12th Ave Sullivan Hall . . . Seattle WA 98122 206-398-4000 398-4058*
Fax: Admissions ■ *Web:* www.law.seattleu.edu

South Texas College of Law
1303 San Jacinto St . . . Houston TX 77002 713-659-8040 646-2906*
Fax: Admissions ■ *Web:* www.stcl.edu

Southern Illinois University School of Law
1209 W Chautauqua Rd . . . Carbondale IL 62901 618-453-8858 453-8921*
Fax: Admissions ■ *TF:* 800-739-9187 ■ *Web:* www.law.siu.edu

Southern Methodist University Dedman School of Law
3300 University Blvd . . . Dallas TX 75205 214-768-2550 768-2549*
Fax: Admissions ■ *TF:* 888-768-5291 ■ *Web:* www.law.smu.edu

Southern University Law Ctr
Two Roosevelt Steptoe Dr PO Box 9294 . . . Baton Rouge LA 70813 225-771-6297 771-2121
TF: 800-537-1135 ■ *Web:* www.sulc.edu

Southwestern University School of Law
3050 Wilshire Blvd . . . Los Angeles CA 90010 213-738-6700 738-6899
Web: www.swlaw.edu

Stanford University Law School
559 Nathan Abbott Way Crown Quadrangle . . . Stanford CA 94305 650-723-2465 723-0838*
Fax: Admissions ■ *Web:* www.law.stanford.edu

Suffolk University Law School 120 Tremont St . . . Boston MA 02108 617-573-8144 523-1367*
Fax: Admissions ■ *Web:* www.suffolk.edu

Syracuse University College of Law
950 Irving Ave . . . Syracuse NY 13244 315-443-1962 443-9568
Web: www.law.syr.edu

Temple University James E Beasley School of Law
1719 N Broad St . . . Philadelphia PA 19122 215-204-7861 204-1185
TF: 800-560-1428 ■ *Web:* www.law.temple.edu

Texas Tech University School of Law
1802 Hartford Ave . . . Lubbock TX 79409 806-742-3990 742-1629
Web: www.law.ttu.edu

Texas Wesleyan University School of Law
1515 Commerce St . . . Fort Worth TX 76102 817-212-4000 212-4141*
Fax: Admissions ■ *TF:* 800-733-9529 ■ *Web:* law.tamu.edu

Thomas Jefferson School of Law
1155 Island Ave . . . San Diego CA 92101 619-297-9700 961-1382
TF: 877-318-6901 ■ *Web:* www.tjsl.edu

Thomas M Cooley Law School 300 S Capitol Ave . . . Lansing MI 48933 517-371-5140 334-5752
Web: www.cooley.edu

Touro College Jacob D Fuchsberg Law Ctr
225 Eastview Dr . . . Central Islip NY 11722 631-421-2244 421-2675
Web: www.tourolaw.edu

Tulane University Law School
6329 Freret St Weinmann Hall . . . New Orleans LA 70118 504-865-5930 865-6710*
Fax: Admissions ■ *TF:* 800-328-6819 ■ *Web:* www.law.tulane.edu

University at Buffalo Law School
John Lord O'Brian Hall . . . Buffalo NY 14260 716-645-2052 645-2064
Web: www.law.buffalo.edu

University of Akron School of Law
150 University Ave . . . Akron OH 44325 330-972-7331 258-2343
TF: 800-655-4884 ■ *Web:* www.uakron.edu

University of Alabama PO Box 870132 . . . Tuscaloosa AL 35487 205-348-6010 348-9046*
Fax: Admissions ■ *TF Admissions:* 800-933-2262 ■ *Web:* www.ua.edu
School of Law 101 Paul W Bryant Dr E . . . Tuscaloosa AL 35401 205-348-5440 348-3971
Web: www.law.ua.edu

University of Arizona James E Rogers College of Law
1201 E Speedway Blvd PO Box 210176 . . . Tucson AZ 85721 520-621-1373 626-1839
Web: www.law.arizona.edu

University of Arkansas at Little Rock William H Bowen School of Law
1201 McMath Ave . . . Little Rock AR 72202 501-324-9903 324-9909
Web: ualr.edu

University of Arkansas School of Law
1045 W Maple St . . . Fayetteville AR 72701 479-575-5601 575-3937*
Fax: Admissions ■ *TF:* 800-295-9118 ■ *Web:* www.law.uark.edu

University of California Berkeley School of Law
2600 Bancroft Way 5 Boalt Hall . . . Berkeley CA 94720 510-642-2274 643-6222*
Fax: Admissions ■ *Web:* www.law.berkeley.edu

University of California Davis School of Law
400 Mrak Hall Dr . . . Davis CA 95616 530-752-0243 754-8371
Web: www.law.ucdavis.edu

University of California Hastings College of the Law
200 McAllister St . . . San Francisco CA 94102 415-565-4600 581-8946*
Fax: Admissions ■ *Web:* www.uchastings.edu

University of Chicago Law School
1111 E 60th St . . . Chicago IL 60637 773-702-9494 834-0942
Web: www.law.uchicago.edu

University of Cincinnati College of Law
2540 Clifton Ave . . . Cincinnati OH 45221 513-556-6805 556-2391
Web: www.law.uc.edu

University of Colorado School of Law
2450 Kittredge Loop Rd . . . Boulder CO 80309 303-492-8047 492-1757
Web: www.colorado.edu/law

University of Connecticut School of Law
45 Elizabeth St . . . Hartford CT 06105 860-570-5100 570-5153*
Fax: Admissions ■ *TF:* 800-633-7867 ■ *Web:* www.law.uconn.edu

University of Dayton School of Law
300 College Pk . . . Dayton OH 45469 937-229-3211 229-4194*
Fax: Admissions ■ *TF:* 800-837-7433 ■ *Web:* www.udayton.edu

University of Denver College of Law
2255 E Evans Ave . . . Denver CO 80208 303-871-6000 871-6378
Web: www.law.du.edu

University of Detroit Mercy School of Law
651 E Jefferson Ave . . . Detroit MI 48226 313-596-0264 *
Fax: Admissions ■ *TF:* 888-726-6921 ■ *Web:* www.law.udmercy.edu

University of Florida Fredric G Levin College of Law
2500 SW Second Ave . . . Gainesville FL 32611 352-273-0890 392-4087*
Fax: Admissions ■ *TF:* 877-429-1297 ■ *Web:* www.law.ufl.edu

University of Georgia School of Law
225 Herty Dr . . . Athens GA 30602 706-542-5191 542-5556
Web: www.law.uga.edu
Hamilton Library 2500 Campus Rd . . . Honolulu HI 96822 808-956-6911 956-7109
Web: www.manoa.hawaii.edu/
William S Richardson School of Law
2515 Dole St . . . Honolulu HI 96822 808-956-7966 956-6402*
Fax: Admissions ■ *Web:* www.hawaii.edu

University of Houston Law Ctr 100 Law Ctr . . . Houston TX 77204 713-743-2100 743-2194*
Fax: Admissions ■ *TF:* 800-252-9690 ■ *Web:* www.law.uh.edu

University of Idaho College of Law
Sixth & Rayburn St PO Box 442321 . . . Moscow ID 83844 208-885-4977 885-5709
TF: 888-884-3246 ■ *Web:* www.uidaho.edu

University of Illinois College of Law
504 E Pennsylvania Ave . . . Champaign IL 61820 217-333-0930 244-1478
TF: 800-369-6151 ■ *Web:* www.law.illinois.edu

University of Iowa College of Law
130 Byington Rd . . . Iowa City IA 52242 319-335-9034 335-9019
TF: 800-553-4692 ■ *Web:* www.law.uiowa.edu

University of Kansas School of Law
1535 W 15th St . . . Lawrence KS 66045 785-864-4550 864-5054
TF: 877-404-5823 ■ *Web:* www.law.ku.edu

University of Kentucky College of Law
620 S Limestone St . . . Lexington KY 40506 859-257-1678 323-1061
TF: 800-888-8189 ■ *Web:* www.law.uky.edu

University of Maine School of Law
246 Deering Ave . . . Portland ME 04102 207-780-4355 780-4239
Web: www.mainelaw.maine.edu

University of Memphis Cecil C Humphreys School of Law
3715 Central Ave . . . Memphis TN 38152 901-678-2421 678-5210
TF: 800-872-3728 ■ *Web:* www.memphis.edu

University of Miami School of Law
1311 Miller Dr . . . Coral Gables FL 33146 305-284-2339 284-3084*
Fax: Admissions ■ *Web:* www.law.miami.edu

University of Michigan Law School
625 S State St . . . Ann Arbor MI 48109 734-764-1358 647-3218*
Fax: Admissions ■ *Web:* www.law.umich.edu

University of Minnesota Law School
229 19th Ave S Walter F Mondale Hall . . . Minneapolis MN 55455 612-625-1000 626-1874*
Fax: Admissions ■ *Web:* www.law.umn.edu

University of Mississippi School of Law
301 Grove Loop PO Box 1848 . . . University MS 38677 662-915-6870 915-1289*
Fax: Admissions ■ *Web:* www.olemiss.edu

University of Missouri Columbia School of Law
203 Hulston Hall . . . Columbia MO 65211 573-882-6487 882-4984
Web: www.law.missouri.edu

University of Missouri Kansas City School of Law
500 E 52nd St . . . Kansas City MO 64110 816-235-1644 235-5276*
Fax: Admissions ■ *Web:* www.law.umkc.edu

University of Montana School of Law
32 Campus Dr . . . Missoula MT 59812 406-243-4311 243-2576*
Fax: Admissions ■ *Web:* www.umt.edu/law

University of Nebraska College of Law
1875 N 42nd St . . . Lincoln NE 68583 402-472-2161 472-5185
Web: www.unl.edu

University of Nevada Las Vegas William S Boyd School of Law
4505 Maryland Pkwy . . . Las Vegas NV 89154 702-895-3671 895-1095
Web: www.law.unlv.edu

University of New Mexico School of Law
1117 Stanford Dr NE . . . Albuquerque NM 87106 505-277-2146 277-0068

University of North Carolina School of Law
160 Ridge Rd . . . Chapel Hill NC 27599 919-962-5106 843-7939
Web: www.law.unc.edu

University of North Dakota School of Law
264 Centennial Dr Stop 9003 . . . Grand Forks ND 58202 701-777-2104
Web: law.und.edu

University of Oklahoma College of Law
300 Timberdell Rd Andrew M Coats Hall . . . Norman OK 73019 405-325-4699 325-7474
Web: www.law.ou.edu

University of Oregon School of Law
1515 Agate St . . . Eugene OR 97403 541-346-3852 346-1564
Web: www.law.uoregon.edu

University of Pennsylvania Law School
3400 Chestnut St . . . Philadelphia PA 19104 215-898-7483 573-2025
Web: www.law.upenn.edu

University of Pittsburgh School of Law
3900 Forbes Ave . . . Pittsburgh PA 15260 412-648-1400 648-2647
Web: www.law.pitt.edu

University of Richmond School of Law
28 W Hampton Way . . . University of Richmond VA 23173 804-289-8740 289-8992
Web: www.law.richmond.edu

University of Saint Thomas School of Law
1000 LaSalle Ave . . . Minneapolis MN 55403 651-962-4892 962-4876*
Fax: Admissions ■ *TF:* 800-328-6819 ■ *Web:* www.stthomas.edu

University of San Diego School of Law
5998 Alcala Pk . . . San Diego CA 92110 619-260-4528 260-2218*
Fax: Admissions ■ *TF:* 800-248-4873 ■ *Web:* www.sandiego.edu/usdlaw

University of San Francisco School of Law
2130 Fulton St . . . San Francisco CA 94117 415-422-6307 422-5442*
Fax: Admissions ■ *Web:* www.usfca.edu/law

University of South Carolina School of Law
701 S Main St . . . Columbia SC 29208 803-777-6605 777-7751*
Fax: Admissions ■ *Web:* www.law.sc.edu

University of South Dakota School of Law
414 E Clark St . . . Vermillion SD 57069 605-677-5443 677-5417
TF: 877-269-6837 ■ *Web:* www.usd.edu/law

University of Southern California Law School
699 Exposition Blvd . . . Los Angeles CA 90089 213-740-7331

University of Tennessee College of Law
1505 Cumberland Ave . . . Knoxville TN 37916 865-974-2521 974-6595
Web: www.law.utk.edu

				Phone	Fax

University of Texas School of Law
727 E Dean Keeton St ... Austin TX 78705 512-471-5151 471-6988
Web: www.utexas.edu/law

University of the District of Columbia David A Clarke School of Law
4200 Connecticut Ave NW ... Washington DC 20008 202-274-7341 274-5583
Web: www.law.udc.edu

University of the Pacific McGeorge School of Law
3200 Fifth Ave. ... Sacramento CA 95817 916-739-7105 739-7134*
**Fax:* Admissions ■ *Web:* www.mcgeorge.edu

University of Toledo College of Law
2801 W Bancroft MS 507 ... Toledo OH 43606 419-530-4131
Web: utoledo.edu/law

University of Utah SJ Quinney College of Law
332 South 1400 East Rm 101 ... Salt Lake City UT 84112 801-581-6833 581-6897
Web: www.law.utah.edu

University of Virginia School of Law
580 Massie Rd ... Charlottesville VA 22903 434-924-7354 924-7536
TF: 877-307-0158 ■ *Web:* www.law.virginia.edu

University of Washington School of Law
William H Gates Hall PO Box 353020 ... Seattle WA 98195 206-543-4078 543-5671
TF: 866-866-0158 ■ *Web:* www.law.washington.edu

University of Wisconsin Law School
975 Bascom Mall ... Madison WI 53706 608-262-2240 262-5485
TF: 866-301-1753 ■ *Web:* www.law.wisc.edu

University of Wyoming College of Law
1000 E University Ave Dept 3035 ... Laramie WY 82071 307-766-6416 766-6417
TF: 800-442-6757 ■ *Web:* www.uwyo.edu

Valparaiso University School of Law
651 College Ave ... Valparaiso IN 46383 219-465-7829 465-7808
TF: 888-825-7652 ■ *Web:* www.valpo.edu

Vanderbilt University Law School
131 21st Ave S ... Nashville TN 37203 615-322-2615 322-6631
Web: law.vanderbilt.edu

Vermont Law School
168 Chelsea St PO Box 96 ... South Royalton VT 05068 802-831-1239 763-7071
TF: 800-227-1395 ■ *Web:* www.vermontlaw.edu

Villanova University School of Law
299 N Spring Mill Rd ... Villanova PA 19085 610-519-7000 519-6291*
**Fax:* Admissions ■ *Web:* www1.villanova.edu

Wake Forest University School of Law
Worrell Professional Ctr
Wake Forest Rd ... Winston-Salem NC 27109 336-758-5435 758-3930*
**Fax:* Admissions ■ *Web:* www.law.wfu.edu

Washington & Lee University School of Law
Sydney Lewis Hall Fourth Fl ... Lexington VA 24450 540-458-8502 458-8586*
**Fax:* Admissions ■ *Web:* www.law.wlu.edu

Washington University School of Law
One Brookings Dr Anheuser-Busch Hall ... Saint Louis MO 63130 314-935-6400 935-8778*
**Fax:* Admissions ■ *Web:* law.wustl.edu

Wayne State University Law School
471 W Palmer St ... Detroit MI 48202 313-577-3937 993-8129*
**Fax:* Admissions ■ *Web:* www.law.wayne.edu

West Virginia University College of Law
PO Box 6130 ... Morgantown WV 26506 304-293-5301
Web: law.wvu.edu

Western New England College School of Law
1215 Wilbraham Rd ... Springfield MA 01119 413-782-3111
TF: 800-325-1122 ■ *Web:* www1.law.wne.edu/

Western State University College of Law
1111 N State College Blvd ... Fullerton CA 92831 714-459-1101 441-1748*
**Fax:* Admissions ■ *TF:* 800-978-4529 ■ *Web:* www.wsulaw.edu

Whittier Law School 3333 Harbor Blvd ... Costa Mesa CA 92626 714-444-4141 444-0250*
**Fax:* Admissions ■ *Web:* www.law.whittier.edu

Widener University Commonwealth Law School
3800 Vartan Way ... Harrisburg PA 17110 717-541-3900 541-3999
TF: 888-943-3637 ■ *Web:* www.law.widener.edu

Widener University School of Law Wilmington
4601 Concord Pk ... Wilmington DE 19803 302-477-2100 477-2224*
**Fax:* Admissions ■ *TF General:* 888-943-3637 ■ *Web:* www.law.widener.edu

Willamette University College of Law
245 Winter St SE ... Salem OR 97301 503-370-6282 370-6087*
**Fax:* Admissions ■ *TF:* 844-232-7228 ■ *Web:* www.willamette.edu/wucl

William & Mary Law School
613 S Henry St ... Williamsburg VA 23185 757-221-3800 221-3261*
**Fax:* Admissions ■ *Web:* www.wm.edu

William Mitchell College of Law
875 Summit Ave ... Saint Paul MN 55105 651-227-9171 290-6414
TF: 888-962-5529 ■ *Web:* www.wmitchell.edu

Yale Law School 127 Wall St ... New Haven CT 06511 203-432-4992 432-2112
Web: www.law.yale.edu

169-2 Medical Schools

Medical schools listed here are accredited, MD-granting members of the Association of American Medical Colleges. Accredited Canadian schools that do not offer classes in English are not included among these listings.

				Phone	Fax

Albert Einstein College of Medicine of Yeshiva University
1300 Morris Pk Ave ... Bronx NY 10461 718-430-2000
Web: www.einstein.yu.edu

Baylor College of Medicine
One Baylor Plz MS BCM365 ... Houston TX 77030 713-798-7766 798-1518
Web: www.bcm.edu

Boston University School of Medicine
715 Albany St ... Boston MA 02118 617-638-8000 638-5258*
**Fax:* Admissions ■ *Web:* www.bumc.bu.edu

Brody School of Medicine at East Carolina University
600 Moye Blvd ... Greenville NC 27834 252-744-1020 744-1926*
**Fax:* Admissions ■ *TF:* 800-722-3281 ■ *Web:* www.ecu.edu/med

Brown Medical School
222 Richmond St First Fl ... Providence RI 02912 401-863-2149 863-5096
Web: brown.edu

Case Western Reserve University School of Medicine (CWRU)
2109 Adelbert Rd ... Cleveland OH 44106 216-368-3450 368-6011
Web: casemed.case.edu

Cincinnati Children's Hospital Medical Ctr
3333 Burnet Ave ... Cincinnati OH 45229 513-636-4200 636-3733*
**Fax:* Admitting ■ *TF:* 800-344-2462 ■ *Web:* www.cincinnatichildrens.org

Creighton University School of Medicine
2500 California Plz ... Omaha NE 68178 402-280-2799 280-1241*
**Fax:* Admissions ■ *TF:* 800-325-4405 ■ *Web:* medschool.creighton.edu

Dalhousie University Faculty of Medicine
1459 Oxford St Rm C-132 ... Halifax NS B3H4H7 902-494-1874 494-6369*
**Fax:* Admissions ■ *Web:* www.medicine.dal.ca

Drexel University College of Medicine
2900 Queen Ln ... Philadelphia PA 19129 215-991-8202 843-1766
Web: www.drexelmed.edu

Duke University School of Medicine
Office of Admissions DUMC 3710 ... Durham NC 27710 919-684-2985 668-3714*
**Fax:* Admissions ■ *TF:* 888-275-3853 ■ *Web:* www.medschool.duke.edu

Eastern Virginia Medical School
700 W Olney Rd PO Box 1980 ... Norfolk VA 23501 757-446-5812 446-5896*
**Fax:* Admissions ■ *Web:* www.evms.edu

Emory University School of Medicine
1440 Clifton Rd NE Rm 115 ... Atlanta GA 30322 404-727-5660 727-5456*
**Fax:* Admissions ■ *Web:* www.med.emory.edu

Florida State University College of Medicine
1115 W Call St ... Tallahassee FL 32306 850-644-1855 645-2846*
**Fax:* Admissions ■ *Web:* www.med.fsu.edu

George Washington University School of Medicine & Health Sciences
2300 'I' St NW Ross Hall 716 ... Washington DC 20037 202-994-3506 994-1753
TF: 866-846-1107 ■ *Web:* smhs.gwu.edu

Georgetown University School of Medicine
3900 Reservoir Rd NW ... Washington DC 20057 202-687-1154 687-3079
Web: som.georgetown.edu

Harvard Medical School 25 Shattuck St ... Boston MA 02115 617-432-1550 432-3307*
**Fax:* Admissions ■ *TF:* 866-606-0573 ■ *Web:* www.hms.harvard.edu

Howard University College of Medicine
520 W St NW ... Washington DC 20059 202-806-6270 806-7934
Web: medicine.howard.edu

Indiana University School of Medicine
340 W Tenth St Ste 6200 ... Indianapolis IN 46202 317-274-8157
Web: www.medicine.iu.edu

Jefferson Medical College of Thomas Jefferson University
1015 Walnut St ... Philadelphia PA 19107 215-955-6983 955-5151
TF: 800-533-3669 ■ *Web:* jefferson.edu/university/jmc

Joan & Sanford Weill Medical College of Cornell University
445 E 69th St ... New York NY 10021 212-746-5454 746-8052*
**Fax:* Admissions ■ *TF:* 800-422-0711 ■ *Web:* weill.cornell.edu

Joan C Edwards School of Medicine at Marshall University
1600 Medical Ctr Dr ... Huntington WV 25701 304-691-1700 691-1726
TF: 877-691-1600 ■ *Web:* www.musom.marshall.edu

Johns Hopkins University School of Medicine
601 N Caroline St ... Baltimore MD 21205 410-955-3080 955-0826
Web: www.hopkinsmedicine.org

Keck School of Medicine of the University of Southern California
1975 Zonal Ave KAM 100 ... Los Angeles CA 90089 323-442-1100 442-2433*
**Fax:* Admissions ■ *Web:* www.usc.edu

Loma Linda University School of Medicine
11175 Campus St ... Loma Linda CA 92350 909-558-4467 558-0359
TF: 800-422-4558 ■ *Web:* www.llu.edu/llu/medicine

Louisiana State University School of Medicine in New Orleans
433 Bolivar St ... New Orleans LA 70112 504-568-6262 568-7701
TF: 844-503-7283 ■ *Web:* www.medschool.lsuhsc.edu

Louisiana State University School of Medicine in Shreveport
1501 Kings Hwy PO Box 33932 ... Shreveport LA 71130 318-675-5069 675-5000
TF: 800-337-3627 ■ *Web:* www.sh.lsuhsc.edu

Loyola University Chicago Stritch School of Medicine
2160 S First Ave Bldg 120 Rm 200 ... Maywood IL 60153 708-216-3229 216-9160*
**Fax:* Admissions ■ *Web:* www.meddean.luc.edu

Mayo Medical School 200 First St SW ... Rochester MN 55905 507-284-2316 284-2634
Web: www.mayo.edu/mms

McMaster University School of Medicine
1200 Main St W
Health Sciences Ctr Rm 3H46-B ... Hamilton ON L8N3Z5 905-525-9140 546-0349
Web: www.fhs.mcmaster.ca

Medical College of Georgia School of Medicine
1120 15th St ... Augusta GA 30912 706-721-0211 721-7279*
**Fax:* Admissions ■ *TF:* 800-736-2273 ■ *Web:* gru.edu

Medical College of Wisconsin
8701 Watertown Plank Rd ... Milwaukee WI 53226 414-456-8296 456-6506
Web: www.mcw.edu

Medical University of South Carolina College of Medicine (MUSC)
171 Ashley Ave ... Charleston SC 29425 843-792-1414
Web: academicdepartments.musc.edu

Meharry Medical College School of Medicine
1005 Doctor D B Todd Junior Blvd ... Nashville TN 37203 615-327-6111 327-6228
Web: www.mmc.edu

Michigan State University College of Human Medicine
965 Fee Rd Rm A-110 ... East Lansing MI 48824 517-353-1730 355-0342
Web: www.humanmedicine.msu.edu

Morehouse School of Medicine
720 Westview Dr SW ... Atlanta GA 30310 404-752-1500 752-1512*
**Fax:* Admissions ■ *Web:* www.msm.edu

New Jersey Medical School
185 S Orange Ave Rm C-653 PO Box 1709 ... Newark NJ 07101 973-972-4631 972-7986
Web: njms.rutgers.edu

New York Medical College Admin Bldg ... Valhalla NY 10595 914-594-4507 594-4976*
**Fax:* Admissions ■ *Web:* www.nymc.edu

New York University School of Medicine
560 First Ave ... New York NY 10016 212-263-7300 263-0720
TF: 855-698-2220 ■ *Web:* www.med.nyu.edu

Northeast Ohio Medical University
4209 State Rt 44 PO Box 95 ... Rootstown OH 44272 330-325-2511 325-8372*
**Fax:* Admissions ■ *TF:* 800-686-2511 ■ *Web:* neomed.edu

Phone | Fax

Northwestern University Feinberg School of Medicine
303 E Chicago Ave . . . . . Chicago IL 60611 312-503-8649 503-6978
Web: www.feinberg.northwestern.edu

Ohio State University College of Medicine & Public Health
370 W Ninth Ave 155 Meiling Hall . . . . . Columbus OH 43210 614-292-2220 247-7959*
**Fax:* Admitting ■ *Web:* www.medicine.osu.edu

Oregon Health & Science University
Bone Marrow Transplant Program (OHSU)
3181 SW Sam Jackson Pk Rd . . . . . Portland OR 97239 503-494-1617 494-7086
TF: 800-799-7233 ■ *Web:* www.ohsu.edu
School of Medicine
3181 SW Sam Jackson Pk Rd L-109 . . . . . Portland OR 97239 503-494-7800 494-4629
TF: 800-775-5460 ■ *Web:* www.ohsu.edu

Pennsylvania State University College of Medicine
500 University Dr Rm C1805 PO Box 850 . . . . . Hershey PA 17033 717-531-4395 531-6225*
**Fax:* Admissions ■ *Web:* www.pennstatehershey.org

Queen's University Faculty of Health Sciences
School of Medicine 68 Barrie St . . . . . Kingston ON K7L3N6 613-533-2542 533-3190
Web: healthsci.queensu.ca

Robert Wood Johnson Medical School
675 Hoes Ln . . . . . Piscataway NJ 08854 732-235-4576 235-5078
Web: www.rwjms.umdnj.edu

Rosalind Franklin University of Medicine & Science
3333 Green Bay Rd . . . . . North Chicago IL 60064 847-578-3205 578-3284
TF: 800-254-0460 ■ *Web:* www.rosalindfranklin.edu

Rush Medical College of Rush University
600 S Paulina St . . . . . Chicago IL 60612 888-352-7874 942-2333*
**Fax Area Code:* 312 ■ **Fax:* Admissions ■ *Web:* www.rushu.rush.edu

Saint Louis University School of Medicine
One North Grand Rm17 . . . . . Saint Louis MO 63103 800-758-3678 977-9825*
**Fax Area Code:* 314 ■ *TF:* 800-758-3678 ■ *Web:* www.slu.edu/colleges/med

Schulich School of Medicine & Dentistry
Western University . . . . . London ON N6A5C1 519-661-3459 661-3797
Web: www.schulich.uwo.ca

Southern Illinois University School of Medicine
520 N Fourth St PO Box 19670 . . . . . Springfield IL 62702 217-545-8000
TF: 800-342-5748 ■ *Web:* www.siumed.edu

Stanford University School of Medicine
291 Campus Dr Rm LK3C02 . . . . . Stanford CA 94305 650-725-3900 725-7368
Web: med.stanford.edu

State University of New York Downstate Medical Ctr
450 Clarkson Ave PO Box 60M . . . . . Brooklyn NY 11203 718-270-1000 270-7592
Web: www.downstate.edu

State University of New York Upstate Medical University
766 Irving Ave . . . . . Syracuse NY 13210 315-464-4570 464-8867
TF: 800-736-2171 ■ *Web:* www.upstate.edu

Stony Brook University Health Sciences Ctr School of Medicine
101 Nichols Rd
Health Sciences Ctr Level 4 Rm 158 . . . . . Stony Brook NY 11794 631-689-8333 444-6032*
**Fax:* Admissions ■ *Web:* www.hsc.stonybrook.edu/som

Temple University School of Medicine
3340 N Broad St SFC 427 . . . . . Philadelphia PA 19140 215-707-3656 707-6932
Web: www.temple.edu/medicine

Texas A & M University System Health Science Ctr
College of Medicine 8447 Hwy 47 3rd Fl . . . . . Bryan TX 77807 979-436-0237
Web: www.medicine.tamhsc.edu

Texas Tech University Health Sciences Ctr
Preston Smith Library of the Health Sciences
3601 Fourth St MS 7781 . . . . . Lubbock TX 79430 806-743-2200 743-2218
Web: www.ttuhsc.edu/libraries/guides/lubbockguide.aspx#welcome
School of Medicine 3601 Fourth St MS 6207 . . . . . Lubbock TX 79430 806-743-3000 743-3021
Web: www.ttuhsc.edu

Tufts University School of Medicine
136 Harrison Ave . . . . . Boston MA 02111 617-636-7000 636-3805
Web: www.tufts.edu

Tulane University School of Medicine
1555 Poydras St Ste 1000 . . . . . New Orleans LA 70118 504-988-5462
Web: tulane.edu

University at Buffalo School of Medicine & Biomedical Sciences
131 Biomedical Education Bldg . . . . . Buffalo NY 14214 716-829-3466 829-3849*
**Fax:* Admissions ■ *Web:* www.wings.buffalo.edu

University of Alberta Faculty of Medicine & Dentistry
2-45 Medical Sciences Bldg . . . . . Edmonton AB T6G2R3 780-492-6350 492-9531
Web: www.med.ualberta.ca

University of Arizona College of Medicine
1501 N Campbell Ave . . . . . Tucson AZ 85724 520-626-4555 626-6252
Web: www.medicine.arizona.edu

University of Arkansas for Medical Sciences
Bone Marrow Transplantation Ctr
4301 W Markham Ave Slot 816 . . . . . Little Rock AR 72205 501-686-8250 526-2273
Web: www.uams.edu
College of Medicine
4301 W Markham St Slot 551 . . . . . Little Rock AR 72205 501-686-5354 686-5873*
**Fax:* Admissions ■ *Web:* www.uams.edu/com

University of British Columbia Faculty of Medicine
317-2194 Health Sciences Mall . . . . . Vancouver BC V6T1Z3 604-822-2421 822-6061
Web: www.med.ubc.ca

University of Calgary Faculty of Medicine
3330 Hospital Dr NW . . . . . Calgary AB T2N4N1 403-220-7448
Web: cumming.ucalgary.ca/intranet

University of California Davis School of Medicine
4610 X St . . . . . Sacramento CA 95817 916-734-4800
TF: 855-221-4673

University of California Irvine School of Medicine
1001 Health Sciences Rd 252 Irvine Hall . . . . . Irvine CA 92697 949-824-6119
TF: 800-824-5388 ■ *Web:* www.som.uci.edu

University of California San Diego School of Medicine
9500 Gilman Dr MC 0602 . . . . . La Jolla CA 92093 858-534-0830 534-6573
Web: som.ucsd.edu

University of Chicago Pritzker School of Medicine
924 E 57th St . . . . . Chicago IL 60637 773-702-1939 702-2598

University of Cincinnati College of Medicine
231 Albert Sabin Way PO Box 670552 . . . . . Cincinnati OH 45267 513-558-5575 558-1100
Web: www.med.uc.edu

University of Connecticut School of Medicine
263 Farmington Ave Rm AG036 MC 3906 . . . . . Farmington CT 06030 860-679-2000 679-1899*
**Fax:* Admissions ■ *Web:* www.medicine.uchc.edu
Hamilton Library 2500 Campus Rd . . . . . Honolulu HI 96822 808-956-6911 956-7109
Web: www.manoa.hawaii.edu/

University of Hawaii at Manoa
John A Burns School of Medicine (JABSOM)
651 Ilalo St Medical Education Bldg . . . . . Honolulu HI 96813 808-692-1000 692-1251
Web: www.jabsom.hawaii.edu

University of Illinois College of Medicine
808 S Wood St Rm 165 . . . . . Chicago IL 60612 312-996-5635 996-6693*
**Fax:* Admissions ■ *Web:* www.uic.edu/depts/mcam

University of Iowa Roy J & Lucille A Carver College of Medicine
200 CMAB . . . . . Iowa City IA 52242 319-335-6707 335-8318
TF: 800-725-8460 ■ *Web:* www.medicine.uiowa.edu

University of Kentucky College of Medicine
Office of Medical Education MN 104 UKMC . . . . . Lexington KY 40536 859-323-6161 323-2076
TF: 800-273-8255 ■ *Web:* www.mc.uky.edu

University of Louisville School of Medicine
323 E Chestnut St Abell Bldg Rm 413 . . . . . Louisville KY 40202 502-852-5193 852-0302
TF: 800-334-8635 ■ *Web:* www.louisville.edu/medschool

University of Manitoba Faculty of Medicine
727 McDermot Ave Rm 260 . . . . . Winnipeg MB R3E3P5 204-789-3557 789-3928
Web: www.umanitoba.ca

University of Maryland School of Medicine
685 W Baltimore St
1-005 Bressler Research Bldg . . . . . Baltimore MD 21201 410-706-7478 706-0467*
**Fax:* Admissions ■ *Web:* www.medschool.umaryland.edu

University of Medicine & Dentistry of New Jersey
Graduate School of Biomedical Sciences (GSBS)
185 S Orange Ave MSB B640 . . . . . Newark NJ 07107 973-972-4511
Web: rbhs.rutgers.edu

University of Minnesota Medical School Twin Cities
420 Delaware St SE Mayo MC 293 . . . . . Minneapolis MN 55455 612-624-5100 626-4911
TF: 800-752-1000 ■ *Web:* www.health.umn.edu

University of Mississippi School of Medicine
2500 N State St . . . . . Jackson MS 39216 601-984-1080 984-1079
TF: 888-815-2005 ■ *Web:* www.umc.edu

University of Missouri-Kansas City School of Medicine
2411 Holmes St . . . . . Kansas City MO 64108 816-235-1111 235-5277
TF: 800-735-2466 ■ *Web:* med.umkc.edu

University of Nebraska School of Medicine
985527 Nebraska Medical Ctr . . . . . Omaha NE 68198 402-559-2259 559-6840
TF: 800-626-8431 ■ *Web:* www.unmc.edu

University of Nevada School of Medicine
1664 N Virginia St
Pennington Medical Education Bldg 357 . . . . . Reno NV 89557 775-784-6063 784-6194
Web: www.unr.edu

University of New Mexico School of Medicine
1 University of New Mexico . . . . . Albuquerque NM 87131 505-272-4766 925-6031
TF: 877-977-2263 ■ *Web:* hsc.unm.edu/som

University of North Dakota School of Medicine & Health Sciences
501 N Columbia Rd . . . . . Grand Forks ND 58203 701-777-5046 777-4942*
**Fax:* Admissions ■ *TF:* 800-225-5863 ■ *Web:* www.med.und.edu

University of Oklahoma College of Medicine
PO Box 26901 . . . . . Oklahoma City OK 73190 405-271-2265 271-3032
Web: www.oumedicine.com

University of Ottawa Faculty of Medicine
451 Smyth Rd . . . . . Ottawa ON K1H8M5 613-562-5700 562-5323
TF: 877-868-8292 ■ *Web:* www.uottawa.ca

University of Pittsburgh School of Medicine
3550 Terr St 518 Scaife Hall . . . . . Pittsburgh PA 15261 412-648-9891 648-8768*
**Fax:* Admissions ■ *Web:* www.medschool.pitt.edu

University of Rochester School of Medicine & Dentistry
601 Elmwood Ave . . . . . Rochester NY 14642 585-275-0017 756-5479*
**Fax:* Admissions ■ *TF:* 888-661-6162 ■ *Web:* www.urmc.rochester.edu/SMD

University of South Alabama College of Medicine
307 N University Blvd . . . . . Mobile AL 36688 251-460-6101 460-6278
Web: www.southalabama.edu

University of South Carolina School of Medicine
6439 Garners Ferry Rd . . . . . Columbia SC 29209 803-216-3300 733-3335
Web: www.med.sc.edu

University of South Dakota School of Medicine
414 E Clark St . . . . . Vermillion SD 57069 605-677-5233

University of South Florida College of Medicine (USF)
12901 Bruce B Downs Blvd . . . . . Tampa FL 33612 813-974-2229 974-4990
TF: 877-338-2577 ■ *Web:* health.usf.edu

University of Tennessee Health Science Ctr College of Medicine
920 Madison Ave . . . . . Memphis TN 38163 901-448-5529
Web: www.uthsc.edu

University of Texas Medical Branch
301 University Blvd . . . . . Galveston TX 77555 409-772-2618 747-2909*
**Fax:* Admissions ■ *TF:* 800-228-1841 ■ *Web:* www.utmb.edu

University of Texas Medical School at San Antonio
7703 Floyd Curl Dr . . . . . San Antonio TX 78229 210-567-4420 567-6962*
**Fax:* Admissions ■ *Web:* som.uthscsa.edu
Hematopoietic Cell Transplant Program
2201 Inwood Rd Second Fl . . . . . Dallas TX 75390 214-645-4673 645-6926
TF: 866-645-6455 ■ *Web:* www.utsouthwestern.edu

University of Texas Southwestern Medical Ctr Dallas
Southwestern Medical School
5323 Harry Hines Blvd . . . . . Dallas TX 75390 214-648-3111 648-3289
TF: 866-648-2455 ■ *Web:* utsouthwestern.edu/education/medical-school/

University of Toledo College of Medicine
2801 W Bancroft . . . . . Toledo OH 43606 419-530-4636 383-6602
TF: 800-586-5336 ■ *Web:* www.utoledo.edu

University of Toronto Faculty of Medicine
500 University Ave Second Fl . . . . . Toronto ON M5G1V7 416-978-6976 978-7144
Web: medicine.utoronto.ca

University of Utah School of Medicine
30 N 1900 E . . . . . Salt Lake City UT 84132 801-581-7201 585-3300
TF: 844-988-7284 ■ *Web:* medicine.utah.edu

	City	State	Zip	Phone	Fax
University of Vermont College of Medicine 89 Beaumont Ave E-126 Given Bldg *TF:* 800-571-0668 ■ *Web:* www.uvm.edu	Burlington	VT	05405	802-656-2156	656-8577
University of Virginia School of Medicine 1300 Jefferson Pk Ave PO Box 800793 *Web:* www.medicine.virginia.edu	Charlottesville	VA	22908	434-924-5571	982-2586
University of Washington School of Medicine A-300 Health Sciences Bldg PO Box 356340 *Web:* www.uwmedicine.org	Seattle	WA	98195	206-543-5560	616-3341
University of Wisconsin Medical School 750 Highland Ave Rm 2130 **Fax:* Admissions ■ *Web:* www.med.wisc.edu	Madison	WI	53705	608-263-4925	262-4226*
Vanderbilt University School of Medicine 215 Light Hall *TF:* 866-263-8263 ■ *Web:* medschool.vanderbilt.edu	Nashville	TN	37232	615-322-2145	343-8397
Virginia Commonwealth University School of Medicine 1101 E Marshall St PO Box 980565 **Fax:* Admissions ■ *TF:* 800-332-8813 ■ *Web:* www.medschool.vcu.edu	Richmond	VA	23298	804-828-9629	828-1246*
Wake Forest University School of Medicine Medical Ctr Blvd *TF:* 800-445-2255 ■ *Web:* www.wakehealth.edu	Winston-Salem	NC	27157	336-716-4264	716-9593
Washington University in Saint Louis School of Medicine 660 S Euclid Ave	Saint Louis	MO	63110	314-362-6858	
Wayne State University School of Medicine 540 E Canfield St 1310 Scott Hall **Fax:* Admitting ■ *Web:* home.med.wayne.edu	Detroit	MI	48201	313-577-1460	577-9420*
West Virginia University School of Medicine Medical Ctr Dr Health Sciences Ctr N Rm 1146 *TF:* 800-543-5650 ■ *Web:* www.hsc.wvu.edu/som	Morgantown	WV	26506	304-293-2408	293-7814
Wright State University Boonshoft School of Medicine 3640 Col Glenn Hwy **Fax:* Admissions ■ *TF:* 800-338-4057 ■ *Web:* medicine.wright.edu	Dayton	OH	45435	937-775-2934	775-3322*
Yale University School of Medicine 333 Cedar St *TF:* 877-925-3637 ■ *Web:* medicine.yale.edu	New Haven	CT	06510	203-785-2643	785-3234

169-3 Theological Schools

Theological schools listed here are members of the Association of Theological Schools (ATS), an organization of graduate schools in the U.S. and Canada that conduct post-baccalaureate professional and academic degree programs to educate persons for the practice of ministry and for teaching and research in the theological disciplines. Listings include ATS accredited member schools, candidates for accredited membership, and associate member schools.

	City	State	Zip	Phone	Fax
Acadia Divinity College 38 Highland Ave *TF:* 866-875-8975 ■ *Web:* www.acadiadiv.ca	Wolfville	NS	B4P2R6	902-585-2210	
American Baptist Seminary of the West 2606 Dwight Way *TF:* 800-799-7233 ■ *Web:* www.absw.edu	Berkeley	CA	94704	510-841-1905	841-2446
Anderson University 1100 E Fifth St **Fax:* Admissions ■ *TF Admissions:* 800-428-6414 ■ *Web:* www.anderson.edu	Anderson	IN	46012	765-649-9071	641-4091*
Andover Newton Theological School 210 Herrick Rd *TF:* 800-964-2687 ■ *Web:* www.ants.edu	Newton Centre	MA	02459	617-964-1100	965-9756
Andrews University Seventh-day Adventist Theological Seminary 4145 E Campus Cir Dr Andrews University *TF:* 800-253-2874 ■ *Web:* www.andrews.edu/sem	Berrien Springs	MI	49104	269-471-3537	471-6202
Aquinas Institute of Theology 23 S Spring Ave *TF:* 800-977-3869 ■ *Web:* www.ai.edu	Saint Louis	MO	63108	314-256-8800	256-8888
Asbury Theological Seminary 204 N Lexington Ave *TF:* 800-227-2879 ■ *Web:* www.asburyseminary.edu	Wilmore	KY	40390	859-858-3581	858-2248
Ashland Theological Seminary 910 Ctr St *Web:* www.ashland.edu	Ashland	OH	44805	419-289-5161	289-5969
Assemblies of God Theological Seminary 1435 N Glenstone Ave *TF:* 800-467-2487 ■ *Web:* www.agts.edu	Springfield	MO	65802	417-268-1000	268-1001
Associated Mennonite Biblical Seminary 3003 Benham Ave *TF:* 800-964-2627 ■ *Web:* www.ambs.edu	Elkhart	IN	46517	574-295-3726	
Athenaeum of Ohio 6616 Beechmont Ave *Web:* www.mtsm.org	Cincinnati	OH	45230	513-231-2223	231-3254
Atlantic School of Theology 660 Francklyn St *Web:* www.astheology.ns.ca	Halifax	NS	B3H3B5	902-423-6939	492-4048
Austin Presbyterian Theological Seminary 100 E 27th St *Web:* www.austinseminary.edu	Austin	TX	78705	512-472-6736	479-0738
Azusa Pacific University 901 E Alosta Ave PO Box 7000 *TF:* 800-825-5278 ■ *Web:* www.apu.edu	Azusa	CA	91702	626-969-3434	812-3096
Bangor Theological Seminary 159 State St *TF:* 800-287-6781 ■ *Web:* www.bts.edu	Portland	ME	04101	207-942-6781	990-1267
Baptist Missionary Assn Theological Seminary 1530 E Pine St *TF:* 800-259-5673 ■ *Web:* www.bmats.edu	Jacksonville	TX	75766	903-586-2501	586-0378
Baptist Theological Seminary at Richmond 8040 Villa Park Dr Ste 250 *TF:* 888-345-2877 ■ *Web:* www.btsr.edu	Richmond	VA	23227	804-355-8135	355-8182
Bethany Theological Seminary 615 National Rd W *TF:* 800-287-8822 ■ *Web:* www.bethanyseminary.edu	Richmond	IN	47374	765-983-1800	983-1840
Bethel Seminary 3949 Bethel Dr *TF:* 800-255-8706 ■ *Web:* seminary.bethel.edu	Saint Paul	MN	55112	651-638-6400	638-6002
Bexley Hall Seminary 583 Sheridan Ave *Web:* www.bexleyseabury.edu	Columbus	OH	43209	614-231-3095	231-3236
Biblical Theological Seminary 200 N Main St *TF:* 800-235-4021 ■ *Web:* www.biblical.edu	Hatfield	PA	19440	215-368-5000	368-2301
Biola University 13800 Biola Ave **Fax:* Admissions ■ *TF Admissions:* 800-652-4652 ■ *Web:* www.biola.edu	La Mirada	CA	90639	562-903-6000	903-4709*
Blessed John XXIII National Seminary 558 S Ave *Web:* www.blessedjohnxxiii.edu	Weston	MA	02493	781-899-5500	899-5500
Briercrest College & Seminary 510 College Dr *Web:* www.briercrest.ca	Caronport	SK	S0H0S0	306-756-3200	756-5500
Byzantine Catholic Seminary of SS Cyril & Methodius 3605 Perrysville Ave *Web:* www.bcs.edu	Pittsburgh	PA	15214	412-321-8383	321-9936
Calvin Theological Seminary 3233 Burton St SE *TF:* 800-388-6034 ■ *Web:* www.calvinseminary.edu	Grand Rapids	MI	49546	616-957-6036	957-8621
Campbell University 450 Leslie Campbell Ave PO Box 546 **Fax:* Admissions ■ *TF:* 800-334-4111 ■ *Web:* www.campbell.edu	Buies Creek	NC	27506	910-893-1290	893-1288*
Canadian Southern Baptist Seminary 200 Seminary View *TF:* 877-922-2727 ■ *Web:* www.csbs.ca	Cochrane	AB	T4C2G1	403-932-6622	932-7049
Carey Theological College 5920 Iona Dr *Web:* www.carey-edu.ca	Vancouver	BC	V6T1J6	604-224-4308	224-5014
Catholic Theological Union 5416 S Cornell Ave *Web:* www.ctu.edu	Chicago	IL	60615	773-324-8000	324-4360
Catholic University of America 620 Michigan Ave NE *Web:* www.cua.edu	Washington	DC	20064	202-319-5000	319-6533
Central Baptist Theological Seminary 6601 Monticello Rd **Fax Area Code:* 412 ■ *TF:* 800-677-2287 ■ *Web:* www.cbts.edu	Shawnee	KS	66226	913-667-5700	788-6510*
Christ The King Seminary 711 Knox Rd *Web:* www.cks.edu	East Aurora	NY	14052	716-652-8900	652-8903
Christian Theological Seminary 1000 W 42nd St *TF:* 800-585-0108 ■ *Web:* www.cts.edu	Indianapolis	IN	46208	317-924-1331	923-1961
Christian Witness Theological Seminary 1975 Concourse Dr **Fax Area Code:* 925 ■ *Web:* www.cwts.edu	San Jose	CA	95131	408-433-2280	676-5220*
Church Divinity School of the Pacific 2451 Ridge Rd *Web:* www.cdsp.edu	Berkeley	CA	94709	510-204-0700	644-0712
Cincinnati Christian University 2700 Glenway Ave *TF:* 800-949-4228 ■ *Web:* www.ccuniversity.edu	Cincinnati	OH	45204	513-244-8100	244-8140
Claremont School of Theology 1325 N College Ave **Fax:* Admissions ■ *TF:* 800-733-5181 ■ *Web:* www.cst.edu	Claremont	CA	91711	909-447-2500	447-6389*
Colgate Rochester Crozer Divinity School 1100 S Goodman St *TF:* 888-937-3732 ■ *Web:* www.crcds.edu	Rochester	NY	14620	585-271-1320	271-8013
Columbia International University 7435 Monticello Rd *TF:* 800-777-2227 ■ *Web:* www.ciu.edu	Columbia	SC	29203	803-754-4100	786-4209
Columbia Theological Seminary 701 S Columbia Dr *Web:* www.ctsnet.edu	Decatur	GA	30030	404-378-8821	377-9696
Concordia Lutheran Seminary 7040 Ada Blvd *Web:* www.concordiasem.ab.ca	Edmonton	AB	T5B4E3	780-474-1468	479-3067
Concordia Seminary 801 Seminary Pl *TF:* 800-822-9545 ■ *Web:* www.csl.edu	Saint Louis	MO	63105	314-505-7000	505-7001
Concordia Theological Seminary 6600 N Clinton St *TF:* 800-481-2155 ■ *Web:* www.ctsfw.edu	Fort Wayne	IN	46825	260-452-2100	452-2121
Cornerstone University 1001 E Beltline Ave NE **Fax:* Admissions ■ *TF Admissions:* 800-787-9778 ■ *Web:* www.cornerstone.edu	Grand Rapids	MI	49525	616-222-1426	222-1418*
Dallas Theological Seminary 3909 Swiss Ave **Fax Area Code:* 214 ■ *TF:* 800-992-0998 ■ *Web:* www.dts.edu	Dallas	TX	75204	800-387-9673	841-3664*
Denver Seminary 6399 S Santa Fe Dr *TF:* 800-922-3040 ■ *Web:* www.denverseminary.edu	Littleton	CO	80120	303-761-2482	761-8060
Dominican House of Studies 487 Michigan Ave NE *Web:* www.dhs.edu	Washington	DC	20017	202-529-5300	636-1700
Dominican School of Philosophy & Theology 2301 Vine St *TF:* 888-450-3778 ■ *Web:* www.dspt.edu	Berkeley	CA	94708	510-849-2030	849-1372
Drew University Theological School 36 Madison Ave *Web:* www.drew.edu	Madison	NJ	07940	973-408-3258	408-3068
Duke University Divinity School 407 Chapel Drive PO Box 90968 *TF:* 800-367-3853 ■ *Web:* www.divinity.duke.edu	Durham	NC	27708	919-660-3400	660-3473
Earlham School of Religion 228 College Ave *TF:* 800-432-1377 ■ *Web:* www.esr.earlham.edu	Richmond	IN	47374	765-983-1423	983-1688
Eastern Mennonite University 1200 Pk Rd **Fax:* Admissions ■ *TF Admissions:* 800-368-2665 ■ *Web:* www.emu.edu	Harrisonburg	VA	22802	540-432-4118	432-4444*
Ecumenical Theological Seminary (ETS) 2930 Woodward Ave *Web:* www.etseminary.org	Detroit	MI	48201	313-831-5200	831-1353
Eden Theological Seminary 475 E Lockwood Ave *TF:* 800-969-3627 ■ *Web:* www.eden.edu	Saint Louis	MO	63119	314-961-3627	918-2626
Episcopal Divinity School 99 Brattle St *TF:* 866-333-8742 ■ *Web:* www.eds.edu	Cambridge	MA	02138	617-868-3450	864-5385
Episcopal Theological Seminary of the Southwest (SSW) 501 E 32nd PO Box 2247 *TF:* 800-252-5400 ■ *Web:* www.ssw.edu	Austin	TX	78705	512-472-4133	472-3098
Erskine Theological Seminary 2 Washington St PO Box 338 *TF:* 888-359-4358 ■ *Web:* www.erskine.edu	Due West	SC	29639	864-379-8885	
Evangelical School of Theology 121 S College St *TF:* 800-532-5775 ■ *Web:* www.evangelical.edu	Myerstown	PA	17067	717-866-5775	866-4667

				Phone	Fax
Franciscan School of Theology					
1712 Euclid Ave	Berkeley	CA	94709	760-547-1800	547-1807
TF: 855-355-1550 ■ *Web:* www.fst.edu					
Fuller Theological Seminary					
135 N Oakland Ave	Pasadena	CA	91182	626-584-5200	795-8767
TF: 800-235-2222 ■ *Web:* www.fuller.edu					
Gardner-Webb University M Christopher White School of Divinity					
110 S Main St PO Box 997	Boiling Springs	NC	28017	704-406-4000	
Web: gardner-webb.edu					
General Theological Seminary 440 W 21st St	New York	NY	10011	212-243-5150	727-3907
TF: 888-487-5649 ■ *Web:* gts.edu					
George Fox Evangelical Seminary					
12753 SW 68th Ave	Portland	OR	97223	503-554-6150	554-6111
TF: 800-493-4937 ■ *Web:* www.georgefox.edu					
Golden Gate Baptist Theological Seminary					
201 Seminary Dr	Mill Valley	CA	94941	415-380-1300	380-1302
TF: 888-442-8701 ■ *Web:* www.ggbts.edu					
Gordon-Conwell Theological Seminary					
130 Essex St	South Hamilton	MA	01982	978-468-7111	468-6691
TF: 800-428-7329 ■ *Web:* www.gordonconwell.edu					
Grace Theological Seminary					
200 Seminary Dr	Winona Lake	IN	46590	574-372-5100	372-5113
TF: 800-544-7223 ■ *Web:* gts.grace.edu					
Graduate Theological Union 2400 Ridge Rd	Berkeley	CA	94709	510-649-2400	649-1730
TF: 800-826-4488 ■ *Web:* www.gtu.edu					
Harding University Graduate School of Religion					
915 E Market Ave	Searcy	AR	72143	501-279-4407	
TF: 800-477-4407 ■ *Web:* harding.edu/bible/faculty					
Hartford Seminary 77 Sherman St	Hartford	CT	06105	860-509-9500	509-9509*
**Fax:* Admissions ■ *TF:* 877-860-2255 ■ *Web:* www.hartsem.edu					
Hellenic College-Holy Cross School of Theology					
50 Goddard Ave	Brookline	MA	02445	617-731-3500	850-1460*
**Fax:* Admissions ■ *Web:* www.hchc.edu					
Hood Theological Seminary					
1810 Lutheran Synod Dr	Salisbury	NC	28144	704-636-7611	636-7699
Web: www.hoodseminary.edu					
Houston Graduate School of Theology					
2501 Central Pkwy	Houston	TX	77092	713-942-9505	942-9506
Web: www.hgst.edu					
Howard University School of Divinity					
1400 Shepherd St NE	Washington	DC	20017	202-806-0500	806-0711
TF: 800-822-6363 ■ *Web:* www.howard.edu					
Iliff School of Theology					
2201 S University Blvd	Denver	CO	80210	303-744-1287	777-0164
TF: 800-678-3360 ■ *Web:* www.iliff.edu					
Interdenominational Theological Ctr					
700 Martin Luther King Jr Dr	Atlanta	GA	30314	404-527-7700	527-0901
TF: 800-908-9946 ■ *Web:* www.itc.edu					
Jesuit School of Theology at Berkeley					
1735 LeRoy Ave	Berkeley	CA	94709	510-549-5000	841-8536
TF: 800-824-0122 ■ *Web:* www.scu.edu					
Kenrick-Glennon Seminary 5200 Glennon Dr	Saint Louis	MO	63119	314-792-6100	792-6500
Web: www.kenrick.edu					
Knox College 59 St George St	Toronto	ON	M5S2E6	416-978-4500	971-2133
Web: www.utoronto.ca					
La Sierra University 4500 Riverwalk Pkwy	Riverside	CA	92515	951-785-2000	785-2901
TF: 800-874-5587 ■ *Web:* www.lasierra.edu					
Lancaster Theological Seminary					
555 W James St	Lancaster	PA	17603	717-393-0654	393-4254
TF: 800-393-0654 ■ *Web:* www.lancasterseminary.edu					
Lexington Theological Seminary					
631 S Limestone St	Lexington	KY	40508	859-252-0361	281-6042
TF: 866-296-6087 ■ *Web:* www.lextheo.edu					
Lincoln Christian College Seminary					
100 Campus View Dr	Lincoln	IL	62656	217-732-3168	732-4078
TF: 888-522-5228 ■ *Web:* lincolnchristian.edu					
Lipscomb University 3901 Granny White Pk	Nashville	TN	37204	615-966-1000	966-1804*
**Fax:* Admissions ■ *TF:* 800-333-4358 ■ *Web:* www.lipscomb.edu					
Logos Evangelical Seminary 9358 Telstar Ave	El Monte	CA	91731	626-571-5110	571-5119
Web: www.logos-seminary.edu					
Louisville Presbyterian Theological Seminary					
1044 Alta Vista Rd	Louisville	KY	40205	502-895-3411	895-1096
TF: 800-264-1839 ■ *Web:* www.lpts.edu					
Luther Seminary 2481 Como Ave	Saint Paul	MN	55108	651-641-3456	641-3425
TF: 800-588-4373 ■ *Web:* www.luthersem.edu					
Lutheran School of Theology at Chicago					
1100 E 55th St	Chicago	IL	60615	773-256-0700	256-0782
TF: 800-635-1116 ■ *Web:* www.lstc.edu					
Lutheran Theological Seminary					
114 Seminary Crescent	Saskatoon	SK	S7N0X3	306-966-7850	966-7852
Web: www.usask.ca					
Lutheran Theological Seminary at Gettysburg					
61 Seminary Ridge	Gettysburg	PA	17325	717-334-6286	334-3469
TF: 800-658-8437 ■ *Web:* www.ltsg.edu					
Lutheran Theological Seminary at Philadelphia					
7301 Germantown Ave	Philadelphia	PA	19119	215-248-4616	248-4577
TF: 800-286-4616 ■ *Web:* www.ltsp.edu					
McCormick Theological Seminary					
5460 S University Ave	Chicago	IL	60615	773-947-6300	288-2612
TF: 800-228-4687 ■ *Web:* www.mccormick.edu					
Meadville Lombard Theological School					
5701 S Woodlawn Ave	Chicago	IL	60637	773-256-3000	327-7002*
**Fax Area Code:* 312 ■ *TF:* 800-848-0979 ■ *Web:* www.meadville.edu					
Memphis Theological Seminary 168 E Pkwy S	Memphis	TN	38104	901-458-8232	452-4051
Web: www.memphisseminary.edu					
Mennonite Brethren Biblical Seminary					
4824 E Butler Ave	Fresno	CA	93727	559-453-2000	251-7212
TF: 800-251-6227 ■ *Web:* seminary.fresno.edu					
Methodist Theological School in Ohio					
3081 Columbus Pk	Delaware	OH	43015	740-363-1146	362-3135
TF: 800-333-6876 ■ *Web:* www.mtso.edu					
Michigan Theological Seminary					
41550 E Ann Arbor Trail	Plymouth	MI	48170	734-207-9581	207-9582
TF: 800-356-6639 ■ *Web:* www.moody.edu					
Mid-America Reformed Seminary 229 Seminary Dr	Dyer	IN	46311	219-864-2400	864-2410
TF: 888-440-6277 ■ *Web:* www.midamerica.edu					
Midwestern Baptist Theological Seminary					
5001 N Oak Trafficway	Kansas City	MO	64118	816-414-3700	414-3799
TF: 877-414-3720 ■ *Web:* www.mbts.edu					
Moravian Theological Seminary 1200 Main St	Bethlehem	PA	18018	610-861-1516	861-1569
TF: 800-843-6541 ■ *Web:* www.moravianseminary.edu					
Mount Angel Seminary One Abbey Dr	Saint Benedict	OR	97373	503-845-3951	845-3126
Web: www.mountangelabbey.org					
Mount Saint Mary's University					
16300 Old Emmitsburg Rd	Emmitsburg	MD	21727	301-447-5214	447-5860*
**Fax:* Admissions ■ *TF Admissions:* 800-448-4347 ■ *Web:* www.msmary.edu					
Multnomah Bible College & Biblical Seminary					
8435 NE Glisan St	Portland	OR	97220	503-255-0332	254-1268
TF: 800-275-4672 ■ *Web:* www.multnomah.edu					
Nashotah House 2777 Mission Rd	Nashotah	WI	53058	262-646-6500	646-6504
TF: 800-627-4682 ■ *Web:* www.nashotah.edu					
Nazarene Theological Seminary					
1700 E Meyer Blvd	Kansas City	MO	64131	816-333-6254	333-6271
TF: 800-831-3011 ■ *Web:* www.nts.edu					
New Brunswick Theological Seminary					
17 Seminary Pl	New Brunswick	NJ	08901	732-247-5241	249-5412
TF: 800-445-6287 ■ *Web:* www.nbts.edu					
New Orleans Baptist Theological Seminary					
3939 Gentilly Blvd	New Orleans	LA	70126	504-282-4455	816-8023
TF: 800-662-8701 ■ *Web:* www.nobts.edu					
New York Theological Seminary					
475 Riverside Dr Ste 500	New York	NY	10115	212-870-1211	870-1236
Web: nyts.edu					
Newman Theological College (NTC) 10012-84 St	Edmonton	AB	T6A0B2	780-392-2450	462-4013
Web: www.newman.edu					
North Park Theological Seminary					
3225 W Foster Ave	Chicago	IL	60625	773-244-6210	244-6244
TF: 800-964-0101 ■ *Web:* www.northpark.edu					
Northern Seminary 660 E Butterfield Rd	Lombard	IL	60148	630-620-2180	620-2190
TF: 800-937-6287 ■ *Web:* www.seminary.edu					
Notre Dame Seminary					
2901 S Carrollton Ave	New Orleans	LA	70118	504-866-7426	866-3119
Web: nds.edu					
NYACK 350 N Highland Ave	Nyack	NY	10960	845-353-2020	
TF: 800-541-6891 ■ *Web:* nyack.edu					
Oakland City University					
138 N Lucretia St	Oakland City	IN	47660	812-749-4781	749-1433
TF: 800-737-5125 ■ *Web:* www.oak.edu					
Oblate School of Theology 285 Oblate Dr	San Antonio	TX	78216	210-341-1366	341-4519
Web: www.ost.edu					
Oral Roberts University 7777 S Lewis Ave	Tulsa	OK	74171	918-495-6161	495-6222*
**Fax:* Admissions ■ *TF:* 800-678-8876 ■ *Web:* www.oru.edu					
Pacific Lutheran Theological Seminary					
2770 Marin Ave	Berkeley	CA	94708	510-524-5264	524-2408
TF: 800-235-7587 ■ *Web:* www.plts.edu					
Pacific School of Religion 1798 Scenic Ave	Berkeley	CA	94709	510-848-0528	845-8948
TF: 800-999-0528 ■ *Web:* www.psr.edu					
Palmer Theological Seminary					
588 N Gulph Rd	King Of Prussia	PA	19406	610-896-5000	649-3834
TF: 800-220-3287 ■ *Web:* www.palmerseminary.edu					
Payne Theological Seminary					
1230 Wilberforce Clifton Rd	Wilberforce	OH	45384	937-376-2946	376-3330
TF: 888-816-8933 ■ *Web:* www.payne.edu					
Pentecostal Theological Seminary					
900 Walker St NE	Cleveland	TN	37311	423-478-1131	478-7711
TF: 800-228-9126 ■ *Web:* www.ptseminary.edu					
Phillips Theological Seminary 901 N Mingo Rd	Tulsa	OK	74116	918-610-8303	610-8404
TF: 800-843-4675 ■ *Web:* www.ptstulsa.edu					
Phoenix Seminary 4222 E Thomas Rd Ste 400	Phoenix	AZ	85018	602-850-8000	850-8080
TF: 888-443-1020 ■ *Web:* www.ps.edu					
Pittsburgh Theological Seminary					
616 N Highland Ave	Pittsburgh	PA	15206	412-362-5610	363-3260
TF: 800-451-4194 ■ *Web:* www.pts.edu					
Pontifical College Josephinum					
7625 N High St	Columbus	OH	43235	614-885-5585	885-2307
TF: 888-252-5812 ■ *Web:* www.pcj.edu					
Princeton Theological Seminary					
64 Mercer St	Princeton	NJ	08540	609-921-8300	924-2973
TF: 800-622-6767 ■ *Web:* www.ptsem.edu					
Protestant Episcopal Theological Seminary in Virginia					
3737 Seminary Rd	Alexandria	VA	22304	703-370-6600	370-6234
TF: 800-941-0083 ■ *Web:* www.vts.edu					
Providence College & Seminary					
10 College Crescent	Otterburne	MB	R0A1G0	204-433-7488	433-3046
TF: 800-668-7768 ■ *Web:* www.providenceuc.ca					
Queen's College Faculty of Theology					
210 Prince Philip Dr Ste 3000	Saint John's	NL	A1B3R6	709-753-0116	753-1214
TF: 877-753-0116 ■ *Web:* www.queenscollegemun.ca					
Queen's Theological College					
Theological Hall 99 University Ave Rm 212	Kingston	ON	K7L3N6	613-533-2110	533-6879
Web: www.queensu.ca					
Reformed Episcopal Seminary 826 Second Ave	Blue Bell	PA	19422	610-292-9852	292-9853
Web: www.reseminary.edu					
Reformed Presbyterian Theological Seminary					
7418 Penn Ave	Pittsburgh	PA	15208	412-731-6000	731-4834
Web: www.rpts.edu					
Reformed Theological Seminary					
5422 Clinton Blvd	Jackson	MS	39209	601-923-1600	923-1654
TF: 800-543-2703 ■ *Web:* www.rts.edu					
Regent College 5800 University Blvd	Vancouver	BC	V6T2E4	604-224-3245	224-3097
TF: 800-663-8664 ■ *Web:* www.regent-college.edu					
Regis College 15 St Mary St	Toronto	ON	M4Y2R5	416-922-5474	922-2898
Web: www.regiscollege.ca					

Phone Fax

Roberts Wesleyan College 2301 Westside Dr. Rochester NY 14624 585-594-6000 594-6371*
*Fax: Admissions ■ TF Admissions: 800-777-4792 ■ Web: www.roberts.edu

Sacred Heart School of Theology
7335 S Hwy 100 Franklin WI 53132 414-425-8300 529-6999
Web: shsst.edu/

Saint Bernard's School of Theology & Ministry
120 French Rd Rochester NY 14618 585-271-3657 271-2045
Web: www.stbernards.edu

Saint Charles Borromeo Seminary
100 E Wynnewood Rd Wynnewood PA 19096 610-667-3394
Web: www.scs.edu

Saint John Vianney Theological Seminary
1300 S Steele St Denver CO 80210 303-282-3427
Web: www.sjvdenver.org

Saint John's Seminary 5012 Seminary Rd Camarillo CA 93012 805-482-2755
Web: www.stjohnsem.edu

Saint Joseph's Seminary 201 Seminary Ave Yonkers NY 10704 914-968-6200 376-2019
Web: www.archny.org

Saint Mary Seminary & Graduate School of Theology
28700 Euclid Ave Wickliffe OH 44092 440-943-7600 943-7577
Web: www.stmarysem.edu

Saint Mary's Seminary & University
5400 Roland Ave. Baltimore MD 21210 410-864-4000 864-4278
Web: www.stmarys.edu

Saint Meinrad School of Theology
200 Hill Dr Saint Meinrad IN 47577 812-357-6611 357-6964
Web: www.saintmeinrad.edu

Saint Patrick's Seminary & University
320 Middlefield Rd Menlo Park CA 94025 650-325-5621 323-5447
Web: www.stpatricksseminary.org

Saint Paul School of Theology
5123 Truman Rd Kansas City MO 64127 800-825-0378 483-9605*
*Fax Area Code: 816 ■ TF: 800-825-0378 ■ Web: www.spst.edu

Saint Peter's Seminary 1040 Waterloo St N London ON N6A3Y1 519-432-1824 432-0964
Web: www.stpetersseminary.ca

Saint Tikhon's Orthodox Theological Seminary
St Tikhon's Rd PO Box 130 South Canaan PA 18459 570-561-1818 937-3100
Web: www.stots.edu

Saint Vincent de Paul Regional Seminary
10701 S Military Trl Boynton Beach FL 33436 561-732-4424 737-2205
Web: www.svdp.edu

Saint Vincent Seminary
300 Fraser Purchase Rd Latrobe PA 15650 724-532-6600 532-5052
Web: www.saintvincentseminary.edu

Samford University 800 Lakeshore Dr Birmingham AL 35229 205-726-3673 726-2171*
*Fax: Admissions ■ TF Admissions: 800-888-7218 ■ Web: www.samford.edu

San Francisco Theological Seminary
105 Seminary Rd San Anselmo CA 94960 415-451-2800 451-2851
TF: 800-447-8820 ■ Web: www.sfts.edu

Seminary of the Immaculate Conception
440 W Neck Rd Huntington NY 11743 631-423-0483 423-2346
Web: icseminary.edu

Seton Hall University Immaculate Conception Seminary
400 S Orange Ave South Orange NJ 07079 973-761-9575 761-9577
Web: www.shu.edu

Shaw University 118 E S St Raleigh NC 27601 919-546-8275 546-8271*
*Fax: Admissions ■ TF Admissions: 800-214-6683 ■ Web: www.shawu.edu

Sioux Falls Seminary 2100 S Summit Sioux Falls SD 57105 605-336-6588 335-9090
TF: 800-440-6227 ■ Web: www.sfseminary.edu

Southeastern Baptist Theological Seminary
120 S Wingate St Wake Forest NC 27587 919-556-3101
TF: 800-284-6317 ■ Web: www.sebts.edu

Southern Baptist Theological Seminary
2825 Lexington Rd Louisville KY 40280 502-897-4011 897-4723*
*Fax: Admitting ■ TF: 800-626-5525 ■ Web: www.sbts.edu

Southwestern Baptist Theological Seminary
PO Box 22740 Fort Worth TX 76122 817-923-1921 921-8758
TF: 877-467-9287 ■ Web: www.swbts.edu

SS Cyril & Methodius Seminary
3535 Indian Trl Orchard Lake MI 48324 248-683-0310 738-6735
Web: sscms.edu

Starr King School for the Ministry
2441 LeConte Ave. Berkeley CA 94709 510-845-6232 845-6273
TF: 866-727-4894 ■ Web: www.sksm.edu

Taylor University College & Seminary
11525 23rd Ave Edmonton AB T6J4T3 780-431-5200 436-9416
TF: 800-567-4988 ■ Web: www.taylor-edu.ca

Toronto School of Theology
47 Queen's Pk Crescent E Toronto ON M5S2C3 416-978-4039 978-7821
Web: www.tst.edu

Trinity Episcopal School for Ministry
311 11th St. Ambridge PA 15003 724-266-3838 266-4617
TF: 800-874-8754 ■ Web: tsm.edu

Trinity International University
2065 Half Day Rd Deerfield IL 60015 847-945-8800 317-8097
TF: 800-822-3225 ■ Web: www.tiu.edu

Trinity Lutheran Seminary 2199 E Main St Columbus OH 43209 614-235-4136 238-0263
TF: 866-610-8571 ■ Web: tlsohio.edu

Trinity Western University 7600 Glover Rd Langley BC V2Y1Y1 604-888-7511 513-2064*
*Fax: Admissions ■ TF: 888-468-6898 ■ Web: www.twu.ca

Tyndale University College & Seminary
25 Ballyconnor Ct. Toronto ON M2M4B3 416-226-6380 226-6746
TF: 877-896-3253 ■ Web: www.tyndale.ca

Union Theological Seminary 3041 Broadway New York NY 10027 212-662-7100 280-1416
TF: 800-251-9489 ■ Web: www.uts.columbia.edu

Union Theological Seminary & Presbyterian School of Christian Education
3401 Brook Rd Richmond VA 23227 804-355-0671
TF: 800-229-2990 ■ Web: upsem.edu

United Theological Seminary 4501 Denlinger Rd. Dayton OH 45426 937-529-2201
Web: www.united.edu

United Theological Seminary of the Twin Cities
3000 Fifth St NW New Brighton MN 55112 651-633-4311 633-4315
TF: 800-937-1316 ■ Web: www.unitedseminary-mn.org

Phone Fax

University of Dubuque Theological Seminary
2000 University Ave Dubuque IA 52001 563-589-3122 589-3110
TF: 800-369-8387 ■ Web: udts.dbq.edu

University of Saint Mary of the Lake Mundelein Seminary
1000 E Maple Ave. Mundelein IL 60060 847-566-6401 566-7330
Web: www.usml.edu

University of Saint Michael's College Faculty of Theology
81 St Mary St Toronto ON M5S1J4 416-926-1300 926-7276
Web: www.utoronto.ca

University of Saint Thomas School of Theology
9845 Memorial Dr Houston TX 77024 713-686-4345 683-8673
Web: www.stthom.edu

University of the South 735 University Ave. Sewanee TN 37383 931-598-1238 598-3248*
*Fax: Admissions ■ TF: 800-522-2234 ■ Web: www.sewanee.edu

Urshan Graduate School of Theology
704 Howder Shell Rd Florissant MO 63031 314-921-9290 921-9203
Web: www.ugst.edu

Vancouver School of Theology 6040 Iona Dr Vancouver BC V6T2E8 604-822-9031 822-9212
TF: 866-822-9031 ■ Web: www.vst.edu

Virginia Union University
1500 N Lombardy St. Richmond VA 23220 804-342-3570 342-3511*
*Fax: Admissions ■ TF: 800-368-3227 ■ Web: www.vuu.edu

Wartburg Theological Seminary
333 Wartburg Pl Dubuque IA 52003 563-589-0200 589-0333
TF: 800-225-5987 ■ Web: www.wartburgseminary.edu

Washington Baptist University
4302 Evergreen Ln Annandale VA 22003 703-333-5904 333-5906
Web: www.wbcs.edu

Washington Bible College/Capital Bible Seminary
6511 Princess Garden Pkwy Lanham MD 20706 301-552-1400 552-2775
TF: 877-793-7227 ■ Web: www.bible.edu

Washington Theological Union
6896 Laurel St NW Washington DC 20012 202-726-8800
Web: www.wtu.edu

Wesley Biblical Seminary 787 E Northside Dr Jackson MS 39206 601-366-8880 366-8832
Web: www.wbs.edu

Wesley Theological Seminary
4500 Massachusetts Ave NW Washington DC 20016 202-885-8600 885-8605
TF: 800-882-4987 ■ Web: wesleyseminary.edu

Western Seminary 5511 SE Hawthorne Blvd. Portland OR 97215 503-517-1800 517-1801
TF: 877-517-1800 ■ Web: www.westernseminary.edu

Western Theological Seminary 101 E 13th St Holland MI 49423 616-392-8555 392-7717
TF: 800-392-8554 ■ Web: www.westernsem.edu

Westminster Theological Seminary
2960 Church Rd Glenside PA 19038 215-887-5511 887-5404
TF: 800-373-0119 ■ Web: www.wts.edu

Westminster Theological Seminary in California
1725 Bear Vly Pkwy Escondido CA 92027 760-480-8474 480-0252
Web: www.wscal.edu

Winebrenner Theological Seminary
950 N Main St Findlay OH 45840 419-434-4200 434-4267
TF: 800-992-4987 ■ Web: www.winebrenner.edu

Yale Divinity School Admissions Office
409 Prospect St New Haven CT 06511 203-432-5360 777-6100
TF: 866-358-3806

170 COLLEGES & UNIVERSITIES - HISTORICALLY BLACK

Historically Black Colleges & Universities (HBCUs) are colleges or universities that were established before 1964 with the intention of serving the African-American community. (Prior to 1964, African-Americans were almost always excluded from higher education opportunities at the predominantly white colleges and universities.)

Phone Fax

Albany State University 504 College Dr Rd Albany GA 31705 229-430-4600 430-1614*

Allen University 1530 Harden St Columbia SC 29204 803-376-5700 376-5733*
*Fax: Mail Rm ■ TF: 877-625-5368 ■ Web: www.allenuniversity.edu

Benedict College 1600 Harden St. Columbia SC 29204 803-253-5000
TF: 800-868-6598 ■ Web: www.benedict.edu

Bennett College 900 E Washington St. Greensboro NC 27401 336-370-8624 517-2166*
*Fax: Admissions ■ TF Admissions: 800-413-5323 ■ Web: www.bennett.edu

Bethune-Cookman College
640 Dr Mary McLeod Bethune Blvd Daytona Beach FL 32114 386-481-2900 481-2601*
*Fax: Admissions ■ TF Admissions: 800-448-0228 ■ Web: www.cookman.edu

Bluefield State College 219 Rock St Bluefield WV 24701 304-327-4000 325-7747*
*Fax: Admissions ■ TF: 800-654-7798 ■ Web: bluefieldstate.edu

Bowie State University 14000 Jericho Pk Rd. Bowie MD 20715 301-860-4000 860-3518
TF: 877-772-6943 ■ Web: www.bowiestate.edu

Central State University
1400 Brush Row Rd PO Box 1004 Wilberforce OH 45384 937-376-6011 376-6648*
*Fax: Admissions ■ TF: 800-388-2781 ■ Web: www.centralstate.edu

Charles R Drew University of Medicine & Science
1731 E 120th St Los Angeles CA 90059 323-563-4800 563-4957*
*Fax: Admissions ■ Web: www.cdrewu.edu

Cheyney University of Pennsylvania
1837 University Cir PO Box 200 Cheyney PA 19319 610-399-2275 399-2099*
*Fax: Admissions ■ TF: 800-243-9639 ■ Web: www.cheyney.edu

Claflin University 400 Magnolia St Orangeburg SC 29115 803-535-5000 535-5385
TF: 800-922-1276 ■ Web: www.claflin.edu

Clark Atlanta University
223 James P Brawley Dr SW Atlanta GA 30314 404-880-8000 880-6174*
*Fax: Admissions ■ TF Admissions: 800-688-3228 ■ Web: www.cau.edu

Clinton Junior College 1029 Crawford Rd Rock Hill SC 29730 803-327-7402 328-6318*
*Fax: Admissions ■ TF: 877-837-9645

Coppin State University 2500 W N Ave Baltimore MD 21216 410-951-3600 523-7351*
*Fax: Admissions ■ TF Admissions: 800-635-3674 ■ Web: www.coppin.edu

Delaware State University 1200 N DuPont Hwy. Dover DE 19901 302-857-6351 857-6352*
*Fax: Admissions ■ TF Admissions: 800-845-2544 ■ Web: www.desu.edu

Elizabeth City State University
1704 Weeksville Rd Elizabeth City NC 27909 252-335-3400 335-3537*
*Fax: Admissions ■ TF Admissions: 800-347-3278 ■ Web: www.ecsu.edu

				Phone	Fax
Fayetteville State University 1200 Murchison Rd — *Fax: Admissions ■ *TF Admissions:* 800-222-2594 ■ *Web:* www.uncfsu.edu	Fayetteville	NC	28301	910-672-1371	672-1414*
Fisk University 1000 17th Ave N — *TF:* 888-702-0022 ■ *Web:* www.fisk.edu	Nashville	TN	37208	615-329-8500	329-8774
Florida Memorial University 15800 NW 42nd Ave — *TF:* 800-822-1362 ■ *Web:* www.fmuniv.edu	Miami Gardens	FL	33054	305-626-3600	
Fort Valley State University 1005 State University Dr — *Fax: Admissions ■ *TF:* 877-462-3878 ■ *Web:* www.fvsu.edu	Fort Valley	GA	31030	478-825-6211	825-6169*
Grambling State University 403 Main St — *TF:* 800-569-4714 ■ *Web:* www.gram.edu	Grambling	LA	71245	318-247-3811	
Hampton University 100 E Queen St — *TF:* 800-624-3341 ■ *Web:* www.hamptonu.edu	Hampton	VA	23668	757-727-5000	
Harris-Stowe State University 3026 Laclede Ave — *Web:* www.hssu.edu	Saint Louis	MO	63103	314-340-3366	340-3555
Hinds Community College 501 E Main St PO Box 1100 — *Fax: Admissions ■ *TF:* 800-446-3722 ■ *Web:* www.hindscc.edu	Raymond	MS	39154	601-857-5261	857-3539*
Howard University 2400 Sixth St NW — *Fax: Admissions ■ *TF:* 800-822-6363 ■ *Web:* www.howard.edu	Washington	DC	20059	202-806-6100	806-4465*
Huston-Tillotson University 900 Chicon St — *Fax: Admissions ■ *TF:* 877-487-8702 ■ *Web:* www.htu.edu	Austin	TX	78702	512-505-3000	505-3192*
Interdenominational Theological Ctr 700 Martin Luther King Jr Dr — *TF:* 800-908-9946 ■ *Web:* www.itc.edu	Atlanta	GA	30314	404-527-7700	527-0901
Jackson State University 1400 John R Lynch St — *Fax: Admissions ■ *TF:* 800-848-6817 ■ *Web:* www.jsums.edu	Jackson	MS	39217	601-979-2121	979-3445*
Jarvis Christian College PO Box 1470 — *Fax: Admissions ■ *Web:* www.jarvis.edu	Hawkins	TX	75765	903-769-5700	769-1282*
Johnson C Smith University 100 Beatties Ford Rd — *Fax: Admissions ■ *TF Admissions:* 800-782-7303 ■ *Web:* www.jcsu.edu	Charlotte	NC	28216	704-378-1000	378-1242*
Kentucky State University 400 E Main St — *Fax: Admissions ■ *TF Admissions:* 800-325-1716 ■ *Web:* www.kysu.edu	Frankfort	KY	40601	502-597-6000	597-5814*
Lane College 545 Ln Ave — *Fax: Admissions ■ *TF Admissions:* 800-960-7533 ■ *Web:* www.lanecollege.edu	Jackson	TN	38301	731-426-7500	426-7559*
Langston University 2013 Langston University PO Box 1500 — *Web:* www.lunet.edu	Langston	OK	73050	405-466-3237	466-3271
Lincoln University 820 Chestnut St B-7 Young Hall — *Fax: Admissions ■ *TF Admissions:* 800-521-5052 ■ *Web:* www.lincolnu.edu	Jefferson City	MO	65102	573-681-5599	681-5889*
Livingstone College 701 W Monroe St — *TF:* 800-835-3435 ■ *Web:* www.livingstone.edu	Salisbury	NC	28144	704-216-6963	216-6215
Meharry Medical College School of Medicine 1005 Doctor D B Todd Junior Blvd — *Web:* www.mmc.edu	Nashville	TN	37203	615-327-6111	327-6228
Miles College 5500 Myron Massey Blvd — *Fax: Admissions ■ *TF Admissions:* 800-445-0708 ■ *Web:* www.miles.edu	Fairfield	AL	35064	205-929-1000	929-1627*
Mississippi Valley State University 14000 Hwy 82 — *TF:* 800-844-6885 ■ *Web:* www.mvsu.edu	Itta Bena	MS	38941	662-254-9041	254-3759
Morehouse College 830 Westview Dr SW — *Fax: Admissions ■ *Web:* www.morehouse.edu	Atlanta	GA	30314	404-681-2800	572-3668*
Morehouse School of Medicine 720 Westview Dr SW — *Fax: Admissions ■ *Web:* www.msm.edu	Atlanta	GA	30310	404-752-1500	752-1512*
Morgan State University 1700 E Cold Spring Ln — *Fax: Admissions ■ *TF:* 800-319-4678 ■ *Web:* www.morgan.edu	Baltimore	MD	21251	443-885-3333	885-8260*
Morris College 100 W College St — *Fax: Admissions ■ *TF Admissions:* 866-853-1345 ■ *Web:* www.morris.edu	Sumter	SC	29150	803-934-3200	773-8241*
Norfolk State University 700 Pk Ave — *Fax: Admissions ■ *TF:* 800-274-1821 ■ *Web:* www.nsu.edu	Norfolk	VA	23504	757-823-8600	823-2078*
North Carolina A & T State University 1601 E Market St — *Fax: Admissions ■ *TF Admissions:* 800-443-8964 ■ *Web:* www.ncat.edu	Greensboro	NC	27411	336-334-7946	334-7478*
North Carolina Central University 1801 Fayetteville St — *Fax: Admissions ■ *TF Admissions:* 877-667-7533 ■ *Web:* www.nccu.edu	Durham	NC	27707	919-530-6100	530-7625*
Oakwood College 7000 Adventist Blvd — *Fax: Admissions ■ *TF:* 800-824-5312 ■ *Web:* www.oakwood.edu	Huntsville	AL	35896	256-726-7356	726-7154*
Paine College 1235 15th St — *Fax: Admissions ■ *TF:* 800-476-7703 ■ *Web:* www.paine.edu	Augusta	GA	30901	706-821-8200	821-8293*
Paul Quinn College 3837 Simpson Stuart Rd — *Fax: Admissions ■ *TF:* 800-433-3243 ■ *Web:* www.pqc.edu	Dallas	TX	75241	214-376-1000	*
Prairie View A & M University PO Box 519 — *Fax: Admissions ■ *TF:* 800-787-7826 ■ *Web:* www.pvamu.edu	Prairie View	TX	77446	936-857-2626	261-1079*
Rust College 150 Rust Ave — *Fax: Admissions ■ *TF:* 888-886-8492 ■ *Web:* www.rustcollege.edu	Holly Springs	MS	38635	662-252-8000	252-2258*
Saint Augustine's College 1315 Oakwood Ave — *Fax: Admissions ■ *TF Admissions:* 800-948-1126 ■ *Web:* www.st-aug.edu	Raleigh	NC	27610	919-516-4016	516-5805*
Saint Paul's College 115 College Dr — *Fax: Admissions ■ *Web:* www.saintpauls.edu	Lawrenceville	VA	23868	434-848-3111	848-6407*
Selma University 1501 Lapsley St — *Web:* selmauniversity.org	Selma	AL	36701	334-872-2533	872-7746
Shaw University 118 E S St — *Fax: Admissions ■ *TF Admissions:* 800-214-6683 ■ *Web:* www.shawu.edu	Raleigh	NC	27601	919-546-8275	546-8271*
Shelton State Community College 9500 Old Greensboro Rd — *Fax: Admissions ■ *Web:* www.sheltonstate.edu	Tuscaloosa	AL	35405	205-391-2211	391-3910*
Shorter College 604 N Locust St	North Little Rock	AR	72114	501-374-6305	374-9333*
South Carolina State University 300 College St NE PO Box 7127 — *TF Admissions:* 800-260-5956 ■ *Web:* www.scsu.edu	Orangeburg	SC	29117	803-536-7000	536-8990
Southern University & A & M College 156 Elton C Harrison Dr PO Box 9757 — *Fax: Admissions ■ *TF Admissions:* 800-256-1531 ■ *Web:* www.subr.edu	Baton Rouge	LA	70813	225-771-5180	771-4762*
Southwestern Christian College PO Box 10 — *TF:* 800-925-9357 ■ *Web:* www.swcc.edu	Terrell	TX	75160	972-524-3341	563-7133
Spelman College 350 Spelman Ln SW — *Fax: Admissions ■ *TF Admissions:* 800-982-2411 ■ *Web:* www.spelman.edu	Atlanta	GA	30314	404-681-3643	270-5201*
Stillman College 3601 Stillman Blvd — *TF:* 800-841-5722 ■ *Web:* www.stillman.edu	Tuscaloosa	AL	35401	205-349-4240	366-8941
Tennessee State University 3500 John A Merritt Blvd PO Box 9609 — *TF Admissions:* 888-463-6878 ■ *Web:* www.tnstate.edu	Nashville	TN	37209	615-963-5000	963-5108
Texas College 2404 N Grand Ave — *Fax: Admissions ■ *TF:* 800-306-6299 ■ *Web:* www.texascollege.edu	Tyler	TX	75702	903-593-8311	593-0588*
Texas Southern University 3100 Cleburne St — *TF:* 800-252-5400 ■ *Web:* www.tsu.edu	Houston	TX	77004	713-313-7011	313-1859
Tougaloo College 500 W County Line Rd — *Fax: Admissions ■ *TF Admissions:* 888-424-2566 ■ *Web:* www.tougaloo.edu	Tougaloo	MS	39174	601-977-7700	977-4501*
Trenholm State Technical College 1225 Air Base Blvd — *TF:* 800-917-2081 ■ *Web:* www.trenholmstate.edu/	Montgomery	AL	36108	334-420-4200	420-4206
Tuskegee University 1200 W Montgomery Rd — *Fax: Admissions ■ *TF Admissions:* 800-622-6531 ■ *Web:* www.tuskegee.edu	Tuskegee	AL	36088	334-727-8011	727-5750*
University of the District of Columbia 4200 Connecticut Ave NW — *Web:* www.udc.edu	Washington	DC	20008	202-274-5000	274-5552
Virginia State University One Hayden Dr — *TF Admissions:* 800-871-7611 ■ *Web:* www.vsu.edu	Petersburg	VA	23806	804-524-5000	524-5055
Virginia Union University 1500 N Lombardy St — *Fax: Admissions ■ *TF:* 800-368-3227 ■ *Web:* www.vuu.edu	Richmond	VA	23220	804-342-3570	342-3511*
Voorhees College 213 Wiggins Dr PO Box 678 — *TF Admissions:* 800-446-6250 ■ *Web:* www.voorhees.edu	Denmark	SC	29042	803-780-1234	753-9077
West Virginia State University Barron Dr Rt 25 E PO Box 1000 — *Fax: Admissions ■ *TF:* 800-987-2112 ■ *Web:* www.wvstateu.edu	Institute	WV	25112	304-766-3000	766-5182*
Wilberforce University 1055 N Bickett Rd PO Box 1001 — *Fax: Admissions ■ *TF Admissions:* 800-367-8568 ■ *Web:* www.wilberforce.edu	Wilberforce	OH	45384	937-376-2911	376-4751*
Wiley College 711 Wiley Ave — *Fax: Admissions ■ *TF Admissions:* 800-658-6889 ■ *Web:* www.wileyc.edu	Marshall	TX	75670	903-927-3300	927-3366*
Winston-Salem State University 601 S ML King Jr Dr 206 Thompson Ctr — *Fax: Admissions ■ *TF Admissions:* 800-257-4052 ■ *Web:* www.wssu.edu	Winston-Salem	NC	27110	336-750-2000	750-2079*
Xavier University of Louisiana 1 Drexel Dr — *TF:* 877-520-7388 ■ *Web:* www.xula.edu	New Orleans	LA	70125	504-486-7411	520-7922

171 COLLEGES & UNIVERSITIES - JESUIT

The institutions listed here are members of the Association of Jesuit Colleges & Universities.

				Phone	Fax
Boston College 140 Commonwealth Ave — *TF:* 800-360-2522 ■ *Web:* www.bc.edu	Chestnut Hill	MA	02467	617-552-3100	552-0798
Canisius College 2001 Main St — *Fax: Admissions ■ *TF:* 800-843-1517 ■ *Web:* www.canisius.edu	Buffalo	NY	14208	716-888-2200	888-3230*
College of the Holy Cross 1 College St — *TF:* 800-442-2421 ■ *Web:* www.holycross.edu	Worcester	MA	01610	508-793-2011	793-3888
Creighton University 2500 California Plz — *Fax: Admissions ■ *TF:* 800-282-5835 ■ *Web:* www.creighton.edu	Omaha	NE	68178	402-280-2700	280-2685*
Fairfield University 1073 N Benson Rd — *Fax: Admissions ■ *Web:* www.fairfield.edu	Fairfield	CT	06824	203-254-4000	254-4199*
College at Lincoln Ctr 113 W 60th St — *TF:* 800-367-3426 ■ *Web:* www.fordham.edu	New York	NY	10023	212-636-6710	636-7002
Georgetown University 37th & 'O' Sts NW — *Web:* www.georgetown.edu	Washington	DC	20057	202-687-3600	687-5084
Gonzaga University 502 E Boone Ave — *Fax: Admissions ■ *TF:* 800-986-9585 ■ *Web:* www.gonzaga.edu	Spokane	WA	99258	509-323-6572	323-5780*
John Carroll University 20700 N Pk Blvd — *Fax: Admissions ■ *TF:* 888-335-6800 ■ *Web:* www.jcu.edu	Cleveland	OH	44118	216-397-1886	397-4981*
Le Moyne College 1419 Salt Springs Rd — *Fax: Admissions ■ *TF Admissions:* 800-333-4733 ■ *Web:* www.lemoyne.edu	Syracuse	NY	13214	315-445-4100	445-4711*
Loyola College 4501 N Charles St — *Fax: Admissions ■ *TF:* 800-221-9107 ■ *Web:* www.loyola.edu	Baltimore	MD	21210	410-617-5012	617-2176*
Loyola Marymount University One LMU Dr — *TF:* 800-568-4636 ■ *Web:* www.lmu.edu	Los Angeles	CA	90045	310-338-2700	338-2797
Monroe Library 6363 St Charles Ave — *Web:* library.loyno.edu	New Orleans	LA	70118	504-864-7111	864-7247
Loyola University					
New Orleans 6363 St Charles Ave CB 18 — *Fax: Admissions ■ *TF Admissions:* 800-456-9652 ■ *Web:* www.loyno.edu	New Orleans	LA	70118	504-865-3240	865-3383*
Cudahy Library 1032 W Sheridan Rd — *Web:* libraries.luc.edu/cudahy	Chicago	IL	60660	773-508-2632	
Lake Shore 6525 N Sheridan Rd — *Web:* www.luc.edu	Chicago	IL	60626	773-508-3075	508-8926
Loyola University Chicago					
Water Tower 820 N Michigan Ave — *Fax: Admissions ■ *TF Admissions:* 800-262-2373 ■ *Web:* www.luc.edu	Chicago	IL	60611	312-915-6500	915-7216*
Marquette University 1217 W Wisconsin Ave — *Fax: Admissions ■ *TF Admissions:* 800-222-6544 ■ *Web:* www.marquette.edu	Milwaukee	WI	53233	414-288-7302	288-3764*
Rockhurst University 1100 Rockhurst Rd — *Fax: Admissions ■ *TF:* 800-842-6776 ■ *Web:* www.rockhurst.edu	Kansas City	MO	64110	816-501-4000	501-4241*
Saint Joseph's University 5600 City Ave — *Fax: Admissions ■ *TF:* 888-232-4295 ■ *Web:* www.sju.edu	Philadelphia	PA	19131	610-660-1000	660-1314*
Saint Louis University 221 N Grand Blvd — *Fax: Admissions ■ *TF:* 800-758-3678 ■ *Web:* www.slu.edu	Saint Louis	MO	63103	314-977-7288	977-7136*
Santa Clara University 500 El Camino Real — *Web:* www.scu.edu	Santa Clara	CA	95053	408-554-4000	554-5255
Seattle University 901 12th Ave — *Fax: Admissions ■ *TF:* 800-426-7123 ■ *Web:* www.seattleu.edu	Seattle	WA	98122	206-296-6000	296-5656*
Spring Hill College 4000 Dauphin St — *Fax: Admissions ■ *TF Admissions:* 800-742-6704 ■ *Web:* badgerweb.shc.edu	Mobile	AL	36608	251-380-4000	460-2186*

Phone | Fax

University of Detroit Mercy
4001 W McNichols Rd .... Detroit MI 48221 313-993-1000 993-3326*
*Fax: Admissions ■ TF Admissions: 800-635-5020 ■ Web: www.udmercy.edu

University of Detroit Mercy School of Dentistry
Corktown Campus 2700 MLK Dr .... Detroit MI 48219 313-494-6611
Web: www.udmercy.edu

University of San Francisco
2130 Fulton St .... San Francisco CA 94117 415-422-5555 422-2217*
*Fax: Admissions ■ TF Admissions: 800-225-5873 ■ Web: www.usfca.edu

University of Scranton
800 Linden St St Thomas Hall .... Scranton PA 18510 570-941-7400 941-5928*
*Fax: Admissions ■ TF: 888-727-2686 ■ Web: scranton.edu

Wheeling Jesuit University
316 Washington Ave .... Wheeling WV 26003 304-243-2000 243-2397*
*Fax: Admissions ■ TF: 800-624-6992 ■ Web: www.wju.edu

Xavier University 3800 Victory Pkwy .... Cincinnati OH 45207 513-745-3000 745-4319*
*Fax: Admissions ■ TF: 800-344-4698 ■ Web: www.xavier.edu

172 COMMODITY CONTRACTS BROKERS & DEALERS

SEE ALSO Investment Advice & Management p. 2590; Securities Brokers & Dealers p. 3151

Phone | Fax

Advantage Futures LLC
231 S Lasalle St Ste 1400 .... Chicago IL 60604 312-800-7000
Web: advantagefutures.com

Applied Research Co 53 W Jackson Blvd Ste 337 .... Chicago IL 60604 312-922-7882
Web: www.appliedresearch.com

Basic Commodities Inc 863 S Orlando Ave .... Winter Park FL 32789 407-629-2000
TF: 800-338-7006 ■ Web: basiccommodities.com

Cedar Petrochemicals Inc
110 Wall St Seventh Fl .... New York NY 10005 212-288-4320
Web: www.cedarpetrochemicals.com

ClearTrade Inc 5415 N Sheridan Rd Ste 5512 .... Chicago IL 60640 773-561-9777
Web: www.cleartrade.com

Commerzbank Capital Markets Corp
2 World Financial Ctr 31st Fl .... New York NY 10281 212-703-4000 266-7235
Web: www.commerzbank.com

Essex Futures Inc 8105 Irvine Ctr Dr Ste 840 .... Irvine CA 92618 949-450-8221
Web: www.essexfutures.com

Farmers Discount Futures 137 S Main St .... West Bend WI 53095 262-334-4406
Web: stewart-peterson.com

GFI Group Inc 55 Water St .... New York NY 10041 212-968-4100 968-2386
NYSE: GFIG ■ TF: 888-750-5884 ■ Web: www.gfigroup.com

Keeley Investment Corp
401 S La Salle St Ste 1201 .... Chicago IL 60605 312-786-5000 786-5002
TF: 800-533-5344 ■ Web: www.keeleyfunds.com

Koch Mineral Services LLC 4111 E 37th St N .... Wichita KS 67220 316-828-5500 828-6997
TF: 800-750-5834

Koch Supply & Trading LP 4111 E 37th St N .... Wichita KS 67220 713-544-4123 828-5739*
*Fax Area Code: 316 ■ TF: 800-245-2243 ■ Web: www.kochoil.com

Kolmar Americas Inc
10 Middle St Penthouse .... Bridgeport CT 06604 203-873-2051
Web: www.kolmargroup.com

Marubeni America Corp 375 Lexington Ave .... New York NY 10017 212-450-0100 450-0700
Web: www.marubeni-usa.com

Mla General Contractor Inc PO Box 624 .... Fallbrook CA 92028 760-723-0210
Web: mlacontractor.com

OptionsXpress Inc 311 W Monroe Ste 1000 .... Chicago IL 60606 312-630-3300 629-5256
TF: 888-280-8020 ■ Web: www.optionsxpress.com

Orion Futures 1905 W Busch Blvd .... Tampa FL 33612 813-876-9662 876-5530

PS International Ltd
1414 Raleigh Rd Ste 205 .... Chapel Hill NC 27517 919-933-7400 933-7441
Web: www.psinternational.net

RJ O'Brien & Assoc
222 S Riverside Plz Ste 900 .... Chicago IL 60606 312-373-5000 373-5238
TF: 866-438-7564 ■ Web: www.rjobrien.com

Rosenthal Collins Group LLC (RCG)
216 W Jackson Blvd Ste 400 .... Chicago IL 60606 312-460-9200 795-7730*
*Fax: Hum Res ■ Web: www.rcgdirect.com

Vestor Capital Corp
10 S Riverside Plz Ste 1400 .... Chicago IL 60606 312-641-2400
Web: www.vestorcapital.com

Viridian Partners LLC
1745 Shea Ctr Dr Ste 190 .... Highlands Ranch CO 80129 303-271-9114
Web: www.viridianpartners.com

Zaner Group LLC 150 S Wacker Dr Ste 2350 .... Chicago IL 60606 312-277-0050 277-0150
TF: 800-621-1414 ■ Web: www.zaner.com

173 COMMUNICATIONS TOWER OPERATORS

SEE ALSO Communications Lines & Towers Construction p. 2087
Listed here are companies that own, operate, lease, maintain, and/or manage towers used by telecommunications services and radio broadcast companies, including free-standing towers as well as antenna systems mounted on monopoles or rooftops. Many of these companies also build their communications towers, but companies that only do the building are classified as heavy construction contractors.

Phone | Fax

American Tower Corp 116 Huntington Ave 11th Fl .... Boston MA 02116 617-375-7500 375-7575
NYSE: AMT ■ TF: 877-282-7483 ■ Web: www.americantower.com

Atlantic Tower Group of Cos Inc
6260 Pine Slash Rd .... Mechanicsville VA 23116 804-550-7490 559-6041
Web: www.atlantic-tower.com

CLS Group 609 S Kelly Ave Ste D .... Edmond OK 73003 405-348-5460 551-8270
Web: www.clsgroup.com

Crown Castle International Corp
1220 Augusta Dr Ste 500 .... Houston TX 77057 713-570-3000
NYSE: CCI ■ TF: 877-486-9377 ■ Web: www.crowncastle.com

Crown Castle USA Inc 2000 Corporate Dr .... Canonsburg PA 15317 724-746-3600 416-2200
TF: 877-486-9377 ■ Web: crowncastle.com

Phone | Fax

LTS Wireless Inc 311 S LHS Dr .... Lumberton TX 77657 409-755-4038 755-7409
Web: www.ltswireless.com

SBA Communications Corp
5900 Broken Sound Pkwy NW .... Boca Raton FL 33487 561-995-7670 995-7626
NASDAQ: SBAC ■ TF: 800-487-7483 ■ Web: www.sbasite.com

Tower Innovations 3266 Tower Dr .... Newburgh IN 47630 812-853-0595 853-6652
TF: 800-664-8222 ■ Web: www.centraltower.com

174 COMMUNITIES - ONLINE

SEE ALSO Internet Service Providers (ISPs) p. 2589

Phone | Fax

America Online Inc (AOL) 22000 AOL Way .... Dulles VA 20166 703-265-1000
Web: www.aol.com

AudienceScience Inc
1120 112th Ave NE Ste 400 .... Bellevue WA 98004 425-201-3900
Web: www.audiencescience.com

Beliefnet Inc 999 Waterside Dr Ste 1900 .... Norfolk VA 23150 800-311-2458
Web: www.beliefnet.com

BlackPlanet.com 205 Hudson St Sixth Fl .... New York NY 10013 212-431-4477 505-3478
Web: www.blackplanet.com

Internet Broadcasting Systems Inc
355 Randolph Ave .... Saint Paul MN 55102 651-365-4000 365-4430
Web: www.ibsys.com

Knot Inc, The 462 Broadway 6th Fl .... New York NY 10013 212-219-8555 219-1929
TF: 800-390-9784 ■ Web: www.xogroupinc.com

lawyers.com
Martindale-Hubbell 121 Chanlon Rd .... New Providence NJ 07974 908-464-6800 464-3553
TF: 800-526-4902 ■ Web: www.lawyers.com

Merit Network Inc 1000 Oakbrook Dr Ste 200 .... Ann Arbor MI 48104 734-764-9430 527-5790
Web: www.merit.edu

Military Advantage Inc
799 Market St Ste 700 .... San Francisco CA 94103 415-820-3434 820-0552
Web: www.military.com

Nominum Inc 2000 Seaport Blvd Ste 400 .... Redwood City CA 94063 650-381-6000 381-6055
Web: www.nominum.com

One Call Concepts Inc 7223 Pkwy Dr Ste 210 .... Hanover MD 21076 410-712-0082 712-0838
Web: www.occinc.com

QuinStreet Inc 950 Tower Ln 6th Fl .... Foster City CA 94404 650-578-7700
Web: www.quinstreet.com

Salon.com 101 Spear St Ste 203 .... San Francisco CA 94105 415-645-9200 645-9204
Web: www.salon.com

Sensitech Inc 800 Cummings Ctr Ste 258x .... Beverly MA 01915 978-927-7033 921-2112
TF: 800-843-8367 ■ Web: www.sensitech.com

SHRM Global Forum 1800 Duke St .... Alexandria VA 22314 703-548-3440 535-6490
TF: 800-283-7476 ■ Web: www.shrm.org/global

Spark Networks PLC
8383 Wilshire Blvd Ste 800 .... Beverly Hills CA 90211 323-836-3000
NYSE: LOV ■ Web: www.spark.net

Trinet Internet Solutions Inc
1423 Powhatan St Bldg 1 .... Alexandria VA 22314 703-548-8900
Web: trinetsolutions.com

WELL, The 1195 Park Ave Ste 206 .... Emeryville CA 94608 415-343-5731
Web: www.well.com

COMPRESSORS - AIR CONDITIONING & REFRIGERATION

SEE Air Conditioning & Heating Equipment - Commercial/Industrial p. 1726

175 COMPRESSORS - AIR & GAS

Phone | Fax

A G Equipment Company Inc 3401 W Albany .... Broken Arrow OK 74012 918-250-7386
Web: www.agequipmentcompany.com

Accessorie Air Compressor Systems Inc
1858 N Case St .... Orange CA 92865 714-634-2292
Web: accessorieair.com

Air Compressor Supply Inc
3916 S I-35 Service Rd .... Oklahoma City OK 73129 405-672-0382
Web: www.aircompressorsupplyinc.com

Air Relief Inc 32 E Powell Rd .... Mayfield KY 42066 270-247-0203
Web: airrelief.com

Airtek Inc PO Box 466 .... Irwin PA 15642 724-863-1350 864-7853
TF: 800-424-7835 ■ Web: www.airtek-inc.com

Ariel Corp 35 Blackjack Rd Ext .... Mount Vernon OH 43050 740-397-0311
Web: www.arielcorp.com

Atlas Copco Comptec LLC 46 School Rd .... Voorheesville NY 12186 518-765-3344
Web: www.atlascopco.us

Bauer Compressors Inc 1328 Azalea Garden Rd .... Norfolk VA 23502 757-855-6006 855-6224
Web: www.bauercomp.com

Bitzer US Inc 4031 Chamblee Rd .... Oakwood GA 30566 770-718-2900
Web: www.bitzerus.com

Blackhawk Equipment Co 6250 W 55th Ave .... Arvada CO 80002 303-421-3000
Web: www.blackhawkequipment.com

Boss Industries Inc 1761 Genesis Dr .... Laporte IN 46350 219-324-7776
Web: www.bossair.com

Brabazon Pumps & Compressor
2484 Century Rd .... Green Bay WI 54303 920-498-6020
Web: www.brabazon.com

Cameron Compression Systems 16250 Port NW Dr .... Houston TX 77041 713-354-1900 354-1923
TF: 800-323-9160 ■ Web: www.c-a-m.com

Cameron Turbocompressor 3101 Broadway .... Buffalo NY 14225 716-896-6600 896-1233
TF: 877-805-7911 ■ Web: www.c-a-m.com

Champion A Gardner Denver Inc
1301 N Euclid Ave .... Princeton IL 61356 815-875-3321 872-0421
Web: www.gardnerdenver.com

Chapin International Inc 700 Ellicott St .... Batavia NY 14021 585-343-3140 344-1775
Web: www.chapinmfg.com

Compressed Air Systems Inc 9303 Stannum St .... Tampa FL 33619 813-626-8177 628-0187
TF: 800-626-8177 ■ Web: www.compressedairsystems.com

Company	City	State	Zip	Phone	Fax
Compression Leasing Services Inc 1935 N Loop Ave	Casper	WY	82601	307-265-3242	
Web: www.compressionleasing.com					
Compressor Engineering Corp (CECO) 5440 Alder Dr	Houston	TX	77081	713-664-7333	664-6444
TF: 800-879-2326 ■ *Web:* www.tryceco.com					
Corken Inc 3805 NW 36th St	Oklahoma City	OK	73112	405-946-5576	948-6664
TF: 800-631-4929 ■ *Web:* www.corken.com					
CSI Compressor Systems Inc 3809 S FM 1788 PO Box 60760	Midland	TX	79711	432-563-1170	757-9604*
**Fax Area Code:* 903 ■ *TF:* 800-676-0654 ■ *Web:* www.compressor-systems.com					
Curtis Dyna-Fog Ltd 17335 US Hwy 31 N	Westfield	IN	46074	317-896-2561	896-3788
TF: 800-544-8990 ■ *Web:* www.dynafog.com					
Curtis-Toledo Inc 1905 Kienlen Ave	Saint Louis	MO	63133	314-383-1300	383-1300
TF: 800-925-5431 ■ *Web:* us.fscurtis.com					
Danfoss Scroll Technologies LLC One Scroll Dr	Arkadelphia	AR	71923	870-246-0700	
Web: www.scrolltech.com					
Danfoss Turbocor Compressors Inc 1769 E Paul Dirac Dr	Tallahassee	FL	32310	850-504-4800	
Web: www.turbocor.com					
Danmar Industries 2303 Oil Ctr Ct	Houston	TX	77073	281-230-1000	230-1010
Web: www.danmarind.com					
Dearing Compressor & Pump Co 3974 Simon Rd	Youngstown	OH	44512	330-783-2258	
Web: www.dearingcomp.com					
Dresser-Rand Co Paul Clark Dr PO Box 560	Olean	NY	14760	716-375-3000	375-3178
Web: www.dresser-rand.com					
Dresser-Rand Co Reciprocating Products Div 100 Chemung St	Painted Post	NY	14870	619-656-4740	937-2100*
**Fax Area Code:* 607 ■ *TF:* 877-590-7858 ■ *Web:* www.dresser-rand.com					
Elliott Group 901 N Fourth St	Jeannette	PA	15644	724-527-2811	600-8442
TF: 800-635-2208 ■ *Web:* www.elliott-turbo.com					
Estis Compression LLC 545 Huey Lenard Loop	West Monroe	LA	71292	318-397-5557	
Web: www.estiscompression.com					
Federal Equipment Co 5298 River Rd	Cincinnati	OH	45233	513-621-5260	621-0524
TF: 877-435-4723 ■ *Web:* www.federalequipment.com					
Fountainhead Group Inc 23 Garden St	New York Mills	NY	13417	315-736-0037	768-4220
TF: 800-311-9903 ■ *Web:* www.thefountainheadgroup.com					
FS-Elliott Company LLC 5710 Mellon Rd	Export	PA	15632	724-387-3200	
Web: www.fs-elliott.com					
Gardner Denver Compressor Div 1800 Gardner Expwy	Quincy	IL	62305	217-222-5400	247-3506*
**Fax Area Code:* 270 ■ *TF:* 800-682-9868 ■ *Web:* www.gardnerdenver.com					
Gardner Denver Inc 1800 Gardner Expy	Quincy	IL	62305	217-222-5400	247-3506*
NYSE: GDI ■ **Fax Area Code:* 270 ■ *TF:* 800-682-9868 ■ *Web:* www.gardnerdenver.com					
Gardner Denver Nash 1800 Gardner Expy	Quincy	IL	62305	217-222-5400	
TF: 800-637-5729 ■ *Web:* www.gardnerdenver.com					
Gardner Denver Nash LLC Alta Vista Business Park 200 Simko Blvd	Charleroi	PA	15022	724-239-1500	
Web: www.gdnash.com					
Gardner Denver Water Jetting Systems Inc 12300 N Houston Rosslyn	Houston	TX	77086	281-448-5800	247-3506*
**Fax Area Code:* 270 ■ *TF General:* 800-682-9868 ■ *Web:* www.gardnerdenver.com					
Gas Technology Energy Concepts LLC 401 William L Gaiter Pkwy Ste 4	Buffalo	NY	14215	800-451-8294	
TF: 800-451-8294 ■ *Web:* www.gas-tec.com					
Gast Mfg Inc 2300 M-139 Hwy PO Box 97	Benton Harbor	MI	49023	269-926-6171	925-8288
TF: 800-665-1196 ■ *Web:* www.gastmfg.com					
Guardair Corp 54 Second Ave	Chicopee	MA	01020	413-594-4400	594-4884
TF: 800-482-7324 ■ *Web:* www.guardaircorp.com					
Industrial Air Centers Inc 731 E Market St	Jeffersonville	IN	47130	812-280-7070	
Web: www.iacserv.com					
Ingersoll Rand Air Solutions Group 800-D Beaty St	Davidson	NC	28036	800-866-5457	
Web: company.ingersollrand.com					
Integrated Flow Systems LLC 43455 Osgood Rd	Fremont	CA	94539	510-659-4900	
ITW Industrial Finishing 195 International Blvd	Glendale Heights	IL	60139	630-237-5000	
ITW Ransburg 320 Phillips Ave	Toledo	OH	43612	419-470-2000	470-2270
TF Cust Svc: 800-233-3366 ■ *Web:* site.ransburg.com					
Kaeser Compressors Inc PO Box 946	Fredericksburg	VA	22404	540-898-5500	898-5520
Web: www.kaeser.com					
Manchester Tank 1000 Corp Centre Dr Ste 300	Franklin	TN	37067	615-370-6300	370-6150
TF: 800-399-5628 ■ *Web:* www.mantank.com					
Master Mfg Co 747 N Yale Ave	Villa Park	IL	60181	630-833-7060	243-8030*
**Fax Area Code:* 320 ■ *TF:* 800-864-1649					
Mattson Spray Equipment 230 W Coleman St	Rice Lake	WI	54868	715-234-1617	236-7032
TF: 800-877-4857 ■ *Web:* www.mattsonspray.com					
McGee Company Inc 1140 S Jason St	Denver	CO	80223	303-777-2615	
Web: www.mcgeecompany.com					
Michigan Automotive Compressor Inc (MACI) 2400 N Dearing Rd	Parma	MI	49269	517-622-7000	
Web: www.michauto.com					
Norwalk Compressor Co 1650 Stratford Ave	Stratford	CT	06615	203-386-1234	386-1300
TF: 800-556-5001 ■ *Web:* www.norwalkcompressor.com					
Pristech Products Inc 6952 Fairgrounds Pkwy Ste 107	San Antonio	TX	78238	210-520-8051	509-7463
Web: www.pristech.com					
Puma Industries Inc 1992 Airways Blvd	Memphis	TN	38114	901-744-7979	
Web: www.pumaairusa.com					
Quincy Compressor 3501 Wismann Ln	Quincy	IL	62305	217-222-7700	222-5109
Web: www.quincycompressor.com					
Riley Industrial Services Inc 2615 San Juan Blvd PO Box 2014	Farmington	NM	87401	505-327-4947	326-0305
Web: www.rileyindustrial.com					
RIX Industries Inc 4900 Industrial Way	Benicia	CA	94510	707-747-5900	
Web: www.rixindustries.com					
Rogers Machinery Company Inc 14650 SW 72nd Ave PO Box 230429	Portland	OR	97224	503-639-0808	
Web: www.rogers-machinery.com					
Sanden International (USA) Inc 601 S Sanden Blvd	Wylie	TX	75098	972-442-8400	
Web: www.sanden.com					
Sauer Compressors USA Inc 64 Log Canoe Cir	Stevensville	MD	21666	410-604-3142	
Web: www.sauerusa.com					
Saylor Beall Mfg Company Inc 400 N Kibbee St	Saint Johns	MI	48879	989-224-2371	224-8788
TF: 800-248-9001 ■ *Web:* www.saylor-beall.com					
Scales Air Compressor Corp 110 Voice Rd	Carle Place	NY	11514	516-248-9096	248-9639
TF: 877-798-0454 ■ *Web:* www.scalesair.com					
SCFM Compressor Systems 3701 S Maybelle Ave	Tulsa	OK	74107	918-663-1309	
Web: www.scfm.com					
SIHI Pumps Inc 303 Industrial Blvd	Grand Island	NY	14072	716-773-6450	773-2330
Web: www.sihi-pumps.com					
Spencer Turbine Co 600 Day Hill Rd	Windsor	CT	06095	860-688-8361	688-0098
TF: 800-232-4321 ■ *Web:* www.spencerturbine.com					
Sullair Corp 3700 E Michigan Blvd	Michigan City	IN	46360	219-879-5451	874-1252*
**Fax:* Mktg ■ *TF:* 800-785-5247 ■ *Web:* www.sullair.com					
Sullivan-Palatek Inc 1201 W US Hwy 20	Michigan City	IN	46360	219-874-2497	872-5043
TF: 800-438-6203 ■ *Web:* www.palatek.com					
Sulzer Metco US Inc 1101 Prospect Ave	Westbury	NY	11590	516-334-1300	338-2414*
**Fax:* Sales ■ *TF:* 877-280-2342 ■ *Web:* www.sulzer.com					
Tafa Inc 146 Pembroke Rd	Concord	NH	03301	603-224-9586	
Web: www.praxair.com					
Technology General Corp 12 Cork Hill Rd	Franklin	NJ	07416	973-827-4143	
Web: www.iconservice.com					
Tecumseh Products Co 1136 Oak Valley Dr	Ann Arbor	MI	48108	734-585-9500	352-3700
NASDAQ: TECU ■ *Web:* www.tecumseh.com					
Thermionics Laboratory 1842 Sabre St	Hayward	CA	94545	510-538-3304	538-2889
TF: 800-962-2310 ■ *Web:* www.thermionics.com					
Tuthill Vacuum Systems 4840 W Kearney St	Springfield	MO	65803	417-865-8715	865-2950
TF: 800-634-2695 ■ *Web:* www.tuthill.com					
Wagner Spray Tech Corp 1770 Fernbrook Ln	Plymouth	MN	55447	763-553-7000	519-3563
TF: 800-328-8251 ■ *Web:* www.wagnerspraytech.com					
Wittemann Company LLC, The One Industry Dr	Palm Coast	FL	32137	386-445-4200	445-7042
Web: www.pureco2nfidence.com					
Zeks Compressed Air Solutions 1302 Goshen Pkwy	West Chester	PA	19380	610-692-9100	692-9192
TF: 800-888-2323 ■ *Web:* www.zeks.com					

176 COMPUTER EQUIPMENT

SEE ALSO Business Machines - Mfr p. 1893; Calculators - Electronic p. 1899; Modems p. 2012; Computer Networking Products & Systems p. 2020; Flash Memory Devices p. 2291; Automatic Teller Machines (ATMs) p. 1829; Point-of-Sale (POS) & Point-of-Information (POI) Systems p. 2951

176-1 Computer Input Devices

Company	City	State	Zip	Phone	Fax
3M Touch Systems 501 Griffin Brook Dr	Methuen	MA	01844	978-659-9000	659-9103
TF: 866-407-6666 ■ *Web:* www.3m.com					
Aten Technology Inc 23 Hubble	Irvine	CA	92618	949-428-1111	428-1100
TF: 888-999-2836 ■ *Web:* www.aten-usa.com					
CH Products 970 Pk Ctr Dr	Vista	CA	92081	760-598-2518	598-2524
Web: www.chproducts.com					
Chicony America Inc 53 Parker	Irvine	CA	92618	949-380-0928	380-8201
Web: www.chicony.com.tw					
Cirque Corp 2463 South 3850 West Ste A	Salt Lake City	UT	84120	801-467-1100	467-0208
TF: 800-454-3375 ■ *Web:* www.cirque.com					
Cortron Inc 59 Technology Dr	Lowell	MA	01851	978-975-5445	975-0357
Web: www.cortroninc.com					
Digit Professional Inc 5050 Seymour Rd	Jackson	MI	49201	734-677-0840	
Web: prodvx.com					
Elo TouchSystems Inc 301 Constitution Dr	Menlo Park	CA	94025	650-361-4700	361-4747
TF: 800-557-1458 ■ *Web:* www.elotouch.com					
Esterline Interface Technologies 600 W Wilbur Ave	Coeur d'Alene	ID	83815	208-765-8000	292-2275
TF: 800-444-5923 ■ *Web:* www.esterline.com					
Fujitsu Components America Inc 250 E Caribbean Dr	Sunnyvale	CA	94089	408-745-4900	745-4970
Web: www.fujitsu.com					
GTCO CalComp Inc 7125 Riverwood Dr	Columbia	MD	21046	410-381-6688	290-9065
Web: gtcocalcomp.com					
Gyration Inc 3601-B Calle Tecate	Camarillo	CA	93012	888-340-0033	987-6665*
**Fax Area Code:* 805 ■ *TF:* 888-340-0033 ■ *Web:* www.gyration.com					
Immersion Corp 30 Rio Robles	San Jose	CA	95134	408-467-1900	467-1901
NASDAQ: IMMR ■ *TF:* 877-223-6273 ■ *Web:* www.immersion.com					
Interlink Electronics Inc 546 Flynn Rd	Camarillo	CA	93012	805-484-8855	484-8989
OTC: LINK ■ *Web:* www.interlinkelec.com					
Kensington Computer Products Group 333 Twin Dolphin Dr Sixth Fl	Redwood Shores	CA	94065	650-572-2700	267-2800
TF: 800-535-4242 ■ *Web:* www.kensington.com					
Kinesis Corp 22030 20th Ave SE Ste 102	Bothell	WA	98021	425-402-8100	402-8181
TF: 800-454-6374 ■ *Web:* www.kinesis-ergo.com					
KYE Systems Corp 1301 NW 84th Ave Ste 127	Doral	FL	33126	305-468-9250	468-9251
TF: 800-488-3111 ■ *Web:* www.geniusnet.com					
Lite-On Trading USA Inc 720 S Hillview Dr	Milpitas	CA	95035	408-946-4873	941-4597
Web: www.us.liteon.com					
Logitech Inc 6505 Kaiser Dr	Fremont	CA	94555	510-795-8500	792-8901
TF Sales: 800-231-7717 ■ *Web:* www.logitech.com					
Macally USA Mace Group Inc 4601 E Airport Dr	Ontario	CA	91761	909-230-6888	230-6889
TF: 800-644-1132 ■ *Web:* www.macally.com					
Mad Catz Interactive Inc 7480 Mission Vly Rd Ste 101	San Diego	CA	92108	619-683-9830	683-9839
NYSE: MCZ ■ *TF:* 800-659-2287 ■ *Web:* www.madcatz.com					
NaturalPoint Inc 33872 SE Eastgate Cir	Corvallis	OR	97333	541-753-6645	753-6689
Web: www.naturalpoint.com					

Company	City	State	ZIP	Phone	Fax
NMB Technologies Corp 9730 Independence Ave *Web:* www.nmbtc.com	Chatsworth	CA	91311	818-341-3355	341-8207
Numonics Corp 101 Commerce Dr PO Box 1005 *TF:* 800-523-6716 ■ *Web:* interactivewhiteboards.com	Montgomeryville	PA	18936	215-362-2766	361-0167
PolyVision Corp 3970 Johns Creek Ct Ste 325 *TF:* 800-620-7659 ■ *Web:* www.polyvision.com	Suwanee	GA	30024	678-542-3100	542-3200
SMART Modular Technologies Inc 39870 Eureka Dr *NASDAQ: SMOD* ■ *TF:* 800-956-7627 ■ *Web:* www.smartm.com	Newark	CA	94560	510-623-1231	623-1434
SMART Technologies Inc 3636 Research Road NW *TSE: SMA* ■ *TF:* 888-427-6278 ■ *Web:* www.smarttech.com	Calgary	AB	T2L1Y1	403-245-0333	245-0366
Synaptics Inc 3120 Scott Blvd Ste 130 *NASDAQ: SYNA* ■ *Web:* www.synaptics.com	Santa Clara	CA	95054	408-454-5100	454-5200
TouchSystems Corp 220 Tradesmen Dr *TF:* 800-320-5944 ■ *Web:* www.touchsystems.com	Hutto	TX	78634	512-846-2424	846-2425
Ultra Electronics Measurement Systems Inc 50 Barnes Pk N Ste 102 *Web:* www.ultra-msi.com	Wallingford	CT	06492	203-949-3500	949-3598
Wacom Technology Corp 1311 SE Cardinal Ct *TF:* 800-922-6613 ■ *Web:* www.wacom.com	Vancouver	WA	98683	360-896-9833	896-9724

176-2 Computers

Company	City	State	ZIP	Phone	Fax
Aberdeen LLC 9130 Norwalk Blvd **Fax:* Sales ■ *TF:* 800-500-9526 ■ *Web:* www.aberdeeninc.com	Santa Fe Springs	CA	90670	562-699-6998	695-5570*
Acer America Corp 333 W San Carlos St Ste 1500 **Fax:* Sales ■ *TF:* 800-253-2687 ■ *Web:* www.acer.com	San Jose	CA	95110	408-533-7700	533-4574*
ACMA Computers Inc 1565 Reliance Way *TF Sales:* 800-800-6328 ■ *Web:* www.acma.com	Fremont	CA	94539	510-651-8886	651-4119
ACME Portable Machines Inc 1330 Mtn View Cir *Web:* www.acmeportable.com	Azusa	CA	91702	626-610-1888	610-1881
Amax Engineering Corp 1565 Reliance Way *TF Cust Svc:* 800-889-2629 ■ *Web:* www.amax.com	Fremont	CA	94539	510-651-8886	651-4119
Apple Inc One Infinite Loop *NASDAQ: AAPL* ■ **Fax:* Mail Rm ■ *TF Cust Svc:* 800-275-2273 ■ *Web:* www.apple.com	Cupertino	CA	95014	408-996-1010	996-0275*
Azul Systems Inc 1600 Plymouth St *TF:* 800-258-4199 ■ *Web:* www.azulsystems.com	Mountain View	CA	94043	650-230-6500	230-6600
BlackBerry Ltd 295 Phillip St *NASDAQ: BBRY* ■ *Web:* ca.blackberry.com	Waterloo	ON	N2L3W8	519-888-7465	888-7884
Bytespeed LLC 3131 24th Ave S *TF:* 877-553-0777 ■ *Web:* www.bytespeed.com	Moorhead	MN	56560	218-227-0445	
Cemtrol Inc 3035 E La Jolla St *Web:* www.cemtrol.com	Anaheim	CA	92806	714-666-6606	666-6616
CG Automation 60 Fadem Rd *Web:* www.qeiinc.com	Springfield	NJ	07081	973-379-7400	379-2138
Chem USA Corp 38507 Cherry St *TF:* 800-866-2436 ■ *Web:* www.chemusa.com	Newark	CA	94560	510-608-8818	608-8828
Comark Corp 93 W St *TF:* 800-280-8522 ■ *Web:* www.comarkcorp.com	Medfield	MA	02052	508-359-8161	359-2267
Corvallis Microtechnology Inc 413 SW Jefferson Ave *Web:* www.cmtinc.com	Corvallis	OR	97333	541-752-5456	752-4117
Cray Inc 901 Fifth Ave Ste 1000 *NASDAQ: CRAY* ■ *Web:* www.cray.com	Seattle	WA	98164	206-701-2000	701-2500
CSP Inc 43 Manning Rd *NASDAQ: CSPI* ■ *TF:* 800-325-3110 ■ *Web:* www.cspi.com	Billerica	MA	01821	978-663-7598	663-0150
CSS Laboratories Inc 1641 McGaw Ave *TF:* 800-852-2680 ■ *Web:* www.csslabs.com	Irvine	CA	92614	949-852-8161	852-0410
Daisy Data Displays Inc 2850 Lewisberry Rd *Web:* www.d3inc.net	York Haven	PA	17370	717-932-9999	932-8000
Datalux Corp 155 Aviation Dr *TF:* 800-328-2589 ■ *Web:* www.datalux.com	Winchester	VA	22602	540-662-1500	662-1682
Dedicated Computing N26 W23880 Commerce Cir *TF:* 877-523-3301 ■ *Web:* www.dedicatedcomputing.com	Waukesha	WI	53188	262-951-7200	523-2222
Dell Inc One Dell Way *NASDAQ: DELL* ■ *TF:* 800-879-3355 ■ *Web:* www.dell.com	Round Rock	TX	78682	512-338-4400	283-6161
Diversified Technology Inc 476 Highland Colony Pkwy *Web:* www.dtims.com	Ridgeland	MS	39157	601-856-4121	
Drive Thru Technology Inc 1755 N Main St *TF:* 800-933-8388 ■ *Web:* www.dttusa.com	Los Angeles	CA	90031	323-576-1400	576-1470
DRS Tactical Systems Inc 1110 W Hibiscus Blvd *Web:* www.drs-ts.com	Melbourne	FL	32901	321-727-3672	725-0496
Ectaco Inc 31-21 31st St *TF:* 800-710-7920 ■ *Web:* www.ectaco.com	Long Island City	NY	11106	718-728-6110	728-4023
Electrovaya Inc 2645 Royal Windsor Dr *TSE: EFL* ■ *TF:* 800-388-2865 ■ *Web:* www.electrovaya.com	Mississauga	ON	L5J1K9	905-855-4610	822-7953
ENGlobal Corp 654 N Sam Houston Pkwy E Ste 400 *NASDAQ: ENG* ■ *Web:* www.englobal.com	Houston	TX	77060	281-878-1000	878-1010
Equus Computer Systems Inc 5801 Clearwater Dr *TF:* 866-378-8727 ■ *Web:* www.equuscs.com	Minnetonka	MN	55343	612-617-6200	617-6298
Franklin Electronic Publishers Inc One Franklin Plz *TF:* 800-266-5626 ■ *Web:* www.franklin.com	Burlington	NJ	08016	609-386-2500	239-5948
Fujitsu America Inc 1250 E Arques Ave *TF:* 800-538-8460 ■ *Web:* www.fujitsu.com	Sunnyvale	CA	94085	408-746-6200	746-6260
Gateway Inc 7565 Irvine Ctr Dr *TF:* 800-846-2000 ■ *Web:* www.gateway.com	Irvine	CA	92618	949-471-7040	471-7041
Granite Microsystems Inc 10202 N Enterprise Dr *Web:* www.granitemicrosystems.com	Mequon	WI	53092	262-242-8800	242-8825
Hewlett-Packard (Canada) Ltd (HP) 5150 Spectrum Way *TF:* 888-447-4636 ■ *Web:* welcome.hp.com	Mississauga	ON	L4W5G1	905-206-4725	
Hewlett-Packard Co 3000 Hanover St *NYSE: HPQ* ■ *TF Sales:* 800-752-0900 ■ *Web:* www.hp.com	Palo Alto	CA	94304	650-857-1501	857-5518
Immecor Corp 2351 Circadian Way *Web:* www.immecor.com	Santa Rosa	CA	95407	707-636-2550	636-2565
International Business Machines Corp (IBM) One New OrchaRd Rd *NYSE: IBM* ■ *TF:* 800-426-4968 ■ *Web:* www.ibm.com	Armonk	NY	10504	914-499-1900	
Keydata International Inc 201 Cir Dr N Ste 101	Piscataway Township	NJ	08854	732-868-0588	
Kontron Mobile Computing Inc 7631 Anagram Dr **Fax Area Code:* 612 ■ *TF:* 888-343-5396 ■ *Web:* kontron.com/	Eden Prairie	MN	55344	952-974-7000	974-7199*
LXE Inc 125 Technology Pkwy *TF:* 800-664-4593 ■ *Web:* www.honeywellaidc.com	Norcross	GA	30092	770-447-4224	447-4405
MaxVision Corp 495 Production Ave *TF:* 800-533-5805 ■ *Web:* www.maxvision.com	Madison	AL	35758	256-772-3058	772-3078
Mercury Computer Systems Inc 201 Riverneck Rd *NASDAQ: MRCY* ■ *TF:* 866-627-6951 ■ *Web:* www.mc.com	Chelmsford	MA	01824	978-967-1401	
Micro Electronics Inc 4119 Leap Rd *Web:* www.microcenter.com	Hilliard	OH	43026	614-850-3000	850-3001
Micro Electronics, Inc. 2701 Charter St Ste A *TF:* 877-636-9793 ■ *Web:* www.microcenter.com	Columbus	OH	43228	614-326-8500	
Micro Express Inc Eight Hammond Dr Ste 105 *TF:* 800-989-9900 ■ *Web:* www.microexpress.net	Irvine	CA	92618	949-460-9911	269-3070
Micro/Sys Inc 3730 Pk Pl *Web:* www.embeddedsys.com	Montrose	CA	91020	818-244-4600	244-4246
Microtech Computers Inc 4921 Legends Dr *TF Tech Supp:* 800-828-9533 ■ *Web:* www.microtechcomp.com	Lawrence	KS	66049	785-841-9513	841-1809
Microway Inc 12 RichaRds Rd *Web:* www.microway.com	Plymouth	MA	02360	508-746-7341	746-4678
Myricom Inc 325 N Santa Anita Ave *Web:* www.myricom.com	Arcadia	CA	91006	626-821-5555	821-5316
Panasonic Corporation of North America Two Riverfront Plaza *TF:* 888-223-1012 ■ *Web:* www.panasonic.com/business/toughbook/contact-toughbook.asp	Newark	NJ	07102	888-223-1012	
Pinnacle Data Systems Inc 6600 Port Rd Ste 100 *TF:* 800-882-8282 ■ *Web:* www.avnetintegrated.com	Groveport	OH	43125	614-748-1150	748-1209
Quantum3D Inc 6330 San Ignacio Ave *TF:* 888-747-1020 ■ *Web:* www.quantum3d.com	San Jose	CA	95119	408-361-9999	361-9980
Roper Mobile Technology 7450 S Priest Dr	Tempe	AZ	85283	480-705-4200	705-4216
Sharp Electronics Corp One Sharp Plz *TF:* 800-237-4277 ■ *Web:* www.sharpusa.com	Mahwah	NJ	07430	201-529-8200	529-8413
Sony Electronics Inc One Sony Dr **Fax:* Hum Res ■ *TF Cust Svc:* 800-222-7669 ■ *Web:* www.sony.com	Park Ridge	NJ	07656	201-930-1000	358-4058*
SRC Computers LLC 4240 N Nevada Ave *Web:* www.srccomp.com	Colorado Springs	CO	80907	719-262-0213	262-0223
Stealth Computer Corp 530 Rowntree Dairy Rd Bldg 4 *TF:* 888-783-2584 ■ *Web:* www.stealth.com	Woodbridge	ON	L4L8H2	905-264-9000	264-7440
Superchips Inc 1790 E Airport Blvd *TF:* 888-227-2447 ■ *Web:* www.superchips.com	Sanford	FL	32773	407-585-7000	585-1900
Systemax Inc 11 Harbor Pk Dr *NYSE: SYX* ■ *TF:* 888-645-0878 ■ *Web:* www.systemax.com	Port Washington	NY	11050	516-608-7000	608-7001
Tangent Inc 191 Airport Blvd *TF:* 800-342-9388 ■ *Web:* www.tangent.com	Burlingame	CA	94010	650-342-9388	342-9380
Technology Advancement Group Inc 22355 Tag Way *TF:* 800-824-7693 ■ *Web:* www.tag.com	Sterling	VA	20166	703-406-3000	406-0305
Toshiba America Inc 1251 Ave of the Americas Ste 4100 *TF:* 800-457-7777 ■ *Web:* www.toshiba.com	New York	NY	10020	212-596-0600	593-3875
Toshiba America Information Systems Inc 9740 Irvine Blvd *TF Cust Svc:* 800-457-7777 ■ *Web:* www.toshiba.com	Irvine	CA	92618	949-583-3000	
TouchStar Solutions LLC *Touchstar Group* 5147 S Garnett Rd Ste D *Web:* www.touchstargroup.com	Tulsa	OK	74146	918-307-7100	307-7190
Transource Computers Corp 2405 W Utopia Rd *TF:* 800-486-3715 ■ *Web:* www.transource.com	Phoenix	AZ	85027	623-879-8882	879-8887
Twinhead Corp 48303 Fremont Blvd **Fax Area Code:* 510 ■ *TF Sales:* 800-995-8946 ■ *Web:* www.twinhead.com.tw	Fremont	CA	94538	800-995-8946	492-0820*
Versalogic Corp 4211 W 11th Ave *TF:* 800-824-3163 ■ *Web:* www.versalogic.com	Eugene	OR	97402	541-485-8575	485-5712
Win Enterprises Inc 300 Willow St S *Web:* www.win-ent.com	North Andover	MA	01845	978-688-2000	
WYSE Technology Inc 3471 N First St *TF:* 800-800-9973 ■ *Web:* www.wyse.com	San Jose	CA	95134	408-473-1200	473-2080

176-3 Modems

Company	City	State	ZIP	Phone	Fax
ActionTec Electronics Inc 760 N Mary Ave *TF Tech Supp:* 888-436-0657 ■ *Web:* www.actiontec.com	Sunnyvale	CA	94085	408-752-7700	541-9003
Avocent Corp 4991 Corporate Dr *TF:* 866-286-2368 ■ *Web:* www.emersonnetworkpower.com	Huntsville	AL	35805	256-430-4000	430-4030
Aztech Labs Inc 4005 Clipper Ct *Web:* www.aztech.com	Fremont	CA	94538	510-683-9800	683-9803
Best Data Products Inc 20740 Plummer St *Web:* diamondmm.com/	Chatsworth	CA	91311	818-773-9600	773-9619
Biscom Inc 321 Billerica Rd *TF:* 800-477-2472 ■ *Web:* www.biscom.com	Chelmsford	MA	01824	978-250-1800	250-4449
Canoga Perkins Corp 20600 Prairie St *TF Tech Supp:* 800-360-6642 ■ *Web:* www.canoga.com	Chatsworth	CA	91311	818-718-6300	718-6312

Company / Address	City	State	ZIP	Phone	Fax
Cermetek Microelectronics Inc 374 Turquoise St	Milpitas	CA	95035	408-752-5000	942-1346
TF: 800-882-6271 ■ *Web:* www.cermetek.com					
Comtech EF Data Corp 2114 W Seventh St	Tempe	AZ	85281	480-333-2200	333-2540
Web: www.comtechefdata.com					
Copia International Ltd 1220 Iroquois Dr Ste 180	Naperville	IL	60563	630-778-8898	778-8848*
**Fax:* Sales ■ *TF Sales:* 800-689-8898 ■ *Web:* www.copia.com					
CXR Larus Corp 894 Faulstich Ct	San Jose	CA	95112	408-573-2700	
TF: 800-999-9946 ■ *Web:* www.cxr.com					
Data-Linc Group 3535 Factoria Blvd SE Ste 100	Bellevue	WA	98006	425-882-2206	867-0865
Web: www.data-linc.com					
Dataforth Corp 3331 E Hemisphere Loop	Tucson	AZ	85706	520-741-1404	741-0762
TF: 800-444-7644 ■ *Web:* www.dataforth.com					
Electronic Systems Technology Inc 415 N Quay St Bldg B-1	Kennewick	WA	99336	509-735-9092	783-5475
OTC: ELST ■ *Web:* www.esteem.com					
Encore Networks Inc 3800 Concorde Pkwy Ste 1500	Chantilly	VA	20151	703-318-7750	787-4625
Web: www.encorenetworks.com					
Engage Communications Inc 9565 Soquel Dr	Aptos	CA	95003	831-688-1021	688-1421
Web: www.engagecom.com					
FreeWave Technologies Inc 1880 S Flatiron Ct Ste F	Boulder	CO	80301	303-444-3862	786-9948
TF Cust Svc: 866-923-6168 ■ *Web:* www.freewave.com					
GRE America Inc 425 Harbor Blvd	Belmont	CA	94002	650-591-1400	591-2001
TF: 800-233-5973 ■ *Web:* www.greamerica.com					
Multi-Tech Systems 2205 Woodale Dr	Mounds View	MN	55112	763-785-3500	785-9074
TF Cust Svc: 800-328-9717 ■ *Web:* www.multitech.com					
Novatel Wireless Inc 9645 Scranton Rd Ste 205	San Diego	CA	92121	888-888-9231	812-3402*
NASDAQ: NVTL ■ **Fax Area Code:* 858 ■ *TF:* 888-888-9231 ■ *Web:* www.novatelwireless.com					
Phoebe Micro Inc 47606 Kato Rd	Fremont	CA	94538	510-360-0800	360-0818
Web: www.phoebemicro.com					
Sierra Wireless Inc 13811 Wireless Way	Richmond	BC	V6V3A4	604-231-1100	231-1109
Web: www.sierrawireless.com					
Teldat Corp 1901 S Bascom Ave Ste 520	Campbell	CA	95008	408-892-9363	369-9915
Web: www.teldat.com					
Teletronics International Inc Two Choke Cherry Rd	Rockville	MD	20850	301-309-8500	309-8851
Web: www.teletronics.com					
Unlimited Systems Corp Inc 9530 Padgett St	San Diego	CA	92126	858-537-5010	550-7330
TF: 800-275-6354 ■ *Web:* www.konexx.com					
US Robotics Corp 1300 E Woodfield Dr Ste 506	Schaumburg	IL	60173	847-874-2000	874-2001
TF: 877-710-0884 ■ *Web:* www.usr.com					
Western Telematic Inc 5 Sterling	Irvine	CA	92618	949-586-9950	583-9514
TF: 800-854-7226 ■ *Web:* www.wti.com					
Wi-LAN Inc 11 Holland Ave Ste 608	Ottawa	ON	K1Y4S1	613-688-4900	688-4894
TSE: WIN ■ *Web:* www.wi-lan.com					
Works Computing Inc 1801 American Blvd E Ste 12	Bloomington	MN	55425	952-746-1580	746-1585
TF: 866-222-4077 ■ *Web:* www.workscomputing.com					
ZyXEL Communications Inc 1130 N Miller St	Anaheim	CA	92806	714-632-0882	632-0858
TF: 800-255-4101 ■ *Web:* www.zyxel.com					

176-4 Monitors & Displays

Company / Address	City	State	ZIP	Phone	Fax
Aydin Displays Inc One Riga Ln	Birdsboro	PA	19508	610-404-7400	404-8190
TF: 866-367-2934 ■ *Web:* www.aydindisplays.com					
Barco Electronic Systems Pvt Ltd 11101 Trade Ctr Dr	Rancho Cordova	CA	95670	916-859-2500	859-2515
TF: 888-414-7226 ■ *Web:* barco.com					
BarcoView LLC 3059 Premiere Pkwy	Duluth	GA	30097	678-475-8000	
Web: www.barco.com					
Conrac Inc 5124 Commerce Dr	Baldwin Park	CA	91706	626-480-0095	480-0077
TF: 800-451-5288 ■ *Web:* www.conrac.us					
Daisy Data Displays Inc 2850 Lewisberry Rd	York Haven	PA	17370	717-932-9999	932-8000
Web: www.d3inc.net					
Daktronics Inc 201 Daktronics Dr	Brookings	SD	57006	605-692-0200	697-4700
NASDAQ: DAKT ■ *TF:* 800-325-8766 ■ *Web:* www.daktronics.com					
Dotronix Inc 160 First St SE	New Brighton	MN	55112	651-633-1742	633-1065
TF: 800-720-7218 ■ *Web:* www.dotronix.com					
Eizo Nanao Technologies Inc 5710 Warland Dr	Cypress	CA	90630	562-431-5011	431-4811
TF: 800-800-5202 ■ *Web:* www.eizo.com					
eMagin Corp 3006 Northup Way Ste 103	Bellevue	WA	98004	425-284-5200	284-5201
NYSE: EMAN ■ *Web:* www.emagin.com					
Envision Peripherals Inc (EPI) 47490 Seabridge Dr	Fremont	CA	94538	510-770-9988	770-1088
TF Tech Supp: 888-838-6388 ■ *Web:* www.aocdisplay.com					
Futaba Corp of America 711 E State Pkwy	Schaumburg	IL	60173	847-884-1444	884-1635
Web: www.futaba.com					
General Digital Corp Eight Nutmeg Rd S	South Windsor	CT	06074	860-282-2900	282-2244
TF: 800-952-2535 ■ *Web:* www.generaldigital.com					
Gunze USA 2113 Wells Branch Pkwy Ste 5400	Austin	TX	78728	512-990-3400	252-1181
Web: www.gunzeusa.com					
Hantronix Inc 10080 Bubb Rd	Cupertino	CA	95014	408-252-1100	252-1123
Web: www.hantronix.com					
ITUS Corp 900 Walt Whitman Rd	Melville	NY	11747	631-549-5900	549-5974
OTC: COPY ■ *Web:* ctipatents.com/					
La Cie Ltd 22985 NW Evergreen Pkwy	Hillsboro	OR	97124	503-844-4500	844-4508*
**Fax:* Mktg ■ *Web:* www.lacie.com					
LG Electronics USA Inc 1000 Sylvan Ave	Englewood Cliffs	NJ	07632	201-816-2000	
TF Tech Supp: 800-180-9999 ■ *Web:* www.lg.com					
Lite-On Trading USA Inc 720 S Hillview Dr	Milpitas	CA	95035	408-946-4873	941-4597
Web: www.us.liteon.com					
NEC Corp of America 10850 Gold Ctr Dr Ste 200	Rancho Cordova	CA	95670	916-463-7000	
TF: 800-632-4636 ■ *Web:* www.necam.com					
NEC Display Solutions of America Inc 500 Pk Blvd Ste 1100	Itasca	IL	60143	630-467-3000	467-3010*
**Fax:* Sales ■ *TF Cust Svc:* 800-632-4662 ■ *Web:* www.necdisplay.com					
OSRAM Sylvania Inc 100 Endicott St	Danvers	MA	01923	978-777-1900	750-2152
Web: www.sylvania.com					
Pioneer Electronics (USA) Inc 1925 E Dominguez St	Long Beach	CA	90810	310-952-2000	952-2402
TF: 800-421-1404 ■ *Web:* www.pioneerelectronics.com					
Planar Systems Inc 1195 NW Compton Dr	Beaverton	OR	97006	503-748-1100	748-1244
NASDAQ: PLNR ■ *TF:* 866-475-2627 ■ *Web:* www.planar.com					
Sharp Electronics Corp One Sharp Plz	Mahwah	NJ	07430	201-529-8200	529-8413
TF: 800-237-4277 ■ *Web:* www.sharpusa.com					
Sharp Microelectronics of the Americas 5700 NW Pacific Rim Blvd	Camas	WA	98607	360-834-2500	834-8903
Web: www.sharpsma.com					
Sony Electronics Inc One Sony Dr	Park Ridge	NJ	07656	201-930-1000	358-4058*
**Fax:* Hum Res ■ *TF Cust Svc:* 800-222-7669 ■ *Web:* www.sony.com					
Tatung Company of America Inc 2850 El Presidio St	Long Beach	CA	90810	310-637-2105	
TF: 800-827-2850 ■ *Web:* www.tatungusa.com					
Trans-Lux Corp 26 Pearl St	Norwalk	CT	06850	203-853-4321	
OTC: TNLX ■ *TF:* 800-243-5544 ■ *Web:* www.trans-lux.com					
Trans-Lux Fair-Play Inc 1700 Delaware Ave	Des Moines	IA	50317	515-265-5305	265-3364
TF: 800-247-0265 ■ *Web:* www.fair-play.com					
Video Display Corp 1868 Tucker Industrial Rd	Tucker	GA	30084	770-938-2080	493-3903
NASDAQ: VIDE ■ *TF Cust Svc:* 800-241-5005 ■ *Web:* www.videodisplay.com					
ViewSonic Corp 381 Brea Canyon Rd	Walnut	CA	91789	909-444-8888	468-1240
TF: 800-888-8583 ■ *Web:* ap.viewsonic.com					
Wells-Gardner Electronics Corp 9500 W 55th St Ste A	McCook	IL	60525	708-290-2100	290-2200
NYSE: WGA ■ *TF:* 800-336-6630 ■ *Web:* www.wellsgardner.com					

176-5 Multimedia Equipment & Supplies

Company / Address	City	State	ZIP	Phone	Fax
Corsair Memory Inc 46221 Landing Pkwy	Fremont	CA	94538	510-657-8747	657-8748
TF: 888-222-4346 ■ *Web:* www.corsair.com					
Creative Labs Inc 1901 McCarthy Blvd	Milpitas	CA	95035	408-428-6600	428-6611
TF Cust Svc: 800-998-1000 ■ *Web:* www.us.creative.com					
Cyber Acoustics LLC 3109 NE 109th Ave	Vancouver	WA	98682	360-883-0333	883-4888
Web: www.cyberacoustics.com					
Kinyo Company Inc 14235 Lomitas Ave	La Puente	CA	91746	626-333-3711	961-9114
TF: 800-735-4696 ■ *Web:* www.kinyo.com					
Matrox Electronic Systems Ltd 1055 St Regis Blvd	Dorval	QC	H9P2T4	514-822-6000	822-6363
Web: www.matrox.com					
SpeakerCraft Inc 940 Columbia Ave	Riverside	CA	92507	951-787-0543	787-8747
TF: 800-448-0976 ■ *Web:* www.speakercraft.com					
VITEC 2200 Century Pkwy Ste 900	Atlanta	GA	30345	404-320-0110	320-3132
Web: vitec.com/					
Vocollect Inc 703 Rodi Rd	Pittsburgh	PA	15235	412-829-8145	829-0972
Web: www.intermec.com					

176-6 Printers

Company / Address	City	State	ZIP	Phone	Fax
Addmaster Corp 225 Huntington Dr	Monrovia	CA	91016	626-358-2395	358-2784
Web: www.addmaster.com					
AMT Datasouth Corp 803 Camarillo Springs Rd Ste D	Camarillo	CA	93012	805-388-5799	484-5282
TF: 800-215-9192 ■ *Web:* www.amtdatasouth.com					
Astro-Med Inc 600 E Greenwich Ave	West Warwick	RI	02893	401-828-4000	822-2430
NASDAQ: ALOT ■ *TF:* 800-343-4039 ■ *Web:* www.astro-medinc.com					
Citizen Systems America Corp 363 Van Ness Way Ste 404	Torrance	CA	90501	310-781-1460	781-9152
TF: 800-421-6516 ■ *Web:* www.citizen-systems.com					
Craden Peripherals Corp 7860 Airport Hwy	Pennsauken	NJ	08109	856-488-0700	488-0925
Web: www.craden.com					
Datamax Corp 4501 Pkwy Commerce Blvd	Orlando	FL	32808	407-578-8007	578-8377
TF: 800-656-2062 ■ *Web:* www.datamaxcorp.com					
Digital Design Inc 67 Sand Pk Rd	Cedar Grove	NJ	07009	973-857-0900	857-9375
TF: 800-967-7746 ■ *Web:* www.genesisinkjet.com/ddiworldwide					
Eastman Kodak Co 343 State St	Rochester	NY	14650	585-724-4000	724-0663
OTC: EKDKQ ■ *Web:* www.kodak.com					
Epson America Inc 3840 Kilroy Airport Way	Long Beach	CA	90806	562-981-3840	290-5220
TF: 800-463-7766 ■ *Web:* www.epson.com					
Fujitsu Components America Inc 250 E Caribbean Dr	Sunnyvale	CA	94089	408-745-4900	745-4970
Web: www.fujitsu.com					
GCC Printers USA 209 Burlington Rd	Bedford	MA	01730	781-275-1115	442-2329*
**Fax Area Code:* 800 ■ *TF Sales:* 800-422-7777 ■ *Web:* www.gccprinters.de/en					
Hewlett-Packard (Canada) Ltd (HP) 5150 Spectrum Way	Mississauga	ON	L4W5G1	905-206-4725	
TF: 888-447-4636 ■ *Web:* welcome.hp.com					
Hewlett-Packard Co 3000 Hanover St	Palo Alto	CA	94304	650-857-1501	857-5518
NYSE: HPQ ■ *TF Sales:* 800-752-0900 ■ *Web:* www.hp.com					
International Business Machines Corp (IBM) One New OrchaRd Rd	Armonk	NY	10504	914-499-1900	
NYSE: IBM ■ *TF:* 800-426-4968 ■ *Web:* www.ibm.com					
Konica Minolta Business Solutions USA Inc 100 Williams Dr	Ramsey	NJ	07446	201-825-4000	
Web: www.kmbs.konicaminolta.us					
Kroy LLC 3830 Kelley Ave	Cleveland	OH	44114	216-426-5600	426-5601
TF Cust Svc: 888-888-5769 ■ *Web:* www.kroy.com					
Lexmark International Inc 740 W New Cir Rd	Lexington	KY	40550	859-232-2000	
NYSE: LXK ■ *TF Cust Svc:* 800-539-6275 ■ *Web:* www.lexmark.com					

Company / Address	City	State	Zip	Phone	Fax
Mutoh America Inc 2602 S 47th St Ste 102	Phoenix	AZ	85034	480-968-7772	968-7990
TF: 800-996-8864 ■ *Web:* www.mutoh.com					
NEC Corp of America 10850 Gold Ctr Dr Ste 200	Rancho Cordova	CA	95670	916-463-7000	
TF: 800-632-4636 ■ *Web:* www.necam.com					
Oce-USA Inc 5450 N Cumberland Ave Sixth Fl	Chicago	IL	60656	773-714-8500	693-7634
TF: 800-877-6232 ■ *Web:* csa.canon.com					
Oki Data Americas Inc 2000 Bishops Gate Blvd	Mount Laurel	NJ	08054	856-235-2600	222-5320
TF Cust Svc: 800-654-3282 ■ *Web:* www.okidata.com					
Pentax Imaging Co 633 17th St Ste 2600	Denver	CO	80202	303-799-8000	
TF: 800-877-0155 ■ *Web:* www.us.ricoh-imaging.com					
Plastic Card Systems Inc 31 Pierce St	Northborough	MA	01532	508-351-6210	
TF: 800-742-2273 ■ *Web:* www.plasticard-systems.com					
Practical Automation Inc 45 Woodmont Rd	Milford	CT	06460	203-882-5640	882-5648
Web: www.practicalautomation.com					
Primera Technology Inc Two Carlson Pkwy N Ste 375	Plymouth	MN	55447	763-475-6676	475-6677
TF: 800-797-2772 ■ *Web:* www.primera.com					
Printek Inc 1517 Townline Rd	Benton Harbor	MI	49022	269-925-3200	925-8539
TF: 800-368-4636 ■ *Web:* www.printek.com					
Printronix Inc 14600 Myford Rd	Irvine	CA	92606	714-368-2300	368-2600
TF: 800-665-6210 ■ *Web:* www.printronix.com					
Ricoh Printing Systems America Inc 2390 Ward Ave Ste A	Simi Valley	CA	93065	805-578-4000	578-4001
Web: www.rpsa.ricoh.com					
RISO Inc Eight New England Executive Park Ste 390	Burlington	MA	01803	978-777-7377	777-2517
TF General: 800-942-7476 ■ *Web:* www.riso.com					
Roland DGA Corp 15363 Barranca Pkwy	Irvine	CA	92618	949-727-2100	727-2112
TF: 800-542-2307 ■ *Web:* www.rolanddga.com					
Sato America Inc 10350A Nations Ford Rd	Charlotte	NC	28273	704-644-1650	644-1662
TF: 888-871-8741 ■ *Web:* www.satoamerica.com					
Seiko Instruments USA Inc 21221 S Western Ave Ste 250	Torrance	CA	90501	310-517-7700	517-7709
TF Sales: 800-688-0817 ■ *Web:* www.seikoinstruments.com					
Seiko Instruments USA Inc Business & Home Office Products Div (SII) 21221 S Western Ave Ste 250	Torrance	CA	90501	310-517-7700	517-7779
Web: labelprinters.sii-thermalprinters.com					
Seiko Instruments USA Inc Micro Printer Div 2990 Lomita Blvd	Torrance	CA	90505	310-517-7778	
TF: 800-688-0817 ■ *Web:* labelprinters.sii-thermalprinters.com					
Sharp Electronics Corp One Sharp Plz	Mahwah	NJ	07430	201-529-8200	529-8413
TF: 800-237-4277 ■ *Web:* www.sharpusa.com					
SiPix Imaging Inc 47485 Seabridge Dr	Fremont	CA	94538	510-743-2849	
Web: www.eink.com					
Star Micronics America Inc 1150 King George's Post Rd	Edison	NJ	08837	732-623-5500	623-5590*
**Fax:* Sales ■ *TF:* 800-782-7636 ■ *Web:* www.starmicronics.com					
Stratix 4920 Avalon Ridge Pkwy	Norcross	GA	30071	770-326-7580	326-7593
TF: 800-883-8300 ■ *Web:* www.stratixcorp.com					
TallyGenicom 15345 Barranca Pkwy Ste 100	Irvine	CA	92618	714-368-2300	222-7629*
**Fax Area Code:* 703 ■ *TF:* 800-436-4266 ■ *Web:* www.tallygenicom.com					
Telpar Inc 187 Crosby Rd Ste 100	Dover	NH	03820	603-750-7237	742-9938
TF: 800-872-4886 ■ *Web:* www.telpar.com					
Toshiba America Inc 1251 Ave of the Americas Ste 4100	New York	NY	10020	212-596-0600	593-3875
TF: 800-457-7777 ■ *Web:* www.toshiba.com					
TransAct Technologies Inc one Hamden Ctr 2319 Whitney Ave Ste 3B	Hamden	CT	06518	203-859-6800	949-9048
NASDAQ: TACT ■ *TF:* 800-243-8941 ■ *Web:* www.transact-tech.com					
Unimark Products 9818 Pflumm Rd	Lenexa	KS	66215	913-649-2424	649-5795
TF Cust Svc: 800-255-6356 ■ *Web:* www.unimark.com					
Xante Corp 2800 Dauphin St Ste 100	Mobile	AL	36606	251-473-6502	473-6503
TF: 800-926-8839 ■ *Web:* xante.com					
Xerox Corp 45 Glover Ave PO Box 4505	Norwalk	CT	06856	203-968-3000	
NYSE: XRX ■ *TF:* 800-327-9753 ■ *Web:* www.xerox.com					
Zebra Technologies Corp 475 Half Day Rd Ste 500	Lincolnshire	IL	60069	847-634-6700	913-8766
NASDAQ: ZBRA ■ *TF:* 800-423-0422 ■ *Web:* www.zebra.com					

176-7 Scanning Equipment

Company / Address	City	State	Zip	Phone	Fax
Accu-Sort Systems Inc 511 School House Rd	Telford	PA	18969	215-723-0981	721-5551
TF: 800-227-2633 ■ *Web:* www.datalogic.com					
AirClic Inc 900 Northbrook Dr Ste 100	Trevose	PA	19053	215-504-0560	504-0565
TF: 800-419-8495 ■ *Web:* www.airclic.com					
BenQ America Corp 15375 Barranca Ste A205	Irvine	CA	92618	949-255-9500	255-9600
TF: 866-600-2367 ■ *Web:* www.benq.us					
BOWE Bell + Howell 760 S Wolf Rd	Wheeling	IL	60090	847-675-7600	340-8852*
**Fax Area Code:* 585 ■ *TF:* 800-220-3030 ■ *Web:* www.bellhowell.net					
CardScan Inc 25 First St Ste 107	Cambridge	MA	02141	617-492-4200	492-6659
TF: 800-942-6739 ■ *Web:* www.cardscan.com					
Computerwise Inc 302 N Winchester Ln	Olathe	KS	66062	913-829-0600	829-0810
TF: 800-255-3739 ■ *Web:* www.computerwise.com					
Datalogic Scanning 959 Terry St	Eugene	OR	97402	541-683-5700	345-7140
TF: 800-695-5700 ■ *Web:* www.datalogic.com					
Eastman Kodak Co 343 State St	Rochester	NY	14650	585-724-4000	724-0663
OTC: EKDKQ ■ *Web:* www.kodak.com					
GTCO CalComp Inc 7125 Riverwood Dr	Columbia	MD	21046	410-381-6688	290-9065
Web: gtcocalcomp.com					
Hewlett-Packard Co 3000 Hanover St	Palo Alto	CA	94304	650-857-1501	857-5518
NYSE: HPQ ■ *TF Sales:* 800-752-0900 ■ *Web:* www.hp.com					
Hitachi Canada Ltd 5450 Explore Dr Suite 501	Mississauga	ON	L4W5N1	905-629-9300	290-0141
TF: 866-797-4332 ■ *Web:* www.hitachi.ca					
iCAD Inc Four Townsend W Ste 17	Nashua	NH	03063	603-882-5200	880-3843
NASDAQ: ICAD ■ *TF:* 866-280-2239 ■ *Web:* www.icadmed.com					
InPath Devices 3610 Dodge St Ste 200	Omaha	NE	68131	402-345-9200	526-5920*
**Fax Area Code:* 888 ■ *TF:* 800-988-1914 ■ *Web:* www.inpath.com					
Microtek Lab Inc 10900 183rd St Ste 290	Cerritos	CA	90703	310-687-5800	903-7832*
**Fax Area Code:* 562 ■ *Web:* www.microtekusa.com/					
Mustek Inc 15271 Barranca Pkwy	Irvine	CA	92618	949-790-3800	247-8960
TF: 800-308-7226 ■ *Web:* www.mustek.com					
Oce-USA Inc 5450 N Cumberland Ave Sixth Fl	Chicago	IL	60656	773-714-8500	693-7634
TF: 800-877-6232 ■ *Web:* csa.canon.com					
Order-Matic Corp 340 S Eckroat St PO Box 25463	Oklahoma City	OK	73129	405-672-1487	672-5349
TF: 800-767-6733 ■ *Web:* www.ordermatic.com					
Peripheral Dynamics Inc 5150 Campus Dr Whitemarsh Industrial Pk	Plymouth Meeting	PA	19462	610-825-7090	834-7708
TF: 800-523-0253 ■ *Web:* www.pdiscan.com					
Ricoh Electronics Inc 1100 Valencia Ave	Tustin	CA	92780	714-566-2500	
Web: www.rei.ricoh.com					
Roland DGA Corp 15363 Barranca Pkwy	Irvine	CA	92618	949-727-2100	727-2112
TF: 800-542-2307 ■ *Web:* www.rolanddga.com					
Scan-Optics Inc 169 Progress Dr	Manchester	CT	06042	860-645-7878	645-7995
TF: 800-543-8681 ■ *Web:* www.scanoptics.com					
Scantron Corp 34 Parker	Irvine	CA	92618	949-639-7500	639-7710
TF: 800-722-6876 ■ *Web:* www.scantron.com					
Stratix 4920 Avalon Ridge Pkwy	Norcross	GA	30071	770-326-7580	326-7593
TF: 800-883-8300 ■ *Web:* www.stratixcorp.com					
Techville Inc 11343 N Central Expwy	Dallas	TX	75243	214-739-7033	
Web: www.umax.com					
Videx Inc 1105 NE Cir Blvd	Corvallis	OR	97330	541-738-5500	738-5501
Web: www.videx.com					
Visioneer Inc 5673 Gibraltar Dr Ste 150	Pleasanton	CA	94588	925-251-6300	416-8600
Web: www.visioneer.com					
Wizcom Technologies Inc Boston Post Rd W 33 Ste 320	Marlborough	MA	01752	508-251-5388	251-5394
TF: 888-777-0552 ■ *Web:* www.wizcomtech.com					
ZBA Inc 94 Old Camplain Rd	Hillsborough	NJ	08844	908-359-2070	595-0909
TF: 800-750-4239 ■ *Web:* www.zbaus.com					

176-8 Storage Devices

Company / Address	City	State	Zip	Phone	Fax
Ampex Data Systems Corp 500 Broadway	Redwood City	CA	94063	650-367-2011	367-3106
Web: www.ampex.com					
Appro International Inc 901 Fifth Ave Ste 1000	Seattle	WA	98164	206-701-2000	299-9174
TF: 800-950-2729 ■ *Web:* www.cray.com					
Apricorn Inc 12191 Kirkham Rd	Poway	CA	92064	858-513-2000	513-2020
TF: 800-458-5448 ■ *Web:* www.apricorn.com					
Atp Electronics Inc 750 N Mary Ave	Sunnyvale	CA	94085	408-732-5000	732-5055
Web: www.atpinc.com					
Avere Systems Inc 5000 Mcknight Rd Ste 404	Pittsburgh	PA	15237	412-894-2570	
TF: 888-882-8373 ■ *Web:* www.averesystems.com					
BlueArc Corp 50 Rio Robles Dr	San Jose	CA	95134	408-576-6600	576-6601
Web: www.hds.com					
BridgeSTOR LLC 18060 Old Coach Dr	Poway	CA	92064	858-375-7076	
TF: 800-280-8204 ■ *Web:* www.bridgestor.com					
Cirrascale Corp 12140 Community Rd	Poway	CA	92064	858-874-3800	874-3838
TF: 888-942-3800 ■ *Web:* www.cirrascale.com					
CMS Peripherals Inc 12 Mauchly Unit E	Irvine	CA	92618	714-424-5520	
TF: 800-327-5773 ■ *Web:* www.cmsproducts.com					
Creative Labs Inc 1901 McCarthy Blvd	Milpitas	CA	95035	408-428-6600	428-6611
TF Cust Svc: 800-998-1000 ■ *Web:* www.us.creative.com					
CRU Acquisitions Group LLC 1000 SE Tech Ctr Dr Ste 160	Vancouver	WA	98683	360-816-1800	816-1831
TF: 800-260-9800 ■ *Web:* www.cru-inc.com					
Cybernetics Inc 111 Cybernetics Way	Yorktown	VA	23693	757-833-9100	833-9300
Web: www.cybernetics.com					
DataDirect Networks 9320 Lurline Ave	Chatsworth	CA	91311	818-700-7600	700-7601
TF: 800-837-2298 ■ *Web:* www.ddn.com					
Datalink Corp 8170 Upland Cir	Chanhassen	MN	55317	952-944-3462	944-7869
NASDAQ: DTLK ■ *TF:* 800-448-6314 ■ *Web:* www.datalink.com					
Digital Peripheral Solutions Inc 8015 E Crystal Dr	Anaheim	CA	92807	877-998-3440	692-5516*
**Fax Area Code:* 714 ■ *TF:* 877-998-3440 ■ *Web:* q-see.com					
Disc Makers 7905 N Rt 130	Pennsauken	NJ	08110	856-663-9030	661-3458
TF: 800-468-9353 ■ *Web:* www.discmakers.com					
Dynamic Network Factory Inc 21353 Cabot Blvd	Hayward	CA	94545	510-265-1122	265-1565
TF: 800-947-4742 ■ *Web:* www.dnfstorage.com					
Edge Electronics Inc 75 Orville Dr	Bohemia	NY	11716	631-471-3343	471-3405
TF: 800-647-3343 ■ *Web:* www.edgeelectronics.com					
FlexPlay Technologies Inc 3350 Peachtree Rd One Capital City Plz Ste 1150	Atlanta	GA	30326	404-835-9900	
Web: www.flexplay.com					
Fujitsu Computer Products of America Inc 1255 E Arques Ave	Sunnyvale	CA	94085	408-746-7000	746-6910
TF: 800-626-4686 ■ *Web:* www.fujitsu.com					
Fusion-io Inc 2855 E Cottonwood Pkwy Ste 100	Salt Lake City	UT	84121	801-424-5500	
Web: www.fusionio.com					
Gridstore Inc 1975 W El Camino Real Ste 306	Mountain View	CA	94040	650-316-5515	
TF: 855-786-7065 ■ *Web:* www.gridstore.com					
H Company Computer Products Inc 16812 Hale Ave	Irvine	CA	92606	949-833-3222	
TF: 800-726-2477 ■ *Web:* www.thinkcp.com					
Headway Technologies Inc 682 S Hillview Dr	Milpitas	CA	95035	408-934-5300	
Web: headway.com					
Hewlett-Packard (Canada) Ltd (HP) 5150 Spectrum Way	Mississauga	ON	L4W5G1	905-206-4725	
TF: 888-447-4636 ■ *Web:* welcome.hp.com					
Hewlett-Packard Co 3000 Hanover St	Palo Alto	CA	94304	650-857-1501	857-5518
NYSE: HPQ ■ *TF Sales:* 800-752-0900 ■ *Web:* www.hp.com					

Phone | Fax

Hie Electronics Inc
321 N Central Expy Ste 260 Mckinney TX 75070 972-542-2327
TF: 888-782-7937 ■ *Web:* www.hie-electronics.com

Hitachi America Ltd Computer Div
2000 Sierra Pt Pkwy Brisbane CA 94005 800-448-2244 244-7776*
**Fax Area Code:* 650 ■ *TF:* 800-448-2244 ■ *Web:* www.hitachi-america.us

Hitachi Data Systems Corp
750 Central Expy Santa Clara CA 95050 408-970-1000 727-8036
TF: 877-437-3849 ■ *Web:* www.hds.com

I/O Magic Corp
20512 Crescent Bay Dr Ste 106 Lake Forest, CA 92630 949-707-4800 855-3550
OTC: IOMG ■ *Web:* www.iomagic.com

Idealstor LLC 1100 Lakeway Dr Ste100 Lakeway TX 78734 512-279-4321
TF: 888-864-3257 ■ *Web:* www.idealstor.com

Imation Corp One Imation Pl Oakdale MN 55128 651-704-4000 704-7100
NYSE: IMN ■ *TF:* 888-466-3456 ■ *Web:* www.imation.com

Infortrend Corp 435 Lakeside Dr Ste 130 Sunnyvale CA 94085 408-988-5088
Web: www.infortrend.com

International Business Machines Corp (IBM)
One New OrchaRd Rd Armonk NY 10504 914-499-1900
NYSE: IBM ■ *TF:* 800-426-4968 ■ *Web:* www.ibm.com

Kanguru Solutions 1360 Main St Millis MA 02054 508-376-4245 376-4462
TF Sales: 888-526-4878 ■ *Web:* www.kanguru.com

La Cie Ltd 22985 NW Evergreen Pkwy Hillsboro OR 97124 503-844-4500 844-4508*
**Fax:* Mktg ■ *Web:* www.lacie.com

LG Electronics USA Inc
1000 Sylvan Ave Englewood Cliffs NJ 07632 201-816-2000
TF Tech Supp: 800-180-9999 ■ *Web:* www.lg.com

Luminex Software Inc 871 Marlborough Ave Riverside CA 92507 951-781-4100 781-4105
TF Sales: 888-586-4639 ■ *Web:* www.luminex.com

Microboards Technology LLC
8150 Mallory Ct PO Box 846 Chanhassen MN 55317 952-556-1600 556-1620
TF: 800-646-8881 ■ *Web:* www.microboards.com

Mitsumi Electronics Corp
40000 Grand River Ave
Novi Technology Ctr Ste 200 Novi MI 48375 248-426-8448
Web: www.mitsumi.com

NEC Corp of America
10850 Gold Ctr Dr Ste 200 Rancho Cordova CA 95670 916-463-7000
TF: 800-632-4636 ■ *Web:* www.necam.com

NexGen Storage Inc
361 Centennial Pkwy Ste 230 Louisville CO 80027 720-245-6300
Web: nexgenstorage.com

Perifitech of Ohio Inc 23108 Felch St Cleveland OH 44128 216-332-0655 332-0656
Web: www.perifitech.com

Pexagon Technology Inc
14 Business Park Dr Ste E Branford CT 06405 203-458-3364
Web: www.pexagontech.com

Phoenix International 812 W Southern Ave Orange CA 92865 714-283-4800 283-1169
Web: www.phenxint.com

Pioneer Electronics (USA) Inc
1925 E Dominguez St Long Beach CA 90810 310-952-2000 952-2402
TF: 800-421-1404 ■ *Web:* www.pioneerelectronics.com

PURE Storage Inc 650 Castro St Ste 400 Mountain View CA 94041 650-290-6088
Web: www.purestorage.com

Qualstar Corp 3990-B Heritage Oak Ct Simi Valley CA 93063 805-583-7744 583-7749
NASDAQ: QBAK ■ *TF:* 800-468-0680 ■ *Web:* www.qualstar.com

Quantum Corp 224 Airport Pkwy Ste 300 San Jose CA 95110 408-944-4000 944-4040
NYSE: QTM ■ *TF Tech Supp:* 800-677-6268 ■ *Web:* www.quantum.com

Quantum/ATL 141 Innovation Dr Irvine CA 92617 949-856-7800 856-7799
TF: 800-677-6268 ■ *Web:* www.quantum.com

Rimage Corp 7725 Washington Ave S Minneapolis MN 55439 952-944-8144 400-0939
TF: 800-553-8312 ■ *Web:* www.qumu.com

SANBlaze Technology Inc
One Monarch Dr Ste 204 Littleton MA 01460 978-679-1400
Web: www.sanblaze.com

Savage IO Inc Eight S Lyon St Batavia NY 14020 585-250-4216
Web: www.savageio.com

Seagate Technology LLC
10200 S De Anza Blvd Cupertino CA 95014 831-438-6550
Web: www.seagate.com

Shaffstall Corp 8531 Bash St Indianapolis IN 46250 317-842-2077 915-9045
TF: 800-357-6250 ■ *Web:* www.shaffstall.com

Sony Electronics Inc One Sony Dr Park Ridge NJ 07656 201-930-1000 358-4058*
**Fax:* Hum Res ■ *TF Cust Svc:* 800-222-7669 ■ *Web:* www.sony.com

Tandberg Data 10225 Westmoor Dr Ste 125 Westminster CO 80021 303-442-4333
TF: 800-392-2983 ■ *Web:* www.tandbergdata.com

TDK USA Corp 525 RXR Plaza PO Box 9302 Uniondale NY 11556 516-535-2600 294-8318*
**Fax:* Sales ■ *TF General:* 800-285-2783 ■ *Web:* www.tdk.com

TEAC America Inc 7733 Telegraph Rd Montebello CA 90640 323-726-0303 727-7656
Web: www.teac.com

Tegile Systems Inc 8000 Jarvis Ave Newark CA 94560 510-791-7900
Web: www.tegile.com

Themis Computer 47200 Bayside Pkwy Fremont CA 94538 510-252-0870 490-5529
Web: www.themis.com

Tintri Inc 2570 W El Camino Real Mountain View CA 94040 650-209-3900
Web: www.tintri.com

Toshiba America Inc
1251 Ave of the Americas Ste 4100 New York NY 10020 212-596-0600 593-3875
TF: 800-457-7777 ■ *Web:* www.toshiba.com

Unitrends Software Corp
Seven Technology Cir Ste 100 Columbia SC 29203 803-454-0300
Web: www.unitrends.com

VeriStor Systems Inc
3308 Peachtree Industrial Blvd Duluth GA 30096 678-990-1593 990-1597
TF: 866-956-2948 ■ *Web:* www.veristor.com

Western Digital Corp 3355 Michelson Dr Ste 100 Irvine CA 92612 949-672-7000 672-5498
NASDAQ: WDC ■ *TF:* 800-832-4778 ■ *Web:* www.wdc.com

177 COMPUTER EQUIPMENT & SOFTWARE - WHOL

SEE ALSO Business Machines - Whol p. 1894; Electrical & Electronic Equipment & Parts - Whol p. 2223

Phone | Fax

A.I.W. Inc 4446 Old Winter Garden Rd Ste 101 Orlando FL 32811 407-521-4576
Web: www.aiwonline.net

AAA Digital Imaging Inc
5706 New Peachtree Rd Chamblee GA 30341 770-451-7861
Web: www.aaadi.com

ABOL Software Inc 413 Creekstone Ridge Woodstock GA 30188 678-494-3172
Web: www.iabol.com

Access Specialties International LLC
15230 Carrousel Way Rosemount MN 55068 651-453-1283
TF: 800-332-1013 ■ *Web:* www.access-specialties.com

Addonics Technologies Inc 1918 Junction Ave San Jose CA 95131 408-573-8580
Web: www.addonics.com

Advanced Clinical Services LLC
10 Pkwy N Ste 350 Deerfield IL 60015 847-267-1176
Web: www.advancedclinical.com

Advanced Web Offset Inc 2260 Oak Ridge Way Vista CA 92081 760-727-1700
Web: www.awoink.com

Ahearn & Soper Inc 100 Woodbine Downs Blvd Rexdale ON M9W5S6 416-675-3999 675-3457
TF: 800-263-4258 ■ *Web:* www.ahearn.com

Alacritech Inc 1995 N First St Ste 200 San Jose CA 95112 408-287-9997
Web: www.alacritech.com

Alexander Open Systems Inc
12851 Foster St Overland Park KS 66213 913-307-2300 307-2380
TF: 800-473-1110 ■ *Web:* www.aos5.com

Alexander's Print Advantage Co
245 South 1060 West Lindon UT 84042 801-224-8666
Web: www.alexanders.com

Allied Group Inc, The 25 Amflex Dr Cranston RI 02921 401-946-6100
TF: 800-556-6310 ■ *Web:* www.thealliedgrp.com

Altametrics Inc 3191 Red Hill Ave Ste 100 Costa Mesa CA 92626 800-676-1281
TF: 800-676-1281 ■ *Web:* www.altametrics.com

Altruent Corp 805 N W St Raleigh NC 27603 919-828-4419
Web: www.altruent.com

American Portwell Technology Inc
44200 Christy St Fremont CA 94538 510-403-3399 403-3184
TF: 877-278-8899 ■ *Web:* www.portwell.com

Amex Inc 2724 Summer St NE Minneapolis MN 55413 612-331-3063 331-3180
Web: www.amexinc.com

Amnet Inc 219 W Colorado Ave Ste 304 Colorado Springs CO 80903 719-442-6683
Web: www.amnet.net

APCON Inc 9255 SW Pioneer Ct Wilsonville OR 97070 503-682-4050
TF: 800-624-6808 ■ *Web:* www.apcon.com

App-Techs Corp 505-B Willow Ln Lancaster PA 17601 717-735-0848
Web: www.app-techs.com

Applied Ceramics Inc 48630 Milmont Dr Fremont CA 94538 510-249-9700
Web: www.appliedceramics.net

Arbitech LLC 15330 Barranca Pkwy Irvine CA 92618 949-376-6650
Web: www.arbitech.com

Arete Inc 65 S Main St Bldg E Pennington NJ 08534 609-737-1212
Web: www.areteinc.com

Arrow Electronics Corp 7459 S Lima St Englewood CO 80112 303-824-4000
NYSE: ARW ■ *Web:* www.arrow.com

Arrow Enterprise Computing Solutions
7459 S Lima St Bldg 2 Englewood CO 80112 303-824-7650
Web: www.arrowecs.com

ASA Tire Systems Inc 651 S Stratford Dr Meridian ID 83642 208-855-0781
TF: 800-241-8472 ■ *Web:* www.asatire.com

ASI Corp 48289 Fremont Blvd Fremont CA 94538 510-226-8000 226-8858*
**Fax:* Sales ■ *TF:* 800-200-0274 ■ *Web:* www.asipartner.com

ATEC Group 1762 Central Ave Ste 1 Albany NY 12205 518-452-3700

Aternity Inc 200 Friberg Pkwy Ste 3000 Westborough MA 01581 508-475-0414
Web: www.aternity.com

Atlantix Global Systems One Sun Ct Norcross GA 30092 770-248-7700 448-7726
TF: 877-552-8526 ■ *Web:* www.atlantixglobal.com

Autostar Solutions Inc
1300 Summit Ave Ste 800 Fort Worth TX 76102 800-682-2215
TF: 800-682-2215 ■ *Web:* www.autostarsolutions.com

AVAD Canada Ltd 205 Courtneypark Dr W Mississauga ON L5W0A5 866-523-2823
TF: 866-523-2823 ■ *Web:* ca.avad.com

Avnet Inc 2211 S 47th St Phoenix AZ 85034 480-643-2000
NYSE: AVT ■ *TF:* 888-822-8638 ■ *Web:* www.avnet.com

Avnet Technology Solutions 8700 S Price Rd Tempe AZ 85284 480-794-6500
TF: 800-409-1483 ■ *Web:* www.ats.avnet.com

Axiom Memory Solutions LLC
19651 Descartes Foothill Ranch CA 92610 949-581-1450
TF: 888-658-3326 ■ *Web:* www.axiommemory.com

Barr Systems LLC 4500 NW 27th Ave Gainesville FL 32606 352-491-3100
Web: www.barrsystems.com

Bay Technical Assoc Inc
5239 Ave A Long Beach Industrial Park MS 39560 228-563-7334
TF: 800-523-2702 ■ *Web:* www.baytech.net

Big Huge Games Inc
1954 Greenspring Dr Ste 520 Timonium MD 21093 410-842-0028

Blueslice Networks Inc
1751 Richardson St Ste 7500 Montreal QC H3K1G6 514-935-9700

BreezeGo Inc 3332 Southside Blvd Jacksonville FL 32216 904-998-4066
Web: www.breezego.com

Burstek 12801 Westlinks Dr Ste 101 Fort Myers FL 33913 239-495-5900
Web: www.burstek.com

Butler Technologies Inc 231 W Wayne St Butler PA 16001 724-283-6656
TF: 800-494-6656 ■ *Web:* www.butlertechnologies.com

C Enterprises LP 2445 Cades Way Vista CA 92081 760-599-5111
Web: www.copierdepot.com

Cabaret Systems Inc 8848 Red Oak Blvd Charlotte NC 28217 704-333-1100
Web: cabaretsystems.com

Phone | Fax

CAD/CAM Consulting Services Inc (CCCS) 996 Lawrence Dr Ste 101 ... Newbury Park CA 91320 805-375-7676 375-7678
TF: 888-375-7676 ■ Web: www.cad-cam.com

Cadec Corp 645 Harvey Rd ... Manchester NH 03103 603-668-1010 623-0604
TF: 800-252-2332 ■ Web: www.cadec.com

Cakewalk Inc 268 Summer St Eighth Fl ... Boston MA 02210 617-423-9004
Web: www.cakewalk.com

Cash Management Solutions Inc 13921 Icot Blvd Ste 710 ... Clearwater FL 33760 727-524-1103
Web: www.cashmgmt.com

CCT Technologies Inc 482 W San Carlos St ... San Jose CA 95110 408-519-3200
Web: www.cland.com

Central Florida Press Inc 4560 L B Mcleod Rd ... Orlando FL 32811 407-843-5811
Web: www.printcfp.com

Champion Solutions Group 791 Pk of Commerce Blvd Ste 200 ... Boca Raton FL 33487 561-997-2900 997-4043
TF: 800-771-7000 ■ Web: www.championsg.com

Chicago Electronic Discovery LLC 1000 Lk St Ste 203 ... Oak Park IL 60301 312-878-1100
Web: www.viaforensics.com

Chief Architect Inc 6500 N Mineral Dr ... Coeur D'Alene ID 83815 208-292-3400
Web: www.chiefarchitect.com

City Press Inc W238 N1650 Rockwood Dr ... Waukesha WI 53188 262-523-3000
Web: www.citypressinc.com

Colorfx Inc 10776 Aurora Ave ... Des Moines IA 50322 800-348-9044
Web: www.colorfxprint.com

Columbia Ultimate Business Systems Inc 4400 NE 77th Ave Ste 100 ... Vancouver WA 98662 360-256-7358 260-1614
TF: 800-488-4420 ■ Web: www.columbiaultimate.com

Columbus Productions Inc 4580 Cargo Dr ... Columbus GA 31907 706-644-1595
Web: www.columbusproductionsinc.com

Column Technologies Inc 1400 Opus Pl Ste 110 ... Downers Grove IL 60515 630-515-6660 271-1508
Web: www.columnit.com

Comprehensive Traffic Systems Inc 4860 Robb St Ste 205 ... Wheat Ridge CO 80033 303-432-3777
TF: 888-353-9002 ■ Web: www.ctsworldwide.net

Computech International Inc 525 Northern Blvd ... Great Neck NY 11021 516-487-0101
Web: www.cti-intl.com

Computer Aided Technology Inc 165 N Arlington Heights Rd Ste 101 ... Buffalo Grove IL 60089 888-308-2284
TF: 888-308-2284 ■ Web: www.cati.com

Computer Connection of Central New York Inc 11206 Cosby Manor Rd ... Utica NY 13502 315-724-2209
TF: 800-566-4786 ■ Web: www.ccny.com

Computer Crafts Inc 57 Thomas Rd ... Hawthorne NJ 07506 973-423-3500
Web: www.computer-crafts.com

Computer Dynamics Inc 3030 Whitehall Pk Dr ... Charlotte NC 28273 866-599-6512 583-9671*
*Fax Area Code: 704 ■ TF: 866-599-6512 ■ Web: www.cdynamics.com

Comstor Inc 14850 Conference Ctr Dr Ste 200 ... Chantilly VA 20151 703-345-5100 345-5572*
*Fax: Sales ■ TF: 800-955-9590 ■ Web: www.comstor.com

Configure Inc 1800 Hamilton Ave Ste 200 ... San Jose CA 95125 408-269-1122
Web: www.configureinc.com

Cordoba Corp 1401 N Broadway ... Los Angeles CA 90012 213-895-0224
Web: www.cordobacorp.com

Coridian Technologies Inc 1725 Lk Dr W ... Chanhassen MN 55317 952-361-9980
Web: coridian.com

Cornell Mayo Assoc Inc 600 Lanidex Plz ... Parsippany NJ 07054 973-887-3069
Web: www.cornell-mayo.com

Corporate Information Technologies Inc 14 Brick Walk Ln ... Farmington CT 06032 860-676-2720
Web: www.corpit.com

Cpu Venturetech 330 Walsh Dr ... Casper WY 82609 307-235-6212
Web: www.cpuventuretech.com

Cranel Inc 8999 Gemini Pkwy ... Columbus OH 43240 614-431-8000 431-8388
TF General: 800-288-3475 ■ Web: www.cranel.com

Crown Micro Inc 48351 Fremont Blvd ... Fremont CA 94538 510-490-8187
TF: 800-963-7070 ■ Web: fremont.mercurynews.com

CS3 Technology 5272 S Lewis Ave Ste 100 ... Tulsa OK 74105 918-496-1600
Web: www.crouchslavin.com

CSF International Inc 1629 Barber Rd ... Sarasota FL 34240 941-379-0881

CSU Industries Inc 15 Hoover St ... Inwood NY 11096 516-239-4310
Web: www.csuindustries.com

D & H Distributing Company Inc 2525 N Seventh St ... Harrisburg PA 17110 800-340-1001 340-1001
TF: 800-340-1001 ■ Web: www.dandh.com

Data Impressions 17418 Studebaker Rd ... Cerritos CA 90703 562-207-9050 207-9053
TF: 800-777-6488 ■ Web: dataimpressions.com

Data Sales Company Inc 3450 W Burnsville Pkwy ... Burnsville MN 55337 952-890-8838 895-3369
TF: 800-328-2730 ■ Web: www.datasales.com

Databit Inc 200 Route 17 ... Mahwah NJ 07430 201-529-8050
Web: www.databitinc.com

Datamaxx Applied Technologies Inc 2001 Drayton Dr ... Tallahassee FL 32311 850-558-8000
Web: www.datamaxx.com

Dataprobe Inc 1B Pearl Ct ... Allendale NJ 07401 201-934-9944
Web: www.dataprobe.com

Daymark Solutions Inc 23 Third Ave ... Burlington MA 01803 781-359-3000
Web: www.daymarksi.com

De Marque inc 400 Boul Jean-Lesage Bureau 540 ... Quebec QC G1K8W1 418-658-9143
TF: 888-458-9143 ■ Web: www.demarque.com

Deccan International 5935 Cornerstone Court W Ste 230 ... San Diego CA 92121 858-764-8400
Web: deccanintl.com

Decision Academic Inc 411 Legget Dr Ste 501 ... Ottawa ON K2K3C9 613-254-9669
Web: www.decisionacademic.com

Dectrader 3305 Grande Vista Dr ... Newbury Park CA 91320 805-480-1888
Web: www.abtinc.com

Delkin Devices Inc 13350 Kirkham Way ... Poway CA 92064 858-391-1234
Web: www.delkin.com

Phone | Fax

Dellas Graphics Inc 835 Canal St ... Syracuse NY 13210 315-474-4641
Web: www.dellasgraphics.com

Delta Computer Group Inc Four Dubon Ct ... Farmingdale NY 11735 631-845-0400
Web: www.deltacomputergroup.com

Desire2Learn Inc 151 Charles SW Ste 400 ... Kitchener ON N2G1H6 519-772-0325 772-0324
TF: 888-772-0325 ■ Web: www.d2l.com

Dieselpoint Inc 117 N Jefferson St ... Chicago IL 60661 773-528-1700
Web: www.dieselpoint.com

DigiLink Inc 840 S Pickett St ... Alexandria VA 22304 703-340-1800
TF: 877-806-3453 ■ Web: www.digilink-inc.com

Digital Impressions Inc 1127 International Pkwy Ste 109 ... Fredericksburg VA 22406 540-752-1011
Web: www.digimpressions.com

Digital Storage Inc 7611 Green Meadows Dr ... Lewis Center OH 43035 740-548-7179 803-8030*
*Fax Area Code: 800 ■ TF: 800-232-3475 ■ Web: www.digitalstorage.com

Dirxion LLC 1859 Bowles Ave Ste 100 ... Fenton MO 63026 636-717-2300
Web: www.dirxion.com

Dlt Solutions 13861 Sunrise Valley Dr Ste 400 ... Herndon VA 20171 703-709-7172 709-8450
TF: 800-262-4358 ■ Web: www.dlt.com

Documation LLC 1556 International Dr ... Eau Claire WI 54701 715-839-8899
Web: documation.com

DPC DATA Inc 103 Eisenhower Pkwy Ste 300 ... Roseland NJ 07068 201-346-0701
TF: 800-996-4747 ■ Web: www.dpcdata.com

DVTel Inc 65 Challenger Rd ... Ridgefield Park NJ 07660 201-368-9700
Web: www.dvtel.com

Dynamic Computer Corp 23400 Industrial Pk Ct ... Farmington Hills MI 48335 248-473-2200 473-2201
TF: 866-257-2111 ■ Web: www.dcc-online.com

Dynamic Digital Depth Inc 2120 Colorado Ave Ste 100 ... Santa Monica CA 90404 310-566-3340
Web: www.ddd.com

DYNAMIC SYSTEMS Inc 124 Maryland St ... El Segundo CA 90245 310-337-4400
Web: www.dynamicsystemsinc.com

E John Schmitz & Sons Inc 37 Loveton Cir ... Sparks MD 21152 410-329-3000
Web: www.schmitzpress.com

e-TechServices.com Inc 5220 SW 91st Terrace ... Gainesville FL 32608 352-332-3200
Web: web2.e-techservices.com

Eastern Computer Exchange Inc 105 Cascade Blvd ... Milford CT 06460 203-877-4334
Web: www.ecei.com

Eastern Data Inc 4386 Park Dr ... Norcross GA 30093 770-279-8888
Web: www.edi-atl.com

EDAC Systems Inc 10970 Pierson Dr ... Fredericksburg VA 22408 540-361-1580
Web: www.edacsystems.com

Electronic Environments Corp 410 Forest St ... Marlborough MA 01752 508-229-1400 303-0579
TF: 800-342-5332 ■ Web: www.eecnet.com

Eleven Wireless Inc 315 SW 11th Ave Third Fl ... Portland OR 97205 503-222-4321
Web: www.elevenwireless.com

Elk River Systems Inc 777 E Main Ste 108 ... Bozeman MT 59715 406-632-4763
TF: 888-771-0809 ■ Web: www.elkriversystems.com

Enseo Inc 1680 Prospect Dr Ste 100 ... Richardson TX 75081 972-234-2513
TF: 800-270-8747 ■ Web: www.enseo.com

EON Reality Inc 39 Parker St Ste 100 ... Irvine CA 92618 949-460-2000
Web: www.eonreality.com

Ergonomic Group Inc 609-3 Cantiague Rock Rd ... Westbury NY 11590 516-746-7777
Web: www.ergogroup.com

ESRI Canada Ltd 12 Concorde Pl Ste 900 ... Toronto ON M3C3R8 416-441-6035
Web: www.esri.ca

EtherCom Corp 1409 Fulton Pl ... Fremont CA 94539 510-440-0242
Web: www.ethercom.com

ExtraView Corp 269 Mt Hermon Rd Ste 207 ... Scotts Valley CA 95066 831-461-7100
Web: www.extraview.com

Exxact Corp 45445 Warm Springs Blvd ... Fremont CA 94539 510-226-7366
Web: www.exxactcorp.com

Ficomp Inc 3015 Advance Ln ... Colmar PA 18915 215-997-2600

Flixster Inc 208 Utah St Fourth Fl ... San Francisco CA 94103 415-255-7215
Web: www.flixster.com

Floodgate Entertainment LLC 55 Moody St Ste 31 ... Waltham MA 02453 781-893-3500

Folgergraphics Inc 2339 Davis Ave ... Hayward CA 94545 510-887-5656
Web: www.folgergraphics.com

FusionOps inc 707 California St ... Mountain View CA 94041 408-524-2222
Web: www.fusionops.com

Gamse Lithographing Company Inc 7413 Pulaski Hwy ... Baltimore MD 21237 410-866-4700
Web: www.gamse.com

Gar Enterprises 418 E Live Oak Ave ... Arcadia CA 91006 626-574-1175 574-0553
Web: www.kgselectronics.com

Gearbox Software LLC 101 E Park Blvd Ste 1200 ... Plano TX 75074 972-312-8202
Web: www.gearboxsoftware.com

General Data Co Inc 4354 Ferguson Dr ... Cincinnati OH 45245 513-752-7978 752-6947*
*Fax: Sales ■ TF: 800-733-5252 ■ Web: www.general-data.com

General Networks Corp 3524 Ocean View Blvd ... Glendale CA 91208 818-249-1962
Web: www.gennet.com

Global Computer Supplies Inc 11 Harbor Pk Dr ... Port Washington NY 11050 800-446-9662
TF: 800-446-9662 ■ Web: www.globalcomputer.com

Good Printers Inc 213 Dry River Rd ... Bridgewater VA 22812 540-828-4663
TF: 800-296-3731 ■ Web: www.goodprinters.com

Gotham Technology Group LLC One Paragon Dr Ste 200 ... Montvale NJ 07645 201-474-4200
Web: www.gothamtg.com

Graphic Connections Group LLC 174 Chesterfield Industrial Blvd ... Chesterfield MO 63005 636-519-8320
Web: www.gcfrog.com

Graphic Management Specialty Products Inc 139 Evergreen Rd PO Box 408 ... Oconto WI 54153 920-835-3299
Web: www.gmsp.com

Company / Address	City	State	Zip	Phone	Fax
Graphic Partners Inc 4300 Il Rt 173 *Web:* www.graphicpartners.com	Zion	IL	60099	847-872-9445	
Graphic Products Inc PO Box 4030 *TF:* 888-326-9244 ■ *Web:* www.graphicproducts.com	Beaverton	OR	97076	503-644-5572	646-0183
GTSI Corp 2553 Dulles View Dr Ste 100 *NASDAQ: GTSI* ■ *TF:* 800-999-4874 ■ *Web:* unicomgov.com	Herndon	VA	20171	703-502-2000	463-5101
Hamer Enterprises 4200-A N Bicentennial Dr *Web:* hecorp.com	Mcallen	TX	78504	956-682-3466	
Harding Poorman 4923 W 78th St *Web:* www.hardingpoorman.com	Indianapolis	IN	46268	317-876-3355	
Harwood International Corp 4713 Gann Store Rd 100 Northshore Office Park *Web:* www.harwood-intl.com	Chattanooga	TN	37343	423-870-5500	
Helmel Engineering Products Inc 6520 Lockport Rd *TF:* 800-237-8266 ■ *Web:* www.helmel.com	Niagara Falls	NY	14305	716-297-8644	297-9405
HOBI International Inc 1202 Nagel Blvd *Web:* www.hobi.com	Batavia	IL	60510	630-761-0500	
Home Automated Living Inc 14401 Sweitzer Ln Sixth Fl *TF:* 800-935-5313 ■ *Web:* www.automatedliving.com	Laurel	MD	20707	301-498-6000	
Horizon USA Data Supplies Inc 1595 Meadow Wood Ln Ste 1 *Web:* www.horizonusa.com	Reno	NV	89502	775-858-2300	
IAR Systems Software Inc 1065 E Hillsdale Blvd Century Plz *Web:* iar.com	Foster City	CA	94404	650-287-4250	
Iceptstechnology Group Inc 1301 Fulling Mill Rd *TF:* 888-477-7989 ■ *Web:* www.icepts.com	Middletown	PA	17057	717-704-1000	704-1010
ICL Imaging Corp 51 Mellen St *Web:* www.icl-imaging.com	Framingham	MA	01702	508-872-3280	
Ideal Printers Inc 645 Olive St *Web:* www.idealprint.com	Saint Paul	MN	55130	651-855-1100	
IndiSoft LLC 5550 Sterrett Pl Ste 311 *Web:* www.indisoft.us	Columbia	MD	21044	410-730-0667	
Industrios Software Inc 2150 Winston Park Dr Ste 214 *Web:* www.industrios.com	Oakville	ON	L6H5V1	905-829-2525	
INETCO Systems Ltd 4664 Lougheed Hwy Ste 258 *Web:* www.inetco.com	Burnaby	BC	V5C5T5	604-451-1567	
Infotel Distributors 6450 Poe Ave Ste 200 *TF:* 888-528-4504 ■ *Web:* www.infoteldistributors.com	Dayton	OH	45414	888-528-4504	
Ingram Micro Inc 1600 E St Andrew Pl *NYSE: IM* ■ **Fax Area Code:* 716 ■ **Fax:* Cust Svc ■ *TF Sales:* 800-456-8000 ■ *Web:* www.ingrammicro.com	Santa Ana	CA	92705	714-566-1000	565-8899*
InLine 600 Lakeshore Pkwy	Birmingham	AL	35209	205-278-8100	
InnQuest Software Corp 5300 W Cypress Ste 160 *Web:* www.innquest.com	Tampa	FL	33607	813-288-4900	
Inserts East Inc 7045 Central Hwy *Web:* www.insertseast.com	Pennsauken	NJ	08109	856-663-8181	
Intcomex Inc 3505 NW 107th Ave Ste 1 *Web:* www.intcomex.com	Miami	FL	33178	305-477-6230	477-5694
Integral Networks Inc 4960 Rocklin Rd Ste 100 *Web:* www.integralnet.biz	Rocklin	CA	95677	916-626-4000	
Integrated Services Inc 15115 SW Sequoia Pkwy Ste 110 *Web:* www.lubenet.com	Portland	OR	97224	503-968-8100	
Intellicomm Inc 2701 Renaissance Blvd *Web:* www.intellicomm.com	King Of Prussia	PA	19406	610-731-0400	
Intelligent Computer Solutions Inc 9350 Eton Ave *TF:* 888-994-4678 ■ *Web:* www.ics-iq.com	Chatsworth	CA	91311	818-998-5805	
InterTech Computer Products Inc 5225 S 39th St *Web:* www.allcovered.com	Phoenix	AZ	85040	602-437-0035	
Island Computer Products Inc 20 Clifton Ave *Web:* www.icpcorp.com	Staten Island	NY	10305	718-556-6700	
Itochu Technology Inc 3945 Freedom Cir Ste 350 *Web:* www.ctc-america.com	Santa Clara	CA	95054	408-727-8810	727-9391
Journey Education Marketing Inc 13755 Hutton Dr Ste 500 *TF:* 800-874-9001 ■ *Web:* www.journeyed.com	Dallas	TX	75234	972-481-2000	245-3585
Kavi Corp 225 SE Main St *Web:* www.kavi.com	Portland	OR	97214	503-234-4220	
Kingdom Inc 719 Lambs Creek Rd *Web:* www.kingdom.com	Mansfield	PA	16933	570-662-7515	
Kirkwood Digital 55 Sixth Rd *Web:* www.nugraphics.com	Woburn	MA	01801	781-938-6164	
Knowledge Reservoir LLC 1800 W Loop S Ste 1000 *Web:* www.knowledge-reservoir.com	Houston	TX	77027	713-586-5950	
Lake Cos Inc, The 2980 Walker Dr *Web:* www.lakeco.com	Green Bay	WI	54311	920-406-3030	406-3040
Las Vegas Color Graphics Inc 4265 W Sunset Rd *Web:* www.lasvegascolor.com	Las Vegas	NV	89118	702-617-9000	
Laser Pros International One International Ln *TF:* 888-558-5277 ■ *Web:* www.laserpros.com	Rhinelander	WI	54501	715-369-5995	369-5910
Leadman Electronic USA Inc 382 Laurelwood Dr *TF:* 877-532-3626 ■ *Web:* www.leadman.com	Santa Clara	CA	95054	408-738-1751	738-2620
Legacy Electronics Inc 1220 N Dakota St P.O. Box 348 *Web:* www.legacyelectronics.com	Canton	SD	57013	949-498-9600	
LendingTools.com Inc 200 N Broadway Ste 700 *Web:* www.lendingtools.com	Wichita	KS	67202	316-267-3200	
Lexy Pacific Corp 611 Vaqueros Ave *Web:* www.lexypacific.com	Sunnyvale	CA	94085	408-331-8818	
Lindsey & Company Inc 2302 Llama Dr *TF:* 800-890-7058 ■ *Web:* www.lindseysoftware.com	Searcy	AR	72143	501-268-5324	
LINQWARE Inc 6161 NE 175th St Ste 205 *Web:* www.lincware.com	Kenmore	WA	98028	425-486-5313	
Loeffler Randall Inc 525 Broadway Fourth Fl *Web:* www.loefflerrandall.com	New York	NY	10012	212-226-8787	
Logical Choice Technologies Inc 1045 Progress Cir	Lawrenceville	GA	30043	770-564-1044	
Long View Systems Corp 3100 255 Fifth Ave SW *TF:* 866-515-6900 ■ *Web:* www.longviewsystems.com	Calgary	AB	T2P3G6	403-515-6900	
M & A Technology Inc 2045 Chenault Dr *TF:* 800-225-1452 ■ *Web:* www.macomp.com	Carrollton	TX	75006	972-490-5803	490-0616
MA Laboratories Inc 2075 N Capitol Ave *Web:* www.malabs.com	San Jose	CA	95132	408-941-0808	941-0909
MacPractice Inc 233 N Eighth St Ste 300 *Web:* www.macpractice.com	Lincoln	NE	68508	402-420-2430	
MasterGraphics Inc 2979 Triverton Pike Dr *Web:* www.mastergraphics.com	Madison	WI	53711	608-256-4884	
Max Group Corp 17011 Green Dr *TF:* 800-256-9040 ■ *Web:* www.maxgroup.com	City of Industry	CA	91745	626-935-0050	935-0056
MedInformatix Inc 5777 W Century Blvd Ste 1700 *Web:* www.medinformatix.com	Los Angeles	CA	90045	310-348-7367	
MeLLmo Inc 120 S Sierra Ave *Web:* www.roambi.com	Solana Beach	CA	92075	858-847-3272	
Merisel Inc 127 W 30th St Fifth Fl *Web:* www.merisel.com	New York	NY	10001	212-594-4800	
Micro Technology Concepts (MTC) 17837 Rowland St *Web:* www.mtcusa.com	City Of Industry	CA	91748	626-839-6800	839-6899
Microland Electronics Corp 1883 Ringwood Ave *Web:* www.microlandusa.com	San Jose	CA	95131	408-441-1688	441-1767
Mimaki USA Inc 150 Satellite Blvd NE Ste A *Web:* www.mimakiusa.com	Suwanee	GA	30024	678-730-0170	
Minicomputer Exchange Inc 150A Charcot Ave *Web:* www.mce.com	San Jose	CA	95131	408-733-4400	
MontaVista Software Inc 2929 Patrick Henry Dr *TF:* 888-624-4846 ■ *Web:* www.mvista.com	Santa Clara	CA	95054	408-572-8000	572-8005
MotionDSP Inc 700 Airport Blvd Ste 270 *Web:* www.motiondsp.com	Burlingame	CA	94010	650-288-1164	
Mythics Inc 1439 N Great Neck Rd *Web:* www.mythics.com	Virginia Beach	VA	23454	757-412-4362	
neoSaej Corp 77 S Bedford St Ste 450 *Web:* www.neosaej.com	Burlington	MA	01803	781-272-1774	
NewWave Technologies Inc 4635 Wedgewood Blvd Ste 107 *Web:* www.newwavetech.com	Frederick	MD	21703	301-624-5300	
NinthDecimal Inc 150 Post St Ste 500 *Web:* www.jiwire.com	San Francisco	CA	94108	415-821-8600	
Novarad Corp 752 East 1180 South Ste 200 *Web:* www.novarad.net	American Fork	UT	84003	801-642-1001	
NuMedics Inc 6950 SW Hampton Rd Ste 221 *Web:* www.numedics.com	Tigard	OR	97223	503-597-3861	
Office Systems of Texas 104 Lockhaven Dr *Web:* www.bizhubhouston.com	Houston	TX	77073	281-443-2996	
Onix Networking Corp 18519 Detroit Ave *TF:* 800-664-9638 ■ *Web:* www.onixnet.com	Lakewood	OH	44107	800-664-9638	
Open Storage Solutions Inc 2 Castleview Dr *TF:* 800-387-3419 ■ *Web:* www.openstore.com	Toronto	ON	L6T5S9	905-790-0660	
Open Systems of Cleveland Inc 22999 Forbes Rd Ste A *TF:* 888-881-6660 ■ *Web:* www.osinc.com	Cleveland	OH	44146	440-439-2332	439-3794
OpenEye Scientific Software Inc Nine Bisbee Court Ste D *Web:* www.eyesopen.com	Santa Fe	NM	87508	505-473-7385	
Pact-One Solutions Inc 8215 S Eastern Ave Ste 101 *TF:* 866-722-8663 ■ *Web:* www.pact-one.com	Las Vegas	NV	89123	866-722-8663	
Palamida Inc 215 Second St Second Fl *Web:* palamida.com	San Francisco	CA	94105	415-777-9400	
Paragon Development Systems Inc 1823 Executive Dr *TF:* 800-966-6090 ■ *Web:* www.pdspc.com	Oconomowoc	WI	53066	800-966-6090	
Pathmaker Group LP 4209 Gateway Dr Ste 100 *Web:* pathmaker-group.com	Colleyville	TX	76034	817-704-3644	
Pc Treasures Inc 3720 Lapeer Rd *Web:* pctreasures.com	Auburn Hills	MI	48326	248-969-7800	
PCI Geomatics Inc 50 W Wilmot St *Web:* www.pcigeomatics.com	Richmond Hill	ON	L4B1M5	905-764-0614	
Peak Technologies Inc 10330 Old Columbia Rd *TF:* 800-926-9212 ■ *Web:* www.peak-ryzex.com	Columbia	MD	21046	800-926-9212	
PerfectForms Inc 1917 Palomar Oaks Way Ste 160 *Web:* www.perfectforms.com	Carlsbad	CA	92008	760-585-1870	
Prism Color Corp 31 Twosome Dr *Web:* www.prismcolorcorp.com	Moorestown	NJ	08057	856-234-7515	
Professional Graphics Inc 25 Perry Ave *Web:* www.progi.net	Norwalk	CT	06850	203-846-4291	
Programmer's Paradise Inc 1157 Shrewsbury Ave Ste C *TF:* 800-441-1511 ■ *Web:* www.techxtend.com	Shrewsbury	NJ	07702	732-389-8950	389-0010
Promark Technology Inc 10900 Pump House Rd Ste B **Fax Area Code:* 301 ■ *TF:* 800-634-0255 ■ *Web:* www.promarktech.com	Annapolis Junction	MD	20701	240-280-8030	725-7869*
Prostar Computer Inc 837 Lawson St *TF:* 888-576-4742 ■ *Web:* www.pro-star.com	City of Industry	CA	91748	626-839-6472	854-3438

Company	City	State	Zip	Phone	Fax
Provantage Corp 7249 Whipple Ave NW *TF:* 800-336-1166 ■ *Web:* www.provantage.com	North Canton	OH	44720	330-494-8715	494-5260
Queen Beach Printers Inc 937 Pine Ave *Web:* www.qbprinters.com	Long Beach	CA	90813	562-436-8201	
Radiological Imaging Technology Inc 5065 List Dr *Web:* www.radimage.com	Colorado Springs	CO	80919	719-590-1077	
Rave Computer Assn Inc 7171 Sterling Ponds Ct *TF:* 800-966-7283 ■ *Web:* www.rave.com	Sterling Heights	MI	48312	586-939-8230	939-7431
Real Asset Management Inc 309 Court Ave Ste 244 *Web:* www.realassetmgt.com	Des Moines	IA	50309	515-699-8564	
Real Time Consultants Inc 777 Corporate Dr Ste 1 *Web:* www.realtimenet.com	Mahwah	NJ	07430	201-512-1777	
Red Line Graphics Inc 6430 S Belmont Ave *Web:* www.redlinegroup.com	Indianapolis	IN	46217	317-784-3777	
Redline Trading Solutions Inc 18 Commerce Way Ste 6800 *Web:* www.redlinetrading.com	Woburn	MA	01801	781-995-3403	
Remcom Inc 315 S Allen St Ste 222 *Web:* www.remcom.com	State College	PA	16801	814-861-1299	
RemoteScan Corp 305 S Fourth St E Ste 200 *Web:* www.remote-scan.com	Missoula	MT	59801	406-721-0319	
Revana Inc 8123 S Hardy Dr *Web:* www.revana.com	Tempe	AZ	85284	480-902-5900	
Rippey Corp 5000 Hillsdale Cir *Web:* www.rippey.com	El Dorado Hills	CA	95762	916-939-4332	939-4338
Rorke Data Inc 7626 Golden Triangle Dr *TF:* 800-328-8147 ■ *Web:* www.rorke.com	Eden Prairie	MN	55344	952-829-0300	829-0988
Rpl Supplies Inc 141 Lanza Ave Bldg 3A *TF:* 800-524-0914 ■ *Web:* www.rplsupplies.com	Garfield	NJ	07026	973-767-0880	772-6601
Sanyo Denki America Inc 468 Amapola Ave *Web:* www.sanyo-denki.com	Torrance	CA	90501	310-783-5400	212-6545
ScanSource Inc Six Logue Ct *NASDAQ: SCSC* ■ *TF:* 800-944-2432 ■ *Web:* www.scansource.com	Greenville	SC	29615	864-288-2432	288-1165
Scivantage Inc 10 Exchange Pl Unit 13 *TF:* 866-724-8268 ■ *Web:* www.scivantage.com	Jersey City	NJ	07302	646-452-0050	452-0049
SDV Solutions Inc 133 Waller Mill Rd Ste 100 *Web:* www.sdvsolutions.us	Williamsburg	VA	23185	757-903-2068	
SED International Inc 4916 N Royal Atlanta Dr *TF Sales:* 800-444-8962 ■ *Web:* www.sedonline.com	Tucker	GA	30084	770-491-8962	
SigmaTEK Systems LLC 1445 Kemper Meadow Dr *Web:* www.sigmanest.com	Cincinnati	OH	45240	513-674-0005	
Smith Micro Technologies Inc 3435 Labore Rd *Web:* smithmicrotech.com	St. Paul	MN	55110	651-482-8718	
Softmart Inc 450 Acorn Ln *TF Cust Svc:* 800-328-1319 ■ *Web:* www.softmart.com	Downingtown	PA	19335	610-518-4000	518-3000
Software House International (SHI) 290 Davidson Ave *TF:* 888-764-8888 ■ *Web:* www.shi.com	Somerset	NJ	08873	888-764-8888	
Solution Systems Inc 3201 Tollview Dr *Web:* www.solsyst.com	Rolling Meadows	IL	60008	847-590-3000	590-0912
Soroc Technology Inc 607 Chrislea Rd *Web:* www.soroc.com	Woodbridge	ON	L4L8A3	905-265-8000	
SouthWare Innovations Inc 1922 Professional Cir *Web:* southware.com	Auburn	AL	36831	334-821-1108	
St Louis Lithographing Co 6880 Heege Rd	St Louis	MO	63123	314-352-1300	
Stardock Systems Inc 15090 N Beck Rd Ste 300 *TF:* 888-782-7362 ■ *Web:* www.stardock.com	Plymouth	MI	48170	734-927-0677	927-0678
Static Control Components Inc 3010 Lee Ave PO Box 152 *TF:* 800-488-2426 ■ *Web:* www.scc-inc.com	Sanford	NC	27331	919-774-3808	774-1287
Stromberg Allen & Co 18504 W Creek Dr *Web:* strombergallen.com	Tinley Park	IL	60477	773-847-7131	
Symco Group Inc 5012 Bristol Industrial Way Ste 105 *Web:* www.symcogroup.com	Buford	GA	30518	770-451-8002	
Symmetry Software Corp 14350 N 87th St Ste 250 *Web:* www.symmetry.com	Scottsdale	AZ	85260	480-596-1500	
Synergy Resources Inc 3500 Sunrise Hwy Bldg 100 Ste 201 *Web:* www.synergyresources.net	Great River	NY	11739	631-665-2050	
SYNNEX Canada 200 Ronson Dr **Fax:* Hum Res ■ *Web:* www.synnex.ca	Etobicoke	ON	M9W5Z9	416-240-7012	240-2622*
Synnex Corp 44201 Nobel Dr *NYSE: SNX* ■ *TF Cust Svc:* 800-756-1888 ■ *Web:* www.synnex.com	Fremont	CA	94538	510-656-3333	668-3777
System Design Advantage LLC 3711 Kennebec Dr *Web:* www.sdallc.com	Eagan	MN	55122	952-703-3500	
Tactical Communications Group LLC Two Highwood Dr Bldg 2 *Web:* g2tcg.com	Tewksbury	MA	01876	978-654-4800	
Talari Networks Inc 20195 Stevens Creek Blvd Ste 220 *Web:* www.talari.com	Cupertino	CA	95014	408-689-0400	
Tanner Research Inc 825 S Myrtle Ave *TF:* 877-325-2223 ■ *Web:* www.tanner.com	Monrovia	CA	91016	626-471-9700	
Tech Data Corp 5350 Tech Data Dr *NASDAQ: TECD* ■ **Fax:* Hum Res ■ *TF:* 800-237-8931 ■ *Web:* www.techdata.com	Clearwater	FL	33760	727-539-7429	538-7054*
Tekla Inc 1075 Big Shanty Rd NW Ste 175 *Web:* www.tekla.com	Kennesaw	GA	30144	770-426-5105	
Telecorp Products Inc 2000 E Oakley Park Rd Ste 101 *Web:* telecorpproducts.com	Walled Lake	MI	48390	248-960-1000	
Teracai Corp 217 Lawrence Rd E *Web:* www.teracai.com	North Syracuse	NY	13212	315-883-3500	
Tharo Systems Inc 2866 Nationwide Pkwy *Web:* www.tharo.com	Brunswick	OH	44212	330-273-4408	
Think Computer Corp 3260 Hillview Ave *TF:* 888-815-8599 ■ *Web:* www.thinkcomputer.com	Palo Alto	CA	94304	415-670-9350	
Third Wave Systems Inc 7900 W 78th St Ste 300 *Web:* www.thirdwavesys.com	Minneapolis	MN	55439	952-832-5515	
TigerDirect Inc 7795 W Flagler St Ste 35 *TF:* 800-800-8300 ■ *Web:* www.tigerdirect.com	Miami	FL	33144	800-800-8300	
TKO Electronics Inc 31113 Via Colinas *Web:* www.tkoelectronics.com	Westlake Village	CA	91362	818-879-2233	
Topdek Inc 2926 NW 72nd Ave **Fax Area Code:* 786 ■ *Web:* www.topdek.com	Miami	FL	33122	305-599-0006	845-8668*
Transcend Information Inc 1645 N Brian St *Web:* www.transcend-info.com	Orange	CA	92867	714-921-2000	921-2111
Transim Technology Corp 433 NW Fourth Ave Ste 200 *Web:* www.transim.com	Portland	OR	97209	503-450-1355	
TransMagic Inc 11859 Pecos St Ste 310 *Web:* transmagic.com	Westminster	CO	80234	303-460-1406	
Transoft Solutions Inc 13575 Commerce Pkwy Ste 250 *Web:* www.transoftsolutions.com	Richmond	BC	V6V2L1	604-244-8387	244-1770
Tributary Systems Inc 3717 Commerce Pl Ste C *Web:* www.tributary.com	Bedford	TX	76021	817-354-8009	
UCI Communications LLC 500 St Michael St *Web:* www.ucicom.com	Mobile	AL	36602	251-457-1404	
Unified Systems Group Inc 1235 64th Ave SE Ste 4a *Web:* www.usg.ca	Calgary	AB	T2H2J7	403-686-8088	
United Systems Inc 4335 N Classen Blvd *Web:* www.unitedsystemsok.com	Oklahoma City	OK	73118	405-523-2162	
Us Micro Corp 7000 Highlnds Pkwy SE *TF:* 888-876-4276 ■ *Web:* www.usmicrocorp.com	Smyrna	GA	30082	770-437-0706	437-0855
Vartek Services Inc 1785 S Metro Pkwy *Web:* www.vartek.com	Dayton	OH	45459	937-226-9708	
Virginia Surety Company Inc 175 W Jackson Blvd 11th Fl	Chicago	IL	60604	312-356-3000	
Virtucom Inc 6610 Bay Cir Ste E *Web:* www.virtucom.com	Norcross	GA	30071	770-908-8100	
Vivid Impact Corp 10116 Bunsen Way *Web:* www.vividimpact.com	Louisville	KY	40299	502-495-6900	
VLN Partners LLP 1212 E Carson St *Web:* www.vlnpartners.com	Pittsburgh	PA	15203	412-381-0183	
WDL Systems 220 Chatham Business Dr *TF Sales:* 800-548-2319 ■ *Web:* www.wdlsystems.com	Pittsboro	NC	27312	919-545-2500	545-2559
WebQA Inc 900 S Frontage Rd Ste 110 *Web:* www.webqa.net	Woodridge	IL	60517	630-985-1300	
West-Com Nurse Call Systems Inc 2200 Cordelia Rd *TF:* 800-761-1180 ■ *Web:* www.westcall.com	Fairfield	CA	94534	707-428-5900	
Westcon Group Inc 520 White Plains Rd 2nd Fl *TF:* 800-527-9516 ■ *Web:* www.westcongroup.com	Tarrytown	NY	10591	914-829-7000	829-7137
Westcon Group, Inc *Westcon Convergence* 520 White Plains Rd Ste 100 *TF:* 877-642-7750 ■ *Web:* www.westcongroup.com	Omaha	NE	68154	877-642-7750	
Westham Trade Co Ltd 3620 NW 114th Ave *TF:* 888-852-5000 ■ *Web:* www.wtrade.com	Doral	FL	33178	305-717-5400	593-0316
Whalley Computer Associates Inc One Whalley Way *Web:* www.wca.com	Southwick	MA	01077	413-569-4200	
Wheal-Grace Corp 300 Ralph St *Web:* www.wheal-grace.com	Belleville	NJ	07109	973-450-8100	
Wintec Industries Inc 675 Sycamore Dr *TF:* 866-989-4683 ■ *Web:* www.wintecindustries.com	Milpitas	CA	95035	408-856-0500	856-0501
Wolf Colorprint Inc 111 Holmes Rd *Web:* www.wolfcolorprint.com	Newington	CT	06111	860-666-1200	
Woot Inc 4121 International Pkwy *TF:* 866-551-6881 ■ *Web:* woot.com	Carrollton	TX	75007	972-417-3959	418-9245
WorldAPP Inc 220 Forbes Rd *Web:* worldapp.com	Braintree	MA	02184	781-849-8118	
Worth Higgins & Assoc Inc 8770 Park Central Dr *Web:* whaprint.com/	Richmond	VA	23227	804-264-2304	
Zones Inc 1102 15th St SW *Web:* www.zones.com	Auburn	WA	98001	253-205-3000	205-2655
Zuercher Technologies LLC 5121 S Solberg Ave Ste 150 *Web:* www.zuerchertech.com	Sioux Falls	SD	57108	605-274-6061	

COMPUTER & INTERNET TRAINING PROGRAMS

SEE Training & Certification Programs - Computer & Internet p. 3247

178 COMPUTER MAINTENANCE & REPAIR

Company	City	State	Zip	Phone	Fax
24hourtek LLC 268 Bush St *Web:* www.24hourtek.com	San Francisco	CA	94104	415-294-4449	
Accram Inc 2901 W Clarendon Ave *TF:* 800-786-0288 ■ *Web:* www.accram.com	Phoenix	AZ	85017	800-786-0288	
Acropolis Computers Inc 915 Whitelaw Ave *Web:* www.acropolistech.com	Wood River	IL	62095	618-254-8733	
Ah Computer Services Inc 7221 Aloma Ave Ste 300 *Web:* ahcomputers.net	Winter Park	FL	32792	407-671-3557	
Aim Computers 1819 Willow Pass Rd *Web:* www.aimcomp.com	Concord	CA	94520	925-687-2822	

Company / Address	City	State	Zip	Phone	Fax
Aixtek 1275 Fairfax Ave Ste 201 *Web:* www.eatonassoc.com	San Francisco	CA	94124	415-282-1188	
Applied Copier Concepts 4260 Piedmont Pkwy Ste 105 *Web:* www.appliedcopierconcepts.com	Greensboro	NC	27410	336-632-9285	
ATCI Consultants 11720 Chairman Dr Ste 108 *Web:* www.atcicomputer.com	Dallas	TX	75243	214-343-0600	343-0716
Ats Tech Solutions Inc 2805 Ramsey Rd *Web:* www.atstech.net	Gainesville	GA	30501	770-538-2900	
Bde Computer Services LLC 399 Lakeview Ave *Web:* www.bdecomputer.com	Clifton	NJ	07011	973-772-8507	
BigByte Corp 47400 Seabridge Dr *Web:* www.bigbytecorp.com	Fremont	CA	94538	510-249-1100	
Brains II Canada Inc 165 Konrad Crescent *Web:* www.brainsii.com	Markham	ON	L3R9T9	905-946-8700	
Brentech Inc 9340 Carmel Mtn Rd Ste C *Web:* www.brentech-inc.com	San Diego	CA	92129	858-484-7314	
Brooks-jeffrey Computer Store 19 Medical Plz *Web:* www.bjmweb.com	Mountain Home	AR	72653	870-425-8064	
Bryley Systems Inc 12 Main St *Web:* www.bryley.com	Hudson	MA	01749	978-562-6077	
Byte Right Support Inc 335 N Charles St *Web:* byterightsupport.com	Baltimore	MD	21201	410-347-2983	
C T S Services Inc 260 Maple St *Web:* www.ctsservices.com	Bellingham	MA	02019	508-528-7720	
C&W Enterprises Inc 2522 SE Federal Hwy *Web:* www.cwnow.com	Stuart	FL	34994	772-287-5215	
CAD & Graphic Supply Inc 2120 Hutton Dr Ste 800 *Web:* www.cadgraphicsupply.com	Carrollton	TX	75006	972-409-7333	
Cascade Computer Maintenance Inc 3240 Commercial St SE *Web:* www.ccmaint.com	Salem	OR	97302	503-581-0081	
Cds - Networks & Services Inc 672 Stratford Blvd *Web:* www.cdsnetworks.com	Kinston	NC	28504	252-523-6664	
Citrus Computers Inc 7512 Ehrlich Rd *Web:* www.citruscomputers.com	Tampa	FL	33625	813-926-9672	
ClickAway Corp 457 E McGlincy Ln Ste 1 *Web:* www.clickaway.com	Campbell	CA	95008	408-626-9400	
Cnic Inc 4418 Monroe Rd E *Web:* www.cnic-inc.com	Charlotte	NC	28205	704-344-0090	
Compciti Business Solutions Inc 261 W 35th St Ste 603 *Web:* www.compciti.com	New York	NY	10001	212-594-4374	
Compu-Fix Inc 920 Thompson Run Rd *Web:* compufix-inc.com	West Mifflin	PA	15122	412-464-0275	
CompuCycle Inc 7700 Kempwood Dr *Web:* www.compucycle.net	Houston	TX	77055	713-869-6700	
Computer Centerline 1500 Broad St *Web:* cclprotech.com	Greensburg	PA	15601	724-838-0852	
Computer Equip Svces 261 W Main St *Web:* netces.com	Bay Shore	NY	11706	631-666-1234	
Computer Heaven 577 Oak Villa Blvd *Web:* computerheaven.com	Baton Rouge	LA	70815	225-923-0999	
Computer Repair & Sales 2930 W Main St *Web:* www.computerrepair.org	Rapid City	SD	57702	605-399-0278	342-6141
Computer Specialists Inc 2101 Gaither Rd Ste 175	Rockville	MD	20850	301-921-2111	
Computer Troubleshooters USA 755 Commerce Dr Ste 605 *TF:* 877-704-1702 ■ *Web:* www.comptroub.com	Decatur	GA	30030	404-477-1302	
ComputerPlus Sales & Service Inc Five Northway Ct *TF:* 800-849-4426 ■ *Web:* www.computer-plus.com	Greer	SC	29651	800-849-4426	
Comware Technical Services Inc 17922 Sky Park Cir Ste E *Web:* comwaretech.com	Irvine	CA	92614	949-851-9600	
CPT of South Florida Inc 2699 Stirling Rd Ste A 101 *Web:* www.cpt-florida.com	Fort Lauderdale	FL	33312	954-963-2775	963-5781
CRSA Computer Rescue Inc 2434 Brockton St *Web:* www.computerrescuesa.com	San Antonio	TX	78217	210-366-4811	
Cru Solutions Inc 7261 Engle Rd Ste 305 *Web:* www.crusolutions.com	Cleveland	OH	44130	440-891-0330	
CRV Inc 3407 Northeast Pkwy Ste 170	San Antonio	TX	78205	210-828-8552	
Data Applications Corp 4408 Sunbelt Dr *Web:* www.data-app.com	Addison	TX	75001	972-250-0973	
Data Exchange Corp 3600 Via Pescador *TF:* 800-237-7911 ■ *Web:* www.dex.com	Camarillo	CA	93012	805-388-1711	389-1726
Dataserv Corp 8625 F St *Web:* www.dataservcorp.com	Omaha	NE	68127	402-339-8700	
DBK Concepts Inc 12905 SW 129 Ave *TF:* 800-725-7226 ■ *Web:* www.dbk.com	Miami	FL	33186	305-596-7226	596-7222
Decatur Computers Inc 1234 N Water St Ste B *Web:* decaturcomputers.com	Decatur	IL	62521	217-475-0226	
DecisionOne Corp 426 W Lancaster Ave *TF:* 800-767-2876 ■ *Web:* decisionone.com	Devon	PA	19333	610-296-6000	296-2910
Desktop Consulting Services 43311 Joy Rd *TF:* 888-600-2731 ■ *Web:* dcs-mi.com	Canton	MI	48187	888-600-2731	
Dhc Communications Inc 125 Hall St *Web:* www.dhc.bc.ca	Nelson	BC	V1L7B4	250-352-0861	
Dhcs Inc 6828 Ranchester Dr *Web:* dhcs-inc.com	Houston	TX	77036	832-426-4829	
Digirati Networks 9255 E River Rd Nw *Web:* www.digirati-networks.com	Minneapolis	MN	55433	763-784-3500	
Digital Dot Systems Inc 13213 F St *Web:* www.ddsine.com	Omaha	NE	68137	402-408-0115	
Digital Rework Depot 1500 Soldiers Field Rd *Web:* digitalrework.com	Brighton	MA	02135	617-562-1444	
DP Solutions Inc 1508 S First St *Web:* www.dpsol.com	Lufkin	TX	75901	936-637-7977	
Eagle Haven Computers Inc 5860 Clearfield Woodland Hwy *Web:* www.eaglehaven.com	Clearfield	PA	16830	814-765-5779	
Eagle Networks Inc 2738 W Bullard Ave *Web:* www.eaglenetworks.com	Fresno	CA	93711	559-448-8877	
Electrosonics 17150 15 Mile Rd *Web:* www.electrosonics.net	Fraser	MI	48026	586-415-5555	
Elementum Solutions 2540 New Butler Rd *Web:* www.elementumsolutions.com	New Castle	PA	16101	724-656-8837	
Emf Inc 60 Foundry St *Web:* www.emfinc.com	Keene	NH	03431	603-352-8400	
Ener-Tel Services Inc 4512 Adobe Dr *Web:* www.ener-tel.com	San Angelo	TX	76903	325-658-8375	
Entre Computer Solutions 8900 N Second St *Web:* www.entrerock.com	Machesney Park	IL	61115	815-399-5664	
Essential Technologies Inc 1107 Hazeltine Blvd Ste 477 *TF:* 800-818-1125 ■ *Web:* www.essentialtechinc.com	Chaska	MN	55318	952-368-9001	368-3334
Eventnet Usa 1129 Se Fourth Ave *Web:* www.eventnetusa.com	Fort Lauderdale	FL	33316	954-467-9898	
Everprint International Inc 18021 Cortney Ct *TF:* 800-984-5777 ■ *Web:* www.everprint.com	City of Industry	CA	91748	800-984-5777	
Ex-Cel Solutions Inc 14618 Grover St **Fax:* Cust Svc ■ *Web:* www.excels.com	Omaha	NE	68144	402-333-6541	333-3124*
Excalibur Data Systems 115 Sagamore Hill Rd *Web:* www.excaliburdata.com	Pittsburgh	PA	15239	724-387-1331	
Expert Laser Service One N St *Web:* www.expertlaserservices.com	Southbridge	MA	01550	508-764-1413	
EZ Systems.com 3480 W Warner Ave Ste A *Web:* www.ezsystems.com	Santa Ana	CA	92704	714-662-4959	
Facet Computers 2103 Court St *Web:* www.facettech.com	Pekin	IL	61554	309-353-4727	
Far Western Graphics Inc 1105 Kern Ave *Web:* www.farwesterngraphics.com	Sunnyvale	CA	94085	408-481-9777	
First Resource Computer Inc 590 Reservoir Ave *Web:* www.frcomputers.com	Cranston	RI	02910	401-941-2500	
Firsttech Corp Two Industrial Dr Ste C *Web:* cafishgrill.com	Keyport	NJ	07735	732-566-1001	
Fortress Computer Pros 11305 Rancho Bernardo Rd Ste 116 *Web:* www.fortresscomputerpros.com	San Diego	CA	92127	858-451-7020	
Gtek Computers LLC 114 Lang Rd Ste B *Web:* www.www.gtek.biz	Portland	TX	78374	361-777-1400	
Gtm Wholesale Liquidators Inc 2025 Gillespie Way Ste 108 *Web:* www.gtmstores.com	El Cajon	CA	92020	619-596-7486	
Hc & C Communications Inc 5427 Telegraph Ave Ste P *Web:* www.hcccom.net	Oakland	CA	94609	510-655-1193	
Helix Technologies Inc 8550 W Main St *Web:* helixtec.net	French Lick	IN	47432	812-936-2525	
Help Me Computers LLC 903 Austin Hwy *Web:* www.helpmecomputers.com	San Antonio	TX	78209	210-822-8817	
IIS Group LLC 1015 Virginia Dr Ste 1 W *TF:* 855-443-5777 ■ *Web:* www.iisgroupllc.com	Fort Washington	PA	19034	855-443-5777	
Ilink Technology Inc 5055 Avenida Encinas Ste 100 *Web:* ilinktechnology.com	Carlsbad	CA	92008	760-216-6560	
Insight Computing LLC 505 San Marin Dr Ste A240 *Web:* www.insight-computing.com	Novato	CA	94945	415-898-5411	
Intag Inc 10805 Sunset Office Dr Ste 300 *Web:* www.appliedws.com	Saint Louis	MO	63127	314-822-1102	
Integranetics 325 Park Plz Dr 2b *Web:* integranetics.net	Owensboro	KY	42301	270-685-6016	
Integration Technologies Group Inc 2745 Hartland Rd Ste 200 *TF:* 800-835-7823 ■ *Web:* www.itgonline.com	Falls Church	VA	22043	703-698-8282	698-0305
Integron Corp 35 Bermar Park *Web:* www.integron.com	Rochester	NY	14624	585-426-6200	
Interactive Services Group Inc 600 Delran Pkwy Ste C **Fax Area Code:* 856 ■ *TF:* 800-566-3310 ■ *Web:* www.isg-service.com	Delran	NJ	08075	800-566-3310	824-9415*
Intermax Computer Associates Inc 242 Big Run Rd *Web:* intermaxcomputer.com	Lexington	KY	40503	859-277-5453	
Intratek Computer Inc 5431 Industrial Dr *TF:* 800-892-8282 ■ *Web:* www.intrapc.com	Huntington Beach	CA	92649	800-892-8282	
Invisible Inc 3610 Mall Dr *Web:* www.invisibleinc.com	Eau Claire	WI	54701	715-835-8082	
Ises Inc 372 Us Hwy 22 W *Web:* www.isesincorporated.com	Whitehouse Station	NJ	08889	908-823-9183	
J&S Electronic Business System Inc 878 Jefferson St *Web:* www.jselectronics.com	Burlington	IA	52601	319-752-5603	
Jaguar Computer Systems Inc 4135 Indus Way *Web:* www.jaguar.net	Riverside	CA	92503	951-273-7950	734-5615
Just Service Inc 2940 N Clark St *Web:* www.justservice.com	Chicago	IL	60657	773-871-7171	
Just Solutions Inc 7300 Pittsford Palmyra Rd (RT 31) PO Box 118 *Web:* www.justinc.com	Fairport	NY	14450	585-203-8910	
Kam Companies Inc 3982 New Vision Dr *Web:* kamcompanies.com	Fort Wayne	IN	46845	260-432-4432	

	City	State	Zip	Phone	Fax
Kaplan Computers LLC 61 Tolland Tpke *Web:* kaplancomputers.com	Manchester	CT	06042	860-643-6474	
Kdt Solutions Inc 1256 Fifth St *Web:* www.kdtsolutions.com	West Palm Beach	FL	33409	561-688-9399	
Konicom Inc 1819 J St *Web:* www.konicom.com	Sacramento	CA	95811	916-441-7373	
L. M. s Technical Services Inc 21 Grand Ave *Web:* www.lmstech.com	Farmingdale	NY	11735	631-694-2034	
Laser & Computer Options Inc 3758 E Grove St *Web:* www.toner-low.com	Phoenix	AZ	85040	480-968-8440	
Ledger Systems Inc 865 Laurel St *Web:* www.ledgersys.com	San Carlos	CA	94070	650-592-6211	
Local.com Corp 7555 Irvine Ctr Dr *Web:* www.local.com	Irvine	CA	92618	949-784-0800	
Lti Network Consulting Group LLC 820 E Terra Cotta Ave Ste 240 *Web:* www.ltinetworkconsulting.com	Crystal Lake	IL	60014	815-356-8888	
M1 Networks Inc 6019 Mcpherson Rd Ste 4 *Web:* m1networks.net	Laredo	TX	78041	956-718-1005	
Markent Personnel Inc 121 E Conant St *Web:* www.markentpersonnel.com	Portage	WI	53901	608-742-7300	
Masterit LLC 8024 Stage Hills Blvd Ste 101 *Web:* www.master-it.com	Memphis	TN	38133	901-377-7891	
Matthijssen Inc 14 Rt 10 *TF:* 800-845-2200 ■ *Web:* www.mattnj.com	East Hanover	NJ	07936	973-887-1100	887-2453
Maybank Systems 525 E Bay St Ste 201 *Web:* maybanksystems.com	Charleston	SC	29403	843-278-0339	
Mike Collins & Associates Inc 6048 Century Oaks Dr *Web:* www.mcollins.com	Chattanooga	TN	37416	423-892-8899	
Mri Technologies 17047 El Camino Real Ste 200 *Web:* mricompany.com	Houston	TX	77058	281-786-2004	
Nations First Office Repair 1555 E Flamingo Rd Ste 202 *Web:* www.laptoprepairs.com	Las Vegas	NV	89119	702-699-5657	699-5468
NCE Computer Group 1866 Friendship Dr *TF Cust Svc:* 800-767-2587 ■ *Web:* www.ncegroup.com	El Cajon	CA	92020	619-212-3000	596-2881
Network Company of California 310 Via Vera Cruz *Web:* tncc.com	San Marcos	CA	92078	760-744-0442	
Network Experts 260 S Beverly Dr Ste 325 *Web:* www.networkexperts.la	Beverly Hills	CA	90212	310-275-1911	
Nexicore 4201 Guardian Street *Web:* www.avnetintegrated.com	Simi Valley	CA	93063	805-306-2500	
Noguska LLC 741 Countyline St *Web:* www.noguska.com	Fostoria	OH	44830	419-435-0404	
Novastar Solutions Com LLC 35200 Plymouth Rd *Web:* www.novastar.net	Livonia	MI	48150	734-453-8003	
Npa Computers Inc 751 Coates Ave *Web:* www.npacomputers.com	Holbrook	NY	11741	631-467-2500	
Ockers Co 830 W Chestnut St *Web:* www.ockers.com	Brockton	MA	02301	508-586-4642	584-9180
On-Site Lasermedic Corp 21540 Prairie St Ste D *Web:* www.onsitelasermedic.com	Chatsworth	CA	91311	818-772-6911	
Orion Communications Inc 7650 Standish Pl Ste 102 *Web:* www.oricomm.com	Rockville	MD	20855	301-921-9056	
Pacific Pharmacy Computers Inc 4167 N Golden State Bouelvard Ste 106 *Web:* www.goppc.com	Fresno	CA	93722	559-276-6168	
Panurgy Inc Three Wing Dr Ste 225 *Web:* www.panurgy.com	Cedar Knolls	NJ	07927	973-625-9686	
PC Innovations 1555 E Henrietta Rd *Web:* www.pcinnovations.com	Rochester	NY	14623	585-340-1555	
Pcage Inc 345 Lancaster Ave *Web:* www.pcageinc.com	Malvern	PA	19355	610-889-4812	
Planetbids Inc 20929 Ventura Blvd *Web:* home.planetbids.com	Woodland Hills	CA	91364	818-992-1771	
Portable CIO 172 Via Serena *Web:* www.theportablecio.com	Alamo	CA	94507	925-552-7953	
Precision Computer Services Inc (PCS) 175 Constitution Blvd S *TF:* 800-340-9890 ■ *Web:* www.precisiongroup.com	Shelton	CT	06484	203-929-0000	929-8800
Pro-data Computer Services Inc 2809 S 160th St Ste 401 *Web:* www.prodatacomputer.com	Omaha	NE	68130	402-697-7575	
ProLender Solutions Inc 6050 Santo Rd Ste 160 *Web:* www.prolender.com	San Diego	CA	92124	619-258-3595	
Ptc Select LLC 2450 N Knoxville Ave *Web:* www.ptcselect.com	Peoria	IL	61604	309-685-8400	
Quick Electronics Inc 10800 76th Ct *Web:* www.automationsource.com	Largo	FL	33777	727-546-9299	
R-Cubed Service & Sales Inc 11126 Shady Trl *Web:* www.rcubed.com	Dallas	TX	75229	972-243-3830	
Raven Computers 5952 Odana Rd *Web:* ravencomputers.com	Madison	WI	53719	608-661-1372	
REACT Computer Services Inc 7654 Plz Ct *Web:* www.reactcomputerservices.com	Willowbrook	IL	60527	630-323-6200	
Realistic Computing Inc Four W Rolling *Web:* www.realistic-computing.com	Baltimore	MD	21228	410-744-8144	
ReliaTech 2300 El Portal Dr Ste G *Web:* streettech.org	San Pablo	CA	94806	510-236-7000	
Rescuecom Corp 2560 Burnet Ave **Fax Area Code:* 315 ■ *TF:* 800-737-2837 ■ *Web:* www.rescuecom.com	Syracuse	NY	13206	800-737-2837	433-5228*
Rockford It 419 N Mulford Rd Ste 2 *Web:* rockfordit.com	Rockford	IL	61107	815-316-7575	
Sanders Software Consulting Inc 3008 W 30th St *Web:* www.sanderssoftware.com	Lawrence	KS	66047	785-865-5111	
Sentinel Technologies Inc 2550 Warrenville Rd *Web:* www.sentinel.com	Downers Grove	IL	60515	630-769-4300	
Service Express Inc 3854 Broadmoor Ave SE *Web:* www.seiservice.com	Grand Rapids	MI	49512	616-698-2221	
Shiloh Service Inc 85 Mtn View Pl *Web:* shilohservice.com	Irwin	PA	15642	724-863-0190	
Simple Pc 101 Grace St *Web:* simple-pc.com	Greenwood	SC	29649	864-229-2447	
Spartan Computer Services Inc 350 W Phillips Rd *Web:* www.spartancomputer.com	Greer	SC	29650	864-848-3810	
Systems Maintenance Services Inc (SMS) 10420 Harris Oaks Blvd Suite C *TF:* 877-405-0330 ■ *Web:* www.sysmaint.com	Charlotte	NC	28269	877-405-0330	
T&s Trading Co 1110 Ortega St *Web:* tandstradingco.com	San Francisco	CA	94122	415-242-1551	
Team One Repair Inc 1911 Satellite Blvd Ste 100 *Web:* www.teamonerepair.net	Buford	GA	30518	678-985-0772	
Tech Team Solutions LLC 106 S Loudoun St *Web:* www.techteamsolutions.com	Winchester	VA	22601	540-667-2000	
Tecinfo Inc 601 N Deer Creek Dr E *Web:* tecinfo.net	Leland	MS	38756	662-686-9009	
Tecnet Canada Inc 3403 Seymour Pl *Web:* www.tecnet.ca	Victoria	BC	V8X1W4	250-475-6066	
Telirite Technical Services Inc 2857 Lakeview Ct *Web:* www.telirite.com	Fremont	CA	94538	510-440-3888	
Throckmorten Enterprises 17433 Hwy 120 *Web:* throck.com	Big Oak Flat	CA	95305	209-962-7308	
Trident Contract Management 2918 Marketplace Dr Ste 206 *Web:* www.trident-it.com	Madison	WI	53719	608-276-1900	
True Tech Systems Inc 270 N Tinman St *Web:* www.truetechsystems.com	Coal City	IL	60416	815-634-0308	
Tsg Networks 10462 San Pablo Ave *Web:* tsgnetworks.com	El Cerrito	CA	94530	512-772-1298	
Turner Techtronics Inc 3200 W Burbank Blvd *Web:* www.turnertech.com	Burbank	CA	91505	818-973-1060	
UCR LLC 1332 Woodman Dr *Web:* www.ucrnet.com	Dayton	OH	45432	937-253-8898	
V2 Systems Inc 9104 Manassas Dr Unit P *Web:* www.v2systems.com	Manassas	VA	20111	703-361-4606	
Vip Technology Solutions Group LLC 12149 S State Hwy 51 *Web:* viptsg.com	Coweta	OK	74429	918-279-7000	
Visual Net Design Lc 212 E Ramsey Rd *Web:* www.vndx.com	San Antonio	TX	78216	210-590-2734	
VITEC Solutions LLC 455 Commerce Dr Ste 3 *Web:* www.vitecsolutions.com	Amherst	NY	14228	716-204-9200	
Voxtechnologies Com 301 S Sherman St *Web:* www.voxtechnologies.com	Richardson	TX	75081	972-234-4343	
W Dm Computer Services Inc 1900 Harrison St Ste 2 *Web:* wdmquincy.com	Quincy	IL	62301	217-228-1950	
Wolf Technology Group Inc One Chick Springs Rd Ste 115 *Web:* www.wolftg.com	Greenville	SC	29609	864-248-6316	
Word-Tech Inc 5625 Foxridge Dr Ste 110 *Web:* www.wordtech.com	Mission	KS	66202	913-722-3334	
Wsb Computer Services Inc 21 Craft St *Web:* www.wsbcs.net	Alamosa	CO	81101	719-589-8940	

179 COMPUTER NETWORKING PRODUCTS & SYSTEMS

SEE ALSO Modems p. 2012; Systems & Utilities Software p. 2049; Telecommunications Equipment & Systems p. 3206

	City	State	Zip	Phone	Fax
Accton Technology Corp 1200 Crossman Ave Ste 130 *Web:* www.accton.com	Sunnyvale	CA	94089	408-747-0994	747-0982
Alcatel-Lucent 600 Mountain Ave *Web:* www.alcatel-lucent.com	Murray Hill	NJ	07974	908-508-8080	508-2576
Allied Telesyn International Corp 19800 N Creek Pkwy Ste 100 **Fax:* Sales ■ *TF:* 800-424-4284 ■ *Web:* www.alliedtelesis.com	Bothell	WA	98011	425-481-3895	481-3899*
American Megatrends Inc (AMI) 5555 Oakbrook Pkwy Bldg 200 *TF:* 800-828-9264 ■ *Web:* www.ami.com	Norcross	GA	30093	770-246-8600	246-8790
ASA Computers Inc 645 National Ave *TF:* 800-732-5727 ■ *Web:* www.asacomputers.com	Mountain View	CA	94043	650-230-8000	230-8090
Asante Technologies Inc 673 S Milpitas Blvd Ste 100 *OTC: ASNL* ■ *TF:* 800-303-9121 ■ *Web:* www.asante.com	Milpitas	CA	95035	408-435-8388	719-8594
Avaya Inc 211 Mt Airy Rd *TF:* 800-237-3239 ■ *Web:* www.avaya.com	Basking Ridge	NJ	07920	908-953-6000	
Axis Communications Inc (ACI) 100 Apollo Dr *TF:* 800-444-2947 ■ *Web:* www.axis.com	Chelmsford	MA	01824	978-614-2000	614-2100
Black Box Corp 1000 Pk Dr *NASDAQ: BBOX* ■ **Fax Area Code:* 800 ■ *TF:* 877-877-2269 ■ *Web:* www.blackbox.com	Lawrence	PA	15055	724-746-5500	321-0746*
Blue Coat Systems Inc 420 N Mary Ave *NASDAQ: BCSI* ■ *TF:* 866-302-2628 ■ *Web:* www.bluecoat.com	Sunnyvale	CA	94085	408-220-2200	220-2250
Brocade Communications Systems Inc 130 Holger Way *NASDAQ: BRCD* ■ *TF:* 800-752-8061 ■ *Web:* www.brocade.com	San Jose	CA	95134	408-333-8000	333-8101
Cambex Corp 337 Tpke Rd *OTC: CBEX* ■ *TF:* 800-325-5565 ■ *Web:* www.cambex.com	Southborough	MA	01772	508-281-0209	281-0214

Company	City	State	Zip	Phone	Fax
Chatsworth Products Inc 31425 Agoura Rd TF: 800-834-4969 ■ Web: www.chatsworth.com	Westlake Village	CA	91361	818-735-6100	735-6199
CIENA Corp Metro Transport Div 1185 Sanctuary Pkwy Web: www.ciena.com	Alpharetta	GA	30009	678-867-5100	867-5101
Cisco Systems Inc 170 W Tasman Dr NASDAQ: CSCO ■ TF: 800-553-6387 ■ Web: www.cisco.com	San Jose	CA	95134	408-526-4000	526-4100
Compex Inc 7918 Jones Branch Dr *Fax Area Code: 714 ■ *Fax: Sales ■ TF: 800-279-8891 ■ Web: www.compex.com.sg	Mclean	VA	22102	703-642-5910	482-0332*
CompuCom Systems Inc 7171 Forest Ln TF Cust Svc: 800-597-0555 ■ Web: www.compucom.com	Dallas	TX	75230	972-856-3600	
Comtrol Corp 6655 Wedgewood Rd Ste 120 TF: 800-926-6876 ■ Web: www.comtrol.com	Maple Grove	MN	55311	763-494-4100	494-4199
Contemporary Control Systems Inc 2431 Curtiss St Web: www.ccontrols.com	Downers Grove	IL	60515	630-963-7070	963-0109
Continental Resources Inc 175 Middlesex Tpke TF: 800-937-4688 ■ Web: www.conres.com	Bedford	MA	01730	781-275-0850	275-6563
Coriant 220 Mill Rd Web: www.coriantamerica.com	Chelmsford	MA	01824	978-250-2900	256-3434
Crossroads Systems Inc 8300 N MoPac Expy NASDAQ: CRDS ■ TF: 800-643-7148 ■ Web: www.crossroads.com	Austin	TX	78759	512-349-0300	795-8309
Crystal Group Inc 850 Kacena Rd TF: 877-279-7863 ■ Web: www.crystalrugged.com	Hiawatha	IA	52233	319-378-1636	393-2338
Cubix Corp 2800 Lockheed Way TF Sales: 800-829-0550 ■ Web: www.cubix.com	Carson City	NV	89706	775-888-1000	888-1002
Cyberdata Corp Three Justin Ct TF: 800-363-8010 ■ Web: www.cyberdata.net	Monterey	CA	93940	831-373-2601	373-4193
D-Link Systems Inc 17595 Mt Herrmann St *Fax Area Code: 866 ■ TF: 800-326-1688 ■ Web: www.dlink.com	Fountain Valley	CA	92708	714-885-6000	743-4905*
Daly Computers Inc 22521 Gateway Ctr Dr TF: 800-955-3259 ■ Web: www.daly.com	Clarksburg	MD	20871	301-670-0381	963-1516
Datacomm Management Sciences Inc 25 Van Zant St	East Norwalk	CT	06855	203-838-7183	838-1751
Dell Inc One Dell Way NASDAQ: DELL ■ TF: 800-879-3355 ■ Web: www.dell.com	Round Rock	TX	78682	512-338-4400	283-6161
Digi International Inc 11001 Bren Rd E NASDAQ: DGII ■ TF: 877-912-3444 ■ Web: www.digi.com	Minnetonka	MN	55343	952-912-3444	912-4991
Dot Hill Systems Corp 1351 S Sunset St NASDAQ: HILL ■ TF: 800-872-2783 ■ Web: www.dothill.com	Longmont	CO	80501	303-845-3200	845-3655
Echelon Corp 550 Meridian Ave NASDAQ: ELON ■ TF: 888-324-3566 ■ Web: www.echelon.com	San Jose	CA	95126	408-938-5200	790-3800
Egenera Inc 80 Central St TF: 866-301-3117 ■ Web: www.egenera.com	Boxborough	MA	01719	978-206-6300	206-6436
Electronics for Imaging Inc 303 Velocity Way NASDAQ: EFII ■ TF: 888-334-8650 ■ Web: w3.efi.com	Foster City	CA	94404	650-357-3500	357-3500
EMC Corp 176 S St NYSE: EMC ■ Web: www.emc.com	Hopkinton	MA	01748	508-435-1000	497-6912
Emulex Corp 3333 Susan St NYSE: ELX ■ TF: 800-854-7112 ■ Web: www.emulex.com	Costa Mesa	CA	92626	714-662-5600	241-0792
Enterasys Networks Inc 50 Minuteman Rd Web: extremenetworks.com	Andover	MA	01810	978-684-1000	
eSoft Inc 295 Interlocken Blvd Ste 500 TF: 888-903-7638 ■ Web: untangle.com/esoft	Broomfield	CO	80021	303-444-1600	444-1640
Extreme Networks Inc 3585 Monroe St NASDAQ: EXTR ■ TF: 888-257-3000 ■ Web: www.extremenetworks.com	Santa Clara	CA	95051	408-579-2800	579-3000
Ezenia! Inc 14 Celina Ave Unit 17 *Fax Area Code: 603 ■ TF: 800-966-2301 ■ Web: www.ezenia.com	Nashua	NH	03063	781-505-2100	880-4978*
F5 Networks Inc 401 Elliott Ave W NASDAQ: FFIV ■ TF: 888-882-4447 ■ Web: www.f5.com	Seattle	WA	98119	206-272-5555	272-5556
Finisar Corp 1389 Moffett Pk Dr NASDAQ: FNSR ■ Web: www.finisar.com	Sunnyvale	CA	94089	408-548-1000	541-6129
Fujitsu Computer Systems Corp 1250 E Arques Ave TF: 800-538-8460 ■ Web: solutions.us.fujitsu.com	Sunnyvale	CA	94085	408-746-6000	
Futurex Inc 864 Old Boerne Rd TF: 800-251-5112 ■ Web: www.futurex.com	Bulverde	TX	78163	830-980-9782	438-8782
General DataComm Inc 6 Rubber Ave Web: www.gdc.com	Naugatuck	CT	06770	203-729-0271	723-2883
High Point Solutions Inc 5 Gail Ct Web: www.highpt.com	Sparta	NJ	07871	973-940-0040	940-0041
iGo Inc 17800 N Perimeter Dr Ste 200 NASDAQ: IGOI ■ TF: 888-205-0093 ■ Web: www.igo.com	Scottsdale	AZ	85255	480-596-0061	596-0349
iLinc Communications Inc 2999 N 44th St Ste 650 TF: 800-767-9054 ■ Web: www.ilinc.com	Phoenix	AZ	85018	602-952-1200	952-0544
IMC Networks Corp 19772 Pauling TF: 800-624-1070 ■ Web: bb-elec.com	Foothill Ranch	CA	92610	949-465-3000	465-3020
Interphase Corp 2901 N Dallas Pkwy Ste 200 NASDAQ: INPH ■ TF: 800-327-8638 ■ Web: www.interphase.com	Plano	TX	75093	214-654-5000	654-5500
Juniper Networks Inc 1194 N Mathilda Ave NYSE: JNPR ■ TF: 888-586-4737 ■ Web: www.juniper.net	Sunnyvale	CA	94089	408-745-2000	745-2100
LightSand Communications Inc 101 E Pk Blvd Ste 600 Web: www.lightsand.com	Plano	TX	75074	972-516-3740	516-3741
Link Computer Corp Inc PO Box 250 Web: www.linkcorp.com	Bellwood	PA	16617	814-742-7700	742-7900
MAPSYS Inc 920 Michigan Ave Web: www.mapsysinc.com	Columbus	OH	43215	614-224-5193	224-6048
Marvell Semiconductor Inc 5488 Marvell Ln TF Cust Svc: 855-627-8355 ■ Web: www.marvell.com	Santa Clara	CA	95054	408-222-2500	
Medical Knowledge Systems Inc 440 Burrough Ste 130 Web: www.mksi.com	Detroit	MI	48202	313-483-0955	731-0591
MTM Technologies Inc 1200 High Ridge Rd OTC: MTMC ■ Web: www.mtm.com	Stamford	CT	06905	203-975-3700	975-3701

Company	City	State	Zip	Phone	Fax
NEC Corp of America 10850 Gold Ctr Dr Ste 200 TF: 800-632-4636 ■ Web: www.necam.com	Rancho Cordova	CA	95670	916-463-7000	
Netplanner Systems Inc 3145 Northwoods Pkwy Ste 800 TF: 800-795-1975 ■ Web: www.netplanner.com	Norcross	GA	30071	770-662-5482	441-3773
Network Appliance Inc 495 E Java Dr NASDAQ: NTAP ■ TF Sales: 800-443-4537 ■ Web: www.netapp.com	Sunnyvale	CA	94089	408-822-6000	822-4422
Network Dynamics Inc 640 Brooker Creek Blvd Ste 410 TF: 877-818-8597 ■ Web: www.ndiwebsite.com	Oldsmar	FL	34677	813-818-8597	818-9659
Network Equipment Technologies Inc 6900 Paseo Padre Pkwy NASDAQ: NWK	Fremont	CA	94555	510-713-7300	574-4000
Overland Storage Inc 4820 Overland Ave NASDAQ: OVRL ■ TF: 800-729-8725 ■ Web: www.overlandstorage.com	San Diego	CA	92123	858-571-5555	571-0982
OvisLink Technologies Corp 20266 Paseo Robles Web: www.ovislink.com	Walnut	CA	91789	909-869-8666	869-8585
Patton Electronics Co 7622 Rickenbacker Dr Web: www.patton.com	Gaithersburg	MD	20879	301-975-1000	869-9293
Peak 10 752 Barret Ave TF: 866-732-5836 ■ Web: www.peak10.com	Louisville	KY	40204	502-315-6015	315-6035
Plaintree Systems Inc 90 Decosta Pl Ste 100 Web: www.plaintree.com	Arnprior	ON	K7S0B5	613-623-3434	623-4647
Polycom Inc 4750 Willow Rd *Fax: Hum Res ■ TF: 800-765-9266 ■ Web: www.polycom.com	Pleasanton	CA	94588	800-765-9266	*
PrimeArray Systems Inc 127 Riverneck Rd TF: 800-433-5133 ■ Web: www.primearray.com	Chelmsford	MA	01824	978-654-6250	654-6249
Quick Eagle Networks Inc 830 Maude Ave	Mountain View	CA	94043	650-962-8282	
Raytheon Computer Products 1001 Boston Post Rd *Fax Area Code: 508 ■ Web: www.raytheon.com	Marlborough	MA	01752	781-522-3000	490-2675*
Ringdale Inc 101 Halmar Cove TF: 888-288-9080 ■ Web: www.ringdale.com	Georgetown	TX	78628	512-288-9080	288-7210
Safari Circuits Inc 411 Washington St TF: 888-694-7230 ■ Web: www.safaricircuits.com	Otsego	MI	49078	269-694-9471	692-2651
SafeNet Inc 4690 Millennium Dr TF Sales: 800-533-3958 ■ Web: www.safenet-inc.com	Belcamp	MD	21017	410-931-7500	931-7524
SARCOM Inc 8337 Green Meadows Dr N Ste A *Fax: Sales ■ TF: 800-700-1000 ■ Web: sarcom.pcm.com	Lewis Center	OH	43035	614-854-1300	854-1800*
Server Technology Inc 1040 Sandhill Dr TF: 800-835-1515 ■ Web: www.servertech.com	Reno	NV	89521	775-284-2000	284-2065
Silicon Graphics Inc (SGI) 900 N McCarthy Blvd Web: www.sgi.com	Milpitas	CA	95035	669-900-8000	
Skyline Network Engineering LLC 6956-F Aviation Blvd Ste C Web: www.skylinenet.net	Glen Burnie	MD	21061	410-795-2700	
SOHOware Inc 1250 Oakmead Pkwy Ste 210 TF: 800-632-1118 ■ Web: www.sohoware.com	Sunnyvale	CA	94085	408-565-9888	565-9889
Solectek Corp 6370 Nancy Ridge Dr Ste 109 TF: 888-299-8057 ■ Web: www.solectek.com	San Diego	CA	92121	858-450-1220	457-2681
SonicWALL Inc 2001 Logic Dr TF: 888-557-6642 ■ Web: www.sonicwall.com	San Jose	CA	95124	408-745-9600	745-9300
Spectrum Communications Cabling Services Inc 226 N Lincoln Ave	Corona	CA	92882	951-371-0549	270-3833
SteelCloud Inc 20110 Ashbrook Pl Ste 270 OTC: SCLD ■ TF: 800-296-3866 ■ Web: www.steelcloud.com	Ashburn	VA	20147	703-674-5500	674-5506
StoneFly Inc 21353 Cabot Blvd TF: 888-786-6335 ■ Web: www.stonefly.com	Hayward	CA	94545	510-265-1616	265-1565
Storage Engine Inc One Sheila Dr Bldg 6A TF: 866-734-8899 ■ Web: www.storageengine.com	Tinton Falls	NJ	07724	732-747-6995	747-6542
Strictly Business Computer Systems Inc 848 Fourth Ave Ste 200 *Fax Area Code: 304 ■ TF: 888-529-0401 ■ Web: www.sbcs.com	Huntington	WV	25701	888-529-0401	781-2590*
Symon Communications Inc 500 N Central Expy Ste 175 TF: 800-827-9666 ■ Web: rmgnetworks.com	Plano	TX	75074	972-578-8484	422-1680
Systech Corp 16510 Via Esprillo TF: 800-800-8970 ■ Web: www.systech.com	San Diego	CA	92127	858-674-6500	613-2400
Systemax Inc 11 Harbor Pk Dr NYSE: SYX ■ TF: 888-645-0878 ■ Web: www.systemax.com	Port Washington	NY	11050	516-608-7000	608-7001
TalkPoint Communications Inc 100 William St TF: 866-323-8660 ■ Web: talkpoint.com/	New York	NY	10038	212-909-2900	909-2901
Technology Integration Group (TIG) 7810 Trade St TF: 800-858-0549 ■ Web: www.tig.com	San Diego	CA	92121	858-566-1900	566-8794
Tekworks Inc 13000 Gregg St Ste B TF: 877-835-9675 ■ Web: www.tekworks.com	Poway	CA	92064	877-835-9675	
Telebyte Inc 355 Marcus Blvd TF: 800-835-3298 ■ Web: www.telebyteusa.com	Hauppauge	NY	11788	631-423-3232	385-8184
TeleSoft International Inc 4029 S Capital of TX Hwy Ste 220 Web: www.telesoft-intl.com	Austin	TX	78704	512-373-4224	788-5660
Telkonet Inc 10200 W Innovation Dr Ste 300 OTC: TKOI ■ TF Sales: 888-703-9398 ■ Web: www.telkonet.com	Milwaukee	WI	53226	414-223-0473	258-8307
Transition Networks Inc 10900 Red Cir Dr TF: 800-526-9267 ■ Web: www.transition.com	Minnetonka	MN	55343	952-941-7600	941-2322
Transource Computers Corp 2405 W Utopia Rd TF: 800-486-3715 ■ Web: www.transource.com	Phoenix	AZ	85027	623-879-8882	879-8887
Trendware International Inc 20675 Manhattan Pl TF: 888-326-6061 ■ Web: www.trendnet.com	Torrance	CA	90501	310-961-5500	961-5511
Ultera Systems Inc 26081 Merit Cir Ste 125 TF: 877-462-7362 ■ Web: www.ultera.com	Laguna Hills	CA	92653	949-367-8800	367-0758
UNICOM 565 Brea Canyon Rd Ste A *Fax: Mktg ■ TF: 800-346-6668 ■ Web: www.unicomlink.com	Walnut	CA	91789	626-964-7873	964-7880*
Unimark Products 9818 Pflumm Rd TF Cust Svc: 800-255-6356 ■ Web: www.unimark.com	Lenexa	KS	66215	913-649-2424	649-5795
US Robotics Corp 1300 E Woodfield Dr Ste 506 TF: 877-710-0884 ■ Web: www.usr.com	Schaumburg	IL	60173	847-874-2000	874-2001

				Phone	Fax
ViewCast Corp 3701 W Plano Pkwy Ste 300 .... Plano *TF:* 800-540-4119 ■ *Web:* www.viewcast.com	TX	75075		972-488-7200	488-7299
Virtela Technology Services Inc 5680 Greenwood Plz Blvd Ste 200 .... Greenwood Village *TF:* 877-803-9629 ■ *Web:* www.virtela.net	CO	80111		720-475-4000	475-4001
Visara International Inc 2700 Gateway Centre Blvd Ste 600 .... Morrisville *TF:* 888-334-4380 ■ *Web:* www.visara.com	NC	27560		919-882-0200	882-0163
WatchGuard Technologies Inc 505 Fifth Ave S Ste 500 .... Seattle *TF Sales:* 800-734-9905 ■ *Web:* www.watchguard.com	WA	98104		206-613-6600	521-8342
WAV Inc 2380 Prospect Dr .... Aurora *TF:* 800-678-2419 ■ *Web:* www.wavonline.com	IL	60504		630-818-1000	818-4450
WideBand Corp 401 W Grand St .... Gallatin *TF:* 888-663-3050 ■ *Web:* www.wband.com	MO	64640		660-663-3000	663-3736
Winchester Systems Inc 101 Billerica Ave Bldg 5 .... North Billerica *TF Cust Svc:* 800-325-3700 ■ *Web:* www.winsys.com	MA	01862		781-265-0200	265-0201
Works Computing Inc 1801 American Blvd E Ste 12 .... Bloomington *TF:* 866-222-4077 ■ *Web:* www.workscomputing.com	MN	55425		952-746-1580	746-1585
World Data Products Inc 121 Cheshire Ln .... Minnetonka *TF:* 888-210-7636 ■ *Web:* www.wdpi.com	MN	55305		952-476-9000	476-1903
Xyratex International 2031 Concourse Dr .... San Jose *Web:* www.xyratex.com	CA	95131		916-375-8181	375-8488
ZT Group International Inc 350 Meadowlands Pkwy .... Secaucus *TF:* 888-984-8899 ■ *Web:* www.ztsystems.com	NJ	07094		201-559-1000	559-1004

180 COMPUTER PROGRAMMING SERVICES - CUSTOM

SEE ALSO Computer Software p. 2040; Computer Systems Design Services p. 2054

			Phone	Fax
2plus2 Partners Inc 5980 Horton St Ste 360 .... Emeryville *Web:* www.2plus2partners.com	CA	94608	510-652-7700	
3CLogic Inc 9201 Corporate Blvd Ste 470 .... Rockville *Web:* www.3clogic.com	MD	20850	240-454-6347	
4 Consulting Inc 1221 Abrams Rd .... Richardson *Web:* www.4ci-usa.com	TX	75081	214-698-8633	
41st Parameter Inc, The 17851 N 85th St Ste 250 .... Scottsdale *Web:* www.the41.com	AZ	85255	480-776-5500	
4th Source Inc 2400 Veterans Blvd Ste 480 .... Kenner *TF:* 855-875-4700 ■ *Web:* www.4thsource.com	LA	70062	855-875-4700	
6k Systems Inc 44084 Riverside Pkwy Ste 340 .... Leesburg *Web:* www.6ksystems.com	VA	20176	703-724-1320	
7 Medical Systems LLC 651 Nicollet Mall Ste 501 .... Minneapolis *Web:* www.7medical.com	MN	55402	612-230-7700	
A L H Group Inc 880 Industrial Way .... San Luis Obispo *Web:* alh.alh-group.com	CA	93401	805-541-8739	
Aaantivirus.com 200 Dillon Ave Ste D .... Campbell *Web:* aaantivirus.com	CA	95008	408-374-8000	
Aaxis Group 6399 Wilshire Blvd Ste 914 .... Los Angeles *Web:* www.aaxiscommerce.com	CA	90048	323-653-1500	
AB Controls Inc 188 Technology Dr Ste K .... Irvine *Web:* www.abcontrols.com	CA	92618	949-341-0977	
Abaris Inc 1255 Treat Blvd Ste 140 .... Walnut Creek *Web:* www.abaris-inc.com	CA	94597	949-333-3500	
Abila Inc 7901 Jones Branch Dr .... Mclean *Web:* avectra.com	VA	22102	703-506-7000	
AbleSys Corp 20954 Corsair Blvd .... Hayward *Web:* www.ablesys.com	CA	94545	510-265-1883	
ABSOFT Corp 2781 Bond St .... Rochester Hills *Web:* absoft.com	MI	48309	248-853-0050	
Abtech 17300 SW Upper Boones Ferry Rd Ste 110 .... Portland *Web:* www.abtech-pdx.com	OR	97224	503-924-1090	
AcademyOne Inc 601 Willowbrook Ln .... West Chester *Web:* www.academyone.com	PA	19382	610-436-5680	
Accelerated Technology Laboratories Inc 496 Holly Grove School Rd .... West End *Web:* www.atlab.com	NC	27376	910-673-8165	
Acceleware Ltd 435 10 Ave SE .... Calgary *Web:* www.acceleware.com	AB	T2G0W3	403-249-9099	
Access Innovations Inc 4725 Indian School Rd NE Ste 100 .... Albuquerque *TF:* 800-926-8328 ■ *Web:* www.accessinn.com	NM	87110	505-265-3591	256-1080
Access Softek Inc 727 Allston Way Ste C .... Berkeley *Web:* www.accessoftek.com	CA	94710	510-848-0606	
Acclaim Systems Inc 110 E Pennsylvania Blvd .... Feasterville *Web:* www.acclaimsystems.com	PA	19053	215-354-1420	
AccuCode Inc 6886 S Yosemite St Ste 100 .... Centennial *TF:* 866-705-9879 ■ *Web:* www.accucode.com	CO	80112	303-639-6111	639-6178
Accumedic Computer Systems Inc 11 Grace Ave Ste 401 .... Great Neck *Web:* www.accumedic.com	NY	11021	516-466-6800	
Accumedscript LLP 1601 Bethel Rd .... Columbus *Web:* www.accumedscript.com	OH	43220	614-804-5656	
Accurate Computer Technology Inc 17821 Sky Park Cir Ste J .... Irvine *Web:* www.accuratecomputer.com	CA	92614	949-261-6677	
Accuzip 3216 El Camino Real .... Atascadero *Web:* www.accuzip.com	CA	93422	805-461-7300	
Ace Technologies Inc 2375 Zanker Rd Ste 250 .... San Jose *Web:* www.acetechnologies.com	CA	95131	408-521-1139	
Achieve IT Solutions Inc 640 Belle Terre Rd Bldg B .... Port Jefferson *Web:* www.achieveits.com	NY	11777	631-543-3200	

			Phone	Fax
Acquidata Inc 400 Garden City Plz Ste 445 .... Garden City *Web:* www.acquidata.com	NY	11530	516-408-3585	
Actsoft Inc 8910 N Dale Mabry Hwy .... Tampa *TF:* 888-732-6638 ■ *Web:* www.actsoft.com	FL	33614	813-936-2331	936-7541
Acuo Technologies LLC 8009 34th Ave S Riverview Office Tower Ste 900 .... Bloomington *Web:* www.acuotech.com	MN	55128	952-905-3440	
Ad Astra Information Systems LLC 6900 W 80th St Ste 300 .... Overland Park *Web:* www.aais.com	KS	66204	913-652-4100	
Ad Solutions Group Inc 1200 Harger Rd Ste 203 .... Oak Brook *Web:* www.adsgroup.net	IL	60523	630-574-4545	
Ada Business Computers 1003 N Mississippi Ave .... Ada *Web:* www.adacomp.com	OK	74820	580-436-2803	
Adapt Software Applications 959 S Coast Dr Ste 100 .... Costa Mesa *Web:* www.adaptcrm.com	CA	92626	714-389-1584	
Adicio Inc One Carlsbad Research Ctr 2382 Faraday Ave Ste 350 .... Carlsbad *Web:* www.adicio.com	CA	92008	760-602-9502	
Adino Inc 360 Alden Ct .... Chicago Heights *Web:* www.adinoinc.com	IL	60411	708-481-1000	
ADMINS Inc 1035 Cambridge St .... Cambridge *Web:* www.admins.com	MA	02141	617-494-5100	
Ads Programming Services One Independence Plz Ste 820 .... Birmingham *Web:* www.adsprogramming.com	AL	35209	205-803-2196	
Advanced Chemistry Development Inc 110 Yonge St 14th Fl .... Toronto *Web:* www.acdlabs.com	ON	M5C1T4	416-368-3435	
Advanced Computer Technologies LLC 101 Market Pl .... Montgomery *Web:* www.actinnovations.com	AL	36117	334-262-6882	
Advanced Computing Solutions Group Inc 19125 Northcreek Pkwy .... Bothell *Web:* www.acsgrp.com	WA	98011	425-609-3165	
Advanced Digital Data Inc Six Laurel Dr .... Flanders *TF:* 800-922-0972 ■ *Web:* www.addsys.com	NJ	07836	973-584-4026	584-3205
Advanced Health Media LLC (AHM) 420 Mountain Ave .... New Providence *Web:* www.ahmdirect.com	NJ	07974	908-393-8700	393-8701
Advanced Solutions International Inc 901 N Pitt St Ste 200 .... Alexandria *Web:* www.advsol.com	VA	22314	703-739-3100	739-3218
Advanced Systems Consultants Inc 4074 E Patterson Rd .... Beavercreek *Web:* ascsoftware.com	OH	45430	937-429-1428	
Advancedware Corp 13844 Alton Pkwy Ste 136 .... Irvine *Web:* advancedware.com	CA	92618	949-609-1240	
AdvanTech Inc 2661 Riva Rd Ste 1030 .... Annapolis *Web:* www.advantech-inc.com	MD	21401	410-266-8000	
Aeon Nexus Corp 174 Glen St .... Glens Falls *Web:* www.aeonnexus.com	NY	12801	518-338-1551	
Aequor Technologies Inc 377 Hoes Ln .... Piscataway *Web:* www.aequor.com	NJ	08854	732-494-4999	
Ag Informaton Systems 306 Primrose Ln .... Mountville *Web:* www.ag-is.com	PA	17554	717-285-7105	
Agb Investigative Services Inc 2033 W 95th St .... Chicago *Web:* agbinvestigative.com	IL	60643	773-445-4300	
AgileAssets Inc 3001 Bee Caves Rd Ste 200 .... Austin *Web:* www.agileassets.com	TX	78746	512-327-4200	
Agiletics Inc 585 S Ronald Reagan Blvd Ste 113 .... Longwood *Web:* agiletics.com	FL	32750	407-834-5115	
Agilysys NV LLC 28925 Fountain Pkwy .... Solon *Web:* www.agilysys.com	OH	44139	770-810-7800	
Agnik LLC 8840 Stanford Blvd Ste 1300 .... Columbia *Web:* www.agnik.com	MD	21045	410-290-0864	
Ahead Hum Res Inc/Prosoft LLC 2209 Heather Ln .... Louisville *Web:* aheadhr.com	KY	40218	502-485-1000	
Airput Inc 3819 Germantown Pk .... Collegeville *Web:* www.airput.com	PA	19426	610-454-5100	
Aisle7 215 NW Park Ave .... Portland *Web:* aisle7.com	OR	97209	503-234-4092	
Alebra Technologies Inc 550 Main St Ste 250 PO Box 120390 .... New Brighton *Web:* www.alebra.com	MN	55112	651-366-6140	
All of E Solutions 2510 W Sixth St .... Lawrence *Web:* allofe.com	KS	66049	785-832-2900	
All Squared Web Design LLC 284 Susquehanna Trl .... Allentown *Web:* allsquared.com	PA	18104	610-351-5416	
Alltech International Inc 8298-B Old Courthouse Rd Centennial Plz - Tysons Corner .... Vienna *Web:* www.alltech.net	VA	22182	703-506-1222	
Alpha Lex Systems Integration 21604 Tribune St .... Chatsworth *Web:* alphalex.com	CA	91311	818-407-9200	
Alpha Net Consulting LLC 3080 Olcott St Ste 235C .... Santa Clara *Web:* anetcorp.com	CA	95054	408-330-0896	
Alphapoint Technology Inc Ste 200 6371 Business Blvd .... Sarasota *Web:* new.alphapoint-us.net	FL	34240	941-907-8822	
Alphinat Inc Ste 680 2000 Peel .... Montreal *Web:* www.alphinat.com	QC	H3A2W5	514-398-9799	

Company	City	State	Zip	Phone	Fax
Alr Systems & Software Inc 11707 M Cir *Web:* www.alrsys.com	Omaha	NE	68137	402-891-1500	
Alta Via Consulting LLC 127 ConKinnon Dr *TF:* 877-258-2842 ■ *Web:* www.altavia.com	Lenoir City	TN	37772	877-258-2842	
Altair Technology Inc 1116 W Blanco Rd *Web:* www.altairtech.com	San Antonio	TX	78232	210-764-9900	497-1329
Altamira Technologies Corp 8201 Greensboro Dr Ste 800 *Web:* www.invertix.com	Mclean	VA	22102	703-813-2100	
Altech Services Inc 1160 Parsippany Blvd Ste 202 *TF:* 888-725-8324 ■ *Web:* www.altechts.com	Parsippany	NJ	07054	888-725-8324	
Altep Inc 7450 Remcon Cir *Web:* www.altep.com	El Paso	TX	79912	915-533-8722	
Altia Inc 7222 Commerce Ctr Dr Ste 240 *Web:* www.altia.com	Colorado Springs	CO	80919	719-598-4299	
Alvarez Technology Group Inc 209 Pajaro St Ste A *Web:* www.alvareztg.com	Salinas	CA	93901	831-753-7677	
Amaram Technology Corp 2123 Mckay St *Web:* www.amaram.com	Falls Church	VA	22043	703-288-4113	
Ambasoft Inc 23505 Crenshaw Blvd Ste 153 *Web:* www.ambasoft.com	Torrance	CA	90505	310-326-4160	
Amer Technology Inc 5717 Northwest Pkwy *Web:* www.amersolutions.com	San Antonio	TX	78249	210-256-7070	
American Hytech Corp Headquarters 125 UPark Rd *Web:* ahc.net	Pittsburgh	PA	15238	412-826-3333	
American Technology Services Inc 2751 Prosperity Ave Sixth Fl *Web:* www.networkats.com	Fairfax	VA	22031	703-876-0300	
AMS.NET Inc 502 Commerce Way *Web:* www.ams.net	Livermore	CA	94550	925-245-6100	
Amtex Enterprises Inc 520 E Weddell Dr Ste 12 *Web:* www.amtexenterprises.com	Sunnyvale	CA	94089	408-734-4050	
Analytical Graphics Inc 220 Vly Creek Blvd *TF:* 800-220-4785 ■ *Web:* www.agi.com	Exton	PA	19341	610-981-8000	981-8001
Analytical Mechanics Associates Inc 303 Butler Farm Rd Ste 104A *Web:* www.ama-inc.com	Hampton	VA	23666	757-865-0000	
Anchor Marketing Inc 2726 17th Ave S *Web:* www.anchorwebsite.com	Grand Forks	ND	58208	701-787-8230	
ANGOSS Software Corp Ste 200 111 George St *Web:* www.angoss.com	Toronto	ON	M5A2N4	416-593-1122	
AnswerOn Inc 1707 Main St Ste 500 *Web:* www.answeron.com	Longmont	CO	80501	720-684-4900	
Antares Development Corp 6243 W Ih 10 870 *Web:* www.antares-corp.com	San Antonio	TX	78201	210-736-2220	
Aparaa Corp 14900 Landmark Blvd Ste 630 *TF:* 888-441-2535 ■ *Web:* www.aparaa.com	Dallas	TX	75254	888-441-2535	
Apex Business Machines & Supplies 352 Riverside Dr *Web:* apexbiz.com	Sudbury	ON	P3E1H7	705-674-4472	
Apex Information Management Consultants Inc 4515 Culver Rd Ste 310 *Web:* www.apeximc.com	Rochester	NY	14622	585-225-8430	
Apex Innovations Inc 19951 W 162nd St *Web:* www.apex-innovations.com	Olathe	KS	66062	913-254-0250	
Apex Software Inc 37 Antrim Rd	Pittston	PA	18640	570-830-5893	
APlus Technologies Inc 10015 Old Columbia Rd Ste B *Web:* www.aplustechnologies.com	Columbia	MD	21046	410-290-6233	
Apollo PACS Inc 7700 Leesburg Pike Ste 419 *Web:* www.apollopacs.com	Falls Church	VA	22043	703-288-1474	
APOS Systems Inc 100 Conestoga College Blvd Ste 1118 *Web:* www.apos.com	Kitchener	ON	N2P2N6	519-894-2767	
Appfluent Technology Inc 6001 Montrose Rd Tenth Fl Ste 1000 *Web:* www.appfluent.com	Rockville	MD	20852	301-770-2888	
Applied Business Software 2847 Gundry Ave *Web:* www.themortgageoffice.com	Signal Hill	CA	90755	562-426-2188	
Applied Cad Knowledge Inc 18 Westech Dr *Web:* www.appliedcad.com	Tyngsboro	MA	01879	978-649-9800	
Applied Integrated Technologies Inc 6305 Ivy Ln Ste 520 *Web:* www.ait-i.com	Greenbelt	MD	20770	301-614-9700	
Applied OLAP Inc 3322 S Memorial Pkwy Ste 647 *Web:* www.appliedolap.com	Huntsville	AL	35801	256-885-4371	
Applied Performance Technologies Inc 400 W Wilson Bridge Rd Ste 250 *Web:* appliedperformance.com	Worthington	OH	43085	614-847-9600	
Applied Software Inc 3919 National Dr Ste 200 *TF:* 888-624-8439 ■ *Web:* www.magview.com	Burtonsville	MD	20866	888-624-8439	
Appolis Inc 333 Washington Ave N *Web:* www.appolis.com	Minneapolis	MN	55401	612-343-0404	
Apprise Software Inc 3101 Emrick Blvd Ste 301 *Web:* www.apprise.com	Bethlehem	PA	18020	610-991-3900	
Appsec Consulting Inc 6110 Hellyer Ave Ste 100 *Web:* www.appsecconsulting.com	San Jose	CA	95138	408-224-1110	
AppTech Corp Ste 102 2011 Palomar Airport Rd *Web:* apptechcorp.com	Carlsbad	CA	92011	760-707-5955	

Company	City	State	Zip	Phone	Fax
Apptricity Corp 5605 N Macarthur Blvd Ste 900 *Web:* www.apptricity.com	Irving	TX	75038	214-596-0601	
Apriva Inc 6900 E Camelback Rd Ste 700 *Web:* www.apriva.com	Scottsdale	AZ	85251	480-421-1210	
Aquarius Imaging LLC 3810 Inverrary Blvd *Web:* www.aquariusimaging.com	Lauderhill	FL	33319	954-777-2729	
Archibus Inc 18 Tremont St *Web:* www.archibus.com	Boston	MA	02108	617-227-2508	227-2509
Archive-cd LLC 910 Beverly Way *Web:* www.archive-cd.com	Jacksonville	OR	97530	541-899-5704	
Archonix Systems LLC 30 Lk Ctr Executive Park 401 Rt 73 N Ste 105 *Web:* www.archonixsystems.com	Marlton	NJ	08053	856-787-0020	
Archway Systems Inc 2134 Main St Ste 160 *Web:* www.archwaysystems.com	Huntington Beach	CA	92648	714-374-0440	
Argo Data Resource Corp 1500 N Greenville Ave *Web:* www.argodata.com	Richardson	TX	75081	972-866-3300	866-3301
Ariel Partners LLC 85 River St Ste 3a *Web:* www.arielpartners.com	Waltham	MA	02453	781-647-2425	
Ariel Software Consultants 2827 W Sherwin Ave *Web:* arielsoftware.com	Chicago	IL	60645	773-764-3434	
Aries Software Design 6210 W Olympic Blvd *Web:* www.aries-software.com	Los Angeles	CA	90048	323-934-1423	
Aristatek Inc 710 E Garfield St Ste 220 *Web:* www.aristatek.com	Laramie	WY	82070	307-721-2126	
Arkansas Data Services 27 Macarthur Dr *Web:* www.ark-data-services.com	Conway	AR	72032	501-327-8000	
Arnima Design 518 N Tampa St Ste 320 *Web:* arnima.com	Tampa	FL	33602	813-341-3500	
Arowana Consulting Inc 1550 Park Ave Ste 202 *Web:* www.arowanaconsulting.com	South Plainfield	NJ	07080	732-412-3567	
Arrayworks Inc 135 Wood Rd	Braintree	MA	02184	781-849-9797	
Arrendale Associates Inc 20484 Chartwell Ctr Dr Ste G *Web:* www.aaita.com	Cornelius	NC	28031	704-895-8025	
Artemis Solutions Group Inc 2501 Coolidge Rd Ste 503 *Web:* artemis-solutions.com	East Lansing	MI	48823	517-336-9925	
Artwork Conversion Software Inc 417 Ingalls St *Web:* www.artwork.com	Santa Cruz	CA	95060	831-426-6163	
Aruba Networks Inc 1344 Crossman Ave *NASDAQ: ARUN* ■ *TF:* 800-943-4526 ■ *Web:* www.arubanetworks.com	Sunnyvale	CA	94089	408-227-4500	752-0626
Asa Solutions Inc 8040 E Morgan Trl Ste 21 *Web:* www.asasolutions.com	Scottsdale	AZ	85258	480-922-9532	
Asc Consulting Inc 5781 Robeys Meadow Ln *Web:* www.ascconsultinginc.com	Fairfax	VA	22030	703-346-8570	
Ascentive LLC 50 S 16th St Ste 3575 *Web:* www.ascentive.com	Philadelphia	PA	19102	215-320-6000	
Aspect Consulting Inc 20140 Vly Forge Cir *Web:* www.aspect-consulting.com	King Of Prussia	PA	19406	610-783-0600	
Aspex Inc 1984 Isaac Newton Sq W *Web:* aspex.com	Reston	VA	20190	703-956-9343	
Aspex Solutions 8001 Lincoln Ave Ste 202 *Web:* www.applitrack.com	Skokie	IL	60077	847-475-2283	
Assette LLC One Faneuil Hall Fourth Fl *Web:* www.assette.com	Boston	MA	02109	617-723-6161	
Assist Cornerstone Technologies Inc 150 West Civic Ctr Dr Ste 601 *TF:* 800-732-0136 ■ *Web:* www.assistcornerstone.com	Sandy	UT	84070	800-732-0136	
At-your-service Software Inc 450 Bronxville Rd *Web:* www.ayssoftware.com	Bronxville	NY	10708	914-337-9030	
Atalasoft Inc 116 Pleasant St Ste 321 *Web:* www.atalasoft.com	Easthampton	MA	01027	413-572-4443	
Atigeo LLC 800 Bellevue Way NE Ste 600 *Web:* www.atigeo.com	Bellevue	WA	98004	425-635-3900	
Atlantic Software Technologies Inc 2435 Hwy 34 *Web:* www.astworld.com	Manasquan	NJ	08736	732-223-8810	
Atlas Systems Inc 244 Clearfield Ave Ste 407 *Web:* www.atlas-sys.com	Virginia Bch	VA	23462	757-467-7872	
Atlatl Inc 3000 Croasdaile Dr *Web:* sehhey.com	Durham	NC	27705	919-384-0514	
Atomic Object LLC 941 Wealthy St SE *Web:* www.atomicobject.com	Grand Rapids	MI	49506	616-776-6020	
Austin Test Inc Dba Bridge 360 10415 Morado Cir	Austin	TX	78759	512-837-8798	
Authentech Software Developers In 11285 Palmer Ln *Web:* authentech.com	Twinsburg	OH	44087	330-425-4538	
Authentify Inc 8745 W Higgins Rd Ste 240 *Web:* www.authentify.com	Chicago	IL	60631	773-243-0300	
Auto Clerk Inc 936 Dewing Ave Ste G *Web:* www.autoclerk.com	Lafayette	CA	94549	925-284-1005	
Autologue Computer Systems Inc 8452 Commonwealth Ave *Web:* www.autologue.com	Buena Park	CA	90621	714-522-3551	
Automated Trading Desk LLC 11 eWall St *Web:* www.atdesk.com	Mount Pleasant	SC	29464	843-789-2000	
Avant Solution, The 29610 Southfield Rd Ste 115 *Web:* avantsolution.com	Southfield	MI	48076	248-423-0052	
Avi Technologies Inc 1 Bank St Ste 401 *Web:* www.avitechnologies.net	Stamford	CT	06901	203-348-1800	

Company	City	State	ZIP	Phone	Fax
Avidian Technologies Inc 2053 152nd Ave NE *Web:* avidian.com	Redmond	WA	98052	206-686-3001	
Avilar Technologies Inc 6760 Alexander Bell Dr Ste 105 *Web:* www.avilar.com	Columbia	MD	21046	410-290-0008	
Avineon Inc 4825 Mark Ctr Dr Ste 700 *Web:* www.avineon.com	Alexandria	VA	22311	703-671-1900	671-1901
Avior Computing Corp Nashua Airport 11 Perimeter Rd *Web:* www.aviorcomputing.com	Nashua	NH	03063	603-886-8145	
Avtech Software Inc 16 Cutler St Cutler Mill *Web:* www.avtech.com	Warren	RI	02885	401-847-6700	
Avval Inc 1255 Windham Pkwy Ste 900-a *Web:* www.avval.com	Romeoville	IL	60446	630-343-6860	
Axcient Inc 1161 San Antonio Rd *TF:* 800-715-2339 ■ *Web:* www.axcient.com	Mountain View	CA	94043	800-715-2339	
Axiom Software Ltd 400 Columbus Ave *Web:* www.axiomsw.com	Valhalla	NY	10595	914-769-8800	
AXIOM Systems Inc 241 E Fourth St Ste 200 *Web:* www.axiom-systems.com	Frederick	MD	21701	301-815-5220	
Axletree Solutions Inc Two King Arthur Court Lakeside W Ste A-1 *Web:* www.axletrees.com	North Brunswick	NJ	08902	732-296-0001	
Axxiem Corp 578 Warburton Ave *Web:* www.axxiem.com	Hastings On Hudson	NY	10706	914-478-7600	
Axxis Inc 1295 Bandana Blvd Ste 120 *Web:* www.axxispetro.com	St. Paul	MN	55108	651-644-8280	
Aylus Networks Inc Six Technology Park Dr *Web:* www.aylus.com	Westford	MA	01886	978-392-4730	
Azteca Systems Inc 11075 South State St Ste 24 *Web:* www.azteca.com	Sandy	UT	84070	801-523-2751	
B Sharp Technologies Inc 23 Lesmill Rd Ste 404 *Web:* www.bsharp.com	Toronto	ON	M3B3P6	416-445-7162	
B Swing Inc 700 Washington Ave N *Web:* www.bswing.com	Minneapolis	MN	55401	612-752-1160	
B&L Associates Inc 13 Tech Cir *Web:* www.bandl.com	Natick	MA	01760	508-651-1404	
Bachmann Software & Service 270 Sparta Ave Ste 104 *Web:* www.bachmannsoftware.com	Sparta	NJ	07871	973-729-9427	
BackOffice Associates LLC 940 Route 28 *Web:* www.boaweb.com	South Harwich	MA	02661	508-430-7100	
BAHAMA Consulting Corp 4651 Nicols Rd Ste 200 *Web:* bahama-consulting.com	Eagan	MN	55122	651-994-7900	
Bahwan CyberTek Inc 209 W Central St 312 *Web:* www.bahwancybertek.com	Natick	MA	01760	508-652-0001	
Bakbone Software Inc 9540 Towne Ctr DrSte 100 *Web:* www.bakbone.com	San Diego	CA	92121	858-450-9009	
Baldwin Hackett & Meeks Inc 11602 W Ctr Rd *Web:* www.bhmi.com	Omaha	NE	68144	402-333-3300	
Bamboo Solutions Corp 11417 Sunset Hills Rd Ste 105 *Web:* www.bamboosolutions.com	Reston	VA	20190	703-964-2002	
Barcontrol Systems & Services Inc 113 Edinburgh Ct *Web:* www.barcontrol.com	Greenville	SC	29607	864-421-0050	
Bare Bones Software Inc 73 Princeton St Ste 206 *Web:* www.barebones.com	North Chelmsford	MA	01863	978-251-0500	
Basis Technology Corp One Alewife Center *Web:* www.basistech.com	Cambridge	MA	02140	617-386-2000	
BasWare Inc 60 Long Ridge Rd *Web:* www.basware.com	Stamford	CT	06902	203-487-7900	
Bay Computer Associates Inc 136 Frances Ave *Web:* www.baycomp.com	Cranston	RI	02910	401-461-1484	
Bayou Microsystems LLC 209 Abby Rd *Web:* www.bayoumicro.com	Thibodaux	LA	70301	985-414-3949	
BCNS Technologies 116 Highwood Ave *Web:* computernetworking-repair.com	Henderson	NV	89015	702-566-5321	
Bcs Engineering 25 Grosvenor St *Web:* www.bcsengineering.com	Athens	OH	45701	740-331-4481	
Beachhead Solutions Inc 1955 The Alameda *Web:* www.beachheadsolutions.com	San Jose	CA	95126	408-496-6936	
Bedrock Prime 1309 N Wilson Rd Ste A *Web:* www.bedrockprime.com	Radcliff	KY	40160	270-351-8043	
Behavior LLC 40 W 27th St Rm 1200 *Web:* www.behaviordesign.com	New York	NY	10001	212-532-4002	
Bellsoft Inc 3545 Cruise Rd Ste 102 *Web:* www.bellsoftinc.com	Lawrenceville	GA	30044	770-935-4152	
BEM Interactive Inc 416 Gallimore Dairy Rd Ste N *Web:* beminteractive.com	Greensboro	NC	27409	336-851-0040	
Bender Rbt Inc 17 Cardinale Ln *Web:* www.benderrbt.com	Queensbury	NY	12804	518-743-8755	
Benedict Group Inc 900 Small Dr *Web:* www.benedictgroup.com	Elizabeth City	NC	27909	252-330-4892	
Benefit Express Services LLC 1700 E Golf Rd Ste 1000 *Web:* www.benefitexpress.info	Schaumburg	IL	60173	847-637-1550	
Benelogic LLC 2118 Greenspring Dr *Web:* www.benelogic.com	Timonium	MD	21093	443-322-2494	
Bennet-Tec Information Systems Inc 50 Jericho Tpke *Web:* www.bennet-tec.com	Jericho	NY	11753	516-997-5596	
BeQuick Software Inc 4280 Professional Ctr Dr Ste 200 *Web:* www.bqsoft.com	Palm Beach Gardens	FL	33410	561-721-9600	
Berkeley Varitronics Systems Inc 255 Liberty St Liberty Corporate Park *Web:* www.bvsystems.com	Metuchen	NJ	08840	732-548-3737	
Berndt Group Ltd, The 3618 Falls Rd *Web:* www.berndtgroup.net	Baltimore	MD	21211	410-889-5854	
Betis Group Inc 6711 Lee Hwy *Web:* www.betis.com	Arlington	VA	22205	703-532-2008	
Bframe Data Systems Inc 3057 Peachtree Industrial Blvd Ste 200 *Web:* www.bframe.com	Duluth	GA	30097	678-387-0100	
Big Creek Software LLC 201 N Third St Ste E *Web:* www.bigcreek.com	Polk City	IA	50226	515-984-6243	
BigLever Software Inc 10500 Laurel Hill Cove *Web:* www.biglever.com	Austin	TX	78730	512-426-2227	
Bill.com Inc 1810 Embarcadero Rd *Web:* www.bill.com	Palo Alto	CA	94303	650-621-7700	
Billpro Management Systems Inc 30575 Euclid Ave *Web:* www.billpro.net	Wickliffe	OH	44092	440-516-3776	
BIPT Inc 5971 Cattleridge Blvd Ste 101 *Web:* focustechnologies.net	Sarasota	FL	34232	941-342-0077	
BIS Computer Solutions Inc 2428 Foothill Blvd *Web:* www.biscomputer.com	La Crescenta	CA	91214	818-248-5023	
Bit by Bit Computing 5233 Mccandlish Rd *Web:* bitbybitcomputing.com	Grand Blanc	MI	48439	810-694-7477	
BitWise Inc 1515 Woodfield Rd Ste 930 *Web:* www.bitwiseglobal.com	Schaumburg	IL	60173	847-969-1500	
Bitzio Inc 9625 Cozycroft Ave Ste a *Web:* bitzio.com	Chatsworth	CA	91311	213-489-1377	
Bizzuka Inc 105 Chapel Dr Ste 300 *Web:* www.bizzuka.com	Lafayette	LA	70506	337-216-4423	
Blackfin Technology Inc 1702 W Fairview Ave *Web:* blackfin.com	Boise	ID	83702	208-338-1581	
Blue Chip Computer Systems 6733 S Sepulveda Blvd Ste 150 *Web:* www.bccs.com	Los Angeles	CA	90045	310-410-0126	
Blue Frog Solutions Inc 555 S Andrews Ave Ste 202 *Web:* www.bluefrogsolutions.com	Pompano Beach	FL	33069	954-788-0700	
Blue Mountain Quality Resources Inc 1963 Cato Ave *Web:* coolblue.com	State College	PA	16801	814-234-2417	
Bluewave Computing LLC 2251 Corporate Plz Pkwy SE *Web:* www.bluewave-computing.com	Smyrna	GA	30080	770-980-9283	
Blueye Corp 1321 N Wood St *Web:* www.blueye.com	Chicago	IL	60622	773-342-1200	
Bluware Inc 16285 Park 10 Pl Ste 300 *Web:* www.bluware.com	Houston	TX	77084	713-335-1500	
BobCAD-CAM Inc 28200 US Hwy 19 N Ste E *Web:* www.bobcad.com	Clearwater	FL	33761	727-442-3554	
Bodhtree Solutions Inc 210 Hammond Ave *Web:* www.bodhtree.com	Fremont	CA	94539	408-954-8700	
Boingo Wireless Inc 10960 Wilshire Blvd Ste 800 *TF:* 800-880-4117 ■ *Web:* www.boingo.com	Los Angeles	CA	90024	310-586-5180	586-4060
Bond Consulting Services 3450 Spring St Ste 108 *Web:* www.bondconsultingservices.com	Long Beach	CA	90806	562-988-3451	
Boost Motor Group Inc 3080 Yonge St *Web:* www.boostmotorgroup.com	Toronto	ON	M4N3N1	416-487-7000	
Boston Logic Technology Partners Inc 81 Wareham St *Web:* www.bostonlogic.com	Boston	MA	02118	617-266-9166	
Boyer & Associates Inc 3525 Plymouth Blvd Ste 207 *Web:* www.boyerassoc.com	Plymouth	MN	55447	763-412-4300	
Bradford Technologies Inc 302 Piercy Rd *Web:* www.bradfordsoftware.com	San Jose	CA	95138	408-360-8520	
BrainX Inc 45 Rincon Dr Ste 103-3B *Web:* www.brainx.com	Camarillo	CA	93012	805-384-1001	
BTM Solutions Inc 572 Yorkville Rd E *Web:* www.btmsolutions.com	Columbus	MS	39702	662-328-2400	
BuildASign.com 11525B Stonehollow Dr Ste 220 *Web:* www.buildasign.com	Austin	TX	78758	512-374-9850	
Bullhorn Inc 33-41 Farnsworth St Fifth Fl *Web:* www.bullhorn.com	Boston	MA	02210	617-478-9100	
Buscomm Inc 11696 Lilburn Park Rd *Web:* www.buscomminc.com	Saint Louis	MO	63146	314-567-7755	
Byrne Software Technologies Inc 1819 Clarkson Rd Ste 200 *Web:* www.byrnesoftware.com	Chesterfield	MO	63017	636-537-2505	
Bytewyze 120 Iowa Ln *Web:* www.bytewyze.com	Cary	NC	27511	919-465-1916	
C R I 8280 Greensboro Dr Ste 400 *Web:* www.cri-solutions.com	Mc Lean	VA	22102	703-356-6956	
C-Sharp Technologies Inc 4700 Coolbrook Dr *Web:* www.c-sharp.com	Hilliard	OH	43026	614-668-7182	
C2k 10555 Jefferson Blvd *Web:* www.c2ktechnologies.com	Culver City	CA	90232	310-279-5530	
CAD Zone Inc, The 4790 SW Watson *Web:* www.cadzone.com	Beaverton	OR	97005	503-641-1342	
Cake Development Corp 1785 E Sahara Ave Ste 490-423 *Web:* www.cakedc.com	Las Vegas	NV	89104	702-425-5085	
Camcad Technologies Inc 1016 Spring Villas Pt Ste 1000 *Web:* www.camcadtech.com	Winter Springs	FL	32708	407-327-4975	
Canton Group, The 2920 Odonnell St *Web:* cantongroup.com	Baltimore	MD	21224	410-675-5708	
Capstone Technology Corp 14300 SE 1st St *Web:* www.capstonetechnology.com	Vancouver	WA	98607	360-619-5010	
Capstone Worldwide Inc 79 W Monroe St Ste 1010 *Web:* capstoneww.com	Chicago	IL	60603	312-854-7300	

Company	City	State	ZIP	Phone	Fax
CareEvolution Inc 320 Miller Ave Ste 195 *Web:* careevolution.com	Ann Arbor	MI	48104	734-678-4788	
CareWatch Inc 3483 Satellite Blvd Ste 211 S *Web:* www.carewatch.com	Duluth	GA	30096	770-409-0244	
Carillon Financials Corp 12221 Merit Dr Ste 550 *Web:* www.carillon.us	Dallas	TX	75251	972-437-2230	
Carina Technology Inc 1300 Meridian St Ste A-13 *Web:* www.carinatek.com	Huntsville	AL	35806	256-704-0422	
Carlson Software Inc 102 W Second St *Web:* www.carlsonsw.com	Maysville	KY	41056	606-564-5028	
Carnegie Learning Inc 437 Grant St *TF:* 888-851-7094 ■ *Web:* www.carnegielearning.com	Pittsburgh	PA	15219	412-690-6284	690-2444
Castellan Inc 16255 Ventura Blvd Ste 930 *Web:* www.castellan.net	Encino	CA	91436	818-789-0088	
Catalpa Systems Inc 53 W Jackson Blvd # 552 *Web:* www.catalpa-systems.com	Chicago	IL	60604	312-663-3658	
Cats Co 2100 W Big Beaver Rd *Web:* www.catscompany.com	Troy	MI	48084	248-816-2287	
Cayuse Technologies LLC 72632 Coyote Rd *Web:* www.cayusetechnologies.com	Pendleton	OR	97801	541-278-8200	
CDM Technologies Inc 2975 McMillan Ave Ste 272 *Web:* www.cdmtech.com	San Luis Obispo	CA	93401	805-541-3750	
Celt Corp 65 Boston Post Rd W *Web:* celtcorp.com	Marlborough	MA	01752	508-624-4474	
Cencotech Inc 141 Adelaide St W Ste 610 *Web:* www.cencotech.com	Toronto	ON	M5H3L5	416-861-1474	
Centriq University 8700 State Line Rd Ste 200 *Web:* www.centriq.com	Leawood	KS	66206	913-696-5300	
Cepstral LLC 1801 E Carson St Second Fl *Web:* www.cepstral.com	Pittsburgh	PA	15203	412-432-0400	
Channelnet Three Harbor Dr Ste 206 *TF:* 800-667-6858 ■ *Web:* www.channelnet.com	Sausalito	CA	94965	415-332-4704	332-1635
Chapman Location Systems 941 Clint Moore Rd *Web:* c3ls.com	Boca Raton	FL	33487	561-995-9004	
Charles River Analytics Inc 625 Mt Auburn St Ste 3 *TF:* 877-547-4600 ■ *Web:* www.cra.com	Cambridge	MA	02138	617-491-3474	868-0780
Chateaux Software Development 50 Riverside Ave Ste 3 *Web:* www.chatsoft.com	Westport	CT	06880	203-222-7118	
Cherryroad Technologies Inc 301 Gibraltar Dr Ste 2C *TF:* 877-402-7804 ■ *Web:* www.cherryroad.com	Morris Plains	NJ	07950	973-402-7802	402-7808
Cimarron Software Services Inc 1115 Gemini *Web:* www.cimarroninc.com	Houston	TX	77058	281-226-5100	226-5190
Cimetrics Inc 141 Tremont St Fl 11 *Web:* www.cimetrics.com	Boston	MA	02111	617-350-7550	
Cipherspace LLC Four Raskin Rd *Web:* www.cipherspace.com	Morristown	NJ	07960	973-630-1050	
Cistera Networks Inc 6509 Windcrest Dr Ste 160 *Web:* web.cistera.com	Plano	TX	75024	972-381-4699	
Cisys Inc 8386 Six Forks Rd *Web:* www.cisys.com	Raleigh	NC	27615	919-870-1436	
Citizant Inc 5180 Parkstone Dr Ste 100 *Web:* citizant.com	Chantilly	VA	20151	703-667-9420	
Clairvia Inc 2525 Meridian Pkwy Ste 150 *Web:* www.atstaff.com	Durham	NC	27713	919-382-8282	
Claricent Inc 22 Preserve way *TF:* 888-325-6496 ■ *Web:* www.claricent.com	Sturbridge	MA	01566	888-325-6496	
Clarity Software Solutions Inc 92 Wall St Ste 1 *Web:* www.clarityssi.com	Madison	CT	06443	203-453-3999	
ClearPoint Inc Five Marine View Plz Ste 501 *Web:* www.clearpointlearning.com	Hoboken	NJ	07030	201-683-9944	
Clients First Business Solutions LLC 670 N Beers St Bldg 4 *TF:* 866-677-6290 ■ *Web:* www.clientsfirst-us.com	Holmdel	NJ	07733	866-677-6290	
Clinicient Inc 708 SW Third Ave Ste 400 *Web:* www.clinicient.com	Portland	OR	97204	503-525-0275	
ClioSoft Inc 39500 Stevenson Pl Ste 110 *Web:* www.cliosoft.com	Fremont	CA	94539	510-790-4732	
CMA Consulting Services Inc 700 Troy Schenectady Rd *TF:* 800-276-6101 ■ *Web:* www.cma.com	Latham	NY	12110	518-783-9003	783-5093
Coastal Software & Consulting Inc 1101 Se 182nd Ave *Web:* www.coastalsoftware.com	Vancouver	WA	98683	360-891-6174	
Coaxis Inc 1515 SE Water Ave Ste 300 *Web:* viewpoint.com	Portland	OR	97214	971-255-4800	
Code Green Networks Inc 385 Moffett Park Dr Ste 105 *Web:* www.codegreennetworks.com	Sunnyvale	CA	94089	408-716-4200	
Code Red Inc 10 Milk St 10th Fl Ste 1050 *Web:* www.coderedinc.com	Boston	MA	02108	617-330-4100	
CogniTech Corp 1060 East 100 South Ste 306 *Web:* www.cognitech-ut.com	Salt Lake City	UT	84102	801-322-0101	
Cognitim Inc 455 N Whisman Rd *Web:* www.cognitim.com	Mountain View	CA	94043	650-404-8000	
Coherent Solutions Inc 1600 Utica Ave S Ste 120 *Web:* www.coherentsolutions.com	Minneapolis	MN	55416	612-279-6262	
CollabNet Inc 8000 Marina Blvd Ste 600 *TF:* 888-532-6823 ■ *Web:* www.collab.net	Brisbane	CA	94005	650-228-2500	228-2501
College Health Services LLC 144 Turnpike Rd Ste 240 *TF:* 866-636-8336 ■ *Web:* www.studenthealth101.com	Southboro	MA	01772	866-636-8336	
Collins Computing Inc 26050 Acero St *Web:* www.collinscomputing.com	Mission Viejo	CA	92691	949-457-0500	

Company	City	State	ZIP	Phone	Fax
Commercial Programming Systems Inc 4400 Coldwater Canyon Ave **Fax Area Code:* 818 ■ *TF:* 888-277-4562 ■ *Web:* www.cpsinc.com	Studio City	CA	91604	323-851-2681	301-1996*
COMPanion Corp 1831 Ft Union Blvd *Web:* www.companioncorp.com	Salt Lake City	UT	84121	801-943-7277	
Companion Professional Services LLC 1301 Gervais St Ste 1700 *TF:* 800-780-1170 ■ *Web:* www.tmfloyd.com	Columbia	SC	29201	803-765-1310	765-1431
Competitive Innovations LLC 2724 Dorr Ave Ste 100G *Web:* www.cillc.com	Fairfax	VA	22031	703-698-5000	
Complete Innovations Inc 475 Cochrane Dr Ste 8 *Web:* www.fleetcomplete.com	Markham	ON	L3R9R5	905-944-0863	
Complete Systems Support Two Rosemar Cir *Web:* www.cssiwv.com	Parkersburg	WV	26104	304-428-2143	
Compli 610 SW Broadway Ste 600 *Web:* www.compli.com	Portland	OR	97205	503-294-2020	
Component Control Inc 1731 Kettner Blvd *Web:* www.componentcontrol.com	San Diego	CA	92101	619-696-5400	
Compu-data International LLC 431 Nursery Rd Ste A300 *Web:* www.cdlac.com	Spring	TX	77380	281-292-1333	
CompuPros Ltd Two Bent Tree Twr 16479 Dallas Pkwy Ste 800 *Web:* www.compupros.com	Addison	TX	75001	972-250-4504	
Compusearch Software Systems Inc 21251 Ridgetop Cir *TF:* 855-817-2720 ■ *Web:* www.compusearch.com	Dulles	VA	20166	703-481-3699	481-3442
Computech Corp 100 W Kirby St Ste 101 *Web:* www.computechcorp.com	Detroit	MI	48202	248-594-6500	
Computek Inc 355 Crawford St *Web:* www.e-computek.com	Portsmouth	VA	23704	757-399-0320	
Computer Aid Inc (CAI) 1390 Ridgeview Dr *TF:* 877-432-7228 ■ *Web:* www.compaid.com	Allentown	PA	18104	610-530-5000	530-5298
Computer Analyst Service & Support 28116 Orchard Lk Rd *Web:* www.cass-tech.com	Farmington Hills	MI	48334	248-538-7374	
Computer Arts Inc 320 SW Fifth Ave *Web:* www.gocai.com	Meridian	ID	83642	208-385-9335	
Computer Express Inc 301 N Ave *Web:* www.computerexpress.com	Wakefield	MA	01880	781-246-4477	
Computer Frontiers Inc 5970 Frederick Crossing Ln Ste 101 *Web:* www.computer-frontiers.com	Frederick	MD	21704	301-601-0624	
Computer Guidance Corp 15035 N 75th St *TF:* 888-361-4551 ■ *Web:* www.computerguidance.com	Scottsdale	AZ	85260	480-444-7000	444-7001
Computer Office Solutions 7266 Sw 48th St *Web:* www.snappydsl.com	Miami	FL	33155	305-663-8620	
Computer Parts Warehouse 4681 Calle Bolero *Web:* www.thecpw.com	Camarillo	CA	93012	805-987-5882	
Computer Team Inc 1049 State St *Web:* www.computerteam.com	Bettendorf	IA	52722	563-355-0426	
ComputerLogic Inc 4951 Forsyth Rd *Web:* www.computerlogic.com	Macon	GA	31210	478-474-5593	
ComputerSmith Inc 457 Lazelle Rd *Web:* computersmith.com	Westerville	OH	43081	614-436-0131	
Computerworks of Chicago Inc 5153 N Clark St *Web:* www.booklog.com	Chicago	IL	60640	773-275-4437	
Computing Integrity Inc 60 Belvedere Ave *Web:* cintegrity.com	Richmond	CA	94801	510-233-5400	
Computrition Inc 19808 Nordhoff Pl **Fax Area Code:* 818 ■ *TF:* 800-222-4488 ■ *Web:* www.computrition.com	Chatsworth	CA	91311	800-222-4488	701-1702*
COMSO Inc 6303 Ivy Ln Ste 300 *Web:* www.comso.com	Greenbelt	MD	20770	301-345-0046	
Comspark International Inc 3265 W Sarazens Cir Ste 201 *Web:* www.comsparkint.com	Memphis	TN	38125	901-758-0261	
Concept Dynamics Ltd 5435 Bull Vly Rd Ste 306 *Web:* cdlweb.net	Mchenry	IL	60050	815-344-1392	
Concurrent EDA LLC 5001 Baum Blvd Ste 640 *Web:* www.concurrenteda.com	Pittsburgh	PA	15213	412-687-8800	
ConEst Software Systems Inc 592 Harvey Rd *Web:* www.conest.com	Manchester	NH	03103	603-437-9353	
CoNetrix LLC 5214 68th St Ste 200 *Web:* www.conetrix.com	Lubbock	TX	79424	806-687-8600	
CONIX Systems Inc 7252 Main St *TF:* 800-332-1899 ■ *Web:* conix.com	Manchester Center	VT	05255	800-332-1899	
Construx Software 11820 Northup Way Ste E-200 *TF:* 866-296-6300 ■ *Web:* www.construx.com	Bellevue	WA	98005	425-636-0100	636-0159
Consult Usa Inc 634 Alpha Dr *Web:* consultusa.com	Pittsburgh	PA	15238	412-963-8621	
Contemporary Software Concepts Inc 455 Pennsylvania Ave Ste 220 *Web:* www.consoftware.com	Fort Washington	PA	19034	610-687-6000	
Continuum Performance Systems Inc 634 Boston Post Rd *Web:* www.continuumperformance.com	Madison	CT	06443	203-245-5000	
Control Systems International Inc 8040 Nieman Rd	Lenexa	KS	66214	913-599-5010	599-5013
Coretechs 50 Woodside Plz Ste 604 *Web:* www.moldex3d.com	Redwood City	CA	94061	650-363-7960	
Corning Data Services Inc 139 Wardell St PO Box 1187 *Web:* corningdata.com	Corning	NY	14830	607-936-4241	
Corporate Systems Engineering LLC 1215 Brookville Way *Web:* www.corporatesystems.com	Indianapolis	IN	46239	317-375-3600	
Corptax LLC 1751 Lk Cook Rd Ste 100 **Fax Area Code:* 847 ■ *TF:* 800-966-1639 ■ *Web:* www.corptax.com	Deerfield	IL	60015	800-966-1639	236-8011*

Phone Fax

Coyote Software Corp
3425 Harvester Rd Ste 216 .... Burlington ON L7N3N1 905-639-8533
Web: coyotecorp.com

Credant Technologies Inc
15303 Dallas Pkwy Ste 1420 .... Addison TX 75001 972-458-5400 458-5454
TF: 800-929-8331 ■ *Web:* www.credant.com

Crescendo Systems Corp 1600 Montgolfier .... Laval QC H7T0A2 450-973-8029
Web: www.crescendo.com

CRM Innovation 8527 Bluejacket St .... Lenexa KS 66214 913-492-2764
Web: www.crminnovation.com

Croop-LaFrance Inc 7647 Main St Fishers .... Victor NY 14564 585-869-6100
Web: www.croop-lafrance.com

Crowdstar Inc 330 Primrose Rd Ste 306 .... Burlingame CA 94010 650-347-4166
Web: crowdstar.com

CRT Systems Inc 742 Anderson Rd N .... Rock Hill SC 29730 803-327-9030
Web: www.crtsys.com

CS Solutions Inc 3440 Federal Dr Ste 100 .... Eagan MN 55122 651-603-8288
Web: www.cssolutionsinc.com

CSG Professional Services Inc
734 NW 14th Ave .... Portland OR 97209 503-292-0859
Web: csgpro.com

CTE Solutions Inc 11 Holland Ave Ste 100 .... Ottawa ON K1Y4S1 613-798-5353
Web: www.ctesolutions.com

CTH Technologies Inc
18w140 Butterfield Rd .... Oakbrook Terrace IL 60181 630-613-7070
Web: www.cthtech.com

CTL Inc 375 Bridgeport Ave .... Shelton CT 06484 203-925-4266
Web: www.ctlinc.com

Culinary Software Services Inc
1900 Folsom St Ste 210 .... Boulder CO 80302 303-447-3334
Web: www.culinarysoftware.com

Curl Inc One Cambridge Ctr 10th Fl .... Cambridge MA 02142 617-761-1200
Web: curl.com

Customer Service Delivery Platform Corp
15615 Alton Pkwy Ste 310 .... Irvine CA 92618 888-741-2737
TF: 888-741-2737 ■ *Web:* www.csdpcorp.com

Cutting Edge 1825 Gillespie Way Ste 100 .... El Cajon CA 92020 619-258-7800
Web: www.cuttedge.com

Cyber-Ark Software Inc 60 Wells Ave Ste 20A .... Newton MA 02459 617-965-1544 965-1644
TF: 888-808-9005 ■ *Web:* cyberark.com

Cyberchrome Inc 3642 Main St .... Stone Ridge NY 12484 845-687-2671
Web: cyberchromeusa.com

CyberMark International Inc
2222 W Parkside Ln Ste 116 .... Phoenix AZ 85027 623-889-3380
Web: www.cybermark.com

Cybersoft North America Inc
1500 S Dairy Ashford St Ste 190 .... Houston TX 77077 281-752-0600
Web: www.csnainc.com

CyberThink Inc 1125 US Hwy 22 Ste 1 .... Bridgewater NJ 08807 908-429-8008 429-8004
Web: www.cyberthink.com

Cyberwolf Inc 1596 Pacheco St Ste 203 .... Santa Fe NM 87505 505-983-6463
Web: www.cyberwolf.com

Cymbel Corp 154 Wells Ave .... Newton MA 02459 617-581-6633
Web: www.cymbel.com

D-Ta Systems Inc 2500 Lancaster Rd .... Ottawa ON K1B4S5 613-745-8713
Web: www.d-ta.com

Data Advantage Group Inc
604 Mission St .... San Francisco CA 94105 415-947-0400
Web: www.dag.com

Data Financial Inc 1100 Glen Oaks Ln .... Mequon WI 53092 262-243-5511
Web: www.datafinancial.com

Data Inc 72 Summit Ave .... Montvale NJ 07645 201-802-9800
Web: www.datainc.biz

Data Integrity Inc 228 Highland Ave .... West Newton MA 02465 617-964-1977 224-2324
Web: www.dii2000.com

Data Management Marketing 3225 Jordan Blvd .... Malabar FL 32950 321-725-8081
Web: www.dmm-marketing.com

Data Paradigm Inc 2323 Bryan St Ste 2600 .... Dallas TX 75201 214-468-0200 722-1860
Web: dataparadigm.com

Data Select Systems Inc
2829 Townsgate Rd Ste 300 .... Westlake Village CA 91361 805-446-2090
Web: www.clcsiii.com

Data Ventures 1475 Central Ave Ste 230 .... Los Alamos NM 87544 505-662-6655
Web: www.dataventures.com

Data3 Corp 2448 E 81st St Ste 700 .... Tulsa OK 74137 918-237-4400
Web: www.datathree.com

Databased Solutions Inc 1200 Route 22 .... Bridgewater NJ 08807 908-314-0000
Web: www.dbsiservices.com

DataCeutics Inc 1610 Medical Dr Ste 300 .... Pottstown PA 19464 610-970-2333
Web: www.dataceutics.com

Dataclarity Corp
7200 Falls Of Neuse Rd Ste 202 .... Raleigh NC 27615 919-256-6700
Web: www.dataclaritycorp.com

Datacor Inc 25 Hanover Rd Ste 300B .... Florham Park NJ 07932 973-822-1551
Web: www.datacorinc.com

Datafirst Corp 5124 Departure Dr .... Raleigh NC 27616 919-876-6650
Web: www.datafirst.com

Dataflux Corp 940 NW Cary Pkwy Ste 201 .... Cary NC 27513 919-447-3000 677-4444
TF: 800-727-0025

Datalink Software Consultants Inc
4745 N Seventh St Ste 200 .... Phoenix AZ 85014 602-279-7788
Web: www.datalinksc.com

Datalogic Software Inc
1501 S 77 Sunshinestrip .... Harlingen TX 78550 956-412-1424
Web: www.vestanotes.com

DataMAX Software Group Inc, The
1101 Investment Blvd Ste 250 .... El Dorado Hills CA 95762 916-939-4065
Web: www.datamaxsg.com

Dataprise Inc
12250 Rockville Pike Second Fl .... Rockville MD 20852 301-945-0700
Web: www.dataprise.com

DataWorks Plus LLC 728 N Pleasantburg Dr .... Greenville SC 29607 864-672-2780
Web: www.dataworksplus.com

Phone Fax

Davis Powers Inc 640 N La Salle Dr Ste 285 .... Chicago IL 60654 312-654-9239
Web: davispowers.com

DAX Technologies Corp
100 Matawan Rd Matawan Ste 300 .... Matawan NJ 07747 732-203-1784
Web: www.daxtechnologies.com

DAZ Systems Inc 880 Apollo St Ste 201 .... El Segundo CA 90245 310-640-1300
Web: www.dazsi.com

Dealogic LLC 120 Broadway Eighth Fl .... New York NY 10271 212-577-4400
Web: www.dealogic.com

Debt Buyers Inc 3080 S Durango Dr Ste 208 .... Las Vegas NV 89117 702-946-8440
Web: www.srcnv.com

deCarta Inc Four N Second St Ste 950 .... San Jose CA 95113 408-294-8400
Web: www.decarta.com

DecisionPoint Systems Inc
19655 Descartes .... Foothill Ranch CA 92610 949-465-0065 215-9642
OTC: DPSI ■ *TF:* 800-336-3670 ■ *Web:* www.decisionpt.com

Decker Wright Corp
628 Shrewsbury Ave Ste E .... Tinton Falls NJ 07701 732-747-9373
Web: www.deckerwright.com

Decurtis Corp 2314 Longmoore Ct .... Orlando FL 32835 407-522-8722
Web: www.decurtis.com

Defined Logic LLC 116 Chestnut St .... Red Bank NJ 07701 732-222-4310
Web: definedlogic.com

Dekker Ltd 3633 Inland Empire Blvd .... Ontario CA 91764 909-384-9000 889-9163

Delta Data Software Inc
700 Brookstone Centre Pkwy .... Columbus GA 31904 706-324-0855
Web: www.deltadatasoft.com

DeltaSoft Inc 624 Courtyard Dr .... Hillsborough NJ 08844 908-595-9777
Web: www.deltasoftinc.com

Demiurge Studios Inc
130 Prospect St First Fl .... Cambridge MA 02139 617-354-7772
Web: demiurgestudios.com

DeNA Global Inc 1 Waters Park Dr Ste 165 .... San Mateo CA 94403 650-638-1026
Web: www.denaglobal.com

Denim Group Ltd
1354 N Loop 1604 E Ste 110 .... San Antonio TX 78232 844-572-4400
TF: 844-572-4400 ■ *Web:* www.denimgroup.com

Denodo Technologies 530 Lytton Ave Ste 301 .... Palo Alto CA 94301 650-566-8833
Web: www.denodo.com

Desco Dental Systems LLC
5005 W Loomis Rd Ste 100 .... Milwaukee WI 53220 414-281-9192
Web: descodental.com

Design Hub Inc 600 W Michigan Ave Ste A .... Saline MI 48176 734-944-8705
Web: www.design-hub.com

Devicenet USA Inc 4000 Moorpark Ave Ste 116 .... San Jose CA 95117 408-557-0413
Web: www.devicenet-usa.com

DeviceVM 1054 S De Anza Blvd Ste 200 .... San Jose CA 95129 408-861-1088
Web: www.devicevm.com

Dh Web Inc 11377 Robinwood Dr Ste D .... Hagerstown MD 21742 301-733-7672
Web: www.dhwebsites.com

Diagnos Inc Ste 340 7005 Taschereau Blvd .... Brossard QC J4Z1A7 450-678-8882
Web: www.diagnos.ca

Digilabs Inc 1032 Elwell Ct Ste 245 .... Palo Alto CA 94303 650-390-9749
Web: www.digi-labs.net

Digital ChoreoGraphics PO Box 8268 .... Newport Beach CA 92658 949-548-1969
Web: www.dcgfx.com

Digital Dogs Inc 16416 N 92nd St Ste 120 .... Scottsdale AZ 85260 480-451-3647
Web: www.digitaldogs.com

Digital I-Ollc 1424 30th St .... San Diego CA 92154 619-423-4433
Web: www.digitalio.com

Digital Intelligence Systems Corp
4151 Lafayette Ctr Dr .... Chantilly VA 20151 703-802-0500
Web: www.disys.com

Digital Motorworks Inc
8601 RR 2222 Ste 400 Bldg I .... Austin TX 78730 512-349-9360
Web: www.digitalmotorworks.com

Digital Pictures 212 N Second St .... Minneapolis MN 55401 612-371-4515
Web: www.digitalpictures.com

Dino Software Corp 1912 Earldale Ct 200 .... Alexandria VA 22306 703-768-2610
Web: www.dino-software.com

Discovery Information Technologies Inc
904 N Memorial Fwy .... Nederland TX 77627 409-727-7080
Web: www.discoveryit.com

Distant Horizon 16612 W 159th St Ste 201 .... Lockport IL 60441 815-836-3410
Web: www.distanthorizon.com

Distek Integration Inc
1110 N County Rd 2350 .... Carthage IL 62321 217-357-3100
Web: www.distek.com

DMI Technology Group 406 Kays Dr .... Normal IL 61761 309-828-4439
Web: www.deskmic.com

Document Storage Systems Inc
12575 US Hwy 1 Ste 200 .... Juno Beach FL 33408 561-284-7000
Web: www.docstorsys.com

Donatech Corp 2094 185th St Ste 110 .... Fairfield IA 52556 641-472-7474
Web: www.donatech.com

Dorian Business Systems Inc 3001 Century Dr .... Rowlett TX 75088 214-556-1912
Web: dorianbusinesssystems.com

Double Infinity Inc
14414 Detroit Ave Ste 102 .... Lakewood OH 44107 216-228-7500
Web: www.doubleinfinity.com

DoubleCheck LLC
101 Gilbraltar Dr Ste 1E .... Morris Plains NJ 07950 973-984-2229
Web: www.doublechecksoftware.com

DrivenBI LLC 221 E Walnut St Ste 229 .... Pasadena CA 91101 626-795-2088
Web: www.drivenbi.com

Droege Computing Services Inc
20 W Colony Pl Ste 120 .... Durham NC 27705 919-403-9459
Web: droegecomputing.com

Droste Consultants Inc
140 Willow St Ste 2 .... North Andover MA 01845 978-686-5775
Web: www.droste1.com

Phone Fax

DSD Business Systems Inc
5120 Shoreham Pl Ste 280 San Diego CA 92122 858-550-5900
Web: www.dsdinc.com

DSG Systems Inc 56 Inverness Dr E Ste 260 Englewood CO 80112 303-790-0453 790-0866
Web: www.dsgsys.com

Duley Hopkins & Assoc Inc
1200 Mtn Creek Rd Chattanooga TN 37405 423-877-1220
Web: dha-us.com

Dunn Solutions Group Inc
5550 W Touhy Ave Ste 400 Skokie IL 60077 847-673-0900
Web: www.dunnsolutions.com

Duo Consulting Inc 641 W Lk Ste 301 Chicago IL 60661 312-529-3000
Web: www.duoconsulting.com

Dynaxys LLC 11911 Tech Rd Silver Spring MD 20904 301-622-0900
Web: www.dynaxys.com

E p Radiological Services Inc
8040 Remmet Ave Ste 1 Canoga Park CA 91304 818-313-9729
Web: www.epradinc.com

e3 Solutions Inc 50 Richmond St E Ste 200 Toronto ON M5C1N7 416-640-7033
Web: e3solutionsinc.com

EADOC 180 Grand Ave Ste 995 Oakland CA 94612 510-903-9658
Web: www.eadocsoftware.com

Eagle Applied Sciences LLC
1826 N Loop 1604 W Ste 350 San Antonio TX 78248 210-477-9242 581-8609
Web: www.eagle-app-sci.com

Eagle Technology Inc 11019 N Towne Sq Rd Mequon WI 53092 262-241-3845
Web: www.eaglecmms.com

Ecalix Inc 44093 S Grimmer Blvd Fremont CA 94538 510-396-0821
Web: www.ecalix.com

ECCO Select Corp 1301 Oak St Ste 400 Kansas City MO 64106 816-960-3800
Web: www.eccoselect.com

Ecd Systems Inc
3821 Falmouth Rd Ste 8a Marstons Mills MA 02648 508-420-6950
Web: www.ecdsystems.com

Echo Assoc Inc 933 Ridge Dr Mclean VA 22101 703-448-0633
Web: callecho.com

Echo Group Inc, The 15 Washington St Conway NH 03818 603-447-8600
Web: www.echoman.com

Edge Systems LLC 3S721 W Ave Ste 200 Warrenville IL 60555 630-810-9669 810-9228
TF Tech Supp: 800-352-3343 ■ *Web:* www.edge.com

Edgenet Inc 3445 Peachtree Rd NE Atlanta GA 30326 615-371-3848 371-3023
TF: 866-865-6602 ■ *Web:* www.edgenet.com

EdgeWave Inc 15333 Ave of Science San Diego CA 92128 858-676-2277
Web: www.stbernard.com

EdTek Services Inc 30 Wascana Ave Toronto ON M5A1V5 647-435-7133 827-1184*
**Fax Area Code:* 888 ■ *Web:* www.edtekservices.com

Education Management Systems Inc
4110 Shipyard Blvd Wilmington NC 28403 910-799-0121
Web: www.mealsplus.com

Effone Software Inc 1294 Kifer Rd Ste 709 Sunnyvale CA 94086 408-830-1010
Web: www.effone.com

eHire LLC
3500 Lenox Rd NE One Alliance Ctr Ste 630 Atlanta GA 30326 404-477-2680
Web: www.ehire.com

ElanTech Inc 7852 Walker Dr Ste 425 Greenbelt MD 20770 301-486-0600
Web: www.ameritasacacia.com

Electrocon International Inc
405 Little Lk Dr Ann Arbor MI 48103 734-761-8612
Web: www.electrocon.com

Elkco Corp 50 Dangelo Dr Ste 5 Marlborough MA 01752 508-842-2111
Web: www.elkco.com

Ellie Mae Inc 4155 Hopyard Rd Ste 200 Pleasanton CA 94588 925-227-7000
Web: elliemae.com

Ellkay 259 Cedar Ln Teaneck NJ 07666 201-791-0606
Web: www.ellkay.com

Emaint Enterprises LLC 438 N Elmwood Rd Marlton NJ 08053 856-810-2700
Web: emaint.com

Embedded Data Systems LLC
2019 Fortune Dr Lawrenceburg KY 40342 502-859-5490
Web: www.embeddeddatasystems.com

Emberex Inc 220 E 11th Ave Ste 6 Eugene OR 97401 541-687-5778
Web: www.emberex.com

Emergency Technologies Inc
8521 Six Forks Rd Ste 110 Raleigh NC 27615 919-676-6200
Web: www.emergencytechnologies.com

Emergin Inc 6400 Congress Ave Ste 1050 Boca Raton FL 33487 561-361-6990
Web: www.emergin.com

Emfluence 106 W 11Th St Ste 2220 Kansas City MO 64105 816-472-5643
Web: www.emfluence.com

EmLogis Inc 9800 Richmond Ave Ste 235 Houston TX 77042 713-785-0960
Web: www.emlogis.com

Empower Financials Inc
305 E Eisenhower Ste 318 Ann Arbor MI 48108 734-747-9393
Web: empowerfin.com

Enabling Technologies Corp
12226 Long Green Pk Glen Arm MD 21057 443-625-5100
Web: www.enablingtechcorp.com

Endeavor Commerce Inc 13140 Coit Ste 450 Dallas TX 75240 214-736-7178
Web: endeavorcpq.com

Energent Inc Ste 208 - 115 King St South Waterloo ON N2J5A3 519-725-0906
Web: www.energent.com

Enfold Systems Inc 4617 Montrose Blvd Houston TX 77006 713-942-2377
Web: www.enfoldsystems.com

EngagePoint Inc 3901 Calverton Blvd Ste 110 Calverton MD 33309 301-388-7900
Web: www.consumerhealthtech.com

enherent Corp Ste 116 100 Wood Ave South Iselin NJ 08830 732-321-1004
Web: www.enherent.com

Enilon Group 945 Foch St Fort Worth TX 76107 817-632-3200
Web: www.enilon.com

Enlightened Inc 1100 15th St N W Ste 300 Washington DC 20005 202-728-7190
Web: www.nlightened.com

Enounce Inc 2666 E Bayshore Rd Palo Alto CA 94303 650-494-6200
Web: www.enounce.com

Phone Fax

Ensyte Energy Software International
770 S Post Oak Ln Ste 330 Houston TX 77056 713-622-2875
Web: www.ensyte.com

Enteo Software Inc 1111 N Plz Dr Ste 102 Schaumburg IL 60173 847-706-9400
Web: www.enteo.com

Entero Corp 1040 Seventh Ave SW Ste 500 Calgary AB T2P3G9 403-261-1820
Web: www.entero.com

Enterprise Computing Solutions Inc
26024 Acero Mission Viejo CA 92691 949-609-1980
Web: www.thinkecs.com

Enterprise Information Services Inc
1945 Old Gallows Rd Ste 500 Vienna VA 22182 703-749-0007
Web: www.goeis.com

Enthought Inc 515 Congress Ave Ste 2100 Austin TX 78701 512-536-1057
Web: www.enthought.com

Envision Technology Advisors LLC
999 Main St Pawtucket RI 02860 401-272-6688
Web: www.envisionsuccess.net

Epac Software Technologies Inc
42 Ladd St East Greenwich RI 02818 401-884-5512
Web: www.epacst.com

Ephibian Inc 3180 N Swan Rd Tucson AZ 85712 520-917-4747
Web: www.ephibian.com

Ephox Corp 135 University Ave Fl 2 Palo Alto CA 94301 650-292-9659
Web: ephox.com

Epitec Inc 24800 Denso Dr Ste 150 Southfield MI 48033 248-353-6800
Web: www.epitecinc.com

Eportation LLC 401 S Second St Ste 305 Philadelphia PA 19147 215-627-2651
Web: www.eportation.com

Eric A. King 301 Grant St Ste 4300 Pittsburgh PA 15219 281-667-4200
Web: www.the-modeling-agency.com

eRIDE Inc
1 Letterman Drive Bldg C Ste 310 San Francisco CA 94129 415-848-7800
Web: www.eride.com

eROI Inc 505 NW Couch Ste 300 Portland OR 97209 503-221-6200
Web: www.eroi.com

Esprida Corp 5180 Orbitor Dr Mississauga ON L4W5L9 905-629-0455
Web: www.esprida.com

Et International 10 Fountainview Dr Newark DE 19713 302-738-1438 738-1436
Web: etinternational.com

ETC ComputerLand 3206 Kochs Ln Quincy IL 62305 217-228-6180
Web: www.etccomputerland.com

ethosIQ LLC 17121 W Rd 201 Houston TX 77095 281-616-5711
Web: www.ethosiq.com

Eti-Net Inc 180 Rene Levesque E Ste 320 Montreal QC H2X1N6 514-395-1200
Web: www.etinet.com

Eureka Software Solutions Inc
3305 Northland Dr Ste 305 Austin TX 78731 512-459-9292
Web: www.eurekasoft.com

Eureka Technocrats Inc 1985 W Big Beaver Rd Troy MI 48084 248-816-1617
Web: www.eurekatek.com

Evans Caseload Inc 1915 Danforth Ave Toronto ON M4C1J5 416-762-0236
Web: caseload.com

Everest Consulting Group Inc
3840 Pk Ave Ste 203 Edison NJ 08820 732-548-2700 548-6200
Web: www.everestconsulting.net

Execusys Inc 6767 N Wickham Rd Melbourne FL 32940 321-253-0077
Web: execusys.com

Experts Exchange LLC PO Box 1062 San Luis Obispo CA 93406 805-787-0603
Web: www.experts-exchange.com

Experts Inc, The
2400 E Commercial Blvd Ste 614 Fort Lauderdale FL 33308 954-493-8040
TF: 888-748-3526 ■ *Web:* www.expertsit.com

Extensis 1800 SW First Ave Ste 500 Portland OR 97201 503-274-2020 274-0530
TF: 800-796-9798 ■ *Web:* www.extensis.com

Externetworks 10 Corporate Pl S Piscataway NJ 08854 732-465-0001
Web: www.externetworks.com

Eyefinity Inc
10875 International Dr Ste 200 Rancho Cordova CA 95670 877-448-0707
TF: 877-448-0707 ■ *Web:* www.eyefinity.com

Fabtrol Systems Inc 1025 Willamette St Ste 300 Eugene OR 97401 541-345-1494
Web: www.fabtrol.com

Fairway Technologies Inc
7825 Fay Ave Ste 100 La Jolla CA 92037 858-454-4471
Web: fairwaytech.com

Femme Comp Inc 14170 Newbrook Dr Ste 100 Chantilly VA 20151 703-961-1818
Web: www.femmecomp.com

Fgm Inc 12021 Sunset Hills Rd Ste 400 Reston VA 20190 703-885-1000 885-0130
Web: www.fgm.com

FieldView Solutions Inc 275 Raritan Ctr Pkwy Edison NJ 08837 732-395-6920
Web: www.fieldviewsolutions.com

FieldWorker Products Ltd
1092 Islington Ave Ste 202 Toronto ON M8Z4R9 416-483-3485
Web: www.fieldworker.com

Filemobile Inc 18 Mowat Ave Second Fl Toronto ON M6K3E8 416-642-9047
Web: www.filemobile.com

FileTrail Inc 111 N Market St Ste 715 San Jose CA 95113 408-289-1300
Web: www.filetrail.com

Fillmore Group Inc, The
8501 La Salle Rd Ste 318 Towson MD 21286 410-465-6335
Web: www.thefillmoregroup.com

Financial Navigator Inc
883 N Shoreline Blvd Ste D-100 Mountain View CA 94043 650-962-0300
Web: www.finnav.com

Financial Software Systems Inc
100 Tournament Dr Ste 300 Horsham PA 19044 215-784-1100
Web: www.finsoftware.com

Fine Technology Solutions
7936 Grado El Tupelo Carlsbad CA 92009 760-274-2370
Web: www.fineonline.com

Fire Engine Red 700 Locust St Apt A4 Philadelphia PA 19106 215-829-1850
Web: fire-engine-red.com

Phone | Fax

First Edge Solutions Inc 1301 W Canal St. Milwaukee WI 53233 414-289-8300
Web: www.firstedgesolutions.com

First Insight Corp
22845 NW Bennett St Bldg B Ste 200. Hillsboro OR 97124 503-707-8600
Web: www.first-insight.com

Five K Computers & Internet Services
104 S Sixth Ave. Yakima WA 98902 509-575-3600
Web: www.fivek.com

Fleet Advantage LLC
401 E Las Olas Blvd 17th Fl. Fort Lauderdale FL 33301 954-615-4400
Web: www.fleetadvantage.net

Fm3 Systems Inc 16602 N 23rd Ave Ste 110. Phoenix AZ 85023 602-288-1416
Web: fm3systems.com

Focus 360 Inc 27721 La Paz Rd. Laguna Niguel CA 92677 949-234-0008
Web: www.focus360.com

Folderwave 238 Littleton Rd Ste 204. Westford MA 01886 978-392-2055
Web: www.folderwave.com

Forcex Inc 1001 Progress Dr. Clarksville TN 37040 931-368-0111
Web: www.forcexinc.com

Foremost Media 1337 Excalibur Dr. Janesville WI 53546 608-758-4841
Web: foremostmedia.com

Formotus Inc 9725 SE 36th St Ste 400. Mercer Island WA 98040 206-973-5060
Web: www.formotus.com

Fortifire Inc 46560 Fremont Blvd Ste 119. Fremont CA 94538 510-651-7770
Web: www.fortifire.com

Freedom Scientific Inc
11800 31st Court N. St. Petersburg FL 33716 727-803-8000
Web: www.freedomscientific.com

Friedman Corp One Pkwy N Ste 400S. Deerfield IL 60015 847-948-7180
Web: www.csisoftware.com

Fulcrum Technologies Inc 712 Aurora Ave N. Seattle WA 98109 206-336-5656
Web: www.fulcrum.net

Full Spectrum Software
225 Tpke Rd Ste 504. Southborough MA 01772 508-620-6400
Web: www.fullspectrumsoftware.com

FusionOne Inc 55 Almaden Blvd Fifth Fl. San Jose CA 95113 408-282-1200
Web: www.fusionone.com

FusionStorm Two Bryant St Ste 150. San Francisco CA 94105 415-623-2626 623-2630
TF: 800-228-8324 ■ *Web:* www.fusionstorm.com

Futrend Technology Inc
8605 Westwood Ctr Dr Ste 502. Vienna VA 22182 703-556-0016
Web: www.futrend.com

Future Computing Solutions Inc
23800 Via Del Rio. Yorba Linda CA 92887 714-692-9120
Web: www.fcsinet.com

Future Tech Enterprise Inc 101-8 Colin Dr. Holbrook NY 11741 631-472-5500 472-6599
Web: www.ftei.com

Future Visions Inc 3424 Stony Spring Cir. Louisville KY 40220 502-499-6337
Web: futurevisions.com

G2 Software Systems Inc
4250 Pacific Hwy #125. San Diego CA 92110 619-222-8025
Web: g2ss.com

Gallagher Systems Group Inc 2502 N Clark St. Chicago IL 60614 773-348-5400

Gates Business Solutions LLC
2418 Crossroads Dr Ste 3600. Madison WI 53718 608-661-0810
Web: www.gatesbusinesssolutions.com

Gavel & Gown Software Inc 365 Bay St Ste 700. Toronto ON M5H2V1 416-977-6633
Web: amicusattorney.com

Gcom Software Inc 24 Madison Ave Ext. Albany NY 12203 518-869-1671
Web: www.gcomsoft.com

GDI Infotech Inc 3775 Varsity Dr. Ann Arbor MI 48108 734-477-6900 477-7100
TF: 800-608-7682 ■ *Web:* www.gdii.com

GeBBS Healthcare Solutions Inc
560 Sylvan Ave Second Fl Ste 2053. Englewood Cliffs NJ 07632 201-227-0088
Web: www.gebbs.com

Gene Codes Corp 775 Technology Dr. Ann Arbor MI 48108 734-769-7249
Web: www.genecodes.com

Genesis Concepts & Consultants LLC
1777 Ne Loop 410 Ste 1009. San Antonio TX 78217 210-451-5100
Web: www.genconcepts.com

Genesisfour Corp 7747 Ten Acre Rd. Andrews SC 29510 843-461-4117 443-1303*
**Fax Area Code:* 978 ■ *TF:* 800-937-4364 ■ *Web:* www.service2k.com

Genova Technologies Inc
4250 River Ctr Court NE Ste A. Cedar Rapids IA 52402 319-378-8455
Web: www.genovatech.com

Gevity Consulting Inc 375 Water St Ste 350. Vancouver BC V6B5C6 604-608-1779
Web: www.global-village.net

GIDEON Informatics Inc
8721 Santa Monica Blvd Ste 234. Los Angeles CA 90069 323-934-0000
Web: www.gideononline.com

Gilltek Systems Intl Inc 2409 S Rural Rd Ste C. Tempe AZ 85282 480-831-5565
Web: www.gilltek.com

Gisbiz Inc 25 Century Blvd Ste 602. Nashville TN 37214 615-465-8287
Web: www.gisbiz.com

Givenhansco Inc
2400 Corporate Exchange Dr Ste 103. Columbus OH 43231 614-310-0060
Web: www.givenhansco.com

GL Communications Inc
818 W Diamond Ave Third Fl. Gaithersburg MD 20878 301-670-4784
Web: www.gl.com

Glaser Technology Inc 123 W Madison St 1100. Chicago IL 60602 312-578-0377
Web: www.glasertechnology.com

Glenbriar Technologies Inc 736-1100 8 Ave SW. Calgary AB T2P3T9 403-233-7300
Web: www.glenbriar.com

Global Micro Solutions Inc
21250 Hawthorne Blvd Ste 540. Torrance CA 90503 310-218-5678
Web: www.geosmart.com

Global Nest LLC 281 State Rt 79 N Ste 208. Morganville NJ 07751 732-333-5848
Web: www.globalnest.com

Global Reach Internet Productions LLC
2321 N Loop Dr Ste 101. Ames IA 50010 515-996-0996
Web: www.globalreach.com

Global Solutions Network Inc
121 Congressional Ln Ste 302. Rockville MD 20852 301-881-7012 881-7014*
**Fax Area Code:* 703 ■ *Web:* www.gsnhome.com

Gloto Corp 8171 Maple Lawn Blvd Ste 250. Fulton MD 20759 301-317-9800
Web: gloto.com

Glu Mobile Inc 500 Howard St Ste 300. San Francisco CA 94105 415-800-6100
Web: www.glu.com

Gnuco LLC 20 N Wacker Dr Ste 1870. Chicago IL 60606 312-669-9600
TF: 800-800-8805 ■ *Web:* www.emergenow.com

Go 2 Group 138 N Hickory Ave. Bel Air MD 21014 410-879-8102
Web: www.go2group.com

Good Design LLC 450 Industrial Park Rd. Deep River CT 06417 860-526-1600
Web: gooddesignusa.com

Gorton Studios 4640 Nicols Rd Ste 205. Saint Paul MN 55122 651-365-7891
Web: gortonstudios.com

Government Systems Technologies Inc
3159 Schrader Rd. Dover NJ 07801 973-361-2627
Web: www.gstiusa.com

GP Solutions Inc 201 N Charles St Ste 2406. Baltimore MD 21201 410-244-8548
Web: www.gpsonline.com

GPC Systems Inc 2108B Gallows Rd. Vienna VA 22182 703-760-9700
Web: www.gpcsystems.com

GPS Insight LLC
21803 N Scottsdale Rd Ste 220. Scottsdale AZ 85255 480-663-9454
Web: www.gpsinsight.com

Grapnel Tech Services LLC
6905 Vista Dr. West Des Moines IA 50266 515-953-5767
Web: www.grapneltech.com

Graycon Group Ltd 325 10th Ave SW. Calgary AB T2R0A5 403-508-2255
Web: www.graycon.com

Great South Texas Corp 814 Arion Pkwy. San Antonio TX 78216 210-369-0300
Web: www.comsoltx.com

Greenleaf Media 2040 Winnebago St Ste 100. Madison WI 53704 608-240-9611
Web: greenleafmedia.com

Gregg Engineering Inc 403 Julie Rivers Dr. Sugar Land TX 77478 281-494-8100
Web: www.greggeng.com

Grid Net Inc 340 Brannan St Ste 501. San Francisco CA 94107 415-442-4623
Web: www.grid-net.com

Grupo -sms 2525 Main St Ste 200. Irvine CA 92614 949-223-9240
Web: www.grupo-sms.com

GSL Solutions Inc 1411 N W Shore Blvd Ste 204. Tampa FL 33607 813-637-8535
Web: www.gslsolutions.com

Gst Information Technology Solutions
13043 166th St. Cerritos CA 90703 562-345-8700 345-8701
TF: 800-833-0128 ■ *Web:* www.gstes.com

Guest-tek Ltd 240, 3030 - Third Ave N.E. Calgary AB T2A6T7 403-509-1010
Web: www.guest-tek.com

Gulo Solutions LLC
1532 N Milwaukee Ave Ste 203. Chicago IL 60622 773-276-8066
Web: www.gulosolutions.com

Gwynn Group 1409 S Lamar St Apt 603. Dallas TX 75215 214-941-7075
Web: www.gwynngroup.com

H & W Computer Systems Inc PO Box 46019. Boise ID 83711 208-377-0336 377-0069
TF: 800-338-6692 ■ *Web:* www.hwcs.com

Hagerman Inc 510 W Washington Blvd. Fort Wayne IN 46802 260-424-1470
Web: www.thehagermangroup.com

HAL Inc 11109 Cutten Rd Ste 200. Houston TX 77066 281-260-8181
Web: www.hal-inc.com

Halden Group, The 5948 Harbour Park Dr. Midlothian VA 23112 804-595-2295
Web: www.haldengroup.com

Hall Mark Global Technologies Inc
262 Chapman Rd Ste 101. Newark DE 19702 302-366-8960
Web: www.hgtechinc.net

Halsted Communications Ltd
13 Commerce Dr. Ballston Spa NY 12020 518-885-8590

Hammer Data Systems LLC 8138 Main St. Garrettsville OH 44231 330-527-4018
Web: www.hammerdata.com

Hanson Information System
2433 W White Oaks Dr. Springfield IL 62704 217-726-2400
Web: hansoninfosys.com

Harmonia Inc 2020 Kraft Dr Ste 1000. Blacksburg VA 24060 540-951-5900
Web: www.harmonia.com

Harmonix Music Systems Inc
625 Massachusetts Ave. Cambridge MA 02139 617-491-6144
Web: harmonixmusic.com

Harvey Software Inc
7050 Winkler Rd Ste 104. Fort Myers FL 33919 800-231-0296
TF: 800-231-0296 ■ *Web:* www.harveysoft.com

Hawk Ridge Systems 5707 Redwood Rd Ste 18. Oakland CA 94619 510-482-6110
Web: hawkridgesys.com

Hbm Integrated 600-1496 Bedford Hwy. Bedford NS B4A1E5 902-835-9611
Web: www.hbmintegrated.com

HDF Group 1800 S Oak St Ste 203. Champaign IL 61820 217-531-6100
Web: www.hdfgroup.org

Health Care Software Inc PO Box 2430. Farmingdale NJ 07727 800-524-1038 938-5380*
**Fax Area Code:* 732 ■ *TF:* 800-524-1038 ■ *Web:* www.hcsinteractant.com

Health Information Designs Inc
391 Industry Dr. Auburn AL 36832 334-502-3262
Web: www.hidinc.com

Healthcare Automation Inc 41 Sharpe Dr. Cranston RI 02920 401-572-3040 572-3350
TF: 800-738-8850 ■ *Web:* www.healthcare-automation.com

Healthco Information Systems Inc
7657 Sw Mohawk St. Tualatin OR 97062 503-612-1666
Web: www.healthcois.com

Helix Computer Systems Inc
700 Harris St. Charlottesville VA 22903 434-963-4900
Web: www.helixsystems.com

Heller Consulting Inc
1736 Franklin St Ste 600. Oakland CA 94611 510-841-4222
Web: www.teamheller.com

Henning Industrial Software Inc
102 First St Ste 211. Hudson OH 44236 330-650-4212
Web: henningsoftware.com

Company	City	State	ZIP	Phone	Fax
Henschen & Associates Inc 432 W Gypsy Ln *Web:* henschen.com	Bowling Green	OH	43402	419-352-5454	
Hensley, Elam & Associates LLC 163 E Main St Ste 401 *Web:* www.hea.biz	Lexington	KY	40507	859-389-8182	
Heuristic Park Inc 1512 Emory Rd Ne *Web:* www.heuristicpark.com	Atlanta	GA	30306	404-373-7786	
Hiasun Inc 5218 Atlantic Ave P.O. Box 785 *Web:* hiasun.com	Mays Landing	NJ	08330	609-625-0565	
Higher One Inc 115 Munson St *Web:* higherone.com	New Haven	CT	06511	203-776-7776	
Highfleet Inc 3600 Odonnell St Ste 600 *Web:* highfleet.com	Baltimore	MD	21224	410-675-1201	
Hitachi ID Systems Inc 500 1401 - First St SE Ste 500 *Web:* www.hitachi-id.com	Calgary	AB	T2G2J3	403-233-0740	
Hive Group Inc, The 2201 N Central Expy Ste 180 *Web:* www.hivegroup.com	Richardson	TX	75080	972-808-0400	
Hobsons Digital Media Inc 331 Jefferson St *Web:* www.hobsons.com	Oakland	CA	94607	510-251-8703	
HolaDoctor Inc 30 Mansell Court Ste 215 *Web:* www.holadoctor.net	Roswell	GA	30076	770-649-0298	
Horizon Software International LLC 2915 Premier Pkwy Ste 300 *Web:* www.horizon-boss.com	Duluth	GA	30097	770-554-6353	
Horton Group 136 Rosa L Parks Blvd *Web:* www.hortongroup.com	Nashville	TN	37203	615-292-0642	
HSMC Orizon 2007 E Prairie Cir *Web:* www.it21.com	Olathe	KS	66062	913-393-4821	
HTC Global Services Inc 3270 W Big Beaver Rd *Web:* htcinc.com	Troy	MI	48084	248-786-2500	
Hubspan Inc 505 Fifth Ave S Ste 350	Seattle	WA	98104	206-838-5400	838-5449
Human Factors International Inc 410 W Lowe Ave *TF:* 800-242-4480 ■ *Web:* www.humanfactors.com	Fairfield	IA	52556	641-472-4480	472-5412
Human Head Studios 1741 Commercial Ave Ste 200 *Web:* humanhead.com	Madison	WI	53704	608-298-0643	
Hx5 LLC 212 Eglin Pkwy Se *Web:* www.hxfive.com	Fort Walton Beach	FL	32548	850-362-6551	
HyperDisk Marketing Inc 18251 McDurmott W Ste A *Web:* www.hyperdisk.com	Irvine	CA	92614	949-442-9850	
I C S Solutions Inc 11964 Oak Creek Pkwy *Web:* www.icss.com	Huntley	IL	60142	847-515-8000	
I. s Outsource Inc 333 First Ave W *Web:* www.isoutsource.com	Seattle	WA	98119	206-374-0251	
iAdvantage Software Inc 404 E Chatham St *Web:* www.iadvantagesoftware.com	Cary	NC	27511	919-469-3888	
Iars Systems Engineers 100 Park Royal S Ste 200 *Web:* www.iars-syseng.com	West Vancouver	BC	V7T1A2	604-926-9270	
Icentrix Corp 11 Red Roof Ln Ste 1a *Web:* www.icentrix.com	Salem	NH	03079	603-893-3922	
Idea Works Inc, The 100 W Briarwood Ln *Web:* www.ideaworks.com	Columbia	MO	65203	573-445-4554	
Ideal Software Systems Inc 4909 29th Ave *Web:* www.idealss.com	Meridian	MS	39305	601-693-1673	
IGEL Technology Inc 5353 NW 35th Ave *Web:* www.igel.com	Fort Lauderdale	FL	33309	954-739-9990	
Ignify Inc 200 Pine Ave Fourth Fl *Web:* www.ignify.com	Long Beach	CA	90802	562-219-2000	
Ignite! Learning Inc 4030 W Braker Ln Ste 175 *Web:* www.ignitelearning.com	Austin	TX	78759	512-697-7000	
Illuminet Inc 4501 Intelco Loop SE *Web:* www.illuminet.com	Olympia	WA	98507	360-493-6000	
iLookabout Corp Ste 408 383 Richmond St *Web:* www.ilookabout.com	London	ON	N6A3C4	519-963-2015	
Image API LLC 2002 Old St Augustine Rd Bldg D *Web:* www.imageapi.com	Tallahassee	FL	32301	850-222-1400	
Image Architects Inc 784 Morris Tpke *Web:* www.imagearch.com	Short Hills	NJ	07078	973-912-9334	
Imaginet Resources Corp 233 Portage Ave *Web:* imaginet.com	Winnipeg	MB	R3B2A7	204-989-6022	
Imec Technologies Inc 6710 N E Arrowhead Dr *Web:* www.imectechnologies.com	Urbana	IL	61802	217-643-7488	
Impact Interactive 5400 Laurel Springs Pkwy Ste 1003 *Web:* www.impact-interactive.com	Suwanee	GA	30024	678-679-6000	
implement.com Corp 701 N 36th St Ste 310 *Web:* www.implement.com	Seattle	WA	98103	206-547-8100	
Implementation & Consulting Services Inc 5066R W Chester Pk *Web:* www.ics-corporate.com	Newtown Square	PA	19073	610-355-7750	
In-Touch Insight Systems Inc 400 March Rd *Web:* www.intouchinsight.com	Ottawa	ON	K2K3H4	613-270-7900	
Inclind Inc Web Development Services 208 W Market St *Web:* www.inclind.com	Georgetown	DE	19947	302-856-2802	
Indigo BioSystems Inc 7820 Innovation Blvd Ste 250 *Web:* www.indigobio.com	Indianapolis	IN	46278	317-493-2400	
INDUS Corp 1951 Kidwell Dr *Web:* www.induscorp.com	Vienna	VA	22182	703-506-6700	
Industrial Logic Inc 829 Bancroft Way *Web:* www.industriallogic.com	Berkeley	CA	94710	510-540-8336	
Infiniedge Software Inc 14320 Infiniedge Way *Web:* www.infiniedge.com	Prairieville	LA	70769	225-677-8902	

Company	City	State	ZIP	Phone	Fax
Infinite Campus Inc 4321 109th Ave NE *Web:* www.infinitecampus.com	Blaine	MN	55449	651-631-0000	
Infitech LLC 7116 Sennet Pl *Web:* www.infitech.net	West Chester	OH	45069	513-779-5700	
Info-Power International Inc 3345 Silverstone Dr *Web:* www.abw.com	Plano	TX	75023	972-424-4447	
Infoaccess.net LLC 8801 E Pleasant Vly Rd *Web:* www.infoaccess.net	Cleveland	OH	44131	216-328-0100	
Infocrossing Inc Two Christie Heights St *Web:* ww2.infocrossing.com	Leonia	NJ	07605	201-840-4700	
InfoExpress Inc 170 S Whisman Rd Ste B *Web:* www.infoexpress.com	Mountain View	CA	94041	650-623-0260	
Informant Technologies Inc 19 Jenkins Ave Ste 200 *Web:* www.informant-tech.com	Lansdale	PA	19446	215-412-9165	
Infosemantics 2605 Sagebrush Dr Ste 207 *Web:* www.infosemantics.com	Flower Mound	TX	75022	469-941-0266	
Infosilem Inc 99 Rue Emilien-marcoux *Web:* www.infosilem.com	Blainville	QC	J7C0B4	450-420-5565	
Infosource Inc 1300 City View Ctr *TF:* 800-393-4636 ■ *Web:* www.infosourcelearning.com	Oviedo	FL	32765	407-796-5200	796-5190
Infostretch Corp 3200 Patrick Henry Sr Ste 250 *Web:* infostretch.com	Santa Clara	CA	95054	408-727-1100	
Ingenuite Inc 7701 S Western Ave Ste 204 *Web:* ingenuite.com	Oklahoma City	OK	73139	405-636-1802	
Ingenuity Systems Inc 1700 Seaport Blvd Third Fl *Web:* www.ingenuity.com	Redwood City	CA	94063	650-381-5100	
inhouseIT 3193 Red Hill Ave *Web:* www.inhouseit.com	Costa Mesa	CA	92626	949-660-5655	
Inine Technologies LLC Three Independence Way Ste 117 *Web:* www.inine.net	Princeton	NJ	08540	609-452-2000	
Inland Productivity Solutions Inc 1153 W Ninth St *Web:* www.inland-prod.com	Upland	CA	91786	909-981-4500	
Inmedius Inc 2247 Babcock Blvd Ste 200 **Fax Area Code:* 412 ■ *TF:* 800-697-7110 ■ *Web:* www.inmedius.com	Pittsburgh	PA	15237	800-697-7110	459-0311*
Innography Inc 3900 N Capital Of Tx Hwy Ste 175	Austin	TX	78746	512-306-8688	
Innovasystems International LLC 2385 Northside Dr Ste 300 *TF:* 866-566-7778 ■ *Web:* www.innovasi.com	San Diego	CA	92108	619-955-5800	955-5801
InnovaTech Inc 1800 Diagonal Rd Ste 240 *Web:* www.innovateteam.com	Alexandria	VA	22314	703-418-3919	
Innovative Data Management Systems LLC 4006 W Azeele St *Web:* idmsystems.com	Tampa	FL	33609	813-207-2025	
Innovative Systems Group Inc 799 Roosevelt Rd *TF:* 800-739-2400 ■ *Web:* www.innovativesys.com	Glen Ellyn	IL	60137	630-858-8500	858-8532
inRESONANCE Inc 32 Industrial Dr E Ste 1 *Web:* www.inresonance.com	Northampton	MA	01060	413-587-0236	
Insequence Inc 750 Jim Parker Dr *Web:* www.insequence.com	Smyrna	TN	37167	615-459-8943	
Insight Technology Solutions Inc 17251 Melford Blvd Ste 100 *Web:* www.insighttsi.com	Bowie	MD	20715	301-860-1121	
Insurance Technology Consultants Inc (ITC) 2090 N Tustin Ave Ste 260 *Web:* www.itc-systems.com	Santa Ana	CA	92705	714-836-0671	836-0737
Insurity Inc 170 Huyshope Ave *Web:* insurity.com	Hartford	CT	06106	860-616-7721	
Integrated Alliances LLC 1777 Larimer St Ste 1905 *Web:* www.integratedalliances.com	Denver	CO	80202	303-683-9600	
Integrated Data Services Inc 34 Spinnaker Ct Ste 35 *Web:* www.idserve.com	Patchogue	NY	11772	631-265-7162	366-4317
Integrated Digital Technologies Corp 1501 S Brand Blvd *Web:* www.idt.edu	Glendale	CA	91204	818-396-3511	
Integrated Document Solutions Inc 3511 W Commercial Blvd *Web:* www.idssite.com	Fort Lauderdale	FL	33309	954-484-0969	
IntegriChain Inc 100 Canal Pointe Blvd Ste 117 *Web:* www.integrichain.com	Princeton	NJ	08540	609-806-5005	
Integrity Systems & Solutions LLC 1247 Highland Ave Ste 202 *Web:* www.integrityss.com	Cheshire	CT	06410	203-271-7971	
Intelligent Software Solutions Inc 5450 Tech Ctr Dr *Web:* www.issinc.com	Colorado Springs	CO	80919	719-452-7000	452-7001
Intellinetics 2190 Dividend Dr *Web:* www.intellinetics.com	Columbus	OH	43228	614-921-8170	
Intepros Consulting Inc 750 Marrett Rd *Web:* www.intepros.com	Lexington	MA	02421	781-761-1140	
Interchange Technologies Inc 8130 Brentwood Industrial Dr *Web:* www.interchangetech.com	Saint Louis	MO	63144	314-647-5440	
Interdynamix 620-10180 101 St Nw *Web:* www.interdynamix.com	Edmonton	AB	T5J3S4	780-423-7005	
Intex Solutions Inc 110 A St *Web:* www.intex.com	Needham	MA	02494	781-449-6222	
Intnet Inc 606 Monterey Pass Rd *Web:* www.intnetinc.com	Monterey Park	CA	91754	626-281-4882	
Intrafinity Inc 60 ADELAIDE St E *Web:* www.intrafinity.com	Toronto	ON	M5C3E4	416-848-9722	

Company	City	State	ZIP	Phone	Fax
InVision Software Inc 110 Lk Ave S Ste 35 *Web:* www.invisionsoft.com	Nesconset	NY	11767	631-360-3400	
IPextreme Inc 54 N Central Ave Ste 204 *Web:* www.ip-extreme.com	Campbell	CA	95008	408-540-0095	
IQMax Inc 11325 N Community House Rd Ste 175 *Web:* iqmax.com	Charlotte	NC	28277	704-377-2202	
IQMS Inc 2231 Wisteria Ln *Web:* www.iqms.com	Paso Robles	CA	93446	805-227-1122	
iRise 2301 Rosecrans Ave Ste 4100 *Web:* www.irise.com	El Segundo	CA	90245	310-426-7800	
Ironspeed 2870 Zanker Rd #210 *Web:* ironspeed.com	San Jose	CA	95134	408-228-3400	
ISBX Corp 3415 S Sepulveda Blvd Ste 370 *Web:* www.isbx.com	Los Angeles	CA	90034	310-437-8010	
Isc Sales Inc 4421 Tradition Trl *Web:* www.iscenclosurecooling.com	Plano	TX	75093	972-964-2700	
isee systems Inc Wheelock Office Park 31 Old Etna Rd Ste 7N *Web:* www.iseesystems.com	Lebanon	NH	03766	603-448-4990	
Isis Papyrus America Inc 301 Bank St *Web:* www.isis-papyrus.com	Southlake	TX	76092	817-416-2345	416-1223
Island Key Computer Ltd 938 Howe St *Web:* www.islandkey.com	Vancouver	BC	V6Z1N9	604-669-8178	
Island Micro Solutions Inc 3375 Koapaka St Ste B282 *Web:* solutionshawaii.com	Honolulu	HI	96819	808-833-6048	
Island Technologies 17408 Chatsworth St Ste 200 *Web:* www.islandtechnologies.net	Granada Hills	CA	91344	818-832-2310	
ISR Info Way Inc 559 Donofrio Dr Ste 101 & 102 *Web:* www.isrinfo.com	Madison	WI	53719	608-827-7884	
ISTT Inc 846 Broadway Ave *Web:* isttechnology.com	Bowling Green	KY	42101	270-781-5096	
It Doctors 2175 Northdale Blvd Nw *Web:* zinncorp.com	Minneapolis	MN	55433	763-267-6980	
Itology.com Ltd 214 - 11 Ave SE Ste 210 *Web:* www.itsportsnet.com	Calgary	AB	T2G0X8	403-226-3040	
IV Most Consulting Inc 25 Meadow Ln *TF:* 800-448-6678 ■ *Web:* www.ivmost.com	Chappaqua	NY	10514	800-448-6678	
Ivenuecom 9925 Painter Ave Ste A *TF:* 800-683-8314 ■ *Web:* www.ivenue.com	Whittier	CA	90605	800-683-8314	
Ivory Consulting Corp 325 Lennon Ln *Web:* www.ivorycc.com	Walnut Creek	CA	94598	925-926-1100	
Iyka Enterprises 3890 E Main St *Web:* www.iyka.com	Saint Charles	IL	60174	630-372-3900	
J L Patterson & Associates 725 W Town And Country Rd Ste 300 *Web:* www.jlpatterson.com	Orange	CA	92868	714-835-6355	
Jaas Systems Ltd 555 Lancaster Ave *Web:* jaas.net	Reynoldsburg	OH	43068	614-759-4167	
JBoss Inc 3340 Peachtree Rd Ste 1200 *Web:* www.redhat.com	Atlanta	GA	30326	404-467-8555	
JDi Data Corp 2400 E Commercial Blvd Ste 322 *Web:* www.jdidata.com	Fort Lauderdale	FL	33308	954-938-9100	
Jfw Enterprises Inc 3350 Pawtucket Ave *Web:* www.wallace1.com	Riverside	RI	02915	401-438-3030	
Jolera Inc 777 Richmond St W Unit 2 *Web:* www.jolera.com	Toronto	ON	M6J0C2	416-410-1011	
JRI America Inc 277 Park Ave *Web:* www.jri-america.com	New York	NY	10172	212-224-4200	
JRL Enterprises Inc 1820 St Charles Ave Ste 203 *Web:* www.icanlearn.com	New Orleans	LA	70130	504-263-1380	
Jtl Technical Services LLC 113 Crosby Rd Ste U8 *Web:* www.jtltechnicalservices.com	Dover	NH	03820	603-834-6570	
Junction Solutions Inc 9785 S Maroon Cir Ste 410 *Web:* junctionsolutions.com	Englewood	CO	80112	303-327-8800	
Justia Inc 1380 Pear Ave Unit 2b *Web:* www.justia.com	Mountain View	CA	94043	650-810-1990	
Justice Systems Inc 4600 McLeod NE *Web:* www.justicesystems.com	Albuquerque	NM	87109	505-883-3987	883-2845
Kallo Inc 15 Allstate Pkwy Ste 600 *Web:* www.kalloinc.ca	Markham	ON	L3R5B4	416-246-9997	
Karpel Computer Systems Inc 5714 S Lindbergh Blvd *Web:* www.apcwarranties.com	Saint Louis	MO	63123	314-892-6300	
KBACE Technologies Inc Six Trafalgar Sq *Web:* www.kbace.com	Nashua	NH	03063	603-821-7000	
Keller Schroeder & Assoc Inc 4920 Carriage Dr *Web:* kellerschroeder.com	Evansville	IN	47715	812-474-6825	
Kelly Computer Systems 1060 La Avenida St *Web:* www.kelly.com	Mountain View	CA	94043	650-960-1010	
Kepware Inc 400 Congress St Fourth Fl *Web:* www.kepware.com	Portland	ME	04101	207-775-1660	
Kestrel Labs Inc 3133 Indian Rd Ste K *Web:* www.kestrellabs.com	Boulder	CO	80301	303-544-0660	
Keycentrix LLC 2420 N Woodlawn Bldg 500 *Web:* www.keycentrix.com	Wichita	KS	67220	316-262-2231	
KEYW Corp 7740 Milestone Pkwy Ste 400 *TF:* 800-340-1001 ■ *Web:* www.keywcorp.com	Hanover	MD	21076	443-733-1600	733-1601
Klein Systems Group Ltd 360-4400 Dominion St *Web:* www.kleinsystems.com	Burnaby	BC	V5G4G3	604-689-7117	
Knowcean Consulting Inc 10605 Stapleford Hall Dr *Web:* knowceanconsulting.com	Potomac	MD	20854	240-672-1699	
Knowledge Relay LLC 5836 Corporate Ave Ste 130 *Web:* www.knowledgerelay.com	Cypress	CA	90630	714-761-6760	
Knowles - Mcniff 12862 Garden Grove Blvd Ste C *TF:* 800-820-5254 ■ *Web:* www.knowles-mcniff.us	Garden Grove	CA	92843	800-820-5254	
Koni Ameri Tech Services Inc 15 Serina Dr *Web:* www.katsi.com	Plainsboro	NJ	08536	732-226-0727	
Kord Technologies Inc 1101 Mcmurtrie Dr NW Bldg A *Web:* kordtechnologies.com	Huntsville	AL	35806	256-489-2346	
Kpit Infosystems Inc 33 Wood Ave S Ste 720 *Web:* www.kpit.com	Iselin	NJ	08830	732-321-0921	
Krillion Inc 607A W Dana St *TF:* 877-784-0805 ■ *Web:* www.krillion.com	Irvine	CA	92618	949-784-0800	784-0880
Kryptiq Corp 1920 NW Amberglen Pkwy Ste 200 *Web:* www.kryptiq.com	Beaverton	OR	97006	503-906-6300	
KSM Technology Partners LLC 2650 Eisenhower Ave *Web:* ksmpartners.com	Norristown	PA	19403	610-628-0550	
KUBRA Data Transfer Ltd 5050 Tomken Rd *Web:* www.kubra.com	Mississauga	ON	L4W5B1	905-624-2220	
KVS Information Systems Inc 821 Maple Rd *Web:* www.kvsinfo.com	Williamsville	NY	14221	716-626-1976	
Kyyba Inc 28230 Orchard Lk Rd Ste 130 *Web:* www.kyyba.com	Farmington Hills	MI	48334	248-813-9665	
LAITEK Inc 18101 Martin Ave *Web:* www.laitek.com	Homewood	IL	60430	708-799-5000	
Lambda Research Corp 25 Porter Rd *Web:* lambdares.com	Littleton	MA	01460	978-486-0766	
Lancet Software Development Inc 11980 Portland Ave South *Web:* www.lancetdatasciences.com	Burnsville	MN	55337	952-230-7360	
Lancore Technologies 11211 Richmond Ave *Web:* www.lancoretech.com	Houston	TX	77082	281-493-5850	
LanXpert Corp 605 Market St Ste 410 *Web:* www.lanxpert.com	San Francisco	CA	94105	415-543-1033	
Laser App Software Inc 3190 Shelby St Ste D 100 *Web:* www.laserapp.com	Ontario	CA	91764	909-985-2174	
Lattice3d 582 Market St Ste 1215 *Web:* www.lattice3d.com	San Francisco	CA	94104	415-274-1670	
LBi Software Inc 7600 Jericho Tpke *Web:* www.lbisoftware.com	Woodbury	NY	11797	516-921-1500	
LCG Inc 6000 Executive Blvd Ste 410 *Web:* lcgsystems.com	Rockville	MD	20852	301-984-4004	
Lead Technologies Inc 1927 S Tryon St Ste 200 *Web:* www.leadtools.com	Charlotte	NC	28203	704-332-5532	
LeadScope Inc 1393 Dublin Rd *Web:* www.leadscope.com	Columbus	OH	43215	614-675-3730	
LeapFrog Systems Inc 33 Arch St 31st Fl *Web:* www.leapfrogsystems.com	Boston	MA	02110	617-224-9700	
Learnframe Inc 12637 South 265 West Ste 300	Draper	UT	84020	801-523-8000	523-8012
Lease Harbor LLC 414 N Orleans St Ste 602 *Web:* leaseharbor.com	Chicago	IL	60654	312-494-9470	
Leaseteam Inc 4139 S 143rd Cir *Web:* leaseteam.com	Omaha	NE	68137	402-493-3445	
Lemko Corp One Pierce Place Ste 700 *Web:* lemko.com	Itasca	IL	60143	630-948-3025	
Levelfield.com Inc 11675 Jollyville Rd Ste 207 *Web:* www.levelfield.com	Austin	TX	78759	512-401-9200	
Lexicon Technologies Inc 2195 Eastview Pkwy *Web:* www.lexicontech.com	Conyers	GA	30013	770-602-1858	
Lextech Global Services 3080 Ogden Ave Ste 200 *Web:* www.lextech.com	Lisle	IL	60532	630-420-9670	
LGB & Associates Inc 10400 Eaton Pl Ste 130 *Web:* www.lgb-inc.com	Fairfax	VA	22030	703-359-6950	
LHS Productions Inc 260 Union St *Web:* www.videobankdigital.com	Northvale	NJ	07647	201-767-2002	
Lieberman Software Corp 1900 Ave of the Stars Ste 425 *Web:* www.liebsoft.com	Los Angeles	CA	90067	310-550-8575	
Life:WIRE Corp 129 Blantyre Ave Main Fl *Web:* www.lifewire.ca	Toronto	ON	M1N2R6	416-690-1516	
Liftoff LLC 1667 Patrice Cir *Web:* www.liftofflearning.com	Crofton	MD	21114	410-419-1591	
Lightwave Management Resources 4707 140th Ave N 316 *Web:* www.sycoretech.com	Clearwater	FL	33762	727-507-0983	
Link-Systems International Inc 4515 George Rd Ste 340 *Web:* www.link-systems.com	Tampa	FL	33634	813-674-0660	
Liquidframeworks 24 E Greenway Plz *Web:* liquidframeworks.com	Houston	TX	77046	713-552-9250	
Litera Corp 5000 Crossmill Rd *Web:* www.litera.com	Mcleansville	NC	27301	336-375-2991	
Loftware Inc 166 Corporate Dr *Web:* www.loftware.com	Portsmouth	NH	03801	603-766-3630	
Logic Choice Technologies LLC 950 E Haverford Rd *Web:* www.logicchoice.com	Bryn Mawr	PA	19010	610-525-1236	
Logical Images Inc 3445 Winton Pl Ste 240 *Web:* www.logicalimages.com	Rochester	NY	14623	585-427-2790	
Logical Innovations Inc 16902 El Camino Real Ste 3C *Web:* www.logical-i2.com	Houston	TX	77058	281-990-8560	
Logicorps 35015 Automation Dr *Web:* www.logicorps.com	Clinton Township	MI	48035	586-792-9900	
LogiSense Corp 181 Groh Ave Ste 201 *Web:* www.logisense.com	Cambridge	ON	N3C1Y8	519-249-0508	

Phone | Fax

LogiSolve LLC 600 Inwood Ave N Ste 275 ... Oakdale MN 55128 763-383-1000
Web: www.logisolve.com

Logix Guru LLC 3821 Old William Penn Hwy ... Murrysville PA 15668 724-733-4500
Web: www.logixguru.com

Long Business Systems Inc
10749 Pearl Rd Ste 2A ... Strongsville OH 44136 440-846-8500
Web: www.lbsi.com

Lpit Solutions Inc
25 Commerce Ave Sw Ste 200 ... Grand Rapids MI 49503 616-632-2225
Web: www.lpitsolutions.com

Lucas Systems Inc 11279 Perry Hwy Fourth Fl ... Wexford PA 15090 724-940-7000
Web: www.lucasware.com

LumenVox LLC 3615 Kearny Villa Rd ... San Diego CA 92123 858-707-7700
Web: www.lumenvox.com

LVM Systems Inc 4262 E Florian Ave ... Mesa AZ 85206 480-633-8200
Web: www.lvmsystems.com

Lymba Corp 1701 N Collins Blvd ... Richardson TX 75080 972-680-0800
Web: www.lymba.com

Lynx Media Inc
12501 Chandler Blvd Ste 202 ... Valley Village CA 91607 818-761-5859
Web: lynxmedia.com

Lynx Medical Systems Inc
15325 SE 30th Pl Ste 200 ... Bellevue WA 98007 425-641-4451
TF: 800-767-5969 ■ *Web:* www.lynxmed.com

Lyynks Inc 1812 W Burbank Blvd Unit 644 ... Burbank CA 91506 818-478-2260
Web: lyynks.com

M2M Data Corp 8668 Concord Ctr Dr ... Englewood CO 80112 303-768-0064
Web: www.m2mdatacorp.com

M2S Inc 12 Commerce Ave ... West Lebanon NH 03784 603-298-5509 298-5055
Web: www.m2s.com

Macdac Engineering 27 Quality Ave ... Somers CT 06071 860-749-5544
Web: www.macdac.com

Machinima Inc 8441 Santa Monica Blvd ... West Hollywood CA 90069 323-301-1529
Web: www.machinima.com

Macro Group Inc, The
1200 Washington Ave S Ste 350 ... Minneapolis MN 55415 612-332-7880
Web: www.macrogroup.net

Macro Solutions 2000 14th St N Ste 900 ... Arlington VA 22201 703-527-9400
Web: www.macrosolutions.com

Magnatron Inc 225 S Peters Rd ... Knoxville TN 37923 865-769-2622
Web: magnatron.com

Mammography Reporting System Inc
9709 Third Ave NE Ste 208 ... Seattle WA 98115 206-633-6145
Web: www.mrsys.com

Management Analysis Inc 2070 Chain Bridge Rd ... Vienna VA 22182 703-506-0505
Web: www.mainet.com

Manifest Solutions Corp
2035 Riverside Dr ... Upper Arlington OH 43221 614-930-2800
Web: www.manifestsc.com

Marathon Digital Services
716 W Pennway St ... Kansas City MO 64108 816-221-7881
Web: www.mysmartplans.com

Marcole Enterprises Inc
2920 Camino Diablo Ste 200 ... Walnut Creek CA 94597 925-933-9792
Web: www.marcole.com

Marquis Software Development Inc
1611 Jaydell Cir Ste G ... Tallahassee FL 32308 850-877-8864
Web: marquisware.com

Mastermedia LLC
1908 Coney Island Ave Ste 200 ... Brooklyn NY 11223 718-376-3700 504-4000
Web: www.mastermediallc.com

Maximum Insights Inc
17295 Chesterfield Airport Rd Ste 200 ... Chesterfield MO 63005 314-878-8700
Web: www.maximuminsights.com

MAXON COMPUTER Inc 2640 Lavery Ct Ste A ... Newbury Park CA 91320 805-376-3333
Web: www.maxon.net

MaxPoint Interactive Inc
3020 Carrington Mill Blvd Ste 300 ... Morrisville NC 27560 800-916-9960
TF: 800-916-9960 ■ *Web:* www.maxpoint.com

Maxwell Geoservices 1168 Hamilton St ... Vancouver BC V6B2S2 604-678-3298
Web: maxwellgeoservices.com

McKissock LP 218 Liberty St ... Warren PA 16365 814-723-6979
Web: www.mckissock.com

McLeod Software Corporation Inc
2550 Acton Rd PO Box 43200 ... Birmingham AL 35243 205-823-5100
Web: www.mcleodsoftware.com

Media Excel Inc
8834 N Capital of Texas Hwy Ste 302 ... Austin TX 78759 512-502-0034 502-0119
Web: www.mediaexcel.com

Medical Information Technology Inc
6423 City W Pkwy ... Eden Prairie MN 55344 952-941-1000
Web: meditech.com

Medivo Inc 55 Broad St 16th Fl ... New York NY 10004 888-362-4321
TF: 888-362-4321 ■ *Web:* www.medivo.com

MedMatica Consulting Associates
18 Barrington Ln ... Chester Springs PA 19425 610-827-1356
Web: www.medmatica.com

Mekanika Inc 3998 FAU Blvd Ste 210 ... Boca Raton FL 33431 561-210-5671
Web: www.mekanika.com

MembersFirst Inc 321 Commonwealth Rd ... Wayland MA 01778 508-653-3399
Web: www.membersfirst.com

MentorMate LLC 3036 Hennepin Ave ... Minneapolis MN 55408 612-823-4000
Web: www.mentormate.com

Menusoft Systems Corp 7370 Steel Mill Dr ... Springfield VA 22150 703-912-3000
Web: www.digitaldining.com

Meridian Technology Group Inc
12909 SW 68th Pkwy Ste 340 ... Portland OR 97223 503-697-1600 697-8600
TF: 800-755-1038 ■ *Web:* www.meridiangroup.com

Mersoft Corp
Corporate Woods Bldg 55 9300 W 110th St
Ste 350 ... Overland Park KS 66210 913-871-6200
Web: www.mersoft.com

Phone | Fax

MetaLogix Inc
9227 Whispering Wind Dr Ste 100 ... Charlotte NC 28277 704-543-1616
Web: www.meta-logix.net

MetroStar Systems Inc
1856 Old Reston Ave Ste 100 ... Reston VA 20190 703-481-9581
Web: www.metrostarsystems.com

Mi-Co LLC 4601 Creekstone Dr Ste 102 ... Durham NC 27703 919-485-4819
Web: www.mi-corporation.com

MI9 Business Intelligence Systems Inc
301-245 Yorkland Blvd ... Toronto ON M2J4W9 416-491-1483
Web: mi9retail.com

Micro Performance Inc 2569 Housley Rd ... Annapolis MD 21401 410-224-3100
Web: www.microperformance.com

Micro Strategies Inc 85 Bloomfield Ave ... Denville NJ 07834 973-625-7721
Web: www.microstrat.com

Microintegration Inc 5005 Lincolnway E ... Mishawaka IN 46544 574-256-6777
Web: www.microintegration.net

MicroPact Inc 12901 Worldgate Dr Ste 800 ... Herndon VA 20170 703-709-6110
Web: www.micropact.com

Microsmarts LLC 600 Plz Dr Ste 545 ... Matteson IL 60443 708-748-7558
Web: microsmartsllc.com

Midwest Medical Insurance Holding Co
7650 Edinborough Way Ste 400 ... Minneapolis MN 55435 952-838-6700
Web: www.mmicgroup.com

Mikal Corp 4382 Mount Carmel Tobasco ... Cincinnati OH 45244 513-528-5100
Web: www.mikal.com

Mil Corp 4000 Mitchellville Rd ... Bowie MD 20716 301-805-8500 805-8505
TF: 800-875-0867 ■ *Web:* www.milcorp.com

Mil-pac Technology 1672 Main St Ste E-254 ... Ramona CA 92065 760-788-3030
Web: milpac.com

Military Personnel Services Corp
6066 Leesburg Pk ... Falls Church VA 22041 571-481-4000
Web: www.mpscrc.com

Miller Energy Inc
3200 S Clinton Ave ... South Plainfield NJ 07080 908-755-6700
Web: www.millerenergy.com

Milton Security Group LLC
2271 W Malvern Ave # 118 ... Fullerton CA 92833 714-515-4011
Web: www.miltonsecurity.com

Mimic Technologies Inc 811 First Ave Ste 408 ... Seattle WA 98104 206-923-3337
Web: www.mimicsimulation.com

MIMICS Inc 2620 Dakota NE ... Albuquerque NM 87110 505-332-9220
Web: www.mimics.com

Mindex Technologies Inc 3495 Winton Pl ... Rochester NY 14623 585-424-3590
Web: mindex.com

Mindfinders Inc
1050 Connecticut Ave Nw Ste 1000 ... Washington DC 20036 202-772-4177
Web: www.themindfinders.com

MindTouch Inc 401 W A St ... San Diego CA 92101 619-795-8459
Web: www.mindtouch.com

Mintec Inc 3544 E Ft Lowell Rd ... Tucson AZ 85716 520-795-3891
Web: minesight.com

Minuteman Group Inc 35 Bedford St Ste 2 ... Lexington MA 02420 781-861-7493
Web: www.minuteman-group.com

Miria Systems Inc
2570 Blvd of the Generals Ste 222 ... Norristown PA 19403 484-446-3300
Web: www.miriasystems.com

MIS Training Institute LLC
153 Cordaville Rd Ste 200 ... Southborough MA 01772 508-879-7999
Web: www.misti.com

Mission Critical Technologies Inc
2041 Rosecrans Ave ... El Segundo CA 90245 310-246-4455 246-9540
Web: www.mctinc.net

Misys International Banking Systems Inc
1180 Ave ... New York NY 10036 212-898-9500
Web: www.misys.com

MJ Partners Inc 1433 43rd Ave ... Kenosha WI 53144 262-553-9696
Web: www.mjpartnersinc.com

Modulant Inc
4130 Faber Pl Dr Ste 204 ... North Charleston SC 29405 843-743-2888
Web: www.modulant.com

Mojo Interactive Inc 1080 Woodcock Rd Ste 108 ... Orlando FL 32803 407-206-0700
Web: www.mojointeractive.com

Momentummedia-mag Inc 31 Dutch Mill Rd ... Ithaca NY 14850 607-257-6970
Web: momentummedia.com

Money Market Directories Inc
401 E Market St PO Box 1608 ... Charlottesville VA 22902 434-977-1450
Web: www.mmdwebaccess.com

Money Tree Software Ltd
2430 NW Professional Wy ... Corvallis OR 97330 541-754-3701 738-6522
TF: 877-421-9815 ■ *Web:* www.moneytree.com

Mortgageflex Systems Inc
1200 Riverplace Blvd Ste 650 ... Jacksonville FL 32207 904-356-2490 356-1099
TF General: 800-326-3539 ■ *Web:* www.mortgageflex.com

MSI Data Systems
10033 N Port Washington Rd Ste 300 ... Mequon WI 53092 262-241-7800
Web: www.msidata.com

MTS Consulting Group Inc 25450 Friar Ln ... Southfield MI 48033 248-875-7424
Web: www.mtsconsultinggroup.com

Multisoft Corp 1723 SE 47th Ter ... Cape Coral FL 33904 239-945-6433
Web: www.multisoft.com

Mutare Software
2060 E Algonquin Rd Ste 701 ... Schaumburg IL 60173 847-496-9002
Web: www.mutare.com

Mutual Mobile Inc 206 E Ninth St Ste 1400 ... Austin TX 78701 512-615-1800
Web: www.mutualmobile.com

MWA Intelligence Inc
15990 N Greenway Hayden Loop Ste C400 ... Scottsdale AZ 85260 480-538-5900
Web: www.mwaintelligence.com

Mynah Technologies 504 Trade Ctr Blvd ... Chesterfield MO 63005 636-728-2000
Web: www.mynah.com

Mysql Inc 20400 Stevens Creek Blvd ... Cupertino CA 95014 408-213-6600
TF: 866-221-0634 ■ *Web:* www.mysql.com

Phone | Fax

N i C s 392 East 12300 South Ste L ..... Draper UT 84020 801-254-3125
Web: www.nicserv.com
Nakisa Inc 733 Cathcart ..... Montreal QC H3B1M6 514-228-2000
Web: www.nakisa.com
Nanonation Inc 301 S 13th St Ste 700 ..... Lincoln NE 68508 402-323-6266
Web: www.nanonation.net
Nasoft USA Inc 417 E Carmel St ..... San Marcos CA 92078 760-410-1210 510-0024
Web: www.nasoft.com
Nauticon Imaging Systems Inc
15878 Gaither Dr ..... Gaithersburg MD 20877 301-279-0123
Web: www.nauticon.com
nCircle Network Security Inc
101 Second St Ste 400 ..... Portland OR 94105 503-276-7500 223-0182
TF: 866-897-8776 ■ *Web:* www.tripwire.com
Ndex Systems Inc 50 Queen St Ste 304 ..... Montreal QC H3C2N5 514-288-0908
Web: www.ndexsystems.com
NearSpace 1301 Redwood Way Ste 240 ..... Petaluma CA 94954 707-795-1784
Web: www.nearspace.com
Nelson Technology Assoc Inc
1051 Hill Meadow Pl ..... Danville CA 94526 925-855-3610
Web: nelsontech.com
Neoris Inc 703 Waterford Way Ste 700 ..... Miami FL 33126 305-728-6000
Web: www.neoris.com
Net Effect Technologies 730 E Cypress Ave ..... Monrovia CA 91016 626-930-0101
Web: www.pay4music.com
Net Endeavor Inc 982 S Main St ..... Pleasant Grove UT 84062 801-796-5582
Web: net-endeavor.com
Netcellent System Inc 4030 Valley Blvd ..... Walnut CA 91789 909-598-9019
Web: elliott.com
Netcetera Consulting Inc
120 Lonsdale Ave ..... North Vancouver BC V7M2E8 604-980-2755
Web: netcetera.ca
Netlink Systems Inc 5959 Shallowford Rd ..... Chattanooga TN 37421 423-855-0065
Web: www.netlink-systems.com
Netology LLC 1200 Summer St Ste 304 ..... Stamford CT 06905 203-975-9630
Web: www.netologyllc.com
Netstar Corp Seven W Sq Lk Rd ..... Bloomfield Hills MI 48302 248-335-5843
Web: www.netstar-corp.com
Nettempo Inc 130 Battery St Ste 500 ..... San Francisco CA 94111 415-992-4900
Web: nettempo.com
Network Data Security Experts Inc
3600 Douglasdale Rd ..... Richmond VA 23221 804-521-7946
Web: www.ndse.net
Network Dynamics Inc
640 Brooker Creek Blvd Ste 410 ..... Oldsmar FL 34677 813-818-8597 818-9659
TF: 877-818-8597 ■ *Web:* www.ndiwebsite.com
Networking Concepts Inc
9881 Broken Land Pkwy Ste 402 ..... Columbia MD 21046 410-381-0100
Web: www.networkingconcepts.com
Neudesic LLC 8105 Irvine Ctr Dr ..... Irvine CA 92618 949-754-4500 754-6800
TF: 800-805-1805 ■ *Web:* www.neudesic.com
Neutral Tandem Inc 550 W Adams St Fl 9 ..... Chicago IL 60661 312-384-8040
Web: www.inteliquent.com
New England Systems & Software Inc
33 Holly Ln ..... Lake George NY 12845 518-377-4057
Web: www.nessnetworks.com
New World Systems Corp 888 W Big Beavr Rd ..... Troy MI 48084 248-269-1000 269-1020
Web: www.newworldsystems.com
Newforma Inc 1750 Elm St ..... Manchester NH 03104 603-625-6212
Web: www.newforma.com
Newfound Technologies Inc
1050 Kingsmill Pkwy ..... Columbus OH 43229 614-318-5000
Web: www.nfti.com
Newgen Software Inc 1364 Beverly Rd Ste 300 ..... Mclean VA 22101 703-749-2855
Web: newgen.net
Nexenta Systems Inc 455 El Camino Real ..... Santa Clara CA 95050 408-791-3300
Web: www.nexenta.com
Nexlan 28 W N St ..... Danville IL 61832 217-431-7236 477-5731
TF: 877-263-9526 ■ *Web:* nexlan.com
nextPoint Inc 4043 N Ravenswood Ave ..... Chicago IL 60613 888-929-6398
TF: 888-929-6398 ■ *Web:* www.nextpoint.com
Nextware Technologies 3726 Seahorn Dr ..... Malibu CA 90265 310-741-9688
Web: www.nextwaretech.com
Nimbleuser 656 Kreag Rd ..... Pittsford NY 14534 585-586-4750
Web: www.nimbleuser.com
Nims & Associates 1445 Technology Ln Ste A8 ..... Petaluma CA 94954 707-781-6300
Web: www.nimsassociates.com
Nirvana Systems Inc 7000 N MoPac Ste 425 ..... Austin TX 78731 512-345-2545
Web: www.omnitrader.com
Nodus Technologies Inc
2099 S State College Blvd Ste 250 ..... Anaheim CA 92806 909-482-4701
Web: www.nodustech.com
Noetix Corp 5010 148th Ave NE Ste 100 ..... Redmond WA 98052 425-372-2699 436-0406*
**Fax Area Code: 866* ■ *TF:* 866-466-3849 ■ *Web:* www.noetix.com
Noldus Information Technology Inc
1503 Edwards Ferry Rd Ne Ste 201 ..... Leesburg VA 20176 703-771-0440
Web: www.noldus.com
Nomadix Inc 30851 Agoura Rd Ste 102 ..... Agoura Hills CA 91301 818-597-1500 597-1502
Web: www.nomadix.com
Norman Technologies LLC
630 Davidson Gateway Dr Ste 250 ..... Davidson NC 28036 704-896-0128
Web: www.normantech.com
Northwest Data Solutions LLC 2627 C St ..... Anchorage AK 99503 907-227-1676
Web: www.nwds-ak.com
Not Rocket Science Inc 251 Hwy 21 ..... Madisonville LA 70447 985-845-2334
Web: www.notrs.com
Nova Development Corp
23801 Calabasas Rd Ste 1018 ..... Calabasas CA 91302 818-591-9600
Web: www.novadevelopment.com
Nova Libra Inc 8609 W Bryn Mawr Ave Ste 208 ..... Chicago IL 60631 773-714-1441
Web: novalibra.com
Novani 15 Forest View Dr ..... San Francisco CA 94132 415-731-1111
Web: www.novani.com

Phone | Fax

November Research Group LLC
475 14th St Ste 250 ..... Oakland CA 94612 415-987-3313
Web: www.novemberresearch.com
Novex Software Developments Inc
8743 Commercial St ..... New Minas NS B4N3C4 902-542-1813
Web: novexsoftware.com
Novosoft Inc 3803 Mount Bonnel Rd ..... Austin TX 78731 512-454-1140
Web: www.novosoft.us
NOW Solutions Inc 101 W Renner Rd Ste 300 ..... Richardson TX 75082 972-437-3339
Web: www.nowsolutions.com
NowDocs International Inc
1985 Lookout Dr ..... North Mankato MN 56003 888-669-3627
TF: 888-669-3627 ■ *Web:* www.nowdocs.com
NuAxis LLC 8603 Westwood Ctr Dr Ste 340 ..... Vienna VA 22182 703-481-7400
Web: nuaxis.com
Nuesoft Technologies Inc
1685 Terrell Mill Rd ..... Marietta GA 30067 678-303-1140
Web: www.nuemd.com
Numeric Technologies Inc 4200 Cantera Dr ..... Warrenville IL 60555 630-955-9060
Web: www.ntsiinc.com
Nylon Technology 350 Seventh Ave Rm 1005 ..... New York NY 10001 212-691-1134
Web: www.nylontechnology.com
O P Solutions Inc 237 First Ave Fifth Fl ..... New York NY 10003 212-979-1000
Web: www.opsolutions.com
OA Systems Inc 10783 Edison Ct ..... Rancho Cucamonga CA 91730 909-466-1605
Web: www.oasite.com
Oasis Computing Inc 1595 16th Ave ..... Richmond Hill ON L4B3N9 905-709-7456
Web: www.oasiscomputing.com
ObjectBuilders Inc
20134 W Vly Forge Cir ..... King Of Prussia PA 19406 610-783-7748
Web: www.objectbuilders.com
Objective Arts Inc 20 N Wacker Ave ..... Chicago IL 60606 312-977-1150
Web: objectivearts.com
Objective Interface Systems Inc
220 Spring St Ste 530 ..... Herndon VA 20170 703-295-6500
Web: www.ois.com
Objective Technologies Inc
712 Heatherglen Dr ..... Southlake TX 76092 817-251-6900
ObjectRiver Inc 21 Pemberton Rd ..... Wayland MA 01778 508-651-0767
Web: www.objectriver.net
Objectwin Technology Inc
14800 St Mary's Ln Ste 100 ..... Houston TX 77079 713-782-8200 782-8283
Web: www.objectwin.com
OC Systems Inc 9990 Fairfax Blvd Ste 270 ..... Fairfax VA 22030 703-359-8160
Web: www.ocsystems.com
Oculis Labs Inc 338 Clubhouse Rd ..... Hunt Valley MD 21031 410-891-1701
Web: www.oculislabs.com
Oden Industries Inc
268 W Hospitality Ln ..... San Bernardino CA 92408 909-386-0310
Web: www.odenindustries.com
Oeconnection LLC 4205 Highlander Pkwy ..... Richfield OH 44286 330-523-1830 523-1700
TF: 888-776-5792 ■ *Web:* www.oeconnection.com
OfficeOps LLC 619 S Vulcan Ave ..... Encinitas CA 92024 760-634-2006
Web: www.office-ops.com
Officepro Inc Eight Granite Pl ..... Gaithersburg MD 20878 301-468-3312
Web: www.officeproinc.com
Omega Airline Software 116 N Eighth St ..... Midlothian TX 76065 972-775-3693
Web: www.omegaair.com
Omnitech Inc 5841 S Corporate Pl ..... Sioux Falls SD 57108 605-336-0888
Web: omnitech-inc.com
On Center Software Inc
8708 Technology Forest Pl Ste 175 ..... The Woodlands TX 77381 281-297-9000
Web: www.oncenter.com
One Point Solutions Inc 43422 W Oaks Dr Ste 294 ..... Novi MI 48377 248-887-8470
Web: www.one-point.com
One Web Systems Inc 6195 Barfield Rd Ste 170 ..... Atlanta GA 30328 404-252-5400
Web: www.targetatlanta.com
Oneshield Inc 62 Forest St Ste 200 ..... Marlborough MA 01752 774-348-1000
Web: oneshield.com
ONRAD Inc 1770 Iowa Ave Ste 280 ..... Riverside CA 92507 951-786-0801
Web: www.onradinc.com
Onramp Access LLC 2916 Montopolis Dr Ste 300 ..... Austin TX 78741 512-322-9200
Web: www.onr.com
Ontario Systems Corp 1150 W Kilgore Ave ..... Muncie IN 47305 765-751-7000 751-7099
Web: www.ontariosystems.com
Open Dental Software
Ste 110 3995 Fairview Industrial Dr SE ..... Salem OR 97302 503-363-5432
Web: www.opendental.com
Openet Telecom Inc 1886 Metro Ctr Dr Ste 310 ..... Reston VA 20190 703-480-1820
Web: www.openet.com
OpenPeak Inc 1750 Clint Moore Rd ..... Boca Raton FL 33487 561-893-7800
Web: www.openpeak.com
Operation Technology Inc 17 Goodyear Ste 100 ..... Irvine CA 92618 949-900-1000
Web: etap.com
OPSWAT Inc 398 Kansas St ..... San Francisco CA 94103 415-590-7300
Web: www.opswat.com
Optical Image Technology Inc
100 Oakwood Ave Ste 700 ..... State College PA 16803 814-238-0038
Web: www.docfinity.com
Optima Global Solutions Inc
3131 Princeton Pike Ste 207 ..... Lawrenceville NJ 08648 609-586-8811
Web: www.optimags.com
Optimal Electronics Corp
8716 N Mo Pac Expy Ste 230 ..... Austin TX 78759 512-372-3415
Web: www.optelco.com
Optimum Solutions Corp 170 Earle Ave ..... Lynbrook NY 11563 516-247-5300
Web: www.oscworld.com
Oracle Applications Users Group
One Piedmont Ctr Ste 400 ..... Atlanta GA 30305 404-240-0897
Web: www.oaug.org
Orange Legal Technologies LLC
30 East Broadway Ste 300 ..... Salt Lake City UT 84111 801-328-4566
Web: www.orangelt.com

Company / Address	City	State	ZIP	Phone	Fax
Orasi Software Inc 114 TownPark Dr Ste 400	Kennesaw	GA	30144	678-819-5300	
Web: www.orasi.com					
Orchard Software Corp					
701 Congressional Blvd Ste 360	Carmel	IN	46032	317-573-2633	573-2633
TF: 800-856-1948 ■ *Web:* www.orchardsoft.com					
Orchestro Ste 350 1760 Old Meadow Rd	Mclean	VA	22102	703-640-3300	
Web: orchestro.com					
OriginLab Corp One Roundhouse Plz	Northampton	MA	01060	413-586-2013	
Web: www.originlab.com					
Ortho Computer Systems Inc 1107 Buckeye Ave	Ames	IA	50010	515-233-1026	
Web: www.ortho2.com					
Other Firm LLC, The 618 NW Glisan St Ste 201	Portland	OR	97209	503-336-5359	
Web: www.theotherfirm.com					
Outa Knoware International 886 Salem Rd	Dracut	MA	01826	978-688-1388	
Web: outaknoware.com					
Overland Rentals Inc					
1901 N State Hwy 360 Ste 340	Grand Prairie	TX	75050	972-602-9819	
Web: m.point-of-rental.com					
Ox International Inc 13111 NW Fwy Fifth Fl	Houston	TX	77040	713-895-6610	
Web: www.oxinternational.com					
P C Whip 4451 Henderson Rd	Hickory	PA	15340	724-356-4070	
Web: www.pcwhip.com					
Pace Computer Solutions Inc					
10480 Little Patuxent Pkwy Ste 760	Columbia	MD	21044	443-539-0290	
Web: www.pace-solutionsinc.com					
Pacific Tech Solutions LLC					
15530 Rckfeld Blvd Ste B4	Irvine	CA	92618	949-830-1623	
Web: www.pts1.com					
PacketTrap Networks Inc					
118 Second St Sixth Fl	San Francisco	CA	94105	415-348-0700	
Web: www.packettrap.com					
Paksys Software LLC 116 Salem Rd	North Brunswick	NJ	08902	732-297-8908	
Web: www.paksys.com					
Paladin Data Systems Corp					
19362 Powder Hill Pl NE	Poulsbo	WA	98370	360-779-2400	779-2600
TF: 800-532-8448 ■ *Web:* www.paladindata.com					
Palmetto GBA LLC 17 Technology Cir AG-905	Columbia	SC	29203	803-735-1034	
Web: www.palmettogba.com					
Panasas Inc 969 W Maude Ave	Sunnyvale	CA	94085	408-215-6800	215-6801
TF: 800-726-2727 ■ *Web:* www.panasas.com					
Pangaea Information Technologies Ltd					
219 W Chicago Ave	Chicago	IL	60654	312-337-5404	
Web: www.pangaeatech.com					
Pangolin Laser Systems Inc					
9501 Satellite Blvd Ste 109	Orlando	FL	32837	407-299-2088	
Web: pangolin.com					
Pangomedia Inc 3003 Minnesota Dr Ste 303	Anchorage	AK	99503	907-868-8092	
Web: pangomedia.com					
PaperThin Inc 300 Congress St Ste 303	Quincy	MA	02169	617-471-4440	
Web: www.paperthin.com					
PaperWise Inc 3171 E Sunshine	Springfield	MO	65804	417-886-7505	
Web: www.paperwise.com					
PAR Excellence Systems Inc					
11500 Northlake Dr	Cincinnati	OH	45249	513-936-9744	
Web: www.parexcellencesystems.com					
Paraben Corp 21690 Red Rum Dr Ste 137	Ashburn	VA	20147	801-796-0944	
Web: www.paraben.com					
Paragon Application Systems Inc					
326 Raleigh St	Holly Springs	NC	27540	919-567-9890	
Web: www.paragonedge.com					
Parity Computing Inc					
6160 Lusk Blvd Ste C205	San Diego	CA	92121	858-535-0516	
Web: www.paritycomputing.com					
Park Place Technologies Inc					
5910 Landerbrook Dr	Cleveland	OH	44124	877-778-8707	
TF: 877-778-8707 ■ *Web:* www.parkplacetechnologies.com					
PASSUR Aerospace Inc					
One Landmark Sq Ste 1900	Stamford	CT	06901	203-622-4086	
Web: www.passur.com					
Patel Consultants Corp 1525 Morris Ave	Union	NJ	07083	908-964-7575	964-3176
Web: www.patelcorp.com					
Patni Americas Inc 116 Pine St Ste 320	Harrisburg	PA	17101	617-914-8000	914-8200
TF: 877-209-0463 ■ *Web:* www.igate.com					
Patriot Managed Care Solutions Inc					
1800 Augusta Dr Ste 220	Houston	TX	77057	713-346-6200	
Web: www.patriotmcs.net					
Patriot Technologies Inc					
5108 Pegasus Ct Ste F	Frederick	MD	21704	301-695-7500	695-4711
TF: 888-417-9899 ■ *Web:* www.patriot-tech.com					
Pattern Insight Inc					
465 Fairchild Dr Ste 209	Mountain View	CA	94043	866-582-2655	
TF: 866-582-2655 ■ *Web:* patterninsight.com					
Pc Focus Computer Co 7500 Mountain Ave	Orangevale	CA	95662	916-988-0404	
Web: www.pcfocus.net					
PC Scale Inc 119 S Fifth St	Oxford	PA	19363	610-932-4006	
Web: www.pcscaletower.com					
PCA Group Inc, The 455 Cayuga Rd Ste 200	Buffalo	NY	14225	716-932-7830	
Web: www.pcatechnologygroup.com					
PCMS Datafit Inc					
25 Merchant St Executive Centre 3 Ste 400	Cincinnati	OH	45246	513-587-3100	
Web: www.pcmsdatafit.com					
Pen-Link Ltd 5936 VanDervoort Dr	Lincoln	NE	68516	402-421-8857	
Web: www.penlink.com					
Pepper Group, The 220 N Smith St Ste 406	Palatine	IL	60067	847-963-0333	
Web: www.peppergroup.com					
Peppler & Associates Inc					
22 E Dundee Rd Ste 26	Barrington	IL	60010	847-382-6866	
Web: peppler.com					
Perforce Software Inc 2320 Blanding Ave	Alameda	CA	94501	510-864-7400	
Web: perforce.com					
Performance Software					
2095 W Pinnacle Peak Rd Ste 120	Phoenix	AZ	85027	623-780-1517	308-8688*
**Fax Area Code:* 602 ■ **Fax:* Sales ■ *Web:* www.psware.com					
Performance Support Inc					
5775 Carmichael Pkwy	Montgomery	AL	36117	334-244-9797	
Web: www.at-psi.com					
PERI Software Solutions Inc 570 Broad St	Newark	NJ	07102	973-735-9500	
Web: www.perisoftware.com					
petroWEB Inc 1825 Blake St	Denver	CO	80202	303-308-9100	
Web: www.petroweb.com					
Petz Enterprises LLC 7575 W Linne Rd	Tracy	CA	95304	209-835-2720	
Web: www.petzent.com					
PFW Systems Corp 850 Medway Park Ct	London	ON	N6G5C6	519-474-3300	
Web: www.pfw.com					
PharmaSys Inc 216 Towne Village Dr	Cary	NC	27513	919-468-2547	
Web: www.pharma-sys.com					
Phunware Inc 7800 Shoal Creek Blvd	Austin	TX	78757	855-521-8485	
TF: 855-521-8485 ■ *Web:* www.phunware.com					
PIC Business Systems Inc					
5119 Beckwith Blvd Ste 106	San Antonio	TX	78249	210-690-9106	
Web: www.picbusiness.com					
Picaboo Corp 1160 Chestnut St	Menlo Park	CA	94025	650-326-3200	
Web: www.picaboo.com					
Pine River Capital Management LP					
601 Carlson Pkwy Ste 330	Minnetonka	MN	55305	612-238-3300	
Web: www.pinerivercapital.com					
Pinnacle Solutions Inc					
426 E New York St Ste 900	Indianapolis	IN	46202	317-423-9143	
Web: www.psiconsultants.com					
Pipkins Inc					
One McBride & Son Ctr Dr Ste 140	Chesterfield	MO	63005	314-469-6106	
Web: www.pipkins.com					
Piston Cloud Computing Inc					
126 Post St Fifth Fl	San Francisco	CA	94108	650-242-5683	
Web: pistoncloud.com					
Pivot Systems Inc 2480 N First St Ste 150	San Jose	CA	95131	408-435-1000	
Web: www.pivotsys.com					
Pixel Systems Inc 103 Carnegie Ctr Ste 300	Princeton	NJ	08540	609-945-3190	
Web: www.pixelsystemsinc.com					
Pixstar Inc 1515 Savannah Rd	Lewes	DE	19958	302-644-8650	
Web: www.pixstar.com					
PKMM Inc 265 E Main St Ste B	Oceanport	NJ	07757	732-935-1927	
Web: pkmminc.com					
Plan B Technologies Inc					
16701 Melford Blvd Ste 300	Bowie	MD	20715	301-860-1006	
Web: www.planbtech.net					
Pointwise Inc 213 S Jennings Ave	Fort Worth	TX	76104	817-377-2807	
Web: www.pointwise.com					
Polar Instruments Inc					
18649 SW Farmington Rd	Beaverton	OR	97007	503-356-5270	
Web: www.polarinstruments.com					
Polaris Health Directions Inc					
444 Oxford Vly Rd Ste 300	Langhorne	PA	19047	215-359-3901	
Web: www.polarishealth.com					
Portable Technology Solutions LLC					
221 David Ct	Calverton	NY	11933	877-640-4152	
TF: 877-640-4152 ■ *Web:* www.ptshome.com					
Porter Lee Corp 1901 Wright Blvd	Schaumburg	IL	60193	847-985-2060	
Web: www.porterlee.com					
Portrait Displays Inc 6663 Owens Dr	Pleasanton	CA	94588	925-227-2700	
Web: www.portrait.com					
Pos Source 535 Harrison Ave	Panama City	FL	32401	850-747-0581	
Web: www.execu-tech.com					
PowerServe International Inc					
959 Broad St Ste 300	Augusta	GA	30901	706-826-1506	
Web: www.powerserve.net					
Practice Technology Inc 1312 E Robinson St	Orlando	FL	32801	407-228-4400	
Web: prevail.net					
Prakat Solutions Inc 6016 Annandale Dr	Fort Worth	TX	76132	817-846-7541	
Web: www.prakat.com					
Praxis Engineering Technologies Inc					
135 National Business Pkwy	Annapolis Junction	MD	20701	301-490-4299	
Web: praxiseng.com					
Predicate Logic Inc 6404 Nancy Ridge Dr	San Diego	CA	92121	858-715-0100	
Web: www.predicate.com					
Preferred Medical Marketing Corp					
15720 John J Delaney Dr Ste 460	Charlotte	NC	28277	704-543-8103	
Web: www.pmmconline.com					
Preferred Strategies LLC 2425 Porter St Ste 20	Soquel	CA	95073	831-465-7164	
Web: www.preferredstrategies.com					
Prelude Systems Inc 3911 Hartzdale Dr	Camp Hill	PA	17011	717-441-2400	
Web: preludeservices.com					
Prenia Corp 16625 Redmond Way Ste M-418	Redmond	WA	98052	425-999-4330	898-8301
Web: www.prenia.com					
PreViser Corp 20849 Cascade Ridge Dr	Mount Vernon	WA	98274	360-941-4715	
Web: www.previser.com					
Primal Fusion Inc 7-258 King St N	Waterloo	ON	N2J2Y9	519-741-1243	
Web: www.primal.com					
Prime Controls LP 1725 Lakepointe D	Lewisville	TX	75057	972-221-4849	420-4842
Web: www.prime-controls.com					
Prince Software Inc 70 Hilltop Rd Ste 2400	Ramsey	NJ	07446	201-934-0022	
Web: www.princesoftware.com					
Prism Microsystems Inc					
8815 Centre Park Dr T hird Fl	Columbia	MD	21045	410-953-6776	
Web: www.eventtracker.com					
Prism Systems Inc 200 Virginia St	Mobile	AL	36603	251-341-1140	
Web: prismsystems.com					
Pro-cad Software Ltd 12 Elbow River Rd	Calgary	AB	T3Z2V2	403-216-3375	
Web: www.procad.com					
Pro-Tek Manufacturing Inc					
4849 Southfront Rd	Livermore	CA	94551	925-454-8100	
Web: www.protekmfg.com					
Procera Networks Inc 47448 Fremont Blvd	Fremont	CA	94538	510-230-2777	
Web: www.proceranetworks.com					

Company	City	State	ZIP	Phone	Fax
Process Control Technology Inc 4335 Piedras Dr W Ste 175 *Web:* www.gopct.com	San Antonio	TX	78228	210-735-9141	735-9775
ProcessMAP Corp 13450 W Sunrise Blvd Ste 160 *Web:* www.processmap.com	Sunrise	FL	33323	954-515-5040	
Productivity Apex Inc 11301 Corporate Blvd Ste 303 *Web:* www.productivityapex.com	Orlando	FL	32817	407-384-0800	
Profit Programming Inc 11350 Mccormick Rd Ste 304 *Web:* www.profitprogramming.com	Hunt Valley	MD	21031	410-316-1000	
Profitsword LLC 9355 Cypress Cove Dr *Web:* www.profitsword.com	Orlando	FL	32819	407-909-8822	
Progeny Linux Systems Inc 9100 Keystone Ste 440	Indianapolis	IN	46240	317-833-0313	833-0315
Progeny Software LLC 130 S Main St Ste 420 *Web:* www.progenygenetics.com	South Bend	IN	46601	574-968-0822	
Promiles Software Development 1900 Texas Ave *Web:* www.promiles.com	Bridge City	TX	77611	409-697-2589	
Promium LLC 3350 Monte Villa Pkwy Ste 220 *Web:* www.promium.com	Bothell	WA	98021	425-286-9200	
Proofpoint Systems Inc 1393 Oak Ave *Web:* proofpoint.net	Los Altos	CA	94024	650-968-7032	
Property Panorama Inc 9475 Pinecone Dr *Web:* propertypanorama.com	Mentor	OH	44060	440-290-2200	
ProSites Inc 27919 Jefferson Ave Ste 103 *Web:* www.prosites.com	Temecula	CA	92590	951-693-9101	
Prosync Technology Group LLC 6021 University Blvd Ste 300 *Web:* www.prosync.com	Ellicott City	MD	21043	410-772-7969	
Protech Systems Group Shadow Creek I - Southwind 3350 Players Club Pkwy *Web:* www.psgi.net	Memphis	TN	38125	901-767-7550	
Proteus Technologies LLC 133 National Business Pkwy *Web:* proteus-technologies.com	Annapolis Junction	MD	20701	443-539-3400	
Providge Consulting LLC 2207 Concord Pike Ste 537 *TF:* 888-927-6583 ■ *Web:* www.providge.com	Wilimington	DE	19803	888-927-6583	
Proware 7621 E Kemper Rd *Web:* www.proware.com	Cincinnati	OH	45249	513-489-5477	
Prowess Inc 1844 Clayton Rd *Web:* www.prowess.com	Concord	CA	94520	925-356-0360	
Proxibid Inc 4411 S 96 St *Web:* www.proxibid.com	Omaha	NE	68127	402-505-7770	
Proximex Corp 300 Santana Row Ste 200 *Web:* www.proximex.com	San Jose	CA	95128	408-215-9000	
Proximo Consulting Services Inc 2500 Plz Five *TF:* 800-236-9250 ■ *Web:* www.proximo.com	Jersey City	NJ	07311	800-236-9250	
Ps Websolutions Inc 906 Carriage Path Se Ste 106 *Web:* www.pswebsolution.com	Smyrna	GA	30082	770-801-8866	
Psychological Software Solutions Inc 4119 Montrose Blvd *Web:* psiwaresolutions.com	Houston	TX	77006	713-965-6941	
Psychology Software Tools Inc Sharpsburg Business Park 311 23rd St Ext Ste 200 *Web:* www.pstnet.com	Sharpsburg	PA	15215	412-271-5040	
Psytech Solutions 1138 Stone Creek Dr *Web:* www.psytechsolutions.net	Hummelstown	PA	17036	717-583-0349	
Public Systems Associates Inc 2431 S Acadian Thruway Ste 570 *Web:* publicsystems.org	Baton Rouge	LA	70808	225-346-0618	
Purvis Systems Inc 88 Silva Ln *Web:* purvis.com	Middletown	RI	02842	401-849-4750	849-0121
Pyramid Software Development Inc 4008 Louetta Rd #404 *Web:* pyramidsdi.com	Spring	TX	77388	281-350-2535	
QFlow Systems LLC 9317 Manchester Rd *Web:* www.qflowsystems.com	St. Louis	MO	63119	314-968-9906	
QHR Corp Ste 300 1620 Dickson Ave *Web:* www.qhrtechnologies.com	Kelowna	BC	V1Y9Y2	250-448-7095	
QSR Automations Inc 2301 Stanley Gault Pkwy *Web:* www.qsrautomation.com	Louisville	KY	40223	502-297-0221	
QStar Technologies Inc 8738 Ortega Park Dr *Web:* www.qstar.com	Navarre	FL	32566	850-243-0900	
Quadramed Inc 12110 Sunset Hills Rd Ste 600 *Web:* www.quadramed.com	Reston	VA	20190	703-709-2300	
Qualnetics Corp 2183 Alpine Way *Web:* www.qualnetics.com	Bellingham	WA	98226	360-733-4151	
Quantia Communications Inc 52 Second Ave *Web:* www.secure.quantiamd.com	Waltham	MA	02451	617-219-6100	
Quantros Inc 475 Sycamore Dr *Web:* www.quantros.com	Milpitas	CA	95035	408-957-3300	
Quantum Aviation Solutions Inc 1720 Epps Bridge Pkwy Ste 108 Number 304 *Web:* www.quantum.aero	Athens	GA	30606	404-348-4839	
Quantum Simulations Inc 5275 Sardis Rd *Web:* quantumsimulations.com	Murrysville	PA	15668	724-733-8603	
Questek Innovations LLC 1820 Ridge Ave *Web:* www.questek.com	Evanston	IL	60201	847-328-5800	
Questionmark Corp Five Hillandale Ave *Web:* www.questionmark.com	Stamford	CT	06902	203-358-3950	
Quick Technologies Inc 2508 Highlander Way Ste 200 *Web:* www.qti.com	Carrollton	TX	75006	214-631-6000	
QuickCompliance Inc 8A Canal Ct *Web:* www.quickcompliance.net	Avon	CT	06001	860-676-9400	
QuickStart Intelligence Inc 16815 Von Karman Ave Ste 100 *Web:* www.quickstart.com	Irvine	CA	92606	800-326-1044	
Quorum Business Solutions Inc 811 Main St Ste 2000 *Web:* www.qbsol.com	Houston	TX	77002	713-430-8601	430-8697
R Z Communications 1400 Smith Rd # B101 *Web:* www.rzaustin.com	Austin	TX	78721	512-386-7336	
R&D Logic Inc 1611 Borel Pl Ste 2 *Web:* www.rdlogic.com	San Mateo	CA	94402	650-571-5255	
Radiant Logic Inc 75 Rowland Way Ste 300 *Web:* www.radiantlogic.com	Novato	CA	94945	415-209-6800	
RADinfo Systems Inc 43676 Trade Ctr Pl Ste 100 *Web:* www.radinfosystems.com	Dulles	VA	20166	703-713-3313	
Radley Corp 23077 Greenfield Rd Ste 440 *Web:* www.radley.com	Southfield	MI	48075	248-559-6858	
RAF Technology Inc 15400 NE 90th St Ste 300 *Web:* www.raf.com	Redmond	WA	98052	425-867-0700	
Raintree Systems Inc 27307 Via Industria *Web:* www.raintreeinc.com	Temecula	CA	92590	951-252-9400	
RamQuest Software Inc 5801 Tennyson Pkwy Ste 500 *Web:* www.ramquest.com	Plano	TX	75024	214-291-1600	
Ramsoft Systems Inc 29777 Telegraph Rd Ste 2250 *Web:* www.ramsoft.net	Southfield	MI	48034	248-354-0100	
Ranch Santa Fe Technology 5961 Kearny Villa Rd	San Diego	CA	92123	858-565-7224	
Rapid Insight Inc 53 Technology Ln Ste 112 *TF:* 888-585-6511 ■ *Web:* www.rapidinsightinc.com	Conway	NH	03818	888-585-6511	
Rapid Software Corp 3079 Parr Ln *Web:* www.rapidsw.com	Grapevine	TX	76051	817-251-0615	
Rata Associates LLC 1916 Boothe Cir *Web:* www.rataassociates.com	Longwood	FL	32750	407-831-7282	
Rave Wireless Inc 50 Speen St *Web:* www.ravemobilesafety.com	Framingham	MA	01701	508-848-2484	
Razorleaf Corp 3766 Fishcreek Rd Ste 291 *Web:* www.razorleaf.com	Stow	OH	44224	330-676-0022	
RBB Innovations 73 Brock St *Web:* rbbinnovations.com	Sault Ste. Marie	ON	P6A3B4	705-942-9053	
RCI Technologies Inc 1133 Green St *Web:* www.rci-technologies.com	Iselin	NJ	08830	732-382-3000	
RDA Corp 303 International Cir Ste 340 *TF:* 888-441-1278 ■ *Web:* www.rdacorp.com	Hunt Valley	MD	21030	410-308-9300	308-9600
Ready-to-run Software Inc 212 Cedar Cv *Web:* www.rtr.com	Lansing	NY	14882	607-533-4002	
ReadyGo Inc 1761 Pilgrim Ave *Web:* www.readygo.com	Mountain View	CA	94040	650-559-8990	
Real Time Information Services Inc 191 W Shaw Ave Ste 106 *Web:* realtimeca.com	Fresno	CA	93704	559-222-6456	
Real Vision Software Inc 3700 Jackson St Ext *Web:* www.realvisionsoftware.com	Alexandria	LA	71303	318-449-4579	
Realdecoy Inc 205 Catherine St *Web:* www.realdecoy.com	Ottawa	ON	K2P1C3	613-234-9330	
Rediker Software Inc 2 Wilbraham Rd *TF:* 800-213-9860 ■ *Web:* www.rediker.com	Hampden	MA	01036	413-566-3463	566-2274
RedMane Technology LLC 8614 W Catalpa Ave Ste 1001 *Web:* www.redmane.com	Chicago	IL	60656	773-693-3919	
Redspin Inc 4690 Carpinteria Ave Ste B *Web:* www.redspin.com	Carpinteria	CA	93013	805-684-6858	
Referentia Systems Inc 155 Kapalulu Pl Ste 200 *Web:* www.referentia.com	Honolulu	HI	96819	808-840-8500	
Regional Economic Models Inc 433 W St *Web:* remi.com	Amherst	MA	01002	413-549-1169	549-1038
REI Systems Inc 45335 Vintage Pk Plz *Web:* www.reisystems.com	Sterling	VA	20166	703-480-9100	689-4680
ReleaseTEAM Inc 1400 W 122nd Ave Ste 202 *Web:* www.releaseteam.com	Denver	CO	80234	720-977-8010	
Reliable Software Resources Inc 22260 Haggerty Rd Ste 285 *Web:* www.rsrit.com	Northville	MI	48167	248-477-3555	
Renewable NRG Systems 110 Riggs Rd *Web:* www.nrgsystems.com	Hinesburg	VT	05461	802-482-2255	
RenoWorks Software Inc 2816 21 St NE *Web:* www.renoworks.com	Calgary	AB	T2E6Z2	403-296-3880	
Rentfrow Inc 5675 Ralston St *Web:* www.rentfrow.com	Ventura	CA	93003	805-650-7677	
Reporting Systems Inc 851 Coho Way Ste 307 *Web:* www.emergencyreporting.com	Bellingham	WA	98225	360-647-6003	
Resolute Technology Solutions Inc 433 Main St Ste 600 *Web:* www.resolutets.com	Winnipeg	MB	R3B1B3	204-927-3520	
Resort Data Processing Inc 211 Eagle Rd *Web:* www.resortdata.com	Avon	CO	81620	970-845-1140	
Resource & Financial Management Systems Inc 3073 Palisades Ct *TF:* 800-701-7367 ■ *Web:* www.rfms.com	Tuscaloosa	AL	35405	800-701-7367	
Resource Data Inc 560 E 34th Ave Ste 100 *Web:* www.resdat.com	Anchorage	AK	99503	907-563-8100	
Rethink Autism Inc 19 W 21st St Ste 403 *Web:* www.rethinkfirst.com	New York	NY	10010	646-257-2919	
RF Engineering Inc 13801 Bison Ct *Web:* www.rfe-inc.com	Silver Spring	MD	20906	301-460-8374	
Rfd & Associates Inc 401 Camp Craft Rd *Web:* www.rfdinc.com	Austin	TX	78746	512-347-9411	
Richter Media Inc 255 W 23rd St Apt 4ce *Web:* www.richtermedia.com	New York	NY	10011	212-802-8588	

	City	State	ZIP	Phone	Fax
Rina Group LLC 8180 Corporate Park Dr Ste 140 — *Web:* www.rinasystems.com	Cincinnati	OH	45242	513-469-7462	
Rivet Software Inc 4340 S Monaco St Ste 100 — *Web:* www.rivetsoftware.com	Denver	CO	80237	720-249-2100	
RLW Inc 2029 Cato Ave — *Web:* www.rlwinc.com	State College	PA	16801	814-867-5122	
Robert Sharp & Associates Inc 3615 Canyon Lk Dr Ste 1 — *Web:* www.thesharpagency.com	Rapid City	SD	57702	605-341-5226	
Robocast Inc 89 Fifth Ave — *Web:* robocast.com	New York	NY	10003	212-620-0007	
Rochester Group Inc, The 600 Park Ave — *Web:* www.rochgrp.com	Rochester	NY	14607	585-271-1110	
Rocket Jones Interactive LLC 204 Walnut St Ste C — *Web:* rocketjones.com	Fort Collins	CO	80524	970-482-5790	
Rockysoft Corp 760 Whalers Way #C-100 — *Web:* www.rockysoft.com	Fort Collins	CO	80525	970-493-0868	
Rolands & Associates Corp 120 Del Rey Gardens Dr — *Web:* www.rolands.com	Del Rey Oaks	CA	93940	831-373-2025	
Rooster Park 901 Thomas St — *Web:* www.roosterpark.com	Seattle	WA	98109	206-801-0189	
Rose International 16401 Swingley Ridge Rd Ste 300 — *Web:* www.roseit.com	Chesterfield	MO	63017	636-812-4000	812-0076
Roshi Tech Inc Five Castleton Ct — *Web:* www.roshitech.com	Merrimack	NH	03054	603-889-2211	
Royal Cyber Inc 55 Shuman Blvd Ste 1025 — *Web:* www.royalcyber.com	Naperville	IL	60563	630-355-6292	
RP Design Web Services 1187 Highland Ave Ste 2 — *Web:* www.rpdesign.com	Cheshire	CT	06410	203-271-7991	
RTT USA Inc 751 N Fair Oaks Ave — *Web:* www.rtt.ag	Pasadena	CA	91103	626-535-9726	
Rtz Associates Inc 150 Grand Ave Ste 201 — *Web:* www.rtzassociates.com	Oakland	CA	94612	510-986-6700	
Rubicon Group Ltd, The 125 Windsor Dr Ste 118 — *Web:* www.rubgrp.com	Oak Brook	IL	60523	630-574-7766	
Runner Technologies Inc 6530 W Rogers Cir Ste 31 — *Web:* www.runnertechnologies.com	Boca Raton	FL	33487	561-395-9322	
S2Tech 720 Spirit 40 Park Dr — *Web:* www.s2tech.com	Chesterfield	MO	63005	636-530-9286	
S3 Ventures 6300 Bridgepoint Pkwy Bldg One Ste 405 — *Web:* www.s3vc.com	Austin	TX	78730	512-258-1759	
Safe Banking Systems LLC 114 Old Country Rd Ste 320 — *Web:* www.safe-banking.com	Mineola	NY	11501	631-547-5400	
Safe Bridge Solutions Inc 8401 Greenway Blvd Ste 100 — *Web:* www.safebridgeinc.com	Madison	WI	53562	608-442-0012	
Safe Passage International Inc 333 Metro Park — *Web:* www.safe-passage.com	Rochester	NY	14623	585-292-4910	
SafeNet Consulting Inc 5810 Baker Rd — *Web:* www.safenetconsulting.com	Minnetonka	MN	55345	952-930-3636	
SAFER Systems LLC 5284 Adolfo Rd Ste 100 — *Web:* www.safersystemv10.com	Camarillo	CA	93012	805-383-9711	
Sagarsoft Inc 78 Eastern Blvd — *Web:* www.sagarsoft.com	Glastonbury	CT	06033	860-633-2025	
Sage Computing Inc 11491 Sunset Hills Rd Ste 350 — *Web:* sagecomputing.com	Reston	VA	20190	703-742-7881	
Sage Data Security LLC 2275 Congress St — *Web:* www.sagedatasecurity.com	Portland	ME	04102	207-879-7243	
Sage Microsystems Inc 18 N Village Ave — *Web:* www.sagemicrosystems.com	Exton	PA	19341	610-524-1300	
SageLogix Inc 9100 E Panorama Dr Ste 100 — *Web:* www.sagelogix.com	Englewood	CO	80112	303-925-0100	
Sales Simplicity Software 325 E Elliot Rd — *Web:* www.salessimplicity.net	Chandler	AZ	85225	480-892-2500	
Salford Systems Inc 9685 Via Excelencia Ste 208 — *Web:* www.salford-systems.com	San Diego	CA	92126	619-543-8880	
Saltech Systems Inc 137 Lynn Ave Ste 200 — *Web:* www.saltechsystems.com	Ames	IA	50014	515-598-4347	
SAMSA Inc 5560 Gratiot Ste D — *Web:* www.samsa.com	Saginaw	MI	48638	989-790-0507	
SAP America Inc 1721 Moon Lake Blvd Ste 300 — *TF:* 800-872-1727 ■ *Web:* www.sap.com	Hoffman Estates	IL	60169	847-230-3800	230-3801
SAPIEN Technologies Inc 841 Latour Court Ste D — *Web:* www.sapien.com	Napa	CA	94558	707-252-8700	
Satcom Direct Inc 1901 Hwy A1A — *Web:* www.satcomdirect.com	Satellite Beach	FL	32937	321-777-3000	
Satcom Resources LLC 101 Eagle Rd Bldg 7 — *Web:* www.satcomresources.com	Avon	CO	81620	970-748-3094	
Satmetrix Systems Inc 1100 Pk Pl — **Fax Area Code: 415* ■ *TF:* 888-800-2313 ■ *Web:* www.satmetrix.com	San Mateo	CA	94403	650-227-8300	618-3421*
Satori Solutions 10901 W Toller Dr Ste 110 — *Web:* www.satorisolutions.com	Littleton	CO	80127	303-215-1921	
Satuit Technologies Inc 100 Grossman Dr — *Web:* satuit.com	Braintree	MA	02184	781-871-7788	
Saturn Systems Inc 314 W Superior St Ste 1015 — *Web:* www.saturnsys.com	Duluth	MN	55802	218-623-7200	
Saylent Technologies Inc 122 Grove St Ste 300 — *Web:* www.saylent.com	Franklin	MA	02038	508-570-2161	
Scadaware Inc 1602 Rhodes Ln — *Web:* www.scadaware.com	Bloomington	IL	61704	309-665-0135	
Scala Inc 350 Eagleview Blvd Ste 350 — *Web:* www.scala.com	Exton	PA	19341	610-363-3350	
Scalability Experts Inc 1203 Crestside Dr — *Web:* www.scalabilityexperts.com	Coppell	TX	75019	469-635-6200	
Scalar Decisions Inc 280 King St E Fourth Fl — *Web:* www.scalar.ca	Toronto	ON	M5A1K7	416-202-0020	
ScaleMP Inc 2175 Lemoine Ave Ste 401 — *Web:* www.scalemp.com	Fort Lee	NJ	07024	201-429-9740	
ScheduleSoft Corp 455 Science Dr Ste 250 — *Web:* www.schedulesoft.com	Madison	WI	53711	608-662-7601	
Schedulicity Inc 424 E Main Ste 201 — *Web:* www.schedulicity.com	Bozeman	MT	59715	406-582-0494	
ScholarOne Inc 375 Greenbrier Dr Ste 200 — *Web:* www.scholarone.com	Charlottesville	VA	22901	434-964-4000	
School Webmasters 2846 E Nora St — *Web:* www.schoolwebmasters.com	Mesa	AZ	85213	602-750-4556	
SchoolCity Inc 2900 Lakeside Dr Ste 270 — *Web:* www.schoolcity.com	Santa Clara	CA	95054	650-934-6123	
Scicom Infrastructure Services Inc 2250 N Druid Hills Rd Ne Ste 238 — *Web:* www.scicominfra.com	Atlanta	GA	30329	404-636-9882	
SDK Software Inc 11320 86th Ave N — *Web:* www.sdksoft.com	Maple Grove	MN	55369	763-657-7272	
SDN Global Inc 11101 Nations Ford Rd — *Web:* www.sdnglobal.com	Pineville	NC	28241	704-588-2233	
Seacoast Laboratory Data Systems Inc 195 New Hampshire Ave Ste 140 — *Web:* www.sldsi.com	Portsmouth	NH	03801	603-431-4114	
SearchSoft Solutions Inc 47 S Meridian St — *Web:* www.searchsoft.net	Indianapolis	IN	46204	317-488-5240	
Second Opinion Software LLC 3830 Del Amo Blvd 101 — *Web:* www.2opinion.com	Torrance	CA	90503	310-538-2800	
SEDONA Corp 1003 W Ninth Ave Second Fl — *Web:* www.sedonacorp.com	King Of Prussia	PA	19406	610-337-8400	
Seilevel Inc 3410 Far W Blvd — *Web:* www.seilevel.com	Austin	TX	78731	512-527-9952	
Selbysoft Inc 8326 Woodland Ave E — *Web:* www.selbysoft.com	Puyallup	WA	98371	253-770-2993	
Selltis LLC 3500 Hwy 190 Ste 200 — *Web:* www.selltis.com	Mandeville	LA	70471	985-727-3455	
Selsoft Inc 1303 Wheatberry Ln — *Web:* www.selsoftinc.com	Allen	TX	75002	217-721-3186	
Senscio Systems Inc 1740 Massachusetts Ave — *Web:* www.senssiosystems.com	Boxborough	MA	01719	978-635-9090	
ServerLogic Corp 2800 Northup Way Ste 120 — *Web:* www.serverlogic.com	Bellevue	WA	98004	425-803-0378	
Service Objects Inc 133 E de la Guerra St Ste 10 — *Web:* www.serviceobjects.com	Santa Barbara	CA	93101	805-963-1700	
Shadow-soft LLC 185 Wentworth Ter — *Web:* www.shadow-soft.com	Alpharetta	GA	30022	770-740-8030	
shared logic group inc, The 6904 Spring Vly Dr Ste 305 — *Web:* www.sharedlogic.com	Holland	OH	43528	419-865-0083	
Shasta Qa 1538 Market St — *Web:* www.shastaqa.com	Redding	CA	96001	530-242-5799	
Shaw Systems Assoc Inc 6200 Savoy Dr Ste 600 — *Web:* www.shawsystems.com	Houston	TX	77036	713-782-7730	782-4158
Shelby Systems Inc 7345 Goodlett Farms Pkwy — *Web:* www.shelbysystems.com	Cordova	TN	38016	901-757-2372	
Sherrill-Lubinski Corp 240 Tamal Vista Blvd — *Web:* www.sl.com	Corte Madera	CA	94925	415-927-8400	
Shoreland Inc 933 N Mayfair Rd Ste 208 — *Web:* www.shoreland.com	Milwaukee	WI	53226	414-290-1900	
Sibble Computer Consulting 1720 Venables St — *Web:* pdscc.com	Vancouver	BC	V5L2H4	604-739-3709	
Sigma Systems Canada Inc 55 York St Ste 1100 — *Web:* www.sigma-systems.com	Toronto	ON	M5J1R7	416-943-9696	
Signiant Inc 152 Middlesex Tpke — *Web:* www.signiant.com	Burlington	MA	01803	781-221-4000	
Signifi Solutions Inc 2100 Matheson Blvd E Ste 100 — *Web:* www.signifi.com	Mississauga	ON	L4W5E1	905-602-7707	
Silanis Technology Inc 8200 Decarie Blvd Third Fl — *Web:* www.silanis.com	Montreal	QC	H4P2P5	514-337-5255	
Silk Software Corp 2522 Chambers Rd Ste 101 — *Web:* www.silksoftware.com	Tustin	CA	92780	714-697-0733	
Silver Oven Studios Inc 953 Islington St — *Web:* www.silveroven.com	Portsmouth	NH	03801	603-570-7300	
Silver Screen Tele-Reality Inc 4144 N Central Expy — *Web:* www.sister.tv	Dallas	TX	75204	972-855-3500	
Simba Technologies Inc 938 W Eigth Ave — *Web:* www.simba.com	Vancouver	BC	V5Z1E5	604-633-0008	
Simcrest Inc 700 Central Expy Ste 310 — *Web:* www.simcrest.com	Allen	TX	75013	214-644-4000	
Simoncomputing Inc 5350 Shawnee Rd Ste 200 — *Web:* simoncomputing.com	Alexandria	VA	22312	703-914-5454	
Simplesoft Inc 257 Castro St Ste 220 — *Web:* www.smplsft.com	Mountain View	CA	94041	650-965-4515	
Sirsi Corp 3300 N Ashton Blvd Ste 500 — *TF:* 800-288-8020 ■ *Web:* www.sirsidynix.com	Lehi	UT	84043	800-288-8020	

Company	City	State	ZIP	Phone	Fax
SiTime Corp 990 Almanor Ave *Web:* www.sitime.com	Sunnyvale	CA	94085	408-328-4400	
Skybox Security Inc 2099 Gateway Pl Ste 450 *Web:* www.skyboxsecurity.com	San Jose	CA	95110	408-441-8060	
Skyline Technologies Inc 1400 Lombardi Ave *Web:* skylinetechnologies.com	Green Bay	WI	54304	920-437-1360	
SmartBen Inc 576 Sigman Rd Ste 100 *Web:* www.smartben.net	Conyers	GA	30013	678-413-0005	
SmarterTools Inc 1903 W Parkside Ln Ste 106 *Web:* www.smartertools.com	Phoenix	AZ	85027	623-434-8050	
Smartronix Inc 44150 Smartronix Way *TF:* 866-442-7767 ■ *Web:* www.smartronix.com	Hollywood	MD	20636	301-373-6000	373-7171
SMD Software Inc 3000 Highwoods Blvd *Web:* www.smdsoftware.com	Raleigh	NC	27604	919-865-0789	
Smooth Fusion Inc 5502 58th St Ste 200 *Web:* www.smoothfusion.com	Lubbock	TX	79414	806-771-3873	
Soft Science 17515 Chatham Way Dr *Web:* softscience.com	Houston	TX	77084	281-861-0832	
Softchalk LLC 22 S Auburn Ave *TF:* 877-638-2425 ■ *Web:* softchalk.com	Richmond	VA	23221	877-638-2425	
Softdocs Inc 920 Hemlock Dr *Web:* www.softdocs.com	Columbia	SC	29201	803-695-6044	
Softech Inc 28104 Orchard Lk Rd Ste 100 *Web:* dentech.com	Farmington Hills	MI	48334	248-855-6130	
Softek Service Inc 1101 14th St Nw Ste 850 *Web:* www.softekdc.com	Washington	DC	20005	202-747-5000	
Softeq Development Corp 14027 Memorial Dr Ste 302 *Web:* www.softeq.com	Houston	TX	77079	713-827-2228	
Softerware Inc 132 Welsh Rd Ste 140 *TF:* 800-220-8111 ■ *Web:* www.softerware.com	Horsham	PA	19044	215-628-0400	628-0585
Softman Products LLC 13470 Washington Blvd *Web:* www.buycheapsoftware.com	Marina Del Rey	CA	90292	310-305-3644	
Softplan Systems Inc 8118 Isabella Ln *Web:* www.softplan.com	Brentwood	TN	37027	615-370-1121	
Softplc Corp 25603 Red Brangus Rd *Web:* www.softplc.com	Spicewood	TX	78669	512-264-8390	
Softrisc Communication Solutions Inc 575 N Pastoria Ave *Web:* www.softrisc.com	Sunnyvale	CA	94085	408-333-9775	
SoftSol Resources Inc 46755 Fremont Blvd *Web:* www.softsol.net	Fremont	CA	94538	510-824-2000	
Softtec Inc 621 Wall St *Web:* host.softtec.com	Sevierville	TN	37862	865-428-2209	
Software & Services of Louisiana LLC 1120 S Pointe Pkwy *Web:* softwareservices.net	Shreveport	LA	71105	318-865-1505	
Software Management Inc 250 Mount Lebanon Blvd Ste 417 *Web:* www.softwaremgt.com	Pittsburgh	PA	15234	412-254-9000	
Software Methods Inc 770 E Market St *Web:* www.software-methods.com	West Chester	PA	19382	610-430-8956	
Software Professionals Inc 1029 Long Prairie Rd Ste A *Web:* www.spius.net	Flower Mound	TX	75022	972-518-0198	
Software Toolbox 148 E Charles St *Web:* www.softwaretoolbox.com	Matthews	NC	28105	704-849-2773	
Sohum Inc 2931 Tahoe Way *Web:* www.sohum.biz	San Jose	CA	95125	408-265-2391	
Solai & Cameron Inc 2335 N Southport Ave *Web:* www.solcam.com	Chicago	IL	60614	773-506-2720	
Soleratec LLC 2430 Auto Park Way Ste 205 *Web:* www.soleratec.com	Escondido	CA	92029	760-743-7200	
Solers Inc 950 N Glebe Rd Ste 1100 *Web:* www.solers.com	Arlington	VA	22203	703-526-0001	908-9353
Soliant Consulting Inc 14 N Peoria St 2H *Web:* www.soliantconsulting.com	Chicago	IL	60607	312-850-3830	
Solix Technologies Inc 4701 Patrick Henry Dr Bldg 20 *Web:* www.solix.com	Santa Clara	CA	95054	408-654-6400	
Solutions Development Corp 12220 Charles St *Web:* www.sdc-world.com	La Plata	MD	20646	301-638-3040	
Sonatype Inc 12501 Prosperity Dr Ste 350 *Web:* www.sonatype.com	Silver Spring	MD	20904	301-684-8080	
Soniya Technology International 3130 De La Cruz Blvd Ste 101 *Web:* www.soniyatech.com	Santa Clara	CA	95054	408-988-7719	
Sonoma Wire Works 101 First St Ste 587 *Web:* www.sonomawireworks.com	Los Altos	CA	94022	650-948-2003	
Sophisticated Business Systems Inc 6600 LBJ Fwy Ste 210 *Web:* www.ateras.com	Dallas	TX	75240	972-664-9005	
Sotech Inc 12011 Guilford Rd *Web:* ultra-sotech.com	Annapolis Junction	MD	20701	301-470-7015	
Source Photonics Inc 20550 Nordhoff St *Web:* www.sourcephotonics.com	Chatsworth	CA	91311	818-773-9044	
South River Technologies Inc 127 Lubrano Dr Ste 202 *Web:* www.southrivertech.com	Annapolis	MD	21401	410-266-0667	
Southeast Computer Solutions Inc 15165 Nw 77th Ave Ste 2009 *Web:* www.southeastcomputers.com	Hialeah	FL	33014	305-556-4697	
Southern Software Inc 150 Perry Dr *Web:* southernsoftware.com	Southern Pines	NC	28387	910-695-0005	
Space Ground System Solutions Inc 4343 Fortune Pl Ste C *Web:* www.sgss.com	Melbourne	FL	32904	321-956-8200	
SPARC LLC 2387 Clements Ferry Rd *Web:* www.sparcedge.com	Charleston	SC	29492	843-471-1231	
Sparta Systems Inc Holmdel Corporate Plz 2137 Hwy 35 *TF:* 888-261-5948 ■ *Web:* www.spartasystems.com	Holmdel	NJ	07733	732-203-0400	203-0375
Spartan Technology Solutions Inc 125 Venture Blvd Ste B *Web:* www.spartantechnology.com	Spartanburg	SC	29306	864-587-1386	
Spoken Translation Inc 1100 W View Dr *Web:* www.spokentranslation.com	Berkeley	CA	94705	510-843-9900	
Spud Software Inc 9468 S Saginaw Rd *Web:* www.spudsoftware.com	Grand Blanc	MI	48439	810-695-0001	
Sql Data Solutions Inc 43 Herkomer St *Web:* www.sqldatasolutionsinc.com	New Hyde Park	NY	11040	516-358-1998	
Square Root Inc 508 Oakland Ave *Web:* www.square-root.com	Austin	TX	78703	512-693-9232	
Squarei Technologies Inc 1315 Oakridge Dr Ste 100 *Web:* www.squarei.com	Fort Collins	CO	80525	970-377-0077	
SSI Group Inc, The 4721 Morrison Dr Ste 100 *Web:* www.thessigroup.com	Mobile	AL	36609	251-345-0000	
Stackframe LLC 114 W First St Ste 246 *Web:* www.stackframe.com	Sanford	FL	32771	407-321-1333	
Stantive Technologies Group Inc Four Cataraqui St Ste 100 *Web:* www.stantive.com	Kingston	ON	K7K1Z7	613-887-2647	
StayinFront Inc 107 Little Falls Rd *Web:* stayinfront.com	Fairfield	NJ	07004	973-461-4800	
Steadmantech 1153 Powderhouse Rd *TF:* 866-772-0882 ■ *Web:* www.steadmantech.com	Vestal	NY	13850	866-772-0882	
Stellar Systems Inc 222 Ne Monroe St *Web:* www.ssinet.com	Peoria	IL	61602	309-677-7350	
Stenograph LLC 1500 Bishop Ct *TF:* 800-323-4247 ■ *Web:* www.stenograph.com	Mount Prospect	IL	60056	847-803-1400	803-1089
StepOne Systems LLC 2801 Liberty Ave Ste 200 *Web:* www.steponesystems.com	Pittsburgh	PA	15222	412-894-8698	
Sterling Resources Inc Six Forest Ave *Web:* sterlingnet.com	Paramus	NJ	07652	201-843-6444	
Stone Bond Technologies LP 1021 Main St Ste 1550 *Web:* www.stonebond.com	Houston	TX	77002	713-622-8798	
Stone Design Corp 2400 Rio Grande Blvd Nw *Web:* www.stone.com	Albuquerque	NM	87104	505-345-4800	
Stone Technologies Inc 550 Spirit of St Louis Blvd *Web:* www.stonetek.com	Chesterfield	MO	63005	636-530-7240	
Stonebranch Inc 950 N Point Pkwy Ste 200 *Web:* www.stonebranch.com	Alpharetta	GA	30005	678-366-7887	
Stoneware Inc 11555 N Meridian St Ste 150 *Web:* www.stone-ware.com	Carmel	IN	46032	317-669-8730	
Strafford Technology 1D Commons Dr *Web:* www.strafford.com	Londonderry	NH	03053	603-434-2550	
Strand Management Solutions 61 Princeton Hightstown Rd *Web:* www.strandmanagement.com	Princeton Junction	NJ	08550	609-799-7715	
Strata Decision Technology LLC 2001 S First St Ste 200 *Web:* www.stratadecision.com	Champaign	IL	61820	217-359-8422	
StreamBase Systems Inc 181 Spring St *Web:* www.streambase.com	Lexington	MA	02421	781-761-0800	
StreamServe Inc Three Van De Graaff Dr *Web:* www.streamserve.com	Burlington	MA	01803	781-863-1510	
StrikeIron Inc 15501 Weston Pkwy Ste 150 *Web:* www.strikeiron.com	Cary	NC	27513	919-467-4545	
Studsvik Scandpower Inc 1087 Beacon St Ste 301 *Web:* www.studsvik.com	Newton	MA	02459	617-965-7450	
Subsystem Technologies Inc 2121 Crystal Dr Ste 680 *Web:* www.subsystem.com	Arlington	VA	22202	703-841-0071	
Subx Inc 428 Fore St *Web:* www.quantrix.com	Portland	ME	04101	207-775-0808	
Success Sciences Inc 17838 N US Hwy 4 *Web:* www.success-sciences.com	Tampa	FL	33549	813-989-9900	
Sudjam 520 E Broadway Ste 202 *Web:* www.sudjam.com	Glendale	CA	91205	818-244-3778	
Summa Technologies Inc 925 Liberty Ave *Web:* summa-tech.com	Pittsburgh	PA	15222	412-258-3300	
Sunplus Data Group Inc 3781 Presidential Pkwy *Web:* www.sunplusdata.com	Atlanta	GA	30340	770-455-3264	
Support Group Inc, The 24 Prime Park Way *Web:* www.supportgroup.com	Natick	MA	01760	508-653-8400	
Sureit Solutions Inc 1801 W Queen Creek Rd Ste 3 *Web:* www.sureitinc.com	Chandler	AZ	85248	480-917-2000	
Surf Merchants 41 W St Fifth Fl *Web:* surfmerchants.com	Boston	MA	02111	617-292-8008	
Survey & Ballot Systems Inc 7653 Anagram Dr *Web:* www.surveyandballotsystems.com	Eden Prairie	MN	55344	952-974-2300	
Sutisoft Inc 4984 El Camino Real Ste 200 *Web:* www.sutisoft.com	Los Altos	CA	94022	650-969-7884	
Symitar Systems Inc 8985 Balboa Ave *Web:* www.symitar.com	San Diego	CA	92123	619-542-6700	
Synergy Business Solutions Inc 16250 SW Upper Boones Ferry Rd *Web:* www.synergybusiness.com	Portland	OR	97224	503-601-4100	
Synergy Development Consulting Inc 11510 Interchange Cir N *Web:* www.syndev.com	Miramar	FL	33025	305-652-5699	
Synre Voice Technologies Inc 200 Cochrane Dr *Web:* www.synrevoice.com	Markham	ON	L3R8E7	905-946-8500	

Phone Fax

Syntell Inc 2954 Boul Laurier Quebec QC G1V4T2 418-266-0900
Web: www.syntell.com

Sysintelli Inc 9466 Black Mtn Rd Ste 140 San Diego CA 92126 858-271-1600
Web: www.sysintelli.com

SysLogic Inc 375 Bishops Way Ste 105 Brookfield WI 53005 262-780-0380
Web: www.syslogicinc.com

System Concepts Inc 15900 N 78th St Scottsdale AZ 85260 480-951-8011
Web: www.foodtrak.com

Systems Application Engineering Inc
3655 Westcenter Dr Houston TX 77042 713-783-6020
Web: www.saesystems.com

Systems Engineering Technologies Corp
6121 Lincolnia Rd Ste 200 Alexandria VA 22312 703-941-7887
Web: www.sytechcorp.com

Systems Exchange Inc 26625 Carmel Ctr Pl Carmel CA 93923 831-649-3800
Web: www.tfdg.com

Systems Integration & Management Inc
2611 Jefferson Davis Hwy Arlington VA 22202 703-412-5068 412-5069
Web: www.simincsd.com

Systems Products & Solutions Inc (SPS)
307 Wynn Dr Huntsville AL 35805 256-319-2135
Web: www.services-sps.com

Systems Resource Management Inc
42 Valley Rd Middletown RI 02842 401-849-2913
Web: www.srminc.net

Systems Technology Group Inc
3155 W Big Beaver Rd Troy MI 48084 248-643-9010 643-9250
Web: www.stgit.com

Systemtec Inc 246 Stoneridge Dr Ste 301 Columbia SC 29210 803-806-8100
Web: systemtec.net

T.S.D. Inc 1620 Turnpike St N Andover MA 01845 978-794-1400
Web: tsdweb.com

Table Trac Inc 6101 Baker Rd Ste 206 Minnetonka MN 55345 952-548-8877
Web: www.tabletrac.com

TABLETmedia Inc 2468 Union St San Francisco CA 94123 415-567-8100
Web: www.tabletmedia.com

Talent Logic Inc 2313 Timber Shadows Kingwood TX 77339 281-358-1858
Web: talentlogic.com

Tallan Inc 175 Capital Blvd Ste 401 Rocky Hill CT 06067 860-633-3693 513-4870
TF: 800-677-3693 ■ *Web:* www.tallan.com

Tamlin Software Developers Inc
5646 Milton St Ste 540 Dallas TX 75206 214-739-6576
Web: www.tamlinsoftware.com

Tanager Inc
10010 Junction Dr Ste 120N Annapolis Junction MD 20701 240-547-3150
Web: www.tanagerinc.com

Tangent Systems Inc
2155 Stnngton Ave Hoffman Estates IL 60195 847-882-3833
Web: www.tangent-systems.com

Tangoe Inc 35 Executive Blvd Orange CT 06477 203-859-9300 859-9427
NASDAQ: TNGO ■ *TF:* 877-571-4737 ■ *Web:* www.tangoe.com

Tapestry Solutions Inc 5643 Copley Dr San Diego CA 92111 858-503-1990
Web: www.tapestrysolutions.com

Targeted Technologies LLC
1735 Hooper Ave Ste 2 Toms River NJ 08753 732-255-9005
Web: targtech.com

Tarigma Corp 6161 Busch Blvd Ste 110 Columbus OH 43229 614-436-3734
Web: www.tarigma.com

Tavant Technologies Inc
3101 Jay St Ste 101 Santa Clara CA 95054 408-519-5400
Web: www.tavant.com

Taylor Data Systems Inc 181 E Evans St Florence SC 29506 843-656-2084
Web: taylordata.com

TBS Communications Inc
1800 Peachtree St Ste 655 Atlanta GA 30309 404-876-6989
Web: www.coolbluei.com

TC Net-Works 23610 Mohican St NW St. Francis MN 55070 612-747-4357
Web: www.tcnet-works.com

Team Automation 2215 First St 104 Simi Valley CA 93065 805-522-3875
Web: www.teamautomation.com

Teamwork Solutions 5005 Horizons Dr Ste 200 Columbus OH 43220 614-457-7100
Web: www.teamsol.com

Tech Friends 1341 County Rd 759 Jonesboro AR 72401 870-933-6386
Web: mytechfriends.com

Tech Heads Inc 7060 SW Beveland Rd Tigard OR 97223 503-639-8542
Web: www.techeads.com

Tech Observer 375 Main St 201 Hackensack NJ 07601 201-489-7705
Web: www.tech-observer.com

Tech-X Corp 5621 Arapahoe Ave Ste A Boulder CO 80303 303-448-0727
Web: www.cusys.edu

TechFlow Inc 6405 Mira Mesa Blvd Ste 250 San Diego CA 92121 858-412-8000
Web: www.techflow.com

Techgene Solutions LLC 4545 Fuller Dr Ste 406 Irving TX 75038 972-580-0247
Web: techgene.com

Technical Differences
5256 S Mission Rd Ste 210 Bonsall CA 92003 760-941-5800
Web: www.people-trak.com

Technical Empowerment Inc 141 Nevada St El Segundo CA 90245 310-524-1700
Web: www.techempower.com

Technical Support Inc 11253 John Galt Blvd Omaha NE 68137 402-331-4977
Web: www.techsi.com

Technical Toolboxes Ltd 3801 Kirby Dr Ste 520 Houston TX 77098 713-630-0505
Web: www.ttoolboxes.com

Technosoft Corp 28411 NW Hwy Ste 640 Southfield MI 48034 248-603-2600 603-2599
Web: www.technosoftcorp.com

Technotraining Inc
328 Office Sq Ln Ste 202 Virginia Beach VA 23462 757-425-0728
Web: www.technotraining.net

Techone Inc 630 Alder Dr Ste 102 Milpitas CA 95035 408-894-8100
Web: www.techone.com

Techrecruiters Inc
675 N Brookfield Rd Ste 205 Brookfield WI 53045 262-781-0920
Web: techrecruiters.biz

Tecplot Inc 3535 Factoria Blvd SE Ste 550 Bellevue WA 98006 425-653-1200
Web: www.tecplot.com

Teksouth Corp 1420 Northbrook Dr Ste 220 Birmingham AL 35071 205-631-1500
Web: www.teksouth.com

Tel Tech Plus Inc 393 Enterprise St San Marcos CA 92078 760-510-1323
Web: www.ttp-us.com

Teldata Communications Inc
19211 Chennault Way Ste A Gaithersburg MD 20879 301-670-0122
Web: www.teldata.net

Telemanager Technologies Inc
211 Warren St Ste 409 Newark NJ 07103 973-679-7500
Web: www.pharmacyshopper.com

Telemessage Inc 468 Great Rd Ste 3 Acton MA 01720 978-263-1015
Web: www.telemessage.com

Telenav Inc 950 De Guigne Dr Sunnyvale CA 94085 408-245-3800
Web: telenav.com

Telenix Corp 9194 Red Branch Rd Columbia MD 21045 410-772-3275
Web: www.telenix.com

TeleSecurity Sciences Inc
7391 Prairie Falcon Rd Ste 150-B Las Vegas NV 89128 702-227-7327
Web: www.telesecuritysciences.com

TELESIS Corp 4700 Corridor Pl Ste D Beltsville MD 20705 240-241-5600
Web: www.telesishq.com

TeleVoice Inc
10497 Town & Country Way Ste 500 Houston TX 77024 281-497-8000
Web: televoice.com

Tell Systems Inc 106 Bridge Ave Bay Head NJ 08742 732-899-0202
Web: www.tellsystems.com

Telliant Systems LLC
3180 N Point Pkwy Ste 108 Alpharetta GA 30005 678-892-2801
Web: www.telliant.com

Telosa Software Inc 610 Cowper St Palo Alto CA 94301 650-853-1100
Web: www.telosa.com

Tempest Development Group Inc
8431 160 St Ste 103 Surrey BC V4N0V6 604-597-2846
Web: www.tempestdg.com

Tempest Technologies LLC
38 S Last Chance Gulch Ste 5a Helena MT 59601 406-495-8731
Web: tempest-av.com

Tenable Network Security Inc
7021 Columbia Gateway Dr Ste 500 Columbia MD 21046 410-872-0555
Web: www.tenable.com

Terasci Industries Inc
5362 Production Dr Huntington Beach CA 92649 714-896-0150
Web: www.terasci.com

TERiX Computer Service Inc
388 Oakmead Pkwy Sunnyvale CA 94085 408-737-1455
Web: www.terix.com

Terra Dotta LLC 501 W Franklin St Ste 105 Chapel Hill NC 27516 877-368-8277
TF: 877-368-8277 ■ *Web:* www.terradotta.com

Terracor Business Solutions
677 St Mary's Rd Winnipeg MB R2M3M6 204-477-5342
Web: terracor.ca

Terranova International 3675 Nordstrom Ln Lafayette CA 94549 925-299-6833
Web: www.terranova4mapping.com

TerraSim Inc
420 Ft Duquesne Blvd One Gateway Ctr
Ste 2050 Pittsburgh PA 15222 412-232-3646
Web: www.terrasim.com

Testware Associates Inc 21 E High St Somerville NJ 08876 908-526-2900
Web: www.testwareinc.com

Tetrad Computer Applications Ltd
1445 W Georgia St Vancouver BC V6G2T3 604-685-2295
Web: www.tetrad.com

TEXbase Inc 895 Technology Blvd Ste 202 Bozeman MT 59718 406-582-8874
Web: www.texbase.com

Thermoanalytics Inc 23440 Airpark Blvd Calumet MI 49913 906-482-9560
Web: www.thermoanalytics.com

Thermoflow Inc 29 Hudson Rd Sudbury MA 01776 978-579-7999
Web: www.thermoflow.com

Thinkmap Inc 599 Broadway Ninth Fl New York NY 10012 212-285-8600
Web: www.thinkmap.com

Third Pillar Systems Inc
Three Waters Park Dr Ste 100 San Mateo CA 94403 650-372-1200
Web: www.thirdpillar.com

Threespot Media LLC 3333 14th St NW Washington DC 20010 202-471-1000
Web: threespot.com

Tier1 Inc 2403 Sidney St Ste 225 Pittsburgh PA 15203 412-381-9201
Web: tier1inc.com

TIES 1667 Snelling Ave N St. Paul MN 55108 651-999-6000
Web: ties.k12.mn.us

Tietronix Software Inc
1331 Gemini Ave Ste 300 Houston TX 77058 281-461-9300
Web: www.tietronix.com

Tigerpaw Software Inc 2201 Thurston Cir Bellevue NE 68005 402-592-4544
Web: www.jamesfoxall.com

Tim Ivey Company Inc 1129 Riders Club Rd Onalaska WI 54650 608-738-8066
Web: timivey.com

Timberline Interactive Inc
Five Park St Ste 2 Middlebury VT 05753 802-388-8377
Web: www.timberlineinteractive.com

Time & Cents Consultants LLC
320 Flintlock Rd Southport CT 06890 203-254-7736
Web: www.timeandcents.com

Time Trak Systems Inc 933 Pine Grove Port Huron MI 48060 810-984-1313
Web: timetrak.com

TimeTECH Canada Inc
7420 Airport Rd Ste 101 Mississauga ON L4T4E5 905-677-7009
Web: www.synerion.com

Timeware Inc 9329 Ravenna Rd Ste D Twinsburg OH 44087 330-963-2700
Web: www.timewareinc.com

Tips Inc 2402 Williams Dr Georgetown TX 78628 512-863-3653 863-5392
Web: tipsweb.com

Company	City	State	Zip	Phone	Fax
Titan Lenders Corp 5353 W Dartmouth Ave Ste 50 *TF:* 866-412-9180 ■ *Web:* www.titanlenderscorp.com	Denver	CO	80227	866-412-9180	
TIW Technology Inc 769 Youngs Hill Rd *Web:* www.tiwcorp.com	Easton	PA	18040	610-258-5161	
Tizbi Inc 800 Saint Mary's St Ste 402 *TF:* 888-729-0951 ■ *Web:* www.tizbi.com	Raleigh	NC	27605	888-729-0951	
Today's Business Computers 213 E Black Horse Pk *Web:* www.tbcusa.com	Pleasantville	NJ	08232	609-645-5132	
Tom Sawyer Software Corp 1997 El Dorado Ave *Web:* www.tomsawyer.com	Berkeley	CA	94707	510-208-4370	
Tone Software Inc 1735 S Brookhurst St *Web:* www.tonesoft.com	Anaheim	CA	92804	714-991-9460	
TopCoder Inc 95 Glastonbury Blvd *TF:* 866-867-2633 ■ *Web:* www.topcoder.com	Glastonbury	CT	06033	860-633-5540	657-4276
Torrid Technologies Inc 1860 Sandy Plains Rd Ste 204-129 *Web:* www.torrid-tech.com	Marietta	GA	30066	770-565-6405	
Total Cad Systems Inc 480 N Sam Houston Pkwy E Ste 234 *Web:* www.tcadsys.com	Houston	TX	77060	281-445-6161	
Total Computing Solutions of America Inc 23430 Hawthorne Blvd Skypark Office Ctr Bldg 3 Ste 300 *Web:* www.tcsamerica.com	Torrance	CA	90505	310-378-9100	
Total Solutions Inc 238 Business Park Blvd Ste G *Web:* www.totalsolutions-inc.com	Madison	AL	35758	256-721-3987	
Touch Networks 2515 152nd Ave Ne *Web:* touchnetworks.com	Redmond	WA	98052	425-881-8806	
Towerstrides Inc 4229 Lafayette Ctr Dr Ste 1200 *Web:* www.towerstrides.com	Chantilly	VA	20151	703-953-1531	
Towerwall 615 Concord St *Web:* www.towerwall.com	Framingham	MA	01702	774-204-0700	
TrackAbout Inc 410 Rouser Rd Ste 400 *Web:* corp.trackabout.com	Moon Township	PA	15108	412-269-1872	
Tracorp Inc 5621 W Beverly Ln *Web:* www.tracorp.com	Glendale	AZ	85306	602-864-1385	
Trade Manage Capital Inc 299 Market St Fourth Fl *Web:* www.yamner.com	Saddle Brook	NJ	07663	201-587-2424	
Transcendent LLC 1040 Cottonwood Ave Ste 300 *Web:* transcendent-llc.com	Hartland	WI	53029	262-953-2750	
TransGaming Inc 431 King St W Ste 600 *Web:* www.transgaming.com	Toronto	ON	M5V1K4	416-979-9900	
Transpara Corp 865 Piemonte Dr Ste 100 *Web:* www.transpara.com	Pleasanton	CA	94566	925-218-6983	
Transzap Inc 633 17th St Ste 2000 *Web:* www.transzap.com	Denver	CO	80202	303-863-8600	
Traveling Computers Inc 210 E Main St *Web:* www.tcinc.net	Riverton	WY	82501	307-856-8676	
Treehouse Software Inc 2605 Nicholson Rd Ste 230 *Web:* www.treehouse.com	Sewickley	PA	15143	724-759-7070	
TRG Networking 11436 Cronhill Dr Ste 4B *Web:* www.trgnetworking.com	Owings Mills	MD	21117	410-363-6980	
Tri-star Data Systems Inc 650 Sentry Pkwy Ste 1 *Web:* tristardatasystems.com	Blue Bell	PA	19422	610-941-2116	
Triad Interactive Inc 1100 H St Nw Ste 1201 *Web:* www.triadinteractive.com	Washington	DC	20036	202-347-0900	347-0930
Triangle MicroWorks Inc 2840 Plz Pl Ste 205 *Web:* www.trianglemicroworks.com	Raleigh	NC	27612	919-870-5101	
Triforce Consulting Svc Inc 650 N Cannon Ave *Web:* triforce-inc.com	Lansdale	PA	19446	215-362-2611	
Trifox Inc 3131 S Bascom Ave *Web:* www.trifox.com	Campbell	CA	95008	408-369-2300	
Trigyn Technologies Inc 100 Metroplex Dr Ste 101 *Web:* www.trigyn.com	Edison	NJ	08817	732-777-0050	
Trilog Group Inc 54 Cummings Park *Web:* www.triloggroup.com	Woburn	MA	01801	781-937-9963	
Triple Point Technology Inc 301 Riverside Ave *Web:* www.tpt.com	Westport	CT	06880	203-291-7979	291-7977
Triware Technologies Inc 76 Brookfield Rd *Web:* www.triware.ca	St John's	NL	A1E3T9	709-579-5000	
Trix Systems Inc 68 Smith St *Web:* www.trixsystems.com	Chelmsford	MA	01824	978-256-4445	
TriZetto Corporation 501 N Broadway 3rd Fl *TF:* 800-969-3666 ■ *Web:* www.trizettoprovider.com	Sacramento	CA	95814	800-969-3666	
Tropics Software Technologies Inc One S School Ave *Web:* www.gotropics.com	Sarasota	FL	34237	941-955-1234	
Truckers Helper LLC, The 630 S Wickham Rd Ste 203 *Web:* www.truckershelper.com	Melbourne	FL	32904	321-956-7331	
True Solutions Inc 5001 Lyndon B Johnson Fwy Ste 125 *Web:* www.truesolutions.com	Dallas	TX	75244	972-770-0900	
Truepoint Solutions LLC 5714 Folsom Blvd Ste 236 *Web:* www.truepointsolutions.com	Sacramento	CA	95819	916-600-4993	
Trusant Technologies LLC 6011 University Blvd *Web:* trusant.com	Ellicott City	MD	21043	410-418-5400	
Trusted Integration Inc 525 Wythe St *Web:* www.trustedintegration.com	Alexandria	VA	22314	703-299-9171	
Trutek 1740 S Main St *Web:* www.trutek.com	Salt Lake City	UT	84115	801-486-6655	
Truven Holding Corp 777 E Eisenhower Pkwy *Web:* www.truvenhealth.com	Ann Arbor	MI	48108	734-913-3000	
Tsa-advet 4722 Campbells Run Rd *Web:* www.tsa.advet.com	Pittsburgh	PA	15205	412-787-0980	
TTG Systems Inc 12310 105 Ave Nw Ste 200 *Web:* www.ttg-inc.com	Edmonton	AB	T5N0Y4	780-462-6365	
Tucson Embedded Systems Inc 5620 N Kolb Rd *Web:* tucsonembedded.com	Tucson	AZ	85750	520-575-7283	575-5563
Turner Consulting Group Inc 306 Florida Ave NW *Web:* www.tcg.com	Washington	DC	20001	202-986-5533	
Twin Oaks Software Development Inc 1463 Berlin Tpke *Web:* www.healthclubsoftware.com	Berlin	CT	06037	860-829-6000	
Twin State Technical Services Ltd 3543 E Kimberly Rd *Web:* www.tsts.com	Davenport	IA	52807	563-441-1504	
Twinstar Inc 8703 Yates Dr Ste 115 *Web:* www.twinstarinc.net	Westminster	CO	80031	303-430-7101	
Tympani LLC 2001 Butterfield Rd Ste 250 *Web:* www.tympani.net	Downers Grove	IL	60515	630-981-5000	
Ultra Electronics Advanced Tactical Systems Inc 4101 Smith School Rd *Web:* www.ultra-ats.com	Austin	TX	78744	512-327-6795	327-8043
Unicentric Inc 3127 Penn Ave *Web:* www.unicentric.com	Pittsburgh	PA	15201	412-697-7200	
Unimax Systems Corporation Inc 430 First Ave N Ste 790 *Web:* www.unimax.com	Minneapolis	MN	55401	612-341-0946	
Union Street Media 444 S Union St Ste 360 *Web:* unionstreetmedia.com	Burlington	VT	05401	802-865-3332	
Unique Business Systems Corp 2901 Ocean Park Blvd # 215 *Web:* www.unibiz.com	Santa Monica	CA	90405	310-396-3929	
United e r p LLC 235 Closter Dock Rd *Web:* www.unitederp.com	Closter	NJ	07624	201-567-6315	
United Systems & Software Inc 300 Colonial Ctr Pkwy Ste 150 PO Box 958444 *TF:* 800-522-8774 ■ *Web:* www.ussincorp.com	Lake Mary	FL	32746	407-875-2120	875-9600
Unity Technologies Inc 795 Folsom St Ste 200 *Web:* unity3d.com	San Francisco	CA	94107	415-539-3162	
Univeris Corp 111 George St Third Fl *Web:* www.univeris.com	Toronto	ON	M5A2N4	416-979-3700	
Unleaded Software Inc 2314 Broadway Unit B *Web:* www.unleadedsoftware.com	Denver	CO	80205	720-221-7126	
Unleashed Technologies 10005 Old Columbia Rd Ste L-261 *Web:* www.unleashed-technologies.com	Columbia	MD	21046	410-864-8980	
Unlimi-Tech Software Inc 1725 St Laurent Blvd Ste 205 *Web:* www.utechsoft.com	Ottawa	ON	K1G3V4	613-667-2439	
Unlimited Innovations Inc 180 N Riverview Dr Ste 320 *Web:* www.uius.com	Anaheim Hills	CA	92808	714-998-0866	
Untangle Inc 100 W San Fernando St Ste 565 *Web:* www.metavize.com	San Jose	CA	95113	408-598-4299	
Upperspace Corp 600 SE 49th St *Web:* www.upperspace.com	Pryor	OK	74361	918-825-4844	
Us Biomedical Information Systems Inc 408 W University Ave Ste 301 *Web:* www.usbmis.com	Gainesville	FL	32601	352-376-0587	
US Networx Inc 6360 I 55 N Ste 310 *Web:* www.usnx.com	Jackson	MS	39211	601-956-4770	
USA Digital Solutions Inc 10835 N 25th Ave Ste 350 *Web:* digisolaz.com	Phoenix	AZ	85029	602-866-8199	
Usmax Corp 382 Gambrills Rd *Web:* www.usmax.com	Gambrills	MD	21054	301-912-1166	
Utilant LLC 475 Ellicott St Ste 5 *Web:* utilant.com	Buffalo	NY	14203	716-923-7440	
V2Soft Inc 300 Enterprise Ct Ste 100 *Web:* www.v2soft.com	Bloomfield Hills	MI	48302	248-904-1700	
Valco Data Systems Inc N57 W13652 Reichert Ave *Web:* valcodata.com	Menomonee Falls	WI	53051	262-781-7731	
Valid8 .com Inc 500 W Cummings Park Ste 6550 *Web:* valid8.com	Woburn	MA	01801	781-938-1221	
Valley Agricultural Software Inc 3950 S K St *Web:* www.vas.com	Tulare	CA	93274	559-686-9496	
Valley Scale Company LLC 751 W Kenwood Ave *Web:* www.thinkvsc.com	Clarksville	IN	47129	812-282-5269	
Valogix Inc 27 Division St Ste 2 *Web:* www.valogix.com	Saratoga Springs	NY	12866	518-450-0309	
ValueCheck Inc 8822 Ridgeline Blvd Ste 100 *Web:* www.valuecheckonline.com	Highlands Ranch	CO	80129	720-283-0737	
ValuSource LLC 4575 Galley Rd Ste 200E *Web:* www.valusourcesoftware.com	Colorado Springs	CO	80915	719-548-4900	
Varden Technologies Inc 77 Franklin St Seventh Fl *Web:* www.vardentech.com	Boston	MA	02110	617-482-5902	
Varen Technologies Inc 9801 Broken Land Pkwy Ste 100 *Web:* www.varentech.com	Columbia	MD	21046	410-290-8008	
Varite Inc 12 S First St Ste 404 *Web:* www.varite.com	San Jose	CA	95113	408-977-0700	
Vecna Technologies Inc 6404 Ivy Ln Ste 500 *Web:* www.vecna.com	Greenbelt	MD	20770	240-965-4500	

Company / Address	City	State	ZIP	Phone	Fax
Vector Consulting 6455 E Johns Crossing *Web:* vectorconsulting.com	Duluth	GA	30097	770-246-0968	
Vector Planning & Services Inc 591 Camino De La Reina Ste 300 *Web:* myvpsi.com	San Diego	CA	92108	619-297-5656	
Vector Software Inc 1351 S County Trl Ste 310 *Web:* www.vectorcast.com	East Greenwich	RI	02818	401-398-7185	
VectorMAX Corp Four Dubon Ct *Web:* www.vectormax.com	Farmingdale	NY	11735	212-937-7706	
Vektrex Electronic Systems Inc 10225 Barnes Canyon Rd *Web:* www.vektrex.com	San Diego	CA	92121	858-558-8282	
Vensiti Inc 1304 W Walnut Hill Ln *Web:* www.vensiti.com	Irving	TX	75038	972-580-7995	
Verecloud Inc 555 Eldorado Blvd Ste 200 *TF:* 877-300-2158 ■ *Web:* www.verecloud.com	Broomfield	CO	80021	877-300-2158	
Verican Inc One Hallidie Plz Ste 404 *Web:* www.verican.com	San Francisco	CA	94102	415-296-7300	
Veridikal Inc 1541 E Hope St *Web:* www.veridikal.com	Mesa	AZ	85203	480-636-1830	
Verisource Services Inc 13201 Northwest Fwy Ste 402 *Web:* www.verisource.com	Houston	TX	77040	713-647-6540	
Verisurf Software Inc 1553 N Harmony Cir *Web:* www.verisurf.com	Anaheim	CA	92807	714-970-1683	
Veritas Medicine Inc 11 Cambridge Ctr *Web:* www.veritasmedicine.com	Cambridge	MA	02142	617-234-1500	
Verix Inc 339 S San Antonio Rd Ste 2G *Web:* www.verix.com	Los Altos	CA	94022	650-691-2700	
Veros Real Estate Solutions LLC 2333 N Broadway Ste 350 *Web:* www.veros.com	Santa Ana	CA	92706	714-415-6300	
Versonix Corp 1175 Saratoga Ave Ste 4 *Web:* versonix.com	San Jose	CA	95129	408-873-3131	
Vertex Software Corp 1515 S Cptl Of Tx Hwy 4 *Web:* www.vertex.com	Austin	TX	78746	512-328-3700	
Vertical Management Systems Inc Seven N Fair Oaks Ave Second Fl *TF:* 800-867-4357 ■ *Web:* www.vmshelp.com	Pasadena	CA	91103	800-867-4357	
Vertical Systems Inc 6500 City W Pkwy Ste 101 *Web:* www.vertsys.com	Eden Prairie	MN	55344	952-934-7533	
Viatron Systems Inc 18233 S Hoover St *Web:* www.viatron.com	Gardena	CA	90248	310-502-6004	
Vibration Research Corp 2385 Wilshere Dr # A *Web:* www.vibrationresearch.com	Jenison	MI	49428	616-669-3028	
VideoMining Corp 403 S Allen St Ste 101 *TF:* 800-898-9950 ■ *Web:* www.videomining.com	State College	PA	16801	800-898-9950	
Viget Labs LLC 400 S Maple Ave *Web:* viget.com	Falls Church	VA	22046	703-891-0670	
VirnetX Holding Corp 308 Dorla Court Ste 206 *Web:* virnetx.com	Zephyr Cove	NV	89448	831-438-8200	
Virtual Training Company Inc 5395 Main St *Web:* www.vtc.com	Stephens City	VA	22655	540-869-8686	
Viscira LLC 200 Vallejo St *Web:* www.viscira.com	San Francisco	CA	94111	415-848-8010	
Visibility Corp 200 Minuteman Rd *Web:* www.visibility.com	Andover	MA	01810	978-269-6500	269-6501
Vision Multimedia Technologies LLC 800 Wyman Park Dr *Web:* www.vmtllc.com	Baltimore	MD	21211	410-889-7770	
Vision Technologies Inc 530 McCormick Dr Ste G *TF:* 866-746-1122 ■ *Web:* www.visiontechnologiesinc.net	Glen Burnie	MD	21061	410-424-2183	424-2208
Visionary Legal Technologies LP 14677 Midway Rd Ste 118 *Web:* www.visionarylegaltechnologies.com	Addison	TX	75001	214-370-4359	
Visionsoft International Inc 1842 Old Norcross Rd Ste 100 *Web:* www.vsiiusa.com	Lawrenceville	GA	30044	770-682-2899	
Vistar Technologies Corp 11924 Forest Hill Blvd Ste 22-127 *Web:* vistartech.com	Wellington	FL	33414	561-792-6644	
Vistrian Inc 562 Valley Way *Web:* www.vistrian.com	Milpitas	CA	95035	408-719-0500	
Visual Learning Systems Inc PO Box 8226 *TF:* 866-968-7857 ■ *Web:* www.vls-inc.com	Missoula	MT	59807	866-968-7857	
Visual Purple LLC 75 Higuera St Ste 240 *Web:* www.visualpurple.com	San Luis Obispo	CA	93401	805-595-7579	
Visual Risk Technology 210 25th Ave N Ste 910 *Web:* www.vrisk.com	Nashville	TN	37203	615-321-4848	
Visualware Inc 937 Sierra Dr *Web:* www.visualware.com	Turlock	CA	95380	209-668-3673	
Vitech Corp 2270 Kraft Dr Ste 1600 *Web:* www.vitechcorp.com	Blacksburg	VA	24060	540-951-3322	
Vivox Inc 2-4 Mercer Rd *Web:* www.vivox.com	Natick	MA	01760	508-650-3571	
Vocera Communications Inc 525 RACE St Ste 150 *Web:* www.vocera.com	San Jose	CA	95126	408-882-5100	
VoiceBox Technologies Inc 11980 NE 24th St Ste 100 *Web:* www.voicebox.com	Bellevue	WA	98005	425-968-7900	
Volare Systems Inc 4351 Canyonbrook Dr *Web:* volaresystems.com	Highlands Ranch	CO	80130	303-532-5838	
Volian Enterprises Inc 122 Kerr Rd *Web:* volian.com	New Kensington	PA	15068	724-335-3744	
Vortx Inc 2245 Ashland St *Web:* www.vortx.com	Ashland	OR	97520	541-201-9965	
VOSINC 2030 Arnold Dr *Web:* www.vosinc.com	Martinez	CA	94553	925-229-6600	
VPIsystems Corp 300 Atrium Dr Fourth Fl *Web:* www.vpisystems.com	Somerset	NJ	08873	732-332-0233	469-7823
Vrp Consulting Inc 268 Bush St Ste 3836 *Web:* www.vrpinc.com	San Francisco	CA	94104	415-225-6466	
VSolvIT LLC 4171 Market St Ste 2 *Web:* www.vsolvit.com	Ventura	CA	93003	805-277-4705	
W a m s Inc 222 S Harbor Blvd *Web:* www.wamsinc.com	Anaheim	CA	92805	714-994-2811	
Wavecrest Computing Inc 2006 Vernon Pl *Web:* www.wavecrest.net	Melbourne	FL	32901	321-953-5351	
Wavefunction Inc 18401 Von Karman Ave *Web:* www.wavefun.com	Irvine	CA	92612	949-955-2120	
Wavelength Datacom LLC 1265 Oakmead Pkwy *Web:* www.wavdata.com	Sunnyvale	CA	94085	408-746-0200	
Web Advanced 49 Discovery Ste 100 *Web:* www.webadvanced.com	Irvine	CA	92618	949-453-1805	
Webaloo LLC 217 Second St N *Web:* www.webaloo.com	Stillwater	MN	55082	651-351-1041	
WebAssist.com Corp 227 N El Camino Real Ste 204 *Web:* www.webassist.com	Encinitas	CA	92024	760-633-4013	
WebEquity Solutions LLC 1010 N 102nd St Ste 100 *Web:* www.webequitysolutions.com	Omaha	NE	68114	402-344-5200	
Webline Designs Inc 3100 47th Ave Ste D *Web:* weblinedesigns.com	Long Island City	NY	11101	718-786-0008	
Webmagic 87 N Raymond Ave Ste 850 *Web:* acids.com	Pasadena	CA	91103	626-792-5552	
WebNet Services Inc 247 Rt 100 *TF:* 866-923-4811 ■ *Web:* www.webnetservices.com	Somers	NY	10589	914-232-6900	232-6901
Weidenhammer Systems Corp 935 Berkshire Blvd *TF:* 866-497-2227 ■ *Web:* www.hammer.net	Reading	PA	19610	610-378-1149	378-9409
Weidt Group Inc, The 5800 Baker Rd Ste 100 *Web:* www.twgi.com	Minnetonka	MN	55345	952-938-1588	
Welligent Inc 5205 Colley Ave *TF:* 888-317-5960 ■ *Web:* www.welligent.com	Norfolk	VA	23508	888-317-5960	
Wellness Layers Inc 336 Atlantic Ave Ste 301 *Web:* www.wellnesslayers.com	East Rockaway	NY	11518	212-537-9498	
Wennsoft Inc 1970 S Calhoun Rd *Web:* www.wennsoft.com	New Berlin	WI	53151	262-821-4100	
Wescon Technology Inc 4655 Old Ironsides Dr Ste 170 *Web:* www.wescongroup.com	Santa Clara	CA	95054	408-727-8818	
West Gulf Maritime Association 1717 E Loop N Ste 200 *Web:* www.wgma.org	Houston	TX	77029	713-678-7655	
WetStone Technologies Inc 20 Thornwood Dr Ste 105 *Web:* www.wetstonetech.com	Ithaca	NY	14850	607-266-8086	
WhatIfSports.com Inc 10200 Alliance Rd *Web:* www.whatifsports.com	Cincinnati	OH	45242	513-333-0313	
White Horse Interactive LLC 3747 NE Sandy Blvd *Web:* www.whitehorse.com	Portland	OR	97232	503-471-4200	
White Stone Group Inc, The 2030 Falling Waters Rd Ste 250 *Web:* www.twsg.com	Knoxville	TN	37922	865-531-4545	
White Ware Inc 22583 Park St *Web:* www.whiteware.com	Dearborn	MI	48124	313-792-1222	
Whole Brain Group LLC, The 109 E Ann St *Web:* www.thewholebraingroup.com	Ann Arbor	MI	48104	734-929-0431	
Winning Solutions Inc 1421 S Bell Ave Ste 105 *Web:* www.winningsolutionsinc.com	Ames	IA	50010	515-239-9900	
Winston Hospitality Inc 3701 National Dr Ste 120 *Web:* www.choate.com	Raleigh	NC	27612	919-334-6910	
Winware Inc 1955 W Oak Cir *TF:* 888-419-1399 ■ *Web:* www.cribmaster.com	Marietta	GA	30062	770-419-1399	419-1968
Wiredrive 4216 3/4 Glencoe Ave *Web:* www.wiredrive.com	Marina Del Rey	CA	90292	310-823-8238	
WireSpring Technologies Inc 1901 W Cypress Creek Rd Ste 100 *Web:* wirespring.com	Fort Lauderdale	FL	33309	954-548-3300	
Wolfe Diversified Industries LLC 223 W Ninth St *Web:* www.wolfediversifiedindustries.com	Anderson	IN	46016	765-683-9374	
Wolfram Research Inc 100 Trade Ctr Dr *TF:* 800-965-3726 ■ *Web:* www.wolfram.com	Champaign	IL	61820	217-398-0700	398-0747
Work Technology Corp 255 Elm St Ste 300 *Web:* www.worktech.com	Somerville	MA	02144	617-625-5888	
Workshare Technology Inc 208 Utah St Ste 350 *Web:* www.workshare.com	San Francisco	CA	94103	415-975-3855	
Worthwhile 9C Caledon Ct *Web:* worthwhile.com	Greenville	SC	29615	864-233-2552	
Wyant Data Systems Inc 245 Century Cir Ste 106 *Web:* www.wyantdata.com	Louisville	CO	80027	303-604-6254	
X-iss 2190 N Loop W Ste 415 *Web:* www.x-iss.com	Houston	TX	77018	713-862-9200	
X3O LLC 11810 Parklawn Dr Ste 208 *Web:* www.x3o.com	Rockville	MD	20852	301-816-9055	
Xcape Solutions Inc 207 Crystal Grove Blvd *Web:* www.xcapesolutions.net	Lutz	FL	33548	813-964-9101	
Xceltech Inc 2136 Gallows Rd *Web:* www.xceltech.com	Dunn Loring	VA	22027	703-208-9120	
Xelas Systems Engineering LLC 8111 Red Farm Ln *Web:* www.xelas-systems.com	Bowie	MD	20715	301-789-1162	

Phone *Fax*

Xenex Enterprises Inc
155 Rexdale Blvd Ste 707 .... Etobicoke ON M9W5Z8 416-345-8138
Web: www.xenex.ca

Xeno Media 18w100 22nd St Ste 128 .... Oakbrook Terrace IL 60181 630-599-1550
Web: www.xenomedia.com

Xiacon Inc 140 Fell Ct Ste 120 .... Hauppauge NY 11788 631-300-3500
Web: www.xiaconinc.com

Xlink Technology Inc 1546 Centre Pointe Dr .... Milpitas CA 95035 408-263-8201
Web: www.xlink.com

XPAND Corp 1941 Roland Clarke Pl .... Reston VA 20191 703-742-0900
Web: www.xpandcorp.com

Xper2go 39180 Liberty St .... Fremont CA 94538 510-585-2500
Web: www.xper2go.com

Xrg Systems Inc 38 Lily Ct .... Danville CA 94506 925-217-1143
Web: xrgsystems.com

XSYS Inc 653 Steele Dr .... Valparaiso IN 46385 219-477-4816
Web: www.xsysinc.com

Xytech Systems Corp
15451 San Fernando Mission Blvd
Ste 400 .... Mission Hills CA 91504 818-698-4900
Web: www.xytechsystems.com

Y-change 43575 Mission Blvd Ste 416 .... Fremont CA 94539 510-573-2205
Web: www.y-change.com

Yang Enterprises Inc 1420 Alafaya Trl Ste 200 .... Oviedo FL 32765 407-365-7374
Web: www.yangenterprises.com

Youngsoft Inc 49197 Wixom Tech Dr .... Wixom MI 48393 248-675-1200 675-1201
TF: 888-470-4553 ■ *Web:* www.youngsoft.com

Z Option Inc 417 Oakbend Dr Ste 200 .... Lewisville TX 75067 972-315-8800
Web: www.zoption.com

Z-Law Software Inc
80 Upton Ave PO Box 40602 .... Providence RI 02940 401-331-3002 421-5334
TF: 800-526-5588 ■ *Web:* www.z-law.com

Zasio Enterprises Inc
12601 W Explorer Dr Ste 250 .... Boise ID 83713 800-513-1000
TF: 800-513-1000 ■ *Web:* www.zasio.com

Zeda Soft 2310 Gravel Dr .... Fort Worth TX 76118 817-616-1000
Web: www.zedasoft.com

Zenith Information Systems Inc
18757 Burbank Blvd .... Tarzana CA 91356 310-826-8634
Web: www.zis.com

Zenoss Inc 11305 Four Points Dr Bldg 1 Ste 300 .... Austin TX 78726 410-990-0274
Web: www.zenoss.com

Zentech Technical Services Inc
14800 Saint Marys Ln Ste 270 .... Houston TX 77079 281-558-0290
Web: www.zentech-usa.com

Zephyr-tec Corp
9651 Business Ctr Dr Ste C .... Rancho Cucamonga CA 91730 909-581-8245
Web: www.zephyr-tec.com

Zethcon Corp 200 W 22nd St Ste 218 .... Lombard IL 60148 847-318-0800
Web: zethcon.com

Zinck Computer Group 131 Ilsley Ave .... Dartmouth NS B3B1T1 902-468-2738
Web: www.zcg.com

Zirous Inc 1503 42nd St Ste 210 .... West Des Moines IA 50266 515-225-9015
Web: www.zirous.com

ZM Financial Systems Inc
5915 Farrington Rd Ste 201 .... Chapel Hill NC 27517 919-493-0029
Web: www.zmfs.com

Zombie Studios 420 Fourth Ave .... Seattle WA 98104 206-623-9655
Web: www.zombie.com

Zoomedia Inc 1620 Montgomery St .... San Francisco CA 94111 415-474-1192
Web: hdmz.com

Zoot Enterprises Inc 555 Zoot Enterprises Ln .... Bozeman MT 59718 406-586-5050
Web: www.zootweb.com

Zoove Corp 2300 Geng Rd Ste 150 .... Palo Alto CA 94303 650-798-2700
Web: www.zoove.com

Zotec Partners LLC 11460 N Meridian St .... Carmel IN 46032 317-705-5050
Web: zotecpartners.com

COMPUTER RESELLERS

SEE Computer Equipment & Software - Whol p. 2015

181 COMPUTER SOFTWARE

SEE ALSO Computer Equipment & Software - Whol p. 2015; Computer Networking Products & Systems p. 2020; Computer Programming Services - Custom p. 2022; Computer Stores p. 2051; Computer Systems Design Services p. 2054; Educational Materials & Supplies p. 2211; Application Service Providers (ASPs) p. 1745

Phone *Fax*

Calypso Technology Inc
595 Market St Ste 1800 .... San Francisco CA 94105 415-817-2400 284-1222
Web: www.calypso.com

Williamson Law Book Co 790 Canning Pkwy .... Victor NY 14564 585-924-3400 924-4153
TF: 800-733-9522 ■ *Web:* www.wlbonline.com

181-1 Business Software (General)

Companies listed here make general-purpose software products that are designed for use by all types of businesses, professionals, and, to some extent, personal users.

Phone *Fax*

1MAGE Software Inc
384 Inverness Pkwy Ste 206 .... Englewood CO 80112 800-844-1468 796-0587*
**Fax Area Code:* 303 ■ *TF:* 800-844-1468 ■ *Web:* www.1mage.com

4D Inc 3031 Tisch Way Ste 900 .... San Jose CA 95128 408-557-4600 261-9879
TF: 800-785-3303 ■ *Web:* www.4d.com

ACI Worldwide 4965 Preston Pk Blvd Ste 800 .... Plano TX 75093 972-599-5600 599-5610
TF: 877-238-3095 ■ *Web:* www.aciworldwide.com

ACOM Solutions Inc 2850 E 29th St .... Long Beach CA 90806 562-424-7899 424-8662
TF: 800-347-3638 ■ *Web:* www.acom.com

Action Technologies Inc
10970 International Blvd Second Fl .... Oakland CA 94603 510-638-8300 638-8115
TF: 800-967-5356 ■ *Web:* www.actiontech.com

Actuate Corp 2207 Bridgepointe Pkwy Ste 500 .... San Mateo CA 94404 650-645-3000
NASDAQ: OTEX ■ *TF Sales:* 800-914-2259 ■ *Web:* www.actuate.com

Adexa Inc 5933 W Century Blvd 12th Fl .... Los Angeles CA 90045 310-642-2100 338-9878
TF: 888-300-7692 ■ *Web:* www.adexa.com

Adobe Systems Inc 345 Pk Ave .... San Jose CA 95110 408-536-6000 537-6000
NASDAQ: ADBE ■ *TF:* 800-833-6687 ■ *Web:* www.adobe.com

AdStar Inc 4553 Glencoe Ave Ste 300 .... Marina del Rey CA 90292 310-577-8255 577-8266
PINK: ADST

Advent Software Inc
600 Townsend St Ste 500 5th Fl .... San Francisco CA 94103 415-543-7696 543-5070
NASDAQ: ADVS ■ *TF:* 800-727-0605 ■ *Web:* www.advent.com

AgilQuest Corp 9407 Hull St Rd .... Richmond VA 23236 804-745-0467 745-6243
TF: 888-745-7455 ■ *Web:* www.agilquest.com

Alpha Software Inc 70 BlanchaRd Rd Ste 206 .... Burlington MA 01803 781-229-4500 272-4876
Web: www.alphasoftware.com

Alterian Inc 35 E Wacker Dr Ste 200 .... Chicago IL 60601 312-704-1700 704-1701
Web: www.sdl.com

American Business Systems Inc
315 Littleton Rd .... Chelmsford MA 01824 800-356-4034 250-8027*
**Fax Area Code:* 978 ■ *TF:* 800-356-4034 ■ *Web:* www.abs-software.com

American Software Inc 470 E Paces Ferry Rd .... Atlanta GA 30305 404-261-4381 264-5206
NASDAQ: AMSWA ■ *TF:* 800-726-2946 ■ *Web:* www.amsoftware.com

Appian Corp 1875 Explorer St Fourth Fl .... Reston VA 20190 703-442-8844 442-8919
Web: www.appian.com

APPX Software Inc
11363 San Jose Blvd Ste 301 .... Jacksonville FL 32223 904-880-5560 880-6635
TF: 800-879-2779 ■ *Web:* www.appx.com

AquiTec International
547 W Jackson Blvd Ninth Fl .... Chicago IL 60661 312-264-1900 264-1991

Architecture Technology Corp (ATC)
9971 Vly View Rd .... Eden Prairie MN 55344 952-829-5864 829-5868
Web: www.atcorp.com

Artemis International Solutions Corp
401 Congress Ave Ste 2650 .... Austin TX 78701 512-201-8222 874-8900
Web: www.aisc.com

Astea International Inc
240 Gibraltar Rd Ste 300 .... Horsham PA 19044 215-682-2500 682-2515
NASDAQ: ATEA ■ *TF:* 800-878-4657 ■ *Web:* www.astea.com

athenahealth Inc 311 Arsenal St .... Watertown MA 02472 617-402-1000 402-1099
NASDAQ: ATHN ■ *TF:* 800-981-5084 ■ *Web:* www.athenahealth.com

Atos Origin 2500 Westchester Ave Ste 300 .... Purchase NY 10577 914-881-3000
TF: 866-875-8902 ■ *Web:* na.atos.net

AttachmateWRQ 1500 Dexter Ave N .... Seattle WA 98109 206-217-7500 217-7515
TF Sales: 800-872-2829 ■ *Web:* www.attachmate.com

Attunity Inc 70 BlanchaRd Rd .... Burlington MA 01803 781-730-4070 896-2760*
**Fax Area Code:* 877 ■ *TF:* 866-288-8648 ■ *Web:* www.attunity.com

Avue Technologies Corp
1145 Broadway Plaza Ste 800 .... Tacoma WA 98402 253-573-1877 573-1876
Web: www.avuetech.com

Baudville Inc 5380 52nd St SE .... Grand Rapids MI 49512 616-698-0889 698-0554
TF Orders: 800-728-0888 ■ *Web:* www.baudville.com

Blackbaud Inc 2000 Daniel Island Dr .... Charleston SC 29492 843-216-6200 216-6100
NASDAQ: BLKB ■ *TF:* 800-468-8996 ■ *Web:* www.blackbaud.com

BMC Software Inc 2101 City W Blvd .... Houston TX 77042 713-918-8800 918-8000
NASDAQ: BMC ■ *TF:* 800-841-2031 ■ *Web:* www.bmc.com

Bottomline Technologies 325 Corporate Dr .... Portsmouth NH 03801 603-436-0700 436-0300
NASDAQ: EPAY ■ *TF:* 800-243-2528 ■ *Web:* www.bottomline.com

Bradmark Technologies Inc
4265 San Felipe St Ste 700 .... Houston TX 77027 713-621-2808 621-1639
TF: 800-621-2808 ■ *Web:* www.bradmark.com

Brady Identification Solutions
6555 W Good Hope Rd .... Milwaukee WI 53223 414-358-6600 292-2289*
**Fax Area Code:* 800 ■ **Fax:* Cust Svc ■ *TF Cust Svc:* 800-537-8791 ■ *Web:* www.bradyid.com

Brainworks Software Inc 100 S Main St .... Sayville NY 11782 631-563-5000 563-6320
TF: 800-755-1111 ■ *Web:* www.brainworks.com

BroadSoft Inc
9737 Washingtonian Blvd Ste 350 .... Gaithersburg MD 20877 301-977-9440
NASDAQ: BSFT ■ *Web:* www.broadsoft.com

Business Computer Design International Inc
950 N York Rd Ste 206 .... Hinsdale IL 60521 630-986-0800 986-0926
Web: www.bcdsoftware.com

CA Inc One CA Plz .... Islandia NY 11749 631-342-6000 342-6800
NASDAQ: CA ■ *TF:* 800-225-5224 ■ *Web:* www.ca.com

CDC Trade Beam Inc Two Waters Pk Dr Ste 100 .... San Mateo CA 94403 650-653-4800
TF: 888-311-1415 ■ *Web:* www.aptean.com

Cicero Inc 8000 Regency Pkwy Ste 542 .... Cary NC 27518 919-380-5000 380-5121
TF: 866-538-3588 ■ *Web:* www.ciceroinc.com

Cincom Systems Inc 55 Merchant St .... Cincinnati OH 45246 513-612-2300 612-2000
TF: 800-224-6266 ■ *Web:* www.cincom.com

Computershare Plans Software
Two Enterprise Dr .... Shelton CT 06484 203-944-7300 944-7325
TF: 888-340-4267 ■ *Web:* www.transcentive.com

Computing Technologies Inc
3028 Javier Rd Ste 400 .... Fairfax VA 22031 703-280-8800 280-8804
Web: www.cots.com

Compuware Corp One Campus Martius St .... Detroit MI 48226 313-227-7300
NASDAQ: CPWR ■ *TF:* 800-292-7432 ■ *Web:* www.compuware.com

Current Analysis Inc
21335 Signal Hill Plz Ste 200 .... Sterling VA 20164 703-404-9200 404-9300
TF: 877-787-8947 ■ *Web:* www.currentanalysis.com

Cyma Systems Inc 2330 W University Dr Ste 4 .... Tempe AZ 85281 800-292-2962 303-2969*
**Fax Area Code:* 480 ■ *TF:* 800-292-2962 ■ *Web:* www.cyma.com

D&B Sales & Marketing Solutions
460 Totten Pond Rd .... Waltham MA 02451 781-672-9200
TF: 866-473-3932 ■ *Web:* www.hoovers.com

Data Direct Technologies 14100 SW Fwy .... Sugar Land TX 77478 281-491-4200

Data Pro Acctg Software Inc
111 Second Ave NE Ste 1200 .... Saint Petersburg FL 33701 727-803-1500 803-1535
TF: 800-237-6377 ■ *Web:* www.dpro.com

Company	City	State	ZIP	Phone	Fax
Datalogics Inc 101 N Wacker Dr Ste 1800 *Web:* www.datalogics.com	Chicago	IL	60606	312-853-8200	853-8282
Datamatics Management Services Inc 330 New Brunswick Ave *TF:* 800-673-0366 ■ *Web:* www.datamaticsinc.com	Fords	NJ	08863	732-738-9600	738-9603
Deltek Inc 13880 Dulles Corner Ln. *NASDAQ: PROJ* ■ *TF:* 800-456-2009 ■ *Web:* www.deltek.com	Herndon	VA	20171	703-734-8606	734-0346
DeskNet Inc 10 Exchange Pl 20th Fl. *Web:* www.desknetinc.com	Jersey City	NJ	07302	201-946-7080	
DLGL Ltd 850 Bd Michele Bohec *Web:* www.dlgl.com	Blainville	QC	J7C5E2	450-979-4646	
Drake Software 235 E Palmer St **Fax Area Code:* 828 ■ *TF:* 800-890-9500 ■ *Web:* www.drakesoftware.com	Franklin	NC	28734	800-890-9500	369-9928*
DST Systems Inc 333 W 11th St. *NYSE: DST* ■ *Web:* www.dstsystems.com	Kansas City	MO	64105	816-435-1000	435-8630
E*Trade Financial Corp Corporate Services 4500 Bohannon Dr *TF:* 800-786-2575 ■ *Web:* us.etrade.com	Menlo Park	CA	94025	650-331-6000	331-6801
eCredit 777 Yamato Rd Ste 500. *TF:* 800-276-2321 ■ *Web:* www.cortera.com	Boca Raton	FL	33431	561-226-9000	
Edge Technologies Inc 3702 Pender Dr Ste 250 *TF:* 888-771-3343 ■ *Web:* www.edge-technologies.com	Fairfax	VA	22030	703-691-7900	691-4020
Elcom International Inc 50 Braintree Hill Park *OTC: ELCO* ■ *Web:* hugedomains.com/domain_profile.cfm?d=elcominternational&e=com	Braintree	MA	02184	781-501-4000	501-4070
EMC Corp Documentum Div 6801 Koll Ctr Pkwy. *Web:* www.emc.com	Pleasanton	CA	94566	925-600-6800	600-6850
EMC Document Sciences Corp 5958 Priestly Dr. *Web:* emc.com/domains/docscience/index.htm	Carlsbad	CA	92008	760-602-1400	602-1450
Equitrac Corp 1000 S Pine Island Rd Ste 900. *Web:* www.equitrac.com	Plantation	FL	33324	954-888-7800	475-7295
eSignal 3955 Pt Eden Way. *TF:* 800-815-8256 ■ *Web:* www.esignal.com	Hayward	CA	94545	510-266-6000	266-6100
Evolutionary Technologies International Inc (ETI) 401 Congress Ave Ste 2560 *Web:* www.eti.com	Austin	TX	78701	800-248-0027	
Exelis Visual Information Solutions 4990 Pearl E Cir. *Web:* www.exelisvis.com	Boulder	CO	80301	303-786-9900	786-9909
Fidessa Financial Corp 17 State St 42nd Fl. *Web:* fidessa.com	New York	NY	10004	212-269-9000	943-0353
FileMaker Inc 5201 Patrick Henry Dr **Fax:* Cust Svc ■ *TF Cust Svc:* 800-325-2747 ■ *Web:* www.filemaker.com	Santa Clara	CA	95054	408-987-7000	987-3932*
Fischer International Systems Corp 5801 Pelican Bay Blvd Ste 300. *TF Tech Supp:* 800-776-7258 ■ *Web:* www.fisc.com	Naples	FL	34108	239-643-1500	643-3772
FlexiInternational Software Inc Two Enterprise Dr *OTC: FLXI* ■ *TF:* 800-353-9492 ■ *Web:* www.flexi.com	Shelton	CT	06484	203-925-3040	925-3044
FrontRange Solutions USA Inc 5675 Gibraltar Dr *TF:* 800-776-7889 ■ *Web:* www.frontrange.com	Pleasanton	CA	94588	925-398-1800	
Gemmar Systems International Inc 11450 Cote de Liesse *Web:* www.gsi.ca	Dorval	QC	H9P1A9	514-631-3336	631-7722
Gemstone Systems Inc 1260 NW Waterhouse Ave Ste 200 *TF:* 800-243-4772 ■ *Web:* www.gemstone.com	Beaverton	OR	97006	503-533-3000	629-8556
Global Shop Solutions Inc 975 Evergreen Cir. *TF Sales:* 800-364-5958 ■ *Web:* www.globalshopsolutions.com	The Woodlands	TX	77380	281-681-1959	681-2663
Global Software Inc 3201 Beechleaf Ct Ste 170 *TF:* 800-326-3444 ■ *Web:* globalsoftwareinc.com	Raleigh	NC	27604	919-872-7800	876-8205
Glovia International Inc 2250 E Imperial Hwy Ste 200 *TF:* 888-245-6842 ■ *Web:* www.glovia.com	El Segundo	CA	90245	310-563-7000	563-7300
Grandite Inc PO Box 47133 *TF:* 866-808-3932 ■ *Web:* www.grandite.com	Quebec	QC	G1S4X1	581-318-2018	703-0924
GSE Systems Inc 1332 Londontown Blvd Ste 200 *NYSE: GVP* ■ *TF Cust Svc:* 800-638-7912 ■ *Web:* www.gses.com	Sykesville	MD	21784	410-970-7800	970-7997
Halogen Software 495 March Rd *TF:* 866-566-7778 ■ *Web:* www.halogensoftware.com	Kanata	ON	K2K3G1	613-270-1011	270-8311
HarrisData 13555 Bishops Ct Ste 300 *TF:* 800-225-0585 ■ *Web:* www.harrisdata.com	Brookfield	WI	53005	262-784-9099	784-5994
HighJump Software 5600 W 83rd St Ste 600 **Fax Area Code:* 507 ■ *TF:* 800-328-3271 ■ *Web:* www.highjump.com	Minneapolis	MN	55437	952-947-4088	213-8852*
Hitachi Consulting Corp 14643 Dallas Pkwy Ste 800 *Web:* www.hitachiconsulting.com	Fremont	TX	75254	214-665-7000	665-7010
HK Systems Inc 2855 S James Dr. *TF:* 800-424-7365 ■ *Web:* www.dematic.com	New Berlin	WI	53151	262-860-7000	860-7010
I-many Inc 1735 Market St 37th Fl *TF:* 877-774-2451 ■ *Web:* www.revitasinc.com	Philadelphia	PA	19103	215-344-1900	344-1919
IBM WebSphere Information Integration 26 Forest St *Web:* www-01.ibm.com/software/data/integration	Marlborough	MA	01752	508-366-3888	
iCIMS Inc 90 Matawan Rd Pkwy 120 Fifth Fl. *TF:* 800-889-4422 ■ *Web:* www.icims.com	Matawan	NJ	07747	732-847-1941	876-0422
Iconixx Software 3420 Executive Ctr Dr Ste 250. **Fax Area Code:* 512 ■ *TF:* 877-426-6499 ■ *Web:* iconixx.com	Austin	TX	78731	877-426-6499	651-3111*
IFS North America Inc 300 Pk Blvd Ste 555 *TF:* 888-437-4968 ■ *Web:* www.ifsworld.com	Chicago	IL	60143	888-437-4968	
Image Process Design 36800 Woodward Ave Ste 300 *Web:* www.ipdsolution.com	Bloomfield Hills	MI	48304	248-723-9733	203-2566
Infoglide Software 6500 River Pl Blvd Bldg 2 *Web:* www.infoglide.com	Austin	TX	78730	512-532-3500	532-3505
Informatica Corp 100 Cardinal Way *NASDAQ: INFA* ■ *TF:* 800-653-3871 ■ *Web:* www.informatica.com	Redwood City	CA	94063	650-385-5000	385-5500
Information & Computing Services Inc (ICS) 1650 Prudential Dr Ste 300 *TF:* 800-676-4427 ■ *Web:* www.icsfl.com	Jacksonville	FL	32207	904-399-8500	398-7855
InfoVista Corp 12950 Worldgate Dr Ste 250 *TF:* 866-921-9219 ■ *Web:* www.infovista.com	Herndon	VA	20170	703-435-2435	435-5122
Innovative Systems Inc 790 Holiday Dr Bldg 11 *TF:* 800-622-6390 ■ *Web:* www.innovativesystems.com	Pittsburgh	PA	15220	412-937-9300	937-9309
Inova Solutions Inc 110 Avon St. *TF:* 800-637-1077 ■ *Web:* www.inovasolutions.com	Charlottesville	VA	22902	434-817-8000	817-8002
Inspiration Software Inc 5125 SW Macadam Ave Ste 145. *TF:* 800-877-4292 ■ *Web:* www.inspiration.com	Beaverton	OR	97239	503-297-3004	297-4676
Integrated Business Systems & Services Inc 1601 Shop Rd Ste E *Web:* www.ibss.net	Columbia	SC	29201	803-736-5595	736-5639
Integrated Decisions & Systems Inc 8500 Normandale Lk Blvd Ste 1200. *Web:* www.ideas.com	Minneapolis	MN	55437	952-698-4200	698-4299
Intellicorp Inc 2900 Lakeside Dr Ste 221 *Web:* www.intellicorp.com	Santa Clara	CA	95054	408-454-3500	454-3529
International Business Machines Corp (IBM) One New OrchaRd Rd *NYSE: IBM* ■ *TF:* 800-426-4968 ■ *Web:* www.ibm.com	Armonk	NY	10504	914-499-1900	
InterraTech Corp PO Box 4. *TF:* 888-589-4889 ■ *Web:* www.interratech.com	Mount Ephraim	NJ	08059	856-854-5100	854-5102
InterSystems Corp One Memorial Dr *Web:* intersystems.com	Cambridge	MA	02142	617-621-0600	494-1631
Intuitive Research & Technology Corp 5030 Bradford Dr NW # 205. *Web:* www.irtc-hq.com	Huntsville	AL	35805	256-922-9300	922-1122
ISG Novasoft (ISGN) 600 A N John Rodes Blvd **Fax Area Code:* 321 ■ *TF:* 800-939-8258 ■ *Web:* www.isgn.com	Melbourne	FL	32934	800-939-8258	255-9366*
JDA Software Group Inc 1615 S Congress Ave Ste 200 *Web:* escalate.com	Delray Beach	FL	33445	561-265-2700	
K-Systems Inc 2104 Aspen Dr. *TF:* 800-221-0204 ■ *Web:* www.ksystemsinc.com	Mechanicsburg	PA	17055	717-795-7711	795-7715
Kalido 1 Wall St Ste 3 *TF:* 866-466-3849 ■ *Web:* www.kalido.com	Burlington	MA	01803	781-202-3200	202-3299
Levi Ray & Shoup Inc 2401 W Monroe St. *Web:* www.lrs.com	Springfield	IL	62704	217-793-3800	787-3286
Logility Inc 470 E Paces Ferry Rd. *TF:* 800-762-5207 ■ *Web:* www.logility.com	Atlanta	GA	30305	404-261-9777	264-5206
Longview Solutions 100 Matsonford Rd Ste 230 **Fax Area Code:* 484 ■ *TF:* 888-456-6484 ■ *Web:* www.longview.com	Radnor	PA	19087	610-977-0995	367-1153*
M2 Technology Inc 21702 Hardy Oak Ste 100. *TF:* 800-267-1760 ■ *Web:* www.m2ti.com	San Antonio	TX	78258	210-566-3773	566-3993
Malvern Systems Inc 81 Lancaster Ave Ste 219. **Fax Area Code:* 610 ■ *TF:* 800-296-9642 ■ *Web:* www.malvernsys.com	Malvern	PA	19355	800-296-9642	889-2254*
Maverick Technologies 265 Admiral Trost Rd PO Box 470 *TF:* 888-917-9109 ■ *Web:* www.mavtechglobal.com	Columbia	IL	62236	618-281-9100	281-9191
Mayflowers Software 44 Stoneymeade Wy *Web:* www.maysoft.com	Acton	MA	01720	978-635-1700	371-1696
Mediagrif Interactive Technologies Inc 1111 St-Charles St W E Tower Ste 255. *TSE: MDF* ■ *TF:* 877-677-9088 ■ *Web:* www.mediagrif.com	Longueuil	QC	J4K5G4	450-449-0102	449-8725
Meridian Systems 1720 Prairie City Rd Ste 120. *TF:* 800-850-2660 ■ *Web:* www.meridiansystems.com	Folsom	CA	95630	916-294-2000	294-2001
Meridium Inc 207 Bullitt Ave SE *Web:* www.meridium.com	Roanoke	VA	24013	540-344-9205	345-7083
MicroBiz Corp 655 Oak Grove Ave Ste 493 Ste 493. **Fax Area Code:* 650 ■ *TF:* 800-937-2289 ■ *Web:* www.microbiz.com	Menlo Park	CA	94025	702-749-5353	440-4740*
Microlink Enterprise Inc 20955 Pathfinder Rd Ste 100 *TF:* 800-829-3688 ■ *Web:* www.microlinkenterprise.com	Diamond Bar	CA	91765	562-205-1888	205-1886
Microsoft Corp One Microsoft Way. *NASDAQ: MSFT* ■ *Web:* www.microsoft.com	Redmond	WA	98052	425-882-8080	936-7329
Microsoft Great Plains Business Solutions 3900 Great Plains Dr S. *TF:* 888-477-7877 ■ *Web:* www.microsoft.com	Fargo	ND	58104	701-281-6500	
Microsystems 3025 Highland Pkwy Ste 450. *Web:* www.microsystems.com	Lombard	IL	60515	630-598-1100	598-9520
Milner Technologies Inc 5125 Peachtree Industrial Blvd. *TF:* 800-592-3766 ■ *Web:* www.comsquared.com	Norcross	GA	30092	770-734-5300	734-5379
Multi-Ad Inc 1720 W Detweiller Dr. *TF:* 800-348-6485 ■ *Web:* www.multiad.com	Peoria	IL	61615	309-692-1530	692-6566
NetMotion Wireless Inc 701 N 34th St Ste 250. *TF:* 877-818-7626 ■ *Web:* www.netmotionwireless.com	Seattle	WA	98103	206-691-5500	691-5501
New Century Education Foundation PO Box 43052 **Fax Area Code:* 609 ■ *TF:* 866-326-1133 ■ *Web:* www.newcenturyeducation.org	Upper Montclair	NJ	07043	866-326-1133	586-8491*
NewlineNoosh Inc 625 Ellis St Ste 300 *TF:* 888-286-6674 ■ *Web:* noosh.com	Mountain View	CA	94043	650-637-6000	965-1377
Newport Wave Inc 15 McLean *TF:* 800-999-2611 ■ *Web:* www.newportwave.com	Irvine	CA	92620	949-651-1099	786-0167
North Atlantic Publishing Systems Inc 66 Commonwealth Ave. *Web:* www.napsys.com	Concord	MA	01742	978-371-8989	371-5678
Novell Inc 1800 S Novell Pl **Fax:* Sales ■ *TF:* 800-529-3400 ■ *Web:* www.novell.com	Provo	UT	84606	801-861-4272	861-3122*
Objectivity Inc 640 W California Ave Ste 210. *TF:* 800-767-6259 ■ *Web:* www.objectivity.com	Sunnyvale	CA	94086	408-992-7100	992-7171
OMD Corp 3705 Missouri Blvd *TF:* 866-440-8664 ■ *Web:* www.omdcorp.com	Jefferson City	MO	65109	573-893-8930	893-3487
OneSCM 6805 Capital of Texas Hwy Ste 370. *TF:* 800-324-5143 ■ *Web:* onescm.com	Austin	TX	78731	512-231-8191	231-0292
Open Systems Inc 4301 Dean Lakes Blvd **Fax Area Code:* 952 ■ *TF Sales:* 800-328-2276 ■ *Web:* www.osas.com	Shakopee	MN	55379	800-328-2276	403-5870*

Company / Address	City	State	ZIP	Phone	Fax
OpenLink Software Inc 10 Burlington Mall Rd Ste 265 *Web:* www.openlinksw.com	Burlington	MA	01803	781-273-0900	229-8030
OpenText Corp 8600 W Bryn Mawr Ave Ste 710 N *TF:* 800-499-6544 ■ *Web:* www.opentext.com	Chicago	IL	60631	773-632-1400	
Oracle Corp 500 Oracle Pkwy *NYSE: ORCL* ■ *TF Sales:* 800-392-2999 ■ *Web:* www.oracle.com	Redwood Shores	CA	94065	650-506-7000	506-7200
Oracle Information Rights Management 500 Oracle Pkwy *Web:* www.oracle.com	Redwood Shores	CA	94065	650-506-7000	
Oracle USA 500 Oracle Pkwy *TF:* 800-392-2999 ■ *Web:* www.oracle.com	Redwood Shores	CA	94065	650-506-7000	
Palisade Corp 798 Cascadilla St *TF:* 800-432-7475 ■ *Web:* www.palisade.com	Ithaca	NY	14850	607-277-8000	277-8001
Paperclip Software Inc One University Plz **Fax:* Hum Res ■ *TF:* 800-929-3503 ■ *Web:* www.paperclip.com	Hackensack	NJ	07601	201-525-1221	525-1511*
Passport Corp 85 Chestnut Ridge Rd *TF:* 800-926-6736 ■ *Web:* www.passportcorp.com	Montvale	NJ	07645	201-573-0038	573-0082
Payspan Inc 7751 Belfort Pkwy Ste 200 *TF:* 877-331-7154 ■ *Web:* www.payspan.com	Jacksonville	FL	32256	877-331-7154	
PDI 3407 S 31st St *Web:* www.profdata.com	Temple	TX	76502	254-771-7100	771-7117
Pegasystems Inc 101 Main St *NASDAQ: PEGA* ■ *Web:* www.pega.com	Cambridge	MA	02142	617-374-9600	374-9620
Pentagon 2000 Software Inc 15 W 34th St Fifth Fl *TF:* 800-643-1806 ■ *Web:* www.pentagon2000.com	New York	NY	10001	212-629-7521	629-7513
PeopleStrategy Inc 5883 Glenridge Dr Ste 200 *TF:* 855-488-4100 ■ *Web:* www.peoplestrategy.com	Atlanta	GA	30328	855-488-4100	
Percussion Software Inc 600 Unicorn Pk Dr *TF:* 800-283-0800 ■ *Web:* www.percussion.com	Woburn	MA	01801	781-438-9900	438-9955
Personnel Data Systems Inc (PDS) 470 Norriftown Rd Ste 202 *TF:* 800-243-8737 ■ *Web:* www.pdssoftware.com	Blue Bell	PA	19422	610-238-4600	238-4550
Pilgrim Quality Solutions 2807 W Busch Blvd *Web:* www.pilgrimsoftware.com	Tampa	FL	33618	813-915-1663	915-1948
Pitney Bowes Group 1 Software 4200 Parliament Pl Ste 600 *TF:* 800-367-6950 ■ *Web:* www.g1.com	Lanham	MD	20706	301-731-2300	731-0360
Planview Inc 8300 N Mopac Ste 300 *TF:* 800-856-8600 ■ *Web:* www.planview.com	Austin	TX	78759	512-346-8600	346-9180
Platform Computing Inc 3760 14th Ave *TF:* 877-528-3676 ■ *Web:* ibm.com/	Markham	ON	L3R3T7	905-948-8448	948-9975
Portrait Software Inc 125 Summer St 16th Fl *TF:* 800-327-8627 ■ *Web:* www.portraitsoftware.com	Boston	MA	02110	617-457-5200	457-5299
Print-O-Stat Inc 1011 W Market St *TF:* 800-711-8014 ■ *Web:* www.printostat.com	York	PA	17404	717-854-7821	846-4084
Process Control Technology Inc 4335 Piedras Dr W Ste 175 *Web:* www.gopct.com	San Antonio	TX	78228	210-735-9141	735-9775
Progress Software Corp 14 Oak Pk *NASDAQ: PRGS* ■ *TF:* 800-477-6473 ■ *Web:* www.progress.com	Bedford	MA	01730	781-280-4000	280-4095
QAD Inc 100 Innovation Pl *NASDAQ: QADB* ■ *TF:* 888-641-4141 ■ *Web:* www.qad.com	Santa Barbara	CA	93108	805-684-6614	565-4202
Quest Software Inc Five Polairis Way *NASDAQ: QSFT* ■ *TF:* 800-306-9329 ■ *Web:* www.quest.com	Aliso Viejo	CA	92656	949-754-8000	754-8999
Quick Solutions Inc 440 Polaris Pkwy Ste 500 *Web:* www.quicksolutions.com	Westerville	OH	43082	614-825-8000	825-8006
Quorum Business Solutions Inc 811 Main St Ste 2000 *Web:* www.qbsol.com	Houston	TX	77002	713-430-8601	430-8697
Realtime Software Corp 24 Deane Rd *TF:* 800-323-1143 ■ *Web:* www.realtimesw.com	Bernardston	MA	01337	847-803-1100	954-4764
Red Wing Software Inc 491 Hwy 19 *TF:* 800-732-9464 ■ *Web:* www.redwingsoftware.com	Red Wing	MN	55066	651-388-1106	388-7950
Redemtech Inc 4115 Leap Rd *TF:* 800-393-7627 ■ *Web:* www.arrowvaluerecovery.com	Hilliard	OH	43026	614-850-3366	
Rentrak Corp 7700 NE Ambassador Pl Third Fl *NASDAQ: RENT* ■ *TF:* 800-929-0070 ■ *Web:* www.rentrak.com	Portland	OR	97220	503-284-7581	
Sage Fixed Assets 2325 Dulles Corner Blvd Ste 700 **Fax Area Code:* 703 ■ *TF:* 800-368-2405 ■ *Web:* na.sage.com	Herndon	VA	20171	800-368-2405	793-2770*
Sand Technology Inc 4115 Rue Sherbrooke Ouest *NYSE: SNDTF* ■ *TF:* 877-468-2538 ■ *Web:* www.sand.com	Westmount	QC	H3Z1B1	514-939-3477	
SAP 100 Consilium Pl *TF:* 888-777-1727 ■ *Web:* www.sap.com	Scarborough	ON	M1H3E3	416-791-7100	791-7101
Sapphire International Inc 101 Merritt Blvd	Trumbull	CT	06611	203-375-8668	
SAS Institute Inc 100 SAS Campus Dr *TF:* 800-727-0025 ■ *Web:* www.sas.com	Cary	NC	27513	919-677-8000	677-4444
Satori Software Inc 1301 5th Ave Ste 2200 *TF:* 800-553-6477 ■ *Web:* www.satorisoftware.com	Seattle	WA	98101	206-357-2900	357-2901
Sciforma Corp 985 University Ave Ste 5 *TF Sales:* 800-533-9876 ■ *Web:* www.sciforma.com	Los Gatos	CA	95032	408-354-0144	354-0122
SDL International 2550 N First St Ste 301 *Web:* www.sdl.com	San Jose	CA	95131	408-743-3600	743-3601
Selectica Inc 2121 S. El Camino Rl 10th Fl *NASDAQ: SLTC* ■ **Fax Area Code:* 408 ■ *TF:* 877-712-9560 ■ *Web:* www.selectica.com	San Mateo	CA	94403	650-532-1500	570-9705*
SERENA Software Inc 1900 Seaport Blvd Second Fl *TF:* 800-457-3736 ■ *Web:* www.serena.com	Redwood City	CA	94063	650-481-3400	481-3700
Silvon Software Inc 900 Oakmont Ln Ste 400 *TF:* 800-874-5866 ■ *Web:* www.silvon.com	Westmont	IL	60559	630-655-3313	655-3377
Siwel Consulting Inc 71 W 23rd St Ste 1907 *Web:* www.siwel.com	New York	NY	10010	212-691-9326	929-6815
Skybridge Global Inc 161 Village Pkwy NE Bldg 7 *Web:* www.skybridgeglobal.com	Marietta	GA	30067	770-373-2300	953-8360
Soffront Software Inc 45437 Warm Springs Blvd *TF:* 800-763-3766 ■ *Web:* www.soffront.com	Fremont	CA	94539	510-413-9000	413-9027
Software AG USA 11700 Plz America Dr Ste 700 *TF:* 877-724-4965 ■ *Web:* www.softwareag.com	Reston	VA	20190	703-860-5050	391-6975
Sophos Inc 3 Van de Graaff Dr 2nd Fl **Fax Area Code:* 781 ■ *TF:* 866-866-2802 ■ *Web:* www.sophos.com	Burlington	MA	01803	866-866-2802	494-5801*
Source Technologies 2910 Whitehall Pk Dr *TF:* 800-922-8501 ■ *Web:* www.sourcetech.com	Charlotte	NC	28273	704-969-7500	969-7595
SP Systems Inc 7500 Greenway Ctr Dr Ste 850 *TF:* 877-327-8732 ■ *Web:* www.sp-systems.com	Greenbelt	MD	20770	301-614-1322	614-1328
Stamps.com Inc 1990 E Grand Ave *NASDAQ: STMP* ■ *TF:* 855-889-7867 ■ *Web:* www.stamps.com	El Segundo	CA	90245	855-889-7867	
StrataCare Inc 17838 Gillette Ave **Fax Area Code:* 949 ■ *TF:* 800-277-6512 ■ *Web:* www.stratacare.com	Irvine	CA	92614	800-277-6512	743-1299*
Superior Software Inc 16055 Ventura Blvd Ste 650 *TF:* 800-421-3264 ■ *Web:* www.superior-software.com	Encino	CA	91436	818-990-1135	783-5846
Sybase Inc 1 Sybase Dr *TF:* 800-792-2735 ■ *Web:* www.sybase.com	Dublin	CA	94568	925-236-5000	236-4321
SYSPRO 959 S Coast Dr Ste 100 *TF:* 800-369-8649 ■ *Web:* www.syspro.com	Costa Mesa	CA	92626	714-437-1000	437-1407
Systar Inc 8618 Westwood Ctr Dr Ste 240 *Web:* www.systar.com	Vienna	VA	22182	703-556-8400	556-8430
Taleo Corp 4140 Dublin Blvd Ste 400 *NYSE: ORCL* ■ *TF:* 800-672-2531 ■ *Web:* www.oracle.com	Dublin	CA	94568	925-452-3000	452-3001
TECSYS Inc 1 Pl Alexis Nihon Ste 800 *TF:* 800-922-8649 ■ *Web:* www.tecsys.com	Montreal	QC	H3Z3B8	514-866-0001	866-1805
Tenrox 401 Congress Avenue *TF:* 855-944-7526 ■ *Web:* www.tenrox.com	Austin	TX	78701	626-796-6640	796-6662
Thomson Tax & Acctg 7322 Newman Blvd *TF Cust Svc:* 800-968-8900 ■ *Web:* cs.thomsonreuters.com	Dexter	MI	48130	800-968-8900	326-1040
Tomax Corp 224 South 200 West *Web:* www.tomax.com	Salt Lake City	UT	84101	801-990-0909	924-3400
Tribridge 4830 W Kennedy Blvd Ste 890 *TF:* 877-744-1360 ■ *Web:* www.tribridge.com	Tampa	FL	33609	877-744-1360	
Trilogy Software Inc 401 Congress Ave Ste 2650 *Web:* www.trilogy.com	Austin	TX	78701	512-874-3100	
Trintech Inc 15851 Dallas Pkwy Ste 900 *TF:* 800-416-0075 ■ *Web:* www.trintech.com	Addison	TX	75001	972-701-9802	701-9337
Tritek Solutions Inc 7617 Little River Tpke Ste 800 *Web:* www.perficient.com	Annandale	VA	22003	703-333-3060	333-3071
Ultimate Software Group Inc 2000 Ultimate Way *NASDAQ: ULTI* ■ *TF:* 800-432-1729 ■ *Web:* www.ultimatesoftware.com	Weston	FL	33326	954-331-7000	
Valiant Solutions Inc 110 Crossways Pk Dr *Web:* www.valiant.com	Woodbury	NY	11797	516-390-1100	390-1111
Validar Inc 800 Maynard Ave S Ste 401 *TF:* 888-784-2929 ■ *Web:* www.validar.com	Seattle	WA	98134	206-264-9151	
Versant Corp 255 Shoreline Dr Ste 450 *NASDAQ: VSNT* ■ *TF:* 888-446-4737 ■ *Web:* actian.com	Redwood City	CA	94065	650-232-2400	232-2401
Vertex Inc 1041 Old Cassatt Rd *TF:* 800-355-3500 ■ *Web:* www.vertexinc.com	Berwyn	PA	19312	610-640-4200	640-5892
VFA Inc 99 Bedford St *TF:* 800-693-3132 ■ *Web:* www.vfa.com	Boston	MA	02111	617-451-5100	350-7087
Vignette Corp 1301 S Mopac Expy Ste 100 *TF:* 800-540-7292 ■ *Web:* www.opentext.com	Austin	TX	78746	512-741-4300	
Visible Systems Corp 201 Spring St *TF Sales:* 888-850-9911 ■ *Web:* www.visible.com	Lexington	MA	02421	781-778-0200	778-0208
Vitria Technology Inc 945 Stewart Dr Ste 200 **Fax Area Code:* 408 ■ *TF:* 877-365-5935 ■ *Web:* www.vitria.com	Sunnyvale	CA	94085	877-365-5935	212-2720*
Wave Systems Corp 480 Pleasant St *NASDAQ: WAVX* ■ *TF:* 800-928-3638 ■ *Web:* www.wave.com	Lee	MA	01238	413-243-1600	243-0045
Wizdom Systems Inc 1300 Iroquois Ave *Web:* www.wizdom.com	Naperville	IL	60563	630-357-3000	357-3059
Worden Bros Inc 4905 Pine Cone Dr *TF:* 800-776-4940 ■ *Web:* www.worden.com	Durham	NC	27707	919-408-0542	408-0545
Xaware Inc 3300 Irvine Ave Ste 261 **Fax Area Code:* 719 ■ *Web:* www.xaware.com	Newport Beach	CA	92660	949-222-2287	325-8943*
ZyLAB North America LLC 7918 Jones Branch Dr Ste 230 **Fax Area Code:* 703 ■ *Web:* www.zylab.com	McLean	VA	22102	866-995-2262	991-2508*

181-2 Computer Languages & Development Tools

Company / Address	City	State	ZIP	Phone	Fax
Amzi! inc 83 Vance Crescent Ext *Web:* www.amzi.com	Asheville	NC	28806	828-350-0350	
Applied Dynamics International Inc 3800 Stone School Rd *TF:* 888-465-4329 ■ *Web:* www.adi.com	Ann Arbor	MI	48108	734-973-1300	668-0012
BSQUARE Corp 110 110th Ave NE Ste 200 *NASDAQ: BSQR* ■ *TF:* 888-820-4500 ■ *Web:* www.bsquare.com	Bellevue	WA	98004	425-519-5900	519-5999
Calypso Technology Inc 595 Market St Ste 1800 *Web:* www.calypso.com	San Francisco	CA	94105	415-817-2400	284-1222
Data Access Corp 14000 SW 119th Ave *TF:* 800-451-3539 ■ *Web:* www.dataaccess.com	Miami	FL	33186	305-238-0012	238-0012
DDC-I Inc 4600 E Shea Blvd Ste 102 *Web:* www.ddci.com	Phoenix	AZ	85028	602-275-7172	252-6054
Diamond Edge Inc 661 W State St Ste A *Web:* www.diamondedge.com/company/reed.html	Pleasant Grove	UT	84062	801-785-8473	
Embarcadero Technologies Inc 100 California St 12th Fl *Web:* www.embarcadero.com	San Francisco	CA	94111	415-834-3131	434-1721
Empress Software Inc 11785 Beltsville Dr *TF:* 866-626-8888 ■ *Web:* www.empress.com	Beltsville	MD	20705	301-220-1919	220-1997
Fgm Inc 12021 Sunset Hills Rd Ste 400 *Web:* www.fgm.com	Reston	VA	20190	703-885-1000	885-0130
FMS Inc 8150 Leesburg Pk Ste 600 *TF:* 866-367-7801 ■ *Web:* www.fmsinc.com	Vienna	VA	22182	703-356-4700	448-3861
Forth Inc 5959 W Century Blvd Ste 700 *TF:* 800-553-6784 ■ *Web:* www.forth.com	Los Angeles	CA	90045	310-999-6784	943-3806

Phone Fax

Green Hills Software Inc 30 W Sola St .... Santa Barbara CA 93101 805-965-6044 965-6343
TF: 800-765-4733 ■ *Web:* www.ghs.com

Instantiations Inc Officers Row Ste 1325B .... Vancouver WA 98661 503-649-3836 649-3836
TF: 855-476-2558 ■ *Web:* www.instantiations.com

Integrated Computer Solutions Inc (ICS)
54 Middlesex Tpke Ste B .... Bedford MA 01730 617-621-0060 621-9555
Web: www.ics.com

LANSA Inc 3010 Highland Pkwy Ste 275 .... Downers Grove IL 60515 630-874-7000 874-7001
Web: www.lansa.com

Lattice Inc 1751 S Naperville Rd Ste 100 .... Wheaton IL 60189 630-949-3250 949-3299
TF Sales: 800-444-4309 ■ *Web:* www.lattice.com

Mix Software Inc 1203 Berkeley Dr .... Richardson TX 75081 972-231-0949
TF: 800-333-0330 ■ *Web:* www.mixsoftware.com

NIS Inc 12995 Thomas Creek Rd .... Reno NV 89511 775-852-0640
Web: nissoftware.net

Numara Software Inc 2202 NW Shore Blvd Ste 650 .... Tampa FL 33607 813-227-4500 227-4501
TF Sales: 800-557-3031 ■ *Web:* www.bmc.com

Primus Software Corp
3061 Peachtree Industrial Blvd Ste 110 .... Duluth GA 30097 770-300-0004 300-0005
Web: www.primussoft.com

Prolifics 114 W 47th St 20th Fl .... New York NY 10036 212-267-7722 608-6753
TF: 800-458-3313 ■ *Web:* www.prolifics.com

Revelation Software 99 Kinderkamack Rd .... Westwood NJ 07675 201-594-1422 722-9815
TF: 800-262-4747 ■ *Web:* www.revelation.com

Rogue Wave Software Inc 5500 Flatiron Pkwy .... Boulder CO 80301 303-473-9118 473-9137
TF: 800-487-3217 ■ *Web:* www.roguewave.com

SemWare Corp 730 Elk Cove Ct .... Kennesaw GA 30152 678-355-9810 355-9812
Web: www.semware.com

Shaw Systems Assoc Inc 6200 Savoy Dr Ste 600 .... Houston TX 77036 713 782 7730 782 4158
Web: www.shawsystems.com

SlickEdit Inc
3000 Aerial Ctr Pkwy Ste 120 .... Morrisville NC 27560 919-473-0070 473-0080
TF: 800-934-3348 ■ *Web:* www.slickedit.com

Sunbelt Computer Systems Inc
13090 Swan Lake Rd CR 468 .... Tyler TX 75704 903-881-0400 881-0440
Web: www.sunbelt-plb.com

Synactive Inc 950 Tower Ln Ste 750 .... Foster City CA 94404 650-341-3310 341-3610
Web: www.synactive.net

Thoroughbred Software International Inc
285 Davidson Ave Ste 302 .... Somerset NJ 08873 732-560-1377 560-1594
TF: 800-524-0430 ■ *Web:* www.thoroughbredsoftware.com

Zortec International
25 Century Blvd Ste 103 .... Nashville TN 37214 615-361-7000 361-3800
TF: 800-361-7005 ■ *Web:* www.zortec.com

181-3 Educational & Reference Software

Phone Fax

Allen Communication Learning Services
55 West 900 South Ste 100 .... Salt Lake City UT 84101 801-537-7800 537-7805
TF: 866-310-7800 ■ *Web:* www.allencomm.com

Atari Inc 417 Fifth Ave Eighth Fl .... New York NY 10016 212-726-6500 252-8603
Web: www.atari.com

Blackboard Inc 1899 L St NW Fifth Fl .... Washington DC 20036 202-463-4860 463-4863
TF: 800-424-9299 ■ *Web:* www.blackboard.com

CompassLearning Inc 203 Colorado St .... Austin TX 78701 512-478-9600 492-6193
TF: 800-232-9556 ■ *Web:* www.compasslearning.com

Fuel Education LLC 7506 Broadway Ext .... Oklahoma City OK 73116 800-222-2811
TF: 800-222-2811 ■ *Web:* www.amered.com

Individual Software Inc
4255 HopyaRd Rd Ste 2 .... Pleasanton CA 94588 925-734-6767 734-8337
TF: 800-822-3522 ■ *Web:* www.individualsoftware.com

Inscape Publishing Inc
6465 Wayzata Blvd Ste 800 .... Minneapolis MN 55426 763-765-2222 765-2277
TF: 877-735-8383 ■ *Web:* everythingdisc.com/

Inspiration Software Inc
5125 SW Macadam Ave Ste 145 .... Beaverton OR 97239 503-297-3004 297-4676
TF: 800-877-4292 ■ *Web:* www.inspiration.com

Language Engineering Co 135 Beaver St Ste 204 .... Waltham MA 02452 781-642-8900
Web: www.lec.com

LDP Inc 75 Kiwanis Blvd PO Box O .... West Hazleton PA 18201 800-522-8413
TF: 800-522-8413 ■ *Web:* www.leaderservices.com

MindPlay Educational Software
440 S Williams Blvd Ste 206 .... Tucson AZ 85711 520-888-1800 888-7904
TF: 800-221-7911 ■ *Web:* www.mindplay.com

Optimum Resource Inc 18 Hunter Rd .... Hilton Head Island SC 29926 843-689-8000 689-8008
TF: 888-784-2592 ■ *Web:* www.stickybear.com

Queue Inc 80 Hathaway Dr .... Stratford CT 06615 800-232-2224 775-2729
TF: 800-232-2224 ■ *Web:* www.queueinc.com

Renaissance Learning Inc
2911 Peach St .... Wisconsin Rapids WI 54494 715-424-3636 424-4242
TF: 800-338-4204 ■ *Web:* renaissance.com

Saba Software Inc 2400 Bridge Pkwy .... Redwood Shores CA 94065 650-581-2500 696-1773
OTC: SABA ■ *TF:* 877-722-2101 ■ *Web:* www.saba.com

Scientific Learning Corp
300 Frank H Ogawa Plz Ste 600 .... Oakland CA 94612 510-444-3500 444-3580
OTC: SCIL ■ *TF:* 888-665-9707 ■ *Web:* www.scilearn.com

Siboney Corp 325 N Kirkwood Rd .... Saint Louis MO 63122 314-822-3163

Tom Snyder Productions Inc 100 Talcott Ave .... Watertown MA 02472 617-926-6000 926-6222
TF: 800-342-0236 ■ *Web:* www.tomsnyder.com

Transparent Language Inc 12 Murphy Dr .... Nashua NH 03062 800-538-8867 262-6476*
**Fax Area Code:* 603 ■ *TF:* 800-538-8867 ■ *Web:* www.transparent.com

Wordsmart Corp 10025 Mesa Rim Rd .... San Diego CA 92121 858-565-8068 202-1820
TF: 800-858-9673

181-4 Electronic Purchasing & Procurement Software

Phone Fax

Apptis Inc 4800 Westfields Blvd .... Chantilly VA 20151 703-579-0471 745-1304
TF: 888-277-8478 ■ *Web:* www.apptis.com

Ariba Inc 807 11th Ave .... Sunnyvale CA 94089 650-390-1000
NASDAQ: ARBA ■ *TF:* 866-772-7422 ■ *Web:* www.ariba.com

CA Inc One CA Plz .... Islandia NY 11749 631-342-6000 342-6800
NASDAQ: CA ■ *TF:* 800-225-5224 ■ *Web:* www.ca.com

Covisint 1 Campus Martius Suite 700 .... Detroit MI 48226 800-229-4125
TF: 800-229-4125 ■ *Web:* www.covisint.com

Elavon Two Concourse Pkwy Ste 300 .... Atlanta GA 30328 678-731-5000 577-0661*
**Fax Area Code:* 865 ■ *TF:* 800-725-1243 ■ *Web:* www.elavon.com

Fiserv Lending Solutions
455 S Gulph Rd Ste 125 .... King of Prussia PA 19406 610-337-8686 337-7206
Web: www.fiservlemans.com

GXS Inc 9711 Washingtonian Blvd .... Gaithersburg MD 20878 301-340-4000 340-5299
TF: 800-560-4347 ■ *Web:* www.gxs.com

International Business Machines Corp (IBM)
One New OrchaRd Rd .... Armonk NY 10504 914-499-1900
NYSE: IBM ■ *TF:* 800-426-4968 ■ *Web:* www.ibm.com

MarketAxess Holdings Inc 299 Pk Ave 10th Fl .... New York NY 10171 212-813-6000 813-6390
NASDAQ: MKTX ■ *Web:* www.marketaxess.com

SciQuest Inc 6501 Weston Pkwy Ste 200 .... Cary NC 27513 919-659-2100 659-2199
TF: 888-638-7322 ■ *Web:* www.sciquest.com

181-5 Engineering Software

Phone Fax

Accelrys Inc 10188 Telesis Ct Ste 100 .... San Diego CA 92121 858-799-5000 799-5100
NASDAQ: ACCL ■ *TF:* 888-249-2284 ■ *Web:* www.accelrys.com

Advanced Visual Systems Inc (AVS) 300 Fifth Ave .... Waltham MA 02451 781-890-4300 890-8287
OTC: AVSC ■ *Web:* www.avs.com

Altium Inc 3207 Grey Hawk Ct Ste 100 .... Carlsbad CA 92010 760-231-0760 231-0761
TF Sales: 800-544-4186 ■ *Web:* www.altium.com

ANSYS Inc 275 Technology Dr .... Canonsburg PA 15317 724-746-3304 514-9494
NASDAQ: ANSS ■ *TF:* 800-937-3321 ■ *Web:* www.ansys.com

Ashlar Inc 9600 Great Hills Trl Ste 150W-1625 .... Austin TX 78759 512-250-2186 250-5811
TF: 800-877-2745 ■ *Web:* www.ashlar.com

Aspen Technology Inc 200 Wheeler Rd .... Burlington MA 01803 781-221-6400 221-6410
NASDAQ: AZPN ■ *TF:* 888-996-7100 ■ *Web:* www.aspentech.com

Autodesk Inc 111 McInnis Pkwy .... San Rafael CA 94903 415-507-5000 507-5100
NASDAQ: ADSK ■ *TF Tech Supp:* 800-964-6432 ■ *Web:* www.autodesk.com

Bentley Systems Inc 685 Stockton Dr .... Exton PA 19341 610-458-5000 458-1060
TF: 800-236-8539 ■ *Web:* www.bentley.com

Bohannan Huston Inc
7500 Jefferson St NE Courtyard 1 .... Albuquerque NM 87109 505-823-1000 798-7988
TF: 800-877-5332 ■ *Web:* www.bhinc.com

CACI MTL Systems Inc 2685 Hibiscus Way .... Beavercreek OH 45431 937-426-3111
Web: www.caci.com

Cadalog Inc 1448 King St .... Bellingham WA 98229 360-647-2426 647-2890
Web: www.cadalog-inc.com

Cadence Design Systems Inc 2655 Seely Ave .... San Jose CA 95134 408-943-1234 428-5001
NASDAQ: CDNS ■ *TF Cust Svc:* 800-746-6223 ■ *Web:* www.cadence.com

CambridgeSoft Corp 100 CambridgePark Dr .... Cambridge MA 02140 617-588-9100 588-9190
TF: 800-315-7300 ■ *Web:* www.cambridgesoft.com

Comarco Inc 25541 Commerce Ctr Dr .... Lake Forest CA 92630 949-599-7400 599-1415
OTC: CMRO ■ *TF:* 800-792-0250 ■ *Web:* www.comarco.com

CSA Inc 280 I- N Cir SE Ste 250 .... Atlanta GA 30339 770-955-3518 956-8748
TF: 800-844-6584 ■ *Web:* www.csaatl.com

Data Description Inc 840 Hanshaw Rd Second Fl .... Ithaca NY 14850 607-257-1000 257-4146*
**Fax:* Sales ■ *Web:* www.datadesk.com

Direct Source Inc 8176 Mallory Ct .... Chanhassen MN 55317 952-934-8000 934-8030
TF: 800-934-8055 ■ *Web:* www.directsource.com

Disk Software Inc 205 Ridgestone Dr .... Murphy TX 75094 972-423-7288
Web: www.disksoft.com

DP Technology Corp 1150 Avenida Acaso .... Camarillo CA 93012 805-388-6000 388-3085
TF: 800-627-8479 ■ *Web:* www.dptechnology.com

Engineered Software Inc
615 Guilford College Rd PO Box 18344 .... Greensboro NC 27409 336-299-4843
Web: www.engsw.com

Evolution Computing
7000 N 16th St Ste 120 514 .... Phoenix AZ 85020 800-874-4028
TF: 800-874-4028 ■ *Web:* www.fastcad.com

Geocomp Corp 1145 Massachusetts Ave .... Boxborough MA 01719 978-635-0012 635-0266
TF Cust Svc: 800-822-2669 ■ *Web:* www.geocomp.com

Gibbs & Assoc 323 Science Dr .... Moorpark CA 93021 805-523-0004 523-0006
TF Cust Svc: 800-654-9399 ■ *Web:* gibbscam.com

Infinite Graphics Inc 4611 E Lake St .... Minneapolis MN 55406 612-721-6283 721-3802
OTC: INFG ■ *TF:* 800-679-0676 ■ *Web:* www.igi.com

Intergraph Corp 19 Interpro Rd .... Madison AL 35758 256-730-2000 730-2048
TF: 800-345-4856 ■ *Web:* www.intergraph.com

Kubotek USA Two Mt Royal Ave Ste 500 .... Marlborough MA 01752 508-229-2020 229-2121
TF: 800-372-3872 ■ *Web:* kubotek3d.com

LINDO Systems Inc 1415 N Dayton St .... Chicago IL 60622 312-988-7422 988-9065
TF Sales: 800-441-2378 ■ *Web:* www.lindo.com

Magma Design Automation Inc
1650 Technology Dr .... San Jose CA 95110 408-565-7500 565-7501
NASDAQ: LAVA ■ *Web:* www.magma-da.com

Mathworks Inc Three Apple Hill Dr .... Natick MA 01760 508-647-7000 647-7001
Web: www.mathworks.in

Mentor Graphics Corp 8005 SW Boeckman Rd .... Wilsonville OR 97070 503-685-7000 685-1204
NASDAQ: MENT ■ *TF:* 800-592-2210 ■ *Web:* www.mentor.com

MSC.Software Corp Two MacArthur Pl .... Santa Ana CA 92707 714-540-8900 784-4056
TF: 800-345-2078 ■ *Web:* www.mscsoftware.com

National Instruments Corp 11500 N Mopac Expy .... Austin TX 78759 512-794-0100 683-8411
NASDAQ: NATI ■ *TF Cust Svc:* 800-433-3488 ■ *Web:* www.ni.com

Numerical Control Computer Sciences
2600 Michelson Dr Ste 1700 .... Irvine CA 92612 949-852-3665 553-1911
Web: www.nccs.com

Parametric Technology Corp (PTC)
140 Kendrick St .... Needham MA 02494 781-370-5000 370-6000
NASDAQ: PTC ■ *TF:* 800-613-7535 ■ *Web:* www.ptc.com

Planit Solutions Inc 3800 Palisades Dr .... Tuscaloosa AL 35405 205-556-9199 556-9210
TF: 800-280-6932 ■ *Web:* www.verosoftware.com

				Phone	Fax
PMS Systems Corp 2800 28th St Ste 109 *TF:* 800-755-3968 ■ *Web:* www.assetsmart.com	Santa Monica	CA	90405	310-450-2566	450-1311
Science Application International Corp Inc (SAIC Inc) 1710 SAIC Dr **Fax:* News Rm ■ *TF:* 866-400-7242 ■ *Web:* www.saic.com	McLean	VA	22102	703-676-4300	676-2269*
Tripos Inc 1699 S Hanley Rd *TF:* 800-323-2960 ■ *Web:* certara.com	Saint Louis	MO	63144	314-647-1099	647-9241
Triton Services Inc 2014 Industrial Dr *Web:* www.tritonsvc.com	Annapolis	MD	21401	443-716-0600	716-0601
Zuken USA 238 Littleton Rd Ste 100 *TF:* 800-447-7332 ■ *Web:* www.zuken.com	Westford	MA	01886	978-692-4900	692-4725

181-6 Games & Entertainment Software

				Phone	Fax
Abacus Software Inc 3413 Roger B Chaffee Memorial Blvd SE *Web:* www.abacuspub.com	Grand Rapids	MI	49546	616-241-3404	
Activision Inc 3100 Ocean Pk Blvd *Web:* www.activision.com	Santa Monica	CA	90405	310-255-2000	479-4005
Apogee Software Inc 1999 S Bascom Ave Ste 250 *Web:* www.apogee.com	Campbell	CA	95008	408-369-9001	369-9018
Bethesda Softworks LLC 1370 Piccard Dr Ste 120 *Web:* www.bethsoft.com	Rockville	MD	20850	301-926-8300	926-8010
Capcom USA Inc 800 Concar Dr Ste 300 *Web:* www.capcom.com	San Mateo	CA	94402	650-350-6500	350-6657
Cyan Worlds Inc 14617 N Newport Hwy *Web:* cyanworlds.com	Mead	WA	99021	509-468-0807	467-2209
Disney Consumer Products 500 S Buena Vista St **Fax Area Code:* 215 ■ **Fax:* Cust Svc ■ *TF PR:* 877-282-8322 ■ *Web:* thewaltdisneycompany.com	Burbank	CA	91521	818-560-1000	553-5402*
Electronic Arts Inc (EA) 209 Redwood Shores Pkwy *NASDAQ: EA* ■ *Web:* www.ea.com	Redwood City	CA	94065	650-628-1500	628-1414
Her Interactive Inc 1150 114th Ave SE Ste 200 *TF Orders:* 800-461-8787 ■ *Web:* www.herinteractive.com	Bellevue	WA	98004	425-460-8787	460-8788
iEntertainment Network Inc 124 Quade Dr P.O. Box 3897 *OTC: IENT* ■ *TF:* 800-395-8425 ■ *Web:* www.ient.com	Cary	NC	27519	919-238-4090	678-8302
Jim Henson Co 1416 N La Brea Ave *Web:* www.henson.com	Hollywood	CA	90028	323-802-1500	802-1825
Lucasfilm Ltd LucasArts Entertainment Div 1110 Gorgas St *Web:* starwars.com/games-apps	San Francisco	CA	94129	415-746-8000	746-8923
MakeMusic! Inc 7615 Golden Triangle Dr Ste M *NASDAQ: MMUS* ■ *TF:* 800-843-2066 ■ *Web:* www.makemusic.com	Eden Prairie	MN	55344	952-937-9611	937-9760
Nintendo of America Inc 4820 150th Ave NE *TF Cust Svc:* 800-255-3700 ■ *Web:* www.nintendo.com	Redmond	WA	98052	425-882-2040	882-3585
NovaLogic Inc 27489 Agoura Rd *Web:* www.novalogic.com	Agoura Hills	CA	91301	818-880-1997	865-6405
Rovi Corp 2830 de la Cruz Blvd *Web:* www.rovicorp.com	Santa Clara	CA	95050	408-562-8400	567-1800
SEGA of America Inc 350 Rhode Island Street Suite 400 *Web:* www.sega.com	San Francisco	CA	94103	415-701-6000	701-6001
Take-Two Interactive Software Inc 622 Broadway *NASDAQ: TTWO* ■ *Web:* www.take2games.com	New York	NY	10012	646-536-2842	536-2926
THQ Inc 29903 Agoura Rd *NASDAQ: THQI* ■ *Web:* thq.com	Agoura Hills	CA	91301	818-871-5000	871-7400
TreyArch 3420 Ocean Pk Blvd Ste 1000 *Web:* www.treyarch.com	Santa Monica	CA	90405	310-581-4700	581-4702
WildTangent Inc 18578 NE 67th Ct Redmond E Office Complex Bldg 5 *Web:* www.wildtangent.com	Redmond	WA	98052	425-497-4500	497-4501

181-7 Internet & Communications Software

				Phone	Fax
@Comm Corp 150 Dow St **Fax Area Code:* 603 ■ *TF:* 800-641-5400 ■ *Web:* www.atcomm.com	Manchester	NH	03101	650-375-8188	628-3140*
Activeworlds Inc 95 Parker St *Web:* www.activeworlds.com	Newburyport	MA	01950	978-499-0222	499-0221
Adaptive Micro Systems Inc 7840 N 86th St *TF:* 800-558-4187 ■ *Web:* www.adaptivedisplays.com	Milwaukee	WI	53224	414-357-2020	357-2029
Akamai Technologies Inc Eight Cambridge Ctr *NASDAQ: AKAM* ■ *TF:* 877-425-2624 ■ *Web:* www.akamai.com	Cambridge	MA	02142	617-444-3000	444-3001
Alexa Internet PO Box 29141 *Web:* www.alexa.com	San Francisco	CA	94129	415-561-6900	561-6795
Amcom Software Inc 10400 Yellow Cir Dr *TF:* 800-852-8935 ■ *Web:* spok.com/	Eden Prairie	MN	55343	952-230-5200	230-5510
Answers Corp 237 W 35th St Ste 1101 *TF:* 888-885-5008 ■ *Web:* www.answers.com	New York	NY	10001	646-502-4778	502-4778
AnyDoc Software Inc 28500 Clemens Road Ste 800 **Fax Area Code:* 813 ■ *TF:* 888-495-2638 ■ *Web:* www.onbase.com/en/product/onbaseanydoc	Westlake	OH	44145	888-495-2638	222-0018*
Apex Voice Communications Inc 21031 Ventura Blvd Second Fl *TF:* 800-727-3970 ■ *Web:* www.apexvoice.com	Woodland Hills	CA	91364	818-379-8400	379-8410
Ariba Inc 807 11th Ave *NASDAQ: ARBA* ■ *TF:* 866-772-7422 ■ *Web:* www.ariba.com	Sunnyvale	CA	94089	650-390-1000	
Asure Softwar 110 Wild Basin Rd *NASDAQ: ASUR* ■ *TF:* 888-323-8835 ■ *Web:* www.asuresoftware.com	Austin	TX	78746	512-437-2700	437-2365
AttachmateWRQ 1500 Dexter Ave N *TF Sales:* 800-872-2829 ■ *Web:* www.attachmate.com	Seattle	WA	98109	206-217-7500	217-7515
Authorize.Net Corp PO Box 8999 *TF:* 877-447-3938 ■ *Web:* www.authorize.net	San Francisco	CA	94128	801-492-6450	492-6489
Automation Technology Inc 2001 Gateway Pl *Web:* www.intertek.com	San Jose	CA	95110	408-350-7020	350-7021
Avanquest Software USA 1333 W 120th Ave *Web:* www.avanquest.com	Westminster	CO	80234	303-450-1139	
Avistar Communications Corp 1875 S Grant St 10th Fl *OTC: AVSR* ■ *TF:* 800-803-0153 ■ *Web:* www.avistar.com	San Mateo	CA	94402	650-525-3300	525-1360
Axeda Systems Inc 25 Forbes Blvd *TF:* 800-613-7535 ■ *Web:* www.axeda.com	Foxboro	MA	02035	508-337-9200	337-9201
Big Sky Technologies 9325 Sky Pk Ct Ste 120 *TF:* 800-736-2751 ■ *Web:* www.bigskytech.com	San Diego	CA	92123	858-715-5000	715-5010
Blast Inc 220 Chatham Business Dr PO Box 818 *TF:* 800-242-5278 ■ *Web:* www.blast.com	Pittsboro	NC	27312	919-533-0143	542-5955
Callware Technologies Inc 9100 S 500 W *TF:* 800-888-4226 ■ *Web:* www.callware.com	Sandy	UT	84070	801-988-6800	
ClickSoftware Inc 35 Corporate Dr Ste 400 *NASDAQ: CKSW* ■ *TF:* 888-438-3308 ■ *Web:* www.clicksoftware.com	Burlington	MA	01803	781-272-5903	272-6409
Continuous Computing Corp 9450 Carroll Pk Dr *Web:* www.ccpu.com	San Diego	CA	92121	858-882-8800	777-3388
Cothern Computer Systems Inc 1640 Lelia Dr Ste 200 *TF:* 800-844-1155 ■ *Web:* www.ccslink.com	Jackson	MS	39216	601-969-1155	969-1184
Cykic Software Inc PO Box 3098 *Web:* www.cykic.com	San Diego	CA	92163	619-459-8799	
DataMotion Inc 35 Airport Rd Ste 120 *TF:* 800-672-7233 ■ *Web:* datamotion.com	Morristown	NJ	07960	973-455-1245	455-0750
DealerTrack Holdings Inc 1111 Marcus Ave Ste M04 *NASDAQ: TRAK* ■ *TF:* 877-357-8725 ■ *Web:* www.dealertrack.com	New Hyde Park	NY	11042	516-734-3600	
Deerfield Communications Co 4241 Old US 27 S PO Box 851 *TF:* 800-599-8856 ■ *Web:* www.deerfield.com	Gaylord	MI	49735	989-732-8856	731-9299
Dynamic Instruments Inc 3860 Calle Fortunada *TF:* 800-793-3358 ■ *Web:* www.dynamicinst.com	San Diego	CA	92123	858-278-4900	278-6700
eAcceleration Corp 1050 NE Hostmark St Ste 100-B *TF Sales:* 800-803-4588 ■ *Web:* www.eacceleration.com	Poulsbo	WA	98370	360-779-6301	598-2450
Education Management Solutions Inc 436 Creamery Way Ste 300 **Fax Area Code:* 484 ■ *TF:* 877-367-5050 ■ *Web:* simulationiq.com/	Exton	PA	19341	610-701-7002	653-1070*
Elance Inc 441 Logue Ave Ste 150 *TF:* 877-435-2623 ■ *Web:* www.elance.com	Mountain View	CA	94043	650-316-7500	316-7501
EXTOL International Inc 529 Terry Reiley Way *TF:* 800-542-7284 ■ *Web:* www.extol.com	Pottsville	PA	17901	570-628-5500	628-6983
FutureSoft Inc 1660 Townhurst Dr Ste E *TF:* 800-989-8908 ■ *Web:* www.futuresoft.com	Houston	TX	77043	281-496-9400	496-1090
GeoTrust Inc 350 Ellis St Bldg J *TF:* 866-511-4141 ■ *Web:* www.geotrust.com	Mountain View	CA	94043	650-426-5010	237-8871
Grassroots Enterprise Inc 1875 Eye St NW Ste 900 *Web:* www.grassroots.com	Washington	DC	20006	202-371-0200	
Hilgraeve Inc 115 E Elm Ave *TF Sales:* 800-826-2760 ■ *Web:* www.hilgraeve.com	Monroe	MI	48162	734-243-0576	243-0645
Hyland Software Inc 28500 Clemens Rd *TF:* 888-495-2638 ■ *Web:* onbase.com/	Westlake	OH	44145	440-788-5000	788-5100
Ikanos Communications 47669 Fremont Blvd *NASDAQ: IKAN* ■ *Web:* www.ikanos.com	Fremont	CA	94538	510-979-0400	979-0500
Imecom Group Eight Governor Wentworth Hwy *TF:* 800-329-9099 ■ *Web:* www.imecominc.com	Wolfeboro	NH	03894	603-569-0600	569-0609
InfoNow Corp 1875 Lawrence St Ste 1200 *TF:* 855-524-3282 ■ *Web:* channelinsight.com	Denver	CO	80202	303-293-0212	293-0213
Information Builders Inc Two Penn Plz *TF:* 800-969-4636 ■ *Web:* www.informationbuilders.com	New York	NY	10121	212-736-4433	967-6406
IntelliNet Technologies Inc 1990 W New Haven Ave Ste 303 *TF:* 888-726-0686 ■ *Web:* diametriq.com/intellinet-tech/	Melbourne	FL	32904	321-726-0686	726-0683
Interact Inc 1225 L St Ste 600 *Web:* www.iivip.com	Lincoln	NE	68508	402-476-8786	
Interactive Intelligence Inc 7601 Interactive Way *NASDAQ: ININ* ■ *TF:* 800-267-1364 ■ *Web:* www.inin.com	Indianapolis	IN	46278	317-872-3000	872-3000
InternetSafety.com Inc 3979 S Main St Ste 230 *TF:* 877-944-8080 ■ *Web:* www.internetsafety.com	Acworth	GA	30101	877-944-8080	
Ion Networks Inc 120 Corporate Blvd Ste A *TF:* 800-722-8986 ■ *Web:* apitech.com	South Plainfield	NJ	07080	908-546-3900	546-3901
Jones Cyber Solutions Ltd 9697 E Mineral Ave *Web:* www.jonescyber.com	Centennial	CO	80112	303-784-3600	784-3797
KANA Software Inc 840 W California Ave Ste 100 **Fax Area Code:* 408 ■ *Web:* www.kana.com	Sunnyvale	CA	94086	650-614-8300	736-7613*
Keynote Systems Inc 777 Mariners Island Blvd *NASDAQ: KEYN* ■ *TF:* 888-539-7978 ■ *Web:* www.keynote.com	San Mateo	CA	94404	650-403-2400	403-5500
Language Automation Inc (LAI) 1660 S Amphlett Blvd Ste 106 *Web:* www.lai.com	San Mateo	CA	94402	650-571-7877	
LassoSoft LLC PO Box 33 *TF:* 888-286-7753 ■ *Web:* www.lassosoft.com	Manchester	WA	98353	954-302-3526	302-3526
LOGIKA Corp 3717 N Ravenswood Ave Ste 244 *Web:* www.logika.net	Chicago	IL	60613	773-529-3482	529-3483
Mark/Space Softworks 1999 S Bascom Ave Ste 325 *TF:* 800-799-1718 ■ *Web:* www.markspace.com	Campbell	CA	95008	408-293-7299	293-7298

Phone | Fax

Metric Stream Inc 2600 E Bayshore Rd .... Palo Alto CA 94303 650-620-2900 565-8542
Web: www.metricstream.com

Mirror Image Internet Inc 2 Highwood Dr........... Tewksbury MA 01876 781-376-1100 376-1110
TF: 800-353-2923 ■ *Web:* www.mirror-image.com

Mize Houser & Co 534 S Kansas Ave Ste 700 .... Topeka KS 66603 785-233-0536 233-1078
Web: www.mizehouser.com

Moai Technologies Inc 100 First Ave 9th Fl.......... Pittsburgh PA 15222 412-454-5550 454-5555
TF: 800-814-1548 ■ *Web:* www.moai.com

MODCOMP Inc 1500 S Powerline Rd............ Deerfield Beach FL 33442 954-571-4600 571-4700
TF: 800-940-1111 ■ *Web:* www.modcomp.com

Momentum Systems Ltd 41 Twosome Dr Ste 9..... Moorestown NJ 08057 856-727-0777 273-3765
TF: 800-279-1384 ■ *Web:* www.momsys.com

NetScout Systems Inc 310 Littleton Rd .... Westford MA 01886 978-614-4000 614-4004
NASDAQ: NTCT ■ *TF:* 800-357-7666 ■ *Web:* www.netscout.com

NetVillage.com LLC 342 Main St....................... Laurel MD 20707 301-498-7797 498-8110
TF: 888-638-8455 ■ *Web:* www.netvillage.com

NICE Systems Inc 301 Rt 17 N 10th Fl.............. Rutherford NJ 07070 201-964-2600 964-2610
TF: 800-994-4498 ■ *Web:* www.nice.com

Northcore Technologies Inc 302 E Mall............. Etobicoke ON M9B6C7 416-640-0400
NYSE: NTI

Nuance Communications Inc One Wayside Rd....... Burlington MA 01803 781-565-5000 565-5012
NASDAQ: NUAN ■ *TF:* 800-654-1187 ■ *Web:* www.nuance.com

ObjectVideo Inc 11600 Sunrise Vly Dr Ste 290 .... Reston VA 20191 703-654-9300 654-9399
Web: www.objectvideo.com

OmTool Ltd Six Riverside Dr......................... Andover MA 01810 978-327-5700 659-1323
OTC: OMTL ■ *TF:* 800-886-7845 ■ *Web:* www.omtool.com

One Touch Systems Inc 2346 Bering Dr.............. San Jose CA 95131 408-436-4600 436-4699
TF: 800-721-8682 ■ *Web:* www.onetouchsys.com

Open Text Corp 275 Frank Tompa Dr .... Waterloo ON N2L0A1 519-888-7111 888-0677
TSE: OTC ■ *TF General:* 800-499-6544 ■ *Web:* www.opentext.com

Open Text Corp (USA)
100 Tri-State International Pkwy 3rd Fl............. Lincolnshire IL 60069 847-267-9330 267-9332
TSE: OTC ■ *TF Sales:* 800-507-5777 ■ *Web:* www.opentext.com

OpenCon Systems Inc 377 Hoes Ln................ Piscataway NJ 08854 732-463-3131 463-3557
Web: www.opencon.com

OpenConnect Systems Inc 2711 LBJ Fwy Ste 700....... Dallas TX 75234 972-484-5200 484-6100
TF: 800-551-5881 ■ *Web:* www.oc.com

OpenTV Corp 275 Sacramento St .... San Francisco CA 94111 415-962-5000 962-5300
Web: www.nagra.com

Openwave Systems Inc One Wall St .... Burlington MA 01803 781-313-1400 480-8100*
**Fax Area Code:* 650 ■ *Web:* www.openwave.com

Paloma Systems Inc 11250 Waples Mill Rd............. Fairfax VA 22030 703-626-5024 591-0985
TF: 855-300-2686 ■ *Web:* www.palomasys.com

PartsRiver Inc 3155 Kearney St Ste 210............... Fremont CA 94538 855-700-7278 413-0079*
**Fax Area Code:* 510 ■ *TF:* 855-700-7278 ■ *Web:* www.partsriver.com

PCTEL Inc 471 Brighton Dr.................... Bloomingdale IL 60108 630-372-6800 372-8077
NASDAQ: PCTI ■ *Web:* www.pctel.com

Powersteering Software Inc 25 First St............ Cambridge MA 02141 617-492-0707 492-9444
TF: 866-390-9088 ■ *Web:* www.powersteeringsoftware.com

Propel Software Corp 1010 Rincon Cir .... San Jose CA 95131 408-571-6300 577-1070
TF: 866-799-4767 ■ *Web:* www.propel.com

QSA ToolWorks LLC 3100 47th Ave .... Long Island City NY 11101 516-935-9151 662-2636*
**Fax Area Code:* 570 ■ *TF:* 800-784-7018 ■ *Web:* www.qsatoolworks.com

Quadbase Systems Inc
275 Saratoga Ave Ste 105........................ Santa Clara CA 95050 408-982-0835 982-0838
Web: www.quadbase.com

Qualcomm Inc 5775 Morehouse Dr................. San Diego CA 92121 858-587-1121 658-2100
NASDAQ: QCOM ■ *Web:* www.qualcomm.com

Selectica Inc 2121 S. El Camino Rl 10th Fl........... San Mateo CA 94403 650-532-1500 570-9705*
NASDAQ: SLTC ■ **Fax Area Code:* 408 ■ *TF:* 877-712-9560 ■ *Web:* www.selectica.com

Sendmail Inc 6475 Christie Ave Ste 350 .... Emeryville CA 94608 510-594-5400 594-5429
TF: 888-594-3150 ■ *Web:* www.sendmail.com

Smith Micro Software Inc
51 Columbia St Ste 200.......................... Aliso Viejo CA 92656 949-362-5800 362-2300
NASDAQ: SMSI ■ *Web:* www.smithmicro.com

Support.com Inc 900 Chesapeake Dr 2nd Fl .... Redwood City CA 94063 650-556-9440 556-1195
NASDAQ: SPRT ■ *TF:* 877-493-2778 ■ *Web:* www.support.com

Surety LLC 12020 Sunrise Vly Dr Ste 250................ Reston VA 20191 571-748-5800 748-5810
TF: 800-298-3115 ■ *Web:* www.surety.com

Sybase Inc 1 Sybase Dr .... Dublin CA 94568 925-236-5000 236-4321
TF: 800-792-2735 ■ *Web:* www.sybase.com

Symantec Corp 350 Ellis St.................. Mountain View CA 94043 650-527-8000 527-8050
NASDAQ: SYMC ■ *TF:* 800-441-7234 ■ *Web:* www.symantec.com

Symphony SMS 14881 Quorum Dr Ste 800.............. Dallas TX 75254 972-581-7300 581-7301
Web: www.tangoe.com

Telenity Inc 755 Main St Ste 7....................... Monroe CT 06468 203-445-2000 268-1860
Web: www.telenity.com

Transend Corp 225 Emerson St..................... Palo Alto CA 94301 650-324-5370 324-5377
Web: www.transend.com

UmeVoice Inc 20C Pimentel Ct Ste 1................... Novato CA 94949 415-883-1500
TF: 888-230-3300 ■ *Web:* www.theboom.com

Vendio Services Inc 2800 Campus Dr Ste 150........ San Mateo CA 94403 650-293-3500
Web: www.vendio.com

Verint Systems Inc 330 S Service Rd .... Melville NY 11747 631-962-9600 962-9300
Web: www.verint.com

Vertical Communications Inc
3940 Freedom Cr Ste 110......................... Santa Clara CA 95054 408-404-1600 969-9601
OTC: VRCC ■ *TF Sales:* 800-914-9985 ■ *Web:* www.vertical.com

Visto Corp
101 Redwood Shores Pkwy Ste 400........... Redwood Shores CA 94065 650-486-6000
Web: www1.good.com

Voxware Inc 300 American Metro Blvd Ste 155......... hamilton NJ 08619 609-514-4100 514-4102
Web: www.voxware.com

WaveLink Corp 1011 Western Ave Ste 601 .... Seattle WA 98104 206-274-4280 652-2329
TF Tech Supp: 888-697-9283 ■ *Web:* www.wavelink.com

Websense Inc 10240 Sorrento Vly Rd............... San Diego CA 92121 858-320-8000 458-2950
NASDAQ: WBSN ■ *TF:* 800-723-1166 ■ *Web:* www.websense.com

Wexcel Inc 222 S Riverside Plz .... Chicago IL 60606 312-347-0955 347-0908

WorldFlash Software Inc
3853 Marcasel Ave.............................. Los Angeles CA 90066 310-775-3633
Web: www.worldflash.com

XAP Corp 3534 Hayden Ave....................... Culver City CA 90232 310-842-9800 842-9898
Web: www.xap.com

YellowBrix Inc 200 North Glebe Rd Ste 1025 .... Arlington VA 22203 703-548-3300 548-9151
TF: 888-325-9366 ■ *Web:* www.yellowbrix.com

Yodlee Inc 3600 Bridge Pkwy Ste 200 .... Redwood City CA 94065 650-980-3600 980-3602
Web: yodlee.com

Zone Alarm 800 Bridge Pkwy .... Redwood City CA 94065 415-633-4500 633-4501
TF: 877-966-5221 ■ *Web:* www.zonealarm.com

181-8 Multimedia & Design Software

Phone | Fax

3D Systems Inc 333 Three D Systems Cir............. Rock Hill SC 29730 803-326-3900
TF: 800-793-3669 ■ *Web:* www.3dsystems.com

ACD Systems International Inc
129-1335 Bear Mtn Pkwy........................... Victoria BC V9B6T9 250-419-6700 419-6742
TF: 800-579-5309 ■ *Web:* www.acdsee.com

Adobe Systems Inc 345 Pk Ave..................... San Jose CA 95110 408-536-6000 537-6000
NASDAQ: ADBE ■ *TF:* 800-833-6687 ■ *Web:* www.adobe.com

Apple Inc One Infinite Loop...................... Cupertino CA 95014 408-996-1010 996-0275*
NASDAQ: AAPL ■ **Fax:* Mail Rm ■ *TF Cust Svc:* 800-275-2273 ■ *Web:* www.apple.com

Auto FX Software 141 Village St Ste 2 .... Birmingham AL 35242 205-980-0056 980-1121
TF: 800-839-2008 ■ *Web:* www.autofx.com

Autodesk 210 King St E .... Toronto ON M5A1J7 416-362-9181 369-6140
Web: www.autodesk.com

Autodessys Inc 2011 Riverside Dr .... Columbus OH 43221 614-488-8838 488-0848
Web: www.formz.com

Avid Technology Inc 65-75 Network Dri .... Burlington MA 01803 978-640-6789 640-3366
NASDAQ: AVID ■ *TF:* 800-949-2843 ■ *Web:* www.avid.com

Brilliant Digital Entertainment Inc
14011 Ventura Blvd Ste 501.................... Sherman Oaks CA 91423 818-386-2179
Web: www.globalfileregistry.com

Chyron Corp 5 Hub Dr............................ Melville NY 11747 631-845-2000 845-3895*
NASDAQ: CHYR ■ **Fax:* Sales ■ *TF:* 800-642-1687 ■ *Web:* chyronhego.com/

Concurrent 4375 River Green Pkwy Ste 100 .... Duluth GA 30096 678-258-4000 258-4300
NASDAQ: CCUR ■ *TF:* 877-978-7363 ■ *Web:* www.ccur.com

Corel Corp 1600 Carling Ave....................... Ottawa ON K1Z8R7 613-728-8200 761-9176
TF Orders: 800-772-6735 ■ *Web:* www.corel.com

Dassault SystŠmes 166 Valley St .... Providence RI 02909 401-276-4400 276-4408
Web: simulia.com

DeLorme Two DeLorme Dr PO Box 298............... Yarmouth ME 04096 207-846-7000 561-5105*
**Fax Area Code:* 800 ■ *TF Sales:* 800-452-5931 ■ *Web:* www.delorme.com

Equilibrium Inc 3 Harbor Dr .... Sausalito CA 94965 415-332-4343 331-8374
TF: 855-378-4542 ■ *Web:* equilibrium.com

eWorkplace Solutions Inc
24461 Ridge Rt Dr Ste 210..................... Laguna Hills CA 92653 949-583-1646 271-4620
TF: 888-477-7989 ■ *Web:* www.batchmaster.com

Fonthead Design Inc 3210 S Lansdowne Dr .... Wilmington DE 19810 302-479-7922 806-1006*
**Fax Area Code:* 866 ■ *Web:* www.fonthead.com

HydroCAD Software Solutions LLC PO Box 477 ...... Chocorua NH 03817 603-323-8666 323-7467
TF: 800-927-7246 ■ *Web:* www.hydrocad.net

Image Labs International PO Box 1545............. Belgrade MT 59714 406-585-7225 388-0998
TF: 800-785-5995 ■ *Web:* www.imagelabs.com

International Microcomputer Software Inc
25 Leveroni Ct .... Novato CA 94949 415-483-8000 884-9023
TF: 800-833-8082 ■ *Web:* www.imsidesign.com

Kofax PLC 15211 Laguna Canyon Rd .... Irvine CA 92618 949-783-1000 727-3144
Web: www.kofax.com

La Cie Ltd 22985 NW Evergreen Pkwy................. Hillsboro OR 97124 503-844-4500 844-4508*
**Fax:* Mktg ■ *Web:* www.lacie.com

Media 100 Inc 450 Donald Lynch Blvd............ Marlborough MA 02210 508-460-1600 460-8627
TF: 888-772-6747 ■ *Web:* www.borisfx.com

MicroVision Development Inc
5541 Fermi Ct Ste 120............................ Carlsbad CA 92008 760-438-7781 438-7406
TF: 800-998-4555 ■ *Web:* www.mvd.com

Minds-Eye-View Inc 103 Remsen St Ste 201 .... Cohoes NY 12047 518-237-1975
Web: www.ipix.com

Mitek Systems Inc 8911 Balboa Ave Ste B .... San Diego CA 92123 858-503-7810 503-7820
Web: www.miteksys.com

Nemetschek North America 7150 Riverwood Dr ...... Columbia MD 21046 410-290-5114 290-8050
TF: 888-646-4223 ■ *Web:* www.vectorworks.net

NewTek Inc 5131 Beckwith Blvd.................. San Antonio TX 78249 210-370-8000 370-8001
TF Cust Svc: 800-862-7837 ■ *Web:* www.newtek.com

Octopus Media LLC 412 Eigth Ave .... New York NY 10001 212-967-5191

Onyx Computing 10 Avon St...................... Cambridge MA 02138 617-876-3876 868-8033
Web: www.onyxtree.com

Overwatch Geospatial Operations
21660 Ridgetop Cir Ste 110......................... Sterling VA 20166 703-437-7651 437-0039
Web: textronsystems.com/company-overview/rebrand

PaceWorks Inc 16780 Lark Ave..................... Los Gatos CA 95032 408-354-5711 884-2281
Web: www.paceworks.com

Patton & Patton Software Corp
1796 W Wimbledon Way .... Tucson AZ 85737 520-638-8738 888-2937
Web: www.patton-patton.com

PC/Nametag 124 Horizon Dr PO Box 8604 .... Verona WI 53593 877-626-3824 233-9787*
**Fax Area Code:* 800 ■ *TF:* 877-626-3824 ■ *Web:* www.pcnametag.com

Peerless Systems Corp
1055 Washington Blvd 8th Fl....................... Stamford CT 06901 203-350-0040
NASDAQ: PRLS ■ *Web:* www.peerless.com

Prediction Systems Inc
309 Morris Ave Ste G.......................... Spring Lake NJ 07762 732-449-6800 449-0897
Web: www.predictsys.com

Presagis 1301 W George Bush Fwy Ste 120.......... Richardson TX 75080 800-361-6424 467-4564*
**Fax Area Code:* 469 ■ *TF:* 800-361-6424 ■ *Web:* www.presagis.com

Quark Inc 1800 Grant St .... Denver CO 80203 800-676-4575 894-3399*
**Fax Area Code:* 303 ■ *TF Cust Svc:* 800-676-4575 ■ *Web:* www.quark.com

RealNetworks Inc 2601 Elliott Ave Ste 1000 .... Seattle WA 98121 206-674-2700 674-2696
NASDAQ: RNWK ■ *TF Cust Svc:* 888-484-8256 ■ *Web:* www.realnetworks.com

Scan-Optics Inc 169 Progress Dr.................. Manchester CT 06042 860-645-7878 645-7995
TF: 800-543-8681 ■ *Web:* www.scanoptics.com

				Phone	Fax
Sigma Design 5521 Jackson St *TF Sales:* 888-990-0900 ■ *Web:* www.arriscad.com	Alexandria	LA	71303	318-449-9900	449-9901
Silicon Graphics Inc (SGI) 900 N McCarthy Blvd. *Web:* www.sgi.com	Milpitas	CA	95035	669-900-8000	
SoftPress Systems Inc 3020 Bridgeway Ste 408 *TF:* 800-853-6454 ■ *Web:* www.softpress.com	Sausalito	CA	94965	415-331-4820	331-4824
Spatial Corp 310 Interlocken Pkwy Ste 200 *Web:* www.spatial.com	Broomfield	CO	80021	303-544-2900	544-3000
TechSmith Corp 2405 Woodlake Dr. *TF:* 800-517-3001 ■ *Web:* www.techsmith.com	Okemos	MI	48864	517-381-2300	381-2336
Telestream Inc 848 Gold Flat Rd Ste 1 *TF:* 877-681-2088 ■ *Web:* www.telestream.net	Nevada City	CA	95959	530-470-1300	470-1301
Three D Graphics Inc 11340 W Olympic Blvd Ste 352 *TF:* 800-913-0008 ■ *Web:* www.threedgraphics.com	Los Angeles	CA	90064	310-231-3330	231-3303
Videotex Systems Inc 10255 Miller Rd *TF:* 800-888-4336 ■ *Web:* www.videotexsystems.com	Dallas	TX	75238	972-231-9200	231-2420
Worlds.com Inc 11 Royal Rd. *TF:* 800-315-2580 ■ *Web:* www.worlds.com	Brookline	MA	02445	617-725-8900	975-3888

181-9 Personal Software

				Phone	Fax
APEX Analytix Inc 1501 Highwoods Blvd Ste 200-A **Fax:* Hum Res ■ *TF:* 866-577-8183 ■ *Web:* www.apexanalytix.com	Greensboro	NC	27410	336-272-4669	387-1775*
Approva Corp 13454 Sunrise Vly Dr Ste 500 *Web:* www.infor.com	Herndon	VA	20171	703-956-8300	956-8350
Corel Corp 1600 Carling Ave. *TF Orders:* 800-772-6735 ■ *Web:* www.corel.com	Ottawa	ON	K1Z8R7	613-728-8200	761-9176
Equis International 90 South 400 West Ste 620 *TF Sales:* 800-882-3040 ■ *Web:* www.metastock.com	Salt Lake City	UT	84101	801-265-9996	265-3999
HowardSoft 7852 Ivanhoe Ave **Fax Area Code:* 800 ■ *Web:* www.howardsoft.com	La Jolla	CA	92037	858-454-0121	248-2937*
Intuit Inc 2632 Marine Way *NASDAQ: INTU* ■ *TF Cust Svc:* 800-446-8848 ■ *Web:* www.intuit.com	Mountain View	CA	94043	650-944-6000	944-5656
Logos Bible Software 1313 Commercial St *Web:* www.logos.com	Bellingham	WA	98225	360-527-1700	527-1701
Micro Logic Corp 666 Godwin Ave *Web:* www.miclog.com	Midland Park	NJ	07432	201-962-7510	
Microsoft Corp One Microsoft Way *NASDAQ: MSFT* ■ *Web:* www.microsoft.com	Redmond	WA	98052	425-882-8080	936-7329
MOTU Inc 1280 Massachusetts Ave. *Web:* www.motu.com	Cambridge	MA	02138	617-576-2760	576-3609
Musicam USA 670 N Beers St Bldg 4 *Web:* www.musicamusa.com	Holmdel	NJ	07733	732-739-5600	739-1818
Nolo.com 950 Parker St *TF:* 800-728-3555 ■ *Web:* www.nolo.com	Berkeley	CA	94710	800-728-3555	645-0895
Radialpoint 2050 Bleury St Ste 300 *TF:* 866-286-2636 ■ *Web:* www.radialpoint.com	Montreal	QC	H3A2J5	514-286-2636	286-0558
Sony Creative Software 1617 Sherman Ave. *TF:* 800-577-6642 ■ *Web:* www.sonycreativesoftware.com	Madison	WI	53704	608-256-3133	250-1745
Stevens Creek Software PO Box 2126 *TF:* 800-823-4279 ■ *Web:* www.stevenscreek.com	Cupertino	CA	95015	408-725-0424	366-1954
Symantec Corp 350 Ellis St. *NASDAQ: SYMC* ■ *TF:* 800-441-7234 ■ *Web:* www.symantec.com	Mountain View	CA	94043	650-527-8000	527-8050

181-10 Professional Software (Industry-Specific)

Companies listed here manufacture software designed for specific professions or business sectors (i.e., architecture, banking, investment, physical sciences, real estate, etc.).

				Phone	Fax
9Dots Management Corp 1010 Spring Mill Ave *Web:* satorigroupinc.com	Conshohocken	PA	19428	610-862-6300	
Access International Group Inc 248 Columbia Tpk *Web:* www.accessig.com	Florham Park	NJ	07932	973-360-0750	
Acentia 3130 Fairview Pk Dr Ste 800 *Web:* acentia.com	Falls Church	VA	22042	703-712-4000	712-4010
ACI Worldwide Inc 6060 Coventry Dr *NASDAQ: ACIW* ■ *Web:* aciworldwide.com/	Elkhorn	NE	68022	402-390-7600	
Adacel Technologies Ltd 9677 Tradeport Dr *Web:* www.adacelinc.com	Orlando	FL	32827	407-581-1560	581-1581
AGFA HealthCare Corp 10 S Academy St *TF:* 877-777-2432 ■ *Web:* www.agfahealthcare.com	Greenville	SC	29601	864-421-1600	421-1414
AIMS Inc 235 Desiard St *TF:* 800-729-2467 ■ *Web:* www.aims1.com	Monroe	LA	71201	318-323-2467	322-3472
Algorithmics Inc 185 Spadina Ave	Toronto	ON	M5T2C6	416-217-1500	971-6100
Allot Communications 300 Tradecenter Ste 4680 *TF:* 877-255-6826 ■ *Web:* www.allot.com	Woburn	MA	01801	781-939-9300	939-9393
Allscripts Healthcare Solutions 222 Merchandise Mart Plz Ste 2024 *NASDAQ: MDRX* ■ *TF:* 800-654-0889 ■ *Web:* www.allscripts.com	Chicago	IL	60654	800-654-0889	
Alternative System Concepts Inc 22 Haverhill Rd PO Box 128 *Web:* www.ascinc.com	Windham	NH	03087	603-437-2234	437-2722
Amdocs Ltd 1390 Timberlake Manor Pkwy *NYSE: DOX* ■ *TF:* 866-426-8003 ■ *Web:* www.amdocs.com	Chesterfield	MO	63017	314-212-7000	212-7500
American Traffic Solutions Inc 42 Oriental St *OTC: NEST*	Providence	RI	02908	401-274-5658	434-5807
Anchor Computer Inc 1900 New Hwy. *TF:* 800-728-6262 ■ *Web:* www.anchorcomputer.com	Farmingdale	NY	11735	631-293-6100	293-0891
ARI Network Services Inc 10850 W Pk Pl Ste 1200 *TF:* 877-805-0803 ■ *Web:* www.arinet.com	Milwaukee	WI	53224	414-973-4300	283-4357
ASI DataMyte Inc 2800 Campus Dr Ste 60 *TF:* 800-207-5631 ■ *Web:* www.asidatamyte.com	Plymouth	MN	55441	763-553-1040	553-1041
Aspyra Inc 4360 Pk Terr Dr Ste 100 *OTC: APYI* ■ *TF:* 800-437-9000 ■ *Web:* www.aspyra.com	Westlake Village	CA	91361	818-449-8671	880-4398
Avantus 15 W Strong St Ste 20A **Fax Area Code:* 800 ■ *TF:* 800-600-2510 ■ *Web:* www.advantagecredit.com	Pensacola	FL	32501	850-470-9336	600-2508*
Avaya Government Solutions Inc 12730 Fair Lakes Cir *TF:* 800-492-6769 ■ *Web:* www.avayagov.com	Fairfax	VA	22033	703-653-8000	653-8001
BatchMaster Software Inc 24461 Ridge Rt Dr Ste 210 *TF:* 800-359-0920 ■ *Web:* www.batchmaster.com	Laguna Hills	CA	92653	949-583-1646	271-4620
Baxter Planning Systems Inc 7801 N Capital of Texas Hwy Ste 250 *Web:* bybaxter.com	Austin	TX	78731	512-323-5959	323-5354
BenefitMall Inc 4851 LBJ Fwy Ste 1100 *TF:* 888-338-6293 ■ *Web:* www.benefitmall.com	Dallas	TX	75244	469-791-3300	791-3313
Brodart Co 500 Arch St. *TF:* 800-233-8467 ■ *Web:* www.brodart.com	Williamsport	PA	17701	570-326-2461	
C-Solutions Inc 1900 Folsom St Ste 205 *Web:* www.gmsworks.com	Boulder	CO	80302	303-786-9461	786-9469
CACI MTL Systems Inc 2685 Hibiscus Way *Web:* www.caci.com	Beavercreek	OH	45431	937-426-3111	
CAM Commerce Solutions Inc 17075 Newhope St Ste A *TF:* 800-726-3282 ■ *Web:* www.camcommerce.com	Fountain Valley	CA	92708	714-241-9241	241-9893
CareCentric Inc 20 Church Street 12th Fl *TF:* 866-467-8263 ■ *Web:* www.carecentrix.com	Hartford	CT	06103	800-808-1902	
Carousel Industries of North America Inc 659 S County Trl. **Fax Area Code:* 860 ■ *TF:* 800-401-0760 ■ *Web:* www.carouselindustries.com	Exeter	RI	02822	800-401-0760	760-5236*
CCH Small Firm Services 225 Chastain Meadows Ct NW Ste 200 **Fax Area Code:* 706 ■ *TF Sales:* 866-345-4171 ■ *Web:* www.taxwise.com	Kennesaw	GA	30144	866-345-4171	236-9168*
Cedara Software Corp 6303 Airport Rd Ste 500 *TF:* 800-724-5970 ■ *Web:* www.merge.com	Mississauga	ON	L4V1R8	905-364-8000	364-8100
Charles River Development Inc Seven New England Executive Pk *Web:* www.crd.com	Burlington	MA	01803	781-238-0099	238-0088
Circa Information Technology 12001 Woodruff Ave. *Web:* www.circausa.com	Downey	CA	90241	562-803-1594	803-5898
CliniComp International 9655 Towne Ctr Dr *TF:* 800-350-8202 ■ *Web:* www.clinicomp.com	San Diego	CA	92121	858-546-8202	546-1801
Cobalt Group Inc 2200 First Ave S Ste 400 **Fax Area Code:* 206 ■ *TF:* 800-909-8244 ■ *Web:* www.cobalt.com	Seattle	WA	98134	800-909-8244	269-6350*
Command Alkon Inc 1800 International Pk Dr Ste 400 *TF:* 800-624-1872 ■ *Web:* www.commandalkon.com	Birmingham	AL	35243	205-879-3282	870-1405
Community Computer Service Inc PO Box 980 *Web:* www.medent.com	Auburn	NY	13021	315-255-1751	255-3539
Computac Inc 162 N Main St. *Web:* www.computac.com	West Lebanon	NH	03784	603-298-5721	298-6189
Computers Unlimited 2407 Montana Ave. *TF:* 800-763-0308 ■ *Web:* www.cu.net	Billings	MT	59101	406-255-9500	255-9595
Construction Software Technologies Inc 4500 W Lake Forest Drive Ste 502 *TF:* 800-364-2059 ■ *Web:* www.isqft.com	Cincinnati	OH	45242	513-645-8004	645-8005
Construction Systems Software Inc 494 Covered Bridge *TF:* 800-531-1035	Schertz	TX	78154	210-979-6494	
CoStar Group Inc Two Bethesda Metro Ctr 10th Fl *NASDAQ: CSGP* ■ *TF:* 800-613-1303 ■ *Web:* www.costar.com	Bethesda	MD	20814	301-215-8300	218-2444
CSG Systems International 9555 Maroon Cir *NASDAQ: CSGS* ■ *Web:* www.csgi.com	Englewood	CO	80112	303-796-2850	200-3333
CSSC Inc 26 Mayfield Ave *Web:* www.csscinc.com	Edison	NJ	08837	732-225-5555	626-6035
Datatel Inc 4375 Fair Lakes Ct **Fax Area Code:* 703 ■ *TF:* 800-223-7036 ■ *Web:* www.ellucian.com	Fairfax	VA	22033	800-223-7036	968-4625*
DealerTrack Holdings Inc 1111 Marcus Ave Ste M04 *NASDAQ: TRAK* ■ *TF:* 877-357-8725 ■ *Web:* www.dealertrack.com	New Hyde Park	NY	11042	516-734-3600	
Deltagen Inc 1900 S Norfolk St Ste 105 *Web:* www.deltagen.com	San Mateo	CA	94403	650-345-7602	
Digineer 505 N Hwy 169 Ste 750 *Web:* www.digineer.com	Plymouth	MN	55441	763-210-2300	210-2301
Digital Harbor Inc 8229 Boone Blvd Ste 730 *Web:* www.digitalharbor.com	Tysons Corner	VA	22182	703-476-7339	
Digital Technology International 1180 N Mountain Springs Pkwy *Web:* newscyclesolutions.com/	Springville	UT	84663	801-853-5000	853-5002
DIS Corp 1315 Cornwall Ave. *TF Cust Svc:* 800-426-8870 ■ *Web:* www.dis-corp.com	Bellingham	WA	98225	360-733-7610	647-6921
Document Security Systems Inc 28 E Main St Ste 1525 *NYSE: DSS* ■ *TF:* 877-407-8031 ■ *Web:* www.dsssecure.com	Rochester	NY	14614	585-325-3610	325-2977
DynTek Inc 4440 Von Karman Ste 200 *Web:* www.dyntek.com	Newport Beach	CA	92660	949-271-6700	271-0801
Eagle Point Software Corp 4131 Westmark Dr *TF:* 800-678-6565 ■ *Web:* www.eaglepoint.com	Dubuque	IA	52002	563-556-8392	556-5321
Ellucian 4375 Fair Lakes Ct. **Fax Area Code:* 703 ■ *TF:* 800-223-7036 ■ *Web:* www.ellucian.com	Fairfax	VA	22033	610-647-5930	968-4625*
Enghouse Systems Ltd 80 Tiverton Ct Ste 800 *TSE: ESL* ■ *TF:* 866-206-0240 ■ *Web:* www.enghouse.com	Markham	ON	L3R0G4	905-946-3200	946-3201
Environmental Systems Research Institute Inc 380 New York St. *TF Sales:* 800-447-9778 ■ *Web:* www.esri.com	Redlands	CA	92373	909-793-2853	793-5953
Envision Telephony Inc 901 Fifth Ave Ste 3300 *Web:* www.envisioninc.com	Seattle	WA	98164	206-225-0800	

Company / Address	City	State	ZIP	Phone	Fax
EPIQ Systems Inc 501 Kansas Ave	Kansas City	KS	66105	913-621-9500	321-1243
NASDAQ: EPIQ ■ *Web:* www.epiqsystems.com					
Equis International 90 South 400 West Ste 620	Salt Lake City	UT	84101	801-265-9996	265-3999
TF Sales: 800-882-3040 ■ *Web:* www.metastock.com					
eResearch Technology Inc 1818 Market St Ste 1000	Philadelphia	PA	19103	215-972-0420	972-0414
NASDAQ: ERT ■ *TF:* 800-704-9698 ■ *Web:* www.ert.com					
Ericsson 1 Telcordia Dr	Piscataway	NJ	08854	732-699-2000	
TF: 800-521-2673 ■ *Web:* www.telcordia.com					
Final Draft Inc 26707 W Agoura Rd Ste 205	Calabasas	CA	91302	818-995-8995	995-4422
TF: 800-231-4055 ■ *Web:* www.finaldraft.com					
Financial Engines Inc 1804 Embarcadero Rd	Palo Alto	CA	94303	650-565-4900	565-4905
NASDAQ: FNGN ■ *TF:* 888-443-8577 ■ *Web:* www.corp.financialengines.com					
First DataBank Inc (FDB) 701 Gateway Blvd Ste 600	South San Francisco	CA	94080	800-633-3453	
TF General: 800-633-3453 ■ *Web:* www.fdbhealth.com					
FishNet Security 2575 E Camelback Rd	Phoenix	AZ	85016	602-343-2300	
TF: 888-732-9406 ■ *Web:* www.fishnetsecurity.com					
Follett Software Co 1391 Corporate Dr	McHenry	IL	60050	815-344-8700	344-8774
TF: 800-323-3397 ■ *Web:* www.follettsoftware.com					
FXCM Inc 32 Old Slip	New York	NY	10005	212-897-7660	229-0004*
NYSE: FXCM ■ **Fax Area Code:* 877 ■ *TF:* 888-503-6739 ■ *Web:* www.fxcm.com					
General Dynamics C4 Systems 400 John Quincy Adams Rd Bldg 80	Taunton	MA	02780	877-449-0600	880-4800*
**Fax Area Code:* 508 ■ *TF:* 877-449-0600 ■ *Web:* www.gdc4s.com					
Geofields Inc 1201 W Peachtree St Ste 2450	Atlanta	GA	30309	404-253-1000	875-2442
Web: www.geofields.com					
GHG Corp 960 Clear Lk City Blvd	Webster	TX	77598	281-488-8806	488-1838
TF: 866-380-4146 ■ *Web:* www.ghg.com					
Glimmerglass Networks Inc 26142 Eden Landing Rd	Hayward	CA	94545	510-723-1900	780-9851
TF: 877-723-1900 ■ *Web:* www.glimmerglass.com					
Global Turnkey Systems Inc 2001 US 46	Parsippany	NJ	07054	973-331-1010	
TF: 800-221-1746 ■ *Web:* www.gtsystems.com					
GoldenSource Corp 22 Cortlandt St	New York	NY	10007	212-798-7100	798-7238
Web: www.thegoldensource.com					
gomembers Inc 1155 Perimeter Center West Bldg 700	Atlanta	GA	30338	855-411-2783	
TF: 888-288-4634 ■ *Web:* www.aptean.com					
Guidance Software Inc 215 N Marengo Ave 2nd Fl	Pasadena	CA	91101	626-229-9191	229-9199
TF: 866-229-9199 ■ *Web:* guidancesoftware.com/					
HRsmart 2929 N Central Expwy Ste 110	Richardson	TX	75080	972-783-3000	853-5319*
**Fax Area Code:* 214 ■ *Web:* www.hrsmart.com					
iHealth Technologies 115 Perimeter Ctr Pl Ste 700	Atlanta	GA	30346	770-379-2800	379-2803
Web: www.ihealthtechnologies.com					
IHS Energy Group 15 Inverness Way E	Englewood	CO	80112	303-736-3000	
TF: 800-447-2273 ■ *Web:* www.ihs.com					
ImageWare Systems Inc 10815 Rancho BernaRdo Rd Ste 310	San Diego	CA	92127	858-673-8600	673-1770
TF: 800-842-4199 ■ *Web:* www.iwsinc.com					
Incyte Corp 1801 Augustine Cut-Off	Wilmington	DE	19803	302-498-6700	425-2750
NASDAQ: INCY ■ *Web:* www.incyte.com					
Info Tech Inc 5700 SW 34th St Ste 1235	Gainesville	FL	32608	352-381-4400	381-4444
TF: 888-352-2439 ■ *Web:* www.infotechfl.com					
Infor Global Solutions 13560 Morris Rd Ste 4100	Alpharetta	GA	30004	678-319-8000	319-8682
TF: 866-244-5479 ■ *Web:* www.infor.com					
Inmagic Inc 600 Unicorn Pk Dr	Woburn	MA	01801	781-938-4444	938-4446
TF: 800-229-8398 ■ *Web:* www.inmagic.com					
Innovative Technologies Corp (ITC) 1020 Woodman Dr Ste 100	Dayton	OH	45432	937-252-2145	254-6853
TF: 800-745-8050 ■ *Web:* www.itc-1.com					
Input 1 LLC 6200 Canoga Ave Ste 400	Woodland Hills	CA	91367	818-713-2303	340-1261
TF: 888-882-2554 ■ *Web:* www.input1.com					
Insurance Information Technologies Inc (INSTEC) 1811 Centre Pt Cir Ste 115	Naperville	IL	60563	630-955-9200	955-9240
Web: www.instec-corp.com					
Intradiem 3650 Mansell Rd Ste 500	Alpharetta	GA	30022	678-356-3500	
TF: 888-566-9457 ■ *Web:* www.intradiem.com					
IPC Systems Inc 3 2nd St 15th Fl	Jersey City	NJ	07311	201-253-2000	253-2361
Web: www.ipc.com					
ISG Technology & Data Center 127 N Seventh St	Salina	KS	67401	785-823-1555	827-3310
Web: www.isgtech.com					
Island Pacific Inc 17310 Red Hill Ave Ste 320	Irvine	CA	92614	800-994-3847	
TF: 800-994-3847 ■ *Web:* www.islandpacific.com					
Ita Software Inc 141 Portland St	Cambridge	MA	02139	617-714-2100	621-3913
Web: www.itasoftware.com					
iWay Software Two Penn Plz	New York	NY	10121	212-736-4433	967-6406
TF: 800-736-6130 ■ *Web:* www.informationbuilders.com					
Jenzabar Inc 101 Huntington Ave Ste 2200	Boston	MA	02199	617-492-9099	492-9081
TF: 800-593-0028 ■ *Web:* www.jenzabar.com					
Kinaxis 700 Silver Seven Rd	Ottawa	ON	K2V1C3	613-592-5780	592-0584
TF General: 877-546-2947 ■ *Web:* www.kinaxis.com					
Knorr Assoc Inc 10 Pk Pl PO Box 400	Butler	NJ	07405	973-492-8500	492-0453
Web: www.knorrassociates.com					
Knovalent 3135 S State St Ste 300	Ann Arbor	MI	48108	734-996-8300	996-2754
Web: www.knovalent.com					
Labware Inc Three Mill Rd Ste 102	Wilmington	DE	19806	302-658-8444	658-7894
Web: www.labware.com					
Land & Legal Solutions Inc 300 S Hamilton Ave	Greensburg	PA	15601	724-853-8992	853-3221
TF: 800-245-7900 ■ *Web:* www.landlegal.com					
Landacorp Inc 500 Orient St Ste 110	Chico	CA	95928	530-891-0853	891-8428
TF: 866-828-8263 ■ *Web:* www.landacorp.com					
Learnsomething Inc 2457 Care Dr	Tallahassee	FL	32308	850-385-7915	385-7964
Web: www.learnsomething.com					
Lumedx Corp 555 12th St Ste 2060	Oakland	CA	94607	510-419-1000	419-3699
TF: 800-966-0699 ■ *Web:* www.lumedx.com					

Company / Address	City	State	ZIP	Phone	Fax
Luminex Molecular Diagnostics 439 University Ave Ste 900	Toronto	ON	M5G1Y8	416-593-4323	593-1066
Web: www.luminexcorp.com					
LynuxWorks Inc 855 Embedded Way	San Jose	CA	95138	408-979-3900	979-3920
TF: 800-255-5969 ■ *Web:* lynx.com/index.php					
Management Information Control Systems Inc (MICS) 2025 Ninth St	Los Osos	CA	93402	805-543-7000	543-0373
TF: 800-838-6427 ■ *Web:* www.bissoftware.com					
Managing Editor Inc 610 York Rd # 250	Jenkintown	PA	19046	215-886-5662	886-5681
Web: www.maned.com					
Manhattan Assoc Inc 2300 Windy Ridge Pkwy 10th Fl	Atlanta	GA	30339	770-955-7070	955-0302
NASDAQ: MANH ■ *TF:* 877-756-7435 ■ *Web:* www.manh.com					
Market Scan Information Systems Inc 811 Camarillo Springs Ste B	Camarillo	CA	93012	800-658-7226	
TF: 800-658-7226 ■ *Web:* www.marketscan.com					
Marshall & Swift 777 S Figueroa St 12th Fl	Los Angeles	CA	90017	213-683-9000	683-9010
TF: 800-544-2678 ■ *Web:* www.marshallswift.com					
McKesson Information Solutions 5995 Windward Pkwy	Alpharetta	GA	30005	404-338-6000	338-5116*
**Fax:* Sales ■ *TF:* 800-981-8601 ■ *Web:* mckesson.com					
MDI Achieve 10900 Hampshire Ave South Ste 100	Bloomington	MN	55438	952-995-9800	995-9735
TF: 800-869-1322 ■ *Web:* www.matrixcare.com					
MEDecision Inc 601 Lee Rd Chesterbrook Corp Ctr	Wayne	PA	19087	610-540-0202	540-0270
Web: www.medecision.com					
Media Cybernetics Inc 4340 E W Hwy Ste 400	Bethesda	MD	20814	301-495-3305	495-5964
TF Sales: 800-263-2088 ■ *Web:* www.mediacy.com					
MedPlus Inc 4690 Pkwy Dr	Mason	OH	45040	513-229-5500	229-5505
TF: 800-444-6235 ■ *Web:* questdiagnostics.com/home/physicians/chartmaxx/mason-bu.html					
Megaputer Intelligence Inc 1600 W Bloomfield Rd Ste E	Bloomington	IN	47403	812-330-0110	330-0150
Web: www.megaputer.com					
Merrick Systems Inc 55 Waugh Dr Ste 400	Houston	TX	77007	713-579-3400	579-3499
TF: 800-842-8389 ■ *Web:* www.p2energysolutions.com					
MicroBilt Corp 1640 Airport Rd Ste 115	Kennesaw	GA	30144	800-884-4747	218-4997*
**Fax Area Code:* 770 ■ *TF:* 800-884-4747 ■ *Web:* www.microbilt.com					
Midrange Software Inc 12716 Riverside Dr	Studio City	CA	91607	818-762-8539	762-6256
TF: 800-737-6766 ■ *Web:* www.midrangesoftware.com					
Minitab Inc Quality Plz 1829 Pine Hall Rd	State College	PA	16801	814-238-3280	238-1702
Web: www.minitab.com					
Mortgage Builders Software 24370 NW Hwy Ste 200	Southfield	MI	48075	800-850-8060	
TF: 800-850-8060 ■ *Web:* www.mortgagebuilder.com					
Mzinga Inc 230 Third Ave	Waltham	MA	02451	781-930-5430	494-6555
TF: 888-694-6428 ■ *Web:* www.mzinga.com					
Navtech Inc 295 Hagey Blvd Ste 200	Waterloo	ON	N2L6R5	519-747-1170	747-1003
Web: www.navtechinc.com					
netGuru Inc 1240 N Van Buren St Ste 104	Anaheim	CA	92807	714-638-4878	414-0200
Web: www.netguru.com					
Netsol Technologies Inc 23901 Calabasas Rd Ste 2072	Calabasas	CA	91302	818-222-9195	222-9197
NASDAQ: NTWK ■ *Web:* www.netsoltech.com					
New England Computer Services Inc 168 Boston Post Rd Stes 6 & 7	Madison	CT	06443	203-245-3999	245-4513
TF Sales: 800-766-6327 ■ *Web:* www.necs.com					
NIC Inc 25501 W Valley Pkwy Ste 300	Olathe	KS	66061	877-234-3468	498-3472*
NASDAQ: EGOV ■ **Fax Area Code:* 913 ■ *TF:* 877-234-3468 ■ *Web:* www.egov.com					
Nissho Electronics USA Corp 226 Airport Pkwy	San Jose	CA	95110	408-969-9700	969-9701
Web: www.nelco.com					
OATSystems Inc 309 Waverley Oaks Rd Ste 306	Waltham	MA	02452	781-907-6100	907-6098
TF: 877-628-7877 ■ *Web:* www.oatsystems.com					
Olson Research Assoc Inc 10290 Old Columbia Rd	Columbia	MD	21046	410-290-6999	290-6726
TF: 888-657-6680 ■ *Web:* www.olsonresearch.com					
OpenTable Inc One Montgomery St Fourth Fl	San Francisco	CA	94103	415-344-4200	
NASDAQ: OPEN ■ *TF:* 800-673-6822 ■ *Web:* www.opentable.com					
Opex Corp 305 Commerce Dr	Moorestown	NJ	08057	856-727-1100	727-1955
TF: 800-835-2362 ■ *Web:* www.opex.com					
OSI Software Inc 777 Davis St Ste 250	San Leandro	CA	94577	510-297-5800	357-8136
Web: www.osisoft.com					
OverDrive Inc One OverDr Wy Unit C	Cleveland	OH	44125	216-573-6886	573-6888
Web: www.overdrive.com					
Packet Design Inc 2455 Augustine Dr	Santa Clara	CA	95054	408-490-1000	562-0080
Web: www.packetdesign.com					
Pason Systems Inc 6130 Third St SE	Calgary	AB	T2H1K4	403-301-3400	301-3499
TSE: PSI ■ *TF:* 877-255-3158 ■ *Web:* www.pason.com					
Passport Health Communications Inc 720 Cool Springs Blvd Ste 200	Franklin	TN	37067	615-661-5657	376-3552
TF: 888-661-5657 ■ *Web:* www.passporthealth.com					
PDF Solutions Inc 333 W San Carlos St Ste 700	San Jose	CA	95110	408-280-7900	280-7915
NASDAQ: PDFS ■ *Web:* www.pdf.com					
Picis Inc 100 Quannapowitt Pkwy Ste 405	Wakefield	MA	01880	781-557-3000	557-3140
Web: picis.com					
PKC Corp One Mill St C13 Ste 355	Burlington	VT	05401	802-658-5351	658-3078
TF: 800-752-5351 ■ *Web:* www.pkc.com					
Planet Payment Inc 670 Long Beach Blvd	Long Beach	NY	11561	516-670-3200	670-3520
NYSE: PLPM ■ *Web:* www.planetpayment.com					
Pragmatics Inc 1761 Business Ctr Dr	Reston	VA	20190	703-761-4033	438-1779
Web: www.pragmatics.com					
ProCard Inc 1819 Denver W Dr Bldg 26 Ste 300	Lakewood	CO	80401	303-279-2255	279-2874
TF: 800-469-6578 ■ *Web:* www.procard.com					
Promodel Corp 3400 Bath Pike Ste 200	Bethlehem	PA	18017	801-223-4600	226-6046
TF: 888-900-3090 ■ *Web:* www.promodel.com					
Pros Holdings Inc 3100 Main St Ste 900	Houston	TX	77002	713-335-5151	335-8144
NYSE: PRO ■ *Web:* www.pros.com					

Company	City	State	ZIP	Phone	Fax
PSI International Inc 4000 Legato Rd Ste 850 *Web:* www.psiint.com	Fairfax	VA	22033	703-621-5825	352-8236
QlikTech International AB 150 N Radnor Chester Rd Ste E220 *NASDAQ: QLIK* ■ **Fax Area Code:* 610 ■ *TF:* 888-828-9768 ■ *Web:* qlik.com/	Radnor	PA	19087	888-828-9768	975-5987*
Quality Systems Inc (QSI) 18111 Von Karman Ave Ste 600 *NASDAQ: QSII* ■ *TF Cust Svc:* 800-888-7955 ■ *Web:* www.qsii.com	Irvine	CA	92612	949-255-2600	255-2605
QUMAS 66 York St *TF Sales:* 800-577-1545 ■ *Web:* www.qumas.com	Jersey City	NJ	07302	973-805-8600	377-8687
Qvidian Corp 175 Cabot St Ste 210 **Fax Area Code:* 978 ■ *TF:* 800-272-0047 ■ *Web:* www.qvidian.com	Lowell	MA	01854	513-631-1155	703-7631*
RainMaker Software Inc 1777 Sentry Pkwy W *TF:* 800-336-0339	Blue Bell	PA	19422	610-567-3409	
Raytheon Company 10 Moulton St **Fax Area Code:* 703 ■ *TF:* 866-230-1307 ■ *Web:* www.bbn.com	Cambridge	MA	02138	617-873-8000	318-5041*
Raytheon Solipsys 8170 Maple Lawn Blvd Ste 300 *Web:* www.solipsys.com	Fulton	MD	20759	240-554-8100	554-8101
Red Wing Software Inc 491 Hwy 19 *TF:* 800-732-9464 ■ *Web:* www.redwingsoftware.com	Red Wing	MN	55066	651-388-1106	388-7950
RESUMate Inc 2500 Packard St Ste 200 *TF Cust Svc:* 800-530-9310 ■ *Web:* www.resumate.com	Ann Arbor	MI	48104	734-477-9402	429-4228
Retail Pro International LLC 400 Plz Dr Ste 200 *OTC: RTPRQ* ■ **Fax Area Code:* 949 ■ *TF:* 800-738-2457 ■ *Web:* www.retailpro.com	Folsom	CA	95630	916-605-7200	476-0177*
Reynolds & Reynolds Co One Reynolds Way *TF:* 800-767-0080 ■ *Web:* www.reyrey.com	Dayton	OH	45430	937-485-2000	
Risk Management Solutions Inc 7575 Gateway Blvd *Web:* www.rms.com	Newark	CA	94560	510-505-2500	505-2501
RiskWatch (RWI) 1237 N Gulfstream Ave *TF:* 800-360-1898 ■ *Web:* riskwatch.com/contact-us	Sarasota	Fl	34236	800-360-1898	
Sapiens International Corp 4000 CentreGreen Way Ste 150 *NASDAQ: SPNS* ■ *TF:* 888-281-1167 ■ *Web:* www.sapiens.com	Cary	NC	27513	919-405-1500	405-1700
Scantron Corp 34 Parker *TF:* 800-722-6876 ■ *Web:* www.scantron.com	Irvine	CA	92618	949-639-7500	639-7710
Schlumberger Information Solutions (SIS) 5599 San Felipe St Ste 100 *Web:* www.slb.com	Houston	TX	77056	713-513-2000	513-2006
Serendipity Systems Inc PO Box 10477 *Web:* www.serendipsys.com	Sedona	AZ	86339	928-282-6831	282-4383
Siemens Product Lifecycle Management Software Inc 5800 Granite Pkwy Ste 600 *TF:* 800-498-5351 ■ *Web:* www.plm.automation.siemens.com	Plano	TX	75024	972-987-3000	987-3397
Simulations Plus Inc 42505 Tenth St W *NASDAQ: SLP* ■ *TF:* 888-266-9294 ■ *Web:* www.simulations-plus.com	Lancaster	CA	93534	661-723-7723	723-5524
SM & A 4695 MacArthur Ct Eighth Fl *Web:* www.smawins.com	Newport Beach	CA	92660	949-975-1550	975-1624
Snap-on Diagnostics 420 Barclay Blvd *TF:* 800-424-7226 ■ *Web:* www1.snapon.com	Lincolnshire	IL	60069	847-478-0700	
Snowbound Software 309 Waverley Oaks Rd Ste 401 *Web:* www.snowbound.com	Waltham	MA	02452	617-607-2000	607-2002
Software Consulting Services LLC 630 Selvaggio Dr Ste 420 *Web:* www.newspapersystems.com	Nazareth	PA	18064	610-746-7700	746-7900
SolidWorks Corp 300 Baker Ave *TF:* 800-693-9000 ■ *Web:* www.solidworks.com	Concord	MA	01742	978-371-5011	371-7303
Spillman Technologies Inc 4625 Lake Pk Blvd *TF General:* 800-860-8026 ■ *Web:* www.spillman.com	Salt Lake City	UT	84120	801-902-1200	902-1210
SQN Banking Systems 65 Indel Ave Second Fl *TF:* 888-744-7226 ■ *Web:* www.sqnsigs.com	Rancocas	NJ	08073	609-261-5500	265-9517
StatSoft Inc 2300 E 14th St *Web:* www.statsoft.com	Tulsa	OK	74104	918-749-1119	749-2217
Stok Software Inc 9230 56th Ave Flushing Ste 287 *Web:* www.stok.com	New York	NY	11373	631-232-2228	
SunGard Trust Systems Inc 5510 77 Ctr Dr *Web:* www.sungard.com	Charlotte	NC	28217	704-527-6300	527-9617
Synergex International Corp 2330 Gold Meadow Way *TF:* 800-366-3472 ■ *Web:* www.synergex.com	Rancho Cordova	CA	95670	916-635-7300	635-6549
Synopsys Inc 700 E Middlefield Rd *NASDAQ: SNPS* ■ *TF:* 800-541-7737 ■ *Web:* www.synopsys.com	Mountain View	CA	94043	650-584-5000	965-8637
System Automation 7110 Samuel Morse Dr Ste 100 *TF:* 800-839-4729 ■ *Web:* www.systemautomation.com	Columbia	MD	21046	301-837-8000	837-8001
System Innovators Inc 10550 Deerwood Pk Blvd Ste 700 **Fax Area Code:* 904 ■ *TF:* 800-963-5000 ■ *Web:* systeminnovators.com	Jacksonville	FL	32256	800-963-5000	281-0075*
Tableau Software Inc 837 N 34th St Ste 400 *Web:* www.tableausoftware.com	Seattle	WA	98103	206-633-3400	633-3004
Thomson Elite 800 Corporate Pointe Ste 150 **Fax Area Code:* 323 ■ *TF Cust Svc:* 800-354-8337 ■ *Web:* www.elite.com	Los Angeles	CA	90230	424-243-2100	642-5400*
TMA Resources Inc 1919 Gallows Rd Fourth Fl *Web:* www.personifycorp.com	Vienna	VA	22182	703-564-5200	564-5201
TMW Systems Inc 21111 Chagrin Blvd *TF:* 800-401-6682 ■ *Web:* www.tmwsystems.com	Beachwood	OH	44122	216-831-6606	831-3606
TradeStation Group Inc 8050 SW Tenth St Ste 2000 *TF:* 800-871-3577 ■ *Web:* www.tradestation.com	Plantation	FL	33324	954-652-7000	652-7300
Transentric 1400 Douglas St Ste 0840 *TF:* 800-877-0328 ■ *Web:* www.transentric.com	Omaha	NE	68179	402-544-6000	501-2984
TransWorks 9910 Dupont Cir Dr E Ste 200 *TF:* 800-435-4691 ■ *Web:* www.trnswrks.com	Fort Wayne	IN	46825	260-487-4400	
TRX Inc 2970 Clairmont Rd Ste 300 *OTC: TRXI* ■ **Fax:* Hum Res ■ *Web:* www.trx.com	Atlanta	GA	30329	404-929-6100	929-5270*
Tyler Technologies Inc 5949 Sherry Ln Ste 1400 *NYSE: TYL* ■ **Fax Area Code:* 972 ■ *TF:* 800-431-5776 ■ *Web:* www.tylertech.com	Dallas	TX	75225	800-431-5776	713-3741*
US Dataworks Inc 1 Sugar Creek Ctr Blvd 5th Fl *OTC: UDWK* ■ *TF:* 888-254-8821 ■ *Web:* www.usdataworks.com	Sugar Land	TX	77478	281-504-8000	565-2567
US Digital Corp 1400 NE 136th Ave *TF:* 800-736-0194 ■ *Web:* www.usdigital.com	Vancouver	WA	98684	360-260-2468	260-2469
Vermont Systems Inc 12 Market Pl *TF:* 877-883-8757 ■ *Web:* www.vermontsystems.com	Essex Junction	VT	05452	802-879-6993	879-5368
Viewlocity Technologies 5339 Alpha Rd Ste 170 *Web:* www.viewlocity.com	Dallas	TX	75240	972-715-0300	
ViPS Inc 1 W Pennsylvania Ave Ste 700 *TF:* 800-242-0230 ■ *Web:* gdit.com/capabilities/health/health-payer-solutions/customer-support	Towson	MD	21204	410-832-8300	
Vital Images Inc 5850 Opus Pkwy Ste 300 *TF:* 800-208-3005 ■ *Web:* www.vitalimages.com	Minnetonka	MN	55343	952-487-9500	487-9510
VoltDelta Resources Inc 560 Lexington Ave 14th Fl *Web:* www.voltdelta.com	New York	NY	10022	212-827-2600	827-2650
Votenet Solutions Inc 1420 K St *Web:* www.votenet.com	Washington	DC	20005	202-737-2277	737-2283
VT MAK 150 Cambridge Park Dr 3rd Fl *Web:* www.mak.com	Cambridge	MA	02140	617-876-8085	876-9208
Wausau Financial Systems Inc 875 Indianhead Dr PO Box 37 *TF:* 800-937-0017 ■ *Web:* www.wausaufs.com	Mosinee	WI	54455	715-359-0427	241-2288
Weather Services International 400 Minuteman Rd *TF:* 800-872-2359 ■ *Web:* www.wsi.com	Andover	MA	01810	978-983-6300	983-6400
Wizsoft Inc 6800 Jericho Tpke Ste 120W *Web:* www.wizsoft.com	Syosset	NY	11791	516-393-5841	393-5842
Wolters Kluwer Financial Services Inc 100 S Fifth St Ste 700 *TF:* 800-552-9408 ■ *Web:* www.wolterskluwerfs.com	Minneapolis	MN	55402	612-656-7700	
Wonderware Corp 26561 Rancho Pkwy S *Web:* wonderware.com	Lake Forest	CA	92630	949-727-3200	727-3270
Worksoft Inc 15851 Dallas Pkwy Ste 855 **Fax Area Code:* 972 ■ *TF:* 866-836-1773 ■ *Web:* www.worksoft.com	Addison	TX	75001	214-239-0400	250-9900*
Xybernet Inc 10640 Scripps Ranch Blvd *TF Cust Svc:* 800-228-9026 ■ *Web:* www.xyber.net	San Diego	CA	92131	858-530-1900	530-1419

181-11 Service Software

Company	City	State	ZIP	Phone	Fax
Alorica Inc 5 Park Plaza Ste 1100 **Fax Area Code:* 909 ■ *Web:* www.alorica.com	Irvine	CA	92614	949-527-4600	606-7708*
Applied Systems Inc 200 Applied Pkwy **Fax:* Hum Res ■ *TF Sales:* 800-999-5368 ■ *Web:* www.appliedsystems.com	University Park	IL	60466	708-534-5575	534-8016*
Aptech Computer Systems Inc 135 Delta Dr *TF:* 800-245-0720 ■ *Web:* www.aptech-inc.com	Pittsburgh	PA	15238	412-963-7440	
ARINC Inc 2551 Riva Rd *TF:* 866-321-6060 ■ *Web:* www.arinc.com	Annapolis	MD	21401	410-266-4000	573-3300
Aristotle Inc 205 Pennsylvania Ave SE **Fax:* Sales ■ *TF Sales:* 800-296-2747 ■ *Web:* www.aristotle.com	Washington	DC	20003	202-543-8345	543-6407*
ASA International Ltd 10 Speen St *Web:* www.asaint.com	Framingham	MA	01701	508-626-2727	626-0645
Automated Financial Systems Inc 123 Summit Dr **Fax Area Code:* 610 ■ *Web:* www.afsvision.com	Exton	PA	19341	484-875-1250	524-7977*
Camstar Enterprise Platform 13024 Ballantyne Corporate Pl Ste 300 *Web:* www.camstar.com	Charlotte	NC	28277	704-227-6600	227-6783
Capital Growth Systems Inc 180 N LaSalle St Ste 2430 *OTC: CGSYQ* ■ *Web:* www.globalcapacity.com	Chicago	IL	60601	312-673-2400	673-2422
CaseSoft Div 5000 Sawgrass Village Cir Ste 21 *Web:* www.casesoft.com	Ponte Vedra Beach	FL	32082	904-273-5000	273-5001
Cerner Corp 2800 Rockcreek Pkwy *NASDAQ: CERN* ■ *TF:* 888-827-7220 ■ *Web:* www.cerner.com	North Kansas City	MO	64117	816-221-1024	274-1742
Datamann Inc 1994 Hartford Ave *TF:* 800-451-4263 ■ *Web:* www.datamann.com	Wilder	VT	05088	802-295-6600	296-3623
DHI Computing Service Inc 1525 West 820 North PO Box 51427 *TF:* 800-992-1344 ■ *Web:* www.dhiprovo.com	Provo	UT	84601	801-373-8518	374-5316
Digital Solutions Inc 955 SE Olson Dr *TF Cust Svc:* 888-464-8770 ■ *Web:* www.accesssystems.com	Waukee	IA	50263	515-987-6227	
DPSI Inc 1801 Stanley Rd Ste 301 *TF:* 800-897-7233 ■ *Web:* www.dpsi.com	Greensboro	NC	27407	336-854-7700	854-7715
Ebix Inc 5 Concourse Pkwy Ste 3200 *NASDAQ: EBIX* ■ *TF:* 800-755-2326 ■ *Web:* www.ebix.com	Atlanta	GA	30328	678-281-2020	281-2019
Firstwave Technologies Inc 6263 N Scottsdale Rd Ste 180 *TF:* 800-540-6061 ■ *Web:* www.firstwave.com	Scottsdale	AZ	85250	678-672-3112	
Fiserv Mortgage Products 3575 Moreau Ct Ste 2 *Web:* fiserv.com	South Bend	IN	46628	574-282-3300	282-3366
Galaxy Hotel Systems LLC 15621 Red Hill Ave Ste 100 *TF:* 800-434-9990 ■ *Web:* www.galaxyhotelsystems.com	Tustin	CA	92780	714-258-5800	258-5880
H & M Systems Software Inc 600 E Crescent Ave Ste 203 *Web:* www.hm-software.com	Upper Saddle River	NJ	07458	201-934-3414	934-9206
IHS Inc 321 Inverness Dr S *NYSE: IHS* ■ *TF:* 800-525-7052 ■ *Web:* www.ihs.com	Englewood	CO	80112	303-790-0600	397-2599
Incontact Inc 7730 S Union Pk Ave Ste 500 *NASDAQ: SAAS* ■ *TF:* 800-363-6177 ■ *Web:* www.incontact.com	Salt Lake City	UT	84047	801-320-3200	320-3330
Insurance Data Processing Inc (IDP) 8101 Washington Ln *TF:* 800-523-6745 ■ *Web:* www.idpnet.com	Wyncote	PA	19095	215-885-2150	887-4621
Jack Henry & Assoc Inc 663 W Hwy 60 PO Box 807 *NASDAQ: JKHY* ■ *TF:* 800-299-4222 ■ *Web:* www.jackhenry.com	Monett	MO	65708	417-235-6652	235-8406

Company	City	State	ZIP	Phone	Fax
Jobscope Corp 355 Woodruff Rd *TF:* 800-443-5794 ■ *Web:* www.jobscope.com	Greenville	SC	29607	864-458-3100	458-3160
Kalibrate Technologies PLC 25B Hanover Rd *TF Cust Svc:* 800-727-6774 ■ *Web:* kalibratetech.com	Florham Park	NJ	07932	973-549-1850	549-1860
Keane Care Inc 8383 158th Ave NE Ste 100 **Fax Area Code:* 425 ■ *TF:* 800-426-2675 ■ *Web:* www.nttdataltc.com	Redmond	WA	98052	800-426-2675	307-2220*
Key Information Systems Inc 21700 Oxnard St Ste 250 *TF:* 877-442-3249 ■ *Web:* www.keyisit.com	Woodland Hills	CA	91367	818-992-8950	992-8970
Kronos Inc 297 Billerica Rd *TF:* 888-293-5549 ■ *Web:* www.kronos.com	Chelmsford	MA	01824	978-250-9800	367-5900
Liquent Inc 101 Gibraltar Rd *Web:* parexel.com/liquent/	Horsham	PA	19044	215-328-4444	328-4360
Management Technology America Ltd 4742 N 24th St Ste 410 *Web:* www.mtanet.com	Phoenix	AZ	85016	602-381-5100	251-0903
Manatron Inc 510 E Milham Ave *TF Cust Svc:* 866-471-2900 ■ *Web:* tax.thomsonreuters.com	Portage	MI	49002	269-567-2900	567-2930
MC Software LLC 2650 Washington Blvd *Web:* www.mcoffice.com	Ogden	UT	84401	801-621-3900	
McCallie Assoc Inc 3906 Raynor Pkwy Ste 200 *Web:* www.mccallie.com	Bellevue	NE	68123	402-291-2203	291-8221
Mediware Information Systems Inc 11711 W 79th St *NASDAQ: MEDW* ■ *TF:* 800-255-0026 ■ *Web:* www.mediware.com	Lenexa	KS	66214	913-307-1000	307-1111
Meta Health Technology Inc 330 Seventh Ave 14th Fl *TF:* 800-334-6840 ■ *Web:* www.streamlinehealth.net	New York	NY	10001	212-695-5870	643-2913
Metafile Information Systems Inc 2900 43rd St NW *TF Sales:* 800-638-2445 ■ *Web:* metaviewer.com	Rochester	MN	55901	507-286-9232	286-9065
MicroMass Communications Inc 11000 Regency Pkwy Ste 300 *Web:* www.micromass.com	Cary	NC	27518	919-851-3182	851-3188
MicroStrategy 1850 Towers Crescent Plz *NASDAQ: MSTR* ■ *TF:* 888-266-0321 ■ *Web:* www.microstrategy.com	Tysons Corner	VA	22182	703-848-8600	848-8610
Mincron Software Systems 333 N Sam Houston Pkwy E Ste 1100 *Web:* www.mincron.com	Houston	TX	77060	281-999-7010	999-6329
Narus Inc 570 Maude Ct	Sunnyvale	CA	94085	408-215-4300	215-4301
Netsmart Technologies Inc 3500 Sunrise Hwy Ste D-122 *TF:* 800-421-7503 ■ *Web:* www.ntst.com	Great River	NY	11739	631-968-2000	968-2123
Newmarket International Inc 75 New Hampshire Ave Ste 300 *Web:* www.newmarketinc.com	Portsmouth	NH	03801	603-436-7500	436-1826
Parallels Holding 500 SW 39th St Ste 200 *Web:* www.parallels.com	Renton	WA	98057	425-282-6400	282-6444
Proscape Technologies Inc 5 Walnut Grove Dr Ste 180 *Web:* www.proscape.com	Horsham	PA	19044	215-441-0300	441-0600
Radware Inc 575 Corporate Dr Lobby 2 *TF:* 888-234-5763 ■ *Web:* www.radware.com	Mahwah	NJ	07430	201-512-9771	512-9774
Real Soft Inc 2540 Rt 130 N Ste 118 *Web:* www.realsoftinc.com	Cranbury	NJ	08512	609-409-3636	409-3637
Right On Computer Software 27 Bowdon Rd Ste B *Web:* www.rightonlibrarysoftware.com	Greenlawn	NY	11740	631-424-7777	424-7207
Sandata Technologies Inc 26 Harbor Pk Dr *TF Sales:* 800-544-7263 ■ *Web:* www.sandata.com	Port Washington	NY	11050	516-484-4400	484-6084
SS & C Technologies Inc 80 Lamberton Rd *TF:* 800-234-0556 ■ *Web:* www.ssctech.com	Windsor	CT	06095	860-298-4500	298-4900
Strictly Business Computer Systems Inc 848 Fourth Ave Ste 200 **Fax Area Code:* 304 ■ *TF:* 888-529-0401 ■ *Web:* www.sbcs.com	Huntington	WV	25701	888-529-0401	781-2590*
Successfactors Inc 1500 Fashion Island Blvd Ste 300 *NYSE: SFSF* ■ *TF:* 800-809-9920 ■ *Web:* www.successfactors.com	San Mateo	CA	94404	650-645-2000	645-2099
SunGard Pentamation Inc 1000 Business Ctr Dr Ste 1 *TF Cust Svc:* 866-965-7732 ■ *Web:* www.sungardps.com	Lake mary	FL	32746	610-691-3616	
Symphony Technology Group LLC (STG) 2475 Hanover St *Web:* www.symphonytg.com	Palo Alto	CA	94304	650-935-9500	935-9501
Synergistics Inc 16 Tech Cir *TF:* 866-455-5222 ■ *Web:* www.millennium-groupinc.com	Natick	MA	01760	508-655-1340	651-2902
Technalysis Inc 7172 Waldemar Dr *Web:* www.technalysis.com	Indianapolis	IN	46268	317-291-1985	291-7281
Teradata 900 E 96th St Ste 400 *Web:* teradata.com/teradata-applications/	Indianapolis	IN	46240	317-814-6465	
TimeValue Software 22 Mauchly *TF Sales:* 800-426-4741 ■ *Web:* www.timevalue.com	Irvine	CA	92618	949-727-1800	727-3268
TMA Systems LLC 5100 E Skelly Dr Ste 900 *TF:* 800-862-1130 ■ *Web:* www.tmasystems.com	Tulsa	OK	74135	918-858-6600	858-6655
Velos Inc 2201 Walnut Ave Ste 208 *Web:* www.velos.com	Fremont	CA	94538	510-739-4010	739-4018
Xactware Solutions Inc One Xactware Plz *TF Sales:* 800-424-9228 ■ *Web:* www.xactware.com	Orem	UT	84097	801-764-5900	932-8013
Xora Inc 850 N Shoreline Blvd *TF:* 877-477-9672 ■ *Web:* www.xora.com	Mountain View	CA	94043	650-314-6460	938-8401

181-12 Systems & Utilities Software

Company	City	State	ZIP	Phone	Fax
ACCESS Systems Americas Inc 1188 E Arques Ave *Web:* www.access-company.com	Sunnyvale	CA	94085	408-400-3000	400-1500
activePDF Inc 27405 Puerta Real Ste 100 *TF:* 866-468-6733 ■ *Web:* www.activepdf.com	Mission Viejo	CA	92691	949-582-9002	582-9004
AEP Networks Inc 347 Elizabeth Ave Ste 100	Somerset	NJ	08873	732-764-8858	764-8862
Allen Systems Group Inc (ASG) 1333 Third Ave S **Fax Area Code:* 800 ■ *TF:* 800-932-5536 ■ *Web:* www.asg.com	Naples	FL	34102	239-435-2200	325-2555*
Apex CoVantage LLC 198 Van Buren St 200 Presidents Plz *Web:* apexcovantage.com	Herndon	VA	20170	703-709-3000	709-0333
Aspect Business Solutions 7550 IH-10 W 14th Fl	San Antonio	TX	78229	210-298-5000	298-5001
Avatier Corp 2603 Camino Ramon Ste 110 *TF:* 800-609-8610 ■ *Web:* www.avatier.com	San Ramon	CA	94583	925-217-5170	275-0853
Basis International Ltd 5901 Jefferson St NE *TF Orders:* 800-423-1394 ■ *Web:* www.basis.com	Albuquerque	NM	87109	505-345-5232	345-5082
BenchmarkQA Inc 7301 Ohms Ln Ste 590 *TF:* 877-425-2581 ■ *Web:* www.benchmarkqa.com	Edina	MN	55439	952-392-2400	392-2382
Beta Systems Software of North America Inc 8300 Greensboro Dr Ste 1150 *Web:* www.betasystems.com	McLean	VA	22102	703-889-1240	889-1241
Blue Lance Inc 410 Pierce St Ste 950 *TF:* 800-856-2583 ■ *Web:* www.bluelance.com	Houston	TX	77002	713-255-4800	622-1370
bNimble Technologies 45987 Paseo Padre Pkwy Ste 7 *Web:* www.bnimbletech.com	Fremont	CA	94539	510-870-2312	445-0625
CA Inc One CA Plz *NASDAQ: CA* ■ *TF:* 800-225-5224 ■ *Web:* www.ca.com	Islandia	NY	11749	631-342-6000	342-6800
CardLogix 16 Hughes Ste 100 *TF:* 866-392-8326 ■ *Web:* www.cardlogix.com	Irvine	CA	92618	949-380-1312	380-1428
Certicom Corp 4701 Tahoe Blvd Bldg A *TF:* 800-561-6100 ■ *Web:* www.certicom.com	Mississauga	ON	L4W0B5	905-507-4220	507-4230
Check Point Software Technologies Ltd 800 Bridge Pkwy *NASDAQ: CHKP* ■ *TF:* 800-429-4391 ■ *Web:* www.checkpoint.com	Redwood City	CA	94065	650-628-2000	654-4233
Cincom Systems Inc 55 Merchant St *TF:* 800-224-6266 ■ *Web:* www.cincom.com	Cincinnati	OH	45246	513-612-2300	612-2000
Citrix Systems Inc 851 W Cypress Creek Rd *NASDAQ: CTXS* ■ *TF:* 800-393-1888 ■ *Web:* www.citrix.com	Fort Lauderdale	FL	33309	954-267-3000	267-9319
Columbia Data Products Inc 925 Sunshine Ln Ste 1080 *TF Sales:* 800-613-6288 ■ *Web:* cdp.com	Altamonte Springs	FL	32714	407-869-6700	862-4725
Communication Intelligence Corp (CIC) 275 Shoreline Dr Ste 500 *OTC: CICI* ■ *Web:* www.cic.com	Redwood Shores	CA	94065	650-802-7888	802-7777
CommuniGate Systems Inc 655 Redwood Hwy Ste 275 *TF:* 800-262-4722 ■ *Web:* www.stalker.com	Mill Valley	CA	94941	415-383-7164	383-7461
ComponentOne LLC 201 S Highland Ave Third Fl 3rd Fl *TF:* 800-858-2739 ■ *Web:* www.componentone.com	Pittsburgh	PA	15206	412-681-4343	681-4384
Condusiv Technologies 7590 N Glenoaks Blvd *TF Sales:* 800-829-6468	Burbank	CA	91504	818-771-1600	252-5512
Crossmatch 720 Bay Rd Ste 100 *TF:* 866-463-7792 ■ *Web:* www.digitalpersona.com	Redwood City	CA	94063	650-474-4000	298-8313
CSI International Inc 8120 State Rt 138 *TF:* 800-795-4914 ■ *Web:* www.csi-international.com	Williamsport	OH	43164	740-420-5400	333-7335
CSP Inc 43 Manning Rd *NASDAQ: CSPI* ■ *TF:* 800-325-3110 ■ *Web:* www.cspi.com	Billerica	MA	01821	978-663-7598	663-0150
CYA Technologies Inc 4 Research Dr	Shelton	CT	06484	203-513-3111	513-3139
DataViz Inc 612 Wheelers Farms Rd *TF:* 800-733-0030 ■ *Web:* www.dataviz.com	Milford	CT	06460	203-874-0085	874-4345
Datawatch Corp 271 Mill Rd *NASDAQ: DWCH* ■ *TF:* 800-445-3311 ■ *Web:* www.datawatch.com	Chelmsford	MA	01824	978-441-2200	441-1114
Descartes Systems Group Inc 120 Randall Dr *TSE: DSG* ■ *TF:* 800-419-8495 ■ *Web:* www.descartes.com	Waterloo	ON	N2V1C6	519-746-8110	747-0082
Digicomp Research Corp 930 Danby Rd *Web:* www.digicomp.com	Ithaca	NY	14850	607-273-5900	273-8779
Digimarc Corp 9405 SW Gemini Dr *NASDAQ: DMRC* ■ *TF:* 800-344-4627 ■ *Web:* www.digimarc.com	Beaverton	OR	97008	503-469-4800	
Distinct Corp 3315 Almaden Expy Ste 10 *Web:* www.distinct.com	San Jose	CA	95118	408-445-3270	445-3274
Diversified International Sciences Corp 4550 Forbes Blvd Ste 300	Lanham	MD	20706	301-731-9070	731-9070
E-Net Corp 300 Valley St Ste 204 *Web:* www.enet.com	Sausalito	CA	94965	415-332-6200	339-9592
EasyLink Services Corp 6025 The Corners Pwy Ste 100 *TF:* 800-209-6245 ■ *Web:* www.easylink.com	Norcross	GA	30092	678-823-4600	
eMag Solutions LLC 3495 Piedmont Rd 11 Piedmont Ctr Ste 500 *TF:* 800-364-9838 ■ *Web:* www.emagsolutions.com	Atlanta	GA	30305	404-995-6060	872-8247
EMC Corp 176 S St *NYSE: EMC* ■ *Web:* www.emc.com	Hopkinton	MA	01748	508-435-1000	497-6912
Empirix Inc 600 Technology Park Dr Ste 100 *Web:* www.empirix.com	Billerica	MA	01821	978-313-7000	313-7001
Entrust Inc 5400 LBJ Fwy Ste 1340 *TF Sales:* 888-690-2424 ■ *Web:* www.entrust.com	Dallas	TX	75240	972-728-0447	728-0440
Esker Inc 1212 Deming Way Ste 350 *TF:* 800-368-5283 ■ *Web:* www.esker.com	Madison	WI	53717	608-828-6000	828-6001
Expert Choice Inc 1501 Lee Hwy Ste 302 *TF:* 888-259-6400 ■ *Web:* www.expertchoice.com	Arlington	VA	22209	703-243-5595	243-5587
F-Secure Inc 1735 Technology Dr Ste 850 **Fax Area Code:* 408 ■ *Web:* www.f-secure.com	San Jose	CA	95110	888-432-8233	350-2339*
FalconStor Software Inc Two Huntington Quad Ste 2S01 *NASDAQ: FALC* ■ *Web:* www.falconstor.com	Melville	NY	11747	631-777-5188	501-7633
FileStream Inc 240 Glen Head Rd Ste 93 *Web:* www.filestream.com	Glen Head	NY	11545	516-759-4100	759-3011
Heroix Corp 165 Bay State Dr *TF:* 800-229-6500 ■ *Web:* www.heroix.com	Braintree	MA	02184	781-848-1701	843-3472
HID Global Corp 611 Center Ridge Dr *TF:* 800-237-7769 ■ *Web:* www.hidglobal.com	Austin	TX	78753	512-776-9000	776-9930

Company / Address	City	State	Zip	Phone	Fax
Hitachi Data Systems Corp 750 Central Expy *TF:* 877-437-3849 ■ *Web:* www.hds.com	Santa Clara	CA	95050	408-970-1000	727-8036
IMS Health 83 Wooster Heights Rd *NYSE: IMS* ■ *Web:* www.imshealth.com	Danbury	ON	06810	203-448-4600	
Infosystems Technology Inc 4 Professional Dr Ste 118 **Fax Area Code:* 301 ■ *Web:* www.rubix.com	Gaithersburg	MD	20879	202-412-0152	869-4667*
Innodata-Isogen Inc Three University Plz Dr *NASDAQ: INOD* ■ *TF:* 877-454-8400 ■ *Web:* www.innodata.com	Hackensack	NJ	07601	201-371-8000	
Innovative Security Systems Inc 1809 Woodfield Dr *Web:* gdc4s.com/pitbull	Savoy	IL	61874	217-355-6308	
International Business Machines Corp (IBM) One New OrchaRd Rd *NYSE: IBM* ■ *TF:* 800-426-4968 ■ *Web:* www.ibm.com	Armonk	NY	10504	914-499-1900	
InterTrust Technologies Corp 920 Stewart Dr Ste 100 *TF:* 800-393-2272 ■ *Web:* www.intertrust.com	Sunnyvale	CA	94085	408-616-1600	616-1626
Intrusion Inc 1101 E Arapaho Rd *TF:* 888-637-7770 ■ *Web:* www.intrusion.com	Richardson	TX	75081	972-234-6400	301-3685
Ipswitch Inc 83 Hartwell Ave *TF:* 800-793-4825 ■ *Web:* www.ipswitch.com	Lexington	MA	02421	781-676-5700	676-5710
Kroll Ontrack Inc 9023 Columbine Rd *TF:* 800-872-2599 ■ *Web:* www.krollontrack.com	Eden Prairie	MN	55347	952-937-5161	937-5750
LapLink Software Inc 600 108th Ave NE Ste 610 *TF:* 800-343-8080 ■ *Web:* www.laplink.com	Bellevue	WA	98004	425-952-6000	952-6002
Lattice Inc 1751 S Naperville Rd Ste 100 *TF Sales:* 800-444-4309 ■ *Web:* www.lattice.com	Wheaton	IL	60189	630-949-3250	949-3299
Lenel System International Inc 1212 Pittsford-Victor Rd *Web:* www.lenel.com	Pittsford	NY	14534	585-248-9720	248-9185
Luminex Software Inc 871 Marlborough Ave *TF Sales:* 888-586-4639 ■ *Web:* www.luminex.com	Riverside	CA	92507	951-781-4100	781-4105
Mainstay 1320 Flynn Rd Ste 401 *TF Orders:* 800-362-2605 ■ *Web:* www.mstay.com	Camarillo	CA	93012	805-484-9400	484-9428
Management Science Assoc Inc 6565 Penn Ave *TF:* 800-672-4636 ■ *Web:* www.msa.com	Pittsburgh	PA	15206	412-362-2000	363-5598
MARX Software Security Inc 2900 Chamblee-Tucker Rd Bldg 9 Ste 100 *TF:* 800-627-9468 ■ *Web:* www.marx.com	Atlanta	GA	30341	770-986-8887	986-8891
McAfee Inc 2821 Mission College Blvd *TF Cust Svc:* 888-847-8766 ■ *Web:* www.mcafee.com	Santa Clara	CA	95054	408-988-3832	970-9727
McCabe Software Inc 3300 N Ridge Rd *TF:* 800-638-6316 ■ *Web:* www.mccabe.com	Ellicott City	MD	21043	410-381-3710	381-7912
Mediafour Corp 1101 Fifth St *Web:* www.mediafour.com	West Des Moines	IA	50265	515-225-7409	225-6370
Micro Logic Corp 666 Godwin Ave *Web:* www.miclog.com	Midland Park	NJ	07432	201-962-7510	
Microsoft Corp One Microsoft Way *NASDAQ: MSFT* ■ *Web:* www.microsoft.com	Redmond	WA	98052	425-882-8080	936-7329
Mindjet Corp 1160 Battery St E Fourth Fl *Web:* www.mindjet.com	San Francisco	CA	94111	415-229-4200	229-4201
Mitem Corp 640 Menlo Ave *TF Sales:* 800-826-4836 ■ *Web:* www.mitem.com	Menlo Park	CA	94025	650-323-1500	323-1511
MTI Systems Inc 59 Interstate D *TF:* 800-644-4318 ■ *Web:* www.mtisystems.com	West Springfield	MA	01089	413-733-1972	739-9250
NetIQ Corp 1233 W Loop S *TF Sales:* 888-323-6768 ■ *Web:* www.netiq.com	Houston	TX	77027	713-548-1700	548-1771
Network Appliance Inc 495 E Java Dr *NASDAQ: NTAP* ■ *TF Sales:* 800-443-4537 ■ *Web:* www.netapp.com	Sunnyvale	CA	94089	408-822-6000	822-4422
New Year Tech Inc 12330 Pinecrest Rd Ste 100 *TF:* 800-525-7767 ■ *Web:* www.nyt1.net	Reston	VA	20191	703-564-0290	564-0296
Norman Data Defense Systems Inc 9302 Lee Hwy *TF:* 888-466-6762 ■ *Web:* www.norman.com	Fairfax	VA	22031	703-267-6109	934-6368
NovaStor Corp 80-B W Cochran St **Fax:* Sales ■ *Web:* www.novastor.com	Simi Valley	CA	93065	805-579-6700	579-6710*
NTP Software 20A NW Blvd Ste 136 *TF:* 800-226-2755 ■ *Web:* www.ntpsoftware.com	Nashua	NH	03063	603-622-4400	263-2375
Numara Software Inc 2202 NW Shore Blvd Ste 650 *TF Sales:* 800-557-3031 ■ *Web:* www.bmc.com	Tampa	FL	33607	813-227-4500	227-4501
Open Door Networks Inc 110 S Laurel St *Web:* www.opendoor.com	Ashland	OR	97520	541-488-4127	
Open Systems Management Inc 1511 Third Ave Ste 905 *Web:* www.osminc.com	Seattle	WA	98101	206-583-8373	
OPNET Technologies Inc 7255 Woodmont Ave *NASDAQ: OPNT* ■ *Web:* riverbed.com/products-solutions/products/opnet.html?redirect=opnet	Bethesda	MD	20814	240-497-3000	497-3001
Optical Research Assoc 3280 E Foothill Blvd *Web:* optics.synopsys.com	Pasadena	CA	91107	626-795-9101	795-9102
Oracle Corp 500 Oracle Pkwy *NYSE: ORCL* ■ *TF Sales:* 800-392-2999 ■ *Web:* www.oracle.com	Redwood Shores	CA	94065	650-506-7000	506-7200
Perceptics Corp 9737 Cogdill Rd Ste 200 **Fax Area Code:* 865 ■ *TF:* 800-448-8544 ■ *Web:* www.perceptics.com	Knoxville	TN	37932	800-448-8544	966-9330*
Pervasive Software Inc 12365 Riata Trace Pkwy Bldg B *NASDAQ: PVSW* ■ *TF:* 800-287-4383 ■ *Web:* www.pervasive.com	Austin	TX	78727	512-231-6000	231-6010
Phoenix Technologies Ltd 915 Murphy Ranch Rd *TF:* 800-677-7305 ■ *Web:* www.phoenix.com	Milpitas	CA	95035	408-570-1000	570-1001
PKWare Inc 648 N Plankinton Ave Ste 220 *Web:* pkware.com/about-us	Milwaukee	WI	53203	414-289-9788	289-9789
Plex Systems Inc 1731 Harmon Rd *Web:* www.plex.com	Auburn Hills	MI	48326	248-391-8001	393-1799
Pragma Systems Inc 13809 Research Blvd Ste 675 *TF:* 800-224-1675 ■ *Web:* www.pragmasys.com	Austin	TX	78750	512-219-7270	219-7110
Process Software Corp 959 Concord St *TF:* 800-722-7770 ■ *Web:* www.process.com	Framingham	MA	01701	508-879-6994	879-0042
RadView Software Inc 111 Deerwood Rd Ste 200 **Fax Area Code:* 925 ■ *TF:* 888-723-8439 ■ *Web:* www.radview.com	San Ramon	CA	94583	908-526-7756	831-4807*
Raxco Software Inc Six Montgomery Village Ave Ste 500 *TF Tech Supp:* 800-546-9728 ■ *Web:* www.raxco.com	Gaithersburg	MD	20879	301-527-0803	519-7711
RDKS Inc 17861 Cartwright Rd **Fax:* Sales ■ *Web:* www.litronic.com	Irvine	CA	92614	949-851-1085	851-8588*
Red Hat Inc 1801 Varsity Dr *NYSE: RHT* ■ *TF:* 888-733-4281 ■ *Web:* www.redhat.com	Raleigh	NC	27606	919-754-3700	754-3701
Relais International 1690 Woodward Dr Ste 215 *TF:* 888-294-5244 ■ *Web:* www.relais-intl.com	Ottawa	ON	K2C3R8	613-226-5571	226-0998
Rhintek Inc 8835 Columbia 100 Pkwy Ste C *Web:* www.rhintek.com	Columbia	MD	21045	410-730-2575	730-5960
RSA Security Inc 174 Middlesex Tpke *TF:* 800-995-5095 ■ *Web:* emc.com/domains/rsa/index.htm	Bedford	MA	01730	781-515-5000	515-5010
ScriptLogic Corp 6000 Broken Sound Pkwy NW *TF:* 800-306-9329 ■ *Web:* www.quest.com	Boca Raton	FL	33487	561-886-2400	886-2499
Serengeti Systems Inc 812 W 11th St Third Fl *TF:* 800-634-3122 ■ *Web:* www.serengeti.com	Austin	TX	78701	512-345-2211	480-8729
Silicon Graphics Inc (SGI) 900 N McCarthy Blvd *Web:* www.sgi.com	Milpitas	CA	95035	669-900-8000	
Simtrol Inc 520 Guthridge Ct **Fax Area Code:* 770 ■ *TF:* 800-423-0769 ■ *Web:* www.simtrol.com	Norcross	GA	30092	678-533-1200	441-1823*
Skyward Inc 5233 Coye Dr *TF:* 800-236-0001 ■ *Web:* www.skyward.com	Stevens Point	WI	54481	715-341-9406	341-1370
Smart Card Integrators Inc (SCI) 2424 N Ontario St *Web:* www.sci-s.com	Burbank	CA	91504	818-847-1022	847-1454
SNMP Research International Inc 3001 Kimberlin Heights Rd *TF:* 877-644-5866 ■ *Web:* www.snmp.com	Knoxville	TN	37920	865-579-3311	579-6565
Software Engineering of America Inc (SEA) 1230 Hempstead Tpke *TF:* 800-272-7322 ■ *Web:* www.seasoft.com	Franklin Square	NY	11010	516-328-7000	354-4015
Software Pursuits Inc 1900 S Norfolk St *TF:* 800-367-4823 ■ *Web:* www.softwarepursuits.com	San Mateo	CA	94403	650-372-0900	372-2912
Stratus Technologies 111 Powdermill Rd *TF:* 800-787-2887 ■ *Web:* www.stratus.com	Maynard	MA	01754	978-461-7000	461-3670
Symantec Corp 350 Ellis St *NASDAQ: SYMC* ■ *TF:* 800-441-7234 ■ *Web:* www.symantec.com	Mountain View	CA	94043	650-527-8000	527-8050
Syncsort Inc 50 Tice Blvd *Web:* www.syncsort.com	Woodcliff Lake	NJ	07677	201-930-9700	882-8305
TeamQuest Corp One TeamQuest Way *TF:* 800-551-8326 ■ *Web:* www.teamquest.com	Clear Lake	IA	50428	641-357-2700	357-2778
TechSmith Corp 2405 Woodlake Dr *TF:* 800-517-3001 ■ *Web:* www.techsmith.com	Okemos	MI	48864	517-381-2300	381-2336
Tecsec Inc 12950 Worldgate Dr Ste 100 **Fax Area Code:* 703 ■ *Web:* www.tecsec.com	Herndon	VA	20170	571-299-4100	506-1484*
Thales e-Security Inc 2200 N Commerce Pkwy Ste 200 *TF:* 888-744-4976 ■ *Web:* www.thales-esecurity.com	Weston	FL	33326	954-888-6200	888-6211
TigerLogic Corp 25-A Technology Dr *NASDAQ: TIGR* ■ *TF:* 800-367-7425 ■ *Web:* tigerlogic.com	Irvine	CA	92618	949-442-4400	250-8187
TrendMicro Inc 10101 N De Anza Blvd *TF:* 800-228-5651 ■ *Web:* www.trendmicro.com	Cupertino	CA	95014	408-257-1500	863-6526
Tripwire Inc 101 SW Main St Ste 1500 *TF General:* 800-874-7947 ■ *Web:* www.tripwire.com	Portland	OR	97204	503-276-7500	223-0182
TurboLinux Inc 600 Townsend St	San Francisco	CA	94103	415-503-4330	
UltraBac Software 15015 Main St Ste 200 *TF:* 866-554-8562 ■ *Web:* www.ultrabac.com	Bellevue	WA	98007	425-644-6000	644-8222
UniSoft Corp 10 Rollins Rd Ste 118 *Web:* www.unisoft.com	Millbrae	CA	94030	650-259-1290	259-1299
VanDyke Software Inc 4848 Tramway Ridge Dr NE Ste 101 *TF:* 800-952-5210 ■ *Web:* www.vandyke.com	Albuquerque	NM	87111	505-332-5700	332-5701
VCG LLC 1805 Old Alabama Rd *TF:* 800-318-4983 ■ *Web:* www.bond-us.com	Roswell	GA	30076	770-246-2300	449-3638
Vendant Inc 26 Parker St *TF:* 800-714-4900 ■ *Web:* www.vedanthealth.com	Newburyport	MA	01950	978-462-0737	462-4755
Vision Solutions Inc 15300 Barranca Pkwy *TF:* 800-683-4667 ■ *Web:* www.visionsolutions.com	Irvine	CA	92618	949-253-6500	253-6501
VisionAIR Inc 5601 Barbados Blvd *TF:* 800-882-2108 ■ *Web:* www.visionair.com	Castle Hayne	NC	28429	910-675-9117	602-6190
Visual Automation Inc 403 S Clinton St Ste 4 *Web:* www.visualautomation.com	Grand Ledge	MI	48837	517-622-1850	622-1761
Webroot Software Inc 2560 55th St *TF:* 800-772-9383 ■ *Web:* www.webroot.com	Boulder	CO	80301	303-442-3813	442-3846
WildPackets Inc 1340 Treat Blvd Ste 500 **Fax:* Sales ■ *TF:* 800-466-2447 ■ *Web:* www.wildpackets.com	Walnut Creek	CA	94597	925-937-3200	937-3211*
Wilson WindowWare Inc 5421 California Ave SW *TF:* 800-762-8383 ■ *Web:* www.windowware.com	Seattle	WA	98136	206-938-1740	935-7129
Wind River Systems Inc 500 Wind River Way *TF:* 800-545-9463 ■ *Web:* www.windriver.com	Alameda	CA	94501	510-748-4100	749-2010
WinZip Computing Inc PO Box 540 *Web:* www.winzip.com	Mansfield	CT	06268	860-429-3542	429-3542
Xinet Inc 2560 Ninth St Ste 312 *Web:* www.northplains.com	Berkeley	CA	94710	510-845-0555	644-2680
XIOtech Corp 9950 Federal Dr Ste 100 *TF:* 866-472-6764 ■ *Web:* xiostorage.com	Colorado Springs	CO	80921	719-388-5500	
Yrrid Software Inc 507 Monroe St *TF:* 800-443-0065 ■ *Web:* www.yrrid.com	Chapel Hill	NC	27516	919-968-7858	968-7856
Zix Corp 2711 N Haskell Ave Ste 2300-LB *NASDAQ: ZIXI* ■ *TF:* 888-771-4049 ■ *Web:* www.zixcorp.com	Dallas	TX	75204	214-370-2000	370-2070
Zone Alarm 800 Bridge Pkwy *TF:* 877-966-5221 ■ *Web:* www.zonealarm.com	Redwood City	CA	94065	415-633-4500	633-4501

182 COMPUTER STORES

SEE ALSO Appliance & Home Electronics Stores p. 1743

Name / Address	City	State	ZIP	Phone	Fax
1 EDI Source Inc 31875 Solon Rd Ste 2 — *Web:* www.1edisource.com	Solon	OH	44139	440-519-7800	
A Matter of Fax 105 Harrison Ave — *TF:* 800-433-3329 ■ *Web:* www.amatteroffax.com	Harrison	NJ	07029	973-482-3700	482-0715
Aberdeen LLC 9130 Norwalk Blvd — **Fax:* Sales ■ *TF:* 800-500-9526 ■ *Web:* www.aberdeeninc.com	Santa Fe Springs	CA	90670	562-699-6998	695-5570*
Ablaze Wireless 4010 Moorpark Ave Ste 201 — *Web:* www.ablazewireless.com	San Jose	CA	95117	408-615-0888	
Accordant Company LLC 365 South St — *Web:* www.accordantco.com	Morristown	NJ	07960	973-887-8900	
Accounting Software Plus LLC 96 N Third St Ste 150 — *Web:* www.acctsoft.com	San Jose	CA	95112	408-280-7587	
ACCUCOM Technical Services Inc 660 N Glenville — *Web:* www.accucom.com	Richardson	TX	75081	972-238-7502	
ADA Station Communication Inc 1079 Linvingston Rd — *Web:* www.adastation.com	Crossville	TN	38555	931-707-5389	
AFIX Technologies Inc 205 N Walnut St — *Web:* www.afix.net	Pittsburg	KS	66762	620-232-6420	
Aim Two Berkeley St — *Web:* www.aim.ca	Toronto	ON	M5A4J5	416-594-9393	
Aktion Associates Inc 1687 Woodlands Dr — *Web:* www.aktion.com	Maumee	OH	43537	419-893-7001	
Aljex Software Inc 463 Union Ave — *Web:* www.alcrest.com	Middlesex	NJ	08846	732-357-8700	
Allplus Computer Systems Corp 3075 NW 107th Ave — *Web:* www.allpluscomputer.com	Doral	FL	33172	305-436-3993	
Amicus Technology 2118 Wilshire Blvd Ste 430 — *Web:* www.amicustech.com	Santa Monica	CA	90403	310-670-4962	
Amika Mobile Corp 700 March Rd Ste 203 — *Web:* www.amikamobile.com	Ottawa	ON	K2K2V9	613-599-4445	
Amptech Inc 201 Glocheski Dr — *Web:* www.amptechinc.com	Manistee	MI	49660	231-464-5492	
Analynk Wireless LLC 790 Cross Pointe Rd — *Web:* www.analynk.com	Columbus	OH	43230	614-755-5091	
Answer Co, The 200-4170 Still Creek Dr — *Web:* www.theanswerco.com	Burnaby	BC	V5C6C6	604-473-9166	
Answer One Inc 2216 Young Dr Ste 3 — *Web:* answerone.biz	Lexington	KY	40505	859-269-3482	
Applied Voice & Speech Technologies Inc 27042 Towne Centre Dr Ste 200 — *Web:* www.avst.com	Foothill Ranch	CA	92610	949-699-2300	
Arbutus Software Inc 6450 Roberts St — *Web:* www.arbutussoftware.com	Burnaby	BC	V5G4E1	604-437-7873	
ASAP Solutions Group LLC 3885 Holcomb Bridge Rd — *Web:* www.myasap.com	Norcross	GA	30092	770-246-1718	
Ascendbridge Solutions 50 Acadia Ave — *Web:* www.ascendbridge.com	Markham	ON	L3R0B3	905-944-0047	
Aspyr Media Inc 1250 S Capital of Texas Hwy Ste 650 — *Web:* www.aspyr.com	Austin	TX	78746	512-708-8100	708-9595
Atiwa Computer Leasing Exchange 6950 Portwest Dr Ste 100 — *Web:* www.atiwa.com	Houston	TX	77024	713-467-9390	
Audcomp Computer Systems 611 Tradewind Dr Ste 100 — *Web:* www.audcomp.com	Ancaster	ON	L9G4V5	905-304-1775	
Automated Medical Systems Inc 2310 N Patterson St Bldg H — *TF:* 800-256-3240 ■ *Web:* automedical.com	Valdosta	GA	31602	800-256-3240	
Azar Computer Software Services Inc 1200 Regal Row — *Web:* www.azarinc.com	Austin	TX	78748	512-476-5085	
BAASS Business Solutions BC Inc 305-9600 Cameron St — *Web:* www.plus.ca	Burnaby	BC	V3J7N3	604-420-1099	
Balihoo Inc 404 S Eighth St Ste 300 — *TF:* 866-446-9914 ■ *Web:* balihoo.com	Boise	ID	83702	866-446-9914	
Barcoding Inc 2220 Boston St — *TF:* 888-412-7226 ■ *Web:* www.barcoding.com	Baltimore	MD	21231	410-385-8532	385-8559
Basic Software Systems 905 N Kings Hwy — *Web:* www.basic-software.com	Texarkana	TX	75501	903-792-4421	
BCS Prosoft Inc 2700 Lockhill Selma — *Web:* www.bcsprosoft.com	San Antonio	TX	78230	210-308-5505	
Beacon Technologies Inc 1441 Donelson Pk — *Web:* beacontech.net	Nashville	TN	37217	615-301-5020	
Beb Software Systems 1806 Swift Ave Ste 207 — *Web:* www.bebsoft.com	Kansas City	MO	64116	816-452-4222	
BEMAS Software Inc Seven The Pines Court Ste B — *Web:* www.bemassoftware.com	St. Louis	MO	63141	314-439-5300	
Best Choice Software Inc 2112 First St W — *Web:* www.bestchoicesoftware.com	Bradenton	FL	34208	941-747-5858	
Bitlab LLC 1144 Parkwood Ave — *Web:* bitlab.com	Park Ridge	IL	60068	847-823-5070	
Bizco Technologies Inc 7950 "O" St — *Web:* www.bizco.com	Lincoln	NE	68510	402-323-4800	
BlueSun Inc 5500 N Service Rd Ste 1107 — *Web:* www.bluesun.ca	Burlington	ON	L7L6W6	905-333-3353	
Boston Electronics Corp 91 Boylston St — *Web:* www.boselec.com	Brookline	MA	02445	617-566-3821	
Bredy Consulting Services 50 Union St — *Web:* www.bnmc.net	Andover	MA	01810	978-482-2020	
C-Team Systems Inc 38 Auriga Dr Unit 12 — *Web:* www.cteam.ca	Ottawa	ON	K2E8A5	613-727-8224	
Canfield Scientific Inc 253 Passaic Ave — *Web:* www.canfieldsci.com	Fairfield	NJ	07004	973-276-0336	
Cannon IV Inc 950 Dorman St — *Web:* www.cannon4.com	Indianapolis	IN	46202	317-951-0500	
Carrier IQ Inc 640 W California Ave Ste 100 — *Web:* www.carrieriq.com	Sunnyvale	CA	94086	650-625-5400	
Carrillo Business Technologies Inc 750 The City Dr S Ste 225 — *TF:* 888-241-7585 ■ *Web:* www.cbtechinc.com	Orange	CA	92868	888-241-7585	
Caselle Inc 1656 South East Bay Blvd Ste 100 — *Web:* www.caselle.com	Provo	UT	84606	801-850-5000	
Cayuse Inc 10700 SW Beaverton-Hillsdale Hwy Park Plz W Bldg III Ste 654 — *Web:* cayuse.com	Beaverton	OR	97005	503-297-2108	
CDW Corp 200 N Milwaukee Ave — *TF:* 800-800-4239 ■ *Web:* www.cdw.com	Vernon Hills	IL	60061	847-465-6000	465-6800
Cendec Systems Inc Ste 315 1615 10th Ave SW — *Web:* cendec.com	Calgary	AB	T3C0J7	403-215-9936	
CenterGate Research Group LLC 420 S Smith Rd — *Web:* www.centergate.com	Tempe	AZ	85281	480-804-8100	
Central Mass Web Design Inc 70 Snake Pond Rd — *Web:* www.centralmasswebdesign.com	Gardner	MA	01440	978-632-5300	
Centric Business Systems Inc 10702 Red Run Blvd — *Web:* www.centricbiz.com	Owings Mills	MD	21117	410-902-3300	
Cepeda Systems & Software Analysis Inc 110 Timber Ridge Cv — *Web:* www.cepedasystems.com	Madison	AL	35758	256-461-7985	
Chenomx Inc 10230 Jasper Ave Ste 4350 — *Web:* www.chenomx.com	Edmonton	AB	T5J4P6	780-432-0033	
Colligo Networks Inc 400-1152 Mainland St — *Web:* www.colligo.com	Vancouver	BC	V6B4X2	604-685-7962	
Colonial Systems Inc 326 Ballardvale St Ste 200 — *Web:* colonialsystems.com	Wilmington	MA	01887	978-657-6508	
Complete Solutions Technology Group LLC 4635 Southwest Fwy Ste 310 — *Web:* www.complete-solutions.com	Houston	TX	77027	713-974-9060	
ComponentArt Inc 511 King St W Ste 400 — *Web:* www.componentart.com	Toronto	ON	M5V1K4	416-622-2923	
Comres Telecom 33 Ne Second St Ste 212 — *Web:* www.comresusa.com	Fort Lauderdale	FL	33301	954-462-9600	
Concepts In Data Management Inc 205 Oxford St E — *TF:* 800-668-8768 ■ *Web:* www.instanetsolutions.com	London	ON	N6A5G6	800-668-8768	
Conference Group LLC, The 254 Chapman Rd Topkis Bldg Ste 102 — *Web:* confgroupinc.com	Newark	DE	19702	302-224-8255	
ConnectWise Inc 4110 George Rd Ste 200 — *TF:* 800-671-6898 ■ *Web:* www.connectwise.com	Tampa	FL	33634	813-463-4700	
CopperLeaf Technologies Inc 4170 Still Creek Dr Ste 450 — *Web:* copperleafgroup.com	Burnaby	BC	V5C6C6	604-639-9700	
Crawford Technologies Inc 45 St Clair Ave W Ste 102 — *Web:* www.crawfordtech.com	Toronto	ON	M4V1K9	416-923-0080	
CTrends Inc 27142 Burbank — *Web:* www.ctrends.com	Foothill Ranch	CA	92610	949-472-9050	
Datel Systems Inc 5636 Ruffin Rd — *Web:* www.datelsys.com	San Diego	CA	92123	858-571-3100	571-0452
Db Technologies Inc 3601 N First St Ste E — *Web:* dbtechnm.com	Bloomfield	NM	87413	505-632-7900	
Ddi System LLC 75 Glen Rd Ste 204ddi — *Web:* ddisys.com	Sandy Hook	CT	06482	203-364-1200	
Dehart Marine Electronics Inc 134 W Carolina Ave — *Web:* dehartmarine.com	Memphis	TN	38103	901-523-0945	
Devcare Solution Ltd 4174 Greensbury Dr — *Web:* www.devcare.com	New Albany	OH	43054	614-221-2277	
Dexter & Chaney Inc 9700 Lk City Way NE — *Web:* www.dexterchaney.com	Seattle	WA	98115	206-364-1400	
DMJ Technologies LLC 140 Henley Ave Ste 5 — *Web:* www.dmjtechnologies.com	New Milford	NJ	07646	201-261-5560	
DOVICO Software Inc 236 St George St Ste 119 — *Web:* www.dovico.com	Moncton	NB	E1C1W1	506-855-4477	
DTM Systems Inc 2323 Boundary Rd Unit 130 — *Web:* www.dtm.ca	Vancouver	BC	V5M4V8	604-257-6700	
Dynamic Business Solutions Inc 30100 Telegraph Rd Ste 322 — *Web:* www.qualitech.net	Bingham Farms	MI	48025	248-646-0093	
East End Computers LLC 30 Long Island Ave — *Web:* www.eastendcomputer.com	Sag Harbor	NY	11963	631-725-4000	
Echoworx Corp 4101 Yonge St Ste 708 — *Web:* www.echoworx.com	Toronto	ON	M2P1N6	416-226-8600	
ElectSolve Technology Solutions & Services Inc 333 E Texas St Ste 520 — *Web:* www.electsolve.com	Shreveport	LA	71101	318-221-2055	
Employee Development Systems Inc 7308 S Alton Way Ste 2J — *Web:* www.employeedevelopmentsystems.com	Centennial	CO	80112	303-221-0710	
Envision Payment Solutions Inc 3039 Premiere Pkwy Ste 600 — *Web:* www.checkcare.com	Duluth	GA	30097	770-709-3000	
EPLAN Software & Services LLC 37000 Grand River Ave Ste 380 — *Web:* www.eplan.de	Farmington Hills	MI	48335	248-945-9204	

Company / Address	City	State	ZIP	Phone	Fax
Erb's Business Machines Inc 4935 Bowling St SW *Web:* www.erbs.com	Cedar Rapids	IA	52404	319-364-5159	
Evident Point Software Corp 160-3751 Shell Rd *Web:* www.evidentpoint.com	Richmond	BC	V6X2W2	604-241-2711	
Executech 12701 Marblestone Dr Ste 150 *Web:* www.esc-techsolutions.com	Woodbridge	VA	22192	571-285-3331	
Express Logic Inc 11423 W Bernardo Ct *Web:* www.expresslogic.com	San Diego	CA	92127	858-613-6640	
Eyelit Inc 5685 Whittle Rd *Web:* www.eyelit.com	Mississauga	ON	L4Z3P8	905-502-6184	
EyeSee360 Inc 300 Fleet St Ste 250 *Web:* eyesee360.com	Pittsburgh	PA	15220	412-922-6002	
FatTail Inc 20969 Ventura Blvd Ste 209 *Web:* adserver.fattail.com	Woodland Hills	CA	91364	818-615-0380	
FDM Software Ltd 949 W Third St Ste 113 *Web:* www.fdmsoft.com	North Vancouver	BC	V7P3P7	604-986-9941	
First Call Computer Solutions Inc 616 S Higgins Ave *Web:* www.firstsolution.com	Missoula	MT	59801	406-721-4592	
FM Communications Inc 1914 Colvin Blvd *Web:* www.fmcommunications.com	Tonawanda	NY	14150	716-832-2026	
Freeman Av 4545 W Davis St *Web:* www.freeman.com	Dallas	TX	75211	214-623-1300	
GameStop Corp 625 Westport Pkwy *NYSE: GME* ■ *TF:* 800-883-8895 ■ *Web:* www.gamestop.com	Grapevine	TX	76051	817-424-2000	424-2002
Garza Enterprises Inc 840 W Rhapsody Dr *Web:* www.costx.com	San Antonio	TX	78216	210-377-3500	
Gateway Inc 7565 Irvine Ctr Dr *TF:* 800-846-2000 ■ *Web:* www.gateway.com	Irvine	CA	92618	949-471-7040	471-7041
Geeks.com 43195 Business Park Dr **Fax Area Code:* 760 ■ *Web:* www.geeks.com	Temecula	CA	92056	951-694-4335	726-7723*
Georgian College of Applied Arts & Technology, The One Georgian Dr *Web:* www.georgianc.on.ca	Barrie	ON	L4M3X9	705-728-1968	
GGA Software Services LLC One Mifflin Pl *Web:* www.ggasoftware.com	Cambridge	MA	02138	617-491-5100	
Gold Key Solutions Inc 28118 Agoura Rd Ste 202 *Web:* www.goldkeysolutions.com	Agoura Hills	CA	91301	818-865-0006	
Gopher Electronics Company Inc 222 Little Canada Rd *Web:* www.gopherelectronics.com	Saint Paul	MN	55117	651-490-4900	
Govconnection Inc 7503 Standish Pl **Fax Area Code:* 603 ■ *TF:* 800-998-0009 ■ *Web:* www.govconnection.com	Rockville	MD	20855	800-998-0009	423-6192*
Gts Communications & Cabling Co 11953 Prospect Rd *Web:* www.gtscommunications.com	Strongsville	OH	44149	440-878-8866	
Hartco Inc 9393 Louis-H-Lafontaine *NYSE: HCI* ■ *Web:* www.hartco.com	Montreal	QC	H1J1Y8	514-354-3810	354-1998
Higher Gear Group Inc, The 145 W Central Rd *Web:* www.highergear.com	Schaumburg	IL	60195	847-843-6800	
Higher Information Group 400 N Blue Ribbon Ave Ste 2 *Web:* higherinfogroup.com	Harrisburg	PA	17112	717-652-3310	
Housing Data Systems 750 W City Hwy 16 *Web:* www.housingdatasystems.com	West Salem	WI	54669	608-786-2366	
ICAM Technologies Corp 21500 Nassr St *Web:* www.icam.com	Sainte-anne-de-bellevue	QC	H9X4C1	514-697-8033	
imageTech Marketing Inc 10388 S Randall St *Web:* www.imagetechmarketing.com	Orange	CA	92869	714-639-5411	
INACOMP Data-Voice System Inc 2424 A Jenks Ave *Web:* www.inacompnet.com	Panama City	FL	32405	850-784-0101	
Indigo Rose Corp 123 Bannatyne Ave Ste 200 *Web:* www.indigorose.com	Winnipeg	MB	R3B0R3	204-946-0263	
Ineo Technology LLC 3340-A Annapolis Ln *Web:* www.ineotechnology.com	Plymouth	MN	55447	612-236-2100	
Innovative Information Solutions Inc 61 I- Ln *TF:* 800-343-8121 ■ *Web:* www.innovativeis.com	Waterbury	CT	06705	203-756-4243	756-4244
Insight Enterprises Inc 6820 S Harl Ave *NASDAQ: NSIT* ■ *TF:* 800-467-4448 ■ *Web:* www.insight.com	Tempe	AZ	85283	480-333-3000	760-3330
Inspironix Inc 3400 Cottage Way *Web:* www.inspironix.com	Sacramento	CA	95825	916-488-3222	
Intalio Inc 644 Emerson St Ste 200 *Web:* www.intalio.com	Palo Alto	CA	94301	650-596-1800	249-0439
Intelex Technologies Inc 905 King St West Ste 600 *Web:* www.intelex.com	Toronto	ON	M6K3G9	416-599-6009	
IPRO Tech Inc 6811 E Mayo Blvd Ste 350 *Web:* www.iprotech.com	Phoenix	AZ	85054	602-324-4776	
J&s Radio Sales Inc 1147 Main St *Web:* www.jsradiosales.com	Willimantic	CT	06226	860-456-2667	
Janssen Consulting Inc 1704 Mission Ave Ste 1 *Web:* www.janssenconsulting.com	Carmichael	CA	95608	916-716-2326	
Jargon Software 716 N First St *Web:* www.jargonsoft.com	Minneapolis	MN	55401	612-338-1175	
Jencess Software & Technologies Inc 4509 - 101 St *Web:* www.jencess.com	Edmonton	AB	T6E5C6	780-434-4444	
Jive Communications Inc 1275 West 1600 North Ste 100 *TF:* 866-768-5429 ■ *Web:* jive.com	Orem	UT	84057	866-768-5429	
Jonah Group Ltd, The 461 King St W Third Fl *Web:* www.jonahgroup.com	Toronto	ON	M5V1K4	416-304-0860	
Karaman Communications Inc 4424 Bragg Blvd Ste 101 *Web:* www.karamancom.com	Fayetteville	NC	28303	910-222-1234	
Key Events Inc 657 Mission St Ste 202 *Web:* www.keyevents.com	San Francisco	CA	94105	415-695-8000	
Khemia Software Co 33080 Industrial Rd *Web:* khemia.com	Livonia	MI	48150	734-513-9940	
KLA Laboratories Inc 6800 Chase Rd *Web:* www.klalabs.com	Dearborn	MI	48126	313-846-3800	
KLJ Computer Solutions Inc 115 Joseph Zatzman Dr *TF:* 888-455-5669 ■ *Web:* www.venueclaims.com	Dartmouth	NS	B3B1N3	888-455-5669	
Knowledge Information Solutions Inc 2877 Guardian Ln Ste 201 *TF:* 877-547-7248 ■ *Web:* www.kisinc.net	Virginia Beach	VA	23452	757-463-0033	463-3971
L S Technologies LLC 4150 Rock Mtn Rd *Web:* www.lstechnologies.com	Fallbrook	CA	92028	760-731-2320	
Lanamark Inc 100 King St W First Canadian Pl 56th Fl *Web:* www.lanamark.com	Toronto	ON	M5X1C9	416-342-1960	
Laser Tek Services Inc 205 19th St N *Web:* www.laserteksservices.com	Fargo	ND	58102	701-239-4033	
Launch Pad 18130 Jorene Rd *TF:* 888-920-3450 ■ *Web:* www.launchpadonline.com	Odessa	FL	33556	888-920-3450	
Lcptracker Inc 850 E Chapman Ave Ste D *Web:* www.lcptracker.com	Orange	CA	92866	714-669-0052	
LD Systems LP 407 Garden Oaks *Web:* www.ldsystems.com	Houston	TX	77018	713-695-9400	
Libertas Technologies LLC 708 Walnut St Ste 400 *Web:* www.libertastechnologies.com	Cincinnati	OH	45202	513-721-7800	
Lieberman Group LLC, The 223 NW Second St Ste 300 *Web:* www.ltnow.com	Evansville	IN	47708	812-434-6600	
Loki Systems Inc 1258-13351 Commerce Pkwy *Web:* www.lokisys.com	Richmond	BC	V6V2X7	604-249-5050	
London Computer Services 1007 Cottonwood Dr *Web:* www.lcs.com	Loveland	OH	45140	513-583-1482	
Lone Wolf Real Estate Technologies Inc 231 Shearson Crescent Ste 310 *Web:* www.lwolf.com	Cambridge	ON	N1T1J5	519-624-1236	
M3 Technology Inc 58 Sawgrass Dr *Web:* www.m3-tec.com	Bellport	NY	11713	631-205-0005	
MACK Technologies Inc 27 Carlisle Rd *Web:* www.macktech.com	Westford	MA	01886	978-392-5500	
Macs at Work Inc 775 Hartford Tpke *Web:* www.macsatwork.com	Shrewsbury	MA	01545	508-845-0709	
MadCap Software Inc 7777 Fay Ave *Web:* www.madcapsoftware.com	La Jolla	CA	92037	858-320-0387	
Magitech Corp 1500 Don Mills Rd Ste 702 *Web:* www.ezgame.com	Toronto	ON	M3B3K4	416-441-1933	
MailChannels Corp 142-757 W Hastings St Ste 612 *Web:* www.mailchannels.com	Vancouver	BC	V6C1A1	604-685-7488	
Mainsaver Software LLC 10803 Thornmint Rd *Web:* www.mainsaver.com	San Diego	CA	92127	858-674-8700	
MC2 Inc 1106 S First St *Web:* www.mc2wi.com	Milwaukee	WI	53204	414-276-2200	
Medflow Inc 6739A Fairview Rd *Web:* medflow.com	Charlotte	NC	28210	704-927-9800	
Medical Priority Consultants Inc 139 E S Temple St *Web:* www.prioritydispatch.net	Salt Lake City	UT	84111	801-363-9127	
Medicat LLC Sandy Springs 1100 Johnson Ferry Rd Ste 240 *Web:* www.medicat.com	Atlanta	GA	30342	404-252-2295	
Medisys for Physicians Inc 7201 Halcyon Summit Dr *Web:* www.medisysinc.com	Montgomery	AL	36117	334-277-6201	
Meritech Inc 4577 Hinckley Industrial Pkwy *Web:* www.meritechinc.com	Cleveland	OH	44109	216-459-8333	
Messaging Architects 180 Peel St Ste 333 *Web:* www.netmail.com	Montreal	QC	H3C2G7	514-392-9220	
Microdea Inc 15 Wertheim Court Ste 301 *Web:* www.microdea.com	Richmond	ON	L4B3H7	905-881-6071	
Momentum Healthware Inc 308-131 Provencher Blvd *Web:* www.momentumhealthware.com	Winnipeg	MB	R2H0G2	204-231-3836	
Moore Oil Company Inc 4033 W Custer Ave *Web:* mooreoil.com	Milwaukee	WI	53209	414-462-3200	
Mphasis Corp 460 Pk Ave S Rm 1101 *Web:* www.mphasis.com	New York	NY	10016	212-686-6655	
NCX Inc 70 E Beaver Creek Rd Unit 2 *Web:* www.ncxinc.ca	Richmond Hill	ON	L4B3B2	905-370-7060	
Netdirective Technologies Inc 5430 Village Dr Ste 103 *Web:* www.netdirective.com	Rockledge	FL	32955	321-205-1830	
Netgain Networks Inc 8378 Attica Dr *Web:* netgainnetworks.com	Riverside	CA	92508	951-656-0194	
Network Depot LLC 12040 S Lakes Dr Ste 202 *Web:* www.networkdepot.com	Reston	VA	20191	703-264-7776	
Neuma Technology Inc #51 - 5450 Canotek Rd *Web:* www.neuma.com	Ottawa	ON	K1J9G3	613-749-9450	
New Tech Solutions Inc 4179 Business Ctr Dr *Web:* www.ntsca.com	Fremont	CA	94538	510-353-4070	
Newegg Inc 16839 E Gale Ave *TF:* 800-390-1119 ■ *Web:* www.newegg.com	City of Industry	CA	91745	626-271-9700	271-9403
NewTech Infosystems Inc 9999 Muirlands Blvd *Web:* www.ntius.com	Irvine	CA	92618	949-421-0720	
Nova Voice & Data Systems Inc 3909 Oceanic Dr Ste 401 *Web:* www.enova.us	Oceanside	CA	92056	760-439-5200	

				Phone	Fax
Novus LLC 338 Commerce Dr — Web: www.novusllc.com	Fairfield	CT	06825	203-331-1112	
Nuventive LLC 9800B McKnight Rd Ste 255 — Web: www.nuventive.com	Pittsburgh	PA	15237	412-847-0280	
NuWave Technology Partners LLC 5268 Azo Ct. — Web: www.nuwavepartners.com	Kalamazoo	MI	49048	269-342-4400	
O p t 918 Mission Ave — Web: www.optcorp.com	Oceanside	CA	92054	760-722-3348	
Office Solutions Inc 217 Mount Horeb Rd — Web: www.osidirect.com	Warren	NJ	07059	732-356-0200	
Omni-Med.com Inc 160 Pope St — Web: www.omnimed.com	Cookshire	QC	J0B1M0	819-875-5411	
Omnivex Corp 3300 Hwy 7 Ste 501 — Web: www.omnivex.com	Concord	ON	L4K4M3	905-761-6640	
Open Automation Software 5077 Bear Mtn Dr — Web: www.opcsystems.com	Evergreen	CO	80439	303-679-0898	
Optessa Inc 5555 Calgary Trl NW Ste 1040 — Web: www.optessa.com	Edmonton	AB	T6H5P9	780-431-8426	
Optiwave Systems Inc Seven Capella Ct — Web: www.optiwave.com	Ottawa	ON	K2E7X1	613-224-4700	
Orion Industries Inc One Orion Park Dr — Web: www.orionindustries.com	Ayer	MA	01432	978-772-6000	
P-Q Controls Inc 95 Dolphin Rd — Web: www.p-qcontrols.com	Bristol	CT	06010	860-583-6994	
Palomino System Innovations Inc 533 College St Ste 404 — Web: www.palominosys.com	Toronto	ON	M6G1A8	416-964-7333	
ParetoLogic Inc 1827 Ft St — Web: www.paretologic.com	Victoria	BC	V8R1J6	250-370-9229	
Patriot Software Inc 2925 E 96th St Ste 100 — Web: patriotsoftware.net	Indianapolis	IN	46240	317-573-5431	
PC Connection Inc 730 Milford Rd Rt 101A — NASDAQ: PCCC ■ TF: 888-213-0607 ■ Web: www.pcconnection.com	Merrimack	NH	03054	603-683-2000	683-5766
PC Connection Inc MacConnection Div 730 Milford Rd Rt 101A — *Fax Area Code: 603 ■ TF: 888-213-0260 ■ Web: www.macconnection.com	Merrimack	NH	03054	888-213-0260	683-5766*
PC Mall Inc 2555 W 190th St — NASDAQ: PCMI ■ TF: 800-555-6255 ■ Web: www.pcm.com	Torrance	CA	90504	310-354-5600	
PC Network Services Inc 109 Nicholson Rd — Web: www.pcnsinc.com	Sewickley	PA	15143	412-928-8670	
Physmark Inc 101 E Pk Blvd Ste 600 — TF: 800-922-7060 ■ Web: www.physmark.com	Plano	TX	75074	972-231-8000	
Pinnacle Corp, The 201A E Abram St — Web: www.pinncorp.com	Arlington	TX	76010	817-795-5555	
Planet Technologies Inc 20400 Observation Dr Ste 204 — Web: go-planet.com	Germantown	MD	20876	301-721-0100	
Pointon Communications 202 South Blvd — Web: www.pointon.com	Baraboo	WI	53913	608-355-0257	
Points North Inc 371 Canal Park Dr Ste 210 — Web: www.points-north.com	Duluth	MN	55802	218-726-1195	
PowerMed Corp 48 Free St — Web: www.powermed.com	Portland	ME	04101	207-772-3920	
PPM 2000 Inc 10025-102A Ave Ste 1200 — Web: www.ppm2000.com	Edmonton	AB	T5J2Z2	780-448-0616	
Primal Technologies Inc 3615 Laird Rd Ste 13 — Web: www.primaltech.com	Mississauga	ON	L5L5Z8	416-548-3395	
ProComp Software Consultants Inc 555 Cincinnati-Batavia Pk — Web: www.procompsoftware.com	Cincinnati	OH	45244	513-685-5245	
Prolifiq Software Inc 4145 SW Watson Ave Ste 450 — Web: prolifiq.com	Beaverton	OR	97005	503-684-1415	
Protis Computers 7212 Mcneil Dr Ste 202 — Web: protis.com	Austin	TX	78729	512-258-1282	
PSI Software Inc 7326 Remcon Cir — Web: www.psisoftware.com	El Paso	TX	79912	915-584-4100	
PYR Software Ltd 9050 Yonge St Ste 300 — Web: www.pyrsoftware.com	Richmond Hill	ON	L4C9S6	905-763-7828	
Qeh2 LLC 401 S Wilcox St Ste 202 — Web: www.qeh2.com	Castle Rock	CO	80104	303-688-7531	
Quatro Systems Inc 231 Gibraltar Rd — Web: www.quatro.com	Horsham	PA	19044	215-672-7100	
Questica Inc 980 Fraser Dr Ste 105 — TF: 877-707-7755 ■ Web: www.questica.com	Burlington	ON	L7L5P5	877-707-7755	
Radio Guys 2061 Fwy Dr Ste D — Web: www.theradioguys.com	Woodland	CA	95776	530-406-0700	
Rainbow Computers Corp 6000 NW 97th Ave Ste 21 — Web: www.rainbowcc.com	Doral	FL	33178	305-592-2611	
Recursion Software Inc 2591 Dallas Pkwy Ste 200 — TF: 800-727-8674 ■ Web: www.recursionsw.com	Frisco	TX	75034	972-731-8800	731-8881
RedSky Technologies Inc 925 W Chicago Ave Ste 300 — Web: www.redskye911.com	Chicago	IL	60642	312-432-4300	
Regional Computer Recycling & Recovery LLC 7318 Victor Mendon Rd — Web: www.ewaste.com	Victor	NY	14564	585-924-3840	
Repeated Signal Solutions Inc 7127 Hollister Ave Ste 109 — Web: www.repeatedsignal.com	Goleta	CA	93117	805-685-6700	
RLM Communications Inc 1027 E Manchester Rd — Web: www.rlm-communications.com	Spring Lake	NC	28390	910-223-1350	
Rushworks 800 Parker Sq Ste 200 — Web: www.rushworks.tv	Flower Mound	TX	75028	972-899-8142	
Saffron Technology Inc 1000 CentreGreen Way Ste 160 — Web: saffrontech.com	Cary	NC	27513	919-468-8201	
SDG Systems LLC 330 Perry Hwy Ste 200 — Web: www.sdgsystems.com	Harmony	PA	16037	724-452-9366	
Sector Micro Computers Inc 399 Hoover Ave Ste 2 — Web: sectormicro.com	Bloomfield	NJ	07003	973-429-1113	
Selectron Technologies Inc 12323 SW 66th Ave — Web: www.selectrontechnologies.com	Portland	OR	97223	503-443-1400	
Service Communications Inc 10675 Willows Rd NE Ste 100 — TF: 800-488-0468 ■ Web: www.servicecommunications.com	Redmond	WA	98052	800-488-0468	
Shamrock Office Solutions Inc 6908 Sierra Ct Ste A — Web: www.shamrockoffice.com	Dublin	CA	94568	925-875-0480	
SHIELDS Electronics Supply Inc 4722 Middlebrook Pk — Web: shieldselectronics.com	Knoxville	TN	37921	865-588-2421	
Side Effects Software Inc 123 Front St W Ste 1401 — Web: www.sidefx.com	Toronto	ON	M5J2M2	416-504-9876	
Silke Communications Inc 680 Tyler St — Web: www.silkecom.com	Eugene	OR	97402	541-687-1611	
Silver Bullet Technology Inc 25 W Cedar St Ste 440 — Web: www.sbullet.com	Pensacola	FL	32502	850-437-5880	
Smart Levels Media Inc 16 Hammond — Web: www.smartlevels.com	Irvine	CA	92618	949-540-0500	
SoftCode Inc 33 Boston Post Rd W Ste 360 — Web: www.softcodeinc.com	Marlborough	MA	01752	774-348-3000	
Softechnologies Inc 1504 W Northwest Blvd Ste C — Web: www.softechnologies.com	Spokane	WA	99205	509-327-4624	
Software Development Forum 111 W Saint John Ste 200 — Web: www.sdforum.org	San Jose	CA	95113	408-414-5950	
Software Enterprises Inc 5380 Twin Hickory Rd — Web: www.softent.com	Glen Allen	VA	23059	804-747-6436	
Software Unlimited Inc 1314 Bedford Ave Ste 201 — Web: medicalmastermind.com	Baltimore	MD	21208	410-602-9250	
SPLICE Software Inc 220-6125 11 St SE — Web: www.splicesoftware.com	Calgary	AB	T2H2L6	403-720-8326	
STC Netcom Inc 11611 Industry Ave — Web: www.stcnetcom.com	Fontana	CA	92337	951-685-8181	
Stealthbits Technologies 55 Harristown Rd Ste 106 — Web: www.stealthbits.com	Glen Rock	NJ	07452	201-447-9300	
Stiehl Communications W5361 County Rd Kk Ste A — Web: www.stiehlcommunications.com	Appleton	WI	54915	920-830-1116	
Stonestreet One LLC 9960 Corporate Campus Dr — Web: www.stonestreetone.com	Louisville	KY	40223	502-708-3500	
Strata Health Solutions Inc 933 - 17 Ave SW Ste 600 — Web: stratahealth.com	Calgary	BC	T2T5R6	403-261-0616	
Strategy Companion Corp 3240 El Camino Real Ste 120 — Web: www.strategycompanion.com	Irvine	CA	92602	714-460-8398	
Sunnking Inc Four Owens Rd — Web: www.sunnking.com	Brockport	NY	14420	585-637-8365	
SydneyPLUS International Library Systems Corp 13562 Maycrest Way Ste 5138 — Web: www.sydneyplus.com	Richmond	BC	V6V2J7	604-278-6717	
Synergy Telcom Inc 8222 Indy Ln — Web: www.synergy-tel.com	Indianapolis	IN	46214	317-713-1652	
Synetra Inc 8180 Lakeview Center — Web: www.synetra.com	Odessa	TX	79765	432-561-7200	
System Solutions Inc 3630 Commercial Ave — Web: www.thessi.com	Northbrook	IL	60062	847-272-6160	
Taurus Software Inc 420 Brewster Ave — Web: taurus.com	Redwood City	CA	94063	650-482-2022	
Tech Depot 55 Corporate Dr Ste 5 — *Fax: Cust Svc ■ Web: www.techdepot.com	Trumbull	CT	06611	203-615-7000	615-7005*
Techpeople Inc 5426 Guadalupe St Ste 211 — Web: www.techpeopleinc.com	Austin	TX	78751	512-493-1400	
Tel-West Communications Inc 7311 E Broadway Ste B — Web: www.telwest.net	Spokane	WA	99212	509-325-8500	
Telserv LLC Seven Progress Dr — Web: www.telserv.com	Cromwell	CT	06416	860-740-3600	
TenAsys Corp 1400 NW Compton Dr Ste 301 — Web: www.tenasys.com	Beaverton	OR	97006	503-748-4720	
Tetrasoft Inc 502 Audubon Pl Ct — Web: www.tetrasoft.us	Ballwin	MO	63021	636-530-7638	
Ticoon Technology Inc 56 The Esplanade Ste 404 — Web: www.ticoon.com	Toronto	ON	M5E1A7	416-513-9524	
Tj Rock Enterprises Inc 5800 Genesis Ln — Web: tjrockcorp.com	Frederick	MD	21703	301-831-4128	
Tlc Office Systems 500 N Chenango St Ste 314 — Web: tlcofficesystems.com	Angleton	TX	77515	979-848-8300	
Top Producer Systems Inc 10651 Shellbridge Way Ste 155 — TF: 800-821-3657 ■ Web: www.topproducer.com	Richmond	BC	V6X2W8	800-821-3657	
Translations.com Inc Three Pk Ave 39th Fl — TF: 800-688-7205 ■ Web: www.translations.com	New York	NY	10016	212-689-1616	685-9797
Triad Productions Inc 1910 Ingersoll Ave — Web: www.triadav.com	Des Moines	IA	50309	515-243-2125	
Tricerat Inc 11500 Cronridge Dr Ste 100 — Web: www.tricerat.com	Owings Mills	MD	21117	410-715-4226	
Trinium Technologies LLC 304 Tejon Pl — Web: www.triniumtech.com	Palos Verdes	CA	90274	310-214-3118	

Company	City	State	Zip	Phone	Fax
Tritech Software Systems 9860 Mesa Rim Rd *Web:* www.tritech.com	San Diego	CA	92121	858-799-7000	799-7010
TriVium Systems Inc 1865 NW 169th Pl Ste 210 *Web:* www.triviumsys.com	Beaverton	OR	97006	503-439-9338	
Tukatech Inc 5527 E Slauson Ave *Web:* www.tukatech.com	Los Angeles	CA	90040	323-726-3836	726-3866
TVL Inc 901 16th St W Ste 200 *Web:* www.tvl.com	North Vancouver	BC	V7P1R2	604-983-2298	
Ultrasource Inc 22 Clinton Dr *Web:* www.ultrasource.com	Hollis	NH	03049	603-881-7799	
V-Soft Inc 888 Saratoga Ave Ste 203 *Web:* v-softinc.com	San Jose	CA	95129	408-342-1700	
V.L.S Systems Inc 4080 Lafayette Ctr Dr Ste 300 *Web:* www.vls-systems.com	Chantilly	VA	20151	703-953-3118	
Valley Office Systems 2050 First St *Web:* www.valleyofficesystems.com	Idaho Falls	ID	83401	208-529-2777	
Varay Systems LLC 201 E Main Dr Ste 700 *Web:* www.varay.com	El Paso	TX	79901	915-496-8555	
Vector Networks Inc 541 10th St Unit 123 *Web:* www.vector-networks.com	Atlanta	GA	30318	770-622-2850	
Vertex Systems Inc 440 Polaris Pkwy Ste 100 *Web:* www.vertexsystems.com	Westerville	OH	43082	614-318-7100	
Vertex Wireless LLC 500 Wegner Dr *Web:* www.vertexwireless.com	West Chicago	IL	60185	630-293-6300	
VistaVu Solutions Inc 7326 10 St NE Ste 350 *Web:* www.vistavusolutions.com	Calgary	AB	T2E8W1	403-263-2727	
Vocantas Inc 750 Palladium Dr Ste 200 *Web:* www.vocantas.com	Ottawa	ON	K2V1C7	613-271-8853	
Voice on the Go Inc 20 Amber St Ste 207 *Web:* www.voiceonthego.com	Markham	ON	L3R5P4	905-305-1355	
Voyager Electronics Corp 3065 101st Ave NE *Web:* www.voyagercorp.com	Blaine	MN	55449	763-571-7766	
Web-Point Communications LLC 3801 Sunset Ave *Web:* www.wpc.net	Rocky Mount	NC	27804	252-557-0056	
WhiteLight Group LLC N14 W24200 Tower Place Ste 203 *Web:* www.whitelightgrp.com	Waukesha	WI	53188	630-571-6705	
Winfund Software Corp Two Gurdwara Rd Ste 206 *Web:* www.winfund.com	Ottawa	ON	K2E1A2	613-526-1969	
World Recycling Co 5600 Columbia Park Rd *Web:* world-recycling.com	Cheverly	MD	20785	301-386-3010	
Worldlink Integration Group Inc 21076 Bake Pkwy Ste 106 *Web:* www.worldlinkintegration.com	Lake Forest	CA	92630	949-861-2830	

183 COMPUTER SYSTEMS DESIGN SERVICES

SEE ALSO Web Site Design Services p. 3296

Companies that plan and design computer systems that integrate hardware, software, and communication technologies.

Company	City	State	Zip	Phone	Fax
1010data Inc 750 Third Ave Fourth Fl *Web:* www.1010data.com	New York	NY	10017	212-405-1010	
30 Dps 118 N Tejon St 304 *Web:* www.30dps.com	Colorado Springs	CO	80903	719-380-9996	
3Gtms Inc Eight Progress Dr *Web:* www.3gtms.com	Shelton	CT	06484	203-567-4610	
3s Global Business Solutions 7923 Nita Ave *Web:* www.3sgbs.com	Canoga Park	CA	91304	818-453-4403	
3sharp LLC 14700 Ne 95th St Ste 210 *Web:* www.3sharp.com	Redmond	WA	98052	425-882-1032	
3T Systems 5990 Greenwood Pl Blvd Ste 350 *Web:* 3tsystems.com	Greenwood Village	CO	80111	303-858-8800	
3tech Corp 2828 W Parker Rd Ste B101 *Web:* www.3tech.com	Plano	TX	75075	972-490-4443	
7strategy LLC 117 N Cooper St *Web:* www.7strategy.com	Olathe	KS	66061	913-638-2130	
A 2000 Network Solutions 237 Goolsby Blvd *Web:* a2000ns.com	Deerfield Beach	FL	33442	954-480-8430	
A D C Legal Systems Inc 1209 Edgewater Dr *Web:* www.adclegal.com	Orlando	FL	32804	407-843-8992	
A Partner in Technology 105 Dresden Ave *Web:* www.apitechnology.com	Gardiner	ME	04345	207-582-0888	
A r C Informatique Inc 1776 Rue Mitis *Web:* www.webdomaine.ca	Chicoutimi	QC	G7K1H4	418-545-9224	
AAE Systems Inc 642 N Pastoria Ave *Web:* www.aaesys.com	Sunnyvale	CA	94085	408-732-1710	
AAJ Technologies 6301 NW Fifth Way Ste 1700 *Web:* www.aajtech.com	Fort Lauderdale	FL	33309	954-689-3984	
Aasys Group 11301 N US Hwy 301 Ste 106 *Web:* www.aasysgroup.com	Thonotosassa	FL	33592	813-246-4757	
Abacus Business Solutions Inc 15301 Roosevelt Blvd Ste 303 *Web:* www.abacus-pos.com	Clearwater	FL	33760	727-524-0177	
Abacus Technology Corp 5454 Wisconsin Ave Ste 1100 *TF:* 800-225-2135 ■ *Web:* www.abacustech.com	Chevy Chase	MD	20815	301-907-8500	907-8508
Absolute Networking Systems Inc 11440 Bluegrass Pkwy *Web:* www.sayyestoans.com	Louisville	KY	40299	502-267-2552	
Acadiana Computer Systems Inc 324 Dulles Dr *Web:* www.acsmd.com	Lafayette	LA	70506	337-981-2494	
AccessIT Group Inc 2000 Vly Forge Cir Ste 106 *Web:* www.accessitgroup.com	King Of Prussia	PA	19406	610-783-5200	
Acg Inc 7007 Corporate Way *Web:* www.acgcbs.com	Dayton	OH	45459	937-433-8122	
Achilles Guard Inc 4201 Spring Vly Rd Ste 1400 *TF:* 866-525-8680 ■ *Web:* www.criticalwatch.com	Dallas	TX	75244	866-525-8680	
Acranet 2139 Tapo St Ste 209 *Web:* www.acranet.com	Simi Valley	CA	93063	805-584-3196	
Acsis Inc Nine E Stow Rd *Web:* www.acsisinc.com	Marlton	NJ	08053	856-673-3000	
Activo Inc 161 Alden Rd Unit 6 *Web:* www.activo.ca	Markham	ON	L3R3W7	905-752-1900	
Acumen Solutions Inc 1660 International Dr Ste 500 *Web:* www.acumensolutions.com	McLean	VA	22102	703-600-4000	600-4001
Acxius Strategic Consulting LLC Ste 300 500 Campus Dr *Web:* www.acxius.com	Morganville	NJ	07751	732-972-7970	
Adaptive Equipment Inc 2512 NE First Blvd Ste 400 *Web:* www.adaptiveequipment.com	Gainesville	FL	32609	352-372-7821	
Adc Information Technologies Inc 950 Michigan Ave *Web:* www.ibswebsite.com	Columbus	OH	43215	614-240-5999	
AdTek Information Systems Inc 500 Fifth Ave Ste 2110 *Web:* www.adtek.com	New York	NY	10110	212-307-1115	
Advanced Data Systems Corp 15 Prospect St	Paramus	NJ	07652	201-368-2001	
Advanced Information Systems Group Inc 11315 Corporate Blvd Ste 210 *TF:* 800-593-8359 ■ *Web:* www.aisg.com	Orlando	FL	32817	407-581-2929	581-2935
Advanced Resource Technologies Inc 1555 King St Ste 400 *Web:* www.team-arti.com	Alexandria	VA	22314	703-682-4740	682-4820
Advent Global Solutions Inc 12777 Jones Rd Ste 445 **Fax Area Code:* 281 ■ *Web:* www.adventglobal.com	Houston	TX	77070	832-678-3889	678-3889*
Aeroflex RAD Inc 5017 N 30th St *Web:* ams.aeroflex.com	Colorado Springs	CO	80919	719-531-0800	
AETEA Information Technology Inc 1445 Research Blvd Ste 300 *TF:* 888-772-3832 ■ *Web:* www.aetea.com	Rockville	MD	20850	301-721-4200	721-1730
Ag Connections Inc 1576 Killdeer Trl *Web:* www.agconnections.com	Murray	KY	42071	270-435-4369	
Agj Systems & Networks Inc 14257 Dedeaux Rd *Web:* www.agjsystems.com	Gulfport	MS	39503	228-392-7133	
AgniTEK LLC 214 N Main St *Web:* www.agnitek.com	Bryan	TX	77803	979-260-8324	
AGSI 3343 Peachtree Rd NE Ste 510 *TF:* 800-768-2474 ■ *Web:* www.agsi.com	Atlanta	GA	30326	404-816-7577	816-7578
Aim Systems 350 Speedvale Ave W *Web:* www.aimsystems.ca	Guelph	ON	N1H7M7	519-837-1072	
AirSage Inc 1330 Spring St NW Ste 400 *Web:* www.airsage.com	Atlanta	GA	30309	404-809-2499	
Alaska Computer Brokers 551 W Dimond Blvd *Web:* www.acbsolutions.net	Anchorage	AK	99515	907-267-4200	
Alexander & Tom Inc 3500 Boston St *Web:* alextom.com	Baltimore	MD	21224	410-327-7400	
Algo Design Inc 3100 Boul Le Carrefour *Web:* www.algodesign.com	Laval	QC	H7T2K7	450-681-2588	
ALI's Database Consultants 1151 Williams Dr *Web:* www.aliconsultants.com	Aiken	SC	29803	803-648-5931	
All Native Systems LLC One Mission Dr PO Box 458 *Web:* www.allnativesystems.com	Winnebago	NE	68071	402-878-2700	878-2560
All Star Consulting Inc 1111 Oak St *Web:* www.all-stars.com	San Francisco	CA	94117	415-552-1400	
All Systems Installation Inc 8300 10th Ave N Ste A *Web:* www.allsysinst.com	Golden Valley	MN	55427	763-593-1330	
Allied Technology Inc 1803 Research Blvd Ste 601 *TF:* 888-294-8560 ■ *Web:* www.alliedtech.com	Rockville	MD	20850	301-309-1234	309-0978
Allstar Tech 1856 Angus St *Web:* allstartech.com	Regina	SK	S4T1Z4	306-522-7827	
Alpac Inc 5752 Cedar Ridge Dr *Web:* alpacinc.com	Ann Arbor	MI	48103	734-623-2866	
AlphaKOR Group Inc 1670 Mercer St *Web:* www.alphakor.com	Windsor	ON	N8X3P7	519-944-6009	
Alphaserve Technologies LLC 104 W 27th St *Web:* www.alphaserveit.com	New York	NY	10001	212-763-5500	
AlphaSoft Services Corp 2035 Lincoln Hwy Ste 1190 *Web:* www.alphasoftservices.com	Edison	NJ	08817	925-952-6300	
Alpine Consulting Inc 1100 E Wdfield Rd *Web:* www.alpineinc.com	Schaumburg	IL	60173	847-605-0788	
Alt-N Technologies Ltd 4550 State Hwy 360 Ste 100 *Web:* www.altn.com	Grapevine	TX	76051	817-601-3222	
Alta Computer Data Services LLC 8823 S Redwood Rd Ste D2 *Web:* alta-acs.com	West Jordan	UT	84088	801-233-0531	
AmberWave Inc 13 Garabedian Dr *Web:* www.amberwave.com	Salem	NH	03079	603-870-8700	870-8607
American Systems Corp 14151 Pk Meadow Dr Ste 500 *TF:* 800-733-2721 ■ *Web:* www.americansystems.com	Chantilly	VA	20151	703-968-6300	968-5151
Amgraf Inc 1501 Oak St *Web:* amgraf.com	Kansas City	MO	64108	816-474-4797	
Amtex Systems Inc 50 Broad St Ste 801 *Web:* www.amtexsystems.com	New York	NY	10004	212-269-6448	269-6458

Company	City	State	ZIP	Phone	Fax
Analystik 1430 Rue Belanger *Web:* www.analystik.ca	Montreal	QC	H2G1A4	514-278-2727	
Analysts International Corp 7700 France Ave S Ste 200 *NASDAQ: ANLY* ■ *TF:* 800-800-5044 ■ *Web:* www.analysts.com	Minneapolis	MN	55435	952-838-3000	897-4555
Animate Systems Inc 133 Richmond St W *Web:* www.animate.com	Toronto	ON	M5H2L3	416-535-2516	
Apache Design Solutions Inc 2645 Zanker Rd *Web:* apache-da.com	San Jose	CA	95134	408-457-2000	
Applied Data Trends Inc 107-A Clinton Ave *Web:* www.adt-it.com	Huntsville	AL	35801	256-319-0700	
Applied Minds LLC 1209 Grand Central Ave *Web:* appliedminds.com	Glendale	CA	91201	818-545-1400	
Applied Science Group Inc 4455 Genesee St Bldg 6 *Web:* www.appliedsciencesgroup.com	Buffalo	NY	14225	716-626-5100	
APPNET.COM 9649 NC Hwy 105 S *Web:* www.appnet.com	Banner Elk	NC	28604	828-963-7286	
Apprio Inc 425 Third St SW Ste 890 *Web:* www.apprioinc.com	Washington	DC	20024	202-684-8266	
Arcane Technologies Inc 918 Monticello Ave *Web:* www.arcane-tech.com	Charlottesville	VA	22902	434-979-7979	
Architel Inc 8350 N Central Expy Ste 250 *Web:* www.architel.com	Dallas	TX	75206	214-550-2000	
ArcSight Inc Five Results Way *Web:* www.arcsight.com	Cupertino	CA	95014	408-864-2600	
Arcsoft Inc 46601 Fremont Blvd *Web:* arcsoft.com	Fremont	CA	94538	510-440-9901	
Area Wide Technologies Inc 2110 Clearlake Blvd Ste 100 *Web:* areawidetech.com	Champaign	IL	61822	217-359-8041	
Argo Systems Inc 2964 Peachtree Rd *Web:* sintecmedia.com	Atlanta	GA	30305	404-869-4575	
Arlington Computer Products Inc 851 Commerce Ct *TF Orders:* 800-548-5105 ■ *Web:* www.arlingtoncp.com	Buffalo Grove	IL	60089	847-541-6333	541-6881
Arrow Strategies LLC 30300 Telegraph Rd Ste 117 *Web:* www.arrowstrategies.com	Bingham Farms	MI	48025	248-502-2500	502-2525
Art & Logic Inc Two N Lk Ave Ste 1050 *Web:* www.artandlogic.com	Pasadena	CA	91101	818-500-1933	
Arx Networks LLC 581 Foster City Blvd Ste 210 *Web:* www.arxnetworks.com	Foster City	CA	94404	650-403-4279	
Ascend Quality Partners 20 Sunysde Ave Ste A195 *Web:* www.ascendquality.com	Mill Valley	CA	94941	415-381-4400	
Ascent Services Group, The 3000 Oak Rd Ste 200 *Web:* www.ascentsg.com	Walnut Creek	CA	94597	925-627-4900	
ASI Computer Systems Inc 5250 Nordic Dr *Web:* www.asicomp.com	Cedar Falls	IA	50613	319-266-7688	
Asi Networks Inc 19331 E Walnut Dr N *Web:* www.asi-networks.com	City Of Industry	CA	91748	909-869-6160	
Aspen Networks Inc 3777 Stevens Creek Blvd *Web:* www.aspen-networks.com	Santa Clara	CA	95051	408-246-4059	
ASSETT Inc 11220 Assett Loop Ste 101 *Web:* www.assett.net	Manassas	VA	20109	703-365-8950	
Atlantic Webworks & Consulting Inc 331 S Swing Rd *Web:* www.atlanticwebworks.com	Greensboro	NC	27409	336-855-8572	
Attention Software Inc 2175 N Academy Cir Ste 100 *Web:* www.attentionsoftware.com	Colorado Springs	CO	80909	719-591-9110	
Attronica Computers Inc 15867 Gaither Dr *Web:* www.attronica.com	Gaithersburg	MD	20877	301-417-0070	
Aumtech Inc 710 Old Bridge Tpke *Web:* aumtech.com	East Brunswick	NJ	08816	732-254-1875	
Aurora Computer Technology Inc Six Schubert St *Web:* auroracomputer.com	Staten Island	NY	10305	718-981-2363	
Automation Image Inc 2650 Vly View Ln Ste 100 *Web:* www.automationimage.com	Dallas	TX	75234	972-247-8816	243-2814
Automation Technologies Inc 8219 Leesburg Pk *Web:* www.ati4it.com	Vienna	VA	22182	703-883-1410	883-1435
Avant Systems Group 815-1661 Portage Ave *Web:* avant.ca	Winnipeg	MB	R3J3T7	204-789-9596	
AVF Consulting Inc 1220-C E Joppa Rd Ste 514 *Web:* www.avfconsulting.com	Baltimore	MD	21286	410-296-5100	
Avl Systems Design LLC 14901 Bristol Park Blvd *Web:* www.avl1.com	Edmond	OK	73013	405-749-1866	
AVS Installations LLC 400 Raritan Ctr Pkwy Ste D *Web:* www.avsillc.com	Edison	NJ	08837	732-634-7903	
AVT Inc 341 Bonnie Cir Ste 102 *TF:* 877-424-3663 ■ *Web:* www.autoretail.com	Corona	CA	92880	877-424-3663	
Axios Products Inc Ste 204 353 Veterans Hwy *Web:* www.axios.com	Commack	NY	11725	631-864-3666	
Axyz Automation Inc 2844 E Kemper Rd *Web:* www.axyz.com	Cincinnati	OH	45241	513-771-7444	
Ayoka LLC 1161 W Corporate Dr Ste 303 *Web:* www.ayokasystems.com	Arlington	TX	76006	817-210-4042	
B Green Innovations Inc 750 Hwy 34 *TF:* 877-996-9333 ■ *Web:* bgreeninnovations.com	Matawan	NJ	07747	732-441-7700	
Banyan Medical Systems Inc 4106 S 87th St *Web:* www.banyanmedicalsystems.com	Omaha	NE	68127	402-403-4400	
Barcom Inc 400B Chickamauga Rd *Web:* www.barcominc.com	Chattanooga	TN	37421	423-855-1822	
Baroan Technologies 385 Falmouth Ave *Web:* www.baroan.com	Elmwood Park	NJ	07407	201-796-0404	
Barry Strock Consulting Associates Inc 154 Rosemont St *Web:* strock.com	Albany	NY	12206	518-797-3954	
Base One Technologies Inc 10 S Division St Ste 5 *Web:* www.base-one.com	New Rochelle	NY	10805	914-633-0200	
Battle Medialab Inc 117 E Boca Raton Rd *Web:* battlemedialab.com	Boca Raton	FL	33432	561-395-1555	
Bay Microsystems Inc 2055 Gateway Pl Ste 650 *Web:* baymicrosystems.com	San Jose	CA	95110	408-437-0400	
Bay State Computers Inc 16901 Melford Blvd Ste 329 *Web:* www.bayst.com	Bowie	MD	20716	301-352-7878	352-6925
Bazon Cox & Associates Inc 1244 Executive Blvd *Web:* www.bazcox.com	Chesapeake	VA	23320	757-410-2128	
Bek Business Solutions 723 Memorial Hwy *Web:* www.bekbusiness.com	Bismarck	ND	58504	701-255-2032	
Bell Techlogix 5777 Decatur Blvd **Fax Area Code:* 888 ■ *TF:* 866-782-2355 ■ *Web:* www.belltechlogix.com	Indianapolis	IN	46241	317-333-7777	890-9494*
Bella Web Design Inc 3605 Sandy Plains Rd Ste 240-121 *Web:* www.bellawebdesign.com	Marietta	GA	30066	770-509-8797	
Benchmark Network Solutions Inc 1931 Evans Rd *Web:* www.benchmark-net.com	Cary	NC	27513	919-678-8595	
Bender Consulting Services Inc Penn Ctr W III Ste 223 *Web:* www.benderconsult.com	Pittsburgh	PA	15276	412-787-8567	
Beta Soft Systems Inc 42808 Christy St Ste 101 *Web:* www.betasoftsystems.com	Fremont	CA	94538	510-744-1700	
bitHeads Inc 1309 Carling Ave *Web:* www.bitheads.com	Ottawa	ON	K1Z7L3	613-722-3232	
Bits n Bytes Computer Systems 3201 Double C Dr *Web:* www.bnbtech.com	Norman	OK	73069	405-292-5408	
Bitworks LLC 126 Tower Rd *Web:* www.bitworksusa.net	Waterbury	CT	06710	203-756-9513	
BizSpeed Inc 3050 Royal Blvd S Ste 130 *Web:* www.bizspeed.com	Alpharetta	GA	30022	678-287-3310	
BlackBag Technologies Inc 300 Piercy Rd *Web:* www.blackbagtech.com	San Jose	CA	95138	408-844-8890	
Blast Advanced Media 950 Reserve Dr Ste 150 *Web:* www.blastam.com	Roseville	CA	95678	916-724-6701	
Blink Reaction LLC 195 US Route 9 S Ste 101 *Web:* www.blinkreaction.com	Manalapan	NJ	07726	732-792-6566	
Blough Tech Inc 119 S Broad St *Web:* www.bloughtech.com	Cairo	GA	39828	229-377-8825	
Blue Tangerine Solutions Inc 1380 Sarno Rd Ste B *Web:* www.bluetangerinesolutions.com	Melbourne	FL	32935	321-309-6900	
Bluelock LLC 6325 Morenci Trl *TF:* 888-402-2583 ■ *Web:* www.bluelock.com	Indianapolis	IN	46268	888-402-2583	
Bluestorm Technologies Inc 455 Court St *Web:* www.bluestormtech.com	Binghamton	NY	13904	607-762-5401	
Blytheco LLC 23161 Mill Creek Dr *TF:* 800-425-9843 ■ *Web:* www.blytheco.com	Laguna Hills	CA	92653	949-583-9500	583-0649
BNL Inc 11760 Armistead Filler Ln *Web:* www.bnlinc.com	Lovettsville	VA	20180	540-822-5569	
Book Systems Inc 4901 University Sq Ste 3 *Web:* www.booksys.com	Huntsville	AL	35816	256-533-9746	
Boxworks Technologies Inc 2065 Pkwy Blve *Web:* boxworks.com	Salt Lake City	UT	84119	801-214-6100	
Boyle Software Inc 42 W 24th St *Web:* www.boylesoftware.com	New York	NY	10010	212-691-0609	
Bradshaw Consulting Services Inc 2170 Woodside Exec Ct *Web:* www.bcs-gis.com	Aiken	SC	29803	803-641-0960	
Brave River Solutions Inc 875 Centerville Rd Bldg 3 *Web:* www.braveriver.com	Warwick	RI	02886	401-828-6611	
Bredet Services Inc 1660 N Service Rd E *Web:* www.bredetservices.com	Oakville	ON	L6H7G3	905-337-7233	
BriarTek Inc 3129 Mount Vernon Ave *Web:* www.briartek.com	Alexandria	VA	22305	703-548-7892	
Bridgeline Digital 80 BlanchaRd Rd *TF:* 800-603-9936 ■ *Web:* www.bridgelinedigital.com	Burlington	MA	01803	781-376-5555	376-5033
Buchanan Technologies Inc 1026 Texan Trl *Web:* www.buchanan.com	Grapevine	TX	76051	972-869-3966	
Buffalo Computer Graphics Inc 3741 Lk Shore Rd *Web:* www.buffalocomputergraphics.com	Blasdell	NY	14219	716-822-8668	
BUILDERadius Inc 16 Biltmore Ave Ste 300 *Web:* www.buildfax.com	Asheville	NC	28801	828-350-9950	
Bull HN Information Systems Inc 285 Billerica Rd *Web:* www.bull.com	Billerica	MA	01824	978-294-6000	244-0085
Burgiss Group LLC, The 111 River St Fl 10th *Web:* burgiss.com	Hoboken	NJ	07030	201-427-9600	
Burgundy Group Inc, The 2420 S Power Rd Ste 103 *Web:* www.tbginc.com	Mesa	AZ	85209	480-325-7700	
Burton Computer Resources Inc 400 N 16th Ave *Web:* www.burtoncomputer.com	Laurel	MS	39440	601-428-0205	
C-double Web Development 5201 College Ave *Web:* c-double.com	Bakersfield	CA	93306	661-872-2738	
CACI International Inc 1100 N Glebe Rd *NYSE: CACI* ■ *TF:* 866-606-3471 ■ *Web:* www.caci.com	Arlington	VA	22201	703-841-7800	841-7882

Phone | Fax

Cad Technology Center
1000 Boone Ave N Ste 200 ... Minneapolis MN 55427 952-941-1181
Web: www.cadtechnologycenter.com

Cadence Technologies Inc
1006 Windward Rdg Pkwy ... Alpharetta GA 30005 770-667-6250
Web: www.cadencetechnologies.com

Cadre Computer Resources Co
201 East Fifth Street Suite 1800 ... Cincinnati OH 45202 513-762-7350 762-6502
TF: 866-762-6700 ■ *Web:* www.ccr.com

Cadsoft Consulting Inc
4578 N First Ave Ste 120 ... Tucson AZ 85718 520-546-2233
Web: cadsoft-consult.com

Calibre Systems Inc
6354 Walker Ln Ste 300 Metro Pk ... Alexandria VA 22310 703-797-8500 797-8501
TF: 888-225-4273 ■ *Web:* www.calibresys.com

Camber Corp 635 Discovery Dr NW ... Huntsville AL 35806 256-922-0200 922-3599
TF: 800-998-7988 ■ *Web:* www.camber.com

Canweb Internet Services 1086 Modeland Rd ... Sarnia ON N7S6L2 519-332-6900
Web: www.canweb.ca

Capgemini US LLC 623 Fifth Ave # 33 ... New York NY 10022 212-314-8000
Web: www.capgemini.com

Capital Datacorp
3600 Madison Ave Ste 65 ... North Highlands CA 95660 916-529-4063
Web: www.capdata.com

CapitalSoft Inc
1702 N Collins Blvd Ste 211 ... Richardson TX 75080 972-220-1560
Web: www.capitalsoft.com

Capitol Computers Inc 151 Water St ... Augusta ME 04330 207-623-2700
Web: www.capcomp.com

CARA Group Inc, The
Drake Oak Brook Plz 2215 York Rd Ste 300 ... Oak Brook IL 60523 630-574-2272
Web: www.caracorp.com

Carolina Computer Training Inc
33 Villa Rd Ste 100 ... Greenville SC 29615 864-527-8100
Web: www.cctbusiness.com

Caron Engineering Inc 1931 Sanford Rd ... Wells ME 04090 207-646-6071
Web: www.caron-eng.com

Catapult Systems Inc
1221 S MoPac Expwy Ste 350 ... Austin TX 78746 512-328-8181 328-0584
TF: 800-528-6248 ■ *Web:* www.catapultsystems.com

Cayman Technologies Inc
12954 Stonecreek Dr Ste E ... Pickerington OH 43147 614-759-9461
Web: www.caymantech.com

Cazarin Web Group 7064 E Fish Lk Rd ... Minneapolis MN 55311 763-420-9992
Web: www.cazarin.com

CBM of America Inc
1455 W Newport Ctr Dr ... Deerfield Beach FL 33442 954-698-9104
Web: www.cbmusa.com

Cbord Group Inc, The 61 Brown Rd ... Ithaca NY 14850 607-257-2410

Cca Medical Inc Six Southridge Ct ... Greenville SC 29607 864-233-2700
Web: www.ccamedical.com

CD Group Inc 5550 Triangle Pkwy ... Norcross GA 30092 678-268-2000 268-2001
Web: www.cdgroup.com

CDMS Inc 550 Sherbrooke W West Tower Ste 250 ... Montreal QC H3A1B9 514-286-2367
Web: www.cdmsfirst.com

Cdo Technologies Inc 5200 Sprngfeld St Ste 320 ... Dayton OH 45431 937-258-0022 258-1614
TF: 866-307-6616 ■ *Web:* www.cdotech.com

Centurion Data Systems
N27w23957 Paul Rd Ste 102 ... Pewaukee WI 53072 262-524-9290
Web: www.cendatsys.com

Ceres Technology Group Inc
2985 Sterling Court Ste A ... Boulder CO 80301 303-440-6963
Web: www.boulderpcs.com

CGI Group Inc
1130 Sherbrooke St W Seventh Fl ... Montreal QC H3A2M8 514-841-3200 841-3299
TSE: GIB/A ■ *TF:* 800-828-8377 ■ *Web:* www.cgi.com

Challenge Training & Consulting Inc
1099 Wall St W Ste 390 ... Lyndhurst NJ 07071 201-636-2420
Web: www.challengetraining.com

Chameleon Consulting Inc 89 Falmouth Rd W ... Arlington MA 02474 781-646-2272
Web: www.chamcon.com

Chaney Systems Inc 5100 S Calhoun Rd ... New Berlin WI 53151 262-679-6000
Web: www.chaney.net

Cherokee Consulting LLC 5057 Bear Mtn Dr ... Evergreen CO 80439 303-674-4857
Web: www.cherokeeconsultingllc.com

Cherokee Information Services Inc
2850 Eisenhower Ave Ste 210 ... Alexandria VA 22314 703-416-0720 416-1045
Web: www.cherokee-inc.com

Chi Corp 5265 Naiman Pkwy ... Cleveland OH 44139 440-498-2300
Web: www.chicorporation.com

CIBER Inc
6363 S Fiddler's Green Cir
Ste 1400 ... Greenwood Village CO 80111 303-220-0100 220-7100
NYSE: CBR ■ *TF:* 800-242-3799 ■ *Web:* www.ciber.com

Cigniti Inc 433 E Las Colinas Blvd Ste 1300 ... Irving TX 75039 972-756-0622
Web: www.cigniti.com

CIM Concepts Inc
100 W Commons Blvd Ste 101 ... New Castle DE 19720 302-613-5400
Web: cimconcepts.com

CIO Solutions 150 Castilian Dr #100 ... Goleta CA 93117 805-692-6700
Web: www.ciosolutions.com

Ckc Laboratories Inc 5046 Sierra Pines Dr ... Mariposa CA 95338 209-966-5240
Web: www.ckc.com

CLAdirect Inc 8600 NW 17th St Ste 140 ... Miami FL 33126 305-418-4253
Web: cladirect.com

Clarkston Consulting 1007 Slater Rd Ste 400 ... Durham NC 27703 919-484-4400 484-4450
TF: 800-652-4274 ■ *Web:* www.clarkstonconsulting.com

Classy Llama Studios LLC
4064 S Lone Pine ... Springfield MO 65804 417-866-8887
Web: www.classyllama.com

Clever Devices Ltd 300 Crossways Pk Dr ... Woodbury NY 11797 516-433-6100
TF: 800-872-6129 ■ *Web:* www.cleverdevices.com

Phone | Fax

CLICK-into Inc 160 Gibson Dr Ste 4 ... Markham ON L3R3K1 905-477-8853
Web: www.click-into.com

Clockwork 4120 Yonge St ... North York ON M2P2B8 416-222-8990
Web: www.clockwork.ca

Cluen Corp, The Seven W 22nd St Fl 5 ... New York NY 10010 212-255-6659
Web: www.cluen.com

Coalfire Systems Inc
361 Centennial Pkwy Ste 150 ... Louisville CO 80027 303-554-6333
Web: www.coalfire.com

Cognitive Technologies Inc
16333 S Great Oaks Dr Ste 201 ... Round Rock TX 78681 703-562-0600
Web: www.cog-ps.com

Cognizant Technology Solutions Corp
500 Frank W Burr Blvd ... Teaneck NJ 07666 201-801-0233 801-0243*
NASDAQ: CTSH ■ **Fax:* Mktg ■ *TF:* 888-937-3277 ■ *Web:* www.cognizant.com

Colibri Ltd 419 E Crossville Rd Ste 102 ... Roswell GA 30075 678-352-1001
Web: www.colibrilimited.com

COLSA Corp 6728 Odyssey Dr ... Huntsville AL 35806 256-964-5555
Web: www.colsa.com

Comit Technologies 1325 Eraste Landry Rd ... Lafayette LA 70506 337-326-5479
Web: www.comittechnologies.com

Comport Consulting Corp 78 Orchard St ... Ramsey NJ 07446 201-236-0505
Web: www.comport.com

Compsys Inc 800 Wilcrest Ste 260 ... Houston TX 77042 713-961-3999

Compu-Cure New Orleans Inc
3528 Holiday Dr ... New Orleans LA 70114 504-486-7741
Web: compucure.com

CompuNet Consulting Group Inc
6535 Shiloh Rd Ste 300 ... Alpharetta GA 30005 678-965-6500
Web: www.ccgi.net

Computech Inc 7735 Old Georgetown Rd ... Bethesda MD 20814 301-656-4030 656-7060
Web: www.computechinc.com

Computek 9383 Charles Smith Ave ... Rancho Cucamonga CA 91730 909-987-8515
Web: www.computek.com

Computer Analytical Systems Inc (CASI)
1418 S Third St ... Louisville KY 40208 502-635-2019
TF: 800-977-3475 ■ *Web:* www.c-a-s-i.com

Computer Generated Solutions Inc
200 Vesey St Three World Financial Ctr
27th Fl ... New York NY 10281 212-408-3800
Web: www.cgsinc.com

Computer Horizons Corp
49 Old Bloomfield Ave ... Mountain Lakes NJ 07046 973-299-4000
NYSE: CHZS

Computer Power Solutions Inc
4644 Katella Ave ... Los Alamitos CA 90720 562-493-4487
Web: www.computerpowersolutions.com

Computer Pundits Corp 6515 Cecilia Cir ... Bloomington MN 55439 952-854-2422
Web: www.computerpundits.com

Computer Sciences Corp 2100 E Grand Ave ... El Segundo CA 90245 310-615-0311
NYSE: CSC ■ *TF:* 866-310-0950 ■ *Web:* www.csc.com

Computer Task Group Inc (CTG) 800 Delaware Ave ... Buffalo NY 14209 716-882-8000 887-7464
OTC: CTG ■ *TF:* 800-992-5350 ■ *Web:* www.ctg.com

Computer Technology Assoc (CTA)
12530 Parklawn Dr Ste 470 ... Rockville MD 20852 301-581-3200 581-3201
Web: www.cta.com

ComResource Inc 1159 Dublin Rd Ste 200 ... Columbus OH 43215 614-221-6348
Web: www.comresource.com

Condortech Services Inc
6621-A Electronic Dr ... Springfield VA 22151 703-916-9200
Web: www.condortech.com

Conduit Corp 3212 W End Ave Ste 500 ... Nashville TN 37203 615-269-5710
Web: www.conduitcorporation.com

Connect Tech Inc 42 Arrow Rd ... Guelph ON N1K1S6 519-836-1291
Web: www.connecttech.com

Consult Dynamics Inc 1016 Delaware Ave ... Wilmington DE 19806 302-654-1019
Web: www.dca.net

Contec Systems Industrial Corp
1566 Medical Dr Ste 310 ... Pottstown PA 19464 610-326-3235
Web: contecsystems.com

Context Creative Inc 317 Adelaide St W ... Toronto ON M5V1P9 416-972-1439
Web: contextcreative.com

Continuum Worldwide Corp 3333 Farnam St Ste 1 ... Omaha NE 68131 402-916-1800
Web: www.continuumww.com

Convio Inc 11501 Domain Dr Ste 200 ... Austin TX 78758 512-652-2600
Web: www.convio.com

Cook Systems International Inc
6799 Great Oaks Rd Atrium II Ste 200 ... Memphis TN 38138 901-757-8877
Web: www.cooksys.com

Corbett Technology Solutions
4151 Lafeyette Ctr Dr Ste 700 ... Chantilly VA 20151 703-631-3377
Web: www.ctsi-usa.com

Corestar International Corp 1044 Sandy Hill Rd ... Irwin PA 15642 724-744-4094
Web: www.corestar-corp.com

Coretelligent LLC 75 Second Ave Ste 210 ... Needham MA 02494 781-247-4900
Web: coretelligent.com

Corstar Communications LLC
40 Saw Mill River Rd ... Hawthorne NY 10532 914-347-2700
Web: www.corstar.com

Corus Group LLC 130 Technology Pkwy ... Norcross GA 30092 770-300-4700
Web: www.corus360.com

Covansys Corp
32605 W 12 Mile Rd Ste 250 ... Farmington Hills MI 48334 248-488-2088 488-2089
TF: 866-310-0950

Covestic Inc 5555 Lakeview Dr Ste 100 ... Kirkland WA 98033 425-803-9889
Web: www.covestic.com

Cr&t Management Inc 116 Mtn Way Dr ... Orem UT 84058 801-222-0930
Web: www.cr-t.com

Creation Engine 348 E Middlefield Rd ... Mountain View CA 94043 650-934-0176
Web: www.creationengine.com

Creative Logistics Solutions Inc
2135 Espey Ct ... Crofton MD 21114 410-793-0708
Web: www.creativelogistics.com

Company	City	State	Zip	Phone	Fax
CRI Advantage Inc 6149 N Meeker Pl Ste 200 *Web:* www.criadvantage.com	Boise	ID	83713	208-343-9192	
CSSI Inc 400 Virginia Ave SW Ste 210 *Web:* www.cssiinc.com	Washington	DC	20024	202-863-2175	
Custom Computer Specialists Inc (CCS) 70 Suffolk Ct *TF:* 800-598-8989 ■ *Web:* www.customonline.com	Hauppauge	NY	11788	631-864-6699	543-2512
Custom Consulting Associates LLC 1112 Sw 118th Pl *Web:* www.cca-llc.net	Oklahoma City	OK	73170	405-691-3417	
Custom Systems & Controls 132 Winter St *Web:* custom-sys.com	Framingham	MA	01702	508-879-4390	
CWPS Inc 14120 A Sullyfield Cir *TF:* 877-297-7472 ■ *Web:* www.cwps.com	Chantilly	VA	20151	877-297-7472	
Cyber Korp Inc 125 Fairfield Way Ste 380 *Web:* www.cyberkorp.com	Bloomingdale	IL	60108	630-980-4416	
CyberCore Technologies LLC 6605 Business Pkwy Meadowridge Business Park *Web:* www.cybercoretech.com	Elkridge	MD	21075	410-560-7177	
Cyberjaz Corp 2276 Todd Rd *Web:* www.cyberjaz.net	Aliquippa	PA	15001	724-857-8083	
Cybersoft 1958 Butler Pk *Web:* www.cybersoft.com	Conshohocken	PA	19428	610-825-6785	
Cybersoft Technologies Inc 4422 Fm 1960 Rd W Ste 300 *Web:* www.cybersofttech.com	Houston	TX	77068	281-895-7717	
Cybertech Systems & Software Inc 3401 Quebec St Ste 3600 *Web:* www.cybertech.com	Denver	CO	80207	303-321-0592	321-0689
Cybrix Group Inc 312 E Seventh Ave *Web:* www.cybrixgroup.com	Tampa	FL	33602	813-630-2744	
CYIOS Corporation Inc Ste 700 1300 PENNSYLVANIA AVE NW *Web:* www.cyios.com	Washington	DC	20004	202-204-3006	
Cypress Networks 114 S Westgate Dr Ste C *Web:* www.cypressnetworks.net	Greensboro	NC	27407	336-808-0131	
Cyquent Inc 5410 Edson Ln Ste 210C *Web:* www.cyquent.com	Rockville	MD	20852	240-292-0230	
D V O Enterprises Inc 620 Windsor Ct *Web:* www.dvo.com	Alpine	UT	84004	801-492-1290	
Dallas Digital Services LLC 5316 Bransford Rd *Web:* www.ddserv.com	Colleyville	TX	76034	817-577-8794	
Data Computer Corporation of America 5310 Dorsey Hall Dr *Web:* www.dcca.com	Ellicott City	MD	21042	410-992-3760	
Data Consulting Group Inc 965 E Jefferson Ave *Web:* www.dcgroupinc.com	Detroit	MI	48207	313-963-7771	
Data Innovations Inc 120 Kimball Ave Ste 100 *Web:* www.datainnovations.com	South Burlington	VT	05403	802-658-2850	
Data Networks Corp 1821 Michael Faraday Dr Ste 401 *Web:* dncx.com	Reston	VA	20190	703-478-2650	
Data Perceptions 174 Bridge St W *Web:* www.dataperceptions.com	Waterloo	ON	N2K1K9	519-749-9319	
Data Recovery Services 1343 Belmont Ave *Web:* drsllc.net	Youngstown	OH	44504	330-259-4900	
Data Systems Analysts Inc (DSA) Eigth Neshaminy Interplex Ste 209 *Web:* www.dsainc.com	Trevose	PA	19053	215-245-4800	245-4375
DataComm Networks Inc 6801 N 54th St *Web:* www.datacomm.com	Tampa	FL	33610	813-873-0674	
DataLink Interactive Inc 1120 Benfield Blvd Ste G *Web:* www.datalinktech.com	Millersville	MD	21108	410-729-0440	
Datamatrix Systems Inc 505 Lincoln Hwy *Web:* www.getdatamatrix.com	East Mckeesport	PA	15035	412-825-3600	
Datapro Inc 770 Ponce De Leon Blvd Second Fl *Web:* www.datapromiami.com	Coral Gables	FL	33134	305-374-0606	
Datapro Solutions Inc 6336 E Utah Ave *Web:* www.dataprosolutionsinc.com	Spokane	WA	99212	509-532-3530	
Dataskill Inc 5675 Ruffin Rd Ste 100 *Web:* www.dataskill.com	San Diego	CA	92123	858-755-3800	
Datatrend Technologies Inc 121 Cheshire Ln Ste 700 *Web:* www.datatrend.com	Minnetonka	MN	55305	952-931-1203	
Datroo Technologies LLC 1049 N Third St Ste 707 *Web:* www.datroo.com	Abilene	TX	79601	325-675-8880	
Dayhuff Group LLC, The 740 Lakeview Plz Blvd Ste 300 *Web:* www.dayhuffgroup.com	Worthington	OH	43085	614-854-9999	
Dcs Netlink 1800 Macauley Ave *Web:* dcsnetlink.com	Rice Lake	WI	54868	715-236-7424	
Dcse Inc 95 Argonaut Ste 260 *Web:* www.dcse.com	Aliso Viejo	CA	92656	949-465-3400	
Decision Systems Plus Inc 1011 E Touhy Ave Ste 170 *Web:* www.motherg.com	Des Plaines	IL	60018	847-699-9960	
Decisive Business Systems Inc 6991 N Park Dr *Web:* www.decisivebiz.com	Pennsauken	NJ	08109	856-910-0900	
Delaney Computer Services 66 Orange Tpke *Web:* dcsny.com	Sloatsburg	NY	10974	845-753-5800	
Dell Perot Systems 370 Southpointe Blvd Fourth Fl	Canonsburg	PA	15317	724-514-5000	
Delta Corporate Services Inc 129 Littleton Rd *TF:* 800-335-8220 ■ *Web:* www.deltacorp.com	Parsippany	NJ	07054	973-334-6260	331-0144
Denali Advance Integration (DAI) 17735 NE 65th St Ste 130 *TF:* 877-467-8008 ■ *Web:* www.denaliai.com	Redmond	WA	98052	425-885-4000	467-1127
Design Strategy Corp 805 Third Ave 11th Fl *TF:* 800-331-8726 ■ *Web:* www.designstrategy.com	New York	NY	10016	212-370-0000	949-3648
Detroit Engineered Products Inc 560 Kirts Blvd Ste 103 *Web:* www.depusa.com	Troy	MI	48084	248-269-7130	
Dew Software Inc 983 Corporate Way *Web:* www.dewsoftware.com	Fremont	CA	94539	510-490-9995	
Dexisive Inc 1801 Robert Fulton Dr Ste 120 *Web:* www.dexisive.com	Reston	VA	20191	703-935-0110	
Dialogic Inc 1504 Mccarthy Blvd *TF:* 800-755-4444 ■ *Web:* www.dialogic.com	Milpitas	CA	95035	408-750-9400	
Digett 105 Falls Court Ste 300 *Web:* digett.com	Boerne	TX	78006	830-249-9494	
Digital Bungalow Inc 209 Essex St *Web:* www.digitalbungalow.com	Salem	MA	01970	978-565-0111	
Digital Celerity LLC 10 Fernwood Dr *Web:* www.digitalcelerity.com	San Francisco	CA	94127	408-812-9999	
Digital Foundry Inc 1707 Tiburon Blvd *Web:* www.digitalfoundry.com	Belvedere Tiburon	CA	94920	415-789-1600	
Digium Inc 445 Jan Davis Dr NW *Web:* www.digium.com	Huntsville	AL	35806	256-428-6000	
Dini Communications 340 Campus Dr *Web:* dini.net	Edison	NJ	08837	732-225-4514	
Dirks Group, The 3802 Hummingbird Rd *Web:* www.dirksgroup.com	Wausau	WI	54401	715-848-9865	
Diverse Technology Solutions Inc 2949 Sunrise Hwy *Web:* www.diverse-technology.com	Islip Terrace	NY	11752	631-224-1200	
DLP Technologies Inc 8080 Reading Rd *Web:* www.netgainit.com	Cincinnati	OH	45237	513-232-7791	
DMC Technology Group Inc 7657 King's Pointe Rd *Web:* www.dmcconsulting.com	Toledo	OH	43617	419-535-2900	
Documentation Strategies Inc 15 Second Ave *Web:* www.docstrats.com	Rensselaer	NY	12144	518-432-1233	
Dominant Systems Corp 3850 Varsity Dr *Web:* domsys.com	Ann Arbor	MI	48108	734-971-1210	
Dowling Consulting Group Inc 4833 Darrow Rd Ste 100 *Web:* www.dowlinggroup.com	Stow	OH	44224	330-656-1136	
Dp Guardian Inc 2270 W Chenango Ave Unit 300 *Web:* www.dpguardian.com	Littleton	CO	80120	303-783-0191	
DPE Systems Inc 425 Pontius Ave N Ste 430 *TF:* 800-541-6566 ■ *Web:* www.dpes.com	Seattle	WA	98109	206-223-3737	223-0859
Dr FirstCom Inc 9420 Key W Ave Ste 230 *Web:* drfirst.com	Rockville	MD	20850	301-231-9510	
Dr Tax Software Inc 3333 Graham Blvd Ste 222 *Web:* www.drtax.ca	Montreal	QC	H3R3L5	514-733-8355	
Drayton, Drayton & Lamar Inc 616 Ponder Pl Dr Ste 2 *Web:* www.ddlinc.com	Evans	GA	30809	706-854-1145	
Druide informatique Inc 1435 rue Saint-Alexandre Bureau 1040 *Web:* www.druide.com	Montreal	QC	H3A2G4	514-484-4998	
Durst Image Technology US LLC 50 Methodist Hill Dr Ste 100 *Web:* www.durstus.com	Rochester	NY	14623	585-486-0340	
Dxm Productions 472 S Shoreline Blvd *Web:* www.dxm.com	Mountain View	CA	94041	650-969-6580	
Dynamic Edge Inc 2245 S State St Ste 1200 *Web:* dynamic-edge.net	Ann Arbor	MI	48104	734-975-0460	
Dynamic Motion Control Inc 1333 N Kingsbury St *Web:* www.dmcinfo.com	Chicago	IL	60642	312-255-8757	
Dyonyx LP 1235 N Loop W *TF General:* 855-749-6758 ■ *Web:* www.dyonyx.com	Houston	TX	77008	713-485-7000	830-5909
Dytech Group 7201 Sandscove Ct Ste 4 *Web:* www.dytech.com	Winter Park	FL	32792	407-678-8300	
E & E It Consulting Services Inc 5026 Arthur Ave *Web:* ene-it-consulting.com	Mechanicsburg	PA	17050	717-975-1664	
EA Consulting Inc 1024 Iron Point Rd *Web:* www.eainc.com	Folsom	CA	95630	916-357-6588	200-0368
Echota Technologies Corp 3286 Northpark Blvd Ste A	Alcoa	TN	37701	865-273-1270	273-1277
Eco-Shift Power Corp 1090 Fountain St North Unit 1 2 *Web:* eco-shiftpower.com	Cambridge	ON	N3H4R7	519-650-9506	
Ecom Enterprises Inc 1230 Oakmead Pkwy Ste 318 *Web:* www.ecomenterprises.com	Sunnyvale	CA	94085	408-720-9194	
Ecom Solutions 7326 Yellowstone Blvd 2 *Web:* www.ecomsolutions.net	Forest Hills	NY	11375	718-793-2828	
Edvance Research Inc 9901 W Interstate 10 Ste 1000 *Web:* edvanceresearch.com	San Antonio	TX	78230	210-558-1902	
EHD Technologies LLC 1600 Westgate Cir *Web:* www.ehdtech.com	Brentwood	TN	37027	615-953-1907	
Elangeni Consulting Inc 219 Intervale Rd *Web:* www.elangeni.com	Boonton	NJ	07005	973-541-1667	
Elara Systems 2880 Sunrise Blvd Ste 200 *Web:* www.elarasystems.com	Rancho Cordova	CA	95742	916-941-9597	

Phone Fax

Electronic Warfare Assoc Inc (EWA Inc)
13873 Pk Ctr Rd Ste 500 Herndon VA 20171 703-904-5700 904-5779
TF General: 888-392-0002 ■ *Web:* www.ewa.com

Elemco Software Integration Group Ltd
245 Atlantic St Central Islip NY 11722 631-234-3099
Web: www.elemcosoftware.com

Em Data Consultants Inc
42 Queen St S Ste 201 Mississauga ON L5M1K4 905-858-8442
Web: www.emdci.com

EMA Design Automation Inc 225 Tech Park Dr Rochester NY 14623 585-334-6001
Web: www.ema-eda.com

eMagine Communications LLC
73 Stevens St East Taunton MA 02718 508-802-9577
Web: www.emagine.com

eMedia Music Corp 664 NE Northlake Way Seattle WA 98105 206-329-5657
Web: www.emediamusic.com

Emotion Studios 85 Liberty Ship Way Sausalito CA 94965 415-331-6975
Web: www.emotionstudios.com

Encompass Iowa LLC
1420 First Ave NE Ste 200 Cedar Rapids IA 52402 319-862-0221
Web: www.encompassiowa.com

Engenius Inc 31077 Schoolcraft Rd Livonia MI 48150 734-522-2120
Web: www.engenius.com

Engine Interactive 1415 10th Ave 4 Seattle WA 98122 206-709-1955
Web: www.enginei.com

Enhanced Telecommunication Inc
6065 Atlantic Blvd Norcross GA 30071 770-242-3620
Web: etisoftware.com

Entre Solutions 51 W Fairmont Ave Savannah GA 31406 912-352-1600
Web: www.entresolutions.com

Eos Systems Inc 10 Kearney Rd Needham MA 02494 781-453-2600
Web: www.eos-systems.com

Epc Consultants Inc 655 Davis St San Francisco CA 94111 415-675-7580
Web: www.epcconsultants.com

Epic Systems Corp 1979 Milky Way Verona WI 53593 608-271-9000
Web: epic.com

Epitomione 4502 Chews Vineyard Ellicott City MD 21043 443-540-2230
Web: www.epitomione.com

Epsilonium Systems Inc 201 E Southern Ave 205 Tempe AZ 85282 480-219-2629
Web: www.epsilonium.com

eSecurityToGo LLC 1109 Quail St Newport Beach CA 92660 949-261-5555
Web: www.esecuritytogo.com

Est Group LLC 1907 Ascension Blvd Ste 100 Arlington TX 76006 817-296-2177
Web: www.est-grp.com

Esti Consulting Services
812 Spadina Cres E Saskatoon SK S7K3H4 306-242-2436
Web: www.esti.ca

Etrafficers 199 East 840 South Orem UT 84058 801-221-9400
Web: www.etrafficers.com

Eventus Solutions Group
98 Inverness Dr E Ste 100 Englewood CO 80112 303-376-6161
Web: www.eventusg.com

eVerge Group Inc 4965 Preston Pk Blvd Ste 700 Plano TX 75093 972-608-1803 608-1893
TF: 888-548-1973 ■ *Web:* www.evergegroup.com

Exacta Corp 16595 W Bluemound Rd Brookfield WI 53005 262-796-0000
Web: exactacorp.com

Excel Computer Corp Six Frost Dr Bangor ME 04401 207-990-3305
Web: www.excelme.com

Excel Technologies LLC 3701 Pender Dr Fairfax VA 22030 703-246-9002
Web: exceltechllc.com

Excella Consulting Inc
2300 Wilson Blvd Ste 630 Arlington VA 22201 703-840-8600
Web: www.excella.com

Exclamake! Inc 225 Prado Rd Ste E2 Sn Luis Obisp CA 93401 805-540-5114
Web: www.exclamake.net

Exobase Corp 3150 De La Cruz Blvd Santa Clara CA 95054 408-235-8808
Web: www.exobase.com

Expert System Applications Inc
5351 Naiman Pkwy Ste C Solon OH 44139 440-248-0110
Web: www.expert-system.com

EZ Micro Solutions Inc 2670 Lehigh St Whitehall PA 18052 610-264-1232
Web: www.ezmicro.com

Facilite Informatique Canada Inc
Five Pl Ville-Marie Ste 1045 Montreal QC H3B2G2 514-284-5636 284-9529
Web: www.facilite.com

Far Ridgeline Engagements Inc
285 W New York Ave Southern Pines NC 28387 910-725-0303
Web: www.frleinc.com

Federal Technology Solutions Inc
16 Hughes St Ste C106 Irvine CA 92618 949-830-8858
Web: www.federalsales.com

FedTek Inc 12700 Black Forest Ln Ste 202 Woodbridge VA 22192 703-551-4718
Web: www.fedtek.com

Feith Systems & Software Inc
425 Maryland Dr Ft Washington PA 19034 215-646-8000
Web: feith.com

FiberPlus Inc 8240 Preston Court Ste C Jessup MD 20794 301-317-3300
Web: www.fiberplusinc.com

Fifth Business Inc
Ste 500 Marathon Oil Tower 5555 San Felipe Houston TX 77056 713-622-5423
Web: www.fifthbusiness.com

Figtree Consulting Inc
101 Gibraltar Dr Ste 3D Morris Plains NJ 07950 973-539-9311
Web: www.figtree.com

Firmwater 20 Maud St Ste 405 Toronto ON M5V2M5 416-815-1496
Web: www.firmwater.com

Focus Technology Solutions Inc 93 Ledge Rd Seabrook NH 03874 603-766-0000
Web: www.focustsi.com

Force 3 Inc 2151 Priest Bridge Dr Ste 7 Crofton MD 21114 301-261-0204 721-5624*
**Fax Area Code:* 410 ■ *TF:* 800-391-0204 ■ *Web:* www.force3.com

Forgentum Inc 9312 W St Manassas VA 20110 703-906-8996
Web: www.forgentum.com

FoxNet Solutions Inc 28 Erb St E Waterloo ON N2J1L6 519-886-8895
Web: www.foxnetsolutions.com

Frontier Computer Corp
1275 Business Pk Dr Traverse City MI 49686 231-929-1386
TF: 866-226-6344 ■ *Web:* www.frontiercomputercorp.com

Frontier Consulting Inc 10101 SW Fwy Ste 202 Houston TX 77074 713-778-0799
Web: www.frontier-consulting.com

Fujitsu Consulting 1250 E Arques Ave Sunnyvale CA 94085 800-831-3183
TF: 800-831-3183 ■ *Web:* fujitsu.com

Fultech Solutions Inc 7837 Bayberry Rd Jacksonville FL 32256 904-992-6624
Web: www.fultechsolutions.com

Fusionworks Inc
120 Condado Ave Pico Ctr Ste 102 San Juan PR 00907 787-721-1039
Web: www.fwpr.com

FYI Systems Inc 35 Waterview Blvd Parsippany NJ 07054 973-331-9050 331-9055
Web: www.fyisolutions.com

G&B Solutions Inc 1861 Wiehle Ave Ste 200 Reston VA 20190 703-883-1140 883-1143
Web: www.gbsolutionsinc.com

G2 Web Services LLC
1750 112th Ave NE Ste C101 Bellevue WA 98004 425-749-4040
Web: www.g2webservices.com

Garvin-Allen Solutions Ltd
Unit 12 155 Chain Lk Dr Halifax NS B3S1B3 902-453-3554
Web: www.garvin-allen.com

Gaslight Media 120 E Lake St Petoskey MI 49770 231-487-0692
Web: gaslightmedia.com

General Dynamics Information Technology
3211 Jermantown Rd Fairfax VA 22030 703-246-0200 995-6750
TF: 800-242-0230 ■ *Web:* www.gdit.com

Genesis Corp 950 Third Ave Fl 26 New York NY 10022 212-688-5522 421-6292
TF: 800-261-1776 ■ *Web:* www.genesis10.com

Geneva Consulting Group Inc
14 Vanderventer Ave Ste 250 Port Washington NY 11050 212-244-9595
Web: www.genevaconsulting.com

Genuitec LLC 2221 Justin Rd Ste 119-340 Flower Mound TX 75028 214-224-0461
Web: www.genuitec.com

GeoLogics Corp 5285 Shawnee Rd Ste 300 Alexandria VA 22312 703-750-4000 750-4010
TF: 800-684-3455 ■ *Web:* geologics.com

Getnet Inc 333 E Indian School Rd Phoenix AZ 85012 602-264-7000
Web: www.getnet.net

Global Consultants Inc 25 Airport Rd Morristown NJ 07960 973-889-5200 292-1643
TF: 877-264-6424 ■ *Web:* www.collabera.com

Global Help Desk Services Inc
2080 Silas Deane Hwy Rocky Hill CT 06067 800-770-1075
TF: 800-770-1075 ■ *Web:* www.ghdsi.com

Global Infotek Inc 1920 Association Dr Ste 200 Reston VA 20191 703-652-1600
Web: globalinfotek.com

Global Management Systems Inc (GMSI)
2201 Wisconsin Ave NW Ste 300 Washington DC 20007 202-471-4674 625-9016
Web: www.gmsi.com

Global Outsourcing Services Inc
40-2 Fleetwood Ct Ronkonkoma NY 11779 631-471-6798
Web: gosservices.com

Global Technology Resources Inc
990 S Broadway Ste 400 Denver CO 80209 303-455-8800 803-6520*
**Fax Area Code:* 888 ■ *TF:* 877-603-1984 ■ *Web:* www.gtri.com

Globalspec Inc 350 Jordan Rd Troy NY 12180 518-880-0200 880-0250
TF: 800-261-2052 ■ *Web:* www.globalspec.com

Glotech 2551 Eltham Ave Ste A Norfolk VA 23513 757-499-3650
Web: glotech.net

Gold Key Technology Solutions Inc
220 S Second St Temple TX 76501 254-774-9035
Web: goldkeytechnology.com

Goldberg Testa & Company Inc
6201 Ft Hamilton Pkwy Brooklyn NY 11219 718-748-4851

Good Dog Design 21 Corte Madera Ave Ste 2 Mill Valley CA 94941 415-383-0110
Web: gooddogdesign.com

GP Strategies Corp
11000 Broken Land Parkway Suite 200 Columbia MD 21044 443-367-9600
TF: 888-843-4784 ■ *Web:* gpstrategies.rwd.com

Granite Information Systems
1490 Union Lk Rd White Lake MI 48386 248-360-8400
Web: graniteinfosys.com

Grantek Systems Integration Inc
4480 Harvester Rd Burlington ON L7L4X2 905-634-0844
Web: grantek.com

Graphics Systems Corp. (GXSC)
W133 N5138 Campbell Dr Menomonee Falls WI 53051 262-790-1080
Web: www.gxsc.com

Green Technology Group, Llc, The
10619 Canterberry Rd Fairfax Station VA 22039 202-285-4748
Web: www.tgtgllc.com

Greenpages Inc 33 Badgers Island W Kittery ME 03904 207-439-7310 439-7334
TF: 888-687-4876 ■ *Web:* www.greenpages.com

Groupe conseil OSI Inc
700 De la Gauchetiere St W Ste 2400 Montreal QC H3B5M2 514-847-1080
Web: www.gcosi.com

Groupe Gsc 7800 Boul Metropolitain E Anjou QC H1K1A1 514-354-4222
Web: groupe-gsc.qc.ca

Groupe Informatique TechSolCom Inc
1450 City Councillors Ste 340 Montreal QC H3A2E6 514-392-9997
Web: www.techsolcom.ca

Groupe SYGIF Inc
120 Montee Industrielle-et-Commerciale Rimouski QC G5M1B1 418-721-5353
Web: groupesygif.ca

Gsat Inc 100 W Oak St Ste 200 Denton TX 76201 469-287-6771
Web: www.gsati.com

Harmonix Technologies Inc
4915 Paseo De Norte Ne A Albuquerque NM 87113 505-205-1585
Web: www.harmonixtechnologies.com

Harris Computer Systems Inc
One Antares Dr Ste 400 Ottawa ON K2E8C4 613-226-5511
Web: www.harriscomputer.com

				Phone	Fax
Harris Technology Services Inc 1603 Golf Course Rd SE *Web:* htsusa.com	Rio Rancho	NM	87124	505-892-7364	
Hartford Computer Group Inc 10440 Little Patuxent Pkwy 3rd Fl *TF:* 800-370-5849 ■ *Web:* www.hcgi.com	Columbia	MD	21044	410-740-3020	740-8732
Hayden Technologies Inc 6075 Lk Forrest Dr *Web:* www.haydentechnologies.com	Atlanta	GA	30328	404-303-9935	
Hedrick Associates Inc 2360 Oak Industrial Dr Ne *Web:* hedrickassoc.com	Grand Rapids	MI	49505	616-454-1218	
Helios & Matheson North America Inc 350 Fifth Ave Ste 7520 *Web:* www.tact.com	New York	NY	10018	212-979-8228	
Henry A Bromelkamp & Co 106 E 24th St *Web:* www.bromelkamp.com	Minneapolis	MN	55404	612-870-9087	
Herrod Technology Inc Po Box 152495 *Web:* herrodtech.com	Arlington	TX	76015	214-202-0999	
Hexaware Technologies Inc 1095 Cranbury Rd *TF:* 866-746-2133 ■ *Web:* www.hexaware.com	Jamesburg	NJ	08831	609-409-6950	409-6910
Hixardt Technologies Inc 119 W Intendencia St *Web:* www.hixardt.com	Pensacola	FL	32502	850-439-3282	
Hlb Systems Solutions 50 Malcolm Rd *Web:* www.hlbsolutions.com	Guelph	ON	N1K1A9	519-822-3450	
Hln Consulting LLC 7072 Santa Fe Canyon Pl *Web:* www.hln.com	San Diego	CA	92129	858-538-2220	
HMS Technologies Inc One Discovery Pl *Web:* www.hmstech.com	Martinsburg	WV	25403	304-596-5583	
Holcomb Enterprises 25108 Marguerite Pkwy B-206 *Web:* www.holcombenterprises.com	Mission Viejo	CA	92692	949-458-0292	
Holman'S of Nevada Inc 4445 S Vly View Blvd *Web:* www.holmansnv.com	Las Vegas	NV	89103	702-222-1818	
Horizon Solutions LLC 2005 Brighton-Henrietta Tl Rd *Web:* hs-e.com	Rochester	NY	14623	585-424-7376	
House of Brick Technologies LLC 9300 Underwood Ave Ste 300 *Web:* www.houseofbrick.com	Omaha	NE	68114	402-445-0764	
Houston Medical Records Inc 2211 Norfolk St Ste 950 *Web:* www.houmedicalbilling.com	Houston	TX	77098	713-850-1190	
Howard Systems International 2777 Summer St **Fax Area Code:* 203 ■ *TF:* 800-326-4860 ■ *Web:* www.howardsystems.com	Stamford	CT	06905	800-326-4860	324-7722*
HUB Technical Services 44 Norfolk Ave Ste 4 *Web:* www.hubtechnical.com	South Easton	MA	02375	508-238-9887	
Huber & Associates Inc 1400 Edgewood Dr *Web:* www.teamhuber.com	Jefferson City	MO	65109	573-634-5000	
Hurd It Communications 2106 Gallows Rd A *Web:* www.hurdit.com	Vienna	VA	22182	703-442-3422	
Hurdman Communications 1344 West 75 North *Web:* www.hurdmanivr.com	Centerville	UT	84014	801-292-7673	
I.M. Systems Group Inc 3206 Tower Oaks Blvd Ste 300 *Web:* www.imsg.com	Rockville	MD	20852	240-833-1889	
i4i Inc 116 Spadina Ave Fifth Fl *Web:* www.i4i.com	Toronto	ON	M5V2K6	416-504-0141	
Ibaset 27442 Portola Pkwy *TF:* 877-422-7381 ■ *Web:* www.ibaset.com	Foothill Ranch	CA	92610	949-598-5200	598-2600
Icc 6406 Odana Rd *Web:* www.iccnow.com	Madison	WI	53719	608-277-8000	
Ice Technologies Inc 411 SE Ninth St *Web:* www.icetechnologies.com	Pella	IA	50219	641-628-8724	
Iconixx Software 3420 Executive Ctr Dr Ste 250 **Fax Area Code:* 512 ■ *TF:* 877-426-6499 ■ *Web:* iconixx.com	Austin	TX	78731	877-426-6499	651-3111*
Iconomics Inc 250 Ferrand Dr Ste 401 *Web:* www.iconomics-inc.com	Toronto	ON	M3C3G8	416-703-6547	
Ideal Integrations Inc 800 Regis Ave *Web:* www.idealintegrations.net	Pittsburgh	PA	15236	412-349-6680	
Idealogical Systems Inc 2900 John St *Web:* www.idealogical.com	Markham	ON	L3R5G3	905-474-0772	
Idesign Solutions Inc 51 Roysun Rd *Web:* www.idesignsol.com	Woodbridge	ON	L4L8P9	416-213-8445	
Imaging Systems Technology Inc 4750 W Bancroft St *Web:* www.isttouch.com	Toledo	OH	43615	419-536-5741	
iMakeNews Inc 200 Fifth Ave *TF:* 866-964-6397 ■ *Web:* www.imninc.com	Waltham	MA	02451	781-890-4700	890-4701
iModules Software Inc 5101 College Blvd Ste 300 *Web:* www.imodules.com	Leawood	KS	66211	913-888-0772	
Impact Makers Inc 1707 Summit Ave Ste 201 *Web:* www.impactmakers.com	Richmond	VA	23230	804-774-2600	
Impulse Point LLC 6810 New Tampa Hwy Ste 400 *Web:* www.impulse.com	Lakeland	FL	33815	863-802-3738	
In-Sys Solutions Inc 14048 W Petronella Dr *Web:* www.in-sys.com	Libertyville	IL	60048	847-996-0400	
InCycle Software Inc 545 Promenade du Centropolis Ste 220 *Web:* www.incyclesoftware.com	Laval	QC	H7T0A3	450-682-4777	
Indotronix International Corp (IIC) 331 Main St *Web:* www.iic.com	Poughkeepsie	NY	12601	845-473-1137	473-1197
Indtai Inc 21525 Ridgetop Cir Ste 280 *Web:* www.indtai.com	Sterling	VA	20166	703-373-3178	

				Phone	Fax
Indusa Technical Corp One TransAm Plz Dr Ste 350 *Web:* www.indusa.com	Oakbrook Terrace	IL	60181	630-424-1800	
Ineoquest Technologies Inc 170 Forbes Blvd *Web:* ineoquest.com	Mansfield	MA	02048	508-339-2497	
Inetsolution 45170 Cass Ave *Web:* www.inetsolution.com	Utica	MI	48317	586-726-9490	
Infinity Software Development Inc 1901 Commonwealth Ln *Web:* www.infinity-software.com	Tallahassee	FL	32303	850-383-1011	383-1015
Info-Link Technologies Inc 601 Pittsburgh Ave *Web:* www.nfolink.net	Mount Vernon	OH	43050	740-393-3100	
InfoGard Laboratories Inc 709 Fiero Ln Ste 25 *Web:* www.infogard.com	San Luis Obispo	CA	93401	805-783-0810	
Inforeem Inc One Quality Pl *Web:* www.inforeem.com	Edison	NJ	08820	732-494-4100	
Information Analysis Inc 11240 Waples Mill Rd Ste 201 *TF:* 800-829-7614 ■ *Web:* www.infoa.com	Fairfax	VA	22030	703-383-3000	293-7979
Information Systems & Networks Corp (ISN) 10411 Motor City Dr Ste700 *Web:* www.isncorp.com	Bethesda	MD	20817	301-469-0400	469-0767
InfoSystems Inc 1317 Hickory Vly Rd *Web:* www.infosystems.biz	Chattanooga	TN	37421	423-624-6551	
Ingenium Corp 7474 Greenway Ctr Dr Maryland Trade Ctr II Ste 800 *Web:* www.ingenium.net	Greenbelt	MD	20770	301-883-9800	
Innonet LLC Five Research Pkwy *Web:* www.innonetllc.com	Old Saybrook	CT	06475	860-395-0700	
Innosphere Systems Development Group Ltd 147 Wyndham St N Ste 306 *Web:* innosphere.ca	Guelph	ON	N1H4E9	519-766-4995	
Innovasic Inc 5635 Jefferson St NE Ste A *Web:* www.innovasic.com	Albuquerque	NM	87109	505-883-5263	
Insight Designs Web Solutions 2006 Broadway St 300 *Web:* www.insightdesigns.com	Boulder	CO	80302	303-449-8567	
Insite Computer Group Inc 8920 Woodbine Ave Ste 104 *Web:* www.insite.ca	Markham	ON	L3R9W9	416-736-8386	
Integral Solutions LLC 450 Wofford St *Web:* www.integralsg.com	Spartanburg	SC	29301	864-574-8161	
Integrated Systems Analysts Inc 2001 N Beauregard St Ste 600 *TF:* 800-929-1024 ■ *Web:* www.isa.com	Alexandria	VA	22311	703-824-0700	578-2626
Integration Partners Inc 80 Hayden Ave *Web:* www.integrationpartners.com	Lexington	MA	02421	781-357-8100	
Integri Net Solutions Inc 10020 W Fairview Ave 10 *Web:* www.insllc.net	Boise	ID	83704	208-376-0500	
Integridata Inc 7690 County 17 Blvd *Web:* www.integridata.com	Cannon Falls	MN	55009	507-263-9260	
Integrity Business Solutions Inc 9470 Annapolis Rd *Web:* www.integritybsi.com	Lanham	MD	20706	301-306-3100	
Integrity Tech Solutions 816 S Eldorado Rd Ste 4 *Web:* integrityts.com	Bloomington	IL	61704	309-662-7723	
Intelect Corp 4000 Dillon St *Web:* intelectcorp.com	Baltimore	MD	21224	410-327-0020	
Intelesys Corp 6797 Dorsey Rd *Web:* www.intelesyscorp.com	Elkridge	MD	21075	410-540-9755	
Intelli-Mine Inc 1200 Quail St Ste 270 *Web:* www.intelli-mine.com	Newport Beach	CA	92660	949-486-2900	
Intellicom Computer Consulting 1702 Second Ave *Web:* www.intellicominc.com	Kearney	NE	68847	308-237-0684	
Intelligent Decisions Inc 21445 Beaumeade Cir *TF:* 800-929-8331 ■ *Web:* www.intelligent.net	Ashburn	VA	20147	703-554-1600	
IntelliSoft Group LLC 61 Spit Brook Rd *TF:* 888-634-4464 ■ *Web:* www.intellisoftgroup.com	Nashua	NH	03060	888-634-4464	
Intelliswift Software Inc 2201 Walnut Ave *Web:* www.intelliswift.com	Fremont	CA	94538	510-490-9240	
Intellisys Technology LLC 1000 Jorie Blvd Ste 200 *Web:* www.intellisystechnology.com	Oak Brook	IL	60523	630-928-1111	
Interactive Business Systems Inc 2625 Butterfield Rd *TF:* 800-555-5427 ■ *Web:* www.ibs.com	Oak Brook	IL	60523	630-571-9100	571-2490
InterDev LLC 2650 Holcomb Bridge Rd Ste 310 *Web:* www.interdev.com	Alpharetta	GA	30022	770-643-4400	
InterNiche Technologies Inc 51 E Campbell Ave Ste 160 *Web:* www.iniche.com	Campbell	CA	95008	408-540-1160	
InterRel Consulting Inc The Rangers Ballpark in Arlington 1000 Ballpark Way Ste 304 *Web:* www.interrel.com	Arlington	TX	76011	972-735-8716	
InterVision Systems Technologies Inc 2250 Walsh Ave *Web:* www.intervision.com	Santa Clara	CA	95050	408-980-8550	
InterWorks Inc 1425 S Sangre Rd *Web:* www.interworks.com	Stillwater	OK	74074	405-624-3214	
Intrepid Control Systems Inc 5700 18 Mile Rd *Web:* www.intrepidcs.com	Sterling Heights	MI	48314	586-731-7950	
Invizeon Corp 113 W Front St Ste 101 *Web:* www.invizeon.com	Missoula	MT	59802	406-543-4059	

Company	City	State	ZIP	Phone	Fax
Inyxa LLC 904 S Roselle Rd Ste 230 *Web:* inyxa.com	Schaumburg	IL	60193	224-425-0429	
IO Integration Inc 20480 Pacifica Dr Ste 1C *Web:* www.iointegration.com	Cupertino	CA	95014	408-996-3420	
IOActive Inc 701 Fifth Ave Ste 6850 *Web:* www.ioactive.com	Seattle	WA	98104	206-784-4313	
Iomer Internet Solutions 10110 107 St Nw *Web:* www.iomer.com	Edmonton	AB	T5J1J4	780-424-3122	
IonIdea Inc 3913 Old Lee Hwy Ste 33B *Web:* www.ionidea.com	Fairfax	VA	22030	703-691-0400	
IQware Inc 600 W Hillsboro Blvd Ste 201 *Web:* www.iqwareinc.com	Deerfield Beach	FL	33441	954-698-5151	
Iris Software Inc 200 Metroplex Dr Ste 300 *Web:* www.irissoftinc.com	Edison	NJ	08817	732-393-0034	393-0035
Irosoft 3100 Boul De La Cote-vertu *Web:* www.irosoft.com	Saint-laurent	QC	H4R2J8	514-920-0020	
ISG Prime LLC 12723 Mill Heights Ct *Web:* www.isgprime.com	Herndon	VA	20171	703-624-9409	
Isis It Inc 88 Vilcom Ctr Dr Ste 180 *Web:* www.isisit.com	Chapel Hill	NC	27514	919-932-6150	
Istech Inc 4691 Raycom Rd *Web:* www.istech-inc.com	Dover	PA	17315	717-764-5565	
IT Prophets LLC 3030 Woodbridge Ln *Web:* www.itprophets.com	Canton	GA	30114	770-335-1410	
IT Weapons 7965 Goreway Dr Unit 1 *Web:* www.itweapons.com	Brampton	ON	L6T5T5	905-494-1040	
Itergy International Inc 2075 University Ste 700 *Web:* www.itergy.com	Montreal	QC	H3A2L1	514-845-5881	
ITSource Technology Inc 1401 Los Gamos Dr Ste 102 *Web:* www.itsourcetek.com	San Rafael	CA	94903	415-472-5700	
J K Datta Consultants Inc 711 W 40th St Ste 355 *Web:* www.datta-consultants.com	Baltimore	MD	21211	410-243-2882	
J2k Technology LLC 62 New Hyde Park Rd *Web:* www.j2ktechnology.com	Garden City	NY	11530	516-488-7625	
Jacer Corp 10400 Eaton Pl Ste 501 *Web:* www.jacer.com	Fairfax	VA	22030	703-352-1964	
Jackson Technical LLC 427 S Boston Ave Ste 1010 *Web:* www.jacksontechnical.com	Tulsa	OK	74103	918-585-8324	
Jacob Technologies Inc 12424 Saint Andrews Dr *Web:* www.sabre-tech.com	Oklahoma City	OK	73120	405-302-5555	
Jaekle Group Inc, The 1410 Highland Rd E *Web:* www.jaeklegroup.com	Macedonia	OH	44056	330-405-9353	
JASINT Consulting & Technologies LLC 7959 Covington Ave *Web:* www.jasint.com	Glen Burnie	MD	21061	410-969-5573	
Jibe Consulting Inc 2501 SW First Ave Ste 300 *Web:* www.jibeconsulting.com	Portland	OR	97201	503-274-0788	
JKL Technologies Inc 501-I S Reno Rd Ste 355 *Web:* www.cos-jkl.com	Newbury Park	CA	91320	805-375-5820	
JMA Information Technology Inc 10551 Barkley Ste 400 *Web:* www.jmait.com	Overland Park	KS	66212	913-722-3252	
Johnson-Laird Inc 850 NW Summit Ave *Web:* www.jli.com	Portland	OR	97210	503-274-0784	
Joint Technology Solution Inc 3919 Old Lee Hwy *Web:* jtsi.net	Fairfax	VA	22030	703-218-0372	
Jonar Systems Inc 5645 Ch Saint-francois *Web:* www.jonar.com	Saint-laurent	QC	H4S1W6	514-335-5525	
Jrm Consultants Inc Po Box 90310 *Web:* www.jrmconsultants.com	Santa Barbara	CA	93190	805-564-3119	
Kanatek Technologies Inc 535 Legget Dr Ste 400 *Web:* www.kanatek.com	Kanata	ON	K2K3B8	613-591-1482	
Karabowicz & Associates 1215 Paramount Pkwy *Web:* karanet.com	Batavia	IL	60510	630-879-1360	
Karcher Group Inc 14221a Willard Rd Ste 1500 *Web:* www.karchergroup.com	Chantilly	VA	20151	703-631-6626	
Kemark Financial Services Inc One Blue Hill Plz 11th Fl *Web:* www.kemarkfinancial.com	Pearl River	NY	10965	845-620-9300	
Kemtah Group Inc 7601 Jefferson St NE Ste 120 *TF:* 877-753-6824 ■ *Web:* www.kemtah.com	Albuquerque	NM	87109	505-346-4900	346-4990
Key Software Systems LLC 5100 Belmar Blvd *Web:* www.keysoftwaresystems.com	Farmingdale	NJ	07727	732-409-6068	
Kezber i Solution 2685 Rue Hertel *Web:* www.kezber.com	Sherbrooke	QC	J1J2J4	819-566-6900	
KForce Government Soultions 2750 Prosperity Ave Ste 300 *TF:* 800-200-7465 ■ *Web:* www.kforcegov.com	Fairfax	VA	22031	703-245-7350	245-7560
Kinsey & Kinsey Inc 26 N Park Blvd *Web:* kinsey.com	Glen Ellyn	IL	60137	630-858-4866	
KMP Designs Inc 7145 W Credit Ave Ste 101 *Web:* www.kmpdesigns.com	Mississauga	ON	L5N6J7	905-812-5635	
Knovation Inc 3630 Park 42 Dr Ste 170F *Web:* www.nettrekker.com	Cincinnati	OH	45241	513-731-4090	
Kutir Corp 37600 Central Ct Ste 280 *Web:* www.kutirtech.com	Newark	CA	94560	510-402-4526	
Lanair Group LLC 620 N Brand Blvd Sixth Fl *Web:* www.lanairgroup.com	Glendale	CA	91203	323-512-7363	
Lancaster Systems Inc 411 Theodore Fremd Ave *Web:* www.lancastersys.com	Rye	NY	10580	914-967-5700	
Lantech LLC 1783 Tribute Rd Ste C *Web:* www.lantechllc.com	Sacramento	CA	95815	916-564-5455	
Lead IT Corp 1999 Wabash Ave Ste 210 *Web:* www.leaditgroup.com	Springfield	IL	62704	217-726-7250	
Learning Worlds Inc 2647 Broadway Ste 5W *Web:* learningworlds.com	New York	NY	10025	212-725-0436	
Lectra USA Inc 889 Franklin Rd SE Bldg 100 *Web:* www.lectra.com	Marietta	GA	30067	770-422-8050	
Ledge Light Technologies Inc 88D Howard St Ste D *Web:* ledgelight.com	New London	CT	06320	860-444-0138	444-0274
Lek Technology Consultants Inc 12788 Gillard Rd *Web:* lekcomp.com	Winter Garden	FL	34787	407-877-6505	
Lextech Inc 202 Wilson Downing Rd *Web:* www.lextechky.com	Lexington	KY	40517	859-278-9230	
Lightburn 220 E Buffalo St *Web:* lightburndesigns.com	Milwaukee	WI	53202	414-347-1866	
Lighthouse Computer Services Inc 6 Blackstone Valley Pl Ste 205 *TF:* 888-542-8030 ■ *Web:* www.lighthousecs.com	Lincoln	RI	02865	401-334-0799	334-0719
Linium LLC 187 Wolf Rd Ste 210 *Web:* www.linium.com	Albany	NY	12205	518-689-3100	
Link Medical Computing Inc 200 Reservoir St *Web:* www.linkmed.com	Needham	MA	02494	781-453-0300	
LinTech Global Inc 31600 W 13 Mile Rd Ste 122 *Web:* www.lintechglobal.com	Farmington Hills	MI	48334	248-851-8877	
LiveTechnology Holdings Inc 16 Sterling Lk Rd LiveTechnology Park *Web:* www.livebuilder.com	Tuxedo Park	NY	10987	845-351-5100	
Livewire LLC 4900 W Clay St *Web:* www.getlivewire.com	Richmond	VA	23230	804-937-9001	
Locus Systems Inc 146 W Beaver Creek Rd Unit 1 *Web:* www.locussystems.com	Richmond Hill	ON	L4B1C2	905-948-0093	
Logic Solutions Inc 2929 Plymouth Rd Ste 207 *Web:* www.logicsolutions.com	Ann Arbor	MI	48105	734-930-0009	
Logicalis Inc 34505 W 12 Mile Rd Ste 210 *Web:* us.logicalis.com	Farmington Hills	MI	48331	248-957-5600	
Logicease Solutions Inc 1 Bay Plaza Ste 520 *TF:* 866-212-3273 ■ *Web:* complianceease.com	Burlingame	CA	94010	650-373-1111	
Logikal Solutions 3915 N 1800e Rd *Web:* www.logikalsolutions.com	Herscher	IL	60941	815-949-1593	949-1012
Login Consulting Services Inc 300 N Continental Blvd Ste 530 *Web:* www.loginconsult.com	El Segundo	CA	90245	310-607-9091	
Logistics Management Resources Inc 4300 Crossings Blvd *Web:* www.lmr-inc.com	Prince George	VA	23875	804-541-6193	541-2559
Look Matters 1815 Rae St Ste 202 *Web:* lookmatters.com	Regina	SK	S4T2E3	306-757-4686	
Lucid Technology 1754 N Wilmot *Web:* www.lucidtec.com	Chicago	IL	60647	312-238-8976	
Lumtron Technologies Inc 820 E Terra Cotta Ave Ste 242 *Web:* www.lumtron.com	Crystal Lake	IL	60014	815-788-0088	
Lynx Computer Technologies Inc Seven Bristol Ct *Web:* lynxnet.com	Wyomissing	PA	19610	610-678-8131	
M Box Design 9234 Deering Ave *Web:* www.mboxdesign.com	Chatsworth	CA	91311	818-700-7770	
M2ns Inc 6037 Frantz Rd Ste 103 *Web:* www.m2ns.com	Dublin	OH	43017	614-798-5177	
Maden Technologies 4601 N Fairfax Dr Ste 1030 *Web:* www.madentech.com	Arlington	VA	22203	703-940-3609	
Magenium Solutions LLC 535 Pennsylvania Ave Ste 103 *Web:* www.magenium.com	Glen Ellyn	IL	60137	630-786-5900	
Magestic Systems Inc 205 Fairview Ave *Web:* www.magestic.com	Westwood	NJ	07675	201-263-0090	
Mainline Information Systems Inc 1700 Summit Lk Dr *TF:* 866-490-6246 ■ *Web:* www.mainline.com	Tallahassee	FL	32317	850-219-5000	
MainSpring Inc 20010 Fisher Ave Ste E PO Box 505 *Web:* www.gomainspring.com	Poolesville	MD	20837	301-948-8077	
Mainstay Technologies 201 Daniel Webster Hwy *Web:* www.mstech.com	Belmont	NH	03220	603-524-4774	
Managed Business Solutions 12325 Oracle Blvd Ste 200 *Web:* www.thinkmbs.com	Colorado Springs	CO	80921	719-314-3400	314-3499
MANDEX Inc 12500 Fair Lakes Cir Ste 125 *Web:* www.mandex.com	Fairfax	VA	22033	703-227-0900	227-0910
Mandli Communications Inc 4801 Tradewinds Pkwy *Web:* mandli.com	Madison	WI	53718	608-835-3500	
Mantra Technologies LLC 1180 Arbor Creek Dr *Web:* www.mantrasys.com	Roswell	GA	30076	770-772-4678	
Marucco, Stoddard, Ferenbach & Walsh Inc 3445 Liberty Dr *Web:* www.msfw.com	Springfield	IL	62704	217-698-3535	
Matricis Informatique Inc 1425 Rene-Levesque Blvd W Ste 240 *Web:* matricis.com	Montreal	QC	H3G1T7	514-394-0011	
Matrix Integration LLC 417 Main St *Web:* www.matrixintegration.com	Jasper	IN	47546	812-634-1550	
Matrix Technologies Inc 1760 Indian Wood Cir *Web:* matrixti.com	Maumee	OH	43537	419-897-7200	

Company	City	State	ZIP	Phone	Fax
Maven Company Inc 1115 Elkton Dr Ste 300 *Web:* www.mavenco.com	Colorado Springs	CO	80907	719-884-0102	
Maverick Mesa Computer Specialties Inc 10814 W Orangewood Ave *Web:* mavmesa.com	Glendale	AZ	85307	623-872-1296	
Maximizer Software Inc 1090 W Pender St 10th Fl *Web:* www.maximizer.com	Vancouver	BC	V6E2N7	604-601-8000	
MCAD Technologies Inc 7450 W Alaska Dr *Web:* www.mcad.com	Lakewood	CO	80226	303-969-8844	
McCracken Financial Solutions Corp Eight Suburban Park Dr *Web:* www.mccrackenfs.com	Billerica	MA	01821	978-439-9000	
Mdl Enterprise Inc 9888 Southwest Fwy *Web:* www.mdlent.com	Houston	TX	77074	713-771-6350	
MediaPro Inc 20021 120th Ave NE Ste 102 *Web:* www.mediapro.com	Bothell	WA	98011	425-483-4700	
Medullan Inc 625 Mount Auburn St Ste 201 *Web:* www.medullan.com	Cambridge	MA	02138	617-547-0273	
Mercom Inc 313 Commerce Dr *TF:* 877-223-8330 ■ *Web:* www.mercomcorp.com	Pawleys Island	SC	29585	843-979-9957	979-9956
Merittech LLC 6700 Kirkville Rd Bldg B Ste 105 *Web:* www.barry-wehmillerinternational.com	East Syracuse	NY	13057	315-234-4545	
Metters Industries Inc 8200 Greensboro Dr Ste 500 *Web:* www.metters.com	McLean	VA	22102	703-821-3300	821-3996
Micro Force Inc 505 Jericho Tpke *Web:* micro-force.com	Huntington Station	NY	11746	631-421-1030	
Micro Source Inc 655 Fairfield Ct *Web:* www.microsrc.com	Ann Arbor	MI	48108	734-669-8833	
Microserv Computer Techs Inc 1808 E 17th St *Web:* www.ida.net	Idaho Falls	ID	83404	208-528-6161	
Microwest Software Systems Inc 10981 San Diego Mson 21 *Web:* www.microwestsoftware.com	San Diego	CA	92108	619-280-0440	
Microworks 6955 South Union Park Ctr Ste 220 *Web:* www.microworks.ca	Midvale	UT	84047	801-487-9400	
Miles Technologies Inc 300 W Route 38 *Web:* www.milestechnologies.com	Moorestown	NJ	08057	856-439-0999	
Mills & Murphy Software Systems Inc 618 94th Ave N *Web:* www.millsmur.com	Saint Petersburg	FL	33702	727-577-1236	
MILVETS Systems Technology Inc 11825 High Tech Ave Ste 150 *Web:* www.milvets.com	Orlando	FL	32817	407-207-2242	
Mindwrap Inc 664h Zachary Taylor Hwy *Web:* www.mindwrap.com	Flint Hill	VA	22627	540-675-3015	
Miragee Corp 2512 Merriwood Dr *Web:* www.miragee.com	Louisville	KY	40299	502-266-8768	
Mobile Technical Services 70 Old Bloomfield Ave *Web:* mtsnj.com	Pine Brook	NJ	07058	973-808-2882	
Moment Design 13 Crosby St Sixth Fl *Web:* www.momentnyc.com	New York	NY	10013	212-625-9744	
Moore Computing LLP 317 N 11th St Ste 502 *Web:* www.moorecomputing.com	Saint Louis	MO	63101	314-621-5585	
MorganFranklin Corp 1753 Pinnacle Dr Ste 1200 *Web:* www.morganfranklin.com	Mclean	VA	22102	703-564-7525	
MSS Technologies Inc 1555 E Orangewood Ave *Web:* www.msstech.com	Phoenix	AZ	85020	602-387-2100	
Multidev Technologies Inc 999 de Maisonneuve W Ste 1100 *Web:* chaindrive.com	Montreal	QC	H3A3L4	514-337-6465	
Multiple Media Inc 465 McGill St Office 1000 *Web:* www.multiple-media.com	Montreal	QC	H2Y2H1	514-276-7660	
Mystikal Solutions LLC 431 Wolf Rd Ste 102 *Web:* www.mystikalsolutions.com	San Antonio	TX	78216	210-979-9300	
Mytech Partners Inc 2420 Long Lk Rd *Web:* www.mytech.com	Roseville	MN	55113	612-659-9800	
N Cell Systems Inc 1907 E Wayzata *Web:* ncell.com	Wayzata	MN	55391	952-746-5125	
N'Ware Technologies Inc 11500 2e Ave *Web:* www.nwaretech.com	Saint-georges	QC	G5Y1W6	418-227-4292	
Nbt Solutions LLC 188 State St Ste 200 *Web:* www.nbtsolutions.com	Portland	ME	04101	617-202-3088	
NCI Inc 11730 Plz America Dr Ste 700 *NASDAQ: NCIT* ■ *Web:* www.nciinc.com	Reston	VA	20190	703-707-6900	707-6901
Nebula Consulting Inc 207 Warwick Way *Web:* www.gonebula.com	North Wales	PA	19454	215-353-3141	
NES Associates LLC 6400 Beulah St Ste 300 *Web:* www.nesassociates.com	Alexandria	VA	22310	703-224-2600	
Net Aspects 2850 Cordelia Rd *Web:* netaspects.com	Fairfield	CA	94534	707-399-8060	
Netblaze Systems Inc 1299 Newell Hill Pl Ste 202 *Web:* www.netblaze.biz	Walnut Creek	CA	94596	925-932-1765	
Netcom Technologies Inc 313 N Berry St **Fax Area Code:* 741 ■ *Web:* netcomtechnologies.net	Brea	CA	92821	714-256-9229	990-3841*
Netessentials Inc 705 Eighth St Ste 1000 *Web:* www.netessentials.net	Wichita Falls	TX	76301	940-767-6387	
Netgain Information Systems Co 220 Reynolds Ave *Web:* www.netgainis.com	Bellefontaine	OH	43311	937-593-7177	
Netlogix Inc 181 Notre Dame St *Web:* netlgx.com	Westfield	MA	01085	413-568-2777	
NetRate Systems Inc 3493 Woods Edge Dr *Web:* www.mcswin.com	Okemos	MI	48864	517-347-4900	
NetStandard Inc 2000 Merriam Ln *Web:* www.netstandard.com	Kansas City	KS	66106	913-262-3888	
Nettech LLC 1851 Hudson Ln *Web:* www.nettech.net	Monroe	LA	71201	318-387-0001	
NetVoyage Corp 2500 West Executive Pkwy Ste 350 *Web:* www.netdocuments.com	Lehi	UT	84043	801-226-6882	
Netway Solutions Inc 240 Palomino Dr *Web:* www.netwaysolutions.com	Salisbury	NC	28146	704-637-6155	
Netwize Inc 702 Confluence Ave *Web:* www.netwize.net	Salt Lake City	UT	84123	801-747-3200	
Network 2000 LLC 2100 N Nimitz Hwy *Web:* www.network2000-hi.com	Honolulu	HI	96819	808-848-0000	
Network America Inc 118 107th Ave *TF:* 877-624-8311 ■ *Web:* ldms.com	Treasure Island	FL	33706	877-624-8311	
Network Center Communications Inc 3247 39th St S *Web:* www.netcentersupply.com	Fargo	ND	58104	701-235-8100	
Network Data Systems Inc 50 E Commerce Dr Ste 120 *Web:* www.network-data.com	Schaumburg	IL	60173	847-385-6700	
Network Directions 2012 E Bradford Ave *Web:* www.net-directions.com	Milwaukee	WI	53211	414-963-8759	
Network Performance Inc 85 Green Mtn Dr *Web:* www.npi.net	South Burlington	VT	05403	802-859-0808	
Network Synergy Corp 126 Monroe Tpke *Web:* www.netsynergy.com	Trumbull	CT	06611	203-261-2201	
Network Vigilance LLC 10731 Treena St Ste 200 *Web:* www.networkvigilance.com	San Diego	CA	92131	858-695-8676	
Networks of Florida 111 N Baylen St *Web:* www.nof.com	Pensacola	FL	32502	850-434-8600	
NetXperts Inc 2680 Bishop Dr Ste 125 *Web:* www.netxperts.com	San Ramon	CA	94583	925-806-0800	
NetXposure Inc 735 SW First Ave Third Fl *Web:* netx.net	Portland	OR	97204	503-499-4342	
Neuro Logic Systems Inc 451 Constitution Ave *Web:* www.neuro-logic.com	Camarillo	CA	93012	805-389-5435	
New Age Technologies Inc 819 W Main St Ste 200 *Web:* www.newat.com	Louisville	KY	40202	502-412-6681	
New Target Inc 815 N Royal St Ste 100 *Web:* www.newtarget.com	Alexandria	VA	22314	703-548-3433	
New Technologies Inc 4380 Baldwin Rd *Web:* www.newtechnologiesinc.com	Holly	MI	48442	810-694-5426	694-1183
New Wave Industries Inc 135 Day St *Web:* www.newwaveindustries.com	Newington	CT	06111	860-953-9283	
NewAgeSys Inc 231 Clarksville Rd Ste 200 *TF:* 888-863-9243 ■ *Web:* www.newagesys.com	Princeton Junction	NJ	08550	609-919-9800	919-9830
Next Eon Com 40 Meriam St *Web:* www.nexteon.com	Wakefield	MA	01880	781-231-3200	
NextGate Solutions Inc 3579 E Foothill Blvd Ste 587 *Web:* www.nextgatesolutions.com	Pasadena	CA	91107	626-376-4100	
Nintex USA LLC 10800 NE Eighth St Ste 210 *Web:* www.nintex.com	Bellevue	WA	98004	425-324-2400	
Nobel Systems Inc 436 E Vanderbilt Way *Web:* www.nobel-systems.com	San Bernardino	CA	92408	909-890-5611	
Northern Data Systems Inc 362 US Route One *Web:* www.ndsys.com	Falmouth	ME	04105	207-781-3236	
Northlan Solutions Inc 2370 County Rd J *Web:* www.2northlan.com	Saint Paul	MN	55110	651-653-4866	
NOTSOLDSEPARATELY.COM Two Friends Ave *Web:* www.notsoldseparately.com	Medford	NJ	08055	856-727-8200	
Novacoast Inc 1505 Chapala St *TF:* 800-949-9933 ■ *Web:* www.novacoast.com	Santa Barbara	CA	93101	800-949-9933	
Novanis 3161 W White Oaks Dr Ste 100 *Web:* www.novanis.com	Springfield	IL	62704	217-698-0999	
NOVIPRO Inc 2055 Peel St Ste 701 *Web:* www.novipro.com	Montreal	QC	H3A1V4	514-744-5353	
Novix Network Specialists Inc 2000 W Main St Ste Jr *Web:* www.novixinc.com	Saint Charles	IL	60174	630-443-0036	
Novo Solutions Inc 516 S Independence Blvd *Web:* www.novosolutions.com	Virginia Beach	VA	23452	757-687-6590	
Nowcom Corp 4751 Wilshire Blvd Ste 115 *Web:* www.nowcom.com	Los Angeles	CA	90010	323-692-4040	
nQueue Inc 7890 S Hardy Dr Ste 105 *TF:* 800-299-5933 ■ *Web:* www.nqueue.com	Tempe	AZ	85284	800-299-5933	
Nth Generation Computing Inc 17055 Camino San Bernardo *Web:* www.nth.com	San Diego	CA	92127	858-451-2383	
NTT DATA, Inc 100 City Sq **Fax Area Code:* 972 ■ *TF:* 800-745-3263 ■ *Web:* americas.nttdata.com	Boston	MA	02129	800-745-3263	624-7940*
Numeric Computer Systems Inc 275 Oser Ave *Web:* www.ncssuite.com	Hauppauge	NY	11788	631-486-9000	
Nutech Information Systems 1010 Summer St Ste 203 *Web:* www.nutechsoft.com	Stamford	CT	06905	203-961-8911	
Nutechs LLC 6785 Telegraph Rd Ste 350 *Web:* www.nutechs.com	Bloomfield Hills	MI	48301	248-593-5700	
nuTravel Technology Solutions LLC 181 Westchester Ave Ste 302 *Web:* www.nutravel.com	Port Chester	NY	10573	914-848-4566	
NuWare Technology Corp Inc 100 Wood Ave S Ste 122 *Web:* www.nuware.com	Iselin	NJ	08830	732-494-0550	494-4586

Company	City	State	ZIP	Phone	Fax
Nvision Networking Inc 7450 N Thornydale Rd *Web:* nvisionnet.com	Tucson	AZ	85741	520-219-6040	
O'Neil Software Inc 11 Cushing Ste 100 *Web:* oneilsoft.com	Irvine	CA	92618	949-458-1234	
Oak Hill Technology Inc 12505-A Trl Dr St *Web:* www.oakhilltech.com	Austin	TX	78737	512-288-0008	
Oakland Consulting Group Inc 9501 Sheridan St Ste 200 *Web:* www.ocg-inc.com	Lanham	MD	20706	301-577-4111	
Oakwood Systems Group Inc 622 Emerson Rd Ste 350 *Web:* www.oakwoodsys.com	Saint Louis	MO	63141	314-824-3000	
Oar Net 1224 Kinnear Rd *Web:* www.oar.net	Columbus	OH	43212	614-292-1956	
Oasis Technology Inc 601 E Daily Dr Ste 226 *Web:* www.oasistechnology.com	Camarillo	CA	93010	805-445-4833	
Oculus VisionTech Inc 507 837 W Hastings St *Web:* www.usvo.com	Vancouver	BC	V6C3N6	604-685-1017	
Odyssey Systems Consulting Group Ltd 201 Edgewater Dr Ste 270 *Web:* www.odysseyconsult.com	Wakefield	MA	01880	781-245-0111	245-5858
Office Automation Technologies 11919 W 48th Ave *Web:* www.oati1.com	Wheat Ridge	CO	80033	303-202-5151	
Official Payments Corp 3550 Engineering Dr *TF:* 877-754-4413 ■ *Web:* www.officialpayments.com	Norcross	GA	30092	770-325-3100	325-3099
Ohio Computer Aided Engineering Inc 1612 Georgetown Rd *Web:* www.simutechgroup.com	Hudson	OH	44236	330-552-2301	
Omnilogic Systems Inc 1420 Broad St *Web:* www.omnilogic.net	Regina	SK	S4R1Y9	306-586-6118	
Omnitech Labs Inc 215 Boul Du Seminaire S *Web:* www.omnitechlabs.net	Saint-jean-sur-richelieu	QC	J3B8W1	450-359-0891	
Oncall Interactive LLC 216 Southfferson Ste 602 *Web:* www.oncallinteractive.com	Chicago	IL	60661	312-226-1259	
Onenet USA Inc 4445 W 77th St Ste 106 *Web:* www.onenetusa.com	Edina	MN	55435	952-960-1000	
ONESPRING LLC 980 Birmingham Rd Ste 501-165 *TF:* 888-472-1840 ■ *Web:* www.onespring.net	Alpharetta	GA	30004	888-472-1840	
OnPath Business Solutions Inc St Joseph's Bldg 1165 Kenaston St *Web:* www.onpath.com	Ottawa	ON	K1B3N9	613-564-6565	
Open Computing Platforms Inc 207 W Los Angeles Ave *Web:* www.wirelessguys.com	Moorpark	CA	93021	805-578-8590	
Oproma Inc 116 Av Gatineau *Web:* www.oproma.com	Gatineau	QC	J8T4J6	819-561-1376	
Opsol Integrators Inc 1566 La Pradera Dr *Web:* www.opsol.com	Campbell	CA	95008	408-364-9915	
Optima Telecom Inc 90 Allstate Pky *Web:* www.optimatele.com	Markham	ON	L3R6H3	905-477-0987	
Optimal Data Group Inc 2967 Sable Ridge Dr *Web:* www.optimal.ca	Gloucester	ON	K1T3S3	613-738-1868	
Oracular Inc 317 City Ctr *Web:* www.oracular.com	Oshkosh	WI	54901	920-303-0470	
Osbee Industries Inc 99 Calvert St 100 *Web:* osbee.com	Harrison	NY	10528	914-777-6611	
OSHEAN Inc 6946 Post Rd Ste 402 *Web:* www.oshean.org	North Kingstown	RI	02852	401-398-7500	
OUTSOURCEIT Inc 6810 Crain Hwy *Web:* www.outsourceitcorp.com	La Plata	MD	20646	301-539-0200	
P C Assistance Inc 3200 S Shackleford Rd Ste 9 *Web:* www.pcassistance.com	Little Rock	AR	72205	501-907-4722	
Pachyderm Consulting LLC 66 W 38th St Apt 11k *Web:* pachyderm.net	New York	NY	10018	212-629-7600	
Pacific Software Publishing Inc 1404 140th Pl NE *Web:* www.pspinc.com	Bellevue	WA	98007	425-957-0808	
Pacificad Inc 159 S Lincoln St *Web:* www.pacificad.com	Spokane	WA	99201	509-326-7789	
Pandell Technology Corp 4838 Richard Rd SW Ste 210 *Web:* www.pandell.com	Calgary	AB	T3E6L1	403-271-0701	
PAR4 Technology 110 Haverhill Rd Ste 502 *Web:* www.par4tech.com	Amesbury	MA	01913	978-388-7711	
Paradata Financial Systems 640 Cepi Dr Ste B *Web:* paradatafinancial.com	Chesterfield	MO	63005	636-530-4545	
Paragon Data Systems Inc 2218 Superior Ave *Web:* www.paragondatasystems.com	Cleveland	OH	44114	216-621-7571	
Parallel Edge Inc 126 E Beechtree Ln *Web:* www.paralleledge.com	Wayne	PA	19087	610-293-0101	
Passageways LLC 1551 Win Hentschel Blvd *Web:* www.passageways.com	West Lafayette	IN	47906	765-497-8829	
Pavliks Com 364 St Vincent St *Web:* www.pavliks.com	Barrie	ON	L4M4A5	705-726-2966	
PC Care Inc 221 Parking Way *Web:* www.pccare-inc.com	Lake Jackson	TX	77566	979-297-1117	
PC Works Plus Inc 109 Stadium Dr *Web:* www.pcworksplus.com	Bellwood	PA	16617	814-742-9750	
PDX Inc & Affiliates 101 Jim Wright Fwy S *Web:* pdxinc.com	Fort Worth	TX	76108	817-246-6760	
PEAK Resources Inc 2750 W Fifth Ave *Web:* www.peakresources.com	Denver	CO	80204	303-934-1200	
Pencilneck Software 896 Cambie St *Web:* www.pencilnecksoftware.com	Vancouver	BC	V6B2P6	604-676-3690	
Penguin Computing Inc 45800 Northport Loop W *Web:* www.penguincomputing.com	Fremont	CA	94538	415-954-2800	
Phacil Inc 601 California St *Web:* phacil.com	San Francisco	CA	94108	703-526-1800	
Phoinix Group Inc, The 16308 Calidonia Ste 100 - 105 *Web:* www.phoinixgroup.com	Tampa	FL	33624	813-962-4000	
Pi Tech 522 Shafor Blvd *Web:* proficientinfotech.com	Dayton	OH	45419	937-299-7722	
Pico Envirotec Inc 222 Snidercroft Rd *Web:* www.picoenvirotec.com	Concord	ON	L4K2K1	905-760-9512	
Pinnacle Technical Resources Inc 5501 Lyndon B Johnson Fwy *Web:* pinnacle1.com	Dallas	TX	75240	214-740-2424	
PIREL Inc 1250 Nobel Ste 190 *Web:* www.pirel.com	Boucherville	QC	J4B5H1	450-449-5199	
Pj Cook Web Designs Inc 2034 Rainbow Farms Dr *Web:* pjcook.com	Safety Harbor	FL	34695	727-712-9493	
Planet Personal Agency Inc 55 Yonge St *Web:* www.planet4it.com	Toronto	ON	M5E1J4	416-363-9888	
Planned Systems International Inc 10632 Lttle Patuxent Pkwy *TF:* 800-275-7749 ■ *Web:* www.plan-sys.com	Columbia	MD	21044	410-964-8000	964-8001
Plaudit Design 2470 University Ave W *Web:* www.plauditdesign.com	Saint Paul	MN	55114	651-646-0696	
Point Alliance Inc 20 Adelaide St E Ste 500 *Web:* www.pointalliance.com	Toronto	ON	M5C2T6	416-943-0001	
Point of Sale System Services Inc Two Shaker Rd Ste F100 *Web:* www.pss-pos.com	Shirley	MA	01464	978-425-3003	
Pointe Technology Group Inc 7272 Pk Cir Dr Ste 200 *TF:* 800-730-6171 ■ *Web:* www.pointetech.com	Hanover	MD	21076	410-712-9425	712-9435
Pomeroy IT Solutions Inc 1020 Petersburg Rd *TF:* 800-846-8727 ■ *Web:* www.pomeroy.com	Hebron	KY	41048	859-586-0600	586-4414
Portland Webworks Inc Five Milk St Second Fl *Web:* www.portlandwebworks.com	Portland	ME	04101	207-773-6600	
Portola Systems Inc 7064 Corline Ct Ste B5 *Web:* www.portolasystems.net	Sebastopol	CA	95472	707-824-8800	
PowerPhone Inc 1321 Boston Post Rd *Web:* www.powerphone.com	Madison	CT	06443	203-245-8911	
PowerVision Inc 260 Harbor Blvd *Web:* powervisionlens.com	Belmont	CA	94002	650-620-9948	
Practice Velocity LLC 10100 Forest Hills Rd *Web:* www.practicevelocity.com	Machesney Park	IL	61115	815-544-7480	
Pragmatix Inc 565 Taxter Rd *Web:* www.pragmatix.com	Elmsford	NY	10523	914-345-9444	
Predictix Inc 1349 W Peachtree St NW Two Midtown Plz Ste 1880 *Web:* www.predictix.com	Atlanta	GA	30309	404-478-2090	
Preferred Systems Solutions Inc 1945 Old Gallows Rd Ste 450 *Web:* www.pssfed.com	Vienna	VA	22182	703-663-2777	663-2780
Premcom Corp 85 Northpointe Pkwy Ste 1 *Web:* www.premcom.com	Amherst	NY	14228	716-691-0791	
Premier Network Solutions Inc 5070 Oaklawn Dr *Web:* prenet.com	Cincinnati	OH	45227	513-631-6381	
Presidio Networked Solutions Inc 7601 Ora Glen Dr Ste 100 *TF:* 800-452-6926 ■ *Web:* www.presidio.com	Greenbelt	MD	20770	301-313-2000	313-2400
Presteligence Inc 8328 Cleveland Ave NW *Web:* www.presteligence.com	Canton	OH	44720	330-305-6960	
Pro It Co 258 W 31st St *Web:* www.proitco.com	Chicago	IL	60616	312-225-6847	
Proactive Networking 9240 NW 63rd St *Web:* www.proactivekc.com	Parkville	MO	64152	816-587-7878	
Procase Consulting 180 Caster Ave Unit 55 *Web:* www.procaseconsulting.com	Woodbridge	ON	L4L5Y7	905-856-7479	
Process Data Control Corp 1803-A W Park Row Dr *Web:* www.pdccorp.com	Arlington	TX	76013	817-459-4488	
Professional Software Engineering Inc 780 Lynnhaven Pkwy Ste 350 *TF:* 800-924-1091 ■ *Web:* www.prosoft-eng.com	Virginia Beach	VA	23452	757-431-2400	463-1071
Progeny Systems Corp 9500 Innovation Dr *Web:* progeny.net	Manassas	VA	20110	703-368-6107	
Progi-media Inc 1040 Boul Michele-bohec *Web:* www.progi-media.com	Blainville	QC	J7C5E2	514-272-0599	
Promedia Technology Services 535 Route 46 *Web:* www.promedianj.com	Little Falls	NJ	07424	973-253-7600	
Pronet Solutions Inc 4313 E Cotton Ctr Blvd Ste 120 *Web:* www.pronetsol.com	Phoenix	AZ	85040	602-650-1100	
Protocol Networks Inc 15 Shore Dr *TF:* 877-676-0146 ■ *Web:* www.protocolnetworks.com	Johnston	RI	02919	877-676-0146	
ProTrak International Inc 237 W 35th St Ste 507 *Web:* www.protrak.com	New York	NY	10001	212-265-9833	
Provade Inc 770 N Jefferson St Ste 230 *Web:* www.provade.com	Milwaukee	WI	53202	414-395-8050	
Psychological Services Inc 2950 N Hollywood Way Ste 200 *Web:* corporate.psionline.com	Burbank	CA	91505	818-847-6180	
Psychsoft PO Box 232 *Web:* www.psych-soft.com	Quincy	MA	02171	617-471-8733	

Company	City	State	ZIP	Phone	Fax
PTS Data Center Solutions Inc 16 Thornton Rd *Web:* www.ptsdcs.com	Oakland	NJ	07436	201-337-3833	
Publish Or Perish Inc 825 E Roosevelt Rd *Web:* www.publishorperish.com	Lombard	IL	60148	630-627-7227	
Punchcut LLC 170 Maiden Ln *Web:* punchcut.com	San Francisco	CA	94108	415-445-8855	
Pup Group Inc Dba Enlighten, The 3027 Miller Rd	Ann Arbor	MI	48103	734-668-6678	
Q.A. Technologies Inc 222 S 15th St Ste 1404 *Web:* www.qat.com	Omaha	NE	68102	402-391-9200	
Qcera Inc 1525 S Sepulveda Blvd *Web:* www.qcera.com	Los Angeles	CA	90025	310-473-7988	
Quadrant 4 System Corp Ste 405 2850 GOLF Rd *Web:* www.qfor.com	Rolling Meadows	IL	60008	732-798-3000	
Quadrus Development Inc 640 - Eighth Ave SW Ste 400 *Web:* www.quadrus.com	Calgary	AB	T2P1G7	403-257-0850	
QVS Software Inc 5950 Six Forks Rd *Web:* qvssoftware.com	Raleigh	NC	27609	919-676-1991	
R & d Industries Inc 812 10th St *Web:* www.audioengineering.com	Milford	IA	51351	712-338-2999	
Radiant Networks Services Inc 13000 Middletown Industrial Blvd Ste D *Web:* www.radiant-networks.com	Louisville	KY	40223	502-379-4800	
Ranac Computer Corp 4181 E 96th St Ste 280 *Web:* ranac.com	Indianapolis	IN	46240	317-844-0141	
Rapier Solutions Inc 3095 Senna Dr *Web:* www.rapiersolutions.com	Matthews	NC	28105	704-321-2271	
RCC Consultants Inc 100 Woodbridge Ctr Dr *Web:* www.rcc.com	Woodbridge	NJ	07095	732-404-2400	
RCO Systems Inc 251 James Jackson Ave *Web:* www.rconet.com	Cary	NC	27513	919-319-3612	
Redman Technologies Inc 10140 88 St Nw *Web:* www.redmantech.com	Edmonton	AB	T5H1P1	780-425-6270	
Relate Corp 900 Avenida Acaso Ste K *Web:* relate.com	Camarillo	CA	93012	805-482-7381	
Rembrandt Group LLC, The Two N Rd Apt 3 *Web:* www.rembrandtgroup.com	Warren	NJ	07059	732-356-1600	
Remote Operations Co 200 Pakerland Dr *Web:* www.roccompany.com	Green Bay	WI	54303	920-437-4466	
Rendersoft Inc 5801 Christie Ave Ste 275 *Web:* www.rendersoftinc.com	Emeryville	CA	94608	510-652-3936	
Research Data Inc 3900 Carolina Ave *Web:* www.researchdata.com	Richmond	VA	23222	804-643-3468	
Revelex Corp 6405 Congress Ave Ste 120 *Web:* www.revelex.com	Boca Raton	FL	33487	561-988-5588	
Rex Black Consulting Services Inc 31520 Beck Rd *Web:* www.rbcs-us.com	Bulverde	TX	78163	830-438-4830	
Rgen Solutions 4156 148th Ave Ne Bldg I *Web:* www.rgensolutions.com	Redmond	WA	98052	425-867-1350	
RhinoCorps Limited Co 1128 Pennsylvania St NE Ste 100 *Web:* www.rhinocorps.com	Albuquerque	NM	87110	505-323-9836	
River Run Computers Inc 2320 W Camden Rd *Web:* www.river-run.com	Milwaukee	WI	53209	414-228-7474	
Rivercrest Technologies Inc 1215 Oak Forest Dr *Web:* www.rcrest.com	Onalaska	WI	54650	608-779-2233	
RiverPoint Group LLC 2200 E Devon Ave Ste 385 *TF:* 800-297-5601 ■ *Web:* www.riverpoint.com	Des Plaines	IL	60018	847-233-9600	233-9602
Rj Computer Networks Inc 9150 Painter Ave Ste 102 *Web:* www.rjcomputers.com	Whittier	CA	90602	562-464-3644	
RJM Systems Inc 88 VilCom Cir McClamroch Hall Ste 187 *Web:* www.sonis.com	Chapel Hill	NC	27514	203-262-2310	
RJT Compuquest Inc 23440 Hawthorne Blvd Ste 210 *Web:* rjtcompuquest.com	Torrance	CA	90505	310-378-6666	
Rolta Tusc Inc 333 E Butterfield Rd Ste 900 *TF:* 800-755-8872 ■ *Web:* www.rolta.com	Lombard	IL	60148	630-960-2909	
Root Group Inc, The 1790 30th St Ste 140 *Web:* www.rootgroup.com	Boulder	CO	80301	303-447-8093	
Royal Technocrats Inc 9896 Bissonnet St Ste 240 *Web:* royaltechnocrats.com	Houston	TX	77036	713-776-8300	
RuggedCom Inc 300 Applewood Crescent *Web:* www.ruggedcom.com	Concord	ON	L4K5C7	905-856-5288	
Sagitec Solutions LLC 422 County Rd D E *Web:* sagitec.com	Little Canada	MN	55117	612-284-7130	
SAI Systems International Inc 12 Progress Dr *Web:* www.saisystems.com	Shelton	CT	06484	203-929-0790	
Sakki Computers Inc 22 Hempstead Tpke Ste B *Web:* www.sakki.com	Farmingdale	NY	11735	516-293-1609	
Saucon Technologies Inc 2455 Baglyos Cir *Web:* www.saucontds.com	Bethlehem	PA	18020	484-241-2500	
Sayers Group LLC 825 Corporate Woods Pkwy *TF:* 800-323-5357 ■ *Web:* www.sayers.com	Vernon Hills	IL	60061	800-323-5357	
SCC Soft Computer Inc 5400 Tech Data Dr *TF:* 800-763-8352 ■ *Web:* www.softcomputer.com	Clearwater	FL	33760	727-789-0100	789-0124
Schuur Solutions 3230 E Imperial Hwy *Web:* schuur.com	Brea	CA	92821	714-986-9990	
Scorpion Design Inc 28480 Ave Stanford Ste 140 *Web:* www.scorpiondesign.com	Valencia	CA	91355	661-702-0100	
Securance LLC 6922 W Linebaugh Ave Ste 101 *TF:* 877-578-0215 ■ *Web:* www.securanceconsulting.com	Tampa	FL	33625	877-578-0215	
SecureInfo Corp 211 N Loop 1604 E Ste 200 *TF:* 888-677-9351 ■ *Web:* www.secureinfo.com	San Antonio	TX	78232	210-403-5600	403-5702
Seitel Leeds & Associates Inc 1200 Post Aly Ste 2 *Web:* www.sla.com	Seattle	WA	98101	206-832-2875	
Select Computing Inc 3001 Broadway St NE Ste 655 *Web:* www.selectcomputing.com	Minneapolis	MN	55413	612-331-5535	
Sendio Inc 4911 Birch St Ste 150 *Web:* www.sendio.com	Newport Beach	CA	92660	949-274-4375	
Sense Corp 2731 Sutton Blvd Ste 200 *Web:* www.sensecorp.com	Saint Louis	MO	63143	314-266-3700	
Servigistics Sns Inc 2300 Windy Ridge Pkwy 450 N Tower	Atlanta	GA	30339	770-565-2340	565-8767
Sgs Technologie LLC 6817 Southpoint Pkwy Ste 2104 *Web:* www.sgstechnologies.net	Jacksonville	FL	32216	904-332-4534	
Shadow Financial Systems Inc 1551 S Washington Ave *Web:* www.shadowfinancial.com	Piscataway	NJ	08854	732-225-6800	
Sharphat Inc 333 Sylvan Ave Ste 320 *Web:* sharphat.com	Englewood Cliffs	NJ	07632	201-503-0020	
Siemens IT Solutions & Services Inc 101 Merritt 7 *Web:* atos.net	Norwalk	CT	06851	817-264-8200	264-8579
Simacor LLC 10700 Hwy 55 Ste 170 *Web:* www.simacor.com	Plymouth	MN	55441	763-544-4415	
Simsmart Technologies Inc Four Pl du Commerce Ste 100 *Web:* www.simsmart.com	Brossard	QC	J4W3B3	450-923-0400	
Skeleton Key 3260 Hampton Ave Ste 200 *Web:* www.skeletonkey.com	Saint Louis	MO	63139	314-353-4300	
Skyline Ultd Inc 16333 S Great Ste 121 *Web:* www.skyline-ultd.com	Round Rock	TX	78681	703-671-9200	
Skyweb Networks 2710 State St *Web:* skywebonline.com	Saginaw	MI	48602	989-792-8681	
Smartech Systems Inc 500 E Brighton Ave *Web:* www.s2ieng.com	Syracuse	NY	13210	315-701-2316	
Smooth Solutions Inc 300-2 Route 17 South *Web:* smoothsolutions.com	Lodi	NJ	07644	973-249-6666	
SMS Data Products Group Inc 1751 Pinnacle Dr 12th Fl **Fax Area Code:* 703 ■ *TF:* 800-331-1767 ■ *Web:* www.sms.com	McLean	VA	22102	800-331-1767	356-4831*
Snap Inc 14900 Bogle Dr Ste 203 *Web:* www.snapinc.net	Chantilly	VA	20151	703-393-6400	
Social & Scientific Systems Inc 8757 Georgia Ave 12th Fl *Web:* www.s-3.com	Silver Spring	MD	20910	301-628-3000	628-3001
Society Consulting LLC 901 104th Ave Ne *Web:* societyconsulting.com	Bellevue	WA	98004	206-420-3500	
Soft-Con Enterprises Inc 6505 Belcrest Rd Ste 120 *Web:* www.softcon1.com	Hyattsville	MD	20782	301-429-0075	
Softassist Inc 700 American Ave *Web:* www.softassist.com	King Of Prussia	PA	19406	610-265-8484	
Softech & Associates Inc 1570 Corporate Dr Ste B *Web:* www.softechis.com	Costa Mesa	CA	92626	714-427-1122	
Softek International Inc 1974 State Rt 27 *Web:* www.softekintl.com	Edison	NJ	08817	732-287-3337	
Softential Inc 607 Herndon Pkwy Ste 202 *Web:* www.softential.com	Herndon	VA	20170	703-650-0001	
Softrim Corp 9210 Estero Park Commons Blvd Ste 5 *Web:* www.softrim.com	Estero	FL	33928	239-449-4444	
Softsolutions Inc 325 Mtn Ave SW *Web:* www.softsolutionsit.com	Roanoke	VA	24016	540-345-1045	
Software Information Systems Inc (SIS) 165 Barr St *TF:* 800-337-6914 ■ *Web:* www.thinksis.com	Lexington	KY	40507	859-977-4747	977-4750
Software Technology Group 555 S 300 E *TF:* 888-595-1001 ■ *Web:* www.softwaretechnologygroup.com	Salt Lake City	UT	84111	801-595-1000	595-1080
Solar Technologies Inc 26180 Enterprise Way Bldg 100	Lake Forest	CA	92630	949-458-1080	
Solid Border Inc 1806 Turnmill St *Web:* www.solidborder.com	San Antonio	TX	78248	210-492-8125	
Solutia Consulting Inc 1241 Amundson Cir *Web:* www.solutia-consulting.com	Stillwater	MN	55082	651-351-0123	
Solution Beacon LLC 14419 Greenwood Ave N Ste 332 *Web:* www.solutionbeacon.com	Seattle	WA	98133	206-366-6606	
Solution Partners Inc 1770 N Park St Ste 100 *Web:* www.solpart.com	Naperville	IL	60563	630-416-1335	
SolutionsIQ Inc 10785 Willows Rd NE Ste 250 *Web:* www.solutionsiq.com	Redmond	WA	98052	425-451-2727	
Solvere LLC 69 Mcadenville Rd *Web:* www.solvere.net	Belmont	NC	28012	704-829-1015	
Somethingcool.com LLC 121a E High St *Web:* somethingcool.com	Potosi	MO	63664	573-436-2665	
Sonit Systems LLC 130 W Field Dr *Web:* www.sonit.com	Archbold	OH	43502	419-446-2151	
Sonos Inc 223 E De La Guerra	Santa Barbara	CA	93101	805-965-3001	
Southeastern Computer Consultants Inc 5166 Potomac Dr Ste 400 *Web:* www.teamscci.com	King George	VA	22485	301-695-5311	695-6101
Spaceflight Systems 47 Constitution Dr *Web:* ssc-nh.com	Bedford	NH	03110	603-472-4934	
Sparkhound Inc 11207 Proverbs Ave *Web:* www.sparkhound.com	Baton Rouge	LA	70816	225-216-1500	

Company	City	State	ZIP	Phone	Fax
Spectraforce Technologies Inc 5511 Capital Ctr Dr Ste 340	Raleigh	NC	27606	919-233-4466	
Web: www.spectraforce.com					
Spherexx LLC 9142 S Sheridan	Tulsa	OK	74133	918-491-7500	
Web: www.spherexx.com					
Sprinklr Inc 29 W 35th St Eighth Fl	New York	NY	10001	917-933-7800	
Web: www.sprinklr.com					
SQA LABS Inc 3404 W Cheryl Dr	Phoenix	AZ	85051	602-439-5500	
Web: www.sqalabs.com					
Squires Group Inc, The 608 Melvin Ave Ste 101	Annapolis	MD	21401	410-224-7779	
Web: www.squiresgroup.com					
SRA International Inc 4300 Fair Lakes Ct	Fairfax	VA	22033	703-803-1500	803-1509
TF: 800-511-6398 ■ *Web:* www.sra.com					
Ssinfotek Inc 9560 Research Dr	Irvine	CA	92618	949-732-3100	
Web: www.ssinfotek.com					
Staffing Technologies LLC 221 Roswell St Ste 200	Alpharetta	GA	30009	678-338-2040	
Web: www.staffingtechnologies.com					
Starcare Systems Inc 107 S W St Ste 108	Alexandria	VA	22314	703-836-0331	
Web: www.starcaresystems.com					
Starpoint Solutions 22 Cortlandt St Ste 14	New York	NY	10007	212-962-1550	962-7175
Web: www.starpoint.com					
Startech Computing Inc 1755 Old W Main St	Red Wing	MN	55066	651-385-0607	
Web: startech-comp.com					
Statera Inc 6501 E Belleview Ave	Englewood	CO	80111	720-346-0070	
Web: statera.com					
STC Network Services Inc 4904 Oak Cir Dr N	Mobile	AL	36609	251-661-7130	
Web: www.stcnetwork.com					
Stefanini TechTeam Inc 27335 W Eleven-Mile Rd	Southfield	MI	48034	248-357-2866	357-2570
TF: 800-522-4451 ■ *Web:* stefanini.com					
Stelvio Inc 430 Rue Sainte-helene	Montreal	QC	H2Y2K7	514-281-8570	
Web: stelvio.com					
Stg International Inc 4900 Seminary Rd Ste 1100	Alexandria	VA	22311	703-578-6030	578-4474
TF: 855-507-0660 ■ *Web:* www.stginternational.com					
STI Computer Services Inc 2700 Van Buren Ave	Eagleville	PA	19403	610-650-9700	
Web: sticomputer.com					
Stockell Consulting Inc 15400 S Outer Forty Ste 105	Chesterfield	MO	63017	636-537-9100	
Web: www.stockellconsulting.com					
Strata Information Group 3935 Harney St Ste 203	San Diego	CA	92110	619-296-0170	
Web: sigcorp.com					
Stratacache Inc Two Emmet St Ste 200	Dayton	OH	45405	937-224-0485	
Web: www.stratacache.com					
Sulaan Solutions Inc 410 N Roosevelt Ave Ste 106	Chandler	AZ	85226	480-626-4041	
Web: www.sulaan.com					
Sumaria Systems Inc 99 Rosewood Dr	Danvers	MA	01923	978-739-4200	739-4850
Web: www.sumariasystems.com					
Summit 7 Systems Inc 300 Voyager Way Ste 300	Huntsville	AL	35806	256-585-6868	
Web: www.summit7systems.com					
Sun Technologies Inc 3700 Mansell Rd Ste 125	Alpharetta	GA	30022	770-418-0434	643-0623
Web: www.suntechnologies.com					
Sunquest Information Systems Inc 250 S Williams Blvd	Tucson	AZ	85711	520-570-2000	
Web: www.sunquestinfo.com					
SupplyFrame Inc 51 W Dayton St Ste 300	Pasadena	CA	91105	626-793-7732	
Web: www.supplyframe.com					
Surecomp Services Inc Two Hudson Pl Fl 4	Hoboken	NJ	07030	201-217-1437	
Web: www.surecomp.com					
Svam International Inc 233 E Shore Rd Ste 201	Great Neck	NY	11023	516-466-6655	466-8260
TF: 800-903-6716 ■ *Web:* www.svam.com					
Swearingen Software Inc 6950 Empire Central Dr	Houston	TX	77040	713-849-2026	
Web: www.swearingensoftware.com					
Swip Systems Inc One Regency Plz Dr Ste 100	Collinsville	IL	62234	618-346-8014	
Web: swipsystems.com					
Sykes Enterprises Inc 400 N Ashley Dr Ste 2800	Tampa	FL	33602	813-274-1000	273-0148
NASDAQ: SYKE ■ *TF:* 800-867-9537 ■ *Web:* www.sykes.com					
Symmetrix Technologies LLC 106 N Denton Tap Rd Ste 210-262	Coppell	TX	75019	972-599-1585	
Web: www.symmetrixtech.com					
Synergy 74130 Country Club Dr Ste 101	Palm Desert	CA	92260	760-601-5244	
Web: www.synergyis.us					
Synergy Associates LLC 550 Clydesdale Trl	Medina	MN	55340	888-763-9920	
TF: 888-763-9920 ■ *Web:* www.synllc.com					
Synergy Data Solutions Inc 1104 S State St Apt A	Champaign	IL	61820	217-356-2522	
Web: synergydata.com					
Syntel Inc 525 E Big Beaver Rd Ste 300	Troy	MI	48083	248-619-2800	619-2888
NASDAQ: SYNT ■ *Web:* www.syntelinc.com					
SYSCOM Inc 400 E Pratt St Inner Harbor Ctr Ste 502	Baltimore	MD	21202	410-539-3737	
Web: www.syscom.com					
Syscon Inc 94 Mcfarland Blvd	Northport	AL	35476	205-758-2000	
Web: www.syscononline.com					
Sysnet Technology Solutions Inc 4320 Stevens Creek Blvd Ste 229	San Jose	CA	95129	408-248-5000	
Web: www.sysnetts.com					
Sysorex Federal Inc 13800 Coppermine Rd Ste 300	Herndon	VA	20171	703-356-2900	
Web: www.sysorex.com					
System Development Integration Inc (SDI) 33 W Monroe St Ste 400	Chicago	IL	60603	312-580-7500	580-7600
Web: www.sdienterprises.com					
Systems Implementers Inc 350 S Williams Blvd	Tucson	AZ	85711	520-795-5729	
Web: www.systemsimplementers.com					
Systima Technologies Inc 1832 180th St SE	Bothell	WA	98012	425-487-4020	
Web: www.systima.com					
Tangible Solutions Inc 1320 Matthews Mint Hill R	Matthews	NC	28105	704-940-4200	
Web: www.tangible.com					
Tantus Technologies Inc 501 School St SW Ste 800	Washington	DC	20024	202-567-2777	
Web: www.tantustech.com					
TASC Inc 4805 Stonecroft Blvd	Chantilly	VA	20151	703-633-8300	449-3400
Web: www.tasc.com					
Tbs Automation Systems Inc 122 E Kings Hwy Ste 504	Maple Shade	NJ	08052	856-424-3247	
Web: tbsauto.com					
TC Computer Service Inc 3303 FM1960 W Ste 100	Houston	TX	77068	713-686-2083	
Web: www.tccsi.com					
Tech Mahindra Americas Inc 2140 Lk Park Blvd Ste 300	Richardson	TX	75080	972-991-2900	
Web: techmahindra.com					
Tech-Pro Inc 3000 Centre Pointe Dr	Roseville	MN	55113	651-634-1400	
Web: www.tech-pro.com					
Techfusion 20 Concord Ln	Cambridge	MA	02138	617-491-1001	
Web: www.techfusion.com					
Technica Corp 22970 Indian Creek Dr Ste 500	Dulles	VA	20166	703-662-2000	662-2001
Web: www.technicacorp.com					
Technical Youth LLC 8395 Keystone Crossing	Indianapolis	IN	46240	317-475-0079	
Web: www.technicalyouth.com					
Technocom Corp 2030 Corte De Nogal Ste 200	Carlsbad	CA	92011	760-438-5115	438-5815
Web: technocom-wireless.com					
Techspeed Inc 280 SW Moonridge Pl	Portland	OR	97225	503-291-0027	
Web: www.techspeed.com					
TECSys Development Inc 1600 10th St Ste B	Plano	TX	75074	972-881-1553	
Web: www.tditechnologies.com					
Teds Inc 235 Mtn Empire Rd	Atkins	VA	24311	276-783-6991	
Web: teds.com					
Tekmark Global Solutions LLC 100 Metroplex Dr Ste 102	Edison	NJ	08817	732-572-5400	
Web: tekmarkinc.com					
TeKONTROL Inc 711 W Amelia St	Orlando	FL	32805	407-398-6575	
Web: www.tekontrol.com					
Teksavers Inc 2120 Grand Ave Pkwy	Austin	TX	78728	512-491-5304	233-2328
Web: teksavers.com					
Teleformix LLC 250 E Devon Ave	Itasca	IL	60143	630-285-6500	
Web: www.teleformix.com					
Telenet Communications Inc 16 Shenandoah Ave	Staten Island	NY	10314	718-370-3900	
Web: www.telenetny.com					
Telos Corp 19886 Ashburn Rd	Ashburn	VA	20147	703-724-3800	724-3868
OTC: TLSRP ■ *Web:* www.telos.com					
Tenlinks 300 Professional Ctr Dr	Novato	CA	94947	415-897-8800	
Web: www.tenlinks.com					
Tenplus Systems 500 Uwharrie Ct Ste C	Raleigh	NC	27606	919-832-5799	
Web: www.tenplus.com					
TeraMach Technologies Inc 1130 Morrison Dr Ste 105	Ottawa	ON	K2H9N6	613-226-7775	
Web: www.teramach.com					
TFC.NET Corp 15211 Lk Maurine Dr	Odessa	FL	33556	813-880-0909	
Web: www.tfc.net					
Tgo Consulting Inc 120-140 Renfrew Dr	Markham	ON	L3R6B3	905-470-6830	
Web: www.tgo.ca					
Thaumaturgix Inc 19 W 44th St Ste 810	New York	NY	10036	212-918-5000	918-5001
Web: www.tgix.com					
Thin Client Computing 34522 N Scottsdale Rd	Scottsdale	AZ	85266	602-432-8649	
Web: www.thinclient.net					
ThruPoint Inc 1040 Ave of the Americas	New York	NY	10018	646-562-6000	562-6100
Titan Solutions Group Inc 11901 W Parmer Ln Ste 400	Cedar Park	TX	78613	512-345-4234	
Web: www.titansolutions.com					
TLX Inc 7944 E Beck Ln Ste 200	Scottsdale	AZ	85260	480-609-8888	
Web: www.tlxinc.com					
Toolworx Information Products Inc 7994 Grand River	Brighton	MI	48114	810-220-5115	
Web: www.toolworx.com					
Toss Corp 1253 Worcester Rd Ste 304	Framingham	MA	01701	508-820-2990	
Web: www.toss.com					
Total Networx Inc 12209 Wood Lk Dr	Burnsville	MN	55337	952-400-6500	
Web: www.totalnetworx.com					
Tracy Time Systems Inc 230 32nd St SE	Grand Rapids	MI	49548	616-241-1661	
Web: www.tracyinc.com					
Transite Technology Inc 1008 Bullard Ct	Raleigh	NC	27615	919-862-1900	
Web: www.transite.com					
Tratum Technologies Inc 1110 Elden St	Herndon	VA	20170	703-456-7000	
Web: tratumtech.com					
TRI-COR Industries Inc 4403 Forbes Blvd Ste 205	Lanham	MD	20706	301-731-6140	306-6740
Web: www.tricorind.com					
Trianz Inc 3979 Freedom Cir Ste 210	Santa Clara	CA	95054	408-387-5800	
Web: www.trianz.com					
Tribridge 4830 W Kennedy Blvd Ste 890	Tampa	FL	33609	877-744-1360	
TF: 877-744-1360 ■ *Web:* www.tribridge.com					
Tridia Corp 1355 Tarrell Mill Rd Bldg1482 Ste 1	Marietta	GA	30067	770-428-5000	
Web: www.tridia.com					
Trillium Teamologies Inc 219 S Main St Ste 300	Royal Oak	MI	48067	248-584-2080	
Web: www.trilliumteam.com					
Trimax Systems Inc 565 Explorer St	Brea	CA	92821	714-255-8590	
Web: www.trimaxsystems.com					

Company	City	State	Zip	Phone	Fax
Trinity Millennium Group Inc 2424 Babcock Rd Ste 300 — *Web:* www.tringroup.com	San Antonio	TX	78229	210-615-1606	
Trioro Inc 642 King St W — *Web:* www.trioro.com	Toronto	ON	M5V1M7	416-977-3333	
Trivalent Group Inc 3145 Prairie St SW Ste 101 — *Web:* www.trivalentgroup.com	Grandville	MI	49418	616-222-9200	
Trivalley Internet Inc 4713 First St Ste 110 — *Web:* www.trivalley.com	Pleasanton	CA	94566	925-417-7600	
Trivera Interactive N88 W16447 Main St Ste 400 — *Web:* www.trivera.com	Menomonee Falls	WI	53051	262-250-9400	
Trofholz Technologies Inc 2207 Plz Dr Ste 100 — *Web:* www.trofholz.com	Rocklin	CA	95765	916-577-1903	
Tsa Inc 2050 W Sam Houston Pkwy N — *Web:* ww.tsa.com	Houston	TX	77043	713-935-1500	
Turn Key Distribution Systems Inc 450 Broadway — *Web:* turnkey.com	Malden	MA	02148	781-322-3000	
Tygart Technology Inc 1543 Fairmont Ave — *Web:* www.tygart.com	Fairmont	WV	26554	304-363-6855	
U r s Information Systems Inc 155 W St Ste 1 — *Web:* www.ursinfo.com	Wilmington	MA	01887	978-657-6100	
U2 Logic 8001 E 88th Ave — *Web:* www.u2logic.com	Henderson	CO	80640	303-768-9601	
Ultimate Technical Solutions Inc 651 Leson Ct — *Web:* www.utsi.us	Harvey	LA	70058	504-367-4957	
UNAPEN Inc Two Barnes Industrial Rd South — *Web:* unapen.com	Wallingford	CT	06492	203-269-2111	
UNICON International Inc 241 Outerbelt St — *Web:* www.unicon-intl.com	Columbus	OH	43213	614-861-7070	
Upnorth Consulting Inc 9100 W Bloomington Fwy — *Web:* upnorth-vet.com	Minneapolis	MN	55431	952-224-8656	
US-Analytics Solutions Group LLC 600 E Las Colinas Blvd Ste 2222 — *TF General:* 877-828-8727 ■ *Web:* www.us-analytics.com	Irving	TX	75039	214-630-0081	630-0082
Userful Corp 200-709 11th Ave SW — *Web:* www.userful.com	Calgary	AB	T2R0E3	403-289-2177	
USfalcon Inc One Copley Pkwy Ste 200 — *Web:* www.usfalcon.com	Morrisville	NC	27560	919-459-1956	
USWired Inc 2107 N First St Ste 250 — *Web:* www.uswired.com	San Jose	CA	95131	408-432-1144	
Utility Integration Solutions Inc 24 Benthill Ct — *Web:* www.uisol.com	Lafayette	CA	94549	925-939-0449	
Utopia Systems Inc 1172 Old Forge Rd — *Web:* www.utopiasystems.com	New Castle	DE	19720	302-777-0772	
V I Engineering Inc 27300 Haggerty Rd — *Web:* viengineering.com	Farmington Hills	MI	48331	248-489-1200	
Valli Information Systems Inc 915 Main St Ste 100 — *Web:* www.valli.com	Caldwell	ID	83605	208-459-3611	
Valuemomentum Inc 3001 Hadley Rd Unit 8 — *Web:* www.valuemomentum.com	South Plainfield	NJ	07080	908-755-0048	
Vanguard Integrity Professionals Inc 6625 S Eastern Ave Ste 100 — *Web:* www.go2vanguard.com	Las Vegas	NV	89119	702-794-0014	
Vantix Systems 10119 97a Ave Nw — *Web:* vantixsystems.com	Edmonton	AB	T5K2T3	780-421-0499	
Vasc Alert LLC 3000 Kent Ave — *Web:* www.vasc-alert.com	West Lafayette	IN	47906	765-775-2525	
Ventera Corp 1881 Campus Commons Dr Ste 350 — *Web:* www.ventera.com	Reston	VA	20191	703-760-4600	390-1113
Ventraq Inc 817 E Gate Dr Ste 101 — *Web:* 1db088.campgn5.com/ventraq	Mount Laurel	NJ	08054	856-866-1000	
Veritaaq Technology House Inc 2327 Saint-Laurent Blvd Ste 100 — *Web:* www.veritaaq.ca	Ottawa	ON	K1G4J8	613-736-6120	
Verity Three Inc 733 Ridgeview Dr — *Web:* www.xamin.com	Mchenry	IL	60050	815-385-4474	
Verma Systems Inc 4111 S Sherwood Forest Blvd — *Web:* www.vermasystems.com	Baton Rouge	LA	70816	225-296-0399	
Vertel Corp 21300 Victory Blvd Ste 700 — *Web:* www.vertel.com	Woodland Hills	CA	91367	818-227-1400	
Vertisoft 990 Boul Pierre-roux E — *Web:* www.vertisoftpme.com	Victoriaville	QC	G6T0K9	819-751-6660	
Victory Enterprises Inc 5200 30th St SW — *Web:* www.victoryenterprises.com	Davenport	IA	52802	563-884-4444	
Video Insight Inc Three Riverway Dr Ste 700 — *Web:* www.video-insight.com	Houston	TX	77056	713-621-9779	
Viewsource 11841 Mason Montgomery Rd Ste C — *Web:* viewsource.com	Cincinnati	OH	45249	513-671-6238	
Viking Networks Inc 4655 Middle Rd B — *Web:* www.vikingnetworks.net	Columbus	IN	47203	812-372-0007	
Virtual Connect Technologies Inc 3089 S Hwy 14 — *Web:* www.virtualconnect.net	Greer	SC	29650	864-288-9595	
Virtual Education Software Inc 300 N Argonne Rd Ste 102 — *Web:* www.virtualeduc.com	Spokane	WA	99212	509-891-7219	
Virtual Enterprises Inc 12405 Grant St — *Web:* www.virtual.com	Thornton	CO	80241	303-301-3000	
Virtual Matrix Corp 7200 France Ave S Ste 324 — *Web:* www.vmatrixcorp.com	Minneapolis	MN	55435	952-835-6400	
Visionary Integration Professionals Inc 80 Iron Pt Cir Ste 100 — *TF:* 800-434-2673 ■ *Web:* trustvip.com/	Folsom	CA	95630	916-985-9625	985-9632
Vistronix Inc 11091 Sunset Hills Rd Ste 700 — *TF:* 800-483-2434 ■ *Web:* www.vistronix.com	Reston	VA	20190	703-463-2059	483-2500
Visual Networks Inc 2092 Gaither Rd — *Web:* www.visualnetworks.com	Rockville	MD	20850	301-296-2300	
Vivid Solutions 2328 Government St — *Web:* www.vividsolutions.com	Victoria	BC	V8T5G5	250-385-6040	
Voyager Systems Inc 360 Route 101 — *Web:* www.voyagersystems.com	Bedford	NH	03110	603-472-5172	
Vvm Inc 5606 W Adams Ave — *Web:* www.vvm.com	Temple	TX	76502	254-771-0070	
W-Industries Inc 11500 Charles Rd — *Web:* www.w-industries.com	Houston	TX	77041	713-466-9463	
Walker Group Inc, The 20 Waterside Dr — *Web:* www.walkersystemssupport.com	Farmington	CT	06032	860-678-3530	
Washington Consulting Group Inc 4915 Auburn Ave Ste 301 — *Web:* www.washcg.com	Bethesda	MD	20814	301-656-2330	656-1996
Water Intelligence PLC 888 E Research Dr Ste 100 — *Web:* www.waterintelligence.co.uk	Palm Springs	CA	92263	760-969-6830	
Waypoint Solutions Group LLC 9305 Monroe Rd Ste L — *Web:* www.waypointsg.com	Charlotte	NC	28270	704-246-1717	
Web Yoga Inc 938 Senate Dr — *Web:* www.webyoga.com	Dayton	OH	45459	937-428-0000	
White Sands Technology Inc 6737 Variel Ave Ste A — *Web:* www.whitesands.com	Canoga Park	CA	91303	818-702-9200	
WidePoint Corp 7926 Jones Branch Dr Ste 124 — **Fax Area Code:* 630 ■ *Web:* www.widepoint.com	Mclean	VA	22102	703-349-2577	629-7559*
Wimmer Solutions Corp 1341 N Northlake Way Ste 300 — *Web:* www.wimmersolutions.com	Seattle	WA	98103	206-324-4594	
Winning Technologies Great Lakes LLC 147 Triad Ctr W — *Web:* www.winningtech.com	O Fallon	MO	63366	636-379-8279	
Wisdom Infotech Ltd 18650 W Corp Dr Ste 120 — *Web:* www.wisdominfotech.com	Brookfield	WI	53045	262-792-0200	792-0202
WISNET.COM 481 E Division St 700 — *Web:* www.wisnet.com	Fond Du Lac	WI	54935	920-921-8391	
WM Software Corp 3660 Ctr Rd Ste 371 — *Web:* www.wmsoftware.com	Brunswick	OH	44212	330-558-0501	
Wolcott Systems Group LLC 1684 Medina Rd Ste 204 — *Web:* www.wolcottgroup.com	Medina	OH	44256	330-666-5900	666-5600
Wood Networks 10260 Robinson Dr — *Web:* www.woodnetworks.com	Tyler	TX	75703	903-592-6986	
Working Machines Corp 2170 Dwight Way — *Web:* www.workingmachines.com	Berkeley	CA	94704	510-704-1100	
Worldcom Exchange Inc Six Delaware Dr — *Web:* www.wei.com	Salem	NH	03079	603-893-0900	
Worx Group LLC, The 18 Waterbury Rd — *Web:* www.theworxgroup.com	Prospect	CT	06712	203-758-3311	
Wurldtech Security Technologies Inc 1090 W Georgia St Ste 1000 — *Web:* www.wurldtech.com	Vancouver	BC	V6E3V7	604-669-6674	
Xfer International Inc 39201 Schoolcraft Rd Ste B 9 — *Web:* www.xfer.com	Livonia	MI	48150	734-927-6666	
Xoriant Corp 1248 Reamwood Ave — *Web:* www.xoriant.com	Sunnyvale	CA	94089	408-743-4400	
Yaana Technologies LLC 542 Gibraltar Dr — *Web:* www.yaanatech.com	Milpitas	CA	95035	408-719-9000	
Yellow Dog Networks 9664 Marion Rd — *Web:* www.yellowdognetworks.com	Kansas City	MO	64137	816-767-9364	
Yojna Inc 32605 W 12 Mile Rd # 275 — *Web:* www.yojna.com	Farmington Hills	MI	48334	248-489-9650	
YouMail Inc 43 Corporate Park Ste 200 — *TF:* 800-374-0013 ■ *Web:* www.youmail.com	Irvine	CA	92606	800-374-0013	
Zel Technologies LLC 54 Old Hampton Ln — *Web:* zeltech.com	Hampton	VA	23669	757-722-5565	
Zenmonics Inc 125 Floyd Smith Office Park Dr Ste 220 — *Web:* www.zenmonics.com	Charlotte	NC	28262	704-971-7315	
Zontec Inc 1389 Kemper Meadow Dr — *Web:* www.zontec-spc.com	Cincinnati	OH	45240	513-648-9695	
ZyQuest Inc 1385 W Main Ave Ste 101 — *TF:* 800-992-0533 ■ *Web:* www.zyquest.com	De Pere	WI	54115	920-499-0533	490-3218

184 CONCERT, SPORTS, OTHER LIVE EVENT PRODUCERS & PROMOTERS

Company	City	State	Zip	Phone	Fax
AMS Entertainment 1120 Coast Village Cir — *Web:* santabarbara.amsentertainment.com	Santa Barbara	CA	93108	805-899-4000	
Cinnabar California Inc 4571 Electronics Pl — *Web:* www.cinnabar.com	Los Angeles	CA	90039	818-842-8190	842-0563
Contemporary Productions LLC 190 Carondelet Plz Ste 1111 — *Web:* www.contemporaryproductions.com	Saint Louis	MO	63105	314-721-9090	721-9091
Executive Visions Inc 7000 Miller Ct E — *Web:* www.executivevisions.com	Norcross	GA	30071	770-416-6100	416-6300
Gilmore Entertainment Group 8901-A Business 17 N — *TF:* 800-843-6779 ■ *Web:* thecarolinaopry.com/	Myrtle Beach	SC	29572	843-913-4000	

Phone | Fax

Harlem Globetrotters International Inc
400 E Van Buren St Ste 300 .... Phoenix AZ 85004 602-258-0000 258-5925
TF: 800-641-4667 ■ *Web:* www.harlemglobetrotters.com

House of Blues Entertainment Inc
7060 Hollywood Blvd .... Hollywood CA 90028 323-769-4600 769-4787
TF: 877-632-7600 ■ *Web:* www.houseofblues.com

IMG Inc 1360 E Ninth St .... Cleveland OH 44114 216-522-1200 522-1145
Web: img.com

JAM Productions Ltd 205 W Goethe .... Chicago IL 60610 312-440-9191 266-9568
Web: www.jamusa.com

Live Nation Inc 9348 Civic Ctr Dr .... Beverly Hills CA 90210 310-867-7000 867-7001
NYSE: LYV ■ *Web:* www.livenation.com

Miss Universe LP
1370 Ave of the Americas 16th Fl .... New York NY 10019 212-373-4999 315-5378
Web: www.missuniverse.com

Production Resource Group 300 Harvestore Dr .... DeKalb IL 60115 815-756-9600 756-9377
Web: www.nocturneproductions.com

Radio City Entertainment LLC 1260 Sixth Ave .... New York NY 10020 212-485-7200 472-0603*
**Fax: PR* ■ *Web:* www.radiocity.com

Speedway Motorsports Inc (SMI)
5555 Concord Pkwy S .... Concord NC 28027 704-455-3239
NYSE: TRK ■ *TF:* 800-461-9330 ■ *Web:* www.speedwaymotorsports.com

Top Rank Inc
3980 Howard Hughes Pkwy Ste 580 .... Las Vegas NV 89169 702-732-2717 733-8232
Web: www.toprank.com

Willy Bietak Productions Inc
1404 Third St Promenade Ste 200 .... Santa Monica CA 90401 310-576-2400 576-2405
Web: www.iceshows.com

World Wrestling Entertainment Inc
1241 E Main St .... Stamford CT 06902 203-352-8600 359-5151
NYSE: WWE ■ *TF:* 866-993-7467 ■ *Web:* wwe.sify.com

185 CONCRETE - READY-MIXED

Phone | Fax

A Teichert & Son Inc
3500 American River Dr .... Sacramento CA 95864 916-484-3011 484-6506
Web: www.teichert.com

AJ Walker Construction Co 421 S 21st St .... Mattoon IL 61938 217-235-5647 235-5939

Alamo Concrete Pavers 1008 Hoefgen .... San Antoino TX 78261 210-534-8821 534-8997
Web: alamopavers.net/

Allied Concrete Products LLC
3900 Shannon St .... Chesapeake VA 23324 757-494-5200
Web: www.alliedconcreteusa.com

Anderson Concrete Corp 400 Frank Rd .... Columbus OH 43207 614-443-0123 443-4001
Web: www.andersonconcrete.com

Arizona Materials LLC 3636 S 43rd Ave .... Phoenix AZ 85009 602-278-4444
Web: www.arizonamaterials.com

AVR Inc 14698 Galaxy Ave .... Apple Valley MN 55124 952-432-7132 432-7530
Web: www.avrconcrete.com

Baccala Concrete Corp 100 Armento St .... Johnston RI 02919 401-231-8300 232-3965
TF: 866-705-2382 ■ *Web:* baccalaconcrete.com

Baker Ready Mix & Building Materials
2800 Frenchmen St .... New Orleans LA 70122 504-947-8081
Web: www.bakerreadymix.com

BARD Materials 2021 325th Ave PO Box 246 .... Dyersville IA 52040 563-875-7145 875-7860
Web: bardmaterials.com

Bode Concrete 385 Mendell St .... San Francisco CA 94124 415-920-7100 920-7106
Web: www.bodegravel.com

Bonded Concrete Inc 303 Rt 155 .... Watervliet NY 12189 518-273-5800 273-0848
TF: 800-252-8589 ■ *Web:* www.bondedconcrete.com

Boston Sand & Gravel Company Inc
100 N Washington St PO Box 9187 .... Boston MA 02114 617-227-9000 523-7947
OTC: BSND ■ *TF:* 800-624-2724 ■ *Web:* www.bostonsand.com

Builders Redi-Mix Inc
30701 W 10 Mile Rd Ste 500
PO Box 2900 .... Farmington Hills MI 48333 888-988-4400
TF: 888-988-4400 ■ *Web:* www.superiormaterialsllc.com

Building Products Corp 950 Freeburg Ave .... Belleville IL 62220 618-233-4427 233-2031
TF: 800-233-1996 ■ *Web:* www.buildingproductscorp.com

CalPortland Co
5975 E Marginal Way S PO Box 1730 .... Seattle WA 98134 206-764-3000 764-3012
TF: 800-750-0123 ■ *Web:* www.calportland.com

Cemex USA 840 Gessner Ste 1400 .... Houston TX 77024 713-650-6200 317-6047*
NYSE: CX ■ **Fax Area Code: 212* ■ *TF:* 888-292-0070 ■ *Web:* www.cemex.com

Cemstone Products Co
2025 Centre Pt Blvd Ste 300 .... Mendota Heights MN 55120 651-688-9292 688-0124
TF: 800-236-7866 ■ *Web:* www.cemstone.com

Centex Materials Inc
3019 Alvin Devane Blvd Ste 100 .... Austin TX 78741 512-460-3003 444-9809
Web: eaglematerials.com

Central Builders Supply Company Inc
125 Bridge Ave PO Box 152 .... Sunbury PA 17801 570-286-6461 286-5108
TF: 800-326-9361 ■ *Web:* centralbuilderssupply.com

Central Concrete Supermix Inc 4300 SW 74th Ave ...... Miami FL 33155 305-262-3250 267-0698
Web: www.supermix.com

Central Concrete Supply Company Inc
755 Stockton Ave .... San Jose CA 95126 408-293-6272 294-3162
TF: 866-404-1000 ■ *Web:* www.centralconcrete.com

Century Ready-Mix Corp
3250 Armand St PO Box 4420 .... Monroe LA 71211 318-322-4444 322-7299
TF: 800-732-3969 ■ *Web:* centuryreadymix.com

Champion Inc
180 Traders Mine Rd PO Box 490 .... Iron Mountain MI 49801 906-779-2300
TF Sales: 800-568-8881 ■ *Web:* www.championinc.com

Chandler Concrete Company Inc
1006 S Church St PO Box 131 .... Burlington NC 27216 336-226-1181 226-2969
Web: www.chandlerconcrete.com

CJ Horner Company Inc 105 W Grand Ave .... Hot Springs AR 71901 501-321-9600
Web: cjhornerinc.com

Clayton Cos, The PO Box 3015 .... Lakewood NJ 08701 800-662-3044 751-7623*
**Fax Area Code: 732* ■ *TF:* 800-662-3044 ■ *Web:* www.claytonco.com

Phone | Fax

Concrete Materials Corp (CMC) 106 Industry Rd .... Richmond KY 40475 859-623-4238 623-4255
Web: www.concretematerialscompany.net

Conproco Corp 17 Production Dr .... Dover NH 03820 603-743-5800
Web: www.conproco.com

Delta Concrete Products Co Inc
425 Florida Blvd .... Denham Springs LA 70726 225-665-6103

Devine Bros Inc 38 Commerce St .... Norwalk CT 06850 203-866-4421 857-4609
Web: www.devinebioheat.com

Dolese Bros Co 20 NW 13th St .... Oklahoma City OK 73103 405-235-2311 297-8329
TF: 800-375-2311 ■ *Web:* dolese.com

Dragon Products Co 960 Ocean Ave .... Portland ME 04103 207-774-6355 761-5694
TF: 800-828-8352 ■ *Web:* www.dragonproducts.com

Dublin Construction Company Inc
305 S Washington St .... Dublin GA 31021 478-272-0721
Web: www.dublinconstruction.com

Dunham Price Inc
210 Mike Hooks Rd PO Box 760 .... Westlake LA 70669 337-433-3900 433-8895
Web: www.dunhamprice.com

Eagle Materials Inc
3811 Turtle Creek Blvd Ste 1100 .... Dallas TX 75219 214-432-2000 432-2100
NYSE: EXP ■ *Web:* www.eaglematerials.com

Eastern Concrete Materials Inc
475 Market St .... Elmwood Park NJ 07407 201-797-7979 791-9631*
**Fax: Sales* ■ *TF:* 800-822-7242 ■ *Web:* www.us-concrete.com

Eastern Industries Inc
4401 Camp Meeting Rd Ste 200 .... Center Valley PA 18034 610-866-0932 867-1886
Web: www.eastern-ind.com

Elkins Builders Supply Co Five 11th St .... Elkins WV 26241 304-636-2640 636-8078
Web: www.wvbuilders.com

Ernst Enterprises Inc 3361 Successful Way .... Dayton OH 45414 937-233-5555 233-9203
TF: 800-353-1555 ■ *Web:* ernstconcrete.com

Federal Materials Concrete
2425 Wayne Sullivan Dr .... Paducah KY 42003 270-442-5496 443-6484
Web: www.fmc1.com

Garrott Bros Continous Mix Inc PO Box 419 .... Gallatin TN 37066 615-452-2385 452-8952
Web: www.garrottbros.com

Geiger Ready Mix Company Inc PO Box 50 .... Leavenworth KS 66048 913-772-4010 772-8661
Web: www.geigerreadymix.com

Geneva Rock Products Inc 302 W 5400 S Ste 200 .... Murray UT 84107 801-281-7900
TF: 855-614-6497 ■ *Web:* www.genevarock.com

Hardaway Concrete Co Inc 2001 Taylor St .... Columbia SC 29204 803-254-4350

Hawaiian Cement 99-1300 Halawa Vly St .... Aiea HI 96701 808-532-3400 532-3499
Web: www.hawaiiancement.com

Hempt Bros Inc 205 Creek Rd .... Camp Hill PA 17011 717-737-3411 761-5019
Web: hemptbros.com

Hilltop Basic Resources Inc
One W Fourth St Ste 1100 .... Cincinnati OH 45202 513-651-5000 684-8222
Web: www.hilltopbasicresources.com

Ideal Ready Mix Company Inc
3902 W Mount Pleasant St .... West Burlington IA 52655 319-754-4747
Web: www.idealrm.com

Ingram Readymix Inc 3580 Fm 482 .... New Braunfels TX 78132 830-625-9156
Web: www.ingramreadymixinc.com

Irving Materials Inc (IMI) 8032 N SR-9 .... Greenfield IN 46140 317-536-6650 326-3105
Web: www.irvmat.com

Irving Ready-Mix Inc 13415 Coldwater Rd .... Fort Wayne IN 46845 260-637-3104

Jackson Ready Mix Concrete Inc
100 W Woodrow Wilson Dr .... Jackson MS 39213 601-354-3801 292-3924
Web: delta-ind.com

Janesville Sand & Gravel Co (JSG)
1110 Harding St .... Janesville WI 53547 608-754-7701
TF: 800-955-7702 ■ *Web:* www.jsandg.com

Jones & Sons Inc PO Box 2357 .... Washington IN 47501 812-254-4731 254-3293
Web: www.jonesandsons.com

King's Material Inc 650 12th Ave SW .... Cedar Rapids IA 52404 319-363-0233 366-0249
TF: 800-332-5298 ■ *Web:* www.kingsmaterial.com

Kirkpatrick Concrete Co
2000-A Southbridge Pkwy Ste 610 .... Birmingham AL 35209 205-423-2600 621-0952
TF: 800-489-0205 ■ *Web:* nationalcement.com

Kloepfer Concrete & Paving Co
505 E Ellis PO Box 875 .... Paul ID 83347 208-438-4525 438-5030
Web: www.kloepfer.com

Knife River Corp 1150 W Century Ave .... Bismarck ND 58503 701-530-1400 530-1451
Web: www.kniferiver.com

Krehling Industries Inc 1399 Hagy Way .... Harrisburg PA 17110 717-232-7936 236-8810
TF: 800-839-1654 ■ *Web:* www.krehlingcountertops.com

Kuert Concrete Inc 3402 Lincoln Way W .... South Bend IN 46628 574-232-9911 232-9977
Web: www.kuert.com

Kuhlman Corp 1845 Indian Woods Cir .... Maumee OH 43537 419-897-6000 897-6061
TF: 800-669-3309 ■ *Web:* www.kuhlman-corp.com

L & L Redi Mix 1939 Rt 206 .... Southampton NJ 08088 609-859-2271
Web: www.llredimix.com

L Suzio Concrete Company Inc
975 Westfield Rd .... Meriden CT 06450 203-237-8421 238-9177
TF: 888-789-4626 ■ *Web:* www.suzioyorkhill.com

Lafarge North America Inc
12950 Worldgate Dr Ste 600 .... Herndon VA 20170 703-480-3600 480-3899
Web: www.lafarge-na.com

Loveland Ready Mix Concrete Inc
644 N County Rd 19 E .... Loveland CO 80537 970-667-1108

Lycon Inc 1110 Harding St PO Box 427 .... Janesville WI 53547 608-754-7701 754-8555
TF: 800-955-8758 ■ *Web:* www.lyconinc.com

Manitou Construction Company Inc
1260 Jefferson Rd .... Rochester NY 14623 585-424-6040

Metro Ready Mix Concrete Inc
1136 Second Ave N .... Nashville TN 37208 615-255-1900
Web: www.mrm1.com

Mid-Continent Concrete Co PO Box 3878 .... Tulsa OK 74102 918-582-8111
TF: 800-225-5422 ■ *Web:* gccusa.com

MMC Materials Inc
1052 Highland Colony Pkwy Ste 201 .... Ridgeland MS 39157 601-898-4000 898-4030
Web: www.mmcmaterials.com

Phone | Fax

National Cement Company of California Inc
15821 Ventura Blvd Ste 475 ... Encino CA 91436 818-728-5200 788-0615
Web: www.vicat.com

Ozark Ready Mix Company Inc
1115 Bluff Dr ... Osage Beach MO 65065 573-348-1181
Web: www.ozarkreadymix.com

Pacific Concrete Industries 7170 Holz Rd ... Lynden WA 98264 360-734-0910

Pennsy Supply Inc 1001 Paxton St ... Harrisburg PA 17104 717-233-4511 238-7312
Web: www.pennsysupply.com

Pine Bluff Sand & Gravel Inc
1501 Heart Wood ... white hall AR 71602 870-534-7120 534-2980
Web: pbsgc.applicantharbor.com

Prairie Group Inc 7601 W 79th St ... Bridgeview IL 60455 708-458-0400 458-6007
TF Sales: 800-649-3690 ■ *Web:* www.prairiegroup.com

Prestige Concrete Products
8529 S Pk Cr Ste 320 ... Orlando FL 32819 407-802-3540 226-0359
Web: prestigeconcreteproducts.com

Ready Mixed Concrete Co 4315 Cuming St ... Omaha NE 68131 402-556-3600 556-5171
Web: lymanrichey.com

RiverStone Group Inc 1701 Fifth Ave ... Moline IL 61265 309-757-8250 757-8257
TF: 800-906-2489 ■ *Web:* www.riverstonegrp.com

RMX Holdings Inc 4602 E Thomas Rd ... Phoenix AZ 85018 602-249-5814
Web: rmxholdings.com

Robar Enterprises Inc 17671 Bear Valley Rd ... Hesperia CA 92345 760-244-5456 244-1819
Web: www.robarenterprises.com

Robertson's Ready Mix Concrete Inc
200 S Main St Ste 200 ... Corona CA 92882 951-493-6500
Web: www.rrmca.com

Rockville Fuel & Feed Company Inc
14901 S Lawn Ln PO Box 1707 ... Rockville MD 20849 301-762-3988 309-3894
Web: rockvilleconcrete.com

Roth Ready Mix Concrete Co 900 Kieley Pl ... Cincinnati OH 45217 513-242-8400
Web: www.cincinnatireadymix.com

S & G Concrete Co 2110 Philadelphia Rd ... Edgewood MD 21040 410-679-0500 679-3293
Web: vulcanmaterials.com

Sequatchie Concrete Service Inc
406 Cedar Ave ... South Pittsburg TN 37380 423-837-7913 837-7479
TF: 800-824-0824 ■ *Web:* www.seqconcrete.com

Shelby Materials PO Box 280 ... Shelbyville IN 46176 800-548-9516 398-2727*
**Fax Area Code:* 317 ■ *TF:* 800-548-9516 ■ *Web:* www.shelbymaterials.com

Silvi Concrete Products Inc
355 Newbold Rd ... Fairless Hills PA 19030 215-295-0777 295-0630
TF: 800-426-6273 ■ *Web:* www.silvi.com

Smith Ready Mix Inc 251 W Lincolnway ... Valparaiso IN 46383 219-462-3191 465-4025
TF: 888-632-5656 ■ *Web:* www.smithreadymix.com

Speedway Redi Mix Inc 1201 N Taylor Rd ... Garrett IN 46738 260-357-6885 357-0238
TF: 800-227-5649 ■ *Web:* www.speedwayredimix.com

Starvaggi Industries Inc
401 Pennsylvania Ave ... Weirton WV 26062 304-748-1400 797-5208
Web: www.starvaggi.com

Stocker Concrete Co
7574 US Rt 36 PO Box 176 ... Gnadenhutten OH 44629 740-254-4626 254-9108
Web: www.stockerconcrete.com

Superior Ready Mix Concrete LP
1508 Mission Rd ... Escondido CA 92029 760-745-0556 740-9556
Web: superiorrm.com

Thomas Bennett & Hunter Inc 70 John St ... Westminster MD 21157 410-848-9030 876-0733
Web: www.tbhconcrete.com

Tilcon Connecticut Inc PO Box 1357 ... New Britain CT 06050 860-224-6010 225-1865
TF: 888-845-2666 ■ *Web:* www.tilconct.com

Titan America Inc 1151 Azalea Garden Rd ... Norfolk VA 23502 757-858-6500 855-7707
TF: 800-468-7622 ■ *Web:* www.titanamerica.com

United Cos of Mesa County Inc
2273 River Rd ... Grand Junction CO 81505 970-243-4900 243-5945
Web: united-gj.com

United Materials LLC
The Woodlands Corporate Ctr E 3949 Forest Pkwy
Ste 400 ... North Tonawanda NY 14120 716-213-5832 213-5850
TF: 888-918-6483 ■ *Web:* www.unitedmaterialsllc.com

US Concrete Inc 2925 Briarpark Dr Ste 1050 ... Houston TX 77042 713-499-6200 499-6201
NASDAQ: USCR ■ *Web:* www.us-concrete.com

VanDerVart Concrete Products
1436 S 15th St ... Sheboygan WI 53081 920-459-2400 459-2410
Web: vandervaartinc.com

Westroc Inc 670 West 220 South ... Pleasant Grove UT 84062 801-785-5600 785-7408
Web: www.westrocinc.com

WG Block Co 1414 Mississippi Blvd ... Bettendorf IA 52722 563-823-2080 823-2071

Willcan Inc PO Box 1357 ... Calhoun GA 30703 706-629-2256 625-0587
Web: www.basicreadymix.com

186 CONCRETE PRODUCTS - MFR

Phone | Fax

A Duchini Inc 2550 McKinley Ave ... Erie PA 16514 814-456-7027 454-0737
TF: 800-937-7317 ■ *Web:* www.duchini.com

Abresist Corp PO Box 38 ... Urbana IN 46990 260-774-3327
TF: 800-348-0717 ■ *Web:* www.abresist.com

AC Miller Concrete Products Inc
31 E Bridge St PO Box 199 ... Spring City PA 19475 610-948-4600 948-9750
TF: 800-229-2922 ■ *Web:* www.acmiller.com

Accord Industries 4001 Forsyth Rd ... Winter Park FL 32792 407-671-6989 679-2297
TF General: 800-876-6989 ■ *Web:* www.universal100.com

Acm Chemistries Inc
3190 Reps Miller Rd Ste 100 ... Norcross GA 30071 770-417-3490
Web: acmchem.com

Acme Block & Brick Inc 248 Dayton Spur Rd ... Crossville TN 38555 931-484-8435
Web: www.acmeblockandbrick.com

Adams Products Co
5701 McCrimmon Pkwy PO Box 189 ... Morrisville NC 27560 919-467-2218 469-0509
TF: 800-672-3131 ■ *Web:* www.adamsproducts.com

Phone | Fax

Advanced Concrete Systems Inc
55 Advanced Ln ... Middleburg PA 17842 570-837-3955
Web: www.yourbasement.com

American Artstone Co 2025 N Broadway St ... New Ulm MN 56073 507-233-3700
Web: www.american-artstone.com

American Concrete Pipe Association
8445 Freeport Pkwy ... Irving TX 75063 972-506-7216 506-7682
Web: www.concrete-pipe.org/

Ameron International Corp
245 S Los Robles Ave ... Pasadena CA 91101 626-683-4000 683-4060
Web: www.nov.com

Amvic Inc 501 McNicoll Ave ... Toronto ON M2H2E2 416-410-5674
Web: www.amvicsystem.com

Angelle Concrete Group LLC
2638 S Sherwood Forest Blvd Ste 200 ... Baton Rouge LA 70816 225-297-4700
Web: www.angelleconcrete.com

Angelus Block Co Inc 11374 Tuxford St ... Sun Valley CA 91352 818-767-8576 768-3124
Web: www.angelusblock.com

ARDEX Inc 400 Ardex Park Dr ... Aliquippa PA 15001 724-203-5000
Web: www.ardex.com

Arkansas Precast Corp 2601 Cory Dr ... Jacksonville AR 72076 501-982-1547 982-4001

Atlantic Concrete Products Inc
8900 Old Rt 13 ... Tullytown PA 19007 215-945-5600 946-3102
TF: 888-318-9473 ■ *Web:* www.atlanticconcrete.com

Basalite Concrete Products LLC
605 Industrial Way ... Dixon CA 95620 707-678-1901 678-6268
TF: 800-776-6690 ■ *Web:* www.basalite.paccoast.com

Bayshore Concrete Products Corp
1134 Bayshore Rd PO Box 230 ... Cape Charles VA 23310 757-331-2300 331-2501
Web: www.usa.skanska.com

Beavertown Block Company Inc
3612 Paxtonville Rd PO Box 337 ... Middleburg PA 17842 570-837-1744 837-1591
Web: www.beavertownblock.com

Binkley & Ober Inc 2742 Lancaster Rd ... Manheim PA 17545 717-569-0441
TF: 800-682-5625 ■ *Web:* www.oldcastlenortheast.com

Black Diamond Paving Inc 41550 Boscell Rd ... Fremont CA 94538 510-770-1150
Web: www.blackdiamondpaving.com

Blakeslee Arpaia Chapman Inc
200 N Branford Rd ... Branford CT 06405 203-488-2500
TF: 800-922-6203 ■ *Web:* bac-inc.com

Blakeslee Prestress Inc
Rt 139 McDermott Rd PO Box 510 ... Branford CT 06405 203-481-5306 481-3562
Web: www.blakesleeprestress.com

BNZ Materials Inc 6901 S Pierce St Ste 260 ... Littleton CO 80128 303-978-1199 978-0308
TF: 800-999-0890 ■ *Web:* www.bnzmaterials.com

Bonsal American Inc
8201 Arrowridge Blvd PO Box 241148 ... Charlotte NC 28273 704-525-1621 529-5261
Web: www.bonsalamerican.com/html/contact.html

Buehner Block Co 2800 SW Temple ... Salt Lake City UT 84115 801-467-5456 467-0866
TF: 800-999-2565 ■ *Web:* www.buehnerblock.com

BuildBlock Building Systems LLC
9701 N Broadway Ext ... Oklahoma City OK 73114 405-840-3386
Web: www.buildblock.com

Burtco Inc 185 Rt 123 ... Westminster Station VT 05159 802-722-3358
Web: burtcoselfstorage.com

By-crete 517 King St ... Lebanon PA 17042 717-866-7690
Web: www.bycrete.com

Carr Concrete Corp Waverly Rd ... Waverly WV 26184 304-464-4013
Web: www.carrconcrete.com

Cary Concrete Products Inc
211 Dean St Ste 1D ... Woodstock IL 60098 815-338-2301 337-5801
Web: www.caryconcrete.com

Cast Systems LLC 19400 Peachland Blvd ... Port Charlotte FL 33948 941-625-3474
Web: www.castsystemsllc.com

Cast-Crete Corp 6324 County Rd 579 ... Seffner FL 33584 813-621-4641
Web: www.castcrete.com

Cement Industries Inc
2925 Hanson St PO Box 823 ... Fort Myers FL 33902 239-332-1440 332-0370
TF: 800-332-1440 ■ *Web:* www.cementindustries.com

Cement Products & Supply Co Inc
516 W Main St ... Lakeland FL 33815 863-686-5141 683-2034
TF: 800-248-2385 ■ *Web:* cementproducts.us

Central Pre-Mix Concrete Co 5111 E Broadway ... Spokane WA 99212 509-534-6221
Web: www.centralpremix.com

Century Group Inc, The
1106 W Napoleon St PO Box 228 ... Sulphur LA 70664 337-527-5266 527-8028
TF: 800-527-5232 ■ *Web:* www.centurygrp.com

CERATECH Inc 1500 N Beauregard St Ste 320 ... Alexandria VA 22311 703-894-1130
Web: www.ceratechinc.com

Chaney Enterprises
12480 Mattawoman Dr PO Box 548 ... Waldorf MD 20604 301-932-5000
TF: 888-244-0411 ■ *Web:* www.chaneyenterprises.com

Ciment Quebec Inc
145 Blvd du Centenaire ... St. Basile De Portneuf QC G0A3G0 418-329-2100
Web: www.bcr.cc

Cinder & Concrete Block Corp
10111 Beaver Dam Rd PO Box 9 ... Cockeysville MD 21030 410-666-2350 666-8781
Web: cinderblockonline.com

Clayton Block Co PO Box 3015 ... Lakewood NJ 08701 800-662-3044 751-7618*
**Fax Area Code:* 732 ■ *TF:* 800-662-3044 ■ *Web:* www.claytonco.com

Clayton Cos, The PO Box 3015 ... Lakewood NJ 08701 800-662-3044 751-7623*
**Fax Area Code:* 732 ■ *TF:* 800-662-3044 ■ *Web:* www.claytonco.com

Coastal Concrete Southeast II LLC
118 Pipemakers Cir Ste 100 ... Pooler GA 31322 912-330-8990
Web: www.coastalconcrete.com

Con Cast Pipe LP 299 Brock Rd S RR#3 ... Guelph ON N1H6H9 800-668-7473
TF: 800-668-7473 ■ *Web:* www.concastpipe.com

Con Forms 777 Maritime Dr ... Port Washington WI 53074 262-284-7800 284-7878
TF: 800-223-3676 ■ *Web:* www.conforms.com

Concast Inc 1010 N Star Dr ... Zumbrota MN 55992 507-732-4095
Web: www.concastinc.com

Concrete Equipment Company Inc 237 N 13th St ... Blair NE 68008 402-426-4181
Web: con-e-co.com

Phone | Fax

Concrete Technology Corp
1123 Port of Tacoma Rd PO Box 2259 Tacoma WA 98401 253-383-3545 572-9386
Web: www.concretetech.com

Concrete Tie Corp 130 E Oris St Compton CA 90222 310-886-1000 638-8363
Web: www.concretetie.net

Construction Products Inc 1631 Ashport Rd Jackson TN 38305 731-668-7305 668-1361
TF: 800-238-8226 ■ *Web:* www.cpi-tn.com

Cook Concrete Products Inc 5461 Eastside Rd Redding CA 96001 530-243-2562 243-6881
Web: www.cookconcreteproducts.com

Coreslab Structures Inc 150 W Placentia Ave Perris CA 92571 951-943-9119 943-7571
Web: www.coreslab.com

Cranesville Block Company Inc
1250 Riverfront Ctr Amsterdam NY 12010 518-684-6000
Web: www.cranesville.com

Creter Vault Corp 417 US Hwy 202 Flemington NJ 08822 908-782-7771
Web: doric-vaults.com

Cretex Concrete Products Wes
725 Bryan Stock Trail Casper WY 82601 307-265-3100 265-0013
Web: www.cretexwest.com/

Cretex Cos 311 Lowell Ave Elk River MN 55330 763-441-2121 441-3585
Web: www.cretexinc.com

Crom Corp 250 SW 36th Terr Gainesville FL 32607 352-372-3436 372-6209
Web: www.cromgnv.com

CXT Inc 3808 N Sullivan Rd Bldg 7 Spokane WA 99216 509-921-8766
Web: www.cxtinc.com

David Kucera Inc 42 Steves Ln Gardiner NY 12525 845-255-1044
Web: davidkucerainc.com

DN Tanks 351 Cypress Ln El Cajon CA 92020 619-440-8181
TF: 800-227-8181 ■ *Web:* www.dntanks.com

Dolese Bros Co 20 NW 13th St Oklahoma City OK 73103 405-235-2311 297-8329
TF: 800-375-2311 ■ *Web:* dolese.com

DuKane Precast Inc 1805 High Grove Ln Naperville IL 60540 630-355-8118
Web: www.dukaneprecast.com

Dura-Stress Inc 11325 County Rd 44 Leesburg FL 34788 352-787-1422 787-0080
TF General: 800-342-9239 ■ *Web:* www.durastress.com

Dutchland Inc PO Box 549 Gap PA 17527 717-442-8282 442-9330
Web: www.dutchlandinc.com

E Dillon & Co
2522 Swords Creek Rd PO Box 160 Swords Creek VA 24649 276-873-6816 873-4208
TF: 800-234-8970 ■ *Web:* www.edillon.com

Echo Rock Ventures 13620 Lincoln Way Ste 380 Auburn CA 95603 530-823-9600 823-9650

Empire Blended Products Inc 250 Hickory Ln Bayville NJ 08721 732-269-4949
Web: empireblended.com

EP Henry Corp 201 Pk Ave Woodbury NJ 08096 856-845-6200 845-0023
TF: 800-444-3679 ■ *Web:* www.ephenry.com

Ernest Maier Inc 4700 Annapolis Rd Bladensburg MD 20710 301-927-8300 779-8924
TF: 888-927-8303 ■ *Web:* www.emcoblock.com

F S Prestress LLC 190 Prestress Rd Princeton LA 71067 318-949-2444
Web: www.fsprestress.com

Fabcon Inc 6111 Hwy 13 W Savage MN 55378 952-890-4444 890-6657
TF: 800-727-4444 ■ *Web:* www.fabcon-usa.com

Featherlite Bldg Products Corp
508 McNeil St Round Rock TX 78681 512-255-2573 255-2572
Web: www.featherlitetexas.com

Federal Block Corp 247 Walsh Ave New Windsor NY 12553 845-561-4108 561-5344
TF: 800-724-1999 ■ *Web:* www.montfortgroup.com

Fencecrete America Inc
15089 Tradesman Dr San Antonio TX 78249 210-492-7911
Web: www.fencecrete.com

Fendt Builders Supply Inc
22005 Gill Rd Farmington Hills MI 48335 248-474-3211 474-8110
Web: www.fendtproducts.com

Fibrebond Corp 1300 Davenport Dr Minden LA 71055 318-377-1030
Web: www.fibrebond.com

Fin Pan Inc 3255 Symmes Rd Hamilton OH 45015 513-870-9200
Web: www.finpan.com

Finfrock Industries Inc 2400 Apopka Blvd Apopka FL 32703 407-293-4000 297-0512
Web: finfrock.com

Fitzgerald Formliners Inc
1500 E Chestnut Ave Santa Ana CA 92701 714-547-6710
Web: www.formliners.com

Fizzano Bros Concrete Products Inc
1776 Chester Pk Crum Lynne PA 19022 610-833-1100 833-5347
Web: www.fizzano.com

Flexicore of Texas PO Box 450049 Houston TX 77245 281-437-5700 437-8913
TF: 888-359-4267 ■ *Web:* www.flexicoreoftexas.com

Florence Concrete Products Inc PO Box 5506 Florence SC 29502 843-662-2549 667-0729
Web: www.florenceconcreteproducts.com

Fountain People Inc 4600 Hwy 123 San Marcos TX 78666 512-392-1155
Web: fountainpeople.com

Fritz Industries Inc 180 Gordon Dr Ste 113 Exton PA 19341 800-345-6202 363-0735*
*Fax Area Code: 610 ■ *TF:* 800-345-6202 ■ *Web:* www.fritztile.com

Gage Brothers Concrete Products Inc
4301 W 12th St Sioux Falls SD 57106 605-336-1180
Web: www.gagebrothers.com

Gary Merlino Construction Co
9125 Tenth Ave S Seattle WA 98108 206-762-9125 763-4178

General Shale Products LLC
3015 Bristol Hwy Johnson City TN 37601 423-282-4661 952-4104
TF: 800-414-4661 ■ *Web:* www.generalshale.com

Geneva Pipe Inc 1465 West 400 North Orem UT 84057 801-225-2416
Web: www.genevapipe.com

George L Throop Co 444 N Fair Oaks Ave Pasadena CA 91103 626-796-0285
Web: www.throop.com

GFRC Cladding Systems LLC 118 N Shiloh Rd Garland TX 75042 972-494-9000 494-1900
Web: www.gfrccladding.com

Giannini Garden Ornaments Inc
225 Shaw Rd South San Francisco CA 94080 650-873-4493
Web: www.gianninigarden.com

Glen-Gery Corp 1166 Spring St PO Box 7001 Wyomissing PA 19610 610-374-4011 374-1622
Web: www.glengerybrick.com

Phone | Fax

Goria Enterprises PO Box 14489 Greensboro NC 27415 800-446-7421 375-5656*
*Fax Area Code: 336 ■ *TF:* 800-446-7421 ■ *Web:* www.goria.biz/contact.htm

Grand Blanc Cement Products 10709 Ctr Rd Grand Blanc MI 48439 810-694-7500 694-2995
TF: 800-875-7500 ■ *Web:* www.grandblanccement.com

Gulf Coast Pre-stress Inc PO Box 825 Pass Christian MS 39571 228-452-9486 452-9495
Web: www.gcprestress.com

H2 Pre-Cast Inc 4919 Contractors Dr East Wenatchee WA 98802 509-884-6644
Web: www.h2precast.com

Hancock Concrete Products Inc
17 Atlantic Ave Hancock MN 56244 320-392-5207 392-5155
TF: 800-321-1558 ■ *Web:* www.hancockconcrete.com

Hanover Pavers Inc 240 Bender Rd Hanover PA 17331 717-637-0500
Web: www.hanoverpavers.com

Hastings Pavement Company LLC
200 Henry St Lindenhurst NY 11757 631-669-0600 669-8052
Web: www.hastingsarchitectural.com

Heldenfels Enterprises Inc
5700 IH-35 S (Exit 199) San Marcos TX 78666 512-396-2376 396-2381
Web: heldenfels.com

High Concrete Structures Inc 125 Denver Rd Denver PA 17517 717-336-9300 336-9301*
*Fax: Sales ■ *TF:* 800-773-2278 ■ *Web:* www.highconcrete.com

High Industries Inc 1853 William Penn Way Lancaster PA 17601 717-293-4444 293-4416
Web: www.high.net

Hy-grade Precast Concrete
2411 First St St Catharines ON L2R6P7 905-684-8568
Web: www.hygradeprecast.com

Isabel Bloom LLC 736 Federal St Ste 2100 Davenport IA 52803 800-273-5436 333-2044*
*Fax Area Code: 563 ■ *TF:* 800-273-5436 ■ *Web:* www.ibloom.com

Jensen Precast 625 Bergin Way Sparks NV 89431 775-359-6200 359-1038
TF: 800-648-1134 ■ *Web:* www.jensenprecast.com

Jersey Precast Corp
853 Nottingham Way Hamilton Township NJ 08638 609-689-3700
Web: www.jerseyprecast.com

Joseph P. Carrara & Sons Inc
167 N Shrewsbury Rd North Clarendon VT 05759 802-775-2301
Web: www.jpcarrara.com

JW Peters Inc 500 W Market St Burlington WI 53105 262-806-9009 763-2779
TF: 866-265-7888 ■ *Web:* journaltimes.com

K & S Contractors Supply Company Inc
1971 Gunnville Rd Lancaster NY 14086 716-759-6911 759-2129

Kieft Bros Inc 837 S Riverside Dr Elmhurst IL 60126 630-832-8090 834-5765
Web: www.kieftbros.com

King's Material Inc 650 12th Ave SW Cedar Rapids IA 52404 319-363-0233 366-0249
TF: 800-332-5298 ■ *Web:* www.kingsmaterial.com

Kistner Concrete Products Inc
8713 Read Rd East Pembroke NY 14056 585-762-8216 762-8315
TF: 800-809-2801 ■ *Web:* www.kistner.com

L M Scofield Co 6533 Bandini Blvd Los Angeles CA 90040 323-720-8810 722-7826
TF: 800-800-9900 ■ *Web:* www.scofield.com

Lafarge North America Inc
12950 Worldgate Dr Ste 600 Herndon VA 20170 703-480-3600 480-3899
Web: www.lafarge-na.com

Lakelands Concrete Products Inc 7520 E Main St Lima NY 14485 585-624-1990 624-2102
Web: www.lakelandsconcrete.com

Landis Block Co
711 N County Line Rd PO Box 64418 Souderton PA 18964 215-723-5506 723-5500
Web: www.landisbc.com

Leavcon Ii Inc 108 American Ave Lansing KS 66043 913-351-1430
Web: www.leavcon.com

Lombard Co 4245 W 123rd St Alsip IL 60803 708-389-1060 389-7120
Web: lombardcompany.com

M-CON Products Inc 2150 Richardson Side Rd Carp ON K0A1L0 613-831-1736 831-2048
Web: www.mconproducts.com

Mack Industries Inc
1321 Industrial Pkwy N Ste 500 Brunswick OH 44212 330-460-7005
Web: www.mackconcrete.com

MantelsDirect 217 N Seminary St Florence AL 35630 888-493-8898
TF: 888-493-8898 ■ *Web:* www.mantelsdirect.com

Mathis-Akins Concrete Block Co Inc
130 Lower Elm St Macon GA 31206 478-746-5154

Metromont Corp PO Box 2486 Greenville SC 29602 864-295-0295 295-0295
TF: 888-295-0383 ■ *Web:* www.metromont.com

Midwest Cast Stone Inc 1610 State Ave Kansas City KS 66102 913-371-3300
Web: www.midwestcaststone.com

Midwest Tile & Concrete Products Inc
4309 Webster Rd Woodburn IN 46797 260-749-5173 493-2477
TF: 800-359-4701 ■ *Web:* www.midwesttile.net

Millenium Products Inc 6346 Heron Pkwy Clarkston MI 48346 239-877-6811
Web: www.milleniumproducts.net

MMC Materials Inc
1052 Highland Colony Pkwy Ste 201 Ridgeland MS 39157 601-898-4000 898-4030
Web: www.mmcmaterials.com

Modern Inc/Environmental & Wastewater
210 Durham Rd Ottsville PA 18942 610-847-5112 847-2468
TF: 888-965-3227 ■ *Web:* www.modcon.com

Molin Concrete Products Co 415 Lilac St Lino Lakes MN 55014 651-786-7722 786-0229
TF: 800-336-6546 ■ *Web:* www.molin.com

Montfort Bros Inc 44 Elm St Fishkill NY 12524 845-896-6225 896-0021
TF: 800-724-1777 ■ *Web:* www.montfortgroup.com

Montfort Group, The 44 Elm St Fishkill NY 12524 845-896-6225 896-0021
TF: 800-724-1777 ■ *Web:* www.montfortgroup.com

Mutual Materials Co 605 119th Ave NE Bellevue WA 98005 425-452-2300 454-7732
TF: 800-477-3008 ■ *Web:* www.mutualmaterials.com

NAPCO Precast LLC 6949 Low Bid Ln San Antonio TX 78250 210-509-9100 509-9111
Web: www.napcosa.com

National Concrete Products Co 939 S Mill St Plymouth MI 48170 734-453-8448 452-6506*
*Fax Area Code: 281

National Oilwell Varco (NOV)
7909 Parkwood Cir Dr Houston TX 77036 713-375-3700
NYSE: NOV ■ *TF:* 888-262-8645 ■ *Web:* www.nov.com

NC Products Corp 920 Withers Rd PO Box 27077 Raleigh NC 27603 919-772-6301 772-1209
TF: 888-965-3227 ■ *Web:* oldcastleprecast.com

Company	City	State	ZIP	Phone	Fax
New Milford Block & Supply 574 Danbury Rd *TF:* 800-724-1888 ■ *Web:* www.montfortgroup.com	New Milford	CT	06776	860-355-1101	355-3772
Nitterhouse Concrete Products Inc 2655 Molly Pitcher Hwy *Web:* www.nitterhouse.com	Chambersburg	PA	17201	717-267-4505	267-4518
Northfield an Oldcastle Co 2200 S Main St *TF:* 800-227-6512 ■ *Web:* northfieldblock.com	West Bend	WI	53095	262-338-5700	306-8257
Norwalk Concrete Industries Inc 80 Commerce Dr *Web:* www.nciprecast.com	Norwalk	OH	44857	419-668-8167	
Oldcastle Inc 900 Ashwood Pkwy Ste 600 *TF:* 800-899-8455 ■ *Web:* www.oldcastle.com	Atlanta	GA	30338	770-804-3363	
Oldcastle Precast Inc 1920 12th St PO Box 312 *Web:* www.oldcastleprecast.com	Folsom	NJ	08037	800-642-3755	
Olson Precast Co (OPC) 2750 Marion Dr *TF:* 800-876-8374	Las Vegas	NV	89115	702-643-4371	643-4510
Orco Block Co Inc 11100 Beach Blvd *TF:* 800-473-6726 ■ *Web:* www.orco.com	Stanton	CA	90680	714-527-2239	895-4021
Phoenix Precast Products Inc 1856 E Deer Vly Rd *Web:* www.phoenixprecastproducts.com	Phoenix	AZ	85024	602-569-6090	
Pontchartrain Materials Corp 3819 France Rd *Web:* www.pontchartrain.com	New Orleans	LA	70126	504-949-7571	944-3338
Pre-Cast Specialties Inc 1380 NE 48th St *TF:* 800-749-4041 ■ *Web:* www.precastspecialties.com	Pompano Beach	FL	33064	954-781-4040	781-3539
Preload Inc 49 Wireless Blvd STE 200 *TF:* 888-773-5623 ■ *Web:* www.preload.com	Hauppauge	NY	11788	631-231-8100	231-8881
Premarc Corp 7505 E M 71	Durand	MI	48429	989-288-2661	
Premier Concrete Products 5102 Galveston Rd *Web:* www.premier-concrete.com	Houston	TX	77017	713-641-2727	641-1112
Prestress Engineering Corp 2220 Rt 176 *Web:* www.pre-stress.com	Prairie Grove	IL	60012	815-459-4545	459-6855
Prestress Services Inc 7855 NW Winchester Rd *Web:* www.prestressservices.com	Decatur	IN	46733	260-724-7117	724-3349
Prestressed Casting Co 1600 S Scenic Ave *Web:* www.prestressedcasting.com	Springfield	MO	65807	417-869-7350	
Puerto Rican Cement Company Inc PO Box 364487 *Web:* www.cemexpuertorico.com	San Juan	PR	00936	787-783-3000	
QUIKRETE Cos 3490 Piedmont Rd Ste 1300 *TF:* 800-282-5828 ■ *Web:* www.quikrete.com	Atlanta	GA	30305	404-634-9100	842-1424
Rancho Bldg Materials Co 4701 Wible Rd	Bakersfield	CA	93313	661-831-0831	831-0244
RCP Block & Brick Inc 8240 Broadway *TF:* 800-794-4727 ■ *Web:* www.rcpblock.com	Lemon Grove	CA	91945	619-460-7250	460-3926
Reading Precast Inc 5494 Pottsville Pike *TF:* 800-724-4881 ■ *Web:* www.readingprecast.com	Leesport	PA	19533	610-926-5000	926-0894
Reading Rock Inc 4600 Devitt Dr *TF:* 800-482-6466 ■ *Web:* www.readingrock.com	Cincinnati	OH	45246	513-874-2345	874-2520
RI Lampus Co 816 RI Lampus Ave PO Box 167 **Fax Area Code:* 724 ■ *TF:* 800-872-7310 ■ *Web:* www.lampus.com	Springdale	PA	15144	412-362-3800	274-2181*
Rinker Materials Corp Concrete Pipe Div 8311 W Carder Ct *TF:* 800-909-7763 ■ *Web:* www.rinkerpipe.com	Littleton	CO	80125	303-791-1600	791-1710
Rockwood Retaining Walls Inc 7200 Hwy 63 N **Fax Area Code:* 507 ■ *TF:* 800-535-2375 ■ *Web:* www.rockwoodwalls.com	Rochester	MN	55906	888-288-4045	529-2879*
Rolling Mix Management Ltd 7209 Railway St SE *Web:* www.rollingmix.com	Calgary	AB	T2H2V6	403-253-6426	
Rotondo Weirich Enterprises Inc 681 Harleysville Pk *Web:* www.rotondoweirich.com	Lederach	PA	19450	215-256-7940	
Royal Concrete Pipe Inc PO Box 430 *TF:* 800-817-3240 ■ *Web:* www.royalenterprises.net	Stacy	MN	55079	651-462-2130	462-6990
SD Ireland Co 193 Industrial Ave *TF:* 800-339-4565 ■ *Web:* www.sdireland.com	Williston	VT	05495	802-863-6222	
Selkirk Canada Corp 375 Green Rd *Web:* www.selkirkcorp.com	Stoney Creek	ON	L8E4A5	905-662-6600	
Seminole Precast Manufacturing Inc 331 Benson Junction Rd *Web:* www.seminoleprecast.com	Debary	FL	32713	386-668-7323	
Sequatchie Concrete Service Inc 406 Cedar Ave *TF:* 800-824-0824 ■ *Web:* www.seqconcrete.com	South Pittsburg	TN	37380	423-837-7913	837-7479
Silver State Materials LLC 4005 Dean Martin Dr *Web:* www.ssmaterials.com	Las Vegas	NV	89103	702-650-5000	
Smith-Midland Corp 5119 Catlett Rd PO Box 300 *OTC:* SMID ■ *Web:* www.smithmidland.com	Midland	VA	22728	540-439-3266	439-1232
Spancrete Industries Inc N 16 W 23415 Stone Ridge Dr PO Box 828 *Web:* www.spancrete.com	Waukesha	WI	53187	414-290-9000	290-9125
Specchem 444 Richmond Ave *Web:* www.specchemllc.com	Kansas City	KS	66101	913-371-8705	
Speed Fab-Crete Corp International PO Box 15580 *Web:* www.speedfab-crete.com	Fort Worth	TX	76119	817-478-1137	561-2544
StressCrete Group 9200 Energy Ln *Web:* www.stresscrete.com	Northport	AL	35476	205-339-0711	
Stubbe's Precast 30 Muir Line *TF:* 866-355-2183 ■ *Web:* www.stubbesprecast.org	Harley	ON	N0E1E0	519-424-2183	424-9058
Superlite Block Co Inc 4150 W Turney Ave *TF:* 800-366-7877 ■ *Web:* www.superliteblock.com	Phoenix	AZ	85019	602-352-3500	352-3813
Terre Hill Silo Company Inc PO Box 10 *TF:* 800-242-1509 ■ *Web:* www.terrehill.com	Terre Hill	PA	17581	717-445-3100	445-3108
Texas Concrete Co 4702 N Vine St *Web:* www.texasconcreteco.com	Victoria	TX	77904	361-573-9145	
Tindall Corp 3076 N Blackstock Rd PO Box 1778 *TF:* 800-849-4521 ■ *Web:* www.tindallcorp.com	Spartanburg	SC	29301	864-576-3230	587-8828
Trenwyth Industries Inc One Connely Rd PO Box 438 *TF Cust Svc:* 800-233-1924 ■ *Web:* www.trenwyth.com	Emigsville	PA	17318	717-767-6868	767-4023
Unistress Corp 550 Cheshire Rd *TF:* 800-927-9468 ■ *Web:* www.unistresscorp.com	Pittsfield	MA	01201	413-499-1441	499-9930
Universal Concrete Products Corp 400 Old Reading Pk Ste 100 *Web:* www.universalconcrete.com	Stowe	PA	19464	610-323-0700	323-4046
Utility Concrete Products 2495 Bungalow Rd *Web:* www.utilityconcrete.com	Morris	IL	60450	815-416-0900	
Valley Blox Inc 210 Stone Spring Rd **Fax:* Acctg ■ *TF:* 800-648-6725 ■ *Web:* valleybuildingsupply.com	Harrisonburg	VA	22801	540-434-6725	434-6514*
Verti-Crete LLC 16500 South 500 West *Web:* www.verti-crete.com	Bluffdale	UT	84065	801-571-2028	
Walters & Wolf Precast 41777 Boyce Rd *Web:* www.waltersandwolf.com	Fremont	CA	94538	510-226-9800	226-0360
Wausau Tile Inc PO Box 1520 *TF:* 800-388-8728 ■ *Web:* www.wausautile.com	Wausau	WI	54402	715-359-3121	355-4627
Wells Concrete Products Inc 835 Hwy 109 NE PO Box 308 *TF:* 800-658-7049 ■ *Web:* www.wellsconcrete.com	Wells	MN	56097	507-553-3138	553-6089
Western Architectural Services LLC 12552 South 125 West Ste B *Web:* www.western-architectural.com	Draper	UT	84020	801-523-0393	
Wieser Concrete Products Inc W3716 US Hwy 10 *TF:* 800-325-8456 ■ *Web:* www.wieserconcrete.com	Maiden Rock	WI	54750	715-647-2311	647-5181
Wingra Stone Co 2975 Kapec Rd PO Box 44284 *TF:* 800-249-6908 ■ *Web:* www.wingrastone.com	Madison	WI	53744	608-271-5555	271-3142
York Bldg Products Co 950 Smile Way *TF:* 800-673-2408 ■ *Web:* www.yorkbuilding.com	York	PA	17404	717-848-2831	854-9156

187 CONFERENCE & EVENTS COORDINATORS

Company	City	State	ZIP	Phone	Fax
Absolute Exhibits Inc 1382 Valencia Ave Ste H *Web:* www.absoluteexhibits.com	Tustin	CA	92780	714-685-2800	
Accent on Cincinnati 915 W Eigth St *Web:* www.accentcinti.com	Cincinnati	OH	45203	513-721-8687	721-1542
Aim Meetings & Events 212 S Henry St Fl 2 *Web:* www.aimmeetings.com	Alexandria	VA	22314	703-549-9500	
Amc Network LLC 825 Gravenstein Hwy N Ste 10 *Web:* www.amcnetwork.com	Sebastopol	CA	95472	707-829-9484	
Arata Expositions Inc 15928 Tournament Dr *Web:* www.arataexpo.com	Gaithersburg	MD	20877	301-921-0800	
ASD 6255 Sunset Blvd 19th Fl *TF:* 888-441-7575 ■ *Web:* www.asdonline.com	Los Angeles	CA	90028	323-817-2200	957-1131
Ashbury Images 1661 Tennessee St Ste 3 *Web:* www.ashburyimages.org	San Francisco	CA	94107	415-885-2742	
Ashton Gardens Houston 21919 Inverness Forest Blvd *Web:* www.ashtongardens.com	Houston	TX	77073	281-362-0011	
Ayers Meetings & Events Inc 19727 Whitewind Dr *Web:* www.ayersme.com	Houston	TX	77094	281-492-7272	
Bell Trans 1900 Industrial Rd *Web:* bell-trans.com	Las Vegas	NV	89102	702-739-7990	
Bixel & Co 8721 Sunset Blvd Ste 101 *Web:* www.bixelco.com	Los Angeles	CA	90069	310-854-3828	854-0115
Briggs Inc 1501 Broadway Ste 406 *Web:* www.briggsnyc.com	New York	NY	10036	212-354-9440	382-1560
Can-do Promotions Inc 6517 Wise Ave Nw *Web:* www.candopromo.com	North Canton	OH	44720	330-494-3527	
Cappa & Graham Inc 401 Terry A Francois Blvd Ste 128 *Web:* www.cappa-graham.com	San Francisco	CA	94158	415-512-6967	512-6982
Carlisle Productions Inc 1000 Bryn Mawr Rd *Web:* www.carlisleevents.com	Carlisle	PA	17013	717-243-7855	
Celebritees Inc 1014 Atlantic Ave *Web:* www.celebritees.net	Savannah	GA	31401	912-233-9941	
Centennial Conferences 901 Front St Ste 130 *Web:* www.centennialconferences.com	Louisville	CO	80027	303-499-2299	499-2599
COMCOR Event & Meeting Production 1040 Bayview Dr # 407 *Web:* www.comcorevents.com	Fort Lauderdale	FL	33304	954-491-3233	
Conference & Logistics Consultants Inc 31 Old Solomans Island Rd *Web:* www.gomeeting.com	Annapolis	MD	21401	410-571-0590	571-0592
Conference & Travel 5655 Coventry Ln *TF:* 800-346-9807 ■ *Web:* www.conftvl.com	Fort Wayne	IN	46804	260-434-6600	436-3177
Conference Consultants 445 El Escarpado	Stanford	CA	94305	650-324-1653	326-7751
Conference Group Inc 1580 Fishinger Rd	Columbus	OH	43221	614-488-2030	488-5747
Conference Hotels Unlimited 51 Harborview Rd *Web:* conferencehotels.com	Hull	MA	02045	781-925-4000	925-2474
Conference Management Assoc Inc 45 Lyme Rd Ste 304	Hanover	NH	03755	603-643-2325	643-1444
Conference Management Services PO Box 2506 *Web:* www.conferencemanagement.net	Monterey	CA	93942	831-622-7772	622-0711
Conference Solutions Inc 520 SW Yamhill St Ste 430 *Web:* www.conferencesolutionsinc.com	Portland	OR	97204	503-244-4294	244-2401
Convention Consultants Historic Savannah Foundation 117 W Perry St *Web:* www.conventionconsultants.net	Savannah	GA	31401	912-234-4088	
Copyworks 4837 First Ave Se Ste 103 *Web:* copyworks.com	Cedar Rapids	IA	52402	319-373-5335	
Courtesy Assoc 2025 M St NW Ste 800 *TF:* 800-647-4689 ■ *Web:* www.courtesyassociates.com	Washington	DC	20036	800-647-4689	

Company	City	State	ZIP	Phone	Fax
Creative Impact Group Inc 801 Skokie Blvd Ste 108 *TF:* 800-445-2171 ■ *Web:* www.creativeimpactgroup.com	Northbrook	IL	60062	847-945-7401	945-7405
Crescent City Consultants 1010 Common St Ste 3010 *Web:* www.ccc-nola.com	New Orleans	LA	70112	504-561-1191	568-0783
CSI Worldwide Inc 40 Regency Plz *Web:* www.csiworldwide.net	Glen Mills	PA	19342	610-558-4500	
D & L Entertainment Services Inc 4120 Main St *Web:* dandlentertainment.com	Dallas	TX	75226	214-634-0757	
Destination Resources 5435 Balboa Blvd Ste 106 *TF:* 800-422-6524 ■ *Web:* www.destinationresources.com	Encino	CA	91316	818-995-7915	990-6129
Destination Services of Colorado Inc (DSC) PO Box 3660 *TF:* 800-372-7686 ■ *Web:* www.dsc-co.com	Avon	CO	81620	970-476-6565	
Eagle Recognition 2706 Mtn Industrial Blvd Ste 300 *Web:* www.eaglerecognition.com	Tucker	GA	30084	770-985-0808	
Event Planning International Corp 10900 Granite St *TF:* 800-940-2164 ■ *Web:* www.epicreg.com	Charlotte	NC	28273	980-233-3777	233-3800
Every Promotional Product 30401 Agoura Rd Ste 102 *Web:* www.everypromotionalproduct.com	Agoura Hills	CA	91301	818-597-9900	
Excel Decorators Inc 3748 Kentucky Ave *Web:* lexusbadexperiences.com	Indianapolis	IN	46221	317-856-1300	
Executive Arrangements 2460 Fairmount Blvd Ste 205 *Web:* www.executivearrangements.com	Cleveland	OH	44106	216-231-9311	
Exhibit Concepts Inc 700 Crossroads Ct *Web:* www.exhibitconcepts.com	Vandalia	OH	45377	937-890-7000	
Exhibits Development Group LLC Landmark Ctr 432 75 W Fifth St *Web:* www.exhibitsdevelopment.com	Saint Paul	MN	55102	651-222-1121	
Experient Inc 2500 E Enterprise Pkwy *Web:* www.experient-inc.com	Twinsburg	OH	44087	330-425-8333	425-3299
Expo Group, The 5931 W Campus Cir Dr *TF:* 800-736-7775 ■ *Web:* www.theexpogroup.com	Irving	TX	75063	972-580-9000	550-7877
ExpoMarketing LLC 2741 Dow Ave *Web:* www.expomarketing.com	Tustin	CA	92780	949-250-3976	
Fotofest Inc 1113 Vine St Ste 101 *Web:* www.fotofest.org	Houston	TX	77002	713-223-5522	
Freddie Georges Production Group 5595 Fresca Dr *Web:* www.freddiegeorges.com	La Palma	CA	90623	714-367-9260	
Freeman Cos 1600 Viceroy Ste 100 *Web:* www.freemanco.com	Dallas	TX	75235	214-445-1000	445-0200
Gavel International Corp 300 Tri State International Ste 320 *TF:* 800-544-2835 ■ *Web:* www.gavelintl.com	Lincolnshire	IL	60069	847-945-8150	945-6569
Genuity Concepts Inc 507 N Church St *Web:* www.genuityconcepts.com	Greensboro	NC	27401	336-379-1850	
GES Exposition Services 7000 Lindell Rd *TF:* 800-443-9767 ■ *Web:* www.ges.com	Las Vegas	NV	89118	702-515-5500	515-5765
Gls Group Inc 27850 Detroit Rd *Web:* glsgroup.com	Westlake	OH	44145	440-899-7770	
Graphic Creations Inc 1809 Lk Ave Ste B *Web:* www.graphiccreations.com	Knoxville	TN	37916	865-522-6221	
Graylyn International Conference Center Inc 1900 Reynolda Rd *Web:* graylyn.com	Winston Salem	NC	27106	336-758-2600	
Great Events & TEAMS Inc 2170 S Parker Rd Ste 290 *TF:* 866-706-7814 ■ *Web:* www.geteams.com	Denver	CO	80231	303-394-2022	394-3450
GT Consultants Inc 3050 Eagle Watch Dr *Web:* www.gtconsultantsinc.com	Woodstock	GA	30189	770-591-1343	
Gtcbio 635 W Foothill Blvd *Web:* gtcbio.com	Monrovia	CA	91016	626-256-6405	
Hartford York 2615 Boeing Way *Web:* www.hartfordyork.com	Stockton	CA	95206	209-982-5462	
Harvey-daco Inc 1370 Pantheon Way Ste 154 *Web:* harvey-daco.com	San Antonio	TX	78232	210-499-4040	
Health Connect Partners Inc 65 Business Park Dr *Web:* www.hlthcp.com	Lebanon	TN	37090	615-449-6234	
Henry V Events 6360 NE ML K Jr Blvd *Web:* www.henryvevents.com	Portland	OR	97211	503-232-6666	
Holiday Models Convention Services 3651 Lindell Rd Ste D140 *Web:* www.holidaymodels.com	Las Vegas	NV	89103	702-373-7039	796-5676
Hughes Production 1625 Berger Ln PO Box 3556 *Web:* www.hughesproduction.com	Jackson	WY	83001	307-733-6505	733-0542
Idegy 3990 Business Park Dr *Web:* idegy.com	Columbus	OH	43204	614-545-5000	
IDG World Expo Three Speen St Ste 320 *Web:* www.idgworldexpo.com	Framingham	MA	01701	508-879-6700	620-6668
Incentive Travel & Meetings (ITM) 970 Clementstone Dr Ste 100 *Web:* www.usaitm.com	Atlanta	GA	30342	404-252-2728	252-8328
International Meeting Managers Inc 4550 Post Oak Pl Ste 342 *TF:* 800-423-7175 ■ *Web:* www.meetingmanagers.com	Houston	TX	77027	713-965-0566	960-0488
International Trade Information Inc (ITI) 900 Las Vegas Blvd S Unit 908 *Web:* www.internationaltradeinformation.com	Las Vegas	NV	89101	818-591-2255	591-2289
Ivey Performance Marketing LLC 5679 SE International Way *Web:* www.ivey.com	Portland	OR	97222	503-794-9800	
JBW Entertainment LLC 2465 S Industrial Park Ave Ste 3 *Web:* www.koolpartyrentals.com	Phoenix	AZ	85282	623-434-8822	
Kerry Group LLC, The 44 Soccer Park Rd *Web:* www.kerrygroup.net	Fenton	MO	63026	636-203-5550	
Key Event Group LLC, The 3815 Hilldale Dr *Web:* www.nashvilledmc.com	Nashville	TN	37215	615-352-6900	385-4976
LEO Events 265 S Front St *Web:* www.leoevents.com	Memphis	TN	38103	901-766-1836	
Lydon Co 143 St Clair Dr	Saint Simons Island	GA	31522	912-638-0901	638-2451
Lynnwood Convention Center 3711 196th St Sw *Web:* lynnwoodcc.com	Lynnwood	WA	98036	425-778-7155	
Management International Inc 1828 SE First Ave **Fax Area Code:* 800 ■ *Web:* www.currentreviews.com	Fort Lauderdale	FL	33316	954-763-8003	425-1995*
Maxcel Co 6600 LBJ Fwy Ste 109 *Web:* www.maxcel.net	Dallas	TX	75240	972-644-0880	680-2488
Meeting Alliance LLC Bank Plz 14 Main St *Web:* www.meetingalliance.com	Robbinsville	NJ	08691	609-208-1908	
Meeting Connection Inc, The 893 High St *TF:* 800-398-2568 ■ *Web:* www.the-meeting-connection.com	Worthington	OH	43085	614-888-2568	888-1684
Meeting Services Unlimited 135 S Mitthoeffer Rd *Web:* www.conventionmanagers.com	Indianapolis	IN	46229	317-841-7171	578-0621
Meetings & Incentives Group 21760 Stevens Creek Blvd *Web:* www.migr.com	Cupertino	CA	95014	408-973-1915	973-9712
Mirror Show Management Inc 855 Hard Rd *Web:* www.mirrorshow.com	Webster	NY	14580	585-232-4020	
MP Assoc Inc 1721 Boxelder St Ste 107 *Web:* www.mpassociates.com	Louisville	CO	80027	303-530-4562	530-4334
National Trade Productions Inc 313 S Patrick St *TF:* 800-687-7469 ■ *Web:* www.ntpshow.com	Alexandria	VA	22314	703-683-8500	836-4486
Nceca 77 Erie Village Sq Unit 280 *Web:* nceca.net	Erie	CO	80516	303-828-2811	
Omnience Inc 1350 Center Dr Ste 100 *Web:* www.meetingconsultants.com	Atlanta	GA	30338	770-399-3199	
On the Scene 500 N Dearborn St Ste 550 *Web:* www.onthescenechicago.com	Chicago	IL	60654	312-661-1440	
Ones We Love Inc 3901 Westerly Pl Ste 205 *Web:* www.owlus.com	Newport Beach	CA	92660	714-658-1033	
Pacific Agenda 2425 NW Overton St	Portland	OR	97210	503-223-8633	
Paramount Convention Services Inc 5015 Fyler Ave *Web:* www.paramountcs.com	Saint Louis	MO	63139	314-621-6677	
Pat Hoey Productions 167 Auburn St *Web:* www.thebostonhomeshow.com	Auburn	MA	01501	508-832-3300	
Paulette Wolf Events & Entertainment Inc 1165 N Clark St Ste 613 *Web:* www.pwe-e.com	Chicago	IL	60610	312-981-2600	
Pearson & Pipkin Inc 1101 Pennsylvania Ave SE Ste 201	Washington	DC	20003	202-547-7177	
Pearson Group 904 Princess Anne St *Web:* pearsonplanners.com	Fredericksburg	VA	22401	540-373-4493	
Pittcon 300 Penn Ctr Blvd Ste 332 *Web:* www.pittcon.org	Pittsburgh	PA	15235	412-825-3220	
Prestige Accommodations International 1231 E Dyer Rd Ste 240 *TF:* 800-321-6338 ■ *Web:* www.meetingplanners.com	Santa Ana	CA	92705	714-957-9100	957-9112
Productions USA Inc 1960 N Lincoln Pk W *Web:* www.productionsusa.com	Chicago	IL	60614	773-296-6200	296-6333
Proteus On-Demand Facilities LLC 6727 Oak Ridge Commerce Way SW *Web:* www.proteusondemand.com	Austell	GA	30168	770-333-1886	
QVC Inscript 210 Rue Lee *Web:* qvc.qc.ca	Quebec	QC	G1K2K6	418-523-1371	
Recourse Communications Inc 112 Intracoastal Pointe Dr *Web:* www.rcirecruitmentsolutions.com	Jupiter	FL	33477	561-686-6800	
Resource Connection Inc 161 S Main St *TF:* 800-649-5228 ■ *Web:* www.resource-connection.com	Middleton	MA	01949	978-777-9333	777-3360
Reverse Logistics Trends Inc 441 West Main St Ste D *Web:* www.reverselogisticstrends.com	Lehi	UT	84043	801-331-8949	
Robustelli Corporate Services 1717 Newfield Ave *Web:* www.rcsltd.com	Stamford	CT	06903	203-322-2790	912-6487
RX Worldwide Meetings Inc 3060 Communications Pkwy Ste 200 *TF:* 800-562-1713 ■ *Web:* www.rx-worldwide.net	Plano	TX	75093	214-291-2920	291-2930
S.A.F.E. Management LLC Arizona 1 Cardinals Dr *Web:* www.safemanagement.net	Glendale	AZ	85305	623-433-7300	
Sand Assoc 3560 Green St *Web:* www.sandassociates.com	Harrisburg	PA	17110	717-238-5558	238-4626
Schneider Group 5400 Bosque Blvd Ste 680 *Web:* www.sgmeet.com	Waco	TX	76710	254-776-3550	776-3767
Seattle Hospitality Group 16 W Harrison St Second Fl *Web:* www.seattlehospitality.com	Seattle	WA	98119	206-623-2090	623-2540
Secretariat PO Box 3509 *Web:* www.secevents.com	Wilmington	DE	19807	302-654-4479	654-4117
Shepard Exposition Services 1531 Carroll Dr NW *Web:* www.shepardes.com	Atlanta	GA	30318	404-720-8600	720-8750
Shreveport Convention Center 400 Caddo St *Web:* shreveportcenter.com	Shreveport	LA	71101	318-841-4000	
Splash!events Inc 210 Hillsdale Ave *Web:* www.splashevents.com	San Jose	CA	95136	408-287-8600	
Steven Restivo Event Services LLC 805 Fourth St Ste 8 *Web:* www.sresproductions.com	San Rafael	CA	94901	415-456-6455	
T3 Expo LLC Eight Lakeville Business Park Unit 1 *TF:* 888-698-3397 ■ *Web:* www.t3expo.com	Lakeville	MA	02347	888-698-3397	

	City	State	Zip	Phone	Fax
TBA Global LLC 220 W 42nd St 10th Fl *Web:* tbaglobal.com	New York	NY	10036	646-445-7000	445-7001
Transeair Travel LLC 2813 McKinley Pl NW *Web:* www.transeairtravel.com	Washington	DC	20015	202-362-6100	362-7411
Travizon Meeting Management 275 Mishawum Rd Ste 300 *TF:* 800-423-2500 ■ *Web:* www.travizon.com	Woburn	MA	01801	888-781-5200	
Universal Odyssey Inc 1601 Dove St Ste 260 *Web:* www.universalodyssey.com	Newport Beach	CA	92660	949-263-1222	263-0983
Van Winkle & Associates Inc 1180 W Peachtree St Nw Ste 400 *Web:* www.vanwinkleassociates.com	Atlanta	GA	30309	404-355-0126	
Vega Group 7220 Washington Ave *TF:* 800-771-2979 ■ *Web:* www.vegagroup.com	New Orleans	LA	70125	504-488-5222	488-5214
Vista Convention Services Inc 6804 Delilah Rd *Web:* www.vistacs.com	Egg Harbor Township	NJ	08234	609-485-2421	
Westbury National Show Systems Ltd 772 Warden Ave *Web:* www.westbury.com	Toronto	ON	M1L4T7	416-752-1371	
Weston & Assoc Inc 110 Thomas St *Web:* www.westoninc.com	Winston-Salem	NC	27101	336-725-1147	725-0551
Willwork Inc 23 Norfolk Ave *Web:* www2.willworkinc.com	South Easton	MA	02375	508-230-3170	
Wilsonwest Inc 1601 Dolores St *Web:* www.wilsonwest.com	San Francisco	CA	94110	415-282-4560	
Wings Unlimited Inc 455 Post Rd Ste 102 *Web:* www.wingsunlimited.net	Darien	CT	06820	203-656-9591	656-1141

188 CONGLOMERATES

SEE ALSO Holding Companies p. 2459

A business conglomerate is defined here as a corporation that consists of many business units in different industries.

	City	State	Zip	Phone	Fax
3M Co 3M Ctr Bldg 225-3S-06 *NYSE: MMM* ■ **Fax:* Mail Rm ■ *TF:* 800-364-3577 ■ *Web:* www.3m.com	Saint Paul	MN	55144	651-733-1110	733-9973*
Aerojet Rocketdyne Holdings Inc Hwy 50 & Aerojet Rd PO Box 537012 *NYSE: GY* ■ *Web:* www.GenCorp.com	Rancho Cordova	CA	95742	916-355-4000	
Alexander & Baldwin Inc 822 Bishop St *NYSE: ALEX* ■ *TF:* 800-454-0477 ■ *Web:* www.alexanderbaldwin.com	Honolulu	HI	96813	808-525-6611	525-6652
Alleghany Corp Seven Times Sq Tower *NYSE: Y* ■ *Web:* www.alleghany.com	New York	NY	10036	212-752-1356	759-8149
Alticor Inc 7575 Fulton St E **Fax:* Hum Res ■ *Web:* www.alticor.com	Ada	MI	49355	616-787-1000	787-4764*
Altria Group Inc 6601 W Broad St *NYSE: MO* ■ *Web:* www.altria.com	Richmond	VA	23230	804-274-2200	484-8231
AMERCO 1325 Airmotive Way Ste 100 *NASDAQ: UHAL* ■ *Web:* www.amerco.com	Reno	NV	89502	775-688-6300	688-6338
Andersons Inc 480 W Dussel Dr *NASDAQ: ANDE* ■ **Fax:* Hum Res ■ *TF:* 800-537-3370 ■ *Web:* www.andersonsinc.com	Maumee	OH	43537	419-893-5050	891-6393*
APi Group Inc 1100 Old Hwy 8 NW **Fax Area Code:* 651 ■ *TF:* 800-223-4922 ■ *Web:* www.apigroupinc.com	New Brighton	MN	55112	800-223-4922	636-0312*
ARAMARK Corp 1101 Market St *TF:* 800-388-3300 ■ *Web:* www.aramark.com	Philadelphia	PA	19107	937-660-4708	
Archer Daniels Midland Co (ADM) 4666 E Faries Pkwy *NYSE: ADM* ■ **Fax:* PR ■ *TF:* 800-637-5843 ■ *Web:* www.adm.com	Decatur	IL	62526	217-424-5200	424-5580*
Ashland Inc 50 E River Ctr Blvd PO Box 391 *NYSE: ASH* ■ *TF:* 877-546-2782 ■ *Web:* www.ashland.com	Covington	KY	41012	859-815-3333	815-3559
Ball Corp 10 Longs Peak Dr *NYSE: BLL* ■ **Fax:* Sales ■ *Web:* www.ball.com	Broomfield	CO	80021	303-469-3131	460-5256*
Berkshire Hathaway Inc 3555 Farnam St Ste 1440 *NYSE: BRK/A* ■ *TF:* 800-223-2064 ■ *Web:* www.berkshirehathaway.com	Omaha	NE	68131	402-346-1400	346-3375
Berwind Group 1500 Market St 3000 Ctr Sq W *Web:* www.berwind.com	Philadelphia	PA	19102	215-563-2800	575-2314
BFC Financial Corp 401 E Las Olas Blvd Ste 800 *OTC: BFCF* ■ *Web:* www.bfcfinancial.com	Fort Lauderdale	FL	33301	954-940-4994	940-5320
Brown-Forman Corp 850 Dixie Hwy PO Box 1080 *NYSE: BFB* ■ *TF:* 800-831-9146 ■ *Web:* www.brown-forman.com	Louisville	KY	40210	502-585-1100	774-7188
Canadian Tire Corp Ltd 2180 Yonge St PO Box 770 Stn K *TSE: CTC* ■ *TF:* 800-387-8803 ■ *Web:* www.corp.canadiantire.ca	Toronto	ON	M4P2V8	416-480-3000	544-7715
Carlson Cos Inc 701 Carlson Pkwy *Web:* www.carlson.com	Minnetonka	MN	55305	763-212-5000	
Chemed Corp 255 E Fifth St Ste 2600 *NYSE: CHE* ■ *TF General:* 800-982-7650 ■ *Web:* www.chemed.com	Cincinnati	OH	45202	513-762-6900	
Clorox Co 1221 Broadway *NYSE: CLX* ■ *TF Cust Svc:* 800-424-9300 ■ *Web:* www.thecloroxcompany.com	Oakland	CA	94612	510-271-7000	832-1463
CSX Corp 500 Water St 15th Fl *NYSE: CSX* ■ *Web:* csx.com	Jacksonville	FL	32202	904-359-3200	
Deere & Co One John Deere Pl *NYSE: DE* ■ *Web:* www.deere.com	Moline	IL	61265	309-765-8000	765-4609
Delaware North Cos Inc 40 Fountain Plz *TF:* 800-828-7240 ■ *Web:* www.delawarenorth.com	Buffalo	NY	14202	716-858-5000	858-5266
Deseret Management Corp 55 N 300 W Ste 800 *Web:* www.deseretmanagement.com	Salt Lake City	UT	84101	801-538-0651	517-4600
Dover Corp 3005 Highland Pkwy Ste 200 *NYSE: DOV* ■ *Web:* www.dovercorporation.com	Downers Grove	IL	60515	630-541-1540	743-2671
Dyson-Kissner-Moran Corp (DKM) 565 Fifth Ave Fourth Fl *Web:* www.dkmcorp.com	New York	NY	10017	212-661-4600	986-7169
EBSCO Industries Inc 5724 Hwy 280 *TF:* 800-527-5901 ■ *Web:* www.ebscoind.com	Birmingham	AL	35242	205-991-6600	995-1636
Empire Company Ltd 115 King St *TSE: EMP.A* ■ *Web:* www.empireco.ca	Stellarton	NS	B0K1S0	902-755-4440	755-6477
Federal Signal Corp 1415 W 22nd St Ste 1100 *NYSE: FSS* ■ *Web:* www.federalsignal.com	Oak Brook	IL	60523	630-954-2000	954-2030
FirstService Corp 1140 Bay St First Service Bldg Ste 4000 *TSE: FSV* ■ *Web:* www.firstservice.com	Toronto	ON	M5S2B4	416-960-9500	960-5333
Fortune Brands Inc 520 Lk Cook Rd *NYSE: FBHS* ■ *TF:* 800-225-2719 ■ *Web:* www.fortunebrands.com	Deerfield	IL	60015	847-484-4400	
Griffon Corp 712 Fifth Ave 18th Fl *NYSE: GFF* ■ *Web:* www.griffoncorp.com	New York	NY	10019	212-957-5000	957-5040
Hallwood Group Inc 3710 Rawlins St Ste 1500 *NYSE: HWG* ■ *Web:* www.hallwood.com	Dallas	TX	75219	214-528-5588	528-8855
Harsco Corp 350 Poplar Church Rd *NYSE: HSC* ■ *TF:* 866-470-3900 ■ *Web:* www.harsco.com	Camp Hill	PA	17011	717-763-7064	763-6424
Hitachi America Ltd 50 Prospect Ave *TF:* 800-448-2244 ■ *Web:* www.hitachi.com	Tarrytown	NY	10591	914-332-5800	332-5555
Holiday Cos 4567 American Blvd W PO Box 1224 *TF:* 800-745-7411 ■ *Web:* www.holidaystationstores.com	Bloomington	MN	55437	952-830-8700	
HT Hackney Co 502 S Gay St PO Box 238 *TF:* 800-406-1291 ■ *Web:* www.hthackney.com	Knoxville	TN	37901	865-546-1291	
IAC/InterActiveCorp 555 W 18th St *NASDAQ: IACI* ■ *Web:* www.iac.com	New York	NY	10011	212-314-7300	314-7309
iHeartMedia, Inc 200 E Basse Rd *TF:* 888-283-6901 ■ *Web:* www.iheartmedia.com	San Antonio	TX	78209	210-822-2828	
Intermec Inc 6001 36th Ave W *NYSE: IN* ■ *TF:* 800-755-5505 ■ *Web:* www.intermec.com	Everett	WA	98203	425-348-2600	267-2983
Jim Pattison Group 1067 W Cordova St Ste 1800 *Web:* www.jimpattison.com	Vancouver	BC	V6C1C7	604-688-6764	687-2601
Johnson & Johnson One Johnson & Johnson Plz *NYSE: JNJ* ■ *TF:* 800-565-0122 ■ *Web:* www.jnj.com	New Brunswick	NJ	08933	732-524-0400	214-0332
Jordan Industries Inc (JII) 1751 Lake Cook Rd Ste 550	Deerfield	IL	60015	847-945-5591	945-5698
Kaman Corp PO Box 1 *NYSE: KAMN* ■ *Web:* www.kaman.com	Bloomfield	CT	06002	860-243-7100	
Kimball International Inc 1600 Royal St *NASDAQ: KBAL* ■ **Fax:* Hum Res ■ *TF:* 800-482-1616 ■ *Web:* www.kimball.com	Jasper	IN	47549	812-482-1600	*
Kluge & Co 810 Seventh Ave Ste 29	New York	NY	10019	212-606-4400	606-4337
Koch Enterprises Inc 14 S 11th Ave *Web:* www.kochenterprises.com	Evansville	IN	47712	812-465-9800	465-9613
Koch Industries Inc PO Box 2256 *Web:* www.kochind.com	Wichita	KS	67201	316-828-3756	
Kohler Co Inc 444 Highland Dr **Fax:* Mktg ■ *TF:* 800-456-4537 ■ *Web:* kohler.com	Kohler	WI	53044	920-457-4441	459-1826*
Kraus-Anderson Co (KA) 523 S Eigth St *TF:* 888-547-3983 ■ *Web:* www.krausanderson.com	Minneapolis	MN	55404	612-305-2934	332-0217
Lancaster Colony Corp 37 W Broad St *NASDAQ: LANC* ■ *Web:* www.lancastercolony.com	Columbus	OH	43215	614-224-7141	
Larry H Miller Group 9350 S 150 E Ste 1000 *Web:* www.lhm.com	Sandy	UT	84070	801-563-4100	264-3198
LDI Ltd 54 Monument Cir Ste 800 *Web:* www.ldiltd.com	Indianapolis	IN	46204	317-237-5400	237-2280
Leucadia National Corp 315 Pk Ave S 20th Fl *NYSE: LUK* ■ *Web:* www.leucadia.com	New York	NY	10010	212-460-1900	598-4869
LGL Group Inc, The 2525 Shader Rd *NYSE: LGL* ■ *Web:* www.lglgroup.com	Orlando	FL	32804	407-298-2000	
Loews Corp 667 Madison Ave **Fax:* Mktg ■ *TF:* 800-235-6397 ■ *Web:* www.loews.com	New York	NY	10065	212-521-2000	*
MacAndrews & Forbes Holdings Inc 35 E 62nd St *Web:* www.macandrewsandforbes.com	New York	NY	10065	212-572-8600	572-8400
Marmon Group LLC, The 181 W Madison St 26th Fl *Web:* www.marmon.com	Chicago	IL	60602	312-372-9500	845-5305
Mars Inc 6885 Elm St *Web:* www.mars.com	McLean	VA	22101	703-821-4900	448-9678
MAXXAM Inc 1330 Post Oak Blvd Ste 2000 *OTC: MAXX* ■ **Fax:* Hum Res ■ *Web:* charleshurwitz.com	Houston	TX	77056	713-975-7600	267-3701*
McRae Industries Inc PO Box 1239 *Web:* www.mcraeindustries.com	Mount Gilead	NC	27306	910-439-6147	439-4190
MDU Resources Group Inc 1200 W Century Ave PO Box 5650 *NYSE: MDU* ■ *TF:* 866-760-4852 ■ *Web:* www.mdu.com	Bismarck	ND	58506	701-530-1000	222-7607
NACCO Industries Inc 5875 Landerbrook Dr Ste 300 *NYSE: NC* ■ *TF:* 877-756-5118 ■ *Web:* www.nacco.com	Cleveland	OH	44124	440-449-9600	
NESCO Inc 6140 Parkland Blvd *Web:* nescoresource.com	Mayfield Heights	OH	44124	440-461-6000	449-3111
Newell Rubbermaid Inc Three Glenlake Pkwy *NYSE: NWL* ■ *TF:* 800-752-9677 ■ *Web:* www.newellrubbermaid.com	Atlanta	GA	30328	770-418-7000	677-8662
Olin Corp 190 Carondelet Plz Ste 1530 *NYSE: OLN* ■ *Web:* www.olin.com	Clayton	MO	63105	314-480-1400	
Onex Corp 161 Bay St PO Box 700 *Web:* www.onex.com	Toronto	ON	M5J2S1	416-362-7711	362-5765
Oxbow Corp 1601 Forum Pl Ste 1400 **Fax:* Hum Res ■ *Web:* www.oxbow.com	West Palm Beach	FL	33401	561-697-4300	697-1876*
PepsiCo Inc 700 Anderson Hill Rd *NYSE: PEP* ■ *TF PR:* 800-433-2652 ■ *Web:* www.pepsico.com	Purchase	NY	10577	914-253-2000	253-2070
Procter & Gamble Co (PG) 1 Procter & Gamble Plaza *NYSE: PG* ■ *Web:* www.pg.com	Cincinnati	OH	45202	513-983-1100	
Raleigh Enterprises 5300 Melrose Ave 4th Fl *Web:* www.raleighenterprises.com	Hollywood	CA	90038	310-899-8900	899-8910
RB Pamplin Corp 805 SW Broadway *Web:* www.pamplin.org	Portland	OR	97205	503-248-1133	
Renco Group 1 Rockefeller Plaza # 29 *Web:* www.rencogroup.net	New York	NY	10020	212-541-6000	541-6197

	City	State	Zip	Phone	Fax
Roll International Corp 11444 W Olympic Blvd 10th Fl *Web:* www.roll.com	Los Angeles	CA	90064	310-966-5700	914-4747
Rowan Companies 2800 Postoak Blvd Ste 5450 *NYSE: RDC* ■ *Web:* www.rowancompanies.com	Houston	TX	77056	713-621-7800	
Sammons Enterprises Inc 5949 Sherry Ln Ste 1900 *Web:* www.sammonsenterprises.com	Dallas	TX	75225	214-210-5000	210-5099
Seaboard Corp 9000 W 67th St *NYSE: SEB* ■ *TF:* 866-676-8886 ■ *Web:* www.seaboardcorp.com	Shawnee Mission	KS	66202	913-676-8800	676-8872
Siemens Corp 527 Madison Ave Ste 8 **Fax:* Mktg ■ *TF:* 800-743-6367 ■ *Web:* www.usa.siemens.com	New York	NY	10022	212-258-4000	258-4099*
Standex International Corp 11 Keewaydin Dr *NYSE: SXI* ■ *TF:* 800-514-5275 ■ *Web:* www.standex.com	Salem	NH	03079	603-893-9701	893-7324
Sten Corp 13828 Lincoln St NE *TF:* 800-328-7958 ■ *Web:* www.stencorporation.com	Ham Lake	MN	55304	952-545-2776	545-2795
Tang Industries Inc 8960 Spanish Ridge Ave *Web:* nmlp.com	Las Vegas	NV	89148	702-734-3700	
TECO Energy Inc 702 N Franklin St *NYSE: TE* ■ *Web:* tecoenergy.com	Tampa	FL	33602	813-228-1111	228-1670
Teleflex Inc 155 S Limerick Rd *NYSE: TFX* ■ *TF:* 866-246-6990 ■ *Web:* www.teleflex.com	Limerick	PA	19468	610-948-5100	
Textron Inc 40 Westminster St *NYSE: TXT* ■ *Web:* www.textron.com	Providence	RI	02903	401-421-2800	
Time Warner Inc One Time Warner Ctr *NYSE: TWX* ■ *Web:* www.timewarner.com	New York	NY	10019	212-484-8000	
Topa Equities Ltd 1800 Ave of the Stars Ste 1400 *Web:* www.topa.com	Los Angeles	CA	90067	310-203-9199	229-9788
Trinity Industries Inc 2525 Stemmons Fwy *NYSE: TRN* ■ *TF:* 800-631-4420 ■ *Web:* www.trin.net	Dallas	TX	75207	214-631-4420	589-8501
United Services Automobile Assn (USAA) 10750 McDermott Fwy *TF:* 800-531-8722 ■ *Web:* www.usaa.com	San Antonio	TX	78288	800-531-8722	531-5717
United Technologies Corp One Financial Plz *NYSE: UTX* ■ **Fax:* Hum Res ■ *Web:* www.utc.com	Hartford	CT	06103	860-728-7000	728-7028*
Universal Corp 9201 Forest Hill Ave PO Box 25099 *NYSE: UVV* ■ *Web:* www.universalcorp.com	Richmond	VA	23260	804-359-9311	254-3582
Valhi Inc 5430 LBJ Fwy Ste 1700 3 Lincoln Ctr *NYSE: VHI* ■ **Fax:* Acctg ■ *Web:* www.valhi.net	Dallas	TX	75240	972-233-1700	448-1445*
Viacom Inc 1515 Broadway 52nd Fl *NASDAQ: VIAB* ■ *Web:* www.viacom.com	New York	NY	10036	212-258-6000	258-6100
Viad Corp 1850 N Central Ave Ste 800 *NYSE: VVI* ■ **Fax:* Hum Res ■ *Web:* www.viad.com	Phoenix	AZ	85004	602-207-4000	207-5455*
Walt Disney Co 500 S Buena Vista St *NYSE: DIS* ■ **Fax:* Mail Rm ■ *Web:* thewaltdisneycompany.com	Burbank	CA	91521	818-560-1000	553-7210*
Watkins Associated Industries 1958 Monroe Dr NE	Atlanta	GA	30324	404-872-3841	
Wesco Financial Corp 301 E Colorado Blvd Ste 300 *CVE: WSC* ■ *Web:* www.wescofinancial.com	Pasadena	CA	91101	626-585-6700	449-1455
Weyerhaeuser Co 33663 Weyerhaeuser Way S *NYSE: WY* ■ *TF:* 800-525-5440 ■ *Web:* www.weyerhaeuser.com	Federal Way	WA	98003	253-924-2345	924-2685
Wirtz Corp 680 N Lk Shore Dr Ste 1900 *Web:* wirtzinsurance.com	Chicago	IL	60611	312-943-7000	943-9017

189 CONSTRUCTION - BUILDING CONTRACTORS - NON-RESIDENTIAL

	City	State	Zip	Phone	Fax
1st Choice Facilities Services Corp 1941 Whitfield Park Loop *TF:* 866-241-0070 ■ *Web:* 1stchoicecorp.com	Sarasota	FL	34243	866-241-0070	
3LK Construction LLC 18401 Weaver St *Web:* www.3lkconstruction.com	Detroit	MI	48228	313-493-9101	
4 Sight Inc 135 Fifth Ave *Web:* www.4sightinc.com	New York	NY	10010	212-253-0525	
A & E Construction Co 152 Garrett Rd *Web:* www.aeconstruction.com	Upper Darby	PA	19082	610-449-3152	449-6325
A D Morgan Corp, The 716 N Renellie Dr *Web:* www.admorgan.com	Tampa	FL	33609	813-832-3033	831-9860
A J Martini Inc Five Lowell Ave *Web:* www.ajmartini.com	Winchester	MA	01890	781-569-6900	
A Morton Thomas & Associates Inc 800 King Farm Blvd Fourth Fl *Web:* www.amtengineering.com	Rockville	MD	20850	301-881-2545	
A R Mays Construction Inc 6900 E Indian School Rd Ste 200 *Web:* www.armays.com	Scottsdale	AZ	85251	480-850-6900	
A Ruiz Construction Company & Assoc Inc 1601 Cortland Ave *Web:* www.aruizconstruction.com	San Francisco	CA	94110	415-647-4010	
A.O.W. Associates Inc 30 Essex St *Web:* aowassoc.com	Albany	NY	12206	518-482-3400	
AAPCO Southeast Inc 506 Webb Rd *Web:* www.aapcogroup.com	Concord	NC	28025	704-784-2690	
Abhe & Svoboda Inc 18100 Dairy Ln *Web:* www.abheonline.com	Jordan	MN	55352	952-447-6025	
Abide International Inc 561 First St W *Web:* www.abideinternational.com	Sonoma	CA	95476	707-935-1577	
Abrams Construction Inc Seven Kent St Ste 2 *TF:* 800-935-9350 ■ *Web:* www.abrams-properties.com	Brookline	MA	02445	617-566-9090	566-9098
Absher Construction Company Inc 1001 Shaw Rd *Web:* absherco.com	Puyallup	WA	98372	253-845-9544	841-0925
Accrete Construction LLC 801 Valley Ave NW *Web:* www.bpci.net	Puyallup	WA	98371	253-922-3399	
ACS Development Corporation Inc 16148 Sand Canyon Ave *Web:* www.acsirvine.com	Irvine	CA	92618	949-263-1920	
Adamo Construction Inc 11980 Woodside Ave Ste 5 *Web:* www.adamoconstruction.com	Lakeside	CA	92040	619-390-6706	
Adler Group Inc 1400 NW 107 Ave *Web:* www.adlergroup.com	Miami	FL	33172	305-392-4000	
Adolfson & Peterson Construction Inc 6701 W 23rd St *Web:* www.a-p.com	Minneapolis	MN	55426	952-544-1561	525-2333
Advanced Industrial Services Inc 3250 Susquehanna Trial *TF:* 800-544-5080 ■ *Web:* www.ais-york.com	York	PA	17406	717-764-9811	764-3144
Aecon Buildings Inc 19020 33rd Ave W Ste 500 *Web:* www.usa.aecon.com	Lynnwood	WA	98036	425-774-2945	
Aecon Group Inc Ste 800 20 Carlson Ct *Web:* www.aecon.com	Toronto	ON	M9W7K6	416-293-7004	
Aerie Inc 139 S Guild Ave Ste 101 *Web:* www.aerieinc.com	Lodi	CA	95240	209-339-9751	
AIC International Inc 736 S Chicago St PO Box 80925 *Web:* www.aicconstruction.com	Seattle	WA	98108	206-762-3340	
Ajax Bldg Corp 1080 Commerce Blvd *Web:* www.ajaxbuilding.com	Midway	FL	32343	850-224-9571	224-2496
AKEA Inc 25105 W Newberry Rd *Web:* www.akeainc.com	Newberry	FL	32669	352-474-6124	
Alan Shintani Inc 94-409 Akoki St *Web:* www.alan-shintani.com	Waipahu	HI	96797	808-841-7631	
Alan Utz & Assoc Inc (AU& A) PO Box 131857 *Web:* www.auainc.com	Tyler	TX	75713	903-566-9797	566-9393
Albert C. Kobayashi Inc 94-535 Ukee St *Web:* www.ack-inc.com	Waipahu	HI	96797	808-671-6460	
Albert M Higley Co 2926 Chester Ave *Web:* www.amhigley.com	Cleveland	OH	44114	216-861-2050	861-0038
Albu & Associates Inc 1460 Minnesota Ave *Web:* www.albu.biz	Winter Park	FL	32789	407-788-1450	
Alcamo Supply Corp 1152 Jericho Tpke *Web:* www.alcamopools.com	Commack	NY	11725	631-543-8820	
Alcan Electrical & Engineering Inc 6670 Arctic Spur Rd *Web:* www.alcanelectric.com	Anchorage	AK	99518	907-563-3787	562-6286
Alex E. Paris Contracting Co 1595 Smith Township State *Web:* www.alexparis.com	Atlasburg	PA	15004	724-947-2235	947-3820
All Pool & Spa Inc 905 Kalanianaole Hwy *Web:* www.allpoolandspa.com	Kailua	HI	96734	808-261-8991	263-6158
Allen Blasting & Coating Inc 814 E Adams St *Web:* allenblastingandcoating.com	New London	IA	52645	319-367-5500	
Allen m p General Contractors Inc 9807 Fair Oaks Blvd *Web:* www.mpallen.com	Fair Oaks	CA	95628	916-904-5000	
Alliance Construction Solutions LLC 2725 Rocky Mtn Ave Ste 100 *Web:* www.allianceconstruction.com	Loveland	CO	80538	970-663-9700	663-9750
AlliedCook Construction Corp Eight US Route 1 *Web:* www.alliedcook.com	Scarborough	ME	04074	207-772-2888	
Allstate Construction Inc 5718 Tower Rd *Web:* www.allstateconstruction.com	Tallahassee	FL	32303	850-514-1004	514-1206
Alpha Bldg Corp 24850 Blanco Rd Ste 200 *Web:* www.alphabuilding.com	San Antonio	TX	78260	210-491-9925	491-9717
Alten Construction Inc 720 12th St *Web:* www.altenconstruction.com	Richmond	CA	94801	510-234-4200	
Alvin H Butz Inc 840 W Hamilton St Ste 600 *Web:* www.butz.com	Allentown	PA	18101	610-395-6871	395-3363
AMEC Construction Management 1979 Lakeside Pkwy Ste 400 *Web:* www.amec.com	Tucker	GA	30084	770-688-2500	688-2501
American Modular Systems Inc 787 Spreckels Ave *Web:* www.americanmodular.com	Manteca	CA	95336	209-825-1921	
American Trademark Construction Services Inc 200 Lau Pkwy *Web:* www.atcs-online.com	Clayton	OH	45315	937-832-8885	
Ameris Bank 24 Second Ave SE PO Box 3668 *TF:* 866-616-6020 ■ *Web:* www.amerisbank.com	Moultrie	GA	31768	866-616-6020	
Anchor Construction Corp 2254 25th Place NE *Web:* www.anchorconst.com	Washington	DC	20018	202-269-6694	
Anchor Tampa Inc 3907 W Osborne Ave *Web:* www.anchortampa.com	Tampa	FL	33614	813-879-8685	
Andersen Construction Company Inc 6712 N Cutter Cir *Web:* www.andersen-const.com	Portland	OR	97217	503-283-6712	283-3607
Angeles Contractor Inc 8461 Commonwealth Ave *Web:* www.angelescontractor.com	Buena Park	CA	90621	714-443-3655	
Ansco & Assoc LLC 16D Oak Branch Dr *Web:* www.anscoinc.com	Greensboro	NC	27407	336-852-3433	852-4027
Apex Homes Inc 7172 Rt 522 *TF:* 800-326-9524 ■ *Web:* www.apexhomesinc.com	Middleburg	PA	17842	570-837-2333	837-2346
Arch-Con Corp 1335 W Gray Ste 300 *Web:* www.arch-con.com	Houston	TX	77019	713-533-1900	
Armada Hoffler 222 Central Pk Ave Ste 2100 *Web:* www.armadahoffler.com	Virginia Beach	VA	23462	757-366-4000	523-0782
Ashland Construction Co 4601 Atlantic Ave *Web:* www.ashlandconstruction.com	Raleigh	NC	27604	919-872-7500	
Asi Constructors Inc 1850 E Platteville Blvd *Web:* www.asiconstructors.com	Pueblo West	CO	81007	719-647-2821	647-2890
Atlas General Contractors LLC 8218 E 121st St S *Web:* www.atlasgc.com	Bixby	OK	74008	918-369-3910	

Company	City	State	ZIP	Phone	Fax
Atmos Tech Industries L L C 1108 Pollack Ave *Web:* www.atmostech.com	Ocean	NJ	07712	732-493-8400	
Auld & White Constructors LLC 4168 Southpoint Pkwy Ste 101 *Web:* www.auld-white.com	Jacksonville	FL	32216	904-296-2555	
Ausland Builders Inc 3935 Highland Ave *Web:* auslandgroup.com	Grants Pass	OR	97526	541-476-3788	
Austin Co 6095 Parkland Blvd *Web:* www.theaustin.com	Cleveland	OH	44124	440-544-2600	544-2661
Austin Commercial Inc 3535 Travis Ste 300 **Fax:* Acctg ■ *Web:* www.austin-ind.com	Dallas	TX	75204	214-443-5700	443-5793*
Auto Builders South Florida 5715 Corporate Way *Web:* www.questcontracting.com	West Palm Beach	FL	33407	561-622-3515	
Aztec Building Systems Inc 3361 Deskin Dr *Web:* www.aztecbuildingsystems.com	Norman	OK	73069	405-329-0255	
B C & G Weithman Construction Company Inc 2171 E Mansfield St *Web:* www.weithman.com	Bucyrus	OH	44820	419-562-8027	
B R Mcmillan & Associates Inc 4030 Hwy 31 W *Web:* www.brmcmillan.com	Cottontown	TN	37048	615-672-2996	
B&B Contractors & Developers Inc 2781 Salt Springs Rd *Web:* www.bbcdonline.com	Youngstown	OH	44509	330-270-5020	270-5035
B. H. Craig Construction Company Inc 835 Wall St *Web:* www.bhcraigconst.com	Florence	AL	35630	256-766-3350	767-0367
Bachmann Construction Company Inc 1201 S Stoughton Rd *Web:* bachmannconstruction.net	Madison	WI	53716	608-222-8869	
Baldwin & Shell Construction Co Inc 1000 W Capitol PO Box 1750 *Web:* www.baldwinshell.com	Little Rock	AR	72201	501-374-8677	375-7649
Balfour Beatty Construction (BBC) 3100 McKinnon St 10th Fl *Web:* balfourbeattyus.com	Dallas	TX	75201	214-451-1000	
Bank of the Orient 233 Sansome St *TF:* 877-275-3342 ■ *Web:* www.bankorient.com/home	San Francisco	CA	94104	415-338-0843	338-0619
Barker-morrissey Contracting Inc 3619 E Speedway Blvd Ste 101 *Web:* www.barkermorrissey.com	Tucson	AZ	85716	520-323-3831	
Barlovento LLC 431 Technology Dr *TF:* 877-498-6039 ■ *Web:* barloventollc.com	Dothan	AL	36303	334-983-9979	983-9983
Barnhill Contracting Co 2311 N Main St *Web:* www.barnhillcontracting.com	Tarboro	NC	27886	252-823-1021	823-0137
Baron Sign Manufacturing 900 W 13th St *Web:* www.baronsign.com	Riviera Beach	FL	33404	561-863-7446	
Barr & Barr Inc 460 W 34th St 16th Fl *Web:* www.barrandbarr.com	New York	NY	10001	212-563-2330	967-2297
Barton Malow Enterprises Inc 26500 American Dr *Web:* www.bartonmalow.com	Southfield	MI	48034	248-436-5000	436-5001
Batson-Cook Co 817 Fourth Ave PO Box 151 *Web:* www.batson-cook.com	West Point	GA	31833	706-643-2500	643-2199
Bay Electric Company Inc 627 36th St *Web:* www.bayelectricco.com	Newport News	VA	23607	757-595-2300	595-6112
Baybutt Construction Corp 25 Avon St *Web:* www.baybutt.com	Keene	NH	03431	603-352-6846	352-6633
Bayland Buildings Inc PO Box 13571 *Web:* baylandbuildings.com	Green Bay	WI	54307	920-498-9300	
Bayley Construction Co 8005 SE 28th St Ste 100 *Web:* www.bayley.net	Mercer Island	WA	98040	206-621-8884	343-7728
Baywood Homes 1140 Sheppard Ave W Ste 13 *TF:* 888-751-2223 ■ *Web:* www.baywoodhomes.com	Toronto	ON	M3K2A2	416-633-7333	633-7491
BBL Construction Services Inc (BBL) 302 Washington Ave Ext *Web:* www.bblinc.com	Albany	NY	12203	518-452-8200	452-2897
BE&K Building Group 5605 Carnegie Blvd Ste 200 *Web:* www.kbrbuildinggroup.com	Charlotte	NC	28209	704-551-2700	551-2799
Beauchamp Construction Co 2100 Ponce De Leon Blvd Ste 825 *Web:* www.beauchampco.com	Coral Gables	FL	33134	305-445-0819	447-0941
Beck & Hofer Construction Inc 618 E Maple St *Web:* beckandhofer.com	Sioux Falls	SD	57104	605-336-0118	
Beck Group, The 1807 Ross Ave Ste 500 *Web:* www.beckgroup.com	Dallas	TX	75201	214-303-6200	303-6300
Becker Arena Products Inc 6611 W Hwy 13 *Web:* www.beckerarena.com	Savage	MN	55378	952-890-2690	
Becker Bros Inc 401 Main St Ste 110 *Web:* bccinc.net	Peoria	IL	61602	309-674-1200	674-5454
Behlen Building Systems 102 W Fourth St *Web:* www.eaglespan.com	Loveland	CO	80537	970-593-0596	
Beitzel Corp 12072 Bittinger Rd *Web:* www.beitzelcorp.com	Grantsville	MD	21536	301-245-4107	
Belrock Construction Ltd 185 Adesso Dr *Web:* www.belrock.com	Concord	ON	L4K3C4	905-669-9481	
Benaka Inc Seven Lawrence St *Web:* www.benakainc.com	New Brunswick	NJ	08901	732-246-7060	
Benchmark Construction Company Inc 4121 Oregon Pike PO Box 806 *Web:* www.benchmarkgc.com	Brownstown	PA	17508	717-626-9559	
Benjamin Development Company Inc 377 Oak St Ste 401 *Web:* www.benjamindevco.com	Garden City	NY	11530	516-745-0150	
Benning Construction Co Inc (BCC) 4695 S Atlanta Rd *Web:* www.benningnet.com	Atlanta	GA	30339	404-792-1911	792-2337
Bergenfield Public School District 225 W Clinton Ave *Web:* www.bergenfield.org	Bergenfield	NJ	07621	201-385-8801	
Berghammer Construction Corp 4750 N 132nd St *Web:* berghammer.com	Butler	WI	53007	262-790-4750	
Berkowsky & Associates Inc 2551 Us Hwy 130 Ste 2 *Web:* www.berkowsky.com	Cranbury	NJ	08512	609-655-2400	
Bernards Bros Inc 555 First St *Web:* www.bernards.com	San Fernando	CA	91340	818-898-1521	
Bethlehem Construction Inc 5505 Tichenal Rd *Web:* www.bethlehemc.com	Cashmere	WA	98815	509-782-1001	
Bette & Cring LLC 22 Century Hill Dr Ste 201 *Web:* www.bettecring.com	Latham	NY	12110	518-213-1010	
Beyer Construction Ltd 3080 S Calhoun Rd *Web:* www.beyer.com	New Berlin	WI	53151	262-789-6040	
Bittenbender Consrtuction Lp 5 N. Columbus Blvd Pier 5 *Web:* www.bittenbenderconstruction.com	Philadelphia	PA	19106	215-925-8900	925-6270
BL Harbert International Inc PO Box 531390 *Web:* blharbert.com	Birmingham	AL	35253	205-802-2800	802-2801
Blach Construction Co 469 El Cmino Real Ste 100 *Web:* www.blach.com	Santa Clara	CA	95050	408-244-7100	244-2220
Blaine Construction Corp 6510 Deane Hill Dr *Web:* www.blaineconstruction.com	Knoxville	TN	37919	865-693-8900	691-7606
BlueScope Construction Inc 1540 Genessee St *Web:* www.bucon.com	Kansas City	MO	64102	816-245-6000	245-6099
BNBuilders Inc 2601 Fourth Ave Ste 350 *Web:* www.bnbuilders.com	Seattle	WA	98121	206-382-3443	
Bockstael Construction (1979) Ltd 1505 Dugald Rd *Web:* www.bockstael.com	Winnipeg	MB	R2J0H3	204-233-7135	
Bognet Construction Associates Inc 1911 N Ft Myer Dr Ste 705 *Web:* www.bognet.com	Arlington	VA	22209	703-807-0007	
Bolton Construction & Service of WNC Inc 169 Elk Mtn Rd *Web:* boltonservicewnc.com	Asheville	NC	28804	828-253-3621	
Bond Bros Inc 145 Spring St *Web:* www.bondbrothers.com	Everett	MA	02149	617-387-3400	389-1412
Bondfield Construction Company Ltd 407 Basaltic Rd *Web:* www.bondfield.com	Concord	ON	L4K4W8	416-667-8422	
Bonnette Page & Stone Corp 91 Bisson Ave *Web:* www.bpsnh.com	Laconia	NH	03246	603-524-3411	524-4641
Boro Developers Inc 400 Feheley Dr *Web:* www.boroconstruction.com	King Of Prussia	PA	19406	610-272-7400	
Bosse Mattingly Constructors Inc 2116 Plantside Dr *Web:* www.bmconstructors.com	Louisville	KY	40299	502-671-0995	
Bowen & Watson Inc PO Box 877 *Web:* www.bowen-watson.com	Toccoa	GA	30577	706-886-3197	886-3010
Boyd Jones Construction Co 4360 Nicholas St *Web:* www.boydjones.biz	Omaha	NE	68131	402-553-1804	
Boyertown Area School District (BASD) 911 Montgomery Ave *Web:* www.boyertownasd.org	Boyertown	PA	19512	610-367-6031	369-7620
Brackett Builders Inc 185 Marybill Dr S *Web:* www.brackettbuilders.com	Troy	OH	45373	937-339-7505	
Bradbury & Stamm Construction Company Inc 7110 Second St NW *Web:* www.bradburystamm.com	Albuquerque	NM	87107	505-765-1200	842-5419
Brae Burn Construction Co PO Box 742288 *Web:* www.braeburnconstruction.com	Houston	TX	77274	713-777-0063	995-9649
Branagh Inc 750 Kevin Ct *Web:* www.branaghinc.com	Oakland	CA	94621	510-638-6455	562-8371
Branch Group Inc PO Box 40004 *Web:* www.branchgroup.com	Roanoke	VA	24022	540-982-1678	
Brannan Paving Coltd 111 Elk Dr PO Box 3403 *TF:* 800-626-7064 ■ *Web:* www.brannanpaving.com	Victoria	TX	77903	361-573-3130	573-6211
Brasfield & Gorrie LLC 3021 Seventh Ave S *TF:* 800-239-8017 ■ *Web:* www.brasfieldgorrie.com	Birmingham	AL	35233	205-328-4000	251-1304
Breiholz Construction Co 202 Des Moines St *Web:* www.breiholz.com	Des Moines	IA	50309	515-288-6077	288-6335
Brice Bldg Company Inc 201 Sunbelt Pkwy	Birmingham	AL	35211	205-930-9911	918-1850
Briohn Building Corp 3885 N Brookfield Rd Ste 200 *Web:* www.briohn.com	Brookfield	WI	53045	262-790-0500	
Bristol Construction Services LLC 111 W 16th Ave Fl 3 *Web:* www.bristol-companies.com	Anchorage	AK	99501	907-563-0013	
Briston Construction LLC 309 E 10th Dr *Web:* www.bristonconstruction.com	Mesa	AZ	85210	480-776-5810	
Brookstone LP 3715 Dacoma St *Web:* www.brookstone-tx.com	Houston	TX	77092	713-683-8800	680-0088
Brycon Corp 134 Rio Rancho Blvd NE *Web:* www.brycon.com	Rio Rancho	NM	87124	505-892-6163	
Brytex Building Systems Inc 5610 97 St *Web:* www.brytex.com	Edmonton	AB	T6E3J1	780-437-7970	
BSI Constructors Inc 6767 SW Ave *Web:* www.bsistl.com	Saint Louis	MO	63143	314-781-7820	781-1354
BT Mancini Co Inc 876 S Milpitas Blvd *TF:* 800-787-6381 ■ *Web:* www.btmancini.com	Milpitas	CA	95035	408-942-7900	945-1360
BT Mancini Co Inc Brookman Div 876 S Milpitas Blvd *TF:* 800-787-6381 ■ *Web:* www.btmancini.com	Milpitas	CA	95035	408-942-7900	
Budreck Truck Lines Inc 8040 S Roberts Rd *TF:* 800-621-0013 ■ *Web:* www.budreck.com	Bridgeview	IL	60455	708-496-0522	496-0568

Phone Fax

Buford-Thompson Co PO Box 151829 Ft Worth Arlington TX 76108 817-467-4981 467-5619
Web: www.buford-thompson.com

BuilderGuru Contracting Inc
2124 Priest Bridge Dr Ste 101 Crofton MD 21114 410-923-1379
Web: www.builderguru.com

Building Bridges at Wilcat Way
1525 Ne Wildcat Way Bentonville AR 72712 479-254-5277
Web: portal.bentonville.k12.ar.us

Bullard Construction Inc
4371 Lindbergh Dr Ste 205 Addison TX 75001 972-661-8474
Web: www.bullardconstruction.com

Bulley & Andrews LLC 1755 W Armitage Ave Chicago IL 60622 773-235-2433 235-2471
Web: www.bulley.com

Burrow Global LLC 6200 Savoy Dr Ste 800 Houston TX 77036 713-963-0930
Web: www.burrowglobal.com

Butler Brothers Supply Division Inc
2001 Lisbon St Lewiston ME 04240 207-784-6875
Web: www.butlerbros.com

Butters Construction & Development Inc
6820 Lyons Technology Ctr Ste 100 Coconut Creek FL 33073 954-312-2415 570-8844
Web: www.butters.com

Bycor General Contractors Inc
6490 Marindustry Pl San Diego CA 92121 858-587-1901
Web: www.bycor.com

C Erickson & Sons Inc
2200 ARCH St Ste 200 Philadelphia PA 19103 215-568-3120 496-9460
Web: www.cerickson.com

C F Evans & Company Inc 125 Regional Pkwy Orangeburg SC 29118 803-536-6443
Web: www.cfevans.com

C Overaa & Company Inc 200 Parr Blvd Richmond CA 94801 510-234-0926 237-2435
Web: www.overaa.com

C T Earle Maintenance Co 7001 Gibsonton Dr Gibsonton FL 33534 813-677-7803

C. Martin Company Inc
3395 W Cheyenne Ave North Las Vegas NV 89032 702-656-8080
Web: www.cmartin.com

C.a. Murren & Sons Co Inc
2275 Loganville Hwy Grayson GA 30017 770-682-2940 682-1802
TF: 800-523-2200 ■ *Web:* www.camurren.com

C.t. Wilson Construction Co PO Box 2011 Durham NC 27702 919-383-2535 382-0044
Web: www.ctwilson.com/

C.W. Brown Inc One Labriola Ct Armonk NY 10504 914-741-1212
Web: www.cwbrown.net

C1S Group Inc 4231 Sigma Rd Ste 110 Dallas TX 75244 972-386-7005
Web: www.c1sinc.com

Ca Lindman Inc 10401 Guilford Rd Jessup MD 20794 301-470-4700 470-4708
TF: 877-737-8675 ■ *Web:* www.calindman.com

Caddell Construction Co Inc
2700 Lagoon Pk Dr Montgomery AL 36109 334-272-7723 272-8844
Web: www.caddell.com

Cadence Mcshane Corp
5057 Keller Springs Rd Ste 500 Addison TX 75001 972-239-2336
Web: www.cadencemcshane.com

Cahill Contractors Inc
425 California St Ste 2200 San Francisco CA 94104 415-986-0600
Web: www.cahill-sf.com

Caliber Construction Inc 240 N Orange Ave Brea CA 92821 714-255-2700
Web: www.caliberconstructioninc.com

Callahan Inc 80 First St Bridgewater MA 02324 508-279-0012
Web: www.callahan-inc.com

Camco Pacific Construction Company Inc
19712 MacArthur Blvd Ste 200 Irvine CA 92612 949-251-1300
Web: www.camcopacific.com

Camosy Construction Inc 43451 N US Hwy 41 Zion IL 60099 847-395-6800 395-6891
Web: www.camosy.com

Capitol Construction Services Inc
10412 Allisonville Rd Ste 100 Fishers IN 46038 317-574-5488
Web: www.capitolconstruct.com

Carbondale Elementary School District 95
925 S Giant City Rd Carbondale IL 62902 618-457-3591 457-2043
Web: www.ces95.org

Cardinal Construction Inc
531 Commercial St PO 897 Waterloo IA 50704 319-232-5400 232-3149
Web: www.cardinalconst.com

Careage Development
4411 Point Fosdick Dr NW Ste 203 Gig Harbor WA 98335 253-853-4457 853-5280
Web: www.careage.com

Carl Belt Inc 11521 Milnor Ave PO Box 1210 Cumberland MD 21502 301-729-8900
Web: www.thebeltgroup.com

Carmel Contractors Inc 8030 England St Charlotte NC 28273 704-552-2338 552-0397
Web: www.carmelcontractors.com

Carroll County School District
605-9 Pine St Hillsville VA 24343 276-730-3200 728-3195
Web: www.ccpsd.k12.va.us

Case Construction LLC 56 Midtown Park W Ste A Mobile AL 36606 251-338-2400
Web: www.casecc.com

Case Contracting Co 2311 Turkey Creek Rd Plant City FL 33566 813-754-3477
Web: www.casecontracting.com

Catamount Constructors Inc
1250 Bergen Pkwy Ste B200 Evergreen CO 80439 303-679-0087
Web: www.catamountconstructors.com

Cavico Corp
17011 Beach Blvd Ste 1230 Huntington Beach CA 92647 714-843-5456 996-5818*
OTC: CAVO ■ *Fax Area Code: 302 ■ *Web:* www.cavicocorp.com

CBS Construction Ltd
150 MacKay Crescent Fort Mcmurray AB T9H4W8 780-743-1810
Web: www.cbsconstruction.ca

CD Moody Construction Company Inc
6017 Redan Rd Lithonia GA 30058 770-482-7778 482-7727
Web: www.cdmoodyconstruction.com

CD Smith Construction Inc
889 E Johnson St PO Box 1006 Fond du Lac WI 54935 920-924-2900 924-2910
Web: www.cd-smith.com

CDI Contractors LLC 3000 Cantrell Rd Little Rock AR 72202 501-666-4300 666-4741
Web: www.cdicon.com

Cedar Grove Composting Inc
7343 E Marginal Way S Seattle WA 98108 206-832-3000 832-3030
TF: 888-832-3008 ■ *Web:* www.cedar-grove.com

Cello & Maudru Construction Company Inc
2505 Oak St Napa CA 94559 707-257-0454
Web: www.cello-maudru.com

Centerpoint Builders Ltd 5339 Alpha Rd Ste 250 Dallas TX 75240 972-220-0500
Web: www.centerpointbuilders.com

CenTex House Leveling 1120 E 52nd St Austin TX 78723 512-444-5438
Web: www.centexhouseleveling.com

Centrix Builders Inc
160 S Linden Ave
Ste 100 S San Francisco San Francisco CA 94080 650-876-9400
Web: www.centrixbuilders.com

Century Concrete Inc
1364 Air Rail Ave Virginia Beach VA 23455 757-460-5366 460-3296
Web: www.centuryconcreteinc.com

CF Jordan Construction LLC 7700 CF Jordan Dr El Paso TX 79912 915-877-3333 877-3999
Web: jordanfosterconstruction.com/

CG Schmidt Inc 11777 W Lake Pk Dr Milwaukee WI 53224 414-577-1177 577-1155
TF: 800-248-1254 ■ *Web:* www.cgschmidt.com

Champion Site Prep LP
455 STATE Hwy 195 Ste A Georgetown TX 78633 512-863-3453
Web: www.idigdirt.com

Chanen Construction Company Inc
3300 N Third Ave Phoenix AZ 85013 602-266-3600
Web: www.srchanen.com

Channel Building Company Inc
355 Middlesex Ave Wilmington MA 01887 978-657-7300
Web: www.channelbuilding.com

Channel Systems Inc 74 98th Ave Oakland CA 94603 510-568-7170
Web: www.channelsystems.com

Charles C Brandt Construction Co
1505 N Sherman Dr Indianapolis IN 46201 317-375-1111 375-4321
Web: www.ccbrandt.com

Charles DeWeese Construction Inc
765 Industrial By Pass PO Box 504 Franklin KY 42135 270-586-9122
Web: www.charlesdeweeseconstruction.com

Charles N. White Construction Company Inc
613 Crescent Cir Ste 100 Ridgeland MS 39157 601-898-5180
Web: www.whiteconst.com

Charles Pankow Builders Ltd
3280 E Foothill Blvd Ste 100 Pasadena CA 91107 626-304-1190 696-1782
Web: www.pankow.com

Chasco Constructors Ltd LLP
2801 E Old Settlers Blvd Round Rock TX 78665 512-244-0600
Web: www.chasco.com

Chicago Records Management Inc
3815 Carnation St Franklin Park IL 60131 847-678-0002
Web: www.chicagorecords.com

Choate Construction Co
8200 Roberts Dr Ste 600 Atlanta GA 30350 678-892-1200 892-1202
Web: www.choateco.com

Chris Woods Construction Company Inc
8068 US Hwy 70 Memphis TN 38133 901-386-3182
Web: www.chriswoodsconstruction.com

Christa Construction LLC
119 Victor Heights Pkwy Victor NY 14564 585-924-3050
Web: www.christa.com

Christman Company Inc 208 N Capitol Ave Lansing MI 48933 517-482-1488 482-3520
Web: www.christmanco.com

Clancy & Theys Construction Co
516 W Cabarrus St Raleigh NC 27603 919-834-3601 834-2439
Web: www.clancytheys.com

Clarion Construction Inc
21067 Commerce Pointe Dr Walnut CA 91789 909-598-4060
Web: www.clarionconst.com

ClariPhy Communications Inc
7585 Irvine Ctr Dr Ste 100 Irvine CA 92618 949-861-3074
Web: www.clariphy.com

Claris Construction Inc 153 S Main St Newtown CT 06470 203-364-9460
Web: www.clarisconstruction.com

Clark & Sullivan Constructors Inc
905 Industrial Way Ste 26 Sparks NV 89431 775-355-8500
Web: www.clarksullivan.com

Clark Construction Group LLC
7500 Old Georgetown Rd Bethesda MD 20814 301-272-8100 272-1928
TF: 800-655-1330 ■ *Web:* www.clarkconstruction.com

Clark Transfer Inc 800A Paxton St Harrisburg PA 17104 717-238-0801
TF: 800-488-7585 ■ *Web:* www.clarktransfer.com

Clarksdale Municipal School District
101 McGuire St PO Box 1088 Clarksdale MS 38614 662-627-8500 627-8542
TF: 877-820-7831 ■ *Web:* www.cmsd.k12.ms.us

Cleary Building Corp
190 Paoli St PO Box 930220 Verona WI 53593 608-845-9700
Web: clearybuilding.com

Clemens Construction Company Inc
1435 Walnut St Seven Fl Philadelphia PA 19102 215-567-5757
Web: www.clemensconstruction.com

Climatec Inc 2851 W Kathleen Rd Phoenix AZ 85053 602-944-3330
Web: www.climatec.com

Clinton Fences Company Inc
2630 Old Washington Rd Waldorf MD 20601 301-645-8808
Web: fencesouthernmd.com

CM Company Inc 431 W McGregor Ct Boise ID 83705 208-384-0800
Web: www.cmcompany.com

Cm Construction Company Inc
12215 Nicollet Ave Burnsville MN 55337 952-895-8223
Web: www.cmconstructionco.com

Company / Address	City	State	Zip	Phone	Fax
Colaianni Construction Inc 2141 State Rt 150	Dillonvale	OH	43917	740-769-2362	
Web: www.colaianniconst.com					
Coleman-Adams Construction Inc 1031 Performance Rd	Forest	VA	24551	434-525-4700	
Web: www.coleman-adams.com					
Comanco 4301 Sterling Commerce Dr	Plant City	FL	33566	813-988-8829	988-8779
Web: www.comanco.net					
Commercial Air 601 Ransdell Rd	Lebanon	IN	46052	765-482-8121	
Web: www.commercialair.com					
Commodore Builders 80 Bridge St	Newton	MA	02458	617-614-3500	965-8354
Web: www.commodorebuilders.com					
Complete Property Services Inc 140 Pine Ave S	Oldsmar	FL	34677	727-793-9777	
Web: www.completeproperty.com					
Con-Real Support Group LP 1900 Ballpark Way Ste 110	Arlington	TX	76006	817-640-4420	
Web: www.con-real.com					
Concord Cos Inc 4215 E McDowell Rd Ste 201	Mesa	AZ	85215	480-962-8080	962-0707
Web: www.concordinc.com					
Condon-Johnson & Assoc Inc 480 Roland Way Ste 200	Oakland	CA	94621	510-636-2100	568-9316
Web: www.condonjohnson.com					
Condotte America Inc 10790 NW 127th St	Medley	FL	33178	305-670-7585	670-7462
Web: www.condotteamerica.com					
Congleton Hacker Co PO Box 22640	Lexington	KY	40522	859-254-6481	253-0442
Web: www.congleton-hacker.com					
Conlan Co, The 1800 Pkwy Pl Ste 1010	Marietta	GA	30067	770-423-8000	423-8010
Web: www.conlancompany.com					
Conlon Construction Company Inc 1100 Rockdale Rd	Dubuque	IA	52003	563-583-1724	
Web: www.conlonco.com					
Conrad Schmitt Studios Inc 2405 S 162nd St	New Berlin	WI	53151	262-786-3030	
Web: www.conradschmitt.com					
Consolidated Distribution Corp 1285 101st St	Lemont	IL	60439	630-972-9800	
Web: www.cdcsupply.com					
Construct Two Group 30 S Ivey Ln	Orlando	FL	32811	407-295-9812	
Web: www.constructtwo.com					
Construction Albert Jean Ltd 4045 Parthenais St	Montreal	QC	H2K3T8	514-522-2121	
Web: www.albertjean.com					
Construction Outfitters International Inc 37450 Interstate 10 W Ste 101	Boerne	TX	78006	830-816-2104	
Web: www.coiworld.com					
Cooper Brothers Construction Company Inc 3005 Citizens Pkwy	Selma	AL	36701	334-874-8267	
Web: cooperbrothersconstruction.com					
Cooper Pugeda Management Inc 65 Mccoppin St	San Francisco	CA	94103	415-543-6515	
Web: www.cpmservices.com					
CORE Construction Services of Arizona Inc 3036 E Greenway Rd	Phoenix	AZ	85032	602-494-0800	
Web: www.coreconstruct.com					
Corna/Kokosing Construction Co 6235 Westerville Rd	Westerville	OH	43081	614-901-8844	212-5599
Web: www.corna.com					
Corporate Construction Ltd 7617 Mineral Pt Rd	Madison	WI	53717	608-827-6001	827-6066
Web: www.corporate-construction.com					
Couvrette Building Systems 8665 Argent St Ste D	Santee	CA	92071	619-938-8000	
Web: www.couvrette.com					
Cox Schepp Construction Inc 2410 Dunavant St	Charlotte	NC	28203	704-716-2100	
Web: www.coxschepp.com					
CPM Constructors Inc 30 Bonney St PO Box B	Freeport	ME	04032	207-865-0000	
Web: www.cpmconstructors.com					
CR Meyer & Sons Co 895 W 20th Ave	Oshkosh	WI	54902	920-235-3350	235-3419
Web: www.crmeyer.com					
Craftcorps Inc 3401 Manor Rd	Austin	TX	78723	512-476-8886	
Web: www.craftcorps.com					
Crawford Merz Anderson Construction Co 2316 Fourth Ave S	Minneapolis	MN	55404	612-874-9011	
Web: www.cmacco.com					
Creative Business Interiors 1535 S 101st St	Milwaukee	WI	53214	414-545-8500	
Web: www.creativebusinessinteriors.com					
Creative Times Dayschool Inc 2878 Commerce Way	Ogden	UT	84401	801-334-7250	
Web: www.creativetimesdayschool.com					
Cresleigh Homes Corp 433 California St Ste 700	San Francisco	CA	94104	415-982-7777	
Web: hotelpurchase.com					
Cressey Development Corp 555 W Eighth Ave Ste 200	Vancouver	BC	V5Z1C6	604-683-1256	
Web: www.cressey.com					
Crossland Construction Company Inc PO Box 45	Columbus	KS	66725	620-429-1414	429-1412
Web: www.crosslandconstruction.com					
Crystal Steel Fabricators Inc - Acdbe 9317 Old Racetrack Rd	Delmar	DE	19940	302-846-0613	
Web: www.crystalsteel.com					
CSM Group Inc 444 W Michigan Ave Ste 100	Kalamazoo	MI	49007	269-746-5600	
Web: www.csmgroup.com					
Culp Construction Co 2320 S Main St	Salt Lake City	UT	84115	801-486-2064	485-4755
Web: www.culpco.com					
Culpepper & Terpening Inc 2980 S 25th St	Fort Pierce	FL	34981	772-464-3537	
Web: www.ct-eng.com					
Cutler Associates Inc 43 Harvard St	Worcester	MA	01609	508-757-7500	
Web: cutlerdb.com					
CW Driver General Contractors Inc 468 N Rosemead Blvd	Pasadena	CA	91107	626-351-8800	351-8880
Web: www.cwdriver.com					
D & D Construction Services of Orlando Inc 2707 Rew Cir	Ocoee	FL	34761	407-654-7545	
Web: www.ddconstructionservices.com					
D & K Landscape Inc 3068 S Highland Dr	Las Vegas	NV	89109	702-361-5855	
Web: dklandscape.com					
D'annunzio & Sons Inc 136 Central Ave Ste 102	Clark	NJ	07066	732-574-1300	574-1244
Web: www.dannunziocorp.com					
D.A.G. Construction Company Inc 4924 Winton Rd	Cincinnati	OH	45232	513-542-8597	
Web: www.dag-cons.com					
D.s.simmons Inc 112 W Chestnut St PO Box 287	Goldsboro	NC	27530	919-734-4700	
Web: www.dssimmons.com					
D4 Construction Services LLC 4121 Main St	Rowlett	TX	75088	972-463-0390	
Web: www.d4cs.com					
Da Pope Inc 1160 Chess Dr Ste 11	Foster City	CA	94404	650-349-5086	
Web: www.dapope.com					
Danco Industrial Contractors Inc 1121 N Beverlye Rd	Dothan	AL	36303	334-792-3985	
Web: www.dancoindustrial.com					
Daniels Corp, The 20 Queen St W Ste 3400	Toronto	ON	M5H3R3	416-598-2129	
Web: www.danielshomes.ca					
Danis Bldg Construction Co 3233 Newmark Dr	Miamisburg	OH	45342	937-228-1225	228-7443
Web: www.danisbuilding.com					
Daryl Flood Inc 450 Airline Dr Ste 100	Coppell	TX	75019	972-471-1496	745-9629
TF: 888-454-9481 ■ *Web:* www.darylflood.com					
Davenport Cos, The 20 N Main St	South Yarmouth	MA	02664	508-398-2293	
Web: www.thedavenportcompanies.com					
David Simpson Construction Company Inc 17177 Gillette Ave Ste A	Irvine	CA	92614	949-250-1348	
Web: www.davidsimpsonconstruction.com					
Davis & Assoc Inc 2852 N Webster Ave	Indianapolis	IN	46219	317-263-9947	238-9209
Web: www.davisassocindy.com					
Daw Construction Group LLC 12552 South 125 West	Draper	UT	84020	801-553-9111	
TF: 800-748-4778 ■ *Web:* www.dawcg.com					
Dawson Construction Inc PO Box 30920	Bellingham	WA	98225	360-756-1000	756-1001
Web: www.dawson.com					
DE Harvey Builders Inc 3630 Westchase Dr	Houston	TX	77242	713-783-8710	
Web: www.harveybuilders.com					
De Jager Construction Inc 75-60th St SW	Wyoming	MI	49548	616-530-0060	
Web: www.dejagerconstruction.com					
Dean Kurtz Construction 1651 Rand Rd	Rapid City	SD	57702	605-343-6665	
Web: www.deankurtzconstruction.com					
Dean Snyder Construction Co 913 N 14th St PO Box 181	Clear Lake	IA	50428	641-357-2283	357-2232
Web: www.deansnyderconst.com					
Deerfield Construction Company Inc 8960 Glendale Milford Rd	Loveland	OH	45140	513-984-4096	984-4180
Web: www.deerfieldconstruction.com					
DEI Inc 1550 Kemper Meadow Dr	Cincinnati	OH	45240	513-825-5800	
Web: www.dei-corp.com					
Deig Bros Lumber & Construction Inc 2804 A St	Evansville	IN	47712	812-423-4201	421-5058
Web: www.deigbros.com					
Deltec Homes Inc 69 Bingham Rd	Asheville	NC	28806	828-253-0483	254-1880
TF: 800-642-2508 ■ *Web:* www.deltechomes.com					
Demar Ltd 6200 Savoy Dr Ste 800	Houston	TX	77036	713-963-0930	963-0941
Web: www.demar-ltd.com					
DeMaria Bldg Company Inc 3031 W Grand Blvd Ste 624	Detroit	MI	48202	313-870-2800	870-2810
Web: www.demariabuild.com					
Denark Construction Inc 1635 Western Ave Ste 105	Knoxville	TN	37921	865-637-1925	
Web: www.denak.com					
Denver Commercial Builders Inc (DCB) 909 E 62nd Ave	Denver	CO	80216	303-287-5525	287-3697
Web: www.dcb1.com					
Desbuild Inc 4744 Baltimore Ave	Hyattsville	MD	20781	301-864-4095	
Web: www.desbuild.com					
Descor Builders 3164 Gold Camp Dr Ste 250	Rancho Cordova	CA	95670	916-463-0191	
Web: www.descorbuilders.com					
Design Partnership, The 1629 Telegraph Ave Ste 500	Oakland	CA	94612	415-777-3737	777-3476
Web: www.dpsf.com					
Designed Mobile Systems Industries PO Box 367	Patterson	CA	95363	209-892-6298	892-5018
Web: www.dmsi-inc.com					
Devcon Construction Inc 690 Gibraltar Dr	Milpitas	CA	95035	408-942-8200	942-8200
Web: www.devcon-const.com					
Devier Construction LLC 1932 Surgi Dr Ste F	Mandeville	LA	70448	985-626-3184	
Web: www.devierconstruction.com					
DEW Construction Corp 277 Blair Park Rd Ste 130	Williston	VT	05495	802-872-0505	
Web: www.dewcorp.com					
Dick Anderson Construction Inc 3424 Hwy 12 East	Helena	MT	59601	406-443-3225	443-1537
Web: www.daconstruction.com					
Dickinson Cameron Construction Company Inc 6184 Innovation Way	Carlsbad	CA	92009	760-438-9114	
Web: www.dickinsoncameron.com					
Diffenbaugh Inc 6865 Airport Dr	Riverside	CA	92504	951-351-6865	351-6880
TF: 800-394-5334 ■ *Web:* www.diffenbaugh.com					
Dimeo Construction Co 75 Chapman St	Providence	RI	02905	401-781-9800	461-4580
Web: dimeo.com					
Dineen Construction Corp 70 Disco Rd Ste 300	Toronto	ON	M9W1L9	416-675-7676	
Web: www.dineen.com					
DL Withers Construction LC 3220 E Harbour Dr	Phoenix	AZ	85034	602-438-9500	438-9600
Web: www.dlwithers.com					

Company	City	State	Zip	Phone	Fax
Dolan Construction Inc 401 S 13th St *Web:* www.dolanconstructioninc.com	Reading	PA	19602	610-372-4664	
Don Chapin Company Inc, The 560 Crazy Horse Canyon Rd *Web:* www.donchapin.com	Salinas	CA	93907	831-449-4273	449-0700
Donahuefavret Contractors Inc 3030 E Causeway Approach *Web:* www.donahuefavret.com	Mandeville	LA	70448	985-626-4431	
Donohoe Cos Inc 2101 Wisconsin Ave NW *Web:* www.donohoe.com	Washington	DC	20007	202-333-0880	342-3924
Doster Construction Co 2100 International Pk Dr *Web:* www.dosterconstruction.com	Birmingham	AL	35243	205-443-3800	951-2612
Doug Hollyhand Construction Co 527 Main Ave *Web:* www.hollyhand.com	Northport	AL	35476	205-345-0955	
DPR Construction Inc 1450 Veterans Blvd *Web:* www.dpr.com	Redwood City	CA	94063	650-474-1450	474-1451
Drahota Commercial LLC 4700 Innovation Dr Bldg C *Web:* www.drahota.com	Fort Collins	CO	80525	970-204-0100	
Drury Co 4072 State Hwy K *Web:* www.druryco.com	Cape Girardeau	MO	63701	573-334-8271	
Drymalla Construction Company Ltd 608 Harbert St PO Box 698 *Web:* www.drymalla.com	Columbus	TX	78934	979-732-5731	
DSP Builders Inc 12000 E 47th Ave Ste 201 *Web:* www.dspbuilders.com	Denver	CO	80239	303-289-0666	
Duffield Aquatic 515 Concord Industrial Dr *Web:* www.duffieldaquatics.com	Seneca	SC	29672	864-882-7900	
Duffield Assoc Inc 5400 Limestone Rd *TF:* 877-732-9633 ■ *Web:* duffnet.com	Wilmington	DE	19808	302-239-6634	239-8485
Dugan & Meyers 11110 Kenwood Rd *Web:* www.dugan-meyers.com	Cincinnati	OH	45242	513-891-4300	891-0704
Dunlap & Company Inc 6325 E 100 South *Web:* www.dunlapinc.com	Columbus	IN	47202	812-376-3021	
Dunn Investment Co 3905 Messer Airport Hwy *Web:* dunnconstruction.com	Birmingham	AL	35222	205-592-8908	
Duplan Construction Inc 390 Industrial St *Web:* duplanconstruction.com	Campbell	CA	95008	408-866-6682	
Dyad Constructors Inc 8505 Holt St *TF:* 800-803-9202 ■ *Web:* www.dyad-inc.com	Houston	TX	77054	713-799-9380	799-2021
E.R. Stuebner Construction Inc 227 Blair Ave *Web:* www.ersconstruction.com	Reading	PA	19601	610-376-6625	
Eagle Environmental Inc 891 West Robinson Dr Ste 4 *Web:* www.cnnct.com	North Salt Lake	UT	84054	801-936-1155	
Eagle River Homes LLC 21 S Groffdale Rd *Web:* www.eagleriverhomes.net	Leola	PA	17540	717-656-2381	
Eastern Construction Company Ltd 505 Consumers Rd Ste 1100 *Web:* www.easternconstruction.com	Toronto	ON	M2J5G2	416-497-7110	
EBC Inc 1095 Valets St *Web:* www.ebcinc.com	L'ancienne-lorette	QC	G2E4M7	418-872-0600	
EBCO General Contractor Ltd 305 W Gillis *Web:* ebcogc.com	Cameron	TX	76520	254-697-8516	
Ebert Inc 23350 County Rd 10 *Web:* www.ebertconst.com	Loretto	MN	55357	763-498-7844	
Ecological Restoration & Management Inc (ER&M) 9475 Deereco Rd Ste 406 *Web:* www.er-m.com	Timonium	MD	21093	410-337-4899	583-5678
Ed Grush, General Contractor Inc 3236 E Willow St *Web:* www.edgrush.com	Signal Hill	CA	90755	562-426-9526	
Ed Taylor Construction South Inc 2713 N Falkenburg Rd *Web:* www.edtaylor.net	Tampa	FL	33619	813-623-3724	621-1439
Edger Enterprises of Elmira Inc 330 E 14th St *Web:* www.edgerenterprises.com	Elmira Heights	NY	14903	607-733-9664	
Edifice Inc 1401 W Morehead St *Web:* www.edificeinc.com	Charlotte	NC	28208	704-332-0900	
EE Reed Construction LP 333 Commerce Green Blvd PO Box 108 *Web:* www.eereed.com	Sugar Land	TX	77478	281-933-4000	933-4852
EI Group Inc, The 2101 Gateway Centre Blvd Ste 200 *Web:* www.ei1.com	Morrisville	NC	27560	919-657-7500	
Ejh Construction Inc 30896 W 8 Mile Rd *Web:* ejhconstruction.com	Farmington Hills	MI	48336	248-478-1400	
Eklunds Inc 2860 Market Loop *Web:* www.eklunds.com	Southlake	TX	76092	817-949-2030	
Elder-Jones Inc 1120 E 80th St Ste 211 *Web:* www.elderjones.com	Minneapolis	MN	55420	952-854-2854	854-2703
Eldor Contracting Corp 30 Corporate Dr *Web:* www.eldor.com	Holtsville	NY	11742	631-218-0010	
Eleven Western Builders Inc 2862 Executive Pl *Web:* www.ewbinc.com	Escondido	CA	92029	760-796-6346	
Elite Retails Services Inc PO Box 618 *Web:* www.elite-construction.com	Lake Jackson	TX	77566	979-285-0712	285-0714
Ellis Stone Construction 3201 Stanley St PO Box 366 *Web:* www.ellisstone.com	Stevens Point	WI	54481	715-345-5000	345-5007
EllisDon Corp 2045 Oxford St *Web:* www.ellisdon.com	London	ON	N5V2Z7	519-455-6770	
Elt Enterprises 1323 Fernbridge Dr *Web:* www.navexglobal.com	Fortuna	CA	95540	707-725-2124	
Emery Air Charter Inc One Airport Cir *Web:* www.emeryair.net	Rockford	IL	61109	815-968-8287	
EMJ Corp 2034 Hamilton Pl Blvd Ste 400 *Web:* www.emjcorp.com	Chattanooga	TN	37421	423-855-1550	855-6857
Energy Services of America Corp 75 W third Ave *OTC: ESOA* ■ *Web:* www.energyservicesofamerica.com	Huntington	WV	25701	304-399-6300	399-1096
Engelberth Construction Inc 463 Mtn View Dr Ste 200 Second Fl *Web:* www.engelberth.com	Colchester	VT	05446	802-655-0100	
Engineering Economics Inc 8700 Monrovia St Ste 310 *Web:* www.eeienginers.com	Lenexa	KS	66215	303-239-8700	
Environamics Inc 1401 Freedom Dr *Web:* www.environamics-inc.com	Charlotte	NC	28208	704-376-3613	
ERC Properties Inc 813 Ft St *Web:* www.erc.com	Barling	AR	72923	479-452-9950	
Erdman Co One Erdman Pl *Web:* www.erdman.com	Madison	WI	53717	608-410-8000	
ESA Construction Inc 3435 Girard Blvd NE Ste A *Web:* www.esaconstruction.com	Albuquerque	NM	87107	505-884-2171	888-3150
Eutaw Construction Company Inc 109 1/2 W Commerce St PO Box 36 *Web:* www.eutawconstruction.com	Aberdeen	MS	39730	662-369-8868	369-7770
Evergreen Engineering Portland LLC 7431 Nw Evergreen Pkwy Ste 210 *Web:* www.evergreenengineering.com	Hillsboro	OR	97124	503-439-8777	
Ewing Construction Company Inc PO Box 4235 *Web:* www.ewingcc.com	Corpus Christi	TX	78469	361-882-6525	882-8424
Express Construction Company Inc 355 118th Ave SE Ste 100 *Web:* www.expressconstruction.net	Bellevue	WA	98005	206-230-8500	
EXXCEL Project Management Inc 328 S Civic Ctr Dr *Web:* www.exxcel.com	Columbus	OH	43215	614-621-4500	
F&H Construction 1115 E Lockeford St *Web:* www.f-hconst.com	Lodi	CA	95240	209-931-3738	
FA Wilhelm Construction Co Inc 3914 Prospect St *Web:* www.fawilhelm.com	Indianapolis	IN	46203	317-359-5411	359-8346
Facility Construction Services Inc 8200 Lovett Ave *Web:* www.fcsdallas.com	Dallas	TX	75227	214-381-0101	275-4744
Facility Group Inc 2233 Lake Pk Dr Ste 100 *Web:* fdgatlanta.com	Smyrna	GA	30080	770-437-2700	437-3900
Fairfield Banchshares Inc 220 E Main St PO Box 429 *Web:* www.fairfieldnb.com	Fairfield	IL	62837	618-842-2107	842-5849
Faith Enterprises Inc 129 S Corona St *Web:* www.faithenterprisesinc.com	Colorado Springs	CO	80903	719-578-8281	
Fassberg Construction Co 17000 Ventura Blvd Ste 200 *Web:* www.fassbergconstruction.com	Encino	CA	91316	818-386-1800	
FBI Buildings Inc 3823 W 1800 S *Web:* www.fbibuildings.com	Remington	IN	47977	219-261-2157	
FCL Builders Inc 1150 Spring Lk Dr *Web:* www.fclbuilders.com	Itasca	IL	60143	630-773-0050	773-4030
Ferguson Construction Co 400 Canal St *Web:* www.ferguson-construction.com	Sidney	OH	45365	937-498-2381	498-1796
Findorff JH & Son Inc 300 S Bedford St *Web:* www.findorff.com	Madison	WI	53703	608-257-5321	257-5306
FIP Construction Inc 308 Farmington Ave *Web:* www.fipconstruction.com	Farmington	CT	06032	203-271-0356	
First Financial Bank 223 N Mill St PO Box 680 *Web:* first-online.com	Pontiac	IL	61764	815-844-3171	842-2958
Fisher Development Inc 601 California St Ste 300 *Web:* www.fisherinc.com	San Francisco	CA	94108	415-228-3060	468-6241
Fite Building Company Inc 3116 Sexton Rd SE Ste A *Web:* www.fitebuilding.com	Decatur	AL	35603	256-353-5759	
Five Star Industries Inc 1308 Wells St Rd *Web:* www.5starind.com	Du Quoin	IL	62832	618-542-5421	
Flintco LLC 1624 W 21st St *TF:* 800-947-2828 ■ *Web:* www.flintco.com	Tulsa	OK	74107	918-587-8451	582-7506
Flow Construction Company Inc 3628 Trousdale Dr Ste E *Web:* flowconstruction.com	Nashville	TN	37204	615-832-0707	
Fluor Constructors International Inc 352 Halton Rd	Greenville	SC	29607	864-234-7335	234-5476
Fluor Daniel Inc Three Polaris Way *Web:* www.fluor.com	Aliso Viejo	CA	92698	949-349-2000	349-2585
Ford Development Corp 11148 Woodward Ln *Web:* www.forddevelopment.com	Cincinnati	OH	45241	513-772-1521	772-1556
Forino Company LP 555 Mtn Home Rd *Web:* www.forino.com	Sinking Spring	PA	19608	610-670-2200	
Fort Hill Construction Inc 8118 Hollywood Blvd *Web:* www.forthill.com	Los Angeles	CA	90069	323-656-7425	
Fortney & Weygandt Inc 31269 Bradley Rd *Web:* www.fortneyweygandt.com	North Olmsted	OH	44070	440-716-4000	716-4010
Foushee & Assoc Inc 3260 118th Ave SE *Web:* www.foushee.com	Bellevue	WA	98005	425-746-1000	746-3737
Francis Tuttle Technology Ctr School District 21 12777 N Rockwell Ave *Web:* www.francistuttle.edu	Oklahoma City	OK	73142	405-717-7799	
Frank L. Blum Construction Co 830 E 25th St *Web:* www.flblum.com	Winston-Salem	NC	27105	336-724-5528	
Frank Rewold & Son Inc 333 E Second St *Web:* frankrewold.com	Rochester	MI	48307	248-651-7242	

Company	City	State	Zip	Phone	Fax
Franklin Electric LP 916 Fulton St *Web:* www.franklinelectric.net	Pittsburgh	PA	15233	412-322-4477	
Fred Olivieri Construction Company Inc 6315 Promway Ave NW *Web:* www.fredolivieri.com	North Canton	OH	44720	330-494-1007	
Frederick Quinn Corp 103 S Church St *Web:* www.fquinncorp.com	Addison	IL	60101	630-628-8500	628-8595
Frize Corp 16605 Gale Ave *Web:* www.frizecorp.com	City Of Industry	CA	91745	626-369-6088	
Fuller Engineering Co 4135 W 99th St *Web:* www.fullerengineering.com	Carmel	IN	46032	317-228-5800	
Furino & Son Inc 66 Columbia Rd *Web:* www.furinoandsons.com	Branchburg	NJ	08876	908-756-7736	756-3783
Fusco Corp 555 Long Wharf Dr Long Wharf Maritime Ctr Ste 14 *Web:* www.fusco.com	New Haven	CT	06511	203-777-7451	
FutureNet Group Inc 12801 Auburn St *Web:* www.futurenetgroup.com	Detroit	MI	48223	313-544-7117	
G & D Transportation Inc 50 Commerce Dr *TF:* 800-451-6680 ■ *Web:* www.gdintegrated.com	Morton	IL	61550	309-266-1472	
G L Wilson Bldg Co 190 Wilson Pk Rd *Web:* www.glwilson.com	Statesville	NC	28625	704-872-2411	872-8281
G.M. Crisalli Associates Inc 843 Hiawatha Blvd W *Web:* gmca.com	Syracuse	NY	13204	315-454-0000	
Gaines Motor Lines Inc 2349 13th Ave SW PO Box 1549 *TF:* 800-438-7311 ■ *Web:* www.gainesml.com	Hickory	NC	28603	828-322-2000	324-7026
Galaxie Defense Marketing Services 5330 Napa St *Web:* www.galaxiemgmt.com	San Diego	CA	92110	619-299-9950	
Gamma Construction Co 2808 Joanel St *Web:* www.gammaconst.com	Houston	TX	77027	713-963-0086	963-0961
Ganneston Construction Corp 3025 N Belfast Ave Rt 3 *Web:* gannestonconstruction.com	Augusta	ME	04330	207-621-8505	
Ganther Construction & Architecture Inc 4825 County Rd A *Web:* www.ganther.com	Oshkosh	WI	54901	920-426-4774	
Garco Construction Inc 4114 E Broadway *Web:* www.garco.com	Spokane	WA	99202	509-535-4688	
Garling Construction Inc 1120 11th St *Web:* www.garlingconstruction.com	Belle Plaine	IA	52208	319-444-3409	444-2437
GE Johnson Construction Co 25 N Cascade Ave Ste 400 *TF:* 800-640-9501 ■ *Web:* www.gejohnson.com	Colorado Springs	CO	80903	719-473-5321	473-5324
Geis Cos, The 10020 Aurora Hudson Rd *Web:* www.geis.us	Streetsboro	OH	44241	330-528-3500	528-0008
Geneva Construction Co (GCCO) 1350 Aurora Ave *Web:* www.genevaconstruction.net	Aurora	IL	60507	630-892-4357	892-7738
George J. Shaw Construction Co 1601 Bellefontaine Ave *Web:* georgeshawconstruction.com	Kansas City	MO	64127	816-231-8200	
George Sollitt Construction 790 N Central Ave *Web:* www.sollitt.com	Wood Dale	IL	60191	630-860-7333	
Gerace Construction Company Inc 4055 S Saginaw Rd *Web:* www.geraceconstruction.com	Midland	MI	48640	989-496-2440	496-2465
Gerald H Phipps 5995 Greenwood Florida Plaza Blvd Ste 100 *TF:* 866-487-2365 ■ *Web:* www.ghpd.com	Greenwood Village	CO	80111	303-571-5377	629-7467
Gerardi Construction Inc 1604 N 19th St *Web:* www.gerardiconstruction.com	Tampa	FL	33605	813-248-4341	
Gerloff Company Inc 14955 Bulverde Rd *TF:* 800-486-3621 ■ *Web:* www.gerloffinc.com	San Antonio	TX	78247	210-490-2777	494-0610
Gibbs Construction LLC 5736 Citrus Blvd Ste 200 *Web:* www.gibbsconstruction.net	New Orleans	LA	70123	504-733-4336	
Gil Haugan Construction Inc 200 E 60th St N *Web:* www.gilhaugan.com	Sioux Falls	SD	57104	605-336-6082	
Gilbane Bldg Co New England Regional Office 7 Jackson Walkway *TF:* 800-445-2263 ■ *Web:* www.gilbaneco.com	Providence	RI	02903	401-456-5800	456-5936
Gilbane Bldg Company Mid-Atlantic Regional Office 7901 Sandy Spring Rd Ste 500 *TF:* 800-445-2263 ■ *Web:* www.gilbaneco.com	Laurel	MD	20707	301-317-6100	317-6155
Gilbane Bldg Company Southwest Regional Office 1331 Lamar St Ste 1170 *TF:* 800-445-2263 ■ *Web:* www.gilbaneco.com	Houston	TX	77010	713-209-1873	651-0541
Gilford Corp 4600 Powder Mill Rd Ste 350 *Web:* www.gilfordcorp.com	Beltsville	MD	20705	301-931-3900	
Gillis Gilkerson Inc 212 W Main St Ste 305 *Web:* www.gillisgilkerson.com	Salisbury	MD	21801	410-749-4821	
Giordano Construction Company Inc 1155 Main St *Web:* www.giordano-construction.com	Branford	CT	06405	203-488-7264	481-5764
Glenn H. Johnson Construction 1776 Winthrop Dr *Web:* www.ghjohnson.com	Des Plaines	IL	60018	847-297-4700	
Golden Sands General Contractors Inc 2500 NW 39 St *Web:* www.goldensandsgc.com	Miami	FL	33142	305-633-3336	
Gomez Construction Co 7100 SW 44th St *Web:* www.gomezconstruction.com	Miami	FL	33155	305-661-7660	661-0504
Gootee Construction Inc 2400 N Arnoult Rd *Web:* www.gootee.com	Metairie	LA	70001	504-831-1909	
Grae-Con Construction Inc PO Box 1778 *Web:* www.graecon.com	Steubenville	OH	43952	740-282-6830	282-6849
Granger Construction Co 6267 Aurelius Rd *Web:* www.grangerconstruction.com	Lansing	MI	48911	517-393-1670	393-1382
Grant Parish School Board (GPSB) 512 Main St PO Box 208 *TF:* 877-277-3812 ■ *Web:* www.gpsb.org	Colfax	LA	71417	318-627-3274	627-5931
Gray Construction 10 Quality St *TF:* 800-814-8468 ■ *Web:* www.gray.com	Lexington	KY	40507	859-281-5000	252-5300
Green Acres Contracting Company Inc 703 Pennsylvania Ave *Web:* www.greenacrescontracting.com	Scottdale	PA	15683	724-887-8096	
Greenway Enterprises Inc PO Box 5553 *Web:* www.greenwayent.com	Helena	MT	59604	406-458-9411	458-6516
GreenWood Inc 160 Milestone Way Ste A *Web:* www.gwood.com	Greenville	SC	29615	864-244-9669	
Greiner Construction Inc 625 Marquette Ave *Web:* www.greinerconstruction.biz	Minneapolis	MN	55402	612-338-1696	
Greystone Construction Co 500 Marschall Rd Ste 300 *Web:* www.greystoneconstruction.com	Shakopee	MN	55379	952-496-2227	
Groupe Plombaction Inc 575 boul Pierre-Roux est *Web:* www.groupeplombaction.com	Victoriaville	QC	G6T1S7	819-752-6064	
Grunley Construction Company Inc 15020 Shady Grove Rd Ste 500 *Web:* www.grunley.com	Rockville	MD	20850	240-399-2000	399-2001
Gulf & Pacific Equities Corp 1300 Bay St Ste 300 *Web:* www.gpequities.com	Toronto	ON	M5R3K8	416-968-3337	
Gulf Seaboard General Contractors Inc 629 N Washington Hwy *Web:* www.gulfseaboard.com	Ashland	VA	23005	804-752-7600	
Gunda Corporation LLC 6161 Savoy Dr Ste 550 *Web:* www.gundacorp.com	Houston	TX	77036	713-541-3530	
Guntersville City Schools Board of Education 4200 Alabama 79 S	Guntersville	AL	35976	256-582-3159	582-6158
Gutirrez Co, The One Wall St *Web:* www.gutierrezco.com	Burlington	MA	01803	781-272-7000	272-3130
Gutknecht Construction Co 2280 Citygate Dr *Web:* www.gutknecht.com	Columbus	OH	43219	614-532-5410	
H & M Construction Company Inc 50 Security Dr *Web:* hmcompany.com	Jackson	TN	38305	731-664-6300	
H C Olsen Construction Company Inc 710 Los Angeles Ave *Web:* www.hcolsen.com	Monrovia	CA	91016	626-359-8900	
H.P. Cummings Construction Co 14 Prospect St PO Box 29 *Web:* www.hpcummings.com	Ware	MA	01082	413-967-6251	
Halbert Construction Company Inc 330 S Magnolia Ave Ste 203 *Web:* www.halbertco.com	El Cajon	CA	92020	619-593-3527	
Halco Products 100 Gordon St Ste 1 *Web:* www.halco-products.com	Elk Grove Village	IL	60007	847-956-1600	
Haley Construction Inc 900 Orange Ave *Web:* www.haleyconstruction.com	Daytona Beach	FL	32114	386-944-0470	944-0471
Haley-Greer Inc 2257 -C Lombardy Ln *Web:* www.haleygreer.com	Dallas	TX	75220	972-556-1177	556-1384
Halfacre Construction Co 7015 Professional Pkwy E *Web:* www.halfacreconstruction.com	Sarasota	FL	34240	941-907-9099	
Hammer & Hand Inc 1020 Se Harrison St *Web:* hammerandhand.com	Portland	OR	97214	503-232-2447	
Hanlin-Rainaldi Construction Corp 6610 Singletree Dr *Web:* www.hanlinrainaldi.com	Columbus	OH	43229	614-436-4204	
Hansen Company Inc, The 5665 Greendale Rd Ste A *Web:* www.hansencompany.com	Johnston	IA	50131	515-270-1117	270-3829
Harbour Contractors Inc 23830 W Main St *Web:* www.harbour-cm.com	Plainfield	IL	60544	815-254-5500	254-5505
Hardaway Group 615 Main St *Web:* www.hardaway.net	Nashville	TN	37206	615-254-5461	254-4518
Hardy Bros Inc 6406 Siloam Rd *TF:* 800-525-5354 ■ *Web:* www.hardybros.com	Siloam	NC	27047	336-374-5050	374-5045
Harkins Builders Inc 2201 Warwick Way *TF:* 800-227-2345 ■ *Web:* www.harkinsbuilders.com	Marriottsville	MD	21104	410-750-2600	480-4299
Harman Construction Inc 1633 Rogers Rd *Web:* harmanconstructioninc.net	Fort Worth	TX	76107	817-336-5780	336-5797
Harper Construction Company Inc 2241 Kettner Blvd Ste 300 *Web:* www.harperconstruction.com	San Diego	CA	92101	619-233-7900	
Harvey Benjamin r Company Inc Contractors Nine Cindy Ln *Web:* www.bharveyco.com	Ocean	NJ	07712	732-493-2300	
Harvey-cleary Builders 207a Perry Pkwy Ste 1 *Web:* www.harveycleary.com	Gaithersburg	MD	20877	301-519-2288	
Haselden Construction LLC 6950 S Potomac St *Web:* www.haselden.com	Centennial	CO	80112	303-751-1478	751-1627
Haskell Co 111 Riverside Ave *TF:* 800-622-4326 ■ *Web:* haskell.com	Jacksonville	FL	32202	904-791-4500	791-4699
Haskell Corp PO Box 917 *Web:* www.haskellcorp.com	Bellingham	WA	98227	360-734-1200	734-5538
Hathaway Dinwiddie Construction Co 275 Battery St Ste 300 *Web:* www.hdcco.com	San Francisco	CA	94111	415-986-2718	956-5669
Hawkins Construction Co 2516 Deer Pk Blvd *Web:* www.hawkins1.com	Omaha	NE	68105	402-342-1607	
Haydon Building Corp 4640 E Cotton Gin Loop *Web:* www.haydonbc.com	Phoenix	AZ	85040	602-296-1496	

Company	City	State	ZIP	Phone	Fax
HBD Construction Inc 5517 Manchester Ave *Web:* www.hbdgc.com	Saint Louis	MO	63110	314-781-8000	
HBE Corp 11330 Olive Blvd *Web:* www.hbecorp.com	Saint Louis	MO	63141	314-567-9000	567-0602
Heartland Bldg Company Inc 117 William St	Middlesex	NJ	08846	732-302-9277	
Hedrick Brothers Construction Company Inc 2200 Centrepark W Dr Ste 100 *Web:* www.hedrickbrothers.com	West Palm Beach	FL	33409	561-689-8880	
Hellas Construction Inc 12710 Research Blvd Ste 240 *Web:* www.hellasconstruction.com	Austin	TX	78759	512-250-2910	
Henderson Corp 575New Jersey 28	Raritan	NJ	08869	908-685-1300	
Hennessy Construction Services Corp 2300 22nd St N *Web:* www.hcsfl.com	Saint Petersburg	FL	33713	727-821-3223	
Henning Construction Company Inc PO Box 394 *Web:* www.henningconstruction.com	Johnston	IA	50131	515-253-0943	253-0942
Hensel Phelps Construction Co 420 Sixth Ave PO Box 0 *TF:* 800-826-6309 ■ *Web:* www.henselphelps.com	Greeley	CO	80632	970-352-6565	352-9311
Herrero Brothers Inc 2100 Oakdale Ave *Web:* www.herrero.com	San Francisco	CA	94124	415-824-7675	
HG Reynolds Co Inc 113 Contract Dr	Aiken	SC	29801	803-641-1401	
HHI Corp 736 W Harrisville Rd *Web:* www.hhicorp.com	Ogden	UT	84404	385-333-4400	
Hi-five Development Services Inc 202 W Main St Ste C *Web:* hifive1.com	Mason	OH	45040	513-336-9280	
Highland Partnership Inc 285 Bay Blvd *Web:* www.highlandpartnership.net	Chula Vista	CA	91910	619-498-2900	
Hilco Transport Inc 7700 Kenmont Rd *Web:* www.hilcotransport.com	Greensboro	NC	27409	336-273-9441	273-9701
Hinderliter Construction Inc 3601 N Saint Joseph Ave *Web:* www.hinderliterconstruction.com	Evansville	IN	47720	812-425-4137	
Hitt Contracting Inc 2900 Fairview Park Dr *Web:* www.hitt-gc.com	Falls Church	VA	22042	703-846-9000	846-9110
HJ Russell & Co 504 Fair St SW *Web:* www.hjrussell.com	Atlanta	GA	30313	404-330-1000	688-5179
Hoar Construction Inc Two Metroplex Dr # 400 *Web:* www.hoar.com	Birmingham	AL	35209	205-803-2121	423-2323
HOF Construction Inc 3137 Jamieson Ave *Web:* www.hofconstruction.com	Saint Louis	MO	63139	314-645-2200	
Hoffman Construction Corp 805 SW Broadway Ste 2100 *Web:* www.hoffmancorp.com	Portland	OR	97205	503-221-8811	221-8934
Hoffman Planning, Design, & Construction Inc 122 E College Ave Ste 1G *Web:* www.hoffman.net	Appleton	WI	54911	920-731-2322	
Hogg Construction 2351 Freedom Way *Web:* www.hoggconstruct.com	York	PA	17402	717-741-0839	
Hohl Industrial Services Inc 770 Riverview Blvd *Web:* www.hohlind.com	Buffalo	NY	14150	716-332-0466	
Holder Construction Co 3333 Riverwood Pkwy Ste 400 *Web:* www.holderconstruction.com	Atlanta	GA	30339	770-988-3000	988-3042
Hollister Construction Co 4887 E La Palma Ave Ste 705 *Web:* www.hollico.net	Anaheim	CA	92807	714-701-1400	
Holloman Corp 333 N Sam Houston Pkwy E Ste 600 *Web:* www.hollomancorp.com	Houston	TX	77060	281-878-2600	272-1227
Hood Construction Company Inc 1050 Shop Rd Ste A *Web:* www.hoodconstruction.com	Columbia	SC	29201	803-765-2940	
Horst Group Inc 320 Granite Run Dr PO Box 3330 *TF:* 800-732-0330 ■ *Web:* www.horstgroup.com	Lancaster	PA	17604	717-581-9800	581-9816
Hospitality Builders Inc 506 S Wilson St *Web:* www.hospitalitybuilders.com	Aberdeen	SD	57401	605-229-5945	
Housley Communications Inc 3550 S Bryant Blvd *TF:* 800-880-9905 ■ *Web:* housleygroup.com	San Angelo	TX	76903	325-944-9905	944-1781
Howard Immel Inc 1820 Radisson St *Web:* www.immel-builds.com	Green Bay	WI	54302	920-468-8208	
Hunt Construction Group 2450 S Tibbs Ave *Web:* www.huntconstructiongroup.com	Indianapolis	IN	46241	317-227-7800	227-7810
Hunzinger Construction Co 21100 Enterprise Ave *Web:* www.hunzinger.com	Brookfield	WI	53045	262-797-0797	797-0474
Hutter Construction Corp 810 Turnpike Rd *Web:* hutterconstruction.com	New Ipswich	NH	03071	603-878-2300	
Hutton Construction Corp 2229 S W St *Web:* www.huttonconstruction.com	Wichita	KS	67213	316-942-8855	
Ideal Builders Inc 1406 Emil St *Web:* www.idealbuildersinc.com	Madison	WI	53713	608-271-8111	
Ideal Interiors Inc 450 Seventh Ave *Web:* www.ideal-interiors.com	New York	NY	10123	212-262-7005	262-7024
IMCO Carbide Tool Inc 28170 Cedar Park Blvd *Web:* www.imcousa.com	Perrysburg	OH	43551	419-661-6313	
Imco General Construction Inc 2116 Buchanan Loop *Web:* imcoconstruction.com	Ferndale	WA	98248	360-671-3936	
Industrial Resources Inc PO Box 2648 *Web:* www.indres.com	Fairmont	WV	26555	304-363-4100	367-9737
Inman-emj Construction 88 Union Ave Ste 400 *Web:* www.inmanconstruction.com	Memphis	TN	38103	901-682-4100	682-0755
Inspec Group LLC 140 SW Arthur St *Web:* www.inspecgroup.com	Portland	OR	97201	503-595-6540	
Interface Construction Corp 8401 Wabash Ave *Web:* www.interfaceconstruction.com	Saint Louis	MO	63134	314-522-1011	522-1022
International Contractors Inc 977 S Rt 83 *Web:* www.iciinc.com	Elmhurst	IL	60126	630-834-8043	
IPAC Services Corp 8701 102 St *Web:* www.ipacservices.com	Clairmont	AB	T0H0W0	780-532-7350	
Irmscher Inc 1030 Osage St	Fort Wayne	IN	46808	260-422-5572	424-1487
Irwin Industries Inc 1580 W Carson St *Web:* www.irwinindustries.com	Long Beach	CA	90810	310-233-3000	834-9402
J & R Builders 84 Miller Woods Dr *Web:* www.betterhomeinspectionsvermont.com	Barre	VT	05641	802-476-3386	
J D H Contracting 8109 Network Dr *Web:* www.jdhcontracting.com	Plainfield	IN	46168	317-839-0520	
J F C Construction Inc 4901 Pacheco Blvd *Web:* www.jfcconstruction.com	Martinez	CA	94553	925-228-0924	
J Kokolakis Contracting Inc 1500 Ocean Ave *Web:* www.jkokolakis.com	Bohemia	NY	11716	631-744-6147	744-6156
J L Wallace Inc 9111 W College Pointe Dr *Web:* www.jlwallaceinc.com	Fort Myers	FL	33919	239-437-1111	
J R Roberts Corp 7745 Greenback Ln Ste 300 *Web:* www.jrroberts.com	Citrus Heights	CA	95610	916-729-5600	
J T Turner Construction Co Inc 2250 E Victory Dr Ste 104 *Web:* www.jttconst.com	Savannah	GA	31404	912-356-5611	356-5615
J.A. Street & Associates Inc 245 Birch St *Web:* www.jastreet.com	Blountville	TN	37617	423-323-8017	
J.I. Garcia Construction Co 5591 N Golden State Blvd #101 *Web:* www.jigarcia.com	Fresno	CA	93722	559-276-7726	
J.R. Abbot Construction Inc 3408 First Ave S *Web:* www.jrabbott.com	Seattle	WA	98134	206-467-8500	447-1885
J.W. Design & Construction Inc 3563 Sueldo St Ste I *Web:* www.jwdci.com	San Luis Obispo	CA	93401	805-544-3130	
JA Tiberti Construction Co 1806 Industrial Rd *Web:* www.tiberti.com	Las Vegas	NV	89102	702-248-4000	382-5361
Jackson Local Schools District (JLSD) 7602 Fulton Dr *Web:* jackson.stark.k12.oh.us	Massillon	OH	44646	330-830-8000	830-8008
Jacob White Construction Co 2000 W Parkwood Ste 100 *Web:* www.jacobwhitecc.com	Friendswood	TX	77546	281-286-6666	
James G Davis Construction Corp 12530 Parklawn Dr Ste 100 *Web:* www.davisconstruction.com	Rockville	MD	20852	301-881-2990	468-3918
Janus Corp 1081 Shary Cir *Web:* www.januscorp.com	Concord	CA	94518	925-969-9200	
Jasmine Engineering Inc 115 E Travis St Ste 1020 *Web:* www.jasmineengineering.com	San Antonio	TX	78205	210-227-3000	
Jayman MasterBUILT Inc 200 3132 - 118 Ave SE *Web:* www.jayman.com	Calgary	AB	T2Z3X1	403-258-3772	
Jaynes Corp 2906 Broadway NE **Fax Area Code: 619* ■ *TF:* 800-393-6343 ■ *Web:* www.jaynescorp.com	Albuquerque	NM	87107	505-345-8591	233-4090*
JCN Construction Company Inc 155 Dow St *Web:* www.jcnconstruction.com	Manchester	NH	03101	603-624-7080	
JE Dunn Construction Co 1001 Locust St *Web:* www.jedunn.com	Kansas City	MO	64106	816-474-8600	460-2769
Jeffrey M. Brown Assoc LLC 2337 Philmont Ave *Web:* www.jmbassociates.com	Huntingdon Valley	PA	19006	215-938-5000	938-5005
Jendoco Construction Corp 2000 Lincoln Rd *Web:* www.jendoco.com	Pittsburgh	PA	15235	412-361-4500	
Jensen Builders Ltd 1175 S 32nd St *Web:* www.jensenbuilders.com	Fort Dodge	IA	50501	515-573-3292	
JESCO Inc 2020 McCullough Blvd *Web:* jescoinc.net	Tupelo	MS	38801	662-842-3240	680-6123
JGA-Beacon Inc 2200 Cook Dr *Web:* www.jgacorp.com	Atlanta	GA	30340	770-246-3400	
JJ Deluca Company Inc 760 W Sproul Rd Ste 300 *Web:* www.jjdeluca.com	Springfield	PA	19064	610-543-6660	
JLC Associates Inc 3198-A Airport Loop Dr *Web:* www.jlcassoc.com	Costa Mesa	CA	92626	714-241-4430	
John Burns Construction Company Inc 17601 Southwest Hwy *Web:* www.jbconstructionco.com	Orland Park	IL	60467	708-326-3500	
John Deklewa & Sons Inc 1273 Washington Pk *Web:* www.deklewa.com	Bridgeville	PA	15017	412-257-9000	257-4486
John E Jones Oil Co Inc 1016 S Cedar PO Box 546 *TF:* 800-323-9821 ■ *Web:* www.jonesoil.net	Stockton	KS	67669	785-425-6746	425-6323
John Gallin & Son Inc 102 Madison Ave Ninth Fl *Web:* www.gallin.com	New York	NY	10016	212-252-8900	
John S Clark Co Inc 210 Airport Rd *Web:* www.jsclark.com	Mount Airy	NC	27030	336-789-1000	789-7609
Joseph A Natoli Construction Corp 293 Changebridge Rd *Web:* www.jnatoli.com	Pine Brook	NJ	07058	973-575-1500	575-8216
Joseph Construction Company Inc 203 Letterman Rd *Web:* www.josephconst.com	Knoxville	TN	37919	865-584-3945	
K L House Construction Company Inc 6409 Acoma Rd SE *Web:* www.klhouse.com	Albuquerque	NM	87108	505-268-4361	268-9266

	City	State	ZIP	Phone	Fax
Kalamazoo Valley Plant Growers Cooperative Inc 8937 Krum Ave *Web:* www.kvpg.com	Galesburg	MI	49053	269-216-1200	
Kapp Construction Co 329 Mt Vernon Ave PO Box 629 *Web:* www.kappconstruction.com	Springfield	OH	45503	937-324-0134	324-3406
Kaufman Lynn Construction Inc 4850 T-Rex Ave Ste 300 *Web:* www.kaufmanlynn.com	Boca Raton	FL	33431	561-361-6700	
Kcc Contractor Inc 2664 E Kearney St *Web:* www.killco.com	Springfield	MO	65803	417-883-1204	887-7338
KCI Construction Co 10315 Lk Bluff Dr *Web:* www.kciconstruction.com	St. Louis	MO	63123	314-894-8888	
Keating Bldg Corp 1600 Arch St Ste 300 *Web:* www.tutorperinibuilding.com	Philadelphia	PA	19103	610-668-4100	668-4060
Keating Daniel J Co 134 N Narberth Ave *Web:* www.djkeating.com	Narberth	PA	19072	610-664-2799	
Keller Inc N216 State Rd 55 *Web:* www.kellerbuilds.com	Kaukauna	WI	54130	920-766-5795	
Kelsey Construction Inc 306 E Princeton St *Web:* www.kelseyconstruction.com	Orlando	FL	32804	407-898-4101	898-0172
Kemp Bros. Construction Inc 10135 Geary Ave *Web:* www.kempbros.com	Santa Fe Springs	CA	90670	562-236-5000	
Ken Brady Construction Company Inc 4001 Turnagain Blvd *Web:* www.kenbrady.com	Anchorage	AK	99517	907-243-4604	
Kenmore Construction Co Inc 700 Home Ave *Web:* www.kenmorecompanies.com	Akron	OH	44310	330-762-9373	762-2135
Kenny Construction Co 2215 Sanders Rd Ste 400 *Web:* www.kennyconstruction.com	Northbrook	IL	60062	847-541-8200	272-5421
Key Construction Inc 741 W Second *Web:* www.keyconstruction.com	Wichita	KS	67203	316-263-9515	
Kickerillo Cos 1306 S Fry Rd **Fax Area Code:* 281 ■ *Web:* www.kickerillo.com	Katy	TX	77450	713-951-0666	492-2018*
Kinco Constructors LLC 12600 Lawson Rd *Web:* www.kincoconstructors.com	Little Rock	AR	72210	501-225-7606	
Kinney Construction Services Inc 120 N Beaver St Ste 100 *Web:* www.kinneyconstruction.net	Flagstaff	AZ	86001	928-779-2820	
Kinsley Construction Inc 1110 E Princess St *Web:* www.rkinsley.com	York	PA	17403	717-741-3841	741-9054
Kirila Contractors Inc 505 Bedford Rd PO Box 179 *Web:* www.kirila.com	Brookfield	OH	44403	330-448-4055	454-4054
Kirtley-Cole Associates LLC 1010 SE Everett Mall Way Ste 102 *Web:* www.kirtley-cole.com	Everett	WA	98208	425-609-0400	
Kitchell Corp 1707 E Highland Ave Ste 100 **Fax:* Hum Res ■ *Web:* www.kitchell.com	Phoenix	AZ	85016	602-264-4411	364-6133*
Kiwi Ii Construction Inc 28177 Keller Rd *Web:* www.kiwiconstruction.com	Murrieta	CA	92563	951-301-8975	
Kjellstrom & Lee Inc 1607 Ownby Ln *Web:* www.kjellstromandlee.com	Richmond	VA	23220	804-288-0082	285-4288
Klassen Corp 2021 Westwind Dr *Web:* www.klassencorp.com	Bakersfield	CA	93301	661-324-3000	
Knutson Construction Services Inc 7515 Wayzata Blvd Ste 300 *Web:* www.knutsonconstruction.com	Minneapolis	MN	55426	763-546-1400	546-2226
Korte Co, The 9225 W Flamingo Rd Ste 100 *Web:* www.korteco.com	Las Vegas	NV	89147	702-228-9551	228-5852
Korth Companies Inc, The 9101 Gaither Rd *Web:* www.korthcos.com	Gaithersburg	MD	20877	301-921-9500	
KPRS Construction Services Inc 2850 Saturn St *Web:* www.kprsinc.com	Brea	CA	92821	714-672-0800	672-0871
Kraemer Bros Inc 925 Pk Ave *Web:* www.kraemerbrothers.com	Plain	WI	53577	608-546-2411	546-2509
Kreis Johnson Construction 160 Village St Ste 100 *Web:* www.johnsonkreis.com	Birmingham	AL	35242	205-981-9030	
Krusinski Construction Co 2107 Swift Dr *Web:* www.krusinski.com	Oak Brook	IL	60523	630-573-7700	
Kustom Fl LLC 265 Hunt Park Cv *TF:* 866-679-0699 ■ *Web:* www.kustom.us	Longwood	FL	32750	866-679-0699	
L Kelley Construction Co 2901 Falling Springs Rd *Web:* www.lkeeley.com	Sauget	IL	62206	314-421-5933	421-2266
L L Pelling Co 1425 W Penn St PO Box 230 *Web:* www.llpelling.com	North Liberty	IA	52317	319-626-4600	626-4605
La Habra City School District (LHCSD) 500 N Walnut St PO Box 307 *Web:* www.lhcsd.k12.ca.us	La Habra	CA	90631	562-690-2305	
Lacy Construction Co 3356 W Old Hwy 30 P O Box 188 *Web:* www.lacygc.com	Grand Island	NE	68801	308-384-2866	
Ladco Company Ltd 200-40 Lakewood Blvd *Web:* www.ladco.mb.ca	Winnipeg	MB	R2J2M6	204-982-5900	
Lakeview Construction Inc 10505 Corp Dr Ste 200 *Web:* www.lvconstruction.com	Pleasant Prairie	WI	53158	262-857-3336	857-3424
Lampasas Isd 207 W Eigth St *Web:* www.lampasas.k12.tx.us	Lampasas	TX	76550	512-556-6224	556-8711
Landau Bldg Co 9855 Rinaman Rd *Web:* www.landau-bldg.com	Wexford	PA	15090	724-935-8800	935-6510
Landis Construction LLC 8300 Earhart Blvd Ste 300 PO Box 4278 *Web:* www.landisllc.com	New Orleans	LA	70118	504-833-6070	833-6662
Lanham Brothers General Contractors 2119 W 3rd St *Web:* www.lanhambros.com	Owensboro	KY	42301	270-683-4591	
Larson-Danielson Construction Company Inc 302 Tyler St *Web:* www.ldconstruction.com	La Porte	IN	46350	219-362-2127	
Lathrop Co 460 W Dussel Dr *Web:* www.turnerconstruction.com	Maumee	OH	43537	419-893-7000	893-1741
Law Company Inc, The 345 Riverview St Ste 300 *Web:* www.law-co.com	Wichita	KS	67203	316-268-0200	268-0210
Lease Crutcher Lewis 107 Spring St *Web:* www.lewisbuilds.com	Seattle	WA	98104	206-622-0500	343-6541
LeChase Construction Services LLC 300 Trolley Blvd *Web:* www.lechase.com	Rochester	NY	14606	585-254-3510	
Lee Kennedy Company Inc 122 Quincy Shore Dr *Web:* www.leekennedy.com	Quincy	MA	02171	617-825-6930	
Lee Lewis Construction Inc 7810 Orlando Ave *Web:* www.leelewis.com	Lubbock	TX	79423	806-797-8400	797-8492
Lehr Construction Company Inc 2115 Frederick Ave *Web:* www.lehrconstruction.com	Saint Joseph	MO	64501	816-232-4431	
Lend Lease Corp 200 Pk Ave 9th Fl *Web:* www.lendlease.com	New York	NY	10166	212-592-6800	592-6988
Leon D. DeMatteis Construction 820 Elmont Rd *Web:* www.dematteisorg.com	Elmont	NY	11003	516-285-5500	
Leonard S. Fiore Inc 5506 Sixth Ave Rear *Web:* www.lsfiore.com	Altoona	PA	16602	814-946-3686	
Leopardo Cos Inc 5200 Prairie Stone Pkwy *Web:* www.leopardo.com	Hoffman Estates	IL	60192	847-783-3000	783-3001
Letsos Co 8435 Westglen Dr PO Box 36927 *Web:* www.letsos.com	Houston	TX	77063	713-783-3200	972-7880
Lettire Construction Corp 334-336 E 110th St *Web:* lettire.com	New York	NY	10029	212-996-6640	
Levine Builders 42-09 235th St *Web:* www.levinebuilders.com	Douglaston	NY	11363	718-281-0550	
Lewis & Michael Inc 1827 Woodman Dr *TF:* 800-543-3524 ■ *Web:* atlaslm.com	Dayton	OH	45420	937-252-6683	258-7862
Lewis Contractors LLC 55 Gwynns Mill Ct *Web:* www.lewis-contractors.com	Owings Mills	MD	21117	410-356-4200	356-7732
Lightner Electronics Inc 1771 Beaver Dam Rd *Web:* www.lightnerelectronics.com	Claysburg	PA	16625	814-239-8323	
Linbeck Construction Corp 3900 Essex Ln Ste 1200 PO Box 22500 **Fax:* Mktg ■ *Web:* www.linbeck.com	Houston	TX	77027	713-621-2350	341-9436*
Lincoln Builders Inc 1910 Farmerville Hwy *Web:* www.lincolnbuilders.com	Ruston	LA	71270	318-255-3822	
Lippert Bros Inc 2211 E I-44 Service Rd PO Box 17450 *Web:* www.lippertbros.com	Oklahoma City	OK	73136	405-478-3580	478-3301
Llewelyn-davies Sahni International Inc 5120 Woodway Dr Ste 8010 *Web:* www.theldnet.com	Houston	TX	77056	713-850-1500	
Lloyd Bilyeu McLellan Construction Company Inc (LBM) 11421 Blankenbaker Access Dr *Web:* www.lbmconstructionco.com	Louisville	KY	40299	502-452-1151	454-0291
Lockerbie & Hole Inc 14940-121A Ave *Web:* www.lockerbiehole.com	Edmonton	AB	T5V1A3	780-452-1250	
Loebl Schlossman & Hackl Inc 233 N Michigan Ave Ste 3000 *Web:* www.lshdesign.com	Chicago	IL	60601	312-565-1800	565-5912
Logan Trucking Inc 3224 Navarre Rd SW *TF:* 800-683-0142 ■ *Web:* www.logantrucking.com	Canton	OH	44706	330-478-1404	478-6706
Lombardi Contracting Corp 7744 Formula Pl *Web:* www.lombardicontracting.com	San Diego	CA	92121	858-566-0060	
Louis P Ciminelli Construction Corp 2421 Main St *Web:* www.lpciminelli.com	Buffalo	NY	14202	716-855-1200	854-6655
Loven Contracting Inc 1100 S Pinnacle St *Web:* www.lovencontracting.com	Flagstaff	AZ	86001	928-774-9040	
Luckett & Farley Architects Engineers & Construction Managers Inc 737 S Third St *Web:* www.luckett-farley.com	Louisville	KY	40202	502-585-4181	587-0488
Lueder Construction Co 9999 J St Ste B *Web:* www.lueder.com	Omaha	NE	68127	402-339-1000	
Lumber One Avon Inc 101 Second St NW PO Box 7 *Web:* www.lumber-one.com	Avon	MN	56310	320-356-7342	
Lusardi Construction Company Inc 1570 Linda Vista Dr *Web:* www.lusardi.com	San Marcos	CA	92078	760-744-3133	744-9064
Lydig Construction Inc 11001 E Montgomery St *Web:* www.lydig.com	Spokane	WA	99206	509-534-0451	535-6622
M.B. Kahn Construction Company Inc 101 Flintlake Rd *Web:* www.mbkahn.com	Columbia	SC	29223	803-736-2950	
M.J. Harris Construction Inc One Riverchase Rdg Ste 300 *Web:* www.mjharris.com	Birmingham	AL	35244	205-380-6800	
MA Angeliades Inc 5-44 47th Ave *Web:* www.ma-angeliades.com	Long Island City	NY	11101	718-786-5555	786-4700
MA Mortenson Co 700 Meadow Ln N *Web:* www.mortenson.com	Minneapolis	MN	55422	763-522-2100	287-5430
Maas Bros Construction Company Inc 410 Water Tower Ct *Web:* www.maasbros.com	Watertown	WI	53094	920-261-1682	
MacDonald-Bedford LLC 2900 Main St Ste 200 *Web:* www.macdonaldbedford.com	Alameda	CA	94501	510-521-4020	
Magil Construction Corp 1655 rue De Beauharnois Ouest *Web:* www.magil.com	Montreal	QC	H4N1J6	514-341-9899	
Mak Design Build Inc 430 F St Ste B *Web:* www.makdesignbuild.com	Davis	CA	95616	530-750-2209	

				Phone	Fax
Make It Right Inc 55 E Huntington Dr *Web:* www.makeitright.net	Arcadia	CA	91006	626-445-0366	
Mall Craft Inc 2225 N Windsor Ave *Web:* www.mallcraft.com	Altadena	CA	91001	626-398-3598	
Maloney & Bell General Contractors Inc 3117 Fite Cir Ste 101 *Web:* www.maloneyandbell.com	Sacramento	CA	95827	916-687-8779	756-2402
Mapp Construction LLC 344 Third St *Web:* mappconstruction.com	Baton Rouge	LA	70801	225-757-0111	
March Associates Inc 601 Hamburg Tpke Ste 300 *Web:* www.marchassociates.com	Wayne	NJ	07470	973-904-0213	
Marco Enterprises Inc 3504 Watkins Ave *Web:* www.marcoenterprises.com	Landover	MD	20785	301-773-5656	773-0422
Mark Cerrone Inc 2368 Maryland Ave *Web:* markcerrone.com	Niagara Falls	NY	14305	716-282-5244	
Market Contractors Ltd of Oregon 10250 NE Marx St *TF:* 800-793-1448 ■ *Web:* www.marketcontractors.com	Portland	OR	97220	503-255-0977	262-4280
Marlborough Public Schools (MPS) 17 Washington St *Web:* www.mps-edu.org	Marlborough	MA	01752	508-460-3509	
Marne Construction Inc 748 N Poplar St *Web:* www.marneconstruction.com	Orange	CA	92868	714-935-0995	
Martin Allgeier & Assoc Inc 7231 E 24th St *Web:* www.amce.com	Joplin	MO	64804	417-680-7200	680-7300
Martin-Harris Construction Co 3030 S Highland Dr *Web:* www.martinharris.com	Las Vegas	NV	89109	702-385-5257	474-8257
Mathiowetz Construction Co 30676 County Rd 24 *Web:* www.mathiowetzconst.com	Sleepy Eye	MN	56085	507-794-6953	794-3514
Matous Construction Ltd 8602 State Hwy 317 *Web:* www.matousconstruction.com	Belton	TX	76513	254-780-1400	780-2599
Matthews Construction Company Inc 210 First Ave S *Web:* www.matthewsconstruction.com	Conover	NC	28613	828-464-7325	465-6747
Max J. Kuney Co 120 N Ralph St PO Box 4008 *Web:* www.maxkuney.com	Spokane	WA	99220	509-535-0651	534-6828
MBA Construction 298 W Bridge St *Web:* www.mbaconstruction.net	Blackfoot	ID	83221	208-785-7171	
McBride Construction Resources Inc 224 Nickerson St *Web:* www.mcbrideconstruction.com	Seattle	WA	98109	206-283-7121	284-5670
McCarthy Bldg Cos Inc 1341 N Rock Hill Rd **Fax:* Mktg ■ *Web:* www.mccarthy.com	Saint Louis	MO	63124	314-968-3300	968-4642*
McGough Construction Co Inc 2737 Fairview Ave N *TF:* 800-552-7670 ■ *Web:* www.mcgough.com	Saint Paul	MN	55113	651-633-5050	633-5673
McIntyre Elwell & Strammer General Contractors Inc 1645 Barber Rd *Web:* www.mesgc.com	Sarasota	FL	34240	941-377-6800	
McKay-Cocker Construction Ltd 1665 Oxford St E *Web:* www.mckaycocker.com	London	ON	N5Y5R9	519-451-5270	
McPherson Concrete Storage Systems Inc 116 N Augustus St *Web:* www.mcphersonconcrete.com	Mcpherson	KS	67460	620-241-4362	
MDC Systems Inc 37 N Vly Rd 3 Sta Sq Ste 100 *Web:* www.mdcsystems.com	Paoli	PA	19301	610-640-9600	
MDS Builders of Texas Inc 2512 S Interstate 35 Ste 110 *Web:* www.mdsbuilders-tx.com	Austin	TX	78704	512-851-1133	
Mechanical Contractor 4165 Brunswick Rd *Web:* www.dmcmemphis.com	Memphis	TN	38133	901-730-4799	
Meehleis Modular Buildings Inc 1303 E Lodi Ave *Web:* www.meehleis.com	Lodi	CA	95240	209-334-4637	
Mehlville School District 3120 Lemay Ferry Rd *Web:* www.mehlvilleschooldistrict.com	Saint Louis	MO	63125	314-467-5000	467-5099
MEP Associates 2720 Arbor Ct Ste A *Web:* www.mepassociates.com	Eau Claire	WI	54701	715-832-5680	
MEP Consulting Engineers Inc 7500 Glenview Dr Ste A *Web:* www.mepce.com	Fort Worth	TX	76118	972-870-9060	
Merced Irrigation District PO Box 2288 *TF:* 855-800-2267 ■ *Web:* mercedid.com/	Merced	CA	95344	209-722-5761	722-6421
Mercer Construction Company Inc 42690 Rio Nedo Way Ste D *Web:* www.mercerconstruction.com	Temecula	CA	92590	951-296-0111	
Messer Construction Co 5158 Fishwick Dr *Web:* www.messer.com	Cincinnati	OH	45216	513-242-1541	242-6467
Met-Con Construction Inc 15760 Acorn Trl *Web:* www.met-con.com	Faribault	MN	55021	507-332-2266	
Metal Masters Inc 3825 Crater Lk Hwy *Web:* www.metalmasters-inc.com	Medford	OR	97504	541-779-1049	
Metropolitan Glass Inc 6400 Franklin St *Web:* www.metroglass.com	Denver	CO	80229	303-853-4527	
Meyer & Najem Inc 13099 Parkside Dr *TF:* 888-578-5131 ■ *Web:* www.meyer-najem.com	Fishers	IN	46038	317-577-0007	577-0286
MGM Mirage Design Group Inc 3260 Industrial Rd *TF:* 800-929-1111 ■ *Web:* www.mgmresortsdiversity.com	Las Vegas	NV	89109	702-650-7400	
MGQ & Associates Inc 3104 N Armenia Ave Ste 4 *Web:* www.mgqassociates.com	Tampa	FL	33607	813-877-8895	
Mid Valley School District 52 Underwood Rd *Web:* www.mvsd.us	Throop	PA	18512	570-307-1150	307-1107
Midstate Construction Corp 1180 Holm Rd *Web:* www.midstateconstruction.com	Petaluma	CA	94954	707-762-3200	762-0700
Milan Engineering Inc 925 S Semoran Blvd Ste 100 *Web:* www.milan-engineering.com	Winter Park	FL	32792	407-678-2055	
Milender White Construction Co 12655 W 54th Dr *Web:* www.milenderwhite.com	Arvada	CO	80002	303-216-0420	
Miller-davis Co 1029 Portage St *Web:* www.miller-davis.com	Kalamazoo	MI	49001	269-345-3561	
Millie & Severson Inc 3601 Serpentine Dr *Web:* www.mandsinc.com	Los Alamitos	CA	90720	562-493-3611	598-6871
Mine & Mill Industrial Supply Company Inc 2500 S Combee Rd **Fax Area Code:* 813 ■ *TF:* 800-282-8489 ■ *Web:* www.minemill.com	Lakeland	FL	33801	863-665-5601	623-6999*
Miron Construction Co Inc 1471 McMahon Dr *Web:* miron-construction.com	Neenah	WI	54956	920-969-7000	969-7393
Modular Connections LLC 1090 Industrial Blvd *Web:* www.modularconnections.com	Bessemer	AL	35022	205-980-4565	
Modular Genius Inc 1201 S Mountain Rd *Web:* www.modulargenius.com	Joppa	MD	21085	888-420-1113	
Momentum Engineering Company LLC 5225 Katy Fwy Ste 605 *Web:* momentumtx.com	Houston	TX	77007	713-910-8300	
Monarch Construction Company Inc PO Box 12249 *Web:* www.monarchconstruction.cc	Cincinnati	OH	45212	513-351-6900	351-0979
Montgomery Martin Contractors LLC 8245 Tournament Dr Ste 300 *Web:* www.montgomerymartin.com	Memphis	TN	38125	901-374-9400	374-9402
Moores Electrical & Mechanical PO Box 119 *Web:* www.mooreselectric.com	Altavista	VA	24517	434-369-4374	369-7402
Morcon Construction Company Inc 5905 Golden Vly Rd *Web:* www.morcon.com	Golden Valley	MN	55422	763-546-6066	
Morganti Group Inc 100 Mill Plain Rd 4th Fl **Fax:* Sales ■ *Web:* www.morganti.com	Danbury	CT	06811	203-743-2675	830-4478*
Morris Group Inc Three Office Pk Cir Ste 302	Mountain Brook	AL	35223	205-871-3500	
Moseley Architects PC 3200 Norfolk St *Web:* www.moseleyarchitects.com	Richmond	VA	23230	804-794-7555	355-5690
Mosser Construction 122 S Wilson Ave *TF:* 800-589-3801 ■ *Web:* www.mosserconstruction.com	Fremont	OH	43420	419-334-3801	
Motor Service Inc 130 Byassee Dr *TF:* 800-966-5080 ■ *Web:* www.motorserviceinc.net	Hazelwood	MO	63042	314-731-4111	731-1213
Multigon Industries Inc 1 Odell Plz *Web:* www.aqua-eez.com	Yonkers	NY	10701	800-289-6858	
Munilla Construction Management LLC 6201 SW 70th St Second Fl *Web:* www.mcm-us.com	Miami	FL	33143	305-541-0000	541-9771
Murnane Bldg Contractors Inc 104 Sharron Ave *Web:* www.murnanebuilding.com	Plattsburgh	NY	12901	518-561-4010	561-5926
Murphy & Sons Inc 9148 Corporate Dr PO Box 492 *Web:* www.murphyandsons.com	Southaven	MS	38671	662-393-3130	393-8111
Muse Concrete Contractors Inc 8599 Commercial Way *Web:* www.museconcrete.com	Redding	CA	96002	530-226-5151	226-5155
MYCON General Contractors Inc 208 E Louisiana Ste 200 *Web:* www.mycon.com	Mckinney	TX	75069	972-529-2444	
Nabholz Construction Corp PO Box 2090 *Web:* www.nabholz.com	Conway	AR	72033	501-505-5800	327-8231
Nastos Construction Inc 1421 Kenilworth Ave NE *Web:* www.nastos.com	Washington	DC	20019	202-398-5500	398-5501
National Fence Systems Inc 1033 Route One *Web:* www.nationalfencesystems.com	Avenel	NJ	07001	732-636-5600	
Near-Cal Corp 512 Chaney St *Web:* www.nearcal.com	Lake Elsinore	CA	92530	951-245-5400	
Neenan Co 2620 E Prospect Rd Ste 100 *Web:* neenan.com	Fort Collins	CO	80525	970-493-8747	493-5869
NeoCom Solutions Inc 10064 Main St *Web:* www.neocom.biz	Woodstock	GA	30188	678-238-1818	
Neumann Brothers Inc 1435 Ohio St *Web:* www.neumannbros.com	Des Moines	IA	50314	515-243-0156	
New Life Service Co. 39 W Fifth St *Web:* www.nlsco.com	Eureka	CA	95501	707-444-8222	
New Philadelphia City School District (NPCS) 248 Front Ave SW *Web:* www.npschools.org	New Philadelphia	OH	44663	330-364-0600	364-9310
NewGround Resources Inc 15450 S Outer Forty Dr Ste 300 *Web:* www.newground.com	Chesterfield	MO	63017	636-898-8100	
Nibbi Bros Inc 180 Hubbell St *Web:* www.nibbi.com	San Francisco	CA	94107	415-863-1820	863-1150
Nicholas & Associates 1001 Feehanville Dr *Web:* www.nicholasquality.com	Mount Prospect	IL	60056	847-394-6200	
Nooter Construction Co 1500 S Second St *Web:* www.nooterconstruction.com	Saint Louis	MO	63104	314-421-7600	
Nor-Son Inc 7900 Hastings Rd *TF:* 800-858-1722 ■ *Web:* www.nor-son.com	Baxter	MN	56425	218-828-1722	828-0487
Norcon Corp 5600 Municipal St *Web:* www.norconcorp.com	Schofield	WI	54476	715-359-5808	
Norfolk Dredging Co 110 Centervilless Tpke N *Web:* www.norfolkdredging.com	Chesapeake	VA	23320	757-547-9391	547-2833
NorSouth 2000 RiverEdge Pkwy Ste 950 *Web:* www.norsouth.com	Atlanta	GA	30328	770-850-8280	850-8230
North Salem Elementary School 140 Zion Hill Rd *Web:* www.sau57.org/northsalem/pages/home.aspx	Salem	NH	03079	603-893-7062	893-7062
Northern Trailer Ltd 3355 Sugarloaf Rd *Web:* www.northerntrailer.com	Kamloops	BC	V2C6C3	250-828-2644	

Company	City	State	Zip	Phone	Fax
Northstar Technology Corp 32 Mauchly Ste C *Web:* www.northstar-technology.com	Irvine	CA	92618	949-788-0738	
Norwood Co 375 Technology Dr *Web:* www.norwdco.com	Malvern	PA	19355	610-240-4400	
NRB Inc 115 S Service Rd W *Web:* www.nrb-inc.com	Grimsby	ON	L3M4G3	905-945-9622	
NTS Communications Inc 1220 Broadway *Web:* www.ntscom.com	Lubbock	TX	79401	806-771-0687	788-3398
Nujak Development Inc 711 N Kentucky Ave *Web:* www.nujak.com	Lakeland	FL	33801	863-686-1565	
Numega Solutions LLC 7426 Alban Sta Blvd Ste A104 *Web:* www.numegasolutions.com	Springfield	VA	22150	703-372-2200	
O & G Industries Inc 112 Wall St *Web:* www.ogind.com	Torrington	CT	06790	860-489-9261	489-9261
O'Connor Constructors Inc 45 Industrial Dr *Fax Area Code: 781 ■ *Web:* www.oconnorconst.com	Canton	MA	02021	617-364-9000	828-8248*
O'Harrow Construction Co 4575 Ann Arbor Rd *Web:* www.oharrow.net	Jackson	MI	49202	517-764-4770	764-5564
O'Neal Construction Inc 525 W William *Web:* www.onealconstruction.com	Ann Arbor	MI	48103	734-769-0770	
Ocean Quest Pools Inc 10208 N Fm 620 *Web:* www.oceanquest.com	Austin	TX	78726	512-258-7379	
Oceanic Companies Inc 91-462 Komohana St *Web:* www.oceaniccompanies.com	Kapolei	HI	96707	808-682-0113	
Oceanside Unified School District (OUSD) 2111 Mission Ave *Web:* www.oside.k12.ca.us	Oceanside	CA	92058	760-966-4000	
Odebrecht Construction Inc 201 Alhambra Cir Ste 1400 *TF:* 800-771-0001 ■ *Web:* www.odebrecht.com.br	Coral Gables	FL	33134	305-341-8800	569-1500
Oliver & Company Inc 1300 S 51st St *Web:* www.oliverandco.net	Richmond	CA	94804	510-412-9090	
Oltmans Construction Co 10005 Mission Mill Rd PO Box 985 *Web:* www.oltmans.com	Whittier	CA	90608	562-948-4242	695-5299
Omega Construction Inc 344 Shelleybrook Dr PO Box 250 *Web:* www.omegaconstruction.com	Pilot Mountain	NC	27041	336-368-5156	
Omni Construction Services Inc 533 Airport Blvd Ste 555 *Web:* www.clearkey.com	Burlingame	CA	94010	650-685-2490	
One Way Building Services Inc 6811 Washington Ave S *Web:* owbs.net	Minneapolis	MN	55439	952-942-0412	
Oneonta City School District 31 Ctr St *Web:* www.oneontacsd.org	Oneonta	NY	13820	607-433-8200	433-8290
Opechee Construction Corp 11 Corporate Dr *Web:* www.opechee.com	Belmont	NH	03220	603-527-9090	
Opp & Seibold General Construction Inc 1220 W Poplar St *Web:* www.oppseibold.com	Walla Walla	WA	99362	509-525-1373	
Opus Group of Cos 10350 Bren Rd W *Web:* www.opus-group.com	Minnetonka	MN	55343	952-656-4444	
Orcutt/Winslow 3003 N Central Ave *TF:* 800-331-5842 ■ *Web:* www.owp.com	Phoenix	AZ	85012	602-257-1764	257-9029
Orion Building Corp 9025 Overlook Blvd Ste 100 *Web:* www.orionbldg.com	Brentwood	TN	37027	615-321-4499	
Osborne Construction Company Inc 10602 NE 38th Pl Ste 100 *Web:* www.osborne.cc	Kirkland	WA	98033	425-827-4221	828-4314
Oscar J Boldt Construction Co 2525 N Roemer Rd *Web:* www.theboldtcompany.com	Appleton	WI	54911	920-739-6321	739-4409
OSI Inc 3950 Birmingham Hwy *Web:* www.osibuildings.com	Montgomery	AL	36108	334-834-3500	
Outside the Lines Inc 529 W Blueridge Ave *Web:* otl-inc.com	Orange	CA	92865	714-637-4747	
Owen-Ames-Kimball Co 300 Ionia Ave NW *Web:* www.owen-ames-kimball.com	Grand Rapids	MI	49503	616-456-1521	458-0770
Ozanne Construction Company Inc 1635 E 25th St *Web:* www.ozanne.com	Cleveland	OH	44114	216-696-2876	696-8613
P & C Construction Co 2133 NW York St *Web:* www.builtbypandc.com	Portland	OR	97210	503-665-0165	667-2565
P A Landers Inc 351 Winter St *TF:* 800-660-6404 ■ *Web:* www.palanders.com	Hanover	MA	02339	781-826-8818	829-8934
P.H. Hagopian Contractor Inc 778 W Town & Country Rd *Web:* www.phhagopian.com	Orange	CA	92868	714-543-4185	
Pacrim Engineering 233 W Cerritos Ave *Web:* www.pacrimengineering.com	Anaheim	CA	92805	714-683-0470	
Palace Construction Company Inc Seven S Galapago St *Web:* www.palaceconst.com	Denver	CO	80223	303-777-7999	777-5256
Pangere Corp 4050 W Fourth Ave *Web:* www.pangere.com	Gary	IN	46406	219-949-1368	944-3028
Paragon Supply Co 160 Reaser Ct *Web:* www.paragon-supply.com	Elyria	OH	44035	440-365-8040	
Parent Co, The PO Box 5036 *Web:* www.theparentco.com	Brentwood	TN	37024	615-221-7000	221-7013
Parkinson Construction Company Inc 3905 Perry St *Web:* www.parkinsonconstruction.com	Brentwood	MD	20722	301-985-6080	
Parkway Construction & Assoc LP 1000 Civic Cir *TF:* 800-869-4567 ■ *Web:* www.parkwayconstruction.com	Lewisville	TX	75067	972-221-1979	219-0061
Paul Hemmer Construction Co 250 Grandview Dr *Web:* www.paulhemmer.com	Fort Mitchell	KY	41017	859-341-8300	
PBG Builders Inc 1000 NorthChase Dr Ste 307 *Web:* www.pbgbuilders.com	Goodlettsville	TN	37072	615-256-2200	
PCL Construction Enterprises Inc 2000 S Colorado Blvd Tower 2 Ste 2-500 *Web:* www.pcl.com	Denver	CO	80222	303-365-6500	
PCL Construction Group Inc 5410 99th St NW *Web:* www.pcl.com	Edmonton	AB	T6E3P4	780-733-5000	
PDC Facilities Inc 700 Walnut Ridge Dr *TF:* 800-545-5998 ■ *Web:* www.pdcbiz.com	Hartland	WI	53029	262-367-7700	367-7744
Peacock Construction Inc PO Box 1818 *Web:* www.peacockconstruction.com	Lafayette	CA	94549	925-283-4550	283-0784
Peaklogix Inc 14409 Justice Rd *Web:* www.peaklogix.com	Midlothian	VA	23113	804-794-5700	
Pence Kelly Construction LLC 2747 Pence Loop SE *TF:* 800-434-6654 ■ *Web:* www.pencekelly.com	Salem	OR	97302	503-399-7223	585-7477
Penfield Fire Company Inc 1838 Penfield Rd *Web:* www.penfieldfire.org	Penfield	NY	14526	585-586-2413	387-6610
Pepper Construction 643 N Orleans St *Web:* www.pepperconstruction.com	Chicago	IL	60610	312-266-4700	266-2792
Perini Corp PO Box 9160 PO Box 9160 *Web:* www.tutorperini.com	Framingham	MA	01701	508-628-2000	
Peris Cos Inc 282 N Washington St *Web:* www.peris.com	Falls Church	VA	22046	703-533-4700	533-4710
Perma-Seal Waterproofing 513 Rogers St *Web:* www.permaseal.net	Downers Grove	IL	60515	630-663-8972	
Perry Construction Group Inc 1440 W 21st St *Web:* www.perryconst.com	Erie	PA	16502	814-459-8551	453-5653
Perspectiva 3401 Louisiana St Ste 270 *Web:* www.perspectiva.net	Houston	TX	77002	713-520-7580	
Petrini Corp 187 Rosemary St *Web:* www.petrinicorp.com	Needham	MA	02494	781-444-1963	
Pettus Mechanical Services 12647 Hwy 72 *Web:* www.pettushvac.com	Rogersville	AL	35652	256-389-8181	
Phipps Houses 902 Broadway 13th Fl *Web:* www.phippsny.org	New York	NY	10010	212-243-9090	727-1639
Phoenix Modular Inc 5139 N Tom Murray Ave *Web:* www.phoenixmodular.com	Glendale	AZ	85301	623-209-3300	
Phoenix Renovation & Restoration Inc 16250 Foster *Web:* www.kcphoenix.com	Overland Park	KS	66085	913-599-0055	
Piedmont Construction Group LLC (PCG) 107 Gateway Dr Ste B *Web:* www.piedmontconstructiongroup.com	Macon	GA	31210	478-405-8907	405-8908
Pierson Co 1200 W Harris St *Web:* www.piersoncompany.com	Eureka	CA	95503	707-268-1800	268-1801
Pierson Construction Inc 4500 N Route E *Web:* www.piersonconstruction.net	Columbia	MO	65202	573-445-8493	
Pinkard Construction Co 9195 W Sixth Ave *Web:* www.pinkardcc.com	Lakewood	CO	80215	303-986-4555	985-5050
Pinkerton & Laws Inc 1165 N Chase Pkwy Ste 100 *Web:* pinkerton-laws.com	Marietta	GA	30067	770-956-9000	618-8688
Pinner Construction Company Inc 1255 S Lewis St *Web:* www.pinnerconstruction.com	Anaheim	CA	92805	714-490-4000	
Pioneer Construction Company Inc 550 Kirtland St SW *Web:* www.pioneerinc.com	Grand Rapids	MI	49507	616-247-6966	247-0186
Pioneer Contract Services Inc 8090 Kempwood Dr *Web:* www.pioneercontract.com	Houston	TX	77055	713-464-8200	464-7100
Pizzagalli Construction Co 193 Tilley Dr *Web:* www.pcconstruction.com	South Burlington	VT	05403	802-658-4100	
PKC Construction 520 W 103rd St # 299 *Web:* www.pkcc.com	Kansas City	MO	64114	913-782-4646	
Plant Process Equipment Inc 280 Reynolds Ave *Web:* www.plant-process.com	League City	TX	77573	281-333-7850	332-6280
Plasteak Inc 3563 Copley Rd *Web:* www.plasteak.com	Copley	OH	44321	330-668-2587	
Plath & Company Inc 1575 Francisco Blvd E *Web:* plathco.com	San Rafael	CA	94901	415-460-1575	
PM Construction Co Inc PO Box 728 *TF:* 800-646-0068 ■ *Web:* www.pmconstruction.com	Saco	ME	04072	207-282-7697	283-4549
PMG Project Management Group LLC 2723 Houston Ave *Web:* www.pmgunited.com	Houston	TX	77009	713-880-2626	
Pointe General Contractors LLC 1200 Premier Dr Ste 120 *Web:* www.pointecentre.com	Chattanooga	TN	37421	423-755-0844	
Polaris Engineering Inc 212 Pine St *Web:* www.polarisengr.com	Lake Charles	LA	70601	337-497-0652	
Polhemus Savery DaSilva Architects Builders 101 Depot Rd *Web:* www.psdab.com	Chatham	MA	02645	508-945-4500	945-9803
Port Jervis City School District PO Box 1104 *TF:* 877-544-6664 ■ *Web:* www.pjschools.org	Port Jervis	NY	12771	845-858-3100	856-1885
Porta-King Building Systems 4133 Shoreline Dr *TF:* 800-284-5346 ■ *Web:* www.portaking.com	Earth City	MO	63045	800-284-5346	
Portable Buildings Inc 3235 Bay Rd *Web:* www.portablebuildingsinc.com	Milford	DE	19963	302-335-1300	
Power Construction Company LLC 8750 W Bryn Mawr Ave Ste 500 *Fax Area Code: 847 ■ *Web:* www.powerconstruction.net	Chicago	IL	60631	312-596-6960	925-1372*
Powers & Sons Construction Company Inc 2636 W 15th Ave *Web:* www.powersandsons.com	Gary	IN	46404	219-949-3100	949-5906

				Phone	Fax
Prava Construction Services Inc 2032 Corte Del Nogal Ste 100	Carlsbad	CA	92011	760-929-9787	
Web: www.pravacsi.com					
Premiere Concrete Inc 11332 Red Lion Rd	White Marsh	MD	21162	410-344-1604	
Web: premierconcrete.biz					
Primary Integration LLC 8180 Greensboro Dr Ste 700	Mclean	VA	22102	703-356-2200	
Web: www.primaryintegration.com					
Prime Contractors Inc 525 N Sam Houston Pkwy E	Houston	TX	77060	281-999-0875	999-0885
TF: 800-692-8378 ■ *Web:* www.primecontractorsinc.com					
Primus Builders Inc 8294 Hwy 92 Ste 210	Woodstock	GA	30189	770-928-7120	928-6548
Web: www.primusbuilders.com					
Prince George County Public Schools 6410 Cts Dr	Prince George	VA	23875	804-733-2700	733-2737
Web: www.pgs.k12.va.us					
Prismatic Development Inc 60 Route 46	Fairfield	NJ	07004	973-882-1133	
Web: www.prisdev.com					
PRO Building Systems Inc 3678 N Peachtree Rd	Atlanta	GA	30341	770-455-1791	
Web: www.probldgsystems.com					
Progressive Contracting Company Inc 10 N Ritters Ln	Owings Mills	MD	21117	410-356-9096	356-9098
Web: www.progressivecci.com					
Promac Inc 1153 Timber Dr	Elgin	IL	60123	847-695-8181	
Web: www.promac.com					
Prosser Wilbert Construction Inc 13730 W 108th St	Lenexa	KS	66215	913-906-0104	
Web: www.prosserwilbert.com					
Provident Construction Inc 12424 E Weaver Pl	Centennial	CO	80111	720-482-0200	
Web: www.providentconstruction.com					
Quadrants Inc 49132 Wixom Tech Dr	Wixom	MI	48393	248-960-3900	960-9867
Web: www.quadrants.com					
Quandel Group Inc 3003 N Front St Ste 203	Harrisburg	PA	17110	717-657-0909	652-6282
Web: www.quandel.com					
Quantum Crossings LLC 111 E Wacker Dr Ste 990	Chicago	IL	60601	312-467-0065	
Web: www.quantumcrossings.com					
Quorex Construction Ltd 142 Cardinal Crescent	Saskatoon	SK	S7L6H6	306-244-3717	
Web: www.quorex.ca					
R & O Construction Co 933 Wall Ave	Ogden	UT	84404	801-627-1403	
Web: www.randoco.com					
R A Burch Construction Company Inc 405 Maple St Bldg B	Ramona	CA	92065	760-788-0800	
Web: www.raburch.com					
R F Stearns Inc 4000 Kruse Way Pl Bldg 3 Ste 100	Lake Oswego	OR	97035	503-601-8700	
Web: www.rfstearns.com					
R W Mercer Co 2322 Brooklyn Rd PO Box 180	Jackson	MI	49204	517-787-2960	787-8111
TF: 877-763-7237 ■ *Web:* www.rwmercer.com					
R Zoppo Corp 160 Old Maple St	Stoughton	MA	02072	781-344-8822	344-7382
Web: www.zoppo.com					
R&h Construction Co 1530 SW Taylor St	Portland	OR	97205	503-228-7177	
Web: www.rhconst.com					
Ra-lin & Associates Bldg Contr 101 Parkwood Cir	Carrollton	GA	30117	770-834-4884	
Web: www.ra-lin.com					
Raco General Contractors 1401 Dalon Rd NE	Atlanta	GA	30306	404-873-3567	876-1394
Web: www.racogc.com					
Rafn Co 1721 132nd Ave NE	Bellevue	WA	98005	425-702-6600	
Web: www.rafn.com					
Ragnar Benson Construction LLC 250 S NW Hwy	Park Ridge	IL	60068	847-698-4900	692-9320
Web: www.ragnarbenson.com					
Ramtech Bldg Systems Inc 1400 Hwy 287 S	Mansfield	TX	76063	855-887-1888	473-3485*
**Fax Area Code:* 817 ■ *TF:* 855-887-1888 ■ *Web:* www.ramtechgroup.com					
Rand Construction Co 1428 W Ninth St	Kansas City	MO	64101	816-421-4143	421-4144
Web: www.randsc.com					
Randolph & Son Builders Inc PO Box 410283	Charlotte	NC	28241	704-588-7116	588-8280
Web: www.randolphbuilders.com					
Ray Angelini Inc 105 Blackwood-Barnsboro Rd	Sewell	NJ	08080	856-228-5566	
Web: www.raiservices.com					
RD Olson Construction 2955 Main St Third Fl	Irvine	CA	92614	949-474-2001	474-1534
Web: www.rdolson.com					
Renaissance Cos, The 8925 E Pima Ctr Pkwy Ste 205	Scottsdale	AZ	85258	480-967-0880	
Web: www.renaissancecos.com					
Renfrow Bros Inc 855 Gossett Rd PO Box 4786	Spartanburg	SC	29307	864-579-0558	522-5958*
**Fax Area Code:* 888 ■ *TF:* 888-522-5958 ■ *Web:* www.renfrowbros.com					
Renier Construction Corp 2164 Citygate Dr	Columbus	OH	43219	614-866-4580	
Web: www.renier.com					
Reno Contracting Inc 1450 Frazee Rd Ste 100	San Diego	CA	92108	619-220-0224	220-0229
Web: www.renocon.com					
Rentenbach Constructors Inc 2400 Sutherland Ave	Knoxville	TN	37919	865-546-2440	546-3414
Web: www.rentenbach.com					
Richard & Richard Construction Company Inc 234 Venture St Ste 100	San Marcos	CA	92078	760-759-2260	
Web: www.rrconstruction.com					
Ricks Barbecue Inc 2367 Hwy 43 S	Leoma	TN	38468	931-852-2324	
TF: 800-544-5864 ■ *Web:* www.ricksbbq.com					
Riddleberger Bros Inc (RBI) 6127 S Valley Pk	Mount Crawford	VA	22841	540-434-1731	432-1691
Web: www.rbiva.com					
Riley Construction Company Inc 5301 99th Ave	Kenosha	WI	53144	262-658-4381	
Web: www.rileycon.com					
Ringland-Johnson Construction PO Box 5165	Rockford	IL	61125	815-332-8600	332-8411
Web: www.ringland.com					
River City Construction LLC 101 Hoffer Ln	East Peoria	IL	61611	309-694-3120	694-1332
Web: www.rccllc.com					
Robert E. Porter Construction Company Inc 1720 W Lincoln St	Phoenix	AZ	85007	602-253-4911	
Web: robertporterconstruction.com					
Robins & Morton Group 400 Shades Creek Pkwy Ste 200	Birmingham	AL	35209	205-870-1000	871-0906
Web: www.robinsmorton.com					
Roche Constructors Inc 361 71st Ave	Greeley	CO	80634	970-356-3611	356-3619
Web: www.rocheconstructors.com					
Rochon Corp 3650 Annapolis Ln N Ste 101	Plymouth	MN	55447	763-559-9393	559-8101
Web: www.rochoncorp.com					
Rockdale Pipeline Inc PO Box 1157	Conyers	GA	30012	770-922-4123	614-5723
Web: www.rockdalepipeline.com					
Roebbelen Construction Inc 1241 Hawks Flight Ct	El Dorado Hills	CA	95762	916-939-4000	939-4028
Web: www.roebbelen.com					
Rogers-o'brien Construction USA 1901 Regal Row	Dallas	TX	75235	214-962-3000	962-3001
Web: www.rogers-obrien.com					
Rough Brothers Inc 5513 Vine St	Cincinnati	OH	45217	513-242-0310	
Web: www.roughbros.com					
Roy Anderson Corp 11400 Reichold Rd	Gulfport	MS	39503	228-896-4000	896-4078
TF: 800-688-4003 ■ *Web:* www.rac.com					
Roy Kirby & Sons Inc 1403 Rome Rd Ste 130	Baltimore	MD	21227	410-536-0808	536-0799
Web: www.roykirby.com					
RSH Architects 363 Vanadium Rd Ste 200	Pittsburgh	PA	15243	412-429-1555	279-7285
Web: www.rsharc.com					
Rudolph & Sletten Inc 1600 Seaport Blvd Ste 350	Redwood City	CA	94063	650-216-3600	599-9112
Web: www.rsconstruction.com					
Ruhlin Company Inc PO Box 190	Sharon Center	OH	44274	330-239-2800	239-1828
Web: www.ruhlin.com					
Ruscilli Construction Co Inc 2041 Arlingate Ln	Columbus	OH	43228	614-876-9484	876-0253
Web: www.ruscilli.com					
Rushforth Construction Company Inc 6021 12th St E Ste 100	Tacoma	WA	98424	253-922-1884	922-2089
Web: a-p.com					
Russo Corp 1421 Mims Ave SW	Birmingham	AL	35211	205-923-4434	
Web: www.russocorp.com					
Rust Orling Architecture Inc 1215 Cameron St	Alexandria	VA	22314	703-836-3205	
Web: www.rustorling.com					
RW Allen LLC 1015 Broad St	Augusta	GA	30901	706-733-2800	733-3879
Web: www.rwallen.com					
RW Setterlin Bldg Co 560 Harmon Ave	Columbus	OH	43223	614-459-7077	459-0960
Web: www.setterlin.com					
Ryan Cos US Inc 50 S Tenth St Ste 300	Minneapolis	MN	55403	612-492-4000	492-3000
Web: www.ryancompanies.com					
Rycon Construction Inc 2525 Liberty Ave	Pittsburgh	PA	15222	412-392-2525	392-2526
TF: 800-883-1901 ■ *Web:* www.ryconinc.com					
S C & A Construction Inc PO Box 7202	Wilmington	DE	19803	302-478-6030	478-3775
Web: www.scaconstructs.com					
S D Deacon Corp 17681 Mitchell N Ste 100	Irvine	CA	92614	949-222-9060	222-0596
Web: www.deacon.com					
Sain Construction Co 713 Vincent St	Manchester	TN	37355	931-728-7644	728-7944
Web: www.sainconstruction.com					
Sambe Construction Company Inc 1650 Hylton Rd	Pennsauken	NJ	08110	856-663-7751	663-5859
Web: www.sambe.net					
Samet Corp 309 Gallimore Dairy Rd Ste 102 PO Box 8050	Greensboro	NC	27409	336-544-2600	544-2638
Web: www.sametcorp.com					
Samuels Group Inc 311 Financial Way St 300	Wausau	WI	54401	715-842-2222	
Web: www.samuelsgroup.net					
Satterfield & Pontikes Construction Inc 11000 Equity Dr Ste 100	Houston	TX	77041	713-996-1300	996-1400
Web: www.satpon.com					
Saugus Union School, The 24930 Ave Stanford	Santa Clarita	MA	91355	661-294-5300	
Web: www.saugususd.org					
Saunders Construction Inc 6950 S Jordan Rd	Centennial	CO	80112	303-699-9000	680-7448
Web: www.saundersci.com					
Saxon Group Inc, The 790 Brogdon Rd PO Box 606	Suwanee	GA	30024	770-271-2174	271-2176
Web: www.thesaxongroupinc.com					
SBBI Inc 3282 State Hwy 82 PO Box 770	Sonoita	AZ	85637	520-455-5983	
Web: www.sbbiaz.com					
SBCC Inc 1711 Dell Ave	Campbell	CA	95008	408-379-5500	
Web: www.sbci.com					
SC Anderson Inc P.O. Box 81747	Bakersfield	CA	93308	661-392-7000	391-9999
Web: www.scanderson.com					
Sc Builders Inc 910 Thompson Pl	Sunnyvale	CA	94085	408-328-0688	
Web: www.scbuildersinc.com					
Scharine Group, The 4213 N Scharine Rd	Whitewater	WI	53190	608-883-2880	
Web: www.thescharinegroup.com					
Schimenti Construction Co 650 Danbury Rd	Ridgefield	CT	06877	914-244-9100	244-9103
Web: www.schimenti.com					
Schmidt Bros. Inc 145 Chesterfield Ln	Maumee	OH	43537	419-826-3671	
Web: www.schmidtbrosinc.com					
Schneider Electric Buildings LLC 1354 Clifford Ave	Loves Park	IL	61111	888-444-1311	
TF: 888-444-1311 ■ *Web:* www.schneider-electric.com					
Scott Builders Inc 8105 - 49 Ave Close	Red Deer	AB	T4P2V5	403-343-7270	346-4310
Web: www.scottbuilders.com					
Scott Swimming Pools Inc 75 Washington Rd	Woodbury	CT	06798	203-263-2108	
Web: www.scottpools.com					
SCR Construction Company Inc 5420 FM 2218 Rd	Richmond	TX	77469	281-344-0700	344-0099
Web: www.scrconstruction.net					
SDB Inc 810 W 1st St	Tempe	AZ	85281	480-967-5810	967-5841
Web: www.sdb.com					

Phone Fax

SDV Construction Inc 6436 Edith Blvd Ne . . . . Albuquerque NM 87107 505-883-3176
Web: www.sdvconstruction.com

Sedalco Inc 2554 E Long Ave. . . . . Fort Worth TX 76137 817-831-2245 831-2248
Web: www.sedalco.com

Sellen Construction Co Inc
227 Westlake Ave N . . . . Seattle WA 98109 206-682-7770 623-5206
Web: www.sellen.com

Septagon Construction 113 E Third St . . . . Sedalia MO 65301 660-827-2115 826-8058
TF: 800-733-5999 ■ *Web:* www.septagon.com

Sfcc Inc 2410 Squire Pl Ste B . . . . Dallas TX 75234 972-484-2480
Web: www.sfccinc.net

Shales McNutt Construction 425 Renner Dr. . . . . Elgin IL 60123 847-622-1214
Web: www.shalesmcnutt.com

Shaw Construction Company LLC 300 Kalamath St . . . . . . Denver CO 80223 303-825-4740 825-6403
Web: www.shawconstruction.net

Shawmut Design & Construction
560 Harrison Ave . . . . Boston MA 02118 617-622-7000 622-7001
Web: www.shawmut.com

Sherrick Aerospace 307 Emery Dr. . . . . Nashville TN 37214 615-872-1050
Web: www.sherrickco.com

Shiel Sexton Company Inc
902 N Capitol Ave. . . . . Indianapolis IN 46204 317-423-6000 423-6300
Web: www.shielsexton.com

Shingobee Builders Inc PO Box 8 . . . . Loretto MN 55357 763-479-1300 479-3267
Web: www.shingobee.com

Shioi Construction Inc 98-724 Kuaho Pl . . . . Pearl City HI 96782 808-487-2441 487-2445
Web: shioihawaii.com

Shoemaker Construction Co
100 Front St Ste 365. . . . . West Conshohocken PA 19428 610-941-5500 941-5525
Web: www.shoemakerco.com

Sigal Construction Corp
2231 Crystal Dr Ste 200 . . . . Arlington VA 22202 703-302-1500 302-1520
Web: www.sigal.com

Sigma Associates Inc 535 Griswold St Ste 500 . . . . Detroit MI 48226 313-963-9700
Web: www.sigmaassociates.com

Signal Point Systems Inc
1270 Shiloh Rd Ste 100 . . . . Kennesaw GA 30144 770-499-0439
Web: sigpoint.com

Singer Group Inc, The 12915 Dover Rd . . . . Reisterstown MD 21136 410-561-7561
Web: www.singergrp.com

Sjostrom & Sons Inc PO Box 5766. . . . . Rockford IL 61125 815-226-0330 226-8868
Web: www.sjostromconstruction.com

Skanska USA Inc 1616 Whitestone Expy . . . . Whitestone NY 11356 718-767-2600 767-2663
Web: www.skanska.com

Skyline Construction
731 Sansome St 4th Fl . . . . San Francisco CA 94111 415-908-1020
Web: www.skylineconst.com

Sletten Construction Company Inc
1000 25th St N . . . . Great Falls MT 59401 406-761-7920 761-0923
Web: www.slettencompanies.com

SLR Contracting & Service Company Inc
260 Michigan Ave. . . . . Buffalo NY 14203 716-896-8148
Web: www.slrcontracting.com

Small Mine Development LLC
967 E Parkcenter Blvd. . . . . Boise ID 83706 208-338-8880 338-8881
Web: www.undergroundmining.com

Smith Tank & Steel Inc 42422 Hwy 30. . . . . Gonzales LA 70737 225-644-8747
Web: www.smith-tank.net

Smoot Construction Co 1907 Leonard Ave. . . . . Columbus OH 43219 614-253-9000
Web: www.smootconstruction.com

Snyder Langston Inc 17962 Cowan St . . . . Irvine CA 92614 949-863-9200 863-1087
TF: 800-899-4122 ■ *Web:* www.snyder-langston.com

Sordoni Construction Co 409 Main St. . . . . Chester NJ 07930 908-879-1130
Web: sordonionline.com

Sordoni Construction Services Inc
45 Owen St. . . . . Forty Fort PA 18704 570-287-3161 287-0298
Web: www.sordoni.com

South Brunswick Public Schools
231 Black Horse Ln PO Box 181. . . . . Monmouth Junction NJ 08852 732-297-7800
Web: www.sbschools.org

South Coast Construction Services
8935 Knight Rd. . . . . Houston TX 77054 713-222-2308
Web: www.sccsi.net

Southeast Connections LLC 2720 Dogwood Dr SE . . . . . Conyers GA 30013 404-659-1422
Web: www.seconnections.com

Speed Fab-Crete Corp International
PO Box 15580 . . . . Fort Worth TX 76119 817-478-1137 561-2544
Web: www.speedfab-crete.com

SPS Corp 3502 Independence Dr . . . . Fort Wayne IN 46808 260-482-3702
Web: www.spscorporation.com

Stanker & Galetto Inc 317 W Elmer Rd . . . . Vineland NJ 08360 856-692-8098
Web: www.stankergaletto.com

Star Consultants Inc 1910 Bethel Rd . . . . Columbus OH 43235 614-538-8445 538-8446
Web: starconsultants.org

Stella May Contracting Inc 1512 Edgewood Rd . . . . . . Edgewood MD 21040 410-679-8306
Web: stellamay.com

Stellar Group 2900 Hartley Rd . . . . Jacksonville FL 32257 904-260-2900 268-4932*
**Fax:* Sales ■ *TF:* 800-488-2900 ■ *Web:* stellar.net

Stenstrom Cos Ltd 2420 20th St PO Box 5866. . . . . Rockford IL 61125 815-398-2420 398-0041
Web: www.rstenstrom.com

Sterling Construction Company Inc
20810 Fernbush Ln . . . . Houston TX 77073 281-821-9091 821-2995
NASDAQ: STRL ■ *Web:* strlco.com/

Stevens Construction Corp PO Box 7726. . . . . Madison WI 53707 608-222-5100 222-5930
Web: www.stevensconstruction.com

Stidham Trucking Inc PO Box 308. . . . . Yreka CA 96097 530-842-4161 842-2047
TF: 800-827-9500 ■ *Web:* www.stidhamtrucking.com

Stiles Construction Co
301 E Las Olas Blvd . . . . Fort Lauderdale FL 33301 954-627-9300 627-9288
Web: www.stiles.com

Story Construction Co 300 S Bell Ave PO Box 1668 . . . . Ames IA 50010 515-232-4358 232-0599
Web: www.storycon.com

Streeter Assoc Inc
101 E Woodlawn Ave PO Box 118 . . . . Elmira NY 14902 607-734-4151 732-2952
TF: 866-493-1640 ■ *Web:* www.streeterassociates.com

Structura Inc
9208 Waterford Centre Blvd Ste 100. . . . . Austin TX 78758 512-495-9702 495-9712
Web: www.structurainc.com

Structure Tone Inc 770 Broadway 9th Fl. . . . . New York NY 10003 212-481-6100 685-9267
Web: www.structuretone.com

Suffolk Construction 65 Allerton St . . . . Boston MA 02119 617-445-3500 541-2128
Web: www.suffolkconstruction.com

Sullivan & McLaughlin Companies Inc
74 Lawley St. . . . . Boston MA 02122 617-474-0500
Web: www.sullymac.com

Sun Builders Co 5870 6 N Hwy Ste 206 . . . . Houston TX 77084 281-815-1020 815-1021
Web: www.sunbuildersco.com

Sun Eagle Corp 461 N Dean Ave. Chandler AZ 85226 480-961-0004 940-0160
Web: www.suneaglecorporation.com

Sun State Builders Inc
1050 W Washington St Ste 214 . . . . Tempe AZ 85281 480-894-1286
Web: www.sunstatebuilders.com

Sundt Construction Inc 2015 W River Rd Ste 101 . . . . Tucson AZ 85704 520-750-4600
TF: 800-467-5544 ■ *Web:* www.sundt.com

Sunpeak Construction Inc
1401 Quail St Ste 105. . . . . Newport Beach CA 92660 949-474-0501
Web: www.sunpeak.com

Swanson Construction Co
3400 Towne Pointe Dr. . . . . Bettendorf IA 52722 563-332-4859
Web: swansonbuilt.com

Swinerton Builders 260 Townsend St. . . . . San Francisco CA 94107 415-421-2980 984-1292
Web: www.swinerton.com

Swinerton Inc 260 Townsend St . . . . San Francisco CA 94107 415-421-2980 984-1292*
**Fax:* Hum Res ■ *Web:* www.swinerton.com

T&G Constructors Inc 8623 Commodity Cir. . . . . Orlando FL 32819 407-352-4443 352-0778
Web: www.t-and-g.com

Taggart Global LLC
4000 Town Ctr Blvd Ste 300 . . . . Canonsburg PA 15317 724-754-9800
Web: www.taggartglobal.com

Taisei Construction Corp
6261 Katella Ave Ste 200 . . . . Cypress CA 90630 714-886-1530 886-1550

Talladega City Schools
501 S St E PO Box 946. . . . . Talladega AL 35160 256-315-5600 315-5606
Web: www.talladega-cs.net

Tanglewood Conservatories 15 Engerman Ave . . . . Denton MD 21629 410-479-4700
Web: www.tanglewoodconservatories.com

Tarlton Corp 5500 W Pk Ave. . . . . Saint Louis MO 63110 314-633-3300 647-1940
Web: www.tarltoncorp.com

Tbi Construction & Construction Management Inc
1960 the Alameda Ste 100 . . . . San Jose CA 95126 408-246-3691 241-9983
Web: strategic-cm.com

TCI Architects/Engineers/Contractors Inc
1718 State Rd 16 . . . . La Crosse WI 54601 608-781-5700 781-5705
Web: www.tciaec.com

TCS Communications LLC
2045 W Union Ave Bldg E . . . . Englewood CO 80110 303-377-3800 377-8300
Web: www.tcscomm.com

Technology Site Planners Inc
8188 Business Way . . . . Plain City OH 43064 614-873-7800
Web: www.techsiteplan.com

Tedco Construction Corp Tedco Pl. . . . . Carnegie PA 15106 412-276-8080 276-6804
Web: www.tedco.com

Telecon Inc 13 500 boul Metropolitain E . . . . Montreal QC H1A3W1 514-644-2333
Web: www.telecon.ca

Tepsco 2909 Aaron St . . . . Deer Park TX 77536 281-604-0309 930-0788
Web: www.tepsco.com

Theatre Projects Consultants Inc
25 Elizabeth St . . . . South Norwalk CT 06854 203-299-0830
Web: www.theatreprojects.com

Thomas & Marker Construction Co
2084 US 68 S PO Box 250 . . . . Bellefontaine OH 43311 937-599-2160 599-6170
Web: www.thomasmarker.com

Thompson Thrift Construction Inc
901 Wabash Ave Ste 300 . . . . Terre Haute IN 47807 812-235-5959 235-8122
Web: www.thompsonthrift.com

ThompsonBrooks Inc 151 Vermont St Ste 9 . . . . . . San Francisco CA 94103 415-581-2600
Web: thompsonbrooks.com

THS Constructors
150 Executive Ctr Dr Ste B108 . . . . Greenville SC 29615 864-254-6066
Web: www.thsconstructors.com

Tiger Construction Ltd
6280 Everson Goshen Rd . . . . Everson WA 98247 360-966-7252
Web: www.hub-4.com

Tilden-Coil Constructors Inc
3612 Mission Inn Ave. . . . . Riverside CA 92501 951-684-5901
Web: www.tilden-coil.com

Tilton Asset Management 510 Boston Post Rd. . . . . Weston MA 02493 781-373-2244
Web: tiltonasset.com

TN Ward Co 129 Coulter Ave PO Box 191 . . . . Ardmore PA 19003 610-649-0400 649-1790
Web: www.tnward.com

Tom Rectenwald Construction Inc
330A Perry Hwy . . . . Harmony PA 16037 724-452-8801
Web: www.tomrectenwald.com

Toney Construction Services Inc
14031 Huffmeister Rd. . . . . Cypress TX 77429 281-304-1778
Web: www.toneyconstruction.com

Top Shop Inc, The 5740 Logan St . . . . Denver CO 80216 303-996-6026
Web: www.tshopinc.com

Torcon Inc 328 Newman Springs Rd. . . . . Red Bank NJ 07701 732-704-9800 704-9810
Web: www.torcon.com

Torti Gallas & Partners Inc
1300 Spring St Ste 400 . . . . Silver Spring MD 20910 301-588-4800 650-2255
Web: www.tortigallas.com

Phone Fax

Tower Lighting of Texas
1251 Rolling Crk ....Spring Branch TX 78070 830-228-4594
Web: www.navacomm.com

Tredyffrin-Easttown School District (TESD)
940 W Valley Rd Ste 1700 ....Wayne PA 19087 610-240-1900
Web: www.tesd.k12.pa.us

Trehel Corp PO Box 1707 ....Clemson SC 29633 864-654-6582 654-7788
TF: 800-319-7006 ■ *Web:* www.trehel.com

Tri-C Construction Company Inc
1765 Merriman Rd ....Akron OH 44313 330-836-2722 869-8373
Web: www.tricc.com

Tri-state Design Construction Inc
7401 Old York Rd ....Elkins Park PA 19027 215-782-8200 782-8282
Web: www.tristatedesign.net

Tribalco LLC 4915 St Elmo Ave Ste 501 ....Bethesda MD 20814 301-652-8450
Web: www.tribalco.com

Tribble & Stephens Construction Ltd
8588 Katy Fwy Ste 100...........................Houston TX 77024 713-465-8550 973-7107
Web: www.tribblestephens.com

Trotter & Morton Ltd 5711 - First St SE...............Calgary AB T2H1H9 403-255-7535
Web: www.trotterandmorton.com

Turelk Inc 3700 Santa Fe Ave PO Box 93101 ....Long Beach CA 90810 310-835-3736 835-5909
Web: www.turelk.com

Turner Construction Co 375 Hudson St.............New York NY 10014 212-229-6000 229-6390*
**Fax:* Mktg ■ *Web:* www.turnerconstruction.com

Turner Universal 336 James Record Rd.............Huntsville AL 35824 256-461-0568 461-6737
Web: www.turnerconstruction.com

Tutor-Saliba Corp 15901 Olden St ....Sylmar CA 91342 818-362-8391 367-5379
Web: www.tutorsaliba.com

TWC Construction Inc
431 Eastgate Rd Third Fl.........................Henderson NV 89011 702-597-3444
Web: www.twcconstruction.com

Tyler 2 Construction Inc
5400 Old Pineville Rd.............................Charlotte NC 28217 704-527-3031
Web: www.tyler2construction.com

U S Government Absentee Shawnee Tribe of Oklahoma
2025 Gordon Cooper Dr..........................Shawnee OK 74801 405-275-4030
Web: www.astribe.com

U S Group Inc 100 Executive Ctr Dr Ste 217 ....Columbia SC 29210 803-798-1420 798-1450
Web: www.usgroupinc.com

Ukpeagvik Inupiat Corp
1250 Agvik St PO Box 890..........................Barrow AK 99723 907-852-4460 852-4459
Web: www.ukpik.com

Unit Company Inc 620 E Whitney Rd...............Anchorage AK 99501 907-349-6666
Web: www.unitcompany.com

Universal Construction Company Inc
11200 W 79th St..................................Lenexa KS 66214 913-342-1150 342-1151
Web: www.universalconstruction.net

University Moving & Storage Co
23305 Commerce Dr ....Farmington Hills MI 48335 248-615-7000 615-8515
TF: 800-448-6683 ■ *Web:* www.universitymoving.com

USM Inc 1880 Markley St.........................Norristown PA 19401 610-278-9000 275-8023
TF: 800-355-4000 ■ *Web:* www.usmservices.com

USS Cal Builders Inc 8051 Main St..................Stanton CA 90680 714-828-4882
Web: www.usscalbuilders.com

UW Marx Inc 20 Gurley Ave.............................Troy NY 12182 518-272-2541 272-1196
Web: www.uwmarx.com

Valley Construction Co 3610 - 78th Ave W ....Rock Island IL 61201 309-787-0292 787-7048
Web: www.valleyconstruction.com

Van Hoose Construction 101 NE 70th St ....Oklahoma City OK 73105 405-848-0415 848-3911
Web: www.vhcon.com

Vandervert Construction Inc
608 E Holland Ave ....Spokane WA 99218 509-467-6654
Web: www.vandervertconstruction.com

Vaughn Construction 10355 Westpark Dr ....Houston TX 77042 713-243-8300 243-8350
Web: www.vaughnconstruction.com

VCI Telcom Inc 1921 W 11th St ....Upland CA 91786 909-946-0905
Web: www.vcicom.com

Veit & Company Inc 14000 Veit Pl ....Rogers MN 55374 763-428-2242
Web: www.veitusa.com

Vesta Properties Ltd 9770 196A St Ste 101A..........Langley BC V1M2X5 604-888-7869
Web: www.vestaproperties.com

Vinco Inc PO Box 907 ....Forest Lake MN 55025 651-982-4642
Web: www.vinco-inc.com

Virtexco Corp 977 Norfolk Sq ....Norfolk VA 23502 757-466-1114 466-1115
TF: 800-766-1082 ■ *Web:* www.virtexco.com

Vissering Construction Co
175 Benchmark Industrial Dr ....Streator IL 61364 815-673-5511
Web: www.vissering.com

VJS Construction Services
W233 N2847 Roundy Cir W ....Pewaukee WI 53072 262-542-9000
Web: www.vjscs.com

Vratsinas Construction (VCC)
216 Louisiana St PO Box 2558...................Little Rock AR 72203 501-376-0017 376-4145
Web: www.vccusa.com/

VRH Construction Corp 320 Grand Ave ....Englewood NJ 07631 201-871-4422 871-6727
Web: www.vrhcorp.com

W E O'Neil Construction Co
2751 N Clybourn Ave ....Chicago IL 60614 773-755-1611
Web: www.weoneil.com

W. L. Butler Construction Inc
204 Franklin St..................................Redwood City CA 94063 650-361-1270 361-8657
Web: www.wlbutler.com

W. Rogers Co 649 Bizzell Dr ....Lexington KY 40510 859-231-6290 233-2066
Web: www.wrogers.com

WA Klinger LLC
2015 E Seventh St PO Box 8800....................Sioux City IA 51102 712-277-3900 277-5300
Web: www.waklinger.com

Wakefield Corp, The PO Box 31198................Knoxville TN 37930 865-675-1550 675-1582
Web: www.thewakefieldcorp.com

Walbridge Aldinger Co 777 Woodward Ave #300 ....Detroit MI 48226 313-963-8000 963-8150
Web: www.walbridge.com

Phone Fax

Walker Industries Holdings Ltd
2800 Thorold Townline Rd ....Niagara Falls ON L2E6S4 905-227-4142
Web: www.walkerind.com

Wallick Construction Company Inc
PO Box 1023 ....Columbus OH 43216 614-863-4640 863-1725
Web: www.wallickcos.com

Walsh Construction Co 2905 SW First Ave ....Portland OR 97201 503-222-4375 274-7676
Web: www.walshconstructionco.com

Walsh Group Inc 929 W Adams St....................Chicago IL 60607 312-563-5400 563-5466
TF: 800-957-1842 ■ *Web:* walshgroup.com

Walton County Board of Education
200 Double Springs Church Rd ....Monroe GA 30656 770-266-4520
Web: www.walton.k12.ga.us

Wantman Group Inc
2035 Vista Pkwy Ste 100 ....West Palm Beach FL 33411 561-687-2220
Web: www.wantmangroup.com

Wanzek Construction Inc 2028 2nd Ave NW........ West Fargo ND 58078 701-282-6171 282-6166
TF: 877-492-6935 ■ *Web:* www.wanzek.com

Ware County Board of Education
1301 Bailey St PO Box 1789.......................Waycross GA 31502 912-283-8656 283-8698
TF: 800-419-3191 ■ *Web:* www.ware.k12.ga.us

Warfel Construction Co
1110 Enterprise Rd.........................East Petersburg PA 17520 717-299-4500 299-4628
Web: www.warfelcc.com

Warren Paving Inc
562 Elks Lk Rd PO Box 572 ....Hattiesburg MS 39403 601-544-7811 544-2005
Web: www.warrenpaving.com

Washington Local Schools
3505 W Lincolnshire Blvd ....Toledo OH 43606 419-473-8251 473-8247
TF: 800-462-3589 ■ *Web:* www.washloc.k12.oh.us

Washtenaw County Road Commission
555 N Zeeb Rd ....Ann Arbor MI 48103 734-761-1500 761-3239
Web: www.wcroads.org

Waterbury Public School District (WPSD)
236 Grand St Ste 1 ....Waterbury CT 06702 203-574-8000 574-8010
Web: www.waterbury.k12.ct.us

Weaver Cooke Construction LLC
8401 Key Blvd ....Greensboro NC 27409 336-378-7900 378-7901
Web: www.weavercooke.com

Weber Group Inc 5233 Progress Way ....Sellersburg IN 47172 812-246-2100 246-2109
Web: webergroupinc.com

Weis Builders Inc 2227 Seventh St NW............. Rochester MN 55901 507-288-2041 288-7979
Web: www.weisbuilders.com

Weitz Company Inc 5901 Thornton Ave............Des Moines IA 50321 515-246-4700
Web: www.weitz.com

Weitz/Cohen Construction Co
4725 S Monaco St Ste 100...........................Denver CO 80237 303-860-6600 860-6698
Web: www.weitz.com

Welbro Bldg Corp
2301 Maitland Ctr Pkwy Ste 250 ....Maitland FL 32751 407-475-0800 475-0801
Web: www.welbro.com

Welch & Rushe Inc
391 Prince George's Blvd ....Upper Marlboro MD 20774 301-430-6000
Web: www.welchandrushe.com

Wesely-thomas Enterprises Inc
250 Lombard St Ste 1.......................Thousand Oaks CA 91360 805-379-2365
Web: www.wtei.com

West Bay Builders Inc 250 Bel Marin Keys Blvd ....Novato CA 94949 415-456-8972 459-0665
Web: www.westbaybuilders.com

West Coast Construction
9021 Rancho Park Ct .... Rancho Cucamonga CA 91730 909-982-6979
Web: www.wccsinc.com

West Construction Inc
318 S Dixie Hwy Ste 4-5......................... Lake Worth FL 33460 561-588-2027 582-9419
Web: www.westconstructioninc.net

Western Builders of Amarillo Inc
700 S Grant St ....Amarillo TX 79101 806-376-4321
Web: www.wbamarillo.com

Western Summit Constructors Inc
9780 Mt Pyramid Ct Ste 100 ....Englewood CO 80112 303-298-9500 325-0304
Web: www.westernsummit.com

WG Yates & Sons Construction Co Inc
1 Gulley Ave PO Box 456 .... Philadelphia MS 39350 601-656-5411 656-8958
Web: www.wgyates.com

Whiting-Turner Contracting Co
300 E Joppa Rd Eighth Fl.........................Towson MD 21286 410-821-1100 337-5770
TF: 800-638-4279 ■ *Web:* www.whiting-turner.com

Wichman Construction 5029 W Grace St.............. Tampa FL 33607 813-282-1179
Web: www.wichmanconstruction.com

Wild Bldg Contractors Inc
225 W First N St Ste 102 ....Morristown TN 37814 423-581-5639 587-4037
Web: www.wildbuilding.com

William A Randolph Inc 820 Lakeside Dr Ste 3 ....Gurnee IL 60031 847-856-0123
Web: www.warandolph.com

William Blanchard Co 199 Mountain Ave...........Springfield NJ 07081 973-376-9100 376-9154
Web: wmblanchard.com

Williams Company of Orlando Inc
2301 Silver Star Rd...............................Orlando FL 32804 407-295-2530 297-0459
Web: www.williamsco.com

Windstar Lines Inc 1903 US Hwy 71 N.................Carroll IA 51401 712-792-4221 792-9615
TF: 888-494-6378 ■ *Web:* www.gowindstar.com

Winter Construction Co 191 Peachtree St NE ....Atlanta GA 30303 404-588-3300
Web: winter-construction.com

Winter Park Construction Co 221 Cir Dr .... Maitland FL 32751 407-644-8923 645-1972
Web: www.wpc.com

WM Brode Co 100 Elizabeth St PO Box 299 ...... Newcomerstown OH 43832 740-498-5121 498-8553
Web: www.wmbrode.com

WM Jordan Company Inc
11010 Jefferson Ave..........................Newport News VA 23601 757-596-6341 596-7425
Web: www.wmjordan.com

Wolverine Bldg Group Inc 4045 Barden SE........Grand Rapids MI 49512 616-949-3360 949-6211
Web: www.wolvgroup.com

Company	City	State	Zip	Phone	Fax
Woodfield Inc 3161 Hwy 376 S *TF:* 800-501-6020 ■ *Web:* www.woodfieldinc.com	Camden	AR	71701	870-231-6020	231-6070
Worth Construction Company Inc 24 Taylor Ave *Web:* www.worthconstruction.com	Bethel	CT	06801	203-797-8788	791-2515
Wright Construction Corp 5811 Youngquist Rd *Web:* www.wrightconstructioncorp.com	Fort Myers	FL	33912	239-481-5000	481-2448
Wright Construction Western Inc 2919 Cleveland Ave *Web:* www.wrightconstruction.ca	Saskatoon	SK	S7K8A9	306-934-0440	
Wright Process Systems 88 Commerce St *Web:* www.wrightps.com	Lodi	CA	95240	209-369-2795	
WS Bellows Construction Corp 1906 Afton St *Web:* www.wsbellows.com	Houston	TX	77055	713-680-2132	680-2614
WS Cumby Inc 938 Lincoln Ave *Web:* www.cumby.com	Springfield	PA	19064	610-328-5353	
Wurzel Builders Ltd 8721 S First St *Web:* wurzelbuilders.com	Austin	TX	78748	512-282-9488	
Yeadon Fabric Structures Ltd Kerr Industrial Park R.R. #3 *Web:* www.yeadondomes.com	Guelph	ON	N1H6H9	519-821-9301	821-9010
Yeargin Potter Shackelford Construction Inc 121 Edinburgh Ct *Web:* www.ypsconst.com	Greenville	SC	29607	864-232-1491	
Yellowridge Construction Ltd 2605 Clarke St Ste 200 *Web:* yellowridge.ca	Port Moody	BC	V3H1Z4	604-936-2605	
Zachry Group 527 Logwood Ave *Web:* zhi.com	San Antonio	TX	78221	210-588-5000	588-5060
Zeeland Public Schools (ZPS) 183 W Roosevelt Ave *Web:* www.zps.org	Zeeland	MI	49464	616-748-3000	748-3033
Ziolkowski Construction Inc 4050 Ralph Jones Dr *Web:* www.zbuild.com	South Bend	IN	46628	574-287-1811	

190 CONSTRUCTION - BUILDING CONTRACTORS - RESIDENTIAL

Company	City	State	Zip	Phone	Fax
Agbayani Construction Corp 88 Dixon Ct *Web:* www.agbayani.com	Daly City	CA	94014	415-221-2065	665-9470
Air Contact Transport Inc PO Box 570 **Fax Area Code:* 973 ■ *TF:* 800-765-2769 ■ *Web:* actovernight.com	Budd Lake	NJ	07828	800-765-2769	691-0127*
Alcan Electrical & Engineering Inc 6670 Arctic Spur Rd *Web:* www.alcanelectric.com	Anchorage	AK	99518	907-563-3787	562-6286
Alexander Company Inc, The 145 E Badger Rd Ste 200 *Web:* www.alexandercompany.com	Madison	WI	53713	608-258-5580	258-5599
Alliance Construction Solutions LLC 2725 Rocky Mtn Ave Ste 100 *Web:* www.allianceconstruction.com	Loveland	CO	80538	970-663-9700	663-9750
Arthur Rutenberg Homes Inc 13922 58th St N *TF:* 800-274-6637 ■ *Web:* www.arthurrutenberghomes.com	Clearwater	FL	33760	727-536-5900	538-9089
Aui Contractors LLC 4775 N Fwy *Web:* www.auigc.com	Fort Worth	TX	76106	817-926-4377	926-4387
Ball Homes LLC 3609 Walden Dr *TF:* 888-268-1101 ■ *Web:* www.ballhomes.com	Lexington	KY	40517	859-268-1191	268-9093
Bar None Auction Inc 4751 Power Inn Rd **Fax Area Code:* 916 ■ *TF:* 866-372-1700 ■ *Web:* www.barnoneauction.com	Sacramento	CA	95826	866-372-1700	383-6865*
Bob Schmitt Homes Inc 9095 Gatestone Rd *Web:* www.bobschmitthomes.com	North Ridgeville	OH	44039	440-327-9495	327-7540
Bozzuto Group 7850 Walker Dr Ste 400 *TF General:* 866-698-7513 ■ *Web:* www.bozzuto.com	Greenbelt	MD	20770	301-220-0100	220-3738
Breeden Homes Inc 366 E 40th Ave *TF Sales:* 800-870-1367 ■ *Web:* www.breedenhomes.com	Eugene	OR	97405	541-686-9431	686-0918
Burnsteads, The 11980 NE 24th St Ste 200 *Web:* www.burnstead.com	Bellevue	WA	98005	425-454-1900	454-4543
Bush Construction Corp 4029 Ironbound Rd Ste 200	Williamsburg	VA	23188	757-220-2874	229-2542
Calcon Constructors Inc 2270 W Bates Ave *Web:* www.calconci.com	Englewood	CO	80110	303-762-1554	762-1948
Capital Pacific Holdings Inc 4100 MacArthur Blvd Ste 150 *Web:* cph-inc.com	Newport Beach	CA	92660	949-622-8400	622-8404
Churchill Development Corp Five Choke Cherry Rd Ste 360 *Web:* www.churchillbuilders.com	Rockville	MD	20850	240-243-1000	
City Dash 949 Laidlaw Ave *Web:* www.citydash.com	Cincinnati	OH	45237	513-562-2000	
Clark-Pacific Corp 1980 S River Rd *Web:* www.clarkpacific.com	West Sacramento	CA	95691	916-371-0305	372-0323
Colson & Colson Construction Co 2260 McGilchrist St SE *Web:* www.colson-colson.com	Salem	OR	97302	503-586-7401	370-4205
Construction Enterprises Inc (CEI) 325 Seaboard Ln Ste 170 *Web:* www.constructionenterprises.com	Franklin	TN	37067	615-332-8880	771-0818
Crossgates Inc 3555 Washington Rd *Web:* www.crossgatesinc.com	McMurray	PA	15317	724-941-9240	941-4339
Damuth Trane 1100 Cavalier Blvd *Web:* www.damuth.com	Chesapeake	VA	23323	757-558-0200	558-9715
Dot-Line Transportation PO Box 8739 *TF:* 800-423-3780 ■ *Web:* www.dotline.net	Fountain Valley	CA	92728	323-780-9010	780-1552
Drees Co 211 Grandview Dr *TF:* 866-265-2980 ■ *Web:* www.dreeshomes.com	Fort Mitchell	KY	41017	859-578-4200	578-4200
DuBois Area School District Inc 500 Liberty Blvd *Web:* www.dasd.k12.pa.us	Du Bois	PA	15801	814-371-2700	
Eid-Co Homes 1701 32nd Ave S *Web:* www.eid-co.com	Fargo	ND	58103	701-237-0510	
Excel Homes Inc 10642 S Susquehanna Trail *TF Sales:* 800-521-8599 ■ *Web:* www.excelhomes.com	Liverpool	PA	17045	717-444-3395	444-7577
Eyde Co 4660 S Hagadorn Ste 660 *TF:* 800-422-3933 ■ *Web:* www.eyde.com	East Lansing	MI	48823	517-351-2480	351-3946
F D Rich Co 222 Summer St *Web:* www.fdrich.com	Stamford	CT	06901	203-359-2900	328-7980
Farmington School District R-7 1022 Ste Genevieve Ave *Web:* www.farmington.k12.mo.us	Farmington	MO	63640	573-701-1300	701-1309
FH Martin Constructors 28740 Mound Rd *Web:* www.fhmartin.com	Warren	MI	48092	586-558-2100	558-2921
Fish Enterprises 905 S Fair Oaks Ave *Web:* www.fishenterprises.com	Pasadena	CA	91105	626-773-8800	773-8820
Forbes Homes Inc 470 Cayuga Rd *Web:* www.forbeshomes.com	Cheektowaga	NY	14225	716-688-5597	688-6674
Fox Ridge Homes Inc 93 Seaboard Ln Ste 201 *Web:* www.foxridgehomes.com	Brentwood	TN	37027	615-377-6840	377-6864
Franklin Development Co 21260 Gathering Oak Ste 101 *Web:* franklincompanies.com	San Antonio	TX	78260	210-694-2223	
Fulton Homes Corp 9140 S Kyrene Rd Ste 202 *Web:* www.fultonhomes.com	Tempe	AZ	85284	480-753-6789	753-5554
Galaxy Builders Ltd 4729 College Pk *Web:* thegalaxycompanies.com	San Antonio	TX	78249	210-493-0550	493-1238
Gioffre Cos Inc 6262 Eiterman Rd *Web:* www.gioffreconstruction.com	Dublin	OH	43016	614-764-0032	764-1620
Green Valley Corp 777 N First St Fifth Fl *Web:* www.barryswensonbuilder.com	San Jose	CA	95112	408-287-0246	998-1737
Grupe Co 3255 W March Ln Ste 400 *Web:* www.grupe.com	Stockton	CA	95219	209-473-6000	473-6001
Hardaway Group 615 Main St *Web:* www.hardaway.net	Nashville	TN	37206	615-254-5461	254-4518
Harkins Builders Inc 2201 Warwick Way *TF:* 800-227-2345 ■ *Web:* www.harkinsbuilders.com	Marriottsville	MD	21104	410-750-2600	480-4299
Harper Corp General Contractors 35 W Ct St Ste 400 *Web:* www.harpercorp.com	Greenville	SC	29601	864-527-2500	527-2536
Hasbrouck Heights Board of Education 379 Blvd *Web:* www.hhschools.org	Hasbrouck Heights	NJ	07604	201-288-6150	
Hawaii Modular Space Inc 91-282 Kalaeloa Blvd *Web:* www.hawaiimodularspace.com	Kapolei	HI	96707	808-682-5559	682-5199
Haywood County School District 900 E Main St *Web:* www.haywoodschools.com	Brownsville	TN	38012	731-772-9613	772-3275
Hernandez Cos Inc 3734 E Anne St *Web:* www.hernandezcompanies.com	Phoenix	AZ	85040	602-438-7825	438-6558
Hitt Contracting Inc 2900 Fairview Park Dr *Web:* www.hitt-gc.com	Falls Church	VA	22042	703-846-9000	846-9110
Hovnanian Enterprises Inc 1806 S Highland Ave *Web:* khov.com	Lombard	IL	60148	630-953-2222	
James A Cummings Inc 3575 NW 53rd St *Web:* www.jamesacummings.com	Fort Lauderdale	FL	33309	954-733-4211	485-9688
JB Sandlin Cos 5137 Davis Blvd *TF:* 800-821-4663 ■ *Web:* sandlinhomes.com	Fort Worth	TX	76180	817-281-3509	656-0719
Jim Walter Homes LLC 3000 Riverchase Galleria Ste 1700 *TF:* 800-643-0202 ■ *Web:* www.jimwalterhomes.com	Birmingham	AL	35244	205-745-2615	
John Cannon Homes Inc 6710 Professional Pkwy W *Web:* www.johncannonhomes.com	Sarasota	FL	34240	941-924-5935	924-4129
Jokake Construction Co 5013 E Washington St Ste 100 *Web:* www.jokake.com	Phoenix	AZ	85034	602-224-4500	667-5500
Joseph J. Henderson & Son Inc 4288 Old Grand Ave PO Box 9 *Web:* www.jjhenderson.com	Gurnee	IL	60031	847-244-3222	244-9572
Kalian Cos 225 Hwy 35 Navesink N *Web:* www.kalian.com	Red Bank	NJ	07701	732-741-0054	741-3404
Kickerillo Cos 1306 S Fry Rd **Fax Area Code:* 281 ■ *Web:* www.kickerillo.com	Katy	TX	77450	713-951-0666	492-2018*
Kopf Builders Inc 420 Avon Belden Rd *Web:* www.kopf.net	Avon Lake	OH	44012	440-933-6908	933-6956
LAS Enterprises Inc 2413 L & A Rd *TF:* 800-264-1527 ■ *Web:* lashome.com	Metairie	LA	70001	504-887-1515	832-0036
Lewis Builders Inc 54 Sawyer Ave *Web:* www.lewisbuilders.com	Atkinson	NH	03811	603-362-5333	362-4936
Lizardos Engineering Assoc Pc 200 Old Country Rd Ste 670 *Web:* www.leapc.com	Mineola	NY	11501	516-484-1020	484-0926
McBride & Son Inc 16091 Swingley Ridge Rd Ste 300 *Web:* www.mcbridehomes.com	Chesterfield	MO	63005	636-537-2000	537-2546
Mercy Housing Inc 1999 Broadway Ste 1000 *TF:* 866-338-0557 ■ *Web:* www.mercyhousing.org	Denver	CO	80202	303-830-3300	
Michaels Group LLC 10 Blacksmith Dr Ste 1 *Web:* www.michaelsgroup.com	Malta	NY	12020	518-899-6311	899-6260
Morgan Group Inc 5606 S Rice Ave *Web:* www.morgangroup.com	Houston	TX	77081	713-361-7200	361-7299
Nordaas American Homes Company Inc 10091 State Hwy 22 *TF:* 800-658-7076 ■ *Web:* nordaashomes.com	Minnesota Lake	MN	56068	507-462-3331	462-3211
Norris School District 6940 Calloway Dr *TF:* 800-877-8339 ■ *Web:* www.norris.k12.ca.us	Bakersfield	CA	93312	661-387-7000	399-9750
NVR Inc 11700 Plz America Dr Ste 500 *NYSE:* NVR ■ *Web:* nvrinc.com	Reston	VA	20190	703-956-4000	956-4750
O'Harrow Construction Co 4575 Ann Arbor Rd *Web:* www.oharrow.net	Jackson	MI	49202	517-764-4770	764-5564

Company	City	State	ZIP	Phone	Fax
Ole South Properties Inc 201 E Main St Ste 300 *Web:* www.olesouth.com	Murfreesboro	TN	37130	615-896-0019	896-9380
Olgoonik Development LLC 3201 C St Ste 700 *TF:* 855-763-2613 ■ *Web:* www.olgoonik.com	Anchorage	AK	99503	907-562-8728	562-8751
Olympus Homes Inc PO Box 2999 *Web:* www.olympushomes.com	Westerville	OH	43086	614-436-4100	
Perry Homes PO Box 34306 *TF:* 800-247-3779 ■ *Web:* www.perryhomes.com	Houston	TX	77234	713-947-1750	944-9106
Prince Telecom Inc 551 Mews Dr Ste A *Web:* www.princetelecom.com	New Castle	DE	19720	302-324-1800	324-0428
Providence Homes Inc 4901 Belfort Rd Ste 140 *TF:* 866-836-0981 ■ *Web:* www.providencehomesinc.com	Jacksonville	FL	32256	904-262-9898	262-9861
Purcell Construction Inc 277 Dennis St *Web:* www.purcellc.com	Humble	TX	77338	281-548-1000	548-2998
Pyramid Construction Inc 275 N Franklin Tpke. *Web:* www.pyramidgroup.biz	Ramsey	NJ	07446	201-327-1919	327-0054
R L Turner Corp 1000 W Oak St. *Web:* www.rlturner.com	Zionsville	IN	46077	317-873-2712	873-1262
Reimers & Jolivette Inc 2344 NW 24th Ave *Web:* reimersandjolivette.com	Portland	OR	97210	503-228-7691	228-2721
Rio Verde Development Inc 25609 N Danny Ln *TF:* 800-233-7103 ■ *Web:* www.theverdes.com	Rio Verde	AZ	85263	480-471-1962	471-0107
Rockford Homes Inc 999 Polaris Pkwy Ste 200 *Web:* www.rockfordhomes.net	Columbus	OH	43240	614-785-0015	785-9181
Rohde Construction Company Inc 4087 Brockton Dr *Web:* rohdeconstruction.com	Kentwood	MI	49512	616-698-0880	698-1850
RS Mowery & Sons Inc 1000 Bent Creek Blvd *Web:* www.rsmowery.com	Mechanicsburg	PA	17050	717-506-1000	506-1010
Russell Construction Company Inc 4600 E 53rd St *Web:* www.russellco.com	Davenport	IA	52807	563-459-4600	
Rust Constructors Inc 2 Perimeter Pk S Ste 300 W *Web:* rustconstructors.azurewebsites.net	Birmingham	AL	35243	205-995-7171	995-3873
Schneider Homes Inc 6510 Southcenter Blvd Ste 1 *Web:* www.schneiderhomes.com	Tukwila	WA	98188	206-248-2471	242-4209
Selmer Co 2200 Woodale Ave. *TF:* 800-992-6538 ■ *Web:* theboldtcompany.com	Green Bay	WI	54313	920-434-0230	
Shaw Construction Company LLC 300 Kalamath St *Web:* www.shawconstruction.net	Denver	CO	80223	303-825-4740	825-6403
Shreve Land Company Inc 624 Travis St Ste 100 *Web:* www.shreveland.com	Shreveport	LA	71101	318-226-0056	226-0064
Shugart Enterprises LLC 221 Jonestown Rd *Web:* www.shugartenterprises.com	Winston Salem	NC	27104	336-765-9661	765-1295
Simpson County School District 176 W Ct St PO Box 127 *Web:* www.simpsoncounty.biz	Mendenhall	MS	39114	601-847-2375	847-2380
Skogman Construction Company Inc 411 First Ave Ste 500 *Web:* www.skogman.com	Cedar Rapids	IA	52401	319-363-8285	366-7257
Smith Bros Construction PO Box 1068 *Web:* www.smithbrothersconstruction.com	Solana Beach	CA	92075	858-350-1445	350-7629
Southern California Boiler Inc 5331 Business Dr *TF:* 800-775-2645 ■ *Web:* www.californiaboiler.com	Huntington Beach	CA	92649	714-891-0701	891-4320
SS Steele & Company Inc 4951 Government Blvd *Web:* www.steelehomes.cc	Mobile	AL	36693	251-661-9600	
Stabile Cos Inc 20 Cotton Rd Ste 200 *Web:* www.stabilecompanies.com	Nashua	NH	03063	603-889-0318	595-2571
Stanmar Inc 321 Commonwealth Rd Ste 201 *Web:* www.stanmar-inc.com	Wayland	MA	01778	508-310-9922	310-0479
Staples Construction Company Inc 1501 Eastman Ave *TF:* 800-881-4650 ■ *Web:* www.staplesconstruction.com	Ventura	CA	93003	805-658-8786	658-8785
Structural Component Systems Inc (SCS) 1255 Front St *TF:* 800-844-5622 ■ *Web:* www.scstruss.com	Fremont	NE	68026	402-721-5622	721-6170
Sunset Development Co One Annabel Ln Ste 201 *Web:* www.bishopranch.com	San Ramon	CA	94583	925-866-0100	866-1330
T&G Constructors Inc 8623 Commodity Cir *Web:* www.t-and-g.com	Orlando	FL	32819	407-352-4443	352-0778
T. Gerding Construction Co PO Box 1082 **Fax Area Code:* 547 ■ *Web:* www.tgerding.com	Corvallis	OR	97339	541-753-2012	754-6654*
TH Properties 345 Main St *TF Sales:* 800-225-5847 ■ *Web:* www.thproperties.com	Harleysville	PA	19438	215-513-4270	511-3202
Thompson Realty Corp 2505 N Plano Rd Ste 3000 *Web:* www.thompson-realty.com	Richardson	TX	75082	972-644-2400	
Thor Construction Inc 5400 Main St NE Ste 203 *Web:* www.thorconstructioninc.com	Minneapolis	MN	55421	763-571-2580	571-2631
Traton Corp 720 Kennesaw Ave NW *Web:* www.tratonhomes.com	Marietta	GA	30060	770-427-9064	427-2714
Triple Crown Corp 5351 Jaycee Ave. *TF:* 877-822-4663 ■ *Web:* www.triplecrowncorp.com	Harrisburg	PA	17112	717-657-5729	657-8125
True Homes LLC 2649 Breckenridge Ctr Dr Ste 104 *Web:* truehomesusa.com	Monroe	NC	28110	704-238-1229	238-1150
Trustmark Construction Corp 841 Sweetwater Ave *Web:* www.trustmarkcorp.com	Florence	AL	35630	256-760-9624	760-0902
Tuttle Construction Inc 880 Shawnee Rd. *Web:* www.tuttlenet.com	Lima	OH	45805	419-228-6262	229-7414
United-Bilt Homes Inc 8500 Line Ave *TF:* 800-551-8955 ■ *Web:* www.ubh.com	Shreveport	LA	71106	318-861-4572	869-0132
Urban Concrete Contractors Ltd 24114 Blanco Rd *Web:* www.urbanconcrete.com	San Antonio	TX	78258	210-490-0090	490-1505
Vantage Homes 1710 Jet Stream Dr Ste 100 *Web:* www.vhco.com	Colorado Springs	CO	80921	719-534-0984	534-0998
Venture Express Inc 131 Industrial Blvd. *Web:* www.ventureexpress.com	La Vergne	TN	37086	615-793-9500	793-9267
Village Green Cos 30833 NW Hwy *TF:* 800-521-2220 ■ *Web:* www.villagegreen.com	Farmington Hills	MI	48334	248-851-9600	851-6161
Voorhees International Inc 1656 Headland Dr. *Web:* www.voorheesintl.com	Saint Louis	MO	63026	636-349-1555	349-5130
Wallick Construction Company Inc PO Box 1023 *Web:* www.wallickcos.com	Columbus	OH	43216	614-863-4640	863-1725
Walsh Group Inc 929 W Adams St. *TF:* 800-957-1842 ■ *Web:* walshgroup.com	Chicago	IL	60607	312-563-5400	563-5466
Walter Toebe Construction Co 29001 Wall St PO Box 930129 *Web:* www.toebe-construction.com	Wixom	MI	48393	248-349-7500	349-4870
Weavertown Environmental Group Two Dorrington Rd *TF:* 800-746-4850 ■ *Web:* www.weavertown.com	Carnegie	PA	15106	724-746-4850	746-9024
Wermers Multi-Family Corp 5120 Shoreham Pl Ste 150 *Web:* www.wermerscompanies.com	San Diego	CA	92122	858-535-1475	535-0171
Western Water Constructors Inc 707 Aviation Blvd *Web:* www.westernwater.com	Santa Rosa	CA	95403	707-540-9640	540-9641
Wexford Homes 135 Keveling Dr *Web:* www.wexfordhomes.com	Saline	MI	48176	734-470-6647	
Wheeler Construction Inc 3255 E Gulf to Lake Hwy. *Web:* www.citrusbuilder.com	Inverness	FL	34453	352-726-0973	637-4959
Wildish Land Co Inc 3600 Wildish Ln PO Box 40310 *Web:* www.wildish.com	Eugene	OR	97408	541-485-1700	683-7722
William Lyon Homes 4695 MacArthur Ct Eighth Fl *Web:* www.lyonhomes.com	Newport Beach	CA	92660	949-833-3600	476-2178
Winchester Homes Inc 6905 Rockledge Dr Ste 800 *Web:* yourhomeyourway.com/winchester/	Bethesda	MD	20817	301-803-4800	474-1609
Wohlsen Construction Co 548 Steel Way PO Box 7066 *Web:* www.wohlsenconstruction.com	Lancaster	PA	17604	717-299-2500	299-3419

191 CONSTRUCTION - HEAVY CONSTRUCTION CONTRACTORS

Company	City	State	ZIP	Phone	Fax
2G - CENERGY Power Systems Technologies Inc 205 Commercial Dr *Web:* www.2g-cenergy.com	St. Augustine	FL	32092	904-579-3217	
Allen & Shariff Corp 7061 Deepage Dr *Web:* www.allenshariff.com	Columbia	MD	21045	410-381-7100	
Apac-ks Wilkerson Crane Rental 12790 E 36th St N *Web:* www.wilkersoncranerental.com	Tulsa	OK	74116	918-437-9500	
Bo-mac Contractors Ltd 1020 Lindbergh Dr *Web:* www.bomaccontractors.com	Beaumont	TX	77707	409-842-2125	
Broda Construction Ltd 4271 - Fifth Ave E *Web:* www.brodaconstruction.com	Prince Albert	SK	S6V7V6	306-764-5337	
Capitol Tunneling Inc 2216 Refugee Rd *Web:* www.capitoltunneling.com	Columbus	OH	43207	614-444-0255	
Chet Morrison Contractors LLC Nine Bayou Dularge Rd *Web:* www.chetmorrison.com	Houma	LA	70363	985-868-1950	
Comer Industries Inc 12730 Virkler Dr *Web:* www.comerindustries.com	Charlotte	NC	28273	704-588-8400	
Currier Construction Inc 36 N 56th St *Web:* www.currierinc.com	Phoenix	AZ	85034	602-274-4370	
Dcr Business Solutions Inc PO Box 297 *Web:* www.dcrservices.com	Mulberry	FL	33860	863-904-1077	428-9027
Elkhorn Construction Inc 71 Allegiance Cir PO Box 809 *Web:* www.elkhornconstruction.com	Evanston	WY	82930	307-789-1595	
Fagor Automation Corp 2250 Estes Ave *Web:* www.fagorautomation.com	Elk Grove Village	IL	60007	847-981-1500	
Floating Island International Inc 10052 Floating Island Way *Web:* www.floatingislandinternational.com	Shepherd	MT	59079	406-373-5200	
Geo-Solutions Inc 1250 Fifth Ave. *Web:* www.geo-solutions.com	New Kensington	PA	15068	724-335-7273	
Golf Creations 18250 Beck Rd *Web:* lohmann.com	Marengo	IL	60152	815-923-1868	
Gulf Engineering LLC 611 Hill St. *Web:* www.gulfengineering.com	Jefferson	LA	70121	504-733-4868	
Halmar International LLC 421 E Route 59 Nanuet *Web:* www.halmarinternational.com	New York	NY	10954	845-735-3511	
Harbor Rail Services of California Inc 1399 N Chrisman Rd *Web:* harborservices.com	Tracy	CA	95304	209-834-2393	
LandTek Group Inc, The 235 County Line Rd *Web:* www.landtekgroup.com	Amityville	NY	11701	631-691-2381	
Larkin Enterprises Inc 317 W Broadway PO Box 405 *Web:* larkinent.com	Lincoln	ME	04457	207-794-8700	

Company	City	State	ZIP	Phone	Fax
Lone Star Railroad Contractors Inc 4201 S Interstate 45 *Web:* www.lonestarrailroad.com	Ennis	TX	75119	972-878-9500	
McNally International Inc 1855 Barton St E *Web:* www.mcnallycorp.com	Hamilton	ON	L8H2Y7	905-549-6561	
Norair Engineering Corp 337 Brightseat Rd Ste 200 *Web:* www.norair.com	Landover	MD	20785	301-499-2202	
Oman Systems Inc 3334 Powell Ave *Web:* www.omanco.com	Nashville	TN	37204	615-385-2500	
Pala Group LLC 16347 Old Hammond Hwy *Web:* www.palagroup.com	Baton Rouge	LA	70895	225-272-5194	
Pease & Sons Inc 10601 Waller Rd E *Web:* www.peaseandsons.com	Tacoma	WA	98448	253-531-7700	
Pinck & Company Inc 98 Magazine St *Web:* pinck-co.com	Boston	MA	02119	617-445-3555	
PNR RailWorks Inc 2595 Deacon St PO Box 2280 *Web:* www.pnrail.com	Abbotsford	BC	V2T4X2	604-850-9166	
Power Grid Engineering LLC 5744 Canton Cove Ste 110 *Web:* www.powergridengineering.com	Winter Springs	FL	32708	321-244-0170	
R&R Contracting Inc 5201 N Washington St *Web:* www.rrcontracting.net	Grand Forks	ND	58203	701-772-7667	
RealEnergy LLC 1500 Soscol Ferry Rd *Web:* realenergy.com	Napa	CA	94558	707-944-2400	
Tecon Services Inc 515 Garden Oaks Blvd *Web:* www.teconservices.com	Houston	TX	77018	713-691-2700	
Thompson Brothers (Construction) LP 411 S Ave PO Box 4300 *Web:* www.thompsonbros.com	Spruce Grove	AB	T7X3B4	780-962-1030	
Utilipath Inc 136 Corporate Pk Dr Ste G *Web:* www.utilipath.com	Mooresville	NC	28117	704-948-1005	658-3929
Vancouver Pile Driving Ltd 20 Brooksbank Ave *Web:* www.vanpile.com	North Vancouver	BC	V7J2B8	604-986-5911	
Voice Construction Ltd 7545 52 St *Web:* www.voiceconst.com	Edmonton	AB	T6B2G2	780-469-1351	
Watts Constructors LLC 737 Bishop St Ste 2900 *Web:* www.wattsconstructors.com	Honolulu	HI	96813	808-543-5201	
White Construction Inc 3900 E White Ave *Web:* www.whiteconstruction.com	Clinton	IN	47842	765-832-8526	
Zellner Construction Services LLC 2926 Ridgeway Rd *Web:* www.zellnerconstruction.com	Memphis	TN	38115	901-794-1100	794-9141

191-1 Communications Lines & Towers Construction

Company	City	State	ZIP	Phone	Fax
Black & Veatch 11401 Lamar Ave *Web:* www.bv.com	Overland Park	KS	66211	913-458-2000	
Cellcom Services Inc 11301 W 218th St	Peculiar	MO	64078	816-779-5660	
CLS Group 609 S Kelly Ave Ste D *Web:* www.clsgroup.com	Edmond	OK	73003	405-348-5460	551-8270
CommStructures Inc 101 E Roberts Rd *Web:* www.commstructures.com	Pensacola	FL	32534	850-968-9293	968-9283
Fluor Daniel Inc Three Polaris Way *Web:* www.fluor.com	Aliso Viejo	CA	92698	949-349-2000	349-2585
Malouf Engineering International Inc 17950 Preston Rd Ste 720 *Web:* www.maloufengineering.com	Dallas	TX	75252	972-783-2578	783-2583
MasTec Inc 800 Douglas Rd 12th Fl *NYSE:* MTZ ■ *TF:* 800-531-5000 ■ *Web:* www.mastec.com	Coral Gables	FL	33134	305-599-1800	406-1960
NAT-COM Inc 2622 Audubon Rd *TF:* 800-486-7947 ■ *Web:* www.nat-com.com	Eagleville	PA	19403	610-666-7947	666-7136
Quanta Services Inc 1360 Post Oak Blvd Ste 2100 *NYSE:* PWR ■ *Web:* www.quantaservices.com	Houston	TX	77056	713-629-7600	629-7676
Seacomm Erectors Inc 32527 SR 2 PO Box 1740 *TF:* 800-497-8320 ■ *Web:* www.seacomm.com	Sultan	WA	98294	360-793-6564	793-4402
Tyco Telecommunications 60 Columbia Rd *Web:* www.tycotelecom.com	Morristown	NJ	07960	973-656-8000	
Utility Services Inc 400 N Fourth St *TF:* 800-638-3278 ■ *Web:* www.montana-dakota.com	Bismarck	ND	58501	701-222-7900	

191-2 Foundation Drilling & Pile Driving

Company	City	State	ZIP	Phone	Fax
Berkel & Co Contractors Inc PO Box 335 *Web:* www.berkelandcompany.com	Bonner Springs	KS	66012	913-422-5125	441-0402
Case Foundation Co 1325 W Lake St *Web:* www.casefoundation.com	Roselle	IL	60172	630-529-2911	529-2995
LG Barcus & Sons Inc 1430 State Ave *TF:* 800-255-0180 ■ *Web:* www.barcus.com	Kansas City	KS	66102	913-621-1100	621-3288
Malcolm Drilling Co Inc 3503 Breakwater Ct *TF:* 800-523-2200 ■ *Web:* www.malcolmdrilling.com	Hayward	CA	94545	510-780-9181	780-9167
WM Brode Co 100 Elizabeth St PO Box 299 *Web:* www.wmbrode.com	Newcomerstown	OH	43832	740-498-5121	498-8553

191-3 Golf Course Construction

Company	City	State	ZIP	Phone	Fax
Barbaron Inc 107 NE Fourth St *Web:* www.barbaron.com	Crystal River	FL	34429	352-795-9010	
Formost Construction Co PO Box 559 *Web:* www.formostconstruction.com	Temecula	CA	92593	951-698-7270	698-6170
Golf Development Construction Inc PO Box 197249 *Web:* www.golfdev.com	Louisville	KY	40259	502-894-8916	893-1932
Golf Visions LLC 344 E Lyndale Ave *Web:* golfvisions.net	Northlake	IL	60164	708-562-5247	562-7497
Golf Works Inc 3660 Stone Ridge Rd *Web:* www.golfworksinc.com	Austin	TX	78746	512-327-8089	327-8169
Harris Miniature Golf 141 W Burk Ave *TF:* 888-294-6530 ■ *Web:* www.harrisminigolf.com	Wildwood	NJ	08260	609-522-4200	729-0100
Johnson Golf Course Builders 497 Golf Rd	South Sioux City	NE	68776	402-494-4687	494-0816
Landscapes Unlimited LLC 1201 Aries Dr *Web:* www.landscapesunlimited.com	Lincoln	NE	68512	402-423-6653	423-4487
MacCurrach Golf Construction Inc 3501 Faye Rd *Web:* www.maccurrachgolf.com	Jacksonville	FL	32226	904-646-1581	
Niebur Golf Inc 1230 Tenderfoot Hill Rd Ste 100 *Web:* www.nieburdevelopment.com	Colorado Springs	CO	80906	719-527-0313	
Prince Contracting LLC 10210 Highland Manor Dr Ste 110 *Web:* www.princeinc.com	Tampa	FL	33610	813-699-5900	699-5901
Ryan Inc Central 2700 E Racine St *Web:* www.ryancentral.com	Janesville	WI	53545	608-754-2291	754-3290
Shapemasters Inc PO Box 11128 *Web:* www.shapemasters.com	Southport	NC	28461	910-278-1434	278-1944
Total Golf Construction Inc 4045 43rd Ave *Web:* www.totalgolfconstruction.com	Vero Beach	FL	32960	772-562-1177	562-2773
Wadsworth Golf Construction Co 13941 Van Dyke Rd *Web:* www.wadsworthgolf.com	Plainfield	IL	60544	815-436-8400	436-8404

191-4 Highway, Street, Bridge, Tunnel Construction

Company	City	State	ZIP	Phone	Fax
A Teichert & Son Inc 3500 American River Dr *Web:* www.teichert.com	Sacramento	CA	95864	916-484-3011	484-6506
Ace Asphalt & Paving Co 115 S Averill Ave *Web:* aceasphaltpaving.com	Flint	MI	48506	810-238-1737	238-4326
Adams Construction Co 523 Rutherford Ave NE *TF:* 800-237-6060 ■ *Web:* www.adamspaving.com	Roanoke	VA	24016	540-982-2366	982-2942
Ajax Paving Industries Inc PO Box 7058 **Fax Area Code:* 813 ■ *TF:* 888-468-5489 ■ *Web:* www.ajaxpaving.com	Troy	MI	48007	248-244-3300	574-8334*
Allan A Myers Inc 1805 Berks Rd PO Box 1340 *TF:* 800-596-6118 ■ *Web:* www.americaninfrastructure.com	Worcester	PA	19490	610-222-8800	222-3300
Allen Company Inc 525 Burbank St PO Box 445 *TF:* 800-876-8600 ■ *Web:* www.allencompany.net	Broomfield	CO	80020	303-469-1857	466-7437
American Bridge Co 1000 American Bridge Way **Fax:* Acctg ■ *Web:* www.americanbridge.net	Coraopolis	PA	15108	412-631-1000	631-2000*
American Civil Constructors Inc 4901 S Windemere St *Web:* www.accbuilt.com	Littleton	CO	80120	303-795-2582	347-1844
American Paving Company Inc 315 N Thorne PO Box 4348 *Web:* www.americanpavingco.com	Fresno	CA	93706	559-268-9886	487-7949
Anderson Bros Construction Company Inc 11325 Hwy 210 E PO Box 668 *Web:* www.andersonbrothers.com	Brainerd	MN	56401	218-829-1768	829-7607
Anderson Columbia Co Inc 871 NW Guerdon St PO Box 1829 *Web:* www.andersoncolumbia.com	Lake City	FL	32056	386-752-7585	755-5430
Angelo Iafrate Construction Co 26300 Sherwood Ave *Web:* www.iafrate.com	Warren	MI	48091	586-756-1070	756-0467
Arrow Road Construction Co 3401 S Busse Rd *Web:* www.arrowroad.com	Mount Prospect	IL	60056	847-437-0700	437-0779
Austin Bridge & Road Inc 6330 Commerce Dr Ste 150 *Web:* www.austin-ind.com	Irving	TX	75063	214-596-7300	596-7395
Autostrade International of Virginia 45305 Catalina Ct Ste 102	Sterling	VA	20166	703-904-8001	
Balfour Beatty Inc 999 Peachtree St NE Ste 200 *Web:* www.balfourbeatty.com	Atlanta	GA	30309	404-875-0356	607-1784
Barber Bros Contracting Company LLC 2636 Dougherty Dr *Web:* www.barber-brothers.com	Baton Rouge	LA	70805	225-355-5611	355-5615
Barnhill Contracting Co 2311 N Main St *Web:* www.barnhillcontracting.com	Tarboro	NC	27886	252-823-1021	823-0137
Barrett Industries Corp Three Becker Farm Rd *Web:* www.barrettpaving.com	Roseland	NJ	07068	973-533-1001	533-1020
Barriere Construction Co LLC 1 Galleria Blvd Ste 1650 *TF:* 866-645-3060 ■ *Web:* www.barriere.com	Metairie	LA	70001	504-581-7283	581-2270
Basic Resources Inc 928 12th St Ste 700	Modesto	CA	95354	209-521-9771	579-9502
Blythe Construction Inc 2911 N Graham St *Web:* www.blytheconstruction.com	Charlotte	NC	28206	704-375-8474	375-7814
Boh Bros Construction Co LLC 730 S Tonti St *TF:* 800-284-3377 ■ *Web:* www.bohbros.com	New Orleans	LA	70119	504-821-2400	821-0714
Border States Paving Inc 4101 N 32nd St *Web:* borderstatespaving.com	Fargo	ND	58102	701-237-4860	237-0233
Borderland Construction Company Inc 400 E 38 St *Web:* borderland-inc.com	Tucson	AZ	85713	520-623-0900	623-0232
BR Amon & Sons Inc W 2950 State Rd 11	Elkhorn	WI	53121	262-723-2547	723-2666

Company	City	State	ZIP	Phone	Fax
Branch Highways Inc 442 Rutherford Ave. *Web:* www.branchhighways.com	Roanoke	VA	24016	540-982-1678	982-4216
Brechan Enterprises Inc 2705 Mill Bay Rd *Web:* www.brechanenterprises.com	Kodiak	AK	99615	907-486-3215	486-4889
Brox Industries Inc 1471 Methuen St *Web:* www.broxindustries.com	Dracut	MA	01826	978-454-9105	805-9720
C.A Rasmussen Inc 28548 Livingston Ave *Web:* www.carasmussen.com	Valencia	CA	91355	661-367-9040	367-9099
Cardi Corp 400 Lincoln Ave. *Web:* www.cardi.com	Warwick	RI	02888	401-739-8300	736-2977
CC Myers Inc 3286 Fitzgerald Rd *Web:* www.ccmyers.com	Rancho Cordova	CA	95742	916-635-9370	635-8961
Central Allied Enterprises Inc 1243 Raff Rd SW *Web:* www.central-allied.com	Canton	OH	44710	330-477-6751	477-1660
Cherry Hill Construction Inc 8211 Washington Blvd *Web:* www.cherryhillconstruction.com	Jessup	MD	20794	410-799-3577	799-5483
Cianbro Corp 335 Hunnewell Ave. **Fax Area Code:* 207 ■ *Web:* www.cianbro.com	Pittsfield	ME	04967	866-242-6276	487-3861*
Civil Constructors Inc 2283 US Hwy 20 E *Web:* www.helmgroup.com	Freeport	IL	61032	815-235-2200	235-2219
CJ Mahan Construction Co 3400 SW Blvd. *Web:* www.cjmahan.com	Grove City	OH	43123	614-875-8200	875-1175
Clark Construction Group LLC 7500 Old Georgetown Rd *TF:* 800-655-1330 ■ *Web:* www.clarkconstruction.com	Bethesda	MD	20814	301-272-8100	272-1928
Clarkson Construction Co 4133 Gardner Ave. *Web:* clarksonconstruction.com	Kansas City	MO	64120	816-483-8800	241-6823
Concrete General Inc 8000 Beechcraft Ave *Web:* www.concretegeneral.com	Gaithersburg	MD	20879	301-948-4450	948-8273
Concrete Materials Inc 1201 W Russell St *Web:* www.concretematerialscompany.com	Sioux Falls	SD	57118	605-357-6000	334-6221
Constructors Inc 1815 Y St *Web:* www.constructorslincoln.com	Lincoln	NE	68508	402-434-1764	434-1799
Crowder Construction Company Inc PO Box 30007 *TF:* 800-849-2966 ■ *Web:* www.crowdercc.com	Charlotte	NC	28230	704-372-3541	376-3573
CS McCrossan Inc PO Box 1240 *Web:* www.mccrossan.com	Maple Grove	MN	55311	763-425-4167	425-1255
Cummins Construction Company Inc 1420 W Chestnut Ave *TF:* 800-375-6001 ■ *Web:* www.cumminsasphalt.com	Enid	OK	73702	580-233-6000	233-9858
Curran Contracting Company Inc 286 Memorial Ct. *Web:* www.currancontracting.com	Crystal Lake	IL	60014	815-455-5100	455-7894
Curran Group Inc 286 Memorial Ct *Web:* www.currangroup.com	Crystal Lake	IL	60014	815-455-5100	455-7894
Cutler Repaving Inc 921 E 27th St *Web:* www.cutlerrepaving.com	Lawrence	KS	66046	785-843-1524	843-3942
CW Matthews Contracting Company Inc 1600 Kenview Dr *Web:* www.cwmatthews.com	Marietta	GA	30061	770-422-7520	422-1068
D & J Enterprises Inc 3495 Lee Rd 10 *Web:* dandjenterprises.com/	Auburn	AL	36832	334-821-1249	
D'Ambra Construction Co Inc 800 Jefferson Blvd *Web:* www.d-ambra.com	Warwick	RI	02886	401-737-1300	732-4725
DA Collins Construction Co Inc 269 Ballard Rd *Web:* www.dacollins.com	Wilton	NY	12831	518-664-9855	
David A Bramble Inc 705 Morgnec Rd *Web:* www.davidabrambleinc.com	Chestertown	MD	21620	410-778-3023	778-3427
David Nelson Construction Co 3483 Alternate 19 *Web:* www.nelson-construction.com	Palm Harbor	FL	34683	727-784-7624	786-8894
Dean Word Company Ltd 1245 River Rd PO Box 310330 *TF:* 800-683-3926 ■ *Web:* www.deanword.com	New Braunfels	TX	78131	830-625-2365	606-5008
Delta Cos Inc 114 S Silver Springs Rd *Web:* www.deltacos.com	Cape Girardeau	MO	63703	573-334-5261	334-9576
Delta Railroad Construction Inc 2648 W Prospect Rd PO Box 1398 *Web:* www.deltarr.com	Ashtabula	OH	44004	440-992-2997	992-1311
Dement Construction Co PO Box 1812 *Web:* www.dementconstruction.com	Jackson	TN	38302	731-424-6306	424-5308
DH Blattner & Sons Inc 392 County Rd 50 *TF:* 800-877-2866 ■ *Web:* www.dhblattner.com	Avon	MN	56310	320-356-7351	356-7392
Dondlinger & Sons Construction Company Inc 2656 S Sheridan *Web:* dondlinger.biz	Wichita	KS	67217	316-945-0555	945-9009
Driggs Co LLC 8700 Ashwood Dr *Web:* www.driggs.net	Capitol Heights	MD	20743	301-350-4000	
Duininck Inc 408 Sixth St PO Box 208 *TF General:* 800-328-8949 ■ *Web:* www.duininckcompanies.com	Prinsburg	MN	56281	800-328-8949	
Dunn Roadbuilders LLC 411 W Oak St PO Box 6560 *Web:* www.dunnroadbuilders.com	Laurel	MS	39441	601-649-4111	425-4644
ECCO III Enterprises Inc 201 Saw Mill River Rd *Web:* www.eccoiii.com	Yonkers	NY	10701	914-963-3600	963-3989
Edward Kraemer & Sons Inc One Plainview Rd. *Web:* www.edkraemer.com	Plain	WI	53577	608-546-2311	546-2130
Elam Construction Inc 556 Struthers Ave *TF:* 800-675-4598 ■ *Web:* www.elamconstruction.com	Grand Junction	CO	81501	970-242-5370	245-7716
English Construction Co Inc 615 Church St. *Web:* www.englishconst.com	Lynchburg	VA	24504	434-845-0301	845-0306
Evans & Assoc Construction Company Inc 3320 N 14th St *Web:* evans-assoc.com	Ponca City	OK	74601	580-765-6693	765-2298
F H Paschen S N Nielsen Inc 8725 W Higgins Rd Ste 200 *Web:* www.fhpaschen.com	Chicago	IL	60631	773-444-3474	693-0064
Facchina Construction Co Inc 102 Centennial St Ste 201 *Web:* www.facchina.com/ContactUs.aspx	La Plata	MD	20646	240-776-7000	776-7001
FCI Constructors Inc 3070 I-70 Business Loop # A *Web:* www.fciol.com	Grand Junction	CO	81504	970-434-9093	434-7583
Flatiron Constructors Inc 10090 E I25 Frontage Rd *Web:* www.flatironcorp.com	Longmont	CO	80504	303-485-4050	485-3922
Fluor Constructors International Inc 352 Halton Rd.	Greenville	SC	29607	864-234-7335	234-5476
FNF Construction Inc 115 S 48th St *Web:* www.fnfinc.com	Tempe	AZ	85281	480-784-2910	829-8607
Fox Contractors Corp 5430 W Ferguson Rd Ste B. *Web:* www.foxcontractors.com	Fort Wayne	IN	46809	260-747-7461	747-7717
Francis O Day Construction Company Inc 850 E Gude Dr *Web:* www.foday.com	Rockville	MD	20850	301-652-2400	340-6592
Fred Weber Inc 2320 Creve Coeur Mill Rd *TF:* 866-739-8855 ■ *Web:* www.fredweberinc.com	Maryland Heights	MO	63043	314-344-0070	344-0970
Gallagher & Burk Inc 344 High St *Web:* www.gallagherandburk.com	Oakland	CA	94601	510-261-0466	261-3806
Gallagher Asphalt Corp 18100 S Indiana Ave *TF:* 800-536-7160 ■ *Web:* www.gallagherasphalt.com	Thornton	IL	60476	708-877-7160	877-5222
George & Lynch Inc 150 Lafferty Ln *Web:* www.geolyn.com	Dover	DE	19901	302-736-3031	734-9743
George Harms Construction Co Inc PO Box 817 *Web:* www.ghcci.com	Farmingdale	NJ	07727	732-938-4004	938-2782
Gilbert Southern Corp 3555 Farnam St. **Fax:* Hum Res ■ *Web:* www.kiewit.com	Omaha	NE	68131	402-342-2052	271-2829*
Glasgow Inc 104 Willow Grove Ave *TF:* 877-222-5514 ■ *Web:* www.glasgowinc.com	Glenside	PA	19038	215-884-8800	884-1465
Godbersen-Smith Construction Company Inc 5784 Iowa 175	Ida Grove	IA	51445	712-364-3388	
Gohmann Asphalt & Construction Inc PO Box 2428	Clarksville	IN	47131	812-282-1349	288-2168
Gowan Construction Inc PO Box 228 *Web:* www.gowanconstruction.com	Oslo	MN	56744	701-699-5171	699-3400
Grace Pacific LLC PO Box 78 *Web:* www.gracepacificcorp.com	Honolulu	HI	96810	808-674-8383	674-1040
Granite Construction Inc 585 W Beach St. *NYSE:* GVA ■ *Web:* www.graniteconstruction.com	Watsonville	CA	95076	831-724-1011	722-9657
Gray & Sons Inc 430 W Padonia Rd *TF:* 800-254-0752 ■ *Web:* www.graynson.com	Timonium	MD	21093	410-771-4311	771-8125
Great Lakes Construction Co 2608 Great Lakes Way *Web:* www.tglcc.com	Hinckley	OH	44233	330-220-3900	220-7670
Gulf Asphalt Corp 4116 US Hwy 231 *Web:* www.gaccontractors.com	Panama City	FL	32404	850-785-4675	769-3456
Halverson Construction Company Inc 620 N 19th St *Web:* www.halversonconstruction.com	Springfield	IL	62702	217-753-0027	753-1904
Hardrives of Delray Inc 2101 S Congress Ave *Web:* www.hardrivespaving.com	Delray Beach	FL	33445	561-278-0456	278-2147
Harper Co 1648 Petersburg Rd *Web:* harperco.com	Hebron	KY	41048	859-586-8890	586-8891
Harper Industries Inc 616 Northview St *TF:* 866-487-9243 ■ *Web:* www.harper1.com	Paducah	KY	42001	270-442-2753	443-9154
Hempt Bros Inc 205 Creek Rd *Web:* hemptbros.com	Camp Hill	PA	17011	717-737-3411	761-5019
Herzog Contracting Corp 600 S Riverside Rd *TF:* 800-541-7846 ■ *Web:* www.herzogcompanies.com	Saint Joseph	MO	64507	816-233-9001	233-9881
Hi-Way Paving Inc 4343 Weaver Ct N *Web:* www.hiwaypaving.com	Hilliard	OH	43026	614-876-1700	876-1899
Hinkle Contracting Corp 395 N Middletown Rd. *Web:* www.hinklecontracting.com	Paris	KY	40361	859-987-3670	987-0727
Hoover Construction Co Inc PO Box 1007 *TF:* 800-741-0970 ■ *Web:* www.hooverconstruction.biz	Virginia	MN	55792	218-741-3280	741-6804
HRI Inc 1750 W College Ave. **Fax Area Code:* 814 ■ *TF:* 877-474-9999 ■ *Web:* www.hrico.com	State College	PA	16801	877-474-9999	238-0131*
Hubbard Construction Co 1936 Lee Rd 3rd Fl *TF:* 800-476-1228 ■ *Web:* www.hubbard.com	Winter Park	FL	32789	407-645-5500	623-3865
Hudson River Construction Co 1800 Church *Web:* www.hudsonriverconstruction.com	Albany	NY	12202	518-434-6677	
Hughes Group Inc 6200 E Hwy 62 Bldg 2501 Ste 100 *Web:* hughesdevelopmentllc.com	Jeffersonville	IN	47130	812-282-4393	283-0142
Hunter Contracting Co 701 N Cooper Rd *TF:* 877-992-0521 ■ *Web:* www.huntercontracting.com	Gilbert	AZ	85233	480-892-0521	892-4932
Hutchens Construction Co 1007 Main St *TF:* 888-728-3482 ■ *Web:* www.hutchensconstruction.com	Cassville	MO	65625	417-847-2489	847-5561
India Globalization Capital Inc 4336 Montgomery Ave *NYSE:* IGC ■ **Fax Area Code:* 240 ■ *Web:* www.indiaglobalcap.com	Bethesda	MD	20814	301-983-0998	465-0273*
J Reese Construction Inc 10805 Thornmint Rd Ste 200 *Web:* www.debinc.com	San Diego	CA	92127	858-592-6500	592-1410
Jack B Parson Cos 2350 South 1900 West *TF:* 888-672-7766 ■ *Web:* www.stakerparson.com	Ogden	UT	84401	801-731-1111	731-8800
James D Morrissey Inc 9119 Frankford Ave. *Web:* www.jdm-inc.com	Philadelphia	PA	19114	215-357-5505	338-3225
James H Drew Corp 8701 Zionsville Rd *TF:* 800-772-7342 ■ *Web:* jameshdrew.com	Indianapolis	IN	46268	317-876-3739	876-3829

Phone Fax

James McHugh Construction Co
1737 S Michigan Ave .... Chicago IL 60616 312-986-8000 431-8518
Web: www.mchughconstruction.com

James W Glover Ltd
248 Sand Island Access Rd .... Honolulu HI 96819 808-591-8977 591-9174
Web: www.gloverltd.com

Jay Dee Contractors Inc 38881 Schoolcraft Rd .... Livonia MI 48150 734-591-3400 464-6868
Web: www.jaydeecontr.com

JB Coxwell Contracting Inc
6741 Lloyd Rd W .... Jacksonville FL 32254 904-786-1120 783-2970
Web: www.jbcoxwell.com

JD Abrams LP 111 Congress Ave Ste 2400 .... Austin TX 78701 512-322-4000 322-4018
Web: www.jdabrams.com

JF Shea Construction Inc 655 Brea Canyon Rd .... Walnut CA 91789 909-594-9500 883-3371
TF: 888-779-7333 ■ *Web:* www.jfshea.com

JF White Contracting Co 10 Burr St .... Framingham MA 01701 508-879-4700 558-0460*
**Fax Area Code:* 617 ■ *TF:* 866-539-4400 ■ *Web:* www.jfwhite.com

JLB Contracting LP 7151 Randol Mill Rd .... Fort Worth TX 76120 817-261-2991 261-3044

John Carlo Inc 20848 Hall Rd .... Clinton Township MI 48038 586-741-5362

John R Jurgensen Co 11641 Mosteller Rd .... Cincinnati OH 45241 513-771-0820 771-2678
Web: www.jrjnet.com

Johnson Bros Corp 5476 Lithia Pinecrest Rd .... Lithia FL 33547 813-685-5101 685-5939
Web: www.johnson-bros.com

K-Five Construction Corp 13769 Main St .... Lemont IL 60439 630-257-5600 257-6788
Web: k-five.com/

Kamminga & Roodvoets Inc
3435 Broadmoor Ave SE .... Grand Rapids MI 49512 616-949-0800 949-1894

Kankakee Valley Construction Company Inc
4356 W SR 17 .... Kankakee IL 60901 815-937-8700 937-0402
Web: www.kvcci.com

KF Jacobsen & Co 4315 SE McLoughlin Blvd .... Portland OR 97202 503-239-5532

Kiewit Corp 3555 Farnam St .... Omaha NE 68131 402-342-2052 271-2829*
**Fax:* Hum Res ■ *Web:* www.kiewit.com

Kiska Construction Corp USA
10-34 44th Dr .... Long Island City NY 11101 718-943-0400 943-0401
Web: www.kiskagroup.com

Knife River Corp 1150 W Century Ave .... Bismarck ND 58503 701-530-1400 530-1451
Web: www.kniferiver.com

Kokosing Construction Company Inc
17531 Waterford Rd PO Box 226 .... Fredericktown OH 43019 740-694-6315 694-1481
TF: 800-800-6315 ■ *Web:* www.kokosing.biz

Koss Construction Co 5830 SW Drury Ln .... Topeka KS 66604 785-228-2928 228-2927
Web: kossconstruction.com

Lake Erie Construction Co
25 S Norwalk Rd PO Box 777 .... Norwalk OH 44857 419-668-3302 668-3314
Web: lec-co.com

Lakeside Industries Inc
6505 226th Pl SE # 200 .... Issaquah WA 98027 425-313-2600 313-2620
Web: www.lakesideind.com

Lane Construction Company Inc One Indian Rd .... Denville NJ 07834 973-586-2700 586-2965
Web: www.thelanegroup.us

Lane Construction Corp 90 Fieldstone Ct .... Cheshire CT 06410 203-235-3351 237-4260
Web: www.laneconstruct.com

Las Vegas Paving Corp 4420 S Decatur Blvd .... Las Vegas NV 89103 702-251-5800 251-1968
Web: www.lasvegaspaving.com

Lawrence Construction Company Inc
9002 N Moore Rd .... Littleton CO 80125 303-791-5642 791-5647
Web: lawrence-construction.com

LC Whitford Company Inc 164 N Main St .... Wellsville NY 14895 585-593-3601 593-1876
Web: www.lcwhitford.com

Lee Construction Co PO Box 7667 .... Charlotte NC 28241 704-588-5272 588-1535
Web: www.leecarolinas.com

Lehigh Asphalt Paving & Construction Co Inc
PO Box 549 .... Tamaqua PA 18252 570-668-4303 668-5910
TF: 877-222-5514 ■ *Web:* www.glasgowinc.com/subsidiaries.aspx

LH Lacy Co 1880 Crown Dr .... Dallas TX 75234 214-357-0146 350-0662
Web: www.lhlacy.com

Lunda Construction Company Inc
620 GebhaRdt Rd .... Black River Falls WI 54615 715-284-9491 284-9146
Web: www.lundaconstruction.com

Manatt's Inc 1775 Old 6 Rd .... Brooklyn IA 52211 641-522-9206 522-5594
TF: 800-532-1121 ■ *Web:* www.manatts.com

Markham Contracting Company Inc
22820 N 19th Ave .... Phoenix AZ 85027 623-869-9100 869-9400
Web: www.markhamcontracting.com

Martin K. Eby Construction Co
610 N Main Ste 500 Ste 500 .... Wichita KS 67203 316-268-3500 268-3649
Web: www.ebycorp.com

Mathy Construction Co Inc 920 Tenth Ave N .... Onalaska WI 54650 608-783-6411 783-4311
TF: 800-822-5246 ■ *Web:* mathy.com

Matich Corp 1596 Harry Sheppard Blvd .... San Bernardino CA 92408 909-382-7400 382-0191
TF: 800-404-4975 ■ *Web:* www.matichicm.com

Maymead Inc 1995 Roan Creek Rd .... Mountain City TN 37683 423-727-2000
Web: www.maymead.com

McCarthy Improvement Company Inc
5401 Victoria Ave .... Davenport IA 52807 563-359-0321 344-3740
Web: www.mccarthyimprovement.com

McCourt Equipment Company Inc 60 K St Ste 2 .... Boston MA 02127 617-269-2330
Web: www.mccourtconstruction.com

MCM Construction Inc
6413 32nd St PO Box 620 .... North Highlands CA 95660 916-334-1221 334-8355
Web: www.mcmconstructioninc.com

McMurry Ready Mix Co
5684 Old W Yellowstone Hwy .... Casper WY 82604 307-473-9581 235-0144
Web: www.mcmurryreadymix.com

Meadow Valley Corp 4602 E Thomas .... Phoenix AZ 85018 602-437-5400 437-1681
Web: www.meadowvalley.com

Merco Inc 1117 Rt 31 S .... Lebanon NJ 08833 908-730-8622 730-6472
Web: www.mercoinc.com

Mica Corp 5750 N Riverside Dr .... Fort Worth TX 76137 817-847-6121 847-6831

Michael Baker Corp
100 Airsite Dr Airsite Business Pk .... Moon Township PA 15108 412-269-6300 463-0503*
NYSE: BKR ■ **Fax Area Code:* 757 ■ *TF:* 800-553-1153 ■ *Web:* www.mbakercorp.com

Michigan Paving & Materials Co
1100 Market Ave SW .... Grand Rapids MI 49503 616-459-9545 784-5040
Web: www.michiganpaving.com

Mid Valley School District 52 Underwood Rd .... Throop PA 18512 570-307-1150 307-1107
Web: www.mvsd.us

Milestone Contractors LP 3410 S 650 E .... Columbus IN 47203 812-579-5248 579-6703
Web: www.milestonelp.com

Mountain States Constructors Inc
3601 Pan American Rd NE .... Albuquerque NM 87107 505-292-0108 790-1503*
**Fax Area Code:* 303

NAB Construction Corp 112-20 14th Ave .... College Point NY 11356 718-762-0001 961-3789
Web: www.nabconstruction.com

Nagle Paving Co 39525 W 13 Mile Rd 300 .... Novi MI 48377 248-553-0600 553-0669
Web: www.naglepaving.com

Nesbitt Contracting Company Inc 100 S Price Rd .... Tempe AZ 85281 480-423-7600 423-7680
Web: www.nesbitts.com

Newell Roadbuilders Inc 13266 US Hwy 31 .... Hope Hull AL 36043 334-288-2702 288-2721

Northern Improvement Co
4000 12th Ave NW PO Box 2846 .... Fargo ND 58108 701-277-1225 277-1516
Web: www.nicnd.com/nic/nic1.html

Oakgrove Construction Inc 6900 Seneca St .... Elma NY 14059 716-652-2200 655-3919
TF: 866-435-1499 ■ *Web:* www.oakgroveconst.com

Odebrecht Construction Inc
201 Alhambra Cir Ste 1400 .... Coral Gables FL 33134 305-341-8800 569-1500
TF: 800-771-0001 ■ *Web:* www.odebrecht.com.br

Oldcastle Materials Inc
900 Ashwood Pkwy Ste 700 .... Atlanta GA 30338 770-522-5600 522-5608
Web: www.apac.com

P Flanigan & Sons Inc 2444 Loch Raven Rd .... Baltimore MD 21218 410-467-5900 467-3127
Web: www.pflanigan.com

Palmer Paving Corp 25 Blanchard St .... Palmer MA 01069 413-283-8354 289-1939
TF: 800-244-8354 ■ *Web:* www.palmerpaving.com

Parsons Corp 100 W Walnut St .... Pasadena CA 91124 626-440-2000 440-2630
TF All: 800-883-7300 ■ *Web:* www.parsons.com

Pavex Inc 4400 Gettysburg Rd .... Camp Hill PA 17011 717-761-1502 761-0329
Web: pavexinc.com

PCiRoads LLC 14123 42nd St NE .... Saint Michael MN 55376 763-497-6100 497-6101
Web: www.pciroads.com

Peckham Industries Inc 20 Haarlem Ave .... White Plains NY 10603 914-949-2000 949-2075
Web: www.peckham.com

Perini Corp PO Box 9160 PO Box 9160 .... Framingham MA 01701 508-628-2000
Web: www.tutorperini.com

Perry Engineering Company Inc
1945 Millwood Pk .... Winchester VA 22602 540-667-4310 667-7618
Web: www.perryeng.com

Peter Baker & Son Co
1349 Rockland Rd PO Box 187 .... Lake Bluff IL 60044 847-362-3663 362-0707
Web: www.peterbaker.com

Petricca Industries Inc 550 Cheshire Rd .... Pittsfield MA 01201 413-442-6926 499-9930
Web: unistresscorp.com

Phillips Contracting Co PO Box 2069 .... Columbus MS 39704 662-328-6250 329-3291
Web: www.phillipscontracting.com

Pike Industries Inc 3 Eastgate Pk Rd .... Belmont NH 03220 603-527-5100 527-5101
TF: 800-283-0803 ■ *Web:* pikeindustries.com

PJ Keating Co 998 Reservoir Rd .... Lunenburg MA 01462 978-582-5200 582-7130
TF: 800-441-4119 ■ *Web:* www.pjkeating.com

PKF-Mark III Inc 17 Black Smith Rd PO Box 390 .... Newtown PA 18940 215-968-5031 968-3829
Web: www.pkfmarkiii.com

Plote Inc 1100 Brandt Dr .... Hoffman Estates IL 60192 847-695-9300 695-9317
Web: www.plote.com

Prince Contracting LLC
10210 Highland Manor Dr Ste 110 .... Tampa FL 33610 813-699-5900 699-5901
Web: www.princeinc.com

Pulice Construction Inc
2033 W Mountain View Rd .... Phoenix AZ 85021 602-944-2241 944-8861
Web: www.pulice.com

Ranger Construction Industries Inc
101 Sansbury's Way .... West Palm Beach FL 33411 561-793-9400 790-4332
TF: 800-969-9402 ■ *Web:* www.rangerconstruction.com

Ray Bell Construction Company Inc
255 Wilson Pake Cir PO Box 363 .... Brentwood TN 37027 615-373-4343 373-9224

Reeves Construction Co Inc 101 Sheraton Ct .... Macon GA 31210 478-474-9092 474-9192
TF: 800-743-0593 ■ *Web:* www.reevescc.com

Reilly Construction Co Inc PO Box 99 .... Ossian IA 52161 563-532-9211 532-9759
Web: www.reilly-construction.com

Reliable Contracting Co Inc
1 Church View Rd .... Millersville MD 21108 410-987-0313 987-8020
TF: 800-492-4357 ■ *Web:* www.reliablecontracting.com

Richard F Kline Inc 7700 Grove Rd .... Frederick MD 21704 301-662-8211 662-0041
Web: www.rfkline.com

Rieth-Riley Construction Co Inc
3626 Elkhart Rd PO Box 477 .... Goshen IN 46526 574-875-5183 875-8405
Web: rieth-riley.com/

Rifenburg Construction Inc 159 Brick Church Rd .... Troy NY 12180 518-279-3265 279-4260
Web: www.rifenburg.com

Rogers Group Inc 421 Great Cir Rd .... Nashville TN 37228 615-242-0585
Web: www.rogersgroupincint.com

Royal Contracting Company Ltd 677 Ahua St .... Honolulu HI 96819 808-839-9006 839-7571
Web: www.royalcontracting.com

RS Audley Inc 609 Rt 3A .... Bow NH 03304 603-224-7724 225-7614
Web: www.audleyconstruction.com

Ruhlin Company Inc PO Box 190 .... Sharon Center OH 44274 330-239-2800 239-1828
Web: www.ruhlin.com

Sargent Corp 378 Bennoch Rd .... Stillwater ME 04489 207-827-4435 827-6150
TF: 800-533-1812 ■ *Web:* www.sargent-corp.com

Schiavone Construction Company Inc
150 Meadowlands Pkwy Third Fl .... Secaucus NJ 07094 201-867-5070 866-6132
Web: www.schiavoneconstruction.com

Scott Construction Inc 560 Munroe Ave .... Lake Delton WI 53940 608-254-2555 254-2249
TF: 800-843-1556 ■ *Web:* www.scottconstruct.com

Scruggs Company Inc PO Box 2065 .... Valdosta GA 31604 229-242-2388 242-7109
TF: 800-230-7263 ■ *Web:* scruggscompany.com

Phone | Fax

Shelly Co 80 Pk Dr. Thornville OH 43076 740-246-6315 246-4715
Web: www.shellyco.com

Sherwood Construction Company Inc
3219 W May St. Wichita KS 67213 316-943-0211 943-3772
Web: www.sherwoodcompanies.com

Shirley Contracting Corp 8435 Backlick Rd. Lorton VA 22079 703-550-8100 550-7897
Web: www.shirleycontracting.com

Sioux Falls Construction Company Inc
800 S Seventh Ave Sioux Falls SD 57101 605-336-1640 334-9342
Web: journeyconstruction.com/

Skanska USA Inc 1616 Whitestone Expy Whitestone NY 11356 718-767-2600 767-2663
Web: www.skanska.com

Sletten Construction Company Inc
1000 25th St N Great Falls MT 59401 406-761-7920 761-0923
Web: www.slettencompanies.com

Sloan Construction Co Inc 250 Plemmons Rd. Duncan SC 29334 864-968-2250 968-2255
Web: www.sloan-construction.com

Staker Parson Cos 2350 South 1900 West Ogden UT 84401 801-731-1111 731-8800
TF: 888-672-7766 ■ *Web:* stakerparson.com

Standard Concrete Products Inc (SCP)
PO Box 1360 Columbus GA 31902 706-322-3274 322-7856
Web: www.standardconcrete.net

Steve P Rados Inc
2002 E McFadden Ave Ste 200 PO Box 15128 Santa Ana CA 92705 714-835-4612 835-2186
Web: www.radoscompanies.com

Suburban Grading & Utilities Inc
1190 Harmony Rd. Norfolk VA 23502 757-461-1800 461-0989
Web: www.suburbangrading.com

Sukut Construction Inc 4010 W Chandler Ave. Santa Ana CA 92704 714-540-5351 545-2438
TF: 888-785-8801 ■ *Web:* www.sukut.com

Sully-Miller Contracting Co Inc
135 S State Collage Blvd Ste 400 Brea CA 92821 714-578-9600 578-2850*
*Fax: Hum Res ■ *Web:* sully-miller.com/

Summers-Taylor Inc 300 W Elk Ave. Elizabethton TN 37643 423-543-3181 543-6189
Web: summerstaylor.com

Sundt Construction Inc 2015 W River Rd Ste 101 Tucson AZ 85704 520-750-4600
TF: 800-467-5544 ■ *Web:* www.sundt.com

Superior Construction Company Inc
2045 E Dunes Hwy PO Box 64888 Gary IN 46401 219-886-3728 885-4328
Web: www.superior-construction.com

Sweeping Services of Texas LP
3324 Roy Orr Blvd Grand Prairie TX 75050 817-268-4100
Web: wastepartners.com

TJ Lambrecht Construction Inc 10 Gougar Rd Joliet IL 60432 815-726-7722 727-6421

Tony Angelo Cement Construction Co
46850 Grand River Ave. Novi MI 48374 248-344-4000 344-4048

Traylor Bros Inc 835 N Congress Ave Evansville IN 47715 812-477-1542 474-3223
TF: 866-895-1491 ■ *Web:* www.traylor.com

Trumbull Corp 1020 Lebanon Rd West Mifflin PA 15122 412-462-9300 462-1074
Web: www.trumbullcorp.com

United Contractors Midwest Inc
PO Box 13420 Springfield IL 62791 217-546-6192 546-1904
Web: www.ucm.biz

Vecellio & Grogan Inc 2251 Robert C Byrd Dr. Beckley WV 25802 304-252-6575 252-4131
TF: 800-255-6575 ■ *Web:* www.vecelliogrogan.com

Walsh Group Inc 929 W Adams St. Chicago IL 60607 312-563-5400 563-5466
TF: 800-957-1842 ■ *Web:* walshgroup.com

Washington Corp PO Box 16630 Missoula MT 59808 406-523-1300 523-1399
TF: 800-832-7329 ■ *Web:* www.washcorp.com

WE Blain & Sons Inc 98 Pearce Rd Mount Olive MS 39119 601-797-4551
Web: blain-co.com

WG Yates & Sons Construction Co Inc
1 Gulley Ave PO Box 456 Philadelphia MS 39350 601-656-5411 656-8958
Web: www.wgyates.com

Williams Bros Construction Company Inc
3800 Milam St Houston TX 77006 713-522-9821 520-5247
Web: www.wbctx.com

Windsor Service 2415 Kutztown Rd. Reading PA 19605 610-929-0716 929-4825
Web: hkgroup.com

Winzinger Inc 1704 Marne Hwy PO Box 537 Hainesport NJ 08036 609-267-8600 267-4079
Web: www.winzinger.com

WM Brode Co 100 Elizabeth St PO Box 299 Newcomerstown OH 43832 740-498-5121 498-8553
Web: www.wmbrode.com

Yantis Co 3611 Paesano's Pkwy Ste 300 San Antonio TX 78231 210-655-3780 655-8526
Web: www.yantiscompany.com

Yonkers Contracting Company Inc
969 Midland Ave. Yonkers NY 10704 914-965-1500 378-8885
Web: www.yonkerscontractingco.com

Zachry Holdings Inc 527 Logwood Ave. San Antonio TX 78221 210-475-8000
Web: www.zachrygroup.com/

191-5 Marine Construction

Phone | Fax

Anderson-Tully 1725 N Washington St. Vicksburg MS 39181 601-629-3283 629-3284
Web: www.andersontully.com

Andrie Inc 561 E Western Ave. Muskegon MI 49442 231-728-2226 726-6747
TF: 800-722-2421 ■ *Web:* www.andrie.com

Bellingham Marine Industries Inc
1001 C St. Bellingham WA 98225 360-676-2800 734-2417
TF: 800-733-5679 ■ *Web:* www.bellingham-marine.com

Choctaw Transportation Co Inc PO Box 585 Dyersburg TN 38025 731-286-0012 285-4668
Web: choctawtrans.com

Civil Constructors Inc 2283 US Hwy 20 E Freeport IL 61032 815-235-2200 235-2219
Web: www.helmgroup.com

Corey Delta Inc 4931 Park Rd PO Box 637 Benicia CA 94510 707-747-7500 745-5619
TF: 800-727-2260 ■ *Web:* www.coreydelta.com

DeSilva Gates Construction Inc
11555 Dublin Blvd Dublin CA 94568 925-829-9220 803-4268
Web: www.desilvagates.com

Dot-Line Transportation PO Box 8739 Fountain Valley CA 92728 323-780-9010 780-1552
TF: 800-423-3780 ■ *Web:* www.dotline.net

Frontier-Kemper Constructors Inc
1695 Allen Rd. Evansville IN 47710 812-426-2741 428-0337
TF: 877-554-8600 ■ *Web:* www.frontierkemper.com

Granite Construction Inc 585 W Beach St. Watsonville CA 95076 831-724-1011 722-9657
NYSE: GVA ■ *Web:* www.graniteconstruction.com

Great Lakes Dredge & Dock Co 2122 York Rd Oak Brook IL 60523 630-574-3000 574-2909
NASDAQ: GLDD ■ *Web:* www.gldd.com

Hawaiian Dredging & Construction Co
201 Merchant St. Honolulu HI 96813 808-735-3211 735-7416
Web: www.hdcc.com

James Steele Construction Co
1410 Sylvan St. Saint Paul MN 55117 651-488-6755 488-4787
Web: www.jamessteeleconstruction.com

JR Filanc Construction Company Inc
740 N Andreasen Dr Escondido CA 92029 760-941-7130 941-3969
TF: 877-225-5428 ■ *Web:* www.filanc.com

Lane Construction Corp 90 Fieldstone Ct. Cheshire CT 06410 203-235-3351 237-4260
Web: www.laneconstruct.com

Luhr Bros Inc 250 W Sand Bank Rd Columbia IL 62236 618-281-4106 281-4288
Web: www.luhr.com

Manson Construction Co 5209 E Marginal Way S. Seattle WA 98134 206-762-0850 764-8590
TF General: 800-262-6766 ■ *Web:* www.mansonconstruction.com

Massman Construction Co
8901 State Line Rd Ste 240 PO Box 8458 Kansas City MO 64114 816-523-1000 333-2109
Web: www.massman.net

McDermott International Inc
757 N Eldridge Pkwy Houston TX 77079 281-870-5000
NYSE: MDR ■ *Web:* www.mcdermott.com

Norris School District 6940 Calloway Dr Bakersfield CA 93312 661-387-7000 399-9750
TF: 800-877-8339 ■ *Web:* www.norris.k12.ca.us

P Gioioso & Sons Inc 50 Sprague St Hyde Park MA 02136 617-364-5800 364-9462
Web: www.pgioioso.com

TG Construction Inc 139 Nevada St. El Segundo CA 90245 310-640-0220 640-2907
Web: www.tgconst.com

Washington Corp PO Box 16630 Missoula MT 59808 406-523-1300 523-1399
TF: 800-832-7329 ■ *Web:* www.washcorp.com

Weeks Marine Inc Four Commerce Dr Cranford NJ 07016 908-272-4010 272-4740
Web: www.weeksmarine.com

191-6 Mining Construction

Phone | Fax

AME Inc 2467 Coltharp Rd. Fort Mill SC 29715 803-548-7766 548-7448
TF: 800-849-7766 ■ *Web:* www.ameonline.com

Frontier-Kemper Constructors Inc
1695 Allen Rd. Evansville IN 47710 812-426-2741 428-0337
TF: 877-554-8600 ■ *Web:* www.frontierkemper.com

Sundt Construction Inc 2015 W River Rd Ste 101 Tucson AZ 85704 520-750-4600
TF: 800-467-5544 ■ *Web:* www.sundt.com

191-7 Plant Construction

Phone | Fax

Angelo Iafrate Construction Co
26300 Sherwood Ave Warren MI 48091 586-756-1070 756-0467
Web: www.iafrate.com

Bancroft Construction Co
1300 N Grant Ave Ste 110 Wilmington DE 19806 302-655-3434 655-4599
Web: www.bancroftconstruction.com

Barton Malow Enterprises Inc
26500 American Dr. Southfield MI 48034 248-436-5000 436-5001
Web: www.bartonmalow.com

Bechtel North America 3000 Post Oak Blvd Houston TX 77056 713-235-2000 960-9031
Web: www.bechtel.com

Bechtel Petroleum & Chemical
3000 Post Oak Blvd Houston TX 77056 713-235-2000 235-4494
Web: www.bechtel.com

Big-D Construction Corp
404 West 400 South Salt Lake City UT 84101 801-415-6000 415-6900
Web: www.big-d.com

Black & Veatch 11401 Lamar Ave Overland Park KS 66211 913-458-2000
Web: www.bv.com

Bowen Engineering Corp
8802 N Meridian St Indianapolis IN 46260 317-842-2616 841-4257
Web: www.bowenengineering.com

Brasfield & Gorrie LLC 3021 Seventh Ave S. Birmingham AL 35233 205-328-4000 251-1304
TF: 800-239-8017 ■ *Web:* www.brasfieldgorrie.com

Brinderson 3330 Harbor Blvd Ste 100 Costa Mesa CA 92626 714-466-7100 466-7320
Web: www.brinderson.com

Cajun Constructors Inc 15635 Airline Hwy Baton Rouge LA 70817 225-753-5857 751-9777
TF: 877-401-5911 ■ *Web:* cajunusa.com

CCC Group Inc 5797 Dietrich Rd. San Antonio TX 78219 210-661-4251 661-6060
Web: www.cccgroupinc.com

Cianbro Corp 335 Hunnewell Ave. Pittsfield ME 04967 866-242-6276 487-3861*
*Fax Area Code: 207 ■ *Web:* www.cianbro.com

Cives Corp 1825 Old Alabama Rd Ste 200 Roswell GA 30076 770-993-4424 998-2361
Web: www.cives.com

Civil Constructors Inc 2283 US Hwy 20 E Freeport IL 61032 815-235-2200 235-2219
Web: www.helmgroup.com

Clark Construction Co 3535 Moores River Dr Lansing MI 48911 517-372-0940 372-0668
Web: www.clarkcc.com

Clark Construction Group LLC
7500 Old Georgetown Rd Bethesda MD 20814 301-272-8100 272-1928
TF: 800-655-1330 ■ *Web:* www.clarkconstruction.com

Day & Zimmermann Group Inc
1818 Market St. Philadelphia PA 19130 215-299-8000
TF: 877-319-0270 ■ *Web:* www.dayzim.com

				Phone	Fax
English Construction Co Inc 615 Church St *Web:* www.englishconst.com	Lynchburg	VA	24504	434-845-0301	845-0306
Fluor Daniel Inc Three Polaris Way *Web:* www.fluor.com	Aliso Viejo	CA	92698	949-349-2000	349-2585
Forcum Lannom Contractors LLC 350 US Hwy 51 Bypass S *Web:* www.forcumlannom.com	Dyersburg	TN	38024	731-287-4700	287-4701
Gilbane Bldg Co Seven Jackson Walkway *TF:* 800-445-2263 ■ *Web:* www.gilbaneco.com	Providence	RI	02903	401-456-5800	
Gray Construction 10 Quality St *TF:* 800-814-8468 ■ *Web:* www.gray.com	Lexington	KY	40507	859-281-5000	252-5300
H & M Construction Company Inc 50 Security Dr *Web:* hmcompany.com	Jackson	TN	38305	731-664-6300	
Haskell Co 111 Riverside Ave *TF:* 800-622-4326 ■ *Web:* haskell.com	Jacksonville	FL	32202	904-791-4500	791-4699
Hoffman Construction Corp 805 SW Broadway Ste 2100 *Web:* www.hoffmancorp.com	Portland	OR	97205	503-221-8811	221-8934
Hunt Construction Group 2450 S Tibbs Ave *Web:* www.huntconstructiongroup.com	Indianapolis	IN	46241	317-227-7800	227-7810
Hunter Contracting Co 701 N Cooper Rd *TF:* 877-992-0521 ■ *Web:* www.huntercontracting.com	Gilbert	AZ	85233	480-892-0521	892-4932
JF White Contracting Co 10 Burr St **Fax Area Code:* 617 ■ *TF:* 866-539-4400 ■ *Web:* www.jfwhite.com	Framingham	MA	01701	508-879-4700	558-0460*
Johnson Bros Corp 5476 Lithia Pinecrest Rd *Web:* www.johnson-bros.com	Lithia	FL	33547	813-685-5101	685-5939
Koch Specialty Plant Services 12221 E Sam Houston Pkwy N *TF:* 800-765-9177 ■ *Web:* www.kochservices.com	Houston	TX	77044	713-427-7700	427-7747
Louis P Ciminelli Construction Corp 2421 Main St *Web:* www.lpciminelli.com	Buffalo	NY	14202	716-855-1200	854-6655
MECS Inc 14522 S Outer 40 Rd *Web:* www.mecsglobal.com	Chesterfield	MO	63017	314-275-5700	275-5701
Northeast Remsco Construction Inc 1433 Hwy 34 S Bldg B1 *TF:* 800-879-8204 ■ *Web:* www.northeastconstruction.org	Farmingdale	NJ	07727	732-557-6100	736-8900
Parsons Corp 100 W Walnut St *TF All:* 800-883-7300 ■ *Web:* www.parsons.com	Pasadena	CA	91124	626-440-2000	440-2630
Performance Contractors Inc 9901 Pecu Ln *Web:* www.performance-br.com	Baton Rouge	LA	70810	225-751-4156	751-8409
Pizzagalli Construction Co 193 Tilley Dr *Web:* www.pcconstruction.com	South Burlington	VT	05403	802-658-4100	
Powell Technologies 3622 Bristol Hwy *Web:* powell-tech.com	Johnson City	TN	37601	423-282-0111	282-1541
Rudolph & Sletten Inc 1600 Seaport Blvd Ste 350 *Web:* www.rsconstruction.com	Redwood City	CA	94063	650-216-3600	599-9112
Sargent Corp 378 Bennoch Rd *TF:* 800-533-1812 ■ *Web:* www.sargent-corp.com	Stillwater	ME	04489	207-827-4435	827-6150
Shook Construction 4977 Northcutt Pl *TF:* 800-664-1844 ■ *Web:* www.shookconstruction.com	Dayton	OH	45414	937-276-6666	276-6676
SJ Amoroso Construction Co Inc 390 Bridge Pkwy *Web:* www.sjamoroso.com	Redwood Shores	CA	94065	650-654-1900	654-9002
Skanska USA Bldg Inc 389 Interpace Pkwy Fifth Fl *Web:* www.usa.skanska.com	Parsippany	NJ	07054	973-753-3500	753-3499
Skanska USA Inc 1616 Whitestone Expy *Web:* www.skanska.com	Whitestone	NY	11356	718-767-2600	767-2663
Todd & Sargent Inc 2905 SE Fifth St *Web:* www.tsargent.com	Ames	IA	50010	515-232-0442	232-0682
Turner Industries Group LLC 8687 United Plaza Blvd Ste 500 **Fax:* Mail Rm ■ *TF:* 800-288-6503 ■ *Web:* www.turner-industries.com	Baton Rouge	LA	70809	225-922-5050	922-5055*
Ventech Engineers Inc 1149 Ellsworth Dr *Web:* www.ventech-eng.com	Pasadena	TX	77506	713-477-0201	477-2420
Walbridge Aldinger Co 777 Woodward Ave #300 *Web:* www.walbridge.com	Detroit	MI	48226	313-963-8000	963-8150
Walsh Group Inc 929 W Adams St *TF:* 800-957-1842 ■ *Web:* walshgroup.com	Chicago	IL	60607	312-563-5400	563-5466
WG Yates & Sons Construction Co Inc 1 Gulley Ave PO Box 456 *Web:* www.wgyates.com	Philadelphia	MS	39350	601-656-5411	656-8958
Whiting-Turner Contracting Co 300 E Joppa Rd Eighth Fl *TF:* 800-638-4279 ■ *Web:* www.whiting-turner.com	Towson	MD	21286	410-821-1100	337-5770
Zachry Holdings Inc 527 Logwood Ave *Web:* www.zachrygroup.com/	San Antonio	TX	78221	210-475-8000	

191-8 Railroad Construction

				Phone	Fax
Acme Construction Co Inc 7695 Bond St *Web:* www.acmerrinc.com	Cleveland	OH	44139	440-232-7474	232-7477
Atlas Railroad Construction LLC 1370 Washington Pike Ste 202 **Fax Area Code:* 585 ■ *TF:* 800-829-4059 ■ *Web:* gwrr.com	Bridgeville	PA	15017	412-677-2020	785-6206*
Campbell Earl Construction Co 6060 Armour Dr	Houston	TX	77020	713-673-6208	672-9614
Parsons Corp 100 W Walnut St *TF All:* 800-883-7300 ■ *Web:* www.parsons.com	Pasadena	CA	91124	626-440-2000	440-2630
RailWorks Corp Five Penn Plz *Web:* www.railworks.com	New York	NY	10001	212-502-7900	
RW Summers Railroad Contractor Inc 3693 E Gandy Rd *Web:* www.rwsummers.net	Bartow	FL	33830	863-533-8107	533-8100
Snelson Company Inc 601 W State St *Web:* www.snelsonco.com	Sedro Woolley	WA	98284	360-856-6511	856-5816
Swanson Contracting Co 11701 S Mayfield Ave *TF:* 800-622-6850 ■ *Web:* www.swansoncontracting.com	Alsip	IL	60803	708-388-0623	388-9986
Trac-Work Inc 104 Creechville Rd PO Box 1338 *Web:* www.trac-work.com	Ennis	TX	75119	972-878-2232	875-2202
Tutor-Saliba Corp 15901 Olden St *Web:* www.tutorsaliba.com	Sylmar	CA	91342	818-362-8391	367-5379
WE Yoder Inc 41 S Maple St *TF:* 800-889-5149 ■ *Web:* www.weyoderinc.com	Kutztown	PA	19530	610-683-7383	683-8638

191-9 Refinery (Petroleum or Oil) Construction

				Phone	Fax
ARB Inc 26000 Commercentre Dr *TF:* 800-622-2699 ■ *Web:* www.arbinc.com	Lake Forest	CA	92630	949-598-9242	454-7190
Austin Industrial Inc 2801 E 13th S PO Box 87888 *TF:* 866-308-2592 ■ *Web:* www.austin-ind.com	La Porte	TX	77571	713-641-3400	641-2424
Bechtel North America 3000 Post Oak Blvd *Web:* www.bechtel.com	Houston	TX	77056	713-235-2000	960-9031
Bechtel Petroleum & Chemical 3000 Post Oak Blvd *Web:* www.bechtel.com	Houston	TX	77056	713-235-2000	235-4494
Fluor Daniel Inc Three Polaris Way *Web:* www.fluor.com	Aliso Viejo	CA	92698	949-349-2000	349-2585
McDermott International Inc 757 N Eldridge Pkwy *NYSE:* MDR ■ *Web:* www.mcdermott.com	Houston	TX	77079	281-870-5000	
Oscar J Boldt Construction Co 2525 N Roemer Rd *Web:* www.theboldtcompany.com	Appleton	WI	54911	920-739-6321	739-4409
Parsons Corp 100 W Walnut St *TF All:* 800-883-7300 ■ *Web:* www.parsons.com	Pasadena	CA	91124	626-440-2000	440-2630
Ref-Chem LP 1128 S Grandview PO Box 2588 *Web:* www.ref-chem.com	Odessa	TX	79761	432-332-8531	332-3325
Snelson Company Inc 601 W State St *Web:* www.snelsonco.com	Sedro Woolley	WA	98284	360-856-6511	856-5816
Turner Industries Group LLC 8687 United Plaza Blvd Ste 500 **Fax:* Mail Rm ■ *TF:* 800-288-6503 ■ *Web:* www.turner-industries.com	Baton Rouge	LA	70809	225-922-5050	922-5055*
Underground Construction Company Inc 5145 Industrial Way *TF:* 800-424-6521 ■ *Web:* www.undergrnd.com	Benicia	CA	94510	707-746-8800	746-1314
Zachry Holdings Inc 527 Logwood Ave *Web:* www.zachrygroup.com/	San Antonio	TX	78221	210-475-8000	

191-10 Water & Sewer Lines, Pipelines, Power Lines Construction

				Phone	Fax
Amzak Corp One N Federal Hwy Ste 400 *Web:* www.amzak.com	Boca Raton	FL	33432	561-953-4164	338-7677
Angelo Iafrate Construction Co 26300 Sherwood Ave *Web:* www.iafrate.com	Warren	MI	48091	586-756-1070	756-0467
Argonaut Constructors Inc 1236 Central Ave *Web:* www.argonautconstructors.com	Santa Rosa	CA	95401	707-542-4862	542-3210
Aubrey Silvey Enterprises Inc 371 Hamp Jones Rd *Web:* www.silvey.com	Carrollton	GA	30117	770-834-0738	834-1055
B Frank Joy LLC 5355 Kilmer Pl *TF:* 800-992-3569 ■ *Web:* www.bfjoy.com	Hyattsville	MD	20781	301-779-9400	699-6013
Balfour Beatty Inc 999 Peachtree St NE Ste 200 *Web:* www.balfourbeatty.com	Atlanta	GA	30309	404-875-0356	607-1784
Bancker Construction Corp 218 Blydenburgh Rd *Web:* www.bancker.com	Islandia	NY	11749	631-582-8880	582-3698
Barnard Construction Company Inc PO Box 99 *Web:* www.barnard-inc.com	Bozeman	MT	59771	406-586-1995	586-3530
Bechtel North America 3000 Post Oak Blvd *Web:* www.bechtel.com	Houston	TX	77056	713-235-2000	960-9031
Bechtel Pipeline 3000 Post Oak Blvd *Web:* www.bechtel.com	Houston	TX	77056	713-235-2000	960-9031
BRB Contractors Inc 3805 NW 25th St *TF:* 800-833-6747 ■ *Web:* www.brbcontractors.com	Topeka	KS	66618	785-232-1245	235-8045
Cajun Constructors Inc 15635 Airline Hwy *TF:* 877-401-5911 ■ *Web:* cajunusa.com	Baton Rouge	LA	70817	225-753-5857	751-9777
Callas Contractors Inc 10549 Downsville Pk *Web:* www.callascontractors.com	Hagerstown	MD	21740	301-739-8400	739-7065
Cianbro Corp 335 Hunnewell Ave **Fax Area Code:* 207 ■ *Web:* www.cianbro.com	Pittsfield	ME	04967	866-242-6276	487-3861*
Cives Corp 1825 Old Alabama Rd Ste 200 *Web:* www.cives.com	Roswell	GA	30076	770-993-4424	998-2361
Contractors Northwest Inc 3731 N Ramsey Rd *Web:* www.contractorsnorthwest.com	Coeur d'Alene	ID	83815	208-667-2456	667-6388
CW Wright Construction Company Inc 11500 Iron Bridge Rd *Web:* www.cwwright.com	Chester	VA	23831	804-768-1054	768-6057
EE Cruz & Co Inc 165 Ryan St The Cruz Bldg **Fax Area Code:* 732 ■ *Web:* eecruz.com	South Plainfield	NJ	07080	908-791-9599	946-7592*
Elkins Constructors Inc 701 W Adams St *TF:* 800-772-1213 ■ *Web:* www.elkinsconstructors.com	Jacksonville	FL	32204	904-353-6500	387-1303
Facchina Construction Co Inc 102 Centennial St Ste 201 *Web:* www.facchina.com/ContactUs.aspx	La Plata	MD	20646	240-776-7000	776-7001

Phone Fax

FCI Constructors Inc
3070 I-70 Business Loop # A Grand Junction CO 81504 970-434-9093 434-7583
Web: www.fciol.com

Frontier-Kemper Constructors Inc
1695 Allen Rd Evansville IN 47710 812-426-2741 428-0337
TF: 877-554-8600 ■ *Web:* www.frontierkemper.com

Garney Cos Inc 1333 NW Vivion Rd Kansas City MO 64118 816-741-4600 741-4488
Web: www.garney.com

Global Industries Ltd 8000 Global Dr Sulphur LA 70665 337-583-5000 583-5100
TF: 800-525-3483 ■ *Web:* lake-charles.gopickle.com

Granite Construction Inc 585 W Beach St Watsonville CA 95076 831-724-1011 722-9657
NYSE: GVA ■ *Web:* www.graniteconstruction.com

GSE Construction Company Inc
1020 Shannon Ct Livermore CA 94550 925-447-0292 447-0962
Web: www.gseconstruction.com

Hall Contracting Corp 6415 Lakeview Rd Charlotte NC 28269 704-598-0818 598-3855
Web: hallcontracting.com

Henkels & McCoy Inc 985 Jolly Rd Blue Bell PA 19422 215-283-7600 283-7659
TF: 800-523-2568 ■ *Web:* www.henkels.com

Hood Corp 3166 Horseless Carriage Rd Norco CA 92860 951-520-4282 520-4385
Web: www.hoodcorp.com

Hubbard Construction Co
1936 Lee Rd 3rd Fl Winter Park FL 32789 407-645-5500 623-3865
TF: 800-476-1228 ■ *Web:* www.hubbard.com

Insituform Technologies Inc
17988 Edison Ave Chesterfield MO 63005 636-530-8000 519-8010
TF Cust Svc: 800-234-2992 ■ *Web:* www.insituform.com

Irish Construction Inc 2641 River Ave Rosemead CA 91770 626-288-8530 573-5136
Web: www.irishteam.com

James White Construction Company Inc
4156 Freedom Way Weirton WV 26062 304-748-8181 748-8183
Web: jameswhiteconstruction.com

Jay Dee Contractors Inc 38881 Schoolcraft Rd Livonia MI 48150 734-591-3400 464-6868
Web: www.jaydeecontr.com

JC Evans Construction Company Inc
8660 183 A Toll Rd Leander TX 78641 512-244-1400 244-1900
Web: www.jcevans.com

JF Shea Construction Inc 655 Brea Canyon Rd Walnut CA 91789 909-594-9500 883-3371
TF: 888-779-7333 ■ *Web:* www.jfshea.com

JF White Contracting Co 10 Burr St Framingham MA 01701 508-879-4700 558-0460*
**Fax Area Code:* 617 ■ *TF:* 866-539-4400 ■ *Web:* www.jfwhite.com

JH Berra Construction Company Inc
5091 Baumgartner Rd Saint Louis MO 63129 314-487-5617
Web: www.jhberra.com

John F Otto Inc 1717 Second St Sacramento CA 95811 916-441-6870 441-6138
Web: www.ottoconstruction.com

Johnson Bros Corp 5476 Lithia Pinecrest Rd Lithia FL 33547 813-685-5101 685-5939
Web: www.johnson-bros.com

JR Filanc Construction Company Inc
740 N Andreasen Dr Escondido CA 92029 760-941-7130 941-3969
TF: 877-225-5428 ■ *Web:* www.filanc.com

Kankakee Valley Construction Company Inc
4356 W SR 17 Kankakee IL 60901 815-937-8700 937-0402
Web: www.kvcci.com

Kimmins Contracting Corp 1501 Second Ave Tampa FL 33605 813-248-3878 579-1081
Web: www.kimmins.com

Kip Inc 25740 Washington Ave Murrieta CA 92562 951-698-7890
Web: www.kipincorporated.com

Kiska Construction Corp USA
10-34 44th Dr Long Island City NY 11101 718-943-0400 943-0401
Web: www.kiskagroup.com

Koch Specialty Plant Services
12221 E Sam Houston Pkwy N Houston TX 77044 713-427-7700 427-7747
TF: 800-765-9177 ■ *Web:* www.kochservices.com

Landmark Structures LP 1665 Harmon Rd Fort Worth TX 76177 817-439-8888 439-9001
TF: 800-888-6816 ■ *Web:* www.teamlandmark.com

Lane Construction Corp 90 Fieldstone Ct Cheshire CT 06410 203-235-3351 237-4260
Web: www.laneconstruct.com

Latex Construction Co PO Box 917 Conyers GA 30012 770-760-0820 760-0852
Web: www.latexconstruction.com

Layne 4520 N State Rd 37 Orleans IN 47452 812-865-3232 865-3075
TF All: 855-529-6301 ■ *Web:* www.layne.com

MasTec Inc 800 Douglas Rd 12th Fl Coral Gables FL 33134 305-599-1800 406-1960
NYSE: MTZ ■ *TF:* 800-531-5000 ■ *Web:* www.mastec.com

McLean Contracting Co 6700 McLean Way Glen Burnie MD 21060 410-553-6700 553-6718
Web: mcleancont.com

Mears Group Inc 4500 N Mission Rd Rosebush MI 48878 989-433-2929 433-2199
TF: 800-632-7727 ■ *Web:* www.mears.net

Michels Corp 817 W Main St Brownsville WI 53006 920-583-3132 583-3429
TF: 877-297-8663 ■ *Web:* www.michels.us

Miller Pipeline Corp
8850 Crawfordsville Rd Indianapolis IN 46234 317-293-0278 293-8502
TF: 800-428-3742 ■ *Web:* www.millerpipeline.com

Miron Construction Co Inc 1471 McMahon Dr Neenah WI 54956 920-969-7000 969-7393
Web: miron-construction.com

Montana Construction Corp Inc 80 Contant Ave Lodi NJ 07644 973-478-5200 478-7604
Web: www.montanaconstructioninc.com

Mountain Cascade Inc PO Box 5050 Livermore CA 94551 925-373-8370 638-1962
Web: www.mountaincascade.com

New River Electrical Corp PO Box 70 Cloverdale VA 24077 540-966-1650 966-1699
Web: www.newriverelectrical.com

Northeast Remsco Construction Inc
1433 Hwy 34 S Bldg B1 Farmingdale NJ 07727 732-557-6100 736-8900
TF: 800-879-8204 ■ *Web:* www.northeastconstruction.org

O'Brien & Gere Technical Services Inc
333 W Washington St Syracuse NY 13202 315-956-6100 463-7554
Web: www.obg.com

Oldcastle Materials Inc
900 Ashwood Pkwy Ste 700 Atlanta GA 30338 770-522-5600 522-5608
Web: www.apac.com

P Gioioso & Sons Inc 50 Sprague St Hyde Park MA 02136 617-364-5800 364-9462
Web: www.pgioioso.com

Phone Fax

Penn Line Service Inc 300 Scottdale Ave Scottdale PA 15683 724-887-9110 887-0545
TF All: 800-448-9110 ■ *Web:* www.pennline.com

Phylway Construction LLC 1074a Hwy 1 Thibodaux LA 70301 985-446-9644
Web: www.phylway.com

Quanta Services Inc
1360 Post Oak Blvd Ste 2100 Houston TX 77056 713-629-7600 629-7676
NYSE: PWR ■ *Web:* www.quantaservices.com

RH White Construction Company Inc
41 Central St Auburn MA 01501 508-832-3295 832-7084
Web: www.rhwhite.com

River City Construction LLC
101 Hoffer Ln East Peoria IL 61611 309-694-3120 694-1332
Web: www.rcclic.com

Satellite Store 7412 Preston Hwy Louisville KY 40219 502-966-0045 969-3499
TF: 800-693-9393 ■ *Web:* www.thesatellitestore.com

Shaw Constructors Inc 36445 Perkins Rd Prairieville LA 70769 225-673-4606 744-6202
Web: cbi.com

Sheehan Pipe Line Construction Co
2431 E 61st St Ste 700 Tulsa OK 74136 918-747-3471 747-9888
Web: www.sheehanpipeline.com

Siciliano Inc 3601 Winchester Rd Springfield IL 62707 217-585-1200 585-1211
Web: www.sicilianoinc.com

Sletten Construction Company Inc
1000 25th St N Great Falls MT 59401 406-761-7920 761-0923
Web: www.slettencompanies.com

Snelson Company Inc 601 W State St Sedro Woolley WA 98284 360-856-6511 856-5816
Web: www.snelsonco.com

Spiniello Cos 354 Eisenhower Pkwy Livingston NJ 07039 973-808-8383 808-9591
Web: www.spiniello.com

Stacy & Witbeck Inc
2800 Harbor Bay Pkwy Ste 240 Alameda CA 94502 510-865-2967 748-1205
Web: www.stacywitbeck.com

Stuart C Irby Co 815 S President St Jackson MS 39201 601-960-7346 960-7277
TF: 866-687-4729 ■ *Web:* www.irby.com

Suburban Grading & Utilities Inc
1190 Harmony Rd Norfolk VA 23502 757-461-1800 461-0989
Web: www.suburbangrading.com

Sumter Utilities Inc 1151 N Pike W Sumter SC 29153 803-469-8585 469-4600
Web: www.sumter-utilities.com

TA Loving Company Inc
400 Patetown Rd PO Box 919 Goldsboro NC 27530 919-734-8400 731-7538
Web: www.taloving.com

TJ Lambrecht Construction Inc 10 Gougar Rd Joliet IL 60432 815-726-7722 727-6421

Tri Dal Ltd 540 Commerce St Southlake TX 76092 817-481-2886 481-8195
Web: www.tridal.com

Underground Construction Company Inc
5145 Industrial Way Benicia CA 94510 707-746-8800 746-1314
TF: 800-424-6521 ■ *Web:* www.undergrnd.com

URS 7633 E 63rd Pl Ste 500 Tulsa OK 74133 918-294-3030 307-8960
TF: 800-564-6253 ■ *Web:* www.flintenergy.com

Utility Services Inc 400 N Fourth St Bismarck ND 58501 701-222-7900
TF: 800-638-3278 ■ *Web:* www.montana-dakota.com

UTILX Corp 22820 Russell Rd Kent WA 98032 253-395-0200 238-4840
Web: www.willbros.com/businessunits/utilx

Walbridge Aldinger Co 777 Woodward Ave #300 Detroit MI 48226 313-963-8000 963-8150
Web: www.walbridge.com

Welded Construction LP 26933 Eckel Rd Perrysburg OH 43551 419-874-3548 874-4883
Web: www.welded-construction.com

West Valley Construction Company Inc
580 McGlincey Ln Campbell CA 95008 800-588-5510 371-3604*
**Fax Area Code:* 408 ■ *TF:* 800-588-5510 ■ *Web:* www.westvalleyconstruction.com

Wharton-Smith Inc PO Box 471028 Lake Monroe FL 32747 407-321-8410 321-4368
TF Help Line: 888-393-0068 ■ *Web:* www.whartonsmith.com

Whitesell-Green Inc 3881 N Palafox St Pensacola FL 32505 850-434-5311 434-5315
Web: www.whitesell-green.com

Willbros Engineers Inc 2087 E 71st St Tulsa OK 74136 918-496-0400 491-9436
Web: www.willbros.com

Yantis Co 3611 Paesano's Pkwy Ste 300 San Antonio TX 78231 210-655-3780 655-8526
Web: www.yantiscompany.com

Yates Construction Company Inc
9220 NC Hwy 65 Stokesdale NC 27357 336-379-8131
Web: www.yatesconstruction.com

192 CONSTRUCTION - SPECIAL TRADE CONTRACTORS

SEE ALSO Swimming Pools p. 3202

192-1 Building Equipment Installation or Erection

Phone Fax

APi Group Inc Specialty Construction Services Group
1100 Old Hwy 8 NW New Brighton MN 55112 800-223-4922 636-0312*
**Fax Area Code:* 651 ■ *TF:* 800-223-4922 ■ *Web:* apigroupinc.com/industries/

AWC Commercial Window Coverings Inc
825 Williamson Ave Fullerton CA 92832 714-879-3880 879-8419
TF: 800-252-2280 ■ *Web:* www.awc-cwc.com

Aycock LLC 8261 Derry St Hummelstown PA 17036 717-566-5066 566-5077
TF: 800-772-5066 ■ *Web:* www.aycockrigging.com

Baltimore Rigging Company Inc, The
8149 Norris Ln PO Box 18401 Dundalk MD 21222 443-696-4001 696-4006
TF: 800-626-2150 ■ *Web:* www.baltimorerigging.com

Bigge Crane & Rigging Company Inc
10700 Bigge St PO Box 1657 San Leandro CA 94577 510-638-8100 639-4053
TF: 888-337-2444 ■ *Web:* bigge.com

Chicago Elevator Co 3260 W Grand Ave Chicago IL 60651 773-227-0737 645-7581
Web: www.chicagoelevator.com

Columbia Elevator Products Company Inc
380 Horace St Bridgeport NY 06610 888-858-1558 937-9181*
**Fax Area Code:* 914 ■ *TF:* 888-858-1558 ■ *Web:* www.columbiaelevator.com

Company	City	State	Zip	Phone	Fax
Commercial Contracting Corp 4260 N Atlantic Blvd. *Web:* www.cccnetwork.com	Auburn Hills	MI	48326	248-209-0500	209-0501
Don R Fruchey Inc 5608 Old Maumee Rd *Web:* www.donrfruchey.com	Fort Wayne	IN	46803	260-749-8502	749-6337
DW Nicholson Corp 24747 Clawiter Rd *Web:* www.dwnicholson.com	Hayward	CA	94545	510-887-0900	783-9948
Elward Construction Co 680 Harlan St. *TF:* 800-933-5339 ■ *Web:* www.elward.com	Lakewood	CO	80214	303-239-6303	239-8719
Fenton Rigging & Contracting Inc 2150 Langdon Farm Rd *Web:* fenton1898.com	Cincinnati	OH	45237	513-631-5500	631-4361
George W Auch Co 735 S Paddock St PO Box 430719 *Web:* www.auchconstruction.com	Pontiac	MI	48341	248-334-2000	334-3404
Integral Automation Inc 16w171 Shore Ct *Web:* www.premiertool.com	Burr Ridge	IL	60527	630-654-4300	654-8519
International Industrial Contracting Corp 35900 Mound Rd *Web:* www.iiccusa.com	Sterling Heights	MI	48310	586-264-7070	264-7088
James Machine Works LLC 1521 Adams St *TF:* 800-259-6104 ■ *Web:* www.jmwinc.net	Monroe	LA	71201	318-322-6104	388-4245
PS Marcato Elevator Co 4411 11th St *Web:* www.psmarcato.com	Long Island City	NY	11101	718-392-6400	
Rigging International 1210 Marina Village Pkwy *Web:* www.sarens.com	Alameda	CA	94501	510-865-2400	865-9450
Sand Steel Bldg Co 101 Browell St PO Box 129	Emerado	ND	58228	701-594-4435	594-4438
Schindler Elevator Corp 20 Whippany Rd. **Fax:* Mail Rm ■ *TF:* 800-225-3123 ■ *Web:* www.schindler.com	Morristown	NJ	07960	973-397-6500	397-3619*
SCI Global Structural Contours Inc PO Box 4970 *Web:* www.sciglobal.com	Greenwich	CT	06830	203-531-4400	531-4403
Thyssen Elevator Co 15141 E Whittier Blvd Ste 505 *Web:* www.thyssenkrupp.com	Whittier	CA	90603	901-365-5600	365-5600
W & H Systems Inc 120 Asia Pl *TF:* 800-966-6993 ■ *Web:* www.whsystems.com	Carlstadt	NJ	07072	201-933-7840	933-2144
Wales Industrial Service Inc PO Box 21628 *Web:* www.walesindustrial.com	Waco	TX	76702	254-772-3310	772-3420
Wyatt Field Service Co 15415 Katy Fwy Ste 800 *Web:* www.wyattfieldservice.com	Houston	TX	77094	281-675-1300	675-1390

192-2 Carpentry & Flooring Contractors

Company	City	State	Zip	Phone	Fax
ACMAT Corp 233 Main St *OTC:* ACMT ■ *Web:* www.acmatcorp.com	New Britain	CT	06051	860-229-9000	
Archadeck 2924 Emerywood Pkwy Ste 101 *TF:* 800-722-4668 ■ *Web:* www.archadeck.com	Richmond	VA	23294	804-353-6999	353-2364
Associated Floors 32 Morris Ave **Fax Area Code:* 212 ■ *TF:* 800-800-4320 ■ *Web:* www.assocint.com	Springfield	NJ	07081	800-800-4320	633-0626*
Bonitz Contracting Company Inc 645 Rosewood Dr PO Box 82 *Web:* www.bonitz.us	Columbia	SC	29202	803-799-0181	748-9223
Carpenter Contractors of America Inc 3900 Ave D NW *TF:* 800-959-8806 ■ *Web:* www.carpentercontractors.com	Winter Haven	FL	33880	863-294-6449	299-9940
Cincinnati Floor Company Inc 5162 Broerman Ave *TF:* 800-886-4501 ■ *Web:* www.cincifloor.com	Cincinnati	OH	45217	513-641-4500	482-4204
Covington Flooring Co Inc 709 First Ave N *Web:* www.covington.com	Birmingham	AL	35203	205-328-2330	328-2496
Custom Stone 2999 Teagarden St. *Web:* www.customstoneusa.com	San Leandro	CA	94577	510-667-0099	667-0099
E&K Companies 343 Carol Ln *TF:* 800-365-5760 ■ *Web:* www.air-tite.net	Elmhurst	IL	60126	630-530-9001	
Frank Novak & Sons Inc 23940 Miles Rd.	Cleveland	OH	44128	216-475-5440	
Interior Construction Services Ltd 2930 Market St. *Web:* www.ics-stl.com	Saint Louis	MO	63103	314-534-6664	534-6663
John H Hampshire Inc 320 W 24th St *Web:* www.jhhampshire.com	Baltimore	MD	21211	410-366-8900	467-7391
Kalman Floor Company Inc 1202 Bergen Pkwy Ste 110 *TF:* 800-525-7840 ■ *Web:* kalmanfloor.com	Evergreen	CO	80439	303-674-2290	674-1238
Meyer & Lundahl 2345 W Lincoln St. *TF:* 800-264-9286 ■ *Web:* www.meyerandlundahl.com	Phoenix	AZ	85009	602-254-9286	258-6943
Overhead Door Company of Sacramento Inc 6756 Franklin Blvd *TF:* 800-929-3667 ■ *Web:* www.overheaddoor.com	Sacramento	CA	95823	916-421-3747	
Rock-Tred Corp 405 Oakwood Ave **Fax:* Cust Svc ■ *Web:* www.rocktred.com	Waukegan	IL	60085	847-673-8200	679-6665*
Sundt Construction 2620 S 55th St. *TF:* 800-280-3000 ■ *Web:* www.sundt.com	Tempe	AZ	85282	480-293-3000	
Tribco Construction Services 200 S Michigan Ave Ste 200	Chicago	IL	60604	312-341-0303	341-1534
Turner-Brooks Inc 28811 John R Rd *Web:* turnerbrooks.com	Madison Heights	MI	48071	248-548-3400	548-9213

192-3 Concrete Contractors

Company	City	State	Zip	Phone	Fax
Alex E. Paris Contracting Co 1595 Smith Township State *Web:* www.alexparis.com	Atlasburg	PA	15004	724-947-2235	947-3820
Allied Contractors Inc 204 E Preston St. *Web:* alliedcontractor.com	Baltimore	MD	21202	410-539-6727	332-4594
Asphalt Specialists Inc 1780 Highwood E. *Web:* www.asipaving.com	Pontiac	MI	48340	248-334-4570	334-4135
Aurora Blacktop Inc 1065 Sard Ave *Web:* aurorablacktop.com	Montgomery	IL	60538	630-892-9389	554-3306
Baker Concrete Construction Inc 900 N Garver Rd *TF:* 800-359-3935 ■ *Web:* www.bakerconcrete.com	Monroe	OH	45050	513-539-4000	539-4380
Barnard Construction Company Inc PO Box 99 *Web:* www.barnard-inc.com	Bozeman	MT	59771	406-586-1995	586-3530
Berglund Construction 8410 S Chicago Ave *Web:* www.berglundco.com	Chicago	IL	60617	773-374-1000	374-0701
Bi-Con Services Inc 10901 Clay Pike Rd *Web:* www.biconservices.com/	Derwent	OH	43733	740-685-2542	685-3863
Blair Concrete Services 1410-B Diggs Dr. **Fax Area Code:* 804 ■ *TF:* 800-815-7395 ■ *Web:* www.donleyinc.com	Raleigh	NC	27603	919-833-9088	560-7828*
Bomel Construction Company Inc 8195 E Kaiser Blvd *Web:* www.bomelconstruction.com	Anaheim Hills	CA	92808	714-921-1660	921-1943
Bowen Engineering Corp 8802 N Meridian St *Web:* www.bowenengineering.com	Indianapolis	IN	46260	317-842-2616	841-4257
Ceco Concrete Construction LLC 9135 Barton *TF:* 800-285-1131 ■ *Web:* www.cecoconcrete.com	Overland Park	KS	66214	913-362-1855	
Cleveland Cement Contractors Inc 4823 Van Epps Rd *Web:* www.clevelandcement.com	Brooklyn Heights	OH	44131	216-741-3954	741-9278
Colorado Asphalt Services Inc 3700 E 56th Ave *Web:* www.coloradoasphalt.com	Commerce City	CO	80022	303-292-3434	292-6267
Culbertson Enterprises Inc (CEI) 600A Snyder Ave *TF:* 800-382-2685	West Chester	PA	19382	610-436-6400	
Daisy Construction Company Inc 3120 New Castle Ave *Web:* www.daisyconstruction.com	New Castle	DE	19720	302-658-4417	658-0618
Damon G Douglas Co 245 Birchwood Ave. **Fax Area Code:* 732 ■ *TF:* 800-724-1759 ■ *Web:* www.dgdco.com	Cranford	NJ	07016	908-272-0100	560-0305*
Dance Bros Inc 825C Hammonds Ferry Rd *Web:* dancebrothers.com	Linthicum	MD	21090	410-789-8200	636-3663
Donley's Inc 5430 Warner Rd *Web:* www.donleyinc.com	Cleveland	OH	44125	216-524-6800	642-3216
Dywidag Systems International 320 Marmon Dr *TF:* 800-457-7633 ■ *Web:* www.dywidag-systems.com	Bolingbrook	IL	60440	630-739-1100	739-5517
Egizii Electric Inc (EEI) 700 N MacArthur Blvd	Springfield	IL	62702	217-528-4001	528-1677
Francis O Day Construction Company Inc 850 E Gude Dr *Web:* www.foday.com	Rockville	MD	20850	301-652-2400	340-6592
Harris Cos Inc 909 Montreal Cir *Web:* www.hmcc.com	Saint Paul	MN	55102	651-602-6500	602-6699
Healy Long & Jevin Inc 2000 Rodman Rd *Web:* www.healylongjevin.com	Wilmington	DE	19805	302-654-8039	654-8153
Hubbard Construction Co 1936 Lee Rd 3rd Fl *TF:* 800-476-1228 ■ *Web:* www.hubbard.com	Winter Park	FL	32789	407-645-5500	623-3865
John Rohrer Contracting Company Inc 2820 Roe Ln Bldg S *Web:* www.johnrohrercontracting.com	Kansas City	KS	66103	913-236-5005	236-7291
Kalman Floor Company Inc 1202 Bergen Pkwy Ste 110 *TF:* 800-525-7840 ■ *Web:* kalmanfloor.com	Evergreen	CO	80439	303-674-2290	674-1238
Landavazo Bros Inc 29280 Pacific St	Hayward	CA	94544	510-581-7104	581-7423
Larson Contracting Inc 508 West Main St *TF:* 800-765-1426 ■ *Web:* www.larsoncontracting.com	Lake Mills	IA	50450	641-592-5800	592-8610
Lindblad Construction Co 717 E Cass St *Web:* www.lindbladconstruction.com	Joliet	IL	60432	815-726-6251	723-4907
Manafort Bros Inc 414 New Britain Ave *TF:* 888-626-2367 ■ *Web:* www.manafort.com	Plainville	CT	06062	860-229-4853	747-4861
Miller & Long Concrete Construction Inc 4824 Rugby Ave *Web:* www.millerandlong.com	Bethesda	MD	20814	301-657-8000	657-8610
Musselman & Hall Contractors LLC 4922 E Blue Banks PO Box 300858 *TF:* 800-257-4255 ■ *Web:* www.musselmanandhall.com	Kansas City	MO	64130	816-861-1234	861-1237
Oldcastle Precast Bldg Systems Div 1401 Trimble Rd **Fax Area Code:* 410 ■ *TF:* 800-523-9144 ■ *Web:* oldcastleprecast.com	Edgewood	MD	21040	800-523-9144	612-1214*
Otto Baum Company Inc 866 N Main St PO Box 161 *Web:* www.ottobaum.com	Morton	IL	61550	309-266-7114	263-1050
Proshot Concrete Inc 4158 Musgrove Dr. *TF:* 800-633-3141 ■ *Web:* www.proshotconcrete.com	Florence	AL	35630	256-764-5941	764-5946
Richard Goettle Inc 12071 Hamilton Ave *Web:* www.goettle.com	Cincinnati	OH	45231	513-825-8100	825-8107
SB Ballard Construction Co 2828 Shipps Corner Rd *Web:* www.sbballard.com	Virginia Beach	VA	23453	757-440-5555	451-2873
Seretta Construction Inc 2604 Clark St *Web:* www.seretta.com	Apopka	FL	32703	407-290-9440	290-9372
Smock Fansler Corp 2910 W Minnesota St. *Web:* www.smockfansler.com	Indianapolis	IN	46241	317-248-8371	244-4507
Suncoast Post-Tension LP 509 N Sam Houston Pkwy Ste 400 E *TF:* 800-847-8886 ■ *Web:* www.suncoast-pt.com	Houston	TX	77060	281-668-1840	668-1862
Superior Gunite Inc 12306 Van Nuys Blvd *Web:* www.shotcrete.com	Lakeview Terrace	CA	91342	818-896-9199	896-6699
TAS Commercial Concrete Construction LLC 19319 Oil Ctr Blvd *Web:* www.tasconcrete.com	Houston	TX	77073	281-230-7500	230-7664
Treviicos Corp 38 Third Ave. *Web:* www.treviicos.com	Charlestown	MA	02129	617-241-4800	737-5810
Weaver-Bailey Contractors Inc PO Box 60 *TF:* 800-253-3385 ■ *Web:* www.weaverbailey.com	El Paso	AR	72045	501-796-2301	796-2372

192-4 Electrical Contractors

Phone | Fax

A E C Group Inc, The 1735 Fifth Ave McKeesport PA 15132 412-678-1440
Web: www.aecgroup.com

A. M. Ortega Construction Inc 10125 Ch Rd Lakeside CA 92040 619-390-1988 390-1941
TF: 800-909-1988 ■ *Web:* www.amortega.com

AC Corp 301 Creek Ridge Rd Greensboro NC 27406 336-273-4472 765-0416
TF: 800-422-7378 ■ *Web:* www.accorporation.com

AC Electric Co
2921 Hangar Way PO Box 81977 Bakersfield CA 93308 661-410-0000 410-0400
Web: www.a-celectric.com

Aldridge Electric Inc 844 E Rockland Rd Libertyville IL 60048 847-680-5200 680-5298
Web: www.aldridge-electric.com

Allan Briteway Electrical Contractors Inc
130 Algonquin Pkwy Whippany NJ 07981 973-781-0022 781-1744
Web: www.allanbriteway.com

Althoff Industries Inc 8001 S Rt 31 Crystal Lake IL 60014 815-455-7000 455-9375*
**Fax:* Sales ■ *TF:* 800-225-2443 ■ *Web:* www.althoffind.com

Anderson Electric Inc PO Box 758 Springfield IL 62705 217-529-5471 529-0412
Web: www.anderson-electric.com

Anixter Inc 2301 Patriot Blvd Glenview IL 60026 224-521-8000 521-8100
TF: 800-264-9837 ■ *Web:* www.anixter.com

Arrow Electric Company Inc
317 Wabasso Ave Louisville KY 40209 502-367-0141 361-8613
TF: 888-999-5591 ■ *Web:* www.arrowelectric.com

Aschinger Electric Co
877 Horan Dr PO Box 26322 Fenton MO 63026 636-343-1211 343-9658
TF: 800-280-4061 ■ *Web:* www.aschinger.com

Athena Engineering Inc 456 E Foothill Blvd San Dimas CA 91773 909-599-0947 599-5018
TF: 877-777-4778 ■ *Web:* www.athenaengineering.net

B & I Contractors Inc 2701 Prince St Fort Myers FL 33916 239-332-4646 332-5928
Web: www.bandicontractors.com

Baker Electric Inc 111 Jackson Ave Des Moines IA 50315 515-288-6774 288-2226
Web: www.bakerelectric.com

Barth Electric Company Inc
1934 N Illinois St Indianapolis IN 46202 317-924-6226 923-6938
TF: 800-666-6226 ■ *Web:* www.barthelectric.com

Bell Electrical Contractors Inc
128 Millwell Dr Maryland Heights MO 63043 314-739-7744 717-2355*
**Fax Area Code:* 800 ■ *TF:* 800-717-2355 ■ *Web:* www.bellelectrical.com

Bergelectric Corp 5650 W Centinela Ave Los Angeles CA 90045 310-337-1377 337-2663
TF: 800-734-2374 ■ *Web:* www.bergelectric.com

Berger Engineering Co 10900 Shady Trl Dallas TX 75220 214-358-4451 351-2954
Web: www.berger-engr.com

Berwick Electric Co
3450 N Nevada Ave Ste 100 Colorado Springs CO 80907 719-632-7683 471-9660
Web: www.berwickelectric.com

Brink Constructors Inc
2950 N Plz Dr PO Box 1186 Rapid City SD 57702 605-342-6966 342-5905
Web: www.brinkred.com

Broadway Electric Service Company Inc
1800 N Central St Knoxville TN 37917 865-524-1851 546-2104
Web: besco.com

Broadway Electrical Company Inc
295 Freeport St Boston MA 02122 617-288-7900 288-4169
Web: www.broadelec.com

Brothers Inc 1000 Sussex Blvd Broomall PA 19008 610-328-0670 328-6218
TF: 866-276-7462 ■ *Web:* www.brotherselectric.com

Bruce & Merrilees Electric Co 930 Cass St New Castle PA 16101 724-652-5566 652-8290
TF: 800-652-5560 ■ *Web:* www.bruceandmerrilees.com

Cache Valley Electric Inc 875 N 1000 W Logan UT 84321 435-752-6405 752-9111
TF: 888-558-0600 ■ *Web:* www.cvelectric.com

Campbell Alliance Group Inc
8045 Arco Corporate Dr Ste 500 Raleigh NC 27617 919-844-7100 844-7560
TF: 888-297-2001 ■ *Web:* www.campbellalliance.com

Cannon & Wendt Electric Co 4020 N 16th St Phoenix AZ 85016 602-279-1681 230-8464
Web: www.cannon-wendt.com

Capital Electric Construction Company Inc
600 Broadway Ste 600 Kansas City MO 64105 816-472-9500 421-4244
Web: www.capitalelectric.com

Center Line Electric Inc 26554 Lawrence Center Line MI 48015 586-757-5505 759-2453
Web: www.centerline-elec.com

Church & Murdock Electric Inc 5709 Wattsburg Rd Erie PA 16509 814-825-3456 825-4043
Web: www.churchandmurdock.com

Cleveland Electric Company Inc
1281 Fulton Industrial Blvd NW Atlanta GA 30336 404-696-4550 696-2849
TF: 800-282-7150 ■ *Web:* www.clevelectric.com

Cleveland Group Inc
1281 Fulton Industrial Blvd Atlanta GA 30336 404-696-4550 505-7792
TF: 800-282-7150 ■ *Web:* www.clevelectric.com

Cochran Electric Company Inc PO Box 33524 Seattle WA 98133 206-367-1900 368-3262
Web: www.cochraninc.com

Collins Electric Co Inc 53 Second Ave Chicopee MA 01020 413-592-9221 592-4157
TF: 877-553-2810 ■ *Web:* www.collinselectricco.com

Commander Electric Inc
500 Johnson Ave PO Box 526 Bohemia NY 11716 631-563-3223 563-8322

Commonwealth Electric Co of Midwest
PO Box 80638 Lincoln NE 68501 402-474-1341 474-0114
Web: www.commonwealthelectric.com

Contemporary Electrical Services Inc
1954 Isaac Newton Sq W Ste 200 Reston VA 20190 703-255-9226
Web: www.cont-elec.com

Continental Electric Company Inc
9501 E Fifth Ave PO Box 2710 Gary IN 46403 219-938-3460 938-3469
Web: www.continentalelectric.com

Cupertino Electric Inc 1132 N Seventh St San Jose CA 95112 408-808-8000 275-8575
Web: www.cei.com

Phone | Fax

Custom Cable Industries Inc
3221 Cherry Palm Dr Tampa FL 33619 813-623-2232 623-3534
TF: 800-552-2232 ■ *Web:* www.mflightwave.com

Daidone Electric Inc 200 Raymond Blvd Newark NJ 07105 973-690-5216 344-3645
Web: daidoneelectric.com

Dashiell Corp 12301 Kurland Dr Ste 400 Houston TX 77034 713-558-6600 558-6694
Web: www.dashiell.com

Davis H Elliot Co Inc 1920 Progress Dr SE Roanoke VA 24013 540-427-5459
Web: www.davishelliot.com

Decker Electric Company Inc
1282 Folsom St San Francisco CA 94103 415-552-1622 861-4257

Del Monte Electric Company Inc 6998 Sierra Ct Dublin CA 94568 925-829-6000 829-6033
Web: www.delmonteelectric.com

Divane Bros Electric Co 2424 Rose St Franklin Park IL 60131 847-455-7143 455-7899
Web: www.divanebros.com

Dorey Electric Co PO Box 10158 Norfolk VA 23513 757-855-3381
Web: www.doreyelectric.com

Ducci Electrical Contractors Inc
427 Goshen Rd Torrington CT 06790 860-489-9267 489-7980
Web: duccielectrical.com

Dycom Industries Inc
11770 US Hwy 1 Ste 101 Palm Beach Gardens FL 33408 561-627-7171 627-7709
NYSE: DY ■ *Web:* www.dycomind.com

Dynalectric Corp 4462 Corporate Ctr Dr Los Alamitos CA 90720 714-828-7000 890-7794*
**Fax Area Code:* 866 ■ **Fax:* Acctg ■ *TF:* 866-890-7794 ■ *Web:* www.kdc-systems.com

E-J Electric Installation Co
46-41 Vernon Blvd Long Island City NY 11101 718-786-9400 937-9120
Web: www.ej1899.com

EC Co PO Box 10286 Portland OR 97296 800-659-3511 241-0807*
**Fax Area Code:* 503 ■ *TF:* 800-462-3370 ■ *Web:* www.e-c-co.com

EC Ernst Inc 132 Log Canoe Cir Stevensville MD 21666 301-350-7770 499-0933
TF: 800-683-7770 ■ *Web:* www.ecernst.com

Edwin L Heim Co 1918 Greenwood St Harrisburg PA 17104 717-233-8711 233-8619
TF: 800-692-7316 ■ *Web:* www.elheim.com

Egizii Electric Inc (EEI)
700 N MacArthur Blvd Springfield IL 62702 217-528-4001 528-1677

ElDeCo Inc 5751 Augusta Rd Greenville SC 29605 864-277-9088 277-2811
Web: www.eldecoinc.com

Electric Resource Contractors Inc
4024 Washington Ave N Minneapolis MN 55412 612-522-6511
Web: eganco.com/

Electrical Contractors Inc 3510 Main St Hartford CT 06120 860-549-2822 549-7948
Web: www.ecincorporated.com

Electrical Corp of America
7320 Arlington Ave Raytown MO 64133 816-737-3206 356-0731
Web: www.ecahq.com

Electronic Contracting Co PO Box 29195 Lincoln NE 68529 402-466-8274 466-0819
TF: 800-366-5320 ■ *Web:* www.eccoinc.com

EMCOR Construction Services Inc
1420 Spring Hill Rd Ste 500 McLean VA 22102 703-556-8000 556-0890
Web: www.emcorgroup.com

EMCOR Group Inc 301 Merritt 7 Sixth Fl Norwalk CT 06851 203-849-7800 849-7900
NYSE: EME ■ *TF:* 866-890-7794 ■ *Web:* www.emcorgroup.com

EMCOR Hyre Electric Co 2655 Garfield Ave Highland IN 46322 219-923-6100 838-3631
Web: www.emcorhyre.com

Engineered Protection Systems Inc
750 Front Ave NW Ste 300 Grand Rapids MI 49504 616-459-0281 459-0553
TF: 800-966-9199 ■ *Web:* www.epssecurity.com

Enterprise Electric Co 4204 Shannon Dr Baltimore MD 21213 410-488-8200 488-6639
Web: www.eecompany.com

Ermco Inc 1625 W Thompson Rd Indianapolis IN 46217 317-780-2923 780-2853
Web: www.ermco.com

Ferndale Electric Company Inc
915 E Drayton Ave Ferndale MI 48220 248-545-4404 545-8140
Web: www.ferndale-electric.com

Ferran Services & Contracting 530 Grand St Orlando FL 32805 407-422-3551 648-0961
Web: www.ferran-services.com

Fisk Electric Co 111 TC Jester Blvd Houston TX 77007 713-868-6111 880-2918
Web: www.fiskcorp.com

Forest Electric Corp Two Penn Plz Fourth Fl New York NY 10121 212-318-1500 318-1518
Web: www.forestelectric.net

Foshay Electric Company Inc
7676 Engineer Rd San Diego CA 92111 858-277-7676 277-2629
Web: www.foshayelectric.com

Fox Electric Ltd 1104 Colorado Ln Arlington TX 76015 817-461-2571 261-7311
Web: www.foxelectric.com

Fox Valley Fire & Safety Company Inc
2730 Pinnacle Dr Elgin IL 60124 847-695-5990 695-3699
Web: www.foxvalleyfire.com

G & M Electrical Contractors Co
1746 N Richmond St Chicago IL 60647 773-278-8200 278-8038
Web: www.gm-electric.com

Gardner-Zemke Company Inc
6100 Indian School Rd NE Albuquerque NM 87110 505-881-0555
Web: gardnerzemke.com

Gaylor Electric
5750 Castle Creek Pkwy N Dr Ste 400 Indianapolis IN 46250 317-843-0577 848-0364
TF: 800-878-0577 ■ *Web:* www.gaylor.com

GEM Inc 6842 Commodore Dr Walbridge OH 43465 419-666-6554 666-7004
TF General: 866-720-2700 ■ *Web:* www.gemindustrial.com

Gibson Electric Company Inc
3100 Woodcreek Dr Downers Grove IL 60515 630-288-3800 743-2100
Web: www.gibsonelec.com

Gill-Simpson Inc 11620 Red Run Blvd Reisterstown MD 21136 410-467-3335 366-4557

Goldfield Corp 1684 W Hibiscus Blvd Melbourne FL 32901 321-724-1700 724-1163
NYSE: GV ■ *Web:* www.goldfieldcorp.com

GR Sponaugle & Sons Inc
4391 Chambers Hill Rd Harrisburg PA 17111 717-564-1515 564-3675
Web: www.grsponaugle.com

Grand-Kahn Electric (GK) 2455 W Grand Ave Chicago IL 60612 312-298-1500 298-1501
Web: www.grandkahn.com

Company / Address	City	State	ZIP	Phone	Fax
Gregory Electric Company Inc					
2124 College St	Columbia	SC	29205	803-748-1122	748-1102
Web: www.gregoryelectric.com					
GSL Electric 8540 S Sandy Pkwy	Sandy	UT	84070	801-565-0088	565-0099
Web: www.gslelectric.com					
Guarantee Electrical Co 3405 Bent Ave	Saint Louis	MO	63116	314-772-5400	772-9261
TF General: 800-854-4326 ■ *Web:* www.geco.com					
Gulf Electric Company Inc of Mobile					
PO Box 2385	Mobile	AL	36652	251-666-0654	666-6323
Web: www.gulfelec.com					
H & H Group Inc 2801 Syene Rd	Madison	WI	53713	608-273-3434	273-9654
Web: www.hhindustries.com					
Hargrove Electric Company Inc					
1522 Market Ctr Blvd	Dallas	TX	75207	214-742-8665	744-0846
Web: www.hargroveelectric.com					
Harlan Electric Co 2695 Crooks Rd	Rochester Hills	MI	48309	248-853-4601	853-4603
Web: www.myrgroup.com					
Hatzel & Buehler Inc 3600 Silverside Rd	Wilmington	DE	19803	302-478-4200	478-2750
Web: www.hatzelandbuehler.com					
HB Frazer Co 514 Shoemaker Rd.	King of Prussia	PA	19406	610-768-0400	992-5070
Web: hbfrazer.com					
Hi-Tech Electric Inc					
11116 W Little York Rd Bldg 8	Houston	TX	77041	832-243-0345	467-0132
Web: www.hitechelectric.com					
Highlines Construction Company Inc					
701 Bridge City Ave PO Box 408	Westwego	LA	70096	504-436-3961	436-4939
Web: www.highlines.com					
Hilscher Clarke Electric Co 519 Fourth St NW	Canton	OH	44703	330-452-9806	452-5867
Web: www.hilscher-clarke.com					
Honshy Electric Company Inc 7345 SW 41st St	Miami	FL	33155	305-264-5500	266-3159
Web: www.honshyelectric.com					
Hooper Corp 2030 Pennsylvania Ave	Madison	WI	53704	608-249-0451	249-7360
TF: 800-242-8511 ■ *Web:* www.hoopercorp.com					
Howe Electric Inc 4682 E Olive Ave	Fresno	CA	93702	559-255-8992	255-9745
Web: www.howe-electric.com					
Hunt Electric Corp 2300 Territorial Rd.	Saint Paul	MN	55114	651-646-2911	643-6575
Web: www.huntelec.com					
Industrial Contractors Inc 701 Ch Dr	Bismarck	ND	58501	701-258-9908	258-9988
TF: 800-467-3089 ■ *Web:* www.icinorthdakota.com					
Industrial Power & Lighting Corp					
701 Seneca St Ste 500	Buffalo	NY	14210	716-854-1811	854-1828
TF: 800-639-3702 ■ *Web:* www.iplcorp.com					
Industrial Specialty Contractors LLC					
20480 Highland Rd	Baton Rouge	LA	70817	225-756-8001	
Web: www.iscgrp.com					
Inglett & Stubbs LLC 5200 Riverview Rd	Mableton	GA	30126	404-881-1199	872-3101
Web: www.inglett-stubbs.com					
Integrated Electrical Services Inc (IES)					
5433 Westheimer Rd Ste 500	Houston	TX	77056	713-860-1500	
NASDAQ: IESC ■ *Web:* ies-corporate.com					
Intermountain Electric Inc (IME)					
5050 Osage St Ste 500	Denver	CO	80221	303-733-7248	722-2410
Web: imelect.com					
Interstates Construction Services Inc					
1520 N Main Ave	Sioux Center	IA	51250	712-722-1662	722-1667
TF: 800-827-1662 ■ *Web:* www.interstates.com					
J & M Brown Company Inc					
267 Amory St PO Box 300227	Jamaica Plain	MA	02130	617-522-6800	522-6422
Web: www.jmbco.com					
JF Electric Inc					
100 Lakefront Pkwy PO Box 570	Edwardsville	IL	62025	618-797-5353	797-5354
Web: www.jfelectric.com					
John A Penney Company Inc 270 Sidney St	Cambridge	MA	02139	617-547-7744	547-4332
Jordano Electric Company Inc					
200 Hudson St	Hackensack	NJ	07601	201-489-4800	489-5071
Web: www.jordanoelectric.com					
Kearney Electric Inc 3609 E Superior Ave	Phoenix	AZ	85040	602-437-0235	437-2914
Web: www.kearneyaz.com					
Kelso-Burnett Co 5200 Newport Dr	Rolling Meadows	IL	60008	847-259-0720	259-0839
Web: www.kelso-burnett.com					
Kirby Electric Inc 415 Northgate D	Warrendale	PA	15086	724-772-1800	772-2227
Web: www.kirbyelectricinc.com					
Kleinknecht Electric Company Inc					
252 W 37th St Ninth Fl	New York	NY	10018	212-728-1800	
Web: www.kecny.com					
Koontz-Wagner Electric Company Inc					
3801 Voorde Dr	South Bend	IN	46628	574-232-2051	288-8510
TF: 800-345-2051 ■ *Web:* www.koontz-wagner.com					
Lake Erie Electric Inc 25730 First St	Westlake	OH	44145	440-835-5565	835-5688
Web: www.lakeerieelectric.com					
Linder & Assoc Inc 840 N Main St PO Box 1202	Wichita	KS	67201	316-265-1616	265-8097
Web: www.linderandassociates.com					
LK Comstock & Company Inc					
Five Penn Plz 12th Fl	New York	NY	10001	212-502-7900	502-1865
Web: www.railworks.com					
Ludvik Electric Co 3900 S Teller St	Lakewood	CO	80235	303-781-9601	783-6349
Web: www.ludvik.com					
Marathon Electrical Contractors Inc					
PO Box 320067	Birmingham	AL	35222	205-323-8500	
Web: www.marathonelectrical.com					
Marrs Electric Inc PO Box 690296	Tulsa	OK	74169	918-437-5802	438-3563
Web: www.marrselectric.com					
Matco Electric Corp 320 N Jensen Rd	Vestal	NY	13850	607-729-4921	729-0932
Web: www.matcoelectric.com					
Mayers Electric Company Inc 4004 Erie Ct	Cincinnati	OH	45227	513-272-2900	272-2904
Web: www.mayerselectric.com					
Meade Electric Company Inc					
9550 W 55th St Ste A	Countryside	IL	60525	708-588-2500	588-2501
Web: www.meadeelectric.com					
Meisner Electric Inc 220 NE First St	Delray Beach	FL	33444	561-278-8362	278-8397
Web: www.mei.cc					
Merit Electric Company Inc 6520 125th Ave N	Largo	FL	33773	727-536-5945	536-9014
TF: 800-330-5945 ■ *Web:* www.meritelectricco.com					
Merit Electrical Inc 17723 Airline Hwy	Prairieville	LA	70769	225-673-8850	673-8838
Web: www.meritelectrical.com					
Metropower Inc PO Box 5228	Albany	GA	31706	229-432-7345	436-3869
Web: www.metropower.com					
Mid-City Electrical Construction					
1099 Sullivant Ave	Columbus	OH	43223	614-221-5153	221-2225
Web: www.midcityelectric.com					
Miller Electric Co 2251 Rosselle St	Jacksonville	FL	32204	904-513-2818	389-8653
TF Sales: 877-540-2160 ■ *Web:* www.mecojax.com					
Miller Engineering Co 1616 S Main St	Rockford	IL	61102	815-963-4878	963-0823
Web: mecogroup.com					
MJ Electric Inc PO Box 686	Iron Mountain	MI	49801	906-774-8000	779-4217
Web: www.mjelectric.com					
MMR Group Inc 15961 Airline Hwy	Baton Rouge	LA	70817	225-756-5090	753-7012
TF: 800-880-5090 ■ *Web:* www.mmrgrp.com					
Mojave Electric Inc 3755 W Hacienda Ave	Las Vegas	NV	89118	702-798-2970	798-3740
Mona Electric Group Inc					
7915 Malcolm Rd Ste 102	Clinton	MD	20735	301-868-8400	868-4178
Web: www.getmona.com					
Morrow-Meadows Corp 231 Benton Ct	City of Industry	CA	91789	909-598-7700	598-3907
Web: www.morrow-meadows.com					
Morse Electric Inc 500 W S St	Freeport	IL	61032	815-266-4200	266-8900
Web: www.themorsegroup.com					
Motor City Electric Co 9440 Grinnell St	Detroit	MI	48213	313-921-5300	921-5310
Web: www.mceco.com					
Msf Electric Inc 10455 Fountaingate Dr	Stafford	TX	77477	281-494-4700	
TF: 866-366-7943 ■ *Web:* www.msfelectric.com					
Muska Electric Co 1985 Oakcrest Ave	Roseville	MN	55113	651-636-5820	636-0916
Web: www.muskaelectric.com					
Muth Electric Inc 1717 N Sanborn PO Box 1400	Mitchell	SD	57301	605-996-3983	996-2203
TF: 800-888-1597 ■ *Web:* www.muthelectric.com					
Mutual Telecom Services Inc					
250 First Ave Ste 301	Needham	MA	02494	800-687-2848	449-1996*
**Fax Area Code: 781* ■ *TF:* 800-687-2848 ■ *Web:* www.blackbox.com					
MYR Group					
1701 W Golf Rd Twr 3 Ste 1012	Rolling Meadows	IL	60008	847-290-1891	290-1892
Web: www.myrgroup.com					
Netsville Inc 72 Cascade Dr	Rochester	NY	14614	585-232-5670	232-4512
TF: 888-638-7845 ■ *Web:* www.netsville.com					
Network Infrastructure Corp					
8945 S Harl Ave Ste 102	Tempe	AZ	85284	480-850-5050	
TF: 866-456-4422 ■ *Web:* www.us.logicalis.com					
New Com Electric 4035 Flossmoor St	Las Vegas	NV	89115	702-876-1116	
Newtron Group, The 8183 W El Cajon Dr	Baton Rouge	LA	70815	225-927-8921	
Web: www.thenewtrongroup.com					
O'Connell Electric Co 830 Phillips Rd	Victor	NY	14564	585-924-2176	924-4973
Web: www.oconnellelectric.com					
Operational Security Systems Inc					
1231 Collier Rd NW Ste D	Atlanta	GA	30318	404-352-0025	350-0815
Web: www.ossatl.com					
Palmer Electric & Showcase Lighting					
875 Jackson Ave	Winter Park	FL	32789	407-646-8700	647-8951
Web: www.palmer-electric.com					
Parsons Electric LLC 5960 Main St NE	Minneapolis	MN	55432	763-571-8000	571-7210
TF: 800-403-4832					
PayneCrest Electric & Communications					
10411 Baur Blvd	Saint Louis	MO	63132	314-996-0400	996-0500
Web: www.payneelectric.com					
Peoples Electric Company Inc					
277 E Fillmore Ave	Saint Paul	MN	55107	651-227-7711	
Web: www.peoplesco.com					
Perlectric 2711 Prosperity Ave	Fairfax	VA	22031	703-352-5151	352-5155
Web: perlectric.com					
Perreca Electric Co 520 Broadway	Newburgh	NY	12550	845-562-4080	562-0801
TF: 800-973-7732 ■ *Web:* www.perreca.com					
Phillips Bros Electrical Contractors Inc					
235 Sweet Spring Rd	Glenmoore	PA	19343	610-458-8578	458-8438
TF: 800-220-5051 ■ *Web:* www.philipsbrothers.com					
Pieper Electric Inc 5070 N 35th St	Milwaukee	WI	53209	414-462-7700	462-7711
TF: 800-424-8802 ■ *Web:* www.pieperpower.com					
Pike Electric Corp 100 Pike Way PO Box 868	Mount Airy	NC	27030	336-789-2171	
NYSE: PIKE ■ *TF:* 800-424-7453 ■ *Web:* www.pikeelectric.com					
Power City Electric Inc 3327 E Olive Ave	Spokane	WA	99202	509-535-8500	535-4665
Web: www.powercityelectric.com					
Premier Electrical Corp					
4401 85th Ave N	Brooklyn Park	MN	55443	763-424-6551	424-5225
Web: www.premiercorp.net					
Pritchard Electric Company Inc					
2425 Eigth Ave	Huntington	WV	25703	304-529-2566	529-2567
Web: www.pritchardelectric.com					
R K Electric Inc 42021 Osgood Rd	Fremont	CA	94539	510-770-5660	770-5684
TF: 800-400-4418 ■ *Web:* www.rkelectric.com					
R2W Inc 5957 McLeod Dr	Las Vegas	NV	89120	702-434-6500	
Web: www.r2west.com					
Ready Electric Company Inc					
3300 Gilmore Industrial Blvd	Louisville	KY	40213	502-893-2511	893-2519
Web: www.readyelec.com					
Rex Moore Electrical Contractors & Engineers					
6001 Outfall Cir	Sacramento	CA	95828	916-372-1300	372-4013
TF: 800-266-1922 ■ *Web:* www.rexmoore.com					
RFI Communications & Security Systems					
360 Turtle Creek Ct	San Jose	CA	95125	408-298-5400	882-4401
TF: 800-341-9292 ■ *Web:* www.rfi.com					
Riggs Distler Company Inc					
9411 Philadelphia Rd Ste M	Baltimore	MD	21237	410-633-0300	633-2119
Web: www.riggsdistler.com					
Roman Electric Company Inc 640 S 70th St	Milwaukee	WI	53214	414-771-5400	471-8693
Web: www.romanelectric.com					
Romanoff Electric Company LLC					
5570 Enterprise Blvd	Toledo	OH	43612	419-726-2627	726-5406
Web: quebe.com					
Rosendin Electric Inc 880 N Mabury Rd	San Jose	CA	95133	408-286-2800	793-5001*
**Fax: Hum Res* ■ *TF General:* 800-540-4734 ■ *Web:* www.rosendin.com					

Company / Address	City	State	ZIP	Phone	Fax
Rydalch Electric Inc 250 Plymouth Ave *Web:* www.rydalchelectric.com	Salt Lake City	UT	84115	801-265-1813	265-2166
Salem Electric Company Inc 3933 Westpoint Blvd PO Box 26784 *Web:* www.salemelectriccoinc.com	Winston-Salem	NC	27114	336-765-0221	765-7286
SASCO Electric 2750 Moore Ave *Web:* www.sasco.com	Fullerton	CA	92833	714-870-0217	738-3571
Schenectady Hardware & Electric Company Inc PO Box 338 *Web:* www.sheinc.com	Schenectady	NY	12301	518-346-2369	372-7549
Schmidt Electric Coy L P 9701 FM 1625 *Web:* www.schmidt-electric.com	Austin	TX	78747	512-243-1450	243-0601
Sesco Lighting Inc 1133 W Morse Blvd Ste 100 *Web:* www.sescolighting.com	Winter Park	FL	32789	407-629-6100	629-6168
Shambaugh & Son LP 7614 Opportunity Dr *TF:* 866-890-7794 ■ *Web:* www.shambaugh.com	Fort Wayne	IN	46825	260-487-7777	487-7701
Shaw Electric Co 22100 Telegraph Rd *Web:* www.shawelectric.com	Southfield	MI	48033	248-228-2000	228-2080
Shawver & Son Inc 144 NE 44th St *TF:* 800-320-5121 ■ *Web:* www.shawver.net	Oklahoma City	OK	73105	405-525-9451	525-6136
Shelley Electric Inc 3619 W 29th St S *Web:* www.shelleyelectric.com	Wichita	KS	67217	316-945-8311	
Smith & Keene Electric Service Inc 833 Live Oak Dr *Web:* www.smithandkeene.com	Chesapeake	VA	23320	757-420-1231	420-5340
Southern Air Inc 2655 Lakeside Dr *TF:* 800-743-1214 ■ *Web:* www.southern-air.com	Lynchburg	VA	24501	434-385-6200	385-9081
Spg Solar Inc 1039 N McDowell Blvd *Web:* www.spgsolar.com	Petaluma	CA	94954	415-883-7657	
Sprig Electric Co 1860 S Tenth St *Web:* www.sprigelectric.com	San Jose	CA	95112	408-298-3134	298-2132
Staff Electric Company Inc W 133 N 5030 Campbell Dr *Web:* staffelectric.com	Menomonee Falls	WI	53051	262-781-8230	781-1680
Staley Inc 8101 Fourche Rd *TF:* 877-616-0661 ■ *Web:* www.staleyinc.com	Little Rock	AR	72209	501-565-3006	565-9674
Starr Electric Company Inc Six Battleground Ct *Web:* www.starrelectric.net	Greensboro	NC	27408	336-275-0241	273-0734
Steiny & Company Inc 221 N Ardmore Ave PO Box 74901 *Web:* www.steinyco.com	Los Angeles	CA	90004	213-382-2331	381-6781
Stoner Electric Inc 1904 SE Ochoco St *Web:* www.stonergroup.com	Milwaukie	OR	97222	503-462-6500	659-4968
Sturgeon Electric Company Inc 12150 E 112th Ave *Web:* www.myrgroup.com	Henderson	CO	80640	303-286-8000	
Sunwest Electric Inc 3064 E Miraloma Ave *Web:* www.sunwestelectric.net	Anaheim	CA	92806	714-630-8700	630-8740
Super Electric Construction Co 4300 W Chicago Ave *Web:* www.superelec.com	Chicago	IL	60651	773-489-4400	235-1455
System Electric Co 1278 Montalvo Way *Web:* www.systemelectric.com	Palm Springs	CA	92262	760-327-7847	323-7247
T & J Electrical Corp 636 Second Ave *Web:* www.tandjelectric.com	Troy	NY	12182	518-237-1893	237-3195
Taft Electric Co 1694 Eastman Ave *Web:* taftelectric.com	Ventura	CA	93003	805-642-0121	644-6488
TEC Corp 2300 Seventh St *Web:* www.tec-corp.com	Sioux City	IA	51105	712-252-4275	
Teknon Corp 15443 NE 95th St *TF:* 800-338-6142 ■ *Web:* www.teknon.com	Redmond	WA	98052	425-895-8535	895-0535
Tennessee Associated Electric 7511 Taggart Ln *Web:* www.tn-associated.com	Knoxville	TN	37938	865-524-3686	522-1553
Terry's Electric Inc 600 N Thacker Ave Ste A *Web:* www.terryselectric.com	Kissimmee	FL	34741	407-572-2100	846-6607
Totem Electric of Tacoma Inc 2332 Jefferson Ave *Web:* www.totemelectric.com	Tacoma	WA	98402	253-383-5022	272-5214
Tri-City Electrical Contractors Inc 430 W Dr *TF:* 800-768-2489 ■ *Web:* tcelectric.com	Altamonte Springs	FL	32714	407-788-3500	682-7353
Triangle Electric Co 29787 Stephenson Hwy *Web:* www.trielec.com	Madison Heights	MI	48071	248-399-2200	399-2612
Van Ert Electric Company Inc 7019 Stewart Ave *Web:* www.vanert.com	Wausau	WI	54401	715-845-4308	848-3671
Vaughn Industries LLC 1201 E Findlay St *Web:* www.vaughnindustries.com	Carey	OH	43316	419-396-3900	
WA Chester LLC 4390 Parliament Pl Ste Q *Web:* wachester.com	Lanham	MD	20706	240-487-1940	487-1941
Wasatch Electric 2455 W 1500 S Ste A *Web:* www.wasatchelectric.com	Salt Lake City	UT	84104	801-487-4511	487-5032
Watson Electrical 1500 Charleston St *Web:* www.watsonelec.com	Wilson	NC	27893	252-237-7511	243-1607
Wayne J Griffin Electric Inc 116 Hopping Brook Rd *Fax Area Code: 508 ■ *TF:* 800-421-0151 ■ *Web:* www.waynejgriffin.com	Holliston	MA	01746	800-421-0151	429-7825*
Wellington Power Corp 40th & Butler Sts *TF:* 800-540-0017 ■ *Web:* www.wellingtonpower.com	Pittsburgh	PA	15201	412-681-0103	681-0109
Welsbach Electric Corp 111-01 14th Ave *TF:* 866-890-7794 ■ *Web:* www.welsbachelectric.com	College Point	NY	11356	718-670-7900	670-7999
West-Fair Electric Contractors Inc 200 Brady Ave *Web:* www.west-fair.com	Hawthorne	NY	10532	914-769-8050	769-7451
White Electrical Construction Co 1730 Chattahoochee Ave *TF:* 888-519-4483 ■ *Web:* white-electrical.com	Atlanta	GA	30318	404-351-5740	355-5823
Williard Limbach 175 Titus Ave Ste 100 *Fax: Cust Svc ■ *Web:* www.limbachinc.com	Warrington	PA	18976	215-488-9700	488-9699*
York River Electric Inc 108 Production Dr *Web:* www.yorkriverelectric.com	Yorktown	VA	23693	757-369-3673	369-3680
Zwicker Electrical Company Inc 360 Pk Ave S Fourth Fl *Web:* www.zwicker-electric.com	New York	NY	10010	212-477-8400	995-8469

192-5 Excavation Contractors

Company / Address	City	State	ZIP	Phone	Fax
Allied Contractors Inc 204 E Preston St *Web:* alliedcontractor.com	Baltimore	MD	21202	410-539-6727	332-4594
Aman Environmental Construction Inc 614 E Edna Pl *Web:* www.amanenvironmental.com	Covina	CA	91723	626-967-4287	332-1877
Anastasi Trucking & Paving Inc 4430 Walden St *Web:* www.anastasitrucking.com	Lancaster	NY	14086	716-683-5003	683-5045
Andrews Excavating Inc Five W Willow Rd *Web:* andrewsexcavating.com	Willow Street	PA	17584	717-464-3329	464-4963
B & B Wrecking & Excavating Inc 4510 E 71st St Ste 6 *Web:* www.bbwrecking.net	Cleveland	OH	44105	216-429-1700	429-1717
Barnard Construction Company Inc PO Box 99 *Web:* www.barnard-inc.com	Bozeman	MT	59771	406-586-1995	586-3530
Berkel & Co Contractors Inc PO Box 335 *Web:* www.berkelandcompany.com	Bonner Springs	KS	66012	913-422-5125	441-0402
Bi-Con Services Inc 10901 Clay Pike Rd *Web:* www.biconservices.com/	Derwent	OH	43733	740-685-2542	685-3863
Borderland Construction Company Inc 400 E 38 St *Web:* borderland-inc.com	Tucson	AZ	85713	520-623-0900	623-0232
BR Kreider & Son Inc 63 Kreider Ln *TF:* 800-689-7651 ■ *Web:* www.brkreider.com	Manheim	PA	17545	717-898-7651	569-8074
Carl Bolander & Sons Company Inc 251 Starkey St *Web:* www.bolander.com	Saint Paul	MN	55107	651-224-6299	223-8197
Case Foundation Co 1325 W Lake St *Web:* www.casefoundation.com	Roselle	IL	60172	630-529-2911	529-2995
CP Ward Inc PO Box 900 *Web:* www.cpward.com	Scottsville	NY	14546	585-889-8800	889-6008
Daisy Construction Company Inc 3120 New Castle Ave *Web:* www.daisyconstruction.com	New Castle	DE	19720	302-658-4417	658-0618
Dywidag Systems International 320 Marmon Dr *TF:* 800-457-7633 ■ *Web:* www.dywidag-systems.com	Bolingbrook	IL	60440	630-739-1100	739-5517
Feutz Contractors Inc 1120 N Main St PO Box 130 *Web:* www.feutzcontractors.com	Paris	IL	61944	217-465-8402	463-2256
Foundation Constructors Inc 81 Big Break Rd PO Box 97 *TF:* 800-841-8740 ■ *Web:* www.foundationpiledriving.com	Oakley	CA	94561	925-754-6633	625-5783
Francis O Day Construction Company Inc 850 E Gude Dr *Web:* www.foday.com	Rockville	MD	20850	301-652-2400	340-6592
Geo-Con Inc 4075 Monroeville Blvd Ste 400 Bldg 2 *Web:* www.geocon.net	Monroeville	PA	15146	412-856-7700	373-3357
George J Igel & Company Inc 2040 Alum Creek Dr *Web:* www.igelco.com	Columbus	OH	43207	614-445-8421	445-8205
Harry C. Crooker & Sons Inc PO Box 5001 *Web:* www.crooker.com	Topsham	ME	04086	207-729-5511	725-4025
Hayward Baker Inc 1130 Annapolis Rd Ste 202 *TF:* 800-456-6548 ■ *Web:* www.haywardbaker.com	Odenton	MD	21113	410-551-8200	551-1900
HT Sweeney & Son Inc 308 Dutton Mill Rd *Web:* htsweeney.com	Brookhaven	PA	19015	610-872-8896	874-6730
Independence Excavating Inc 5720 Schaaf Rd *TF:* 800-524-3478 ■ *Web:* www.indexc.com	Independence	OH	44131	216-524-1700	524-1701
J Fletcher Creamer & Son Inc 101 E Broadway *TF:* 800-835-9801 ■ *Web:* www.jfcson.com	Hackensack	NJ	07601	201-488-9800	488-2901
Kamminga & Roodvoets Inc 3435 Broadmoor Ave SE	Grand Rapids	MI	49512	616-949-0800	949-1894
Luburgh Inc 4174 E Pk	Zanesville	OH	43701	740-452-3668	454-7225
M Rondano Inc 49 E Ave *Web:* www.rondano.com	Norwalk	CT	06851	203-846-1577	846-9564
Manafort Bros Inc 414 New Britain Ave *TF:* 888-626-2367 ■ *Web:* www.manafort.com	Plainville	CT	06062	860-229-4853	747-4861
Markham Contracting Company Inc 22820 N 19th Ave *Web:* www.markhamcontracting.com	Phoenix	AZ	85027	623-869-9100	869-9400
McAninch Corp 4001 Delaware Ave Ste 125 *Web:* www.mcaninchcorp.com	West Des Moines	IA	50266	515-267-2500	267-2550
McGowan-Stauffer Inc 1400 Stn St *Web:* www.mcgowan-stauffer.com	Coraopolis	PA	15108	412-264-3500	264-3200
Merlyn Contractors Inc PO Box 917 *Web:* www.merlyn.us	Novi	MI	48376	248-349-3800	347-2966
Moretrench American Corp 100 Stickle Ave PO Box 316 *TF:* 800-394-6673 ■ *Web:* www.moretrench.com	Rockaway	NJ	07866	973-627-2100	627-3950
Nicholson Construction Co 12 McClane St *TF:* 800-388-2340 ■ *Web:* www.nicholsonconstruction.com	Cuddy	PA	15031	412-221-4500	221-3127
Noralco Corp 1920 Lincoln Rd *Web:* www.noralco.com	Pittsburgh	PA	15235	412-361-6678	361-6535
Oldcastle Materials Inc 900 Ashwood Pkwy Ste 700 *Web:* www.apac.com	Atlanta	GA	30338	770-522-5600	522-5608

Phone Fax

Ortiz Enterprises Inc Six Cushing Way Ste 200 Irvine CA 92618 949-753-1414 753-1477
Web: www.ortizent.com

Park Construction Company Inc
1481 81st Ave NE Minneapolis MN 55432 763-786-9800 786-2952
Web: www.parkconstructionco.com

Pavex Inc 4400 Gettysburg Rd Camp Hill PA 17011 717-761-1502 761-0329
Web: pavexinc.com

Perry Engineering Company Inc
1945 Millwood Pk Winchester VA 22602 540-667-4310 667-7618
Web: www.perryeng.com

Phillips & Jordan Inc 6621 Wilbanks Rd Knoxville TN 37912 865-688-8342 688-8369
TF: 800-955-0876 ■ *Web:* www.pandj.com

Pleasant Excavating Co Inc
24024 Frederick Rd Ste 200 Clarksburg MD 20871 301-428-0800 428-3922
TF: 800-842-1180 ■ *Web:* pleasantsconstruction.com

PT Ferro Construction Co 700 Rowell Ave Joliet IL 60433 815-726-6284 726-5614
Web: www.ptferro.com

Raymond Excavating Co Inc
800 Gratiot Blvd Marysville MI 48040 810-364-6881 364-2930
TF: 800-837-6770 ■ *Web:* www.raymondexcavating.com

Richard Goettle Inc 12071 Hamilton Ave Cincinnati OH 45231 513-825-8100 825-8107
Web: www.goettle.com

Ruttura & Sons Construction Co Inc
200 Cabot St West Babylon NY 11704 631-454-0291 454-8804
Web: www.ruttura.com

Ryan Inc Central 2700 E Racine St Janesville WI 53545 608-754-2291 754-3290
Web: www.ryancentral.com

Seubert Excavators Inc 604 King St Cottonwood ID 83522 208-962-3501

Shoosmith Bros Inc 11800 Lewis Rd Chester VA 23831 804-748-5823 748-8482
Web: www.shoosmith.com

Sierrita Mining & Ranching Company Inc
9333 White Hills Loop Sahuarita AZ 85629 520-625-1204

Soil Engineering Construction Inc
927 Arguello St Redwood City CA 94063 650-367-9595 367-8139
Web: soilengineeringconstruction.com

Stroer & Graff Inc 1830 Phillips Ln Antioch CA 94509 925-778-0200 778-6766

Subsurface Constructors Inc
110 Angelica St Saint Louis MO 63147 314-421-2460 421-2479
Web: www.subsurfaceconstructors.com

Super Excavators Inc
N 59 W 14601 Bobolink Ave Menomonee Falls WI 53051 262-252-3200 252-8079
Web: www.superexcavators.com

Terra Engineering & Construction Corp
2201 Vondron Rd Madison WI 53718 608-221-3501 221-4075
Web: whyterra.com

TJ Lambrecht Construction Inc 10 Gougar Rd Joliet IL 60432 815-726-7722 727-6421

Union Engineering Company Inc
3658 N Ventura Ave Ventura CA 93001 805-648-3373

Urban Foundation/Engineering LLC
32-33 111th St East Elmhurst NY 11369 718-478-3021 899-4967
TF: 800-843-6664 ■ *Web:* www.dfi.org

Velting Contractors Inc 3060 Breton Rd SE Kentwood MI 49512 616-949-6660 949-8168
Web: www.velting.com

192-6 Glass & Glazing Contractors

Phone Fax

Benson Industries LLC
1650 NW Naito Pkwy Ste 250 Portland OR 97209 503-226-7611 226-0070
TF: 800-999-5113 ■ *Web:* www.bensonglobal.com

Cartner Glass Systems Inc
2508 Westinghouse Blvd Charlotte NC 28273 704-588-1976 588-9440

Culbertson Enterprises Inc (CEI)
600A Snyder Ave West Chester PA 19382 610-436-6400
TF: 800-382-2685

Enclos Corp 2770 Blue Water Rd Eagan MN 55121 651-796-6100 994-6360
TF: 888-234-2966 ■ *Web:* www.enclos.com

General Glass Company Inc
5797 MacCorkle Ave SE Charleston WV 25304 304-925-2171 925-8915

Giroux Glass Inc 850 W Washington Blvd Los Angeles CA 90015 213-747-7406 747-8778
TF: 800-684-5277 ■ *Web:* www.girouxglass.com

Karas & Karas Glass Company Inc
455 Dorchester Ave Boston MA 02127 617-268-8800 269-0536
TF: 800-888-1235 ■ *Web:* www.karasglass.com

Lafayette Glass Company Inc 2841 Teal Rd Lafayette IN 47905 765-474-1402 474-3382
Web: www.lafayetteglass.com

Lee & Cates Glass Inc 5355 Shawland Rd Jacksonville FL 32254 904-358-8555 358-8777
TF: 888-844-1989 ■ *Web:* www.leeandcatesglass.com

Lynbrook Glass & Architectural Metals Corp
941 Motor Pkwy Hauppauge NY 11788 631-582-3060 582-3974
Web: www.lynbrookglass.com

Masonry Arts Inc 2105 Third Ave N Bessemer AL 35020 205-428-0780
Web: www.masonryarts.com

National Glass & Metal Company Inc
1424 Easton Rd Ste 400 Horsham PA 19044 215-938-8880 938-7028
Web: www.ngmco.com

Sashco Inc 720 S Rochester Ave Ste D Ontario CA 91761 909-937-8222 937-8223
TF: 800-600-3232 ■ *Web:* www.sashcoinc.com

Sound Glass Sales Inc 5501 75th St W Tacoma WA 98499 253-473-7477 473-0849
TF: 800-468-9949 ■ *Web:* www.soundglass.com

Waltek & Company Ltd 2130 Waycorss Rd Cincinnati OH 45240 513-577-7980 577-7990
Web: www.walteklted.com

Walters & Wolf 41450 Boscell Rd Fremont CA 94538 510-490-1115 651-7172
Web: www.waltersandwolf.com

192-7 Masonry & Stone Contractors

Phone Fax

Brisk Waterproofing Company Inc
720 Grand Ave Ridgefield NJ 07657 201-945-0210 945-7841
TF: 800-325-2801 ■ *Web:* www.briskwaterproofing.com

Bruns-Gutzwiller Inc 305 John St Batesville IN 47006 812-934-2105 934-2107
Web: www.bruns-gutzwiller.com

Caretti Inc
4590 Industrial Pk Rd PO Box 331 Camp Hill PA 17011 717-737-6759 737-6880
Web: www.carettimasonry.com

Culbertson Enterprises Inc (CEI)
600A Snyder Ave West Chester PA 19382 610-436-6400
TF: 800-382-2685

Dee Brown Inc (DBI)
4101 S Shiloh Rd PO Box 570335 Dallas TX 75357 214-321-6443 328-1039*
**Fax:* Tech Supp ■ *Web:* www.deebrowncompanies.com

Design Masonry Inc
20703 Santa Clara St Canyon Country CA 91351 661-298-1013 298-0117
Web: www.designmasonry.com

Edgar Boettcher Mason Contractors Inc
Yard 3803 N Euclid Bay City MI 48706 989-684-4807 684-4824
Web: www.boettchermasonry.com

Evans-Mason Inc 1021 S Grand Ave E Springfield IL 62703 217-522-3396 522-3190
Web: evans-mason.com

Gallegos Corp PO Box 821 Vail CO 81658 970-926-3737 926-3727
TF: 800-425-5346 ■ *Web:* www.gallegoscorp.com

International Chimney Corp
55 S Long St Williamsville NY 14221 800-828-1446 634-3983*
**Fax Area Code:* 716 ■ *TF:* 800-828-1446 ■ *Web:* www.internationalchimney.com

JD Long Masonry Inc
7044 Colchester Park Dr PO Box 1457 Manassas VA 20112 703-550-8880 730-5210
Web: www.jdlongmasonry.net/gallery.htm

John J Smith Masonry Co 9200 Green Pk Rd Saint Louis MO 63123 314-894-9500 894-1172
Web: www.smithmasonry.com

Kauai Builders Ltd 3988 Halau St Lihue HI 96766 808-245-2911 245-1769

Kretschmar & Smith Inc 6293 Pedley Rd Riverside CA 92509 951-361-1405 361-1381
Web: kandsmasonry.com

Leonard Masonry Inc 5925 Fee Fee Rd Hazelwood MO 63042 314-731-5500 731-3366
Web: www.leonardmasonry.com

Lindblad Construction Co 717 E Cass St Joliet IL 60432 815-726-6251 723-4907
Web: www.lindbladconstruction.com

Manganaro Corp New England 52 Cummings Pk Woburn MA 01801 781-937-8880 937-8882
Web: www.manganaro.com

Masonry Arts Inc 2105 Third Ave N Bessemer AL 35020 205-428-0780
Web: www.masonryarts.com

MB Haynes Corp 187 Deaverview Rd Asheville NC 28806 828-254-6141 253-8136
Web: www.mbhaynes.com

Mid-Continental Restoration Company Inc
401 E Hudson Rd PO Box 429 Fort Scott KS 66701 620-223-3700 223-5052
TF: 800-835-3700 ■ *Web:* www.midcontinental.com

Montana Stone Gallery LLC 6900 Kestrel Dr Missoula MT 59808 406-541-7625
Web: www.montanastonegallery.com

Otto Baum Company Inc 866 N Main St PO Box 161 Morton IL 61550 309-266-7114 263-1050
Web: www.ottobaum.com

Pyramid Masonry Contractors Inc
2330 Mellon Ct Decatur GA 30035 770-987-4750 981-7142
Web: pyramidmasonry.net

Ron Kendall Masonry Inc
101 Benoist Farms Rd West Palm Beach FL 33411 561-793-5924 795-2621
TF: 866-844-1404 ■ *Web:* www.ronkendallmasonry.com

Schiffer Mason Contractors Inc
2190 Delhi NE PO Box 250 Holt MI 48842 517-694-2566 694-1936
Web: www.schiffermasonry.com

Seedorff Masonry Inc
408 W Mission St Strawberry Point IA 52076 563-933-2296 933-4114
Web: www.seedorff.com

Snow Jr & King Inc 2415 Church St Norfolk VA 23504 757-627-8621 622-3883
Web: www.snowjrandking.com

Sun Valley Masonry Inc 10828 N Cave Creek Rd Phoenix AZ 85020 602-943-6106 997-6857
Web: www.svmasonry.com

Treviicos Corp 38 Third Ave Charlestown MA 02129 617-241-4800 737-5810
Web: www.treviicos.com

WASCO Inc 1122 Second Ave N Ste B Nashville TN 37208 615-244-9090 726-2643
Web: www.wascomasonry.com

192-8 Painting & Paperhanging Contractors

Phone Fax

Ascher Bros Company Inc 3033 W Fletcher St Chicago IL 60618 773-588-0001 588-5350
Web: www.ascherbrothers.com

Askins Family LTP 208 S Blanding St Lake City SC 29560 843-394-8555 394-8333

Avalotis Co 400 Jones St Verona PA 15147 412-828-9666
Web: www.avalotis.com

Benise-Dowling & Assoc Inc
5068 Snapfinger Woods Dr Decatur GA 30035 770-981-4237 593-0342
Web: www.benise-dowling.com

Borbon Inc 7312 Walnut Ave Buena Park CA 90620 714-994-0170 994-0641
Web: www.borbon.net

Brock Services LLC 1675 Spindletop Rd Beaumont TX 77705 409-833-7571 839-4705
TF: 800-600-9675 ■ *Web:* www.brockgroup.com

CertaPro Painters Ltd 150 Green Tree Rd Ste 1003 Oaks PA 19456 800-689-7271 650-9997*
**Fax Area Code:* 610 ■ *TF:* 800-689-7271 ■ *Web:* www.certapro.com

E Caligari & Son Inc 1333 Ingleside Rd Norfolk VA 23502 757-853-4511 855-9424
Web: www.ecaligariandson.com

F D Thomas Inc PO Box 4663 Medford OR 97501 541-664-3010 664-1105
Web: www.fdthomas.com

George E Masker Inc 887 71st Ave Oakland CA 94621 510-568-1206 638-2530
Web: www.maskerpainting.com

Goodman Decorating Co
3400 Atlanta Industrial Pkwy NW Atlanta GA 30331 404-965-3626 965-2558
Web: www.goodman-decorating.com

Hartman-Walsh Painting Co
7144 N Market St Saint Louis MO 63133 314-863-1800 863-6964
Web: www.hartmanwalsh.com

Hess Sweitzer Inc 2805 S 160th St New Berlin WI 53151 262-641-9100 272-5328
TF: 800-491-4377 ■ *Web:* www.hesssweitzer.com

Company	City	State	ZIP	Phone	Fax
JP Carroll Company Inc 310 N Madison Ave *Web:* myhomepro.org	Los Angeles	CA	90004	323-660-9230	
K2 Industrial Services 5233 Hohman Ave *TF:* 866-524-6387 ■ *Web:* www.k2industrial.com	Hammond	IN	46320	219-933-5300	933-5301
Long Painting Co 21414 68th Ave S *TF:* 800-678-5664 ■ *Web:* www.longpainting.com	Kent	WA	98032	253-234-8050	234-0034
Madias Bros Inc 12850 Evergreen Rd	Detroit	MI	48223	313-272-5330	272-5345
Midwest Pro Painting Inc 12845 Farmington Rd *TF:* 800-860-6757 ■ *Web:* www.mpp-inc.com	Livonia	MI	48150	734-427-1040	427-0209
ML McDonald LLC 50 Oakland St PO Box 315 *TF:* 800-733-6243 ■ *Web:* www.mlmcdonald.com	Watertown	MA	02471	617-923-0900	926-8418
National Services Group Inc 1682 Langley Ave *TF:* 800-394-6000 ■ *Web:* www.nationalservicesgroup.com	Irvine	CA	92614	714-564-7900	564-8725
NLP Enterprises Inc PO Box 349 *Web:* www.nlpentinc.com	Owings Mills	MD	21117	410-356-7500	356-7525
Peter King Corp 11040 N 19th Ave *Web:* petekingaz.com	Phoenix	AZ	85029	602-944-4441	943-4876
Specialty Finishes Inc 1545 Marietta Blvd NW *Web:* www.specialtyfinishes.com	Atlanta	GA	30318	404-351-1062	351-0535
TMI Coatings Inc 3291 Terminal Dr *TF:* 800-328-0229 ■ *Web:* www.tmicoatings.com	Saint Paul	MN	55121	651-452-6100	452-0598
Vulcan Painters Inc PO Box 1010 *Web:* www.vulcan-group.com	Bessemer	AL	35021	205-428-0556	424-2267

192-9 Plastering, Drywall, Acoustical, Insulation Contractors

Company	City	State	ZIP	Phone	Fax
Acousti Engineering Co of Florida Inc 4656 34th St SW *TF:* 800-434-3467 ■ *Web:* www.acousti.com	Orlando	FL	32811	407-425-3467	425-5108
Allied Construction Services & Color Inc 2122 Fleur Dr PO Box 937 *TF:* 800-365-4855 ■ *Web:* www.alliedconst.com	Des Moines	IA	50304	515-288-4855	288-2069
Anning Johnson Company Inc 1959 Anson Dr *Web:* www.anningjohnson.com	Melrose Park	IL	60160	708-681-1300	681-1310
APi Construction Co 1100 Old Hwy 8 NW *TF:* 800-223-4922 ■ *Web:* www.apiconst.com	New Brighton	MN	55112	651-636-4320	636-0312
Baker Triangle 415 Highway 80 East PO Box 850227 *TF:* 800-458-3480 ■ *Web:* www.bakerdrywall.com	Mesquite	TX	75150	972-289-5534	289-4580
Bayside Interiors Inc 3220 Darby Common *Web:* www.baysideinteriors.com	Fremont	CA	94539	510-438-9171	438-9375
BHN Corp 435 Madison Ave *TF:* 800-238-9046 ■ *Web:* www.bhncorp.com	Memphis	TN	38103	901-521-9500	521-9507
Burnham Industrial Contractors Inc 3229 Babcock Blvd *Web:* www.burnhamindustrial.net	Pittsburgh	PA	15237	412-366-6622	366-7540
Cannon Constructors Inc 17000 Ventura Blvd Ste 301 *Web:* www.cannongroup.com	Encino	CA	91316	818-906-6200	906-6220
CE Thurston & Sons Inc 3335 Croft St *TF:* 800-444-7713 ■ *Web:* www.cethurston.com	Norfolk	VA	23513	757-855-7700	855-1214
Central Ceilings Inc 36 Norfolk Ave *Web:* www.centralceilings.com	South Easton	MA	02375	508-238-6985	238-2191
Circle B Company Inc 5636 S Meridian St *Web:* circlebco.com	Indianapolis	IN	46217	317-787-5746	780-2654
Circle Group, The 1275 Alderman Dr *Web:* www.thecirclegroup.com	Alpharetta	GA	30005	678-356-1000	
Cleveland Construction Inc 8620 Tyler Blvd *Web:* www.clevelandconstruction.com	Mentor	OH	44060	440-255-8000	205-1138
Davenport Insulation Inc 7400 Gateway Ct *TF:* 855-626-6459 ■ *Web:* mascocs.com	Manassas	VA	20109	703-631-7744	631-8730
Daw Technologies Inc 1600 West 2200 South Ste 201 *Web:* www.dawtech.com	Salt Lake City	UT	84119	801-977-3100	973-6640
Drywall Contractors Inc 2920 N Arlington Ave *Web:* www.drywallpartners.com	Indianapolis	IN	46218	317-546-6605	
E&K Companies 343 Carol Ln *TF:* 800-365-5760 ■ *Web:* www.air-tite.net	Elmhurst	IL	60126	630-530-9001	
Entrx Corp 800 Nicollet Mall Ste 2690	Minneapolis	MN	55402	612-333-0614	338-7332
FL Crane & Sons Inc 508 S Spring St PO Box 428 *TF:* 800-748-9523 ■ *Web:* www.flcrane.com	Fulton	MS	38843	662-862-2172	862-2649
Group Builders Inc 511 Mokauea St *Web:* www.groupbuilders.net	Honolulu	HI	96819	808-832-0888	832-0890
Henderson-Johnson Co Inc 918 Canal St PO Box 6964 *Web:* www.hjcoinc.com	Syracuse	NY	13210	315-479-5561	479-5585
Interior Construction Services Ltd 2930 Market St *Web:* www.ics-stl.com	Saint Louis	MO	63103	314-534-6664	534-6663
Irex Contracting Group 120 N Lime St **Fax Area Code:* 717 ■ *TF:* 800-487-7255 ■ *Web:* www.irexcontracting.com	Lancaster	PA	17608	800-487-7255	399-5135*
ISI Insulation Specialties Inc 2142 Rheem Dr Ste A **Fax Area Code:* 410	Pleasanton	CA	94588	925-846-7990	439-3769*
Jacobson & Company Inc 1079 E Grand St PO Box 511 *Web:* www.jacobsoncompany.com	Elizabeth	NJ	07207	908-355-5200	355-8680
KHS & S Contractors Inc 5422 Bay Ctr Dr Ste 200 *TF:* 866-991-7277 ■ *Web:* www.khss.com	Tampa	FL	33609	813-628-9330	628-4339
Kramig Insulation 323 S Wayne Ave *TF:* 888-579-0079 ■ *Web:* www.kramiginsulation.com	Cincinnati	OH	45215	513-761-4010	761-0362
Land Coast Insulation Inc 4017 Second St *TF:* 800-333-9424 ■ *Web:* www.landcoast.com	New Iberia	LA	70560	337-367-7741	367-7744
Lotspeich Co 16101 NW 54th Ave *Web:* www.lotspeich.com	Miami	FL	33014	305-624-7777	624-4517
Luse Holdings Inc 3990 Enterprise Ct *Web:* luse.com	Aurora	IL	60504	630-862-2600	862-2674
M Ecker & Co 9525 W Bryn Mawr Ave Ste 900 *Web:* www.eckerusa.com	Rosemont	IL	60018	847-994-6000	233-9715
Manganaro Corp New England 52 Cummings Pk *Web:* www.manganaro.com	Woburn	MA	01801	781-937-8880	937-8882
Marek Bros Co 3701 Piney Woods *Web:* www.marekbros.com	Houston	TX	77018	713-681-9213	681-0446
Midwest Drywall Company Inc 1351 S Reca Ct *Web:* www.mwdw.com	Wichita	KS	67209	316-722-9559	722-9682
ML McDonald LLC 50 Oakland St PO Box 315 *TF:* 800-733-6243 ■ *Web:* www.mlmcdonald.com	Watertown	MA	02471	617-923-0900	926-8418
National Acoustics Inc 13-06 43rd Ave *Web:* nationalacoustics.com	Long Island City	NY	10001	212-695-1252	695-4539
Paul J Krez Co 7831 N Nagle Ave *Web:* www.krezgroup.com	Morton Grove	IL	60053	847-581-0017	965-7841
Precision Walls Inc 1230 NE MaynaRd Rd *TF:* 800-849-9255 ■ *Web:* www.precisionwalls.com	Cary	NC	27513	919-832-0380	839-1402
Shields Inc 2625 Hope Church Rd *Web:* www.shieldsinc.com	Winston-Salem	NC	27103	336-765-9040	765-3715
South Valley Drywall Inc 12362 Dumont Way *Web:* www.southvalleydrywall.com	Littleton	CO	80125	303-791-7212	470-0116
Spectrum Interiors Inc 2652 Crescent Springs Rd *Web:* www.spectruminterior.com	Crescent Springs	KY	41017	859-331-2696	331-4322
Thorne Assoc Inc 1450 W Randolph St *Web:* www.thorneassociates.com	Chicago	IL	60607	312-738-5230	738-5249
TJ McCartney Inc Three Capitol St Ste 1 *Web:* www.tjminc.com	Nashua	NH	03063	603-889-6380	880-0770
Turner-Brooks Inc 28811 John R Rd *Web:* turnerbrooks.com	Madison Heights	MI	48071	248-548-3400	548-9213
Waco Inc 5450 Lewis Rd PO Box 829 *Web:* www.wacoinc.net	Sandston	VA	23150	804-222-8440	226-3241
Walldesign Inc 5940 Key Ct *Web:* www.walldesigninc.com	Loomis	CA	95650	916-660-0102	
Western Partitions Inc 8300 SW Hunziker Rd *TF:* 800-783-0315 ■ *Web:* www.westernpartitions.com	Tigard	OR	97223	503-620-1600	624-5781
Wyatt Inc 4545 Campbells Run Rd *Web:* www.wyattinc.com	Pittsburgh	PA	15205	412-787-5800	787-5845

192-10 Plumbing, Heating, Air Conditioning Contractors

Company	City	State	ZIP	Phone	Fax
A & B Mechanical Contractors Inc 272 West 3620 South *Web:* abmechanicalcontractors.com	Salt Lake City	UT	84115	801-263-1700	
AC Corp 301 Creek Ridge Rd *TF:* 800-422-7378 ■ *Web:* www.accorporation.com	Greensboro	NC	27406	336-273-4472	765-0416
Accent Plumbing Inc 21101 Fm 685	Pflugerville	TX	78660	512-251-2819	
ACCO Engineered Systems 6265 San Fernando Rd *TF Cust Svc:* 800-998-2226 ■ *Web:* www.accoair.com	Glendale	CA	91201	818-243-1727	247-6533
Action Inc 1308 Church St *Web:* action-mechanical.com	Barling	AR	72923	479-452-5723	
Adkins & Kimbrough Mechanical 4415 Turin Dr *Web:* jadkinsmechanical.com	Bessemer	AL	35020	205-432-4000	
Adrian L Merton Inc 9011 E Hampton Dr *Web:* almertoninc.com	Capitol Heights	MD	20743	301-336-2700	
Advance Mechanical Contractors 1301 E Burnett St *Web:* advancemechanicalcontractors.com	Signal Hill	CA	90755	562-426-1725	
Advance Mechanical Systems Inc 425 Algonquin Rd *Web:* www.jfahern.com	Arlington Heights	IL	60005	847-593-2510	593-2536
Air Comfort Corp 2550 Braga Dr *TF:* 800-466-3779 ■ *Web:* www.aircomfort.com	Broadview	IL	60155	708-345-1900	345-2730
Air Con Refrigeration & Heating Inc 123 Lake St	Waukegan	IL	60085	847-336-4128	336-4949
Air Controls Bozeman Inc 7510 Shedhorn Dr *Web:* aircontrolsbozeman.com	Bozeman	MT	59718	406-587-6292	
Aire Serv Heating & Air Conditioning Inc 5387 Texas 6 Fwy Ste 101 **Fax Area Code:* 716 ■ *TF:* 855-983-0630 ■ *Web:* www.aireserv.com	Woodway	TX	76712	254-523-3600	782-2013*
Airtrol Inc 3960 N St *Web:* airtrolmechanical.com	Baton Rouge	LA	70806	225-383-2617	343-7986
AJ Perri Inc 1138 Pine Brook Rd *Web:* ajperri.com	Tinton Falls	NJ	07724	732-982-8700	
Al Gordon Plumbing & Heating LC 3855 W Airline Hwy *Web:* algordonplumbing.com	Waterloo	IA	50703	319-233-3991	
Alaka'i Mechanical Corp 2655 Waiwai Loop *TF:* 800-600-1085 ■ *Web:* www.alakaimechanical.com	Honolulu	HI	96819	808-834-1085	834-1800
Albert Arno Inc 5000 Claxton Ave *Web:* albertarnostl.com	St Louis	MO	63120	314-383-2700	
Aldag Honold Mechanical Inc 3509 S Business Dr *Web:* www.aldaghonold.com	Sheboygan	WI	53082	920-458-5558	458-3750
All Hvac Service Company Inc 9030 Ft Hamilton Pkwy *Web:* allhvac.com	Brooklyn	NY	11209	718-833-0148	
Allen'S Tri-State Mechanical 404 S Hayden St *Web:* allenstristate.com	Amarillo	TX	79101	806-376-8345	
Allied Fire Protection LP PO Box 2842 *TF:* 800-604-2600 ■ *Web:* www.alliedfireprotection.com	Pearland	TX	77588	281-485-6803	412-9668
Allied Mechanical Services Inc 5688 E MI Ave Ste A *TF:* 888-237-3017 ■ *Web:* www.alliedmechanical.com	Kalamazoo	MI	49048	269-344-0191	344-0196
ALLPoints Inc 909 Lunt Ave *Web:* allpointsinc.net	Schaumburg	IL	60193	847-585-0160	

Company	City	State	ZIP	Phone	Fax
Althoff Industries Inc 8001 S Rt 31 *Fax: Sales ■ TF: 800-225-2443 ■ Web: www.althoffind.com	Crystal Lake	IL	60014	815-455-7000	455-9375*
American Mechanical Services 13300 Mid Atlantic Blvd Web: www.amsofusa.com	Laurel	MD	20708	301-206-5070	206-2520
American Residential Services LLC 9010 Maier Rd Ste 105 TF: 866-399-2885 ■ Web: www.ars.com	Laurel	MD	20723	901-271-9700	
Anderson Rowe & Buckley Inc 2833 Third St	San Francisco	CA	94107	415-282-1625	282-0752
Anron Heating & Air Conditioning Inc 440 Wyandanch Ave Web: anronac.com	West Babylon	NY	11704	631-643-3433	491-6983
AO Reed & Co 4777 Ruffner St Web: www.aoreed.com	San Diego	CA	92111	858-565-4131	292-6958
Arden Engineering Constructors LLC 505 Narragansett Pk Dr Web: www.ardeneng.com	Pawtucket	RI	02861	401-727-3500	727-3540
Armistead Mechanical Inc 168 Hopper Ave TF: 800-587-5267 ■ Web: www.armisteadmechanical.com	Waldwick	NJ	07463	201-447-6740	447-6744
Arnold Refrigeration Inc 1122 N Cherry Web: arnoldrefrigeration.com	San Antonio	TX	78202	210-225-5493	225-2605
ASA Controls Inc 10051 Simonson Rd Ste 8 Web: asacontrols.com	Harrison	OH	45030	513-353-3101	
Atlantic Constructors Inc 1401 Battery Brooke Pkwy Web: www.atlanticconstructors.com	Richmond	VA	23237	804-222-3400	222-6638
Atlas Welding & Boiler Repair Inc 2373 Tiebout Ave	Bronx	NY	10458	718-365-6600	367-5658
Atmac Mechanical Services LP 1201 Summit Ave Web: atmacmech.com	Plano	TX	75074	214-428-1544	
August Arace & Sons Inc 642 Third Ave Web: www.augustarace.com	Elizabeth	NJ	07202	908-354-1626	
Azco Inc PO Box 567 Web: www.azco-inc.com	Appleton	WI	54912	920-734-5791	734-7432
B & I Contractors Inc 2701 Prince St Web: www.bandicontractors.com	Fort Myers	FL	33916	239-332-4646	332-5928
B-G Mechanical Service Inc 12 Second Ave TF: 800-992-7386 ■ Web: www.bgmechanical.com	Chicopee	MA	01020	413-888-1500	594-2983
Baker Group 4224 Hubbell Ave TF: 855-262-4000 ■ Web: www.thebakergroup.com	Des Moines	IA	50317	515-262-4000	266-1025
Barry Assoc Inc 17 Halls Mill Rd	Preston	CT	06365	860-889-8943	
Baumann & De Groot Inc 116 Lakewood Ste 10 Web: 396heat.com	Holland	MI	49424	616-355-6550	
Bay Mechanical Inc 2696 Reliance Dr Ste 200 TF: 888-229-6324 ■ Web: www.baymechanical.com	Virginia Beach	VA	23452	757-468-6700	468-0377
BC Plumbing Co 1215 S Seventh St Web: bcplumbing.net	Louisville	KY	40203	502-634-9725	
BCH Mechanical Inc 6354 118th Ave N Web: www.bchmechanical.com	Largo	FL	33773	727-546-3561	545-1801
Beasley Heating & Air 57 Wc Beasley Ln	Coats	NC	27521	919-894-4248	
Benjamin Plumbing Inc 5396 King James Way Web: benjaminplumbing.com	Madison	WI	53719	608-271-7071	
Bernhard Mechanical Contractors Inc 10321 Airline Hwy Web: www.bernhardmechanical.com	Baton Rouge	LA	70816	225-293-2791	296-0931
Beutler Air Conditioning Service 855 National Dr Ste 109 *Fax Area Code: 916 ■ TF: 866-559-0108 ■ Web: www.beutlerairconditioningandheating.com	Sacramento	CA	95834	866-559-0108	646-2200*
Biggs Plumbing Co 1615 Dungan Ln Web: biggsplumbing.com	Austin	TX	78754	512-837-5955	837-3108
BMW Constructors Inc 1740 W Michigan St Web: www.bmwcnstrs.com	Indianapolis	IN	46222	317-267-0400	267-0459
Bradham Bros Inc 6128 Rozzelles Ferry Rd Web: bradhambrothers.com	Charlotte	NC	28214	704-392-8056	
Bradley Plumbing & Heating Inc 431 Hackel Dr	Montgomery	AL	36117	334-271-0700	
Bratcher Heating & Air Conditioning Inc 1210 Ft Jesse Rd Web: bratchercomfort.com	Normal	IL	61761	309-454-1611	
Brewer-Garrett Company (Inc) 6800 Eastland Rd Web: www.brewer-garrett.com	Cleveland	OH	44130	440-243-3535	243-9993
Brown Sprinkler Corp 4705 Pinewood Rd *Fax Area Code: 580 ■ Web: www.brownsprinkler.com	Louisville	KY	40218	502-968-6274	625-4398*
Btu Management Inc 534 La Crosse St Web: btumanagement.com	Mauston	WI	53948	608-847-4600	
Butcher Air Conditioning Company Inc 101 Boyce St Web: butcherac.com	Broussard	LA	70518	337-837-2000	
Butters-Fetting Company Inc 1669 S First St Web: www.buttersfetting.com	Milwaukee	WI	53204	414-645-1535	645-7622
C & R Mechanical 12825 Pennridge Dr TF: 800-524-3828 ■ Web: www.crmechanical.com	Bridgeton	MO	63044	314-739-1800	739-1721
Calvert Plumbing & Heating Company Inc 5806 York Rd Web: calvertinc.com	Baltimore	MD	21212	410-323-5400	
Campito Plumbing & Heating Inc Three Hemlock St	Latham	NY	12110	518-785-0994	785-0769
Cape Coral Plumbing Inc 5812 Enterprise Pkwy Web: capecoralplumbing.com	Fort Myers	FL	33905	239-693-4714	
Capron Company Inc 411 N Stonestreet Ave Web: capron.com	Rockville	MD	20850	301-424-9500	
Cattrell Cos Inc 906 Franklin St Web: cattrell.com	Toronto	OH	43964	740-537-2481	
CCI Mechanical Inc 758 S Redwood Rd Web: ccimechanical.com	Salt Lake City	UT	84104	801-973-9000	975-7204
Central Air Conditioning Inc 3435 W Harry St Web: www.centralairco.com	Wichita	KS	67213	316-945-0797	945-3174

Company	City	State	ZIP	Phone	Fax
Central Heating And 2317 Nc Hwy 11 N Web: centralheatairconditioning.com	Kinston	NC	28501	252-527-6676	
Central Mechanical Construction Company Inc 631 Pecan Cir Web: www.centralmechanical.com	Manhattan	KS	66502	785-537-2437	537-2491
Central Systems Htg & A/C Inc 2857 Wbound 40 Hwy	Blue Springs	MO	64015	816-228-2022	
Chad Stephens Inc Dba Comfort Solutions 1470 Wall Ave	Ogden	UT	84404	801-393-2206	
Champion Industrial Contractors Inc 1420 Coldwell Ave PO Box 4399 Web: championindustrial.com	Modesto	CA	95350	209-524-6601	524-6931
Chapman Corp 331 S Main St Web: www.chapmancorporation.com	Washington	PA	15301	724-228-1900	228-4311
Charles P. Blouin Inc 203 New Zealand Rd Web: www.cpblouin.com	Seabrook	NH	03874	603-474-3400	474-7118
Chas Roberts Heating & Air Conditioning Inc 9828 N 19th Ave Web: www.chasroberts.com	Phoenix	AZ	85021	602-331-2686	997-0068
Chilmar Corp 5724 Belair Rd Web: chilmar.com	Baltimore	MD	21206	410-426-5482	
Christianson Air Conditioning & Plumbing 1950 Louis Henna Blvd Web: www.christiansonco.com	Round Rock	TX	78664	512-246-5200	246-5201
Cinfab Mechanical Inc 5240 Lester Rd Web: www.cinfab.com	Cincinnati	OH	45213	513-396-6100	396-7574
Clima-Tech 875 W Mcgregor Ct Ste 180 Web: clima-tech.com	Boise	ID	83705	208-377-9755	
Climate Design Air ConditioningIn 12530 47th Way N Web: climatedesign.com	Clearwater	FL	33762	727-572-9100	
Climate Engineers Inc 883 Shaver Rd Ne Web: climate-engr.com	Cedar Rapids	IA	52402	319-364-1569	
Coastal Mechanical Services LLC 394 E Dr TF: 866-584-9528 ■ Web: www.coastalmechanical.com	Melbourne	FL	32904	321-725-3061	984-0718
Cobb Mechanical Contractors 2906 W Morrison TF General: 800-808-2622 ■ Web: www.cobbmechanical.com	Colorado Springs	CO	80904	719-471-8958	389-0127
Collins Plumbing Inc 8130 Commercial St Web: collinsplumbing.com	La Mesa	CA	91942	619-469-0800	
ColonialWebb Contractors Co 2820 Ackley Ave TF: 877-208-3894 ■ Web: www.colonialwebb.com	Richmond	VA	23228	804-916-1400	264-5083
Comfort Group Inc, The 659 Thompson Ln Web: www.thecomfortgroup.com	Nashville	TN	37204	615-263-2900	263-2939
Comfort Systems USA 9745 Bent Oak Dr *Fax Area Code: 713	Houston	TX	77040	832-590-5700	856-9720*
Comfort Systems USA Inc 675 Bering Ste 400 NYSE: FIX ■ TF: 800-723-8431 ■ Web: www.comfortsystemsusa.com	Houston	TX	77057	713-830-9600	830-9696
Correct Temp Inc 268 Hampstead Rd Web: correcttemp.com	Methuen	MA	01844	978-688-8700	
Corrigan Co 3545 Gratiot St Web: www.corriganco.com	Saint Louis	MO	63103	314-771-6200	771-8537
Cox Engineering Co 35 Industrial Dr Web: coxengineering.com	Canton	MA	02021	781-302-3300	302-3444
Critchfield Mechanical Inc 1901 Junction Ave Web: www.cmihvac.com	San Jose	CA	95131	408-437-7000	437-7199
Cullum Mechanical Construction Inc 3325 Pacific Ave Web: www.culluminc.com	North Charleston	SC	29418	843-554-6645	
CW Plumbing & Design Inc 41683 Date St	Murrieta	CA	92562	951-894-7703	
D J Heating & Air Conditioning Inc 1409 Rt 9W	Marlboro	NY	12542	845-236-4436	
Dauenhauer & Son Plumbing & Piping Company Inc 3416 Robards Ct Web: www.dauenhauerplumbing.com	Louisville	KY	40218	502-451-2882	
Dave Droegkamp Heating Air Conditioning & Sheet Metal Inc 540 Norton Dr Web: davedroegkamp.com	Hartland	WI	53029	262-367-2820	
Davis Contractors Ltd 5205 Fm 236	Cuero	TX	77954	361-275-5721	
Dean Custom Air LLC 120 Logan Rd Web: deancustomair.com	Bluffton	SC	29909	843-706-2850	
DeBra-Kuempel 3976 Southern Ave TF: 800-395-5741 ■ Web: www.debra-kuempel.com	Cincinnati	OH	45227	513-271-6500	271-4676
Dee Plumbing Inc 3828 W 128th Pl Web: deeplumbing.com	Alsip	IL	60803	708-389-8075	
Dehart Plumbing Heating & Air Inc 311 Bitritto Way Web: dehartinc.com	Modesto	CA	95356	209-523-4578	
Delta Fire Sprinklers Inc 111 Tech Dr Web: delta-fire.com	Sanford	FL	32771	407-328-3000	
Delta Technology Corp 1223 Valentine Ave Se	Pacific	WA	98047	253-863-8415	
Dmi Corp PO Box 53 Web: www.deckermechanical.com	Cedar Hill	TX	75104	972-291-9907	299-6437
Doody Mechanical Inc 7450 Flying Cloud Dr Web: www.metromech.com	Eden Prairie	MN	55344	952-941-7010	
Dorvin D Leis Company Inc 202 Lalo St Web: www.leisinc.com	Kahului	HI	96732	808-877-3902	877-5168
Downey Inc 2203 W Michigan St	Milwaukee	WI	53233	414-933-3123	
Downing Heating & Air Conditioning Inc 3070 Kerner Blvd Ste K Web: downinghvac.com	San Rafael	CA	94901	415-485-1011	
Dunbar Mechanical Inc 2806 N Reynolds Rd TF: 800-719-2201 ■ Web: www.dunbarmechanical.com	Toledo	OH	43615	419-537-1900	537-8840
Dupree Plumbing Company Inc 869 Worley Dr Web: www.dupreeplumbing.com	Marietta	GA	30066	770-428-2291	
E Mitchell Inc 1580 Indiana St	San Francisco	CA	94107	415-826-2929	
Eastern Mechanical Services Inc 3 Starr St Web: emsinc.us	Danbury	CT	06810	203-792-7668	748-0385
Edward J Meloney Inc 22 Madison Ave	Lansdowne	PA	19050	610-626-4900	

	City	State	Zip	Phone	Fax
Elliott & Bradley Plumbing Inc 10030 Windisch Rd *Web:* elliottandbradley.com	West Chester	OH	45069	513-772-0050	
EM Duggan Inc 140 Will Dr *Web:* emduggan.com	Canton	MA	02021	781-828-2292	828-0991
EMCOR Group Inc 301 Merritt 7 Sixth Fl *NYSE:* EME ■ *TF:* 866-890-7794 ■ *Web:* www.emcorgroup.com	Norwalk	CT	06851	203-849-7800	849-7900
Engineering & Refrigeration Inc 56 Baldwin Ave *Web:* dupont.com	Jersey City	NJ	07306	201-333-4200	
Enting Water Conditioning Inc 3211 Dryden Rd *Web:* enting.com	Dayton	OH	45439	937-294-5100	
ERP Group Inc 88 Farwell St	West Haven	CT	06516	203-931-0490	
EW Tompkins Company Inc 126 Sheridan Ave *Web:* www.thetompkinsgroup.com	Albany	NY	12210	518-462-6577	462-6570
Fagan Co 3125 Brinkerhoff Rd PO Box 15238 *Web:* www.faganco.com	Kansas City	KS	66115	913-621-4444	621-1735
Farmer & Irwin Corp 3300 Ave K *Web:* www.fandicorp.com	Riviera Beach	FL	33404	561-842-5316	842-5999
FE Moran 2265 Carlson Dr *Web:* femoran.com	Northbrook	IL	60062	847-498-4800	498-9091
Ferran Services & Contracting 530 Grand St *Web:* www.ferran-services.com	Orlando	FL	32805	407-422-3551	648-0961
Fisher Air Heating & Air Conditioning Services 239 Viking Ave *Web:* fisherair.com	Brea	CA	92821	714-529-9600	
Fisher Container Corp 1111 Busch Pkwy *TF:* 800-837-2247 ■ *Web:* www.fishercontainer.com	Buffalo Grove	IL	60089	847-541-0000	541-0075
Fitzgerald Contractors Inc 7103 St Vincent Ave *TF:* 800-259-3264 ■ *Web:* www.fitzgeraldcontractors.com	Shreveport	LA	71106	318-869-3262	865-9640
Foulk Bros Plumbing & Heating Co 322 W Seventh St *Web:* foulkbros.com	Sioux City	IA	51103	712-258-3388	
Fountain Construction Co 5655 Hwy 18 W *Web:* www.fountainconstruction.com	Jackson	MS	39209	601-373-4162	373-4300
Fox Service Co PO Box 19047 *TF:* 866-668-4749 ■ *Web:* www.foxservice.com	Austin	TX	78760	512-442-6782	
Frank Lill & Son Inc 785 Old Dutch Road *TF:* 800-756-0490 ■ *Web:* www.franklillandson.com	Victoriaville	NY	14564	585-265-0490	265-1842
Frank M Booth Inc 222 Third St *Web:* www.frankbooth.com	Marysville	CA	95901	530-742-7134	742-8109
FW Spencer & Son Inc 99 S Hill Dr *Web:* www.fwspencersoninc.com	Brisbane	CA	94005	415-468-5000	468-4579
G E Tignall & Company Inc 14 Mccann Ave *Web:* getignall.com	Cockeysville	MD	21030	410-666-3000	
Gay WW Mechanical Contractor Inc 524 Stockton St *Web:* wwgmc.com	Jacksonville	FL	32204	904-388-2696	389-4901
GEM Inc 6842 Commodore Dr *TF General:* 866-720-2700 ■ *Web:* www.gemindustrial.com	Walbridge	OH	43465	419-666-6554	666-7004
General Hydronics Inc 1001 Zuni Dr	Alamogordo	NM	88310	575-437-6512	
George H Wilson Inc 250 Harvey W Blvd *Web:* www.geohwilson.com	Santa Cruz	CA	95060	831-423-9522	423-9903
Getzschman Heating LLC 1700 E 23rd St *Web:* getzschman.com	Fremont	NE	68025	402-721-6301	
Gillette Air Conditioning Company Inc 1215 San Francisco *Web:* www.gillette-ac.com	San Antonio	TX	78201	210-735-9235	736-1932
Godwin Plumbing Inc 3703 Division Ave *Web:* godwinplumbing.com	Grand Rapids	MI	49548	616-243-3131	
Gold Mechanical Inc 4735 W Division St *Web:* goldmechanical.com	Springfield	MO	65802	417-873-9770	
Gowan Inc 5550 Airline Dr *Web:* www.gowaninc.com	Houston	TX	77076	713-696-5400	695-1726
Goyette Mechanical Co 3842 Gorey Ave *TF:* 877-469-3883 ■ *Web:* www.goyettemechanical.com	Flint	MI	48501	810-743-6883	743-9090
GR Sponaugle & Sons Inc 4391 Chambers Hill Rd *Web:* www.grsponaugle.com	Harrisburg	PA	17111	717-564-1515	564-3675
Grant Supply Company Inc 901 Joyce Kilmer Ave *Web:* grantsupply.com	North Brunswick	NJ	08902	732-545-1018	
Green Mechanical Construction Inc 322 W Main St *Web:* gmci.com	Glasgow	KY	42141	270-651-8978	
Greg'S Heating & Air Cond Inc 2115 Pacific Blvd Se *Web:* gregsheating.com	Albany	OR	97321	541-926-8950	
Griffith ID Inc 735 S Market St *Web:* www.idgriffith.com	Wilmington	DE	19801	302-656-8253	656-8268
Grunau Company Inc 1100 W Anderson Ct *TF:* 800-365-1920 ■ *Web:* www.grunau.com	Oak Creek	WI	53154	414-216-6900	768-7950
H & H Group Inc 2801 Syene Rd *Web:* www.hhindustries.com	Madison	WI	53713	608-273-3434	273-9654
H & R Mechanical Contractors Inc 106 Demand Ct *Web:* hrmech.com	Georgetown	KY	40324	502-863-4955	
HACI Mechanical Contractors Inc 2108 W Shangri La Rd *Web:* www.hacimechanical.com	Phoenix	AZ	85029	602-944-1555	678-0266
Hampshire Fire Protection Company Inc Eight N Wentworth Ave *Web:* www.hampshirefire.com	Londonderry	NH	03053	603-432-8221	
Hanna Plumbing & Supply Co 643 S Santa Fe Ave	Vista	CA	92083	760-726-2002	
Harder Mechanical Contractors Inc 2148 NE M L King Blvd *TF:* 800-392-3729 ■ *Web:* www.hardercompanies.com	Portland	OR	97212	503-281-1112	287-5284
Hardy Corp 350 Industrial Dr *TF:* 800-289-4822 ■ *Web:* www.hardycorp.com	Birmingham	AL	35211	205-252-7191	326-6268
Harford Refrigeration Company Inc 7915 Philadelphia Rd *Web:* harfordrefrigeration.com	Rosedale	MD	21237	410-698-1076	
Harold G Butzer Inc 730 Wicker Ln *TF:* 800-769-1065 ■ *Web:* hgbutzer.com	Jefferson City	MO	65109	573-636-4115	636-7053
Harris & Hart Inc 1759 West 1200 South	Ogden	UT	84404	801-731-0577	
Harry Grodsky & Company Inc 33 Shaws Ln *Web:* www.grodsky.com	Springfield	MA	01104	413-785-1947	737-9870
Haslett Heating & Cooling Inc 920 King Ave *Web:* haslettmechanical.com	Columbus	OH	43212	614-299-2133	
Haury Plumbing & Heating Inc 1816 N Market St	Sparta	IL	62286	618-443-2416	
HE Neumann Inc 100 Middle Creek Rd *TF:* 800-627-5312 ■ *Web:* www.heneumann.com	Triadelphia	WV	26059	304-232-3040	232-7858
Heating & Plumbing Engineers Inc 407 Fillmore Pl *Web:* www.hpeinc.com	Colorado Springs	CO	80907	719-633-5414	633-4031
Heide & Cook Ltd 1714 Kanakanui St *Web:* www.heidecook.com	Honolulu	HI	96819	808-841-6161	841-4889
Heritage Mechanical Services Inc 305 Suburban Ave **Fax Area Code:* 631 ■ *Web:* www.heritagemech.com	Deer Park	NY	11729	516-558-2000	667-8613*
Herman Goldner Co Inc 7777 Brewster Ave *TF:* 800-355-5997 ■ *Web:* www.goldner.com	Philadelphia	PA	19153	215-365-5400	492-6486
High Purity Systems Inc 8432 Quarry Rd *Web:* www.highpurity.com	Manassas	VA	20110	703-330-5094	
Hill Mechanical Group 11045 Gage Ave *Web:* www.hillgrp.com	Franklin Park	IL	60131	847-451-5000	451-5011
HiMEC Mechanical 1400 Seventh St NW *Web:* www.himec.com	Rochester	MN	55901	507-281-4000	281-5206
Holaday-Parks Inc 4600 S 134 Pl PO Box 69208 *Web:* www.holadayparks.com	Seattle	WA	98168	206-248-9700	248-8700
Hooper Corp 2030 Pennsylvania Ave *TF:* 800-242-8511 ■ *Web:* www.hoopercorp.com	Madison	WI	53704	608-249-0451	249-7360
Horwitz/NSI 4401 Quebec Ave N *Web:* www.horwitzinc.com	New Hope	MN	55428	763-533-1900	235-9810
Hubbard & Drake General Mechanical Contractors Inc PO Box 1867 *TF:* 800-353-9245 ■ *Web:* www.hubbarddrake.com	Decatur	AL	35602	256-353-9244	350-5043
Humphrey Company Ltd 4439 W 12th St *Web:* www.humphreyltd.com	Houston	TX	77055	713-686-8606	686-7619
Hurckman Mechanical Industries Inc PO Box 10977 *Web:* www.hurckman.com	Green Bay	WI	54307	920-499-8771	499-6769
I & M Heating & Appliance Service Inc 1628 S Michigan St *Web:* iandmheatingandcooling.com	South Bend	IN	46613	574-288-3351	
IHP Industrial Inc 1701 S Eigth St *Web:* ihpindustrial.com	Saint Joseph	MO	64503	816-364-1581	232-4473
IMCOR-Interstate Mechanical Corp 1841 E Washington St *TF:* 800-628-0211 ■ *Web:* www.imcor-az.com	Phoenix	AZ	85034	602-257-1319	271-0674
Independent Mechanical Industries Inc 4155 N Knox Ave *Web:* www.independentmech.com	Chicago	IL	60641	773-282-4500	282-2046
Industrial Air Inc 428 Edwardia Dr PO Box 8769 *Web:* www.industrialairinc.com	Greensboro	NC	27409	336-292-1030	855-7763
Industrial Contractors Inc 701 Ch Dr *TF:* 800-467-3089 ■ *Web:* www.icinorthdakota.com	Bismarck	ND	58501	701-258-9908	258-9988
Industrial Piping Inc 800 Culp Rd *TF:* 800-951-0988 ■ *Web:* www.goipi.com	Pineville	NC	28134	704-588-1100	588-5614
Interstate Mechanical Contractors Inc 3200 Henson Rd *Web:* interstatemechanical.com	Knoxville	TN	37921	865-588-0180	602-4124
J A Sauer Co 4559 Peoples Rd *Web:* jasauerco.com	Pittsburgh	PA	15237	412-931-7200	
J F Jacobs Inc 31523 W 8 Mile Rd *Web:* jfjacobsinc.net	Livonia	MI	48152	248-476-7888	
J J Plumbing LLC 3414 A St Se Ste 104 *Web:* jjplumbingllc.com	Auburn	WA	98002	253-939-1390	
J Lawrence Hall Company Inc 17 Progress Ave *Web:* jlawrencehall.com	Nashua	NH	03062	603-882-2021	
J-Berd Mechanical Contractors Inc 3308 Southway Dr *Web:* j-berd.com	St Cloud	MN	56301	320-656-0847	
Jack Laurence Corp 12831 W Golden Ln	San Antonio	TX	78249	210-696-0273	
Jackson & Blanc Inc 7929 Arjons Dr *Web:* www.jacksonandblanc.com	San Diego	CA	92126	858-831-7900	527-1502
Jacobs Mechanical Inc 1366 Hopple St *Web:* jacobsmech.com	Cincinnati	OH	45225	513-681-6800	
Jamar Co 4701 Mike Colalillo Dr *Web:* www.jamarcompany.com	Duluth	MN	55807	218-628-1027	628-1174
James Craft & Son Inc 2780 York Haven Rd PO Box 8 *Web:* www.jamescraftson.com	York Haven	PA	17370	717-266-6629	266-6623
James E Conner Jr Plumbing 505 Rt 168 Stes B And C *Web:* jameseconnerjrplumbing.com	Turnersville	NJ	08012	856-784-0004	
Janazzo Services Corp 140 Norton St Rt 10 PO Box 469 *TF:* 800-297-3931 ■ *Web:* www.janazzo.com	Milldale	CT	06467	860-621-7381	621-7529
JC Higgins Corp 70 Hawes Way *Web:* www.jchigginscorp.com	Stoughton	MA	02072	781-341-1500	344-6075
JF Ahern Co 855 Morris St *TF:* 800-532-0155 ■ *Web:* www.jfahern.com	Fond du Lac	WI	54935	920-921-9020	921-8632
JH Kelly 821 Third Ave *Web:* www.jhkelly.com	Longview	WA	98632	360-423-5510	423-9170
John Bouchard & Sons Co 1024 Harrison St *Web:* www.jbouchard.com	Nashville	TN	37203	615-256-0112	256-2427
John E Green Co 220 Victor Ave *Web:* www.johnegreen.com	Highland Park	MI	48203	313-868-2400	868-0011

				Phone	Fax
John Hoadley & Sons Inc 672 Union St *Web:* hoadleyandsons.com	Rockland	MA	02370	781-878-8098	
John W Danforth Co 300 Colvin Woods Pkwy *TF:* 800-888-6119 ■ *Web:* www.jwdanforth.com	Tonawanda	NY	14150	716-832-1940	832-2388
Johnson Contracting Company Inc 2750 Morton Dr *Web:* www.jccinc.com	East Moline	IL	61244	309-755-0601	752-7056
Joy Equipment Protection Inc 5690 Casitas Pass Rd *Web:* joyequipment.com	Carpinteria	CA	93014	805-684-0805	
JR Barto Heating/Air- Conditioning/Sheet Metal Inc 300 N G St *Web:* jrbarto.com	Lompoc	CA	93436	805-736-5160	
JR Pierce Plumbing Co 14481 Wicks Blvd *Web:* jrpierceplumbing.com	San Leandro	CA	94577	510-483-5473	
Kaiser Air Cond & Sheet Metal Inc 600 Pacific Ave *Web:* kaiserac.com	Oxnard	CA	93030	805-988-1800	
Karls Mechanical Contractors Inc 954 Forward Ave *Web:* karlsmechanical.com	Chilton	WI	53014	920-849-2050	
Kenron Industrial A/C Inc 299 Gregory St *Web:* kenron.com	Rochester	NY	14620	585-442-5600	
Kings Aire Inc 1035 Kessler Dr *Web:* kingsaire.com	El Paso	TX	79907	915-592-2997	
Kinseth Plumbing & Heating Inc 148 E Main St *Web:* kinsethplumbing.com	Belmond	IA	50421	641-444-4428	
KLM Mechanical Service Inc 1409 E Bluelick Rd *Web:* klm-mechanical.com	Shepherdsville	KY	40165	502-955-2062	
Kreider Ayers & Assoc Inc 1130 Patterson Ave SW	Roanoke	VA	24016	540-343-7612	
Kuhlman Inc N 56 W 16865 Ridgewood Dr *TF:* 800-781-9229 ■ *Web:* www.kuhlmaninc.com	Menomonee Falls	WI	53051	262-252-9400	252-9401
Lawman Heating & Cooling Inc PO Box 599 *Web:* www.lawmanhc.com	Sackets Harbor	NY	13685	315-646-2919	
Lawson Mechanical Contractors 6090 S Watt Ave *Web:* www.lawsonmechanical.com	Sacramento	CA	95829	916-381-5000	381-5073
Leardon Boiler Works Inc 479 Walton Ave	Bronx	NY	10451	718-585-5314	
Lee Co Inc 331 Mallory Stn Rd *TF:* 888-567-7747 ■ *Web:* www.leecompany.com	Franklin	TN	37067	615-567-1000	567-1026
Lightfoot Air Conditioning & Refrigeration 1414 W Oak *Web:* lightfootair.com	Palestine	TX	75801	903-723-2665	
Limbach Facility Services LLC 31 35th St *Web:* www.limbachinc.com	Pittsburgh	PA	15201	412-359-2100	359-2235
Long Building Technologies Inc 5001 S Zuni St *Web:* long.com	Littleton	CO	80120	303-975-2100	
Lutz Frey Corp 1195 Ivy Dr *TF:* 800-280-6794 ■ *Web:* www.freylutz.com	Lancaster	PA	17601	717-898-6808	898-3421
MA Ogg Heating & Air Conditioning 4721 Arrow Hwy Ste B	Montclair	CA	91763	909-624-8608	
MacDonald-Miller Facility Solutions Inc 7717 Detroit Ave SE *TF:* 800-962-5979 ■ *Web:* www.macmiller.com	Seattle	WA	98106	206-763-9400	767-6773
Mallory & Evans Inc 646 Kentucky St *Web:* www.malloryandevans.com	Scottdale	GA	30079	404-297-1000	297-1075
Mared Mechanical Contractors Corp 4230 W Douglas Ave *Web:* maredmechanical.com	Milwaukee	WI	53209	414-536-0411	
Martin Petersen Company Inc 9800 55th St *Web:* mpcmech.com	Kenosha	WI	53144	262-658-1326	658-1048
Martz Plumbing & Heating Inc 216 W Fifth St	Waynesboro	PA	17268	717-762-6115	
McCarl's Inc 1413 Ninth Ave *Web:* www.mccarl.com	Beaver Falls	PA	15010	724-843-5660	843-3180
McClure Co 4101 N Sixth St *TF:* 800-382-1319 ■ *Web:* www.mcclureco.com	Harrisburg	PA	17110	717-232-9743	236-5239
McCrea Equipment Company Inc 4463 Beech Rd *TF:* 800-597-0091 ■ *Web:* mccreaway.com	Temple Hills	MD	20748	301-423-4585	899-9476
McKenney's Inc 1056 Moreland Industrial Blvd SE *TF:* 877-440-4204 ■ *Web:* www.mckenneys.com	Atlanta	GA	30316	404-622-5000	624-8665
McKinstry Co 5005 Third Ave S *TF:* 800-669-6223 ■ *Web:* www.mckinstry.com	Seattle	WA	98134	206-762-3311	762-2624
McNutt Service Group Inc 39 Loop Rd *Web:* www.mcnuttservicegroup.com	Arden	NC	28704	828-693-0933	
Meccon Industries Inc 2703 Bernice Rd *Web:* www.meccon.com	Lansing	IL	60438	708-474-8300	474-9550
Mechanical Service Corp 41 S Jefferson Rd *Web:* mscnj.com	Whippany	NJ	07981	973-884-5000	
Mechanical Construction Company LLC 3001 17th St *Web:* www.mccgroup.com	Metairie	LA	70002	504-833-8291	831-4760
Mechanical Inc 2283 US Rt 20 E *TF:* 877-426-6628 ■ *Web:* www.helmgroup.com	Freeport	IL	61032	815-235-2200	235-1940
Merit Electrical Inc 17723 Airline Hwy *Web:* www.meritelectrical.com	Prairieville	LA	70769	225-673-8850	673-8838
Mid-State Contracting LLC 2001 County Hwy U *Web:* www.midstatecontracting.com	Wausau	WI	54402	715-675-2388	675-6971
Midwest Mechanical Group 801 Parkview Blvd *TF:* 800-214-3680 ■ *Web:* www.midwestmech.com	Lombard	IL	60148	630-850-2300	655-0730
Miller Engineering Co 1616 S Main St *Web:* mecogroup.com	Rockford	IL	61102	815-963-4878	963-0823
Miscor Group Ltd 800 Nave Rd SE *OTC:* MIGL ■ *Web:* www.miscor.com	Massillon	OH	44646	330-830-3500	830-3520
Mitchell Plumbing & Heating Company Inc 801 N Rowley St 1328	Mitchell	SD	57301	605-996-7583	
MJ Flaherty Co One Gateway Ctr Ste 450 *Web:* www.mjflaherty-hvac.com	Newton	MA	02458	617-969-1492	964-0176
MJ Mechanical Services Inc 2040 Military Rd *Web:* tonawandaboilerrepair.com	Tonawanda	NY	14150	716-874-9200	
MM Comfort Systems 18103 NE 68th St *Web:* mmcomfortsystems.com	Redmond	WA	98052	425-881-7920	
MMC Corp 10955 Lowell Ste 350 *Web:* mmccorp1932.com	Overland Park	KS	66210	913-469-0101	469-8780
Mock Plumbing & Mechanical Inc PO Box 22456 *Web:* www.mocksavannah.com	Savannah	GA	31403	912-232-1104	232-6284
Mollenberg-Betz Inc 300 Scott St *Web:* www.mollenbergbetz.com	Buffalo	NY	14204	716-614-7473	614-7465
Monterey Mechanical Co 8275 San Leandro St *Web:* www.montmech.com	Oakland	CA	94621	510-632-3173	632-0732
Moore J & Co 118 Naylon Ave *Web:* www.jmoore.com	Livingston	NJ	07039	973-992-6970	992-8860
Morrison Construction Co 1834 Summer St *Web:* www.mcco.com	Hammond	IN	46320	219-932-5036	933-7302
Mountain Air Conditioning & Heating Corp 735 S Broadway	Hicksville	NY	11801	516-935-0149	
Mr Rooter Corp 1010 N University Parks Dr **Fax Area Code:* 254 ■ *TF:* 877-766-8305 ■ *Web:* www.mrrooter.com	Waco	TX	76707	800-583-8003	745-2501*
Multiple Ventilation Products Inc 1313 Bigley Ave *Web:* mvphvac.net	Charleston	WV	25302	304-720-8686	
Murphy & Miller Inc 600 W Taylor St *Web:* www.murphymiller.com	Chicago	IL	60607	312-427-8900	427-0324
Murphy Co Mechanical Contractors & Engineers 1233 N Price Rd *TF:* 888-838-4038 ■ *Web:* www.murphynet.com	Saint Louis	MO	63132	314-997-6600	997-4536
MYR Group 1701 W Golf Rd Twr 3 Ste 1012 *Web:* www.myrgroup.com	Rolling Meadows	IL	60008	847-290-1891	290-1892
Nagelbush Mechanical Inc 1800 NW 49th St Ste 110 *Web:* www.nagelbush.com	Fort Lauderdale	FL	33309	954-736-3000	748-7881
National HVAC Service Ltd 101 Bradford Rd Ste 340 *TF:* 800-281-3608 ■ *Web:* www.nationalhvacservice.com	Wexford	PA	15090	724-935-9390	935-9533
Nitro Electric Co LLC 4300 First Ave 2nd Fl **Fax:* Acctg ■ *Web:* www.nitro-electric.com	Nitro	WV	25143	304-722-7701	757-1213*
NV Heathorn Co 1155 Beecher St *Web:* www.nvheathorn.com	San Leandro	CA	94577	510-569-9100	569-9106
Oak Brook Mechanical Services Inc 961 S Rt 83 *Web:* omshvac.com	Elmhurst	IL	60126	630-941-3555	941-0294
Oasis Air Conditioning Heating & Sheet Metal Inc 1931 Grimes St	Fallon	NV	89406	775-423-5258	
Oregon Equipment Service Corpora 180 NE Irving Ave *Web:* oregonequipmentservice.com	Bend	OR	97701	541-388-2235	
Ouellette Plumbing & Heating 36 Dorset Ln	Williston	VT	05495	802-878-6004	
P & D Mechanical Inc 627 Old Hartford Rd	Colchester	CT	06415	860-537-0617	
P1 Group Inc 2151 Haskell Ave Bldg 1 *TF:* 800-376-2911 ■ *Web:* www.p1group.com	Lawrence	KS	66046	785-843-2910	843-2884
Pace Mechanical Services Inc 301 Merritt Seven *TF:* 866-890-7794 ■ *Web:* www.emcorgroup.com	Norwalk	CT	06851	203-849-7800	849-7900
Pacific Mechanical Corp 2501 Annalisa Dr *Web:* www.pmcorporation.com	Concord	CA	94520	925-827-4940	827-0519
Palmer & Sicard Inc 140 Epping Rd *Web:* palmerandsicard.com	Exeter	NH	03833	603-778-1841	778-0119
Par Plumbing Company Inc 60 N Prospect Ave *Web:* www.parplumbing.com	Lynbrook	NY	11563	516-887-4000	593-9089
PC Godfrey Inc 1816 Rozzells Ferry Rd *Web:* pcgodfreyservice.com	Charlotte	NC	28208	704-334-8604	376-5186
PC Jackson Plumbing 3908 Corporation Cir	Charlotte	NC	28216	704-391-1017	
Penguin Air Conditioning Corp 26 W St *Web:* www.penguinac.com	Brooklyn	NY	11222	718-706-6500	706-2536
Performance Contracting Group Inc 16400 College Blvd *TF:* 800-255-6886 ■ *Web:* www.pcg.com	Lenexa	KS	66219	913-888-8600	492-8723
Piedmont Mechanical Inc 116 John Dodd Rd *TF:* 800-849-5725 ■ *Web:* www.piedmontmechanical.com	Spartanburg	SC	29303	864-578-9114	578-5314
Pierce Assoc Inc 4216 Wheeler Ave PO Box 9050 *Web:* www.pierceassociates.com	Alexandria	VA	22304	703-751-2400	751-2479
Pipco Cos Ltd, The 1409 W Altorfer Dr	Peoria	IL	61615	309-692-4060	
Pleune Service Co 750 Himes Se *Web:* pleuneservice.com	Grand Rapids	MI	49548	616-243-6374	
Plyler Construction 3505 Texoma Pkwy PO Box 912406 *Web:* www.plylerbuilds.com	Sherman	TX	75091	903-893-6393	892-3523
Poole & Kent Corp 4530 Hollins Ferry Rd *Web:* www.poole-kent.com	Baltimore	MD	21227	410-247-2200	247-2331
Postler & Jaeckle Corp 615 S Ave *TF:* 800-724-4252 ■ *Web:* www.postlerandjaeckle.com	Rochester	NY	14620	585-546-7450	546-4316
Power Piping Co 436 Butler St *Web:* powerpipingcompany.com	Pittsburgh	PA	15223	412-323-6200	323-6334
Power Process Piping Inc 45780 Port St *Web:* www.ppphq.com	Plymouth	MI	48170	734-451-0130	451-0763
Precision Piping & Mechanical Inc 5201 Middle Mt Vernon Rd *Web:* www.ppmiconstruction.com	Evansville	IN	47712	812-425-5052	425-5067
Pritchett Controls Inc 6980 Muirkirk Meadows Dr *Web:* pritchettcontrols.com	Beltsville	MD	20705	301-470-7300	
Pro-Tec Refrigeration Inc 3640 N 39th Ave *Web:* protecref.com	Phoenix	AZ	85019	602-222-9881	

Phone *Fax*

Process Construction Inc
1421 Queen City Ave .... Cincinnati OH 45214 513-251-2211 251-2267
Web: www.processconstruction.com

PSF Industries Inc 65 S Horton St.................... Seattle WA 98134 206-622-1252 682-1070
TF General: 800-426-1204 ■ *Web:* www.psfindustries.com

Questec Constructors Inc
1390 Boone Industrial Dr Ste 260.................. Columbia MO 65202 573-875-0260
Web: questec.us

Ralph Warner & Sons Inc Plumbing & Heating
161 Berlin St................................ Southington CT 06489 860-628-6826

Ray L Hellwig Plumbing & Heating Inc
1301 Laurelwood Rd.......................... Santa Clara CA 95054 408-727-5612 727-4382
Web: www.rlhellwig.com

Reedy Industries Inc 2440 Ravine Way Ste 200........ Glenview IL 60025 847-729-9450 729-0558
Web: www.reedyindustries.com

Regional Heating & Air Conditioning Inc
2525 Won Rd .... Colorado Springs CO 80910 719-392-6171

Reigel Plumbing & Heating Inc
1701 S Galvin Ave .... Marshfield WI 54449 715-387-3411
Web: reigelplumbing.com

Remco Inc 195 Hempt Rd..................... Mechanicsburg PA 17050 717-697-0389
Web: remcopa.com

Riggs Distler Company Inc
9411 Philadelphia Rd Ste M....................... Baltimore MD 21237 410-633-0300 633-2119
Web: www.riggsdistler.com

RJH Air Conditioning & Refrige
12232 Distribution Pl........................... Beltsville MD 20705 301-776-7270
Web: rjhhvacr.com

RK Mechanical Inc 3800 Xanthia St .... Denver CO 80238 303-355-9696 355-8666
TF: 877-576-9696 ■ *Web:* www.rkmi.com

Robert Gibb & Sons Inc 205 SW 40th St .... Fargo ND 58103 701-282-5900 281-0819
Web: www.robertgibb.com

Robert Jones Plumbing Inc 6071 SR- 128 .... Cleves OH 45002 513-353-2230 353-2247
Web: robertjonesplumbing.com

Rock Hill Mechanical Corp 524 Clark Ave .... Saint Louis MO 63122 314-966-0600 966-3679
Web: www.rhmcorp.com

Roth Bros Inc PO Box 4209 .... Youngstown OH 44515 330-793-5571 793-3930
TF: 800-872-7684 ■ *Web:* www.rothbros.com

Roth Heating Company Inc 400 W Drexel Ave........ Oak Creek WI 53154 414-764-4700
Web: rothheating.com

Roto-Rooter Inc
255 E Fifth St 2500 Chemed Ctr.................... Cincinnati OH 45202 513-762-6690 762-6590
TF: 800-768-6911 ■ *Web:* www.rotorooter.com

RW Warner Inc 217 Monroe Ave...................... Frederick MD 21701 301-662-5387 698-0451
TF: 800-854-5387 ■ *Web:* www.rwwarner.com

Saber Plumbing Co 325 Market Pl................. Escondido CA 92029 760-480-5716
Web: saberplumbing.com

Sauer Inc 11223 Phillips Pkwy Dr E .... Jacksonville FL 32256 904-262-6444
Web: www.sauer-inc.com

SB Ballard Construction Co
2828 Shipps Corner Rd .... Virginia Beach VA 23453 757-440-5555 451-2873
Web: www.sbballard.com

Schambach Plumbing & Heating Inc
40W899 Russell Rd .... Elgin IL 60124 847-464-5373

Schoppe Company Inc 352 Van Buren Ave........ Salt Lake City UT 84115 801-467-5466
Web: schoppe.net

Schweizer Dipple Inc 7227 Div St .... Cleveland OH 44146 440-786-8090 786-8099
Web: www.schweizer-dipple.com

Shambaugh & Son LP 7614 Opportunity Dr......... Fort Wayne IN 46825 260-487-7777 487-7701
TF: 866-890-7794 ■ *Web:* www.shambaugh.com

Shaw-Winkler Inc 4910 Dawn Ave.............. East Lansing MI 48823 517-351-5720
Web: shawwinkler.com

Shook & Fletcher Mechanical Contractors Inc
2915 Richard Arrington Jr Blvd N.................. Birmingham AL 35203 205-252-9400 252-9407
Web: shook-fletcher.com

Sigman Heating & Air Conditioning
6200 Old Saint Louis Rd.......................... Belleville IL 62223 618-234-4343
Web: sigmanhvacr.com

Silvertip Inc 600 St Mary St...................... Lewisburg PA 17837 570-523-1206
Web: silvertip-inc.com

Smith & Oby Co 7676 Northfield Rd............... Walton Hills OH 44146 440-735-5333 735-5334
Web: www.smithandoby.com

Sojam LLC Dba Martin J Braun Co
6325 Erdman Ave............................... Baltimore MD 21205 410-488-3990

Southern Air Inc 2655 Lakeside Dr................ Lynchburg VA 24501 434-385-6200 385-9081
TF: 800-743-1214 ■ *Web:* www.southern-air.com

Southern Industrial Constructors Inc
6101 Triangle Dr.................................. Raleigh NC 27617 919-782-4600 782-2935
TF: 866-890-7794 ■ *Web:* www.southernindustrial.com

Southland Industries
7421 Orangewood Ave .... Garden Grove CA 92841 714-901-5800 901-5811
Web: www.southlandind.com

Spengler Company Inc 1402 Frontage Rd .... Ofallon IL 62269 618-632-4433
Web: spenglerco.com

Stratz Heating & Cooling Inc
20960 19 Mile Rd................................ Big Rapids MI 49307 231-796-3717
Web: stratzheatingandcooling.com

Stromberg Sheet Metal Works Inc
6701 Distribution Dr............................ Beltsville MD 20705 301-931-1000 931-1020
Web: www.strombergmetals.com

Sturdevant Refrigeration & Air Conditioning Inc
475 Hukilike St.................................. Kahului HI 96732 808-871-6404
Web: www.sturdevantair.com

Sturm Heating Inc 1112 N Nelson St.................. Spokane WA 99202 509-325-4505
Web: sturmheating.com

SubZero Constructors Inc
30055 Comercio..................... Rancho Santa Margarita CA 92688 949-216-9500 216-9539
Web: www.szero.com

Summers Heating & Air Conditio
6031 Rising Sun Ave .... Philadelphia PA 19111 215-722-3716
Web: summersquality.com

Phone *Fax*

Systems Contracting Corp
214 N Washington Ave Ste 700 .... El Dorado AR 71730 870-862-1315
Web: tsg.bz

TA Caid Industries Inc 2275 E Ganley Rd .... Tucson AZ 85706 520-294-3126 294-8180
Web: www.caid.com

Tatro Plumbing Company Inc
1285 Acraway Ste 300 .... Garden City KS 67846 620-277-2167
Web: tatroplumbing.com

TDIndustries 13850 Diplomat Dr....................... Dallas TX 75234 972-888-9500
Web: www.tdindustries.com

Telgian Corp 11230 Sorrento Vly Rd .... San Diego CA 92121 858-795-1000 795-1001
Web: www.telgian.com

Thorpe Heating & Cooling Inc
8402 Us Hwy 98 N .... Lakeland FL 33809 863-858-2577
Web: thorpeac.com

Tom Rostron Co Inc
2490 Tiltons Corner Rd........................ Wall Township NJ 07719 732-223-8221
Web: tomrostron.com

Trautman & Shreve Inc 4406 Race St .... Denver CO 80216 303-295-1414 295-0324
Web: www.trautman-shreve.com

Trouble Free Plumbing Inc 802 Willow St............... Pekin IL 61554 309-347-5309 347-6140
Web: troublefreeinc.com

University Mechanical & Engineering Contractors Inc
1168 Fesler St .... El Cajon CA 92020 619-956-2500 956-2300
Web: www.umec.com

US Engineering Co 3433 Roanoke Rd .... Kansas City MO 64111 816-753-6969 931-5773
Web: www.usengineering.com

US Home Services 9260 Marketplace Dr .... Miamisburg OH 45342 937-898-0826
Web: directenergy.com

Vals Plumbing & Heating Inc 413 Front St .... Salinas CA 93901 831-424-1633
Web: valsplumbing.com

Vasey Commercial Heating & Air Company Nditioning Inc
10830 Andrade Dr .... Zionsville IN 46077 317-873-2512
Web: vasey.biz

Vermont Heating & Ventilating Company Inc
16 Tigan St Ste A .... Winooski VT 05404 802-655-8805 655-8809
Web: www.vhv.com

Victoria Air Conditioning Ltd 513 Profit Dr .... Victoria TX 77901 361-578-5241
Web: victoriaair.com

Viglione Heating & Cooling Inc
259 Commerce St.............................. East Haven CT 06512 203-787-8588
Web: viglione.biz

Walter N Yoder & Sons Inc
16200 McMullen Hwy SW PO Box 1337 .... Cumberland MD 21502 301-729-0610 729-1517
Web: wnyoder.com

Ward Systems & Services Inc 2121 Cee Gee .... San Antonio TX 78217 210-824-7683

Warwick Plumbing & Heating Corp
11048 Warwick Blvd........................ Newport News VA 23601 757-599-6111 595-9739
Web: www.wphcorp.com

Way Engineering Ltd 5308 Ashbrook Dr............... Houston TX 77081 713-666-3541 666-8455
Web: wayeng.com

Wayne Crouse Inc 3370 Stafford St................. Pittsburgh PA 15204 412-771-5176 771-2357
Web: www.waynecrouse.com

WB Guimarin & Co Inc
1124 Bluff Industrial Blvd .... Columbia SC 29202 803-256-0515 252-8239
Web: www.wbguimarin.com

WB Wallis & Co 540 Kentucky St .... Scottdale GA 30079 404-294-1722
Web: wbwallis.com

WD Manor Mechanical Contractors Inc
1838 N 23rd Ave.................................. Phoenix AZ 85009 602-253-0703 253-3659
Web: www.wdmanor.com

Weather Champions Ltd 158 Dikeman St .... Brooklyn NY 11231 718-522-0300
Web: wechamps.com

Webb Heating & Air Conditioning 170 Webb Way...... Advance NC 27006 336-998-2121
Web: webbhvac.com

Weeks Service Co 1306 Hwy 3 S .... League City TX 77573 281-332-9555 332-9558
Web: weeksservicecompany.com

Wellington Power Corp 40th & Butler Sts........... Pittsburgh PA 15201 412-681-0103 681-0109
TF: 800-540-0017 ■ *Web:* www.wellingtonpower.com

Western Air & Refrigeration Co
15914 S Avalon Blvd .... Compton CA 90220 310-327-4400
Web: www.limbachinc.com

WG Tomko Inc 2559 Rt 88.......................... Finleyville PA 15332 724-348-2000 348-7001
Web: www.wgtomko.com

William E Walter Inc 1917 Howard Ave .... Flint MI 48503 810-232-7459 232-8698
TF: 800-681-3320 ■ *Web:* www.williamewalter.com

Williard Limbach 175 Titus Ave Ste 100............ Warrington PA 18976 215-488-9700 488-9699*
**Fax:* Cust Svc ■ *Web:* www.limbachinc.com

Worth & Company Inc
6263 Kellers Church Rd .... Pipersville PA 18947 267-362-1100 362-1130
TF: 800-220-5130 ■ *Web:* www.worthandcompany.com

Yearout Mechanical & Engineering Inc
8501 Washington St NE .... Albuquerque NM 87113 505-884-0994 883-5073
Web: www.yearout.com

Young Plumbing & Heating Co
750 S Hackett Rd .... Waterloo IA 50701 319-234-4411 234-4540
Web: www.youngphc.com

192-11 Remodeling, Refinishing, Resurfacing Contractors

Phone *Fax*

A J Johns Inc 3225 Anniston Rd .... Jacksonville FL 32246 904-641-2055 641-2102
Web: www.ajjohns.com

Bathcrest Inc 5195 W 4700 S.................. Salt Lake City UT 84118 801-957-1400
TF: 800-826-6790 ■ *Web:* www.bathcrest.com

California Closet Co 610A DuBois St............... San Rafael CA 94901 415-256-8500 256-8501
TF General: 888-336-9707 ■ *Web:* www.californiaclosets.com

Closet Factory 12800 S Broadway.................. Los Angeles CA 90061 310-516-7000 516-8065
TF: 800-838-7995 ■ *Web:* www.closetfactory.com

Phone Fax

DreamMaker Bath & Kitchen by Worldwide
510 N Valley Mills Dr Ste 304 .... Waco TX 76710 800-583-2133
TF: 800-583-2133 ■ *Web:* www.dreammaker-remodel.com

Handyman Connection Inc 11115 Kenwood Rd ...... Cincinnati OH 45242 513-771-3003 771-6439
TF: 800-884-2639 ■ *Web:* www.handymanconnection.com

Kitchen Tune-Up Inc 813 Cir Dr .... Aberdeen SD 57401 605-225-4049
TF: 800-333-6385 ■ *Web:* www.kitchentuneup.com

Miracle Method US Corp
4239 N Nevada Ave Ste 115 .... Colorado Springs CO 80907 719-594-9091 594-9282
TF: 800-444-8827 ■ *Web:* www.miraclemethod.com

Perma-Glaze Inc 1638 Research Loop Rd Ste 160 .... Tucson AZ 85710 520-722-9718 296-4393
TF: 800-332-7397 ■ *Web:* www.permaglaze.com

Re-Bath LLC 16879 N 75th Ave Ste 101 .... Peoria AZ 85382 800-426-4573
TF: 800-426-4573 ■ *Web:* rebath.com

192-12 Roofing, Siding, Sheet Metal Contractors

Phone Fax

A Zahner Sheet Metal Company Inc
1400 E Ninth St .... Kansas City MO 64106 816-474-8882 474-7994
Web: www.azahner.com

AC Dellovade Inc 108 Cavasina Dr .... Canonsburg PA 15317 724-873-8190 873-8187
Web: www.acdellovade.com

All-South Subcontractors Inc
2678 Queenstown Rd .... Birmingham AL 35210 205-836-8111 836-4227
TF: 800-873-8110 ■ *Web:* www.allsouthsub.com

Anson Industries Inc 1959 Anson Dr .... Melrose Park IL 60160 708-681-1300 681-1310
Web: www.ansonindustries.com

B & M Roofing of Colorado Inc
3768 Eureka Way .... Frederick CO 80516 303-443-5843 938-9642
Web: www.bmroofing.com

Baker Roofing Co 517 Mercury St .... Raleigh NC 27603 919-828-2975 828-9352
TF: 800-849-4096 ■ *Web:* www.bakerroofing.com

Beldon Enterprises Inc PO Box 13380 .... San Antonio TX 78213 210-341-3100 341-2959
TF: 800-688-7663 ■ *Web:* www.beldon.com

BHW Sheet Metal Co 113 Johnson St .... Jonesboro GA 30236 770-471-9303 478-7923
Web: bhwsm.com

Birdair Inc 65 Lawrence Bell Dr .... Amherst NY 14221 716-633-9500 633-9850
TF: 800-622-2246 ■ *Web:* www.birdair.com

Bonland Industries Inc 50 Newark-Pompton Tpke .... Wayne NJ 07470 973-694-3211 628-1120
TF: 800-232-6600 ■ *Web:* www.bonlandhvac.com

Brazos Urethane Inc 1031 Sixth St N .... Texas City TX 77590 409-965-0011 948-1511
TF: 866-527-2967 ■ *Web:* www.brazosurethane.com

BT Mancini Co Inc 876 S Milpitas Blvd .... Milpitas CA 95035 408-942-7900 945-1360
TF: 800-787-6381 ■ *Web:* www.btmancini.com

Centimark Corp 12 Grandview Cir .... Canonsburg PA 15317 800-558-4100 743-7770*
**Fax Area Code:* 724 ■ *TF:* 800-558-4100 ■ *Web:* www.centimark.com

Charles F Evans Company Inc 800 Canal St .... Elmira NY 14901 607-734-8151 733-5422
Web: evansroofingcompany.com

Commercial Siding & Maintenance Co, The
8059 Crile Rd .... Painesville OH 44077 440-352-7800 352-7048
TF: 800-229-4276 ■ *Web:* www.commercialsiding.com

Construction Services Inc 2214 S Lincoln St .... Amarillo TX 79109 806-373-1732 373-9472

Crown Corr Inc 7100 W 21st Ave .... Gary IN 46406 219-949-8080 944-9922
Web: www.crowncorr.com

DC Taylor Co 312 29th St NE .... Cedar Rapids IA 52402 319-363-2073 363-8311
TF: 800-876-6346 ■ *Web:* www.dctaylorco.com

Dee Cramer Inc 4221 E Baldwin Rd .... Holly MI 48442 810-579-5000 579-2664
TF: 888-342-6995 ■ *Web:* www.deecramer.com

Dix Corp 4024 S Grove Rd .... Spokane WA 99224 509-838-4455 838-4464
Web: www.dixcorp.com

Douglass Colony Group Inc
5901 E 58th Ave .... Commerce City CO 80022 303-288-2635 288-8602
Web: www.douglasscolony.com

Elmsford Sheet Metal Work Inc
23 Arlo Ln .... Cortlandt Manor NY 10567 914-739-6300 739-1285
Web: www.elmsfordsheetmetal.com

Enterprise Roofing & Sheet Metal Co
1021 Irving St .... Dayton OH 45419 937-298-8664 298-4516
Web: www.enterpriserfg.com

Flynn Canada Ltd 1390 Spruce St .... Winnipeg MB R3E2V7 204-786-6951 788-4584
TF General: 877-856-8566 ■ *Web:* www.flynn.ca

Fort Roofing & Sheet Metal Works Inc
14 W Oakland Ave .... Sumter SC 29150 803-773-9391 773-7711
Web: www.fortroofing.com

Gowan Inc 5550 Airline Dr .... Houston TX 77076 713-696-5400 695-1726
Web: www.gowaninc.com

Hahnel Bros Co (HBC)
46 Strawberry Ave PO Box 1160 .... Lewiston ME 04243 207-784-6477 782-9859
Web: www.hahnelbrosco.com

Heidler Roofing Services Inc 2120 Alpha Dr .... York PA 17408 717-792-3549 792-4660
TF: 866-792-3549 ■ *Web:* www.heidlerroofing.com

Henry C Smither Roofing Company Inc
6850 E 32nd St PO Box 26057 .... Indianapolis IN 46226 317-545-1304 546-4764
Web: www.smitherroofing.com

IG Inc 720 S Sara Rd .... Mustang OK 73137 405-376-9393 376-3933
TF: 800-654-8433 ■ *Web:* www.igok.com

Jamar Co 4701 Mike Colalillo Dr .... Duluth MN 55807 218-628-1027 628-1174
Web: www.jamarcompany.com

John J Campbell Company Inc
6012 Resources Dr .... Memphis TN 38134 901-372-8400
Web: www.campbellroofing.com

Johnson Contracting Company Inc
2750 Morton Dr .... East Moline IL 61244 309-755-0601 752-7056
Web: www.jccinc.com

Jottan Inc PO Box 166 .... Florence NJ 08518 609-447-6200 447-6200
TF: 800-364-4234 ■ *Web:* www.jottan.com

JP Patti Company Inc
365 Jefferson St PO Box 539 .... Saddle Brook NJ 07663 973-478-6200 478-2175
Web: www.jppatti.com

Ketcher & Co Inc 1717 E 5th .... North Little Rock AR 72114 501-372-5216 372-0949
Web: ketcherco.com

LE Schwartz & Son Inc 279 Reid St .... Macon GA 31206 478-745-6563 745-2711
Web: www.leschwartz.com

M Gottfried Roofing Inc 89 Research Dr .... Stamford CT 06906 203-323-8173 359-2498
Web: www.mgottfried.com

Midland Engineering 52369 SR 933 N .... South Bend IN 46637 574-272-0200 272-7400
Web: www.midlandengineering.com

Miller-Thomas-Gyekis Inc 3341 Stafford St .... Pittsburgh PA 15204 412-331-4610 331-8871

National International Roofing Corp
11317 Smith Dr .... Huntley IL 60142 847-669-3444 669-3173
TF: 800-221-7663 ■ *Web:* www.nir.com

North American Roofing Services Inc
41 Dogwood Rd .... Asheville NC 28806 828-687-7767 687-1230
TF: 800-876-5602 ■ *Web:* www.naroofing.com

Olsson Roofing Company Inc 740 S Lake St .... Aurora IL 60506 630-892-0449 892-1556
Web: www.olssonroofing.com

Orndorff & Spaid Inc
11722 Old Baltimore Pk .... Beltsville MD 20705 301-937-5911 937-0310
Web: www.osroofing.com

R.A. Smith National Inc
16745 W Bluemound Rd Ste 200 .... Brookfield WI 53005 262-781-1000 781-8466
Web: www.rasmith.com

RD Herbert & Sons Company Inc
1407 Third Ave N .... Nashville TN 37208 615-242-3501 256-4056
Web: www.rdherbert.com

Schreiber Corp 29945 Beck Rd .... Wixom MI 48393 248-926-1500 926-1788
TF: 800-558-2706 ■ *Web:* www.schreiberroofing.com

Schust Engineering Inc 701 North St .... Auburn IN 46706 800-686-9297 482-9291*
**Fax Area Code:* 260 ■ *TF:* 800-686-9297 ■ *Web:* www.schustengineering.com

Sechrist-Hall Co 102 Omaha .... Corpus Christi TX 78408 361-884-5264

Silktown Roofing Inc 27 Pleasant St .... Manchester CT 06040 860-647-0198
Web: www.silktownroofing.com

Snyder Roofing & Sheet Metal Inc
12650 SW Hall Blvd .... Tigard OR 97223 503-620-5252 684-3310
Web: snyder-builds.com

Standard Roofing Co
516 N McDonough St PO Box 1309 .... Montgomery AL 36102 334-265-1262 834-3004
TF: 800-239-5705 ■ *Web:* www.standardtaylor.com

Superior Roofing & Sheet Metal Co Inc
3405 S 500 W .... Salt Lake City UT 84115 801-266-1473 266-1522
Web: www.superior-roof.l7marketing.com

TDIndustries 13850 Diplomat Dr .... Dallas TX 75234 972-888-9500
Web: www.tdindustries.com

Tecta America Co 15002 Wicks Blvd .... San Leandro CA 94577 510-686-4951
Web: www.tectaamerica.com

Tri-State Roofing & Sheet Metal Group
PO Box 5310 .... Vienna WV 26105 304-295-3311 295-6991
Web: www.tri-stateservicegroup.com

Turner Roofing & Sheet Metal Inc
1200 E Memphis St .... Broken Arrow OK 74012 918-258-2585 251-9913
Web: www.turnerroofing.com

US Industries Inc 1701 First Ave .... Evansville IN 47710 812-425-2428
TF: 800-456-8721

Western Fireproofing Company of Kansas Inc
1501 Westport Rd .... Kansas City MO 64111 816-561-7667
Web: www.westernfireproofing.com

192-13 Sprinkler System Installation (Fire Sprinklers)

Phone Fax

Active Fire Sprinkler Corp 63 Flushing Ave .... Brooklyn NY 11205 718-834-8300

Advance Fire Protection Company Inc
1451 W Lambert Rd .... La Habra CA 90631 562-691-0918 691-5482
Web: firesprinkleradvisoryboard.org

All-South Subcontractors Inc
2678 Queenstown Rd .... Birmingham AL 35210 205-836-8111 836-4227
TF: 800-873-8110 ■ *Web:* www.allsouthsub.com

APi Group Inc Fire Protection Group
1100 Old Hwy 8 NW .... New Brighton MN 55112 800-223-4922 636-0312*
**Fax Area Code:* 651 ■ *TF:* 800-223-4922 ■ *Web:* apigroupinc.com

August Winter & Sons Inc 2323 N Roemer Rd .... Appleton WI 54911 920-739-8881 739-2230
TF: 800-236-8882 ■ *Web:* www.augustwinter.com

Brendle Sprinkler Co Inc 3635 S Montgomery St .... Tacoma WA 98409 334-270-8571 277-7967
TF: 800-392-8021

Cosco Fire Protection Inc
1075 W Lambert Rd Bldg D .... Brea CA 92821 714-989-1800 989-1801
TF: 800-485-3795 ■ *Web:* www.coscofire.com

Crisp-Ladew Fire Protection Co
5201 Saunders Rd .... Fort Worth TX 76119 817-572-3663
Web: crisp-ladew.com

FE Moran 2265 Carlson Dr .... Northbrook IL 60062 847-498-4800 498-9091
Web: femoran.com

Fire Protection Co 12828 S Ridgeway Ave .... Alsip IL 60803 708-371-4300 371-4340

Fire Protection Systems Inc
22 Industrial Pk Dr .... Hendersonville TN 37075 615-822-3600 822-3427
Web: www.fireprotectionsys.com

Firetrol Protection Systems Inc
3696 West 900 South Ste A .... Salt Lake City UT 84104 801-485-6900 485-6902
Web: www.firetrol.net

Geo M Robinson & Co 1461 Atteberry Ln .... San Jose CA 95131 408-432-6264

High Point Sprinkler Inc
Two Regency Industrial Blvd .... Thomasville NC 27360 336-475-6181

JF Ahern Co 855 Morris St .... Fond du Lac WI 54935 920-921-9020 921-8632
TF: 800-532-0155 ■ *Web:* www.jfahern.com

John E Green Co 220 Victor Ave .... Highland Park MI 48203 313-868-2400 868-0011
Web: www.johnegreen.com

McDaniel Fire Systems 1055 W Joliet Rd .... Valparaiso IN 46385 219-462-0571 611-2907*
**Fax Area Code:* 800 ■ *Web:* www.mcdanielfire.com

Company	City	State	ZIP	Phone	Fax
National Automatic Sprinkler Industries 8000 Corporate Dr *TF:* 800-638-2603 ■ *Web:* www.nasifund.org	Landover	MD	20785	301-577-1700	429-4709
Oliver Fire Protection & Security 501 Feheley Dr *Web:* www.oliverfps.com	King of Prussia	PA	19406	610-277-1331	277-2837
Patti & Sons Inc Eight Berry St *Web:* pattispray.com	Brooklyn	NY	11211	718-963-3700	388-8671
SA Comunale Company Inc 2900 Newpark Dr *TF:* 800-776-7181 ■ *Web:* www.sacomunale.com	Barberton	OH	44203	330-706-3040	861-0860
Security Fire Protection Co Inc 4495 Mendenhall Rd S *TF:* 888-274-8595 ■ *Web:* www.securityfire.com	Memphis	TN	38141	901-362-6250	366-7869
Tyco Fire & Security 6600 Congress Ave *Web:* www.tyco.com	Boca Raton	FL	33487	561-912-6000	
Viking Automatic Sprinkler Co 301 York Ave *Web:* www.vikingsprinkler.com	Saint Paul	MN	55130	651-558-3300	558-3310
Wayne Automatic Fire Sprinklers Inc 222 Capital Ct *Web:* www.waynefire.com	Ocoee	FL	34761	407-656-3030	656-8026
Western States Fire Protection Co 7020 S Tucson Way *Web:* www.wsfp.com	Centennial	CO	80112	303-792-0022	790-3875
Wiginton Fire Systems 699 Aero Ln *Web:* www.wiginton.net	Sanford	FL	32771	407-585-3200	585-3280

192-14 Structural Steel Erection

Company	City	State	ZIP	Phone	Fax
Adams & Smith Inc 1380 W Ctr St *Web:* www.adamsandsmith.com	Lindon	UT	84042	801-785-6900	785-6400
Advance Tank & Construction Co 3700 E County Rd 64 PO Box 219 *Web:* www.advancetank.com	Wellington	CO	80549	970-568-3444	568-3435
Albach Company Inc 301 E Prosper St *Web:* www.albachco.com	Chalmette	LA	70043	504-271-1113	
Albany Steel Inc 566 Broadway *TF:* 800-342-9317 ■ *Web:* www.albanysteel.net	Albany	NY	12204	518-436-4851	436-1458
Allstate Steel Company Inc 130 S Jackson Ave *Web:* www.allstatesteel.com	Jacksonville	FL	32220	904-781-6040	783-3421
Arben Group LLC 175 Marble Ave *Web:* arbengroup.com	Pleasantville	NY	10570	914-741-5459	741-2923
Area Erectors Inc 2323 Harrison Ave *Web:* www.areaerectors.com	Rockford	IL	61104	815-398-6700	398-6787
Ben Hur Construction Co 3783 Rider Trail S *Web:* www.benhurconstruction.com	Saint Louis	MO	63045	314-298-8007	298-9671
Bosworth Steel Erectors Inc 4001 Jaffee St *Web:* www.bosworthsteel.com	Dallas	TX	75216	214-371-3700	371-1020
Bratton Corp 2801 E 85th St *Web:* www.brattonsteel.com	Kansas City	MO	64132	816-363-1014	361-8021
Brunton Enterprises Inc 8815 Sorensen Ave *Web:* www.plas-tal.com	Santa Fe Springs	CA	90670	562-945-0013	696-7620
Canron Construction Inc 4600 NE 138th Ave *Web:* supremegroup.com	Portland	OR	97230	503-255-8634	253-3907
CBI Services Inc 24 Read's Way *TF:* 800-642-8675 ■ *Web:* www.cbi.com	New Castle	DE	19720	302-325-8400	323-0788
CE Toland & Son 5300 Industrial Way *Web:* cetoland.com	Benicia	CA	94510	707-747-1000	747-5300
Central Maintenance & Welding Inc (CMW) 2620 E Keysville Rd *TF:* 877-704-7411 ■ *Web:* www.cmw.cc	Lithia	FL	33547	813-737-1402	737-1820
Century Steel Erectors Co 210 Washington Ave PO Box 490 *TF:* 888-601-8801 ■ *Web:* www.centurysteel.com	Dravosburg	PA	15034	412-469-8800	469-0813
Chicago Bridge & Iron Co 6001 Rogerdale Rd *NYSE: CBI* ■ *TF General:* 866-235-5687 ■ *Web:* www.cbi.com	Houston	TX	77072	713-485-1000	485-1005
Dix Corp 4024 S Grove Rd *Web:* www.dixcorp.com	Spokane	WA	99224	509-838-4455	838-4464
Fenton Rigging & Contracting Inc 2150 Langdon Farm Rd *Web:* fenton1898.com	Cincinnati	OH	45237	513-631-5500	631-4361
Fought & Company Inc PO Box 23759 *Web:* www.fought.org	Tigard	OR	97281	503-639-3141	620-3279
High Industries Inc 1853 William Penn Way *Web:* www.high.net	Lancaster	PA	17601	717-293-4444	293-4416
High Steel Structures Inc 1915 Old Philadelphia Pike PO Box 10008 *Web:* www.highsteel.com	Lancaster	PA	17605	717-390-4270	399-4102
Highland Tank & Manufacturing Co One Highland Rd *Web:* www.highlandtank.com	Stoystown	PA	15563	814-893-5701	893-6126
Lafayette Steel Erector Inc 313 Westgate Rd *TF:* 877-234-9435 ■ *Web:* www.l-s-e.com	Lafayette	LA	70506	337-234-9435	234-0217
Midwest Steel & Equipment Company Inc 9825 Moers Rd *Web:* www.midwest-steel.com	Houston	TX	77075	713-991-7843	991-4745
Midwest Steel Inc 2525 E Grand Blvd *Web:* www.midweststeel.com	Detroit	MI	48211	313-873-2220	873-2222
Pittsburg Tank & Tower Co Inc 1 Watertank Pl **Fax:* Sales ■ *TF:* 800-222-5555 ■ *Web:* www.watertank.com	Henderson	KY	42420	270-826-9000	827-4417*
Rebar Engineering Inc 10706 Painter Ave	Santa Fe Springs	CA	90670	562-946-2461	941-7740
Ryan Iron Works Inc 1830 Broadway *Web:* www.ryanironworks.net	Raynham	MA	02767	508-822-8001	823-1359
Schuff Steel Co 420 S 19th Ave *TF:* 800-435-8528 ■ *Web:* www.schuff.com	Phoenix	AZ	85009	602-252-7787	452-4465
Shurtleff & Andrews Corp 1875 West 500 South *Web:* www.shurtleff-slc.com	Salt Lake City	UT	84104	801-973-9096	973-2248
Southeastern Construction & Maintenance Company Inc 1150 Pebbledale Rd PO Box 1055 *Web:* www.southeasternconst.com	Mulberry	FL	33860	863-428-1511	428-1110
Sure Steel Inc 7528 Cornia Dr	South Weber	UT	84405	801-917-5800	917-5799
Tampa Steel Erecting Co 5127 Bloomingdale Ave *Web:* tampasteelerecting.com	Tampa	FL	33619	813-677-7184	677-8364
Walden Structures Inc 801 Opal Ave *Web:* www.waldenstructures.com	Mentone	CA	92359	909-389-9100	
Waldinger Corp 2601 Bell Ave *TF:* 800-473-4934 ■ *Web:* www.waldinger.com	Des Moines	IA	50321	515-284-1911	323-5150
Washington Ornamental Iron Works Inc 17926 S Broadway *Web:* washingtoniron.com	Gardena	CA	90248	310-327-8660	329-4180
Williams Industries Inc 8624 JD Reading Dr *OTC: WMSI* ■ *Web:* www.wmsi.com	Manassas	VA	20109	703-335-7800	335-7802
WO Grubb Steel Erection Inc 5120 Jefferson Davis Hwy *TF:* 866-964-7822 ■ *Web:* www.wogrubb.com	Richmond	VA	23234	804-271-9471	271-2539
Zimkor Industries Inc 7011 W Titan Rd *Web:* www.zimkor.com	Littleton	CO	80125	303-791-1333	791-1340

192-15 Terrazzo, Tile, Marble, Mosaic Contractors

Company	City	State	ZIP	Phone	Fax
Belfi Bros & Company Inc 4310 Josephine St PO Box 9582 *Web:* www.belfibrothers.com	Philadelphia	PA	19124	215-289-2766	289-9208

192-16 Water Well Drilling

Company	City	State	ZIP	Phone	Fax
Alsay Inc 6615 Gant St *TF:* 800-833-5969 ■ *Web:* alsaywater.com	Houston	TX	77066	281-444-6960	444-7081
Kelley Dewatering & Construction Co 5175 Clay Ave SW *Web:* www.kelleydewatering.com	Grand Rapids	MI	49548	616-538-8010	538-0708
Ohio Drilling Co 2405 Bostic Blvd SW *Web:* ohiodrilling.com	Massillon	OH	44647	330-832-1521	832-5302
Ots-Nj LLC (OTS) 340 Bismark Rd *Web:* www.otstel.com	Jackson	NJ	08527	732-833-0600	833-1169
Raba-Kistner Consultants Inc 12821 W Golden Ln *TF:* 866-722-2547 ■ *Web:* www.rkci.com	San Antonio	TX	78249	210-699-9090	699-6426
Rosencrantz-Bemis Water Well Co 1105 Hwy 281 Bypass *TF:* 800-466-2467 ■ *Web:* kansaswaterwelldrilling.com	Great Bend	KS	67530	620-793-5512	793-5176
Tri-State Drilling Inc 16940 Hwy 55 W *TF:* 800-383-1033 ■ *Web:* www.tristatedrilling.com	Plymouth	MN	55446	763-553-1234	553-9778
Water Resources International Inc 1100 Alakea St Ste 2900 *Web:* www.brninc.com	Honolulu	HI	96813	808-531-8422	531-7181

192-17 Wrecking & Demolition Contractors

Company	City	State	ZIP	Phone	Fax
Allied Erecting & Dismantling Company Inc 2100 Poland Ave *TF:* 800-624-2867 ■ *Web:* www.aed.cc	Youngstown	OH	44502	330-744-0808	744-3218
Barnard Construction Company Inc PO Box 99 *Web:* www.barnard-inc.com	Bozeman	MT	59771	406-586-1995	586-3530
Bi-Con Services Inc 10901 Clay Pike Rd *Web:* www.biconservices.com/	Derwent	OH	43733	740-685-2542	685-3863
Bierlein Cos Inc 2000 Bay City Rd *TF:* 800-336-6626 ■ *Web:* www.bierlein.com	Midland	MI	48642	989-496-0066	496-0144
Cherry Demolition 6131 Selinsky Rd *TF:* 800-444-1123 ■ *Web:* www.cherrycompanies.com	Houston	TX	77048	713-987-0000	987-0629
Dustrol Inc 1200 E Main PO Box 309 *Web:* www.dustrol.com	Towanda	KS	67144	316-536-2262	536-2789
Edgerton Contractors Inc 545 W Ryan Rd PO Box 901 *Web:* www.edgertoncontractors.com	Oak Creek	WI	53154	414-764-4443	764-9788
Ferma Corp 1265 Montecito Ave *TF:* 877-337-6211 ■ *Web:* www.fermacorp.com	Mountain View	CA	94043	650-961-2742	968-3945
James White Construction Company Inc 4156 Freedom Way *Web:* jameswhiteconstruction.com	Weirton	WV	26062	304-748-8181	748-8183
Kimmins Contracting Corp 1501 Second Ave *Web:* www.kimmins.com	Tampa	FL	33605	813-248-3878	579-1081
Kipin Industries Inc 4194 Green Garden Rd *TF:* 800-782-8050 ■ *Web:* www.kipin.com	Aliquippa	PA	15001	724-495-6200	495-2219
Manafort Bros Inc 414 New Britain Ave *TF:* 888-626-2367 ■ *Web:* www.manafort.com	Plainville	CT	06062	860-229-4853	747-4861
Mercer Wrecking Recycling Corp 1519 Calhoun St *Web:* mercergroup.com	Trenton	NJ	08638	609-393-6775	
Midwest Steel & Equipment Company Inc 9825 Moers Rd *Web:* www.midwest-steel.com	Houston	TX	77075	713-991-7843	991-4745
National Wrecking Co 2441 N Leavitt St *Web:* www.nationalwrecking.com	Chicago	IL	60647	773-384-2800	384-0403
NCM 404 N Berry St *TF:* 800-283-2933 ■ *Web:* ncmgroup.com	Brea	CA	92821	714-672-3500	

Phone Fax

Noralco Corp 1920 Lincoln Rd ... Pittsburgh PA 15235 412-361-6678 361-6535
Web: www.noralco.com

O'Rourke Wrecking Co 660 Lunken Pk Dr ... Cincinnati OH 45226 513-871-1400 871-1313
TF: 800-354-9850 ■ *Web:* www.orourkewrecking.com

Patuxent Cos 2124 Priest Bridge Dr Ste 18 ... Crofton MD 21114 410-793-0181
TF: 800-628-4942 ■ *Web:* www.patuxentcompanies.com

Plant Reclamation 912 Harbour Way S ... Richmond CA 94804 510-233-6552 237-6739
Web: www.plantreclamation.com

Robinette Demolition Inc
0 S 560 Hwy 83 ... Oakbrook Terrace IL 60181 630-833-7997 833-8047
Web: www.rdidemolition.com

Siciliano Inc 3601 Winchester Rd ... Springfield IL 62707 217-585-1200 585-1211
Web: www.sicilianoinc.com

US Dismantlement LLC 2600 S Throop St ... Chicago IL 60608 312-328-1400 328-1477
Web: www.usdllc.com

193 CONSTRUCTION MACHINERY & EQUIPMENT

SEE ALSO Industrial Machinery, Equipment, & Supplies p. 2554; Material Handling Equipment p. 2720

Phone Fax

Acco Material Handling Solutions LLC
76 Acco Dr PO Box 792 ... York PA 17405 717-741-4863
Web: www.accolifting.com

Allen Engineering Corp 819 S Fifth St ... Paragould AR 72450 870-236-7751
Web: www.alleneng.com

Allied Construction Products LLC
3900 Kelley Ave ... Cleveland OH 44114 216-431-2600 431-2601
TF Cust Svc: 800-321-1046 ■ *Web:* www.alliedcp.com

Allis Roller LLC 9800 S 60th St ... Franklin WI 53132 414-423-9000
Web: www.allis-roller.com

Altec Industries Inc 210 Inverness Ctr Dr ... Birmingham AL 35242 205-991-7733 408-8601
Web: altec.com

Ashland Industries Inc
1115 Rail Dr PO Box 717 ... Ashland WI 54806 715-682-4622
Web: www.ashlandind.com

Asphalt Drum Mixers Inc (ADM) One ADM Pkwy ... Huntertown IN 46748 260-637-5729 637-3164
Web: www.admasphaltplants.com

Astec Industries Inc 1725 Shepherd Rd ... Chattanooga TN 37421 423-899-5898 899-4456
NASDAQ: ASTE ■ *Web:* www.astecindustries.com

Atlantic Construction Fabrics Inc
2831 CaRdwell Rd ... Richmond VA 23234 804-271-2363 743-7779
TF: 800-448-3636 ■ *Web:* www.acfenvironmental.com

Automation Engineering LLC 1100 W Grand Ave ... Salina KS 67401 785-309-0505
Web: www.bcd.com

Bandit Industries Inc 6750 W Millbrook Rd ... Remus MI 49340 989-561-2270 561-2273
TF: 800-952-0178 ■ *Web:* www.banditchippers.com

Barnhart Crane & Rigging Co 1701 Dunn Ave ... Memphis TN 38106 901-775-3000
TF: 800-727-0149 ■ *Web:* www.barnhartcrane.com

Bay Shore Systems Inc 14206 N Ohio St ... Rathdrum ID 83858 208-687-3311 687-4153
TF: 888-569-3745 ■ *Web:* eventbrite.com/e/

Bid-Well Corp PO Box 97 ... Canton SD 57013 800-843-9824 987-2605*
**Fax Area Code:* 605 ■ *TF:* 800-843-9824 ■ *Web:* www.terex.com

Bihler of America Inc 85 Industrial Rd ... Phillipsburg NJ 08865 908-213-9001 329-9111
Web: www.bihler.com

Boart Longyear Co 2640 W 1700 S ... Salt Lake City UT 84104 801-972-6430 977-3374
TF: 800-453-8740 ■ *Web:* www.boartlongyear.com

Bomag Americas Inc 2000 Kentville Rd ... Kewanee IL 61443 309-853-3571 852-0350
TF: 800-782-6624 ■ *Web:* www.bomag.com

BradenCarco Gearmatic Paccar Winch Div
800 E Dallas St ... Broken Arrow OK 74012 918-251-8511 259-1575
Web: www.paccarwinch.com

Burns Power Tools 350 Mariano Bishop Blvd ... Fall River MA 02721 508-675-0381
Web: www.burnstools.com

Caron Compactor Co 1204 Ullrey Ave ... Escalon CA 95320 209-838-2062 838-1404
TF: 800-542-2766 ■ *Web:* www.caroncompactor.com

Caterpillar Engine Systems Inc
100 NE Adams St ... Peoria IL 61629 309-675-1000

Caterpillar Inc 100 NE Adams St ... Peoria IL 61629 309-675-1000 675-4332*
NYSE: CAT ■ **Fax:* PR ■ *Web:* www.cat.com

Cemen Tech Inc 1700 N 14th St ... Indianola IA 50125 515-961-7407 961-7409
TF: 800-247-2464 ■ *Web:* www.cementech.com

Central Mine Equipment Company Inc
4215 Rider Trl N ... Earth City MO 63045 314-291-7700 291-4880
TF: 800-325-8827 ■ *Web:* www.cmeco.com

Centurion Industries Inc 1107 N Taylor Rd ... Garrett IN 46738 260-357-6665 357-6761
TF: 888-832-4466 ■ *Web:* www.centurionind.com

Charles Machine Works Inc PO Box 66 ... Perry OK 73077 580-336-4402
TF Cust Svc: 800-654-6481 ■ *Web:* www.ditchwitch.com

Chemgrout Inc 805 E 31st St ... La Grange Park IL 60526 708-354-7112 354-3881
Web: www.chemgrout.com

Chicago Slitter Company Inc, The
1025 W Thorndale Ave ... Itasca IL 60143 630-875-9800
Web: www.therdigroup.com

Clm Equipment Company Inc 3135 Hwy 90 E ... Broussard LA 70518 337-837-6693
Web: www.clmequipment.com

Contractors Equipment Supply Company Inc
2000 E Overland Rd ... Meridian ID 83642 208-888-3337
Web: www.cescoequip.com

Crane Carrier (Canada) Ltd 11523 186 St ... Edmonton AB T5S2W6 780-443-2493
Web: pacifictruck.com

CRC Evans Pipeline International Inc
10700 E Independence St ... Tulsa OK 74116 918-438-2100 438-6237
TF: 800-664-9224 ■ *Web:* www.crc-evans.com

DB & S Lumber Co 78 Accord Park Dr ... Norwell MA 02061 781-878-3345
Web: www.dbslumber.com

Deep South Crane & Rigging
15324 Airline Hwy ... Baton Rouge LA 70817 225-753-4371
Web: www.deepsouthcrane.com

Deepwell Services LLC 719 W New Castle St ... Zelienople PA 16063 724-473-0687
Web: deepwellservices.com

Phone Fax

Demag Cranes & Components 29201 Aurora Rd ... Solon OH 44139 440-248-2400
TF: 866-920-3000 ■ *Web:* www.demagcranes.us

DENIS CIMAF Inc 188 de l'Eglise ... Roxton Falls QC J0H1E0 450-548-7007 548-7008
Web: www.deniscimaf.com

Derr & Gruenewald Construction Co (DGCC)
11100 E 108th Ave ... Brighton CO 80601 303-287-3456 287-3459
Web: www.dgccsteel.com

Dynapac USA Inc 2100 N First St PO Box 462288 ... Garland TX 75040 972-496-7400 496-7425
Web: www.dynapac.com

E-Z Trench Manufacturing Inc 2315 Hwy 701 S ... Loris SC 29569 843-756-6444
Web: www.eztrench.com

Eagle Iron Works 129 E Holcomb Ave ... Des Moines IA 50313 515-243-1123 243-8214
Web: www.eagleironworks.com

ED Etnyre & Co 1333 S Daysville Rd ... Oregon IL 61061 815-732-2116 732-7400
TF: 800-995-2116 ■ *Web:* www.etnyre.com

Elgin National Industries Inc
2001 Butterfield Rd ... Downers Grove IL 60515 630-434-7200 434-7272
Web: www.elginindustries.com

Enventure Global Technology LLC
15995 N Barkers Landing Ste 350 ... Houston TX 77079 281-552-2200
Web: www.enventuregt.com

Erie Strayer Co 1851 Rudolph Ave ... Erie PA 16502 814-456-7001 452-3422
Web: www.eriestrayer.com

Esco Corp 2141 NW 25th Ave ... Portland OR 97210 503-228-2141 226-8071
TF: 800-523-3795 ■ *Web:* www.escocorp.com

F&M Mafco Inc PO Box 11013 ... Cincinnati OH 45211 513-367-2151 367-0363
TF: 800-333-2151 ■ *Web:* www.fmmafco.com

Flint Equipment Company - West Columbia
3464 Sunset Blvd ... West Columbia SC 29169 803-794-9340
Web: www.flintequipco.com

Gencor Industries Inc
5201 N Orange Blossom Trail ... Orlando FL 32810 407-290-6000 578-0577*
NASDAQ: GENC ■ **Fax:* Sales ■ *TF General:* 888-887-1266 ■ *Web:* www.gencor.com

GES Global Energy Services Inc
3220 Cypress Creek Pkwy ... Houston TX 77068 888-523-6797
Web: www.global-energy.ca

Gradall Industries Inc
406 Mill Ave SW ... New Philadelphia OH 44663 330-339-2211 339-8468
Web: www.gradall.com

Gulf Crane Services Inc 73413 Bollfield Dr ... Covington LA 70435 985-892-0056
Web: www.gulfcraneservices.com

Guntert & Zimmerman Construction Div Inc
222 E Fourth St ... Ripon CA 95366 209-599-0066
Web: www.guntert.com

Gyrodata Inc 23000 Northwest Lk Dr ... Houston TX 77095 281-213-6300
Web: www.gyrodata.com

H & E Equipment Services Inc
11100 Mead Rd ... Baton Rouge LA 70809 225-298-5200
NASDAQ: HEES ■ *TF:* 866-467-3682 ■ *Web:* www.he-equipment.com

H&R Agri-Power Inc 4900 Eagle Way ... Hopkinsville KY 42240 270-886-3918
Web: www.hragripower.com

Harlo Corp 4210 Ferry St SW ... Grandville MI 49468 616-538-0550
Web: www.harlocorporation.com

Henke Manufacturing Corp 3070 Wilson Ave ... Leavenworth KS 66048 913-682-9000
Web: www.henkemfg.com

Hensley Industries Inc
2108 Joe Field Rd PO Box 29779 ... Dallas TX 75229 972-241-2321 241-0915*
**Fax:* Cust Svc ■ *TF:* 888-406-6262 ■ *Web:* www.hensleyind.com

Highway Equipment Co 1330 76th Ave SW ... Cedar Rapids IA 52404 319-363-8281 286-3350
Web: www.highwayequipment.com

Hunter Heavy Equipment Inc 2829 Texas Ave ... Texas City TX 77590 409-945-2382 945-9145
TF: 800-562-7368 ■ *Web:* www.hunterheavyequipment.com

Hunting Energy Services Inc
Two Northpoint Dr Ste 400 ... Houston TX 77060 281-442-7382
Web: www.huntingplc.com

Inquipco 2730 N Nellis Blvd ... Las Vegas NV 89115 702-644-1700
TF: 800-598-3465 ■ *Web:* www.inquipco.com

Integrated Drilling Equipment Co
25311 I-45 N Woodpark Business Ctr Bldg No 6 ... Spring TX 77380 281-465-9393
Web: www.ide-rig.com

J J Curran Crane Co 865 S Ft St ... Detroit MI 48217 313-842-1700
Web: www.jjcurran.com

Jakes Crane & Rigging Inc
6109 Dean Martin Dr ... Las Vegas NV 89118 702-872-5253
Web: www.jakescrane.com

James E Roberts-obayashi Corp 20 Oak Ct ... Danville CA 94526 925-820-0600
Web: www.jerocorp.com

Jennmar Corp 258 Kappa Dr ... Pittsburgh PA 15238 412-963-9071 963-9767
Web: www.jennmar.com

Jensen Mixers International Inc
5354 S Garnett Rd ... Tulsa OK 74146 918-627-5770
Web: www.jensenmixers.com

JH Fletcher & Co Inc 402 High St ... Huntington WV 25705 304-525-7811 525-3770
TF: 800-327-6203 ■ *Web:* www.jhfletcher.com

JLG Industries Inc One JLG Dr ... McConnellsburg PA 17233 717-485-5161 485-6417
Web: www.jlg.com

John Deere Construction & Forestry
1515 Fifth Ave ... Moline IL 61265 309-765-0227 748-0117*
**Fax:* Cust Svc ■ *Web:* deere.com

Kawasaki Construction Machinery Copr of America
60 Amlajack Blvd ... Newnan GA 30265 770-218-5884
Web: www.kawasakiloaders.com

Kor-it Inc 2442 Rice Ave ... West Sacramento CA 95691 888-727-4560
TF: 888-727-4560 ■ *Web:* www.kor-it.com

Kress Corp 227 W Illinois St ... Brimfield IL 61517 309-446-3395 446-9625
Web: www.kresscarrier.com

LA Pipeline Rental & Industrial Supply LLC
3210 E Napoleon St ... Sulphur LA 70663 337-533-8184
Web: www.lapipelinerentals.com

Liebherr-America Inc 4100 Chestnut Ave ... Newport News VA 23607 757-245-5251 928-8700
TF: 866-879-6312 ■ *Web:* liebherr.com

Company	City	State	Zip	Phone	Fax
Link-Belt Construction Equipment Co 2651 Palumbo Dr *Web:* www.linkbelt.com	Lexington	KY	40583	859-263-5200	
Liquid Waste Technology LLC 1750 Madison Ave *Web:* www.lwtpithog.com	New Richmond	WI	54017	715-246-2888	
Machine Maintenance Inc 2300 Cassens Dr *Web:* www.lubyequipment.com	Fenton	MO	63026	636-343-9970	
Man Lift Mfg Co 5707 S Pennsylvania Ave *Web:* www.manliftengineering.com	Cudahy	WI	53110	414-486-1760	
Manitowoc Company Inc 2400 S 44th St *NYSE:* MTW ■ *Web:* www.manitowoc.com	Manitowoc	WI	54220	920-684-4410	652-9778
Mayville Engineering Company Inc 715 S St *Web:* www.mecinc.com	Mayville	WI	53050	920-387-4500	387-2682
McLellan Equipment Inc 251 Shaw Rd *TF:* 800-848-8449 ■ *Web:* mclellanindustries.com	South San Francisco	CA	94080	650-873-8100	589-7398
Meyer Products 18513 Euclid Ave **Fax:* Sales ■ *Web:* www.meyerproducts.com	Cleveland	OH	44112	216-486-1313	486-1321*
Mi-Jack Products Inc 3111 W 167th St *Web:* www.mi-jack.com	Hazel Crest	IL	60429	708-596-5200	
Midland Machinery Company Inc 101 Cranbrook Ext *Web:* www.midlandmachinery.com	Tonawanda	NY	14150	716-692-1200	692-1206
Midwestern Industries Inc 915 Oberlin Rd SW *TF Cust Svc:* 877-474-9464 ■ *Web:* www.midwesternind.com	Massillon	OH	44647	330-837-4203	837-4210
Miken Specialties Ltd 431 Commerce St *Web:* www.mikenspecialties.com	Clute	TX	77531	979-265-9599	265-9094
Millcraft Industries Inc 95 W Beau St Ste 600 *Web:* www.millcraftinv.com	Washington	PA	15301	724-229-8800	229-8800
Mixer Systems Inc 190 Simmons Ave *Web:* www.mixersystems.com	Pewaukee	WI	53072	262-691-3100	
Mr Crane Inc 647 N Hariton St *TF:* 800-672-7263 ■ *Web:* www.mrcrane.com	Orange	CA	92868	714-633-2100	
Nexgen Enterprises Inc 1099 Greenleaf Ave *Web:* gonexgen.com/	Elk Grove Village	IL	60007	847-303-9800	303-9801
Nordco Inc 245 W Forest Hill Ave *Web:* www.nordco.com	Oak Creek	WI	53154	414-766-2180	766-2379
North American Equipment Upfitters Inc Six Sutton Cir *Web:* www.naeuinc.com	Hooksett	NH	03106	603-624-6288	
Pace Engineering Inc 4800 Beidler Rd *Web:* www.paceparts.net	Willoughby	OH	44094	440-942-1234	
Palmer Steel Supplies Inc 4300 Acapulco Ave *Web:* www.palmersteel.com	Mcallen	TX	78503	956-686-6575	686-7022
Pengo Corp 500 E Hwy 10 *TF Cust Svc:* 800-599-0211 ■ *Web:* www.pengoattachments.com	Laurens	IA	50554	712-845-2540	845-2497
Pennsylvania Crusher Corp 600 Abbott Dr *Web:* terrasource.com/	Broomall	PA	19008	610-544-7200	543-0190
Peri Formwork Systems Inc 7135 Dorsey Run Rd *Web:* www.peri-usa.com	Elkridge	MD	21075	410-712-7225	
Pettibone Corp 2626 Warrenville Rd Ste 300 *Web:* pettibonellc.com	Downers Grove	IL	60515	630-353-5000	353-5026
Pierce Pacific Manufacturing Inc 4424 NE 158th PO Box 30509 *TF:* 800-760-3270 ■ *Web:* www.piercepacific.com	Portland	OR	97294	503-808-9110	808-9111
Precision Husky Corp 850 Markeeta Spur Rd *Web:* www.precisionhusky.com	Moody	AL	35004	205-640-5181	640-1147
Prime Systems Inc 416 Mission St *Web:* www.primeuv.com	Carol Stream	IL	60188	630-681-2100	
Putzmeister America 1733 90th St *TF:* 800-553-3414 ■ *Web:* www.putzmeister.com	Sturtevant	WI	53177	800-553-3414	
Radwell International Inc 111 Mt Holly Bypass *Web:* www.radwellinternational.com	Lumberton	NJ	08048	609-288-9393	
Ramsey Winch Company Inc 1600 N Garnett Rd *TF:* 800-777-2760 ■ *Web:* www.ramsey.com	Tulsa	OK	74116	918-438-2760	438-6688
Reco Equipment Inc 41245 Reco Rd *TF:* 800-686-7326 ■ *Web:* www.recoequip.com	Belmont	OH	41245	740-782-1314	782-1020
REED LLC 13822 Oaks Ave *Web:* www.reedmfg.com	Chino	CA	91710	909-287-2100	
Richland LLC 1905 Mines Rd *Web:* www.richlandllc.com	Pulaski	TN	38478	931-424-3900	
RKI Inc 2301 Central Pkwy *TF:* 800-346-8988 ■ *Web:* www.rki-us.com	Houston	TX	77092	713-688-4414	688-8982
Roadtec Inc 800 Manufacturers Rd PO Box 180515 *TF:* 800-272-7100 ■ *Web:* www.roadtec.com	Chattanooga	TN	37405	423-265-0600	267-7104
Robertson Transformer Co 13611 Thornton Rd *TF:* 800-323-5633 ■ *Web:* www.robertsontransformer.com	Blue Island	IL	60406	708-388-2315	388-2420
Rotary Drilling Tools USA LP 9022 Vincik Ehlert PO Box 73 *Web:* www.rdt-usa.co	Beasley	TX	77417	979-387-3223	
Rotochopper Inc 217 W St *Web:* www.rotochopper.com	Saint Martin	MN	56362	320-548-3586	
Rovibec Inc 591 rang St-Joseph *Web:* www.rovibec.com	Sainte-monique	QC	J0G1N0	819-289-2260	289-2203
Sauber Manufacturing Co 10 N Sauber Rd *Web:* www.saubermfg.com	Virgil	IL	60151	630-365-6600	
Scomi Oiltools Inc 6818 N Sam Houston Pkwy W *Web:* www.scomigroup.com.my	Houston	TX	77064	281-260-6016	
Shamokin Filler Company Inc PO Box 568 *Web:* www.shamokinfiller.com	Shamokin	PA	17872	570-644-0437	
Shelby Industries Inc 175 McDaniels Rd *Web:* www.shelbyindustries.com	Shelbyville	KY	40065	502-633-2040	633-2186
Shimpo 1701 Glenlake Ave *Web:* www.nidec-shimpo.com	Itasca	IL	60143	630-924-7138	
Simco Drilling Equipment Inc PO Box 448 *TF:* 855-222-8570 ■ *Web:* www.simcodrill.com	Osceola	IA	50213	641-342-2166	342-6764
Star Su Company LLC 5200 Prairie Stone Pkwy Ste 100 *Web:* www.star-su.com	Hoffman Estates	IL	60192	847-649-1450	
Stephens Manufacturing Co 711 W Fourth St *Web:* www.stephensmfg.com	Tompkinsville	KY	42167	270-487-6774	
Superwinch Inc 359 Lake Rd *TF:* 800-323-2031 ■ *Web:* www.superwinch.com	Dayville	CT	06241	860-928-7787	928-1143
Swenson Spreader Co 127 Walnut St *TF:* 888-825-7323 ■ *Web:* www.swensonproducts.com	Lindenwood	IL	61049	815-393-4455	393-4964
Terex Corp 200 Nyala Farm Rd *NYSE:* TEX ■ *Web:* www.terex.com	Westport	CT	06880	203-222-7170	222-7976
Terex Roadbuilding 8236 W I-40 Service Rd *Web:* www.terex.com	Oklahoma City	OK	73128	405-787-6020	
Test Mark Industries Inc 995 N Market St *Web:* www.testmark.net	East Palestine	OH	44413	330-426-2200	
Thermal Technologies Inc 130 Northpoint Ct *Web:* www.irisndt.us	Blythewood	SC	29016	803-691-8000	
Thrustmaster of Texas Inc PO Box 840189 *Web:* thrustmaster.net	Houston	TX	77284	713-937-6295	937-7962
Treeline Well Services Inc 750 333 - 11th Ave SW *Web:* www.treelinewell.com	Calgary	AB	T2R1L9	403-266-2868	
Tulsa Winch Group 11135 S James Ave *Web:* www.team-twg.com	Jenks	OK	74037	918-298-8300	298-8301
United Rotary Brush Corp 15607 W 100th Ter *Web:* www.united-rotary.com	Lenexa	KS	66219	913-888-8450	
Varel International 1625 W Crosby Dr Ste 124 *TF:* 800-827-3526 ■ *Web:* www.varelintl.com	Carrollton	TX	75006	972-242-1160	242-8770
Volvo Construction Equipment of North America Inc 312 Volvo Way *Web:* www.volvoce.com	Shippensburg	PA	17257	717-532-9181	
VT LeeBoy Inc 500 Lincoln County Pkwy Extention *Web:* www.leeboy.com	Lincolnton	NC	28092	704-966-3300	
Wacker Neuson N 92 W 15000 Anthony Ave **Fax Area Code:* 800 ■ *TF:* 800-770-0957 ■ *Web:* products.wackerneuson.com	Menomonee Falls	WI	53051	262-255-0500	822-0710*
Web Equipment 464 Central Rd *TF:* 800-225-3858 ■ *Web:* www.webequipment.com	Fredericksburg	VA	22401	540-657-5855	
Wenzel Downhole Tools Ltd 717- Seventh Ave SW Ste 1000 *Web:* www.downhole.com	Calgary	AB	T2P0Z3	403-262-3050	
Western Products Inc 7777 N 73rd St **Fax:* Cust Svc ■ *Web:* www.westernplows.com	Milwaukee	WI	53223	414-354-2310	354-2310*
Wilco Marsh Buggies & Draglines Inc 1304 Macarthur Ave *Web:* www.wilcomarshbuggies.com	Harvey	LA	70058	504-341-3409	
Wingenback Inc Bay F Century Park 707 Barlow Trl *Web:* www.wingenback.com	Calgary	AB	T2E8C2	403-221-8120	291-5114
Xcaliber LP 5051 Fm 2920 *TF:* 866-620-8586 ■ *Web:* www.xcaliberlp.com	Spring	TX	77388	281-219-8100	
Young Corp 3231 Utah Ave S *TF:* 800-321-9090 ■ *Web:* www.youngcorp.com	Seattle	WA	98134	206-624-1071	682-6881
Ziebell Water Service Products 2001 Pratt Blvd *Web:* www.ziebellproducts.com	Elk Grove Village	IL	60007	847-364-0670	
Zimmerman Industries Inc 196 Wabash Rd *Web:* www.zimmermanindustries.com	Ephrata	PA	17522	717-733-6166	

194 CONSTRUCTION MATERIALS

SEE ALSO Home Improvement Centers p. 2475

194-1 Brick, Stone, Related Materials

Company	City	State	Zip	Phone	Fax
Accent Marble & Granite Inc 21609 N 12th Ave Ste 800 *Web:* accentmarblegranite.com	Phoenix	AZ	85027	623-582-1501	
AHI Supply Inc PO Box 884 *TF:* 800-873-5794 ■ *Web:* www.ahi-supply.com	Friendswood	TX	77549	281-331-0088	331-9813
All Tile Inc 1201 Chase Ave *TF:* 877-255-8453 ■ *Web:* www.alltile.com	Elk Grove Village	IL	60007	847-979-2500	
Allen Refractories Co (Inc) 131 Shackelford Rd *Web:* www.allenrefractories.com	Pataskala	OH	43062	740-927-8000	927-9404
Alley-Cassetty Cos Inc Two Oldham St *Web:* www.alley-cassetty.com	Nashville	TN	37213	615-244-0440	254-4553
Architectural Ceramics Inc 800 E Gude Dr Ste F *Web:* www.architecturalceramics.net	Rockville	MD	20850	301-762-4140	762-2497
Arley Wholesale Inc 700 N S Rd *Web:* www.arleywholesale.com	Scranton	PA	18504	570-344-9874	
Atlas Construction Supply Inc 4640 Brinnell St *TF:* 877-588-2100 ■ *Web:* www.atlasform.com	San Diego	CA	92111	858-277-2100	277-0585
Bedrock International LLC 9929 Lackman Rd *Web:* www.kcstone.com	Lenexa	KS	66219	913-438-7625	
Bierschbach Equipment & Supply Co PO Box 1444 *TF:* 800-843-3707 ■ *Web:* bierschbach.com	Sioux Falls	SD	57101	605-332-4466	332-4522
Castelli Marble Inc 3958 Superior Ave E *Web:* www.castellimarble.com	Cleveland	OH	44114	216-361-1222	361-1797

				Phone	Fax
Century Roof Tile 23135 Saklan Rd	Hayward	CA	94545	510-780-9489	
TF: 888-233-7548 ■ *Web:* www.centuryrooftile.com					
ClarkWestern Dietrich Building Systems LLC 9100 Centre Pointe Dr Ste 210	West Chester	OH	45069	513-870-1100	
Web: www.clarkdietrich.com					
Clay Ingels Company LLC 914 Delaware Ave	Lexington	KY	40505	859-252-0836	
Web: www.clay-ingels.com					
Colonial Materials of Fayetteville Inc 570 Belt Blvd	Fayetteville	NC	28301	910-485-5099	
Web: colonialmaterials.com					
Commercial Ready Mix Products Inc PO Box 189	Winton	NC	27986	252-358-5461	358-4912
Web: www.crmpinc.com					
Consolidated Brick & Bldg Supls Inc 127 W 24th St Fl 3	New York	NY	10011	212-645-6700	
Web: www.consolidatedbrick.com					
Contempo Ceramic Tile Corp 3732 South 300 West	Salt Lake City	UT	84115	801-262-1717	
Web: contempotile.com					
Corriveau-Routhier Inc 266 Clay St	Manchester	NH	03103	603-627-3805	627-3805
Web: www.corriveaurouthier.com					
CSC Home & Hardware 1580 Earl L Core Rd	Morgantown	WV	26505	304-292-1340	
Web: www.wvcsc.com					
E-Z Mix Inc 11450 Tuxford St	Sun Valley	CA	91352	818-768-0568	
Web: www.ezmixinc.com					
East Coast Sales Company Inc 554 N State Rd	Briarcliff Manor	NY	10510	914-923-5000	
Web: www.ecsceramics.com					
Engler Meier & Justus Inc 1030 Vandustrial Dr	Westmont	Il	60559	630-852-4600	
Web: www.westmontint.com					
FAYBLOCK Materials Inc 130 Builders Blvd	Fayetteville	NC	28302	910-323-9198	
TF: 800-326-9198 ■ *Web:* www.fayblock.com					
FG Wilson Inc 10431 N Commerce Pkwy	Miramar	FL	33025	954-433-2212	
Web: www.fgwilsonmiami.com					
Foothill Ready Mix Inc 11415 State Hwy 99W	Red Bluff	CA	96080	530-527-2565	
Web: foothillreadymix.com					
Foundation Technologies Inc 1400 Progress Industrial Blvd	Lawrenceville	GA	30043	678-407-4640	
TF: 800-773-2368 ■ *Web:* www.foundationtechnologies.com					
Frank Thompson Transport Inc PO Box 1876	El Dorado	AR	71731	870-862-5426	
Fullen Dock & Warehouse Inc 382 Klinke Rd	Memphis	TN	38127	901-358-9544	357-2879
TF: 800-467-7104 ■ *Web:* www.fullendock.com					
Fyfe Co LLC 8380 Miralani Dr Ste A	San Diego	CA	92126	858-642-0694	444-2982
Web: www.fyfeco.com					
Garden State Tile Distributors Inc 5001 Industrial Rd	Farmingdale	NJ	07727	732-938-6675	
Web: www.gstile.com					
Gerrity Stone Inc 225 Merrimac St Ste B	Woburn	MA	01801	781-938-1820	
Web: www.gerritystone.com					
Granicor Inc 300 Rue De Rotterdam	St AuguSt in	QC	G3A1T4	418-878-3530	878-3208
Web: www.granicor.com					
Granite Construction Inc 585 W Beach St	Watsonville	CA	95076	831-724-1011	722-9657
NYSE: GVA ■ *Web:* www.graniteconstruction.com					
Graniterock Co 350 Technology Dr PO Box 50001	Watsonville	CA	95077	831-768-2000	768-2201
TF: 888-762-5100 ■ *Web:* www.graniterock.com					
Guaranteed Supply Company of South Carolina Inc 1211 Rotherwood Rd	Greensboro	NC	27406	336-273-6140	
Web: www.guaranteedsupply.com					
Gypsum Supply Company Inc 859 74th St	Byron Center	MI	49315	616-583-9300	
Web: www.gypsum-supply.com					
Henry Products Inc 302 S 23rd Ave	Phoenix	AZ	85009	602-253-3191	254-2325
TF: 800-525-5533 ■ *Web:* www.henryproducts.com					
Hudson Liquid Asphalts Inc 89 Ship St	Providence	RI	02903	401-274-2200	274-2220
Iberia Tiles Corp 2975 NW 77 Ave	Miami	FL	33122	305-591-3880	591-4341
Web: www.iberiatiles.com					
In-O-Vate Technologies Inc 810 Saturn St Ste 21	Jupiter	FL	33477	561-743-8696	
TF: 888-443-7937 ■ *Web:* www.dryerbox.com					
Indital USA Ltd 7947 Mesa Dr	Houston	TX	77028	713-694-6065	
Web: www.indital.com					
Inter Tile 74824 42nd Ave	Palm Desert	CA	92260	760-773-1001	
Web: www.intertile.com					
Intrepid Enterprises Inc 1848 Industrial Blvd	Harvey	LA	70058	504-348-2861	340-7018
Web: intrepidstone.com					
Jaeckle Wholesale Inc 4101 Owl Creek Dr	Madison	WI	53718	608-838-5400	523-2553*
**Fax Area Code:* 800 ■ *TF:* 800-236-7225 ■ *Web:* www.jaeckledistributors.com					
Jarco Supply LLC 100 Ag Dr	Youngsville	NC	27596	919-562-0123	
Web: jarcosupply.com					
Jeffrey Court Inc 620 Parkridge Ave	Norco	CA	92860	951-340-3383	
Web: www.jeffreycourt.com					
Kamco Supply Corp of Boston 181 New Boston St	Woburn	MA	01801	781-938-0909	
Web: www.kamcoboston.com					
Kencove Farm Fence Inc 344 Kendall Rd	Blairsville	PA	15717	724-459-8991	
Web: www.charleskendall.com					
Kobrin Builders Supply Inc 1924 W Princeton St	Orlando	FL	32804	407-843-1000	649-8600
TF: 800-273-5511 ■ *Web:* www.kobrinbuilderssupply.com					
L Thorn Co Inc 6000 Grant Line Rd PO Box 198	New Albany	IN	47150	812-246-4461	246-2678
TF: 800-662-4594 ■ *Web:* www.lthorn.com					
Lang Stone Co Inc PO Box 360747	Columbus	OH	43219	614-235-4099	
Web: www.langstone.com					
Lyman-Richey Corp 4315 Cuming St	Omaha	NE	68131	402-558-2727	556-5171
TF: 800-727-8432 ■ *Web:* www.lymanrichey.com					
Lynx Brand Fence Products 4330 76 Ave SE	Calgary	AB	T2C2J2	403-273-4821	
Web: www.lynxfence.com					
Marble Systems Inc 2737 Dorr Ave	Fairfax	VA	22031	703-204-1818	
Web: www.marblesystems.com					
Materials Mktg Ltd 120 W Josephine St	San Antonio	TX	78212	210-731-8453	
Web: www.mstoneandtile.com					
Meadow Burke LLC 531 S Us Hwy 301	Tampa	FL	33619	813-248-1944	
Web: www.meadowburke.com					
Merrimac Tile Company Inc 18 Tsienneto Rd	Derry	NH	03038	603-432-2544	
Web: www.merrimactile.com					
Mixcor Aggregates Inc 6303 43 St	Leduc	AB	T9E0G8	780-986-6721	
Web: www.mixcor.ca					
Nemo Tile Co 17702 Jamaica Ave	Jamaica	NY	11432	718-291-5969	
Web: www.nemotile.com					
Patene Building Supplies Ltd 641 Speedvale Ave W	Guelph	ON	N1K1E6	519-822-1890	
Web: www.patene.com					
Potvin & Bouchard Inc 3900 Rue Colbert St-Jean Cp550	Jonquiere	QC	G7X7W4	418-547-4752	
Web: www.potvinbouchard.qc.ca					
Preferred Sands LLC 100 Matsonford Rd One Radnor Corporate Ctr	Radnor	PA	19087	610-834-1969	
Web: preferredsands.com					
PRL Glass Systems Inc 251 Mason Way	City Of Industry	CA	91746	626-961-5890	
Web: www.prlglass.com					
Quick Crete Products 731 Parkridge Ave	Norco	CA	92860	909-737-6240	
Web: www.quickcrete.com					
Reimers-kaufman Concrete Prods 6200 Cornhusker Hwy	Lincoln	NE	68507	402-434-1855	434-1877
Web: www.reimerskaufman.com					
Rio Grande Co 201 Santa Fe Dr	Denver	CO	80223	303-825-2211	629-0417
Web: www.riograndeco.com					
Robert F Henry Tile Company Inc 1008 Lagoon Business Loop	Montgomery	AL	36117	334-269-2518	
Web: www.henrytile.com					
Saf-t-co Supply 1300 E Normandy Pl	Santa Ana	CA	92705	714-547-9975	667-7985
Web: www.saftco.com					
Safety Seal 8100 Belvedere Rd	West Palm Beach	FL	33411	561-790-5801	
Stone Connection Inc 3045 Business Park Dr	Norcross	GA	30071	770-662-0188	
Web: www.stoneconnection.com					
Stone Source LLC 215 Pk Ave S	New York	NY	10003	212-979-6400	979-6989
Web: www.stonesource.com					
Stony Point Rock Quarry Inc 7171 Stony Point Rd	Cotati	CA	94931	707-795-1775	
Web: sprqinc.com					
Superior Concrete Block Company Inc 401 Mckinzie St S	Mankato	MN	56001	507-387-7068	
Web: www.cencrete.com					
Synergy Ceramics Gp LLC 5200 Tennyson Pkwy Ste 400	Plano	TX	75024	972-608-0515	
Web: synergyceramics.com					
Terrazzo & Marble Supply Company of Illinois 77 Wheeling Rd	Wheeling	IL	60090	847-353-8000	353-8001
Web: www.tmsupply.com					
Tri-State Brick & Stone of New York Inc 333 Seventh Ave Fifth Fl	New York	NY	10001	212-686-3939	686-4387
Web: btsbm.com					
United Marble & Granite Inc 2163 Martin Ave Ste B	Santa Clara	CA	95050	408-347-3300	
Web: www.umgslabs.com					
Universal Minerals International Inc 4620 S Coach Dr	Tucson	AZ	85714	520-748-9362	
Web: www.mrrinc.com					
Vimco Inc 300 Hansen Access Rd	King Of Prussia	PA	19406	610-768-0500	768-0586
TF Cust Svc: 888-468-4626 ■ *Web:* www.vimcoinc.com					
WF Saunders & Sons Inc PO Box A	Nedrow	NY	13120	315-469-3217	469-3940
Web: www.saundersconcrete.com					
Zeiser Wilbert Vault Inc 750 Howard St	Elmira	NY	14904	607-733-0568	
Web: zeiserwilbertvault.com					
Zircoa Inc 31501 Solon Rd	Solon	OH	44139	440-248-0500	
Web: www.zircoa.com					

194-2 Construction Materials (Misc)

				Phone	Fax
Acoustical Material Services Inc 1620 S Maple Ave	Montebello	CA	90640	323-721-9011	721-2476
TF: 888-531-1416 ■ *Web:* www.a-m-s.com					
Alliance Wood Group Engineering LP 330 Barker Cypress Rd	Houston	TX	77094	281-828-6000	215-8506*
**Fax Area Code:* 713 ■ *TF:* 866-313-0052					
American Fence Inc 2502 N 27th Ave	Phoenix	AZ	85009	602-272-2333	734-0580
TF: 888-691-4565 ■ *Web:* www.americanfence.com					
APi Group Inc Materials Distribution Group 1100 Old Hwy 8 NW	New Brighton	MN	55112	800-223-4922	636-0312*
**Fax Area Code:* 651 ■ *TF:* 800-223-4922 ■ *Web:* www.apigroupinc.com					
Arabel Inc 16301 NW 49th Ave	Hialeah	FL	33014	305-623-8302	624-0714
TF Sales: 800-759-5959 ■ *Web:* www.arabel.com					
Basic Components Inc 1201 S Second Ave	Mansfield	TX	76063	817-473-7224	473-3388
TF: 800-452-1780 ■ *Web:* www.basiccomp.com					
Brooks Construction Company Inc 6525 Ardmore Ave	Fort Wayne	IN	46809	260-478-1990	747-7086
Web: www.brooks1st.com					
Buchheit Inc 33 Perry County Rd 540	Perryville	MO	63775	573-547-1010	547-1001
Web: www.buchheitonline.com					
Builders Hardware & Specialty Company Inc 2002 W 16th St	Erie	PA	16505	814-453-4736	488-8909*
**Fax Area Code:* 412 ■ *Web:* www.builders-hardware.net					
Chemung Supply Corp PO Box 527	Elmira	NY	14903	607-733-5506	732-5379
TF: 800-733-5508 ■ *Web:* www.chemungsupply.com					
Clyde Cos Inc 730 North 1500 West	Orem	UT	84057	801-802-6900	802-6906
Web: www.clydeinc.com					
Concrete Materials Inc 1201 W Russell St	Sioux Falls	SD	57118	605-357-6000	334-6221
Web: www.concretematerialscompany.com					
CR Laurence Company Inc 2503 E Vernon Ave PO Box 58923	Los Angeles	CA	90058	323-588-1281	262-3299*
**Fax Area Code:* 800 ■ *TF:* 800-421-6144 ■ *Web:* www.crlaurence.com					

	City	State	Zip	Phone	Fax
DS Brown Co 300 E Cherry St *TF:* 800-848-1730 ■ *Web:* www.dsbrown.com	North Baltimore	OH	45872	419-257-3561	257-2200
Eastern Wholesale Fence Co Inc 274 Middle Island Rd *Web:* www.easternfence.com	Medford	NY	11763	631-698-0975	698-6408
Empire Bldg Materials Inc PO Box 220 **Fax Area Code:* 406 ■ *TF:* 800-332-4577 ■ *Web:* www.empireinc.com	Bozeman	MT	59771	800-548-8201	587-3144*
Fargo Glass & Paint Company Inc 1801 Seventh Ave N *Web:* fargoglass.com	Fargo	ND	58102	701-235-4441	235-3435
Gossen /Corp 2030 W Bender Rd *TF:* 800-558-8984 ■ *Web:* www.gossencorp.com	Milwaukee	WI	53209	414-228-9800	228-9077
H Myers John & Son Inc 2200 Monroe St *Web:* www.jhmson.com	York	PA	17404	717-792-2500	792-5115
J O Galloup Co 135 Manufacturers Dr *TF:* 888-755-3110 ■ *Web:* www.galloup.com	Holland	MI	49424	269-965-4005	965-3263
Kuriyama of America Inc 360 E State Pkwy *TF:* 800-800-0320 ■ *Web:* www.kuriyama.com	Schaumburg	IL	60173	847-755-0360	885-0996
Lummus Supply Co 1554 Bolton Rd NW *Web:* www.lummus-supply.com	Atlanta	GA	30331	404-794-1501	794-4519
Penrod Co 2809 S Lynnhaven Rd Ste 350 *TF:* 800-537-3497 ■ *Web:* www.thepenrodcompany.com	Virginia Beach	VA	23452	757-498-0186	498-1075
Powers Products Co PO Box 1187 *Web:* www.powersproducts.com	Cheyenne	WY	82003	307-634-5190	632-2335
Robert N Karpp Company Inc 480 E First St *TF:* 800-244-5886 ■ *Web:* www.karpp.com	Boston	MA	02127	617-269-5880	269-2387
Rose & Walker Supply Lafayette Inc (RWS) 3565 US Hwy 52 S *Web:* www.roseandwalkersupply.com	Lafayette	IN	47905	765-471-7070	474-7507
Spates Fabricators 85435 Middleton *Web:* www.spates.com	Thermal	CA	92274	760-397-4122	397-4724
Star Sales & Distributing Corp 29 Commerce Way *TF:* 800-222-8118 ■ *Web:* www.starsales.com	Woburn	MA	01801	781-933-8830	933-2145
T H Rogers Lumber Co, The PO Box 5770 *Web:* www.throgers.com	Edmond	OK	73083	405-330-2181	330-2186

194-3 Lumber & Building Supplies

	City	State	Zip	Phone	Fax
84 Lumber Co 1019 Rt 519 *TF:* 800-664-1984 ■ *Web:* www.84lumber.com	Eighty Four	PA	15330	724-228-8820	
AC Houston Lumber Co 2912 E La Madre Way **Fax Area Code:* 208 ■ *Web:* www.houstonlumber.com	Las Vegas	NV	89081	702-633-5000	726-5673*
Alamo Lumber Co 10800 Sentinel Dr *TF:* 855-828-9792 ■ *Web:* alamo.doitbest.com/	San Antonio	TX	78217	210-352-1300	
Allied Bldg Products Corp 15 E Union Ave *TF:* 800-541-2198 ■ *Web:* www.alliedbuilding.com	East Rutherford	NJ	07073	201-507-8400	507-3855
Alpine Lumber Co 1120 W 122nd Ave Ste 301 *TF:* 800-499-1634 ■ *Web:* www.alpinelumber.com	Denver	CO	80234	303-451-8001	451-5232
American Direct Procurement Inc 11000 Lakeview Ave *Web:* www.americandirectco.com	Lenexa	KS	66219	913-677-5588	
American International Forest Products LLC (AIFP) 5560 SW 107th Ave *TF:* 800-366-1611 ■ *Web:* www.lumber.com	Beaverton	OR	97005	503-641-1611	641-2800
Arnold Lumber Co 251 Fairgrounds Rd *TF:* 800-339-0116 ■ *Web:* www.arnold.myeshowroom.com	West Kingston	RI	02892	401-783-2266	792-3610
Auburn Corp 10490 164th Pl **Fax Area Code:* 708 ■ *TF:* 800-393-1826 ■ *Web:* www.auburncorp.com	Orland Park	IL	60467	800-393-1826	349-9461*
Babcock Lumber Company Inc 2220 Palmer St PO Box 8348 *TF:* 800-553-4441 ■ *Web:* www.babcocklumber.com	Pittsburgh	PA	15218	412-351-3515	351-1522
Baille Lumber Co 4002 Legion Dr PO Box 6 *TF:* 800-950-2850 ■ *Web:* www.baillie.com	Hamburg	NY	14075	716-649-2850	649-2811
Banner Supply Co 7195 NW 30th St *TF:* 888-511-4004 ■ *Web:* www.bannersupply.com	Miami	FL	33122	305-593-2946	477-2775
Bayer Built Woodworks Inc 24614 Hwy 71 *Web:* www.bayerbuilt.com	Belgrade	MN	56312	320-254-3651	254-3601
Beavertooth Oak Inc 401 S Fir St *TF:* 800-306-1942 ■ *Web:* www.beavertooth.net	Medford	OR	97501	541-779-1942	776-0944
Bender Lumber Company Inc 3120 Brock Ln *Web:* www.benderlumber.com	Bedford	IN	47421	812-279-9737	279-1659
Big C Lumber Inc 50860 Princess Way PO Box 176 *TF:* 888-297-0010 ■ *Web:* www.bigclumber.com	Granger	IN	46530	574-277-4550	271-3823
Big Creek Lumber 3564 Hwy 1 *Web:* www.big-creek.com	Davenport	CA	95017	831-457-5015	423-2800
Birmingham International Forest Products LLC 300 Riverhills Business Pk *TF:* 800-767-2437 ■ *Web:* www.bifp.com	Birmingham	AL	35242	205-972-1500	972-1461
Boise Cascade Bldg Materials Distribution Div 1111 W Jefferson Ste 300 PO Box 50 *TF:* 800-367-4611 ■ *Web:* www.bc.com	Boise	ID	83728	208-384-7700	384-7291
Britton Lumber Company Inc Seven Ely Rd PO Box 389 *TF:* 800-343-5300 ■ *Web:* www.brittonlumber.com	Fairlee	VT	05045	802-333-4388	333-4295
Brookside Lumber & Supply Co 500 Logan Rd PO Box 327 *Web:* www.brooksidelumber.com	Bethel Park	PA	15102	412-835-7610	835-8672
Buckeye Pacific LLC 4386 SW Macadam Ave Ste 200 *TF:* 800-767-9191 ■ *Web:* www.buckeyepacific.com	Portland	OR	97207	503-274-2284	274-2284
Builders FirstSource Inc 2001 Bryan St Ste 1600 *NASDAQ: BLDR* ■ *Web:* www.bldr.com	Dallas	TX	75201	214-880-3500	880-3599
Builders General Supply Co 15 Sycamore Ave **Fax Area Code:* 732 ■ *TF:* 800-570-7227 ■ *Web:* www.buildersgeneral.com	Little Silver	NJ	07739	800-570-7227	741-1095*
Campbellsport Bldg Supply Inc 227 W Main St PO Box 510 *Web:* www.drexelteam.com	Campbellsport	WI	53010	920-533-4412	533-4333
Causeway Lumber Co 3318 SW Second Ave *TF:* 800-375-5050 ■ *Web:* www.causewaylumber.com	Fort Lauderdale	FL	33315	954-763-1224	467-2389
Champion Lumber Co 1313 Chicago Ave Ste 100 *Web:* www.championlumber.net	Riverside	CA	92507	951-684-5670	275-0825
Chelsea Lumber Co One Old Barn Cir *TF:* 800-875-9126 ■ *Web:* www.chelsealumber.com	Chelsea	MI	48118	734-475-9126	475-7320
Chicago Lumber Company of Omaha, The 1324 Pierce St PO Box 3487 *TF:* 800-642-8210 ■ *Web:* www.clc-omaha.com	Omaha	NE	68103	402-342-0840	344-8323
Cleary Millwork Company Inc 235 Dividend Rd *TF:* 800-486-7600 ■ *Web:* www.clearymillwork.com	Rocky Hill	CT	06067	860-721-0520	
CNC Assoc Ny Inc 101 Kentile Rd *Web:* www.cncassociates.com	South Plainfield	NJ	07080	718-416-3853	
Counter Pro Inc 210 Lincoln St *TF:* 800-899-2444 ■ *Web:* counterproincusa.com	Manchester	NH	03103	603-647-2444	647-6770
Coventry Lumber Inc 2030 Nooseneck Hill Rd *TF:* 800-390-0919 ■ *Web:* www.coventrylumber.com	Coventry	RI	02816	401-821-2800	828-2870
Creative Pultrusions Inc 214 Industrial Ln *TF:* 888-274-7855 ■ *Web:* www.creativepultrusions.com	Alum Bank	PA	15521	814-839-4186	839-4276
Custom Builder Supply Company Inc PO Box 413 *Web:* www.custombuildersupply.com	Williamsburg	VA	23187	757-229-5150	253-7568
Doka USA Ltd 214 Gates Rd *TF:* 877-365-2872 ■ *Web:* www.doka.com	Little Ferry	NJ	07643	201-329-7839	641-6254
Door Systems Inc PO Box 511 *TF:* 800-545-3667 ■ *Web:* doorsys.com	Framingham	MA	01704	508-875-3508	
Falmouth Lumber Inc 670 Teaticket Hwy *Web:* www.falmouthlumber.com	East Falmouth	MA	02536	508-548-6868	457-0649
Forest City Trading Group LLC 10250 SW Greenburg Rd Ste 200 PO Box 4209 *TF:* 800-767-3284 ■ *Web:* www.fctg.com	Portland	OR	97223	503-246-8500	246-1116
Forest Products Group Inc, The 1033 Dublin Rd *Web:* www.forestproductsgroup.com	Columbus	OH	43215	614-488-9743	
Foxworth-Galbraith Lumber Co 4965 Preston Pk Blvd Ste 400 *TF:* 800-688-8082 ■ *Web:* www.foxgal.com	Plano	TX	75093	972-665-2400	454-4251
Frank Miller Lumber Company Inc 1690 Frank Miller Rd *Web:* www.frankmiller.com	Union City	IN	47390	765-964-3196	964-6618
Frank Paxton Lumber Co 7455 Dawson Rd **Fax:* Sales ■ *TF:* 800-325-9800 ■ *Web:* www.paxtonwood.com	Cincinnati	OH	45243	513-984-8200	984-9060*
Genesee Reserve Supply Inc 200 Jefferson Rd PO Box 20619 *Web:* www.geneseereserve.com	Rochester	NY	14602	585-292-7040	292-7046
Gerretsen Bldg Supply Co 1900 NE Airport Rd *Web:* www.gerretsen.com	Roseburg	OR	97470	541-672-2636	464-6230
Great Lakes Gypsum & Supply 33900 Concord Rd	Livonia	MI	48150	734-421-1170	421-5237
Great Lakes Veneer Inc 222 S Parkview Ave PO Box 476 *Web:* www.greatlakesveneer.com	Marion	WI	54950	715-754-2501	754-2582
Guardian Building Products (GBPD) 979 Batesville Rd *TF:* 800-569-4262 ■ *Web:* guardian-distribution.com	Greer	SC	29651	864-297-6101	281-3558
H. W. Culp Lumber Co PO Box 235 *Web:* www.culplumber.com	New London	NC	28127	704-463-7311	463-4100
Hagle Lumber Company Inc 3100 Somis Rd PO Box 120 *Web:* www.haglelumber.com	Somis	CA	93066	805-987-3887	987-7564
Hatch & Bailey Company Inc One Meadow St Ext *Web:* www.hatchandbailey.com	Norwalk	CT	06854	203-866-5515	854-1712
Hawaii Planing Mill Ltd (HPM) 16-166 Melekahiwa St *TF:* 877-841-7633 ■ *Web:* www.hpmhawaii.com	Keaau	HI	96749	808-966-5693	966-7564
Holt & Bugbee Co 1600 Shawsheen St *TF:* 800-325-6010 ■ *Web:* www.holtandbugbee.com	Tewksbury	MA	01876	978-851-7201	851-3941
Howard Lumber Co 475 Columbia Industrial Blvd PO Box 1039 *TF:* 800-868-3227 ■ *Web:* howardlumbercompany.com	Evans	GA	30809	706-868-8400	868-9989
Hutchison Inc 7460 Hwy 85 PO Box 1158 *TF:* 800-525-0121 ■ *Web:* www.hutchison-inc.com	Adams City	CO	80022	303-287-2826	289-3286
Huttig Bldg Products Inc (HBP) 555 Maryville University Dr Ste 400 *OTC: HBPI* ■ *TF:* 800-325-4466 ■ *Web:* www.huttig.com	Saint Louis	MO	63141	314-216-2600	216-2601
Idaho Pacific Lumber Co (IdaPac) 7255 Franklin Rd *TF:* 800-231-2310 ■ *Web:* www.idapac.com	Boise	ID	83709	208-375-8052	375-3054
Jb Wholesale Roofing & Bldg Supplies Inc 21524 Nordhoff St PO Box 5289 *TF General:* 800-464-2461 ■ *Web:* www.jbroofing.com	Chatsworth	CA	91311	818-998-0440	527-1587
Jewett-Cameron Trading Company Ltd 32275 NW Hillcrest PO Box 1010 *NASDAQ: JCTCF* ■ *TF:* 800-547-5877 ■ *Web:* www.jewettcameron.com	North Plains	OR	97133	503-647-0110	647-2272
Kight Home Ctr 5521 Oak Grove Rd *Web:* www.kighthomecenter.com	Evansville	IN	47715	812-479-8281	473-7763
Kimal Lumber Co 400 Riverview Dr *Web:* www.kimallumber.com	Nokomis	FL	34275	941-484-9721	484-9593
Kleet Lumber Company Inc 777 Pk Ave *TF:* 800-696-5533 ■ *Web:* www.kleet.com	Huntington	NY	11743	631-427-7060	427-4384
Lumbermen's Merchandising Corp 137 W Wayne Ave **Fax Area Code:* 484 ■ *Web:* www.lmc.net	Wayne	PA	19087	610-293-7000	293-7098*
Lyman Lumber Co 300 Morse Ave PO Box 40 *Web:* www.lymanlumber.com	Excelsior	MN	55331	952-470-3600	470-3670
Lyon & Billard Co, The 38 Gypsy Ln *Web:* www.lyon-billard.com	Meriden	CT	06451	203-235-4487	235-9736
Magbee Contractors Supply 1065 Bankhead Hwy *Web:* www.magbee.com	Winder	GA	30680	678-425-2600	425-2602

Phone Fax

Magnolia Forest Products Inc
13252 I- 55 S PO Box 99 .... Terry MS 39170 800-366-6374 878-2590*
*Fax Area Code: 601 ■ TF: 800-366-6374 ■ Web: www.magnoliaforest.com

Markraft Cabinets Inc
2705 Castle Creek Ln .... Wilmington NC 28401 910-762-1986 762-1985
Web: www.markraft.com

Matheus Lumber Company Inc
15800 Woodinville-Redmond Rd NE
PO Box 2260 .... Woodinville WA 98072 425-489-3000 822-4028
TF: 800-284-7501 ■ Web: www.matheuslumber.com

Matt's Building Materials 404 E Expy 83 .... Pharr TX 78577 956-787-5561
Web: www.mattsbuildingmaterials.com

Mattingly Lumber & Millwork Inc 410 E St. .... Madison IL 62040 636-343-3877 343-4141
Web: www.mattinglylumber.com

McCray Lumber Co 10741 El Monte Ln. .... Overland Park KS 66211 913-341-6900 341-1881
Web: www.mccraylumber.com

Mead Clark Lumber Co
Hearn Ave & Dowd Dr PO Box 529 .... Santa Rosa CA 95402 707-576-3333 523-0350
TF: 800-585-9663 ■ Web: www.meadclark.com

MID-AM Bldg Supply Inc
1615 Omar Bradley Dr PO Box 645 .... Moberly MO 65270 660-263-2140 263-7892
TF: 800-892-5850 ■ Web: www.midambuilding.com

Mid-South Bldg Supply Inc
7940 Woodruff Ct .... Springfield VA 22151 703-321-8500 321-9308
Web: www.msbs.net

Millard Lumber Inc 12900 I St PO Box 45445 .... Omaha NE 68145 402-896-2800 896-2865
TF: 800-228-9260 ■ Web: millardlumber.com

Musser Lumber Company Inc
200 Shoal Ridge Dr .... Rural Retreat VA 24368 276-686-5113 686-5169
Web: www.musserlumber.com

Nalco Real Estate Corp 24595 Groesbeck Hwy .... Warren MI 48089 586-775-8200 775-4110

Nassau Suffolk Lumber & Supply Corp
2000 Ocean Ave .... Ronkonkoma NY 11716 631-467-2020 467-2720
Web: www.nassausuffolklumber.com

National Industrial Lumber Co
1 Chicago Ave. .... Elizabeth PA 15037 800-289-9352 384-3955*
*Fax Area Code: 412 ■ TF: 800-289-9352 ■ Web: www.nilco.net/about-us/locations

Ohio Valley Supply Co
3512 Spring Grove Ave. .... Cincinnati OH 45223 513-681-8300 853-3307
TF: 800-696-5608 ■ Web: www.ovsco.com

Omega Products International
1681 California Ave .... Corona CA 92881 951-737-7447 520-2594
TF: 800-600-6634 ■ Web: www.omega-products.com

Orgain Building Supply Co 65 Commerce St .... Clarksville TN 37040 931-647-1567 648-4482
Web: www.orgainbuilding.com

Pacific Source Inc PO Box 2323 .... Woodinville WA 98072 888-343-1515 486-1445*
*Fax Area Code: 425 ■ TF: 888-343-1515 ■ Web: www.pacsource.com

Pacific Wood Laminates Inc
885 Railroad Ave PO Box 820 .... Brookings OR 97415 541-469-4177 469-9105
Web: www.pacificwoodlaminates.com

Palmer-Donavin Manufacturing Co
1200 Steelwood Rd. .... Columbus OH 43212 614-486-9657 486-5073
TF: 800-589-4412 ■ Web: www.palmerdonavin.com

Park Avenue Building & Roofing Supplies LLC
2120 Atlantic Ave .... Brooklyn NY 11233 718-403-0100 596-5085
Web: www.parkavebenmoore.com

Parker Lumber Co Inc 2192 Eastex Fwy .... Beaumont TX 77703 409-898-7000 347-0942
Web: www.parkersbuildingsupply.com

Parker Lumber Co of Port Arthur Inc
2948 Gulfway Dr. .... Port Arthur TX 77642 409-983-2745 983-3993
TF: 855-828-9792 ■ Web: www.parkerlumber.com

Parksite Inc 1563 Hubbard Ave .... Batavia IL 60510 630-761-9490 761-6820
TF: 800-338-3355 ■ Web: www.parksite.com

Product Distributors Inc
4200 Beach Dr Ste 2 Ste 2 .... Rapid City SD 57702 605-341-6500 341-1976
Web: www.forpd.com

Pyramid Interiors Distributors Inc
PO Box 181058 .... Memphis TN 38181 901-375-4197
TF: 800-456-0592 ■ Web: www.pyramidinteriors.com

Quality Plywood Specialties Inc
4500 110th Ave N. .... Clearwater FL 33762 727-572-0500 571-3623
TF: 888-722-1181 ■ Web: www.qualityplywoodspec.com

Quality Wholesale Bldg Inc
11701 KinaRd Rd .... North Little Rock AR 72117 501-945-3442 945-0506

Raymond Bldg Supply Corp
7751 Bayshore Rd .... North Fort Myers FL 33917 239-731-8300 731-3299
TF: 877-731-7272 ■ Web: www.rbsc.net

Reliable Wholesale Lumber Inc
7600 Redondo Cir .... Huntington Beach CA 92648 714-848-8222 847-1605
TF: 877-795-4638 ■ Web: www.rwli.net

Richmond International Forest Products Inc
4050 Innslake Dr Ste 100 .... Glen Allen VA 23060 804-747-0111 270-4547
TF: 800-767-0111 ■ Web: www.rifp.com

Ridout Lumber Co 125 Henry Farrar Dr .... Searcy AR 72143 501-268-3929
Web: www.ridoutlumber.com

Rigidply Rafters Inc 701 E Linden St .... Richland PA 17087 717-866-6581
Web: www.rigidply.com

Riverhead Bldg Supply Corp 1093 Pulaski St. .... Riverhead NY 11901 631-727-3650 727-7713
TF: 800-378-3650 ■ Web: www.rbscorp.com

Riverside Forest Products Inc
2912 Professional Pkwy .... Augusta GA 30907 706-855-5500 863-3362
TF: 888-855-8733 ■ Web: www.riversideforest.com

RP Lumber Company Inc 514 E Vandalia St .... Edwardsville IL 62025 618-656-1514 656-6785
Web: www.rplumber.com

Russin Lumber Corp 21 Leonards Dr. .... Montgomery NY 12549 845-457-4000 457-4010
TF: 800-724-0010 ■ Web: www.russinlumber.com

Schoeneman Bros Co 4000 S Western Ave .... Sioux Falls SD 57103 605-339-0745 336-2529
Web: www.schoenemans.com

Seaboard International Forest Products LLC
22F Cotton Rd Ste F .... Nashua NH 03063 603-881-3700 598-2280
TF: 800-669-6800 ■ Web: www.sifp.com

Seigle's 1331 Davis Rd .... Elgin IL 60123 847-742-2000 697-6521
Web: www.seigles.com

Phone Fax

Service Construction Supply Inc
PO Box 13405 .... Birmingham AL 35202 205-252-3158 252-5720
TF: 866-729-4968 ■ Web: www.serviceconstructionsupply.com

Solar Industries Inc PO Box 27337 .... Tucson AZ 85726 520-519-8258
TF: 800-449-2323 ■ Web: www.solarindustriesinc.com

Spellman Hardwoods Inc 4645 N 43rd Ave .... Phoenix AZ 85031 602-272-2313 930-7668*
*Fax Area Code: 623 ■ TF: 800-624-5401 ■ Web: www.spellmanhardwoods.com

Sprenger Midwest Inc 700 S Fourth Ave .... Sioux Falls SD 57104 605-334-7705 334-5205
Web: www.sprengermidwest.com

Stan's Lumber Inc 226 E Main St .... Twin Lakes WI 53181 262-877-2181 723-3472
TF: 800-535-2890 ■ Web: alexlbr.com

Stevenson Lumber 501 Division .... Adrian MI 49221 517-265-5151 265-5534

Stock Bldg Supply 8020 Arco Corporate Dr. .... Raleigh NC 27617 919-431-1000 431-1700
TF: 877-734-6365 ■ Web: www.stockbuildingsupply.com

Stock Building Supply 8020 Arco Corporate Dr .... Raleigh NC 27617 919-431-1000
Web: www.carolinaholdings.com

Sunderland Bros Co 9700 J St .... Omaha NE 68127 402-339-2220 339-4455
Web: www.sunderlands.com

Timber Products Co
305 S Fourth St PO Box 269 .... Springfield OR 97477 541-747-4577 744-4296
TF: 800-547-9520 ■ Web: www.timberproducts.com

Timberline Forest Products LLC PO Box 1568 .... Sherwood OR 97140 503-590-5485 590-7421
Web: www.timberlineforestproducts.com

Tischler Und Sohn 6 Suburban Ave .... Stamford CT 06901 203-674-0600 674-0601
Web: www.tischlerwindows.com

Tri-state Forest Products Inc
2105 Sheridan Ave .... Springfield OH 45505 937-323-6325 323-6888
TF: 800-949-6325 ■ Web: www.tsfpi.com

Tulnoy Lumber Inc 1620 Webster Ave .... Bronx NY 10457 718-901-1700 299-8920
Web: www.tulnoylumber.com

US Lumber Group Inc
2160 Satellite Blvd Ste 450 .... Duluth GA 30097 678-474-4577 474-4575
Web: www.uslumber.com

Verhalen Inc 500 Pilgrim Way PO Box 11968 .... Green Bay WI 54304 920-431-8900 431-8901
TF: 800-895-0071 ■ Web: www.verhaleninc.com

Viking Forest Products LLC
7615 Smetana Ln .... Eden Prairie MN 55344 952-941-6512 941-4633
TF: 800-733-3801 ■ Web: www.vikingforest.com

VNS Corp 325 Commerce Loop PO Box 1659 .... Vidalia GA 30475 912-537-8964 537-4839
Web: www.vnscorp.com

Warren Trask Co 1481 Central St. .... Stoughton MA 02072 781-341-2426 341-3522
Web: www.wtrask.com

Western Lumber Cy LLC 2240 Tower E Ste 200 .... Medford OR 97504 541-779-5121 779-0155
TF: 800-633-5554 ■ Web: www.westernlumber.com

Wheeler Lumber LLC 9330 James Ave S. .... Bloomington MN 55431 952-929-7854 929-2909
TF: 800-328-3986 ■ Web: www.wheeler-con.com

White Cap Industries Inc 1723 S Ritchie St. .... Santa Ana CA 92705 714-258-3300 258-3289
TF: 800-944-8322 ■ Web: www.whitecap.com

Wilson Lumber Co Inc
4818 Meridian St PO Box 3159 .... Huntsville AL 35811 256-852-7411 851-9904
Web: www.wilsonlumber.net

Window Rama Enterprises Inc
71 Heartland Blvd .... Edgewood NY 11717 800-695-7262
TF: 800-897-7262 ■ Web: www.windowrama.com

Wright Do-it Ctr 1306 N Market .... Sparta IL 62286 618-443-5335 687-1030
Web: www.wrightdoit.com

WT Harvey Lumber Co 800 15th St PO Box 310 .... Columbus GA 31902 706-322-8204 323-2433
Web: www.harveylumber.com

Zeeland Lumber & Supply Co 146 E Washington .... Zeeland MI 49464 616-772-2119 772-6409
Web: www.zeelandlumber.com

194-4 Roofing, Siding, Insulation Materials

Phone Fax

ABC Seamless 3001 Fiechtner Dr .... Fargo ND 58103 701-293-5952 293-3107
TF: 800-732-6577 ■ Web: www.abcseamless.com

ABC Supply Company Inc One ABC Pkwy. .... Beloit WI 53511 608-362-7777 362-6215
TF: 888-492-1047 ■ Web: www.abcsupply.com

B & L Wholesale Supply Inc 70 Hartford St .... Rochester NY 14605 585-546-6616 546-7326
Web: www.blwholesale.com

Beacon Roofing Supply Inc One Lakeland Pk Dr. .... Peabody MA 01960 978-535-7668 535-7358
NASDAQ: BECN ■ TF: 877-645-7663 ■ Web: www.beaconroofingsupply.com

Best Distributing Company Inc PO Box 128 .... Goldsboro NC 27533 919-735-1651
Web: www.bestdist.com

Brunswick Floors 3550 Darien Hwy .... Brunswick GA 31525 912-265-0222
Web: www.brunswickfloors.com

Burbank Roofing Supply Inc
700 N Victory Blvd .... Burbank CA 91502 818-840-8851 840-8234
Web: www.roofingdealer.com

Carlisle Cos Inc
13925 Ballantyne Corporate Pl Ste 400 .... Charlotte NC 28277 704-501-1100 501-1190
NYSE: CSL ■ TF: 800-248-5995 ■ Web: www.carlisle.com

Carlisle SynTec 1285 Ritner Hwy PO Box 7000 .... Carlisle PA 17013 717-245-7000 245-7053
TF: 800-479-6832 ■ Web: www.carlislesyntec.com

Crane Composites Inc 23525 W Eames St. .... Channahon IL 60410 815-467-8600 467-8666*
*Fax: Hum Res ■ TF: 800-435-0080 ■ Web: www.cranecomposites.com

E O Wood Company Inc PO Box 7416 .... Fort Worth TX 76111 817-834-8811 831-0834
Web: www.eowood.com

EJ Bartells Co 700 Powell Ave SW PO Box 4160 .... Renton WA 98057 425-228-4111 228-8807
TF: 800-468-9528 ■ Web: www.ejbartells.com

Fire Brick Engineers Co 2400 S 43rd St. .... Milwaukee WI 53219 414-383-6000
Web: www.firebrickengineers.com

Frank Roberts & Sons Inc
1130 Robertsville Rd .... Punxsutawney PA 15767 814-938-5000 938-0880
TF: 800-262-8955 ■ Web: frankrobertsandsons.com

General Insulation Company Inc
278 Mystic Ave Ste 209 .... Medford MA 02155 781-391-2070 391-3094
TF: 800-442-6662 ■ Web: www.generalinsulation.com

Harvey Industries Inc 1400 Main St. .... Waltham MA 02451 800-598-5400 398-7715*
*Fax Area Code: 781 ■ TF: 800-598-5400 ■ Web: www.harveybp.com

				Phone	Fax
Howred Corp 7887 San Felipe St Ste 122 *TF:* 800-535-5053 ■ *Web:* www.howred.com	Houston	TX	77063	713-781-3980	784-3985
James Hardie Bldg Products 26300 La Alameda Ave Ste 400 *TF:* 888-542-7343 ■ *Web:* www.jameshardie.com	Mission Viejo	CA	92691	949-348-1800	367-1294
Jenkins Brick & Tile Company LLC 201 Sixth St N *Web:* www.jenkinsbrick.com	Montgomery	AL	36104	334-834-2210	
JPS Industries Inc 55 Beattie Pl # 1510 *Web:* jps-industries.com	Greenville	SC	29601	864-239-3900	271-9939
Lansing Bldg Products 8501 Sanford Dr *TF:* 800-768-5762 ■ *Web:* lansingbp.com/	Richmond	VA	23228	804-266-8771	266-0166
MacArthur Co 2400 Wycliff St *TF:* 800-777-7507 ■ *Web:* www.macarthurco.com	Saint Paul	MN	55114	651-646-2773	642-9630
McClure-Johnston Co 201 Corey Ave *TF:* 800-232-0018 ■ *Web:* www.cassadymcclure.com	Braddock	PA	15104	412-351-4300	351-1480
Norandex Bldg Materials Distribution Inc 300 Executive Pkwy W Ste 100 *TF:* 800-528-0942 ■ *Web:* www.norandex.com	Hudson	OH	44236	800-528-0942	
North Carolina Foam Industries Inc 1515 Carter St *TF:* 800-346-8229 ■ *Web:* www.ncfi.com	Mount Airy	NC	27030	336-789-9161	789-9586
North Coast Roofing Systems 701 Brazos St Ste 1050 *Web:* www.shelterdistribution.com	Austin	TX	78701	972-369-8000	
Oberfields LLC 1165 Alum Creek Dr *TF:* 800-845-7644 ■ *Web:* www.oberfields.com	Columbus	OH	43209	614-252-0955	
Olympia Tile International Inc 1000 Lawrence Ave W *TF:* 800-268-1613 ■ *Web:* www.olympiatile.com	Toronto	ON	M6A1C6	416-785-6666	
Onduline North America Inc 4900 Ondura Dr *TF:* 800-777-7663 ■ *Web:* www.ondura.com	Fredericksburg	VA	22407	540-898-7000	898-4991
Owens Corning One Owens Corning Pkwy *NYSE: OC* ■ *Web:* www.owenscorning.com	Toledo	OH	43659	419-248-8000	325-1538
Pacific Coast Bldg Products Inc 10600 White Rock Rd Bldg B Ste 100 *Web:* www.paccoast.com	Rancho Cordova	CA	95670	916-631-6500	631-6685
Pfister Maintenance Inc 80 E Fifth St *Web:* www.pfisterroofing.com	Paterson	NJ	07524	973-569-9330	
Philadelphia Reserve Supply Co 200 Mack Dr *TF:* 800-347-7726 ■ *Web:* www.prsco.org	Croydon	PA	19021	215-785-3141	785-5806
Plastatech Engineering Ltd 725 Morley Dr *TF:* 800-892-9358 ■ *Web:* www.plastatech.com	Saginaw	MI	48601	989-754-6500	754-1626
Roofing & Insulation Supply Inc 12221 Merit Dr Ste 1015 *Web:* www.risris.com	Dallas	TX	75251	972-239-8309	239-8310
Roofing Products & Bldg Supply Company Inc 4955 River Rd *Web:* www.rfgproducts.com	Jefferson	LA	70121	504-733-0404	733-0360
Roofing Supply Group 8319 N Lamar Blvd *Web:* www.roofingsupplygroup.com	Austin	TX	78753	512-834-4347	834-4352
Roofing Wholesale Co Inc 1918 W Grant St *TF Cust Svc:* 800-528-4532 ■ *Web:* www.rwc.org	Phoenix	AZ	85009	602-258-3794	256-0932
SG Wholesale Roofing Supplies Inc 1101 E Sixth St *TF Cust Svc:* 888-747-8500 ■ *Web:* www.sgroof.com	Santa Ana	CA	92701	714-568-1906	568-1915
Shook & Fletcher Insulation Co 4625 Valleydale Rd *TF:* 888-829-2575 ■ *Web:* www.shookandfletcher.com	Birmingham	AL	35242	205-991-7606	991-7745
Spec Bldg Materials Inc 4300 W Ave *TF:* 800-588-3892 ■ *Web:* speccorp.com	San Antonio	TX	78213	210-342-2727	340-0688
Specialty Products & Insulation Co (SPI) 1650 Manheim Pk Ste 202 *TF:* 800-788-7764 ■ *Web:* www.spi-co.com	Lancaster	PA	17601	717-569-3900	519-4046
Standard Roofings Inc 100 Pk Rd *Web:* www.abcsupply.com/	Tinton Falls	NJ	07724	732-542-5200	389-4982
Supreme Systems Inc 1355 N Walton Walker Blvd *Web:* www.supremeroofing.com	Dallas	TX	75211	214-330-8913	
Toitures GGR Inc 34 Trudel Cp 333 *Web:* www.toituresggr.com	Amos	QC	J9T3A7	819-727-3348	
Variform Inc 5020 Weston Pkwy Ste 400 **Fax Area Code:* 816 ■ *TF:* 800-800-2244 ■ *Web:* variform.plygem.com	Cary	NC	27513	888-975-9436	903-6942*
Warko Roofing Company Inc 18 Morgan Dr *Web:* www.thewarkogroup.com	Reading	PA	19608	610-796-4545	796-4547
Wesco Cedar Inc PO Box 520 *TF:* 800-547-2511 ■ *Web:* www.wescocedar.com	Creswell	OR	97426	541-688-5020	688-5024

195 CONSULTING SERVICES - ENVIRONMENTAL

SEE ALSO Recyclable Materials Recovery p. 3046; Remediation Services p. 3048; Waste Management p. 3293

				Phone	Fax
A & A Maintenance Enterprise Inc 965 Midland Ave *Web:* www.aamaintenance.com	Yonkers	NY	10704	914-969-0009	
A G Miller Company Inc 53 Batavia St *Web:* www.agmiller.com	Springfield	MA	01109	413-732-9297	734-1236
Aadfw Inc 2161 Regal Pkwy *Web:* www.aadfwinc.com	Euless	TX	76040	817-540-0153	540-0886
Aarcher 910 Commerce Rd *Web:* www.aarcherinc.com	Annapolis	MD	21401	410-897-9100	
ACS Manufacturing Inc 1601 Commerce Blvd *Web:* www.acsmanufacturing.com	Denison	TX	75020	903-462-2001	
Ameresco Inc 111 Speen St Ste 410 *TF:* 866-263-7372 ■ *Web:* www.ameresco.com	Framingham	MA	01701	508-661-2200	661-2201
AmeriPark LLC 3200 Cobb Galleria Pkwy Ste 299 *Web:* www.ameripark.com	Atlanta	GA	30339	678-303-5962	
Arcadis 630 Plz Dr Ste 200 *Web:* www.arcadis-us.com	Highlands Ranch	CO	80129	720-344-3500	344-3535
ARISE Technologies Corp 65 Northland Rd *Web:* www.arisetech.com	Waterloo	ON	N2V1Y8	519-725-2244	
Arizona Energy Masters 219 W Lone Cactus *Web:* www.arizonaenergymasters.com	Phoenix	AZ	85027	602-427-0007	
AshBritt Inc 565 E Hillsboro Blvd Ste 103 *Web:* www.ashbritt.com	Deerfield Beach	FL	33441	954-545-3535	
Ashbrook Simon-Hartley LP 11600 E Hardy *Web:* www.as-h.com	Houston	TX	77093	281-449-0322	
ATC Assoc Inc 104 E 25th St 10th Fl *TF:* 800-476-5886 ■ *Web:* cardno.com/cardnoatc	New York	NY	10010	212-353-8280	353-8306
Avogadro Group LLC, The 2825 Verne Roberts Cir *Web:* www.avogadrogroup.com	Antioch	CA	94509	925-680-4300	
Badger Express LLC 181 Quality Ct *TF:* 800-972-0084 ■ *Web:* www.badgerexpress.com	Fall River	WI	53932	920-484-5808	484-5818
Basic Systems Inc 9255 Cadiz Rd *Web:* www.bsinaturalgas.com	Cambridge	OH	43725	740-432-3001	
Blade Energy Partners Ltd 2600 Network Blvd Ste 550 *TF:* 800-849-1545 ■ *Web:* www.blade-energy.com	Frisco	TX	75034	972-712-8407	712-8408
BlazeTech Corp 29B Montvale Ave *Web:* www.blazetech.com	Woburn	MA	01801	781-759-0700	
Blue Pillar Inc 9025 N River Rd Ste 150 *TF:* 888-234-3212 ■ *Web:* bluepillar.com	Indianapolis	IN	46240	888-234-3212	
Blue Water Satellite Inc 440 E Poe Rd Ste 203 *Web:* www.bluewatersatellite.com	Bowling Green	OH	43402	419-728-0060	
Brighter Planet Inc 36 Main St *Web:* brighterplanet.com	Middlebury	VT	05753	802-458-0441	
Brightergy LLC 1617 Main St Third Fl *Web:* brightergy.com	Kansas City	MO	64108	816-866-0555	
Broad Oak Energy II LLC 1707 Market Pl Ste 320 *Web:* www.broadoakenergy.com	Irving	TX	75063	972-444-8808	
Burnaby Lake Greenhouses Ltd 17250 80 Ave *Web:* www.burlake.com	Surrey	BC	V4N6J6	604-576-2088	
Buzas Greenhouses 3927 Newburg Rd *Web:* buzasgreenhouseandfarm.com	Easton	PA	18045	610-252-5289	
C. F. Bean LLC 619 Engineers Rd *Web:* www.cfbean.com	Belle Chasse	LA	70037	504-587-8700	
Caravan Facilities Management LLC 1400 Weiss St *TF:* 855-211-7450 ■ *Web:* www.caravanfm.com	Saginaw	MI	48602	855-211-7450	
Cardinal Group Inc, The 406 King St E *Web:* www.cardinalgroup.ca	Toronto	ON	M5A1L4	416-971-4494	
CH2M Hill Cos Ltd 9191 S Jamica St **Fax Area Code:* 720 ■ *Web:* www.ch2m.com	Englewood	CO	80112	303-771-0900	286-9250*
Chicago Parking Meters LLC 2735 N Ashland Ave *Web:* www.chicagometers.com	Chicago	IL	60614	773-935-2178	
Chicanos Por La Causa Inc 1112 E Buckeye Rd *Web:* www.cplc.org	Phoenix	AZ	85034	602-257-0700	256-2740
Clark Pest Control Inc 555 N Guild Ave *TF:* 877-918-9988 ■ *Web:* www.clarkpest.com	Lodi	CA	95240	877-918-9988	
Clear Comfort Water LLC 4888 Pearl E Cir Ste 100W *Web:* clearcomfort.com	Boulder	CO	80301	303-872-4477	
Climate Registry, The 523 W Sixth St Ste 445 *TF:* 866-523-0764 ■ *Web:* www.theclimateregistry.org	Los Angeles	CA	90014	866-523-0764	
CoaLogix Inc 11707 Steele Creek Rd *Web:* www.coalogix.com	Charlotte	NC	28273	704-827-8933	
COCAT LLC 4905 Lima St *Web:* www.cocat.com	Denver	CO	80239	303-333-0392	
Compaction Technologies Inc 1171 Northland Dr Ste 121 *TF:* 877-860-6900 ■ *Web:* www.compactiontechnologies.com	Mendota Heights	MN	55120	877-860-6900	
Covino Environmental Assoc Inc 300 Wildwood Ave *Web:* www.covinoinc.com	Woburn	MA	01801	781-933-2555	932-9402
Cox Mclain Environmental Consulting Inc 6010 Balcones Dr Ste 210 *Web:* www.coxmclain.com	Austin	TX	78731	512-338-2223	
Cramer Fish Sciences 300 Se Arrow Creek Ln *Web:* www.fishsciences.net	Gresham	OR	97080	503-491-9577	
Direct Supply Inc 6767 N Industrial Rd *Web:* www.directsupply.com	Milwaukee	WI	53223	414-358-2805	358-7411
DPRA Inc 200 Research Dr *Web:* www.dpra.com	Manhattan	KS	66503	785-539-3565	537-0272
Draper Aden Assoc Inc 2206 S Main St Ste A *Web:* www.daa.com	Blacksburg	VA	24060	540-552-0444	552-0291
Durisol Inc 67 Frid St *Web:* www.armtec.com	Hamilton	ON	L8P4M3	905-521-0999	
Earth Networks Inc 12410 Milestone Ctr Dr Ste 300 *Web:* www.aws.com	Germantown	MD	20876	301-250-4000	
Earth Resource Systems LLC 16285 Laconia Ln *Web:* www.earthresourcesystems.com	Milton	GA	30004	404-513-5429	
Earth Systems Services Inc 895 Aerovista Pl Ste 102 *TF:* 866-781-0112 ■ *Web:* www.earthsystems.com	San Luis Obispo	CA	93401	805-781-0112	781-0180
Earthcon Consultants Inc 1880 W Oak Pkwy Bldg 100 Ste 106 *Web:* www.premiercorp-usa.com	Marietta	GA	30062	770-973-2100	
Eastern Janitorial Services Inc 23 N Michigan Ave *Web:* www.easternjs.com	Kenilworth	NJ	07033	908-298-8120	
Ecology & Environment Inc 368 Pleasant View Dr *NASDAQ: EEI* ■ *Web:* www.ene.com	Lancaster	NY	14086	716-684-8060	684-0844
Ehs-International Inc 13228 NE 20th St Ste 100 *Web:* www.ehsintl.com	Bellevue	WA	98005	425-455-2959	646-7247

Phone Fax

Energy Worldnet
1210 S Bus Hwy 81/287 Decatur Decatur TX 76234 940-626-1941
Web: www.energyworldnet.com
EnerNex Corp 620 Mabry Hood Rd Ste 300 Knoxville TN 37932 865-218-4600
Web: www.enernex.com
Entact LLC 3129 Bass Pro Dr Grapevine TX 76051 972-580-1323 550-7464
Web: www.entact.com
Entec Services Inc 30 Monroe Dr Pelham AL 35124 205-358-1011
Web: www.entecservices.com
Enviro Clean Services LLC 11717 N Morgan Rd Yukon OK 73099 405-373-4545
Web: www.envirocleanps.com
Environmental & Safety Designs Inc
5724 Summer Trees Dr Memphis TN 38134 901-372-7962 372-2454
TF: 800-588-7962 ■ *Web:* www.ensafe.com
Environmental Standards Inc
1140 Vly Forge Rd Valley Forge PA 19482 610-935-5577
Web: www.envstd.com
EnviroTrac Ltd Five Old Dock Rd Yaphank NY 11980 631-924-3001
Web: www.envirotrac.com
Eureka Resources LLC 419 Second St Williamsport PA 17701 570-323-2535
Web: www.eureka-resources.com
Fauske & Assoc LLC 16w070 83rd St Burr Ridge IL 60527 630-323-8750 986-5481
TF: 877-328-7531 ■ *Web:* www.fauske.com
First Environment Inc 91 Fulton St Boonton NJ 07005 973-334-0003 334-0928
TF: 800-486-5869 ■ *Web:* www.firstenvironment.com
Fishbio Environmental LLC 3188 Wood Creek Dr Chico CA 95928 530-342-9262
Web: www.fishbio.com
Ganaraska Region Conservation 2216 28 Hwy Port Hope ON L1A3V8 905-885-8173
Web: www.grca.on.ca
GEEP Ecosys Inc 220 John St Barrie ON L4N2L2 705-725-1919
Web: www.geepecosys.com
Gershman, Brickner & Bratton Inc
8550 Arlington Blvd Ste 304 Fairfax VA 22031 703-573-5800
Web: www.gbbinc.com
Giant Resource Recovery Company Inc
654 Judge St PO Box 352 Harleyville SC 29488 803-496-2200
Web: www.grr-giant.com
Gilman & Pastor LLP 63 Atlantic Ave Third Fl Boston MA 02110 617-742-9700 291-3258*
**Fax Area Code:* 508 ■ *TF:* 877-428-7374 ■ *Web:* www.gilmanlawllp.com
Glacial Energy 2701 N Dallas Pkwy Ste 120 Plano TX 75093 877-569-2841
TF: 877-569-2841 ■ *Web:* www.glacialenergy.com
GLE Associates Inc 4300 W Cypress St Ste 400 Tampa FL 33607 813-241-8350
Web: www.gleassociates.com
Great Ecology 2231 Broadway Ste 4 New York NY 10024 212-579-6800
Web: www.greatecology.com
Green Seal Environmental Inc
114 State Rd Ste B1 Sagamore Beach MA 02562 508-888-6034
Web: www.gseenv.com
GreenerU Inc One Moody St Waltham MA 02453 781-891-3750
Web: greeneru.com
Greenland International Consulting Ltd
120 Hume St Collingwood ON L9Y1V5 705-444-8805
Web: www.grnland.com
Heath Consultants Inc 9030 Monroe Rd Houston TX 77061 713-844-1300 844-1309
TF: 800-432-8487 ■ *Web:* www.heathus.com
Hemet, California 445 E Florida Ave Hemet CA 92543 951-765-2330
Web: www.cityofhemet.org
HKA Enterprises Inc 337 Spartangreen Blvd Duncan SC 29334 864-661-5100
Web: www.hkaa.com
Hotel Cleaning Services Inc 9609 N 22nd Ave Phoenix AZ 85021 602-588-0864
Web: www.hotelcleaningservices.com
Hydrozonix LLC 8940 Gall Blvd Zephyrhills FL 33541 813-780-4380
Web: www.hydrozonix.com
IESI NY Corp 325 Casanova St Bronx NY 10474 718-542-5659
Web: progressivewaste.com
Inland Technologies Inc 14 Queen St PO Box 253 Truro NS B2N5C1 902-895-6346
Web: www.inlandgroup.ca
ISN Global Enterprises Inc Po Box 1391 Claremont CA 91711 909-670-0601
Web: isnglobal.com
J Frank Schmidt & Son Company Inc
9500 SE 327th Ave Boring OR 97009 503-663-4128
Web: www.jfschmidt.com
JM Sorge Inc 57 Fourth St Somerville NJ 08876 908-218-0066
Web: www.jmsorge.com
John Holmlund Nursery LLC 29285 SE Hwy 212 Boring OR 97009 503-663-6650
Web: www.jhnsy.com
Karbone Inc 130 W 42nd St 9th Fl New York NY 10036 646-291-2900 219-7168
TF: 800-728-2056 ■ *Web:* www.karbone.com
KB Environmental Sciences Inc
9500 Koger Blvd N Ste 211 Saint Petersburg FL 33702 727-578-5152
Web: www.kbenv.com
Kellermeyer Bergensons Services LLC
1575 Henthorne Dr Maumee OH 43537 419-867-4300
Web: www.kbs-clean.com
Kemron Environmental Services Inc
8521 Leesburg Pike Ste 175 Vienna VA 22182 703-893-4106 893-1741
TF: 888-429-3516 ■ *Web:* kemron.com
LG Chem Power Inc 1857 Technology Dr Troy MI 48083 248-307-1800
Web: www.lgcpi.com
Liesch Associates Inc 13400 15th Ave N Minneapolis MN 55441 763-489-3100
Web: www.liesch.com
Logees Greenhouses Ltd 141 N St Danielson CT 06239 860-774-8038
Web: www.logees.com
Los Alamos Technical Assoc Inc
999 Central Ave Ste 300 Los Alamos NM 87544 505-662-9080 662-1757
TF: 800-888-1745 ■ *Web:* www.lata.com
LP Amina Inc
13850 Ballantyne Corporate Pl Ste 125 Charlotte NC 28277 704-944-5425
Web: www.lpamina.com
Lynn Water & Sewer Commission 400 Parkland Ave Lynn MA 01905 781-596-2400
Web: www.lynnwatersewer.org
Maxymillian Technologies Inc 1801 E St Pittsfield MA 01201 413-499-3050 443-0511
Web: www.maxymillian.com

Phone Fax

Medallion Laboratories
9000 Plymouth Ave N Minneapolis MN 55427 763-764-4453 764-4010
TF: 800-245-5615 ■ *Web:* www.medallionlabs.com
Micah Group 389 Waller Ave Ste 210 Lexington KY 40504 859-260-7760
TF: 877-260-7760 ■ *Web:* www.micahgroup.com
Micromidas Inc
930 Riverside Pkwy Ste 10 West Sacramento CA 95605 916-231-9329
Web: www.micromidas.com
Mondre Energy Inc
1800 John F Kennedy Blvd Ste 1504 Philadelphia PA 19103 215-988-0577
Web: www.mondreenergy.com
Moran Environmental Recovery LLC
75-D York Ave Randolph MA 02368 781-815-1100
Web: www.moranenvironmental.com
MPS Group Inc 2920 Scotten St Detroit MI 48210 313-841-7588 489-0653*
**Fax Area Code:* 248 ■ *TF:* 800-741-8779 ■ *Web:* www.mpsgrp.com
Mwh Global Inc
380 Interlocken Crescent Ste 200 Broomfield CO 80021 303-533-1900 533-1901
TF: 866-257-5984 ■ *Web:* www.mwhglobal.com
MyClean Inc 247 W 35th Ninth Fl New York NY 10018 646-912-8473
Web: www.myclean.com
Nal Property Inspection
10416 Investment Cir Rancho Cordova CA 95670 916-361-0555
Web: www.nal1.com
Native Environmental LLC 3250 S 35th Ave Phoenix AZ 85009 602-254-0122
Web: www.nativeaz.com
Navarro Research & Engineering Inc
669 Emory Valley Rd Oak Ridge TN 37830 865-220-9650 220-9651
TF: 866-681-5265 ■ *Web:* www.navarro-inc.com
Neal Mast & Son Inc Greenhouses
1780 4 Mile Rd Nw Grand Rapids MI 49544 616-784-3323
Web: www.nealmastgreenhouses.com
Neo Corp 289 Silkwood Dr Canton NC 28716 800-822-1247
TF: 800-822-1247 ■ *Web:* www.neocorporation.com
Next Step Living Inc 21 Drydock Ave Second Fl Boston MA 02210 866-867-8729
TF: 866-867-8729 ■ *Web:* nextstepliving.com
Norman Scott Company Inc
126 29th St Dr SE Cedar Rapids IA 52403 319-363-8561 363-2106
Web: www.in-tolerance.com
Normandeau Assoc Inc 25 Nashua Rd Bedford NH 03110 603-472-5191 472-7052
Web: www.normandeau.com
North Wind Inc 1425 Higham St Idaho Falls ID 83402 208-528-8718
Web: www.northwind-inc.com
NTS Inc 526 Chestnut St Virginia MN 55792 218-741-4290
Web: www.netechnical.com
Nuka Research & Planning Group LLC
1451 N Boone Ln Seldovia AK 99663 907-234-7821
Web: www.nukaresearch.com
Oil Mop LLC 131 Keating Dr Belle Chasse LA 70037 504-394-6110
Web: www.oilmop.com
Olive Hill Greenhouses Inc
3508 Olive Hill Rd Fallbrook CA 92028 760-728-4596
Web: olivehill.net
Omaha Public Power District 444 S 16th St Mall Omaha NE 68102 402-636-2000
Web: www.oppd.com
Onsite Energy Corp 2701 Loker Ave W Ste 107 Carlsbad CA 92010 760-931-2400
Web: www.onsitenergy.com
Ontario Clean Water Agency 1 Yonge St Toronto ON M5E1E5 416-314-5600 314-8300
TF: 800-515-2759 ■ *Web:* www.ocwa.com
P E La Moreaux & Assoc Inc PO Box 2310 Tuscaloosa AL 35403 205-752-5543 752-4043
TF: 800-682-6338 ■ *Web:* www.pela.com
Parsons Infrastructure & Technology
100 W Walnut St Pasadena CA 91124 626-440-4000 830-0287*
**Fax Area Code:* 256 ■ *TF:* 800-300-0287 ■ *Web:* www.parsons.com
Partner Assessment Corp
2154 Torrance Blvd Ste 200 Torrance CA 90501 800-419-4923
TF: 800-419-4923 ■ *Web:* www.partneresi.com
Paul Davis Systems Canada Ltd
38 Crockford Blvd Toronto ON M1R3C2 416-299-8890
Web: www.pds.ca
PEER Consultants PC 888 17th St NW Ste 850 Washington DC 20006 202-478-2060
Web: www.peercpc.com
Pegasus Sustainability Solutions Inc
2693 Research Park Dr Ste 201 Fitchburg WI 53711 608-210-4202
Web: www.pegasus-sustainability.com
Perma-Fix Environmental Services Inc
8302 Dunwoody Pl Ste 250 Atlanta GA 30350 770-587-9898 587-9937
NASDAQ: PESI ■ *TF:* 800-365-6066 ■ *Web:* www.perma-fix.com
PermaTreat Inc 505 Lafayette Blvd Fredericksburg VA 22401 540-373-6655
Web: www.permatreat.com
Portage Inc 1075 S Utah Ave Ste 200 Idaho Falls ID 83402 208-528-6608 523-8860
Web: www.portageinc.com
Potesta & Associates Inc
7012 MacCorkle Ave SE Charleston WV 25304 304-342-1400
Web: potesta.com
Prestige Maintenance USA Ltd
1808 10th St Ste 300 Plano TX 75074 972-578-9801
Web: www.prestigeusa.net
Pro Park America Inc One Union Pl Hartford CT 06103 860-527-2378
Web: www.propark.com
PSC 5151 San Felipe Ste 1100 Houston TX 77056 800-726-1300 985-5318*
**Fax Area Code:* 713 ■ *TF:* 800-726-1300 ■ *Web:* www.pscnow.com
R E I Consultants Inc PO Box 286 Beaver WV 25813 304-255-2500 255-2572
TF: 800-999-0105 ■ *Web:* www.reiclabs.com
Ramboll Environ 4350 N Fairfax Dr Ste 300 Arlington VA 22203 703-516-2300 516-2345
Web: www.environcorp.com
Randys Environmental Services
4351 US Hwy 12 SE PO Box 169 Delano MN 55328 763-972-3335 972-6042
Web: www.randyssanitation.com
RECON Environmental Inc 1927 Fifth Ave San Diego CA 92101 619-308-9333
Web: www.recon-us.com
Red River Sanitors Inc 1522 Corporate Dr Shreveport LA 71107 318-222-6070
Web: www.sanitors.com

Company / Address	City	State	Zip	Phone	Fax
Regreen Inc 2928 N Main St *TF:* 855-573-4733 ■ *Web:* regreencorp.com	Los Angeles	CA	90031	855-573-4733	
Reliance Trading Corporation of America 55 Watermill Ln *Web:* beautysilk.com	Great Neck	NY	11021	516-466-6240	
RJN Group Inc 200 W Front St *TF:* 800-227-7838 ■ *Web:* www.rjn.com	Wheaton	IL	60187	630-682-4700	682-4754
S & ME Inc 3201 Spring Forest Rd *TF Cust Svc:* 800-849-2517 ■ *Web:* www.smeinc.com	Raleigh	NC	27616	919-872-2660	876-3958
Sabre Companies LLC, The 1891 New Scotland Rd *Web:* www.thesabrecompanies.com	Slingerlands	NY	12159	518-514-1572	
Sage Environmental Consulting LP 4611 Bee Caves Rd Ste 100 *Web:* www.sageenvironmental.com	Austin	TX	78746	512-327-0288	
Sanexen Environmental Services Inc 1471 Lionel-Boulet Blvd Ste 32 *Web:* www.sanexen.com	Varennes	QC	J3X1P7	450-652-9990	
Save the World Air Inc Ste 500 735 State St *Web:* www.stwa.com	Santa Barbara	CA	93101	805-845-3581	
SENES Consultants Ltd 121 Granton Dr Unit 12 *Web:* www.senes.ca	Richmond Hill	ON	L4B3N4	905-764-9380	
Shalewater Solutions Inc 37 Grande Meadows Dr Ste 201 *Web:* www.shalewater.com	Bridgeport	WV	26330	304-592-2794	
SHIFT Energy Inc 75 Prince William St *Web:* www.shiftenergy.com	Saint John	NB	E2L2B2	506-642-9422	
SNC-Lavalin Operations & Maintenance Inc 304 The E Mall Ste 900 *Web:* www.snclavalinom.com	Toronto	ON	M9B6E2	416-207-4700	
Source Intelligence LLC 1921 Palomar Oaks Way Ste 205 *TF:* 877-916-6337 ■ *Web:* www.sourceintelligence.com	Carlsbad	CA	92008	877-916-6337	
Southern Landscape Professionals Inc 8625 Mount Pleasant Church Rd *Web:* www.southernlandscapepros.com	Willow Spring	NC	27592	919-552-1156	
Southwest Hazard Control Inc 1953 W Grant Rd *Web:* swhaz.com	Tucson	AZ	85745	520-622-3607	
Spherix Inc 6430 Rockledge Dr Ste 503 *NASDAQ: SPEX* ■ *TF:* 855-816-0624 ■ *Web:* www.spherix.com	Bethesda	MD	20817	301-897-2540	897-2567
SpotHero Inc 200 S Wacker Dr *Web:* spothero.com	Chicago	IL	60606	312-566-7768	
Stella Group Ltd, The 1616 H St NW Ste 1020 *Web:* www.thestellagroupltd.com	Washington	DC	20006	202-347-2214	
Sullivan International Group Inc 2750 Womble Rd *TF:* 888-744-1432 ■ *Web:* www.onesullivan.com	San Diego	CA	92106	619-260-1432	260-1421
Sunora Energy Solutions 2342 E University Dr *Web:* sunoraenergy.com	Phoenix	AZ	85034	602-772-5220	
Sustainable Resources Group Inc 440 Creamery Way Ste 150 *Web:* www.sustainableresourcesgroup.com	Exton	PA	19341	610-840-9200	
SWCA Inc 3033 N Central Ave Ste 145 *TF:* 800-828-8517 ■ *Web:* www.swca.com	Phoenix	AZ	85012	602-274-3831	274-3958
Team Industrial Services Inc 25 Bodrington Ct *Web:* www.teamindustrial.com	Markham	ON	L6G1B6	905-940-9334	
TechLaw Inc 14500 Avion Pkwy Ste 300 *Web:* www.techlawinc.com	Chantilly	VA	20151	703-818-1000	
Tetra Tech EC Inc 1000 the American Rd **Fax Area Code:* 303 ■ *TF:* 800-580-3765 ■ *Web:* www.tteci.com	Morris Plains	NJ	07950	973-630-8000	980-3539*
Tetra Tech Geo 21335 Signal Hill Plaza Ste 100 *Web:* www.geotransinc.com	Sterling	VA	20164	703-444-7000	
Tetra Tech Inc 3475 E Foothill Blvd *NASDAQ: TTEK* ■ *Web:* www.tetratech.com	Pasadena	CA	91107	626-351-4664	351-5291
Tidewater Environmental Services Inc 38 Romney St Ste 202 *Web:* www.tidewaterenvironmental.com	Charleston	SC	29403	843-762-3750	
TRC Cos Inc 21 Griffin Rd N *TF:* 800-365-8254 ■ *Web:* www.trcsolutions.com	Windsor	CT	06095	860-298-9692	298-6399
U.S. Facilities Inc 30 N 41 St Ste 400 *TF:* 800-236-6241 ■ *Web:* www.usfacilitiesinc.com	Philadelphia	PA	19104	800-236-6241	
USA Synthetic Fuel Corp Ste 1600 312 Walnut St *Web:* www.usasfc.com	Cincinnati	OH	45202	513-762-7870	
Utility Service Company Inc 535 Courtney Hodges Blvd *TF:* 855-526-4413 ■ *Web:* www.utilityservice.com	Perry	GA	31069	478-987-0303	
Vertex Engineering Services Inc 400 Libbey Pkwy *TF:* 888-298-5162 ■ *Web:* vertexeng.com	Weymouth	MA	02189	781-952-6000	335-3543
Vivint Solar Inc 4931 North 300 West *TF:* 877-404-4129 ■ *Web:* www.vivintsolar.com	Provo	UT	84604	877-404-4129	
Western Technologies Inc 3737 E Broadway Rd *TF:* 800-580-3737 ■ *Web:* www.wt-us.com	Phoenix	AZ	85040	602-437-3737	470-1341
Whitman Strategy Group LLC, The PO Box 1621 *Web:* www.whitmanstrategygroup.com	New Brunswick	NJ	08903	646-330-4850	
Woolpert Inc 4454 Idea Ctr Blvd *Web:* www.woolpert.com	Dayton	OH	45430	937-461-5660	461-0743
WorleyParsons Corp 6330 W Loop S *Web:* www.worleyparsons.com	Bellaire	TX	77401	713-407-5000	350-1300
WSP Environment & Energy LLC 11190 Sunrise Vly Dr Ste 300 *Web:* www.wspgroup.com	Reston	VA	20191	703-709-6500	
XENCO Laboratories Inc 4143 Greenbriar Dr Ste I *Web:* www.xenco.com	Stafford	TX	77477	281-240-4200	
Yardmaster Inc 1447 N Ridge Rd *Web:* www.yardmaster.com	Painesville	OH	44077	440-357-8400	
YPSILANTI Michigan Community Utilities Authority 2777 State Rd *Web:* www.ycua.org	Ypsilanti	MI	48198	734-484-4600	
Zerowait Corp 707 Kirkwood Hwy *TF:* 888-811-0808 ■ *Web:* www.zerowait.com	Wilmington	DE	19805	302-996-9408	738-4302
Zia Engineering & Environmental Consultants LLC 755 S Telshor Blvd Ste F-201 *Web:* www.ziaeec.com	Las Cruces	NM	88011	575-532-1526	

196 CONSULTING SERVICES - HUMAN RESOURCES

SEE ALSO Professional Employer Organizations (PEOs) p. 2975

Company / Address	City	State	Zip	Phone	Fax
180 Business Solutions 1000 W Wilshire Blvd Ste 203 *Web:* 180business.com	Oklahoma City	OK	73116	405-840-4180	
A.S.G. Staffing Inc 231 W Grand Ave Ste 102 *Web:* www.asgstaffing.com	Bensenville	IL	60106	630-787-6150	
Aasgard Summit Management Services Inc 4017 13th Ave W *Web:* aasgardsummit.net	Seattle	WA	98119	206-284-0475	
Abacus Group LLC 14 Penn Plz *Web:* www.abacusnyc.com	New York	NY	10122	212-812-8444	
ACRT Inc 1333 Home Ave *TF:* 800-622-2562 ■ *Web:* www.acrtinc.com	Akron	OH	44310	330-945-7500	945-7200
Administrative Resource Options Inc 200 W Adams St Ste 2000 *Web:* www.aroptions.com	Chicago	IL	60606	312-634-0300	
Advantage Sci LLC 222 N Sepulveda Blvd Ste 1780 *Web:* www.advantagesci.com	El Segundo	CA	90245	310-536-9876	
Aegis Group 41451 W 11 Mile Rd *Web:* www.aegis-group.com	Novi	MI	48375	248-344-1450	
Afterburner Inc 55 Ivan Allen Junior Blvd Ste 525 *Web:* www.afterburnerseminars.com	Atlanta	GA	30308	404-835-3500	
Alliance For Employee Growth & Development Inc, The 80 Cottontail Ln Ste 320 *TF:* 800-323-3436 ■ *Web:* www.employeegrowth.com	Somerset	NJ	08873	800-323-3436	
Alpine Access Inc 1120 Lincoln St Ste 1400 *TF General:* 866-279-0585 ■ *Web:* www.alpineaccess.com	Denver	CO	80203	303-279-0585	279-0584
Applied Clinical Intelligence LLC 251 St Asaphs Rd 3 Bala Plz W Ste 402 *Web:* www.aciclinical.com	Bala Cynwyd	PA	19004	484-429-7200	
Ard Group Inc 116 John St Apt 602 *Web:* www.ardcareers.com	New York	NY	10038	212-571-1111	
Arthur J Gallagher & Co 2 Pierce Pl *NYSE: AJG* ■ *TF:* 888-285-5106 ■ *Web:* www.ajg.com	Itasca	IL	60143	630-773-3800	285-4000
Ashtead Technology Inc 19407 Pk Row Ste 170 *TF:* 800-242-3910 ■ *Web:* www.ashtead-technology.com	Houston	TX	77084	281-398-9533	
Assess It 12137 Travertine Ct *Web:* assessit.com	Poway	CA	92064	858-689-0017	
Atlantic Personnel Search Inc 9624 Pennsylvania Ave *Web:* www.atlanticpersonnel.com	Upper Marlboro	MD	20772	301-599-2108	
B. E. Smith Inc 9777 Ridge Dr *TF:* 800-467-9117 ■ *Web:* www.besmith.com	Lenexa	KS	66219	800-467-9117	
Bedford Consulting Group Inc 145 Adelaide St W Ste 400 *Web:* www.bedfordgroup.com	Toronto	ON	M5H4E5	416-963-9000	
Benz Communications LLC 209 Mississippi St *TF:* 888-550-5251 ■ *Web:* www.benzcommunications.com	San Francisco	CA	94107	888-550-5251	
Berkhemer Clayton Inc 241 S Figueroa St Ste 300 *Web:* www.berkhemerclayton.com	Los Angeles	CA	90012	213-621-2300	
Berks & Beyond Employment Services Inc 926 Penn Ave *Web:* www.berksandbeyond.com	Wyomissing	PA	19610	610-376-9675	
Bessire & Associates Inc 7621 Little Ave Ste 106 *Web:* bessire.com	Charlotte	NC	28226	704-341-1423	
Biko Ltd Co 3920 Ravens Crest Dr *Web:* www.bikotech.biz	Plainsboro	NJ	08536	617-910-0160	
Blackwell Consulting Services Inc 100 S Wacker Dr *Web:* www.bcsinc.com	Chicago	IL	60606	312-553-0730	553-0745
Buyer Advertising Inc 189 Wells Ave *Web:* www.buyerads.com	Newton	MA	02459	857-404-0860	
Cadmus Group Inc 57 Water St *Web:* www.cadmusgroup.com	Watertown	MA	02472	617-673-7000	673-7001
Caldwell Partners International Inc, The 165 Ave Rd *Web:* www.caldwellpartners.com	Toronto	ON	M5R3S4	416-920-7702	
Caliper Corporation Inc 506 Carnegie Ctr Ste 300 *Web:* www.calipercorp.com	Princeton	NJ	08543	609-524-1400	
Carlyle & Conlan 430 Davis Dr Ste 230 *Web:* www.ccesearch.com	Morrisville	NC	27560	919-474-0771	
Carnow Conibear & Assoc Ltd 600 W Van Buren Ste 500 *TF:* 800-860-4486 ■ *Web:* www.ccaltd.com	Chicago	IL	60607	312-782-4486	782-5145
CarterBaldwin Inc 200 Mansell Court E Ste 450 *Web:* www.carterbaldwin.com	Roswell	GA	30076	678-448-0000	
Cedarstone Partners Inc 209 E Liberty Dr *Web:* www.cedarstonepartners.com	Wheaton	IL	60187	630-580-5750	
CEO Inc 412 Louise Ave *Web:* ceohr.com	Charlotte	NC	28204	704-372-4701	

Company	City	State	Zip	Phone	Fax
Certus International Inc Nine Cedarwood Dr Ste 8 *Web:* www.certusintl.com	Bedford	NH	03110	603-627-1212	
Challenger Gray & Christmas Inc 150 S Wacker Dr Ste 2800 *Web:* www.challengergray.com	Chicago	IL	60606	312-332-5790	332-4843
Charon Planning Corp 2600 Kelly Rd Ste 300 *Web:* www.charonplanning.com	Warrington	PA	18976	267-482-8300	
Chernoff Diamond & Company LLC 725 RXR Plz E Tower *Web:* www.chernoffdiamond.com	Uniondale	NY	11556	516-683-6100	
Citystaff Inc 1701 K St Nw Ste 500 *Web:* www.citystaffdc.com	Washington	DC	20006	202-861-4200	
Clark Consulting 2100 Ross Ave *TF:* 800-999-3125 ■ *Web:* www.clarkconsulting.com	Dallas	TX	75201	214-871-8717	720-6050
Coleman Lew & Associates Inc 326 W Tenth St *Web:* www.colemanlew.com	Charlotte	NC	28202	704-377-0362	
Collaborative Consulting LLC 70 BlanchaRd Rd Ste 500 *TF:* 877-376-9900 ■ *Web:* collaborative.com	Burlington	MA	01803	781-565-2600	565-2700
Comcentric Inc 10463 Park Meadows Dr Ste 208 *Web:* www.comcentric.com	Lone Tree	CO	80124	303-805-4700	
Compensation Solutions Inc 500 Valley Rd *Web:* csihro.com	Wayne	NJ	07470	201-405-1115	
CONTAX Inc 893 Yonge St *Web:* www.contax.com	Toronto	ON	M4W2H2	416-927-1913	
Courtland Associates Inc 22500 Orchard Lk Rd *Web:* courtlandmi.com	Farmington	MI	48336	248-888-3535	
Crown Advisors Inc 100 McKnight Park Dr Ste 110 *Web:* www.crownsearch.com	Pittsburgh	PA	15237	412-348-1540	
CyberCoders Inc 6591 Irvine Ctr Dr Ste 200 *Web:* www.cybercoders.com	Irvine	CA	92618	949-885-5151	
Davies Park 10060 Jasper Ave Nw *Web:* www.daviespark.com	Edmonton	AB	T5J3R8	780-420-9900	
DB Consulting Group Inc 8403 Colesville Rd *Web:* www.dbconsultinggroup.com	Silver Spring	MD	20910	301-589-4020	
Demand Planning LLC 10g Roessler Rd Ste 508 *Web:* demandplanning.net	Woburn	MA	01801	781-995-0685	
Development Dimensions International 1225 Washington Pike *TF Mktg:* 800-933-4463 ■ *Web:* www.ddiworld.com	Bridgeville	PA	15017	412-257-0600	220-2942
dicentra Inc 27 Prince Arthur Ave *Web:* www.dicentra.com	Toronto	ON	M5R1B2	416-361-3400	
DuffyGroup Inc 4727 E Union Hills Dr Ste 200 *Web:* www.duffygroupinc.com	Phoenix	AZ	85050	602-861-5840	
E3 Services Conseils Inc 19 Le Royer St W Ste 304 *Web:* e3sc.com	Montreal	QC	H2Y1W4	514-281-1737	
Ecology and Environment Inc 368 Pleasant View Dr *Web:* www.ene.com	Lancaster	NY	14086	716-684-8060	684-0844
EdgeLink LLC 115 SW Ash St Ste 321 *Web:* www.edgelink.com	Portland	OR	97204	503-246-3989	
EGGers Consulting Company Inc 11272 Elm St Eggers Plz *Web:* www.eggersconsulting.com	Omaha	NE	68144	402-333-3480	
Emergo Group Inc 816 Congress Ave Ste 1400 *Web:* www.emergogroup.com	Austin	TX	78701	512-327-9997	
Employer Plan Services Inc 2180 N Loop W Ste 400 *Web:* www.epsibenefitsinc.com	Houston	TX	77018	713-351-3500	
Engineering Services Network Inc 2450 Crystal Dr Ste 1015 *Web:* www.esncc.com	Arlington	VA	22202	703-412-3640	
Er Marketing 512 Delaware St *Web:* www.ermarketing.net	Kansas City	MO	64105	816-471-1400	
Ergometrics 18720 33rd Ave W Ste 200 *Web:* www.ergometrics.org	Lynnwood	WA	98037	425-774-5700	
Essential Personnel Inc 3415 W State St Ste B *Web:* www.essentialpersonnelinc.com	Grand Island	NE	68803	308-381-4400	
Et Search Inc 1250 Prospect St Ste 101 *Web:* www.etsearch.com	La Jolla	CA	92037	858-459-3443	
Exceed Resources Inc 294 New Rd *Web:* www.exceedresourcesinc.com	Monmouth Junction	NJ	08852	732-329-2742	
Exceed Staffing LLC 305 21st St Ste 242 *Web:* www.exceedstaffing.com	Galveston	TX	77550	409-770-9000	
Excel Staffing Companies 1700 Louisiana Boulvard NE Ste 210 *Web:* www.excelstaff.com	Albuquerque	NM	87110	505-262-1871	
Executive Resources International LLC 63 Atlantic Ave *Web:* erisearch.net	Boston	MA	02110	617-742-8970	
Findley Davies One Seagate # 2050 *Web:* www.findleydavies.com	Toledo	OH	43604	419-255-1360	259-5685
Floyd Browne Group 3875 Embassy Parkway *TF General:* 800-325-7647 ■ *Web:* ctconsultants.com	Akron	OH	44333	330-375-0800	665-0620
FPMI Solutions Inc 1033 N Fairfax St Ste 200 *TF:* 888-644-3764 ■ *Web:* www.fpmi.com	Alexandria	VA	22314	888-644-3764	
Frederic W Cook & Co 90 Pk Ave 35th Fl *Web:* www.fwcook.com	New York	NY	10016	212-986-6330	986-3836
Gabriel Roeder Smith & Co 1 Towne Sq Ste 800 *TF:* 800-521-0498 ■ *Web:* www.gabrielroeder.com	Southfield	MI	48076	248-799-9000	799-9020
Gaming Laboratories International Inc 600 Airport Rd *Web:* www.gaminglabs.com	Lakewood	NJ	08701	732-942-3999	942-0043
Genesis Global Group Inc 28 Highland Rd *Web:* www.g3global.com	Westport	CT	06880	203-222-1795	
Geomet Technologies LLC 20251 Century Blvd *TF:* 877-407-8033 ■ *Web:* www.geomet.com	Germantown	MD	20874	301-428-9898	428-9482
Global Search Network Inc 118 S Fremont Ave *Web:* www.globalsearchnetwork.com	Tampa	FL	33606	813-832-8300	
Globe Consultants Inc 3112 Porter St Ste D *TF:* 800-208-0663 ■ *Web:* www.globeconsultants.com	Soquel	CA	95073	800-208-0663	
Goodwill Industries of Akron Ohio Inc, The 570 E Waterloo Rd *TF:* 800-989-8428 ■ *Web:* www.goodwillakron.org	Akron	OH	44319	330-724-6995	
GRA Inc 2317 Falling Creek Rd *Web:* www.gra3.com	Silver Spring	MD	20904	301-989-9659	
H r Office Inc, The 2437 Commercial Blvd Ste 5 *Web:* www.thehrofficeinc.com	State College	PA	16801	814-238-3750	
Hamilton Grey Executive Search 250 Kenilworth Ave *Web:* www.hamgrey.com	Glen Ellyn	IL	60137	630-858-4900	
Hanley Wood Market Intelligence 555 Anton Blvd Ste 950 **Fax Area Code:* 480 ■ *TF:* 800-938-8839 ■ *Web:* www.metrostudy.com	Costa Mesa	CA	92626	714-540-8500	452-0833*
Harrington Group, The 873 Inverness Cir *Web:* harringtongroup.net	Spartanburg	SC	29306	864-585-5850	
Hay Group Inc 1650 Arch St Ste 2300 *TF:* 800-716-4429 ■ *Web:* www.haygroup.com	Philadelphia	PA	19107	215-861-2000	861-2111
Hayes & Wiesel Independent Solutions Inc 78365 United States Hwy 111 Ste 316 *Web:* www.hwisolutions.com	La Quinta	CA	92253	760-347-5505	
Hire Dynamics LLC 1845 Satellite Blvd Ste 800 *Web:* www.hiredynamics.com	Duluth	GA	30097	678-482-0200	
Hobbs & Towne Inc 1288 Vly Forge Rd PMB 269 PO Box 987 *Web:* hobbstowne.com	Valley Forge	PA	19482	610-783-4600	
Hudson RPO 10 S Wacker Dr Ste 2600 *NASDAQ: HSON* ■ *Web:* us.hudson.com	Chicago	IL	60606	312-795-4275	795-4288
Huthwaite Inc 901 N Glebe Rd Ste 200 *TF:* 800-851-3842 ■ *Web:* www.huthwaite.com	Arlington	VA	22203	703-467-3800	467-3801
Impact Management Services 29792 Telegraph Rd Ste 150 *Web:* www.theimpactanswer.com	Southfield	MI	48034	248-262-5200	
Impact Science & Technology Inc 85 NW Blvd	Nashua	NH	03063	603-459-2255	
Independent Roofing Consultants 2901 Tullman St Ste 100 *Web:* www.irctech.com	Santa Ana	CA	92705	949-476-8626	476-9810
Indiggo Associates Inc 4600 E W Hwy Ste 875 *Web:* www.indiggoassociates.com	Bethesda	MD	20814	240-314-0533	
InfoMart Inc 1582 Terrell Mill Rd *Web:* www.infomart-usa.com	Marietta	GA	30067	770-984-2727	
Infusive Solutions Inc 411 Fifth Ave Rm 702 *Web:* www.infusivesolutions.com	New York	NY	10016	212-566-1400	
Insight 444 Scott Dr *TF:* 800-467-4448 ■ *Web:* www.insight.com	Bloomingdale	IL	60108	800-467-4448	
Insight Global Inc (IGI) 4170 Ashford Dunwoody Rd Ste 580 *TF:* 888-336-7463 ■ *Web:* www.insightglobal.net	Atlanta	GA	30319	404-257-7900	257-1004
Iowa Employment Solutions 430 E Grand Ave *Web:* www.iowaemploymentsolutions.com	Des Moines	IA	50309	515-281-9700	
ITAC Solutions LLC 700 Montgomery Hwy Ste 148 *Web:* www.itacsolutions.com	Birmingham	AL	35216	205-326-0004	
ITR Group Inc 2520 Lexington Ave S Ste 500 *TF:* 866-290-3423 ■ *Web:* www.itrgroupinc.com	Saint Paul	MN	55120	866-290-3423	
Johnson, Grossnickle & Associates LLC 29 S Park Blvd *Web:* www.jgacounsel.com	Greenwood	IN	46143	317-215-2400	
K2 Partnering 821 Sansome St *Web:* k2partnering.com	San Francisco	CA	94111	415-391-1035	
Kazak Composites Inc 10f Gill St *Web:* plasan-na.com	Woburn	MA	01801	781-932-5667	932-5671
Kelchner Inc 50 Advanced Dr *Web:* www.kelchner.com	Springboro	OH	45066	937-704-9890	
Ken Leiner Associates Inc 11510 Georgia Ave Ste 105 *Web:* www.kla-inc.com	Silver Spring	MD	20902	301-933-8800	
Kenexa Corp 650 Swedesford Rd Second Fl *NYSE: KNXA* ■ *Web:* www.kenexa.com	Wayne	PA	19087	610-971-9171	971-9181
Kimmel & Associates Inc 25 Page Ave *Web:* www.kimmel.com	Asheville	NC	28801	828-251-9900	
Kincannon & Reed LLC 40 Stoneridge Dr Ste 101 *Web:* www.krsearch.com	Waynesboro	VA	22980	540-941-3460	
Lanmark Staffing Co 1002 Green Ave *Web:* lanmarkstaffing.com	Orange	TX	77630	409-886-7676	
Lee Hecht Harrison LLC 50 Tice Blvd *TF:* 800-611-4544 ■ *Web:* www.lhh.com	Woodcliff Lake	NJ	07677	800-611-4544	
LifeCourse Associates Inc 9080 Eaton Park Rd *TF:* 866-537-4999 ■ *Web:* www.lifecourse.com	Great Falls	VA	22066	866-537-4999	
LJ Kushner & Associates LLC 36 W Main St Ste 302 *Web:* ljkushner.com	Freehold	NJ	07728	732-577-8100	
Longnecker & Associates 11011 Jones Rd Ste 200 *Web:* www.longnecker.com	Houston	TX	77070	281-378-1350	
LSA Assoc Inc 20 Executive Pk Ste 200 *Web:* www.lsa-assoc.com	Irvine	CA	92614	949-553-0666	553-8076
Magellan Search Group Inc 620 W Germantown Pike Ste 300 *Web:* www.magellangroup.com	Plymouth Meeting	PA	19462	610-941-0100	
Magis Group LLC, The 106 Brinker Rd *Web:* themagisgroup.com	Barrington	IL	60010	847-756-4200	

Phone | Fax

Mandrake Management Consultants
55 St Clair Ave W Ste 401 .... Toronto ON M4V2Y7 416-922-5400
Web: www.mandrake.ca

Martin Partners LLC
224 S Michigan Ave Ste 620 .... Chicago IL 60604 312-922-1800
Web: www.martinpartners.com

Mc Connell Consulting Group
5004 Warren St Nw.......... Washington DC 20016 202-223-0207
Web: mcconnellconsultinggroup.com

Mercer LLC 400 W Market St .... Louisville KY 40202 502-561-4500 561-4747
TF: 800-333-3070 ■ *Web:* www.mercer.com

Mice Groups Inc, The
1730 S Amphlett Blvd Ste 100 .... San Mateo CA 94402 650-655-7632
Web: www.micegroups.com

Michael C. Fina Corporate Sales
3301 Hunters Point Ave .... Long Island City NY 11101 800-999-3462
TF: 800-999-3462 ■ *Web:* www.mcfrecognition.com

Mid-Michigan Industries Inc (MMI)
2426 Pkwy Dr.......... Mount Pleasant MI 48858 989-773-6918 773-1317
Web: www.mmionline.com

Mission Search International Inc
2203 N Lois Ave Ste 1225 .... Tampa FL 33607 813-870-9500
Web: www.missionsearchusa.com

Modern Management Inc
253 Commerce Dr Ste 105.......... Grayslake IL 60030 847-945-7400 543-7710
TF: 800-323-1331 ■ *Web:* www.modernmanagement.com

Montgomery County Intermediate Unit 23
1605 W Main St Ste B .... Norristown PA 19403 610-539-8550
Web: www.mciu.org

Morgan Samuels Co
6420 Wilshire Blvd Ste 1100 .... Los Angeles CA 90048 310-205-2200
Web: morgansamuels.com

Msys Inc 140 Iowa Ln Ste 201.......... Cary NC 27511 919-380-9783
Web: www.msysinc.com

National Ctr for Retirement Benefits Inc
666 Dundee Rd Ste 1200 .... Northbrook IL 60062 800-666-1000 564-4944*
**Fax Area Code:* 847 ■ *TF:* 800-666-1000 ■ *Web:* www.ncrb.com

NPAworldwide 1680 Viewpond Dr SE.......... Grand Rapids MI 49508 616-455-6555
Web: www.npaworldwide.com

Nurse Staffing LLC 1700 Route 23 N Ste 100 .... Wayne NJ 07470 973-709-1009
Web: www.nursesapply.com

Options Group Inc 121 E 18th St.......... New York NY 10003 212-982-0900
Web: www.optionsgroup.com

Parker Remick Inc 1106 Harris Ave Ste 201.......... Bellingham WA 98225 360-527-2555
Web: www.parkerremick.com

Pasha Corporate Housing
10447 Roselle St Ste 1.......... San Diego CA 92121 858-622-1881
Web: www.pchousing.com

Pembrooke Occupational Health Inc
2307 N Parham Rd.......... Richmond VA 23229 804-346-1010
TF: 888-378-4832 ■ *Web:* www.pembrooke.com

PerformTech Inc 810 King St.......... Alexandria VA 22314 703-548-0320
Web: www.performtech.com

Personnel Decisions International Corp
33 S Sixth St Ste 4900.......... Minneapolis MN 55402 612-339-0927 337-8217
TF: 800-344-2415 ■ *Web:* www.personneldecisions.com

Personnel Policy Service Inc
159 Saint Matthews Ave Ste 5 .... Louisville KY 40207 502-899-5102
Web: www.ppspublishers.com

Point B Communications 750 N Orleans Ste 550.......... Chicago IL 60610 312-867-7750
Web: pointbcommunications.com

Premium Retail Services Inc
618 Spirit Dr.......... Chesterfield MO 63005 636-728-0592
Web: www.premiumretail.com

Prescott Legal Search Inc
3900 Essex Ln Ste 1110.......... Houston TX 77027 713-439-0911
Web: www.prescottlegal.com

Pridestaff Inc 7535 N Palm Ave Ste 101.......... Fresno CA 93711 559-432-7780
Web: www.pridestaff.com

Purcell International Group
500 S Kraemer Blvd Ste 102.......... Brea CA 92821 714-524-0640
Web: www.purcellintl.com

Qualigence Inc 35200 Schoolcraft Rd.......... Livonia MI 48150 734-432-6300
Web: www.qualigence.com

Quantus Software 32-62 Scurfield Blvd .... Winnipeg MB R3Y1M5 866-478-1308
TF: 866-478-1308 ■ *Web:* www.quantussoftware.com

Razorfish Platforms 7750 Paragon Rd.......... Dayton OH 45459 937-723-2300
Web: technologyplatforms.razorfish.com

Recruitech International Inc
120 Gibraltar Rd Ste 218 .... Horsham PA 19044 215-293-1300
Web: www.recruitech.com

Resources Unlimited Co 7931 Nw 54th Ave .... Johnston IA 50131 515-270-0694
Web: www.resourcesunlimited.com

Ricklin-Echikson Assoc 374 Millburn Ave.......... Millburn NJ 07041 973-376-2020 376-2072
TF: 800-544-2317 ■ *Web:* www.r-e-a.com

Right Management Consultants Inc
1818 Market St 33rd Fl.......... Philadelphia PA 19103 215-988-1588 988-0150
TF: 800-237-4448 ■ *Web:* www.right.com

Rjr Innovations 1400 St Laurent Blvd.......... Ottawa ON K1K4H4 613-233-1915
Web: www.rjrinnovations.com

Roger Grace Associates LLC 109 Greenfield Ct .... Naples FL 34110 239-596-8738
Web: www.rgrace.com

Roux Assoc Inc 209 Shafter St.......... Islandia NY 11749 631-232-2600 232-9898
TF: 800-322-7689 ■ *Web:* www.rouxinc.com

Runzheimer International Runzheimer Pk .... Rochester WI 53167 262-971-2200 971-2254
TF: 800-558-1702 ■ *Web:* www.runzheimer.com

Searchlogix Group, The
2950 Cherokee St Nw Ste 900 .... Kennesaw GA 30144 770-517-2660
Web: searchlogixgroup.com

Searchwide Inc 320 Myrtle St W.......... Stillwater MN 55082 651-275-1370
Web: searchwide.com

Seaton Companies, The 860 W Evergreen Ave .... Chicago IL 60642 312-915-0700
Web: www.staffmanagement.com

Segal Co 333 W 34th St.......... New York NY 10001 212-251-5000 365-3243*
**Fax Area Code:* 646 ■ *Web:* www.segalco.com

Selection Management Systems Inc
155 Tri County Pkwy Ste 150.......... Cincinnati OH 45246 513-522-8764
Web: www.selection.com

Senior Housing Management Inc
208 35th St Dr SE Ste 500.......... Cedar Rapids IA 52403 319-363-6094
Web: www.seniorhousingcompanies.com

Sharp Sky Partners
520 Baker Bldg 706 Second Ave South.......... Minneapolis MN 55402 612-339-3444
Web: www.sharpsky.com

Source Group Inc, The
3478 Buskirk Ave Ste 100.......... Pleasant Hill CA 94523 925-944-2856
Web: www.thesourcegroup.net

Stanley Hunt DuPree & Rhine Inc (SHDR)
7701 Airport Ctr Dr.......... Greensboro NC 27409 800-768-4873
TF: 888-999-4701 ■ *Web:* www.shdr.com

Superior Environmental Corp 1128 Franklin Ct .... Marne MI 49435 616-667-4000 667-3668
TF: 877-667-4142 ■ *Web:* www.superiorenvironmental.com

Synechron Inc 1 Corporate Pl S Suite 200 .... Piscataway NJ 08854 212-619-5200 619-5210
Web: www.synechron.com

TalentQuest Inc 1275 Peachtree St NE Ste 400.......... Atlanta GA 30309 404-266-9368
Web: www.talentquest.com

Tct Computing Group Inc Po Box 402 .... Bel Air MD 21014 410-893-5800
Web: www.tctcomputing.com

Tech Center Inc 265 S Main St .... Akron OH 44308 330-762-6212
Web: www.techcenterinc.com

TerraFirma 600 Grant St Ste 700 .... Denver CO 80203 303-861-0388 923-1191*
**Fax Area Code:* 602

Think Resources Inc 225 Scientific Dr.......... Norcross GA 30092 770-390-9888
Web: www.thinkresources.com

Thornmark Asset Management Inc
119 Spadina Ave Ste 701 .... Toronto ON M5V2L1 416-204-6200
Web: www.thornmark.com

Total Resource Management Inc
510 King St Ste 300.......... Alexandria VA 22314 703-548-4285 548-3641
TF: 877-548-5100 ■ *Web:* www.trmnet.com

TRACOM Group, The 6675 S Kenton St Ste 118.......... Centennial CO 80111 303-470-4900
Web: www.tracomcorp.com

Transhire
3601 W Commercial Blvd Ste 12 .... Fort Lauderdale FL 33309 954-484-5401
Web: www.transhiregroup.com

Trendtec Inc 2381 Zanker Rd.......... San Jose CA 95131 408-435-9500
Web: www.trendtec.com

United Way of Central Md Inc, The
100 S Charles St PO Box 1576.......... Baltimore MD 21203 410-547-8000 547-8289
Web: www.uwcm.org

Uptime Group Inc, The 200 Violet St Ste 150.......... Golden CO 80401 303-757-4611
Web: www.theuptimegroup.com

Valerie Frederickson & Co
800 Menlo Ave Ste 220 .... Menlo Park CA 94025 650-614-0220
Web: www.vfandco.com

Vantige Inc 100 W Rd Ste 300.......... Towson MD 21204 410-337-4774
Web: www.vantigeinc.com

Whitaker Medical Ltd
1200 Enclave Pkwy Ste 200.......... Houston TX 77077 281-870-1000
Web: www.whitakermedical.com

workforcetactix Inc 954 Ridgebrook Rd Ste 200 .... Sparks MD 21152 443-212-1540
Web: www.workforcetactix.com

ZE PowerGroup Inc 130 - 5920 No Two Rd .... Richmond BC V7C4R9 604-244-1469
Web: www.ze.com

197 CONSULTING SERVICES - MANAGEMENT

SEE ALSO Management Services p. 2704; Association Management Companies p. 1754

Phone | Fax

1secureaudit LLC 1600 Tysons Blvd Fl 8.......... Mc Lean VA 22102 703-245-3020
TF: 800-321-0706 ■ *Web:* www.1secureaudit.com

3 Kings Environmental Inc
1311 SE Grace Ave.......... Battle Ground WA 98604 360-666-5464
Web: www.3kingsenvironmental.com

360 Press Solutions 2009 Windy Ter.......... Cedar Park TX 78613 512-381-2360
Web: www.360presssolutions.com

360 Solutions LLC 2114 Austin Ave.......... Waco TX 76701 254-755-7000
TF: 877-755-7888 ■ *Web:* www.360solutions.com

3plus Logistics Co
20250 S Alameda St.......... Rancho Dominguez CA 90221 310-667-5160
Web: e3pl.com

89 Degrees Inc 25 Mall Rd.......... Burlington MA 01803 781-221-5400
Web: www.89degrees.com

A C e International Company Inc
85 Independence Dr.......... Taunton MA 02780 508-884-9600
TF: 800-223-4685 ■ *Web:* www.aceintl.com

a i Solutions Inc 10001 Derekwood Ln Ste 215.......... Lanham MD 20706 301-306-1756 306-1754
Web: www.ai-solutions.com

A y r Consulting Group 3708 Rodale Way Ste 200.......... Dallas TX 75287 972-820-8400
Web: ayrconsulting.com

A1 Roof Trusses Ltd Co
4451 Saint Lucie Blvd.......... Fort Pierce FL 34946 772-409-1010
Web: www.a1truss.com

Abacus Automation Inc 264 Shields Dr.......... Bennington VT 05201 802-442-3662
Web: abacusautomation.com

Abacus Planning Group Inc
2500 Devine St Ste 101 .... Columbia SC 29205 803-933-0054 498-0798*
**Fax Area Code:* 913 ■ *Web:* www.abacusplanninggroup.com

ABACUS Project Management Inc
3030 N Central Ave Ste 1207 .... Phoenix AZ 85012 602-265-6870
Web: www.abacuspm.com

Abba Technologies Inc
1501 San Pedro Dr NE.......... Albuquerque NM 87110 505-889-3337 889-3338
TF: 888-222-2832 ■ *Web:* www.abbatech.com

Phone Fax

ABeam Consulting (USA) Ltd
8445 Freeport Pkwy Fourth Fl. Irving TX 75063 972-929-3130
Web: www.abeam.com

Abrams Consulting Group Inc
3020 Wchester Ave Ste 307 Purchase NY 10577 914-696-5100
Web: www.abramsconsulting.com

ABS Group of Cos Inc
Abs Plz 16855 Northchase Dr. Houston TX 77060 281-673-2800
Web: www.abs-group.com

AC Group Inc 118 Lyndsey Dr Montgomery TX 77316 281-413-5572
Web: www.acgroup.org

AC Lordi Corp 101 Lindenwood Dr First Fl Malvern PA 19355 610-738-0100
Web: www.aclordi.com

AC Square Inc 371 Foster City Blvd Foster City CA 94404 650-293-2730
Web: www.acsquare.com

Academic Keys LLC 1066 Storrs Rd Ste D Storrs CT 06268 860-429-0218
Web: www.academickeys.com

Academy Leadership LLC
10120 Vly Forge Cir King Of Prussia PA 19406 610-783-0630
Web: www.academyleadership.com

Acadia Enviromental Technology
48 Free St Ste L05 Portland ME 04101 207-780-1230
Web: www.acadiaenvironmental.com

Acai Solutions LLC
1285 Ave Of Americas 35th Fl New York NY 10019 212-554-4460
Web: www.acaisolutions.com

ACC Environmental Consultants Inc
7977 Capwell Dr Ste 100 Oakland CA 94621 510-638-8400
Web: www.accenv.com

Accelero Health Partners LLC
380 Southpointe Blvd Plz II Ste 400 Canonsburg PA 15317 724-743-3760
Web: www.accelerohealth.com

Accenture Inc 5450 Explorer Dr Ste 400 Mississauga ON L4W5M1 416-641-5000 641-5099
Web: www.accenture.com

Access Highway Inc 96 Carleton Ave Central Islip NY 11722 631-232-9119

Acclivus Corp 14500 Midway Rd Dallas TX 75244 972-385-1277 386-6720
Web: www.acclivus.com

Accucom Consulting Inc 250 Post Rd E Westport CT 06880 203-221-1212 221-1946
Web: accucomci.com

Accumyn LLC 1415 Congress St Ste 200 Houston TX 77002 713-800-2550
Web: www.accumyn.com

Accuvoice Inc 343 Wainwright Dr Northbrook IL 60062 847-559-7272

Achievement Incentives & Meetings
64 River Rd East Hanover NJ 07936 973-386-9500
Web: www.aimtrav.com

ACM Capital Partners LLC
200 S Biscayne Blvd Seventh Fl Miami FL 33131 305-960-8851
Web: www.acmcapitalpartners.com

Acorn Consulting 803 Curtis St Menlo Park CA 94025 650-329-8923
Web: www.acorn-od.com

Acquest International 909 Third Ave 27th Fl New York NY 10022 212-719-1500
Web: www.acquestinternational.com

ACS Assoc Inc 2145 Edge Hill Rd Huntingdon Valley PA 19006 215-784-0661

Action Learning Systems Inc
135 S Rosemead Blvd Pasadena CA 91107 626-744-5344
Web: www.actionlearningsystems.com

Active Environmental Technologies Inc
203 Pine St Mount Holly NJ 08060 609-702-1500
Web: www.active-env.com

Acumentra Health Inc
2020 SW Fourth Ave Ste 520 Portland OR 97201 503-279-0100
Web: www.acumentra.org

AcuTech Group Inc 1919 Gallows Rd Ste 900 Vienna VA 22182 703-676-3180
Web: www.acutech-consulting.com

Adaptek Systems Inc 14224 Plank St Fort Wayne IN 46818 260-637-8660
Web: www.adapteksystems.com

adaQuest Inc 14450 NE 29th Pl Ste Ste 220 Bellevue WA 98007 425-284-7800
Web: www.adaquest.com

Addx Corp 4900 Seminary Rd Ste 570 Alexandria VA 22311 703-933-7637 933-7638
Web: www.addxcorp.com

Adiligy LLC 845 Third Ave Sixth Fl New York NY 10022 646-290-5288
Web: www.adiligy.com

Adizes 6404 Via Real Carpinteria CA 93013 805-565-2901
Web: www.adizes.com

Administrative Controls Management Inc
525 Avis Dr Ste 2 Ann Arbor MI 48108 734-995-9640
Web: www.acmpm.com

Advanced Analytical Consulting Group Inc
211 Congress St Boston MA 02110 617-338-2224
Web: www.aacg.com

Advanced Electronics
2601 Manhattan Beach Blvd Redondo Beach CA 90278 310-725-0410
Web: www.advancedelectronics.com

Advanced Energy Corp
909 Capability Dr Ste 2100 Raleigh NC 27606 919-857-9000
Web: www.advancedenergy.org

Advanced Recovery Service
5434 King Ave Ste 200 Pennsauken NJ 08109 856-488-8860
Web: www.advancedrecoveryservice.com

Advancement LLC 32200 Solon Rd Solon OH 44139 440-248-8550
TF: 866-364-3370 ■ *Web:* www.advancementllc.com

Advantage Consulting Inc
7611 Little River Tpke Ste 204 W Annandale VA 22003 703-642-5153
Web: www.acibiz.com

Advantage Performance Group Inc
700 Larkspur Landing Cir Larkspur CA 94939 415-925-6832 925-9512
TF: 800-494-6646 ■ *Web:* www.advantageperformance.com

Adventive Mktg Inc
417 S Arlington Heights Rd Arlington Heights IL 60005 847-590-1110
Web: www.adventivemarketing.com

Advisory Board Co, The 2445 M St NW Washington DC 20037 202-266-5600 672-5700
NASDAQ: ABCO ■ *TF:* 800-784-8669 ■ *Web:* www.advisory.com

Phone Fax

Advus Corp 16 E 34th St 15th Fl New York NY 10016 212-400-7922
Web: www.advus.com

AFC Industries Inc 13-16 133rd Pl College Point NY 11356 718-747-0237
TF: 800-663-3412 ■ *Web:* www.afcindustries.com

Affect Strategies Inc 60 W 38th St Fourth Fl New York NY 10018 212-398-9680
Web: www.affectstrategies.com

Affiliated Power Purchasers International LLC
224 Phillip Morris Dr Ste 402 Salisbury MD 21804 800-520-6685
TF: 800-520-6685 ■ *Web:* www.appienergy.com

Affinitas Corp 1015 N 98th St Ste 100 Omaha NE 68114 402-505-5000
TF: 800-369-6495 ■ *Web:* www.affinitas.net

Affinity Consultants Inc 222 N Canal St Canal Fulton OH 44614 330-854-9066
Web: www.affinityconsultants.com

Affinity Management Group LLC
10205 Westheimer Rd Ste 460 Houston TX 77042 713-452-3100
Web: www.affinity-mgt.com

Affinity Wealth Management Inc
1702 Lovering Ave Wilmington DE 19806 302-652-6767
Web: www.affinitywealth.com

AFIMAC Inc 8160 Parkhill Dr Milton ON L9T5V7 905-693-0746
Web: afimacglobal.com

AFrame Digital Inc
1889 Preston White Dr Ste 101 Reston VA 20191 571-308-0147
Web: www.aframedigital.com

AFYA Inc 8101 Sandy Spring Rd Ste 301 Laurel MD 20707 301-957-3040
Web: www.afyainc.com

Agcall Inc 251 Midpark Blvd SE Calgary AB T2X1S3 403-256-1229 254-2371
Web: www.agcall.com

Ageatia Technology Consultancy Services Inc
850 E Higgins Rd Ste 125 Schaumburg IL 60173 847-517-8415
Web: www.ageatia.com

Airbus North America Holdings
198 Van Buren St Ste 300 Herndon VA 20170 703-834-3400 834-3593
TF: 888-340-2375 ■ *Web:* www.airbus.com

AirStar International Inc
5273 N Commerce Ave Unit 11 Moorpark CA 93021 805-553-9996
Web: www.airstarintl.com

AK Capital LLC 445 Park Ave Fl 9 New York NY 10022 212-333-8634
Web: www.akcapital.com

Alan Davis & Assoc Inc 538 Main Rd Hudson QC J0P1J0 450-458-3535
Web: www.alandavis.com

Alaska Permanent Capital Management Co
900 W Fifth Ave Ste 601 Anchorage AK 99501 907-272-7575
Web: www.apcm.net

Alba Spectrum Technologies 1715 Wabansia Chicago IL 60622 773-384-9264
Web: www.albaspectrum.com

Albert Moving & Storage Inc
4401 Barnett Rd Wichita Falls TX 76310 940-696-7000
Web: www.albertmovingandstorage.com

Albright Stonebridge Group
555 Thirteenth St NW Ste 300 W Washington DC 20004 202-637-8600
Web: www.albrightstonebridge.com

ALCO Sales & Service Co
6851 High Grove Blvd Burr Ridge IL 60527 630-655-1900
Web: www.alcosales.com

Alego Health 24651 Center Ridge Rd., Ste 400 Westlake OH 44145 440-918-4570
Web: www.alegohealth.com

Aleut Management Services LLC
5540 Tech Ctr Dr Ste 100 Colorado Springs CO 80919 719-531-9090
Web: www.aleutmgt.com

Alexander Street Press LLC 3212 Duke St Alexandria VA 22314 703-212-8520
Web: alexanderstreet.com

Alia Conseil Inc
Place Iberville III 2960 Laurier Blvd Ste 214 Quebec QC G1V4S1 418-652-1737
Web: www.aliaconseil.com

Alimansky Capital Group Inc 12 E 44th St Ph New York NY 10017 212-832-7300
Web: www.alimansky.com

Aliron International Inc
5231 Massachusetts Ave Bethesda MD 20816 301-229-1900
Web: www.aliron.com

All4 Inc 2393 Kimberton Rd Kimberton PA 19442 610-933-5246
Web: www.all4inc.com

Allant Group Inc, The
2056 Westings Ave Ste 500 Naperville IL 60563 800-367-7311 355-3090*
**Fax Area Code:* 630 ■ *TF:* 800-367-7311 ■ *Web:* www.allantgroup.com

Alliance Geotechnical Group Inc
3228 Halifax St Dallas TX 75247 972-444-8889
Web: www.aggengr.com

Alliance Solutions Group Inc
11838 Rock Landing Dr Ste 125 Newport News VA 23606 757-223-7233
Web: www.asg-inc.org

Alliant Co-op Data Solutions LLC
301 Fields Ln N Ctr Brewster NY 10509 845-276-2600
Web: www.alliantdata.com

Allied Business Consulting
295 Durham Ave Ste 212 South Plainfield NJ 07080 908-222-7015 834-0930
Web: www.abcincus.com

ALLogistx International, Inc.
2130 Huntington Dr Ste 205 South Pasadena CA 91030 323-254-9550
Web: allogistx.com

Allsup Inc 300 Allsup Pl Belleville IL 62223 800-854-1418 236-5778*
**Fax Area Code:* 618 ■ *TF:* 800-854-1418 ■ *Web:* www.allsup.com

AllTek Staffing & Resource Group Inc
600 Davidson Rd Pittsburgh PA 15239 412-573-0077
Web: www.alltekstaffing.com

Almaco 99 M Ave Nevada IA 50201 515-382-3506
Web: www.almaco.com

Alpha & Omega Financial Management Consultants Inc
8580 La Mesa Blvd Ste 100 La Mesa CA 91942 800-755-5060
TF: 800-755-5060 ■ *Web:* www.alpha-omega-inc.com

Alpha Corp 21351 Ridgetop Cir Ste 200 Dulles VA 20166 703-450-0800 450-0043
Web: www.alphacorporation.com

Phone | Fax

Alpha Investment Consulting Group LLC
111 E Kilbourn Ave Ste 1600 .... Milwaukee WI 53202 414-319-4100
Web: www.alpha-investment.com

Alphamicron Inc 1950 SR- 59 Ste 100 .... Kent OH 44240 330-676-0648 676-0649
Web: www.alphamicron.com

Alphaport Inc 18013 Cleveland Pkwy Ste 170 .... Cleveland OH 44135 216-619-2400
Web: www.alpha-port.com

Alpine Innovations 275 North 950 East .... Lehi UT 84043 801-766-4994
TF: 866-489-6788 ■ *Web:* www.alpineproducts.com

Alster Communications 3062 N Cir .... Anchorage AK 99507 907-344-9674
Web: alster.com

Altair Customer Intelligence
341 Cool Springs Blvd Ste 450 .... Franklin TN 37067 615-468-6938
TF: 800-241-6631 ■ *Web:* www.altairci.com

Altair Engineering Inc 1820 E Big Beaver Rd .... Troy MI 48083 248-614-2400 614-2411
TF: 888-222-7822 ■ *Web:* www.altair.com

Altamont Environmental Inc 231 Haywood St .... Asheville NC 28801 828-281-3350
Web: www.altamontenvironmental.com

AltaTerra Ltd 530 Lytton Ave Second Fl .... Palo Alto CA 94301 650-362-0440
Web: www.altaterra.net

AltEnergy LLC 137 Rowayton Ave .... Rowayton CT 06853 203-299-1400
Web: www.altenergyllc.com

Altfest Personal Wealth Management
425 Park Ave 24th Fl .... New York NY 10022 212-406-0850
Web: www.altfest.com

Altman Weil Inc PO Box 625 .... Newtown Square PA 19073 610-359-9900 359-0467
TF: 866-886-3600 ■ *Web:* www.altmanweil.com

Altoros Systems 830 Stewart Dr Ste 119 .... Sunnyvale CA 94085 650-395-7002
TF: 855-258-6767 ■ *Web:* www.altoros.com

Altus Alliance LLC
719 Second Ave The Millennium Tower 14th Fl .... Seattle WA 98104 206-438-1890
Web: www.altusalliance.com

Alvarez & Marsal Holdings LLC
600 Lexington Ave Sixth Fl .... New York NY 10022 212-759-4433 759-5532
Web: www.alvarezandmarsal.com

Ambit Consulting 310-1847 Broadway W .... Vancouver BC V6J1Y6 604-662-3130
Web: ambit-consulting.com

Amerex Energy Services LLC
One Sugar Creek Ctr Blvd Ste 700 .... Sugar Land TX 77478 281-340-5247
Web: www.amerexenergy.com

American Cybersystems Inc (ACS)
2400 Meadowbrook Pkwy .... Duluth GA 30096 770-493-5588 270-6248*
**Fax Area Code:* 877 ■ *Web:* www.acsicorp.com

American Executive Management Inc
30 Federal St .... Salem MA 01970 978-744-5923
Web: www.americanexecutive.us

American Geothermal Systems Inc
8650 Spicewood Springs Rd .... Austin TX 78759 512-219-1465
Web: www.amgeosystems.com

American Journal of Pathology
9650 Rockville Pk .... Bethesda MD 20814 301-634-7130
Web: www.asip.org

American Mktg Services & Consultant
939 Tower Rd .... Mundelein IL 60060 847-566-4545
Web: amscinc.com

American National Logistics Inc
202 N San Jacinto St .... Rockwall TX 75087 972-772-3132
Web: www.anlinc.com

American Partners Inc 1005 Main St Ste 2205 .... Pawtucket RI 02860 401-312-4262
Web: www.americanpartnersinc.com

Americorp Financial LLC 877 S Adams Rd .... Birmingham MI 48009 248-723-4500
Web: www.eamericorp.com

Amherst Capital Partners LLC
Brown St Centre 255 E Brown St Ste 120 .... Birmingham MI 48009 248-642-5660

Ami Adini & Assoc Inc 4609 Russell Ave .... Los Angeles CA 90027 323-913-4073
TF: 888-400-4260 ■ *Web:* www.amiadini.com

Amidyne Group Inc 165 Pony Dr. .... Newmarket ON L3Y7B5 905-954-0841
Web: amidynegroup.com

Amino Transport Inc 223 NE Loop 820 Ste 101 .... Hurst TX 76053 800-304-3360
TF: 800-304-3360 ■ *Web:* www.aminotransport.com

Amirit Technologies Inc
271 Us Hwy 46 Ste C103 .... Fairfield NJ 07004 973-575-7557 828-0205
Web: amirit.com

Ammunition Group
1500 Sansome St Ste 110 .... San Francisco CA 94111 415-632-1170
Web: www.ammunitiongroup.com

Amotec Inc 1220 W 6th St .... Cleveland OH 44113 440-250-4600
Web: www.amotecinc.com

AMVC Management Services LLC 508 Market St. ...... Audubon IA 50025 712-563-2080
Web: www.amvcms.com

AnaJet LLC 3050 Redhill Ave .... Costa Mesa CA 92626 714-662-3200
Web: www.anajet.com

Analysis Group Inc 111 Huntington Ave 10th Fl .... Boston MA 02199 617-425-8000 425-8001
Web: www.analysisgroup.com

Anchor Benefit Consulting Inc
2400 Maitland Ctr Pkwy Ste 111 .... Maitland FL 32751 407-667-8766
Web: anchorbenefit.com

Anchor QEA LLC 720 Olive Way Ste 1900 .... Seattle WA 98101 206-287-9130 287-9131
TF: 800-887-8681 ■ *Web:* www.anchorqea.com

Anderson LeNeave & Co
6000 Fairview Rd Ste 625 .... Charlotte NC 28210 704-552-9212
Web: www.andersonleneave.com

Andrews Logistics Inc
2445 E Southlake Blvd Ste 300 .... Southlake TX 76092 817-527-2770
Web: www.andrewslogistics.com

Ann Mcgee-cooper & Assoc Inc 4236 Hockaday Dr. ...... Dallas TX 75229 214-357-8550
Web: www.amca.com

Another 9 LLC 777 Old Saw Mill River Rd .... Tarrytown NY 10591 914-909-1800
Web: www.another9.com

Answerport Inc 241 N Broadway Ste 401 .... Milwaukee WI 53202 414-289-9100
Web: www.answerport.com

Antaean Solutions LLC
11700 Preston Rd Ste 600-213 .... Dallas TX 75230 214-987-3439
Web: www.antaeans.com

Antarctica Asset Management Ltd
57 E 11th St .... New York NY 10003 212-925-1419
Web: www.antarcticaam.com

Anthem Mktg Corp 549 W Randolph Ste 700 .... Chicago IL 60661 312-441-0382
Web: www.anthemedge.com

APN Consulting Inc 475 Wall St .... Princeton NJ 08540 609-924-3400
Web: www.apnconsultinginc.com

Apple Spice Junction West Valley
2235 South 1300 West Ste A .... Salt Lake City UT 84119 801-359-8821
Web: www.applespice.com

Apples of Gold Center for Learning
604 Liberty St Ste 123 .... Pella IA 50219 641-620-1160

Applied Educational Systems Inc 208 Bucky Dr .... Lititz PA 17543 717-627-7710
Web: www.aeseducation.com

Applied Energy Group Inc
1377 Motor Pkwy Ste 401 .... Islandia NY 11749 631-434-1414
Web: www.appliedenergygroup.com

Aqua Finance Inc One Corporate Dr Ste 300 .... Wausau WI 54401 715-848-5425
Web: www.aquafinance.com

Aquantia Corp 700 Tasman Dr .... Milpitas CA 95035 408-228-8300
Web: www.aquantia.com

Archimede Gruden USA Inc 51 Newark St Ste 302 ..... Hoboken NJ 07030 201-798-0222

Ardent Sound Inc 33 S Sycamore St .... Mesa AZ 85202 480-649-1806
Web: www.ardentsound.com

Ardmore Banking Advisors Inc
44 E Lancaster Ave Second Fl
44 E Lancaster Ave Second Fl .... Ardmore PA 19003 610-649-4643
Web: www.ardmoreadvisors.com

ARG Recovery LLC 3308 Preston Rd Ste 350-215 .... Plano TX 75093 972-335-2090
Web: www.argrecovery.com

Argent Wealth Management
13 Riverside Rd Riverside Office Pk .... Weston MA 02493 781-290-4900
Web: www.argentwm.com

Argus Management Corp
15 Keith Hill Rd Ste 100 .... Grafton MA 01519 508-839-1828
Web: www.arguscorp.net

Ariel Group Inc, The
1050 Waltham St Ste 600 .... Lexington MA 02421 781-761-9000
Web: www.arielgroup.com

Arlington Capital Management Inc
21 S Evergreen Ave Ste 210 .... Arlington Heights IL 60005 847-670-4030
Web: www.arlington-capital.com

Armortex Inc 5926 Corridor Pkwy .... Schertz TX 78154 210-661-8306 661-8308
Web: www.armortex.com

Arthur D Little Inc 1 Federal St Ste 2810 .... Boston MA 02110 617-532-9550 261-6630
Web: www.adlittle.com

Arthur Langhus Layne LLC 1718 S Cheyenne .... Tulsa OK 74119 918-382-7581
Web: www.all-llc.com

Arthur W Wood Company Inc
50 Congress St Ste 300 .... Boston MA 02109 617-542-0500
Web: www.arthurwood.com

Artifex Technology Consulting Inc
614 George Washington Hwy .... Lincoln RI 02865 401-723-6644
TF: 888-278-4339 ■ *Web:* www.artifextech.com

Ascend Advisory Group LLC 6760 Perimeter Dr .... Dublin OH 43016 614-784-6000
Web: www.ascendadvisory.com

Ascent Capital Management LLC
975 S W Colorado Ste 200 .... Bend OR 97702 541-382-4847
Web: www.ascentcap.com

Asian American Business Development Center Inc
80 Wall St Ste 418 .... New York NY 10005 212-966-0100
Web: www.aabdc.com

Asian Inc Social Svc Crdntr
1167 Mission St Fl 4 .... San Francisco CA 94103 415-928-5910
Web: www.asianinc.org

Aspen Environmental Group
5020 Chesebro Rd Ste 200 .... Agoura Hills CA 91301 818-597-3407
Web: www.aspeneg.com

Aspire Financial Search Inc
220 Commerce Dr Ste 200 .... Ft Washington PA 19034 215-654-8050
Web: www.aspire-1.com

ASR Analytics LLC 1389 Canterbury Way .... Potomac MD 20854 301-738-9502
Web: www.asranalytics.com

ASR Constructors Inc 5230 Wilson St .... Riverside CA 92509 951-779-6580
Web: asrconstructors.com

Asset Based Lending Consultant
1641 NW 71st Ter .... Hollywood FL 33024 954-962-0099
TF: 800-861-5711 ■ *Web:* www.ablc.net

Associated Industries Management Services Inc
1206 N Lincoln Ste 200 .... Spokane WA 99201 509-326-6885
Web: www.aiin.com

Astek Corp 5055 Corporate Plz Dr .... Colorado Springs CO 80919 719-260-1625
Web: www.simtek.com

ASU Group, The 2120 University Park Dr .... Okemos MI 48805 517-349-2212
Web: www.asugroup.com

AT Kearney Inc 227 W Adams St Ste 2500 .... Chicago IL 60606 312-648-0111 223-6200
Web: www.atkearney.com

Atlanta International Consulting Group (aicg)
1401 Peachtree St Ne Ste 500 .... Atlanta GA 30309 404-872-4884
Web: www.aicginc.com

Atlas Brown Investment Advisors Inc
333 E Main St - 400 .... Louisville KY 40202 502-271-2900
Web: www.atlasbrown.com

Atlas Scientific Technologies Inc
2430 University Blvd W .... Jacksonville FL 32217 904-731-0241
Web: www.atlasscitech.com

Audax Labs 101 Huntington Ave .... Boston MA 02199 617-859-1500
Web: www.audaxgroup.com

Audio Advisor 3427 Kraft Ave SE .... Grand Rapids MI 49512 616-254-8870 254-8875
TF: 800-942-0220 ■ *Web:* www.audioadvisor.com

Phone Fax

Audio Visual Dynamics Eight Budd St . . . Morristown NJ 07960 973-993-8500
Web: www.audiovisualdynamics.com
Audit Integrity Inc
11111 Santa Monica Blvd Ste 220 . . . Los Angeles CA 90025 310-444-8820
August Mack Environmental Inc
1302 N Meridian St Ste 300 . . . Indianapolis IN 46202 317-916-8000
Web: www.augustmack.com
Auroros Inc 5809 Vly Mist Ct . . . Raleigh NC 27613 919-841-0553
Web: www.aurorosinc.com
Aurotech Inc 6909 Timber Creek Ct . . . Clarksville MD 21029 301-854-1326
Web: www.aurotechcorp.com
Austin Ribbon & Computer Supplies Inc (ARC)
9211 Waterford Centre Blvd Ste 202 . . . Austin TX 78758 512-452-0651 452-0691
TF: 800-783-7459 ■ *Web:* arc-is.com
Automation & Control Technology Inc
6141 Avery Rd . . . Dublin OH 43016 614-495-1120
Web: www.autocontroltech.com
Automotive Quality & Logistics Inc
14744 Jib St . . . Plymouth MI 48170 734-459-1670
Web: www.aql-inc.com
Avanti Corp 5520 Cherokee Ave Ste 205 . . . Alexandria VA 22312 703-916-1660
Web: www.avanticorporation.com
Avanti Environmental Inc
10842 Noel St Ste 108 . . . Los Alamitos CA 90720 714-730-3320
Web: www.avantienvironmental.com
Avenger Aircraft & Services LLC
103 N Main St Ste 106 . . . Greenville SC 29601 864-232-8073
Web: www.avengeraircraft.com
Avery Point Mktg Solutions 244 Upton Rd . . . Colchester CT 06415 860 537 2440
Avoca Group 179 Nassau St Ste 3a . . . Princeton NJ 08542 609-252-9020 252-9022
Web: www.theavocagroup.com
Avs Group 3120 S Ave . . . La Crosse WI 54601 608-787-8101
Web: www.avsgroup.com
Award Solutions Inc 2100 Lakeside Blvd . . . Richardson TX 75082 972-664-0727 664-0729
Web: awardsolutions.com
Axiom Resource Management Inc
5203 Leesburg Pk Ste 300 . . . Falls Church VA 22041 703-208-3000
TF: 800-566-9305 ■ *Web:* www.axiom-rm.com
Axios Inc 801 Broadway Ave NW Ste 200 . . . Grand Rapids MI 49504 616-949-2525
Web: www.axiosincorporated.com
Axis Teknologies
8800 Roswell Rd Bldg A Ste 265 . . . Sandy Springs GA 30350 678-441-0260
Web: www.axisteknologies.com
Azavar Technologies 234 S Wabash Ave Fl 6 . . . Chicago IL 60604 312-583-0100
Web: www.azavar.com
Aztec Energy Partners Inc
1951 Honey Creek Commons . . . Conyers GA 30013 770-760-1100
Web: aztec-energy.com/
B Ma Media Group 4091 Erie St . . . Willoughby OH 44094 440-975-4262
Web: www.bmamedia.com
B27 Resources 1417 Gables Ct . . . Plano TX 75075 214-473-8580
Web: www.b27resources.com/b27//gp.nsf/viewsub?openform&page=B27Locations
Baa Indianapolis LLC
2500 S High School Rd Ste 100 . . . Indianapolis IN 46241 317-487-5025
Web: www.indianapolisairport.com
Bad Boy Inc 102 Industrial Dr . . . Batesville AR 72501 870-698-0090
Web: www.badboymowers.com
BAE Systems Analytical Solutions Inc
308 Voyager Way . . . Huntsville AL 35806 256-890-8000
Web: www.mevatec.com
Bain & Co 131 Dartmouth St . . . Boston MA 02116 617-572-2000 572-2427
Web: www.bain.com
Banda Group International LLC
1799 E Queen Creek Rd Ste 1 . . . Chandler AZ 85286 480-636-8734
Web: www.bandagroupintl.com
Bankers Business Management Services Inc
8121 Georgia Ave Ste 950 . . . Silver Spring MD 20910 301-565-0601
Web: www.bankersbms.com
Bar Green Inc 619 E Winghouse Blvd . . . Charlotte NC 28273 704-552-6483 552-1403
Web: www.bargreeninc.com
Barnes & Conti Assoc Inc
940 Dwight Way Ste 15 . . . Berkeley CA 94710 510-644-0911
Web: www.barnesconti.com
Barnes Communications Inc 1 Yonge St Ste 1504 . . . Toronto ON M5E1E5 416-367-5000 367-5390
Web: www.barnesir.com
Bay Area Economics 1285 66th St . . . Emeryville CA 94608 510-547-9380
Web: www.bae1.com
Bay Dynamics Inc 595 Market St Ste 920 . . . San Francisco CA 94105 415-912-3130
Web: www.baydynamics.com
BC One Call Ltd 4259 Canada Way Ste 222 . . . Burnaby BC V5G1H1 604-257-1900
Web: www.bconecall.bc.ca
BCS Inc 8920 Stephens Rd Ste 200 . . . Laurel MD 20723 410-997-7778
Web: www.bcs-hq.com
Beachwood Systems Consulting Inc
13315 Broadway Ave . . . Cleveland OH 44125 216-823-1800
Web: www.beachsys.com
Beacon Assoc Inc 900-A S Main St Ste 102 . . . Bel Air MD 21014 410-638-7279 638-7662
TF: 877-846-5046 ■ *Web:* www.beaconassociates.net
Beacon Financial Partners
25800 Science Park Dr Ste 200 . . . Beachwood OH 44122 216-910-1850
Web: www.beaconplanners.com
Beacon Occupational Health & Safety Services Inc
800 Cordova St . . . Anchorage AK 99501 907-222-7612
Web: www.beaconohss.com
Beacon Partners Inc 97 Libbey Pkwy Ste 310 . . . Weymouth MA 02189 781-982-8400
Web: www.beaconpartners.com
Beam Interactive & Relationship Mktg LLC
24 School St Ste 403 . . . Boston MA 02108 617-523-0500
Web: www.beamland.com
BeamPines Inc 232 Madison Ave 10th Fl . . . New York NY 10016 212-476-4100
Web: www.beampines.com
Becker''s ASC Review 77 Wacker . . . Chicago IL 60611 312-750-6016
TF: 800-417-2035 ■ *Web:* www.beckersasc.com

Phone Fax

Becton Healthcare Resources Inc
5674 Stoneridge Dr Ste 116 . . . Pleasanton CA 94588 925-520-0005
Web: www.bhrcorp.org
Beeson & Assoc Inc 7711 Cambridge Ct . . . Crestwood KY 40014 502-241-8460
Behavioral Science Technology Inc
417 Bryant Cir . . . Ojai CA 93023 805-646-0166
TF: 800-548-5781 ■ *Web:* www.bstsolutions.com
Bekker Compliance Consulting Partners LLC
1133 Sixth Ave Ste 203 . . . San Diego CA 92101 818-836-1291
Web: www.bccp-llc.com
Benchmark Technologies International Inc
411 Hackensack Ave Fl 8 . . . Hackensack NJ 07601 201-996-0077
Web: www.btiworld.com
Benedetto Guitars Inc 10 Mall Ter Ste A . . . Savannah GA 31406 912-692-1400
Web: benedettoguitars.com
Benefitdecisions Inc 125 S Wacker Ste 2075 . . . Chicago IL 60606 312-606-4800
Web: www.benefitdecisions.com
Benemax Inc Seven W Mill St . . . Medfield MA 02052 800-528-1530
TF: 800-528-1530 ■ *Web:* www.benemax.com
Benjamin Schlesinger & Assoc LLC
3 Bethesda Metro Ctr Ste 700 . . . Bethesda MD 20814 301-951-7266
Web: www.bsaenergy.com
Benson Mktg Group
2700 Napa Vly Corporate Dr Ste H . . . Napa CA 94558 707-254-9292
Web: www.bensonmarketing.com
Berkeley Communications Corp 1321 67th St . . . Emeryville CA 94608 510-644-1599
TF: 877-237-5266 ■ *Web:* www.berkcom.com
Bernzott Capital Advisors
888 W Ventura Blvd Ste B . . . Camarillo CA 93010 805-389-9445
Web: www.bernzott.com
Bertling Logistics Inc 19054 Kenswick Dr . . . Humble TX 77338 281-774-2300
Web: www.bertling.com
Beta-tech Consulting Inc 1553 Markham Way . . . Sacramento CA 95818 916-443-0300
Web: beta-techconsulting.com
Betacom Inc 5620 E Fowler Ave Ste F . . . Temple Terrace FL 33617 813-985-4097
Web: www.betacominc.com
BGR Holding LLC
The Homer Bldg Eleventh Fl S 601 Thirteenth St NW
. . . Washington DC 20005 202-333-4936
Web: www.bgrdc.com
BIA Financial Network Inc
15120 Enterprise Ct . . . Chantilly VA 20151 703-818-2425
TF: 800-331-5086 ■ *Web:* www.bia.com
Biggins Lacy Shapiro & Company LLC
47 Hulfish St Ste 400 . . . Princeton NJ 08542 609-924-9775
Web: www.blsstrategies.com
Bingham Osborn & Scarborough LLC
345 California St Ste 1100 . . . San Francisco CA 94104 415-781-8535
Web: www.bosinvest.com
BIO Analytics 65 Broad St . . . Stamford CT 06901 203-327-0800
Web: www.bio4analytics.com
Bioline USA Inc 305 Constitution Dr . . . Taunton MA 02780 508-880-8990
Web: www.bioline.com
Biondo Investment Advisors LLC
540 Routes 6 & 209 . . . Milford PA 18337 570-296-5525
Web: www.thebiondogroup.com
Biostat International Inc
14506 University Point Pl Ste A . . . Tampa FL 33613 813-979-1619
Web: biostatinternational.com/
BioXcel Corp 780 E Main St . . . Branford CT 06405 203-433-4086
Web: www.bioxcel.com
Bizfin 50 Mclaughlin Dr . . . Greensburg PA 15601 724-836-6827
Web: www.bizfin.com
Bizphyx Inc 1910 Poplar Dr . . . Wylie TX 75098 972-429-5560
Web: www.bizphyx.com
Black Letter Discovery Inc
33 New Montgomery St Ste 950 . . . San Francisco CA 94105 415-946-2470
Web: www.blackletterdiscovery.com
Blaine Tech Services Inc 1680 Rogers Ave . . . San Jose CA 95112 408-573-0555
TF: 800-545-7558 ■ *Web:* www.blainetech.com
Blanton & Assoc Inc
5 Lakeway Centre Ct Ste 200 . . . Austin TX 78734 512-264-1095 264-1531
TF: 888-863-5881 ■ *Web:* www.blantonassociates.com
Blood Group Alliance Inc
1300 Division Rd Ste 102 . . . West Warwick RI 02893 401-381-0600
Blue Door Consulting 21 W New York Ave . . . Oshkosh WI 54901 920-230-2583
Web: www.bluedoorconsulting.com
Blue Garnet Assoc LLC
8055 W Manchester Ave Ste 430 . . . Playa Del Rey CA 90293 310-439-1930
Web: www.bluegarnet.net
Blue Magnet Partners LLC
11030 Jones Bridge Rd Ste 206 . . . Alpharetta GA 30022 770-265-9858
Web: www.bluemagnetpartners.com
Blue Ridge Grain & Mktg Inc
2545 Flintridge Rd Ste 120 . . . Gainesville GA 30501 770-535-2864
Blue Ridge Partners Management Consulting LLC
1350 Beverly Rd Ste 115 . . . Mclean VA 22101 703-448-1881
Web: www.blueridgepartners.com
Blue Tent Mktg 218 E Valley Rd Ste 205 . . . Carbondale CO 81623 970-704-3240
Web: bluetent.com/
Bluepoint Leadership Development Ltd
25 Whitney Dr . . . Milford OH 45150 513-683-4702
Web: www.bluepointleadership.com
Bluestone Energy Services LLC
136 Longwater Dr Ste 103 . . . Norwell MA 02061 781-982-2888
Web: www.bluestoneenergy.com
Blumberg Capital 580 Howard St Ste 101 . . . San Francisco CA 94105 415-905-5000
Web: www.blumbergcapital.com
BlumbergExcelsior Inc 16 Court St 14th Fl . . . Brooklyn NY 11241 212-431-5000
Web: www.blumberg.com
Boa Technology Inc 1760 Platte St . . . Denver CO 80202 303-455-5126
Web: www.boatechnology.com

Company / Address	City	State	Zip	Phone	Fax
Bob Hart Consulting LLC 5126 W Evans Creek Rd	Rogue River	OR	97537	541-582-8890	
Bockorny Group Inc 1101 16th St Northwest Ste 500	Washington	DC	20036	202-659-9111	
Web: www.bockornygroup.com					
Bollard Group LLC, The One Joy St	Boston	MA	02108	617-720-5800	
Web: www.bollard.com					
Bon Secours Virginia HealthSource Inc 7229 Forest Ave Ste 208	Richmond	VA	23226	804-673-2727	
Web: richmond.bonsecours.com					
Bonanza Trade & Supply 6853 Lankershim Blvd	North Hollywood	CA	91605	818-765-6577	
TF: 888-965-6577 ■ *Web:* www.stonetooling.com					
Boomer Consulting 610 Humboldt St	Manhattan	KS	66502	785-537-2358	
TF: 800-739-9998 ■ *Web:* www.boomer.com					
Boomer Project 2601 Floyd Ave	Richmond	VA	23220	804-358-8981	
Web: www.boomerproject.com					
Boomtown Internet Group Inc 111 Rosemary Ln	Glenmoore	PA	19343	888-454-3330	
Web: www.boomtownig.com					
Booz Allen Hamilton Inc 8283 Greensboro Dr	McLean	VA	22102	703-902-5000	902-3333
TF: 866-390-3908 ■ *Web:* www.boozallen.com					
Bordercomm Partners LP 6842 Industrial Ave	El Paso	TX	79915	915-779-3000	
Web: bordercomm.com					
Bortz Media & Sports Group Inc 5105 DTC Pkwy Ste 200	Greenwood Village	CO	80111	303-893-9902	893-9913
Web: www.bortz.com					
Boston Consulting Group Inc 53 State St Sixth Fl	Boston	MA	02109	617-973-1200	973-1399
Web: www.bcg.com					
Boston Event Guide.com 475 Hillside Ave Ste 6	Needham Hgts	MA	02494	781-444-7771	
Web: www.bostoneventguide.com					
Boston Market Strategies Inc 500 Cummings Ctr Ste 3150	Beverly	MA	01915	781-245-7773	
Web: www.bmsi3.com					
Boundless Network Inc 200 E Sixth St Ste 300	Austin	TX	78701	512-472-9200	472-9204
Web: www.boundlessnetwork.com					
Boykin Management Co 8015 W Kenton Cir Ste 220	Huntersville	NC	28078	704-896-2880	
Web: www.boykin.com					
Brakke Consulting Inc 2735 Villa Creek Ste 140	Dallas	TX	75234	972-243-4033	
TF: 877-399-6354 ■ *Web:* www.brakkeconsulting.com					
Brand Advisor 512 Union St	San Francisco	CA	94133	415-393-0800	
Web: www.brandadvisors.com					
Brand Electric Inc 6274 E 375 S	Lafayette	IN	47905	765-296-3437	
Web: www.brandelectric.com					
Brand Integrity 60 Park Ave	Rochester	NY	14607	585-442-5404	
Web: www.brandintegrity.com					
Brattle Group Inc, The 44 Brattle St	Cambridge	MA	02138	617-864-7900	
Web: www.brattle.com					
Braverman Financial Associates 2173 Embassy Dr	Lancaster	PA	17603	717-399-4030	
Web: www.bravermanfinancial.com					
Bread Loaf Corp 1293 Rt 7 S	Middlebury	VT	05753	802-388-9871	388-3815
Web: breadloaf.com					
Breakthrough Management Group Inc 1921 Corporate Ctr Cir	Longmont	CO	80501	303-827-0010	
Web: www.bmgi.com					
BridgePortfoliocom Inc 411 N Lasalle Ste 400	Chicago	IL	60654	312-321-9139	
Web: www.bridgeportfolio.com					
Brokers Logistics Ltd 1000 Hawkins Blvd	El Paso	TX	79915	915-778-7751	778-1358
Web: www.brokerslogistics.com					
Brookstone Capital Management 1751 S Naperville Rd	Wheaton	IL	60189	630-653-1400	
Web: www.brookstonecm.com					
Brownlie & Braden LLC 2820 Lincoln Plz 500 N Akard	Dallas	TX	75201	214-219-4650	
Web: www.brownliebraden.com					
Bryn Mawr Capital Management Inc One Town Pl Ste 200	Bryn Mawr	PA	19010	484-380-8100	
Web: www.brynmawrcap.com					
BTAS Inc 3572 Dayton-Xenia Rd Ste 210	Beavercreek	OH	45432	937-431-9431	
Web: www.btas.com					
BTS USA Inc 300 Stamford Pl Ste 425	Stamford	CT	06902	203-316-2740	
TF: 800-445-7089 ■ *Web:* www.bts.com					
Bucher & Christian Consulting Inc 10 W Market St Ste 1300	Indianapolis	IN	46204	317-423-8980	
TF: 866-363-1132 ■ *Web:* www.bcforward.com					
Building Performance Institute Inc 107 Hermes Rd Ste 110	Malta	NY	12020	518-899-2727	
TF: 877-274-1274 ■ *Web:* www.bpi.org					
Bull & Bear Capital Advisors Inc 8659 Nathans Cove Ct	Jacksonville	FL	32256	904-363-3600	
Web: www.bullbearcapital.com					
Bull Mktg Group LLC 79 S Milwaukee Ave	Wheeling	IL	60090	847-520-1182	
Web: bullmarketinggroup.com					
Bulldawg Mktg Inc 115 Eastbend Ct	Mooresville	NC	28117	704-660-6441	
Web: www.bulldawgmarketing.com					
Bullseye Database Mktg LLC 5546 S 104th E Ave	Tulsa	OK	74146	918-587-1731	
Web: www.bullseyedm.com					
Bullseye Strategy LLC 1700 E Las Olas Blvd Ste 301	Fort Lauderdale	FL	33301	954-591-8999	
Web: www.bullseyestrategy.com					
Bundy Group 24 Walnut Ave	Roanoke	VA	24016	540-342-2151	
Web: www.bundyandcompany.com					
Burchfield Group Inc, The 1295 Northland Dr Ste 350	St Paul	MN	55120	651-389-5640	
TF: 800-778-1359 ■ *Web:* www.burchfieldgroup.com					
Burdeshaw Associates Ltd 4701 Sangamore Rd Ste N100	Bethesda	MD	20816	301-229-5800	
Web: www.burdeshaw.com					
Burl Capital LLC One International Pl Seventh Fl	Boston	MA	02110	617-936-3358	
Web: www.burlcapital.com					
Burnham Nationwide Inc The Burnham Ctr 111 W Washington St Ste 450	Chicago	IL	60602	312-407-7990	
Web: burnhamnationwide.com					
Burton-Taylor International Consulting LLC 1319 Thornapple Dr Mezzanine Level	Osprey	FL	34229	646-201-4152	
Web: www.burton-taylor.com					
Busek Company Inc 11 Tech Cir	Natick	MA	01760	508-655-5565	
Web: www.busek.com					
Bush Consulting Group 136 S Broadway Ave Second Fl	Salem	OH	44460	330-337-6104	
Web: bushconsultinggroup.com					
Business Advancement Inc 178 Sycamore Terr	Glen Rock	NJ	07452	201-612-1228	
Web: www.businessadvance.com					
Business Leaders for Michigan 600 Renaissance Ctr Ste 1760	Detroit	MI	48243	313-259-5400	
Web: www.businessleadersformichigan.com					
Business Resource Group (BRG) 10440 N Central Expy Ste 1150	Dallas	TX	75231	214-777-5100	777-5101
TF: 888-391-9166 ■ *Web:* www.brg.com					
Business Training Library Inc 285 Chesterfield Business Pkwy	Chesterfield	MO	63005	636-534-1000	
Web: www.bizlibrary.com					
BusinessBroker Network LLC 375 Northridge Rd Ste 475	Atlanta	GA	30350	770-391-5061	
Web: www.businessbroker.net					
Businesspersons Between Jobs Inc 601 Claymont Dr	Ballwin	MO	63011	636-394-1440	
Web: bbj.org					
BUSlink Media 440 Cloverleaf Dr	Baldwin Park	CA	91706	626-336-1888	
Web: www.buslink.com					
C & C Reservoirs Inc 10333 Harwin Dr Ste 270	Houston	TX	77036	713-776-3872	
Web: www.ccreservoirs.com					
C Myers Corp 8222 S 48th St Ste 275	Phoenix	AZ	85044	602-840-0606	
Web: www.cmyers.com					
C4 Planning Solutions LLC 4914 Deans Bridge Rd	Blythe	GA	30805	706-592-1520	
Web: www.c4plans.com					
Cabot Advisory Group LLC, The 90 Washington Vly Rd	Bedminster	NJ	07921	908-719-8966	
California Primary Care Association 1231 I St Ste 400	Sacramento	CA	95814	916-440-8170	
Web: www.cpca.org					
Callahan Financial Planning Co 3157 Farnam St Ste 7112	Omaha	NE	68131	402-341-2000	
Web: www.callahanfp.com					
Calliope Learning 1581H Hillside Ave	Victoria	BC	V8T2C1	250-213-6239	
Web: www.calliopelearning.com					
Callisto Integration 635 Fourth Line Ste 16	Oakville	ON	L6L5B3	905-339-0059	
TF: 800-387-0467 ■ *Web:* www.aseco.net					
CALMAC Manufacturing Corp 3-00 Banta Pl	Fair Lawn	NJ	07410	201-797-1511	
Web: www.calmac.com					
Calnet Inc 12359 Sunrise Vly Dr Ste 270	Reston	VA	20191	703-547-6800	547-6806
TF General: 877-322-5638 ■ *Web:* www.calnet.com					
Cambay Group Inc, The 2999 Oak Rd Ste 400	Walnut Creek	CA	94597	925-933-1405	
Web: www.cambaygroup.com					
Cambria Consulting Inc One Bowdoin Sq	Boston	MA	02114	617-523-7500	
Web: www.cambriaconsulting.com					
Cambria Solutions Inc 1050 20th St Ste 275	Sacramento	CA	95811	916-326-4446	
Web: www.cambriasolutions.com					
Cambridge Financial Services Group Inc 83 Mason St	Greenwich	CT	06830	203-869-0033	
Web: www.cambridgegroup.net					
Cambridge Meridian Group Inc 50 Church St Fifth Fl	Cambridge	MA	02138	617-876-7400	
Web: www.cambridgemeridian.com					
Campaign Consultation Inc 2819 Saint Paul St	Baltimore	MD	21218	410-243-7979	
Web: www.campaignconsultation.com					
Canadian Enerdata Ltd 86 Ringwood Dr Ste 201	Stouffville	ON	L4A1C3	905-642-8167	
Web: www.enerdata.com					
Canadian Urban Institute 555 Richmond St W	Toronto	ON	M5V3B1	416-365-0816	
Web: www.canurb.com					
Canaudit Inc 2139 Tapo St Ste 206	Simi Valley	CA	93063	805-583-3723	
Web: www.canaudit.com					
Cape Fox Corp PO Box 8558	Ketchikan	AK	99901	907-225-5163	
Web: www.capefoxcorp.com					
CapGen Financial Grou 120 W 45th St Ste 1010	New York	NY	10036	212-542-6868	
Web: www.capgen.com					
Capital Advisors Ltd LLC 20600 Chagrin Blvd Ste 1115	Shaker Heights	OH	44122	216-295-7900	
Web: www.capitaladvisorsltd.com					
Capital Consulting Corp 2810 Old Lee Hwy Ste 245	Fairfax	VA	22031	703-876-0400	
Web: www.capconcorp.com					
Capital Investment Advisors Inc 200 Sandy Springs Pl Ne Ste 300	Atlanta	GA	30328	404-531-0018	
Web: www.yourwealth.com					
Capitol Archives & Record Storage Inc 133 Laurel St	Hartford	CT	06106	860-951-8981	
Web: www.capitolarchives.com					
Capri Capital Partners LLC 875 N Michigan Ave Ste 3430	Chicago	IL	60611	312-573-5300	
Web: www.capricap.com					
Capstrat Inc 1201 Edwards Mill Rd Fourth Fl	Raleigh	NC	27607	919-828-0806	
Web: capstrat.com					
Carana Corp 4350 Fairfax Dr Ste 900	Arlington	VA	22203	703-243-1700	
Web: www.carana.com					

Phone Fax

Cardiosolutions Inc 75 Mill St.................... Stoughton MA 02072 781-344-0801
Web: www.cardiosolutionsinc.com

Carepro Health Services
1014 Fifth Ave SE............................Cedar Rapids IA 52403 319-363-4554
Web: careprohealthservices.com

Carlisle & Company Inc 30 Monument Sq Ste 225..... Concord MA 01742 978-318-0500
Web: www.carlisle-co.com

Carlson Capital Management Inc
11 Bridge Sq................................... Northfield MN 55057 507-645-8887
Web: carlsoncap.com

Carolina Financial Group 185 W Main St............. Brevard NC 28712 828-393-0088
Web: www.carofin.com

Carr Management Inc One Tara Blvd Ste 303........... Nashua NH 03062 603-888-1315
Web: www.carrmanagement.com

Carroll County Economic Development
111 N Mason St................................ Carrollton MO 64633 660-542-8760

Carter Express Inc 4020 W 73rd St.................Anderson IN 46011 800-738-7705
Web: www.carter-express.com

CartwrightDownes Inc 950 Lee St Ste 110......... Des Plaines IL 60016 847-685-2700 685-2727
TF: 800-323-2049 ■ *Web:* www.cartwrightdownes.com

Cascade Financial Management Inc
950 17th St Ste 950...............................Denver CO 80202 800-353-0008
TF: 800-353-0008 ■ *Web:* www.cascade-inc.com

Catalyst Mktg Design Inc 930 S Calhoun St........ Fort Wayne IN 46802 260-422-4888
Web: catalystgetsit.com

Catalytic Combustion Corp 709 21st Ave.............Bloomer WI 54724 715-568-2882
Web: www.catalyticcombustion.com

Catapult Direct Mktg LLC
300 Orchard City Dr Ste 131........................Campbell CA 95008 408-369-8111
Web: www.catapultdata.com

Cato Research Ltd 4364 S Alston Ave.................Durham NC 27713 919-361-2286 361-2290
Web: www.cato.com

Cavalier Logistics Management Inc
45085 Old Ox Rd.................................. Dulles VA 20166 703-733-4010
Web: www.cavlog.com

Caxton Growth Partners
5755 Granger Rd Ste 100...................... Independence OH 44131 216-867-9780
Web: www.caxtongrowth.com

CBI Group LLC
Casho Mill Professional Ctr 1501 Casho Mill Rd
Ste 9.. Newark DE 19711 302-266-0860
Web: www.thecbigroup.com

CBI Research Inc 600 Unicorn Park Dr................ Woburn MA 01801 339-298-2100
Web: www.cbinet.com

CCG Facilities Integration Inc
1500 S Edgewood St.............................Baltimore MD 21227 410-525-0010
Web: www.ccgfacilities.com

Cedar Management Consulting International LLC
250 Park Ave 7th Fl..............................New York NY 10177 212-572-6314
Web: www.cedar-consulting.com

Ceeva Inc 643 First Ave Ste 300.................... Pittsburgh PA 15219 412-690-2300
TF: 866-233-8248 ■ *Web:* www.ceeva.com

Cenergistic Inc 5950 Sherry Ln Ste 900................ Dallas TX 75225 214-346-5950
TF: 888-782-7937 ■ *Web:* www.cenergistic.com

Center for Civic Education
5145 Douglas Fir Rd............................ Calabasas CA 91302 818-591-9321
Web: www.civiced.org

Center for Collaborative 33 Harrison Ave # 6...........Boston MA 02111 617-421-0134
Web: www.ccebos.org

Center for Cultural Interchange
746 N La Salle Dr Ste 1............................Chicago IL 60654 312-944-2544
Web: www.cci-exchange.com

Center for Professional
992 Old Eagle School Rd Ste 913...................... Wayne PA 19087 610-688-1708
Web: www.cfpie.com

Centris Consulting Inc 800 James Ave............... Scranton PA 18510 570-963-1136
Web: www.centrisconsulting.com

Century Health Solutions Inc
2951 SW Woodside Dr..............................Topeka KS 66614 785-233-1816
TF: 800-227-0089 ■ *Web:* www.century-health.com

CFI Group 625 Avis Dr............................ Ann Arbor MI 48108 734-930-9090 930-0911
Web: www.cfigroup.com

CFM Partners Inc 4435 Macomb St NW...........Washington DC 20016 202-364-2380
Web: www.cfmpartners.com

CFO Strategies LLC 2221 Arbutus St............ Newport Beach CA 92660 949-338-9394

CGLA Infrastructure Inc
1827 Jefferson Pl NW Ste 1......................Washington DC 20036 202-776-0990
Web: www.cg-la.com

Cgn & Assoc Inc 415 SW Washington St................ Peoria IL 61602 309-495-2100 495-2370
TF: 888-746-4246 ■ *Web:* www.cgnglobal.com

ChaCha Search Inc 14550 Clay Terr Blvd Ste 130........Carmel IN 46032 317-660-6680
TF: 800-224-2242 ■ *Web:* www.chacha.com

Chambers Group Inc
Five Hutton Centre Dr Ste 750..................... Santa Ana CA 92707 949-261-5414
Web: www.chambersgroupinc.com

Champion College Services Inc
4600 S Mill Ave Ste 180.............................. Tempe AZ 85282 480-947-7375
TF: 800-761-7376 ■ *Web:* www.championcollegeservices.com

Chao & Company Ltd 8460 Tyco Rd Ste E...............Vienna VA 22182 703-847-4380
Web: www.chaoco.com

Charter Trust Co 90 N Main St...................... Concord NH 03301 603-224-1350
Web: www.chartertrust.com

CHC Consulting 1700 E Garry Ave Ste 210............ Santa Ana CA 92705 949-250-0004
Web: chcconsulting.com

Checchi & Company Consulting Inc
1899 L St NW Ste 800..........................Washington DC 20036 202-452-9700 466-9070
Web: www.checchiconsulting.com

Chem Space Assoc Inc 655 William Pitt Way......... Pittsburgh PA 15238 412-828-3191
Web: www.lcms.com

ChemADVISOR Inc
811 Camp Horne Rd Stone Quarry Crossing
Ste 220... Pittsburgh PA 15237 412-847-2000
Web: www.chemadvisor.com

Chemonics International Inc 1717 H St NW.......Washington DC 20006 202-955-3300
Web: www.chemonics.com

Chief Manufacturing Inc
6436 City W Pkwy Ste 700........................... Prairie MN 55378 952-894-6280
Web: www.chiefmfg.com

Children's Educational Network Inc
283 S Escondido Blvd.......................... Escondido CA 92025 760-233-2863
Web: www.childrenseducationalnetwork.com

Childrens Education Connection Inc
6301 Hwy 39.................................... Meridian MS 39305 601-485-2856
Web: childrenseducationconnection.com

CHP & Assoc Consulting Engineers Inc
7660 Woodway Dr Ste 400..........................Houston TX 77063 713-977-3430 977-3828
Web: buryinc.com/news/detail/bury-acquires-chp-and-associates

Christensen Roberts Solutions
Eight Lunar Dr.................................Woodbridge CT 06525 203-389-4440
Web: www.crsol.com

Chrysalis Consulting LLC
11711 N Pennsylvania St............................Carmel IN 46032 317-844-1400
Web: www.chrysalisglobal.com

CIMdata Inc 3909 Research Park Dr................ Ann Arbor MI 48108 734-668-9922
Web: www.cimdata.com

Cinetic Media Inc 555 W 25th St Fourth Fl...........New York NY 10001 212-204-7979
Web: www.cineticmedia.com

Cipher Systems LLC 2661 Riva Rd Ste 1000.......... Annapolis MD 21401 410-412-3326 897-1066
TF: 888-899-1523 ■ *Web:* www.cipher-sys.com

CipherMax Inc 3 Results Way..................... Cupertino CA 95014 408-861-3697 861-3650

Circadian Technologies Inc
Two Main St Ste 310.............................. Stoneham MA 02180 781-439-6300 439-6399
TF: 800-284-5001 ■ *Web:* www.circadian.com

Cirrus Assoc LLC 11757 Katy Fwy Ste 1300............Houston TX 77079 281-854-2383
Web: www.cirrusassociates.com

City of New Westminster
511 Royal Ave.............................New Westminster BC V3L1H9 604-527-4605
Web: www.newwestcity.ca

CL Services Inc 600 S Central Ave Ste 300...........Hapeville GA 30354 678-686-0933
Web: www.clservicesinc.com

Claritee Group LLC
2300 Computer Rd Ste C13.....................Willow Grove PA 19090 215-657-5170
Web: www.clariteegroup.com

Clark & Wamberg LLC
102 S Wynstone Park Dr.....................North Barrington IL 60010 847-304-5800
Web: www.clarkwamberg.com

Clarus Mktg Group LLC
100 Roscommon Dr Ste 100...................... Middletown CT 06457 860-358-9198
Web: www.clarusmarketing.com

Classroom Inc 245 Fifth Ave 20th Fl................New York NY 10016 212-545-8400
Web: www.classroominc.org

Clear Blue Skies Communications
Two Thatcher St................................ Hyde Park MA 02136 617-361-3229

ClearBridge Compensation Group LLC
515 Madison Ave 32nd Fl..........................New York NY 10022 212-886-1022
Web: www.clearbridgecomp.com

ClearCreek Partners 1743 Wazee St Ste 375...........Denver CO 80202 303-383-1100
Web: www.clearcreekpartners.com

Clearedge Mktg LLC 415 N Lasalle St Ste 202..........Chicago Il 60654 312-731-3149
Web: www.clearedgemarketing.com

CLEAResult 4301 Westbank Dr Ste 300................ Austin TX 78746 512-327-9200
Web: www.rsgrp.com

Client Mktg Systems Inc 880 Price St............Pismo Beach CA 93449 805-773-7981
Web: climark.com

Client Success Group Inc
5166 Sunny Creek Dr............................. San Jose CA 95135 408-531-1907
Web: www.clientsuccessgroup.com

Cliffwater LLC
4640 Admiralty Way
Ste 1101 Marina Twr........................ Marina Del Rey CA 90292 310-448-5000
Web: www.cliffwater.com

Cline Resource & Development Co
430 Harper Park Dr................................ Beckley WV 25801 304-255-7458
Web: www.clineres.com

CLX Logistics LLC
1777 Sentry Pkwy W Abington Hall Ste 300............ Blue Bell PA 19422 215-461-3805
Web: www.chemlogix.com

CMF Associates LLC
325 Chestnut St Ste 410........................ Philadelphia PA 19106 215-531-7500
Web: www.cmfassociates.com

CMS Innovative Consultants
Eight Fletcher Pl.................................Melville NY 11747 631-425-3000
Web: www.cmsav.com

Co-Sales Co 2700 N Third St Ste 1000...............Phoenix AZ 85004 602-254-5555
Web: www.co-sales.com

Coalesce Mktg & Design Inc
4321 W College Ave Ste 250....................... Appleton WI 54914 920-380-4444
Web: www.coalescemarketing.com

Coastal Logistics Group Inc
50 Sonny Perdue Dr............................Garden City GA 31408 912-964-0707
Web: www.clg-sav.com

Coates Field Service Inc
4800 N Santa Fe............................Oklahoma City OK 73118 405-528-5676
Web: www.coatesfieldservice.com

Cogenix Consulting Ltd
401-50 Burnhamthorpe Rd W.................... Mississauga ON L5B3C2 905-803-9132

Cogistics Inc 2525 Drane Field Rd Ste 25............. Lakeland FL 33811 863-647-9389
Web: www.cogistics.com

Cohasset Assoc Inc
505 N Lk Shore Dr Apt 3806.........................Chicago IL 60611 312-527-1550
Web: www.cohasset.com

Cohen Asset Management Inc
1900 Ave of the Stars Ste 500.....................Los Angeles CA 90067 310-860-0598
Web: www.cohenasset.com

Phone Fax

Coles Mktg Communications Inc
3950 Priority Way S Dr Ste 106 .... Indianapolis IN 46240 317-571-0051
Web: www.colesmarketing.com

Collins Consulting 630 Woofter Ave .... Colby KS 67701 785-462-8352
Web: collins.net

Colony Group LLC, The Two Atlantic Ave .... Boston MA 02110 617-723-8200
Web: www.thecolonygroup.com

Colt International Inc 300 Flint Ridge Rd .... Webster TX 77598 281-280-2100
Web: www.coltinternational.com

Command Consulting Group LLC
1919 M St NW STE 200 .... Washington DC 20036 202-207-2930
Web: www.commandcg.com

Communispond Inc 12 Barns Ln .... East Hampton NY 11937 631-907-8010
TF: 800-529-5925 ■ *Web:* www.communispond.com

Community Care Inc 1555 S Layton Blvd .... Milwaukee WI 53215 414-385-6600
Web: www.communitycareinc.org

Compass Career Management Solutions LLC
8509 Crown Crescent Ct Ste 100 .... Charlotte NC 28227 704-849-2500
Web: www.compasscareer.com

Compass Mktg Solutions LLC 808 P St Ste 300 .... Lincoln NE 68508 402-438-3222
Web: compassventures.com

Compensation Resources Inc
310 Rt 17 N .... Upper Saddle River NJ 07458 201-934-0505 934-0737
TF: 877-934-0505 ■ *Web:* www.compensationresources.com

Compensia Inc 1731 Technology Dr Ste 810 .... San Jose CA 95110 408-876-4025
Web: www.compensia.com

Complete Healthcare Communications Inc
One Dickinson Dr Ste 200 .... Chadds Ford PA 19317 610-358-3600
Web: www.chcinc.com

Compliance Corp
21617 S Essex Dr Ste 34 .... Lexington Park MD 20653 301-863-8070 863-8290
Web: www.compliancecorporation.com

Compliance Professional Resources LLC
11 Hanover Sq Ste 501 .... New York NY 10005 212-257-6500
Web: www.complianceprofessionalresources.com

Compliance Services Group Inc
7619 University Ave .... Lubbock TX 79423 806-748-0040 748-0030
Web: www.csg.net

Comprehensive Consulting Group
1800 Walt Whitman Rd Ste 130 .... Melville NY 11747 631-249-0500
Web: www.ccg1800.com

Comprehensive Financial Planning Inc
1075 Main Ave Ste 216 .... Durango CO 81301 970-385-5227
Web: www.compfinancial.com

Comprehensive Loss Management Inc
15800 32nd Ave N Ste 106 .... Minneapolis MN 55447 763-551-1022
Web: www.clmi-training.com

Comprehensive Pharmacy Services Inc (CPS)
6409 N Quail Hollow Rd .... Memphis TN 38120 901-748-0470 748-4069
TF: 800-968-6962 ■ *Web:* www.cpspharm.com

Compu- Vision Consulting Inc
2050 SR- 27 Ste 202 .... North Brunswick NJ 08902 732-422-1500
Web: www.compuvis.com

Computech Consulting Inc
707 West 700 South Ste 201 .... Woods Cross UT 84087 801-298-2155
Web: www.i4.net

Computer Management Technologies Inc
731 Gratiot Ave .... Saginaw MI 48602 989-791-4860 791-4928
Web: www.cmtonline.com

Computer Resource Solutions One Pierce Pl .... Itasca IL 60143 630-467-1010
Web: www.crscorp.com

Computer Training Systems
200 W Douglas Ave Ste 230 .... Wichita KS 67202 316-265-1585
Web: www.ctsys.com

Computerized Assessments & Learning LLC
1202 E 23rd St Ste B .... Lawrence KS 66046 785-856-3850
Web: www.caltesting.org

Comspec Corp 822 N Elm St Ste 105 .... Greensboro NC 27401 336-370-1456
Web: comspeccorp.net

Comtel 750 Ensminger Rd Ste 100 .... Tonawanda NY 14150 716-874-5500
Web: www.comtel.us

Concensus Consulting LLC 103 Fox Trot Dr .... Mars PA 16046 724-898-1888
Web: concensus.com

Concentric Energy Advisors Inc
293 Boston Post Rd W Ste 500 .... Marlborough MA 01752 508-263-6200
Web: www.ceadvisors.com

Condor Capital Management Inc
1973 Washington Vly Rd .... Martinsville NJ 08836 732-356-7323
Web: www.condorcapital.com

Condor Earth Technologies Inc PO Box 3905 .... Sonora CA 95370 209-532-0361 532-0773
TF: 800-800-0490 ■ *Web:* www.condorearth.com

Consolidated Chassis Management LLC
500 International Dr .... Budd Lake NJ 07828 973-298-8900
Web: www.ccmpool.com

Consolidated Construction Management Services Inc
Nine Professional Cir Ste 204 .... Colts Neck NJ 07722 732-303-1997
Web: www.ccmscorp.com

Consortia Consulting Inc
233 S 13th St Ste 1225 .... Lincoln NE 68508 402-441-4315
Web: www.consortiaconsulting.com

Constat Corp 1860 Blake St Ste 650 .... Denver CO 80202 303-572-1051
Web: constat.com

Consultants & Builders Inc
3850 Peachtree Industrial Blvd .... Duluth GA 30096 770-729-8183
Web: www.consultantsandbuilders.com

Consumer Electronics Assn 1919 S Eads St .... Arlington VA 22202 703-907-7600
Web: www.ce.org

Consumer Sales Solutions
537 Douglas Ave Ste 1 .... Dunedin FL 34698 727-733-8700
Web: bk.com/

Container Consulting Service Inc
455 Mayock Rd .... Gilroy CA 95020 408-842-1919
Web: www.ccs-packaging.com

Phone Fax

Contemporary Benefits Design Inc
1956 Wellness Blvd .... Monroe NC 28110 704-847-1007
Web: www.contemporarybenefits.com

Continental Shelf Assoc Inc
8502 SW Kansas Ave .... Stuart FL 34997 772-219-3000 219-3010
Web: www.conshelf.com

Contoural Inc 5150 El Camino Real Ste D-30 .... Los Altos CA 94022 650-390-0800
Web: www.contoural.com

Contract Land Staff LLC
2245 Texas Dr Ste 200 .... Sugar Land TX 77479 281-240-3370 240-5009
TF: 800-874-4519 ■ *Web:* www.contractlandstaff.com

Conway MacKenzie Inc
401 S Old Woodward Ave Ste 340 .... Birmingham MI 48009 248-433-3100
Web: www.conwaymackenzie.com

Cook & Co 12 Masterton Rd .... Bronxville NY 10708 914-779-4838
Web: www.cook-co.com

Coradix Technology Consulting Ltd
151 Slater St .... Ottawa ON K1P5H3 613-234-0800 234-0988
Web: www.coradix.com

CoreTech 660 American Ave .... King of Prussia PA 19406 800-220-3337
TF: 800-220-3337 ■ *Web:* xsellresources.com

Cornelius & Assoc Inc 631 Harden St Ste G .... Columbia SC 29205 803-779-3354
Web: www.collegiateproject.com

Corner Alliance Inc 1620 L St NW Ste 200 .... Washington DC 20036 202-754-8120
Web: www.corneralliance.com

Cornerstone Consulting & Technology
44 Montgomery St Ste 3360 .... San Francisco CA 94104 415-705-7800
Web: www.cornerstoneconcilium.com

Cornerstone Systems Inc
3250 Players Club Pkwy .... Memphis TN 38125 901-842-0660
TF: 855-288-7720 ■ *Web:* www.cornerstone-systems.com

Corporate Benefit Strategies Inc
5001 Plainfield Ave Ne Ste A .... Grand Rapids MI 49525 616-365-2413
Web: www.cbscobra.com

Corporate Dynamics Inc 1630 W Diehl Rd .... Naperville IL 60563 630-778-9991
Web: www.corpdyn.com

Corporate Executive Board Co
1919 N Lynn St .... Arlington VA 22209 571-303-3000 303-3100
NYSE: CEB ■ *TF:* 866-913-2632 ■ *Web:* www.executiveboard.com

Corporate Finance Group Inc
15 Broad St Fifth Fl .... Boston MA 02109 617-531-8270
Web: www.cfgi.com

Corporate Ink Public Relations Ltd
90 Washington St .... Newton MA 02458 617-969-9192
Web: www.corporateink.com

Corridor Capital LLC
12400 Wilshire Blvd Ste 645 .... Los Angeles CA 90025 310-442-7000
Web: www.corridorcapital.com

Corridor Group Inc, The
6405 Metcalf Ste 108 .... Overland Park KS 66202 913-362-0600
Web: www.corridorgroup.com

Corybant PO Box 19136 .... Boulder CO 80308 303-447-1988
Web: www.corybant.com

Coskata Inc 4575 Weaver Pkwy Ste 100 .... Warrenville IL 60555 630-657-5800

Cosmos Consulting Group Inc 212 E Ohio St .... Chicago IL 60611 312-222-0700

Cosmos Sports 1690 Bonhill Rd .... Mississauga ON L5T1C8 905-564-4660 564-4881
Web: www.cosmossports.com

Country Aircheck 1102 17th Ave S Ste 205 .... Nashville TN 37212 615-320-1450
Web: countryaircheck.com

COVELLO GROUP Inc, The
1660 Olympic Blvd Ste 300 .... Walnut Creek CA 94596 925-933-2300
Web: www.covellogroup.com

Cowin & Company Inc 301 Industrial Dr .... Birmingham AL 35219 205-945-1300
Web: www.cowin-co.com

CRA International Inc
200 Clarendon St Ste T-33 .... Boston MA 02116 617-425-3000 425-3132
NASDAQ: CRAI ■ *Web:* www.crai.com

Cradlerock Group LLC, The 65 High St 402 .... Stamford CT 06905 203-324-0088
Web: www.cradlerock.com

Crandall Engineering Ltd
1077 St. George Blvd .... Moncton NB E1E4C9 506-857-2777 857-2753
Web: www.crandallnb.com

Crane Metamarketing Ltd
831 Christopher Robin Rd .... Alpharetta GA 30005 770-642-2082
Web: www.cranesnest.com

Creative Advantage Inc 246 W End Ave Ste 9G .... New York NY 10023 212-475-9300
Web: www.creativeadvantage.com

Creative Assoc International Inc
5301 Wisconsin Ave NW Ste 700 .... Washington DC 20015 202-966-5804 363-4771
Web: www.creativeassociatesinternational.com

Creative Educational Concepts
116 Dennis Dr .... Lexington KY 40503 859-260-1717
Web: www.ceconcepts.net

Creative Energy Options Inc
45 Country Pl Ln .... White Haven PA 18661 570-636-3858
Web: www.retreatpa.com

Creative Management Services LLC
Three Alpine Ct .... Chestnut Ridge NY 10977 845-639-8600
Web: www.mc-2online.com

Crescendo Consulting Group
48 Free St Ste 206 .... Portland ME 04101 207-774-2345
Web: www.crescendocg.com

CRG Consulting 301 Moodie Dr Ste 325 .... Ottawa ON K2H9C4 613-596-2910 820-4718
Web: www.thecrg.com

Critical Path Strategies Inc 33 Fm 474 .... Boerne TX 78006 830-249-1977
Web: criticalpathstrategies.com

Cross X Platform LLC
2570 Blvd Of The Generals Ste X .... Audubon PA 19403 610-539-2297
Web: www.crossxplatform.com

Crosscheck Compliance LLC
810 W Washington Blvd Fifth Fl .... Chicago IL 60607 312-346-4600
Web: www.crosscheckcompliance.com

Phone Fax

CSBA 1667 K St Nw Ste 900 .... Washington DC 20006 202-331-7990
Web: www.csbaonline.org

CSI Latina Financial Inc 2100 Coral Way Ste 706 .... Miami FL 33145 305-860-1616
Web: www.csilatina.com

Cso Insights 36 Tamal Vista Blvd .... Corte Madera CA 94925 415-924-3500
Web: www.csoinsights.com

CTI Consulting
20410 Observation Dr Ste 203 .... Germantown MD 20876 301-528-8591 528-2037
Web: www.countertech.com

CU America Financial Services
450 E 22nd St Ste 240 .... Lombard IL 60148 630-620-5200
Web: www.cuamerica.com

Culturalink Inc 922 E Wayne St .... South Bend IN 46617 574-233-3700

Curbstone Financial Management Corp
741 Chestnut St .... Manchester NH 03104 603-624-8462
Web: www.curbstonefinancial.com

Cyon Research Corp 8220 Stone Trail Dr .... Bethesda MD 20817 301-365-9085 365-4586
Web: www.cyonresearch.com

D & S Mktg Systems Inc 1205 38th St .... Brooklyn NY 11218 718-633-8383
Web: dsmarketing.com

D Hilton Assoc Inc 9450 Grogans Mill Rd .... Spring TX 77380 281-292-5088
TF: 800-367-0433 ■ *Web:* www.dhilton.com

D2M Inc 935 Benecia Ave .... Sunnyvale CA 94085 650-567-9995
Web: www.d2m-inc.com

DA Kreuter Assoc Inc 555 N Ln Ste 5020 .... Conshohocken PA 19428 610-834-1100 834-7722
Web: www.dakassociates.com

Daland Corp 9313 Eat 34th St N Ste 100 .... Wichita KS 67226 316-681-1081
Web: www.dalandcorp.com

DANSR Inc 818 W Evergreen Ave .... Chicago IL 60642 312-475-0464
Web: www.dansr.com

Danville Signal Processing Inc
38570 100th Ave .... Cannon Falls MN 55009 507-263-5854
Web: www.danvillesignal.com

Danya International Inc
8737 Colesville Rd Ste 1100 .... Silver Spring MD 20910 301-565-2142
Web: www.danya.com

Data Communication Solutions Inc
10125 Crosstown Cir Ste 235 .... Eden Prairie MN 55344 952-941-5466
Web: www.dcs-is-edi.com

Data Mktg Network Inc 701 Murfreesboro Pk .... Nashville TN 37210 615-313-7000
Web: dnicorp.com/

Data Partners Inc 12857 Banyan Creek Dr .... Fort Myers FL 33908 239-267-8762
Web: www.data-partners.com

Data Stream Mobile Technologies
11531 Interchange Cir S .... Miramar FL 33025 954-271-1240
Web: www.dswltech.net

Data Technology Services
1300 N Berard St .... Breaux Bridge LA 70517 337-332-4347
Web: www.dtscom.com

Datanomics 991 US Hwy 22 W Ste 301 .... Bridgewater NJ 08807 908-707-8200
Web: www.datanomics.com

Datatime Consulting 109 Forrest Ave .... Narberth PA 19072 610-668-9640
Web: www.datatimeconsult.com

David Allen Co 407 Bryant Cir Ste F .... Ojai CA 93023 805-646-8432
Web: gettingthingsdone.com/

David Kurlan & Assoc Inc 114 Turnpike Rd .... Westborough MA 01581 508-389-9350
Web: www.salesdevelopmentspecialists.com

David Powell Inc 3190 Clearview Way Ste 100 .... San Mateo CA 94402 650-357-6000
Web: www.davidpowell.com

Davies Consulting Inc
6935 Wisconsin Ave Ste 600 .... Chevy Chase MD 20815 301-652-4535 907-9355
TF: 800-811-8336 ■ *Web:* www.daviescon.com

Dawnbreaker Inc 3161 Union St .... North Chili NY 14514 585-594-0025
Web: www.dawnbreaker.com

Dawson Logistics Inc 431 N Vermilion .... Danville IL 61832 217-442-7036
Web: www.dawsonlogistics.com

Day Enterprises Inc 1912 S Ridge Ave .... Kannapolis NC 28083 704-933-2218
Web: www.carfare.com

DB Root & Company Inc
436 Seventh Ave Ste 2800 .... Pittsburgh PA 15219 412-227-2800
Web: www.dbroot.com

dbaDIRECT Inc 7310 Turfway Rd Ste 300 .... Florence KY 41042 859-283-2520
Web: www.dbadirect.com

dBrn Assoc Inc 189 Curtis Rd .... Hewlett Neck NY 11598 516-569-4557
Web: www.dbrnassociates.com

Dcc Lee Enterprises dba McDonald's
12276 San Jose Blvd Ste 601 .... Jacksonville FL 32223 904-288-6750
Web: www.mcdjax.com

DDF CPA Group 107A Edwards Rd .... Starke FL 32091 904-964-7404
Web: www.ddfcpa.com

Dean & Co 8065 Leesburg Pk Ste 500 .... Vienna VA 22182 703-506-3900 506-3905
Web: www.dean.com

Deca Aviation Engineering Ltd
7050 Telford Way .... Mississauga ON L5S1V7 905-405-1371
Web: deca-aviation.com

Decca Design 476 S 1st St .... San Jose CA 95113 408-947-1411
Web: www.decdesign.com

Dechert-Hampe & Co (DHC)
33332 Valle Rd .... San Juan Capistrano CA 92675 949-429-1999
Web: www.dechert-hampe.com

Deegit Inc 1111 Plz Dr Ste 370 .... Schaumburg IL 60173 847-330-1985
Web: www.deegit.com

DeFoe Corp 800 S Columbus Ave .... Mount Vernon NY 10550 914-699-7440
Web: www.defoecorp.com

DeHayes Consulting Group
2999 Douglas Blvd Ste 320 .... Roseville CA 95661 916-782-8321
Web: www.dcgcorp.com

Dell 8270 Willow Oaks Corporate Dr Ste 300 .... Fairfax VA 22031 703-289-8000
TF: 877-219-6982 ■ *Web:* www.dell.com

Deloitte Consulting LLP 25 Broadway 3rd Fl .... New York NY 10004 212-618-4000 850-1485*
**Fax Area Code:* 866 ■ *Web:* www.deloitte.com

DeMoss Capital Inc 25 E Main St Ste 201 .... Chattanooga TN 37408 423-756-4800
Web: www.demosscapital.com

Phone Fax

Deprince Race & Zollo Inc
250 Pk Ave S Ste 250 Ste 250 .... Winter Park FL 32789 407-420-9903 841-8778
Web: www.drz-inc.com

Desert Whale Jojoba Company Inc
2101 E Beverly Dr .... Tucson AZ 85719 520-882-4195
Web: www.desertwhale.com

DevTech Systems Inc
1700 N Moore St Ste 1720 .... Arlington VA 22209 703-312-6038 312-6039
Web: www.devtechsys.com

DG Capital Management Inc
800 Boylston St 16th Fl .... Boston MA 02199 857-453-6705
Web: www.dgcap.com

Dimension Capital Management
1221 Brickell Ave Ste 2450 .... Miami FL 33131 305-371-2776
Web: www.dimensioncapital.com

Direct Mktg Solutions Inc
8534 NE Alderwood Rd .... Portland OR 97220 503-281-1400
Web: www.resultsdm.com

Diversicare Leasing Corp
1621 Galleria Blvd .... Brentwood TN 37027 615-771-7575
Web: www.advocat.com

Diversified Lenders Inc 5607 S Ave Q .... Lubbock TX 79412 800-288-3024
TF: 800-288-3024 ■ *Web:* www.diversifiedlenders.com

DK Consultants LLC 1307 Carpers Farm Way .... Vienna VA 22182 703-438-3648
Web: www.dkconsult.net

DM Transportation Management Services Inc
PO Box 621 .... Boyertown PA 19512 610-367-0162 369-0270
TF: 888-399-0162 ■ *Web:* www.dmtrans.com

DME-Direct Inc 28486 Westinghouse Pl Ste 120 .... Valencia CA 91355 877-721-7701
TF: 877-721-7701 ■ *Web:* www.dme-direct.com

Dock Street Asset Management Inc
263 Glenville Rd .... Greenwich CT 06831 203-532-9470
Web: www.dockstreet.net

Dodge Communications Inc
11675 Rainwater Dr Ste 300 .... Alpharetta GA 30009 770-998-0500
Web: www.dodgecommunications.com

Doherty Enterprises Inc Seven Pearl Ct .... Allendale NJ 07401 201-818-4669
Web: www.dohertyinc.com

Domus Inc 123 Ave Of The Arts Ste 1980 .... Philadelphia PA 19109 215-772-2805
Web: www.domusinc.com

Douglas Wilson Cos Inc 450 B St Ste 1900 .... San Diego CA 92101 619-641-1141
Web: www.douglaswilson.com

Drew Wireless 459 Collindale Ave Nw .... Grand Rapids MI 49504 616-453-7200
Web: www.drewwireless.com

DrugLogic Inc 11490 Commerce Park Dr Ste 320 .... Reston VA 20191 703-821-3200
Web: www.druglogic.com

DWQ Assoc Ltd 38 N Ct St 2nd Fl .... Providence RI 02903 401-273-5220
Web: www.dwqassociates.com

Eagle Financial Management Services LLC
400 Travis St Ste 518 .... Shreveport LA 71101 318-675-0826
Web: www.eaglefms.net

EagleOne Case Management Solutions Inc
80 Burr Ridge Pkwy Ste 121 .... Burr Ridge IL 60527 630-655-0800
Web: www.eagleonecms.com

EAI Inc Environmental Management Service
50 Prescott St .... Jersey City NJ 07304 201-395-0010
Web: www.eaienviro.com

EBA Engineering Consultants Ltd
14940-123 Ave .... Edmonton AB T5V1B4 780-451-2121 454-5688
Web: www.eba.ca

ECG Management Consultants Inc
1111 Third Ave Ste 2700 .... Seattle WA 98101 206-689-2200 689-2209
TF: 800-729-7635 ■ *Web:* www.ecgmc.com

Echo Global Logistics Inc
600 W Chicago Ave Ste 725 .... Chicago IL 60654 800-354-7993
TF: 800-354-7993 ■ *Web:* www.echo.com

Eckler Ltd 110 Sheppard Ave E Ste 900 .... Toronto ON M2N7A3 416-429-3330
Web: www.eckler.ca

Edge Biosystems Inc 201 Perry Pkwy Ste 5 .... Gaithersburg MD 20877 301-990-2685 326-2685*
**Fax Area Code:* 800 ■ *Web:* www.edgebio.com

Edgewood Management LLC
535 Madison Ave 15th Fl .... New York NY 10022 212-652-9100
Web: www.edgewood.com

EDS Manufacturing Inc 765 N Target Range Rd .... Nogales AZ 85621 520-287-9711
Web: www.edsmanufacturing.com

Effective Training Inc 14143 Farmington Rd .... Livonia MI 48154 734-744-5940
Web: www.etinews.com

eHDL Inc 3106 Commerce Pkwy .... Miramar FL 33025 954-331-6500
Web: www.ehdl.com

Ehlers & Assoc Inc 3060 Centre Pointe Dr .... Roseville MN 55113 651-697-8500
TF: 800-552-1171 ■ *Web:* www.ehlers-inc.com

ElectroChem Inc 400 W Cummings Pk .... Woburn MA 01801 781-938-5300
Web: www.fuelcell.com

Eltrex Industries 65 Sullivan St .... Rochester NY 14605 585-454-6100

EMC Corp Documentum Div
6801 Koll Ctr Pkwy .... Pleasanton CA 94566 925-600-6800 600-6850
Web: www.emc.com

Employees Only Inc
3256 University Dr Ste 25 .... Auburn Hills MI 48326 248-276-0950
Web: www.employeesonly.net

Encore Consumer Capital
111 Pine St Ste 1825 .... San Francisco CA 94111 415-296-9850
Web: www.encoreconsumercapital.com

Energy & Resource Solutions Inc
120 Water St Ste 350 .... North Andover MA 01845 978-521-2550
Web: www.ers-inc.com

Energy Automation Systems Inc
145 Anderson Ln .... Hendersonville TN 37075 615-822-7250
Web: www.energyautomation.com

EnerVision Inc
4170 Ashford Dunwoody Rd Ste 550 .... Atlanta GA 30319 678-510-2900
TF: 888-999-8840 ■ *Web:* www.enervision-inc.com

	City	State	Zip	Phone	Fax
England Logistics Inc 1325 South 4700 West; TF: 800-848-7810 ■ Web: www.englandlogistics.com	Salt Lake City	UT	84104	801-656-4500	
EnSolve Biosystems Inc 5805 Departure Dr Ste B; Web: www.ensolve.com	Raleigh	NC	27616	919-954-6196	
Envision Group 990 W 190th St Ste 220; Web: www.envisiongroup.com	Torrance	CA	90502	310-523-2000	
EP Wealth Advisors Inc 21515 Hawthorne Blvd Ste 1200; Web: www.epwealth.com	Torrance	CA	90503	310-543-4559	
EQUIS Hospitality Management LLC 1034 S Brentwood Blvd Ste 2020; Web: www.equishospitality.com	St. Louis	MO	63117	314-932-3200	
Equity Communications LLC 1512 Grand Ave Ste 200; Web: www.equitycommunications.com	Santa Barbara	CA	93103	805-897-1880	
Eskridge & Assocs 1609 Wildwood Dr; Web: www.eskridgeassociates.com	Round Rock	TX	78681	512-244-7023	
Essex Radez LLC 440 S LaSalle St Ste 1111; Web: www.essexradez.com	Chicago	IL	60605	312-212-1815	
eStrategy Solutions Inc 6601 Vaught Ranch Rd Ste 100; Web: www.esslearning.com	Austin	TX	78730	512-451-0100	
Ethis Communications Inc 80 Maiden Ln Ste 2201; Web: www.ethiscommunications.com	New York	NY	10038	212-791-1440	
Eubel Brady & Suttman Asset Management Inc 10100 Innovation Dr Ste 410; Web: www.ebs-asset.com	Dayton	OH	45342	937-291-1223	
Euclid Discoveries LLC 30 Monument Sq Ste 212; Web: www.eucliddiscoveries.com	Concord	MA	01742	978-369-8303	
Evensky & Katz LLC 2333 Ponce De Leon Blvd Ph Ste 1100; Web: www.evensky.com	Coral Gables	FL	33134	305-448-8882	
ExaDigm Inc 2871 Pullman St; TF: 800-933-0064 ■ Web: www.exadigm.com	Santa Ana	CA	92705	949-486-0320	
Extra Mile Mktg Inc 12600 SE 38th St Ste 205; Web: www.extramilemarketing.com	Bellevue	WA	98006	425-746-1572	
Fagen Inc 501 W Hwy 212 PO Box 159; Web: www.fageninc.com	Granite Falls	MN	56241	320-564-3324	
Fairview Advisors LLC 3838 Tamiami Trl N Ste 416; Web: www.fairviewadvisors.com	Naples	FL	34103	239-213-1107	
Fairway Consulting Group 300 Merrick Rd Ste 404; Web: fcgsearch.com/	Lynbrook	NY	11563	516-596-2800	
Far Hills Group LLC 1180 Ave Of The Americas 18th Fl; Web: www.farhills.com	New York	NY	10036	212-840-7779	
Farrar Scientific LLC 30765 State Rt 7; Web: www.farrarscientific.com	Marietta	OH	45750	740-374-8300	
Faulk & Winkler LLC 6811 Jefferson Hwy; TF: 800-927-6811	Baton Rouge	LA	70806	225-927-6811	
FCG Advisors LLC One Main St Ste 202; Web: www.fcgadvisors.com	Chatham	NJ	07928	973-635-7374	
FemmePharma Inc 37 W Ave Second Fl; Web: www.femmepharma.com	Wayne	PA	19087	610-995-0801	
Ferrell Capital Management LLC 4 Greenwich Office Park; Web: www.ferrellcapital.com	Greenwich	CT	06831	203-862-9500	
Financial Advisory Service Inc 4747 W 135th St Ste 100; Web: www.faskc.com	Leawood	KS	66224	913-239-2300	
Financial Management Professionals Inc 6034 W Courtyard Dr Ste 380; Web: www.fmprofessionals.com	Austin	TX	78730	512-329-5174	
Fine Furniture Design & Mktg LLC 1107 N Main St; Web: www.ffdm.com	High Point	NC	27262	336-883-9918	
Fingerpaint Mktg Inc 395 Broadway; Web: fingerpaintmarketing.com	Saratoga Springs	NY	12866	518-693-6960	
FinSer Corp One Alamo Ctr 106 S St Mary'S St Ste 600; Web: www.finser.com	San Antonio	TX	78205	210-224-5492	
First Clinical Research LLC 2249 Sutter St; Web: www.firstclinical.com	San Francisco	CA	94115	650-465-0119	
First Command Financial Services Inc One FirstComm Plz; Web: www.firstcommand.com	Fort Worth	TX	76109	817-731-8621	
First Financial Equity Corp 7373 N Scottsdale Rd Ste D-120; Web: ffec.com	Scottsdale	AZ	85253	480-951-0079	
First Manhattan Consulting Group 90 Pk Ave 18th Fl; Web: www.fmcg.com	New York	NY	10016	212-557-0500	338-9296
First Niagara RISK Management 1215 Manor Dr; TF: 800-421-0004 ■ Web: www.firstniagara.com	Mechanicsburg	PA	17055	717-795-8666	
Fisher & Arnold Inc 9180 Crestwyn Hills Dr; TF: 888-583-9724 ■ Web: www.fisherarnold.com	Memphis	TN	38125	901-748-1811	
Fisher International Inc 50 Water St; Web: www.fisheri.com	Norwalk	CT	06854	203-854-5390	854-5070
Flex-Pay Business Services Inc 723 Coliseum Dr Ste 200; TF: 800-457-2143 ■ Web: www.flex-pay.com	Winston-Salem	NC	27106	336-773-0128	
FlexEnergy Inc 30 New Hampshire Ave; Web: www.flexenergy.com	Portsmouth	NH	03801	603-430-7000	
Fluor Corp 6700 Las Colinas Blvd; TF: 800-405-6637 ■ Web: www.fluor.com	Irving	TX	75039	469-398-7000	398-7255
FMI Corp 5171 Glenwood Ave Ste 200; TF General: 800-669-1364 ■ Web: www.fminet.com	Raleigh	NC	27612	919-787-8400	785-9320
Food Management Associates Inc 22349 La Palma Ave Ste 115; Web: www.foodmgt.com	Yorba Linda	CA	92887	714-694-2828	
Foodbuy LLC 1105 Lakewood Pkwy; Web: www.foodbuy.com	Alpharetta	GA	30009	678-256-8000	
Franchoice Inc 7500 Flying Cloud Dr; TF: 877-396-4238 ■ Web: www.franchoice.com	Eden Prairie	MN	55344	952-345-8400	942-5793
Frazier & Deeter LLC 600 Peachtree St Ste 1900; Web: www.frazierdeeter.com	Atlanta	GA	30308	404-253-7500	
Front Runner Consulting LLC 6850 O'Bannon Bluff; TF: 877-328-3360 ■ Web: www.frontrunnerconsulting.com	Loveland	OH	45140	513-697-6850	
Fry Consultants 2100 Powers Ferry Rd Ste 125; Web: www.fryconsultants.com	Atlanta	GA	30339	770-226-8888	226-8899
FST Logistics Inc 2040 Atlas St; Web: www.fstlogistics.com	Columbus	OH	43228	614-529-7900	
Fulcrum International Ltd 280 Railroad Ave; Web: www.fulcrum-intl.com	Greenwich	CT	06830	203-869-8181	
Fulenwider Enterprises Inc 104 Mull St; Web: www.fulenwider.net	Morganton	NC	28655	828-437-8000	
Fusion Solutions Inc 16901 N Dallas Pkwy Ste 114; TF: 888-817-1951 ■ Web: www.fusionsolutionsinc.com	Dallas	TX	75001	972-764-1708	
GA Repple & Co 101 Normandy Rd; Web: www.garepple.com	Casselberry	FL	32707	407-339-9090	
Galtere Ltd 515 Madison Ave 35th Fl; Web: www.galtere.com	New York	NY	10022	212-598-1837	
Garcia & Assoc Inc One Saunders Ave; Web: www.garciaandassociates.com	San Anselmo	CA	94960	415-458-5803	
Gargiulo Inc 15000 Old 41 N; Web: www.gargiulo.com	Naples	FL	34110	239-597-3131	
Garnett & Helfrich Capital 1200 Park Pl Ste 330; Web: www.garnetthelfrich.com	San Mateo	CA	94403	650-234-4200	
Gateway Communications Services 220 Log Canoe Cir; Web: www.gatewaycsi.com	Stevensville	MD	21666	410-670-4399	
Gavin de Becker & Assoc 11684 Ventura Blvd Ste 440; Web: www.gavindebecker.com	Studio City	CA	91604	818-505-0177	506-0426
Genesys Venture Inc 4-1250 Waverley St; Web: www.genesysventure.com	Winnipeg	MB	R3T6C6	204-487-2328	
Geneva Capital LLC 522 Broadway St Ste 4; TF: 800-408-9352 ■ Web: www.gogenevacapital.com	Alexandria	MN	56308	800-408-9352	
Geneva Venture Group 101 California St Ste 2710; Web: www.genevagroup.com	San Francisco	CA	94111	415-433-4646	
Genex Services Inc 440 E Swedesford Rd Ste 1000; TF: 888-464-3639 ■ Web: www.genexservices.com	Wayne	PA	19087	610-964-5100	964-1919
Geocom Inc 366 Madison Ave 10th Fl; Web: www.geocom-inc.com	New York	NY	10017	212-949-0712	
GEOSYS Inc 3030 Harbor Ln Ste 202; Web: www.geosys.com	Plymouth	MN	55447	763-557-0092	
Gerken Capital Associates 110 Tiburon Blvd Ste 5; Web: gerkencapital.com	Mill Valley	CA	94941	415-383-1464	
GESD Capital Partners 221 Main St Ste 1450; Web: www.gesd.net	San Francisco	CA	94105	415-477-8200	
Ginac Group Inc, The 8834 N Capital of Texas Hwy Ste 200	Austin	TX	78759	512-943-6801	
Global Change Assoc Inc 2576 Broadway; Web: www.global-change.com	New York	NY	10025	212-316-0223	
Global Equity Capital LLC 6260 Lookout Rd; Web: www.globalequitycap.com	Boulder	CO	80301	303-531-1000	
Global Experiences Inc 209 W St; Web: www.globalexperiences.com	Annapolis	MD	21401	410-267-7306	
Global Inventures Inc 2400 Camino Ramon Bishop Ranch 6 Ste 375; Web: www.inventures.com	San Ramon	CA	94583	925-275-6690	
Global Mktg Group Worldwide LLC 16-00 Rt 208; Web: www.gmgww.com	Fair Lawn	NJ	07410	201-475-7755	
Global Public Affairs Inc 50 O'Connor St Ste 901; Web: globalpublicaffairs.ca	Ottawa	ON	K1P6L2	613-782-2336	
Global SATCOM Technology Inc 9141 Arbuckle Dr; Web: www.globalsatcom.com	Gaithersburg	MD	20877	301-963-0088	
Global Stock Trends Corp One Park Place 621 NW 53rd St Ste 240; Web: www.globalstocktrends.com	Boca Raton	FL	33487	401-885-4606	
Global Strategy Group LLC 895 Broadway Fifth Fl; Web: www.globalstrategygroup.com	New York	NY	10003	212-260-8813	
Global Ventures Inc 2106 145th Ave SE; Web: www.globalventuresinc.com	Bellevue	WA	98007	206-292-1428	
GlobalPhone Corp 137 N Washington St; Web: www.gphone.com	Falls Church	VA	22046	703-533-2122	
Globe Mktg Services Inc 133 NW 122nd St; Web: globeontheweb.com	Oklahoma City	OK	73114	405-755-8282	
Globe Tax Services Inc 90 Broad St 16th Fl; Web: www.globetax.com	New York	NY	10004	212-747-9100	
Goldin Associates LLC 350 Fifth Ave The Empire State Bldg Ste 1810; Web: www.goldinllc.com	New York	NY	10118	212-593-2255	
Goodman Networks Inc 6400 International Ste 1000; Web: www.goodmannetworks.com	Plano	TX	75093	972-406-9692	406-9291

Phone Fax

Gordon L Seaman Inc 29 Old Dock Rd Yaphank NY 11980 631-567-8000
Web: www.gordonlseaman.com

Gradient Corp 20 University Rd Cambridge MA 02138 617-395-5000 395-5001
Web: www.gradientcorp.com

Grande Communications Networks LLC
401 Carlson Cir San Marcos TX 78666 512-878-4000
Web: mygrande.com

Grant Thornton LLP 175 W Jackson Blvd 20th Fl Chicago IL 60604 312-856-0200 602-8099
Web: www.grantthornton.com

Great Plains Tribal Chairmen's Health Board
1770 Rand Rd Rapid City SD 57702 605-721-1922
Web: www.aatchb.org

Great Point Partners LLC
165 Mason St Third Fl Greenwich CT 06830 203-971-3300
Web: www.greatpointpartnersllc.com

Greater Ny Dental Meeting
518 Fifth Ave Fl 3 New York NY 10036 212-398-6922
Web: www.gnydm.com

Greek Peak Mountain Resort 2000 NYS Rt 392 Cortland NY 13045 607-835-6300
Web: www.greekpeak.net

Greenwich Assoc LLC 6 High Ridge Pk Stamford CT 06905 203-629-1200 629-1229
TF: 800-704-1027 ■ *Web:* www.greenwich.com

GREYHAWK North America LLC
260 Crossways Park Dr Woodbury NY 11797 516-921-1900
Web: www.greyhawk.com

Gries Financial LLC
1801 E Ninth St Ste 1600 Cleveland OH 44114 216-861-1148
Web: www.gries.com

Groton Partners LLC 640 Fifth Ave Ste 1700 New York NY 10019 212-430-1800
Web: www.grotonpartners.com

Groupe Sante Sedna Inc
1010 Sherbrooke W Ste 2405 Montreal QC H3A2R7 514-844-8760
Web: www.groupesedna.ca

GrowthForce LLC 800 Rockmead Ste 200 Kingwood TX 77339 281-358-2007
Web: growthforce.com/

Guttman Development Strategies Inc
400 Valley Rd Ste 103 Mt. Arlington NJ 07856 973-770-7177
Web: www.guttmandev.com

GW & Wade LLC 93 Worcester St Wellesley MA 02481 781-239-1188
Web: www.gwwade.com

Haitian American Community Development
181 NE 82 St Miami FL 33138 305-759-2542
Web: www.littlehaitihousing.org

Harrison Scott Publications Inc
Five Marine View Plz Ste 400 Hoboken NJ 07030 201-659-1700
Web: www.hspnews.com

Hart Hotels Inc 617 Dingens St Buffalo NY 14206 716-893-6551
Web: www.harthotels.com

Hatch Ltd 2800 Speakman Dr Mississauga ON L5K2R7 905-855-7600 855-8270
Web: www.hatch.ca

Hay Group Inc 1650 Arch St Ste 2300 Philadelphia PA 19107 215-861-2000 861-2111
TF: 800-716-4429 ■ *Web:* www.haygroup.com

Hazmat Environmental Group Inc
60 Commerce Dr Buffalo NY 14218 716-827-7200 827-7217
Web: www.hazmatinc.com

Health Dimensions Group
4400 Baker Rd Ste 100 Minneapolis MN 55343 763-537-5700
Web: www.healthdimensionsgroup.com

Health Integrated Inc 10008 N Dale Mabry Hwy Tampa FL 33618 813-388-4000
Web: www.healthintegrated.com

Health Management Services Inc
9100 Southwest Fwy Ste 114 Houston TX 77074 713-541-2727
Web: www.hmssleep.com

Healthcare Analytics 125-310 Village Blvd Princeton NJ 08540 609-452-2488 452-2668
Web: www.gbshealthcareanalytics.com

Healthcasts Meded 55 E Ninth St Apt 7I New York NY 10003 212-533-1111
Web: www.healthcastsmeded.com

Healthforce Partners Inc
18323 Bothell Everett Hwy Bothell WA 98012 425-806-5700 806-5701
TF: 877-437-2497 ■ *Web:* www.healthforcepartners.com

HealthInsight Inc
756 E Winchester St Ste 200 Salt Lake City UT 84107 801-892-0155
Web: www.healthinsight.org

Healthy Companies International Inc
2101 Wilson Blvd Ste 1002 Arlington VA 22201 703-351-9901
Web: healthycompanies.com

Hefren - Tillotson Inc 308 Seventh Ave Pittsburgh PA 15222 412-434-0990
Web: www.hefren.com

Helix Enterprises Inc 4300 Forbes Blvd Ste 140 Lanham MD 20706 301-429-0880
Web: helixenterprises.com

HELIX Environmental Planning Inc
7578 El Cajon Blvd Ste 200 La Mesa CA 91942 619-462-1515
Web: www.helixepi.com

Herbal Magic Inc 1867 Yonge St Ste 700 Toronto ON M4S1Y5 416-487-7009
Web: www.herbalmagic.ca

Heritage Financial Consultants LLC
307 International Cir Ste 390 Hunt Valley MD 21030 410-785-0033
Web: heritageconsultants.com

Herman Weissker Inc 1645 Brown Ave Riverside CA 92509 951-826-8800
Web: www.hermanweissker.com

Hicaps Inc 600 N Regional Rd Greensboro NC 27409 336-665-1234
Web: www.hicaps.com

High Ridge Partners 140 S Dearborn Ste 420 Chicago IL 60603 312-456-5636
Web: www.high-ridge.com

HighVista Strategies LLC
200 Clarendon St John Hancock Tower 50th Fl Boston MA 02116 617-406-6500
Web: www.highvistastrategies.com

Homrich & Berg Inc 3060 Peachtree Rd Ste 830 Atlanta GA 30305 404-264-1400
Web: www.homrichberg.com

Horan Capital Management LLC
230 Schilling Cir Ste 234 Hunt Valley MD 21031 410-494-4380
Web: www.horancm.com

Human Resource Development Press Inc
22 Amherst Rd Amherst MA 01002 413-253-3488
TF: 800-822-2801 ■ *Web:* www.hrdpressonline.com

Huntington Hotel Group LLC
105 Decker Ct Ste 500 Irving TX 75062 972-510-1200
Web: www.huntingtonhotelgroup.com

I-Behavior Inc 2051 Dogwood St Ste 220 Louisville CO 80027 303-228-5000
Web: www.i-behavior.com

IBCC Industries Inc 3200 S Third St Milwaukee WI 53207 414-486-5460
Web: www.ibccind.com

IBT Enterprises LLC
1770 Indian Trail Rd Ste 300 Norcross GA 30093 770-381-2023 381-2123
TF: 877-242-8428 ■ *Web:* www.ibtenterprises.com

ICF International Inc 9300 Lee Hwy Fairfax VA 22031 703-934-3000 934-3740
NASDAQ: ICFI ■ *Web:* www.icfi.com

Idaho Innovation Center Inc
2300 N Yellowstone Hwy Ste 100 Idaho Falls ID 83401 208-523-1026
Web: www.iictr.com

Ideal Innovations Inc
950 N Glebe Rd Ste 800 Arlington VA 22203 703-528-9101 528-1913
Web: www.idealinnovations.com

In-Store Broadcasting Network LLC
175 S Main St Ste 220 Salt Lake City UT 84111 801-596-9344
Web: instoreaudionetwork.com/

Inca Engineers Inc 400 112th Ave NE Ste 400 Bellevue WA 98004 425-635-1000 635-1150
TF: 800-825-4622 ■ *Web:* www.incainc.com

Independent Equipment Company
2471 McMullen Booth Rd Ste 309 Clearwater FL 33759 727-796-7733
Web: www.iecvalue.com

Independents Service Co 2710 Market St Hannibal MO 63401 573-221-4615
Web: www.isco.net

Indiana Health Information Exchange Inc
846 N Senate Ave Ste 110 Indianapolis IN 46202 317-644-1750
Web: www.ihie.org

Infodata Corp 181 Waukegan Rd Ste 300 Northfield IL 60093 847-486-0000 386-7166
Web: www.infodatacorp.com

Informa Research Services Inc
26565 Agoura Rd Ste 300 Calabasas CA 91302 818-880-8877
Web: www.informars.com

Initiative for a Competitive Inner City
200 High St Fl 3 Boston MA 02110 617-292-2363
Web: www.icic.org

Innovation Capital LLC
222 N Sepulveda Blvd Ste 1300 El Segundo CA 90245 310-335-9333
Web: www.innovation-capital.com

Innovative Resources Consultant Group Inc
One Pk Plz Ste 600 Irvine CA 92614 949-252-0590 252-0592
Web: www.ircginc.com

Insight Environmental Consultants Inc
5500 Ming Ave Ste 360 Bakersfield CA 93309 661-282-2200
Web: www.insenv.com

Integrated Decisions & Systems Inc
8500 Normandale Lk Blvd Ste 1200 Minneapolis MN 55437 952-698-4200 698-4299
Web: www.ideas.com

Integrated Health Management Services LLC
2632 E Thomas Rd Ste 103 Phoenix AZ 85016 602-522-3240
Web: www.ihmsllc.com

Integrated Mktg Services Inc
279 Wall St Research Pk Princeton NJ 08540 609-683-9055
Web: www.imsworld.com

Integrated Title Insurance Services LLC
6925 South Union Park Ctr Ste 160 Midvale UT 84047 801-307-0160
Web: www.itstitle.com

Integrity Interactive Corp
51 Sawyer Rd Ste 510 Waltham MA 02453 781-891-9700

Intellex Consulting Services Inc
Four Apple Row Kennett Square PA 19348 610-388-3939
Web: www.intellexinc.com

Intellimed International Corp
1825 E Northern Ave Ste 175 Phoenix AZ 85020 602-230-0333
Web: www.intellimed.com

Interaction Assoc 625 Mt Auburn St Cambridge MA 02138 617-234-2700 234-2727
Web: www.interactionassociates.com

Interactive Motion Technologies Inc
80 Coolidge Hill Rd Watertown MA 02472 617-926-4800
Web: www.interactive-motion.com

Investment Management & Consulting Group
97A Exchange St Portland ME 04101 207-774-6552
Web: www.imcgrp.com

Investor Group Services LLC
855 Boylston St 10th Fl Boston MA 02116 617-371-4000
Web: www.igsboston.com

IQ BackOffice LLC
2121 Rosecrans Ave Ste 3350 El Segundo CA 90245 310-322-2868
Web: www.iqbackoffice.com

Iridian Asset Management LLC 276 Post Rd W Westport CT 06880 203-341-9000
Web: www.iridian.com

Irvine Technology Corp
201 E Sandpointe Ave Ste 300 Santa Ana CA 92707 866-322-4482 434-8869*
**Fax Area Code: 714* ■ *TF:* 866-322-4482 ■ *Web:* www.irvinetechcorp.com

IVG Energy Ltd 20 E Greenway Pl Ste 400 Houston TX 77046 713-554-3700
Web: www.ivgenergy.com

iWay Software Two Penn Plz New York NY 10121 212-736-4433 967-6406
TF: 800-736-6130 ■ *Web:* www.informationbuilders.com

iXP Corp
Princeton Forrestal Village 103 Main St Princeton NJ 08540 609-759-5100
Web: www.ixpcorp.com

Jadoo Power Systems Inc
181 Blue Ravine Rd Ste 120 Folsom CA 95630 916-608-9044
Web: www.jadoopower.com

Janson Media Inc 88 Semmens Rd Harrington Park NJ 07640 845-359-8488
Web: www.janson.com

Company	City	State	ZIP	Phone	Fax
JANUS Research Group Inc 600 Ponder Pl Dr *Web:* janusresearch.com	Evans	GA	30809	706-364-9100	
Jay Cashman Inc 549 S St *Web:* www.jaycashman.com	Quincy	MA	02269	617-890-0600	
JB&A Inc 5203 Leesburg Pk Ste 1401 *Web:* www.jb-a-inc.com	Falls Church	VA	22041	703-399-2850	
JBCStyle Inc 108 W 39th St Seventh Fl *Web:* www.jbcstyle.com	New York	NY	10018	212-355-3197	
Jeff Zell Consultants Inc 1031 Fourth Ave *Web:* www.jeffzell.com	Coraopolis	PA	15108	412-262-2022	
Jeffrey Slocum & Assoc Inc 43 Main St S E Ste 148 *Web:* www.jslocum.com	Minneapolis	MN	55414	612-338-7020	
Jet Support Services Inc 180 N Stetson 29th Fl *Web:* www.jetsupport.com	Chicago	IL	60601	312-644-4444	
JH Technology Inc 5107 Lena Rd Ste 9 *Web:* www.jhtechnology.com	Bradenton	FL	34211	941-927-0300	
JJDS Environmental Inc 40 Woodview Dr *Web:* www.jjdsenvironmental.com	Doylestown	PA	18901	267-880-2325	
JM Search & Company Inc 1045 First Ave Ste 110 *Web:* www.jmsearch.com	King Of Prussia	PA	19406	610-964-0200	
John Snow Inc 44 Farnsworth St *Web:* www.jsi.com	Boston	MA	02210	617-482-9485	482-0617
Johnson Rice & Company LLC 639 Loyola Ave Ste 2775 *Web:* www.jrco.com	New Orleans	LA	70113	504-525-3767	
Journey Communications 418 Fourth St Ne *Web:* www.journeygroup.com	Charlottesville	VA	22902	434-961-2500	
Julie Morgenstern Enterprises LLC 850 Seventh Ave *Web:* www.juliemorgenstern.com	New York	NY	10019	212-586-8084	544-0755
Kaiser Assoc 1615 L St NW 13th Fl *Web:* www.kaiserassociates.com	Washington	DC	20036	202-454-2000	454-2001
KAMedData.com Inc 4400 Bayou Blvd Ste 12 *Web:* www.kameddata.com	Pensacola	FL	32503	850-477-2475	
Kamsky Assoc Inc 563 Park Ave *Web:* www.kamsky.com	New York	NY	10065	212-317-1116	
Kaya Assoc Inc 101 Quality Cir Ste 120 *Web:* www.kayacorp.com	Huntsville	AL	35806	256-382-8084	382-8089
KCB Management 117 E Colorado Blvd Ste 400 *Web:* www.kcbm.com	Pasadena	CA	91105	626-356-0944	
Keel Point Advisors LLC 8065 Leesburg Pk Ste 300 *Web:* www.keelpoint.com	Vienna	VA	22182	703-807-2020	
Ken Blanchard Companies Inc, The 125 State Pl *Web:* www.kenblanchard.com	Escondido	CA	92029	760-839-8070	
Kepner-Tregoe Inc PO Box 704 *TF:* 800-537-6378 ■ *Web:* www.kepner-tregoe.com	Princeton	NJ	08542	609-921-2806	497-0130
Kessler & Assoc Inc 31800 NW Hwy *Web:* www.kesslercpa.com	Farmington Hills	MI	48334	248-855-4224	855-4405
Keystone Equities Group, The 1003 B Egypt Rd *TF:* 800-715-9905 ■ *Web:* www.keystoneequities.com	Oaks	PA	19456	610-415-6300	
Keystone Fruit Marketing Inc 11 N Carlisle St Ste 102 PO Box 189 *TF:* 800-779-1156 ■ *Web:* www.keystonefruit.com	Greencastle	PA	17225	717-597-2112	597-4096
Kimley-Horn & Associates Inc 3001 Weston Pkwy *Web:* www.kimley-horn.com	Cary	NC	27513	919-677-2000	
King Chapman & Broussard Consulting Group Inc 3355 W Albama St Ste 1255 *Web:* www.kcbcg.com	Houston	TX	77098	713-223-7233	223-7260
Kinsight LLC 600 University Park Pl Ste 501 *Web:* www.kinsight.com	Birmingham	AL	35209	205-871-3334	
Kipp Foundation 135 Main St Ste 1700 *TF:* 866-345-5477 ■ *Web:* www.kipp.org	San Francisco	CA	94105	415-399-1556	
Kline & Company Inc 150 Clove Rd Seventh Fl *TF:* 800-290-5214 ■ *Web:* www.klinegroup.com	Little Falls	NJ	07424	973-435-6262	435-6291
Kmea 964 Fifth Ave *Web:* www.kmea.net	San Diego	CA	92101	619-342-7377	
Knight Electronics Inc 10557 Metric Dr *TF:* 800-323-2439 ■ *Web:* www.orionfans.com	Dallas	TX	75243	214-340-0265	
Knight Facilities Management Inc 5360 Hampton Pl *Web:* www.knightfm.com	Saginaw	MI	48604	989-793-8820	399-9096
Knowledge Anywhere Inc 3015 112th Ave NE Ste 210 *Web:* www.knowledgeanywhere.com	Bellevue	WA	98004	425-454-4454	
KnowledgeBank Inc 1481 Chain Bridge Rd Ste 201 *Web:* www.knowledgebank.us.com	Mclean	VA	22101	703-448-8070	
Kozeny-Wagner Inc 951 W Outer Rd *Web:* www.kozenywagner.com	Arnold	MO	63010	636-296-2012	
KPMG LLP 333 Base St Ste 4600 *Web:* www.kpmg.com	Toronto	ON	M5H2S5	416-777-8500	777-8818
KPMG LLP US Three Chestnut Ridge Rd *Web:* www.kpmg.com	Montvale	NJ	07645	201-307-7000	307-7575
Kraus Manning Inc 7233 Lk Ellenor Dr Ste 100 *Web:* www.kraus-manning.com	Orlando	FL	32809	407-251-0085	
Kroll Inc 600 Third Ave *Web:* www.kroll.com	New York	NY	10016	212-593-1000	593-2631
Krueger-Gilbert Health Physics Inc 1118 Baldwin Mll Rd PO Box 410 *Web:* kruegergilbert.com	Jarrettsville	MD	21084	410-692-9806	
Kurt Salmon Assoc Inc 1355 Peachtree St NE Ste 900 *Web:* www.kurtsalmon.com	Atlanta	GA	30309	404-892-0321	898-9590
L E Peabody & Assoc Inc 1501 Duke St Ste 200 *Web:* www.lepeabody.com	Alexandria	VA	22314	703-836-0100	836-0285
La Jolla Sports Club Inc 7825 Fay Ave *Web:* www.lajollasportsclub.com	La Jolla	CA	92037	858-456-2595	
Lachman Consultant Services Inc 1600 Stewart Ave Ste 604 *Web:* www.lachmanconsultants.com	Westbury	NY	11590	516-222-6222	
Lamont Engineers 548 Main St *TF:* 800-882-9721 ■ *Web:* www.lamontengineers.com	Cobleskill	NY	12043	518-234-4028	234-4613
Lang Asset Management Inc 171 Village Pkwy NE Bldg 8A Ste 1080 *Web:* www.langasset.com	Marietta	GA	30067	404-256-4100	256-1473
Larrabee Ventures Inc 15165 Ventura Blvd Ste 450 *Web:* www.larrabeeventures.com	Sherman Oaks	CA	91403	818-789-6020	
Latigo Partners LP 450 Park Ave Ste1200 *Web:* www.latigopartners.com	New York	NY	10022	212-754-1610	
Lavista Assoc Inc 3105 Northwoods Pl *Web:* www.lavista.com	Norcross	GA	30071	770-448-6400	
Leehar Distributors Inc 701 Emerson Rd Ste 301 *Web:* www.ldirx.com	Creve Coeur	MO	63141	314-652-3121	
Legacy Capital LLC 433 Metairie Rd Ste 405 *Web:* legacycapital.com	Metairie	LA	70005	504-837-3450	
Legacy Financial Partners LLC 1912 21st Ave S *Web:* www.legacy-fp.com	Nashville	TN	37212	615-292-5351	
Legend Group Inc, The 4600 E Park Dr Ste 300 *Web:* www.legendgroup.com	Palm Beach Gardens	FL	33410	561-694-0110	
LEK Consulting 28 State St 16th Fl *TF:* 800-929-4535 ■ *Web:* www.lek.com	Boston	MA	02109	617-951-9500	951-9392
Leopard Communications Inc 555 17th St Ste 300 *Web:* www.leopard.com	Denver	CO	80202	303-527-2900	530-3480
Leuthold Weeden Capital Management LLC 33 S Sixth St Ste 4600 *Web:* www.leutholdfunds.com	Minneapolis	MN	55402	612-332-9141	
Lewin Group 3130 Fairview Pk Dr Ste 800 *TF:* 877-227-5042 ■ *Web:* www.lewin.com	Falls Church	VA	22042	703-269-5500	269-5501
Lewtan Technologies Inc 410 Totten Pond Rd 4th Fl *Web:* www.lewtan.com	Waltham	MA	02451	781-895-9800	890-3684
Lexipol LLC 6B Liberty Ste 200 *Web:* www.lexipol.com	Aliso Viejo	CA	92656	949-484-4444	
LifePlans Inc 51 Sawyer Rd Ste 340 *Web:* www.lifeplansinc.com	Waltham	MA	02453	781-893-7600	647-3552
LifeSafe Services LLC 5971 Powers Ave Ste 108 *Web:* www.lifesafeservices.com	Jacksonville	FL	32217	904-730-4800	
Limited Management 1230 Pottstown Pike Ste 6 *Web:* www.ltdmgmt.com	Glenmoore	PA	19343	610-330-2727	458-8039
Line Systems Inc 1645 W Chester Pk *Web:* www.linesystems.com	West Chester	PA	19382	610-355-9700	
Liquidhub Inc 500 E Swedesford Rd Ste 300 *Web:* www.liquidhub.com	Wayne	PA	19087	484-654-1400	654-1401
Liquidia Technologies Inc 419 Davis Dr Ste 100 *Web:* www.liquidia.com	Morrisville	NC	27560	919-328-4400	
Livingstone Partners LLC 443 N Clark Ste 200 *Web:* www.livingstonepartners.com	Chicago	IL	60654	312-670-5900	
Lochridge Group 420 Boylston St *Web:* www.lochridge.com	Boston	MA	02116	617-267-5959	267-8438
Lockwood International Inc 10203 Wallisville Rd *Web:* www.lockwoodint.com	Houston	TX	77013	713-675-8186	675-2733
Loftus Engineering Inc 233 S Mccrea St Ste 700 *Web:* www.applied-e-s.com	Indianapolis	IN	46225	317-352-5822	
Logical Automation Inc 1011 Alcon St *Web:* www.logicalautomation.com	Pittsburgh	PA	15220	412-444-0400	
Logile Inc 1333 Corporate Dr Ste 310 *Web:* www.logile.com	Irving	TX	75038	972-550-6000	
Logisticz 10400 Eaton Pl Ste 315 *Web:* www.decisionanalysis.net	Fairfax	VA	22030	703-691-0380	
Long International 10029 Whistling Elk Dr *Web:* www.long-intl.com	Littleton	CO	80127	303-972-2443	972-6980
Lordi Consulting LLC 1900 Market St Ste 805 *Web:* www.lordiconsulting.com	Philadelphia	PA	19103	215-568-2300	
Loring Ward International Ltd 3055 Olin Ave Ste 2000 *Web:* www.loringward.com	San Jose	CA	95128	408-260-3100	
Lucas Engineering & Management Services Inc 1201 Jadwin Ave Ste 102 *Web:* www.lucasinc.com	Richland	WA	99352	509-942-1080	
Lucidity Consulting Group LP 8605 Freeport Pkwy Ste 150 **Fax Area Code:* 972 ■ *Web:* www.luciditycg.com	Irving	TX	75063	214-451-2500	608-4901*
Lynda.com Inc 6410 Via Real *TF:* 888-335-9632 ■ *Web:* www.lynda.com	Carpinteria	CA	93013	805-477-3900	
M Floyd John & Assoc Inc (JMFA) 125 N Burnett Dr **Fax Area Code:* 281 ■ *TF:* 800-809-2307 ■ *Web:* www.jmfa.com	Baytown	TX	77520	800-809-2307	424-8864*
M&N Trading LLC 952 W Lake St *Web:* www.mntrading.com	Chicago	IL	60607	312-568-5000	568-5010
Mac Pizza Management Inc 3104 Texas Ave S *Web:* www.macpizzamgmt.com	College Station	TX	77845	979-695-9912	695-0553
Macadam Capital Partners 4800 SW Macadam Ave Ste 311 *Web:* www.macadamcapital.com	Portland	OR	97239	503-225-0889	
MacMillin Company Inc, The 17 Elm St *Web:* www.macmillin.com	Keene	NH	03431	603-352-3070	

Phone Fax

Mahoney Assoc Inc
2455 E Sunrise Blvd Ste 300 .... Fort Lauderdale FL 33304 954-564-4300
Web: www.mahoneyandassociates.com

Maine Pointe LLC 470 Atlantic Ave Fourth Fl .... Boston MA 02210 617-273-8450
Web: www.mainepointe.com

Manchester Capital Management LLC
3657 Main St PO Box 416 .... Manchester VT 05254 802-362-4410
Web: www.mcmllc.com

Manex Resource Group Inc
1100 - 1199 W Hastings St .... Vancouver BC V6E3T5 604-684-9384
Web: www.manexresourcegroup.com

Mariner Wealth Advisors
1 Giralda Farms Ste 130............................ Madison NJ 07940 973-984-3352
Web: www.brintoneaton.com

Market Metrics Inc 53 State St Ste 6.................. Boston MA 02109 617-376-0550
Web: www.marketmetrics.com

Marketing Werks Inc 130 E Randolph St.............. Chicago IL 60601 312-228-0800 228-0801
Web: www.marketingwerks.com

Mars & Co 124 Mason St .... Greenwich CT 06830 203-629-9292 629-9432
Web: www.marsandco.com

Marsh Berry & Company Inc 4420 Sherwin Rd...... Willoughby OH 44094 440-354-3230
TF: 800-426-2774 ■ *Web:* www.marshberry.com

Marshall & Stevens Inc
355 S Grand Ave Ste 1750 .... Los Angeles CA 90071 213-612-8000 612-8010
TF: 800-950-9588 ■ *Web:* www.marshall-stevens.com

Marshall Communications Corp
20098 Ashbrook Pl Ste 260 .... Ashburn VA 20147 571-223-2010
Web: www.marshallcomm.com

Marvin F Poer & Company Inc
12700 Hillcrest Rd Ste 125........................... Dallas TX 75230 972-770-1100
Web: www.mfpoer.com

Maryland Health Enterprises Inc
3300 N Ridge Rd Ste 390........................ Ellicott City MD 21043 410-750-7500
Web: www.lorienhealth.com

MAXIMUS Inc 11419 Sunset Hills Rd.................. Reston VA 20190 703-251-8500 251-8240
NYSE: MMS ■ *TF:* 800-629-4687 ■ *Web:* www.maximus.com

Mazars Harel Drouin LLP
215 Saint Jacques Bureau 1200..................... Montreal QC H2Y1M6 514-845-9253
Web: www.mazars.ca

Mazzone & Associates Inc
75 Fourteenth St NE Office Tower at the Four Seasons
Ste 2800... Atlanta GA 30309 404-931-8545
Web: www.globalmna.com

MBL International Corp
Four H Constitution Way............................ Woburn MA 01801 781-939-6964
TF: 800-200-5459 ■ *Web:* www.mblintl.com

McBee Assoc Inc 997 Old Eagle School Rd Ste 205....... Wayne PA 19087 610-964-9680 964-7987
TF: 800-767-6203 ■ *Web:* www.mcbeeassociates.com

McDonald Information Service Inc
215 14th St... Jersey City NJ 07310 201-659-2600
Web: www.callmis.com

McDonald Partners LLC 959 W St Clair Ave .... Cleveland OH 44113 216-912-0567
Web: www.mcdonald-partners.com

McKinsey & Company Inc 55 E 52nd St .... New York NY 10022 212-446-7000 446-8575
Web: www.mckinsey.com

McManus Wealth Building & Management
1930 17th St Ste 210 .... Boulder CO 80302 303-544-0355
Web: www.mcmanusandyou.com

MedExpert International Inc
1300 Hancock St .... Redwood City CA 94063 650-326-6000
Web: www.medexpert.com

Media Breakaway LLC
1490 W 121st Ave Ste 201 .... Westminster CO 80234 303-464-8164 464-8218
Web: www.mediabreakaway.com

Medical Communications Media Inc
54 Friends Ln Ste 125 .... Newtown PA 18940 267-364-0556
Web: cmecorner.com

Medical Doctor Assoc Inc
145 Technology Pkwy NW .... Norcross GA 30092 770-246-9191 246-0882
TF: 800-780-3500 ■ *Web:* www.mdainc.com

Medifit Corporate Services Inc
25 Hanover Rd .... Florham Park NJ 07932 973-593-9000 593-9007
TF: 888-723-6334 ■ *Web:* www.medifit.com

MediLodge Group, The 64500 Van Dyke........... Washington MI 48095 586-752-5008
Web: www.lcsnet.com

Medlink Corp
10393 San Diego Mission Rd Ste 120 .... San Diego CA 92108 619-640-4660
Web: www.medlink.com

Medweb California LLC 667 Folsom St.......... San Francisco CA 94107 415-541-9980
Web: www.medweb.com

MEMdata LLC 1601 Sebesta .... College Station TX 77845 979-695-1950 695-1954
Web: www.memdata.com

Mercer Inc 1166 Ave of the Americas................. New York NY 10036 212-345-5000 345-7414
Web: www.mercer.com

Metropolitan Professional Services Inc
39670 Mount Gilead Rd .... Leesburg VA 20175 703-737-7303
Web: www.mps-inc.com

MGT of America Inc 2123 Centre Pt Blvd .... Tallahassee FL 32308 850-386-3191 385-4501
Web: www.mgtamer.com

MilesTek Corp 1506 Interstate 35 W .... Denton TX 76207 940-484-9400
TF: 800-958-5173 ■ *Web:* www.milestek.com

Milestone Advisors LLC
6053 N College Ave .... Indianapolis IN 46220 317-581-1820
Web: www.milestoneadvisors.net

Milliman USA 1301 Fifth Ave Ste 3800................. Seattle WA 98101 206-624-7940 340-1380*
**Fax:* Mktg ■ *Web:* in.milliman.com

Mindlance Inc 80 River St Ste 4b .... Hoboken NJ 07030 201-386-5400 386-0553
Web: www.mindlance.com

Miratek Corp Inc 8201 Lockheed Dr Ste 218 .... El Paso TX 79925 915-772-2852 772-1764
Web: miratek.us

Mitsubishi Power Systems Inc
100 Colonial Ctr Pkwy .... Lake Mary FL 32746 407-688-6201 688-6481
TF: 800-445-9723 ■ *Web:* www.mpshq.com

MMC Group LLC Seven Clark Ct Ste 110 .... Kendall Park NJ 08824 732-821-6652
Web: www.careerxroads.com

Mobile Video Services Ltd
1620 I St NW Ste 1000 10th Fl.................... Washington DC 20006 202-331-8882
Web: www.mobilevideo.net

Modspace Financial Services Canada Ltd
2300 N Park Dr.................................. Brampton ON L6S6C6 905-794-3900
Web: www.modspace.ca

Mojix Inc 11075 Santa Monica Blvd Ste 350.......... Los Angeles CA 90025 310-479-9021
Web: www.mojix.com

Monarch Dental Corp 7989 Belt Line Rd Ste 90.......... Dallas TX 75248 972-702-9017
Web: www.monarchdental.com

Mongoose Atlantic Inc 61 Broadway Rm 3024........ New York NY 10006 212-968-0196
Web: www.mongooseatlantic.com

Monroe Financial Partners Inc
100 N Riverside Plz Ste 1620........................ Chicago IL 60606 312-327-2530 327-2540
TF: 800-766-5560 ■ *Web:* www.monroefp.com

Monsoon Capital LLC
4720 Montgomery Ln Ste 410 .... Bethesda MD 20814 301-222-8000
Web: www.monsooncapital.com

Morgan Creek Capital Management LLC
301 W Barbee Chapel Rd Ste 200.................. Chapel Hill NC 27517 919-933-4004
Web: www.morgancreekcap.com

Morley Company Inc 2717 Schust .... Saginaw MI 48603 989-791-2565 497-1874
TF: 800-323-1492 ■ *Web:* www.morleytravel.com

Morton Consulting LLC 4701 Cox Rd Ste 214 .... Glen Allen VA 23060 804-290-4272
Web: www.mortonconsulting.com

Motivano Inc 5810 W Cypress St Ste H................ Tampa FL 33607 866-664-4621
TF: 066-664-4621 ■ *Web:* www.motivano.com

Mount Hood Equity Partners LP
4800 SW Meadows Rd Ste 300 .... Lake Oswego OR 97035 503-639-0915

Mount Yale Capital Group LLC
8000 Norman Ctr Dr Ste 630 .... Minneapolis MN 55437 952-897-5390
Web: www.mtyale.com

MultiLingual Solutions Inc
11 N Washington St Ste 300........................ Rockville MD 20850 301-424-7444
Web: www.mlsolutions.com

Musselman Hotels LLC 2912 Eastpoint Pkwy .... Louisville KY 40223 502-426-3006
Web: www.musselmanhotels.com

Muzea Insider Consulting Services LLC
1575 Delucchi Ln Ste 204 .... Reno NV 89502 775-850-9480
TF: 866-642-6427 ■ *Web:* www.smartinsider.net

Mx Group, The 7020 High Grove Blvd .... Burr Ridge IL 60527 800-827-0170 654-0302*
**Fax Area Code:* 630 ■ *TF:* 800-827-0170 ■ *Web:* www.themxgroup.com

Mzinga 10 Burlington Mall Rd Ste 111 .... Burlington MA 01803 888-694-6428 494-6555*
**Fax Area Code:* 781 ■ *TF:* 888-694-6428 ■ *Web:* www.mzinga.com

NANA Development Corp 909 W Ninth Ave .... Anchorage AK 99501 907-265-4100
Web: www.nana-dev.com

Nathan Assoc Inc 2101 Wilson Blvd Ste 1200 .... Arlington VA 22201 703-516-7700 351-6162
Web: www.nathaninc.com

National Economic Research Assoc Inc
50 Main St 14th Fl .... White Plains NY 10606 914-448-4000 448-4040
Web: www.nera.com

National Product Services Inc
105 Decker Ct Ste 700 .... Irving TX 75062 972-373-9484
Web: www.npsinet.com

Navigant Consulting Inc
30 S Wacker Dr Ste 3100 .... Chicago IL 60606 312-583-5700 583-5701*
NYSE: NCI ■ **Fax:* Mktg ■ *TF:* 888-461-9425 ■ *Web:* www.navigant.com

Navigy Inc
4800 Deerwood Campus Pkwy DCC9-1............ Jacksonville FL 32246 904-363-5490
Web: www.navigy.net

Navitaire Inc 333 S Seventh St Ste 500............. Minneapolis MN 55402 612-317-7000 317-7575
TF: 877-216-6787 ■ *Web:* www.navitaire.com

Neace Lukens Inc 2305 River Rd.................... Louisville KY 40206 502-894-2100 894-8602
TF: 888-499-8092 ■ *Web:* www.neacelukens.com

Neshaminy Constructors Inc
1839 Bustleton Pk .... Feasterville PA 19053 215-322-2700
Web: www.nci3.com

Netspeed Learning Solutions
3016 Ne Blakeley St Ste 100.......................... Seattle WA 98105 206-517-5271
Web: www.netspeedlearning.com

Network Innovations Inc 4424 Manilla Rd SE.......... Calgary AB T2G4B7 403-287-5000
TF: 888-466-2772 ■ *Web:* www.networkinv.com

Newbn Inc 14240 Proton Rd.......................... Dallas TX 75244 972-404-8192
Web: www.newbenefits.com

Newport Real Estate Services Inc
3184 Airway Ave Ste H........................... Costa Mesa CA 92626 714-850-0085
Web: www.nres.net

Newton & Associates Inc
1806 Rocky River Rd .... Charlotte NC 28213 704-597-4384
Web: www.newtonandassociates.com

Nexant Inc 44 S Broadway Fifth Fl .... White Plains NY 10601 914-609-0300 609-0399
Web: www.nexant.com

NextMark Inc 33 S Main St 3rd Fl.................... Hanover NH 03755 603-643-1307
Web: www.nextmark.com

North Central Pennsylvania Regional Planning & Development Commission
651 Montmorenci Rd .... Ridgway PA 15853 814-773-3162 772-7045
TF: 800-942-9467 ■ *Web:* www.ncentral.com

Northern Management Services Inc
607 Church St .... Sandpoint ID 83864 208-263-1363
Web: www.nmsinc.com

Northern Oak Capital Management Inc
555 E Wells St Ste 1625.......................... Milwaukee WI 53202 414-278-0590
Web: www.northern-oak.com

Northwestern Management Services LLC
951 Broken Sound Pkwy Ste 185 .... Boca Raton FL 33487 561-999-9650
Web: www.gentledentalgroup.com

Novotus LLC 5508 Parkcrest Dr Ste 100............... Austin TX 78731 512-733-2244 540-1074*
**Fax Area Code:* 866 ■ *TF:* 800-856-0143 ■ *Web:* www.novotus.com

Nth Degree Financial Solutions
1500 Noyes St .... Evanston IL 60201 847-328-0907
Web: www.nthdegreefinancial.com

Phone Fax

O M V Medical Inc 6940 Carroll Ave .... Takoma Park MD 20912 301-270-9212 270-9335
Web: www.omvmedical.com

O'Brien & Company Inc 811 First Ave Ste 380........... Seattle WA 98104 206-621-8626
Web: www.obrienandco.com

O'Neill & Assoc LLC Thirty-One New Chardon St ....Boston MA 02114 617-646-1000
Web: www.oneillandassoc.com

Oak Creek Energy Systems Inc
500 La Terraza Blvd.............................. Escondido CA 92025 760-975-0910
Web: www.oces.com

Oakwood Capital Management LLC
12121 Wilshire Blvd Ste 1250 ....Los Angeles CA 90025 310-772-2600
Web: www.oakwoodcap.com

Occupational Health Dynamics
197 Cahaba Vly Pkwy.............................. Pelham AL 35124 205-980-0180
Web: www.ohdusa.com

Oleet & Co LLC 452 5th Ave Fourth Fl ....New York NY 10018 212-235-2200 540-3300*
**Fax Area Code:* 802 ■ *Web:* www.oleet.com

Omniture Inc 250 Brannan St.................. San Francisco CA 94107 408-536-6000
Web: www.adobe.com

Onsite Occupational Health & Safety Inc
101 N Hart St ....Princeton IN 47670 812-770-4480
Web: www.onsiteohs.com

Ontility LLC 3403 N Sam Houston Pkwy Ste 300 ....Houston TX 77086 281-854-1400
Web: www.ontility.com

Optima Group Inc 2150 Post Rd .... Fairfield CT 06824 203-255-1066
Web: www.optimagroupinc.com

Organizational Dynamics Inc
790 Boston Rd Ste 201..............................Billerica MA 01821 978-671-5454 671-5005
TF: 800-634-4636 ■ *Web:* www.orgdynamics.com

Orion Development Group
177 Beach 116th St Ste 4..................... Rockaway Park NY 11694 718-474-4600
Web: www.odgroup.com

Orion Mobility LLC
4 Mountainview Terrace Ste 101..................... Danbury CT 06810 203-762-0365 834-9625
TF: 800-476-7787 ■ *Web:* www.orionmobility.com

Orr Group, The
110 S Stratford Rd Ste 402.................... Winston-salem NC 27104 336-722-7881
Web: www.theorrgroup.com

Ortloff Engineers Ltd 415 W Wall Ave Ste 2000.........Midland TX 79701 432-685-0277 685-0258
Web: www.ortloff.com

Osi Consulting Inc
5950 Canoga Ave Ste 300 .... Woodland Hills CA 91367 818-992-2700 992-8700
Web: www.osius.com

OSS.Net Inc PO Box 369................................Oakton VA 22124 703-266-6390
Web: www.oss.net

OZ Systems Inc 2001 Ne Green Oaks Blvd ....Arlington TX 76006 817-385-0390
Web: www.spassociates.com

Pacific Material Handling Solutions Inc
3428 Arden Rd .... Hayward CA 94545 510-786-0215
Web: www.pmhsi.com

Pacrim Hospitality Services Inc
30 Damascus Rd...................................... Bedford NS B4A0C1 902-404-7474
TF: 877-680-7666 ■ *Web:* www.pacrimhospitality.com

Palladium Group Inc 55 Old Bedford Rd Ste 100........ Lincoln MA 01773 781-259-3737 259-3389
TF: 800-773-2399 ■ *Web:* www.thepalladiumgroup.com

Palmaz Scientific Inc
2100 McKinney Ave Ste 1700........................ Dallas TX 75201 214-520-9292
Web: www.palmazscientific.com

Panthera Global Inc 155 N Wacker Dr 42nd Fl.........Chicago IL 60606 312-214-4660

Paradigm Learning Inc 2701 N Rocky Pt Dr .... Tampa FL 33607 813-287-9330 287-9331
Web: www.paradigmlearning.com

Paric Corp 77 Westport Plz Ste 250 .... St. Louis MO 63146 636-561-9500
Web: www.paric.com

Parsec Financial Management Inc
Six Wall St .... Asheville NC 28801 828-255-0271
Web: www.parsecfinancial.com

Parthenon Group 50 Rowes Wharf 14th Fl ....Boston MA 02110 617-478-2550
Web: www.parthenon.com

PathGroup Inc 5301 Virginia Way Ste 320...........Brentwood TN 37027 615-221-4500
Web: www.pathgroup.com

Patten & Patten Inc 520 Lookout St............. Chattanooga TN 37403 423-756-3480
Web: www.patteninc.com

PDM Healthcare 24700 Ctr Ridge Rd Ste 110......... Cleveland OH 44145 440-871-1721
Web: www.pdmhealthcare.com

Pencor Inc 1361 13th Ave S Ste 250 .... Jacksonville Beach FL 32250 904-242-4245 242-0521
Web: www.pencor-inc.com

Pension Consulting Alliance Inc
514 NW 11th Ave Ste 203............................Portland OR 97209 503-226-1050
Web: www.pensionconsulting.com

Penske Vehicle Services Inc 1225 E Maple Rd .... Troy MI 48083 248-729-5400
TF: 877-210-5290 ■ *Web:* penskevehicleservices.com

Performance Indicator LLC
116 John St/South Mill First Fl .... Lowell MA 01852 978-459-4500
Web: www.performanceindicator.com

Permedion Inc 350 Worthington Rd Ste H...........Westerville OH 43082 614-895-9900
Web: hmspermedion.com

Perry Johnson Registrars Inc
26555 Evergreen Rd Ste 1340 .... Southfield MI 48076 248-358-3388
Web: www.pjr.com

Persimmon Group, The 11 E Fifth St Ste 300 .... Tulsa OK 74103 918-592-4121
Web: www.thepersimmongroup.com

PharmaSeq Inc
11 Deer Park Dr Ste 104.................. Monmouth Junction NJ 08852 732-355-0100 355-0102
Web: www.pharmaseq.com

Philip Crosby Assoc 306 Dartmouth St.................Boston MA 02116 877-276-7295
TF: 877-276-7295 ■ *Web:* www.philipcrosby.com

Phillips Financial Management LLC
6920 Pointe Inverness Way Ste 230................ Fort Wayne IN 46804 260-420-7732
Web: www.1phillips.com

Pindler & Pindler Inc 11910 Poindexter Ave ....Moorpark CA 93021 805-531-9090
Web: www.pindler.com

Pinnacle Management Systems Inc
8500 North Stemmons Freeway Ste 6010................ Dallas TX 75247 703-382-9161 975-9991*
**Fax Area Code:* 888 ■ *TF:* 888-975-1119 ■ *Web:* www.pinnaclemanagement.com

Pinnacle Performance Improvement Worldwide (PPIW)
101 Main St ....Pepperell MA 01463 978-925-9797 925-9798
TF: 800-368-3408 ■ *Web:* www.pinnaclecg.com

Pinnacle Products International Inc
668 Stony Hill Rd Ste 302 .... Yardley PA 19067 215-891-8460
Web: www.pinnacleint.com

Pinney Assoc Inc Three Bethesda Metro Ctr .... Bethesda MD 20814 301-718-8440 718-0034
Web: www.pinneyassociates.com

Pipitone Group 3933 Perrysville Ave................ Pittsburgh PA 15214 412-321-0879
Web: pipitonegroup.com

Plan Administrators Inc 1300 Enterprise Dr........... De Pere WI 54115 920-339-2974
Web: www.pai.com

Plank Enterprises Inc 4404 Anderson Dr............ Eau Claire WI 54703 715-839-1225
Web: www.plankenterprises.com

Plastic Technologies Inc 1440 Timberwolf Dr.......... Holland OH 43528 419-867-5400
Web: www.plastictechnologies.com

Platinum Systems Specialists Inc
4715 Yender Ave.. Lisle IL 60532 630-375-6800 375-9069
Web: www.platinum-universe.com

PM Environmental Inc 3340 Ranger Rd ....Lansing MI 48906 517-321-3331
Web: www.pmenv.com

Pma Consultants LLC 1 Woodward Ave Ste 1400......... Detroit MI 48226 313-963-8863 963-8918
Web: www.pmaconsultants.com

Pollock Planning Assoc Inc
232 Juniper Way............................ Mountainside NJ 07092 908-789-4226
Web: www.pollockplanning.com

Porter Henry & Company Inc 455 E 86th St ....New York NY 10028 212-953-5544
Web: www.porterhenry.com

PPI Construction Management Inc
8200 NW 15th Pl Ste B..........................Gainesville FL 32606 352-331-1141
Web: www.ppicm.com

Pragmatek Consulting Group
8500 Normandale Lake Blvd Ste 1060 ....Bloomington MN 55437 612-333-3164 378-2914
TF: 800-833-3164 ■ *Web:* www.pragmatek.com

Prairie Cardiovascular Consultants Ltd
619 E Mason St ....Springfield IL 62701 217-788-0706
Web: www.prairiecardiovascular.com

Precision Automation Company Inc
1841 Old Cuthbert Rd...........................Cherry Hill NJ 08034 856-428-7400
Web: www.precisionautomationinc.com

Presidio Group Inc, The
5295 South 300 West Ste 550 .... Salt Lake City UT 84107 801-924-1400
TF: 800-924-1404 ■ *Web:* www.presidio-group.com

Press Ganey Associates Inc
404 Columbia Pl.............................. South Bend IN 46601 800-232-8032
TF: 800-232-8032 ■ *Web:* www.pressganey.com

Primesource Staffing LLC
400 S Colorado Blvd Ste 400.........................Denver CO 80246 303-869-2990 869-2997
Web: www.primesourcestaffing.com

Princeton Capital Management Inc
47 Hulfish St Ste 500..............................Princeton NJ 08542 609-924-6867
Web: www.pcminvest.com

PRISM Mktg Services Inc
222 W College Ave Ste 2A .... Appleton WI 54911 920-380-2380
Web: www.prism-mktg.com

Pritchett LLC 13355 Noel Rd Ste 1650 .... Dallas TX 75240 214-239-9600 239-9650
TF: 800-992-5922 ■ *Web:* www.pritchettnet.com

Proactive Communications Inc
100 E Whitestone Blvd Ste 148.....................Cedar Park TX 78613 254-699-0067
Web: www.proactivecommo.com

Professional Bank Services Inc
6200 Dutchmans Ln Ste 305 ....Louisville KY 40205 502-451-6633 451-6755
TF: 800-523-4778 ■ *Web:* www.probank.com

Professional Research Consultants Inc
11326 P St ....Omaha NE 68137 402-592-5656 592-3019
TF: 800-428-7455 ■ *Web:* www.prccustomresearch.com

Profile Mktg Research Inc
4020 S 57th Ave Ste 101 .... Lake Worth FL 33463 561-965-8300
Web: radius-global.com

Program Planning Professionals
1340 Eisenhower Pl .... Ann Arbor MI 48108 734-741-7770 741-1343
TF: 877-728-2331 ■ *Web:* www.pcubed.com

Progressive Mktg Products Inc
3130 E Miraloma Ave............................. Anaheim CA 92806 714-632-7100
TF: 800-368-9700 ■ *Web:* www.mounts.com

Projects Plus Inc 254 W 29th St 5th Fl..............New York NY 10001 212-997-0100
Web: www.projectsplusinc.com

ProManage LLC 150 N Michigan Ave Ste 2930..........Chicago IL 60603 312-456-0665
Web: www.promanageplan.com

Promontory Financial Group LLC
1201 Pennsylvania Ave NW Ste 617................Washington DC 20004 202-384-1200
Web: www.promontory.com

Promontory Point Capital
322 E Michigan St Ste 500........................Milwaukee WI 53202 414-225-0484
Web: www.promontorypointcapital.com

Prophet Equity LLC 1460 Main St Ste 200 .... South Lake TX 76092 817-898-1500
Web: www.prophetequity.com

Protected Investors of America Inc
235 Montgomery St Ste 1050................... San Francisco CA 94104 800-786-2559
TF: 800-786-2559 ■ *Web:* www.protectedinvestors.com

PsyMax Solutions LLC
25550 Chagrin Blvd Ste 100...................... Cleveland OH 44122 216-896-9991
Web: www.psymaxsolutions.com

Public Consulting Group Inc 148 State St.............Boston MA 02109 800-210-6113 426-4632*
**Fax Area Code:* 617 ■ *TF:* 800-210-6113 ■ *Web:* www.publicconsultinggroup.com

Public Resources Advisory Group Inc
40 Rector St Ste 1600..............................New York NY 10006 212-566-7800
Web: www.pragadvisors.com

Purple Cows Inc 3210 N Canyon Rd Ste 307..............Provo UT 84604 801-344-8532
Web: www.purplecows.com

	City	State	Zip	Phone	Fax
Q Analysts LLC 5201 Great America Pkwy *Web:* www.qanalysts.com	Santa Clara	CA	95054	408-907-8500	
QSL Print Communications Inc 3000 Pierce Pkwy *Web:* www.qslprinting.com	Springfield	OR	97477	541-687-1184	
Quadel Consulting 1200 G St NW Ste 700 *TF:* 866-640-1019 ■ *Web:* www.quadel.com	Washington	DC	20005	202-789-2500	898-0632
Quality Built LLC 401 SE 12th St Ste 200 *Web:* www.qualitybuilt.com	Fort Lauderdale	FL	33316	954-358-3500	
Quality Business Solutions Inc 12701 Whitewater Dr Ste 180 *Web:* www.qbs.com	Hopkins	MN	55343	952-564-3088	
Quality Group Inc, The 5825 Glenridge Dr Ste 3-101 *Web:* www.thequalitygroup.net	Atlanta	GA	30328	404-843-9525	
Quest Turnaround Advisors LLC 800 Westchester Ave Ste S-520 *Web:* www.qtadvisors.com	Rye Brook	NY	10573	914-253-8100	
Questor 700 E Maple Rd 2nd Fl *Web:* questor.com	Birmingham	MI	48009	248-593-1930	723-3907
Quorum Health Resources LLC 105 Continental Pl *Web:* www.qhr.com	Brentwood	TN	37027	615-371-7979	
R L Hulett & Company Inc 8000 Maryland Ave Ste 245 *Web:* www.rlhulett.com	St Louis	MO	63105	314-721-0607	
R W Rog & Company Inc 630 Johnson Ave Ste 103 *Web:* www.rwroge.com	Bohemia	NY	11716	631-218-0077	
Radiant Communication Inc 5512 Merrick Rd Ste 123 *Web:* www.rccny.com	Massapequa	NY	11758	516-798-0465	
Radio Communications Co 8035 Chapel Hill Rd *Web:* www.rccws.com	Cary	NC	27513	919-467-2421	
Rapid Ratings Pty Ltd 86 Chambers St Ste 701 *Web:* www.rapidratings.com	New York	NY	10007	646-233-4600	
Rath & Strong Inc 1666 Massachusetts Ave PO Box 170 *TF:* 800-622-2025 ■ *Web:* www.rathstrong.com	Lexington	MA	02420	781-861-1700	861-1424
Raytheon Professional Services LLC 1200 S Jupiter Rd *Web:* raytheon.com/ourcompany/rps/	Garland	TX	75042	972-205-5100	
Raytrans Management Inc 1501 Reedsdale St Ste 3001 *Web:* www.raytrans.com	Pittsburgh	PA	15233	412-321-0100	
RCI Consultants Inc 17314 State Hwy 249 Ste 350 *Web:* www.rcigroup.us	Houston	TX	77064	281-970-4221	970-4241
Red Level Networks LLC 24371 Catherine Industrial Dr Ste 223 *Web:* www.redlevelnetworks.com	Novi	MI	48375	248-412-8200	
Redmond Co, The W228 N745 Westmound Dr *Web:* www.theredmondco.com	Waukesha	WI	53186	262-549-9600	
Reed Group Ltd 10155 Westmoor Dr Ste 210 *Web:* www.reedgroup.com	Westminster	CO	80021	303-247-1860	247-1863
Regency Hotel Management LLC 3211 W Sencore Dr *Web:* www.regency-mgmt.com	Sioux Falls	SD	57107	605-334-2371	
Renewable Choice Energy Inc 4775 Walnut St Ste 230 *Web:* www.renewablechoice.com	Boulder	CO	80301	303-468-0405	
Resort Parks International 2901 Cherry Ave *Web:* resortparks.com	Signal Hill	CA	90755	562-595-8818	
Resources For Living Ltd 4407 Monterey Oaks Blvd *Web:* www.rfl.com	Austin	TX	78749	512-358-8400	
Respira Medical Inc 521 Progress Dr BWI Tech Park Ste A - C *Web:* www.respiramedical.com	Linthicum	MD	21090	443-200-0055	
RETax Funding LP 14785 Preston Rd Ste 495 *Web:* www.retaxfunding.com	Dallas	TX	75254	972-855-3550	
Revere Group, The 325 N LaSalle Ste 325 *TF:* 800-745-3263 ■ *Web:* americas.nttdata.com	Chicago	IL	60654	312-873-3400	
RGBS Enterprises 2842 Richmond Ter *Web:* www.rgbse.com	Staten Island	NY	10303	718-981-0734	
RHR International LLP 233 S Wacker Dr 95th Fl *TF:* 800-892-4496 ■ *Web:* rhrinternational.com	Chicago	IL	60606	312-924-0800	924-0801
RINET Company LLC 101 Federal St 14th Fl *Web:* www.rinetco.com	Boston	MA	02110	617-488-2700	
Rippe Keane Mktg Inc 5950 Seminole Centre Ct Ste 220 *Web:* www.rippekeane.com	Madison	WI	53711	608-277-9097	
Rising Tide Capital Inc 334 Martin Luther King Dr *Web:* risingtidecapital.org	Jersey City	NJ	07305	201-432-4316	
Risk Management Services Co (RMSC) 9100 Marksfield Rd **Fax Area Code:* 888 ■ *Web:* www.rmsc.com	Louisville	KY	40222	502-326-5900	326-5909*
RM Strategic Marketing 800 W End Ave *Web:* www.rmstrategicmarketing.com	New York	NY	10025	212-961-1120	
Robert E Nolan Company Inc 92 Hopmeadow St *TF:* 800-653-1941 ■ *Web:* www.renolan.com	Weatogue	CT	06089	860-658-1941	651-3465
Robert Group Inc, The 3108 Los Feliz Blvd *Web:* www.therobertgroup.com	Los Angeles	CA	90039	323-669-9100	
Robert Half Management Resources (RHIMR) 2884 Sand Hill Rd Ste 200 *TF:* 888-400-7474 ■ *Web:* www.roberthalf.com	Menlo Park	CA	94025	650-234-6000	234-6999
Robinson & Maites Inc 35 E Wacker Dr Ste 3500 *Web:* radiant-1.com	Chicago	IL	60601	312-372-9333	
Robson Forensic Inc 354 N Prince St *TF:* 800-813-6736 ■ *Web:* www.robsonforensic.com	Lancaster	PA	17603	717-293-9050	
Rodheim Mktg Group 125 E Baker St Ste 143	Costa Mesa	CA	92626	714-557-5100	
Roff Enterprises Inc 438 N Frederick Ave *Web:* www.hhcgroup.com	Gaithersburg	MD	20877	301-963-0762	
Roland Berger & Partners 230 Pk Ave Ste 112 *Web:* www.rolandberger.com	New York	NY	10169	212-651-9660	756-8750
Romar Learning Solutions LLC 28420 Hardy Toll Rd Ste 150 *Web:* www.romarlearning.com	Spring	TX	77373	281-292-5508	
Roscoe Medical Inc 21973 Commerce Pkwy *Web:* www.roscoemedical.com	Strongsville	OH	44149	440-572-1962	
Rose Displays Ltd 35 Congress St *TF:* 800-631-9707 ■ *Web:* www.rosedisplays.com	Salem	MA	01970	978-219-8100	
RoseRyan Inc 35473 Dumbarton Ct *Web:* www.roseryan.com	Newark	CA	94560	510-456-3056	
Round Table Wealth Management 319 Lenox Ave *Web:* www.roundtableservices.com	Westfield	NJ	07090	908-789-7310	
Roy Jorgensen Assoc Inc 3735 Buckeystown Pk *Web:* www.royjorgensen.com	Buckeystown	MD	21717	301-831-1000	
Royal Paper Corp 10232 Palm Dr *Web:* www.royal-paper.com	Santa Fe Springs	CA	90670	562-903-9030	944-6000
Royce Associates A LP 35 Carlton Ave *Web:* www.royceintl.com	East Rutherford	NJ	07073	201-438-5200	
RSI Logistics Inc 2419 Science Pkwy *Web:* www.rsilogistics.com	Okemos	MI	48864	517-349-7713	
RTD Financial Advisors Inc 30 S 17th St United Plz Ste 1620 *Web:* www.rtdfinancial.com	Philadelphia	PA	19103	215-557-3800	
Ruhof Corp, The 393 Sagamore Ave *Web:* www.ruhof.com	Mineola	NY	11501	516-294-5888	
Ryan Group Inc, The 14110 Dallas Pkwy *Web:* www.ryangroupinc.com	Dallas	TX	75254	972-385-7781	
Sage Financial Group 300 Barr Harbor Dr Five Tower Bridge Ste 200 *Web:* www.sagefinancial.com	West Conshohocken	PA	19428	484-342-4400	
SageView Advisory Group LLC 1920 Main St Ste 800 *Web:* www.sageviewadvisory.com	Irvine	CA	92614	949-955-1395	
SAK Management Services LLC One Northfield Plz Ste 480 *Web:* www.sakmgmt.com	Northfield	IL	60093	773-202-0000	
Sambatek Inc 12800 Whitewater Dr Ste 300 *Web:* www.sambatek.com	Minnetonka	MN	55343	763-476-6010	
Sandy Corp 300 E Big Beaver Rd Ste 500 *TF:* 866-876-0606 ■ *Web:* www.gpstrategies.com	Troy	MI	48083	248-729-4628	729-4701
Sanli Pastore & Hill Inc Sanli Pastore & Hill 1990 S Bundy Dr Ste 800 *Web:* www.sphvalue.com	Los Angeles	CA	90025	310-571-3400	
Sapient Corp 131 Dartmouth St 3rd Fl *NASDAQ: SAPE* ■ *TF:* 866-796-6860 ■ *Web:* www.sapient.com	Boston	MA	02116	617-621-0200	621-1300
Savage & Assoc Inc 4427 Talmadge Rd *Web:* www.savageandassociates.com	Toledo	OH	43623	419-475-8665	
Savant Capital LLC 190 Buckley Dr *Web:* www.savantcapital.com	Rockford	IL	61107	815-227-0300	
Savino Del Bene USA Inc 1905 S Mt Prospect Rd Ste D *Web:* www.savinodelbene.com	Des Plaines	IL	60018	847-390-3600	
SBW Consulting Inc 2820 Northup Way Ste 230 *Web:* www.sbwconsulting.com	Bellevue	WA	98004	425-827-0330	
Scalable Display Technologies Inc 585 Massachusetts Ave Fourth Fl *Web:* www.scalabledisplay.com	Cambridge	MA	02139	617-864-9300	
Schaffer Consulting 707 Summer Street *Web:* www.schafferresults.com	Stamford	CT	06901	203-322-1604	316-0591
Schahet Hotels Inc 9333 N Meridian St *Web:* www.schahethotels.com	Indianapolis	IN	46260	317-848-9000	
Schweppe Inc 376 W N Ave (Route 64) *Web:* www.chefsaver.com	Lombard	IL	60148	630-627-3550	
Scorelogix LLC Two Reads Way Ste 226 *Web:* www.scorelogix.com	New Castle	DE	19720	302-328-1210	
Scott Madden & Assoc Inc 2626 Glenwood Ave Ste 480 *TF:* 800-321-9774 ■ *Web:* www.scottmadden.com	Raleigh	NC	27608	919-781-4191	781-2537
SCP Construction LLC 5340 W Luke Ave *Web:* www.scpaz.com	Glendale	AZ	85301	623-931-9131	
SeaMates International Inc 316 Main St PO Box 436 *Web:* www.seamates.com	East Rutherford	NJ	07073	201-896-8899	
Secova Inc 5000 Birch St W Tower Ste 1400 *TF:* 800-257-0011 ■ *Web:* www.secova.com	Newport Beach	CA	92660	714-384-0530	384-0600
Sedlak Management Consultants Inc Metropolitan Plz 22901 Millcreek Blvd Ste 600 *Web:* www.jasedlak.com	Highland Hills	OH	44122	216-206-4700	206-4840
Selerix Systems Inc 2851 Craig Dr Ste 300 *Web:* www.selerix.com	Mckinney	TX	75070	469-452-7076	
Self Opportunity Inc 808 Office Park Cir *Web:* www.selfopportunity.com	Lewisville	TX	75057	214-222-1500	
Selling Source LLC 325 E Warm Springs Rd Ste 200 *TF:* 800-251-6147 ■ *Web:* sellingsource.com	Las Vegas	NV	89119	702-407-0707	407-0711
Seneca Partners Inc 300 Park St Ste 400 *Web:* www.senecapartners.com	Birmingham	MI	48009	248-723-6650	
Sequent Energy Management LP 1200 Smith St Ste 900 *Web:* www.sequentenergy.com	Houston	TX	77002	832-397-1700	397-1722
SES Advisors Inc 10 Shurs Ln Ste 102 *Web:* www.sesadvisors.com	Philadelphia	PA	19127	215-508-1600	

Company / Address	City	State	Zip	Phone	Fax
Setpoint Systems Inc 2835 Commerce Way *Web:* www.setpointusa.com	Ogden	UT	84401	801-621-4117	
Sharkey Howes & Javer Inc 720 S Colorado Blvd Ste 600 S Twr *Web:* www.shwj.com	Denver	CO	80246	303-639-5100	
Shenkman Capital Management Inc 461 Fifth Ave 22nd Fl *Web:* www.shenkmancapital.com	New York	NY	10017	212-867-9090	
Sherman International Corp 367 Mansfield Ave *Web:* www.shermaninternational.com	Pittsburgh	PA	15220	412-928-2880	
Shoreline Partners LLC 6310 Greenwich Dr Ste 120 *Web:* www.shoreline.com	San Diego	CA	92122	858-587-9800	
Sierra Group, The 588 N Gulph Rd # 110 *Web:* www.thesierragroup.com	King Of Prussia	PA	19406	610-992-0288	
SigmaBleyzer 123 N Post Oak Ln Ste 410 *Web:* www.sigmableyzer.com	Houston	TX	77024	713-621-3111	
Signature Financial Management Inc 101 W Main St Ste 700 *Web:* www.signatureus.com	Norfolk	VA	23510	757-625-7670	
Signature Inc 5115 Parkcenter Ave *Web:* signatureworldwide.com	Dublin	OH	43017	614-766-5101	
Simply Healthcare Plans Inc 1701 Ponce De Leon Blvd Ste 300 *Web:* www.simplyhealthcareplans.com	Coral Gables	FL	33134	305-408-5890	
Sirius Solution LLC 1233 W Loop S *TF:* 800-585-1085 ■ *Web:* www.sirsol.com	Houston	TX	77027	713-888-0488	888-0235
SiriusDecisions Inc 187 Danbury Rd *Web:* www.siriusdecisions.com	Wilton	CT	06897	203-665-4000	
Skillman Corp, The 3834 S Emerson Ave Bldg A *Web:* www.skillman.com	Indianapolis	IN	46203	317-783-6151	
Social Communications Co 380 Altair Wy Ste 100 *Web:* www.sococo.com	Sunnyvale	CA	94086	650-425-7801	
Solving International 1755 The Exchange Ste 380 *Web:* www.solving-int.com	Atlanta	GA	30339	770-988-2600	988-2626
Sorrento Pacific Financial LLC 10150 Meanley Dr First Fl *Web:* www.mybd.com	San Diego	CA	92131	858-805-7900	
Specialty Construction Management Inc 1314 Eigth St Nw *Web:* www.specialtyconstruction.net	Washington	DC	20001	202-832-7250	
Specialty Sales & Mktg Inc 6725 Millcreek Dr Ste 5 *Web:* www.specialtysales.ca	Mississauga	ON	L5N5V3	905-816-0011	
Spectrum Financial System Inc 163 McKenzie Rd *TF:* 800-525-0555 ■ *Web:* www.spectrumfinancialinc.com	Mooresville	NC	28115	704-663-4466	663-0611
SpenDifference LLC 12015 E 46th Ave Ste 300 *Web:* www.spendifference.com	Denver	CO	80239	303-531-2680	
Ssci 3065 Kent Ave *TF:* 800-375-2179 ■ *Web:* www.ssci-inc.com	West Lafayette	IN	47906	765-463-0112	463-4722
Stablex Canada Inc 760 Blvd Industriel *Web:* www.stablex.com	Blainville	QC	J7C3V4	450-430-9230	430-4642
Staff Management Group LLC 172 New St *Web:* www.tandemstaffingsolutions.com	New Brunswick	NJ	08901	732-246-0099	
Standing Dog Interactive 6060 N Central Expy Ste 350 *Web:* www.standingdog.com	Dallas	TX	75206	214-696-9600	
Stanley-Laman Group Ltd 1235 Westlakes Dr Ste 295 *Web:* www.stanleylaman.com	Berwyn	PA	19312	610-993-9100	
Starbridge Media Group Inc 6723 Whittier Ave Ste 300 *Web:* www.starbridgemedia.com	Mclean	VA	22101	703-760-0051	
State Street Consultants Inc 22 Batterymarch St *Web:* www.statestreetconsultants.com	Boston	MA	02109	617-482-1234	
Stelera Wireless LLC 13431 Bdwy Extn Ste 102 *Web:* www.stelerawireless.com	Oklahoma City	OK	73114	405-751-3525	
Stem International Inc 4692 Millennium Dr Ste 400 *Web:* www.stemint.com	Belcamp	MD	21017	410-272-9080	272-9085
Stertil-Koni USA Inc 200 Log Canoe Cir *Web:* www.stertil-koni.com	Stevensville	MD	21666	410-643-9001	
Stewart Environmental Consultants LLC 3801 Automation Way Ste 200 *TF:* 800-373-1348 ■ *Web:* www.stewartenv.com	Fort Collins	CO	80525	970-226-5500	
Stockbridge Risk Management Inc 40 Cutter Mill Rd *Web:* www.stockbridgegroup.com	Great Neck	NY	11021	516-487-1700	487-1146
Stone House Consulting LLC 126 Thornton Rd *Web:* www.stonehouseconsulting.com	Thornton	PA	19373	610-358-1791	
Storm Technologies Inc 411 N Depot St *Web:* www.stormeng.com	Albemarle	NC	28002	704-983-2040	
Strategic Advisors Inc 400 Southpointe Blvd Plz I Ste 440 *Web:* www.strategicad.com	Canonsburg	PA	15317	724-743-5800	
Strategic Decisions Group 745 Emerson St *Web:* www.sdg.com	Palo Alto	CA	94301	650-475-4400	475-4401
Strategic Employee Services Inc 11410 Kingston Pk Ste 100 *Web:* www.seshr.com	Knoxville	TN	37934	865-671-0534	675-0186
Strategic Public Partners Inc 88 E Broad St Ste 1320 *Web:* www.1spp.com	Columbus	OH	43215	614-222-8490	
Strategic Resources Inc 7927 Jones Branch Dr *Web:* www.sri-hq.com	McLean	VA	22102	703-749-3040	749-3046
Stratosphere Multimedia LLC 551 Madison Ave Seventh Fl *TF:* 888-212-0700 ■ *Web:* www.stratosphere-nyc.com	New York	NY	10022	212-702-0700	
Straw Hat Cooperative Corp 18 Crow Canyon Ct Ste 270 *Web:* www.strawhatpizza.com	San Ramon	CA	94583	925-837-3400	
Sullivan- Bille & Co 600 Clark Rd Fourth Fl *Web:* www.sullivanbillepc.com	Tewksbury	MA	01876	978-970-2900	
Summit Envirosolutions Inc 1217 Bandana Blvd N *Web:* www.summite.com	St Paul	MN	55108	651-644-8080	
Summit Health Inc 27175 Haggerty Rd *Web:* www.summithealth.com	Novi	MI	48377	248-799-8303	
Summit Publications Inc 404 S Jefferson St *Web:* www.bestlocalsearch.com	Kearney	MO	64060	816-628-5492	
Sumnicht & Associates W6240 Communication Ct Ste 1 *Web:* www.sumnicht.com	Appleton	WI	54914	920-731-4455	
Sunrise Labs Inc Five Dartmouth Dr *Web:* www.sunriselabs.com	Auburn	NH	03032	603-644-4500	622-9797
SYMMEDRx LLC 10955 Lowell Ave Ste 600 *Web:* www.symmedrx.com	Overland Park	KS	66210	913-338-4900	
Syndicated Capital Inc 1299 Ocean Ave Ste 210 *Web:* www.computercafe.com	Santa Monica	CA	90401	310-255-4490	
Synectic Solutions Inc 1701 Pacific Ave Ste 260 *Web:* www.synecsolu.com	Oxnard	CA	93033	805-483-4800	
Sysorex Global Holding Corporation 405 Clyde Ave *Web:* www.sysorex.com	Mountain View	CA	94043	650-967-2200	
Systech Solutions Inc 700 N Brand Blvd Ste 800 *Web:* www.systechusa.com	Glendale	CA	91203	818-550-9690	550-9692
System of Systems Analytics Inc 11250 Waples Mill Rd Ste 201c *Web:* www.sosacorp.com	Fairfax	VA	22030	703-349-7057	
System Planning Corp (SPC) 3601 Wilson Blvd *Web:* www.sysplan.com	Arlington	VA	22201	703-351-8200	
Talemed Inc 6279 Tri Ridge Blvd Ste 110 *Web:* www.talemed.com	Loveland	OH	45140	513-774-7300	
Tata Consultancy Services Ltd (TCS) 101 Pk Ave 26th Fl *Web:* www.tcs.com	New York	NY	10178	212-557-8038	867-8652
Tbm Consulting Group Inc 4400 Ben Franklin Blvd *TF:* 866-532-6826 ■ *Web:* www.tbmcg.com	Durham	NC	27704	919-471-5535	471-5135
Tech Usa Inc 8334 Veterans Hwy *TF:* 888-584-8181 ■ *Web:* www.techusa.net	Millersville	MD	21108	410-729-4328	987-9080
Technology & Business Integrators 136 Summit Ave Ste 205 *Web:* www.tbicentral.com	Montvale	NJ	07645	201-573-0400	
Technology Commercialization Group LLC 1009 Slater Rd Ste 450 *Web:* www.t-c-group.com	Durham	NC	27703	919-941-0700	
Technomic Inc 300 S Riverside Plaza Ste 1200 *Web:* www.technomic.com	Chicago	IL	60606	312-876-0004	876-1158
Techsico Enterprise Solutions Inc 910 S Hudson Ave *Web:* www.techsico.com	Tulsa	OK	74112	918-585-2347	
Tel-Adjust Inc 29000 Inkster Rd Ste 115 *Web:* www.teladjust.com	Southfield	MI	48034	248-208-1600	208-0805
Tele-Measurements Inc 145 Main Ave *TF:* 800-223-0052 ■ *Web:* www.telemeasurements.com	Clifton	NJ	07014	973-473-8822	
Telesoft Corp 1661 E Camelback Rd Ste 300 *Web:* www.telesoft.com	Phoenix	AZ	85016	602-308-2100	308-1300
Tenera Environmental 971 Dewing Ave Ste 101 *Web:* www.tenera.com	Lafayette	CA	94549	925-962-9769	
Termnet Merchant Services Inc 1601 Dodge St Ste 1600 **Fax Area Code: 770* ■ *TF:* 800-228-2443 ■ *Web:* tsys.com/tms/atlanta/index.cfm	Omaha	NE	68102	800-228-2443	431-3012*
Terra Nova Asset Management LLC 777 Third Ave *Web:* www.terranovausa.com	New York	NY	10017	212-355-1234	
Terrahealth Inc 5710 W Hausman Ste 108 *Web:* www.terrahealth.com	San Antonio	TX	78249	210-475-9881	475-9397
Tessada & Associates Inc 8001 Forbes Pl Ste 310 *Web:* www.tessada.com	Springfield	VA	22151	703-564-1210	
Testmax 927 Lincoln Rd Ste 209 *Web:* www.testmax.net	Miami Beach	FL	33139	305-673-5728	
TheraTogs Inc 305 Society Dr Ste 3-C *Web:* www.theratogs.com	Telluride	CO	81435	970-728-7078	
Thomson ISI ResearchSoft 2141 Palomar Airport Rd Ste 350 *TF:* 800-722-1227 ■ *Web:* www.refman.com	Carlsbad	CA	92009	760-438-5526	
Thyssen Krupp Hearn 59 I- Dr *TF:* 877-854-7178 ■ *Web:* www.tkmna.com	Wentzville	MO	63385	636-332-1772	
TIDAL BASIN HOLDINGS INC 300 N Washington St Ste 500 *Web:* www.tidalbasin-gc.com	Alexandria	VA	22314	703-683-8551	
Tom McCall & Assoc Inc 20180 Governors Hwy Ste 100 *TF:* 800-715-5474 ■ *Web:* www.tmccall.com	Olympia Fields	IL	60461	708-747-5707	747-5890
Tompkins International 6870 Perry Creek Rd *TF:* 800-789-1257 ■ *Web:* tompkinsinc.com	Raleigh	NC	27616	919-876-3667	872-9666
Total Technology Ventures LLC 1230 Peachtree St Ne Ste 1150 *Web:* www.ttvatlanta.com	Atlanta	GA	30309	404-347-8400	
Traffic Management Inc 1710 Douglas Dr N Ste 270 *Web:* www.trafficmgmt.com	Minneapolis	MN	55422	763-544-3455	

				Phone	Fax
Transition Partners Co 11732 Bowman Green Dr Web: www.tpco.us	Reston	VA	20190	703-736-0550	
Transportation Management Services Inc 16600 Table Mtn Pkwy Web: www.imagitas.com	Golden	CO	80403	303-287-8600	
Travelclick Seven Times Sq 38th Fl TF: 866-674-4549 ■ Web: www.travelclick.com	New York	NY	10036	212-817-4800	
Treesdale Partners LLC 1325 Ave of the Americas Ste 2302 Web: www.treesdalellc.com	New York	NY	10019	212-299-5525	
TrestleTree Inc 3715 Business Dr Ste 202 Web: www.trestletree.com	Fayetteville	AR	72703	479-582-0777	
Triage Consulting Group 221 Main St Ste 1100 Web: www.triageconsulting.com	San Francisco	CA	94105	415-512-9400	512-9404
TrialCard Inc 6501 Weston Pkwy Ste 370 Web: corp.trialcard.com	Cary	NC	27513	919-845-0774	
Tribal Solutions Inc 10875 John W Elliott Dr Ste 400 Web: www.tribalsolutionsinc.com	Frisco	TX	75033	972-984-1000	
Triumph Enterprises Inc 11325 Random Hills Rd Ste 340 Web: www.triumph-enterprises.com	Fairfax	VA	22030	703-563-4400	
Troon Golf LLC 15044 N Scottsdale Rd Ste 300 Web: www.troongolf.com	Scottsdale	AZ	85254	480-606-1000	
Trotter Wellness Ltd 2124 Kohler Memorial Dr Ste 300 Web: www.trotterwellness.com	Sheboygan	WI	53081	920-457-3036	
Trout & Partners Ltd Eight Wahneta Rd Web: www.troutandpartners.com	Old Greenwich	CT	06870	203-637-7001	637-7071
True Partners Consulting LLC 225 W Wacker Dr Ste 1600 Web: www.tpctax.com	Chicago	IL	60606	312-235-3300	
Tunnell Consulting 900 E Eigth Ave Ste 106 Web: www.tunnellconsulting.com	King of Prussia	PA	19406	610-337-0820	337-1884
Tunstall Consulting Inc 13153 N Dale Mabry Hwy Ste 200 Web: www.tunstallconsulting.com	Tampa	FL	33618	813-968-4461	961-2315
UcompassCom Inc 3019 Shannon Lakes N Ste 203 Web: www.ucompass.com	Tallahassee	FL	32309	850-297-1800	
ULC Robotics Inc 55 Corbin Ave Web: www.ulcrobotics.com	Bay Shore	NY	11706	631-667-9200	
UMS Group Inc 300 Interpace Pkwy Ste C380 Web: www.umsgroup.com	Parsippany	NJ	07054	973-335-3555	335-7738
United Rebar Inc 8301 Galena Ave Web: unitedrebar.com	Sacramento	CA	95828	916-379-9900	379-9909
University Research Company LLC 7200 Wisconsin Ave Ste 600 Web: www.urc-chs.com	Bethesda	MD	20814	301-654-8338	941-8427
Urban Science 400 Renaissance Ctr Ste 2900 TF: 800-321-6900 ■ Web: www.urbanscience.com	Detroit	MI	48243	313-259-9900	259-9901
Urology Healthcare Group Inc 720 Cool Springs Blvd Ste 500 Web: www.cimplify.net	Franklin	TN	37067	615-261-6700	
Utility Technologies International Corp 4700 Homer Ohio Ln Web: www.uti-corp.com	Groveport	OH	43125	614-482-8080	
V2 Capital LLC 2700 Patriot Blvd Ste 140 Web: www.v2capital.com	Glenview	IL	60026	847-201-3620	
Validation Systems Inc 988 San Antonio Rd Web: www.validationsystems.com	Palo Alto	CA	94303	650-856-4874	
Vanport Manufacturing Inc 28590 Se Wally Rd Web: www.vanport-intl.com	Boring	OR	97009	503-663-4466	
VARIS LLC 9245 Sierra College Blvd Web: www.varis1.com	Roseville	CA	95661	916-294-0860	
Vawter Financial Ltd 1161 Bethel Rd Ste 304 Web: www.vawterfinancial.com	Columbus	OH	43220	614-451-1002	
VCFO Holdings Inc 6836 Austin Ctr Blvd Bldg 1 Ste 280 Web: www.vcfo.com	Austin	TX	78731	512-345-9441	
VCNA Prairie Inc 7601 W 79th St PO Box 1123 Web: www.prairie.com	Bridgeview	IL	60455	708-458-0400	
VDC Research Group Inc 679 Worcester Rd Ste 2 Web: www.vdcresearch.com	Natick	MA	01760	508-653-9000	653-9836
Veber Partners LLC 605 N W 11th Ave Web: www.veber.com	Portland	OR	97209	503-229-4400	
Verity International Ltd 200 King St W Ste 1301 TF: 877-623-2396 ■ Web: www.verityintl.com	Toronto	ON	M5H3T4	416-862-8422	
Vermillion Financial Advisors Inc 16 Executive Ct Ste 3 Web: www.vermillionfinancial.com	South Barrington	IL	60010	847-382-9999	
Vermont Composites Inc 25 Performance Dr Web: www.vtcomposites.com	Bennington	VT	05201	802-442-9964	445-2921
Vesta Hospitality LLC 900 Washington St Ste 760 Web: www.vestahospitality.com	Vancouver	WA	98660	360-737-0442	
Viatech Systems Inc 1749 Old Meadow Rd 650 Web: www.viatech-systems.net	McLean	VA	22102	703-917-0550	917-0558
Viccs Inc 11821 Parklawn Dr Ste 224 Web: www.viccs.com	Rockville	MD	20852	301-984-1355	984-1360
Virginia Society of Professional Engineers 6160 Kempsville Cir Ste 240 Web: www.vspe.org	Norfolk	VA	23502	757-455-5800	
Virtu Financial Inc 645 Madison Ave Web: www.virtu.com	New York	NY	10022	212-418-0100	
Vital Mktg LLC 115 E 23rd St 10th Fl Web: www.vitalmarketing.com	New York	NY	10010	212-995-9525	
Vital Wave Consulting 555 Bryant St Ste 226 Web: www.vitalwaveconsulting.com	Palo Alto	CA	94301	650-964-1316	
VoiceAge Corp 750 Lucerne Rd Ste 250 Web: www.voiceage.com	Montreal	QC	H3R2H6	514-737-4940	
Wainscot Media LLC 110 Summit Ave Web: www.wainscotmedia.com	Montvale	NJ	07645	201-571-2244	
Wakely Consulting Group Inc 17757 US 19 Ste 310 Web: www.wakely.com	Clearwater	FL	33764	727-507-9858	507-9658
Waller Financial Planning Group Inc 941 Chatham Ln Ste 212 Web: www.waller.com	Columbus	OH	43221	614-457-7026	
Walsh Brothers Inc 210 Commercial St Web: www.walshbrothers.com	Boston	MA	02109	617-878-4800	
Walter Greenblatt & Associates LLC 430 Nassau St Web: www.wgreenblatt.com	Princeton	NJ	08540	609-497-1282	
Washington Group Consultants LLC PO Box A TF: 800-236-7323 ■ Web: www.washingtongroup.com	Fairfax	VA	22031	703-591-6600	591-6602
Watermark Capital Partners LLC 272 E Deerpath Rd Ste 320 Web: www.watermarkcap.com	Lake Forest	IL	60045	847-482-8600	
Watermark Learning Inc 7300 Metro Blvd Ste 207 TF: 800-646-9362 ■ Web: www.watermarklearning.com	Minneapolis	MN	55439	952-921-0900	
WCD Consultants LLC 23 Rt 31 N Ste B26 Web: www.wcdgroup.com	Pennington	NJ	08534	609-730-0007	730-0011
WealthTrust LLC 8434 E Shea Blvd Ste 600 Web: www.wealthtrust.com	Scottsdale	AZ	85260	480-339-5221	
Weeden & Company LP 145 Mason St Web: www.weedenco.com	Greenwich	CT	06830	203-861-7670	
Welocalize Inc 241 E Fourth St Ste 207 TF: 800-370-9515 ■ Web: www.welocalize.com	Frederick	MD	21701	301-668-0330	668-0335
West Coast Asset Management Inc 1205 Coast Village Rd Web: www.wcam.com	Montecito	CA	93108	805-653-5333	
West Coast Dental Services Inc 12121 Wilshire Blvd Ste 1111 Web: www.westcoastdental.com	Los Angeles	CA	90025	310-820-9933	
West Coast Financial LLC 1525 State St Ste 104 Web: www.wcfinc.com	Santa Barbara	CA	93101	805-962-9131	
West Monroe Partners LLC 222 W Adams St TF: 800-828-6708 ■ Web: www.westmonroepartners.com	Chicago	IL	60606	312-602-4000	
Westcare Management Inc 3155 River Rd S Ste 100 TF: 800-541-3732 ■ Web: www.westcaremgt.com	Salem	OR	97302	800-541-3732	
Westport Resources Management Inc 55 Greens Farms Rd Web: www.westportresources.com	Westport	CT	06880	203-226-0222	
Whimsy Inc 1901 S Busse Rd Web: www.whimsytrucking.com	Mount Prospect	IL	60056	847-690-1246	
White Oaks Wealth Advisors Inc 80 S Eighth St IDS Ctr Ste 1725 Web: www.whiteoakswealth.com	Minneapolis	MN	55402	612-455-6900	
White Shield Inc 320 N 20th Ave Web: www.whiteshield.com	Pasco	WA	99301	509-547-0100	
Whitsons Food Service Corp 1800 Motor Pkwy Web: www.whitsons.com	Islandia	NY	11749	631-424-2700	
Wildlands Inc 3855 Atherton Rd Web: www.wildlandsinc.com	Rocklin	CA	95765	916-435-3555	
Wind River Financial Inc 18500 W Corporate Dr Web: www.windriverfinancial.com	Brookfield	WI	53045	262-792-1119	
Windmill International Inc Two Robinson Rd Web: www.windmill-intl.com	Nashua	NH	03060	603-888-5502	888-5512
Witzenmann USA LLC 2200 Centerwood Dr Web: www.witzenmann.us	Warren	MI	48091	586-756-1900	
Wk Dickson & Co Inc 616 Colonnade Dr Web: www.wkdickson.com	Charlotte	NC	28205	704-334-5348	334-0078
WM Smith Securities Inc 1700 Lincoln St Ste 2545 Web: www.wmsmith.com	Denver	CO	80203	303-831-9696	
Wolgast Corp 4835 Towne Centre Rd Ste 203 Web: www.wolgastcorporation.com	Saginaw	MI	48604	989-790-9120	
Women's Mktg Inc 1221 Post Rd E Ste 201 Web: www.womensmarketing.com	Westport	CT	06880	203-256-0880	
WorkCare.com 300 S Harbor Blvd Ste 600 TF: 800-455-6155 ■ Web: www.workcare.com	Anaheim	CA	92805	800-455-6155	
Worldtech International LLC 1901 N Beauregard St Ste 380 Web: www.worldtech-int.com	Alexandria	VA	22311	703-778-5444	
XMaLpha Technologies LLC 935 Arbogast St Web: www.xmalpha.com	Shoreview	MN	55126	651-484-0471	
Zachary Scott & Co 1200 Fifth Ave Ste 1500 Web: www.zacharyscott.com	Seattle	WA	98101	206-224-7380	
Zeiders Enterprises Inc 2750 Killarney Dr Ste 100 Web: www.zeiders.com	Woodbridge	VA	22192	703-496-9000	580-6339

198 CONSULTING SERVICES - MARKETING

				Phone	Fax
1-2-1 Marketing Services Group Inc 20195 S Diamond Lk Rd Ste 700 Web: www.121msg.com	Rogers	MN	55374	763-428-8123	
2020 Companies LLC 3575 Lone Star Cir Ste 300 Web: www.2020companies.com	Fort Worth	TX	76177	817-490-0100	
220 Marketing 3405 Kenyon St Ste 501 TF: 877-220-6584 ■ Web: www.220marketing.com	San Diego	CA	92110	877-220-6584	

Phone | Fax

3 Media Web Solutions Inc
1900 W Park Dr Ste 280 Westborough MA 01581 508-845-8900
Web: www.3mediaweb.com

360 Bc Group Inc 25562 Gloriosa Dr Mission Viejo CA 92691 949-916-9120
Web: www.360businessconsulting.com

5th Business 5100 Orbitor Dr Ste 100 Mississauga ON L4W4Z4 905-275-2220
Web: www.5thbusiness.com

6s Marketing 1120 Hamilton St Vancouver BC V6B2S2 604-642-6765
Web: www.6smarketing.com

7Summits LLC
1110 Old World Third St Ste 500 Milwaukee WI 53203 866-705-6372
TF: 866-705-6372 ■ *Web:* www.7summitsagency.com

919 Marketing Company Inc
102 Avent Ferry Rd Holly Springs NC 27540 919-557-7890
Web: www.919marketing.com

A.D.D. Marketing Inc 6600 Lexington Ave Los Angeles CA 90038 323-790-0500
Web: www.addmarketing.com

Accelerant Sales Group LLC Two Skyline Dr Montville NJ 07045 973-331-0600
Web: www.accelerantsales.com

Ace Ranking 953 Mission St Ste 120 San Francisco CA 94103 415-536-3929
Web: www.acerankings.com

Achieve LLC 233 McCrea St Ste 200 Indianapolis IN 46225 317-637-3000
Web: www.achieveguidance.com

Aci Event Group 652 Hayes St San Francisco CA 94102 415-553-7880
Web: www.acieventgroup.com

Acosta Sales & Marketing Co
665 W N Ave Ste 300 Lombard IL 60148 630-620-7600 281-9966*
**Fax Area Code: 904* ■ *TF General:* 888-281-9810 ■ *Web:* www.acosta.com

AcrobatAnt LLC 1336 E 15th St Tulsa OK 74120 918-938-7901
Web: www.acrobatant.com

Action Lead Solutions
2232 N Clybourn Ave Third Fl Chicago IL 60614 773-661-1570
Web: actionleadsolutions.com

ACTON Marketing LLC 3401 NW 39th St Lincoln NE 68524 402-470-2909
Web: www.acton.com

AD-EX International Inc
1301 Glendale-Milford Rd Cincinnati OH 45215 513-771-2339
Web: www.adex-intl.com

Adams & Associates of Nevada Inc
10395 Double R Blvd Reno NV 89521 775-348-0900
Web: www.adamsaai.com

Adams Group Inc, The 925 Gervais St Columbia SC 29201 803-765-1223
Web: www.adamsgroup.com

Adams Unlimited 80 Broad St Ste 3202 New York NY 10004 212-956-5900
Web: adams-pr.com

Advisors Excel LLC
1300 SW Arrowhead Rd Ste 200 Topeka KS 66604 866-363-9595
TF: 866-363-9595 ■ *Web:* www.advisorsexcel.com

Aerotronics Marketing Inc
5331 Derry Ave Ste O Agoura Hills CA 91301 818-735-6633
Web: www.aerotronics.net

AgileCat LLC 4390 Main St Second Fl Philadelphia PA 19127 215-508-2082
Web: www.agilecat.com

AIS RealTime 4440 Bowen Blvd SE Grand Rapids MI 49508 877-314-1100
TF: 877-314-1100 ■ *Web:* www.aisservice.com

Albert Risk Management Consultants
72 River Park St Ste 3 Needham Heights MA 02494 781-449-2866
Web: www.albertrisk.com

Albion International Services
2520 Nw 97th Ave Ste 110 Doral FL 33172 305-406-1000
Web: www.albionstaffing.com

All Terrain 2675 W Grand Ave Chicago IL 60612 312-421-7672
Web: www.allterrain.net

Allout Marketing Inc
1905 Wayzata Blvd Ste 130 Wayzata MN 55391 952-404-0800
Web: www.alloutsuccess.com

Alloy Education Two LAN Dr Ste 100 Westford MA 01886 978-692-5092
Web: www.alloyeducation.com

Alpha Marketing Inc 510 Glenwood Ave Ste 321 Raleigh NC 27603 919-836-2169
Web: www.alphamarketing.com

Altitude Marketing 417 State Rd Second Fl Emmaus PA 18049 610-421-8601
Web: altitudemarketing.com

Americhip Inc 19032 S Vermont Ave Los Angeles CA 90248 310-323-3697
Web: www.americhip.com

Amerivon Holdings LLC
2815 Townsgate Rd Ste 225 Westlake Village CA 91361 805-719-4800
Web: www.amerivon.com

AMPERAGE Marketing 6711 Chancellor Dr Cedar Falls IA 50613 319-268-9151
Web: www.meandv.com

Analytical Group Inc, The 16638 N 90th St Scottsdale AZ 85260 480-483-7505
Web: www.analyticalgroup.com

Angie Brewer & Associates LC
9104 58th Dr E Bradenton FL 34202 941-757-4300
Web: www.angiebrewer.com

Apex Asset Management LLC
1891 Santa Barbara Dr Ste 204 Lancaster PA 17601 717-519-1770
Web: www.apexasset.com

Apparel Media Group Co
155 N Michigan Ave Ste 417 Chicago IL 60601 312-729-5195
Web: www.apparelmedia.com

Argo Marketing Group 64 Lisbon St Lewiston ME 04240 207-514-0744
Web: argomarketing.com

Armstrong Partnership LP 23 Prince Andrew Pl Toronto ON M3C2H2 416-444-3050
Web: www.armstrongpartnership.com

Arrowhead Promotion & Fulfillment Company Inc
1105 SE Eighth St Grand Rapids MN 55744 218-327-1165
Web: www.apfco.com

ASL Marketing Two Dubon Ct Farmingdale NY 11735 516-248-6100
Web: www.aslmarketing.com

Aspasie Inc 221 Saint-Georges Saint-barnabe-nord QC G0X2K0 819-264-2075
Web: www.aspasie.qc.ca

ASTONE Inc 2300 Tulare St Ste 210 Fresno CA 93721 559-375-7100
Web: www.astoneagency.com

Phone | Fax

Atomic Leads Inc 4926 Windy Hill Dr Raleigh NC 27609 919-439-4900
Web: www.atomicleads.com

Augeo Affinity Marketing Inc
2561 Territorial Rd St. Paul MN 55114 651-917-9143
Web: www.augeomarketing.com

Autopacific Inc 2991 Dow Ave Tustin CA 92780 714-838-4234
Web: www.autopacific.com

Avideon Corp PO Box 4830 Baltimore MD 21211 443-957-1986
Web: www.avideon.com

Axiom Marketing Inc 624 E Park Ave Libertyville IL 60048 847-362-5656
Web: www.axmarketing.com

Azul Partners Inc 421 W Melrose Ste 10C Chicago IL 60657 773-525-7406
Web: www.azulpartners.com

Backus Turner International
316 NE Fourth St Ft. Lauderdale FL 33301 305-573-9996
Web: www.backusturner.com

Baesman Group Inc 274 Marconi Blvd Columbus OH 43215 614-771-2300
Web: www.baesman.com

Ballard Direct 516 Pelhamdale Ave Pelham NY 10803 914-738-3701
Web: www.ballarddirect.com

Band Digital Inc 150 N Michigan Ave Ste 300 Chicago IL 60601 312-981-6000
Web: banddigital.com

Bay MarketForce LLC 2410 S Main St Ste C West Bend WI 53095 262-355-5612
Web: www.baymarketforce.com

BDS Marketing Inc 10 Holland Irvine CA 92618 949-472-6700
Web: www.bdsmktg.com

Becker Media 2633 Telegraph Ave Ste 110 Oakland CA 94612 510-465-6200
Web: www.beckermedia.net

Beezley Management LLC
23632 Calabasas Rd Ste 105 Calabasas CA 91302 818-591-8555
Web: www.beezleymanagement.com

Bellomy Research Inc 175 Sunnynoll Ct Winston Salem NC 27106 800-443-7344
TF: 800-443-7344 ■ *Web:* www.bellomyresearch.com

Benevity Social Ventures Inc
1110 First St SW Calgary AB T2R0V1 403-237-7875
Web: www.benevity.com

Best Image Marketing Inc 2222 Park Pl Blvd Clearlake CA 95422 707-995-5050
Web: connect.homes.com

BeTuitive 116 W Illinois St Fl 6e Chicago IL 60654 312-832-1500
Web: www.betuitive.com

Beverage Marketing Corp
850 Third Ave 18th Fl New York NY 10022 212-688-7640 826-1255
TF: 800-275-4630 ■ *Web:* www.beveragemarketing.com

Bill Good Marketing Inc
12393 South Gateway Park Pl Ste 600 Draper UT 84020 801-572-1480
Web: www.billgood.com

BioVid Corp Five Vaughn Dr Ste 111 Princeton NJ 08540 609-750-1400
Web: biovid.com

Blane Canada Ltd 1506 Cadet Ct Wheaton IL 60189 630-462-9222
Web: www.blanecanada.com

Blue Lotus Creative 7971 Columbia St Vancouver BC V5Z2X5 604-306-8701
Web: www.bluelotuscreative.com

Blue Rooster Marketing Inc
1300 N Northlake Way Ste 100 Seattle WA 98103 206-632-7730
Web: www.bluerooster.com

Blue Telescope 236 W 30 St Seventh Fl New York NY 10001 212-675-7702
Web: www.blue-telescope.com

Bluedog Design LLC 403 N Carpenter St Chicago IL 60642 312-243-1101
Web: www.bluedogdesign.com

Bluegrass Promotional Marketing LLC
13325 S Point Blvd Ste 100 Charlotte NC 28273 704-529-0999
Web: www.bluegrassltd.com

BlueRush Media Group Corp 75 Sherbourne St Toronto ON M5A2P9 416-203-0618
Web: www.bluerush.ca

Boomers & Beyond Inc
1998 Ruffin Mill Rd Colonial Heights VA 23834 804-524-9888 524-9889
TF: 800-958-8324 ■ *Web:* www.firststreetonline.com

Brains On Fire Inc 148 River St Greenville SC 29601 864-676-9663
Web: www.brainsonfire.com

Brand Iron 2240 Blake St Denver CO 80205 303-534-1901
Web: brandiron.net

BrightHouse LLC 790 Marietta St Atlanta GA 30318 404-240-2500
Web: www.thinkbrighthouse.com

Broadway Marketing Ltd 80 Fuller Rd Albany NY 12205 518-489-3226
Web: www.broadwaymarketing.com

Brogan & Partners Advertising Consultancy Inc
800 N Old Woodward Ave Ste 100 Birmingham MI 48009 248-341-8200
Web: www.brogan.com

Builder Homesite Inc 11900 Ranch Rd 620 N Austin TX 78750 512-371-3800
Web: www.builderhomesite.com

Business Efficacy 6130 Blue Cir Dr Hopkins MN 55343 952-217-0425
Web: www.businessefficacy.com

Business-to-Business Marketing Communications Inc
900 Ridgefield Dr Ste 270 Raleigh NC 27609 919-872-8172 872-8875
Web: www.btbmarketing.com

C-4 Analytics LLC 999 Broadway Ste 500 Saugus MA 01906 617-250-8888
Web: www.c-4analytics.com

C.J. Driscoll & Associates
2636 Via Carrillo Palos Verdes Estates CA 90274 310-544-5046
Web: www.cjdriscoll.com

Cadmium Cd LLC 19 Newport Dr Ste 101 Forest Hill MD 21050 410-638-9239
Web: www.cadmiumcd.com

Calmare Therapeutics Inc 1375 Kings Hwy Fairfield CT 06824 203-368-6044 368-5399
Web: www.competitivetech.net

Campus Special LLC, The
3575 Koger Blvd Ste 300 Duluth GA 30096 800-365-8520
TF: 800-365-8520 ■ *Web:* www.campusspecial.com

Canary Marketing Inc
600 San Ramon Vly Blvd Ste 200 Danville CA 94526 925-314-1888
Web: www.canarymarketing.com

Cdr Assessment Group Inc 1644 S Denver Ave Tulsa OK 74119 918-488-0722
Web: cdrassessmentgroup.com

Company / Address	City	State	Zip	Phone	Fax
CellTrust Corp 14822 N 73rd St Bldg B Ste 113 *Web:* www.celltrust.com	Scottsdale	AZ	85260	480-515-5200	
Centrus Group Inc 1653 Merriman Rd Ste 211 *Web:* centrusgroup.com	Akron	OH	44313	330-864-5800	
Ceridian Benefits Services Inc 3201 34th St South *Web:* www.ceridian-benefits.com	St. Petersburg	FL	33711	727-864-3300	
Cheshire Marketing Inc 3209 Guess Rd Ste 108 *Web:* www.cheshiremarketing.com	Durham	NC	27705	919-479-2008	
Classical Marketing LLC 150 N Martingale Rd Ste 800 *Web:* classicalmarketing.com	Schaumburg	IL	60173	847-969-1696	
Client Focused Media Inc 100 Festival Park Ave *Web:* cfmedia.net	Jacksonville	FL	32202	904-232-3001	
Cohn 2881 N Speer Blvd *Web:* www.cohnmarketing.com	Denver	CO	80211	303-839-1415	
Common Interest Management Services Inc 315 Diablo Rd Ste 221 *Web:* www.commoninterest.com	Danville	CA	94526	925-743-3080	
ComNet Marketing Group Inc 1214 Stowe Ave *TF:* 877-581-2565 ■ *Web:* www.comnetmarketing.com	Medford	OR	97501	877-581-2565	
Compu-Mail LLC 3235 Grand Island Blvd *Web:* www.compu-mail.com	Grand Island	NY	14072	716-775-8001	
ComStar Networks LLC 1820 NE Jensen Beach Blvd Ste 564 *TF:* 800-516-1595 ■ *Web:* www.comstarnetwork.com	Jensen Beach	FL	34957	800-516-1595	
Concept Studio LLC, The 165 Kings Hwy N *Web:* www.tcspromo.com	Westport	CT	06880	203-227-7444	
Content Firm LLC, The 26 Academy Dr E *Web:* evanschuman.com	Whippany	NJ	07981	973-993-8098	
Cooper Thomas LLC 923 V St Nw *Web:* cooperthomas.com	Washington	DC	20001	202-387-8366	
Coupons.com Inc 400 Logue Ave *Web:* www.couponsinc.com	Mountain View	CA	94043	650-605-4600	
Creor Group LLC Po Box 110398 *Web:* creorgroup.com	Campbell	CA	95011	408-248-4822	
Crimson Consulting Group 4970 El Camino Real Ste 200 *Web:* www.crimson-consulting.com	Los Altos	CA	94022	650-960-3600	960-3737
Crossmark Inc 5100 Legacy Dr *TF:* 877-699-6275 ■ *Web:* www.crossmark.com	Plano	TX	75024	469-814-1000	814-1355
Crucial Interactive Inc 21 Camden St Fifth Fl *Web:* www.crucialinteractive.com	Toronto	ON	M5V1V2	416-645-0135	
Crunch Brands One First Ave Bldg 34 *Web:* crunchbrands.com	Charlestown	MA	02129	617-241-5553	
Culture22 Communications LLC 935B N Plum Grove Rd *Web:* www.culture22.com	Schaumburg	IL	60173	847-517-9022	
Customer Elation Inc 9065 Lyndale Ave South *Web:* www.customerelation.com	Bloomington	MN	55420	952-653-0801	
D A Crowley & Associates Inc Three OVERLOOK DR UNIT 2 *Web:* www.dacrowley.com	Amherst	NH	03031	603-673-7050	
D Side Advisors 12601 Easton Dr *Web:* dside.com	Saratoga	CA	95070	408-255-4620	
D.Trio Marketing Group 401 N Third St Ste 480 *Web:* www.dtrio.com	Minneapolis	MN	55401	612-436-0323	
D3Logic Inc 89 Commercial Way *Web:* www.d3logic.com	East Providence	RI	02914	401-435-4300	
Dane Media LLC 385 Sylvan Ave Ste 24 *TF:* 888-233-2863 ■ *Web:* www.danemedia.com	Englewood Cliffs	NJ	07632	888-233-2863	
Data Banque Ltd 5500 Brooktree Rd Ste 200 *Web:* www.databanque.com	Wexford	PA	15090	412-548-1030	
Datamart Direct Inc 6405 Muirfield Dr *Web:* www.datamartdirect.com	Hanover Park	IL	60133	630-307-7100	
Davis Brand Capital LLC 154 Krog St Ste 100 *Web:* davisbrandcapital.com	Atlanta	GA	30307	404-347-7778	
Day Vision Marketing 2222 S 12th St Ste D *Web:* www.dayvision.com	Allentown	PA	18103	610-403-3999	
Daymon Assoc Inc 700 Fairfield Ave *Web:* www.daymon.com	Stamford	CT	06902	203-352-7500	352-7947
DCI Marketing Inc 2727 W Good Hope Rd *TF:* 800-778-4805 ■ *Web:* www.dci-artform.com	Milwaukee	WI	53209	414-228-7000	228-4366
dDirect Inc 2707 Peachtree Sq *Web:* www.ddirect.com	Atlanta	GA	30360	678-530-0034	
Delaney Meeting & Event Planning One Mill St Ste 315 *Web:* www.delaneymeetingevent.com	Burlington	VT	05401	802-865-5202	
Deloitte Digital 837 N 34th St Ste 100 *Web:* www.ubermind.com	Seattle	WA	98103	206-633-1167	
Delta Marketing Dynamics 100 N Salina St Ste 500 *Web:* deltamarketingdynamics.com	Syracuse	NY	13202	315-492-2905	
Deniro Marketing LLC 6777 Embarcadero Dr Ste 3 *Web:* www.datinggold.com	Stockton	CA	95219	209-477-7676	
Design Compendium Inc, The 155 20th St *Web:* www.designcompendium.com	Brooklyn	NY	11232	718-499-7722	
Deskey 120 E Eighth St *Web:* www.deskey.com	Cincinnati	OH	45202	513-721-6800	
Direct Tech Inc 13259 Millard Ave Ste 306 *Web:* www.direct-tech.com	Omaha	NE	68137	402-895-2100	
Djs Marketing Group Inc 2398 S Dixie Hwy *Web:* www.djs-marketing.com	Miami	FL	33133	305-860-9500	
DMI Music & Media Solutions 35 W Dayton St *Web:* www.dmimusic.com	Pasadena	CA	91105	626-795-0432	
Do My Own Pest Control 4260 Communications Dr *Web:* www.domyownpestcontrol.com	Norcross	GA	30093	770-840-8831	
Doneger Group, The 463 Seventh Ave *Web:* www.doneger.com	New York	NY	10018	212-564-1266	
Dreamspan Product Innovation LLC 11645 N Cave Creek Rd *Web:* www.dreamspan.com	Phoenix	AZ	85020	602-354-7640	
E-power Marketing Inc 111 N Main St Ste 405 *Web:* www.epower.com	Oshkosh	WI	54901	920-303-1244	
East Tennessee Human Resource Agency Inc 9111 Cross Park Dr Ste A-250 *Web:* www.ethra.org	Knoxville	TN	37923	865-691-2551	
ebQuickstart 3000 S IH 35 Ste 320 *Web:* www.ebquickstart.com	Austin	TX	78704	512-637-9696	
Ecity Interactive Inc 1501 Walnut St Fl 2 *Web:* ecityinteractive.com	Philadelphia	PA	19102	215-557-0767	
Eclipse Marketing Services Inc 490 Headquarters Plz N Tower 10th Fl *TF:* 800-837-4648 ■ *Web:* www.eclipse2.com	Morristown	NJ	07960	800-837-4648	
Economic Consulting Services LLC 2001 L St NW *Web:* www.economic-consulting.com	Washington	DC	20036	202-466-7720	466-2710
EdgeCore LLC 1025 Technology Pkwy Ste A *Web:* www.edgecore.com	Cedar Falls	IA	50613	319-277-3700	
eGumBall Inc 8687 Research Dr Ste 200 *TF:* 800-890-8940 ■ *Web:* www.egumball.com	Irvine	CA	92618	800-890-8940	
Eire Direct Marketing 720 N Franklin St Ste 310 *Web:* www.eiredirect.com	Chicago	IL	60654	312-640-4000	
Emarketingwerx Inc 5335 W 138th St *Web:* www.emarketingwerx.com	Hawthorne	CA	90250	310-686-2314	
Emerald Hospitality Associates Inc 2001 Crocker Rd Ste 300 *Web:* www.emeraldhospitality.com	Westlake	OH	44145	440-239-9848	
Entegral Energy Marketing Inc 1228 Kensington Rd NW Ste 205 *Web:* www.entegralenergy.com	Calgary	AB	T2N3P3	403-283-1133	
Environics Analytics Group Ltd 33 Bloor St E Ste 400 *Web:* www.environicsanalytics.ca	Toronto	ON	M4W3H1	416-969-2733	
Envision Marketing Inc 26941 Cabot Rd Ste 121 *Web:* www.envisionmarketing.net	Laguna Hills	CA	92653	949-367-7818	
Ernst-Van Praag Inc 433 Plaza Real Ste 275 *Web:* www.evpconsulting.com	Boca Raton	FL	33432	561-447-0557	447-0527
ESN Interactive 6255 W Sunset Blvd Ste 1110 *Web:* www.esninteractive.com	Los Angeles	CA	90028	323-337-0600	
Ethos Marketing & Design 907 Main St *Web:* ethos-marketing.com	Westbrook	ME	04092	207-856-2610	
EtQ Management Consultants Inc 399 Conklin St Ste 208 *Web:* www.etq.com	Farmingdale	NY	11735	516-293-0949	
Eventsful Inc 305 E 40th St Apt 6f *Web:* www.eventsful.com	New York	NY	10016	212-682-8405	
Eview 360 Corp 39255 Country Club Dr Ste B-30 *Web:* www.eview360.com	Farmington Hills	MI	48331	248-306-5191	
Experience Corp, The 127A E 71st St *Web:* richardattiasassociates.com	New York	NY	10021	212-794-8801	
Extole Inc 274 Brannan St Ste 602 *Web:* www.extole.com	San Francisco	CA	94107	415-625-0500	
Eyeball Digital Inc 187 Lafayette St *Web:* www.eyeballnyc.com	New York	NY	10013	212-431-5324	
Eze Castle Integration Inc 260 Franklin St 12th Fl *TF:* 800-752-1382 ■ *Web:* www.eci.com	Boston	MA	02110	617-217-3000	217-3001
F & H. Solutions Group LLC 1300 19th St Nw Ste 700 *Web:* fhsolutionsgroup.com	Washington	DC	20036	202-719-2000	
Faith Popcorn's BrainReserve 885 Second Ave 16th Fl 1 Dad Hammarskjold Plz *TF:* 800-873-6337 ■ *Web:* www.faithpopcorn.com	New York	NY	10017	212-772-7778	
Fast Horse 240 Ninth Ave N *Web:* www.fasthorseinc.com	Minneapolis	MN	55401	612-332-8009	
FinCo Management LLC 18 Doaks Ln *Web:* www.fincomanagement.com	Marblehead	MA	01945	781-639-6000	
Find & Convert 36181 E Lk Rd Ste 188 *Web:* www.findandconvert.com	Palm Harbor	FL	34685	727-234-0952	
Finity Communications Inc 1314 Nw Irving St Apt 710 *Web:* www.finity.com	Portland	OR	97209	503-808-9240	
Fitch Inc 585 S Front St Ste 50 *Web:* www.fitch.com	Columbus	OH	43215	614-885-3453	885-4289
Fixation Marketing Inc 4340 East-West Hwy Ste 200 *Web:* www.fixation.com	Bethesda	MD	20814	240-207-2009	
Forward Branding & Identity 34 May St *Web:* www.forwardbranding.com	Webster	NY	14580	585-872-9222	
FourCubed LLC 509 First Ave NE *Web:* fourcubed.com	Minneapolis	MN	55413	612-454-1509	
Frantz Group Inc, The 1245 Cheyenne Ave *Web:* www.thefrantzgroup.com	Grafton	WI	53024	262-204-6000	
Fresh Consulting LLC 914 140th Ave NE Ste 201 *Web:* www.freshconsulting.com	Bellevue	WA	98005	425-502-8480	
Fulcrum Analytics Inc 70 W 40th St 10th Fl *TF:* 888-245-9450 ■ *Web:* www.fulcrum-mktg.com	New York	NY	10018	212-651-7000	651-7049
Fulfillment Solutions Advantage Inc, The 80 Ambassador Dr *Web:* www.thefsagroup.com	Mississauga	ON	L5T2Y9	905-696-8884	
Gannett Offset 7950 Jones Branch Dr *TF:* 800-255-1457 ■ *Web:* www.gannett.com	McLean	VA	22107	703-750-8673	658-8359

Company	City	State	Zip	Phone	Fax
GasPedal LLC 333 W N Ave Ste 500 *Web:* www.gaspedal.com	Chicago	IL	60610	312-932-9000	
Gc Marketing Services 10 E 23rd St Ste 300 *Web:* www.gcmarketingservices.com	New York	NY	10010	212-780-5200	
George P. Johnson Co 3600 Giddings Rd *Web:* www.gpj.com	Auburn Hills	MI	48326	248-475-2500	
Gifting Services LLC 7494-B Santa Monica Blvd *Web:* www.giftingservices.com	West Hollywood	CA	90046	323-874-4156	
GLS Companies Inc 6845 Winnetka Cir *Web:* www.glsmn.com	Brooklyn Park	MN	55428	763-535-7277	
Gold Stars Speakers Bureau 7478 N La Cholla Blvd *Web:* www.goldstars.com	Tucson	AZ	85741	520-742-4384	
Goldense Group Inc 1346 South St *Web:* www.goldensegroupinc.com	Needham	MA	02492	781-444-5400	
Gorilla Marketing 4100 Flat Rock Dr Ste A *Web:* www.gorillamarketing.net	Riverside	CA	92505	951-353-8133	
Gravity Group 107 E Water St *Web:* www.gravitygroup.com	Harrisonburg	VA	22801	540-433-3071	
Grayrose Marketing Group 9631 Ne Colfax St *Web:* www.grayrose.com	Portland	OR	97220	503-281-1922	
Great Falls Marketing LLC 121 Mill St *TF:* 800-221-8895 ■ *Web:* www.greatfallsmarketing.com	Auburn	ME	04210	800-221-8895	
Group for Organizational Effectiveness Inc, The 727 Waldens Pond Rd *Web:* groupoe.com	Albany	NY	12203	518-456-7738	
Group iii Marketing of Plymouth Inc 1907 Wayzata Blvd Ste 200 *Web:* www.group3marketing.com	Wayzata	MN	55391	952-475-3269	
Hanapin Marketing LLC 501 N Morton St Ste 212 *Web:* www.hanapinmarketing.com	Bloomington	IN	47404	812-330-3134	
Hansa GCR LLC 308 SW First Ave *Web:* www.hansagcr.com	Portland	OR	97204	503-241-8036	
Harte-Hanks Market Intelligence 9980 Huennekens St **Fax Area Code: 858* ■ *TF:* 800-854-8409 ■ *Web:* www.citdb.com	San Diego	CA	92121	800-854-8409	452-7491*
Hcpro Inc 75 Sylvan St Ste A-10 *TF:* 800-650-6787 ■ *Web:* www.hcpro.com	Danvers	MA	01923	800-650-6787	
Healthmark Services 217 Lakewood Rd *Web:* www.healthmarkservices.com	Van Buren	AR	72956	479-471-9797	
Heinzeroth Marketing Group 415 Y Blvd Ste 3 *Web:* www.heinzeroth.com	Rockford	IL	61107	815-967-0929	
High Tide Creative 245 Craven St *Web:* www.hightidecreative.com	New Bern	NC	28560	252-671-7087	
Hollis Marketing 2130 Brenner St *Web:* hollismarketing.com	Saginaw	MI	48602	989-797-3300	
Holsted Marketing Inc 135 Madison Ave *Web:* www.holstedmarketing.com	New York	NY	10016	212-686-8537	
Home Team Marketing LLC 812 Huron Rd E Ste 205 *Web:* www.hometeammarketing.com	Cleveland	OH	44115	216-566-8326	
Hr Alliance LLC 580 W Main St *Web:* hralliancewithyou.com	Wytheville	VA	24382	276-223-1718	
Hr Answers Inc 7659 SW Mohawk St *Web:* www.hranswers.com	Tualatin	OR	97062	503-885-8614	
Hr Consultants Inc 160 Jari Dr Ste 180 *Web:* www.hrconsults.com	Johnstown	PA	15904	814-266-3818	
Hunter Business Group LLC 4650 N Port Washington Rd *TF:* 800-423-4010 ■ *Web:* www.hunterbusiness.com	Milwaukee	WI	53212	414-203-8060	203-8225
ICiDigital Inc 4000 Westchase Blvd Ste 280 *Web:* www.icidigital.com	Raleigh	NC	27607	919-883-9467	
ICS Marketing Services Inc 4225 Legacy Pkwy *Web:* www.icshq.com	Lansing	MI	48911	517-394-1890	
Image Matters LLC 201 Loudoun St SW *Web:* www.imagemattersllc.com	Leesburg	VA	20175	703-669-5510	
Impact Planning Group 11 Grumman Hill Rd *Web:* www.impactplan.com	Wilton	CT	06897	203-854-1011	854-4888
In Touch Marketing Inc 2793 Deerhaven Dr *Web:* intouchmarketinginc.net	Cincinnati	OH	45244	513-474-6317	
Initial Outfitters Inc 209 Alabama St *Web:* www.initialoutfitters.com	Auburn	AL	36832	334-887-1856	
Innotrac Corp 6465 E Johns Crossing *NASDAQ: INOC* ■ *TF:* 800-322-2885 ■ *Web:* www.innotrac.com	Johns Creek	GA	30097	678-584-4000	475-5840
Inquiry Systems Inc 1195 Goodale Blvd *Web:* www.inquirysys.com	Columbus	OH	43212	614-464-3800	
Insider Marketing 10801 E Northwest Hwy *Web:* www.insidermarketing.com	Dallas	TX	75238	214-348-4350	
Insight Marketing Design Inc 401 E Eighth St Ste 304 *Web:* insightmarketingdesign.com	Sioux Falls	SD	57103	605-275-0011	
Insights in Marketing LLC 444 Skokie Blvd Ste 200 *Web:* www.insightsinmarketing.com	Wilmette	IL	60091	847-853-0500	
Insigniam Performance 1205 N Coast Hwy Ste D *Web:* insigniam.com	Laguna Beach	CA	92651	949-494-4553	
Intellimar Inc 7560 Main St *Web:* www.intellimar.com	Sykesville	MD	21784	410-552-9940	552-9939
IntelliShop LLC 2025 Michael Owens Way *Web:* www.intelli-shop.com	Perrysburg	OH	43551	419-872-5103	
Intrinzic Inc One Levee Way Ste 3121 *Web:* www.intrinzicinc.com	Newport	KY	41071	859-261-2200	
Invenio Marketing Solutions Inc 2201 Donley Dr Ste 200 *Web:* www.inveniomarketing.com	Austin	TX	78758	512-990-2000	
InVision Communications Inc 1280 Civic Dr Third Fl *Web:* www.iv.com	Walnut Creek	CA	94596	925-944-1211	
iORMYX Inc 1100-D Elden St Ste 304 *Web:* www.iormyx.com	Herndon	VA	20170	703-456-7010	
Ipsenault Co, The 3791 River Rd N Ste F *Web:* ipsenault.com	Keizer	OR	97303	503-390-8968	
Ivie & Associates Inc 601 Silveron Blvd Ste 200 *Web:* www.ivieinc.com	Flower Mound	TX	75028	972-899-5000	
IZ ON Media LLC 600 Harrison St Fourth Fl *Web:* www.izonmedia.com.	San Francisco	CA	94107	415-808-3500	
J C Marketing Associates Inc 467 Main St *Web:* jcmarketingassociates.com	Wakefield	MA	01880	781-245-7070	
J Hl Mail Marketing 3100 Borham Ave *Web:* www.jhl.com	Stevens Point	WI	54481	715-341-0581	
J-dak Inc 6257 Hwy 76 E *Web:* jdak.com	Springfield	TN	37172	615-382-5651	
J. Knipper & Company Inc One Healthcare Way *Web:* www.knipper.com	Lakewood	NJ	08701	732-905-7878	
J. Stokes & Associates Inc 1444 N Main St *Web:* jstokes.com	Walnut Creek	CA	94596	925-933-1624	
James Gutheim & Associates Inc 16400 Ventura Blvd Ste 312 *Web:* gutheim.com	Encino	CA	91436	818-784-7189	
JD Events LLC 5520 Park Ave Ste 305 *Web:* www.jdevents.com	Trumbull	CT	06611	203-371-6322	
Kahler Slater Inc 111 W Wisconsin Ave *Web:* www.kahlerslater.com	Milwaukee	WI	53203	414-272-2000	
KARMA Media Labs LLC 10215 Santa Monica Blvd *Web:* www.karmamedialabs.com	Los Angeles	CA	90067	310-722-7027	
Karo Group Inc 308-611 Alexander St *Web:* www.karo.com	Vancouver	BC	V6A1E1	604-255-6100	
KELYN Group LLC, The 137 Stone Root Ln Ste 1 *Web:* www.thekelyngroup.com	Concord	MA	01742	978-369-7000	
Kempton Group, The Two Garfield Pl Ste 1501 *Web:* tkg-marketing.com	Cincinnati	OH	45202	513-651-5556	
Kern Organization Inc 20955 Warner Ctr Ln *Web:* kernagency.com	Woodland Hills	CA	91367	818-703-8775	
Kesselman Jones 3411 Candelaria Rd Ne Ste G *Web:* www.kessjones.com	Albuquerque	NM	87107	505-266-3461	
Khong Guan Corp 30068 Eigenbrodt Way *TF:* 877-889-8968 ■ *Web:* kgcusa.squarespace.com	Union City	CA	94587	510-487-7800	487-0301
Krt Marketing Inc 3685 Mt Diablo Blvd Ste 255 *Web:* www.krtmarketing.com	Lafayette	CA	94549	925-284-0444	
Kuczmarski & Assoc 2001 N Halsted Ste 201 *Web:* www.kuczmarski.com/contact-2	Chicago	IL	60614	312-988-1539	
Ky-ani Sun Inc 1070 Riverwalk Dr Ste 350 *Web:* www.kyani.net	Idaho Falls	ID	83402	208-529-9872	
L b L Strategies Ltd 6321 N Avondale Ave Ste 214 *Web:* lblstrategies.com	Chicago	IL	60631	773-774-0240	
Landajob Advertising & Marketing Talent 222 W Gregory Blvd Ste 304 *Web:* www.landajobnow.com	Kansas City	MO	64114	816-523-1881	
Landor Assoc Ltd 1001 Front St *TF:* 888-252-6367 ■ *Web:* www.landor.com	San Francisco	CA	94111	415-365-1700	365-3190
Lansberg, Gersick & Associates LLC 100 Whitney Ave Apt 1 *Web:* www.lgassoc.com	New Haven	CT	06510	203-497-8855	
Launch Two W 45th St *Web:* www.321launch.com	New York	NY	10036	212-845-5800	
LaVERDAD Hispanic Marketing Solutions 7817 Cooper Rd *Web:* www.laverdadmarketing.com	Cincinnati	OH	45242	513-891-1430	
LeadMD Inc 9383 E Bahia Dr Ste 225 *Web:* www.leadmd.com	Scottsdale	AZ	85260	480-278-7205	
Left Brain DGA 3130 Alpine Rd Ste 288-154 *Web:* www.leftbraindga.com	Portola Valley	CA	94028	650-561-3435	
Legendary Marketing 3729 S Lecanto Hwy *Web:* www.legendarymarketing.com	Lecanto	FL	34461	352-527-3553	
Lexicon Branding Inc 30 Liberty Ship Way Ste 3360 *Web:* www.lexiconbranding.com	Sausalito	CA	94965	415-332-1811	332-2528
Lexnet Consulting Group Inc 101 Lucas Vly Rd Ste 249 *Web:* lexnetcg.com	San Rafael	CA	94903	415-472-3100	
Licensing Resource Group LLC 442 Century Ln Ste 100 *Web:* lrgusa.com	Holland	MI	49423	616-395-0676	
Lift Agency Inc 205 Industrial Pkwy N Unit 1 *Web:* www.getlift.com	Aurora	ON	L4G4C4	416-438-5438	
Liquid Agency Inc 448 S Market St *Web:* www.liquidagency.com	San Jose	CA	95113	408-850-8800	
Lloyd Schuh Advertising Inc 2207 Cantrell Rd *Web:* www.lscmarketing.com	Little Rock	AR	72202	501-374-2332	
Lmd 14409 Greenview Dr Ste 200 *Web:* www.lmdagency.com	Laurel	MD	20708	301-498-6656	
LocBox 400 Second St Ste 400 *TF:* 855-256-2269 ■ *Web:* app.locbox.com	San Francisco	CA	94107	855-256-2269	
Loop Consulting Group 9485 Sw 72nd St Ste A204 *Web:* loopconsulting.com	Miami	FL	33173	305-271-9915	
Lorel Marketing Group LLC 235 S 17th St *Web:* www.lorel.com	Philadelphia	PA	19103	610-337-2343	
LoyaltyExpress Inc 53 Commerce Way *Web:* www.loyaltyexpress.com	Woburn	MA	01801	781-938-1175	
LRG Marketing Communications Inc 48 Burd St Ste105 *Web:* lrgmarketing.com	Nyack	NY	10960	845-358-1801	

Company	City	State	ZIP	Phone	Fax
M45 Marketing Services Inc 524 W Stephenson St *Web:* m45.com	Freeport	IL	61032	815-297-0166	
MacroSoft Inc Two Sylvan Way Third Fl. *Web:* www.macrosoftinc.com	Parsippany	NJ	07054	973-889-0500	
Magic Logix Inc 16610 Dallas Pkwy Ste 2200 *Web:* www.magiclogix.com	Dallas	TX	75248	214-694-2162	
Magicomm LLC 15 Alexander Rd *Web:* www.magicomm.biz	Billerica	MA	01821	978-964-1900	
Magnani & Associates Advertising Inc 200 S Michigan Ave Ste 500 *Web:* www.magnani.com	Chicago	IL	60604	312-957-0770	
Marcom Gurus 2083 Louise Ln *Web:* marcomgurus.com	Los Altos	CA	94024	650-564-0011	
MarketBridge Inc 4350 East-West Hwy Sixth Fl. **Fax Area Code:* 301 ■ *TF:* 888-468-6658 ■ *Web:* www.market-bridge.com	Bethesda	MD	20814	240-752-1800	907-3282*
Marketing Management Group Inc 561 Seventh Ave Ste 1700 *Web:* www.mmgus.com	New York	NY	10018	212-768-9660	
Marketing Results 2900 W Horizon Ridge Pkwy Ste 200 *Web:* www.marketingresults.net	Henderson	NV	89052	702-361-3850	
MarketingProfs LLC 419 N Larchmont Blvd #295 *TF:* 866-557-9625 ■ *Web:* www.marketingprofs.com	Los Angeles	CA	90004	866-557-9625	
Marnell Companies LLC 222 Via Marnell Way *Web:* www.marnellcompanies.com	Las Vegas	NV	89119	702-739-2000	
Martin Group LLC, The 477 Main St *Web:* tmgbrandfuel.com	Buffalo	NY	14203	716-853-2757	
Martin Investment Management LLC 1007 Church St Ste 530 *Web:* www.martin-investments.com	Evanston	IL	60201	847-424-9124	
Mass Connections Inc 13131 E 166th St *Web:* www.massconnections.com	Cerritos	CA	90703	562-365-0200	
Massini Group 1323 NE Orenco Stn Pkwy Ste 300 *Web:* www.massini-group.com	Hillsboro	OR	97124	503-640-9800	640-9888
Maturehealth Communications 502 Centennial Ave *Web:* www.maturehealth.com	Cranford	NJ	07016	908-709-8080	
Mcdaniels Marketing Communications 11 Olt Ave *Web:* www.mcdanielsmarketing.com	Pekin	IL	61554	309-346-4230	
McDill Associates 4800 Leapfrog Ln *Web:* jacobsheart.org	Soquel	CA	95073	831-462-3198	
Mcdowell Group Inc 9360 Glacier Hwy Ste 201 *Web:* www.mcdowellgroup.net	Juneau	AK	99801	907-586-6126	
Mclellan Creative 695 Mistletoe Rd Ste M2 *Web:* www.mclellancreative.com	Ashland	OR	97520	541-488-2270	
Meridia Audience Response 5207 Militia Hill Rd Ste 100 *Web:* www.meridiaars.com	Plymouth Meeting	PA	19462	610-260-6800	
Meridian One Corp 5775 General Washington Dr *Web:* www.meridianone.com	Alexandria	VA	22312	703-461-5200	
Merkle Inc 50 Chestnut Ridge Road, Ste. 120 *Web:* www.analytici.com	Montvale	NJ	07645	201-571-2000	
Metrix Marketing Inc 40 Wildbriar Rd *Web:* www.metrix-marketing.com	Rochester	NY	14623	585-334-0890	
MFR Consultants Inc 128 Chestnut St *Web:* www.mfrconsultants.com	Philadelphia	PA	19106	215-238-9270	
Michael Allen Co Nine Old Kings Hwy South *Web:* www.michaelallencompany.com	Darien	CT	06820	203-662-5100	
Midlantic Marketing 118 Commons Ct *Web:* www.midlantic.net	Chadds Ford	PA	19317	610-361-0500	
Military Sales & Service Co 5301 S Westmoreland Rd *Web:* mssco.com	Dallas	TX	75237	214-330-4621	330-1740
Miller Heiman Inc 10509 Professional Cir Ste 100 *Web:* www.millerheiman.com	Reno	NV	89521	775-827-4411	
Millstone Medical Outsourcing LLC 580 Commerce Dr *Web:* www.millstonemedical.com	Fall River	MA	02720	508-679-8384	679-8414
Missouri Enterprise 1706 E 10th St *TF:* 800-956-2682 ■ *Web:* www.missourienterprise.org	Rolla	MO	65401	800-956-2682	
Mitchell Group The Conslțnt 1816 11th St Nw *Web:* www.the-mitchellgroup.com	Washington	DC	20001	202-745-1919	
Mobiquity Networks Inc 600 Old Country Rd Ste 541 *Web:* www.mobiquitynetworks.com	Garden City	NY	11530	516-256-7766	
Mood Media Corp 1703 W Fifth St Ste 600 *Web:* www.moodmedia.com	Austin	TX	78703	416-510-2800	
Moosylvania Marketin LC 7303 Marietta Ave *Web:* www.moosylvania.com	St. Louis	MO	63143	314-644-7900	
Morris & Mcdaniel Inc Consultants 117 S Saint Asaph St *Web:* www.morrisandmcdaniel.com	Alexandria	VA	22314	703-836-3600	
Morrison Agency Inc, The 3365 Piedmont Rd Ste 1400 Tower Walk at Tower Pl *Web:* www.morrisonagency.com	Atlanta	GA	30305	404-233-3405	261-8384
Mosteller & Associates 2433 Morgantown Rd Ste 100 *Web:* www.mostellerhr.com	Reading	PA	19607	610-779-3870	
Motive 620 16th St Ste 200 *Web:* thinkmotive.com	Denver	CO	80202	303-302-2100	
Murdoch Marketing 217 E 24th St Ste 220 *Web:* www.murdochmarketing.com	Holland	MI	49423	616-392-4893	
Mym Austin Inc 13206 Mansfield Dr Bldg A *Web:* mymaustin.com	Austin	TX	78732	512-266-7777	
N.A.Williams Co 2900 A Paces Ferry Rd. *Web:* www.nawilliams.com	Atlanta	GA	30339	770-433-2282	
National Food Laboratory Inc 6363 Clark Ave *Web:* www.thenfl.com	Dublin	CA	94568	925-828-1440	833-9239
NCompass International Inc 8223 Santa Monica Blvd. *Web:* www.ncompassinternational.com	West Hollywood	CA	90046	323-785-1700	
Nelson Ink 330 Second St N *Web:* nelsonink.com	Middle River	MN	56737	218-222-3831	
Nethawk Interactive Inc 1185 Park Ave *Web:* www.nethawk.net	Emeryville	CA	94608	510-595-2220	
Netmark.com 1930 N Woodruff Ave *TF:* 800-935-5133 ■ *Web:* www.netmark.com	Idaho Falls	ID	83401	800-935-5133	
Netsertive Inc 2400 Perimeter Park Dr Ste 100 *TF:* 800-940-4351 ■ *Web:* www.netsertive.com	Research Triangle Region	NC	27560	800-940-4351	
New Angle Media 2601 E Thomas Rd Ste 235 *Web:* www.newanglemedia.com	Phoenix	AZ	85016	602-840-5530	
newBrandAnalytics Inc 1250 23rd St NW Ste 450 *Web:* www.newbrandanalytics.com	Washington	DC	20037	202-800-7850	
NexAge Technologies USA Inc 75 Lincoln Hwy Ste 101 *Web:* www.nexageusa.com	Iselin	NJ	08830	732-494-4944	
Next Marketing Inc 2820 Peterson Pl *Web:* www.nextmarketing.com	Norcross	GA	30071	770-225-2200	
Next Steps Marketing One Polk St Fl 2 *Web:* www.nextstepsmarketing.com	San Francisco	CA	94102	415-773-1841	
Nielsen Media Research Ltd 160 McNabb St *Web:* www.nielsenmedia.ca	Markham	ON	L3R4B8	905-475-9595	
Niven Marketing Group, The 955 Kimberly Dr *Web:* www.niven.net	Carol Stream	IL	60188	630-580-6000	580-5690
NMV The Marketing Firm Inc 11300 Coloma Rd Ste B-14 *Web:* www.nmvinc.com	Gold River	CA	95670	916-852-7716	
Nordis Direct 4401 NW 124th Ave *Web:* www.nordisdirect.com	Coral Springs	FL	33065	954-323-5500	
Northern Response International Ltd 50 Staples Ave Richmond Hill *Web:* www.northernresponse.com	Toronto	ON	L4B0A7	905-737-6698	
Notions Marketing Corp 1500 Buchanan Ave Sw *Web:* notions-marketing.com	Grand Rapids	MI	49507	616-243-8424	
nParallel LLC 13120 County Rd 6 *Web:* www.nparallel.com	Minneapolis	MN	55441	763-231-4800	
Nu Image Marketing 1271 N Tustin Ave *Web:* nimarketing.com	Anaheim	CA	92807	714-575-8947	
Obi Creative 2920 Farnam St *Web:* obiinc.net	Omaha	NE	68131	402-493-7999	
Oglethorpe Inc 18302 Highwoods Preserve Pkwy Ste 114 *Web:* www.oglethorpeinc.com	Tampa	FL	33647	813-978-1933	
Ohana Companies LLC, The 1405 Foulk Rd Foulkstone Plz Ste 200 *Web:* www.everybodywins.com	Wilmington	DE	19803	302-225-5505	
Omgeo LLC 55 Thomson Pl *TF:* 866-496-6436 ■ *Web:* www.omgeo.com	Boston	MA	02210	866-496-6436	
On Track Marketing Inc 1910 W N Ave *Web:* www.otmarketing.com	Chicago	IL	60622	773-235-0017	
Optiem 1370 W Sixth St Third Fl *Web:* www.optiem.com	Cleveland	OH	44113	216-574-8700	
Opus Events Agency 9309 SW Nimbus Ave *Web:* www.opuseventsagency.com	Beaverton	OR	97008	971-223-0777	
OrangeSoda Inc 732 E Utah Vly Dr *Web:* www.orangesoda.com	American Fork	UT	84003	801-610-2500	
Orbit Design 2560 Sheridan Blvd Ste 4 *Web:* www.orbit-design.com	Denver	CO	80214	303-433-1616	
P W Feats Inc Three E Read St Fl 1 *Web:* www.featsinc.com	Baltimore	MD	21202	410-727-5575	
Page Group Inc, The 8905 Fairview Rd Ste 401 *Web:* www.pagegroup.com	Silver Spring	MD	20910	301-565-4020	
Parks Productions Ltd 116 Premier Dr Orion Mi *Web:* www.parkspro.com	Orion	MI	48359	248-370-9200	
Patpatia & Associates Inc 1803 Sixth St Ste A *Web:* patpatia.com	Berkeley	CA	94710	510-559-7140	
Paulsen Marketing Inc 3510 S First Ave Cir *Web:* www.paulsen.ag	Sioux Falls	SD	57105	605-336-1745	
PayStream Advisors Inc 2923 S Tryon St Ste 240 *Web:* www.paystreamadvisors.com	Charlotte	NC	28203	704-523-7357	
PDI Inc 300 Interpace Pkwy Morris Corp Ctr 1 Bldg A *NASDAQ: PDII* ■ *TF:* 800-242-7494 ■ *Web:* www.pdi-inc.com	Parsippany	NJ	07054	800-242-7494	
Peak Sales & Marketing Inc 4751 Lindle Rd Ste 128 *Web:* www.peaksalesmkt.com	Harrisburg	PA	17111	717-986-0301	
Pedowitz Group, The 810 Mayfield Rd *TF:* 855-738-6584 ■ *Web:* www.pedowitzgroup.com	Milton	GA	30009	855-738-6584	
Penny Group Inc, The 1328 Harding Pl *Web:* thepennygroup.com	Charlotte	NC	28204	704-372-1400	
Pentera Inc 8650 Commerce Park Pl Ste G *Web:* www.pentera.com	Indianapolis	IN	46268	317-875-0910	
Peppers & Rogers Group 901 Main Ave # 212 *Web:* www.1to1media.com	Norwalk	CT	06851	203-642-5121	642-5126
PharMethod Inc 1170 Wheeler Way *Web:* www.pharmethod.com	Langhorne	PA	19047	215-354-1212	
Piranha Marketing Inc 4440 S Rural Rd Bldg F *Web:* joepolish.com	Tempe	AZ	85282	480-858-0008	

	City	State	ZIP	Phone	Fax
Planogramming Solutions Inc 9080 Golfside Dr	Jacksonville	FL	32256	904-448-0834	
Web: www.planogrammingsolutions.com					
Points International Ltd 171 John St Fifth Fl	Toronto	ON	M5T1X3	416-595-0000	
Web: www.points.com					
Populus Group LLC 850 Stephenson Hwy Ste 500	Troy	MI	48083	248-581-1100	581-1170
Web: www.populusgroup.com					
Practical Imagination Enterprising 18 Losey Rd	Ringoes	NJ	08551	908-237-2246	
Web: www.practical-imagination.com					
Pragma Corp, The 116 E Broad St	Falls Church	VA	22046	703-237-9303	
Web: www.pragmacorp.com					
Pragmatic Marketing Inc 8910 E Raintree Dr	Scottsdale	AZ	85260	480-515-1411	
Web: www.pragmaticmarketing.com					
Premier Direct Marketing Inc 7725 National Tpke Unit 100	Louisville	KY	40214	502-367-6441	
Web: premierdm.net					
Pricing Advisor Inc 3535 Roswell Rd Ste 59	Marietta	GA	30062	770-509-9933	
Web: pricingsociety.com					
Prime Concepts Group Inc 1807 S Eisenhower St	Wichita	KS	67209	316-942-1111	
Web: www.primeconcepts.com					
Printfection LLC 3700 Quebec St Unit 100-136	Denver	CO	80207	866-459-7990	
TF: 866-459-7990 ■ *Web:* www.printfection.com					
Pro-mail Associates Inc 22404 66th Ave S	Kent	WA	98032	206-282-2400	
Web: www.pmadm.com					
ProOrbis LLC 112 Moores Rd Ste 400	Malvern	PA	19355	610-240-0200	
Web: www.proorbis.com					
Prospect Smarter Inc 2502 N Rocky Point Dr Ste 500	Tampa	FL	33607	813-699-9996	
Web: www.prospectsmarter.com					
Prospectiv Direct Inc 40 Harvard Mill Sq Ste 1	Wakefield	MA	01880	781-305-2100	
Web: www.prospectiv.com					
PSD Global LLC 505 N Mansfield St	Alexandria	VA	22304	703-531-8773	
Web: www.psdglobal.com					
Public Impact 504 Dogwood Dr	Chapel Hill	NC	27516	919-240-7955	
Web: www.publicimpact.com					
Public Policy Institute 1231 Lincoln Dr	Carbondale	IL	62901	618-453-4009	
Web: www.siu.edu					
Quala-Tel Enterprises 9925 Business Park Ave Ste A	San Diego	CA	92131	858-577-2900	
Web: www.qualatel.com					
Quixote Group Research Marketing 3107 Brassfield Rd Ste 100	Greensboro	NC	27410	336-605-0363	
Web: www.quixotegroup.com					
Rainmaker Marketing Corp 15519 Dawnbrook Dr	Houston	TX	77068	281-537-1200	
Web: www.rainmakermarketing.com					
Ramapo Sales & Marketing Inc 4760 Goer Dr Ste F	North Charleston	SC	29406	843-747-2577	
Web: www.ramaposales.com					
Rassak Experience 221 11th St	San Francisco	CA	94103	415-621-4300	
Web: rassak.com					
Raven One to One Marketing 2650 Lehigh St	Whitehall	PA	18052	484-240-6500	
Web: raven121.com					
RAZR Marketing Inc 10590 Wayzata Blvd	Minnetonka	MN	55305	763-404-6100	
Web: www.razrmarketing.com					
Red Cloud Promotions 1600 Sawtelle Blvd Ste 108	Los Angeles	CA	90025	310-444-5583	
Web: redcloudpromotions.com					
Red Feather Marketing Group Inc 332 Main St	Madison	NJ	07940	973-966-1399	
Web: www.red-feather.com					
Reese Military Sales Inc 2820 Bransford Ave	Nashville	TN	37204	615-298-5774	
Web: reesemilitarysales.com					
Regalix Inc 1121 San Antonio Rd Ste B200	Palo Alto	CA	94303	650-331-1167	
Web: www.regalix.com					
Rely Services Inc 2354 Hassell Rd Ste B	Hoffman Estates	IL	60169	847-310-8750	
Web: relyservices.com					
Rennhack Marketing Services Inc 752 Port America Pl	Grapevine	TX	76051	817-481-6516	
Web: www.rennhack.com					
REVShare Corp 32836 Wolf Store Rd	Temecula	CA	92592	951-302-2091	
Web: www.revshare.com					
Ries & Ries 2195 River Cliff Dr	Roswell	GA	30076	770-643-0880	643-0051
Web: www.ries.com					
Riovida Networks 6979 Exeter Dr	Oakland	CA	94611	510-336-2636	
Web: www.riovida.net					
Rome Group Inc, The 14 N Newstead Ave	Saint Louis	MO	63108	314-533-0930	
Web: www.theromegroup.com					
Ronin Corp Two Research Way Second Fl	Princeton	NJ	08540	609-452-0060	452-0091
Web: ronin.com					
Ross Marketing Inc 2214 Main St Ste A	Cedar Falls	IA	50613	319-266-5881	
Web: rossmarketing.net					
RPM Direct LLC 24 Arnett Ave Ste 100	Lambertville	NJ	08530	609-566-7150	
Web: www.rpmdirectllc.com					
RS Consulting USA 39 S LaSalle St	Chicago	IL	60603	312-368-0800	
Web: www.rsconsulting-usa.com					
RTC Inc 2800 Golf Rd	Rolling Meadows	IL	60008	847-640-2400	
Web: www.rtc.com					
Rymax Corp 19 Chapin Rd Bldg B	Pine Brook	NJ	07058	973-808-4066	
Web: www.rymaxinc.com					
S. Emerson Group Inc 407 E Lancaster Ave	Wayne	PA	19087	610-971-9600	
Web: www.emersongroup.com					
S.H. Hirth & Associates Inc 36 W 44th St Ste 610	New York	NY	10036	212-997-1187	
Web: www.shhirthandassociates.com					
Sales Evolution LLC 2837 Dogwood Ln	Broomall	PA	19008	610-353-8686	
Web: www.salesevolution.com					
Sales Readiness Group Inc 8015 SE 28th St Ste 206	Mercer Island	WA	98040	800-490-0715	
TF: 800-490-0715 ■ *Web:* www.salesreadinessgroup.com					
Salt Branding LLC 1265 Battery St Fl 2	San Francisco	CA	94111	415-616-1500	
Web: saltbranding.com					
Sandra Hartog & Associates Inc 280 First St	Brooklyn	NY	11215	718-832-2118	
Web: www.sandrahartogassoc.com					
Scarsin Corp Two Brock St W Ste 201	Uxbridge	ON	L9P1P2	905-852-0086	
Web: www.scarsin.com					
Schmidt Consulting Services Inc 405 McKnight Park Dr	Pittsburgh	PA	15237	412-367-1226	
Web: www.schmidtcs.com					
School Photo Marketing 35 Vanderburg Rd	Marlboro	NJ	07746	732-431-0440	
Web: www.schoolphotoonline.com					
Scientia Global Inc 2210 Front St Ste 204	Melbourne	FL	32901	321-733-1971	
Web: www.scientiaglobal.com					
Selling Simplified Inc 7400 E Orchard Rd Ste 350S	Greenwood Village	CO	80111	720-638-8500	
Web: sellingsimplified.com					
Senior Marketing Specialist 801 Gray Oak Dr	Columbia	MO	65201	573-443-3155	
Web: www.smsteam.net					
Seroka & Associates N17w24222 Riverwood Dr Ste 170	Waukesha	WI	53188	262-523-3740	
Web: www.seroka.com					
Sid Factor 7 Inc 1827 Pearl St Ste 1	Boulder	CO	80302	303-449-5323	
Web: sidfactor.com					
Sid Lee Inc 75 Rue Queen Bureau 1400	Montreal	QC	H3C2N6	514-282-2200	
Web: www.sidlee.com					
Signet Inc 1801 Shelby Oaks Dr N Ste 12	Memphis	TN	38134	901-387-5555	
Web: www.gosignet.com					
Silicon Alley Group One Austin Ave Fl 2	Iselin	NJ	08830	732-326-1600	
Web: sag-inc.com					
SilverTech Inc 196 Bridge St	Manchester	NH	03104	603-669-6600	
Web: www.silvertech.com					
Sitkins Group Inc 6700 Winkler Rd Ste 4	Fort Myers	FL	33919	239-337-2555	
Web: www.sitkins.com					
Sixth Sense Media 4220 NC Hwy 55 Ste 340	Durham	NC	27713	919-484-2442	
Web: www.sixthsensemedia.com					
Sixth Star Entertainment & Marketing Inc 21 NW Fifth St	Fort Lauderdale	FL	33301	954-462-6760	
Web: www.sixthstar.com					
Skillpath Seminars 6900 Squibb Rd	Mission	KS	66201	913-362-3900	
Web: www.skillpath.com					
Smartsearch Marketing 4450 Arapahoe Ave Ste 100	Boulder	CO	80303	303-444-3134	
Web: smartsearchmarketing.com					
Smithgeiger LLC 31365 Oak Crest Dr Ste 150	Westlake Village	CA	91361	818-874-2000	
Web: smithgeiger.com					
SOAP Group, The PO Box 7828	Portland	ME	04112	207-772-0066	
Web: www.thesoapgroup.com					
Softresources LLC 11411 Ne 124th St Ste 270	Kirkland	WA	98034	425-216-4030	
Web: www.softresources.com					
Somerset Management Group LLC 80 Veronica Ave Ste 3	Somerset	NJ	08873	732-296-8200	
Web: somersetmgmt.com					
Sonawane Webdynamics Inc 44031 Pipeline Plz Ste 305	Ashburn	VA	20147	703-723-9191	
Web: www.sonawane.com					
Sound Impressions Music Marketing L.L.C 14290 Gillis Rd Ste A	Dallas	TX	75244	888-512-9119	
TF: 888-512-9119 ■ *Web:* www.fancorps.com					
Special Audience Marketing Inc 6700 Manchaca Rd	Austin	TX	78745	512-441-6484	
Web: specialaudience.com					
Spencer Hall Inc 11321 Terwilligerscreek Dr	Cincinnati	OH	45249	513-683-9724	
Web: www.spencerhall.com					
St Meyer & Hubbard Inc 10N865 Williamsburg Dr	Elgin	IL	60124	847-717-4328	
Web: www.stmeyerandhubbard.com					
Stafford Communications Group Inc 309 South St Ste 3	New Providence	NJ	07974	908-464-7740	
Web: www.staffcom.com					
Starmark International Inc 210 S Andrews Ave	Fort Lauderdale	FL	33301	954-874-9000	874-9010
Web: www.starmark.com					
Stevens & Tate Inc 1900 S Highland Ave Ste 200	Lombard	IL	60148	630-627-5200	
Web: www.stevens-tate.com					
Stone Coast Fund Services LLC Two Portland Sq	Portland	ME	04101	207-699-2680	
Web: www.stone-coast.com					
Stoptech Ltd 365 Industrial Dr	Harrison	OH	45030	513-202-5500	
Web: stoptechltd.com					
stratton gilmore group 37 Old Shore Rd	Madison	WI	53704	608-249-3610	
Web: strattongilmoregroup.com					
Strider Marketing 3755 S Capital Of Texas Hwy Ste 210	Austin	TX	78704	512-707-5120	
Web: www.striderbikes.com					
StringCan Interactive LLC 7525 E Camelback Rd Ste 201	Scottsdale	AZ	85251	480-612-0360	
Web: www.stringcaninteractive.com					
Stuart Maue Mitchell & James Ltd 3850 Mckelvey Rd	Bridgeton	MO	63044	314-291-3030	
Web: www.smmj.com					
Suarez Corp Industries 7800 Whipple Ave NW	North Canton	OH	44720	330-494-5504	
TF: 800-764-0008 ■ *Web:* www.suarez.com					
Success Associates LLC 26 Kings Vly Ct	Damascus	MD	20872	301-391-6161	
Web: www.successassociates.com					
Summit Direct Mail Inc 1655 Terre Colony Ct	Dallas	TX	75212	469-916-5170	
Web: www.summitdm.com					

Phone Fax

Sunbelt Sales & Marketing Associates Inc
170 Ottley Dr ... Atlanta GA 30324 404-892-8778
Web: www.filmloc.com

Sundog Inc 2000 44th St SW Fl 6 ... Fargo ND 58103 701-235-5525
Web: www.sundoginteractive.com

Surgem LLC 555 Kinderkamack Rd Ste 4 ... Oradell NJ 07649 201-834-1100
Web: www.surgemllc.com

Suss Consulting
801 Old York Rd Noble Plz Ste 305 ... Jenkintown PA 19046 215-884-5900 884-1637
TF: 888-984-5900 ■ *Web:* www.sussconsulting.com

Swiss Knife Shop 10 Northern Blvd Ste 8 ... Amherst NH 03031 603-732-0069
Web: www.swissknifeshop.com

Symbolist 1090 Texan Trl ... Grapevine TX 76051 800-498-6885
TF: 800-498-6885 ■ *Web:* www.symbolist.com

Symetri Internet Marketing
6520 Airport Ctr Dr Ste 208 ... Greensboro NC 27409 336-285-0940
Web: www.symetri.com

Syndyne Corp 12109 Ne 95th St ... Vancouver WA 98682 360-256-8466
Web: syndyne.com

Synergy Direct Response 130 E Alton Ave ... Santa Ana CA 92707 714-754-5733
Web: www.synergydr.com

Tactician Corp 305 N Main St ... Andover MA 01810 978-475-4475
Web: www.tactician.com

Tahzoo LLC 3128 M St Nw ... Washington DC 20007 202-621-7160
Web: www.tahzoo.com

Tartan Marketing 10467 93rd Ave N ... Osseo MN 55369 763-391-7575
Web: www.tartanmarketing.com

TASC Technical Services LLC 73 Newton Rd ... Plaistow NH 03865 877-304-8272
TF: 877 304 8272 ■ *Web:* www.tasctech.com

TDH Marketing & Communications Inc
8153 Garnet Dr ... Dayton OH 45458 937-438-3434
Web: www.tdh-marketing.com

Team Epic LLC 230 East Ave ... Norwalk CT 06855 203-831-2100
Web: www.teamvelocity.com

Team Marketing Inc 6810 N State Rd 7 ... Coconut Creek FL 33073 561-995-0690
Web: www.teaminc.net

Technical Communities Inc
1000 Cherry Ave Ste 100 ... San Bruno CA 94066 650-624-0525 624-0535
TF: 888-665-2765 ■ *Web:* www.technicalcommunities.com

Techno Source USA Inc 20 W 22nd St Ste 1101 ... New York NY 10010 212-929-5200
Web: www.technosourcehk.com

TechSearch International Inc
4801 Spicewood Springs Rd Ste 150 ... Austin TX 78759 512-372-8887
Web: www.techsearchinc.com

Tenet Partners 122 W 27th St 9th Fl ... New York NY 10001 212-329-3030 329-3031
Web: www.corebrand.com

Thobe Group Inc 2727 Raintree Dr ... Carrollton TX 75006 972-245-9444 245-9063
TF: 888-462-3477 ■ *Web:* www.thobe.com

Three Deep Marketing 180 E Fifth Ste 910 ... Saint Paul MN 55101 651-789-7701
Web: www.threedeepmarketing.com

Three Ships Media 111 E Hargett St ... Raleigh NC 27601 919-576-0460
Web: www.three-ships.com

Through Smoke Creative Inc
480 Gate 5 Rd Studio 340 ... Sausalito CA 94965 415-289-7500
Web: www.throughsmoke.com

Tompkins Research & Management Consulting Inc
203 Redstone Hill ... Plainville CT 06062 860-747-0497
Web: www.trmc.com

TOP Marketing U.S.A. LLC 1332 Baur Blvd ... St. Louis MO 63132 314-262-8550
Web: www.topmarketingusa.com

TowerData Inc 379 Park Ave S Fifth Fl ... New York NY 10016 646-742-1771
Web: www.towerdata.com

TR Design Inc Six Windsor St ... Andover MA 01810 978-470-1444
Web: www.trdesign.com

Transcosmos America Inc
879 W 190th St Ste 1050 ... Gardena CA 90248 310-630-0072
Web: www.transcosmos.net

Travers Collins & Co 726 Exchange St Ste 500 ... Buffalo NY 14210 716-842-2222
Web: www.traverscollins.com

Trident Marketing 1930 N Poplar St ... Southern Pines NC 28387 910-693-3000
Web: www.tridentmarketing.com

Trio Solutions Inc
505 Belle Hall Pkwy Unit 202 ... Mount Pleasant SC 29464 843-216-0442
Web: triohrsolutions.com

Truebridge Inc 105 Beach St Ste 3 ... Boston MA 02111 617-956-5020
Web: www.truebridge.com

Tvc Marketing 3200 W Wilshire Blvd ... Oklahoma City OK 73116 405-843-2722
Web: www.tvcmatrix.com

Twin City Sales & Marketing
361 W End Blvd ... Winston-salem NC 27101 336-685-1501
Web: www.twincitysam.com

TWOBOLT Marketing Technologies Inc
1110 Central Ave ... Pawtucket RI 02861 401-724-7600
Web: www.twobolt.com

United Marketing Group LLC
929 N Plum Grove Rd ... Schaumburg IL 60173 847-240-2005 438-5788*
**Fax Area Code:* 630 ■ *TF:* 800-513-7000 ■ *Web:* www.unitedmarket.com

Upp Entertainment Marketing Inc
3401 Winona Ave ... Burbank CA 91504 818-526-0111
Web: www.upp.net

V12 Group Inc 141 W Front St Ste 410 ... Red Bank NJ 07701 732-842-1001
Web: www.v12groupinc.com

Vanguard Management Group 9300 N 16th St ... Tampa FL 33612 813-930-8036
Web: www.vanguardmanagementgroup.com

Venture Solutions Inc 1170 Grey Fox Rd ... Arden Hills MN 55112 651-494-1740
Web: www.venturesolutions.com

VeraData.com LLC
7680 Cambridge Manor Pl Ste 200 ... Fort Myers FL 33907 800-561-9927
TF: 800-561-9927 ■ *Web:* www.veradata.com

Verequest 401 Queens Quay W ... Toronto ON M5V2Y2 416-362-6777
Web: www.verequest.com

ViewCentral 900 E Hamilton Ave ... Campbell CA 95008 408-626-3800 369-0910
OTC: RMKR ■ *TF:* 800-631-1545 ■ *Web:* www.rainmakersystems.com

Phone Fax

Vikus Corp 2255 Center St Ste 107 ... Chattanooga TN 37421 423-954-3378
Web: www.vikus.com

Vip Sports Marketing Inc
811 W Evergreen Ave Ste 305 ... Chicago IL 60642 312-951-0700
Web: www.vipsm.com

Vista Hill Management LLC 1201 W Swann Ave ... Tampa FL 33606 813-253-5400
Web: www.vistahillmanagement.com

Vistex Inc 2300 Barrington Rd Ste 550 ... Hoffman Estates IL 60169 847-490-0420
Web: www.vistex.com

Vistra Communications LLC
15436 N Florida Ave Ste 160 ... Tampa FL 33613 813-961-4700
Web: www.consultvistra.com

W Ca Logistics 643 Bodey Cir Unit A ... Urbana OH 43078 937-653-6382
Web: www.wcalogistics.com

Waife & Associates Inc 62 Warren St ... Needham MA 02492 781-449-7032
Web: www.waife.com

Wasabi Rabbit Inc 19 Fulton St Ste 307 ... New York NY 10038 646-366-0000
Web: www.wasabirabbit.com

Wayne Reaves Software & Websites Inc
6211 Thomaston Rd ... Macon GA 31220 478-474-8779
Web: www.waynereaves.com

Web Clients LLC 2300 Vartan Way Ste 100 ... Harrisburg PA 17110 717-346-3600
Web: www.webclients.net

Web Decisions LLC
303 Pisgah Church Rd Ste 2A ... Greensboro NC 27455 336-545-7817
Web: www.webdecisions.com

Web Talent Marketing 322 N Arch St Ste 120 ... Lancaster PA 17603 717-283-4045
Web: www.webtalentmarketing.com

Wellness International Network Ltd
5800 Democracy Dr ... Plano TX 75024 972-312-1100 430-4674*
**Fax Area Code:* 800 ■ *Web:* www.wellnessinternational.com

West Park Direct 2728 Euclid Ave Fl 2 ... Cleveland OH 44115 216-589-0200
Web: www.westparkdirect.com

Westland Financial Services Inc
1717 Kettner Blvd Ste 200 ... San Diego CA 92101 619-238-8144
Web: westlandinc.com

Wilkin Guge Marketing
3237 E Guasti Rd Ste 220 ... Ontario CA 91761 909-390-1239
Web: www.wilkinguge.com

Willems Marketing 120 N Morrison St Ste 200 ... Appleton WI 54911 920-831-6580
Web: www.willemsmarketingandevents.com

Workbook LLC 6762 Lexington Ave ... Los Angeles CA 90038 323-856-0008
Web: www.workbook.com

WorkPlace Media Inc 9325 Progress Pkwy ... Mentor OH 44060 440-639-9100
Web: www.cccsfw.org

World Steel Dynamics Inc
456 Sylvan Ave ... Englewood Cliffs NJ 07632 201-503-0900
Web: www.worldsteeldynamics.com

WSI Internet 5580 Explorer Dr Ste 600 ... Mississauga ON L4W4Y1 905-678-7588 678-7242
TF: 888-678-7588 ■ *Web:* www.wsicorporate.com

Xenium Resources 7401 Sw Washo Ct Ste 200 ... Tualatin OR 97062 503-612-1555
Web: www.xeniumresources.com

ZGM Collaborative Marketing Inc
1324 17th Ave SW Ste 500 ... Calgary AB T2T5S8 403-770-2250
Web: www.zgm.ca

Zionist Organization of America Inc
Four E 34th St Fl 3 ... New York NY 10016 212-481-1500
Web: zoa.org

ZS Assoc 1800 Sherman Ave Ste 700 ... Evanston IL 60201 847-492-3600 864-6280
Web: www.zsassociates.com

199 CONSULTING SERVICES - TELECOMMUNICATIONS

Phone Fax

2020 Exhibits Inc 10550 S Sam Huston Pkwy W ... Houston TX 77071 713-354-0900
Web: www.2020exhibits.com

352-MEDIA 422 Sw 140th Ter ... Newberry FL 32669 352-374-9657
Web: www.352media.com

360 Cloud Solutions LLC
14350 N 87th St Ste 165 ... Scottsdale AZ 85260 480-295-3420
Web: www.360cloudsolutions.com

3E Company Inc 3207 Grey Hawk Ct ... Carlsbad CA 92010 760-602-8700
Web: www.3ecompany.com

4patientcare One World Trade Ctr Ste 800 ... Long Beach CA 90831 562-861-1800
Web: 4patientcare.com

A G Wassenaar Inc 2180 S Ivanhoe St Ste 5 ... Denver CO 80222 303-759-8100
Web: www.agwassenaar.com

A3 Communications Inc 1038 Kinley Rd Bldg B ... Irmo SC 29063 803-744-5000
Web: a3communications.com

Aacom Inc 201 Stuyvesant Ave ... Lyndhurst NJ 07071 201-438-2244
Web: www.aacomnj.com

Ab Ovo Inc 2320-H Walsh Ave ... Santa Clara CA 95051 408-567-9090
Web: www.abovoinc.com

Accent Information Systems Inc
585 Sunbury Rd ... Delaware OH 43015 740-548-7378
Web: www.accentservices.com

Accuscreen Systems 1038 Main St ... Baton Rouge LA 70802 225-343-8378
Web: www.accuscreensystems.com

Actuarial Research Corp
6928 Little River Tpke Ste E ... Annandale VA 22003 703-941-7400
Web: www.aresearch.com

Acuity Audio Visual 11301 Industrial Rd ... Manassas VA 20109 703-361-6080
Web: www.acuityav.com

Acuity Inc 12930 Worldgate Dr Ste 100 ... Herndon VA 20170 703-766-0977
Web: www.myacuity.com

ADB Consulting & CRO Inc
8569 Pines Blvd Ste 215 ... Pembroke Pines FL 33024 954-517-1970
Web: www.adbccro.com

Adistec 7620 NW 25 St Unit 7 ... Miami FL 33122 786-221-2300
Web: www.adistec.com

	City	State	ZIP	Phone	Fax
Advance Communications & Consulting Inc 8803 Swigert Ct Unit A	Bakersfield	CA	93311	661-664-0177	
Web: www.advancecomm.net					
Adventace 2166 Chardonnay Cir	Gibsonia	PA	15044	724-443-2383	
Web: www.adventace.com					
Aerial Innovations Inc 3703 W Azeele St	Tampa	FL	33609	813-254-7339	
Web: www.flythis.com					
Aether Consulting Inc 8369 Windstone Ct	Goodrich	MI	48438	586-939-8028	
Web: aetherconsulting.com					
Affinion Loyalty Group Inc 7814 Carousel Ln	Richmond	VA	23294	804-217-8090	
Web: affinion.com					
Affinity 2600 N Mayfair Rd	Milwaukee	WI	53226	414-258-0200	
Web: www.affinityit.com					
AHC Inc 2230 N Fairfax Dr Ste 100	Arlington	VA	22201	703-486-0626	
Web: www.ahcinc.org					
Air Chek Inc 1936 Butler Bridge Rd	Mills River	NC	28759	828-684-0893	
Web: www.radon.com					
Air-Transport IT Services Inc 5950 Hazeltine National Dr Ste 210	Orlando	FL	32822	407-370-4664	
Web: www.airit.com					
Ajilon Communications 970 Peachtree Industrial Blvd Ste 200	Suwanee	GA	30024	678-482-5103	482-8849
TF: 800-843-6910					
Alacrinet Inc 530 Lytton Ave Second Fl	Palo Alto	CA	94301	650-646-2670	
Web: www.alacrinet.com					
Alchemic Dream Inc 442 Ave Willow	Shawinigan	QC	G9N1X2	819-840-9607	
Web: www.alchemicdream.com					
Alevistar Group Presidential Blvd	Bala Cynwyd	PA	19004	610-617-7800	
Web: www.alevistar.com					
Allegro Consultants Ltd 9800 JEB Stuart Pkwy Ste 106	Glen Allen	VA	23059	804-553-1130	
Web: www.allegroconsultants.com					
Allied Consultants Inc 1304 W Ave	Austin	TX	78701	512-236-8535	
Web: www.alliedconsultants.com					
AllSector Technology Group Inc 345 Hudson St	New York	NY	10014	212-366-8480	
Web: www.allsector.com					
Alogic US LLC 1845 Ferguson Rd	Allison Park	PA	15101	412-635-2500	
Web: www.alogic-us.com					
Alpha I Marketing Corp 65 W Red Oak Ln	White Plains	NY	10604	914-697-5300	
Web: www.alpha1marketing.com					
Altamont Capital Partners 400 Hamilton Ave Ste 230	Palo Alto	CA	94301	650-264-7750	
Web: www.altamontcapital.com					
AltaRock Energy Inc 2320 Marinship Way Ste 300	Sausalito	CA	94965	415-331-0130	
Web: www.altarockenergy.com					
Alto Consulting & Training 7210 Metro Blvd	Minneapolis	MN	55439	952-831-6604	
Web: www.altoconsulting.com					
American Ecotech LLC 100 Elm St Unit 16	Warren	RI	02885	401-247-0100	
Web: www.americanecotech.com					
AMITA Corp 1420 Blair Pl Ste 500	Ottawa	ON	K1J9L8	613-742-6482	
Web: www.amita.com					
AMTEL 900 Lafayette St Ste 506	Santa Clara	CA	95050	408-615-0522	
Web: www.amtelnet.com					
Anacom Inc 3000 Tasman Dr	Santa Clara	CA	95054	408-519-2062	
Web: www.anacominc.com					
Ananke Inc One Richmond Sq Ste 165W	Providence	RI	02906	401-331-2780	
Web: www.ananke.com					
AndPlus LLC 1881 Worcester Rd Ste 201	Framingham	MA	01701	508-425-7533	
Web: www.andplus.com					
ANEXIO Technology Services Inc One Bank of America Plz 421 Fayetteville St	Raleigh	NC	27601	941-556-3410	
Web: www.anexio.com					
Angarai International Inc 7331 Hanover Pkwy Ste C & D	Greenbelt	MD	20770	410-472-5000	
Web: www.angarai-intl.com					
Aok Networking LLC 820 Clark St	Oviedo	FL	32765	407-249-1989	
Web: www.aoknetworking.com					
Apex Computer Systems Inc 13875 Cerritos Corp Dr Ste A	Cerritos	CA	90703	562-926-6820	
Web: www.acsi2000.com					
Applied Power Technologies Inc 470 Vandell Way Ste A	Campbell	CA	95008	408-342-0790	
Web: www.apt4power.com					
Aptude Inc 1387 Wind Energy Pass	Batavia	IL	60510	630-692-6700	
Web: www.bluetech.com					
Aquaterra Technologies Inc 122 S Church St	West Chester	PA	19382	610-431-5733	
Web: aquaterra-tech.com					
Aquilent Inc 1100 W St	Laurel	MD	20707	301-939-1000	
Web: www.aquilent.com					
Arbor Solutions Inc 1345 Monroe Ave NW	Grand Rapids	MI	49505	616-451-2500	
Web: www.arbsol.com					
Arc Aspicio LLC 3318 Lorcom Ln	Arlington	VA	22207	703-465-2060	
Web: www.arcaspicio.com					
Arcadia Solutions LLC 20 Blanchard Rd Unit 10	Burlington	MA	01803	781-202-3600	
Web: www.arcadiasolutions.com					
Arxis Technology Inc 2468 Tapo Canyon Rd	Simi Valley	CA	93063	805-306-7800	
Web: www.arxistechnology.com					
ASCC Inc 130 Wisconsin Ave	Cranberry Township	PA	16066	724-772-2722	
Web: asccinc.com					
Ascendum Solutions LLC 10290 Alliance Rd	Cincinnati	OH	45242	513-792-5100	
Web: www.ascendum.com					
Associated Communications & Research Services Inc (ACRS) 817 NE 63rd St	Oklahoma City	OK	73105	405-843-9966	843-9852
Web: www.acrsokc.com					
Astatech Inc 2525 Pearl Buck Rd	Bristol	PA	19007	215-785-2656	
Web: www.astatechinc.com					
Atrion Networking Corp 30 Service Ave	Warwick	RI	02886	401-736-6400	633-6766
TF: 800-890-4526 ■ *Web:* www.atrion.net					
ATS Group LLC 1200 Atwater Dr Ste 170	Malvern	PA	19355	484-320-4302	
Web: www.theatsgroup.com					
Attac Consulting Group 535 W William St Ste 303	Ann Arbor	MI	48103	734-214-2990	
Web: attacconsulting.com					
Autoscan Inc 4040 23rd Ave W	Seattle	WA	98199	206-282-1616	
Web: www.autoscaninc.com					
Avancent Consulting Corp 1896 Kentucky Ave	Winter Park	FL	32789	407-897-8664	
Web: www.avancent.com					
Avantia Inc 9655 Sweet Vly Dr	Valley View	OH	44125	216-901-9366	
Web: eavantia.com					
Avantica Technologies 2680 Bayshore Pkwy Ste 416	Mountain View	CA	94043	650-248-9678	
Web: www.avantica.net					
Avesta Computer Services Ltd 23 Emmet Ct	Piscataway	NJ	08854	201-369-9400	
Web: www.avestacs.com					
AXIA Consulting LLC 1799 W Fifth Ave Ste 320	Columbus	OH	43212	614-675-4050	
Web: www.axiaconsulting.net					
Axian Inc 9600 Sw Nimbus Ave	Beaverton	OR	97008	503-644-6106	
Web: www.axian.com					
Aztech Technologies Inc Five McCrea Hill Rd	Ballston Spa	NY	12020	518-885-5385	
Web: www.aztechtech.com					
B D N Industrial Hygiene Consultants Inc 8105 Valleywood Ln Ofc B	Portage	MI	49024	269-329-1237	
Web: bdnihc.com					
B i d Designs 1525 Perimeter Pkwy Nw Ste 265	Huntsville	AL	35806	256-489-2815	
Web: bid-designs.com					
B2 Environmental Inc 10838 Old Mill Rd Ste A	Omaha	NE	68154	402-330-0763	
Web: www.b2environmental.com					
Bailiwick Data Systems Inc 4260 Norex Dr	Chaska	MN	55318	952-556-5502	
Web: www.bailiwick.com					
Baka Communications Inc 630 The East Mall	Etobicoke	ON	M9B4B1	416-641-2800	
Web: www.baka.ca					
BalancePoint Inc 9201 Ward Pkwy Ste 200	Kansas City	MO	64114	816-268-1400	
Web: www.balancepointcorp.com					
Bank Advisory Group LLC, The 15100 Gebron Dr	Austin	TX	78734	512-263-8800	
Web: www.bankadvisory.com					
Barbaricum LLC 819 Seventh St NW	Washington	DC	20001	202-393-0873	
Web: barbaricum.com					
Barish & O'Brien Consulting LLC 572 N Broadway	White Plains	NY	10603	914-428-8600	
Web: www.barish-obrien.com					
Barrio Logan College Institute 1807 Main St	San Diego	CA	92113	619-232-4686	
Web: blci.org					
Becterm Inc 4780 Boul Henri-bourassa	Quebec	QC	G1H3A7	418-622-6777	
Web: becterm.com					
Benefitvision Inc 4522 RFD	Long Grove	IL	60047	800-810-2200	
TF: 800-810-2200 ■ *Web:* www.benefitvision.com					
Bensinger Consulting 625 W Deer Vly Rd Ste 103	Phoenix	AZ	85027	602-237-8500	
Web: www.bensingerconsulting.com					
BestIT.com Inc 3724 N Third St	Phoenix	AZ	85012	602-667-5613	
Web: www.bestit.com					
Bestmark Inc 5605 Green Cir Dr Ste 200	Minnetonka	MN	55343	952-922-3890	
Web: www.bestmark.com					
Betach Solutions Inc 12 Manning Close NE	Calgary	AB	T2E7N6	403-984-2473	
Web: www.betach.com					
Big Bang ERP Inc 105 De Louvain W	Montreal	QC	H2N1A3	514-360-4408	
Web: www.bigbangerp.com					
Bio Medware 3526 W Liberty Rd Ste 100	Ann Arbor	MI	48103	734-913-1098	
Web: www.biomedware.com					
Bio-west Inc 1063 West 1400 North	Logan	UT	84321	435-752-4202	
Web: bio-west.com					
Biodiversity Research Institute 19 Flaggy Meadow Rd	Gorham	ME	04038	207-839-7600	
Web: www.briloon.org					
Biota Pacific Environmental Sciences Inc 10516 E Riverside Dr	Bothell	WA	98011	425-402-6887	
Web: connectory.com					
BITS 6082 Franconia Rd	Alexandria	VA	22310	703-822-0970	
Web: www.thebitsgroup.com					
BizTech Inc 1150 First Ave Ste 320	King Of Prussia	PA	19406	610-592-0600	
Web: www.biztech.com					
Blue Skies Consulting LLC 100 Blue Skies Dr Belen Alexander Airport (E80)	Belen	NM	87002	505-864-3700	
Web: www.blueskies.aero					
Bluemetal Architects Inc 44 Pleasant St	Watertown	MA	02472	866-252-0111	
TF: 866-252-0111 ■ *Web:* www.bluemetal.com					
Bossa Nova Technologies LLC 606 Venice Blvd Ste B	Venice	CA	90291	310-577-8113	
Web: www.bossanovatech.com					
Botnay Bay Computer 177 Bartlett St	Portsmouth	NH	03801	603-436-6035	
Web: botnaybay.com					
Brad Montgomery Productions Inc 6574 S Zeno Ct	Aurora	CO	80016	303-691-0726	
Web: www.bradmontgomery.com					
Braxton Technologies LLC Six N Tejon St Ste 220	Colorado Springs	CO	80903	719-380-8488	
Web: www.braxtontech.com					
Brazos Telecommunications Inc 109 N Ave D	Olney	TX	76374	940-564-5659	
Web: www.brazostelephone.com					
Bridgeforce Inc 155 Stanton Christiana Rd	Newark	DE	19702	302-325-7100	
Web: www.bridgeforce.com					
Bright Innovation LLC 333 E Carson St Ste 527	Pittsburgh	PA	15219	412-325-6705	
Web: www.bright-innovation.com					

	City	State	ZIP	Phone	Fax
BrightMove Inc 320 High Tide Dr # 201	Saint Augustine	FL	32080	877-482-8840	
TF: 877-482-8840 ■ *Web:* www.brightmove.com					
Brimtek Inc 21660 Red Rum Dr Ste 105	Ashburn	VA	20147	571-918-4921	
Web: www.brimtek.com					
Broadband Specialists Inc 1700 Peachtree Rd	Balch Springs	TX	75180	972-329-1280	
Web: www.bsicable.com					
Brookman LLC 1821 South St NW	Washington	DC	20009	301-515-0450	
Web: www.brookman.com					
Brubaker & Associates Inc 7626 Hammerly Blvd	Houston	TX	77055	713-464-4666	
Web: www.brubakerandassociates.com					
Bryant Christie Inc 500 Union St Ste 701	Seattle	WA	98101	206-292-6340	
Web: www.bryantchristie.com					
BTI Group 1901 S Bascom Ave Ste 400	San Jose	CA	95008	408-246-1102	
Web: www.btigroupma.com					
BTR Solutions LLC 1300 Thorndale Ave	Elk Grove Village	IL	60007	847-750-9350	
Web: www.belmont-technology.com					
Bts Consulting Group Ltd 355 Glen Arms Dr	Danville	CA	94526	925-837-1730	
Web: btsconsultinggroup.com					
Bugcrowd Inc 145 Ninth St #105	San Francisco	CA	94103	650-260-8443	
Web: bugcrowd.com					
C p Environmental Group Inc 1092 Fifth Ave	New Kensington	PA	15068	724-594-1900	
Web: www.cpeg-inc.com					
Cage Inc 6440 N Beltline Rd Ste 125	Irving	TX	75063	972-550-1001	
Web: www.cage-inc.com					
Caine Real Estate Group 111 Williams St	Greenville	SC	29601	864-250-2850	
Web: www.cbcaine.com					
Calder Bateman 10241 109 St Nw	Edmonton	AB	T5J1N2	780-426-3610	
Web: www.calderbateman.com					
Calibre Computer Solutions LLC 318 W Glendale St	Princeton	IN	47670	812-386-8919	
Web: www.calibreforhome.com					
Cameron-cole LLC 200 E Government St Ste 100	Pensacola	FL	32502	850-434-1011	
Web: www.cameron-cole.com					
Campaign Services Inc 117 N Saint Asaph St	Alexandria	VA	22314	703-684-3435	
Web: campaignsolutions.com					
Campos Market Research 216 Blvd Of The Allies	Pittsburgh	PA	15222	412-471-8484	
Web: www.campos.com					
Canadian Professional Sales Association 310 Front St W Ste 800	Toronto	ON	M5V3B5	416-408-2685	
Web: www.cpsa.com					
Candoris Technologies LLC Nine E Main St	Annville	PA	17003	717-228-1600	
Web: www.candoris.com					
CAP Index Inc 150 John Robert Thomas Dr The Commons at Lincoln Center	Exton	PA	19341	610-903-3000	
Web: capindex.com					
Capital Hill Group 45 O'Connor St Ste 1540	Ottawa	ON	K1P1A4	613-235-0221	
Web: www.capitalhill.ca					
Cardiff Park Advisors 2257 Vista La Nisa	Carlsbad	CA	92009	760-632-7855	
Web: www.cardiffpark.com					
Carlisle & Gallagher Consulting Group Inc 212 S Tryon St Ste 800	Charlotte	NC	28281	704-936-1600	
Web: www.cgcginc.com					
Carnegie East House For Seniors 1844 Second Ave	New York	NY	10128	212-410-0033	
Web: carnegieeast.org					
Casey, Quirk & Associates LLC 17 Old King's Hwy S Ste 200	Darien	CT	06820	203-899-3000	
Web: www.caseyquirk.com					
Cash Flow Solutions Inc 5166 College Corner Pk	Oxford	OH	45056	513-524-2320	
Web: www.followthefrog.com					
Casson-Mark Corp 10515 Markison Rd	Dallas	TX	75238	214-340-0880	
Web: www.cmarkcorp.com					
Catalyst IT Services Inc 502 S Sharp St	Baltimore	MD	21201	410-385-2500	
Web: www.catalystitservices.com					
Cc Coaching & Consulting Inc 5595 S Sycamore St	Littleton	CO	80120	303-984-9000	
Web: www.cccandc.com					
CC Intelligent Solutions Inc 7701 Six Forks Rd	Raleigh	NC	27615	919-844-2111	
Web: www.ccis-inc.com					
CCS Presentation Systems Inc 17350 N Hartford Dr	Scottsdale	AZ	85255	480-348-0100	
Web: www.ccsprojects.com					
Celerity Consulting Group Inc Two Gough St Ste 300	San Francisco	CA	94103	415-986-8850	
Web: www.celerityconsulting.net					
Celigo LLC 230 Twin Dolphin Dr Ste A	Redwood City	CA	94065	650-579-0210	
Web: www.celigo.com					
Cella Consulting LLC 4350 E W Hwy Ste 307	Bethesda	MD	20814	301-280-0313	
Web: www.cellaconsulting.com					
Chameleon Group LLC 951 Islington St	Portsmouth	NH	03801	603-570-4300	
Web: www.chameleonsales.com					
Chamness Technology Inc 2255 Little Wall Lk Rd	Blairsburg	IA	50034	515-325-6133	
Web: www.chamnesstechnology.com					
Change Companies, The 5221 Sigstrom Dr	Carson City	NV	89706	775-885-2610	
Web: www.changecompanies.net					
Channel Solutions LLC 3145 E Chandler Blvd Ste 110	Phoenix	AZ	85048	866-501-9690	
TF: 866-501-9690 ■ *Web:* www.cscorp-us.com					
Chase & Associates Cpas PC 9293 Corporate Cir	Manassas	VA	20110	703-361-7114	
Web: www.chaseadvisors.com					
Chase Enterprises Inc 6509 W Reno Ave	Oklahoma City	OK	73127	405-495-1722	
Web: www.chappellsupply.com					
CHP International Inc 1040 N Blvd Ste 220	Oak Park	IL	60301	708-848-9650	
Web: www.chpinternational.com					
Chuck Schubert & Associates 17197 N Laurel Park Dr Ste 114	Livonia	MI	48152	734-953-5600	
Web: csasoftware.com					
Cibola Systems Corp 180 S Cypress St	Orange	CA	92866	714-480-0272	
Web: www.cibolasystems.com					
Ciris Energy Inc 9155 E Nichols Ave Ste 200	Centennial	CO	80112	303-649-2000	
Web: www.cirisenergy.com					
Civic Resource Group LLC 915 Wilshire Blvd Ste 1680	Los Angeles	CA	90017	213-225-1170	
Web: www.civicresource.com					
Cj Brown Energy PC 4245 Union Rd Ste 204b	Buffalo	NY	14225	716-565-9190	
Web: www.cjbrownenergy.com					
Clarite Consulting 20 Tower Hill Rd	Mountain Lakes	NJ	07046	973-541-0051	
Web: www.clariteconsulting.com					
Clear Resolution Consulting LLC 5523 Research Park Dr Ste 240	Baltimore	MD	21228	443-543-5260	
Web: www.crctoday.com					
ClearConnex Inc 1021 Main Campus Rd Ste 300	Raleigh	NC	27606	760-845-4028	
Web: www.clearconnex.com					
ClearEdge IT Solutions LLC 10620 Guilford Rd Ste 200	Jessup	MD	20794	443-212-4700	
Web: www.clearedgeit.com					
Clearview International LLC 6606 LBJ Fwy Ste 135	Dallas	TX	75240	972-419-5991	
Web: www.clearviewfocus.com					
Click Optimize Creative Group 700 Blue Ridge Rd Ste 107	Raleigh	NC	27606	919-301-8406	
Web: cocg.co					
Clinical Meeting Management Inc 313 Cedar St	Bastrop	TX	78602	512-303-6610	
Web: www.cmmglobal.com					
Coastal Healthcare Consulting Inc 6808 220th St SW Ste 204	Mountlake Terrace	WA	98043	206-324-6540	
Web: www.coastalhealthcare.com					
Cokeva Inc 9000 Foothils Blvd	Roseville	CA	95747	916-462-6000	
Web: www.cokeva.com					
Coleman Hines Inc 20830 N Tatum Blvd Ste 330	Phoenix	AZ	85050	480-346-5800	
Web: colemanhines.com					
Colocenters Inc 2001 Sixth Ave Ste 1800	Seattle	WA	98121	206-777-7600	
Web: www.colocenters.com					
Comaintel Inc 121 Second Ave	Grand-mere	QC	G9T7G1	819-538-6583	
Web: www.comaintel.com					
Compass Computer Group Inc 9408 Ravenna Rd	Twinsburg	OH	44087	330-963-0800	
Web: ccgi.cc					
Compqsoft Inc 505N Sam Houston Pkwy E Ste 682	Houston	TX	77060	281-914-4428	
Web: www.compqsoft.com					
CompuOne Corp 9883 F Pacifc Hts Blvd	San Diego	CA	92121	858-404-7000	
Web: www.compuone.com					
Compusoft Integrated Solutions Inc 31500 W 13 Mile Rd Ste 200	Farmington Hills	MI	48334	248-538-9494	
Web: www.compusoft-is.com					
ComSci LLC 485B Rt 1 S Ste 100	Iselin	NJ	08830	732-632-8000	632-1830
Web: www.comsci.com					
Concepts of Independence Inc 120 Wall St Ste 1010	New York	NY	10005	212-293-9999	
Web: www.coiny.org					
Concepts to Operations Inc 801 Compass Way Ste 217	Annapolis	MD	21401	410-224-8911	
Web: www.concepts2ops.com					
Conde Group Inc 4141 Jutland Dr Ste 130	San Diego	CA	92117	800-838-0819	
TF: 800-838-0819 ■ *Web:* www.condegroup.com					
Contava Inc 4103 97 St Nw	Edmonton	AB	T6E6E9	780-434-7564	
Web: www.contava.com					
Contex Americas Inc 15737 Crabbs Branch Way	Derwood	MD	20855	240-399-5600	
Web: www.contex.com					
Cordev Inc 146 B Hillwood Ave Ste 146 B	Falls Church	VA	22046	703-237-2802	
Web: www.cordev.net					
Core Management Resources Group Inc 515 Mulberry St	Macon	GA	31201	478-741-3521	
Web: www.corehealthbenefits.com					
Core Mississippi Operations LLC 12091 Bricksome Ave Ste B	Baton Rouge	LA	70816	225-756-2673	
Web: www.coreoccupational.com					
Core Vision IT Solutions 600 Dakota Ste D	Crystal Lake	IL	60012	855-788-5835	
TF: 855-788-5835 ■ *Web:* www.cvits.com					
Corporate It Solutions Inc 661 Pleasant St	Norwood	MA	02062	888-521-2487	
TF: 888-521-2487 ■ *Web:* www.corpitsol.com					
Cost Control Associates Inc 310 Bay Rd	Queensbury	NY	12804	518-798-4437	
Web: www.costcontrolassociates.com					
Covetrix It Consulting Group 18333 Preston Rd Ste 550	Dallas	TX	75252	214-575-9583	
Web: www.covetrix.com					
Craig Roberts Assoc Inc 4230 Avondale Ave Ste 202	Dallas	TX	75219	214-526-6470	
Web: www.craigroberts.com					
Credent Technologies LLC 30 Brookfield St Ste A	South Windsor	CT	06074	860-436-6391	
Web: www.credenttech.com					
CRM Dynamics Inc 245 Glenforest Rd	Toronto	ON	M4N2A5	866-740-2424	
TF: 866-740-2424 ■ *Web:* www.crmdynamics.ca					
CrossRealms Inc 55 W Monroe St Ste 3330	Chicago	IL	60603	312-278-4445	
Web: www.crossrealms.com					
Crunchy Logistics 189 S Orange Ave Ste 2000	Orlando	FL	32801	407-476-2044	
Web: crunchy.co					
Crystal Communications Ltd 1525 Lakeville Dr Ste 230	Kingwood	TX	77339	281-361-5199	
Web: www.crystalcomltd.com					

Company	City	State	ZIP	Phone	Fax
Crystal Technologies Group Inc 1566 Mcdaniel Dr *Web:* crystaltechnologies.com	West Chester	PA	19380	610-430-2005	
Cs&S Computer Systems Inc 1440 W University Dr *Web:* www.css-computers.com	Tempe	AZ	85281	480-968-8585	
CSI Group Inc, The 11 Farview Ter *Web:* thecsigroup.com	Paramus	NJ	07652	201-587-1400	
CT Solutions Inc 3900 Jermantown Rd *Web:* www.ctsols.com	Fairfax	VA	22030	703-289-1560	
Cura Hospitality Inc 2970 Corporate Court Ste 5 *Web:* www.curahospitality.com	Orefield	PA	18069	610-530-7300	
Customized Energy Solutions Ltd 1528 Walnut St 22nd Fl *Web:* ces-ltd.com	Philadelphia	PA	19102	215-875-9440	
Cyber City Inc 224 W 30th St Rm 1100 *Web:* cybercityinc.com	New York	NY	10001	212-633-0649	
Cybersearch Ltd 800 E Northwest Hwy *Web:* www.cybsearch.com	Palatine	IL	60074	847-357-0200	
Cycom Canada Corp 3500 Pharmacy Ave Ste 1 *Web:* www.cycom.com	Scarborough	ON	M1W2T6	416-494-5040	
Cygnus Corporation Inc 5640 Nicholson Ln Ste 300 *Web:* www.cygnusc.com	Rockville	MD	20852	301-231-7537	
Cynergy Solutions LLC 543 Country Club Dr Ste 538 *Web:* www.cynergysolutions.net	Simi Valley	CA	93065	805-416-1610	
Dakota Analytics Inc 205 Fifth Ave SW Ste 600 *Web:* www.dakotaanalytics.com	Calgary	AB	T2P2V7	403-264-6999	
Dalby, Wendland & Company PC 464 Main St *Web:* dalbycpa.com	Grand Junction	CO	81502	970-243-1921	
Daman Consulting Inc 1250 S Capial Of Texas Hw *Web:* damaninc.com	Austin	TX	78746	512-329-6646	
Dan's Excavating Inc 12955 23 Mile Rd *Web:* www.dansexc.com	Shelby	MI	48315	586-254-2040	
Data Concepts LLC 4405 Cox Rd *Web:* www.dataconcepts-inc.com	Glen Allen	VA	23060	804-968-4700	
Data Path 318 McHenry Ave *Web:* mydatapath.com	Modesto	CA	95354	209-521-0055	
Database Network Specialists Inc 12485 SW 137 Ave *Web:* www.dns-inc.com	Miami	FL	33186	305-593-9934	
DataMentors LLC 2319-104 Oak Myrtle Ln *Web:* www.datamentors.com	Wesley Chapel	FL	33544	813-960-7800	
Davidson Institute for Talent Development 9665 Gateway Dr *Web:* www.ditd.org	Reno	NV	89521	775-852-3483	
dcVAST Inc 1319 Butterfield Rd Ste 504 *Web:* www.dcvast.com	Downers Grove	IL	60515	630-964-6060	
Decypher Technologies Ltd 200 Concord Plz Dr *Web:* www.decypherpsigov.com	San Antonio	TX	78216	210-735-9900	
DelaGet LLC 6608 Flying Cloud Dr *TF:* 866-264-5050 ■ *Web:* www.delaget.com	Eden Prairie	MN	55344	866-264-5050	
Delaware Power Systems Corp 11782 Hammersmith Way Ste 118 *Web:* www.delpowersys.com	Richmond	BC	V7A5E2	604-247-2800	
Delcom Group LP 2525B E SH 121 Ste 400 *Web:* www.delcomgroup.com	Lewisville	TX	75056	214-389-5500	
Delta Risk LLC 106 S St Mary's St Ste 428 *Web:* www.delta-risk.net	San Antonio	TX	78205	210-293-0707	
Denver Cyber Security 8100 E Union Ave Ste 2008 *Web:* www.denvercybersecurity.com	Denver	CO	80237	303-997-5506	
Designhammer Media Group LLC 1912 E Nc Hwy 54 Ste 201 *Web:* designhammer.com	Durham	NC	27713	919-544-0086	
Detechtion Technologies 1100-8th Ave SW Ste 277 *Web:* www.detechtion.com	Calgary	AB	T2P3T8	403-250-9220	
Detectent Inc 120 W Grand Ave Ste 104 *Web:* www.detectent.com	Escondido	CA	92025	760-233-4030	
DIGICON Corp 9601 Blackwell Rd 1st Fl Conference Rm *Web:* www.digicon.com	Rockville	MD	20850	301-721-6300	869-8081
Digicorp Inc 3315 N 124th St Ste E *Web:* digicorp-inc.com	Brookfield	WI	53005	262-402-6100	
Digital Evidence Group Inc 1726 M St NW Ste 1010 *Web:* www.digitalevidencegroup.com	Washington	DC	20036	202-232-0646	
Dimension Consulting Inc 2620 Second Ave Ste 9D *Web:* www.dimcon.com	San Diego	CA	92103	703-636-0933	
Directec Corp 1650 Lyndon Farm Ct Ste 202 *Web:* www.directec.com	Louisville	KY	40223	502-357-5000	
Distant Focus Corp 4114b Fieldstone Rd *Web:* distantfocus.com	Champaign	IL	61822	217-351-2655	
DMR Consulting Inc 7504 McElvey Rd *Web:* www.dmrcinc.com	Panama City Beach	FL	32407	850-230-3767	
Document Access Systems 9019 Forest Hill Ave Ste 9C *TF:* 866-544-9876 ■ *Web:* www.documentaccess.net	Richmond	VA	23235	866-544-9876	
Domital Corp 8858 NW 18th Terrace *Web:* www.domital.com	Doral	FL	33172	305-594-0873	
DPM Consulting Services Inc 507 E Maple Rd *Web:* www.dpmcs.com	Troy	MI	48083	248-740-8735	
DRT Strategies Inc 4245 N Fairfax Dr Ste 800 *Web:* www.drtstrategies.com	Arlington	VA	22203	571-482-2500	
Due North Consulting Inc 105 Owens Pkwy Ste C *Web:* duenorthmedia.com	Birmingham	AL	35244	205-989-9394	
Dvp Technologies LLC 123 Hillcrest Dr *Web:* www.dvptech.com	Southbury	CT	06488	203-262-6005	
Dynamics Edge Inc 2635 N First St Ste #148 *TF:* 800-453-5961 ■ *Web:* www.dynamicsedge.com	San Jose	CA	95134	800-453-5961	
Dynamis Inc 3707 Henson Rd *Web:* dynamis-inc.com	Knoxville	TN	37921	865-588-5422	
E r o Resources Corp 1842 Clarkson St *Web:* www.eroresources.com	Denver	CO	80218	303-830-1188	
e-ternity Business Continuity Consultants Inc 2425 Matheson Blvd E Eighth Fl *Web:* www.e-ternity.ca	Mississauga	ON	L4W5K4	416-410-2142	
e-Zsigma (Canada) Inc One Dundas St W Ste 2500 *Web:* www.ezsigmagroup.com	Toronto	ON	M5G1Z3	416-593-8026	
Earthbalance Corp 2579 N Toledo Blade Blvd *Web:* www.earthbalance.com	North Port	FL	34289	941-426-7878	
Eastex Environmental Lab Inc 1119 S University Dr *Web:* www.eastexlabs.com	Nacogdoches	TX	75961	936-569-8879	
EB Computing 19 Piping Rock Dr *Web:* www.eb-computing.com	Ossining	NY	10562	914-523-8142	
ebi consulting inc 21 B St *Web:* www.ebiconsulting.com	Burlington	MA	01803	781-273-2500	
Echo Technology Solutions 216 11th St *Web:* www.echots.com	San Francisco	CA	94103	415-857-3246	
Ecs & r 3237 Us Hwy 19 *Web:* www.ecsr.net	Cochranton	PA	16314	814-425-7773	
Edify Technologies Inc 2200 S Main St Ste 306 *Web:* www.edifytech.com	Lombard	IL	60148	630-932-9308	
Edtec Central LLC 22620 Woodward Ave Ste C *Web:* edtec.net	Ferndale	MI	48220	248-582-8100	
Eduworks Corp 136 Sw Washington Ave Ste 203 *Web:* eduworks.com	Corvallis	OR	97333	541-753-0844	
Edwards Industries LLC 6085 Marshalee Dr Ste 140 *Web:* www.edwps.com	Elkridge	MD	21075	443-561-0180	
Efk Group LLC 1027 S Clinton Ave *Web:* www.efkgroup.com	Trenton	NJ	08611	609-393-5838	
eFulgent Datawarehousing Solutions 10000 N 31st Ave Ste C203 *Web:* www.efulgent.net	Phoenix	AZ	85051	602-439-5503	
Egen Solutions Inc 40 Shuman Blvd Ste 302 *Web:* www.egeni.com	Naperville	IL	60563	847-224-5844	
Eh Krohl Consulting Inc 3704 Duxford Dr *Web:* www.fdacompliance.com	Raleigh	NC	27614	919-676-4801	
Elan Technologies 5143 Kennedy Ave *Web:* elantech.net	Cincinnati	OH	45213	513-322-0463	
ELI Inc 2675 Paces Ferry Rd Se Ste 470 *Web:* www.eliinc.com	Atlanta	GA	30339	770-319-7999	
Elk Environmental Services 1420 Clarion St *Web:* www.elkenv.com	Reading	PA	19601	610-372-4760	
Ellis Management Services Inc 4324 N Beltine Rd *Web:* www.epmsonline.com	Irving	TX	75038	972-256-3767	
Ellumen Inc 1401 Wilson Blvd Ste 1200 *Web:* www.ellumen.com	Arlington	VA	22209	703-253-5555	
Elm Consulting 60 State St Ste 201 *Web:* www.elmgroup.com	Peoria	IL	61602	309-673-7648	
Embience Inc 6450 Lusk Blvd E202203 *Web:* www.embience.com	San Diego	CA	92121	858-366-0415	
Emgence Technologies Inc 11440 W Bernardo Ct *Web:* www.emgence.com	San Diego	CA	92127	858-753-1985	
Emission Monitoring Service Inc 400 S Hwy 146 *Web:* www.emsi-air.com	Baytown	TX	77520	281-428-1140	
EMMsphere 102 W Third St Ste 1200 *Web:* www.marketspheremarketing.com	Winston-salem	NC	27101	336-608-3060	
empathylogic.com 15732 Los Gatos Blvd #434 *Web:* www.empathylogic.com	Los Gatos	CA	95032	408-940-3951	
Encari LLC 250 Pkwy Dr Ste 150 *Web:* www.encari.com	Lincolnshire	IL	60069	847-947-8448	
Endsight 1440 Fourth St Ste B *Web:* www.endsight.net	Berkeley	CA	94710	510-280-2000	
Endurance IT Services 4646 Princess Anne Rd Ste 104 *Web:* www.endurance-it.com	Virginia Beach	VA	23462	757-216-3671	
Energy Market Innovations 83 Columbia St Ste 400 *Web:* emiconsulting.com	Seattle	WA	98104	206-621-1160	
Enform 1538 25 Ave Ne *Web:* www.enform.ca	Calgary	AB	T2E8Y3	403-250-9606	
Enviroapplications Inc 2831 Camino Del Rio S Ste 214 *Web:* www.enviroapplications.com	San Diego	CA	92108	619-291-3636	
Envirosafe Services of Ohio Inc 876 Otter Creek Rd *Web:* envirosafeservices.com	Oregon	OH	43616	419-698-3500	
Envirosep Fluid & Heat Recovery Systems 31 Aviation Blvd *Web:* www.envirosep.com	Georgetown	SC	29440	843-546-7400	
Envirotech Financial Inc 1851 E First St Ste 900 *Web:* etfinancial.com	Santa Ana	CA	92705	714-532-2731	
Epicom Corp 211 E Seventh St Ste 110 *Web:* www.epicom.com	Austin	TX	78701	512-481-9000	
Equity Methods LLC 15300 N 90th St Ste 400 *Web:* www.equitymethods.com	Scottsdale	AZ	85260	480-428-3344	

	City	State	Zip	Phone	Fax
Ergos Technology Partners Inc 3831 Golf Dr *Web:* www.ergos.com	Houston	TX	77018	713-621-9220	
Ericsson 1 Telcordia Dr *TF:* 800-521-2673 ■ *Web:* www.telcordia.com	Piscataway	NJ	08854	732-699-2000	
ERP International LLC 603 Seventh St Ste 203 *Web:* www.erpinternational.com	Laurel	MD	20707	301-490-0080	
ESI Information Technologies 1550 Metcalfe St Ste 1100 *Web:* www.esitechnologies.com	Montreal	QC	H3A1X6	514-745-3311	
Essdack 1500 E 11th Ave Ste 200 *Web:* www.essdack.org	Hutchinson	KS	67501	620-663-9566	
Etek It Services Inc 830 E Higgins Rd Ste 102 *Web:* etekit.com	Schaumburg	IL	60173	847-969-0200	
Etelint Consulting Inc 1683 Moongate Cres *Web:* www.etelintconsulting.com	Mississauga	ON	L5M4T2	905-826-3977	
Etera Consulting 1100 17th St NW Ste 605 *Web:* www.eteraconsulting.com	Washington	DC	20036	202-349-0177	
Events Forum Inc Two Oxford Xing Ste 4 *Web:* www.eventsforum.net	New Hartford	NY	13413	315-792-7600	
Everglades Technologies One Union Sq W Ste 302 *Web:* www.etny.net	New York	NY	10003	212-741-0000	
Evogi Group Inc, The 20645 N Pima Rd Bldg N Ste 130 *TF:* 888-277-5573 ■ *Web:* www.evogi.com	Scottsdale	AZ	85255	888-277-5573	
Evoke Research & Consulting LLC 1000 Wilson Blvd Ste 2500 *Web:* www.evokeconsulting.com	Arlington	VA	22209	703-415-1007	
Exalt Integrated Technologies 401 Bombay Ln *Web:* www.exaltit.com	Roswell	GA	30076	770-217-4688	
Excalibur Technology Corp 700 Fox Glen Lowr Level *Web:* www.excaltech.com	Barrington	IL	60010	847-842-9570	
Excel Management Systems Inc 691 N High St Second Fl *Web:* www.emsi.com	Columbus	OH	43215	614-224-4007	
Eyak Technology LLC 201 E Third Ave Ste 200 *Web:* www.eyaktek.com	Anchorage	AK	99501	907-276-4472	
Facility Programming & Consulting Inc 100 W Houston St Ste 1100 *Web:* www.facilityprogramming.com	San Antonio	TX	78205	210-228-9600	
Faneuil Inc Two Eaton St Ste 1002 *Web:* www.faneuil.com	Hampton	VA	23669	757-722-3235	
Fentress Inc 945 Sunset Vly Dr *Web:* www.fentress.com	Sykesville	MD	21784	301-854-4885	
Fineline Technologies Inc 3145 Medlock Bridge Rd *Web:* www.finelinetech.com	Norcross	GA	30071	678-969-0835	
Fitt Telecommunications Inc 1740 W Sam Houston Pkwy N *Web:* fittcom.com	Houston	TX	77043	281-497-8181	
Formatech It Services 3263 Claremont Way # B *Web:* www.formatech-it.com	Napa	CA	94558	707-258-1492	
Fortin Consulting Inc 215 Hamel Rd *Web:* www.fortinconsulting.com	Hamel	MN	55340	763-478-3606	
Fortistar LLC One N Lexington Ave *Web:* www.fortistar.com	White Plains	NY	10601	914-421-4900	
Fortrust LLC 4300 Brighton Blvd *Web:* www.fortrustdatacenter.com	Denver	CO	80216	720-264-2000	
Foxboro Consulting Inc 17 Crowne Pond Ln *Web:* www.foxboro.net	Wilton	CT	06897	203-761-4901	
FPT USA Corp 155 Bovet Rd Ste 303 *Web:* fpt-software.com	San Mateo	CA	94402	650-349-5000	
Frank Lynn & Associates Inc 500 Park Blvd Ste 1300 *Web:* www.franklynn.com	Itasca	IL	60143	312-263-7888	
FranNet LLC 10302 Brookridge Village Blvd Ste 201 *Web:* www.frannet.com	Louisville	KY	40291	502-753-2380	
Freed & Associates 412 Yale Ave *Web:* www.freedassociates.com	Berkeley	CA	94708	510-525-1853	
FreshAddress Inc 36 Crafts St *Web:* www.freshaddress.com	Newton	MA	02458	617-965-4500	
Futureproof LLC 2803 Saint Philip St *Web:* www.futureproofnola.com	New Orleans	LA	70119	504-822-8995	
G Stephens Inc 133 N Summit St *Web:* www.gstephensinc.com	Akron	OH	44304	330-762-1386	
GameChanger Products LLC 2207 Harbor Bay Pkwy *Web:* gamechanger.net	Alameda	CA	94502	510-521-7985	
Gantec Corp 1111 Plz Dr Ste 310 *Web:* www.gantecusa.com	Schaumburg	IL	60173	847-885-7655	
Genesys Engineering PC 629 Fifth Ave Bldg 3 *Web:* www.genesysengineering.net	Pelham	NY	10803	914-251-0540	
Gentech Systems Management LLC Nine Lamont Ave *Web:* www.gentech.com	Trenton	NJ	08619	609-890-2522	
Geostat Environmental LLC 115 E Marlin St *Web:* www.geostatenvironmental.com	Mcpherson	KS	67460	620-241-6090	
Gh Package Product & Testing Consulting Inc 4090 Thunderbird Ln *Web:* www.ghtesting.com	Fairfield	OH	45014	513-870-0080	
Gila River Telecommunications Inc 7065 W Allison Dr *Web:* www.gilanet.net	Chandler	AZ	85226	520-796-3333	
Gladstein Neandross & Associates LLC 3015 Main St Ste 300 *Web:* www.gladstein.org	Santa Monica	CA	90405	310-314-1934	
Global Environment & Technology Foundation 2900 S Quincy St Ste 375 *Web:* www.getf.org	Arlington	VA	22206	703-379-2713	
Global Inflight Products 8918 152nd Ave Ne *Web:* www.gipusa.com	Redmond	WA	98052	425-558-2778	
Global IT Communications Inc 6720 Bright Ave *Web:* globalit.com	Whittier	CA	90601	562-698-2500	
Global Productivity Solutions LLC 19176 Hall Rd Ste 250 *Web:* www.gpsqtc.com	Clinton Township	MI	48038	586-412-9609	
Globex International Inc 115 Route 46 W Bldg C *Web:* www.globexintl.com	Mountain Lakes	NJ	07046	973-541-1144	
GNC Consulting Inc 21195 S LaGrange Rd *Web:* www.gnc-consulting.com	Frankfort	IL	60423	815-469-7255	
Go Pro Management Inc 22 Cynthia Rd *Web:* www.gopromanagement.com	Needham	MA	02494	781-444-5753	
Greenbusch Group Inc 1900 W Nickerson St Ste 201 *Web:* www.greenbusch.com	Seattle	WA	98119	206-378-0569	
Greene Consulting Associates LLC Waterstone Bldg 4751 Best Rd Ste 450 *Web:* www.greeneconsults.com	Atlanta	GA	30337	404-324-4600	
Greening of Detroit 1418 Michigan Ave *Web:* greeningofdetroit.com	Detroit	MI	48216	313-237-8733	
Greenstar Environmental Solutions LLC Six Gellatly Dr *Web:* www.greenstarsolutions.com	Wappingers Falls	NY	12590	845-223-9944	
Greenview Data Inc 8178 Jackson Rd *Web:* www.greenviewdata.com	Ann Arbor	MI	48103	734-426-7500	
Greenwood King Properties 2 Inc 1616 S Voss Rd Ste 900 *Web:* www.greenwoodking.com	Houston	TX	77057	713-784-0888	
Greystone Healthcare Management Corp 4042 Park Oaks Blvd Ste 300 *Web:* www.greystonehealth.com	Tampa	FL	33610	813-635-9500	
Groff NetWorks LLC 11 State St *Web:* www.groffnetworks.com	Troy	NY	12180	518-320-8906	
GSPANN Technologies Inc 362 Fairview Way *Web:* www.gspann.com	Milpitas	CA	95035	408-263-3435	
GSS Infotech Inc 1699 Wall St Ste 201 *Web:* www.gssinfotech.com	Mt. Prospect	IL	60056	847-640-3700	
Guidant Partners 1410 Donelson Pike Ste B5 *Web:* www.guidantpartners.com	Nashville	TN	37217	615-327-9111	
Gurus Information Technology Services LLC 517 Georges Rd *Web:* www.gurusit.com	North Brunswick	NJ	08902	732-247-7747	
H I M on Call Inc 1033 Hamilton St *Web:* www.himoncall.com	Allentown	PA	18101	610-435-5724	
H2O Consulting Inc 5870 Hwy 6 N Ste 215 *Web:* h2oconsulting.net	Houston	TX	77084	281-861-6215	
H3 Solutions Inc 10432 Balls Ford Rd Ste 230 *Web:* www.h3s-inc.com	Manassas	VA	20109	703-335-2311	
Haberfeld Associates Inc 206 S 13th St Ste 1500 *Web:* www.haberfeld.com	Lincoln	NE	68508	402-475-1191	
Hanover Research 1700 K St NW Eighth Fl *Web:* www.hanoverresearch.com	Washington	DC	20006	202-559-0050	
Harvey Hohauser & Associates 5600 New King Dr Ste 355 *Web:* www.hohauser.com	Troy	MI	48098	248-641-1400	
Hays Financial Consulting LLC Atlanta Financial Ctr 3343 Peachtree Rd Ste 200 *Web:* haysconsulting.net	Atlanta	GA	30326	404-926-0060	
HCI Group, The 6440 Southpoint Pkwy Ste 300 *Web:* thehcigroup.com	Jacksonville	FL	32216	904-337-6300	
HCL America Inc 330 Potrero Ave *Web:* www.hcl.com	Sunnyvale	CA	94085	408-733-0480	
Heritage Global Solutions Inc 230 N Maryland Ave *Web:* www.heritageglobalsolutions.com	Glendale	CA	91206	818-547-4474	
Hernandez Consulting LLC 3221 Tulane Ave *Web:* www.hernandezconsulting.com	New Orleans	LA	70119	504-305-8571	
Hicks & Company Inc 1504 W Fifth St *Web:* hicksenv.com	Austin	TX	78703	512-478-0858	
Hile Group 1100 Beech St Ste 15 *Web:* www.hilegroup.com	Normal	IL	61761	309-888-4453	
Himebaugh Consulting Inc 4940 Munson St Nw Ste 2100 *Web:* www.hcd.net	Canton	OH	44718	330-493-9700	
Hoop Group, The 1930 Heck Ave Ste 4 *Web:* www.hoopgroup.com	Neptune	NJ	07753	732-502-2255	
Horizon Consulting Inc 44135 Woodridge Pkwy Ste 100 *Web:* horizon-inc.com	Lansdowne	VA	20176	703-726-6430	
Horsley Witten Group Inc 90 Route 6A Ste 1 *Web:* www.horsleywitten.com	Sandwich	MA	02563	508-833-6600	
HPM Inc 3231 Osgood Common *Web:* www.hpmnetworks.com	Fremont	CA	94539	510-353-0770	
Hr Strategies & Solutions 49663 Draper Cir Ste 200 *Web:* www.yourhrteam.net	Plymouth	MI	48170	734-455-1185	
HR&A Advisors Inc 99 Hudson St Third Fl *Web:* www.hraadvisors.com	New York	NY	10013	212-977-5597	
Hrd Discount Book Society 2002 Renaissance Blvd *Web:* www.hrdqstore.com	King Of Prussia	PA	19406	610-279-2002	
Hunt Conference Group Inc 611 S Main St Ste 461 *Web:* www.huntconferencegroup.com	Grapevine	TX	76051	817-410-4660	

	City	State	Zip	Phone	Fax
Hunter Benefits Consulting Group Inc 119 E Palatine Rd Ste 104 *Web:* hunterbenefits.com	Palatine	IL	60067	847-776-2125	
Hydro Geo Chem Inc 6340 E Thomas Rd Ste 224 *Web:* www.hgcinc.com	Scottsdale	AZ	85251	480-421-1501	
I Macc 900 E Diehl Rd Ste 110 *Web:* imacc.net	Naperville	IL	60563	630-527-9052	
I.T. Blueprint Solutions Consulting Inc 170-422 Richards St. *TF:* 866-261-8981 ■ *Web:* www.itblueprint.ca	Vancouver	BC	V6B2Z4	866-261-8981	
Ibi Global Inc 200 Lime Quarry Rd *Web:* www.ibiglobal.com	Madison	AL	35758	256-774-5444	
ICI Services Corp 500 Viking Dr Ste 400 *Web:* www.icisrvcs.com	Virginia Beach	VA	23452	757-340-6970	
IDT|RPM Consulting Services 963 Hawthorn Dr. *Web:* www.idt-inc.com	Itasca	IL	60143	630-875-1100	
IeSmart Systems LLC 15200 E Hardy Rd *Web:* www.iesmartsystems.com	Houston	TX	77032	281-447-6278	
Ifocus Consulting Inc 100 39th St Ste 201 *Web:* ifocus-consulting.com	Astoria	OR	97103	503-338-7443	
ikaSystems Corp 134 Turnpike Rd *Web:* www.ikasystems.com	Southborough	MA	01772	508-229-0600	
Illumen Group Inc 1338 S Valentia St Ste 130 *Web:* www.illumen.com	Denver	CO	80247	303-743-8700	
Illuminous Enterprises Inc 3225 Belle River Dr. *Web:* www.illuminousinc.com	Hacienda Heights	CA	91745	626-968-0585	
Imanami Corp 2301 Armstrong St Ste 211 *Web:* imanami.com	Livermore	CA	94551	925-371-3000	
iMethods LLC 10748 Deerwood Park Blvd Ste 150 *TF:* 888-306-2261 ■ *Web:* www.imethods.com	Jacksonville	FL	32256	888-306-2261	
iMomentous 20 Gibraltar Rd Ste 109 *TF:* 888-985-7755 ■ *Web:* www.imomentous.com	Horsham	PA	19044	888-985-7755	
IMPRES Technology Solutions Inc 10330 Pioneer Blvd Ste 280 *Web:* www.imprestechnology.com	Santa Fe Springs	CA	90670	562-298-4030	
Inbound Call Experts LLC 700 Banyan Trl Ste 200 *Web:* www.inboundcallexperts.com	Boca Raton	FL	33431	561-705-0700	
Indus Instruments 721 Tristar Dr Ste C *Web:* www.indusinstruments.com	Webster	TX	77598	281-286-1130	
Infogrow Corp 2140 Front St *TF:* 800-897-9807 ■ *Web:* www.infogrowcorp.com	Cuyahoga Falls	OH	44221	800-897-9807	
Infoquest Consulting Group Inc 2540 Us Hwy 130 Ste 118 *Web:* www.infoquestgroup.com	Cranbury	NJ	08512	609-409-5151	
Infosmart Systems Inc 5850 Town and Country Blvd Ste 1102 *Web:* www.infosmartsys.com	Frisco	TX	75034	972-267-5900	
Infotrends/CAP Ventures Inc 97 Libbey Industrial Pkwy Ste 300 *Web:* www.capv.com	Weymouth	MA	02189	781-616-2100	616-2121
InfoZen Inc 6700A Rockledge Dr Ste 300 *Web:* www.infozen.com	Bethesda	MD	20817	301-605-8000	
Intact Info Solutions LLC 1370 Vly Vista Dr Ste 265 *Web:* www.intactinfo.com	Diamond Bar	CA	91765	909-396-9200	
Intega IT 108-1900 Merivale Rd *Web:* www.intega.ca	Ottawa	ON	K2G4N4	613-260-1114	
Integra Information Technologies Inc 101 South 27th St. *Web:* www.integrainfotech.com	Boise	ID	83702	208-336-2720	
integraSoft Inc 2547 Tech Dr *Web:* integrasoft.com	Bettendorf	IA	52722	563-332-5030	
Intelimax Media Inc Harbour CentreSte 2320 555 W Hastings St PO Box 12022 *Web:* www.intelimax.com	Vancouver	BC	V6B4N4	604-742-1111	
Interact One Inc 4665 Cornell Rd Ste 255 *Web:* www.interactone.com	Cincinnati	OH	45241	513-469-7042	
InterBase Corp 22485 La Palma Ave Ste 200D *Web:* www.interbasecorp.com	Yorba Linda	CA	92887	714-701-3600	
Intervoice Inc 17811 Waterview Pkwy. *Web:* www.intervoice.com	Dallas	TX	75252	972-454-8000	
Intone Networks Inc 499 Ernston Rd Ste A7 *Web:* www.intonenetworks.com	Parlin	NJ	08859	732-721-3002	
IntraEdge Inc 80 N McClintock Dr Ste 2 *Web:* www.intraedge.com	Chandler	AZ	85226	480-240-5240	
Investigator Support Services 1320 N Milwaukee Ave Fl 2 *Web:* www.researchsite.net	Chicago	IL	60622	773-278-1567	
INW Solutions 4500 Holland Office Park Ste #301 *Web:* www.inwsolutions.com	Virginia Beach	VA	23452	757-563-3572	
Iomosaic Corp 93 Stiles Rd Ste 102 *Web:* www.iomosaic.com	Salem	NH	03079	603-893-7009	
IPC Technologies Inc 7200 Glen Forest Dr Ste 100 *Web:* www.ipctech.com	Richmond	VA	23226	804-622-7288	
Itech Consulting Partners LLC 30 Church Hill Rd Ste 4 *Web:* www.itechcp.com	Newtown	CT	06470	203-270-0051	
itelligence Inc 10856 Reed Hartman Hwy *Web:* itelligencegroup.com	Cincinnati	OH	45242	513-956-2000	
ITERA International Energy Corp 9995 Gate Pkwy N Ste 400 *Web:* iterausa.com	Jacksonville	FL	32246	904-996-8800	
J K Consulting 990 E Ninth St. *Web:* www.jkconsulting.net	Lockport	IL	60441	815-588-4530	
J L a Consulting 1013 N Causeway Blvd. *Web:* www.jlaconsulting.net	Metairie	LA	70001	504-835-9639	
J Wda 2359 Fourth Ave Ste 300 *Web:* www.jwdainc.com	San Diego	CA	92101	619-233-6777	
JCG Technologies Inc 50 S Belcher Rd *Web:* jcgtech.com	Clearwater	FL	33765	727-461-3776	
Jcms Inc 1741 Whitehorse Mercerville Rd *Web:* www.jcms.com	Mercerville	NJ	08619	609-631-0700	
Jdk Consulting 16752 Addison St *Web:* www.jdkconsulting.com	Encino	CA	91436	818-705-8050	
Jerkins Creative Consulting 1002 Vale St # 1002 *Web:* jccservices.com	Benton	IL	62812	618-435-3739	
Jlack Consulting Inc 15 Toilsome Ln Ste 2 *Web:* www.jlack.com	East Hampton	NY	11937	631-324-9980	
JMP IT Services 535 W 152 St. *Web:* www.jmpits.com	New York	NY	10031	646-397-8117	
Jones Environmental Inc 708 Milam St Ste 100 *Web:* www.jonesenvironmentalinc.com	Shreveport	LA	71101	318-226-8444	
JVKellyGroup Inc 145 E Main St. *Web:* www.jvkg.com	Huntington	NY	11743	631-427-2888	
Jzanus Healthcare Financial Service 170 Jericho Tpke *Web:* www.artlink.net	Floral Park	NY	11001	516-326-0808	
K&R Negotiation Associates LLC 908 Ethan Allen Hwy. *Web:* www.negotiators.com	Ridgefield	CT	06877	203-431-7693	
K.D. Analytical Consulting Inc 4460 Linglestown Rd *Web:* www.kdanalytical.com	Harrisburg	PA	17112	717-343-2984	
Kaava Consulting Inc 15190 Sw 136th St Ste 24 *Web:* kaavainc.com	Miami	FL	33196	305-255-5151	
Kalba International Inc 116 McKinley Ave *Web:* www.kalbainternational.com	New Haven	CT	06515	203-397-2199	
KAMM Consulting Inc 1407 W Newport Ctr Dr *Web:* www.kammconsulting.com	Deerfield Beach	FL	33442	954-949-2200	
Kaseya Corp 400 Totten Pond Rd Ste 200 *TF:* 877-926-0001 ■ *Web:* www.kaseya.com	Waltham	MA	02451	877-926-0001	
KBTS Technologies Inc 41461 W 11 Mile Rd *Web:* kbtstech.com	Novi	MI	48375	248-374-1230	
KDC Technologies 27201 Tourney Rd Ste 201 *TF:* 877-532-1112 ■ *Web:* www.kdctechnologies.com	Valencia	CA	91355	877-532-1112	
Kenton Groupcom LLC 4454 Fairway Oaks Dr Ste 400 *Web:* www.kentongroup.com	Mulberry	FL	33860	651-451-3465	
Keysource Group Inc, The 1330 Corporate Dr Ste 200 *Web:* www.thekeysource.com	Hudson	OH	44236	330-342-4630	
Kingery Construction Co 201 N 46th St. *Web:* www.kccobuilders.com	Lincoln	NE	68503	402-465-4200	
Kingsley Consulting Group Ltd 701 Papworth Ave Ste 207 *Web:* kingsleygroup.com	Metairie	LA	70005	504-834-6484	
Kinsbursky Brothers Inc 125 E Commercial *Web:* www.kinsbursky.com	Anaheim	CA	92801	714-738-8516	
Kinsley & Associates 5401 S Prince St Ste 105 *Web:* kinsleyassociates.com	Littleton	CO	80120	303-798-3664	
Kln Klein Product Development Inc 19787 56 Ave *Web:* klnklein.com	Langley	BC	V3A3X8	604-530-1491	
Kms Consulting Services Inc 92 Broadway Ste 206 *Web:* kmssolutions.com	Greenlawn	NY	11740	631-912-0200	
Knack Systems LLC One Woodbridge Ctr Ste 335 *Web:* www.knacksystems.com	Woodbridge	NJ	07095	732-596-0110	
KRAMER aerotek Inc 580 Utica Ave *Web:* www.krameraerotek.com	Boulder	CO	80304	303-247-1762	
Krell Institute 1609 Golden Aspen Dr *Web:* www.krellinst.org	Ames	IA	50010	515-956-3696	
KRW Consulting Group LLC 1881 Commerce Dr Ste 111 *Web:* www.krweng.com	Elk Grove Village	IL	60007	847-734-0128	
Kwame Building Group Inc, The 1204 Washington Ave 200 *Web:* www.kwamebuildinggroup.com	Saint Louis	MO	63103	314-862-5344	
Kyra InfoTech Inc 4454 Florida National Dr. *Web:* www.kyrainfotech.com	Lakeland	FL	33813	863-686-2271	
L D Reeves & Associates Inc 1889 Manzana Ave *Web:* www.ldreeves.com	Punta Gorda	FL	33950	941-575-3555	
Labat-Anderson Inc 8000 Westpark Dr Ste 400 *Web:* www.labat.com	Mclean	VA	22102	703-506-9600	
Lane Group LLC, The 14-25 Plz Rd *Web:* www.tlgmeetings.com	Fair Lawn	NJ	07410	201-398-9230	
Lanlogic Inc 248 Rickenbacker Cir. *Web:* www.lanlogic.com	Livermore	CA	94551	925-273-2300	
LANSolutions LLC 6359 Nancy Ridge Dr. *Web:* www.lansolutions.net	San Diego	CA	92121	858-587-8000	
Larta Institute 606 S Olive St Ste 650 *Web:* www.larta.org	Los Angeles	CA	90014	213-694-2826	
LAURUS Systems Inc 3460 Ellicott Ctr Dr Ste 101 *Web:* www.laurussystems.com	Ellicott City	MD	21043	410-465-5558	
Lawrence Behr Assoc Inc 3400 Tupper Dr PO Box 8026 *TF:* 800-522-4464 ■ *Web:* www.lbagroup.com/associates	Greenville	NC	27834	252-757-0279	752-9155

Company / Address	City	State	ZIP	Phone	Fax
Lazorpoint LLC The Caxton Bldg 812 Huron Rd Ste 800 — *Web:* www.lazorpoint.com	Cleveland	OH	44115	216-325-5200	
Le Groupe Genitique Inc 2655 Blvd du Royaume Faubourg Sagamie Ste 480 — *Web:* www.genitique.com	Jonquiere	QC	G7S4S9	418-548-4626	
LED Supply Co 747 Sheridan Blvd Unit 8E — *TF:* 877-595-4769 ■ *Web:* ledsupplyco.com	Lakewood	CO	80214	877-595-4769	
Levementum Inc 55 N Arizona Place# 203 — *Web:* www.levementum.com	Chandler	AZ	85225	480-320-2500	
Lew Edwards Group, The 5454 Broadway — *Web:* lewedwardsgroup.com	Oakland	CA	94618	510-594-0224	
Lewis & Ellis Inc 2929 N Central Expy Ste 200 — *Web:* www.lewisellis.com	Richardson	TX	75080	972-850-0850	
Lightopia LLC 1043 N Coast Hwy — *Web:* www.lightopiaonline.com	Laguna Beach	CA	92651	949-715-5575	
Linguagraphics 194 Park Pl — *Web:* www.linguagraphics.com	Brooklyn	NY	11238	718-789-2782	
Lloyd's Register Americas Inc 1330 Enclave Pkwy Ste 200 — *Web:* www.cdlive.lr.org	Houston	TX	77077	281-675-3100	
Lme Consulting 4625 Ladera Way — *Web:* www.lmeconsulting.com	Carmichael	CA	95608	916-601-1961	
Loffler Companies Inc 1101 E 78th St Ste 200 — *Web:* www.loffler.com	Bloomington	MN	55420	952-925-6800	
LRA Worldwide Inc 300 Welsh Rd Bldg 1 Ste 200 — *Web:* www.lraworldwide.com	Horsham	PA	19044	215-957-1999	
Lucidview LLC 80 Rolling Links Blvd — *Web:* www.lucidview.com	Oak Ridge	TN	37830	865-220-8440	
Luther Consulting LLC 423 Massachusetts Ave — *Web:* www.lutherconsulting.com	Indianapolis	IN	46204	317-636-0282	
Lyceum Kennedy French & American School One Cross Rd — *Web:* lyceumkennedy.org	Ardsley	NY	10502	914-479-0722	
Lylab Technology Solutions Inc 526 Cumberland St — *Web:* www.lylab.net	Lebanon	PA	17042	717-279-8595	
Magnolia Consulting LLC 5135 Blenheim Rd — *Web:* www.magnoliaconsulting.org	Charlottesville	VA	22902	434-984-5540	
Making Waves Education Program 200 24th St — *Web:* www.making-waves.org	Richmond	CA	94804	510-237-3434	
Makor Solutions LLC 7430 W 27th St — *Web:* www.makorsolutions.com	St. Louis Park	MN	55426	952-922-2975	
Malibu Technologies Inc 48700 Structural Dr — *Web:* www.malibutech.com	Chesterfield	MI	48051	586-598-9900	
Management Network Group Inc (TMNG) 7300 College Blvd Ste 302 — *NASDAQ: CRTN* ■ *Web:* cartesian.com/	Overland Park	KS	66210	913-345-9315	
Maple Lake Ltd 60 Columbia Way Ste 502 — *Web:* www.txtgroup.com	Markham	ON	L3R0C9	905-513-7480	
Market Force Information Inc 248 Centennial Pkwy Ste 150 — *Web:* www.marketforce.com	Louisville	CO	80027	303-402-6920	
Marlin Environmental Inc 3935 Commerce Dr — *Web:* marlinenv.com	Saint Charles	IL	60174	630-443-6649	
Marlo Plastic Products Inc 289 State Route 33 — *Web:* marloplasticproducts.com	Manalapan	NJ	07726	732-792-1988	
Marvin Huffaker Consulting Inc 1311 W Chandler Blvd Ste 160 — *Web:* www.redjuju.com	Chandler	AZ	85224	480-988-7215	
Mather Economics LLC 43 Woodstock St Historic Roswell District — *Web:* www.mathereconomics.com	Roswell	GA	30075	770-993-4111	
Matt Construction Corp 9814 Norwalk Blvd Ste 100 — *Web:* www.mattconstruction.com	Santa Fe Springs	CA	90670	562-903-2277	
Max Environmental Technologies Inc 1815 Washington Rd — *Web:* www.maxenvironmental.com	Pittsburgh	PA	15241	412-343-4900	
Max Technical Training 4900 Pkwy Dr Ste 160 — *Web:* www.maxtrain.com	Mason	OH	45040	513-322-8888	
Mccann Systems LLC 290 Fernwood Ave — *Web:* www.mccannsystems.com	Edison	NJ	08837	732-346-9600	
MCM Services Group 1300 Corporate Ctr Curve — *TF:* 888-507-6262 ■ *Web:* www.mcmservicesgroup.com	Eagan	MN	55121	888-507-6262	
McVeigh Associates Ltd 275 Dixon Ave — *Web:* www.mcveigh.com	Amityville	NY	11701	631-789-8833	
Med Legal Consulting Source Inc 201 S Santa Fe Ave Ste 100 — *Web:* elevateservices.com	Los Angeles	CA	90012	213-347-0203	
Medical Specialties Managers Inc One City Blvd W Ste 1100 — *Web:* www.msmnet.com	Orange	CA	92868	714-571-5000	
MediRevv Inc 2600 University Pkwy — *TF:* 888-665-6310 ■ *Web:* www.medirevv.com	Coralville	IA	52241	888-665-6310	
Medisolv Inc 10420 Little Patuxent Pkwy Ste 400 — *Web:* www.medisolv.com	Columbia	MD	21044	443-539-0505	
meltmedia 1255 W Rio Salado Pkwy Ste 209 — *Web:* www.meltmedia.com	Tempe	AZ	85281	602-340-9440	
Menlo Scientific Ltd 5161 Rain Cloud Dr — *Web:* www.sysid-labs.com	Richmond	CA	94803	510-758-9014	
Mercury Z 1150 Se Maynard Rd Ste 140 — *TF:* 877-548-4052 ■ *Web:* www.mercuryz.com	Cary	NC	27511	877-548-4052	
Meridian Associates Inc One E Erie St Ste 240 — *Web:* www.meridianai.com	Chicago	IL	60611	312-335-8050	
Meridian Institute 105 Village Pl — *Web:* www.merid.org	Dillon	CO	80435	970-513-8340	
MetaOption LLC 574 Newark Ave Ste 210 — *Web:* www.metaoption.com	Jersey City	NJ	07306	201-377-3150	
Michael Brandman Associates 220 Commerce Ste 200 — *Web:* www.firstcarbonsolutions.com	Irvine	CA	92602	714-508-4100	
Michell Consulting Group Inc 8240 NW 52nd Ter Ste 410 — *Web:* www.michellgroup.net	Doral	FL	33166	305-592-5433	
Midego Inc 4710 Olley Ln — *Web:* midego.publishpath.com	Fairfax	VA	22032	571-331-4158	
Mind Drivers LLC The Mill 381 Brinton Lk Rd — *Web:* www.minddrivers.com	Thornton	PA	19373	610-361-1000	
MIRUS Restaurant Solutions 820 Gessner Rd Ste 1600 — *Web:* www.mirus.com	Houston	TX	77024	713-468-7300	
MIS Inc 222 W Highland Dr — *Web:* www.mis-inc.net	Lakeland	FL	33813	863-669-1100	
MOBI Wireless Management LLC 6100 W 96th St Ste 150 — *TF:* 855-259-6624 ■ *Web:* mobiwm.com	Indianapolis	IN	46278	855-259-6624	
More Effective Consulting LLC 10 Chestnut Cir — *Web:* www.moreeffective.com	Mont Vernon	NH	03057	603-801-3923	
MoreDirect Inc 1001 Yamato Rd Ste 200 — *Web:* www.moredirect.com	Boca Raton	FL	33431	561-237-3300	
Morphix Business Consulting PO Box 5217 Stn A — *Web:* www.morphix.biz	Calgary	AB	T2H1X3	403-520-7710	
Mosaic Event Management Inc 67 Haight St — *Web:* www.mosaicevents.com	San Francisco	CA	94102	415-908-2650	
Mr.Copy Inc 5657 Copley Dr — *Web:* www.mrcopy.com	San Diego	CA	92111	858-573-6300	
MTE Consultants Inc 520 Bingemans Centre Dr — *Web:* www.mte85.com	Kitchener	ON	N2B3X9	519-743-6500	
MultiLing Corp 86 North University Ave Third Fl — *Web:* www.multiling.com	Provo	UT	84601	801-377-2000	
MX Consulting Services Inc 544 Paramount Dr Ste 1 — *Web:* www.mxcsi.com	Raynham	MA	02767	508-821-5855	
Mxn Corp 1025 Rose Creek Dr Ste 620 — *Web:* mxncorp.com	Woodstock	GA	30189	770-926-1884	
N & b Team Consulting Inc 3625 Nw 82nd Ave Ste 207 — *Web:* nbteamconsulting.com	Doral	FL	33166	305-514-2404	
Nation Consulting LLC 5027 W N Ave Ste 201 — *Web:* www.nation-consulting.com	Milwaukee	WI	53208	414-344-1733	
Native Seeds-search 3584 E River Rd — *Web:* www.nativeseeds.org	Tucson	AZ	85718	520-622-0830	
Natl Elevator Industrial Educational Program 11 Larsen Way — *Web:* www.neiep.org	Attleboro Falls	MA	02763	508-699-2200	
NavCom Technology Inc 20780 Madrona Ave — *Web:* www.navcomtech.com	Torrance	CA	90503	310-381-2000	
Navigant Healthcare Cymetrix 2875 Michelle Dr Ste 250 — *Web:* www.cymetrix.com	Irvine	CA	92606	714-361-6800	
Necando Solutions Inc 620 St-Jacques Ste 500 — *Web:* necando.com	Montreal	QC	H3C1C7	514-360-4000	
Neko Industries Inc 3017 Douglas Blvd Ste 300 — *Web:* www.nekoind.com	Roseville	CA	95661	916-774-7125	
Nelrod Co 3109 Lubbock Ave — *Web:* www.nelrod.com	Fort Worth	TX	76109	817-922-9000	
Nennie & Associates 340 W Exchange St — *Web:* www.nenniandassoc.com	Sycamore	IL	60178	815-899-9421	
Neos LLC 20 Church St — *Web:* www.neosllc.com	Hartford	CT	06103	860-519-5601	
Net Matrix Solutions 10235 W Little York Rd Ste 435 — *Web:* www.netmatrixsolutions.com	Houston	TX	77040	281-598-2600	
Net Source Inc 8020 Shaffer Pkwy — *Web:* www.netsourcestorage.com	Littleton	CO	80127	303-948-3360	
Net World Technology Corp 65 S College St — *Web:* networldtechnology.com	Carlisle	PA	17013	717-249-7232	
Netlink Software Group America Inc 999 Tech Row — *TF:* 800-485-4462 ■ *Web:* netlink.com	Madison Heights	MI	48071	800-485-4462	
Network Designs Integration Services Inc 48890 Milmont Dr Ste 101 — *Web:* www.network-designs.com	Fremont	CA	94538	510-249-9549	
Neutron Inc 220 Reese Rd — *Web:* www.neutronet.com	State College	PA	16801	814-237-0902	
Nevada Crystal Premium LLC 6185 S Vly View Blvd — *Web:* nevadacrystalpremium.com	Las Vegas	NV	89118	702-892-0535	
Newdea Inc 4B Inverness Court E Ste 110 — *Web:* www.newdea.com	Englewood	CO	80112	720-249-3030	
NextRidge Inc 12 Elmwood Rd — *Web:* www.nextridgeinc.com	Albany	NY	12204	518-292-6505	
Nextrio LLC 4803 E Fifth St — *Web:* www.nextrio.com	Tucson	AZ	85711	520-545-7100	
Nfocus Consulting Inc 1594 Hubbard Dr — *Web:* www.n-focus.com	Lancaster	OH	43130	740-654-5809	
Ninety Five 5 LLC 1767 Lakewood Ranch Blvd Ste 209 — *Web:* www.nf5.com	Bradenton	FL	34211	484-323-2413	

Company / Address	City	State	ZIP	Phone	Fax
Nordisk Systems Inc 13475 SE Johnson Rd *Web:* nordisksystems.com	Milwaukie	OR	97222	503-353-7555	
North Fork Crow River Wsd 100 Prairie Ave S *Web:* crowriver.org	Brooten	MN	56316	320-346-2869	
Northspan Group Inc, The 221 W First St *Web:* www.ardc.org	Duluth	MN	55802	218-722-5545	
Nova Corp 601 Norland Ave Ste 201 *Web:* www.nova-dine.com	Chambersburg	PA	17201	717-262-9750	
Nova Partners Inc 855 El Cmino Real Ste 307 *Web:* www.novapartners.com	Palo Alto	CA	94301	650-324-5324	
Novotech Technologies Corp 57 Iber Rd Unit 2 *Web:* www.novotech.com	Ottawa	ON	K2S1E7	613-280-1900	
Noxent Inc 6400 Boul Taschereau Bur 220 *Web:* www.noxent.com	Brossard	QC	J4W3J2	450-926-0662	
Nucar Consulting Inc 313 N Dupont Hwy *Web:* www.nucarconsulting.com	Odessa	DE	19730	302-696-6000	
Oasis Ranch Management 86235 Ave 52 *Web:* seaviewsales.com	Coachella	CA	92236	760-398-8850	
Object Edge Inc 315 Lennon Ln *Web:* www.objectedge.com	Walnut Creek	CA	94598	925-943-5558	
Object Systems Group Inc 8600 Freeport Pkwy Ste 400 *Web:* www.osgcorp.com	Irving	TX	75063	972-650-2026	
Objectiva Software Solutions Inc 505 Lomas Santa Fe Dr Ste 170 *Web:* www.objectivasoftware.com	Solana Beach	CA	92075	760-230-6607	
Oceanus Partners 16540 Pointe Village Dr Ste 208 *TF:* 888-496-1117 ■ *Web:* www.workcompadvisorygroup.com	Lutz	FL	33558	888-496-1117	
Omnikron Systems 6301 Owensmouth Ave Ste 720 *Web:* www.omnikron.com	Woodland Hills	CA	91367	818-591-7890	
Omnipress 2600 Anderson St *Web:* omnipress.com	Madison	WI	53704	608-246-2600	
OmniVue Business Solutions LLC 1355 Windward Concourse Ste 200 *Web:* www.omnivue.net	Alpharetta	GA	30005	770-587-0095	
One Eighty Consulting Inc 413 N Meridian St *Web:* 180consultinginc.com	Tallahassee	FL	32301	850-412-0300	
One Source Safety & Health Inc 140 S Village Ave Ste 130 *Web:* 1ssh.com	Exton	PA	19341	610-524-5525	
Opal Financial Group Inc 10 E 38th St Fourth Fl *Web:* www.opalgroup.net	New York	NY	10016	212-532-9898	
Optimal Satcom Inc 11180 Sunrise Vly Dr Ste 200 *Web:* optimalsatcom.com	Reston	VA	20191	703-657-8800	
Optimal Strategix Group Inc Ste 118 140 Terry Dr *Web:* www.optimalstrategix.com	Newtown	PA	18940	215-867-1880	
OPTIO LLC 390 Spaulding Ave SE *TF:* 888-981-3282 ■ *Web:* www.optiodata.com	Ada	MI	49301	888-981-3282	
ORR Associates Inc 2801 M St NW *Web:* www.oai-usa.com	Washington	DC	20007	202-338-6100	
Overture Partners LLC 57 Wells Ave # 22 *Web:* www.overturepartners.com	Newton	MA	02459	617-614-9600	
P3 North America Inc 1957 Crooks Rd Ste B *Web:* www.p3-group.com	Troy	MI	48084	248-792-2277	
Pacotech Inc 1739 Nina Lee Ln *Web:* www.pacotech.com	Houston	TX	77018	713-688-0404	
Palitto Consulting Services Inc 600 Weber Dr *Web:* www.palittoconsulting.com	Wadsworth	OH	44281	330-335-7271	
Palo Alto Networks Inc 4401 Great America Pkwy *Web:* www.paloaltonetworks.com	Santa Clara	CA	95054	408-753-4000	
Pams Inc 3361 Pomona Blvd *Web:* www.pamsinc.com	Pomona	CA	91768	909-869-7267	
Parallax Consulting LLC 325 Wood Rd Ste 107 *Web:* parallax-consulting.com	Braintree	MA	02184	781-535-6004	
Parallax Press 2236 Sixth St *Web:* www.parallax.org	Berkeley	CA	94710	510-540-6411	
Partner Harvard Medical International Inc 131 Dartmouth St Fifth Fl *Web:* www.phmi.partners.org	Boston	MA	02116	617-535-6400	
Pathway Health Services Inc 2025 Fourth St *Web:* www.pathwayhealth.com	White Bear Lake	MN	55110	651-407-8699	
Patricia Egen Consulting LLC 803 Creek Overlook *Web:* www.egenconsulting.com	Chattanooga	TN	37415	423-875-2652	
Peak Environmental Inc 74 Main St Ste 2 *Web:* www.peak-environmental.com	Woodbridge	NJ	07095	732-326-1010	
Peduzzi Associates Ltd 221 S Alfred St *Web:* www.pal-aerospace.com	Alexandria	VA	22314	703-836-7990	
Penncomp 2050 N Loop West Ste 200 *Web:* www.penncomp.com	Houston	TX	77018	713-669-0965	
Persimmon Technologies Corp 200 Harvard Mill Sq Ste 110 *Web:* www.persimmontech.com	Wakefield	MA	01880	781-587-0677	
Personnel Systems Associates Inc 7551 E Moonridge Ln *Web:* personnelsystems.com	Anaheim	CA	92808	714-281-8337	
Pervasive Solutions 117 Victor Heights Pkwy *Web:* www.pervasivesolutions.net	Victor	NY	14564	585-300-0440	
Pete Fowler Construction Services 931 Calle Negocio Ste J *Web:* www.petefowler.com	San Clemente	CA	92673	949-240-9971	
PhishLabs PO Box 20877 *Web:* www.phishlabs.com	Charleston	SC	29413	843-628-3368	
Plan First Technologies Inc 120 Groton Ave *Web:* www.p1tech.net	Cortland	NY	13045	607-756-9347	
Planaxis Inc 505 de Maisonneuve Blvd W *Web:* www.planaxis.com	Montreal	QC	H3A3C2	514-878-2295	
Plasco Energy Group Inc 1000 Innovation Dr Ste 400 *Web:* www.plascoenergygroup.com	Ottawa	ON	K2K3E7	613-591-9438	
Platinum Vault Inc 10554 Norwalk Blvd *Web:* www.hartleymedical.com	Santa Fe Springs	CA	90670	562-903-1494	
PlusOne Solutions Inc 3501 Quadrangle Blvd Ste 120 *Web:* www.plusonesolutions.net	Orlando	FL	32817	407-359-5929	
PMOLink LLC 2001 Lakeshore Dr *Web:* www.pmolink.com	Mandeville	LA	70448	985-674-5968	
Pollution Control Corp 500 W Country Club Rd *TF:* 800-966-1265 ■ *Web:* www.pollutioncontrolcorp.com	Chickasha	OK	73018	800-966-1265	
Portable Church Industries Inc 1923 Ring Dr *Web:* www.portablechurch.com	Troy	MI	48083	248-585-9540	
Potomac Communications Group Inc 1133 20th St Nw Ste 400 *Web:* www.pcgpr.com	Washington	DC	20036	202-466-7391	
Potomac Healthcare Solutions LLC 1549 Old Bridge Rd Ste 201 *Web:* www.potomachealthcare.com	Woodbridge	VA	22192	703-436-9009	
PotomacWave Consulting Inc 107 S W St Ste 770 *Web:* www.potomacwave.com	Alexandria	VA	22314	703-623-5144	
Power Depot Inc 3553 NW 78th Ave *Web:* www.powerdepot.com	Miami	FL	33122	305-592-7100	
Preclinomics Inc 7918 Zionsville Rd *Web:* www.preclinomics.com	Indianapolis	IN	46268	317-872-6001	
PremierComm LLC 415 N Prince St Ste 200 *Web:* www.premiercommllc.com	Lancaster	PA	17603	717-431-7100	
Prism Consulting Inc 1150 Hancock St Ste 400 *Web:* www.prismconsultinginc.com	Quincy	MA	02169	617-328-9896	
Proactive Management Consulting LLC 2700 Cumberland Pkwy SE *Web:* www.proactive-management.com	Atlanta	GA	30339	770-319-7468	
Procurri LLC 5825 Peachtree Corners E Ste A *Web:* www.procurri.com	Norcross	GA	30092	770-817-9092	
Product Safety Consulting Inc 605 Country Club Dr Ste I *Web:* productsafetyinc.com	Bensenville	IL	60106	630-238-0188	
Profit Recovery Partners LLC 18231 W McDurmott *Web:* www.prpllc.com	Irvine	CA	92614	949-851-2777	
Project Consulting Services Inc 3300 W Esplanade Ave S Ste 500 *Web:* www.projectconsulting.com	Metairie	LA	70002	504-833-5321	
Project X Ltd 25 Rumsey Rd *Web:* www.pxltd.ca	Toronto	ON	M4G1N7	416-422-8900	
ProSource Solutions LLC 4199 Kinross Lakes Pkwy Ste 150 *TF:* 866-549-0279 ■ *Web:* www.prosource-corp.com	Richfield	OH	44286	866-549-0279	
Psa Constructors Inc 1516 E Hillcrest St *Web:* www.psaonline.com	Orlando	FL	32803	407-898-9119	
Public Data Works Inc 2720 Reynolda Rd *Web:* www.publicdataworks.com	Winston-salem	NC	27106	336-725-4456	
Public Sector Consultants Inc 600 W Saint Joseph St Ste 10 *Web:* www.pscinc.com	Lansing	MI	48933	517-484-4954	
PV-Tron Inc 8810 Blvd Langelier *Web:* www.pvtron.com	Saint-L,onard	QC	H1P3H2	514-723-2131	
Pyramid Healthcare Solutions Inc 14141 46th St N Ste 1212 *Web:* www.pyramidhs.com	Clearwater	FL	33762	727-431-3000	
Quadlogic Controls Corp 3300 Northern Blvd Fl 2 *Web:* www.quadlogic.com	Long Island City	NY	11101	212-930-9300	
Quality Management Solutions LLC 146 Lowell St Ste 300B *TF:* 800-645-6430 ■ *Web:* www.qmsinc.com	Wakefield	MA	01889	800-645-6430	
QualPro Inc 3117 Pellissippi Pkwy *Web:* www.qualproinc.com	Knoxville	TN	37931	865-927-0491	
Quantum Information Systems Solutions Inc 2805 Pontiac Lk Rd Ste 2C *Web:* www.qinfosys.com	Waterford	MI	48328	248-393-3621	
Quartech Systems Ltd 2160 Springer Ave Ste 200 *Web:* www.quartech.com	Burnaby	BC	V5B3M7	604-291-9686	
Qubera Solutions Inc Ste C 220 Twin Dolphin Dr *Web:* www.quberasolutions.com	Redwood City	CA	94065	650-294-4460	
R2 Unified Technologies 980 N Federal Hwy Ste 410 *Web:* www.r2ut.com	Boca Raton	FL	33432	561-515-6800	
Rader Solutions Ltd 260 La Rue France *Web:* radersolutions.com	Lafayette	LA	70508	337-205-4652	
Radgov Inc 1500 W Cypress Creek Rd *Web:* www.radgov.com	Fort Lauderdale	FL	33309	954-938-2800	
Raffa Consulting Economists Inc 17 S Osceola Ave Ste 200 *Web:* raffaconsulting.com	Orlando	FL	32801	407-648-5141	
Rage Administrative & Marketing Services Inc 1313 N Webb Rd Ste 200 *Web:* www.rage-inc.com	Wichita	KS	67206	316-634-1888	
Red Path Consulting Group 9220 Bass Lake Rd *Web:* redpathcg.com	Minneapolis	MN	55428	763-432-3604	
Redapt Inc 12226 134th CT NE Bldg D *Web:* www.redapt.com	Redmond	WA	98052	425-882-0400	

Phone Fax

Redhawk Network Security LLC
62958 Layton Ave Ste One . . . . Bend OR 97701 541-382-4360
Web: www.redhawksecurity.com

RedLegg 902 S Randall Rd Ste C 319 . . . . St. Charles IL 60174 877-811-5040
TF: 877-811-5040 ■ *Web:* www.redlegg.com

Research into Action Inc
3934 Ne Mlking Jr Blvd Ste 300 . . . . Portland OR 97212 503-287-9136
Web: researchintoaction.com

Resolve Inc 1255 23rd St NW Ste 875 . . . . Washington DC 20037 202-944-2300
Web: www.resolv.org

Response Design Corp 5541 Simpson Ave . . . . Ocean City NJ 08226 609-398-3230
Web: www.responsedesign.com

Revention Inc
1315 W Sam Houston Pkwy North Ste 100 . . . . Houston TX 77043 877-738-7444
TF: 877-738-7444 ■ *Web:* www.revention.com

Rhein Consulting Laboratories
4475 Sw Scholls Ferry Rd Ste 101 . . . . Portland OR 97225 503-292-1988
Web: www.rheinlabs.com

Richard Carlton Consulting Inc
1941 Rollingwood Dr . . . . Fairfield CA 94534 707-422-4053
Web: www.rcconsulting.com

Rigel Networks LLC
1500 Quail St Ste 280 . . . . Newport Beach CA 92660 949-891-2571
Web: www.rigelnetworks.com

Rimkus Consulting Group Inc
Eight Greenway Plz Ste 500 . . . . Houston TX 77046 713-621-3550
Web: www.rimkus.com

Ris Corp 5905 Weisbrook Ln Ste 101 . . . . Knoxville TN 37909 865-588-4456
Web: www.ris-corp.com

Risetime Inc 547 W Jackson Eighth Fl . . . . Chicago IL 60661 312-362-9930
Web: www.risetime.com

Rls Logistics 2260 Industrial Way . . . . Vineland NJ 08360 856-691-2040
Web: www.rlslogistics.com

RMG Financial Consulting Inc
813 E Ballard Ave . . . . Colbert WA 99005 509-468-2956
Web: www.rmgfinancial.com

Robert Frances Group 120 Post Rd W Ste 201 . . . . Westport CT 06880 203-429-8950
Web: www.rfgonline.com

Robert Rippe & Associates Inc
6117 Blue Cir Dr . . . . Minnetonka MN 55343 952-933-0313
Web: www.rrippe.com

Roi Communications Inc
5274 Scotts Vly Dr . . . . Scotts Valley CA 95066 831-430-0170
Web: www.roico.com

Root Inc 5470 Main St . . . . Sylvania OH 43560 800-852-1315
TF: 800-852-1315 ■ *Web:* www.rootinc.com

Rose Shattuck & Associates LLC
3109 Poplarwood Ct Ste 301 . . . . Raleigh NC 27604 919-256-1675
Web: shattuckconsulting.com

Rouis & Company LLP 51 Sullivan St . . . . Wurtsboro NY 12790 845-888-5656
Web: www.rouiscpas.com

Rouse Consulting Group Inc 422 16th St . . . . Moline IL 61265 309-762-3589
Web: www.go2rcg.com

Rsi Corp 543 Main St . . . . Kiowa KS 67070 620-825-4600
Web: www.rsicorp.com

RTP Technology Corp 95 N Rte 17 Ste 108 . . . . Paramus NJ 07410 201-796-2266
Web: www.rtptech.com

Rue & Associates Inc
7264 Hanover Green Dr . . . . Mechanicsville VA 23111 804-730-7455
Web: www.rueassociates.com

Rulesware LLC 10 N Martingale Rd Ste 400 . . . . Schaumburg IL 60173 312-224-8501
Web: www.rulesware.com

Ryad Consulting Inc 4876 Township Trce . . . . Marietta GA 30066 770-650-8468
Web: ryadconsulting.com

S & L International
150 E Colorado Blvd Ste 350 . . . . Pasadena CA 91105 626-405-0999
Web: www.slinternational.com

Sabertooth Technologies
5944 Coral Ridge Dr # 215 . . . . Coral Springs FL 33076 954-635-5545
Web: www.stooth.net

Sabio Information Technologies Inc
8200 NW 27th St Ste 115 . . . . Miami FL 33122 305-499-9088
Web: www.sabioit.com

Sabretech Consulting LLC 154 Lewis St . . . . Hillsdale MI 49242 517-437-7150
Web: www.sabretechllc.com

Safety Center Inc 3909 Bradshaw Rd . . . . Sacramento CA 95827 916-366-7233
Web: www.safetycenter.org

Safeway Industrial Services LLC
308 E Air Depot Rd . . . . Glencoe AL 35905 256-492-3704
Web: www.safewayind.com

Samsung Information Systems America Inc
75 W Plumeria Dr . . . . San Jose CA 95134 408-544-5700
Web: www.sisa.samsung.com

SatisfYd 47 E Chicago Ave Ste 310 . . . . Naperville IL 60540 800-562-9557
TF: 800-562-9557 ■ *Web:* satisfyd.com

Saturn Infotech Inc 1120 Welsh Rd Ste 110 . . . . North Wales PA 19454 267-337-6779
Web: saturninfotech.com

Scheig Associates 4227 Burnham Dr . . . . Gig Harbor WA 98332 253-858-3534
Web: www.scheig.com

School Loop Inc 49 Powell St . . . . San Francisco CA 94102 650-351-5060
Web: www.schoolloop.com

SchoolSpring Inc Four Elsom Pkwy . . . . South Burlington VT 05403 802-660-8567
Web: www.schoolspring.com

Scireg Inc 12733 Directors Loop . . . . Woodbridge VA 22192 703-494-6500
Web: www.scireg.com

Scribe Inc 842 S Second St . . . . Philadelphia PA 19147 215-336-5092
Web: scribenet.com

SDLC Partners LP
2790 Mosside Blvd Ste 705 . . . . Monroeville PA 15146 412-373-1950
Web: www.sdlcpartners.com

Sea Shepherd Conservation Society
1225 Wold Rd . . . . Friday Harbor WA 98250 360-370-5650
Web: www.seashepherd.org

Selection Resource Inc
3231 Central Park W Ste 109 . . . . Toledo OH 43617 419-893-8905
Web: selectionresource.com

SemiTorr Inc 10655 Manhasset Dr . . . . Tualatin OR 97062 503-682-7052
Web: www.semitorrinc.com

Senes Oak Ridge Center for Risk Analysis Inc
102 Donner Dr . . . . Oak Ridge TN 37830 865-483-6111
Web: senes.com

Sequel Data Systems Inc
11824 Jollyville Rd Ste 400 . . . . Austin TX 78759 512-918-8841
Web: www.sequeldata.com

Sera-Brynn LLC 5806 Harbour View Blvd Ste 204 . . . . Suffolk VA 23435 757-243-1257
Web: sera-brynn.com

Sererra Consulting Group LLC
5430 Trabuco Rd Ste 150 . . . . Irvine CA 92620 877-276-3774
TF: 877-276-3774 ■ *Web:* www.sererra.com

Serti Informatique Inc 7555 Beclard St . . . . Montreal QC H1J2S5 514-493-1909
Web: www.serti.com

Service Technologies Inc 1284 Logan Cir NW . . . . Atlanta GA 30318 404-355-6262
Web: servicetechnologies.net

ServIT Inc 3721 Cherokee St . . . . Kennesaw GA 30144 770-499-6300
Web: www.servit.net

Sevatec Inc 3112 Fairview Park Dr . . . . Falls Church VA 22042 571-766-1300
Web: www.sevatec.com

Seven Degrees 891 Laguna Canyon Rd . . . . Laguna Beach CA 92651 949-376-1555
Web: www.seven-degrees.com

Shearer & Associates Inc
4960 Corporate Dr Ste 100 . . . . Huntsville AL 35805 256-830-1031
Web: shearerassociates.us

Sierra Business Council 10116 Jibboom St . . . . Truckee CA 96161 530-582-4800
Web: www.sbcouncil.org

Sign Biz Inc 24681 La Plz Ste 270 . . . . Dana Point CA 92629 949-234-0408
Web: www.signbiz.com

Signal Securities Inc 700 Throckmorton St . . . . Fort Worth TX 76102 817-877-4256
Web: www.signalsecurities.com

Signal-tech 4985 Pittsburgh Ave . . . . Erie PA 16509 814-835-3000
Web: www.signal-tech.com

Silicon Engines Ltd
3550 W Salt Creek Ln . . . . Arlington Heights IL 60005 847-637-1180
Web: siliconengines-ltd.com

Simon Consulting LLC
3200 N Central Ave Ste 2460 . . . . Phoenix AZ 85012 602-279-7500
Web: www.simonconsulting.net

Simon-kucher & Partners LLC
One Canal Park Ste 7 . . . . Cambridge MA 02141 617-231-4500
Web: www.simon-kucher.com

Simple Computer Repair LLC
10525 S Eastern Ave Ste 140 . . . . Henderson NV 89052 702-614-3186
Web: www.simplecomputerrepair.com

Simplicity Consulting Inc
11250 Kirkland Way Ste 203 . . . . Kirkland WA 98033 888-252-0385
TF: 888-252-0385 ■ *Web:* www.simplicityconsultinginc.com

Simplion Technologies Inc
1525 McCarthy Blvd Ste 228 . . . . Milpitas CA 95035 408-935-8686
Web: www.simplion.com

Sims & Steele Consulting
44 Merrimon Ave Ste 3a . . . . Asheville NC 28801 828-254-9004
Web: simsandsteele.com

SinglePoint Solutions Inc
9710 Park Plz Ave Ste 201 . . . . Louisville KY 40241 502-212-4017
Web: www.sptsolutions.com

Sivad Business Solutions LLC
2021 Aldbury Ln . . . . Woodstock GA 30189 678-215-1705
Web: www.sivadsolutions.com

Skidata Inc One Harvard Way Ste 5 . . . . Hillsborough NJ 08844 908-243-0000
Web: www.skidata.com

Sky I T Group LLC 330 Seventh Ave . . . . New York NY 10001 212-868-7800
Web: www.skyitgroup.com

SlickData 252 Nassau St Second Fl . . . . Princeton NJ 08542 609-736-0036
Web: www.slickdata.com

Smart Safety Group
2535 Camino Del Rio S Ste 125 . . . . San Diego CA 92108 619-491-3099
Web: www.smartsafetygroup.com

SmarTek21 LLC 12910 Totem Lk Blvd NE Ste 200 . . . . Kirkland WA 98034 425-242-3786
Web: www.smartek21.com

SOAProjects Inc
495 N Whisman Rd Ste 100 . . . . Mountain View CA 94043 650-960-9900
Web: soaprojects.com

SoftNice Inc 5050 Tilghman St Ste 115 . . . . Allentown PA 18104 610-871-0400
Web: www.softnice.com

Solutions Plus 755 Se Main St . . . . Simpsonville SC 29681 864-967-6782
Web: www.splus.net

Solvera Solutions Inc 201 - 1853 Hamilton St . . . . Regina SK S4P2C1 306-757-3510
Web: www.solvera.ca

Somerset Consulting Group Inc
3103 Bee Caves Rd Ste 120 . . . . Austin TX 78746 512-327-0090
Web: www.somersetcg.com

Sonoma Technical Support Services
8840 210th St Ste 342 . . . . Langley BC V1M2Y2 866-898-3123
TF: 866-898-3123 ■ *Web:* www.sonomaservices.com

Soundearth 2811 Fairview Ave E . . . . Seattle WA 98102 206-306-1900
Web: www.soundearthinc.com

Source Data Products Inc
18350 Mount Langley St . . . . Fountain Valley CA 92708 714-593-0387
Web: www.source-data.com

Source One Technical Solutions LLC
1952 Route 22 E . . . . Bound Brook NJ 08805 732-748-8643
Web: www.source1tek.com

South Alabama Regional Planning Commission
110 Beauregard St . . . . Mobile AL 36633 251-433-6541
Web: www.sarpc.org

Southland Safety LLC 403 Hubbard Dr . . . . Henderson TX 75652 903-657-8669
Web: southlandsafety.com

				Phone	Fax
Spd Foundation 5655 S Yosemite St Ste 305 *Web:* spdfoundation.net	Greenwood Village	CO	80111	303-794-1182	
Spearhead Staffing LLC 991 Route 22 W Ste 200 Third Fl. *Web:* www.spearheadstaffing.com	Bridgewater	NJ	08807	908-864-8081	
Spectral Sciences Inc Four Fourth Ave *Web:* www.spectral.com	Burlington	MA	01803	781-273-4770	
Spire Consulting Group LLC 114 W Seventh St Ste 600 *Web:* www.spireconsultinggroup.com	Austin	TX	78701	512-637-0845	
Spire Technologies Inc 2140 SW Jefferson St Ste 300 *Web:* www.spiretech.com	Portland	OR	97201	503-222-3086	
Spokane Neighborhood Action Programs 212 W Second Ave *Web:* www.snapwa.org	Spokane	WA	99201	509-744-3370	
Sri Quality Sys 300 Northpointe Cir Ste 304 *Web:* www.sriregistrar.com	Seven Fields	PA	16046	724-934-9000	
Staffcentrix LLC 33 Woodstock Meadows *Web:* www.staffcentrix.com	Woodstock	CT	06281	860-928-6969	
Stahl Consulting Group PA 8626 N Himes Ave *Web:* www.stahlconsulting.com	Tampa	FL	33614	813-936-0313	
Stanard & Associates Inc 309 W Washington St Ste 1000 *Web:* stanard.com	Chicago	IL	60606	312-553-0213	
Stanfield Systems Inc 718 Sutter St Ste 108 *Web:* www.www.stanfieldsystems.com	Folsom	CA	95630	916-608-8006	
Star Trax Inc 24463 W 10 Mile Rd *Web:* startrax.com	Southfield	MI	48033	248-263-6300	
Sterliteusa 1117 Lake St *Web:* sterliteusa.com	Oak Park	IL	60301	708-383-4003	
Stillmeadow Inc 12852 Park One Dr. *Web:* www.stillmeadow.com	Sugar Land	TX	77478	281-240-8828	
Stohl Environmental LLC 4169 Allendale Pkwy 100 *Web:* www.stohlenvironmental.com	Blasdell	NY	14219	716-312-0070	
storyminers Inc 1862 Wilkenson Crossing *Web:* www.mikewittenstein.com	Marietta	GA	30066	770-425-9830	
StrateGen Consulting LLC 2150 Allston Way Ste 210 *Web:* strategen.com	Berkeley	CA	94704	510-665-7811	
Strategic Development Solutions LLC 11150 W Olympic Blvd Ste 910 *Web:* www.sdsgroup.com	Los Angeles	CA	90064	310-914-5333	
Street Solutions Inc 2930 Plz Five *Web:* www.streetsolutions.com	Jersey City	NJ	07311	201-763-9500	
Strickland General Agency Inc 2963 Gulf To Bay Blvd *Web:* www.sgainfl.com	Clearwater	FL	33759	727-669-8886	
Stroudwater Associates Inc 50 Sewall St Ste 102 *Web:* www.stroudwaterassociates.com	Portland	ME	04102	207-221-8250	
Sts Consulting Services LLC 434 E Loop 281 Ste 105 *Web:* ststx.com	Longview	TX	75605	903-247-1787	
Summit Environmental Consultants Inc 640 Main St *Web:* www.summitenv.com	Lewiston	ME	04240	207-795-6009	
Superior Communications Inc 704 E Gude Dr *Web:* www.scicommo.com	Rockville	MD	20850	301-762-7878	762-6870
Superna Business Consulting Inc 104 Schneider Rd *Web:* www.superna.net	Kanata	ON	K2K1Y2	613-792-1199	
Surfrider Foundation 942 Calle Negocio Ste 150 *Web:* www.surfrider.org	San Clemente	CA	92673	949-492-8170	
Survival Strategies Inc 335 N Third St *Web:* www.survivalstrategies.com	Burbank	CA	91502	818-276-1000	
Swift Media Group 717 Forest Ave Ste 200n *Web:* swiftmediagroup.com	Lake Forest	IL	60045	847-283-0272	
Switchfast Technologies 4043 N Ravenswood Ste 203 *Web:* www.switchfast.com	Chicago	IL	60613	773-241-3007	
Synercomm Inc 3265 Gateway Rd Ste 650 *Web:* www.synercomm.com	Brookfield	WI	53045	262-860-4220	
Synertel 3450 Third St Ste 2B *Web:* www.synertel.com	San Francisco	CA	94124	415-970-0100	
SyNet Technology Solutions Inc 205 Hallene Rd Ste 101 *Web:* www.synetinc.com	Warwick	RI	02886	401-736-6450	
System Improvements Inc 238 S Peters Rd Ste 301 *Web:* www.taproot.com	Knoxville	TN	37923	865-539-2139	
Systems Plus Computers Inc 12 Centerra Pkwy Ste 20 *Web:* www.spci.com	Lebanon	NH	03766	603-643-5800	
Talent Plus Inc One Talent Plus Way *Web:* www.talentplus.com	Lincoln	NE	68506	402-489-2000	
TalentSmart Inc 11526 Sorrento Vly Rd *Web:* www.talentsmart.com	San Diego	CA	92121	858-509-0582	
Tallgrass Restoration LLC 2221 Hammond Dr *Web:* www.tallgrassrestoration.com	Schaumburg	IL	60173	847-925-9830	
TayganPoint Consulting Group Inc 243 N Union St Ste 210 *Web:* www.tayganpoint.com	Lambertville	NJ	08530	609-460-4211	
Te21 Inc 1184 Clements Ferry Rd Ste G *Web:* www.te21.com	Charleston	SC	29492	843-579-2520	
Teachers' Curriculum Institute 3735 Bradview Dr Ste 100 *Web:* teachtci.com	Sacramento	CA	95827	916-366-3686	
Team Work Consulting Inc 22550 Mccauley Rd *Web:* www.teamworkconsulting.com	Shaker Heights	OH	44122	216-360-1790	
Techblocks Inc 399 Applewood Crescent Ste 400 *Web:* tblocks.com	Vaughan	ON	L4K4J3	416-775-1919	
Techforce Inc 3445 Breckinridge Blvd. *Web:* www.techforce.net	Duluth	GA	30096	678-597-2300	
Technical Assurance Inc 38112 Second St. *Web:* www.technicalassurance.com	Willoughby	OH	44094	440-953-3147	
Technolab International Corp 2020 NE 163 St *Web:* www.technolabcorp.com	Miami	FL	33162	305-433-2973	
Technology Futures Inc (TFI) 13740 Research Blvd (N Hwy 183) Ste C-1 *TF:* 800-835-3887 ■ *Web:* www.tfi.com	Austin	TX	78750	512-258-8898	258-0087
Technomedia Solutions LLC 4545 36th St *Web:* www.gotechnomedia.com	Orlando	FL	32811	407-351-0909	
Technossus LLC 17885 Von Karman Ave Ste 410 *Web:* www.technossus.com	Irvine	CA	92614	949-769-3500	
Techwave Consulting Inc One E Uwchlan Ave *Web:* techwavenet.com	Exton	PA	19341	484-872-8707	
Tel Tec Security Systems Inc 5020 Lisa Marie Ct *Web:* www.tel-tec.com	Bakersfield	CA	93313	661-397-5511	
TELCOR Inc 7101 A St. *Web:* www.telcor.com	Lincoln	NE	68510	402-489-1207	
Teledyne Controls 1365 Corporate Ctr Curv *Web:* www.teledynecontrols.com	Eagan	MN	55121	651-994-1000	
Telephone Doctor Inc 30 Hollenberg Ct. *Web:* www.telephonedoctor.com	Bridgeton	MO	63044	314-291-1012	
Telephony Partners LLC 320 W Kennedy Blvd Ste 650 *Web:* www.thinkacuity.com	Tampa	FL	33606	813-769-4690	
Telesolv Consulting LLC 1210 Florida Ave Ne *Web:* telesolvconsulting.com	Washington	DC	20002	202-558-5639	
Telnet Inc 7630 Standish Pl *Web:* www.telnet-inc.com	Rockville	MD	20855	301-840-7110	
thinkASG 15265 Alton Pkwy Ste 300 *TF:* 800-991-9274 ■ *Web:* www.thinkasg.com	Irvine	CA	92618	800-991-9274	
Thinkwrap Commerce Inc 303 Moodie Dr Ste 200 *Web:* www.thinkwrap.com	Ottawa	ON	K2H9R4	613-751-4441	
Tiburon Strategic Advisors LLC 1735 Tiburon Blvd *Web:* www.tiburonadvisors.com	Tiburon	CA	94920	415-789-2540	
Tiburon Technologies Inc 6200 Rockside Woods Blvd Ste 200 *Web:* www.tiburontech.com	Cleveland	OH	44131	440-808-8730	
Tierra Right of Way Services Ltd 1575 E River Rd Ste 201 *Web:* www.tierra-row.com	Tucson	AZ	85718	520-319-2106	
Tilson Technology Management 245 Commercial St *Web:* www.tilsontech.com	Portland	ME	01410	207-591-6427	
Todd Herman & Associates PA 620 Green Vly Rd Ste 104 *Web:* www.toddherman.com	Greensboro	NC	27408	336-297-4200	
Tom Hopkins International Inc 7531 E Second St *Web:* www.tomhopkins.com	Scottsdale	AZ	85251	480-949-0786	
Tonka-Tek Inc 4100 Shoreline Dr Ste 2 *Web:* www.tonkatek.com	Spring Park	MN	55384	612-435-3705	
Total Event Resources 1920 Thoreau Dr N Ste 105 *Web:* www.total-event.com	Schaumburg	IL	60173	847-397-2200	
ToxServices LLC 1367 Connecticut Ave Nw Ste 300 *Web:* toxservices.com	Washington	DC	20036	202-429-8787	
Tradescape Inc 520 S El Camino Real Ste 640 *TF:* 800-697-6068 ■ *Web:* www.tradescape.biz	San Mateo	CA	94402	800-697-6068	
Training Modernization Group Inc 9737 Peppertree Rd *Web:* www.tmgva.com	Spotsylvania	VA	22553	540-295-9313	
Tri-basin Natural Resources District 1723 Burlington St *TF:* 877-995-6688 ■ *Web:* tribasinnrd.org	Holdrege	NE	68949	877-995-6688	
Tri-com Consulting Group LLC, The 333 Industrial Park Rd *Web:* www.tricomgroup.com	Middletown	CT	06457	860-635-9600	
Trincon Group LLC 1683 Old Henderson Rd *Web:* trincon.com	Columbus	OH	43220	614-442-0590	
Trinity Systems Technologies Inc 5885 Cumming Hwy Ste 108-273 *TF:* 888-828-5655 ■ *Web:* www.trinitysystemstech.com	Sugar Hill	GA	30518	888-828-5655	
Trio Media Group LLC 182 Hilderbrand Dr Ste 100 *Web:* triomediagroup.com	Atlanta	GA	30328	404-255-1970	
Triple-I Corp, The 6330 Lamar Ave Ste 230 *Web:* www.triplei.com	Overland Park	KS	66202	913-563-7200	
Triton Environmental Inc 385 Church St Ste 201 *Web:* www.tritonenvironmental.com	Guilford	CT	06437	203-458-7200	
TriVista Business Group Inc 15 Enterprise Ste 410 *Web:* www.trivista.com	Aliso Viejo	CA	92656	949-218-4830	
TRM Technologies Inc 280 Albert St Ste 1000 10th Fl *Web:* www.trm.ca	Ottawa	ON	K1P5G8	613-722-8843	
True North Strategic Advisors LLC 347 W Berry St Ste 100 *Web:* www.truenorthsa.com	Fort Wayne	IN	46802	260-420-5050	
TrueCloud 2147 E Baseline Rd *TF:* 866-990-8783 ■ *Web:* www.truecloud.com	Tempe	AZ	85283	866-990-8783	

Name / Address	City	State	Zip	Phone	Fax
TruMethods LLC 609 Oldershaw Ave *Web:* www.trumethods.com	Moorestown	NJ	08057	856-316-4900	
Turning Point Inc, The 1835 W State Rt 89A Ste 4 *Web:* www.turningpoint.com	Sedona	AZ	86336	928-203-9711	
Unintech Consulting Engineers Inc 2431 E Evans Rd *Web:* www.unintech.com	San Antonio	TX	78259	210-641-6003	
Unison Systems Inc 6130 Greenwood Plz Blvd Ste 100 *Web:* www.unisonsystems.com	Greenwood Village	CO	80111	303-623-8800	
Unisys Corp 801 Lakeview Dr Ste 100 *Web:* www.unisys.com	Blue Bell	PA	19422	215-986-4011	
Urban Strategies LLC 2341 Ninth St S *Web:* www.urbanstrategies.us	Arlington	VA	22204	202-368-3408	
Ursa Institute 390 Fourth St Fl 1 *Web:* www.cus-united.org	San Francisco	CA	94107	415-777-1922	
USC Consulting Group LLC 3000 Bayport Dr Ste 1010 *Web:* www.usccg.com	Tampa	FL	33607	813-636-4004	
Usman Trade 10535 Rockley Rd Ste 103 *Web:* usmantrade.com	Houston	TX	77099	281-933-7200	
Utility Sales Assoc Inc 930 E Oak St *Web:* www.utilitysales.net	Lake In The Hills	IL	60156	847-658-8965	
V t i Valtronics Inc 3463 Double Springs Rd *Web:* www.val-tronics.com	Valley Springs	CA	95252	209-754-0707	
V2Solutions Inc 2340 Dr Walsh Ave *Web:* www.v2solutions.com	Santa Clara	CA	95051	408-550-2340	
VAC-TRON Equipment LLC 27137 S Hwy 33 *Web:* www.vactron.com	Okahumpka	FL	34762	352-728-2222	
VAE Inc 12005 Sunrise Vly Dr Ste 202 *Web:* www.vaeit.com	Reston	VA	20191	703-942-6727	
Value Consulting LLC 23475 Rock Haven Way Ste 200 *Web:* www.valconusa.com	Sterling	VA	20166	703-723-0100	
Velocite Systems Inc 810 Cromwell Park Dr Ste K *Web:* www.velocitesystems.com	Glen Burnie	MD	21061	443-572-0015	
Vensai Technologies 2450 Atlanta Hwy Ste 1002 *Web:* www.vensaiinc.com	Cumming	GA	30040	770-888-4804	
Verinon Technology Solutions Ltd 3395 N Arlington Heights Rd *Web:* www.verinon.com	Arlington Heights	IL	60004	847-577-5256	
Verologix LLC Ste 700 6 Centerpointe Dr *TF:* 800-403-8041 ■ *Web:* www.verologix.com	La Palma	CA	90623	800-403-8041	
Vested Group, The 1001 E 15th St Ste 200 *Web:* thevested.com	Plano	TX	75074	972-429-9025	
Veteran Corps of America 220 E State St Ste 2F *Web:* www.veterancorps.com	O'fallon	IL	62269	703-691-8385	
Vintage IT Services 1210 W Fifth St *Web:* www.vintageits.com	Austin	TX	78703	512-481-1117	
Visitec Marketing Associates Inc 2020 Dean St Unit H *Web:* www.visitec.com	St. Charles	IL	60174	630-762-0300	
Vista Projects Ltd 6020 Second St SE Ste B29 *Web:* www.vistaprojects.com	Calgary	AB	T2H2L8	403-255-3455	
ViWo Inc 10801 National blvd 410 *TF:* 877-958-5174 ■ *Web:* www.viwoinc.com	Los Angeles	CA	90064	877-958-5174	
Vode Lighting LLC 1206 E Macarthur St Ste 3 *Web:* vode.com	Sonoma	CA	95476	707-996-9898	
W d Communications 227 E Bergen Pl Ste 6 *Web:* wdcommunications.com	Red Bank	NJ	07701	732-530-2076	
WAC Consulting Inc 367 W Main St *Web:* www.wacinc.com	Northborough	MA	01532	508-393-7731	
Wainhouse Research LLC 34 Duckhill Ter *Web:* www.wainhouse.com	Duxbury	MA	02332	781-934-6165	
WALZ Postal Solutions Inc 27398 Via Industria *Web:* www.walzgroup.com	Temecula	CA	92590	951-491-6800	
Warm Training Center Inc 4835 Michigan Ave *Web:* www.warmtraining.org	Detroit	MI	48210	313-894-1030	
Warner Consulting Inc 5106 Berryessa St *Web:* warner-consulting.com	Oceanside	CA	92056	760-806-7722	
Watershed Co, The 750 Sixth St S *Web:* www.watershedco.com	Kirkland	WA	98033	425-822-5242	
Watson Institute, The 301 Campmeeting Rd *Web:* www.thewatsoninstitute.org	Sewickley	PA	15143	412-741-1958	
Wcm Group Inc, The 110 S Bender Ave *Web:* wcmgroup.com	Humble	TX	77338	281-446-7070	
WebeDoctor 471 W Lambert Rd Ste 102 *Web:* webedoctor.com	Brea	CA	92821	714-990-3999	
Welch Global Consulting 10084 Oak Knoll Ter *Web:* www.welchgc.com	Colorado Springs	CO	80920	970-292-6600	
West Side Telecommunications 1449 Fairmont Rd *Web:* westsidetelecommunications.net	Morgantown	WV	26501	304-983-2211	
Western Reserve Partners LLC 200 Public Sq Ste 3750 *Web:* wesrespartners.com	Cleveland	OH	44114	216-589-0900	
Whitney, Bradley & Brown Inc 11790 Sunrise Vly Dr *Web:* www.readyroom.com	Reston	VA	20191	703-448-6081	
Wi-fi Guys LLC 7265 Hwy 1 *Web:* www.wi-figuys.com	Finland	MN	55603	218-353-7798	
Wilogic Inc 15896 Manufacture Ln *Web:* www.wilogic.com	Huntington Beach	CA	92649	714-230-8487	
Wilson Consulting Group 100 Old Schoolhouse Ln *Web:* wcg-pc.com	Mechanicsburg	PA	17055	717-591-3070	
Windfall Assoc 981 Chestnut St *Web:* www.windfall-assoc.com	Newton Upper Falls	MA	02464	617-969-1790	969-1777
WingSwept 645 Poole Dr *Web:* www.wingswept.com	Garner	NC	27529	919-779-0954	
Wipro Inc 1300 Crittenden Ln Ste 200 *Web:* www.wipro.com	Mountain View	CA	94043	650-316-3555	
Wireless Facilities Inc (WFI) 4800 Westfields Blvd Ste 200 *NASDAQ:* WFII ■ *TF:* 877-566-7277 ■ *Web:* lcc.com/index.php/en/wfi	Chantilly	VA	20151	703-563-7100	563-7200
WOG LLC 23 S Harrison St *Web:* www.whiteoak-group.com	Easton	MD	21601	410-690-3511	
Wolf Consulting Inc 3875 Franklin Towne Court Ste 110 *Web:* www.wolfconsulting.com	Murrysville	PA	15668	724-325-2900	
Wostmann & Associates Inc 226 Seward St Ste 210 *Web:* www.wostmann.com	Juneau	AK	99801	907-586-6167	
Xantrion Inc 651 20th St *Web:* www.xantrion.com	Oakland	CA	94612	510-272-4701	
Xp3 Corp 745 N Aurora Rd *Web:* xp3hornet.com	Aurora	OH	44202	330-562-8490	
xRM3 Inc 2604-b El Camino Real #251 *Web:* xrmcubed.com	Carlsbad	CA	92008	760-585-4250	
YASH Technologies Inc 605-17th Ave *Web:* www.yash.com	East Moline	IL	61244	309-755-0433	
Yellow Pencil Inc 503 10158 - 103 St. *Web:* yellowpencil.com	Edmonton	AB	T5J0X6	780-423-5917	
YourAmigo Inc 4708 Del Valle Pkwy *Web:* www.youramigo.com	Pleasanton	CA	94566	510 813 1355	
Yoush Consulting Inc 7481 Woodbine Ave Ste 204 *Web:* www.yoush.com	Markham	ON	L3R2W1	905-307-6263	
Youth Frontiers Inc 6009 Excelsior Blvd *Web:* www.youthfrontiers.org	Minneapolis	MN	55416	952-922-0222	
Zbeta Consulting Inc 851 Irwin St Ste 305 *Web:* www.zbetaconsulting.com	San Rafael	CA	94901	415-259-0422	
zedSuite 210 Water St Ste 400 *Web:* www.zedsuite.com	St. John's	NL	A1C1A9	709-722-7213	
Zencos Consulting LLC 1400 Crescent Green Ste 140 *Web:* www.zencos.com	Cary	NC	27518	919-459-4600	
Zestron Corp 11285 Assett Loop *Web:* www.zestron.com	Manassas	VA	20109	703-393-9880	

200 CONSUMER INFORMATION RESOURCES - GOVERNMENT

Name / Address	City	State	Zip	Phone	Fax
Afterschool.gov 370 L'Enfant Promenade SW *Web:* www.acf.hhs.gov	Washington	DC	20447	202-401-9215	205-9688
Alzheimer's Disease Education & Referral Ctr PO Box 8250 *TF:* 800-438-4380 ■ *Web:* www.nia.nih.gov/alzheimers	Silver Spring	MD	20907	301-495-1080	495-3334
National Center for Immunization & Respiratory Diseases 1600 Clifton Rd NE MS E-05 *TF:* 800-232-4636 ■ *Web:* www.cdc.gov/vaccines	Atlanta	GA	30333	800-232-4636	
Centers for Disease Control & Prevention *Travelers Health* 1600 Clifton Rd NE **Fax Area Code:* 888 ■ *TF:* 800-232-4636 ■ *Web:* wwwnc.cdc.gov/travel	Atlanta	GA	30333	800-232-4636	232-3299*
Consumer Product Safety Commission (CPSC) 4340 E W Hwy Ste 502 *TF:* 800-638-2772 ■ *Web:* www.cpsc.gov	Bethesda	MD	20814	301-504-7923	504-0051
Corp for National & Community Service *AmeriCorps USA* 1201 New York Ave NW *TF:* 800-833-3722 ■ *Web:* www.nationalservice.gov	Washington	DC	20525	202-606-5000	
Learn & Serve America 1201 New York Ave NW *TF:* 800-833-3722 ■ *Web:* www.nationalservice.gov	Washington	DC	20525	202-606-5000	
Education Resource Information Ctr (ERIC) c/o CSC 655 15th St NW Ste 500 *TF:* 800-538-3742 ■ *Web:* www.usa.gov	Washington	DC	20005	800-538-3742	
Eldercare Locator 1730 Rhode Island Ave NW Ste 1200 **Fax Area Code:* 202 ■ *TF:* 800-677-1116 ■ *Web:* www.eldercare.gov	Washington	DC	20036	800-677-1116	872-0057*
Energy Efficiency & Renewable Energy Information Ctr 1000 Independence Ave SW **Fax Area Code:* 360 ■ *TF:* 877-337-3463 ■ *Web:* energy.gov	Washington	DC	20585	202-586-4849	236-2023*
FedWorld.gov National Technical Information Service 5285 Port Royal Rd *TF:* 800-553-6847 ■ *Web:* fedworld.ntis.gov	Alexandria	VA	22312	703-605-6000	
Foster Grandparent Program c/o Senior Corps 1201 New York Ave NW *TF:* 800-424-8867 ■ *Web:* www.nationalservice.gov	Washington	DC	20525	202-606-5000	
Grants.gov *Dept of Health & Human Services* 200 Independence Ave SW HHH Bldg *TF:* 800-518-4726 ■ *Web:* www.grants.gov	Washington	DC	20201	800-518-4726	
Homeland Security Information Ctr National Technical Information Service 5301 Shawnee Rd *Web:* www.ntis.gov/hs	Alexandria	VA	22312	703-605-6000	487-4639
National Clearinghouse for Alcohol & Drug Information 11426 Rockville Pk PO Box 2345 *TF:* 800-729-6686 ■ *Web:* samhsa.gov	Rockville	MD	20847	800-729-6686	
National Institute for Literacy (NIFL) 1775 'I' St NW Ste 730 *TF:* 800-228-8813 ■ *Web:* www.lincs.ed.gov	Washington	DC	20006	202-233-2025	233-2050
National Mental Health Information Ctr PO Box 42557 **Fax Area Code:* 240 ■ *TF:* 800-487-4889 ■ *Web:* www.samhsa.gov	Washington	DC	20015	800-487-4889	747-5470*

	Phone	Fax
National Women's Health Information Ctr 200 Independence Ave S.W .... Washington DC 20201	800-994-9662	
TF: 800-994-9662 ■ Web: www.womenshealth.gov		
President's Council on Physical Fitness Sports & Nutrition 1101 Wootton Pkwy .... Rockville MD 20852	240-276-9567	276-9860
Web: www.fitness.gov		
Project Safe Neighborhoods *Office of Justice Programs* 810 Seventh St NW .... Washington DC 20531	202-616-6500	305-1367
TF: 888-744-6513 ■ Web: www.bja.gov		
PubMed US National Library of Medicine 8600 Rockville Pike .... Bethesda MD 20894	888-346-3656	402-1384*
*Fax Area Code: 301 ■ TF: 888-346-3656 ■ Web: www.ncbi.nlm.nih.gov		
Recreation.gov 1849 C St NW .... Washington DC 20240	202-208-4743	
TF: 877-444-6777 ■ Web: www.recreation.gov		
Retired & Senior Volunteer Program (RSVP) 1201 New York Ave NW .... Washington DC 20525	202-606-5000	
TF: 800-833-3722 ■ Web: www.nationalservice.gov		
Senior Corps 1201 New York Ave NW .... Washington DC 20525	202-606-5000	
TF: 800-833-3722 ■ Web: www.nationalservice.gov		
US Dept of Labor Women's Bureau 200 Constitution Ave NW Rm S-3002 .... Washington DC 20210	202-693-6710	693-6710
TF: 800-827-5335 ■ Web: www.dol.gov/wb		
USA Freedom Corps 1201 New York Ave NW .... Washington DC 20005	202-606-5000	
TF: 800-833-3722 ■ Web: www.nationalservice.gov		
USDA Ctr for Nutrition Policy & Promotion 3101 Pk Ctr Dr Fl 10 .... Alexandria VA 22302	703-305-7600	305-3300
Web: www.choosemyplate.gov		
White House Office 1600 Pennsylvania Ave NW .... Washington DC 20500	202-456-1414	
Web: www.whitehouse.gov		

201 CONTAINERS - METAL (BARRELS, DRUMS, KEGS)

	Phone	Fax
Actron Steel Inc 2866 Cass Rd .... Traverse City MI 49684	231-947-3981	
American Metal Crafters LLC 695 High St .... Middletown CT 06457	860-343-1960	
Web: www.americanmetalcraftersllc.com		
Berenfield Containers Inc 4555 Lk Forest Dr Ste 205 .... Cincinnati OH 45242	513-618-3780	618-3781
Web: www.berenfield.com		
C&C Fabrication Company Inc One Fabrication Dr .... Lacey's Spring AL 35754	256-881-7300	
Web: www.ccfab.com		
Cendrex Inc 11303 26th Ave .... Montreal QC H1E6N6	514-493-1489	
Web: www.cendrex.com		
Champion Co 400 Harrison St .... Springfield OH 45505	937-324-5681	324-2397
TF Sales: 800-328-0115 ■ Web: www.championspd.com		
Champion Container Corp 180 Essex Ave PO Box 90 .... Avenel NJ 07001	732-636-6700	855-8663
Web: www.championcontainer.com		
Chicago Steel Container Corp 1846 S Kilbourn Ave .... Chicago IL 60623	773-277-2244	277-1585
Web: chicagosteelcontainer.com		
Columbia Metal Spinning Company Inc 4351 N Normandy Ave .... Chicag IL 60634	773-685-2800	
Web: www.cmspinning.com		
Conco Inc 4000 Oaklawn Dr .... Louisville KY 40219	502-969-1333	962-2190
Web: www.concocontainers.com		
Container Research Corp (CRC) 1 Hollow Hill Rd .... Glen Riddle PA 19037	610-459-2160	
TF: 844-220-9574 ■ Web: www.crc-flex.com		
Csi Industries Inc 6910 W Ridge Rd .... Fairview PA 16415	814-474-9353	474-5797
TF: 800-937-9033 ■ Web: www.flo-bin.com		
DeWys Manufacturing Inc 15300 Eigth Ave .... Marne MI 49435	616-677-5281	
Web: www.dewysmfg.com		
Ductmate Industries Inc 210 Fifth St .... Charleroi PA 15022	724-258-0500	
Web: www.ductmate.com		
Erie Engineered Products Inc 908 Niagara Falls Blvd .... North Tonawanda NY 14120	716-694-2020	694-4339
Web: www.containers-cases.com		
Fabricated Metals LLC 6300 Kenjoy Dr .... Louisville KY 40214	502-363-2625	
Web: www.fabricatedmetals.com		
Fiba Technologies Inc 1535 Grafton Rd PO Box 360 .... Millbury MA 01527	508-887-7100	754-2254
Web: www.fibatech.com		
Gardner Manufacturing Inc 1201 W Lake St .... Horicon WI 53032	920-485-4303	
Web: www.gardnermfg.com		
General Steel Drum LLC 4500 S Blvd .... Charlotte NC 28209	704-525-7160	
Web: www.generalsteeldrum.com		
Geometrica Inc 12300 Dundee Ct Ste 200 .... Cypress TX 77429	832-220-1200	482-0879
Web: www.geometrica.com		
Greentree Toyota Scion 87 Federal Rd .... Danbury CT 06811	203-730-4040	
Web: www.greentree.com		
Greif Inc 425 Winter Rd .... Delaware OH 43015	740-549-6000	657-6592
NYSE: GEF ■ TF: 877-781-9797 ■ Web: www.greif.com		
Harper Motors Inc 200 Hwy 531 .... Minden LA 71055	318-377-0395	
Web: www.harperminden.com		
Highlands Diversified Services Inc 250 Westinghouse Dr .... London KY 40741	606-878-1856	
Web: www.hds-usa.com		
Imperial Industries Inc 505 Industrial Pk Ave .... Rothschild WI 54474	715-359-0200	355-5349
TF: 800-558-2945 ■ Web: www.imperialind.com		
Impulse Manufacturing Inc 55 Impulse Industrial Dr .... Dawsonville GA 30534	706-216-1700	
Web: www.impulsemfg.com		
Industrial Container Services 7152 First Ave S .... Seattle WA 98108	206-763-2345	763-2699
TF: 800-273-3786 ■ Web: www.iconserv.com		
Innovative Fluid Handling Systems 3300 E Rock Falls Rd .... Rock Falls IL 61071	815-626-1018	626-1438
TF: 800-435-7003 ■ Web: www.ifhgroup.com		
Justrite Manufacturing Co 2454 E Dempster St Ste 300 .... Des Plaines IL 60016	847-298-9250	298-9261
TF: 800-798-9250 ■ Web: www.justritemfg.com		
Klune Industries Inc 7323 Coldwater Canyon Ave .... North Hollywood CA 91605	818-503-8100	
Web: www.klunev.com		
Lebus International Inc 215 Industrial Dr .... Longview TX 75602	903-758-5521	757-7782
Web: www.lebus-intl.com		
McKey Perforating Company Inc 3033 S 166th St .... New Berlin WI 53151	262-786-2700	
Web: www.mckey.com		
Meyer Steel Drum Inc 3201 S Millard Ave .... Chicago IL 60623	773-376-8376	376-7060
Web: www.meyersteeldrum.com		
Mi-T-M Corp 8650 Enterprise Dr .... Peosta IA 52068	563-556-7484	
Web: www.mitm.com		
Mid-America Steel Drum Co Inc 8570 S Chicago Rd .... Oak Creek WI 53154	414-762-1114	762-1623
Web: www.midamericasteeldrum.com		
Midwest Products & Engineering Inc 10597 W Glenbrook Ct .... Milwaukee WI 53224	414-355-0310	
Web: www.mpe-inc.com		
Modern Aire Manufacturing Corp 7319 Lankershim Blvd .... North Hollywood CA 91605	818-765-9870	
Web: www.modernaire.com		
Myers Container Corp 8435 NE Killingsworth .... Portland OR 97220	503-501-5830	501-5831
TF: 800-406-9377 ■ Web: www.myerscontainer.com		
North Coast Container Corp 8806 Crane Ave .... Cleveland OH 44105	216-441-6214	441-6239
Web: www.ncc-corp.com		
Northwest Chevrolet 2516 Duss Ave .... Ambridge PA 15003	724-266-3380	
Web: www.wrightcars.com		
Norton Packaging Inc 20670 Cosair Blvd .... Hayward CA 94545	510-786-3445	782-5329
Web: www.nortonpackaging.com		
Packaging Specialties Inc 300 Lake Rd .... Medina OH 44256	330-723-6000	725-8180
TF: 800-344-9271 ■ Web: www.packspec.com		
PCI Industries Inc 5101 Blue Mound Rd .... Fort Worth TX 76106	817-509-2300	
Web: www.pci-industries.com		
Penn Metal Fabricators Inc 2103 New Germany Rd .... Ebensburg PA 15931	814-472-6000	
Web: www.pennmetalfab.com		
Quadra Tech Inc 864 E Jenkins Ave .... Columbus OH 43207	614-443-0630	
Web: www.quadra-techinc.com		
R&M Manufacturing Company LLC 200 Centennial Dr .... Buffalo MN 55313	763-574-9225	
Web: www.rmmco.com		
Rice Motor Company LLC 2630 Battleground Ave .... Greensboro NC 27408	336-288-1190	
Web: ricetoyota.com		
Self Industries Inc 3491 Mary Taylor Rd .... Birmingham AL 35235	205-655-3284	655-3288
Web: selfindustries.com		
Skolnik Industries Inc 4900 S Kilbourn Ave .... Chicago IL 60632	773-735-0700	
Web: www.skolnik.com		
Smith Industries Inc 2781 Gunter Park Dr E .... Montgomery AL 36109	334-277-8520	
Web: www.jrsmith.com		
Stackbin Corp 29 Powderhill Rd .... Lincoln RI 02865	401-333-1600	333-1952
TF Sales: 800-333-1603 ■ Web: www.stackbin.com		
Stainless Metals Inc 60-01 31 Ave .... Woodside NY 11377	718-784-1454	784-4719
Web: www.stainlessmetals.com		
Textainer Equipment Management Ltd 650 California St Fl 16 .... San Francisco CA 94108	415-434-0551	434-0599
Web: www.textainer.com		
United Skys 702 Magna Dr .... Round Lake IL 60073	847-546-7776	
Web: unitedskys.com		
USA Container Company Inc 1776 S Second St .... Piscataway NJ 08854	732-752-7722	
TF: 888-752-7722 ■ Web: www.usacontainer.com		
Von Duprin Inc 2720 Tobey Dr .... Indianapolis IN 46219	800-999-0408	
TF: 800-999-0408 ■ Web: us.allegion.com		
Westmor Industries LLC 3 Development Dr .... Morris MN 56267	320-589-2100	
Web: westmor-ind.com/		
Worthington Dealership Group 5548 Paseo Del Norte .... Carlsbad CA 92008	760-431-1222	
Web: www.calworthington.com		
Wrobel Engineering Company Inc 154 Bodwell St .... Avon MA 02322	508-586-8338	
Web: www.wrobeleng.com		
Young Bros Stamp Works Inc 1415 Howard Ave .... Muscatine IA 52761	563-263-3575	
Web: mw-radio.com		

202 CONTAINERS - PLASTICS (DRUMS, CANS, CRATES, BOXES)

	Phone	Fax
Akro-Mils Inc 1293 S Main St .... Akron OH 44301	800-253-2467	761-6348*
*Fax Area Code: 330 ■ TF: 800-253-2467 ■ Web: www.akro-mils.com		
Beden-Baugh Products Inc 105 Lisbon Rd .... Laurens SC 29360	864-682-3136	682-9302
TF: 866-598-5794 ■ Web: www.naclsolutions.com		
Belco Mfg Company Inc 2303 Taylors Vly Rd .... Belton TX 76513	254-933-9000	939-2644
TF: 800-251-8265 ■ Web: www.belco-mfg.com		
Berry Plastics Corp 101 Oakley St .... Evansville IN 47710	812-424-2904	424-0128
TF: 877-662-3779 ■ Web: www.berryplastics.com		
Brentwood Industries Inc 610 Morgantown Rd .... Reading PA 19611	610-374-5109	376-6022
Web: www.brentwoodindustries.com		
Buckhorn Inc 55 W Techne Ctr Dr .... Milford OH 45150	513-831-4402	831-5474
TF: 800-543-4454 ■ Web: www.buckhorninc.com		
Case Design Corp 333 School Ln .... Telford PA 18969	215-703-0130	703-0139
TF: 800-847-4176 ■ Web: www.casedesigncorp.com		
Champion Container Corp 180 Essex Ave PO Box 90 .... Avenel NJ 07001	732-636-6700	855-8663
Web: www.championcontainer.com		

Company	City	State	ZIP	Phone	Fax
Chem-Tainer Industries Inc 361 Neptune Ave. *TF:* 800-275-2436 ■ *Web:* www.chemtainer.com	West Babylon	NY	11704	631-661-8300	661-8209
Comar Inc One Comar Pl. *Web:* www.comar.com	Buena	NJ	08310	856-692-6100	692-9251
Custom-Pak Inc 1131 Roosevelt St. *Web:* www.custom-pak.com	Clinton	IA	52732	563-242-1801	244-5362
ECS Composites Inc 3560 Rogue River Hwy *Web:* www.ecscase.com	Grants Pass	OR	97527	541-476-8871	474-2479
Fibrenetics Inc Two Cutters Dock Rd *Web:* www.fibglass.com	Woodbridge	NJ	07095	732-636-5670	636-6624
Fort Recovery Industries Inc 2440 Ohio 49 *Web:* www.fortrecoveryindustries.com	Fort Recovery	OH	45846	419-375-4121	375-4194
Gatekeeper Systems Inc 8 Studebaker *TF:* 888-808-9433 ■ *Web:* www.gatekeepersystems.com	Irvine	CA	92618	949-453-1940	453-8148
Handley Industries Inc 2101 Brooklyn Rd *TF:* 800-870-5088 ■ *Web:* www.handleyind.com	Jackson	MI	49203	517-787-8821	787-3946
Hedwin Corp 1600 Roland Heights Ave **Fax:* Cust Svc ■ *TF:* 800-638-1012 ■ *Web:* www.hedwin.com	Baltimore	MD	21211	410-467-8209	889-5189*
HGI Skydyne 100 River Rd. **Fax Area Code:* 845 ■ *TF:* 800-428-2273 ■ *Web:* www.skydyne.com	Port Jervis	NY	12771	800-428-2273	856-8378*
Iroquois Products of Chicago 2220 W 56th St. **Fax Area Code:* 773 ■ *TF:* 800-453-3355 ■ *Web:* www.iroquoisproducts.com	Chicago	IL	60636	800-453-3355	436-4908*
Jewel Case Corp 110 Dupont Dr *TF:* 800-441-4447 ■ *Web:* www.jewelcase.com	Providence	RI	02907	401-943-1400	943-1426
McConkey Co 1615 Puyallup St PO Box 1690 *TF:* 800-426-8124 ■ *Web:* www.mcconkeyco.com	Sumner	WA	98390	253-863-8111	863-5833
Meese Orbitron Dunne Co (MOD) 4920 State Rd	Ashtabula	OH	44004	440-998-1202	
Menasha Corp 1645 Bergstrom Rd *TF:* 800-558-5073 ■ *Web:* www.menasha.com	Neenah	WI	54956	920-751-1000	751-1236
Molded Fiber Glass Tray Co 6175 US Hwy 6 *TF Sales:* 800-458-6050 ■ *Web:* www.mfgtray.com	Linesville	PA	16424	814-683-4500	683-4504
Myers Industries Inc 1293 S Main St. *NYSE: MYE* ■ **Fax:* Acctg ■ *Web:* www.myersindustries.com	Akron	OH	44301	330-253-5592	761-6156*
ORBIS Corp 1055 Corporate Ctr Dr *TF:* 800-999-8683 ■ *Web:* www.orbiscorporation.com	Oconomowoc	WI	53066	262-560-5000	560-5841
Owens-Illinois Inc One Michael Owens Way *NYSE: OI* ■ **Fax Area Code:* 419 ■ *Web:* www.o-i.com	Perrysburg	OH	43551	567-336-5000	247-1082*
Paragon Mfg Company Inc 2001 N 15th Ave *Web:* www.paragonmanufacturing.com	Melrose Park	IL	60160	708-345-1717	345-1721
Pelican Products Inc 147 N Main St *TF:* 800-542-7344 ■ *Web:* www.pelican.com/	South Deerfield	MA	01373	413-665-2163	665-4801
Plano Molding Co 431 E S St *TF:* 800-226-9868 ■ *Web:* www.planomolding.com	Plano	IL	60545	630-552-3111	552-8989
Plas-Tanks Industries Inc 39 Standen Dr *TF:* 800-247-6709 ■ *Web:* www.plastanks.com	Hamilton	OH	45015	513-942-3800	942-3993
Plastic Enterprises Company Inc 401 SE Thomson Dr *Web:* ipl-plastics.com/afficher.aspx?section=313&langue=en	Lee's Summit	MO	64082	816-246-8200	246-8119
Plastic Forming Company Inc 20 S Bradley Rd *TF:* 800-732-2060 ■ *Web:* www.pfccases.com	Woodbridge	CT	06525	203-397-1338	389-0420
Plastican Inc 196 Industrial Rd PO Box 868 *Web:* www.bwaycorp.com	Leominster	MA	01453	978-537-4911	537-6376
Plastics Research Corp 1400 S Campus Ave *Web:* www.prccal.com	Ontario	CA	91761	909-391-2006	391-2205
Rehrig Pacific Co 4010 E 26th St *TF:* 800-421-6244 ■ *Web:* www.rehrigpacific.com	Los Angeles	CA	90023	323-262-5145	269-8506
River Bend Industries 2421 16th Ave S *TF:* 800-365-3070 ■ *Web:* www.riverbendind.com	Moorhead	MN	56560	218-236-1818	236-6168
Rocket Box Inc 125 E 144th St *TF:* 800-762-5521 ■ *Web:* www.rocketbox.com	Bronx	NY	10451	718-292-5370	402-2021
Rotonics Manufacturing Inc 6770 Brighton Blvd. *Web:* www.snyderplasticsolutions.com	Commerce City	CO	80022	303-227-9300	
RPM Industries Inc 26 Aurelius Ave *TF:* 800-669-3676 ■ *Web:* www.rpmindustriesinc.com	Auburn	NY	13021	315-255-1105	252-1167
Schaefer Systems International Inc 10021 Westlake Dr *TF:* 800-876-6000 ■ *Web:* ssi-schaefer.us	Charlotte	NC	28241	704-944-4500	588-1862
Snyder Industries Inc 4700 Fremont St *Web:* www.snydernet.com	Lincoln	NE	68504	402-467-5221	465-1220
Specialty Plastic Fabricators Inc 9658 196th St. *TF:* 800-747-9509 ■ *Web:* www.spfinc.com	Mokena	IL	60448	708-479-5501	479-5598
Stack-On Products Co 1360 N Old Rand Rd *TF:* 800-323-9601 ■ *Web:* www.stack-on.com	Wauconda	IL	60084	847-526-1611	526-6599
Toter Inc PO Box 5338. *TF:* 800-424-0422 ■ *Web:* www.toter.com	Statesville	NC	28677	704-872-8171	878-0734
Tulip Corp 714 E Keefe Ave *Web:* www.tulipcorp.com	Milwaukee	WI	53212	414-963-3120	962-1825
Unifuse LLC 2092 New York 9G *Web:* www.unifuse.com	Staatsburg	NY	12580	845-889-4000	889-4002
US Plastic Corp 1390 Newbrecht Rd. *TF:* 800-537-9724 ■ *Web:* www.usplastic.com	Lima	OH	45801	419-228-2242	228-5034
Xerxes Corp 7901 Xerxes Ave S Ste 201 *Web:* www.xerxes.com	Minneapolis	MN	55431	952-887-1890	887-1870

203 CONTAINERS - WOOD

SEE ALSO Pallets & Skids p. 2853

Company	City	State	ZIP	Phone	Fax
Abbot & Abbot Box Corp 37-11 Tenth St **Fax Area Code:* 718 ■ *TF:* 888-525-7186 ■ *Web:* www.abbotbox.com	Long Island City	NY	11101	888-525-7186	392-8439*
Associated Pallets Inc 71 Premium Dr *Web:* www.associatedpallet.com	South Carrollton	KY	42374	270-754-4087	
Bonsai Artransport Inc 509 Mccormick Dr Ste O *Web:* www.bonsai-finearts.com	Glen Burnie	MD	21061	410-768-2787	
Buckeye Diamond Logistics Inc 15 Sprague Rd *Web:* www.buckeyediamond.com	South Charleston	OH	45368	937-462-8361	
Case Crating & Packing 3340A Greens Rd Ste 900 *Web:* www.casecratingandpacking.com	Houston	TX	77032	713-862-7283	
Commercial Lumber & Pallet Co 135 Long Ln *Web:* www.clcpallets.com	City Of Industry	CA	91746	626-968-0631	
Demptos Napa Cooperage 1050 Soscol Ferry Rd *Web:* www.demptos.fr	Napa	CA	94558	707-257-2628	257-1622
Dove Manufacturing Plant 1 2525 N Sixth St *Web:* knoxcountyarc.com	Vincennes	IN	47591	812-886-4312	
Elberta Crate & Box Co 606 Dothan Hwy *Web:* www.elberta.net	Bainbridge	GA	39818	229-246-2266	246-0387
Franklin Crates Inc PO Box 279 *Web:* www.franklincrates.com	Micanopy	FL	32667	352-466-3141	466-0708
Greif Inc 425 Winter Rd *NYSE: GEF* ■ *TF:* 877-781-9797 ■ *Web:* www.greif.com	Delaware	OH	43015	740-549-6000	657-6592
Independent Stave Company Inc 1078 S Jefferson PO Box 104 *Web:* independentstavecompany.com	Lebanon	MO	65536	417-588-4151	588-3344
Johnston's Trading Inc 11 N Pioneer Ave Ste 101 *Web:* johnstontrading.com	Woodland	CA	95776	530-661-6152	661-0566
Liberty Bell Equipment Corp 3201 S 76th St *Web:* www.medcotool.com	Philadelphia	PA	19153	215-492-6700	
Maine Bucket Co 21 Fireslate Pl *Web:* mainebucket.com	Lewiston	ME	04240	207-784-6700	
Mele & Co 2007 Beechgrove Pl. *TF:* 800-635-6353 ■ *Web:* www.melejewelrybox.com	Utica	NY	13501	315-733-4600	733-3183
Monte Package Company Inc 3752 Riverside Rd *TF:* 800-653-2807 ■ *Web:* www.montepkg.com	Riverside	MI	49084	269-849-1722	849-0185
Northwest Pallet Supply Co 3648 Morreim Dr *Web:* www.northwestpallet.com	Belvidere	IL	61008	815-544-6001	
Pallet Factory Inc, The 3740 Arnold Rd *Web:* www.thepalletfactory.com	Memphis	TN	38118	901-795-8300	
Pallet Services Inc 12926 Farm to Market Rd **Fax Area Code:* 253 ■ *TF:* 800-769-2245 ■ *Web:* www.palletservices.com	Mount Vernon	WA	98273	800-769-2245	627-5119*
Pomona Box Co 301 W Imperial Hwy PO Box 536 *Web:* www.pomonabox.com	La Habra	CA	90631	714-871-0932	871-3483
Southwest Forest Products Inc 2828 S 35th Ave *Web:* www.southwestforestproducts.com	Phoenix	AZ	85009	602-278-1009	
Stearnswood Inc 320 Third Ave NW *Web:* www.stearnswood.com	Hutchinson	MN	55350	320-587-2137	587-7646
Texas Basket Co 100 Myrtle Dr *TF:* 800-657-2200 ■ *Web:* www.texasbasket.com	Jacksonville	TX	75766	903-586-8014	586-0988
TKV Containers Inc 4582 E Harvey Ave	Fresno	CA	93702	559-251-5551	
Wisconsin Box Company Inc 929 Townline Rd *TF:* 800-876-6658 ■ *Web:* www.wisconsinbox.com	Wausau	WI	54402	715-842-2248	842-2240

204 CONTROLS - INDUSTRIAL PROCESS

Company	City	State	ZIP	Phone	Fax
3D Instruments LP 2900 E White Star Ave *Web:* www.3dinstruments.com	Anaheim	CA	92806	714-399-9200	
3PS Inc 1300 Arrow Point Dr *Web:* www.3psinc.com	Cedar Park	TX	78613	512-610-5200	
ADA-ES Inc 8100 Southpark Way Ste B. *NASDAQ: ADES* ■ *TF:* 888-822-8617 ■ *Web:* www.adaes.com	Littleton	CO	80120	303-734-1727	734-0330
ADS Environmental Services 4940 Research Dr *TF:* 800-633-7246 ■ *Web:* www.adsenv.com	Huntsville	AL	35805	256-430-3366	430-6633
Advanced Systems Integrators 45 Craig Dr Apt 4S *Web:* www.asiopen.com	West Springfield	MA	01108	413-230-5010	
AeroControlex Group 313 Gillett St *Web:* www.aerocontrolex.com	Painesville	OH	44077	440-352-6182	354-2912
Air Logic Power Systems LLC 1745 S 38th St Ste 100 *Web:* www.alpsleak.com	Milwaukee	WI	53215	414-671-3332	
ALL-TEST Pro LLC 123 Spencer Plain Rd *TF:* 800-952-8776 ■ *Web:* www.alltestpro.com	Old Saybrook	CT	06475	860-399-4222	
Alpha Technologies Services LLC 3030 Gilchrist Rd *TF:* 800-356-9886 ■ *Web:* www.alpha-technologies.com	Akron	OH	44305	330-745-1641	848-7326
Altech Environment USA Corp 2623 Kaneville Ct *Web:* www.altechusa.com	Geneva	IL	60134	630-262-4400	
AMETEK Automation & Process Technologies 1080 N Crooks *TF:* 800-635-0289 ■ *Web:* www.ametekapt.com	Clawson	MI	48017	248-435-0700	435-8120
AMETEK Power Instruments 50 Fordham Rd **Fax:* Cust Svc ■ *Web:* www.ametekpower.com	Wilmington	MA	01887	978-988-4903	988-4944*
AMETEK Process & Analytical Instruments THERMOX Div 150 Freeport Rd *Web:* www.ametekpi.com	Pittsburgh	PA	15238	412-828-9040	826-0399
Amot Controls Corp 8824 Fallbrook Dr **Fax Area Code:* 713 ■ *Web:* www.amotusa.com	Houston	TX	77064	281-940-1800	559-9419*
Anderson Instrument Co 156 Auriesville Rd *TF:* 800-833-0081 ■ *Web:* www.andinst.com	Fultonville	NY	12072	518-922-5315	922-8997
Applied Microstructures Inc 1020 Rincon Cir *TF:* 877-683-2678 ■ *Web:* www.appliedmst.com	San Jose	CA	95131	408-907-2885	

				Phone	Fax

Arcet Equipment Company Inc
1700 Chamberlayne Ave — Richmond VA 23222 — 800-388-0302
TF: 800-388-0302 ■ *Web:* www.arcet.com

ARi Industries Inc 381 Ari Ct — Addison IL 60101 — 630-953-9100
TF: 800-237-6725 ■ *Web:* www.ariindustries.com

Arzel Zoning Technology Inc
4801 Commerce Pkwy — Cleveland OH 44128 — 216-831-6068
TF: 800-611-8312 ■ *Web:* www.arzelzoning.com

ASCO Valve Inc 50-60 Hanover Rd — Florham Park NJ 07932 — 973-966-2000
Web: www.ascovalve.com

Athena Controls Inc 5145 Campus Dr — Plymouth Meeting PA 19462 — 610-828-2490 — 828-7084
TF: 800-782-6776 ■ *Web:* www.athenacontrols.com

ATI Industrial Automation Export Co
1031 Goodworth Dr — Apex NC 27539 — 919-772-0115 — 772-8259
Web: www.ati-ia.com

Auburn Systems LLC
Eight Electronics Ave Ste 1 — Danvers MA 01923 — 978-777-2460
Web: www.auburnsys.com

Automation Nth 491 Waldron Rd — La Vergne TN 37086 — 615-793-7704
Web: www.automationnth.com

Automation Products Group Inc (APG)
1025 West 1700 North — Logan UT 84321 — 435-753-7300 — 753-7490
TF: 888-525-7300 ■ *Web:* www.apgsensors.com

Automation Service 13871 Parks Steed Dr — Earth City MO 63045 — 314-785-6600 — 785-6610
TF: 800-325-4808 ■ *Web:* www.automationservice.com

Automation Systems Interconnect Inc
4700 Wport Dr Ste 500 — Mechanicsburg PA 17055 — 717-249-5581
Web: www.asi-ez.com

Azonix Corp 900 Middlesex Tpke Bldg 6 — Billerica MA 01821 — 978-670-6300 — 670-8855
TF: 800-967-5558 ■ *Web:* www.azonix.com

Bacharach Inc 621 Hunt Vly Cir — New Kensington PA 15068 — 724-334-5000 — 334-5001
TF: 800-736-4666 ■ *Web:* www.bacharach-inc.com

Barksdale Inc 3211 Fruitland Ave — Los Angeles CA 90058 — 323-589-6181 — 589-3463
TF: 800-835-1060 ■ *Web:* www.barksdale.com

BECS Technology Inc
9487 Dielman Rock Island Industrial Dr — Saint Louis MO 63132 — 314-567-0088
Web: www.becs.com

Bio-Chem Fluidics Inc 85 Fulton St — Boonton NJ 07005 — 973-263-3001
Web: www.biochemfluidics.com

Blue-White Industries Ltd
5300 Business Dr — Huntington Beach CA 92649 — 714-893-8529 — 894-9492
Web: www.bluwhite.com

Brookfield Engineering Lab Inc
11 Commerce Blvd — Middleboro MA 02346 — 508-946-6200 — 946-6262
TF: 800-628-8139 ■ *Web:* www.brookfieldengineering.com

Brooks Instrument 250 Andrews Rd — Trevose PA 19053 — 215-357-0893
Web: www.keyinstruments.com

Budzar Industries Inc
38241 Willoughby Pkwy — Willoughby OH 44094 — 440-918-0505
Web: www.budzar.com

Buhler Inc 13105 12th Ave N — Plymouth MN 55441 — 763-847-9900 — 847-9911
TF: 800-722-7483 ■ *Web:* www.buhlergroup.com

Cal-Bay Systems Inc 3070 Kerner Blvd Ste B — San Rafael CA 94901 — 415-258-9400

Campbell Scientific Inc 815 West 1800 North — Logan UT 84321 — 435-753-2342 — 750-9540
Web: www.campbellsci.com

Canfield Connector Div 8510 Foxwood Ct — Youngstown OH 44514 — 800-554-5071
TF: 800-554-5071 ■ *Web:* www.canfieldconnector.com

Cec Controls Co Inc 14555 Barber Ave — Warren MI 48088 — 586-779-0222 — 779-0266
TF: 877-924-0303 ■ *Web:* www.ceccontrols.com

Celesco Transducer Products Inc
20630 Plummer St — Chatsworth CA 91311 — 818-701-2750
TF: 800-423-5483 ■ *Web:* www.celesco.com

Celtech Corp 1300 Terminal Dr — Carlsbad NM 88220 — 575-887-2044
Web: www.aseholdings.com

Cephasonics Inc 160 Saratoga Ave Ste 180 — Santa Clara CA 95051 — 408-249-4629
Web: www.cephasonics.com

Cincinnati Test Systems Inc 5555 Dry Fork Rd — Cleves OH 45002 — 513-367-6699 — 367-5426
TF: 800-850-3189 ■ *Web:* www.cincinnati-test.com

Clearsign Combustion Corp
12870 Interurban Ave S — Seattle WA 98168 — 206-673-4848
Web: www.clearsign.com

Cleveland Electric Labortories
1776 Enterprise Pkwy — Twinsburg OH 44087 — 330-425-4747
Web: www.clevelandelectriclabs.com

Colloidal Dynamics Pty Ltd
5150 Palm Vly Rd Ste 303 — Ponte Vedra Beach FL 32082 — 904-686-1536
Web: www.colloidal-dynamics.com

Compressor Controls Corp 4725 121st St — Des Moines IA 50323 — 515-270-0857 — 270-1331
Web: www.cccglobal.com

Conax Buffalo Technologies LLC
2300 Walden Ave — Buffalo NY 14225 — 716-684-4500 — 684-7433
TF: 800-223-2389 ■ *Web:* www.conaxtechnologies.com

Control Gaging Inc 5200 Venture Dr — Ann Arbor MI 48108 — 734-668-6750
Web: www.controlgaging.com

Cooper Atkins Corp 33 Reeds Gap Rd — Middlefield CT 06455 — 860-349-3473 — 349-8994
TF Sales: 800-835-5011 ■ *Web:* cooper-atkins.com/default.asp

Corelis Inc
Alondra Corporate Ctr 13100 Alondra Blvd — Cerritos CA 90703 — 562-926-6727
Web: www.corelis.com

Crane Company Dynalco Controls Div
3690 NW 53rd St — Fort Lauderdale FL 33309 — 954-739-4300 — 484-3376
TF: 800-368-6666 ■ *Web:* www.dynalco.com

Crest Semiconductors Inc
2001 Gateway Pl 610 W — San Jose CA 95110 — 408-441-0303
Web: www.slicex.com

Cresta Technology Corp
3900 Freedom Cir Ste 201 — Santa Clara CA 95054 — 408-486-5610
Web: www.crestatech.com

CUES Inc 3600 Rio Vista Ave — Orlando FL 32805 — 407-849-0190
Web: www.cuesinc.com

Custom Control Manufacturer of Kansas Inc
5601 Merriam Dr — Merriam KS 66203 — 913-722-0343
Web: www.customcontrolmfr.com

Custom Control Sensors Inc
21111 Plummer St — Chatsworth CA 91311 — 818-341-4610 — 709-0426
Web: www.ccsdualsnap.com

Custom Sensors & Technologies (CST)
14401 Princeton Ave — Moorpark CA 93021 — 805-552-3599
Web: www.cstsensors.com

Daniel Measurement & Control Inc
5650 Brittmoore Rd — Houston TX 77041 — 713-467-6000 — 827-3880
TF: 800-518-1623 ■ *Web:* www.emersonprocess.com

Davidson Instruments Inc
9391 Grogan's Mill Rd — The Woodlands TX 77380 — 281-362-4900
Web: www.davidson-instruments.com

Daytronic Corp 2566 Kohnle Dr — Miamisburg OH 45342 — 937-293-2566
Web: www.daytronic.com

DCG Systems Inc 45900 Northport Loop E — Fremont CA 94538 — 510-897-6800
Web: www.dcgsystems.com

Del Mar Scientific Acquisition Ltd
4951 Airport Pkwy Ste 803 — Addison TX 75001 — 972-661-5160
Web: www.delmarscientific.com

DENT Instruments Inc 925 SW Emkay Dr — Bend OR 97702 — 541-388-4774
Web: www.dentinstruments.com

Dexter Research Center Inc
7300 Huron River Dr — Dexter MI 48130 — 734-426-3921
Web: www.dexterresearch.com

Dickson Co 930 S Westwood Ave — Addison IL 60101 — 630-543-3747 — 543-0498
TF: 800-757-3747 ■ *Web:* www.dicksondata.com

Digalog Systems Inc 3180 S 166th St — New Berlin WI 53151 — 262-797-8000
Web: www.digalogsystems.com

Dwyer Instruments Inc
102 Indiana Hwy 212 PO Box 373 — Michigan City IN 46360 — 219-879-8000 — 872-9057
Web: www.dwyer-inst.com

Eico Inc 1054 Yosemite Dr — Milpitas CA 95035 — 408-945-9898
Web: www.eico.net

Eldridge Products Inc 2700 Garden Rd Bldg A — Monterey CA 93940 — 831-648-7777
TF: 800-321-3569 ■ *Web:* www.epiflow.com

Electro Optical Industries Inc
859 Ward Dr — Santa Barbara CA 93111 — 805-964-6701 — 967-8590
Web: www.electro-optical.com

Emerson Process Management
8100 W Florissant Ave Annex K — Saint Louis MO 63136 — 314-553-1847 — 553-1982
Web: www.emersonprocess.com

Emulation Technology Inc 759 Flynn Rd — Camarillo CA 93012 — 805-383-8480
TF: 800-232-7837 ■ *Web:* www.emulation.com

Encoder Products Co 464276 Hwy 95 S PO Box 249 — Sagle ID 83860 — 208-263-8541 — 263-0541
TF: 800-366-5412 ■ *Web:* www.encoder.com

Endress+Hauser Inc 2350 Endress Pl — Greenwood IN 46143 — 317-535-7138 — 535-8498
TF: 888-363-7377 ■ *Web:* www.us.endress.com

Enerac Inc 67 Bond St — Westbury NY 11590 — 516-997-2100
Web: www.enerac.com

Enmetric Systems Inc 617 Mtn View Ave Ste 5 — Belmont CA 94002 — 650-762-5757
Web: www.enmetric.com

ERDCO Engineering Corp 721 Custer Ave — Evanston IL 60202 — 847-328-0550
Web: www.erdco.com

Fairchild Industrial Products Co
3920 Westpoint Blvd — Winston-Salem NC 27103 — 336-659-3400 — 659-9323*
**Fax:* Sales ■ *TF:* 800-334-8422 ■ *Web:* www.fairchildproducts.com

Fast Heat Inc 776 Oaklawn Ave — Elmhurst IL 60126 — 630-833-5400 — 833-2040
TF: 877-747-8575 ■ *Web:* www.fastheat.com

Fluid Components International
1755 La Costa Meadows Dr — San Marcos CA 92078 — 760-744-6950 — 736-6250
TF: 800-863-8703 ■ *Web:* www.fluidcomponents.com

Forney Corp 3405 Wiley Post Rd — Carrollton TX 75006 — 972-458-6100 — 458-6650
TF Cust Svc: 800-356-7740 ■ *Web:* www.forneycorp.com

Fred Knapp Engraving Company Inc
5102 Douglas Ave — Racine WI 53402 — 262-639-9035
Web: www.air-logic.com

FTI Flow Technology Inc 8930 S Beck Ave Ste 107 — Tempe AZ 85284 — 480-240-3400
Web: www.ftimeters.com

GainSpan Corp 3590 N First St Ste 300 — San Jose CA 95134 — 408-627-6500
Web: www.gainspan.com

Galvanic Applied Sciences USA Inc
41 Wellman St — Lowell MA 01851 — 978-848-2701
Web: www.galvanic.com

GE Infrastructure Sensing
1100 Technology Pk Dr — Billerica MA 01821 — 978-437-1000 — 437-1031
TF: 800-833-9438 ■ *Web:* www.ge-mcs.com

Gefran ISI Inc Eight Lowell Ave — Winchester MA 01890 — 781-729-5249
TF: 888-888-4474 ■ *Web:* www.gefran.com

Gems Sensors Inc One Cowles Rd — Plainville CT 06062 — 860-747-3000 — 747-4244
TF: 800-378-1600 ■ *Web:* www.gemssensors.com

General Devices Company Inc
1410 S Post Rd — Indianapolis IN 46239 — 317-897-7000
TF: 800-821-3520 ■ *Web:* www.generaldevices.com

Geotech Environmental Equipment Inc
2650 E 40th Ave — Denver CO 80205 — 303-320-4764 — 322-7242
TF: 800-833-7958 ■ *Web:* www.geotechenv.com

Geotest - Marvin Test Systems Inc
1770 Kettering — Irvine CA 92614 — 949-263-2222
Web: marvintest.com

GF Piping Systems 3401 Aero Jet Ave — El Monte CA 91731 — 626-571-2770 — 573-2057
Web: www.gfps.com

GfG Instrumentation Inc
1194 Oak Vly Dr Ste 20 — Ann Arbor MI 48108 — 734-769-0573
TF: 800-959-0329 ■ *Web:* www.gfg-inc.com

Greenvity Communications Inc
673 S Milpitas Blvd Ste 204 — Milpitas CA 95035 — 408-935-9434
Web: www.greenvity.com

Guided Wave Inc 3033 Gold Canal Dr — Rancho Cordova CA 95670 — 916-638-4944
Web: www.guidedwave.com

Halma Holdings Inc
11500 Northlake Dr Ste 306 — Cincinnati OH 45249 — 513-772-5501
Web: www.halma.com

Company	City	State	Zip	Phone	Fax
Hammond Manufacturing Company Ltd 394 Edinburgh Rd N *Web:* www.hammfg.com	Guelph	ON	N1H1E5	519-822-2960	
Harco Laboratories Inc 186 Cedar St *Web:* www.harcolabs.com	Branford	CT	06405	203-483-3700	483-0391
Harding Instruments 9431 41 Ave NW Edmonton Alberta Canada T6E 5X7 *Web:* www.harding.ca	Edmonton	AB	T6E5X7	780-462-7100	
Hart Scientific Inc 799 E Utah Vly Dr *TF:* 800-438-4278 ■ *Web:* us.flukecal.com	American Fork	UT	84003	801-763-1600	763-1010
Healthspace USA Inc 4860 Cox Rd Ste 200 *Web:* www.healthspace.ca	Glen Allen	VA	23060	804-935-8532	
Heraeus Electro-Nite Co One Summit Sq Ste 100 *Web:* www.heraeus-electro-nite.com	Langhorne	PA	19047	215-944-9000	944-9000
HO Trerice Co 12950 W Eight-Mile Rd *TF:* 888-873-7423 ■ *Web:* www.trerice.com	Oak Park	MI	48237	248-399-8000	399-7246
Hoffland Environmental Inc 10391 Silver Springs Rd *Web:* www.hoffland.net	Conroe	TX	77303	936-856-4515	856-4589
Honeywell Automation & Control Solutions 11 W Spring St *Web:* www.honeywell.com	Freeport	IL	61032	815-235-5500	
HSQ Technology 26227 Research Rd *TF:* 800-486-6684 ■ *Web:* www.hsq.com	Hayward	CA	94545	510-259-1334	259-1391
Industrial Scientific Corp 7848 Steubenville Pk *TF:* 800-338-3287 ■ *Web:* www.indsci.com	Oakdale	PA	15071	412-788-4353	788-8353
INFICON Inc Two Technology Pl *Web:* www.inficon.com	East Syracuse	NY	13057	315-434-1100	437-3803
Intelligent Instrumentation Inc 419 NE 10th Ave **Fax Area Code:* 520 ■ *TF:* 800-685-9911 ■ *Web:* www.instrument.com	Portland	OR	97232	503-928-3188	573-0522*
Invisa Inc 1800 Second St Ste 965 *Web:* www.invisa.com	Sarasota	FL	34236	941-870-3950	
IO Industries Inc 1510 Woodcock St *Web:* www.ioindustries.com	London	ON	N6H5S1	519-663-9570	663-9571
IO Semiconductor Inc 4350 Executive Dr Ste 200 *Web:* www.iosemi.com	San Diego	CA	92121	858-373-0440	
ISCO Inc 4700 Superior St PO Box 82531 **Fax:* Cust Svc ■ *TF:* 800-228-4250 ■ *Web:* www.isco.com	Lincoln	NE	68501	402-464-0231	465-3022*
ITT Industries Inc 1133 Westchester Ave *NYSE:* ITT ■ *TF:* 800-254-2823 ■ *Web:* www.itt.com	White Plains	NY	10604	914-641-2000	696-2950
JMS Southeast Inc 105 Temperature Ln *Web:* www.jms-se.com	Statesville	NC	28677	704-873-1835	
Keller America Inc 813 Diligence Dr Ste 120 *Web:* www.kelleramerica.com	Newport News	VA	23606	757-596-6680	
King Instrument Company Inc 12700 Pala Dr *Web:* www.kinginstrumentco.com	Garden Grove	CA	92841	714-891-0008	
Kistler-Morse Corp 150 Venture Blvd *TF:* 800-426-9010 ■ *Web:* www.kistlermorse.com	Spartanburg	SC	29306	864-574-2763	574-8063
Lake Monitors Inc 8809 Industrial Dr *TF:* 800-850-6110 ■ *Web:* www.lakemonitors.com	Franksville	WI	53126	262-884-9800	884-9810
Lake Shore Cryotronics 575 McCorkle Blvd *TF:* 877-969-0010 ■ *Web:* www.lakeshore.com	Westerville	OH	43082	614-891-2243	818-1600
LaMotte Co 802 Washington Ave *TF:* 800-344-3100 ■ *Web:* www.lamotte.com	Chestertown	MD	21620	410-778-3100	778-6394
Larson Davis Inc 3425 Walden Ave *Web:* www.larsondavis.com	Depew	NY	14043	716-926-8243	
Lime Instruments LLC 1187 Brittmoore Rd *Web:* www.limeinst.net	Houston	TX	77043	713-781-1883	
Linear Laboratories 42025 Osgood Rd *TF:* 800-536-0262 ■ *Web:* www.linearlabs.com	Fremont	CA	94539	510-226-0488	226-1112
Liquid Controls LLC 105 Albrecht Dr *Web:* www.lcmeter.com	Lake Bluff	IL	60044	847-295-1050	
Lucas Labs 393 Tomkins Ct Ste J *Web:* www.signatone.com	Gilroy	CA	95020	408-848-2851	
Lynntech Inc 2501 Earl Rudder Fwy S Ste 100 *Web:* www.lynntech.com	College Station	TX	77845	979-764-2200	
Magnetrol International Inc 5300 Belmont Rd *TF:* 800-624-8765 ■ *Web:* magnetrol.com	Downers Grove	IL	60515	630-969-4000	969-9489
Mahr Federal Inc 1144 Eddy St *TF Orders:* 800-343-2050 ■ *Web:* www.mahrfederal.com	Providence	RI	02905	401-784-3100	784-3246
Malema Engineering Corp 1060 S Rogers Cir *TF:* 800-637-6418 ■ *Web:* www.malema.com	Boca Raton	FL	33487	561-995-0595	995-0622
MAMAC Systems Inc 8189 Century Blvd *TF:* 800-843-5116 ■ *Web:* www.mamacsys.com	Minneapolis	MN	55317	952-556-4900	
Mark-10 Corp 11 Dixon Ave *Web:* www.mark-10.com	Copiague	NY	11726	631-842-9200	
Marsh Bellofram Corp 8019 Ohio River Blvd *TF:* 800-727-5646 ■ *Web:* www.marshbellofram.com	Newell	WV	26050	304-387-1200	387-1212
Maxcess International Corp 222 W Memorial Rd *Web:* www.maxcessintl.com	Oklahoma City	OK	73114	405-755-1600	
Maxitrol Co 23555 Telegraph Rd PO Box 2230 *Web:* www.maxitrol.com	Southfield	MI	48033	248-356-1400	356-0829
McCrometer Inc 3255 W Stetson Ave *TF:* 800-220-2279 ■ *Web:* www.mccrometer.com	Hemet	CA	92545	951-652-6811	652-3078
Measurement Technology Northwest Inc 4211 24th Ave W *Web:* www.mtnw-usa.com	Seattle	WA	98199	206-634-1308	
Mensor Corp 201 Barnes Dr *Web:* www.mensor.com	San Marcos	TX	78666	512-396-4200	396-1820
Metron Inc 1505 W Third Ave *Web:* www.metroninc.com	Denver	CO	80223	303-592-1903	534-1947
Micro Lithography Inc 1257 Elko Dr *Web:* www.mliusa.com	Sunnyvale	CA	94089	408-747-1769	
Micro Motion Inc 7070 Winchester Cir *TF:* 800-522-6277 ■ *Web:* www2.emersonprocess.com/en-us/brands/micromotion	Boulder	CO	80301	303-530-8400	
MicroMod Automation Inc 75 Town Centre Dr *TF:* 800-480-1975 ■ *Web:* www.micmod.com	Rochester	NY	14623	585-321-9200	
Minco Products Inc 7300 Commerce Ln NE **Fax:* Sales ■ *Web:* www.minco.com	Minneapolis	MN	55432	763-571-3121	571-0927*
MKS Instruments Inc 2 Tech Dr Ste 201 *TF:* 800-428-9401 ■ *Web:* www.mksinst.com	Andover	MA	01810	978-645-5500	557-5100
Mocon Inc 7500 Boone Ave N Ste 111 *NASDAQ:* MOCO ■ *Web:* www.mocon.com	Minneapolis	MN	55428	763-493-6370	493-6358
Monarch Instrument Inc 15 Columbia Dr *Web:* www.monarchinstrument.com	Amherst	NH	03031	603-883-3390	
Moore Industries International Inc 16650 Schoenborn St *TF:* 800-999-2900 ■ *Web:* www.miinet.com	North Hills	CA	91343	818-894-7111	891-2816
NDC Infrared Engineering 5314 N Irwindale Ave *Web:* www.ndc.com	Irwindale	CA	91706	626-960-3300	939-3870
Nearfield Systems Inc 19730 Magellan Dr *TF:* 800-334-7384 ■ *Web:* www.nearfield.com	Torrance	CA	90502	310-525-7000	
Noren Products Inc 1010 Obrien Dr *Web:* www.norenproducts.com	Menlo Park	CA	94025	650-322-9500	324-1348
Noshok Inc 1010 W Bagley Rd *Web:* www.noshok.com	Berea	OH	44017	440-243-0888	243-3472
NRD LLC 2937 Alt Blvd PO Box 310 *TF:* 800-525-8076 ■ *Web:* www.nrdstaticcontrol.com	Grand Island	NY	14072	716-773-7634	773-7744
Octasic Inc 4101 Molson St Ste 300 *Web:* www.octasic.com	Montreal	QC	H1Y3L1	514-282-8858	
Omega Engineering Inc One Omega Dr PO Box 4047 **Fax:* Cust Svc ■ *TF:* 800-826-6342 ■ *Web:* www.omega.com	Stamford	CT	06907	203-359-1660	359-7700*
ONICON Inc 1500 N Belcher Rd *Web:* www.btumeter.com	Clearwater	FL	33765	727-447-6140	
Onset Computer Corp PO Box 3450 *TF:* 800-564-4377 ■ *Web:* www.onsetcomp.com	Pocasset	MA	02559	508-759-9500	759-9100
Opto 22 Inc 43044 Business Park Dr *Web:* www.opto22.com	Temecula	CA	92590	951-695-3000	
OPW Fuel Management Systems 6900 Santa Fe Dr **Fax:* Cust Svc ■ *TF:* 800-547-9393 ■ *Web:* www.opwglobal.com	Hodgkins	IL	60525	708-485-4200	485-4630*
Orange Research Inc 140 Cascade Blvd *TF:* 800-989-5657 ■ *Web:* www.orangeresearch.com	Milford	CT	06460	203-877-5657	
Orion Instruments LLC 2105 Oak Villa Blvd *TF:* 866-556-7466 ■ *Web:* www.orioninstruments.com	Baton Rouge	LA	70815	225-906-2343	906-2344
PakSense Inc 6223 N Discovery Pl *TF:* 877-832-0720 ■ *Web:* www.paksense.com	Boise	ID	83713	208-489-9010	
Palmer Wahl Instrumentation Group 234 Old Weaverville Rd *Web:* www.instrumentationgroup.com	Asheville	NC	28804	828-658-3131	
Paper Machine Components 11 Old Sugar Hollow Rd *Web:* www.pmc1.com	Danbury	CT	06810	203-792-8686	
Parker Hannifin Corp 6035 Parkland Blvd *Web:* parker.com	Cleveland	OH	44124	216-896-3000	514-6738
Parker Hannifin Corp Veriflo Div 250 Canal Blvd *TF:* 800-272-7537 ■ *Web:* parker.com	Richmond	CA	94804	510-235-9590	232-7396
PdMA Corp 5909-C Hampton Oaks Pkwy *TF:* 800-476-6463 ■ *Web:* www.pdma.com	Tampa	FL	33610	813-621-6463	
Pearpoint Inc 72055 Corporate Way *TF:* 800-688-8094 ■ *Web:* spx.com/en/pearpoint/	Thousand Palms	CA	92276	760-343-7350	
Pentair 7433 Harwin Dr *TF:* 800-545-6258 ■ *Web:* pentairthermal.com	Houston	TX	77036	800-545-6258	
Photon Dynamics Inc 5970 Optical Ct	San Jose	CA	95138	408-226-9900	
Portage Electric Products Inc 7700 Freedom Ave NW *TF:* 888-464-7374 ■ *Web:* www.pepiusa.com	North Canton	OH	44720	330-499-2727	499-1853
Porter Instrument Company Inc 245 Township Line Rd PO Box 907 *TF:* 888-723-4001 ■ *Web:* www.porterinstrument.com	Hatfield	PA	19440	215-723-4000	723-2199
Potter Electric Signal Company Inc 5757 Phantom Dr Ste 125 *TF:* 800-325-3936 ■ *Web:* www.pottersignal.com	Hazelwood	MO	63042	314-878-4321	595-6999
Pressure Profile Systems Inc 5757 Century Blvd Ste 600 *TF:* 888-249-2464 ■ *Web:* www.pressureprofile.com	Los Angeles	CA	90045	310-641-8100	
Proportion-Air Inc 8250 N 600 W PO Box 218 *Web:* www.proportionair.com	Mccordsville	IN	46055	317-335-2602	
Proteus Industries 340 Pioneer Way *Web:* www.proteusind.com	Mountain View	CA	94041	650-964-4163	
Pyromation Inc 5211 Industrial Rd *Web:* www.pyromation.com	Fort Wayne	IN	46825	260-484-2580	482-6805
Q-Lab Corp 800 Canterbury Rd *Web:* www.q-lab.com	Westlake	OH	44145	440-835-8700	
Qualitrol Company LLC 1385 Fairport Rd *Web:* www.qualitrolcorp.com	Fairport	NY	14450	585-586-1515	377-0220
Quantenna Communications Inc 3450 W Warren Ave *Web:* www.quantenna.com	Fremont	CA	94538	510-743-2260	
RACO Mfg & Engineering Company Inc 1400-62nd St *Web:* www.racoman.com	Emeryville	CA	94608	510-658-6713	
Radian Research Inc 3852 Fortune Dr *Web:* www.radianresearch.com	Lafayette	IN	47905	765-449-5500	
RAE Systems 3775 N First St *TF:* 877-723-2878 ■ *Web:* www.raesystems.com	San Jose	CA	95134	408-952-8200	952-8480
Raven Industries Inc 205 E Sixth St *NASDAQ:* RAVN ■ *TF:* 800-243-5435 ■ *Web:* www.ravenind.com	Sioux Falls	SD	57104	605-336-2750	335-0268

	City	State	Zip	Phone	Fax
Raytheon Network Centric Systems (NCS) 2501 W University Dr *Web:* www.raytheon.com	McKinney	TX	75071	781-522-3000	
Red Lion Controls Inc 20 Willow Springs Cir *Web:* www.redlion-controls.com	York	PA	17406	717-767-6511	
Renco Encoders Inc 26 Coromar Dr *Web:* www.renco.com	Goleta	CA	93117	805-968-1525	685-7965
REOTEMP Instrument Corp 10656 Roselle St *Web:* www.reotemp.com	San Diego	CA	92121	858-784-0710	
Research Inc 7128 Shady Oak Rd *Web:* pcscontrols.com/	Eden Prairie	MN	55344	952-941-3300	941-3628
Restek Corp 110 Benner Cir *Web:* www.restek.com	Bellefonte	PA	16823	814-353-1300	
Robertshaw Industrial Products 1602 Mustang Dr *TF:* 800-228-7429 ■ *Web:* www.robertshawindustrial.com	Maryville	TN	37801	865-981-3100	981-3168
Rochester Gauges Inc of Texas 11616 Harry Hines Blvd *TF:* 800-821-1829 ■ *Web:* www.rochestergauges.com	Dallas	TX	75229	972-241-2161	620-1403
Ronan Engineering Co 21200 Oxnard St **Fax Area Code:* 818 ■ *TF:* 800-327-6626 ■ *Web:* www.ronan.com	Woodland Hills	CA	91367	800-327-6626	992-6435*
Roper Industries Inc 6901 Professional Pkwy Ste 200 *NYSE:* ROP ■ *TF:* 888-227-3565 ■ *Web:* www.roperind.com	Sarasota	FL	34240	941-556-2601	
Rosemount Analytical Inc Process Analytical Div 6565 P Davis Industrial Pkwy **Fax Area Code:* 330 ■ *TF:* 800-433-6076 ■ *Web:* www.emersonprocess.com	Solon	OH	44139	440-914-1261	684-4434*
Rosemount Inc 8200 Market Blvd *Web:* www.rosemount.com	Chanhassen	MN	55317	952-906-8888	
RTP Corp 1834 SW Second St *Web:* www.rtpcorp.com	Pompano Beach	FL	33069	954-974-5500	975-9815
Sabina Motors & Controls Inc 1440 N Burton Pl *Web:* www.sabinadrives.com	Anaheim	CA	92806	714-956-0480	956-0486
Sable Systems International Inc 6000 S Ea Ste 1 *Web:* www.sablesys.com	Las Vegas	NV	89119	702-269-4445	
Santa Barbara Infrared Inc 30 S Calle Cesar Chavez Ste D *Web:* www.sbir.com	Santa Barbara	CA	93103	805-965-3669	
Scienscope Inc 5751 Schaefer Ave *Web:* www.scienscope.com	Chino	CA	91710	909-590-7273	
Scully Signal Co 70 Industrial Way *TF:* 800-272-8559 ■ *Web:* www.scully.com	Wilmington	MA	01887	617-692-8600	692-8620
See Water Inc 121 N Dillon St *TF:* 888-733-9283 ■ *Web:* www.seewaterinc.com	San Jacinto	CA	92583	951-487-8073	487-0557
Sensidyne Inc 16333 Bay Vista Dr *TF:* 800-451-9444 ■ *Web:* www.sensidyne.com	Clearwater	FL	33760	727-530-3602	539-0550
Sensory Analytics LLC 4413-C W Market St *Web:* www.sensoryanalytics.com	Greensboro	NC	27407	336-315-6090	315-6030
Sensus USA Inc 8601 Six Forks Rd Stes 300 & 700 *Web:* www.sensus.com	Raleigh	NC	27615	919-845-4000	
Siemens Milltronics Process Instruments Inc 1954 Technology Dr *Web:* www.automation.siemens.com	Peterborough	ON	K9J6X7	705-745-2431	
Sierra Instruments Inc Five Harris Ct Bldg L *TF:* 800-866-0200 ■ *Web:* www.sierrainstruments.com	Monterey	CA	93940	831-373-0200	373-4402
Signature Control Systems Inc 25 Manzanita *Web:* www.signaturecontrol.com	Littleton	CO	80127	720-641-1131	
SJE-Rhombus 22650 County Hwy 6 PO Box 1708 *TF:* 800-746-6287 ■ *Web:* www.sjerhombus.com	Detroit Lakes	MN	56502	218-847-1317	847-4617
SOR Inc 14685 W 105th St *TF:* 800-676-6794 ■ *Web:* sorinc.com	Lenexa	KS	66215	913-888-2630	888-0767
SpectraSensors Inc 4333 W Sam Houston Pkwy N *Web:* www.spectrasensors.com	Houston	TX	77043	713-300-2700	
Spectronics Corp 956 Brush Hollow Rd *TF:* 800-274-8888 ■ *Web:* www.spectroline.com	Westbury	NY	11590	800-274-8888	491-6868
Spectrum Controls Inc PO Box 5533 *Web:* www.spectrumcontrols.com	Bellevue	WA	98006	425-746-9481	641-9473
Spirax Sarco Inc 1150 Northpoint Blvd *TF:* 800-883-4411 ■ *Web:* www.spiraxsarco.com/us	Blythewood	SC	29016	803-714-2000	714-2222
Sterling Inc 2900 S 160th St *TF Cust Svc:* 800-783-7835 ■ *Web:* www.sterlco.com	New Berlin	WI	53151	262-641-8600	641-8653
Sutron Corp 22400 Davis Dr *NASDAQ:* STRN ■ *Web:* www.sutron.com	Sterling	VA	20164	703-406-2800	406-2801
Taylor Precision Products LLC 2311 W 22nd St **Fax Area Code:* 630 ■ *TF:* 866-843-3905 ■ *Web:* www.taylorusa.com	Oak Brook	IL	60523	866-843-3905	954-1275*
Teledyne Advanced Pollution Instrumentation 9480 Carroll Pk Dr *TF:* 800-324-5190 ■ *Web:* www.teledyne-api.com	San Diego	CA	92121	858-657-9800	657-9816
Teledyne Monitor Labs Inc (TML) 35 Inverness Dr E *TF:* 800-422-1499 ■ *Web:* www.monitorlabs.com	Englewood	CO	80112	303-792-3300	799-4853
Temptime Corp 116 American Rd *Web:* www.temptimecorp.com	Morris Plains	NJ	07950	973-984-6000	
Tevet LLC 85 Spring St S *Web:* www.tevetllc.com	Mosheim	TN	37818	678-905-1300	
Thermo Fisher Scientific Inc 81 Wyman St PO Box 9046 *NYSE:* TMO ■ *TF:* 800-678-5599 ■ *Web:* www.thermofisher.com	Waltham	MA	02454	781-622-1000	622-1207
Thermo Probe Inc 613 E Court St *Web:* www.thermoprobe.net	Jackson	MS	39201	601-939-1831	
Tiger Optics LLC 250 Titus Ave *Web:* www.tigeroptics.com	Warrington	PA	18976	215-343-6600	
Titan Logix Corp 4130 - 93 St *Web:* www.titanlogix.com	Edmonton	AB	T6E5P5	780-462-4085	450-8369
Transcat Inc 35 Vantage Pt Dr *NASDAQ:* TRNS ■ *TF:* 800-800-5001 ■ *Web:* www.transcat.com	Rochester	NY	14624	585-352-9460	352-1486
Tritech Group Ltd 5413 - 271 St *Web:* www.tritechgroup.ca	Langley	BC	V4W3Y7	604-607-8878	
Troxler Electronic Laboratories Inc 3008 E Cornwallis Rd PO Box 12057 *TF:* 877-876-9537 ■ *Web:* www.troxlerlabs.com	Research Triangle Park	NC	27709	919-549-8661	549-0761
TSI Inc 500 CaRdigan Rd *TF:* 800-874-2811 ■ *Web:* www.tsi.com	Shoreview	MN	55126	651-483-0900	490-3824
TTE Lab Services 77 Main St Ste 1 *Web:* www.pipettes.com	Hopkinton	MA	01748	508-435-7301	
Unicontrol Inc 1111 Brookpark Rd *Web:* www.unicontrolinc.com	Cleveland	OH	44109	216-398-4414	
United Electric Controls Co 180 Dexter Ave *Web:* www.ueonline.com	Watertown	MA	02472	617-926-1000	926-2568
Uson LP 8640 N Eldridge Pkwy *Web:* www.uson.com	Houston	TX	77041	281-671-2000	671-2001
Vacuum Instrument Corp 2099 Ninth Ave *Web:* www.vicleakdetection.com	Ronkonkoma	NY	11779	631-737-0900	
Veeder-Root 125 Powder Forest Dr *TF:* 888-262-7539 ■ *Web:* www.veeder.com	Simsbury	CT	06070	860-651-2700	651-2719
Venture Measurement Company LLC 150 Venture Blvd *Web:* www.venturemeasurement.com	Spartanburg	SC	29306	864-574-8960	578-7308
VIEW Micro-Metrology Inc 1711 W 17th St *Web:* www.viewmm.com	Tempe	AZ	85281	480-295-3150	
Visualant Inc 500 Union St Ste 420 *Web:* www.visualant.net	Seattle	WA	98101	206-903-1351	
Weed Instrument Company Inc 707 Jeffrey Way *Web:* weedinstrument.com	Round Rock	TX	78665	512-434-2900	
Wika Instrument Corp 1000 Wiegand Blvd *TF:* 888-945-2872 ■ *Web:* www.wika.us	Lawrenceville	GA	30043	770-513-8200	338-5118
Wilmington Instrument Company Inc 332 N Fries Ave *Web:* www.calcert.com	Wilmington	CA	90744	310-834-1133	
Wilmington Research & Development Corp 50 Parker St *Web:* www.wrdcorp.com	Newburyport	MA	01950	978-499-0100	
Winland Electronics Inc 1950 Excel Dr *NYSE:* WEX ■ *TF:* 800-635-4269 ■ *Web:* www.winland.com	Mankato	MN	56001	507-625-7231	387-2488
World Energy Alternatives LLC 2 Constitution Ctr *TF:* 800-829-3676 ■ *Web:* www.worldenergy.net	Boston	MA	02129	617-889-7300	
World Energy Labs (2) Inc 365 E Middlefield Rd *Web:* www.worldenergylabs.com	Mountain View	CA	94043	650-900-4600	
XiTRON Technologies Inc 7507 Convoy Ct *Web:* www.xitrontech.com	San Diego	CA	92111	858-530-8099	
Yokogawa Corp of America 12530 W Airport Blvd *TF:* 800-888-6400 ■ *Web:* www.yokogawa.com/us	Sugar Land	TX	77478	281-340-3800	340-3838
YSI Inc 1700-1725 Brannum Ln *TF Cust Svc:* 800-765-4974 ■ *Web:* www.ysi.com	Yellow Springs	OH	45387	937-767-7241	767-9353
ZK Celltest Inc 256 Gibraltar Dr Ste 109 *TF:* 800-837-8235 ■ *Web:* www.zk.com	Sunnyvale	CA	94089	408-752-0449	
Zolo Technologies Inc 4946 N 63rd St *Web:* www.zolotech.com	Boulder	CO	80301	303-604-5800	
ZTEC Instruments Inc 7715 Tiburon St Ne *Web:* www.ztecinstruments.com	Albuquerque	NM	87109	505-342-0132	

205 CONTROLS - TEMPERATURE - RESIDENTIAL & COMMERCIAL

	City	State	Zip	Phone	Fax
Alerton 6670 185th Ave NE *Web:* www.alerton.com	Redmond	WA	98052	425-869-8400	869-8445
APCOM Inc 125 SE Pkwy *Web:* www.apcom-inc.com	Franklin	TN	37064	615-794-5574	791-0660
Automated Logic Corp 1150 Roberts Rd N *Web:* www.automatedlogic.com	Kennesaw	GA	30144	770-429-3000	429-3001
Azonix Corp 900 Middlesex Tpke Bldg 6 *TF:* 800-967-5558 ■ *Web:* www.azonix.com	Billerica	MA	01821	978-670-6300	670-8855
CAPP/USA 201 Marple Ave **Fax Area Code:* 800 ■ **Fax:* Sales ■ *TF:* 800-356-8000 ■ *Web:* www.cappusa.com	Clifton Heights	PA	19018	610-394-1100	237-3292*
Channel Products Inc 7100 Wilson Mills Rd *Web:* www.channelproducts.com	Chesterland	OH	44026	440-423-0113	423-1502
Clean Coal Technologies Inc 12th Fl 295 Madison Ave *Web:* www.cleancoaltechnologiesinc.com	New York	NY	10017	646-710-3549	
Cooper Atkins Corp 33 Reeds Gap Rd *TF Sales:* 800-835-5011 ■ *Web:* cooper-atkins.com/default.asp	Middlefield	CT	06455	860-349-3473	349-8994
DeltaTRAK Inc PO Box 398 *TF:* 800-962-6776 ■ *Web:* www.deltatrak.com	Pleasanton	CA	94566	925-249-2250	249-2251
Emerson Climate Technologies - Retail Solutions 1065 Big Shanty Rd NW Ste 100 *TF:* 800-829-2724 ■ *Web:* www.emersonclimate.com	Kennesaw	GA	30144	770-425-2724	425-9319
Eurotherm USA 44621 Guilford Dr Ste 100 *Web:* www.eurotherm.com	Ashburn	VA	20147	703-724-7300	724-7301
Hallcrest Inc 1820 Pickwick Ln *TF General:* 800-527-1419 ■ *Web:* www.hallcrest.com	Glenview	IL	60026	847-998-8580	998-6866
Hansen Technologies Corp 6827 High Grove Blvd *TF:* 800-426-7368 ■ *Web:* www.hantech.com	Burr Ridge	IL	60527	630-325-1565	325-1572
HSQ Technology 26227 Research Rd *TF:* 800-486-6684 ■ *Web:* www.hsq.com	Hayward	CA	94545	510-259-1334	259-1391
Johnson Controls Systems 9410 Bunsen Pkwy Ste 100-B *TF:* 800-765-7773 ■ *Web:* www.johnsoncontrols.com	Louisville	KY	40220	502-671-7300	499-2135
Kidde-Fenwal Inc 400 Main St *TF Hum Res:* 800-872-6527 ■ *Web:* www.kidde-fenwal.com	Ashland	MA	01721	508-881-2000	
KMC Controls Inc 19476 Industrial Dr *TF:* 877-444-5622 ■ *Web:* www.kmc-controls.com	New Paris	IN	46553	574-831-5250	831-5252

Phone Fax

Nailor Industries of Texas Inc
4714 Winfield Rd .... Houston TX 77039 281-590-1172 590-3086
Web: www.nailor.com

Novar Controls Corp
6060 Rockside Woods Blvd Ste 400 .... Cleveland OH 44131 800-348-1235 682-1614*
**Fax Area Code:* 216 ■ *TF:* 800-348-1235 ■ *Web:* www.novar.com

Phoenix Controls Corp 75 Discovery Way .... Acton MA 01720 978-795-1285 795-1111
Web: www.phoenixcontrols.com

Portage Electric Products Inc
7700 Freedom Ave NW .... North Canton OH 44720 330-499-2727 499-1853
TF: 888-464-7374 ■ *Web:* www.pepiusa.com

Prentke Romich Co 1022 Heyl Rd .... Wooster OH 44691 330-262-1984 263-4829
TF: 800-848-8008 ■ *Web:* www.prentrom.com

Residential Control Systems
11481 Sunrise Gold Cir Ste 1 .... Rancho Cordova CA 95742 916-635-6784 635-7668
TF: 888-727-4822 ■ *Web:* www.rcstechnology.com

Sabine River Authority of Texas PO Box 579 .... Orange TX 77631 409-746-2192 746-3780
Web: www.sra.dst.tx.us

Siemens Bldg Technologies Inc
1000 Deerfield Pkwy .... Buffalo Grove IL 60089 847-215-1000 215-1093
TF General: 800-877-7545 ■ *Web:* www.buildingtechnologies.siemens.com

SPX Corp Robinair Div 655 Eisenhower Dr .... Owatonna MN 55060 507-455-7000
TF: 800-628-6496 ■ *Web:* www.robinair.com

Taylor Precision Products LLC
2311 W 22nd St .... Oak Brook IL 60523 866-843-3905 954-1275*
**Fax Area Code:* 630 ■ *TF:* 866-843-3905 ■ *Web:* www.taylorusa.com

Therm-O-Disc Inc 1320 S Main St .... Mansfield OH 44907 419-525-8500 525-8344*
**Fax:* Sales ■ *Web:* www.thermodisc.com

WAKO Electronics USA Inc
2105 Production Dr .... Louisville KY 40299 502-429-8866 429-8869
Web: www.wako-usa.com

Watlow Winona 1241 Bundy Blvd .... Winona MN 55987 507-454-5300 452-4507
TF: 800-928-5692 ■ *Web:* www.watlow.com

Weiss Instruments Inc 905 Waverly Ave .... Holtsville NY 11742 631-207-1200 207-0900
Web: www.weissinstruments.com

Xylem 8200 N Austin Ave .... Morton Grove IL 60053 847-966-3700 983-5954
Web: unitedstates.xylemappliedwater.com

206 CONTROLS & RELAYS - ELECTRICAL

Phone Fax

ABB SSAC 8242 Loop Rd .... Baldwinsville NY 13027 315-638-1300 638-0333
TF Tech Supp: 800-377-7722 ■ *Web:* www.ssac.com

Absolute Electronics Inc
W137 N8589 Landover Ct .... Menomonee Falls WI 53051 262-250-1151
Web: www.absoluteelectronics.net

Allied Controls Inc 150 E Aurora St .... Waterbury CT 06708 203-757-4200
TF: 800-788-0955 ■ *Web:* alliedcontrols.com

American Relays Inc
10306 Norwalk Blvd .... Santa Fe Springs CA 90670 562-944-0447 944-0590
Web: www.americanrelays.com

American Zettler Inc 75 Columbia .... Aliso Viejo CA 92656 949-831-5000 831-8642
Web: www.azettler.com

AMETEK National Controls Corp
1725 Western Dr .... West Chicago IL 60185 630-231-5900 231-1377
TF: 800-323-2593 ■ *Web:* www.nationalcontrols.com

AMX Corp 3000 Research Dr .... Richardson TX 75082 469-624-8585
TF: 855-269-8585 ■ *Web:* www.amx.com

Anaheim Automation 910 E Orangefair Ln .... Anaheim CA 92801 714-992-6990 992-0471
TF Sales: 800-345-9401 ■ *Web:* www.anaheimautomation.com

Artisan Controls Corp
111 Canfield Ave Bldg B15-18 .... Randolph NJ 07869 973-598-9400
Web: www.artisancontrols.com

Automation & Control Services Inc
2440 Ontario St .... Schererville IN 46375 219-558-2060
Web: www.automationcontrolservices.com

Balboa Instruments Inc 1382 Bell Ave .... Tustin CA 92780 714-384-0382
Web: www.balboainstruments.com

Barantec Inc 777 Passaic Ave Fl 4 .... Clifton NJ 07012 973-779-8774 779-8768
Web: www.barantec.com

Basler Electric Co 12570 SR- 143 PO Box 269 .... Highland IL 62249 618-654-2341 654-2351
Web: www.basler.com

Bright Image Corp 2830 S18th Ave .... Broadview IL 60155 888-449-5656 449-1155*
**Fax Area Code:* 708 ■ *TF:* 888-449-5656 ■ *Web:* www.touchandglow.com

Bus-tech Inc 26 Crosby Dr .... Bedford MA 01710 781-272-8200

Cambridge Viscosity Inc 101 Stn Landing .... Medford MA 02155 303-893-0552
Web: hugedomains.com/domain_profile.cfm?d=cambridgeapplied&e=com

Cleveland Motion Controls Inc
7550 Hub Pkwy .... Cleveland OH 44125 216-524-8800 642-2199
TF: 800-321-8072 ■ *Web:* www.cmccontrols.com

Connor-Winfield Corp 2111 Comprehensive Dr .... Aurora IL 60505 630-851-4722
Web: www.conwin.com

Contrex Inc 8900 Zachary Ln N .... Maple Grove MN 55369 763-424-7800
TF: 800-342-4411 ■ *Web:* www.contrexinc.com

Control Masters Inc 5235 Katrine Ave .... Downers Grove IL 60515 630-968-2390 968-3260
Web: www.controlmasters.com

Control Resources Inc 11 Beaver Brook Rd .... Littleton MA 01460 978-486-4160
Web: www.controlres.com

Converteam Inc 610 Epsilon Dr .... Pittsburgh PA 15238 412-967-0765 967-7660
Web: www.gepowerconversion.com

Coto Technology USA 66 Whitecap Dr .... North Kingstown RI 02852 401-943-2686 942-0920
Web: www.cotorelay.com

Crydom Inc
2320 Paseo de las Americas Ste 201 .... San Diego CA 92154 619-210-1550
Web: www.crydom.com

D & R Technology LLC
400 E Fullerton Ave .... Carol Stream IL 60188 630-614-7201
Web: www.d-r-t.com

Datacom Systems Inc Nine Adler Dr .... East Syracuse NY 13057 315-463-9541
Web: www.datacomsystems.com

Phone Fax

Digi-Data Corp 11101 W 120th Ave Ste 350 .... Broomfield CO 80021 303-604-9020 604-9017
Web: www.digidata.com

Digital Control Systems Inc
7401 SW Capitol Hwy .... Portland OR 97219 503-246-8110
Web: www.dcs-inc.net

DST Controls 651 Stone Rd .... Benicia CA 94510 707-745-5117 745-8952
TF: 800-251-0773 ■ *Web:* www.dstcontrols.com

Ducommun Inc 23301 Wilmington Ave .... Carson CA 90745 310-513-7280 513-7279
NYSE: DCO ■ *TF:* 800-667-6589 ■ *Web:* www.ducommun.com

Duct-O-Wire Co 345 Adams Cir .... Corona CA 92882 951-735-8220 735-2372
TF: 800-752-6001 ■ *Web:* www.ductowire.com

Durex Industries Inc 190 Detroit St .... Cary IL 60013 847-639-5600 639-2199
Web: www.durexindustries.com

Easter Owens Electric Co 6692 Fig St .... Arvada CO 80004 303-431-0111
Web: www.easter-owens.com

Eaton Corp 1111 Superior Ave Eaton Ctr .... Cleveland OH 44114 216-523-5000
Web: www.eaton.com

ELCON Inc 600 Twin Rail Dr .... Minooka IL 60447 815-467-9500
Web: www.elconinc.net

Electric Motor & Contracting Co Inc
3703 Cook Blvd .... Chesapeake VA 23323 757-487-2121 487-5983
Web: www.emc-co.com

Electric Regulator Corp 6189 El Camino Real .... Carlsbad CA 92009 760-438-7873 438-0437
TF: 800-458-6566 ■ *Web:* www.electricregulator.com

Electrical & Electronics 3881 Danbury Rd .... Brewster NY 10509 914-769-5000 769-3641
Web: www.eecontrols.com

Electrical Design & Control Co
2200 Stephenson Hwy .... Troy MI 48083 248-743-2400
Web: www.edandc.com

Electro-Matic Products Co 2235 N Knox Ave .... Chicago IL 60639 773-235-4010 235-7317
Web: www.em-chicago.com

Electroid Co 45 Fadem Rd .... Springfield NJ 07081 973-467-8100 467-2606
Web: www.electroid.com

Electronic Theatre Controls Inc
3031 Pleasantview Rd .... Middleton WI 53562 608-831-4116 836-1736
TF: 800-688-4116 ■ *Web:* www.etcconnect.com

Enercon Engineering Inc One Altorfer Ln .... East Peoria IL 61611 309-694-1418 694-3703
TF: 800-218-8831 ■ *Web:* www.enercon-eng.com

Energy Conversion Technologies Inc
1271 Denison St Unit 56-59 .... Markham ON L3R4B5 905-947-4300
Web: www.energyconversiontech.com

FAS Controls Inc 1100 Airport Rd .... Shelby NC 28150 704-482-9582
Web: www.fascontrols.com

FSI Technologies Inc 668 E Western Ave .... Lombard IL 60148 630-932-9380 932-0016
TF: 800-468-6009 ■ *Web:* www.fsinet.com

Fujitsu Components America Inc
250 E Caribbean Dr .... Sunnyvale CA 94089 408-745-4900 745-4970
Web: www.fujitsu.com

FXC Corp 3410 S Susan St .... Santa Ana CA 92704 714-556-7400 641-5093
Web: www.pia.com

G & L Motion Control Inc
672 S Military Rd .... Fond Du Lac WI 54935 920-921-7100
Web: www.glcontrols.com

GE Digital Energy 650 Markland St .... Markham ON L6C0M1 905-294-6222
TF: 877-605-6777 ■ *Web:* www.gedigitalenergy.com

Genesis International Inc
1040 Fox Chase Industrial Dr .... Arnold MO 63010 636-282-0011
Web: www.genesis-international.com

Gentec Inc 2625 Dalton .... Quebec QC G1P3S9 418-651-8000
Web: gentec.ca

GET Engineering Corp 9350 Bond Ave .... El Cajon CA 92021 619-443-8295 443-8613
TF: 877-494-1820 ■ *Web:* www.getntds.com

Glendinning Marine Products 740 Century Cir .... Conway SC 29526 843-399-6146 399-5005
TF: 800-500-2380 ■ *Web:* www.glendinningprods.com

Globe Electronic Hardware Inc 34-24 56th St .... Woodside NY 11377 718-457-0303 457-7493
TF: 800-221-1505 ■ *Web:* www.globelectronics.com

Governors America Corp 720 Silver St .... Agawam MA 01001 413-786-5600
Web: www.governors-america.com

Guardian Electric Mfg Company Inc
1425 Lake Ave .... Woodstock IL 60098 815-334-3600 337-0377
TF: 800-762-0369 ■ *Web:* www.guardian-electric.com

Hamlin Electronics Inc 612 E Lake St .... Lake Mills WI 53551 920-648-3000 648-3001
Web: www.hamlin.com

Harold Beck & Sons Inc 11 Terry Dr .... Newtown PA 18940 215-968-4600
Web: www.haroldbeck.com

Hasco Relays & Electronics International Corp
906 Jericho Tpke .... New Hyde Park NY 11040 516-328-9292
Web: www.hascorelays.com

HF scientific Inc 3170 Metro Pkwy .... Fort Myers FL 33916 239-337-2116
Web: www.hfscientific.com

High Country Tek Inc 208 Gold Flat Ct .... Nevada City CA 95959 530-265-3236
Web: www.highcountrytek.com

Honeywell Automation & Control Solutions
11 W Spring St .... Freeport IL 61032 815-235-5500
Web: www.honeywell.com

Honeywell Sensing & Control 11 W Spring St .... Freeport IL 61032 815-235-5500
TF Cust Svc: 800-537-6945 ■ *Web:* www.honeywell.com

Hubbell Industrial Controls
4301 Cheyenne Dr .... Archdale NC 27263 336-434-2800 434-2803
Web: www.hubbell-icd.com

Hydrolevel Co 83 Water St .... New Haven CT 06511 203-776-0473
Web: www.hydrolevel.com

Icm Controls Corp
7313 William Barry Blvd .... North Syracuse NY 13212 315-233-5266 233-5276
TF: 800-365-5525 ■ *Web:* www.icmcontrols.com

IDEC Corp 1175 Elko Dr .... Sunnyvale CA 94089 408-747-0550 744-9055
TF: 800-262-4332 ■ *Web:* www.idec.com

Imperial Irrigation District (IID) PO Box 937 .... Imperial CA 92251 760-482-9600 482-9611
TF: 800-303-7756 ■ *Web:* www.iid.com

Inertia Dynamics Inc
31 Industrial Pk Rd .... New Hartford CT 06057 860-482-4444 693-6463
TF: 800-800-6445 ■ *Web:* www.idicb.com

	City	State	Zip	Phone	Fax
Infitec Inc 6500 Badgley Rd *Web:* www.infitec.com	East Syracuse	NY	13057	315-433-1150	
Intermatic Inc 7777 Winn Rd *Web:* www.intermatic.com	Spring Grove	IL	60081	815-675-7000	675-7001
Jennings Technology Co 970 McLaughlin Ave *Web:* www.jenningstech.com	San Jose	CA	95122	408-292-4025	286-1789
Joslyn Clark Corp 2100 W Broad St **Fax Area Code:* 803 ■ *TF:* 800-476-6952 ■ *Web:* www.danaherspecialtyproducts.com	Elizabethtown	NC	28337	800-476-6952	285-0885*
JR Merritt Controls Inc 55 Sperry Ave *Web:* www.jrmerritt.com	Stratford	CT	06615	203-381-0100	
K/E Electric Supply Co 146 N Groesbeck Hwy *Web:* www.keelectric.com	Mount Clemens	MI	48043	586-469-3005	469-3006
KB Electronics Inc 12095 NW 39th St *TF:* 800-221-6570 ■ *Web:* www.kbelectronics.com	Coral Springs	FL	33065	954-346-4900	346-3377
KEMCO Industries LLC 70 Keyes Ct *Web:* www.kemco.com	Sanford	FL	32773	407-322-1230	
Keytroller LLC 3907 W Martin Luther King Blvd *Web:* www.keytroller.com	Tampa	FL	33614	813-877-4500	
Kobelt Manufacturing Company Ltd 8238 129th St *Web:* www.kobelt.com	Surrey	BC	V3W0A6	604-572-3935	590-8313
Leach International Corp 6900 Orangethorpe Ave *TF:* 800-232-7700 ■ *Web:* www.esterline.com	Buena Park	CA	90622	714-736-7598	739-1713
Lutron Electronics Company Inc 7200 Suter Rd *TF Tech Supp:* 800-523-9466 ■ *Web:* www.lutron.com	Coopersburg	PA	18036	610-282-6280	282-6253
Mac Products Inc 60 Pennsylvania Ave PO Box 469 *Web:* www.macproducts.net	Kearny	NJ	07032	973-344-0700	344-5368
Magnet Schultz of America Inc 401 Plaza Dr *Web:* www.magnet-schultz.com	Westmont	IL	60559	630-789-0600	789-0614
MagneTek Inc N49 W13650 Campbell Dr *NASDAQ: MAG* ■ *TF:* 800-288-8178 ■ *Web:* www.magnetek.com	Menomonee Falls	WI	53051	800-288-8178	298-3503
Marquardt Switches Inc 2711 US 20 *Web:* us.marquardt.com/	Cazenovia	NY	13035	315-655-8050	655-8042
Martin Automatic Inc 1661 Northrock Ct *Web:* www.martinauto.com	Rockford	IL	61103	815-654-4800	654-4810
Maxcess International, Inc. 222 W Memorial Rd PO Box 26508 *TF:* 800-333-3433 ■ *Web:* www.fife.com	Oklahoma City	OK	73114	405-755-1600	755-8425
McDade-Woodcock Inc 2404 Claremont Ave NE PO Box 11592 *Web:* mwieic.com/	Albuquerque	NM	87107	505-884-0155	884-6073
Moog Inc Jamison Rd *NYSE: MOG/A* ■ *TF:* 800-336-2112 ■ *Web:* www.moog.com	East Aurora	NY	14052	716-652-2000	687-4457
Mosebach Manufacturing Co 1417 Mclaughlin Run Rd *Web:* www.mosebachresistors.com	Pittsburgh	PA	15241	412-220-0200	
Networks Electronic Co 9750 De Soto Ave *Web:* www.networkselectronic.com	Chatsworth	CA	91311	818-341-0440	718-7133
Novaspect Inc 1124 Tower Rd *Web:* www.novaspect.com	Schaumburg	IL	60173	847-956-8020	885-8200
OEM Controls Inc 10 Controls Dr *Web:* www.oemcontrols.com	Shelton	CT	06484	203-929-8431	929-3867
OMRON Corp One Commerce Dr *TF:* 800-556-6766 ■ *Web:* www.omron247.com	Schaumburg	IL	60173	847-843-7900	843-7787
OMRON Scientific Technologies Inc 6550 Dumbarton Cir *TF:* 888-510-4357 ■ *Web:* www.sti.com	Fremont	CA	94555	510-608-3400	744-1440
Ormec Systems Corp 19 Linden Pk *TF:* 800-656-7632 ■ *Web:* www.ormec.com	Rochester	NY	14625	585-385-3520	385-5999
Panasonic Electric Works Corp of America 629 Central Ave *TF:* 800-276-6289 ■ *Web:* www.pewa.panasonic.com	New Providence	NJ	07974	908-464-3550	464-4128
Parker Hannifin Corp Electromechanical Automation Div 5500 Business Pk Dr *TF:* 800-358-9068 ■ *Web:* www.parkermotion.com	Rohnert Park	CA	94928	707-584-7558	584-8015
Parker McCrory Manufacturing Co 2000 Forest Ave *TF:* 800-662-1038 ■ *Web:* www.parmakusa.com	Kansas City	MO	64108	816-221-2000	221-9879
Payne Engineering Co Rt 29 PO Box 70 *TF Orders:* 800-331-1345 ■ *Web:* www.payneng.com	Scott Depot	WV	25560	304-757-7353	757-7305
Peerless Instrument Company Inc 1966-D Broadhollow Rd *Web:* www.peerless.cwfc.com	Farmingdale	NY	11735	631-396-6500	396-6555
Pepperl Fuchs Inc 1600 Enterprise Pkwy *Web:* www.pepperl-fuchs.us	Twinsburg	OH	44087	330-425-3555	425-4607
Phasetronics Inc 1600 Sunshine Dr *Web:* www.phasetronics.com	Clearwater	FL	33765	727-573-1819	
Pine Instrument Co 101 Industrial Dr *Web:* www.pineinst.com	Grove City	PA	16127	724-458-6391	458-4648
Polytron Corp 4400 Wyland Dr *TF:* 888-228-0246 ■ *Web:* www.polytron-corp.com	Elkhart	IN	46516	574-522-0246	522-0457
Precision Governors Inc 2322 Seventh Ave *Web:* www.precisiongovernors.com	Rockford	IL	61104	815-229-5300	
Precision Multiple Controls Inc 33 Greenwood Ave *Web:* www.precisionmulticontrols.com	Midland Park	NJ	07432	201-444-0600	445-8575
Premier System Integrators Inc 140 Weakley Ln PO Box 329 *Web:* www.premier-system.com	Smyrna	TN	37167	615-355-7200	355-7210
PVA Tepla America Inc 251 Corporate Terr *TF Sales:* 800-527-5667 ■ *Web:* pvateplaamerica.com	Corona	CA	92879	951-371-2500	
RAM Industrial Services Inc 5460B Pottsville Pk *Web:* www.ramindustrialservices.com	Leesport	PA	19533	610-916-8000	
RCI Custom Products 801 NE St Ste 2A *TF:* 800-546-4724 ■ *Web:* www.rcicustom.com	Frederick	MD	21701	301-620-9130	620-9103
Relay Specialties Inc 17 Raritan Rd *Web:* www.relayspec.com	Oakland	NJ	07436	201-337-1000	
Rockford Systems Inc 4620 Hydraulic Rd **Fax: Sales* ■ *TF Cust Svc:* 800-922-7533 ■ *Web:* www.rockfordsystems.com	Rockford	IL	61109	815-874-7891	874-6144*
Sendec Corp 72 Perinton Pkwy *TF:* 800-295-8000 ■ *Web:* apitech.com	Fairport	NY	14450	585-425-3390	425-3392
Sequence Controls Inc 150 Rosamond St *Web:* www.sequencecontrols.com	Carleton	ON	K7C1V2	613-257-7356	
Snaptron Inc 2468 E Ninth St *Web:* www.snaptron.com	Loveland	CO	80537	970-686-5682	
SOR Inc 14685 W 105th St *TF:* 800-676-6794 ■ *Web:* sorinc.com	Lenexa	KS	66215	913-888-2630	888-0767
South/Shore Controls Inc 4485 N Ridge Rd *Web:* www.southshorecontrols.com	Perry	OH	44081	440-259-2500	259-2500
Sparton 27 Hale Spring Rd *TF:* 800-443-4132 ■ *Web:* www.beckwood.com	Plaistow	NH	03865	603-382-3840	
Spectra Precision Inc 10355 Westmoor Dr Ste 100 *Web:* www.spectraprecision.com	Westminster	CO	80021	720-587-4700	
Sprecher + Schuh 15910 International Plaza Dr *TF:* 877-721-5913 ■ *Web:* www.sprecherschuh.com	Houston	TX	77032	281-442-9000	442-1570
SSI Technologies Inc PO Box 5011 *Web:* www.ssitechnologies.com	Janesville	WI	53547	608-373-2000	
Statek Corp 512 N Main St *Web:* www.statek.com	Orange	CA	92868	714-639-7810	997-1256
Static Controls Corp 30460 S Wixom Rd *Web:* www.scccontrols.com	Wixom	MI	48393	248-926-4400	926-4412
Struthers-Dunn 407 E Smith St Ste B *Web:* www.struthers-dunn.com	Timmonsville	SC	29161	843-346-4427	346-4465
Sturdy Corp 1822 Carolina Beach Rd *TF:* 800-721-3282 ■ *Web:* www.sturdycorp.com	Wilmington	NC	28401	910-763-2500	763-2650
Super Talent Technology Corp 2077 N Capitol Ave *Web:* www.supertalent.com	San Jose	CA	95132	408-934-2560	
Systems East Inc 30 Basil Sawyer Dr *Web:* systemseastinc.com	Hampton	VA	23666	757-766-8400	
Systems Machines Automation Components Corp 5807 Van Allen Way *Web:* www.smac-mca.com	Carlsbad	CA	92008	760-929-7575	929-7588
Tech/Ops Sevcon Inc 155 Northboro Rd *NASDAQ: SEV* ■ *Web:* www.techopssevcon.com	Southborough	MA	01772	508-281-5500	
Time Mark Corp 11440 E Pine St *TF:* 800-862-2875 ■ *Web:* www.time-mark.com	Tulsa	OK	74116	918-438-1220	437-7584
Time-O-Matic Inc 1015 Maple St *TF:* 800-637-2645 ■ *Web:* www.watchfiresigns.com	Danville	IL	61832	217-442-0611	442-1020
Tornatech Inc 7075, Place Robert-Joncas Ste 132 *Web:* www.tornatech.com	Saint-laurent	QC	H4M2Z2	514-334-0523	334-5448
Transdyn Inc 4256 Hacienda Dr # 100 *Web:* kapsch.net/ktc	Pleasanton	CA	94588	925-225-1600	225-1610
Triumph Controls Inc 205 Church Rd *TF:* 800-322-2885 ■ *Web:* triumphgroup.com	North Wales	PA	19454	215-699-4861	699-2595
Trombetta 8111 N 87th St *Web:* www.trombetta.com	Milwaukee	WI	53224	414-410-0300	355-3882
Unico Inc 3725 Nicholson Rd *Web:* www.unicous.com	Franksville	WI	53126	262-886-5678	504-7396
Ventek Inc 4030 W First St Ste 100 *Web:* www.ventek-inc.com	Eugene	OR	97402	541-344-5578	
Wago Corp N120 W19129 Freistadt Rd **Fax Area Code:* 262 ■ *TF:* 800-346-7245 ■ *Web:* www.wago.us	Germantown	WI	53022	800-346-7245	255-3232*
Whitepath Fab Tech Inc 16402 Hwy 515 N *Web:* www.whitepath.com	Ellijay	GA	30540	706-276-2511	276-2524
Whittaker Controls Inc 12838 Saticoy St *Web:* www.whittakercontrols.com	North Hollywood	CA	91605	818-765-8160	759-2190
Woodward Controls Inc 6250 W Howard St *Web:* www.woodward.com	Niles	IL	60714	847-967-7730	
X-COM Systems LLC 12345-B Sunrise Vly Dr *TF:* 800-342-8408 ■ *Web:* www.xcomsystems.com	Reston	VA	20191	703-390-1087	
Yaskawa America Inc 2121 Norman Dr S **Fax: Mktg* ■ *TF:* 800-927-5292 ■ *Web:* www.yaskawa.com	Waukegan	IL	60085	847-887-7000	887-7310*

207 CONVENIENCE STORES

SEE ALSO Gas Stations p. 2354; Grocery Stores p. 2439

	City	State	Zip	Phone	Fax
7-Eleven Inc 1722 Routh Ste 100 *TF:* 800-255-0711 ■ *Web:* www.7-eleven.com	Dallas	TX	75221	972-828-7011	828-1067
A & E Stores Inc 1000 Huyler St *Web:* www.aestores.com	Teterboro	NJ	07608	201-393-0600	393-0233
Cafepress.com Inc 1850 Gateway Dr Ste 300 *Web:* www.cafepress.com	Foster City	CA	94404	650-655-3120	240-0260
Casey's General Stores Inc One Convenience Blvd *NASDAQ: CASY* ■ *Web:* www.caseys.com	Ankeny	IA	50021	515-965-6100	965-6160
Cracker Barrel Convenience Stores Inc 12221 Industriplex Blvd *Web:* crackerbarrelcstores.com	Baton Rouge	LA	70809	225-753-3200	753-3200
Crown Coco Inc 1717 Broadway St	Minneapolis	MN	55413	612-331-9344	
Dairy Barn Stores Inc 544 Elwood Rd *Web:* www.dairybarn.com	East Northport	NY	11731	631-368-8050	266-2547
Dixie Gas & Oil Corp 229 Lee Hwy P O Box 900 *Web:* www.dixiegas.com	Verona	VA	24482	540-248-6273	
E-Z Mart Stores 602 W Falvey Ave PO Box 1426 *TF:* 800-234-6502 ■ *Web:* www.ezmart.com	Texarkana	TX	75501	903-832-6502	832-3731
Fkg Oil Co 721 W Main *TF:* 800-873-3546 ■ *Web:* www.mymotomart.com	Belleville	IL	62220	618-233-6754	233-1327
Go-Mart Inc 915 Riverside Dr *Web:* gomart.com	Gassaway	WV	26624	304-364-8000	
Heathco'S Pizza & Variety 375 Court St *Web:* heathcos.com	Auburn	ME	04210	207-689-9175	

				Phone	Fax
Heritage Dairy Stores Inc 376 Jessup Rd *Web:* www.heritages.com	Thorofare	NJ	08086	856-845-2855	845-8392
Holiday Stationstores 4567 American Blvd W *TF:* 800-745-7411 ■ *Web:* www.holidaystationstores.com	Bloomington	MN	55437	952-830-8700	
Hollar Co 2012 Rainbow Dr *Web:* shell.com	Gadsden	AL	35901	256-547-1644	547-1494
Jet Food Stores of Georgia 1106 S Harris St	Sandersville	GA	31082	478-552-2588	552-8758
JFM Inc 4276 Lakeland Dr *Web:* www.jfminc.net	Flowood	MS	39232	601-664-7177	664-7272
Johnny Quick Food Stores 96 Shaw Ave Ste 240 *Web:* www.johnnyquik.com	Clovis	CA	93612	559-297-6830	297-7519
Krause Gentle Corp 6400 Westown Pkwy *Web:* www.kumandgo.com	West Des Moines	IA	50266	515-226-0128	457-0178
Kwik Trip Inc 1626 Oak St PO Box 2107 *Web:* www.kwiktrip.com	La Crosse	WI	54602	608-781-8988	781-7517
Lassus BROS Handy Dandy 1800 Magnavox Way *TF General:* 800-686-2836 ■ *Web:* www.lassus.com	Fort Wayne	IN	46804	260-436-1415	436-0340
Leading Market Technologies Inc Bldg 100 One Kendall Sq *Web:* www.lmtech.com	Cambridge	MA	02139	617-494-4747	
Li'l Thrift Food Marts Inc 1007 Arsenal Ave *Web:* www.shortstopfoodmarts.com	Fayetteville	NC	28305	910-433-4490	
Loaf N' Jug Mini Mart 442 Keeler Pkwy *TF:* 866-562-3658 ■ *Web:* www.loafnjug.com	Pueblo	CO	81001	719-948-3071	
Love's Travel Stops & Country Stores Inc 10601 N Pennsylvania Ave *TF:* 800-388-0983 ■ *Web:* www.loves.com	Oklahoma City	OK	73120	800-388-0983	
Mac's Convenience Stores Inc 305 Milner Ave Ste 400 4th Fl **Fax Area Code:* 416 ■ *TF:* 800-268-5574 ■ *Web:* www.macs.ca	Toronto	ON	M1B3V4	800-268-5574	291-4947*
Maverik Inc 880 W Center St **Fax Area Code:* 307 ■ *TF Cust Svc:* 800-789-4455 ■ *Web:* www.maverik.com	North Salt Lake	UT	84054	877-936-5557	885-3832*
Miller & Holmes Inc 2311 O'Neil Rd *Web:* mhgas.com	Hudson	WI	54016	715-377-1730	
Open Pantry Food Marts 10505 Corporate Dr Ste 101 *TF:* 800-242-3358 ■ *Web:* www.openpantry.com	Pleasant Prairie	WI	53158	262-857-1156	857-9667
Pantry Inc 305 Gregson Dr *NASDAQ: PTRY* ■ *TF:* 877-798-4792 ■ *Web:* www.thepantry.com	Cary	NC	27511	919-774-6700	776-5303
Plaid Pantries Inc 10025 SW Allen Blvd *TF:* 800-677-5243 ■ *Web:* www.plaidpantry.com	Beaverton	OR	97005	503-646-4246	646-3071
Presto Food Stores Inc 1513 James L Redman Pkwy	Plant City	FL	33563	813-754-3511	752-5494
Quik Stop Markets Inc 4567 Enterprise St *Web:* quikstop.com	Fremont	CA	94538	510-657-8500	657-1544
QuikTrip Corp 4705 S 129th E Ave *TF:* 800-441-0253 ■ *Web:* www.quiktrip.com	Tulsa	OK	74134	918-615-7700	615-7377
Rocky Top Markets LLC 1324 Lawnville Rd	Kingston	TN	37763	865-717-0700	
Scaffs Inc 134 Se Colburn Ave *Web:* scaffs.com	Lake City	FL	32025	386-752-7344	
Seven-Eleven Hawaii Inc 1755 Nuuanu Ave	Honolulu	HI	96817	808-526-1711	
Sheetz Inc 5700 Sixth Ave *TF:* 800-487-5444 ■ *Web:* www.sheetz.com	Altoona	PA	16602	814-941-5106	941-5105
Speedway LLC 500 Speedway Dr *TF Cust Svc:* 800-643-1948 ■ *Web:* www.speedway.com	Enon	OH	45323	937-864-3001	
Stop In Food Stores Inc 3000 Ogden Rd *Web:* petroleummarketers.com	Roanoke	VA	24018	540-772-4700	
Stripes Convenience Stores 4525 Ayers St *NYSE: SUSS* ■ *TF:* 800-569-3585 ■ *Web:* www.susser.com	Corpus Christi	TX	78415	361-884-2464	884-2494
Tedeschi Food Shops Inc 14 Howard St *Web:* www.tedeschifoodshops.com	Rockland	MA	02370	781-878-8210	878-0476
Tom Thumb Food Stores Inc 97 W Okeechobee Rd *Web:* tomthumb.com	Hialeah	FL	33010	305-885-5451	885-0144
Uppy's Convenience Stores Inc 1011 Boulders Spring Dr *Web:* circlekmacs.com	Richmond	VA	23225	804-204-1534	
Valdak Corp 1149 36th Ave S *Web:* www.valleydairy.com	Grand Forks	ND	58201	701-746-8371	772-9464
Wawa Inc 260 W Baltimore Pike **Fax:* Hum Res ■ *TF:* 800-444-9292 ■ *Web:* www.wawa.com	Media	PA	19063	610-358-8000	358-8808*
Xtramart 221 Quinebaug Rd *TF:* 800-243-6366 ■ *Web:* www.xtramart.com	North Grosvenordale	CT	06255	800-243-6366	

208 CONVENTION CENTERS

SEE ALSO Performing Arts Facilities p. 2900; Stadiums & Arenas p. 3192

Listings are alphabetized by city names within state groupings.

				Phone	Fax
Venuworks Inc 4611 Mortensen Rd Ste 111 *Web:* www.venuworks.com	Ames	IA	50014	515-232-5151	
DataCo LLC 85 W Algonquin Rd Ste 360 *Web:* www.datacosolutions.com	Arlington Heights	IL	60005	847-290-0636	
Rolex Watch Usa Inc 2651 N Harwood St Ste 500 *Web:* www.rolex.com	Dallas	TX	75201	214-871-0500	
One Broward Executive Offices One E Broward Blvd Ste 700 *Web:* onebroward.com	Fort Lauderdale	FL	33301	954-745-5800	
Green Lake Conference Center W2511 State Rd 23 *Web:* www.glcc.org	Green Lake	WI	54941	920-294-3323	
Accesso Partners LLC 1140 E Hallandale Beach Blvd *Web:* www.accessopartners.com	Hallandale Beach	FL	33009	954-454-4665	
Nrccua 3651 Ne Ralph Powell Rd *Web:* www.nrccua.org	Lees Summit	MO	64064	816-434-4720	
Ivanhoe Cambridge Inc 1001 Sq Victoria bureau C-500 *Web:* www.ivanhoecambridge.com	Montreal	QC	H2Z2B5	514-841-7600	
Lied Lodge & Conference Center 2700 Sylvan Rd *Web:* liedlodge.org	Nebraska City	NE	68410	402-873-8733	
WLA Investments Inc 1301 Dove St Ste 1080 *Web:* www.wlainvestments.com	Newport Beach	CA	92660	949-851-2020	
Koch Development Co 222 S Central Ave Ste 300 *Web:* www.rentstlouis.com	St. Louis	MO	63105	314-333-5624	
Chair-man Mills Inc 184 Railside Rd *Web:* www.chairmanmills.com	Toronto	ON	M3A3R4	416-391-0400	

Alabama

				Phone	Fax
Birmingham-Jefferson Convention Complex 2100 Richard Arrington Jr Blvd N *Web:* www.bjcc.org	Birmingham	AL	35203	205-458-8400	328-8523
Von Braun Ctr 700 Monroe St *Web:* www.vonbrauncenter.com	Huntsville	AL	35801	256-533-1953	551-2203

Alaska

				Phone	Fax
William A Egan Civic & Convention Ctr 555 W Fifth Ave *Web:* www.anchorageconventioncenters.com	Anchorage	AK	99501	907-263-2800	263-2858
Carlson Ctr 2010 2nd Ave *Web:* www.carlson-center.com	Fairbanks	AK	99701	907-451-7800	451-1195
Centennial Hall Convention Ctr 101 Egan Dr *TF:* 800-478-4176 ■ *Web:* www.juneau.org	Juneau	AK	99801	907-586-5283	586-1135

Arizona

				Phone	Fax
Glendale Civic Ctr 5750 W Glenn Dr *Web:* www.glendaleciviccenter.com	Glendale	AZ	85301	623-930-4300	930-4319
Mesa Convention Ctr 263 N Ctr St *Web:* www.mesaconventioncenter.com	Mesa	AZ	85201	480-644-2178	644-2617
Phoenix Convention Ctr 100 N Third St *TF:* 800-282-4842 ■ *Web:* www.phoenixconventioncenter.com	Phoenix	AZ	85004	602-262-6225	495-3642
Tucson Convention Ctr 260 S Church Ave *Web:* tucsonaz.gov/	Tucson	AZ	85701	520-791-4101	791-5572
Yuma Civic Ctr 1440 W Desert Hills Dr *TF:* 800-410-2554 ■ *Web:* www.yumaaz.gov	Yuma	AZ	85365	928-373-5040	344-9121

Arkansas

				Phone	Fax
Fort Smith Convention Ctr 55 S Seventh St *Web:* www.fortsmith.org	Fort Smith	AR	72901	479-788-8932	788-8930
Hot Springs Convention Ctr (HSCVB) 134 Convention Blvd PO Box 6000 *TF:* 800-625-7576 ■ *Web:* www.hotsprings.org	Hot Springs	AR	71902	501-321-2277	955-2600
Statehouse Convention Ctr 426 W Markham PO Box 3232 *TF:* 800-844-4781 ■ *Web:* littlerockmeetings.com/convention-center/	Little Rock	AR	72203	501-376-4781	374-2255

British Columbia

				Phone	Fax
Vancouver Convention & Exposition Centre (VCEC) 1055 Canada Pl *TF:* 866-785-8232 ■ *Web:* www.vancouverconventioncentre.com	Vancouver	BC	V6C0C3	604-689-8232	647-7232

California

				Phone	Fax
Anaheim Convention Ctr 800 W Katella Ave *Web:* www.anaheimconventioncenter.com	Anaheim	CA	92802	714-765-8950	765-8965
Rabobank Arena Theater & Convention Ctr 1001 Truxtun Ave *Web:* rabobankarena.com	Bakersfield	CA	93301	661-852-7300	861-9904
Carson Ctr 801 E Carson St *Web:* www.carsoncenter.com	Carson	CA	90745	310-835-0212	835-0160
Cow Palace 2600 Geneva Ave *Web:* www.cowpalace.com	Daly City	CA	94014	415-404-4100	404-4111
Fresno Convention Ctr 848 M St *Web:* www.fresnoconventioncenter.com	Fresno	CA	93721	559-445-8100	445-8110
Bren Events Ctr 100 Bren Events Ctr *Web:* www.bren.uci.edu	Irvine	CA	92697	949-824-5050	824-5097
Long Beach Convention & Entertainment Ctr 300 E Ocean Blvd *Web:* www.longbeachcc.com	Long Beach	CA	90802	562-436-3636	436-9491
California Market Ctr 110 E Ninth St *TF:* 800-225-6278 ■ *Web:* www.californiamarketcenter.com	Los Angeles	CA	90079	213-630-3600	630-3708
Los Angeles Convention Ctr 1201 S Figueroa St *Web:* www.lacclink.com	Los Angeles	CA	90015	213-741-1151	765-4266
Shrine Auditorium & Exposition Ctr 665 W Jefferson Blvd *Web:* www.shrineauditorium.com	Los Angeles	CA	90007	213-748-5116	742-9922
Modesto Centre Plaza 1000 L St *Web:* www.modestogov.com/prnd/facilities/mcp	Modesto	CA	95354	209-577-6444	544-6729
Monterey Conference Ctr One Portola Plz *TF Sales:* 800-742-8091 ■ *Web:* www.montereyconferencecenter.com	Monterey	CA	93940	831-646-3770	646-3777

Phone Fax

Oakland Convention Ctr 1001 Broadway Oakland CA 94607 510-451-4000 835-3466
TF: 800-228-9290 ■ *Web:* marriott.com

Ontario Convention Ctr
2000 E Convention Ctr Way Ontario CA 91764 909-937-3000 937-3080
TF: 800-455-5755 ■ *Web:* www.ontariocc.org

Palm Springs Convention Ctr
277 N Avenida Caballeros Palm Springs CA 92262 760-325-6611 778-4102
TF: 800-898-7256 ■ *Web:* www.palmspringscc.com

Sacramento Convention Ctr 1400 J St Sacramento CA 95814 916-808-5291 808-7687
Web: www.sacramentoconventioncenter.com

NOS Events Ctr 689 SE St San Bernardino CA 92408 909-888-6788 889-7666
Web: www.nosevents.com

San Diego Convention Ctr 111 W Harbor Dr San Diego CA 92101 619-525-5000 525-5005
TF: 800-525-7322 ■ *Web:* www.sdccc.org

Concourse Exhibition Ctr 635 Eigth St San Francisco CA 94103 415-490-5800 490-5885
Web: www.sfdesigncenter.com

Moscone Ctr 747 Howard St San Francisco CA 94103 415-974-4000 974-4073
Web: www.moscone.com

Nob Hill Masonic Ctr
1111 California St San Francisco CA 94108 415-776-7457 776-3945
Web: www.sfmasoniccenter.com

San Jose Convention Center (SJC)
150 W San Carlos St San Jose CA 95110 408-792-4194 277-3535
TF: 800-726-5673 ■
Web: www.sanjose.org/plan-a-meeting-event/venues/convention-center

Santa Clara Convention Ctr
5001 Great America Pkwy Santa Clara CA 95054 408-748-7000 748-7013
Web: www.santaclara.org

Santa Monica Civic Auditorium
1855 Main St Santa Monica CA 90401 310-458-8551 394-3411
TF: 866-728-3229 ■ *Web:* smgov.net/departments/ccs/civicauditorium

Visalia Convention Ctr 303 E Acequia Ave Visalia CA 93291 559-713-4000 713-4804
TF: 800-640-4888 ■ *Web:* www.ci.visalia.ca.us

Colorado

Phone Fax

Colorado Springs City Auditorium
221 E Kiowa St Colorado Springs CO 80903 719-385-5969 385-6584
TF: 800-888-4748 ■ *Web:* www.springsgov.com

Colorado Convention Ctr 700 14th St Denver CO 80202 303-228-8000 228-8103
Web: www.denverconvention.com

Two Rivers Convention Ctr 159 Main St Grand Junction CO 81501 970-263-5700 263-5720
Web: www.tworiversconvention.com

Connecticut

Phone Fax

XL Ctr One Civic Ctr Plz Hartford CT 06103 860-249-6333 241-4226
Web: www.xlcenter.com

District of Columbia

Phone Fax

Washington Convention Ctr Authority
801 Mt Vernon Pl NW Washington DC 20001 202-249-3000
TF: 800-368-9000 ■ *Web:* www.dcconvention.com

Florida

Phone Fax

Ocean Ctr 101 N Atlantic Ave Daytona Beach FL 32118 386-254-4500 254-4512
TF: 800-858-6444 ■ *Web:* www.oceancenter.com

Greater Fort Lauderdale-Broward County Convention Ctr
1950 Eisenhower Blvd Fort Lauderdale FL 33316 954-765-5900 763-9551
Web: www.ftlauderdalecc.com

Harborside Event Ctr 1375 Monroe St Fort Myers FL 33901 239-321-8110 344-5926
TF: 800-294-9516 ■ *Web:* www.fmharborside.com

Prime Osborn Convention Ctr
1000 Water St Jacksonville FL 32204 904-630-4000 630-4029
Web: www.jaxevents.com/primeosbornconventioncenter

Lakeland Ctr 701 W Lime St Lakeland FL 33815 863-834-8100 834-8101
Web: www.thelakelandcenter.com

Miami Beach Convention Ctr
1901 Convention Ctr Dr Miami Beach FL 33139 305-673-7311 673-7435
Web: www.miamibeachconvention.com

Orange County Convention Ctr (OCCC)
9800 International Dr Orlando FL 32819 407-685-9800 685-9876
TF: 800-345-9845 ■ *Web:* www.occc.net

Manatee Convention Ctr 1 Haben Blvd Palmetto FL 34221 941-722-3244 729-1820
TF: 800-822-2017 ■ *Web:* www.bradentongulfislands.com

Turnbull Conference Ctr
555 W Pensacola St
FSU Ctr for Professional Development Tallahassee FL 32306 850-644-3801 644-2589
Web: alwayslearning.fsu.edu

Tampa Convention Ctr 333 S Franklin St Tampa FL 33602 813-274-8511 274-7430
TF: 866-790-4111 ■ *Web:* www.tampagov.net

Palm Beach County Convention Ctr
650 Okeechobee Blvd West Palm Beach FL 33401 561-366-3000 366-3001
Web: www.palmbeachfl.com

Georgia

Phone Fax

AmericasMart 240 Peachtree St NW Ste 2200 Atlanta GA 30303 404-220-3000 220-3030
TF: 800-285-6278 ■ *Web:* www.americasmart.com

Cobb Galleria Centre Two Galleria Pkwy Atlanta GA 30339 770-955-8000 955-7719
Web: www.cobbgalleria.com

Georgia World Congress Ctr
285 Andrew Young International Blvd NW Atlanta GA 30313 404-223-4200 223-4211
Web: www.gwcc.com

Georgia International Convention Ctr
2000 Convention Ctr Concourse College Park GA 30337 770-997-3566 994-8559
TF: 888-331-4422 ■ *Web:* www.gicc.com

Columbus Georgia Convention & Trade Ctr
801 Front Ave Columbus GA 31901 706-327-4522 327-0162
Web: www.columbusga.org/tradecenter

Northwest Georgia Trade & Convention Ctr
2211 Dug Gap Battle Rd Dalton GA 30720 706-272-7676 278-5811
TF: 800-824-7469 ■ *Web:* www.nwgtcc.com

Gwinnett Ctr 6400 Sugarloaf Pkwy Duluth GA 30097 770-813-7500 813-7501
Web: www.gwinnettcenter.com

Georgia Mountains Ctr
301 Main St SW PO Box 2496 Gainesville GA 30501 770-534-8420
Web: www.gainesville.org

Jekyll Island Convention Ctr
1 N Beachview Dr Jekyll Island GA 31527 912-635-5203
TF: 877-453-5955 ■ *Web:* www.jekyllisland.com

Savannah International Trade & Convention Ctr
One International Dr Savannah GA 31421 912-447-4000 447-4722*
**Fax:* Sales ■ *TF:* 888-644-6822 ■ *Web:* www.savtcc.com

Hawaii

Phone Fax

Hawaii Convention Ctr 1801 Kalakaua Ave Honolulu HI 96815 808-943-3500 943-3599
TF: 800-295-6603 ■ *Web:* www.meethawaii.com

Idaho

Phone Fax

Boise Centre on the Grove 850 W Front St Boise ID 83702 208-336-8900 336-8803
Web: www.boisecentre.com

Illinois

Phone Fax

McCormick Place 2301 S Lk Shore Dr Chicago IL 60616 312-791-7000 791-6543
Web: www.mccormickplace.com

Merchandise Mart
222 Merchandise Mart Plz Ste 470 Chicago IL 60654 312-527-4141
TF: 800-677-6278 ■ *Web:* www.merchandisemart.com/mmart

Navy Pier 600 E Grand Ave Chicago IL 60611 312-595-5400
TF: 800-595-7437 ■ *Web:* www.navypier.com

Gateway Ctr One Gateway Dr Collinsville IL 62234 618-345-8998 345-9024
TF: 800-289-2388 ■ *Web:* gatewaycenter.com

Exposition Gardens 1601 W Northmoor Rd Peoria IL 61614 309-691-6332 691-2372
Web: www.expogardensinc.com

Oakley-Lindsay Ctr 300 Civic Ctr Plaza Ste 237 Quincy IL 62301 217-223-1000 223-1330
Web: www.oakleylindsaycenter.com

Quad City Conservation Alliance Expo Ctr
2621 Fourth Ave Rock Island IL 61201 309-788-5912 788-9619
TF: 877-734-1565 ■ *Web:* www.qccaexpocenter.com

Donald E Stephens Convention Ctr
5555 N River Rd Rosemont IL 60018 847-692-2220 696-9700
Web: www.rosemont.com

Prairie Capital Convention Ctr (PC3)
One Convention Ctr Plz Springfield IL 62701 217-788-8800 788-0811
Web: springfieldpc3.com/

Indiana

Phone Fax

Bloomington Monroe County Convention Ctr
302 S College Ave Bloomington IN 47403 812-336-3681 349-2981
Web: www.bloomingtonconvention.com

Evansville Auditorium & Convention Ctr
715 Locust St Evansville IN 47708 812-435-5770 435-5500
TF: 844-381-4751 ■ *Web:* centre.evansvillegis.com

Grand Wayne Convention Ctr
120 W Jefferson Blvd Fort Wayne IN 46802 260-426-4100 420-9080
Web: www.grandwayne.com

Indiana Convention Ctr & Lucas Oil Stadium (ICCLOS)
100 S Capitol Ave Indianapolis IN 46225 317-262-3400 262-3685
Web: www.icclos.com

Horizon Convention Ctr 401 S High St Muncie IN 47305 765-288-8860 751-9190
TF: 888-288-8860 ■ *Web:* www.horizonconvention.com

Century Ctr 120 S St Joseph St South Bend IN 46601 574-235-9711 235-9185
Web: www.centurycenter.org

Iowa

Phone Fax

US Cellular Ctr 370 First Ave E Cedar Rapids IA 52401 319-398-5211 362-2102
TF: 800-745-3000 ■ *Web:* www.uscellularcenter.com

RiverCenter Adler Theatre 136 E Third St Davenport IA 52801 563-326-8500 326-8505
Web: www.riverctr.com

Polk County Convention Complex
730 Third St Des Moines IA 50309 515-564-8001 564-8001
Web: www.iowaeventscenter.com

Sioux City Convention Ctr 801 Fourth St Sioux City IA 51101 712-279-4800 279-4900
TF: 800-593-2228 ■ *Web:* www.visitsiouxcity.org/convention-center

Tyson Events Ctr 401 Gordon Dr Sioux City IA 51101 712-279-4850 279-4903
TF: 800-593-2228 ■ *Web:* www.tysoncenter.com

Kansas

Phone Fax

Kansas Expocentre One Expocentre Dr Topeka KS 66612 785-235-1986 235-2967
TF: 800-745-3000 ■ *Web:* www.ksexpo.com

				Phone	Fax
Century II Performing Arts & Convention Ctr 225 W Douglas Ave. *Web:* www.century2.org	Wichita	KS	67202	316-264-9121	303-8688

Kentucky

				Phone	Fax
Frankfort Convention Ctr 405 Mero St. *TF:* 800-426-7866 ■ *Web:* www.frankfortconventioncenter.com	Frankfort	KY	40601	502-564-5335	564-3310
Lexington Convention Ctr 430 W Vine St. *Web:* www.lexingtoncenter.com	Lexington	KY	40507	859-233-4567	253-2718
Kentucky International Convention Ctr 221 S Fourth St. *TF:* 800-701-5831 ■ *Web:* www.kyconvention.org	Louisville	KY	40202	502-595-4381	584-9711

Louisiana

				Phone	Fax
Baton Rouge River Ctr 275 S River Rd. *Web:* www.brrivercenter.com	Baton Rouge	LA	70802	225-389-3030	389-4954
Bossier Civic Ctr 620 Benton Rd. *TF:* 800-522-4842 ■ *Web:* www.bossiercity.org	Bossier City	LA	71111	318-741-8900	741-8910
Pontchartrain Ctr 4545 Williams Blvd. *TF:* 800-745-3000 ■ *Web:* www.pontchartraincenter.com	Kenner	LA	70065	504-465-9985	468-6692
Cajundome & Convention Ctr 444 Cajundome Blvd. *Web:* www.cajundome.com	Lafayette	LA	70506	337-265-2100	265-2311
Monroe Civic Ctr 401 Lea Joyner Expy. *Web:* ci.monroe.la.us	Monroe	LA	71201	318-329-2225	329-2548
Ernest N Morial Convention Ctr 900 Convention Ctr Blvd. *Web:* www.mccno.com	New Orleans	LA	70130	504-582-3023	582-3088
Festival Plaza 101 Crockett St Ste A. *TF:* 888-458-4748 ■ *Web:* www.shreveportla.gov	Shreveport	LA	71101	318-673-5100	673-5105

Maine

				Phone	Fax
Augusta Civic Ctr 16 Cony St. *Web:* www.augustamaine.gov	Augusta	ME	04330	207-626-2405	626-5968
Cross Insurance Center 515 Main St. *Web:* www.crossinsurancecenter.com	Bangor	ME	04401	207-561-8300	

Maryland

				Phone	Fax
Baltimore Convention Ctr One W Pratt St. *Web:* www.bccenter.org	Baltimore	MD	21201	410-649-7000	649-7008

Massachusetts

				Phone	Fax
Boston Convention & Exhibition Ctr 415 Summer St. *Web:* massconvention.com	Boston	MA	02210	617-954-2000	954-2299
Exchange Conference Ctr 212 Northern Ave. *Web:* www.exchangeconferencecenter.com	Boston	MA	02210	617-790-1900	790-1922
John B Hynes Veterans Memorial Convention Ctr 900 Boylston St. *TF:* 800-392-6089 ■ *Web:* massconvention.com	Boston	MA	02115	617-954-2000	954-2299
MassMutual Ctr 1277 Main St. *Web:* www.massmutualcenter.com	Springfield	MA	01103	413-787-6610	787-6645
DCU Ctr 50 Foster St. *Web:* www.dcucenter.com	Worcester	MA	01608	508-755-6800	929-0111

Michigan

				Phone	Fax
Cobo Conference & Exhibition Ctr 1 Washington Blvd. *Web:* www.cobocenter.com	Detroit	MI	48226	313-877-8777	877-8577
DeVos Place 303 Monroe Ave. *Web:* www.devosplace.org	Grand Rapids	MI	49503	616-742-6500	742-6590
Lansing Ctr 333 E Michigan Ave. *Web:* www.lepfa.com	Lansing	MI	48933	517-483-7400	483-7439
Horizons Conference Ctr 6200 State St. *Web:* www.horizonscenter.com	Saginaw	MI	48603	989-799-4122	799-4188

Minnesota

				Phone	Fax
Duluth Entertainment Convention Ctr 350 Harbor Dr. *TF:* 800-628-8385 ■ *Web:* www.decc.org	Duluth	MN	55802	218-722-5573	722-4247
Earle Brown Heritage Ctr 6155 Earle Brown Dr. *Web:* www.earlebrown.com	Minneapolis	MN	55430	763-569-6300	569-6320
Minneapolis Convention Ctr 1301 Second Ave S. *Web:* www.minneapolis.org	Minneapolis	MN	55403	612-335-6000	335-6757
Mayo Civic Ctr 30 Civic Ctr Dr SE. *TF:* 800-422-2199 ■ *Web:* www.mayociviccenter.com	Rochester	MN	55904	507-328-2220	328-2221
Saint Paul RiverCentre 175 W Kellogg Blvd. *Web:* www.rivercentre.org	Saint Paul	MN	55102	651-265-4800	265-4899

Mississippi

				Phone	Fax
Mississippi Coast Coliseum & Convention Ctr 2350 Beach Blvd. *TF:* 800-726-2781 ■ *Web:* mscoastcoliseum.com	Biloxi	MS	39531	228-594-3700	594-3812
James M Trotter Convention Ctr 402 Second Ave N	Columbus	MS	39701	662-328-4164	329-5166
Natchez Convention Ctr 211 Main St. *TF:* 888-475-9144 ■ *Web:* www.natchezconventioncenter.org	Natchez	MS	39120	601-442-5880	

Missouri

				Phone	Fax
Jack Lawton Webb Convention Ctr 5300 S Range Line Rd	Joplin	MO	64804	417-781-4000	623-7400
Kansas City Convention & Entertainment Centers 301 W 13th St. *TF:* 800-821-7060 ■ *Web:* visitkc.com/convention-center/index.aspx	Kansas City	MO	64105	816-513-5000	513-5001
America's Ctr Convention Ctr 701 Convention Plz. *Web:* www.explorestlouis.com/americascenter/public.asp	Saint Louis	MO	63101	314-342-5036	342-5040
Saint Louis Executive Conference Ctr 701 Convention Plz. *TF:* 800-325-7962 ■ *Web:* www.explorestlouis.com	Saint Louis	MO	63101	314-342-5050	342-5053
Springfield Exposition Ctr 635 E St Louis St. *Web:* www.upspringfield.com	Springfield	MO	65806	417-522-3976	864-3077

Montana

				Phone	Fax
MetraPark PO Box 2514. *TF:* 800-366-8538 ■ *Web:* www.metrapark.com	Billings	MT	59103	406-256-2400	256-2479
City of Great Falls PO Box 5021 Great Falls Civic Ctr. *Web:* www.greatfallsmt.net	Great Falls	MT	59403	406-771-0885	
Helena Civic Ctr 340 Neill Ave. *Web:* www.helenaciviccenter.com	Helena	MT	59601	406-447-8481	447-8480

Nebraska

				Phone	Fax
Pershing Ctr 226 Centennial Mall S.	Lincoln	NE	68508	402-441-8744	441-7913

Nevada

				Phone	Fax
Elko Convention & Visitors Authority 700 Moren Way. *TF:* 800-248-3556 ■ *Web:* www.elkocva.com	Elko	NV	89801	775-738-4091	738-2420
Henderson Convention Ctr 200 S Water St. *TF:* 877-775-5252 ■ *Web:* www.visithenderson.com	Henderson	NV	89015	702-267-2171	267-2177
Las Vegas Convention Ctr 3150 Paradise Rd. **Fax:* Mktg ■ *TF:* 877-847-4858 ■ *Web:* www.lvcva.com	Las Vegas	NV	89109	702-892-0711	892-2824*
Sands Expo & Convention Ctr 201 Sands Ave. *Web:* www.sandsexpo.com	Las Vegas	NV	89169	702-733-5556	733-5568
Reno-Sparks Convention Ctr 4590 S Virginia St. *TF:* 800-367-7366 ■ *Web:* www.visitrenotahoe.com	Reno	NV	89502	775-827-7600	827-7701

New Jersey

				Phone	Fax
New Jersey Convention & Exposition Ctr 97 Sunfield Ave. *TF:* 800-367-0070 ■ *Web:* www.njexpocenter.com	Edison	NJ	08837	732-417-1400	
Meadowlands Exposition Ctr 355 Plaza Dr. *TF:* 888-560-3976 ■ *Web:* www.mecexpo.com	Secaucus	NJ	07094	201-330-7773	330-1172
Garden State Exhibit Ctr 50 Atrium Dr. *Web:* www.gsec.com	Somerset	NJ	08873	732-469-4000	563-4500
Wildwoods Convention Ctr 4501 Boardwalk. *TF:* 800-992-9732 ■ *Web:* www.wildwoodsnj.com	Wildwood	NJ	08260	609-729-9000	846-2631

New Mexico

				Phone	Fax
Albuquerque Convention Ctr 401 Second St NW. *Web:* www.albuquerquecc.com	Albuquerque	NM	87102	505-768-4575	768-3239

New York

				Phone	Fax
Office of General Services Corning Tower 41st Fl Empire State Plz. *TF:* 877-426-6006 ■ *Web:* ogs.ny.gov	Albany	NY	12242	518-474-3899	457-3081
Buffalo Niagara Convention Ctr 153 Franklin St Convention Ctr Plz. *TF:* 800-995-7570 ■ *Web:* www.buffaloconvention.com	Buffalo	NY	14202	716-855-5555	855-3158
Jacob K Javits Convention Ctr 655 W 34th St. *Web:* www.javitscenter.com	New York	NY	10001	212-216-2000	216-2588
Rochester Riverside Convention Ctr 123 E Main St. *Web:* www.rrcc.com	Rochester	NY	14604	585-232-7200	232-1510
Saratoga Springs City Ctr 522 Broadway. *Web:* saratogacitycenter.org	Saratoga Springs	NY	12866	518-584-0027	584-0117
Oncenter Complex 800 S State St. *TF:* 800-776-7548 ■ *Web:* www.oncenter.org	Syracuse	NY	13202	315-435-8000	435-8099

North Carolina

	City	State	Zip	Phone	Fax
Asheville Civic Ctr 87 Haywood St *TF:* 888-464-4218 ■ *Web:* www.ashevillenc.gov	Asheville	NC	28801	828-259-5743	259-5777
Charlotte Convention Ctr 501 S College St *Web:* www.charlotteconventionctr.com	Charlotte	NC	28202	704-339-6000	339-6024
Metrolina Expo Trade Ctr 7100 Statesville Rd *Web:* www.metrolinatradeshowexpo.com	Charlotte	NC	28269	704-596-4650	295-1983
Park Expo & Conference Ctr, The 800 Briar Creek Rd *Web:* www.ppm-nc.com	Charlotte	NC	28205	704-333-7709	
Greensboro Coliseum Complex 1921 W Lee St *Web:* www.greensborocoliseum.com	Greensboro	NC	27403	336-373-7400	373-2170
International Home Furnishings Ctr 210 E Commerce Ave	High Point	NC	27260	336-888-3700	882-1873
Raleigh Convention Ctr 500 S Salisbury St *Web:* www.raleighconvention.com	Raleigh	NC	27601	919-996-8500	
Benton Convention Ctr 301 W Fifth St *Web:* twincityquarter.com	Winston-Salem	NC	27101	336-727-2976	727-2879

North Dakota

	City	State	Zip	Phone	Fax
Bismarck Civic Ctr 315 S Fifth St *Web:* www.bismarckciviccenter.com	Bismarck	ND	58504	701-355-1370	222-6599
Fargo Civic Ctr 207 N Fourth St *Web:* www.cityoffargo.com	Fargo	ND	58102	701-241-1480	241-1483
Alerus Ctr 1200 42nd St S *Web:* www.aleruscenter.com	Grand Forks	ND	58201	701-792-1200	746-6511

Ohio

	City	State	Zip	Phone	Fax
John S Knight Ctr 77 E Mill St *TF:* 800-245-4254 ■ *Web:* www.johnsknightcenter.org	Akron	OH	44308	330-374-8900	374-8971
Duke Energy Ctr 525 Elm St *Web:* www.duke-energycenter.com	Cincinnati	OH	45202	513-419-7300	419-7327
International Exposition Ctr 1-X Ctr Dr *TF:* 855-436-8683 ■ *Web:* www.ixcenter.com	Cleveland	OH	44135	216-676-6000	
Franklin County Veterans Memorial 300 W Broad St	Columbus	OH	43215	614-221-4341	221-8422
Greater Columbus Convention Ctr 400 N High St *TF:* 800-626-0241 ■ *Web:* www.columbusconventions.com	Columbus	OH	43215	614-827-2500	221-7239
Dayton Convention Ctr 22 E Fifth St *Web:* www.daytonconventioncenter.com	Dayton	OH	45402	937-333-4700	333-4711
Sharonville Convention Ctr 11355 Chester Rd *TF:* 800-294-3179 ■ *Web:* www.sharonvilleconventioncenter.com	Sharonville	OH	45246	513-771-7744	772-5745
SeaGate Convention Centre 401 Jefferson Ave *Web:* www.toledo-seagate.com	Toledo	OH	43604	419-255-3300	255-7731

Oklahoma

	City	State	Zip	Phone	Fax
Cherokee Strip Conference Ctr 123 W Maine St	Enid	OK	73701	580-616-7362	
Cox Business Services Convention Ctr One Myriad Gardens *Web:* www.coxconventioncenter.com	Oklahoma City	OK	73102	405-602-8500	602-8505
Expo Square 4145 E 21st St *TF:* 877-781-2660 ■ *Web:* www.exposquare.com	Tulsa	OK	74114	918-744-1113	744-8725
Tulsa Convention Ctr 100 Civic Ctr *TF:* 800-678-7177 ■ *Web:* www.coxcentertulsa.com	Tulsa	OK	74103	918-894-4350	

Ontario

	City	State	Zip	Phone	Fax
Metro Toronto Convention Centre 255 Front St W **Fax:* Hum Res ■ *Web:* www.mtccc.com	Toronto	ON	M5V2W6	416-585-8000	585-8262*

Oregon

	City	State	Zip	Phone	Fax
Lane Events Ctr 796 W 13th Ave *Web:* www.atthefair.com	Eugene	OR	97402	541-682-4292	682-3614
Florence Events Ctr 715 Quince St *TF:* 888-968-4086 ■ *Web:* www.ci.florence.or.us	Florence	OR	97439	541-997-1994	902-0991
City of Pendleton 500 SW Dorion Ave *TF:* 800-238-5355 ■ *Web:* www.pendleton.or.us	Pendleton	OR	97801	541-966-0201	966-0251
Oregon Convention Ctr 777 NE Martin Luther King Jr Blvd *TF:* 800-791-2250 ■ *Web:* www.oregoncc.org	Portland	OR	97232	503-235-7575	235-7417
Portland Metropolitan Exposition Ctr 2060 N Marine Dr *Web:* www.expocenter.org	Portland	OR	97217	503-736-5200	736-5201
Oregon State Fair & Expo Ctr 2330 17th St NE *Web:* oregonstatefair.org	Salem	OR	97301	503-947-3247	947-3206
Salem Conference Ctr 200 Commercial St SE *TF Sales:* 877-589-1700 ■ *Web:* salemconventioncenter.org	Salem	OR	97301	503-589-1700	589-1715
Seaside Civic & Convention Ctr 415 First Ave *TF:* 800-394-3303 ■ *Web:* www.seasideconvention.com	Seaside	OR	97138	503-738-8585	738-0198

Pennsylvania

	City	State	Zip	Phone	Fax
Valley Forge Convention Ctr 1160 First Ave *Web:* www.vfconventioncenter.com	King of Prussia	PA	19406	610-768-3215	
Hampton Inn Philadelphia Ctr City-Convention Ctr 1301 Race St *TF:* 800-426-7866 ■ *Web:* www3.hilton.com	Philadelphia	PA	19107	215-665-9100	665-9200
Pennsylvania Convention Ctr 1101 Arch St *TF:* 800-428-9000 ■ *Web:* www.paconvention.com	Philadelphia	PA	19107	215-418-4700	418-4747
David L Lawrence Convention Ctr 1000 Ft Duquesne Blvd *Web:* www.pittsburghcc.com	Pittsburgh	PA	15222	412-565-6000	565-6008
Stetson Convention Services Inc 2900 Stayton St *Web:* www.stetsonexpo.com	Pittsburgh	PA	15212	412-223-1090	223-1094

Rhode Island

	City	State	Zip	Phone	Fax
Rhode Island Convention Ctr One Sabin St *Web:* www.riconvention.com	Providence	RI	02903	401-458-6000	458-6500

South Carolina

	City	State	Zip	Phone	Fax
Charleston Area Convention Ctr Complex (CACC) 5001 Coliseum Dr *Web:* www.charlestonconventioncenter.com	Charleston	SC	29418	843-529-5000	529-5010
Carolina First Ctr One Exposition Dr *Web:* www.tdconventioncenter.com	Greenville	SC	29607	864-233-2562	255-8600
Myrtle Beach Convention Ctr 2101 N Oak St *TF:* 800-537-1690 ■ *Web:* www.myrtlebeachconventioncenter.com	Myrtle Beach	SC	29577	843-918-1225	918-1243

South Dakota

	City	State	Zip	Phone	Fax
Rushmore Plaza Civic Ctr 444 Mt Rushmore Rd N *TF:* 800-468-6463 ■ *Web:* www.gotmine.com	Rapid City	SD	57701	605-394-4115	394-4119

Tennessee

	City	State	Zip	Phone	Fax
Chattanooga Convention Ctr 1150 Carter St PO Box 6008 *TF:* 800-962-5213 ■ *Web:* www.chattconvention.org	Chattanooga	TN	37402	423-756-0001	267-5291
Knoxville Convention Ctr 701 Henley St *Web:* www.kccsmg.com	Knoxville	TN	37902	865-522-5669	329-0422
Memphis Cook Convention Ctr 3205 Elvis Presley Blvd *Web:* www.memphistravel.com	Memphis	TN	38116	901-543-5333	
Nashville Convention Ctr 601 Commerce St *Web:* www.nashvilleconventionctr.com	Nashville	TN	37203	615-742-2000	742-2014

Texas

	City	State	Zip	Phone	Fax
Amarillo Civic Ctr 401 S Buchanan St *Web:* www.civicamarillo.com	Amarillo	TX	79101	806-378-4297	378-4234
Arlington Convention Ctr 1200 Ballpark Way *Web:* www.arlingtontx.gov	Arlington	TX	76011	817-459-5000	459-5091
Austin Convention Ctr 500 E Cesar Chavez St *Web:* www.austinconventioncenter.com	Austin	TX	78701	512-404-4000	404-4416
Palmer Events Ctr 900 Barton Springs Rd *Web:* www.austinconventioncenter.com	Austin	TX	78704	512-404-4500	404-4422
Beaumont Civic Ctr Complex 701 Main St *TF:* 800-782-3081 ■ *Web:* beaumontcityevents.com/	Beaumont	TX	77701	409-838-3435	838-3715
Bell County Expo Ctr 301 W Loop 121 *Web:* www.bellcountyexpo.com	Belton	TX	76513	254-933-5353	933-5354
American Bank Ctr 1901 N Shoreline Blvd *Web:* www.americanbankcenter.com	Corpus Christi	TX	78401	361-826-4700	826-4905
Dallas Convention Ctr 650 S Griffin St *TF:* 877-850-2100 ■ *Web:* www.dallasconventioncenter.com	Dallas	TX	75202	214-939-2750	939-2700
Dallas Market Ctr 2100 Stemmons Fwy Ste 113 *TF:* 800-325-6587 ■ *Web:* www.dallasmarketcenter.com	Dallas	TX	75207	214-655-6100	749-5479
El Paso Convention & Performing Arts Ctr One Civic Ctr Plz *TF:* 800-351-6024 ■ *Web:* www.visitelpaso.com	El Paso	TX	79901	915-534-0600	534-0687
Fort Worth Convention Ctr 1201 Houston St *TF:* 866-630-2588 ■ *Web:* fortworthtexas.gov	Fort Worth	TX	76102	817-392-6338	392-2756
Moody Gardens Convention Ctr Seven Hope Blvd *TF:* 888-388-8484 ■ *Web:* www.moodygardenshotel.com	Galveston	TX	77554	409-741-8484	683-4928
Grapevine Convention Ctr, The 1209 S Main St *TF:* 866-782-7897 ■ *Web:* www.grapevinetexasusa.com	Grapevine	TX	76051	817-410-3459	410-3090
George R Brown Convention Ctr 1001 Avenida de Las Americas *TF:* 800-427-4697 ■ *Web:* www.houstonconventionctr.com	Houston	TX	77010	713-853-8000	853-8090
Maude Cobb Convention Ctr 100 Grand Blvd PO Box 1952 *Web:* www.maudecobb.longviewtexas.gov	Longview	TX	75604	903-237-1230	
Lubbock Memorial Civic Ctr 1501 MacDavis Ln *Web:* www.mylubbock.us/departmental-websites/departments/civic-center/home	Lubbock	TX	79401	806-775-2242	775-3240

				Phone	Fax
Plano Centre 2000 E Springcreek Pkwy *Web:* plano.gov	Plano	TX	75074	972-422-0296	424-0002
Robert A "Bob" Bowers Civic Ctr 3401 Cultural Ctr Dr *Web:* www.portarthur.net	Port Arthur	TX	77642	409-985-8801	985-3125
San Angelo Convention Ctr Coliseum & Auditorium 500 Rio Concho Dr *Web:* cosatx.us	San Angelo	TX	76903	325-653-9577	659-0900
Henry B Gonzalez Convention Ctr 200 E Market St *TF:* 877-504-8895 ■ *Web:* www.sahbgcc.com	San Antonio	TX	78205	210-207-8500	223-1495
South Padre Island Convention Centre 7355 Padre Blvd *TF:* 800-657-2373 ■ *Web:* www.sopadre.com	South Padre Island	TX	78597	956-761-3000	761-3024
Frank W Mayborn Civic & Convention Ctr 3303 N Third St *Web:* ci.temple.tx.us	Temple	TX	76501	254-298-5720	298-5388
Oil Palace, The 10408 Hwy 64 E *Web:* www.oilpalace.com	Tyler	TX	75707	903-566-2122	566-4206
MPEC (Multi-Purpose Events Ctr) 1000 Fifth St *Web:* www.wfmpec.com	Wichita Falls	TX	76301	940-716-5500	716-5509

Utah

				Phone	Fax
Golden Spike Event Ctr 1000 North 1200 West *Web:* www.goldenspikeeventcenter.com	Ogden	UT	84404	801-399-8798	392-1995
Ogden Eccles Conference Ctr 2415 Washington Blvd *TF:* 866-472-4627 ■ *Web:* oeccutah.com	Ogden	UT	84401	801-689-8600	689-8651
Salt Palace Convention Ctr 100 W Temple *Web:* www.saltpalace.com	Salt Lake City	UT	84101	801-534-4777	

Virginia

				Phone	Fax
Greater Richmond Convention Ctr 403 N Third St *Web:* www.richmondcenter.com	Richmond	VA	23219	804-783-7300	780-2577

Washington

				Phone	Fax
Meydenbauer Ctr 11100 NE Sixth St *Web:* www.meydenbauer.com	Bellevue	WA	98004	425-637-1020	637-0166
Three Rivers Convention Ctr & Coliseum 7016 W Grandbridge Blvd *Web:* www.threeriversconventioncenter.com	Kennewick	WA	99336	509-737-3700	735-9431
Ocean Shores Convention Ctr 120 W Chance a La Mer Ave *TF:* 800-874-6737 ■ *Web:* www.oceanshoresconventioncenter.com	Ocean Shores	WA	98569	360-289-4411	289-4412
Bell Harbor International Conference Ctr 2211 Alaskan Way Pier 66 *TF:* 888-772-4422 ■ *Web:* www.bellharbor.com	Seattle	WA	98121	206-441-6666	441-6665
Washington State Convention 800 Convention Pl *Web:* wscc.com/	Seattle	WA	98101	206-694-5000	694-5399
Spokane Ctr 720 W Mallon Ave *Web:* www.spokanecenter.com	Spokane	WA	99201	509-279-7000	279-7050
Greater Tacoma Convention & Trade Ctr 1500 Broadway *TF:* 800-745-3000 ■ *Web:* www.tacomaconventioncenter.com	Tacoma	WA	98402	253-830-6601	573-2363
Yakima Convention Ctr 10 N Eigth St *TF:* 800-221-0751 ■ *Web:* www.visityakima.com	Yakima	WA	98901	509-575-6062	575-6252

West Virginia

				Phone	Fax
Charleston Civic Ctr & Coliseum 200 Civic Ctr Dr *Web:* www.charlestonwvciviccenter.com	Charleston	WV	25301	304-345-1500	345-3492

Wisconsin

				Phone	Fax
La Crosse Ctr 300 Harborview Plz *Web:* www.lacrossecenter.com	La Crosse	WI	54601	608-789-7400	789-7444
Alliant Energy Ctr of Dane County 1919 Alliant Energy Ctr Way *Web:* www.alliantenergycenter.com	Madison	WI	53713	608-267-3976	267-0146
Monona Terrace Community & Convention Ctr One John Nolen Dr *Web:* www.mononaterrace.com	Madison	WI	53703	608-261-4000	261-4049
Frontier Airlines Ctr 400 W Wisconsin Ave *TF:* 800-745-3000 ■ *Web:* wisconsincenter.org	Milwaukee	WI	53203	414-908-6000	908-6010

Wyoming

				Phone	Fax
Casper Events Ctr 1 Events Dr *TF:* 800-442-2256 ■ *Web:* www.casperwy.gov	Casper	WY	82601	307-235-8441	235-8445

209 CONVENTION & VISITORS BUREAUS

SEE ALSO Travel & Tourism Information - Canadian p. 3257; Travel & Tourism Information - Foreign Travel p. 3257

Listings are alphabetized by city names.

				Phone	Fax
Aberdeen Convention & Visitors Bureau 10 Railroad Ave SW PO Box 78 *TF:* 800-645-3851 ■ *Web:* www.visitaberdeensd.com	Aberdeen	SD	57401	605-225-2414	225-3573
Abilene Convention & Visitors Bureau 1101 N First St *TF:* 800-727-7704 ■ *Web:* www.abilenevisitors.com	Abilene	TX	79601	325-676-2556	676-1630
Abingdon Convention & Visitors Bureau 335 Cummings St *TF:* 800-435-3440 ■ *Web:* visitabingdonvirginia.com	Abingdon	VA	24210	276-676-2282	676-3076
Akron/Summit County Convention & Visitors Bureau 77 E Mill St *TF:* 800-245-4254 ■ *Web:* www.visitakron-summit.org	Akron	OH	44308	330-374-8900	374-7626
Albany County Convention & Visitors Bureau 25 Quackenbush Sq *TF:* 800-258-3582 ■ *Web:* www.albany.org	Albany	NY	12207	518-434-1217	434-0887
Albany Visitors Assn 300 Second Ave SW *TF:* 800-526-2256 ■ *Web:* www.albanyvisitors.com	Albany	OR	97321	541-928-0911	926-1500
Albuquerque Convention & Visitors Bureau 20 First Plz Ste 601 *TF:* 800-733-9918 ■ *Web:* visitalbuquerque.org/	Albuquerque	NM	87102	505-842-9918	247-9101
Alexandria Convention & Visitors Assn 221 King St *TF:* 800-388-9119 ■ *Web:* www.visitalexandriava.com	Alexandria	VA	22314	703-746-3301	838-4683
Alexandria/Pineville Area Convention & Visitors Bureau (APACVB) 707 Main St PO Box 1070 *TF:* 800-551-9546 ■ *Web:* alexandriapinevillela.com/	Alexandria	LA	71301	318-442-9546	443-1617
Allegan County Tourist & Recreational Council 3255 122nd Ave Ste 103 *TF:* 888-425-5342 ■ *Web:* www.visitallegancounty.com	Allegan	MI	49010	269-686-9088	673-0454
Lehigh Valley Visitor Ctr 840 Hamilton St Ste 200 *TF:* 800-747-0561 ■ *Web:* www.discoverlehighvalley.com	Allentown	PA	18101	610-882-9200	
Alpena Area Convention & Visitors Bureau 235 W Chisholm St *TF:* 800-425-7362 ■ *Web:* www.alpenacvb.com	Alpena	MI	49707	989-354-4181	356-3999
Alton Regional Convention & Visitors Bureau (ARCVB) 200 Piasa St *TF:* 800-258-6645 ■ *Web:* www.visitalton.com	Alton	IL	62002	618-465-6676	465-6151
Amana Colonies Convention & Visitors Bureau 622 46th Ave *TF:* 800-579-2294 ■ *Web:* www.amanacolonies.com	Amana	IA	52203	319-622-7622	622-6395
Amarillo Convention & Visitor Council 1000 S Polk St PO Box 9480 *TF:* 800-692-1338 ■ *Web:* www.visitamarillotx.com	Amarillo	TX	79105	806-374-1497	373-3909
Lorain County Visitors Bureau 8025 Leavitt Rd *TF:* 800-334-1673 ■ *Web:* www.visitloraincounty.com	Amherst	OH	44001	440-984-5282	984-7363
Anaheim/Orange County Visitor & Convention Bureau 800 W Katella Ave PO Box 4270 *TF:* 855-405-5020 ■ *Web:* www.anaheimoc.org	Anaheim	CA	92802	714-765-8888	991-8963
Anchorage Convention & Visitors Bureau 524 W Fourth Ave *TF:* 800-445-8667 ■ *Web:* www.anchorage.net	Anchorage	AK	99501	907-276-4118	278-5559
Anderson/Madison County Visitors & Convention Bureau 6335 S Scatterfield Rd *TF:* 800-533-6569 ■ *Web:* www.heartlandspirit.com	Anderson	IN	46013	765-643-5633	643-9083
Steuben County Tourism Bureau 430 N Wayne St Ste 1B *TF:* 888-665-5668 ■ *Web:* www.lakes101.org	Angola	IN	46703	260-665-5386	665-2268
Ann Arbor Area Convention & Visitors Bureau 120 W Huron St *TF:* 800-888-9487 ■ *Web:* www.visitannarbor.org	Ann Arbor	MI	48104	734-995-7281	995-7283
Southernmost Illinois Tourism Bureau PO Box 378 *TF:* 800-248-4373 ■ *Web:* www.southernmostillinois.com	Anna	IL	62906	618-833-9928	
Annapolis & Anne Arundel County Conference & Visitors Bureau (AAACCVB) 26 W St *TF:* 888-302-2852 ■ *Web:* www.visitannapolis.org	Annapolis	MD	21401	410-280-0445	263-9591
Fox Cities Convention & Visitors Bureau 3433 W College Ave *TF:* 800-236-6673 ■ *Web:* www.foxcities.org	Appleton	WI	54914	920-734-3358	734-1080
Arkansas City Convention & Visitors Bureau 106 S Summit St PO Box 795 *Web:* www.arkcity.org	Arkansas City	KS	67005	620-442-0230	441-0048
Arlington Convention & Visitors Bureau 1905 E Randol Mill Rd *TF:* 800-433-5374 ■ *Web:* www.experiencearlington.org	Arlington	TX	76011	817-265-7721	265-5640
Asheville Area Convention & Visitors Bureau 36 Montford Ave *TF:* 800-257-5583 ■ *Web:* www.exploreasheville.com	Asheville	NC	28801	828-258-6101	
Aspen Chamber Resort Assn 425 Rio Grande Pl *TF:* 800-670-0792 ■ *Web:* www.aspenchamber.org	Aspen	CO	81611	970-925-1940	920-1173
Athens Convention & Visitors Bureau 300 N Thomas St *TF:* 800-653-0603 ■ *Web:* www.visitathensga.com	Athens	GA	30601	706-357-4430	546-8040
Athens County Convention & Visitors Bureau 667 E State St *TF:* 800-878-9767 ■ *Web:* www.athensohio.com	Athens	OH	45701	740-592-1819	593-7365
Atlanta Convention & Visitors Bureau 233 Peachtree St NE Ste 1400 *TF:* 800-285-2682 ■ *Web:* www.atlanta.net	Atlanta	GA	30303	404-521-6600	
Cobb Travel & Tourism One Galleria Pkwy *TF:* 800-451-3480 ■ *Web:* www.travelcobb.org	Atlanta	GA	30339	678-303-2622	303-2625
Atlantic City Convention & Visitors Authority 2314 Pacific Ave *TF:* 888-228-4748 ■ *Web:* www.atlanticcitynj.com	Atlantic City	NJ	08401	609-348-7100	

	City	State	ZIP	Phone	Fax
Auburn-Opelika Tourism Bureau 714 E Glenn Ave *TF:* 866-880-8747 ■ *Web:* www.aotourism.com	Auburn	AL	36830	334-887-8747	821-5500
Augusta Metropolitan Convention & Visitors Bureau 1450 Greene St Ste 110 *TF:* 800-726-0243 ■ *Web:* visitaugusta.com/	Augusta	GA	30901	706-823-6600	823-6609
Aurora Area Convention & Visitors Bureau 43 W Galena Blvd *TF:* 800-477-4369 ■ *Web:* www.enjoyaurora.com	Aurora	IL	60506	630-897-5581	897-5589
Austin Convention & Visitors Bureau 301 Congress Ave Ste 200 *TF:* 800-926-2282 ■ *Web:* www.austintexas.org	Austin	TX	78701	512-474-5171	583-7282
Catalina Island Visitors Bureau One Green Pier PO Box 217 *Web:* www.catalinachamber.com	Avalon	CA	90704	310-510-1520	510-7607
Baker County Visitors & Convention Bureau 490 Campbell St *TF:* 800-523-1235 ■ *Web:* www.visitbaker.com	Baker City	OR	97814	541-523-3356	523-9187
Greater Bakersfield Convention & Visitors Bureau 515 Truxtun Ave *TF:* 866-425-7353 ■ *Web:* www.visitbakersfield.com	Bakersfield	CA	93301	661-852-7282	325-7074
Baltimore Area Convention & Visitors Assn (BACVA) 100 Light St 12th Fl *TF:* 877-225-8466 ■ *Web:* www.baltimore.org	Baltimore	MD	21202	410-659-7300	727-2308
Bandera County Convention & Visitors Bureau 126 State Hwy 16 S PO Box 171 *TF:* 800-364-3833 ■ *Web:* www.banderacowboycapital.com	Bandera	TX	78003	830-796-3045	796-4121
Greater Bangor Convention & Visitors Bureau 40 Harlow St *TF:* 800-916-6673 ■ *Web:* www.visitbangormaine.com	Bangor	ME	04401	207-947-5205	942-2146
Clermont County Convention & Visitors Bureau (CCCVB) 410 E Main St PO Box 100 *TF:* 800-796-4282 ■ *Web:* www.visitclermontohio.com	Batavia	OH	45103	513-732-3600	732-2244
Baton Rouge Convention & Visitors Bureau 359 Third St *TF:* 800-527-6843 ■ *Web:* www.visitbatonrouge.com	Baton Rouge	LA	70801	225-383-1825	346-1253
Battle Creek/Calhoun County Convention & Visitors Bureau 77 E Michigan Ave Ste 100 *TF:* 800-397-2240 ■ *Web:* www.battlecreekvisitors.org	Battle Creek	MI	49017	269-962-2240	962-6917
Beaumont Convention & Visitors Bureau 505 Willow St *TF:* 800-392-4401 ■ *Web:* www.beaumontcvb.com	Beaumont	TX	77701	409-880-3749	880-3750
Greene County Convention & Visitors Bureau 1221 Meadowbridge Dr *TF:* 800-733-9109 ■ *Web:* www.greenecountyohio.org	Beavercreek	OH	45434	937-429-9100	429-7726
Washington County Visitors Assn 11000 SW Stratus St Ste 170 *TF:* 800-537-3149 ■ *Web:* www.oregonswashingtoncounty.com	Beaverton	OR	97008	503-644-5555	644-9784
Southern West Virginia Convention & Visitors Bureau 1406 Harper Rd *TF:* 800-847-4898 ■ *Web:* www.visitwv.com	Beckley	WV	25801	304-252-2244	252-2252
Bedford County Visitors Bureau 131 S Juliana St *TF:* 800-765-3331 ■ *Web:* www.visitbedfordcounty.com	Bedford	PA	15522	814-623-1771	623-1671
Gaston County Travel & Tourism 620 N Main St *TF:* 800-849-9994 ■ *Web:* www.gastongov.com	Belmont	NC	28012	704-825-4044	
Beloit Convention & Visitors Bureau 500 Public Ave *TF:* 800-423-5648 ■ *Web:* www.visitbeloit.com	Beloit	WI	53511	608-365-4838	365-6850
Bucks County Conference & Visitors Bureau (BCCVB) 3207 St Rd *TF:* 800-836-2825 ■ *Web:* www.visitbuckscounty.com	Bensalem	PA	19020	215-639-0300	642-3277
Southwestern Michigan Tourism Council 2300 Pipestone Rd *Web:* www.swmichigan.org	Benton Harbor	MI	49022	269-925-6301	925-7540
Gatheringguide.com 531 Grizzly Peak Blvd *Web:* www.gatheringguide.com	Berkeley	CA	94708	510-524-8200	
Beverly Hills Conference & Visitors Bureau 239 S Beverly Dr *TF:* 800-345-2210 ■ *Web:* lovebeverlyhills.com	Beverly Hills	CA	90212	310-248-1000	248-1020
Greater Big Rapids Convention & Visitors Bureau 246 N State St *TF:* 800-999-9069 ■ *Web:* www.bigrapids.org	Big Rapids	MI	49307	231-796-7640	796-0832
Big Spring Convention & Visitor Bureau 215 W Third St PO Box 3359 *TF:* 866-222-7100 ■ *Web:* www.bigspringtx.com	Big Spring	TX	79720	432-264-6032	264-6047
Billings Convention & Visitors Bureau 815 S 27th St PO Box 31177 *TF:* 800-735-2635 ■ *Web:* www.visitbillings.com	Billings	MT	59107	406-245-4111	245-7333
Mississippi Gulf Coast Convention & Visitors Bureau 2350 Beach Blvd Ste A *TF:* 888-467-4853 ■ *Web:* www.gulfcoast.org	Biloxi	MS	39531	228-896-6699	896-6788
Greater Binghamton Convention 49 Ct St Second Fl PO Box 995 *Web:* greaterbinghamtonchamber.com	Binghamton	NY	13902	607-772-8860	722-4513
Greater Birmingham Convention & Visitors Bureau 2200 Ninth Ave N *TF:* 800-458-8085 ■ *Web:* birminghamal.org	Birmingham	AL	35203	205-458-8000	458-8086
Bismarck-Mandan Convention & Visitors Bureau 1600 Burnt Boat Dr *TF:* 800-767-3555 ■ *Web:* www.discoverbismarckmandan.com	Bismarck	ND	58503	701-222-4308	222-0647
Bloomington Convention & Visitors Bureau (BCVB) 7900 International Dr Ste 990 *TF:* 800-346-4289 ■ *Web:* www.bloomingtonmn.org	Bloomington	MN	55425	952-858-8500	858-8854
Bloomington-Normal Area Convention & Visitors Bureau 3201 CIRA Dr Ste 201 *TF:* 800-433-8226 ■ *Web:* www.bloomingtonnormalcvb.org	Bloomington	IL	61704	309-665-0033	661-0743
Bloomington/Monroe County Convention & Visitors Bureau 2855 N Walnut St *TF:* 800-800-0037 ■ *Web:* www.visitbloomington.com	Bloomington	IN	47404	812-334-8900	334-2344
Columbia-Montour Visitors Bureau 121 Papermill Rd *TF:* 800-847-4810 ■ *Web:* www.itourcolumbiamontour.com	Bloomsburg	PA	17815	570-784-8279	784-1166
Mercer County Convention & Visitors Bureau 704 Bland St PO Box 4088 *TF:* 800-221-3206 ■ *Web:* www.visitmercercounty.com	Bluefield	WV	24701	304-325-8438	324-8483
Boise Convention & Visitors Bureau 1199 Main St *TF:* 800-635-5240 ■ *Web:* www.boise.org	Boise	ID	83702	208-344-7777	344-6236
North Carolina High Country Host 1700 Blowing Rock Rd *TF:* 800-438-7500 ■ *Web:* www.highcountryhost.com	Boone	NC	28607	828-264-1299	265-0550
Greater Boston Convention & Visitors Bureau (GBCVB) Two Copley Pl Ste 105 *TF:* 888-733-2678 ■ *Web:* www.bostonusa.com	Boston	MA	02116	617-536-4100	424-7664
Bottineau Convention & Visitor Bureau 519 Main St Ste 100 *Web:* www.bottineau.com	Bottineau	ND	58318	701-228-3849	228-5130
Boulder Convention & Visitors Bureau 2440 Pearl St *TF:* 800-444-0447 ■ *Web:* www.bouldercoloradousa.com	Boulder	CO	80302	303-442-2911	938-2098
Brenham/Washington County Convention & Visitor Bureau 314 S Austin St *TF:* 888-273-6426 ■ *Web:* www.brenhamtexas.com	Brenham	TX	77833	979-836-3695	836-2540
Greater Bridgeport Conference & Vistors Ctr 164 W Main St *TF:* 800-368-4324 ■ *Web:* www.greater-bridgeport.com	Bridgeport	WV	26330	304-842-7272	842-1941
Minneapolis Northwest 6200 Shingle Creek Pkwy Ste 130 *TF:* 800-541-4364 ■ *Web:* www.minneapolisnorthwest.com	Brooklyn Center	MN	55430	763-852-7500	566-6526
Northwest Pennsylvania's Great Outdoors Visitors Bureau 2801 Maplevale Rd *TF:* 800-348-9393 ■ *Web:* www.visitpago.com	Brookville	PA	15825	814-849-5197	849-1969
Brownsville Convention & Visitors Bureau 650 Ruben M Torres Sr Blvd *TF:* 800-626-2639 ■ *Web:* brownsville.org/	Brownsville	TX	78521	956-546-3721	
Brunswick & The Golden Isles of Georgia Visitors Bureau Four Glynn Ave *TF:* 800-933-2627 ■ *Web:* www.goldenisles.com	Brunswick	GA	31520	912-265-0620	265-0629
Buena Park Convention & Visitors Office 6601 Beach Blvd **Fax Area Code:* 714 ■ *TF:* 800-541-3953 ■ *Web:* www.visitbuenapark.com	Buena Park	CA	90621	800-541-3953	522-3319*
Buffalo Niagara Convention & Visitors Bureau 617 Main St Ste 200 *TF:* 800-283-3256 ■ *Web:* www.visitbuffaloniagara.com	Buffalo	NY	14203	716-852-2356	852-0131
San Mateo County Convention & Visitors Bureau 111 Anza Blvd Ste 410 *TF:* 800-288-4748 ■ *Web:* www.smccvb.com	Burlingame	CA	94010	650-348-7600	348-7687
Burlington/Alamance County Convention & Visitors Bureau 610 S Lexington Ave PO Box 519 *TF:* 800-637-3804 ■ *Web:* www.visitalamance.com	Burlington	NC	27216	336-570-1444	228-1330
Vermont Convention Bureau 60 Main St Ste 100 *TF:* 877-264-3503 ■ *Web:* www.vermont.org	Burlington	VT	05401	802-860-0606	863-1538
Cadillac Area Visitors Bureau 201 N Mitchell St *TF:* 800-225-2537 ■ *Web:* www.cadillacmichigan.com	Cadillac	MI	49601	231-775-0657	779-5933
Tourism Calgary 200 238 11th Ave SE *TF:* 800-661-1678 ■ *Web:* www.visitcalgary.com	Calgary	AB	T2G0X8	403-263-8510	262-3809
Cambridge Office for Tourism Inc Four Brattle St Ste 208 *Web:* www.cambridgeusa.org	Cambridge	MA	02138	617-441-2884	
Finger Lakes Visitors Connection 25 Gorham St *TF:* 877-386-4669 ■ *Web:* www.visitfingerlakes.com	Canandaigua	NY	14424	585-394-3915	394-4067
Canton/Stark County Convention & Visitors Bureau 222 Market Ave N *TF:* 800-552-6051 ■ *Web:* www.visitcantonstark.com	Canton	OH	44702	330-454-1439	456-3600
Cape Girardeau Convention & Visitors Bureau 400 Broadway Ste 100 *TF:* 800-777-0068 ■ *Web:* www.visitcape.com	Cape Girardeau	MO	63701	573-335-1631	334-6702
Carlsbad Convention & Visitors Bureau 400 Carlsbad Village Dr *TF:* 800-227-5722 ■ *Web:* www.visitcarlsbad.com	Carlsbad	CA	92008	760-434-6093	434-6056
Hamilton County Convention & Visitors Bureau Inc 37 E Main St *TF:* 800-776-8687 ■ *Web:* www.visithamiltoncounty.com	Carmel	IN	46032	317-848-3181	848-3191
Carrington Convention & Visitors Bureau 871 Main St PO Box 439 *TF:* 800-641-9668 ■ *Web:* www.cgtn-nd.com	Carrington	ND	58421	701-652-2524	652-2391
Carson City Convention & Visitors Bureau 1900 S Carson St Ste 100 *Web:* www.visitcarsoncity.com	Carson City	NV	89701	775-687-7410	687-7416
Convention & Buiness Bruae One Friendship Plz Ste 1 PO Box 200397	Cartersville	GA	30120	770-387-1357	607-3104
Casper Area Convention & Visitors Bureau 992 N Poplar St *TF:* 800-852-1889 ■ *Web:* visitcasper.com/	Casper	WY	82601	307-234-5362	261-9928
Cedar City-Brian Head Tourism & Convention Bureau 581 N Main St Ste A *TF:* 800-354-4849 ■ *Web:* www.scenicsouthernutah.com	Cedar City	UT	84721	435-586-5124	586-4022
Cedar Rapids Area Convention & Visitors Bureau 119 First Ave SE PO Box 5339 *TF:* 800-735-5557 ■ *Web:* www.cedar-rapids.com	Cedar Rapids	IA	52401	319-398-5009	398-5089
Champaign County Convention & Visitors Bureau 108 S Neil St *TF:* 800-369-6151 ■ *Web:* www.visitchampaigncounty.org	Champaign	IL	61820	217-351-4133	359-1809
Chapel Hill/Orange County Visitors Bureau 501 W Franklin St **Fax Area Code:* 919 ■ *TF:* 888-968-2060 ■ *Web:* www.visitchapelhill.org	Chapel Hill	NC	27516	888-968-2060	968-2062*
Charleston Area Convention & Visitors Bureau 423 King St *TF:* 800-868-8118 ■ *Web:* www.charlestoncvb.com	Charleston	SC	29403	843-853-8000	853-0444
Charleston Convention & Visitors Bureau 601 Morris St Ste 204 *Web:* www.charlestonwv.com	Charleston	WV	25301	304-344-5075	344-1241

				Phone	Fax
Charlotte Convention & Visitors Bureau 500 S College St Ste 300 *TF:* 800-722-1994 ■ *Web:* www.charlottesgotalot.com	Charlotte	NC	28202	704-334-2282	342-3972
Chattanooga Area Convention & Visitors Bureau 215 Broad St. *TF:* 800-322-3344 ■ *Web:* www.chattanoogafun.com	Chattanooga	TN	37402	423-756-8687	265-1630
Chautauqua County Visitors Bureau Chautauqua Main Gate Rt 394 PO Box 1441 *TF:* 800-242-4569 ■ *Web:* www.tourchautauqua.com	Chautauqua	NY	14722	716-357-4569	357-2284
Cherokee Tribal Travel & Promotions 498 Tsali Blvd PO Box 460 *TF:* 877-440-9990 ■ *Web:* nc-cherokee.com	Cherokee	NC	28719	828-359-6492	554-6475
Chesapeake Conventions & Tourism Bureau (CCT) 860 Greenbrier Cir Ste 101 *TF:* 888-889-5551 ■ *Web:* www.visitchesapeake.com	Chesapeake	VA	23320	757-502-4898	502-8016
Randolph County Tourism Committee 1 Taylor St Courthouse *Web:* www.randolphco.org	Chester	IL	62233	618-826-5000	826-3750
Cheyenne Area Convention & Visitors Bureau 121 W 15th St Ste 202 *TF:* 800-426-5009 ■ *Web:* www.cheyenne.org	Cheyenne	WY	82001	307-778-3133	778-3190
Chicago Convention & Tourism Bureau 2301 S Lk Shore Dr McCormick Complex Lakeside Ctr *Web:* www.choosechicago.com	Chicago	IL	60616	312-567-8500	
Chicago Office of Tourism & Culture 78 E Washington St 4th Fl *TF:* 866-966-5335 ■ *Web:* www.choosechicago.com	Chicago	IL	60602	312-744-2400	
Chula Vista Convention & Visitors Bureau 233 Fourth Ave *Web:* www.chulavistaconvis.com	Chula Vista	CA	91910	619-426-2882	420-1269
Greater Cincinnati Convention & Visitors Bureau 525 Vine St Ste 1500 *TF:* 800-543-2613 ■ *Web:* www.cincyusa.com	Cincinnati	OH	45202	513-621-2142	621-5020
Pickaway County Visitors Bureau 325 W Main St *TF:* 800-283-4678 ■ *Web:* www.pickaway.com	Circleville	OH	43113	740-474-3636	420-9181
Clarksville/Montgomery County Tourist Commission 25 Jefferson St Ste 300 *TF:* 800-530-2487 ■ *Web:* www.clarksvillepartnership.com	Clarksville	TN	37040	931-647-2331	645-1574
Clear Lake Convention & Visitors Bureau 205 Main Ave PO Box 188 *TF:* 800-285-5338 ■ *Web:* www.clearlakeiowa.com	Clear Lake	IA	50428	641-357-2159	357-8141
Ranch at Ucross, The 2673 Us Hwy 14 *Web:* blairhotels.com	Clearmont	WY	82835	307-737-2281	
Visit St Petersburg Clearwater 13805 58th St N Ste 2-200 *TF:* 877-352-3224 ■ *Web:* www.visitstpeteclearwater.com	Clearwater	FL	33760	727-464-7200	464-7222
Cleveland/Bradley Convention & Visitors Bureau 225 Keith St PO Box 2275 *Web:* www.clevelandchamber.com	Cleveland	TN	37320	423-472-6587	472-2019
Positively Cleveland Visitors Ctr 100 Public Sq Ste 100 *TF:* 800-321-1001 ■ *Web:* thisiscleveland.com/	Cleveland	OH	44113	216-875-6680	621-5967
Clinton Convention & Visitors Bureau 721 S Second St *Web:* www.clintoniowatourism.com	Clinton	IA	52732	563-242-5702	242-5803
Brevard County Tourism Development 430 Brevard Ave Ste 150 *TF:* 877-572-3224 ■ *Web:* brevardcounty.us	Cocoa Village	FL	32922	321-433-4470	433-4476
Park County Travel Council (PCTC) 836 Sheridan Ave PO Box 2454 *TF:* 800-393-2639 ■ *Web:* www.yellowstonecountry.org	Cody	WY	82414	307-587-2297	527-6228
Colby Convention & Visitors Bureau 350 S Range Ste 10 *TF:* 800-611-8835 ■ *Web:* www.oasisontheplains.com	Colby	KS	67701	785-460-7643	460-4509
Bryan/College Station Convention & Visitors Bureau (BCSCVB) 715 University Dr E *TF:* 800-777-8292 ■ *Web:* www.visitaggieland.com	College Station	TX	77840	979-260-9898	260-9800
Colorado Springs Convention & Visitors Bureau 515 S Cascade Ave *TF:* 800-888-4748 ■ *Web:* www.visitcos.com	Colorado Springs	CO	80903	719-635-7506	635-4968
Columbia Convention & Visitors Bureau 300 S Providence Rd *TF:* 800-652-0987 ■ *Web:* www.visitcolumbiamo.com	Columbia	MO	65203	573-875-1231	443-3986
Columbia Metropolitan Convention & Visitors Bureau 1101 Lincoln St PO Box 15 *TF:* 800-264-4884 ■ *Web:* www.columbiacvb.com	Columbia	SC	29202	803-545-0000	545-0013
Columbus Area Visitors Ctr 506 Fifth St. *TF:* 800-468-6564 ■ *Web:* www.columbus.in.us	Columbus	IN	47201	812-378-2622	372-7348
Columbus Convention & Visitors Bureau 318 7th St N *TF:* 800-327-2686 ■ *Web:* visitcolumbusms.org/	Columbus	MS	39701	662-329-1191	329-8969
Greater Columbus Convention & Visitors Bureau 277 W Nationwide Blvd Ste 125 *TF:* 866-397-2657 ■ *Web:* www.experiencecolumbus.com	Columbus	OH	43215	614-221-6623	221-5618
Polk County Travel & Tourism 20 E Mills St PO Box 308 *TF:* 800-440-7848 ■ *Web:* www.nc-mountains.org	Columbus	NC	28722	828-894-2324	894-6142
New Hampshire Div of Travel & Tourism Development 172 Pembroke Rd PO Box 1856 *TF:* 800-262-6660 ■ *Web:* www.visitnh.gov	Concord	NH	03302	603-271-2665	271-6870
Coos Bay-North Bend Visitor & Convention Bureau 50 Central Ave *TF:* 800-824-8486 ■ *Web:* www.oregonsadventurecoast.com	Coos Bay	OR	97420	541-269-0215	269-2861
Iowa City/Coralville Area Convention & Visitors Bureau 900 First Ave Hayden Fry Way *TF:* 800-283-6592 ■ *Web:* www.iowacitycoralville.org	Coralville	IA	52241	319-337-6592	337-9953
Corinth Area Convention & Visitors Bureau 215 N Fillmore St *TF:* 800-748-9048 ■ *Web:* www.corinth.net	Corinth	MS	38834	662-287-8300	286-0102
Corpus Christi Convention & Visitors Bureau 101 N Shoreline Blvd Ste 430 *TF:* 800-678-6232 ■ *Web:* www.visitcorpuschristitx.org	Corpus Christi	TX	78401	361-881-1888	887-9023
Corvallis Tourism 420 NW Second St *TF:* 800-334-8118 ■ *Web:* www.visitcorvallis.com	Corvallis	OR	97330	541-757-1544	753-2664
Council Grove/Morris County Chamber of Commerce & Tourism 207 W Main St *Web:* www.councilgrove.com	Council Grove	KS	66846	620-767-5413	767-5553
Northern Kentucky Convention & Visitors Bureau (NKYCVB) 50 E RiverCenter Blvd Ste 200 *TF:* 877-659-8474 ■ *Web:* meetnky.com/	Covington	KY	41011	859-261-4677	261-5135
Montgomery County Visitors & Convention Bureau 218 E Pike St *TF:* 800-866-3973 ■ *Web:* www.crawfordsville.org	Crawfordsville	IN	47933	765-362-5200	362-5215
Crescent City-Del Norte County Chamber of Commerce (CCDNCVB) 1001 Front St *TF:* 800-343-8300 ■ *Web:* delnorte.org/	Crescent City	CA	95531	707-464-3174	464-3561
Dallas Convention & Visitors Bureau 325 N St Paul St Ste 700 *TF:* 800-232-5527 ■ *Web:* www.visitdallas.com	Dallas	TX	75201	214-571-1000	571-1000
Central Florida Visitors & Convention Bureau 101 Adventure Ct *TF:* 800-828-7655 ■ *Web:* www.visitcentralflorida.org	Davenport	FL	33837	863-420-2586	420-2593
Tucker County Convention & Visitors Bureau 410 William Ave *TF:* 800-782-2775 ■ *Web:* www.canaanvalley.org	Davis	WV	26260	304-259-5315	259-4210
Dayton/Montgomery County Convention & Visitors Bureau One Chamber Plz Ste A *TF:* 800-221-8235 ■ *Web:* daytoncvb.com	Dayton	OH	45402	937-226-8211	226-8294
Decatur Area Convention & Visitors Bureau 202 E N St *TF:* 800-331-4479 ■ *Web:* www.decaturcvb.com	Decatur	IL	62523	217-423-7000	423-7455
Decatur/Morgan County Convention & Visitors Bureau (DMCCVB) 719 Sixth Ave SE PO Box 2349 *TF:* 800-232-5449 ■ *Web:* www.decaturcvb.org	Decatur	AL	35602	256-350-2028	350-2054
Wicomico County Convention & Visitors Bureau 8480 Ocean Hwy *TF:* 800-332-8687 ■ *Web:* www.wicomicotourism.org	Delmar	MD	21875	410-548-4914	548-0490
Denver Metro Convention & Visitors Bureau 1555 California St Ste 300 *TF:* 800-480-2010 ■ *Web:* www.denver.org	Denver	CO	80202	303-892-1112	892-1636
Greater Des Moines Convention & Visitors Bureau 400 Locust St Ste 265 *TF:* 800-451-2625 ■ *Web:* www.catchdesmoines.com	Des Moines	IA	50309	515-286-4960	244-9757
Detroit Metropolitan Convention & Visitors Bureau 211 W Fort St Ste 1000 *TF:* 877-424-5554 ■ *Web:* www.visitdetroit.com	Detroit	MI	48226	313-202-1800	202-1833
Dickinson Convention & Visitors Bureau 72 E Museum Dr. *TF:* 800-279-7391 ■ *Web:* www.visitdickinson.com	Dickinson	ND	58601	701-483-4988	483-9261
Dothan Area Convention & Visitors Bureau 3311 Ross Clark Cir PO Box 8765 *TF:* 888-449-0212 ■ *Web:* www.dothanalcvb.com	Dothan	AL	36301	334-794-6622	712-2731
Kent County & Greater Dover Delaware Convention & Visitors Bureau 435 N DuPont Hwy *TF:* 800-233-5368 ■ *Web:* www.visitdover.com	Dover	DE	19901	302-734-1736	734-0167
DuQuoin Tourism Commission 20 N Chestnut St PO Box 1037 *TF:* 800-455-9570 ■ *Web:* www.duquointourism.org	Du Quoin	IL	62832	618-542-8338	542-2098
Dublin Convention & Visitors Bureau Nine S High St *TF:* 800-245-8387 ■ *Web:* www.irishisanattitude.com	Dublin	OH	43017	614-792-7666	760-1818
Atlanta's Gwinnett Convention & Visitors Bureau (GCVB) 6500 Sugarloaf Pkwy Ste 200 *TF:* 888-494-6638 ■ *Web:* www.gcvb.org	Duluth	GA	30097	770-623-3600	623-1667
Duluth Convention & Visitors Bureau 21 W Superior St Ste 100 *TF:* 800-438-5884 ■ *Web:* www.visitduluth.com	Duluth	MN	55802	218-722-4011	722-1322
Durango Area Tourism Office 111 S Camino del Rio *TF:* 800-525-8855 ■ *Web:* www.durango.org	Durango	CO	81301	970-247-3500	385-7884
Durham Convention & Visitors Bureau 101 E Morgan St *TF:* 800-446-8604 ■ *Web:* durham-nc.com	Durham	NC	27701	919-687-0288	683-9555
Eagan Convention & Visitors Bureau 1501 Central Pkwy *TF:* 866-324-2620 ■ *Web:* www.eaganmn.com	Eagan	MN	55121	651-675-5546	675-5545
Talbot County Tourism Office 11 S Harrison St *Web:* www.tourtalbot.org	Easton	MD	21601	410-770-8000	770-8057
Visit Eau Claire 4319 Jeffers Rd Ste 201 *TF:* 888-523-3866 ■ *Web:* www.visiteauclaire.com	Eau Claire	WI	54703	715-831-2345	831-2340
Effingham Convention & Visitors Bureau 201 E Jefferson Ave *TF:* 800-772-0750 ■ *Web:* www.effinghamil.com	Effingham	IL	62401	217-342-5305	342-2746
El Paso Convention & Visitors Bureau One Civic Ctr Plz *TF:* 800-351-6024 ■ *Web:* www.visitelpaso.com	El Paso	TX	79901	915-534-0600	534-0600
Elgin Area Convention & Visitors Bureau 77 S Riverside Dr Ste 1 *TF:* 800-217-5362 ■ *Web:* www.northernfoxrivervalley.com	Elgin	IL	60120	847-695-7540	695-7668
Elkhart County Convention & Visitors Bureau 219 Caravan Dr. *TF:* 800-250-4827 ■ *Web:* www.amishcountry.org	Elkhart	IN	46514	574-262-8161	262-3925
Howard County Tourism Council 8267 Main St Side Entrance *TF:* 800-243-3425 ■ *Web:* www.howardcountymd.gov	Ellicott City	MD	21043	410-313-1900	313-1902
Grays Harbor Tourism PO Box 1229 *TF:* 800-621-9625 ■ *Web:* visitgraysharbor.com	Elma	WA	98541	360-482-2651	482-3297
VisitErie 208 E Bayfront Pkwy Ste 103 *TF:* 800-524-3743 ■ *Web:* www.visiteriepa.com	Erie	PA	16507	814-454-1000	459-0241
Travel Lane County PO Box 10286 *TF:* 800-547-5445 ■ *Web:* www.eugenecascadescoast.org	Eugene	OR	97440	541-484-5307	343-6335
Humboldt County Convention & Visitors Bureau 1034 Second St *TF:* 800-346-3482 ■ *Web:* www.redwoods.info	Eureka	CA	95501	707-443-5097	443-5115

Name / Address	City	State	Zip	Phone	Fax
Evansville Convention & Visitors Bureau 401 SE Riverside Dr *TF:* 800-433-3025 ■ *Web:* www.visitevansville.com	Evansville	IN	47713	812-421-2200	421-2207
Fairbanks Convention & Visitors Bureau 101 Dunkel St Ste 111 *TF:* 800-327-5774 ■ *Web:* www.explorefairbanks.com	Fairbanks	AK	99701	907-456-5774	459-3757
Jefferson County Visitor's Bureau PO Box 274 *Web:* www.visitoregontrail.org	Fairbury	NE	68352	402-729-3000	729-3076
Fairfax County Convention & Visitors Bureau (FXVA) 3702 Pender Dr Ste 420 *TF:* 800-732-4732 ■ *Web:* www.fxva.com	Fairfax	VA	22030	703-790-0643	790-5097
Convention & Visitors Bureau of Marion County 1000 Cole St Ste A *TF:* 800-834-7365 ■ *Web:* www.marioncvb.com	Fairmont	WV	26554	304-368-1123	333-0155
Fairmont Convention & Visitors Bureau 323 E Blue Earth Ave *TF:* 800-657-3280 ■ *Web:* visitfairmontmn.com	Fairmont	MN	56031	507-235-8585	235-8411
Tourism Bureau Southwestern Illinois 10950 Lincoln Trail *TF:* 800-442-1488 ■ *Web:* www.thetourismbureau.org	Fairview Heights	IL	62208	618-397-1488	397-1945
Fargo-Moorhead Convention & Visitors Bureau 2001 44th St S *TF:* 800-235-7654 ■ *Web:* www.fargomoorhead.org	Fargo	ND	58103	701-282-3653	282-4366
Farmington Convention & Visitors Bureau 3041 E Main St *TF:* 800-448-1240 ■ *Web:* www.farmingtonnm.org	Farmington	NM	87402	505-326-7602	327-0577
Fayetteville Area Convention & Visitors Bureau (FACVB) 245 Person St *TF:* 800-255-8217 ■ *Web:* www.visitfayettevillenc.com	Fayetteville	NC	28301	910-483-5311	484-6632
Flagstaff Convention & Visitors Bureau 323 W Aspen Ave *TF:* 800-217-2367 ■ *Web:* www.flagstaffarizona.org	Flagstaff	AZ	86001	928-779-7611	556-1305
Florence Convention & Visitors Bureau 3290 W Radio Dr *TF General:* 800-325-9005 ■ *Web:* www.visitflo.com	Florence	SC	29501	843-664-0330	665-9480
Tropical Everglades Visitor Assn 160 US Hwy Ste 1 *TF:* 800-272-6232 ■ *Web:* www.tropicaleverglades.com	Florida City	FL	33034	305-245-9180	247-4335
Fond du Lac Convention & Visitors Bureau 171 S Pioneer Rd *TF:* 800-937-9123 ■ *Web:* www.fdl.com	Fond du Lac	WI	54935	920-923-3010	929-6846
Fort Collins Convention & Visitors Bureau 19 Old Town Sq Ste 137 *TF:* 800-274-3678 ■ *Web:* www.visitftcollins.com	Fort Collins	CO	80524	970-232-3840	232-3841
Greater Fort Lauderdale Convention & Visitors Bureau 100 E Broward Blvd Ste 200 *TF:* 800-227-8669 ■ *Web:* www.sunny.org	Fort Lauderdale	FL	33301	954-765-4466	765-4467
Fort Madison 614 Ninth St *TF:* 800-210-8687 ■ *Web:* fortmadison.com	Fort Madison	IA	52627	319-372-5471	372-6404
Lee County Visitors & Convention Bureau 12800 University Dr Ste 550 *TF:* 800-237-6444 ■ *Web:* www.fortmyers-sanibel.com	Fort Myers	FL	33907	239-338-3500	334-1106
Fort Smith Convention & Visitors Bureau 2 N 'B' *TF:* 800-637-1477 ■ *Web:* www.fortsmith.org	Fort Smith	AR	72901	479-783-8888	784-2421
Fort Wayne/Allen County Convention & Visitors Bureau 927 S Harrison St *TF:* 800-767-7752 ■ *Web:* www.visitfortwayne.com	Fort Wayne	IN	46802	260-424-3700	424-3914
Fort Worth Convention & Visitors Bureau 111 W Fourth St Ste 200 *TF:* 800-433-5747 ■ *Web:* www.fortworth.com	Fort Worth	TX	76102	817-336-8791	698-7823
Frankenmuth Convention & Visitors Bureau 635 S Main St *TF:* 800-386-8696 ■ *Web:* www.frankenmuth.org	Frankenmuth	MI	48734	989-652-6106	652-3841
Frankfort/Franklin County Tourist & Convention Commission 100 Capitol Ave *TF:* 800-960-7200 ■ *Web:* www.visitfrankfort.com	Frankfort	KY	40601	502-875-8687	227-2604
Williamson County Convention & Visitors Bureau 400 Main St Ste 200 *Web:* www.visitwilliamson.com	Franklin	TN	37064	615-791-7554	
Tourism Council of Frederick County Inc 151 S East St *Web:* www.visitfrederick.org	Frederick	MD	21701	301-600-2888	
Fredericksburg Chamber of Commerce 302 E Austin St *TF:* 888-997-3600 ■ *Web:* www.fredericksburg-texas.com	Fredericksburg	TX	78624	830-997-6523	997-8588
Dodge County Convention & Visitors Bureau 338 N Main St *Web:* www.fremontne.org	Fremont	NE	68025	402-753-6414	721-1511
Fremont/Sandusky County Convention & Visitors Bureau 712 N St Ste 102 *TF:* 800-255-8070 ■ *Web:* www.sanduskycounty.org	Fremont	OH	43420	419-332-4470	332-4359
Fresno & Clovis Convention & Visitors Bureau 1550 E Shaw Ave Ste 101 *TF:* 800-788-0836 ■ *Web:* www.playfresno.org	Fresno	CA	93710	559-981-5500	445-0122
Alachua County Visitors & Convention Bureau 30 E University Ave *TF:* 866-778-5002 ■ *Web:* www.visitgainesville.com	Gainesville	FL	32601	352-374-5260	338-3213
Galena/Jo Daviess County Convention & Visitors Bureau (GJDCCVB) 101 Bouthillier St *Web:* www.galena.org	Galena	IL	61036	815-777-3557	777-3566
Galesburg Area Convention & Visitors Bureau 2163 E Main St *TF:* 800-916-3330 ■ *Web:* www.visitgalesburg.com	Galesburg	IL	61401	309-343-2485	343-2521
Finney County Convention & Visitors Bureau 1511 E Fulton Terr *TF:* 866-267-4638 ■ *Web:* www.gardencity.net	Garden City	KS	67846	620-275-1900	276-3290
Georgetown Convention & Visitors Bureau 1101 N College St *TF:* 800-436-8696 ■ *Web:* www.visit.georgetown.org	Georgetown	TX	78626	512-930-3545	930-3697
Gettysburg Convention & Visitors Bureau 571 W Middle St PO Box 4117 *TF:* 800-337-5015 ■ *Web:* destinationgettysburg.com/index.asp	Gettysburg	PA	17325	717-334-6274	334-1166
Greater Grand Forks Convention & Visitors Bureau 4251 Gateway Dr *TF:* 800-866-4566 ■ *Web:* www.visitgrandforks.com	Grand Forks	ND	58203	701-746-0444	746-0775
Grand Junction Visitors & Convention Bureau 740 Horizon Dr *TF:* 800-962-2547 ■ *Web:* www.visitgrandjunction.com	Grand Junction	CO	81506	970-244-1480	243-7393
Grand Rapids/Kent County Convention & Visitors Bureau 171 Monroe Ave NW Ste 700 *TF:* 800-678-9859 ■ *Web:* www.experiencegr.com	Grand Rapids	MI	49503	616-459-8287	459-7291
Grants Pass Visitors & Convention Bureau 1995 NW Vine St *TF:* 800-547-5927 ■ *Web:* www.visitgrantspass.org	Grants Pass	OR	97526	541-476-5510	476-9574
Houma Area Convention & Visitors Bureau 114 Tourist Dr *TF:* 800-688-2732 ■ *Web:* www.houmatravel.com	Gray	LA	70359	985-868-2732	
Greeley Convention & Visitors Bureau 902 Seventh Ave *TF:* 800-449-3866 ■ *Web:* www.greeleychamber.com	Greeley	CO	80631	970-352-3567	352-3572
Packer Country Visitor & Convention Bureau 1901 S Oneida St *TF:* 888-867-3342 ■ *Web:* www.greenbay.com	Green Bay	WI	54304	920-494-9507	405-1271
Putnam County Convention & Visitors Bureau 12 W Washington St *TF:* 800-829-4639 ■ *Web:* www.coveredbridgecountry.com	Greencastle	IN	46135	765-653-8743	
Greensboro Area Convention & Visitors Bureau 2200 Pinecroft Rd Ste 200 *TF:* 800-344-2282 ■ *Web:* visitgreensboronc.com	Greensboro	NC	27407	336-274-2282	230-1183
Greater Greenville Convention & Visitors Bureau 148 River St Ste 222 *TF:* 800-351-7180 ■ *Web:* www.visitgreenvillesc.com	Greenville	SC	29601	864-421-0000	421-0005
Greenville-Pitt County Convention & Visitors Bureau (GPCCVB) 303 SW Greenville Blvd PO Box 8027 *TF:* 800-537-5564 ■ *Web:* www.visitgreenvillenc.com	Greenville	NC	27835	252-329-4200	329-4205
Greenwood Convention & Visitors Bureau 111 E Market St *TF:* 800-748-9064 ■ *Web:* www.gcvb.com	Greenwood	MS	38930	662-453-9197	453-5526
Alabama Gulf Coast Convention & Visitors Bureau 3150 Gulf Shores Pkwy PO Box 457 *TF:* 800-745-7263 ■ *Web:* www.gulfshores.com	Gulf Shores	AL	36547	251-968-7511	968-6095
Lake County Convention & Visitors Bureau 5465 W Grand Ave Ste 100 *TF:* 800-525-3669 ■ *Web:* www.visitlakecounty.org	Gurnee	IL	60031	847-662-2700	662-2702
Hagerstown/Washington County Convention & Visitors Bureau 16 Public Sq *TF:* 888-257-2600 ■ *Web:* www.marylandmemories.org	Hagerstown	MD	21740	301-791-3246	791-2601
Hampton Conventions & Visitors Bureau 1919 Commerce Dr Ste 290 *TF:* 800-487-8778 ■ *Web:* visithampton.com	Hampton	VA	23666	757-722-1222	896-4600
Hannibal Convention & Visitors Bureau 505 N Third St *TF:* 866-263-4825 ■ *Web:* www.visithannibal.com	Hannibal	MO	63401	573-221-2477	221-6999
Jefferson County Convention & Visitors Bureau 37 Washington Ct *TF:* 866-435-5698 ■ *Web:* www.discoveritallwv.com	Harpers Ferry	WV	25425	304-535-2627	
Hershey Harrisburg Region Visitors Bureau 17 S Second St *TF:* 877-727-8573 ■ *Web:* www.visithersheyharrisburg.org	Harrisburg	PA	17101	717-231-7788	231-2808
Long Island Convention & Visitors Bureau & Sports Commission 330 Motor Pkwy Ste 203 **Fax Area Code:* 631 ■ *TF:* 877-386-6654 ■ *Web:* www.discoverlongisland.com	Hauppauge	NY	11788	877-386-6654	951-3439*
Hays Convention & Visitors Bureau 2700 Vine St PO Box 490 *TF:* 800-569-4505 ■ *Web:* www.haysusa.com	Hays	KS	67601	785-628-8202	628-1471
Alpine Helen/White County Convention & Visitors Bureau 726 Bruckenstrasse PO Box 730 *TF:* 800-858-8027 ■ *Web:* www.helenga.org	Helen	GA	30545	706-878-2181	878-4032
Henderson County Tourist Commission 101 N Water St Ste B *TF:* 800-648-3128 ■ *Web:* www.hendersonky.org	Henderson	KY	42420	270-826-3128	826-0234
Henderson County Travel & Tourism 201 S Main St *TF:* 800-828-4244 ■ *Web:* www.historichendersonville.org	Hendersonville	NC	28792	828-693-9708	697-4996
Huntingdon County Visitors Bureau 6993 Seven Pt Rd Ste 2 *TF:* 888-729-7869 ■ *Web:* www.raystown.org	Hesston	PA	16647	814-658-0060	658-0068
Hickory Metro Convention & Visitors Bureau 1960 13th Ave Dr SE *TF:* 800-509-2444 ■ *Web:* www.hickorymetro.com	Hickory	NC	28602	828-322-1335	322-8983
High Point Convention & Visitors Bureau 300 S Main St *TF:* 800-720-5255 ■ *Web:* www.highpoint.org	High Point	NC	27260	336-884-5255	884-5256
Hilton Head Island Visitors & Convention Bureau 1 Chamber Dr PO Box 5647 *TF:* 800-523-3373 ■ *Web:* www.hiltonheadisland.org	Hilton Head Island	SC	29938	843-785-3673	785-7110
Holland Area Convention & Visitors Bureau 76 E Eigth St *TF:* 800-506-1299 ■ *Web:* www.holland.org	Holland	MI	49423	616-394-0000	394-0122
Hawaii Visitors & Convention Bureau 2270 Kalakaua Ave Ste 801 *TF:* 800-464-2924 ■ *Web:* www.gohawaii.com	Honolulu	HI	96815	800-464-2924	
Hot Springs Convention & Visitors Bureau 134 Convention Blvd *TF:* 800-543-2284 ■ *Web:* www.hotsprings.org	Hot Springs	AR	71901	501-321-2277	321-2136
Greater Houston Convention & Visitors Bureau 901 Bagby St Ste 100 *TF:* 800-446-8786 ■ *Web:* www.visithoustontexas.com	Houston	TX	77002	713-437-5200	227-6336
Cabell-Huntington Convention & Visitors Bureau PO Box 347 *TF:* 800-635-6329 ■ *Web:* www.wvvisit.org	Huntington	WV	25708	304-525-7333	525-7345
Huntington County Visitors & Convention Bureau 407 N Jefferson St *TF:* 800-848-4282 ■ *Web:* www.visithuntington.org	Huntington	IN	46750	260-359-8687	359-9754

			Phone	Fax
Huntington Beach Marketing & Visitors Bureau 301 Main St Ste 208 . . . . Huntington Beach *TF:* 800-729-6232 ■ *Web:* www.surfcityusa.com	CA	92648	714-969-3492	845-4990
Huntsville/Madison County Convention & Visitor's Bureau 500 Church St Ste 1 . . . . Huntsville *TF:* 800-843-0468 ■ *Web:* www.huntsville.org	AL	35801	256-551-2230	551-2324
Huron Chamber & Visitors Bureau 1725 Dakota Ave S . . . . Huron *TF:* 800-487-6673 ■ *Web:* www.huronsd.com	SD	57350	605-352-0000	352-8321
Hurricane Convention & Visitors Bureau 3255 Teays Vly Rd PO Box 1086 . . . . Hurricane *TF:* 877-487-7982 ■ *Web:* www.hurricanewv.com	WV	25526	304-562-5896	562-5858
Greater Hutchinson Convention & Visitors Bureau 117 N Walnut St PO Box 519 . . . . Hutchinson *TF:* 800-691-4262 ■ *Web:* www.hutchchamber.com	KS	67504	620-662-3391	662-2168
Incline Village/Crystal Bay Visitors Bureau 969 Tahoe Blvd . . . . Incline Village *TF:* 800-468-2463 ■ *Web:* www.gotahoenorth.com	NV	89451	775-832-1606	832-1605
Indiana County Tourist Bureau 2334 Oakland Ave Ste 68 . . . . Indiana *TF:* 877-746-3426 ■ *Web:* www.visitindianacountypa.org	PA	15701	724-463-7505	465-3819
Indianapolis Convention & Visitors Assn 200 S Capitol Ave Ste 300 . . . . Indianapolis *TF:* 800-862-6912 ■ *Web:* www.visitindy.com	IN	46225	317-262-3000	
Western Upper Peninsula Convention & Visitor Bureau 405 N Lake St PO Box 706 . . . . Ironwood *TF:* 800-522-5657 ■ *Web:* www.explorewesternup.com	MI	49938	906-932-4850	932-3455
Irving Convention & Visitors Bureau 222 W Las Colinas Blvd Ste 1550 . . . . Irving *TF:* 800-247-8464 ■ *Web:* www.irvingtexas.com	TX	75039	972-252-7476	257-3153
Ithaca/Tompkins County Convention & Visitors Bureau 904 E Shore Dr . . . . Ithaca *TF:* 800-284-8422 ■ *Web:* www.visitithaca.com	NY	14850	607-272-1313	272-7617
Jackson County Convention & Visitors Bureau 141 S Jackson St . . . . Jackson *TF:* 800-245-5282 ■ *Web:* www.experiencejackson.com	MI	49201	517-764-4440	780-3688
Metro Jackson Convention & Visitors Bureau 111 E Capitol St Ste 102 . . . . Jackson *TF:* 800-354-7695 ■ *Web:* www.visitjackson.com	MS	39202	601-960-1891	960-1827
Jacksonville Convention & Visitors Bureau 310 E State St . . . . Jacksonville *TF:* 800-593-5678 ■ *Web:* www.jacksonvilleil.org	IL	62650	217-243-5678	
Onslow County Tourism 1099 Gum Branch Rd . . . . Jacksonville **Fax Area Code:* 910 ■ *TF:* 800-932-2144 ■ *Web:* www.onlyinonslow.com	NC	28540	800-932-2144	347-4705*
Visit Jacksonville 208 N Laura St Ste 1 . . . . Jacksonville *TF:* 800-733-2668 ■ *Web:* www.visitjacksonville.com	FL	32202	904-798-9111	798-9103
Jamestown Promotions & Tourism Ctr 404 Louis L'Amour Ln . . . . Jamestown *TF:* 800-222-4766 ■ *Web:* www.tourjamestown.com	ND	58401	701-251-9145	251-9146
Jefferson City Convention & Visitors Bureau 100 E High St PO Box 2227 . . . . Jefferson City *TF:* 800-769-4183 ■ *Web:* www.visitjeffersoncity.com	MO	65101	573-632-2820	638-4892
Clark-Floyd Counties Convention & Tourism Bureau 315 Southern Indiana Ave . . . . Jeffersonville *TF:* 800-552-3842 ■ *Web:* www.sunnysideoflouisville.org	IN	47130	812-282-6654	282-1904
Johnson City Convention & Visitors Bureau 601 E Main St . . . . Johnson City *Web:* www.johnsoncitytn.org	TN	37601	423-461-8000	461-8047
Greater Johnstown/Cambria County Convention & Visitors Bureau 416 Main St Ste 100 . . . . Johnstown *TF:* 800-237-8590 ■ *Web:* www.visitjohnstownpa.com	PA	15901	814-536-7993	539-3370
Heritage Corridor Convention & Visitors Bureau 339 W Jefferson St . . . . Joliet *TF:* 800-926-2262 ■ *Web:* www.heritagecorridorcvb.com	IL	60435	815-727-2323	727-2324
Joplin Convention & Visitors Bureau 222 W Third St . . . . Joplin *Web:* www.visitjoplinmo.com	MO	64801	417-625-4789	624-7948
Juneau Convention & Visitors Bureau 101 Egan Dr . . . . Juneau *TF:* 888-581-2201 ■ *Web:* www.traveljuneau.com	AK	99801	907-586-1737	586-6304
Kalamazoo County Convention & Visitors Bureau 141 E Michigan Ave Ste 100 . . . . Kalamazoo *TF:* 800-888-0509 ■ *Web:* www.discoverkalamazoo.com	MI	49007	269-488-9000	488-0050
Flathead Convention & Visitors Bureau 15 Depot Pk . . . . Kalispell *TF:* 800-543-3105 ■ *Web:* www.fcvb.org	MT	59901	406-756-9091	257-2500
Cabarrus County Convention & Visitors Bureau 3003 Dale Earnhardt Blvd . . . . Kannapolis *TF:* 800-848-3740 ■ *Web:* www.visitcabarrus.com	NC	28083	704-782-4340	782-4333
Kansas City Convention & Visitors Assn 1100 Main St Ste 2200 . . . . Kansas City *TF:* 800-767-7700 ■ *Web:* www.visitkc.com	MO	64105	816-221-5242	691-3805
Kansas City Kansas Convention & Visitors Bureau Inc 901 N Eigth St PO Box 171517 . . . . Kansas City *TF:* 800-264-1563 ■ *Web:* www.visitkansascityks.com	KS	66117	913-321-5800	371-3732
Chester County Tourist Bureau 300 Greenwood Rd . . . . Kennett Square *Web:* www.brandywinevalley.com	PA	19348	484-770-8550	770-8557
Tri-Cities Visitor & Convention Bureau 7130 W Grandridge Blvd Ste B . . . . Kennewick *TF:* 800-254-5824 ■ *Web:* www.visittri-cities.com	WA	99336	509-735-8486	783-9005
Kenosha Area Convention & Visitors Bureau 812 56th St . . . . Kenosha *TF:* 800-654-7309 ■ *Web:* www.kenoshacvb.com	WI	53140	262-654-7307	654-0882
Kerrville Convention & Visitors Bureau 2108 Sidney Baker St . . . . Kerrville *TF:* 800-221-7958 ■ *Web:* www.kerrvilletexascvb.com	TX	78028	830-792-3535	792-3230
Ketchikan Visitors Bureau 131 Front St . . . . Ketchikan *TF:* 800-770-3300 ■ *Web:* www.visit-ketchikan.com	AK	99901	907-225-6166	225-4250
Key West Visitors Ctr 510 Greene St 1st Fl . . . . Key West *TF General:* 800-533-5397 ■ *Web:* www.keywestchamber.org	FL	33040	305-294-2587	294-7806
Monroe County Tourist Development Council 1201 White St Ste 102 . . . . Key West *TF:* 800-242-5229 ■ *Web:* www.fla-keys.com	FL	33040	305-296-1552	296-6962
Killeen Civic & Conference Ctr & Visitors Bureau 3601 S WS Young Dr . . . . Killeen *Web:* www.visitkilleen.com	TX	76542	254-501-3888	
Valley Forge Convention & Visitors Bureau 1000 First Ave Ste 101 . . . . King of Prussia *TF General:* 888-847-4883 ■ *Web:* www.valleyforge.org	PA	19406	610-834-1550	834-0202
Kingsport Convention & Visitors Bureau (KCVB) 400 Clinchfield St Ste 100 . . . . Kingsport *TF:* 800-743-5282 ■ *Web:* www.visitkingsport.com	TN	37660	423-392-8820	392-8833
Kinston Convention & Visitors Bureau 301 N Queen St . . . . Kinston *TF:* 800-869-0032 ■ *Web:* www.visitkinston.com	NC	28501	252-523-2500	527-1914
Armstrong County Tourist Bureau 125 Market St Ste 2 . . . . Kittanning *TF:* 888-265-9954 ■ *Web:* www.armstrongcounty.com	PA	16201	724-543-4003	545-3119
Discover Klamath 205 Riverside Dr Ste B . . . . Klamath Falls *TF:* 800-445-6728 ■ *Web:* www.discoverklamath.com	OR	97601	541-882-1501	850-0125
Knoxville Tourism & Sports Corp 301 S Gay St . . . . Knoxville *TF:* 800-727-8045 ■ *Web:* visitknoxville.com/	TN	37902	865-523-7263	673-4400
Lake Barkley Tourist Commission 82 Days Inn Dr . . . . Kuttawa *TF:* 800-355-3885 ■ *Web:* www.lakebarkley.org	KY	42055	270-388-5300	388-5301
La Crosse Area Convention & Visitors Bureau 410 Veterans Memorial Dr . . . . La Crosse *TF:* 800-658-9424 ■ *Web:* www.explorelacrosse.com	WI	54601	608-782-2366	782-4082
Lafayette Convention & Visitors Commission 1400 NW Evangeline Thwy . . . . Lafayette *TF:* 800-346-1958 ■ *Web:* www.lafayettetravel.com	LA	70501	337-232-3737	232-0161
Lafayette-West Lafayette Convention & Visitors Bureau 301 Frontage Rd . . . . Lafayette *TF:* 800-872-6648 ■ *Web:* www.homeofpurdue.com	IN	47905	765-447-9999	447-5062
Laguna Beach Visitors & Conference Bureau 381 Forest Ave . . . . Laguna Beach *TF:* 800-877-1115 ■ *Web:* visitlagunabeach.com/	CA	92651	949-497-9229	376-0558
Southwest Louisiana Convention & Visitors Bureau 1205 N Lakeshore Dr . . . . Lake Charles *TF:* 800-456-7952 ■ *Web:* www.visitlakecharles.org	LA	70601	337-436-9588	494-7952
Seminole County Convention & Visitors Bureau 1515 International Pkwy Suite 1013 . . . . Lake Mary *TF:* 800-800-7832 ■ *Web:* www.visitseminole.com	FL	32746	407-665-2900	665-2920
Lake Placid Convention & Visitors Bureau 49 Parkside Dr . . . . Lake Placid *TF:* 800-447-5224 ■ *Web:* www.lakeplacid.com	NY	12946	518-523-2445	523-2605
Chicago Southland Convention & Visitors Bureau 2304 173rd St . . . . Lansing *TF:* 888-895-8233 ■ *Web:* www.cscvb.com	IL	60438	708-895-8200	895-8288
Greater Lansing Convention & Visitors Bureau 500 E Michigan Ave Ste 180 . . . . Lansing *TF:* 888-252-6746 ■ *Web:* www.lansing.org	MI	48912	517-487-0077	487-5151
Prince George's County Conference & Visitors Bureau 9200 Basil Ct Ste 101 . . . . Largo *Web:* www.visitprincegeorges.com	MD	20774	301-925-8300	925-2053
Las Cruces Convention & Visitors Bureau 211 N Water St . . . . Las Cruces *TF:* 800-429-9488 ■ *Web:* www.lascrucescvb.org	NM	88001	575-541-2444	541-2164
Las Vegas Convention & Visitors Authority 3150 Paradise Rd . . . . Las Vegas *TF:* 877-847-4858 ■ *Web:* www.lvcva.com	NV	89109	702-892-0711	837-0315
Leavenworth Convention & Visitors Bureau 518 Shawnee St PO Box 44 . . . . Leavenworth *TF:* 800-844-4114 ■ *Web:* www.visitleavenworthks.com	KS	66048	913-682-4113	682-8170
Boone County Convention & Visitors Bureau PO Box 644 . . . . Lebanon *Web:* www.boonecvb.com	IN	46052	765-484-8572	
Lenexa Convention & Visitors Bureau 11180 Lackman Rd . . . . Lenexa *Web:* www.lenexa.org	KS	66219	913-888-1414	888-3770
Greenbrier County Convention & Visitors Bureau 540 N Jefferson St Ste N . . . . Lewisburg *TF:* 800-833-2068 ■ *Web:* www.greenbrierwv.com	WV	24901	304-645-1000	647-3001
Juniata River Valley Visitors Bureau (JRVVB) Historic Courthouse 1 W Market St Ste 103 . . . . Lewistown *Web:* www.juniatarivervalley.org	PA	17044	717-248-6713	248-6714
Lexington Convention & Visitors Bureau 301 E Vine St . . . . Lexington *TF:* 800-845-3959 ■ *Web:* www.visitlex.com	KY	40507	859-233-7299	254-4555
Laurel Highlands Visitors Bureau 120 E Main St . . . . Ligonier *TF:* 800-333-5661 ■ *Web:* www.laurelhighlands.org	PA	15658	724-238-5661	238-3673
Lima/Allen County Convention & Visitors Bureau 144 S Main St Ste 101 . . . . Lima *TF:* 888-222-6075 ■ *Web:* www.lima-allencvb.com	OH	45801	419-222-6075	222-0134
Abraham Lincoln Tourism Bureau of Logan County 1555 Fifth St . . . . Lincoln *Web:* tourlogancounty.com	IL	62656	217-732-8687	735-9205
Lincoln Convention & Visitors Bureau 1135 M St Ste 300 . . . . Lincoln *TF:* 800-423-8212 ■ *Web:* www.lincoln.org	NE	68508	402-434-5335	436-2360
Lincoln City Visitor & Convention Bureau 801 SW Hwy 101 Ste 401 . . . . Lincoln City *TF:* 800-452-2151 ■ *Web:* www.oregoncoast.org	OR	97367	541-996-1274	994-2408
Lisle Convention & Visitors Bureau 925 Burlington Ave . . . . Lisle *TF:* 800-733-9811 ■ *Web:* stayinlisle.com	IL	60532	630-769-1000	769-1006
Western CT Convention & Visitors Bureau PO Box 968 . . . . Litchfield *Web:* www.northwestct.com	CT	06759	860-567-4506	567-5214
Little Rock Convention & Visitors Bureau 426 W Markham St PO Box 3232 . . . . Little Rock *TF:* 800-844-4781 ■ *Web:* www.littlerock.com	AR	72203	501-376-4781	374-2255

Name / Address	City	State	Zip	Phone	Fax
Lodi Conference & Visitors Bureau 115 S School St Ste 5 *TF:* 800-798-1810 ■ *Web:* www.visitlodi.com	Lodi	CA	95240	209-365-1195	365-1191
London/Laurel County Tourist Commission 140 Faith Assembly Church Rd *TF:* 800-348-0095 ■ *Web:* www.laurelkytourism.com	London	KY	40741	606-878-6900	877-1689
Long Beach Convention & Visitors Bureau 301 E Ocean Blvd *TF:* 800-452-7829 ■ *Web:* www.visitlongbeach.com	Long Beach	CA	90802	562-436-3645	435-5653
Cowlitz County Tourism 1900 Seventh Ave *Web:* www.visitmtsthelens.com	Longview	WA	98632	360-577-3137	578-2660
Los Angeles Convention & Visitors Bureau 333 S Hope St 18th Fl *Web:* www.discoverlosangeles.com	Los Angeles	CA	90071	213-624-7300	
Louisville & Jefferson County Convention & Visitors Bureau 401 W Main St Ste 2300 *TF:* 800-626-5646 ■ *Web:* www.gotolouisville.com	Louisville	KY	40202	502-584-2121	584-6697
Greater Merrimack Valley Convention & Visitors Bureau 40 French St Second Fl *TF:* 800-443-3332 ■ *Web:* www.merrimackvalley.org	Lowell	MA	01852	978-459-6150	459-4595
Lubbock Convention & Visitors Bureau 1500 Broadway St Sixth Fl *TF:* 800-692-4035 ■ *Web:* www.visitlubbock.org	Lubbock	TX	79401	806-747-5232	747-1419
Lumberton Area Visitors Bureau 3431 Lackey St *TF:* 800-359-6971 ■ *Web:* www.lumberton-nc.com	Lumberton	NC	28360	910-739-9999	739-9777
Mackinaw Area Visitors Bureau 10800 US 23 *TF:* 800-666-0160 ■ *Web:* www.mackinawcity.com	Mackinaw City	MI	49701	231-436-5664	436-5991
Macomb Area Convention & Visitors Bureau 201 S Lafayette St *Web:* www.makeitmacomb.com	Macomb	IL	61455	309-833-1315	833-3575
Macon-Bibb County Convention/Visitors Bureau 450 Martin Luther King Jr Blvd *TF:* 800-768-3401 ■ *Web:* www.maconga.org	Macon	GA	31201	478-743-1074	745-2022
Greater Madison Convention & Visitors Bureau 615 E Washington Ave *TF:* 800-373-6376 ■ *Web:* www.visitmadison.com	Madison	WI	53703	608-255-2537	258-4950
Madison Convention & Visitors Bureau 115 E Jefferson St *TF:* 800-709-7406 ■ *Web:* www.madisonga.org	Madison	GA	30650	706-342-4454	342-4455
Saint Tammany Parish Tourist & Convention Commission 68099 Hwy 59 *TF:* 800-634-9443 ■ *Web:* www.louisiananorthshore.com	Mandeville	LA	70471	985-892-0520	892-1441
Manhattan Convention & Visitors Bureau 501 Poyntz Ave *TF:* 800-759-0134 ■ *Web:* www.manhattancvb.org	Manhattan	KS	66502	785-776-8829	776-0679
Manitowoc Area Visitor & Convention Bureau PO Box 966 **Fax Area Code:* 920 ■ *TF:* 800-627-4896 ■ *Web:* www.manitowoc.info	Manitowoc	WI	54221	800-627-4896	683-4876*
Greater Mankato Growth 1961 Premier Dr *TF:* 800-697-0652 ■ *Web:* www.greatermankato.com	Mankato	MN	56001	507-385-6640	345-4451
Mansfield/Richland County Convention & Visitors Bureau 124 N Main St *TF:* 800-642-8282 ■ *Web:* www.mansfieldtourism.com	Mansfield	OH	44902	419-525-1300	524-7722
Outer Banks Visitors Bureau One Visitor Ctr Cir *TF:* 877-629-4386 ■ *Web:* www.outerbanks.org	Manteo	NC	27954	252-473-2138	473-5777
Marion-Grant County Convention & Visitors Bureau 428 S Washington St Ste 261 *TF:* 800-662-9474 ■ *Web:* www.showmegrantcounty.com	Marion	IN	46953	765-668-5435	668-5424
Williamson County Tourism Bureau 1602 Sioux Dr *TF General:* 800-433-7399 ■ *Web:* www.visitsi.com	Marion	IL	62959	618-997-3690	997-1874
Marquette Country Convention & Visitors Bureau 337 W Washington St *TF:* 800-544-4321 ■ *Web:* www.travelmarquettemichigan.com	Marquette	MI	49855	906-228-7749	228-3642
Marshall Area Convention & Visitors Bureau 317 W Main St *Web:* www.marshall-mn.org	Marshall	MN	56258	507-532-4484	532-4485
Marshfield Convention & Visitors Bureau 700 S Central Ave PO Box 868 *TF:* 800-422-4541 ■ *Web:* www.marshfieldchamber.com	Marshfield	WI	54449	715-384-3454	387-8925
Mason City Convention & Visitors Bureau 2021 Fourth St SW Hwy 122 W *TF:* 800-423-5724 ■ *Web:* www.visitmasoncityiowa.com	Mason City	IA	50401	641-422-1663	423-5725
Brandywine Conference & Visitors Bureau 1501 N Providence Rd *TF:* 800-343-3983 ■ *Web:* www.brandywinecvb.org	Media	PA	19063	610-565-3679	627-9207
Melbourne Regional Chamber of East Central Florida 1005 E Strawbridge Ave *TF:* 855-894-4673 ■ *Web:* melbourneregionalchamber.com/	Melbourne	FL	32901	321-724-5400	725-2093
Memphis Convention & Visitors Bureau 47 Union Ave *TF:* 888-633-9099 ■ *Web:* www.memphistravel.com	Memphis	TN	38103	901-543-5300	543-5350
Merced Conference & Visitors Bureau (MCVB) 710 W 16th St *TF:* 800-446-5353 ■ *Web:* visitmerced.travel	Merced	CA	95340	209-384-2791	
Meridian/Lauderdale County Tourism Bureau 212 Constitution Ave PO Box 5313 *TF:* 888-868-7720 ■ *Web:* www.visitmeridian.com	Meridian	MS	39301	601-482-8001	486-4988
Greater Miami Convention & Visitors Bureau 701 Brickell Ave Ste 2700 *TF:* 800-933-8448 ■ *Web:* www.miamiandbeaches.com	Miami	FL	33131	305-539-3000	530-5859
LaPorte County Convention & Visitors Bureau 4073 S Franklin St *TF:* 800-634-2650 ■ *Web:* www.michigancitylaporte.com	Michigan City	IN	46360	219-872-5055	872-3660
Middletown Convention-Visitors (MCVB) 4935 Riverview Ave *Web:* gettothebc.com	Middletown	OH	45042	513-422-3030	
Midland County Convention & Visitors Bureau 300 Rodd St Ste 101 *TF:* 800-444-9979 ■ *Web:* gogreat.com/	Midland	MI	48640	989-839-0340	835-3701
Visit Milledgeville 200 W Hancock St *TF:* 800-653-1804 ■ *Web:* www.visitmilledgeville.org	Milledgeville	GA	31061	478-452-4687	453-4440
Greater Milwaukee Convention & Visitors Bureau 648 N Plankinton Ave Ste 425 *TF:* 800-554-1448 ■ *Web:* www.visitmilwaukee.org	Milwaukee	WI	53203	414-273-7222	273-5596
Meet Minneapolis 250 Marquette Ave Ste 1300 *TF:* 800-445-7412 ■ *Web:* www.minneapolis.org	Minneapolis	MN	55401	612-767-8000	335-5839
Minot Convention & Visitors Bureau 1020 S Broadway *TF:* 800-264-2626 ■ *Web:* www.visitminot.org	Minot	ND	58701	701-857-8206	857-8228
Modesto Convention & Visitors Bureau 1150 Ninth St Ste C *TF:* 888-640-8467 ■ *Web:* www.visitmodesto.com	Modesto	CA	95354	209-526-5588	526-5586
Quad Cities Convention & Visitors Bureau 1601 River Dr Ste 110 *TF:* 800-747-7800 ■ *Web:* www.visitquadcities.com	Moline	IL	61265	309-277-0937	764-9443
Monterey County Convention & Visitors Bureau PO Box 1770 *TF:* 888-221-1010 ■ *Web:* www.seemonterey.com	Monterey	CA	93942	831-657-6400	648-5373
Montgomery Area Chamber of Commerce Convention & Visitor Bureau 300 Water St *TF:* 800-240-9452 ■ *Web:* www.visitingmontgomery.com	Montgomery	AL	36104	334-261-1100	261-1111
Montrose Visitor & Convention Bureau 1519 E Main St *TF:* 888-212-8294 ■ *Web:* www.visitmontrose.com	Montrose	CO	81401	970-249-5000	964-4073
Greater Morgantown Convention & Visitors Bureau 68 Donley St *TF:* 800-458-7373 ■ *Web:* www.tourmorgantown.com	Morgantown	WV	26501	304-292-5081	291-1354
Knox County Convention & Visitors Bureau 107 S Main St *TF:* 800-837-5282 ■ *Web:* www.visitknoxohio.org	Mount Vernon	OH	43050	740-392-6102	392-7840
Mount Vernon Convention & Visitors Bureau 200 Potomac Blvd *TF:* 800-252-5464 ■ *Web:* www.mtvernon.com	Mount Vernon	IL	62864	618-242-3151	242-6849
Muncie Visitors Bureau 3700 S Madison St *TF:* 800-568-6862 ■ *Web:* visitmuncie.org/muncie-sports-plex/	Muncie	IN	47302	765-284-2700	284-3002
Muskegon County Convention & Visitors Bureau 610 W Western Ave *TF:* 800-250-9283 ■ *Web:* www.visitmuskegon.org	Muskegon	MI	49440	231-724-3100	724-1398
Myrtle Beach Area Convention Bureau 1200 N Oak St *TF:* 800-356-3016 ■ *Web:* www.visitmyrtlebeach.com	Myrtle Beach	SC	29577	843-626-7444	448-3010
Nacogdoches Convention & Visitors Bureau 200 E Main St *TF:* 888-653-3788 ■ *Web:* www.visitnacogdoches.org	Nacogdoches	TX	75961	936-564-7351	462-7688
Napa Valley Conference & Visitors Bureau 600 Main St *Web:* www.visitnapavalley.com	Napa	CA	94559	707-251-5895	
Greater Naples Marco Island Everglades Convention & Visitors Bureau 2800 Horseshoe Dr *TF:* 800-688-3600 ■ *Web:* www.paradisecoast.com	Naples	FL	34104	239-252-2384	252-2404
Brown County Convention & Visitors Bureau 10 N Van Buren St PO Box 840 *TF:* 800-753-3255 ■ *Web:* www.browncounty.com	Nashville	IN	47448	812-988-7303	988-1070
Nashville Convention & Visitors Bureau (NCVB) 150 Fourth Ave N Ste G250 *TF:* 800-657-6910 ■ *Web:* www.visitmusiccity.com	Nashville	TN	37219	615-259-4730	259-4126
Natchez Convention & Visitors Bureau 640 S Canal St *TF:* 800-647-6724 ■ *Web:* www.visitnatchez.org	Natchez	MS	39120	601-446-6345	442-0814
Craven County Convention & Visitors Bureau 203 S Front St *TF:* 800-437-5767 ■ *Web:* www.visitnewbern.com	New Bern	NC	28560	252-637-9400	637-0250
Greater New Braunfels Chamber of Commerce Inc, The 390 S Seguin Ave PO Box 311417 *TF:* 800-572-2626 ■ *Web:* innewbraunfels.com	New Braunfels	TX	78130	830-625-2385	625-7918
Lawrence County Tourist Promotion Agency 229 S Jefferson St *TF:* 888-284-7599 ■ *Web:* www.visitlawrencecounty.com	New Castle	PA	16101	724-654-8408	654-2044
Jefferson Convention & Visitors Bureau 1221 Elmwood Pk Blvd Ste 411 *TF:* 877-572-7474 ■ *Web:* www.experiencejefferson.com	New Orleans	LA	70123	504-731-7083	731-7089
New Orleans Metropolitan Convention & Visitors Bureau 2020 St Charles Ave *TF:* 800-672-6124 ■ *Web:* www.neworleanscvb.com	New Orleans	LA	70130	504-566-5011	566-5046
NYC & Co 810 Seventh Ave Third Fl *Web:* www.nycgo.com	New York	NY	10019	212-484-1200	397-1931
Newberry Area Tourism Assn, The PO Box 308 *TF:* 800-831-7292 ■ *Web:* www.newberrytourism.com	Newberry	MI	49868	906-293-5562	
Newport County Convention & Visitors Bureau 23 America's Cup Ave *TF:* 800-976-5122 ■ *Web:* discovernewport.org/	Newport	RI	02840	401-849-8048	849-0291
Newport Beach Conference & Visitors Bureau 1200 Newport Ctr Dr Ste 120 *TF:* 800-942-6278 ■ *Web:* www.visitnewportbeach.com	Newport Beach	CA	92660	949-719-6100	719-6101
Newport News Tourism Development Office 700 Town Ctr Dr Ste 320 *TF:* 888-493-7386 ■ *Web:* www.newport-news.org	Newport News	VA	23606	757-926-1400	926-1441
Newton Convention & Visitor Bureau 300 E 17th St S Ste 400 *TF:* 800-798-0299 ■ *Web:* www.visitnewton.com	Newton	IA	50208	641-792-0299	791-0879
Niagara Tourism & Convention Corp 10 Rainbow Blvd *TF:* 877-325-5787 ■ *Web:* www.niagara-usa.com	Niagara Falls	NY	14303	716-282-8992	285-0809
Nome Convention & Visitors Bureau 301 Front St PO Box 240 HP-N *Web:* www.visitnomealaska.com	Nome	AK	99762	907-443-6624	443-5832
Norfolk Area Chamber of Commerce 405 Madison Ave *Web:* www.norfolk.ne.us	Norfolk	NE	68701	402-371-4862	371-0182
Norfolk Convention & Visitors Bureau 232 E Main St *TF:* 800-368-3097 ■ *Web:* www.visitnorfolktoday.com	Norfolk	VA	23510	757-664-6620	622-3663

Bureau / Address	City	State	Zip	Phone	Fax
Norman Convention & Visitors Bureau 309 E Main St *TF:* 800-767-7260 ■ *Web:* www.visitnorman.com	Norman	OK	73069	405-366-8095	366-8096
Greater New Haven Convention & Visitors Bureau 127 Washington Ave *Web:* rexdevelopment.org	North Haven	CT	06473	203-777-8550	782-7755
Lincoln County Convention & Visitor's Bureau 315 W Eugene Ave *Web:* www.visitnorthplatte.com	North Platte	NE	69101	308-532-4729	532-5914
North Ridgeville Visitors Bureau 34845 Lorain Rd *Web:* www.nrchamber.com	North Ridgeville	OH	44039	440-327-3737	327-1474
DuPage Convention & Visitors Bureau 915 Harger Rd Ste 240 *TF:* 800-232-0502 ■ *Web:* www.discoverdupage.com	Oak Brook	IL	60523	630-575-8070	575-8078
Oak Park Area Convention & Visitors Bureau 1118 Westgate *TF:* 888-625-7275 ■ *Web:* www.visitoakpark.com	Oak Park	IL	60301	708-524-7800	524-7473
Oak Ridge Convention & Visitors Bureau 102 Robertsville Rd Ste C *TF:* 800-887-3429 ■ *Web:* www.oakridgevisitor.com	Oak Ridge	TN	37830	865-482-7821	481-3543
Yosemite Sierra Visitors Bureau 40637 Hwy 41 *Web:* www.yosemitethisyear.com	Oakhurst	CA	93644	559-683-4636	683-5697
Oakland Convention & Visitors Bureau 481 Water St *Web:* www.visitoakland.org	Oakland	CA	94607	510-839-9000	839-5924
Ocean City Convention & Visitors Bureau 4001 Coastal Hwy *TF:* 800-626-2326 ■ *Web:* www.ococean.com	Ocean City	MD	21842	410-289-8181	723-8655
Oconomowoc Convention & Visitors Bureau 174 E Wisconsin Ave *TF:* 888-936-7463 ■ *Web:* www.oconomowoc-wi.gov	Oconomowoc	WI	53066	262-569-2186	569-2164
Odessa Convention & Visitors Bureau 700 N Grant Ave Ste 200 *TF:* 800-780-4678 ■ *Web:* www.odessacvb.com	Odessa	TX	79761	432-333-7871	333-7858
Ogden/Weber Convention & Visitors Bureau 2438 Washington Blvd *TF:* 800-255-8824 ■ *Web:* www.visitogden.com	Ogden	UT	84401	801-778-6250	399-0783
Oklahoma City Convention & Visitors Bureau 123 Pk Ave *TF:* 800-225-5652 ■ *Web:* www.visitokc.com	Oklahoma City	OK	73102	405-297-8912	297-8888
McDowell County Tourism Development Authority 25 W Main St *TF:* 888-233-6111 ■ *Web:* www.mcdowellnc.org	Old Fort	NC	28762	828-668-4282	668-4924
Olympia Lacey Tumwater Visitor & Convention Bureau 103 Sid Snyder Ave SW *TF:* 877-704-7500 ■ *Web:* www.visitolympia.com	Olympia	WA	98501	360-704-7544	704-7533
Greater Omaha Convention & Visitors Bureau 1001 Farnam St Ste 200 *TF:* 866-937-6624 ■ *Web:* www.visitomaha.com	Omaha	NE	68102	402-444-4660	444-4511
Onalaska Ctr for Commerce & Tourism 1101 Main St *TF:* 800-873-1901 ■ *Web:* www.discoveronalaska.com	Onalaska	WI	54650	608-781-9570	781-9572
Ontario Convention & Visitors Bureau 2000 E Convention Ctr Way *TF:* 800-455-5755 ■ *Web:* www.ontariocc.org	Ontario	CA	91764	909-937-3000	937-3080
Orlando/Orange County Convention & Visitors Bureau Inc 6700 Forum Dr Ste 100 *TF:* 800-972-3304 ■ *Web:* www.visitorlando.com	Orlando	FL	32821	407-363-5872	370-5000
Lake of the Ozarks Convention & Visitors Bureau 5815 Hwy 54 PO Box 1498 *TF:* 800-386-5253 ■ *Web:* www.funlake.com	Osage Beach	MO	65065	573-348-1599	348-2293
Ottawa Tourism & Convention Authority 130 Albert St Ste 1800 *TF:* 800-363-4465 ■ *Web:* www.ottawatourism.ca	Ottawa	ON	K1P5G4	613-237-5150	237-7339
Ottawa Visitors Ctr 106 W Lafayette St *TF:* 888-688-2924 ■ *Web:* pickusottawail.com	Ottawa	IL	61350	815-434-2737	434-4530
Overland Park Convention & Visitors Bureau 9001 W 110th St Ste 100 *TF:* 800-262-7275 ■ *Web:* www.visitoverlandpark.com	Overland Park	KS	66210	913-491-0123	491-0015
Owensboro-Davies County Tourist Commission 215 E Second St *TF:* 800-489-1131 ■ *Web:* www.visitowensboro.com	Owensboro	KY	42303	270-926-1100	926-1161
Oxford Convention & Visitors Bureau 102 Ed Perry Blvd *TF:* 800-758-9177 ■ *Web:* visitoxfordms.com	Oxford	MS	38655	662-232-2367	
Oxnard Convention & Visitors Bureau 1000 Town Ctr Dr Ste 130 *TF:* 800-269-6273 ■ *Web:* www.visitoxnard.com	Oxnard	CA	93036	805-385-7545	385-7571
Panama City Beach Convention & Visitors Bureau 17001 Panama City Beach Pkwy *TF:* 800-722-3224 ■ *Web:* www.visitpanamacitybeach.com	Panama City Beach	FL	32413	850-233-5070	233-5072
Park City Chamber of Commerce/Convention & Visitors Bureau 1910 Prospector Ave PO Box 1630 *TF:* 800-453-1360 ■ *Web:* www.visitparkcity.com	Park City	UT	84060	435-649-6100	649-4132
Greater Parkersburg Convention & Visitors Bureau 350 Seventh St *TF:* 800-752-4982 ■ *Web:* www.greaterparkersburg.com	Parkersburg	WV	26101	304-428-1130	428-8117
Pasadena Convention & Visitors Bureau 300 E Green St *TF:* 800-307-7977 ■ *Web:* www.visitpasadena.com	Pasadena	CA	91101	626-795-9311	795-9656
Pensacola Convention & Visitors Bureau 1401 E Gregory St *TF:* 800-874-1234 ■ *Web:* www.visitpensacola.com	Pensacola	FL	32502	850-434-1234	432-8211
Peoria Area Convention & Visitors Bureau 456 Fulton St Ste 300 *TF:* 800-747-0302 ■ *Web:* www.peoria.org	Peoria	IL	61602	309-676-0303	676-8470
Perry Area Convention & Visitors Bureau 101 Gen Courtney Hodges Blvd PO Box 1609 *Web:* www.perryga.com	Perry	GA	31069	478-988-8000	988-8005
Petoskey Area Visitors Bureau 401 E Mitchell St *TF:* 800-845-2828 ■ *Web:* www.petoskeyarea.com	Petoskey	MI	49770	231-348-2755	348-1810
Philadelphia Convention & Visitors Bureau 1700 Market St Ste 3000 *Web:* www.discoverphl.com	Philadelphia	PA	19103	215-636-3300	636-3327
Greater Phoenix Convention & Visitors Bureau 400 E Van Buren St Ste 600 *TF:* 877-225-5749 ■ *Web:* www.visitphoenix.com	Phoenix	AZ	85004	602-254-6500	253-4415
Pigeon Forge Dept of Tourism P.O. Box 1390 *TF:* 800-251-9100 ■ *Web:* www.mypigeonforge.com	Pigeon Forge	TN	37868	865-453-8574	429-7362
Pine Bluff Convention & Visitors Bureau (PBCVB) One Convention Ctr Plz *TF:* 800-536-7660 ■ *Web:* www.pinebluffcvb.org	Pine Bluff	AR	71601	870-536-7600	850-2105
Greater Pittsburgh Convention & Visitors Bureau 120 Fifth Ave Fifth Ave Pl, 1st Level *TF:* 800-359-0758 ■ *Web:* www.visitpittsburgh.com	Pittsburgh	PA	15222	412-281-7711	644-5512
Plano Convention & Visitors Bureau 2000 E Spring Creek Pkwy *TF:* 800-817-5266 ■ *Web:* www.visitplano.com	Plano	TX	75074	972-941-5840	424-0002
Ponca City Tourism 420 E Grand Ave PO Box 1109 *TF:* 866-763-8092 ■ *Web:* www.poncacitytourism.com	Ponca City	OK	74602	580-765-4400	765-2798
North Olympic Peninsula Visitor & Convention Bureau 338 W First St Ste 104 PO Box 670 *TF:* 800-942-4042 ■ *Web:* www.olympicpeninsula.org	Port Angeles	WA	98362	360-452-8552	452-7383
Port Arthur Convention & Visitors Bureau 3401 Cultural Ctr Dr *TF:* 800-235-7822 ■ *Web:* www.portarthurtexas.com	Port Arthur	TX	77642	409-985-7822	985-5584
Lake Erie Shores & Islands Welcome Ctr 770 SE Catawba Rd *TF:* 800-441-1271 ■ *Web:* www.shoresandislands.com	Port Clinton	OH	43452	419-734-4386	734-9798
Indiana Dunes the Casual Coast 1215 N State Rd 49 *TF:* 800-283-8687 ■ *Web:* www.indianadunes.com	Porter	IN	46304	219-926-2255	929-5395
Greater Portland Convention & Visitors Bureau 94 Commercial St Ste 300 *Web:* www.visitportland.com	Portland	ME	04101	207-772-4994	874-9043
Travel Portland 1000 SW Broadway Ste 2300 *TF:* 800-962-3700 ■ *Web:* www.travelportland.com	Portland	OR	97205	503-275-9750	275-9774
Providence Warwick Convention & Visitors Bureau 10 Memorial Blvd *TF:* 800-233-1636 ■ *Web:* www.goprovidence.com	Providence	RI	02903	401-456-0200	351-2090
Utah Valley Convention & Visitors Bureau 111 S University Ave *TF:* 800-222-8824 ■ *Web:* www.utahvalley.com	Provo	UT	84601	801-851-2100	851-2109
Plumas County Visitors Bureau 550 Crescent St *TF:* 800-326-2247 ■ *Web:* www.plumascounty.org	Quincy	CA	95971	530-283-6345	283-5465
Quincy Area Convention & Visitors Bureau (QACVB) 532 Gardner Expy *TF:* 800-978-4748 ■ *Web:* www.seequincy.com	Quincy	IL	62301	217-214-3700	
Greater Raleigh Convention & Visitors Bureau 421 Fayetteville St Mall Ste 1505 *TF:* 800-849-8499 ■ *Web:* www.visitraleigh.com	Raleigh	NC	27602	919-834-5900	831-2887
Palm Springs Desert Resorts Convention & Visitors Authority 70-100 Hwy 111 *TF:* 800-967-3767 ■ *Web:* www.visitgreaterpalmsprings.com	Rancho Mirage	CA	92270	760-770-9000	779-9001
Rapid City Convention & Visitors Bureau 444 Mt Rushmore Rd N *TF:* 800-487-3223 ■ *Web:* www.visitrapidcity.com	Rapid City	SD	57701	605-718-8484	348-9217
Reading & Berks County Visitors Bureau 2525 N 12th St Ste 101 *TF:* 800-443-6610 ■ *Web:* www.gogreaterreading.com	Reading	PA	19605	610-375-4085	375-9606
Rehoboth Beach Convention Ctr 229 Rehoboth Ave *TF:* 888-743-3628 ■ *Web:* www.cityofrehoboth.com	Rehoboth Beach	DE	19971	302-227-4641	227-4643
Reno-Sparks Convention & Visitors Authority PO Box 837 *TF:* 800-443-1482 ■ *Web:* www.visitrenotahoe.com	Reno	NV	89504	775-827-7600	827-7678
Richardson Convention & Visitors Bureau 411 W Arapaho Rd Ste 105 *TF:* 888-690-7287 ■ *Web:* www.richardsontexas.org	Richardson	TX	75080	972-744-4034	744-5834
Richmond Metropolitan Convention & Visitors Bureau 401 N Third St *TF:* 800-370-9004 ■ *Web:* visitrichmondva.com	Richmond	VA	23219	804-782-2777	780-2577
Richmond/Wayne County Convention & Tourism Bureau 5701 National Rd E *TF:* 800-828-8414 ■ *Web:* www.visitrichmond.org	Richmond	IN	47374	765-935-8687	935-0440
Ridgecrest Area Convention & Visitors Bureau (RACVB) 139 Balsam St Ste 1700 *TF:* 800-847-4830 ■ *Web:* www.visitdeserts.com	Ridgecrest	CA	93555	760-375-8202	375-9850
Rising Sun/Ohio County Convention Tourism & Visitors Commission 120 N Walnut St PO Box 112 *Web:* www.enjoyrisingsun.com	Rising Sun	IN	47040	812-438-4933	438-4932
Riverside Convention & Visitors Bureau 3750 University Ave Ste 175 *TF:* 888-748-7733 ■ *Web:* www.riversidecvb.com	Riverside	CA	92501	951-222-4700	222-4712
Roanoke Valley Convention & Visitors Bureau 101 Shenandoah Ave NE *TF:* 800-635-5535 ■ *Web:* www.visitroanokeva.com	Roanoke	VA	24016	540-342-6025	342-7119
Tunica County Convention & Visitors Bureau 13625 Hwy 61 N **Fax Area Code:* 662 ■ *TF:* 888-488-6422 ■ *Web:* www.tunicatravel.com	Robinsonville	MS	38664	888-488-6422	363-1493*
Rochester Convention & Visitors Bureau 30 Civic Ctr Dr SE Ste 200 *TF:* 800-634-8277 ■ *Web:* www.rochestercvb.org	Rochester	MN	55904	507-288-4331	288-9144
Visit Rochester 45 E Ave Ste 400 *TF:* 800-677-7282 ■ *Web:* www.visitrochester.com	Rochester	NY	14604	585-279-8300	232-4822
Rockhill-York County Convention & Visitors Bureau 452 S Anderson Rd *TF:* 888-702-1320 ■ *Web:* www.visityorkcounty.com	Rock Hill	SC	29730	803-329-5200	329-0145
Rockford Area Convention & Visitors Bureau 102 N Main St *TF:* 800-521-0849 ■ *Web:* www.gorockford.com	Rockford	IL	61101	815-963-8111	963-4298

				Phone	Fax

Conference & Visitors Bureau of Montgomery County MD Inc
111 Rockville Pk Ste 800 .... Rockville MD 20850 240-777-2060 777-2065
TF: 877-789-6904 ■ *Web:* www.visitmontgomery.com

Greater Rome Convention & Visitors Bureau
402 Civics Ctr Dr .... Rome GA 30161 706-295-5576 236-5029
TF: 800-444-1834 ■ *Web:* www.romegeorgia.org

Rosemont Convention Bureau
9301 Bryn Mawr Ave .... Rosemont IL 60018 847-823-2100 696-9700
Web: www.rosemont.com

Historic Roswell Convention & Visitors Bureau
617 Atlanta St.................................... Roswell GA 30075 770-640-3253 640-3252
TF: 800-776-7935 ■ *Web:* www.visitroswellga.com

Wausau Central Wisconsin Convention & Visitors Bureau (CWCVB)
10204 Pk Plz Ste B............................Rothschild WI 54474 715-355-8788 359-2306
TF: 888-948-4748 ■ *Web:* www.visitwausau.com

Sacramento Convention & Visitors Bureau
1608 'I' St .... Sacramento CA 95814 916-808-7777 808-7788
TF: 800-292-2334 ■ *Web:* visitsacramento.com/

Greater Saint Charles Convention & Visitors Bureau
230 S Main St................................Saint Charles MO 63301 636-946-7776 949-3217
TF: 800-366-2427 ■ *Web:* www.historicstcharles.com

Saint Cloud Area Convention & Visitors Bureau
525 Hwy 10 S Ste 1 .... Saint Cloud MN 56304 320-251-4170 656-0401
TF: 800-264-2940 ■ *Web:* www.granitecountry.com

Saint Joseph Convention & Visitors Bureau
109 S Fourth St .... Saint Joseph MO 64501 816-233-6688 233-9120
TF: 800-785-0360 ■ *Web:* www.stjomo.com

Auglaize & Mercer Counties Convention & Visitors Bureau
900 Edgewater Dr .... Saint Marys OH 45885 419-394-1294 394-1642
TF: 800-860-4726 ■ *Web:* www.seemore.org

Saint Paul RiverCentre Convention & Visitors Authority
175 W Kellogg Blvd .... Saint Paul MN 55102 651-265-4800
Web: www.rivercentre.org

City Of Salem 101 S Broadway .... Salem IL 62881 618-548-2222 548-5330
Web: www.salemil.us

Salem Convention & Visitors Assn
181 High St NE.................................... Salem OR 97301 503-581-4325 581-4540
TF: 800-874-7012 ■ *Web:* www.travelsalem.com

North of Boston Convention & Visitors Bureau (NBCVB)
I-95 Southbound Exit 60 PO Box 5193................Salisbury MA 01952 978-465-6555 977-7758
Web: www.northofboston.org

Rowan County Convention & Visitors Bureau
204 E Innes St Ste 120............................Salisbury NC 28144 704-638-3100 642-2011
TF: 800-332-2343 ■ *Web:* www.visitsalisburync.com

Salt Lake Convention & Visitors Bureau
90 SW Temple.............................. Salt Lake City UT 84101 801-534-4900 541-4955*
**Fax Area Code:* 800 ■ *TF:* 800-541-4955 ■ *Web:* www.visitsaltlake.com

San Angelo Chamber of Commerce
418 W Ave B.................................... San Angelo TX 76903 325-655-4136 658-1110
TF: 800-252-1381 ■ *Web:* www.sanangelo.org

San Antonio Convention & Visitors Bureau
203 S St Marys St Ste 200.......................San Antonio TX 78205 210-207-6700 207-6768
TF: 800-447-3372 ■ *Web:* www.visitsanantonio.com

San Bernardino Convention & Visitors Bureau
1955 Hunts Ln Ste 102....................... San Bernardino CA 92408 909-891-1151 891-1873
TF: 800-867-8366 ■ *Web:* www.san-bernardino.org

San Diego Convention & Visitors Bureau
2215 India St .... San Diego CA 92101 619-232-3101 696-9371
Web: www.sandiego.org

San Francisco Convention & Visitors Bureau
201 Third St Ste 900......................... San Francisco CA 94103 415-974-6900 227-2602
TF: 855-847-6272 ■ *Web:* www.sanfrancisco.travel

San Jose Convention & Visitors Bureau
408 Almaden Blvd .... San Jose CA 95110 408-295-9600 277-3535
TF: 800-726-5673 ■ *Web:* www.sanjose.org

Puerto Rico Convention Bureau
100 Convention Blvd .... San Juan PR 00907 787-725-2110 725-2133
TF: 800-214-0420 ■ *Web:* www.prconvention.com

Marin Convention & Visitors Bureau
1 Mitchell Blvd Ste B .... San Rafael CA 94903 415-925-2060 925-2063
TF: 866-925-2060 ■ *Web:* www.visitmarin.org

Santa Barbara Visitors Bureau & Film Commission
1601 Anacapa St............................ Santa Barbara CA 93101 805-966-9222 966-1728
TF: 800-676-1266 ■ *Web:* www.santabarbaraca.com

Santa Clara Convention/Visitors Bureau
1850 Warburton Ave............................ Santa Clara CA 95050 408-244-9660 244-9202
TF: 800-272-6822 ■ *Web:* www.santaclara.org

Santa Cruz County Conference & Visitors Council
303 Water St Ste 100 ....Santa Cruz CA 95060 831-425-1234 425-1260
TF: 800-833-3494 ■ *Web:* www.santacruz.org

Santa Fe Convention Ctr 201 W Marcy St .... Santa Fe NM 87501 505-955-6200 955-6222
TF: 800-777-2489 ■ *Web:* www.santafe.org

Santa Maria Valley Convention & Visitors Bureau
614 S Broadway ....Santa Maria CA 93454 805-925-2403 928-7559
Web: www.santamaria.com

Santa Monica Convention & Visitors Bureau
1920 Main St Ste B........................... Santa Monica CA 90405 310-319-6263 319-6273
TF: 800-544-5319 ■ *Web:* www.santamonica.com

Visit Sarasota County 1777 Main St Ste 302 .... Sarasota FL 34236 941-955-0991 951-2956
TF: 800-522-9799 ■ *Web:* www.visitsarasota.org

Saratoga Convention & Tourism Bureau
60 Railroad Pl Ste 301 ....Saratoga Springs NY 12866 518-584-1531 584-2969
Web: www.discoversaratoga.org

Sault Sainte Marie Convention & Visitors Bureau
1808 Ashmun St...........................Sault Sainte Marie MI 49783 906-632-3366 632-6161
TF: 800-647-2858 ■ *Web:* www.saultstemarie.com

Savannah Area Convention & Visitors Bureau
101 E Bay St.................................... Savannah GA 31401 912-644-6400 644-6499
TF: 877-728-2662 ■ *Web:* www.visitsavannah.com

Greater Woodfield Convention & Visitors Bureau
1375 E Woodfield Rd Ste 120..................... Schaumburg IL 60173 847-490-1010 490-1212
TF: 800-847-4849 ■ *Web:* www.chicagonorthwest.com

Scottsdale Convention & Visitors Bureau
4343 N Scottsdale Rd Ste 170 .... Scottsdale AZ 85251 480-421-1004 421-9733
TF: 800-782-1117 ■ *Web:* www.experiencescottsdale.com

Lackawanna County Convention & Visitors Bureau
99 Glenmaura National Blvd....................... Scranton PA 18507 570-496-1701
TF: 800-229-3526 ■ *Web:* www.visitnepa.org

Seattle's Convention & Visitors Bureau
701 Pike St Ste 800 .... Seattle WA 98101 206-461-5800 461-5855
TF: 866-732-2695 ■ *Web:* www.visitseattle.org

Seward Convention & Visitors Bureau
2001 Seward Hwy................................... Seward AK 99664 907-224-8051 224-5353
Web: seward.com/

Visit MercerCounty PA 50 N Water Ave ....Sharon PA 16146 724-346-3771 346-0575
TF: 800-637-2370 ■ *Web:* www.visitmercercountypa.com

Shelby County Office of Tourism
315 E Main St...................................Shelbyville IL 62565 217-774-2244 774-2224
TF: 800-874-3529 ■ *Web:* www.lakeshelbyville.com

Shepherdsville-Bullitt County Tourist & Convention Commission
395 Paroquet Springs Dr ....Shepherdsville KY 40165 502-543-8687 543-4889
TF: 800-526-2068 ■ *Web:* www.travelbullitt.org

Shipshewana/LaGrange County Convention & Visitors Bureau
350 S Van Buren St Ste H.......................Shipshewana IN 46565 260-768-4008 768-4091
TF: 800-254-8090 ■ *Web:* www.backroads.org

Shreveport-Bossier Convention & Tourist Bureau
629 Spring St...................................Shreveport LA 71101 318-222-9391 222-0056
TF: 800-551-8682 ■ *Web:* www.shreveport-bossier.org

Sioux City Tourism Bureau 801 Fourth St .... Sioux City IA 51101 712-279-4800 279-4900
TF: 800-593-2228 ■ *Web:* www.visitsiouxcity.org

Sioux Falls Convention & Visitors Bureau
200 N Phillips Ave Ste 102...................... Sioux Falls SD 57104 605-336-1620 336-6499
TF: 800-333-2072 ■ *Web:* visitsiouxfalls.com

Sitka Convention & Visitors Bureau
303 Lincoln St Ste 4................................. Sitka AK 99835 907-747-5940 747-3739
TF: 800-557-4852 ■ *Web:* www.sitka.org

Skagway Visitor Information
245 Broadway PO Box 1029........................ Skagway AK 99840 907-983-2855 983-3854
TF: 888-762-1898 ■ *Web:* www.skagway.com

Johnston County Convention & Visitors Bureau
235 E Market St .... Smithfield NC 27577 919-989-8687 989-6295
TF: 800-441-7829 ■ *Web:* www.johnstoncountync.org

South Bend/Mishawaka Convention & Visitors Bureau
401 E Colfax Ave Ste 310........................ South Bend IN 46617 574-234-0051 289-0358
TF: 800-519-0577 ■ *Web:* www.visitsouthbend.com

Lake Tahoe Visitors Authority
3066 Lk Tahoe Blvd .... South Lake Tahoe CA 96150 530-544-5050
TF: 800-288-2463 ■ *Web:* www.tahoesouth.com

South Padre Island Convention & Visitors Bureau
7355 Padre Blvd........................ South Padre Island TX 78597 956-761-6433 761-9462
TF: 800-767-2373 ■ *Web:* www.sopadre.com

South Sioux City Convention & Visitors Bureau
3900 Dakota Ave Ste 11 .... South Sioux City NE 68776 402-494-1307 494-5010
TF: 866-494-1307 ■ *Web:* visitsouthsiouxcity.com

Convention & Visitors Bureau-Village of Pinehurst Southern Pines Aberdeen Area
10677 Hwy 15-501.......................... Southern Pines NC 28387 910-692-3330 692-2493
TF: 800-346-5362 ■ *Web:* www.homeofgolf.com

Spartanburg Convention & Visitors Bureau
298 Magnolia St.................................Spartanburg SC 29306 864-594-5050
Web: www.visitspartanburg.com

Spokane Convention & Visitors Bureau
801 W Riverside Ste 301 .... Spokane WA 99201 509-624-1341 623-1297
TF: 800-662-0084 ■ *Web:* www.visitspokane.com

Central Illinois Tourism Development Office
700 E Adams St ....Springfield IL 62701 217-525-7980 525-8004
Web: visitlandoflincoln.com

Greater Springfield Convention & Visitors Bureau
1441 Main St ....Springfield MA 01103 413-787-1548 781-4607
TF: 800-723-1548 ■ *Web:* www.valleyvisitor.com

Springfield Convention & Visitors Bureau
109 N Seventh St ....Springfield IL 62701 217-789-2360 544-8711
TF: 800-545-7300 ■ *Web:* www.visitspringfieldillinois.com

Springfield Missouri Convention & Visitors Bureau
815 E St Louis St Ste 100........................Springfield MO 65806 417-881-5300 881-2231
TF: 800-678-8767 ■ *Web:* www.springfieldmo.org

Centre County Convention & Visitors Bureau
800 E Pk Ave...................................State College PA 16803 814-231-1400 231-8123
TF: 800-358-5466 ■ *Web:* www.visitpennstate.org

Stevens Point Area Convention & Visitors Bureau
340 Div St N................................... Stevens Point WI 54481 715-344-2556 344-5818
Web: www.stevenspointarea.com

Pocono Mountains Vacation Bureau
1004 Main St .... Stroudsburg PA 18360 570-421-5791 421-6927
TF: 800-722-9199 ■ *Web:* www.800poconos.com

Racine County Convention & Visitors Bureau
14015 Washington Ave........................... Sturtevant WI 53177 262-884-6400 884-6404
TF: 800-272-2463 ■ *Web:* realracine.com

Superior/Douglas County Convention & Visitors Bureau
305 Harborview Pkwy............................. Superior WI 54880 715-392-7151 392-3810
TF: 800-942-5313 ■ *Web:* www.superiorchamber.org

Tacoma Regional Convention & Visitor Bureau
1516 Pacific Ave Ste 500 .... Tacoma WA 98402 253-627-2836 627-8783
TF: 800-272-2662 ■ *Web:* www.traveltacoma.com

North Lake Tahoe Resort Assn
100 N Lake Blvd ....Tahoe City CA 96145 530-581-6900 581-1686
TF: 800-824-6348 ■ *Web:* www.gotahoenorth.com

North Lake Tahoe Visitors & Convention Bureau
PO Box 1757 ....Tahoe City CA 96145 530-581-8700 581-1686
TF: 800-462-5196 ■ *Web:* www.gotahoenorth.com

Chambers of Commerce / Tourism
106 E Jefferson St.............................. Tallahassee FL 32301 850-606-2305 606-2301
TF: 800-628-2866 ■ *Web:* www.visittallahassee.com

Tampa Bay & Co 401 E Jackson St Ste 2100 .... Tampa FL 33602 813-223-1111 229-6616
TF: 877-230-0078 ■ *Web:* www.visittampabay.com

	City	State	ZIP	Phone	Fax
Tempe Convention & Visitors Bureau 51 W Third St Ste 105 *TF:* 866-914-1052 ■ *Web:* www.tempetourism.com	Tempe	AZ	85281	480-894-8158	968-8004
Terre Haute Convention & Visitors Bureau 5353 E Margaret Dr **Fax Area Code: 812* ■ *TF:* 800-366-3043 ■ *Web:* www.terrehaute.com	Terre Haute	IN	47803	800-366-3043	234-6750*
Thief River Falls Convention & Visitors Bureau (TRFCVB) 102 Main Ave N *TF:* 800-657-3700 ■ *Web:* www.visittrf.org	Thief River	MN	56701	218-686-9785	
City of Thomasville Tourism Authority 144 E Jackson St *TF:* 800-533-4587 ■ *Web:* www.thomasvillega.com	Thomasville	GA	31792	229-226-3424	228-4188
Three Lakes Information Bureau 1704 Superior St PO Box 268 *TF:* 800-972-6103 ■ *Web:* www.threelakes.com	Three Lakes	WI	54562	715-546-3344	546-2103
River Country Tourism Bureau PO Box 214 **Fax Area Code: 269* ■ *TF:* 800-447-2821 ■ *Web:* www.rivercountry.com	Three Rivers	MI	49093	800-447-2821	651-4342*
Greater Toledo Convention & Visitors Bureau 401 Jefferson Ave *TF:* 800-243-4667 ■ *Web:* www.dotoledo.org	Toledo	OH	43604	419-321-6404	255-7731
Tomah Convention & Visitors Bureau 901 Kilbourn Ave PO Box 625 *TF:* 800-948-6624 ■ *Web:* www.tomahwisconsin.com	Tomah	WI	54660	608-372-2166	372-2167
Travel Industry Assn of Kansas 919 S Kansas Ave *Web:* www.tiak.org	Topeka	KS	66612	785-233-9465	232-5705
Visit Topeka Inc 618 S Kansas Ave *TF:* 800-235-1030 ■ *Web:* www.visittopeka.com	Topeka	KS	66603	785-234-1030	234-8282
Toronto Convention & Visitors Assn 207 Queen's Quay W Ste 405 PO Box 126 *TF:* 800-499-2514 ■ *Web:* www.seetorontonow.com	Toronto	ON	M5J1A7	416-203-2600	203-6753
Smoky Mountain Visitors Bureau 7906 E Lamar Alexander Pkwy *TF:* 800-525-6834 ■ *Web:* www.smokymountains.org	Townsend	TN	37882	865-448-6134	448-9806
Baltimore County Visitor Ctr 400 Washington Ave *Web:* www.enjoybaltimorecounty.com	Towson	MD	21204	410-887-2849	
Traverse City Convention & Visitors Bureau 101 W Grandview Pkwy *TF:* 800-940-1120 ■ *Web:* www.traversecity.com	Traverse City	MI	49684	231-947-1120	947-2621
Atlanta's DeKalb Convention & Visitors Bureau 1957 Lakeside Pkwy Ste 510 *TF:* 800-999-6055 ■ *Web:* www.visitatlantasdekalbcounty.com	Tucker	GA	30084	770-492-5000	492-5033
Metropolitan Tucson Convention & Visitors Bureau 100 S Church Ave *TF:* 800-638-8350 ■ *Web:* www.visittucson.org	Tucson	AZ	85701	520-624-1817	884-7804
Tulsa Convention & Visitors Bureau One W Third St Ste 100 **Fax Area Code: 918* ■ *TF:* 800-558-3311 ■ *Web:* www.visittulsa.com	Tulsa	OK	74103	800-558-3311	592-6244*
Turlock Convention & Visitors Bureau 115 S Golden State Blvd *Web:* www.visitturlock.org	Turlock	CA	95380	209-632-2221	632-5289
Colbert County Tourism & Convention Bureau 719 Hwy 72 W PO Box 740425 *TF:* 800-344-0783 ■ *Web:* www.colbertcountytourism.org	Tuscumbia	AL	35674	256-383-0783	383-2080
Tyler Convention & Visitors Bureau (TCVB) 315 N Broadway *TF:* 800-235-5712 ■ *Web:* www.visittyler.com	Tyler	TX	75702	903-592-1661	592-1268
Oneida County Convention & Visitors Bureau PO Box 551 *TF:* 800-426-3132 ■ *Web:* www.oneidacountytourism.com	Utica	NY	13503	315-724-7221	724-7335
Vail Valley Tourism Bureau PO Box 1130 *TF:* 800-525-3875 ■ *Web:* www.visitvailvalley.com	Vail	CO	81658	970-476-1000	476-6008
Vallejo Convention & Visitors Bureau 289 Mare Island Way *TF General:* 866-921-9277 ■ *Web:* www.visitvallejo.com	Vallejo	CA	94590	707-642-3653	644-2206
Greater Vancouver Convention & Visitors Bureau 200 Burrard St *Web:* www.tourismvancouver.com	Vancouver	BC	V6C3L6	604-682-2222	682-1717
Southwest Washington Convention & Visitors Bureau 1220 Main S Ste 220 *TF:* 877-600-0800 ■ *Web:* www.visitvancouverusa.com	Vancouver	WA	98660	360-750-1553	750-1553
Ventura Visitors & Convention Bureau 101 S California St *TF:* 800-333-2989 ■ *Web:* www.ventura-usa.com	Ventura	CA	93001	805-648-2075	648-2150
Iron Range Tourism Bureau 403 N First St *TF:* 800-777-8497 ■ *Web:* www.ironrange.org	Virginia	MN	55792	218-749-8161	749-8055
Virginia Beach Convention & Visitor Bureau (VBCVB) 2101 Parks Ave Ste 500 *TF:* 800-700-7702 ■ *Web:* www.visitvirginiabeach.com	Virginia Beach	VA	23451	757-385-4700	437-4747
Visalia Convention & Visitors Bureau PO Box 2734 *TF:* 800-524-0303 ■ *Web:* www.visitvisalia.org	Visalia	CA	93279	559-334-0141	713-4800
Waco Convention & Visitors Bureau 100 Washington Ave *TF:* 800-321-9226 ■ *Web:* www.wacoheartoftexas.com	Waco	TX	76701	254-750-5810	750-5801
Kallman Worldwide Inc Four N St Ste 800 *Web:* kallman.com	Waldwick	NJ	07463	201-251-2600	
Warren County Visitors Bureau 22045 Rt 6 *TF:* 800-624-7802 ■ *Web:* www.wcvb.net	Warren	PA	16365	814-726-1222	726-7266
Kosciusko County Convention & Visitors Bureau (KOSCVB) 111 Capital Dr *TF:* 800-800-6090 ■ *Web:* www.koscvb.org	Warsaw	IN	46582	574-269-6090	269-2405
Washington DC Convention & Tourism Corp 901 Seventh St NW 4th Fl *TF:* 800-422-8644 ■ *Web:* washington.org	Washington	DC	20001	202-789-7000	
Waterloo Convention & Visitor Bureau 500 Jefferson St *TF:* 800-728-8431 ■ *Web:* www.waterloocvb.org	Waterloo	IA	50701	319-233-8350	233-2733
Tioga County Visitors Bureau 2053 Rt 660 PO Box 139 *TF:* 888-846-4228 ■ *Web:* www.visittiogapa.com	Wellsboro	PA	16901	570-724-0635	723-1016
West Branch Area Chamber of Commerce 422 W Houghton Ave *Web:* wbacc.com	West Branch	MI	48661	989-345-2821	
West Hollywood Convention & Visitors Bureau 8687 Melrose Ave Ste M38 *TF:* 800-368-6020 ■ *Web:* www.visitwesthollywood.com	West Hollywood	CA	90069	310-289-2525	289-2529
Monroe-West Monroe Convention & Visitors Bureau 601 Constitution Dr PO Box 1436 *TF:* 800-843-1872 ■ *Web:* www.monroe-westmonroe.org	West Monroe	LA	71292	318-387-5691	324-1752
Palm Beach County Convention & Visitors Bureau 1555 Palm Beach Lakes Blvd Ste 800 *TF:* 800-554-7256 ■ *Web:* www.palmbeachfl.com	West Palm Beach	FL	33401	561-233-3000	233-3009
Wheeling Convention & Visitors Bureau 1401 Main St *TF:* 800-828-3097 ■ *Web:* www.wheelingcvb.com	Wheeling	WV	26003	304-233-7709	233-1470
Westchester County Tourism & Film 148 Martine Ave Ste 104 *Web:* westchestergov.com	White Plains	NY	10601	914-995-8500	995-8505
Wichita Convention & Visitors Bureau 515 Main St Ste 115 *TF:* 800-288-9424 ■ *Web:* www.gowichita.com	Wichita	KS	67202	316-265-2800	265-0162
Williamsburg Destination Marketing Committee 421 N Boundary St PO Box 3495 *TF:* 800-368-6511 ■ *Web:* www.visitwilliamsburg.com	Williamsburg	VA	23187	757-229-6511	229-2047
Martin County Travel & Tourism Authority 100 E Church St PO Box 382 *TF:* 800-776-8566 ■ *Web:* www.visitmartincounty.com	Williamston	NC	27892	252-792-6605	792-8710
Cape Fear Coast Convention & Visitors Bureau 505 Nutt St Unit A *TF:* 877-406-2356 ■ *Web:* www.wilmingtonandbeaches.com	Wilmington	NC	28401	910-341-4030	341-4029
Greater Wilmington Convention & Visitors Bureau 100 W Tenth St Ste 20 **Fax Area Code: 302* ■ *TF:* 800-489-6664 ■ *Web:* www.visitwilmingtonde.com	Wilmington	DE	19801	800-489-6664	652-4726*
Wilson Visitors Bureau 209 Broad St *TF:* 800-497-7398 ■ *Web:* www.wilson-nc.com	Wilson	NC	27893	252-243-8440	243-7550
Winnemucca Convention & Visitors Authority 50 W Winnemucca Blvd *TF:* 800-962-2638 ■ *Web:* www.winnemucca.nv.us	Winnemucca	NV	89445	775-623-5071	623-5087
Winona Convention & Visitors Bureau 160 Johnson St *TF:* 800-657-4972 ■ *Web:* visitwinona.com	Winona	MN	55987	507-452-0735	454-0006
Winston-Salem Convention & Visitors Bureau 200 Brookstown Ave *TF:* 866-728-4200 ■ *Web:* www.visitwinstonsalem.com	Winston-Salem	NC	27101	336-728-4200	728-4220
Wisconsin Dells Visitors & Convention Bureau 701 Superior St PO Box 390 *TF:* 800-223-3557 ■ *Web:* www.wisdells.com	Wisconsin Dells	WI	53965	608-254-8088	254-4293
Wayne County Convention & Visitors Bureau 428 W Liberty St *TF:* 800-362-6474 ■ *Web:* wccvb.com	Wooster	OH	44691	330-264-1800	264-1141
Worcester County Convention & Visitors Bureau 30 Elm St Second Fl *TF:* 866-755-7439 ■ *Web:* www.centralmass.org	Worcester	MA	01609	508-755-7400	754-2703
Mahoning County Convention & Visitors Bureau 21 W Boardman St *TF:* 800-447-8201 ■ *Web:* www.youngstownlive.com	Youngstown	OH	44503	330-740-2130	740-2144
Ypsilanti Area Convention & Visitors Bureau 106 W Michigan Ave *TF:* 800-265-9045 ■ *Web:* www.ypsilanti.org	Ypsilanti	MI	48197	734-483-4444	483-0400
Yuma Convention & Visitors Bureau 201 N Fourth Ave *TF:* 800-293-0071 ■ *Web:* www.visityuma.com	Yuma	AZ	85364	928-783-0071	783-1897
Zanesville-Muskingum County Convention & Visitors Bureau 205 N Fifth St *TF:* 800-743-2303 ■ *Web:* www.zmchamber.com	Zanesville	OH	43701	740-455-8282	454-2963

210 CONVEYORS & CONVEYING EQUIPMENT

SEE ALSO Material Handling Equipment p. 2720

	City	State	ZIP	Phone	Fax
Airfloat LLC 2230 Brush College Rd *TF:* 800-888-0018 ■ *Web:* www.airfloat.com	Decatur	IL	62526	217-423-6001	422-1049
Alba Manufacturing Inc 8950 Seward Rd *Web:* www.albamfg.com	Fairfield	OH	45011	513-874-0551	
Allied Uniking Corporation Inc 4750 Cromwell Ave	Memphis	TN	38118	901-365-7240	
Allor Manufacturing Inc 12534 Emerson Dr *TF:* 888-244-4028 ■ *Web:* allorplesh.com	Brighton	MI	48116	248-486-4500	486-4040
AMF Bakery Systems 2115 W Laburnum Ave *TF:* 800-225-3771 ■ *Web:* www.amfbakery.com	Richmond	VA	23227	804-355-7961	355-1074
Arrowhead Conveyor Corp 3255 Medalist Dr PO Box 2408 *Web:* www.arrowheadconveyor.com	Oshkosh	WI	54903	920-235-5562	235-3638
Automated Conveyor Systems Inc 3850 Southland Dr *Web:* www.automatedconveyors.com	West Memphis	AR	72301	870-732-5050	732-5191
Automatic Systems Inc 9230 E 47th St *TF:* 800-366-3488 ■ *Web:* www.asi.com	Kansas City	MO	64133	816-356-0660	356-5730
Automation & Modular Components Inc 10301 Enterprise Dr *Web:* www.amcautomation.com	Davisburg	MI	48350	248-922-4740	
Automation Tool Co 101 Mill Dr *Web:* www.automationtool.com	Cookeville	TN	38501	931-528-5417	
Automotion Inc 11000 Lavergne Ave *Web:* www.automotionconveyors.com	Oak Lawn	IL	60453	708-229-3700	229-3799
Beltservice Corp 4143 Rider Trl N *TF:* 800-727-2358 ■ *Web:* www.beltservice.com	Earth City	MO	63045	314-344-8500	344-8511
Bilt-Rite Conveyors 735 Industrial Loop Rd *TF:* 800-558-3616 ■ *Web:* www.bilt-rite.com	New London	WI	54961	920-982-6600	982-7750
BW Container Systems 1305 Lakeview Dr *TF:* 800-527-0494 ■ *Web:* www.fleetinc.com	Romeoville	IL	60446	630-759-6800	759-2299

Company	City	State	ZIP	Phone	Fax
C & M Conveyor 4598 SR 37 *TF:* 800-551-3195 ■ *Web:* www.cmconveyor.com	Mitchell	IN	47446	812-849-5647	849-6126
Caddy Corp of America 509 Sharptown Rd *Web:* www.caddycorp.com	Bridgeport	NJ	08014	856-467-4222	467-5511
Cambelt International Corp 2820 West 1100 South *TF:* 855-226-2358 ■ *Web:* www.cambelt.com	Salt Lake City	UT	84104	801-972-5511	972-5522
Cambridge Inc 105 Goodwill Rd PO Box 399 *TF:* 800-638-9560 ■ *Web:* www.cambridge-intl.com	Cambridge	MD	21613	410-228-3000	901-4979
Can Lines Engineering 9839 Downey Norwalk Rd PO Box 7039 *TF:* 800-233-4597 ■ *Web:* www.canlines.com	Downey	CA	90241	562-861-2996	869-5293
Carrier Vibrating Equipment Inc 3400 Fern Vly Rd *TF:* 800-547-7278 ■ *Web:* www.carriervibrating.com	Louisville	KY	40213	502-969-3171	969-3172
Chantland-Pvs Co, The PO Box 69 *Web:* www.chantlandpulley.com	Humboldt	IA	50548	515-332-4040	332-4923
Christianson Systems Inc 20421 15th St SE PO Box 138 *TF:* 800-328-8896 ■ *Web:* www.christianson.com	Blomkest	MN	56216	320-995-6141	995-6145
CIGNYS 68 Williamson St *Web:* www.cignys.com	Saginaw	MI	48601	989-753-1411	753-4386
Co-Op Country Farmers Elevator 340 Dupont Ave NE *Web:* www.coopcountry.com	Renville	MN	56284	320-329-8377	
Con-Vey Keystone 526 NE Chestnut Roseburg *Web:* www.con-vey.com	Roseburg	OR	97470	541-672-5506	672-2513
Conveyor Components Co 130 Seltzer Rd *TF Cust Svc:* 800-233-3233 ■ *Web:* www.conveyorcomponents.com	Croswell	MI	48422	810-679-4211	679-4510
Conveyor Engineering & Manufacturing Co 1345 76th Ave SW *Web:* www.conveyoreng.com	Cedar Rapids	IA	52404	319-364-5600	
Conveyor Technologies Inc 5313 Womack Rd *Web:* www.conveyor-technologies.com	Sanford	NC	27330	919-776-7227	
Conveyors Inc 620 S Fourth Ave *Web:* www.conveyorsinc.net	Mansfield	TX	76063	817-473-4645	473-3024
Cyclonaire Corp PO Box 366 *TF:* 800-445-0730 ■ *Web:* www.cyclonaire.com	York	NE	68467	402-362-2000	362-2001
Daifuku North American Holdings Co 6700 Tussing Rd *Web:* www.daifuku.com	Reynoldsburg	OH	43068	614-863-1888	
Dakota Fabricating Inc 12111 W Northern Ave *Web:* www.dakotafab.com	Glendale	AZ	85307	623-935-7805	
Dearborn Mid-West Conveyor Co (DMWCC) 20334 Superior Rd *Web:* www.dmwcc.com	Taylor	MI	48180	734-288-4400	288-1914
Dematic 507 Plymouth Ave NE **Fax Area Code:* 616 ■ *TF Cust Svc:* 877-725-7500 ■ *Web:* www.dematic.com	Grand Rapids	MI	49505	877-725-7500	913-7701*
Dynamic Air Inc 1125 Willow Lk Blvd *Web:* www.dynamicair.com	Saint Paul	MN	55110	651-484-2900	484-7015
Engineered Products Inc 500 Furman Hall Rd *TF:* 888-301-1421 ■ *Web:* www.engprod.com	Greenville	SC	29609	864-234-4888	234-4860
Eriez Manufacturing Company Inc 2200 Asbury Rd *Web:* www.eriez.com	Erie	PA	16506	814-835-6000	
Essmueller Co 334 Ave A PO Box 1966 *TF:* 800-325-7175 ■ *Web:* www.essmueller.com	Laurel	MS	39440	601-649-2400	649-4320
Evana Automation 5825 Old Boonville Hwy *TF:* 800-468-6774 ■ *Web:* www.evanaautomation.com	Evansville	IN	47715	812-479-8246	
Fame Industries Inc 51100 Grand River Ave *Web:* www.fameind.com	Wixom	MI	48393	248-348-7760	348-2120
FATA Automation Inc 6050 Nineteen Mile Rd *Web:* www.fatainc.com	Sterling Heights	MI	48314	586-323-9400	
Feeco International Inc 3913 Algoma Rd *TF:* 800-373-9347 ■ *Web:* www.feeco.com	Green Bay	WI	54311	920-468-1000	469-5110
Flexible Steel Lacing Co 2525 Wisconsin Ave *TF:* 800-323-3444 ■ *Web:* www.flexco.com	Downers Grove	IL	60515	630-971-0150	971-1180
Fred D Pfening Co 1075 W Fifth Ave *Web:* www.pfening.com	Columbus	OH	43212	614-294-1633	
Garvey Corp 208 S Rt 73 *TF:* 800-257-8581 ■ *Web:* www.garvey.com	Blue Anchor	NJ	08037	609-561-2450	561-2328
General Kinematics Corp 5050 Rickert Rd *Web:* generalkinematics.com	Crystal Lake	IL	60014	815-455-3222	455-2285
Grasan Equipment Co 440 S Illinois Ave *Web:* www.grasan.com	Mansfield	OH	44907	419-526-4440	524-2176
Hansen Manufacturing Corp 5100 W 12th St *TF:* 800-328-1785 ■ *Web:* www.hiroller.com	Sioux Falls	SD	57107	605-332-3200	
Hapman 6002 E N Ave *TF:* 800-427-6260 ■ *Web:* www.hapman.com	Kalamazoo	MI	49048	269-343-1675	349-2477
Hohl Machine & Conveyor Company Inc 1580 Niagara St *Web:* www.hohlmachine.com	Buffalo	NY	14213	716-882-7210	
Horsley Co, The 1630 South 4800 West Ste D *Web:* www.horsleyco.com	Salt Lake City	UT	84104	801-401-5500	
Hustler Conveyor Co 4101 Crusher Dr *Web:* www.ampulverizer.com	O'fallon	MO	63368	636-441-8600	
Hytrol Conveyor Company Inc 2020 Hytrol St **Fax Area Code:* 800 ■ *Web:* www.hytrol.com	Jonesboro	AR	72401	870-935-3700	852-3233*
I J White Corp 20 Executive Blvd *Web:* www.ijwhite.com	Farmingdale	NY	11735	631-293-2211	
Illinois Crane Inc 1621 W Chanute Rd *Web:* www.illinoiscrane.com	Peoria	IL	61615	309-692-0856	
Industrial Kinetics Inc 2535 Curtiss St *Web:* www.iki.com	Downers Grove	IL	60515	630-655-0300	
Intelligrated Products 475 E High St PO Box 899 **Fax Area Code:* 740 ■ *TF:* 866-936-7300 ■ *Web:* www.intelligrated.com	London	OH	43140	513-701-7300	490-0281*
Interroll Corp 3000 Corporate Dr **Fax Area Code:* 800 ■ *TF Sales:* 800-830-9680 ■ *Web:* www.interroll.es	Wilmington	NC	28405	910-799-1100	830-9679*
Intralox LLC 8715 Bollman Pl *Web:* www.intralox.com	Savage	MD	20763	301-575-2200	575-2266
IPS Group Inc 4343 Easton Rd *Web:* www.continentalscrew.com	Saint Joseph	MO	64503	816-233-1800	
Jorgensen Conveyors Inc 10303 N Baehr Rd *TF:* 800-325-7705 ■ *Web:* www.jorgensenconveyors.com	Mequon	WI	53092	262-242-3089	242-4382
Joy Global Inc 177 Thorn Hill Rd Thorn Hill Industrial Park *Web:* www.joy.com	Warrendale	PA	15086	724-779-4500	
Kice Industries Inc 5500 N Mill Heights Dr *TF:* 877-289-5423 ■ *Web:* www.kice.com	Wichita	KS	67219	316-744-7151	744-7355
Knight Global 1140 Centre Rd *Web:* www.knight-ind.com	Auburn Hills	MI	48326	248-377-4950	377-2135
KWS Mfg Company Ltd 3041 Conveyor Dr *TF:* 800-543-6558 ■ *Web:* www.kwsmfg.com	Burleson	TX	76028	817-295-2247	447-8528
Laitram LLC 200 Laitram Ln *TF:* 800-535-7631 ■ *Web:* www.laitram.com	Harahan	LA	70123	504-733-6000	733-2143
LEWCO Inc 706 Lane St	Sandusky	OH	44870	419-625-4014	
Martin Engineering One Martin Pl *TF:* 800-544-2947 ■ *Web:* www.martin-eng.com	Neponset	IL	61345	309-594-2384	594-2432
Master Solutions Inc 20 Wolf Bridge Rd *Web:* www.mastersi.com	Carlisle	PA	17013	717-243-6849	
Mayfran International Inc 6650 Beta Dr *Web:* www.mayfran.com	Cleveland	OH	44143	440-461-4100	461-5565
Metzgar Conveyor Co Inc 901 Metzgar Dr NW *TF:* 888-266-8390 ■ *Web:* www.metzgarconveyors.com	Comstock Park	MI	49321	616-784-0930	784-4100
Millard Manufacturing Corp 10602 Olive St *Web:* www.millardmfg.com	Omaha	NE	68128	402-331-8010	
Miller Transfer 3833 State Rt 183 *Web:* www.millertransfer.com	Rootstown	OH	44272	330-325-2521	
Multi-fab Products LLC N90 W14507 Commerce Dr *Web:* www.multi-fab.com	Menomonee Falls	WI	53051	262-502-1707	
Nercon Engineering & Manufacturing Inc 3972 S US Hwy 45 *Web:* www.nerconconveyors.com	Oshkosh	WI	54902	920-233-3268	233-3159
NKC of America Inc 1584 E Brooks Rd *TF:* 800-532-6727 ■ *Web:* nkc-j.co.jp	Memphis	TN	38116	901-396-5353	396-2339
Nol-tec Systems Inc 425 Apollo Dr *Web:* www.nol-tec.com	Circle Pines	MN	55014	651-780-8600	780-4400
Nordstrong Equipment Ltd Five Chester Ave *Web:* www.nordstrongequipment.com	Winnipeg	MB	R2L1W5	204-667-1553	
Novi Precision Products Inc 11777 E Grand River Ave *Web:* www.noviprecision.com	Brighton	MI	48116	810-227-1024	227-6160
Overhead Conveyor Co 1330 Hilton Rd *Web:* www.occ-conveyor.com	Ferndale	MI	48220	248-547-3800	547-8344
Pflow Industries 6720 N Teutonia Ave *Web:* www.pflow.com	Milwaukee	WI	53209	414-352-9000	
Prab Inc 5944 E Kilgore Rd *TF:* 800-968-7722 ■ *Web:* www.prab.com	Kalamazoo	MI	49048	269-382-8200	349-2477
Price Rubber Corp 2733 Gunter Park Dr W *Web:* www.pricerubber.com	Montgomery	AL	36109	334-277-5470	
Railex Corp 89-02 Atlantic Ave *Web:* www.railexcorp.com	Ozone Park	NY	11416	718-845-5454	738-1020
Ralphs-pugh Company Inc 3931 Oregon St *Web:* www.ralphs-pugh.com	Benicia	CA	94510	707-745-6363	
Rapat Corp 919 Odonnel St *TF:* 800-325-6377 ■ *Web:* www.rapat.com	Hawley	MN	56549	218-483-3344	483-3535
Rapid Industries 4003 Oaklawn Dr *TF:* 800-727-4381 ■ *Web:* www.rapidindustries.com	Louisville	KY	40219	502-968-3645	968-6331
Renold Jeffrey 2307 Maden Dr *TF:* 800-251-9012 ■ *Web:* www.renoldjeffrey.com	Morristown	TN	37813	423-586-1951	581-2399
Richards-Wilcox Inc 600 S Lake St **Fax Area Code:* 630 ■ *TF:* 800-253-5668 ■ *Web:* www.richardswilcox.com	Aurora	IL	60506	800-253-5668	897-6994*
Roll-A-Way Conveyor Inc 2335 N Delaney Rd *Web:* www.roll-away.com	Gurnee	IL	60031	847-336-5033	336-6542
Ryson International Inc 300 Newsome Dr *Web:* www.ryson.com	Yorktown	VA	23692	757-898-1530	898-1580
Schroeder Industries LLC 580 W Pk Rd *TF:* 800-722-4810 ■ *Web:* www.schroederindustries.com	Leetsdale	PA	15056	724-318-1100	318-1200
Screw Conveyor Corp 700 Hoffman St *Web:* www.screwconveyor.com	Hammond	IN	46327	219-931-1450	931-0209
Shick Tube Veyor Corp 4346 Clary Blvd *TF:* 877-744-2587 ■ *Web:* www.shickusa.com	Kansas City	MO	64130	816-861-7224	921-1901
Shuttleworth Inc 10 Commercial Rd *TF:* 800-444-7412 ■ *Web:* www.shuttleworth.com	Huntington	IN	46750	260-356-8500	359-7810
Southern Systems Inc 4101 Viscount Ave *Web:* www.ssiconveyors.com	Memphis	TN	38118	901-362-7340	360-8002
Stewart Systems 808 Stewart Ave *TF:* 800-966-5808 ■ *Web:* www.stewart-systems.com	Plano	TX	75074	972-422-5808	509-8734
Superior Industries LLC 315 E State Hwy 28 PO Box 684 *Web:* www.superior-ind.com	Morris	MN	56267	320-589-2406	
Sweet Mfg Company Inc 2000 E Leffel Ln *TF Cust Svc:* 800-334-7254 ■ *Web:* www.sweetmfg.com	Springfield	OH	45505	937-325-1511	322-1963
Swisslog 10825 E 47th Ave *TF:* 800-525-1841 ■ *Web:* www.swisslog.com	Denver	CO	80239	303-371-7770	373-7870
T K F Inc 726 Mehring Way *Web:* www.tkf.com	Cincinnati	OH	45203	513-241-5910	
Tekno Inc One Wall St *Web:* www.tekno.com	Cave City	KY	42127	270-773-4181	
TGW-Ermanco Inc 6870 Grand Haven Rd *Web:* www.tgw-group.com	Spring Lake	MI	49456	231-798-4547	798-8322
Thomas Conveyor Co 555 N Burleson Blvd *TF:* 800-433-2217 ■ *Web:* www.thomasconveyor.com	Burleson	TX	76028	817-295-7151	447-3840
Trans-Global Solutions Inc 11811 East Fwy Ste 630 *Web:* www.tgsgroup.com	Houston	TX	77029	713-453-0341	453-2756

Company	City	State	Zip	Phone	Fax
Transco Industries Inc 5534 NE 122nd Ave PO Box 20429 *TF:* 800-545-9991 ■ *Web:* www.transco-ind.com	Portland	OR	97230	503-256-1955	256-0723
Uni-Pak Corp 1015 N Ronald Reagan Blvd *Web:* www.unipak.com	Longwood	FL	32750	407-830-9300	830-4106
United Conveyor Corp 2100 Norman Dr W *Web:* www.unitedconveyor.com	Waukegan	IL	60085	847-473-5900	473-5959
Unitrak Corporation Ltd 299 Ward St *Web:* www.unitrak.com	Port Hope	ON	L1A4A4	905-885-8168	
Universal Industries Inc 5800 Nordic Dr *TF:* 800-553-4446 ■ *Web:* www.universalindustries.com	Cedar Falls	IA	50613	319-277-7501	277-2318
VAC-U-MAX 69 William St *Web:* www.aeromechanical.com	Belleville	NJ	07109	973-759-4600	
W & H Systems Inc 120 Asia Pl *TF:* 800-966-6993 ■ *Web:* www.whsystems.com	Carlstadt	NJ	07072	201-933-7840	933-2144
Warehouse Systems Inc 655 Academy Dr *Web:* www.warehousesys.com	Northbrook	IL	60062	847-562-9526	
WASP Inc PO Box 249 *Web:* www.waspinc.com	Glenwood	MN	56334	320-634-5126	634-5881
Webb-Stiles Co 675 Liverpool Dr PO Box 464 *Web:* www.webb-stiles.com	Valley City	OH	44280	330-225-7761	225-5532
Western Pneumatics Inc PO Box 21340 *Web:* www.westernp.com	Eugene	OR	97402	541-461-2600	461-2606
Westfalia Technologies Inc 3655 Sandhurst Dr *TF:* 800-673-2522 ■ *Web:* www.westfaliausa.com	York	PA	17406	717-764-1115	764-1118
Westmont Industries 10805 Painter Ave *Web:* www.westmont.com	Santa Fe Springs	CA	90670	562-944-6137	946 5209
Whirl Air Flow Corp 20055 177th St *TF:* 800-373-3461 ■ *Web:* www.whirlair.com	Big Lake	MN	55309	763-262-1200	262-1212
White Conveyors Inc 10 Boright Ave *Web:* www.white-conveyors.com	Kenilworth	NJ	07033	908-686-5700	
White Systems Inc 30 Boright Ave *Web:* www.whitesystems.com	Kenilworth	NJ	07033	908-272-6700	
Wire Belt Company of America 154 Harvey Rd *TF Cust Svc:* 800-922-2637 ■ *Web:* www.wirebelt.com	Londonderry	NH	03053	603-644-2500	644-3600
WPS Industries Inc 228 Industrial St *Web:* www.wpsindustries.com	West Monroe	LA	71292	318-812-2800	
Young Industries Inc 16 Painter St *TF:* 800-546-3165 ■ *Web:* www.younginds.com	Muncy	PA	17756	570-546-3165	546-1888

211 CORD & TWINE

Company	City	State	Zip	Phone	Fax
40-Up Tackle Co 16 Union Ave PO Box 442 *Web:* www.40uptackleco.com	Westfield	MA	01086	413-562-0385	
Algoma Net Co 1525 Mueller St *Web:* www.algomanet.com	Algoma	WI	54201	920-487-5577	487-2852
All Line Inc 16851 E Parkview Ave Unit 2 *TF:* 800-843-5733 ■ *Web:* www.alllinerope.com	Fountain Hills	AZ	85268	480-306-6001	306-6001
Ashaway Line & Twine Manufacturing Co 24 Laurel St *TF:* 800-556-7260 ■ *Web:* www.ashawayusa.com	Ashaway	RI	02804	401-377-2221	377-9091
Atkins & Pearce Inc 1 Braid Way *TF:* 800-837-7477 ■ *Web:* www.braidway.com	Covington	KY	41017	859-356-2001	356-2395
Bridon Cordage LLC 909 E 16th St *TF:* 800-533-6002 ■ *Web:* www.bridoncordage.com	Albert Lea	MN	56007	507-377-1601	
Brownell & Company Inc 423 E Haddam-Moodus Rd *Web:* www.brownellco.com	Moodus	CT	06469	860-873-8625	873-1944
Carron Net Company Inc 1623 17th St PO Box 177 *TF:* 800-558-7768 ■ *Web:* www.carronnet.com	Two Rivers	WI	54241	920-793-2217	793-2122
Cordage Source, The *Bridgeline Ltd* 70 Dundas St *Web:* cordages.com	Deseronto	ON	K0K1X0	519-745-7391	745-4290
Cortland Line Company Inc 3736 Kellogg Rd *Web:* www.cortlandline.com	Cortland	NY	13045	607-756-2851	753-8835
Flow Tek Inc PO Box 2018 *Web:* www.monic.com	Boulder	CO	80306	303-530-3050	
Gladding Braided Products LLC 110 Country Rd *Web:* gladdingbraid.com	South Otselic	NY	13155	315-653-7211	653-4492
I & I Sling Inc PO Box 2423 *TF:* 800-874-3539 ■ *Web:* www.slingmax.com	Aston	PA	19014	610-485-8500	494-5835
James Thompson & Company Inc 381 Pk Ave S # 718 *Web:* www.jamesthompson.com	New York	NY	10016	212-686-4242	686-9528
New England Ropes Inc 848 Airport Rd *TF:* 800-333-6679 ■ *Web:* www.neropes.com	Fall River	MA	02720	508-678-8200	679-2363
Pacific Fibre & Rope Company Inc 903 Flint St PO Box 187 *TF:* 800-825-7673 ■ *Web:* www.pacificfibre.com	Wilmington	CA	90744	310-834-4567	
Pelican Rope Works Inc 4001 W Carriage Dr *TF:* 800-464-7673 ■ *Web:* www.pelicanrope.com	Santa Ana	CA	92704	714-545-0116	545-7673
PlymKraft Inc 479 Export Cir *TF:* 800-992-0854 ■ *Web:* www.plymkraft.com	Newport News	VA	23601	757-595-0364	595-3993
Puget Sound Rope Corp 1012 Second St *TF:* 888-525-8488 ■ *Web:* www.cortlandcompany.com	Anacortes	WA	98221	360-293-8488	293-8480
Rockford Manufacturing Co 3901 Little River Rd	Rockford	TN	37853	865-970-3131	
Rocky Mount Cord Co 381 N Grace St *TF Orders:* 800-342-9130 ■ *Web:* www.rmcord.com	Rocky Mount	NC	27804	252-977-9130	977-9123
Samson Rope Technologies Inc 2090 Thornton Rd **Fax Area Code:* 800 ■ *TF Cust Svc:* 800-227-7673 ■ *Web:* www.samsonrope.com	Ferndale	WA	98248	360-384-4669	299-9246*

212 CORK & CORK PRODUCTS

SEE ALSO Office & School Supplies p. 2833

Company	City	State	Zip	Phone	Fax
Amorim Cork Composites 26112 110th St *Web:* www.amorimcorkcomposites.com/index.php	Trevor	WI	53179	262-862-2311	
Expanko Inc 180 Gordon Dr Ste 113 **Fax Area Code:* 610 ■ *TF:* 800-345-6202 ■ *Web:* www.expanko.com	Exton	PA	19341	800-345-6202	363-0735*
Manton Industrial Cork Products Inc 415 Oser Ave Unit U *TF:* 800-663-1921 ■ *Web:* www.mantoncork.com	Hauppauge	NY	11788	631-273-0700	273-0038
Maryland Cork Co Inc 505 Blue Ball Rd PO Box 126 *TF:* 800-662-2675 ■ *Web:* www.marylandcork.com	Elkton	MD	21922	410-398-2955	392-9433

213 CORPORATE HOUSING

Company	City	State	Zip	Phone	Fax
Alikar Gardens Resort, The 1123 Verde Dr *TF:* 800-456-1123 ■ *Web:* www.alikar.com	Colorado Springs	CO	80910	719-475-2564	471-5835
Churchill Corporate Services 56 Utter Ave *TF:* 800-941-7458 ■ *Web:* www.furnishedhousing.com	Hawthorne	NJ	07506	973-636-9400	636-0179
Cincinnati Metropolitan Housing Authority 16 W Central Pkwy *Web:* www.cintimha.com	Cincinnati	OH	45202	513-421-2642	
Coast to Coast Corporate Housing 10773 Los Alamitos Blvd *TF:* 800-451-9466 ■ *Web:* www.ctchousing.com	Los Alamitos	CA	90720	562-795-0250	795-0251
ExecSuite Third Ave SW Ste 702 *TF:* 800-667-4980 ■ *Web:* www.execsuite.ca	Calgary	AB	T2P3B4	403-294-5800	294-5959
Klein & Company Corporate Housing Services Inc 914 Washington Ave *TF:* 800-208-9826 ■ *Web:* www.kleinandcompany.com	Golden	CO	80401	303-796-2100	796-2101
Marriott International Inc 10400 Fernwood Road *NASDAQ: MAR* ■ **Fax Area Code:* 336 ■ **Fax:* Mail Rm ■ *TF:* 800-450-4442 ■ *Web:* www.marriott.com	Bethesda	MD	20817	301-380-3000	665-6522*
ExecuStay Corp 2222 Corinth Ave *TF:* 800-990-9292 ■ *Web:* www.executstay.com	Los Angeles	CA	90064	800-990-9292	
Oakwood Crystal City 400 15th St S *TF:* 877-969-5142 ■ *Web:* www.oakwood.com	Arlington	VA	22202	703-920-9550	271-0190
Oakwood Worldwide 2222 Corinth Ave *TF:* 800-888-0808 ■ *Web:* www.oakwood.com	Los Angeles	CA	90064	310-478-1021	444-2210
SuiteAmerica 4970 Windplay Dr Ste C-1 *TF:* 800-410-4305 ■ *Web:* www.suiteamerica.com	El Dorado Hills	CA	95762	916-941-7970	941-7989
Windsor Corporate Suites 3516 Stearns Hills Rd *Web:* www.windsorcommunities.com	Waltham	MA	02451	781-899-5100	893-0046

214 CORRECTIONAL & DETENTION MANAGEMENT (PRIVATIZED)

SEE ALSO Correctional Facilities - Federal p. 2167; Correctional Facilities - State p. 2168; Juvenile Detention Facilities p. 2610

Company	City	State	Zip	Phone	Fax
Colorado Correctional Industries 2862 S Cir Dr *TF Cust Svc:* 800-685-7891 ■ *Web:* www.coloradoci.com	Colorado Springs	CO	80906	719-226-4206	226-4220
Corrections Corp of America 10 Burton Hills Blvd *NYSE: CXW* ■ *TF:* 800-624-2931 ■ *Web:* www.cca.com	Nashville	TN	37215	615-263-3000	263-3000
Youth Services International 6000 Cattleridge Dr Ste 200 *Web:* www.youthservices.com	Sarasota	FL	34232	941-953-9199	953-9198

215 CORRECTIONAL FACILITIES - FEDERAL

SEE ALSO Correctional & Detention Management (Privatized) p. 2167; Correctional Facilities - State p. 2168; Juvenile Detention Facilities p. 2610

Company	City	State	Zip	Phone	Fax
Administrative-Maximum US Penitentiary					
Florence PO Box 8500 *TF:* 877-623-8426 ■ *Web:* www.bop.gov/locations/institutions/flm	Florence	CO	81226	719-784-9464	784-5290
Beaumont 5830 Knauth Rd *Web:* www.bop.gov	Beaumont	TX	77705	409-727-0101	720-5000
Federal Correctional Complex					
Coleman 846 NE 54th Terr *TF:* 877-623-8426 ■ *Web:* www.bop.gov	ÿColeman	FL	33521	352-689-5000	689-5027
Bastrop 1341 Hwy 95 N PO Box 730 *Web:* www.bop.gov	Bastrop	TX	78602	512-321-3903	304-0117
Big Spring 1900 Simler Ave *Web:* www.bop.gov/locations/institutions/big	Big Spring	TX	79720	432-466-2300	466-2576
Butner Old NC Hwy 75 PO Box 1000 *TF:* 877-623-8426 ■ *Web:* www.bop.gov	Butner	NC	27509	919-575-4541	575-5023
Cumberland 14601 Burbridge Rd SE **Fax:* Hum Res ■ *Web:* www.bop.gov/	Cumberland	MD	21502	301-784-1000	784-1008*
Danbury Rt 37 *TF:* 877-623-8426 ■ *Web:* www.bop.gov	Danbury	CT	06811	203-743-6471	312-5110
Edgefield 501 Gary Hill Rd PO Box 723 *Web:* bop.gov	Edgefield	SC	29824	803-637-1500	637-9840
El Reno PO Box 1000 *Web:* fedcrimlaw.com	El Reno	OK	73036	405-262-4875	
Englewood 9595 W Quincy Ave *TF:* 877-623-8426 ■ *Web:* www.bop.gov	Littleton	CO	80123	303-985-1566	763-2553
Fairton 655 Fairton-Millville Rd PO Box 280 *TF:* 877-623-8426 ■ *Web:* www.bop.gov	Fairton	NJ	08320	856-453-1177	453-4015

				Phone	Fax
Florence 5880 State Hwy 67 S *Web:* usmarshals.gov	Florence	CO	81226	719-784-9100	784-9504
Federal Correctional Institution					
Forrest City 1400 Dale Bumpers Rd PO Box 8000 *TF:* 877-623-8426 ■ *Web:* www.bop.gov	Forrest City	AR	72335	870-630-6000	494-4496
Jesup 2600 Hwy 301 S *Web:* bop.gov	Jesup	GA	31599	912-427-0870	427-1125
Loretto PO Box 1000 *TF:* 877-623-8426 ■ *Web:* www.bop.gov	Loretto	PA	15940	814-472-4140	472-6046
Manchester 805 Fox Hollow Rd PO Box 4000 *TF:* 877-623-8426 ■ *Web:* www.bop.gov	Manchester	KY	40962	606-598-1900	599-4115
McKean 6975 Rt 59 PO Box 8000 *TF:* 877-623-8426 ■ *Web:* www.bop.gov	Lewis Run	PA	16738	814-362-8900	363-6821
Milan PO Box 9999 *Web:* www.bop.gov/locations/institutions/mil	Milan	MI	48160	734-439-1511	439-0949
Morgantown 446 Greenbag Rd *Web:* www.bop.gov	Morgantown	WV	26501	304-296-4416	284-3613
Oxford PO Box 500 *Web:* www.bop.gov	Oxford	WI	53952	608-584-5511	584-6371
Pekin 2600 S Second St *Web:* bop.gov	Pekin	IL	61554	309-346-8588	477-4685
Phoenix 37900 N 45th Ave	Phoenix	AZ	85086	623-465-9757	465-5199
Ray Brook 128 Ray Brook Rd PO Box 300 *Web:* www.bop.gov	Ray Brook	NY	12977	518-897-4000	897-4216
Safford 1529 W Hwy 366 PO Box 9000 *Web:* www.bop.gov	Safford	AZ	85546	928-428-6600	348-1331
Talladega 565 E Renfroe Rd *Web:* bop.gov	Talladega	AL	35160	256-315-4100	315-4495
Tallahassee 501 Capital Cir NE *Web:* federalprisoncalls.net	Tallahassee	FL	32301	850-878-2173	216-1299
Terminal Island 1299 Seaside Ave *Web:* www.bop.gov	San Pedro	CA	90731	310-831-8961	732-5335
Yazoo City 2225 Haley Barbour Pkwy PO Box 5050 *TF:* 877-623-8426 ■ *Web:* www.bop.gov	Yazoo City	MS	39194	662-751-4800	751-4958
Honolulu 351 Elliot St PO Box 30080 *Web:* bop.gov	Honolulu	HI	96820	808-838-4200	838-4510
Houston 1200 Texas Ave	Houston	TX	77002	713-221-5400	
Federal Detention Ctr					
Oakdale PO Box 5060 *Web:* www.bop.gov	Oakdale	LA	71463	318-335-4466	215-2046
Philadelphia PO Box 572 *Web:* www.bop.gov	Philadelphia	PA	19106	215-521-4000	521-7220
SeaTac PO Box 13901 *TF:* 877-623-8426 ■ *Web:* www.bop.gov/locations/institutions/set/index.jsp	Seattle	WA	98198	206-870-5700	870-5717
Butner Old N Carolina Hwy 75 *Web:* www.bop.gov	Butner	NC	27509	919-575-3900	575-4801
Federal Medical Ctr					
Lexington 3301 Leestown Rd *Web:* bop.gov	Lexington	KY	40511	859-255-6812	253-8821
Federal Prison Camp (FPC)					
Bryan 1100 Ursuline Ave PO Box 2147 **Fax:* Warden ■ *Web:* www.bop.gov/	Bryan	TX	77805	979-823-1879	821-3316*
Duluth 6902 Airport Rd PO Box 1400 *TF:* 877-623-8426 ■ *Web:* www.bop.gov	Duluth	MN	55814	218-722-8634	733-4701
Montgomery Maxwell AFB *TF:* 877-623-8426 ■ *Web:* www.bop.gov/locations/institutions/mon	Montgomery	AL	36112	334-293-2100	293-2326
Medical Ctr for Federal Prisoners Springfield 1900 W Sunshine St *TF:* 877-623-8426 ■ *Web:* www.bop.gov/	Springfield	MO	65807	417-862-7041	837-1717
Chicago 71 W Van Buren St *TF:* 877-623-8426 ■ *Web:* www.bop.gov	Chicago	IL	60605	312-322-0567	322-1120
Metropolitan Correctional Ctr					
New York 150 Pk Row *Web:* bop.gov	New York	NY	10007	646-836-6300	836-7751
US Penitentiary (USP)					
Allenwood PO Box 3500 *Web:* www.bop.gov/locations/institutions/alp	White Deer	PA	17887	570-547-0963	547-9201
Atwater 1 Federal Way PO Box 019001 *TF:* 877-623-8426 ■ *Web:* www.bop.gov/locations/institutions/atw	Atwater	CA	95301	209-386-0257	386-4635
Lewisburg 2400 Robert Miller Dr	Lewisburg	PA	17837	570-523-1251	522-7745
Pollock 1000 Airbase Rd PO Box 1000 *Web:* bop.gov	Pollock	LA	71467	318-561-5300	561-5391

216 CORRECTIONAL FACILITIES - STATE

SEE ALSO Correctional & Detention Management (Privatized) p. 2167; Correctional Facilities - Federal p. 2167; Juvenile Detention Facilities p. 2610

Alabama

				Phone	Fax
Bibb Country Correctional Facility 565 Bibb Ln *Web:* doc.alabama.gov	Brent	AL	35034	205-926-5252	926-9928
Bullock County Correctional Facility 104 Bullock Dr PO Box 5107 *Web:* alabama.gov	Union Springs	AL	36089	334-738-5625	738-5020
Elmore Correctional Ctr 3520 Marion Spillway Rd *Web:* www.doc.state.al.us	Elmore	AL	36025	334-567-1460	567-1804
Holman Correctional Facility 866 Ross Rd PO Box 3700 *Web:* www.doc.state.al.us	Atmore	AL	36503	251-368-8173	368-1095
Kilby Correctional Facility 12201 Wares Ferry Rd *Web:* doc.alabama.gov	Montgomery	AL	36117	334-215-6600	
Limestone Correctional Facility 28779 Nick Davis Rd	Harvest	AL	35749	256-233-4600	233-1930
Saint Clair Correctional Facility 1000 St Clair Rd	Springville	AL	35146	205-467-6111	467-2474
Staton Correctional Facility 2690 Marion Spillway Rd PO Box 56 *Web:* doc.state.al.us	Elmore	AL	36025	334-567-2221	
Tutwiler Prison for Women 8966 US Hwy 231 *Web:* doc.state.al.us	Wetumpka	AL	36092	334-567-4369	514-6576
Ventress Correctional Facility Hwy 239 N PO Box 767 *Web:* alabama.gov	Clayton	AL	36016	334-775-3331	
William E Donaldson Facility 100 Warrior Ln. *Web:* doc.state.al.us	Bessemer	AL	35023	205-436-3681	436-3399

Alaska

				Phone	Fax
Anchorage Correctional Complex 1400 E Fourth Ave *Web:* www.correct.state.ak.us	Anchorage	AK	99501	907-269-4100	269-4208
Anvil Mountain Correctional Ctr 1810 Ctr Creek Rd PO Box 730 *Web:* www.correct.state.ak.us	Nome	AK	99762	907-443-2241	443-5195
Fairbanks Correctional Ctr 1931 Eagan Ave. *TF:* 877-741-0741 ■ *Web:* correct.state.ak.us	Fairbanks	AK	99701	907-458-6700	458-6751
Hiland Mountain Correctional Ctr Library 9101 Hesterberg Rd *Web:* correct.state.ak.us	Eagle River	AK	99577	907-694-9511	694-4507
Ketchikan Correctional Ctr 1201 Schoenbar Rd *Web:* www.correct.state.ak.us	Ketchikan	AK	99901	907-228-7350	225-7031
Lemon Creek Correctional Ctr 2000 Lemon Creek Rd *Web:* www.correct.state.ak.us	Juneau	AK	99801	907-465-6200	465-6224
Palmer Correctional Ctr PO Box 919 *TF:* 877-741-0741 ■ *Web:* www.correct.state.ak.us/institutions/palmer	Palmer	AK	99645	907-745-5054	746-1574
Spring Creek Correctional Ctr 3600 Bette Cato PO Box 2109 *Web:* www.correct.state.ak.us/corrections	Seward	AK	99664	907-224-8200	224-8062
Wildwood Correctional Ctr 10 Chugach Ave *Web:* www.correct.state.ak.us	Kenai	AK	99611	907-260-7200	260-7208
Yukon-Kuskokwim Correctional Ctr 1000 Chief Eddie Hoffman Hwy PO Box 400 *Web:* www.correct.state.ak.us	Bethel	AK	99559	907-543-5245	543-3097

Arizona

				Phone	Fax
Arizona State Prison Complex-Douglas 6911 N BDI Blvd PO Box 3867	Douglas	AZ	85607	520-364-7521	364-7445
Arizona State Prison Complex-Eyman 4374 E Butte Ave PO Box 3500 *TF:* 866-333-2039 ■ *Web:* corrections.az.gov	Florence	AZ	85132	520-868-0201	868-0276
Arizona State Prison Complex-Florence 1305 E Butte Ave PO Box 629 *Web:* corrections.az.gov	Florence	AZ	85132	520-868-4011	868-5333
Arizona State Prison Complex-Lewis 26700 S Hwy 85 PO Box 70 *Web:* azcorrections.gov	Buckeye	AZ	85326	623-386-6160	386-7332
Arizona State Prison Complex-Perryville 2105 N Citrus Rd	Goodyear	AZ	85395	623-853-0304	853-0425
Arizona State Prison Complex-Phoenix 2500 E Van Buren PO Box 52109 *Web:* azcorrections.gov	Phoenix	AZ	85072	602-685-3100	685-3124
Arizona State Prison Complex-Safford 896 S Crook Rd PO Box 2222 *Web:* corrections.az.gov	Safford	AZ	85546	928-428-4698	428-3235
Arizona State Prison Complex-Winslow 2100 S Hwy 87 *Web:* az.gov	Winslow	AZ	86047	928-289-9551	289-2951
Arizona State Prison Complex-Yuma 7125 E Juan Sanchez Blvd *Web:* corrections.az.gov	San Luis	AZ	85349	928-627-8871	627-6703

Arkansas

				Phone	Fax
Arkansas Department of Correction 302 Wackenhut Way *Web:* www.adc.arkansas.gov	Newport	AR	72112	870-523-2639	523-6202
Arkansas Dept of Corrections Cummins Unit Hwy 388 PO Box 500 *Web:* adc.arkansas.gov	Grady	AR	71644	870-850-8899	850-8861
Arkansas Dept of Corrections Delta Regional Unit 425 W Capitol Ave Ste 1620 *Web:* www.arkansas.gov	Little Rock	AR	72201	501-324-8900	
Arkansas Dept of Corrections East Arkansas Regional Unit 326 Lee 601 PO Box 180 *Web:* adc.arkansas.gov/pages/default.aspx	Brickeys	AR	72320	870-295-4700	295-6564
Arkansas Dept of Corrections Maximum Security Unit 2501 State Farm Rd *TF:* 866-801-3435 ■ *Web:* www.arkansas.gov	Tucker	AR	72168	501-842-3800	842-1977
Arkansas Dept of Corrections North Central Unit 10 Prison Cir HC 62 PO Box 300 *Web:* adc.arkansas.gov	Calico Rock	AR	72519	870-297-4311	297-4322
Arkansas Dept of Corrections Tucker Unit 2400 State Farm Rd PO Box 240 *TF:* 800-682-7377 ■ *Web:* adc.arkansas.gov	Tucker	AR	72168	501-842-2519	842-3958
Arkansas Dept of Corrections Varner Unit Hwy 388 PO Box 600 *Web:* adc.arkansas.gov	Grady	AR	71644	870-575-1800	479-3803

Phone Fax

Arkansas Dept of Corrections Wrightsville Unit
PO Box 1000 ....Wrightsville AR 72183 501-897-5806 897-5716
Web: adc.arkansas.gov

California

Phone Fax

Avenal State Prison One Kings Hwy PO Box 39..........Avenal CA 93204 559-386-0587 386-0907
Web: cdcr.ca.gov

California Correctional Institution
24900 Hwy 202 PO Box 1031......................Tehachapi CA 93581 661-822-4402 823-5020
Web: www.cdcr.ca.gov

California Men's Colony (CMC)
Hwy 1 PO Box 8101........................San Luis Obispo CA 93409 805-547-7900
Web: www.cdcr.ca.gov

California State Prison Corcoran
4001 King Ave PO Box 8800 ....Corcoran CA 93212 559-992-8800 386-7461
Web: www.cdcr.ca.gov

California State Prison Los Angeles County
44750 60th St W.................................Lancaster CA 93536 661-729-2000 729-6930
Web: cdcr.ca.gov

California State Prison Solano
2100 Peabody Rd PO Box 4000.....................Vacaville CA 95687 707-451-0182 454-3200

Calipatria State Prison 7018 Blair Rd...............Calipatria CA 92233 760-348-7000 348-7188
Web: cdcr.ca.gov

Centinela State Prison
2302 Brown Rd PO Box 731.........................Imperial CA 92251 760-337-7900 337-7692
Web: cdcr.ca.gov

Central California Women's Facility (CCWF)
23370 Rd 22 PO Box 1501.......................Chowchilla CA 93610 559-665-5531
Web: www.cdcr.ca.gov/facilities_locator/ccwf.html

Chuckawalla Valley State Prison (CVSP)
19025 Wiley's Well Rd PO Box 2289 ....Blythe CA 92226 760-922-5300 922-6855
Web: cdcr.ca.gov

Folsom State Prison 300 Prison Rd..................Represa CA 95671 916-985-2561 351-3010
Web: cdcr.ca.gov

High Desert State Prison (HDSP)
475-750 Rice Canyon Rd PO Box 750...............Susanville CA 96127 530-251-5100
Web: www.cdcr.ca.gov

Ironwood State Prison
19005 Wiley's Well Rd PO Box 2229 ....Blythe CA 92225 760-921-3000
Web: www.cdcr.ca.gov/facilities_locator/isp.html

Mule Creek State Prison 4001 Hwy 104 ....Ione CA 95640 209-274-4911 274-4861
TF: 877-256-6877 ■ *Web:* cdcr.ca.gov

Pelican Bay State Prison (PBSP)
5905 Lake Earl Dr PO Box 7000..................Crescent City CA 95531 707-465-1000 465-4376
TF: 877-256-6877 ■ *Web:* www.cdcr.ca.gov

Pleasant Valley State Prison
24863 W Jayne Ave PO Box 8500 ....Coalinga CA 93210 559-935-4900 386-7461
TF: 877-256-6877 ■ *Web:* www.cdcr.ca.gov

RJ Donovan Correctional Facility at Rock Mountain
480 Alta Rd....................................San Diego CA 92179 619-661-6500 661-6253
TF: 877-256-6877 ■ *Web:* cdcr.ca.gov

Salinas Valley State Prison 31625 Hwy 101 N.........Soledad CA 93960 831-678-5500 678-5503
Web: cdcr.ca.gov

Valley State Prison for Women
21633 Ave 24 PO Box 99........................Chowchilla CA 93610 559-665-6100
Web: cdcr.ca.gov

Colorado

Phone Fax

Arkansas Valley Correctional Facility (AVCF)
12750 Colorado 96 PO Box 1000.....................Crowley CO 81033 719-267-3520 267-5024
Web: www.doc.state.co.us

Delta Correctional Ctr 4102 Saw Mill Mesa Rd...........Delta CO 81416 970-874-7614 874-7614
Web: doc.state.co.us

Denver Women's Correctional Facility
3600 Havana St PO Box 392005.......................Denver CO 80239 303-371-4804
Web: www.doc.state.co.us

Fremont Correctional Facility (FCF)
E US Hwy 50 Evans Blvd PO Box 999...............Canon City CO 81215 719-269-5002 269-5020
Web: www.doc.state.co.us

Limon Correctional Facility 49030 State Hwy 71........Limon CO 80826 719-775-9221 775-7607
Web: www.colorado.gov/pacific/cdoc/search/site/Limon%20Correctional%20Facility

Rifle Correctional Ctr 200 County Rd 219................Rifle CO 81650 970-625-1700 625-1706
Web: doc.state.co.us

Sterling Correctional Facility
12101 Hwy 61 PO Box 6000.........................Sterling CO 80751 970-521-5010
Web: www.doc.state.co.us

Connecticut

Phone Fax

Brooklyn Correctional Institution
59 Hartford Rd ....Brooklyn CT 06234 860-779-2600 779-2394
Web: ct.gov

Corrections Dept 1106 N Ave.....................Bridgeport CT 06606 203-579-6131 579-6693
Web: ct.gov

Corrigan Correctional Institution
986 Norwich-New London Tpke....................Uncasville CT 06382 860-848-5700 848-5821
Web: www.ct.gov

Enfield Correctional Institution
289 Shaker Rd PO Box 1500 ....Enfield CT 06082 860-763-7300
Web: www.ct.gov

Garner Correctional Institution
50 Nunnawauk Rd.................................Newtown CT 06470 203-270-2800 270-1826
Web: ct.gov

Gates Correctional Institution
131 N Bridebrook Rd ....Niantic CT 06357 860-691-4700 691-4745
Web: www.ct.gov

Hartford Correctional Ctr 177 Weston St ....Hartford CT 06120 860-240-1800 566-2725
Web: ct.gov

New Haven Correctional Ctr 245 Whalley Ave.......New Haven CT 06511 203-789-7111 974-4167

Northern Correctional Institution
287 Bilton Rd ....Somers CT 06071 860-763-8600 763-8651
Web: ct.gov

Willard-Cybulski Correctional Institution
391 Shaker Rd ....Enfield CT 06082 860-763-6100 763-6111
Web: ct.gov

York Correctional Institution 201 W Main St...........Niantic CT 06357 860-451-3001 451-3200
Web: www.ct.gov

Delaware

Phone Fax

Baylor Women's Correctional Institution
660 Baylor Blvd ....New Castle DE 19720 302-577-3004 577-7099

Sussex Corrections Institution
23203 Dupont Blvd PO Box 500...................Georgetown DE 19947 302-856-5280

Florida

Phone Fax

Apalachee Correctional Institution
35 Apalachee Dr ....Sneads FL 32460 850-718-0688 593-6445
Web: dc.state.fl.us

Avon Park Correctional Institution
County Rd 64 E PO Box 1100......................Avon Park FL 33826 863-453-3174 453-1511
Web: dc.state.fl.us

Baker Correctional Institution
20706 US Hwy 90...............................Sanderson FL 32087 386-719-4500 758-5759
Web: myflorida.com

Bay Correctional Facility
5400 Bayline Dr ....Panama City FL 32404 850-769-1455 769-1942
Web: dc.state.fl.us

Brevard Correctional Institution 855 Camp Rd.........Cocoa FL 32927 321-634-6000 634-6066
Web: dc.state.fl.us

Calhoun Correctional Institution
19562 SE Institutional Dr Unit 1.................Blountstown FL 32424 850-237-6500 237-6508
Web: dc.state.fl.us

Charlotte Correctional Institution
33123 Oil Well Rd............................Punta Gorda FL 33955 941-833-2300 575-5747
Web: dc.state.fl.us

Corrections Department
16415 Spring Hill Dr ....Brooksville FL 34604 352-754-6715 544-2307

Cross City Corrections Dept 568 NE 255 St.........Cross City FL 32628 352-498-4444
Web: dc.state.fl.us

Desoto Correctional Institution
13617 SE Hwy 70...................................Arcadia FL 34266 863-494-3727 494-1740
Web: dc.state.fl.us

Florida Department of Corrections 8784 W US 27.......Mayo FL 32066 386-294-4500 829-4534*
**Fax Area Code:* 904

Florida State Prison 7819 NW 228 St ....Raiford FL 32026 904-368-2500 368-2732
Web: dc.state.fl.us

Gainesville Correctional Institution
2845 NE 39th Ave..............................Gainesville FL 32609 352-955-2001 334-1675

Gulf Correctional Institution
500 Ike Steele Rd ....Wewahitchka FL 32465 850-639-1100 639-1182
Web: dc.state.fl.us

Hamilton Correctional Institution
10650 SW 46th St ....Jasper FL 32052 386-792-5409

Jackson Correctional Institution
5563 Tenth St.....................................Malone FL 32445 850-569-5260 569-5996
Web: dc.state.fl.us

Lake City Correctional Facility
7906 E US Hwy 90...............................Lake City FL 32055 386-755-3379 752-7202
Web: www.cca.com

Lake Correctional Institution
19225 US Hwy 27................................Clermont FL 34711 352-394-6146
Web: dc.state.fl.us

Lancaster Correctional Institution
3449 SW SR 26 ....Trenton FL 32693 352-463-4100 463-3476
Web: dc.state.fl.us

Liberty Correctional Institution
11064 NW Dempsey Barron Rd ....Bristol FL 32321 850-643-9400 643-9412
Web: dc.state.fl.us

Lowell Correctional Institution-Women's Unit
11120 NW Gainesville Rd.............................Ocala FL 34482 352-401-5301 401-5331
Web: dc.state.fl.us

Madison Correctional Institution
382 SW MCI Way...................................Madison FL 32340 850-973-5300 973-3666
Web: dc.state.fl.us

Moore Haven Correctional Facility
1282 E SR 78 NW PO Box 718501................Moore Haven FL 33471 863-946-2420 946-3437
Web: dc.state.fl.us

New River West Correctional Institution
7819 NW 228th St ....Raiford FL 32026 904-368-3000 368-2732
Web: dc.state.fl.us

Okaloosa Correctional
3189 Little Silver Rd.............................Crestview FL 32539 850-682-0931 689-7803
Web: dc.state.fl.us

Okeechobee Correctional Institution
3420 NE 168th St..............................Okeechobee FL 34972 863-462-5400 462-5402
TF: 800-574-5729 ■ *Web:* dc.state.fl.us

Putnam Correctional Institution
128 Yelvington Rd ....East Palatka FL 32131 386-326-6800 312-2219
Web: www.myflorida.com

Quincy Correctional Institution
2225 Pat Thomas Pkwy ....Quincy FL 32351 850-627-5400 875-3572
Web: dc.state.fl.us

Facility	City	State	ZIP	Phone	Fax
Santa Rosa Correctional Institution 5850 E Milton Rd *Web:* dc.state.fl.us	Milton	FL	32583	850-983-5800	983-5907
South Bay Correctional Facility 600 US Hwy 27 S *TF:* 800-574-5729 ■ *Web:* dc.state.fl.us	South Bay	FL	33493	561-992-9505	992-9551
Sumter Correctional Institution 9544 County Rd 476 B *Web:* dc.state.fl.us	Bushnell	FL	33513	352-793-2525	793-3542
Taylor Correctional Institution 8501 Hampton Springs Rd *Web:* dc.state.fl.us	Perry	FL	32348	850-838-4000	838-4024
Tomoka Correctional Institution 3950 Tiger Bay Rd *Web:* dc.state.fl.us	Daytona Beach	FL	32124	386-323-1070	323-1006
Union Correctional Institution 7819 NW 228th St *Web:* dc.state.fl.us	Raiford	FL	32026	386-431-2000	431-2010
Zephyrhills Correctional Institution 2739 Gall Blvd	Zephyrhills	FL	33541	813-782-5521	780-0134

Georgia

Facility	City	State	ZIP	Phone	Fax
Baldwin State Prison Laying Farm Rd PO Box 218 *Web:* dcor.state.ga.us	Hardwick	GA	31034	478-445-5218	445-6507
Calhoun State Prison 27823 Main St PO Box 249 *Web:* www.dcor.state.ga.us	Morgan	GA	39866	229-849-5000	849-5017
Dooly State Prison 1412 Plunkett Rd PO Box 750	Unadilla	GA	31091	478-627-2000	627-2140
Hancock State Prison 701 Prison Blvd PO Box 339 *Web:* dcor.state.ga.us	Sparta	GA	31087	706-444-1000	444-1137
Lee Arrendale State Prison 2023 Gainesville Hwy *Web:* dcor.state.ga.us	Alto	GA	30510	706-776-4700	
Lee State Prison 153 Pinewood Rd *Web:* dcor.state.ga.us	Leesburg	GA	31763	229-759-6453	759-3065
Phillips State Prison 2989 W Rock Quarry Rd *Web:* dcor.state.ga.us	Buford	GA	30519	770-932-4500	932-4544
Pulaski State Prison Upper River Rd Rt 2 PO Box 839 *Web:* www.dcor.state.ga.us	Hawkinsville	GA	31036	478-783-6000	783-6008
Rogers State Prison 1978 Georgia Hwy 147	Reidsville	GA	30453	912-557-7771	557-7051
Rutledge State Prison 7175 Manor Rd	Columbus	GA	31907	706-568-2340	568-2126
Smith State Prison 9676 Hwy 301 N PO Box 726 *Web:* www.dcor.state.ga.us	Glennville	GA	30427	912-654-5000	654-5131
Valdosta State Prison 3259 Valtech Rd PO Box 310 *Web:* www.dcor.state.ga.us	Valdosta	GA	31603	229-333-7900	333-5387
Walker State Prison 97 Kevin Lake PO Box 98 *Web:* www.dcor.state.ga.us	Rock Spring	GA	30739	706-764-3600	764-3613
Ware State Prison 3620 N Harris Rd *Web:* dcor.state.ga.us	Waycross	GA	31501	912-285-6400	287-6520
West Central State Prison 4600 Fulton Mill Rd *Web:* www.dcor.state.ga.us	Macon	GA	31208	478-471-2908	471-2068

Hawaii

Facility	City	State	ZIP	Phone	Fax
Waiawa Correctional Facility 94-560 Kamehameha Hwy *Web:* hawaii.gov	Waipahu	HI	96797	808-677-6150	

Idaho

Facility	City	State	ZIP	Phone	Fax
Idaho Maximum Security Institution (IMSI) PO Box 51 *Web:* www.idoc.idaho.gov	Boise	ID	83707	208-338-1635	
Idaho State Correctional Institution PO Box 14 *Web:* idoc.idaho.gov	Boise	ID	83707	208-336-0740	334-2748
North Idaho Correctional Institution 236 Radar Rd	Cottonwood	ID	83522	208-962-3276	962-7119
Pocatello Women's Correctional Ctr 1451 Fore Rd *Web:* idoc.idaho.gov	Pocatello	ID	83204	208-236-6360	236-6362

Illinois

Facility	City	State	ZIP	Phone	Fax
Big Muddy River Correctional Ctr 251 N Hwy 37 PO Box 1000 *Web:* illinois.gov	Ina	IL	62846	618-437-5300	437-5627
Centralia Correctional Ctr 9330 Shattuc Rd PO Box 1266 *Web:* www2.illinois.gov	Centralia	IL	62801	618-533-4111	533-4112
Danville Correctional Ctr 3820 E Main St *Web:* www2.illinois.gov	Danville	IL	61834	217-446-0441	446-5347
Dixon Correctional Ctr 2600 N Brinton Ave	Dixon	IL	61021	815-288-5561	288-0118
East Moline Correctional Ctr 100 Hillcrest Rd *Web:* idoc.state.il.us	East Moline	IL	61244	309-755-4511	755-2589
Graham Correctional Ctr 12078 Illinois Rt 185 PO Box 499 *Web:* www2.illinois.gov	Hillsboro	IL	62049	217-532-6962	532-6799
Hill Correctional Ctr 600 S Linwood Rd	Galesburg	IL	61401	309-343-4212	
Jacksonville Correctional Ctr 2268 E Morton Ave *Web:* illinois.gov	Jacksonville	IL	62650	217-245-1481	
Logan Correctional Ctr 1096 1350th St *Web:* idoc.state.il.us	Lincoln	IL	62656	217-735-5581	735-1077
Menard Correctional Ctr 711 Kaskaskia St *Web:* idoc.state.il.us	Menard	IL	62259	618-826-5071	
Pinckneyville Correctional Ctr 5835 SR- 154 *Web:* illinois.gov	Pinckneyville	IL	62274	618-357-9722	357-2083
Pontiac Correctional Ctr 700 W Lincoln St *Web:* illinois.gov	Pontiac	IL	61764	815-842-2816	842-3420
Robinson Correctional Ctr 13423 E 1150th Ave *Web:* www2.illinois.gov	Robinson	IL	62454	618-546-5659	544-2166
Shawnee Correctional Ctr 6665 SR 146 E *Web:* idoc.state.il.us	Vienna	IL	62995	618-658-8331	658-8822
Southwestern Correctional Ctr 950 Kings Hwy *Web:* idoc.state.il.us	East Saint Louis	IL	62203	618-394-2200	394-2228
Stateville Correctional Ctr 16830 S Broadway St PO Box 112 *Web:* www.illinois.gov	Joliet	IL	60434	815-727-3607	727-5511
Taylorville Correctional Ctr 1144 Illinois Rt 29 PO Box 1000 *Web:* illinois.gov	Taylorville	IL	62568	217-824-4004	824-4042
Vandalia Correctional Ctr Rt 51 N PO Box 500 *Web:* www.illinois.gov	Vandalia	IL	62471	618-283-4170	283-9147
Vienna Correctional Ctr 6695 SR 146 E *Web:* idoc.state.il.us	Vienna	IL	62995	618-658-8371	658-3609
Western Illinois Correctional Ctr 2500 Illinois 99 *Web:* www.illinois.gov	Mount Sterling	IL	62353	217-773-4441	

Indiana

Facility	City	State	ZIP	Phone	Fax
Henryville Correctional Facility PO Box 148 *Web:* www.in.gov/idoc/2398.htm	Henryville	IN	47126	812-294-4372	294-1523
Indiana State Prison One Pk Row	Michigan City	IN	46360	219-874-7258	
Indiana Women's Prison 2596 N Girls School Rd *Web:* in.gov	Indianapolis	IN	46214	317-244-3387	244-4670
Madison Correctional Facility 800 MSH Busstop Dr *Web:* in.gov	Madison	IN	47250	812-265-6154	265-2142
Miami Correctional Facility 3038 W 850 S *Web:* in.gov	Bunker Hill	IN	46914	765-689-8920	689-7479
New Castle Correctional Facility 1000 Van Nuys Rd	New Castle	IN	47362	765-593-0111	778-3395
Plainfield Correctional Facility 727 Moon Rd *Web:* in.gov	Plainfield	IN	46168	317-839-2513	837-1875
Putnamville Correctional Facility 1946 W Hwy 40 **Fax:* Warden ■ *Web:* in.gov	Greencastle	IN	46135	765-653-8441	653-7461*
Rockville Correctional Facility 811 W 50 N *Web:* in.gov	Rockville	IN	47872	765-569-3178	569-3178
Wabash Valley Correctional Facility PO Box 1111 *Web:* www.in.gov/idoc/2409.htm	Carlisle	IN	47838	812-398-5050	398-5065

Iowa

Facility	City	State	ZIP	Phone	Fax
Clarinda Correctional Facility 1800 N 16th St Ste 1 *Web:* www.doc.state.ia.us	Clarinda	IA	51632	712-542-5634	542-4844
Fort Dodge Correctional Facility 1550 L St *Web:* www.doc.state.ia.us/InstitutionDescriptions	Fort Dodge	IA	50501	515-574-4700	
Iowa Correctional Institution for Women 420 Mill St SW PO Box 700 *Web:* mitchellvilleprison.org/	Mitchellville	IA	50169	515-725-5042	725-5015
Iowa State Penitentiary Ave E & 1st St PO Box 409 *Web:* iaprisonind.com	Fort Madison	IA	52627	319-372-1908	372-2856
Newton Correctional Facility 307 S 50th Ave W PO Box 218 *Web:* doc.state.ia.us	Newton	IA	50208	641-792-7552	791-1683

Kansas

Facility	City	State	ZIP	Phone	Fax
El Dorado Correctional Facility 1737 SE Hwy 54 PO Box 311 *Web:* www.dc.state.ks.us	El Dorado	KS	67042	316-321-7284	321-5349
Hutchinson Correctional Facility PO Box 1568 *Web:* www.doc.ks.gov/facilities/hcf	Hutchinson	KS	67504	620-662-2321	662-8662
Topeka Correctional Facility 815 SE Rice Rd *TF:* 888-317-8204 ■ *Web:* dc.state.ks.us	Topeka	KS	66603	785-296-3317	
Winfield Correctional Facility 1806 Pine Crest Cir *Web:* dc.state.ks.us	Winfield	KS	67156	620-221-6660	221-9229

Kentucky

Facility	City	State	Zip	Phone	Fax
Blackburn Correctional Complex 3111 Spurr Rd *Web:* corrections.ky.gov	Lexington	KY	40511	859-246-2366	246-2376
Eastern Kentucky Correctional Complex 200 Rd to Justice *Web:* www.corrections.ky.gov	West Liberty	KY	41472	606-743-2800	743-2811
Green River Correctional Complex 1200 River Rd *Web:* corrections.ky.gov/	Central City	KY	42330	270-754-5415	
Kentucky Correctional Institution for Women 3000 Ash Ave *TF:* 877-687-6818 ■ *Web:* corrections.ky.gov	Pewee Valley	KY	40056	502-241-8454	243-0079
Kentucky State Reformatory 3001 W Hwy 146 *Web:* corrections.ky.gov	LaGrange	KY	40032	502-222-9441	222-8115
Luther Luckett Correctional Complex Dawkins Rd PO Box 6 *TF:* 800-511-1670 ■ *Web:* www.corrections.ky.gov	LaGrange	KY	40031	502-222-0363	222-8112
Western Kentucky Correctional Complex 374 New Bethel Church Rd *Web:* corrections.ky.gov	Fredonia	KY	42411	270-388-9781	388-0031

Louisiana

Facility	City	State	Zip	Phone	Fax
Allen Correctional Ctr 3751 Lauderdale Woodyard Rd *Web:* doc.la.gov	Kinder	LA	70648	337-639-2942	639-2944
Avoyelles Correctional Ctr 1630 Prison Rd *Web:* doc.la.gov	Cottonport	LA	71327	318-876-2891	876-4220
C Paul Phelps Correctional Ctr 14925 Hwy 27 N PO Box 1056 *TF:* 888-524-3578 ■ *Web:* www.doc.la.gov	Dequincy	LA	70633	337-786-7963	786-4524
Catahoula Correctional Ctr 499 Columbia Rd *Web:* lasallecorrections.com	Harrisonburg	LA	71340	318-744-2121	744-2126
David Wade Correctional Ctr 670 Bell Hill Rd	Homer	LA	71040	318-927-0400	
Dixon Correctional Institute 5568 Hwy 68 *Web:* doc.louisiana.gov	Jackson	LA	70748	225-634-1200	634-4543
Louisiana State Penitentiary 17544 Tunica Trace *Web:* doc.la.gov	Angola	LA	70712	225-655-4411	
Vernon Correctional Facility 2294 Slagle Rd	Leesville	LA	71446	337-238-4522	238-4208

Maine

Facility	City	State	Zip	Phone	Fax
Downeast Correctional Dept 64 Base Rd	Machiasport	ME	04655	207-255-1100	255-1176
Maine Correctional Ctr 17 Mallison Falls Rd *Web:* maine.gov	Windham	ME	04062	207-893-7000	893-7001

Maryland

Facility	City	State	Zip	Phone	Fax
Eastern Correctional Institution 30420 Revells Neck Rd	Westover	MD	21890	410-845-4000	845-4055
Jessup Correctional Institution 7804 House of Correction Rd	Jessup	MD	20794	410-799-0100	
Maryland Correctional Adjustment Ctr 401 E Madison St	Baltimore	MD	21202	410-539-5445	332-4561
Maryland Correctional Institution for Women (MCI-W) 7943 Brockbridge Rd	Jessup	MD	20794	410-379-3800	799-6146
Maryland Correctional Institution-Hagerstown 18601 Roxbury Rd *Web:* msa.maryland.gov	Hagerstown	MD	21746	301-733-2800	797-2872
Maryland Correctional Training Ctr 18800Roxbury Rd *Web:* dbm.maryland.gov	Hagerstown	MD	21746	301-791-7200	797-8574
Roxbury Correctional Institution 18701 Roxbury Rd **Fax Area Code:* 301	Hagerstown	MD	21746	240-420-3000	797-0795*
Western Correctional Institution 13800 McMullen Hwy	Cumberland	MD	21502	301-729-7000	729-7063

Massachusetts

Facility	City	State	Zip	Phone	Fax
Bay State Correctional Ctr 28 Clark St *Web:* mass.gov	Norfolk	MA	02056	508-668-1687	668-1687
Massachusetts Correctional Institution-Cedar Junction 2405 Main St *Web:* www.mass.gov	Walpole	MA	02071	508-668-2100	660-8008
Massachusetts Correctional Institution-Framingham PO Box 9007 *Web:* www.mass.gov	Framingham	MA	01704	508-532-5100	532-5104
Massachusetts Correctional Institution-Plymouth (MCI) One Bumps Pond Rd *Web:* www.mass.gov/	South Carver	MA	02366	508-291-2441	
North Central Correctional Institution at Gardner 500 Colony Rd	Gardner	MA	01440	978-630-6000	630-6040
Old Colony Correctional Ctr One Admin Rd *Web:* mass.gov	Bridgewater	MA	02324	508-279-6000	279-6754
Souza-Baranowski Correctional Ctr PO Box 8000 *Web:* www.mass.gov	Shirley	MA	01464	978-514-6500	514-6529

Michigan

Facility	City	State	Zip	Phone	Fax
Alger Correctional Facility N 6141 Industrial Pk Dr PO Box 600 *Web:* www.michigan.gov/corrections	Munising	MI	49862	906-387-5000	
Baraga Correctional Facility 13924 Wadaga Rd *Web:* www.michigan.gov/corrections	Baraga	MI	49908	906-353-7070	
Carson City Correctional Facility 10274 Boyer Rd *Web:* www.michigan.gov/corrections	Carson City	MI	48811	989-584-3941	
Central Michigan Correctional Facility 320 N Hubbard *Web:* www.michigan.gov/corrections	Saint Louis	MI	48880	989-681-6668	
Charles E Egeler Correctional Facility 3855 Cooper St *TF:* 855-444-3911 ■ *Web:* www.michigan.gov/corrections	Jackson	MI	49201	517-780-5600	780-5814
Chippewa Correctional Facility 4269 W M-80 *Web:* www.michigan.gov/corrections	Kincheloe	MI	49784	906-495-2275	495-5787
Cooper Street Correctional Facility 3100 Cooper St *Web:* www.michigan.gov/corrections	Jackson	MI	49201	517-780-6175	780-6179
Earnest C Brooks Correctional Facility 2500 S Sheridan Dr *Web:* www.michigan.gov/corrections	Muskegon Heights	MI	49444	231-773-9200	777-2097
G Robert Cotton Correctional Facility 3500 N Elm Rd *TF:* 855-444-3911 ■ *Web:* www.michigan.gov/corrections	Jackson	MI	49201	517-780-5000	780-5100
Gus Harrison Correctional Facility 2727 E Beecher St *Web:* www.michigan.gov	Adrian	MI	49221	517-265-3900	263-4401
Hiawatha Correctional Facility 4533 W Industrial Pk Dr *Web:* www.michigan.gov	Kincheloe	MI	49786	906-495-5661	495-5291
Huron Valley Correctional Facility 3201 Bemis Rd *TF:* 855-444-3911 ■ *Web:* www.michigan.gov	Ypsilanti	MI	48197	734-572-9900	572-9499
Ionia Maximum Correctional Facility 1576 W Bluewater Hwy *Web:* www.michigan.gov/corrections	Ionia	MI	48846	616-527-6331	527-6863
Kinross Correctional Facility 16770 S Watertower Dr *Web:* www.michigan.gov/corrections	Kincheloe	MI	49788	906-495-2282	495-5837
Lakeland Correctional Facility 141 First St *Web:* www.michigan.gov/corrections	Coldwater	MI	49036	517-278-6942	279-0327
Macomb Correctional Facility 34625 26th Mile Rd *Web:* michigan.gov	New Haven	MI	48048	586-749-4900	749-4927
Marquette Branch Prison 1960 US Hwy 41 S *Web:* www.michigan.gov/corrections	Marquette	MI	49855	906-226-6531	226-6557
Michigan Reformatory 1727 Bluewater Hwy *Web:* www.michigan.gov/corrections	Ionia	MI	48846	616-527-2500	527-7155
Mound Correctional Facility 17601 Mound Rd *Web:* www.michigan.gov/corrections	Detroit	MI	48212	313-368-8300	368-8972
Muskegon Correctional Facility 2400 S Sheridan Dr **Fax Area Code:* 231 ■ *Web:* www.michigan.gov/corrections	Muskegon	MI	48909	517-335-1426	773-3657*
Newberry Correctional Facility 13747 E County Rd 428 *Web:* www.michigan.gov/corrections	Newberry	MI	49868	906-293-6200	293-0011
Oaks Correctional Facility 1500 Caberfae Hwy *Web:* www.michigan.gov/corrections	Manistee	MI	49660	231-723-8272	728-4278
Richard A Handlon Correctional Facility 1728 Bluewater Hwy *Web:* www.michigan.gov/corrections	Ionia	MI	48846	616-527-3100	527-2991
Riverside Correctional Facility 777 W Riverside Dr *Web:* www.michigan.gov	Ionia	MI	48846	616-527-0110	527-2936
Saginaw Correctional Facility 9625 Pierce Rd *Web:* www.michigan.gov	Freeland	MI	48623	989-695-9880	695-6662
Saint Louis Correctional Facility 8585 N Croswell Rd *Web:* www.michigan.gov	Saint Louis	MI	48880	989-681-6444	681-2425
Thumb Correctional Facility 3225 John Conley Dr *TF:* 855-444-3911 ■ *Web:* www.michigan.gov	Lapeer	MI	48446	810-667-2045	667-2048

Minnesota

Facility	City	State	Zip	Phone	Fax
Minnesota Correctional Facility-Fairbault 1101 Linden Ln **Fax:* Warden ■ *TF:* 800-657-3830 ■ *Web:* www.doc.state.mn.us	Faribault	MN	55021	507-334-0700	332-4538*
Minnesota Correctional Facility-Lino Lakes 7525 Fourth Ave	Lino Lakes	MN	55014	651-717-6100	
Minnesota Correctional Facility-Moose Lake 1000 Lk Shore Dr	Moose Lake	MN	55767	218-485-5000	485-5010
Minnesota Correctional Facility-Rush City 7600 525th St	Rush City	MN	55069	320-358-0400	358-0538
Minnesota Correctional Facility-Shakopee 1010 W Sixth Ave *Web:* www.doc.state.mn.us	Shakopee	MN	55379	952-496-4440	496-4476
Minnesota Correctional Facility-Stillwater 970 Picket St N	Bayport	MN	55003	651-779-2700	351-3600

Mississippi

Facility	City	State	ZIP	Phone	Fax
Central Mississippi Correctional Facility 3794 Hwy 468 *Web:* mdoc.state.ms.us	Pearl	MS	39208	601-932-2880	932-6202
Issaquena County Correctional Facility PO Box 220 *Web:* www.mdoc.state.ms.us	Mayersville	MS	39113	662-873-2153	873-2956
Marion/Walthall Correctional Facility 503 S Main St *Web:* mdoc.state.ms.us	Columbia	MS	39429	601-736-3621	736-4473
Marshall County Correctional Facility 833 W St	Holly Springs	MS	38635	662-252-7111	
Mississippi State Penitentiary Hwy 49 W PO Box 1057 *TF:* 800-844-0898 ■ *Web:* mdoc.state.ms.us	Parchman	MS	38738	662-745-6611	745-8912
South Mississippi Correctional Institution 22689 Hwy 63 N PO Box 1419 *Web:* mdoc.state.ms.us	Leakesville	MS	39451	601-394-5600	394-4451
Wilkinson County Correctional Ctr 2999 US 61 N *Web:* www.cca.com	Woodville	MS	39669	601-888-3199	888-3235
Winston County Correctional Facility PO Box 1437 *Web:* www.mdoc.state.ms.us	Louisville	MS	39339	662-773-2528	773-4989

Missouri

Facility	City	State	ZIP	Phone	Fax
Algoa Correctional Ctr 8501 No More Victims Rd **Fax:* Warden ■ *TF:* 800-392-1111 ■ *Web:* mo.gov	Jefferson City	MO	65102	573-751-3911	526-1385*
Boonville Correctional Ctr 1216 E Morgan St **Fax:* Warden ■ *TF:* 800-392-8486 ■ *Web:* doc.mo.gov	Boonville	MO	65233	660-882-6521	882-7825*
Central Missouri Correctional Ctr 2600 Hwy 179	Jefferson City	MO	65109	573-751-2053	
Chillicothe Correctional Ctr 3151 Litton Rd *TF:* 800-392-8486 ■ *Web:* doc.mo.gov	Chillicothe	MO	64601	660-646-4032	646-1217
Farmington Correctional Ctr 1012 W Columbia St *Web:* mo.gov	Farmington	MO	63640	573-218-7100	
Jefferson City Correctional Ctr 8200 No More Victims Rd *Web:* mo.gov	Jefferson City	MO	65101	573-751-3224	
Missouri Eastern Correctional Ctr 18701 Old Hwy 66 *Web:* mo.gov	Pacific	MO	63069	636-257-3322	257-5296
Moberly Correctional Ctr 5201 S Morley *Web:* www.doc.mo.gov	Moberly	MO	65270	660-263-3778	
Northeast Correctional Ctr 13698 County Rd 46 *Web:* mo.gov	Bowling Green	MO	63334	573-324-9975	324-5183
Ozark Correctional Ctr 929 Honor Camp Ln	Fordland	MO	65652	417-767-4491	
Potosi Correctional Ctr 11593 State Hwy O *Web:* mo.gov	Mineral Point	MO	63660	573-438-6000	438-6006
Tipton Correctional Ctr 619 N Osage Ave *Web:* doc.mo.gov	Tipton	MO	65081	660-433-2031	
Western Missouri Correctional Ctr 609 E Pence Rd *Web:* mo.gov	Cameron	MO	64429	816-632-1390	632-2562

Montana

Facility	City	State	ZIP	Phone	Fax
Montana State Prison 400 Conley Lk Rd *TF:* 888-739-9122 ■ *Web:* www.cor.mt.gov	Deer Lodge	MT	59722	406-846-1320	
Montana Women's Prison 701 S 27th St *Web:* mt.gov	Billings	MT	59101	406-247-5100	247-5161

Nebraska

Facility	City	State	ZIP	Phone	Fax
Lincoln Correctional Ctr 3216 W Van Dorn St PO Box 22800 *Web:* www.corrections.nebraska.gov	Lincoln	NE	68522	402-479-6175	
Nebraska Correctional Ctr for Women 1107 Recharge Rd *TF:* 877-634-8463 ■ *Web:* www.corrections.nebraska.gov	York	NE	68467	402-362-3317	362-3892
Nebraska State Penitentiary 4201 S 14th St *TF:* 877-634-8463 ■ *Web:* www.corrections.nebraska.gov	Lincoln	NE	68502	402-471-3161	471-4326
Omaha Correctional Ctr 2323 Ave J PO Box 11099	Omaha	NE	68110	402-595-3963	595-2227

Nevada

Facility	City	State	ZIP	Phone	Fax
Ely State Prison 4569 NV-90 *Web:* doc.nv.gov	Ely	NV	89301	775-289-8800	684-3399
Lovelock Correctional Ctr 1200 Prison Rd *Web:* doc.nv.gov	Lovelock	NV	89419	775-273-1300	273-4277
Northern Nevada Correctional Ctr 1721 Snyder Dr PO Box 7000 *Web:* doc.nv.gov	Carson City	NV	89702	775-887-9297	
Warm Springs Correctional Ctr 3301 E Fifth St PO Box 7007 *Web:* doc.nv.gov	Carson City	NV	89702	775-684-3000	

New Hampshire

Facility	City	State	ZIP	Phone	Fax
New Hampshire State Prison 281 N State St PO Box 14 *Web:* www.nh.gov/nhdoc/facilities/concord.html	Concord	NH	03302	603-271-1801	271-4092
New Hampshire State Prison for Women 317 Mast Rd *TF:* 800-639-1122	Goffstown	NH	03045	603-668-6137	679-5869
Northern New Hampshire Correctional Facility 138 E Milan Rd *Web:* nh.gov	Berlin	NH	03570	603-752-2906	752-0405

New Jersey

Facility	City	State	ZIP	Phone	Fax
Bayside State Prison 4293 Rt 47 *Web:* state.nj.us	Leesburg	NJ	08327	856-785-0040	785-2559
East Jersey State Prison 1100 Woodbridge Ave Lock Bag R *Web:* state.nj.us	Rahway	NJ	07065	732-499-5010	499-5022
New Jersey State Prison PO Box 861 *Web:* www.state.nj.us	Trenton	NJ	08625	609-292-9700	
South Woods State Prison 215 Burlington Rd S *Web:* state.nj.us	Bridgeton	NJ	08302	856-459-7000	459-7140
Southern State Correctional Facility 4295 Rt 47 PO Box 150	Delmont	NJ	08314	856-785-1300	785-1236

New Mexico

Facility	City	State	ZIP	Phone	Fax
Central New Mexico Correctional Facility 1525 Morris Rd	Los Lunas	NM	87031	505-865-1622	383-3510
Guadalupe County Correctional Facility S Hwy 54 PO Box 520 **Fax Area Code:* 505 ■ *Web:* geogroup.com	Santa Rosa	NM	88435	575-472-1001	472-1006*
New Mexico Women's Correctional Facility 1700 Old US Hwy PO Box 800 *Web:* corrections.state.nm.us	Grants	NM	87020	505-287-2941	285-6828
Penitentiary of New Mexico 4311 Hwy 14 *Web:* corrections.state.nm.us	Santa Fe	NM	87505	505-827-8205	827-8220
Roswell Correctional Ctr 578 W Chickasaw Rd **Fax Area Code:* 505 ■ *Web:* www.corrections.state.nm.us	Hagerman	NM	88232	575-625-3100	625-3190*
Southern New Mexico Correctional Facility 1983 Joe R Silva Blvd *Web:* corrections.state.nm.us	Las Cruces	NM	88004	575-523-3200	523-3349
Torrance County Detention Ctr 209 E Allen Ayers	Estancia	NM	87016	505-384-2711	

New York

Facility	City	State	ZIP	Phone	Fax
Adirondack Correctional Facility 196 Ray Brook Rd PO Box 110 *Web:* www.doccs.ny.gov	Ray Brook	NY	12977	518-891-1343	
Albion Correctional Facility 3595 State School Rd *Web:* nicic.gov	Albion	NY	14411	585-589-5511	
Altona Correctional Facility 555 Devil Den Rd *Web:* www.doccs.ny.gov/faclist.html	Altona	NY	12910	518-236-7841	
Arthur Kill Correctional Facility 2911 Arthur Kill Rd *Web:* metro.org	Staten Island	NY	10309	718-356-7333	
Attica Correctional Facility 639 Exchange St PO Box 149 *Web:* www.doccs.ny.gov/faclist.html	Attica	NY	14011	585-591-2000	
Auburn Correctional Facility 135 State St PO Box 618 *Web:* www.doccs.ny.gov/faclist.html	Auburn	NY	13021	315-253-8401	
Bare Hill Correctional Facility 181 Brand Rd	Malone	NY	12953	518-483-8411	483-8411
Bayview Correctional Facility 550 W 20th St *Web:* doccs.ny.gov	New York	NY	10011	212-255-7590	
Bedford Hills Correctional Facility 247 Harris Rd *Web:* www.doccs.ny.gov/faclist.html	Bedford Hills	NY	10507	914-241-3100	
Buffalo Correctional Facility 3052 Wende Rd PO Box 300 *Web:* ci.buffalo.ny.us	Alden	NY	14004	716-937-3786	
Camp Georgetown Correctional Facility 3191 Crumbhill Rd	Georgetown	NY	13072	315-837-4446	
Cape Vincent Correctional Facility 36560 New York 12E	Cape Vincent	NY	13618	315-654-4100	654-4103
Cayuga Correctional Facility 2202 State Rt 38A PO Box 1150 *Web:* www.doccs.ny.gov	Moravia	NY	13118	315-497-1110	
Chateaugay Correctional Facility 7874 SR 11 PO Box 320 *Web:* doccs.ny.gov	Chateaugay	NY	12920	518-497-3300	
Clinton Correctional Facility 1156 Cook St *Web:* www.doccs.ny.gov/faclist.html	Dannemora	NY	12929	518-492-2511	
Collins Correctional Facility Middle Rd PO Box 490 *Web:* www.doccs.ny.gov	Collins	NY	14034	716-532-4588	
Coxsackie Correctional Facility 11260 Rt 9W PO Box 200 *Web:* www.doccs.ny.gov	Coxsackie	NY	12051	518-731-2781	
Eastern Correctional Facility 30 Institution Rd PO Box 338 *Web:* doccs.ny.gov	Napanoch	NY	12458	845-647-7400	

Phone | Fax

Elmira Correctional Facility 1879 Davis St . . . Elmira NY 14901 607-734-3901
Web: doccs.ny.gov

Franklin Correctional Facility
62 Bare Hill Rd PO Box 10 . . . Malone NY 12953 518-483-6040

Fulton Correctional Facility 1511 Fulton Ave. . . . Bronx NY 10457 718-583-8000

Gouverneur Correctional Facility
112 Scotch Settlement Rd. . . . Gouverneur NY 13642 315-287-7351 287-7351

Gowanda Correctional Facility S Rd PO Box 350 . . . Gowanda NY 14070 716-532-0177
Web: www.doccs.ny.gov

Great Meadow Correctional Facility
11739 SR 22 PO Box 51 . . . Comstock NY 12821 518-639-5516
Web: doccs.ny.gov

Green Haven Correctional Facility
594 Rt 216 . . . Stormville NY 12582 845-221-2711
Web: www.doccs.ny.gov

Greene Correctional Facility
165 Plank Rd PO Box 8 . . . Coxsackie NY 12051 518-731-2741
Web: www.doccs.ny.gov

Lakeview Shock Incarceration Ctr
9300 Lake Ave PO Box T . . . Brocton NY 14716 716-792-7100
Web: ncjrs.gov

Lincoln Correctional Facility
31-33 W 110th St . . . New York NY 10026 212-860-9400 860-2099
Web: doccs.ny.gov

Livingston Correctional Facility
7005 Sonyea Rd . . . Sonyea NY 14556 585-658-3710
Web: doccs.ny.gov

Lyon Mountain Correctional Facility
3864 SR 374 . . . Lyon Mountain NY 12952 518-735-4546

Marcy Correctional Facility 9000 Old River Rd . . . Marcy NY 13403 315-768-1400

Mid-State Correctional Facility PO Box 216 . . . Marcy NY 13403 315-768-8581
Web: www.prisontalk.com

Moriah Shock Incarceration Correctional Facility
75 Burhart Ln PO Box 999 . . . Mineville NY 12956 518-942-7561
Web: www.doccs.ny.gov

Oneida Correctional Facility 6100 School Rd . . . Rome NY 13440 315-339-6880

Orleans Correctional Facility
3531 Gaines Basin Rd . . . Albion NY 14411 585-589-6820

Riverview Correctional Facility
1110 Tibbits Dr PO Box 158 . . . Ogdensburg NY 13669 315-393-8400
Web: doccs.ny.gov

Rochester Correctional Facility
470 Ford St . . . Rochester NY 14608 585-454-2280

Sing Sing Correctional Facility
354 Hunter St . . . Ossining NY 10562 914-941-0108
Web: www.doccs.ny.gov

Southport Correctional Facility
236 Bob Masia Dr PO Box 2000 . . . Pine City NY 14871 607-737-0850
Web: www.doccs.ny.gov

Sullivan Correctional Facility
325 Riverside Dr PO Box 116 . . . Fallsburg NY 12733 845-434-2080
Web: www.doccs.ny.gov

Summit Correctional Facility
137 Eagle Heights Rd . . . Summit NY 12175 518-287-1721

Taconic Correctional Facility
250 Harris Rd . . . Bedford Hills NY 10507 914-241-3010 722-6220*
**Fax Area Code:* 718 ■ *Web:* doccs.ny.gov

Ulster Correctional Facility
750 Berme Rd PO Box 800 . . . Napanoch NY 12458 845-647-1670

Upstate Correctional Facility
309 Bare Hill Rd PO Box 2000 . . . Malone NY 12953 518-483-6997
Web: doccs.ny.gov

Wallkill Correctional Facility
50 McKendrick Rd . . . Wallkill NY 12589 845-895-2021
Web: www.doccs.ny.gov/faclist.html

Washington Correctional Facility
72 Lock 11 Rd . . . Comstock NY 12821 518-639-4486
Web: www.doccs.ny.gov/faclist.html

Watertown Correctional Facility
23147 Swan Rd . . . Watertown NY 13601 315-782-7490

Wende Correctional Facility
3040 Wende Rd PO Box 1187 . . . Alden NY 14004 716-937-4000
Web: www.doccs.ny.gov/faclist.html

Wyoming Correctional Facility
3203 Dunbar Rd PO Box 501 . . . Attica NY 14011 585-591-1010
Web: www.doccs.ny.gov/faclist.html

North Carolina

Phone | Fax

Anson Correctional Ctr
1019 Old Prison Camp Rd PO Box 189 . . . Polkton NC 28135 704-694-7500 694-9655
Web: www.doc.state.nc.us/dop

Avery/Mitchell Correctional Ctr
600 Amity Pk Rd . . . Spruce Pine NC 28777 828-765-0229 765-0946
Web: doc.state.nc.us/

Brown Creek Correctional Institution
248 Prison Camp Rd PO Box 310 . . . Polkton NC 28135 704-694-2622 694-2709
Web: www.doc.state.nc.us

Buncombe Correctional Ctr
2988 Riverside Dr PO Box 18089 . . . Asheville NC 28814 828-645-7630
Web: www.doc.state.nc.us

Carteret Correctional Facility
1084 Orange St PO Box 220 . . . Newport NC 28570 252-223-5100 223-3069
Web: www.doc.state.nc.us

Catawba Correctional Ctr 1347 Prison Camp Rd . . . Newton NC 28658 828-466-5521 466-5523

Central Prison 1300 Western Blvd . . . Raleigh NC 27606 919-733-0800 715-2645
Web: www.ncdps.gov/index2.cfm?a=000003,002240,002381,002252

Craggy Correctional Ctr 2992 Riverside Dr . . . Asheville NC 28804 828-645-5315 658-2183
Web: ncdps.gov

Davidson Correctional Ctr 1400 Thomason St . . . Lexington NC 27292 336-249-7528 249-6962
Web: www.doc.state.nc.us

Phone | Fax

Durham Correctional Ctr 3900 Guess Rd . . . Durham NC 27705 919-477-2314 471-2257

Fountain Correctional Ctr for Women
300 Fountain School Rd PO Box 1435 . . . Rocky Mount NC 27802 252-442-9712 442-1413
Web: www.ncdps.gov/Search.cfm?q=Fountain+Correctional+Ctr+for+Women

Franklin Correctional Ctr
5918 NC 39 Hwy S PO Box 155 . . . Bunn NC 27508 919-496-6119 496-6032
Web: www.ncdps.gov/index2.cfm?a=000003,002240,002381,002253

Gaston Correctional Ctr 520 Justice Ct . . . Dallas NC 28034 704-922-3861 922-1491
Web: www.doc.state.nc.us

Greene Correctional Institution
2699 Hwy 903 N PO Box 39 . . . Maury NC 28554 252-747-3676 747-4432
Web: doc.state.nc.us

Harnett Correctional Institution
1210 McNeil St . . . Lillington NC 27546 910-893-2751 893-6432
Web: www.ncdps.gov/index2.cfm?a=000003,002391,002934

Hoke Correctional Institution
243 Old Hwy 211 . . . Raeford NC 28376 910-944-7612 944-4752
Web: www.doc.state.nc.us

Hyde Correctional Ctr
620 Prison Rd PO Box 278 . . . Swanquarter NC 27885 252-926-1810 926-2306
Web: www.doc.state.nc.us

Johnston Correctional Institution
2465 US 70 W . . . Smithfield NC 27577 919-934-8386 934-9150

Lumberton Correctional Institution
75 Legend Rd . . . Lumberton NC 28359 910-618-5574
Web: www.ncdps.gov

Marion Correctional Institution
355 Old Glenwood Rd PO Box 2405 . . . Marion NC 28752 828-659-7810 652-0115
Web: ncdps.gov

Nash Correctional Institution
2869 US 64 Alt PO Box 600 . . . Nashville NC 27856 252-459-4455 459-7728
Web: www.ncdps.gov/Search.cfm?q=Nash+Correctional+Institution

Neuse Correctional Institution
701 Stevens Mill Rd . . . Goldsboro NC 27530 919-731-2023

New Hanover Correctional Ctr
330 Div Dr PO Box 240 . . . Wilmington NC 28402 910-251-2666 251-2670
Web: www.doc.state.nc.us

North Carolina Correctional Institution for Women
1034 Bragg St . . . Raleigh NC 27610 919-733-4340 733-8031
Web: doc.state.nc.us

North Piedmont Correctional Ctr for Women
1420 Raleigh Rd PO Box 1227 . . . Lexington NC 27292 336-242-1259
Web: www.doc.state.nc.us

Odom Correctional Institution
485 Odom Prison Rd . . . Jackson NC 27845 252-534-5611 574-2011

Orange Correctional Ctr
2110 Clarence Walters Rd . . . Hillsborough NC 27278 919-732-9301 644-1395

Pasquotank Correctional Institution
527 Commerce Dr . . . Elizabeth City NC 27906 252-331-4881 331-4866
Web: ncdps.gov

Pender Correctional Institution
906 Penderlea Hwy . . . Burgaw NC 28425 910-259-8735
Web: www.ncdps.gov

Raleigh Correctional Ctr for Women
1201 S State St . . . Raleigh NC 27610 919-733-4248 733-9737

Randolph Correctional Ctr
2760 US Hwy 220 PO Box 4128 . . . Asheboro NC 27203 336-625-2578 625-5717
Web: www.ncdps.gov/Search.cfm?q=Randolph+Correctional+Ctr

Robeson Correctional Ctr
NC Hwy 711 PO Box 1979 . . . Lumberton NC 28359 910-618-5535 618-5532
Web: doc.state.nc.us/

Rowan Correctional Ctr
4201 Mail Service Ctr PO Box 1207 . . . Raleigh NC 27699 919-838-4000 733-8272
Web: www.ncdps.gov

Rutherford Correctional Ctr
549 Ledbetter Rd PO Box 127 . . . Spindale NC 28160 828-286-4121 286-9285
Web: www.doc.state.nc.us

Sampson Correctional Institution
700 NW Blvd Hwy 421N . . . Clinton NC 28328 910-592-2151 592-2543
Web: www.ncdps.gov

Sanford Correctional Ctr 417 Prison Camp Rd . . . Sanford NC 27330 919-776-4325 774-1866
Web: www.ncdps.gov/index2.cfm?a=000003,002240,002381,002297

Southern Correctional Institution
272 Glen Rd PO Box 786 . . . Troy NC 27371 910-572-3784
Web: www.ncdps.gov

Wake Correctional Ctr 1000 Rock Quarry Rd . . . Raleigh NC 27610 919-733-7988 733-9166
TF: 866-719-0108 ■ *Web:* ncdps.gov

Wilkes Correctional Ctr
404 Statesville Rd . . . North Wilkesboro NC 28659 336-667-4533 667-4095
Web: wilkesprisonministry.org

Ohio

Phone | Fax

Allen Correctional Institution
2238 NW St PO Box 45010 . . . Lima OH 45801 419-224-8000 224-5828
Web: www.drc.state.oh.us

Dayton Correctional Institution
4104 Germantown St PO Box 17399 . . . Dayton OH 45417 937-263-0060 263-1322
Web: www.drc.ohio.gov

Grafton Correctional Institution
2500 S Avon Beldon Rd . . . Grafton OH 44044 440-748-1161 748-2521
Web: drc.ohio.gov

Lebanon Correctional Institution
3791 State Rt 63 PO Box 56 . . . Lebanon OH 45036 513-932-1211 932-1320
Web: www.drc.ohio.gov/public/leci.htm

London Correctional Institution 1580 SR 56 . . . London OH 43140 740-852-2454 852-4854
Web: www.drc.ohio.gov

Lorain Correctional Institution
2075 Avon Belden Rd . . . Grafton OH 44044 440-748-1049 748-2191
TF: 888-988-4768 ■ *Web:* drc.ohio.gov

				Phone	Fax
Mansfield Correctional Institution 1150 N Main St PO Box 788 *Web:* www.drc.ohio.gov	Mansfield	OH	44901	419-525-4455	524-8022
Noble Correctional Institution 15708 McConnelsville Rd *Web:* drc.ohio.gov	Caldwell	OH	43724	740-732-5188	732-2651
North Central Correctional Institution 670 Marion Williamsport PO Box 1812 *Web:* www.drc.ohio.gov/public/ncci.htm	Marion	OH	43302	740-387-7040	387-5575
Ohio Reformatory for Women 1479 Collins Ave *Web:* drc.ohio.gov	Marysville	OH	43040	937-642-1065	642-7603
Ohio State Penitentiary 878 Coitsville HubbaRd Rd. *Web:* drc.ohio.gov	Youngstown	OH	44505	330-743-0700	742-5144
Pickaway Correctional Institution PO Box 209 *Web:* www.drc.ohio.gov	Orient	OH	43146	614-877-4362	877-4514
Richland Correctional Institution 1001 Olivesburg Rd *Web:* ohio.gov	Mansfield	OH	44905	419-526-2100	521-2810
Ross Correctional Institution 16149 SR 104 PO Box 7010 *Web:* drc.ohio.gov	Chillicothe	OH	45601	740-774-7050	774-7065
Southeastern Correctional Institution 5900 B I S Rd *Web:* ohio.gov	Lancaster	OH	43130	740-653-4324	653-0779
Southern Ohio Correctional Facility 1724 SR 728 PO Box 45699 *Web:* drc.ohio.gov	Lucasville	OH	45699	740-259-5544	259-2882
Toledo Correctional Institution 2001 E Central Ave PO Box 80033 *Web:* drc.ohio.gov	Toledo	OH	43608	419-726-7977	726-7157
Trumbull Correctional Institution 5701 Burnett Rd *Web:* drc.ohio.gov	Leavittsburg	OH	44430	330-898-0820	898-0848
Warren Correctional Institution 5787 S Rt 63 PO Box 120 *Web:* www.drc.ohio.gov	Lebanon	OH	45036	513-932-3388	933-0150

Oklahoma

				Phone	Fax
Cimarron Correctional Facility 3200 S Kings Hwy *Web:* www.cca.com	Cushing	OK	74023	918-225-3336	225-3363
Davis Correctional Facility 6888 E 133Rd Rd *Web:* cca.com	Holdenville	OK	74848	405-379-6400	379-6496
Great Plains Correctional Facility 700 Sugar Creek Dr *Web:* www.geogroup.com/	Hinton	OK	73047	405-542-3711	
Howard McLeod Correctional Ctr 1970 E Whippoorwill Ln *Web:* www.ok.gov	Atoka	OK	74525	580-889-6651	889-2264
James Crabtree Correctional Ctr 216 N. Murray St *Web:* www.ok.gov/	Helena	OK	73741	580-852-3221	
Jess Dunn Correctional Ctr PO Box 316 *Web:* www.ok.gov	Taft	OK	74463	918-682-7841	682-4372
John Lilley Correctional Ctr 105150 N 3670 Rd PO Box 407971 *Web:* www.ok.gov	Boley	OK	74829	918-667-3381	667-3959
Joseph Harp Correctional Ctr 16161 Moffat Rd PO Box 548 *Web:* www.ok.gov	Lexington	OK	73051	405-527-5593	527-4841
Lawton Correctional Facility 8607 SE Flower Mound Rd	Lawton	OK	73501	580-351-2778	351-2641
Mabel Bassett Correctional Ctr 29501 Kickapoo Rd	McLoud	OK	74851	405-964-3020	964-3014
Oklahoma State Penitentiary Corner of W & Stonewall PO Box 97 *Web:* www.ok.gov	McAlester	OK	74502	918-423-4700	423-3862
Oklahoma State Reformatory 1700 E First St PO Box 514 *Web:* www.ok.gov	Granite	OK	73547	580-480-3700	480-3997

Oregon

				Phone	Fax
Coffee Creek Correctional Facility 24499 SW Grahams Ferry Rd *Web:* www.oregon.gov	Wilsonville	OR	97070	503-570-6400	570-6417
Columbia River Correctional Institution 9111 NE Sunderland Ave *Web:* www.oregon.gov	Portland	OR	97211	503-280-6646	280-6012
Oregon State Correctional Institution 3405 Deer Pk Dr SE *Web:* www.oregon.gov/doc/ops/prison/pages/osci.aspx	Salem	OR	97310	503-373-0101	378-8919
Oregon State Penitentiary 2605 State St *Web:* oregon.gov	Salem	OR	97310	503-378-2453	378-3897
Powder River Correctional Facility 3600 13th St. *Web:* oregon.gov	Baker City	OR	97814	541-523-6680	523-6678
Santiam Correctional Institution 4005 Aumsville Hwy SE *Web:* www.oregon.gov	Salem	OR	97317	503-378-2144	378-8235
Snake River Correctional Institution 777 Stanton Blvd *Web:* www.oregon.gov/	Ontario	OR	97914	541-881-5000	881-5009
South Fork Forest Camp (SFFC) 48300 Wilson River Hwy *Web:* www.oregon.gov	Tillamook	OR	97317	503-842-2811	842-7943
Two Rivers Correctional Institution 82911 Beach Access Rd *Web:* oregon.gov	Umatilla	OR	97882	541-922-2001	

Pennsylvania

				Phone	Fax
Quehanna Motivational Boot Camp 4395 Quehanna Hwy Staff. *Web:* www.portal.state.pa.us/portal/server.pt/community/hide_quehanna/11404	Karthaus	PA	16845	814-263-4125	
SCI-Coal Township 1 Kelley Dr *TF:* 800-322-4472	Coal Township	PA	17866	570-644-7890	
SCI-Dallas 1000 Follies Rd. *Web:* www.cor.state.pa.us	Dallas	PA	18612	570-675-1101	820-4842
SCI-Graterford PO Box 246. **Fax Area Code:* 484 ■ *Web:* www.portal.state.pa.us	Graterford	PA	19426	610-489-4151	961-7907*
SCI-Greene 169 Progress Dr Staff *Web:* www.portal.state.pa.us/portal/server.pt/community/hide_greene/11373	Waynesburg	PA	15370	724-852-2902	
SCI-Greensburg 165 SCI Ln *Web:* www.portal.state.pa.us	Greensburg	PA	15601	724-837-4397	
SCI-Houtzdale PO Box 1000 *Web:* www.portal.state.pa.us	Houtzdale	PA	16698	814-378-1000	
SCI-Huntingdon 1100 Pike St	Huntingdon	PA	16652	814-643-2400	946-7380
SCI-Mahanoy 301 Morea Rd	Frackville	PA	17932	570-773-2158	
SCI-Muncy PO Box 180 *Web:* www.portal.state.pa.us	Muncy	PA	17756	570-546-3171	
SCI-Pittsburgh 3001 Beaver Rd. *Web:* www.cor.pa.gov/Facilities/CommunityCorrections/Pages/RegionIIIFacilities.aspx#.Vd7L7Ha1Gko	Pittsburgh	PA	15233	412-761-1955	766-8225
SCI-Retreat 660 SR 11 *Web:* portal.state.pa.us	Hunlock Creek	PA	18621	570-735-8754	733-1041
SCI-Rockview One Rockview Pl PO Box A. *Web:* www.portal.state.pa.us	Bellefonte	PA	16823	814-355-4874	355-6026
SCI-Smithfield 1120 Pike St PO Box 999 *Web:* www.portal.state.pa.us	Huntingdon	PA	16652	814-643-6520	
SCI-Somerset 1590 Walters Mill Rd	Somerset	PA	15510	814-443-8100	443-8137
SCI-Waymart PO Box 256 Ste 6 *Web:* www.portal.state.pa.us/portal/server.pt/community/hide_waymart/11432	Waymart	PA	18472	570-488-5811	
State Correctional Institution of Albion 10745 Rt 18 *Web:* portal.state.pa.us	Albion	PA	16475	814-756-5778	756-9737

Rhode Island

				Phone	Fax
Donald W Wyatt Detention Facility 950 High St *Web:* www.wyattdetention.com	Central Falls	RI	02863	401-729-1190	729-1194

South Carolina

				Phone	Fax
Allendale Correctional Institution 1057 Revolutionary Trl PO Box 1151 *Web:* doc.sc.gov	Fairfax	SC	29827	803-632-2561	632-2498
Broad River Correctional Institution 4460 Broad River Rd. *Web:* www.doc.sc.gov	Columbia	SC	29210	803-896-2234	
Evans Correctional Institution 610 Hwy 9 W **Fax Area Code:* 803 ■ *Web:* doc.sc.gov	Bennettsville	SC	29512	843-479-4181	896-4977*
Goodman Correctional Institution 4556 Broad River Rd. *TF:* 866-230-7761 ■ *Web:* doc.sc.gov	Columbia	SC	29210	803-896-8565	896-1671
Kershaw Correctional Institution 4848 Gold Mine Hwy *Web:* www.doc.sc.gov/	Kershaw	SC	29067	803-896-3301	
Kirkland Correctional Institution 4344 Broad River Rd. *Web:* doc.sc.gov	Columbia	SC	29210	803-896-1521	896-1766
Leath Correctional Institution 2809 Airport Rd **Fax Area Code:* 803 ■ *Web:* doc.sc.gov	Greenwood	SC	29649	864-229-5709	896-1766*
Lee Correctional Institution 990 Wisacky Hwy *TF:* 877-846-3472	Bishopville	SC	29010	803-428-2800	896-1766
Lieber Correctional Institution PO Box 205 *Web:* www.doc.sc.gov/institutions/lieber.jsp	Ridgeville	SC	29472	843-875-3332	
MacDougall Correctional Institution 1516 Old GilliaRd Rd *Web:* doc.sc.gov	Ridgeville	SC	29472	843-688-5251	688-4047
McCormick Correctional Institution 386 Redemption Way *Web:* doc.sc.gov	McCormick	SC	29899	864-443-2114	443-2114
Stevenson Correctional Institution 4546 Broad River Rd. *Web:* doc.sc.gov	Columbia	SC	29210	803-896-8575	896-1222
Trenton Correctional Institution 84 Greenhouse Rd *Web:* www.doc.sc.gov	Trenton	SC	29847	803-896-3000	
Turbeville Correctional Institution PO Box 252 *Web:* www.doc.sc.gov/institutions/turbeville.jsp	Turbeville	SC	29162	843-659-4800	
Walden Correctional Institution 4340 Broad River Rd. *Web:* doc.sc.gov	Columbia	SC	29210	803-896-8580	896-1225
Women's Correctional Institution 4450 Broad River Rd.	Columbia	SC	29210	803-896-8590	896-1226

South Dakota

Facility	City	State	Zip	Phone	Fax
Jameson Annex 1600 N Dr PO Box 5911 *Web:* www.doc.sd.gov	Sioux Falls	SD	57117	605-367-5051	367-5585
Mike Durfee State Prison 1412 Wood St. *TF:* 800-537-0025 ■ *Web:* doc.sd.gov	Springfield	SD	57062	605-369-2201	369-2813
South Dakota State Penitentiary 1600 N Dr PO Box 5911 *Web:* doc.sd.gov	Sioux Falls	SD	57117	605-367-5051	367-5038

Tennessee

Facility	City	State	Zip	Phone	Fax
Hardeman County Correctional Facility 2520 Union Springs Rd PO Box 549 *Web:* www.cca.com	Whiteville	TN	38075	731-254-6000	254-6060
Northeast Correctional Complex 5249 Hwy 67 W PO Box 5000 *Web:* tn.gov	Mountain City	TN	37683	423-727-7387	727-5415
Northwest Correctional Complex 960 SR 212 *Web:* tn.gov	Tiptonville	TN	38079	731-253-5000	253-5150
Riverbend Maximum Security Institution 7475 Cockrill Bend Blvd *TF:* 800-770-8277 ■ *Web:* tn.gov	Nashville	TN	37243	615-350-3100	350-3400
South Central Correctional Facility 555 Forest Ave PO Box 279 *TF:* 800-251-3589 ■ *Web:* www.state.tn.us	Clifton	TN	38425	931-676-5372	676-5104
Tennessee Prison for Women 3881 Stewarts Ln *Web:* tn.gov	Nashville	TN	37243	615-741-1255	253-5388
Wayne County Boot Camp PO Box 182 *TF:* 855-876-7283 ■ *Web:* www.tennessee.gov	Clifton	TN	38425	931-676-3345	676-3350
West Tennessee State Penitentiary 480 Green Chapel Rd PO Box 1150 *Web:* www.tn.gov	Henning	TN	38041	731-738-5044	

Texas

Facility	City	State	Zip	Phone	Fax
Bartlett State Jail 1018 Arnold Dr	Bartlett	TX	76511	254-527-3300	527-4489
Bradshaw State Jail 3900 W Loop 571 N PO Box 9000 *Web:* www.cca.com	Henderson	TX	75653	903-655-0880	655-0500
Cole State Jail 3801 Silo Rd *Web:* tdcj.state.tx.us	Bonham	TX	75418	903-583-1100	583-7903
Criminal Justice Department 3901 State Jail Rd.	El Paso	TX	79938	915-856-0046	849-4795
Dominguez State Jail 6535 Cagnon Rd *Web:* tdcj.state.tx.us	San Antonio	TX	78252	210-675-6620	677-0316
Hutchins State Jail 1500 E Langdon Rd *Web:* tdcj.state.tx.us	Dallas	TX	75241	972-225-1304	
Kegans State Jail 707 Top St *Web:* tdcj.state.tx.us	Houston	TX	77002	713-224-6584	224-6212
Lindsey State Jail 1620 FM 3344 *Web:* tdcj.state.tx.us	Jacksboro	TX	76458	940-567-2272	567-2292
Lopez State Jail 1203 El Cibolo Rd *Web:* tdcj.state.tx.us	Edinburg	TX	78542	956-316-3810	316-7447
Lychner State Jail 2350 Atascocita Rd	Humble	TX	77396	281-454-5036	454-4163
Plane State Jail 904 FM 686 *Web:* tdcj.state.tx.us	Dayton	TX	77535	936-258-2476	257-4449
Travis County State Jail 8101 FM 969 *Web:* tdcj.state.tx.us	Austin	TX	78724	512-926-4482	
Willacy County State Jail 1695 S Buffalo Dr	Raymondville	TX	78580	956-689-4900	689-4001
Woodman State Jail 1210 Coryell City Rd *Web:* tdcj.state.tx.us	Gatesville	TX	76528	254-865-9398	

Utah

Facility	City	State	Zip	Phone	Fax
Central Utah Correctional Facility 255 East 300 North *Web:* corrections.utah.gov	Gunnison	UT	84634	435-528-6000	528-6051
Iron County Utah State Correctional Facility 2136 N Main St *Web:* ironsheriff.net	Cedar City	UT	84721	435-867-7555	
Utah State Prison 14425 Bitterbrush Ln *Web:* corrections.utah.gov	Draper	UT	84020	801-576-7000	

Vermont

Facility	City	State	Zip	Phone	Fax
Chittenden Regional Correctional Facility Seven Farrell St *Web:* www.doc.state.vt.us	South Burlington	VT	05403	802-863-7356	863-7473
Northeast Regional Correctional Facility 1270 W Rt 5	Saint Johnsbury	VT	05819	802-748-8151	748-6604
Northern State Correctional Facility 2559 Glen Rd *Web:* vermont.gov	Newport	VT	05855	802-334-3364	334-3367
Northwest State Correctional Facility 3649 Lower Newton Rd *Web:* doc.state.vt.us	Swanton	VT	05488	802-524-6771	527-7534
Southeast State Correctional Facility 546 State Farm Rd *Web:* www.doc.state.vt.us	Windsor	VT	05089	802-674-6717	674-2249

Virginia

Facility	City	State	Zip	Phone	Fax
Augusta Correctional Ctr 1821 Estaline Vly Rd *Web:* vadoc.virginia.gov	Craigsville	VA	24430	540-997-7000	997-7017
Bland Correctional Ctr 256 Bland Farm Rd *Web:* vadoc.virginia.gov	Bland	VA	24315	276-688-3341	
Buckingham Correctional Ctr 1349 Correctional Ctr Rd *Web:* vadoc.virginia.gov	Dillwyn	VA	23936	434-391-5980	983-1752
Deep Meadow Correctional Ctr 3500 Woods Way *Web:* vadoc.virginia.gov	State Farm	VA	23160	804-598-5503	
Deerfield Correctional Ctr 21360 Deerfield Dr **Fax Area Code:* 870 ■ *TF:* 800-560-4292 ■ *Web:* vadoc.state.va.us	Capron	VA	23829	434-658-4368	850-8488*
Greensville Correctional Ctr 901 Corrections Way *Web:* vadoc.virginia.gov	Jarratt	VA	23870	434-535-7000	535-7640
Haynesville Correctional Ctr 421 Barnfield Rd PO Box 129 *Web:* www.vadoc.virginia.gov	Haynesville	VA	22472	804-333-3577	
Lawrenceville Correctional Ctr 1607 Planters Rd *Web:* vadoc.virginia.gov	Lawrenceville	VA	23868	434-848-9349	848-0232
Lunenburg Correctional Ctr 690 Falls Rd PO Box 1424 *Web:* vadoc.virginia.gov	Victoria	VA	23974	434-696-2045	
Nottoway Correctional Ctr 2892 Schutt Rd PO Box 488 *Web:* vadoc.virginia.gov	Burkeville	VA	23922	434-767-5543	
Red Onion State Prison 10800 H Jack Rose Hwy PO Box 970 *Web:* vadoc.virginia.gov	Pound	VA	24279	276-796-7510	
Saint Brides Correctional Ctr 701 Sanderson Rd	Chesapeake	VA	23322	757-421-6600	
Sussex I State Prison 24414 Musselwhite Dr *Web:* vadoc.state.va.us	Waverly	VA	23891	804-834-9967	834-9995
Sussex II State Prison 24427 Musselwhite Dr *Web:* vadoc.state.va.us	Waverly	VA	23891	804-834-2678	834-4073
Virginia Department of Corrections 12352 Coffeewood Dr *Web:* vadoc.state.va.us	Mitchells	VA	22729	540-829-6483	
Wallens Ridge State Prison 272 Dogwood Dr PO Box 759 *Web:* vadoc.virginia.gov	Big Stone Gap	VA	24219	276-523-3310	

Washington

Facility	City	State	Zip	Phone	Fax
Airway Heights Corrections Ctr 11919 W Sprague Ave PO Box 1899 *Web:* www.doc.wa.gov	Airway Heights	WA	99001	509-244-6700	244-6710
Cedar Creek Correctional Ctr 12200 Bordeaux Rd PO Box 37 *Web:* www.doc.wa.gov/facilities/prison/cccc	Littlerock	WA	98556	360-359-4100	
Clallam Bay Corrections Ctr 1830 Eagle Crest Way *Web:* doc.wa.gov	Clallam Bay	WA	98326	360-963-2000	963-3292
Coyote Ridge Corrections Ctr 1301 N Ephrata St *Web:* www.doc.wa.gov	Connell	WA	99326	509-543-5800	543-5801
Hawaii Health Matters PO Box 88900 *Web:* www.hawaiihealthmatters.org	Steilacoom	WA	98388	253-512-6600	
Larch Corrections Ctr 15314 NE Dole Vly Rd *Web:* doc.wa.gov	Yacolt	WA	98675	360-260-6300	686-3892
Olympic Corrections Ctr 11235 Hoh Mainline *Web:* doc.wa.gov	Forks	WA	98331	360-374-6181	
Washington Corrections Ctr for Women 9601 Bujacich Rd NW	Gig Harbor	WA	98332	253-858-4200	858-4289
Washington State Penitentiary 1313 N 13th Ave *Web:* doc.wa.gov	Walla Walla	WA	99362	509-525-3610	
Washington State Reformatory 16550 177th Ave SE PO Box 777 *Web:* www.doc.wa.gov	Monroe	WA	98272	360-794-2600	

West Virginia

Facility	City	State	Zip	Phone	Fax
Denmar Correctional Ctr HC 64 PO Box 125 *Web:* wvdoc.com	Hillsboro	WV	24946	304-653-4201	653-4855
Mount Olive Correctional Complex One Mtnside Way	Mount Olive	WV	25185	304-442-7213	442-7225
Northern Regional Correctional Facility 112 Northern Regional Correctional Dr. *TF:* 866-984-8463 ■ *Web:* www.wvdoc.com	Moundsville	WV	26041	304-843-4067	843-4073
Pruntytown Correctional Ctr PO Box 159 *Web:* www.wvdoc.com	Grafton	WV	26354	304-265-6111	265-6120
Saint Mary's Correctional Ctr 2880 N Pleasants Hwy *Web:* www.wvdoc.com/wvdoc/prisonsandfacilities/saintmaryscorrectionalcenter/tabid/56/default.aspx	Saint Marys	WV	26170	304-684-5500	684-5506

Wisconsin

Facility	City	State	Zip	Phone	Fax
Columbia Correctional Institution 2925 Columbia Dr PO Box 950 *Web:* doc.wi.gov	Portage	WI	53901	608-742-9100	742-9111

Phone Fax

Fox Lake Correctional Institution
PO Box 147 ... Fox Lake WI 53933 920-928-3151 928-6929
Web: doc.wi.gov

Green Bay Correctional Institution
2833 Riverside Dr ... Green Bay WI 54307 920-432-4877 432-5388
Web: doc.wi.gov

Kettle Moraine Correctional Institution
PO Box 31 ... Plymouth WI 53073 920-526-3244 526-3989
Web: doc.wi.gov

Oakhill Correctional Institution
5212 County Hwy M PO Box 140 ... Oregon WI 53575 608-835-3101 835-6082
Web: doc.wi.gov/familiesvisitors/findfacility/oakhillcorrectionalinstitution

Oshkosh Correctional Institution
1730 W Snell Rd PO Box 3530 ... Oshkosh WI 54903 920-231-4010 236-2615
Web: doc.wi.gov

Prairie du Chien Correctional Institution
500 E Parrish St ... Prairie du Chien WI 53821 608-326-7828 326-5960
Web: doc.wi.gov

Racine Correctional Institution
2019 Wisconsin St ... Sturtevant WI 53177 262-886-3214 886-3514
Web: doc.wi.gov

Taycheedah Correctional Institution (WWCS)
751 County Rd PO Box 1947 ... Fond Du Lac WI 54935 920-929-3800 929-2946
Web: doc.wi.gov

Waupun Correctional Institution
200 S Madison St ... Waupun WI 53963 920-324-5571 324-7250
Web: doc.wi.gov/familiesvisitors/findfacility/waupuncorrectionalinstitution

Wisconsin Secure Program Facility
1101 Morrison Dr ... Boscobel WI 53805 608-375-5656 375-5595

Wyoming

Phone Fax

Honor Conservation Camp 40 Pippin Rd ... Newcastle WY 82701 307-746-4436 746-9316
Wyoming Honor Farm 40 Honor Farm Rd ... Riverton WY 82501 307-856-9578 856-2505
Wyoming State Penitentiary 2900 S Higley Rd ... Rawlins WY 82301 307-328-1441
Wyoming Women's Ctr 1000 W Griffith PO Box 300 ... Lusk WY 82225 307-334-3693 334-2254
Web: doc.state.wy.us

217 COSMETICS, SKIN CARE, AND OTHER PERSONAL CARE PRODUCTS

SEE ALSO Perfumes p. 2914

Phone Fax

AHAVA North America 330 7th Avenue ... New York NY 10001 800-366-7254 696-9789*
**Fax Area Code:* 212 ■ *TF:* 800-366-7254 ■ *Web:* www.ahavaus.com

Aire-Master of America Inc 1821 N State Hwy Cc ... Nixa MO 65714 417-725-2691 725-5737
TF: 800-525-0957 ■ *Web:* www.airemaster.com

Apothecary Products
11750 12th Ave S Burnsville ... Burnsville MN 55337 800-328-2742 328-1584
TF: 800-328-2742 ■ *Web:* www.apothecaryproducts.com

Arizona Natural Resources
2525 E BeaRdsley Rd ... Phoenix AZ 85050 602-569-6900 569-9697
Web: www.arizonanaturalresources.com

At Last Naturals Inc 401 Columbus Ave ... Valhalla NY 10595 800-527-8123 747-3791*
**Fax Area Code:* 914 ■ *TF:* 800-527-8123 ■ *Web:* www.atlastnaturals.com

Autumn Harp Inc 26 Thompson Dr ... Essex Junction VT 05452 802-857-4600 857-4601
Web: www.autumnharp.com

Aveda Corp 4000 Pheasant Ridge Dr ... Blaine MN 55449 763-951-4000 783-4110
TF: 800-644-4831 ■ *Web:* www.aveda.com

Avon Products Inc 1345 Ave of the Americas ... New York NY 10017 212-282-7000 282-6035
NYSE: AVP ■ *TF Cust Svc:* 800-367-2866 ■ *Web:* www.avon.com

Bath & Body Works Seven Limited Pkwy E ... Reynoldsburg OH 43068 800-395-1001
TF: 800-395-1001 ■ *Web:* www.bathandbodyworks.com

Bath-and-Body.com 1073 Exchange St ... Boise ID 83716 208-345-5136

BeautiControl Inc
2121 Midway Rd PO Box 815189 ... Carrollton TX 75006 972-458-0601 960-7923*
**Fax:* Sales ■ *TF:* 800-232-8841 ■ *Web:* shop.beauticontrol.com

Belcam Inc Delagar Div 27 Montgomery St ... Rouses Point NY 12979 518-297-3366 297-3366
TF: 800-328-3006 ■ *Web:* www.belcamshop.com

BeneFit Cosmetics 225 Bush St ... San Francisco CA 94104 415-781-8153
TF Cust Svc: 800-781-2336 ■ *Web:* www.benefitcosmetics.com

Body Shop, The 5036 One World Way ... Wake Forest NC 27587 919-554-4900 554-4361
Web: www.thebodyshop.in

Borghese Inc 3 E 54th St 20th Fl ... New York NY 10022 212-659-5300
Web: www.borghese.com

Bradford Soap Works Inc
200 Providence St ... West Warwick RI 02893 401-821-2141 821-1660
Web: www.bradfordsoap.com

Bronner Bros Inc 2141 Powers Ferry Rd ... Marietta GA 30067 770-988-0015 953-0848
TF: 800-241-6151 ■ *Web:* www.bronnerbros.com

CBI Laboratories 4201 Diplomacy Rd ... Fort Worth TX 76155 972-241-7546 352-1094*
**Fax Area Code:* 800 ■ *TF:* 800-822-7546 ■ *Web:* www.cbiskincare.com

CCA Industries Inc
200 Murray Hill Pkwy ... East Rutherford NJ 07073 201-935-3232
NYSE: CAW ■ *TF Cust Svc:* 800-524-2720 ■ *Web:* www.ccaindustries.com

Chattem Inc 1715 W 38th St PO Box 2219 ... Chattanooga TN 37409 423-821-4571 821-0395
Web: www.chattem.com

Church & Dwight Company Inc
469 N Harrison St ... Princeton NJ 08543 609-683-5900
NYSE: CHD ■ *Web:* www.churchdwight.com

Clinique Laboratories Inc
767 Fifth Ave 37th Fl ... New York NY 10153 212-572-3983
TF: 800-419-4041 ■ *Web:* www.clinique.com

Color Factory, The 11312 Penrose St ... Sun Valley CA 91352 818-767-2889 767-4062
Web: www.colorfactoryla.com

Combe Inc 1101 Westchester Ave ... White Plains NY 10604 914-694-5454
TF: 800-431-2610 ■ *Web:* www.combe.com

Cosmetic Essence Inc 2182 Hwy 35 ... Holmdel NJ 07733 732-888-7788 888-6086
Web: www.cosmeticessence.com

Cosmolab Inc 1100 Garrett Pkwy ... Lewisburg TN 37091 931-359-6253 359-8465
Web: www.cosmolab.com

Phone Fax

Cosrich Group Inc 12243 Branford St ... Sun Valley CA 91352 818-686-2500 897-7590
Web: www.cosrich.com

Coty Inc Two Pk Ave 17th Fl ... New York NY 10016 212-479-4300 336-6064*
**Fax Area Code:* 866 ■ *Web:* www.coty.com

Crabtree & Evelyn Ltd 102 Peake Brook Rd ... Woodstock CT 06281 860-928-2761 928-1296
TF: 800-272-2873 ■ *Web:* www.crabtree-evelyn.com

DEB Inc 2815 Coliseum Centre Dr Ste 600 ... Charlotte NC 28217 704-263-4240 263-9601
TF: 800-248-7190 ■ *Web:* www.debgroup.com

Farouk Systems Inc 250 Pennbright Dr ... Houston TX 77090 281-876-2000 876-1700
TF: 800-237-9175 ■ *Web:* www.farouk.com

Forever Living Products International Inc
7501 E McCormick Pkwy ... Scottsdale AZ 85258 480-998-8888 905-8451
TF: 888-440-2563 ■ *Web:* www.foreverliving.com

Fruit of The Earth Inc
3101 High Rver Rd Ste 175 ... Fort Worth TX 76155 972-790-0808 790-1322
TF: 800-527-7731 ■ *Web:* www.fote.com

GOJO Industries Inc One GOJO Plz Ste 500 ... Akron OH 44311 330-255-6000 329-4656*
**Fax Area Code:* 800 ■ *TF:* 800-321-9647 ■ *Web:* www.gojo.com

Guest Supply Inc
4301 US Hwy 1 PO Box 902 ... Monmouth Junction NJ 08852 609-514-9696 514-2692
TF Cust Svc: 800-446-7819 ■ *Web:* www.guestsupply.com

Gurwitch Products LLC 8 Greenway Plz ... Stafford TX 77046 281-275-7000 275-7070
TF: 888-637-2437 ■ *Web:* www.lauramercier.com

H2O Plus Inc 845 W Madison St ... Chicago IL 60607 312-850-9283 633-1440
TF Cust Svc: 800-242-2284 ■ *Web:* www.h2oplus.com

Hillshire Brands PO Box 3901 ... Peoria IL 61612 800-323-7117
TF: 800-323-7117 ■ *Web:* www.hillshirebrands.com

Imperial Distributors Inc 33 Sword St ... Auburn MA 01501 508-756-5156 756-0085
Web: www.imperialdist.com

Jafra Cosmetics International
2451 Townsgate Rd ... Westlake Village CA 91361 805-449-3000 449-3253
TF: 800-551-2345 ■ *Web:* www.jafra.com

Jan Marini Skin Research Inc
6951 Via Del Oro ... San Jose CA 95119 408-362-0130 362-0140
TF: 800-347-2223 ■ *Web:* www.janmarini.com

John Amico Haircare Products
4731 W 136th St ... Crestwood IL 60445 708-824-4000 824-0413
TF: 800-676-5264 ■ *Web:* www.johnamico.com

John Paul Mitchell Systems
1888 Century Park E ste 1600 ... Los Angeles CA 90067 800-793-8790 248-2780*
**Fax Area Code:* 310 ■ *TF Cust Svc:* 800-793-8790 ■ *Web:* www.paulmitchell.com

Johnson & Johnson Consumer Products Co
199 Grandview Rd ... Skillman NJ 08558 908-874-1000
TF: 866-565-2229 ■ *Web:* www.johnsonsbaby.com

Johnson & Johnson Inc 7101 Notre-Dame E ... Montreal QC H1N2G4 514-251-5100 251-6233
TF: 800-361-8990 ■ *Web:* www.jnjcanada.com

Kao Brands Co 2535 Spring Grove Ave ... Cincinnati OH 45214 513-421-1400 455-5497
TF: 800-742-8798 ■ *Web:* www.kaobrands.com

Key West Aloe 13095 N Telecom Pkwy ... Tampa FL 33637 305-293-1885 363-1443*
**Fax Area Code:* 786 ■ *TF:* 800-445-2563 ■ *Web:* www.keywestaloe.com

Kolmar Laboratories Inc 20 W King St ... Port Jervis NY 12771 845-856-5311 856-0640
Web: www.kolmar.com

L Brands Inc 3 Limited Pkwy ... Columbus OH 43230 614-415-7000
NYSE: LTD ■ *Web:* lb.com/

L'Oreal USA 575 Fifth Ave ... New York NY 10017 212-818-1500
TF: 800-322-2036 ■ *Web:* www.lorealusa.com

Lee Pharmaceuticals Inc
1434 Santa Anita Ave ... South El Monte CA 91733 626-442-3141 442-6994
OTC: LPHM

Luster Products Inc 1104 W 43rd St ... Chicago IL 60609 773-579-1800 579-1912
TF: 800-621-4255 ■ *Web:* www.lusterproducts.com

Mana Products Inc 32-02 Queens Blvd ... Long Island City NY 11101 718-361-2550 786-3204
TF Cust Svc: 800-221-3071 ■ *Web:* www.manaproducts.com

Markwins International Corp
22067 Ferrero Pkwy ... Walnut CA 91789 909-595-8898
Web: www.markwins.com

Mary Kay Inc PO Box 799045 ... Dallas TX 75379 972-687-6300 687-1608*
**Fax:* Cust Svc ■ *TF Cust Svc:* 800-627-9529 ■ *Web:* www.marykay.com

Maybelline New York
575 Fifth Ave PO Box 1010 ... New York NY 10017 800-944-0730
TF: 800-944-0730 ■ *Web:* www.maybelline.com

Merle Norman Cosmetics Inc
9130 Bellanca Ave ... Los Angeles CA 90045 310-641-3000 641-7144
TF: 800-421-6648 ■ *Web:* www.merlenorman.com

Neutrogena Corp 5760 W 96th St ... Los Angeles CA 90045 310-642-1150
TF: 800-582-4048 ■ *Web:* www.neutrogena.com

Nutramax Laboratories Inc
2208 Lakeside Blvd ... Edgewood MD 21040 410-776-4000
TF: 800-925-5187 ■ *Web:* www.nutramaxlabs.com

Obagi Medical Products Inc
3760 Kilroy Airport Way Ste 500 ... Long Beach CA 90806 562-628-1007 628-1008
TF: 800-636-7546 ■ *Web:* www.obagi.com

Origins Natural Resources Inc 767 Fifth Ave ... New York NY 10153 800-674-4467
TF Cust Svc: 800-674-4467 ■ *Web:* www.origins.com

Orly International Inc 7710 Haskell Ave ... Los Angeles CA 91406 818-994-1001 994-1144
Web: www.orlybeauty.com

Paramount Cosmetics Inc 93 Entin Rd Ste 4 ... Clifton NJ 07014 973-472-2323 472-5005
TF: 800-522-9880 ■ *Web:* www.paramountcosmetics.net

Person & Covey Inc 616 Allen Ave ... Glendale CA 91201 800-423-2341 547-9821*
**Fax Area Code:* 818 ■ *TF:* 800-423-2341 ■ *Web:* www.personandcovey.com

Personal Products Co
One Johnson & Johnson Plaza ... New Brunswick NJ 08933 732-524-0400
Web: www.jnj.com/our_company/family_of_companies

Peter Thomas Roth Labs LLC
460 Pk Ave 16th Fl ... New York NY 10022 212-581-5800 581-5810
Web: www.peterthomasroth.com

Pfizer Inc 235 E 42nd St ... New York NY 10017 212-733-2323 573-7851
NYSE: PFE ■ *TF:* 800-879-3477 ■ *Web:* www.pfizer.com

Philosophy Inc 3809 E Watkins ... Phoenix AZ 85034 800-568-3151 736-0600*
**Fax Area Code:* 480 ■ *TF:* 800-568-3151 ■ *Web:* www.philosophy.com

Prescriptives Inc 767 Fifth Ave ... New York NY 10153 866-290-6471
TF: 866-290-6471 ■ *Web:* www.prescriptives.com

Phone Fax

Prestige Brands International Inc
660 White Plains Rd Ste 250 .... Tarrytown NY 10591 914-524-6800 524-6815
Web: www.prestigebrandsinc.com

Prestige Cosmetics Corp 1601 Green Rd ...... Pompano Beach FL 33064 954-480-9202 480-9220
TF General: 800-722-7488 ■ *Web:* www.prestigecosmetics.com

Qosmedix 95-Q Executive Dr........................ Edgewood NY 11717 631-242-3270 242-3291
Web: www.qosmedix.com

Revlon Consumer Products Corp
1501 Williamsboro St................................ Oxford NC 27565 212-527-4000 527-4995
TF: 800-473-8566 ■ *Web:* www.revlon.com

Rozelle Cosmetics 4260 Loop Rd................... Westfield VT 05874 802-744-2270 744-2236
TF: 800-451-4216 ■ *Web:* www.rozelle.com

Scolding Locks Corp 1520 W Rogers Ave............. Appleton WI 54914 920-733-5561 733-8800
TF: 800-537-9707 ■ *Web:* www.scoldinglocks.com

Sebastian International Inc
6109 DeSoto Ave .... Woodland Hills CA 91367 818-999-5112
Web: wellainteractive.com

sephora.com Inc
525 Market St First Market Twr 32nd Fl .... San Francisco CA 94105 415-284-3300
TF Cust Svc: 877-737-4672 ■ *Web:* www.sephora.com

SkinMedica Inc 5770 Armada Dr .... Carlsbad CA 92008 760-448-3600
TF: 866-577-3072 ■ *Web:* www.skinmedica.com

Sothys USA Inc 1500 NW 94th Ave .... Miami FL 33172 305-594-4222 592-5785
TF: 800-325-0503 ■ *Web:* www.sothys-usa.com

Star Nail Products Inc 29120 Ave Paine............... Valencia CA 91355 661-257-7827 257-5856
TF: 800-762-6245 ■ *Web:* www.starnail.com

Tom's of Maine Inc 302 Lafayette Ctr .... Kennebunk ME 04043 800-985-3874 985-2196*
**Fax Area Code:* 207 ■ *TF:* 800-367-8667 ■ *Web:* www.tomsofmaine.com

Twincraft Inc Two Tigan St .... Winooski VT 05404 802-655-2200
Web: www.twincraft.com

ULTA Beauty 1000 Remington Blvd Ste 120 .... Bolingbrook IL 60440 630-410-4800 226-8210
TF: 866-983-8582 ■ *Web:* www.ulta.com

Urban Decay 833 W 16th St .... Newport Beach CA 92663 949-631-4504
TF: 800-784-8722 ■ *Web:* www.urbandecay.com

Vi-Jon Labs Inc 8515 Page Ave .... Saint Louis MO 63114 314-427-1000 427-1010
TF: 800-424-9300 ■ *Web:* www.vijon.com

Victoria Vogue Inc 90 Southland Dr................ Bethlehem PA 18017 610-865-1500 865-6089
Web: businessfinder.lehighvalleylive.com

Wahl Clipper Corp 2900 Locust St.................... Sterling IL 61081 815-625-6528 625-0091
TF: 800-767-9245 ■ *Web:* www.wahl.com

WE Bassett Co 100 Trap Falls Rd Ext .... Shelton CT 06484 203-929-8483 929-8963
TF: 800-394-8746 ■ *Web:* www.trim.com

Wella Corp 6109 DeSoto Ave .... Woodland Hills CA 91367 818-999-5112
TF: 800-829-4422 ■ *Web:* www.wella.com

Zotos International Inc 100 Tokeneke Rd.............. Darien CT 06820 203-655-8911 656-7784
TF: 888-242-4247 ■ *Web:* www.zotos.com

218 CREDIT CARD PROVIDERS & RELATED SERVICES

Companies listed here include those that issue credit cards as well as companies that provide services to these companies (i.e., rewards programs, theft prevention, etc.).

Phone Fax

Advanta Medical Solutions LLC
10830 Guilford Rd Ste 312................. Annapolis Junction MD 20701 240-554-1200
Web: www.advantamedicalsolutions.com

American Advisors Group
3800 W Chapman Ave Third Fl .... Orange CA 92868 949-724-1707
Web: www.aag.com

American Express Company Inc
World Financial Ctr 200 Vesey St.................... New York NY 10285 212-640-2000 640-0404
NYSE: AXP ■ *TF:* 800-528-4800 ■ *Web:* www.americanexpress.com

Applied Card Systems 50 Applied Card Way .... Glen Mills PA 19342 866-227-5627 840-2758*
**Fax Area Code:* 484 ■ *TF:* 866-227-5627 ■ *Web:* www.appliedcard.com

Bank of America Card Services
One Commercial Pl Second Fl .... Norfolk VA 23510 757-441-4770
TF: 800-732-9194 ■ *Web:* locators.bankofamerica.com

Capital One Financial Corp
1680 Capital One Dr................................ McLean VA 22102 800-926-1000 290-7335*
NYSE: COF ■ **Fax Area Code:* 877 ■ *TF:* 800-655-2265 ■ *Web:* www.capitalone.com

Celtic Financial Group LLC
60 Cutter Mill Rd Ste 402.......................... Great Neck NY 11021 516-466-0550
Web: www.celticfinancial.com

Chevron Texaco Credit Card Ctr PO Box P .... Concord CA 94524 800-243-8766 827-6367*
**Fax Area Code:* 925 ■ *TF:* 800-243-8766 ■ *Web:* www.chevrontexacocards.com

Diners Club International 111 W Monroe .... Chicago IL 60603 800-234-6377
TF: 800-234-6377 ■ *Web:* www.dinersclubus.com

Discover Financial Services
2500 Lk Cook Rd .... Riverwoods IL 60015 224-405-0900
Web: www.discoverfinancial.com

Green Dot Corp 3465 E Foothill Blvd .... Pasadena CA 91107 626-765-2000
Web: www.greendotcorp.com

Intersections Inc
3901 Stonecroft Blvd PO Box 222455 .... Chantilly VA 20151 703-488-6100 488-6223
NASDAQ: INTX ■ *TF:* 800-695-7536 ■ *Web:* www.intersections.com

Loan Science 12001 Ventura Pl Ste 200............. Studio City CA 91604 818-286-2525
Web: www.loanscience.com

MasterCard Inc 2000 Purchase St .... Purchase NY 10577 914-249-2000 *
NYSE: MA ■ **Fax:* Hum Res ■ *TF:* 800-100-1087 ■ *Web:* www.mastercard.com

Moneris Solutions Corp 3300 Bloor St W .... Toronto ON M8X2X2 416-734-1000
Web: www.moneris.com

Rewards Network 2 N Riverside Plaza Suite 200 .... Chicago IL 60606 866-559-3463
TF: 877-392-7313 ■ *Web:* www.rewardsnetwork.com

Saks Inc 12 E 49th St.............................. New York NY 10017 212-940-5305 940-4849
Web: www.saksincorporated.com

Transaction Network Services Inc.
10740 Parkridge Blvd Ste 100 .... Reston VA 20191 703-453-8300 453-8599
TF: 800-240-2824 ■ *Web:* www.tnsi.com

Unifund CCR Partners Inc
10625 Techwoods Cir............................ Cincinnati OH 45242 513-489-8877
Web: www.unifund.com

Phone Fax

Vesta Corp 11950 SW Garden PL...................... Portland OR 97223 503-790-2500 790-2525
Web: www.trustvesta.com

Visa Inc PO Box 8999 .... San Francisco CA 94128 650-432-3200
NYSE: V ■ *TF:* 866-765-9644 ■ *Web:* www.visa.co.in

Wright Express Corp 97 Darling Ave............ South Portland ME 04106 207-773-8171
NYSE: WEX ■ *TF:* 800-761-7181 ■ *Web:* www.wexinc.com

219 CREDIT & FINANCING - COMMERCIAL

SEE ALSO Credit & Financing - Consumer p. 2178; Banks - Commercial & Savings p. 1848

Phone Fax

AFCO Credit Corp 14 Wall St........................ New York NY 10005 212-401-4400 401-4436
TF: 800-288-6901 ■ *Web:* afco.com

Ag Georgia Farm Credit PO Box 1820 .... Perry GA 31069 478-987-8300
Web: www.aggeorgia.com

Agricredit Acceptance LLC
8001 Birchwood Ct Ste C PO Box 2000 .... Johnston IA 50131 515-314-9203 334-5870
TF: 800-577-8504 ■ *Web:* www.agricredit.com

Alexander Capital Corp
396 Orofino Dr Ste 150......................... Castle Rock CO 80108 303-814-0475

Amada Capital Corp 7025 Firestone Blvd........... Buena Park CA 90621 714-739-2111 739-4099
Web: www.amadacapital.com

American AgCredit (ACA) PO Box 1120 .... Santa Rosa CA 95402 707-545-1200 545-9400
TF: 800-800-4865 ■ *Web:* www.agloan.com

American Capital Strategies Ltd
Two Bethesda Metro Ctr 14th Fl .... Bethesda MD 20814 301-951-6122 654-6714
NASDAQ: ACAS ■ *Web:* www.americancapital.com

AMRESCO Commercial Finance LLC
412 E Parkcenter Blvd................................ Boise ID 83706 208-333-2000 333-2050
Web: www.amresco.com

Arkansas Capital Corp Group
200 S Commerce St Ste 400...................... Little Rock AR 72201 501-374-9247 374-9425
TF: 800-216-7237 ■ *Web:* www.arcapital.com

ATEL Capital Group
600 California St Sixth Fl .... San Francisco CA 94108 415-989-8800 989-3796
TF: 800-543-2835 ■ *Web:* www.atel.com

Automotive Finance Corp (AFC)
13085 Hamilton Crossing Blvd........................ Carmel IN 46032 865-384-8250 550-5439*
**Fax Area Code:* 866 ■ *TF:* 888-335-6675 ■ *Web:* www.afcdealer.com

AutoStar 114 Ave of the Americas Ste 39 .... New York NY 10036 212-930-9400
TF: 800-288-6782 ■ *Web:* www.autostar.com

Bank of America Business Capital
200 Glastonbury Blvd.......................... Glastonbury CT 06033 860-659-3200
Web: corp.bankofamerica.com

BMO Financial Corp
1 First Canadian Place 11th Fl .... Toronto ON M5X1A1 416-359-4440 765-8169*
**Fax Area Code:* 312 ■ *TF:* 800-553-0332 ■ *Web:* www.bmo.com

Bombardier Capital Group
261 Mountain View Dr 4th Fl .... Colchester VT 05446 802-764-5232 764-5244*
**Fax:* Sales ■ *TF:* 800-949-5568 ■ *Web:* www.bombardier.com

BTM Capital Corp 111 Huntington Ave .... Boston MA 02199 617-573-9000 345-5153

Capital Business Credit LLC
1700 Broadway 19th Fl.......................... New York NY 10019 212-887-7900 887-7968
Web: www.capitalbusinesscredit.com

Cascade Federal Credit Union 18020 80th Ave S .... Kent WA 98032 425-251-8888 251-0299
TF: 800-562-2853 ■ *Web:* www.cascadefcu.org

CCO Mortgage Corp PO Box 3410.................. Glen Allen VA 23058 800-234-6002
Web: www.ccomortgage.com

CDC Small Business Finance Corp
2448 Historic Decatur Rd Ste 200.................. San Diego CA 92106 619-291-3594 291-6954
TF: 800-611-5170 ■ *Web:* cdcloans.com

CIT Group Inc 505 Fifth Ave .... New York NY 10017 212-771-0505 382-6871
NYSE: CIT ■ *Web:* www.cit.com

Co-op Finance Assn Inc, The
10100 N Ambassador Dr Ste 315
PO Box 901532 .... Kansas City MO 64153 816-214-4200 214-4221
TF: 877-835-5232 ■ *Web:* www.cfafs.com

Colonial Farm Credit Aca
7104 Mechanicsville Tpke PO Box 727 .... Mechanicsville VA 23111 804-746-4581 746-3159
TF: 800-777-8908 ■ *Web:* www.colonialfarmcredit.com

Connell Equipment Leasing Co
200 Connell Dr.......................... Berkeley Heights NJ 07922 908-673-3700 673-3800
Web: connellequipmentleasing.com

Connell Finance Company Inc
200 Connell Dr.......................... Berkeley Heights NJ 07922 908-673-3700 673-3800
Web: connellco.com

CSA Financial Corp 343 Commercial St .... Boston MA 02109 617-357-1700 357-1720
Web: www.csafinancial.com

Dexia CLF 445 Pk Ave Seventh Fl .... New York NY 10022 212-515-7000 753-5522
Web: www.dexia.com

DLL 1111 Old Eagle School Rd .... Wayne PA 19087 610-386-5000
Web: www.dllgroup.com

Equity Funding 12505 Bel-Red Rd Ste 200 .... Bellevue WA 98005 425-283-1040 283-1054
TF: 866-332-3863 ■ *Web:* www.equity-funding.com

Farm Credit Leasing (FCL)
600 Hwy 169 S Ste 300 .... Minneapolis MN 55426 952-417-7800 417-7801
TF: 800-444-2929 ■ *Web:* www.farmcreditleasing.com

Farm Credit Of Central Florida Aca
115 S Missouri Ave Ste 400........................ Lakeland FL 33815 863-682-4117 688-9364
TF: 800-533-2773 ■ *Web:* www.farmcreditcfl.com

Farm Credit Of Northwest Florida Aca
5052 Hwy 90 .... Marianna FL 32446 850-526-4910 482-6597
TF: 800-527-0647 ■ *Web:* www.farmcredit-fl.com

Financial Pacific Co
3455 S 344th Way Ste 300...................... Federal Way WA 98001 800-447-7107 447-7106
TF: 800-447-7107 ■ *Web:* www.finpac.com

First Carolina Corporate Credit Union
7900 Triad Ctr Dr Ste 410..................... Greensboro NC 27409 800-585-4317 299-7842*
**Fax Area Code:* 336 ■ *TF:* 800-585-4317 ■ *Web:* www.firstcarolina.org

	City	State	Zip	Phone	Fax
First Community Financial Corp (FCFC) 4000 N Central Ave Ste 100 *OTC: FMFP* ■ **Fax Area Code:* 312 ■ *TF:* 877-777-4778 ■ *Web:* capitalsource.com	Phoenix	AZ	85012	602-265-7715	577-7907*
First South FarmCredit 713 S Pear OrchaRd Rd Ste 300 *TF:* 800-955-1722 ■ *Web:* www.firstsouthfarmcredit.com	Ridgeland	MS	39158	601-977-8381	977-8358
Ford Motor Credit Co One American Rd PO Box 1732 *TF:* 800-727-7000 ■ *Web:* credit.ford.com	Dearborn	MI	48121	313-322-3000	
GE Healthcare Financail Services 500 W Monroe *Web:* www.gehealthcarefinance.com	Chicago	IL	60661	312-697-3999	
GE Vendor Financial Services 10 Riverview Dr *TF:* 800-626-2000 ■ *Web:* www.ge.com/capital/vendor	Danbury	CT	06810	203-373-2039	
Grandbridge Real Estate Capital LLC 200 S College St Ste 2100 *Web:* www.gbrecap.com	Charlotte	NC	28202	704-332-4454	332-1931
Green Tree Servicing LLC 345 St Peter St *TF:* 800-643-0202 ■ *Web:* www.gtservicing.com	Saint Paul	MN	55102	800-423-9527	
Greenstone Farm Credit Services Aca 3515 West Road *TF:* 800-444-3276 ■ *Web:* www.greenstonefcs.com	East Lansing	MI	48823	800-968-0061	
Imh Financial Corp 4900 N Scottsdale Rd Ste 5000 *TF:* 800-510-6445 ■ *Web:* www.imhfc.com	Scottsdale	AZ	85251	480-840-8400	
Imperial PFS (UPAC) 8245 Nieman Rd *TF:* 800-877-7848	Lenexa	KS	66214	913-894-6150	
iStar Financial Inc 1114 Ave of the Americas 39th Fl *NYSE: STAR* ■ *TF:* 888-603-5847 ■ *Web:* www.istarfinancial.com	New York	NY	10036	212-930-9400	
Jackson Purchase Ag Credit Assn PO Box 309 *Web:* rivervalleyagcredit.com	Mayfield	KY	42066	270-247-5613	247-6043
John Deere Credit Co 6400 NW 86th St *TF:* 800-275-5322 ■ *Web:* www.deere.com/en_us/jdc	Johnston	IA	50131	515-267-3000	267-3292
Key Equipment Finance 1000 S McCaslin Blvd *TF:* 888-301-6238 ■ *Web:* www.kefonline.com	Superior	CO	80027	888-301-6238	
Kraus-Anderson Capital Inc 523 S Eigth St Ste 523 *TF:* 888-547-3983 ■ *Web:* krausandersoncapital.com	Minneapolis	MN	55404	612-305-2934	305-2932
Lawfinance Group Inc 1401 Los Gamos Dr Ste 140 *TF:* 800-572-1986 ■ *Web:* www.lawfinance.com	San Rafael	CA	94903	415-446-2300	446-2301
Marquette Commercial Finance 1600 W 82nd St Ste 250 *Web:* www.marqcfi.com	Bloomington	MN	55431	952-703-7474	881-3653
Marquette Financial Cos 60 S Sixth St Ste 3800 *Web:* www.marquette.com	Minneapolis	MN	55402	612-661-3880	
Medallion Financial Corp 437 Madison Ave 38th Fl *NASDAQ: TAXI* ■ **Fax:* PR ■ *TF:* 877-633-2554 ■ *Web:* www.medallionfinancial.com	New York	NY	10022	212-328-2100	328-2121*
MicroFinancial Inc 16 New England Executive Pk Ste 200 *NASDAQ: MFI* ■ *TF:* 877-868-3800 ■ *Web:* www.microfinancial.com	Burlington	MA	01803	781-994-4800	994-4938
New York Business Development Corp (NYBDC) 50 Beaver St Sixth Fl *TF:* 800-923-2504 ■ *Web:* www.nybdc.com	Albany	NY	12207	518-463-2268	463-0240
ORIX USA Corp 1717 Main St Ste 900 *Web:* www.orix.com	Dallas	TX	75201	214-237-2000	237-2018
PACCAR Financial Corp 777 106th Ave NE *Web:* www.paccarfinancial.com	Bellevue	WA	98004	425-468-7100	468-8220
Park Community Federal Credit Union PO Box 18630 *TF:* 800-626-2870 ■ *Web:* www.parkcommunity.com	Louisville	KY	40261	502-968-3681	964-6704
PDS Gaming Corp 6280 Annie Oakley Dr *TF:* 800-479-3612 ■ *Web:* www.pdsgaming.com	Las Vegas	NV	89120	702-736-0700	740-8692
Philip Morris Capital Corp 225 High Ridge Rd Ste 300-W **Fax Area Code:* 914 ■ *Web:* www.philipmorriscapitalcorp.com	Stamford	CT	06905	203-348-1350	335-8287*
Phoenix American Inc 2401 Kerner Blvd **Fax Area Code:* 415 ■ *TF:* 866-895-5050 ■ *Web:* www.phxa.com	San Rafael	CA	94901	866-895-5050	485-4891*
Phoenix Growth Capital Corp 2401 Kerner Blvd **Fax Area Code:* 415 ■ *TF:* 866-895-5050 ■ *Web:* www.phxa.com	San Rafael	CA	94901	866-895-5050	485-4813*
Phoenix Leasing Inc 2401 Kerner Blvd **Fax Area Code:* 415 ■ *TF:* 866-895-5050 ■ *Web:* www.phxa.com	San Rafael	CA	94901	866-895-5050	485-4813*
Pinnacle Business Finance Inc 615 Commerce St Ste 101 **Fax Area Code:* 800 ■ *TF:* 800-566-1993 ■ *Web:* www.pinnaclecap.com	Tacoma	WA	98402	253-284-5600	821-5903*
Pioneer Credit Co 1870 Executive Pk NW *Web:* www.pioneercredit.net	Cleveland	TN	37312	423-476-6511	559-8439
PMC Commercial Trust 17950 Preston Rd Ste 600 *NASDAQ: CMCT* ■ *TF:* 800-486-3223 ■ *Web:* cimgroup.com/pmc/	Dallas	TX	75252	972-349-3200	349-3265
Priority Capital Inc 174 Green St *TF:* 800-761-2118 ■ *Web:* prioritycapital.com	Melrose	MA	02176	781-321-8778	321-4108
Private Export Funding Corp 280 Pk Ave Fourth Fl W *Web:* www.pefco.com	New York	NY	10017	212-916-0300	286-0304
Public Financial Management Inc (PFM) One Keystone Plz Ste 300 *Web:* www.pfm.com	Harrisburg	PA	17101	717-232-2723	233-6073
Puerto Rico Farm Credit Aca PO Box 363649 *TF:* 800-981-3323 ■ *Web:* prfarmcredit.com/	San Juan	PR	00936	787-753-0579	250-8414
Republic Financial Corp 3300 S Parker Rd Ste 500 *TF:* 888-822-8766 ■ *Web:* www.republic-financial.com	Aurora	CO	80014	303-751-3501	751-4777
Rockville Financial Inc 1645 Ellington Rd *NASDAQ: RCKB* ■ *Web:* www.rockvillebank.com	South Windsor	CT	06074	860-291-3600	
Schroder Investment Management North America Inc (SIMNA) 875 Third Ave 22nd Fl **Fax Area Code:* 212 ■ *TF:* 800-730-2932 ■ *Web:* www.schroders.com/us	New York	NY	10022	800-730-2932	632-2954*
Siemens Financial Services Inc 170 Wood Ave S *TF:* 800-327-4443 ■ *Web:* finance.siemens.com	Iselin	NJ	08830	732-590-6500	
Snap-on Credit LLC 950 Technology Way Ste 301 *TF:* 877-777-8455 ■ *Web:* www.snaponcredit.com	Libertyville	IL	60048	877-777-8455	777-9375
Southgroup & Financial Services Inc 795 Woodlands Pkwy Ste 101 *Web:* www.southgroup.net	Ridgeland	MS	39157	601-914-3220	914-3188
Sta International 1400 Old Country Rd Ste 411 *TF:* 866-970-9882 ■ *Web:* www.stacollect.com	Westbury	NY	11590	516-997-2400	997-2632
Taycor LLC 6065 Bristol Pkwy *TF:* 800-322-9738 ■ *Web:* www.taycor.com	Culver City	CA	90230	310-895-7704	568-9922
Textron Financial Corp 40 Westminster St *Web:* www.textronfinancial.com	Providence	RI	02903	401-621-4200	621-5037
Tyndall Federal Credit Union Inc PO Box 59760 *TF:* 888-896-3255 ■ *Web:* tyndall.org/	Panama City	FL	32412	850-769-9999	747-4215
Verizon Credit Inc 201 N Tampa St *TF:* 800-483-7988 ■ *Web:* www.verizon.com	Tampa	FL	33602	813-229-6000	
Watson Group Financial Corp 6501 Highland Rd *TF:* 800-666-1572 ■ *Web:* www.watsongrp.com	Waterford	MI	48327	248-666-2700	666-1572
Wells Fargo 420 Montgomery St *NYSE: WFC* ■ *TF:* 800-877-4833 ■ *Web:* www.wellsfargo.com	San Francisco	CA	94104	800-877-4833	
Wells Fargo Equipment Finance Inc 733 Marquette Ave Ste 700 *TF:* 877-322-8228 ■ *Web:* www.wellsfargo.com/com/financing/equipment-financing	Minneapolis	MN	55402	612-667-9876	667-9711
Western Agcredit PO Box 95850 *TF:* 800-824-9198 ■ *Web:* www.westernagcredit.com	South Jordan	UT	84095	801-571-9200	576-0600
Winthrop 11100 Wayzata Blvd Ste 800 *Web:* www.winthropresources.com	Minneapolis	MN	55305	952-936-0226	
Xerox Financial Services Inc 800 Long Ridge Rd *TF:* 800-275-9376 ■ *Web:* xerox.com	Stamford	CT	06904	203-968-3000	

220 CREDIT & FINANCING - CONSUMER

SEE ALSO Credit & Financing - Commercial p. 2177; Credit Unions p. 2179; Banks - Commercial & Savings p. 1848

	City	State	Zip	Phone	Fax
Acacia Capital Corp 101 S Ellsworth Ave Ste 300 *Web:* www.acacia-capital.com	San Mateo	CA	94401	650-372-6400	
Allied Home Mortgage Capital Corp 6110 Pinemont Dr	Houston	TX	77092	713-353-0400	
Atlantic Bay Mortgage Group 596 Lynnhaven Pkwy Ste 102 *TF:* 866-877-3143 ■ *Web:* www.atlanticbay.com	Virginia Beach	VA	23452	757-213-1660	
Budget Finance Co 1849 Sawtelle Blvd *TF:* 800-225-6267 ■ *Web:* www.bfcloans.com	Los Angeles	CA	90025	310-696-4050	
Capital Access Group 150 California St Ste 250 *Web:* www.capitalaccess.com	San Francisco	CA	94111	415-217-7600	
Collegiate Funding Services LLC 10304 Spotsylvania Ave *Web:* htyp.org	Fredericksburg	VA	22408	540-374-1600	
Continental Currency Services Inc (CCS) PO Box 10970 *Web:* www.ccurr.com	Santa Ana	CA	92711	714-667-6699	569-0882
Corpfinance International Ltd 229 Niagara St *Web:* www.corpfinance.ca	Toronto	ON	M6J2L5	416-364-6191	
Credit Acceptance Corp 25505 W 12 Mile Rd *TF:* 800-634-1506 ■ *Web:* www.credaccept.com	Southfield	MI	48034	248-353-2700	
DAS Acquisition Company LLC 12140 Woodcrest Executive Dr Ste 150 *Web:* www.usa-mortgage.com	St Louis	MO	63141	314-628-2000	
Dent-A-Med Inc 203 E Emma Ave	Springdale	AR	72764	479-750-6700	
DHI Mortgage Co Ltd 10700 Pecan Park Blvd Suite 450 *TF:* 800-315-8434 ■ *Web:* www.dhimortgage.com	Austin	TX	78750	512-502-0545	502-0031
Dollar Loan Ctr LLC 6122 W Sahara Ave *TF:* 866-550-4352 ■ *Web:* www.dontbebroke.com	Las Vegas	NV	89146	702-693-5626	364-5627
Enerbank USA Inc 1245 E Brickyard Rd Ste 600 *Web:* www.enerbank.com	Salt Lake City	UT	84106	888-390-1220	
Farm Credit of The Virginias Aca 106 Sangers Ln *TF:* 800-559-1016 ■ *Web:* www.farmcreditofvirginias.com	Staunton	VA	24401	540-886-3435	886-3437
Farm Credit West 1478 Stone Pt Dr Ste 450 *Web:* www.farmcreditwest.com	Roseville	CA	95661	860-741-4380	
Finance Factors Ltd 1164 Bishop St *TF:* 800-648-7136 ■ *Web:* www.financefactors.com	Honolulu	HI	96813	808-548-4940	548-5148
Finance of America Mortgage 300 Welsh Rd Bldg 5 *Web:* www.gatewayfunding.com	Horsham	PA	19044	215-591-0222	
First Insurance Funding Corp 450 Skokie Blvd Ste 1000 *TF:* 800-837-3707 ■ *Web:* www.firstinsurancefunding.com	Northbrook	IL	60062	800-837-3707	837-3709
Ford Motor Credit Co One American Rd PO Box 1732 *TF:* 800-727-7000 ■ *Web:* credit.ford.com	Dearborn	MI	48121	313-322-3000	
Franklin American Mortgage Company Inc 501 Corporate Centre Dr Ste 400 *Web:* www.franklinamerican.com	Franklin	TN	37067	615-778-1000	
Franklin Credit Management Corp 101 Hudson St *TF:* 800-255-5897 ■ *Web:* www.franklincredit.com	Jersey City	NJ	07302	201-604-1800	839-4512
Gateway Mortgage Group LLC 6910 E 14th St *TF:* 877-406-8109 ■ *Web:* www.gatewayloan.com	Tulsa	OK	74112	918-712-9000	

Company	Address	City	State	Zip	Phone	Fax
General Motors Acceptance Corp (GMAC)	200 Renaissance Ctr	Detroit	MI	48265	877-320-2559	428-4622*
	**Fax Area Code: 800* ■ *TF:* 800-200-4622 ■ *Web:* www.ally.com					
Green Tree Servicing LLC	345 St Peter St	Saint Paul	MN	55102	800-423-9527	
	TF: 800-643-0202 ■ *Web:* www.gtservicing.com					
Guaranteed Rate Inc	3940 N Ravenswood	Chicago	IL	60613	773-290-0505	
	TF: 866-934-7283 ■ *Web:* www.guaranteedrate.com					
Harley-Davidson Financial Services Inc	PO Box 21489	Carson City	NV	89721	888-691-4337	
	TF: 888-691-4337 ■ *Web:* www.harley-davidson.com					
iMortgage Services Inc	2570 Boyce Plz Rd Boyce Plz Iii Ste 210	Pittsburgh	PA	15241	412-220-7330	
	Web: www.imortgageservices.com					
Imperial Finance & Trading	701 Pk of Commerce Blvd Ste 301	Boca Raton	FL	33487	888-364-6775	704-0772*
	**Fax Area Code: 866* ■ *TF:* 888-364-6775 ■ *Web:* www.imprl.com					
MCAP Financial Corp	1140 W Pender St Ste 1400	Vancouver	BC	V6E4G1	604-681-8805	
	Web: mcap.com					
Mercedes-Benz Financial Services USA LLC	PO Box 685	Roanoke	TX	76262	800-654-6222	267-6745*
	**Fax Area Code: 877* ■ *TF:* 800-654-6222 ■ *Web:* www.mbfs.com					
Ministry Partners Investment Company LLC	915 W Imperial Hwy Ste 120	Brea	CA	92821	714-671-5720	
	Web: www.ministrypartners.org					
Mortgage Intelligence Inc	5770 Hurontario St Ste 600	Mississauga	ON	L5R3G5	866-304-8455	
	Web: www.mortgageintelligence.ca					
Nationwide Title Clearing Inc	2100 Alternate 19 N	Palm Harbor	FL	34683	727-771-4000	
	Web: www.nationwidetitleclearing.com					
Nelnet Inc	121 S 13th St Ste 201	Lincoln	NE	68501	402-458-2370	458-2399
	NYSE: NNI ■ *TF:* 888-486-4722 ■ *Web:* www.nelnet.com					
New York City Housing Development Corp	110 William St	New York	NY	10038	212-227-5500	227-6865
	Web: www.nychdc.com					
Nicholas Financial Inc	2454 McMullen Booth Rd Bldg C	Clearwater	FL	33759	727-726-0763	726-2140
	NASDAQ: NICK ■ *TF:* 800-237-2721 ■ *Web:* nicholasfinancial.com					
Ontario Centres of Excellence Inc	156 Front St W Ste 200	Toronto	ON	M5J2L6	416-861-1092	
	TF: 866-759-6014 ■ *Web:* www.oce-ontario.org					
Paramount Equity Mortgage Inc	8781 Sierra College Blvd	Roseville	CA	95661	916-290-9999	
	Web: www.paramountequity.com					
PreCash Inc	1800 W Loop S Ste 1400	Houston	TX	77027	713-600-2200	
	TF: 800-773-2274 ■ *Web:* www.precash.com					
Prestige Financial Services Inc	1420 S 500 W	Salt Lake City	UT	84115	801-844-2100	844-2600
	TF: 888-822-7422 ■ *Web:* www.gopfs.com					
Prime Rate Premium Finance Corp	2141 Enterprise Dr PO Box 100507	Florence	SC	29501	843-669-0937	292-1080
	TF Cust Svc: 800-777-7458 ■ *Web:* www.primeratepfc.com					
Redwood Credit Union	PO Box 6104	Santa Rosa	CA	95406	707-545-4000	
	TF: 800-479-7928 ■ *Web:* www.redwoodcu.org					
Regional Acceptance Corp	1424 E Fire Tower Rd	Greenville	NC	27858	252-321-7700	353-1852
	TF: 877-722-7299 ■ *Web:* www.regionalacceptance.com					
Republic Finance	7031 Commerce Cir	Baton Rouge	LA	70809	225-927-0005	
	Web: www.republicfinance.com					
Rpm Mortgage Inc	3240 Stone Vly Rd W	Alamo	CA	94507	925-295-9300	
	Web: rpm-mtg.com					
Sallie Mae	12061 Bluemont Way	Reston	VA	20190	703-810-3000	848-1949*
	**Fax Area Code: 800* ■ *TF Cust Svc:* 888-272-5543 ■ *Web:* www.salliemae.com					
Security Finance Corp	PO Box 811	Spartanburg	SC	29304	864-582-8193	582-2532
	TF All: 800-395-8195 ■ *Web:* www.security-finance.com					
Select Portfolio Servicing Inc	3815 SW Temple	Salt Lake City	UT	84115	800-258-8602	
	TF: 800-258-8602 ■ *Web:* www.spservicing.com					
SLM Corp	12061 Bluemont Way	Reston	VA	20190	703-810-3000	
	NASDAQ: SLM ■ *TF Cust Svc:* 888-272-5543 ■ *Web:* www.salliemae.com					
Sotheby's Financial Services Inc	1334 York Ave	New York	NY	10021	212-606-7000	894-1141
	Web: www.sothebys.com					
Standard Management Co	6151 W Century Blvd Ste 300	Los Angeles	CA	90045	310-410-2300	
	Web: www.strdmgmt.com					
Stann Financial LLC	4021 N Saint Peters Pkwy	St Peters	MO	63304	636-447-8770	
	Web: www.stannfinancial.com					
Toyota Financial Services	19001 S Western Ave	Torrance	CA	90501	212-715-7386	
	TF Cust Svc: 800-874-8822 ■ *Web:* www.toyotafinancial.com					
Triad Financial Services Inc	4336 Pablo Oaks Ct	Jacksonville	FL	32224	800-522-2013	
	Web: www.triadfs.com					
United Finance Co	515 E Burnside St	Portland	OR	97214	503-232-5153	238-6453
	Web: www.unitedfinance.com					
Wallick & Volk Mortgage	222 E 18th St	Cheyenne	WY	82001	307-634-5941	
	TF: 800-280-8655 ■ *Web:* www.wvmb.com					
Watson Mortgage Corp	6206 Atlantic Blvd Ste 1	Jacksonville	FL	32211	904-645-7111	
	Web: watsonmortgagecorp.com					
WebBank Corp	215 S State St Ste 800	Salt Lake City	UT	84111	801-456-8350	
	Web: www.webbank.com					
Wells Fargo Education Financial Services	PO Box 5185	Sioux Falls	SD	57117	800-658-3567	456-0561
	TF: 800-658-3567 ■ *Web:* www.wellsfargo.com					
Wells Fargo Financial Inc	800 Walnut St	Des Moines	IA	50309	515-280-7741	427-1729*
	**Fax Area Code: 704* ■ *Web:* wellsfargo.com					
Western Funding Inc	PO Box 94858	Las Vegas	NV	89193	702-434-1990	434-4286
	Web: www.westernfundinginc.com					
WFS Financial Inc	23 Pasteur	Irvine	CA	92618	949-753-3866	
	Web: www.wellsfargodealerservices.com					

221 CREDIT REPORTING SERVICES

SEE ALSO

Company	Address	City	State	Zip	Phone	Fax
Advantage Credit Inc	32065 Castle Ct Ste 300	Evergreen	CO	80439	303-670-7993	
	Web: www.advcredit.com					
Argus Research Co	61 Broadway Ste 1910	New York	NY	10006	212-425-7500	
	Web: www.argusresearch.com					
Baltimore Credit & Collection Services Inc	6400 Baltimore National Pk Ste 469	Catonsville	MD	21228	410-549-6444	
	Web: www.bccs2.com					
Building Industry Credit Association	2351 W Third St	Los Angeles	CA	90057	213-251-1100	
	Web: www.bica.com					
CBCInnovis Inc	250 E Town St	Columbus	OH	43215	614-222-4343	
	Web: www.cbcinnovis.com					
Coface Services North America Inc	50 Millstone Rd	East Windsor	NJ	08520	609-469-0400	490-1582
	TF: 877-626-3223 ■ *Web:* www.coface-usa.com					
Community Bankers Merchant Services Inc	908 S Old Missouri Rd	Springdale	AZ	72764	479-725-1000	
	Web: www.merchantprocessing.com					
Constellation Technology Corp	7887 Bryan Dairy Rd Ste 100	Largo	FL	33777	727-547-0600	
	TF: 800-335-7355 ■ *Web:* www.contech.com					
Credit Bureau of Connecticut Inc, The	600 Saw Mill Rd	West Haven	CT	06516	203-931-2000	
	Web: www.avantus.com					
Creditors Bureau Associates	420 College St	Macon	GA	31201	478-750-1111	
	Web: www.cbamacon.com					
Data Facts Inc	8520 Macon Rd Ste 2	Cordova	TN	38018	901-685-7599	
	Web: www.datafacts.com					
Equifax Credit Marketing Services	1550 Peachtree St NW	Atlanta	GA	30309	404-885-8000	
	NYSE: EFX ■ *TF Sales:* 800-660-5125 ■ *Web:* www.equifax.com					
Equifax Inc	1550 Peachtree St NW	Atlanta	GA	30309	404-885-8000	
	NYSE: EFX ■ *TF Sales:* 888-202-4025 ■ *Web:* www.equifax.com					
Experian Information Solutions Inc	475 Anton Blvd	Costa Mesa	CA	92626	714-830-7000	
	TF Cust Svc: 888-397-3742 ■ *Web:* www.experian.com					
Fitch Ratings Inc	One State St Plz	New York	NY	10004	212-908-0500	
	TF: 800-753-4824 ■ *Web:* www.fitchratings.com					
Holloway Credit Solutions LLC	1286 Carmichael Way	Montgomery	AL	36106	334-396-1200	
	Web: hollowaycredit.com					
Incharge Institute of America Inc	5750 Major Blvd	Orlando	FL	32819	407-291-7770	
	Web: www.incharge.org					
Kroll Factual Data Inc	5200 Hahns Peak Dr	Loveland	CO	80538	970-663-5700	929-3297*
	**Fax Area Code: 800* ■ *TF:* 800-929-3400 ■ *Web:* www.krollfactualdata.com					
Merchants Credit Bureau	955 Green St	Augusta	GA	30901	706-823-6246	823-6253
	TF: 800-426-5265 ■ *Web:* www.mcbusa.com					
Moody's Corp	250 Greenwich St 7 World Trade Ctr	New York	NY	10007	212-553-0300	
	NYSE: MCO ■ *Web:* www.moodys.com					
NACM South Texas Inc	10887 S Wilcrest Dr	Houston	TX	77099	281-228-6100	
	Web: www.nacmsouthtexas.org					
Screeningone Inc	2233 W 190th St	Torrance	CA	90504	888-327-6511	
	TF: 888-327-6511 ■ *Web:* www.screeningone.com					
Strategic Information Resources Inc	155 Brookdale Dr	Springfield	MA	01104	413-736-4511	
	Web: www.backgrounddecision.com					
Tele-Track	5550 Peach Tree Pkwy Ste 600	Norcross	GA	30092	770-449-8809	449-6647
	TF: 800-729-6981 ■ *Web:* www.corelogic.com					
TENA Companies Inc	251 W Lafayette Frontage Rd	Saint Paul	MN	55107	651-293-1234	
	Web: www.tenaco.com					
TransUnion LLC	555 W Adams St	Chicago	IL	60661	866-922-2100	
	TF: 866-922-2100 ■ *Web:* www.transunion.com					
Trudiligence LLC	3190 S Wadsworth Blvd Ste 260	Lakewood	CO	80227	303-692-8445	
	Web: www.trudiligence.com					

222 CREDIT UNIONS

Company	Address	City	State	Zip	Phone	Fax
1st Advantage Federal Credit Union	110 Cybernetics Way	Yorktown	VA	23693	757-877-2444	
	Web: 1stadvantage.org					
1st Midamerica Credit Union	731 E Bethalto Dr	Bethalto	IL	62010	618-258-3168	
	Web: 1stmidamerica.org					
66 Federal Credit Union	PO Box 1358	Bartlesville	OK	74005	918-336-7662	337-7634
	TF: 800-897-6991 ■ *Web:* www.truitycu.org					
Affinity Federal Credit Union	73 Mountain View Blvd PO Box 621	Basking Ridge	NJ	07920	800-325-0808	
	TF: 800-325-0808 ■ *Web:* www.affinityfcu.org					
Air Force Federal Credit Union	1560 Cable Ranch Rd Ste 200	San Antonio	TX	78245	210-673-5610	673-5102
	TF: 800-227-5328 ■ *Web:* www.airforcefcu.com					
Alabama Credit Union	220 Paul Bryant Dr E	Tuscaloosa	AL	35401	205-348-5944	
	Web: alabamacu.com					
Alabama One Credit Union	1215 Veterans Memorial Pkwy	Tuscaloosa	AL	35404	205-759-1595	
	Web: alabamaone.org					

				Phone	Fax
Alaska USA Federal Credit Union 4000 Credit Union Dr PO Box 196613 *TF:* 800-525-9094 ■ *Web:* www.alaskausa.org	Anchorage	AK	99503	907-563-4567	561-0773
Allegacy Federal Credit Union 1691 Westbrook Plaza Dr *TF:* 800-782-4670 ■ *Web:* www.allegacyfcu.org	Winston-Salem	NC	27103	336-774-3400	774-3475
America First Credit Union 1344 West 4675 South **Fax:* Hum Res ■ *TF:* 800-999-3961 ■ *Web:* www.americafirst.com	Ogden	UT	84405	801-627-0900	778-8079*
American Airlines Employees Federal Credit Union 4151 Amon Carter Blvd PO Box 155489 *TF:* 800-533-0035 ■ *Web:* www.aacreditunion.org	Fort Worth	TX	76155	817-952-4500	
American Eagle Federal Credit Union 417 Main St *TF:* 800-842-0145 ■ *Web:* www.americaneagle.org	East Hartford	CT	06118	860-568-2020	568-2020
Americo Federal Credit Union 4101 Main St *Web:* americofcu.com	Erie	PA	16511	814-899-6608	
Americu Credit Union 1916 Black River Blvd *Web:* americu.org	Rome	NY	13440	315-356-3000	
Amoco Federal Credit Union PO Box 889 *TF:* 800-231-6053 ■ *Web:* www.amocofcu.org	Texas City	TX	77592	409-948-8541	948-3944
Andrews Federal Credit Union (AFCU) 5711 Allentown Rd *TF:* 800-487-5500 ■ *Web:* www.andrewsfcu.org	Suitland	MD	20746	301-702-5500	702-5330
ANG Federal Credit Union PO Box 170204 *TF:* 800-237-6211 ■ *Web:* www.angfcu.org	Birmingham	AL	35217	205-841-4525	841-4545
APCO Employees Credit Union 750 17th St N *TF:* 800-249-2726 ■ *Web:* www.apcocu.org	Birmingham	AL	35203	205-257-3601	
Apple Federal Credit Union 4029 Ridge Top Rd *Web:* applefcu.org	Fairfax	VA	22030	703-788-4800	
Argentine Santa Fe Industries Credit Union 4150 Kansas Ave	Kansas City	KS	66106	913-342-9039	
Arizona Federal Credit Union PO Box 60070 *TF:* 800-523-4603 ■ *Web:* www.arizonafederal.org	Phoenix	AZ	85082	602-683-1000	683-1903
Arkansas Federal Credit Union 2424 Marshall Rd *Web:* afcu.org	Jacksonville	AR	72076	501-982-1000	
Ascend Federal Credit Union 520 Airpark Dr PO Box 1210 *TF:* 800-342-3086 ■ *Web:* www.ascendfcu.org	Tullahoma	TN	37388	931-455-5441	454-1311
Ascentra Credit Union 1710 Grant St *Web:* ascentra.org	Bettendorf	IA	52722	563-355-0152	
Atlanta Postal Credit Union 501 Pulliam St SW Ste 350 *TF:* 800-849-8431 ■ *Web:* www.apcu.com	Atlanta	GA	30312	404-768-4126	768-0815
Autotruck Federal Credit Union 3611 Newburg Rd PO Box 18890 *TF:* 800-459-2328 ■ *Web:* www.autotruckfcu.org	Louisville	KY	40218	502-459-8981	458-0371
Bank-Fund Staff Federal Credit Union PO Box 27755 *TF:* 800-923-7328 ■ *Web:* www.bfsfcu.org	Washington	DC	20038	202-458-4300	522-1528
BayPort Credit Union Inc 3711 Huntington Ave *TF:* 800-928-8801 ■ *Web:* www.bayportcu.org/home.html	Newport News	VA	23607	757-928-8850	380-8127
Beacon Credit Union PO Box 627 *TF:* 800-762-3136 ■ *Web:* www.beaconcu.org	Wabash	IN	46992	260-563-7443	
Bellco First Federal Credit Union 7600 E OrchaRd Rd Ste 400N *TF:* 800-235-5261 ■ *Web:* www.bellco.org	Greenwood Village	CO	80111	303-689-7800	
Belvoir Federal Credit Union 14040 Central Loop *Web:* belvoircreditunion.org	Woodbridge	VA	22193	703-730-1800	
Bethpage Federal Credit Union 899 S Oyster Bay Rd **Fax Area Code:* 516 ■ *TF:* 800-628-7070 ■ *Web:* www.bethpagefcu.com	Bethpage	NY	11714	800-628-7070	349-6828*
BlueCross BlueShield of Tennessee Inc One Cameron Hill Cir *Web:* www.bcbst.com	Chattanooga	TN	37402	423-755-5600	
Boulder Valley Credit Union Inc 5505 Arapahoe Ave *TF:* 800-783-8850 ■ *Web:* www.bvcu.org	Boulder	CO	80303	303-442-8850	440-0838
Bramco Inc 1801 Watterson Trl *Web:* www.bramco.com	Louisville	KY	40232	502-493-4300	
Campus Federal Credit Union PO Box 98036 **Fax Area Code:* 602 ■ *TF:* 888-769-8841 ■ *Web:* www.campusfederal.org	Baton Rouge	LA	70898	225-769-8841	659-2197*
Campus USA Credit Union PO Box 147029 *TF:* 800-367-6440 ■ *Web:* www.campuscu.com	Gainesville	FL	32614	352-335-9090	
Caribe Federal Credit Union 195 Oneil St *Web:* caribefederal.com	San Juan	PR	00918	787-474-5147	
Cataract Savings & Credit Union Ltd 7172 Dorchester Rd *Web:* www.cataractsavings.on.ca	Niagara Falls	ON	L2G5V6	905-357-5222	
CFCU Community Credit Union 1030 Craft Rd *Web:* mycfcu.com	Ithaca	NY	14850	607-257-8500	
Chartway Federal Credit Union 160 Newtown Rd **Fax:* Hum Res ■ *TF:* 800-678-8765 ■ *Web:* www.chartway.com	Virginia Beach	VA	23462	757-552-1000	671-7691*
Chicago Patrolmen'S Federal Credit Union 1407 W Washington Blvd *Web:* cpdfcu.com	Chicago	IL	60607	312-726-8814	
Citadel Federal Credit Union 520 Eagleview Blvd *TF:* 800-666-0191	Exton	PA	19341	610-380-6000	380-6070
Citizens Equity First Credit Union 5401 W Dirksen Pkwy *TF Cust Svc:* 800-633-7077 ■ *Web:* www.cefcu.com	Peoria	IL	61607	309-633-7000	633-3621
Class Act Federal Credit Union 3620 Fern Vly Rd *TF:* 800-292-2960 ■ *Web:* www.classact.org	Louisville	KY	40219	502-964-7575	966-2061
Coast Central Credit Union Inc 2650 Harrison Ave *TF:* 800-974-9727 ■ *Web:* www.coastccu.org	Eureka	CA	95501	707-445-8801	442-2532
Coastal Federal Credit Union 1000 St Albans Dr *TF:* 800-868-4262 ■ *Web:* www.coastal24.com	Raleigh	NC	27609	919-420-8000	
Collins Community Credit Union 1150 42nd St Ne *Web:* collinscu.org	Cedar Rapids	IA	52402	319-393-9000	
Commonwealth Credit Union PO Box 978 *TF:* 800-228-6420 ■ *Web:* www.ccuky.org	Frankfort	KY	40602	502-564-4775	
Community America Credit Union (CACU) 9777 Ridge Dr *TF:* 800-892-7957 ■ *Web:* www.cacu.com	Lenexa	KS	66219	913-905-7000	905-7111
Community Resource Federal Credit Union 20 Wade Rd *TF:* 888-783-2211 ■ *Web:* www.communityresource.coop	Latham	NY	12110	518-783-2211	783-2266
Communitywide Federal Credit Union 1555 W Western Ave *Web:* www.comwide.com	South Bend	IN	46619	574-239-2700	
Contra Costa Federal Credit Union PO Box 509 *TF:* 888-387-8632 ■ *Web:* www.contracostafcu.org	Martinez	CA	94553	925-228-7550	
Coors Credit Union 816 Washington Ave *TF:* 800-770-6414 ■ *Web:* www.coorscu.org	Golden	CO	80401	303-279-6414	279-6336
Coosa Pines Federal Credit Union 17591 Plant Rd *TF:* 800-237-9789 ■ *Web:* www.coosapinesfcu.org	Childersburg	AL	35044	256-378-5559	378-3881
CP Federal Credit Union 1100 Clinton Rd *Web:* cpfederal.com	Jackson	MI	49202	517-784-7101	
Credit Union Acceptance Company LLC 9601 Jones Rd Ste 108 *Web:* www.cuac.net	Houston	TX	77065	281-970-2822	
Credit Union of Southern California PO Box 200 **Fax Area Code:* 714 ■ *TF:* 866-287-6225 ■ *Web:* www.cusocal.org	Whittier	CA	90608	562-698-8326	990-5492*
Credit Union of Texas PO Box 517028 *TF:* 800-314-3828 ■ *Web:* www.cuoftexas.org	Dallas	TX	75251	972-263-9497	301-1980
Credit.com Inc 160 Spear St Ste 1020 *Web:* www.credit.com	San Francisco	CA	94105	415-901-1550	
Dearborn Federal Credit Union 400 Town Ctr Dr *TF:* 888-336-2700 ■ *Web:* www.dfcufinancial.com	Dearborn	MI	48126	313-336-2700	336-2700
Deer Valley Federal Credit Union 16215 N 28th Ave *TF:* 800-579-5051 ■ *Web:* deervalleycu.org	Phoenix	AZ	85053	602-375-7300	375-7333
Delta Employees Credit Union 1025 Virginia Ave *TF:* 800-544-3328 ■ *Web:* www.deltacommunitycu.com	Atlanta	GA	30354	404-715-4725	677-4776
Denver Fire Dept Federal Credit Union (DFDFCU) 2201 Federal Blvd *TF:* 866-880-7770 ■ *Web:* www.dfdfcu.com	Denver	CO	80211	303-228-5300	228-5333
Desert Schools Federal Credit Union 148 N 48th St *TF:* 800-456-9171 ■ *Web:* www.desertschools.org	Phoenix	AZ	85034	602-433-7000	634-2993
Digital Employees' Federal Credit Union 220 Donald Lynch Blvd *TF:* 800-328-8797 ■ *Web:* www.dcu.org	Marlborough	MA	01752	508-263-6700	263-6392
Direct Federal Credit Union PO Box 9123 *TF:* 800-449-7728 ■ *Web:* www.direct.com	Needham	MA	02494	781-455-6500	455-9922
Dover Federal Credit Union 1075 Silver Lk Blvd *Web:* doverfcu.com	Dover	DE	19904	302-678-8000	
Dow Chemical Employees' Credit Union 600 E Lyon Rd *TF:* 800-835-7794 ■ *Web:* www.dcecu.org	Midland	MI	48640	989-835-7794	832-4883
Duca Financial Services Credit Union Ltd 5290 Yonge St *Web:* duca.com	Toronto	ON	M2N5P9	416-223-8502	
Dupaco Community Credit Union 3999 Pennsylvania Ave *Web:* dupaco.com	Dubuque	IA	52002	563-557-7600	
Educational Employees Credit Union PO Box 5242 *TF:* 800-538-3328 ■ *Web:* www.myeecu.org	Fresno	CA	93755	559-437-7700	451-0198
Educators Credit Union (ECU) 1400 N Newman Rd PO Box 81040 *TF:* 800-236-5898 ■ *Web:* www.ecu.com	Racine	WI	53406	262-260-9393	884-7233
Eglin Federal Credit Union 838 Eglin Pkwy NE *TF:* 800-367-6159 ■ *Web:* eglinfcu.org	Fort Walton Beach	FL	32547	850-862-0111	862-0111
Ent Federal Credit Union 7250 Campus Dr *TF:* 800-525-9623 ■ *Web:* www.ent.com	Colorado Springs	CO	80920	719-574-1100	388-9065
Evansville Teachers Federal Credit Union PO Box 5129 *TF:* 800-800-9271 ■ *Web:* www.etfcu.org	Evansville	IN	47716	812-477-9271	473-9704
FAA Credit Union PO Box 26406 *TF:* 800-448-1990 ■ *Web:* www.faaecu.org	Oklahoma City	OK	73126	405-682-1990	
Faa Federal Credit Union 3920 Whitebrook Dr *Web:* faafcu.org	Memphis	TN	38118	901-366-0066	
Fairwinds Federal Credit Union 3087 N Alafaya Trl **Fax:* Acctg ■ *TF:* 800-443-6887 ■ *Web:* www.fairwinds.org	Orlando	FL	32826	407-277-5045	658-7937*
Fedchoice Federal Credit Union 10001 Willowdale Rd *Web:* fedchoice.org	Lanham	MD	20706	301-699-6100	
Federation des caisses populaires acadiennes ltee, The 295 St Pierre Blvd *Web:* www.caissepopulaireacadienne.com	Caraquet	NB	E1W1B7	506-726-4000	
Finance Ctr Federal Credit Union PO Box 26501 *TF:* 800-473-2328 ■ *Web:* www.fcfcu.com	Indianapolis	IN	46226	317-916-7700	916-6206
Financial Partners Credit Union PO Box 7005 *TF:* 800-950-7328 ■ *Web:* www.fpcu.org	Downey	CA	90241	562-923-0311	904-4285

				Phone	Fax
Firefighters Community Credit Union Inc 2300 St Clair Ave NE *TF:* 800-621-4644 ■ *Web:* www.ffcommunity.com	Cleveland	OH	44114	216-621-4644	694-3600
First Community Credit Union (FCCU) PO Box 1030 *TF:* 800-767-8880 ■ *Web:* www.firstcommunity.com	Chesterfield	MO	63006	636-728-3333	537-4448
First Florida Credit Union 500 W First St *Web:* firstflorida.org	Jacksonville	FL	32202	904-359-6800	
Fort Knox Federal Credit Union PO Box 900 *TF:* 800-756-3678 ■ *Web:* www.fkfcu.org	Radcliff	KY	40159	502-942-0254	
Fort Worth City Credit Union PO Box 100099 *TF:* 888-732-3085 ■ *Web:* www.fwccu.org	Fort Worth	TX	76185	817-732-2803	377-7966
Fort Worth Community Credit Union 1905 Forest Ridge Dr PO Box 210848 *TF:* 800-817-8234 ■ *Web:* www.ftwccu.org	Bedford	TX	76021	817-835-5000	835-5235
Forum Credit Union PO Box 50738 *TF:* 800-382-5414 ■ *Web:* www.forumcu.com	Indianapolis	IN	46250	317-558-6000	558-6319
Founders Federal Credit Union 607 N Main St *TF Tech Supp:* 888-918-7403 ■ *Web:* www.foundersfcu.com	Lancaster	SC	29720	803-289-5927	289-5088
Fox Communities Credit Union 3401 E Calumet St *Web:* foxcu.org	Appleton	WI	54915	920-993-9000	
Georgia Cu Affiliates 6705 Sugarloaf Pkwy Ste 200 *Web:* gcua.org	Duluth	GA	30097	770-476-9625	
Georgia's Own Credit Union 1155 Peachtree St NE Ste 400 PO Box 105205 *TF:* 800-533-2062 ■ *Web:* www.georgiasown.org/	Atlanta	GA	30309	404-874-1166	881-2950
Gesa Credit Union 51 Gage Blvd PO Box 500 *TF:* 888-946-4372 ■ *Web:* www.gesa.com	Richland	WA	99352	509-946-1611	
Greater Texas Federal Credit Union 6411 N Lamar Blvd *Web:* gtfcu.org	Austin	TX	78752	512-458-2558	
Greylock Federal Credit Union 150 W St *TF:* 800-207-5555 ■ *Web:* greylock.org	Pittsfield	MA	01201	413-236-4000	443-0292
GTE Federal Credit Union PO Box 172599 *TF:* 888-871-2690 ■ *Web:* www.gtefinancial.org	Tampa	FL	33672	813-871-2690	
Guadalupe Credit Union 3601 Mimbres Ln *TF:* 800-540-5382 ■ *Web:* www.guadalupecu.org	Santa Fe	NM	87507	505-982-8942	216-0497
Guardian Credit Union 4501 W Greenfield Ave *Web:* guardiancu.org	West Milwaukee	WI	53214	414-546-7450	
Hamilton City Employees Federal Credit Union 309 Ct St *TF:* 800-264-5578 ■ *Web:* www.allwealth.org	Hamilton	OH	45011	513-868-5881	867-7339
Harbor Credit Union 800 Weise St *Web:* harborcu.com	Green Bay	WI	54302	920-431-6688	
HarborOne Credit Union 770 Oak St PO Box 720 *TF:* 800-244-7592 ■ *Web:* www.harborone.com	Brockton	MA	02301	508-895-1000	895-1674
Hilco Federal Credit Union 120 Texas Dr *Web:* hilcocu.com	Kerrville	TX	78028	830-257-8238	
Holley Credit Union 1107 Mineral Wells Ave *Web:* holleycreditunion.org	Paris	TN	38242	731-644-9031	
Hoosier Hills Credit Union 630 Lincoln Ave *Web:* hoosierhillscu.org	Bedford	IN	47421	812-279-6644	
Horizon Credit Union 13224 E Mansfield Ste 300 *Web:* hzcu.org	Spokane Valley	WA	99216	509-928-6494	
Hudson Valley Federal Credit Union 159 Barnegat Rd *TF:* 800-468-3011 ■ *Web:* www.hvfcu.org	Poughkeepsie	NY	12601	845-463-3011	463-3613
Hughes Federal Credit Union Inc PO Box 11900 *TF:* 866-760-3156 ■ *Web:* www.hughesfcu.org	Tucson	AZ	85734	520-794-8341	
I B M Southeast Employees Federal Credit Union PO Box 5090 *TF:* 888-567-8688 ■ *Web:* www.ibmsecu.org	Boca Raton	FL	33431	561-982-4700	
Indiana Credit Union League 5975 Castle Creek Parkway N Ste 300 *TF:* 800-285-5300 ■ *Web:* icul.org	Indianapolis	IN	46250	317-594-5300	
Indiana Members Credit Union (IMCU) 7110 W Tenth St *TF:* 800-556-9268 ■ *Web:* www.imcu.com	Indianapolis	IN	46214	317-248-8556	
Interra Credit Union 300 W Lincoln Ave *Web:* interracu.com	Goshen	IN	46526	574-534-2506	
Island Federal Credit Union 120 Motor Pkwy *TF:* 800-475-5263 ■ *Web:* www.islandfcu.org	Hauppauge	NY	11788	631-851-1100	
Keesler Federal Credit Union PO Box 7001 *TF:* 888-533-7537 ■ *Web:* www.kfcu.org	Biloxi	MS	39534	228-385-5500	385-5535
Kern Schools Federal Credit Union PO Box 9506 *TF:* 800-221-3311 ■ *Web:* www.ksfcu.org	Bakersfield	CA	93389	661-833-7900	833-7989
KeyPoint Credit Union 2805 Bowers Ave *TF:* 888-255-3637 ■ *Web:* www.kpcu.com/	Santa Clara	CA	95051	408-731-4100	731-4485
Kim Central Credit Union 625 Deerwood Ave *Web:* kimcentral.org	Neenah	WI	54956	920-720-2572	
Kinecta Federal Credit Union 1440 Rosecrans Ave PO Box 10003 **Fax:* Hum Res ■ *TF:* 800-854-9846 ■ *Web:* www.kinecta.org	Manhattan Beach	CA	90266	310-643-5400	643-8350*
L & N Federal Credit Union 9265 Smyrna Pkwy *TF:* 800-443-2479 ■ *Web:* www.lnfcu.com	Louisville	KY	40229	502-368-5858	
La Capitol Federal Credit Union PO Box 3398 *TF:* 800-522-2748 ■ *Web:* www.lacapfcu.org	Baton Rouge	LA	70821	225-342-5055	342-9135
Lafayette Federal Credit Union (Inc) 3535 University Blvd W *TF:* 800-888-6560 ■ *Web:* www.lfcu.org	Kensington	MD	20895	301-929-7990	
Landmark Credit Union 5445 S Westridge Dr PO Box 510910 *TF:* 800-801-1449 ■ *Web:* www.landmarkcu.com	New Berlin	WI	53151	262-796-4500	782-3422

				Phone	Fax
Langley Federal Credit Union 1055 W Mercury Blvd *TF:* 800-826-7490 ■ *Web:* www.langleyfcu.org	Hampton	VA	23666	757-827-7200	825-7557
Leominster Credit Union 20 Adams St *TF:* 800-649-4646 ■ *Web:* www.leominstercu.com	Leominster	MA	01453	978-537-8021	
Local Government Federal Credit Union 323 W Jones St Ste 600 *TF:* 888-732-8562 ■ *Web:* www.lgfcu.org	Raleigh	NC	27603	919-857-2150	755-0193
Lockheed Federal Credit Union (LFCU) 2340 Hollywood Way *TF:* 800-328-5328 ■ *Web:* logixbanking.com	Burbank	CA	91505	818-565-2020	846-4379
Los Angeles Federal Credit Union PO Box 53032 *TF:* 877-695-2328 ■ *Web:* www.lafcu.org	Los Angeles	CA	90053	818-242-8640	242-5812
Los Angeles Police Federal Credit Union PO Box 10188 *TF:* 877-695-2732 ■ *Web:* www.lapfcu.org	Van Nuys	CA	91410	818-787-6520	786-9508
Matanuska Valley Fcu 1020 S Bailey St *Web:* mvfcu.coop	Palmer	AK	99645	907-745-4891	
Mazuma Credit Union 9300 Troost Ave *Web:* mazuma.org	Kansas City	MO	64131	816-361-4194	
Member One Federal Credit Union 202 Fourth Ne *Web:* memberonefcu.com	Roanoke	VA	24016	540-982-8811	
Members Group Inc, The 1500 NW 118th St *Web:* www.themembersgroup.com	Des Moines	IA	50325	515-457-2000	
Meriwest Credit Union PO Box 530953 **Fax Area Code:* 408 ■ *TF:* 877-637-4937 ■ *Web:* www.meriwest.com	San Jose	CA	95153	877-637-4937	363-3330*
Michigan Schools & Government Credit Union 40400 Garfield Rd	Clinton Township	MI	48038	586-263-8800	
Midwest America Federal Credit Union 1104 Medical Pk Dr *TF:* 800-348-4738 ■ *Web:* www.mwafcu.org	Fort Wayne	IN	46825	260-482-3334	423-8298
Miramar Federal Credit Union PO Box 261370 *TF:* 800-640-1228 ■ *Web:* www.miramarfcu.org	San Diego	CA	92196	858-695-9494	271-1537
Mission City Federal Credit Union 1391 Franklin St *Web:* missioncityfcu.org	Santa Clara	CA	95050	408-244-5818	
Mission Federal Credit Union PO Box 919023 *TF:* 800-500-6328 ■ *Web:* www.missionfed.com	San Diego	CA	92121	858-524-2850	546-7637
Missoula Federal Credit Union 3600 Brooks St *Web:* missoulafcu.org	Missoula	MT	59801	406-523-3300	
Mountain America Credit Union PO Box 9001 *TF:* 800-748-4302 ■ *Web:* www.macu.com	West Jordan	UT	84084	801-325-6228	325-6395
Municipal Credit Union PO Box 3205 *TF:* 866-512-6109 ■ *Web:* www.nymcu.org	New York	NY	10007	212-693-4900	416-7051
Mutual Savings Credit Union Inc 2040 Valleydale Rd *Web:* www.mutualsavings.org	Birmingham	AL	35244	205-682-1100	
Nassau Financial Federal Credit Union 1325 Franklin Ave Ste 500 *TF:* 800-216-2328 ■ *Web:* www.nassaufinancial.org	Garden City	NY	11530	516-742-4900	
Neighbors Federal Credit Union PO Box 2831 *TF:* 866-819-2178 ■ *Web:* www.neighborsfcu.org	Baton Rouge	LA	70821	225-819-2178	819-8923
New England Federal Credit Union PO Box 527 *TF:* 800-400-8790 ■ *Web:* www.nefcu.com	Williston	VT	05495	802-879-8790	879-8557
New Orleans Firemens Federal Credit Union PO Box 689 *TF:* 800-647-1689 ■ *Web:* www.noffcu.org	Metairie	LA	70004	504-889-9090	889-9082
North American Van Lines Inc 5001 US Hwy 30 W *Web:* www.northamerican.com	Fort Wayne	IN	46818	260-429-2511	
North Country Federal Credit Union Inc 69 Swift St Ste 100 *TF:* 800-660-3258 ■ *Web:* www.northcountry.org	South Burlington	VT	05403	802-657-6847	864-9849
North Island Credit Union 5898 Copley Dr *TF Cust Svc:* 800-848-5654 ■ *Web:* www.northislandcu.com	San Diego	CA	92111	619-656-6525	656-4050
NuUnion Credit Union 501 S Capitol Ave *TF:* 888-267-7200 ■ *Web:* www.laketrust.org	Lansing	MI	48933	517-267-7200	267-7095
Odjfs Federal Credit Union 4020 E Fifth Ave *Web:* www.odjfscu.com	Columbus	OH	43219	614-466-3416	
Oil Capital Community Credit Union 4132 E 51st St *Web:* www.oilcapital.com	Tulsa	OK	74135	918-743-4080	
Oklahoma Federal Credit Union 517 NE 36th St *TF:* 800-522-8510 ■ *Web:* okfcu.com	Oklahoma City	OK	73105	405-524-6467	524-1067
Orange County's Credit Union PO Box 11777 *TF:* 888-354-6228 ■ *Web:* orangecountyscu.org	Santa Ana	CA	92711	714-755-5900	
Owensboro Federal Credit Union 717 Harvard Dr PO Box 1189 *TF:* 800-264-1054 ■ *Web:* www.ofcuonline.com	Owensboro	KY	42302	270-683-1054	685-3987
Pacific Marine Credit Union M C X Complex *TF:* 800-736-4500 ■ *Web:* www.pmcu.com	Camp Pendleton	CA	92055	760-430-7511	
Pacific NW Federal Credit Union (PNWFCU) 12106 NE Marx St *TF:* 866-692-8669 ■ *Web:* www.pnwfcu.org	Portland	OR	97220	503-256-5858	253-5858
Pacific Service Federal Credit Union PO Box 8191 *TF:* 888-858-6878 ■ *Web:* www.pacificservice.org	Walnut Creek	CA	94596	925-296-6200	296-6209
Partners 1St Federal Credit Union 1330 Directors Row *Web:* partners1stcu.org	Fort Wayne	IN	46808	260-471-8336	
Pawtucket Credit Union 1200 Central Ave *Web:* pcu.org	Pawtucket	RI	02861	401-722-2212	
Pearl Harbor Federal Credit Union (PHFCU) 94-449 Ukee St **Fax Area Code:* 808 ■ *TF:* 800-987-5583 ■ *Web:* www.phfcu.com	Waipahu	HI	96797	800-987-5583	218-6299*

	Phone	Fax
Pennsylvania State Employees Credit Union One Credit Union Pl ....Harrisburg PA 17110 *TF:* 800-237-7328 ■ *Web:* www.psecu.com	717-234-8484	772-2272
Pentagon Federal Credit Union 2930 Eisenhower Ave ....Alexandria VA 22314 *TF:* 800-247-5626 ■ *Web:* www.penfed.org	800-247-5626	253-6589
People First Federal Credit Union 2141 Downyflake Ln ....Allentown PA 18103 *Web:* peoplefirstcu.org	610-797-7440	
Pine Bluff Cotton Belt Federal Credit Union 1703 River Pines Blvd ....Pine Bluff AR 71601 *TF:* 888-249-1904 ■ *Web:* www.pbcottonbeltfcu.coop	870-535-6365	535-0765
Pittsford Federal Cu 1321 Pittsford Mendon Rd ....Mendon NY 14506 *Web:* pittsfordfcu.org	585-624-7474	
Police & Fire Federal Credit Union 901 Arch St....Philadelphia PA 19107 *TF:* 800-228-8801 ■ *Web:* www.pffcu.org	215-931-0300	931-2926
Portland Teachers Credit Union PO Box 3750....Portland OR 97208 *TF:* 800-527-3932 ■ *Web:* www.onpointcu.com	503-228-7077	273-2698
Premier America Credit Union 19867 Prairie St PO Box 2178 ....Chatsworth CA 91313 *TF:* 800-772-4000 ■ *Web:* www.premier.org	818-772-4000	772-4175
Premier Members Federal Credit Union 5495 Arapahoe Ave....Boulder CO 80303 **Fax Area Code:* 307 ■ *TF:* 800-468-0634 ■ *Web:* premiermembers.org	303-657-7000	777-7252*
Prime Financial Credit Union 5656 S Packard Ave ....Cudahy WI 53110 *Web:* primefinancialcu.org	414-486-4500	
Primeway Federal Credit Union 12811 Northwest Fwy....Houston TX 77040 *Web:* primewayfcu.com	713-799-6200	
Provident Central Credit Union 303 Twin Dolphin Dr....Redwood City CA 94065 *TF:* 800-632-4600 ■ *Web:* www.providentcu.org	650-508-0300	508-7202
Randolph-Brooks Federal Credit Union PO Box 2097 ....Universal City TX 78148 *TF:* 800-580-3300 ■ *Web:* www.rbfcu.org	210-945-3300	945-3764
Red Canoe Credit Union 1418 15th Ave....Longview WA 98632 *Web:* redcanoecu.com	360-425-2130	
Redstone Federal Credit Union 220 Wynn Dr NW ....Huntsville AL 35893 **Fax:* Cust Svc ■ *TF:* 800-234-1234 ■ *Web:* www.redfcu.org	256-837-6110	722-3655*
Rhode Island State Employees Credit Union 160 Francis St ....Providence RI 02903 *TF:* 855-322-7428 ■ *Web:* www.ricreditunion.org	401-751-7440	331-5907
Rockland Federal Credit Union 241 Union St....Rockland MA 02370 *TF:* 800-562-7328 ■ *Web:* www.rfcu.com	781-878-0232	792-3866
Rogue Credit Union 1370 Center Dr ....Medford OR 97501 *Web:* roguefcu.org	541-858-7328	
RTN Federal Credit Union 600 Main St Ste 3....Waltham MA 02452 *TF:* 800-338-0221 ■ *Web:* www.rtn.org	781-736-9900	736-9856
SAC Federal Credit Union (SAFCU) 11515 S 39th St PO Box 1149....Bellevue NE 68123 *TF:* 800-228-0392 ■ *Web:* www.sacfcu.com	402-292-8000	829-0149
Safe 1 Credit Union PO Box 2203....Bakersfield CA 93303 *TF:* 800-322-4529 ■ *Web:* www.safe1.org	661-327-3818	
SAFE Credit Union 3720 Madison Ave....North Highlands CA 95660 *TF:* 800-733-7233 ■ *Web:* www.safecu.org	916-979-7233	348-8340
Safeamerica Credit Union 6001 Gibraltar Dr ....Pleasanton CA 94588 *TF:* 800-972-0999 ■ *Web:* www.safeamerica.com	925-734-4111	
San Antonio Federal Credit Union PO Box 1356 ....San Antonio TX 78295 *TF:* 800-234-7228 ■ *Web:* www.sacu.com	210-258-1234	258-1543
San Diego County Credit Union 6545 Sequence Dr ....San Diego CA 92121 **Fax Area Code:* 858 ■ *TF:* 877-732-2848 ■ *Web:* www.sdccu.com	877-732-2848	597-6509*
San Francisco Federal Credit Union 770 Golden Gate Ave ....San Francisco CA 94102 *TF:* 800-852-7598 ■ *Web:* www.sanfranciscofcu.com	415-775-5377	775-5340
Sb1 Federal Credit Union PO Box 7480....Philadelphia PA 19101 *TF:* 800-806-9465 ■ *Web:* www.sb1fcu.org	215-569-3700	
Schools Financial Credit Union 1485 Response Rd Ste 126....Sacramento CA 95815 *TF:* 800-962-0990 ■ *Web:* www.schools.org	916-569-5400	331-2242
Secure First Credit Union PO Box 170070 ....Birmingham AL 35217 *TF:* 877-520-2115 ■ *Web:* www.securefirstcu.org	205-520-2115	520-2110
Security Service Federal Credit Union 16211 La Cantera Pkwy ....San Antonio TX 78256 *TF:* 800-527-7328 ■ *Web:* www.ssfcu.org	210-476-4000	444-3000
Selco Community Credit Union 299 E 11th Ave ....Eugene OR 97401 *Web:* www.selco.org	541-686-8000	686-4367
Seven Seventeen Credit Union Inc 3181 Larchmont Ave NE....Warren OH 44483 *Web:* www.sscu.net	330-372-8100	372-8337
Sharefax Credit Union Inc 1147 Old SR- 74....Batavia OH 45103 *Web:* sharefax.org	513-753-2440	
Solarity Credit Union 110 N Fifth Ave....Yakima WA 98902 *Web:* solaritycu.org	509-248-1720	
South Carolina Federal Credit Union PO Box 190012 ....North Charleston SC 29419 *TF:* 800-845-0432 ■ *Web:* www.scfederal.org	843-797-8300	
Space Coast Credit Union 8045 N Wickham Rd PO Box 419001....Melbourne FL 32941 *TF:* 800-447-7228 ■ *Web:* www.sccu.com	321-752-2222	723-3716
St Anne's Credit Union of Fall River 286 Oliver St....Fall River MA 02724 *Web:* www.stannes.com	508-324-7300	673-1542
Stanford Federal Credit Union 1860 Embarcadero Rd ....Palo Alto CA 94303 **Fax Area Code:* 866 ■ *TF:* 888-723-7328 ■ *Web:* www.sfcu.org	650-723-2509	579-9764*
Star One Federal Credit Union PO Box 3643....Sunnyvale CA 94088 *TF:* 866-543-5202 ■ *Web:* www.starone.org	408-543-5202	543-5203
State Employees Credit Union of Maryland Inc 971 Corporate Blvd....Linthicum MD 21090 *TF:* 800-879-7328 ■ *Web:* www.secumd.org	410-487-7328	
State Employees Federal Credit Union 700 Patroon Creek Blvd Patroon Creek Corporate Ctr....Albany NY 12206 **Fax:* Hum Res ■ *TF:* 800-727-3328 ■ *Web:* www.sefcu.com	518-452-8234	464-5363*
State Employees' Credit Union (SECU) PO Box 29606 ....Raleigh NC 27626 *TF:* 888-732-8562 ■ *Web:* www.ncsecu.org	919-857-2150	857-2000
Sunstate Federal Credit Union (Inc) PO Box 1162 ....Gainesville FL 32602 *Web:* www.sunstatefcu.org	352-381-5200	
Teachers Credit Union (TCU) PO Box 1395....South Bend IN 46624 *TF:* 800-552-4745 ■ *Web:* www.tcunet.com	574-284-6247	
Teachers Federal Credit Union (TFCU) 2410 N Ocean Ave PO Box 9029 ....Farmingville NY 11738 *TF:* 800-341-4333 ■ *Web:* www.teachersfcu.org	631-698-7000	698-7004
Tech Credit Union 10951 Broadway....Crown Point IN 46307 *TF:* 800-276-8324 ■ *Web:* www.techcu.org	219-663-5120	662-4384
Telcoe Federal Credit Union 820 Lousiana St....Little Rock AR 72201 *TF:* 800-482-9009 ■ *Web:* telcoe.com	501-375-5321	375-6233
Texans Credit Union 777 E Campbell Rd ....Richardson TX 75081 *TF:* 800-843-5295 ■ *Web:* www.texanscu.org	972-348-2000	348-2200
Texas Dow Employees Credit Union (TDECU) 1001 FM 2004....Lake Jackson TX 77566 *TF:* 800-839-1154 ■ *Web:* www.tdecu.org	979-297-1154	299-0212
Tower Federal Credit Union 7901 Sandy Spring Rd ....Laurel MD 20707 **Fax:* Cust Svc ■ *TF:* 800-787-8328 ■ *Web:* www.towerfcu.org	301-497-7000	497-8930*
Transwest Credit Union 37 West 1700 South....Salt Lake City UT 84115 *Web:* transwestcu.com	801-487-1692	
Travis Federal Credit Union One Travis Way....Vacaville CA 95687 *TF:* 800-877-8328 ■ *Web:* www.traviscu.org	707-449-4000	
Trugrocer Federal Credit Union 501 E Highland St....Boise ID 83706 *Web:* trugrocer.com	208-385-5200	
Truliant Federal Credit Union 3200 Truliant Way....Winston-Salem NC 27103 *TF:* 800-822-0382 ■ *Web:* www.truliantfcu.org	336-659-1955	659-3540
Tulsa Federal Credit Union 9323 E 21st St....Tulsa OK 74129 *Web:* tulsafederalcu.org	918-610-0200	
Tyco Electronics Federal Credit Union PO Box 3449 ....Redwood City CA 94064 **Fax Area Code:* 800 ■ *TF:* 888-673-3288 ■ *Web:* www.reachcu.coop	888-673-3288	280-8926*
U S Employees O C Federal Credit Union PO Box 44000....Oklahoma City OK 73144 *TF:* 800-227-6366 ■ *Web:* www.usecreditunion.org	405-685-6200	685-6235
Ukrainian National Federal Credit Union 215 Second Ave PO Box 160....New York NY 10003 *TF:* 866-859-5848 ■ *Web:* www.ukrnatfcu.org	212-533-2980	995-5204
Union Special Corp One Union Special Plz....Huntley IL 60142 *Web:* www.unionspecial.com	847-669-5101	
United Nations Federal Credit Union (UNFCU) 24-01 44th Rd Ct Sq Pl ....Long Island City NY 11101 *TF:* 800-891-2471 ■ *Web:* www.unfcu.org	347-686-6000	686-6400
Unitus Community Credit Union PO Box 1937....Portland OR 97207 *TF:* 800-452-0900 ■ *Web:* www.unitusccu.com	503-227-5571	423-8345
University & State Employees Credit Union 10120 Pacific Heights Blvd Ste 100....San Diego CA 92121 *TF:* 866-873-2448 ■ *Web:* www.usecu.org	858-795-6100	795-6007
University of Hawaii Federal Credit Union PO Box 22070....Honolulu HI 96823 *TF:* 800-927-3397 ■ *Web:* www.uhfcu.com	808-983-5500	
University of Hawaii Foundation, The 2444 Dole St Bachman Hall 105....Honolulu HI 96822 *TF:* 866-846-4262 ■ *Web:* www.uhfoundation.org	808-956-8849	
US Alliance Federal Credit Union 600 Midland Ave....Rye NY 10580 **Fax Area Code:* 914 ■ *TF:* 800-431-2754 ■ *Web:* usalliance.org	800-431-2754	881-3464*
US New Mexico Federal Credit Union (USNMFCU) 3939 Osuna Rd NE PO Box 129....Albuquerque NM 87109 *TF:* 888-342-8766 ■ *Web:* www.usnmfcu.org	505-342-8888	342-8975
Valley First Credit Union PO Box 1411....Modesto CA 95353 *TF:* 877-549-4567 ■ *Web:* www.valleyfirstcu.org	209-549-8500	524-1741
Vantage Credit Union (VCU) PO Box 4433....Bridgeton MO 63044 *TF:* 800-522-6009 ■ *Web:* www.vcu.com	314-298-0055	
Verity Credit Union PO Box 75974....Seattle WA 98175 *TF:* 800-444-4589 ■ *Web:* www.veritycu.com	206-440-9000	361-5300
Vermont Federal Credit Union 84 Pine St....Burlington VT 05402 *Web:* vermontfederal.org	802-658-0225	
Virginia Credit Union 7500 Boulders View Dr ....Richmond VA 23225 *TF:* 800-285-5051 ■ *Web:* www.vacu.org	804-323-6000	608-8619
Visions Federal Credit Union (VFUC) 24 McKinley Ave....Endicott NY 13760 *TF:* 800-242-2120 ■ *Web:* www.visionsfcu.org	607-754-7900	786-1718
Vons Employees Federal Credit Union 4455 Arden Dr PO Box 8023 ....El Monte CA 91731 *Web:* vonsefcu.org	626-444-1972	350-5850
Vystar Credit Union 1802 Kernan Blvd S ....Jacksonville FL 32246 *TF:* 800-445-6289 ■ *Web:* vystarcu.org	904-777-6000	908-2488
Washington State Employees Credit Union 400 E Union Ave....Olympia WA 98501 *TF:* 800-562-0999 ■ *Web:* www.wsecu.org	360-943-7911	754-1385
Wescom Credit Union 123 S Marengo Ave PO Box 7058 ....Pasadena CA 91101 *TF:* 888-493-7266 ■ *Web:* www.wescom.org	626-535-1000	
Westby Co-op Credit Union 501 N Main St....Westby WI 54667 *Web:* www.wccucreditunion.coop	608-634-3118	
Westconsin Credit Union 3333 Schneider Ave Se....Menomonie WI 54751 *Web:* westconsincu.org	715-235-3403	

Phone Fax

Westerra Credit Union 3700 E Alameda Ave .... Denver CO 80209 303-321-4209

White River Credit Union 1499 Garrett St .... Enumclaw WA 98022 360-825-4833
Web: www.whiterivercu.com

Whitehall Credit Union 5025 E Main St....... Columbus OH 43213 614-866-5025
Web: whitehallcu.org

Williams Lake & District Credit Union
139 N Third Ave .... Williams Lake BC V2G2A5 250-392-4135
Web: www.wldcu.com

Wings Financial Credit Union
14985 Glazier Ave Ste 100 .... Apple Valley MN 55124 952-997-8000 997-8124
TF: 800-692-2274 ■ *Web:* www.wingsfinancial.com

Workers' Credit Union
815 Main St PO Box 900 .... Fitchburg MA 01420 978-345-1021 343-5825
TF: 800-221-4020 ■ *Web:* www.wcu.com

Wright-Patt Credit Union Inc
2455 Executive Pk Blvd PO Box 286....... Fairborn OH 45324 937-912-7000 912-8002
TF: 800-762-0047 ■ *Web:* www.wpcu.coop

Y-12 Federal Credit Union
501 Lafayette Dr PO Box 2512 .... Oak Ridge TN 37830 865-482-1043
TF: 800-482-1043 ■ *Web:* www.y12fcu.org

Yolo Federal Credit Union 266 W Main St....... Woodland CA 95695 530-668-2700
Web: yolofcu.org

223 CRUISE LINES

SEE ALSO Casinos p. 1904; Cruises - Riverboat p. 2183; Ports & Port Authorities p. 2954; Travel Agencies p. 3253

Phone Fax

Baja Expeditions Inc 3096 Palm St....... San Diego CA 92104 858-581-3311 430-9473
TF: 800-843-6967 ■ *Web:* www.bajaex.com

Blount Small Ship Adventures 461 Water St....... Warren RI 02885 401-247-0955 247-2350
TF: 800-556-7450 ■ *Web:* blountsmallshipadventures.com

Bluewater Adventures Ltd
252 E First St Ste 3....... North Vancouver BC V7L1B3 604-980-3800 980-1800
TF: 888-877-1770 ■ *Web:* www.bluewateradventures.ca

Carnival Cruise Lines 3655 NW 87th Ave....... Miami FL 33178 305-599-2600 406-4700
TF: 800-764-7419 ■ *Web:* carnival.com

China Ocean Shipping Co Americas Inc (COSCO)
100 Lighting Way .... Secaucus NJ 07094 201-422-0500 422-8956
TF: 800-242-7354 ■ *Web:* www.cosco-usa.com

Costa Cruise Lines 200 S Pk Rd Ste 200....... Hollywood FL 33021 954-266-5600 266-5880*
**Fax:* Hum Res ■ *TF:* 800-462-6782 ■ *Web:* www.costacruise.com

Cruise West 3826 18th Ave W Suite 401 .... Seattle WA 98119 206-283-9322
TF: 888-862-8881 ■ *Web:* www.un-cruise.com

Crystal Cruises Inc
2049 Century Pk E Ste 1400....... Los Angeles CA 90067 310-785-9300 785-0011*
**Fax:* Hum Res ■ *Web:* www.crystalcruises.com

Cunard Line Ltd 24303 Town Ctr Dr Ste 200 .... Valencia CA 91355 661-753-1000
TF: 800-728-6273 ■ *Web:* cunard.co.uk/

Discovery Cruises Inc 1775 NW 70th Ave....... Miami FL 33126 305-597-0336
TF: 800-866-8687 ■ *Web:* www.discoverycruiseline.com

Great Lakes Cruise Co 3270 Washtenaw Ave....... Ann Arbor MI 48104 888-891-0203 677-1428*
**Fax Area Code:* 734 ■ *TF:* 888-891-0203 ■ *Web:* www.greatlakescruising.com

Holland America Line 300 Elliott Ave W....... Seattle WA 98119 206-281-3535 281-7110
TF: 800-426-0327 ■ *Web:* www.hollandamerica.com

Hurtigruten 405 Pk Ave .... New York NY 10022 212-319-1300 319-1390
TF: 866-552-0371 ■ *Web:* www.hurtigruten.us

Lindblad Expeditions 96 Morton St Ninth Fl .... New York NY 10014 212-765-7740 265-3770
TF: 800-397-3348 ■ *Web:* www.expeditions.com

Maine Windjammer Cruises PO Box 617 .... Camden ME 04843 207-236-2938 236-3229
TF: 800-736-7981 ■ *Web:* www.mainewindjammercruises.com

MSC Cruises USA Inc
6750 N Andrews Ave Ste 100....... Fort Lauderdale FL 33309 954-772-6262
Web: www.msccruises.com

Oceania Cruises Inc 8300 NW 33rd St Ste 308 .... Miami FL 33122 305-514-2300 514-2222
TF: 800-531-5619 ■ *Web:* www.oceaniacruises.com

Princess Cruises 24844 Rockefeller Ave....... Santa Clarita CA 91355 661-753-0000 284-4771*
**Fax:* Sales ■ *TF:* 800-774-6237 ■ *Web:* www.princess.com

Rockport Schooner Cruises PO Box 272 .... Belfast ME 04915 207-338-3088
TF: 866-732-2473 ■ *Web:* www.wanderbirdcruises.com

Royal Caribbean International
1050 Caribbean Way....... Miami FL 33132 305-539-6000
TF: 800-327-6700 ■ *Web:* www.royalcaribbean.com

Sea Cloud Cruises Inc 282 Grand Ave Ste 3....... Englewood NJ 07631 201-227-9404 227-9424
TF: 888-732-2568 ■ *Web:* www.seacloud.com

SeaDream Yacht Club
601 Brickell Key Dr Ste 1050 .... Miami FL 33131 305-631-6110 631-6110
TF: 800-707-4911 ■ *Web:* www.seadream.com

Silversea Cruises 110 E Broward Blvd .... Fort Lauderdale FL 33301 954-522-4477 356-5881
TF: 800-722-9955 ■ *Web:* www.silversea.com

Star Clippers Inc 760 NW 107th Ave....... Miami FL 33172 305-442-0550
TF Resv: 800-442-0556 ■ *Web:* www.starclippers.com

Travel Dynamics International 132 E 70th St....... New York NY 10021 212-517-7555 774-1560
TF: 800-257-5767 ■ *Web:* traveldynamics.com/

Windstar Cruises 2101 Fourth Ave Ste 210....... Seattle WA 98121 206-292-9606 733-2790
TF Resv: 800-258-7245 ■ *Web:* www.windstarcruises.com

224 CRUISES - RIVERBOAT

SEE ALSO Casinos p. 1904; Cruise Lines p. 2183

Phone Fax

American Cruise Lines
741 Boston Post Rd Ste 200....... Guilford CT 06437 203-453-6800 453-0417
TF: 800-814-6880 ■ *Web:* www.americancruiselines.com

Englund Marine & Industrial Supply Company Inc
95 Hamburg Ave PO Box 296....... Astoria OR 97103 503-325-4341 325-6421
TF: 800-228-7051 ■ *Web:* www.englundmarine.com

French Country Waterways Ltd PO Box 2195 .... Duxbury MA 02331 781-934-2454 934-9048
TF: 800-222-1236 ■ *Web:* www.fcwl.com

Gateway Clipper Fleet 350 W Stn Sq Dr....... Pittsburgh PA 15219 412-355-7980 355-7987
Web: www.gatewayclipper.com

Spirit of Dubuque 500 E Third St....... Dubuque IA 52001 563-583-8093 585-0634
Web: www.dubuqueriverrides.com

Uniworld 17323 Ventura Blvd .... Encino CA 91316 818-382-7820
TF: 800-733-7820 ■ *Web:* uniworldcruises.in

Victoria Cruises Inc 57-08 39th Ave .... Woodside NY 11377 212-818-1680 818-9889
TF Cust Svc: 800-348-8084 ■ *Web:* www.victoriacruises.com

Viking River Cruises
5700 Canoga Ave Ste 200 .... Woodland Hills CA 91367 818-227-1234 227-1237
TF Cust Svc: 877-668-4546 ■ *Web:* www.vikingrivercruises.com

225 CUTLERY

SEE ALSO Silverware p. 3175

Phone Fax

Atlanta Cutlery Corp 2147 Gees Mill Rd .... Conyers GA 30013 770-922-3700 760-8993
TF: 800-883-0300 ■ *Web:* www.atlantacutlery.com

Buck Knives Inc 660 S Lochsa St .... Post Falls ID 83854 208-262-0500 262-0555
TF: 800-326-2825 ■ *Web:* www.buckknives.com

Crescent Manufacturing Co 1310 Majestic Dr....... Fremont OH 43420 419-332-6484 332-6564
TF: 800-537-1330 ■ *Web:* www.crescentblades.com

Cutco Corp 1116 E State St....... Olean NY 14760 716-372-3111
TF: 800-828-0448 ■ *Web:* www.cutco.com

Dexter-Russell Inc 44 River St....... Southbridge MA 01550 508-765-0201 764-2897
TF: 800-343-6042 ■ *Web:* knives.dexter1818.com/

Douglas/Quikut Co 118 E Douglas Rd .... Walnut Ridge AR 72476 800-982-5233 886-2911*
**Fax Area Code:* 870 ■ *TF:* 800-982-5233 ■ *Web:* www.douglasquikut.com

Fiskars Brands Inc 2537 Daniels St .... Madison WI 53718 866-348-5661
TF: 866-348-5661 ■ *Web:* www2.fiskars.com

Gerber Legendary Blades Inc
14200 SW 72nd Ave....... Portland OR 97224 503-639-6161
Web: gerbergear.com

KA-BAR Knives Inc 200 Homer St....... Olean NY 14760 716-372-5952 790-7188
TF: 800-282-0130 ■ *Web:* www.kabar.com

KAI USA ltd 18600 SW Teton Ave .... Tualatin OR 97062 503-682-1966 682-7168
Web: kershaw.kaiusaltd.com

Lamson & Goodnow Mfg Co 45 Conway St....... Shelburne Falls MA 01370 413-625-0201 625-9816
TF: 800-872-6564 ■ *Web:* www.lamsonsharp.com

Master Cutlery Inc 700 Penhorn Ave .... Secaucus NJ 07094 201-271-7600 271-7666
TF: 888-271-7229 ■ *Web:* www.mastercutlery.com

Midwest Tool & Cutlery Co Inc
1210 Progress St PO Box 160 .... Sturgis MI 49091 269-651-7964 651-4412
TF: 800-782-4659 ■ *Web:* www.midwestsnips.com

Millers Forge Inc 1411 Capital Ave....... Plano TX 75074 972-422-2145 881-0639
Web: www.millersforge.com

Ontario Knife Co 26 Empire St....... Franklinville NY 14737 716-676-5527 299-2618*
**Fax Area Code:* 800 ■ *TF:* 800-222-5233 ■ *Web:* www.ontarioknife.com

Pacific Handy Cutter Inc 17819 Gillette Ave .... Irvine CA 92614 714-662-1033 662-7595
TF Cust Svc: 800-229-2233 ■ *Web:* www.pacifichandycutter.com

Professional Cutlery Direct LLC
242 Branford Rd....... North Branford CT 06471 800-792-6650 296-8039
TF: 800-792-6650 ■ *Web:* unoallavolta.com/artisantable/c/300/

Queen Cutlery Co 507 Chestnut St .... Titusville PA 16354 814-827-3673 676-5535*
**Fax Area Code:* 716 ■ *TF Sales:* 800-222-5233 ■ *Web:* www.queencutlery.com

Rada Manufacturing Co PO Box 838....... Waverly IA 50677 319-352-5454 352-0770
TF: 800-311-9691 ■ *Web:* www.radacutlery.com

Swiss Army Brands Inc 7 Victoria Dr PO Box 874 .... Monroe CT 06468 203-929-6391
TF Cust Svc: 800-442-2706 ■ *Web:* www.victorinox.com

Wenger North America Inc 15 Corporate Dr .... Orangeburg NY 10962 845-365-3500 425-4700
TF Cust Svc: 800-431-2996 ■ *Web:* www.wengerna.com

WR Case & Sons Cutlery Co
50 Owens Way PO Box 4000 .... Bradford PA 16701 800-523-6350 368-1736*
**Fax Area Code:* 814 ■ *TF:* 800-523-6350 ■ *Web:* www.wrcase.com

Zippo Manufacturing Co 33 Barbour St....... Bradford PA 16701 814-368-2700
Web: www.zippo.com

226 CYLINDERS & ACTUATORS - FLUID POWER

SEE ALSO Automotive Parts & Supplies - Mfr p. 1839

Phone Fax

Advance Automation Company Inc
3526 N Elston Ave .... Chicago IL 60618 773-539-7633 539-7299
Web: www.advanceautomationco.com

American Cylinder Company Inc
481 S Governors Hwy....... Peotone IL 60468 708-258-3935 258-3980
Web: www.americancylinder.com

Atlas Cylinder Corp 500 S Wolf Rd....... Des Plaines IL 60016 847-298-2400 294-2655
Web: parker.com

Beaver Aerospace & Defense Inc
11850 Mayfield St .... Livonia MI 48150 734-853-5003 853-5043
Web: www.beaver-online.com

BEI Technologies 2470 Coral St....... Vista CA 92081 760-597-6300
Web: www.beikimco.com

Best Metal Products Co
3570 Raleigh Dr SE PO Box 888440....... Grand Rapids MI 49512 616-942-7141 942-0949
Web: www.bestmetalproducts.com

Bosch Rexroth Corp
5150 Prairie Stone Pkwy....... Hoffman Estates IL 60192 847-645-3600 645-6201
TF: 800-860-1055 ■ *Web:* www.boschrexroth-us.com

Clippard Instrument Lab 7390 Colerain Ave .... Cincinnati OH 45239 513-521-4261 521-4464
TF: 877-245-6247 ■ *Web:* www.clippard.com

Columbus Hydraulics Co PO Box 250 .... Columbus NE 68601 402-564-8544 564-0129
Web: www.columbushydraulics.com

Commercial Honing Co Inc 8608 Sultana Ave .... Fontana CA 92335 909-829-1211 829-7631
Web: www.commercialhoning.com

Control Line Equipment Inc
14750 Industrial Pkwy .... Cleveland OH 44135 216-433-7766
Web: www.control-line.com

Phone Fax

Cunningham Manufacturing Co 318 S Webster St ...... Seattle WA 98108 206-767-3713 762-3457
TF: 800-767-0038 ■ *Web:* www.cunninghamcylinders.com

Dynex Rivett Inc 770 Capitol Dr .... Pewaukee WI 53072 262-691-0300 691-0312
Web: www.dynexhydraulics.com

Eckel Mfg Company Inc 8035 N County Rd W.......... Odessa TX 79764 432-362-4336 362-1827
TF: 800-654-4779 ■ *Web:* www.eckel.com

Energy Mfg Co Inc 204 Plastic Ln.......... Monticello IA 52310 319-465-3537 465-5279
Web: www.energymfg.com

Fabco-Air Inc 3716 NE 49th Ave .... Gainesville FL 32609 352-373-3578 375-8024
Web: www.fabco-air.com

Galland Henning Nopak Inc
1025 S 40th St .... West Milwaukee WI 53215 414-645-6000 645-6048
Web: www.nopak.com

General Engineering Co
26485 Hillman Hwy PO Box 549 .... Abingdon VA 24212 276-628-6068 628-4311
Web: generalengr.com

Great Bend Industries Inc 8701 Sixth St.......... Great Bend KS 67530 620-792-4368 792-3935
Web: www.greatbendindustries.com

Hader/Seitz Inc
15600 W Lincoln Ave PO Box 510260 .... New Berlin WI 53151 877-388-2101 641-5310*
*Fax Area Code: 262 ■ *TF:* 877-388-2101 ■ *Web:* www.haderind.com/seitz.htm

Hannon Hydraulics LLC 625 N Loop 12.......... Irving TX 75061 972-438-2870 554-4047
TF: 800-333-4266 ■ *Web:* www.hannonoffshore.com

Helac Corp 225 Battersby Ave.......... Enumclaw WA 98022 360-825-1601 825-1603
TF: 800-327-2589 ■ *Web:* www.helac.com

Hol-Mac Corp 2730-A Hwy 15 PO Box 349.......... Bay Springs MS 39422 601-764-4121 764-3438
TF: 800-844-3019 ■ *Web:* www.hol-mac.com

Humphrey Products Co
5070 E N Ave PO Box 2008 .... Kalamazoo MI 49048 269-381-5500 381-4113
TF: 800-477-8707 ■ *Web:* www.humphrey-products.com

Hydac Technology Corp
2260-2280 City Line Rd.......... Bethlehem PA 18017 610-266-0100
Web: www.hydacusa.com

ITT Industries Inc Engineered Valves Div
33 Centerville Rd .... Lancaster PA 17603 717-509-2200 509-2336
TF: 800-366-1111 ■ *Web:* www.engvalves.com

JARP Industries Inc 1051 Pine St PO Box 923.......... Schofield WI 54476 715-359-4241 355-4960
Web: www.jarpind.com

Linak Us Inc 2200 Stanley Gault Pkwy .... Louisville KY 40223 502-253-5595 253-5596
Web: www.linak-us.com

Luxfer Gas Cylinders 3016 Kansas Ave.......... Riverside CA 92507 951-684-5110 328-1117
TF: 800-764-0366 ■ *Web:* luxfer.com

Lynair Inc 3515 Scheele Dr.......... Jackson MI 49202 517-787-2240 787-4521
Web: www.lynair.com

Micromatic LLC 525 Berne St.......... Berne IN 46711 260-589-2136 589-8966
TF: 800-333-5752 ■ *Web:* www.micromaticllc.com

Moog Flo-Tork Inc 1701 N Main St PO Box 68.......... Orrville OH 44667 330-682-0010 683-6857
Web: flotork.com

Motion Systems Corp 600 Industrial Way W.......... Eatontown NJ 07724 732-222-1800 389-9191
Web: actuator.com/

Norris Cylinder Co 4818 W Loop 281 .... Longview TX 75603 903-757-7633 237-7654
TF: 800-527-8418 ■ *Web:* www.norriscylinder.com

Parker Hannifin Corp Automation Actuator Div
135 Quadral Dr.......... Wadsworth OH 44281 330-336-3511 334-3335
TF: 800-272-7537 ■ *Web:* www.parker.com

Parker Hannifin Corp Cylinder Div
500 S Wolf Rd.......... Des Plaines IL 60016 847-298-2400 294-2655
TF: 800-272-7537 ■ *Web:* parker.com

Parker Hannifin Corp Oildyne Div
5520 Hwy 169 N.......... Minneapolis MN 55428 763-533-1600 533-0082
Web: parker.com

Parker Instrumentation Group
6035 Parkland Blvd .... Cleveland OH 44124 216-896-3000 896-4022
TF: 800-272-7537 ■ *Web:* parker.com

PHD Inc 9009 Clubridge Dr .... Fort Wayne IN 46809 260-747-6151 747-6754
TF: 800-624-8511 ■ *Web:* www.phdinc.com

Quincy Ortman Cylinders
3501 Wismann Ln PO Box C-2.......... Quincy IL 62305 217-277-0321 222-1773
Web: www.ortmanfluidpower.com

Sargent Controls & Aerospace
5675 W Burlingame Rd.......... Tucson AZ 85743 520-744-1000 744-9494
TF: 800-230-0359 ■ *Web:* www.sargentaerospace.com

Seabee Corp 712 First St NW.......... Hampton IA 50441 641-456-4871 456-2387
Web: www.seabeecylinders.com

Sheffer Corp 6990 Cornell Rd .... Cincinnati OH 45242 513-489-9770 489-3034*
*Fax: Sales ■ *Web:* www.sheffercorp.com

Southwestern Controls
6720 Sands Point Dr Ste 100.......... Houston TX 77074 713-777-2626 988-1750
Web: www.swcontrols.com

Standex International Corp Custom Hoists Div
771 County Rd 30A W PO Box 98 .... Hayesville OH 44838 419-368-4721 368-4209
TF: 800-837-4668 ■ *Web:* www.customhoists.com

Tactair Fluid Controls Inc 4806 W Taft Rd.......... Liverpool NY 13088 315-451-3928 451-8919
Web: www.tactair.com

Texas Hydraulics Inc PO Box 1067.......... Temple TX 76503 254-778-4701 774-9940
Web: www.texashydraulics.com

Tol-O-Matic Inc 3800 County Rd 116.......... Hamel MN 55340 763-478-8000 478-8080
TF: 800-328-2174 ■ *Web:* www.tolomatic.com

Wabash Technologies
1375 Swan St PO Box 829 .... Huntington IN 46750 260-355-4100 355-4265*
*Fax: Sales ■ *TF:* 800-487-6865 ■ *Web:* www.wabashtech.com

227 DATA COMMUNICATIONS SERVICES FOR WIRELESS DEVICES

Companies listed here deliver data such as customized news or stock information, other personalized content, and/or multimedia, audio, and video from the Internet to wireless devices (cellular phones, Personal Digital Assistants, pagers, laptop computers).

Phone Fax

281 Com 1302 Us Hwy 281 .... Marble Falls TX 78654 830-798-9041
Web: www.281.com

2lemetry Inc 1321 15th St Ste 200 .... Denver CO 80202 720-606-2646
Web: 2lemetry.com

4comm Inc 40 Burt Dr Ste 4.......... Deer Park NY 11729 631-254-1000
Web: 4commny.com

7thOnline Inc 24 W 40th St 11th Fl.......... New York NY 10018 212-997-1717
Web: www.7thonline.com

Accel Networks LLC 4905 34th StS #227.......... St. Petersburg FL 33711 877-406-8585
TF: 877-406-8585 ■ *Web:* www.accel-networks.com

Addictive Mobility Inc Two Pardee Ave Ste 101 .... Toronto ON M6K3H5 416-535-0706
Web: addictivemobility.com

ADEX Corp 1035 Windward Ridge Pkwy Ste 500.......... Alpharetta GA 30005 678-393-7900
Web: www.adextelecom.com

Advanced C4 Solutions Inc
4017 W Dr Martin Luther King Junior Blvd.......... Tampa FL 33614 813-282-3031
Web: www.ac4s.com

ADVATEL 24821 Elena Dr Ste 222.......... Laguna Hills CA 92653 949-716-3625
Web: www.advatel.net

Air2Web Inc 1230 Peachtree St NE.......... Atlanta GA 30309 404-942-5300

AirRoamer Inc Adelaide St W Ste 354 - 157 .... Toronto ON M5H4E7 647-258-6589
Web: www.airroamer.com

AldeaVision Solutions Inc
8550 Cote de Liesse Blvd Ste 200 .... St. Laurent QC H4T1H2 514-344-5432
Web: www.aldeavision.com

AlertPay Inc 8255 Mtn Sights Ste 100.......... Montreal QC H4P2B5 514-748-5774
Web: www.alertpay.com

Altius Broadband Inc
3314 Papermill Rd Ste 100.......... Phoenix MD 21131 410-667-1638
Web: www.altiuscomm.com

Ansatel Communications Inc 940 Kingsway .... Vancouver BC V5V3C4 604-566-8699
Web: ansatel.com

AOL Canada Inc 99 Spadina Ave Ste 200.......... Toronto ON M5V3P8 416-263-8100
Web: www.aol.ca

Archi-Tech Systems Inc
275 Phillips Blvd Ste 140.......... Ewing NJ 08618 609-882-2447
Web: www.archi-tech.com

Argent Associates Inc 140 Fieldcrest Ave .... Edison NJ 08837 732-512-9009
Web: www.argentassociates.com

Ascedia Inc 161 S First St.......... Milwaukee WI 53204 414-292-3200
Web: www.ascedia.com

Authenex Inc 1413 Grant Rd .... Mountain View CA 94040 650-641-1198
Web: www.authenex.com

Auto Data Direct Inc
1379 Cross Creek Cir.......... Tallahassee FL 32301 850-877-8804
Web: www.add123.com

Avotus Corp 409 Matheson Blvd E.......... Mississauga ON L4Z2H2 905-890-9199
Web: www.avotus.com

Azimuth Systems Inc 35 Nagog Pk.......... Acton MA 01720 978-263-6610 263-5352
Web: www.azimuthsystems.com

B2B2C Inc 1575 Henri-Bourassa Blvd W Ste 255.......... Montreal QC H3M3A9 514-908-5420
Web: www.b2b2c.ca

BestTransport.com Inc
400 W Wilson Bridge Rd Ste 100.......... Columbus OH 43085 614-888-2378
Web: www.besttransport.com

BlackBerry 295 Phillip St.......... Waterloo ON N2L3W8 519-888-7465 888-7884
TF: 877-255-2377 ■ *Web:* www.blackberry.net

Blast Communications Inc
1444 N Farnsworth Ave Ste 600.......... Aurora IL 60505 630-375-9600
Web: www.blastcomm.com

Broadcast Microwave Services Inc (BMS)
12367 Crosthwaite Cir.......... Poway CA 92064 858-391-3050 391-3049
TF: 800-669-9667 ■ *Web:* bms-inc.com

Broadcast Technical Services Inc
7219 Gessner Dr.......... Houston TX 77040 832-467-0002
Web: www.btshouston.com

Buyatab Online Inc 204 - 576 Seymour St.......... Vancouver BC V6B3K1 888-267-0447
TF: 888-267-0447 ■ *Web:* www.buyatab.com

C5 Group Inc 1329 Bay St.......... Toronto ON M5R2C4 416-927-0718
Web: www.c5groupinc.com

Calpop Com Inc 600 W Seventh St Third Fl .... Los Angeles CA 90017 213-627-1937
Web: calpop.com

Carousel Industries of North America Inc
659 S County Trl.......... Exeter RI 02822 800-401-0760 760-5236*
*Fax Area Code: 860 ■ *TF:* 800-401-0760 ■ *Web:* www.carouselindustries.com

Catalyst Communications Technologies Inc
2107 Graves Mill Rd Mail Stop D.......... Forest VA 24551 434-582-6146
Web: www.catcomtec.com

CaTECH Systems Ltd 201 Whitehall Dr Unit 4.......... Markham ON L3R9Y3 905-944-0000
Web: www.catech-systems.com

CHARGED.fm 10 Jay St .... Brooklyn NY 11201 646-490-2700
Web: www.charged.fm

chatr wireless 333 Bloor St E Eighth Fl.......... Toronto ON M4W1G9 800-485-9745
TF: 800-485-9745 ■ *Web:* www.chatrwireless.com

Clevest Solutions Inc
13911 Wireless Way Ste 100 .... Richmond BC V6V3B9 604-214-9700
Web: www.clevest.com

CodeExcellence.com Inc 3553 31 St NW.......... Calgary AB T2L2K7 403-800-2071
Web: www.codeexcellence.com

Cognify 3170 tyrol dr.......... Laguna Beach CA 92651 415-531-5400
Web: www.cognify.com

Colba.Net Telecom Inc
6465 TransCanada Hwy Ville St-Laurent.......... Montreal QC H4T1S3 514-856-3500
Web: www.colba.net

Cologix Inc 2300 15th St Ste 300.......... Denver CO 80202 720-230-7000
Web: www.cologix.com

Com-Net Services Inc 8232 W Darryl Dr .... Baton Rouge LA 70815 225-928-1231
Web: www.comnetserv.com

ComCanada Communications Inc
232-1027 Davie St.......... Vancouver BC V6E4L2 604-998-4500
Web: www.comcanada.ca

Commerx Computer Systems Inc
2880 Argentia Rd Unit 1.......... Mississauga ON L5N7X8 905-542-9400
Web: www.commerx.ca

Phone | Fax

Commodity Systems Inc
200 W Palmetto Park Rd Ste 200 — Boca Raton FL 33432 — 561-392-8663
Web: www.csidata.com

Condo Control Central
First Canadian Pl 100 King St W Ste 5700 — Toronto ON M5X1C7 — 888-762-6636
TF: 888-762-6636 ■ *Web:* www.condocontrolcentral.com

Conxxus LLC 330 W Ottawa — Paxton IL 60957 — 217-379-2026
Web: www.conxxus.com

Copper Valley Telephone Cooperative Inc
329 Fairbanks Dr — Valdez AK 99686 — 907-835-2231
Web: www.cvinternet.net

Coranet Corp Two Washington St Ste 701 — New York NY 10004 — 212-635-2770
Web: coranet.com

Cti Communication Technologies
18110 chesterfield airport rd. — Chesterfield MO 63005 — 636-537-7200
Web: www.cti-stl.com

Data Conversion Laboratory Inc
61-18 190th St Ste 205 — Fresh Meadows NY 11365 — 718-357-8700
Web: dclab.com

Dial800 LLC 9911 Pico Blvd Ste 1200 — Los Angeles CA 90035 — 800-342-5800
TF: 800-342-5800 ■ *Web:* www.dial800.com

Digital Map Products Inc
18831 Von Karman Ave Ste 200 — Irvine CA 92612 — 949-333-5111
Web: www.digitalmapproducts.com

Digital Networks Group Inc
100 Columbia Ste 100 — Aliso Viejo CA 92656 — 949-428-6333
Web: www.digitalnetworksgroup.com

Discover Communications Inc
30 Victoria Crescent — Brampton ON L6T1E4 — 905-455-5600
Web: www.getconnected.ca

Dissolve Inc 425 78 Ave SW — Calgary AB T2V5K5 — 650-450-9048
Web: www.dissolve.com

Dna Communications 601 First ave. — Rochelle IL 61068 — 815-561-9180
Web: www.dnacom.com

Dot VN Inc 9449 Balboa Ave Ste 114 — San Diego CA 92123 — 858-571-2007
Web: www.dotvn.com

Doublehorn Communications 1802 W Sixth St — Austin TX 78703 — 214-283-1400
Web: www.doublehorn.com

Dovetail Communications Inc
30 E Beaver Creek Rd Ste 202 — Richmond Hill ON L4B1J2 — 905-886-6640
Web: dvtail.com

dPi Teleconnect LLC 1330 Capital Pkwy — Carrollton TX 75006 — 972-488-5500
Web: www.unitytelecom.com

DriverDO LLC 734 Massachusetts St. — Lawrence KS 66044 — 844-366-6837
TF: 844-366-6837 ■ *Web:* www.driverdo.com

Dtreds LLC 1329 Shepard Dr Ste 2 — Sterling VA 20164 — 877-694-7766
TF: 877-694-7766 ■ *Web:* www.dtreds.com

DXStorm.com Inc 824 Winston Churchill Blvd — Oakville ON L6J7X2 — 905-842-8262
Web: www.dxstorm.com

Dynamic Mobile Data Systems Inc
285 Davidson Ave Ste 501 — Somerset NJ 08873 — 732-537-0016 — 302-9558

EDge Interactive Inc 67 Mowat Ave Ste 533 — Toronto ON M6K3E3 — 416-494-3343
Web: www.edgeip.com

EDULINX Canada Corp
Two Robert Speck Pkwy 14th Fl — Mississauga ON L4Z1H8 — 905-306-2995
Web: www.studentaid.alberta.ca

Emergency Communications for SW British Columbia Inc
3301 E Pender St — Vancouver BC V5K5J3 — 604-215-5000
Web: www.ecomm.bc.ca

Ensource Inc 7970 Bayberry Rd Ste 5 — Jacksonville FL 32256 — 904-448-6901
Web: www.ensource.net

Everbridge Inc 500 N Brand Blvd Ste 1000 — Glendale CA 91203 — 818-230-9700
Web: www.everbridge.com

Fibernetics Corp 605 Boxwood Dr — Cambridge ON N3E1A5 — 519-489-6700
Web: www.fibernetics.ca

Fibre Noire Internet Inc
550 Ave Beaumont Ste 320 — Montreal QC H3N1V1 — 514-907-3002
Web: m.fibrenoire.ca

FileTrek Software Inc 16 Fitzgerald Rd Ste 150 — Ottawa ON K2H8R6 — 613-226-9445
Web: filetrek.com

FONEX Data Systems Inc
5400 Ch St-Francois — St-Laurent QC H4S1P6 — 514-333-6639
Web: www.fonex.com

FreshGrade Inc 301-1447 Ellis St — Kelowna BC V1Y2A3 — 877-957-7757
TF: 877-957-7757 ■ *Web:* web.freshgrade.com

FundThrough Inc 260 Spadina Ave Ste 400 — Toronto ON M5T2E4 — 800-766-0460
TF: 800-766-0460 ■ *Web:* www.fundthrough.com

Gabriels Technology Solutions Inc
250 Hudson St Rm 1002 — New York NY 10013 — 212-741-0700
Web: www.gabriels.net

Giles Craig Communications Inc
504 Snidow St — Pembroke VA 24136 — 540-544-2288
Web: www.pemtel.com

Gistics Inc 4171 Piedmont Ave Ste 210 — Oakland CA 94611 — 510-450-9999
Web: gistics.com

Glint Inc 808 Winslow St — Redwood City CA 94063 — 650-817-7240
Web: www.glintinc.com

Global Relay Communications Inc
220 cambie St. — Vancouver BC V6B2M9 — 604-484-6630
Web: www.globalrelay.com

GreenSky Trade Credit LLC
1797 Northeast Expy Ste 100 — Atlanta GA 30329 — 866-936-0602
TF: 866-936-0602 ■ *Web:* www.greenskycredit.com

Groupe Maskatel Inc 3455 Blvd Choquette — St-hyacinthe QC J2S7Z8 — 450-250-5050
Web: www.maskatel.ca

Hamilton Telecommunications
509 N Dewey St — North Platte NE 69101 — 308-534-4341
Web: www.nque.com

Handy Networks LLC 1801 Calif St Ste 240 — Denver CO 80202 — 303-414-6910
Web: www.handynetworks.com

Hay Communications 72863 Blind Line Rr 1 — Zurich ON N0M2T0 — 519-236-4333
Web: www.hay.net

HiBeam Internet & Voice
400 S Woods Mill Rd Ste 305 — Chesterfield MO 63017 — 636-203-9400
Web: www.myhibeam.com

Hotwire Communications LLC
One Belmont Ave Ste 1100 — Bala Cynwyd PA 19004 — 800-409-4733
TF: 800-409-4733 ■ *Web:* hotwirecommunications.com

Hover Networks Inc
40 Gardenville Pkwy Ste 102 — Buffalo NY 14224 — 716-650-5650
Web: www.hovernetworks.com

Huxley Communications Cooperative
102 n main ave — Huxley IA 50124 — 515-597-2212
Web: www.huxcomm.net

iLeads.com LLC
567 San Nicolas Dr Ste 180 — Newport Beach CA 92660 — 877-245-3237
TF: 877-245-3237 ■ *Web:* www.ileads.com

Immediatek Inc(NDA) Ste 200 3301 Airport Fwy — Bedford TX 76021 — 888-661-6565
TF: 888-661-6565 ■ *Web:* www.immediatek.com

Inspire Communications Inc 1414 Montauk Ct — Bartlett IL 60103 — 630-233-1331
Web: inspiredcom.com

Interlinc Direct Corp 1-65 Superior Blvd — Mississauga ON L5T2X9 — 905-677-2620
Web: www.interlincdirect.com

Intermec Technologies Corp 6001 36th Ave W — Everett WA 98203 — 425-348-2600 — 355-9551
TF Sales: 800-934-3163 ■ *Web:* www.intermec.com

InterStar Communications Inc 102 Sampson St — Clinton NC 28329 — 910-564-4638
Web: www.intrstar.net

Ituran USA Inc
1700 NW 64th St Ste 100 — Fort Lauderdale FL 33309 — 954-484-3806
Web: www.ituranusa.com

Itx Corp 1169 Pittsford Victor Rd Ste 100 — Pittsford NY 14534 — 585-899-4888
Web: www.itx.com

Jatom Systems Inc 99 Michael Cowpland Dr — Kanata ON K2M1X3 — 613-591-5910
Web: www.jsitelecom.com

Kin Communications Inc
736 Granville St Ste 100 — Vancouver BC V6Z1G3 — 604-684-6730
Web: www.kincommunications.com

Kineto Wireless Inc 670 McCarthy Blvd — Milpitas CA 95035 — 408-546-0660
Web: www.kineto.com

Koplar Communications International Inc
50 Maryland Dr Ste 300 — Saint Louis MO 63108 — 314-345-1000
Web: www.koplar.com

Kuboo Inc Ste 101 7740 E Evans Rd — Scottsdale AZ 85260 — 480-385-3893
Web: www.safecom.net

Larson Data Communications Inc
305 N Lawler St — Mitchell SD 57301 — 605-996-5521
Web: larsondata.com

Laurel Highland Total Communications Inc
4157 Main St — Stahlstown PA 15687 — 724-593-2411
Web: www.lhtc.co

Lead Intelligence Inc 201 S Maple Ave Ste 150 — Ambler PA 19002 — 267-460-7287
Web: www.leadid.com

LemonStand eCommerce Inc
912-525 Seymour St — Vancouver BC V6B3H7 — 604-558-0555
Web: lemonstand.com

Link America Inc 3002 Century Dr — Rowlett TX 75088 — 972-463-0050
Web: www.linkam.com

Lytro 200 W Evelyn Ste 120 — Mountain View CA 94041 — 650-316-8888
Web: www.lytro.com

MarketQuiz Inc
12500 San Pedro Ave Ste 657 — San Antonio TX 78216 — 210-494-7770
Web: www.marketquiz.com

Masergy Communications Inc
2740 N Dallas Pkwy Ste 260 — Plano TX 75093 — 214-442-5700 — 442-5756
TF: 866-588-5885 ■ *Web:* www.masergy.com

MediaCore Inc 26 Bastion Sq Ste 205 — Victoria BC V8W1H9 — 250-590-9394
Web: mediacore.com

MedTel.com Inc 353 Third Ave Ste 190 — New York NY 10010 — 212-777-7722
Web: www.medtel.com

Metalink Technologies Inc
417 Wayne Ave Ste 101 — Defiance OH 43512 — 419-782-3472
Web: www.metalink.net

Meteorcomm LLC 1201 SW Seventh St — Renton WA 98057 — 253-872-2521 — 872-7662
Web: www.meteorcomm.com

Metro 1 120 NE 27 St Ste 200 — Miami FL 33137 — 305-571-9991 — 571-9661
Web: www.metro1.com

MFour Mobile Research Inc
3525 Hyland Ave Ste 240 — Costa Mesa CA 92626 — 714-754-1234
Web: mfour.com

Mig Communications 800 Hearst Ave — Berkeley CA 94710 — 510-845-7549
Web: www.migcom.com

Modulis Inc 6250 Blvd Monk — Montreal QC H4E3H7 — 514-284-2020
Web: www.modulis.com

Mornington Communications Co-operative Ltd
16 Mill St Rr 2 — Milverton ON N0K1M0 — 519-595-8331
Web: mornington.ca

Namecheap Inc
11400 W Olympic Blvd Ste 200 — Los Angeles CA 90064 — 661-310-2107
Web: www.namecheap.com

Netfast Communications Inc
989 Ave of the Americas 12th Fl — New York NY 10018 — 212-792-5200
Web: www.netfast.com

Netkrom Technologies Inc 2134 Nw 99th Ave — Miami FL 33172 — 305-418-2232
Web: www.netkrom.com

NetLine Corp 750 University Ave Ste 200 — Los Gatos CA 95032 — 408-340-2200
Web: www.netline.com

Netricom Inc 575 Blvd Morgan — Baie-d'urfe QC H9X3T6 — 514-457-4488
Web: www.netricom.com

Network Earth Inc 14 Cambridge Ct — Wappingers Falls NY 12590 — 888-201-5160
TF: 888-201-5160 ■ *Web:* www.netearth.com

Nitel Inc 1101 W Lk St Sixth Fl — Chicago IL 60607 — 888-450-2100
TF: 888-450-2100 ■ *Web:* www.nitelusa.com

NKTelco Inc 301 W S St PO Box 219 — New Knoxville OH 45871 — 419-753-2457
Web: www.nktelco.net

Company	City	State	Postal Code	Phone	Fax
Nonfiction Studios Inc 318 11 Ave Se *Web:* www.nonfiction.ca	Calgary	AB	T2G0Y2	403-686-8887	
NTG Clarity Networks Inc Ste 202 2820 Fourteenth Ave *Web:* www.ntgclarity.com	Markham	ON	L3R0S9	905-305-1325	
NthGen Software Inc 4711 Yonge St Ste 506 *Web:* www.nthgensoftware.com	Toronto	ON	M2N6K8	416-900-0941	
Ocean Executive Inc 4-4 Nafthal Dr *Web:* www.oceanexecutive.com	Bridgewater	NS	B4V3V5	646-436-2355	
Oil-Law Records Corp Eight N W 65th St *Web:* www.oil-law.com	Oklahoma City	OK	73116	405-840-1631	
Okanjo Partners Inc 220 E Buffalo St Ste 303 *Web:* www.okanjo.com	Milwaukee	WI	53202	414-810-1760	
Omnis Network LLC 3655 Torrance Blvd Ste 230 *Web:* www.omnis.com	Torrance	CA	90503	310-316-9600	
Ontash & Ermac Inc 876 Kndrkamak Rd Ste 201 *Web:* www.ontash.com	River Edge	NJ	07661	201-265-2189	
Optical & Telecommunication Solutions Inc 16835 Addison Rd Ste 105 *Web:* www.optelsol.com	Addison	TX	75001	972-931-0360	
Optimum Computer Solutions Inc 780 Westridge Rd *Web:* www.ocscorp.com	The Woodlands	TX	77380	281-364-0539	
Outreach Communications 2801 Glenda St *Web:* www.outreachcom.com	Haltom City	TX	76117	817-288-7200	
Oxford Media Group 70 Wellington St S *Web:* oxfordmediagroup.com	Woodstock	ON	N4S3H6	519-539-9762	
PacketVideo Corp 10350 Science Ctr Dr Ste 210 *Web:* www.pv.com	San Diego	CA	92121	858-731-5300	
Parago Inc 700 State Hwy 121 Bypass Ste 200 *TF:* 866-219-7533 ■ *Web:* www.parago.com	Lewisville	TX	75067	866-219-7533	
Permabit Technology Corp 10 Canal Park Third Fl *Web:* www.permabit.com	Cambridge	MA	02141	617-252-9600	
Pilar Services Inc 13910 Laurel Lakes Ave *Web:* www.pilarservices.net	Laurel	MD	20707	301-362-1569	
Pinger Inc 97 S Second St Ste 210 *Web:* www.pinger.com	San Jose	CA	95113	408-271-5700	
Piquniq Management Corp 6613 Brayton Dr *Web:* www.alaska.net	Anchorage	AK	99507	907-522-5234	
PocketiNet Communications Inc 45 Terminal Loop Rd Ste 210 *Web:* www.pocketinet.com	Walla Walla	WA	99362	509-526-5026	
Powered By Search Inc 505 Consumers Rd Ste 507 *Web:* www.poweredbysearch.com	Toronto	ON	M2J4V8	416-840-9044	
Pure Brand Communications LLC 2401 Larimer St *Web:* www.pure-brand.com	Denver	CO	80205	303-625-1085	
Purple Forge Corp 900 Greenbank Rd Ste 315 *Web:* www.purpleforge.com	Ottawa	ON	K2J4P6	613-216-2148	
Radixx Solutions International Inc 6310 Hazeltine National Dr *Web:* www.radixx.com	Orlando	FL	32822	407-856-9009	
Redline Communications Inc 302 Town Centre Blvd Third Fl *Web:* rdlcom.com	Markham	ON	L3R0E8	905-479-8344	
Remote Dynamics Inc 400 Chisholm Pl Ste 411 *Web:* citysearch.com/guide/dallas-tx-metro	Plano	TX	75075	214-440-5200	440-5208
Rhiza Inc 5850 Ellsworth Ave Ste 200 *Web:* rhiza.com	Pittsburgh	PA	15232	412-488-0600	
RightsTrade LLC 11846 Ventura Blvd Ste 120 *Web:* www.rightstrade.com	Studio City	CA	91604	818-766-2607	
Rightway Gate Inc 5858 Edison Pl *Web:* www.rwgusa.com	Carlsbad	CA	92008	760-736-3700	
RigNet Inc 1880 S Dairy Ashford Rd Ste 300 *Web:* www.rig.net	Houston	TX	77077	281-674-0100	
Ringgold Telephone Company Inc 200 Evitt Pkwy PO Box 869 *Web:* www.rtctel.com	Ringgold	GA	30736	706-965-2345	
RIWI Corp, The Banting & Best Centre for Innovation & Entrepreneurship 100 College St Ste 311 *Web:* riwi.com	Toronto	ON	M5G1L5	416-205-9984	
Roam Mobility Inc 400 - 311 Water St *TF:* 888-762-6487 ■ *Web:* www.roammobility.com	Vancouver	BC	V6B1B8	888-762-6487	
Rockynet.com Inc 1919 Fourteenth St Ste 617 *Web:* www.rockynet.com	Boulder	CO	80302	303-444-7052	
Sandler Partners 1200 Artesia Blvd Ste 305 *Web:* www.sandlerpartners.com	Hermosa Beach	CA	90254	310-796-1393	
Satellite Management Services Inc 4529 E Bwy Rd *Web:* www.smstv.com	Phoenix	AZ	85040	602-386-4444	
SimpleSignal Inc 34232 Pacific Coast Hwy *Web:* www.simplesignal.com	Dana Point	CA	92629	949-487-3333	
Single Digits Inc Four Bedford Farms Dr Ste 210 *Web:* www.singledigits.com	Bedford	NH	03110	603-580-1539	
Siren Telephone Company Inc 7723 W Main St *Web:* sirentel.com	Siren	WI	54872	715-349-2224	
Skycasters LLC 1520 S Arlington St # 100 *Web:* www.satellite-asp.com	Akron	OH	44306	330-785-2100	
Skyway West 3644 Beach Ave *Web:* www.skywaywest.com	Roberts Creek	BC	V0N2W2	604-482-1225	
Skyy Consulting Inc 1335 Fourth St Ste 200 *Web:* www.callfire.com	Santa Monica	CA	90401	213-221-2289	
Smart Cabling Solutions Inc 1250 N Winchester St *Web:* www.thinkscs.com	Olathe	KS	66061	913-390-9501	
Soleo Communications Inc WillowBrook Office Park 300 WillowBrook Dr *Web:* www.soleo.com	Fairport	NY	14450	585-641-4300	
SoundConnect LLC One Batterymarch Park Ste 104 *TF:* 888-827-4462 ■ *Web:* www.sound-connect.com	Quincy	MA	02169	888-827-4462	
Spin Games LLC 100 N Arlington Ave Ste 370 *Web:* www.spingames.net	Reno	NV	89501	775-420-3550	
SPROUT Wellness Solutions Inc 366 Adelaide St W Ste 301 *TF:* 866-535-5027 ■ *Web:* www.sproutatwork.com	Toronto	ON	M5V1R9	866-535-5027	
SSI Micro Ltd 356B Old Airport Rd *Web:* www.ssimicro.com	Yellowknife	NT	X1A3T4	867-669-7500	
StockCharts.com Inc 11241 Willows Rd Ste 140 *Web:* www.stockcharts.com	Redmond	WA	98052	425-881-2606	
Superheat Fgh Services Inc 680 Industrial Pk Dr *TF:* 888-508-3226 ■ *Web:* www.superheatfgh.com	Evans	GA	30809	888-508-3226	
Synchronoss Technologies Inc 200 Crossing Blvd *NASDAQ: SNCR* ■ *TF:* 866-620-3940 ■ *Web:* www.synchronoss.com	Bridgewater	NJ	08807	866-620-3940	
Talena Inc 830 Hillview Ct *Web:* www.talena-inc.com	Milpitas	CA	95035	408-649-6338	
Telebroad LLC 452 Broadway *Web:* www.telebroad.com	Brooklyn	NY	11211	212-444-9911	
Telebyte Communications Inc 6816 50 Ave *Web:* www.telebyte.ca	Red Deer	AB	T4N4E3	403-346-9966	
Teleco 5221 Oleander Dr *Web:* www.teleco-ilm.com	Wilmington	NC	28403	910-791-7000	
TeleCommunication Systems Inc 275 W St Ste 400 *NASDAQ: TSYS* ■ *TF:* 800-810-0827 ■ *Web:* www.telecomsys.com	Annapolis	MD	21401	410-263-7616	263-7617
TELUS Mobility 200 Consilium Pl Ste 1600 *Web:* mobility.telus.com	Scarborough	ON	M1H3J3	604-291-2355	
TeraGo Networks Inc 55 Commerce Vly Dr W Ste 800 *Web:* www.terago.ca	Thornhill	ON	L3T7V9	905-707-0788	
TextureMedia Inc 6604 N Lamar Blvd *Web:* www.naturallycurly.com	Austin	TX	78752	512-371-7545	
Thescore Inc 500 King St W Fourth Fl *Web:* corporate.thescore.com	Toronto	ON	M5V1L9	416-479-8812	
Threshold Communications Inc 16541 Redmond Way Ste C *Web:* www.thresholdcommunications.com	Redmond	WA	98052	206-812-6200	
Tierzero 700 Wilshire Blvd Sixth Fl *Web:* www.tierzero.com	Los Angeles	CA	90017	213-784-1400	
Totelcom Communications LLC 6100 Hwy 16 S PO Box 290 *Web:* totelcom.net	De Leon	TX	76444	254-893-1000	
Trade Service Company LLC 15092 Ave of Science *TF:* 800-854-1527 ■ *Web:* www.tradeservice.com	San Diego	CA	92128	800-854-1527	
Transtelco Inc 500 W Overland Ave Ste 310 *Web:* www.transtelco.net	El Paso	TX	79901	915-534-8100	
TrouveMoiUnPro Inc 736 Wellington Ste 100 *TF:* 855-360-1390 ■ *Web:* www.smartreno.com	Montreal	QC	H3C1T4	855-360-1390	
Trulioo Inc 300 - 420 W Hastings St *TF:* 888-773-0179 ■ *Web:* www.trulioo.com	Vancouver	BC	V6B1L1	888-773-0179	
Underline Communications LLC 12 W 27th St 14th Fl *Web:* www.underlinecom.com	New York	NY	10001	212-994-4340	
Uniserve Communications Corp Ste 330 333 Terminal Ave *Web:* www.uniserve.com	Vancouver	BC	V6A4C1	604-396-3900	
Upstream Communications Gp LLC 1609 shoal creek blvd *Web:* getupstream.com	Austin	TX	78701	512-583-7134	
Usablenet Inc 142 W 57th St Seventh Fl *Web:* www.usablenet.com	New York	NY	10019	212-965-5388	
USBid Inc 2320 Commerce Park Dr *Web:* www.usbid.com	Palm Bay	FL	32905	321-725-9565	
Used-Car-Parts.com Inc 1980 Highland Pk *Web:* www.car-part.com	Fort Wright	KY	41017	859-344-1925	
Visionpoint LLC 152 Rockwell Rd *Web:* www.visionpointllc.com	Newington	CT	06111	860-436-9673	
Vistanet Communications 6804 Villa Hermosa Dr *Web:* vistacommunications.net	El Paso	TX	79912	915-587-1500	
Vitac Corp 101 Hillpointe Dr *Web:* www.vitac.com	Canonsburg	PA	15317	724-514-4000	
Vitelity Communications LLC 7900 E Union Ave Ste 1100 *Web:* www.vitelity.com	Denver	CO	80237	720-257-5400	
Westman Communications Group 1906 Park Ave *Web:* www.westmancom.com	Brandon	MB	R7B0R9	204-725-4300	
Whitecourt Communications 4214 42 Ave *Web:* whitecourtcommunications.ca	Whitecourt	AB	T7S0A3	780-778-3778	
Wireless Analytics LLC 230 N St Ste 4 *TF:* 888-588-5550 ■ *Web:* www.wirelessanalytics.com	Danvers	MA	01923	888-588-5550	
XipLink Inc 3981 St Laurent Blvd Ste 800 *Web:* www.xiplink.com	Montreal	QC	H2W1Y5	514-848-9640	
ZapTel Corp 1440 Hicks Rd *Web:* www.zaptel.com	Rolling Meadows	IL	60008	847-342-2000	
Zimmerman Associates Inc 10600 Arrowhead Dr Ste 325 *Web:* www.zai-inc.com	Fairfax	VA	22030	703-883-0506	
Zingle Inc 5235 Avenida Encinas Ste A *TF:* 877-946-4536 ■ *Web:* www.zingle.me	Carlsbad	CA	92008	877-946-4536	
Zone Communication Group LLC 911 W Eighth St *Web:* www.zonecg.com	Cincinnati	OH	45203	513-579-9663	

				Phone	Fax
Zyme Solutions Inc 240 Twin Dolphin Dr Ste E *TF:* 888-200-6629 ■ *Web:* www.zymesolutions.com	Redwood Shores	CA	94065	888-200-6629	

228 DATA PROCESSING & RELATED SERVICES

SEE ALSO Electronic Transaction Processing p. 2236; Payroll Services p. 2899

				Phone	Fax
1Cloud 25 Lowell St Ste 407 *Web:* www.spectraaccess.com	Manchester	NH	03101	603-296-0760	
360 Services Inc 12623 Newburgh Rd *Web:* 360inc.com	Livonia	MI	48150	734-591-9360	
5280 Solutions Inc 8740 Lucent Blvd Ste 400 *Web:* www.5280solutions.com	Highlands Ranch	CO	80129	303-696-5280	
A t Secure Net 2001 Columbus St *Web:* atsecure.net	Bakersfield	CA	93305	661-872-4807	
Aboundi Inc Four Bud Way Unit 10 *Web:* www.aboundi.com	Nashua	NH	03063	603-889-8188	
Abtronics Inc 211 Dixon Ave *Web:* www.abtronics.com	Molalla	OR	97038	503-829-6100	
Accretive Technologies Inc 330 Research Ct Ste 250 *Web:* www.accretive.com	Norcross	GA	30092	678-328-2440	
Accura Engineering 3342 International Park Dr Se *Web:* www.accuraengineering.com	Atlanta	GA	30316	404-241-8722	
Ace Mailing Corp 2757 16th St *Web:* www.acemailingsf.com	San Francisco	CA	94103	415-863-4223	
ACH Payment Solutions Inc 6919 Treymore Ct *Web:* www.achpaymentsolutions.com	Sarasota	FL	34243	941-360-8859	
ACI Communications 5115 Douglas Fir Rd Ste A *Web:* www.acicommunications.com	Calabasas	CA	91302	818-223-3600	223-3609
ACI Merchant Services Inc 136 E Watson Ave Ste 204 *Web:* acimerchant.com	Langhorne	PA	19047	215-741-6970	
Acroamatics Inc 5385 Holli Ste 105 *Web:* www.acroamatics.com	Santa Barbara	CA	93111	805-967-9909	
ActForex Inc 110 Wall St Seventh Fl *Web:* www.actforex.com	New York	NY	10005	212-425-7111	
ActiFi Inc 3030 Harbor Ln Ste 216 *Web:* www.actifi.com	Plymouth	MN	55447	763-550-0223	
ActiveStrategy Inc 620 W Germantown Pk	Plymouth Meeting	PA	19462	484-690-0700	
Activsupport Inc 900 Cherry Ave Fl 4 *Web:* www.activsupport.com	San Bruno	CA	94066	415-979-9284	
ADEC Solutions USA 10 Monument St PO Box 275 *Web:* www.adecsolutions-usa.com	Deposit	NY	13754	607-467-4600	467-4632
Advansoft International Inc 415 W Golf Rd Ste 55 *Web:* www.adso.com	Arlington Heights	IL	60005	847-952-0000	
Advantis Medical Inc 2121 Southtech Dr Ste 600 *Web:* www.advantismedical.com	Greenwood	IN	46143	317-859-2300	
Adxstudio Inc 200 - 1445 Park St *Web:* www.adxstudio.com	Regina	SK	S4N4C5	306-569-6500	
Affiliated Computer Services Inc (ACS) 2828 N Haskell Ave *Web:* services.xerox.com/	Dallas	TX	75204	214-841-6111	
Affinigent Inc Four Kent Rd Ste 200 *Web:* www.affinigent.com	York	PA	17402	717-600-0033	
AG Dealer Ltd 44 Byward Market Sq Ste 230 *Web:* www.agdealer.com	Ottawa	ON	K1N7A2	613-596-8022	
Akcelerant Software LLC 100 Lindenwood Dr Ste 100 *Web:* www.akcelerant.com	Malvern	PA	19355	610-232-2800	
Allegiance Consultinginc 2601 Blake St Ste 110 *Web:* www.acinow.net	Denver	CO	80205	720-947-9201	
ALLiGACOM 4220 de Rouen Ste 200 *Web:* www.alligacom.com	Montreal	QC	H1V3T2	514-899-0003	
Allison Royce & Associates Inc 70 NE Loop 410, Ste 760 *Web:* allisonroyce.com	San Antonio	TX	78216	210-564-7000	564-7001
Altapacific Technology Group Inc 1525 E Shaw Ave Ste 200 *Web:* www.altapacific.com	Fresno	CA	93710	559-439-5700	
Ambient Consulting LLC 5500 Wayzata Blvd Ste 1250 *Web:* www.ambientconsulting.com	Minneapolis	MN	55416	763-582-9000	582-7901
Amec Foster Wheeler 1002 Walnut St Ste 200 *Web:* amec.com	Boulder	CO	80302	303-443-7839	
Ameritox Ltd 300 E Lombard St Ste 1610 *Web:* www.ameritox.com	Baltimore	MD	21201	443-220-0115	
AMSplus Inc 400 Washington St *Web:* www.amsplus.com	Braintree	MA	02184	781-843-1223	
Annese & Associates Inc 747 Pierce Rd Ste 2 *Web:* www.annese.com	Clifton Park	NY	12065	518-371-9000	
Applicantpro 3688 campus dr *Web:* www.applicantpro.com	Eagle Mountain	UT	84005	801-766-0174	
Applied Imaging Inc 5282 E Paris SE *Web:* www.appliedimaging.com	Grand Rapids	MI	49512	616-554-5200	
Applied Innovations Corp 6401 N Congress Ave Ste 200 *Web:* www.appliedi.net	Boca Raton	FL	33487	561-981-8196	
Applied Services & Information Systems Inc 209 Business Park Dr *Web:* www.asisinfo.net	Virginia Beach	VA	23462	757-498-0100	
Appperfect Corp 20065 Stevens Creek Blvd Ste 2A *Web:* www.appperfect.com	Cupertino	CA	95014	408-252-4100	
Apx Power Markets Inc 224 Airport Pkwy Ste 600 *Web:* www.apx.com	San Jose	CA	95110	408-517-2100	517-2985
ARCON Corp 260 Bear Hill Rd Ste 200 *Web:* www.arcon.com	Waltham	MA	02451	781-890-3330	
Argos Systems Inc 19 Crosby Dr *Web:* www.argos.com	Bedford	MA	01730	781-271-9111	
Argus Connection Inc 1111 W N Carrier Pkwy Ste 300 *Web:* www.argusx.com	Grand Prairie	TX	75050	469-471-0035	
Arkham Graphics 1424 Fourth St Ste 212 *Web:* www.arkhamgraphics.com	Santa Monica	CA	90401	310-393-5390	
Armed Forces Financial Network LLC 11601 Roosevelt Blvd TA-94 *Web:* www.affn.org	Saint Petersburg	FL	33716	727-227-2880	
Artbeats Software Inc 1405 N Myrtle Rd *Web:* www.artbeats.com	Myrtle Creek	OR	97457	541-863-4429	
Aspen Group Inc, The 1100 Wayne Ave Ste 1200 *Web:* www.theaspengroupinc.com	Silver Spring	MD	20910	301-650-6200	
Assessment Technology Inc 6700 E Speedway Blvd *TF:* 800-367-4762 ■ *Web:* www.ati-online.com	Tucson	AZ	85710	520-323-9033	
AtHomeNet Inc PO Box 1405 *Web:* www.athomenet.com	Suwanee	GA	30024	770-904-7930	
Atlantech Online Inc 1010 Wayne Ave Ste 630 *Web:* www.atlantech.net	Silver Spring	MD	20910	301-589-3060	
AtNetPlus Inc 1000 Campus Dr Ste 700 *Web:* www.atnetplus.com	Stow	OH	44224	330-945-5685	
Audiokinetic Inc 409 St-Nicolas St Ste 300 *Web:* www.audiokinetic.com	Montreal	QC	H2Y2P4	514-499-9100	
Augmentum Inc 1065 E Hillsdale Blvd Ste 413 *Web:* augmentum.com	Foster City	CA	94404	650-578-9221	
Automatic Data Processing Inc (ADP) One ADP Blvd *NASDAQ:* ADP ■ *TF:* 800-225-5237 ■ *Web:* www.adp.com	Roseland	NJ	07068	973-994-5000	974-5390
AutoVision Wireless Inc 360 Deerhide Crescent *TF:* 866-514-8030 ■ *Web:* www.autovisionwireless.com	Toronto	ON	M9M2Y6	416-747-4444	747-4443
Axis Technical Group Inc 300 S Ahrbor Blvd *Web:* axistechnical.com	Anaheim	CA	92805	714-491-2636	
Ayalogic Inc 530 S Main St Ste 1731	Akron	OH	44311	330-253-2700	
Bankcard Central Inc 105 E Fifth St *Web:* www.bankcardcentral.com	Kansas City	MO	64106	816-221-1133	
Baracci Solutions Inc 24 Boul De La Concorde E *Web:* www.baracci.com	Laval	QC	H7G4X2	450-662-8700	
Beanstalk Data 656 michael wylie dr *TF:* 800-892-3997 ■ *Web:* beanstalkdata.com	Charlotte	NC	28217	800-892-3997	
Beanstream Internet Commerce Inc 2659 Douglas St Ste 302 *Web:* www.beanstream.com	Victoria	BC	V8T4M3	250-472-2326	472-2330
Beasley Direct Marketing Inc 15227 Perry Ln *Web:* www.beasleydirect.com	Morgan Hill	CA	95037	408-782-0046	
Believe Wireless LLC 9722 Groffs Mill Dr Ste 112 *Web:* www.believewireless.com	Owings Mills	MD	21117	410-902-0070	
Belwave Communications 4132 Edgehill Rd *Web:* belwave.com	Fort Worth	TX	76116	817-737-3124	
Berkadia Commercial Mortgage LLC 118 Welsh Rd *Web:* www.berkadia.com	Horsham	PA	19044	215-328-3200	
Bing Design 126 E Ctr College St *Web:* www.bingdesign.com	Yellow Springs	OH	45387	937-767-2521	
Biobridges LLC 167 Worcester St Ste 211 *Web:* www.biobridges.com	Wellesley	MA	02481	781-416-0909	
BlackInk IT 277 E 12th St *Web:* www.integrate.net	Indianapolis	IN	46202	317-472-8000	
Blade Technologies Inc 10820 Sunset Office Dr Ste 101 *Web:* www.bladetechinc.com	St. Louis	MO	63127	314-752-7999	
Blekko Inc 100 Marine Pkwy Ste 275 *Web:* blekko.com	Redwood City	CA	94065	650-631-3845	
Blizzard Internet Marketing Inc 50629 Hwy 6 *Web:* www.blizzardinternet.com	Glenwood Springs	CO	81601	970-928-7875	
Blue Fountain Media Inc 102 Madison Ave Second Fl *Web:* www.bluefountainmedia.com	New York	NY	10016	212-260-1978	
Blue Mine Group 12626 High Bluff Dr Ste 450 *Web:* blueminegroup.com	San Diego	CA	92130	858-792-2633	
Blue Rock Technologies 800 Kirts Blvd *Web:* www.bluerocktech.com	Troy	MI	48084	248-786-6100	
Bluechip Athletic Solutions LLC 3525 Piedmont Rd Piedmont Ctr Bldg Eight Ste 719 *Web:* bas-llc.net	Atlanta	GA	30305	404-941-2510	
Bluegrassnet Development Corp 321 E Breckinridge St *Web:* www.bluegrass.net	Louisville	KY	40203	502-589-4638	
BlueTie Inc 2480 Browncroft Blvd Ste 2b *TF:* 800-258-3843 ■ *Web:* www.bluetie.com	Rochester	NY	14625	585-586-2000	586-2268
BNSF Logistics LLC 4700 S Thompson Ste A202 *Web:* www.bnsflogistics.com	Springdale	AR	72764	888-285-4514	
Borer Financial Communication LLC 615 Fifth St Ste 210 *Web:* www.borerfinancial.com	Carlstadt	NJ	07072	201-939-9297	

Company	City	State	ZIP	Phone	Fax
BP Logix Inc 410 S Melrose Dr Ste 100 *Web:* www.bplogix.com	Vista	CA	92081	760-643-4121	
Brainstorm Internet Inc 640 Main Ave Ste 201 *Web:* www.gobrainstorm.net	Durango	CO	81301	970-247-1442	
Brandx Internet LLC 927 Sixth St Apt 4 *Web:* www.brandx.net	Santa Monica	CA	90403	310-395-5500	
Brewster Technology 1591 Rt 22 Bldg 1 *Web:* www.brewstertech.net	Brewster	NY	10509	845-279-9400	
Brilliant Store Inc 933 Corporate Way *Web:* www.brilliant-electronics.com	Fremont	CA	94539	510-668-0398	
Broadjam Inc 6401 Odana Rd *Web:* www.broadjam.com	Madison	WI	53719	608-271-3633	
Browsersoft Inc 450 Navajo Ln. *Web:* browsersoft.com	Shawnee Mission	KS	66217	913-851-2453	
Btm Global Consulting 310 Fourth ave s *Web:* www.btmgcs.com	Minneapolis	MN	55415	612-238-8800	
BusinessEdge Solutions Inc One Tower Ctr Blvd *Web:* emc.com/domains/businessedge/index.htm	East Brunswick	NJ	08816	732-828-3200	
C7 Data Centers Inc 357 South 670 West Ste 100 *Web:* www.c7.com	Lindon	UT	84042	801-822-5300	
Cadence Group Inc 1095 Zonolite Rd Ste 105 *Web:* www.cadence-group.com	Atlanta	GA	30306	404-874-0544	
Cambey & West Inc 120 N Route 9W *Web:* www.cambeywest.com	Congers	NY	10920	845-267-3490	
Capax Global LLC 590 Headquarters Plaza *Web:* www.capaxglobal.com	Morristown	NJ	07960	973-401-0660	
Capricorn Systems Inc 3569 Habersham At N *Web:* www.capricornsys.com	Tucker	GA	30084	678-514-1080	514-1081
Carahsoft Technology Corp 12369 Sunrise Vly Dr Ste D2 *TF:* 888-662-2724 ■ *Web:* www.carahsoft.com	Reston	VA	20191	703-871-8500	871-8505
Cardtronics GP Inc 3110 Hayes Rd Ste 300 *Web:* www.cardtronics.com	Houston	TX	77082	281-596-9988	
Casher Assoc Inc 110 Pond Brook Rd *Web:* www.casherassociates.com	Newton	MA	02467	617-527-3927	
Cass Information Systems Inc 13001 Hollenberg Dr *NASDAQ: CASS* ■ *Web:* www.cassinfo.com	Bridgeton	MO	63044	314-506-5500	506-5560
Castles Information Network 301 Alamo Dr *Web:* www.castles.com	Vacaville	CA	95688	707-455-3401	
Catylist Inc 211 W Upper Wacker Dr Ste 450	Chicago	IL	60606	312-595-9209	
CBE Technologies Inc 215 N Brow St *Web:* www.cbetech.com	East Providence	RI	02914	401-453-1234	
CCC Information Services Inc 222 Merchandise Mart Plz *TF:* 800-621-8070 ■ *Web:* ccc.cccis.com	Chicago	IL	60654	800-621-8070	
Central Service Assn 93 S Coley Rd *TF:* 877-842-5962 ■ *Web:* www.csa1.com	Tupelo	MS	38801	662-842-5962	840-1329
Central Valley Broadband LLC 1624 Santa Clara Dr Ste 250 *Web:* www.calwisp.com	Roseville	CA	95661	530-852-0318	
Centurion Service Group LLC 1400 N 25th Ave *Web:* www.centurionservice.com	Melrose Park	IL	60160	708-761-6655	
Certain Affinity 3107 oak creek dr *Web:* www.certainaffinity.com	Austin	TX	78727	512-524-8510	
ChallengePost Inc 425 W 13th St Ste 504 *Web:* challengepost.com	New York	NY	10014	212-675-6164	
Chelsio Communications Inc 370 San Aleso Ave Ste 100 *Web:* www.chelsio.com	Sunnyvale	CA	94085	408-962-3600	
Chrisian Inc 17561 Hillside Ave *Web:* www.chrisian.com	Jamaica	NY	11432	718-465-9151	
Churchill & Harriman LLC 239 Wall St *Web:* chus.com	Princeton	NJ	08540	609-921-3551	
Ciao Systems Inc 4326 Lorcom Ln *Web:* www.ciaosoftware.com	Arlington	VA	22207	703-524-9356	
CitiusTech Inc Two Research Way Second Fl *TF:* 877-248-4871 ■ *Web:* www.citiustech.com	Princeton	NJ	08540	877-248-4871	
Civica Software Inc 20101 SW Birch St Ste 250 *Web:* www.civicasoft.com	Newport Beach	CA	92660	949-851-1600	
Claimsnet.com Inc 14860 Montfort Dr Ste 250 *TF:* 800-356-1511 ■ *Web:* www.claimsnet.com	Dallas	TX	75254	972-458-1701	458-1737
Claris Networks LLC 6100 Lonas Dr *Web:* clarisnetworks.com	Knoxville	TN	37909	865-251-5555	
Clear Government Solutions Inc 11850 Baltimore Ave *Web:* www.cleargovsolutions.com	Beltsville	MD	20705	301-289-3030	
Clear Wireless LLC 4400 Carillon Point *Web:* www.clear.com	Kirkland	WA	98033	425-216-7600	
CNC Software Inc 671 Old Post Rd *Web:* www.mastercam.com	Tolland	CT	06084	860-875-5006	
Cogeco Data Services LP 413 Horner Ave *Web:* www.cogecodata.com	Toronto	ON	M8W4W3	416-599-3282	
Collective Technologies LLC 9433 Bee Caves Rd *TF:* 800-994-1640 ■ *Web:* www.colltech.com	Austin	TX	78733	512-263-5500	263-0606
Colosseum Online Inc 800 Petrolia Rd *Web:* www.colosseum.com	Toronto	ON	M3J3K4	416-739-7873	
Commercial Computer Service Inc 2916 W Sixth St *Web:* minimaxgolf.com	Fort Worth	TX	76107	817-335-6411	870-1532
Communication Data Services 1901 Bell Ave *TF:* 866-897-7987 ■ *Web:* www.cds-global.com	Des Moines	IA	50315	515-246-6837	246-6687
Compact Information Systems Inc 7120 185th Ave NE Ste 150 *Web:* www.compactlists.com	Redmond	WA	98052	425-869-1379	
Complete Data Solutions LLC 7115 Leesburg Pk Ste 317 *Web:* know-your-data.com	Falls Church	VA	22043	703-536-3282	

Company	City	State	ZIP	Phone	Fax
Computer Consultants Inc (CCI) 43252 Woodward Ave Ste 240 *TF:* 800-693-1066 ■ *Web:* www.ccitalent.com	Bloomfield Hills	MI	48302	248-858-7701	858-7724
Computer Engineering 296 East 3900 South *Web:* www.thinkcei.com	Salt Lake City	UT	84107	801-293-8420	
Computer Fulfillment 24 Cook St *Web:* www.computerfulfillment.com	Billerica	MA	01821	978-671-0440	671-0450
Computer Services Inc 3901 Technology Dr *OTC: CSVI* ■ *TF:* 800-545-4274 ■ *Web:* www.csiweb.com	Paducah	KY	42001	270-442-7361	575-9569
Comtech Mobile Datacom Corp 20430 Century Blvd *Web:* www.comtechmobile.com	Germantown	MD	20874	240-686-3300	
Concord Document Services Inc 1321 W 12th St *Web:* www.copying.la	Los Angeles	CA	90015	213-745-3175	
Conenza Inc 810 Third Ave Ste 220 *Web:* www.conenza.com	Seattle	WA	98104	206-792-4247	
Connecticut On-Line Computer Ctr Inc 135 Darling Dr *Web:* www.cocc.com	Avon	CT	06001	860-678-0444	677-1169
Continental Graphics Corp 4060 N Lakewood Blvd Bldg 801 5th Fl *TF:* 800-862-5691 ■ *Web:* www.cdgnow.com	Long Beach	CA	90808	714-503-4200	827-5111
Convergence LLC Six Journey Ste 160 *Web:* www.convergence.net	Aliso Viejo	CA	92656	949-716-8322	
Coon Valley Telecommunications 105 Central Ave *Web:* www.coonvalleytel.com	Coon Valley	WI	54623	608-452-3101	
Cornwell Data Services Inc 352 Evelyn St *Web:* cornwelldirect.com	Paramus	NJ	07652	201-261-1050	
Cott Systems Inc 2800 Corporate Exchange Dr Ste 300 *Web:* www.cottsystems.com	Columbus	OH	43231	614-847-4405	
CPT Group Inc 16630 Aston St *Web:* www.cptgroup.com	Irvine	CA	92606	949-852-8240	
Creative Breakthroughs Inc 2075 W Big Beaver Rd Ste 700 *Web:* www.cbihome.com	Troy	MI	48084	248-519-4000	
Crispin Corp 600 Wade Ave Ste 320 *Web:* www.crispincorp.com	Raleigh	NC	27605	919-845-7744	
Critical Mention Inc 521 Fifth Ave 16th Fl *Web:* www.criticalmention.com	New York	NY	10175	212-398-1141	
Cronus Technologies 250 Second Ave S *Web:* www.cfactorworks.com	Saskatoon	SK	S7K1K9	306-652-5798	
Cross Circuit Electronics Inc 3020 Scott Blvd *Web:* www.cross-circuit.com	Santa Clara	CA	95054	408-654-9637	
Crosscom National LLC 900 Deerfield Pkwy *TF:* 888-471-6050 ■ *Web:* www.crosscomnational.com	Buffalo Grove	IL	60089	847-520-9200	419-4884
CrossView Inc 3333 Bowers Ave Ste 253 *Web:* www.crossview.com	Santa Clara	CA	95054	408-748-1410	
Cst Data 10725 John Price Rd *Web:* cstdata.com	Charlotte	NC	28273	704-927-3282	
CU*Answers 6000 28th St SE Ste 100 *Web:* www.cuanswers.com	Grand Rapids	MI	49546	616-285-5711	
Custom Processing Services Inc Two Birchmont Dr *Web:* www.customprocessingservices.com	Reading	PA	19606	610-779-7001	
Customer Paradigm Inc 5353 Manhattan Cir Ste 103 *Web:* www.customerparadigm.com	Boulder	CO	80303	303-499-9318	
Cyber Pro Systems Inc One World Trade Ctr Ste 2400 *Web:* www.mdxnet.com	Long Beach	CA	90831	562-256-3800	
Cyberonic Internet Communications Inc 544 Pleasant St *Web:* www.cyberonic.com	Worcester	MA	01602	508-751-4801	
Cyberspace Solutions LLC 12021 Sunset Hills Rd Ste 110 *Web:* www.cspacesol.com	Reston	VA	20190	703-472-5715	
D K Global 420 Missouri Ct *Web:* www.dkglobal.net	Redlands	CA	92373	909-747-0201	
D Net Internet Service 208 E Palmer St *Web:* www.dnet.net	Franklin	NC	28734	828-349-3638	
Dantom Systems Inc 29241 Beck Rd *TF:* 866-536-2376 ■ *Web:* www.dantomsystems.com	Wixom	MI	48393	248-567-7300	567-7301
Dark Field Technologies Inc 70 Robinson Blvd *Web:* www.darkfield.com	Orange	CT	06477	203-298-0731	
Dash Inc W176 N9830 Rivercrest Dr *Web:* dashdev.com	Germantown	WI	53022	262-345-5600	
Data Dash Inc 3928 Delor St *Web:* www.datadash.com	Saint Louis	MO	63116	314-832-5788	
Data Dimensions Corp 400 Midland Ct *Web:* datadimensions.com	Janesville	WI	53546	608-757-1100	
Data Lab 7333 N Oak Pk Ave *Web:* www.data-lab.com	Niles	IL	60714	847-647-6678	
Data Reduction Systems Corp 1323 Burnet Ave *Web:* www.drscorp.com	Union	NJ	07083	908-687-5636	
Data Services Inc 31516 Winterplace Pkwy *Web:* www.dataservicesinc.com	Salisbury	MD	21804	410-546-2206	
Data Solutions International Inc 5900 Baker Rd Ste 100 *Web:* www.datasolutionsinc.com	Minnetonka	MN	55345	952-943-8137	
Data Supplies Inc 11300 Lakefield Dr *Web:* datasuppliesinc.com	Duluth	GA	30097	770-476-4455	
DataBank 12000 Baltimore Ave *TF:* 800-873-9426 ■ *Web:* www.databankimx.com	Beltsville	MD	20705	301-837-0197	
Dataflo Corp 2722 S 87th Ave *Web:* www.mydataflo.com	Omaha	NE	68124	402-861-9454	
Datamark Inc 123 W Mills Ave Ste 400 *Web:* www.datamark.net	El Paso	TX	79901	800-477-1944	

Phone Fax

DataSite Northwest Inc
21086 24th Ave S Ste 120 . . . Seatac WA 98198 206-859-2800
Web: www.datasitenw.com

Datasoft Inc 700 Plz Dr . . . Secaucus NJ 07094 201-319-0494
Web: tradeblazer.com/

Datavalet Technologies Inc
5275 ch Queen-Mary . . . Montreal QC H3W1Y3 514-385-4448
Web: www.datavalet.com

Datavault Inc 110 Long Hill Rd . . . West Brookfield MA 01585 508-637-1416
Web: www.datavault.com

Dataxport 10950 Pellicano Dr Ste C4 . . . El Paso TX 79935 915-771-9090
Web: www.dataxport.net

Datex Billing Services Inc
2333 N Sheridan Way . . . Mississauga ON L5K1A7 905-822-2300
Web: www.datex.ca

Datrose Inc 660 Basket Rd . . . Webster NY 14580 585-265-1780
Web: datrose.com

Davissa Telephone Systems Inc
23800 Commerce Park . . . Cleveland OH 44122 216-464-6633
Web: www.davissa.com

DAZ Productions Inc
12637 South 265 West Ste 300 . . . Draper UT 84020 801-495-1777
Web: www.daz3d.com

Dbnet Systems Inc 3602 Keenland Dr . . . Marietta GA 30062 770-509-3638
Web: www.dbnetsystems.com

Decentrix Inc 1200 17th St Ste 500 . . . Denver CO 80202 303-899-4000
Web: www.decentrix.net

Delvinia Inc 370 King St West Fifth Fl . . . Toronto ON M5V1J9 416-364-1455
Web: www.delvinia.com

Desert Dog Marketing LLC
4641 N 12th St Ste 200 . . . Phoenix AZ 85014 800-506-0398
TF: 800-506-0398 ■ *Web:* www.pinnaclecart.com

Destiny Solutions Inc 40 Holly St . . . Toronto ON M4S3C3 416-480-0500
Web: www.destinysolutions.com

Devtopia Digital 220 King St W Ste 300 . . . Toronto ON M5H1K4 416-239-8192
Web: www.devtopia.com

Dexrex LLC Six University Dr Ste 201 . . . Amherst MA 01002 413-461-3031

Digital Footprints International LLC
1142 Broadway Ste 310 . . . Tacoma WA 98402 253-590-4100
Web: www.internetidentity.com

Dini Group, The 7469 Draper Ave . . . La Jolla CA 92037 858-454-3419
Web: www.dinigroup.com

Direct Online Marketing 4727 Jacob St . . . Wheeling WV 26003 304-214-4850
Web: www.directom.com

Directory One Inc 9135 Katy Fwy Ste 204 . . . Houston TX 77024 713-465-0051
Web: www.directoryone.com

DirectWest Corp
2550 Sandra Schmirler Way Ste 200 . . . Regina SK S4W1A1 306-777-0333
Web: www.directwest.com

Discovery Research Group
6975 Union Pk Ctr Ste 150 . . . Midvale UT 84047 800-678-3748 748-2784*
**Fax Area Code:* 801 ■ *TF:* 800-678-3748 ■ *Web:* www.discoveryresearchgroup.com

Doc 2 E-file Inc 4500 S Wayside Dr Ste 102 . . . Houston TX 77087 713-649-2006
Web: www.doc2e-file.com

Docufree Corp 1175 Northmeadow Pkwy Ste 140 . . . Roswell GA 30076 770-643-2900
TF: 877-220-4350

DOmedia LLC
274 Marconi Blvd One Marconi Pl Ste 400 . . . Columbus OH 43215 614-324-2583
Web: domedia.com

Dominknow Learning Systems 40 Sunset Blvd . . . Perth ON K7H2Y4 613-264-0096
Web: www.dominknow.com

Doon Technologies Inc
200 Middlesex-Essex Tpke Ste 309 . . . Iselin NJ 08830 732-404-1334
Web: www.doontec.com

Dovetail Internet Technologies LLC
40 Southbridge St Ste 210 . . . Worcester MA 01608 508-845-6465
Web: www.dovetailinternet.com

DoxTek Inc 264 W Center St . . . Orem UT 84057 877-705-7226
TF: 877-705-7226 ■ *Web:* www.doxtek.com

DPF Data Services Group Inc
1990 Swarthmore Ave . . . Lakewood NJ 08701 732-370-8840 370-1751
TF: 800-431-4416 ■ *Web:* www.dpfdata.com

Dundee Internet Service Inc 168 Riley St . . . Dundee MI 48131 734-529-5331
Web: dundee.net

DuVoice Corp 608 State St S Ste 100 . . . Kirkland WA 98033 425-889-9790
Web: www.duvoice.com

DWS Inc 102 Kimball Ave Ste 2 . . . South Burlington VT 05403 802-861-6004
Web: www.dwsincorporated.com

E Commerce Partners Dotnet Corp
59 Franklin St . . . New York NY 10013 212-334-3390
Web: www.ecommercepartners.net

E Ink Holdings Inc 733 Concord Ave . . . Cambridge MA 02138 617-499-6000 499-6200
TF: 866-311-1999 ■ *Web:* www.eink.com

E-cubed Media Synthesis Ltd 3807 William St . . . Burnaby BC V5C3J1 604-294-1556
Web: www.e-cubed.net

Ease Technologies Inc
10320 Little Patuxent Pkwy Ste 1104 . . . Columbia MD 21044 301-854-0010
Web: www.easetech.com

East Coast Datacom Inc
245 Gus Hipp Blvd Ste 3 . . . Rockledge FL 32955 321-637-9980
Web: www.ecdata.com

Easy Dynamics Inc 2003 11th st nw . . . Washington DC 20001 202-558-7275
Web: www.easydynamics.com

EasyStreet Online Services Inc
9705 SW Sunshine Ct . . . Beaverton OR 97005 503-646-8400
Web: www.easystreet.com

Ebix BPO 151 N Lyon Ave . . . Hemet CA 92543 951-658-4000
Web: www.certsonline.com

eBlox Inc 404 W 30th St Ste A . . . Austin TX 78705 512-867-1001
Web: www.eblox.com

eDaptive Systems
400 Red Brook Blvd Ste 120 . . . Owings Mills MD 21117 410-327-3366
Web: www.edaptivesys.com

Phone Fax

Edcor Data Services Corp
3310 W Big Beaver Ste 305 . . . Troy MI 48084 248-530-4200
Web: www.edcor.com

EDGE Technology Services Inc
100 Roscommon Dr Ste 120 . . . Middletown CT 06457 860-635-3342
Web: edgets.com

Effective Data Inc 1515 E Wdfield Rd . . . Schaumburg IL 60173 847-969-9300
Web: effective-data.com

Efficient Forms LLC
10394 W Chatfield Ave Bldg 3 Ste 109 . . . Littleton CO 80127 303-785-8600
Web: www.efficientforms.com

eGov Strategies LLC
233 S Mccrea St Ste 600 . . . Indianapolis IN 46225 317-634-3468
Web: www.egovstrategies.com

Electric Pulp Inc 4901 S Isabel Pl . . . Sioux Falls SD 57108 605-988-0177
Web: www.janelarson.com

Electric Rain 3100 Carbon Pl Ste 102 . . . Boulder CO 80301 303-543-8233
Web: www.erain.com

Elkhartnet 3124 S Main St . . . Elkhart IN 46517 574-524-1000
Web: www.elkhart.net

Elysium Inc
100 Galleria Officentre Ste 426 . . . Southfield MI 48034 248-799-9800
Web: www.elysiuminc.com

Emerging Health Information Technology LLC
Three Odell Plz . . . Yonkers NY 10701 914-457-6300
Web: emerginghealthit.com

Enhanced Software Products Inc
1811 N Hutchinson Rd . . . Spokane WA 99212 509-534-1514
Web: www.espsolution.net

Entap Inc 136 E Market St . . . Indianapolis IN 46204 317-634-9523
Web: www.entap.com

Envision Online Media Inc
1150 Morrison Dr Ste 201 . . . Ottawa ON K2H8S9 613-594-2804
Web: www.envisiononline.ca

EPIQ Technologies Inc
4711 Viewridge Ave Ste 230 . . . San Diego CA 92123 858-467-9961
Web: www.epiqtech.com

Equifax Inc 1550 Peachtree St NW . . . Atlanta GA 30309 404-885-8000
NYSE: EFX ■ *TF Sales:* 888-202-4025 ■ *Web:* www.equifax.com

Essentialtalk Network 1289 Highfield Cres Se . . . Calgary AB T2G5M2 403-537-9690
Web: www.essentialtalk.com

eWomenNetwork Inc 14900 Landmark Blvd Ste 540 . . . Dallas TX 75254 972-620-9995
Web: www.ewomennetwork.com

Examination Management Services Inc
15333 N Pima Rd Ste 330 . . . Scottsdale AZ 85260 214-689-3600 689-3644
Web: www.emsinet.com

Exceed Technologies Inc 2605 Cleda Dr . . . Columbus MS 39701 662-328-8333
Web: www.exceedtech.net

Fair Isaac Corp 2665 Long Lake Rd Bldg C . . . Roseville MN 55113 612-758-5200 758-5201
NYSE: FICO ■ *TF Cust Svc:* 888-342-6336 ■ *Web:* www.fico.com

Fakhoury Law Group Pc 3290 w big beaver rd . . . Troy MI 48084 248-643-4900
Web: www.employmentimmigration.com

Federico Consulting Inc 333 W Shaw Ave . . . Fresno CA 93704 559-224-5922
Web: www.federico.net

Financial Services Inc 21 Harristown Rd . . . Glen Rock NJ 07452 201-652-6000
Web: www.insidefsi.net

FinditQuick.com Inc
1817 Saunders Settlement Rd . . . Niagara Falls NY 14304 716-297-5292
Web: www.finditquick.com

First Class Solutions Inc
11426 Dorsett Rd . . . Maryland Heights MO 63043 314-209-7800
Web: www.firstclasssolutions.com

Flight Landata Inc 250 Clark St . . . North Andover MA 01845 978-682-7767
Web: www.flightlandata.com

Flightline Data Services Inc
138 Peachtree Ct . . . Fayetteville GA 30215 770-487-3482
Web: www.flightline.com

Flightpath Inc 36 W 25Th St Ninth Fl . . . New York NY 10010 212-674-5600
Web: www.flightpath.com

Flw International 1147 W Ohio St . . . Chicago IL 60642 312-239-2174
Web: www.flwint.net

Flynn Systems Corp 74 Northeastern Blvd . . . Nashua NH 03062 603-598-4444
Web: www.flynn.com

Forte Data Systems Inc 3330 Paddock Pkwy . . . Suwanee GA 30024 678-208-0206
Web: www.fortedata.com

FotoKem Industries Inc 2801 W Alameda Ave . . . Burbank CA 91505 818-846-3101
Web: www.fotokem.com

Fpweb.net LC 1714 Gilsinn Ln . . . Fenton MO 63026 636-600-8960
Web: www.fpweb.net

Fractal Analytics Ltd 1840 Gateway Dr . . . San Mateo CA 94404 650-378-1284
Web: www.fractalanalytics.com

Fred Flare Inc 300f Kingsland Ave . . . Brooklyn NY 11222 718-599-9221

Freedom Consulting Group Inc
9891 Broken Land Pkwy Ste 106 . . . Columbia MD 21046 410-290-9035
Web: freedomconsultinggroup.com

Freight Security Net Inc
7501 N Capital of Texas Hwy Ste A-140 . . . Austin TX 78731 512-329-0292
Web: www.freightsecurity.net

Fusionist LLC 438 Amapola Ave Ste 225 . . . Torrance CA 90501 310-787-7877
Web: www.fusionist.com

Gage E Services LLC
601 S Phillips Ave Ste 100 . . . Sioux Falls SD 57104 605-332-1242
Web: www.geshosting.com

Gaggle Net 1319 n veterans pkwy . . . Bloomington IL 61704 309-665-0572
Web: www.gaggle.net

Galatea Associates LLC
20 Holland St Ste 405 . . . Somerville MA 02144 617-623-5466
Web: www.galatea-associates.com

GenArts Inc 955 Massachusetts Ave . . . Cambridge MA 02139 617-492-2888
Web: www.genarts.com

Genetec Inc 2280 Alfred-Nobel Blvd Ste 400 . . . Montreal QC H4S2A4 514-332-4000
TF: 866-684-8006 ■ *Web:* www.genetec.com

	City	State	Zip	Phone	Fax
GEOSPAN Corp 10900 73rd Ave N Ste 136 *TF:* 800-436-7726 ■ *Web:* www.geospan.com	Minneapolis	MN	55369	763-493-9320	
Geotrace Technologies Inc 12141 Wickchester Ln Ste 200 *Web:* www.geotrace.com	Houston	TX	77079	281-497-8440	
Giact Systems Inc 700 Central Expy S *Web:* www.motio.com	Allen	TX	75013	214-644-0450	
GigaCrete Inc 6775 Speedway Blvd Ste M105 *Web:* www.gigacrete.com	Las Vegas	NV	89115	702-643-6363	
Glance Networks Inc 1167 Massachusetts Ave *TF:* 877-452-6236 ■ *Web:* www.glance.net	Arlington	MA	02476	781-646-8505	
Global Data Consultants LLC 1144 Kennebec Dr *Web:* gdcitsolutions.com	Chambersburg	PA	17201	717-262-2080	
Global Geophysical Services Inc 13927 S Gessner Rd *NYSE: GGS* ■ *Web:* www.globalgeophysical.com	Missouri City	TX	77489	713-972-9200	972-1008
Global Graphics Software Inc 31 Nagog Pk Ste 315 *Web:* www.globalgraphics.com	Acton	MA	01720	978-849-0011	
Global Health Care Exchange LLC (GHX) 1315 W Century Dr *TF:* 800-968-7449 ■ *Web:* www.ghx.com	Louisville	CO	80027	720-887-7000	887-7200
Globat LLC 11684 Ventrura Blvd Ste 825 *Web:* www.globat.com	Studio City	CA	91604	323-874-9000	
Goold Health Systems Inc PO Box 1090 *TF:* 800-832-9672 ■ *Web:* www.ghsinc.com	Augusta	ME	04332	207-622-7153	
Grant Street Group Inc 429 Forbes Ave 1800 Allegheny Bldg *Web:* www.grantstreet.com	Pittsburgh	PA	15219	412-391-5555	
Green Idea 950 page st *Web:* www.greenidea.com	San Francisco	CA	94117	415-863-2157	
GreenGeeks LLC 5739 Kanan Rd Ste 300 *Web:* www.greengeeks.com	Agoura Hills	CA	91301	310-496-8946	
Greystar Development & Construction LP 750 Bering Dr Ste 400 *Web:* www.greystar.com	Houston	TX	77057	713-966-5000	
Grid Dynamics Consulting Services Inc 4600 Bohannon Dr Ste 220 *Web:* www.griddynamics.com	Menlo Park	CA	94025	650-523-5000	
Gtess Corp 2435 N Central Expwy Ste 500 *Web:* www.banctec.com	Richardson	TX	75080	972-792-5500	
Habanero Consulting Group Inc 510-1111 Melville St *Web:* www.habaneroconsulting.com	Vancouver	BC	V6E3V6	604-709-6201	
Halfaker & Associates LLC 2900 S Quincy St Ste 375 *Web:* www.halfakerandassociates.com	Arlington	VA	22206	703-434-3900	
Hartley Data Service Inc (HDS) 1807 Glenview Rd Ste 201 *Web:* hartleydata.com	Glenview	IL	60025	847-724-9280	729-2199
Haug Communications Inc 622 Neptune Dr *Web:* www.bbwi.net	Seneca	KS	66538	785-336-3579	
Havanet Communications 1190 Sw 170th Ave Unit 101 *Web:* www.hevanet.com	Beaverton	OR	97006	503-531-9048	
Health Management Systems Inc 401 Pk Ave S *TF:* 877-467-0184 ■ *Web:* www.hms.com	New York	NY	10016	212-857-5000	857-5004
Healthbridge 11300 Cornell Park Dr Ste 360 *Web:* www.healthbridge.org	Blue Ash	OH	45242	513-469-7222	
Healthcare Administrative Partners LLC 112 Chesley Dr *Web:* www.hapusa.com	Media	PA	19063	610-892-8889	
Healthpac Computer Systems Inc 1010 E Victory Dr *Web:* www.healthpac.net	Savannah	GA	31405	912-341-7420	
Hidden Variable Studios LLC 1800 S Brand Blvd Ste 204 *Web:* www.hiddenvariable.com	Glendale	CA	91204	818-985-4263	
Hiebing Group, The 315 Wisconsin Ave *Web:* www.hiebing.com	Madison	WI	53703	608-256-6357	
High Standards Technology 17000 El Camino Real *Web:* www.weredown.com	Houston	TX	77058	281-990-9422	
Hillcraft Ltd 2202 Advance Rd *Web:* hillcraft.com	Madison	WI	53718	608-221-3220	
Hivelocity Ventures Corp 8010 Woodland Ctr Blvd Ste 700 *Web:* www.hivelocity.net	Tampa	FL	33614	813-471-0355	
Hme Providers Inc 1410 White Dr *Web:* www.hmeproviders.com	Titusville	FL	32780	321-267-7576	
HomeAway.com Inc 1011 W Fifth St Ste 300 *Web:* www.homeaway.com	Austin	TX	78703	512-782-0805	
HUGE Inc 45 Main St Second Fl *Web:* www.hugeinc.com	Brooklyn	NY	11201	718-625-4843	
Hyperion Inc 1660 Intl Dr *Web:* www.hyperioninc.com	Mclean	VA	22102	703-848-8850	
I Sc International 9700 W Bluemound Rd *Web:* www.iscinternational.com	Milwaukee	WI	53226	414-476-7755	
I-netlink 942 Douglas St *Web:* www.infometrics.net	Brandon	MB	R7A7B2	204-578-5600	
i4DM 8227 Cloverleaf Dr Ste 312 *Web:* www.i4dm.com	Millersville	MD	21108	410-729-7920	
Icio Inc 1373 Ridge Commons Blvd *Web:* www.icioinc.com	Hanover	MD	21076	410-903-4166	
ICON Laboratories Inc 123 Smith St *Web:* iconplc.com	Farmingdale	NY	11735	631-777-8833	
ICTV Brands Inc 489 Devon Park Dr Ste 315 *Web:* ictvonline.com	Wayne	PA	19087	484-598-2300	
Icvm Group Inc 50 Love Ln *Web:* www.icvmgroup.com	Mattituck	NY	11952	631-298-5505	
Idm Computer Solutions Inc 5559 Eureka Dr *Web:* idmcomp.com	Hamilton	OH	45011	513-892-8600	
Image Data Inc 18 Petra Ln *Web:* www.imgdata.com	Albany	NY	12205	518-862-2740	
Imagecat Inc 400 Oceangate Ste 1050 *Web:* www.imagecatinc.com	Long Beach	CA	90802	562-628-1675	
Imagenet LLC 6411 S 216th St *Web:* www.imagenet.com	Kent	WA	98032	253-395-0110	
ImageSource Inc 612 Fifth Ave SW *Web:* www.imagesourceinc.com	Olympia	WA	98501	360-943-9273	
IMC Inc 11480 Commerce Park Dr *Web:* www.imc.com	Reston	VA	20191	703-871-8700	
Impact Solutions Consulting Inc 1300 Ridenour Blvd NW Ste 210 *Web:* www.impactsc.com	Kennesaw	GA	30152	770-795-9525	
Impatica Inc 2430 Don Reid Dr Ste 200 *Web:* www.impatica.com	Ottawa	ON	K1H1E1	613-736-9982	
Incontrol Technology Inc 1651 e main st *Web:* incontroltechnology.com	El Cajon	CA	92021	619-654-3799	
Infi Net Solutions Inc 6430 S 84th St *Web:* www.omahait.com	Omaha	NE	68127	402-895-5777	
Influxis 28110 Ave Stanford Unit D *Web:* www.influxis.com	Valencia	CA	91355	661-775-3936	
InfoMine Inc 580 Hornby St Ste 900 *Web:* www.infomine.com	Vancouver	BC	V6C3B6	604-683-2037	
Infosec Inc 14001c Saint Germain Dr *Web:* www.infosecinc.com	Centreville	VA	20121	703-825-1202	
Infotech Global Inc 371 Hoes Ln *Web:* www.igiusa.com	Piscataway	NJ	08854	732-271-0600	
Infutor Data Solutions Inc 15129 S Route 59 *Web:* www.infutor.com	Plainfield	IL	60544	312-348-7900	
IngletBlair LLC 6207 Bee Cave Rd Ste 110 *Web:* www.ingletblair.com	Austin	TX	78746	512-732-0498	
Inmediata Health Group Corp 342 Calle San Luis Ste 203 *Web:* www.inmediata.com	San Juan	PR	00920	787-774-0606	
Innotap 50 Berrywood Ln *Web:* innotap.com	Dresher	PA	19025	215-237-1937	
Innovasium Inc 55 Albert St Ste 200 *Web:* www.innovasium.com	Markham	ON	L3P2T4	905-479-5555	
Input Solutions Inc 9250 Gaither Rd *Web:* www.inputsolutions.com	Gaithersburg	MD	20877	301-948-6620	
Inspired eLearning Inc 613 NW Loop 410 Ste 530 *TF:* 800-631-2078 ■ *Web:* www.inspiredelearning.com	San Antonio	TX	78216	210-579-0224	
INTEG Process Group Inc 2919 E Hardies Rd First Fl *Web:* www.integpg.com	Gibsonia	PA	15044	724-933-9350	
Integrated Solution Group Inc, The 10 Cedar St *Web:* www.intsolgrp.com	Woburn	MA	01801	781-938-0712	
IntelliStance LLC 213 Court St *Web:* www.marketstance.com	Middletown	CT	06457	860-704-6381	
Interactive Tracking Systems Inc 820 51st St E Ste 150 *Web:* www.itracks.com	Saskatoon	SK	S7K0X8	306-665-5026	
Interface Multimedia Inc 8505 Fenton St *Web:* www.ifmm.com	Silver Spring	MD	20910	301-585-0068	
International Procurement Agency Inc 4322 Avondale Ln Nw *Web:* www.usaipa.com	Canton	OH	44708	330-477-5020	
Internet Applications Group 999 Commercial St Ste 210 *Web:* inapp.com	Palo Alto	CA	94303	650-424-0496	
Internet Creations Inc 2000 Waterview Dr Ste 100 *Web:* www.internetcreations.com	Hamilton	NJ	08691	609-570-7200	
Internet Employment Linkage Inc 1010 Lk St Ste 611 *Web:* www.ielinc.net	Oak Park	IL	60301	708-848-4351	
Internet Nebraska Inc 1719 N Cotner Blvd *Web:* www.inebraska.com	Lincoln	NE	68505	402-434-8680	
introNetworks Inc 1482 E Valley Rd Ste 446 *Web:* www.intronetworks.com	Santa Barbara	CA	93108	805-722-1040	
inXile entertainment Inc 2727 Newport Blvd Ste 200 *Web:* www.inxile-entertainment.com	Newport Beach	CA	92663	949-675-3690	
Iostudio LLC 565 Marriott Dr Ste 700 *Web:* www.iostudio.com	Nashville	TN	37214	615-256-6282	
IP Fabrics Inc 14976 NW Greenbrier Pkwy *Web:* www.ipfabrics.com	Beaverton	OR	97006	503-444-2400	
IPS Worldwide LLC 265 Clyde Morris Blvd Ste 100 *Web:* www.ipsww.com	Ormond Beach	FL	32174	386-672-7727	
Iqr Consulting Inc 1915 gardenview cir *Web:* iqrconsulting.com	Santa Rosa	CA	95403	707-921-7071	
IRA Services Trust Co 1160 Industrial Rd Ste 1 *Web:* www.ierinc.com	San Carlos	CA	94070	650-593-2221	
ISD Inc 2500 W Higgins Rd Ste 250 *Web:* www.isdinc.com	Hoffman Estates	IL	60169	847-519-1150	
ISS Software Solutions Inc Five Great Vly Pkwy Ste 120 *Web:* www.intsoftinc.com	Malvern	PA	19355	610-560-4300	
IT-Lifeline Inc 23403 E Mission Ave *Web:* www.itlifeline.net	Liberty Lake	WA	99019	509-984-1600	
ITRenew Inc 8356 Central Ave *Web:* www.itrenew.com	Newark	CA	94560	408-744-9600	
Ives Group Inc Nine Main St Ste 2F *Web:* www.ivesinc.com	Sutton	MA	01590	508-476-7007	
Ivic Design 5125 Rue Du Trianon *Web:* qc.yepplocal.com	Montreal	QC	H1M2S5	514-352-1212	

Phone Fax

Ivision Inc 1430 W Peachtree St NW Atlanta GA 30309 678-999-3002
Web: ivision.com
iWeb Group Inc 3185 Hochelaga Montreal QC H1W1G4 514-286-4242
Web: iweb.com
Jacquette Consulting Inc 710 Providence Rd Malvern PA 19355 610-644-4485
Web: www.jacquette.com
Jasper Design Automation Inc
707 California St Mountain View CA 94041 650-966-0200
Web: www.jasper-da.com
Jdm Systems Consultants Inc
33117 Hamilton Ct Farmington Hills MI 48334 248-324-1937
Web: www.jdmconsulting.com
JP Digital Imaging Inc 230 Polaris Ave Mountain View CA 94043 650-965-0803
Web: www.jpdigital.com
K2 Communications 880 Apollo St Ste 239 El Segundo CA 90245 310-524-9100
Web: k2communications.com
K2Share LLC 1005 University Dr E College Station TX 77840 979-260-0030
Web: k2share.com
Keane Inc 210 Porter Dr Ste 315 San Ramon CA 94583 925-838-8600 241-9507*
**Fax Area Code:* 617
Kell Partners 303 camp craft rd West Lake Hills TX 78746 512-732-2276
Web: www.kellpartners.com
Kelser Corp 111 Roberts St Ste D East Hartford CT 06108 860-528-9819 291-9088
TF: 800-647-5316 ■ *Web:* www.kelsercorp.com
Key Computing 74 Merrick Rd Amityville NY 11701 631-264-0660
Web: keycomputing.com
Keycom Communications 1144 Solana Ave Winter Park FL 32789 407-949-0600
Web: www.keycom.net
Keylogic Systems Inc
3168 Collins Ferry Rd Morgantown WV 26505 304-296-9100
Web: keylogic.com
Keystone Information Systems
1000 S Lenola Rd Maple Shade NJ 08052 856-722-0700
Web: www.keyinfosys.com
Kinsail Corp 1420 Beverly Rd Ste 150 Mclean VA 22101 703-994-4194
Web: www.kinsail.com
Kirtley Technology Corp 9s531 Wilmette Ave Darien IL 60561 630-512-0213
Web: kirtleytech.com
Klein Managment Systems Inc
259 S Middletown Rd Nanuet NY 10954 845-623-7778
Web: kleinmgmt.com
Koniag Services Inc
4100 Lafayette Dr Ste 303 Chantilly VA 20151 703-488-9300
Web: www.ksikoniag.com
Krueger Associates Inc 105 Commerce Dr Aston PA 19014 610-532-4700
Web: www.nfsrv.com
L & e Meridan 7400 Fullerton Rd Springfield VA 22153 703-913-0300
Web: www.l-e.com
L Tech Network Services Inc
9926 Pioneer Blvd Ste 101 Santa Fe Springs CA 90670 562-222-1121
Web: www.ltechnet.com
La Touraine Inc 625 Broadway Ste 700 San Diego CA 92101 619-237-5014
Web: latouraineinc.com
Lake Data Center Inc 800 Lloyd Rd Wickliffe OH 44092 440-944-2020
Web: www.lakedata.com
Learning Enhancement Corp
200 S Wacker Dr Ste 3100 Chicago IL 60606 312-455-1758
TF: 877-272-4610 ■ *Web:* www.mybrainware.com
Leatherup Com 955 Venice Blvd Los Angeles CA 90015 213-763-6185
Web: www.leatherup.com
Lexnet 108 Wind Haven Dr Ste A Nicholasville KY 40356 859-266-1141
Web: www.lexnetinc.com
Lifeline Data Centers LLC
401 N Shadeland Ave Indianapolis IN 46219 317-423-2591
Web: www.lifelinedatacenters.com
LifePics Inc 5777 Central Ave Ste 120 Boulder CO 80301 303-413-9500
Web: www.lifepics.com
Light Styles Internet LLC
1843 S Broadway Ave Ste 104 Boise ID 83706 208-433-3900
Web: www.lightingshowroom.com
Listengage.com Five Edgell Rd Ste 30a Framingham MA 01701 508-935-2275
Web: www.listengage.com
Little Apple Technologies 112 S Broadway Manhattan MT 59741 406-284-3174
Web: littleappletech.com
Livesmart 360 LLC 2829 cattlemen rd Sarasota FL 34232 941-371-1010
Web: www.livesmart360.com
LoganBritton Inc 1700 Park St Ste 111 Naperville IL 60563 630-799-0262
Web: www.loganbritton.com
Login Inc 4003 E Speedway Blvd Tucson AZ 85712 520-618-3000
Web: www.login.com
Long Lines LLC 501 Fourth St PO Box 67 Sergeant Bluff IA 51054 712-271-4000
Web: www.longlines.com
Lord Whalen LLC 371 Van Ness Way Ste 110 Torrance CA 90501 310-676-3300
Web: www.institutionalriskanalytics.com
Lowe-Martin Company Inc 400 Hunt Club Rd Ottawa ON K1V1C1 613-741-0962
Web: www.lmgroup.com
Lumension Security Inc
8660 E Hartford Dr Ste 300 Scottsdale AZ 85255 888-725-7828 970-6323*
**Fax Area Code:* 480 ■ *TF:* 888-725-7828 ■ *Web:* www.lumension.com
Lunarline Inc 3300 N Fairfax Dr Ste 308 Arlington VA 22201 571-481-9300
Web: www.lunarline.com
MaddenCo Inc 4847 E Virginia Ste G Evansville IN 47715 812-474-6245
Web: www.maddenco.com
Magmic Inc 126 York St Ottawa ON K1N5T5 613-241-3571
Web: www.magmic.com
MajescoMastek 105 Fieldcrest Ave Ste 208 Edison NJ 08837 732-590-6400
Web: www.mastek.com
Makro Technologies Inc
One Washington Pk Ste 1502 Newark NJ 07102 973-481-0100
Web: www.makrotech.com
marblemedia Inc 74 Fraser Ave Ste 100 Toronto ON M6K3E1 416-646-2711
Web: www.marblemedia.com

Phone Fax

Marketware Inc 7070 Union Park Ctr Ste 300 Midvale UT 84047 801-944-4230
Web: marketware.com
Mass Media Inc 883 Patriot Dr Moorpark CA 93021 805-531-9399
Web: www.massmedia.com
Mathtech Inc
6402 Arlington Blvd Ste 1200 Falls Church VA 22042 703-875-8866
Web: mathtechinc.com
Mcf Technology Solutions LLC
30400 Detroit Rd Westlake OH 44145 440-201-6050
Web: www.mcftech.com
MecSoft Corp 18019 Sky Park Cir Ste KL Irvine CA 92614 949-654-8163
Web: www.mecsoft.com
MediConnect Global Inc
10897 South Riverfront Pkwy Ste 500 South Jordan UT 84095 801-545-3700
Web: www.mediconnect.net
MedPricer.com Inc
2351 Boston Post Rd Ste 208 Guilford CT 06437 203-453-4554
Web: www.medpricer.com
MegaPath Inc 6800 Koll Ctr Pkwy Ste 200 Pleasanton CA 94566 925-201-2500
Web: www.megapath.com
Melissa DATA Corp
22382 Avenida Empresa Rancho Santa Margarita CA 92688 949-858-3000
Web: www.melissadata.com
Memorial Hermann Health Network Providers Inc
9301 SW Fwy Ste 5000 Houston TX 77074 713-448-6464
Web: www.mhhnp.org
Meridian Midwest Payment 402 S Patterson Ave Joplin MO 64801 417-781-5050
Web: meridian-midwest.com
MerITec Services Inc
12770 Cimarron Path Ste 118 San Antonio TX 78249 210-694-4635
Web: www.meritecservices.com
Merkle Response Services Inc
100 Jamison Ct Hagerstown MD 21740 301-790-3100
Web: www.merkleresponseservices.com
Merritt Technical Associates Inc
114 Saint Johns Rd Wilton CT 06897 203-834-0010
Web: www.merritt-tech.com
MessageSolution Inc
1851 McCarthy Blvd Ste 105 Milpitas CA 95035 408-383-0100
Web: www.messagesolution.com
Metasense Inc Two Keystone Ave Ste 500 Cherry Hill NJ 08003 856-873-9950
Web: www.metasenseusa.com
MIB Inc 50 Braintree Hill Park Braintree MA 02184 781-329-4500 329-3379
Web: www.mib.com
Microwave Applications Group
3030 Industrial Pkwy Santa Maria CA 93455 805-928-5711
Web: magsmx.com
Mid America Computer Corp PO Box 700 Blair NE 68008 402-426-6222 533-5369
TF: 800-622-2502 ■ *Web:* www.maccnet.com
Mile High Shooting Accessories LLC
3731 Monarch St Erie CO 80516 303-255-9999
Web: milehighshooting.com
Mod43 Inc 7946 N Lilley Rd Canton MI 48187 734-416-1009
Web: mod43.com
Modern Earth 449 Provencher Blvd Winnipeg MB R2J0B8 204-885-2469
Web: www.modernearth.net
Mohawk Internet Technologies Rte 138 Kahnawake QC J0L1B0 450-638-4007
Web: mohawkinternettechnologies.com
Moja Inc 7010 Infantry Ridge Rd Manassas VA 20109 703-369-4339
Web: www.moja.net
Momentum Capital Partners
1227 W Magnolia Ave Ste 300 Fort Worth TX 76104 817-920-7599 920-9606
Web: www.mocappartners.com
Moog Animatics 3200 Patrick Henry Dr Santa Clara CA 95054 408-748-8721
Web: www.animatics.com
Mudiam Inc 7100 regency Sq blvd Houston TX 77036 713-484-7266
Web: www.mudiaminc.com
Murphy Industries Inc 1650 Cascade Dr Marion OH 43302 740-387-7890
Web: www.acc-net.com
Musictoday LLC 5391 Three Notched Rd Crozet VA 22932 434-244-7200
Web: www.musictoday.com
N-Dimension Solutions Inc
9030 Leslie St Unit 300 Richmond Hill ON L4B1G2 905-707-8884
Web: www.n-dimension.com
Nakina Systems Inc 80 Hines Rd Ste 200 Ottawa ON K2K2T8 613-254-7351
Web: www.nakinasystems.com
Natel Telecommunications Lc
907 W Burlington Ave Fairfield IA 52556 641-469-6220
Web: www.natel.net
NeST Technologies Corp
44901 Falcon Pl Ste 116 Sterling VA 20166 703-653-1100
Web: www.nesttech.com
Net Solutions Technology Center
38 Sams Point Rd Ab Beaufort SC 29907 843-525-6469
Web: www.easierway.com
Netcom Systems Inc 200 Metroplex Dr Edison NJ 08817 732-393-6100
Web: www.netcom-sys.com
NetQuest Corp 523 Fellowship Rd Ste 205 Mt Laurel NJ 08054 856-866-0505
Web: www.netquestcorp.com
Network Magic Unlimited 1723 21st St Santa Monica CA 90404 310-449-1411
Web: www.netmagicu.com
NeuCo Inc 12 Post Office Sq Fourth Fl Boston MA 02109 617-587-3100
Web: www.neuco.net
Nevada Automotive Test Center
605 Ft Churchill Rd Silver Springs NV 89429 775-629-2000
Web: www.natc-ht.com
New West Technologies Inc
4606 SE Division St Portland OR 97206 503-235-4656
Web: www.newestech.com
Nexcess.net LLC 21700 Melrose Ave Southfield MI 48075 866-639-2377
TF: 866-639-2377 ■ *Web:* www.nexcess.net

Company / Address	City	State	ZIP	Phone	Fax
nexDimension Technology Solutions LLC 10060 Medlock Bridge Rd Ste 100 — *Web:* www.nexdimension.net	Johns Creek	GA	30097	770-475-1575	
NexTalk Inc 10757 River Front Pkwy Ste 290 — *Web:* www.nextalk.com	South Jordan	UT	84095	801-274-6001	
NextCorp Ltd 7701 Las Colinas Ridge Ste 100 — *Web:* www.nextcorp.com	Irving	TX	75063	214-574-6398	
Nextpage Inc 13997 S Minuteman Dr Ste 300	Draper	UT	84020	801-748-4400	748-4410
Nexus Management Inc Four Industrial Pkwy Ste 101 — *Web:* enablesit.us/	Brunswick	ME	04011	207-319-1100	
Nexxus Marketing Group LLC, The 11 Sylvan St — *Web:* www.thenexxusgroup.com	Danvers	MA	01923	978-762-3900	
Nimble Assessment Systems Inc Three Bridge St Ste B101 — *Web:* nimble.tools	Newton	MA	02458	617-431-4441	
Nimbus Design 2363 Broadway St — *Web:* www.nimbusdesign.com	Redwood City	CA	94063	650-365-7568	
Nourtek Services Corp 100 decker ct — *Web:* www.nourtek.com	Irving	TX	75062	972-717-2700	
Novaces LLC Poydras Ctr 650 Poydras St Ste 2320 — *Web:* www.novaces.com	New Orleans	LA	70130	504-544-6888	
Novologix Inc 10400 Viking Dr	Eden Prairie	MN	55344	952-826-2500	
O'neil Data Systems Inc 12655 Beatrice St — *Web:* www.oneildata.com	Los Angeles	CA	90066	310-448-6400	
Oasis Systems Inc 24 Hartwell Ave — *Web:* www.oasissystems.com	Lexington	MA	02421	781-676-7333	676-7353
Objectstream Inc 7725 W Reno Ave Ste 307 — *Web:* www.objectstream.com	Oklahoma City	OK	73127	405-942-4477	
Observera Inc 3856 Dulles S Court Ste I — *Web:* www.observera.com	Chantilly	VA	20151	703-378-3153	
Oly Penn. Inc 245 E Washington St — *Web:* startpage.olypen.com	Sequim	WA	98382	360-683-1456	
Omeda Communications 555 Huehl Rd — *Web:* omeda.com	Northbrook	IL	60062	847-564-8900	
One Source Networks Inc 14402 Blanco Rd Ste 300 — *Web:* www.onesourcenetworks.com	San Antonio	TX	78216	210-679-4600	
One Technologies LP 8144 Walnut Hill Ln Ste 600 — *Web:* www.onetechnologies.net	Dallas	TX	75231	888-550-8471	
Online Business Applications Inc 9018 Heritage Pkwy Ste 600 — *Web:* www.irmsonline.com	Woodridge	IL	60517	630-243-9810	
onShore Networks LLC 1407 W Chicago Ave — *Web:* www.onshore.com	Chicago	IL	60642	312-850-5200	
Opal Soft 1288 Kifer Rd # 201 — *Web:* www.opalsoft.com	Sunnyvale	CA	94086	408-267-2211	
Open Logic Corp 28345 Beck Rd Ste 308 — *Web:* www.open-logix.com	Wixom	MI	48393	248-869-0080	
Openface Inc 3445 Av Du Parc — *Web:* www.openface.com	Montreal	QC	H2X2H6	514-281-8585	
Opinion Access Corp 47-10 32nd Pl — *Web:* www.opinionaccess.com	Long Island City	NY	11101	718-729-2622	
Optimetra Inc 4420 Red Rock Ranch Dr — *Web:* www.optimetra.com	Monument	CO	80132	719-481-2956	
Orchid Suites Inc 1806 T St Nw # 200 — *Web:* www.orchidconnect.com	Washington	DC	20009	202-265-1671	
Original Media LLC 38 E 29th St Fifth Fl — *Web:* www.originalmedia.com	New York	NY	10016	212-683-3086	
Oristech Inc Po Box 310069 — *Web:* www.oristech.com	New Braunfels	TX	78131	830-620-7422	
Oski Technology Inc 2513 E Charleston Rd Ste 203 — *Web:* www.oskitechnology.com	Mountain View	CA	94043	408-216-7728	
Ovation Networks Inc 222 Third Ave Se Ste 276 — *Web:* www.ovationnetworks.com	Cedar Rapids	IA	52401	319-365-6200	
Overture Technologies Inc 6900 Wisconsin Ave Ste 200 — *Web:* home.overturecorp.com	Bethesda	MD	20815	301-492-2140	
P K W Associates Inc 705 E Ordnance Rd Ste 108 — *Web:* www.pkwassoc.com	Baltimore	MD	21226	443-773-1000	
P Murphy & Assoc Inc 2301 W Olive Ave — *Web:* www.pmurphy.com	Burbank	CA	91506	818-841-2002	
P2i Inc 1236 Main St — *Web:* www.p2ionline.com	Hellertown	PA	18055	610-814-0550	
Palm Pictures LLC 110 E 25th St — *Web:* www.palmpictures.com	New York	NY	10010	646-790-1211	
PASCO Inc 1140 Terex Rd — *Web:* pasco-group.com	Hudson	OH	44236	330-655-7000	
Passport Online Inc 9786 Sw Nimbus Ave — *Web:* www.passportonlineinc.com	Beaverton	OR	97008	503-626-7766	
Paytrace 7100 carolina ln — *Web:* paytrace.com	Vancouver	WA	98664	360-326-8330	
PCC Technology Group LLC Two Barnard Ln — *Web:* www.pcctg.com	Bloomfield	CT	06002	860-242-3299	
PenTeleData 540 Delaware Ave PO Box 197 — *TF:* 800-281-3564 ■ *Web:* www.penteledata.net	Palmerton	PA	18071	800-281-3564	
Peraso Technologies Inc 144 Front St W Ste 685 — *Web:* www.perasotech.com	Toronto	ON	M5J2L7	416-637-1048	
Photo Den Vision & Sound 315 SE Seventh St — *Web:* photoden.com	Grants Pass	OR	97526	541-479-1833	
Photodex Corp 11100 Metric Blvd Ste 400 — *Web:* www.photodex.com	Austin	TX	78758	512-419-7000	
Pinnacle Business Systems Inc 3824 S Blvd St Ste 200 — *TF:* 800-311-0757 ■ *Web:* www.pbsnow.com	Edmond	OK	73013	800-311-0757	444-3439
Pinpoint Data 339 Somerset St — *Web:* www.couponchek.com	North Plainfield	NJ	07060	908-756-9400	
Pipeline Interactive Inc 941 Cumberland St — *Web:* www.pipelineinteractive.com	Lebanon	PA	17042	717-273-5665	
Pixeled Business Systems Inc 350 W Ninth Ave Ste 106 — *Web:* www.pixeled.com	Escondido	CA	92025	858-566-6060	
PlasmaNet Inc 420 Lexington Ave Ste 2435 — *Web:* freelotto.com	New York	NY	10170	212-931-6760	
Poka Lambro Telephone Cooperative Inc 560 US Hwy 87 — *Web:* www.poka.com	Wilson	TX	79381	806-924-7234	
Pool 4 Tool America LLC 34119 W 12 Mile Rd Ste 320 — *Web:* www.pool4tool.com	Farmington Hills	MI	48331	248-244-0851	
PowerMetal Technologies Inc 2726 Loker Ave W — *Web:* www.powermetalinc.com	Carlsbad	CA	92010	760-607-0404	
Premier Management Corp 8894 Stanford Blvd Ste 405 — *Web:* premgtcorp.com	Columbia	MD	21045	443-656-3550	
Presentek Inc 987 University Ave Ste 11 — *Web:* www.presentek.com	Los Gatos	CA	95032	408-354-1264	
Pricon Inc 1831 W Lincoln Ave — *Web:* www.pricon.com	Anaheim	CA	92801	714-758-8832	
Prime Care Technologies Inc 6650 Sugarloaf Pkwy Ste 400 — *Web:* primecaretech.com	Duluth	GA	30097	770-870-2888	
Printco Graphics Inc 14112 Industrial Rd — *Web:* www.printcographics.com	Omaha	NE	68144	402-593-1080	
Printmail Systems Inc 23 Friends Ln — *TF:* 800-910-4844 ■ *Web:* www.printmailsystems.com	Newtown	PA	18940	215-860-4250	860-2204
Prism Visual Software Inc One Sagamore Hl Dr Ste 2B — *Web:* www.prismvs.com	Port Washington	NY	11050	516-944-5920	
PRISMHR 50 Resnik Rd Ste 200 — *TF:* 877-837-4311 ■ *Web:* www.fwdco.com	Plymouth	MA	02360	508-747-7261	
Pro Net Communications Inc Ste 350-1122 Mainland St — *Web:* www.pro.net	Vancouver	BC	V6B5L1	604-606-0660	
ProducersWEB Inc Eight Penn Ctr 1628 John F Kennedy Blvd Ste 1850 — *Web:* www.producersweb.com	Philadelphia	PA	19103	215-561-2686	
Projectools Company Inc 5890 Hwy 159 w — *Web:* www.projectools.com	Bellville	TX	77418	979-865-8341	
Prologic Technology Systems Inc 9600 N Mopac Express Way Ste 300 — *Web:* www.prologic-tech.com	Austin	TX	78759	512-328-9496	
Prospection Inc 1750 Av De Vitre — *Web:* www.prospection.qc.ca	Quebec	QC	G1J1Z6	418-521-2248	
Protogate Inc 12225 World Trade Dr — *Web:* www.protogate.com	San Diego	CA	92128	858-451-0865	
PRWT Services Inc 1835 Market St Eighth Fl — *Web:* www.prwt.com	Philadelphia	PA	19103	215-569-8810	569-9893
Puppet Labs 308 SW Second Ave Fifth Fl — *Web:* www.puppetlabs.com	Portland	OR	97204	503-575-9775	
Pyramid Consulting Inc 11100 Atlantis Pl — *Web:* www.pyramidci.com	Alpharetta	GA	30022	678-514-3500	
QC Data International Inc 8000 E Maplewood Ave Ste 300 — *Web:* www.qcdata.com	Greenwood Village	CO	80111	303-783-8888	
Qlan Corp 23232 Peralta Dr 117 — *Web:* www.griffinoptometric.com	Laguna Hills	CA	92653	949-597-8560	
QUESTAR LLC 2905 W Service Rd — *Web:* questarweb.com	Eagan	MN	55121	651-688-0089	
Radius Technology Group Inc 804 Pershing Dr Ste 1 — *Web:* www.radius360.net	Silver Spring	MD	20910	301-565-3400	
Rally Software Development Corp 3333 Walnut St — *Web:* rallydev.com	Boulder	CO	80301	303-565-2800	
Ramco Systems Corp 3150 Brunswick Pk Ste 130 — *TF:* 800-472-6261 ■ *Web:* www.ramco.com	Lawrenceville	NJ	08648	609-620-4800	
Ramius Corp 201-227 Rue Montcalm — *Web:* www.ramius.net	Gatineau	QC	J8Y3B9	613-230-3808	
Randr Inc 3764 Ninth St — *Web:* www.randrinc.com	Riverside	CA	92501	951-369-3427	
Rangam Consultants Inc 370 Campus Dr Ste 103 — **Fax Area Code:* 877 ■ *TF:* 877-583-7054 ■ *Web:* www.rangam.com	Somerset	NJ	08873	908-704-8843	606-6587*
Raptr Inc 701 N Shoreline Blvd — *Web:* raptr.com	Mountain View	CA	94043	650-215-1328	
Rassai 500 Throckmorton St Ste 375 — *Web:* www.rassai.com	Fort Worth	TX	76102	817-332-0069	
Raven Software Corp 8496 Greenway Blvd — *Web:* www.ravensoft.com	Middleton	WI	53562	608-833-5791	
Ray Allen Inc 400 W Erie St Ste 303 — *Web:* www.rayalleninc.com	Chicago	IL	60654	312-428-4915	
RCF Information Systems Inc 4200 Colonel Glenn Hwy Glenn Tech Ctr Ste 100 — *Web:* rcfinfo.com	Beavercreek	OH	45431	937-427-5680	
Real Intent Inc 990 Almanor Ave Ste 220 — *Web:* www.realintent.com	Sunnyvale	CA	94085	408-830-0700	
Reality Technology Inc 2444 Washington St Ste 215 — *Web:* www.reality-technology.com	Denver	CO	80205	303-757-1107	

	City	State	Zip	Phone	Fax
Reallygreatrate Inc 423 S Pacific Coast Hwy Ste 202 *Web:* www.reallygreatrate.com	Redondo Beach	CA	90277	310-540-8900	
Red Clay Interactive 22 Buford Village Way Ste 221 *Web:* www.redclayinteractive.com	Buford	GA	30518	770-297-2430	
Red Storm Entertainment Inc 2000 Centregreen Way Ste 300 *Web:* www.redstorm.com	Cary	NC	27513	919-460-1776	
RedTail Solutions Inc 69 Milk St Ste 100 *Web:* redtailsolutions.com	Westborough	MA	01581	508-983-1900	
Reed Technology & Information Services Inc Seven Walnut Grove Dr *Web:* www.reedtech.com	Horsham	PA	19044	215-441-6400	
REGEN Energy Inc 15 Belfield Rd Ste 5 *Web:* www.regenenergy.com	Toronto	ON	M9W1E8	416-934-1040	
Renesys Corp 1155 Elm St Ste 510 *Web:* dyn.com/performance-assurance/	Manchester	NH	03101	603-643-9300	
Renew Data Corp 9500 Arboretum Blvd *TF:* 888-811-3789 ■ *Web:* www.renewdata.com	Austin	TX	78759	512-276-5500	276-5555
RESOLUTE Partners LLC 37 W Center St Ste 301 *Web:* www.resolutepartners.com	Southington	CT	06489	860-628-6800	
Resource Technology Management Inc 950 N Orlando Ave *Web:* www.rtm-inc.com	Winter Park	FL	32789	407-998-8000	
Respondus Inc 8201 164th Ave NE Ste 200 PO Box 3247 *Web:* www.respondus.com	Redmond	WA	98052	425-497-0389	
Richweb Inc 4235 Innslake Dr Ste 201 *Web:* www.richweb.com	Glen Allen	VA	23060	804-747-8592	
Right Systems Inc 2600 Willamette Dr NE Ste C *TF:* 800-571-1717 ■ *Web:* www.rightsys.com	Lacey	WA	98516	360-956-0414	956-0336
Riverbed Technology Inc 199 Fremont St *NASDAQ: RVBD* ■ *Web:* www.riverbed.com	San Francisco	CA	94105	415-247-8800	247-8801
Ross Group Inc 2730 Indian Ripple Rd *Web:* www.rossgroupinc.com	Dayton	OH	45440	937-427-3069	
Rugged Systems Inc 13000 Danielson St Q *Web:* www.coresystemsusa.com	Poway	CA	92064	858-391-1006	
Rurbanc Data Services Inc 7622 N SR- 66 *Web:* www.rdsiweb.com	Defiance	OH	43512	419-783-8800	784-6542
Ryantech Inc 1794 Olympic Pkwy Ste 250 *Web:* www.ryantechinc.com	Park City	UT	84098	435-647-0118	
Ryte Byte Inc s4125a rocky point rd *Web:* www.rytebyteinc.com	Baraboo	WI	53913	608-356-6822	
Sable Networks Inc 3171 Jay St *Web:* www.sablenetworks.com	Santa Clara	CA	95054	408-727-5514	
Saepio Technologies Inc 4601 Madison Ave Fourth Fl *Web:* www.saepio.com	Kansas City	MO	64112	816-777-2100	
Safe Systems Inc 11395 Old Roswell Rd *Web:* www.safesystems.com	Alpharetta	GA	30009	770-752-0550	
Sagerock.com 129 N Summit St *Web:* www.sagerock.com	Akron	OH	44304	330-379-9000	
SalePoint Inc 9909 Huennekens St Ste 205 *Web:* www.salepoint.com	San Diego	CA	92121	858-546-9400	
Scicom Data Services Ltd 10101 Bren Rd E *TF:* 800-488-9087	Minnetonka	MN	55343	952-933-4200	936-4132
Screenz 5212 N Clark St *Web:* screenz.com	Chicago	IL	60640	773-681-0093	
Seagull Scientific Inc 1616 148th Ave Se *Web:* seagullscientific.com	Bellevue	WA	98007	425-641-1408	
SecureOne Data Solutions LLC 2801 N 33rd Ave Ste 1 *Web:* www.datacenteraz.com	Phoenix	AZ	85009	602-415-1111	
Seguin Services Inc 3100 S Central Ave *Web:* www.seguin.org	Cicero	IL	60804	708-222-4250	
SevenTwenty Strategies 1220 19th St NW Ste 300 *Web:* www.720strategies.com	Washington	DC	20036	202-962-3955	
SHAZAM Inc 6700 Pioneer Pkwy *Web:* www.shazam.net	Johnston	IA	50131	515-288-2828	
Shipcom Wireless Inc 11200 Richmond Ave Ste 552 *Web:* www.shipcomwireless.com	Houston	TX	77082	281-558-5252	
Shop Floor Automations Inc 5360 Jackson Dr *Web:* www.shopfloorautomations.com	La Mesa	CA	91942	619-461-4000	
Sigma Solutions Inc 422 E Ramsey Rd *Web:* www.sigmasolinc.com	San Antonio	TX	78216	210-348-9876	348-9124
SILVACO Inc 4701 Patrick Henry Dr Bldg 2 *Web:* www.silvaco.com	Santa Clara	CA	95054	408-567-1000	
Simplifile LC 4844 North 300 West Ste 202 *Web:* simplifile.com	Provo	UT	84604	801-373-0151	
Six Red Marbles LLC 10 City Sq Third Fl Charlestown *Web:* www.sixredmarbles.com	Boston	MA	02129	857-588-9000	
Skybank Financial Services Corp 1444 Biscayne Blvd Ste 309 *TF:* 800-617-9980 ■ *Web:* www.skybankfinancial.com	Miami	FL	33132	800-617-9980	
Smart Web Concepts Inc 701 Riverside Ave Ste 3 *Web:* boostlogics.com	Roseville	CA	95678	916-782-2288	
Smart Wireless Inc 5035 SE McLoughlin Blvd *Web:* www.smartwireless.com	Portland	OR	97202	503-236-8440	
Smartorg Inc 855 oak grove ave *Web:* www.smartorg.com	Menlo Park	CA	94025	650-328-1612	
Smh Colocation 2463 W La Palma Ave Ste 205 *Web:* www.smhcolocation.com	Anaheim	CA	92801	949-722-8600	
Smilebox Inc 15809 Bear Creek Pkwy *Web:* www.smilebox.com	Redmond	WA	98052	360-797-5269	
Societe Grics 5100 Rue Sherbrooke E *Web:* grics.ca	Montreal	QC	H1V3R9	514-251-3700	

	City	State	Zip	Phone	Fax
Sof Tec Solutions Inc 384 Inverness Pkwy # 211 *TF:* 888-376-3832 ■ *Web:* www.softecinc.com	Englewood	CO	80112	303-662-1010	662-1060
Softcom Technology Consulting Inc 10 Bay St *Web:* www.softcom.biz	Toronto	ON	M5J2R8	416-957-7400	
Softlayer Technologies Inc 4849 Alpha Rd *TF Sales:* 866-398-7638 ■ *Web:* www.softlayer.com	Dallas	TX	75244	214-442-0600	442-0601
Sorteo Games Inc 6725 Mesa Ridge Rd Ste 202 *Web:* www.sorteogames.com	San Diego	CA	92121	858-554-0297	
SourceMedical Solutions Inc 100 Grandview Pl Ste 400 *TF:* 866-245-8093 ■ *Web:* www.sourcemed.net	Birmingham	AL	35243	866-245-8093	
South Point Systems Inc 1019 Us Hwy 431 *Web:* www.southpoint.net	Boaz	AL	35957	256-593-1337	
Southern Data Systems Inc 1245 Land O Lakes Dr *Web:* www.southern-data.com	Roswell	GA	30075	770-993-7103	
Sparta Consulting Inc 111 Woodmere Rd Ste 200 *Web:* www.spartaconsulting.com	Folsom	CA	95630	916-985-0300	
Spectrum Data Inc 131 N Third St *Web:* www.spectrumdata.org	Oregon	IL	61061	815-732-6567	
Splashdot Inc 609 Hastings St W *Web:* www.splashdot.com	Vancouver	BC	V6B4W4	604-899-0597	
SportsDirect Inc 211 Horseshoe Lk Dr *Web:* www.sportsdirectinc.com	Halifax	NS	B3S1E1	902-835-3320	
SQAD Inc 303 S Broadway Ste 210 *Web:* www.sqad.com	Tarrytown	NY	10591	914-524-7600	
SRA OSS Inc 5300 Stevens Creek Blvd Ste 460 *Web:* www.sraoss.com	San Jose	CA	95129	408-855-8200	
SRB Education Solutions Inc 200 Town Centre Blvd Ste 400 *Web:* www.srbeducationsolutions.com	Markham	ON	L3R8G5	905-943-7706	943-7713
Standard Data Corp 26 Journal Sq *Web:* www.standarddata.com	Jersey City	NJ	07306	201-533-4433	533-8236
Stark Services 12444 Victory Blvd Third Fl *Web:* www.starkservices.com	North Hollywood	CA	91606	818-985-2003	
Statco 8870 Business Park Dr *Web:* www.statco.com	Austin	TX	78759	512-795-5000	
Steadfast Networks Inc 350 E Cermak Rd Ste 240 *Web:* www.steadfast.net	Chicago	IL	60616	312-602-2689	
Stockgroup Media Inc 750 W Pender St Ste 500 *Web:* www.stockhouse.com	Vancouver	BC	V6C2T7	604-331-0995	
Storm Internet Services Inc 1760 Courtwood Crescent *Web:* www.storm.ca	Ottawa	ON	K2C2B5	613-567-6585	567-3227
Stratagem Inc 10922 N Cedarburg Rd *Web:* www.stratagemconsulting.com	Mequon	WI	53092	262-532-2700	
Strategic Power Systems Inc 11016 Rushmore Dr Frenette Bldg Ste 275 *Web:* www.spsinc.com	Charlotte	NC	28277	704-544-5501	
StreamingEdge (USA) Inc 75 Park Pl 4-th Fl *Web:* www.streamingedge.com	New York	NY	10007	212-791-6026	
Strictly Technology LLC 5381 nw 33rd ave *Web:* www.strictlyeducation.com	Fort Lauderdale	FL	33309	954-606-5440	
SunGard Data Systems Inc 680 E Swedesford Rd **Fax Area Code: 740* ■ *TF:* 866-264-4829 ■ *Web:* www.sungard.com	Wayne	PA	19087	800-468-7483	376-7112*
Sunhillo Corp 444 Kelley Dr *Web:* www.sunhillo.com	West Berlin	NJ	08091	856-767-7676	
Sunrise Systems Inc 16 Pearl St Ste 101 *Web:* www.sunrisesys.com	Metuchen	NJ	08840	732-603-2200	
SupraNet Communications Inc 8000 Excelsior Dr *Web:* www.supranet.net	Madison	WI	53717	608-836-0282	
Syclone Designs Inc 32 Jack Heard Dr Ste 200 *Web:* syclone.net	Dawsonville	GA	30534	706-265-4394	
symplr 616 Cypress Creek Pkwy Ste 800 *Web:* www.vcsdatabase.com	Houston	TX	77090	281-863-9500	
Synergon Solutions Inc 1335 Gateway Dr *Web:* www.synergon.net	Melbourne	FL	32901	321-728-2674	
Synergy Networks Inc 10970 S Cleveland Ave Ste 406 *Web:* www.snworks.com	Fort Myers	FL	33907	239-790-7000	
Systems House, The 1033 Us Hwy 46 Ste A202 *Web:* tshinc.com	Clifton	NJ	07013	973-777-8050	
Systems Insight Inc 514 Madison Ave 200 *Web:* www.systemsinsight.com	Covington	KY	41011	859-291-9026	
Systemsmith Inc 18436 Hawthorne Blvd #208 *Web:* cognistix.com	Torrance	CA	90504	310-921-2735	
TAG Online Inc Six Prospect Village Plz First Fl *Web:* www.tagonline.com	Clifton	NJ	07013	973-783-5583	
Talario LLC 815 Medary Ave *Web:* www.talario.com	Brookings	SD	57006	605-692-9877	
Tango Media Group 326 Carlaw Ave *Web:* www.tangomediagroup.com	Toronto	ON	M4M3N8	416-204-6269	
Taskstream LLC 71 W 23rd St *TF:* 800-311-5656 ■ *Web:* taskstream.com	New York	NY	10010	212-868-2700	
Tax Management Associates Inc 2225 Coronation Blvd *Web:* www.tma1.com	Charlotte	NC	28227	704-847-1234	
TDEC 8120 Woodmont Ave Ste 550 *Web:* www.tdec.com	Bethesda	MD	20814	301-718-0703	718-1615
TechSkills LLC 108 Wild Basin Rd Ste 150 *Web:* www.techskills.com	Austin	TX	78746	512-328-4235	
Techsmart Solutions Inc 305 W Magnolia St 218 *Web:* onlinepchelp.com	Fort Collins	CO	80521	970-498-0808	

				Phone	Fax
Techsol4u Inc 95 w 11th st *Web:* www.techsol4u.com	Tracy	CA	95376	209-833-3212	
Techware Distribution Inc 7720 W 78th St. *TF:* 800-295-0083 ■ *Web:* www.techwaredist.com	Minneapolis	MN	55439	952-944-0083	
Tecnicard Inc 3191 Coral Way Ste 800 *TF:* 800-317-6020 ■ *Web:* www.tecnicard.com	Miami	FL	33145	305-442-0018	442-9937
Telecom Ottawa Ltd 100 Maple Grove Rd *Web:* www.telecomottawa.com	Ottawa	ON	K2V1B8	613-225-4631	
Telehouse International Corporation of America Inc The Teleport 7 Teleport Dr. *Web:* telehouse.com	Staten Island	NY	10311	718-355-2500	
Telesto Group LLC 1060 State Rd Ste 102 *Web:* www.telestogroup.com	Princeton	NJ	08540	609-503-4201	
Telogical Systems LLC 7900 Westpark Dr *Web:* telogicalsystems.com	Mclean	VA	22102	703-734-7776	
Teradata Corp 10000 Innovation Dr. *NYSE: TDC* ■ *TF:* 866-548-8348 ■ *Web:* in.teradata.com	Dayton	OH	45342	866-548-8348	
TigerLead Solutions LLC 1554 S Sepulveda Blvd Ste 102 *Web:* www.tigerlead.com	Los Angeles	CA	90025	310-312-9800	
Timberlake Membership Software LLC 11230 Waples Mill Rd Ste 105 *Web:* www.timberlakepublishing.com	Fairfax	VA	22030	703-591-4232	
Total Immersion Software Inc One Enterprise Pkwy Ste 330	Hampton	VA	23666	757-224-6250	
Townsend Security 724 columbia st nw *Web:* townsendsecurity.com	Olympia	WA	98501	360-359-4400	
TPG Marine Enterprises LLC 212 W Tenth St Ste D-395 *Web:* www.tpgmarine.com	Indianapolis	IN	46202	317-631-0234	
Trend 660 American Ave Ste 203 *Web:* www.trendmls.com	King Of Prussia	PA	19406	610-783-4650	
Tribal Nova Inc 4200 Boul Saint-Laurent Ste 1203 *Web:* www.tribalnova.com	Montreal	QC	H2W2R2	514-598-0444	
TriTech Enterprise Systems Inc 1869 Brightseat Rd *Web:* www.tritechenterprise.com	Hyattsville	MD	20785	301-918-8250	
Triton-Tek Inc 445 W Erie St Ste 208 *TF:* 866-387-4866 ■ *Web:* www.triton-tek.com	Chicago	IL	60654	312-467-9201	
Triveni Digital Inc 40 Washington Rd *Web:* www.trivenidigital.com	Princeton Junction	NJ	08550	609-716-3500	716-3503
UDP Inc 2426 Cee Gee *Web:* udp.com	San Antonio	TX	78217	210-828-6171	
Ultra Logistics Inc 17-17 Rt 208 N Ste 160 *Web:* www.ultralogistics.com	Fair Lawn	NJ	07410	201-703-5110	
Unicon Group Ltd 1734 Gilsinn Ln. *Web:* www.unicongl.com	St. Louis	MO	63026	636-394-2012	
UniFocus LP 2455 McIver Ln *Web:* www.unifocus.com	Carrollton	TX	75006	972-512-5000	
UnitedLayer Inc 200 Paul Ave Ste 110 *Web:* www.unitedlayer.com	San Francisco	CA	94124	415-349-2100	
Uptick Marketing Inc 201 Summit Pkwy *Web:* www.infomedia.com	Birmingham	AL	35209	205-823-4440	
Urban Web Design 102-19 Dallas Rd *Web:* urbanweb.net	Victoria	BC	V8V5A6	250-380-1296	
US Alliance Group Inc 30052 Aventura Ste B *Web:* www.usag-inc.com	Rancho Santa Margarita	CA	92688	949-888-4408	
US Internet Corp 12450 Wayzata Blvd Ste 224 *Web:* www.usinternet.com	Minnetonka	MN	55305	952-253-3262	
V-fluence Interactive Public Realtions Inc 7770 Regents Rd *Web:* www.v-fluence.com	San Diego	CA	92122	858-453-9900	
Valley Techlogic Inc 261 Business Park Way *Web:* www.valleytechlogic.com	Atwater	CA	95301	209-384-8324	
Vam USA LLC 19210 Hardy Rd *TF:* 800-634-6612 ■ *Web:* www.vam-usa.com	Houston	TX	77041	713-479-3200	
Vangent Inc 4250 N Fairfax Dr	Arlington	VA	22203	703-284-5600	284-5628
VEITS Group LLC 425 Metro Pl N Ste 330 *Web:* www.veitsgroup.com	Dublin	OH	43017	614-467-5414	
Versasuite 13401 Pond Springs Rd *Web:* www.unisoftinc.com	Austin	TX	78729	512-249-8774	
Versatile Systems Inc 19105 36th Ave W Ste 213 *NYSE: CVE* ■ **Fax Area Code:* 425 ■ *Web:* www.versatile.com	Lynnwood	WA	98036	800-262-1622	778-8577*
Vertafore Inc 11724 NE 195th St. *TF:* 800-444-4813 ■ *Web:* www.vertafore.com	Bothell	WA	98011	425-402-1000	402-9569
Virtual Technology Services LLC 806 W Curtis Dr *Web:* www.vts-llc.com	Midwest City	OK	73110	405-733-3500	
VISI Inc 10290 W 70th St. *Web:* www.visi.com	Minneapolis	MN	55344	612-395-9000	
Visicom Media Inc 6200 Blvd Taschereau Ste 304 *Web:* software.visicommedia.com	Brossard	QC	J4W3J8	450-672-0401	
Visionet Systems Inc Four Cedarbrook Dr Bldg B *Web:* www.visionetsystems.com	Cranbury	NJ	08512	609-452-0700	
Visp.net 301 NE Sixth St. *Web:* www.visp.net	Grants Pass	OR	97526	541-955-6900	
VITAL Network Services Inc 14520 McCormick Dr. *Web:* www.vital-ns.com	Tampa	FL	33626	813-818-5100	
Vitamin Usa LLC 1809 S Main St Ste 1 *Web:* www.vitaminusa.com	Findlay	OH	45840	419-423-9875	
VP Solutions Inc 929 Worcester Rd *Web:* www.vpsi.com	Framingham	MA	01701	508-370-0388	
WAND Inc 820 16th St Ste 605 *Web:* www.wandinc.com	Denver	CO	80202	303-623-1200	
Web Age Solutions Inc 439 University Ave Ste 820 *TF:* 866-206-4644 ■ *Web:* www.webagesolutions.com	Toronto	ON	M5G1Y8	866-206-4644	
Web Direct Brands Inc 13100 State Rd 54 *Web:* www.webdirectbrands.com	Odessa	FL	33556	813-920-7259	
Web Full Circle Inc 207 Regncy Ex Pk Dr Ste 150 *Web:* www.webfullcircle.com	Charlotte	NC	28217	980-322-0518	
Web Your Business Inc 1714 Topaz Dr 145 *Web:* www.webyourbusiness.com	Loveland	CO	80537	970-593-6260	
WebLinc LLC 22 S Third St Second Fl *Web:* weblinc.com	Philadelphia	PA	19106	215-925-1800	
WebLink International Inc 3905 W Vincennes Rd Ste 210 *Web:* www.weblinkinternational.com	Indianapolis	IN	46268	317-872-3909	
WebmasterWorld Inc 3801 N Capital of Texas Hwy e240-181 *Web:* www.webmasterworld.com	Austin	TX	78746	512-231-8107	
WebRing Inc 500 A St Ste 2 *Web:* www.webring.com	Ashland	OR	97520	541-488-9895	
WebWisdom.com Inc Syracuse Technology Garden 235 Harrison St Ste 303 *Web:* www.collabworx.com	Syracuse	NY	13202	315-579-4330	
Welsh Consulting 31 Milk St Ste 805 *Web:* www.welsh.com	Boston	MA	02109	617-695-9800	
Wesucceed Solutions Inc 175 Olde Haof Day *Web:* www.wesucceed.com	Lincolnshire	IL	60069	847-229-8130	
WhippleHill Communications Inc Five E Point Dr Bldg C *Web:* www.whipplehill.com	Bedford	NH	03110	603-669-5979	
WiBand Communications Corp 187 Commerce Dr. **Fax Area Code:* 780 ■ *Web:* www.wiband.com	Winnipeg	MB	R3P1A2	204-633-6333	430-4079*
Williams Records Management 1925 E Vernon Ave *TF Cust Svc:* 800-207-3267 ■ *Web:* www.williamsdatamanagement.com	Los Angeles	CA	90058	323-234-3453	233-5451
Winbeam Inc 302 W Otterman St *Web:* www.winbeam.com	Greensburg	PA	15601	724-219-0400	
WinterGreen Research Inc Six Raymond St *Web:* www.wintergreenresearch.com	Lexington	MA	02421	781-863-5078	
WisdomTools LLC 501 N Morton St Indiana University Research Pk Ste 206 *Web:* www.wisdomtools.com	Bloomington	IN	47404	812-856-4202	
Wisetek Providers Inc 11211 Waples Mill Rd *Web:* www.wisepro.com	Fairfax	VA	22030	703-766-8850	
WMW Communications Inc 135 N Magnolia Ave Ste D *Web:* www.ao.net	Orlando	FL	32801	407-895-1200	
Woodberry Graphics 11110 Pepper Rd Ste J *Web:* www.woodberrygraphics.com	Hunt Valley	MD	21031	410-584-9790	
Woodwing Usa 615 Griswold St Ste 1800 *Web:* www.woodwing.com	Detroit	MI	48226	313-962-0542	
Worldwide Revenue Solutions Inc 555 Republic Dr Ste 440 *Web:* www.wrsol.com	Plano	TX	75074	972-424-2200	
Wrightsoft Corp 131 Hartwell Ave *TF:* 800-225-8697 ■ *Web:* www.wrightsoft.com	Lexington	MA	02421	800-225-8697	
XE.com Inc 1145 Nicholson Rd Ste 200 *Web:* www.xe.com	Newmarket	ON	L3Y9C3	416-214-5606	
Xiologix 8215 SW Tualatin Sherwood *Web:* xiologix.com	Tualatin	OR	97062	503-691-4364	
Yakabod Inc Two N Market St Ste 300 *Web:* www.yakabod.com	Frederick	MD	21701	301-662-4554	
Z3 Technologies Inc 11400 W Bluemond Rd *Web:* www.z3tech.com	Wauwatosa	WI	53226	414-607-9767	
Z57 Internet Solutions 10045 Mesa Rim Rd **Fax Area Code:* 858 ■ *TF:* 800-899-8148 ■ *Web:* www.z57.com	San Diego	CA	92121	800-899-8148	869-9931*
Zapata Technology Inc 1450 Greene St Ste 500 *Web:* www.zapatatechnology.com	Augusta	GA	30901	706-955-4809	
Zedo Inc 850 Montgomery St Ste 150 *Web:* zedo.com	San Francisco	CA	94133	415-348-1975	
Zedx Inc 369 Rolling Ridge Dr *Web:* www.zedxinc.com	Bellefonte	PA	16823	814-357-8490	
Zion Software LLC 2842 Main St Ste 325 *Web:* www.zionsoftware.com	Glastonbury	CT	06033	860-432-6258	
ZirMed Inc 888 W Market St. *Web:* methodcare.com	Louisvill	KY	40202	312-787-7376	

229 DATING SERVICES

				Phone	Fax
50000 Feet Inc 1700 W Irving Park Rd Ste 110 *Web:* www.50000feet.com	Chicago	IL	60613	773-529-6760	
A Total Tan 1400 Teal Rd Ste 4 *Web:* atotaltan.net	Lafayette	IN	47905	765-474-1514	
AA Party Rentals Inc 6404 216th St SW *Web:* www.aaparty.com	Mountlake Terrace	WA	98043	425-640-5547	
Adventure Quest Laser Tag 1200 S Clearview Pkwy Ste 1106 *Web:* www.lasertagnola.com	New Orleans	LA	70123	504-207-4444	
Aloha United Way Inc 200 N Vineyard Blvd Ste 700 *Web:* www.auw.org	Honolulu	HI	96817	808-536-1951	
Art Craft Display Inc 500 Business Centre Dr *Web:* artcraftdisplay.com	Lansing	MI	48917	517-485-2221	
ASA Entertainment LLC 201 N Riverside Dr Ste C *Web:* www.asaentertainment.com	Indialantic	FL	32903	321-722-9300	

				Phone	Fax
Ashley Madison Agency, The 2300 Yonge St *Web:* www.ashleymadison.com	Toronto	ON	M4P1E4	416-483-1317	
Atom Group LLC, The 125 Brewery Ln Ste 6 *Web:* www.theatomgroup.com	Portsmouth	NH	03801	603-501-0003	
Austin Enviro Group 6802 Manzanita St *Web:* www.aegaustin.com	Austin	TX	78759	512-913-0077	
Balnea Spa 319 chemin du Lac Gale *Web:* www.balnea.ca	Bromont-sur-le-lac	QC	J2L2S5	450-534-0604	
Beckers Tax Service & Financial Management Company Inc 7010 Champions Plz Dr *Web:* tenfortyplus.com	Houston	TX	77069	281-397-7777	
Buffalo Design Collaborative Group, The 443 Delaware Ave Fl 2 *Web:* www.schneiderdesign.com	Buffalo	NY	14202	716-923-7000	
Caledon Laboratories Ltd 40 Armstrong Ave *Web:* www.caledonlabs.com	Georgetown	ON	L7G4R9	905-877-0101	
Cambridge Credit Counseling Corp 67 Hunt St *Web:* www.cambridge-credit.org	Agawam	MA	01001	413-821-8900	
Cantey Hanger LLP 600 W Sixth St Ste 300 *Web:* www.canteyhanger.com	Fort Worth	TX	76102	817-877-2863	
Carbon Design Systems Inc 125 Nagog Park *Web:* www.carbondesignsystems.com	Acton	MA	01720	978-264-7300	
Career Training Education 970 Klamath Ln *Web:* www.sutter.k12.ca.us	Yuba City	CA	95993	530-822-5120	
Cfj Manufacturing 5001 N Fwy Ste E *Web:* www.cfjmanufacturinglp.com	Fort Worth	TX	76106	817-625-9559	
Clinic of Distinctive 638 11 Ave Sw *Web:* distinctivetherapy.com	Calgary	AB	T2R0E2	403-294-0036	
Clink Events LLC 3006 Bee Cave Rd Ste C-250 *Web:* www.clinkevents.com	Austin	TX	78746	512 236-0264	
Cornerstar Inc 10145 Nw Ash St *Web:* www.cornerstar.com	Portland	OR	97229	503-546-0500	
Corvallis Peter Productions 2200 N Interstate Ave *Web:* www.petercorvallis.com	Portland	OR	97227	503-222-1665	
Counterparts LLC 2012 N 117th Ave Ste 105 *Web:* www.mycounterparts.com	Omaha	NE	68164	402-932-2220	
Creative Monograms 122 N 30th St *Web:* www.creativemonograms.com	Billings	MT	59101	406-259-9925	
Des Moines Golf & Country Club Educational Corp 1600 Jordan Creek Pkwy *Web:* www.dmgcc.org	West Des Moines	IA	50266	515-440-7500	
Digiscribe International LLC 150 Clearbrook Rd Ste 125 *TF:* 800-686-7577 ■ *Web:* www.digiscribe.info	Elmsford	NY	10523	800-686-7577	
Eharmony.com Inc 2401 Colorado Ave *Web:* www.eharmony.com	Santa Monica	CA	90404	424-258-1199	
Elle K Associates Inc 11900 Castlegate Ct *Web:* ellekassociates.com	Rockville	MD	20852	301-984-4494	
Equal Vision Records 136 Fuller Rd *Web:* www.equalvision.com	Albany	NY	12205	518-458-8250	
Express Immigration & Paralegal Services 10143 Sepulveda Blvd *Web:* www.expressimmigration.org	Mission Hills	CA	91345	818-894-4611	
Fandango Productions LLC 4601 Hollins Ferry Rd *Web:* www.fandangoevents.com	Baltimore	MD	21227	410-539-7236	
Fine Hospitality Group LLC 545 W Lambert Rd Ste D *Web:* www.finehospitality.com	Brea	CA	92821	714-990-8800	
Forest Preserve Dist of Dupage County 1717 31st St *Web:* www.dupageforest.com	Oak Brook	IL	60523	630-616-8424	
Friendfinder Network Inc 6800 Broken Sound Pkwy Ste 200 *TSE:* FFN ■ *TF:* 800-388-0760 ■ *Web:* ffn.com	Boca Raton	FL	33487	561-912-7000	912-7038
Gloria Ferrer Caves & Vineyards 23555 Arnold Dr *Web:* www.gloriaferrer.com	Sonoma	CA	95476	707-996-7256	
Great Expectations 14180 Dallas Pkwy Ste 100 *Web:* www.ge-dating.com	Dallas	TX	75254	972-448-7900	448-7969
Hartmann Studios Inc 100 W Ohio Ave *Web:* www.hartmannstudios.com	Richmond	CA	94804	510-232-5030	
Herlache Enterprises 6417 W 87th St Ste 3 *Web:* telassist.com	Oak Lawn	IL	60453	708-430-1440	
Hirease Inc 695 S Bennett St *Web:* www.hirease.com	Southern Pines	NC	28387	910-693-1764	
iGov Technologies Inc 9211 Palm River Rd Ste 110 *Web:* www.igov.com	Tampa	FL	33619	813-612-9470	
Intersyn Technologies LP 2736 Albans *Web:* www.intersyn.com	Houston	TX	77005	713-866-4808	
It's Just Lunch! Inc 101 W Grand Ave Ste 501 *Web:* www.itsjustlunch.com	Chicago	IL	60611	312-644-9999	
Jepson Technologies Inc 14526 Weddington St Apt 102 *Web:* jepsontech.com	Sherman Oaks	CA	91411	818-990-0601	
Joester Loria Group Inc, The 860 Broadway Third Fl *Web:* joesterloriagroup.com	New York	NY	10003	212-683-5150	
M Eg Enterprises 262 W Broadway *Web:* www.meg-enterprises.com	Waukesha	WI	53186	262-522-3220	
MaxVal Group Inc 2251 Grant Rd *Web:* www.maxval.com	Los Altos	CA	94024	650-472-0644	
MEMStaff Inc Eight Pine St *Web:* www.memstaff.com	Newburyport	MA	01950	617-996-9263	
MerlinOne Inc 17 Whitney Rd *Web:* www.merlinone.com	Quincy	MA	02169	617-328-6645	
Momentum Inc 1520 Fourth Ave Ste 300 *Web:* www.momentumbuilds.com	Seattle	WA	98101	206-267-1900	
Murphy Harpst Children's Centers 338 W Third St Sw *Web:* murphyharpst.org	Rome	GA	30165	706-232-5663	
Nexus Business Solutions 157 S Kalamazoo Mall Dr Ste 105 *Web:* www.nexusbusiness.com	Kalamazoo	MI	49007	269-373-1500	
Noerr Programs Corp, The 6632 Fig St *Web:* www.noerrprograms.com	Arvada	CO	80004	303-642-7147	
Nvms Inc 9255 Center St Ste 200 *Web:* www.nvms.com	Manassas	VA	20110	703-361-6262	
Omni Cubed Inc 1390 Broadway Ste B155 *TF:* 877-311-1976 ■ *Web:* omnicubed.com	Placerville	CA	95667	877-311-1976	
Ownersite Technologies LLC 1425 Market Blvd Ste 330-179 *Web:* www.ownersite.com	Roswell	GA	30076	404-402-7117	
People Skills International 2910 Baily Ave *Web:* www.idagreene.com	San Diego	CA	92105	619-262-9951	
Promocentric Inc 102 Tide Mill Rd Ste 1 *Web:* www.promocentric.net	Hampton	NH	03842	603-758-6377	
Psychic Readings by Sylvia 546 Rogers St *Web:* www.keen.com	Lowell	MA	01852	978-937-0998	
Realhome.com Inc 1100 Summer St *Web:* www.ahahome.com	Stamford	CT	06905	203-323-7715	
Red Lodge Mountain Resort 305 Ski Run Rd *Web:* m.redlodgemountain.com	Red Lodge	MT	59068	406-446-2610	
Seva Technologies LLC 1618 Mahan Ctr Blvd *Web:* www.sevatechnologies.com	Tallahassee	FL	32308	850-391-4832	
Siena Engineering Group Inc 50 Mall Rd Ste 203 *Web:* sienaengineeringgroup.com	Burlington	MA	01803	781-221-8400	
Smi Travel Inc 1170 Nikki View Dr *Web:* smitrav.com	Brandon	FL	33511	813-315-9840	
Solomon Group 825 Girod St *Web:* www.solomongroup.com	New Orleans	LA	70113	504-252-4500	
Spa Douce Heure 110 338 Rte *Web:* www.spadouceheure.com	Les Coteaux	QC	J7X1A2	450-267-4949	
Spark Networks PLC 8383 Wilshire Blvd Ste 800 *NYSE:* LOV ■ *Web:* www.spark.net	Beverly Hills	CA	90211	323-836-3000	
Spring Meadows Golf Cntry Clb 59 Lewiston Rd *Web:* www.springmeadowsgolf.com	Gray	ME	04039	207-657-2586	
Stoelt Productions 6464 W Sunset Blvd Ste 830 *Web:* www.stoeltproductions.com	Los Angeles	CA	90028	323-463-3700	
Sunrise Wood Designs 720 107th St *Web:* sunrisewooddesigns.com	Arlington	TX	76011	817-701-4101	
Synch-Solutions Inc 211 W Wacker Dr Ste 300 *Web:* www.synch-solutions.com	Chicago	IL	60606	312-252-3700	
Tarrytown House Estate & Conference Center 49 E Sunnyside Ln *Web:* www.tarrytownhouseestate.com	Tarrytown	NY	10591	914-591-8200	
Tauber-Arons Inc 13848 Ventura Blvd *Web:* www.tauberaronsinc.com	Sherman Oaks	CA	91423	323-851-2008	
U.S. Claims Services Inc 3801 Pegasus Dr Ste 101 *Web:* www.usclaimsservices.com	Bakersfield	CA	93308	661-399-1108	
United Human Capital Solutions One Centerpointe Dr Ste 345 *Web:* www.uhcsolutions.com	Lake Oswego	OR	97035	503-443-6008	
Veer Right Management Group Inc 3195 Airport Blvd Nw Ste D *Web:* www.veerright.com	Wilson	NC	27896	252-237-5900	
Vulcan Value Partners LLC Three Protective Ctr 2801 Hwy 280 S Ste 300 *Web:* www.vulcanvaluepartners.com	Birmingham	AL	35223	205-803-1582	
Wedding Experience 2600 Sw Third Ave Ste 200 *Web:* www.theweddingexperience.com	Miami	FL	33129	305-421-1260	
William Charles Executive Search Partners 5550 Cascade Rd Se Ste 200 *Web:* www.william-charles.com	Grand Rapids	MI	49546	616-464-4355	
Wine Country Party & Events LLC 22674 Broadway Ste A *Web:* www.winecountryparty.com	Sonoma	CA	95476	707-940-6060	
World Class Incentives 426 N Rand Rd *Web:* www.worldclassincentives.com	North Barrington	IL	60010	847-381-1800	
Z 2 Systems 7151 W Gunnison St Apt W *Web:* www.z2systems.com	Harwood Heights	IL	60706	708-867-8181	

230 DENTAL ASSOCIATIONS - STATE

SEE ALSO Health & Medical Professionals Associations p. 1796

				Phone	Fax
Alabama Dental Assn 836 Washington Ave *Web:* www.aldaonline.org	Montgomery	AL	36104	334-265-1684	262-6218
Alaska Dental Society 9170 Jewel Lake Rd Ste 203 *Web:* www.akdental.org	Anchorage	AK	99502	907-563-3003	563-3009
Arizona Dental Assn 3193 N Drinkwater Blvd *TF:* 800-866-2732 ■ *Web:* www.azda.org	Scottsdale	AZ	85251	480-344-5777	344-1442
Arkansas State Dental Assn 7480 Hwy 107 Ste 205 *Web:* www.arkansasdentistry.org	Sherwood	AR	72120	501-834-7650	834-7657
California Dental Assn 1201 K St *TF:* 800-736-7071 ■ *Web:* www.cda.org	Sacramento	CA	95853	916-443-0505	443-2943
Colorado Dental Assn 3690 S Yosemite St Ste 400 *TF:* 866-777-4771 ■ *Web:* www.cdaonline.org	Denver	CO	80237	303-740-6900	740-7989
Delaware State Dental Society 200 Continental Dr Ste 111 *Web:* www.delawarestatedentalsociety.org	Newark	DE	19713	302-368-7634	368-7669

	City	State	Zip	Phone	Fax
District of Columbia Dental Society 502 C St NE	Washington	DC	20002	202-547-7613	546-1482
Web: www.dcdental.org					
Florida Dental Assn 1111 E Tennessee St	Tallahassee	FL	32308	850-681-3629	561-0504
TF: 800-877-9922 ■ *Web:* www.floridadental.org					
Georgia Dental Assn 7000 Peachtree Dnwdy Rd NE Ste 200 Bldg 17	Atlanta	GA	30328	404-636-7553	633-3943
TF: 800-432-4357 ■ *Web:* www.gadental.org					
Hawaii Dental Assn 1345 S Beretania St Ste 301	Honolulu	HI	96814	808-593-7956	593-7636
TF: 800-359-6725 ■ *Web:* www.hawaiidentalassociation.net					
Idaho State Dental Assn 1220 W Hays St	Boise	ID	83702	208-343-7543	
Web: theisda.org					
Illinois State Dental Society 1010 S Second St	Springfield	IL	62704	217-525-1406	525-8872
TF: 888-286-2447 ■ *Web:* www.isds.org					
Indiana Dental Assn 401 W Michigan St	Indianapolis	IN	46202	317-634-2610	634-2612
TF: 800-562-5646 ■ *Web:* www.indental.org					
Iowa Dental Assn 8797 NW 54th Ave Ste 100	Johnston	IA	50131	515-331-2298	334-8007
TF: 800-828-2181 ■ *Web:* www.iowadental.org					
Louisiana Dental Assn 7833 Office Pk Blvd	Baton Rouge	LA	70809	225-926-1986	926-1886
TF: 800-388-6642 ■ *Web:* www.ladental.org					
Maine Dental Assn 29 Assn Dr	Manchester	ME	04351	207-622-7900	
Web: www.medental.org					
Maryland State Dental Assn 6410 Dobbin Rd	Columbia	MD	21045	410-964-2880	964-0583
Web: www.msda.com					
Massachusetts Dental Society Two Willow St Ste 200	Southborough	MA	01745	508-480-9797	480-0002
TF: 800-342-8747 ■ *Web:* www.massdental.org					
Michigan Dental Assn 3657 Okemos Rd Ste 200	Okemos	MI	48864	517-372-9070	372-0008*
**Fax:* PR ■ *TF:* 800-589-2632 ■ *Web:* www.smilemichigan.com					
Minnesota Dental Assn 1335 Industrial Blvd Ste 200	Minneapolis	MN	55413	612-767-8400	767-8500
TF: 800-950-3368 ■ *Web:* www.mndental.org					
Mississippi Dental Assn 2630 Ridgewood Rd Ste C	Jackson	MS	39216	601-982-0442	366-3050
TF: 866-982-0442 ■ *Web:* www.msdental.org					
Missouri Dental Assn 3340 American Ave	Jefferson City	MO	65109	573-634-3436	635-0764
TF: 800-688-1907 ■ *Web:* www.modental.org					
Montana Dental Assn 17 1/2 S Last Chance Gulch PO Box 1154	Helena	MT	59624	406-443-2061	443-1546
TF: 800-257-4988 ■ *Web:* www.mtdental.com					
Nebraska Dental Assn 7160 S 29th St Ste 1	Lincoln	NE	68516	402-476-1704	476-2641
TF: 888-789-2614 ■ *Web:* www.nedental.org					
Nevada Dental Assn 8863 W Flamingo Rd Ste 102	Las Vegas	NV	89147	702-255-4211	255-3302
TF: 800-962-6710 ■ *Web:* www.nvda.org					
New Hampshire Dental Society 23 S State St	Concord	NH	03301	603-225-5961	226-4880
Web: www.nhds.org					
New Jersey Dental Assn 1 Dental Plaza PO Box 6020	North Brunswick	NJ	08902	732-821-9400	821-1082
Web: www.njda.org					
New Mexico Dental Assn 9201 Montgomery Blvd NE Ste 601	Albuquerque	NM	87111	505-294-1368	294-9958
TF: 888-997-2583 ■ *Web:* www.nmdental.org					
New York State Dental Assn 20 Corporate Woods Blvd #602	Albany	NY	12211	518-465-0044	465-3219
TF: 800-255-2100 ■ *Web:* www.nysdental.org					
North Carolina Dental Society 1600 Evans Rd	Cary	NC	27513	919-677-1396	677-1397
TF: 800-662-8754 ■ *Web:* www.ncdental.org					
North Dakota Dental Assn PO Box 1332	Bismarck	ND	58502	701-223-8870	223-0855
TF: 800-444-1330 ■ *Web:* www.nddental.com					
Ohio Dental Assn 1370 Dublin Rd	Columbus	OH	43215	614-486-2700	486-0381
TF: 800-497-6076 ■ *Web:* www.oda.org					
Oklahoma Dental Assn 317 NE 13th St	Oklahoma City	OK	73104	405-848-8873	848-8875
TF: 800-876-8890 ■ *Web:* www.okda.org					
Oregon Dental Assn PO Box 3710	Wilsonville	OR	97070	503-620-3230	218-2009
TF: 800-452-5628 ■ *Web:* www.oregondental.org					
Pennsylvania Dental Assn 3501 N Front St	Harrisburg	PA	17110	717-234-5941	232-7169
Web: www.padental.org					
Riverside Dental Group 7251 Magnolia Ave	Riverside	CA	92504	951-689-5031	813-9510
Web: www.riversidedentalgroup.com					
South Carolina Dental Assn 120 Stonemark Ln	Columbia	SC	29210	803-750-2277	750-1644
TF: 800-327-2598 ■ *Web:* www.scda.org					
South Dakota Dental Assn 804 N Euclid Ave Ste 103	Pierre	SD	57501	605-224-9133	224-9168
TF: 866-551-8023 ■ *Web:* www.sddental.org					
Tennessee Dental Assn (TDA) 660 Bakers Bridge Ave Ste 300	Franklin	TN	37067	615-628-0208	
Web: www.tenndental.org					
Texas Dental Assn 1946 S IH-35 Ste 400	Austin	TX	78704	512-443-3675	443-3031
TF: 800-832-1145 ■ *Web:* www.tda.org					
Utah Dental Assn 1151 East 3900 South Ste 160	Salt Lake City	UT	84124	801-261-5315	261-1235
Vermont State Dental Society 100 Dorset St Ste 18	South Burlington	VT	05403	802-864-0115	864-0116
TF: 800-300-3046 ■ *Web:* www.vsds.org					
Virginia Dental Assn (VDA) 3460 Mayland Ct Ste 110	Richmond	VA	23233	804-288-5750	288-1880
TF: 877-726-0850 ■ *Web:* www.vadental.org					
West Virginia Dental Assn 2016 1/2 Kanawha Blvd E	Charleston	WV	25311	304-344-5246	344-5316
Web: www.wvdental.org					
Wisconsin Dental Assn 6737 W Washington St Ste 2360	West Allis	WI	53214	414-276-4520	864-2997*
**Fax Area Code:* 800 ■ *TF:* 800-364-7646 ■ *Web:* www.wda.org					
Wyoming Dental Assn (WYDA) 259 S Ctr Ste 201	Casper	WY	82601	307-237-1186	237-1186
Web: www.wyda.org					

231 DENTAL EQUIPMENT & SUPPLIES - MFR

	City	State	Zip	Phone	Fax
3D Medical Manufacturing Inc 1006 W 15th St	Riviera Beach	FL	33404	561-842-7175	
Web: www.3dmedicalmfg.com					
3M ESPE Dental Products Div 3M Ctr Bldg 0275-02-SE-03	Saint Paul	MN	55144	651-575-5144	733-2481
TF: 800-634-2249 ■ *Web:* 3m.com					
3M Unitek 2724 Peck Rd	Monrovia	CA	91016	800-634-5300	
TF: 800-634-5300 ■ *Web:* www.3m.com					
A-dec Inc 2601 Crestview Dr	Newberg	OR	97132	503-538-7478	538-0276
TF Cust Svc: 800-547-1883 ■ *Web:* a-dec.com/en					
Accutron Inc 1733 Parkside Ln	Phoenix	AZ	85027	623-780-2020	
TF: 800-531-2221 ■ *Web:* www.accutron-inc.com					
ACTEON North America Inc 124 Gaither Dr Ste 140	Mount Laurel	NJ	08054	856-222-9988	
Web: www.acteongroup.com					
AdDent Inc 43 Miry Brook Rd	Danbury	CT	06810	203-778-0200	
Web: www.addent.com					
Air Techniques Inc 1295 Walt Whitman Rd	Melville	NY	11747	516-433-7676	
TF: 888-247-8481 ■ *Web:* www.airtechniques.com					
Alfa Medical Equipment Specialists Inc 59 Madison Ave	Hempstead	NY	11550	516-489-3855	
Web: www.sterilizers.com					
Align Technology Inc 2560 Orchard Pkwy	San Jose	CA	95131	408-470-1000	470-1010
NASDAQ: ALGN ■ *Web:* www.aligntech.com					
Alpha Pro Tech Ltd 60 Centurian Dr Ste 112	Markham	ON	L3R9R2	905-479-0654	
TF: 800-749-1363 ■ *Web:* www.alphaprotech.com					
Am-touch Dental 28703 Industry Dr	Valencia	CA	91355	661-294-1213	
Web: www.amtouch.com					
American Medical Technologies Inc 5655 Bear Ln	Corpus Christi	TX	78405	361-289-1145	
OTC: ADLI ■ *TF:* 800-359-1959 ■ *Web:* www.americanmedicaltech.com					
American Orthodontics Corp 1714 Cambridge Ave	Sheboygan	WI	53081	920-457-5051	457-1485
TF: 800-558-7687 ■ *Web:* www.americanortho.com					
Argen Corp, The 5855 Oberlin Dr	San Diego	CA	92121	858-455-7900	
Web: www.argen.com					
Arges Imaging Inc 129 N Hill Ave	Pasadena	CA	91106	626-529-3766	
Aribex Inc 744 South 400 East	Orem	UT	84097	801-226-5522	
Web: aribex.com					
Barnhardt Mfg Co 1100 Hawthorne Ln	Charlotte	NC	28205	800-277-0377	342-1892*
**Fax Area Code:* 704 ■ *TF:* 800-277-0377 ■ *Web:* www.barnhardt.net					
Bicon LLC 501 Arborway	Boston	MA	02130	617-524-4443	
TF: 800-882-4266 ■ *Web:* www.bicon.com					
Brasseler USA One Brasseler Blvd	Savannah	GA	31419	800-841-4522	927-8671*
**Fax Area Code:* 912 ■ *TF:* 800-841-4522 ■ *Web:* www.brasselerusa.com					
Buffalo Dental Manufacturing Company Inc 159 Lafayette Dr	Syosset	NY	11791	516-496-7200	
Web: www.buffalodental.com					
Centrix Inc 770 River Rd	Shelton	CT	06484	203-929-5582	
TF: 800-235-5862 ■ *Web:* www.centrixdental.com					
Closure Medical Corp 5250 Greens Dairy Rd	Raleigh	NC	27616	919-876-7800	790-1041
Web: www.closuremed.com					
Coltene/Whaledent Inc 235 Ascot Pkwy	Cuyahoga Falls	OH	44223	330-916-8800	916-7077
TF: 800-221-3046 ■ *Web:* www.coltene.com					
Darby Group Cos Inc 300 Jericho Quad	Jericho	NY	11753	516-683-1800	688-2880
TF: 888-683-5001 ■ *Web:* www.darbygroup.com					
DCI International 305 N Springbrook Rd	Newberg	OR	97132	503-538-8343	
Web: www.dcionline.com					
Den-Mat Corp 2727 Skyway Dr	Santa Maria	CA	93455	805-922-8491	922-6933
TF: 800-433-6628 ■ *Web:* www.denmat.com					
DEN-TAL-EZ Group Inc Two W Liberty Blvd Ste 160	Malvern	PA	19355	610-725-8004	725-9898
TF: 866-383-4636 ■ *Web:* dentalez.com					
DEN-TAL-EZ Inc Equipment Div 2500 Hwy 31 S	Bay Minette	AL	36507	251-937-6781	937-0461
TF: 800-383-4636 ■ *Web:* dentalez.com					
DENTCA Inc 3608 Griffith Ave	Los Angeles	CA	90011	323-232-7505	
Web: www.dentca.com					
DenTek Oral Care Inc 307 Excellence Way	Maryville	TN	37801	865-983-1300	
Web: www.dentek.com					
Dentsply Caulk 38 W Clarke Ave	Milford	DE	19963	302-422-4511	422-3480*
**Fax:* Acctg ■ *TF:* 800-532-2855 ■ *Web:* www.caulk.com					
DENTSPLY International 221 W Philadelphia St P.O. Box 872	York	PA	17405	717-845-7511	
TF: 800-800-2888 ■ *Web:* www.professional.dentsply.com					
Dentsply International Inc 221 W Philadelphia St PO Box 872	York	PA	17405	717-845-7511	849-4762
NASDAQ: XRAY ■ *TF:* 800-877-0020 ■ *Web:* www.dentsply.com					
Dentsply International Inc Rinn Div 1212 Abbott Dr	Elgin	IL	60123	847-742-1115	544-0787*
**Fax Area Code:* 800 ■ *TF:* 800-323-0970 ■ *Web:* www.rinncorp.com					
Dentsply International Inc Tulsa Dental Div 5100 E Skelly Dr Ste 300	Tulsa	OK	74135	918-493-6598	493-6599
TF: 800-662-1202 ■ *Web:* www.tulsadentalspecialties.com					
Dexta Corp 962 Kaiser Rd	Napa	CA	94558	707-255-2454	
Web: www.dexta.com					
Essential Dental Systems Inc 89 Leuning St Ste 8	South Hackensack	NJ	07606	201-487-9090	
Web: www.edsdental.com					
G & H Wire Company Inc 2165 Earlywood Dr	Franklin	IN	46131	317-346-6655	
TF: 800-526-1026 ■ *Web:* www.ghwire.com					
GC America Inc 3737 W 127th St	Alsip	IL	60803	708-597-0900	371-5103*
**Fax:* Cust Svc ■ *TF Cust Svc:* 800-323-7063 ■ *Web:* www.gcamerica.com					
Great Lakes Orthodontic Laboratories Div 200 Cooper Ave	Tonawanda	NY	14150	800-828-7626	
TF: 800-828-7626 ■ *Web:* www.greatlakesortho.com					
Heraeus 300 Heraeus Way	South Bend	IN	46614	800-431-1785	522-1545
TF General: 800-431-1785 ■ *Web:* heraeus-kulzer-us.com					

Phone Fax

Heraeus Kulzer LLC 99 Business Park Dr . . . . Armonk NY 10504 914-219-9000
Web: btnativedirect.com

Hu-Friedy Mfg Company Inc 3232 N Rockwell St . . . . Chicago IL 60618 773-975-6100
TF: 800-483-7433 ■ *Web:* www.hu-friedy.com

Hygenic Corp 1245 Home Ave . . . . Akron OH 44310 330-633-8460 633-9359
TF: 800-321-2135 ■ *Web:* www.hygenic.com

Inter-Med Inc 2200 Northwestern Ave . . . . Racine WI 53404 262-636-9755
Web: www.vista-dental.com

Isolite Systems 111 Castilian Dr . . . . Santa Barbara CA 93117 805-560-9888
TF: 800-560-6066 ■ *Web:* www.isolitesystems.com

Issaquah Dental Lab Inc 640 NW Gilman Blvd . . . . Issaquah WA 98027 425-392-5125
Web: www.issaquah-dl.com

KAB Dental 34842 Mound Rd . . . . Sterling Heights MI 48310 586-983-2502
Web: www.kabdental.com

Keystone Dental Inc 144 Middlesex Tpke . . . . Burlington MA 01803 781-328-3490
TF: 866-902-9272 ■ *Web:* www.keystonedental.com

Kinetic Instrument Inc 17 Berkshire Blvd . . . . Bethel CT 06801 203-743-0080
Web: www.kineticinc.com

Lancer Orthodontics Inc
1493 Poinsettia Bldg 143 . . . . Vista CA 92081 760-744-5585 598-0418
NYSE: LANZ ■ *TF Cust Svc:* 800-854-2896 ■ *Web:* www.lancerortho.com

Lang Dental Manufacturing Co 175 Messner Dr . . . . . . Wheeling IL 60090 847-215-6622
Web: www.langdental.com

LifeCore Biomedical LLC 3515 Lyman Blvd. . . . . Chaska MN 55318 952-368-4300 368-3411
TF Cust Svc: 800-752-2663 ■ *Web:* www.lifecore.com

M & M Innovations 7424 Blythe Island Hwy . . . . Brunswick GA 31523 912-265-7110
TF: 800-688-3384 ■ *Web:* www.drgeorges.com

Metrex Research Corp 1717 W Collins Ave. . . . . Orange CA 92867 714-516-7788
Web: www.metrex.com

Microbrush International Ltd
1376 Cheyenne Ave . . . . Grafton WI 53024 262-375-4011
Web: www.microbrush.com

Midwest Dental Equipment Services & Supplies
2700 Commerce St. . . . . Wichita Falls TX 76301 800-766-2025 551-3514*
**Fax Area Code:* 888 ■ *TF:* 800-766-2025 ■ *Web:* www.mwdental.com

Miltex Inc 589 Davies Dr . . . . York PA 17402 717-840-9335
Web: www.miltex.com

Myotronics-noromed Inc 5870 S 194th St . . . . Kent WA 98032 206-243-4214
TF: 800-426-0316 ■ *Web:* www.myotronics.com

Net32 Inc 250 Towne Village Dr . . . . Cary NC 27513 919-468-1177
TF: 800-517-1997 ■ *Web:* www.net32.com

Nobel Biocare USA Inc
22715 Savi Ranch Pkwy . . . . Yorba Linda CA 92887 714-282-4800 998-9236
TF: 800-993-8100 ■ *Web:* www.nobelbiocare.com

Novalab Group Inc 2350 Power St. . . . . Drummondville QC J2C7Z4 819-474-2580
Web: www.novadent.com

OraMetrix Inc
2350 Campbell Creek Blvd Ste 400 . . . . Richardson TX 75082 972-728-5500
Web: www.orametrix.com

ORMCO Corp 1717 W Collins Ave. . . . . Orange CA 92867 714-516-7400 317-6012*
**Fax Area Code:* 800 ■ *TF Cust Svc:* 800-854-1741 ■ *Web:* www.ormco.com

OrthoAccel Technologies Inc
8275 El Rio St Ste 100 . . . . Houston TX 77054 832-631-1659
Web: www.acceledent.com

Pentron Clinical Technologies LLC
53 N Plains Industrial Rd . . . . Wallingford CT 06492 800-243-3969
TF: 800-243-3969 ■ *Web:* www.pentron.com

Practicon Inc 1112 Sugg Pkwy . . . . Greenville NC 27834 252-752-5183
Web: www.practicon.com

Premier Dental Products Co
1710 Romano Dr PO Box 4500. . . . . Plymouth Meeting PA 19462 610-239-6000 239-6171
TF: 888-773-6872 ■ *Web:* www.premusa.com

PRIMUS Sterilizer Company LLC 6565 S 118th St . . . . Omaha NE 68137 402-344-4200
Web: www.primus-sterilizer.com

Quantum Dental Technologies Inc
748 Briar Hill Ave . . . . Toronto ON M6B1L3 866-993-9910
TF: 866-993-9910 ■ *Web:* www.thecanarysystem.com

Radius Toothbrush 207 Railroad St. . . . . Kutztown PA 19530 610-683-9400
Web: radiustoothbrush.com

Rocky Mountain Orthodontics Inc (RMO Inc)
650 W Colfax Ave. . . . . Denver CO 80204 303-592-8200 592-8200*
**Fax:* Hum Res ■ *TF:* 800-525-6375 ■ *Web:* www.rmortho.com

S s White Burs Inc 1145 Towbin Ave . . . . Lakewood NJ 08701 732-905-1100
Web: www.sswhiteburs.com

Sirona Dental Systems LLC
4835 Sirona Dr Ste 100 . . . . Charlotte NC 28273 704-587-0453
Web: cereconline.com/ecomaxl/index.php?site=cerec_20_years

Southern Implants Inc Five Holland Bldg 209 . . . . Irvine CA 92618 949-273-8505
Web: www.southernimplants.us

Stern Empire Dental Lab 1805 W 34th St. . . . . Houston TX 77018 713-688-1301
Web: www.sternempire.com

Sterngold Dental LLC 23 Frank Mossberg Dr. . . . . Attleboro MA 02703 508-226-5660
Web: www.sterngold.com

Sunstar Americas Inc 4635 W Foster Ave . . . . Chicago IL 60630 888-777-3101 553-2014*
**Fax Area Code:* 800 ■ *TF:* 888-777-3101 ■ *Web:* www.gumbrand.com

Therapeutic Solutions International Inc
4093 Oceanside Blvd Ste B. . . . . Oceanside CA 92056 760-295-7208
Web: www.therapeuticsolutionsint.com

TP Orthodontics Inc 100 Ctr Plz . . . . La Porte IN 46350 219-785-2591 324-3029
TF: 800-348-8856 ■ *Web:* www.tportho.com

Trident Labs Inc 12000 Aviation Blvd . . . . Hawthorne CA 90250 310-915-9121
Web: www.tridentlab.com

Water Pik Inc 1730 E Prospect Rd . . . . Fort Collins CO 80553 800-525-2774
TF: 800-525-2774 ■ *Web:* www.waterpik.com

Whip Mix Corp
361 Farmington Ave PO Box 17183 . . . . Louisville KY 40217 502-637-1451
Web: www.whipmix.com

Young Dental Manufacturing LLC
13705 Shoreline Court E . . . . Earth City MO 63045 314-344-0010
Web: www.youngdental.com

Zest Anchors LLC 2061 Wineridge Pl. . . . . Escondido CA 92029 760-743-7744
Web: www.zestanchors.com

Phone Fax

Zimmer Orthopaedic Surgical Products Inc
200 W Ohio Ave . . . . Dover OH 44622 330-343-8801
Web: zimmer.com

232 DEPARTMENT STORES

Phone Fax

Ammar's Inc 710 S College Ave . . . . Bluefield VA 24605 276-322-4686 326-1060
Web: www.magicmartstores.com

Ann & Hope Inc 1 Ann & Hope Way . . . . Cumberland RI 02864 877-228-7824
Web: www.curtainandbathoutlet.com

Apex Co 100 Main St . . . . Pawtucket RI 02860 401-729-7200
Web: www.theapexcompanies.com

Beall's Inc 1806 38th Ave E . . . . Bradenton FL 34208 941-747-2355 746-1171
Web: www.beallsinc.com

Belk Inc 2801 W Tyvola Rd . . . . Charlotte NC 28217 704-357-1000
OTC: BLKIB ■ *Web:* www.belk.com

Bloomingdale's 1000 Third Ave . . . . New York NY 10022 212-705-2000 705-2805
TF: 800-950-0047 ■ *Web:* www.bloomingdales.com

Bob's Sporting Goods 1111 Hudson St. . . . . Longview WA 98632 360-425-3870 636-4334
TF: 800-292-5551 ■ *Web:* www.bobsmerch.com

Bon-Ton Stores Inc 2801 E Market St . . . . York PA 17402 717-757-7660
NASDAQ: BONT ■ *TF:* 800-945-4438 ■ *Web:* www.bonton.com

BootBarn Inc 620 Pan American Dr . . . . Livingston TX 77351 936-327-2405
Web: www.baskins.com

Boscov's Dept Stores 4500 Perkiomen Ave . . . . Reading PA 19606 610-779-2000 370-3495
Web: www.boscovs.com

Boston Store Inc 2400 N Mayfair Rd . . . . Milwaukee WI 53226 414-453-7500
Web: www.bostonstore.com

Bracker's Dept Store 68 N Morley Ave. . . . . Nogales AZ 85621 520-287-3631 287-7137

Browning Arms Co one Browning Pl . . . . Morgan UT 84050 801-876-2711
Web: www.browning.com

Century 21 Dept Stores 22 Cortlandt St. . . . . New York NY 10007 212-227-9092 267-4271*
**Fax:* Hum Res ■ *Web:* www.c21stores.com

Cookies The Kids Department Store
510 Fulton St . . . . Brooklyn NY 11201 718-797-3300
Web: www.cookieskids.com

Diesel USA Inc 923 N Rush St . . . . Chicago IL 60611 312-255-0157
Web: www.diesel.com

Dillard's Inc 1600 Cantrell Rd . . . . Little Rock AR 72201 501-376-5200 399-7271*
NYSE: DDS ■ **Fax:* Acctg ■ *Web:* www.dillards.com

DTLR Holding Inc 1300 Mercedes Dr. . . . . Hanover MD 21076 410-850-5911
Web: www.dtlr.com

Fred's Inc 4300 New Getwell Rd . . . . Memphis TN 38118 901-365-8880
NASDAQ: FRED ■ *TF:* 800-374-7417 ■ *Web:* www.fredsinc.com

Glik Co 3248 Nameoki Rd. . . . . Granite City IL 62040 618-876-1065 876-7819
Web: www.gliks.com

Good's Store 1338 Main St. . . . . East Earl PA 17519 717-354-4026
Web: www.goodsstores.com

Gordman 12100 W Ctr Rd . . . . Omaha NE 68144 402-691-4000 691-4269
TF: 800-456-7463 ■ *Web:* www.gordmans.com

JC Penney Co Inc 6501 Legacy Dr. . . . . Plano TX 75024 972-431-1000 431-9140*
NYSE: JCP ■ **Fax:* Cust Svc ■ *Web:* www.jcpenney.com

Jones & Jones Inc 4500 N Tenth St Ste 90 . . . . McAllen TX 78504 956-687-1171 631-3345

Kohl's Corp
N 56 W 17000 Ridgewood Dr. . . . . Menomonee Falls WI 53051 262-703-7000
NYSE: KSS ■ *TF:* 855-564-5705 ■ *Web:* www.kohls.com

Lancaster Sales Co
1375 Old Logan Rd Rt 33S. . . . . Lancaster OH 43130 740-653-5334 653-2783

Langstons Co 2034 NW Seventh St . . . . Oklahoma City OK 73106 405-235-9536
TF: 800-658-2831 ■ *Web:* www.langstons.com

Lord & Taylor 424 Fifth Ave. . . . . New York NY 10018 212-391-3344 391-3262
TF: 800-223-7440 ■ *Web:* www.lordandtaylor.com

Macy's 151 W 34th St . . . . New York NY 10001 212-695-4400 494-1057
Web: www.macys.com

Macy's Inc Seven W Seventh St . . . . Cincinnati OH 45202 513-579-7000 579-7555
NYSE: M ■ *TF:* 800-261-5385 ■ *Web:* www.federated-fds.com

Marine Corps Community Services
3044 Catlin Ave . . . . Quantico VA 22134 703-784-3809
TF: 866-400-8753 ■ *Web:* www.usmc-mccs.org

Mast General Store & Annex Nc
3565 Nc Hwy 194 S . . . . Banner Elk NC 28604 828-963-6511
Web: www.mastgeneralstore.com

Masters Inc 5741 NW Cornelius Pass Road. . . . . Hillsboro OR 97124 503-531-3308 531-9153
TF: 877-652-5656

Mc-Caulou's Inc 3512 Mount Diablo Blvd . . . . Lafayette CA 94549 925-283-3380
Web: www.mccaulous.com

MH King Co 1032 Idaho Ave . . . . Burley ID 83318 208-678-7181
Web: kingsdiscount.com

Neiman Marcus Group Inc 1618 Main St. . . . . Dallas TX 75201 214-743-7600 573-5320
Web: neimanmarcuscareers.com

Pants Store, The 8029 Parkway Dr . . . . Leeds AL 35094 205-699-6166
Web: www.pantsstore.com

Peebles Inc 1 Peebles St . . . . South Hill VA 23970 434-447-5200
TF: 800-723-4548 ■ *Web:* stagestores.com/store/?brand=peebles

Proffitt & Goodson Inc
Old Kingston Pl 4800 Old Kingston Pk
Ste 200 . . . . Knoxville TN 37919 865-584-1850
Web: www.proffittgoodson.com

Reitmans (Canada) Ltd 250 Sauve St W . . . . Montreal QC H3L1Z2 514-384-1140
TSE: RET.A ■ *Web:* www.reitmans.ca

RH Reny Inc 731 Rt 1. . . . . Newcastle ME 04553 207-563-3177 563-5681
Web: www.renys.com

Sav-Mart Co 1729 N Wenatchee Ave . . . . Wenatchee WA 98801 509-663-1671 662-3788
Web: www.savemart.com/contact-us-163

Sears Canada Inc 290 Yonge St Ste 700. . . . . Toronto ON M5B2C3 416-362-1711
TSE: SCC ■ *TF:* 877-987-3277 ■ *Web:* www.sears.ca

Sears Roebuck & Co 3333 Beverly Rd . . . . Hoffman Estates IL 60179 847-286-2500
Web: www.sears.com

Shopko LLC 700 Pilgrim Way . . . . Green Bay WI 54304 920-429-2211
Web: www.shopko.com

Phone | Fax

Sierra Trading Post Inc 5025 Campstool Rd .... Cheyenne WY 82007 307-775-8050
Web: www.sierratradingpost.com

SmartBargains Inc 101 S State Rd 7 Ste 201.........Hollywood FL 33023 877-222-6660
TF: 877-222-6660 ■ *Web:* www.smartbargains.com

Stein Mart Inc 1200 Riverplace Blvd ....Jacksonville FL 32207 904-346-1500 398-4341
NASDAQ: SMRT ■ *Web:* www.steinmart.com

Target Corp 1000 Nicollet Mall.................. Minneapolis MN 55403 612-304-6073 304-6073*
NYSE: TGT ■ **Fax:* Hum Res ■ *TF Cust Svc:* 800-440-0680 ■ *Web:* www.target.com

Tongass Trading Co 201 Dock St ....Ketchikan AK 99901 907-225-5101 247-0481
TF: 800-235-5102 ■ *Web:* www.tongasstrading.com

Trading Union Inc 401 N Nordic Dr................Petersburg AK 99833 907-772-3881 772-9309
Web: acehardware.com

Von Maur Inc 6565 Brady St....................... Davenport IA 52806 563-388-2200 388-2242
Web: www.vonmaur.com

Wal-Mart Puerto Rico Inc PO Box 4960.............. Caguas PR 00726 787-653-7777
Web: www.walmartpr.com

Wal-Mart Stores Inc 702 SW Eigth St .... Bentonville AR 72716 479-273-4000
NYSE: WMT ■ *TF Cust Svc:* 800-925-6278 ■ *Web:* corporate.walmart.com

Wal-Mart Stores Inc Supercenter Div
702 SW Eigth St.............................. Bentonville AR 72716 479-273-4000
TF: 800-925-6278 ■ *Web:* corporate.walmart.com

Walmart.com 7000 Marina Blvd.................... Brisbane CA 94005 800-925-6278
TF: 800-925-6278 ■ *Web:* www.walmart.com

233 DEVELOPMENTAL CENTERS

Residential facilities for the developmentally disabled.

Phone | Fax

Altoona Ctr 1020 Green Ave........................ Altoona PA 16601 814-946-2700 946-1420
Web: www.myaltoonacenterfornursingcare.com

Caswell Developmental Ctr 2415 W Vernon Ave .... Kinston NC 28504 252-208-4000 208-4288*
**Fax:* Acctg ■ *Web:* caswellcenter.org

Central Virginia Training Ctr
521 Colony Rd...........................Madison Heights VA 24572 434-947-6000 *
**Fax:* Hum Res ■ *Web:* www.cvtc.dbhds.virginia.gov

Development Counsellors International Ltd (DCI)
215 Pk Ave S Ste 10...............................New York NY 10003 212-725-0707 725-2254
Web: www.aboutdci.com

Glenwood Resource Ctr 711 S Vine St .... Glenwood IA 51534 712-527-4811 527-2329
Web: dhs.iowa.gov

Lanterman Developmental Ctr 3530 Pomona Blvd .....Pomona CA 91769 909-595-1221 598-4352
Web: www.dds.ca.gov

Parsons State Hospital & Training Ctr
2601 Gabriel St..................................Parsons KS 67357 620-421-6550 421-3623
Web: kdads.ks.gov

Porterville Developmental Ctr (PDC)
26501 Ave 140 PO Box 2000 .... Porterville CA 93258 559-782-2222 784-5630
Web: www.dds.ca.gov/Porterville/Index.cfm

Productive Alternatives Inc
1205 N Tower Rd ....Fergus Falls MN 56537 218-998-5630 736-2541
TF: 800-627-3529 ■ *Web:* www.paiff.org

Sonoma Developmental Ctr 15000 Arnold Dr..........Eldridge CA 95431 707-938-6000 938-3605*
**Fax:* Admitting ■ *TF:* 800-862-0007 ■ *Web:* www.dds.ca.gov

Woodward Resource Ctr 1251 334th St .... Woodward IA 50276 515-438-2600 *
**Fax:* Hum Res ■ *TF:* 888-229-9223 ■ *Web:* www.dhs.state.ia.us

234 DIAGNOSTIC PRODUCTS

SEE ALSO Medicinal Chemicals & Botanical Products p. 2736; Pharmaceutical Companies p. 2921; Pharmaceutical Companies - Generic Drugs p. 2924; Biotechnology Companies p. 1869

Phone | Fax

3-V Biosciences Inc
1050 Hamilton Ct Ste 200 .... Menlo Park CA 94025 650-561-8600
Web: www.3vbio.com

A & A Pharmachem Inc 4-77 Auriga Dr .... Ottawa ON K2E7Z7 613-228-2600
Web: www.aapharmachem.com

A & Z Pharmaceutical Inc 180 Oser Ave .... Hauppauge NY 11788 631-952-3802 952-3900
TF: 800-810-9819 ■ *Web:* www.azpharmaceutical.com

A & Z Pharmaceutical LLC
2275 Swallow Hill Rd Bldg 1200 .... Pittsburgh PA 15220 412-279-8000
Web: www.azpharm.com

Abaxis Inc 3240 Whipple Rd.......................Union City CA 94587 510-675-6500 441-6150
NASDAQ: ABAX ■ *TF:* 800-822-2947 ■ *Web:* www.abaxis.com

Abbott Laboratories Abbott Diagnostics Div
100 Abbott Pk Rd .... Abbott Park IL 60064 847-937-6100
TF: 800-387-8378 ■ *Web:* www.abbottdiagnostics.com

Acceleron Pharma Inc 128 Sidney St ....Cambridge MA 02139 617-649-9200
Web: www.acceleronpharma.com

ACCU-BREAK Pharmaceuticals Inc
1000 S Pine Island Rd Ste 430..................... Plantation FL 33324 954-236-7351
Web: www.accubreakpharmaceuticals.com

Accurate Chemical & Scientific Corp
300 Shames Dr.................................Westbury NY 11590 516-333-2221 997-4948
TF: 800-645-6264 ■ *Web:* www.accuratechemical.com

Actinobac Biomed Inc 15 Pelham Rd .... Kendall Park NJ 08824 732-371-2694
Web: www.actinobac.com

ADH Health Products Inc 215 N Rt 303 ....Congers NY 10920 845-268-0027 268-2988
Web: www.adhhealth.com

Advanced Biotechnologies Inc (ABI)
9108 Guilford Rd ....Columbia MD 21046 410-792-9779 497-9773*
**Fax Area Code:* 301 ■ *TF:* 800-426-0764 ■ *Web:* www.abionline.com

Advanced Distribution Systems Inc
105-107 Stonehurst Ct.........................Northvale NJ 07647 201-767-7350
Web: www.ads-outsource.com

Advanced Vision Research Inc 660 Main St.......... Woburn MA 01801 781-932-8327
Web: www.theratears.com

Adynxx Inc 731 Market St Ste 420 .... San Francisco CA 94103 415-512-7740
Web: www.adynxx.com

Phone | Fax

Aerial BioPharma LLC
9001 Aerial Ctr Pkwy Aerial Ctr Executive Pk
Ste 110..Morrisville NC 27560 919-460-9500
Web: www.aerialbio.com

Aerpio Therapeutics Inc
9987 Carver Rd Ste 420 .... Cincinnati OH 45242 513-985-1920
Web: www.aerpio.com

Afferent Pharmaceuticals Inc
2929 Campus Dr Ste 230.........................San Mateo CA 94403 650-286-1276
Web: www.afferentpharma.com

Akers Biosciences Inc 201 Grove Rd...............Thorofare NJ 08086 856-848-8698
Web: www.akersbiosciences.com

Akorn Inc 1925 W Field Ct .... Lake Forest IL 60045 847-279-6100 279-6123
NASDAQ: AKRX ■ *TF:* 800-932-5676 ■ *Web:* www.akorn.com

Alder Biopharmaceuticals Inc
11804 N Creek Pkwy S.............................Bothell WA 98011 425-205-2900
Web: www.alderbio.com

ALerCHEK Inc 15 Oak St Ste 302 ....Springvale ME 04083 207-490-2266 490-2210
TF: 877-282-9542 ■ *Web:* www.alerchek.com

Alere Inc 51 Sawyer Rd Ste 200 .... Waltham MA 02453 781-647-3900 647-3939
TF: 877-441-7440 ■ *Web:* www.alere.com

Alere San Diego Inc 9975 Summers Ridge Rd .... San Diego CA 92121 781-647-3900
TF: 800-286-2111 ■ *Web:* alere.com

Alinea Pharmaceuticals Inc
One Memorial Dr Ste 1225.......................Cambridge MA 02142 617-914-0123

Alk - Abello Pharmaceuticals Inc
35-151 Brunel Rd............................ Mississauga ON L4Z2H6 905-290-9952
Web: www.alk-abello.com

Allermed Laboratories Inc 7203 Convoy Ct......... San Diego CA 92111 800-221-2748 292-5934*
**Fax Area Code:* 858 ■ *TF:* 800-221-2748 ■ *Web:* www.allermed.com

Alnara Pharmaceuticals Inc 840 Memorial Dr.......Cambridge MA 02139 617-349-3690
Web: www.seasidetherapeutics.com

Aloha Medicinals Inc 2300 Arrowhead Dr .... Carson City NV 89706 775-886-6300
TF: 877-835-6091 ■ *Web:* www.alohamedicinals.com

Alphora Research Inc
2395 Speakman Dr Ste 2001 .... Mississauga ON L5K1B3 905-403-0477
Web: www.alphoraresearch.com

Altheus Therapeutics Inc
755 Research Pkwy Ste 435 ....Oklahoma City OK 73104 405-319-8180
Web: www.altheustherapeutics.com

AMAG Pharmaceuticals Inc 61 Mooney St..........Cambridge MA 02138 617-497-2070
AMEX: AVM

Ambion Inc 2130 Woodward St......................... Austin TX 78744 512-651-0200 651-0190
TF: 866-952-3559 ■ *Web:* www.lifetechnologies.com

American Qualex Scientific Products (AQSP)
920-A Calle Negocio .... San Clemente CA 92673 949-492-8298
Web: www.aqsp.com

Amresco Inc 6681 Cochran Rd........................Solon OH 44139 440-349-1313 349-3255
TF: 800-448-4442 ■ *Web:* www.amresco-inc.com

AnaSpec Inc 34801 Campus Dr...................Fremont CA 94555 510-791-9560 791-9572
TF: 800-452-5530 ■ *Web:* www.anaspec.com

AntiCancer Inc 7917 Ostrow St.................... San Diego CA 92111 858-654-2555 268-4175
TF: 800-511-2555 ■ *Web:* www.anticancer.com

Ardelyx Inc 34175 Ardenwood Blvd ....Fremont CA 94555 510-745-1700
Web: www.ardelyx.com

Ascend Laboratories 180 Summit Ave Ste 200 .... Montvale NJ 07645 201-476-1977
Web: www.ascendlaboratories.com

Ascend Therapeutics Inc
607 Herndon Pkwy Ste 110 .... Herndon VA 20170 703-471-4744
TF: 888-412-5751 ■ *Web:* www.ascendtherapeutics.com

Ascenta Therapeutics Inc
101 Lindenwood Dr Ste 405.........................Malvern PA 19355 610-408-0301 725-1515

Ash Stevens Inc 5861 John C Lodge Fwy .... Detroit MI 48202 313-872-6400
Web: www.ashstevens.com

Athena Diagnostics Inc
377 Plantation St 2nd Fl.......................... Worcester MA 01605 508-756-2886 753-5601
TF: 800-394-4493 ■ *Web:* www.athenadiagnostics.com

Avid Radiopharmaceuticals Inc
3711 Market St Seventh Fl........................ Philadelphia PA 19104 215-298-0700
Web: www.avidrp.com

AxioMx Inc 688 E Main St.......................... Branford CT 06405 203-208-1918
Web: www.axiomxinc.com

Aylward Enterprises Inc 401 Industrial Dr............New Bern NC 28562 252-633-5757
Web: www.aylward.com

Azevan Pharmaceuticals Inc 116 Research Dr....... Bethlehem PA 18015 610-419-1057
Web: www.azevan.com

Bachem-Peninsula Laboratories Inc
305 Old County Rd.............................San Carlos CA 94070 650-801-6090 595-4071
TF: 800-922-1516 ■ *Web:* www.bachem.com

Baker Cummins 4400 Biscayne Blvd .... Miami FL 33173 800-226-8629 474-6696*
**Fax Area Code:* 866 ■ *TF:* 800-226-8629 ■ *Web:* www.bakercummins.com

Baxter Corp 7125 Mississauga Rd .... Mississauga ON L5N0C2 905-369-6000
TF: 866-234-2345 ■ *Web:* www.baxter.ca

BD Diagnostics Seven Loveton Cir.......................Sparks MD 21152 410-316-4000 316-4066
TF: 800-666-6433 ■ *Web:* www.bd.com

Bdf 91 Washington St .... Morristown NJ 07960 973-898-9800
Web: www.bdf.com

Beckman Coulter Genomics 36 Cherry Hill Dr.........Danvers MA 01923 978-867-2600
TF: 800-361-7780 ■ *Web:* www.beckmangenomics.com

Becton Dickinson & Co One Becton Dr ....Franklin Lakes NJ 07417 201-847-6800 847-4882*
NYSE: BDX ■ **Fax:* Cust Svc ■ *TF Cust Svc:* 888-237-2762 ■ *Web:* www.bd.com

Bee-alive Inc Seven New Lk Rd................ Valley Cottage NY 10989 845-268-0960
Web: www.beealive.com

Berlex Laboratories Inc Six W Belt .... Wayne NJ 07470 973-694-4100
TF: 888-842-2937 ■ *Web:* www.berlex.com

Bexion Pharmaceuticals LLC 632 Russell St .... Covington KY 41011 859-757-1652
Web: www.bexionpharma.com

Bio-Pharm Inc 2091 Hartel St ....Levittown PA 19057 215-949-3711
Web: www.bio-pharminc.com

Bio-Rad Laboratories 1000 Alfred Nobel Dr........... Hercules CA 94547 510-724-7000 741-5824*
NYSE: BIO ■ **Fax:* Cust Svc ■ *TF:* 800-424-6723 ■ *Web:* www.bio-rad.com

Phone Fax

Biocell Laboratories Inc
2001 University Dr .... Rancho Dominguez CA 90220 310-537-3300
TF: 800-222-8382 ■ *Web:* www.biocell.com

Biofilm Inc 3225 Executive Ridge .... Vista CA 92081 760-727-9030
Web: astroglide.com

BioGenex Laboratories Inc
4600 Norris Canyon Rd .... San Ramon CA 94583 925-275-0550 275-0580
TF: 800-421-4149 ■ *Web:* www.biogenex.com

Biohelix Corp 500 Cummings Ste 5550 .... Beverly MA 01915 978-927-5056
TF: 866-800-5458 ■ *Web:* www.biohelix.com

Biomerica Inc 1533 Monrovia Ave .... Newport Beach CA 92663 949-645-2111
OTC: BMRA ■ *TF Cust Svc:* 800-854-3002 ■ *Web:* www.biomerica.com

BioMerieux Inc 595 Anglum Rd .... Hazelwood MO 63042 314-731-8500 325-1598*
**Fax Area Code:* 800 ■ *TF:* 800-634-7656 ■ *Web:* www.biomerieux.com

Bionostics Inc Seven Jackson Rd .... Devens MA 01434 978-772-7070 772-7072
TF General: 800-776-3856 ■ *Web:* www.bionostics.com

BioSource International Inc 542 Flynn Rd .... Camarillo CA 93012 805-987-0086
TF: 800-242-0607 ■ *Web:* www.lifetechnologies.com

BiosPacific Inc 5980 Horton St Ste 225 .... Emeryville CA 94608 510-652-6155 652-4531
TF: 800-344-6686 ■ *Web:* www.biospacific.com

Biosynexus Inc 9298 Gaither Rd .... Gaithersburg MD 20877 301-330-5800
Web: www.biosynexus.com

Boiron-Borneman Inc 6 Campus Blvd .... Newtown Square PA 19073 610-325-7464
Web: www.boironusa.com/

Boreal Genomics Inc 5150 El Camino Real .... Los Altos CA 94022 604-822-8268
TF: 800-681-5644 ■ *Web:* www.borealgenomics.com

Burlington Drug Co Inc 91 Catamount Dr .... Milton VT 05468 802-893-5105
TF: 800-338-8703 ■ *Web:* www.burlingtondrug.com

Caldwell Consumer Health LLC Eight Elmer St .... Madison NJ 07940 973-360-1090
Web: bleedinggums.com

Calmoseptine Inc 16602 Burke Ln .... Huntington Beach CA 92647 714-840-3405
Web: www.calmoseptine.com

Calypte Biomedical Corp 15875 SW 72nd Ave .... Portland OR 97224 503-726-2227 601-6299
OTC: CBMC ■ *Web:* www.calypte.com

Cancap Pharmaceutical Ltd
13111 Vanier Pl Ste 180 .... Richmond BC V6V2J1 604-278-2188 278-2210
TF: 877-998-2378 ■ *Web:* www.cancappharma.com

Cancer Genetics Inc
Meadows Office Complex 201 Rt 17 N
Second Fl .... Rutherford NJ 07070 201-528-9200
TF: 888-334-4988 ■ *Web:* www.cancergenetics.com

Cangene bioPharma Inc 1111 S Paca St .... Baltimore MD 21230 410-843-5000
TF: 800-441-4225 ■ *Web:* emergentcontractmanufacturing.com

Capricorn Products LLC 12 Rice St .... Portland ME 04103 207-321-0014
Web: www.capricornproducts.com

Carlsbad Technology Inc
5922 Farnsworth Ct Ste 102 .... Carlsbad CA 92008 760-431-8284
Web: www.carlsbadtechnologyinc.com

Carma Laboratories Inc 5801 W Airways Ave .... Franklin WI 53132 414-421-7707
Web: www.mycarmex.com

Catalent Pharma Solutions Inc
14 Schoolhouse Rd .... Somerset NJ 08873 732-537-6200
Web: www.catalent.com

Cedarlane Laboratories Inc
4410 Paletta Ct .... Burlington ON L7L5R2 905-878-8891 288-0020*
**Fax Area Code:* 289 ■ *TF:* 800-268-5058 ■ *Web:* www.cedarlanelabs.com

Cellectar Inc 3301 Agriculture Dr .... Madison WI 53716 608-441-8120
Web: www.cellectar.com

Centaur Pharmaceuticals Inc
1220 Memorex Dr .... Santa Clara CA 95050 408-822-1600
Web: www.centpharm.com

Centice Corp 215 Southport Dr Ste 1000 .... Morrisville NC 27560 919-653-0424
Web: www.centice.com

Centrix Pharmaceutical Inc
31 Inverness Ctr Pkwy Ste 270 .... Birmingham AL 35242 205-991-9870
Web: www.cenrx.com

Ceptaris Therapeutics Inc
101 Lindenwood Dr Ste 400 .... Malvern PA 19355 610-975-9290

Cerexa Inc 2100 Franklin St Ste 900 .... Oakland CA 94612 510-285-9200
Web: www.cerexa.com

Cetylite Industries 9051 River Rd .... Pennsauken NJ 08110 856-665-6111
Web: www.cetylite.com

Chematics Inc PO Box 293 .... North Webster IN 46555 574-834-2406 834-7427
TF: 800-348-5174 ■ *Web:* www.chematics.com

ChemGenes Corp 33 Industrial Way .... Wilmington MA 01887 978-694-4500
Web: www.chemgenes.com

Chiral Quest Inc
7 Deer Park Dr Ste C1 .... Monmouth Junction NJ 08852 732-274-0399
Web: www.chiralquest.com

ChiRhoClin Inc 4000 Blackburn Ln Ste 270 .... Burtonsville MD 20866 301-476-8388
Web: www.chirhoclin.com

Cholestech Corp 9975 Summers Ridge Rd .... San Diego CA 92121 510-732-7200
TF: 800-733-0404 ■ *Web:* www.alere.com

Chromaprobe Inc 378 Fee Fee Rd .... Maryland Heights MO 63043 314-738-0001 738-0001
TF: 888-964-1400 ■ *Web:* www.chromaprobe.com

Clarus Therapeutics Inc
555 Skokie Blvd Ste 340 .... Northbrook IL 60062 847-562-4300
Web: www.clarustherapeutics.com

Clinilabs Inc 423 W 55th St Fourth Fl .... New York NY 10019 646-215-6400
Web: www.clinilabs.com

CLINIQA Corp 288 Distribution St .... San Marcos CA 92078 760-744-1900
Web: www.cliniqa.com

CNS Therapeutics Inc 332 Minnesota St W1750 .... St Paul MN 55101 651-207-6959
Web: www.gablofen.com

Cobalt Pharmaceuticals Inc
6500 Kitimat Rd .... Mississauga ON L5N2B8 905-814-1820
Web: actavis.ca

CoDa Therapeutics Inc
10505 Sorrento Vly Rd Ste 395 .... San Diego CA 92121 858-677-0474
Web: codatherapeutics.com/

Cody Laboratories Inc 601 Yellowstone Ave .... Cody WY 82414 307-587-7099
Web: www.codylabs.com

Collegium Pharmaceutical Inc
400 Highland Corporate Dr .... Cumberland RI 02864 401-762-2000
Web: collegiumpharma.com

CoMentis Inc 280 Utah Ave Ste 275 .... South San Francisco CA 94080 650-869-7600
Web: www.athenagen.com

Cornerstone Pharmaceuticals Inc
One Duncan Dr .... Cranbury NJ 08512 609-409-7050
Web: www.cornerstonepharma.com

County Line Pharmaceuticals LLC
13890 Bishops Dr Ste 410 .... Brookfield WI 53005 262-439-8109
Web: www.countylinepharma.com

CST Technologies Inc
55 Northern Blvd Ste 200 .... Great Neck NY 11021 516-482-9001 482-0186
TF: 800-448-4407 ■ *Web:* www.cstti.com

Daisy Blue Naturals
2610 Yh Hanson Ave Ste 101 .... Albert Lea MN 56007 507-373-0229
Web: daisybluenaturals.com

DakoCytomation 6392 Via Real .... Carpinteria CA 93013 805-566-6655 566-6688
TF Cust Svc: 800-400-3256 ■ *Web:* www.dako.com

DesigneRx Pharmaceuticals Inc
4941 Allison Pkwy Ste B .... Vacaville CA 95688 707-451-0441
Web: www.drxpharma.com

Diagnostics Biochem Canada Inc (DBC)
41 Byron Ave .... Dorchester ON N0L1G2 519-268-8872 268-7167
Web: www.dbc-labs.com

Diamond Drugs Inc 645 Kolter Dr .... Indiana PA 15701 724-349-1111
TF: 800-882-6337 ■ *Web:* www.diamondpharmacy.com

DiaSorin Inc 1951 NW Ave .... Stillwater MN 55082 651-439-9710 351-5669
TF: 855-677-0600 ■ *Web:* www.diasorin.com

Digestive Care Inc 1120 Win Dr .... Bethlehem PA 18017 610-882-0349
TF: 877-882-5950 ■ *Web:* www.digestivecare.com

Dik Drug Company LLC 160 Tower Dr .... Burr Ridge IL 60527 630-655-4000
Web: www.dikdrug.com

Dishman USA Inc 550 Union Ave Ste 9 .... Middlesex NJ 08846 732-560-4300
Web: www.wheelerjobin.com

DMS Pharmaceutical Group Inc
810 Busse Hwy .... Park Ridge IL 60068 847-518-1100
TF: 877-788-1100 ■ *Web:* www.dmspharma.com

DuPont Qualicon
Henry Clay Rd Bldg 400 Rt 141
PO Box 80357 .... Wilmington DE 19880 302-695-5300 351-6454
TF: 800-863-6842 ■ *Web:* dupont.com

Eco Lips 329 10th Ave SE Ste 213 .... Cedar Rapids IA 52401 319-364-2477
Web: www.ecolips.com

Edgemont Pharmaceuticals LLC
1250 Capital of Texas Hwy S Bldg 3 Ste 400 .... Austin TX 78746 512-550-8555
TF: 888-594-4332 ■ *Web:* www.edgemontpharma.com

Edimer Pharmaceuticals Inc
55 Cambridge Pkwy Ste 102W .... Cambridge MA 02142 617-758-4300
Web: www.edimerpharma.com

EDP Biotech Corp 6701 Baum Dr Ste 110 .... Knoxville TN 37919 865-246-0514
Web: www.edpbiotech.com

Emcure Pharmaceuticals USA INC
21/B Cotters Ln .... East Brunswick NJ 08816 732-238-7880
Web: www.emcureusa.com

Emmaus Medical Inc
20725 S Western Ave Ste 136 .... Torrance CA 90501 310-214-0065
Web: emmausmedical.com

Enzo Biochem Inc 527 Madison Ave .... New York NY 10022 212-583-0100 583-0150
NYSE: ENZ ■ *TF:* 800-522-5052 ■ *Web:* www.enzo.com

Enzo Life Sciences Inc 10 Executive Blvd .... Farmingdale NY 11735 631-694-7070
TF: 800-942-0430 ■ *Web:* www.enzolifesciences.com

Epiomed Therapeutics Inc 25 Mauchly Ste 316 .... Irvine CA 92618 949-398-7357
Web: www.epiomed.com

Euro-Pharm International Canada Inc
9400 Boul Langelier .... Montreal QC H1P3H8 514-323-8757 323-6325
Web: www.euro-pharm.com

Euthymics Bioscience 43 Thorndike St .... Cambridge MA 02141 617-758-0300
Web: www.euthymics.com

EXACT Sciences Corp 441 Charmany Dr .... Madison WI 53719 608-284-5700 284-5701
NASDAQ: EXAS ■ *Web:* www.exactsciences.com

Exalpha Biologicals Inc
Five Clock Tower Pl Ste 255 .... Maynard MA 01754 800-395-1137 461-0436*
**Fax Area Code:* 978 ■ *TF:* 800-395-1137 ■ *Web:* www.exalpha.com

Exoxemis Inc 6029 N 16th St .... Omaha NE 68110 402-884-2316

Face Stockholm Ltd 324 Joslen Blvd .... Hudson NY 12534 518-828-6600
TF: 888-334-3223 ■ *Web:* www.facestockholm.com

FibroGen Inc 409 Illinois St .... San Francisco CA 94158 415-978-1200
Web: www.fibrogen.com

Fitzgerald Industries International Inc
30 Sudbury Rd Ste 1A N .... Acton MA 01720 978-371-6446
Web: www.fitzgerald-fii.com

Galera Therapeutics Inc
101 Lindenwood Dr Ste 405 .... Malvern PA 19355 610-725-1500
Web: www.galeratx.com

Gen-Probe Inc 10210 Genetic Ctr Dr .... San Diego CA 92121 858-410-8000 288-3141*
**Fax Area Code:* 800 ■ *TF:* 800-523-5001 ■ *Web:* www.hologic.com

GenBio 15222 Ave of Science Ste A .... San Diego CA 92128 858-592-9300 592-9400
TF Tech Supp: 800-288-4368 ■ *Web:* www.genbio.com

Genus Oncology LLC
Three Hawthorn Pkwy Ste 250 .... Vernon Hills IL 60061 847-549-6500
Web: genusoncology.com

Gibson Laboratories Inc 1040 Manchester St .... Lexington KY 40508 859-254-9500 253-1476
TF: 800-477-4763 ■ *Web:* gibsonbioscience.com

Golden Bridge International Inc
9700 Harbour Pl Ste 129 .... Mukilteo WA 98275 425-493-1801
Web: www.gbi-inc.com

Golden State Medical Supply Inc
5187 Camino Ruiz .... Camarillo CA 93012 805-477-9866
TF: 800-284-8633 ■ *Web:* www.gsms.us

Goodwin Biotechnology Inc
1850 NW 69th Ave .... Plantation FL 33313 954-327-9656 587-6378
TF: 800-814-8600 ■ *Web:* www.goodwinbio.com

Company	City	State	Zip	Phone	Fax
Graceway Pharmaceuticals LLC 340 Martin Luther King Junior Blvd Ste 500	Bristol	TN	37620	423-274-2100	
Green Pharmaceuticals Inc 591 Constitution Ave Ste A *Web:* snorestop.com	Camarillo	CA	93012	805-388-0600	
Guerbet LLC 1185 W Second St *TF:* 877-729-6679 ■ *Web:* www.guerbet-us.com	Bloomington	IN	47403	812-333-0059	
Guy & O'Neill Inc 617 Tower Dr *Web:* www.guyandoneill.com	Fredonia	WI	53021	262-692-2469	
Haemotec Inc 383 Joseph Carrier	Vaudreuil-Dorion	QC	J7V5V5	450-424-3615	
HALO Pharmaceutical Inc 30 N Jefferson Rd *Web:* www.halopharma.com	Whippany	NJ	07981	973-428-4000	
Hanford Pharmaceuticals LLC 304 Oneida St *Web:* www.hanford.com	Syracuse	NY	13202	315-476-7418	
Harlan Bioproducts for Science Inc (HBPS) 298 S Carroll Rd *TF:* 800-793-7287 ■ *Web:* www.harlan.com	Indianapolis	IN	46229	800-793-7287	
Health Freedom Nutrition LLC 255 Bell St Ste 200 *Web:* www.hfn-usa.com	Reno	NV	89503	775-324-1967	
Healthy n Fit International 435 Yorktown Rd *Web:* behealthyfit.com	Croton On Hudson	NY	10520	914-271-6040	
Helena Laboratories Inc 1530 Lindbergh Dr *TF:* 800-231-5663 ■ *Web:* www.helena.com	Beaumont	TX	77704	409-842-3714	842-3094
Hemagen Diagnostics Inc 9033 Red Branch Rd *OTC: HMGN* ■ **Fax Area Code:* 410 ■ *TF:* 800-436-2436 ■ *Web:* www.hemagen.com	Columbia	MD	21045	443-367-5500	997-7812*
hermo Fisher Scientific Inc 8365 Valley Pike PO Box 307 **Fax Area Code:* 540 ■ *TF:* 800-528-0494 ■ *Web:* www.thermofisher.com	Middletown	VA	22645	800-556-2323	869-8126*
Hitachi Chemical Diagnostics 630 Clyde Ct *TF:* 800-233-6278 ■ *Web:* www.hcdiagnostics.com	Mountain View	CA	94043	650-961-5501	969-2745
Honeys Place Inc 640 Glenoaks Blvd *TF:* 800-910-3246 ■ *Web:* www.honeysplace.com	San Fernando	CA	91340	818-256-1101	
Hospira Boulder Inc 4876 Sterling Dr *Web:* hospira.com	Boulder	CO	80301	303-938-1250	
Hovione LLC 40 Lake Dr *Web:* www.hovione.com	East Windsor	NJ	08520	609-918-2600	
HumanZyme Inc 2201 W Campbell Park Dr Ste 24 *Web:* www.humanzyme.com	Chicago	IL	60612	312-738-0127	
Huvepharma Inc 525 Wpark Dr Ste 230 *Web:* www.huvepharma.com	Peachtree City	GA	30269	770-486-7212	
Hycor Biomedical Inc 7272 Chapman Ave **Fax Area Code:* 714 ■ *TF Cust Svc:* 800-382-2527 ■ *Web:* www.hycorbiomedical.com	Garden Grove	CA	92841	800-382-2527	933-3222*
IDEXX Laboratories Inc One IDEXX Dr *NASDAQ: IDXX* ■ *TF:* 800-548-6733 ■ *Web:* www.idexx.com	Westbrook	ME	04092	207-556-0300	556-4346
ImmucorGamma Inc 3130 Gateway Dr PO Box 5625 *NASDAQ: BLUD* ■ *TF Cust Svc:* 800-829-2553 ■ *Web:* www.immucor.com	Norcross	GA	30091	770-441-2051	441-3807
Immuno-Mycologics Inc (IMMY) 2700 Technology Pl **Fax Area Code:* 405 ■ *TF:* 800-654-3639 ■ *Web:* www.immy.com	Norman	OK	73071	800-654-3639	364-1058*
ImmunoDiagnostics Inc One Presidential Way Ste 104 *TF:* 800-573-1700 ■ *Web:* www.immunodx.com	Woburn	MA	01801	781-938-6300	938-7300
Immunovision Inc 1820 Ford Ave *TF:* 800-541-0960 ■ *Web:* www.immunovision.com	Springdale	AR	72764	479-751-7005	751-7002
InnoZen Inc 6429 Independence Ave *Web:* www.innozen.com	Woodland Hills	CA	91367	805-822-5091	
Inotek Pharmaceuticals Corp 33 Hayden Ave Second Fl *Web:* inotekpharma.com/	Lexington	MA	02421	978-232-9660	
Inova Diagnostics Inc 9900 Old Grove Rd *TF:* 800-545-9495 ■ *Web:* www.inovadx.com	San Diego	CA	92131	858-586-9900	586-9911
InSite Vision Inc 965 Atlantic Ave *OTC: INSV* ■ *Web:* www.insitevision.com	Alameda	CA	94501	510-865-8800	865-5700
Interleukin Genetics Inc 135 Beaver St 3rd Fl *OTC: ILIU* ■ *TF Cust Svc:* 800-826-6762 ■ *Web:* www.ilgenetics.com	Waltham	MA	02452	781-398-0700	398-0720
Intermax Pharmaceuticals Inc 228 Sherwood Ave *Web:* synthopharmaceuticals.com	Farmingdale	NY	11735	631-777-3318	
International Immunology Corp 25549 Adams Ave *TF:* 800-843-2853 ■ *Web:* www.iicsera.com	Murrieta	CA	92562	951-677-5629	677-6752
International Isotopes Inc 4137 Commerce Cir *OTC: INIS* ■ *TF:* 800-699-3108 ■ *Web:* www.intisoid.com	Idaho Falls	ID	83401	208-524-5300	524-1411
InVitro International 17751 Sky Pk Cir Ste G *TF:* 800-246-8487 ■ *Web:* www.invitrointl.com	Irvine	CA	92614	949-851-8356	851-4985
Invivis Pharmaceuticals Inc 547 Meadow Rd *Web:* www.invivis.com	Bridgewater	NJ	08807	908-818-9393	
Invivoscribe Technologies Inc 6330 Nancy Ridge Dr Ste 106 *TF:* 866-623-8105 ■ *Web:* www.invivoscribe.com	San Diego	CA	92121	858-224-6600	
Iso-Tex Diagnostics Inc PO Box 909 **Fax Area Code:* 281 ■ *TF:* 800-477-4839 ■ *Web:* www.isotexdiagnostics.com	Friendswood	TX	77549	800-477-4839	482-1070*
Jackson ImmunoResearch Laboratories Inc 872 W Baltimore Pk PO Box 9 *TF:* 800-367-5296 ■ *Web:* www.jacksonimmuno.com	West Grove	PA	19390	610-869-4024	869-0171
Jean Brown Assoc Inc 1045 East 3900 South Ste 100 *Web:* www.jeanbrownresearch.com	Salt Lake City	UT	84124	801-261-2000	
Jenken Biosciences Inc 2 Davis Dr Research Triangle Pk *Web:* www.jenkenbio.com	Research Triangle Park	NC	27709	919-765-0032	
Kalos Therapeutics Inc 4370 La Jolla Village Dr Ste 400 *Web:* www.kalostpx.com	San Diego	CA	92122	858-552-6890	
Kamiya Biomedical Co 12779 Gateway Dr *Web:* www.kamiyabiomedical.com	Seattle	WA	98168	206-575-8068	575-8094
Kc Pharmaceuticals Inc 3201 Producer Way *Web:* kc-ph.com	Pomona	CA	91768	909-598-9499	
Kern Health Systems 9700 Stockdale Hwy *TF:* 888-466-2219 ■ *Web:* www.kernfamilyhealthcare.com	Bakersfield	CA	93311	661-664-5000	
Keysource Medical Inc 7820 Palace Dr *Web:* www.keysourcemedical.com	Cincinnati	OH	45249	513-469-7881	
Kibow Biotech Inc 4781 W Chester Pike Newtown Business Ctr *TF:* 888-271-2560 ■ *Web:* www.kibowbiotech.com	Newtown Square	PA	19073	610-353-5130	
Kirkegaard & Perry Laboratories Inc 910 Clopper Rd *TF:* 800-638-3167 ■ *Web:* www.kpl.com	Gaithersburg	MD	20878	301-948-7755	948-0169
KMI Diagnostics Inc 8201 Central Ave NE Ste P *TF:* 888-564-3424 ■ *Web:* www.kmidiagnostics.com	Minneapolis	MN	55432	763-231-3313	780-2988
Kohl & Frisch Ltd 7622 Keele St *TF:* 800-265-2520 ■ *Web:* www.kohlandfrisch.com	Concord	ON	L4K2R5	800-265-2520	
Kolltan Pharmaceuticals Inc 300 George St Ste 530 *Web:* www.kolltan.com	New Haven	CT	06511	203-773-3000	
Kowa Pharmaceuticals America Inc 530 Industrial Park Blvd *Web:* www.kowapharma.com	Montgomery	AL	36117	334-288-1288	
KVK-TECH Inc 110 Terry Dr Ste 200 *Web:* www.kvktech.com	Newtown	PA	18940	215-579-1842	
Laboratoire Du-var Inc 1460 Rue Graham-Bell *Web:* www.du-var.com	Boucherville	QC	J4B6H5	450-641-4740	641-4743
Lantheus Medical Imaging Inc 331 Treble Cove Rd Bldg 200-2 *Web:* www.lantheus.com	North Billerica	MA	01862	978-667-9531	
Lawton's Drug Stores Ltd 236 Brownlow Ave Ste 270 *TF:* 866-990-1599 ■ *Web:* www.lawtons.ca	Dartmouth	NS	B3B1V5	902-468-1000	
LifeScan Inc 1000 Gibraltar Dr *TF:* 800-227-8862 ■ *Web:* www.lifescan.com	Milpitas	CA	95035	408-263-9789	946-6070
Lightning Powder Company Inc 13386 International Pkwy *Web:* www.redwop.com	Jacksonville	FL	32218	904-485-1836	741-5407
Lipo Technologies Inc 707 Harco Dr *Web:* www.lipotechnologies.com	Englewood	OH	45315	937-264-1222	
LipoScience Inc 2500 Sumner Blvd *TF:* 877-547-6837 ■ *Web:* www.liposcience.com	Raleigh	NC	27616	919-212-1999	
LNK International Inc 22 Arkay Dr *Web:* www.lnkintl.com	Hauppauge	NY	11788	631-435-3500	
MabVax Therapeutics Inc 11588 Sorrento Vly Rd Ste 20 *Web:* www.mabvax.com	San Diego	CA	92121	858-259-9405	
Maine Biotechnology Services Inc 1037 R Forest Ave *TF:* 800-925-9476 ■ *Web:* www.mainebiotechnology.com	Portland	ME	04103	207-797-5454	797-5595
Mallinckrodt Inc 675 McDonnell Blvd *TF:* 800-778-7898	Hazelwood	MO	63042	314-654-2000	
Marianna Industries Inc 11222 "I" St *TF:* 800-228-9060 ■ *Web:* www.mariannaind.com	Omaha	NE	68137	402-593-0211	
MCR American Pharmaceuticals Inc 16255 Aviation Loop *Web:* www.mcramerican.com	Brooksville	FL	34604	352-754-8587	
Medical Analysis Systems Inc 46360 Fremont Blvd *TF:* 800-232-3342 ■ *Web:* www.thermofisher.com/	Fremont	CA	94538	510-979-5000	979-5002
Mediderm Laboratories 2001 S Barrington Ave *Web:* www.twaian.com	Los Angeles	CA	90025	310-445-0600	
Medinox Inc 6120 Paseo Del Norte Ste B-2 *Web:* www.medinox.com	Carlsbad	CA	92009	760-603-8989	
MEDTOX Diagnostics Inc 1238 Anthony Rd **Fax Area Code:* 651 ■ *TF:* 800-334-1116 ■ *Web:* www.medtox.com	Burlington	NC	27215	336-226-6311	286-6222*
Memory Pharmaceuticals Corp 100 Philips Pkwy *Web:* www.memorypharma.com	Montvale	NJ	07645	201-802-7100	
Meridian Bioscience Inc 3471 River Hills Dr *NASDAQ: VIVO* ■ *TF Cust Svc:* 800-543-1980 ■ *Web:* www.meridianbioscience.com	Cincinnati	OH	45244	513-271-3700	272-5421
Miller Drug Inc 210 State St *Web:* www.millerdrug.com	Bangor	ME	04401	207-947-8369	
Miragen Therapeutics Inc 6200 Lookout Rd Ste 100 *Web:* www.miragentherapeutics.com	Boulder	CO	80301	303-531-5952	
Mirari Biosciences Inc 9610 Medical Ctr Dr Ste 240 *Web:* www.miraribiosciences.com	Rockville	MD	20850	240-447-6456	
Moderna Therapeutics Inc 320 Bent St *Web:* www.modernatx.com	Cambridge	MA	02141	617-714-6500	
Monobind Inc 100 N Pt Dr *TF:* 800-854-6265 ■ *Web:* www.monobind.com	Lake Forest	CA	92630	949-951-2665	951-3539
MonoSol Rx Inc 30 Technology Dr *Web:* www.monosolrx.com	Warren	NJ	07059	732-564-5000	
Mork Process Inc 4278 Hudson Dr *Web:* www.morkusa.com	Stow	OH	44224	330-928-3728	
Moss Inc PO Box 189 *TF:* 800-932-6677 ■ *Web:* www.mosssubstrates.com	Pasadena	MD	21123	410-768-3442	768-3971
Nanocopoeia Inc 1246 W University Ave Ste 463 *Web:* www.nanocopeia.com	St Paul	MN	55104	651-209-1184	
National Diagnostics Inc 305 Patton Dr *TF:* 800-526-3867 ■ *Web:* www.nationaldiagnostics.com	Atlanta	GA	30336	404-699-2121	699-2077
Neci 334 Hecla St *TF:* 888-648-7283 ■ *Web:* www.nitrate.com	Lake Linden	MI	49945	906-296-1000	
Neogen Corp 620 Lesher Pl *NASDAQ: NEOG* ■ *TF:* 800-234-5333 ■ *Web:* www.neogen.com	Lansing	MI	48912	517-372-9200	372-2006
NeuroGenetic Pharmaceuticals Inc 445 Marine View Ave Ste 101 *Web:* www.neurogeneticpharmaceuticals.com	Del Mar	CA	92014	858-461-4480	

Phone | Fax

New Century Pharmaceuticals Inc
895 Martin Rd . . . Huntsville AL 35824 256-461-0024
Web: www.newcenturypharm.com

New Horizons Diagnostics Corp
9110 Red Branch Rd . . . Columbia MD 21045 410-992-9357 992-0328
TF: 800-888-5015 ■ *Web:* www.nhdiag.com

NexGenix Pharmaceuticals Holdings Inc
152 W 57th St Ste 11B . . . New York NY 10019 212-974-3006
Web: www.nexgenixpharm.com

Noction Inc 1294 Lawrence Sta Rd . . . Sunnyvale CA 94089 650-618-9823
Web: www.noction.com

Norgenix Pharmaceuticals LLC
101 W Saint John St Ste 307 . . . Spartanburg SC 29306 864-580-2660
Web: www.norgenixpharma.com

Novartis Vaccines & Diagnostics
One Health Plz Bldg 122 . . . East Hanover NJ 07936 862-778-8300
NYSE: NVS ■ *TF:* 888-644-8585 ■ *Web:* www.novartis-vaccines.com

Novocol Pharmaceutical of Canada Inc
25 Wolseley Ct . . . Cambridge ON N1R6X3 519-623-4800 623-4290
Web: www.septodont.ca

Nulab Inc 2180 Calumet St . . . Clearwater FL 33765 727-446-1126
Web: www.nulabinc.com

Nuron Biotech Inc One E Uwchlan Ave Ste 302 . . . Exton PA 19341 610-968-6700

NuTech Inc 1301 Clinic Dr . . . Tyler TX 75701 903-592-8115
Web: www.nutechrx.com

Nutraceutics Corp 2900 Brannon Ave . . . Saint Louis MO 63139 314-664-6684
Web: www.nutraceutics.com

Odan Laboratories Ltd
325 Stillview Ave . . . Pointe-Claire QC H9R2Y6 514-428-1628 428-9783
TF: 800-387-9342 ■ *Web:* www.odanlab.com

Ohmx Corp 1801 Maple Ave Ste 6143 . . . Evanston IL 60201 847-491-8500
Web: www.ohmxbio.com

Oligasis LLC 3350 W Bayshore Rd Ste 150 . . . Palo Alto CA 94303 650-354-0920
Web: www.oligasis.com

Omega Biologicals Inc 910 Technology Blvd . . . Bozeman MT 59718 406-586-3790 586-3792
Web: omegabiologicals.com

Oncogenex Technologies Inc
1001 W Broadway Ste 400 . . . Vancouver BC V6H4B1 604-736-3678
Web: oncogenex.com

Ondine Biomedical Inc
1100 Melville St Ste 910 . . . Vancouver BC V6E4A6 604-669-0555 669-0533
TF: 800-564-6253 ■ *Web:* www.ondinebio.com

OraSure Technologies Inc 220 E First St . . . Bethlehem PA 18015 610-882-1820 882-1830
NASDAQ: OSUR ■ *TF:* 800-869-3538 ■ *Web:* www.orasure.com

Oriel Therapeutics Inc
630 Davis Dr Ste 120 . . . Morrisville NC 27560 919-313-1290

Orion Genomics LLC 4041 Forest Park Ave . . . Saint Louis MO 63108 314-615-6977
Web: www.oriongenomics.com

Ortho-Clinical Diagnostics Inc
1001 US Rt 202 N PO Box 350 . . . Raritan NJ 08869 800-828-6316 453-3660*
**Fax Area Code:* 585 ■ **Fax:* Cust Svc ■ *TF:* 800-828-6316 ■ *Web:* www.orthoclinical.com

Oxford Biomedical Research Inc
2165 Avon Industrial Dr . . . Rochester Hills MI 48309 248-852-8815 852-4466
TF: 800-692-4633 ■ *Web:* www.oxfordbiomed.com

Pacific Biometrics Inc
645 Elliott Ave W Ste 300 . . . Seattle WA 98119 206-298-0068
TF: 800-767-9151 ■ *Web:* www.pacbio.com

Pacific Nutritional Inc 6317 NE 131st Ave . . . Vancouver WA 98682 360-253-3197
Web: www.pacnut.com

Paramount Beauty Distributing Assoc Inc
41 Mercedes Way Ste 34 . . . Edgewood NY 11717 631-242-3737
Web: paramountbeauty.com

Parchem Trading Ltd 415 Huguenot St . . . New Rochelle NY 10801 914-654-6800
TF: 800-282-3982 ■ *Web:* www.parchem.com

ParinGenix Inc 1792 Bell Tower Ln Ste 200 . . . Weston FL 33326 954-315-3660

PBA Health 6300 Enterprise Rd . . . Kansas City MO 64120 816-245-5700
Web: pbahealth.com

Pearl Therapeutics Inc 200 Saginaw Dr . . . Redwood City CA 94063 650-305-2600
Web: www.pearltherapeutics.com

Peloton Therapeutics Inc
2330 Inwood Rd Ste 226 . . . Dallas TX 75235 972-629-4100
Web: www.pelotontherapeutics.com

Peptides International Inc
11621 Electron Dr . . . Louisville KY 40299 502-266-8787 267-1329
TF: 800-777-4779 ■ *Web:* www.pepnet.com

PerkinElmer Inc 940 Winter St . . . Waltham MA 02451 203-925-4602 944-4904
NYSE: PKI ■ *Web:* www.perkinelmer.com

Permeon Biologics Inc
1 Kendall Sq Bldg 1400 W Ste 14203 . . . Cambridge MA 02139 617-945-7780 595-5589*
**Fax Area Code:* 650 ■ *Web:* www.permeonbio.com

Pfizer Centre Source 7000 Portage Rd . . . Kalamazoo MI 49001 269-833-5844
Web: www.pfizercentresource.com

Phadia US Inc 4169 Commercial Ave . . . Portage MI 49002 269-492-1940
TF: 800-346-4364 ■ *Web:* www.phadia.com

Phage Pharmaceuticals Inc
6868 Nancy Ridge Dr Ste 100 . . . San Diego CA 92121 858-427-9100

Pharmaceutical Assoc Inc
1700 Perimeter Rd . . . Greenville SC 29605 864-277-7282
TF: 888-233-2334 ■ *Web:* www.paipharma.com

Pharmaceutical Innovations Inc
897 Frelinghuysen Ave . . . Newark NJ 07114 973-242-2900 242-0578
Web: www.pharminnovations.com

Pharmaceutical Technologies Inc 14301 Fnb Pkwy . . . Omaha NE 68154 402-964-9030

Pharmaceutics International Inc
10819 Gilroy Rd . . . Hunt Valley MD 21031 410-584-0001
Web: www.pharm-int.com

Pharmakon Compounding Inc
801 Congressional Blvd . . . Carmel IN 46032 317-818-1059
Web: pharmakonrx.net

Pharmalucence Inc 29 Dunham Rd . . . Billerica MA 01821 781-275-7120
TF: 800-221-7554 ■ *Web:* www.pharmalucence.com

Pharmametrics 220 Commerce Dr Ste 405 . . . Ft Washington PA 19034 215-274-1315
Web: pharmametricsinc.com

Pharmasave Drugs (National) Ltd
8411 - 200th St Ste 201 . . . Langley BC V2Y0E7 604-455-2400 455-2493
Web: www.pharmasave.com

Pharmascience Inc
6111 Royalmount Ave Ste 100 . . . Montreal QC H4P2T4 514-340-9800 342-7764
TF: 866-853-1178 ■ *Web:* www.pharmascience.com

Pharmetics Inc 3695 AutoRt Des Laurentides . . . Laval QC H7L3H7 450-682-8580
TF: 877-472-4433 ■ *Web:* www.pharmetics.com

PhaseBio Pharmaceuticals Inc
One Great Vly Pkwy Ste 30 . . . Malvern PA 19355 610-981-6500
Web: www.phasebio.com

Pherin Pharmaceuticals Inc
4962 El Camino Real Ste 223 . . . Los Altos CA 94022 650-961-2703
Web: www.pherin.com

Phoenix Pharmaceuticals Inc 330 Beach Rd . . . Burlingame CA 94010 650-558-8898
TF: 800-988-1205 ■ *Web:* www.phoenixpeptide.com

Phylonix Pharmaceuticals Inc
100 Inman St Ste 300 . . . Cambridge MA 02139 617-441-6700
Web: www.phylonix.com

Pierre Fabre Dermo Cosmetique 8 Campus Dr . . . Parsippany NJ 07054 973-898-1042
Web: www.pierre-fabre.com

PlantForm Corp 1920 Yonge St Suite 200 . . . Toronto ON M4S3E2 416-452-7242
Web: www.plantformcorp.com

PLx Pharma Inc 8285 El Rio Ste 130 . . . Houston TX 77054 713-842-1249
Web: www.plxpharma.com

Pointe Scientific Inc
5449 Research Dr PO Box 87188 . . . Canton MI 48188 734-487-8300 483-1592
TF: 800-445-9853 ■ *Web:* www.pointescientific.com

Polaris Pharmaceuticals Inc
9373 Towne Centre Dr Ste 150 . . . San Diego CA 92121 858-452-6688
Web: www.polarispharma.com

Polymedco Inc 510 Furnace Dock Rd . . . Cortlandt Manor NY 10567 914-739-5400 739-5890
TF: 800-431-2123 ■ *Web:* www.polymedco.com

PolyPeptide Laboratories Inc 365 Maple Ave . . . Torrance CA 90503 310-782-3569
TF: 800-338-4965 ■ *Web:* www.polypeptide.com

Polysciences Inc 400 Valley Rd . . . Warrington PA 18976 215-343-6484 343-0214
TF Cust Svc: 800-523-2575 ■ *Web:* www.polysciences.com

Prasco LLC 6125 Commerce Ct . . . Mason OH 45040 513-618-3333
TF: 866-469-1414 ■ *Web:* www.prasco.com

Prescription Supply Inc 2233 Tracy Rd . . . Northwood OH 43619 419-661-6600
Web: www.prescriptionsupply.com

Press Chemical & Pharmaceutical Laboratories Inc
4231 Donlyn Ct . . . Columbus OH 43232 614-863-2802

ProCertus BioPharm Inc
510 Charmany Dr Ste 175 B . . . Madison WI 53719 608-277-7950
Web: www.procertus.com

Product Quest Mfg LLC 330 Carswell Ave . . . Daytona Beach FL 32117 386-239-8787
Web: www.productquestmfg.com

Promega Corp 2800 Woods Hollow Rd . . . Madison WI 53711 608-274-4330 277-2516
TF: 800-356-9526 ■ *Web:* promega.com/

Proteon Therapeutics Inc 200 W St . . . Waltham MA 02451 781-890-0102
Web: www.proteontherapeutics.com

Proteos Inc 4717 Campus Dr . . . Kalamazoo MI 49008 269-372-3480
Web: www.proteos.net

Prozyme Inc 3832 Bay Ctr Pl . . . Hayward CA 94545 510-638-6900 638-6919
TF: 800-457-9444 ■ *Web:* www.prozyme.com

Psyadon Pharmaceuticals Inc
20451 Seneca Meadows Pkwy . . . Germantown MD 20876 301-919-2020
Web: www.psyadonrx.com

PTC Therapeutics Inc
100 Corporate Ct . . . South Plainfield NJ 07080 908-222-7000
Web: www.ptcbio.com

Public Health Solutions 220 Church St Fl 5 . . . New York NY 10013 646-619-6400
Web: www.healthsolutions.org

Purdue Pharma 575 Granite Ct . . . Pickering ON L1W3W8 905-420-6400 420-4193
Web: www.purdue.ca

Qst Consultations Ltd 11275 Edgewater Dr . . . Allendale MI 49401 616-895-5461
Web: qstconsultations.com

Quadris Medical 2030 Lookout Dr . . . North Mankato MN 56003 507-385-2709
Web: quadrismedical.com

Quality Biological Inc
7581 Lindbergh Dr . . . Gaithersburg MD 20879 301-840-9331 840-0743
TF: 800-443-9331 ■ *Web:* www.qualitybiological.com

Quantimetrix Corp
2005 Manhattan Beach Blvd . . . Redondo Beach CA 90278 310-536-0006 536-9977
TF: 800-624-8380 ■ *Web:* quantimetrix.com

Quark Pharmaceuticals Inc 6501 Dumbarton Cir . . . Fremont CA 94555 510-402-4020
Web: quarkpharma.com/

Quidel Corp 10165 McKellar Ct . . . San Diego CA 92121 858-552-1100 453-4338
NASDAQ: QDEL ■ *TF:* 800-874-1517 ■ *Web:* www.quidel.com

R & D Systems Inc 614 McKinley Pl NE . . . Minneapolis MN 55413 612-379-2956 656-4400
TF: 800-343-7475 ■ *Web:* www.rndsystems.com

R X Canada 6711 Mississauga Rd . . . Mississauga ON L5N2W3 905-821-2270
Web: www.rxcanada.ca

Radient Pharmaceuticals Corp
2492 Walnut Ave Ste 100 . . . Tustin CA 92780 714-505-4461 505-4464
OTC: RXPC

Raritan Pharmaceuticals Inc
Eight Joanna Ct . . . East Brunswick NJ 08816 732-432-8200
Web: www.raritanpharm.com

Rasi Laboratories Inc 20 Roosevelt Ave . . . Somerset NJ 08873 732-873-8500
Web: www.rasilaboratories.com

Research & Diagnostic Antibodies
2645 W Cheyenne Ave . . . North Las Vegas NV 89032 702-638-7800 638-7801
TF: 800-858-7322 ■ *Web:* www.rdabs.com

Reviva Pharmaceuticals Inc
3900 Freedom Circle Ste 101 . . . Santa Clara CA 95054 408-960-2209
Web: www.revivapharma.com

RGR Pharma ltd 103 Crystal Harbour Dr . . . Lasalle ON N9J3R6 519-734-6600
Web: www.rgrpharma.com

Rhodes Technologies Inc 498 Washington St . . . Coventry RI 02816 401-262-9200
Web: www.rhodestec.com

Company / Address	City	State	ZIP	Phone	Fax
Rising Pharmaceuticals Inc Three Pearl Ct Stes A/B *Web:* www.risingpharma.com	Allendale	NJ	07401	201-961-9000	
Roche Diagnostics Corp (RDC) 9115 Hague Rd PO Box 50457 *TF Cust Svc:* 800-428-5076 ■ *Web:* www.roche-diagnostics.us	Indianapolis	IN	46250	317-521-2000	521-2090
Rockland Immunochemicals Inc PO Box 326 *TF:* 800-656-7625 ■ *Web:* www.rockland-inc.com	Gilbertsville	PA	19525	610-369-1008	367-7825
RxMosaic Healthcare 711 Third Ave Fl 19 *Web:* rxmosaichealth.com	New York	NY	10017	212-336-7500	
SA Scientific Ltd 4919 Golden Quail *Web:* www.ntextechnologies.com	San Antonio	TX	78240	210-699-8800	699-6545
Saladax Biomedical Inc 116 Research Dr *Web:* www.saladax.com	Bethlehem	PA	18015	610-419-6731	
Sammann Co Inc 9935 N Us Hwy 12 E *TF:* 800-348-2508 ■ *Web:* www.peeperspecs.com	Michigan City	IN	46360	219-872-4413	872-4695
San-Mar Laboratories Inc Four Warehouse Ln *Web:* processtechnologies.com/	Elmsford	NY	10523	914-592-3130	
Sanofi-Aventis US LLC 55 Corporate Dr *Web:* sanofi.us/	Bridgewater	NJ	08807	908-981-5000	
Santen Inc 2100 Powell St Ste 1600 *Web:* www.santeninc.com	Emeryville	CA	94608	415-268-9100	
Saskatchewan Health Research Foundation 253-111 Research Dr *Web:* www.shrf.ca	Saskatoon	SK	S7N3R2	306-975-1680	
Scantibodies Laboratory Inc 9336 Abraham Way *Web:* www.scantibodies.com	Santee	CA	92071	619-258-9300	258-9366
SCIMEDX Corp 100 Ford Rd *TF:* 800-221-5598 ■ *Web:* www.scimedx.com	Denville	NJ	07834	973-625-8822	625-8796
Scivolutions Inc 2260 Raeford Ct	Gastonia	NC	28052	704-853-0100	
Scripps Laboratories Inc 6838 Flanders Dr *Web:* www.scrippslabs.com	San Diego	CA	92121	858-546-5800	546-5812
Sigma-Aldrich Corp 3050 Spruce St *NASDAQ: SIAL* ■ **Fax Area Code:* 800 ■ *TF:* 800-325-3010 ■ *Web:* www.sigmaaldrich.com	Saint Louis	MO	63103	314-771-5765	325-5052*
Sinapis Pharma Inc 3610 Holly Grove Ave *Web:* www.sinapispharma.com	Jacksonville	FL	32217	904-619-0043	
Southern Biotechnology Assoc Inc 160A Oxmoor Blvd *TF:* 800-722-2255 ■ *Web:* www.southernbiotech.com	Birmingham	AL	35209	205-945-1774	945-8768
Specialty Medical Supplies 3882 NW 124th Ave *Web:* www.specialtymedicalsupplies.com	Coral Springs	FL	33065	954-752-5603	
St Renatus LLC 1000 Centre Ave *TF:* 888-686-2314 ■ *Web:* www.st-renatus.com	Fort Collins	CO	80526	970-282-0156	
Stanbio Laboratory LP 1261 N Main St *TF:* 800-531-5535 ■ *Web:* www.stanbio.com	Boerne	TX	78006	830-249-0772	
Stason Pharmaceuticals Inc 11 Morgan *Web:* www.stason.com	Irvine	CA	92618	949-380-4327	
Stat Pharmaceuticals Inc 9545 Pathway St Ste A	Santee	CA	92071	619-956-4200	
Straight Arrow Products Inc 2020 Highland Ave *TF:* 800-827-9815 ■ *Web:* straightarrowinc.com	Bethlehem	PA	18020	610-882-9606	
Strategic Diagnostics Inc 111 Pencader Dr *NASDAQ: SDIX* ■ *TF:* 800-544-8881 ■ *Web:* www.sdix.com	Newark	DE	19702	302-456-6789	456-6770
Streck Inc 7002 S 109th St *TF:* 800-228-6090 ■ *Web:* www.streck.com	Omaha	NE	68128	402-333-1982	
Sun Pharmaceutical Industries Inc 270 Prospect Plains Rd *Web:* www.sunpharma.com	Cranbury	NJ	08512	609-495-2800	
Sunovion Pharmaceuticals Inc 84 Waterford Dr *TF:* 888-394-7377 ■ *Web:* www.sunovion.com	Marlborough	MA	01752	508-481-6700	
Super Thrifty Drugs Canada Ltd 381 Park Ave E *Web:* www.superthrifty.com	Brandon	MB	R7A7A5	204-728-1522	
SurModics Inc 9924 W 74th St *NASDAQ: SRDX* ■ *TF:* 866-787-6639 ■ *Web:* www.surmodics.com	Eden Prairie	MN	55344	952-829-2700	500-7001
Swiss Caps USA Inc 14193 SW 119th Ave *Web:* aenova.de/	Miami	FL	33186	305-234-0102	
Syndax Pharmaceuticals Inc 400 Totten Pond Rd Ste 110 *Web:* www.syndax.com	Waltham	MA	02451	781-419-1400	
Synergent Biochem Inc 12026 Centralia Rd Ste H *Web:* www.synergentbiochem.com	Hawaiian Gardens	CA	90716	562-809-3389	809-6191
Syntrix Biosystems Inc 215 Clay St NW Ste B-5 *Web:* www.syntrixbio.com	Auburn	WA	98001	253-833-8009	
Tec Laboratories Inc 7100 Tec Labs Way SW *TF:* 800-482-4464 ■ *Web:* www.teclabsinc.com	Albany	OR	97321	541-926-4577	
Techne Corp 614 McKinley Pl NE *NASDAQ: TECH* ■ *TF:* 800-343-7475 ■ *Web:* bio-techne.com/	Minneapolis	MN	55413	612-379-8854	379-6580
Teco Diagnostics 1268 N Lakeview Ave *TF:* 800-222-9880 ■ *Web:* www.tecodiagnostics.com	Anaheim	CA	92807	714-463-1111	463-1169
Teikoku Pharma USA Inc 1718 Ringwood Ave *Web:* www.teikokuusa.com	San Jose	CA	95131	408-501-1800	
Ther-Rx Corp One Corporate Woods Dr *Web:* lumarahealth.com	Bridgeton	MO	63044	314-646-3700	
Theracrine Inc One Memorial Dr Seventh Fl	Cambridge	MA	02142	617-218-1605	
Theragenics Corp 5203 Bristol Industrial Way *NYSE: TGX* ■ *TF:* 800-458-4372 ■ *Web:* www.theragenics.com	Buford	GA	30518	770-271-0233	831-5294
TheraVida Inc 177 Bovet Rd Ste 600 *Web:* www.theravida.com	San Mateo	CA	94402	650-638-2335	
Thermo Scientific 12076 Santa Fe Dr PO Box 14428 **Fax Area Code:* 800 ■ *TF:* 800-255-6730 ■ *Web:* www.remel.com	Lenexa	KS	66215	913-888-0939	621-8251*
Theron Pharmaceuticals Inc 365 San Aleso Ave *Web:* www.theronpharma.com	Sunnyvale	CA	94085	408-792-7424	
Time-Cap Labs Inc Seven Michael Ave *Web:* www.timecaplabs.com	Farmingdale	NY	11735	631-753-9090	
Tocagen Inc 3030 Bunker Hill St Ste 230 *Web:* www.tocagen.com	San Diego	CA	92109	858-412-8400	
Tokai Pharmaceuticals Inc One Broadway 14th Fl *Web:* www.tokaipharmaceuticals.com	Cambridge	MA	02142	617-225-4305	
TOLMAR Holding Inc 701 Centre Ave *Web:* www.tolmar.com	Fort Collins	CO	80526	970-212-4500	
Torrent Pharma Inc 5380 Holiday Ter Ste 40 *Web:* www.mtnl.net.in	Kalamazoo	MI	49009	269-544-2299	
Townley Inc 389 Fifth Ave Rm 1100 *Web:* www.townleygirl.com	New York	NY	10016	212-779-0544	
Tragara Pharmaceuticals Inc 3152 Lionshead Ave Ste 120 *Web:* www.tragarapharma.com	Carlsbad	CA	92010	760-208-6900	
Trana Discovery Inc 2054-260 Kildaire Farm Rd *TF:* 866-390-3452 ■ *Web:* www.tranadiscovery.com	Cary	NC	27518	866-390-3452	
Trevena Inc 1018 W Eighth Ave Ste A *Web:* www.trevenainc.com	King Of Prussia	PA	19406	610-354-8840	
Triad Isotopes Inc 4205 Vineland Rd Ste L1 *TF:* 866-310-0086 ■ *Web:* www.triadisotopes.com	Orlando	FL	32811	407-455-6700	
Triarco Industries LLC 400 Hamburg Tpke *Web:* www.triarco.com	Wayne	NJ	07470	973-942-5100	
Triclinic Labs 1201 Cumberland Ave Ste S *Web:* www.tricliniclabs.com	West Lafayette	IN	47906	765-588-6200	
Trinity Biotech PLC 5919 Farnsworth Ct *NASDAQ: TRIB* ■ *TF:* 800-331-2291 ■ *Web:* www.trinitybiotech.com	Carlsbad	CA	92008	760-929-0500	929-0124
TVAX Biomedical Inc 8006 Reeder St *Web:* www.tvaxbiomedical.com	Lenexa	KS	66214	913-492-2221	
Tyger Scientific Inc 324 Stokes Ave *TF:* 888-329-8990 ■ *Web:* www.tygersci.com	Ewing	NJ	08638	609-434-0143	
Uman Pharma Inc 100 De L'Industrie Blvd *TF:* 877-444-9989 ■ *Web:* www.umanpharma.com	Candiac	QC	J5R1J1	450-444-9989	
Unique Pharmaceuticals Ltd 5920 S General Bruce Dr Ste 500 *Web:* www.upisolutions.com	Temple	TX	76502	254-933-0874	
Utak Laboratories Inc 25020 Ave Tibbitts *TF:* 800-235-3442 ■ *Web:* www.utak.com	Valencia	CA	91355	661-294-3935	294-9272
Valeo Pharma Inc 16667 Hymus Blvd Kirkland *TF:* 888-694-0865 ■ *Web:* www.valeopharma.com	Montreal	QC	H9H4R9	514-694-0150	
Valley Wholesale Drug Company Inc 1401 W Fremont St PO Box 2065 *Web:* www.vwdco.com	Stockton	CA	95203	209-466-0131	
VersaPharm Inc 1775 W Oak Pkwy Ste 800 *Web:* www.versapharm.com	Marietta	GA	30062	770-499-8100	
Verus Pharmaceuticals Inc 12671 High Bluff Dr Ste 200 *Web:* www.veruspharm.com	San Diego	CA	92130	858-436-1600	
Viamet Pharmaceuticals Inc 2250 Perimeter Park Dr Ste 320 *Web:* www.viamet.com	Morrisville	NC	27560	919-467-8539	
Victus Inc 4918 SW 74th Ct *Web:* www.victus.com	Miami	FL	33155	305-663-2129	
VIRxSYS Corp 200 Perry Pkwy Ste 1A *Web:* www.virxsys.com	Gaithersburg	MD	20877	301-987-0480	
VistaPharm Inc 2224 Cahaba Vly Dr Ste B3 *Web:* www.vistapharm.com	Birmingham	AL	35242	205-981-1387	
Vitae Pharmaceuticals Inc 502 W Office Ctr Dr *Web:* www.vitaepharma.com	Fort Washington	PA	19034	215-461-2000	
Wako Chemicals USA Inc 1600 Bellwood Rd *TF:* 800-992-9256 ■ *Web:* www.wakousa.com	Richmond	VA	23237	804-271-7677	271-7791
Webco Hawaii Inc 2840 Mokumoa St *Web:* www.awdhi.com	Honolulu	HI	96819	808-839-4551	
World Wide Packaging LLC 15 Vreeland Rd Ste 4 *TF:* 800-950-0390 ■ *Web:* www.wwpinc.com	Florham Park	NJ	07932	973-805-6500	805-6510
Worthington Biochemical Corp 730 Vassar Ave *TF:* 800-445-9603 ■ *Web:* www.worthington-biochem.com	Lakewood	NJ	08701	732-942-1660	942-9270
Xeris Pharmaceuticals Inc 3208 Red River St Ste 300 *TF:* 888-570-4781 ■ *Web:* xerispharma.com	Austin	TX	78705	888-570-4781	
Xttrium Laboratories Inc 415 W Pershing Rd *Web:* www.xttrium.com	Chicago	IL	60609	773-268-5800	
Zepto Metrix Corp 872 Main St *TF Cust Svc:* 800-274-5487 ■ *Web:* www.zeptometrix.com	Buffalo	NY	14202	716-882-0920	882-0959
ZLB Bioplasma Inc 801 N Brand Blvd Ste 1150	Glendale	CA	91203	818-244-2952	
Zymeworks Inc 540-1385 W 8th Ave *Web:* www.zymeworks.com	Vancouver	BC	V6H3V9	604-678-1388	737-7077

235 DISPLAYS - EXHIBIT & TRADE SHOW

Company / Address	City	State	ZIP	Phone	Fax
3D Exhibits Inc 2900 Lively Blvd *TF:* 800-471-9617 ■ *Web:* www.3dexhibits.com	Elk Grove Village	IL	60007	847-250-9000	860-8165
CB Displays International 5141 S Procyon *Web:* www.cbdisplays.com	Las Vegas	NV	89118	702-739-9301	739-8154
Derse Exhibits Inc 3800 W Canal St *TF:* 800-562-2300 ■ *Web:* www.derse.com	Milwaukee	WI	53208	414-257-2000	257-1145
Design & Production Inc 7110 Rainwater Pl *Web:* www.d-and-p.com	Lorton	VA	22079	703-550-8640	339-0296
Downing Displays Inc 550 Techne Ctr Dr *TF:* 800-883-1800 ■ *Web:* www.downingdisplays.com	Milford	OH	45150	513-248-9800	248-2605
Exhibits & More 7843 Goguen Dr *Web:* www.exhibitsandmore.com	Liverpool	NY	13090	315-652-0383	652-8020
Expon Exhibits 909 Fee Dr *TF:* 800-783-9766 ■ *Web:* www.exponexhibits.com	Sacramento	CA	95815	916-924-1600	924-1622
Gilbert Displays Inc 110 Spagnoli Rd *TF:* 855-577-1100 ■ *Web:* www.gilbertdisplays.com	Melville	NY	11747	631-577-1100	577-1139
Group360 Inc 1227 Washington Ave *Web:* www.group360.com	Saint Louis	MO	63103	314-260-6360	

Phone Fax

Hadley Exhibits Inc 1700 Elmwood Ave .... Buffalo NY 14207 716-874-3666 874-9994
Web: hadleyexhibitsinc.com

HB Stubbs Co 27027 Mound Rd .... Warren MI 48092 586-574-9700 574-9741
Web: www.hbstubbs.com

Lynch Exhibits 7 Campus Dr .... Burlington NJ 08016 609-387-1600 239-1669
Web: www.lynchexhibits.com

Marketechs Exhibit Design 3425 Woodbridge Cir......... York PA 17406 717-764-2588
Web: www.marketechs.com

MG Design Assoc Corp 8778 100th St .... Pleasant Prairie WI 53158 262-947-8890 947-8898
Web: www.mgdesign.com

Siegel Display Products 300 Sixth Ave N .... Minneapolis MN 55401 612-340-1493 230-5598*
**Fax Area Code:* 800 ■ *TF:* 800-626-0322 ■ *Web:* www.siegeldisplay.com

Sparks Exhibits & Environments
10232 Palm Dr .... Santa Fe Springs CA 90670 562-941-0101
Web: www.sparksonline.com

236 DISPLAYS - POINT-OF-PURCHASE

SEE ALSO Signs p. 3174

Phone Fax

Acrylic Design Assoc 6050 Nathan Ln N .... Plymouth MN 55442 763-559-8395 559-2589
TF: 800-445-2167 ■ *Web:* www.acrylicdesign.com

AMD Industries Inc 4620 W 19th St .... Cicero IL 60804 708-863-8900 863-2065
TF: 800-367-9999 ■ *Web:* www.amdpop.com

Apco Products Inc PO Box 236........................ Essex CT 06426 860-767-2108 767-7259
Web: www.apco-products.com

Archbold Container Corp
800 W Barre Rd PO Box 10......................... Archbold OH 43502 419-445-8865 446-2529
TF: 800-446-2520 ■ *Web:* www.archboldcontainer.com

Arlington Display Industries
19303 W Davison St................................ Detroit MI 48223 313-837-1212 837-3425
Web: www.arlingtondisplay.com

Array Marketing 45 Progress Ave .... Toronto ON M1P2Y6 416-299-4865 292-9759
TF: 800-295-4120 ■ *Web:* www.arraymarketing.com

Art-Phyl Creations 16250 NW 48th Ave .... Hialeah FL 33014 305-624-2333 621-4093
TF: 800-327-8318 ■ *Web:* hookstoresales.com

Artkraft Strauss LLC 1776 Broadway Ste 1810......... New York NY 10019 212-265-5155 265-5159
Web: www.artkraft.com

Cannon Equipment Co 15100 Business Pkwy .... Rosemount MN 55068 651-322-6300 322-1583
Web: www.cannonequipment.com

Chicago Display Marketing Corp 2021 W St....... River Grove IL 60171 708-842-0001 681-0010*
**Fax Area Code:* 800 ■ *TF:* 800-681-4340 ■ *Web:* www.chicagodisplay.com

Colony Inc 2500 Galvin Dr .... Elgin IL 60123 847-426-5300
TF: 800-735-1300 ■ *Web:* www.colonydisplay.com

Concept Display & Packaging Corp
20 River Ter Ste 361.............................. New York NY 10282 212-566-2359
Web: www.conceptdisplaycorp.com

Display Smart LLC 801 W 27th Terr.................. Lawrence KS 66046 785-843-1869 843-1874
TF: 888-843-1870 ■ *Web:* www.display-smart.com

Display Technologies LLC
1111 Marcus Ave Ste M68...................... Lake Success NY 11042 800-424-4220 321-1932*
**Fax Area Code:* 718 ■ *TF:* 800-424-4220 ■ *Web:* www.display-technologies.com

Felbro Inc 3666 E Olympic Blvd .... Los Angeles CA 90023 323-263-8686 263-8874
TF: 800-733-5276 ■ *Web:* www.felbrodisplays.com

Frank Mayer & Assoc Inc 1975 Wisconsin Ave......... Grafton WI 53024 855-294-2875 377-3449*
**Fax Area Code:* 262 ■ *TF:* 855-294-2875 ■ *Web:* www.frankmayer.com

Harbor Industries Inc 14130 172nd Ave........... Grand Haven MI 49417 616-842-5330 842-1385
TF: 800-968-6993 ■ *Web:* www.harbor-ind.com

Hunter Display 14 Hewlett Ave.............. East Patchogue NY 11772 631-475-5900 475-5950
TF: 800-767-2110 ■ *Web:* www.hunterdisplays.com

IDEAL 4800 S Austin Ave .... Chicago IL 60638 708-594-3100 594-3109
Web: www.idealpop.com

Ideal Wire Works Inc 820 S Date Ave................ Alhambra CA 91803 626-282-0844
Web: www.idealwireworks.com

Kosakura & Assoc Three Holland .... Irvine CA 92618 949-529-3400 529-3411
Web: www.kosakura.com

Lakeshore Display Company Inc
2031 Washington Ave PO Box 983................. Sheboygan WI 53081 920-457-3695 457-5673
Web: www.lakeshoredisplay.com

Lingo Manufacturing Co 7400 Industrial Rd .... Florence KY 41042 859-371-2662 371-0283
TF Cust Svc: 800-354-9771 ■ *Web:* www.lingomfg.com

MDI Worldwide 38271 W 12-Mile Rd.......... Farmington Hills MI 48331 248-553-1900 488-5700*
**Fax:* Sales ■ *TF Sales:* 800-228-8925 ■ *Web:* www.mdiworldwide.com

Millrock
RiverRun Commercial 4660 Early Rd.......... Mt. Crawford VA 22841 540-437-3458
Web: www.riverruncommercial.com

Mpo Videotronics Inc 5069 Maureen Ln .... Moorpark CA 93021 805-499-8513 499-8206
Web: www.mpo-video.com

Nashville Display 306 Hartmann Dr .... Lebanon TN 37087 615-743-2900 743-2901
TF: 800-251-1150 ■ *Web:* www.nashvilledisplay.com

New Dimensions Research Corp
260 Spagnoli Rd.................................. Melville NY 11747 631-694-1356 694-6097
TF: 800-637-8870 ■ *Web:* www.ndrc.com

Ovation Instore 57-13 49th Pl....................... Maspeth NY 11378 718-628-2600 386-8171
TF: 800-553-2202 ■ *Web:* www.ovationinstore.com

Rapid Displays 4300 W 47th St .... Chicago IL 60632 773-927-1091 927-1091
TF: 800-356-5775 ■ *Web:* www.rapiddisplays.com

Service Products Inc 5900 W 51st St................ Chicago IL 60638 773-767-2360 496-1818*
**Fax Area Code:* 708 ■ *Web:* www.serviceproductsinc.com

Thorco Industries Inc 1300 E 12th St................. Lamar MO 64759 417-682-3375 682-1326
TF: 800-445-3375 ■ *Web:* www.thorco.com

Trans World Marketing Corp
360 Murray Hill Pkwy....................... East Rutherford NJ 07073 201-935-5565 559-2011
Web: www.transworldmarketing.com

United Displaycraft 333 E Touhy Ave .... Des Plaines IL 60018 847-375-3800 375-3801
TF General: 877-632-8767 ■ *Web:* www.uniteddisplaycraft.com

Universal Display & Fixtures Co
726 E Hwy 121 .... Lewisville TX 75057 972-221-5022 221-6624
TF: 800-235-0701

Visual Marketing Inc 154 W Erie St.................. Chicago IL 60654 312-664-9177 664-9473
TF: 800-662-8640 ■ *Web:* www.vmichicago.com

Phone Fax

Vulcan Industries Inc 300 Display Dr................. Moody AL 35004 205-640-2400 640-2412
TF: 888-444-4417 ■ *Web:* www.vulcanind.com

DOOR & WINDOW GLASS

SEE Glass - Flat, Plate, Tempered p. 2357

237 DOORS & WINDOWS - METAL

SEE ALSO Shutters - Window (All Types) p. 3173

Phone Fax

AK Draft Seal Ltd 7470 Buller Ave .... Burnaby BC V5J4S5 604-451-1080
Web: www.draftseal.com

Allan Window Technologies Ltd 131 Caldari Rd ...... Concord ON L4K3Z9 905-738-8600
Web: www.allanwindows.com

Allmetal Inc One Pierce Pl Ste 900 .... Itasca IL 60143 630-250-8090
Web: www.allmetalinc.com

Alweather Windows & Doors Ltd 27 Troop Ave...... Dartmouth NS B3B2A7 902-468-2605
Web: www.awwd.ca

American Physical Security Group LLC
1030 Goodworth Dr .... Apex NC 27539 919-363-1894
Web: www.americanpsg.com

Amsco Windows Inc 1880 S 1045 W .... Salt Lake City UT 84104 801-978-5000 974-0498
TF: 800-748-4661 ■ *Web:* www.amscowindows.com

Anemostat 1220 Watsoncenter Rd PO Box 4938.......... Carson CA 90745 310-835-7500 835-0448
TF: 877-423-7426 ■ *Web:* www.anemostat.com

Asi Technologies Inc 5848 N 95th Ct.............. Milwaukee WI 53225 414-464-6200 464-9863
TF: 800-558-7068 ■ *Web.* www.asidoors.com

ASSA ABLOY 110 Sargent Dr...................... New Haven CT 06511 800-377-3948 777-9042*
**Fax Area Code:* 203 ■ **Fax:* Sales ■ *TF:* 800-377-3948 ■ *Web:* www.assaabloydss.com

Atkinson's Mirror and Glass 909 N Orchard St........... Boise ID 83706 208-375-3762 375-3774
Web: www.atkinsonsmirrorandglass.com

Atrium Cos Inc 3890 W NW Hwy Ste 500 .... Dallas TX 75220 214-630-5757 630-5001
Web: atrium.com

AWP Yale Ogron Mfg 8130 NW 74th Ave .... Medley FL 33166 305-887-2646 883-1309
Web: www.awpwindowsanddoors.com

Babcock-Davis 9300 73rd Ave N .... Brooklyn Park MN 55428 763-488-9247 488-9248
TF: 888-412-3726 ■ *Web:* www.babcockdavis.com

Ceco Door 9159 Telecom Dr .... Milan TN 38358 731-686-8345 686-4211
Web: www.cecodoor.com

Champion Aluminum Corp 140 Eileen Way............ Syosset NY 11791 516-921-6200 921-6370
Web: www.championwindows.com

Clopay Bldg Products Inc 8585 Duke Blvd .... Mason OH 45040 800-225-6729
TF: 800-225-6729 ■ *Web:* www.clopaydoor.com

Columbia Mfg Corp 14400 S San Pedro St............ Gardena CA 90248 310-327-9300 323-9862
TF: 800-729-3667 ■ *Web:* www.columbiamfg.com

Cook & Boardman Inc 9347 D Ducks Ln Ste A......... Charlotte NC 28273 704-334-8683 334-9366
Web: www.cookandboardman.com

Cookson Co 2417 S 50th Ave......................... Phoenix AZ 85043 602-272-4244 233-2132
TF: 800-294-4358 ■ *Web:* www.cooksondoor.com

Cornell Iron Works Inc 24 Elmwood Rd.......... Mountain Top PA 18707 570-474-6773 474-9973
TF: 800-233-8366 ■ *Web:* www.cornelliron.com

Cornell Storefront Systems Inc
140 Maffet St .... Wilkes-barre PA 18705 570-706-2775
Web: www.cornellstorefronts.com

Curries Co 1502 12th St NW...................... Mason City IA 50401 641-423-1334 424-8305
Web: www.curries.com

Dawson Metal Company Inc 825 Allen St.......... Jamestown NY 14701 716-664-3815 664-3485
Web: www.dawsonmetal.com

Deansteel Manufacturing Co 111 Merchant .... San Antonio TX 78204 210-226-8271
Web: www.deansteel.com

Dominion Bldg Products
6949 Fairbanks N Houston Rd .... Houston TX 77040 800-826-2617 466-8177*
**Fax Area Code:* 713 ■ *TF:* 800-826-2617 ■ *Web:* www.dominionproducts.com

Door Components Inc 7980 Redwood Ave .... Fontana CA 92336 909-770-5700
TF: 866-989-3667 ■ *Web:* www.doorcomponents.com

Drew Industries Inc 200 Mamaroneck Ave .... White Plains NY 10601 914-428-9098
NYSE: DW ■ *Web:* www.drewindustries.com

Dunbarton Corp PO Box 8577 .... Dothan AL 36304 800-633-7553 793-7022*
**Fax Area Code:* 334 ■ *TF:* 800-633-7553 ■ *Web:* www.dunbarton.com

Dynaflair Corp 8147 Eagle Palm Dr .... Riverview FL 33569 813-248-8100
Web: www.dynaflair.com

Eagle Window & Door Inc 2045 Kerper Blvd .... Dubuque IA 52001 563-556-2270
Web: www.eaglewindow.com

EFCO Corp 1000 County Rd............................ Monett MO 65708 417-235-3193 235-7313
TF: 800-221-4169 ■ *Web:* www.efcocorp.com

Electric Power Door 522 W 27th St .... Hibbing MN 55746 218-263-8366
Web: www.electricpowerdoor.com

Elixir Industries Inc
24800 Chrisanta Dr Ste 210.................... Mission Viejo CA 92691 949-860-5000 860-5011
TF: 800-421-1942 ■ *Web:* www.elixirind.com

EMCO Enterprises Inc
2121 E Walnut St PO Box 853 .... Des Moines IA 50317 515-265-6101

Fimbel Architectural Door Specialties LLC
PO Box 96 .... Whitehouse NJ 08888 908-534-1732
Web: www.fimbelads.com

Fleming Door Products Ltd
101 Ashbridge Cir .... Woodbridge ON L4L3R5 800-263-7515 427-1668*
**Fax Area Code:* 905 ■ *TF:* 800-263-7515 ■ *Web:* www.flemingdoor.com

General Aluminum Company of Texas LLP
1001 W Crosby Rd .... Carrollton TX 75006 972-242-5271 242-7322
TF: 800-727-0835 ■ *Web:* www.miwd.com

GlassCraft Door Co 2002 Brittmoore Rd.............. Houston TX 77043 713-690-8282 690-2919
TF: 800-766-2196 ■ *Web:* www.gcdoor.com

Graham Architectural Products Corp
1551 Mt Rose Ave..................................... York PA 17403 717-849-8100 849-8148
TF: 800-755-6274 ■ *Web:* www.grahamwindows.com

Habersham Metal Products Co
264 Stapleton Rd .... Cornelia GA 30531 706-778-2212 778-2769
Web: www.habershammetal.com

Phone | Fax

Hehr International Inc 3333 Casitas Ave .... Los Angeles CA 90039 323-663-1261 666-2372
Web: www.hehrintl.com

Hope's Windows Inc
84 Hopkins Ave PO Box 580 .... Jamestown NY 14702 716-665-5124 665-3365
Web: www.hopeswindows.com

Hufcor Inc 2101 Kennedy Rd .... Janesville WI 53545 608-756-1241 756-1246
TF: 800-356-6968 ■ *Web:* www.hufcor.com

Hygrade Metal Moulding Manufacturing Corp
1990 Highland Ave .... Bethlehem PA 18020 610-866-2441 866-3761
TF: 800-645-9475 ■ *Web:* www.hygrademetal.com

International Revolving Door Co
2138 N Sixth Ave .... Evansville IN 47710 812-425-3311 426-2682
TF: 800-745-4726 ■ *Web:* www.internationalrevolvingdoors.com

International Window Corp
5625 E Firestone Blvd .... South Gate CA 90280 562-928-6411 928-3492
TF: 800-477-4032 ■ *Web:* www.intlwindow.com

J T Walker Industries Inc
861 N Hercules Ave .... Clearwater FL 33765 727-461-0501 443-7167

Jamison Door Co 55 JV Jamison Dr PO Box 70 ...... Hagerstown MD 21740 301-733-3100 329-5155*
**Fax Area Code:* 240 ■ *TF:* 800-532-3667 ■ *Web:* www.jamison-door.com

Jantek Industries 230 Rt 70 .... Medford NJ 08055 609-654-1030 654-1083
TF: 888-782-7937 ■ *Web:* jantekwindows.com

Joyce Windows 1125 Berea Industrial Pkwy .... Berea OH 44017 440-239-9100
TF: 800-824-7988 ■ *Web:* www.joycewindows.com

Kane Manufacturing Corp 515 N Fraley St .... Kane PA 16735 814-837-6464 837-6230
TF: 800-952-6399 ■ *Web:* www.kanesterling.com

Kawneer Company Inc 555 Guthridge Ct .... Norcross GA 30092 770-449-5555 734-1560
Web: www.kawneer.com

Kinro Inc 2703 College Ave .... Goshen IN 46528 574-535-1125
Web: www.kinro.com

Krieger Specialty Products Co
4880 Gregg Rd .... Pico Rivera CA 90660 562-695-0645 692-0146
TF: 866-203-5060 ■ *Web:* www.kriegerproducts.com

LaForce Inc 1060 W Mason St .... Green Bay WI 54303 920-497-7100 497-4955
TF: 800-236-8858 ■ *Web:* www.laforceinc.com

Liberty Glass & Metal Industries Inc
339 Riverside Dr .... North Grosvenordale CT 06255 860-923-3623
Web: www.libertywindowsystems.com

Lockheed Window Corp Rt 100 PO Box 166 .... Pascoag RI 02859 401-568-3061 568-2273
TF: 800-537-3061 ■ *Web:* www.lockheedwindow.com

Logan Square Aluminum Supply Inc
2500 N Pulaski Rd .... Chicago IL 60639 773-235-2500
Web: www.remodelerssupply.com

Loxcreen Co Inc, The
1630 Old Dunbar Rd PO Box 4004 .... West Columbia SC 29172 803-822-8200 822-8547
TF: 800-330-5699 ■ *Web:* www.loxcreen.com

M-D Bldg Products Inc
4041 N Santa Fe Ave .... Oklahoma City OK 73118 405-528-4411
TF Cust Svc: 800-654-8454 ■ *Web:* www.mdteam.com

Mannix Architectural Window Products
345 Crooked Hill Rd .... Brentwood NY 11717 631-231-0800 231-0571
Web: mannixwindows.com

McKeon Door Co 44 Sawgrass Dr .... Bellport NY 11713 631-803-3000 803-3030
TF: 800-266-9392 ■ *Web:* www.mckeondoor.com

Megadoor Inc 611 Hwy 74 S Ste 100 .... Peachtree City GA 30269 770-631-9086
Web: www.megadoor.com

MI Windows & Doors Inc 650 W Market St .... Gratz PA 17030 717-365-3300 365-3780
TF: 800-727-0835 ■ *Web:* www.miwd.com

Mid-America Precision Products LLC
1927 W Fourth St .... Joplin MO 64801 417-623-2285
Web: www.midampp.com

Milgo Industrial Inc 68 Lombardi St .... Brooklyn NY 11222 718-388-6476 963-0614
Web: www.milgo-bufkin.com

MM Systems Corp 50 MM Way .... Pendergrass GA 30567 706-824-7500 824-7501
TF: 800-241-3460 ■ *Web:* www.mmsystemscorp.com

Moss Supply Company Inc 5001 N Graham St .... Charlotte NC 28269 704-596-8717 598-9012
TF: 800-438-0770 ■ *Web:* www.mosssupply.com

Napoleon Spring Works 111 Weires Dr .... Archbold OH 43502 419-445-1010
Web: www.lynx-nsw.com

National Guard Products Inc 4985 E Raines Rd .... Memphis TN 38118 800-647-7874 255-7874
TF: 800-647-7874 ■ *Web:* www.ngpinc.com

Northeast Bldg Products Corp
4280 Aramingo Ave .... Philadelphia PA 19124 215-535-7110 288-9880
Web: www.nbpcorporation.com

Nystrom Inc 9300 73rd Ave N .... Minneapolis MN 55428 763-488-9200 317-8770*
**Fax Area Code:* 800 ■ *TF:* 800-547-2635 ■ *Web:* www.nystrom.com

O'Keeffe's Inc 325 Newhall St .... San Francisco CA 94124 415-822-4222 822-5222
TF: 888-653-3333 ■ *Web:* www.okeeffes.com

Optimum Technologies Inc
570 Joe Frank Harris Pkwy PO Box 1537 .... Cartersville GA 30120 770-386-3470 382-9047
Web: www.otitech.com

Optimum Window Manufacturing 28 Canal St .... Ellenville NY 12428 845-647-1900
Web: www.optimumwindow.com

Overhead Door Corp
2501 S State Hwy 121 Bus Ste 200 .... Lewisville TX 75067 469-549-7100 549-7281
TF: 800-275-3290 ■ *Web:* www.overheaddoor.com

Overly Manufacturing Co 574 W Otterman St .... Greensburg PA 15601 724-834-7300 830-2871
TF: 800-979-7300 ■ *Web:* www.overly.com

Peelle Co 373 Nesconset Hwy Ste 311 .... Hauppauge NY 11788 905-846-4545 846-2161
TF: 800-787-5020 ■ *Web:* www.peelledoor.com

Peerless Products Inc 2403 S Main St .... Fort Scott KS 66701 620-223-4610 224-3107
TF: 800-279-9999 ■ *Web:* www.peerless-usa.com

PGT Industries 1070 Technology Dr .... Nokomis FL 34275 941-480-1600 486-8369
TF: 800-282-6019 ■ *Web:* www.pgtindustries.com

Phillips Manufacturing Co 4949 S 30th St .... Omaha NE 68107 402-339-3800
Web: www.phillipsmfg.com

Pioneer Industries Inc 171 S Newman St .... Hackensack NJ 07601 201-933-1900 933-9580
Web: www.pioneerindustries.com

Portal Inc 10 Tracy Dr .... Avon MA 02322 508-588-3030
Web: www.portalincorporated.com

Quaker Window Products Inc
504 S Hwy 63 PO Box 128 .... Freeburg MO 65035 800-347-0438 744-5586*
**Fax Area Code:* 573 ■ *TF:* 800-347-0438 ■ *Web:* www.quakerwindows.com

Raynor Garage Doors 1101 E River Rd .... Dixon IL 61021 815-288-1431 288-3720*
**Fax:* Cust Svc ■ *TF:* 800-472-9667 ■ *Web:* www.raynor.com

RC Aluminum Industries 2805 NW 75th Ave .... Miami FL 33122 305-592-1515 392-2184

Rebco Inc 1171-1225 Madison Ave .... Paterson NJ 07509 973-684-0200 684-0118
TF: 800-777-0787 ■ *Web:* www.rebcoinc.com

Reese Enterprises Inc 16350 Asher Ave .... Rosemount MN 55068 651-423-1126 423-2662
TF: 800-328-0953 ■ *Web:* www.reeseusa.com

Richards-Wilcox Inc 600 S Lake St .... Aurora IL 60506 800-253-5668 897-6994*
**Fax Area Code:* 630 ■ *TF:* 800-253-5668 ■ *Web:* www.richardswilcox.com

Rochester Colonial Manufacturing Inc
1794 Lyell Ave .... Rochester NY 14606 585-254-8191
Web: www.rochestercolonial.com

Rytec Corp One Cedar Pkwy .... Jackson WI 53037 262-677-9046
Web: www.rytecdoors.com

Seaway Manufacturing Corp 2250 E 33rd St .... Erie PA 16510 814-898-2255
Web: www.seawaymfg.com

Sellmore Industries Inc 815 Smith St .... Buffalo NY 14206 716-854-1600 856-4509
Web: www.sellmoreind.com

Silver Line Bldg Products
1 Silver Line Dr .... North Brunswick NJ 08902 732-247-2030
TF Sales: 800-234-4228 ■ *Web:* www.silverlinewindows.com

Smith & DeShields Inc 165 NW 20th St .... Boca Raton FL 33431 561-395-0808
Web: www.smithanddeshields.com

Southeastern Aluminum Products Inc
6701 Suemac Pl .... Jacksonville FL 32254 904-781-8200 224-8068
TF Sales: 800-243-8200 ■ *Web:* www.southeasternaluminum.com

Southeastern Metals Mfg Company Inc
11801 Industry Dr .... Jacksonville FL 32218 904-757-4200
TF: 800-874-0335 ■ *Web:* www.semetals.com

Special-Lite Inc PO Box 6 .... Decatur MI 49045 269-423-7068 423-7610
TF: 800-821-6531 ■ *Web:* www.special-lite.com

Stanley Access Technologies
65 Scott Swamp Rd .... Farmington CT 06032 860-677-2861 339-7923*
**Fax Area Code:* 877 ■ **Fax:* Cust Svc ■ *TF:* 800-722-2377 ■ *Web:* www.stanleyaccesstechnologies.com

Steelcraft Mfg Co 9017 Blue Ash Rd .... Cincinnati OH 45242 513-745-6400 451-7754*
**Fax Area Code:* 800 ■ *TF Cust Svc:* 877-613-8766 ■ *Web:* us.allegion.com/

Steves & Sons Inc 203 Humble Ave .... San Antonio TX 78225 210-924-5111 924-0470*
**Fax:* Sales ■ *TF Sales:* 800-617-8586 ■ *Web:* www.stevesdoors.com

Sun Windows Inc 1515 E 18th St .... Owensboro KY 42303 270-684-0691
Web: www.sunwindows.com

Super Sky Products Inc 10301 N Enterprise Dr .... Mequon WI 53092 262-242-2000 242-7409
TF: 800-558-0467 ■ *Web:* www.supersky.com

Taylor Bldg Products 631 N First St .... West Branch MI 48661 989-345-5110 345-5116
TF: 800-248-3600 ■ *Web:* www.taylordoor.com

Tempco Products Co 301 E Tempco Ave .... Robinson IL 62454 618-544-3175
Web: www.tempcoproducts.com

Therma-Tru Corp 1750 Indian Wood Cir .... Maumee OH 43537 419-891-7400 891-7411
TF: 800-537-8827 ■ *Web:* www.thermatru.com

Thermo-Twin Industries Inc
1155 Allegheny Ave .... Oakmont PA 15139 412-826-1000 826-8188
TF: 800-641-2211 ■ *Web:* www.thermotwin.com

TRACO 71 Progress Ave .... Cranberry Township PA 16066 724-776-7000 776-7014
TF: 800-992-4444 ■ *Web:* www.alcoa.com

Traditional Door Design & Millwork Ltd
261 Regina Rd .... Woodbridge ON L4L8M3 416-747-1992
Web: www.traditionaldoor.com

Tubelite Inc 4878 Mackinaw Trl .... Reed City MI 49677 800-866-2227
TF: 800-866-2227 ■ *Web:* www.tubeliteinc.com

Wayne-Dalton Corp One Door Dr PO Box 67 .... Mount Hope OH 44660 330-674-7015 763-8047
TF: 800-827-3667 ■ *Web:* www.wayne-dalton.com

West Window Corp 226 Industrial Pk Dr .... Martinsville VA 24112 276-638-2394 638-2300
TF: 800-446-4167 ■ *Web:* www.westwindow.com

Western Window Systems 5621 S 25th St .... Phoenix AZ 85040 602-268-1300 243-3119
Web: westernwindowsystems.com

Willo Products Company Inc
714 Willo Industrial Dr SE .... Decatur AL 35601 256-353-7161 350-8436
Web: www.willoproducts.com

Won-Door Corp 1865 South 3480 West .... Salt Lake City UT 84104 801-973-7500 974-5273
TF: 800-453-8494 ■ *Web:* www.wondoor.com

Young Windows Inc 680 Colwell Ln .... Conshohocken PA 19428 610-828-5422 828-2144
Web: www.youngwindows.com

238 DOORS & WINDOWS - VINYL

Phone | Fax

American Exteriors LLC
1169 W Littleton Blvd .... Littleton CO 80120 303-794-6369 730-5744
TF: 800-794-6369 ■ *Web:* www.amext.com

Amerimax Bldg Products Inc 5208 Tennyson Pkwy .... Plano TX 75024 469-366-3200 448-8391*
**Fax Area Code:* 800 ■ *TF:* 800-448-4033 ■ *Web:* www.amerimaxbp.com

Associated Materials Inc Alside Div
PO Box 2010 .... Akron OH 44309 800-922-6009
TF Cust Svc: 800-922-6009 ■ *Web:* www.alside.com

CertainTeed Corp 750 E Swedesford Rd .... Valley Forge PA 19482 610-341-7000 341-7777
TF Prod Info: 800-782-8777 ■ *Web:* www.certainteed.com

Champion Window Mfg Inc
12121 Champion Way .... Cincinnati OH 45241 513-346-4600 346-4614
TF: 877-424-2674 ■ *Web:* www.championwindow.com

Chelsea Bldg Products 565 Cedar Way .... Oakmont PA 15139 800-424-3573 826-1598*
**Fax Area Code:* 412 ■ *TF:* 800-424-3573 ■ *Web:* www.chelseabuildingproducts.com

Fortune Brands Home & Hardware Inc
520 Lk Cook Rd .... Deerfield IL 60015 847-484-4400
Web: www.fortunebrands.com

Harry G Barr Co 6500 S Zero St .... Fort Smith AR 72903 479-646-7891 646-8591
TF: 800-829-2277 ■ *Web:* www.weatherbarr.com

Larson Manufacturing Co 2333 Eastbrook Dr .... Brookings SD 57006 605-692-6115
TF Cust Svc: 800-352-3360 ■ *Web:* www.larsondoors.com

Moss Supply Company Inc 5001 N Graham St .... Charlotte NC 28269 704-596-8717 598-9012
TF: 800-438-0770 ■ *Web:* www.mosssupply.com

PGT Industries 1070 Technology Dr .... Nokomis FL 34275 941-480-1600 486-8369
TF: 800-282-6019 ■ *Web:* www.pgtindustries.com

Phone Fax

Ply Gem Windows 615 Carson St....Bryan TX 77801 979-779-1051 822-3259
Web: www.alenco.com

Provia Door Inc 2150 SR- 39....Sugarcreek OH 44681 330-852-4711 852-2107
TF General: 800-669-4711 ■ *Web:* www.proviaproducts.com

Quanex Building Products Corp
1900 W Loop S Ste 1500....Houston TX 77027 713-961-4600
TF Cust Svc: 888-475-0633 ■ *Web:* quanex.com

Rehau Inc 1501 EdwaRds Ferry Rd NE....Leesburg VA 20176 703-777-5255 777-3053
TF: 800-247-9445 ■ *Web:* www.rehau.com

Royal Group, The 30 Royal Group Crescent....Woodbridge ON L4H1X9 905-264-0701 850-9184
TF: 800-263-2353 ■ *Web:* www.royalbuildingproducts.com

RubbAir Door Div Eckel Industries Inc
100 Groton Shirley Rd....Ayer MA 01432 978-772-0480 772-7114
TF: 800-966-7822 ■ *Web:* www.rubbair.com

Soft-Lite LLC 10250 Philipp Pkwy....Streetsboro OH 44241 330-528-3400 528-3501
TF: 800-551-1953 ■ *Web:* www.soft-lite.com

Statewide Remodeling Inc
2940 N Hwy 360 Ste 300....Grand Prairie TX 75050 214-677-9000
TF: 800-317-8283 ■ *Web:* www.statewideremodeling.com

Superseal Mfg Co Inc PO Box 795....South Plainfie NJ 07080 908-561-5910 561-7885
TF: 800-433-4873 ■ *Web:* www.supersealwindows.com

Thermal Industries Inc 3700 Haney C....Murrysville PA 15668 724-733-3880 733-3880
TF: 800-245-1540 ■ *Web:* www.thermalindustries.com

Veka Inc 100 Veka Dr....Fombell PA 16123 724-452-1000 452-1007
TF: 800-654-5589 ■ *Web:* www.vekainc.com

VINYLMAX LLC 2921 McBride Ct....Hamilton OH 45011 513-772-2247 672-8381
Web: www.vinylmax.com

Weather Shield Manufacturing Inc
One Weather Shield Plz PO Box 309....Medford WI 54451 715-748-2100 222-2146*
**Fax Area Code:* 800 ■ *TF:* 800-222-2995 ■ *Web:* www.weathershield.com

West Window Corp 226 Industrial Pk Dr....Martinsville VA 24112 276-638-2394 638-2300
TF: 800-446-4167 ■ *Web:* www.westwindow.com

Windsor Windows & Doors
900 S 19th St....West Des Moines IA 50265 515-223-6660 224-1938*
**Fax:* Cust Svc ■ *TF:* 800-218-6186 ■ *Web:* www.windsorwindows.com

239 DOORS & WINDOWS - WOOD

SEE ALSO Millwork p. 2760; Shutters - Window (All Types) p. 3173

Phone Fax

1st United Door Technologies Inc
7255 S Kyrene Ste 104....Tempe AZ 85283 480-705-6632
Web: www.firstudt.com

A B C Doors 5100 S Willow....Houston TX 77035 713-729-9700
Web: www.abcdoors.com

Algoma Hardwoods Inc 1001 Perry St....Algoma WI 54201 920-487-5221 487-3636
TF: 800-678-8910 ■ *Web:* www.algomahardwoods.com

Allmar Inc 287 Riverton Ave....Winnipeg MB R2L0N2 204-668-1000 668-3029
TF: 800-230-5516 ■ *Web:* www.allmar.com

Andersen Corp 100 Fourth Ave N....Bayport MN 55003 651-264-5150 264-5107*
**Fax:* Hum Res ■ *TF:* 888-888-7020 ■ *Web:* www.andersenwindows.com

Burton Lumber Corp 835 Wilson Rd....Chesapeake VA 23324 757-545-4613 545-8852
Web: burton-lumber.com

Combination Door Co 1000 Morris St....Fond du Lac WI 54935 920-922-2050 922-2917
Web: www.combinationdoor.com

Construction Metals LLC 13169 B Slover Ave....Fontana CA 92337 909-390-9880
Web: www.constructionmetals.com

DIRTT Environmental Solutions Ltd
7303 - 30th St SE....Calgary AB T2C1N6 403-723-5000
Web: www.dirtt.net

Endura Products Inc 8817 W Market St....Colfax NC 27235 336-668-2472
TF: 800-334-2006 ■ *Web:* www.enduraproducts.com

EverMark LLC 1050 Northbrook Pkwy....Suwanee GA 30024 678-455-5188
Web: www.evermark-lnl.com

Fene-Tech Inc 264 St-Beno T Est....Amqui QC G5J2C5 418-629-4675 629-3982
Web: www.fene-tech.com

General Doors Corp One Monroe St PO Box 205....Bristol PA 19007 215-788-9277 788-9450
Web: www.general-doors.com

Great Day Improvements LLC
700 E Highland Rd....Macedonia OH 44056 330-468-0700
TF: 800-230-8301 ■ *Web:* www.greatdayimprovements.com

Haley Bros Inc 6291 Orangethorpe Ave....Buena Park CA 90620 714-670-2112 994-6971
TF: 800-854-5951 ■ *Web:* www.haleybros.com

Industrial Door Company Inc
360 Coon Rapids Blvd....Minneapolis MN 55433 763-786-4730 786-9186
TF: 888-798-0199 ■ *Web:* www.idc-automatic.com

Jenkins Mfg Company Inc 1608 Frank Akers Rd....Anniston AL 36207 256-831-7000 261-6116*
**Fax Area Code:* 800 ■ *TF:* 800-633-2323 ■ *Web:* www.monarchwindows.com

King Sash & Door Inc
2799 Hope Church Rd....Winston-Salem NC 27127 336-774-3071 774-3081
Web: www.kingsashanddoor.com

Larson Manufacturing Co 2333 Eastbrook Dr....Brookings SD 57006 605-692-6115
TF Cust Svc: 800-352-3360 ■ *Web:* www.larsondoors.com

Lincoln Wood Products Inc
1400 W Taylor St PO Box 375....Merrill WI 54452 800-967-2461 536-7090*
**Fax Area Code:* 715 ■ *TF:* 800-967-2461 ■ *Web:* www.lincolnwindows.com

Marvin Windows & Doors PO Box 100....Warroad MN 56763 218-386-1430 386-1904
TF: 888-537-7828 ■ *Web:* www.marvin.com

Masonite International Corp
201 N Franklin St Ste 300....Tampa FL 33602 813-877-2726 739-0204
TF: 800-895-2723 ■ *Web:* www.masonite.com

Mathews Bros Co 22 Perkins Rd....Belfast ME 04915 207-338-6490 338-6300
TF: 800-615-2004 ■ *Web:* www.mathewsbrothers.com

Mohawk Flush Doors Inc
980 Pt Township Dr PO Box 112....Northumberland PA 17857 570-473-3557 473-3737
Web: www.mohawkdoors.com

National Vinyl LLC Seven Coburn St....Chicopee MA 01013 413-420-0548
TF: 800-424-5300 ■ *Web:* www.nvpwindows.com

Pella Corp 102 Main St....Pella IA 50219 641-621-1000 621-6950
TF Cust Svc: 877-473-5527 ■ *Web:* www.pella.com

Phone Fax

Quaker Window Products Inc
504 S Hwy 63 PO Box 128....Freeburg MO 65035 800-347-0438 744-5586*
**Fax Area Code:* 573 ■ *TF:* 800-347-0438 ■ *Web:* www.quakerwindows.com

RAM Industries Inc 13119 Mula Ct....Stafford TX 77477 281-495-9056
Web: www.ramind.com

Semling-Menke Company Inc PO Box 378....Merrill WI 54452 715-536-9411 536-3067
TF: 800-333-2206 ■ *Web:* www.semcowindows.com

SNE Enterprises Inc 880 Southview Dr....Mosinee WI 54455 715-693-7000 748-6508*
**Fax:* Hum Res ■ *TF:* 800-826-5509 ■ *Web:* crestlinewindows.com

Steves & Sons Inc 203 Humble Ave....San Antonio TX 78225 210-924-5111 924-0470*
**Fax:* Sales ■ *TF Sales:* 800-617-8586 ■ *Web:* www.stevesdoors.com

Trustile Doors LLC 1780 E 66th Ave....Denver CO 80229 303-286-3931 288-6521
TF: 866-442-5302 ■ *Web:* www.trustile.com

Vancouver Door Company Inc 203 Fifth St NW....Puyallup WA 98371 253-845-9581 845-3364
TF: 800-999-3667 ■ *Web:* www.vancouverdoorco.com

Weather Shield Manufacturing Inc
One Weather Shield Plz PO Box 309....Medford WI 54451 715-748-2100 222-2146*
**Fax Area Code:* 800 ■ *TF:* 800-222-2995 ■ *Web:* www.weathershield.com

WIL-C-MEEK Corp PO Box 1746....Springfield MO 65804 417-521-2801 521-2870
Web: meeks.com

Windsor Windows & Doors
900 S 19th St....West Des Moines IA 50265 515-223-6660 224-1938*
**Fax:* Cust Svc ■ *TF:* 800-218-6186 ■ *Web:* www.windsorwindows.com

240 DRUG STORES

SEE ALSO Health Food Stores p. 2453

Phone Fax

4D Pharmacy Management Systems Inc
2520 Industrial Row Dr....Troy MI 48084 248-540-8066
Web: www.4dpharmacy.com

Advanced Lifeline Services Pharmacy Inc
9900 Shelbyville Rd Ste 2b....Louisville KY 40223 502-423-7525
Web: www.alspharmacy.com

Advanced Optical Systems Inc
6767 Old Madison Pike Nw Ste 410....Huntsville AL 35806 256-971-0036
Web: www.aos-inc.com

Advanced Pharmacy Concepts Inc
6899 Post Rd....North Kingstown RI 02852 401-295-7660
Web: www.apc-rx.com

Allergychoices Inc 2800 National Dr Ste 100....Onalaska WI 54650 608-793-1580
Web: allergychoices.com

Alpha Tech Pet Inc
789 Massachusetts Ave Ste 20....Lexington MA 02420 781-861-7179
Web: www.alphatechpet.com

Alternatives for Industry Inc
2251 Whitfield Park Ave....Sarasota FL 34243 941-739-6566
Web: www.afi-tools.com

American GNC Corp 888 E Easy St....Simi Valley CA 93065 805-582-0582
Web: www.americangnc.com

Apothecary Shoppe, The
1002 East South Temple....Salt Lake City UT 84102 801-521-6353
Web: www.mygnp.com

Apple Valley Medical Clinic Ltd
14655 Galaxie Ave....Apple Valley MN 55124 952-432-6161
Web: www.applevalleymedicalcenter.com

Aquatrol Inc 237 N Euclid Way Ste H....Anaheim CA 92801 714-533-3381
Web: aquatrol.com

Arbor Centers for Eyecare
2640 183rd St Ste 2....Homewood IL 60430 708-798-6633
TF: 866-798-6633 ■ *Web:* www.arboreyecare.com

Arizona Home Care LLC 1626 S Edward Dr....Tempe AZ 85281 602-252-5000
Web: www.azhomecare.com

ARJ Infusion Services Inc 10049 Lakeview Ave....Lenexa KS 66219 913-451-8804
Web: www.arjinfusion.com

ARW Optical Corp 2021 Capital Dr....Wilmington NC 28405 910-452-7373
Web: arwoptical.com

Assured Pharmacy Inc 11100 Ash St Ste 200....Leawood KS 66211 913-602-8344
OTC: APHYQ ■ *Web:* www.assuredrxservices.com

Balcones Dermatology Associates pa
7800 N Mopac Expy Ste 315....Austin TX 78759 512-459-4869
Web: www.balconesdermatology.com

BCP Veterinary Pharmacy 1614 Webster St....Houston TX 77003 713-771-1144
Web: www.bcpvetpharm.com

Bellevue Drug Co 254 Bellevue Ave....Hammonton NJ 08037 609-561-0825
Web: bellevuedrug.com

Berr Pet Supply Inc 929 N Market Blvd....Sacramento CA 95834 916-921-0145
Web: berrpet.com

Bi-Mart Corp 220 S Seneca Rd....Eugene OR 97402 541-344-0681
Web: www.bimart.com

Blue Valley Public Safety Inc
509 James Rollo Dr....Grain Valley MO 64029 816-847-7502
Web: www.bvpsonline.com

Borak Inc Dba Northfield Pharm
601 Water St S....Northfield MN 55057 507-663-0344

Braswell Drugs Inc 1107 S Tyler St....Covington LA 70433 985-892-0818

Brevard Eye Center Inc 665 S Apollo Blvd....Melbourne FL 32901 321-984-3200
Web: www.brevardeye.com

Brite Pharmacy Inc Dba Vital Script
83 17/19 37th Ave....Jackson Heights NY 11372 718-424-1101

Buffalo Pharmacies Inc 1479 Kensington Ave....Buffalo NY 14215 716-832-0599
Web: www.buffalopharmacies.com

C Stuart Inc Dba Columbia Pharmacy
2840 Long Beach Blvd....Long Beach CA 90806 562-426-0303

Cajahs Mountain Discount Drug Inc
2006 Connelly Springs Rd....Lenoir NC 28645 828-726-8632

Calgary Co-Operative Association Ltd
110151 86th Ave SE Ste 110....Calgary AB T2H3A5 403-219-6025
Web: www.calgarycoop.com

Care Service Inc 34099 Melinz Pkwy Unit F....Eastlake OH 44095 440-954-7709
Web: www.diabeticexpress.com

Phone Fax

Carepoint Inc 215 E Bay St Ste 304................Charleston SC 29401 843-853-6999
Web: carepoint.com
Centric Health Resources Inc
17877 Chesterfield Airport Rd ....Chesterfield MO 63005 636-519-2400
Web: www.centrichealthresources.com
CHEM Rx 750 Park Pl...........................Long Beach NY 11561 516-889-8770
Web: www.chemrx.net
Classic Care Pharmacy Corp 1320 Heine Ct.........Burlington ON L7L6L9 905-631-9027
Web: www.classiccare.ca
Classic Optical Laboratories Inc
3710 Belmont Ave.............................Youngstown OH 44505 330-759-8245
Web: www.classicoptical.com
Cloneys Pharmacy Inc 525 Fifth St ....Eureka CA 95501 707-443-1614
Web: cloneys.com
Community Pharmacies LP 16 Commerce Dr Ste 1.....Augusta ME 04332 800-730-4840
TF: 800-730-4840 ■ *Web:* www.communityrx.com
Complete Rx Ltd 3100 S Gessner Rd Ste 640..........Houston TX 77063 713-355-1196 355-5404
Web: completerx.com
CVS Corp One CVS Dr..........................Woonsocket RI 02895 401-765-1500 765-1500*
**Fax:* Cust Svc ■ *TF Cust Svc:* 888-607-4287 ■ *Web:* www.cvs.com
DailyMe Inc 4000 Hollywood Blvd Ste 745-S..........Hollywood FL 33021 954-922-2999
Web: www.dailyme.com
Data Rx Management 305 W Woodard St.............Denison TX 75020 903-465-0798
Web: www.data-rx.com
Davila Pharmacy Inc
1423 Guadalupe St Ste 108 ....San Antonio TX 78207 210-226-5293 224-9257
Web: www.davilapharmacy.com
Davis Ethical Pharmacy
124 N Long Beach Rd....................... Rockville Centre NY 11570 516-764-3200
Discount Drug Mart Inc 211 Commerce Dr............ Medina OH 44256 330-725-2340 722-2990
TF: 800-833-6278 ■ *Web:* www.discount-drugmart.com
Doc's Drugs 230 Comet Dr.......................Braidwood IL 60408 815-458-6104 458-6158
Web: www.docsdrugs.com
Dons Pharmacy 32 S Frederick Ave ....Oelwein IA 50662 319-283-5254
Dougherty's Holdings Inc
16250 Dallas Pkwy Ste 102 .... Dallas TX 75248 972-860-0200 860-0290
Web: www.doughertysholdings.com
Drugstore.com Inc 411 108th Ave NE Ste 1400.........Bellevue WA 98004 800-378-4786 372-3800*
**Fax Area Code:* 425 ■ *TF:* 800-378-4786 ■ *Web:* www.drugstore.com
Empson Drug Co 212 N Main St.................. Ashland City TN 37015 615-792-4644
Estates Pharmacy Inc 169-01 Hillside Ave ....Jamaica NY 11432 718-739-0311
Esther Pharmacy Inc 71 S Broadway ....Yonkers NY 10701 914-965-2661
Web: estherpharmacy.com
Eye Care for Animals 372 S Milwaukee Ave ....Wheeling IL 60090 847-215-3933
Web: www.eyecareforanimals.com
Eye Center Surgeons & Associates Ll
401 Meridian St N Ste 200........................ Huntsville AL 35801 256-705-3937
Web: www.eyecentersurgeons.com
Fagen Pharmacy 915 S Halleck St PO Box 662..........Demotte IN 46310 219-987-6468 987-7226
Web: www.fagenpharmacy.com
Findleys Pharmacy Inc 136 W Main St..............Somerset PA 15501 814-445-7939
Web: findleyspharmacy.com
Flare Industries Inc
16310 Bratton Lnn Bldg 3 Ste 350 .... Austin TX 78728 512-836-9473
Web: www.flareindustries.com
Fraser Hearing & Optical Center
32925 Groesbeck Hwy .... Fraser MI 48026 586-293-8888
Web: www.fraseroptical.com
Fruth Pharmacy Inc 4016 Ohio River Rd.......... Point Pleasant WV 25550 304-675-1612 675-7338
TF: 800-438-5390 ■ *Web:* www.fruthpharmacy.com
Gemmel Pharmacy Group Inc 143 N Euclid Ave........ Ontario CA 91762 909-988-0591
Web: www.gemmelrx.com
General Hearing Corp
175 Brookhollow Esplanade.........................Harahan LA 70123 504-733-3767
Web: www.generalhearing.com
Geneva Woods Pharmacy Inc
501 W International Airport Rd Ste 1A ....Anchorage AK 99518 907-565-6100
Web: www.genevawoods.com
Gloyer'S Pharmacy Inc 1010 W Main St ....Tomball TX 77375 281-351-5454
Web: gloyersrx.com
Good Day Pharmacy 2033 Boise Ave................. Loveland CO 80538 970-669-7500
Web: www.gooddaypharmacy.com
Grandview Pharmacy Inc 2230 N Park Rd .... Connersville IN 47331 765-827-0847
Web: www.grandviewpharmacy.com
Graymark Healthcare Inc
210 Pk Ave Ste 1350 ....Oklahoma City OK 73102 405-601-5300
NASDAQ: GRMH ■ *Web:* fdnh.com
GT Distributors Inc 100 McFarland Ave.............Rossville GA 30741 706-866-2764
Web: www.gtdist.com
Hallmark Pharmacy
1316 Sycamore School Rd Ste 130 ....Fort Worth TX 76134 817-293-2441
Harmon Stores Inc 650 Liberty Ave...................... Union NJ 07083 866-427-6661 688-0376*
**Fax Area Code:* 908 ■ *TF:* 866-427-6661 ■ *Web:* www.harmondiscount.com
Hartig Drug Co 703 Main St PO Box 709.............Dubuque IA 52001 563-588-8700 588-8750
Web: www.hartigdrug.com
Health Care Unlimited Inc
1100 E Laurel Ave Ste 100..........................Mcallen TX 78501 956-994-9911
Web: www.hcuinc.com
Highlander Charter School, The
42 Lexington Ave .... Providence RI 02907 401-831-7323
Web: www.highlandercharter.org
Horton & Converse Pharmacy
120 Newport Ctr Dr Ste 250.................... Newport Beach CA 92660 949-640-1231
Web: www.hortonandconverse.com
In Focus Optical 202 Cherry St .... Milford CT 06460 203-882-7278
Web: www.infocussystems.com
International Eyecare Center Inc
2445 Broadway......................................Quincy IL 62301 217-222-8800
Web: www.iec2020.com
Interstate Optical Co 680 Lindaire Ln............. Mansfield OH 44901 419-529-6800
Web: interstateoptical.com

Irsfeld Pharmacy PC 33 Ninth St W .... Dickinson ND 58601 701-483-4858
Web: irsfeldpharmacy.com
Janoka Inc Dba The Medicine Shoppe
542 S Eufaula Ave.................................. Eufaula AL 36027 334-687-0021
Jean Coutu Group (PJC) Inc
530 Rue Beriault............................... Longueuil QC J4G1S8 450-646-9760
TSE: PJC.A ■ *TF:* 877-695-6175 ■ *Web:* www.jeancoutu.com
Katz Group
10104 103rd Ave Ste 1702 Bell Tower .... Edmonton AB T5J0H8 780-990-0505
TF: 866-323-9695 ■ *Web:* www.katzgroup.ca
Kinney Drugs Inc 520 E Main St .... Gouverneur NY 13642 315-287-3600
Web: www.kinneydrugs.com
Kizer Pharmacy LLC 1117 S Miles Ave Ste 1 ....Union City TN 38261 731-885-2226
KMC Exim Corp One Harbor Park Dr............ Port Washington NY 11050 516-621-6565
Kontos Inc Dba Alexander'S Pharmacy
505 Nashua Rd...................................... Dracut MA 01826 978-957-0330
Kopp Drug 1405 13th Ave .... Altoona PA 16601 814-949-9512
KPS Health Plans Inc
400 Warren Ave PO Box 339....................... Bremerton WA 98337 360-377-5576
Web: www.kpshealthplans.com
LA Central Pharmacy Inc
2221 Beverly Blvd.............................Los Angeles CA 90057 213-483-3929
Web: mycentralpharmacy.com
Lacey Drug Company Inc 4797 S Main St ....Acworth GA 30101 770-974-3131
Web: laceydrug.com
Lachman Imports Inc 230 Fifth Ave Ste 900...........New York NY 10001 212-532-1030
Web: www.guinotusa.com
Lee Silsby Compounding Pharmacy
3216 Silsby Rd...........................Cleveland Heights OH 44118 216-321-4300 321-4303
TF: 800-918-8831 ■ *Web:* www.leesilsby.com
Lehan Drugs Inc 1407 S Fourth St......................Dekalb IL 60115 815-758-0911
Web: lehandrugs.com
Lewis Drug Inc 4409 E 26th St.................... Sioux Falls SD 57103 605-367-2000 367-2876
Web: www.lewisdrug.com
Liberty Drug & Surgical Inc 195 Main St .... Chatham NJ 07928 973-635-6200 635-6208
TF: 877-816-0111 ■ *Web:* www.libertydrug.com
Los Altos Pharmacy Inc 255 Second St..............Los Altos CA 94022 650-948-1212
Web: www.losaltospharmacy.com
Love Stores 144 W 72nd St......................New York NY 10023 212-877-5351
Web: www.lovestoresnyc.com
Luzerne Optical Laboratories Ltd
180 N Wilkes Barre Blvd......................... Wilkes-barre PA 18702 570-822-3183
Web: www.luzerneoptical.com
Mabiles Corner Pharmacy 100 Gulf St .... Coushatta LA 71019 318-932-5727
Majestic Drug Company Inc
4996 Main St Rt 42..........................South Fallsburg NY 12779 845-436-0011
Web: www.majesticdrug.com
Martin Avenue Pharmacy
1247 Rickert Dr Ste 100 .... Naperville IL 60540 630-355-6400
Web: www.critterchronicle.com
Mast Drug Company Inc 1910 Ross Mill Rd..........Henderson NC 27537 252-438-3112 492-4096
Web: www.mastdrug.com
Medical Center Pharmacy 513b N Grand Ave.........Doniphan MO 63935 573-996-3784
Web: www.medicalcenterrx.com
Medical Park Pharmacy Inc 301 Penny Ln ......Morehead City NC 28557 252-726-0777
Web: www.medicalparkpharmacy.net
Medicap Pharmacies Inc
1 Rider Trail Plaza Dr ....Earth City MO 63045 314-993-6000
TF: 800-407-8055 ■ *Web:* www.medicap.com
MedMeme LLC 224 W 35th St Ste 600 ....New York NY 10001 212-725-5990
Web: www.medmeme.com
Mehron Inc
100 Red Schoolhouse Rd Ste C2 ....Spring Valley NY 10977 845-426-1700
Web: www.mehron.com
Mission Pharmacy Services LLC
201 N Jefferson St Ste 300........................ Kittanning PA 16201 877-758-2039
TF: 877-758-2039 ■ *Web:* www.missionpharmacy.com
Mission Road Pharmacy Inc
1155 N Mission Rd.............................Los Angeles CA 90033 323-227-4646
Web: mrpscripts.com
Monitor Pharmacy Inc 2981 Midland Rd.............Bay City MI 48706 989-684-2343
Web: monitorpharmacy.com
Moreland Plaza Pharmacy Inc
827 W Moreland Blvd........................... Waukesha WI 53188 262-542-4488
Moye's Pharmacy 4467 N Henry Blvd.............Stockbridge GA 30281 770-474-0704
Web: www.moyespharmacy.com
Navarro Discount Pharmacies 9400................. Miami FL 33178 305-633-3000
Web: www.navarro.com
Neighborcare Health 2101 E Yesler Way............... Seattle WA 98122 206-461-7801
Web: www.neighborcare.org
New Era Optical Co 5575 N Lynch Ave ....Chicago IL 60630 773-725-9600
Web: www.neweraopt.com
Nucara Pharmacy 209 E San Marnan Dr.............. Waterloo IA 50702 319-236-8891
Web: www.nucara.com
NuFACTOR Inc 41093 County Ctr Dr Ste B............Temecula CA 92591 951-296-2516
Web: www.nufactor.com
Nutri Pet Research Inc
227 State Rt 33 Ste 10 ....Manalapan NJ 07726 732-786-8822
Web: www.nuprosupplements.com
Nutritional Parental Home Care Inc
660 University Blvd Ste A.........................Birmingham AL 35401 205-345-4566 342-3254
Web: www.nphc.net
Oak Hill Pharmacy Inc 1924 E Morgan Ave .... Evansville IN 47711 812-425-4422
Web: oakhillpharmacy.com
Ocean Eyes Optical Inc 2907 Ocean Ave............. Brooklyn NY 11235 718-332-1017
Web: coolframes.com
Ocu-ease Optical Products Inc
920 San Pablo Ave .... Pinole CA 94564 510-724-0384
Web: www.ocuease.com
Oncology Plus Inc 1070 E Brandon Blvd.............Brandon FL 33511 877-410-0779
TF: 877-410-0779 ■ *Web:* www.oncologyplus.com

Phone | Fax

Optical Physics Co 26610 Agoura Rd Ste 240 Calabasas CA 91302 818-880-2907
Web: www.opci.com
Oronoque Pharmacy Inc 7365 Main St Stratford CT 06614 203-378-1111
Owens Healthcare 2025 Court St Ste A Redding CA 96001 530-339-7950
Web: www.owensmedicalsupply.com
Patient First Renal Solutions
11555 Heron Bay Blvd Coral Springs FL 33076 954-473-4717
Web: pfrenal.com
PBM Plus Inc 300 Techne Ctr Dr Ste B Milford OH 45150 513-248-3071
Web: www.pbmplus.com
Penobscot Community Health Center Inc
103 Maine Ave Bangor ME 04401 207-992-9200
Web: pchcbangor.org
Pet Health Pharmacy 12012 N 111th Ave Youngtown AZ 85363 623-214-2791
Web: www.pethealthpharmacy.com/
Pharma eMarket LLC 15 E Ridge Pk Ste 225 Conshohocken PA 19428 610-862-0909
Web: www.monitorforhire.com
Pharmaceutical Advisors LLC
316 Wall St Second Fl Princeton NJ 08540 609-688-1330
Web: www.pharmadvisors.com
Pharmacy Outcomes Specialists LLC
41 E Main St Ste 200 Lake Zurich IL 60047 847-540-9590
Web: www.pharmout.com
Pharmacy Providers of OK 45 Ne 52nd St Oklahoma City OK 73105 405-557-5700
Web: www.ppok.com
Phipps Pharmacy Inc 205 B Hospital Dr Mckenzie TN 38201 731-352-0820
Web: phippspharmacy.com
Pilot Process Systems 306 Keystone Dr Telford PA 18969 215-453-8010
Web: www.bioskids.com
Premium Rx National LLC 11736 Parklawn Dr Rockville MD 20852 301-230-0908
Pro-tech Security Sales 1313 W Bagley Rd Berea OH 44017 440-239-0100
Web: www.protechsales.com
Ragan & Massey Inc 100 Ponchatoula Pkwy Ponchatoula LA 70454 985-386-6042
Web: raganandmassey.com
Ralston Drug & Discount Liquor
3147 Southmore Blvd Houston TX 77004 713-524-3045 524-5981
Red Cross Pharmacy 425 Main St Forest City PA 18421 570-785-5400
Web: www.rcrx.com
Red Cross Pharmacy Inc 52 E Arrow St Marshall MO 65340 660-886-5535
Web: redcrosspharmacy.com
REM Optical Company Inc
10941 La Tuna Canyon Rd Sun Valley CA 91352 818-504-3950
Web: www.remeyewear.com
Revolution Eyewear Inc
997 Flower Glen St Simi Valley CA 93065 800-986-0010
Web: www.revolutioneyewear.com
Rite Aid Corp 30 Hunter Ln Camp Hill PA 17011 717-761-2633 975-3754
NYSE: RAD ■ *TF:* 800-748-3243 ■ *Web:* www.riteaid.com
Ritzman Pharmacies Inc 8614 Hartman Rd Wadsworth OH 44281 330-335-2318 335-3222
Web: ritzmanrx.com
Rodman's Discount Food & Drugs
4301 Randolph Rd Silver Spring MD 20906 301-946-3100 946-8329
Web: www.rodmans.com
Rotz Pharmacy Inc 1338 Amherst St Winchester VA 22601 540-662-8312
Web: rotzpharmacy.com
Rx Advantage Inc 7101 Hwy 90 Ste 300 Daphne AL 36526 251-625-6100
Web: www.rxadvantage-inc.com
Rx Inc Dba Lo Cost Pharmacy 612 E 69th St Savannah GA 31405 912-352-0375
Rx.com 4710 Mercantile Dr Fort Worth TX 76137 817-547-1000
Web: www.rx.com
RXD Pharmacies Inc 724 Haddon Ave Collingswood NJ 08108 856-858-9292 854-1359
Rxusa Inc 81 Seaview Blvd Port Washington NY 11050 516-467-2500 467-2539
TF: 800-764-3648 ■ *Web:* www.rxusa.com
Saar's Inc 32199 State Rt 20 Oak Harbor WA 98277 360-675-3000
Web: www.saarsmarketplacefoods.com
Safeguard Products Inc 2710 Division Hwy New Holland PA 17557 717-354-4586
Web: www.safeguardproducts.com
Sama Eye Wear 8460 Santa Monica Blvd West Hollywood CA 90069 323-822-3955
Web: www.samaeyewear.net
Sav-Mor Drug Stores 43155 W Nine-Mile Rd Novi MI 48376 248-348-1570 348-4316
Web: www.sav-mor.com
ScriptRx Inc 312 Clematis St Ste 301 West Palm Beach FL 33401 561-805-5935
Web: www.scriptrx.com
Select Rx 11414 E 51st St Ste A Tulsa OK 74146 918-461-8103
Web: www.selectrx.com
Senior Care Pharmacy
4455 Morris Park Dr Ste A Mint Hill NC 28227 704-545-8641
Web: www.seniorcarepharmacy.net
Setzer Pharmacy Inc 1685 Rice St St Paul MN 55113 651-488-0251
Web: setzerrx.com
Shiraz Specialty Pharmacy
205 E Casino Rd Ste B17 Everett WA 98208 425-356-3276
Web: www.shirazpharmacy.com
Shoppers Drug Mart Inc 243 Consumers Rd Toronto ON M2J4W8 416-493-1220
TSE: SC ■ *Web:* www1.shoppersdrugmart.ca
Shore Drugs Inc 30 E Main St Bay Shore NY 11706 631-665-3000
Skyemed Pharmacy
1332 N Federal Hwy Ste 2 Pompano Beach FL 33062 866-778-8255
Web: www.skyemed.com
Slope Drugs & Surgical Supply Inc
406 Fifth Ave Brooklyn NY 11215 718-788-8899
Smart Eye Care Center 255 Western Ave Augusta ME 04330 207-622-5800
Web: www.smarteyecare.com
Stout'S Drug Store Inc 217 Chicago Ave Savanna IL 61074 815-273-2713
Web: stoutsdrugstore.com
Symons Capital Management Inc
650 Washington Rd Ste 800 Pittsburgh PA 15228 412-344-7690
Web: www.symonscapital.com
Theis Distributing Co 17984 Red Iron Schertz TX 78154 210-651-4403 651-4861
Web: www.theisco.com

Phone | Fax

Thrifty White Stores
6055 Nathan Lane N Ste 200 Plymouth MN 55442 763-513-4300
TF: 800-642-3275 ■ *Web:* www.thriftywhite.com
Total Life Care Pharmacy
2731 Manhattan Blvd Ste B17 Harvey LA 70058 504-355-4191
Web: www.tlcrxpharmacy.com
Transcript Pharmacy Inc
2506 Lakeland Dr Ste 201 Jackson MS 39232 866-420-4041
Web: www.transcriptpharmacy.com
Upstate Pharmacy Ltd 40 N America Dr West Seneca NY 14224 716-675-3784
Web: www.upstatepharmacy.com
US Script Inc 2425 W Shaw Ave Fresno CA 93711 559-244-3700
Web: www.usscript.com
VirtuOx Inc 5850 Coral Ridge Dr Ste 304 Coral Springs FL 33076 954-344-7075
Web: www.virtuox.net
Vision Source LP 23824 Hwy 59 N Ste 101 Kingwood TX 77339 281-312-1111
Web: www.visionsource.com
Vitacost.com Inc
5400 Broken Sound Blvd NW Ste 500 Boca Raton FL 33487 800-381-0759
TF: 800-381-0759 ■ *Web:* www.vitacost.com
Vitamin Shoppe Inc 2101 91st St North Bergen NJ 07047 201-868-5959 852-7153*
NYSE: VSI ■ **Fax Area Code:* 800 ■ *TF:* 800-223-1216 ■ *Web:* www.vitaminshoppe.com
Voss Pharmacy Inc 3303 S Halsted St Chicago IL 60608 773-254-5221
Walgreen Co 200 Wilmot Rd Deerfield IL 60015 847-940-2500 236-0862
TF Cust Svc: 800-925-4733 ■ *Web:* www.walgreens.com
West Coast Cosmetics Inc
21050 Superior St Chatsworth CA 91311 818-349-8510
Web: www.westcoastcosmetics.com
White'S Pharmacy of Dalton LLC
2955B Cleveland Hwy Dalton GA 30721 706-259-9707
Whitney Lab 1095 N Us Hwy 1 Ste 1 Ormond Beach FL 32174 386-673-4770
Web: www.methadonehelp.com
Xerimis Inc 102 Executive Dr Moorestown NJ 08057 856-727-9940
Web: www.xerimis.com
Zitomer Pharmacy Inc 969 Madison Ave Fl 1 New York NY 10021 212-737-5560
Web: www.zitomer.com

DRUGS - MFR

SEE Vitamins & Nutritional Supplements p. 3286; Biotechnology Companies p. 1869; Pharmaceutical Companies p. 2921; Medicinal Chemicals & Botanical Products p. 2736; Pharmaceutical Companies - Generic Drugs p. 2924; Diagnostic Products p. 2198

241 DRUGS & PERSONAL CARE PRODUCTS - WHOL

Companies listed here distribute pharmaceuticals, over-the-counter (OTC) drugs, and/or personal care products typically found in drug stores.

Phone | Fax

Aaipharma Services Corp
2320 Scientific Park Dr Wilmington NC 28405 910-254-7000
Web: aaipharma.com
Agion Technologies Inc 60 Audubon Rd Wakefield MA 01880 781-224-7100 246-3340
Web: www.agion-tech.com
Altamont Pharmacy Inc 12 N Third St Altamont IL 62411 618-483-5614
Web: altamontpharmacy.com
Ambient Healthcare Inc 15851 SW 41st St Ste 600 Davie FL 33331 954-796-3338
Web: www.ambienthealth.com
Ambrx Inc 10975 N Torrey Pines Rd La Jolla CA 92037 858-875-2400
Web: www.ambrx.com
AmerisourceBergen Corp
1300 Morris Dr Ste 100 PO Box 959 Chesterbrook PA 19087 610-727-7000 727-3600
NYSE: ABC ■ *TF:* 800-829-3132 ■ *Web:* www.amerisourcebergen.net
Aqua Pharmaceuticals LLC
158 W Gay St Ste 310 West Chester PA 19380 610-644-7000
Web: www.aquapharm.com
AquaCap Inc Four Hillman Dr Ste 190 Chadds Ford PA 19317 610-361-2800
Astrup Drug Inc 1305 First Ave SW Austin MN 55912 507-433-4586
Web: www.astrupdrug.com
Auspex Pharmaceuticals Inc
3366 N Torrey Pines Ct Ste 225 La Jolla CA 92037 858-558-2400
TF: 800-487-7671 ■ *Web:* www.auspexpharma.com
Bach Pharma Inc 800 Turnpike St Ste 300 North Andover MA 01845 978-794-5510
Web: www.bachpharma.com
Bedford Road Pharmacy Inc
11306 Bedford Rd Ne Cumberland MD 21502 301-777-1771 777-0119
TF: 800-788-6693 ■ *Web:* www.pharmacareofcumberland.com
BioMotiv LLC 3605 Warrensville Ctr Rd Cleveland OH 44122 216-455-3200
TF: 800-477-6307 ■ *Web:* www.biomotiv.com
Buffalo Supply Inc 1650A Coal Creek Dr Lafayette CO 80026 800-366-1812
TF: 800-366-1812 ■ *Web:* www.buffalosupply.com
Cadeau Express Inc 3494 E Sunset Rd Las Vegas NV 89120 702-433-1333
TF: 800-240-0301 ■ *Web:* www.cadeauexpress.com
Camp Drugstore 600 Ferguson Wood River IL 62095 618-254-6223
Camphor Technologies Inc
183 Providence New London North Stonington CT 06359 860-535-0241 760-6539
Web: www.camphortech.com
Capellon Pharmaceuticals Ltd
7509 Flagstone St Fort Worth TX 76118 817-595-5820
Web: www.capellon.com
Cardinal Health Distribution 7000 Cardinal Pl Dublin OH 43017 614-757-5000 757-6000
Web: www.cardinal.com
Cardinal Health Nuclear Pharmacy Services
7000 Cardinal Pl Dublin OH 43017 614-757-5000 757-6000
TF: 800-326-6457 ■ *Web:* www.cardinalhealth.com
Carolina Medical Products Company Inc
8026 Us Hwy 264A Farmville NC 27828 252-753-7111
Web: www.carolinamedical.com
Charles Bowman & Company Inc
3328 John F Donnelly Dr Holland MI 49424 616-786-4000 786-2864
Web: www.charlesbowman.com

Company	City	State	Zip	Phone	Fax
Complete Pharmacy Care Inc 4206 Dalrock Rd *Web:* www.completepharmacycare.com	Rowlett	TX	75088	972-675-3300	
Connetics Corp 3160 Porter Dr *Web:* www.olux.com	Palo Alto	CA	94304	650-843-2800	
Contract Pharmacy Services Inc 125 Titus Ave *Web:* www.contractrx.com	Warrington	PA	18976	267-487-9000	487-9050
Correct Rx Pharmacy Services Inc 803-A Barkwood Ct *Web:* www.correctrxpharmacy.com	Linthicum	MD	21090	410-636-9500	
CritiTech Inc 1321 Wakarusa Dr Ste 2102 *Web:* www.crititech.com	Lawrence	KS	66049	785-841-7120	
Dakota Drug Inc 28 Main St N *TF:* 800-437-2018 ■ *Web:* www.dakdrug.com	Minot	ND	58703	701-852-2141	857-1134
Danco Investors Group Lp 112 Second Ave N	Nashville	TN	37201	615-251-9521	
Drais Pharmaceuticals Inc 520 Us Hwy 22 Ste 201 *Web:* www.draispharma.com	Bridgewater	NJ	08807	908-895-1200	
DRAXIMAGE Inc 16751 Transcanada Hwy *TF:* 888-633-5343 ■ *Web:* www.draximage.com	Kirkland	QC	H9H4J4	514-630-7080	
Duchesnay Inc 950 Boul Mich'Le-Bohec *Web:* www.duchesnay.com	Blainville	QC	J7C5E2	450-433-7734	433-2211
Eagle Vision Pharmaceutical Corp 175 Krauser Rd *Web:* www.eaglevpc.com	Downingtown	PA	19335	610-458-2346	
Fabre-Kramer Pharmaceuticals Inc 5847 San Felipe Ste 2000 *Web:* www.fabrekramer.com	Houston	TX	77057	713-975-6900	
Familiprix Inc 6000 Rue Armand-Viau *Web:* www.familiprix.com/en	Quebec	QC	G2C2C5	418-847-3311	
Familymeds Inc 312 Farmington Ave *Web:* www.familymeds.com	Farmington	CT	06032	888-787-2800	
Ferring Pharmaceuticals Inc 100 Interpace Pkwy Third Fl *TF:* 888-337-7464 ■ *Web:* www.ferringusa.com	Parsippany	NJ	07054	973-796-1600	
FoldRx Pharmaceuticals Inc 100 Acorn Park Dr Fifth Fl *Web:* www.foldrx.com	Cambridge	MA	02140	617-252-5500	
Forever Spring 2629 E Craig Rd Ste E *TF:* 800-523-4334 ■ *Web:* www.foreverspring.com	Las Vegas	NV	89030	702-633-4283	633-4182
Forte Research Systems Inc 1200 John Q Hammons Dr Ste 300	Madison	WI	53717	608-826-6000	
Franck's Pharmacy Inc 7518 Soquel Dr *Web:* www.francks.com	Aptos	CA	95003	831-685-1100	
Frank W Kerr Co 43155 W Nine Mile Rd *Web:* www.fwkerr.com	Novi	MI	48376	248-349-5000	
Freedom Pharmaceuticals Inc 801 W New Orleans St *Web:* freedomrxinc.com	Broken Arrow	OK	74011	918-615-6228	
Garden State Orthopaedic Center Inc Nine Post Rd Ste Op1 *Web:* www.gardenstateortho.com	Oakland	NJ	07436	201-337-5566	
Gavis Pharmaceuticals LLC 400 Campus Dr *TF:* 866-403-7592 ■ *Web:* www.gavispharma.com	Somerset	NJ	08873	908-603-6080	
Gentell 3600 Boundbrook Ave *Web:* www.gentell.com	Feasterville Trevose	PA	19053	215-788-2700	
Health Coalition Inc 8320 NW 30th Terr *Web:* healthcoalition.com	Doral	FL	33122	305-662-2988	
Iden Cosmetics Inc 15500 Texaco St *Web:* www.idencosmetics.com	Paramount	CA	90723	562-630-2580	
Iredale Mineral Cosmetics Ltd 28 Church St **Fax Area Code:* 210 ■ *TF:* 877-869-9420 ■ *Web:* www.janeiredale.com	Great Barrington	MA	01230	413-528-1078	932-9801*
J&B Medical Supply Co Inc 50496 W Pontiac Trail *TF:* 800-980-0047 ■ *Web:* www.jandbmedical.com	Wixom	MI	48393	248-896-6210	
JM Smith Corp 101 W Saint John St Ste 305 *Web:* www.jmsmithcorp.com	Spartanburg	SC	29306	864-582-1216	
Kinray Inc 152-35 Tenth Ave *TF:* 800-854-6729 ■ *Web:* www.kinray.com	Whitestone	NY	11357	718-767-1234	767-4706
Kohll's Pharmacy & Homecare Inc 12759 Q St *Web:* www.kohlls.com	Omaha	NE	68137	402-895-6812	
Lawrenceburg Medical Supply Inc 753 W Broadway	Lawrenceburg	KY	40342	502-839-4557	
Lil' Drug Store Products Inc 1201 Continental Pl Ne *TF:* 800-553-5022 ■ *Web:* www.lildrugstore.com	Cedar Rapids	IA	52402	800-553-5022	
London Drugs Ltd 12251 Horseshoe Way *TF:* 888-991-2299 ■ *Web:* www.londondrugs.com	Richmond	BC	V7A4X5	604-272-7400	
Masters Pharmaceutical Inc 11930 Kemper Springs Dr *Web:* mastersrx.com	Cincinnati	OH	45240	513-354-2690	
Mechanical Servants Inc 2755 Thomas St *TF:* 800-351-2000 ■ *Web:* www.cvalet.com	Melrose Park	IL	60160	708-615-9439	486-1501
Methapharm Inc 11772 W Sample Rd *TF:* 800-287-7686 ■ *Web:* www.methapharm.com	Coral Springs	FL	33065	954-341-0795	
MorphoSys USA Inc 4350 Lassiter At N Hills Ave Ste 250 *Web:* www.abdserotec.com	Raleigh	NC	27609	919-878-7978	
Morris & Dickson Co Ltd 410 Kay Ln *TF:* 800-388-3833 ■ *Web:* www.morrisdickson.com	Shreveport	LA	71115	318-797-7900	798-6007
Myoderm Inc 48 E Main St *Web:* www.myoderm.com	Norristown	PA	19401	610-233-3300	
Neil Medical Group Inc 2545 Jetport Rd *TF:* 800-735-9111 ■ *Web:* www.neilmedical.com	Kinston	NC	28504	800-735-9111	
North Carolina Mutual Wholesale Drug Co 816 Ellis Rd *TF:* 800-800-8551 ■ *Web:* www.mutualdrugcompany.com/?page_id=26	Durham	NC	27703	919-596-2151	596-1453
Omegachem Inc 480 rue Perreault *Web:* www.omegachem.com	St-romuald	QC	G6W7V6	418-837-4444	
Pamlab LLC 4099 Hwy 190 E Service Rd *TF:* 844-639-9725 ■ *Web:* pamlab.com	Covington	LA	70433	985-893-4097	893-6195
PanOptica Inc 150 Morristown Rd Ste 205 *Web:* panopticapharma.com	Bernardsville	NJ	07924	908-766-2202	
Park Compounding Pharmacy Inc 280 N W Lake Blvd Ste 100 *Web:* parkcompounding.com	Westlake Village	CA	91362	805-497-8258	
Parmed Pharmaceuticals Inc 4220 Hyde Pk Blvd **Fax Area Code:* 800 ■ *TF:* 800-727-6331 ■ *Web:* www.parmed.com	Niagara Falls	NY	14305	716-284-5666	727-6330*
Pharmacommunications Group Inc 100 Renfrew Dr *Web:* www.pharmacommunications.com	Markham	ON	L3R9R6	905-477-3100	
PharmaForce Inc 960 Crupper Ave *Web:* www.pharmaforceinc.com	Columbus	OH	43229	614-436-2222	
PharmaLogic Inc One S Ocean Blvd Ste 206 *Web:* www.pharmalogic.info	Boca Raton	FL	33432	561-416-0085	
Pharmgate LLC 161 N Franklin Tpke *Web:* www.pharmgate.com	Ramsey	NJ	07446	201-327-3800	327-3802
Phillips Drugstore Inc 123 E State St *Web:* www.phillipsrx.com	Mauston	WI	53948	608-847-5949	
Plant Sciences Inc 342 Green Valley Rd *Web:* www.plantsciences.com	Watsonville	CA	95076	831-728-7771	728-4967
Plasma Services Group Inc 1840 County Line Rd Ste 100 *Web:* plasmaservicesgroup.com	Huntingdon Valley	PA	19006	215-355-1288	
Procter & Gamble 1 or 2 Procter & Gamble Plaza *Web:* pg.com	Cincinnati	OH	45202	513-983-1100	983-1100
Procurity Inc 160 Eagle Dr *Web:* www.procurity.ca	Winnipeg	MB	R2R1V5	204-632-5506	
Putney Inc One Monument Sq Ste 400 *Web:* www.putneyvet.com	Portland	ME	04101	207-828-0880	
QoL meds LLC 4900 Perry Hwy Bldg 2 *Web:* www.qolmeds.com	Pittsburgh	PA	15229	412-931-3131	
Quality King Distributors Inc 35 Sawgrass Drive Suite 3 *Web:* www.qkd.com	Bellport	NY	11713	631-737-5555	439-2202
QVL Pharmacy Holdings Inc 4141 Blue Lk Cir Ste 124 *Web:* www.qvlpharmacy.com	Dallas	TX	75244	972-788-2653	
ReceptoPharm Inc 1537 NW 65th Ave *Web:* www.receptopharm.com	Plantation	FL	33313	954-321-8988	
Reese Pharmaceutical Co 10617 Frank Ave **Fax Area Code:* 216 ■ *TF:* 800-321-7178 ■ *Web:* www.reesechemical.com	Cleveland	OH	44106	800-321-7178	231-6444*
RG Shakour Inc 254 Tpke Rd **Fax Area Code:* 508 ■ *Web:* interiorsbyrgshakour.com	Westborough	MA	01581	800-661-2030	366-9171*
RT Oncology Services Corp 11988 El Camino Real Ste 500 *Web:* www.raintreeoncology.com	San Diego	CA	92130	858-436-7450	
Rx Scan 2478 Lackey Old State Rd *Web:* rxscan.com	Delaware	OH	43015	740-548-1725	
SaveMart Pharmacy 241 W Roseville Rd *Web:* www.savemartpa.com	Lancaster	PA	17601	717-569-7384	
Sheldon's Express Pharmacy Inc 843 Fairview Ave *Web:* www.sheldonsexpresspharmacy.com	Bowling Green	KY	42101	270-842-4515	
Sigma Tau Pharmasource Inc 6925 Guion Rd *Web:* www.sigmataupharmasource.com	Indianapolis	IN	46268	317-347-2800	
Silver Spur Corp 16010 Shoemaker Ave *Web:* www.silverspurcorp.com	Cerritos	CA	90703	562-921-6880	
Sothys USA Inc 1500 NW 94th Ave *TF:* 800-325-0503 ■ *Web:* www.sothys-usa.com	Miami	FL	33172	305-594-4222	592-5785
Sova Pharmaceuticals Inc 11099 N Torrey Pines Rd Ste 290 *Web:* www.sovapharma.com	La Jolla	CA	92037	858-750-4700	750-4701
Sprout Pharmaceuticals Inc 4208 Six Forks Rd *Web:* sproutpharma.com	Raleigh	NC	27609	919-882-0850	
Strategic Pharmaceutical Solut 17014 NE Sandy Blvd *Web:* vetsource.com	Portland	OR	97230	503-802-7400	
superDimension Inc 161 Cheshire Ln Ste 100 *Web:* superdimension.com	Minneapolis	MN	55441	763-210-4000	
SynDevRx Inc One Broadway 14th Fl *Web:* www.syndevrx.com	Cambridge	MA	02142	617-401-3110	
Syndexa Pharmaceuticals Corp 480 Arsenal St Bldg 1 *Web:* www.syndexa.com	Watertown	MA	02472	617-607-7283	
Syreon Corp 260 - 1401 W Eighth Ave *Web:* www.syreon.com	Vancouver	BC	V6H1C9	604-676-5900	
Takeda Pharmaceuticals USAInc One Takeda Pkwy *Web:* takedajobs.com	Deerfield	IL	60015	224-554-6500	
Tri-Med Pharmacy Services LLC 260 W Main St Ste 217 *Web:* www.trimedrx.com	Hendersonville	TN	37075	615-826-9393	
UNFI Specialty Distribution Services 88 Huntoon Memorial Hwy *TF:* 877-476-8749 ■ *Web:* unfi.com	Leicester	MA	01524	508-892-8171	892-4827
US WorldMeds LLC 4010 Dupont Cir Ste L-07 *TF:* 888-900-8796 ■ *Web:* www.usworldmeds.com	Louisville	KY	40207	502-815-8000	
Value Drug Co 1 Golf View Dr *Web:* valuedrugco.com	Altoona	PA	16635	814-944-9316	
Value Drug Mart Assoc Ltd 16504 - 121A Ave *TF:* 888-554-8258 ■ *Web:* www.valuedrugmart.com	Edmonton	AB	T5V1J9	780-453-1701	
Victory Pharma Inc 11682 El Camino Real *TF:* 866-427-6819 ■ *Web:* www.victorypharma.com	San Diego	CA	92130	858-720-4500	720-4501
Viroxis Corp 12621 Silicon Dr Ste 100 *Web:* www.viroxis.com	San Antonio	TX	78249	210-558-8896	
Zafgen Inc 175 Portland St Fourth Fl *Web:* www.zafgen.com	Boston	MA	02114	617-622-4003	
Zeta Pharmaceuticals Inc One Paragon Dr *Web:* www.zetapharm.com	Montvale	NJ	07645	201-930-4934	

242 DUDE RANCHES

SEE ALSO Resorts & Resort Companies p. 3058

Name / Address	City	State	Zip	Phone	Fax
320 Guest Ranch Inc 205 Buffalo Horn Creek Rd *Web:* www.320ranch.com	Gallatin Gateway	MT	59730	406-995-4283	
63 Ranch PO Box 979 **Fax Area Code:* 406 ■ *TF:* 888-395-5151 ■ *Web:* 63ranch.com	Livingston	MT	59047	888-395-5151	222-6363*
7 D Ranch 7D Ranch PO Box 100 *TF:* 888-587-9885 ■ *Web:* www.7dranch.com	Cody	WY	82414	307-587-9885	587-9885
Absaroka Ranch PO Box 929 *Web:* www.absarokaranch.com	Dubois	WY	82513	307-455-2275	455-2275
Air Ivanhoe Ltd Ivanhoe Lk Air Base *Web:* www.air-ivanhoe.com	Foleyet	ON	P0M1T0	705-899-2155	
Aspen Canyon Ranch 13206 County Rd 3 *Web:* www.aspencanyon.com	Parshall	CO	80468	970-725-3600	725-0040
Bar Lazy J Guest Ranch 447 County Rd 3 PO Box N *TF:* 800-396-6279 ■ *Web:* www.barlazyj.com	Parshall	CO	80468	970-725-3437	725-0121
Black Mountain Ranch 4000 Conger Mesa Rd *TF:* 800-967-2401 ■ *Web:* www.blackmtnranch.com	McCoy	CO	80463	970-653-4226	653-4227
Bonanza Creek Country Guest Ranch 523 Bonanza Creek Rd *TF:* 800-476-6045 ■ *Web:* www.bonanzacreekcountry.com	Martinsdale	MT	59053	406-572-3366	572-3366
Brooks Lake Lodge & Guest Ranch 458 Brooks Lk Rd **Fax Area Code:* 307 ■ *TF:* 866-213-4022 ■ *Web:* www.brookslake.com	Dubois	WY	82513	866-213-4022	455-2221*
Brush Creek Ranch 66 Brush Creek Ranch Rd *Web:* www.brushcreekranch.com	Saratoga	WY	82331	307-327-5284	327-5970
C Lazy U Ranch 3640 Colorado Hwy 125 PO Box 379 *Web:* www.clazyu.com	Granby	CO	80446	970-887-3344	887-3917
Caliente Resorts LLC 21240 Gran Via Blvd. *Web:* www.calienteresort.com	Land O Lakes	FL	34637	813-996-3700	
Camp Arrowhead 20 Arrowhead Rd *Web:* www.rochesterymca.org	Pittsford	NY	14534	585-383-4590	
Camp Chewonki 485 Chewonki Neck Rd *Web:* www.chewonki.org	Wiscasset	ME	04578	207-882-7323	
Camp Lebanon 1205 Acorn Rd *Web:* camplebanon.org	Burtrum	MN	56318	320-573-2125	
Camp Ocean Pines Inc 1473 Randall Dr. *Web:* campoceanpines.org	Cambria	CA	93428	805-927-0254	
Camp Rocky Point 1586 Hanna Dr *Web:* gsnetx.org	Denison	TX	75020	903-465-5270	
Camp Simcha 430 White Rd *Web:* campsimcha.org	Glen Spey	NY	12737	845-856-1432	
Camp Sunshine 35 Acadia Rd. *Web:* campsunshine.org	Casco	ME	04015	207-655-3800	
Camp Tawonga 131 Steuart St Ste 460 *Web:* tawonga.org	San Francisco	CA	94105	415-543-2267	
Cheley Colorado Camps Inc 601 Steele St *Web:* www.cheley.com	Denver	CO	80206	303-377-3616	
Cherokee Park Ranch 436 Cherokee Hills Dr *TF:* 800-628-0949 ■ *Web:* www.cherokeeparkranch.com	Livermore	CO	80536	970-493-6522	493-5802
Circle Z Ranch PO Box 194 **Fax Area Code:* 520 ■ *TF:* 888-854-2525 ■ *Web:* www.circlez.com	Patagonia	AZ	85624	888-854-2525	394-2058*
CM Ranch 167 Fish Hatchery Rd PO Box 217 *TF:* 800-455-0721 ■ *Web:* www.cmranch.com	Dubois	WY	82513	307-455-2331	455-3984
Colorado Cattle Company & Guest Ranch 70008 County Rd 132 *Web:* www.coloradocattlecompany.com	New Raymer	CO	80742	970-437-5345	437-5432
Colorado Trails Ranch 12161 County Rd 240 *TF:* 800-323-3833 ■ *Web:* www.coloradotrails.com	Durango	CO	81301	970-247-5055	385-7372
Concordia Language Villages 8659 Thorsonveien Rd *Web:* concordialanguagevillages.org	Bemidji	MN	56601	218-586-8600	
Coulter Lake Guest Ranch 80 County Rd 273 *TF:* 800-858-3046 ■ *Web:* www.coulterlake.com	Rifle	CO	81650	970-625-1473	
Crossed Sabres Ranch 829 N Fork Hwy *Web:* crossedsabresranch.com	Cody	WY	82414	307-587-3750	
Dedham Country Day School 90 Sandy Vly Rd *Web:* www.dedhamcountryday.org	Dedham	MA	02026	781-329-0850	
Deer Valley Ranch 16825 County Rd 162 *Web:* www.deervalleyranch.com	Nathrop	CO	81236	719-395-2353	395-2394
Drowsy Water Ranch PO Box 147 *TF:* 800-845-2292 ■ *Web:* www.drowsywater.com	Granby	CO	80446	970-725-3456	725-3611
Dryhead Schively Ranch 1062 Rd 15 *TF:* 800-628-9081 ■ *Web:* www.dryheadranch.com	Lovell	WY	82431	307-548-6688	548-2322
Eatons' Ranch 270 Eatons' Ranch Rd. *TF:* 800-210-1049 ■ *Web:* eatonsranch.com	Wolf	WY	82844	307-655-9285	655-9269
Echo Canyon Guest Ranch 12507 Echo Canyon Rd.	La Veta	CO	81055	719-742-5261	
Elk Mountain Ranch PO Box 910 *TF:* 800-432-8812 ■ *Web:* elkmtn.com	Buena Vista	CO	81211	800-432-8812	
Elkhorn Ranch Montana 33133 Gallatin Rd. *Web:* www.elkhornranchmt.com	Gallatin Gateway	MT	59730	406-995-4291	
Flying E Ranch 2801 W Wickenburg Way *TF:* 888-684-2650 ■ *Web:* www.flyingeranch.com	Wickenburg	AZ	85390	928-684-2690	684-5304
Fresh Air Fund 633 Third Ave 14th Fl *TF:* 800-367-0003 ■ *Web:* www.freshair.org	New York	NY	10017	800-367-0003	
G Bar M Ranch PO Box 29 *Web:* www.gbarm.com	Clyde Park	MT	59018	406-686-4423	
Grapevine Canyon Ranch Inc PO Box 302 *TF:* 800-245-9202 ■ *Web:* www.gcranch.com	Pearce	AZ	85625	520-826-3185	826-3636
Greenhorn Creek Guest Ranch 2116 Greenhorn Ranch Rd *TF:* 800-334-6939 ■ *Web:* www.greenhornranch.com	Quincy	CA	95971	530-283-0930	
Gros Ventre River Ranch PO Box 151 *Web:* grosventreriverranch.com	Moose	WY	83012	307-733-4138	733-4272
Guided Discoveries Inc 232 W Harrison Ave *Web:* guideddiscoveries.org	Claremont	CA	91711	909-625-6194	
Harbor Health Systems LLC One Venture Ste 130 *Web:* www.harborsys.com	Irvine	CA	92618	949-273-7020	
Hawley Mountain Guest Ranch PO Box 4 *TF:* 877-496-7848 ■ *Web:* www.hawleymountain.com	McLeod	MT	59052	406-932-5791	932-5715
Heart Six Ranch 16985 Buffalo Vly Rd PO Box 70 **Fax Area Code:* 307 ■ *TF:* 888-543-2477 ■ *Web:* heartsix.com	Moran	WY	83013	888-543-2477	543-0918*
Hideout at Flitner Ranch Resort PO Box 206 *TF:* 800-354-8637 ■ *Web:* www.thehideout.com	Shell	WY	82441	307-765-2080	765-2681
High Meadows Camp 1055 Willeo Rd *Web:* highmeadows.org	Roswell	GA	30075	770-993-7975	
Home Ranch PO Box 822 *TF:* 800-688-2982 ■ *Web:* www.homeranch.com	Clark	CO	80428	970-879-1780	879-1795
Homeplace Ranch RR 1 Site 2 *TF:* 877-931-3245 ■ *Web:* www.homeplaceranch.com	Priddis	AB	T0L1W0	403-969-4444	931-3245
Horn Creek Conference Grounds Association 6758 County Rd 130 *Web:* www.horncreek.org	Westcliffe	CO	81252	719-783-2205	
Horse Prairie Ranch 3300 Bachelor Mountain Rd *TF:* 888-726-2454 ■ *Web:* www.ranchlife.com	Dillon	MT	59725	406-681-3166	
Horton Haven Christian Camp 3711 Reed Harris Rd. *Web:* www.hortonhaven.org	Lewisburg	TN	37091	931-364-7656	
Hunewill Cir H Ranch 1110 Hunewill Ranch Rd *Web:* www.hunewillranch.com	Bridgeport	CA	93517	760-932-7710	932-1933
Kay El Bar Guest Ranch PO Box 2480 *TF:* 800-684-7583 ■ *Web:* www.kayelbar.com	Wickenburg	AZ	85358	928-684-7593	684-4497
Kieve Camp 42 Kieve Rd *Web:* kieve.org	Nobleboro	ME	04555	207-563-5172	
Laramie River Dude Ranch 25777 County Rd 103 *TF:* 800-551-5731 ■ *Web:* www.lrranch.com	Jelm	WY	82063	970-435-5716	435-5731
Latigo Ranch PO Box 237 *TF:* 800-227-9655 ■ *Web:* www.latigotrails.com	Kremmling	CO	80459	970-724-9008	
Lazy K Bar Ranch PO Box 1550 *Web:* lkbranch.com	Big Timber	MT	59011	406-537-9450	
Lazy L & B Ranch 1072 E Fork Rd *TF Cust Svc:* 800-453-9488 ■ *Web:* www.lazylb.com	Dubois	WY	82513	307-455-2839	455-2849
Lone Mountain Ranch 750 Lone Mtn Ranch Rd PO Box 160069 *TF:* 800-514-4644 ■ *Web:* www.lonemountainranch.com	Big Sky	MT	59716	406-995-4644	995-4670
Long Hollow Ranch 71105 Holmes Rd *TF:* 877-923-1901 ■ *Web:* www.lhranch.com	Sisters	OR	97759	541-923-1901	610-1993
Lost Valley Ranch 29555 Goose Creek Rd *Web:* ranchweb.com/dude-ranches/guest-ranches/lost-valley-ranch-co-usa	Sedalia	CO	80135	303-647-2311	
Lozier's Box R Ranch 552 Willow Creek Rd PO Box 100 *TF:* 800-822-8466 ■ *Web:* www.boxr.com	Cora	WY	82925	307-367-4868	367-6260
Maranatha Bible Camp Inc 16800 E Maranatha Rd *Web:* www.maranathacamp.org	Maxwell	NE	69151	308-582-4513	
McGinnis Meadows Cattle & Guest Ranch 6220 Mcginnis Meadows Rd *Web:* www.mmgranch.net	Libby	MT	59923	406-293-5000	293-5005
Mountain Sky Guest Ranch PO Box 1219 *TF:* 800-548-3392 ■ *Web:* www.mtnsky.com	Emigrant	MT	59027	406-333-4911	333-4537
Nantahala Outdoor Center Inc 13077 Hwy 19 W *Web:* www.noc.com	Bryson City	NC	28713	828-488-2176	
New Life Camp 701 Mayhew Rd *Web:* newlifecamp.org	Rose City	MI	48654	989-685-2949	
New York-New Jersey Trail Conference 156 Ramapo Vly Rd Rt 202 *Web:* nynjtc.org	Mahwah	NJ	07430	201-512-9348	
Nine Quarter Cir Ranch 5000 Taylor Fork Rd *Web:* www.ninequartercircle.com	Gallatin Gateway	MT	59730	406-995-4276	995-4276
North Fork Ranch (NFR) 55395 Hwy 285 PO Box B *TF:* 800-843-7895 ■ *Web:* www.northforkranch.com	Shawnee	CO	80475	303-838-9873	838-1549
Pali Adventures Summer Camp 30778 Hwy 18 *Web:* www.paliadventures.com	Running Springs	CA	92382	909-867-5743	
Paradise Guest Ranch PO Box 790 **Fax Area Code:* 720 ■ *Web:* www.paradiseranch.com	Buffalo	WY	82834	307-684-7876	862-2126*
Peaceful Valley Ranch 475 Peaceful Vly Rd *TF:* 800-955-6343 ■ *Web:* www.peacefulvalley.com	Lyons	CO	80540	303-747-2881	747-2167
Pine Butte Guest Ranch 351 S Fork Rd *TF:* 877-812-3698 ■ *Web:* www.nature.org	Choteau	MT	59422	406-466-2158	466-5462
Prescott Pines Camp 855 E Schoolhouse Gulch Rd *Web:* prescottpines.org	Prescott	AZ	86303	928-445-5225	
Price Canyon Ranch PO Box 39 *TF:* 800-727-0065 ■ *Web:* www.pricecanyon.com	Rodeo	NM	88056	520-558-2383	731-9453
ProCamps Inc 4600 McAuley Pl Fourth Fl *Web:* www.procamps.com	Cincinnati	OH	45242	513-793-2267	
R Lazy S Ranch PO Box 308 *Web:* www.rlazys.com	Teton Village	WY	83025	307-733-2655	734-1120
Rainbow Trout Ranch (RTR) 1484 FDR 250 PO Box 458 *TF:* 800-633-3397 ■ *Web:* www.rainbowtroutranch.com	Antonito	CO	81120	719-376-5659	376-5659
Rancho de la Osa Guest Ranch PO Box 1 *TF:* 800-872-6240 ■ *Web:* www.ranchodelaosa.com	Sasabe	AZ	85633	520-823-4257	823-4238
Ranger Creek Ranch PO Box 47 *Web:* www.rangercreekranch.net	Shell	WY	82441	307-765-4636	
Rawah Ranch 11447 N County Rd 103 *TF:* 800-820-3152 ■ *Web:* www.rawahranch.com	Glendevey	CO	82063	800-820-3152	
Red Rock Ranch, The PO Box 38 *Web:* www.theredrockranch.com	Kelly	WY	83011	307-733-6288	733-6287
Rich Ranch 939 Cottonwood Lakes Rd *TF:* 800-532-4350 ■ *Web:* www.richranch.com	Seeley Lake	MT	59868	406-677-2317	677-3530
Rimrock Dude Ranch 2728 Northfork Rt. *Web:* www.rimrockranch.com	Cody	WY	82414	307-587-3970	527-5014

Phone Fax

Rock Springs Guest Ranch 64201 Tyler Rd .... Bend OR 97701 541-382-1957
Web: www.rockspings.com

Seven Lazy P Guest Ranch PO Box 178 .... Choteau MT 59422 406-466-2044 466-2903
Web: www.sevenlazyp.com

Smith Fork Ranch 45362 Needle Rock Rd .... Crawford CO 81415 970-921-3454 921-3475
Web: www.smithforkranch.com

Star Island Corp, The 30 Middle St .... Portsmouth NH 03801 603-430-6272
Web: starisland.org

Sundance Trail Guest Ranch
17931 Red Feather Lakes Rd .... Red Feather Lakes CO 80545 970-224-1222 224-1222
TF: 800-357-4930 ■ *Web:* www.sundancetrail.com

Sweet Grass Ranch 460 Rein Ln .... Big Timber MT 59011 406-537-4477 537-4477
Web: www.sweetgrassranch.com

Sylvan Dale Guest Ranch
2939 N County Rd 31 D .... Loveland CO 80538 970-667-3915 635-9336
TF: 877-667-3999 ■ *Web:* www.sylvandale.com

T Cross Ranch LLC
82 Parque Creek Rd PO Box 638 .... Dubois WY 82513 307-455-2206 455-2720
TF: 877-827-6770 ■ *Web:* www.tcross.com

Tadmor Camp 43943 Mcdowell Creek Dr .... Lebanon OR 97355 541-451-4270
Web: tadmor.org

Tanque Verde Ranch 14301 E Speedway .... Tucson AZ 85748 520-296-6275
TF: 800-234-3833 ■ *Web:* www.tanqueverderanch.com

Tarryall River Ranch 270015 County Rd 77 .... Lake George CO 80827 719-748-1214 748-1319
TF: 800-408-8407 ■ *Web:* tarryallranch.com

Telenet Voip Inc 850 N Park View Dr .... El Segundo CA 90245 310-253-9000
Web: www.telenetvoip.com

Thousand Pines Christian Camp & Conference Center
359 Thousnd Pines Rd .... Crestline CA 92325 909-338-2705
Web: www.thousandpines.com

Three Bars Cattle & Guest Ranch
9500 Wycliffe Perry Creek Rd .... Cranbrook BC V1C7C7 250-426-5230
TF: 877-426-5230 ■ *Web:* www.threebarsranch.com

Trail Creek Ranch
7100 W Trl Creek Rd PO Box 10 .... Wilson WY 83014 307-733-2610
Web: www.jacksonholetrailcreekranch.com

Triangle C Dude Ranch 3737 Hwy 26 .... Dubois WY 82513 307-455-2225 455-2031
TF: 800-661-4928 ■ *Web:* www.trianglec.com

Triangle X Ranch Two Triangle X Ranch Rd .... Moose WY 83012 307-733-2183 733-8685
Web: www.trianglex.com

Triple J Wilderness Ranch
91 Mortimer Rd PO Box 310 .... Augusta MT 59410 406-562-3653 562-3836
TF: 800-826-1300 ■ *Web:* www.triplejranch.com

Triple R Ranch PO Box 124 .... Keystone SD 57751 605-666-4605
Web: www.rrrranch.com

Tumbling River Ranch
3715 Pk County Rd 62 PO Box 30 .... Grant CO 80448 303-838-5981 838-5133
TF: 800-654-8770 ■ *Web:* www.tumblingriver.com

Two Bars Seven Ranch PO Box 67 .... Tie Siding WY 82084 307-742-6072
Web: www.twobarssevenranch.com

UXU Ranch 1710 North Fork Highway .... Cody WY 82414 307-587-2143
Web: www.uxufamilyduderanch.com

Vee Bar Guest Ranch 38 Vee Bar Ranch Rd .... Laramie WY 82070 307-745-7036 745-7433
TF: 800-483-3227 ■ *Web:* www.veebar.com

Vista Verde Guest & Ski Ranch
PO Box 770465 .... Steamboat Springs CO 80477 970-879-3858 879-6814
TF: 800-526-7433 ■ *Web:* www.vistaverde.com

Wapiti Meadow Ranch 1667 Johnson Creek Rd .... Cascade ID 83611 208-633-3217 633-3219
Web: www.wapitimeadowranch.com

Waunita Hot Springs Ranch
8007 County Rd 887 PO Box 7 D .... Gunnison CO 81230 970-641-1266 641-0650
Web: www.waunita.com

White Stallion Ranch 9251 W Twin Peaks Rd .... Tucson AZ 85743 520-297-0252 744-2786
TF: 888-977-2624 ■ *Web:* www.wsranch.com

Whiteys Fish Camp 2032 County Rd 220 .... Orange Park FL 32003 904-269-4198
Web: www.whiteysfishcamp.com

Wilderness Trails Ranch 1766 County Rd 302 .... Durango CO 81303 970-247-0722 247-1006
TF: 800-527-2624 ■ *Web:* www.wildernesstrails.com

Wind River Ranch PO Box 3410 .... Estes Park CO 80517 970-586-4212 586-2255
TF: 800-523-4212 ■ *Web:* www.windriverranch.com

Wyman Center Inc 600 Kiwanis Dr .... Eureka MO 63025 636-938-5245
Web: wymancenter.org

243 DUPLICATION & REPLICATION SERVICES

Phone Fax

Andrew T Johnson Company Inc 15 Tremont Pl .... Boston MA 02108 617-742-1610 523-0719
Web: www.andrewtjohnson.com

ARC 1981 N Broadway Ste 385 .... Walnut Creek CA 94596 925-949-5100 949-5101
NYSE: ARC ■ *Web:* www.e-arc.com

ARC Global Document Management
1431 NW 17th Ave .... Portland OR 97209 503-227-3424 223-4254
Web: www.e-arc.com

Avery Dennison Microreplication Div
207 Goode Ave .... Glendale CA 91203 626-304-2000 304-2192
Web: www.averydennison.com

Campbell Blueprint & Supply Company Inc
3124 Broad Ave .... Memphis TN 38112 901-327-7385
Web: memphisreprographics.com

Corporate Disk Co 4610 Crime Pkwy .... McHenry IL 60050 815-331-6000 333-6030
TF: 800-634-3475 ■ *Web:* www.disk.com

Dering Corp, The
1702 Hempstead Rd PO Box 10755 .... Lancaster PA 17601 717-394-4200
Web: www.echodatamedia.com

Digital Video Services 4592 40th St SE .... Grand Rapids MI 49512 616-975-9911 975-9696
TF: 800-747-8273 ■ *Web:* www.dvs.com

Illinois Blueprint Corp 800 SW Jefferson Ave .... Peoria IL 61605 309-676-1300 676-1310
Web: www.illinoisblue.com

Online Copy Corp 48815 Kato Rd .... Fremont CA 94539 510-226-6810 226-7543
TF: 800-833-4460 ■ *Web:* onlinecopycorp.com

Phone Fax

Standard Digital Imaging 4426 S 108th St .... Omaha NE 68137 402-592-1292 592-8003
TF: 800-642-8062 ■ *Web:* www.standardsharev3.com

Thomas Reprographics 600 N Central Expy .... Richardson TX 75080 972-231-7227 231-0623
TF: 800-877-3776 ■ *Web:* www.thomasrepro.com

Victory Studios 2247 15th Ave W .... Seattle WA 98119 206-282-1776 282-3535
Web: www.victorystudios.com

244 DUTY-FREE SHOPS

SEE ALSO Gift Shops p. 2357

Phone Fax

Ambassador Duty Free Store 707 Patricia St .... Windsor ON N9B3B8 519-977-9100 977-7811
Web: www.ambassadordutyfree.com

Baja Duty Free (BDF) 4590 Border Village Rd .... San Ysidro CA 92173 619-428-6671 428-6673
TF: 877-438-8937 ■ *Web:* www.bajadutyfree.com

Duty Free Americas Inc
6100 Hollywood Blvd Seventh Fl .... Hollywood FL 33024 954-986-7700 965-6800
Web: www.dutyfreeamericas.com

Niagara Duty Free Shop 5726 Falls Ave .... Niagara Falls ON L2G7T5 905-374-3700 374-7503
TF: 877-642-4337 ■ *Web:* www.niagaradutyfree.com

Peace Bridge Duty Free Inc
One Peace Bridge Plz PO Box 339 .... Fort Erie ON L2A5N1 800-361-1302 871-6335*
**Fax Area Code: 905* ■ *TF:* 800-361-1302 ■ *Web:* www.dutyfree.ca

Starboard Cruise Services Inc 8400 NW 36th St .... Miami FL 33166 786-845-7300 845-1112
TF: 800-540-4785 ■ *Web:* www.starboardcruise.com

Tunnel Duty Free Shop Inc 465 Goyeau St .... Windsor ON N9A1H1 519-252-2713 252-1688
TF: 800-669-2105 ■ *Web:* www.tunneldutyfree.com

EDUCATIONAL INSTITUTIONS

SEE Preparatory Schools - Boarding p. 2959; Preparatory Schools - Non-boarding p. 2962; Children's Learning Centers p. 1948; Colleges - Tribal p. 1978; Colleges & Universities - Historically Black p. 2008; Colleges & Universities - Jesuit p. 2009

245 EDUCATIONAL INSTITUTION OPERATORS & MANAGERS

Phone Fax

Academic Approach LLC, The
342 W Armitage Ave .... Chicago IL 60614 773-348-8914
Web: www.academicapproach.com

Access College Foundation
7300 Newport Ave Ste 500 .... Norfolk VA 23505 757-962-6113
Web: www.accesscollege.org

AdvancePath Academics Inc
4125 Ironbound Rd Ste 201 .... Williamsburg VA 23188 757-208-0900
Web: www.advancepath.com

Aiesec Canada Inc
161 Eglinton Ave East Ste 402 .... Toronto ON M4P1J5 416-368-1001
Web: aiesec.ca

Apollo Group Inc 4025 E Elwood St .... Phoenix AZ 85040 800-990-2765
NASDAQ: APOL ■ *TF:* 800-990-2765 ■ *Web:* www.apollo.edu

Aqua Data Inc 95 Fifth Ave .... Pincourt QC J7V5K8 514-425-1010
Web: www.aquadata.com

Aqua Rehab Inc 2145 rue Michelin .... Laval QC H7L5B8 450-687-3472
Web: www.aquarehab.com

Avenue100 Media Solutions Inc
10 Presidential Way .... Woburn MA 01801 781-683-3300
Web: avenue100.com

Axonify Inc 460 Phillip St Ste 300 .... Waterloo ON N2L5J2 519-585-1200
Web: www.axonify.com

Bridgepoint Education Inc
13500 Evening Creek Dr N Ste 600 .... San Diego CA 92128 858-668-2586 408-2903
NYSE: BPI ■ *TF:* 866-475-0317 ■ *Web:* www.bridgepointeducation.com

Cambium Learning Group Inc
17855 Dallas Pkwy Ste 400 .... Dallas TX 75287 214-932-9500
Web: www.cambiumlearning.com

Capella Education Co
225 S Sixth St Ninth Fl .... Minneapolis MN 55402 612-339-8650 977-5058
NASDAQ: CPLA ■ *TF Cust Svc:* 888-227-3552 ■ *Web:* www.capella.edu

Career Education Corp (CEC)
2895 Greenspoint Pkwy Ste 600 .... Hoffman Estates IL 60196 847-781-3600 781-3610
NASDAQ: CECO ■ *TF:* 877-559-9222 ■ *Web:* www.careered.com

Carney, Sandoe & Associates, Limited Partnership
44 Bromfield St .... Boston MA 02108 617-542-0260
Web: www.carneysandoe.com

Ccrc Community Link 1665 N Fourth St .... Breese IL 62230 618-526-8800
Web: www.community-links.net

Center of Vocational Alternative For Men
3770 N High St .... Columbus OH 43214 614-294-7117
Web: www.cova.org

Charter Schools USA
6245 N Federal Hwy Fifth Fl .... Fort Lauderdale FL 33308 954-202-3500 202-3512
Web: www.charterschoolsusa.com

Chicago Lighthouse, The 1850 W Roosevelt Rd .... Chicago IL 60608 312-666-1331
Web: www.chicagolighthouse.com

Choice Solutions Inc 420 Lakeside Ave .... Marlborough MA 01752 508-229-0044
Web: www.choicep20.com

ClevrU Corp 1-564 Weber St N .... Waterloo ON N2L5C8 519-746-1898
Web: www.clevru.com

Connect-colleges of Ontario 655 Bay St .... Toronto ON M5G2K4 416-351-0330
Web: www.collegesontario.org

Corinthian Colleges Inc
6 Hutton Centre Dr Ste 400 .... Santa Ana CA 92707 916-431-6959 373-4412*
NASDAQ: COCO ■ **Fax Area Code: 727* ■ *TF:* 888-370-7589 ■ *Web:* www.cci.edu

Custom Learning Designs Inc 375 Concord Ave .... Belmont MA 02478 617-489-1702
Web: www.cldinc.com

DeVRY Inc 3005 Highland Pkwy .... Downers Grove IL 60515 630-515-7700
NYSE: DV ■ *Web:* devryeducationgroup.com/

Phone | Fax

Early Learning Coalition of Miami Dade & Monroe
2555 Ponce De Leon Blvd Ste 500 ... Coral Gables FL 33134 305-646-7220
Web: www.elcmdm.org

East Harlem Tutorial Program
2050 Second Ave ... New York NY 10029 212-831-0650
Web: ehtp.org

East Side House Inc 337 Alexander Ave ... Bronx NY 10454 718-665-5250
Web: www.eastsidehouse.org

eCornell 950 Danby Rd Ste 150 ... Ithaca NY 14850 607-330-3200
Web: www.ecornell.com

Ecra Group 5600 N River Rd Ste 750 ... Rosemont IL 60018 847-318-0072
Web: www.ecragroup.com

Education Management Corp (EDMC)
210 Sixth Ave 33rd Fl ... Pittsburgh PA 15222 412-562-0900 562-0598
NASDAQ: EDMC ■ *TF:* 800-275-2440 ■ *Web:* www.edmc.edu

Elenco Electronics Inc 150 W Carpenter Ave ... Wheeling IL 60090 847-541-3800
Web: www.elenco.com

Energy & Environmental Building Alliance, The
6520 Edenvale Blvd Ste 112 ... Eden Prairie MN 55346 952-881-1098
Web: www.eeba.org

Engage Learning Systems 110 Spadina Ave ... Toronto ON M5V2K4 416-368-0188
Web: www.engagelearn.com

Fund for American Studies, The
1706 New Hampshire Ave NW ... Washington DC 20009 202-986-0384
Web: www.tfas.org

Goodwill Easter Seals of Gulf Coast
2448 Gordon Smith Dr ... Mobile AL 36617 251-471-1581
Web: gesgc.org

Higher Education Assistance Group Inc, The
60 Walnut St Ste 400 ... Wellesley Hills MA 02481 617-928-1975
Web: www.heag.us

Holy Family Institute
8235 Ohio River Blvd ... Pittsburgh PA 15202 412-766-4030
Web: www.hfi-pgh.org

Imagine Schools 1005 N Glebe Rd Ste 610 ... Arlington VA 22201 703-527-2600 527-0038
Web: imagineschools.com

Indiana Dunes Environmental Learning Center Inc
700 Howe Rd ... Chesterton IN 46304 219-395-9555
Web: www.duneslearningcenter.org

ITT Educational Services Inc
13000 N Meridian St ... Carmel IN 46032 317-706-9200 706-9327
NYSE: ESI ■ *TF:* 800-388-3368 ■ *Web:* www.ittesi.com

Krm Information Services Inc
200 Spring St ... Eau Claire WI 54703 715-833-5207
Web: www.krm.com

Lake County Educational Service Ctr
382 Blackbrook Rd ... Painesville OH 44077 440-350-2563 350-2566

Lambda Solutions Inc 350 321 Water St ... Vancouver BC V6B1B8 604-687-2444
Web: www.lambdasolutions.net

Laureate Education Inc 650 S Exeter Street ... Baltimore MD 21202 410-843-6100 843-8780
TF: 866-452-8732 ■ *Web:* www.laureate.net

Leona Group LLC
4660 S Hagadorn Rd Ste 500 ... East Lansing MI 48823 517-333-9030 333-4559
TF: 800-656-6763 ■ *Web:* www.leonagroup.com

LifeLearn Inc 367 Woodlawn Rd W Unit 9 ... Guelph ON N1H7K9 519-767-5043
Web: www.lifelearn.com

Lingo Media Corp 151 Bloor St W Ste 703 ... Toronto ON M5S1S4 416-927-7000
Web: www.lingomedia.com

Literacy Council of Tyler
1530 Loop 323 SSW Rm 120 ... Tyler TX 75711 903-533-0330
Web: www.lcotyler.org

Loyalist Group Ltd 1255 Bay St Eighth Fl ... Toronto ON M5R2A9 416-969-9800
Web: www.loyalistgroup.com

MetaMetrics Inc 1000 Park Forty Plz Dr Ste 120 ... Durham NC 27713 919-547-3400
Web: www.lexile.com

Metro Ecsu 3055 Old Hwy 8 Ste 302 ... Minneapolis MN 55418 612-706-0811
Web: www.ecsu.k12.mn.us

Midtown Educational Foundation
718 S Loomis St ... Chicago IL 60607 312-738-8300
Web: midtown-metro.org

Mind Gym (USA) Inc 13 W 36th St ... New York NY 10018 646-649-4333
Web: us.themindgym.com

N r s i 179 Lafayette Dr ... Syosset NY 11791 516-921-5500
Web: nrsi.com

NACCME-PrincetonCME
300 Rike Dr Ste A ... Millstone Township NJ 08535 609-371-1137
Web: www.naccme.com

National Equity Project
1720 Broadway Fourth Fl ... Oakland CA 94612 510-208-0160
Web: www.nationalequityproject.org

National Heritage Academies
3850 Broadmoor Ave SE Ste 201 ... Grand Rapids MI 49512 877-223-6402 222-1701*
**Fax Area Code:* 616 ■ *TF General:* 877-223-6402 ■ *Web:* www.nhaschools.com

Nebraska Student Loan Program Inc 1300 O St ... Lincoln NE 68508 402-475-8686
Web: nslp.org

New World Educational Center
1313 N Second St Ste 200 ... Phoenix AZ 85004 602-238-9577
Web: www.nweccharter.com

Nobel Learning Communities Inc
1615 W Chester Pike Ste 200 ... West Chester PA 19382 484-947-2000 947-2004
Web: www.nobellearning.com

Noel-Levitz Inc 2350 Oakdale Blvd ... Coralville IA 52241 319-626-8380
Web: www.noellevitz.com

Ohio Restaurant Association
1525 Bethel Rd Ste 201 ... Columbus OH 43220 614-442-3535
Web: www.ohiorestaurant.org

Orbis Education Services Inc
11595 N Meridian Ste 400 ... Carmel IN 46032 317-663-0260
Web: www.orbiseducation.com

Pacific Resources for Education & Learning
900 Ft St Mall Ste 1300 ... Honolulu HI 96813 808-441-1300
Web: www.prel.org

Phone | Fax

Precept Medical Communications Inc
Three Mtn View Rd Third Fl ... Warren NJ 07059 908-605-4800
Web: preceptmedical.com

Princeton Review Inc, The
Ste 550 111 Speen St ... Framingham MA 01701 508-663-5050
Web: www.princetonreview.com

Project Adventure Conference Center
719 Cabot St ... Beverly MA 01915 978-524-4500
Web: www.pa.org

Reach Out & Read 29 Mystic Ave ... Somerville MA 02145 617-629-8042
Web: www.reachoutandread.org

RM Educational Software Inc
310 Barnstable Rd Ste 101 A&B ... Hyannis MA 02601 508-862-0700
Web: www.rmeducation.com

Safe & Civil Schools 2451 Willamette St ... Eugene OR 97405 541-345-1442
Web: www.safeandcivilschools.com

Sales Performance International Inc
6201 Fairview Rd Ste 400 ... Charlotte NC 28210 704-227-6500
Web: www.spisales.com

Scenarios Usa 80 Hanson Pl Ste 305 ... Brooklyn NY 11217 718-230-4381
Web: scenariosusa.org

Schoolwires Inc
330 Innovation Blvd Ste 301 ... State College PA 16803 877-427-9413
TF: 877-427-9413 ■ *Web:* www.schoolwires.com

Sigmatech Inc 4901-C Corporate Dr ... Huntsville AL 35805 256-382-1188
Web: www.sigmatech.com

State Legislative Leaders Foundation
1645 Falmouth Rd Bldg D ... Centerville MA 02632 508-771-3821
Web: sllf.org

Strayer Education Inc 2303 Dulles Stn Blvd ... Herndon VA 20171 703-247-2500
NASDAQ: STRA ■ *Web:* www.strayereducation.com

Streambox Inc 1848 Westlake Ave N Ste 200 ... Seattle WA 98109 206-956-0544
Web: www.streambox.com

Summer Search 500 Sansome St Ste 350 ... San Francisco CA 94111 415-362-0500
Web: www.summersearch.org

Sylvan Learning Centers 1001 Fleet St ... Baltimore MD 21202 888-338-2283 843-8057*
**Fax Area Code:* 410 ■ *TF:* 888-338-2283 ■ *Web:* sylvanlearning.com

Symposia Medicus
399 Taylor Blvd Ste 201 ... Pleasant Hill CA 94523 925-969-1789
Web: symposiamedicus.org

Take Charge America Inc 20620 N 19th Ave ... Phoenix AZ 85027 623-266-6100
Web: www.takechargeamerica.org

Tlg Technologies for Learning Group Inc
101-110 Princess St ... Winnipeg MB R3B1K7 204-940-4550
Web: tlg.ca

Turnaround for Children Inc
25 W 45th St Sixth Fl ... New York NY 10036 646-786-6200
Web: turnaroundusa.org

United Bronx Parents Inc 773 Prospect Ave ... Bronx NY 10455 718-991-7100
Web: www.ubpinc.org

Vertical Alliance Group Inc
1730 Galleria Oaks ... Texarkana TX 75503 903-792-3866
Web: www.verticalag.com

Work In Progress Coaching 102 Alta Verdi Dr ... Aptos CA 95003 831-685-1480
Web: www.wipcoaching.com

246 EDUCATIONAL MATERIALS & SUPPLIES

SEE ALSO Educational & Reference Software p. 2043; Office & School Supplies p. 2833

Phone | Fax

American Educational Products Inc
401 Hickory St PO Box 2121 ... Fort Collins CO 80522 970-484-7445 484-1198
TF: 800-289-9299 ■ *Web:* www.amep.com

Carolina Biological Supply Co
2700 York Rd ... Burlington NC 27215 336-584-0381 584-7686
TF: 800-334-5551 ■ *Web:* www.carolina.com

Carson-Dellosa Publishing Company Inc
7027 Albert Pick Rd ... Greensboro NC 27409 336-632-0084 808-3271
TF: 800-321-0943 ■ *Web:* www.carsondellosa.com

Center Enterprises Inc 30 Shield St ... West Hartford CT 06110 860-953-4423 953-2948
TF Orders: 800-542-2214 ■ *Web:* www.centerenterprises.com

Chenille Kraft Co 65 Ambrogio Dr PO Box 269 ... Gurnee IL 60031 800-621-1261 249-2906*
**Fax Area Code:* 847 ■ *TF:* 800-621-1261 ■ *Web:* www.chenillekraft.com

Claridge Products & Equipment Inc
601 Hwy 62 65 ... Harrison AR 72601 870-743-2200 743-1908
TF: 800-434-4610 ■ *Web:* www.claridgeproducts.com

Creative Teaching Press Inc 6262 Katella Ave ... Cypress CA 92649 714-895-5047 895-6547
TF: 800-444-4287 ■ *Web:* www.creativeteaching.com

Delta Education LLC 80 NW Blvd ... Nashua NH 03063 603-889-8899 880-6520
TF: 800-258-1302 ■ *Web:* www.delta-education.com

Didax Inc 395 Main St ... Rowley MA 01969 978-948-2340 948-2813
TF: 800-458-0024 ■ *Web:* www.didax.com

Education Ctr Inc 3515 W Market St Ste 200 ... Greensboro NC 27403 336-854-0309 547-1587
TF: 800-714-7991 ■ *Web:* www.theeducationcenter.com

Educational Insights Inc
380 N Fairway Dr ... Vernon Hills IL 60061 800-995-4436 995-0506
TF: 800-995-4436 ■ *Web:* www.educationalinsights.com

Educational Supplies Inc
1506 S Salisbury Blvd ... Salisbury MD 21801 410-543-2519 860-0584
Web: www.educationalsuppliesinc.com

Educators Resource Inc 2575 Schillingers Rd ... Semmes AL 36575 800-868-2368 868-6212*
**Fax:* Cust Svc ■ *TF Cust Svc:* 800-868-2368 ■ *Web:* www.erdealer.com

Evan-Moor Educational Publishers Inc
18 Lower Ragsdale Dr ... Monterey CA 93940 831-649-5901 649-6256
TF: 800-777-4362 ■ *Web:* www.evan-moor.com

Excelligence Learning Corp
2 Lower Ragsdale Dr Ste 125 ... Monterey CA 93940 831-333-5572 333-5630
TF: 800-627-2829 ■ *Web:* excelligence.com/?domainredirect=true&

Fisher Science Education
4500 Turnberry Dr ... Hanover Park IL 60133 800-766-7000 955-0740
TF: 800-955-1177 ■ *Web:* www.fishersci.com

				Phone	Fax
Frog Street Press Inc 800 Industrial Blvd Ste 100 *TF:* 800-884-3764 ■ *Web:* www.frogstreet.com	Grapevine	TX	76051	800-884-3764	759-3828
Ghent Manufacturing Inc 2999 Henkle Dr *TF:* 800-543-0550 ■ *Web:* www.ghent.com	Lebanon	OH	45036	513-932-3445	932-9252
Great Source Education Group 181 Ballardvale St *TF:* 800-289-4490 ■ *Web:* www.hmhco.com	Wilmington	MA	01887	800-289-4490	289-3994
Guidecraft USA 55508 Hwy 19 W PO Box U *TF:* 800-524-3555 ■ *Web:* www.guidecraft.com	Winthrop	MN	55396	507-647-5030	647-3254
Hayes School Publishing Co Inc 321 Pennwood Ave **Fax Area Code:* 513 ■ *TF:* 800-926-0704 ■ *Web:* www.hayespub.com	Pittsburgh	PA	15221	412-371-2373	527-4526*
Incentive Publications Inc 2400 Crestmoor Dr *TF Mktg:* 800-967-5325 ■ *Web:* www.incentivepublications.com	Nashville	TN	37215	615-385-2934	
Kaplan Early Learning Co 1310 Lewisville-Clemmons Rd **Fax Area Code:* 800 ■ *TF:* 800-334-2014 ■ *Web:* www.kaplanco.com	Lewisville	NC	27023	336-766-7374	452-7526*
Learning Resources 380 N Fairway Dr *TF:* 800-222-3909 ■ *Web:* www.learningresources.com	Vernon Hills	IL	60061	847-573-8400	573-8425
Learning Works 181 Brackett St *Web:* www.learningworks.me	Portland	ME	04102	207-775-0105	780-1701
Learning Wrap-Ups Inc 1660 W Gordon Ave Ste 4 *TF:* 800-992-4966 ■ *Web:* www.learningwrapups.com	Layton	UT	84041	801-497-0050	497-0063
McDonald Publishing 567 Hanley Industrial Ct *TF:* 800-722-8080 ■ *Web:* www.mcdonaldpublishing.com	Saint Louis	MO	63144	314-781-7400	781-7480
McGraw-Hill Cos Inc SRA/McGraw-Hill Div 8787 Orion Pl *TF:* 800-334-7344 ■ *Web:* www.mheonline.com/segment/view/1	Columbus	OH	43240	800-334-7344	
National School Products 1523 Old Niles Ferry Rd **Fax Area Code:* 800 ■ *TF:* 800-627-9393 ■ *Web:* www.nationalschoolproducts.com	Maryville	TN	37803	865-984-3960	289-3960*
Questar Assessment Inc 5550 Upper 147th St W PO Box 382 *OTC: QUSA* ■ *TF Cust Svc:* 800-800-2598 ■ *Web:* www.questarai.com	Apple Valley	MN	55124	800-471-5448	
Rock 'N Learn Inc 105 Commercial Cir *TF:* 800-348-8445 ■ *Web:* www.rocknlearn.com	Conroe	TX	77304	936-539-2731	539-2659
Roylco Inc 3251 Abbeville Hwy PO Box 13409 *TF:* 800-362-8656 ■ *Web:* www.roylco.com	Anderson	SC	29624	864-296-0043	296-6736
Scholastic News 557 Broadway **Fax:* PR ■ *TF Orders:* 800-724-6527 ■ *Web:* www.scholastic.com/scholasticnews	New York	NY	10012	212-343-6100	343-6930*
School Specialty Inc PO Box 1579 *NASDAQ: SCHS* ■ *TF:* 888-388-3224 ■ *Web:* www.schoolspecialty.com	Appleton	WI	54912	920-734-5712	882-5603
Teacher Created Resources 6421 Industry Way **Fax Area Code:* 800 ■ *TF:* 888-343-4335 ■ *Web:* www.teachercreated.com	Westminster	CA	92683	888-343-4335	525-1254*
Teaching & Learning Co 1204 Buchanan St *Web:* www.lorenzeducationalpress.com	Carthage	IL	62321	937-228-6118	223-2042
TREND Enterprises Inc 300 Ninth Ave SW *TF Cust Svc:* 800-860-6762 ■ *Web:* www.trendenterprises.com	New Brighton	MN	55112	651-631-2850	582-3500
World*Class Learning Materials PO Box 639 *TF:* 800-638-6470 ■ *Web:* www.wclm.com	Candler	NC	28715	800-638-6470	638-6499

247 EDUCATIONAL TESTING SERVICES - ASSESSMENT & PREPARATION

				Phone	Fax
ACT Inc 500 ACT Dr PO Box 168 *Web:* www.act.org	Iowa City	IA	52243	319-337-1000	337-1735
Alpine Testing Inc 51 W Ctr St *Web:* www.alpinetesting.com	Orem	UT	84057	844-625-7463	
Applied Measurement Professionals Inc (AMP) 18000 W 105th St *Web:* www.goamp.com	Olathe	KS	66061	913-895-4600	895-4650
Barron's Educational Series Inc 250 Wireless Blvd *TF:* 800-645-3476 ■ *Web:* www.barronseduc.com	Hauppauge	NY	11788	631-434-3311	434-3723
Castle Worldwide Inc 900 Perimeter Pk Rd Ste G *TF:* 800-655-4845 ■ *Web:* www.castleworldwide.com	Morrisville	NC	27560	919-572-6880	361-2426
College Board 45 Columbus Ave **Fax:* PR ■ *TF:* 800-927-4302 ■ *Web:* www.collegeboard.org	New York	NY	10023	212-713-8000	713-8282*
Educational Testing Service Rosedale Rd *Web:* www.ets.org	Princeton	NJ	08541	609-921-9000	734-5410
General Educational Development Testing Service *American Council on Education* One Dupont Cir NW *Web:* www.acenet.edu	Washington	DC	20036	202-939-9300	
H & H Publishing Company Inc 1231 Kapp Dr *TF:* 800-366-4079 ■ *Web:* www.hhpublishing.com	Clearwater	FL	33765	727-442-7760	442-2195
Human Resources Research Organization (HumRRO) 66 Canal Ctr Plz Ste 400 *Web:* www.humrro.org	Alexandria	VA	22314	703-549-3611	549-9025
Kaplan Inc 6301 Kaplan University Ave *TF Cust Svc:* 800-258-2432 ■ *Web:* www.kaplan.com	Fort Lauderdale	FL	33309	954-515-3993	
McGraw-Hill Cos Inc CTB/McGraw-Hill Div 20 Ryan Ranch Rd *TF:* 800-538-9547 ■ *Web:* www.ctb.com	Monterey	CA	93940	831-393-0700	393-6528
Pearson Vue 5601 Green Vly Dr *Web:* www.pearsonvue.com	Bloomington	MN	55437	952-681-3000	681-3899
Praxis Series Online Educational Testing Service Teaching & Learning Div (ETS) PO Box 6051 *TF:* 800-772-9476 ■ *Web:* www.ets.org	Princeton	NJ	08541	609-771-7395	530-0581
Professional Examination Service 475 Riverside Dr Ste 600 *Web:* www.proexam.org	New York	NY	10115	212-367-4200	367-4266
Prometric 1501 S Clinton St *TF:* 866-776-6387 ■ *Web:* www.prometric.com	Baltimore	MD	21224	443-455-8000	
Riverside Publishing Co 3800 Golf Rd Ste 200 *TF Cust Svc:* 800-323-9540 ■ *Web:* www.riversidepublishing.com	Rolling Meadows	IL	60008	630-467-7000	467-7192
TestTakers One Plz Rd Ste 204 *Web:* www.ttprep.com	Greenvale	NY	11548	516-626-6100	

248 ELECTRIC COMPANIES - COOPERATIVES (RURAL)

SEE ALSO Utility Companies p. 3270

Companies listed here are members of the National Rural Electric Cooperative Association; most are consumer-owned, but some are public power districts. In addition, the companies listed are electricity distribution cooperatives. Companies that generate and/or transmit electricity, but do not distribute it, are not included.

Alabama

				Phone	Fax
Baldwin County Electric Membership Corp 19600 Hwy 59 *TF:* 800-837-3374 ■ *Web:* www.baldwinemc.org	Summerdale	AL	36580	251-989-6247	989-0148
Central Alabama Electric Co-op 1802 Hwy 31 N *TF:* 800-545-5735 ■ *Web:* caec.coop	Prattville	AL	36067	334-365-6762	
Cherokee Electric Co-op 1550 Clarence Chestnut Bypass PO Box 0 *TF:* 800-952-2667 ■ *Web:* www.cherokee.coop	Centre	AL	35960	256-927-5524	927-2278
Coosa Valley Electric Co-op 69220 Alabama Hwy 77 PO Box 837 *TF:* 800-273-7210 ■ *Web:* www.coosavalleyec.com	Talladega	AL	35160	256-362-4180	761-2615
Covington Electric Co-op Inc 18836 US Hwy 84 *TF:* 800-239-4121 ■ *Web:* www.cov-elect.com	Andalusia	AL	36421	334-222-4121	222-1546
Cullman Electric Co-op 1749 Eva Rd NE PO Box 1168 *TF:* 800-242-1806 ■ *Web:* www.cullmanec.com	Cullman	AL	35055	256-737-3201	737-3218
Dixie Electric Co-op 9100 Atlanta Hwy *TF:* 888-349-4332 ■ *Web:* website not working	Montgomery	AL	36117	334-288-1163	
Franklin Electric Co-op Inc 225 Franklin St NW *TF:* 800-410-2732 ■ *Web:* areapower.coop	Russellville	AL	35653	256-332-2730	
Joe Wheeler Electric Membership Corp PO Box 460 *TF:* 800-239-6518 ■ *Web:* www.jwemc.org	Trinity	AL	35673	256-552-2300	355-0631
North Alabama Electric Co-op 41103 US Hwy 72 *TF:* 800-572-2900 ■ *Web:* www.naecoop.com	Stevenson	AL	35772	256-437-2281	437-2286
Pea River Electric Co-op 1311 W Roy Parker Rd PO Box 969 *TF:* 800-264-7732 ■ *Web:* www. peariver .com	Ozark	AL	36360	334-774-2545	774-2548
Sand Mountain Electric Co-op 402 Main St W *TF:* 877-843-2512 ■ *Web:* www.smec.coop	Rainsville	AL	35986	256-638-2153	638-4957
South Alabama Electric Co-op (SAEC) PO Box 449 *TF:* 800-556-2060 ■ *Web:* www.southaec.com	Troy	AL	36081	334-566-2060	566-8949
Southern Pine Electric Co-op 2134 S Blvd PO Box 528 *Web:* www.southernpine.org	Brewton	AL	36427	251-867-5415	867-5219
Tallapoosa River Electric Co-op 15163 US Hwy 431 S PO Box 675 *TF:* 800-332-8732 ■ *Web:* www.trec.coop	Lafayette	AL	36862	334-864-9331	864-0817
Tombigbee Electric Co-op Inc 7686 US Hwy PO Box 610 *TF:* 800-621-8069 ■ *Web:* www.tombigbee.net	Guin	AL	35563	205-468-3325	468-3338

Alaska

				Phone	Fax
Alaska Village Electric Co-op Inc 4831 Eagle St *Web:* www.avec.org	Anchorage	AK	99503	907-561-1818	562-4086
Barrow Utilities & Electric Co-op Inc (BUECI) 1295 Agvik St PO Box 449 *Web:* www.bueci.org	Barrow	AK	99723	907-852-6166	852-6372
Chugach Electric Assn Inc 5601 Electron Dr *TF:* 800-478-7494 ■ *Web:* www.chugachelectric.com	Anchorage	AK	99518	907-563-7494	562-0027
Copper Valley Electric Assn Inc (CVEA) Mile 187 Glenn Hwy PO Box 45 *TF:* 866-835-2832 ■ *Web:* www.cvea.org	Glennallen	AK	99588	907-822-3211	822-5586
Cordova Electric Co-op Inc 705 Second St PO Box 20 *Web:* www.cordovaelectric.com	Cordova	AK	99574	907-424-5555	424-5527
Golden Valley Electrical Assn Inc 758 Illinois St *TF:* 800-770-4832 ■ *Web:* www.gvea.com	Fairbanks	AK	99701	907-452-1151	458-6365
Homer Electric Assn Inc 3977 Lake St *TF:* 800-478-8551 ■ *Web:* www.homerelectric.com	Homer	AK	99603	907-235-8551	235-3313
Kodiak Electric Assn Inc 515 E Marine Way *Web:* www.kodiakelectric.com	Kodiak	AK	99615	907-486-7700	486-7717
Kotzebue Electric Assn Inc PO Box 44 *Web:* www.kea.coop	Kotzebue	AK	99752	907-442-3491	442-2482
Naknek Electric Assn Inc One School Rd *Web:* www.nea.coop	Naknek	AK	99633	907-246-4261	246-6242
Nushagak Electric & Telephone Co-op Inc 557 Kenny Wren Rd *TF:* 800-478-5296 ■ *Web:* www.nushtel.com	Dillingham	AK	99576	907-842-5251	842-2799
Yakutat Power Inc Forrest Hwy PO Box 129	Yakutat	AK	99689	907-784-3248	784-3922

Arizona

				Phone	Fax
Duncan Valley Electric Co-op Inc PO Box 440 *TF:* 800-669-2503 ■ *Web:* www.dvec.org	Duncan	AZ	85534	928-359-2503	359-2370

				Phone	Fax
Graham County Electric Inc 9 W Center St *TF:* 800-577-9266 ■ *Web:* azgcec.coop	Pima	AZ	85543	928-485-2451	485-9491
Navopache Electric Co-op Inc 1878 W White Mtn Blvd *TF:* 800-543-6324 ■ *Web:* www.navopache.org	Lakeside	AZ	85929	928-368-5118	368-6038
Sulphur Springs Valley Electric Co-op Inc PO Box 820 *TF:* 877-877-6861 ■ *Web:* www.ssvec.org	Willcox	AZ	85644	520-384-2221	384-5223
Tohono O'odham Utility Authority PO Box 816 *Web:* www.toua.net	Sells	AZ	85634	520-383-2236	383-2218
Trico Electric Coop 8600 W Tangerine Rd *Web:* www.trico.org	Marana	AZ	85653	520-744-2944	

Arkansas

				Phone	Fax
Arkansas Valley Electric Co-op Corp 1811 W Commercial St PO Box 47 *TF:* 800-468-2176 ■ *Web:* www.avecc.com	Ozark	AR	72949	479-667-2176	667-5238
Ashley-Chicot Electric Co-op Inc 307 E Jefferson St *TF:* 800-281-5212 ■ *Web:* www.ashley-chicot.com	Hamburg	AR	71646	870-853-5212	853-2531
C & L Electric Co-op Corp 900 Church St PO Box 9 *Web:* www.clelectric.com	Star City	AR	71667	870-628-4221	628-4676
Carroll Electric Co-op Corp 920 Hwy 62 Spur *TF:* 800-432-9720 ■ *Web:* www.carrollecc.com	Berryville	AR	72616	870-423-2161	423-4815
Clay County Electric Co-op Corp 300 N Missouri Ave *TF:* 800-521-2450 ■ *Web:* www.claycountyelectric.com	Corning	AR	72422	870-857-3521	857-3523
Craighead Electric Co-op Corp 4314 Stadium Blvd PO Box 7503 *TF:* 800-794-5012 ■ *Web:* www.craigheadelectric.coop	Jonesboro	AR	72403	870-932-8301	972-5674
First Electric Co-op Corp 1000 S JP Wright Loop Rd *TF:* 800-489-7405 ■ *Web:* www.firstelectric.coop	Jacksonville	AR	72076	501-982-4545	982-8450
Mississippi County Electric Co-op 510 N Broadway St *TF:* 800-439-4563 ■ *Web:* www.mceci.com	Blytheville	AR	72315	870-763-4563	763-0513
North Arkansas Electric Co-op Inc 225 S Main St *Web:* www.naeci.com	Salem	AR	72576	870-895-3221	895-6279
Ouachita Electric Co-op Corp 700 Bradley Ferry Rd PO Box 877 *Web:* www.oecc.com	Camden	AR	71711	870-836-5791	836-5794
Ozarks Electric Co-op Corp 3641 W Wedington Dr *TF:* 800-521-6144 ■ *Web:* www.ozarksecc.com	Fayetteville	AR	72704	479-521-2900	444-0943
Petit Jean Electric Co-op 270 Quality Dr PO Box 37 *TF:* 800-786-7618 ■ *Web:* www.pjecc.com	Clinton	AR	72031	501-745-2493	745-4150
Rich Mountain Electric Co-op Inc 515 Janssen PO Box 897 *TF:* 877-828-4074 ■ *Web:* www.rmec.com	Mena	AR	71953	479-394-4140	394-1211
South Central Arkansas Electric Co-op 1140 Main St *TF:* 800-814-2931 ■ *Web:* www.scaec.com	Arkadelphia	AR	71923	870-246-6701	246-8223
Southwest Arkansas Electric Co-op 2904 E Ninth St *Web:* www.swrea.com	Texarkana	AR	71854	870-772-2743	773-2161
Woodruff Electric Co-op PO Box 1619 *TF:* 888-559-6400 ■ *Web:* woodruffelectric.coop	Forrest City	AR	72336	870-633-2262	633-0629

California

				Phone	Fax
Anza ElectricCo-op Inc 58470 Hwy 371 PO Box 391909 *Web:* www.anzaelectric.org	Anza	CA	92539	951-763-4333	763-5297
Brightsource Energy Inc 1999 Harrison St Ste 2150 *Web:* www.brightsourceenergy.com	Oakland	CA	94612	510-550-8161	550-8165
Plumas-Sierra Rural Electric Co-op 73233 SR 70 Ste A *TF:* 800-555-2207 ■ *Web:* www.psrec.coop	Portola	CA	96122	530-832-4261	832-5761
Surprise Valley Electric Co-op 22595 US 395 *TF:* 866-843-2667 ■ *Web:* www.surprisevalleyelectric.org	Alturas	CA	96101	530-233-3511	233-2190
Trinity County California 11 Court St Rm 230 PO Box 1613 **Fax:* Admin ■ *Web:* www.trinitycounty.org	Weaverville	CA	96093	530-623-1382	623-8365*
Truckee Donner Public Utility District (TDPUD) 11570 Donner Pass Rd PO Box 309 *Web:* www.tdpud.org	Truckee	CA	96160	530-587-3896	587-5056
Yuba County Water Agency 1220 F St *Web:* www.ycwa.com	Marysville	CA	95901	530-741-6278	741-6541

Colorado

				Phone	Fax
Delta-Montrose Electric Assn 11925 6300 Rd *Web:* www.dmea.com	Montrose	CO	81401	970-249-4572	240-6801
Empire Electric Assn Inc 801 N Broadway *TF:* 800-709-3726 ■ *Web:* www.eea.coop	Cortez	CO	81321	970-565-4444	565-9198
Grand Valley Rural Power Lines Inc 845 22 Rd PO Box 190 *TF:* 877-760-7435 ■ *Web:* www.gvp.org	Grand Junction	CO	81505	970-242-0040	
Gunnison County Electric Assn Inc 37250 W Hwy 50 PO Box 180 *TF:* 800-726-3523 ■ *Web:* www.gcea.coop	Gunnison	CO	81230	970-641-3520	641-5302
Highline Electric Assn 1300 S Interocean Ave *TF:* 800-816-2236 ■ *Web:* www.hea.coop	Holyoke	CO	80734	970-854-2236	854-3652
Holy Cross Energy PO Box 2150 *TF:* 877-833-2555 ■ *Web:* www.holycross.com	Glenwood Springs	CO	81602	970-945-5491	945-4081
Intermountain Rural Electric Assn 5496 Hwy 85 **Fax Area Code:* 720 ■ *TF:* 800-332-9540 ■ *Web:* www.irea.coop	Sedalia	CO	80135	303-688-3100	733-5872*
KC Electric Assn 422 Third Ave *TF:* 800-700-3123 ■ *Web:* www.kcelectric.coop	Hugo	CO	80821	719-743-2431	743-2396
La Plata Electric Assn Inc 45 Stewart St *TF:* 888-839-5732 ■ *Web:* www.lpea.com	Durango	CO	81303	970-247-5786	247-2674
Morgan County Rural Electric Assn 20169 US Hwy 34 *TF:* 877-495-6487 ■ *Web:* www.mcrea.org	Fort Morgan	CO	80701	970-867-5688	867-3277
Mountain Parks Electric Inc 321 W Agate Ave *TF:* 877-887-3378 ■ *Web:* www.mpei.com	Granby	CO	80446	970-887-3378	887-3996
Mountain View Electric Assn Inc 1655 Fifth St *TF:* 800-388-9881 ■ *Web:* www.mvea.org	Limon	CO	80828	719-775-2861	775-9513
Poudre Valley Rural Electric Assn Inc 7649 Rea Pkwy *TF:* 800-432-1012 ■ *Web:* www.pvrea.com	Fort Collins	CO	80528	970-226-1234	226-2123
San Isabel Electric 893 E Enterprise Dr *TF:* 800-279-7432 ■ *Web:* www.siea.com	Pueblo West	CO	81007	719-547-2160	547-2229
San Luis Valley Rural Electric Co-op 3625 US Hwy 160 W *TF:* 800-332-7634 ■ *Web:* www.slvrec.com	Monte Vista	CO	81144	719-852-3538	852-4333
San Miguel Power Assn Inc 170 W Tenth Ave *TF:* 800-864-7256 ■ *Web:* www.smpa.com	Nucla	CO	81424	970-864-7311	864-7257
Sangre de Cristo Electric Assn 29780 US Hwy 24 *TF:* 800-933-3823 ■ *Web:* www.myelectric.coop	Buena Vista	CO	81211	719-395-2412	395-8742
Southeast Colorado Power Assn (SECPA) 901 W 3rd *TF:* 800-332-8634 ■ *Web:* www.secpa.com	La Junta	CO	81050	719-384-2551	384-7320
United Power Inc 500 Co-op Way *TF:* 800-468-8809 ■ *Web:* www.unitedpower.com	Brighton	CO	80603	303-659-0551	659-2172
White River Electric Assn (WREA) PO Box 958 *TF:* 800-922-1987 ■ *Web:* www.white-river-electric-association.org	Meeker	CO	81641	970-878-5041	878-5766
Y-W Electric Assn Inc 250 Main Ave PO Box Y *TF:* 800-660-2291 ■ *Web:* ywelectric.coop	Akron	CO	80720	970-345-2291	345-2154
Yampa Valley Electric Assn Inc 32 Tenth St *TF:* 888-873-9832 ■ *Web:* www.yvea.com	Steamboat Springs	CO	80487	970-879-1160	879-7270

Delaware

				Phone	Fax
Delaware Electric Co-op Inc PO Box 600 *TF:* 800-282-8595 ■ *Web:* www.delaware.coop	Greenwood	DE	19950	302-349-3147	349-3147

Florida

				Phone	Fax
Central Florida Electric Co-op Inc 1124 N Young Blvd *TF:* 800-227-1302 ■ *Web:* www.cfec.com	Chiefland	FL	32644	352-493-2511	493-4499
Choctawhatchee Electric Co-op Inc 1350 W Baldwin Ave *TF:* 800-342-0990 ■ *Web:* www.chelco.com	DeFuniak Springs	FL	32435	850-892-2111	892-9243
Clay Electric Co-op Inc 7450 State Rd 100 *TF:* 800-224-4917 ■ *Web:* www.clayelectric.com	Keystone Heights	FL	32656	352-473-8000	473-1403
Escambia River Electric Co-op Inc 3425 Florida 4 *TF:* 800-235-3848 ■ *Web:* www.erec.net	Jay	FL	32565	850-675-4521	675-8415
Florida Keys Electric Co-op Assn 91630 Overseas Hwy *TF:* 800-858-8845 ■ *Web:* www.fkec.com	Tavernier	FL	33070	305-852-2431	853-5381
Gulf Coast Electric Co-op Inc 722 Florida 22 *TF:* 800-333-9392 ■ *Web:* www.gcec.com	Wewahitchka	FL	32465	850-639-2216	639-5061
Lee County Electric Co-op Inc 4980 Bayline Dr PO Box 3455 *TF:* 800-282-1643 ■ *Web:* www.lcec.net	North Fort Myers	FL	33917	239-995-2121	995-7904
Peace River Electric Co-op Inc 210 Metheny Rd PO Box 1310 **Fax Area Code:* 863 ■ *TF:* 800-282-3824 ■ *Web:* www.preco.org	Wauchula	FL	33873	800-282-3824	773-3737*
Sumter Electric Co-op Inc PO Box 301 **Fax:* Mktg ■ *TF:* 800-732-6141 ■ *Web:* www.secoenergy.com	Sumterville	FL	33585	352-793-3801	793-6603*
Suwannee Valley Electric Co-op PO Box 160 *TF:* 800-752-0025 ■ *Web:* www.svec-coop.com	Live Oak	FL	32064	386-362-2226	364-5008
Talquin Electric Co-op Inc 1640 W Jefferson St *TF:* 888-271-8778 ■ *Web:* www.talquinelectric.com	Quincy	FL	32351	850-627-7651	627-2553
West Florida Electric Co-op 5282 Peanut Rd *TF:* 800-342-7400 ■ *Web:* westflorida.coop	Graceville	FL	32440	850-263-3231	263-3726
Withlacoochee River Electric Co-op PO Box 278 *Web:* www.wrec.net	Dade City	FL	33526	352-567-5133	521-5971

Georgia

				Phone	Fax
Altamaha Electric Membership Corp 611 W Liberty Ave PO Box 346 *TF:* 800-822-4563 ■ *Web:* www.altamahaemc.com	Lyons	GA	30436	912-526-8181	526-4235
Amicalola Electric Membership Corp 544 Hwy 515 S *TF:* 800-282-7411 ■ *Web:* www.amicalolaemc.com	Jasper	GA	30143	706-253-5200	253-5251
Canoochee Electric Membership Corp 342 E Brazell St *TF:* 800-342-0134 ■ *Web:* www.canoocheeemc.com	Reidsville	GA	30453	800-342-0134	

	City	State	ZIP	Phone	Fax
Carroll Electric Membership Corp 155 N Hwy 113 — *Web:* www.cemc.com	Carrollton	GA	30117	770-832-3552	832-0240
Central Georgia Electric Membership Corp 923 S Mulberry St — **Fax:* Cust Svc ■ *TF:* 800-222-4877 ■ *Web:* www.cgemc.com	Jackson	GA	30233	770-775-7857	504-7877*
Coastal Electric Co-op 1265 S Coastal Hwy PO Box 109 — *TF:* 800-421-2343 ■ *Web:* www.coastalemc.com	Midway	GA	31320	912-884-3311	884-2362
Cobb Electric Membership Corp 1000 EMC Pkwy PO Box 369 — **Fax Area Code:* 678 ■ **Fax:* Hum Res ■ *Web:* www.cobbemc.com	Marietta	GA	30061	770-429-2100	355-3363*
Coweta-Fayette Electric Membership Corp 807 Collinsworth Rd — *TF:* 877-746-4362 ■ *Web:* www.utility.org	Palmetto	GA	30268	770-502-0226	251-9788
Crisp County Power Commission Inc PO Box 1218 — *Web:* www.crispcountypower.com	Cordele	GA	31010	229-273-3811	
Diverse Power Inc 1400 S Davis Rd — *TF:* 800-845-8362 ■ *Web:* www.diversepower.com	LaGrange	GA	30241	706-845-2000	845-2020
Excelsior Electric Membership Corp 986 SE Broad St — *Web:* www.excelsioremc.com	Metter	GA	30439	912-685-2115	685-5782
Flint Energies 103 Macon Rd — *TF:* 800-342-3616 ■ *Web:* www.flintenergies.com	Reynolds	GA	31076	478-847-3415	847-5181
Grady Electric Membership Corp (EMC) 1499 US Hwy 84 W PO Box 270 — *TF:* 800-942-4362 ■ *Web:* www.gradyemc.com	Cairo	GA	39828	229-377-4182	377-7176
Greystone Power Corp 4040 Bankhead Hwy — *Web:* www.greystonepower.com	Douglasville	GA	30134	770-942-6576	489-0940
Habersham Electric Membership Corp 6135 Georgia 115 — **Fax Area Code:* 800 ■ *TF:* 800-640-6812 ■ *Web:* www.habershamemc.com	Clarkesville	GA	30523	706-754-2114	640-6813*
Hart Electric Membership Corp 1071 Elberton Hwy — **Fax Area Code:* 800 ■ *TF:* 800-241-4109 ■ *Web:* www.hartemc.com	Hartwell	GA	30643	706-376-4714	486-3277*
Irwin Electric Membership Corp 915 W Fourth St — *TF:* 800-237-3745 ■ *Web:* www.irwinemc.com	Ocilla	GA	31774	229-468-7415	468-7009
Jackson Electric Membership Corp 850 Commerce Rd — *TF:* 800-462-3691 ■ *Web:* www.jacksonemc.com	Jefferson	GA	30549	706-367-5281	367-6102
Jefferson Energy Co-op 3077 Hwy 17 PO Box 457 — *TF:* 888-634-7336 ■ *Web:* www.jeffersonenergy.com	North Wrens	GA	30833	706-547-2167	547-5075
Little Ocmulgee Electric Membership Corp 26 W Railroad Ave — *Web:* www.littleocmulgeeemc.com	Alamo	GA	30411	912-568-7171	
Middle Georgia Electric Membership Corp 600 Tippettville Rd — *TF:* 800-342-0144 ■ *Web:* mgemc.com	Vienna	GA	31092	229-268-2671	268-7215
Mitchell Electric Membership Corp 475 Cairo Rd — *TF:* 800-479-6034 ■ *Web:* www.mitchellemc.com	Camilla	GA	31730	229-336-5221	336-7088
North Georgia Electric Membership Corp 1850 Cleveland Hwy — *Web:* www.ngemc.com	Dalton	GA	30721	706-259-9441	259-9625
Ocmulgee Electric Membership Corp 5722 Eastman St — *TF:* 800-342-5509 ■ *Web:* www.ocmulgeeemc.com	Eastman	GA	31023	478-374-7001	374-0759
Oconee Electric Membership Corp 3445 US Hwy 80 W — *TF:* 800-522-2930 ■ *Web:* www.oconeeemc.com	Dudley	GA	31022	478-676-3191	676-4200
Okefenoke Rural Electric Membership Corp (REMC) 14384 Cleveland St PO Box 602 — *TF:* 800-262-5131 ■ *Web:* www.oremc.com	Nahunta	GA	31553	912-462-5131	462-6100
Pataula Electric Membership Corp 211 Barkley St	Cuthbert	GA	39840	229-732-3171	
Planters Electric Membership Corp 1740 Hwy 25 N PO Box 979 — *TF:* 888-397-3742 ■ *Web:* www.plantersemc.com	Millen	GA	30442	478-982-4722	982-4798
Rayle Electric Membership Corp 616 Lexington Ave — *Web:* www.rayleemc.com	Washington	GA	30673	706-678-2116	678-5381
Sawnee Electric Membership Corp 543 Atlantic Hwy — *Web:* www.sawnee.com	Cumming	GA	30028	770-887-2363	
Slash Pine Electric Membership Corp 794 W Dame Ave — *Web:* slashpineemc.com	Homerville	GA	31634	912-487-5201	487-2948
Snapping Shoals Electric Membership Corp 14750 Brown Bridge Rd — *TF:* 888-999-1416 ■ *Web:* ssemc.com	Covington	GA	30016	770-786-3484	385-2720
Sumter Electric Membership Corp 1120 Felder St — *TF:* 800-342-6978 ■ *Web:* www.sumteremc.com	Americus	GA	31709	229-924-8041	924-4982
Three Notch Electric Membership Corp PO Box 295 — *TF:* 800-239-5377 ■ *Web:* www.threenotchemc.com	Donalsonville	GA	39845	229-524-5377	
Tri-County Electric Membership Corp PO Box 487 — *TF:* 866-254-8100 ■ *Web:* www.tri-countyemc.com	Gray	GA	31032	478-986-8100	986-4733
Tri-State Electric Membership Corp (TSEMC) 2310 Blue Ridge Dr — *TF:* 800-351-1111 ■ *Web:* www.tsemc.net	Blue Ridge	GA	30513	706-492-3251	492-7617
Upson County Electric Membership Corp 607 E Main St — *Web:* www.upsonemc.com	Thomaston	GA	30286	706-647-5475	647-8545
Walton EMC 842 Hwy 78 NW PO Box 260 — *Web:* www.waltonemc.com	Monroe	GA	30655	770-267-2505	267-1223
Washington Electric Membership Corp 258 N Harris St — *TF:* 800-552-2577 ■ *Web:* www.washingtonemc.com	Sandersville	GA	31082	478-552-2577	552-1879

Idaho

	City	State	ZIP	Phone	Fax
Clearwater Power Co 4230 Hatwai Rd PO Box 997 — *TF:* 888-743-1501 ■ *Web:* www.clearwaterpower.com	Lewiston	ID	83501	208-743-1501	746-3902
Fall River Rural Electric Co-op Inc 1150 N 3400 E — *TF:* 800-632-5726 ■ *Web:* www.frrec.com	Ashton	ID	83420	208-652-7431	652-7825
Idaho County Light & Power Co-op 1065 Hwy 13 PO Box 300 — *TF:* 877-212-0424 ■ *Web:* www.iclp.coop	Grangeville	ID	83530	208-983-1610	983-1432
Kootenai Electric Co-op Inc 2451 W Dakota Ave — *TF:* 800-240-0459 ■ *Web:* www.kec.com	Hayden	ID	83835	208-765-1200	772-5858
Raft River Rural Electric Co-op Inc 155 N Main St PO Box 617 — *TF:* 800-342-7732 ■ *Web:* www.rrelectric.com	Malta	ID	83342	208-645-2211	645-2300
Salmon River Electric Co-op Inc 1130 Main St PO Box 384 — *TF:* 877-806-2283 ■ *Web:* www.srec.org	Challis	ID	83226	208-879-2283	879-2596

Illinois

	City	State	ZIP	Phone	Fax
Adams Electric Co-op 700 Eastwood St PO Box 247 — *TF:* 800-232-4797 ■ *Web:* www.adamselectric.coop	Camp Point	IL	62320	217-593-7701	593-7120
Clinton County Electric Co-op Inc 475 N Main St PO Box 40 — *TF:* 800-526-7282 ■ *Web:* cceci.com	Breese	IL	62230	618-526-7282	526-4561
Coles-Moultrie Electric Co-op 104 DeWitt Ave E PO Box 709 — *TF:* 888-661-2632 ■ *Web:* www.cmec.coop	Mattoon	IL	61938	217-235-0341	234-8342
Corn Belt Energy Corp One Energy Way — *TF:* 800-879-0339 ■ *Web:* www.cornbeltenergy.com	Bloomington	IL	61705	309-662-5330	663-4516
Eastern Illini Electric Co-op 330 W Ottawa PO Box 96 — *TF:* 800-824-5102 ■ *Web:* eiec.org	Paxton	IL	60957	217-379-2131	379-2936
Egyptian Electric Co-op Assn PO Box 38 — *TF:* 800-606-1505 ■ *Web:* www.eeca.coop	Steeleville	IL	62288	618-965-3434	965-3111
Illinois Rural Electric Co-op Two S Main St — *Web:* e-co-op.com	Winchester	IL	62694	217-742-3128	742-3831
Jo-Carroll Energy 793 US Hwy 20 W — *TF:* 800-858-5522 ■ *Web:* www.jocarroll.com	Elizabeth	IL	61028	815-858-2207	858-3731
McDonough Power Co-op 1210 W Jackson St — *Web:* mcdonoughpower.com	Macomb	IL	61455	309-833-2101	833-2104
Menard Electric Co-op 14300 State Hwy 97 PO Box 200 — *TF:* 800-872-1203 ■ *Web:* www.menard.com	Petersburg	IL	62675	217-632-7746	632-2578
MJM Electric Co-op Inc (MJMEC) 264 NE St PO Box 80 — *TF:* 800-648-4729 ■ *Web:* www.mjmec.coop	Carlinville	IL	62626	217-854-3137	854-3918
Norris Electric Co-op 8543 N State Hwy 130 PO Box 6000 — *TF:* 877-783-8765 ■ *Web:* www.norriselectric.com	Newton	IL	62448	618-783-8765	783-3673
Rural Electric Convenience Co-op Co 3973 W SR 104 PO Box 19 — *TF:* 800-245-7322 ■ *Web:* www.recc.coop	Auburn	IL	62615	217-438-6197	438-3212
Shelby Electric Co-op (SEC) Rt 128 N Sixth St PO Box 560 — *TF:* 800-677-2612 ■ *Web:* www.shelbyelectric.coop	Shelbyville	IL	62565	217-774-3986	774-3330
SouthEastern Illinois Electric Co-op 585 Hwy 142 S PO Box 251 — *TF:* 800-833-2611 ■ *Web:* www.seiec.com	Eldorado	IL	62930	618-273-2611	273-3886
Southern Illinois Electric Co-op 7420 US Hwy 51 S — *TF:* 800-762-1400 ■ *Web:* www.siec.coop	Dongola	IL	62926	618-827-3555	827-3585
Southwestern Electric Co-op Inc 525 US Rt 40 PO Box 549 — **Fax Area Code:* 618 ■ *TF:* 800-637-8667 ■ *Web:* www.sweci.com	Greenville	IL	62246	800-637-8667	664-4179*
Spoon River Electric Co-op Inc (SREC) 930 S Fifth Ave PO Box 340 — *TF:* 877-404-2572 ■ *Web:* www.srecoop.org	Canton	IL	61520	309-647-2700	647-7354
Wayne-White Counties Electric Co-op 1501 W Main St — *TF:* 888-871-7695 ■ *Web:* www.wwcec.com	Fairfield	IL	62837	618-842-2196	
Western Illinois Electrical Co-op 524 N Madison St PO Box 338 — *TF:* 800-576-3125 ■ *Web:* www.wiec.net	Carthage	IL	62321	217-357-3125	357-3127

Indiana

	City	State	ZIP	Phone	Fax
Bartholomew County Rural Electric Membership Corp 1697 W. Deaver Rd — *TF:* 800-927-5672 ■ *Web:* www.bcremc.com	Columbus	IN	47201	812-372-2546	372-2112
Boone County Rural Electric Membership Corp 1207 Indianapolis Ave — *TF:* 800-897-7362 ■ *Web:* www.bremc.com	Lebanon	IN	46052	765-482-2390	482-7869
Clark County REMC 7810 State Rd 60 PO Box 411 — *TF:* 800-462-6988 ■ *Web:* www.theremc.com	Sellersburg	IN	47172	812-246-3316	246-3947
Crawfordsville Electric Light & Power 808 Lafayette Ave — *Web:* metronetinc.com/crawfordsville	Crawfordsville	IN	47933	765-362-1900	
Daviess-Martin County REMC 12628 E 75 N PO Box 430 — *TF:* 800-762-7362 ■ *Web:* www.dmremc.com	Loogootee	IN	47553	812-295-4200	295-4216
Decatur County Rural Electric Membership Corp 1430 W Main St PO Box 46 — *TF:* 800-844-7362 ■ *Web:* www.dcremc.com	Greensburg	IN	47240	812-663-3391	663-8572

Phone / Fax

Dubois Rural Electric Co-op Inc
1400 Energy Dr. Jasper IN 47547 812-482-5454
Web: www.duboisrec.com

Fulton County Rural Electric Membership Corp
1448 W State Rd 14 PO Box 230 Rochester IN 46975 574-223-3156 223-4353
TF: 800-286-2265 ■ *Web:* faqs.org

Hendricks Power Co-op 86 N County Rd 500 E. Avon IN 46123 317-745-5473 745-6865
TF: 800-876-5473 ■ *Web:* www.hendrickspower.com

Jackson County Rural Electric Membership Corp
274 E Base Rd Brownstown IN 47220 812-358-4458 358-5719
TF: 800-288-4458 ■ *Web:* www.jacksonremc.com

Jasper County Rural Electric Membership Corp
280 E 400 S Rensselaer IN 47978 219-866-4601 866-2199
TF: 888-866-7362 ■ *Web:* www.jasperremc.com

Jay County Rural Electric Membership Corp
484 S 200 W PO Box 904 Portland IN 47371 260-726-7121 726-6240
TF: 800-835-7362 ■ *Web:* www.jayremc.com

Johnson County Rural Electric Membership Corp
750 International Dr Franklin IN 46131 317-736-6174 736-8185
TF: 800-382-5544 ■ *Web:* www.jcremc.com

Kosciusko County Rural Electric Membership Corp
370 S 250 E Warsaw IN 46582 574-267-6331 267-7273
Web: radarfrog.gatehousemedia.com

LaGrange County Rural Electric Membership Corp
1995 E US Hwy 20 LaGrange IN 46761 260-463-7165 463-4329
TF: 877-463-7165 ■ *Web:* www.lagrangeremc.com

Marshall County REMC
11299 12th Rd PO Box 250 Plymouth IN 46563 574-936-3161 935-4162
Web: www.marshallremc.com

Miami-Cass County Rural Electric Membership Corp
3086 W 100 N PO Box 168 Peru IN 46970 765-473-6668 473-8770
TF General: 800-844-6668 ■ *Web:* mcremc.coop

Noble REMC 300 Weber Rd PO Box 137 Albion IN 46701 260-636-2113 636-3319
TF: 800-933-7362 ■ *Web:* www.nobleremc.com

Northeastern REMC 4901 E Pk 30 Dr. Columbia City IN 46725 260-244-6111 625-3407
Web: www.nremc.com

Orange County Rural Electric Membership Corp
7133 N State Rd 337 PO Box 208 Orleans IN 47452 812-865-2229 865-2061
TF: 888-337-5900 ■ *Web:* www.myremc.coop

Parke County Rural Electric Membership Corp
119 W High St Rockville IN 47872 765-569-3133 569-3360
TF: 800-537-3913 ■ *Web:* www.parkecountyremc.com

Rush Shelby Energy Inc 2777 S 840 W PO Box 55 Manilla IN 46150 765-544-2600 544-2620
TF General: 800-706-7362 ■ *Web:* www.rse.coop

South Central Indiana Rural Electric Membership Corp
300 Morton Ave PO Box 3100 Martinsville IN 46151 765-342-3344 342-1335
TF: 800-264-7362 ■ *Web:* www.sciremc.com

Southeastern Indiana Rural Electric Membership Corp
712 S Buckeye St Osgood IN 47037 812-689-4111 689-6987
TF: 800-737-4111 ■ *Web:* www.seiremc.com

Southern Indiana Rural Electric Co-op Inc
1776 Tenth St PO Box 219 Tell City IN 47586 812-547-2316 547-6853
TF: 800-323-2316 ■ *Web:* www.sirec.com

Steuben County Rural Electric Membership Corp
1212 S Wayne St Angola IN 46703 260-665-3563 665-7495
TF: 888-233-9088 ■ *Web:* www.remcsteuben.com

Tipmont Rural Electric Membership Corp
403 S Main St. Linden IN 47955 800-726-3953 339-4865*
*Fax Area Code: 765 ■ *TF:* 800-726-3953 ■ *Web:* www.tipmont.org

United Rural Electric Membership Corp
4563 E Markle Rd Markle IN 46770 260-758-3155 758-3157
TF: 800-542-6339 ■ *Web:* www.unitedremc.com

Wabash County Rural Electric Membership Corp
350 Wedcor Ave Wabash IN 46992 260-563-2146 563-1523
TF: 800-563-2146 ■ *Web:* www.wabashremc.com

Wabash Valley Power Assn Inc
722 N High School Rd Indianapolis IN 46214 317-481-2800 243-6416
Web: www.wvpa.com

Warren County Rural Electric Membership Corp
15 Midway St PO Box 37 Williamsport IN 47993 765-762-6114 762-6117
TF: 800-872-7319 ■ *Web:* www.wcremc.com

White County Rural Electric Membership Corp
302 N Sixth St Monticello IN 47960 574-583-7161 583-4156
TF: 800-844-7161 ■ *Web:* www.cwremc.com

Whitewater Valley Rural Electric Membership Corp
101 Brownsville Ave Liberty IN 47353 765-458-5171 458-5938
TF: 800-529-5557 ■ *Web:* www.wwvremc.com

WIN Energy Rural Electric Membership Corp
3981 S US Hwy 41 Vincennes IN 47591 812-882-5140 886-0306
TF: 800-882-5140 ■ *Web:* www.winenergyremc.com

Iowa

Phone / Fax

Access Energy Co-op
1800 W Washington St. Mount Pleasant IA 52641 319-385-1577 385-6873
TF: 866-242-4232 ■ *Web:* www.accessenergycoop.com

Allamakee-Clayton Electric Co-op (ACEC)
229 Hwy 51 PO Box 715 Postville IA 52162 563-864-7611 864-7820
TF: 888-788-1551 ■ *Web:* www.acrec.com

Butler County Rural Electric Co-op
521 N Main PO Box 98 Allison IA 50602 319-267-2726 267-2566
TF: 888-267-2726 ■ *Web:* www.butlerrec.coop

Calhoun County Electric Co-op Assn
1015 Tonawanda St PO Box 312 Rockwell City IA 50579 712-297-7112 297-7211
TF: 800-821-4879 ■ *Web:* www.calhounrec.coop

Chariton Valley Electric Co-op
2090 Hwy 5 PO Box 486 Albia IA 52531 641-932-7126 932-2534
TF: 800-475-1702 ■ *Web:* www.cvrec.com

Consumers Energy 2074 242nd St Marshalltown IA 50158 641-752-1593 752-5738
TF: 800-696-6552 ■ *Web:* www.consumersenergy.net

Corn Belt Power Co-op
1300 13th St N PO Box 508 Humboldt IA 50548 515-332-2571 332-1375
Web: www.cbpower.coop

East-Central Iowa Rural Electric Co-op
2400 Bing Miller Ln Urbana IA 52345 319-443-4343 443-4359
TF: 877-850-4343 ■ *Web:* www.ecirec.com

Eastern Iowa Light & Power Co-op
600 E Fifth St PO Box 3003 Wilton IA 52778 563-732-2211 732-2219
TF: 800-728-1242 ■ *Web:* www.easterniowa.com

Franklin Rural Electric Co-op
1560 Hwy 65 PO Box 437 Hampton IA 50441 641-456-2557 456-5183
TF: 800-750-3557 ■ *Web:* www.franklinrec.coop

Grundy County Rural Electric Co-op
102 E 'G' Ave. Grundy Center IA 50638 319-824-5251 824-3118
TF: 800-390-7605 ■ *Web:* www.grundycountyrecia.com

Harrison County Rural Electric Co-op
61 Fourth St Woodbine IA 51579 712-647-2727 647-2242
Web: www.hcrec.coop

Hawkeye REC 24049 Iowa 9 Cresco IA 52136 563-547-3801 547-4033
TF: 800-658-2243 ■ *Web:* www.hawkeyerec.com

Heartland Power Co-op
216 Jackson St PO Box 65 Thompson IA 50478 641-584-2251 584-2253
TF: 888-584-9732 ■ *Web:* www.heartlandpower.com

Humboldt County Rural Electric Co-op (HCREC)
1210 13th St N Humboldt IA 50548 515-332-1616 332-3007
TF: 800-452-1111 ■ *Web:* www.midlandpower.coop

Iowa Lakes Electric Co-op 702 S First St Estherville IA 51334 712-362-7870 362-2819
TF: 800-225-4532 ■ *Web:* www.ilec.coop

Linn County Rural Electric Co-op 5695 Rcc Dr Marion IA 52302 319 377 1587 377 5875
Web: www.linncountyrec.com

Lyon Rural Electric Co-op
116 S Marshall St. Rock Rapids IA 51246 712-472-2506 472-3925
TF: 800-658-3976 ■ *Web:* www.lyonrec.coop

Maquoketa Valley Rural Electric Co-op
109 N Huber St. Anamosa IA 52205 319-462-3542 462-3217
TF: 800-927-6068 ■ *Web:* www.mvec.com

Midland Power Co-op
1005 E Lincolnway PO Box 420 Jefferson IA 50129 515-386-4111 386-2385
TF: 800-833-8876 ■ *Web:* www.midlandpower.coop

Nishnabotna Valley Rural Electric Co-op
1317 Chatburn Ave. Harlan IA 51537 712-755-2166 755-2351
TF: 800-234-5122 ■ *Web:* www.nvrec.com

North West REC
1505 Albany Pl SE PO Box 435 Orange City IA 51041 712-707-4935 707-4934
TF: 800-383-0476 ■ *Web:* www.nwrec.com

Northwest Iowa Power Co-op (NIPCO)
31002 County Rd C38 PO Box 240 Le Mars IA 51031 712-546-4141 546-8795
Web: www.nipco.coop

Osceola Electric Co-op Inc
1102 Egret Dr PO Box 127 Sibley IA 51249 712-754-2519
TF: 888-754-2519 ■ *Web:* www.osceolaelectric.com

Pella Co-op Electric Assn 2615 Washington St. Pella IA 50219 641-628-1040
TF: 800-619-1040 ■ *Web:* pella-cea.org

Raccoon Valley Electric Co-op
28725 Hwy 30 PO Box 486 Glidden IA 51443 712-659-3649 659-3716
TF: 800-253-6211 ■ *Web:* www.rvec.coop

Southern Iowa Electric Co-op Inc
22458 Hwy 2 PO Box 70 Bloomfield IA 52537 641-664-2277 664-3502
TF: 800-607-2027 ■ *Web:* www.sie.coop

Southwest Iowa Rural Electric Co-op
1801 Grove Ave Corning IA 50841 641-322-3165 322-5274
TF: 888-591-1261 ■ *Web:* www.swiarec.coop

TIP Rural Electric Co-op
612 W Des Moines St PO Box 534 Brooklyn IA 52211 641-522-9221 522-9271
TF: 800-934-7976 ■ *Web:* www.tiprec.com

Western Iowa Power Co-op 809 Iowa 39 Denison IA 51442 712-263-2943 263-8655
TF: 800-253-5189 ■ *Web:* www.wipco.com

Woodbury County Rural Electric Co-op Assn
1495 Humboldt Ave Moville IA 51039 712-873-3125 873-5377
TF: 800-469-3125 ■ *Web:* woodburyrec.com

Kansas

Phone / Fax

Ark Valley Electric Co-op Assn
10 E Tenth St. South Hutchinson KS 67504 620-662-6661 665-0148
TF: 888-297-9212 ■ *Web:* www.arkvalley.com

Bluestem Electric Co-op Inc
614 E Hwy 24 PO Box 5 Wamego KS 66547 785-456-2212 456-2003
TF: 800-558-1580 ■ *Web:* www.bluestemelectric.com

Brown-Atchison Electric Co-op Assn Inc
1712 Central Ave PO Box 230 Horton KS 66439 785-486-2117 486-3910
Web: www.baelectric.com

Butler Rural Electric Co-op Assn Inc
216 S Vine St PO Box 1242 El Dorado KS 67042 316-321-9600 321-9980
TF: 800-464-0060 ■ *Web:* www.butler.coop

Caney Valley Electric Co-op Assn Inc, The
401 Lawrence St PO Box 308 Cedar Vale KS 67024 620-758-2262 758-2926
TF: 800-310-8911 ■ *Web:* www.caneyvalley.com

CMS Electric Co-op Inc 509 E Carthage St. Meade KS 67864 620-873-2184 873-5303
TF: 800-794-2353 ■ *Web:* www.cmselectric.com

Doniphan Electric Co-op Assn Inc
101 N Main PO Box 699 Troy KS 66087 785-985-3523 985-2298
Web: www.donrec.org

DS&O Electric Cooperative Inc
129 W Main St PO Box 286 Solomon KS 67480 785-655-2011 655-2805
TF: 800-376-3533 ■ *Web:* www.dsoelectric.com

Flint Hills Rural Electric Co-op Assn Inc
1564 S 1000 Rd Council Grove KS 66846 620-767-5144 767-6311
Web: www.flinthillsrec.com

Heartland Rural Electric Co-op
110 Enterprise St Girard KS 66743 620-724-8251 724-8253
TF: 888-835-9585 ■ *Web:* www.heartland-rec.com

				Phone	Fax
Kaw Valley Electric Co-op Inc 1100 SW Auburn Rd	Topeka	KS	66615	785-478-3444	478-1088
TF: 800-794-2011 ■ *Web:* www.kawvalleyelectric.coop					
Lane-Scott Electric Co-op Inc 410 S High	Dighton	KS	67839	620-397-5327	397-5997
TF: 800-407-2217 ■ *Web:* www.lanescott.coop					
Leavenworth-Jefferson Electric Co-op Inc 507 N Union St	McLouth	KS	66054	888-796-6111	796-6164*
**Fax Area Code:* 913 ■ *TF:* 888-796-6111 ■ *Web:* www.ljec.coop					
Lyon-Coffey Electric Co-op Inc 1013 N 4th PO Box 229	Burlington	KS	66839	620-364-2116	364-5122
TF: 800-748-7395 ■ *Web:* www.lyon-coffey.coop					
Midwest Energy Inc 1330 Canterbury Dr	Hays	KS	67601	785-625-3437	625-1494
TF: 800-222-3121 ■ *Web:* www.mwenergy.com					
Nemaha-Marshall Electric Co-op 402 Prairie St PO Box O	Axtell	KS	66403	785-736-2345	736-2348
TF Cust Svc: 866-736-2347 ■ *Web:* www.nemaha-marshall.coop					
Pioneer Electric Co-op Inc 1850 W Oklahoma St PO Box 368	Ulysses	KS	67880	620-356-1211	356-1669
TF: 800-794-9302 ■ *Web:* www.pioneerelectric.coop					
Prairie Land Electric Co-op Inc 14935 US Hwy 36	Norton	KS	67654	785-877-3323	877-3572
TF: 800-577-3323 ■ *Web:* www.prairielandelectric.com					
Radiant Electric Co-op Inc 100 N 15th St	Fredonia	KS	66736	620-378-2161	378-3164
TF: 800-821-0956 ■ *Web:* radiantec.coop					
Rolling Hills Electric Co-op Inc 122 W Main St PO Box 307	Mankato	KS	66956	785-378-3151	378-3219
TF: 877-906-5903 ■ *Web:* www.rollinghills.coop					
Sedgwick County Electric Co-op 1355 S 383rd St W PO Box 220	Cheney	KS	67025	316-542-3131	542-3943
TF: 866-542-4732 ■ *Web:* www.sedgwickcountyelectric.coop					
Sumner-Cowley Electric Co-op Inc 2223 N A St PO Box 220	Wellington	KS	67152	620-326-3356	326-6579
TF: 888-326-3356 ■ *Web:* www.sucocoop.com					
Twin Valley Electric Co-op Inc 501 S Huston Ave PO Box 385	Altamont	KS	67330	620-784-5500	784-2464
TF: 866-784-5500 ■ *Web:* www.twinvalleyelectric.coop					
Victory Electric Co-op Assn Inc 3230 N 14th Ave	Dodge City	KS	67801	620-227-2139	227-8819
TF: 800-279-7915 ■ *Web:* www.victoryelectric.net					
Western Co-op Electric Assn Inc 635 S 13th St	WaKeeney	KS	67672	785-743-5561	743-2717
TF: 800-330-1025 ■ *Web:* www.westerncoop.com					
Wheatland Electric Co-op Inc 101 S Main St	Scott City	KS	67871	620-872-5885	872-7170
TF: 800-762-0436 ■ *Web:* www.weci.net					

Kentucky

				Phone	Fax
Big Sandy Rural Electric Co-op Corp 504 11th St	Paintsville	KY	41240	606-789-4095	789-5454
TF: 888-789-7322 ■ *Web:* www.bigsandyrecc.com					
Blue Grass Energy Co-op Corp 1201 Lexington Rd	Nicholasville	KY	40356	859-885-4191	885-2854
TF: 888-546-4243 ■ *Web:* www.bgenergy.com					
Clark Energy Co-op Inc 2640 Ironworks Rd	Winchester	KY	40391	859-744-4251	744-4218
TF: 800-992-3269 ■ *Web:* www.clarkenergy.com					
Cumberland Valley Electric Inc 6219 N US Hwy 25 E	Gray	KY	40734	800-513-2677	523-2698*
**Fax Area Code:* 606 ■ *TF:* 800-513-2677 ■ *Web:* www.cumberlandvalley.coop					
Farmers Rural Electric Co-op Corp 504 S Broadway St	Glasgow	KY	42141	270-651-2191	651-7332
TF: 800-253-2191 ■ *Web:* www.farmersrecc.com					
Fleming Mason Energy Co-op 1449 Elizaville Rd	Flemingsburg	KY	41041	606-845-2661	845-1008
TF: 800-464-3144 ■ *Web:* www.fmenergy.com					
Grayson Rural Electric Co-op Corp 109 Bagby Pk	Grayson	KY	41143	606-474-5136	474-5862
TF: 800-562-3532 ■ *Web:* www.graysonrecc.com					
Hickman-Fulton Counties Rural Electric Co-op Corp 1702 Moscow Ave PO Box 190	Hickman	KY	42050	270-236-2521	236-3028
TF: 800-633-1391 ■ *Web:* www.hfrecc.com					
Inter-County Energy Co-op 1009 Hustonville Rd	Danville	KY	40422	859-236-4561	236-3627
TF: 888-266-7322 ■ *Web:* www.intercountyenergy.net					
Jackson Energy Co-op 115 Jackson Energy Ln	McKee	KY	40447	606-364-1000	364-1007
TF: 800-262-7480 ■ *Web:* www.jacksonenergy.com					
Jackson Purchase Energy Corp 2900 Irvin Cobb Dr	Paducah	KY	42002	270-442-7321	442-5337
TF: 800-633-4044 ■ *Web:* www.jpenergy.com					
Kenergy Corp 6402 Old Corydon Rd	Henderson	KY	42419	270-826-3991	826-3999
TF: 800-844-4832 ■ *Web:* www.kenergycorp.com					
Licking Valley Rural Electric Co-op Corp 271 Main St	West Liberty	KY	41472	606-743-3179	743-2415
Web: lvrecc.com					
Meade County Rural Electric Co-op Corp 1351 Kentucky 79	Brandenburg	KY	40108	270-422-2162	422-4705
Web: www.mcrecc.coop					
Nolin Rural Electric Co-op Corp 411 Ring Rd	Elizabethtown	KY	42701	270-765-6153	735-1053
Web: www.nolinrecc.com					
Owen Electric Co-op Inc 8205 Hwy 127 N PO Box 400	Owenton	KY	40359	502-484-3471	484-2661
TF: 800-372-7612 ■ *Web:* www.owenelectric.com					
Pennyrile Rural Electric Co-op Corp 2000 Harrison St PO Box 2900	Hopkinsville	KY	42241	270-886-2555	885-6469
TF Cust Svc: 800-297-4710 ■ *Web:* www.precc.com					
Salt River Electric Co-op Corp 111 W Brashear Ave	Bardstown	KY	40004	502-348-3931	348-1993
TF: 800-221-7465 ■ *Web:* www.srelectric.com					
Shelby Energy Co-op Inc 620 Old Finchville Rd	Shelbyville	KY	40065	502-633-4420	633-2387
TF: 800-292-6585 ■ *Web:* www.shelbyenergy.com					
South Kentucky Rural Electrical Co-op 925 N Main St PO Box 910	Somerset	KY	42502	606-678-4121	679-8279
TF: 800-264-5112 ■ *Web:* www.skrecc.com					
Taylor County RECC 625 W Main St PO Box 100	Campbellsville	KY	42719	270-465-4101	789-3625
TF: 800-931-4551 ■ *Web:* www.tcrecc.com					
Warren Rural Electric Co-op Corp 951 Fairview Ave	Bowling Green	KY	42101	270-842-6541	781-3299
TF: 866-319-3234 ■ *Web:* www.wrecc.com					
West Kentucky Rural Electric Co-op Corp PO Box 589	Mayfield	KY	42066	270-247-1321	247-8496
TF: 877-495-7322 ■ *Web:* www.wkrecc.com					

Louisiana

				Phone	Fax
Beauregard Electric Co-op Inc 1010 E First St	DeRidder	LA	70634	337-463-6221	463-2809
TF: 800-367-0275 ■ *Web:* www.beci.org					
Claiborne Electric Co-Op Inc 12525 Hwy 9 PO Box 719	Homer	LA	71040	318-927-3504	368-3011
Concordia Electric Co-op Inc 1865 Hwy 84 W PO Box 98	Jonesville	LA	71343	318-339-7969	339-7462
TF: 800-617-6282 ■ *Web:* www.concordiaelectric.com					
Dixie Electric Membership Corp (DEMCO) PO Box 15659	Baton Rouge	LA	70895	225-261-1221	261-1383
TF: 800-262-0221 ■ *Web:* www.demco.org					
Jefferson Davis Electric Co-op 906 N Lk Arthur Ave PO Drawer 1229	Jennings	LA	70546	337-824-4330	824-8936
TF: 800-256-5332 ■ *Web:* www.jdec.org					
Northeast Louisiana Power Co-op Inc 1411 Landis St	Winnsboro	LA	71295	318-435-4523	435-3887
Web: nelpco.coop					
Pointe Coupee Electric Membership Corp 2506 False River Dr PO Box 160	New Roads	LA	70760	225-638-3751	638-8124
TF: 800-738-7232 ■ *Web:* www.pcemc.org					
Southwest Louisiana Electric Membership Corp 3420 NE Evangeline Thruway	Lafayette	LA	70509	337-896-5384	896-2533
TF: 888-275-3626 ■ *Web:* www.slemco.com					
Washington-Saint Tammany Electric Co-op 950 Pearl St PO Box N	Franklinton	LA	70438	985-839-3562	839-4315
TF: 866-672-9773 ■ *Web:* www.wste.coop					

Maine

				Phone	Fax
Eastern Maine Electric Co-op Inc 21 Union St	Calais	ME	04619	207-454-7555	454-8376
TF: 800-696-7444 ■ *Web:* www.emec.com					

Maryland

				Phone	Fax
Choptank Electric Co-op Inc 24820 Meeting House Rd PO Box 430	Denton	MD	21629	877-892-0001	479-3516*
**Fax Area Code:* 410 ■ *TF:* 877-892-0001 ■ *Web:* www.choptankelectric.com					

Massachusetts

				Phone	Fax
Intergen 30 Corporate Dr	Burlington	MA	01803	781-993-3000	993-3005
Web: www.intergen.com					
Taunton Municipal Lighting Plant PO Box 870	Taunton	MA	02780	508-824-5844	
Web: www.tmlp.com					

Michigan

				Phone	Fax
Cherryland Electric Co-op 5930 US 31 S PO Box 298	Grawn	MI	49637	231-486-9200	943-8204
TF: 800-442-8616 ■ *Web:* www.cecelec.com					
Grand Haven Board of Lightand & Power (GHBLP) 1700 Eaton Dr	Grand Haven	MI	49417	616-846-6250	846-3114
Web: www.ghblp.org					
Great Lakes Energy Co-op 1323 Boyne Ave	Boyne City	MI	49712	888-485-2537	582-6213*
**Fax Area Code:* 231 ■ **Fax:* Cust Svc ■ *TF:* 888-485-2537 ■ *Web:* www.gtlakes.com					
HomeWorks Tri-County Electric Co-op 7973 E Grand River Ave PO Box 350	Portland	MI	48875	517-647-7554	647-4856
TF: 800-848-9333 ■ *Web:* www.homeworks.org					
Midwest Energy Co-op 901 E State St	Cassopolis	MI	49031	800-492-5989	
TF: 800-492-5989 ■ *Web:* www.teammidwest.com					
Ontonagon County Rural Assn 500 James K Paul St	Ontonagon	MI	49953	906-884-4151	
Web: countrylines.com					
Presque Isle Electric & Gas Co-op PO Box 308	Onaway	MI	49765	989-733-8515	733-2247
TF: 800-423-6634 ■ *Web:* www.pieg.com					
Thumb Electric Co-op (TEC) 2231 Main St	Ubly	MI	48475	989-658-8571	

Minnesota

				Phone	Fax
Agralite Electric Co-op 320 Hwy 12 SE	Benson	MN	56215	320-843-4150	843-3738
TF: 800-950-8375 ■ *Web:* www.agralite.coop					
Arrowhead Electric Co-op Inc 5401 W Hwy 61 PO Box 39	Lutsen	MN	55612	218-663-7239	663-7850
TF: 800-864-3744 ■ *Web:* www.aecimn.com					
Beltrami Electric Co-op Inc 4111 Technology Dr NW	Bemidji	MN	56601	218-444-2540	444-3676
TF: 800-955-6083 ■ *Web:* www.beltramielectric.com					
Benco Electric Co-op 20946 549 Ave PO Box 8	Mankato	MN	56002	507-387-7963	387-1269
TF: 888-792-3626 ■ *Web:* www.benco.org					

Company / Address	City	State	ZIP	Phone	Fax
Brown County Rural Electric Assn 24386 State Hwy 4 PO Box 529 *TF:* 800-658-2368 ■ *Web:* www.browncountyrea.coop	Sleepy Eye	MN	56085	507-794-3331	794-4282
Clearwater-Polk Electric Co-op 315 Main Ave N *TF:* 888-694-3833 ■ *Web:* www.clearwater-polk.com	Bagley	MN	56621	218-694-6241	694-6245
Connexus Energy Co-op 14601 Ramsey Blvd *TF:* 877-382-4357 ■ *Web:* www.connexusenergy.com	Ramsey	MN	55303	763-323-2650	323-2603
Crow Wing Co-op Power & Light Co Hwy 371 N PO Box 507 *TF:* 800-648-9401 ■ *Web:* www.cwpower.com	Brainerd	MN	56401	218-829-2827	825-2209
Dakota Electric Assn 4300 220th St W *TF:* 800-874-3409 ■ *Web:* www.dakotaelectric.com	Farmington	MN	55024	651-463-6144	463-6144
East Central Energy PO Box 39 **Fax Area Code:* 320 ■ *TF:* 800-254-7944 ■ *Web:* www.eastcentralenergy.com	Braham	MN	55006	800-254-7944	396-4114*
Federated Rural Electric Assn 77100 US Hwy 71 PO Box 69 *TF:* 800-321-3520 ■ *Web:* www.federatedrea.com	Jackson	MN	56143	507-847-3520	728-8366
Freeborn-Mower Co-op Services 2501 E Main St *TF:* 800-734-6421 ■ *Web:* www.fmcs.coop	Albert Lea	MN	56007	507-373-6421	369-0259
Goodhue County Co-op Electric Assn 1410 Northstar Dr *TF:* 800-927-6864 ■ *Web:* www.gccea.com	Zumbrota	MN	55992	507-732-5117	732-5110
Great River Energy 12300 Elm Creek Blvd *TF:* 888-521-0130 ■ *Web:* www.greatriverenergy.com	Maple Grove	MN	55369	763-445-5000	445-5050
Itasca-Mantrap Co-op Electrical Assn 16930 County Rd 6 *Web:* www.itasca-mantrap.com	Park Rapids	MN	56470	218-732-3377	732-5890
Lake Country Power 2810 Elida Dr **Fax Area Code:* 218 ■ *TF:* 800-421-9959 ■ *Web:* www.lakecountrypower.com	Grand Rapids	MN	55744	800-421-9959	326-8136*
Lake Region Co-op Electrical Assn 1401 S Broadway PO Box 643 *TF:* 800-552-7658 ■ *Web:* www.lrec.coop	Pelican Rapids	MN	56572	218-863-1171	863-1172
Lyon-Lincoln Electric Co-op Inc (LLEC) 205 W Hwy 14 PO Box 639 *TF:* 800-927-6276 ■ *Web:* www.llec.coop	Tyler	MN	56178	507-247-5505	247-5508
McLeod Co-op Power Assn 1231 Ford Ave N *TF:* 800-494-6272 ■ *Web:* www.mcleodcoop.com	Glencoe	MN	55336	320-864-3148	864-4850
Meeker Co-op Light & Power Assn 1725 E US Hwy 12 PO Box 68 *TF:* 800-232-6257 ■ *Web:* www.meeker.coop	Litchfield	MN	55355	320-693-3231	693-2980
Mille Lacs Electric Co-op PO Box 230 *TF:* 800-450-2191 ■ *Web:* www.mlecmn.net	Aitkin	MN	56431	218-927-2191	927-6822
Minnesota Valley Co-op Light & Power Assn 501 S First St *TF:* 800-247-5051 ■ *Web:* www.mnvalleyrec.com	Montevideo	MN	56265	320-269-2163	269-2302
Minnesota Valley Electric Co-op 125 Minnesota Vly Electric Dr PO Box 77024 *TF:* 800-282-6832 ■ *Web:* www.mvec.net	Jordan	MN	55352	952-492-2313	492-8281
Nobles Co-op Electric 22636 US Hwy 59 PO Box 788 *TF:* 800-776-0517 ■ *Web:* www.noblesce.coop	Worthington	MN	56187	507-372-7331	372-5148
North Itasca Electric Co-op Inc 301 Main Ave PO Box 227 *TF:* 800-762-4048 ■ *Web:* www.northitascaelectric.com	Bigfork	MN	56628	218-743-3131	743-3644
North Star Electric Co-op 441 State Hwy 172 NW PO Box 719 *TF:* 888-634-2202 ■ *Web:* www.northstarelectric.coop	Baudette	MN	56623	218-634-2202	634-2203
People's Energy Co-op 1775 Lk Shady Ave S *TF:* 800-214-2694 ■ *Web:* www.peoplesrec.com	Oronoco	MN	55960	507-367-7000	367-7001
PKM Electric Co-op Inc 406 N Minnesota St *TF:* 800-552-7366 ■ *Web:* www.pkmcoop.com	Warren	MN	56762	218-745-4711	745-4713
Red Lake Electric Co-op Inc 412 International Dr PO Box 430 *TF:* 800-245-6068 ■ *Web:* www.redlakeelectric.com	Red Lake Falls	MN	56750	218-253-2168	253-2630
Red River Valley Co-op Power Assn 109 Second Ave E *TF:* 800-788-7784 ■ *Web:* www.rrvcoop.com	Halstad	MN	56548	218-456-2139	456-2102
Redwood Electric Co-op 60 Pine St PO Box 15 *Web:* www.greatriverenergy.com	Clements	MN	56224	507-692-2214	
Renville-Sibley Co-op Power Assn 103 Oak St PO Box 68 *TF:* 800-826-2593 ■ *Web:* www.renville-sibley.coop	Danube	MN	56230	320-826-2593	826-2679
Roseau Electric Co-op Inc 1107 Third St NE *TF:* 888-847-8840 ■ *Web:* roseauelectric.coop	Roseau	MN	56751	218-463-1543	463-3713
South Central Electric Assn 71176 Tiell Dr PO Box 150 *TF:* 888-805-7232 ■ *Web:* www.southcentralelectric.com	Saint James	MN	56081	507-375-3164	375-3166
Southern Minnesota Municipal Power Agency 500 First Ave SW *Web:* www.smmpa.com	Rochester	MN	55902	507-285-0478	292-6414
Stearns ElectricAssn 900 E Kraft Dr *TF:* 800-962-0655 ■ *Web:* www.stearnselectric.org	Melrose	MN	56352	320-256-4241	256-3618
Steele-Waseca Co-op Electric (SWCE) 2411 W Bridge St PO Box 485 *TF:* 800-526-3514 ■ *Web:* www.swce.com	Owatonna	MN	55060	507-451-7340	446-4242
Todd-Wadena Electric Co-op 550 Ash Ave NE PO Box 431 *TF:* 800-321-8932 ■ *Web:* www.toddwadena.coop	Wadena	MN	56482	218-631-3120	631-4188
Traverse Electric Co-op Inc 1618 Broadway PO Box 66 *TF:* 800-927-5443 ■ *Web:* www.traverseelectric.com	Wheaton	MN	56296	320-563-8616	563-4863
Wild Rice Electric Co-op Inc 502 N Main PO Box 438 *TF:* 800-244-5709 ■ *Web:* www.wildriceelectric.com	Mahnomen	MN	56557	218-935-2517	935-2519
Wright-Hennepin Co-op Electric Assn 6800 Electric Dr PO Box 330 *TF:* 800-943-2667 ■ *Web:* www.whe.org	Rockford	MN	55373	763-477-3000	477-3054

Mississippi

Company / Address	City	State	ZIP	Phone	Fax
Alcorn County Electric Power Assn 1909 S Tate St *TF:* 866-448-3046 ■ *Web:* ace-power.com	Corinth	MS	38834	662-287-4402	287-4088
Central Electric Power Assn 104 E Main St *Web:* www.centralepa.com	Carthage	MS	39051	601-267-5671	267-6032
Coahoma Electric Power Assn 340 Hopson St *Web:* coahomaepa.com	Lyon	MS	38645	662-624-8321	624-8327
Coast Electric Power Assn 18020 Hwy Ste 603 *TF Cust Svc:* 800-624-3348 ■ *Web:* www.coastepa.com	Kiln	MS	39556	228-363-7000	
Delta Electric Power Assn 1700 Hwy 82 W *Web:* deltaepa.com	Greenwood	MS	38930	662-453-6352	453-6359
Dixie Electric Power Assn PO Box 88 *TF:* 888-465-9209 ■ *Web:* www.dixieepa.com	Laurel	MS	39441	601-425-2535	425-2535
East Mississippi Electric Power Assn (EMEPA) 2128 Hwy 39 N PO Box 5517 *Web:* www.emepa.com	Meridian	MS	39302	601-581-8600	482-0701
Four County Electric Power Assn 5265 S Frontage Rd *Web:* www.4county.org	Columbus	MS	39701	662-327-8900	327-8790
Magnolia Electric Power Assn PO Box 747 *Web:* www.magnoliaepa.com	McComb	MS	39649	601-684-4011	684-5535
Monroe County Electric Power Assn 601 N Main St *TF:* 866-656-2962	Amory	MS	38821	662-256-7196	
North East MS EPA 10 PR 2050 PO Box 1037 *TF:* 877-234-6331 ■ *Web:* northeastpower.org	Oxford	MS	38655	662-234-6331	234-0046
Pearl River Valley Electric Power Assn 1422 Hwy 13 N PO Box 1217 *TF:* 855-277-8372 ■ *Web:* www.prvepa.com	Columbia	MS	39429	601-736-2666	736-9702
Pontotoc Electric Power Assn 12 S Main St *Web:* pepa.com	Pontotoc	MS	38863	662-489-3211	489-5156
Prentiss County Electric Power Assn 302 W Church St *Web:* www.pcepa.com	Booneville	MS	38829	662-728-4433	728-4059
Singing River Electric Power Assn Inc 11187 Old Hwy 63 PO Box 767 *Web:* www.singingriver.com	Lucedale	MS	39452	601-947-4211	947-6548
South Mississippi Electric Power Assn (SMEPA) 7037 US Hwy 49 *Web:* www.smepa.coop	Hattiesburg	MS	39402	601-268-2083	
Southern Pine Electric Power Assn 110 Risher St PO Box 60 *TF:* 800-231-5240 ■ *Web:* www.spepa.com	Taylorsville	MS	39168	601-785-6511	785-4980
Southwest Mississippi Electric Power Assn 18671 Hwy 61 PO Box 5 *TF:* 800-287-8564 ■ *Web:* www.southwestepa.com	Lorman	MS	39096	800-287-8564	
Tallahatchie Valley Electric Power Assn 250 Power Dr *Web:* www.tvepa.com	Batesville	MS	38606	662-563-4742	563-8615
Yazoo Valley Electric Power Assn PO Box 8 *TF:* 800-281-5098 ■ *Web:* yazoovalley.com	Yazoo City	MS	39194	662-746-4251	751-1060

Missouri

Company / Address	City	State	ZIP	Phone	Fax
Associated ElectricCo-op Inc 2814 S Golden PO Box 754 *Web:* www.aeci.org	Springfield	MO	65801	417-881-1204	885-9252
Atchison-Holt Electric Co-op 18585 Industrial Rd PO Box 160 *TF:* 888-744-5366 ■ *Web:* www.ahec.coop	Rock Port	MO	64482	660-744-5344	
Barry Electric Co-op 4015 Main St PO Box 307 *TF:* 866-847-2333 ■ *Web:* www.barryelectric.com	Cassville	MO	65625	417-847-2131	847-5524
Barton County Electric Co-op 91 W Hwy 160 PO Box 459 *TF:* 800-286-5636 ■ *Web:* www.bartonelectric.com	Lamar	MO	64759	417-682-5636	682-5276
Boone Electric Co-op 1413 Rangeline St *TF:* 800-225-8143 ■ *Web:* www.booneelectric.coop	Columbia	MO	65201	573-449-4181	
Callaway Electric Co-op 1313 Co-op Dr PO Box 250 *TF:* 888-642-4840 ■ *Web:* www.callawayelectric.com	Fulton	MO	65251	573-642-3326	
Central Missouri ElectricCo-op Inc 22702 Hwy 65 PO Box 939 *Web:* www.cmecinc.com	Sedalia	MO	65302	660-826-2900	826-7180
Co-Mo Electric Co-op Inc 29868 Hwy 5 PO Box 220 *TF:* 800-781-0157 ■ *Web:* www.co-mo.coop	Tipton	MO	65081	660-433-5521	433-5631
Consolidated Electric Co-op 3940 E Liberty St *TF:* 800-621-0091 ■ *Web:* www.consolidatedelectric.com	Mexico	MO	65265	573-581-3630	581-0990
Crawford Electric Co-op Inc 10301 N Service Rd PO Box 10 *TF:* 800-677-2667 ■ *Web:* www.crawfordelec.com	Bourbon	MO	65441	573-732-4415	732-5409
Cuivre River Electric Co-op 1112 E Cherry St *TF:* 800-392-3709 ■ *Web:* www.cuivre.com	Troy	MO	63379	636-528-8261	528-7696
Farmers' Electric Co-op 201 W Business 36 PO Box 680 *TF:* 800-279-0496 ■ *Web:* www.fec-co.com	Chillicothe	MO	64601	660-646-4281	646-3569
Gascosage Electric Co-op 803 S Hwy 28 PO Box G *TF:* 866-568-8243 ■ *Web:* www.gascosage.com	Dixon	MO	65459	573-759-7146	759-6020
Grundy Electric Co-op Inc 4100 Oklahoma Ave *TF:* 800-279-2249 ■ *Web:* www.grundyec.com	Trenton	MO	64683	660-359-3941	359-6030
Howard Electric Co-op 205 Hwy 5 & 240 N PO Box 391 *TF:* 877-352-0122 ■ *Web:* www.howardelectric.com	Fayette	MO	65248	660-248-3311	248-3543
Howell-Oregon Electric Co-op Inc 6327 N US Hwy 63 PO Box 649 *TF:* 855-385-9903 ■ *Web:* www.hoecoop.org	West Plains	MO	65775	417-256-2131	256-4571

	City	State	ZIP	Phone	Fax
Intercounty Electric Co-op 102 Maple Ave *Web:* www.ieca.coop	Licking	MO	65542	573-674-2211	
Laclede Electric Co-op 1400 E Rt 66 *TF:* 800-299-3164 ■ *Web:* www.lacledeelectric.com	Lebanon	MO	65536	417-532-3164	532-8321
Lewis County Rural Electric Co-op 18256 Hwy 16 PO Box 68 *TF:* 888-454-4485 ■ *Web:* www.lewiscountyrec.org	Lewistown	MO	63452	573-215-4000	215-4004
Macon Electric Co-op 31571 Bus Hwy 36 E PO Box 157 *TF:* 800-553-6901 ■ *Web:* www.maconelectric.com	Macon	MO	63552	660-385-3157	385-3334
N W Electric Power Co-op PO Box 565 *Web:* www.nwepc.com	Cameron	MO	64429	816-632-2121	632-3114
New-Mac Electric Co-op Inc 12105 E Hwy 86 *Web:* www.newmac.com	Neosho	MO	64850	417-451-1515	451-9042
Northeast Missouri Electric Power Co-op 3705 Business 61 PO Box 191 *Web:* www.northeast-power.coop	Palmyra	MO	63461	573-769-2107	769-4358
Osage Valley Electric Co-op Assn 1321 N Orange St *TF:* 800-889-6832 ■ *Web:* www.osagevalley.com	Butler	MO	64730	660-679-3131	679-3142
Ozark Border Electric Co-op 3281 S Westwood *TF:* 800-392-0567 ■ *Web:* www.ozarkborder.org	Poplar Bluff	MO	63901	573-785-4631	785-1853
Pemiscot-Dunklin Electric Co-op Hwy 412 W PO Box 509 *TF:* 800-558-6641 ■ *Web:* www.pemdunk.com	Hayti	MO	63851	573-757-6641	757-6656
Platte-Clay Electric Co-op Inc 1000 W Hwy 92 PO Box 100 *TF:* 800-431-2131 ■ *Web:* www.pcec.coop	Kearney	MO	64060	816-628-3121	628-3141
Ralls County Electric Co-op 17594 Hwy 19 PO Box 157 *TF:* 877-985-8711 ■ *Web:* www.rallscountyelectric.com	New London	MO	63459	573-985-8711	985-3658
Sac Osage Electric Co-op Inc 4815 E Hwy 54 PO Box 111 *TF:* 800-876-2701 ■ *Web:* www.sacosage.com	El Dorado Springs	MO	64744	417-876-2721	876-5368
Se-Ma-No Electric Co-op 601 N Business 60 *Web:* semano.com	Mansfield	MO	65704	417-924-3243	924-8215
Three Rivers Electric Co-op 1324 E Main St PO Box 918 *Web:* www.threeriverselectric.com	Linn	MO	65051	573-644-9000	897-3511
Webster Electric Co-op 1240 Spur Dr *TF:* 800-643-4305 ■ *Web:* www.websterec.com	Marshfield	MO	65706	417-859-2216	859-4579
White River Valley Electric Co-op Inc 2449 State Hwy 76 E *TF:* 800-879-4056 ■ *Web:* www.whiteriver.org	Branson	MO	65616	417-335-9335	335-9250

Montana

	City	State	ZIP	Phone	Fax
Beartooth Electric Co-op Inc 1306 N Broadway St PO Box 1110 *TF:* 800-472-9821 ■ *Web:* beartoothec.coopwebbuilder2.com	Red Lodge	MT	59068	406-446-2310	446-3934
Big Flat Electric Co-op Inc 333 S Seventh St *TF:* 800-242-2040 ■ *Web:* www.bigflatelectric.com	Malta	MT	59538	406-654-2040	654-2292
Fergus Electric Co-op Inc 84423 US Hwy 87 *Web:* www.ferguselectric.coop	Lewistown	MT	59457	406-538-3465	538-7391
Flathead Electric Co-op Inc 2510 Hwy 2 E *TF:* 800-735-8489 ■ *Web:* www.flatheadelectric.com	Kalispell	MT	59901	406-751-4483	752-4283
Glacier Electric Co-op Inc 410 E Main St *TF:* 800-347-6795 ■ *Web:* www.glacierelectric.com	Cut Bank	MT	59427	406-873-5566	873-2071
Goldenwest Electric Co-op Inc 119 1 Ave SW	Wibaux	MT	59353	406-796-8146	
Hill County Electric Co-op Inc PO Box 2330 *TF:* 877-394-7804 ■ *Web:* www.hcelectric.com	Havre	MT	59501	877-394-7804	
Lincoln Electric Co-op Inc (LEC) 500 Osloski Rd PO Box 628 *TF:* 800-442-2994 ■ *Web:* www.lincolnelectric.coop	Eureka	MT	59917	406-889-3301	889-3874
Lower Yellowstone Rural Electric Assn Inc 3200 W Holly St PO Box 1047 *Web:* www.lyrec.com	Sidney	MT	59270	406-488-1602	488-6524
Marias River Electric Co-op Inc PO Box 729 *Web:* www.mariasriverec.com	Shelby	MT	59474	406-434-5575	434-2531
McCone Electric Co-op Inc 110 Main St *TF:* 800-684-3605 ■ *Web:* www.mcconeelectric.coop	Circle	MT	59215	406-485-3430	485-3397
Mid Yellowstone Elec Co-Op Inc 203 Elliott PO Box 386	Hysham	MT	59038	406-342-5521	342-5511
Missoula Electric Co-op Inc 1700 W Broadway *TF:* 800-352-5200 ■ *Web:* www.missoulaelectric.com	Missoula	MT	59808	406-541-4433	541-6318
Park Electric Co-op Inc 5706 US Hwy 89 S PO Box 1119 *TF:* 888-298-0657 ■ *Web:* www.parkelectric.coop	Livingston	MT	59047	406-222-3100	222-3418
Ravalli County Electric Co-op Inc 1051 Eastside Hwy *Web:* www.ravallielectric.com	Corvallis	MT	59828	406-961-3001	961-3230
Sheridan Electric Co-op Inc PO Box 227 *TF:* 800-553-4344 ■ *Web:* www.sheridanelectric.coop	Medicine Lake	MT	59247	406-789-2231	789-2234
Southeast Electric Co-op Inc (SECO) 110 S Main St *TF:* 888-485-8762 ■ *Web:* www.seecoop.com	Ekalaka	MT	59324	406-775-8762	775-8763
Sun River Electric Co-op Inc 310 First Ave S PO Box 309 *TF:* 800-452-7516 ■ *Web:* www.sunriverelectric.coop	Fairfield	MT	59436	406-467-2527	
Vigilante Electric Co-op Inc 225 E Bannack St *Web:* www.vec.coop	Dillon	MT	59725	406-683-2327	683-4328
Yellowstone Valley Electric Co-op 150 Co-op Way *TF:* 800-736-5323 ■ *Web:* www.yvec.com	Huntley	MT	59037	406-348-3411	348-3414

Nebraska

	City	State	ZIP	Phone	Fax
Burt County Public Power District 613 N 13th St PO Box 209 *TF:* 888-835-1620 ■ *Web:* www.burtcoppd.com	Tekamah	NE	68061	402-374-2631	374-1605
Butler County Rural Public Power District 1331 N Fourth St *TF:* 800-230-0569 ■ *Web:* www.butlerppd.com	David City	NE	68632	402-367-3081	367-6114
Cedar-Knox Public Power District 56272 W Hwy 84 PO Box 947 *Web:* www.cedarknoxppd.com	Hartington	NE	68739	402-254-6291	
Chimney Rock Public Power District 805 W Eigth St PO Box 608 *TF:* 877-773-6300 ■ *Web:* www.crppd.com	Bayard	NE	69334	308-586-1824	586-2511
Cornhusker Public Power District 23169 235th Ave PO Box 9 *Web:* www.cornhusker-power.com	Columbus	NE	68602	402-564-2821	564-9907
Cuming County Public Power District 500 S Main St *TF:* 877-572-2463 ■ *Web:* www.ccppd.com	West Point	NE	68788	402-372-2463	372-5832
Custer Public Power District 625 E SE St PO Box 10 *TF:* 888-749-2453 ■ *Web:* www.custerpower.com	Broken Bow	NE	68822	308-872-2451	872-2378
Dawson Public Power District 75191 Rd 433 *TF:* 800-752-8305 ■ *Web:* www.dawsonpower.com	Lexington	NE	68850	308-324-2386	324-2907
Elkhorn Rural Public Power District 206 N Fourth St *TF:* 800-675-2185 ■ *Web:* www.erppd.com	Battle Creek	NE	68715	402-675-2185	675-6275
Howard Greeley Rural Power 422 Howard Ave PO Box 105 *TF:* 800-280-4962 ■ *Web:* www.howardgreeleyrppd.com	Saint Paul	NE	68873	308-754-4457	754-4230
KBR Rural Public Power District 374 N Pine St PO Box 187 *TF:* 800-672-0009 ■ *Web:* kbrpower.com	Ainsworth	NE	69210	402-387-1120	387-1033
Loup Public Power District (LPPD) 2404 15th St PO Box 988 *TF:* 866-869-2087 ■ *Web:* www.loup.com	Columbus	NE	68602	402-564-3171	564-0970
McCook Public Power District 1510 N Hwy 83 *TF:* 800-658-4285 ■ *Web:* www.mppdonline.com	McCook	NE	69001	308-345-2500	345-4772
Midwest Electric Co-op Corp 104 Washington Ave *TF:* 800-451-3691 ■ *Web:* www.midwestecc.com	Grant	NE	69140	308-352-4356	352-4957
Nebraska Public Power District 1414 15th St PO Box 499 *TF:* 877-275-6773 ■ *Web:* www.nppd.com	Columbus	NE	68602	402-564-8561	563-5551
Niobrara Valley Electric Membership Corp 427 N Fourth St *Web:* www.nvemc.org	O'Neill	NE	68763	402-336-2803	336-4858
Norris Public Power District 606 Irving St PO Box 399 *TF:* 800-858-4707 ■ *Web:* www.norrisppd.com	Beatrice	NE	68310	402-223-4038	228-2895
North Central Public Power District 1409 Main St PO Box 90 *TF:* 800-578-1060 ■ *Web:* www.ncppd.com	Creighton	NE	68729	402-358-5112	358-5129
Northeast Nebraska Public Power District 1410 W Seventh St PO Box 350 *TF:* 800-750-9277 ■ *Web:* www.nnppd.com	Wayne	NE	68787	402-375-1360	
Northwest Rural Public Power District 5613 State Hwy 87 PO Box 249 *TF:* 800-847-0492 ■ *Web:* www.nrppd.com	Hay Springs	NE	69347	308-638-4445	638-4448
Perennial Public Power District 2122 S Lincoln Ave *TF:* 800-289-0288 ■ *Web:* www.perennialpower.com	York	NE	68467	402-362-3355	362-3623
Polk County Rural Public Power District 115 W 3rd St PO Box 465 *TF:* 888-242-5265 ■ *Web:* www.pcrppd.com	Stromsburg	NE	68666	402-764-4381	764-4382
Seward County Rural Public Power District 3111 Progressive Rd PO Box 69 *Web:* www.sewardppd.com	Seward	NE	68434	402-643-2951	646-4695
South Central Public Power District (SCPPD) 275 S Main St PO Box 406 *TF:* 800-557-5254 ■ *Web:* www.southcentralppd.com	Nelson	NE	68961	402-225-2351	225-2353
Southern Public Power District (SPPD) 4550 W Husker Hwy PO Box 1687 *TF:* 800-652-2013 ■ *Web:* www.southernpd.com	Grand Island	NE	68803	308-384-2350	384-5018
Southwest Public Power District 221 S Main St PO Box 289 *TF:* 800-379-7977 ■ *Web:* www.swppd.com	Palisade	NE	69040	308-285-3295	
Stanton County Public Power District 807 Douglas St *TF:* 877-439-2300 ■ *Web:* www.scppd.net	Stanton	NE	68779	402-439-2228	439-7000
Twin Valleys Public Power District 1145 Nasby St *TF:* 800-658-4266 ■ *Web:* www.twinvalleysppd.com	Cambridge	NE	69022	308-697-3315	697-4877
Wheat Belt Public Power District 2104 Illinois St *TF:* 800-261-7114 ■ *Web:* www.wheatbelt.com	Sidney	NE	69162	308-254-5871	254-2384

Nevada

	City	State	ZIP	Phone	Fax
Overton Power District # 5 615 N Moapa Vly Blvd PO Box 395 *TF:* 888-409-6735 ■ *Web:* opd5.com	Overton	NV	89040	702-397-2512	
Valley Electric Assn Inc 800 E Hwy 372 PO Box 237 *TF:* 800-742-3330 ■ *Web:* www.vea.coop	Pahrump	NV	89048	775-727-5312	727-6320
Wells Rural Electric Co 1451 Humboldt Ave *Web:* www.wrec.coop	Wells	NV	89835	775-752-3328	752-3407

New Hampshire

				Phone	Fax
New Hampshire Electric Co-op 579 Tenney Mtn Hwy *TF:* 800-698-2007 ■ *Web:* www.nhec.com	Plymouth	NH	03264	603-536-1800	536-8682

New Jersey

				Phone	Fax
Sussex Rural Electric Co-op 64 County Rt 639 PO Box 346 *TF:* 877-504-6463 ■ *Web:* www.sussexrec.com	Sussex	NJ	07461	973-875-5101	875-4114

New Mexico

				Phone	Fax
Central Valley Electric Co-op Inc 1505 N 13th St PO Box 230 **Fax Area Code:* 505 ■ *Web:* www.cvecoop.org	Artesia	NM	88211	575-746-3571	746-4219*
Columbus Electric Co-op Inc 900 N Gold St PO Box 631 *TF:* 800-950-2667 ■ *Web:* www.columbusco-op.org	Deming	NM	88031	505-546-8838	546-3128
Continental Divide ElectricCo-op Inc (CDEC) 200 E High St PO Box 1087 *Web:* www.cdec.coop	Grants	NM	87020	505-285-6656	287-2234
Jemez Mountains Electric Co-op PO Box 128 *TF:* 888-755-2105 ■ *Web:* www.jemezcoop.org	Espanola	NM	87532	505-753-2105	753-6958
Mora-San Miguel Electric Co-op PO Box 240 **Fax Area Code:* 505 ■ *TF:* 800-421-6773 ■ *Web:* www.moraelectric.org	Mora	NM	87732	575-387-2205	387-5975*
Northern Rio Arriba Electric Co-op 1135 Camino Escondido PO Box 217 **Fax Area Code:* 505 ■ *Web:* www.noraelectric.org	Chama	NM	87520	575-756-2181	756-2200*
Otero County Electric Co-op Inc 202 Burro Ave PO Box 227 **Fax Area Code:* 505 ■ *TF:* 800-548-4660 ■ *Web:* www.ocec-inc.com	Cloudcroft	NM	88317	575-682-2521	682-3109*
Roosevelt County Electric Co-op Inc (RCEC) 121 N Main St *Web:* www.rcec.org/content/office-location	Portales	NM	88130	575-356-4491	
Sierra Electric Co-op 610 Hwy 195 PO Box 290 **Fax Area Code:* 505 ■ *Web:* www.sierraelectric.org	Elephant Butte	NM	87935	575-744-5231	744-5819*
Socorro Electric Co-op Inc 215 Manzanares Ave PO Box H **Fax Area Code:* 505 ■ *TF:* 800-351-7575 ■ *Web:* www.socorroelectric.com	Socorro	NM	87801	575-835-0560	835-4449*
Springer Electric Co-op Inc 408 Maxwell Ave PO Box 698 *TF:* 800-288-1353 ■ *Web:* www.springercoop.com	Springer	NM	87747	505-483-2421	483-2692

New York

				Phone	Fax
Delaware County Electric Co-op (DCEC) 39 Elm St PO Box 471 *Web:* www.dce.coop	Delhi	NY	13753	607-746-2341	746-7548
Oneida-Madison Electric Co-op Inc 6630 State Rt 20 *TF:* 866-632-9992 ■ *Web:* www.oneida-madison.coop	Bouckville	NY	13310	315-893-1851	893-1857
Otsego Electric Co-op Inc (OEC) 3192 County Hwy 11 PO Box 128 *Web:* www.otsegoec.coop	Hartwick	NY	13348	607-293-6622	293-6624
Steuben Rural Electric Co-op Inc Nine Wilson Ave *TF:* 800-843-3414 ■ *Web:* www.steubenrec.com	Bath	NY	14810	607-776-4161	776-2293

North Carolina

				Phone	Fax
Albemarle Electric Membership Corp P.O. Box 69 *TF:* 800-215-9915 ■ *Web:* www.aemc.coop/	Hertford	NC	27944	252-426-5735	426-8270
Blue Ridge Electric Membership Corp 1216 Blowing Rock Blvd *TF:* 800-451-5474 ■ *Web:* blueridgeemc.com	Lenoir	NC	28645	828-758-2383	758-2699
Brunswick Electric Membership Corp 795 Ocean Hwy PO Box 226 *TF:* 800-842-5871 ■ *Web:* www.bemc.org	Shallotte	NC	28459	910-754-4391	755-4299
Cape Hatteras Electric Co-op 47109 Light Plant Rd PO Box 9 *TF:* 800-454-5616 ■ *Web:* www.chec.coop	Buxton	NC	27920	252-995-5616	995-4088
Carteret-Craven Electric Co-op (CCEC) 1300 Hwy 24 W PO Box 1490 *TF:* 800-682-2217 ■ *Web:* www.carteretcravenelectric.coop	Newport	NC	28570	252-247-3107	247-0235
Central Electric Membership Corp 128 Wilson Rd *TF:* 800-446-7752 ■ *Web:* www.centralelectriconline.com	Sanford	NC	27331	919-774-4900	774-1860
Cogentrix Energy Inc 9405 Arrowpoint Blvd *Web:* www.cogentrix.com	Charlotte	NC	28273	704-525-3800	529-5313
Edgecombe-Martin County Electric Membership Corp NC Hwy 33 E *TF:* 800-445-6486 ■ *Web:* www.ememc.com	Tarboro	NC	27886	252-823-2171	
EnergyUnited Electric Membership Corp PO Box 1831 *TF:* 800-522-3793 ■ *Web:* www.energyunited.com	Statesville	NC	28687	704-873-5241	878-0161
Four County Electric Membership Corp 1822 NC Hwy 53 W PO Box 667 *TF:* 888-368-7289 ■ *Web:* www.fourcty.org	Burgaw	NC	28425	910-259-2171	259-1860
French Broad Electric Membership Corp 3043 Nc 213 Hwy *Web:* www.frenchbroademc.com	Marshall	NC	28753	828-649-2051	649-2989
Halifax Electric Membership Corp 208 Whitfield St *Web:* www.halifaxemc.com	Enfield	NC	27823	252-445-5111	445-2398
Haywood Electric Membership Corp 376 Grindstone Rd *TF:* 800-951-6088 ■ *Web:* www.haywoodemc.com	Waynesville	NC	28785	828-452-2281	
Jones-Onslow Electric Membership Corp 259 Western Blvd *TF:* 800-682-1515 ■ *Web:* www.joemc.com	Jacksonville	NC	28546	910-353-1940	353-8000
Lumbee River Electric Membership Corp PO Box 830 *TF:* 800-683-5571 ■ *Web:* www.lumbeeriver.com	Red Springs	NC	28377	910-843-4131	843-6422
Pee Dee Electric Membership Corp (PDEMC) 575 US Hwy 52 S *TF:* 800-992-1626 ■ *Web:* www.pdemc.com	Wadesboro	NC	28170	704-694-2114	694-9636
Piedmont Electric Membership Corp 2500 Nc Hwy 86 S *Web:* www.pemc.coop	Hillsborough	NC	27278	919-732-2123	644-1030
Randolph Electric Membership Corp 879 McDowell Rd PO Box 40 *TF:* 800-672-8212 ■ *Web:* www.randolphemc.com	Asheboro	NC	27204	336-625-5177	626-1551
Roanoke Electric Co-op 518 NC 561 W *TF:* 800-433-2236 ■ *Web:* www.roanokeelectric.com	Aulander	NC	27805	252-539-4600	539-4612
Rutherford Electric Membership Corp 186 Hudlow Rd PO Box 1569 *TF:* 800-521-0920 ■ *Web:* www.remc.com	Forest City	NC	28043	828-245-1621	248-2319
South River Electric Membership Corp 17494 US 421 S PO Box 931 *TF:* 800-338-5530 ■ *Web:* www.sremc.com	Dunn	NC	28335	910-892-8071	230-2981
Surry-Yadkin Electric Membership Corp 510 S Main St. *TF:* 800-682-5903 ■ *Web:* www.syemc.com	Dobson	NC	27017	336-356-8241	356-9744
Tideland Electric Membership Corp 25831 Hwy 264 E *TF:* 800-637-1079 ■ *Web:* www.tidelandemc.com	Pantego	Nc	27860	252-943-3046	943-3510
Union Power Co-op 1525 N Rocky River Rd *TF:* 800-922-6840 ■ *Web:* www.union-power.com	Monroe	NC	28110	704-289-3145	296-0408
Wake Electric 100 S Franklin St PO Box 1229 *TF:* 800-474-6300 ■ *Web:* www.wemc.com	Wake Forest	NC	27588	919-863-6300	863-6379

North Dakota

				Phone	Fax
Basin Electric Power Co-op 1717 E IH- Ave *Web:* www.basinelectric.com	Bismarck	ND	58501	701-223-0441	224-5336
Burke-Divide Electric Co-op Inc (BDEC) 9549 Hwy 5 W *Web:* www.bdec.coop	Columbus	ND	58727	701-939-6671	939-6666
Capital Electric Co-op Inc 4111 State St *Web:* www.capitalelec.com	Bismarck	ND	58503	701-223-1513	223-1557
Cass County Electric Co-op Inc 4100 32nd Ave SW *TF:* 800-248-3292 ■ *Web:* www.kwh.com	Fargo	ND	58104	701-356-4400	356-4500
Central Power Electric Co-op Inc 525 20th Ave SW *Web:* www.centralpwr.com	Minot	ND	58701	701-852-4407	
Dakota Valley Electric Co-op 7296 Hwy 281 *TF:* 800-342-4671 ■ *Web:* www.dakotavalley.com	Edgeley	ND	58433	701-493-2281	493-2454
KEM Electric Co-op Inc 107 S Broadway *TF:* 800-472-2673 ■ *Web:* www.kemelectric.com	Linton	ND	58552	701-254-4666	254-4975
McKenzie Electric Co-op Inc 908 Fourth Ave NE *Web:* www.mckenzieelectric.com	Watford City	ND	58854	701-444-9288	444-3002
McLean Electric Co-op Inc 4031 Hwy 37 Bypass NW *TF:* 800-263-4922 ■ *Web:* www.mcleanelectric.com	Garrison	ND	58540	701-463-2291	337-5303
Mor-Gran-Sou Electric Co-op Inc 202 Sixth Ave W *TF:* 800-750-8212 ■ *Web:* www.morgransou.com	Flasher	ND	58535	701-597-3301	597-3915
Mountrail-Williams Electric Co-op 218 58th St W PO Box 1346 *TF:* 800-279-2667 ■ *Web:* www.mwec.com	Williston	ND	58802	701-577-3765	577-3777
Nodak Electric Co-op Inc 4000 32nd Ave S *TF:* 800-732-4373 ■ *Web:* www.nodakelectric.com	Grand Forks	ND	58201	701-746-4461	795-6701
North Central Electric Co-op Inc 538 11th St W *TF:* 800-247-1197 ■ *Web:* www.nceci.com	Bottineau	ND	58318	701-228-2202	228-2592
Northern Plains Electric Co-op 1515 W Main St *TF:* 800-882-2500 ■ *Web:* www.nplains.com	Carrington	ND	58421	701-652-3156	
Slope Electric Co-op Inc 116 E 12th St PO Box 338 *TF:* 800-559-4191 ■ *Web:* www.slopeelectric.coop	New England	ND	58647	701-579-4191	579-4193
Verendrye Electric Co-op Inc 615 Hwy 52 *TF:* 800-472-2141 ■ *Web:* www.verendrye.com	Velva	ND	58790	701-338-2855	624-0353

Ohio

				Phone	Fax
Adams Rural Electric Co-op Inc 4800 SR 125 *TF:* 800-283-1846 ■ *Web:* www.adamsrec.com	West Union	OH	45693	937-544-2305	544-3877
Buckeye Rural Electric Co-op PO Box 200 *TF:* 800-231-2732 ■ *Web:* www.buckeyerec.com	Rio Grande	OH	45674	740-379-2025	379-2048
Butler Rural Electric Co-op Inc (BREC) 3888 Still-Beckett Rd *TF:* 800-255-2732 ■ *Web:* www.butlerrural.coop	Oxford	OH	45056	513-867-4400	867-4422
Carroll Electric Co-op Inc 350 Canton Rd NW *TF:* 800-232-7697 ■ *Web:* cecpower.coop	Carrollton	OH	44615	330-627-2116	627-7050

	City	State	ZIP	Phone	Fax
Darke Rural Electric Co-op Inc 1120 Fort Jefferson Rd *TF:* 866-692-6330 ■ *Web:* darkecountyohio.com	Greenville	OH	45331	937-548-4114	
Denier Electric Co Inc 10891 SR- 128 *TF:* 800-676-3282 ■ *Web:* www.denier.com	Harrison	OH	45030	513-738-2641	738-5855
Firelands Electric Co-op Inc One Energy Pl PO Box 32 *TF:* 800-533-8658 ■ *Web:* www.firelandsec.com	New London	OH	44851	419-929-1571	929-8550
Frontier Power Co 770 S 2nd St PO Box 280 *TF:* 800-624-8050 ■ *Web:* www.frontier-power.com	Coshocton	OH	43812	740-622-6755	622-0711
Guernsey-Muskingum Electric Co-op 17 S Liberty St *Web:* www.gmenergy.com	New Concord	OH	43762	740-826-7661	826-7171
Hancock-Wood Electric Co-op Inc (HWEC) 1399 Business Pk Dr S PO Box 190 *TF:* 800-445-4840 ■ *Web:* www.hwe.coop	North Baltimore	OH	45872	419-257-3241	257-3024
Holmes-Wayne Electric Co-op Inc 6060 Ohio 83 *TF:* 866-674-1055 ■ *Web:* www.hwecoop.com	Millersburg	OH	44654	330-674-1055	674-1869
Logan County Co-op Power & Light Assn Inc 1587 County Rd 32 N *Web:* www.loganrec.com	Bellefontaine	OH	43311	937-592-4781	592-5746
Lorain-Medina Rural Electric Co-op Inc 22898 W Rd *TF:* 800-222-5673 ■ *Web:* www.lmre.org	Wellington	OH	44090	440-647-2133	647-4870
Mid Ohio Energy Co-op Inc 555 W Franklin St *TF:* 888-382-6732 ■ *Web:* www.midohioenergy.com	Kenton	OH	43326	419-673-7289	673-8388
North Western Electric Co-op Inc 04125 State Rt 576 PO Box 391 *TF:* 800-647-6932 ■ *Web:* www.nwec.com	Bryan	OH	43506	419-636-5051	636-0194
Paulding-Putman Electric Co-op 910 N Williams St *TF:* 800-686-2357 ■ *Web:* www.ppec.coop	Paulding	OH	45879	419-399-5015	399-3026
Pioneer Electric Co-op 344 W US Rt 36 PO Box 1307 *TF:* 800-762-0997 ■ *Web:* www.pioneerec.com	Piqua	OH	45356	937-773-2523	773-7549
South Central Power Company Inc 2780 Coon Path Rd *TF:* 800-282-5064 ■ *Web:* www.southcentralpower.com	Lancaster	OH	43130	740-653-4422	681-4488
Union Rural Electric Co-op Inc 15461 US 36E *TF:* 800-642-1826 ■ *Web:* www.ure.com	Marysville	OH	43040	937-642-1826	969-8442
Washington Electric Co-op Inc 406 Colegate Dr *TF:* 877-594-9324 ■ *Web:* www.weci.org	Marietta	OH	45750	740-373-2141	373-2941

Oklahoma

	City	State	ZIP	Phone	Fax
Alfalfa Electric Co-op Inc 121 E Main St *TF:* 888-736-3837 ■ *Web:* www.alfalfaelectric.com	Cherokee	OK	73728	580-596-3333	596-2464
Caddo Electric Co-op PO Box 70 *TF:* 800-522-6543 ■ *Web:* www.caddoelectric.com	Binger	OK	73009	405-656-2322	656-2327
Canadian Valley Electric Co-op 11277 S 356 PO Box 751 *TF:* 877-382-3680 ■ *Web:* www.canadianvalley.org	Seminole	OK	74868	405-382-3680	382-8808
Central Rural Electric Co-op 3304 S Boomer Rd PO Box 1809 *TF:* 800-375-2884 ■ *Web:* www.crec.coop	Stillwater	OK	74076	405-372-2884	372-8559
Choctaw Electric Co-op Inc 1033 N 4250 Rd *TF:* 800-780-6486 ■ *Web:* www.choctawelectric.com	Hugo	OK	74743	580-326-6486	326-2492
Cimarron Electric Co-op PO Box 299 *TF:* 800-375-4121 ■ *Web:* www.cimarronelectric.com	Kingfisher	OK	73750	405-375-4121	375-4209
Cookson Hills Electric Co-op Inc 1002 E Main St *TF:* 800-328-2368 ■ *Web:* www.cooksonhills.com	Stigler	OK	74462	918-967-4614	
Cotton Electric Co-op Inc 226 N Broadway *TF:* 800-522-3520 ■ *Web:* www.cottonelectric.com	Walters	OK	73572	580-875-3351	875-3101
East Central Oklahoma Electric Co-op Inc 2001 S Wood Dr PO Box 1178 *TF:* 800-783-9317 ■ *Web:* www.ecoec.com	Okmulgee	OK	74447	918-756-0833	756-6539
Harmon Electric Assn Inc (HEA) 114 N First St PO Box 393 *TF:* 800-643-7769 ■ *Web:* www.harmonelectric.com	Hollis	OK	73550	580-688-3342	688-2981
Indian Electric Co-op Inc 2506 E Hwy 64 *TF:* 800-482-2750 ■ *Web:* www.iecok.com	Cleveland	OK	74020	918-358-2514	358-2518
Kay Electric Co-op (KEC) 300 W Doolin Ave *TF:* 800-535-1079 ■ *Web:* www.kayelectric.coop	Blackwell	OK	74631	580-363-1260	363-2308
Kiamichi Electric Co-op Inc (KEC) 966 SW Hwy 2 PO Box 340 *TF:* 800-888-2731 ■ *Web:* www.kiamichielectric.org	Wilburton	OK	74578	918-465-2338	465-2405
Kiwash Electric Co-op Inc 120 W First St *TF:* 888-832-3362 ■ *Web:* www.kiwash.coop	Cordell	OK	73632	580-832-3361	832-5174
Lake Region Electric Co-op Inc 516 S Lake Region Rd *TF:* 800-364-5732 ■ *Web:* www.lrecok.coop	Hulbert	OK	74441	918-772-2526	
Northeast Oklahoma Electric Co-op Inc 443857 E Hwy 60 PO Box 948 *TF:* 800-256-6405 ■ *Web:* www.neelectric.com	Vinita	OK	74301	918-256-6405	256-9380
Northfork Electric Co-op 311 E Madden St PO Box 400 *Web:* www.nfecoop.com	Sayre	OK	73662	580-928-3366	928-3105
Northwestern Electric Co-op Inc 2925 William Ave *TF:* 800-375-7423 ■ *Web:* www.nwecok.coop	Woodward	OK	73802	580-256-7425	254-2858
Oklahoma Electric Co-op 242 24th Ave NW *Web:* www.okcoop.org	Norman	OK	73069	405-321-2024	217-6900
People's Electric Co-op 1600 N Country Club Rd *Web:* www.peoplesec.com	Ada	OK	74820	580-332-3031	
Rural Electric Co-op Inc (REC) 801 N Industrial Heights PO Box 609 *TF:* 800-259-3504 ■ *Web:* www.recok.coop	Lindsay	OK	73052	405-756-3104	756-8957
Southeastern Electric Co-op Inc 1514 E Hwy 70 PO Box 1370 *TF:* 866-924-1315 ■ *Web:* www.se-coop.com	Durant	OK	74702	580-924-2170	924-6402
Southwest Rural Electric Assn 700 N Broadway PO Box 310 *TF:* 800-256-7973 ■ *Web:* www.swre.com	Tipton	OK	73570	580-667-5281	667-5284
Stillwater Utilities Authority PO Box 1449 *Web:* www.stillwater.org	Stillwater	OK	74076	405-372-0025	
Tri-County Electric 302 E Glaydas St PO Box 880 *TF:* 800-522-3315 ■ *Web:* www.tri-countyelectric.coop	Hooker	OK	73945	580-652-2418	652-3151
Verdigris Valley Electric Co-op 8901 E 146th St N *TF:* 800-870-5948 ■ *Web:* www.vvec.com	Collinsville	OK	74021	918-371-2584	371-9873
Western Farmers Electric Co-op 701 NE Seventh St *Web:* www.wfec.com	Anadarko	OK	73005	405-247-3351	247-4451

Oregon

	City	State	ZIP	Phone	Fax
Blachly-Lane Inc PO Box 70 *TF:* 800-446-8418 ■ *Web:* www.blachlylane.coop	Junction City	OR	97448	541-688-8711	688-8958
Central Electric Co-op Inc (CEC) 2098 Hwy 97 N	Redmond	OR	97756	541-548-2144	
Columbia Basin Electric Co-op 171 W Linden Way *Web:* cbec.cc	Heppner	OR	97836	541-676-9146	
Columbia Power Co-op Assn 311 Wilson St PO Box 97	Monument	OR	97864	541-934-2311	934-2312
Consumers Power Inc (CPI) 6990 W Hills Rd PO Box 1180 *TF:* 800-872-9036 ■ *Web:* www.cpi.coop	Philomath	OR	97370	541-929-3124	929-8673
Coos-Curry Electric Co-op Inc 43050 Hwy 101 PO Box 1268 *Web:* www.ccec.coop	Port Orford	OR	97465	541-332-3931	332-3501
Harney Electric Co-op Inc 277 Lottery Ln PO Box 587 *Web:* www.harneyelectric.org	Hines	OR	97738	541-573-2061	
Lane Electric Co-op 787 Bailey Hill Rd PO Box 21410 *Web:* www.laneelectric.com	Eugene	OR	97402	541-484-1151	484-7316
Midstate Electric Co-op Inc 16755 Finley Butte Rd *TF:* 800-722-7219 ■ *Web:* www.midstateelectric.coop	La Pine	OR	97739	541-536-2126	536-1423
Northern Wasco County People's Utility District 2345 River Rd *Web:* nwasco.com	The Dalles	OR	97058	541-296-2226	298-3320
Oregon Trail Electric ConsumersCo-op Inc (OTEC) 4005 23rd St PO Box 226 *Web:* www.otecc.com	Baker City	OR	97814	541-523-3616	524-2865
Salem Electric 633 Seventh St NW *Web:* www.salemelectric.com	Salem	OR	97304	503-362-3601	371-2956
Tillamook People's Utility District 1115 Pacific Ave *TF:* 800-422-2535 ■ *Web:* www.tpud.org	Tillamook	OR	97141	503-842-2535	842-4161
Umatilla Electric Co-op Assn 750 W Elm Ave *Web:* www.umatillaelectric.com	Hermiston	OR	97838	541-567-6414	567-8142
Wasco Electric Co-op Inc 105 E Fourth St *Web:* www.wascoelectric.com	The Dalles	OR	97058	541-296-2740	296-7781
West Oregon Electric Co-op Inc 652 Rose Ave PO Box 69 *TF:* 800-777-1276 ■ *Web:* www.westoregon.org	Vernonia	OR	97064	503-429-3021	429-8440

Pennsylvania

	City	State	ZIP	Phone	Fax
Adams Electric Co-op Inc 1338 Biglerville Rd PO Box 1055 *TF:* 888-232-6732 ■ *Web:* www.adamsec.coop	Gettysburg	PA	17325	717-334-2171	334-3980
Bedford Rural Electric Co-op Inc 8846 Lincoln Hwy *TF:* 800-808-2732 ■ *Web:* www.bedfordrec.com	Bedford	PA	15522	814-623-5101	623-7983
Citizens' Electric Co 1775 Industrial Blvd PO Box 551 *TF:* 877-487-9384 ■ *Web:* www.citizenselectric.com	Lewisburg	PA	17837	570-524-2231	524-5887
Claverack Rural Electric Co-op Inc 32750 W US 6 *TF:* 800-326-9799 ■ *Web:* www.claverack.com	Wysox	PA	18854	570-265-2167	265-6019
New Enterprise Rural Electric Co-op Inc 3596 Brumbaugh Rd *TF:* 800-270-3177 ■ *Web:* www.newenterpriserec.com	New Enterprise	PA	16664	814-766-3221	766-3319
Northwestern Rural Electric Co-op Assn Inc 22534 State Rte Ste 86 **Fax Area Code:* 814 ■ *TF:* 800-352-0014 ■ *Web:* www.northwesternrec.com	Cambridge Springs	PA	16403	800-472-7910	398-8064*
REA Energy Co-op Inc 75 Airport Rd *TF:* 800-211-5667 ■ *Web:* www.reaenergy.com	Indiana	PA	15701	724-349-4800	349-7151
Somerset Rural Electric Co-op 223 Industrial Pk Rd PO Box 270 *TF:* 800-443-4255 ■ *Web:* www.somersetrec.com	Somerset	PA	15501	814-445-4106	445-5526
Sullivan County Rural Electric Co-op Inc (SCREC) 5675 Rt 87 PO Box 65 *TF:* 800-570-5081 ■ *Web:* www.screc.com	Forksville	PA	18616	570-924-3381	924-3383
Tri-County Rural Electric Co-op Inc PO Box 526 *Web:* www.tri-countyrec.com	Mansfield	PA	16933	570-662-2175	
United Electric Co-op Inc 29 United Rd *Web:* www.prea.com/	Du Bois	PA	15801	814-371-8570	
Valley Rural Electric Co-op Inc 10700 Fairgrounds Rd PO Box 477 *TF:* 800-432-0680 ■ *Web:* www.valleyrec.com	Huntingdon	PA	16652	814-643-2650	643-1678

Name / Address	City	State	Zip	Phone	Fax
Warren Electric Co-op Inc (WEC) 320 E Main St PO Box 208 *TF:* 800-364-8640 ■ *Web:* www.warrenec.coop	Youngsville	PA	16371	814-563-7548	563-7012

South Carolina

Name / Address	City	State	Zip	Phone	Fax
Aiken Electric Co-op Inc 2790 Wagener Rd. *TF Tech Supp:* 877-264-5368 ■ *Web:* aikenco-op.org	Aiken	SC	29802	803-649-6245	641-8310
Berkeley Electric Co-op Inc 551 Rembert C Dennis Blvd *Web:* www.becsc.com	Moncks Corner	SC	29461	843-761-8200	572-1280
Black River Electric Co-op 1121 N Pike Rd W PO Box 130 *Web:* www.blackriver.coop	Sumter	SC	29151	803-469-8060	469-8320
Broad River Electric Co-op Inc 811 Hamrick St *TF:* 866-687-2667 ■ *Web:* www.broadriverelectric.com	Gaffney	SC	29342	864-489-5737	487-7808
Coastal Electric Co-op Inc 2269 Jefferies Hwy *TF:* 866-708-0913 ■ *Web:* www.coastal.coop	Walterboro	SC	29488	843-538-5700	538-5081
Edisto Electric Co-op Inc 896 Calhoun St *TF:* 800-433-3292 ■ *Web:* www.edistoelectric.com	Bamberg	SC	29003	803-245-5141	245-0188
Horry Electric Co-op Inc 2774 Cultra Rd *Web:* www.horryelectric.com	Conway	SC	29526	843-369-2211	369-6040
Laurens Electric Co-op Inc 2254 S Carolina 14 **Fax Area Code:* 864 ■ *TF:* 800-942-3141 ■ *Web:* laurenselectric.com	Laurens	SC	29360	800-942-3141	683-5178*
Little River Electric Co-op Inc (LRECI) PO Box 220 *TF:* 800-459-2141 ■ *Web:* www.lreci.coop	Abbeville	SC	29620	864-366-2141	366-4524
Lynches River Electric Co-op Inc 1104 W McGregor St *TF:* 800-922-3486 ■ *Web:* www.lynchesriver.com	Pageland	SC	29728	843-672-6111	672-6118
Mid-Carolina Electric Co-op Inc PO Box 669 *TF Cust Svc:* 888-813-8000 ■ *Web:* www.mcecoop.com	Lexington	SC	29071	803-749-6555	749-6466
Newberry Electric Co-op Inc 882 Wilson Rd *TF:* 800-479-8838 ■ *Web:* www.nec.coop	Newberry	SC	29108	803-276-1121	276-4121
Pee Dee Electric Co-op Inc PO Box 491 *Web:* www.peedeeelectric.com	Darlington	SC	29540	843-665-4070	669-7931
Santee Electric Co-op Inc 424 Sumter Hwy *TF:* 800-922-1604 ■ *Web:* www.santee.org	Kingstree	SC	29556	843-355-6187	355-0609
Tri-County Electric Co-op 6473 Old State Rd PO Box 217 *TF:* 877-874-1215 ■ *Web:* tri-countyelectric.net	Saint Matthews	SC	29135	803-874-1215	
York Electric Co-op Inc PO Box 150 *TF:* 800-582-8810 ■ *Web:* www.yorkelectric.net	York	SC	29745	803-684-4247	684-6306

South Dakota

Name / Address	City	State	Zip	Phone	Fax
Black Hills Electric Co-op 25191 Co-op Way PO Box 792 *TF:* 800-742-0085 ■ *Web:* www.bhec.com	Custer	SD	57730	605-673-4461	673-3147
Bon Homme Yankton Electric Assn 134 S Lidice St *TF:* 800-925-2929 ■ *Web:* www.byelectric.com	Tabor	SD	57063	605-463-2507	463-2419
Butte Electric Co-op PO Box 137 *TF:* 800-928-8839 ■ *Web:* www.butteelectric.com	Newell	SD	57760	605-456-2494	456-2496
Cam-Wal Electric Co-op Inc 404 W Scranton St PO Box 135 **Fax Area Code:* 605 ■ *TF:* 800-269-7676 ■ *Web:* www.cam-walnet.com	Selby	SD	57472	800-269-7676	649-7031*
Charles Mix Electric Assn Inc 440 Lake St *TF:* 800-208-8587 ■ *Web:* www.cme.coop	Lake Andes	SD	57356	605-487-7321	487-7868
Cherry-Todd Electric Co-op Inc 625 W Second St *Web:* cherry-todd.com	Mission	SD	57555	605-856-4416	
Clay-Union Electric Corp 1410 E Cherry St PO Box 317 *TF:* 800-696-2832 ■ *Web:* www.clayunionelectric.coop	Vermillion	SD	57069	605-624-2673	624-5526
Codington-Clark Electric Co-op 3520 Ninth Ave SW PO Box 880 *TF:* 800-463-8938 ■ *Web:* www.codingtonclarkelectric.coop	Watertown	SD	57201	605-886-5848	886-5934
Dakota Energy Co-op Inc PO Box 830 *TF:* 800-353-8591 ■ *Web:* www.dakotaenergy.coop	Huron	SD	57350	605-352-8591	352-8578
Douglas Electric Co-op Inc 400 Main Ave	Armour	SD	57313	605-724-2323	724-2972
FEM Electric Assn Inc PO Box 468 *TF:* 800-587-5880 ■ *Web:* www.femelectric.coop	Ipswich	SD	57451	605-426-6891	426-6791
Grand Electric Co-op Inc 801 Coleman Ave PO Box 39 *TF:* 800-592-1803 ■ *Web:* www.grandelectric.coop	Bison	SD	57620	605-244-5211	244-7288
H-D Electric Co-op Inc 423 Third Ave S *TF:* 800-781-7474 ■ *Web:* h-delectric.coop	Clear Lake	SD	57226	605-874-2171	874-8173
Kingsbury Electric Co-op Inc 511 Us Hwy 14	De Smet	SD	57231	605-854-3522	854-3465
Lake Region Electric Assn Inc 1212 Main St *TF:* 800-657-5869 ■ *Web:* www.lakeregion.coop	Webster	SD	57274	605-345-3379	345-4442
Moreau-Grand Electric Co-op Inc 405 Ninth St *TF:* 800-952-3158 ■ *Web:* www.mge.coop	Timber Lake	SD	57656	605-865-3511	865-3340
Northern Electric Co-op Inc 39456 133nd St *TF:* 800-529-0310 ■ *Web:* www.northernelectric.coop	Bath	SD	57427	605-225-0310	225-1684
Oahe Electric Co-op Inc 102 S Cranford St PO Box 216 *TF:* 800-640-6243 ■ *Web:* www.oaheelectric.com	Blunt	SD	57522	605-962-6243	962-6306
Rosebud Electric Co-op Inc 512 Rosebud Ave PO Box 439 *Web:* www.rosebudelectric.com	Gregory	SD	57533	605-835-9624	835-9649
Sioux Valley-Southwestern Electric Co-op Inc 47092 SD Hwy 34 PO Box 216 *TF:* 800-234-1960 ■ *Web:* www.siouxvalleyenergy.com	Colman	SD	57017	605-534-3535	256-1693
Union County Electric Co-op Inc 122 W Main St *Web:* unioncounty.coop	Elk Point	SD	57025	605-356-3395	356-3397
West Central Electric Co-op Inc 204 Main St PO Box 17 *TF:* 800-242-9232 ■ *Web:* www.wce.coop	Murdo	SD	57559	605-669-2472	669-2358
West River Electric Assn Inc 1200 W Fourth Ave PO Box 412 **Fax Area Code:* 605 ■ *TF:* 888-279-2135 ■ *Web:* www.westriver.com	Wall	SD	57790	888-279-2135	279-2630*
Whetstone Valley Electric Co-op 1101 E Fourth Ave *TF:* 800-568-6631 ■ *Web:* whetstone.coop	Milbank	SD	57252	605-432-5331	432-5951

Tennessee

Name / Address	City	State	Zip	Phone	Fax
Appalachian Electric Co-op 1109 Hill Dr. *Web:* aecoop.org	New Market	TN	37820	865-475-2032	475-0888
Caney Fork Electric Co-op Inc 920 Smithville Hwy PO Box 272 *TF:* 888-505-3030 ■ *Web:* www.caneyforkec.com	McMinnville	TN	37110	931-473-3116	473-4939
Chickasaw Electric Co-op 17970 US Hwy 64 E PO Box 459 *TF:* 866-465-3591 ■ *Web:* chickasaw.coop	Somerville	TN	38068	901-465-3591	465-5392
Cumberland Electric Membership Corp 1940 Madison St *Web:* www.cemc.org	Clarksville	TN	37043	931-645-2481	552-4730
Duck River Electric Membership Corp 305 Learning Way PO Box 89 *Web:* www.dremc.com	Shelbyville	TN	37160	931-684-4621	685-0013
Fayetteville Public Utilities 408 W College St *TF:* 800-379-2534 ■ *Web:* www.fayelectric.com	Fayetteville	TN	37334	931-433-1522	433-0646
Forked Deer Electric Co-op Inc PO Box 67 *Web:* www.forkeddeer.com	Halls	TN	38040	731-836-7508	
Gibson Electric Membership Corp 1207 S College St PO Box 47 *Web:* www.gibsonemc.com	Trenton	TN	38382	731-855-4740	855-3944
Greeneville Light & Power System PO Box 1690 *TF:* 866-466-1438 ■ *Web:* www.glps.net	Greeneville	TN	37744	423-636-6200	636-6206
Holston Electric Co-op Inc 1200 W Main St *Web:* www.holstonelectric.com	Rogersville	TN	37857	423-272-8821	272-6051
La Follette Utilities Board 302 N Tennessee Ave PO Box 1411 *TF:* 800-352-1340 ■ *Web:* www.lub.org	La Follette	TN	37766	423-562-3316	566-0580
Middle Tennessee Electric Membership Corp 555 New Salem Rd *Web:* www.mtemc.com	Murfreesboro	TN	37129	615-890-9762	895-3594
Mountain Electric Co-op Inc PO Box 180 *TF Cust Svc:* 800-638-3788 ■ *Web:* www.mountainelectric.com	Mountain City	TN	37683	423-727-1800	727-1822
Newport Utilities PO Box 519 *Web:* www.newportutilities.com	Newport	TN	37822	423-625-2800	623-5767
Pickwick Electric Co-op 530 Mulberry Ave *TF:* 800-372-8258 ■ *Web:* www.pickwick-electric.com	Selmer	TN	38375	731-645-3411	645-7167
Plateau Electric Co-op 16200 Scott Hwy PO Box 4669 *Web:* www.plateauelectric.com	Oneida	TN	37841	423-569-8591	569-5726
Powell Valley Electric Co-op 325 Straight Creek Rd PO Box 1528 *Web:* billing.pve.coop	New Tazewell	TN	37825	423-626-5204	
Sequachee Valley Electric Co-op 512 Cedar Ave PO Box 31 *TF:* 800-923-2203 ■ *Web:* www.svalleyec.com	South Pittsburg	TN	37380	423-837-8605	837-9836
Southwest Tennessee Electric Membership Corp 1009 E Main St *TF:* 800-772-0472 ■ *Web:* www.stemc.com	Brownsville	TN	38012	731-772-1322	772-1037
Tennessee Valley Electric Co-op 590 Florence Rd *TF:* 866-925-4916 ■ *Web:* www.tvec.com	Savannah	TN	38372	731-925-4916	925-4919
Upper Cumberland Electric Membership Corp 138 Gordonsville Hwy *TF:* 800-261-2940 ■ *Web:* www.ucemc.com	South Carthage	TN	37030	615-735-2940	735-2603
Volunteer Energy Co-op (VEC) PO Box 277 *Web:* www.vec.org	Decatur	TN	37322	423-334-5721	334-7003

Texas

Name / Address	City	State	Zip	Phone	Fax
Bandera Electric Co-op Inc 3172 State Hwy 16 N **Fax Area Code:* 830 ■ *TF:* 866-226-3372 ■ *Web:* banderaelectric.com	Bandera	TX	78003	866-226-3372	460-3030*
Bartlett Electric Co-op Inc 27492 Texas 95 *Web:* www.bartlettec.coop	Bartlett	TX	76511	254-527-3551	527-3221
Big Country Electric Co-op 1010 W S First St PO Box 518 *TF:* 888-662-2232 ■ *Web:* bigcountry.net/	Roby	TX	79543	325-776-2244	
Bowie-Cass Electric Co-op Inc 117 N St *TF:* 800-794-2919 ■ *Web:* www.bcec.com	Douglassville	TX	75560	903-846-2311	846-2406
Central Texas Electric Co-op Inc (CTEC) 386 Friendship Ln PO Box 553 *TF General:* 800-900-2832 ■ *Web:* www.ctec.coop	Fredericksburg	TX	78624	830-997-2126	997-9034
Coleman County Electric Co-op Inc 3300 N Hwy 84 PO Box 860 *TF:* 800-560-2128 ■ *Web:* www.colemanelectric.org	Coleman	TX	76834	325-625-2128	625-4600
Comanche Electric Co-op Assn 201 W Wrights Ave *TF:* 800-915-2533 ■ *Web:* www.ceca.coop	Comanche	TX	76442	325-356-2533	356-3038
Concho Valley Electric Co-op Inc 2530 Pulliam St PO Box 3388 *Web:* www.cvec.coop	San Angelo	TX	76902	325-655-6957	655-6950

	City	State	ZIP	Phone	Fax
Cooke County Electric Co-op 11799 W US Hwy 82 PO Box 530 *Fax: Cust Svc ■ *TF:* 800-962-0296 ■ *Web:* www.cceca.com	Muenster	TX	76252	940-759-2211	759-4122*
CoServ Electric 7701 S Stemmons Fwy *TF:* 800-274-4014 ■ *Web:* coserv.com	Corinth	TX	76210	940-321-7800	270-6640
Deaf Smith Electric Co-op Inc 1501 E First St *TF:* 800-687-8189 ■ *Web:* Www.dsec.org	Hereford	TX	79045	806-364-1166	
Deep East Texas Electric Co-op Inc 880 Texas Hwy 21 E PO Box 736 *TF:* 800-392-5986 ■ *Web:* www.deepeast.com	San Augustine	TX	75972	936-275-2314	275-2135
Fannin County Electric Co-op Inc 1530 Silo Rd *Web:* www.fcec.coop	Bonham	TX	75418	903-583-2117	
Farmers Electric Co-op Inc 2000 E I-30 *TF:* 800-541-2662 ■ *Web:* www.fecelectric.com	Greenville	TX	75402	903-455-1715	455-8125
Fayette Electric Co-op Inc 357 N Washington St *TF:* 800-874-8290 ■ *Web:* www.fayette.coop	La Grange	TX	78945	979-968-3181	968-6752
Fort Belknap Electric Co-op Inc 1302 W Main PO Box 486 *Web:* www.fortbelknapec.com	Olney	TX	76374	940-564-2343	564-3247
Grayson-Collin Electric Co-op (GCEC) PO Box 548 *TF:* 800-967-5235 ■ *Web:* www.gcec.net	Van Alstyne	TX	75495	903-482-7100	482-5906
Greenbelt Electric Co-op Inc PO Box 948 *TF:* 800-527-3082 ■ *Web:* www.greenbeltelectric.coop	Wellington	TX	79095	806-447-2536	447-2434
Guadalupe Valley Electric Co-op Inc 825 E Sarah Dewitt Dr *TF:* 800-223-4832 ■ *Web:* www.gvec.org	Gonzales	TX	78629	830-857-1200	857-1205
Guadalupe-Blanco River Authority (GBRA) 933 E Ct St *Web:* www.gbra.org	Seguin	TX	78155	830-379-5822	379-9718
Hamilton County Electric Co-op Assn 420 N Rice St PO Box 753 *TF:* 800-595-3401 ■ *Web:* www.hamiltonelectric.coop	Hamilton	TX	76531	254-386-3123	386-8757
Hilco Electric Co-op Inc 115 E Main PO Box 127 *TF:* 800-338-6425 ■ *Web:* www.hilco.org	Itasca	TX	76055	254-687-2331	687-2428
J-A-C Electric Co-op Inc 1784 FM 172 PO Box 278 *Web:* www.jacelectric.com	Bluegrove	TX	76352	940-895-3311	895-3321
Jackson ElectricCo-op Inc 8925 State Hwy 111 S *Web:* www.jecec.com	Ganado	TX	77962	361-771-4400	771-4406
Jasper-Newton Electric Co-op Inc (JNEC) 812 S Margaret Ave *Web:* www.jnec.com	Kirbyville	TX	75956	409-423-2241	423-3648
Karnes Electric Co-op Inc 1007 N Hwy 123 *TF:* 888-807-3952 ■ *Web:* www.karnesec.org	Karnes City	TX	78118	830-780-3952	780-2347
Lamar County Electric Co-op Assn 1485 N Main St *TF:* 800-252-8080 ■ *Web:* www.lamarelectric.com	Paris	TX	75460	903-784-4303	
Lamb County Electric Co-op Inc 2415 S Phelps Ave *TF:* 800-365-9000 ■ *Web:* www.lcec.coop	Littlefield	TX	79339	806-385-5191	385-5197
Lighthouse Electric Co-op Inc PO Box 600 *TF:* 800-657-7192 ■ *Web:* www.lighthouse.coop	Floydada	TX	79235	806-983-2814	983-2804
Lyntegar Electric Co-op Inc PO Box 970 *Web:* lyntegar.coop	Tahoka	TX	79373	806-561-4588	561-4724
Magic Valley Electric Co-op Inc 1 3/4 Mile W Hwy 83 PO Box 267 *TF:* 866-225-5683 ■ *Web:* www.magval.com	Mercedes	TX	78570	956-903-3048	565-0457
McLennan County Electric Co-op 1111 Johnson Dr PO Box 357 *TF:* 800-840-2957 ■ *Web:* www.hotec.coop/	McGregor	TX	76657	254-840-2871	840-4250
Medina Electric Co-op Inc PO Box 370 *TF:* 866-632-3532 ■ *Web:* www.medinaec.org	Hondo	TX	78861	830-741-3334	426-2796
Navarro County Electric Co-op Inc 3800 Texas 22 PO Box 616 *TF:* 800-771-9095 ■ *Web:* navarroec.com	Corsicana	TX	75110	903-874-7411	874-8422
Navasota Valley Electric Co-op Inc 2281 E US Hwy 79 PO Box 848 *TF:* 800-443-9462 ■ *Web:* www.navasotavalley.com	Franklin	TX	77856	979-828-3232	828-5563
North Plains Electric Co-op Inc 14585 Hwy 83 N PO Box 1008 *TF:* 800-272-5482 ■ *Web:* www.npec.org	Perryton	TX	79070	806-435-5482	435-7225
Nueces Electric Co-op (NEC) 709 E Main St PO Box 260970 *TF:* 800-632-9288 ■ *Web:* www.nueceselectric.org	Robstown	TX	78380	361-387-2581	387-4139
Panola-Harrison Electric Co-op 410 E Houston St PO Box 1058 *TF:* 800-972-1093 ■ *Web:* www.phec.us	Marshall	TX	75670	903-935-7936	935-3361
Pedernales Electric Co-op Inc PO Box 1 *TF:* 888-554-4732 ■ *Web:* www.pec.coop	Johnson City	TX	78636	830-868-7155	868-4767
Rio Grande Electric Co-op Inc Hwy 90 & State Hwy 131 PO Box 1509 *TF:* 800-749-1509 ■ *Web:* www.riogrande.coop	Brackettville	TX	78832	830-563-2444	563-2450
Rusk County ElectricCo-op Inc 3162 State Hwy 43 E *Web:* www.rcelectric.org	Henderson	TX	75652	903-657-4571	657-5377
Sam Houston Electric Co-op Inc 1157 E Church St *TF:* 800-458-0381 ■ *Web:* www.samhouston.net	Livingston	TX	77351	936-327-5711	328-1244
San Bernard Electric Co-op Inc 309 W Main St *TF:* 800-364-3171 ■ *Web:* www.sbec.org	Bellville	TX	77418	979-865-3171	865-9706
San Patricio Electric Co-op Inc 402 E Sinton St *TF:* 888-740-2220 ■ *Web:* www.sanpatricioelectric.org	Sinton	TX	78387	361-364-2220	364-3467
South Plains Electric Co-op Inc PO Box 1830 *TF:* 800-658-2655 ■ *Web:* www.spec.coop	Lubbock	TX	79408	806-775-7766	775-7796
Southwest Texas Electric Co-op Inc 101 E Gillis St PO Box 677 *TF:* 800-643-3980 ■ *Web:* www.swtec.com	Eldorado	TX	76936	325-853-2544	853-3141
Swisher Electric Co-op Inc 401 SW Second St PO Box 67 *TF:* 800-530-4344 ■ *Web:* www.swisherelectric.org	Tulia	TX	79088	806-995-3567	995-2249
Taylor Electric Co-op Inc (TEC) 226 County Rd 287 Bldg A PO Box 250 *Web:* www.taylorelectric.com	Merkel	TX	79536	325-793-8500	793-1309
Texas Electric Co-ops Inc 1122 Colorado St 24th Fl *TF:* 800-301-2860 ■ *Web:* www.texas-ec.org	Austin	TX	78701	512-454-0311	486-6237
Tri-County Electric Co-op Inc 600 NW Pkwy *TF:* 800-367-8232 ■ *Web:* www.tcectexas.com	Azle	TX	76020	817-444-3201	444-3542
Trinity Valley Electric Co-op Inc (TVEC) 1800 Hwy 243 E PO Box 888 *TF:* 800-766-9576 ■ *Web:* www.tvec.net	Kaufman	TX	75142	972-932-2214	932-6466
United Co-op Services 3309 N Main St *Web:* www.united-cs.com	Cleburne	TX	76033	817-556-4000	556-4068
Victoria Electric Co-op Inc (VEC) 102 S Ben Jordan St *TF:* 800-344-8377 ■ *Web:* www.victoriaelectric.coop	Victoria	TX	77901	361-573-2428	573-5753
Wharton County Electric Co-op Inc (WCEC) 1815 E Jackson St *TF:* 800-460-6271 ■ *Web:* www.wcecnet.net	El Campo	TX	77437	979-543-6271	543-6259
Wise Electric Co-op Inc 1900 N Trinity St *TF:* 888-627-9326 ■ *Web:* www.wiseec.com	Decatur	TX	76234	940-627-2167	626-3060
Wood County Electric Co-op Inc 501 S Main St *TF:* 800-762-2203 ■ *Web:* www.wcec.org	Quitman	TX	75783	903-763-2203	763-5693

Utah

	City	State	ZIP	Phone	Fax
Dixie-Escalante Rural Electric Assn 71 E Hwy 56 *TF:* 800-874-0904 ■ *Web:* www.dixiepower.com	Beryl	UT	84714	435-439-5311	439-5352
Flowell Electric Assn Inc 495 North 3200 West	Fillmore	UT	84631	435-743-6214	743-5722
Garkane Energy Co-op Inc 120 West 300 South PO Box 465 *TF:* 800-747-5403 ■ *Web:* www.garkaneenergy.com	Loa	UT	84747	435-836-2795	836-2497
Moon Lake Electric Assn Inc 800 West Hwy 40 PO Box 278 *Web:* www.mleainc.com	Roosevelt	UT	84066	435-722-5400	722-3752

Vermont

	City	State	ZIP	Phone	Fax
Vermont Electric Co-op Inc 42 Wescom Rd *TF:* 800-832-2667 ■ *Web:* www.vermontelectric.coop	Johnson	VT	05656	802-635-2331	635-7645
Washington Electric Co-op 40 Church Street *TF:* 800-932-5245 ■ *Web:* www.washingtonelectric.coop	East Montpelier	VT	05602	802-223-5245	

Virginia

	City	State	ZIP	Phone	Fax
BARC Electric Co-op 84 High St PO Box 264 *Fax Area Code: 540 ■ *TF:* 800-846-2272 ■ *Web:* www.barcelectric.com	Millboro	VA	24460	800-846-2272	997-9011*
Central Virginia Electric Co-op 800 Co-op Way PO Box 247 *TF:* 800-367-2832 ■ *Web:* www.forcvec.com	Lovingston	VA	22949	434-263-8336	263-8339
Community Electric Co-op 52 W Windsor Blvd *TF:* 855-700-2667 ■ *Web:* www.comelec.coop	Windsor	VA	23487	757-242-6181	242-3923
Craig-Botetourt Electric Co-op State Rt 615	New Castle	VA	24127	540-864-5121	
Mecklenburg Electric Co-op 11633 Hwy Ninety Two *TF:* 800-989-4161 ■ *Web:* www.meckelec.org	Chase City	VA	23924	434-372-6100	372-6102
Northern Neck Electric Co-op Inc 85 St Johns St PO Box 288 *TF:* 800-243-2860 ■ *Web:* www.nnec.coop	Warsaw	VA	22572	804-333-3621	
Northern Virginia Electric Co-op PO Box 2710 *TF:* 888-335-0500 ■ *Web:* www.novec.com	Manassas	VA	20108	703-335-0500	392-1546
Old Dominion Electric Co-op (ODEC) 4201 Dominion Blvd *Web:* odec.com	Glen Allen	VA	23060	804-747-0592	747-3742
Prince George Electric Co-op 7103 General Mahone Hwy PO Box 168 *Web:* www.pgec.coop	Waverly	VA	23890	804-834-2424	834-3544
Southside Electric Co-op Inc 2000 W Virgina Ave *TF:* 800-552-2118 ■ *Web:* www.sec.coop	Crewe	VA	23930	434-645-7721	645-1147

Washington

	City	State	ZIP	Phone	Fax
Benton Rural Electric Assn (BREA) 402 Seventh St PO Box 1150 *TF:* 800-221-6987 ■ *Web:* www.bentonrea.org	Prosser	WA	99350	509-786-2913	786-0291
Big Bend Electric Co-op 1373 N Hwy 261 PO Box 348 *TF:* 866-844-2363 ■ *Web:* www.bbec.org	Ritzville	WA	99169	509-659-1700	659-1404
Columbia Rural Electric Assn Inc 115 E Main St *TF:* 800-642-1231 ■ *Web:* www.columbiarea.com	Dayton	WA	99328	509-382-2578	382-2736
Elmhurst Mutual Power & Light Co 120 132nd St S *Web:* www.elmhurstmutual.org	Tacoma	WA	98444	253-531-4646	531-8969
Energy Northwest 76 N Power Plant Loop *TF:* 800-468-6883 ■ *Web:* www.energy-northwest.com	Richland	WA	99354	509-372-5000	372-5205

Phone Fax

Inland Power & Light Company Inc
10110 W Hallett Rd. . . . Spokane WA 99224 509-747-7151 747-7987
TF: 800-747-7151 ■ *Web:* www.inlandpower.com

Nespelem Valley Electric Co-op Inc
1009 F St . . . . Nespelem WA 99155 509-634-4571 634-8138
TF: 866-377-8642 ■ *Web:* www.nvec.org

OHOP Mutual Light Co 34014 Mountain Hwy E . . . . Eatonville WA 98328 253-847-4363 847-2877
Web: ohop.coop

Okanogan County Electric Co-op
93 W Chewuch Rd . . . . Winthrop WA 98862 509-996-2228 996-2241
Web: okanoganelectriccoop.com

Orcas Power & Light Co-op 183 Mt Baker Rd . . . . Eastsound WA 98245 360-376-3500 376-3505
Web: www.opalco.com

Parkland Light & Water Co 12918 Pk Ave . . . . Tacoma WA 98444 253-531-5666 531-2684
Web: www.plw.coop

Peninsula Light Co 13315 Goodnough Dr NW. . . . Gig Harbor WA 98332 253-857-5950 857-3100
TF: 888-809-8021 ■ *Web:* www.penlight.org

Public Utility District #1 of Ferry County
686 S Clark Ave PO Box 1039 . . . . Republic WA 99166 509-775-3325 775-3326
Web: www.fcpud.com

Tanner Electric Co
45710 SE North Bend Way . . . . North Bend WA 98045 425-888-0623 888-5688
TF: 800-472-0208 ■ *Web:* tannerelectric.coop

Wisconsin

Phone Fax

Adams-Columbia Electric Co-op
401 E Lake St. . . . Friendship WI 53934 608-339-3346 339-7756
TF: 800-831-8629 ■ *Web:* acecwi.com

Barron Electric Co-op 1434 State Hwy 25 N. . . . Barron WI 54812 715-537-3171
TF: 800-322-1008 ■ *Web:* www.barronelectric.com

Bayfield Electric Co-op Inc
7400 Iron River Dam Rd. . . . Iron River WI 54847 715-372-4287 372-4318
TF: 800-278-0166 ■ *Web:* www.bayfieldelectric.com

Chippewa Valley Electric Co-op
317 S Eigth St. . . . Cornell WI 54732 715-239-6800 239-6160
TF: 800-300-6800 ■ *Web:* www.cvecoop.com

Clark Electric Co-op
124 N Main St PO Box 190. . . . Greenwood WI 54437 715-267-6188 267-7355
TF: 800-272-6188 ■ *Web:* www.cecoop.com

Dairyland Power Co-op 3200 E Ave S . . . . La Crosse WI 54601 608-788-4000 787-1420
Web: www.dairynet.com

Dunn Energy Co-op PO Box 220 . . . . Menomonie WI 54751 715-232-6240 232-6244
TF: 800-924-0630 ■ *Web:* www.dunnenergy.com

Jackson Electric Co-op
N6868 County Rd F PO Box 546 . . . . Black River Falls WI 54615 715-284-5385 284-7143
TF: 800-370-4607 ■ *Web:* www.jackelec.com

Jump River Electric Co-op PO Box 99. . . . Ladysmith WI 54848 715-532-5524 532-3065
TF: 866-273-5111 ■ *Web:* www.jrec.net

Oakdale Electric Co-op PO Box 128 . . . . Oakdale WI 54649 608-372-4131 372-5173
TF: 800-241-2468 ■ *Web:* www.oakdalerec.com

Oconto Electric Co-op
7478 Rea Rd PO Box 168. . . . Oconto Falls WI 54154 920-846-2816 846-4327
TF: 800-472-8410 ■ *Web:* www.ocontoelectric.com

Pierce Pepin Co-op Services
W7725 US Hwy 10 PO Box 420. . . . Ellsworth WI 54011 715-273-4355 273-4476
TF: 800-924-2133 ■ *Web:* www.piercepepin.com

Polk-Burnett Electric Co-op (PBEC)
1001 State Rd 35 . . . . Centuria WI 54824 715-646-2191 646-2404
TF: 800-421-0283 ■ *Web:* www.polkburnett.com

Price Electric Co-op
508 N Lake Ave PO Box 110. . . . Phillips WI 54555 715-339-2155 339-2921
TF: 800-884-0881 ■ *Web:* price-electric.com

Richland Electric Co-op
1027 N Jefferson St . . . . Richland Center WI 53581 608-647-3173 647-4265
TF: 800-242-8511 ■ *Web:* rec.coop/

Riverland Energy Co-op
N28988 State Rd 93 PO Box 277 . . . . Arcadia WI 54612 608-323-3381 323-3014
TF: 800-411-9115 ■ *Web:* www.riverlandenergy.com

Saint Croix Electric Co-op 1925 Ridgeway St . . . . Hammond WI 54015 715-796-7000 796-7070
TF: 800-924-3407 ■ *Web:* www.scecnet.net

Scenic Rivers Energy Co-op
231 N Sheridan St . . . . Lancaster WI 53813 608-723-2121 723-2688
TF: 800-236-2141 ■ *Web:* www.scenicriversenergy.com

Taylor Electric Co-op N1831 State Hwy 13. . . . Medford WI 54451 715-678-2411 678-2555
TF: 800-862-2407 ■ *Web:* www.taylorelectric.org

Vernon Electric Co-op 110 Saugstad Rd . . . . Westby WI 54667 608-634-3121 634-7481
TF: 800-447-5051 ■ *Web:* www.vernonelectric.org

Wyoming

Phone Fax

Big Horn Rural Electric Co-op
208 S Fifth St PO Box 270. . . . Basin WY 82410 307-568-2419 568-2402
TF: 800-564-2419 ■ *Web:* www.bighornrea.com

Bridger Valley Extreme Access
40014 Business Loop 1-80 PO Box 399. . . . Mountain View WY 82939 307-786-2800 786-4362
TF: 800-276-3481 ■ *Web:* bvea.coop

Carbon Power & Light Inc
100 E Willow Ave PO Box 579 . . . . Saratoga WY 82331 307-326-5206
TF: 800-359-0249 ■ *Web:* www.carbonpower.com

Garland Light & Power Co 755 Hwy 14A. . . . Powell WY 82435 307-754-2881 754-5320
Web: garlandpower.org

High Plains Power Inc
1775 E Monroe PO Box 713. . . . Riverton WY 82501 307-856-9426 856-4207
TF: 800-445-0613 ■ *Web:* www.highplainspower.org

High West Energy Inc (HWE)
6270 County Rd 212. . . . Pine Bluffs WY 82082 307-245-3261 245-9292
TF: 888-834-1657 ■ *Web:* www.highwestenergy.com

Lower Valley Energy 236 N Washington PO Box 188. . . . Afton WY 83110 307-885-3175 885-5787
TF: 800-882-5875 ■ *Web:* www.lvenergy.com

Phone Fax

Powder River Energy Corp (PRE)
221 Main St PO Box 930 . . . . Sundance WY 82729 800-442-3630 283-3527*
*Fax Area Code: 307 ■ *TF:* 800-442-3630 ■ *Web:* www.precorp.coop

Wheatland Rural Electric Assn
2154 S St PO Box 1209 . . . . Wheatland WY 82201 307-322-2125 322-5340
TF: 800-344-3351 ■ *Web:* www.wheatlandrea.com

Wyrulec Co 3978 US Hwy 26/85 . . . . Torrington WY 82240 307-837-2225 837-2115
TF: 800-628-5266 ■ *Web:* www.wyrulec.com

249 ELECTRICAL & ELECTRONIC EQUIPMENT & PARTS - WHOL

Phone Fax

360 Systems Inc 3281 Grande Vista Dr . . . . Newbury Park CA 91320 818-991-0360
Web: 360systems.com

A1 Teletronics Inc 1010 118th Ave N . . . . Saint Petersburg FL 33716 727-576-5001
Web: www.a1teletronics.com

ACF Components & Fasteners Inc
31012 Huntwood Ave . . . . Hayward CA 94544 510-487-2100 471-7018
TF Cust Svc: 800-227-2901 ■ *Web:* www.acfcom.com

ADDvantage Technologies Group Inc
1221 E Houston . . . . Broken Arrow OK 74012 918-251-9121 251-0792
NASDAQ: AEY ■ *Web:* www.addvantagetechnologies.com

Adi American Distributors Inc
Two Emery Ave Ste 1 . . . . Randolph NJ 07869 973-328-1181 328-2302
TF: 800-877-0510 ■ *Web:* www.americandistr.com

Advance Electrical Supply Co
263 N Oakley Blvd . . . . Chicago IL 60612 312-421-2300 421-0926
Web: www.advanceelectrical.com

Advanced MP Technology
1010 Calle Sombra. . . . San Clemente CA 92673 949-492-3113 492-9589
TF: 800-492-3113 ■ *Web:* www.advancedmp.com

AE Petsche Company Inc 2112 W Div St. . . . Arlington TX 76012 817-461-9473 277-2887
Web: www.aepetsche.com

Aesco Electronics Inc 2230 Picton Pkwy. . . . Akron OH 44312 330-245-2630 245-2631
TF: 877-442-6987 ■ *Web:* www.aesco.com

Algo Communication Products Ltd
4500 Beedie St . . . . Burnaby BC V5J5L2 604-438-3333 437-5726
Web: www.algo.ca

Allan Crawford Associates Ltd
5805 Kennedy Rd . . . . Mississauga ON L4Z2G3 905-890-2010
Web: www.aca.ca

Allied Electronics Inc
7151 Jack Newell Blvd S . . . . Fort Worth TX 76118 817-595-3500 595-6404
TF: 866-433-5722 ■ *Web:* www.alliedelec.com

Allstar Magnetics LLC 6205 NE 63rd St. . . . Vancouver WA 98661 360-693-0213 693-0639
TF: 800-356-5977 ■ *Web:* www.allstarmagnetics.com

Alltronics LLC 2761 Scoll Blvd . . . . Santa Clara CA 95050 408-778-3868
Web: www.alltronics.com

Altura Communication Solutions LLC
1335 S Acacia Ave . . . . Fullerton CA 92831 714-948-8400
Web: www.alturacs.com

Amazing Video Network, The 802 Cochrane Dr . . . . Markham ON L3R8C9 905-947-8791
Web: www.amazingvideonetwork.com

America II Electronics Inc
2600 118th Ave N. . . . Saint Petersburg FL 33716 727-573-0900 572-9696
TF: 800-767-2637 ■ *Web:* www.americaii.com

American Electric Supply Inc 1872 W Pomona Rd . . . . Corona CA 92880 951-734-7910 737-9906
Web: www.amelect.com

American Technology Corp
15378 Ave of Science Ste 100 . . . . San Diego CA 92128 858-676-1112 676-1120
NASDAQ: LRAD ■ *Web:* www.lradx.com

Amerinet Inc Two City Pl Dr Ste 400 . . . . St. Louis MO 63141 877-711-5700
TF: 877-711-5700 ■ *Web:* www.amerinet-gpo.com

Anadigm Inc 2036 N Gilbert Rd Ste 2-417. . . . Mesa AZ 85203 480-422-0191
Web: www.anadigm.com

Anixter International Inc 2301 Patriot Blvd. . . . Glenview IL 60025 224-521-8000 252-0003*
NYSE: AXE ■ *Fax Area Code: 512 ■ *TF:* 800-492-1212 ■ *Web:* www.anixter.com

Ansett Aircraft Spares & Services Inc
12675 Encinitas Ave. . . . Sylmar CA 91342 818-362-1100
Web: www.ansettspares.com

Area 51 Esg Inc 51 Post. . . . Irvine CA 92618 949-387-0051
TF: 877-476-8751 ■ *Web:* www.area51esg.com

Argo International Corp 160 Chubb Ave . . . . Lyndhurst NJ 07071 201-561-7010 463-9561*
*Fax Area Code: 315 ■ *TF:* 877-274-6468 ■ *Web:* www.argointl.com

Arizona Components Company Inc
2901 W McDowell Rd. . . . Phoenix AZ 85009 602-269-5655 278-6375
Web: www.azcompco.com

Astrex Inc 205 Express St. . . . Plainview NY 11803 516-433-1700 433-1796
TF: 800-633-6360 ■ *Web:* www.astrex.net

Audio Acoustics Inc 800 N Cedarbrook Ave. . . . Springfield MO 65802 417-869-0770
Web: www.a-a-i.com

Audio-technica Us Inc 1221 Commerce Dr . . . . Stow OH 44224 330-686-2600 688-3752
TF: 800-667-3745 ■ *Web:* www.audio-technica.com

Austin Aerotech Repair Services Inc
2005 Windy Ter. . . . Cedar Park TX 78613 512-335-6000
Web: www.austinaerotech.com

Avnet Inc 2211 S 47th St. . . . Phoenix AZ 85034 480-643-2000
NYSE: AVT ■ *TF:* 888-822-8638 ■ *Web:* www.avnet.com

Axcesor Inc 2260 Dakota Dr. . . . Grafton WI 53024 262-375-7530
Web: www.axcesor.com

B&D Industries Inc 9720 Bell Ave Se . . . . Albuquerque NM 87123 505-299-4464
Web: www.banddindustries.com

Barbey Electronics Corp
210 Corporate Dr PO Box 2 . . . . Reading PA 19605 610-916-7955 916-1975
TF: 800-822-2251 ■ *Web:* www.barbeyele.com

Barnett Inc 801 W Bay St. . . . Jacksonville FL 32204 904-384-6530
TF: 888-803-4467 ■ *Web:* www.e-barnett.com

Bates Technologies Inc 9059 Technology Ln. . . . Fishers IN 46038 317-841-2400
Web: www.batestech.com

BaySpec Inc 1101 McKay Dr . . . . San Jose CA 95131 408-512-5928
Web: www.bayspec.com

Phone Fax

Beacon Electric Supply 9630 Chesapeake Dr .... San Diego CA 92123 858-279-9770 279-9908
Web: www.beaconelectric.com

Bearcom Inc 4009 Distribution Dr Ste 200 .... Garland TX 75041 800-527-1670
TF Sales: 800-527-1670 ■ *Web:* www.bearcom.com

Becker Electric Supply Inc 1341 E Fourth St .... Dayton OH 45402 937-226-1341 226-1790
TF: 800-762-9515 ■ *Web:* www.beckerelectric.com

Benfield Electric Supply Company Inc
25 Lafayette Ave .... North White Plains NY 10603 914-948-6660 993-0558
Web: www.benfieldelectric.com

Bertech-Kelex 640 Maple Ave .... Torrance CA 90503 310-787-0337 787-0854
Web: www.bertech.com

Beyond Components 5 Carl Thompson Rd .... Westford MA 01886 800-971-4242 929-2302
TF: 800-971-4242 ■ *Web:* www.beyondcomponents.com

Billows Electric Supply Co
9100 State Rd .... Philadelphia PA 19136 215-332-9700 338-8320
TF: 877-519-7302 ■ *Web:* www.billows.com

Bisco Industries Inc 1500 N Lakeview Ave .... Anaheim CA 92807 800-323-1232
TF: 800-323-1232 ■ *Web:* www.biscoind.com

Border States Electric Supply 105 25th St N .... Fargo ND 58102 701-293-5834 237-9488
TF: 800-800-0199 ■ *Web:* www.borderstates.com

Brightstar Corp 9725 NW 117th Ave Ste 300 .... Miami FL 33178 305-421-6000 513-3959
Web: brightstar.com/

Broadfield Distributing Inc
67A Glen Cove Ave .... Glen Cove NY 11542 516-676-2378 671-3092
TF: 800-634-5178 ■ *Web:* www.broadfield.com

Broken Arrow Electric Supply Inc
2350 W Vancouver .... Broken Arrow OK 74012 918-258-3581 251-3799
Web: www.baes.com

Buckles-Smith 801 Savaker Ave .... San Jose CA 95126 408-280-7777 280-0729
TF: 800-833-7362 ■ *Web:* www.buckles-smith.com

Burst Communication Inc
8200 S Akron St Ste 108 .... Centennial CO 80112 303-649-9600 649-9890
TF: 800-891-8593 ■ *Web:* www.burstvideo.com

Butler Supply Inc 965 Horan Dr. .... Fenton MO 63026 636-349-9000 349-7877
TF: 800-850-9949 ■ *Web:* www.butlersupply.com

Byram Laboratories Inc One Columbia Rd. .... Branchburg NJ 08876 800-766-1212
TF: 800-766-1212 ■ *Web:* www.byramlabs.com

C R International Inc
9105 Whiskey Bottom Rd Ste J. .... Laurel MD 20723 301-210-1540
Web: www.cri-inc.net

Cadex Electronics Inc 22000 Fraserwood Way .... Richmond BC V6W1J6 604-231-7777 231-7755
Web: www.cadex.com

California Eastern Laboratories Inc (CEL)
4590 Patrick Henry Dr .... Santa Clara CA 95054 408-988-3500 988-0279
Web: www.cel.com

Capital Electric Supply Co
7310 W Roosevelt Ste 2 .... Phoenix AZ 85043 623-936-6789 936-6262
Web: www.capitalelectricsupplyco.com

Carlton Bates Co 3600 W 69th St .... Little Rock AR 72209 501-562-9100 562-9200
TF: 800-482-9313 ■ *Web:* www.carltonbates.com

Cell-Tel Government Systems Inc
8226-B Phillips Hwy Ste 290 .... Jacksonville FL 32256 904-363-1111 363-0032
TF: 800-737-7545 ■ *Web:* www.cell-tel.com

Central Wholesale Electrical Distributors Inc
6611 Preston Ave .... Livermore CA 94551 925-245-9310
Web: cwed.com

Centratel LLC 141 NW Greenwood Ave Ste 200. .... Bend OR 97701 541-383-8383
Web: www.centratel.com

Century Fasteners Corp 50-20 Ireland St .... Elmhurst NY 11373 718-446-5000 426-8119
TF: 800-221-0769 ■ *Web:* www.centuryfasteners.com

CK Technologies Inc 3629 Vista Mercado .... Camarillo CA 93012 805-987-4801
Web: www.ckt.com

Classic Components Corp 23605 Telo Ave .... Torrance CA 90505 310-539-5500
Web: www.class-ic.com

Clean Air Solutions Inc 826 Bayridge Pl .... Fairfield CA 94534 707-864-9499
Web: www.cleanroomspecialists.com

Cms Communications Inc 722 Goddard Ave .... Chesterfield MO 63005 800-755-9169
TF: 800-755-9169 ■ *Web:* www.crowson.com

Codale Electric Supply Inc
5225 West 2400 South PO Box 702070 .... Salt Lake City UT 84120 801-975-7300 977-8833
TF: 800-300-6634 ■ *Web:* www.codale.com

Codan US Inc 8430 Kao Cir .... Manassas VA 20110 703-361-2721
Web: www.codan.com.au

Commodity Components International Inc
100 Summit St .... Peabody MA 01960 978-538-0020 538-3633
TF: 800-424-7364 ■ *Web:* www.cci-inc.com

Communications Supply Corp (CSC)
200 E Lies Rd .... Carol Stream IL 60188 630-221-6400 221-6420
TF: 800-468-2121 ■ *Web:* www.gocsc.com

Component InterTechnologies Inc
2426 Perry Hwy .... Hadley PA 16130 724-253-3161
Web: www.cit-hadley.com

Components Distributors Inc
2601 Blake St Ste 200 .... Denver CO 80205 800-777-7334 294-0998*
**Fax Area Code:* 720 ■ *Web:* www.cdiweb.com

Computer Solutions Inc 4217 S 84th St .... Omaha NE 68127 402-339-7441
Web: www.csimicro.com

Comstock Telcom 5445 Equity Ave. .... Reno NV 89502 775-856-2227
Web: www.comstocktel.com

Comtel Corp 39810 Grand River Ave Ste 180 .... Novi MI 48375 248-888-4730 888-4743
TF: 800-335-2505 ■ *Web:* www.comtel.com

Consolidated Electrical Distributors Inc (CED)
9201 J St .... Omaha NE 68127 402-592-7500 592-5870
Web: www.ced-aec.com

Corporate Telephone Services 184 W Second St .... Boston MA 02127 617-625-1200 625-1201
TF: 800-274-1211 ■ *Web:* corptelserv.com

Cortelco Inc 1703 Sawyer Rd. .... Corinth MS 38834 662-287-5281 287-3889
TF: 800-288-3132 ■ *Web:* www.cortelco.com

Crescent Electric Supply Co
7750 Dunleith Dr .... East Dubuque IL 61025 815-747-3145 747-7720
Web: www.cesco.com

Cross Automation Inc
2001 Oak Pkwy PO Box 1026 .... Belmont NC 28012 704-523-2222 523-6500
TF General: 800-272-7537 ■ *Web:* www.cross-automation.com

Crum Electric Supply Co 1165 W English Ave .... Casper WY 82601 307-266-1278 577-1312
TF: 800-726-2239 ■ *Web:* www.crum.com

Dakota Supply Group (DSG) 2601 Third Ave N. .... Fargo ND 58102 701-237-9440 237-6504
TF: 800-437-4702 ■ *Web:* www.dakotasupplygroup.com

Data Panel Sales 7313 Washington Ave S. .... Minneapolis MN 55439 952-941-3511
Web: www.datapanel.com

Dee Electronics Inc 2500 16th Ave SW. .... Cedar Rapids IA 52404 319-365-7551 365-8506
TF: 800-747-3331 ■ *Web:* www.dee-inc.com

Delta Controls Corp 585 Fortson St .... Shreveport LA 71107 318-424-8471
Web: www.deltacnt.com

Deltrol Corp 2740 S 20th St .... Milwaukee WI 53215 414-671-6800
Web: www.deltrol.com

Dependable Component Supply Corp
1003 E Newport Ctr Dr .... Deerfield Beach FL 33442 954-283-5800 283-5802
TF: 800-336-7100 ■ *Web:* www.dependonus.com

Desco Inc 1205 Lincolnton Rd PO Box 1809 .... Salisbury NC 28147 704-633-6331 637-6966
Web: www.descoinc.com

Digi-Key Corp 701 Brooks Ave S .... Thief River Falls MN 56701 218-681-6674 681-3380
TF: 800-344-4539 ■ *Web:* www.digikey.com

Dii Computers Inc 2425 Blair Mill Rd .... Willow Grove PA 19090 215-657-5055
Web: www.d2computers.com

Diversified Electronics Co Inc
PO Box 566 .... Forest Park GA 30298 404-361-4840 361-6327
TF: 800-646-7278 ■ *Web:* www.diversifiedelectronics.com

Dolphin Technology Inc
2025 Gateway Pl Ste 270 .... San Jose CA 95110 408-392-0012
Web: www.dolphin-ic.com

Dominion Electric Supply Company Inc
5053 Lee Hwy .... Arlington VA 22207 703-536-4400 741-0423
TF: 800-525-5006 ■ *Web:* www.dominionelectric.com

Dow Electronics Inc 8603 E Adamo Dr .... Tampa FL 33619 813-626-5195 628-4990
TF: 800-627-2900 ■ *Web:* www.dowelectronics.com

Duke Communications
1781 Jamestown Rd Ste 170 .... Williamsburg VA 23185 757-253-9000
Web: www.widomaker.com

E Sam Jones Distributor Inc 4898 S Atlanta Rd .... Smyrna GA 30080 404-351-3250 351-4140
TF: 800-624-9849 ■ *Web:* www.esamjones.com

Earl & Brown Co Inc 5825 SW Arctic Dr .... Beaverton OR 97005 503-670-1170 432-9237*
**Fax Area Code:* 866 ■ *Web:* www.earlbrown.com

eASIC Corp 2585 Augustine Dr Ste 100 .... Santa Clara CA 95054 408-855-9200
Web: www.easic.com

Eck Supply Co 1405 W Main St .... Richmond VA 23220 804-359-5781 358-1353
Web: www.ecksupply.com

Elecraft Inc Po Box 69 .... Aptos CA 95001 831-763-4211
Web: www.elecraft.com

Electric Supply & Equipment Co
1812 E Wendover Ave. .... Greensboro NC 27405 336-272-4123 274-4632
TF: 800-632-0268 ■ *Web:* www.ese-co.com

Electric Supply Inc 4407 N Manhattan Ave. .... Tampa FL 33614 813-872-1894 874-1680
TF: 800-678-1894 ■ *Web:* www.electricsupplyinc.com

Electrical Wholesale Supply Company of Utah
158 East 4500 South .... Salt Lake City UT 84107 801-268-2555 268-2555
Web: www.borderstates.com/

Electro Brand Inc
1127 S Mannheim Rd Ste 305 .... Westchester IL 60154 708-338-4400
TF: 800-982-3954 ■ *Web:* www.electrobrand-usa.com

Electro Dynamics Crystal Corp
9075 Cody St .... Overland Park KS 66214 913-888-1750
Web: www.electrodynamics.com

Electro-Matic Products Inc
23409 Industrial Pk Ct .... Farmington Hills MI 48335 248-478-1182 478-1472
TF: 888-879-1088 ■ *Web:* www.electro-matic.com

ElectroTech Inc 7101 Madison Ave W .... Minneapolis MN 55427 763-544-4288 542-8102
TF: 800-544-4288 ■ *Web:* www.electrotech-inc.com

Elliott Electric Supply Co
2526 N Stallings Dr PO Box 630610 .... Nacogdoches TX 75963 936-569-1184 569-1836
TF: 877-777-0242 ■ *Web:* www.elliottelectric.com

EM Microelectronic-US Inc
5475 Mark Dabling Blvd Ste 200 .... Colorado Springs CO 80918 719-593-2883
Web: www.emmicroelectronic.com

Emergency Radio Service Inc PO Box 110 .... Ligonier IN 46767 260-894-4145 894-7581
Web: www.ers2way.com

Enetics Inc 830 Canning Pkwy .... Victor NY 14564 585-924-5010
Web: www.enetics.com

EnGenius Technologies Inc 1580 Scenic Ave .... Costa Mesa CA 92626 714-432-8668
Web: www.engeniustech.com

Englewood Electrical Supply 716 Belvedere Dr. .... Kokomo IN 46901 765-452-4087 221-9056*
**Fax Area Code:* 702 ■ *TF:* 800-417-7543 ■ *Web:* wesco.com

EPIR Technologies Inc
590 Territorial Dr Unit B .... Bolingbrook IL 60440 630-771-0203
Web: www.epir.com

Eric Electronics 2220 Lundy Ave. .... San Jose CA 95131 408-432-1111 433-0570
TF General: 800-495-3742 ■ *Web:* www.ericnet.com

ESL ElectroScience Inc
416 E Church Rd .... King Of Prussia PA 19406 610-272-8000
Web: www.electroscience.com

Estech Systems Inc 3701 East Plano Pkwy .... Plano TX 75074 972-422-9700 422-9705
Web: www.esi-estech.com

Evans Enterprises Inc
1536 S Western Ave .... Oklahoma City OK 73109 405-631-1344 631-8948
TF: 800-423-8267 ■ *Web:* www.goevans.com

EWD Solutions 2434 Mciver Ln .... Carrollton TX 75006 972-247-2470
Web: www.ewdsolutions.com

Ewing-Foley Inc 10061 Bubb Rd Ste A .... Cupertino CA 95014 408-342-1200
Web: www.ewingfoley.com

Extrel CMS LLC 575 Epsilon Dr .... Pittsburgh PA 15238 412-963-7530
Web: www.extrel.com

Facility Solutions Group (FSG)
4401 Westgate Blvd Ste 310 .... Austin TX 78745 512-440-7985 440-0399
TF: 800-854-6465 ■ *Web:* www.fsgconnect.com

	City	State	ZIP	Phone	Fax

Famous Enterprises Inc 109 N Union St ... Akron OH 44304 330-762-9621
Web: www.famous-supply.com

FD Lawrence Electric Company Inc
3450 Beekman St ... Cincinnati OH 45223 513-542-1100 542-2422
TF Cust Svc: 800-582-4490 ■ *Web:* www.fdlawrence.com

Feldman Bros Electrical Supply Co
26 Maryland Ave. ... Paterson NJ 07503 973-742-7329 742-2220
Web: www.feldmanbros.com

Fiber Instruments Sales Inc 161 Clear Rd ... Oriskany NY 13424 315-736-2206 736-2285
TF Sales: 800-500-0347 ■ *Web:* www.fiberinstrumentsales.com

Fiber Optic Center New Trust
23 Centre St ... New Bedford MA 02740 508-992-6464
Web: www.focenter.com

Fiber-Span LLC 3434 Rt 22West Ste 140 ... Branchburg NJ 08876 908-253-9080
Web: www.fiber-span.com

Fidelitone Inc 1260 Karl Ct ... Wauconda IL 60084 847-487-3300 469-6581
Web: www.fidelitone.com

Flame Enterprises Inc 21500 Gledhill St ... Chatsworth CA 91311 818-700-2905 700-9168
TF: 800-854-2255 ■ *Web:* www.flamecorp.com

Floyd Bell Inc 720 Dearborn Park Ln ... Columbus OH 43085 614-294-4000
Web: www.floydbell.com

Foxcom Inc 136 Main St Ste 300b ... Princeton NJ 08540 609-514-1800 514-1881
TF: 866-663-7284 ■ *Web:* www.foxcom.com

Friedman Electric 1321 Wyoming Ave ... Exeter PA 18643 570-654-3371 655-6194
TF: 800-545-5517 ■ *Web:* www.friedmanelectric.com

Fromm Electric Supply Corp
2101 Centre Ave PO Box 15147 ... Reading PA 19605 610-374-4441 374-8756
TF: 800-360-4441 ■ *Web:* www.frommelectric.com

FSG Lighting 4401 Westgate Blvd Ste 310 ... Austin TX 78745 512-440-7985 440-0399
TF: 800-854-6465 ■ *Web:* www.fsgi.com

FTG Inc 725 Marshall Phelps Rd ... Windsor CT 06095 860-610-6000 610-6001
TF: 888-610-6020 ■ *Web:* www.farmstead.com

Future Electronics 237 Hymus Blvd ... Pointe-Claire QC H9R5C7 514-694-7710 695-3707
TF Cust Svc: 800-675-1619 ■ *Web:* www.futureelectronics.com

Futurecom Systems Group Inc
3277 Langstaff Rd. ... Concord ON L4K5P8 905-660-5548
Web: www.futurecom.com

Galco Industrial Electronics Inc
26010 Pinehurst Dr ... Madison Heights MI 48071 248-542-9090 542-8031
TF: 888-783-4611 ■ *Web:* www.galco.com

GBH Communications Inc 1309 S Myrtle Ave ... Monrovia CA 91016 800-222-5424
TF: 800-222-5424 ■ *Web:* www.gbh.com

George R Peters Assoc Inc PO Box 850 ... Troy MI 48099 248-524-2211 524-1758
TF: 800-929-5972 ■ *Web:* www.grpeters.com

Graybar Electric Co Inc 34 N Meramec Ave. ... Saint Louis MO 63105 314-573-9200 573-9455
TF: 800-472-9227 ■ *Web:* www.graybar.com

Gross Electric Inc 2807 N Reynolds Rd ... Toledo OH 43615 419-537-1818 537-6627
TF: 800-824-7268 ■ *Web:* www.grosselectric.com

Grove-Madsen Industries 390 E Sixth St ... Reno NV 89512 775-322-3400 322-3495
Web: www.g-m-i.net

Gsolutionz Inc 625 E Santa Clara St Ste 100 ... Ventura CA 93001 805-662-1500
Web: www.gsolutionz.com

Halbrook & Miller Inc
2307 Springlake Rd Ste 518 ... Dallas TX 75234 972-243-4772
Web: tmtel.com

Hamamatsu Corp 360 Foothill Rd ... Bridgewater NJ 08807 908-231-0960
Web: www.hamamatsu.com

Hammond Electronics Inc 1230 W Central Blvd ... Orlando FL 32805 407-849-6060 872-0826
TF Sales: 800-929-3672 ■ *Web:* www.hammondelec.com

Hardware Specialty Company Inc
48-75 36th St ... Long Island City NY 11101 718-361-9393 706-0238
Web: www.hardwarespecialty.com

Hartford Electric Supply Co (HESCO)
30 Inwood Rd Ste 1 ... Rocky Hill CT 06067 860-236-6363 236-0233
TF: 800-969-5444 ■ *Web:* www.hesconet.com

Hawking Technologies Inc 35 Hammond Ste 150 ... Irvine CA 92618 949-206-6900
Web: www.hawkingtech.com

Headsets Direct Inc 1454 W Gurley St Ste A ... Prescott AZ 86305 928-777-9100
Web: www.headsetsdirect.com

Heartland Label Printers Inc
1700 Stephen St ... Little Chute WI 54140 800-236-7914 788-7739*
**Fax Area Code:* 920 ■ *TF General:* 800-236-7914 ■ *Web:* www.hbs.net

Heilind Electronics Inc 58 Jonspin Rd ... Wilmington MA 01887 978-657-4870 658-0278
TF: 800-400-7041 ■ *Web:* www.heilind.com

Hi-Line Inc 2121 Vly View Ln ... Dallas TX 75234 972-247-6200
Web: www.hi-line.com

Hi-Techniques Inc 2515 Frazier Ave. ... Madison WI 53713 608-221-7500
Web: www.hi-techniques.com

HICO America Sales & Technology Inc
Three Penn Ctr W Ste 300 ... Pittsburg PA 15276 412-787-1170
Web: www.hicoamerica.com

Higgins Electric Inc. of Dothan
1350 Columbia Hwy. ... Dothan AL 36301 334-793-4859
Web: www.higginselectric.com

Hite Co 3101 Beale Ave ... Altoona PA 16601 814-944-6121 944-3052
TF: 800-252-3598 ■ *Web:* www.hiteco.com

HITEC Group Ltd 1743 Quincy Ave Unit 155 ... Naperville IL 60540 800-288-8303
TF: 800-288-8303 ■ *Web:* www.hitec.com

HL Dalis Inc 35-35 24th St ... Long Island City NY 11106 718-361-1100 392-7654
TF: 800-453-2547 ■ *Web:* www.hldalis.com

Hotan Corp 751 N Canyons Pkwy ... Livermore CA 94551 925-290-1000
Web: www.hotan.com

Houston Wire & Cable Co (HWC) 10201 N Loop E ... Houston TX 77029 713-609-2100 609-2101
TF: 800-468-9473 ■ *Web:* www.houwire.com

Hutton Communications Inc 2520 Marsh Ln ... Carrollton TX 75006 972-417-0100 417-0180
Web: www.hol4g.com

IBS Electronics Inc 3506 W Lk Ctr Dr Ste D ... Santa Ana CA 92704 714-751-6633 751-8159
TF: 800-527-2888 ■ *Web:* www.ibselectronics.com

ICX Global Inc 8206 E Park Meadows Dr ... Lone Tree CO 80134 720-873-8400
Web: www.icxglobal.com

IMS Inc 340 Progress Dr ... Manchester CT 06040 860-649-4415 649-0806
TF General: 800-264-9837 ■ *Web:* www.imswire.com

Independent Electric Supply Inc
1370 Bayport Ave ... San Carlos CA 94070 650-594-9440 594-0484
TF: 855-437-4968 ■ *Web:* www.iesupply.com

Industrial Electric Wire & Cable Inc (IEWC)
5001 S Towne Dr ... New Berlin WI 53151 262-782-2323 957-1600
TF: 800-344-2323 ■ *Web:* www.iewc.com

Infosat Communications Inc 3130-114 Ave SE ... Calgary AB T2Z3V6 403-543-8188
Web: www.infosat.com

InfoSonics Corp 4350 Executive Dr Ste 100 ... San Diego CA 92121 858-373-1600 373-1503
NASDAQ: IFON ■ *Web:* www.infosonics.com

Insulectro 20362 Windrow Dr ... Lake Forest CA 92630 949-587-3200 454-0066
Web: www.insulectro.com

Integrated Components Source (ICS)
3977 Camino Ranchero ... Camarillo CA 93012 805-822-5100 483-1300
Web: www.yourdrive.com

Inter-Technical LLC PO Box 535 ... Elmsford NY 10523 914-347-2474 347-7230
Web: www.inter-technical.com

International Electrical Sales Corp (IESCO)
7540 NW 66th St ... Miami FL 33166 305-591-8390 591-3294
Web: www.iescomia.com

Interstate Connecting Components Inc
120 Mt Holly By Pass ... Lumberton NJ 08048 888-899-1990 722-9425*
**Fax Area Code:* 856 ■ *TF:* 888-899-1990 ■ *Web:* www.connecticc.com

Interstate Electrical Supply Inc
2300 Second Ave ... Columbus GA 31901 706-324-1000 576-5821
TF: 800-903-4409 ■ *Web:* www.interstate-electrical.com

Jaco Electronics Inc 415 Oser Ave. ... Hauppauge NY 11788 877-373-5226 231-1051*
OTC: JACO ■ **Fax Area Code:* 631 ■ *TF:* 877-373-5226 ■ *Web:* www.jacoelect.com

Janesway Electronic Corp 404 N Terr Ave ... Mount Vernon NY 10552 914-699-6710 699-6969
TF: 800-431-1348 ■ *Web:* www.janesway.com

Jasco Products Inc 10 E Memorial Rd ... Oklahoma City OK 73114 405-752-0710 752-1537
TF: 800-654-8483 ■ *Web:* www.jascoproducts.com

JH Larson Co 10200 51st Ave N ... Plymouth MN 55442 763-545-1717 545-1144
TF: 800-292-7970 ■ *Web:* www.jhlarson.com

Joliet Avionics Inc
43w730 Us Hwy 30 Ste A ... Sugar Grove IL 60554 630-584-3200
Web: www.jaair.com

JOWA USA Inc 59 Porter Rd ... Littleton MA 01460 978-486-9800
Web: www.consiliumus.com

Justin Electronics Corp
400 Oser Ave Ste 800 ... Hauppauge NY 11788 631-951-4900 951-4747
Web: www.justinelectronics.com

K G B Communictions L L C 3219 N Geronimo Ave ... Tucson AZ 85705 520-743-3300
Web: www.kgbcommunications.com

Kansas City Electrical Supply Co (KCES)
10900 MidAmerica Ave. ... Lenexa KS 66219 913-563-7002 563-7052
TF: 866-271-6456 ■ *Web:* www.kcelectricalsupply.com

Kehoe Component Sales Inc 34 Foley Dr ... Sodus NY 14551 800-228-7223
TF: 800-228-7223 ■ *Web:* www.paceelectronics.com

Kendall Electric Inc
131 Grand Trunk Ave ... Battle Creek MI 49037 269-963-5585
TF: 800-632-5422 ■ *Web:* www.kendallelectric.com

Kiddesigns Inc 1299 Main St ... Rahway NJ 07065 732-574-9000
Web: www.kiddesigns.com

Kikusui America Inc
1633 Bayshore Hwy Ste 331 ... Burlingame CA 94010 650-259-5900
Web: www.kikusuiamerica.com

Kirby Risk Corp 1815 Sagamore Pkwy N ... Lafayette IN 47904 765-448-4567
Web: www.kirbyrisk.com

KJB Security Products Inc
841-B Fessiers Pkwy ... Nashville TN 37210 615-620-1370
Web: www.kjbsecurity.com

Kovalsky-Carr Electric Supply Company Inc
208 St Paul St. ... Rochester NY 14604 585-325-1950 546-6904
Web: www.kovalskycarr.com

La Clef De Sol Inc 840 rue Bouvier ... Quebec QC G2J1A3 418-627-0840
Web: www.laclefdesol.com

Laipac Technology Inc
20 Mural St Unit 5 ... Richmond Hill ON L4B1K3 905-762-1228 763-1737
Web: www.laipac.com

Lazo Technologies Inc 611 W Mockingbird Ln. ... Dallas TX 75247 214-652-9898 652-9889
Web: www.lazotech.com

Leff Electric 4700 Spring Rd ... Cleveland OH 44131 216-432-3000 432-0051
TF: 800-686-5333 ■ *Web:* www.leffelectric.com

Lester Sales Co Inc 4312 W Minnesota St ... Indianapolis IN 46241 317-244-7811 248-2369
TF: 800-544-6183 ■ *Web:* www.lestersalesco.com

Lewis Electric Supply Company Inc
1306 Second St PO Box 2237 ... Muscle Shoals AL 35662 256-383-0681 383-0834
TF: 800-239-0681 ■ *Web:* www.lesupply.com

LeWiz Communications Inc
1376 N Fourth St Ste 300 ... San Jose CA 95112 408-452-9800
Web: www.lewiz.com

Loeb Electric Co 1800 E Fifth Ave ... Columbus OH 43219 614-294-6351 294-7640
Web: www.loebelectric.com

Lowe Electric Supply Co
1525 Forsyth St PO Box 4767 ... Macon GA 31208 478-743-8661 742-3374
TF: 800-868-8661 ■ *Web:* www.loweelectric.com

Loyd's Electric Supply Inc (LES)
838 Stonetree Dr. ... Branson MO 65616 417-334-2171 334-6635
TF: 800-492-4030 ■ *Web:* www.loydselectric.com

Ludeca Inc 1425 NW 88th Ave ... Doral FL 33172 305-591-8935
Web: www.ludeca.com

Macnica Americas Inc
380 Stevens Ave Ste 206 ... Solana Beach CA 92075 760-707-0120
Web: www.macnica-na.com

Madison Electric Co 31855 Van Dyke Ave ... Warren MI 48093 586-825-0200 825-0225
Web: www.madisonelectric.com

Main Electric Supply Co 6700 S Main St. ... Los Angeles CA 90003 323-753-5131 753-7750
Web: www.mainelectricsupply.com

Maltby Electric Supply Company Inc
336 Seventh St ... San Francisco CA 94103 415-863-5000 863-5011
TF: 800-339-0668 ■ *Web:* www.maltbyelec.com

Company / Address	City	State	Zip	Phone	Fax
Mars Electric Co 38868 Mentor Ave *TF:* 800-288-6277 ■ *Web:* www.mars-electric.com	Willoughby	OH	44094	440-946-2250	946-3214
Marsh Electronics Inc 1563 S 101st St *TF Cust Svc:* 800-236-8327 ■ *Web:* www.marshelectronics.com	Milwaukee	WI	53214	414-475-6000	771-2847
Maurice Electrical Supply Co 500 Penn St NE *Web:* www.mauriceelectric.com	Washington	DC	20002	202-675-9400	547-1956
Mayer Electric Supply Co 3405 Fourth Ave S PO Box 1328 *TF:* 866-637-1255 ■ *Web:* www.mayerelectric.com	Birmingham	AL	35222	205-583-3500	322-2625
McNaughton-McKay Electric Company Inc 1357 E Lincoln Ave *TF:* 888-626-2785 ■ *Web:* www.mc-mc.com	Madison Heights	MI	48071	248-399-7500	399-6828
Metro Wire & Cable Co 6636 Metropolitan Pkwy *TF:* 800-633-1432 ■ *Web:* www.metrowire.net	Sterling Heights	MI	48312	586-264-3050	264-7390
Michigan Chandelier Company Inc 20855 Telegraph Rd *Web:* www.michand.com	Southfield	MI	48033	248-353-0510	353-0973
MicroRam Electronics Inc 222 Dunbar Ct *Web:* www.microram.com	Oldsmar	FL	34677	813-854-5500	
Mid-Coast Electric Supply Inc (MCESI) 1801 Stolz St PO Box 2505 *Web:* www.mcesi.com	Victoria	TX	77901	361-575-6311	575-5515
Mid-Island Electrical Supply 59 Mall Dr *TF:* 877-324-2636 ■ *Web:* www.mid-island.com	Commack	NY	11725	631-864-4242	864-6644
Mid-South Electronics Inc (MSI) 2620 E Meighan Blvd PO Box 322 *Web:* koller-craftsouth.com	Gadsden	AL	35903	256-492-8997	
Midcom Data Technologies Inc 33493 W 14 Mile Rd Ste 150 *Web:* www.midcomdata.com	Farmington Hills	MI	48331	248-661-0100	
Midtown Electric Supply Corp 157 W 18th St *Web:* www.midtownelectric.com	New York	NY	10011	212-255-3388	255-3177
Minnesota Electric Supply Co 1209 E Hwy 12 *TF:* 800-992-8830 ■ *Web:* willmar.minnesota.com	Willmar	MN	56201	320-235-2255	214-4247
Mobile Communication of Gwinnett Inc 2241 Tucker Industrial Rd *Web:* www.callmc.com	Tucker	GA	30084	770-963-3748	
Mouser Electronics Corp 1000 N Main St *TF:* 800-346-6873 ■ *Web:* mouser.in/	Mansfield	TX	76063	817-804-3888	804-3899
Murdock Industrial Supply 1111 E 1st *TF:* 800-362-2422 ■ *Web:* www.mcos.com	Wichita	KS	67202	316-262-4476	263-8100
Music People Inc 154 Woodlawn Rd Ste C **Fax Area Code:* 860 ■ *TF:* 800-289-8889 ■ *Web:* www.musicpeopleinc.com	Berlin	CT	06037	800-289-8889	828-1353*
NAC Group Inc 10001 16th St N Metropointe Commerce Park *Web:* www.newadvg.com	St. Petersburg	FL	33716	727-576-0550	
NACB Group Inc 10 Starwood Dr *TF:* 800-370-2737 ■ *Web:* www.ncabgroup.com	Hampstead	NH	03841	603-329-4551	329-5033
Nave Communications Co 8215 Dorsey Run Rd *Web:* www.ncctel.com	Jessup	MD	20794	301-725-6283	
Nedco Electronics 594 American Way **Fax Area Code:* 800 ■ *TF:* 800-605-2323 ■ *Web:* www.nedcoelectronics.com	Payson	UT	84651	801-465-1790	605-3836*
Nedco Supply Inc 4200 W Spring Mtn Rd *Web:* www.nedco.com	Las Vegas	NV	89102	702-367-0400	362-8365
Nelson Electric Supply Co Inc 926 State St *TF:* 800-806-3576 ■ *Web:* www.nelson-electric.com	Racine	WI	53404	262-635-5050	637-2465
NEP Electronics Inc 805 Mittel Dr *TF:* 800-284-7470 ■ *Web:* www.nepelectronics.com	Wood Dale	IL	60191	630-595-8500	595-8706
Newton Instrument Company Inc 111 East A St *Web:* www.enewton.com	Butner	NC	27509	919-575-6426	
NF Smith & Assoc LP 5306 Hollister Rd *TF:* 800-468-7866 ■ *Web:* globalpurchasing.com	Houston	TX	77040	713-430-3000	430-3099
Nora Lighting Inc 6505 Gayhart St **Fax Area Code:* 800 ■ *TF:* 800-686-6672 ■ *Web:* www.noralighting.com	Commerce	CA	90040	323-767-2600	500-9955*
North American Communications Resource Inc 3844 Hwy 149 *TF:* 888-321-6227 ■ *Web:* www.nacr.com	Eagan	MN	55121	651-994-6800	994-6801
Northern Video Systems Inc 3625 Cincinnati Ave *TF:* 800-366-4472 ■ *Web:* www.tri-ed.com	Rocklin	CA	95765	916-543-4000	543-4020
Norvell Electronics Inc PO Box 701027 *TF:* 800-893-0593 ■ *Web:* www.norvell.com	Dallas	TX	75370	972-858-3713	490-7245
Nsync Services Inc 850 Greenview Dr *TF:* 866-706-7962 ■ *Web:* www.nsyncservices.com	Grand Prairie	TX	75050	972-641-7426	641-8093
Nu Horizons Electronics Corp 70 Maxess Rd **Fax Area Code:* 256 ■ *TF:* 800-432-5742 ■ *Web:* www.arrow.com	Melville	NY	11747	631-396-5000	864-3349*
Nu-Lite Electrical Wholesalers 850 Edwards Ave *TF:* 800-256-1603 ■ *Web:* www.nulite.com	Harahan	LA	70123	504-733-3300	736-1617
Omni Cable Corp Two Hagerty Blvd *Web:* www.omnicable.com	West Chester	PA	19382	610-701-0100	701-9870
One Link Wireless 7321 Broadway Ext *Web:* www.onelinkwireless.com	Oklahoma City	OK	73116	405-840-2345	
OneSource Distributors 3951 Oceanic Dr *Web:* www.1sourcedist.com	Oceanside	CA	92056	760-966-4500	966-4599
Orban Inc 8350 E Evans Rd Ste C-4 *Web:* www.orban.com	Scottsdale	AZ	85260	480-403-8300	
Orlando Diefenderfer Co 116 S Second St *Web:* www.diefenderfer.com	Allentown	PA	18105	610-434-9595	
Paige Electric Company LP 1160 Springfield Rd *TF:* 800-327-2443 ■ *Web:* www.paigeelectric.com	Union	NJ	07083	908-687-7810	687-2722
Parrish-Hare Electrical Supply LP 1211 Regal Row PO Box 560547 *Web:* www.parrish-hare.com	Dallas	TX	75247	214-905-1001	951-8101
Path Master Inc 1960 Midway Dr *TF:* 855-738-2722 ■ *Web:* www.pathmasterinc.com	Twinsburg	OH	44087	330-425-4994	425-9338
Pathcom Wireless Inc 315 First St East *Web:* www.pathcom.ca	Cochrane	AB	T4C1Z2	403-932-2559	932-2468
Peerless Electronics Inc 700 Hicksville Rd *TF:* 800-285-2121 ■ *Web:* www.peerlesselectronics.com	Bethpage	NY	11714	516-594-3500	593-2179
PEI-Genesis 2180 Hornig Rd *TF:* 800-675-1214 ■ *Web:* www.peigenesis.com	Philadelphia	PA	19116	215-673-0400	552-8022
Peter Parts Electronics Inc 6285 Dean Pkwy *Web:* www.peterparts.com	Ontario	NY	14519	585-265-2000	
PFT Alexander Inc 3250 E Grant St *Web:* www.pft-alexander.com	Signal Hill	CA	90755	562-595-1741	
Platt Electric Supply 10605 SW Allen Blvd *TF:* 800-257-5288 ■ *Web:* www.platt.com	Beaverton	OR	97005	503-641-6121	277-7497
Powell Electronics Inc 200 Commodore Dr *TF:* 800-235-7880 ■ *Web:* www.powell.com	Swedesboro	NJ	08085	856-241-8000	241-8630
Power & Telephone Supply Company Inc 2673 Yale Ave *TF Cust Svc:* 800-238-7514 ■ *Web:* www.ptsupply.com	Memphis	TN	38112	901-866-3300	320-3082
Precise Tool & Gage Company Inc 30540 Se 84th St Unit 2 *Web:* www.precisetoolco.com	Preston	WA	98050	425-222-9567	
Priority Wire & Cable Inc PO Box 398 *TF General:* 800-945-5542 ■ *Web:* www.prioritywire.com	North Little Rock	AR	72115	501-372-5444	372-3988
Professional Electric Products Co (PEPCO) 33210 Lakeland Blvd *TF:* 800-872-7000 ■ *Web:* www.pepconet.com	Eastlake	OH	44095	440-946-3790	942-5883
Projections Unlimited Inc 15311 Varrenca Pkwy **Fax Area Code:* 949 ■ *TF Cust Svc:* 800-551-4405 ■ *Web:* www.gopui.com	Irvine	CA	92618	714-544-2700	789-0626*
QED Inc 1661 W Third Ave *TF:* 800-700-5011 ■ *Web:* www.qedelectric.com	Denver	CO	80223	303-825-5011	893-5019
Quebe Holdings Inc 1985 Founders Dr *Web:* www.quebe.com	Dayton	OH	45420	937-222-2290	
Queen City Electrical Supply Company Inc Third & Walnut St PO Box 1288 *Web:* www.queencityelec.com	Allentown	PA	18105	610-439-0525	439-8637
Radiophone Engineering Inc 534 W Walnut St *Web:* www.radiophonewireless.com	Springfield	MO	65806	417-862-6653	
Ralph Pill Electrical Supply Co 50 Von Hillern Street *TF:* 800-897-1769 ■ *Web:* www.needco.com	Boston	MA	02125	617-265-8800	288-1776
Rawson Inc 2010 McAllister **Fax Area Code:* 713 ■ *Web:* www.rawsonlp.com	Houston	TX	77092	800-779-1414	684-1418*
RCI Sound Systems 10721 Hanna St *Web:* www.rcisound.com	Beltsville	MD	20705	301-931-9001	
Reagan Wireless Corp 720 S Powerline Rd Ste D *TF:* 877-724-3266 ■ *Web:* www.reaganwireless.com	Deerfield Beach	FL	33442	954-596-2355	596-0070
Real Time Systems Inc 103 Industrial Loop Ste 1100 *Web:* www.real-time-sys.com	Fredericksburg	TX	78624	830-990-2340	
Red Peacock International Inc 1945 Gardena Ave *Web:* www.redpeacock.com	Glendale	CA	91204	818-265-7722	265-7750
Regency Lighting Co 9261 Jordan Ave **Fax Area Code:* 818 ■ *TF:* 800-284-2024 ■ *Web:* www.regencylighting.com	Chatsworth	CA	91311	800-284-2024	901-0118*
Renco Electronics Inc 595 International Pl *TF:* 800-645-5828 ■ *Web:* www.rencousa.com	Rockledge	FL	32955	321-637-1000	637-1600
Rexel Canada Inc 5600 Keaton Crescent *Web:* www.rexel.ca	Mississauga	ON	L5R3G3	905-712-4004	
Rexel Inc 14951 Dallas Pkwy PO Box 9085 *Web:* www.rexelusa.com	Dallas	TX	75254	972-387-3600	991-1831
Rexel Ryall Electrical Supplies 11775 E 45th Ave *TF:* 888-739-3577 ■ *Web:* www.rexelusa.com	Denver	CO	80239	303-629-7721	825-7608
Richardson Electronics Ltd 40 W 267 Keslinger Rd PO Box 393 *NASDAQ: RELL* ■ *TF Sales:* 800-348-5580 ■ *Web:* www.rell.com	LaFox	IL	60147	630-208-2200	208-2550
Rochester Electronics Inc 16 Malcolm Hoyt Dr *Web:* www.rocelec.com	Newburyport	MA	01950	978-462-9332	462-9512
Rochester Industrial Control Inc 6400 Furnace Rd *Web:* www.rochesterindustrial.com	Ontario	NY	14519	315-524-4555	
Rohde & Schwarz Inc 6821 Benjamin Franklin Dr *Web:* www.rohde-schwarz.com	Columbia	MD	21046	410-910-7800	
Rondout Electric Inc 33 Arlington Ave *Web:* rondoutelectric.net	Poughkeepsie	NY	12603	845-471-4810	471-1903
RS Electronics Inc 34443 Schoolcraft Rd **Fax Area Code:* 800 ■ *TF:* 866-600-6040 ■ *Web:* www.carltonbates.com/content/rs-electronics	Livonia	MI	48150	734-525-1155	544-2570*
Rumsey Electric Co 15 Colwell Ln *TF:* 800-462-2402 ■ *Web:* www.rumsey.com	Conshohocken	PA	19428	610-832-9000	941-8181
S K C Communication Products Inc 8320 Hedge Ln Terr **Fax Area Code:* 800 ■ *TF:* 800-882-7779 ■ *Web:* www.skccom.com	Shawnee Mission	KS	66227	913-422-4222	454-4752*
Sager Electronics Inc 19 Lorena Dr *TF:* 800-724-3780 ■ *Web:* www.sager.com	Middleboro	MA	02346	508-947-8888	947-0869
Sandusky Electric Inc 1513 Sycamore Line PO Box 2353 *TF:* 800-356-1243 ■ *Web:* www.sanduskyelectric.com	Sandusky	OH	44870	419-625-4915	625-9438
Santek Components LLC 1060 Holland Ave Ste A *Web:* www.santekcomp.com	Clovis	CA	93612	559-294-6015	
Schuster Electronics Inc 2057-D E Aurora Rd **Fax Area Code:* 330 ■ *TF:* 800-521-1358 ■ *Web:* www.schusterusa.com	Twinsburg	OH	44087	800-521-1358	425-1863*
Sciemetric Instruments Inc 359 Terry Fox Dr Ste 100 *Web:* www.sciemetric.com	Ottawa	ON	K2K2E7	613-254-7054	
Scott Electric 1000 S Main St PO Box S **Fax Area Code:* 800 ■ *TF:* 800-442-8045 ■ *Web:* www.scottelectricusa.com	Greensburg	PA	15601	724-834-4321	426-9598*

Company	City	State	Zip	Phone	Fax
Secured Digital Applications Inc 230 Pk Ave 10th Fl *Web:* www.digitalapps.net	New York	NY	10169	212-551-1747	808-3020
SED International Inc 4916 N Royal Atlanta Dr *TF Sales:* 800-444-8962 ■ *Web:* www.sedonline.com	Tucker	GA	30084	770-491-8962	
SED Systems 18 Innovation Blvd *Web:* www.sedsystems.ca	Saskatoon	SK	S7K3P7	306-931-3425	933-1486
Semi Dice Inc PO Box 3002 *Web:* www.semidice.com	Los Alamitos	CA	90720	562-594-4631	430-5942
SemiProbe Inc 276 E Allen St *Web:* www.semiprobe.com	Winooski	VT	05404	802-860-7000	
Sennheiser Electronics Corp One Enterprise Dr *TF:* 877-736-6434 ■ *Web:* en-us.sennheiser.com	Old Lyme	CT	06371	860-434-9190	434-1759
Sensorlink Corp 1360 Stonegate Way *Web:* www.sensorlink.com	Ferndale	WA	98248	360-595-1000	
Service Electric Supply Inc 15424 Oakwood Dr *Web:* www.servelectric.com	Romulus	MI	48174	734-229-9100	229-9101
Shanor Electric Supply Inc 1276 Military Rd *Web:* www.shanorelectric.com	Kenmore	NY	14217	716-876-0711	876-7375
Shealy Electrical Wholesalers Inc 422 Fairforest Way *Web:* www.shealyelectrical.com	Greenville	SC	29607	864-242-6880	235-6097
Shearer Equipment 7762 Cleveland Rd *Web:* www.shearerequipment.com	Wooster	OH	44691	330-345-9023	345-9348
Shepherd Electric Supply 7401 Pulaski Hwy *TF Sales:* 800 253 1777 ■ *Web:* www.shepherdelec.com	Baltimore	MD	21237	410-866-6000	866-6001
Sierra Electronics 690 E Glendale Ave Ste B *Web:* www.sierraelectronics.com	Sparks	NV	89431	775-359-1121	
Signalink Technologies Inc Units 13 & 14 2550 Acland Rd *Web:* www.signalink.com	Kelowna	BC	V1X7L4	250-491-3883	
Silego Technology Inc 1715 Wyatt Dr *Web:* www.silego.com	Santa Clara	CA	95054	408-327-8800	
Singing Machine Company Inc, The 6601 Lyons Rd Bldg A-7 *OTC: SMDM* ■ *TF:* 866-670-6888 ■ *Web:* www.singingmachine.com	Coconut Creek	FL	33073	954-596-1000	596-2000
Skywalker Communications Inc 9390 Veterans Memorial Pkwy *TF:* 800-844-9555 ■ *Web:* www.skywalker.com	O'Fallon	MO	63366	636-272-8025	272-8214
Skyway Towers LLC 20525 Amberfield Dr Ste 102 *Web:* www.skywaytowers.com	Land O'lakes	FL	34638	813-960-6200	
SMAR International Corp 6001 Stonington St Ste 100 *Web:* www.smar.com	Houston	TX	77040	713-849-2021	849-2022
Sommer Electric Corp 818 Third St NE *TF:* 800-766-6373 ■ *Web:* www.sommerelectric.com	Canton	OH	44704	330-455-9454	455-6561
Sonepar USA 510 Walnut St Ste 400 *Web:* www.sonepar-usa.com	Philadelphia	PA	19106	215-399-5900	
Sound Inc 1550 Shore Rd *Web:* www.soundinc.com	Naperville	IL	60563	630-369-2900	
SOURCE Inc 14060 Proton Rd *Web:* www.source.com	Dallas	TX	75244	972-371-2600	
Sousley Sound & Communications 1005 Tieton Dr *Web:* www.sousley.com	Yakima	WA	98902	509-248-4848	
South Dade Electrical Supply 13100 SW 87th Ave *Web:* www.south-dade.com	Miami	FL	33176	305-238-7131	251-5254
South Western Communications Inc 4871 Rosebud Ln *Web:* www.swc.net	Newburgh	IN	47630	812-477-6495	
Southern Controls Inc 3511 Wetumpka Hwy *TF:* 800-392-5770 ■ *Web:* www.southerncontrols.com	Montgomery	AL	36110	800-392-5770	
Spectra Integrated Systems Inc 8100 Arrowridge Blvd *TF:* 800-443-7561 ■ *Web:* www.sitechma.com	Charlotte	NC	28273	704-525-7099	523-8558
Spectra Merchandising International Inc 4230 N Normandy Ave *TF:* 800-777-5331 ■ *Web:* www.spectraintl.com	Chicago	IL	60634	773-202-8408	202-8409
Springfield Electric Supply Co 700 N Ninth St *TF:* 800-747-2101 ■ *Web:* www.springfieldelectric.com	Springfield	IL	62702	217-788-2100	788-2134
Standard Electric Co 2650 Trautner Dr PO Box 5289 *TF:* 800-322-0215 ■ *Web:* www.standardelectricco.com	Saginaw	MI	48603	989-497-2100	497-2101
Standard Electric Supply Co 222 N Emmber Ln PO Box 651 *TF:* 800-776-8222 ■ *Web:* www.standardelectricsupply.com	Milwaukee	WI	53233	414-272-8100	272-8111
Stanion Wholesale Electric Co 812 S Main St PO Box F *TF:* 866-782-6466 ■ *Web:* www.stanion.com	Pratt	KS	67124	620-672-5678	672-6220
State Electric Supply Company Inc 2010 Second Ave *TF Cust Svc:* 800-624-3417 ■ *Web:* www.stateelectric.com	Huntington	WV	25703	304-523-7491	525-8917
Steiner Electric Co 1250 Touhy Ave *TF:* 800-783-4637 ■ *Web:* www.stnr.com	Elk Grove Village	IL	60007	847-228-0400	228-1352
Stereo Advantage Co 5195 Main St *Web:* www.theadvantage.com	Williamsville	NY	14221	716-204-2340	632-7349
Steven Engineering Inc 230 Ryan Way **Fax Area Code: 888* ■ *TF:* 800-258-9200 ■ *Web:* www.stevenengineering.com	South San Francisco	CA	94080	650-588-9200	258-9200*
Stokes Electric Company Inc 1701 McCalla Ave *TF:* 800-999-0351 ■ *Web:* www.stokeselec.com	Knoxville	TN	37915	865-525-0351	971-4149
Stoneway Electric Supply Co 402 N Perry St *TF:* 800-841-1408 ■ *Web:* www.stoneway.com	Spokane	WA	99202	509-535-2933	534-4512
Storage Battery Systems Inc (SBS) N56 W16665 Ridgewood Dr *TF:* 800-554-2243 ■ *Web:* www.sbsbattery.com	Menomonee Falls	WI	53051	262-703-5800	703-3073
Summit Electric Supply Co 2900 Stanford NE *TF:* 800-824-4400 ■ *Web:* www.summit.com	Albuquerque	NM	87107	505-346-9000	346-1616
Surface Mount Distribution Inc (SMD) 1 Oldfield *TF:* 800-820-7634 ■ *Web:* www.smdinc.com	Irvine	CA	92618	949-470-7700	470-7777
SVT 7699 Lochlin Dr *Web:* www.sportviewtechnologies.com	Brighton	MI	48116	248-437-0041	
Swift Electrical Supply Co 100 Hollister Rd *Web:* www.swiftelectrical.com	Teterboro	NJ	07608	201-462-0900	
SYN-FAB Inc 7863 Schillinger Park Rd *Web:* www.synfab.com	Mobile	AL	36608	251-633-4942	
Syn-Tech Inc 3100 Ridgelake Dr Ste 101 *TF:* 800-535-7619 ■ *Web:* www.syntech-inc.com	Metairie	LA	70002	504-835-7825	835-7853
Tacoma Electric Supply Inc 1311 S Tacoma Way *TF:* 800-422-0540 ■ *Web:* www.tacomaelectric.com	Tacoma	WA	98409	253-475-0540	475-0707
Taitron Components Inc 28040 W Harrison Pkwy *NASDAQ: TAIT* ■ *TF:* 800-247-2232 ■ *Web:* www.taitroncomponents.com	Valencia	CA	91355	661-257-6060	257-6415
Talley Inc 12976 Sandoval St *Web:* www.talleycom.com	Santa Fe Springs	CA	90670	562-906-8000	
TCT Inc 11911 County Rd 125 W *Web:* www.tctinc.com	Odessa	TX	79765	432-561-8449	
TeL Systems 7235 Jackson Rd *TF:* 800-686-7235 ■ *Web.* www.telsystemsusa.com	Ann Arbor	MI	48103	734-761-4506	761-9776
Tele-Communications Inc 5125 W 140th St **Fax Area Code: 330* ■ *TF:* 877-841-8914	Brookpark	OH	44142	216-267-0800	869-8515*
Teleco Inc 430 Woodruff Rd Ste 300 *TF:* 800-800-6159 ■ *Web:* www.teleco.com	Greenville	SC	29607	864-297-4400	297-9983
Telephone Warehouse 1936 E McDowell Rd *Web:* www.telephonewarehouse.com	Phoenix	AZ	85006	602-254-5515	
Telesource Services LLC 1450 Highwood E *TF:* 800-525-4300 ■ *Web:* www.telesourcenet.com	Pontiac	MI	48340	248-335-3000	335-0470
Telmar Technology 901 Jupiter Rd *TF:* 866-835-6276 ■ *Web:* www.telmarnt.com	Plano	TX	75074	972-836-0400	836-0430
Tempest Telecom Solutions LLC 136 W Canon Perdido Ste 100 *Web:* www.tempesttelecom.com	Santa Barbara	CA	93101	805-879-4800	
Terry-Durin Co 409 Seventh Ave SE *TF:* 800-332-8114 ■ *Web:* www.terrydurin.com	Cedar Rapids	IA	52401	319-364-4106	364-2562
Terrycomm 4155 Dow Rd Ste N *Web:* terrycomm.com	Melbourne	FL	32934	321-253-6067	
TESSCO Technologies Inc 11126 McCormick Rd *NASDAQ: TESS* ■ *TF:* 800-472-7373 ■ *Web:* www.tessco.com	Hunt Valley	MD	21031	410-229-1000	527-0005
Thorpe Electric Supply Co 27 Washington St *Web:* www.thorpeelectric.com	Rensselaer	NY	12144	518-462-5496	462-3891
Toa Canada Corp 6150 Kennedy Rd Unit 3 *Web:* www.toacanada.com	Mississauga	ON	L5T2J4	905-564-3570	
Tomba Communications LLC 718 Barataria Blvd *Web:* www.tomba.com	Marrero	LA	70072	504-340-2448	
Total Fire & Safety Inc 7909 Carr St *Web:* www.totalfire.com	Dallas	TX	75227	214-381-6116	381-4633
Transfer Devices Inc 45778 Northport Loop W *Web:* www.transferdevices.com	Fremont	CA	94538	510-445-1060	
Trebor International Inc 8100 South 1300 West *Web:* www.treborintl.com	West Jordan	UT	84088	801-561-0303	
Tredent Data Systems Inc 3241 Grande Vista Dr *Web:* www.tredent.com	Newbury Park	CA	91320	805-375-4911	
Trembly Assoc Inc 119 Quincy St NE *Web:* www.trembly.com	Albuquerque	NM	87108	505-266-8616	255-0635
Tri-Ed Distribution Inc 135 Crossways Pk Dr W *TF:* 888-874-3336 ■ *Web:* www.tri-ed.com	Woodbury	NY	11797	516-941-2800	
Tri-State Armature & Electrical Works Inc 330 GE Patterson PO Box 466 *TF:* 800-238-7654 ■ *Web:* www.tristatearmature.com	Memphis	TN	38126	901-527-8412	521-1065
Tri-State Utility Products Inc 1030 Atlanta Industrial Dr *TF:* 800-282-7985 ■ *Web:* www.tristateutility.com	Marietta	GA	30066	770-427-3119	427-3945
Trident Micro Systems Two Trident Dr *Web:* www.tridentms.com	Arden	NC	28704	828-684-7474	
TTI Inc 2441 NE Pkwy **Fax: Hum Res* ■ *TF Sales:* 800-225-5884 ■ *Web:* www.ttiinc.com	Fort Worth	TX	76106	817-740-9000	740-9898*
TURCK Chartwell Canada Inc 140 Duffield Dr *Web:* chartwell.ca	Markham	ON	L6G1B5	905-513-7100	
Turnkey Technologies Inc 2500 Main St Ext Ste 10 *Web:* www.turn-keytechnologies.com	Sayreville	NJ	08872	732-553-9100	
Turtle & Hughes Inc 1900 Lower Rd *Web:* turtle.com	Linden	NJ	07036	732-574-3600	574-3723
Tystar Corp 7050 Lampson Ave Ste 702 *Web:* www.tystar.com	Garden Grove	CA	92841	310-781-9219	
Unical Enterprises Inc 16960 Gale Ave *Web:* www.unical-usa.com	City Of Industry	CA	91745	626-965-5588	
Unique Communications Inc 3650 Coral Ridge Dr *TF:* 800-881-8182 ■ *Web:* www.uniquecommunications.com	Coral Springs	FL	33065	954-735-4002	735-2612
United Electrical Sales Ltd 4496 36th St *TF:* 800-432-5126 ■ *Web:* www.uesfl.com	Orlando	FL	32811	407-246-1992	246-1588

Company	City	State	ZIP	*Phone*	*Fax*
United Lighting & Supply Co 121 Chestnut Ave SE PO Box 307 *Web:* www.unitedlighting.com	Fort Walton Beach	FL	32548	850-244-8155	244-5629
United Utility Supply Co-op Inc 4515 Bishop Ln *TF:* 800-366-4887 ■ *Web:* www.uus.org	Louisville	KY	40218	502-957-2568	815-6378
Universal Remote Control Inc 500 Mamaroneck Ave *Web:* www.universalremote.com	Harrison	NY	10528	914-835-4484	
Upchurch Electrical Supply Co 2355 N Gregg St PO Box 8340 *Web:* www.upchurchelectrical.com	Fayetteville	AR	72703	479-521-2823	521-6673
Utility Lines Inc 206 W Walnut St *Web:* www.utilitylines.com	Davidson	NC	28036	704-896-8866	896-8868
Valex Corp 6080 Leland St *Web:* www.valex.com	Ventura	CA	93003	805-658-0944	
Valley Electric Supply Corp 1361 N State Rd PO Box 724 *TF:* 800-825-7877 ■ *Web:* www.vesupply.com	Vincennes	IN	47591	812-882-7860	882-7893
Van Meter Industrial Inc 850 32nd Ave SW *TF:* 800-247-1410 ■ *Web:* www.vanmeterinc.com	Cedar Rapids	IA	52404	319-366-5301	366-4709
Venkel Ltd 5900 Shepherd Mtn Cove *TF:* 800-950-8365 ■ *Web:* www.venkel.com	Austin	TX	78730	512-794-0081	794-0087
Versa Electronics 3943 Quebec Ave N *Web:* www.versaelectronics.com	Minneapolis	MN	55427	763-557-6737	557-8073
Viking Electric Supply Inc 451 Industrial Blvd W *TF:* 800-435-3345 ■ *Web:* www.vikingelectric.com	Minneapolis	MN	55413	612-627-1300	627-1313
Virginia West Electric Supply Co (WVES) 250 12-th St W *TF:* 800-624-3433 ■ *Web:* www.wvaelectric.com	Huntington	WV	25704	304-525-0361	525-2726
Voss Lighting PO Box 22159 *TF:* 866-292-0529 ■ *Web:* www.vosslighting.com	Lincoln	NE	68542	402-328-2281	
Vsa Inc 6929 Seward Ave *TF:* 800-888-2140 ■ *Web:* www.vsa1.com	Lincoln	NE	68507	402-467-3668	325-8033
Vyrian Inc 9894 Bissonnet St Ste 918 *Web:* www.vyrian.com	Houston	TX	77036	281-404-3420	
Wabash Electric Supply Inc 1400 S Wabash St *TF:* 800-552-7777 ■ *Web:* www.wabashelectric.com	Wabash	IN	46992	260-563-4146	563-4140
Walters Wholesale Electric Co 2825 Temple Ave *TF:* 800-700-5483 ■ *Web:* www.walterswholesale.com	Signal Hill	CA	90755	562-988-3100	988-3150
Warshauer Electric Supply Co 800 Shrewsbury Ave **Fax:* Sales ■ *Web:* www.warshauer.com	Tinton Falls	NJ	07724	732-741-6400	741-3866*
Weinstock Lamp Company Inc 34-30 Steinway St *Web:* www.weinstocklighting.com	Long Island City	NY	11101	718-729-4848	729-4848
Weldylamont Assoc Inc 1040 W NW Hwy *Web:* www.weldy-lamont.com	Mount Prospect	IL	60056	847-398-4510	398-0597
Werner Electric Supply Co 2341 Industrial Dr *TF:* 800-236-5026 ■ *Web:* www.wernerelectric.com	Neenah	WI	54956	920-729-4500	729-4484
Wes-Garde Components Group Inc 190 Elliott St *TF:* 800-554-8866 ■ *Web:* www.wesgarde.com	Hartford	CT	06114	860-525-6907	527-6047
WESCO Distribution Inc 225 W Stn Sq Dr Ste 700 *Web:* www.wesco.com	Pittsburgh	PA	15219	412-454-2200	454-2505
West-Lite Supply Company Inc 12951 166th St **Fax Area Code:* 562 ■ *TF:* 800-660-6678 ■ *Web:* www.west-lite.com	Cerritos	CA	90703	800-660-6678	802-0154*
Western Electrical Sales Inc (WES) 521 Glide Ave Unit A *Web:* www.wesisales.com	West Sacramento	CA	95691	916-372-1001	372-1172
Western Extralite Co 1470 Liberty St *TF:* 800-279-8833 ■ *Web:* www.westernextralite.com	Kansas City	MO	64102	816-421-8404	421-6211
Wheatstone Corp 600 Industrial Dr *Web:* www.wheatstone.com	New Bern	NC	28562	252-638-7000	
White Radio LP 5228 Everest Dr *Web:* www.whiteradio.com	Mississauga	ON	L4W2R4	905-632-6894	
Whitlock Group 12820 W Creekk Pkwy Ste M *TF:* 800-726-9843 ■ *Web:* www.whitlock.com	Richmond	VA	23238	804-273-9100	273-9380
Wholesale Electric Supply Company LP 4040 Guls Fwy *Web:* www.wholesaleelectric.com	Houston	TX	77004	713-748-6100	749-8415
Wholesale Electric Supply Inc 1400 Waterall St *Web:* www.netwes.com	Texarkana	TX	75501	903-794-3404	794-3400
Wieland Electric Inc (WEI) 49 International Rd *TF:* 800-943-5263 ■ *Web:* www.wielandinc.com	Burgaw	NC	28425	910-259-5050	259-3691
Wild Woods Inc 3575 Cahuenga Blvd W Ste 400 *Web:* www.wwoods.com	Los Angeles	CA	90068	323-878-0400	
Williams Supply Inc 210 Seventh St *TF:* 800-533-6969 ■ *Web:* www.williams-supply.com	Roanoke	VA	24016	540-343-9333	342-3254
Willow Electrical Supply Inc 3828 River Rd *Web:* www.willowelectric.com	Schiller Park	IL	60176	847-801-5010	801-5020
Winncom Technologies Corp 30700 Carter St Ste A *Web:* www.winncom.com	Solon	OH	44139	440-498-9510	498-9511
Wiremasters Inc 1788 N Pt Rd *TF:* 800-635-5342 ■ *Web:* www.wiremasters.net	Columbia	TN	38401	615-791-0281	791-6182
Womack Electric Supply Co 518 Newton St *Web:* www.womackelectric.com	Danville	VA	24541	434-793-5134	792-8256
World Electric Supply Orlando Inc 4501 SW 34th St *Web:* www.worldelectricsupply.com	Orlando	FL	32811	407-447-2000	447-2008
World Micro Components Inc 205 Hembree Park Dr Ste 105 *Web:* www.worldmicro.com	Roswell	GA	30076	770-698-1900	
WorldViz LLC 614 Santa Barbara St *Web:* www.worldviz.com	Santa Barbara	CA	93101	805-966-0786	
WSA Distributing Inc 7222 Opportunity Rd *Web:* www.wsadistributing.com	San Diego	CA	92111	858-560-7800	
WW Grainger Inc 100 Grainger Pkwy *NYSE: GWW* ■ *TF:* 888-361-8649 ■ *Web:* www.grainger.com	Lake Forest	IL	60045	847-535-1000	
Xanga.Com Inc 555 Eigth Ave Ste 21F *Web:* www.xanga.com	New York	NY	10018	212-695-4940	
XP Power 990 Benicia Ave *TF:* 800-253-0490 ■ *Web:* www.xppower.com	Sunnyvale	CA	94085	408-732-7777	732-2002
Yucca Tele Communications Is The Subsidiary 201 W Second St *Web:* www.yucca.net	Portales	NM	88130	575-226-2255	
Zack Electronics Inc 1070 Hamilton Rd *TF:* 800-466-0449 ■ *Web:* www.zackelectronics.com	Duarte	CA	91010	626-303-0655	303-8694

250 ELECTRICAL EQUIPMENT FOR INTERNAL COMBUSTION ENGINES

SEE ALSO Motors (Electric) & Generators p. 2776; Automotive Parts & Supplies - Mfr p. 1839

Company	City	State	ZIP	*Phone*	*Fax*
Altronic Inc 712 Trumbull Ave *Web:* www.altronicinc.com	Girard	OH	44420	330-545-9768	545-9005
American Electronic Components 1101 Lafayette St *TF:* 888-847-6552 ■ *Web:* www.aecsensors.com	Elkhart	IN	46516	574-295-6330	293-8013
Andover Inc PO Box 4848 *Web:* www.andovercoils.com	Lafayette	IN	47903	765-447-1157	447-1150
Autotronic Controls Corp 1490 Henry Brennan Dr *TF:* 800-213-3083 ■ *Web:* www.msdignition.com	El Paso	TX	79936	915-857-5200	857-3344
CE Niehoff & Co 2021 Lee St *TF Tech Supp:* 800-643-4633 ■ *Web:* www.ceniehoff.com	Evanston	IL	60202	847-866-6030	492-1242
CPX Inc 410 Kent St **Fax Area Code:* 317 ■ *Web:* www.cpxinc.com	Kentland	IN	47951	812-718-5335	569-0909*
Edge Products 1080 S Depot Dr *TF:* 888-360-3343 ■ *Web:* www.edgeproducts.com	Ogden	UT	84404	801-476-3343	476-3348
Electricfil Corp (EFI) 11880 Belden Ct *Web:* www.electricfil.com	Livonia	MI	48150	734-425-2774	425-3669
EMB Corp 1203 Hawkins Dr *Web:* www.embcorp.com	Elizabethtown	KY	42701	270-737-1996	737-1909
ETCO Inc Automotive Products Div 3004 62nd Ave E *TF:* 800-689-3826 ■ *Web:* www.etco.com	Bradenton	FL	34203	941-756-8426	758-7195
Fargo Assembly of Pennsylvania Inc 800 W Washington St PO Box 550 *Web:* www.fargopa.com	Norristown	PA	19404	610-272-6850	272-6858
Fisher Electric Technology 2801 72nd St N *Web:* www.fisherelectric.com	Saint Petersburg	FL	33710	727-345-9122	345-2904
Flight Systems Inc 505 Fishing Creek Rd *TF:* 800-403-3728 ■ *Web:* www.flightsystems.com	Lewisberry	PA	17339	717-932-9900	932-9925
Goodall Manufacturing Co 7558 Washington Ave S *TF:* 800-328-7730 ■ *Web:* www.goodallmfg.com	Eden Prairie	MN	55344	952-941-6666	941-2617
Hitachi Automotive Systems Americas Inc 955 Warwick Rd *Web:* www.hap.com	Harrodsburg	KY	40330	859-734-9451	734-5309
Ignition Systems & Controls LP 6300 W Hwy 80 *TF:* 800-777-5559 ■ *Web:* www.ignition-systems.com	Midland	TX	79706	432-697-6472	697-0563
Interconnect Wiring Harnesses Inc 5024 W Vickery Blvd *Web:* www.interconnect-wiring.com	Fort Worth	TX	76107	817-377-9473	732-8667
Kelly Aerospace 1404 E S Blvd *Web:* www.kellyaerospace.com	Montgomery	AL	36116	334-286-8551	227-8596
KRA International LLC 1810 Clover Rd *Web:* www.krainternational.com	Mishawaka	IN	46545	574-259-3550	255-1079
M & G Electronics Corp 889 Seahawk Cir *Web:* www.mgelectronic.com	Virginia Beach	VA	23452	757-468-6000	468-5442
Mitsubishi Electric Automotive America Inc 4773 Bethany Rd *Web:* www.meaa-mea.com	Mason	OH	45040	513-398-2220	398-1121
Motorcar Parts & Accessories 2929 California St *TF:* 800-890-9988 ■ *Web:* www.motorcarparts.com	Torrance	CA	90503	310-212-7910	212-7581
NGK Spark Plugs Inc 46929 Magellan *TF:* 877-473-6767 ■ *Web:* www.ngksparkplugs.com	Wixom	MI	48393	248-926-6900	926-6910
Precision Parts & Remanufacturing Co 4411 SW 19th St *TF:* 800-654-3846 ■ *Web:* www.pprok.com	Oklahoma City	OK	73108	405-681-2592	681-2596
Prestolite Wire Corp 200 Galleria Officentre Ste 212 *TF:* 800-498-3132 ■ *Web:* www.prestolitewire.com	Southfield	MI	48034	248-355-4422	386-4462
Prettl Electric Corp 1721 White Horse Rd *Web:* www.prettl.com	Greenville	SC	29605	864-220-1010	220-1020
RE Phelon Company Inc 2063 University Pkwy *Web:* fenix-mfg.com/	Aiken	SC	29801	803-649-1381	648-7309
Remy International Inc 600 Corp Dr *NYSE: REMY* ■ *TF:* 800-372-3555 ■ *Web:* www.remyinc.com	Pendleton	IN	46064	765-778-6499	
Standard Motor Products Inc 37-18 Northern Blvd *NYSE: SMP* ■ *Web:* www.smpcorp.com	Long Island City	NY	11101	718-392-0200	729-4549
Syncro Corp PO Box 890 *Web:* www.syncrocorp.com	Arab	AL	35016	256-931-7800	931-7920
Transpo Electronics Inc 2150 Brengle Ave **Fax Area Code:* 407 ■ *TF:* 800-327-6903 ■ *Web:* www.waiglobal.com	Orlando	FL	32808	800-327-6903	298-4519*
Van Bergen & Greener Inc 1818 Madison St *TF:* 800-621-3889 ■ *Web:* www.starterdrives.com	Maywood	IL	60153	708-343-4700	343-9425

251 ELECTRICAL SIGNALS MEASURING & TESTING INSTRUMENTS

Company	City	State	ZIP	Phone	Fax
3M Telecommunications Div 6801 River Pl Blvd *TF:* 800-426-8688 ■ *Web:* 3m.com/	Austin	TX	78726	800-426-8688	626-0329
Aeroflex 400 New Century Pkwy **Fax:* Cust Svc ■ *TF:* 800-843-1553 ■ *Web:* www.aeroflex.com	New Century	KS	66031	913-764-2452	782-5104*
Aetrium Inc 2350 Helen St *Web:* www.aetrium.com	North Saint Paul	MN	55109	651-770-2000	770-7975
Allied Motion Technologies Inc 495 Commerce Dr Ste 3 *NASDAQ: AMOT* ■ **Fax Area Code:* 303 ■ *TF:* 888-392-5543 ■ *Web:* www.alliedmotion.com	Amherst	NY	14228	716-242-8634	799-8521*
Analog Devices Inc Three Technology Way *NASDAQ: ADI* ■ *TF:* 800-262-5643 ■ *Web:* www.analog.com	Norwood	MA	02062	781-329-4700	461-3113
Anritsu Co 490 Jarvis Dr *TF:* 800-267-4878 ■ *Web:* globalmap.anritsu.com	Morgan Hill	CA	95037	408-778-2000	776-1744
Associated Equipment Corp 5043 Farlan Ave *TF:* 800-949-1472 ■ *Web:* associatedequip.com	Saint Louis	MO	63115	314-385-5178	385-3254
Beede Electrical Instrument Co 88 Village St *Web:* www.beede.com	Penacook	NH	03303	603-753-6362	753-6201
BEI Precision Systems & Space Company Inc 1100 Murphy Dr *Web:* www.beiprecision.com	Maumelle	AR	72113	501-851-4000	851-5452
BI Technologies Corp 4200 Bonita Pl *Web:* www.bitechnologies.com	Fullerton	CA	92835	714-447-2300	447-2745
Bird Electronic Corp 30303 Aurora Rd *TF:* 866-695-4569 ■ *Web:* birdrf.com	Solon	OH	44139	440-248-1200	248-5426
Bird Technologies Group Inc 30303 Aurora Rd *TF:* 866-695-4569 ■ *Web:* birdrf.com	Solon	OH	44139	440-248-1200	248-5426
Bruel & Kjaer Instruments Inc 2815 Colonnades Ct Ste A *TF:* 800-332-2040 ■ *Web:* www.bkhome.com	Norcross	GA	30071	770-209-6907	448-3246
Cascade Microtech Inc 2430 NW 206th Ave *NASDAQ: CSCD* ■ *TF:* 800-854-8400 ■ *Web:* www.cmicro.com	Beaverton	OR	97006	503-601-1000	601-1010
Chatsworth Data Corp 9735 Lurline Ave **Fax Area Code:* 877 ■ *TF:* 877-380-6855 ■ *Web:* www.chatsworthdata.com	Chatsworth	CA	91311	818-350-5072	380-6855*
Cohu Inc 12367 Crosthwaite Cir *NASDAQ: COHU* ■ *TF:* 800-685-5050 ■ *Web:* www.cohu.com	Poway	CA	92064	858-848-8100	848-8185
Communications Manufacturing Co (CMC) 2234 Colby Ave *TF Orders:* 800-462-5532 ■ *Web:* www.gotocmc.com	Los Angeles	CA	90064	310-828-3200	
Curtis Instruments Inc 200 Kisco Ave *TF:* 800-777-3433 ■ *Web:* www.curtisinstruments.com	Mount Kisco	NY	10549	914-666-2971	666-2971
CXR Larus Corp 894 Faulstich Ct *TF:* 800-999-9946 ■ *Web:* www.cxr.com	San Jose	CA	95112	408-573-2700	
CyberOptics Corp 5900 Golden Hills Dr *NASDAQ: CYBE* ■ *TF Cust Svc:* 800-746-6315 ■ *Web:* www.cyberoptics.com	Minneapolis	MN	55416	763-542-5000	542-5100
Delta Design Inc 12367 Crosthwaite Cir **Fax:* Sales ■ *TF:* 877-660-6853 ■ *Web:* cohuseg.com/	Poway	CA	92064	858-848-8000	848-8180*
Desco Industries Inc 3651 Walnut Ave *Web:* desco.descoindustries.com	Chino	CA	91710	909-627-8178	627-7449
DIT-MCO International Corp 5612 Brighton Terr *TF:* 800-821-3487 ■ *Web:* www.ditmco.com	Kansas City	MO	64130	816-444-9700	444-6843
Doble Engineering Co Inc 85 Walnut St *TF:* 800-759-5219 ■ *Web:* www.doble.com	Watertown	MA	02472	617-926-4900	926-0528
Dranetz-BMI 1000 New Durham Rd *TF:* 800-372-6832 ■ *Web:* www.dranetz.com	Edison	NJ	08818	732-287-3680	248-1834
DRS Test & Energy Management Inc 110 Wynn Dr *Web:* www.drs-tem.com	Huntsville	AL	35805	256-895-2000	895-2356
EADS North American Defense Test & Services Inc 4 Goodyear **Fax:* Sales ■ *TF Cust Svc:* 800-722-2528	Irvine	CA	92618	949-859-8999	*
EDAC Technologies Corp 1806 New Britain Ave *NASDAQ: EDAC* ■ *Web:* www.edactechnologies.com	Farmington	CT	06032	860-678-8140	674-2718
Electro-Metrics Corp 231 Enterprise Rd *Web:* www.electro-metrics.com	Johnstown	NY	12095	518-762-2600	762-2812
Everett Charles Technologies (ECT) 700 E Harrison Ave *Web:* www.ectinfo.com	Pomona	CA	91767	909-625-5551	624-9746
Everett Charles Technologies Inc Test Equipment Div 700 E Harrison Ave *Web:* www.ectinfo.com	Pomona	CA	91767	909-625-5551	624-9746
EXFO Inc 400 Godin Ave *NASDAQ: EXFO* ■ *TF:* 800-663-3936 ■ *Web:* www.exfo.com	Quebec	QC	G1M2K2	418-683-0211	683-2170
Fluke Biomedical 6920 Seaway Blvd *TF:* 800-443-5853 ■ *Web:* www.flukebiomedical.com	Everett	WA	98203	425-446-6945	446-5629
Fluke Corp 6920 Seaway Blvd *TF:* 877-355-3225 ■ *Web:* www.fluke.com	Everett	WA	98203	425-446-6100	446-5116
Fluke Networks Inc 6920 Seaway Blvd *TF:* 800-283-5853 ■ *Web:* www.flukenetworks.com	Everett	WA	98203	425-446-4519	446-5043
Frequency Electronics Inc 55 Charles Lindbergh Blvd *NASDAQ: FEIM* ■ *Web:* www.freqelec.com	Uniondale	NY	11553	516-794-4500	794-4340
Giga-Tronics Inc 4650 Norris Canyon Rd *NASDAQ: GIGA* ■ *TF:* 800-726-4442 ■ *Web:* www.gigatronics.com	San Ramon	CA	94583	925-328-4650	328-4700
Gleason M & M Precision Systems Corp 300 Progress Rd *TF:* 800-727-6333 ■ *Web:* www.gleason.com	Dayton	OH	45449	937-859-8273	859-4452
Gold Line Connector Inc PO Box 500 *Web:* www.gold-line.com	West Redding	CT	06896	203-938-2588	938-8740
Greenlee Textron 1390 Aspen Way *TF:* 800-642-2155 ■ *Web:* greenlee.com	Vista	CA	92081	760-598-8900	598-5634
Hickok Inc 10514 Dupont Ave *OTC: HICKA* ■ *TF:* 800-342-5080 ■ *Web:* www.hickok-inc.com	Cleveland	OH	44108	216-541-8060	761-9879
Hipotronics Inc 1650 Rt 22 PO Box 414 *Web:* www.hipotronics.com	Brewster	NY	10509	845-279-8091	279-2467
Hughes Corp Weschler Instruments Div 16900 Foltz Pkwy *TF:* 800-557-0064 ■ *Web:* www.weschler.com	Cleveland	OH	44149	440-238-2550	238-0660
ILX Lightwave Corp 31950 E Frontage Rd *TF:* 800-459-9459 ■ *Web:* www.newport.com	Bozeman	MT	59715	406-586-1244	586-9405
IMPulse NC Inc 100 IMPulse Way *Web:* www.impulsenc.com	Mount Olive	NC	28365	919-658-2200	658-2268
ISEC Inc 33 Inverness Dr *Web:* www.isecinc.com	Englewood	CO	80112	303-790-1444	
Itron Inc 2111 N Molter Rd *NASDAQ: ITRI* ■ *TF:* 800-635-5461 ■ *Web:* www.itron.com	Liberty Lake	WA	99019	509-924-9900	891-3355
Ixia 26601 W Agoura Rd *NASDAQ: XXIA* ■ *TF:* 877-367-4942 ■ *Web:* www.ixiacom.com	Calabasas	CA	91302	818-871-1800	871-1805
Keithley Instruments Inc 28775 Aurora Rd *TF:* 800-552-1115 ■ *Web:* www.keithley.com	Cleveland	OH	44139	440-248-0400	248-6168
KLA-Tencor Corp One Technology Dr *NASDAQ: KLAC* ■ *TF:* 800-600-2829 ■ *Web:* www.kla-tencor.com	Milpitas	CA	95035	408-875-3000	875-4144
Knopp Inc 1307 66th St *TF:* 800-227-1848 ■ *Web:* www.knoppinc.com	Emeryville	CA	94608	510-653-1661	653-2202
Kuka Assembly & Test 5675 Dixie Hwy *Web:* www.kukaat.com	Saginaw	MI	48601	989-777-2111	777-5620
L-3 Electrodynamics Inc 1200 Hicks Rd *Web:* www.l-3com.com/edi	Rolling Meadows	IL	60008	847-660-1750	660-1751
Landis Gyr Inc 2800 Duncan Rd *TF:* 888-390-5733 ■ *Web:* www.landisgyr.com	Lafayette	IN	47904	765-742-1001	742-0936
LeCroy Corp 700 Chestnut Ridge Rd *NASDAQ: LCRY* ■ *TF:* 800-553-2769 ■ *Web:* teledynelecroy.com	Chestnut Ridge	NY	10977	845-425-2000	425-8967
LTS Corp 7250 Woodmont Ave Ste 340 *Web:* www.ltscorporation.com	Bethesda	MD	20814	301-652-2121	951-9624
Megger 4271 Bronze Way *TF:* 800-723-2861 ■ *Web:* www.megger.com	Dallas	TX	75237	214-333-3201	331-7399
Micro Control Co 7956 Main St NE *TF:* 800-328-9923 ■ *Web:* www.microcontrol.com	Minneapolis	MN	55432	763-786-8750	786-6543
Monroe Electronics Inc 100 Housel Ave *TF:* 800-821-6001 ■ *Web:* www.monroe-electronics.com	Lyndonville	NY	14098	585-765-2254	765-9330
Nartron Corp 5000 N US 131 *Web:* www.nartron.com	Reed City	MI	49677	231-832-5525	832-3876
National Instruments Corp 11500 N Mopac Expy *NASDAQ: NATI* ■ *TF Cust Svc:* 800-433-3488 ■ *Web:* www.ni.com	Austin	TX	78759	512-794-0100	683-8411
Newport Electronics Inc 2229 S Yale St *TF Cust Svc:* 800-639-7678 ■ *Web:* www.newportinc.com	Santa Ana	CA	92704	714-540-4914	546-3022
NH Research Inc 16601 Hale Ave *Web:* www.nhresearch.com	Irvine	CA	92606	949-474-3900	474-7062
PerkinElmer Inc 940 Winter St *NYSE: PKI* ■ *Web:* www.perkinelmer.com	Waltham	MA	02451	203-925-4602	944-4904
Phase Matrix Inc 109 Bonaventura Dr *TF:* 877-447-2736 ■ *Web:* www.phasematrix.net	San Jose	CA	95134	408-428-1000	428-1500
Phenix Technologies Inc 75 Speicher Dr *Web:* www.phenixtech.com	Accident	MD	21520	301-746-8118	895-5570
Precision Flow Technologies Inc PO Box 149 *Web:* www.precisionflowtechnologies.com	Saugerties	NY	12477	845-247-0810	247-8764
Prime Technology LLC 344-352 Twin Lakes Rd PO Box 185 *Web:* www.primetechnology.com	North Branford	CT	06471	203-481-5721	481-8937
Prominent Fluid Controls Inc 136 Industry Dr *Web:* www.prominent.us	Pittsburgh	PA	15275	412-787-2484	787-0704
Radiodetection Corp 154 Portland Rd *TF:* 877-247-3797 ■ *Web:* spx.com/en/radiodetection/	Bridgton	ME	04009	207-647-9495	647-9496
Rodale Electronics Inc 20 Oser Ave *Web:* www.rodaleelectronics.com	Hauppauge	NY	11788	631-231-0044	231-1345
Schlumberger Ltd 5599 San Felipe Ste 100 *NYSE: SLB* ■ *Web:* www.slb.com	Houston	TX	77056	713-513-2000	513-2006
Schweitzer E O Mfg Company Inc 450 Enterprise Pkwy *TF:* 888-870-7350 ■ *Web:* www.eosmfg.com	Lake Zurich	IL	60047	847-362-8304	362-8396
Sencore Inc 3200 W Sencore Dr *Web:* www.sencore.com	Sioux Falls	SD	57107	605-339-0100	335-6379
Simpson Electric Co 520 Simpson Ave *Web:* www.simpsonelectric.com	Lac Du Flambeau	WI	54538	715-588-3311	588-1248
Snap-on Diagnostics 420 Barclay Blvd *TF:* 800-424-7226 ■ *Web:* www1.snapon.com	Lincolnshire	IL	60069	847-478-0700	
TEGAM Inc 10 Tegam Way *TF:* 800-666-1010 ■ *Web:* www.tegam.com	Geneva	OH	44041	440-466-6100	466-6110
Teradyne Inc 600 Riverpark Dr *NYSE: TER* ■ *Web:* www.teradyne.com	North Reading	MA	01864	978-370-2700	
Teradyne Inc Assembly Test Div 600 Riverpark Dr *Web:* teradyne.com	North Reading	MA	01864	978-370-2700	
Teradyne Inc Industrial/Consumer Div 600 Riverpark Dr *Web:* teradyne.com	North Reading	MA	01864	978-370-2700	
Teradyne Inc Semiconductor Test Div 600 Riverpark Dr *Web:* www.teradyne.com/std	North Reading	MA	01864	978-370-2700	370-8630
Test Electronics 821 Smith Rd *Web:* www.testelectronics.com	Watsonville	CA	95076	831-763-2000	763-2085
Trek Inc 11601 Maple Ridge Rd **Fax:* Sales ■ *TF:* 800-367-8735 ■ *Web:* www.trekinc.com	Medina	NY	14103	585-798-3140	798-3106*
Trilithic Inc 9710 Pk Davis Dr *TF:* 800-344-2412 ■ *Web:* www.trilithic.com	Indianapolis	IN	46235	317-895-3600	423-7604
Trio-Tech International 14731 Califa St *NYSE: TRT* ■ *Web:* www.triotech.com	Van Nuys	CA	91411	818-787-7000	787-9130
Tyco Electronics Corp Corcom Div 620 S Butterfield Rd *Web:* www.corcom.com	Mundelein	IL	60060	847-680-7400	680-8169
Wems Electronics Inc 4650 W Rosecrans Ave *Web:* www.wems.com	Hawthorne	CA	90250	310-644-0251	644-5334

Phone Fax

Wireless Telecom Group Inc 25 Eastmans Rd ...... Parsippany NJ 07054 973-386-9696 386-9191
NYSE: WTT ■ *Web:* www.wirelesstelecomgroup.com
Xcerra Corporation 1355 California Cir .... Milpitas CA 95035 408-635-4300 635-4985
NASDAQ: XCRA ■ *TF:* 800-451-2400 ■ *Web:* www.ltxc.com
Yokogawa Corp of America
12530 W Airport Blvd.......................... Sugar Land TX 77478 281-340-3800 340-3838
TF: 800-888-6400 ■ *Web:* www.yokogawa.com/us
Zetec Inc 8226 Bracken Pl SE Ste 100 .... Snoqualmie WA 98065 425-974-2700 974-2701
TF: 800-643-1771 ■ *Web:* www.zetec.com

252 ELECTRICAL SUPPLIES - PORCELAIN

Phone Fax

American Technical Ceramics Corp
One Norden Ln .... Huntington Station NY 11746 631-622-4700 622-4748
Web: www.atceramics.com
Associated Ceramics & Technology Inc
400 N Pike Rd.................................... Sarver PA 16055 724-353-1585 353-1050
Web: www.associatedceramics.com
Ceradyne Inc 3169 Redhill Ave .... Costa Mesa CA 92626 714-549-0421 549-5787*
NYSE: MMM ■ **Fax:* Sales ■ *TF:* 877-992-7749 ■ *Web:* solutions.3m.com/
CeramTec North America Corp Technology Pl......... Laurens SC 29360 864-682-3215 682-1140
Web: www.ceramtec.com
CoorsTek Inc 600 Ninth St.......................... Golden CO 80401 303-278-4000 271-7009
TF: 800-821-6110 ■ *Web:* www.coorstek.com
CPS Technologies Corp 111 S Worcester St............ Norton MA 02766 508-222-0614 222-0220
OTC: CPSH ■ *Web:* www.alsic.com
Du-Co Ceramics Co
155 S Rebecca St PO Box 568 .... Saxonburg PA 16056 724-352-1511 352-1266
Web: www.du-co.com
Electrical Distributors Co
1135 Auzerais Ave .... San Jose CA 95126 408-293-5818 287-1152
Web: www.electdist.com
Fair-Rite Products Corp
One Commerical Row PO Box J .... Wallkill NY 12589 845-895-2055 895-2629
TF: 888-324-7748 ■ *Web:* www.fair-rite.com
Ferronics Inc 45 O'Connor Rd .... Fairport NY 14450 585-388-1020 388-0036
Web: www.ferronics.com
Hadron Technologies Inc 4941 Allison St Ste 15 .... Arvada CO 80002 303-431-7798 431-6168
Web: www.hadrontechnologies.com
International Ceramic Engineering
235 Brooks St.................................. Worcester MA 01606 508-853-4700 852-4101
TF: 800-779-3321 ■ *Web:* www.intlceramics.com
Kyocera Industrial Ceramics Corp
5713 E Fourth Plain Rd........................... Vancouver WA 98661 360-696-8950 696-9804
TF: 800-826-0527 ■ *Web:* americas.kyocera.com
LAPP Insulator Co 130 Gilbert St..................... Le Roy NY 14482 585-768-6221 768-6219*
**Fax:* Cust Svc ■ *Web:* www.lappinsulators.com
Maryland Ceramic & Steatite Company Inc
PO Box 527 .... Bel Air MD 21014 410-838-4114 457-4333
Web: www.marylandceramic.com
Medler Eelectric Company Inc 2155 Redman Dr......... Alma MI 48801 800-229-5740 463-4522*
**Fax Area Code:* 989 ■ *TF:* 800-229-5740 ■ *Web:* www.medlerelectric.com
Nu-Tec Tooling Company Inc
13115 State Rt 405.............................. Watsontown PA 17777 570-538-2571
Web: www.nutectool.com
Paramont EO Inc 1000 Davey Rd Ste 100........... Woodridge IL 60517 708-345-0000 345-0816
Web: www.paramont-eo.com
Power & Composite Technologies LLC (PCT)
200 Wallins Corners Rd .... Amsterdam NY 12010 518-843-6825 843-6723
Web: www.pactinc.com
Revere Electric Supply Co
2501 W Washington Blvd .... Chicago IL 60612 312-738-3636 738-2725
Web: www.revereelectric.com
Saint-Gobain Advanced Ceramics Latrobe
4702 Rt 982 .... Latrobe PA 15650 724-539-6000 539-6070
TF: 800-438-7237 ■ *Web:* www.wrt.saint-gobain.com
Sunbelt Transfomer Ltd
1922 S Martin Luther King Jr Dr..................... Temple TX 76504 254-771-3777 771-5719
TF: 800-433-3128 ■ *Web:* www.sunbeltusa.com
Superior Technical Ceramics Corp
600 Industrial Pk Rd.......................... Saint Albans VT 05478 802-527-7726 527-1181
Web: www.ceramics.net
Trans-Tech Inc 5520 Adamstown Rd............... Adamstown MD 21710 301-695-9400 695-7065
Web: www.trans-techinc.com
Victor Insulators Inc 280 Maple Ave .... Victor NY 14564 585-924-2127 924-7906
Web: www.victorinsulators.com

253 ELECTROMEDICAL & ELECTROTHERAPEUTIC EQUIPMENT

SEE ALSO Medical Instruments & Apparatus - Mfr p. 2729

Phone Fax

ABIOMED Inc 22 Cherry Hill Dr .... Danvers MA 01923 978-777-5410 777-8411
NASDAQ: ABMD ■ *TF:* 800-422-8666 ■ *Web:* www.abiomed.com
Adaptive Switch Laboratories Inc
125 Spur 191 Ste C .... Spicewood TX 78669 830-798-0005
Web: www.asl-inc.com
Affymetrix Inc 3420 Central Expy .... Santa Clara CA 95051 408-731-5000 731-5380
NASDAQ: AFFX ■ *TF:* 888-362-2447 ■ *Web:* www.affymetrix.com
Alere Medical Inc 51 Sawyer Rd Ste 200 .... Waltham MA 02453 781-647-3900
Web: www.alere.com
ALR Technologies Inc
7400 Beaufont Springs Dr Ste 300................. Richmond VA 23225 804-554-3500
Web: www.alrt.com
ALung Technologies Inc 2500 Jane St Ste 1 .... Pittsburgh PA 15203 412-697-3370
Web: www.alung.com
Amedica Corp 1885 West 2100 South .... Salt Lake City UT 84119 801-839-3500
Web: www.amedicacorp.com
Arobella Medical LLC 5929 Baker Rd Ste 470 .... Minnetonka MN 55345 952-345-6840
Web: www.advcircuit.com

Phone Fax

Arrhythmia Research Technology Inc
25 Sawyer Passway .... Fitchburg MA 01420 978-345-0181 342-0168
AMEX: HRT ■ *Web:* www.arthrt.com
Artel 25 Bradley Dr.............................. Westbrook ME 04092 207-854-0860
Web: www.artel-usa.com
Astro-Med Inc 600 E Greenwich Ave .... West Warwick RI 02893 401-828-4000 822-2430
NASDAQ: ALOT ■ *TF:* 800-343-4039 ■ *Web:* www.astro-medinc.com
AutoMedx Inc 12321 Middlebrook Rd Ste 150 ...... Germantown MD 20874 301-916-9508
Web: www.automedx.biz
Avancen MOD Corp
1156 Bowman Rd Ste 200 .... Mount Pleasant SC 29464 800-607-1230
TF: 800-607-1230 ■ *Web:* www.avancen.com
Axiobionics 6111 Jackson Rd Ste 200............... Ann Arbor MI 48103 734-327-2946
Web: www.axiobionics.com
Beacon Medaes 1800 Overview Dr .... Rock Hill SC 29730 803-817-5600 817-5750
Web: www.beaconmedaes.com
Bio Medical Innovations 814 Airport Way .... Sandpoint ID 83864 800-201-3958
TF: 800-201-3958 ■ *Web:* www.leadlok.com
BioForce Nanosciences
1615 Golden Aspen Dr Ste 101 .... Ames IA 50010 515-233-8333 231-5022*
**Fax Area Code:* 540 ■ *Web:* www.bioforcenano.com
Bovie Medical Corp
734 Walt Whitman Rd Ste 207 .... Melville NY 11747 631-421-5452 421-5821
NYSE: BVX ■ *TF:* 800-888-4999 ■ *Web:* www.boviemedical.com
BSD Medical Corp (BSDM)
2188 West 2200 South....................... Salt Lake City UT 84119 801-972-5555 972-5930
NASDAQ: BSDM
BTE Technologies Inc 7455-L New Ridge Rd .... Hanover MD 21076 410-850-0333
Web: www.btetech.com
Camag Scientific Inc
515 Cornelius Harnett Dr .... Wilmington NC 28401 910-343-1830
Web: www.camagusa.com
Cardiac Science Corp 3303 Monte Villa Pkwy........... Bothell WA 98021 425-402-2000 402-2001*
**Fax:* Cust Svc ■ *TF Cust Svc:* 800-426-0337 ■ *Web:* www.cardiacscience.com
Cardiogenesis Corp 11 Musick .... Irvine CA 92618 949-420-1800
Web: www.cardiogenesis.com
Care Fusion 1100 Bird Ctr Dr .... Palm Springs CA 92262 760-778-7200
Web: www.viasyshealthcare.com
CAS Medical Systems Inc 44 E Industrial Rd.......... Branford CT 06405 203-488-6056 488-9438
NASDAQ: CASM ■ *TF:* 800-227-4414 ■ *Web:* www.casmed.com
CNS Response Inc 85 Enterprise Ste 410.............Aliso Viejo CA 92656 949-420-4400
Web: www.cnsresponse.com
Conmed Corp 525 French Rd .... Utica NY 13502 315-797-8375 438-3051*
NASDAQ: CNMD ■ **Fax Area Code:* 800 ■ **Fax:* Cust Svc ■ *TF:* 800-448-6506 ■ *Web:* www.conmed.com
Cook Medical Inc 1186 Montgomery Ln............ Vandergrift PA 15690 724-845-8621 845-2848
TF General: 800-245-4715 ■ *Web:* www.cookmedical.com
COSMED USA Inc 2211 N Elston Ave Ste 305 .... Chicago IL 60614 773-645-8113
Web: www.cosmed.it
Criticare Systems Inc N7W22025 Johnson Dr .... Waukesha WI 53186 262-798-8282 798-8290
TF: 800-458-4615 ■ *Web:* www.csiusa.com
CVAC Systems Inc 43397 Business Park Dr D2.......... Temecula CA 92590 951-699-2086
Web: www.cvacsystems.com
Cytosorbents Corp
Seven Deer Park Dr Ste K................ Monmouth Junction NJ 08852 732-329-8885
Web: www.cytosorbents.com
Delsys Inc 650 Beacon St Fl 6.......................... Boston MA 02215 617-236-0599
Web: www.delsys.com
Draeger Medical Inc 3135 Quarry Rd.................. Telford PA 18969 800-437-2437 723-5935*
**Fax Area Code:* 215 ■ *TF:* 800-437-2437 ■ *Web:* www.draeger.com
Dynatronics Corp 7030 Pk Centre Dr .... Salt Lake City UT 84121 801-568-7000 221-1919*
NASDAQ: DYNT ■ **Fax Area Code:* 800 ■ *TF:* 800-874-6251 ■ *Web:* www.dynatronics.com
EBR Systems Inc 686 W Maude Ave Ste 102 .... Sunnyvale CA 94085 408-720-1906
Web: www.ebrsystems.com
Eigen Video 13366 Grass Vly Ave Ste A............. Grass Valley CA 95945 530-274-1240
Web: www.eigen.com
Fisher & Paykel Healthcare Inc
15365 Barranca Pkwy................................ Irvine CA 92618 949-453-4000 453-4001
TF: 800-446-3908 ■ *Web:* www.fphcare.co.nz
Flowmetrics Inc 9201 Independence Ave........... Chatsworth CA 91311 818-407-3420
Web: flowmetrics.com
Futrex Inc 130 Western Maryland Pkwy .... Hagerstown MD 21740 301-733-9368
Web: www.futrex.com
Gambro Renal Products 14143 Denver W Pkwy ...... Lakewood CO 80401 303-232-6800 222-6810
TF: 800-525-2623 ■ *Web:* www.gambro.com
GE Healthcare Information Technologies
8200 W Tower Ave .... Milwaukee WI 53223 414-355-5000
TF: 800-558-5102 ■ *Web:* gehealthcare.com
GN ReSound North America
8001 E Bloomington Fwy .... Bloomington MN 55420 888-735-4327
TF: 888-735-4327 ■ *Web:* www.gnresound.com
Hansen Medical Inc
800 E Middlefield Rd .... Mountain View CA 94043 650-404-5800
Web: hansenmedical.com
HealthTronics Inc 9825 Spectrum Dr Bldg 3 .... Austin TX 78717 512-328-2892 439-8303
TF: 888-252-6575 ■ *Web:* www.healthtronics.com
HeartWare Inc
4750 Wiley Post Way Ste 120............... Salt Lake City UT 84116 801-355-6255 355-7622
NASDAQ: WHRT ■ *Web:* heartware.com
Higgins Supply Company Inc 18-23 S St .... Mcgraw NY 13101 607-836-6474 836-6913
Web: www.higginssupply.com
Hillenbrand Industries Inc
One Batesville Blvd.............................. Batesville IN 47006 812-934-7500 934-7613
NYSE: HI ■ *Web:* www.hillenbrand.com
Honeywell HomMed LLC
3400 Intertech Dr Ste 200......................... Brookfield WI 53045 262-783-5440
Web: www.hommed.com
Impact Instrumentation Inc
27 Fairfield Pl.............................. West Caldwell NJ 07006 973-882-1212
Web: www.impactinstrumentation.com
Imperium Inc 5901-F Ammendale Rd .... Beltsville MD 20705 301-431-2900
Web: www.imperiuminc.com

				Phone	Fax
Inovio Pharmaceuticals Inc 1787 Sentry PkwyW Bldg 18 . . . . . Blue Bell *NASDAQ: INOVIO* ■ *TF:* 877-446-6846 ■ *Web:* www.inovio.com	PA	19422		267-440-4200	
Invivo Therapeutics Holdings Corp One Kendall Sq Ste B14402 . . . . . Cambridge *Web:* www.invivotherapeutics.com	MA	02139		617-863-5500	
IVY Biomedical Systems Inc 11 Business Pk Dr . . . . . Branford *TF:* 800-247-4614 ■ *Web:* www.ivybiomedical.com	CT	06405		203-481-4183	481-8734
Kelyniam Global Inc 97 River Rd . . . . . Canton *TF:* 800-280-8192 ■ *Web:* www.kelyniam.com	CT	06019		800-280-8192	
Lifeline Scientific Inc One Pierce Pl Ste 475W . . . . . Itasca *Web:* lifeline-scientific.com	IL	60143		847-294-0300	
LiteCure LLC 250 Corporate Blvd Ste B . . . . . Newark *Web:* www.litecure.com	DE	19702		302-709-0408	
MAQUET Cardiac Assist 15 Law Dr . . . . . Fairfield *TF:* 800-777-4222 ■ *Web:* ca.maquet.com	NJ	07004		973-244-6100	
Masimo Corp 40 Parker . . . . . Irvine *TF:* 800-326-4890 ■ *Web:* www.masimo.com	CA	92618		949-297-7000	297-7001
Medical Education Technologies Inc (METI) 6300 Edgelake Dr . . . . . Sarasota *TF:* 866-462-7920 ■ *Web:* www.caehealthcare.com	FL	34240		941-377-5562	377-5590
Medical Graphics Corp 350 Oak Grove Pkwy. . . . . Saint Paul *NASDAQ: ANGN* ■ *TF:* 800-950-5597 ■ *Web:* mgcdiagnostics.com	MN	55127		651-484-4874	379-8227
Medtronic Inc 710 Medtronic Pkwy NE. . . . . Minneapolis *NYSE: MDT* ■ *TF Cust Svc:* 800-328-2518 ■ *Web:* www.medtronic.com	MN	55432		763-514-4000	514-4879
Medtronic of Canada Ltd 6733 Kitimat Rd . . . . . Mississauga *TF:* 800-268-5346 ■ *Web:* www.medtronic.com	ON	L5N1W3		905-826-6020	826-6620
Medtronic Perfusion Systems 7611 Northland Dr . . . . . Brooklyn Park *TF:* 800-328-3320 ■ *Web:* www.medtronic.com	MN	55428		763-391-9000	391-9100
MedX Health Corp 220 Superior Blvd . . . . . Mississauga *Web:* www.medxhealth.com	ON	L5T2L2		905-670-4428	
Mennen Medical Corp 950 Industrial Hwy. . . . . SouthHampton *Web:* www.mennenmedical.com	PA	18966		215-259-1020	675-6212
Meridian Medical Technologies Inc 6350 Stevens Forest Rd Ste 301. . . . . Columbia *TF:* 800-638-8093 ■ *Web:* www.meridianmeds.com	MD	21046		443-259-7800	259-7801
MetaStat Inc Eight HILLSIDE Ave Ste 207. . . . . Montclair *Web:* www.metastat.com	NJ	07042		973-744-7618	
Millennium Dental Technologies Inc 10945 S St Ste 104-A. . . . . Cerritos *Web:* www.millenniumdental.com	CA	90703		562-860-2908	
Misonix Inc 1938 NEW Hwy . . . . . Farmingdale *Web:* www.misonix.com	NY	11735		631-694-9555	
Mortara Instrument Inc 7865 N 86th St. . . . . Milwaukee *TF:* 800-231-7437 ■ *Web:* www.mortara.com	WI	53224		414-354-1600	354-4760
National Magnetic Sensors Inc 141 Summer St. . . . . Plantsville *Web:* www.nationalmagnetic.com	CT	06479		860-621-6816	
Natus Medical Inc 1501 Industrial Rd. . . . . San Carlos *NASDAQ: BABY* ■ *TF:* 800-255-3901 ■ *Web:* www.natus.com	CA	94070		650-802-0400	802-0401
NeuroMetrix 62 Fourth Ave . . . . . Waltham *NASDAQ: NURO* ■ *TF:* 888-786-7287 ■ *Web:* www.neurometrix.com	MA	02451		781-890-9989	890-1556
Neuromonics Inc 2810 Emrick Blvd . . . . . Bethlehem *TF:* 866-606-3876 ■ *Web:* www.neuromonics.com	PA	18020		866-606-3876	
Newport Medical Instruments Inc 1620 Sunflower Ave . . . . . Costa Mesa *Web:* www.newportnmi.com	CA	92626		714-427-5811	
Non-Invasive Monitoring Systems Inc 4400 Biscayne Blvd . . . . . Miami *Web:* www.nims-inc.com	FL	33137		305-575-4200	
NovaTract Surgical Inc 170 Ft Path Rd Ste 13. . . . . Madison *Web:* www.novatract.com	CT	06443		203-533-9710	
O-two Medical Technologies Inc 7575 Kimbel St. . . . . Mississauga *Web:* www.otwo.com	ON	L5S1C8		905-677-9410	677-2035
Oscor Inc 3816 DeSoto Blvd . . . . . Palm Harbor **Fax:* Cust Svc ■ *TF Cust Svc:* 800-726-7267 ■ *Web:* www.oscor.com	FL	34683		727-937-2511	934-9835*
OSI Systems Inc 12525 Chadron Ave . . . . . Hawthorne *NASDAQ: OSIS* ■ *Web:* www.osi-systems.com	CA	90250		310-978-0516	644-1727
Osprey Medical Inc 7600 Executive Dr . . . . . Eden Prairie *Web:* www.ospreymed.com	MN	55344		952-955-8230	
Pacific Biosciences Inc 1380 Willow Rd. . . . . Menlo Park *Web:* www.pacificbiosciences.com	CA	94025		650-521-8000	
Paradigm Medical Industries Inc 4273 South 590 West . . . . . Salt Lake City *OTC: PDMI* ■ *TF:* 800-742-0671 ■ *Web:* www.paradigm-medical.com	UT	84123		801-977-8970	977-8973
Philips Respironics Georgia Inc 175 Chastain Meadows Ct . . . . . Kennesaw *Web:* www.healthcare.philips.com	GA	30144		770-499-1212	
Physio-Control Inc 11811 Willows Rd NE . . . . . Redmond **Fax:* Acctg ■ *TF:* 800-442-1142 ■ *Web:* www.physio-control.com	WA	98052		425-867-4000	881-2405*
Positron Corp 530 Oakmont Ln . . . . . Westmont *Web:* www.positron.com	IL	60559		317-576-0183	
PP Systems International Inc 110 Haverhill Rd Ste 301 . . . . . Amesbury *Web:* www.ppsystems.com	MA	01913		978-834-0505	
ProUroCare Medical Inc 6440 Flying Cloud Dr Ste 101 . . . . . Eden Prairie *Web:* www.prourocare.com	MN	55344		952-476-9093	
Pyng Medical Corp 210, 13480 Crestwood Pl. . . . . Richmond *Web:* www.pyng.com	BC	V6V2J9		604-303-7964	303-7987
Respironics Novametrix LLC Five Technology Dr. . . . . Wallingford *TF:* 800-345-6443 ■ *Web:* www.respironics.com	CT	06492		724-387-4000	
Richard Wolf Medical Instruments Corp 353 Corporate Woods Pkwy . . . . . Vernon Hills *TF:* 800-323-9653 ■ *Web:* www.richardwolfusa.com	IL	60061		847-913-1113	913-1488
Rockwell Medical Inc 30142 Wixom Rd . . . . . Wixom *NASDAQ: RMTI* ■ *TF:* 800-449-3353 ■ *Web:* www.rockwellmed.com	MI	48393		248-960-9009	960-9119
SensorMedics Corp 22745 Savi Ranch Pkwy. . . . . Yorba Linda **Fax:* Mktg ■ *TF:* 800-231-2466 ■ *Web:* www.carefusion.com	CA	92887		714-283-2228	283-8439*
Siemens Medical Solutions Inc 51 Valley Stream Pkwy . . . . . Malvern **Fax Area Code:* 610 ■ *TF:* 800-888-7436 ■ *Web:* healthcare.siemens.com	PA	19355		800-225-5336	219-3124*
Solta Medical Inc 25881 Industrial Blvd . . . . . Hayward *TF:* 877-782-2286 ■ *Web:* www.thermage.com	CA	94545		877-782-2286	
SonarMed Inc 12220 N Meridian St Ste 150 . . . . . Carmel *Web:* www.sonarmed.com	IN	46032		317-489-3161	
Spacelabs Health Care 35301 SE Center St . . . . . Snoqualmie *TF:* 800-522-7025 ■ *Web:* www.spacelabshealthcare.com	WA	98065		425-396-3300	396-3301
SpectraScience Inc 11568 Sorrento Vly Rd Ste 11 . . . . . San Diego *Web:* www.spectrascience.com	CA	92121		858-847-0200	
SQI Diagnostics Inc 36 Meteor Dr. . . . . Toronto *Web:* www.sqidiagnostics.com	ON	M9W1A4		416-674-9500	
Starkey Labs-Canada Co 7310 Rapistan Ct . . . . . Mississauga *Web:* www.starkeycanada.ca	ON	L5N6L8		905-542-7555	
Sunshine Heart Inc 7651 ANAGRAM Dr. . . . . Eden Prairie *Web:* www.sunshineheart.com	MN	55344		952-345-4200	
TechniScan Inc 3216 S Highland Dr Ste 200. . . . . Salt Lake City *Web:* www.techniscanmedicalsystems.com	UT	84106		801-521-0444	
Tensys Medical Inc 5825 Oberlin Dr Ste 100 . . . . . San Diego *Web:* www.tensysmedical.com	CA	92121		858-552-1941	
Theralase Technologies Inc 1945 Queen St E . . . . . Toronto *Web:* www.theralase.com	ON	M4L1H7		416-699-5273	
Thoratec Corp 6035 Stoneridge Dr . . . . . Pleasanton *NASDAQ: THOR* ■ *TF:* 800-528-2577 ■ *Web:* www.thoratec.com	CA	94588		925-847-8600	847-8574
Vasomedical Inc 180 Linden Ave . . . . . Westbury *OTC: VASO* ■ *TF:* 800-455-3327 ■ *Web:* www.vasomedical.com	NY	11590		516-997-4600	997-2299
VasSol Inc 348 Lathrop Ave . . . . . River Forest *Web:* www.vassolinc.com	IL	60305		708-366-7000	
Verisante Technology Inc 2309 W 41st Ave Ste 306 . . . . . Vancouver *Web:* www.verisante.com	BC	V6M2A3		604-605-0507	
Vicor Technologies Inc (NDA) 399 Autumn Dr . . . . . Bangor *Web:* www.vicortech.com	PA	18013		570-897-5797	
VitaSound Audio Inc 175 Longwood Rd S Ste 400A . . . . . Hamilton *Web:* vitasound.com	ON	L8P0A1		905-667-7205	
Watermark Medical LLC 1641 Worthington Rd Ste 320 . . . . . West Palm Beach *TF:* 877-710-6999 ■ *Web:* www.watermarkmedical.com	FL	33409		877-710-6999	
Welch Allyn Medical Products 4341 State St Rd. . . . . Skaneateles Falls *TF:* 800-289-2500 ■ *Web:* www.welchallyn.com	NY	13152		315-685-4100	685-4091
Welch Allyn Monitoring Inc 8500 SW Creekside Pl . . . . . Beaverton *TF Cust Svc:* 800-289-2500 ■ *Web:* welchallyn.com	OR	97008		503-530-7500	526-4200
Zecotek Photonics Inc 21331 Gordon Way Unit 1120 . . . . . Richmond *Web:* www.zecotek.com	BC	V6W1J9		604-233-0056	
Zeltiq Aesthetics Inc 4698 Willow Rd Ste 100. . . . . Pleasanton *Web:* www.zeltiq.com	CA	94588		925-474-2500	
ZOLL Medical Corp 269 Mill Rd. . . . . Chelmsford *TF:* 800-348-9011 ■ *Web:* www.zoll.com	MA	01824		978-421-9655	421-0025
Zynex Inc 9990 PARK MEADOWS Dr . . . . . Lone Tree *Web:* www.zynexmed.com	CO	80124		303-703-4906	

254 ELECTRONIC BILL PRESENTMENT & PAYMENT SERVICES

SEE ALSO Application Service Providers (ASPs) p. 1745

			Phone	Fax
401 K Advisors LLC 1000 Skokie Blvd Ste 160 . . . . . Wilmette *Web:* 401kadvisorschicago.com	IL	60091	847-256-4300	
Alpha Card Services Inc 475 Veit Rd. . . . . Huntingdon Valley *TF:* 866-253-2227 ■ *Web:* www.alphacardservices.com	PA	19006	866-253-2227	
Arcus Capital Partners LLC 3050 Peachtree Rd NW Two Buckhead Plz Ste 340. . . . . Atlanta *Web:* www.arcuscp.com	GA	30305	404-949-2111	
Arthur Financial Services LLC 1205 Sam Bass Rd Ste 200 . . . . . Round Rock *Web:* www.arthurfinancial.com	TX	78681	512-218-6948	
Benefit Coordinators Corporation of California Two Robinson Plz Ste 200 . . . . . Pittsburgh *Web:* www.benxcel.com	PA	15205	412-276-1111	
BGCantor Market Data LP 199 Water St One Seaport Plz. . . . . New York *Web:* www.bgcmarketdata.com	NY	10038	212-829-4840	
BlueWater Partners LLC 146 Monroe Ctr St NW Ste 701 . . . . . Grand Rapids *Web:* www.bluewaterpartners.com	MI	49503	616-988-9444	
Capital Merchant Solutions Inc 3005 Gill St Ste 2. . . . . Bloomington *Web:* www.takecardstoday.com	IL	61704	309-452-5990	
Carbon Credit Capital LLC 561 Broadway Ste 6A. . . . . New York *Web:* www.carboncreditcapital.com	NY	10012	212-925-5697	
Check Cashing Place Inc, The 945 Fifth Ave. . . . . San Diego *Web:* www.tccpca.com	CA	92112	619-239-6151	
Crossbeam Capital LLC 7920 Norfolk Ave Ste 501. . . . . Bethesda *Web:* www.crossbeamcapital.com	MD	20814	240-223-0821	
Financial Transmission Network Inc 13220 Birch Dr Ste 120 . . . . . Omaha *Web:* www.ftni.com	NE	68164	402-502-8777	
FIX Flyer LLC 225 Broadway Ste 1600 . . . . . New York *TF:* 888-349-3593 ■ *Web:* www.fixflyer.com	NY	10007	888-349-3593	

				Phone	Fax
Flores Financial Services 314 Sage St Ste 100 *Web:* rflores.com	Lake Geneva	WI	53147	262-248-2771	
Freedman Financial Associates Inc Eight Essex Ctr Dr Third Fl *Web:* www.freedmanfinancial.com	Peabody	MA	01960	978-531-8108	
Gough Financial Group Inc 9415 E Harry St Ste 602 *Web:* www.goughfinancialgroup.com	Wichita	KS	67207	316-683-8400	
Heartland Payment Systems Inc 90 Nassau St Second Fl *NYSE: HPY* ■ *TF:* 888-798-3131 ■ *Web:* www.heartlandpaymentsystems.com	Princeton	NJ	08542	609-683-3831	683-3815
Ifrah Financial Services Inc Little Rock Location - Main 17300 Chenal Pkwy Ste 150 *Web:* www.ifrahfinancial.com	Little Rock	AR	72223	501-821-7733	
Kelly Financial Group LLC 102 Halls Rd *Web:* hammondiles.com	Old Lyme	CT	06371	860-434-6677	
Konsultek 2230 Point Blvd Ste 800 *Web:* www.konsultek.com	Elgin	IL	60123	847-426-9355	
Landmark Financial Group LLC 181 Old Post Rd *Web:* landmark-mortgage.com	Southport	CT	06890	203-254-8422	
Lear Capital Inc 1990 S Bundy Dr Ste 600 *TF:* 800-576-9355 ■ *Web:* www.learcapital.com	Los Angeles	CA	90025	800-576-9355	
Local Investment Commission 3100 Broadway St Ste 1100 *Web:* www.kclinc.org	Kansas City	MO	64111	816-889-5050	
Loring, Wolcott & Coolidge Fiduciary Advisors LLP 230 Congress St *Web:* www.lwcotrust.com	Boston	MA	02110	617-523-6531	
Mcnamara Financial Services Inc Marshfield Professional Ctr 1020 Plain St Ste 200 *Web:* www.mcnamarafinancial.com	Marshfield	MA	02050	781-834-2010	
Mdic Investment Advisory Service LLC 116 Kraft Ave Ste8 *Web:* www.mdicinc.com	Bronxville	NY	10708	914-793-4095	
Money Movers Inc 5880 Lone Pine Rd *Web:* moneymovers.com	Sebastopol	CA	95472	707-829-5577	
Netvantage Inc 6510 Hamilton Ave Ste1 *Web:* www.netvantageinc.com	Cincinnati	OH	45224	513-729-0207	
Orion Advisor Services LLC 17605 Wright St *Web:* www.orionadvisor.com	Omaha	NE	68130	402-496-3513	
PayPal Inc PO Box 45950 *Web:* www.paypal.com	Omaha	NE	68145	402-935-2050	537-5734
RDM Corp 608 Weber St N Ste 4 *Web:* www.rdmcorp.com	Waterloo	ON	N2V1K4	519-746-8483	
Riata Financial Services Inc 245 Landa St *Web:* riatafinancial.com	New Braunfels	TX	78130	830-606-5100	
Sather Financial Group Inc 120 E Constitution St *Web:* www.satherfinancial.com	Victoria	TX	77901	361-570-1800	
Scully Capital Services Inc 1730 M St Nw Ste 204 *Web:* www.scullycapital.com	Washington	DC	20036	202-775-3434	
T-Chek Systems Inc 14800 Charlson Rd *Web:* www.tchek.com	Eden Prairie	MN	55347	952-934-3413	
Toussaint Capital Partners LLC 13 Broadway Ste 2 *Web:* www.toussaintcapital.com	Freehold	NJ	07728	212-328-1800	
U.S. Bankcard Services Inc 17171 E Gale Ave Ste 110 *TF:* 888-888-8872 ■ *Web:* www.usbsi.com	City Of Industry	CA	91745	888-888-8872	
USA Technologies Inc Ste 140 100 Deerfield Ln Chester *TF:* 800-633-0340 ■ *Web:* www.usatech.com	Malvern	PA	19355	800-633-0340	
Value Payment Systems LLC 2207 Crestmoor Rd Ste 200 *Web:* www.valuepaymentsystems.com	Nashville	TN	37215	615-730-6367	
Waldron Wealth Management LLC 1150 Old Pond Rd *Web:* www.waldronprivatewealth.com	Bridgeville	PA	15017	412-221-1005	
Wingate Financial Group Inc 450 Bedford St *Web:* www.wingatewealthadvisors.com	Lexington	MA	02420	781-862-7100	

255 ELECTRONIC COMMUNICATIONS NETWORKS (ECNS)

SEE ALSO Securities Brokers & Dealers p. 3151; Securities & Commodities Exchanges p. 3159

ECNs are computerized trade-matching systems that unite best bid and offer prices and provide anonymity to investors.

				Phone	Fax
Acme Packet Inc 100 Crosby Dr *NASDAQ: APKT* ■ *Web:* www.acmepacket.com	Burlington	MA	01803	781-328-4400	275-8800
Archipelago Holdings LLC 100 S Wacker Dr Ste 1800 *Web:* www.tradearca.com	Chicago	IL	60606	312-960-1696	960-1369
Bloomberg Tradebook 731 Lexington Ave *Web:* www.bloombergtradebook.com	New York	NY	10022	212-617-7070	
Bluesocket Inc One Burlington Woods Dr Ste 210 *Web:* www.adtran.com	Burlington	MA	01803	781-328-0888	
Comm-Works Holdings LLC 1405 Xenium Ln N Ste 120 *TF:* 800-853-8090 ■ *Web:* www.comm-works.com	Minneapolis	MN	55441	763-258-5800	475-6656
Entropic Communications Inc 6290 Sequence Dr *NASDAQ: ENTR* ■ *TF:* 888-510-1765 ■ *Web:* www.entropic.com	San Diego	CA	92121	858-768-3600	768-3601
Layer 3 Communications LLC 1555 Oakbrook Dr Ste 100 *TF:* 866-535-3924 ■ *Web:* www.layer3com.com	Norcross	GA	30093	770-225-5300	225-5298
Network Telephone Services Inc 21135 Erwin St *TF:* 800-742-5687 ■ *Web:* www.nts.net	Woodland Hills	CA	91367	818-992-4300	
NYFIX Inc 11 Wall St *Web:* www.nyse.com	New York	NY	10005	212-656-3000	
OTC Markets Group Inc 304 Hudson St Second Fl *OTC: OTCM* ■ *Web:* www.otcmarkets.com	New York	NY	10013	212-896-4400	868-3848
Vector Resources Inc 3530 Voyager St *Web:* www.vectorusa.com	Torrance	CA	90503	310-436-1000	436-1060

256 ELECTRONIC COMPONENTS & ACCESSORIES - MFR

SEE ALSO Printed Circuit Boards p. 2963; Semiconductors & Related Devices p. 3166

				Phone	Fax
10C Technologies Inc 14285 Midway Rd Ste 125 *Web:* www.10ctech.com	Addison	TX	75001	972-385-2486	
2D2C Inc 250 Pkwy Dr Ste 150 *Web:* www.2d2c.com	Lincolnshire	IL	60069	847-543-0980	
3M Electrical Products Div 6801 River Pl Blvd 3M Austin Ctr **Fax Area Code: 800* ■ *Web:* 3m.com/	Austin	TX	78726	512-984-1800	245-0329*
3M Electronic Handling & Protection Div 6801 River Pl Blvd *TF:* 800-328-1368 ■ *Web:* 3m.com/	Austin	TX	78726	800-328-1368	
3M Interconnect Solutions Div 6801 River Pl Blvd *TF:* 800-225-5373 ■ *Web:* www.3m.com	Austin	TX	78726	512-984-1800	984-3417
A.J. Antunes & Co 180 Kehoe Blvd *Web:* www.ajantunes.com	Carol Stream	IL	60188	630-784-1000	
Aavid Thermalloy LLC 70 Commercial St Ste 200 *TF:* 855-322-2843 ■ *Web:* www.aavid.com	Concord	NH	03301	603-224-9988	223-1790
AccuSpec Electronics LLC 8140 Hawthorne Dr *Web:* accuspecelectronic.com	Erie	PA	16509	814-464-2000	
Actown-Electrocoil Inc 2414 Highview St *Web:* acmetransformer.com	Spring Grove	IL	60081	815-675-6641	675-2050
Adco Circuits 2868 Bond St *Web:* www.adcocircuits.com	Rochester Hills	MI	48309	248-853-6620	853-6698
Advanced Bionics LLC 28515 Westinghouse Pl *TF:* 877-829-0026 ■ *Web:* www.advancedbionics.com	Valencia	CA	91355	661-362-1400	362-1503
AEM Inc 6610 Cobra Way *Web:* www.aem-usa.com	San Diego	CA	92121	858-481-0210	
Aeroflex Inc 35 S Service Rd PO Box 6022 *TSE: ARX* ■ *TF:* 800-843-1553 ■ *Web:* www.aeroflex.com	Plainview	NY	11803	516-694-6700	694-0658
Aerovox Inc 167 John Vertente Blvd *Web:* www.aerovox.com	New Bedford	MA	02745	508-994-9661	995-3000
AESP Inc 16295 NW 13th Ave *TF:* 800-446-2377 ■ *Web:* www.aesp.com	Miami	FL	33169	305-944-7710	949-4483
AJB Software Design Inc 5255 Solar Dr *Web:* www.ajbsoftware.com	Mississauga	ON	L4W5B8	905-282-1877	
Alacron Inc 71 Spit Brook Rd Ste 200 *Web:* www.alacron.com	Nashua	NH	03060	603-891-2750	
Aldelo LP 4641 Spyres Way Ste 4 *TF:* 800-801-6036 ■ *Web:* www.aldelo.com	Modesto	CA	95356	209-338-5488	
Alion Inc 870 Harbour Way S *Web:* www.alion.co	Richmond	CA	94804	510-965-0868	
Alliance Fiber Optic Products Inc 275 Gibralter Dr *NASDAQ: AFOP* ■ *Web:* www.afop.com	Sunnyvale	CA	94089	408-736-6900	736-2466
Alpha Group, The 3767 Alpha Way **Fax: Sales* ■ *TF:* 800-322-5742 ■ *Web:* www.alpha.com	Bellingham	WA	98226	360-647-2360	671-4936*
Alvesta 500 Oakmead Pkwy *Web:* www.alvesta.com	Sunnyvale	CA	94085	408-331-4800	
American Bright Optoelectronics Corp 13815-C Magnolia Ave *Web:* www.americanbrightled.com	Chino	CA	91710	909-628-5050	
American International Inc 1040 Avendia Acaso *TF:* 800-336-6500 ■ *Web:* www.aius.net	Camarillo	CA	93012	805-388-6800	388-7950
American Power Conversion Corp (APC) 132 Fairgrounds Rd *TF Cust Svc:* 800-788-2208 ■ *Web:* www.apc.com	West Kingston	RI	02892	401-789-5735	789-3710
AMETEK Automation & Process Technologies 1080 N Crooks *TF:* 800-635-0289 ■ *Web:* www.ametekapt.com	Clawson	MI	48017	248-435-0700	435-8120
Ametek HDR Power Systems Inc 3563 Interchange Rd *TF:* 888-797-2685 ■ *Web:* www.hdrpower.com	Columbus	OH	43204	614-308-5500	308-5506
AMETEK Solidstate Controls 875 Dearborn Dr *TF:* 800-635-7300 ■ *Web:* www.solidstatecontrolsinc.com	Columbus	OH	43085	614-846-7500	885-3990
Ametek TSE 108 Fifth Ave NW *Web:* ametekemc.com	Arlington	MN	55307	507-964-2237	964-2465
Amphenol Aerospace 40-60 Delaware Ave *TF:* 800-678-0141 ■ *Web:* www.amphenol-aerospace.com	Sidney	NY	13838	607-563-5011	563-5157
Amphenol Interconnect Products Corp (AIPC) 20 Valley St **Fax: Hum Res* ■ *TF:* 888-275-2472 ■ *Web:* www.amphenol-aipc.com	Endicott	NY	13760	607-754-4444	786-4234*
Amphenol PCD 72 Cherry Hill Dr **Fax: Sales* ■ *Web:* www.amphenolpcd.com	Beverly	MA	01915	978-624-3400	927-1513*
Amphenol RF Four Old Newtown Rd *TF:* 800-627-7100 ■ *Web:* www.amphenolrf.com	Danbury	CT	06810	203-743-9272	796-2032
Amphenol Sine Systems 44724 Morley Dr *Web:* www.sineco.com	Clinton Township	MI	48036	586-465-3131	
Amphenol Spectra-Strip 720 Sherman Ave *TF:* 800-846-6400 ■ *Web:* www.spectra-strip.com	Hamden	CT	06514	203-281-3200	281-5872

Phone | Fax

Amphenol-Tuchel Electronics
6900 Haggerty Rd Ste 200 ... Canton MI 48187 734-451-6400 451-7197
TF: 800-380-8052 ■ *Web:* www.amphenol.info
AmRad Engineering Inc 32 Hargrove Grade ... Palm Coast FL 32137 386-445-6000 445-6871
TF: 800-445-6033 ■ *Web:* www.americanradionic.com
Anaren Microwave Inc 6635 Kirkville Rd ... East Syracuse NY 13057 315-432-8909 432-9121
NASDAQ: ANEN ■ *TF:* 800-544-2414 ■ *Web:* www.anaren.com
Antec Inc 47900 Fremont Blvd ... Fremont CA 94538 510-770-1200 770-1288
TF: 800-222-6832 ■ *Web:* www.antec.com
API Delevan 270 Quaker Rd ... East Aurora NY 14052 716-652-3600 652-4814
Web: www.delevan.com
Ardica Technologies Inc
2325 Third St Ste 424 ... San Francisco CA 94107 415-568-9270
Web: www.ardica.com
Aries Electronics Inc
62-A Trenton Ave PO Box 130 ... Frenchtown NJ 08825 908-996-6841 996-3891
Web: www.arieselec.com
Arradiance Inc 142 N Rd Ste F-150 ... Sudbury MA 01776 978-369-8291
Web: www.arradiance.com
ASC Capacitors 301 W O St ... Ogallala NE 69153 308-284-3611 284-8324
Web: www.ascapacitor.com
Atotech USA Inc 1750 Overview Dr ... Rock Hill SC 29730 803-817-3500 817-3666
Web: www.atotech.com/en
AudioQuest Inc 2621 White Rd ... Irvine CA 92614 949-585-0111
TF: 800-747-2770 ■ *Web:* www.audioquest.com
Auric Systems International 85 Grove St ... Peterborough NH 03458 603-924-6079
Web: www.auricsystems.com
AVG Automation 4140 Utica St ... Bettendorf IA 52722 877-774-3279 359-9094*
**Fax Area Code:* 563 ■ *TF:* 877-774-3279 ■ *Web:* avg.net/Index.htm
Avionic Instruments Inc 1414 Randolph Ave ... Avenel NJ 07001 732-388-3500 382-4996
TF: 800-468-3571 ■ *Web:* www.avionicinstruments.com
Avnet Electronics Marketing Inc
2211 S 47th St ... Phoenix AZ 85034 480-643-2000
TF: 888-822-8638 ■ *Web:* avnetexpress.avnet.com
AVX Corp 801 17th Ave S ... Myrtle Beach SC 29577 843-448-9411 444-0424
NYSE: AVX ■ *Web:* www.avx.com
B & K Electric Wholesale
1225 S Johnson Dr ... City Of Industry CA 91745 626-965-5040
Web: www.bk-electric.com
Ballard Power Systems Inc 9000 Glenlyon Pkwy ... Burnaby BC V5J5J8 604-454-0900 412-4700
NASDAQ: BLDP ■ *Web:* www.ballard.com
Banner Engineering Corp 9714 Tenth Ave N ... Minneapolis MN 55441 763-544-3164 544-3213
TF: 888-373-6767 ■ *Web:* www.bannerengineering.com
Beacon Power Corp 65 Middlesex Rd ... Tyngsboro MA 01879 978-694-9121 649-7186
TF: 888-938-9112 ■ *Web:* www.beaconpower.com
BEI Technologies Inc Industrial Encoder Div
7230 Hollister Ave ... Goleta CA 93117 805-968-0782 968-3154
TF Sales: 800-350-2727 ■ *Web:* www.beiied.com
Bel Stewart Connector
11118 Susquehanna Trl S ... Glen Rock PA 17327 717-235-7512 235-7954
Web: www.belfuse.com
Bergquist Co 18930 W 78th St ... Chanhassen MN 55317 952-835-2322 835-4156
TF: 800-347-4572 ■ *Web:* www.bergquistcompany.com
BH Electronics Inc 12219 Wood Lk Dr ... Burnsville MN 55337 952-894-9590 894-9380
Web: www.bhelectronics.com
Bright View Technologies
5151 Mccrimmon Pkwy Ste 200 ... Morrisville NC 27560 919-228-4370
Web: www.brightviewtechnologies.com
C & D Technologies Inc
1400 Union Meeting Rd PO Box 3053 ... Blue Bell PA 19422 215-619-2700 619-7899
TF: 800-543-8630 ■ *Web:* www.cdtechno.com
C&D Technologies 11 Cabot Blvd ... Mansfield MA 02048 508-339-3000 339-6356
TF: 800-233-2765 ■ *Web:* www.murata-ps.com
Califone International Inc
1145 Arroyo St Ste A ... San Fernando CA 91340 818-407-2400 407-2405
TF: 800-722-0500 ■ *Web:* www.califone.com
Camesa Inc 1615 Spur 529 ... Rosenberg TX 77471 281-342-4494
TF: 800-866-0001 ■ *Web:* www.camesainc.com
Canadian Solar Solutions Inc
67A Sparks St Ste 300 ... Ottawa ON K1P5A5 519-954-2057
Web: canadiansolar.com
Canara Inc 181 Third St Ste 150 ... San Rafael CA 94901 415-839-7270
Web: www.canara.com
Celestica Inc 844 Don Mills Rd ... Toronto ON M3C1V7 416-448-5800 448-4810
NYSE: CLS ■ *TF:* 888-899-9998 ■ *Web:* www.celestica.com
CENTROSOLAR America Inc
8350 E Evans Rd Ste E-1 ... Scottsdale AZ 85260 480-348-2555
Web: www.centrosolaramerica.com
Chromasun Inc 1050 N Fifth St Ste 10 ... San Jose CA 95112 650-521-6872
Web: www.chromasun.com
Circuit Assembly Corp 18 Thomas St ... Irvine CA 92618 949-855-7887 855-4298
Web: www.circuitassembly.com
City Electric Supply Inc 315 E Prentiss St ... Iowa City IA 52240 319-338-7561
Web: www.cityelectricsupply.net
Clary Corp 150 E Huntington Dr ... Monrovia CA 91016 626-359-4486 305-0254
TF: 800-551-6111 ■ *Web:* www.clary.com
Clinton Electronics Corp 6701 Clinton Rd ... Loves Park IL 61111 815-633-1444
Web: www.clintonelectronics.com
Cobra Wire & Cable Inc 2930 Turnpike Dr ... Hatboro PA 19040 215-674-8773
Web: www.cobrawire.com
Coilcraft Inc 1102 Silver Lk Rd ... Cary IL 60013 847-639-2361 639-1469
TF: 800-322-2645 ■ *Web:* www.coilcraft.com
Coils Inc 11716 Algonquin Rd PO Box 247 ... Huntley IL 60142 847-669-5115
Color Kinetics Distribution Inc
1247 Norwood Ave ... Itasca IL 60143 630-285-9772
Web: www.colorkinetics.com
Comdel Inc 11 Kondelin Rd ... Gloucester MA 01930 978-282-0620 282-4980
TF: 800-468-3144 ■ *Web:* www.comdel.com
Communications & Power Industries Inc EIMAC Div (CPI)
607 Hansen Way ... Palo Alto CA 94304 800-414-8823 846-3276*
**Fax Area Code:* 650 ■ *TF:* 800-414-8823 ■ *Web:* cpii.com/division.cfm/9

Communications & Power Industries LLC
607 Hansen Way ... Palo Alto CA 94303 650-846-2900 846-3276*
**Fax:* PR ■ *TF:* 800-231-4818 ■ *Web:* www.cpii.com
Conelec of Florida LLC 3045 Tech Park Way ... Deland FL 32724 386-873-3800
Web: www.conelec.net
Conesys Inc 2280 208th St ... Torrance CA 90501 310-618-3737
Web: www.conesys.com
Cooper Industries 600 Travis St Ste 5400 ... Houston TX 77002 713-209-8400 209-8995
NYSE: ETN ■ *TF:* 866-853-4293 ■ *Web:* www.cooperindustries.com
Corning Gilbert Inc 5310 W Camelback Rd ... Glendale AZ 85301 623-245-1050 934-5160
TF Cust Svc: 800-528-0199 ■ *Web:* www.corning.com
Cornucopia Tool & Plastics Inc
448 Sherwood Rd PO Box 1915 ... Paso Robles CA 93447 805-369-0030 369-0033
TF: 800-235-4144 ■ *Web:* www.cornucopiaplastics.com
Cougar Components Corp 927 Thompson Pl ... Sunnyvale CA 94085 408-522-3838 522-3839
Web: www.cougarcorp.com
Creswell-Richardson Supply
900 Appling St ... Chattanooga TN 37406 423-894-4117
Web: www.creswellrichardson.com
Crystek Crystals Corp
12730 Commonwealth Dr ... Fort Myers FL 33913 239-561-3311 561-3311
TF: 800-237-3061 ■ *Web:* www.crystek.com
CTS Corp 905 W Blvd N ... Elkhart IN 46514 574-293-7511 293-6146
NYSE: CTS ■ *TF:* 800-757-6686 ■ *Web:* www.ctscorp.com
Cyber Power Systems Inc
4241 12th Ave E Ste 400 ... Shakopee MN 55379 952-403-9500 403-0009
TF: 877-297-6937 ■ *Web:* www.cyberpowersystems.com
Cyberex 5900 Eastport Blvd ... Richmond VA 23231 804-236-3300 236-3300
TF: 800-238-5000 ■ *Web:* www.tnbpowersolutions.com
Data Device Corp 105 Wilbur Pl ... Bohemia NY 11716 631-567-5600 259-0246*
**Fax Area Code:* 414 ■ *TF Cust Svc:* 800-332-5757 ■ *Web:* www.ddc-web.com
DataCan Services Corp
7485-45 Ave Close Ste 102 ... Red Deer AB T4P4C2 403-352-2245
Web: www.datacan.ca
Deep Imaging Technologies Inc
990 Village Sq Dr ... Tomball TX 77375 281-290-0492
Web: deepimaging.com
Delta Electronics Manufacturing Corp
416 Cabot St ... Beverly MA 01915 978-927-1060 922-6430
Web: www.deltarf.com
Delta Group Inc 4801 Lincoln Rd NE ... Albuquerque NM 87109 505-883-7674 888-5460
Web: www.deltagroupinc.com
Delta Products Corp 4405 Cushing Pkwy ... Fremont CA 94538 510-668-5100 668-0680
Web: www.delta-americas.com
Diamond Antenna & Microwave Corp
59 Porter Rd ... Littleton MA 01460 978-486-0039 486-0079
Web: www.diamondantenna.com
Dielectric Laboratories Inc 2777 US Rt 20 ... Cazenovia NY 13035 315-655-8710 655-0445
TF: 800-656-9499 ■ *Web:* www.dovercmp.com
Digital Light Innovations
3201 Industrial Terr Ste 120 ... Austin TX 78758 512-617-4700
Web: www.dlinnovations.com
Digital Power Corp 41324 Christy St ... Fremont CA 94538 510-353-4023 657-2635
TF: 866-344-7697 ■ *Web:* www.digipwr.com
DigitalOptics Corp 3025 Orchard Pkwy ... San Jose CA 95134 408-473-2500
Web: www.doc.com
Dimation Inc 505 W Travelers Trl ... Burnsville MN 55337 952-746-3030
Web: www.dimation.com
DOW Kokam LLC 2125 Ridgewood Dr ... Midland MI 48642 989-698-3300
Web: dev.dowkokam.com
Dow-Key Microwave Corp 4822 McGrath St ... Ventura CA 93003 805-650-0260 650-1734
TF: 800-266-3695 ■ *Web:* www.dowkey.com
DRS Laurel Technologies 246 Airport Rd ... Johnstown PA 15904 814-534-8900 534-8815
Web: www.drs.com
DSA Encore LLC 50 Pocono Rd ... Brookfield CT 06804 203-740-4200
Web: www.dsaencore.com
Dynalloy Inc 14762 Bentley Cir ... Tustin CA 92780 714-436-1206 436-0511
Web: www.dynalloy.com
Dynamic Source Manufacturing Inc
Unit 117 2765 - 48th Ave NE ... Calgary AB T3J5M9 403-516-1888
Web: www.dynamicsourcemfg.com
e-Merchant Processing Inc 3125 Sterling Cir ... Boulder CO 80301 303-577-0330
Eby Co 4300 H St ... Philadelphia PA 19124 215-537-4700 537-4780
TF: 800-329-3430 ■ *Web:* www.ebycompany.com
eGtran Corp 829 Flynn Rd ... Camarillo CA 93012 805-482-1088
Web: www.egtran.com
Electrex Inc PO Box 948 ... Hutchinson KS 67504 800-319-3676 669-3740*
**Fax Area Code:* 620 ■ *TF:* 800-319-3676 ■ *Web:* www.electrexinc.com
Electro-Mechanical Corp One Goodson St ... Bristol VA 24201 276-669-4084 669-1869
Web: www.electro-mechanical.com
Electrocube Inc 3366 Pomona Blvd ... Pomona CA 91768 909-595-4037 357-8099*
**Fax Area Code:* 626 ■ *TF:* 800-515-1112 ■ *Web:* www.electrocube.com
Electronic Instrumentation & Technology Inc (EIT)
108 Carpenter Dr ... Sterling VA 20164 703-478-0700 478-0291
Web: www.eit.com
Electroswitch Corp 180 King Ave ... Weymouth MA 02188 781-335-5200 335-4253
Web: www.electroswitch.com
Elma Electronic Inc 44350 Grimmer Blvd ... Fremont CA 94538 510-656-3400 656-3783
Web: www.elma.com
ELSAG North America LLC Seven Sutton Pl ... Brewster NY 10509 336-379-7135
Web: www.elsag.com
Emerging Power Inc 200 Holt St ... Hackensack NJ 07601 201-441-3590
Web: www.emergingpower.com
Emerson Network Power Connectivity Solutions
1050 Dearborn Dr ... Columbus OH 43085 614-888-0246 841-6882
TF: 800-275-3500 ■ *Web:* www.emersonnetworkpower.com
EMF Corp 505 Pokagon Trl ... Angola IN 46703 260-665-9541
Web: www.emfusa.com
Emrise Corp 2530 Meridian Pkwy ... Durham NC 27713 919-806-4722
Web: www.emrise.com
Emrise Electronics Corp
9485 Haven Ave Ste 100 ... Rancho Cucamonga CA 91730 909-987-9220
Web: www.emrise.com

Phone | Fax

Energy Conversion Devices Inc
2956 Waterview Dr .... Rochester Hills MI 48309 248-293-0440
OTC: ENERQ

Enevate Corp 101 Theory Ste 200 .... Irvine CA 92617 949-243-0399
Web: www.enevate.com

ENrG Inc 155 Rano St Ste 300 .... Buffalo NY 14207 716-873-2939
Web: www.enrg.com

Eoff Electric Company Inc
3241 NW Industrial St .... Portland OR 97210 503-222-9411
Web: www.eoff.com

EPCOS Inc 485-B Rt 1 S Ste 200 .... Iselin NJ 08830 732-906-4300
Web: www.epcos.com

eSilicon Corp 501 Macara Ave .... Sunnyvale CA 94085 408-616-4600 991-9567
Web: www.esilicon.com

Espey Mfg & Electronics Corp
233 Ballston Ave .... Saratoga Springs NY 12866 518-245-4400 245-4421
NYSE: ESP ■ *Web:* www.espey.com

Exatron Inc 2842 Aiello Dr .... San Jose CA 95111 408-629-7600
Web: www.exatron.com

Fabrinet USA Inc 4104 24th St Ste 345 .... San Francisco CA 94114 408-888-4601
Web: www.fabrinet.com

Fawn Industries Inc
1920 Greenspring Dr Ste 140 .... Timonium MD 21093 410-308-9200 308-9202
Web: fawnplastics.com

Filnor Inc 227 N Freedom Ave PO Box 2328 .... Alliance OH 44601 330-821-7667 829-3175
Web: www.filnor.com

Forbes Snyder Tristate Cash
54 Northampton St .... Easthampton MA 01027 413-529-2950
TF: 800-222-4064 ■ *Web:* www.forbes-snyder.com

Foxlink International Inc 925 W Lambert Rd Ste C .... Brea CA 92821 714-256-1777 256-1700
Web: www.foxlink.com

Franklin Empire Inc 8421 Darnley Rd .... Montreal QC H4T2B2 514-341-9720 341-3907
TF: 800-361-5044 ■ *Web:* www.feinc.com

FRC Component Products Inc
1511 S Benjamin Ave .... Mason City IA 50401 641-424-0370
Web: frccorp.com

FuelCell Energy Inc Three Great Pasture Rd .... Danbury CT 06810 203-825-6000 825-6100
NASDAQ: FCEL ■ *Web:* www.fuelcellenergy.com

Fujitsu Components America Inc
250 E Caribbean Dr .... Sunnyvale CA 94089 408-745-4900 745-4970
Web: www.fujitsu.com

Full Swing Golf Inc 10890 Thornmint Rd .... San Diego CA 92127 858-675-1100
Web: www.fullswinggolf.com

General Microcircuits Inc
1133 N Main St PO Box 748 .... Mooresville NC 28115 704-663-5975 663-6569
Web: www.gmimfg.com

GoMotion Inc 10 Kendrick Rd Unit 3 .... Wareham MA 02571 508-322-7695
Web: www.gomotiongear.com

Greatbatch Inc 10000 Wehrle Dr .... Clarence NY 14031 716-759-5600 759-2562
NYSE: GB ■ *Web:* www.greatbatch.com

Greenlee Textron 1390 Aspen Way .... Vista CA 92081 760-598-8900 598-5634
TF: 800-642-2155 ■ *Web:* greenlee.com

Guestlogix Inc 111 Peter St Ste 302 .... Toronto ON M5V2H1 416-642-0349
Web: www.guestlogix.com

GW Lisk Company Inc Two S St .... Clifton Springs NY 14432 315-462-2611 462-7661
Web: www.gwlisk.com

Harco Laboratories Inc 186 Cedar St .... Branford CT 06405 203-483-3700 483-0391
Web: www.harcolabs.com

HCC Industries Inc 4232 Temple City Blvd .... Rosemead CA 91770 626-443-8933
Web: www.hccindustries.com

Heliene Inc 520 Allen'S Side Rd .... Sault Ste Marie ON P6A6K4 705-575-6556
TF: 855-363-2797 ■ *Web:* www.heliene.ca

Heraeus Shin-Etsu America Inc
4600 NW Pacific Rim Blvd .... Camas WA 98607 360-834-4004 834-3115
Web: sehamerica.com

Herley New England 10 Sonar Dr .... Woburn MA 01801 781-729-9450 729-9547
Web: kratosepd.com/page/moved/herley

Herley-CTI Inc 9 Whippany Rd .... Whippany NJ 07981 973-884-2580 887-6245
TF: 866-606-5867 ■ *Web:* kratosepd.com/page/moved/herley

HiRel Systems 11100 Wayzata Blvd Ste 501 .... Minnetonka MN 55305 952-544-1344 544-1345
TF: 888-604-5888 ■ *Web:* www.hirelsystems.com

Hirose Electric (USA) Inc
2688 Westhills Ct .... Simi Valley CA 93065 805-522-7958 522-3217
Web: www.hirose.com

Hitachi Canada Ltd
5450 Explore Dr Suite 501 .... Mississauga ON L4W5N1 905-629-9300 290-0141
TF: 866-797-4332 ■ *Web:* www.hitachi.ca

Hitachi High Technologies America Inc
10 N Martingale Rd Ste 500 .... Schaumburg IL 60173 847-273-4141 273-4407
Web: www.hitachi-hta.com

Honeywell Electronic Materials
1349 Moffett Pk Dr .... Sunnyvale CA 94089 408-962-2000 962-2257
Web: www51.honeywell.com

Hubbell Power Systems Inc 210 N Allen St .... Centralia MO 65240 573-682-5521 682-8714
TF: 800-346-3062 ■ *Web:* www.hubbellpowersystems.com

Hunting Innova 8383 N Sam Houston Pkwy W .... Houston TX 77064 281-653-5500 653-5501
Web: www.hunting-intl.com

Hutchinson Technology Inc
40 W Highland Pk Dr .... Hutchinson MN 55350 320-587-3797 587-1810
NASDAQ: HTCH ■ *Web:* www.htch.com

Illinois Capacitor Inc 3757 W Touhy Ave .... Lincolnwood IL 60712 847-675-1760 673-2850
TF: 800-263-9275 ■ *Web:* www.illinoiscapacitor.com

IMP Holdings LLC 409 Growth Pkwy .... Angola IN 46703 260-665-6112
Web: www.indianamarine.com

Innergy Power Corp Inc
9051 Siempre Viva Rd Bldg 6 Ste A .... San Diego CA 92154 619-710-0758
Web: www.innergypower.com

Inrad Optics Inc 181 Legrand Ave .... Northvale NJ 07647 201-767-1910
Web: www.inradoptics.com

Instantel Inc 309 Legget Dr .... Ottawa ON K2K3A3 613-592-4642
Web: www.instantel.com

Integrated Magnetics Inc 11248 Playa Ct .... Culver City CA 90230 310-391-7213
TF: 800-421-6692 ■ *Web:* www.intemag.com

Integrated Microwave Corp
11353 Sorrento Valley Rd .... San Diego CA 92121 858-259-2600 755-8679
Web: www.imcsd.com

Interconnect Devices Inc (IDI)
5101 Richland Ave .... Kansas City KS 66106 913-342-5544 342-7043
TF: 866-433-5722 ■ *Web:* www.idinet.com

International Resistive Company Inc (IRC)
736 Greenway Rd .... Boone NC 28607 828-264-8861 264-8865
Web: www.irctt.com

Interpoint Corp PO Box 97005 .... Redmond WA 98073 425-882-3100 882-1990
TF: 800-822-8782 ■ *Web:* www.interpoint.com

inTEST Corp 804 E Gate Dr Ste 200 .... Mount Laurel NJ 08054 856-505-8800 505-8801
NYSE: INTT ■ *Web:* www.intest.com

InVue Security Products Inc
10715 Sikes Pl Ste 200 .... Charlotte NC 28277 704-206-7849
Web: www.alphaworld.com

ipDataTel LLC 13110 SW Fwy .... Sugar Land TX 77478 713-452-2700
TF: 866-896-1818 ■ *Web:* www.ipdatatel.com

Iterna 2600 Beverly Dr .... Aurora IL 60502 630-585-7400
Web: iternacorp.com

ITT Exelis Inc 1650 Tysons Blvd Ste 1700 .... McLean VA 22102 703-790-6300 790-6360
Web: exelisinc.com

ITT Industries Inc 1133 Westchester Ave .... White Plains NY 10604 914-641-2000 696-2950
NYSE: ITT ■ *TF:* 800-254-2823 ■ *Web:* www.itt.com

JAE Electronics Inc 142 Technology Dr Ste 100 .... Irvine CA 92618 949-753-2600 753-2699
TF: 800-523-7278 ■ *Web:* www.jae.com

Jameson LLC 1451 Old N Main St .... Clover SC 29710 803-222-6400
Web: www.jamesonllc.com

Jenkins Electric Inc 5933 Brookshire Blvd .... Charlotte NC 28216 800-438-3003
TF: 800-438-3003 ■ *Web:* www.jenkins.com

Jewell Instruments LLC 850 Perimeter Rd .... Manchester NH 03103 603-669-6400 669-5962
TF: 800-227-5955 ■ *Web:* jewellinstruments.com

Johanson Mfg Corp 301 Rockaway Valley Rd .... Boonton NJ 07005 973-334-2676 334-2954*
**Fax: Sales* ■ *TF:* 800-477-1272 ■ *Web:* www.johansonmfg.com

Joule Unlimited Inc 18 Crosby Dr .... Bedford MA 01730 781-533-9100
Web: www.jouleunlimited.com

K & L Microwave Inc 2250 Northwood Dr .... Salisbury MD 21801 410-749-2424 749-1598
Web: www.klmicrowave.com

Kaiser Systems Inc (KSI) 126 Sohier Rd .... Beverly MA 01915 978-922-9300 922-8374
Web: www.kaisersys.com

Kathrein Inc Scala Div 555 Airport Rd .... Medford OR 97504 541-779-6500
Web: kathrein.de/en/

KEMET Corp PO Box 5928 .... Greenville SC 29606 864-963-6300 963-6322
NYSE: KEM ■ *Web:* www.kemet.com

Kepco Inc 131-38 Sanford Ave .... Flushing NY 11355 718-461-7000 767-1102
TF: 800-526-2324 ■ *Web:* www.kepcopower.com

Key Tronic Corp 4424 N Sullivan Rd .... Spokane WA 99214 509-928-8000 927-5555
NASDAQ: KTCC ■ *Web:* www.keytronic.com

Knowles Corporation 1151 Maplewood Dr .... Itasca IL 60143 630-250-5100 250-0575
Web: www.knowlesinc.com

KOA Speer Electronics Inc 199 Bolivar Dr .... Bradford PA 16701 814-362-5536
Web: www.evalue-tech.com

L-3 Communications Corp Display Systems Div
1355 Bluegrass Lakes Pkwy .... Alpharetta GA 30004 770-752-7000 752-5525
Web: www.l-3com.com

L-3 Narda Microwave-West 107 Woodmere Rd .... Folsom CA 95630 916-351-4500
Web: www.nardamicrowave.com

L-Com Inc 45 Beechwood Dr .... North Andover MA 01845 978-682-6936
Web: www.l-com.com

La Marche Mfg Co 106 Bradrock Dr .... Des Plaines IL 60018 847-299-1188 299-3061
TF: 888-232-9562 ■ *Web:* www.lamarchemfg.com

Larco 210 NE Tenth Ave PO Box 547 .... Brainerd MN 56401 218-829-9797 829-0139
TF Cust Svc: 800-523-6996 ■ *Web:* larco.com/

Lenexpo Inc 1293 Mtn View Alviso Rd Ste A .... Sunnyvale CA 94089 408-962-0515
TF: 877-536-3976 ■ *Web:* www.atlona.com

Lexel Imaging Systems Inc
1501 Newtown Pike .... Lexington KY 40511 859-243-5500 243-5555
TF: 800-397-8121 ■ *Web:* www.lexelimaging.com

LHV Power Corp 10221 Buena Vista Ave .... Santee CA 92071 619-258-7700
Web: www.lhvpower.com

Light Engines LLC 29 Library Ln S .... Sturbridge MA 01566 508-347-0111

LogiCan Technologies Inc 150 Karl Clark Rd .... Edmonton AB T6N1E2 780-450-4400
Web: www.logican.com

Logitek Inc 110 Wilbur Pl .... Bohemia NY 11716 631-567-1100 567-1823
Web: www.naii.com

Lorch Microwave Inc 1725 N Salisbury Blvd .... Salisbury MD 21802 410-860-5100
Web: www.lorch.com

Lucix Corp 800 Avenida Acaso .... Camarillo CA 93012 805-987-3677
Web: www.lucix.com

Lumex Inc 290 E Helen Rd .... Palatine IL 60067 847-359-2790 359-8904
TF: 800-278-5666 ■ *Web:* www.lumex.com

Luminit LLC 1850 W 205th St .... Torrance CA 90501 310-320-1066
Web: www.luminitco.com

Lynn Electronics Corp 154 Railroad Dr .... Ivyland PA 18974 215-355-8200
Web: www.lynnelec.com

Magmotor Technologies Inc 10 Coppage Dr .... Worcester MA 01603 508-459-5991
Web: www.inverpower.com

MagneTek Inc N49 W13650 Campbell Dr .... Menomonee Falls WI 53051 800-288-8178 298-3503
NASDAQ: MAG ■ *TF:* 800-288-8178 ■ *Web:* www.magnetek.com

Magtech Industries Corp
5625-A S Arville St .... Las Vegas NV 89119 702-364-9998
Web: www.magtechind.com

Maida Development Co 201 S Mallory St .... Hampton VA 23663 757-723-0785 722-1194
Web: www.maida.com

Marlow Industries Inc 10451 Vista Pk Rd .... Dallas TX 75238 214-340-4900 340-7728
TF: 877-627-5691 ■ *Web:* www.marlow.com

Maxwell Technologies Inc
5271 Viewridge Ct Ste 100 .... San Diego CA 92123 858-503-3300 503-3301
NASDAQ: MXWL ■ *TF:* 877-511-4324 ■ *Web:* www.maxwell.com

MC10 Inc Nine Camp St Second Fl .... Cambridge MA 02140 617-234-4448 234-0093
Web: www.mc10inc.com

Company	City	State	ZIP	Phone	Fax
McDonald Technologies International Inc 2310 McDaniel Dr *Web:* www.mcdonald-tech.com	Carrollton	TX	75006	972-421-4100	241-2643
Meggitt Safety Systems Inc 1915 Voyager Ave *Web:* www.meggitt.com	Simi Valley	CA	93063	805-584-4100	578-3400
Merrimac Industries Inc 41 Fairfield Pl **Fax:* Sales ■ *Web:* www.craneae.com	West Caldwell	NJ	07006	973-575-1300	575-0531*
Methode Electronics Inc 7401 W Wilson Ave *NYSE: MEI* ■ *TF:* 877-316-7700 ■ *Web:* www.methode.com	Chicago	IL	60706	708-867-6777	867-6999
Micro-coax Inc 206 Jones Blvd *TF:* 800-223-2629 ■ *Web:* www.micro-coax.com	Pottstown	PA	19464	610-495-0110	495-6656
MicroPlanet Technology Corp 15530 Woodinville-Redmond Rd NE Ste B100 *Web:* www.microplanet.com	Woodinville	WA	98072	425-984-2740	
Microwave Engineering Corp 1551 Osgood St *Web:* www.microwaveeng.com	North Andover	MA	01845	978-685-2776	975-4363
Microwave Filter Company Inc 6743 Kinne St *Web:* www.microwavefilter.com	East Syracuse	NY	13057	315-438-4700	
Miteq Inc 100 Davids Dr *Web:* www.miteq.com	Hauppauge	NY	11788	631-436-7400	436-7430
Mitsubishi Electric & Electronics USA Inc *Elevator & Escalator Div* 5665 Plz Dr *Web:* www.mitsubishielectric.com/elevator	Cypress	CA	90630	714-220-4700	220-4812
Molex Inc 2222 Wellington Ct *NASDAQ: MOLX* ■ *TF Cust Svc:* 800-786-6539 ■ *Web:* www.molex.com	Lisle	IL	60532	630-969-4550	969-1352
Morey Corp 100 Morey Dr *Web:* www.moreycorp.com	Woodridge	IL	60517	630-754-2300	754-2001
MS Kennedy Corp 4707 Dey Rd *Web:* www.mskennedy.com	Liverpool	NY	13088	315-701-6751	701-6752
MTI-Milliren Technologies Inc Two New Pasture Rd *Web:* www.mti-milliren.com	Newburyport	MA	01950	978-465-6064	
MtronPTI 1703 E Hwy 50 *TF:* 800-762-8800 ■ *Web:* www.mtronpti.com	Yankton	SD	57078	605-665-9321	665-1709
Multi-Fineline Electronix Inc (Mflex) 3140 E Coronado St *NASDAQ: MFLX* ■ *Web:* www.mflex.com	Anaheim	CA	92806	714-238-1488	
Murata Electronics North America Inc 2200 Lake Pk Dr *TF:* 800-704-6079 ■ *Web:* www.murata.com	Smyrna	GA	30080	770-436-1300	436-3030
Namco Controls Corp 2100 W Broad St **Fax Area Code:* 803 ■ *TF:* 800-390-6405 ■ *Web:* www.danaherspecialtyproducts.com	Elizabethtown	NC	28337	910-862-2511	285-0885*
Netcom Inc 599 S Wheeling Rd *Web:* www.netcominc.com	Wheeling	IL	60090	847-537-6300	537-2700
NewComLink Inc 3900 N Capital Of Texas Hwy Ste 150 *Web:* www.newcomlink.com	Austin	TX	78746	512-501-1240	
Newport Corp 1791 Deere Ave *NASDAQ: NEWP* ■ **Fax:* Sales ■ *TF Sales:* 800-222-6440 ■ *Web:* www.newport.com	Irvine	CA	92606	949-863-3144	253-1680*
Niles Audio Corp 1969 Kellog Ave *TF:* 800-289-4434 ■ *Web:* www.nilesaudio.com	Carlsbad	CA	92008	760-710-0992	
Nortech Systems Inc 1120 Wayzata Blvd E Ste 201 *NASDAQ: NSYS* ■ **Fax Area Code:* 218 ■ *TF:* 800-237-9576 ■ *Web:* www.nortechsys.com	Wayzata	MN	55391	952-345-2244	818-1096*
Nortek Security & Control LLC 1950 Camino Vida Roble Ste 150 *TF Cust Svc:* 800-421-1587 ■ *Web:* www.linearcorp.com	Carlsbad	CA	92008	760-438-7000	931-1340
Novacap Inc 25111 Anza Dr *Web:* knowlescapacitors.com/novacap	Valencia	CA	91355	661-295-5920	295-5928
Novacentrix Corp 200-B Parker Dr Ste 580 *Web:* www.novacentrix.com	Austin	TX	78728	512-491-9500	491-0002
NWL Transformers Inc 312 Rising Sun Rd *TF:* 800-742-5695 ■ *Web:* www.nwl.com	Bordentown	NJ	08505	609-298-7300	298-1982
O M Jones Inc PO Box 4375 *Web:* www.micro-tronics.net	Sonora	CA	95370	209-532-1008	532-1009
Oeco LLC 4607 SE International Way *Web:* www.oeco.com	Milwaukie	OR	97222	503-659-5999	653-6310
Ohmite Manufacturing Co 1600 Golf Rd Ste 850 *TF:* 866-964-6483 ■ *Web:* www.ohmite.com	Rolling Meadows	IL	60008	847-258-0300	574-7501
OK International 12151 Monarch St *TF:* 800-495-1775 ■ *Web:* www.okinternational.com	Garden Grove	CA	92841	714-799-9910	799-9533
On-Line Strategies Inc 7920 Belt Line Rd Ste 1150 *Web:* www.olsdallas.com	Dallas	TX	75254	214-466-1000	
Onyx EMS LLC 2920 Kelly Ave *TF:* 800-258-7989 ■ *Web:* sparton.com	Watertown	SD	57201	605-886-2519	886-5123
Oppenheimer Precision Products 173 Gibraltar Rd *Web:* www.oppiprecision.com	Horsham	PA	19044	215-674-9100	675-5139
Oren Elliott Products Inc 128 W Vine St *Web:* www.orenelliottproducts.com	Edgerton	OH	43517	419-298-2306	298-3545
OSI Systems Inc 12525 Chadron Ave *NASDAQ: OSIS* ■ *Web:* www.osi-systems.com	Hawthorne	CA	90250	310-978-0516	644-1727
OSRAM Sylvania Inc 100 Endicott St *Web:* www.sylvania.com	Danvers	MA	01923	978-777-1900	750-2152
PACE Inc 255 Air Tool Dr *Web:* www.paceworldwide.com	Southern Pines	NC	28387	910-695-7223	
Panamax Inc 1690 Corporate Cir *TF:* 800-472-5555 ■ *Web:* www.panamax.com	Petaluma	CA	94954	707-283-5900	283-5901
Para Systems Inc *Minuteman UPS* 1455 LeMay Dr *TF:* 800-238-7272 ■ *Web:* www.minutemanups.com	Carrollton	TX	75007	972-446-7363	446-9011
PCB Group Inc 3425 Walden Ave *TF:* 800-828-8840 ■ *Web:* www.pcb.com	Depew	NY	14043	716-684-0001	684-0987
PerkinElmer Inc 940 Winter St *NYSE: PKI* ■ *Web:* www.perkinelmer.com	Waltham	MA	02451	203-925-4602	944-4904
PG Life Link Inc 167 Gap Way *TF:* 800-287-4123 ■ *Web:* pglifelink.com/	Erlanger	KY	41018	859-283-5900	372-6272
PhyleTec LLC 4150 Grange Hall Rd *Web:* www.phyletec.com	Holly	MI	48442	248-634-4000	
Piller Inc 45 Turner Rd **Fax Area Code:* 845 ■ *TF:* 800-597-6937 ■ *Web:* www.piller.com	Middletown	NY	10941	800-597-6937	692-0295*
Plastronics Socket Co Inc 2601 Texas Dr *TF Cust Svc:* 800-582-5822 ■ *Web:* www.plastronics.com	Irving	TX	75062	972-258-2580	
Plug Power Inc 968 Albany-Shaker Rd *NASDAQ: PLUG* ■ *TF:* 877-474-1993 ■ *Web:* www.plugpower.com	Latham	NY	12110	518-782-7700	782-9060
Polyflon Co One WillaRd Rd *Web:* www.polyflon.com	Norwalk	CT	06851	203-840-7555	840-7565
Positronic Industries Inc 423 N Campbell Ave PO Box 8247 *TF:* 800-641-4054 ■ *Web:* www.connectpositronic.com	Springfield	MO	65801	417-866-2322	866-4115
Post Glover Resistors Inc 4750 Olympic Blvd Bldg B *TF Cust Svc:* 800-537-6144 ■ *Web:* www.postglover.com	Erlanger	KY	41018	859-283-0778	283-2978
Power-One Inc 740 Calle Plano *NASDAQ: PWER* ■ *Web:* www.power-one.com	Camarillo	CA	93012	805-987-8741	388-0476
Precision Cable Assemblies LLC 16830 Pheasant Dr *Web:* www.pca-llc.com	Brookfield	WI	53005	262-784-7887	784-0681
Precision Devices Inc 8840 N Greenview Dr *TF:* 800-274-9825 ■ *Web:* www.pdixtal.com	Middleton	WI	53562	608-831-4445	831-3343
Precision Interconnect Corp 10025 SW Freeman Ct *TF:* 800-522-6752 ■ *Web:* www.te.com	Wilsonville	OR	97070	503-685-9300	685-9305
Progressive Dynamics Inc 507 Industrial Rd *Web:* www.progressivedyn.com	Marshall	MI	49068	269-781-4241	781-7802
Proton Onsite 10 Technology Dr *Web:* www.protononsite.com	Wallingford	CT	06492	203-678-2000	949-8016
Pulse Engineering Inc 12220 World Trade Dr *Web:* www.pulseelectronics.com	San Diego	CA	92128	858-674-8100	674-8262
Q-tech Corp 10150 Jefferson Blvd *Web:* www.q-tech.com	Culver City	CA	90232	310-836-7900	836-2157
Q-tran Inc 304 Bishop Ave *Web:* www.q-tran.com	Bridgeport	CT	06610	203-367-8777	367-8771
Qual-Tron Inc (QTI) 9409 E 55th Pl *Web:* www.qual-tron.com	Tulsa	OK	74145	918-622-7052	664-8557
QualiTau Inc 830 Maude Ave *Web:* qualitau.com	Mountain View	CA	94043	408-522-9200	
Qualitel Corp 11831 Beverly Pk Rd *TF:* 800-647-7706 ■ *Web:* www.qualitelcorp.com	Everett	WA	98204	425-423-8388	423-8398
Quartzdyne Inc 4334 W Links Dr *Web:* www.quartzdyne.com	Salt Lake City	UT	84120	801-266-6958	266-7985
Raritan Computer Inc 400 Cottontail Ln *TF:* 800-724-8090 ■ *Web:* www.raritan.com	Somerset	NJ	08873	732-764-8886	764-8887
Record USA 4324 Phil Hargett Ct *TF Sales:* 800-438-1937 ■ *Web:* www.record-usa.com	Monroe	NC	28105	704-289-9212	289-2024
Regal Research & Mfg Co Inc 1200 E Plano Pkwy *Web:* www.regalresearch.com	Plano	TX	75074	972-494-0359	272-0220
Revionics Inc 2998 Douglas Blvd Ste 350 *Web:* www.revionics.com	Roseville	CA	95661	916-797-6051	
RF Industries 7610 Miramar Rd Bldg 6000 *NASDAQ: RFIL* ■ *TF:* 800-233-1728 ■ *Web:* www.rfindustries.com	San Diego	CA	92126	858-549-6340	549-6345
Ruhle Cos Inc 99 Wall St *Web:* www.ruhle.com	Valhalla	NY	10595	914-761-2600	761-0405
S & K Electronics Inc 56301 US Hwy 93 *Web:* www.skecorp.com	Ronan	MT	59864	406-883-6241	883-6228
S V Microwave Inc 2400 Centre Pk W Dr *Web:* www.svmicrowave.com	West Palm Beach	FL	33409	561-840-1800	842-6277
Samtec Inc 520 Parkeast Blvd *TF:* 800-726-8329 ■ *Web:* www.samtec.com	New Albany	IN	47150	812-944-6733	948-5047
Schott Corp 1401 Air Wing Rd *Web:* www.schottcorp.com	San Diego	CA	92154	507-223-5572	223-5055
Schumacher Electric Corp 801 E Business Ctr Dr **Fax Area Code:* 847 ■ *TF:* 800-621-5485 ■ *Web:* www.batterychargers.com	Mount Prospect	IL	60056	800-621-5485	298-1698*
Scosche Industries Inc PO Box 2901 *Web:* www.scosche.com	Oxnard	CA	93034	805-486-4450	486-9996
Seiko Instruments USA Inc 21221 S Western Ave Ste 250 *TF Sales:* 800-688-0817 ■ *Web:* www.seikoinstruments.com	Torrance	CA	90501	310-517-7700	517-7709
Semicon Assoc 695 Laco Dr *Web:* www.semiconassociates.com	Lexington	KY	40510	859-255-3664	255-6829
Semiconductor Circuits Inc 49 Range Rd *Web:* www.dcdc.com	Windham	NH	03087	603-893-2330	893-6280
Sendec Corp 72 Perinton Pkwy *TF:* 800-295-8000 ■ *Web:* apitech.com	Fairport	NY	14450	585-425-3390	425-3392
Sharp Microelectronics of the Americas 5700 NW Pacific Rim Blvd *Web:* www.sharpsma.com	Camas	WA	98607	360-834-2500	834-8903
Shelly Assoc Inc 17171 Murphy Ave *Web:* www.shellyinc.com	Irvine	CA	92614	949-417-8070	417-8075
Shogyo International Corp 6851 Jericho Tpke *Web:* www.shogyo.com	Syosset	NY	11791	516-921-9111	921-3777
Sierra Nevada Corp (SNC) 444 Salomon Cir *Web:* www.sncorp.com	Sparks	NV	89434	775-331-0222	331-0370
Sigma Electronics Inc 1027 Commercial Ave *TF:* 866-569-2681 ■ *Web:* www.sigmatechsys.com	East Petersburg	PA	17520	717-569-2926	569-4056
Signal Transformer Company Inc 500 Bayview Ave *TF:* 866-239-5777 ■ *Web:* www.signaltransformer.com	Inwood	NY	11096	516-239-5777	239-7208
Silent Power Inc 8175 Industrial Park Rd Ste 100 *Web:* www.silentpwr.com	Baxter	MN	56425	218-454-3030	
Simplex Inc 5300 Rising Moon Rd *TF:* 800-637-8603 ■ *Web:* www.simplexdirect.com	Springfield	IL	62711	217-483-1600	483-1616
SL Power Electronics Inc 6050 King Dr Bldg A **Fax Area Code:* 858 ■ *TF:* 800-235-5929 ■ *Web:* www.slpower.com	Ventura	CA	93003	805-486-4565	712-2040*

Phone | Fax

Smart Electronics & Assembly Inc
2000 W Corporate Way. . . . . Anaheim CA 92801 714-991-6500
Web: www.smartelec.com
Smart Power Systems Inc 1760 Stebbins Dr. . . . . Houston TX 77043 713-464-8000 984-0841
TF: 800-241-6880 ■ *Web:* www.smartpowersystems.com
SMK Electronics Corp USA
1055 Tierra Del Rey . . . . . Chula Vista CA 91910 619-216-6400 216-6498
Web: www.smk.co.jp
SMTC Corp 635 Hood Rd. . . . . Markham ON L3R4N6 905-479-1810 479-1877
NASDAQ: SMTX ■ *Web:* www.smtc.com
SNC Mfg Company Inc 101 W Waukau Ave. . . . . Oshkosh WI 54902 920-231-7370 231-1090
TF: 800-558-3325 ■ *Web:* www.sncmfg.com
Sorenson Communications Inc
4192 Riverboat Rd Ste 100. . . . . Salt Lake City UT 84123 801-287-9400 287-9401
Web: www.sorenson.com
Spang & Co 110 Delta Dr . . . . . Pittsburgh PA 15238 412-963-9363 696-0333
Web: www.spang.com
Spectrum Control Inc 8031 Avonia Rd. . . . . Fairview PA 16415 814-474-2207 474-2208
Web: eis.apitech.com//
Spellman High Voltage Electronics Corp
475 Wireless Blvd. . . . . Hauppauge NY 11788 631-435-1600 435-1620*
**Fax:* Sales ■ *Web:* www.spellmanhv.com
Spinnaker Microwave Inc 3281 Kifer Rd. . . . . Santa Clara CA 95051 408-732-9828
Web: hunter-technology.com
Standex Electronics Inc
4538 Camberwell Rd . . . . . Cincinnati OH 45209 513-871-3777 871-3779
TF: 866-782-6339 ■ *Web:* www.standexelectronics.com
STATS ChipPAC Test Services Inc
46429 Landing Pkwy . . . . . Fremont CA 94538 408-586-0600 586-0601
Web: www.statschippac.com
Stevens Water Monitoring Systems
12067 NE Glenn Widing Dr Ste 106. . . . . Portland OR 97220 503-469-8000 469-8100
TF: 800-452-5272 ■ *Web:* www.stevenswater.com
Sumida America Inc
1251 N Plum Grove Rd Ste 150 . . . . . Schaumburg IL 60173 847-545-6700 545-6721
Web: www.sumida.com
Superconductor Technologies Inc (STI)
460 Ward Dr. . . . . Santa Barbara CA 93111 805-690-4500 967-0342
NASDAQ: SCON ■ *TF:* 800-727-3648 ■ *Web:* www.suptech.com
Switchcraft Inc 5555 N Elston Ave. . . . . Chicago IL 60630 773-792-2700 792-2129
Web: www.switchcraft.com
SynQor Inc 155 Swanson Rd. . . . . Boxborough MA 01719 978-849-0600 849-0601
Web: www.synqor.com
Sypris Electronics LLC 10901 N McKinley Dr . . . . . Tampa FL 33612 813-972-6000 972-6704
TF: 800-937-9220 ■ *Web:* www.sypris.com
Sypris Solutions Inc
101 Bullitt Ln Ste 450. . . . . Louisville KY 40222 502-329-2000 329-2050
NASDAQ: SYPR ■ *TF:* 800-588-9119 ■ *Web:* www.sypris.com
System Sensor 3825 Ohio Ave. . . . . Saint Charles IL 60174 630-377-6580 377-6495
TF Tech Supp: 800-736-7672 ■ *Web:* www.systemsensor.com
Taiyo Yuden (USA) Inc
1930 N Thoreau Dr Ste 190 . . . . . Schaumburg IL 60173 847-925-0888 925-0899
TF: 800-348-2496 ■ *Web:* www.t-yuden.com
TDI-Transistor Devices Inc
85 Horsehill Rd. . . . . Cedar Knolls NJ 07927 973-267-1900 267-2047
TF: 800-488-6724 ■ *Web:* www.tdipower.com
TDK Corp of America 475 Half Day Rd . . . . . Lincolnshire IL 60069 847-699-2299 803-6296
Web: www.tdk.com
TDK-Lambda Americas Inc 405 Essex Rd. . . . . Neptune NJ 07753 732-922-9300 922-1441
Web: www.us.tdk-lambda.com/hp
Teledyne Electronic Safety Products
19735 Dearborn St . . . . . Chatsworth CA 91311 818-718-6640 998-3312
Web: www.teledynesafetyproducts.com
Telonic Berkeley Inc 1080 La Mirada Ct . . . . . Vista CA 92081 760-744-8350 744-8360
TF Sales: 800-311-8805 ■ *Web:* www.telonicberkeley.com
Threshold Financial Technologies Inc
3269 American Dr. . . . . Mississauga ON L4V1X5 905-678-7373
TF: 888-414-3733 ■ *Web:* www.threshold-fti.com
Times Microwave Systems Inc PO Box 5039. . . . . Wallingford CT 06492 203-949-8400 949-8423
TF: 800-867-2629 ■ *Web:* www.timesmicrowave.com
Toshiba America Inc
1251 Ave of the Americas Ste 4100 . . . . . New York NY 10020 212-596-0600 593-3875
TF: 800-457-7777 ■ *Web:* www.toshiba.com
Total Technologies Ltd Nine Studebaker . . . . . Irvine CA 92618 949-465-0200 465-0212
TF: 800-669-4885 ■ *Web:* www.total-technologies.com
TRAK Microwave Corp 4726 Eisenhower Blvd . . . . . Tampa FL 33634 813-901-7200 901-7491
TF: 888-283-8444 ■ *Web:* www.trak.com
Transcend Technologies Group Inc
3101 Zinfandel Dr Ste 200 . . . . . Rancho Cordova CA 95670 916-421-4000
Web: www.transcendtechgroup.com
Tri Source Inc 84 Platt Rd. . . . . Shelton CT 06484 203-926-9460 567-8181
Web: www.trisourceinc.com
Triton Systems Inc 21405 B St . . . . . Long Beach MS 39560 228-575-3100
TF: 866-787-4866 ■ *Web:* www.tritonatm.com
TSI Power Corp 1103 W Pierce Ave . . . . . Antigo WI 54409 715-623-0636 623-2426
TF: 800-874-3160 ■ *Web:* www.tsipower.com
Tyco Electronics Corp 1050 Westlakes Dr . . . . . Berwyn PA 19312 610-893-9800
Web: www.te.com
United Chemi-Con Inc 9801 W Higgins Rd. . . . . Rosemont IL 60018 847-696-2000 696-9278
TF: 800-344-4539 ■ *Web:* www.chemi-con.com
Usi Electronics Inc
2775 W Cypress Creek Rd . . . . . Fort Lauderdale FL 33309 954-493-8111 493-8212
TF: 800-874-8111 ■ *Web:* www.usielectronics.com
Usmilcom Inc 1952 E Mcfadden Ave. . . . . Santa Ana CA 92705 714-835-3545
Web: www.usmilcom.com
V-TEK Inc 751 Summit Ave . . . . . Mankato MN 56002 507-387-2039
Web: www.vtekusa.com
Valpey Fisher Corp 75 S St. . . . . Hopkinton MA 01748 508-435-6831 435-5289
TF: 800-982-5737 ■ *Web:* www.ctsvalpey.com
Viasystems Group Inc
101 S Hanley Rd Ste 400 . . . . . Saint Louis MO 63105 314-727-2087 746-2233
Web: www.viasystems.com
Viatran Corp 3829 Forest Pkwy Ste 500. . . . . Wheatfield NY 14120 716-629-3800 693-9162
TF: 800-688-0030 ■ *Web:* www.viatran.com
Vicor Corp 25 Frontage Rd . . . . . Andover MA 01810 978-470-2900 475-6715
NASDAQ: VICR ■ *TF:* 800-869-5300 ■ *Web:* www.vicorpower.com
Vishay Intertechnology Inc 63 Lancaster Ave. . . . . Malvern PA 19355 610-644-1300 296-0657
NYSE: VSH ■ *TF:* 800-567-6098 ■ *Web:* www.vishay.com
Wakefield Thermal Solutions Inc 33 Bridge St . . . . . Pelham NH 03076 603-635-2800 635-1900
Web: www.wakefield-vette.com
Wellex Corp 551 Brown Rd. . . . . Fremont CA 94539 510-743-1818 743-1899
Web: www.wellex.com
Western Electronics LLC 1550 S Tech Ln . . . . . Meridian ID 83642 208-955-9700 465-9798*
**Fax Area Code:* 303 ■ *TF:* 888-857-5775 ■ *Web:* www.westernelectronics.com
Wilmore Electronics Company Inc
607 US 70-A E PO Box 1329 . . . . . Hillsborough NC 27278 919-732-9351 732-9359
Web: www.wilmoreelectronics.com
Wireless Xcessories Group Inc
1840 County Line Rd Ste 301. . . . . Huntingdon Valley PA 19006 215-322-4600 233-0220*
OTC: WIRX ■ **Fax Area Code:* 888 ■ *TF:* 800-233-0013 ■ *Web:* www.wirexgroup.com
World Electronics Sales & Service Inc
3000 Kutztown Rd. . . . . Reading PA 19605 610-939-9800 939-9895
TF: 800-523-0427 ■ *Web:* www.world-electronics.com
Xantrex Technology Inc 3700 Gilmore Way. . . . . Burnaby BC V5G4M1 604-422-8595 420-1591
TF: 800-670-0707 ■ *Web:* www.xantrex.com
Yazaki North America Inc 6801 N Haggerty Rd. . . . . Canton MI 48187 734-983-1000
Web: www.yazaki-na.com
Z Communications Inc 14118 Stowe Dr Ste B. . . . . Poway CA 92064 858-621-2700 486-1927
TF: 877-808-1226 ■ *Web:* www.zcomm.com
Zentech Manufacturing Inc 6980 Tudsbury Rd . . . . . Baltimore MD 21244 443-348-4500
Web: www.zentechman.com
Ziptronix Inc 5400 Glenwood Ave Ste G-05. . . . . Raleigh NC 27612 919-459-2400 459-2401
Web: www.ziptronix.com

257 ELECTRONIC ENCLOSURES

Phone | Fax

A & J Mfg Co 14831 Franklin Ave . . . . . Tustin CA 92780 714-544-9570 544-4215
Web: www.aj-racks.com
American Electric Technologies Inc (AETI)
1250 Wood Branch Park Dr Ste 600. . . . . Houston TX 77087 713-644-8182 838-1066*
NASDAQ: AETI ■ **Fax Area Code:* 409 ■ *Web:* www.aeti.com
APW Ltd PO Box 806 . . . . . Pewaukee WI 53072 262-523-7600 523-7624
Buckeye ShapeForm 555 Marion Rd . . . . . Columbus OH 43207 614-445-8433 445-8224
TF: 800-728-0776 ■ *Web:* www.buckeyeshapeform.com
Bud Industries Inc 4605 E 355th St. . . . . Willoughby OH 44094 440-946-3200 951-4015
Web: www.budind.com
Crenlo LLC 1600 Fourth Ave NW. . . . . Rochester MN 55901 507-289-3371 287-3405*
**Fax:* Sales ■ *Web:* www.crenlo.com
Dawson Metal Company Inc 825 Allen St. . . . . Jamestown NY 14701 716-664-3815 664-3485
Web: www.dawsonmetal.com
Electrol Specialties Co 441 Clark St. . . . . South Beloit IL 61080 815-389-2291 389-2294
Web: www.esc4cip.com
Emcor Enclosures 1600 Fourth Ave NW . . . . . Rochester MN 55901 507-289-3371 287-3405*
**Fax:* Sales ■ *Web:* www.crenlo.com
Equipto Electronics Corp 351 Woodlawn Ave. . . . . Aurora IL 60506 630-897-4691 897-5314
TF: 800-204-7225 ■ *Web:* www.equiptoelec.com
Gerome Mfg Co Inc
80 Laurel View Dr PO Box 1089. . . . . Smithfield PA 15478 724-438-8544 437-5608
Web: www.geromemfg.com
Global MetalForm LP 733 Davis St. . . . . Scranton PA 18505 570-346-3871 346-1612
Web: www.markreuther.com/global401web
I-Bus Corp 3350 Scott Blvd Bldg 54 . . . . . Santa Clara CA 95054 408-450-7880 450-7881
Web: www.ibus.com
JMR Electronics Inc 8968 Fullbridht Ave . . . . . Chatsworth CA 91311 818-993-4801 993-9173*
**Fax:* Hum Res ■ *Web:* www.jmr.com
Macase Industrial Corp 3005 Ctr Pl Ste 100. . . . . Norcross GA 30093 770-840-8840 840-7006
Web: www.macase.com/macase
National Mfg Company Inc 12 River Rd . . . . . Chatham NJ 07928 973-635-8846 635-7810
Web: www.natlmfg.com
Omega Tool 308 S Mtn View Ave . . . . . San Bernardino CA 92408 909-888-0440 889-8740
Web: www.omegatool-usa.com
Optima Electronic Packaging Systems
1775 MacLeod Dr. . . . . Lawrenceville GA 30043 770-496-4000 496-4041*
**Fax:* Sales ■ *Web:* optimastantron.com/en/optima-stantron/
Pentair Inc 5500 Wayzata Blvd Ste 800 . . . . . Minneapolis MN 55416 763-545-1730 656-5400
NYSE: PNR ■ *Web:* www.pentair.com
Stahlin Non-Metallic Enclosure
505 W Maple St . . . . . Belding MI 48809 616-794-0700 794-3378
Web: www.stahlin.com
TRI MAP International Inc
111 Val Dervin Pkwy. . . . . Stockton CA 95206 209-234-0100 234-5990
TF: 888-687-4627 ■ *Web:* www.trimapintl.com
Universal Enclosure Systems
1146 S Cedar Ridge Dr. . . . . Duncanville TX 75137 972-298-0531 298-0614
Web: www.universalenclosures.com
Zero Manufacturing Inc
500 West 200 North . . . . . North Salt Lake UT 84054 801-298-5900 292-9450
TF: 800-959-5050 ■ *Web:* www.zerocases.com

258 ELECTRONIC TRANSACTION PROCESSING

Phone | Fax

Alliance Data Systems Corp 7500 Dallas Pkwy . . . . . Plano TX 75024 214-494-3000
NYSE: ADS ■ *Web:* www.alliancedata.com
Avid Payment Solutions
950 S Old Woodward Ste 220. . . . . Birmingham MI 48009 888-855-8644 671-9773*
**Fax Area Code:* 866 ■ *TF:* 888-855-8644 ■ *Web:* www.avidpays.com
Chase Paymentech Solutions LLC
14221 Dallas Pkwy. . . . . Dallas TX 75254 800-708-3740 849-2148*
**Fax Area Code:* 214 ■ *TF Cust Svc:* 800-708-3740 ■ *Web:* www.chasepaymentech.com

	Phone	Fax
Covera Solutions Inc 1021 Watervliet-Shaker Rd PO Box 13539 . . . Albany NY 12205 *Fax Area Code: 518 ■ TF: 866-526-8372 ■ Web: www.coverasolutions.com	866-526-8372	437-8286*
Elavon Two Concourse Pkwy Ste 300 . . . Atlanta GA 30328 *Fax Area Code: 865 ■ TF: 800-725-1243 ■ Web: www.elavon.com	678-731-5000	577-0661*
Euronet Worldwide Inc 3500 College Blvd . . . Leawood KS 66211 NASDAQ: EEFT ■ Web: www.euronetworldwide.com	913-327-4200	327-1921
Global Payments Inc 10 Glenlake Pkwy N Twr . . . Atlanta GA 30328 NYSE: GPN ■ TF: 800-560-2960 ■ Web: www.globalpaymentsinc.com	770-829-8000	
Litle & Co 900 Chelmsford St . . . Lowell MA 01851 Web: www.litle.com	978-275-6500	937-7250
National Bankcard Systems 2600 Via Fortuna Ste 240 . . . Austin TX 78746 Web: enbs.com	512-494-9200	
National Processing Co 5100 Interchange Way . . . Louisville KY 40229 TF General: 877-300-7757 ■ Web: www.npc.net	800-683-2289	
Protegrity USA Inc 5 High Ridge Pk . . . Stamford CT 06905 Web: www.protegrity.com	203-326-7200	348-1251

259 ELEVATORS, ESCALATORS, MOVING WALKWAYS

	Phone	Fax
2H Offshore Inc 15990 N Barkers Landing Ste 200 . . . Houston TX 77079 Web: www.2hoffshore.com	281-258-2000	
2is Inc 75 W St . . . Walpole MA 02081 Web: www.2is-inc.com	508-850-7520	
3 u Technologies 11681 Leonidas Horton Rd . . . Conroe TX 77304 Web: www.3utech.com	936-441-3043	
4 Front 517 Seventh St . . . Rapid City SD 57701 Web: www.4front.biz	605-342-9470	
4g Unwired Inc 551 S Apollo Blvd Ste 100 . . . Melbourne FL 32901 Web: www.4gunwired.com	321-726-4183	
A-P-T Research Inc 4950 Research Dr NW . . . Huntsville AL 35805 Web: www.apt-research.com	256-327-3373	
Able Services 868 Folsom St . . . San Francisco CA 94107 TF: 800-461-9577 ■ Web: www.ableserve.com	415-546-6534	
Abna Engineering Inc 4140 Lindell Blvd . . . Saint Louis MO 63108 Web: abnacorp.com	314-454-0222	
Abonmarche Consultants Inc 361 First St . . . Manistee MI 49660 Web: www.abonmarche.com	231-723-1198	
ABOUT-Consulting LLC 330 Kennett Pike Ste 205 . . . Chadds Ford PA 19317 Web: www.about-consulting.com	610-388-9455	
Abx Engineering 880 Hinckley Rd . . . Burlingame CA 94010 TF: 800-366-4588 ■ Web: www.abxengineering.com	650-552-2322	
Accent Controls Inc 400 NW Platte Vly Dr . . . Riverside MO 64150 Web: www.accentcontrols.com	816-483-6330	
Accipiter Radar Technologies Inc 576 Hwy 20 W . . . Fonthill ON L0S1C0 Web: www.accipiterradar.com	905-228-6888	
Accutemp Engineering Inc 108 School St . . . Watertown MA 02472 Web: www.accutemp-eng.com	617-926-1221	
ACES Systems 10737 Lexington Dr . . . Knoxville TN 37932 Web: www.acessystems.com	865-671-2003	
Ackerman-practicon Inc 801 E Charleston Rd . . . Palo Alto CA 94303 Web: www.apcts.com	650-965-1000	
Acme Worldwide Enterprises Inc 1710 Randolph Ct SE . . . Albuquerque NM 87106 Web: www.acme-worldwide.com	505-243-0400	
Acoustics by Design Inc 124 Fulton St E Ste 200 . . . Grand Rapids MI 49503 Web: www.acousticsbydesign.com	616-241-5810	
Action Facilities Management Inc 115 Malone Dr . . . Morgantown WV 26501 Web: www.actionfacilities.com	304-599-6850	
Adams Communication & Engineering Technology Inc 11637 Terr Dr Ste 201 . . . Waldorf MD 20602 Web: www.adamscomm.com	301-861-5000	
Adaptive Flight Inc 885 Franklin Rd Ste 330 . . . Marietta GA 30067 Web: www.adaptiveflight.com	770-951-8755	
ADF Engineering Inc 228 Byers Rd Ste 202 . . . Miamisburg OH 45342 Web: www.adfengineering.com	937-847-2700	
Advanced Dynamics Corp Ltd 1700 Marie Victorin . . . St Bruno QC J3V6B9 Web: www.advanceddynamics.com	450-653-7220	
Advanced Rotorcraft Technology Inc 1330 Charleston Rd . . . Mountain View CA 94043 Web: www.flightlab.com	650-968-1464	
Advanced Testing Technologies Inc 110 Ricefield Ln . . . Hauppauge NY 11788	631-231-8777	
Advantage Engineering LLC 910 Century Dr . . . Mechanicsburg PA 17055 Web: www.cmxengineering.com	717-458-0800	
Advantage Plastics & Engineering Inc 4524 Bishop Ln . . . Louisville KY 40218 Web: www.advantageplastics.net	502-473-7331	
AE Works Ltd 6587 Hamilton Ave . . . Pittsburgh PA 15206 Web: www.ae-works.com	412-287-7333	
AEC Engineering Inc 400 First Ave N Ste 400 . . . Minneapolis MN 55401 Web: www.aecengineering.com	612-332-8905	
Aegir Systems 2151 Alessandro Dr Ste 211 . . . Ventura CA 93001 Web: www.aegir.com	805-648-2660	
Aegis Labs Inc 32565 B Golden Lantern St Ste 372 . . . Dana Point CA 92629 Web: www.aegislabsinc.com	949-751-8089	
Aerocon Engineering Co 7716 Kester Ave . . . Van Nuys CA 91405 Web: www.aeroconengineering.com	818-785-2743	
Aerospec Inc 505 E Alamo Dr . . . Chandler AZ 85225 Web: www.aerospecinc.com	480-892-7195	
Afram Corp 1601 Olive St . . . Saint Louis MO 63103 Web: www.aframcorp.com	314-645-6299	
AGRA Foundations Ltd 7708 Wagner Rd . . . Edmonton AB T6E5B2 Web: www.agra.com	780-468-3392	
Air Liquide Group 2700 Post Oak Blvd . . . Houston TX 77056 Web: www.us.airliquide.com	713-624-8000	
Alabama Goodwill Industries Inc 2350 Green Springs Hwy S . . . Birmingham AL 35205	205-323-6331	
Alabama Graphics & Engineering Supply Inc 2801 Fifth Ave S . . . Birmingham AL 35233 Web: www.algraphics.com	205-252-8505	
Albert A Webb Assoc 3788 Mccray St . . . Riverside CA 92506 Web: www.webbassociates.com	951-686-1070	
All Star Team Service LLC Two Industrial Park Dr Ste B . . . Waldorf MD 20602 Web: www.weclean2please.com	240-607-6209	
All-points Technology Corp PC Three Saddlebrook Dr . . . Killingworth CT 06419 Web: www.allpointstech.com	860-663-1697	
Allana Buick & Bers Inc 990 Commercial St . . . Palo Alto CA 94303 Web: www.abbae.com	650-543-5600	
Allied Corrosion Industries Inc 1550 Cobb Industrial Dr . . . Marietta GA 30066 TF: 800-241-0809 ■ Web: www.alliedcorrosion.com	770-425-1355	
Allied Resources Corp 106 Pitkin St . . . East Hartford CT 06108 Web: www.alliedr.com	860-290-6665	
Alloy Hardfacing & Engineering Company Inc 20425 Johnson Memorial Dr . . . Jordan MN 55352 Web: alloyhardfacing.com	952-492-5569	
Ally Plm Solutions Inc 9155 Governors Way . . . Cincinnati OH 45249 Web: www.allyplm.com	513-984-0480	
Alpha Consulting Engineers Inc 115 Limekiln Rd . . . New Cumberland PA 17070 Web: alphacei.com	717-770-2500	
Alpha Testing Inc 2209 Wisconsin St Ste 100 . . . Dallas TX 75229 Web: alphatesting.com	972-620-8911	620-1302
Alphion Corp 196 Princeton Hightstown Rd Bldg 1A . . . Princeton Junction NJ 08550 Web: www.alphion.com	609-936-9001	
Alpine Building Maintenance Inc 3006 W Division St . . . Arlington TX 76012 Web: www.bksassociates.com	817-795-6470	
ALSTOM Power Inc 175 Addison Rd . . . Windsor CT 06095 Web: www.alstom.com	860-688-1911	
Alt & Witzig Engineering Inc 4105 W 99th St . . . Carmel IN 46032 Web: www.ascet.org	317-875-7000	
Alum-A-Lift Inc 7909 US Hwy 78 . . . Winston GA 30187 Web: www.alum-a-lift.com	770-489-0328	
Alvine Engineering Inc 1102 Douglas On The Mall . . . Omaha NE 68102 Web: www.alvine.com	402-346-7007	
American Aerospace Advisors Inc 1007 Ford St . . . Bridgeport PA 19405 Web: americanaerospace.com	610-225-2604	225-3781
American Aerospace Controls Inc 570 Smith St . . . Farmingdale NY 11735 TF: 888-873-8559 ■ Web: www.a-a-c.com	631-694-5100	
American Combustion Industries Inc 7100 Holladay Tyler Rd Ste 233 . . . Glenn Dale MD 20769 Web: www.aci.com	301-779-3400	
American SensoRx Inc 31 N Monroe St . . . Ridgewood NJ 07410 Web: www.americansensorx.com	201-447-8999	
AMT Machine Systems Ltd 868 Fwy Dr N . . . Columbus OH 43229 Web: www.amtmachinesystems.com	614-635-8050	
Ana Properties 3630 N Josey Ln Ste 217 . . . Carrollton TX 75007	972-939-0610	
Analytical Design Service Corp 540 Avis Dr Ste E . . . Ann Arbor MI 48108 Web: www.adsc-usa.com	734-761-2626	
Anderson Cleaning 144 Garing Rd . . . Chicora PA 16025	724-445-2849	
Anderson Economic Group LLC 1555 Watertower Pl Ste 100 . . . East Lansing MI 48823 Web: aeg1.com	517-333-6984	
Anderson Pacific Engineering Construction Inc 1390 Norman Ave . . . Santa Clara CA 95054 Web: www.andpac.com	408-970-9900	
Anderson Perry & Assoc Inc 1901 N Fir St . . . La Grande OR 97850 Web: www.andersonperry.com	541-963-8309	
Andrews Hammock Powell Inc 250 Charter Ln . . . Macon GA 31210 Web: www.ahpengr.com	478-405-8301	
Antioch International Inc 410 Winding View . . . New Braunfels TX 78132 Web: www.antioch-intl.com	402-289-2217	
Aon Fire Protection Engineering Corp 1000 Milwaukee Ave Fifth Fl . . . Glenview IL 60025 Web: www.aonfpe.com	847-953-7700	
Apex Geoscience Inc 2120 Brandon Dr . . . Tyler TX 75703 TF: 800-755-8461 ■ Web: www.apexgeo.com	903-581-8080	581-8081
Apogee Consulting Group PA 1151 Kildaire Farm Rd Ste 120 . . . Cary NC 27511 Web: www.acg-pa.com	919-858-7420	
Applied Mfg Technologies Inc 219 Kay Industrial Dr . . . Orion MI 48359 Web: www.robotprogrammers.com	248-409-2000	
Applied Physics Systems Inc 281 E Java Dr . . . Sunnyvale CA 94089 Web: www.appliedphysics.com	650-965-0500	
Applied Systems Engineering Inc 1480 Hickory St Ste 106 . . . Niceville FL 32578 Web: aseifl.com	850-729-7550	

Phone Fax

AQUA TERRA Consultants Inc
2685 Marine Way Ste 1314 ... Mountain View CA 94043 650-962-1864
Web: www.aquaterra.com

Aquaveo LLC 3210 N Canyon Rd Ste 300 ... Provo UT 84604 801-691-5528
Web: www.aquaveo.com

Arcca Inc 2288 Second St Pk ... Penns Park PA 18943 215-598-9750
Web: www.arcca.com

Archibald Gray & McKay Ltd 553 Southdale Rd E ... London ON N6E1A2 519-685-5300
Web: www.agm.on.ca

Architectual Engineering Consultants Inc
40801 Hwy 6 24 Ste 214 ... Avon CO 81620 970-748-8520
Web: www.aec-vail.com

ARDL Inc 400 Aviation Dr ... Mount Vernon IL 62864 618-244-3235
Web: www.ardlinc.com

Areias Systems Inc
5900 Butler Ln Ste 280 ... Scotts Valley CA 95066 831-440-9800
Web: www.areiasys.com

Arizon Structures 11880 Dorsett Rd ... St. Louis MO 63043 314-739-0037
Web: www.arizoncompanies.com

Arkansas Power Electronics International Inc
535 W Research Ctr Blvd Ste 209 ... Fayetteville AR 72701 479-443-5759
Web: apei.net

Armstrong Consultants Inc
861 Rood Ave ... Grand Junction CO 81501 970-242-0101
Web: www.armstrongconsultants.com

Arnold & Assoc 14275 Midway Rd Ste 170 ... Addison TX 75001 972-991-1144
Web: www.elarnoldandassociates.com

Arnold Engineering Inc 345 Cessna Cir Ste 102 ... Corona CA 92880 951-898-0999
Web: www.arnoldeng.com

Arora & Assoc PC
1200 Lenox Dr Ste 200 ... Lawrence Township NJ 08648 609-844-1111
Web: www.arorapc.com

Arrayent Inc 2317 Broadway St Ste 140 ... Redwood City CA 94063 650-260-4520
Web: www.arrayent.com

Art Anderson Assoc Inc 202 Pacific Ave ... Bremerton WA 98337 360-479-5600
Web: www.artanderson.com

Artisan Industries Inc 73 Pond St ... Waltham MA 02451 781-893-6800
Web: www.artisanind.com

Arup North America Ltd
560 Mission St Ste 700 ... San Francisco CA 94105 415-957-9445
Web: www.arup.com

Ascendant Engineering Solutions
13091 Pond Springs Rd Ste 925 ... Austin TX 78729 512-371-5704
Web: aesaustin.com

Associated Engineering Group Ltd
10909 Jasper Ave Ste 1000 ... Edmonton AB T5J5B9 780-451-7666 454-7698
Web: www.ae.ca

Astrodyne Corp 375 Forbes Blvd ... Mansfield MA 02048 508-964-6300
TF: 800-823-8082 ■ *Web:* www.astrodyne.com

Athavale Lystad & Assoc Inc
6001 Montrose Rd Ste 1030 ... Rockville MD 20852 301-816-3237
Web: www.alaengr.com

Atlantic Inertial Systems Inc
250 Knotter Dr ... Cheshire CT 06410 203-250-3676
Web: www.atlanticinertial.com

Aucoin & Assoc Inc 433 N C C Duson St ... Eunice LA 70535 337-457-7366

Audient Inc 20532 Crescent Bay Dr ... Lake Forest CA 92630 949-830-9412

Auto Comm Engineering Corp 109 Evergreen Dr ... Houma LA 70364 985-876-1855
Web: auto-comm.com

Availink Inc 20201 Century Blvd Ste 160 ... Germantown MD 20874 301-515-6716
Web: www.availink.com

Avatar Engineering Inc 14360 W 96th Ter ... Lenexa KS 66215 913-897-6757
Web: avatar-eng.com

Aviles Engineering Corp 5790 Windfern Rd ... Houston TX 77041 713-895-7645 895-7943
Web: www.avilesengineering.com

Avt Simulation Inc
2603 Challenger Tech Ct Ste 180 ... Orlando FL 32826 407-381-5311
Web: www.avtsim.com

Axens North America Inc
650 College Rd E Ste 1200 ... Princeton NJ 08540 609-243-8700
Web: www.axens.net

Axis Engineering Technologies Inc
One Broadway Fl 14 ... Cambridge MA 02142 617-225-4414
Web: www.axisetech.com

Aztec Communications Ltd 6830 Barney Rd ... Houston TX 77092 713-462-6707
Web: www.azteccom.com

Aztec Facility Services Inc
11000 S Wilcrest Dr Ste 125 ... Houston TX 77099 281-668-9000
Web: www.aztec1.com

Azure Green Consultants LLC
409 E Pioneer Ste A ... Puyallup WA 98372 253-770-3144
Web: www.azuregreenconsultants.com

B & W Fluid Dynamics Inc 901 Seaco Ave ... Deer Park TX 77536 281-534-9300

B G m Engineering Inc
14100 Simone Dr ... Shelby Township MI 48315 586-532-8670
Web: bgmengineering.net

B M Ross & Assoc Ltd 62 N St ... Goderich ON N7A2T4 519-524-2641
TF: 888-524-2641 ■ *Web:* www.bmross.net

Babcock Power Services Inc
Five Neponset St ... Worcester MA 01606 508-852-7100
Web: babcockpower.com

Baird Hampton & Brown Inc
6300 Ridglea Pl Ste 700 ... Fort Worth TX 76116 817-338-1277 338-9245
Web: www.bhbinc.com

Baisch Engineering Inc 809 Hyland Ave ... Kaukauna WI 54130 920-766-3521
Web: www.baisch.com

Bala Consulting Engineers Inc
443 S Gulph Rd ... King Of Prussia PA 19406 610-649-8000
Web: www.bala.com

Bancography Inc 2301 First Ave N Ste 103 ... Birmingham AL 35203 205-251-3227
Web: www.bancography.com

Barge Cauthen & Assoc Inc
6606 Charlotte Pk Ste 210 ... Nashville TN 37209 615-356-9911
Web: bargecauthen.com

Barnett Contracting Inc 7703 Bagby Ave ... Waco TX 76712 254-666-7117 666-7119
Web: www.barnettcontracting.com

Barnett Tool & Engineering 2238 Palma Dr ... Ventura CA 93003 805-642-9435
Web: www.barnettclutches.com

Bartlett Holdings Inc 60 Industrial Park Rd ... Plymouth MA 02360 508-746-6464
Web: www.excelscaffold.com

Basin Holdings US LLC
The Chrysler Bldg 405 Lexington Ave 71st Fl ... New York NY 10174 212-695-7376
Web: www.basinholdings.com

Bastion Technologies Inc
17625 El Camino Real Ste 330 ... Houston TX 77058 281-283-9330 283-9333
Web: www.bastiontechnologies.com

Bat Assoc Inc 5151 Brook Hollow Pkwy Ste 250 ... Norcross GA 30071 770-242-3908
Web: www.batassociates.com

Bayside Engineering Inc 110 N 11th St Ste 100 ... Tampa FL 33602 813-314-0314
Web: www.baysideng.com

BBC Engineering Inc 8650 Business Park Dr ... Shreveport LA 71105 318-798-3344
Web: forteandtablada.com/company_history_bbce.asp

BCER Engineering Inc 5420 Ward Rd Ste 200 ... Arvada CO 80002 303-422-7400
Web: www.bcer.com

BDS Engineering Inc
6859 Federal Blvd Ste A ... Lemon Grove CA 91945 619-582-4992
Web: www.bdsengineering.com

Beardsley Design Assoc Architecture Engineering & Landscape Architecture PC
64 S St ... Auburn NY 13021 315-253-7301
Web: www.beardsley.com

BEARSCH COMPEAU KNUDSON Architects & Engineers PC
41 Chenango St ... Binghamton NY 13901 607-772-0007
Web: www.bckpc.com

Becht Engineering Company Inc
22 Church St PO Box 300 ... Liberty Corner NJ 07938 908-580-1119
Web: www.becht.com

Behnke Erdman & Whitaker Engineering Inc
2303 Camino Ramon Ste 220 ... San Ramon CA 94583 925-867-3330
Web: www.bewengineering.com

Benesyst Inc 800 Washington Ave N 8th Fl ... Minneapolis MN 55401 800-422-4661
TF: 866-786-3366 ■ *Web:* www.benesyst.net

Benton & Assoc Inc 1970 W Lafayette Ave ... Jacksonville IL 62650 217-245-4146
Web: www.bentonassociates.com

Best Maids 842 Lemay Ferry Rd ... Saint Louis MO 63125 314-544-6180

BHE Environmental Inc
11733 Chesterdale Rd ... Cincinnati OH 45246 513-326-1500 326-1550
Web: www.powereng.com

Big Enterprises Inc 105 Paul Mellon Ct Ste 15 ... Waldorf MD 20602 301-843-9380

Big Sky Engineering Inc 429 Venture Ct ... Verona WI 53593 608-848-9898
Web: www.bigskyeng.com

Bihrle Applied Research Inc 81 Research Dr ... Hampton VA 23666 757-766-2416
Web: www.bihrle.com

Binkley & Barfield Inc 1710 Seamist Dr ... Houston TX 77008 713-869-3433
Web: www.binkleybarfield.com

Biokinetics & Assoc Ltd 2470 Don Reid Dr ... Ottawa ON K1H1E1 613-736-0384
Web: www.biokinetics.com

BioMimetic Systems Inc
810 Memorial Dr Ste 106 ... Cambridge MA 02139 617-758-2505
Web: www.biomimetic-systems.com

BL Harbert International LLC
820 Shades Creek Pkwy Ste 3000 ... Birmingham AL 35209 404-841-4000
Web: www.bharbert.com

Bleyl & Assoc
1715 S Capital Of Texas Hwy Ste 109 ... Austin TX 78746 512-328-7878 328-7884
Web: bleylengineering.com

Blue Line Engineering Co
525 E Colorado Ave ... Colorado Springs CO 80903 719-447-1373
Web: www.bluelineengineering.com

Bluestone Engineering Inc
1990 N California Blvd Ste 830 ... Walnut Creek CA 94596 925-932-7053
Web: www.bergersongroup.com

Bms Communications Inc 4133 Guardian St ... Simi Valley CA 93063 805-526-1141

Bocook Engineering Inc 312 10th St ... Paintsville KY 41240 606-789-5961
Web: bocook.com

Bohler Engineering PC 35 Technology Dr ... Warren NJ 07059 908-668-8300
Web: www.atlantictraffic.com

Bond Tool & Engineering
6190 N Riverview Dr ... Kalamazoo MI 49004 269-344-5164
Web: www.bondtool.com

Boomerang Management Enterprises LLC
1935 Samco Rd Ste 104 ... Rapid City SD 57702 605-718-2666
Web: boomerangme.com

Borghesi Building & Engineering Company Inc
2155 E Main St ... Torrington CT 06790 860-482-7613
Web: www.borghesibuilding.com

Bouthillette Parizeau 9825 Verville St ... Montreal QC H3L3E1 514-383-3747 383-8760
Web: www.bpa.ca

Bowne AE & T Group 235 E Jericho Tpke ... Mineola NY 11501 516-746-2350
Web: www.bownegroup.com

Boyle Energy Services & Technology Inc
28 Locke Rd ... Concord NH 03301 603-227-5200
Web: www.boyleenergy.com

Bragg's Electric Construction Company Inc
3000 Cantrell Rd ... Little Rock AR 72202 501-666-6166
Web: cdicon.com

Brandon Assocs Ltd 26 Sarah Dr ... Farmingdale NY 11735 631-293-1414
Web: www.brandonassociates.com

Breen Energy Solutions LLC 104 Broadway St ... Carnegie PA 15106 412-431-4499
Web: www.breenes.com

BRIC Engineered Systems Ltd
1101 Wentworth St W Ste D1 ... Oshawa ON L1J8P7 905-436-8867
TF: 800-937-5135 ■ *Web:* www.briceng.com

	Phone	Fax
Bridgers & Paxton Consulting Engineers Inc 4600-C Montgomery Blvd Ne .... Albuquerque NM 87109 *Web:* www.bpce.com	505-883-4111	
Brittain Engineering 56 Third St NW .... Hickory NC 28601 *Web:* www.brittainengineering.com	828-328-1813	
Brooks Borg Skiles Architecture Engineering 317 Sixth Ave Ste 400 .... Des Moines IA 50309 *Web:* www.bbsae.com	515-244-7167	
Brooks Harbour & Assoc Inc 9342 Lindale Ave .... Baton Rouge LA 70815 *Web:* www.arthursrestaurant.com	225-927-7430	
Brooks-ransom Assoc 7415 N Palm Ave Ste 100 .... Fresno CA 93711 *Web:* www.brooksransom.com	559-449-8444	
Bryan A Stirrat & Assoc Inc 1360 Vly Vista Dr .... Diamond Bar CA 91765 *Web:* www.bas.com	909-860-7777	
Building Earth Sciences Inc 5545 Derby Dr .... Irondale AL 35210 *Web:* www.buildingandearth.com	205-836-6300	
Burlington Engineering Inc 220 W Grove Ave .... Orange CA 92865 *Web:* www.burlingtoneng.com	714-921-4045	
Burns Cooley Dennis Inc 551 Sunnybrook Rd .... Ridgeland MS 39157 *Web:* www.bcdgeo.com	601-856-9911	
Burns Engineering Inc 10201 Bren Rd E .... Minnetonka MN 55343 *TF:* 800-328-3871 ■ *Web:* www.burnsengineering.com	952-935-4400	
Burrell Consultng Group Inc 1001 Enterprise Way Ste 100 .... Roseville CA 95678 *Web:* www.burrellcg.com	916-783-8898	
Butier Engineering Inc 17782 17th St Ste 107 .... Tustin CA 92780 *Web:* www.butier.com	714-832-7222	
C & b Consulting Engineers 449 10th St .... San Francisco CA 94103 *Web:* www.cbengineers.com	415-437-7330	
C & C Technologies Inc 730 E Kaliste Saloom Rd .... Lafayette LA 70508 *Web:* www.cctechnol.com	337-210-0000	
C C Tatham & Assoc Ltd 115 Sandford Fleming Dr Ste 200 .... Collingwood ON L9Y5A6 *Web:* www.cctatham.com	705-444-2565	
Caen Engineering Inc 675 N Eckhoff St Ste G .... Orange CA 92868 *Web:* www.caeneng.com	714-456-0800	
Caldera Engineering 695 South 320 West .... Provo UT 84601 *Web:* www.calderaengineering.com	801-356-2862	
Cam Services Inc 5664 Selmaraine Dr .... Culver City CA 90230 *Web:* www.camservices.com	310-390-3552	
Cameron Engineering & Assoc LLP 100 Sunnyside Blvd Ste 100 .... Woodbury NY 11797 *Web:* www.cameronengineering.com	516-827-4900	
Campos Engineering Inc 7430 Greenville Ave .... Dallas TX 75231 *Web:* www.camposengineering.com	214-696-6291	
Canard Aerospace Corp 250 Fuller St S Ste 201 .... Shakopee MN 55379 *Web:* www.canardaero.com	952-944-7990	
Cannon Building Svc Inc 1640 Sierra Madre Cir Ste 6 .... Placentia CA 92870 *Web:* www.cannonbuilding.com	714-630-9570	
Canyon Engineering Products Inc 28909 Ave Williams .... Valencia CA 91355 *Web:* www.canyonengineering.com	661-294-0084	
Cape Design Engineering Co 191 Center St Ste 201 .... Cape Canaveral FL 32920 *Web:* www.cdeco.com	321-799-2970	
Capital Engineering LLC 6933 Indianpolis Blvd .... Hammond IN 46324 *Web:* www.capital-eng.com	219-844-1984	
Cardinal Building Maintenance 4952 W 128th Pl .... Alsip IL 60803 *Web:* www.cardinalmaintenance.com	708-385-3575	
Carillion Canada Inc 7077 Keele St Fourth Fl .... Concord ON L4K0B6 *Web:* www.carillion.ca	905-532-5200	
Carlile Macy Inc 15 Third St .... Santa Rosa CA 95401 *Web:* www.carlilemacy.com	707-542-6451	
Carlson Group Inc 34 Executive Pk Ste 250 .... Irvine CA 92614 *Web:* www.carlson-dc.com	949-251-0455	
Carnahan Proctor & Cross Inc 6101 W Atlantic Blvd Ste 200 .... Margate FL 33063 *Web:* www.carnahan-proctor.com	954-972-3959	
Carr Engineering Inc 12500 Castlebridge Dr .... Houston TX 77065 *Web:* carrengineeringinc.com	281-894-8955	
Carroll & Blackman Inc 3120 Fannin St .... Beaumont TX 77701 *Web:* www.cbieng.com	409-833-3363	833-0317
Carsan Engineering Inc 221 Corporate Cir Ste H .... Golden CO 80401	303-237-9608	
Caruso Turley Scott Inc 1215 W Rio Salado Pkwy Ste 200 .... Tempe AZ 85281 *Web:* www.ctsaz.com	480-774-1700	
Cary Kopczynski & Company Inc PS Bellevue Pl 10500 Eighth St Ste 800 .... Bellevue WA 98004 *Web:* www.ckcps.com	425-455-2144	
Cascadian Building Maintenance Ltd 7415 129th Ave SE .... Newcastle WA 98056 *Web:* www.cascadian.org	425-264-0474	
Casne Engineering Inc 10604 NE 38th Pl Ste 205 .... Kirkland WA 98033 *Web:* www.casne.com	425-522-1000	
Castle Breckenridge Management 5185 Comanche Dr Ste D .... La Mesa CA 91942 *Web:* www.cbmgmt.com	619-697-3191	
Cator Ruma & Assoc Co 896 Tabor St Ste 1 .... Lakewood CO 80401 *Web:* catorruma.com	303-232-6200	
CB Engineering Pacific Inc 909 Seventh Ave Ste 201 .... Kirkland WA 98033 *Web:* www.cb-pacific.com	425-822-1702	
CBCL Ltd 1489 Hollis St .... Halifax NS B3J2R7 *Web:* www.cbcl.ca	902-421-7241	
Cemcon Ltd 2280 White Oak Cir Ste 100 .... Aurora IL 60502 *Web:* www.cemcon.com	630-862-2100	

	Phone	Fax
CF Roark Welding & Engineering Company Inc 136 N Green St .... Brownsburg IN 46112 *Web:* www.roarkfab.com	317-852-3163	
CFW Associated Engineers Inc 9200 Leesgate Rd Ste 200 .... Louisville KY 40222 *Web:* cfwengineers.com	502-423-0805	
CGA Engineers Inc 8179 E 41st St .... Tulsa OK 74145 *Web:* cgaengineers.com	918-749-5800	
CH Perez & Assoc Consulting Engineers in 9594 NW 41st St Ste 201 .... Doral FL 33178 *Web:* p-a.cc	305-592-1070	
Chemi-Source Inc 2665 Vista Pacific Dr .... Oceanside CA 92056 *Web:* www.mrm-usa.com	760-477-8177	
Chester Engineers Inc 1555 Coraopolis Heights Rd .... Moon Township PA 15108 *Web:* www.chester-engineers.com	412-809-6600	
Chi Engineering Services Inc 430 W Rd .... Portsmouth NH 03801 *Web:* www.chiengineering.com	603-433-5654	
Chisholm Fleming & Assoc 317 Renfrew Dr Ste 301 .... Markham ON L3R9S8 *TF:* 888-241-4149 ■ *Web:* www.chisholmfleming.com	905-474-1458	
Choice One Engineering Corp 440 E Hoewisher Rd .... Sidney OH 45365 *Web:* choiceoneengineering.com	937-497-0200	
City of Clarksville 199 10th St .... Clarksville TN 37040 *TF:* 800-342-1003 ■ *Web:* www.cityofclarksville.com	931-645-7464	
City of Vacaville Inc, The 650 Merchant St .... Vacaville CA 95688 *Web:* www.ci.vacaville.ca.us	707-449-5100	
Clarion Technologies Inc 170 College Ave Ste 300 .... Holland MI 49423 *Web:* www.clariontechnologies.com	616-698-7277	
Clarity Innovations Inc 1001 SE Water Ave Ste 262 .... Portland OR 97214 *Web:* www.clarity-innovations.com	503-248-4300	
Clark Contractors Inc 19651 Descartes .... Foothill Ranch CA 92610 *Web:* www.clarkcontractors.com	949-581-6577	
Clark Dietz Inc 125 W Church St .... Champaign IL 61820 *Web:* www.clark-dietz.com	217-373-8900	
Clark Patterson Engineers Surveyor & Architects PC 205 St Paul St Ste 500 .... Rochester NY 14604 *Web:* www.clarkpattersonlee.com	585-454-4570	
Clean Ones Corp PO Box 40008 .... Portland OR 97204 *TF:* 800-367-4587 ■ *Web:* www.cleanones.com	503-224-5211	
Clear Align LLC 2550 Blvd Of The Generals Ste 280 .... Eagleville PA 19403 *Web:* www.clearalign.com	484-956-0510	
Clearview Cleaning Service 1804 Windermere Ave .... Wilmington DE 19804	302-994-5215	
Clifton Assoc Ltd 340 Maxwell Cres .... Regina SK S4N5Y5 *Web:* www.clifton.ca	306-721-7611	
Clouse Engineering Inc 1642 E Orangewood Ave .... Phoenix AZ 85020 *Web:* clouseaz.com	602-395-9300	
Cme Assoc Inc 32 Crabtree Ln .... Woodstock CT 06281 *Web:* www.cmeengineering.com	860-928-7848	
CNC Engineering Inc 19 Bacon Rd .... Enfield CT 06082 *Web:* www.cnc1.com	860-749-1780	
Coastal Planning & Engineering Inc 2481 NW Boca Raton Blvd .... Boca Raton FL 33431 *Web:* cbi.com/markets/infrastructure/maritime/	561-391-8102	
Cobb Architects LLC 67 Washtington St .... Charleston SC 29403 *Web:* www.cobbarchitecture.com	843-856-7333	
Cobb Fendley & Assoc Inc 13430 Northwest Fwy Ste 1100 .... Houston TX 77040 *Web:* www.cobfen.com	713-462-3242	462-3262
Cobra Engineering Inc 23801 La Palma Ave .... Yorba Linda CA 92887 *Web:* www.cobrausa.com/	714-692-8180	692-5019
Colorado Energy Management LLC 2575 Park Ln Ste 200 .... Lafayette CO 80026 *Web:* www.coloradoenergy.com	303-442-5112	
Columbia Energy & Environmental Services Inc 1806 Terminal Dr .... Richland WA 99354 *Web:* columbia-energy.com	509-946-7111	
Columbia Northwest Engineering 249 N Elder St .... Moses Lake WA 98837 *Web:* www.cnweng.com	509-766-1226	
Colwill Engineering Mep & Fp 4750 E Adamo Dr .... Tampa FL 33605 *Web:* www.colwillengineering.com	813-241-2525	
Comfort - Air Engineering Inc 11403 Jones Maltsberger Rd .... San Antonio TX 78216 *Web:* www.comfort-air.com	210-494-1691	
Command Post Technologies Inc 1039 Champions Way .... Suffolk VA 23435 *Web:* commandposttech.com	757-338-3039	
Common Sense Advisory Inc 100 Merrimack St .... Lowell MA 01852 *Web:* commonsenseadvisory.com	978-275-0500	
Composite Engineering Inc 5381 Raley Blvd .... Sacramento CA 95838 *Web:* www.compositeeng.com	916-991-1990	
Compton Engineering 156 Nixon St .... Biloxi MS 39530 *Web:* www.comptonengineering.com	228-432-2133	
Computer Age Engineering Inc 867 E 38th St .... Marion IN 46953 *Web:* www.caeweb.com	765-674-8551	
Concord Engineering Group 520 S Burnt Mill Rd .... Voorhees NJ 08043 *Web:* www.concord-engineering.com	856-427-0200	
Consolidated Engineering Company Inc 1971 Mccollum Pkwy NW .... Kennesaw GA 30144 *Web:* www.cec-intl.com	770-422-5100	
Continental Glass Systems Inc 325 W 74th Pl .... Hialeah FL 33014 *Web:* www.cgsfl.com	305-231-1101	
Controlled Contamination Services LLC 4182 Sorrento Valley Blvd .... San Diego CA 92121 *TF:* 888-263-9886 ■ *Web:* www.cleanroomcleaning.com	858-457-7598	

Phone Fax

Conveyor Dynamics Inc
1111 W Holly St Ste A — Bellingham WA 98225 360-671-2200
Web: www.conveyor-dynamics.com

Conway & Owen Inc
1455 Bluegrass Lakes Pkwy Ste 200 — Alpharetta GA 30004 678-350-9000
Web: www.conway-owen.com

Cornerstone Commissioning Inc
11 Cold Spring Dr — Boxford MA 01921 978-887-8177
Web: www.cxhvac.com

Corporate Image Maintenance
2116 S Wright St — Santa Ana CA 92705 714-966-5325

Corradino Group 200 s Fifth st — Louisville KY 40202 502-587-7221 587-2636
TF: 800-880-8241 ■ *Web:* www.corradino.com

Corrpro Canada Inc 10848 - 214 St — Edmonton AB T5S2A7 780-447-4565
TF: 800-661-8390 ■ *Web:* www.corrpro.ca

Corzo Castella Carballo Thompson Salman PA
901 Ponce De Leon Blvd Ste 900 — Coral Gables FL 33134 305-445-2900
Web: www.c3ts.com

Cosentini Assoc Inc
Two Pennsylvania Plz Third Fl — New York NY 10121 212-615-3600
Web: www.cosentini.com

County Engineers Assn of Ohio
6500 Busch Blvd Ste 100 — Columbus OH 43229 614-221-0707
Web: www.ceao.org

Creative Engineering LLC 38 Milburn St — Bronxville NY 10708 914-771-5540
Web: www.creativeengineering.com

Creative Engineers Inc 361 N E St — York PA 17403 443-807-1202
Web: www.creativeengineers.com

CRL Technologies Inc 5247 Brawner Pl — Alexandria VA 22304 703-297-9900
Web: www.crltechnologies.com

CRW Assoc 16980 Via Tazon Ste 320 — San Diego CA 92127 858-451-3030

Crw Engineering Group LLC
3940 Arctic Blvd Ste 300 — Anchorage AK 99503 907-562-3252
Web: www.crweng.com

Csw Stuber Stroeh Engineering Group Inc
1310 Redwood Way Ste 220 — Petaluma CA 94954 707-795-4764

CTI & Assoc Inc 51331 W Pontiac Trl — Wixom MI 48393 248-486-5100
Web: cticompanies.com

CTI Consultants Inc 13500 E Boundary Rd — Midlothian VA 23112 804-622-8630
Web: www.cti-consultants.com

D & R International Ltd 1300 Spring St — Silver Spring MD 20910 301-588-9387
Web: www.drintl.com

Dacallc 2255 Button Gwinnett Dr — Atlanta GA 30340 770-451-6433
Web: dacapainting.com

Dade Moeller & Assoc Inc
1835 Terminal Dr Ste 200 — Richland WA 99354 509-946-0410
Web: www.moellerinc.com

Daimler Vans Mfg LLC
8501 Palmetto Commerce Pkwy — Ladson SC 29456 843-695-5000
Web: daimler.com

Dalager Engineering Co 936 Railroad Ave — Bath SD 57427 605-229-2412
Web: dalagerengineering.com

Danlaw Inc 41131 Vincenti Ct — Novi MI 48375 248-476-5571
Web: www.danlawinc.com

Dare Enterprices Inc 700 River Ave Ste 215 — Pittsburgh PA 15212 412-231-6100
Web: www.dareent.com

Dare Mighty Things Inc
1000 Market St Ste 102 — Portsmouth NH 03801 603-431-4331
Web: www.daremightythings.com

Data Fusion Corp 10190 Bannock St — Northglenn CO 80260 720-872-2145
Web: www.datafusion.com

Data Science Automation Inc
375 Valleybrook Rd Ste 106 — Mc Murray PA 15317 724-942-6330
Web: www.dsautomation.com

David Mason & Assoc
800 S Vandeventer Ave — Saint Louis MO 63110 314-534-1030
Web: www.davidmason.com

Day Automation Systems Inc 7931 Rae Blvd — Victor NY 14564 585-924-4630
Web: dayautomation.com

Daylor Consulting Group Inc 10 Forbes Rd — Braintree MA 02184 781-849-7070
Web: www.daylor.com

DBA Engineering Ltd 401 Hanlan Rd — Vaughan ON L4L3T1 905-851-0090
Web: www.dbaeng.com

Decimal Engineering Inc
2640 N Powerline Rd — Pompano Beach FL 33069 954-975-7992 975-7994
Web: www.decimal.net

Degree Controls Inc 18 Meadowbrook Dr — Milford NH 03055 603-672-8900
TF: 877-334-7332 ■ *Web:* www.degreec.com

Delco Automation Inc 3735 Thatcher Ave — Saskatoon SK S7R1B8 306-244-6449 665-7500
Web: delcoautomation.com

Delcross Technologies LLC 301 N Neil St — Champaign IL 61820 217-363-3396 363-3398
Web: www.delcross.com

Delphi Engineering Group Inc
485 E 17th St Ste 400 — Costa Mesa CA 92627 949-515-1490
Web: www.delphieng.com

Delta Engineers & Architects PC
184 Court St — Binghamton NY 13901 607-231-6600
Web: www.deltaengineers.com

Denham-Blythe Company Inc 100 Trade St — Lexington KY 40511 859-255-7405
Web: www.denhamblythe.com

Derector Robert Assoc 19 W 44th St Fl 10 — New York NY 10036 212-764-7272
Web: www.derector.com

Diamond d General Engineering Inc
32500 State Hwy 16 — Woodland CA 95695 530-662-2042
Web: www.ddge.net

Dickerson Engineering Inc 8101 N Milwaukee Ave — Niles IL 60714 847-966-0290
Web: www.danaenterprises.com

Differentiation Strategies Inc
3349 Southgate Ct SW — Cedar Rapids IA 52404 319-365-3489

Digital Force Technologies LLC
9455 Waples St Ste 100 — San Diego CA 92121 858-546-1244
Web: www.digitalforcetech.com

Dileo Engineering LLC 2241 W Larkspur Dr — Phoenix AZ 85029 602-395-0756

Phone Fax

Dimension Energy Services
One Fluor Daniel Dr Ste D1-7-50 — Sugar Land TX 77478 832-564-4500
Web: www.dimensionenergyservices.com

Dimensional Control Systems Inc
580 Kirts Blvd Ste 309 — Troy MI 48084 248-269-9777
Web: 3dcs.com

Dirt Pros of Fort Lauderdale PO Box 16453 — Plantation FL 33318 954-318-2477
TF: 877-750-7767 ■ *Web:* www.dirtpros.com

DJ & A PC 3203 S Russell St — Missoula MT 59801 406-721-4320
TF: 800-398-3522 ■ *Web:* www.djanda.com

DJL Construction Inc
1550 Ampere St Ste 200 — Boucherville QC J4B7L4 450-641-8000 655-1201
Web: www.djl.ca

DLB Associates Consulting Engineers PC
265 Industrial Way W — Eatontown NJ 07724 732-774-2000
Web: www.dlbassociates.com

DNB Engineering Inc 5969 Robinson Ave — Riverside CA 92503 951-637-2630
Web: www.dnbenginc.com

Donohue & Assoc Inc 3311 Weeden Creek Rd — Sheboygan WI 53081 920-208-0296
Web: www.donohue-associates.com

Door Engineering Corp 1234 Ballentine Blvd — Norfolk VA 23504 757-622-5355
Web: www.dooreng.com

DoubleStar Inc 1161 Mcdermott Dr Ste 200 — West Chester PA 19380 610-719-1900
Web: www.doublestarinc.com

Dougherty Sprague Environmental Inc
3902 Industrial St Ste A — Rowlett TX 75088 972-412-8666
Web: www.dsei.com

Dungan Engineering pa 1574 Hwy 98 E — Columbia MS 39429 601-731-2600
Web: dunganeng.com

Dynamic Design Solutions Inc
3565 Centre Cir — Fort Mill SC 29715 803-548-3609
TF: 866-337-2010 ■ *Web:* www.dynamicdesignsolutionsinc.com

Dynamic Security Concepts Inc
Hamilton Plz Ste 10 6090 Danenhauer Ln — Mays Landing NJ 08330 609-625-3942
Web: www.dscinc.net

Dynamic Test Solutions Inc
4360 W Chandler Blvd Ste 1 — Chandler AZ 85226 480-632-0312
Web: www.dynamic-test.com

E & a Consulting Group Inc 330 N 117th St — Omaha NE 68154 402-895-4700
Web: www.eacg.com

E C S 2741 S 21st Ave — Broadview IL 60155 708-338-9700
Web: escalatorparts.com

E I Team Inc 2060 Sheridan Dr — Buffalo NY 14223 716-876-4669
Web: www.eiteam.com

E Sciences Inc 34 E Pine St — Orlando FL 32801 407-481-9006
Web: www.esciencesinc.com

EBB Associates Inc 1064 W Ocean View Ave — Norfolk VA 23503 757-588-3939
Web: www.ebbweb.com

EC Source Services LLC 6644 E Thomas Rd Ste 103 — Mesa AZ 85215 480-245-7200
Web: ecsourceservices.com/

ECM Consultants Inc 4409 Utica St Ste 200 — Metairie LA 70006 504-885-4080
Web: ecmconsultants.com

Ecom Engineering Inc
1796 Tribute Rd Ste 100 — Sacramento CA 95815 916-641-5600
Web: www.ecomeng.com

EDM International Inc
4001 Automation Way — Fort Collins CO 80525 970-204-4001
Web: www.edmlink.com

Edminster Hinshaw Russ & Assoc Inc
10555 Woffice Dr — Houston TX 77042 713-784-4500
Web: www.ehrainc.com

Elcon Assoc Inc 12670 NW Barnes Rd — Portland OR 97229 503-644-2490
Web: elconassociates.com

Electrical Consultants Inc 3521 Gabel Rd — Billings MT 59102 406-259-9933
Web: www.electricalconsultantsinc.com

Elevator Equipment Corp 4035 Goodwin Ave — Los Angeles CA 90039 323-245-0147 245-9771
TF: 888-577-3326 ■ *Web:* www.elevatorequipment.com

Elevator Research & Manufacturing Corp
1417 Elwood St — Los Angeles CA 90021 213-746-1914
Web: www.elevatorresearch.com

Eleven Engineering Inc
10150 - 100 St Ste 900 — Edmonton AB T5J0P6 780-425-6511
Web: elevenengineering.com

EM Research Inc 1301 Corporate Blvd — Reno NV 89502 775-345-2411
Web: www.emresearch.com

Emc2 3518 Riverside Dr Ste 202 — Upper Arlington OH 43221 614-459-3200
Web: www.emc-sq.com

Ems-tech Inc 699 Dundas St W — Belleville ON K8N4Z2 613-966-6611
Web: ems-tech.net

ENE Systems Inc 480 Neponset St Ste 11D — Canton MA 02021 781-828-6770
Web: enesystems.com

ENERActive Solutions LLC
700 Mattison Ave Ste A — Asbury Park NJ 07712 732-988-8850
Web: www.eneractivesolutions.com

Engineer Sales Co 2500 25th Ave N — Saint Petersburg FL 33713 727-323-2100
Web: www.engineersales.com

Engineering & Utility Contractors Assn
17 Crow Canyon Ct Ste 100 — San Ramon CA 94583 925-855-7900

Engineering Data Design Corp
105 Daventry Ln Ste 100 — Louisville KY 40223 502-412-4000
Web: ed2c.com

Engineering Specialists Inc
21360 Gateway Ct — Brookfield WI 53045 262-783-8000
Web: www.engspec.com

Engineery System Solutions
4943 N 29th E Ste A — Idaho Falls ID 83401 208-552-9874
Web: www.es2eng.com

Enginetics Aerospace Corp
7700 New Carlisle Pk — Huber Heights OH 45424 937-878-3800
Web: www.enginetics.com

Enginuity Works Corp 2195 Defoor Hills Rd Nw — Atlanta GA 30318 678-739-0001
Web: www.enginuityworks.com

Company	City	State	Zip	Phone	Fax
ENGStudios Inc 1931 Newport Blvd Ste B	Costa Mesa	CA	92627	949-642-2325	
Web: engstudios.com					
Ensign Engineering p C 1111 Calhoun Ave	Bronx	NY	10465	718-863-5590	
Web: www.ensignengineering.com					
Environment Control 3430 N First Ave	Tucson	AZ	85719	520-292-3992	
Web: www.environmentcontrol.com					
Environmental Assessment & Remediation Management Inc					
4097 Trl Creek Rd	Riverside	CA	92505	951-735-5575	
Web: www.earmanagement.com					
Environmental Health & Engineering Inc					
117 Fourth Ave	Needham	MA	02494	781-247-4300	
TF: 800-825-5343 ■ *Web:* www.eheinc.com					
Equinox Engineering Ltd 909-5 Ave SW 10th Fl	Calgary	AB	T2P3G5	403-205-3833	
Web: www.equinox-eng.com					
Equity Exploration Consultants Ltd					
1-2075 Brigantine Dr	Coquitlam	BC	V3K7B8	604-522-9807	
Eran Engineering Inc 2672 Dow Ave	Tustin	CA	92780	714-543-2966	
ESE Inc PO Box 1107	Marshfield	WI	54449	715-387-4778	
TF: 800-236-4778 ■ *Web:* www.ese1.com					
ESEA a California Corp					
280 Second St Ste 270	Los Altos	CA	94022	650-941-4175	
Web: esea.com					
ESI FME Engineers 1800 E 16th St Ste B	Santa Ana	CA	92701	714-835-2800	
Web: www.esifme.com					
Espo Engineering 855 Midway Dr	Willowbrook	IL	60527	630-789-2525	
Web: www.espocorp.com					
Essig Research Inc 497 Cir Fwy	Cincinnati	OH	45246	513-942-7100	
Web: www.essig.com					
Esys Corp 1670 N Opdyke Rd	Auburn Hills	MI	48326	248-754-1900	
Web: esysautomation.com					
Etic Engineering 2285 Morello Ave	Pleasant Hill	CA	94523	925-602-4710	
Web: www.eticeng.com					
Evans-Hamilton Inc 4608 Union Bay Pl N E	Seattle	WA	98105	206-526-5622	
Web: www.evanshamilton.com					
Excalibur Engineering Services Inc					
962 East 2100 North	North Logan	UT	84341	435-787-9599	
Web: www.excalibur-engineering-services.com					
EXCEL Services Corp					
11921 Rockville Pk Ste 100	Rockville	MD	20852	301-984-4400	
Web: www.excelservices.com					
exidacom LLC 64 N Main St	Sellersville	PA	18960	215-453-1720	
Web: www.exida.com					
Expressworks International Inc					
5619 Scotts Vly Dr	Scotts Valley	CA	95066	831-440-9300	
Web: www.expressworks.com					
Facility Masters Inc 1604 Kerley Dr	San Jose	CA	95112	408-436-9090	
Web: www.facilitymasters.com					
Fala Technologies Inc					
430 Old Neighborhood Rd	Kingston	NY	12401	845-336-4000	
Web: www.falatech.com					
Falcon Crest Aviation Supply Inc					
8318 Braniff	Houston	TX	77061	713-644-2290	
TF: 800-833-8229 ■ *Web:* www.falconcrestaviation.com					
Fard Engineers Inc 309 Lennon Ln Ste 200	Walnut Creek	CA	94598	925-932-5505	
Web: www.fard.com					
FCX Systems Inc 400 Fcx Ln	Morgantown	WV	26501	304-983-0400	
Web: www.fcxinc.com					
Felsburg Holt & Ullevig Inc					
6300 S Syracuse Way Ste 600	Centennial	CO	80111	303-721-1440	
Web: www.fhueng.com					
Fibertek Inc 13605 Dulles Technology Dr	Herndon	VA	20171	703-471-7671	
Web: www.fibertek.com					
Fiberutilities Group LLC					
Armstrong Centre 222 Third Ave S E					
Ste 500	Cedar Rapids	IA	52401	319-364-3200	
Web: fiberutilities.com					
Figg Engineering Group 424 N Calhoun St	Tallahassee	FL	32301	850-224-7400	
Web: www.figgbridge.com					
Finley Engineering Company Inc 104 E 11th St	Lamar	MO	64759	417-682-5531	
Web: www.fecinc.com					
Fitzgerald & Halliday Inc 72 Cedar St	Hartford	CT	06106	860-247-7200	247-7206
Web: www.fhiplan.com					
Five Star Professional Maids 8714 N 52nd Ave	Omaha	NE	68152	402-502-3100	
Fluid Engineering Div 1432 Walnut St	Erie	PA	16502	814-453-5014	
Web: www.fluideng.com					
FMHC Corp 1700 Sherwin Ave Ste 600	Des Plaines	IL	60018	773-380-3800	
Web: www.fmhc.com					
Forster Electrical Engineering Inc					
550 N Burr Oak Ave	Oregon	WI	53575	608-835-9009	
Web: www.forstereng.com					
Fortemedia Inc 810 E Arques Ave	Sunnyvale	CA	94085	408-861-8088	
Web: www.fortemedia.com					
Forza Silicon Corp 2947 Bradley St Ste 130	Pasadena	CA	91107	626-796-1182	
Web: www.forzasilicon.com					
Foster-Miller Inc 350 Second Ave	Waltham	MA	02451	781-684-4000	
Web: www.qinetiq-na.com					
Frakes Engineering Inc					
7950 Castleway Dr Ste 160	Indianapolis	IN	46250	317-577-3000	
Web: www.frakesengineering.com					
Fraser - A Weston & Sampson Co 22 High St	Rensselaer	NY	12144	518-463-4400	
Web: www.jkfraser.com					
FTN Assoc Ltd Three Innwood Cir Ste 220	Little Rock	AR	72211	501-225-7779	
Web: cxpdatacenter.com					
Fujitec America Inc 7258 Innovation Way	Mason	OH	45040	513-932-8000	
Web: www.fujitecamerica.com					
Fuscoe Engineering Inc					
16795 Von Karman Ave Ste 100	Irvine	CA	92606	949-474-1960	
Web: www.fuscoe.com					
Fusion Design 440 N Central Ave	Campbell	CA	95008	408-378-9980	
Web: www.fusionnet.com					
FUTEK Advanced Sensor Technology Inc					
10 Thomas	Irvine	CA	92618	949-465-0900	
TF: 800-233-8835 ■ *Web:* www.futek.com					
Future Test Inc 1535 W Parkside Ln	Phoenix	AZ	85027	623-580-0162	
Web: www.futuretest.com					
Futureguard Building Products Inc					
101 Merrow Rd	Auburn	ME	04211	207-795-6536	
Web: www.futureguard.net					
FVB Energy Inc 3901 Hwy 7 Ste 300	Vaughan	ON	L4L8L5	905-265-9777	
Web: www.fvbenergy.com					
Gamma Engineering Inc 601 Airport Dr	Mansfield	TX	76063	817-477-2193	473-8198
Web: www.gammaeng.com					
Gartech Enterprises Inc 3037 W State Rd 256	Austin	IN	47102	812-794-4796	
Web: gartechenterprises.com					
Gas Unlimited 15999 City Walk	Sugar Land	TX	77479	281-295-5600	
Web: www.gasunlim.com					
Gausman & Moore Assoc 1700 Hwy 36 W	Roseville	MN	55113	651-639-9606	639-9618
Web: www.gausman.com					
Gayesco International LP 2859 Wside Dr	Pasadena	TX	77502	713-941-8540	
Web: www.gayesco.com					
GC Engineering Inc					
10010 Indian School Rd Ne	Albuquerque	NM	87112	505-275-0022	
Web: www.occamconsultinggroup.com					
GCI Technologies Inc 1301 Precision Dr	Plano	TX	75074	972-423-8411	
Web: gcitechnologies.com					
GEC Inc 8282 Goodwood Blvd	Baton Rouge	LA	70806	225-612-3000	
Web: www.gecinc.com					
Gedeon Grc Consulting					
6901 Jericho Tpke Ste 216	Syosset	NY	11791	516-873-7010	
Web: gedeongrc.com					
GEL Group Inc, The 2040 Savage Rd	Charleston	SC	29407	843-556-8171	
Web: www.gel.com					
Gemma Power Systems LLC 769 Hebron Ave	Glastonbury	CT	06033	860-659-0509	
Web: www.gemmapower.com					
Geo Strata Environmental Consultants Inc					
4718 College Pk	San Antonio	TX	78249	210-492-7282	
Geocal Inc 7290 S Fraser St	Centennial	CO	80112	303-337-0338	
Web: www.geocal.us					
Geotek Engineering & Testing Services Inc					
909 E 50th St N	Sioux Falls	SD	57104	605-335-5512	
TF: 800-354-5512 ■ *Web:* www.geotekeng.com					
Gertsch-Baker Engineering & Design Inc					
104 S Fourth St Ste 100	Laramie	WY	82070	307-742-6116	
Web: www.gertschbaker.com					
Gibson Engineering Company Inc 90 Broadway	Norwood	MA	02062	781-769-3600	
Web: www.gibsonengineering.com					
Giffin Koerth Inc 40 University Ave Ste 800	Toronto	ON	M5J1T1	416-368-1700	
TF: 800-564-5313 ■ *Web:* www.giffinkoerth.com					
Giles Engineering Assoc Inc					
N8 W22350 Johnson Rd Ste A1	Waukesha	WI	53186	262-544-0118	
TF: 800-782-0610 ■ *Web:* www.gilesengr.com					
Ginn Group Inc, The					
200 Westpark Dr Ste 100	Peachtree City	GA	30269	404-669-9214	
Web: www.theginngroup.com					
gkkworks Construction Services Inc					
2355 Main St Ste 220	Irvine	CA	92614	949-250-1500	
Web: gkkworks.com					
Glen G Shaheen & Associates					
1022 S Purpera Ave	Gonzales	LA	70737	225-644-5523	
Web: www.gsaengineers.com					
Global Performance Holdings Inc					
30 Patewood Dr Patewood Plaza I Ste 200	Greenville	SC	29615	864-288-3009	404-2388
Web: mustangeng.com/pages/default.aspx					
Global Systems Technologies Inc					
109 Floral Vale Blvd	Yardley	PA	19067	215-579-8200	
Web: www.gstpa.com					
Globex Corp 3620 Stutz Dr	Canfield	OH	44406	330-533-0030	
TF: 800-533-8610 ■ *Web:* www.globexcorp.com					
Glumac Inc 150 California St	San Francisco	CA	94111	415-398-7667	
Web: www.glumac.com					
GMI Building Services Inc 8001 Vickers St	San Diego	CA	92111	866-803-4464	
TF: 866-803-4464 ■ *Web:* www.gmiweb.com					
Goetting & Assoc Inc					
12042 Blanco Rd Ste 200	San Antonio	TX	78216	210-530-7000	
Web: www.goetting.com					
Gompers Center Inc 6601 N 27th Ave	Phoenix	AZ	85017	602-336-0061	
Web: www.gomperscenter.org					
Goodwill of the East Bay 1301 30Th Ave	Oakland	CA	94601	510-698-7200	
Web: www.eastbaygoodwill.org					
Goodwin - Lasiter Inc					
1609 S Chestnut St Ste 202	Lufkin	TX	75901	936-637-4900	
Web: glstexas.com					
Gotech Inc 8383 Bluebonnet Blvd	Baton Rouge	LA	70810	225-766-5358	
Web: www.gotech-inc.com					
Govind Development LLC 9359 Ih 37	Corpus Christi	TX	78409	361-241-2777	
Web: www.govinddevelopment.com					
GPA Technologies Inc 2368 Eastman Ave Ste 8	Ventura	CA	93003	805-643-7878	643-7474
Web: www.gpatech.com					
Gray & Osborne Inc 701 Dexter Ave N Ste 200	Seattle	WA	98109	206-284-0860	
Web: www.g-o.com					
Green Valley Consulting Engineers					
335 Tesconi Cir	Santa Rosa	CA	95401	707-579-0388	
Web: www.gvalley.com					
Greenlancer Energy Inc 1150 Griswold St	Detroit	MI	48226	313-312-5101	
Web: www.greenlancer.com					
Greer Galloway Group Inc, The					
973 Crawford Dr	Peterborough	ON	K9J3X1	705-743-5780	743-9592
Web: www.greergalloway.com					
Griffon Aerospace Inc 106 Commerce Cir	Madison	AL	35758	256-258-0035	
Web: www.griffon-aerospace.com					
Groom Energy Solutions LLC 96 Swampscott Rd	Salem	MA	01970	978-306-6052	
Web: www.groomenergy.com					
Group Delta Consultants					
370 Amapola Ave Ste 212	Torrance	CA	90501	310-320-5100	
Web: www.groupdelta.com					

Company / Address	City	State	ZIP	Phone	Fax
Gryphon International Engineering Services Inc A CHA Co 80 King St Ste 404 *Web:* www.gryphoneng.com	Saint Catharines	ON	L2R7G1	905-984-8383	
GS Engineering Consultants Inc 2080 N Talbot Rd RR 1 *Web:* www.gsengineering.ca	Windsor	ON	N9A6J3	519-737-9162	
GT Technologies Inc 5859 Executive Dr *Web:* www.gttechnologies.com	Westland	MI	48185	734-467-8371	
Guy Engineering Services Inc 10759 E Admiral Pl *Web:* guyengr.com	Tulsa	OK	74116	918-437-0282	
H&S Constructors Inc 1616 Valero Way *Web:* www.hsconstructors.com	Corpus Christi	TX	78469	361-289-5272	
Hanover Engineering Assoc Inc 252 Brodhead Rd Ste 100 *Web:* www.hanovereng.com	Bethlehem	PA	18017	610-691-5644	
Hansen Thorp Pellinen Olson Inc 7510 Market Pl Dr *Web:* www.htpo.com	Eden Prairie	MN	55344	952-829-0700	
Hargis Engineers Inc 1201 Third Ave Ste 600 *Web:* www.hargis.biz	Seattle	WA	98101	206-448-3376	
Harper Houf Peterson Righ 205 SE Spokane St *Web:* www.hhpr.com	Portland	OR	97202	503-221-1131	
Harris & Sloan Consulting Group Inc 2295 Gateway Oaks Dr Ste 165 *Web:* www.hscgi.com	Sacramento	CA	95833	916-921-2800	
Hart Engineering Corp 800 Scenic View Dr *Web:* www.hartcompanies.com	Cumberland	RI	02864	401-658-4600	
Harwood Engineering Consultant 255 N 21st St *Web:* www.hecl.com	Milwaukee	WI	53233	414-475-5554	
Haulsey Engineering Inc 10755 Scripps Poway Pkwy Ste 466 *Web:* www.haulseyengr.com	San Diego	CA	92131	858-271-1780	
Haumiller Engineering 445 Renner Dr *Web:* www.haumiller.com	Elgin	IL	60123	847-695-9111	
Hermary Opto Electronics Inc 104-1500 Hartley Ave *Web:* hermaryopto.com	Coquitlam	BC	V3K7A1	604-517-4625	517-2195
HESS Construction + Engineering Services Inc 804 W Diamond Ave Ste 300 *TF:* 800-544-6056 ■ *Web:* www.hessedu.com	Gaithersburg	MD	20878	301-670-9000	
HH Angus & Assoc Ltd 1127 Leslie St *TF:* 866-955-8201 ■ *Web:* www.hhangus.com	Toronto	ON	M3C2J6	416-443-8200	
Highland Associates Ltd 102 Highland Ave *Web:* www.highlandassociates.com	Clarks Summit	PA	18411	570-586-4334	
Highland Engineering & Surveying Inc 1426 Memorial Dr *Web:* highland-engineering.com	Oakland	MD	21550	301-334-6185	
HighRes Biosolutions Inc 299 Washington St *Web:* www.highresbio.com	Woburn	MA	01801	781-932-1912	
Hollister-Whitney Elevator Corp 2603 N 24th St *Web:* www.hollisterwhitney.com	Quincy	IL	62305	217-222-0466	222-0493
Hope Amundson 1301 3rd Ave Ste 300 *Web:* hope-amundson.com	San Diego	CA	92101	619-232-4673	
Hopper Engineering Assoc Inc 300 Vista Del Mar *Web:* www.hopperengineering.com	Redondo Beach	CA	90277	310-373-5573	
Hoque & Assoc Inc 4325 S 34th St *Web:* www.hoqueandassociates.com	Phoenix	AZ	85040	480-921-1368	
Horner & Shifrin Inc 5200 Oakland Ave *Web:* www.hornershifrin.com	St Louis	MO	63110	314-531-4321	
Horrocks Engineers Inc 2162 Grove Pkwy Ste 400 *Web:* horrocksengineers.com/	Pleasant Grove	UT	84062	801-763-5100	
Host Engineering Inc 593 Aa Deakins Rd *Web:* hosteng.com	Jonesborough	TN	37659	423-913-2587	
Howerton Engineering & Surveying 404 Main St *Web:* www.howertoneng.com	Greenup	KY	41144	606-473-5684	
Hunt Guillot & Assoc LLC 603 Reynolds Dr *TF:* 866-255-6825 ■ *Web:* www.hga-llc.com	Ruston	LA	71270	318-255-6825	
Hurst Rosche Engineers Inc 601 N Bruns Ln Ste B *Web:* hurst-rosche.com	Springfield	IL	62702	217-787-1199	
Hutchison Engineering Inc 1801 W Lafayette Ave *Web:* hutchisoneng.com	Jacksonville	IL	62650	217-245-7164	
Hy-capacity Engineering & Manufacturing Inc 1404 13th St S *Web:* www.hy-capacity.com	Humboldt	IA	50548	515-332-2125	
Hyatt Die Cast & Engineering Corp 4656 Lincoln Ave *Web:* www.hyattdiecast.com	Cypress	CA	90630	714-826-7550	
Hydroscience Engineers Inc 10569 Old Plrville Rd *Web:* hydroscience.com	Sacramento	CA	95827	916-364-1490	
Hyundai Repair by Rally Sport Engineering Inc 2136 Newport Blvd *Web:* hyundairepair.net	Costa Mesa	CA	92627	949-548-0978	
Idea Engineering Inc 32 E Sola St *Web:* www.ideaengineering.com	Santa Barbara	CA	93101	805-963-5399	
IJ Research Inc 2919 Tech Ctr Dr *Web:* www.ijresearch.com	Santa Ana	CA	92705	714-546-8522	
Imagize LLC 2855 Telegraph Ave Ste 517 *Web:* www.imagizellc.com	Berkeley	CA	94705	510-540-0260	
Impact Engineering Solutions Inc 13400 Bishops Lnn Ste 30 *Web:* www.impactengsol.com	Brookfield	WI	53005	262-317-8100	317-8101
INCERTEC LLC 160 83rd Ave NE *Web:* www.incertec.com	Fridley	MN	55432	763-717-7016	
Inclinator Company of America 601 Gibson Blvd *Web:* www.inclinator.com	Harrisburg	PA	17104	717-939-8420	
Infinity Engineering Consultants L L C 2626 Canal St Ste 202 *Web:* www.infinityec.com	New Orleans	LA	70119	504-304-0548	
InfoTech Enterprises America Inc 330 Roberts St Ste 102 *TF:* 866-746-2133 ■ *Web:* cyient.com/	East Hartford	CT	06108	860-528-5430	
Infrastructure & Energy Alternatives LLC Two Westbrook Corporate Ctr Ste 200 *Web:* iea.net	Westchester	IL	60154	708-397-4200	
Infratech Corp 2036 Baker Ct *Web:* www.infratechcorp.com	Kennesaw	GA	30144	770-792-8700	
Ingenium Technologies Corp 4216 Maray Dr *Web:* www.ingeniumtech.com	Rockford	IL	61107	815-399-8803	
Innova Engineering Inc Two Park Plz Ste 510 *Web:* www.innovaengineering.com	Irvine	CA	92614	949-975-9965	
Insight Product Development 4660 N Ravenswood Ave *Web:* www.insightpd.com	Chicago	IL	60640	773-907-9500	
Integrated Industrial Technologies 221 Seventh St Ste 200 *Web:* www.isquaredt.com	Pittsburgh	PA	15238	412-828-1200	
Integrated Management Services PA 126 E Amite St *Web:* www.imsengineers.com	Jackson	MS	39201	601-968-9194	
Integrated Solutions Inc 16602 N 23rd Ave Ste 109 *Web:* www.isiaz.com	Phoenix	AZ	85023	602-437-5209	
InterDesign Group Inc 141 E Ohio St *Web:* www.interdesign.com	Indianapolis	IN	46204	317-263-9655	
Interlink Network Systems Inc Nine Colburn Rd *Web:* www.ilinknet.com	East Brunswick	NJ	08816	732-846-2226	
Intertek AIM 601 W California Ave	Sunnyvale	CA	94086	408-745-7000	
InTren Inc 18202 W Union Rd *Web:* www.intren.com	Union	IL	60180	815-923-2300	
Invotec Engineering Inc 10909 Industry Ln *Web:* www.invotec.com	Miamisburg	OH	45342	937-886-3232	
IOS Technologies Inc 3978 Sorrento Vly Blvd Ste 200 *Web:* www.ios3d.com	San Diego	CA	92121	858-202-3360	
Isaacson & Arfman Consulting Engineering Assoc pa 128 Monroe St Ne *Web:* iacivil.com	Albuquerque	NM	87108	505-268-8828	
ISC Engineering 1730 Evergreen St *Web:* www.iscengineering.com	Duarte	CA	91010	909-596-3315	
ISG Resources 11539 Park Woods Cir *Web:* www.isg-resources.com	Alpharetta	GA	30005	770-667-8830	
ITB Group Ltd 39555 Orchard Hill Pl Ste 225 *Web:* itbgroup.com	Novi	MI	48375	248-380-6310	
Itc Engineering Services Inc 9959 Calaveras Rd *Web:* www.itcemc.com	Sunol	CA	94586	925-862-2944	
J f Sato & Assoc Inc 5878 S Rapp St *Web:* www.jfsato.com	Littleton	CO	80120	303-797-1200	
J H i Engineering 3420 SW Macadam Ave *Web:* www.jhiengineering.com	Portland	OR	97239	503-223-7799	
J r Miller & Assoc 2700 Saturn St *Web:* www.jrma.com	Brea	CA	92821	714-524-1870	
J2 Engineering Inc 6921 Pistol Range Rd *Web:* www.j2-eng.com	Tampa	FL	33635	813-888-8861	
JA Woollam Company Inc 645 M St Ste 102 *Web:* www.jawoollam.com	Lincoln	NE	68508	402-477-7501	
Jackson & Tull Chartered Engineers 12201 Distribution Way *Web:* www.jnt.com	Beltsville	MD	20705	301-937-8255	
James Posey Assoc Inc 3112 Lord Baltimore Dr *Web:* www.jamesposey.com	Baltimore	MD	21244	410-265-6100	
James Tool Machine & Engineering Inc 130 Reep Dr *Web:* www.jamestool.com	Morganton	NC	28655	828-584-8722	
Jan-pro Cleaning Systems Mpls 1011 First St S *Web:* janprotwincities.com	Hopkins	MN	55343	952-238-1005	
Janitronics Inc 1988 Central Ave *Web:* www.janitronicsinc.com	Albany	NY	12205	518-456-8484	
JC General Contractors Inc 8250 N Loop Dr Ste A *Web:* www.jc-general.com	El Paso	TX	79907	915-598-8008	
JCM Engineering Corp 2690 E Cedar St *Web:* www.jcmcorp.com	Ontario	CA	91761	909-923-3730	
Jedson Engineering 705 Central Ave Ste B *Web:* www.jedson.com	Cincinnati	OH	45202	513-965-5999	
Jeo Consulting Group Inc 142 W 11th St *Web:* www.pdiowa.com	Wahoo	NE	68066	402-443-4661	
JET Engineering Inc 1241 Park Pl Ne Ste E *Web:* www.jetinc.net	Cedar Rapids	IA	52402	319-294-6106	
Jet Parts Engineering Inc 4772 Ohio Ave S *Web:* www.jetpartsengineering.com	Seattle	WA	98134	206-281-0963	
JK Scanlan Company Inc 15 Research Rd Falmouth Technology Park *Web:* www.jkscanlan.com	East Falmouth	MA	02536	508-540-6226	
JL Richards & Assoc Ltd 864 Lady Ellen Pl *Web:* www.jlrichards.ca	Ottawa	ON	K1Z5M2	613-728-3571	
JLR The Engineering Solutions Co 11611 Airport Rd Ste 201 *Web:* www.jlrcom.com	Everett	WA	98204	425-353-8089	

Company / Address	City	State	ZIP	Phone	Fax
JM Turner Engineering Inc 1325 College Ave *TF:* 800-514-4220 ■ *Web:* www.jmteng.com	Santa Rosa	CA	95404	707-528-4503	
Johnson Engineering Inc 2122 Johnson St *TF:* 866-367-4400 ■ *Web:* www.johnsonengineering.com	Fort Myers	FL	33901	239-334-0046	334-3661
Joyner Keeny & Assoc 1051 N Winstead Ave *Web:* joynerkeeny.com	Rocky Mount	NC	27804	252-977-3124	
Js Dyer & Assoc Inc 8891 Research Dr Ste 200	Irvine	CA	92618	949-296-8858	
JWS & Assoc Inc 10305 Latting Rd	Cordova	TN	38016	901-754-1239	
Kaback Enterprises Inc 45 W 25th St *Web:* www.kaback.com	New York	NY	10010	212-645-5100	
Kalsi Engineering Inc 745 Park Two Dr *Web:* www.kalsi.com	Sugar Land	TX	77478	281-240-6500	240-0255
Kapitan Engineering Inc 802 Franklin St *Web:* kapitan-eng.com	Sauk City	WI	53583	608-643-6477	
KASL Consulting Engineers Inc 7777 Greenback Ln Ste 104 *Web:* www.kasl.com	Citrus Heights	CA	95610	916-722-1800	
Keane Circuits Inc 341 Avondale Ave *Web:* www.keanecircuits.com	Haddonfield	NJ	08033	856-795-1181	
Keller Assoc Engineering Inc 131 SW Fifth Ave Ste A *Web:* www.kellerassociates.com	Meridian	ID	83642	208-288-1992	
Kelly Collins & Gentry Inc 1700 N Orange Ave Ste 400 *Web:* kcgcorp.com	Orlando	FL	32804	407-898-7858	
Kelly's Janitorial Service Inc 228 Hazel Ave *TF:* 800-227-0366 ■ *Web:* www.kellysjanitorial.com	Ewing	NJ	08638	609-771-0365	
KHAFRA Engineering Consultants Inc 230 Peachtree St N W Ste 200 *Web:* www.khafra.com	Atlanta	GA	30303	404-525-2120	
Ki Ho Military Acquisition Consulting Inc 5501 Backlick Rd *Web:* www.kihomac.com	Springfield	VA	22151	703-960-5450	
Kiefner & Assoc Inc 585 Scherers Ct *Web:* www.kiefner.com	Worthington	OH	43085	614-888-8220	
Kim Engineering Inc 11127 New Hampshire Ave *Web:* www.kimengineering.com	Silver Spring	MD	20904	301-754-2882	
Kinetic Systems Inc 20 Arboretum Rd *Web:* homepage.eircom.net	Boston	MA	02131	617-522-8700	
Kiss Janitorial 13498 Pond Springs Rd *Web:* www.kisscleaning.com	Austin	TX	78729	512-258-7003	250-1225
Kjeldsen Sinnock & Neudeck Inc 711 N Pershing Ave *Web:* www.ksninc.com	Stockton	CA	95203	209-946-0268	
Kleen Polymers Inc 145 Rainbow St *Web:* www.kleenpolymers.com	Wadsworth	OH	44281	330-336-4212	
Klewin Construction Inc 444 Brickell Ave Ste 900	Miami	FL	33131	305-709-0700	
Knighthawk Engineering Inc 17625 El Camino Real Ste 412 *Web:* www.knighthawk.com	Houston	TX	77058	281-282-9200	
Knudsen-smith Engineering Inc 2525 W Greenway Rd Ste 302	Phoenix	AZ	85023	602-347-7447	
KPG PS 753 Ninth Ave N *Web:* www.kpg.com	Seattle	WA	98109	206-286-1640	
Krech Ojard & Assoc pa 227 W 1st St Ste 200 *Web:* www.krechojard.com	Duluth	MN	55802	218-727-3282	727-1216
KS Industries LP 6205 District Blvd *Web:* www.ksindustrieslp.com	Bakersfield	CA	93313	661-617-1700	
Kussmaul Electronics Company Inc 170 Cherry Ave *TF:* 800-346-0857 ■ *Web:* www.kussmaul.com	West Sayville	NY	11796	631-567-0314	
KZF Design Inc 700 Broadway St *Web:* www.kzf.com	Cincinnati	OH	45202	513-621-6211	
L & W Engineering Inc 107 Industrial Pkwy *Web:* www.lw-eng.com	Middlebury	IN	46540	574-825-5351	
L2 Consulting Services Inc 2100 E Hwy 290 *Web:* www.l2aviation.com	Dripping Springs	TX	78620	512-894-3414	
LA Fuess Partners Inc 3333 Lee Pkwy Ste 300 *Web:* www.lafp.com	Dallas	TX	75219	214-871-7010	
Lamb-star Engineering LP 5700 W Plano Pkwy Ste 1000 *Web:* www.lamb-star.com	Plano	TX	75093	214-440-3600	
Lan Assoc Engineering Planning Architecture Surveying Inc 445 Godwin Ave Ste 2 *Web:* www.lan-nj.com	Midland Park	NJ	07432	201-447-6400	
Landa & Assoc Inc 5128 E Thomas Rd Ste 100 *Web:* www.landaandassociates.com	Phoenix	AZ	85018	602-443-5515	
Lanmark Engineering & Surveying Inc 9330 Vanguard Dr Ste 131	Anchorage	AK	99507	907-562-6050	
LARON Inc 4255 Santa Fe Dr *TF:* 800-248-3430 ■ *Web:* www.laron.com	Kingman	AZ	86401	928-757-8424	
LEA Group Holdings Inc 625 Cochrane Dr Ste 900 *Web:* www.lea.ca	Markham	ON	L3R9R9	905-470-0015	
Lifeport Inc 1610 Heritage St *Web:* www.lifeport.com	Woodland	WA	98674	360-225-1212	225-1214
Lilja Corp 229 Rickenbacker Cir *Web:* www.liljacorp.com	Livermore	CA	94551	925-455-2300	
Lin Engineering Inc 16245 Vineyard Blvd *Web:* www.linengineering.com	Morgan Hill	CA	95037	408-919-0200	
Loadmaster Universal Rigs Inc 6935 Brittmoore Rd *Web:* www.loadmastereng.com	Houston	TX	77041	281-598-7240	
Lochmueller Group 6200 Vogel Rd *TF:* 800-423-7411 ■ *Web:* www.blainc.com	Evansville	IN	47715	812-479-6200	
Los Gatos Research Inc 67 E Evelyn Ave Ste 3 *Web:* www.lgrinc.com	Mountain View	CA	94041	650-965-7772	

Company / Address	City	State	ZIP	Phone	Fax
Lotek Wireless Inc 115 Pony Dr *Web:* www.lotek.com	Newmarket	ON	L3Y7B5	905-836-6680	836-6455
Mabbett & Associates Inc Five Alfred Cir *Web:* www.mabbett.com	Bedford	MA	01730	781-275-6050	
MacLellan Services Inc 3120 Wall St Ste 100 *Web:* www.maclellan-usa.com	Lexington	KY	40513	859-219-5400	
MadgeTech Inc Six Warner Rd *Web:* www.madgetech.com	Warner	NH	03278	603-456-2011	
Mainstream Engineering Corp 200 Yellow Pl *Web:* www.mainstream-engr.com	Rockledge	FL	32955	321-631-3550	
Makai Ocean Engineering Inc 41-305 Kalanianaole Hwy *Web:* www.makai.com	Waimanalo	HI	96795	808-259-8871	
ManTech Advanced Systems International Inc 12015 Lee Jackson Hwy *Web:* www.mantech.com	Fairfax	VA	22033	703-218-6000	
Martec Ltd 1888 Brunswick St Ste 400 *Web:* www.martec.com	Halifax	NS	B3J3J8	902-425-5101	
Matot Inc 2501 Van Buren St *TF:* 800-369-1070 ■ *Web:* www.matot.com	Bellwood	IL	60104	708-547-1888	547-1608
Matrix Composites Inc 275 Barnes Blvd *Web:* www.matrixcomp.com	Rockledge	FL	32955	321-633-4480	
Matrix Energy Services Inc 3221 Ramos Cir *TF:* 800-556-2123 ■ *Web:* www.matrixescorp.com	Sacramento	CA	95827	916-363-9283	
Matrix LLC 19 Ave D *TF:* 800-338-5603 ■ *Web:* www.cleanforhealth.com	Johnson City	NY	13790	607-766-0700	
Maverick Construction Corp One Westinghouse Plz *Web:* www.maverickcorporation.com	Boston	MA	02136	617-361-6700	
McCall & Associates Inc 3308 Country Club Rd *Web:* www.mccallinc.com	Valdosta	GA	31605	229-242-2551	
McDowell & Assoc Inc 21355 Hatcher Ave *Web:* www.mcdowasc.com	Ferndale	MI	48220	248-399-2066	
McGiffert & Associates LLC 2814 Stillman Blvd *Web:* www.mcgiffert.com	Tuscaloosa	AL	35401	205-759-1521	
McGregor Metalworking Cos 2100 S Yellow Springs St *Web:* mcgregormetal.com	Springfield	OH	45506	937-325-5561	
McInnis Brothers Construction Inc 119 Pearl St *Web:* www.mcinnisbrothers.com	Minden	LA	71055	318-377-6134	
McQ Inc 1551 Forbes St *Web:* www.mcqinc.com	Fredericksburg	VA	22405	540-373-2374	
MDS Aero Support Corp 1220 Old Innes Rd Ste 200 *Web:* www.mdsaero.ca	Ottawa	ON	K1B3V3	613-744-7257	
Meda Ltd 1575 Lauzon Rd *Web:* www.medagroup.com	Windsor	ON	N8S3N4	519-944-7221	944-6862
Metal Master Sales Corp 1159 N Main St *Web:* www.metalmaster.com	Glendale Heights	IL	60139	630-858-4750	
Metric Precision Machine & Engineering LLC 350 W Compton Blvd *Web:* metric-precision.com/	Gardena	CA	90248	310-515-2584	
Metro-Clean Corp 936 W Greenfield Ave	Milwaukee	WI	53204	414-671-6660	
Mid-South Engineering Co 1658 Malvern Ave *Web:* www.mseco.com	Hot Springs	AR	71901	501-321-2276	
Minnesota Elevator Inc 19336 607th Ave *Web:* meielevatorsolutions.com	Mankato	MN	56001	507-245-3060	245-3956
Mitsubishi Electric & Electronics USA Inc *Elevator & Escalator Div* 5665 Plz Dr *Web:* www.mitsubishielectric.com/elevator	Cypress	CA	90630	714-220-4700	220-4812
MMI Engineering Ltd 475 14th St Ste 400 *Web:* www.mmiengineering.com	Oakland	CA	94612	510-836-3002	
Mobile Office Acquisition Corp 9155 Harrison Park Court - NEW *Web:* www.pacvan.com	Indianapolis	IN	46216	317-791-2030	
Moffitt Corp Inc 1351 13th Ave S Ste 130 *TF:* 800-474-3267 ■ *Web:* www.moffitthvac.com	Jacksonville Beach	FL	32250	904-241-9944	
Molding International & Engineering Inc 42136 Avenida Alvarado *Web:* www.mie.com	Temecula	CA	92590	951-296-5010	
Monitor Elevator Products Inc 125 Ricefield Ln *Web:* www.januselevator.com	Hauppauge	NY	11788	800-527-9156	
Motion Control Engineering Inc 11380 White Rock Rd *TF:* 800-444-7442 ■ *Web:* www.mceinc.com	Rancho Cordova	CA	95742	916-463-9200	
MVA Engineering Group Ltd 246 Waterloo St *Web:* www.mva.on.ca	London	ON	N6B2N4	519-668-4698	
Navmar Applied Sciences Corp 65 W St Rd Bldg C *Web:* www.nasc.com	Warminster	PA	18974	215-675-4900	
Neany Inc 44010 Commerce Ave Ste A *Web:* www.neanyinc.com	Hollywood	MD	20636	301-373-8700	
NELSON & Associates Interior Design & Space Planning Inc The NELSON Bldg 222-230 Walnut St *Web:* www.nelsononline.com	Philadelphia	PA	19106	215-925-6562	
Nexus Engineering Inc 1400 Lone Palm Ave *Web:* www.nexusengineering.net	Modesto	CA	95351	209-572-7399	
North American Cable Equipment Inc 1085 Andrew Dr Ste A *Web:* www.northamericancable.com	West Chester	PA	19380	610-429-1821	
Northstar Industries LLC 126 Merrimack St *Web:* www.northstarind.com	Methuen	MA	01844	978-975-5500	
Nth Consultants Ltd 41780 6 Mile Rd *Web:* www.nthconsultants.com	Northville	MI	48168	248-553-6300	

Company / Address	City	State	ZIP	Phone	Fax
NuVision Engineering Inc River Park Commons 2403 Sidney St Ste 700 *Web:* www.nuvisioneng.com	Pittsburgh	PA	15203	412-586-1810	
Oblong Industries Inc 923 E Third St Ste 111 *Web:* oblong.com	Los Angeles	CA	90013	213-683-8863	
Omicron Architecture Engineering Construction Ltd 595 Burrard St Three Bentall Centre Fifth Fl PO Box 49369 *Web:* www.omicronaec.com	Vancouver	BC	V7X1L4	604-632-3350	
OMNI Engineering Services Inc 370 W Second St Ste 100 *Web:* omnimn.com	Winona	MN	55987	507-454-5293	
Optimum Engineering Solutions Inc Three Country Club Executive Park Ste 2 *Web:* www.openso.com	Glen Carbon	IL	62034	618-288-3131	
Opus International Consultants (Canada) Ltd 210-889 Harbourside Dr *Web:* www.opusinternational.ca	North Vancouver	BC	V6E4E6	604-990-4800	990-4805
Otis Elevator Co 10 Farm Springs Rd *Web:* www.otisworldwide.com	Farmington	CT	06032	860-676-6000	998-3910
P&R Enterprises Inc 5681 Columbia Pk Ste 101 *Web:* www.p-and-r.com	Falls Church	VA	22041	703-931-1000	
Parametric Solutions Inc 900 E Indiantown Rd Ste 200 *Web:* www.psnet.com	Jupiter	FL	33477	561-747-6107	
Paramount Building Solutions Inc 401 W Baseline Rd Ste 209 *Web:* www.paramountbldgsol.com	Tempe	AZ	85283	480-348-1177	
PCCI 300 N Lee St *Web:* www.pccii.com	Alexandria	VA	22314	703-684-2060	
Pensar Development Inc 900 E Pine St Ste 201 *Web:* www.pensardevelopment.com	Seattle	WA	98122	206-284-3134	
Piasecki Aircraft Corp 519 W Second St *Web:* www.piasecki.com	Essington	PA	19029	610-521-5700	
Piedmont Geotechnical 3000 Northfield Pl *Web:* www.ascomputer.com	Roswell	GA	30076	770-752-9205	
PIKA Technologies Inc 535 Legget Dr Ste 400 *Web:* www.pikatechnologies.com	Ottawa	ON	K2K3B8	613-591-1555	591-9295
Pinnacle Asset Integrity Services One Pinnacle Way *Web:* www.pinnacleais.com	Pasadena	TX	77504	281-598-1330	
Planned Environments Inc 2219 Wlake Dr Ste 100 *Web:* www.plannedenvironmentsinc.com	Austin	TX	78746	512-474-0806	
Potelco Inc 14103 Stewart Rd *Web:* www.potelco.net	Sumner	WA	98390	253-863-0484	
Power Quality Engineering Inc 3061 W Whitestone Blvd *Web:* www.pqeinc.com	Cedar Park	TX	78613	512-267-6656	
Process Plus LLC 1340 Kemper Meadow Dr *Web:* www.processplus.com	Cincinnati	OH	45240	513-742-7590	
Protochips Inc 617 Hutton St Ste 111 *Web:* www.protochips.com	Raleigh	NC	27606	919-341-2612	
Radiant Technologies Inc 2835 Pan American Fwy Ne *Web:* www.ferrodevices.com	Albuquerque	NM	87107	505-842-8007	
Radius Engineering Inc 1042 West 2780 South *Web:* www.radiuseng.com	Salt Lake City	UT	84119	801-886-2624	
Raisbeck Engineering Inc 4411 S Ryan Way *Web:* www.raisbeck.com	Seattle	WA	98178	206-723-2000	
Ralph S Inouye Company Ltd 2831 Awaawaloa St *Web:* www.rsinouye.com	Honolulu	HI	96819	808-839-9002	
Read Jones Christoffersen Ltd 1285 W Broadway Ste 300 *Web:* www.rjc.ca	Vancouver	BC	V6H3X8	604-738-0048	
Red Cedar Technology Inc 4572 S Hagadorn Rd Ste 3-A *Web:* www.redcedartech.com	East Lansing	MI	48823	517-664-1137	
Rescan Environmental Services Ltd Sixth Fl 1111 W Hastings St *Web:* erm.com/canada	Vancouver	BC	V6E2J3	604-689-9460	
RETEL Services Inc 5871 Glenridge Dr NE Ste 110 *Web:* www.retelservices.com	Atlanta	GA	30328	404-343-2375	
Rhinestahl Corp 7687 Innovation Way *Web:* www.rhinestahl.com	Mason	OH	45040	513-229-5300	
Ricon Corp 7900 Nelson Rd *TF:* 800-322-2884 ■ *Web:* www.riconcorp.com	Panorama City	CA	91402	818-267-3000	267-3001
Ripon Printers Inc 656 S Douglas St *Web:* www.riponprinters.com	Ripon	WI	54971	920-748-3136	
RJ Burnside & Assoc Ltd 15 Townline *Web:* www.rjburnside.com	Orangeville	ON	L9W3R4	519-941-5331	
RM Mechanical Inc 5998 W Gowen Rd *Web:* www.rmmechanical.net	Boise	ID	83709	208-362-0131	
Rutheford & Chekene 55 Second St Ste 600 *Web:* www.ruthchek.com	San Francisco	CA	94105	415-568-4400	
S W Cole Engineering Inc 37 Liberty Dr *Web:* www.swcole.com	Bangor	ME	04401	207-848-5714	
S&ME Inc 6190 Enterprise Ct	Dublin	OH	43016	614-793-2226	
SAI Engineering Inc 13662 Office Pl Ste 101 *Web:* www.saimep.com	Woodbridge	VA	22192	703-590-8200	
Sauer Holdings Inc 30 51st St *Web:* sauerholdings.com	Pittsburgh	PA	15201	412-687-4100	
Schindler Elevator Corp 20 Whippany Rd **Fax:* Mail Rm ■ *TF:* 800-225-3123 ■ *Web:* www.schindler.com	Morristown	NJ	07960	973-397-6500	397-3619*
Schumacher Elevator Co One Schumacher Way PO Box 393 *TF:* 800-779-5438 ■ *Web:* www.schumacherelevator.com	Denver	IA	50622	319-984-5676	984-6316
Scientific Systems Company Inc 500 W Cummings Pk Ste 3000 *Web:* www.ssci.com	Woburn	MA	01801	781-933-5355	
Sematic USA 7852 Bavaria Rd *Web:* sematic.com	Twinsburg	OH	44087	216-524-0100	524-9710
Service Elements Inc 15029 N Thompson Peak Pkwy Ste B111-444 *Web:* www.serviceelements.com	Scottsdale	AZ	85260	480-538-0123	
Shenandoah Electronic Intelligence Inc 220 University Blvd *Web:* www.sei-inc.com	Harrisonburg	VA	22801	540-434-7075	
Sheppard T Powell Assoc LLC 1915 Aliceanna St *Web:* www.stpa.com	Baltimore	MD	21231	410-327-3500	
Sigma Space Corp 4600 Forbes Blvd *Web:* www.optotraffic.com	Lanham	MD	20706	301-552-6000	
Solid State Scientific Corp 27-2 Wright Rd *Web:* www.solidstatescientific.com	Hollis	NH	03049	603-465-5686	
Solusia Inc 3343 Peachtree Rd NE Ste 530 *Web:* www.solusia.com	Atlanta	GA	30326	404-601-1100	
SpaceAge Control Inc 38850 20th St E *Web:* www.spaceagecontrol.com	Palmdale	CA	93550	661-273-3000	
Stephenson Engineering Ltd 2550 Victoria Park Ave Ste 602 *Web:* www.stephenson-eng.com	Toronto	ON	M2J5A9	416-635-9970	
Suburban Motors Grafton Inc 139 N Main St *Web:* www.suburbanharley.com	Thiensville	WI	53092	262-242-2464	
Swenson Say Faget Inc 2124 Third Ave Ste 100 *Web:* swensonsayfaget.com	Seattle	WA	98121	206-443-6212	
Syscor Controls & Automation Inc 201 - 60 Bastion Sq *Web:* www.syscor.com	Victoria	BC	V8W1J2	250-361-1681	361-1682
Technical Systems Integration Inc 816 Greenbrier Cir Ste 208 *TF:* 800-566-8744 ■ *Web:* www.tecsysint.com	Chesapeake	VA	23320	757-424-5793	
Technology for Energy Corp 10737 Lexington Dr *Web:* www.tec-usa.com	Knoxville	TN	37932	865-966-5856	
Telefactor Robotics LLC 1094 New Dehaven Ave *Web:* www.chattenassociates.com	West Conshohocken	PA	19428	610-940-6040	
Teleflex Turbine Services Corp 12661 Challenger Pkwy Ste 250 *Web:* www.turbinetech.com	Orlando	FL	32826	407-677-0813	
Telesto Solutions Inc 2950 E Harmony Rd Ste 200 *Web:* www.telesto-inc.com	Fort Collins	CO	80528	970-484-7704	
Thomas J Dyer Company Inc 5240 Lester Rd *Web:* www.groteenterprises.com	Cincinnati	OH	45213	513-321-8100	
Thompson Engineering Inc 2970 Cottage Hill Rd Ste 190 *Web:* www.tcocompanies.com	Mobile	AL	36606	251-666-2443	
ThyssenKrupp Access Inc 4001 E 138th St *TF:* 800-669-9047 ■ *Web:* www.tkaccess.com	Grandview	MO	64030	816-763-3100	763-4467
Ticom Geomatics Inc 9130 Jollyville Rd Ste 100 *Web:* www.ticom-geo.com	Austin	TX	78759	512-345-5006	
Tidy Building Services Inc 609 W William David Pkwy Ste 202 *Web:* www.tidyusa.com	Metairie	LA	70005	504-838-9843	
Triumph Structures - Los Angeles Inc 17055 E Gale Ave *Web:* www.triumphgroup.com	City Of Industry	CA	91745	626-965-1630	
TTL Inc 3516 Greensboro Ave *Web:* www.ttlinc.com	Tuscaloosa	AL	35401	205-345-0816	
Tulloch Engineering Inc 200 Main St *Web:* www.tulloch.ca	Thessalon	ON	P0R1L0	705-842-3372	
Tundra Engineering Associates Ltd 1331 Macleod Trail SE *Web:* www.tundraeng.com	Calgary	AB	T2G1E1	403-777-2477	
Underground Imaging Technologies LLC 308 Wolf Rd *Web:* www.uit-systems.com	Latham	NY	12110	518-783-9848	
United Consulting Group Ltd 625 Holcomb Bridge Rd *Web:* www.unitedconsulting.com	Norcross	GA	30071	770-209-0029	
United Infrastructure Group Inc 1691 Turnbull Ave *Web:* uig.net	North Charleston	SC	29405	843-529-3010	
United Services Inc 462 Forest St PO Box 1067 *Web:* www.unitedservicesinc.net	Kearny	NJ	07032	201-955-1300	
Vaughn Coltrane Pharr & Associates Inc 2060 E Exchange Pl *Web:* www.vcae.com	Tucker	GA	30084	770-938-2600	
Veneklasen Associates 1711 16Th St *Web:* www.veneklasen-assoc.com	Santa Monica	CA	90404	310-450-1733	
VersaTech Automation Services LLC 11349 FM 529 Rd *Web:* www.vtechas.com	Houston	TX	77041	713-939-6100	
Vidaris Inc 360 Park Ave S *Web:* www.vidaris.com	New York	NY	10010	212-689-5389	
VPT Inc 1971 Kraft Dr *Web:* vptpower.com/	Blacksburg	VA	24060	540-552-5000	552-5003
VTI Instruments Corp 2031 Main St *Web:* www.vtiinstruments.com	Irvine	CA	92614	949-955-1894	
Walker Engineering Inc 8451 Dunwoody Pl *Web:* www.walkerengineer.com	Atlanta	GA	30350	770-641-7306	
Ward Engineering Company Inc 1353 S Seventh St PO Box 2498 *Web:* www.wardengr.com	Louisville	KY	40201	502-637-6521	
Warren & Panzer Engineers PC 228 E 45th St *Web:* www.warrenpanzer.com	New York	NY	10017	212-922-0077	

				Phone	Fax
Watson Industries Inc 3041 Melby Rd. Web: www.watson-gyro.com	Eau Claire	WI	54703	715-839-0628	
Watthour Engineering Company Inc 333 Crosspark Dr. Web: www.watthour.com	Pearl	MS	39208	601-933-0900	
Waupaca Elevator Co Inc 1726 N BallaRd Rd. TF: 800-238-8739 ■ Web: www.waupacaelevator.com	Appleton	WI	54911	920-991-9082	991-9087
Waveguide Consulting One W Court Sq. Web: www.waveguide.com	Decatur	GA	30030	404-815-1919	
Weatherford Aerospace Inc 1020 E Columbia St. Web: www.weatherfordaerospace.com	Weatherford	TX	76086	817-594-5464	594-7450
Wells & Associates 1420 Spring Hill Rd Ste 610. Web: www.mjwells.com	Tysons	VA	22102	703-917-6620	
Western Commercial Services LLC 2311 Industrial Rd. Web: www.westerncommercial.net	Las Vegas	NV	89102	702-384-7907	
Westfield Engineering & Services Inc 8310 McHard Rd. Web: www.westfieldengineering.com	Houston	TX	77053	281-438-2047	
Wickham Glass Co 4747 N Webb Rd. Web: www.wickhamglass.com	Wichita	KS	67226	316-262-3403	
Wiebe Forest Engineering Ltd 3613 - 33rd St NW. Web: www.wfe.ca	Calgary	AB	T2L2A7	403-670-7300	
Williams Engineering Canada Inc 10065 Jasper Ave Ste 200. Web: www.williamsengineering.com	Edmonton	AB	T5J3B1	780-409-5300	
Windermere Information Technology Systems LLC 2000 Windermere Ct. Web: www.witsusa.com	Annapolis	MD	21401	410-266-1700	
Wineman Technology Inc 1668 Champagne Dr N. Web: www.winemantech.com	Saginaw	MI	48604	989-771-3000	
WorkingBuildings LLC 1230 Peachtree St NE 300 Promenade. Web: www.workingbuildings.com	Atlanta	GA	30309	678-990-8001	
WSB & Associates Inc 701 Xenia Ave S Ste 300. Web: www.wsbeng.com	Minneapolis	MN	55416	763-541-4800	
Wynston Hill Capital LLC 488 Madison Ave 24th Fl. Web: www.wynstonhill.com	New York	NY	10022	212-521-1900	208-0978
XCG Consultants Ltd 2620 Bristol Cir Ste 300. Web: www.xcg.com	Oakville	ON	L6H6Z7	905-829-8880	
York Building Services Inc 99 Grand St Ste 3. TF: 855-443-9675 ■ Web: yorkbuildingservices.com	Moonachie	NJ	07074	855-443-9675	

260 EMBASSIES & CONSULATES - FOREIGN, IN THE US

SEE ALSO Travel & Tourism Information - Foreign Travel p. 3257

Foreign embassies in the U.S. generally include consular services among their functions. These embassy-based consulates are listed here only if their address differs from the embassy's.

				Phone	Fax
Afghanistan Embassy 2341 Wyoming Ave NW. TF: 866-323-8609 ■ Web: www.embassyofafghanistan.org	Washington	DC	20008	202-483-6410	483-6488
Algeria Embassy 2118 Kalorama Rd NW. Web: www.algerianembassy.org	Washington	DC	20008	202-265-2800	986-5906
Andorra Embassy Two United Nations Plz 27th Fl. Web: www.state.gov/r/pa/ei/bgn/3164.htm	New York	NY	10017	212-750-8064	750-6630
Angola Embassy 2108 16th St NW. Web: www.angola.org	Washington	DC	20009	202-785-1156	822-9049
Antigua & Barbuda 305 E 47th St Sixth Fl. Web: antigua-barbuda.org	New York	NY	10017	212-541-4117	757-1607
Embassy 3216 New Mexico Ave NW. TF: 866-978-7299 ■ Web: www.antigua-barbuda.org	Washington	DC	20016	202-362-5122	362-5225
Argentina					
Consulate General 245 Peachtree Ctr Ave Ste 2101	Atlanta	GA	30303	404-880-0805	880-0806
Consulate General 2200 W Loop S Ste 1025. Web: www.chous.mrecic.gov.ar	Houston	TX	77027	713-871-8935	
Consulate General 5055 Wilshire Blvd Ste 210. Web: clang.mrecic.gob.ar	Los Angeles	CA	90036	323-954-9155	934-9076
Consulate General 12 W 56th St. Web: www.congenargentinany.com	New York	NY	10019	212-603-0400	541-7746
Embassy 1600 New Hampshire Ave NW. Web: www.embassyofargentina.us	Washington	DC	20009	202-238-6400	332-3171
Armenia Embassy 2225 R St NW. Web: www.armeniaemb.org	Washington	DC	20008	202-319-1976	319-2982
Australia					
Consulate General 1000 Bishop St PH. TF: 866-343-3086 ■ Web: www.usa.embassy.gov.au/whwh/hawaiicg.html	Honolulu	HI	96813	808-529-8100	529-8142
Consulate General 2029 Century Pk E Ste 3150. Web: www.losangeles.consulate.gov.au	Los Angeles	CA	90067	310-229-2300	277-2258
Consulate General 150 E 42nd St 34th Fl. Web: www.newyork.usa.embassy.gov.au	New York	NY	10017	212-351-6500	351-6501
Embassy 2005 Massachusetts Ave NW. TF: 800-345-6541 ■ Web: www.visahq.com	Washington	DC	20036	202-558-2216	318-0771
Australian Consulate General					
Consulate General 123 N Wacker Dr Ste 1330. Web: australia.visahq.com	Chicago	IL	60606	312-419-1480	419-1499
Austria 600 Third Ave 31st Fl. *Fax Area Code: 212 ■ Web: advantageaustria.org	New York	NY	10016	917-542-8400	949-1840*
Consulate General 3524 International Ct NW. *Fax Area Code: 312 ■ Web: www.austria.org	Washington	DC	20008	202-895-6700	222-4113*
Consulate General 11859 Wilshire Blvd Ste 501. TF: 800-255-2414 ■ Web: www.austria.org	Los Angeles	CA	90025	310-444-9310	477-9897
Consulate General 31 E 69th St. Web: aussenministerium.at/newyorkgk/	New York	NY	10021	212-933-5140	585-1992
Embassy 3524 International Ct NW. TF: 800-255-2414 ■ Web: www.austria.org	Washington	DC	20008	202-895-6700	895-6750
Azerbaijan Embassy 2741 34th St NW. Web: www.azembassy.us	Washington	DC	20008	202-337-3500	337-5911
Consulate General 25 SE Second Ave. Web: bahamas.com	Miami	FL	33131	305-373-6295	373-6312
Consulate General 231 E 46th St. Web: www.bahamasny.net	New York	NY	10017	212-421-6420	688-5926
Bahamas					
Embassy 2220 Massachusetts Ave NW. TF: 800-883-7421 ■ Web: nassau.usembassy.gov	Washington	DC	20008	202-319-2660	319-2668
Bahrain 866 Second Ave 14th & 15th Fls	New York	NY	10017	212-223-6200	
Embassy 3502 International Dr NW. Web: www.bahrainembassy.org	Washington	DC	20008	202-342-1111	362-2192
Bangladesh Consulate General 4201 Wilshire Blvd Ste 605. Web: www.bangladeshconsulatela.com	Los Angeles	CA	90010	323-932-0100	932-9703
Barbados					
Consulate General 2121 Poncedaleon Blvd Ste 1300. Web: www.foreign.gov.bb	Coral Gables	FL	33134	305-442-1994	455-7975
Belarus Embassy 1619 New Hampshire Ave NW. Web: embassies.mfa.gov.by	Washington	DC	20009	202-986-1606	986-1805
Belgium					
Consulate General 230 Peachtree St NW Ste 2710. Web: www.diplomatie.belgium.be/united_states	Atlanta	GA	30303	404-659-2150	
Consulate General 1065 Ave of the Americas 22nd Fl. Web: www.diplomatie.be/newyork	New York	NY	10018	212-586-5110	582-9657
Consulate General 6100 Wilshire Blvd Ste 1200. Web: www.diplomatie.be/losangeles	Los Angeles	CA	90048	323-857-1244	936-2564
Embassy 3330 Garfield St NW. Web: www.diplobel.us	Washington	DC	20008	202-333-6900	333-3079
Belize Embassy 2535 Massachusetts Ave NW. Web: embassyofbelize.org	Washington	DC	20008	202-332-9636	332-6888
Benin Embassy 2124 Kalorama Rd NW. Web: www.beninembassy.us	Washington	DC	20008	202-232-6656	265-1996
Bolivarian Republic of Venezuela					
Consulate General 545 Boylston St Third Fl. Web: newyork.embavenez-us.org	Boston	MA	02116	617-266-9368	
Bolivia 801 Second Ave 4th Fl, Rm 42	New York	NY	10017	212-682-8132	
Consulate General 211 E 43rd St Ste 1004	New York	NY	10017	212-687-0530	687-0532
Embassy 3014 Massachusetts Ave NW. Web: www.bolivia-usa.org	Washington	DC	20008	202-483-4410	328-3712
Bosnia & Herzegovina					
Embassy 2109 E St NW. Web: www.bhembassy.org	Washington	DC	20037	202-337-1500	337-1502
Botswana Embassy 1531 New Hampshire Ave NW. Web: www.botswanaembassy.org	Washington	DC	20036	202-244-4990	244-4164
Brazil 747 Third Ave 9th Fl. Web: www.un.int	New York	NY	10017	212-372-2600	371-5716
Consulate General 300 Montgomery St Ste 300	San Francisco	CA	94104	415-981-8170	
Consulate General 175 Purchase St Ste 810. Web: www.consulatebrazil.org	Boston	MA	02110	617-542-4000	542-4318
Consulate General 1233 W Loop S Ste 1150. TF: 800-326-2289 ■ Web: houston.itamaraty.gov.br	Houston	TX	77027	713-961-3063	961-3070
Consulate General 8484 Wilshire Blvd Ste 711. TF: 877-782-5477 ■ Web: losangeles.itamaraty.gov.br	Beverly Hills	CA	90211	323-651-2664	651-1274
Consulate General 80 SW Eigth St 26th Fl. Web: miami.itamaraty.gov.br	Miami	FL	33130	305-285-6200	285-6240
Embassy 3006 Massachusetts Ave NW. Web: washington.itamaraty.gov.br	Washington	DC	20008	202-238-2700	
Brunei Darussalam					
Embassy 3520 International Ct NW. Web: www.bruneiembassy.org	Washington	DC	20008	202-237-1838	885-0560
Bulgaria 11 E 84th St	New York	NY	10028	212-737-4790	472-9865
Consulate General 121 E 62nd St. Web: bulgaria-embassy.org	New York	NY	10021	212-935-4646	319-5955
Embassy 1621 22nd St NW. TF: 800-961-6836 ■ Web: www.bulgaria-embassy.org	Washington	DC	20008	202-387-0174	234-7973
Burkina Faso Embassy 2005 Massachusetts Ave NW. TF: 800-345-6541 ■ Web: www.visahq.com	Washington	DC	20008	202-332-5577	667-1882
Burundi Embassy 2233 Wisconsin Ave NW Ste 212. Web: www.burundiembassy-usa.org	Washington	DC	20007	202-342-2574	342-2578
Cambodia Embassy 4530 16th St NW. Web: www.embassyofcambodia.org	Washington	DC	20011	202-726-7742	726-8381
Cameroon Embassy 3400 International Dr NW. Web: www.cameroonembassyusa.org/	Washington	DC	20008	202-265-8790	387-3826
Canada					
Consulate General 1175 Peachtree St NE 100 Colony Sq Ste 1700. Web: can-am.gc.ca	Atlanta	GA	30361	404-532-2000	532-2050
Consulate General 200 S Biscayne Blvd Ste 1600. Web: canadainternational.gc.ca	Miami	FL	33131	305-579-1600	374-6774
Consulate General 500 N Akard St Ste 2900. TF: 800-267-8376 ■ Web: www.canadainternational.gc.ca	Dallas	TX	75201	214-922-9806	922-9815
Consulate General 1251 Ave of the Americas Concourse Level. TF: 800-267-8376 ■ Web: www.canadainternational.gc.ca	New York	NY	10020	212-596-1628	596-1790
Consulate General 180 N Stetson Ave Ste 2400. Web: chicago.gc.ca	Chicago	IL	60601	312-616-1860	616-1877
Consulate General 701 Fourth Ave S Ninth Fl. Web: www.canadainternational.gc.ca	Minneapolis	MN	55415	612-333-4641	332-4061

	City	State	ZIP	Phone	Fax
Consulate General 1251 Ave of the Americas	New York	NY	10020	212-596-1628	
Web: can-am.gc.ca					
Embassy 501 Pennsylvania Ave NW	Washington	DC	20001	202-682-1740	682-7726
TF: 800-567-6868 ■ *Web:* can-am.gc.ca					
Cape Verde 27 E 69th St	New York	NY	10021	212-472-0333	794-1398
Embassy 3415 Massachusetts Ave NW	Washington	DC	20007	202-965-6820	965-1207
TF: 800-343-2347 ■ *Web:* www.virtualcapeverde.net					
Consulate General 866 UN Plz Ste 601	New York	NY	10017	212-980-3366	888-5288
Web: chileabroad.gov.cl					
Consulate General 870 Market St Ste 1058	San Francisco	CA	94102	415-982-7662	982-2384
Web: www.chile-usa.org					
Chile					
Embassy 1732 Massachusetts Ave NW	Washington	DC	20036	202-785-1746	887-5579
Web: www.chile-usa.org					
Chile Mission 885 Second Ave 40th Fl	New York	NY	10017	917-322-6800	832-0236*
**Fax Area Code:* 212					
China 350 E 35th St	New York	NY	10016	212-655-6100	634-7626
Web: www.china-un.org					
Consulate General 1450 Laguna St	San Francisco	CA	94115	415-852-5941	
Web: www.chinaconsulatesf.org					
Consulate General 100 W Erie St	Chicago	IL	60654	312-803-0095	803-0110
Web: www.chinaconsulatechicago.org					
Consulate General 3417 Montrose Blvd	Houston	TX	77006	713-520-1462	521-3064
Web: houston.china-consulate.org					
Consulate General 443 Shatto Pl	Los Angeles	CA	90020	213-807-8088	807-1961
Web: losangeles.china-consulate.org					
Embassy 2201 Wisconsin Ave NW Ste 110	Washington	DC	20007	202-337-1956	588-9760
Web: www.china-embassy.org					
Colombia 140 E 57th St	New York	NY	10022	212-355-7776	355-7776
Web: www.colombiaun.org					
Consulate General 500 N Michigan Ave Ste 2040	Chicago	IL	60611	312-923-1196	923-1197
Web: nuevayork.consulado.gov.co					
Consulate General 5851 San Felipe Ste 300	Houston	TX	77057	713-527-8919	529-3395
Web: www.colhouston.org					
Embassy 2118 Leroy Pl NW	Washington	DC	20008	202-387-8338	232-8643
Web: www.colombiaemb.org					
Comoros Embassy					
866 United Nations Plaza Ste 418	New York	NY	10017	212-750-1637	937-0692
Consulate General of Honduras					
Consulate General 365 Canal St Ste 1580	New Orleans	LA	70130	504-522-3118	
Consulate General of Liberia					
866 UN Plz Ste 480	New York	NY	10017	212-687-1033	687-1035
Web: www.liberianconsulate-ny.com					
Consulate General of Paraguay					
801 Second Ave Ste 600	New York	NY	10017	212-682-9441	682-9443
Web: www.consulparny.com					
Consulate General of Romania					
Consulate General 11766 Wilshire Blvd Ste 560	Los Angeles	CA	90025	310-444-0043	
Web: www.consulateromania.org					
Consulate General of Switzerland					
633 Third Ave 30th Fl	New York	NY	10017	212-599-5700	212-4266
Web: www.eda.admin.ch/newyork					
Consulate General of the Republic of Suriname					
6303 Blue Lagoon Dr Ste 325	Miami	FL	33126	305-265-4655	265-4599
Web: www.scgmia.com					
Costa Rica					
Consulate General 1605 W Olympic Blvd Ste 400	Los Angeles	CA	90015	213-380-7915	380-5639
Web: www.costarica-embassy.org					
Consulate General 2114 S St NW	Washington	DC	20008	202-480-2200	265-4795
Web: www.costarica-embassy.org					
Consulate General 2730 SW Third Ave Ste 401	Miami	FL	33129	305-871-7485	522-0119*
**Fax Area Code:* 786 ■ *Web:* www.costarica-embassy.org					
Consulate General 2112 S St NW	Washington	DC	20008	202-265-4795	265-4795
Web: www.costarica-embassy.org					
Embassy 2114 S St NW	Washington	DC	20008	202-499-2991	265-4795
Web: www.costarica-embassy.org					
Croatia					
Consulate General 737 N Michigan Ave Ste 1030	Chicago	IL	60611	312-482-9902	482-9987
Web: www.croatiaemb.org					
Consulate General 369 Lexington Ave	New York	NY	10017	212-599-3066	599-3106
Consulate General 11766 Wilshire Blvd Ste 1250	Los Angeles	CA	90025	310-477-1009	477-1866
Web: www.croatiaemb.org					
Embassy 2343 Massachusetts Ave NW	Washington	DC	20008	202-588-5899	588-8936
Web: www.croatiaemb.org					
Cyprus 13 E 40th St	New York	NY	10016	212-481-6023	685-7316
Web: www.un.int					
Consulate General 13 E 40th St	New York	NY	10016	212-686-6016	686-3660
Web: cyprusembassy.net					
Embassy 2211 R St NW	Washington	DC	20008	202-462-5772	483-6710
Web: www.cyprusembassy.net					
Consulate General 10990 Wilshire Blvd Ste 1100	Los Angeles	CA	90024	310-473-0889	473-9813
Web: www.mzv.cz/losangeles					
Consulate General 321 E 73rd St	New York	NY	10021	646-422-3344	422-3311
Web: www.mzv.cz/consulate.newyork					
Czech Republic					
Embassy 3900 Spring of Freedom St NW	Washington	DC	20008	202-274-9100	966-8540
Web: www.mzv.cz					
Democratic & Popular Republic of Algeria, The					
Embassy - Consular Section 2118 Kalorama Rd NW	Washington	DC	20008	202-265-2800	667-2174
Web: www.embassy.org					
Consulate General 875 N Michigan Ave Ste 3950	Chicago	IL	60611	800-345-6541	787-8744*
**Fax Area Code:* 312 ■ *TF:* 800-345-6541 ■ *Web:* denmark.visahq.com					
Denmark					
Embassy 3200 Whitehaven St NW	Washington	DC	20008	202-234-4300	328-1470
Web: usa.um.dk					
Dominica					
Embassy 3216 New Mexico Ave NW	Washington	DC	20016	202-364-6781	364-6791
Dominican Republic					
Consulate General 8770 W Bryn Mawr Ave Triangle Plz	Chicago	IL	60631	773-714-4924	
Web: www.domrep.org					
Consulate General 1038 Brickell Ave	Miami	FL	33131	305-358-3220	358-2318
Web: www.domrep.org					
Consulate General 1501 Broadway Ste 410	New York	NY	10036	212-768-2480	768-2677
Web: www.domrep.org					
Consulate General 500 N Brand Blvd Ste 960	Glendale	CA	91203	818-504-6605	504-6617
Web: www.consulatedrwest.com					
Consulate General 1715 22nd St NW	Washington	DC	20008	202-332-6280	387-2459
Web: www.domrep.org					
Embassy 1715 22nd St NW	Washington	DC	20008	202-332-6280	265-8057
Web: www.domrep.org					
Ecuador					
Consulate General 400 Market St Fourth Fl	Newark	NJ	07105	973-344-6900	344-0008
Web: www.consuladoecuadornj.com					
Consulate General 8484 Wilshire Blvd Ste 500	Beverly Hills	CA	90211	323-297-1150	297-1152
Web: cancilleria.gob.ec					
Consulate General 30 S Michigan Ave	Chicago	IL	60603	312-338-1002	338-1004
Consulate General 4200 Westheimer Rd Ste 218	Houston	TX	77027	713-572-8731	572-8732
Web: consuladoecuadornewyork.com					
Consulate General 1101 Brickell Ave Ste M102	Miami	FL	33131	305-373-8520	539-8313
Web: www.ecuador.org					
Consulate General 800 Second Ave Ste 600	New York	NY	10017	212-808-0170	808-0188
Web: www.consuladoecuadornewyork.com					
Embassy 2535 15th St NW	Washington	DC	20009	202-234-7200	234-3429
Web: www.ecuador.org					
Egypt 304 E 44th St	New York	NY	10017	212-503-0300	949-5999
Web: egyptembassy.net					
Consulate General 500 N Michigan Ave Ste 1900	Chicago	IL	60611	312-828-9162	828-9167
Web: egypt.embassy-online.net					
Consulate General 1110 Second Ave Ste 201	New York	NY	10022	212-759-7120	308-7643
Web: www.egypt-nyc.com					
Embassy 3521 International Ct NW	Washington	DC	20008	202-895-5400	244-4319
Web: www.egyptembassy.net					
El Salvador					
Consulate General 3450 Wilshire Blvd Ste 250	Los Angeles	CA	90010	213-383-5776	383-8599
Web: www.elsalvador.org					
Consulate General 1400 16th St Ste 100	Washington	DC	20036	202-595-7500	270-9683*
**Fax Area Code:* 713 ■ *Web:* www.elsalvador.org					
Consulate General 2600 Douglas Rd Ste 104	Coral Gables	FL	33134	305-774-0840	774-0850
Web: www.elsalvador.org					
Embassy 1400 16th St NW Ste 100	Washington	DC	20036	202-595-7500	232-3763
Web: www.elsalvador.org					
Embassy of Bosnia & Herzegovina					
Consulate General 2109 E St NW	Washington	DC	20037	202-337-1500	337-2909
Web: www.bhembassy.org					
Embassy of Hungary 3910 Shoemaker St NW	Washington	DC	20008	202-362-6730	
Embassy of Israel					
Consulate General 3514 International Dr Ste 1308	Washington	DC	20008	202-364-5500	297-4855*
**Fax Area Code:* 312 ■ *Web:* www.israelemb.org					
Embassy of Syria 2215 Wyoming Ave NW	Washington	DC	20008	202-232-6313	265-4585
Web: www.syrianembassy.us					
Estonia 305 E 47th St Sixth Fl	New York	NY	10017	212-883-0640	514-0099*
**Fax Area Code:* 646 ■ *Web:* www.un.estemb.org					
Consulate General 305 E 47th St 3 Dag Hammarskjold Pl Ste 6B	New York	NY	10016	212-883-0636	883-0648
Web: www.nyc.estemb.org					
Embassy 2131 Massachusetts Ave NW	Washington	DC	20008	202-588-0101	588-0108
Web: www.estemb.org					
Ethiopia Embassy 3506 International Dr NW	Washington	DC	20008	202-364-1200	587-0195
Web: www.ethiopianembassy.org					
Fiji Embassy 2000 M St NW Ste 710	Washington	DC	20036	202-337-8320	466-8325
TF: 800-932-3454 ■ *Web:* www.fijiembassydc.com					
Consulate General 11900 W Olympic Blvd Ste 580	Los Angeles	CA	90064	310-203-9903	481-8981
Web: www.finland.org					
Consulate General 866 UN Plz Ste 250	New York	NY	10017	212-750-4400	750-4418
Web: www.finland.org					
Finland					
Embassy 3301 Massachusetts Ave NW	Washington	DC	20008	202-298-5800	298-6030
Web: www.finland.org					
France 1 Dag Hammarskjold Plaza # 36	New York	NY	10017	212-937-0564	421-6889
Web: www.un.int					
Consulate General 1340 Poydras St Ste 1710	New Orleans	LA	70112	504-569-2870	569-2871
Web: www.consulfrance-nouvelleorleans.org					
Consulate General 1395 Brickell Ave Ste 1050	Miami	FL	33131	305-403-4185	403-4187
TF: 877-624-8737 ■ *Web:* www.consulfrance-miami.org					
Consulate General 205 N Michigan Ave Ste 3700	Chicago	IL	60601	312-327-5200	327-5201
TF: 888-642-2787 ■ *Web:* www.consulfrance-chicago.org					
Consulate General 777 Post Oak Blvd Ste 600	Houston	TX	77056	713-572-2799	572-2911
TF: 888-902-5322 ■ *Web:* www.consulfrance-houston.org					
Consulate General 10390 Santa Monica Blvd Ste 410	Los Angeles	CA	90025	310-235-3200	479-4813
Web: www.consulfrance-losangeles.org					
Consulate General 934 Fifth Ave	New York	NY	10021	212-606-3600	606-3614
TF: 800-772-1213 ■ *Web:* www.consulfrance-newyork.org					
Consulate General 540 Bush St	San Francisco	CA	94108	415-397-4330	433-8357
TF: 800-843-3779 ■ *Web:* www.consulfrance-sanfrancisco.org					
Consulate General 3475 Piedmont Rd NE Ste 1840	Atlanta	GA	30305	404-495-1660	495-1661
TF: 866-347-2523 ■ *Web:* www.consulfrance-atlanta.org					
Consulate General 31 St James Ave Ste 750	Boston	MA	02116	617-832-4400	
Web: www.consulfrance-boston.org					
Embassy 4101 Reservoir Rd NW	Washington	DC	20007	202-944-6000	944-6175
TF: 800-622-6232 ■ *Web:* www.ambafrance-us.org					

	City	State	Zip	Phone	Fax
Gambia Embassy 2233 Wisconsin Ave NW Georgetown Plz Ste 240	Washington	DC	20007	202-785-1399	342-0240
Web: www.gambiaembassy.us					
Germany					
Consulate General 1960 Jackson St.	San Francisco	CA	94109	415-775-1061	775-0187
Web: www.germany.info					
Consulate General 1330 Post Oak Blvd Ste 1850.	Houston	TX	77056	713-627-7770	627-0506
Web: germany.info					
Consulate General 676 N Michigan Ave Ste 3200	Chicago	IL	60611	312-202-0480	202-0466
Web: germany.info					
Consulate General 285 Peachtree Ctr Ave NE Ste 901	Atlanta	GA	30303	404-659-4760	659-1280
TF: 866-687-8561 ■ *Web:* germany.info					
Consulate General 6222 Wilshire Blvd Ste 500	Los Angeles	CA	90048	323-930-2703	930-2805
Web: germany.info					
Consulate General 100 Biscayne Blvd Ste 2200	Miami	FL	33132	305-358-0290	358-0307
Web: germany.info					
Consulate General 871 UN Plz	New York	NY	10017	212-610-9700	610-9702
Web: germany.info					
Embassy 4645 Reservoir Rd NW	Washington	DC	20007	202-298-4000	
Web: www.germany.info					
Ghana 19 E 47th St	New York	NY	10017	212-832-1300	751-6743
Web: www.un.int/ghana					
Consulate General 19 E 47th St	New York	NY	10017	212-832-1300	751-6743
Web: ghanaconsulatenewyork.org					
Embassy 3512 International Dr NW	Washington	DC	20008	202-686-4520	686-4527
Web: www.ghanaembassy.org					
Greece 866 Second Ave 13th Fl	New York	NY	10017	212-888-6900	888-4440
Web: www.mfa.gr					
Consulate General 12424 Wilshire Blvd Ste 800	Los Angeles	CA	90025	310-826-5555	826-8670
Web: www.mfa.gr					
Consulate General 650 N St Clair St	Chicago	IL	60611	312-335-3915	335-3958
Web: www.mfa.gr					
Consulate General 86 Beacon St	Boston	MA	02108	617-523-0100	523-0511
Web: www.mfa.gr					
Consulate General 69 E 79th St	New York	NY	10075	212-988-5500	734-8492
Web: www.mfa.gr					
Consulate General 2441 Gough St	San Francisco	CA	94123	415-775-2102	776-6815
Web: www.mfa.gr					
Embassy 2217 Massachusetts Ave	Washington	DC	20008	202-939-1300	939-1324
Web: www.mfa.gr/usa/en/the-embassy					
Grenada					
Embassy 1701 New Hampshire Ave NW	Washington	DC	20009	202-265-2561	265-2468
Web: www.grenadaembassyusa.org					
Guatemala 57 Pk Ave	New York	NY	10016	212-679-4760	685-8741
Web: www.un.int					
Consulate General 3013 Fountain View Dr Ste 210	Houston	TX	77057	713-953-9531	953-9383
Embassy 2220 R St NW	Washington	DC	20008	202-745-4953	745-1908
Web: www.consulateofguatemalaindenver.org					
Guinea Embassy 2112 Leroy Pl NW	Washington	DC	20008	202-986-4300	986-4800
Web: www.guineaembassyusa.com					
Guyana					
Consulate General 308 W 38th St Ste 402	New York	NY	10001	212-947-5110	947-5163
Web: www.guyana.org					
Embassy 2490 Tracy Pl NW	Washington	DC	20008	202-265-6900	232-1297
Web: guyana.org					
Haiti					
Consulate General 815 2nd Ave 6th Fl	New York	NY	10017	212-697-9767	
Web: www.embassypages.com/missions/embassy21725/					
Consulate General 220 S State St Ste 2110	Chicago	IL	60604	312-922-4004	922-7122
Web: www.haitianconsulate.org					
Consulate General 259 SW 13th St	Miami	FL	33130	305-859-2003	854-7441
Web: haiti.org					
Consulate General 545 Boylston St Rm 201	Boston	MA	02116	617-266-3660	778-6898
Embassy 2311 Massachusetts Ave NW	Washington	DC	20008	202-332-4090	745-7215
Web: www.haiti.org					
Holy See					
Apostolic Nunciature 3339 Massachusetts Ave NW	Washington	DC	20008	202-333-7121	337-4036
Web: www.holyseemission.org					
Honduras					
Consulate General 4439 W Fullerton Ave	Chicago	IL	60639	773-342-8281	342-8293
Web: hondurasemb.org					
Consulate General 7400 Harwin Dr Ste 200	Houston	TX	77036	713-785-5932	785-5931
Web: www.consuladohondurashouston.org					
Consulate General 3550 Wilshire Blvd Ste 410	Los Angeles	CA	90010	213-383-9244	383-9306
Web: www.consulate-los-angeles.com/honduras.html					
Consulate General 870 Market St Ste 875	San Francisco	CA	94102	415-392-0076	392-6726
Web: www.hondurasemb.org					
Embassy 3007 Tilden St NW	Washington	DC	20008	202-966-7702	966-9751
TF: 800-375-5283 ■ *Web:* www.hondurasemb.org					
Hungary Consulate General 223 E 52nd St	New York	NY	10022	212-752-0669	755-5986
Web: www.mfa.gov.hu/kulkepviselet/US/en					
Consulate General 800 Third Ave 36th Fl	New York	NY	10022	646-282-9360	282-9369
Web: www.iceland.is/iceland-abroad					
Iceland					
Embassy House of Sweden 2900 K St NW Ste 509	Washington	DC	20007	202-265-6653	265-6656
Web: www.iceland.is/iceland-abroad/us					
India					
Consulate General 540 Arguello Blvd	San Francisco	CA	94118	415-668-0662	668-9764
TF: 866-978-0055 ■ *Web:* www.cgisf.org					
Consulate General 455 N Cityfront Plz Dr Ste 850	Chicago	IL	60611	312-595-0405	595-0417
Web: www.indianconsulate.com					
Embassy 2107 Massachusetts Ave NW	Washington	DC	20008	202-939-7000	265-4351
Web: www.indianembassy.org					
Embassy - Consular Wing 2536 Massachusetts Ave NW	Washington	DC	20008	202-939-9806	
Web: www.indianembassy.org					
Indonesia 325 E 38th St	New York	NY	10016	212-972-8333	972-9780
Web: www.indonesiamission-ny.org					
Consulate General 211 W Wacker Dr Eighth Fl	Chicago	IL	60606	312-920-1880	920-1881
Web: www.indonesiachicago.org					
Consulate General Five E 68th St	New York	NY	10021	212-879-0600	570-6206
Web: www.kemlu.go.id					
Embassy 2020 Massachusetts Ave NW	Washington	DC	20036	202-775-5200	775-5365
Web: www.embassyofindonesia.org					
Ireland One Dag Hammarskjold Plz # 885	New York	NY	10017	212-421-6934	752-4726
Web: www.un.int					
Consulate General 100 Pine St 33rd Fl	San Francisco	CA	94111	415-392-4214	392-0885
Web: consulateofirelandsanfrancisco.org					
Embassy 2234 Massachusetts Ave NW	Washington	DC	20008	202-462-3939	232-5993
TF: 866-560-1050 ■ *Web:* www.dfa.ie/irish-embassy/usa/					
Israel					
Consulate General 100 Biscayne Blvd Ste 1800	Miami	FL	33132	305-925-9400	925-9451
Web: www.israelemb.org					
Consulate General 1100 Spring St NW Ste 440	Atlanta	GA	30309	404-487-6500	957-9555*
**Fax Area Code: 207* ■ *Web:* www.israelemb.org					
Consulate General 456 Montgomery St Ste 2100	San Francisco	CA	94104	415-844-7500	844-7555
Web: www.israelemb.org					
Embassy 3514 International Dr NW	Washington	DC	20008	202-364-5500	364-5429
Web: www.israelemb.org					
Italy					
Consulate General 600 Atlantic Ave 17th Fl	Boston	MA	02210	617-722-9201	722-9407
TF: 888-225-5427 ■ *Web:* www.consboston.esteri.it					
Consulate General 2590 Webster St	San Francisco	CA	94115	415-292-9200	931-7205
Web: www.conssanfrancisco.esteri.it					
Consulate General 4000 Ponce de Leon Ste 590	Coral Gables	FL	33146	305-374-6322	374-7945
Web: www.consmiami.esteri.it					
Consulate General 150 S Independence Mall W Public Ledger Bldg Ste 1026	Philadelphia	PA	19106	215-592-7329	592-9808
TF: 800-531-0840 ■ *Web:* www.consfiladelfia.esteri.it					
Consulate General 1300 Post Oak Blvd Ste 660	Houston	TX	77056	713-850-7520	850-9113
TF: 800-637-9314 ■ *Web:* www.conshouston.esteri.it					
Consulate General 12400 Wilshire Blvd Ste 300	Los Angeles	CA	90025	310-820-0622	820-0727
TF: 800-313-7133 ■ *Web:* www.conslosangeles.esteri.it					
Consulate General 690 Pk Ave	New York	NY	10021	212-737-9100	249-4945
Web: www.consnewyork.esteri.it					
Embassy 3000 Whitehaven St NW	Washington	DC	20008	202-612-4400	518-2154
TF: 800-222-1222 ■ *Web:* www.ambwashingtondc.esteri.it					
Jamaica Embassy 1520 New Hampshire Ave NW	Washington	DC	20036	202-452-0660	452-0036
Web: www.embassyofjamaica.org					
Japan					
Consulate General 3601 C St Ste 1300	Anchorage	AK	99503	907-562-8424	562-8434
Web: www.anchorage.us.emb-japan.go.jp					
Consulate General 3438 Peachtree Rd Phipps Tower Ste 850	Atlanta	GA	30326	404-240-4300	240-4311
Web: www.atlanta.us.emb-japan.go.jp					
Consulate General 1742 Nuuanu Ave	Honolulu	HI	96817	808-543-3111	543-3170
Web: www.honolulu.us.emb-japan.go.jp					
Consulate General 737 N Michigan Ave Ste 1100	Chicago	IL	60611	312-280-0400	280-9568
Web: www.chicago.us.emb-japan.go.jp					
Consulate General 50 Fremont St Ste 2300	San Francisco	CA	94105	415-777-3533	974-3660
Web: www.sf.us.emb-japan.go.jp					
Consulate General 1801 W End Ave Ste 900	Nashville	TN	37203	615-340-4300	340-4311
Web: www.nashville.us.emb-japan.go.jp					
Consulate General 400 Renaissance Ctr Ste 1600	Detroit	MI	48243	313-567-0120	567-0274
Web: www.detroit.us.emb-japan.go.jp					
Consulate General Wells Fargo Ctr 1300 SW Fifth Ave Ste 2700	Portland	OR	97201	503-221-1811	224-8936
Web: www.portland.us.emb-japan.go.jp					
Consulate General 1225 17th St Ste 3000	Denver	CO	80202	303-534-1151	534-3393
Web: www.denver.us.emb-japan.go.jp					
Consulate General 350 S Grand Ave Ste 1700	Los Angeles	CA	90071	213-617-6700	617-6727
Web: www.la.us.emb-japan.go.jp					
Consulate General 299 Pk Ave 18th Fl	New York	NY	10171	212-371-8222	371-1294
Web: www.ny.us.emb-japan.go.jp					
Consulate General 601 Union St Ste 500	Seattle	WA	98101	206-682-9107	624-9097
Web: www.seattle.us.emb-japan.go.jp					
Consulate General 80 SW Eigth St Brickell Bay View Ctr Ste 3200	Miami	FL	33130	305-530-9090	530-0950
Web: www.miami.us.emb-japan.go.jp					
Consulate General 600 Atlantic Ave Federal Reserve Plz 14th Fl	Boston	MA	02210	617-973-9772	542-1329
Web: www.boston.us.emb-japan.go.jp					
Embassy 2520 Massachusetts Ave NW	Washington	DC	20008	202-238-6700	328-2187
Web: us.emb-japan.go.jp					
Jordan					
Embassy 3504 International Dr NW	Washington	DC	20008	202-966-2664	966-3110
Web: www.jordanembassyus.org					
Kazakhstan					
Consulate 305 E 47th St Third Fl	New York	NY	10017	212-888-3024	888-3025
Web: www.kazconsulny.org					
Embassy 1401 16th St NW	Washington	DC	20036	202-232-5488	232-5845
Web: www.kazakhembus.com					
Kenya Embassy 2249 R St NW	Washington	DC	20008	202-387-6101	462-3829
TF: 888-502-2642 ■ *Web:* www.kenyaembassy.com					
Korea Republic of					
Consulate General 2756 Pali Hwy	Honolulu	HI	96817	808-595-6109	595-3046
Web: usa-honolulu.mofat.go.kr					

Phone Fax

Consulate General
455 N City Front Plz Dr NBC Tower Ste 2700 ....Chicago IL 60611 312-822-9485 822-9849
Web: usa-chicago.mofat.go.kr
Consulate General 3243 Wilshire Blvd......... Los Angeles CA 90010 213-385-9300 385-1849
Web: south-korea.embassy-online.net
Consulate General 460 Pk Ave.................New York NY 10022 646-674-6000
Consulate General 2033 Sixth Ave Ste 1125 ....Seattle WA 98121 206-441-1011
TF: 800-375-5283
Kuwait Embassy 2940 Tilden St NW ....Washington DC 20008 202-966-0702 966-0517
TF: 800-688-9889 ■ *Web:* www.kuwaitembassy.us
Lao People's Democratic Republic Embassy
2222 S St NW.................................Washington DC 20008 202-332-6416 332-4923
Web: www.laoembassy.com
Latvia Embassy 2306 Massachusetts Ave NW........Washington DC 20008 202-328-2840 328-2860
Web: www.mfa.gov.lv
Lebanon 866 UN Plz Rm 531-533...................New York NY 10017 212-355-5460 838-2819
Web: www.un.int/wcm/content/site/lebanon
Consulate General Nine E 76th St ....New York NY 10021 212-744-7905 794-1510
Web: www.lebconsny.org
Embassy 2560 28th St NW ....Washington DC 20008 202-939-6300 939-6324
Web: www.lebanonembassyus.org
Lesotho Embassy 2511 Massachusetts Ave NW ......Washington DC 20008 202-797-5533 234-6815
Web: lesothoemb-usa.gov.ls
Consulate General
866 United Nations Plaza Ste 249 ....New York NY 10017 212-687-1025 599-3189
Web: liberianconsulate-ny.com
Liberia
Embassy 5201 16th St NW ....Washington DC 20011 202-723-0437 723-0436
Web: www.liberianembassyus.org
Liechtenstein Embassy
2900 K St NW Ste 602B........................Washington DC 20007 202-331-0590
Web: www.liechtensteinusa.org
Consulate General
420 Fifth Ave Ste 304 3rd Fl ....New York NY 10018 212-354-7840 354-7911
Web: usa.mfa.lt
Lithuania
Embassy 2622 16th St NW ....Washington DC 20009 202-234-5860 328-0466
Web: www.usa.mfa.lt
Luxembourg
Consulate General 17 Beekman Pl...............New York NY 10022 212-888-6664 888-6116
Web: newyork-cg.mae.lu/en
Consulate General
One Sansome St Ste 830....................San Francisco CA 94104 415-788-0816 788-0985
Web: sanfrancisco.mae.lu
Embassy 2200 Massachusetts Ave NW ....Washington DC 20008 202-265-4171 328-8270
Web: washington.mae.lu
Madagascar Embassy
2374 Massachusetts Ave NW.....................Washington DC 20008 202-265-5525 265-3034
Web: www.madagascar-embassy.org
Malaysia
Consulate General 550 S Hope St Ste 400...... Los Angeles CA 90071 213-892-1238 892-9031
Web: www.malaysianconsulatela.com
Consulate General 313 E 43rd St...............New York NY 10017 212-490-2722 490-2049
Web: kln.gov.my
Embassy 3516 International Ct NW ....Washington DC 20008 202-572-9700 572-9882
Web: kln.gov.my
Mali Embassy 2130 R St NW ....Washington DC 20008 202-332-2249 332-6603
Web: www.maliembassy.us
Malta Embassy 2017 Connecticut Ave NW ....Washington DC 20008 202-462-3611 387-5470
Web: www.malta-citizenship.info
Marshall Islands Embassy
2433 Massachusetts Ave NW....................Washington DC 20008 202-234-5414 232-3236
Web: www.rmiembassyus.org
Mauritania Embassy 2129 Leroy Pl NW ....Washington DC 20008 202-232-5700
Web: www.mauritaniaembassy.com
Mauritius Embassies 1709 N St NW ....Washington DC 20036 202-244-1491 966-0983
Web: www.maurinet.com/embasydc.html
Mexico
Consulate General 5350 Leesdale Dr Ste 100 .... Denver CO 80246 303-331-1110 331-0169
Web: consulmex.sre.gob.mx/denver
Consulate General 1700 Chantilly Dr NE...........Atlanta GA 30324 404-266-2233 266-2302
Web: consulmexatlanta.org
Consulate General 571 N Grand Ave ....Nogales AZ 85621 520-287-2521 287-3175
Web: www.sre.gob.mx
Consulate General 800 Brazos St Ste 330 .... Austin TX 78701 512-478-2866 478-8008
Web: www.sre.gob.mx
Consulate General 1010 Eigth St..............Sacramento CA 95814 916-441-3287
Web: www.mexico.us/consulate.htm
Consulate General 910 E San Antonio St........... El Paso TX 79901 915-533-3644 532-7163
Web: www.sre.gob.mx
Consulate General 127 Navarro St............ San Antonio TX 78205 210-227-9145
Consulate General 1612 Farragut St ....Laredo TX 78040 956-723-0990 723-1741
Web: www.sre.gob.mx
Consulate General 204 S Ashland Ave............ Chicago IL 60607 312-738-2383
Consulate General 27 E 39th St.................New York NY 10016 212-217-6400
Consulate General 4506 Carolinas St .... Houston TX 77004 713-271-6800 271-3201
TF: 877-639-4835 ■ *Web:* www.sre.gob.mx
Consulate General
1911 Pennsylvania Ave Centro Col ....Washington DC 20006 202-728-1600 728-1698
Web: embamex.sre.gob.mx/eua/
Consulate General 532 Folsom St...........San Francisco CA 94105 415-354-1700
Web: www.consulmexsf.com
Embassy 1911 Pennsylvania Ave NW ....Washington DC 20006 202-728-1600 728-1766
Web: embamex.sre.gob.mx
Micronesia
Consulate 1725 N St NW Ste 910 ....Washington DC 20036 202-223-4383 223-4391
TF: 877-730-9753 ■ *Web:* www.fsmembassydc.org
Moldova Embassy 2101 S St NW ....Washington DC 20008 202-667-1130 667-2624
Web: www.embassy.org
Mongolia Embassy 2833 M St NW................Washington DC 20007 202-333-7117 298-9227
Web: www.mongolianembassy.us

Phone Fax

Consulate General 10 E 40th St 24th Fl...........New York NY 10016 212-758-2625 779-7441
Web: www.moroccanconsulate.com
Morocco
Embassy 1601 21st St NW...................Washington DC 20009 202-462-7979 265-0161
Web: embassywashingtondc.com
Mozambique Embassy
1525 New Hampshire Ave NW ....Washington DC 20036 202-293-7146 835-0245
Web: www.embamoc-usa.org
Myanmar Embassy 2300 S St NW................Washington DC 20008 202-332-3344 332-4351
Web: www.mewashingtondc.com
Nepal 820 Second Ave Ste 17B ....New York NY 10017 212-370-3988 953-2038
Embassy 2131 Leroy Pl NW..................Washington DC 20008 202-667-4550 667-5534
Web: www.nepalembassyusa.org
Netherlands
Consulate General 666 Third Ave 19th Fl..........New York NY 10017 877-388-2443 246-9679*
**Fax Area Code:* 212 ■ *TF:* 877-388-2443 ■ *Web:* ny.the-netherlands.org
Consulate General 303 E Wacker Dr Ste 2600...... Chicago IL 60601 312-856-0110 856-9218
TF: 877-388-2443 ■ *Web:* chicago.embassytools.com
Embassy 4200 Linnean Ave NW...............Washington DC 20008 877-388-2443 362-3430*
**Fax Area Code:* 202 ■ *TF:* 877-388-2443 ■ *Web:* dc.the-netherlands.org
Consulate General
2425 Olympic Blvd Ste 600-E .... Santa Monica CA 90404 310-566-6555 566-6556
Web: www.nzcgla.com
New Zealand
Embassy 37 Observatory Cir NW.............Washington DC 20008 202-328-4800 667-5227
TF: 855-844-2835 ■ *Web:* www.nzembassy.com
Nicaragua 820 Second Ave Ste 801 ....New York NY 10017 212-490-7997 286-0815
Web: www.un.int
Consulate General 8989 Westheimer St........... Houston TX 77063 713-789-2762
Web: www.consuladodenicaragua.com
Consulate General 820 Second Ave Ste 802 ....New York NY 10017 212-986-6562 983-2646
Web: consuladonicamiami.com
Embassy 1627 New Hampshire Ave NW ....Washington DC 20009 202-939-6570
Web: consuladodenicaragua.com
Niger Embassy 2204 R St NW ....Washington DC 20008 202-483-4224 483-3169
Web: www.embassyofniger.org
Consulate General 828 Second Ave.............New York NY 10017 212-850-2200 687-1476
Web: www.nigeriahouse.com
Nigeria
Embassy 3519 International Ct NW ....Washington DC 20008 202-986-8400
Web: www.nigeriaembassyusa.org
Norway 825 Third Ave 39th Fl ....New York NY 10022 646-430-7510
Web: www.norway-un.org
Consulate General 3410 W Dallas St............. Houston TX 77019 713-620-4200 620-4290
Web: www.norway.org/Embassy
Consulate General
901 Marquette Ave Ste 2750 .... Minneapolis MN 55402 612-332-3338 332-1386
Web: www.norway.org
Consulate General 825 Third Ave 38th Fl..........New York NY 10022 646-430-7599 754-0583*
**Fax Area Code:* 212 ■ *Web:* www.norway.org/embassy
Embassy 2720 34th St NW ....Washington DC 20008 202-333-6000 337-0870
Web: www.norway.org
Oman Embassy 2535 Belmont Rd NW ....Washington DC 20008 202-387-1980 745-4933
Web: www.omani.info
Pakistan
Consulate General
10850 Wilshire Blvd Ste 1250.................Los Angeles CA 90024 310-441-5114 441-9256
Web: www.pakconsulatela.org
Consulate General 12 E 65th St................New York NY 10065 212-879-5800 517-6987
Web: www.pakistanconsulateny.org
Embassy 3517 International Ct NW ....Washington DC 20008 202-243-6500 686-1534
Web: www.embassyofpakistanusa.org
Palau
Embassy 1701 Pennsylvania Ave NW Ste 300....Washington DC 20006 202-349-8598 349-8597
Web: palauembassy.com
Panama
Consulate General 5775 Blue Lagoon Dr Ste 200 ..... Miami FL 33126 305-447-3700 447-4142
Web: embassyofpanama.org
Consulate General
1100 Poydras St Ste 2615................. New Orleans LA 70163 504-525-3458 524-8960
Web: www.consulateofpanama.com
Embassy 2862 McGill Terr NW ....Washington DC 20008 202-483-1407 483-8413
Web: embassyofpanama.org
Papua New Guinea Embassy
1779 Massachusetts Ave NW Ste 805 ....Washington DC 20036 202-745-3680 745-3679
Web: www.pngembassy.org
Paraguay 801 Second Ave Ste 702....................New York NY 10017 212-687-3490 818-1282
Web: www.paraguayun.com
Consulate General 25 SE Second Ave Suite 705 ...... Miami FL 33131 305-374-9090 374-5522
Web: www.consulparmiami.org
Embassy 2400 Massachusetts Ave NW ....Washington DC 20008 202-483-6960 234-4508
Peru
Consulate General 1001 S Monaco Pkwy Ste 210.... Denver CO 80224 303-355-8555 355-8555
Web: www.consuladoperu.com
Consulate General
870 Market St Ste 1067....................San Francisco CA 94102 415-362-7136 362-2836
TF: 877-714-7378 ■ *Web:* www.consuladoperu.com
Consulate General 100 Hamilton Plaza .... Paterson NJ 07505 973-278-3324 278-0254
TF: 877-714-7378 ■ *Web:* www.consuladoperu.com
Consulate General 5177 Richmond Ave Ste 695 .... Houston TX 77056 713-355-9517 355-9377
TF: 800-444-1027 ■ *Web:* www.consuladoperu.com
Consulate General
3450 Wilshire Blvd Ste 800...................Los Angeles CA 90010 213-252-5910 252-8130
TF: 800-444-1027 ■ *Web:* www.consuladoperu.com
Consulate General 444 Brickell Ave Ste M135........Miami FL 33131 877-714-7378 381-6027*
**Fax Area Code:* 305 ■ *TF:* 877-714-7378 ■ *Web:* www.consuladoperu.com
Consulate General 180 N Michigan Ave Ste 1830... Chicago IL 60601 312-782-1599 704-6969
TF: 877-714-7378 ■ *Web:* www.consuladoperu.com
Consulate General 241 E 49th St...............New York NY 10017 646-735-3828 735-3866
Web: www.consuladoperu.com
Philippines 556 Fifth Ave Fifth Fl...................New York NY 10036 212-764-1300 840-8602
Web: www.un.int

	City	State	Zip	Phone	Fax
Consulate General 447 Sutter St 6th Fl Philippine Ctr Bldg	San Francisco	CA	94108	415-433-6666	421-2641
TF: 877-700-0669 ■ *Web:* www.philippinessanfrancisco.org					
Consulate General 30 N Michigan Ave Ste 2100	Chicago	IL	60602	312-332-6458	332-3657
TF: 888-259-7838 ■ *Web:* www.chicagopcg.com					
Consulate General 3600 Wilshire Blvd Ste 500	Los Angeles	CA	90010	213-639-0980	639-0990
TF: 800-527-2820 ■ *Web:* www.philippineconsulatela.org					
Consulate General 556 Fifth Ave	New York	NY	10036	212-764-1330	764-6010
TF: 866-589-1878 ■ *Web:* www.newyorkpcg.org					
Embassy 1600 Massachusetts Ave NW	Washington	DC	20036	202-467-9300	467-9417
TF: 888-373-7888 ■ *Web:* www.philippineembassy-usa.org					
Poland					
Embassy 2640 16th St NW	Washington	DC	20009	202-234-3800	588-0565
Web: www.polandembassy.org					
Qatar 809 UN Plz Fourth Fl	New York	NY	10017	212-486-9335	758-4952
Web: www.un.org					
Consulate General 1990 Post Oak Blvd Ste 900	Houston	TX	77056	713-355-8221	355-8184
Web: cgqh.net					
Embassy 2555 M St NW	Washington	DC	20037	202-274-1600	237-0061
Web: www.qatarembassy.net					
Romania 573-577 Third Ave	New York	NY	10016	212-682-3273	
Web: www.un.int					
Consulate General 200 E 38th St	New York	NY	10016	212-682-9123	
Web: newyork.mae.ro/en					
Royal Thai Consulate General					
Consulate General 351 E 52nd St	New York	NY	10022	212-754-1770	754-1907
Web: www.thaiconsulnewyork.com					
Russia					
Consulate General 600 University St 1 Union Sq Ste 2510	Seattle	WA	98121	206-728-1910	728-1871
Web: www.netconsul.org					
Consulate General 2790 Green St	San Francisco	CA	94123	415-928-6878	929-0306
Web: www.consulrussia.org					
Consulate General Nine E 91st St	New York	NY	10128	212-348-0926	
Web: ruscon.org					
Embassy 2650 Wisconsin Ave NW	Washington	DC	20007	202-298-5700	298-5735
Web: www.russianembassy.org					
Rwanda Embassy 1875 Connecticut Ave N W	Washington	DC	20009	202-232-2882	232-4544
Web: www.rwandaembassy.org					
Saint Kitts & Nevis Embassy 3216 New Mexico Ave NW	Washington	DC	20016	202-686-2636	686-5740
Web: www.stkittsnevis.org					
Saint Lucia 800 Second Ave Ninth Fl	New York	NY	10017	212-697-9360	697-4993
Web: www.un.int/stlucia					
Consulate General 800 Second Ave Ninth Fl	New York	NY	10017	212-697-9360	697-4993
Web: www.un.int/stlucia/consulate.htm					
Embassy 3216 New Mexico Ave NW	Washington	DC	20016	202-364-6792	783-6580*
**Fax Area Code:* 770 ■ *TF:* 800-456-3984 ■ *Web:* stlucia.org					
Saint Vincent & the Grenadines					
Consulate General 801 Second Ave 21st Fl	New York	NY	10017	212-687-4490	949-5946
Web: www.ny.consulate.gov.vc					
Embassy 3216 New Mexico Ave NW	Washington	DC	20016	202-364-6730	364-6736
Web: www.embsvg.com					
Consulate General 5718 Westheimer Rd Ste 1500	Houston	TX	77057	713-785-5577	273-6937
Web: www.saudiembassy.net					
Consulate General 866 Second Ave Fifth Fl	New York	NY	10017	212-752-2740	688-2719
Web: www.saudiembassy.net					
Saudi Arabia					
Embassy 601 New Hampshire Ave NW	Washington	DC	20037	202-342-3800	944-5983
Web: www.saudiembassy.net					
Consulate General 201 E Ohio St Ste 200	Chicago	IL	60611	312-670-6707	670-6787
Web: www.scgchicago.org					
Serbia					
Embassy 2134 Kalorama Rd NW	Washington	DC	20008	202-332-0333	332-3933
Web: www.serbiaembusa.org					
Seychelles					
Embassy 800 Second Ave Ste 400C	New York	NY	10017	212-972-1785	972-1786
Web: seychellesembassy.com					
Singapore					
Consulate General 595 Market St Ste 2450	San Francisco	CA	94105	415-543-4775	543-4788
Web: www.mfa.gov.sg					
Embassy 3501 International Pl NW	Washington	DC	20008	202-537-3100	537-0876
Web: www.mfa.gov.sg					
Slovakia Embassy 3523 International Ct NW	Washington	DC	20008	202-237-1054	237-6438
Web: www.mzv.sk/washington					
Slovenia					
Consulate General 120 E 56th St Ste 320	New York	NY	10022	212-370-3006	
Web: www.newyork.consulate.si					
Embassy 2410 California St NW	Washington	DC	20036	202-386-6601	386-6633
Web: washington.embassy.si					
South Africa 333 E 38th St Ninth Fl	New York	NY	10016	212-213-5583	692-2498
Web: www.southafrica-newyork.net					
Consulate General 200 S Michigan Ave Ste 600	Chicago	IL	60604	312-939-7929	939-2588
Web: www.sachicago.pwpsystems.com					
Consulate General 333 E 38th St Ninth Fl	New York	NY	10016	212-213-4880	213-0102
Web: www.southafrica-newyork.net					
Embassy 3051 Massachusetts Ave NW	Washington	DC	20008	202-232-4400	265-1607
Web: www.saembassy.org					
South African Consulate-General 6300 Wilshire Blvd Ste 600	Los Angeles	CA	90048	323-651-0902	323-5969
Web: www.dirco.gov.za					
Spain					
Consulate General 1405 Sutter St	San Francisco	CA	94109	415-922-2995	931-9706
Consulate General 150 E 58th St 30th Fl	New York	NY	10155	212-355-4080	644-3751
Web: spainculturenewyork.org					
Embassy 2375 Pennsylvania Ave NW	Washington	DC	20037	202-452-0100	833-5670
Web: www.spainemb.org					
Consulate General 3250 Wilshire Blvd Ste 1405	Los Angeles	CA	90010	213-387-0210	387-0216
Web: www.srilankaconsulatela.com					
Sri Lanka					
Embassy 2148 Wyoming Ave NW	Washington	DC	20008	202-483-4025	232-7181
Web: www.slembassyusa.org					
Sudan Embassy 2210 Massachusetts Ave NW	Washington	DC	20008	202-338-8565	667-2406
Web: www.sudanembassy.org					
Suriname Embassy 4301 Connecticut Ave NW Ste 460	Washington	DC	20008	202-244-7488	244-5878
Web: www.surinameembassy.org					
Consulate General 505 Sansome St Ste 1010	San Francisco	CA	94111	415-788-2631	788-6841
Web: www.swedenabroad.com/en-gb/embassies/san-francisco					
Consulate General 445 Pk Ave Fl 21	New York	NY	10022	212-888-3000	888-3125
Web: www.swedenabroad.com					
Sweden					
Embassy 2900 K St NW	Washington	DC	20007	202-467-2600	467-2699
Web: www.swedenabroad.com					
Consulate General 456 Montgomery St Ste 1500	San Francisco	CA	94104	415-788-2272	788-1402
Web: www.eda.admin.ch/sanfrancisco					
Consulate General 11766 Wilshire Blvd Ste 1400	Los Angeles	CA	90025	310-575-1145	575-1982
Web: www.eda.admin.ch/losangeles					
Switzerland					
Embassy 2900 Cathedral Ave NW	Washington	DC	20008	202-745-7900	387-2564
Web: www.swissemb.org					
Tajikistan					
Embassy 1005 New Hampshire Ave	Washington	DC	20037	202-223-6090	223-6091
Web: www.tjus.org					
Tanzania 307 East 53rd Street 4th Floor	New York	NY	10022	212-697-3612	697-3618
Web: www.tanzania-un.org					
Embassy 1232 22nd St NW	Washington	DC	20037	202-939-6125	797-7408
Web: www.tanzaniaembassy-us.org					
Thailand 351 E 52nd St	New York	NY	10022	212-754-2230	688-3029
Web: un.int					
Consulate General 611 N Larchmont Blvd Second Fl	Los Angeles	CA	90004	323-962-9574	962-2128
Web: www.thaiconsulatela.org					
Embassy 1024 Wisconsin Ave NW Ste 401	Washington	DC	20007	202-944-3600	944-3611
Web: www.thaiembdc.org					
Tonga					
Consulate General 360 Post St Ste 604	San Francisco	CA	94108	415-781-0365	781-3964
Web: www.tongaconsul.com					
Trinidad & Tobago Embassy 1708 Massachusetts Ave NW	Washington	DC	20036	202-467-6490	785-3130
Web: www.ttembassy.com					
Turkey 821 UN Plz 10th Fl	New York	NY	10017	212-949-0150	949-0086
Web: www.un.int/turkey					
Consulate General 455 N Cityfront Plz Dr Ste 2900	Chicago	IL	60611	312-263-0644	263-1449
Web: www.chicago.cg.mfa.gov.tr					
Consulate General 1990 Post Oak Blvd Ste 1300	Houston	TX	77056	713-622-5849	623-6639
TF: 888-566-7656 ■ *Web:* www.houston.cg.mfa.gov.tr					
Consulate General 6300 Wilshire Blvd Ste 2010	Los Angeles	CA	90048	323-655-8832	655-8681
TF: 800-874-8875 ■ *Web:* www.losangeles.cg.mfa.gov.tr					
Consulate General 825 Third Ave 28th Fl	New York	NY	10022	646-430-6560	983-1293*
**Fax Area Code:* 212 ■ *Web:* www.newyork.cg.mfa.gov.tr					
Embassy 2525 Massachusetts Ave NW	Washington	DC	20008	202-612-6700	319-1639
TF: 877-367-8875 ■ *Web:* www.washington.emb.mfa.gov.tr/default.aspx					
Turkmenistan					
Embassy 2207 Massachusetts Ave NW	Washington	DC	20008	202-588-1500	280-1003
Uganda Embassy 5911 16th St NW	Washington	DC	20011	202-726-7100	726-1727
Web: washington.mofa.go.ug					
Ukraine 220 E 51st St	New York	NY	10022	212-759-7003	355-9455
Consulate General 10 E Huron St	Chicago	IL	60611	312-642-4388	642-4385
Web: www.ukrchicago.com					
United Arab Emirates Embassy 3522 International Ct NW	Washington	DC	20008	202-243-2400	243-2432
Web: www.uae-embassy.org					
United Kingdom					
Consulate General 133 Peachtree St NE	Atlanta	GA	30303	404-954-7700	954-7702
Web: www.gov.uk					
Consulate General One Broadway	Cambridge	MA	02142	617-245-4500	621-0220
Web: www.gov.uk					
Consulate General 625 N Michigan Ave Ste 2200	Chicago	IL	60611	312-970-3800	970-3852
Web: www.gov.uk					
Consulate General 1000 Louisiana St Ste 1900	Houston	TX	77002	713-659-6270	659-7094
Web: www.gov.uk					
Consulate General 845 Third Ave	New York	NY	10022	212-745-0200	754-3062
Web: www.gov.uk					
Consulate General One Sansome St Ste 850	San Francisco	CA	94104	415-617-1300	
Web: www.gov.uk					
Embassy 3100 Massachusetts Ave NW	Washington	DC	20008	202-588-6500	
Web: www.gov.uk					
Uruguay 866 UN Plz Ste 322	New York	NY	10017	212-752-8240	593-0935
Web: www.un.int/uruguay					
Consulate General 429 Santa Monica Blvd Ste 400	Santa Monica	CA	90401	310-394-5777	394-5140
Web: www.conurula.org					
Embassy 1913 'I' St NW	Washington	DC	20006	202-331-1313	331-8142
Web: mrree.gub.uy					
Consulate General 801 Second Ave 20th Fl	New York	NY	10017	212-754-7403	
Web: www.uzbekconsulny.org					
Uzbekistan					
Embassy 1746 Massachusetts Ave NW	Washington	DC	20036	202-887-5300	293-6804
Web: www.uzbekistan.org					
Venezuela 335 E 46th St	New York	NY	10017	212-557-2055	557-3528
Web: www.un.int					
Consulate General 2401 Fountain View Dr Ste 220	Houston	TX	77057	713-974-0028	974-1413
Web: venezuela-us.org/houston/					

Phone | Fax

Vietnam
Consulate General
1700 California St Ste 580 — San Francisco CA 94109 — 415-922-1707 — 922-1848
Web: www.vietnamconsulate-sf.org
Embassy 1233 20th St NW Ste 400 — Washington DC 20036 — 202-861-0737 — 861-0917
Web: vietnamembassy-usa.org
Zambia Embassy 2419 Massachusetts Ave NW — Washington DC 20008 — 202-265-9717 — 332-0826
Web: www.zambiaembassy.org
Zimbabwe Embassy
1608 New Hampshire Ave NW — Washington DC 20009 — 202-332-7100 — 483-9326

261 EMBROIDERY & OTHER DECORATIVE STITCHING

Phone | Fax

BMG Conveyor Services of Florida Inc
5010 16th Ave South — Tampa FL 33619 — 813-247-3620
Web: www.bmgtampa.com
Branded Emblem Co Inc 7920 Foster St — Overland Park KS 66204 — 913-648-0573 — 648-7444
TF: 800-448-2267 ■ *Web:* www.campdavid.com
Carolace Embroidery Company Inc
65 Railroad Ave Unit 3 — Ridgefield NJ 07657 — 201-945-2151
Web: www.carolace.com
CR Daniels Inc 3451 Ellicott Ctr Dr — Ellicott City MD 21043 — 410-461-2100 — 461-2987
TF: 800-933-2638 ■ *Web:* www.crdaniels.com
Duck River Textile Inc
1000 New County Rd Ste 2 — Secaucus NJ 07094 — 201-533-1000
Web: duckrivertextile.com
EmbroidMe Inc 2121 Vista Pkwy — West Palm Beach FL 33411 — 561-640-7367 — 640-6062
TF: 877-877-0234 ■ *Web:* www.embroidme.com
Fabri-Quilt Inc 901 E 14th Ave — North Kansas City MO 64116 — 816-421-2000 — 471-2853
TF: 800-279-0622 ■ *Web:* www.fabri-quilt.com
FlagZone LLC 105A Industrial Dr — Gilbertsville PA 19525 — 800-976-4201
TF: 800-976-4201 ■ *Web:* www.theflagzone.com
G&G Outfitters Inc 4901 Forbes Blvd — Lanham MD 20706 — 301-731-2099
Web: www.ggoutfitters.com
Gensco Equipment (1990) Inc 53 Carlaw Ave — Toronto ON M4M2R6 — 416-465-7521
Web: www.genscoequip.com
Herrschners Inc 2800 Hoover Rd — Stevens Point WI 54481 — 715-341-8686 — 341-2250
TF: 800-713-1239 ■ *Web:* www.herrschners.com
Jubilee Embroidery Company Inc 411 Hwy 601 — Lugoff SC 29078 — 803-438-2934
Kasbar National Industries Inc
370 Reed Rd Ste 200 — Broomall PA 19008 — 610-544-7117 — 544-9799
Web: milliken.com
Lion Bros Company Inc
10246 Reisterstown Rd — Owings Mills MD 21117 — 410-363-1000 — 363-0181
TF Cust Svc: 800-365-6543 ■ *Web:* www.lionbrothers.com
Luv N' Care Ltd 3030 Aurora Ave — Monroe LA 71201 — 800-588-6227
TF: 800-588-6227 ■ *Web:* www.nuby.com
Monarch Textile Rental Services Inc
2810 Foundation Dr — South Bend IN 46628 — 574-233-9433
Web: www.monarchlinen.com
Moritz Embroidery Works Inc
1455 Industrial Pk PO Box 187 — Mount Pocono PA 18344 — 570-839-9600 — 839-9430
TF: 800-533-4183 ■ *Web:* www.moritzembroidery.com
MP Global Products Inc 2500 Old Hadar Rd — Norfolk NE 68701 — 402-379-9695
Web: www.mpglobalproducts.com
National Emblem Inc 17036 S Avalon Blvd — Carson CA 90746 — 310-515-5055 — 515-5966
TF: 800-877-6185 ■ *Web:* www.nationalemblem.com
Osgood Textile Company Inc
333 Park St — West Springfield MA 01089 — 413-737-6488
Web: www.osgoodtextile.com
Penn Emblem Co 10909 Dutton Rd — Philadelphia PA 19154 — 800-793-7366 — 632-6166*
**Fax Area Code:* 215 ■ *TF:* 800-793-7366 ■ *Web:* www.pennemblem.com
Saint Louis Embroidery
1759 Scherer Pkwy — Saint Charles MO 63303 — 636-724-2200
TF: 800-457-6676 ■ *Web:* patch.com/stcharles
Schweizer Emblem Co 1022 Busse Hwy — Park Ridge IL 60068 — 847-292-1022 — 292-1028
TF Cust Svc: 800-942-5215 ■ *Web:* www.schweizer-emblem.com
Silkscreening by Classic Graphix
12152 Woodruff Ave — Downey CA 90241 — 562-940-0806
Web: www.classicgraphix.com
SK Textile Inc 2938 E 54th St — Vernon CA 90058 — 323-581-8986
Web: www.sktextile.com
Stahls' Inc 20600 Stephens St — St. Clair Shores MI 48080 — 586-772-5551
Web: www.stahls.com
Stitchmaster LLC 309-B S Regional Rd — Greensboro NC 27409 — 336-852-6448
Web: www.stitchmaster.com
Superior Pleating & Stitching
3671 E Olympic Blvd — Los Angeles CA 90023 — 323-261-3964 — 261-0122
Web: superiorpleating.webs.com
Thread Logic 18190 Dairy Ln Ste 204 — Jordan MN 55352 — 952-224-9575
Web: thread-logic.com
Todd Rutkin Inc 5801 S Alameda St — Los Angeles CA 90001 — 323-584-9225
Web: toddrutkin.com

262 EMPLOYMENT OFFICES - GOVERNMENT

Phone | Fax

Employment & Training Administration
200 Constitution Ave NW — Washington DC 20210 — 866-487-2365
Web: www.doleta.gov
US Dept of Labor 200 Constitution Ave NW — Washington DC 20210 — 202-693-4700 — 693-4754
Web: www.dol.gov/vets
Alaska Employment Security Div PO Box 115509 — Juneau AK 99811 — 907-465-2712 — 465-4537
Web: www.labor.state.ak.us/esd/home.htm
Arizona Employment Administration
PO Box 6123 — Phoenix AZ 85005 — 602-542-3957 — 542-2491
Web: www.azdes.gov
Arkansas Dept of Workforce Services
2 Capitol Mall — North Little Rock AR 72201 — 501-682-2121 — 682-2273
Web: www.arkansas.gov
California Employment Development Dept
800 Capitol Mall MIC 83 — Sacramento CA 95814 — 916-654-8210 — 657-5294
Web: www.edd.ca.gov
Colorado Labor & Employment Dept
633 17th St Ste 201 — Denver CO 80203 — 303-318-8000
TF: 800-390-7936 ■ *Web:* www.coworkforce.com
Connecticut Labor Dept
200 Folly Brook Blvd — Wethersfield CT 06109 — 860-263-6000 — 263-6699
Web: www.ctdol.state.ct.us
Delaware Employment & Training Div
4425 N Market St — Wilmington DE 19802 — 302-761-8085
Web: www.delawareworks.com
Aging Office 441 Fourth St NW Ste 900 S — Washington DC 20001 — 202-724-5622 — 724-4979
Web: www.dcoa.dc.gov
Florida Workforce Florida Inc
1580 Waldo Palmer Ln Ste 1 — Tallahassee FL 32303 — 850-921-1119 — 921-1101
Web: careersourceflorida.com
Georgia Employment Services Div
148 Andrew Young International Blvd NE — Atlanta GA 30303 — 404-232-3515
Web: www.dol.state.ga.us
Hawaii Workforce Development Div
201 Merchant St Ste 1805 — Honolulu HI 96813 — 808-695-4620 — 695-4618
Web: www.hawaii.gov
Idaho Labor Dept 317 W Main St — Boise ID 83735 — 208-332-3570 — 334-6300
Web: labor.idaho.gov/dnn/idl
Indiana Workforce Development Dept
10 N Senate Ave — Indianapolis IN 46204 — 317-232-7670 — 233-4793
TF: 800-891-6499 ■ *Web:* www.in.gov
Iowa Workforce Development
1000 E Grand Ave — Des Moines IA 50319 — 515-281-5387 — 281-4698
TF: 800-562-4692 ■ *Web:* www.iowaworkforce.org
Kentucky Workforce Investment Dept
500 Mero St Fl 3 — Frankfort KY 40601 — 502-564-4286
Web: www.workforce.ky.gov
Louisiana Workforce Commission
1001 N 23rd St — Baton Rouge LA 70802 — 225-342-3111 — 342-7960
TF: 877-529-6757 ■ *Web:* www.laworks.net
Maine Employment Services Bureau
55 State House Station — Augusta ME 04330 — 207-623-7981 — 287-5933
Web: www.mainecareercenter.com
Maryland Workforce Development Div
1100 N Eutaw St Rm 616 — Baltimore MD 21201 — 410-767-2400 — 767-2986
Web: www.dllr.state.md.us/employment
Massachusetts Workforce Development Dept
1 Ashburton Pl Rm 1301 — Boston MA 02108 — 617-626-7100 — 727-1090
Web: www.mass.gov
Michigan Career Education & Workforce Programs
201 N Washington Sq Victor Office Center — Lansing MI 48913 — 517-335-5858 — 373-0314
TF: 888-253-6855 ■ *Web:* www.michigan.gov/mdcd
Minnesota Public Safety Dept
445 Minnesota St — Saint Paul MN 55101 — 651-201-7000 — 282-6555
Web: www.dps.mn.gov
Mississippi Employment Security Commission
1235 Echelon Pkwy PO Box 1699 — Jackson MS 39215 — 601-321-6000 — 321-6004
TF: 888-844-3577 ■ *Web:* www.mdes.ms.gov
Montana Workforce Services Div PO Box 1728 — Helena MT 59624 — 406-444-4100 — 444-3037
Web: wsd.dli.mt.gov
Nebraska Workforce Development - Dept of Labor
550 S 16th St PO Box 94600 — Lincoln NE 68509 — 402-471-2600 — 471-9867
Web: dol.nebraska.gov
Nevada Dept of Employment Training & Rehabilitation
500 E Third St — Carson City NV 89713 — 775-684-3911 — 684-3908
Web: www.nvdetr.org
New Hampshire Employment Security (NHES)
32 S Main St — Concord NH 03301 — 603-224-3311 — 228-4145
TF: 800-852-3400 ■ *Web:* www.nh.gov
New Jersey Workforce New Jersey
1 John Fitch Plz Fl 3 — Trenton NJ 08611 — 609-292-2305 — 695-1174
Web: lwd.dol.state.nj.us
New Mexico Dept of Workforce Solutions
301 W DeVargas — Santa Fe NM 87501 — 505-827-7434 — 827-7346
Web: www.dws.state.nm.us
New York Labor Dept WA Harriman Campus Bldg 12 — Albany NY 12240 — 518-457-9000 — 457-6908
TF: 888-469-7365 ■ *Web:* www.labor.ny.gov
North Carolina Employment Security Commission
700 Wade Ave PO Box 25903 — Raleigh NC 27605 — 919-707-1010 — 733-9420
Web: desncc.com/deshome
Ohio Workforce Developement Office
4020 E Fifth Ave PO Box 1618 — Columbus OH 43219 — 888-296-7541 — 644-7102*
**Fax Area Code:* 614 ■ *TF:* 888-296-7541 ■ *Web:* www.jfs.ohio.gov/owd
Oklahoma Employment Security Commission
PO Box 52003 — Oklahoma City OK 73152 — 405-557-5400 — 557-5355
Web: www.ok.gov
Oregon Employment Dept 875 Union St NE — Salem OR 97311 — 503-451-2400 — 947-1472
Web: www.oregon.gov
Pennsylvania Workforce Investment Board
901 N Seventh St Ste 103 — Harrisburg PA 17120 — 717-772-4966
Web: www.paworkforce.state.pa.us
Rhode Island Labor & Training Dept
1511 Pontiac Ave — Cranston RI 02920 — 401-462-8000 — 462-8872
Web: www.dlt.state.ri.us
South Dakota Career Ctr Div
116 W Missouri Ave — Pierre SD 57501 — 605-773-3372 — 773-6680
Web: www.sdjobs.org
Tennessee Labor & Workforce Development Dept
220 French Landing Dr — Nashville TN 37243 — 615-741-6642 — 741-5078
Web: www.state.tn.us
Texas Workforce Commission 101 E 15th St — Austin TX 78778 — 512-463-2222
Web: twc.state.tx.us

Name / Address	City	State	ZIP	Phone	Fax
Administrative Office of the Courts PO Box 140241 *Web:* www.utcourts.gov	Salt Lake City	UT	84114	801-578-3800	578-3843
Vermont Labor Dept 5 Green Mountain Dr *Web:* www.labor.vermont.gov	Montpelier	VT	05601	802-828-4000	828-4022
Virginia Employment Commission 703 E Main St *Web:* www.vec.virginia.gov	Richmond	VA	23219	804-786-1485	225-3923
Washington Employment Security Dept 212 Maple Pk Ave SE *Web:* www.esd.wa.gov	Olympia	WA	98504	360-902-9500	
Wisconsin Workforce Development Dept 201 E Washington Ave *Web:* dwd.wisconsin.gov	Madison	WI	53702	608-266-3131	266-1784

263 EMPLOYMENT SERVICES - ONLINE

Name / Address	City	State	ZIP	Phone	Fax
3C Consulting Corp 850 W Jackson Blvd *Web:* www.3ccomp.com	Chicago	IL	60607	312-226-8118	
A One Staffing LLC 3639 New Getwell Rd Ste 1 *Web:* www.aonestaffing.com	Memphis	TN	38118	901-367-5757	
A Pavillion Agency Inc 15 E 40 St Ste 400 *Web:* pavillionagency.com	New York	NY	10016	212-889-6609	
A-Check America Inc 1501 Research Park Dr *Web:* www.acheckamerica.com	Riverside	CA	91204	951-750-1501	
A-Star Staffing Inc 2835 Camino Del Rio S Ste 220 *Web:* www.astarstaffing.com	San Diego	CA	92108	619-574-7600	
A.B. Data Ltd 600 A B Data Dr *Web:* abdata.com	Milwaukee	WI	53217	414-961-6400	
A.D. Susman & Associates Inc 1308 N First St *Web:* www.adsusman.com	Bellaire	TX	77401	713-668-7998	
A.J. O'Neal & Associates Inc 109 Falkenburg Rd N *Web:* www.ajoneal.com	Tampa	FL	33619	813-654-4199	
A1 Staffing & Recruiting Agency Inc 7465 NW 23rd St *Web:* www.a1staffingok.com	Bethany	OK	73008	405-787-7600	
Abba Staffing & Consulting Services 2350 Airport Fwy Ste 130 *Web:* www.abbastaffing.com	Bedford	TX	76022	817-354-2800	
Abbott Smith 11697 W Grand Ave *Web:* www.abbottsmith.com	Northlake	IL	60164	708-223-1153	
Abeln, Magy, Underberg & Associates Inc 800 E Wayzata Blvd Ste 200 *Web:* www.abelnmagy.com	Wayzata	MN	55391	952-476-4938	
Accu Personnel Inc 911 Kings Hwy N *Web:* www.accustaffing.com	Cherry Hill	NJ	08034	856-482-2222	
Active Staffing Services 41 W 33rd St Fl 3 *Web:* www.activestaffing.com	New York	NY	10001	212-244-6444	
Ad-Vance Talent Solutions Inc 3911 Gulf Park Loop Ste 103 *Web:* ad-vance.com	Bradenton	FL	34203	941-739-8883	
Adams & Garth Staffing 2119 Berkmar Dr *Web:* adamsandgarth.com	Charlottesville	VA	22901	434-974-7878	
Add Staff Inc 2118 Hollow Brook Dr *Web:* www.addstaffinc.com	Colorado Springs	CO	80918	719-528-8888	
Adguide Publications Inc 3109 W 50 St Ste 121 *Web:* www.collegerecruiter.com	Minneapolis	MN	55410	952-848-2211	
ADP National Account Services 4125 Hopyard Rd *Web:* westnsc.adp.com	Pleasanton	CA	94588	925-737-3500	
ADP Screening & Selection Services Inc 301 Remington St *Web:* www.adpselect.com	Fort Collins	CO	80524	970-484-7722	
Advance Employment Services 416 Elmwood Rd *Web:* www.advanceteam.com	Lansing	MI	48917	517-887-0377	
Advantage RN LLC 8892 Beckett Rd *Web:* www.advantagern.com	West Chester	OH	45069	513-874-8717	
Aes, an Employment Source Inc 1335 N Main St *Web:* www.anemploymentsource.com	Meridian	ID	83642	208-887-7740	
agriCAREERS Inc 613 Main St PO Box 140 *Fax Area Code: 712 ■ *TF:* 800-633-8387 ■ *Web:* www.agricareersinc.com	Massena	IA	50853	800-633-8387	779-3366*
Aim Personnel Service 183 Whiting St 13 *Web:* aimpersonnel.com	Hingham	MA	02043	781-740-8808	
Airetel Staffing Inc 415 Montgomery Rd *Web:* www.airetel.com	Altamonte Springs	FL	32714	407-788-2015	
Alar Staffing Corp 1901 E Fourth St Ste 150 *Web:* www.alarstaffing.com	Santa Ana	CA	92705	714-667-3100	
Alaska Executive Search Inc 821 N St Ste 204 *Web:* www.akexec.com	Anchorage	AK	99501	907-276-5707	
Albertini Group Inc 5550 LBJ Fwy Ste 700 *Web:* www.kingsleygate.com	Dallas	TX	75240	972-726-5550	
All-Star Recruiting LLC 4400 W Sample Rd Ste 250 *TF:* 800-928-0229 ■ *Web:* www.allstarrecruiting.com	Coconut Creek	FL	33073	800-928-0229	
Alliance Legal Staffing Solutions 2909 Cole Ave Ste 230 *Web:* www.alliancelegal.com	Dallas	TX	75204	214-954-1250	
Alpha Rae Personnel Inc 347 W Berry St Ste 7 *Web:* www.alpha-rae.com	Fort Wayne	IN	46802	260-426-8227	
Alpha Search Advisory Partners LLC 14 Tower Pl First Fl *Web:* www.alphasearchadvisory.com	Roslyn	NY	11576	516-626-7896	
Andcor Companies Inc 825 Wayzata Blvd E *Web:* www.andcor.com	Wayzata	MN	55391	952-404-8060	
Andiamo Partners 90 Broad St Ste 1501 *Web:* www.andiamopartners.com	New York	NY	10004	212-488-1595	
APA Search Inc One Byram Brook Pl Ste 103 *Web:* www.apasearch.com	Armonk	NY	10504	914-273-6000	
Arbor Associates Inc 15 Court Sq Ste 1050 *Web:* www.arbor-associates.com	Boston	MA	02108	617-227-8829	
Arrow Staffing Services 499 W State St *Web:* www.arrowstaffing.com	Redlands	CA	92373	909-792-1252	
Artists for Humanity Inc 100 W 2nd St *Web:* www.afhboston.org	Boston	MA	02127	617-268-7620	
Artizen Inc 200 Main St Ste #21A *Web:* www.artizen.com	Redwood City	CA	94063	650-261-9400	
Arvon Inc 196 Business Park Dr *Web:* www.arvon.com	Virginia Beach	VA	23462	757-499-9900	
Asap Personnel Services Inc 10301 N Rodney Parham Rd Ste E1 *Web:* m.asapworksforme.com	Little Rock	AR	72227	501-537-2727	
Ascot Staffing 1939 Harrison St Ste 150 *Web:* www.ascotstaffing.com	Oakland	CA	94612	510-839-9520	
Asereth Medical Services Inc 257 Fair Oaks Ave Ste 100 *Web:* www.asereth.com	Pasadena	CA	91105	626-449-0099	
Ashton Staffing Inc 3590 Cherokee St Ste 303 *Web:* www.ashtonstaffing.com	Kennesaw	GA	30144	770-419-1776	
Asset Staffing Inc 150 SE Second Ave Ste 712 *Web:* www.assetstaffing.com	Miami	FL	33131	305-371-5969	
Atrium Staffing Services Ltd 71 Fifth Ave Third Fl *Web:* www.atriumstaff.com	New York	NY	10003	212-292-0550	
Avenue Staffing 7000 57th Ave N Ste 120 *Web:* www.avenuestaffing.com	Minneapolis	MN	55428	763-537-6104	
Avjobs Inc PO Box 260830 *Fax Area Code: 888 ■ *Web:* www.avjobs.com	Littleton	CO	80163	303-683-2322	624-8691*
B2B Staffing Services Inc 4141 Ball Rd #150 *Web:* www.b2bstaffingservices.com	Cypress	CA	90630	714-243-4104	
Backtrack Inc 8850 Tyler Blvd *Web:* backtracker.com	Mentor	OH	44060	440-205-8280	
Baltimore Teachers Union 5800 Metro Dr Ste 100 *Web:* www.baltimoreteachers.org	Baltimore	MD	21215	410-358-6600	
BANK W Holdings LLC Five Bedford Farms Dr Ste 304 *Web:* www.bankwholdings.com	Bedford	NH	03110	603-792-2345	
Barton Staffing Solutions Inc 723 Aurora Ave *Web:* bartonstaffing.com	Aurora	IL	60505	630-897-3591	
Bcg Attorney Search 175 S Lk Ave Unit 200 *Web:* www.bcgsearch.com	Pasadena	CA	91101	310-416-9090	
Bear Staffing Services Inc 47 S Broad St *Web:* www.bearstaff.com	Woodbury	NJ	08096	856-848-0082	
BECO Inc 200 S Prospect *Web:* www.becogroup.com	Park Ridge	IL	60068	847-825-8000	
BelFlex Staffing Network 127 E Fourth St *Web:* www.belflex.com	Cincinnati	OH	45202	513-241-8367	
Bergen Briller Group LLC, The 1787 Wrightstown Rd *Web:* www.bbgsearch.com	Newtown	PA	18940	215-369-4190	
Berman & Larson Associates 12 N State Rt 17 Ste 209 *Web:* jobsbl.com	Paramus	NJ	07652	201-909-0906	
Beyond 1060 First Ave Ste 100 *TF:* 800-227-7469 ■ *Web:* www.beyond.com	King of Prussia	PA	19406	610-878-2800	878-2801
Beyond.com Inc 1060 First Ave Ste 100 *Web:* www.beyond.com	King of Prussia	PA	19406	610-878-2800	
Bowen Workforce Solutions Inc 602 12 Ave Sw Ste 700 *Web:* www.bowenworks.ca	Calgary	AB	T2R1J3	403-262-1156	
Boyle Ogata Bregman 17461 Derian Ave Ste 202 *Web:* www.bobsearch.com	Irvine	CA	92614	949-474-0115	
Brickforce Staffing Inc Two Ethel Rd *Web:* www.brickforce.com	Edison	NJ	08817	732-819-7770	
Bridge Personnel Services 2800 W Higgins Rd Ste 680 *Web:* www.bridgepersonnel.com	Hoffman Estates	IL	60195	847-885-9696	
Broadband Express LLC 374 Westdale Ave *Web:* www.broadbandexpress.com	Westerville	OH	43082	614-823-6464	
Brockton Area Workforce Investment Board Inc 34 School St Second Fl *Web:* bawib.org	Brockton	MA	02301	508-584-3234	
Broome Employment Center 171 Frnt St *Web:* co.broome.ny.us	Binghamton	NY	13905	607-778-2136	
BSG Team Ventures Inc 224 Clarendon St Ste 41 *Web:* www.bostonsearchgroup.com	Boston	MA	02116	617-266-4333	
Buckman Enochs Coss & Associates 590 Enterprise Dr *Web:* becsearch.com	Lewis Center	OH	43035	614-825-6215	
Burning Glass International Inc One Lewis Wharf *Web:* www.burning-glass.com	Boston	MA	02110	617-227-4800	
Buzz Co, The 62 W Huron St Ste 2W *Web:* www.buzzco.com	Chicago	IL	60654	312-255-0808	
Bwbacon Group 621 kalamath st *Web:* www.bwbacon.com	Denver	CO	80204	303-593-1425	
Caler Group Inc, The 23337 Lago Mar Cir *Web:* www.calergroup.com	Boca Raton	FL	33433	561-394-8045	
Callos & Associates 6547 E Livingston Ave *Web:* www.callos.com	Reynoldsburg	OH	43068	614-575-4900	
Cameron Tucker Consulting 8700 Crownhill Blvd *Web:* www.camerontucker.com	San Antonio	TX	78209	210-348-7333	

Phone | Fax

Canon Recruiting Group LLC
26531 Summit Cir .... Santa Clarita CA 91350 661-252-7400
Web: www.canonrecruiting.com

Capital Workforce Partners
One Union Pl Third Fl .... Hartford CT 06103 860-522-1111
Web: www.capitalworkforce.org

CapitolWorks Inc 2000 P St NW .... Washington DC 20036 202-785-2020
Web: www.capitolworks.com

Cardinal Services Inc 1721 Indian Wood Cir A .... Maumee OH 43537 419-893-5400
Web: www.cardinalstaffing.com

Care Resources Inc 1026 Cromwell Bridge Rd .... Baltimore MD 21286 410-583-1515
Web: www.careresourcesinc.com

Career Alliance Inc 711 N Saginaw St Ste 300 .... Flint MI 48503 810-233-5974
Web: www.careeralliance.org

Career Exposure inc 805 SW Broadway .... Portland OR 97205 503-221-7779

Career Foundations Inc
4011 Westchase Blvd Ste 270 .... Raleigh NC 27607 919-828-1000
Web: www.careerfoundations.com

CareSource Home Health & Hospice LLC
1624 East 4500 South .... Salt Lake City UT 84117 801-266-7200
Web: www.ecaresource.com

Carney Group, The 925 Harvest Dr Ste 240 .... Blue Bell PA 19422 215-646-6200
Web: www.carneyjobs.com

Carolinas Constructions Solutions Inc
6712 Old Pineville Rd .... Charlotte NC 28217 704-578-1567
Web: www.staffccs.com

Carter Group LLC, The
1621 University Blvd South .... Mobile AL 36609 251-342-0999
Web: www.thecartergroup.com

CASCO International Inc 4205 E Dixon Blvd .... Shelby NC 28152 704-482-9591
Web: www.cashort.com

Catalyst Awareness Inc 355 Elmira Rd N Ste 127 .... Guelph ON N1K1S5 866-749-3697
TF: 866-749-3697 ■ *Web:* catalystawareness.com

Celerity Staffing Solutions
6273 University Ave .... Middleton WI 53562 608-238-3410
Web: www.celeritystaffing.com

Chameleon Technologies Inc
520 Kirkland Way Ste 101 .... Kirkland WA 98033 425-827-1173
Web: www.chameleontechinc.com

Chandler Group Executive Search Inc
4165 Shoreline Dr Ste 220 .... Spring Park MN 55384 952-471-3000
Web: www.chandgroup.com

Charm City Concierge Inc 1437 E Ft Ave .... Baltimore MD 21230 410-727-4569
Web: www.charmcityconcierge.com

Chatham Search International Inc
Three Lion Gardiner .... Cromwell CT 06416 860-635-5538
Web: www.chathamct.com

Chicago Nannies Inc 500 Auvergne Pl .... River Forest IL 60305 708-366-2161
Web: www.chicagonanniesinc.com

Children First Home Healthcare Service
4448 Edgewater Dr .... Orlando FL 32804 407-513-3000
Web: www.childrenfirsthomecare.com

Choctaw Management Services Enterprise
2101 W Arkansas St .... Durant OK 74701 580-924-8280
Web: www.cmse.net

Chronicle of Higher Education Career Network, The
1255 23rd St NW Seventh Fl .... Washington DC 20037 202-466-1000
Web: chroniclevitae.com

Clark Personnel Service 1180 Montlimar Dr .... Mobile AL 36609 251-471-6777
Web: www.clarkpersonnel.com

Clearbridge Technology Group
Six Fortune Dr .... Billerica MA 01821 781-916-2284
Web: www.clearbridgetech.com

ClearStaff Inc 7501 S Lemont Rd Ste 220 .... Woodridge IL 60517 630-985-0100
Web: www.stanfordproducts.com

Coast Personnel 2295 De La Cruz Blvd .... Santa Clara CA 95050 408-653-2100
Web: www.coastjobs.com

Coddington Group LLC, The 115 W St Ste 300 .... Annapolis MD 21401 410-263-6200
Web: www.coddingtongroup.com

College Nannies & Tutors Inc
1415 Wayzata Blvd E .... Wayzata MN 55391 952-476-0613
Web: www.collegenannies.com

ComputerJobs.com Inc 1995 N Pk Pl SE .... Atlanta GA 30339 770-850-0045 850-0369
TF: 800-850-0045 ■ *Web:* www.computerjobs.com

Condustrial Inc 105 East N St .... Greenville SC 29601 864-235-3619
Web: www.condustrial.com

Conexess Group LLC 4336 Kenilwood Dr .... Nashville TN 37204 615-242-1014
Web: www.conexess.com

Controllers Group Inc 1818 The Alameda .... San Jose CA 95126 408-294-0004
Web: www.controllersgroup.net

Crist|Kolder Associates LLC
3250 Lacey Rd Ste 450 .... Downers Grove IL 60515 630-321-1110
Web: www.cristassociates.com

Crowe-Innes & Associates 1120 Mar W Ste D .... Tiburon CA 94920 415-789-1422
Web: www.croweinnes.com

CSS International Inc
115 River Landing Dr Daniel Island .... Charleston SC 29492 843-849-8712
Web: www.cssus.com

Culinary Services of America Inc
7280 Melrose Ave .... Los Angeles CA 90046 323-965-7582
Web: www.culinarystaffing.com

D N Schwartz & Co 160 W 71st St Ste 12H .... New York NY 10023 212-787-5017
Web: www.dnschwartz.com

Dako Services Inc 2966 Industrial Row .... Troy MI 48084 248-655-0100
Web: www.dakogroup.com

David Aplin & Associates Ltd
2300 Oxford Tower 10235-101 St .... Edmonton AB T5J3G1 780-428-6663
Web: www.aplin.com

Dax Safety & Staffing Solutions LLC
307 Nw 110th Ter .... Kansas City MO 64155 816-935-9137
Web: daxsafety.com

Phone | Fax

Delta Dallas Protech LP
15950 N Dallas Pkwy Ste 500 .... Dallas TX 75248 972-788-2300
Web: www.deltadallas.com

Depaul Industries
4950 NE Martin Luther King Junior Blvd .... Portland OR 97211 503-281-1289
Web: www.depaulindustries.com

Dice Inc 4101 NW Urbandale Dr .... Urbandale IA 50322 515-280-1144 280-1452
TF: 877-386-3323 ■ *Web:* www.dice.com

Diedre Moire Corporation Inc
510 Horizon Center .... Robbinsville NJ 08691 609-584-9000
Web: www.diedremoire.com

DISCO International Inc
15 W 44th St Fifth Fl .... New York NY 10036 212-382-0025
Web: discointer.com

Diversity Advertising Inc
11271 Ventura Blvd Ste 151 .... Studio City CA 91604 818-530-4852
Web: www.hispanic-jobs.com

Domari & Associates Inc
135 Triple Diamond Blvd Unit 100 .... North Venice FL 34275 941-488-4440
Web: www.domarijobs.com

Dployit Inc 14673 Midway Rd Ste 108 .... Addison TX 75001 214-550-6124
Web: www.dployit.com

DreamJobs 6545 W Central Ave Ste 102 .... Toledo OH 43617 567-455-5500
Web: www.dreamjobsna.com

Drivestaff 110 E Schiller St Ste 208 .... Elmhurst IL 60126 630-941-3748
Web: www.drivestaff.com

E-ventexe 8775 Sierra College Blvd Ste 300 .... Roseville CA 95661 916-458-5820
Web: www.e-ventexe.com

Eastern Design Services
25 Woods Lk Rd Ste 322 .... Greenville SC 29607 864-271-1228
Web: easterndesign.com

Eliassen Group LLC 30 Audubon Rd .... Wakefield MA 01880 781-246-1600
Web: www.eliassen.com

Emerge Financial Wellness Inc
530 Church St Ste 301 .... Nashville TN 37219 800-791-1725
TF: 800-791-1725 ■ *Web:* www.emergebenefit.com

EmplawyerNet 2331 Westwood Blvd. .... Los Angeles CA 90064 800-270-2688
TF: 800-270-2688 ■ *Web:* www.emplawyernet.com

Emplicity 9851 Irvine Ctr Dr .... Irvine CA 92618 714-668-1388
Web: www.emplicity.com

Employco USA Inc 350 E Ogden Ave .... Westmont IL 60559 630-920-0000
Web: www.employco.com

EmploymentGuide.com 150 Granby St .... Norfolk VA 23510 877-876-4039
TF: 877-876-4039 ■ *Web:* www.employmentguide.com

Escamilla & Sons Inc 23820 Potter Rd .... Salinas CA 93908 831-771-5400
Web: www.esons.com

Esquire Inc 21241 Bentura Blvd .... Woodland Hills CA 91364 818-712-9700
Web: www.esquiresearch.com

Ethan Allen Personnel Group Inc
59 Academy St .... Poughkeepsie NY 12601 845-471-9700
Web: www.eaworkforce.com

ettain group Inc
127 W Worthington Ave Ste 100 .... Charlotte NC 28203 704-525-5499
Web: www.ettaingroup.com

Evins Personnel Consultants Inc
2013 W Anderson Ln .... Austin TX 78757 512-454-9561
Web: www.evinspersonnelconsultants.com

Evolve Digital Labs 2315 pine st .... Saint Louis MO 63103 314-260-7455
Web: evolvedigitallabs.com

Excel Partners Inc 1177 Summer St .... Stamford CT 06905 203-978-6200
Web: www.excel-partners.com

ExecUNet Inc 295 Westport Ave .... Norwalk CT 06851 203-750-1030 840-8320
TF: 800-637-3126 ■ *Web:* www.execunet.com

Executrade 9917 112 St Nw .... Edmonton AB T5K1L6 780-944-1122
Web: www.executrade.com

Expanxion 860 Hampshire Rd Ste I .... Westlake Village CA 91361 805-496-3500
Web: expanxion.com

Expert Recruiters 883 Helmcken St .... Vancouver BC V6Z1B1 604-689-3600
Web: www.expertrecruiters.com

Fahrenheit Group LLC, The
1700 Bayberry Court Ste 201 .... Richmond VA 23226 804-955-4440
Web: thefahrenheitgroup.com

Federal Staffing Resources LLC
2200 Somerville Rd Ste 300 .... Annapolis MD 21401 410-990-0795
Web: fsrpeople.com

Fetch Recruiting Inc
21143 Hawthorne Blvd Ste 322 .... Torrance CA 90503 310-375-4384
Web: fetchrecruiting.com

Filter Talent 1505 Fifth Ave Ste 600 .... Seattle WA 98101 206-682-6005
Web: www.filtertalent.com

Flesher & Associates Inc
445 S San Antonio Rd Ste 103 .... Los Altos CA 94022 650-917-9900
Web: www.flesher.com

Flexible Resources Inc
78 Harvard Ave Ste 200 .... Stamford CT 06902 203-351-1180
Web: www.flexibleresources.com

Focus Industrial Workforces 8651 Hauser Ct .... Lenexa KS 66215 913-268-1222
Web: www.workatfocus.com

Forward Edge LLC 3428 Hauck Rd Ste K .... Cincinnati OH 45241 513-761-3343
Web: www.forward-edge.net

FSO Onsite Outsourcing 19 W 44th St Ninth Fl .... New York NY 10036 212-204-1193
Web: www.fso.co

Fusion Recruitment Group Ltd
777 Hornby St Ste 2088 .... Vancouver BC V6Z1S4 604-678-5627
Web: www.fusion-recruitment.com

Future Force Inc 15800 NW 57th Ave .... Miami Lakes FL 33014 305-557-4900
Web: www.futureforcepersonnel.com

G-Force Protective Services & Training Academy Inc
14331 SW 120 St Ste 103 .... Miami FL 33186 305-380-1212
Web: www.gforcemiami.com

Galaxy Software Solutions Inc
5820 N Lilley Rd Ste 8 .... Canton MI 48187 734-983-9030
Web: www.galaxy-soft.com

	City	State	Zip	Phone	Fax
Garms Group, The 830 W Route 22 Ste 250 *Web:* garms.com	Lake Zurich	IL	60047	847-382-7200	
Generate Content LLC 1545 26th St Ste 200 *Web:* www.defymedia.com	Santa Monica	CA	90404	310-255-0460	
Global HR Research LLC 24201 Walden Ctr Dr Ste 206 *Web:* www.ghrr.com	Bonita Springs	FL	34134	239-274-0048	
Global LT Inc 1871 Woodslee Dr *Web:* www.global-lt.com	Troy	MI	48083	248-786-0999	
Good Jobs Inc, The 2120 E Jarvis St *Web:* www.thegoodjobs.com	Milwaukee	WI	53211	414-949-5627	
Goodwill Keystone Area Inc 1150 Goodwill Dr *Web:* www.yourgoodwill.org	Harrisburg	PA	17101	717-232-1831	
Grahall LLC 50 Fairlee Rd *Web:* www.grahall.com	Waban	MA	02468	917-453-4341	
Graham Personnel Services 2100 w cornwallis dr *Web:* www.grahamjobs.com	Greensboro	NC	27408	336-288-9330	
Grapevine Executive Recruiters Inc 269 Richmond St W *Web:* www.grapevinerecruiters.com	Toronto	ON	M5V1X1	416-581-1445	
Greenridge Business Systems Corp 2701 - 83 Garry St *Web:* www.greenridge.ca	Winnipeg	MB	R3C4J9	204-775-3500	
Greer Management Group Inc 3109 Charles B Root Wynd *Web:* www.thegreergroup.com	Raleigh	NC	27612	919-571-0051	
Gsp International Inc 90 Woodbridge Ctr Dr Ste 110 *Web:* gspintl.com	Woodbridge	NJ	07095	732-602-0100	
Gunther Douglas Inc 3400 Mariposa St *Web:* www.guntherdouglas.com	Denver	CO	80211	303-534-4441	
Guru.com 5001 Baum Blvd Ste 760 *Web:* www.guru.com	Pittsburgh	PA	15213	412-687-1316	687-4466
H Ka Staffing Services 800 Waukegan Rd Ste 200 *Web:* www.hkastaffing.com	Glenview	IL	60025	847-998-9300	
Happy Faces Personnel Group Inc 4333 Lynburn Dr. *Web:* www.happyfaces.net	Tucker	GA	30084	770-414-9071	
Harvard Student Agencies Inc 67 Mt Auburn St *Web:* www.hsa.net	Cambridge	MA	02138	617-495-3030	
Haskel Thompson & Associates LLC 12734 Kenwood Ln Ste 74 *Web:* haskelthompson.com	Fort Myers	FL	33907	239-437-4600	
Hds Inc. Professional Driver Services 2621 S 51st Ave *Web:* hdsdrivers.com	Phoenix	AZ	85043	602-484-7901	
Headquist International 230 Florence St Ste 1 *Web:* hedquistintl.com	Crystal Lake	IL	60014	815-479-1700	
HealthCareSource Inc 100 Sylvan Rd Ste 100 *TF:* 800-869-5200 ■ *Web:* www.healthcaresource.com	Woburn	MA	01801	800-869-5200	829-6600
HealthForce Ontario Marketing & Recruitment Agency 163 Queen St E *Web:* www.healthforceontario.ca	Toronto	ON	M5A1S1	416-862-2200	
Helping Hand Nursing Service Inc 8305 S Saginaw St *Web:* www.helpinghandhealthcare.com	Grand Blanc	MI	48439	810-606-8400	
Hire Source Inc, The 24 Wooster Ave Ste 1 *Web:* thehiresource.com	Waterbury	CT	06708	203-757-4000	
Hired 1200 Plymouth Ave N *Web:* www.hired.org	Minneapolis	MN	55411	612-529-3342	
Hodges-Mace Benefits Group Inc 5775-D Glenridge Dr Ste 350 *Web:* www.hodgesmace.com	Atlanta	GA	30328	404-574-6110	
Hotel Pro Staffing LLC 1950 N Park Pl Se Ste 425 *Web:* www.gohotelpro.com	Atlanta	GA	30339	770-937-9007	
Hotline to HR Inc 110 Confederation Pkwy Second Fl *Web:* www.hotlinetohr.com	Concord	ON	L4K4T8	416-619-7867	
Howard E. Nyhart Company Inc, The 8415 Allison Pointe Blvd Ste 300 *Web:* www.nyhart.com	Indianapolis	IN	46250	317-845-3500	
HR Advisors Inc 25411 Cabot Rd Ste 212 *Web:* www.hradvisors.com	Laguna Hills	CA	92653	949-497-7329	
HR Works Inc 200 WillowBrook Ofc Park *Web:* www.hrworks-inc.com	Fairport	NY	14450	585-381-8340	
HR1 Services Inc 2030 Powers Ferry Rd Nw #120 *Web:* www.hr1.com	Atlanta	GA	30339	770-541-7823	
HRCG Inc 1202 E Dover Dr *Web:* ezpublishtest.hrconsultinggroup.com	Provo	UT	84604	801-765-4417	
Hughes Agency, The 700 E 13th St *Web:* www.yesafety.com	North Little Rock	AR	72114	501-791-3303	
Idea Foundry 4551 Forbes Ave Ste 200 *Web:* ideafoundry.org	Pittsburgh	PA	15213	412-682-3067	
Ignite Technical Resources Ltd 1295 - 355 Burrard St *Web:* www.ignitetechnical.com	Vancouver	BC	V6C2G8	604-687-6795	
iMatch LLC 1417 Fourth Ave Ste 810 *Web:* www.imatch.com	Seattle	WA	98101	206-262-1661	
Industry Specific Solutions LLC 24901 Northwestern Hwy Ste 502 *TF:* 877-356-3450 ■ *Web:* www.isscompanies.com	Southfield	MI	48075	877-356-3450	
InjuryFree Inc 20250 144Th Ave NE Ste 305 *Web:* www.ergostat.com	Woodinville	WA	98072	206-363-7676	
InnoSource Inc 6085 Emerald Pkwy *Web:* www.innosourceinc.com	Dublin	OH	43016	614-775-1400	
Intellect Resources Inc 3824 N Elm St Ste 102 *TF:* 877-554-8911 ■ *Web:* www.intellectresources.com	Greensboro	NC	27455	877-554-8911	
International Foundation of Employee Benefit Plans (IFEBP) 18700 W Bluemound Rd *TF:* 888-334-3327 ■ *Web:* www.ifebp.org	Brookfield	WI	53045	262-786-6700	786-8670
Island Staffing 3156 Vista Way Ste 203 *Web:* www.islandstaffing.us	Oceanside	CA	92056	760-547-5018	
Istaff Inc 1325 Satellite Blvd Nw Ste 801 *Web:* www.istaff.com	Suwanee	GA	30024	770-962-9604	
Its Technologies Inc 7060 Spring Meadows Dr W Ste D *Web:* wehireengineers.com	Holland	OH	43528	419-842-2100	
J. s Firm LLC 8205 Camp Bowie W Blvd Ste 214 *Web:* www.jsfirm.com	Fort Worth	TX	76116	817-560-0300	
Jack of All Trades Personnel Services 2701 Franklin Ave *Web:* www.joatwaco.com	Waco	TX	76710	254-754-7997	
Jacob Group, The 6190 Virginia Pkwy One Jacob Pl Ste 100 *Web:* www.jacobgroup.com	Mckinney	TX	75071	214-544-9030	
James Farris Associates Ltd 909 NW 63rd St *Web:* www.jamesfarris.com	Oklahoma City	OK	73116	405-525-5061	
JCSI Corporate Staffing Two South St *Web:* www.jcsi.net	Grafton	MA	01519	774-760-1800	
JDA Professional Services Inc 701 N Post Oak Rd Ste 610 *Web:* www.jdapsi.com	Houston	TX	77024	713-548-5400	
Jet Professionals LLC 114 Charles A Lindbergh Dr Teterboro Airport *Web:* www.jet-professionals.com	Teterboro	NJ	07608	201-393-6900	
Jobboom Inc 800 rue du Sq Victoria Mezzanine - Bureau 5 *Web:* www.jobboom.com	Montreal	QC	H4Z0A3	514-504-2539	
JobDig Inc 5051 Hwy 7 Ste 240 *Web:* www.jobdig.com	Saint Louis Park	MN	55416	952-929-5627	
JobMonkey Inc PO Box 3956 *TF:* 800-230-1095 ■ *Web:* www.jobmonkey.com	Seattle	WA	98124	800-230-1095	
Jobpostings.ca 100-25 Imperial St *TF:* 877-900-5627 ■ *Web:* www.jobpostings.ca	Toronto	ON	M5P1B9	877-900-5627	
JobTarget LLC 225 State St Ste 300 *Web:* www.jobtarget.com	New London	CT	06320	860-440-0635	
Josephine's Personnel Services Inc 2158 Ringwood Ave *Web:* www.jps-inc.com	San Jose	CA	95131	408-943-0111	
JSMN International Inc 591 Summit Ave Ste 522 *Web:* www.jsmninc.com	Jersey City	NJ	07306	201-792-6800	
Judys Staffing Services Inc 3070 Harrodsburg Rd *Web:* www.judysstaffing.com	Lexington	KY	40503	859-223-5005	
JUNO Healthcare Staffing System Inc 411 Fifth Ave Ste 1006 *Web:* www.junohealthcare.com	New York	NY	10016	212-685-5866	
K a Hamilton & Assoc 159 Perry Hwy Ste 100 *Web:* rcn.com	Pittsburgh	PA	15229	412-459-0122	
Kane Partners LLC 1816 W Point Pike Ste 221 *Web:* www.kanepartners.net	Lansdale	PA	19446	215-699-5500	
Kavaliro Staffing Services 12001 Research Pkwy Ste 344 *Web:* www.kavaliro.com	Orlando	FL	32826	407-243-6006	
Kaye Personnel Inc 1868 Marlton Pike E *Web:* kayepersonnel.com	Cherry Hill	NJ	08003	856-489-1200	
Keller Augusta Partners LLC 45 Newbury St Ste 204 *Web:* www.kelleraugusta.com	Boston	MA	02116	617-247-0505	
Kendall & Davis Company Inc 3668 S Geyer Rd Ste 100 *TF:* 866-675-3755 ■ *Web:* www.kendallanddavis.com	St. Louis	MO	63127	866-675-3755	
Key Corporate Services LLC 9746 Olympia Dr *Web:* www.keycorporateservices.com	Fishers	IN	46037	317-598-1950	
Kipe Technology Resources 14725 SW Millikan Way *Web:* www.kipetech.com	Beaverton	OR	97006	503-590-7000	
Koren Rogers 701 Westchester Ave Ste 212W *Web:* www.korenrogers.com	White Plains	NY	10604	914-686-5800	
Kovasys Inc 3575 St Laurent Blvd Ste 511 *TF:* 888-568-2747 ■ *Web:* www.kovasys.com	Montreal	QC	H2X2T7	888-568-2747	
KPM VIPER Consulting LLC South Shore Executive Park 10 Forbes Rd *Web:* www.kpm-us.com	Braintree	MA	02184	781-380-3520	
Kreuzberger & Associates 1000 Fourth St *Web:* www.kreuzberger.com	San Rafael	CA	94901	415-459-2300	
KSPH LLC 4191 Innslake Dr Ste 211 *Web:* www.ksphllc.com	Glen Allen	VA	23060	804-418-6290	
KWCG Inc 12255 Pkwy Centre Dr *TF:* 877-464-5924 ■ *Web:* www.kwcg.us	San Diego	CA	92064	877-464-5924	
Landmark Staffing Resources Inc 2901 E Enterprise Ave Ste 600 *Web:* www.landmarkstaffing.com	Appleton	WI	54913	920-731-3130	
Lawton Group, The 4747 Viewridge Ave Ste 210 *Web:* www.tlcstaffing.com	San Diego	CA	92123	858-569-6260	
Life Advantages LLC 600 First Ave N Ste 307 *Web:* www.lifeadvantages.com	St. Petersburg	FL	33701	727-381-9446	
Life Style Staffing 6765 W Greenfield Ave *Web:* www.lifestylestaffing.com	Milwaukee	WI	53214	414-475-0090	

Phone | Fax

Link Executive Search Inc
730 Second Ave S US Trust Bldg Ste 400 .... Minneapolis MN 55402 612-884-7000
Web: link-us.net

Ll Roberts Group 7475 Skillman St Ste 102c .... Dallas TX 75231 214-221-6463
Web: www.llroberts.com

Lorelei Personnel Inc One Auer Ct .... East Brunswick NJ 08816 732-390-1170
Web: www.loreleipersonnel.com

LyonsHR 1941 Florence Blvd .... Florence AL 35630 256-767-5900
Web: www.lyonshr.com

Madison & Associates Inc
4108 Holly Rd .... Virginia Beach VA 23451 757-425-9950
Web: www.tdmadison.com

Maglio & Company Whlse Fruits
4287 N Port Washington Rd .... Milwaukee WI 53212 414-906-8800
Web: www.maglioproduce.com

Majesty Hospitality Staffing
908 Town And Country Blvd .... Houston TX 77024 713-984-7598
Web: www.majestyhospitalitystaffing.com

Mancino Burfield Edgerton
12 Roszel Rd Ste C-101 .... Princeton NJ 08540 609-520-8400
Web: www.mbels.com

MarketPro Inc 53 Perimeter Ctr E Ste 200 .... Atlanta GA 30346 404-222-9992
Web: marketproinc.com

Mason & Blair LLC 1762 Technology Dr Ste 206 .... San Jose CA 95110 408-436-6300
Web: www.masonblair.com

Maven Group LLC, The 320 N Salem St Ste 204 .... Apex NC 27502 919-386-1010
Web: www.themavengroup.com

Maxsys 173 Dalhousie St .... Ottawa ON K1N7C7 613-562-9943
Web: maxsys.ca

Mcdermott & Bull Executive Search
Two Venture Ste 100 .... Irvine CA 92618 949-753-1700
Web: www.mbsearch.net

MDT Labor LLC 2325 Paxton Church Rd Ste B .... Harrisburg PA 17110 888-454-9202
TF: 888-454-9202 ■ *Web:* www.mdttechnical.com

Meador Staffing Services Inc
722 Fairmont Pkwy Ste A .... Pasadena TX 77504 713-941-0616
Web: www.meador.com

Medpoint Search 4011 Garrott St .... Houston TX 77006 713-524-4443
Web: www.medpointsearch.com

Mega Force Staffing Services Inc
1001 Hay St .... Fayetteville NC 28305 910-484-0133
Web: www.megaforce.com

Melwood Horticultural Training Center In
5606 Dower House Rd .... Upper Marlboro MD 20772 301-599-8000
Web: www.melwood.org

Metasys Technologies Inc
3460 Summit Ridge Pkwy Ste 401 .... Duluth GA 30096 678-218-1600
Web: www.metasysinc.com

Mike Ferry Organization, The
7220 S Cimarron Rd Ste 300 .... Las Vegas NV 89113 702-982-6260
Web: www.mikeferry.com

Miller Resources International Inc
83 Stultz Rd .... Dayton NJ 08810 609-395-1800
Web: www.millerjobs.com

Milliner & Associates LLC
4181 E 96th St Ste 120 .... Indianapolis IN 46240 317-218-1195
Web: www.millinerandassoc.com

Mind Your Business Inc (myb)
305 Eighth Ave E .... Hendersonville NC 28792 828-698-9899
Web: www.mybinc.com

Mindseeker 20130 Lakeview Ctr Plz .... Ashburn VA 20147 571-313-5950
Web: www.mindseeker.com

MonsterTRAK 11845 W Olympic Blvd Ste 500 .... Los Angeles CA 90064 310-474-3377
Web: college.monster.com

Moore Temporaries Inc 184 Pleasant Vly St .... Methuen MA 01844 978-682-4994
Web: www.moorestaffing.com

Morales Group Inc 5628 W 74th St .... Indianapolis IN 46278 317-472-7600
Web: moralesgroup.net

Morgan Hunter Companies
7600 W 110th St .... Overland Park KS 66210 913-491-3434
Web: www.morganhunter.com

Mosaic Company Inc, The
555 S Renton Village Pl .... Renton WA 98057 425-254-1724
Web: www.themosaiccompany.com

Mosse & Mosse Insurance Associates LLC
50 Salem St Bldg B .... Lynnfield MA 01940 781-224-1709
Web: www.mosseandmosse.com

Mundy Contract Maintenance Inc
11150 S Wilcrest .... Houston TX 77099 281-530-8711
Web: www.mundycos.com

Myra Binstock Legal Search
121 Squire Hill Rd .... Upper Montclair NJ 07043 973-783-6006
Web: www.myrabinstock.com

N-Tier Solutions Inc 2596 Landmark Dr .... Winston Salem NC 27103 336-765-3500
Web: www.n-tiersolutions.com

National Diversity Newspaper Job Bank
c/o Morris Communications 725 Broad St .... Augusta GA 30901 706-724-0851
TF: 800-622-6358 ■ *Web:* www.morris.com

National Older Worker Career Center
3811 N Fairfax Dr Ste 900 .... Arlington VA 22203 703-558-4200
Web: www.nowcc.org

NationJob Inc 920 Morgan St Ste T .... Des Moines IA 50309 800-292-7731 243-5384*
**Fax Area Code:* 515 ■ *TF:* 800-292-7731 ■ *Web:* www.nationjob.com

Net-Temps Inc
55 Middlesex St Ste 220 .... North Chelmsford MA 01863 978-251-7272 251-7250
TF: 800-307-0062 ■ *Web:* www.net-temps.com

Netchex 1100 N Causeway Blvd Ste 1 .... Mandeville LA 70471 985-220-1410
Web: www.netchexonline.com

Newport Strategic Search Inc
175 Calle Magdalena .... Encinitas CA 92024 760-274-0100
Web: www.newportsearch.com

Nine Star Enterprises Inc 730 I St .... Anchorage AK 99501 907-279-7827
Web: www.ninestar.com

Phone | Fax

Northwest Software Inc
1800 Nw 169th Pl Ste B150 .... Beaverton OR 97006 503-629-5947
Web: www.nwsi.com

Nova Management Inc 659 Abrego St Ste 5 .... Monterey CA 93940 831-373-4544
Web: www.novamanagement.com

Nowhirecom 21220 Kelly Rd .... Eastpointe MI 48021 586-778-8491
Web: www.nowhire.com

NSTAR Global Services Inc 120 Partlo St .... Garner NC 27529 877-678-2766
TF: 877-678-2766 ■ *Web:* www.nstarglobalservices.com

Olesky Associates Inc
865 Washington St Ste 3 .... Newtonville MA 02460 781-235-4330
Web: www.olesky.com

Oliver Staffing Inc
350 Lexington Ave Ste 401 .... New York NY 10016 212-634-1234
Web: www.oliverstaffing.com

Olympic Staffing Services 588 S Grand Ave .... Covina CA 91724 626-447-3558
Web: www.olystaffing.com

ON Search Partners LLC 6240 SOM Ctr Rd Ste 230 .... Solon OH 44139 440-318-1006
Web: www.onpartners.com

One Stop Career Center
359 Bill France Blvd .... Daytona Beach FL 32114 386-323-7001
Web: www.careersourcefv.com

OneSource Inc 1124 Hwy 315 .... Wilkes-barre PA 18702 570-825-3411
Web: www.onesourcehrsolutions.com

Ongig Inc 708 Montgomery St .... San Francisco CA 94111 415-857-2304
Web: www.ongig.com

Onug Communications Inc 3315 Atlantic Ave .... Raleigh NC 27604 919-876-5455
Web: onugsolutions.com

OperationsInc LLC
992 High Ridge Rd Second Fl .... Stamford CT 06905 203-322-0538
Web: www.operationsinc.com

Opti Staffing Group 2550 Denali Ste 715 .... Anchorage AK 99503 907-677-9675
Web: optistaffing.com

Outsource Staffing Inc 2611 Laurel St .... Beaumont TX 77702 409-813-2900
Web: outsourcestaffinginc.com

Pace Staffing Network Inc
2275-116th Ave NE Ste 200 .... Bellevue WA 98004 425-454-1075
Web: www.pacestaffing.com

Paladin Partners 838 Kirkland Ave .... Kirkland WA 98033 425-260-5354
Web: www.paladinpartners.com

Palo Alto Staffing Services
2471 E Bayshore Rd Ste 525 .... Palo Alto CA 94303 650-493-0223
Web: wehire.com

PCI Group LLC
10801 W Charleston Blvd Ste 650 .... Las Vegas NV 89135 702-515-7490
Web: www.hillpci.com

Penda Aiken Inc 330 Livingston St .... Brooklyn NY 11217 718-643-4880
Web: www.pendaaiken.com

Penmac Staffing Services Inc
447 South Ave .... Springfield MO 65806 417-831-9100
Web: www.penmac.com

Penski Inc 50 Market St .... Potsdam NY 13676 315-265-8860
Web: www.penski.com

People Plus Industrial Inc 1095 Nebo Rd .... Madisonville KY 42431 270-825-8939
Web: www.peopleplusinc.com

Peoplecomm Inc 148 Woodbine Ave .... Northport NY 11768 631-239-5498
Web: cardbrowser.com

Peoplelink Staffing Solutions LLC
431 E Colfax Ave Ste 200 .... South Bend IN 46617 574-232-5400
Web: www.peoplelinkstaffing.com

Perfect Fit Placement Inc 1263 Berlin Tpke .... Berlin CT 06037 860-828-3127
Web: www.perfectfitplacement.com

Perkins Group Inc, The
10701 McMullen Creek Pkwy Ste D .... Charlotte NC 28226 704-543-1111
Web: www.perkinsgroup.com

Peterson's Nelnet LLC 121 S 13th St Ste 201 .... Lincoln NE 68508 609-896-8669 896-4565
TF: 877-338-7772 ■ *Web:* www.essayedge.com

PHC Northwest Inc 5312 Ne 148th Ave .... Portland OR 97230 503-261-1266
Web: www.phcnw.com

Pinnacle Group International 130 Water St .... New York NY 10005 212-968-1200
Web: www.pinnaclegroup.com

Placement Strategies Inc
6965 El Camino Real Ste 105-200 .... Carlsbad CA 92009 909-597-0668
Web: www.placementstrategies.com

Platinum HR Management LLC 4512 Farragut Rd ..... Brooklyn NY 11203 718-859-1600
Web: www.platinumhrm.com

Platinum Personnel 1475 Ellis St .... Kelowna BC V1Y2A3 250-979-7200
Web: www.platinumpersonnel.ca

Polk Works One-stop Centers
500 E Lk Howard Dr .... Winter Haven FL 33881 863-508-1100
Web: www.careersourcepolk.com

Preference Personnel Inc 2600 Ninth Ave S .... Fargo ND 58103 701-293-6905
Web: www.preferencepersonnel.com

Premier Nursing Services Inc
444 W Ocean Blvd Ste 1050 .... Long Beach CA 90802 562-437-4313
Web: www.premiernursing.com

Priority Staffing Solutions Inc
42 W 38th St Rm 503 .... New York NY 10018 212-213-2277
Web: www.prioritystaff.com

PRN Health Services Inc
4321 W College Ave Ste 200 .... Appleton WI 54914 888-830-8811
TF: 888-830-8811 ■ *Web:* www.prnhealthservices.com

Pro-Tem Solutions Inc
249 E Ocean Blvd Ste 500 .... Long Beach CA 90802 562-216-6400
Web: www.pro-temsolutions.com

Procel Temporary Services
2447 Pacific Coast Hwy Ste 207 .... Hermosa Beach CA 90254 310-372-0560
Web: www.procelnurses.com

Profiles Placement 20 S Charles St .... Baltimore MD 21201 410-244-6400
Web: careerprofiles.com

Company	City	State	ZIP	Phone	Fax
Project Connect 1025 W Johnson St 141 Educational Science Bldg *Web:* careers.education.wisc.edu	Madison	WI	53706	608-262-1755	262-9074
Psi Personnel LLC 252 W Swamp Rd Ste 22 *Web:* www.psipersonnel.com	Doylestown	PA	18901	215-345-6778	
Psychiatrists Only LLC 2970 Clairmont Rd Ste 650 *Web:* www.psyonly.com	Atlanta	GA	30329	404-315-7889	
Quad656 LLC 656 E Swedesford Rd *Web:* www.quad656.com	Wayne	PA	19087	610-687-6441	
Qualified Staffing Services 5361 Gateway Centre Ste D *Web:* www.q-staffing.com	Flint	MI	48507	810-230-0368	
Qualitek Services Inc 700 N Wickham Rd Ste 101 *Web:* www.qualitek.biz	Melbourne	FL	32935	321-259-2400	
Quorum Associates LLC 1005 Chapman St. *Web:* www.quorumassociates.com	Yorktown Heights	NY	10598	914-320-6251	
RCS Corp 955 Colony Pkwy *Web:* www.rcscorporation.com	Aiken	SC	29803	803-641-0100	
Reardon Associates Inc 450 Washington St Ste LL5 *Web:* www.reardonassociates.com	Dedham	MA	02026	781-329-2660	
Recruitmilitary LLC 422 W Loveland Ave *Web:* recruitmilitary.com	Loveland	OH	45140	513-683-5020	
RecruitWise 704 S Illinois Ave Ste C-202 *Web:* www.recruitwise.jobs	Oak Ridge	TN	37830	865-425-0405	
Reel Group Inc 15740 Park Row Ste 450 *Web:* www.reelgroup.com	Houston	TX	77084	832-358-2663	
Regional Personnel Services Inc 502 Us Hwy 22 Ste 1 *Web:* www.regionalpersonnel.com	Lebanon	NJ	08833	908-534-8113	
Renhill Staffing Services of Texas Inc 102 Rilla Vista Dr *Web:* www.renhillmgmt.com	San Antonio	TX	78216	210-828-0508	
Resource Mfg 7033 Commonwealth Ave Ste 4 *Web:* www.resourcemfg.com	Jacksonville	FL	32220	904-693-3686	
Response Staffing Solutions Inc 56 W 45th St Second Fl *Web:* www.responseco.com	New York	NY	10036	212-983-8870	
Reveal Global Intelligence 10800 Sikes Place Ste 205 *Web:* www.revealglobal.com	Charlotte	NC	28277	704-844-6000	
Richmar Associates Inc 283 Brokaw Rd *Web:* www.richmar1.com	Santa Clara	CA	95050	408-727-6070	
RightStaff Inc 4919 McKinney Ave *Web:* www.rightstaffinc.com	Dallas	TX	75205	214-953-0900	
Riverside Staffing Services Inc 2322 E Kimberly Rd Paul Revere Sq Ste 130N *Web:* www.riversidestaffing.com	Davenport	IA	52807	563-355-5212	
Rolinc Staffing 333 W Hampden Ave Ste 545 *Web:* rolinc.com	Englewood	CO	80110	303-781-0055	
Royall & Company Inc 1920 E Parham Rd *Web:* www.royall.com	Richmond	VA	23228	804-741-8965	
Rubicon Programs 2500 Bissell Ave *Web:* www.rubiconprograms.org	Richmond	CA	94804	510-235-1516	
Rumpf Corp, The 701 Jefferson Ave. *Web:* www.job1usa.com	Toledo	OH	43604	419-255-5005	
Run Consultants LLC 925 N Point Pkwy Ste 160 *TF:* 866-457-2193 ■ *Web:* www.runconsultants.com	Alpharetta	GA	30005	866-457-2193	
S2Verify LLC Box 2597 *Web:* www.s2verify.com	Roswell	GA	30077	770-649-8282	
Salus Group Benefits Inc 37525 Mound Rd *TF:* 866-991-9907 ■ *Web:* www.salusgroupbenefits.com	Sterling Heights	MI	48310	866-991-9907	
Sanford Rose Associates International Inc 19111 N Dallas Pkwy Ste 201 *Web:* www.sanfordrose.com	Dallas	TX	75287	972-616-7870	
Savela & Associates Inc 3595 Grandview PkwySte 450 *Web:* www.savela.com	Birmingham	AL	35243	205-444-0080	
Search Wizards Inc PO Box 191387 *Web:* www.searchwizards.net	Atlanta	GA	31119	404-846-9500	
Searchpros Staffing 6363 Auburn Blvd Ste C *Web:* www.searchprosmsp.com	Citrus Heights	CA	95621	916-721-6000	
Select Group LLC, The 5420 Wade Park Blvd Ste 100 *Web:* www.selectgroup.com	Raleigh	NC	27607	919-459-1400	
Serviko Inc 2670 Rue Duchesne *Web:* www.serviko.com	Saint-laurent	QC	H4R1J3	514-332-2600	
Set & Service Resources LLC 8303 Six Forks Rd Ste 207 *Web:* www.sasrlink.com	Raleigh	NC	27615	919-787-5571	
Sharf Woodward & Associates Inc 5900 Sepulveda Blvd *Web:* www.swjobs.com	Sherman Oaks	CA	91411	818-989-2200	
Silverman McGovern Staffing & Recruiting 284 W Exchange St. *Web:* www.silvermanmcgovern.com	Providence	RI	02903	401-632-0580	
Sirius Technical Services Inc 6215 Rangeline Rd Ste 102 *Web:* www.siriustechnical.com	Theodore	AL	36582	251-443-1166	
Skillforce Inc 405 Williams Court Ste 100 *TF:* 866-581-8989 ■ *Web:* www.skillforce.com	Baltimore	MD	21220	866-581-8989	
SkillStorm Commercial Services LLC 6414 NW Fifth Way *Web:* www.skillstorm.com	Ft Lauderdale	FL	33309	954-566-4647	
Smart Staffing Service Inc 95 Washington St *Web:* www.smart-tek.net	Foxboro	MA	02035	508-698-9988	

Company	City	State	ZIP	Phone	Fax
Social Work p.r.n. Inc 10680 Barkley Ste 100 *Web:* www.socialworkprn.com	Overland Park	KS	66212	913-648-2984	
Sockwell Partners Inc 800 E Blvd Ste 200 *Web:* www.sockwell.com	Charlotte	NC	28203	704-372-1865	
Solutions Staffing 1237 Dublin Rd *Web:* www.solutionsstaffing.com	Columbus	OH	43215	614-732-5800	
Source One Personnel Inc Two Carnegie Rd. *Web:* www.source1-financial.com	Lawrenceville	NJ	08648	609-895-9700	
Source2 Inc 1245 W Fairbanks Ave Ste 400 *Web:* www.source2.com	Winter Park	FL	32803	407-893-3711	
SourcePoint Staffing LLC 1520 S 108th St. *Web:* www.sourcepointstaffing.com	Milwaukee	WI	53214	414-755-8600	
Southern Healthcare Agency Inc PO Box 320999 *Web:* www.southernhealthcare.com	Flowood	MS	39232	601-933-0037	
Sparks IT Solutions 1775 Greensboro Sta Pl Tower II Ste 300 *Web:* www.sparksitsolutions.com	Mclean	VA	22102	703-821-2650	
Spencer Gray LLC 2744 Villas Way *Web:* spencergray.com	San Diego	CA	92108	619-281-3900	
Spherion Canada One Queen St E Ste 901 *Web:* www.spherion.ca	Toronto	ON	M5C2W5	604-273-1440	
Sprocket Staffing Services 35 Colby Ave. *TF:* 800-269-1441 ■ *Web:* sprocketstaffing.com	Manasquan	NJ	08736	800-269-1441	
Staffing 360 Solutions Inc Ste 1526 641 Lexington Ave. *Web:* www.staffing360solutions.com	New York	NY	10022	212-634-6462	
Staffing Options & Solutions Inc 6249 S E St Ste E *Web:* www.staffingoptionsandsolutions.com	Indianapolis	IN	46227	317-791-2456	
Staffworks Group 20505 W 12 Mile Rd *TF:* 877-304-9690 ■ *Web:* staffworksgroup.com	Southfield	MI	48076	877-304-9690	
StartUpHire LLC 415 Church St Ste 203 *Web:* www.startuphire.com	Vienna	VA	22180	703-865-6350	
Steno Employment Services Inc 8560 Vineyard Ave Ste 208 *Web:* stenoinc.com	Rancho Cucamonga	CA	91730	909-476-1404	
Suh'dutsing Technologies LLC 600 North 100 East *Web:* www.suhdutsingllc.com	Cedar City	UT	84721	435-867-0604	
Synergy Employment Group. Inc 14 Greenfield Rd *Web:* www.synergyempgroup.com	Lancaster	PA	17602	717-824-4005	
Synergy Legal Staffing 500 E Morehead St Ste 101 *Web:* www.synergylegalstaffing.com	Charlotte	NC	28202	704-366-4540	
Tacoma Goodwill Industries 714 S 27th St. *Web:* tacomagoodwill.org	Tacoma	WA	98409	253-573-6500	
Talent Connections LLC 4805 W Village Way Ste 2401 *Web:* www.talentconnections.net	Smyrna	GA	30080	770-552-1550	
Talent Zoo Inc 1736 Defoor Pl Nw *Web:* www.talentzoo.com	Atlanta	GA	30318	404-607-1955	
TalentFusion Inc 343 Huntington Rd *Web:* www.talentfusion.com	Worthington	MA	01098	413-238-0138	
TalentLens Inc 19500 Bulverde Rd *TF:* 888-298-6227 ■ *Web:* talentlens.com	San Antonio	TX	78259	888-298-6227	
Targeted Job Fairs Inc 4441 Glenway Ave. *TF:* 800-695-1939 ■ *Web:* www.targetedjobfairs.com	Cincinnati	OH	45205	800-695-1939	
Taylor & Hill Inc 9941 Rowlett Rd *Web:* www.taylorandhill.com	Houston	TX	77075	713-941-2671	
Taylor Hodson Inc 133 W 19th St *Web:* www.taylorhodson.com	New York	NY	10011	212-924-8300	
TDB Communications Inc 10901 W 84 Ter Ste 105 *Web:* www.tdbcommunications.com	Lenexa	KS	66214	913-327-7400	
Teach Away Inc 147 Liberty St. *Web:* www.teachaway.com	Toronto	ON	M6K3G3	416-628-1386	
Teachers on Reserve LLC 604 Sonora Ave *Web:* teachersonreserve.com	Glendale	CA	91201	818-502-5800	
Tech-ed Services Inc 6121 Sebring Dr. *Web:* www.teservices.com	Columbia	MD	21044	410-772-5840	
Temps Plus Inc 268 N Lincoln Ave Ste 12 *Web:* www.tempsplus.com	Corona	CA	92882	951-549-8309	
Terry Neese Personnel Services 2709 W I 44 Service Rd *Web:* tneesepersonnel.com	Oklahoma City	OK	73112	405-942-8551	
ThinkBRQ LLC 20 Hicksville Rd Ste 7 *Web:* www.thinkbrq.com	Massapequa	NY	11758	516-541-3100	
Thomas Employment 8320 Tyler Blvd. *Web:* thomasemployment.com	Mentor	OH	44060	440-974-2010	
Tiffany Stuart Solutions Inc 390 Diablo Rd Ste 220 *Web:* www.go2dynamic.com	Danville	CA	94526	925-855-3600	
Time Services Inc 6422 Lima Rd. *Web:* www.timeservices.com	Fort Wayne	IN	46818	260-489-2020	
Titan Recruitment Solutions Ltd 355 Burrard St *Web:* titanrecruitment.com	Vancouver	BC	V6C2G8	604-687-6785	
TNS Employee Insights 65 Oakwood Rd *Web:* www.foresightint.com	Lake Zurich	IL	60047	847-726-4677	
Toberson Group, The 884 Woods Mill Rd Ste 101 *Web:* www.toberson.com	Ballwin	MO	63011	636-891-9774	
Topaz International Inc Three Regent St Ste 305 *Web:* topattorneys.com	Livingston	NJ	07039	973-597-0500	
Total Hr 2529 Foothill Blvd Ste 1 *Web:* www.totalhrmgmt.com	La Crescenta	CA	91214	818-248-0049	
Tpi Staffing Inc 21840 Northwest Fwy Ste E *Web:* www.tpistaffing.com	Cypress	TX	77429	281-890-2220	
Tradesmen International Inc 9760 Shepard Rd *Web:* www.tradesmeninternational.com	Macedonia	OH	44056	440-349-3432	

				Phone	Fax
TransTech IT Staffing 248 Spring Lk Dr *Web:* www.trans-tech.com	Itasca	IL	60143	630-250-8880	
Tri Starr Services of Pennsylvania Inc 2201 Oregon Pk *Web:* www.tristarrjobs.com	Lancaster	PA	17601	717-560-2111	
Tricom Technical Services 9240 Glenwood St *Web:* www.tricomts.com	Overland Park	KS	66212	913-652-0600	
Trillium Talent Resources Group 99 Sheppard Ave W *Web:* www.trilliumhr.com	Toronto	ON	M2N1M4	416-497-2624	
TriMech Services LLC 4461 Cox Rd Ste 302 *Web:* www.trimech.com	Glen Allen	VA	23060	804-257-9965	
TS Consulting International 20300 S Vermont Ave Ste 265 *Web:* www.tsconsult.com	Torrance	CA	90502	310-965-9810	
Tula International Inc PO Box 550628 *Web:* www.tulainternational.com	Atlanta	GA	30355	404-543-2835	
Turnkey Sports & Entertainment Inc Nine Tanner St *Web:* turnkeyse.com	Haddonfield	NJ	08033	856-685-1450	
Ultimate Placements LLC One Park Centre Ste 305A *Web:* www.ultimateplacements.com	Wadsworth	OH	44281	330-334-0285	
Unique Employment Services Inc 4646 Corona Dr Ste 100 *Web:* www.uniquehr.com	Corpus Christi	TX	78411	361-852-6392	
United Information Technologies Corp 2818 Corporate Pkwy *Web:* www.uitonline.com	Algonquin	IL	60102	847-658-1222	
United Personnel Services Inc 1331 Main St Ste 23 *Web:* www.unitedpersonnel.com	Springfield	MA	01103	413-736-0800	
United Staffing Systems Inc 130 William St Fifth Fl *Web:* www.unitedstaffing.com	New York	NY	10038	212-743-0200	
United Talent LLC 500 Leon Sullivan Way *Web:* www.unitedtalentwv.com	Charleston	WV	25301	304-556-1190	
Urpan Technologies Inc 341 Cobalt Way Ste 208 *Web:* www.urpantech.com	Sunnyvale	CA	94085	408-245-0006	
USAFact Inc 6240 Box Springs Blvd Ste B *Web:* www.usafact.com	Riverside	CA	92507	951-656-7800	
VanderHouwen & Associates Inc 6342 SW Macadam Ave *Web:* www.vanderhouwen.com	Portland	OR	97239	503-299-6811	
Vault Inc 132 W 31st St 17th Fl *Web:* www.vault.com	New York	NY	10001	212-366-4212	366-6117
Vector Technical Inc 38033 Euclid Ave Ste T-9 *Web:* www.vectortechnicalinc.com	Willoughby	OH	44094	440-946-8800	
VerisVisalign 920 S Broad St *Web:* www.verisassociates.com	Lansdale	PA	19446	215-393-5001	
VetJobs Inc PO Box 71445 *Web:* www.vetjobs.com	Marietta	GA	30007	770-993-5117	
Victory Search Group 20701 N Scottsdale Rd Ste 107-300 *Web:* www.victorysearchgroup.com	Scottsdale	AZ	85255	480-585-0073	
Visiont 2650 106th St Ste 215 *Web:* www.visiont-solutions.com	Urbandale	IA	50322	515-331-0010	
VISTA Staffing Solutions Inc 275 East 200 South *Web:* www.vistastaff.com	Salt Lake City	UT	84111	801-487-8190	
Walker Elliott 11200 Westheimer Ste 365 *Web:* www.walker-elliott.com	Houston	TX	77042	713-482-3750	
Waterstone Group Inc, The 1145 W Main Ave Ste 209 *Web:* www.waterstonegroup.net	De Pere	WI	54115	920-964-0333	
WCG International Consultants Ltd Five - 915 Ft St *Web:* www.wcgservices.com	Victoria	BC	V8V3K3	250-389-0699	
Westways Staffing Services Inc 2050 W Chapman Ave Ste 122 *Web:* www.westwaysstaffing.com	Orange	CA	92868	714-712-4150	
Wfa Staffing 9001 N 76th St Ste 201 *Web:* wfastaffing.com	Milwaukee	WI	53223	414-365-3651	
Wood Personnel Services 1139 Nw Broad St Ste 107 *Web:* wpscareers.com	Murfreesboro	TN	37129	615-890-8400	
Workforce Alliance Inc 1951 N Military Trl Ste D *Web:* www.careersourcepbc.com	West Palm Beach	FL	33409	561-340-1060	
Workplace Benefit Solutions LLC 1667 Elm St Ste 3 *Web:* www.workplacebenefitsolutions.com	Manchester	NH	03101	603-668-0400	
Workplace Group Inc, The 10 Ridgedale Ave *Web:* www.workplacegroup.com	Florham Park	NJ	07932	973-377-4665	
Workplace Staffing Services 650 Graham Rd Ste 106 *Web:* www.workplacestaff.com	Cuyahoga Falls	OH	44221	330-926-1880	
York Employment Services Inc 990 Ontario Blvd *Web:* www.yorkemployment.com	Ontario	CA	91761	909-581-0181	
Zachary Piper LLC 1521 Westbranch Dr Ste 400 *Web:* www.zacharypiper.com	Mclean	VA	22012	703-649-4001	

264 ENGINEERING & DESIGN

SEE ALSO Surveying, Mapping, Related Services p. 3201

				Phone	Fax
219 Design 67 E Evelyn Ave Ste 11 *Web:* www.219design.com	Mountain View	CA	94041	650-969-4219	
7 Layers Inc 15 Musick *Web:* www.7layers.com	Irvine	CA	92618	949-716-6512	
804 Technology LLC 5381 Hwy N Ste 201 *Web:* 804technology.com	Saint Charles	MO	63304	636-928-0330	
89 North Inc One Mill St Unit 285 *Web:* www.89north.com	Burlington	VT	05401	802-881-0302	
A & N Associates Inc 6716 Alexander Bell Dr Ste 118 *Web:* www.anassoc.com	Columbia	MD	21046	410-872-0050	
A Epstein & Sons International Inc 600 W Fulton St *Web:* www.epsteinglobal.com	Chicago	IL	60661	312-454-9100	454-9100
A H Lundberg Associates Inc 13201 Bel Red Rd *Web:* www.lundbergassociates.com	Bellevue	WA	98005	425-283-5070	
A&S Engineers Inc Main Link Business Park 10377 Stella Link *Web:* www.ainsworth-sherwood.com	Houston	TX	77025	713-942-2700	
A.C. Coy Co 395 Vly Brook Rd *Web:* www.accoy.com	Mcmurray	PA	15317	724-820-1820	
Aae Inc 1815 E Heim Ave Ste 100 *Web:* www.aaeinc.com	Orange	CA	92865	714-940-0100	
Aavispro LLC 113 Amberwood Ct *Web:* www.aavispro.com	Bethel Park	PA	15102	412-833-5444	
Abha Architects Inc 1621 N Lincoln St *Web:* abha.com	Wilmington	DE	19806	302-658-6426	
Abraxas Energy Consulting LLC 811 Palm St *Web:* www.abraxasenergy.com	San Luis Obispo	CA	93401	805-547-2050	
Academy Solutions Group LLC 6700 Alexander Bell Dr Ste 195 *Web:* www.asg-llc.com	Columbia	MD	21046	410-290-0871	
Acrion Technologies Inc 7777 Exchange St Ste 5 *Web:* www.acrion.com	Cleveland	OH	44125	216-573-1185	
Acta Inc 2790 Skypark Dr Ste 310 *Web:* www.actainc.com	Torrance	CA	90505	310-530-1008	
Acumen Enterprises Inc 1504 Falcon *Web:* acumen-enterprises.com	Desoto	TX	75115	972-572-0701	
Adams Rehmann & Heggan Assoc 850 S White Horse Pk *Web:* arh-us.com	Hammonton	NJ	08037	609-561-0482	
ADAPT Corp 1733 Woodside Rd Ste 220 *Web:* www.adaptsoft.com	Redwood City	CA	94061	650-306-2400	
Adc Engineering Inc 1226 Yeamans Hall Rd Ste F *Web:* www.adcengineering.com	Hanahan	SC	29410	843-566-0161	
ADD Inc 311 Summer St *Web:* www.addinc.com	Boston	MA	02210	617-234-3100	661-7118
ADEX Machining Technologies LLC 260 Feaster Rd *Web:* adexmt.com	Greenville	SC	29615	864-416-3100	
Adjeleian Allen Rubeli Ltd 75 Albert St Ste 1005 *Web:* www.aar.on.ca	Ottawa	ON	K1P5E7	613-232-5786	
Adobe Associates Inc 1220 N Dutton Ave *Web:* www.adobeinc.com	Santa Rosa	CA	95401	707-541-2300	
Advanced Design Corp 9447B Lorton Market St *Web:* www.advdesign.com	Lorton	VA	22079	703-550-5510	
Advanced Engineering & Environmental Services Inc 2016 S Washington St *Web:* www.ae2s.com	Grand Forks	ND	58201	701-746-8087	
Advanced Government Solutions Inc 16901 Melford Blvd Ste 101 *Web:* www.usgcinc.com	Bowie	MD	20715	240-260-4040	
Advanced Sciences & Technologies LLC 20 E Taunton *Web:* adv-sci-tech.com	Berlin	NJ	08009	856-719-9001	
Advanced Technology & Research Corp 6650 Eli Whitney Dr *Web:* www.atrcorp.com	Columbia	MD	21046	443-766-7888	
AECOM Technology Corp 555 S Flower St 37th Fl *Web:* www.aecom.com	Los Angeles	CA	90071	213-593-8000	593-8730
Aecometric Corp 374 Ohio Rd *Web:* aecometric.com	Richmond Hill	ON	L4C2Z9	905-883-9555	
Aegis Technologies Group Inc, The 410 Jan Davis Dr *Web:* aegistg.com	Huntsville	AL	35806	256-922-0802	
Aegis Technology Inc 3300 Westminster Ave *Web:* www.aegistech.net	Santa Ana	CA	92703	714-265-1238	
Aeplog Inc 12800 Middle Brook Rd	Germantown	MD	20874	301-528-2800	
Aero-Metric Inc 4020 Technology Pkwy *Web:* aerometric.com	Sheboygan	WI	53083	920-457-3631	
Affiliated Engineers Inc (AEI) 5802 Research Pk Blvd *Web:* www.aeieng.com	Madison	WI	53719	608-238-2616	238-2614
Agi Goldratt Institute 442 Orange St *Web:* www.goldratt.com	New Haven	CT	06511	203-624-9026	
Aging Aircraft Consulting LLC 64 Green St *Web:* www.agingaircraftconsulting.com	Warner Robins	GA	31093	478-923-8786	
Agnew Associates Inc 3223 S Loop 289 320 *Web:* www.agnewassociates.com	Lubbock	TX	79423	806-799-0753	

				Phone	Fax
AGRA Industries Inc 1211 W Water St	Merrill	WI	54452	715-536-9584	
Web: www.agraind.com					
AGUIRRE Corp 10670 N Central Expwy Sixth Fl	Dallas	TX	75231	972-788-1508	788-1583
Web: www.aguirreroden.com					
AHA Consulting Engineers Inc 24 Hartwell Ave Third Fl	Lexington	MA	02421	781-372-3000	
Web: www.aha-engineers.com					
AHJ Engineers PC 5418 N Eagle Rd Ste 140	Boise	ID	83713	208-323-0199	
Web: ahjengineers.com					
Ahtna Engineering Services LLC 110 W 38th Ave Ste 100	Anchorage	AK	99503	907-646-2969	
Web: www.ahtnaes.com					
AI Signal Research Inc 3411 Triana Blvd SW	Huntsville	AL	35805	256-551-0008	551-0099
Web: www.aisignal.com					
AIA Engineers Ltd 15310 Park Row	Houston	TX	77084	281-493-4140	
Web: www.aiaengineering.com					
Aillet/Fenner/Jolly/Mcclelland Inc 3003 Knight St Ste 120	Shreveport	LA	71105	318-425-7452	
Web: afjmc.com					
Aim Engineering & Surveying Inc 5300 Lee Blvd	Lehigh Acres	FL	33971	239-332-4569	
Web: aimengineering.com					
Ainley & Associates Ltd 280 Pretty River Pkwy	Collingwood	ON	L9Y4J5	705-445-3451	
Web: www.ainleygroup.com					
Air Diffusion Systems 3964 Grove Ave	Gurnee	IL	60031	847-782-0044	
Web: airdiffusion.com					
Aircon Engineering Inc Seven Williams St	Cumberland	MD	21502	301-722-7269	
Web: www.airconeng.com					
Airflow Sciences Corp 12190 Hubbard St	Livonia	MI	48150	734-525-0300	
Web: www.airflowsciences.com					
AirPol Inc 1000A Lake St Ste 103	Ramsey	NJ	07446	973-599-4400	428-6048
Web: www.airpol.com					
AKRF Inc 440 Pk Ave S	New York	NY	10016	212-696-0670	779-9721
TF: 800-899-2573 ■ Web: www.akrf.com					
Alan Plummer & Assoc Inc 1320 S University Dr	Fort Worth	TX	76107	817-806-1700	870-2536
Web: www.apaienv.com					
Albert Kahn Assoc Inc 7430 Second Ave Albert Kahn Bldg	Detroit	MI	48202	313-202-7000	202-7001
Web: www.albertkahn.com					
Alion Science & Technology 1750 Tysons Blvd Ste 1300	McLean	VA	22102	703-918-4480	250-0810*
*Fax Area Code: 913 ■ TF: 877-439-9227 ■ Web: www.alionscience.com					
Alisto Engineering Group Inc 2737 N Main St Ste 200	Walnut Creek	CA	94597	925-279-5000	
Web: www.alisto.com					
Allen & Hoshall Inc 1661 International Dr Ste 100	Memphis	TN	38120	901-820-0820	683-1001
Web: www.allenhoshall.com					
Alliance Support Partners Inc 5036 Commercial Cir Ste C	Concord	CA	94520	925-363-5382	
Web: asp-support.com					
Alliance Water Resources Inc 206 S Keene St	Columbia	MO	65251	573-874-8080	
Web: alliancewater.com					
Allied Power Group LLC 10131 Mills Rd	Houston	TX	77070	281-444-3535	
Web: www.alliedpg.com					
Alpine Engineering & Design Inc 111 W Canyon Crest Rd	Alpine	UT	84004	801-763-8484	
Web: www.alpineeng.com					
AM Kinney 150 E Fourth St Ste 6	Cincinnati	OH	45202	513-421-2265	
TF: 800-265-3682 ■ Web: www.amkinney.com					
Ambrose Engineering Inc W66n215 Commerce Ct	Cedarburg	WI	53012	262-377-7602	
Web: ambeng.com					
AMCS Corp 135 US Hwy 202-206 Ste 12	Bedminster	NJ	07921	908-719-6560	
Web: www.amcscorp.com					
American Consulting Inc 7260 Shadeland Stn	Indianapolis	IN	46256	317-547-5580	543-0270
Web: www.structurepoint.com					
American Engineering Testing Inc 550 Cleveland Ave N	Saint Paul	MN	55114	651-659-9001	659-1379
TF: 800-972-6364 ■ Web: www.amengtest.com					
Amico Group 2199 Blackacre Dr RR #1	Oldcastle	ON	N0R1L0	519-737-1577	
Web: www.amicoaffiliates.com					
Ammann & Whitney Inc 96 Morton St	New York	NY	10014	212-462-8500	929-5356
Web: www.ammann-whitney.com					
Amory Engineers PC PO Box 1768 25 Depot St	Duxbury	MA	ot St	781-934-0178	
Web: amoryengineers.com					
Ams Mechanical Systems Inc 140 E Tower Dr	Burr Ridge	IL	60527	630-887-7700	887-0770
TF: 800-794-5033 ■ Web: www.amsmechanicalsystems.com					
Amset Technical Consulting 1864 S Elmhurst Rd	Mount Prospect	IL	60056	847-229-1155	
Web: www.amsetusa.com					
Ana Consultants LLC 5000 Thompson Terr	Colleyville	TX	76034	817-335-9900	
Anamet Inc 26102 Eden Landing Rd	Hayward	CA	94545	510-887-8811	
Web: anametinc.com					
Anderson Engineering of New Prague Inc 20526 330th St	New Prague	MN	56071	507-364-7373	
Web: aenpi.com					
Anderson, Eckstein & Westrick Inc 51301 Schoenherr Rd	Shelby Township	MI	48315	586-726-1234	
Web: www.aewinc.com					
Antonucci & Assoc Arch & Engrs 50 Fifth Ave	Pelham	NY	10803	914-636-4000	
Web: www.aa-ae.com					
Anvil Corp 1675 W Bakerview Rd	Bellingham	WA	98226	360-671-1450	
TF: 877-412-6845 ■ Web: www.anvilcorp.com					
Apex Companies LLC 15850 Crabbs Branch Way Ste 200	Rockville	MD	20855	301-417-0200	975-0169
Web: www.apexenv.com					
Apollo Professional Svc 29 Stiles Rd Ste 302	Salem	NH	03079	866-277-3343	
TF: 866-277-3343 ■ Web: www.apollopros.com					
Applied Control Engineering Inc 700 Creek View Rd	Newark	DE	19711	302-738-8800	
Web: ace-net.com					
Applied Flow Technology Corp 2955 Professional Pl Ste 301	Colorado Springs	CO	80904	719-686-1000	
Web: www.aft.com					
Applied Math Modeling Inc 75 S Main St Ste 7 PO Box 144	Concord	NH	03301	603-369-3793	
Web: www.koolsim.com					
Applied Technology & Management Inc 5550 NW 111th Blvd	Gainesville	FL	32653	800-275-6488	375-0995*
*Fax Area Code: 352 ■ TF: 800-275-6488 ■ Web: www.appliedtm.com					
APS Technology Inc Seven Laser Ln	Wallingford	CT	06492	860-613-4450	284-7428*
*Fax Area Code: 203 ■ Web: www.aps-tech.com					
Aqua Science Engineers Inc 55 Oak Ct Ste 220	Danville	CA	94526	925-820-9391	
Web: aquascienceengineers.com					
Aquafor Beech Ltd 2600 Skymark Ave Bldg 6 Ste 202	Mississauga	ON	L4W5B2	905-629-0099	
Web: www.aquaforbeech.com					
Aqualified LLC 4550 Atwater Ct Ste 211	Buford	GA	30518	770-422-1349	
Web: www.aqualified.com					
Aquatech Consultancy Inc One Commercial Blvd Ste 201	Novato	CA	94949	415-884-2121	
Web: www.noleak.com					
Arcadis 630 Plz Dr Ste 200	Highlands Ranch	CO	80129	720-344-3500	344-3535
Web: www.arcadis-us.com					
Arcata Assoc Inc 2588 Fire Mesa St	Las Vegas	NV	89128	702-642-9500	968-2237
Web: www.arcataassoc.com					
Arcsine Engineering 950 Executive Way	Redding	CA	96002	530-222-7204	
Web: www.arc-sine.com					
Arctic Engineering Company Inc 8410 Minnesota St	Merrillville	IN	46410	219-947-4999	
Web: arcticengineering.com					
Ardmore Associates LLC 33 N Dearborn St Ste 1720	Chicago	IL	60602	312-795-1400	
Web: www.ardmoreassociates.com					
ARGO Systems LLC 1362 Mellon Rd Ste 100	Hanover	MD	21076	410-768-2444	
Web: www.argo-sys.com					
Argon Technologies Inc 4612 Wesley St	Greenville	TX	75401	903-455-5036	
Web: www.argontech.com					
Aria Group Inc 17395 Daimler St	Irvine	CA	92614	949-475-2915	
Web: www.aria-group.com					
Arias & Associates Inc 142 Chula Vista Dr	San Antonio	TX	78232	210-308-5884	
Web: www.ariasinc.com					
Arion Systems Inc 15040 Conference Ctr Dr Ste 200	Chantilly	VA	20151	703-815-1130	
Web: arionsys.com					
Arkel International Inc 1048 Florida Blvd	Baton Rouge	LA	70802	225-343-0525	336-1849
Web: www.arkel.com					
Arnold Sanders Consulting Engineers Inc 12651 Mcgregor Blvd Ste 103	Fort Myers	FL	33919	239-267-3666	
Web: arnoldsanders.com					
Arquitectonica International Corp 2900 Oak Ave Ste 1100	Miami	FL	33133	305-372-1812	372-1175
Web: arquitectonica.com					
Array Healthcare Facilities Solutions 2520 Renaissance Blvd Ste 110	King of Prussia	PA	19406	610-270-0599	270-0995
Web: www.array-architects.com					
Arro Consulting Inc 108 W Airport Rd	Lititz	PA	17543	717-569-7021	
Web: www.thearrogroup.com					
Arsee Engineers Inc 9715 Kincaid Dr	Fishers	IN	46037	317-594-5152	
Web: arsee-engineers.com					
Arthur Dyson & Assoc 764 P St Ste B	Fresno	CA	93721	559-486-3582	486-3582
Web: www.arthurdyson.com					
Arw Engineers Inc 1594 West Park Cir Ste 100	Ogden	UT	84404	801-782-6008	
Web: www.arwengineers.com					
ASCG Inc 300 W 31st Ave	Anchorage	AK	99503	907-339-6500	339-5327
Web: www.whpacific.com					
ASG Renaissance 22226 Garrison St	Dearborn	MI	48124	313-565-4700	565-4701
TF: 800-238-0890 ■ Web: www.asgren.com					
ASI Automation LLC 475 Applejack Ct	Sparta	MI	49345	616-887-8201	
Astorino 227 Fort Pitt Blvd	Pittsburgh	PA	15222	412-765-1700	765-1711
TF: 800-518-0464 ■ Web: Www.astorino.com					
Ata Engineering Inc 11995 El Camino Real Ste 200	San Diego	CA	92130	858-480-2000	
Web: ata-e.com					
Atlantic Testing Laboratories Ltd PO Box 29	Canton	NY	13617	315-386-4578	386-1012
Web: www.atlantictesting.com					
AtlasPower Inc 10 Futurity Pl	Tijeras	NM	87059	505-286-9625	
Web: www.atlaspower.com					
Atrenta Inc 2077 Gateway Pl Ste 300	San Jose	CA	95110	408-453-3333	453-3322
Web: www.atrenta.com					
ATSI Inc 415 Commerce Dr	Amherst	NY	14228	716-691-9200	
Web: atsi.com					
Atsim Inc 1825 George Ave Ste 1F	Annapolis	MD	21401	410-990-1711	
Austin Co 6095 Parkland Blvd	Cleveland	OH	44124	440-544-2600	544-2661
Web: www.theaustin.com					
Austrian & Assoc Inc 2530 Superior Ave Ste 202	Cleveland	OH	44114	216-621-6631	
Web: austrianassociates.com					
Automatan Inc 2911 Apache Dr	Plover	WI	54467	715-341-6501	
Web: www.automatan.com					
Automation Services & Controls Inc 16765 Park Cir Dr	Chagrin Falls	OH	44023	440-543-8146	
Web: www.ascdrives.com					
Avion Solutions Inc 4905 Research Dr NW	Huntsville	AL	35805	256-721-7006	
Web: avionsolutions.com					
Avionics Test & Analysis Corp 4540 E Hwy 20 Ste 6	Niceville	FL	32578	850-897-4553	897-4331
Web: avtest.com					

Phone | Fax

Axis Inc 3008 W Willow Knolls Dr, Peoria IL 61614 309-691-3988
Web: axis-inc.com

Ayres Assoc Inc 3433 Oakwood Hills Pkwy, Eau Claire WI 54701 715-834-3161 831-7500
Web: www.ayresassociates.com

Azimuth Inc
3741 Morgantown Industrial Park, Morgantown WV 26501 304-292-3700
Web: www.azimuthinc.com

Aztec Engineering Group Inc
4561 E Mcdowell Rd, Phoenix AZ 85008 602-454-0402
Web: aztec.us

Aztech Innovations Inc 805 Bayridge Dr, Kingston ON K7P1T5 613-384-9400
Web: www.aztechinc.com

B & W Engineering Corp 3303 Harbor Blvd, Costa Mesa CA 92626 714-540-9975
Web: b-w-engineering.com

B G Consultants Inc 4806 Vue Du Lac Pl, Manhattan KS 66503 785-537-7448 537-8793
Web: www.bgcons.com

B Jcc Inspections 1000 Banks Draw, Rexford MT 59930 406-882-4825
Web: www.bjccinspections.com

B W Smith Structural Engineers
12435 Ventura Ct, Studio City CA 91604 818-505-9409

B.R. Fries & Associates Inc 34 W 32nd St, New York NY 10001 212-563-3300
Web: www.brfries.com

BA Consulting Group Ltd
45 St Clair Ave W Ste 300, Toronto ON M4V1K9 416-961-7110
Web: www.bagroup.com

Bachelor Controls Inc 123 N Washington Ave, Sabetha KS 66534 785-284-3482
Web: bachelorcontrols.com

Ballard Group Inc, The
2525 S Wadsworth Blvd Ste 200, Lakewood CO 80227 303-988-4514
Web: www.theballardgroup.com

Ballinger 833 Chestnut St Ste 1400, Philadelphia PA 19107 215-446-0900 446-0901
Web: www.ballinger-ae.com

Bantu Inc 8133 Lessburg Pk Ste 250, Vienna VA 22182 703-766-4577 828-1726*
**Fax Area Code:* 888 ■ *Web:* www.bantu.com

Bar Engineering Company Ltd 6004 50 Ave, Lloydminster AB T9V2T9 780-875-1665
Web: www.bareng.ca

Bard Rao + Athanas Consulting Engineers Inc
10 Guest St The Arsenal on the Charles, Boston MA 02135 617-254-0016 924-9339
Web: www.brplusa.com

Barge Waggoner Sumner & Cannon
211 Commerce St Ste 600, Nashville TN 37201 615-254-1500 255-6572
Web: www.bargewaggoner.com

Barnett Engineering Ltd 7710 5 St Se Ste 215, Calgary AB T2H2L9 403-255-9544
Web: barnett-engg.com

Barr Engineering Co 4700 W 77th St, Minneapolis MN 55435 952-832-2600 832-2601
TF: 800-632-2277 ■ *Web:* www.barr.com

Bartlett & West Engineers Inc
1200 SW Executive Dr, Topeka KS 66615 785-272-2252
TF: 888-200-6464 ■ *Web:* www.bartwest.com

Barton & Loguidice PC 290 Elwood Davis Rd, Liverpool NY 13088 315-457-5200
Web: bartonandloguidice.com

Baskerville-Donovan Inc 449 W Main St, Pensacola FL 32502 850-438-9661
Web: baskervilledonovan.com

Bass, Nixon & Kennedy Inc
6310 Chapel Hill Rd 250, Raleigh NC 27607 919-851-4422
Web: www.bnkinc.com

Batta Environmental Associates Inc
Delaware Industrial Park 6 Garfield Way, Newark DE 19713 302-737-3376
Web: www.battaenv.com

Baxter & Woodman Inc 8678 Ridgefield Rd, Crystal Lake IL 60012 815-459-1260 455-0450
Web: baxterwoodman.com/

Bayer-Risse Engineering Inc 78 Rt 173 W, Hampton NJ 08827 908-735-2255
Web: bayer-risse.com

BBG-BBGM 1825 K Street NW Ste 300, Washington DC 20006 202-452-1644 452-1647
Web: www.bbg-bbgm.com

Bcc Engineering Inc 7300 N Kendall Dr Ste 400, Miami FL 33156 305-670-2350
Web: www.bcceng.com

Bcg Engineering & Consulting Inc
3012 26th St, Metairie LA 70002 504-454-3866
Web: www.bcgengineers.com

Beam Engineering For Advanced
809 S Orlando Ave, Winter Park FL 32789 407-629-1282
Web: www.beamco.com

Beam, Longest & Neff LLC
8126 Castleton Rd, Indianapolis IN 46250 317-849-5832
Web: www.b-l-n.com

Becher-Hoppe Associates Inc 330 Fourth St, Wausau WI 54403 715-845-8000
Web: www.becherhoppe.com

Bechtel Corp 50 Beale St, San Francisco CA 94105 415-768-1234 768-9038
Web: www.bechtel.com

Bechtel North America 3000 Post Oak Blvd, Houston TX 77056 713-235-2000 960-9031
Web: www.bechtel.com

Beckart Environmental Inc 6900 46th St, Kenosha WI 53144 262-656-7680
Web: beckart.com

BEI Engineering Group Inc Dba Banks Engineering
10511 Six Mile Cypress Pkwy, Fort Myers FL 33966 239-939-5490

Belcan Corp 10200 Anderson Way, Cincinnati OH 45242 513-891-0972
TF: 800-423-5226 ■ *Web:* www.belcan.com

Bellamy Management Services LLC
901 D St Sw Ste 1009, Washington DC 20024 202-863-2270
Web: www.bms-llc.com

Bellevue Mechanical Inc 1331 120th Ave NE, Bellevue WA 98005 425-453-2140
Web: www.bellevuemechanical.com

Belstar Inc 8408 Arlington Blvd Ste 200, Fairfax VA 22031 703-645-0280
Web: www.belstar.com

Belt Collins 2153 N King St Ste 200, Honolulu HI 96819 808-521-5361 538-7819
Web: www.beltcollins.com

Bender Engineering Inc 28 Hammond Ste D, Irvine CA 92618 949-458-7560
Web: www.maintstar.com

Benesch 205 N Michigan Ave Ste 2400, Chicago IL 60601 312-565-0450 565-2947
Web: web.benesch.com

Bennett & Pless Inc 3395 NE Expy Ne Ste 110, Atlanta GA 30341 678-990-8700
Web: www.bennett-pless.com

Berg-Oliver Associates Inc
14701 St Mary's Ln Ste 400, Houston TX 77079 281-589-0898
Web: www.bergoliver.com

Berger/ABAM Engineers Inc
33301 Ninth Ave S Ste 300, Federal Way WA 98003 206-431-2300 431-2250
Web: www.abam.com

Bergmann Assoc Inc
28 E Main St 200 1st Federal Plaza, Rochester NY 14614 585-232-5135 325-8303
TF: 800-724-1168 ■ *Web:* www.bergmannpc.com

Bermello Ajamil & Partners 2601 S Bayshore Dr, Miami FL 33133 305-859-2050 859-9638
Web: www.bamiami.com

Berryman & Henigar
11590 W Bernardo Ct Ste 100, San Diego CA 92127 858-451-6100 451-2846
TF: 800-272-9829 ■ *Web:* us.kompass.com

Bertsche Engineering Corp
711 Dartmouth Ln, Buffalo Grove IL 60089 847-537-8757
Web: www.bertsche.com

Beyer Blinder Belle Architects & Planners LLC
41 E 11th St Second Fl, New York NY 10003 212-777-7800 475-7424
Web: www.beyerblinderbelle.com

Beyond Hello Inc 3230 University Ave Ste 7, Madison WI 53705 608-232-1414
Web: beyondhello.com

Bezek-Durst-Seiser Inc 3330 C St Ste 200, Anchorage AK 99503 907-562-6076
Web: bdsak.com

Bfa Systems Inc 990 Explorer Blvd NW, Huntsville AL 35806 256-922-8791
Web: bfasystems.com

BHE Consulting 276 Libbey Industrial Pkwy, Weymouth MA 02189 781-340-5871
Web: www.bheconsulting.com

Biff Duncan Associates Inc
450 Shrewsbury Plz, Shrewsbury NJ 07702 732-876-0263
Web: www.biffduncan.com

Biggs Cardosa Assoc Inc 865 The Alameda, San Jose CA 95126 408-296-5515
Web: biggscardosa.com

Bills Engineering Inc
1124 Ft St Mall Ste 200, Honolulu HI 96813 808-792-2022
Web: billsengineering.com

Bionetics Corp, The
101 Production Dr Ste 100, Yorktown VA 23693 757-873-0900
TF: 800-868-0330 ■ *Web:* www.bionetics.com

Bionomic Industries Inc 777 Corporate Dr, Mahwah NJ 07430 201-529-1094
Web: bionomicind.com

Biopass Medical Systems Inc
9720 W Sample Rd, Coral Springs FL 33065 954-575-1588
Web: www.biopass.com

Birket Engineering Inc 162 W Plant St, Winter Garden FL 34787 407-290-2000
Web: www.birket.com

Bissell Professional Group Inc
3512 N Croatan Hwy, Kitty Hawk NC 27949 252-261-3266
Web: www.bissellprofessionalgroup.com

Bissett Resource Consultants Ltd
250 839 - 5 Ave SW, Calgary AB T2P3C8 403-294-1888
Web: www.bissettres.com

BIT Systems Inc 45200 Business Ct, Sterling VA 20166 703-742-7660
Web: www.bit-sys.com

BKF Engineers 255 Shoreline Dr Ste 200, Redwood City CA 94065 650-482-6300 482-6399
Web: www.bkf.com

BL Cos 355 Research Pkwy, Meriden CT 06450 203-630-1406 630-2615
TF: 800-301-3077 ■ *Web:* www.blcompanies.com

Blackwell Engineering 566 E Market St, Harrisonburg VA 22801 540-432-9555
Web: www.blackwellengineering.com

Blair, Church & Flynn Consulting Engineers
451 Clovis Ave Ste 200, Clovis CA 93612 559-326-1400
Web: www.bcf-engr.com

Bliss & Nyitray Inc
800 S Douglas Rd Ste 300, Coral Gables FL 33134 305-442-7086
Web: www.bniengineers.com

BMC Group Inc 600 First Ave Ste 300, Seattle WA 98104 206-516-3300
Web: www.bmcgroup.com

Bme Assocs 10 Liftbridge Ln E, Fairport NY 14450 585-377-7360
Web: www.bmepc.com

Bmt Fleet Technology Ltd 311 Legget Dr, Kanata ON K2K1Z8 613-592-2830
Web: www.fleetech.com

BNA Consulting Inc 635 S State St, Salt Lake City UT 84111 801-532-2196
Web: www.bnaconsulting.com

Bojo Engineering 473 Sapena Ct Ste 19, Santa Clara CA 95054 408-844-8211
Web: www.bojoinc.com

Bollinger, Lach & Associates Inc
333 Pierce Rd Ste 200, Itasca IL 60143 630-438-6400
Web: www.bollingerlach.com

Bolton & Menk Inc 1960 Premier Dr, Mankato MN 56001 507-625-4171 625-4177
Web: www.bolton-menk.com

Bombard Electric LLC 3570 W Post Rd, Las Vegas NV 89118 702-263-3570
Web: www.bombardelectric.com

BOS Solutions Ltd 635-8th Ave SW Ste 1200, Calgary AB T2P3M3 403-234-8103
Web: www.bos-solutions.com

Boston Engineering Corp 300 Bear Hill Rd, Waltham MA 02451 781-466-8010
Web: www.boston-engineering.com

Boston Industrial Consulting 89 Newbury St, Danvers MA 01923 978-739-0399
Web: bicinc.com

Boswell Engineering
330 Phillips Ave, South Hackensack NJ 07606 201-641-0770 641-1831
Web: www.boswellengineering.com

Boucher & James Inc
1456 Ferry Rd Bldg Ste 500, Doylestown PA 18901 215-345-9400
Web: bjengineers.com

Boudreau-Espley-Pitre Corp
1040 Lorne St Unit 3, Sudbury ON P3C4R9 705-675-7720
Web: www.bestech.com

Bow Engineering & Development Inc
1953 S Beretania St Ph A, Honolulu HI 96826 808-941-8853
Web: www.bowengineering.com

Bowser Morner Inc 1419 Miami St, Toledo OH 43605 419-691-4800
Web: www.bowser-morner.com

Company	City	State	ZIP	Phone	Fax
Bracewell Engineering Inc 6200 Harwood Ave *Web:* bracewellengineering.com	Oakland	CA	94618	510-654-5442	
Brander Construction Technology Inc 2357 W Mason St *Web:* brandercti.com	Green Bay	WI	54303	920-499-0260	
Braun Intertec Corp 11001 Hampshire Ave S *TF:* 800-279-6100 ■ *Web:* www.braunintertec.com	Bloomington	MN	55438	952-995-2000	995-2020
Breault Research Organization Inc 6400 E Grant Rd Ste 350 *Web:* www.breault.com	Tucson	AZ	85715	520-721-0500	
Bresslergroup 1216 Arch St 7th Fl *Web:* www.bresslergroup.com	Philadelphia	PA	19107	215-561-5100	561-5101
Bricmont Inc 500 Technology Dr Southpointe Industrial Pk *TF:* 888-274-2462 ■ *Web:* www.andritz.com	Canonsburg	PA	15317	724-746-2300	746-9420
Brierley Associates LLC 990 S Broadway Ste 222 *Web:* brierleyassociates.com	Denver	CO	80209	303-703-1405	
Brinjac Engineering Inc 114 N Second St Ste 1 *TF:* 877-274-6526 ■ *Web:* www.brinjac.com	Harrisburg	PA	17101	717-233-4502	233-0833
Broaddus & Associates Inc 1301 S Capital of Texas Hwy Ste A 302 *Web:* www.broaddusassociates.com	Austin	TX	78746	512-329-8822	
Brock Solutions Inc 86 Ardelt Ave *TF:* 877-702-7625 ■ *Web:* www.brocksolutions.com	Kitchener	ON	N2C2C9	519-571-1522	571-1721
Brooke Ocean Technology Ltd 11-50 Thornhill Dr *Web:* www.brooke-ocean.com	Dartmouth	NS	B3B1S1	902 468 2928	
Brooks & Sparks Inc 21020 Park Row Dr *Web:* www.brooksandsparks.com	Katy	TX	77449	281-578-9595	
Brown & Caldwell Consulting Engineers 201 N Civic Dr Ste 115 *Web:* www.brownandcaldwell.com	Walnut Creek	CA	94596	925-937-9010	937-9026
Brown & Gay Engineers Inc 10777 Westheimer Rd Ste 400 *Web:* www.browngay.com	Houston	TX	77042	281-558-8700	558-9701
Bruce E Brooks & Associates Inc 2209 Chestnut St *Web:* www.brucebrooks.com	Philadelphia	PA	19103	215-569-0400	
BRUNS-PAK Corp 999 New Durham Rd *Web:* bruns-pak.com	Edison	NJ	08817	732-248-4455	
BSA Life Structures 9365 Counselors Row *Web:* www.bsalifestructures.com	Indianapolis	IN	46240	317-819-7878	819-7288
BSK & Assoc 550 W Locust Ave Ste B *Web:* www.bskinc.com	Fresno	CA	93650	559-497-2880	
Buffalo Engineering PC 4245 Union Rd *Web:* buffaloengineering.com	Cheektowaga	NY	14225	716-633-5300	
Buford Goff & Assoc Inc 1331 Elmwood Ave *Web:* bgainc.com	Columbia	SC	29201	803-254-6302	
Building Leaders Inc 4619 N Ravenswood Ave Ste 200b *Web:* www.buildingleaders.com	Chicago	IL	60640	773-769-4409	
Bulldog Automation 653 Riverside St *Web:* bulldogautomation.com	Portland	ME	04103	207-772-9561	
Burgess & Niple Inc 5085 Reed Rd *TF:* 800-282-1761 ■ *Web:* www.burgessniple.com	Columbus	OH	43220	614-459-2050	451-1385
Burk-Kleinpeter Inc (BKI) 4176 Canal St *Web:* www.bkiusa.com	New Orleans	LA	70119	504-486-5901	483-6298
Burkett & Wong Engineers Inc 3434 Fourth Ave *Web:* burkett-wong.com	San Diego	CA	92103	619-299-5550	
Burkett Engineering Inc 105 E Robinson St Ste 501 *Web:* burkettengineering.com	Orlando	FL	32801	407-246-1260	
Burns & McDonnell 9400 Ward Pkwy *Web:* www.burnsmcd.com	Kansas City	MO	64114	816-333-9400	822-3412
Burns, Delatte & Mccoy Inc 320 Westcott St Ste 100 *Web:* www.bdmi-ce.com	Houston	TX	77007	713-861-3016	
Bursich Associates Inc 2129 E High St *Web:* www.bursich.com	Pottstown	PA	19464	610-323-4040	
Burtech Pipeline 102 Second St *Web:* www.burtechpipeline.com	Encinitas	CA	92024	760-634-2822	
Butler Fairman & Seufert Inc 8450 Wfield Blvd Ste 300 *Web:* bfsengr.com	Indianapolis	IN	46240	317-713-4615	
Byce & Associates Inc 487 Portage St *Web:* www.byce.com	Kalamazoo	MI	49007	269-381-6170	
Byers Engineering Co 6285 Barfield Rd 4th Fl *Web:* www.byers.com	Atlanta	GA	30328	404-843-1000	843-2000
C & S Companies (CSCOS) 499 Col Eileen Collins Blvd *TF:* 877-277-6583 ■ *Web:* www.cscos.com	Syracuse	NY	13212	315-455-2000	455-9667
C S Davidson Inc 38 N Duke St *Web:* csdavidson.com	York	PA	17401	717-846-4805	
C. P. Richards Construction Company Inc 2680 ABCO Ct *Web:* www.cprichardsconstruction.com	Lithonia	GA	30058	678-244-1450	
C2AE 725 Prudden St *Web:* www.c2ae.com	Lansing	MI	48906	517-371-1200	
C3 Corp 3300 E Venture Dr *Web:* www.c3ingenuity.com	Appleton	WI	54911	920-749-9944	
Cabem Technologies LLC Six Lasden Brothers Way *Web:* www.cabem.com	Franklin	MA	02038	508-541-3123	
Cable Aml Inc 2271 W 205th St Ste 101 *Web:* cableaml.com	Torrance	CA	90501	310-222-5599	
Calder Richards Consulting Engineers 634 South 400 West Ste 100 *Web:* crceng.com	Salt Lake City	UT	84101	801-466-1699	
Caldwell Richards Sorensen Inc 2060 East 2100 South *Web:* crsengineers.com	Salt Lake City	UT	84109	801-359-5565	
Callison Architecture Inc 1420 Fifth Ave Ste 2400 *Web:* www.callison.com	Seattle	WA	98101	206-623-4646	623-4625
Caloris Engineering LLC 8649 Commerce Dr *Web:* caloris.com	Easton	MD	21601	410-822-6900	
Calvin Giordano & Assoc Inc 1800 Eller Dr Ste 600 *Web:* cgasolutions.com	Fort Lauderdale	FL	33316	954-921-7781	
Campbell Grinder Co 1226 Pontaluna Rd *Web:* www.campbellgrinder.com	Spring Lake	MI	49456	231-798-6464	798-6466
Cannon Design 2170 Whitehaven Rd *TF:* 800-340-9511 ■ *Web:* www.cannondesign.com	Grand Island	NY	14072	716-773-6800	773-5909
Capital Excavation Co 2967 Business Park Dr *Web:* capitalexcavation.com	Buda	TX	78610	512-440-1717	440-0844
Caribou Road Services Ltd 5110 52nd Ave *Web:* www.caribouroads.com	Pouce Coupe	BC	V0C2C0	250-786-5440	
Carlo Gavazzi Inc 750 Hastings Ln *Web:* www.gavazzionline.com	Buffalo Grove	IL	60089	847-465-6100	
Carlson, Brigance & Doering Inc 5501 W William Cannon Dr *Web:* cbdeng.com	Austin	TX	78749	512-280-5160	
Carman-Dunne PC Two Lakeview Ave *Web:* carman-dunne.com	Lynbrook	NY	11563	516-599-5563	
Carollo Engineers 2700 Ygnacio Vly Rd Ste 300 *TF:* 800 523-5826 ■ *Web:* www.carollo.com	Walnut Creek	CA	94598	925-932-1710	930-0208
Carroll Engineering Corp 949 Easton Rd Ste 100 *Web:* www.carrollengineering.com	Warrington	PA	18976	215-343-5700	343-0875
Carter & Sloope Inc 6310 Peake Rd *Web:* cartersloope.com	Macon	GA	31210	478-477-3923	
CAS Inc PO Box 11190 *TF:* 800-729-8686 ■ *Web:* cascares.cas-inc.com	Huntsville	AL	35814	256-971-6126	922-4207
Casco Bay Engineering Inc 424 Fore St *Web:* cascobayengineering.com	Portland	ME	04101	207-842-2800	
Cashin Assoc PC 1200 Veterans Memorial Hwy *Web:* cashinassociates.com	Hauppage	NY	11788	631-348-7600	
Cass Construction Inc 1100 Wagner Dr *Web:* www.cassconstruction.com	El Cajon	CA	92020	619-590-0929	
Cates Engineering Ltd 7500 Iron Bar Ln Ste 209 *Web:* www.cateseng.com	Gainesville	VA	20155	571-261-9280	
Caviness Lambert Engineering LLC 25 E Court St Ste 202 *Web:* www.cl-e.com	Greenville	SC	29601	864-242-5844	
CDH Energy Corp 2695 Bingley Rd PO Box 641 *Web:* www.cdhenergy.com	Cazenovia	NY	13035	315-655-1063	
CDI Corporation 1717 Arch St 35th Fl *TF:* 866-472-2203 ■ *Web:* www.cdicorp.com	Philadelphia	PA	19103	215-569-2200	636-1177
CDM Smith Inc 50 Hampshire St *Web:* cdmsmith.com	Cambridge	MA	02139	617-452-6000	345-3901
CDR Maguire 8669 NW 36 St Ste 340 *Web:* www.cdrmaguire.com	Doral	FL	33166	786-235-8534	
Centra Technology Inc 25 Burlington Mall Rd *Web:* www.centratechnology.com	Burlington	MA	01803	781-272-7887	272-7836
Century Engineering Inc 10710 Gilroy Rd *Web:* www.centuryeng.com	Hunt Valley	MD	21031	443-589-2400	
Cerami & Associates Inc 404 Fifth Ave *Web:* www.ceramiassociates.com	New York	NY	10018	212-370-1776	
Ces Network Services Inc 920 County Rd 376 *Web:* www.cesnetser.com	Barksdale	TX	78828	972-241-3683	
Cesare Joseph a & Associates Geotechnical Engineeering Consu 7108 S Alton Way Bldg B *Web:* www.jacesare.com	Centennial	CO	80112	303-220-0300	
Ceso Inc 8534 Yankee St Ste 2B *Web:* cesoinc.com	Dayton	OH	45458	937-435-8584	
CET Engineering Services 1240 N Mountain Rd *Web:* ghd.com	Harrisburg	PA	17112	717-541-0622	
CH Guernsey & Co 5555 N Grand Blvd *Web:* www.guernsey.us	Oklahoma City	OK	73112	405-416-8100	416-8111
Chamlin & Assoc Inc 3017 Fifth St *Web:* chamlin.com	Peru	IL	61354	815-223-3344	
Charles Gojer & Associates Inc 11615 Forest Central Dr *Web:* www.cgojer.com	Dallas	TX	75243	214-340-1199	
Chastain-Skillman Inc 4705 Old Rd 37 *Web:* www.chastainskillman.com	Lakeland	FL	33813	863-646-1402	647-3806
Chaudhary & Assoc Inc 211 Gateway Rd W Ste 204 *Web:* chaudhary.com	Napa	CA	94558	707-255-2729	
Chehayeb & Assoc Inc 3702 W Azeele St *Web:* chehayeb.com	Tampa	FL	33609	813-876-1415	
Chemic Engineers & Constructors Inc 4820 Fm 2004 Rd *Web:* chemic.com	Hitchcock	TX	77563	409-986-6504	
Chemical & Industrial Engineering Inc 1930 Bishop Ln Ste 800 *Web:* www.cieng.com	Louisville	KY	40218	502-451-4977	451-9574
Chemstress Consultant Co 39 S Main St *Web:* www.chemstress.com	Akron	OH	44308	330-535-5591	535-1431
ChemTech Consultants Inc 1370 Washington Pk *Web:* www.chemtech88.com	Bridgeville	PA	15017	412-221-1360	221-5685
Chemtex International Inc 1979 Eastwood Rd *TF:* 877-243-6839 ■ *Web:* www.chemtex.com	Wilmington	NC	28403	910-509-4400	509-4567
Chester Valley Engineers Inc 83 Chestnut Rd *Web:* www.chesterv.com	Paoli	PA	19301	610-644-4623	

Company / Address	City	State	ZIP	Phone	Fax
Chevron Energy Solutions 345 California St 18th Fl *Fax Area Code: 925 ■ TF: 800-368-8357 ■ Web: www.chevronenergy.com	San Francisco	CA	94104	415-733-4500	790-3987*
Chiang Patel & Yerby 1820 Regal Row Ste 200 *Web:* www.cpyi.com	Dallas	TX	75235	214-638-0500	638-3723
Chilton Engineering & Surveying Ltd 421 Court St *Web:* farrwestengineering.com	Elko	NV	89801	775-738-2121	
CHL Systems 476 Meetinghouse Rd *Web:* www.chlsystems.com	Souderton	PA	18964	215-723-7284	723-9115
Chs Engineers Inc 12507 Bel Red Rd Ste 101 *Web:* www.chsengineers.com	Bellevue	WA	98005	425-637-3693	
CIMA Technologies 1035 Eastside Rd *Web:* cima-technologies.com	El Paso	TX	79915	915-775-1919	
Ciorba Group Inc 5507 N Cumberland Ave Ste 402 *Web:* www.ciorba.com	Chicago	IL	60656	773-775-4009	
Cirtec Medical Systems LLC 55 Deer Park Dr *Web:* cirtecmed.com	East Longmeadow	MA	01028	413-525-5700	
Citygate GIS LLC 125 Cathedral St *Web:* www.citygategis.com	Annapolis	MD	21401	410-295-3333	
Civil & Environmental Consultants Inc 333 Baldwin Rd *TF:* 800-365-2324 ■ *Web:* www.cecinc.com	Pittsburgh	PA	15205	412-429-2324	429-2114
Civil Consulting Group Pllc 1515 Heritage Dr *Web:* civilgroup.net	Mckinney	TX	75069	972-569-9193	
Civil Dynamics Inc 109a Route 515 *Web:* www.civildynamics.com	Stockholm	NJ	07460	973-697-3496	
Civil Site Design Group PLLC 630 Southgate Ave Ste A *Web:* www.civil-site.com	Nashville	TN	37203	615-248-9999	
Civil Works Engineers Inc 3151 Airway Ave *Web:* civilworksengineers.com	Costa Mesa	CA	92626	714-966-9060	
Civiltec Engineering Inc 118 W Lime Ave *Web:* www.civiltec.com	Monrovia	CA	91016	626-357-0588	
Civiltech Engineering Inc 450 E Devon Ave Ste 300 *Web:* civiltechinc.com	Itasca	IL	60143	630-773-3900	
Civtech Designs Inc 11012 Rhodenda Pl *Web:* civtechdesigns.com	Upper Marlboro	MD	20772	240-244-5517	
Ckgp/Pw & Assoc Inc 989 Chicago Rd *Web:* ckgppw.com	Troy	MI	48083	248-577-0400	
Clark Builders Ltd 4703 - 52 Ave *Web:* www.clarkbuilders.com	Edmonton	AB	T6B3R6	780-395-3300	
Clark Engineering Corp 621 Lilac Dr N *Web:* www.clark-eng.com	Minneapolis	MN	55422	763-545-9196	
Cleary Zimmermann Engineers Inc 1344 S Flores St *Web:* www.clearyzimmermann.com	San Antonio	TX	78204	210-447-6100	
Cleland Site Prep Inc PO Box 3822 *Web:* www.clelandsiteprep.com	Bluffton	SC	29910	843-987-0500	
Close Jensen & Miller PC 1137 Silas Deane Hwy	Wethersfield	CT	06109	860-563-9375	
Clough Harbour & Assoc (CHA) Three Winners Cir PO Box 5269 *TF:* 800-836-0817 ■ *Web:* www.cloughharbour.com	Albany	NY	12205	518-453-4500	458-1735
Clyde Bergemann Bachmann Inc 416 Lewiston Junction Rd *Web:* www.cbpg.com	Auburn	ME	04210	207-784-1903	
Cma Engineers 35 Bow St *Web:* cmaengineers.com	Portsmouth	NH	03801	603-431-6196	
CMG Environmental 67 Hall Rd *Web:* cmgenv.com	Sturbridge	MA	01566	774-241-0901	
Cmj Engineering & Testing Inc 7636 Pebble Dr *Web:* www.cmjengr.com	Fort Worth	TX	76118	817-284-9400	
Cng Engineering PLLC 1917 N New Braunfels Ave Ste 201 *Web:* cngengineering.com	San Antonio	TX	78208	210-224-8841	
COACT Inc 9140 Guilford Rd Ste N *Web:* www.coact.com	Columbia	MD	21046	301-498-0150	
Code Environmental Services Inc 400 Middlesex Ave *Web:* www.codeenvironmental.com	Carteret	NJ	07008	732-969-2700	
Coe & Van Loo Consultants Inc 4550 N 12th St *Web:* www.cvlci.com	Phoenix	AZ	85014	602-264-6831	
Coffey Geotechnics Inc 20 Meteor Dr *Web:* www.coffey.com.au	Etobicoke	ON	M9W1A4	416-213-1255	
Cohesionforce Inc 360C Quality Cir *Web:* cohesionforce.com	Huntsville	AL	35806	256-562-0600	
Colbert, Matz, Rosenfelt Inc 2835 Smith Ave Ste G *Web:* www.cmrengineers.com	Baltimore	MD	21209	410-653-3838	
Coler & Colantonio Inc 101 Accord Pk Dr *Web:* www.col-col.com	Norwell	MA	02061	781-982-5400	982-5490
Columbia Telecommunications Corp 10613 Concord St *Web:* www.ctcnet.us	Kensington	MD	20895	301-933-1488	
Columbus Engineering Consultants Ltd 840 Michigan Ave *Web:* ceceng.net	Columbus	OH	43215	614-228-3500	
Colvin Engineering Assoc Inc 244 West 300 North *Web:* cea-ut.com	Salt Lake City	UT	84103	801-322-2400	
Commonwealth Assoc Inc PO Box 1124 *Web:* www.cai-engr.com	Jackson	MI	49204	517-788-3000	788-3003
Compass Systems Inc 21471 Great Mills Rd *Web:* www.compass-sys-inc.com	Lexington Park	MD	20653	301-737-4640	

Company / Address	City	State	ZIP	Phone	Fax
Composite Technology Development Inc 2600 Campus Dr *Web:* www.ctd-materials.com	Lafayette	CO	80026	303-664-0394	
Composites Innovation Centre 158 Commerce Dr *Web:* www.compositesinnovation.ca	Winnipeg	MB	R3P0Z6	204-262-3400	
Compumation Inc 205 W Grand Ave *Web:* www.compumation.com	Bensenville	IL	60106	630-860-1921	
Computational Engineering International Inc 2166 N Salem St Ste 101 *Web:* ceisoftware.com	Apex	NC	27523	919-363-0883	
Comsearch 19700 Janelia Farm Blvd *Web:* www.comsearch.com	Ashburn	VA	20147	703-726-5500	726-5600
Con-Tech Carpentry LLC 366 W Fourth St *Web:* www.contechcarpentry.com	Eureka	MO	63025	636-938-4748	
Concept Systems Inc 1957 Fescue St Se *Web:* conceptsystemsinc.com	Albany	OR	97322	541-791-8140	
Concepts NREC 217 Billings Farm Rd *TF:* 888-299-8057 ■ *Web:* www.conceptsnrec.com	White River Junction	VT	05001	802-296-2321	296-2325
Coneco Engineers & Scientists Inc Four First St *Web:* www.coneco.com	Bridgewater	MA	02324	508-697-3191	
Conewago Enterprises Inc 660 Edgegrove Rd *Web:* www.conewago.com	Hanover	PA	17331	717-632-7722	
Configure One Inc 900 Jorie Blvd Ste 190 *Web:* www.configureone.com	Oak Brook	IL	60523	630-368-9950	
Connexsys Engineering Inc 3075 Research Dr *Web:* www.connexsysinc.com	Richmond	CA	94806	510-243-2050	
Control Point Corp 110 Castilian Dr Ste 200 *Web:* control-pt.com	Goleta	CA	93117	805-882-1884	
Converse Consultants 222 E Huntington Dr Ste 211 *Web:* www.converseconsultants.com	Monrovia	CA	91016	626-930-1200	930-1212
Cook Coggin Engineers Inc 703 Crossover Rd *Web:* cookcoggin.com	Tupelo	MS	38801	662-842-7381	
Cook Flatt & Strobel Engineers 9229 Ward Pkwy *Web:* cfse.com	Kansas City	MO	64114	816-333-4477	
Coon Engineering Inc (CEI) 2832 W Wilshire Blvd *Web:* www.coonengineering.com	Oklahoma City	OK	73116	405-842-0363	842-0364
Cooper Carry Inc 191 Peachtree St NE Ste 2400 *Web:* www.coopercarry.com	Atlanta	GA	30303	404-237-2000	237-0276
Cooper Zietz Engineers Inc 620 S W Fifth Ave Ste 1225 *Web:* www.coopercm.com	Portland	OR	97204	503-253-5429	
Corestates Inc 4191 Pleasant Hill Rd *Web:* www.core-eng.com	Duluth	GA	30096	770-242-9550	
Corgan Assoc Inc 401 N Houston St *Web:* www.corgan.com	Dallas	TX	75202	214-748-2000	
Corrosion Probe Inc 12 Industrial Park Rd *Web:* www.cpiengineering.com	Centerbrook	CT	06409	860-767-4402	
Corrpro Cos Inc 1055 W Smith Rd *TF:* 800-443-3516 ■ *Web:* www.corrpro.com	Medina	OH	44256	330-723-5082	722-7654
Costello Inc 9990 Richmond Ave Ste 450 *Web:* www.costelloinc.com	Houston	TX	77042	713-783-7788	
Costich Engineering & Land Surveying PC 217 Lake Ave *Web:* costich.com	Rochester	NY	14608	585-458-3020	
Cox & Dinkins Inc 724 Beltline Blvd *Web:* coxanddinkins.com	Columbia	SC	29205	803-254-0518	
CPH Engineers 500 W Fulton St PO Box 2808 *Fax Area Code: 407 ■ *TF:* 866-609-0688 ■ *Web:* www.cphengineers.com	Sanford	FL	32771	866-609-0688	330-0639*
Craig Test Boring Company Inc 5435 Harding Hwy *Web:* craigtestboring.com	Mays Landing	NJ	08330	609-625-4862	
Craven Thompson & Associates Inc 3563 NW 53rd St *Web:* www.craventhompson.com	Fort Lauderdale	FL	33309	954-739-6400	
Crawford Consulting Services Inc 239 Highland Ave *Web:* www.crawfordconsultingservices.com	East Pittsburgh	PA	15112	412-823-0400	
Crawford Murphy & Tilly Inc 2750 W Washington St *Web:* www.cmtengr.com	Springfield	IL	62702	217-787-8050	787-8054
Crenshaw Consulting Engineers Inc 3516 Bush St Ste 200 *Web:* www.crenshawconsulting.com	Raleigh	NC	27609	919-871-1070	
Crew Engineers Inc 1250 Rt 23 N *Web:* crewengineers.com	Butler	NJ	07405	973-492-3300	
Crist Engineers Inc 1405 N Pierce St *Web:* cristengineers.com	Little Rock	AR	72207	501-664-1552	
Cromwell Architect Engineers Inc 101 S Spring St *Web:* www.cromwell.com	Little Rock	AR	72201	501-372-2900	
Crossey Engineering Ltd 2255 Sheppard Ave E Ste E-331 *Web:* www.cel.ca	Toronto	ON	M2J4Y1	416-497-3111	
Crossroad Engineers 3417 Sherman Dr *Web:* www.crossroadengineers.com	Beech Grove	IN	46107	317-780-1555	
Crystal Engineering Solutions Inc 645 Executive Dr *Web:* www.crystaleng.com	Troy	MI	48083	248-588-1390	
CSA Engineering Inc 2565 Leghorn St *Web:* www.csaengineering.com	Mountain View	CA	94043	650-210-9000	
CSI Technologies LLC 2202 Oil Ctr Ct *Web:* www.csi-tech.net	Houston	TX	77073	281-784-7990	
CSS-Dynamac Corp 10301 Democracy Ln Ste 300 *TF:* 800-888-4612 ■ *Web:* www.css-dynamac.com	Fairfax	VA	22030	703-691-4612	691-4615
CT Consultants Inc 8150 Sterling Ct *TF:* 800-925-0988 ■ *Web:* www.ctconsultants.com	Mentor	OH	44060	440-951-9000	951-7487

Company	City	State	ZIP	Phone	Fax
CTA Architects Engineers 13 N 23rd St *Web:* www.ctagroup.com	Billings	MT	59101	406-248-7455	248-3779
Ctl Engineering Inc PO Box 44548 *TF:* 866-366-3832 ■ *Web:* www.ctleng.com	Columbus	OH	43204	614-276-8123	276-6377
CTL/Thompson Inc 1971 W 12th Ave *Web:* www.ctlthompson.com	Denver	CO	80204	303-825-0777	825-4252
Cubex Inc 9794 Charlotte Hwy *Web:* cubexinc.com	Fort Mill	SC	29707	803-547-0748	
Curtain Wall Design & Consulting Inc 8070 Park Ln Ste 400 *Web:* cdc-usa.com	Dallas	TX	75231	972-437-4200	
Custom Engineering Inc 12760 E Us Hwy 40 *Web:* www.customengr.com	Independence	MO	64055	816-350-1473	
D & S Engineering Inc 70 Spring St *Web:* dsenginc.com	Millinocket	ME	04462	207-723-6871	
D. Crupi & Sons Ltd 85 Passmore Ave Agincourt *Web:* www.crupigroup.com	Toronto	ON	M1V4S9	416-291-1986	
D3 Technical Services LLC 4600 W Kearney Ste 100 *Web:* www.d3tech.net	Springfield	MO	65803	417-831-7171	
D3 Technologies Inc 4838 Ronson Ct *TF:* 866-487-2365 ■ *Web:* www.d3tech.com	San Diego	CA	92111	858-571-1685	571-8563
Daniel Consultants Inc 8950 State Rt 108 229 *Web:* www.danielconsultants.com	Columbia	MD	21045	410-995-0090	
Dannenbaum Engineering Corp 3100 W Alabama *Web:* www.dannenbaum.com	Houston	TX	77098	713-520-9570	
Darr & Collins LLC 1425 NW 150th St *Web:* darrcollins.com	Edmond	OK	73013	405-285-2400	
Dataline LLC 7918 Jones Branch Dr Ste 650 *TF:* 800-666-9858 ■ *Web:* www.dataline.co.uk	McLean	VA	22102	703-847-7412	847-7419
Datasyst Engineering & Testing Services Inc S14W33511 Hwy 18 *Web:* www.datasysttest.com	Delafield	WI	53018	262-968-4003	
Datum Engineers Inc 6516 Forest Park Rd *Web:* datumengineers.com	Dallas	TX	75235	214-358-0174	
Datum Inspection Services Inc 21442 N 20th Ave *Web:* datum-inspection.com	Phoenix	AZ	85027	602-997-1340	
David Evans & Assoc Inc (DEA) 2100 SW River Pkwy *TF:* 800-721-1916 ■ *Web:* www.deainc.com	Portland	OR	97201	503-223-6663	223-2701
David L Adams Assoc Inc 1536 Ogden St	Denver	CO	80218	303-455-1900	
David Stires Assoc LLC 678 Us Hwy 202/206 N *Web:* dastires.com	Bridgewater	NJ	08807	908-252-7000	
Davis & Floyd Inc 1319 Hwy 72 221 E *Web:* www.davisfloyd.com	Greenwood	SC	29649	864-229-5211	229-7844
Davroc & Associates Ltd 2051 Williams Pkwy Units 20 and 21 *Web:* www.davroc.com	Brampton	ON	L6S5T4	905-792-7792	
Dayton T Brown Inc 1175 Church St *TF:* 800-232-6300 ■ *Web:* www.daytontbrown.com	Bohemia	NY	11716	631-589-6300	589-0046
DC Engineering PC 440 E Corporate Dr Ste 103 *Web:* www.dcengineering.net	Meridian	ID	83642	208-288-2181	
DCS Corp 6909 Metro Park Dr Ste 500 *Web:* dcscorp.com	Alexandria	VA	22310	571-227-6000	
Defense Group Inc 307 Annandale Rd Ste 110 *TF:* 877-233-5789 ■ *Web:* www.defensegroupinc.com	Falls Church	VA	22042	703-532-0802	532-0806
Degenkolb Engineers 225 Montgomery Ste 500 *Web:* www.degenkolb.com	San Francisco	CA	94104	415-392-6952	981-3157
Deighton Associates Ltd 223 Brock St N Unit 7 *Web:* www.deighton.com	Whitby	ON	L1N4H6	905-697-2644	
Delco Electric Inc One Nw 132Nd St *Web:* www.delcoelectric.com	Oklahoma City	OK	73114	405-302-0099	
Delex Systems Inc 1953 Gallows Rd Ste 700 *Web:* www.delex.com	Vienna	VA	22182	703-734-8300	893-5338
Delixus Inc 1160 Ridgemont Pl *Web:* www.delixus.com	Concord	CA	94521	925-672-2623	
Delon Hampton & Assoc Chartered 900 Seventh St NW Ste 800 *Web:* www.delonhampton.com	Washington	DC	20001	202-898-1999	371-2073
Delphinus Engineering Inc 650 Baldwin Tower *Web:* www.delphinus.com	Eddystone	PA	19022	610-874-9160	
Deltawrx 21700 Oxnard St Ste 530 *Web:* www.deltawrx.com	Woodland Hills	CA	91367	818-227-9300	
Depotstar Inc 6180 140th Ave NW *Web:* www.depotstar.com	Ramsey	MN	55303	763-506-9990	
Derek Engineering Inc 2800 Constant Comment Pl *Web:* www.derekengineering.com	Louisville	KY	40299	502-266-0041	
Desai Nasr Consulting Engineers Inc 6765 Daly Rd *Web:* www.desainasr.com	West Bloomfield	MI	48322	248-932-2010	
Design 3 Engineering Inc 1211 24th St W Ste 7	Billings	MT	59102	406-245-5599	
Design Integrity Inc 1155 W Fulton Market Second Fl *Web:* www.designintegrity.com	Chicago	IL	60607	312-942-0602	
Design Systems Inc 38799 W 12 Mile Rd	Farmington Hills	MI	48331	248-489-4300	
Designers Midwest 9563 Montgomery Rd Ste 2 *Web:* www.designeers.com	Cincinnati	OH	45242	513-793-6670	
DesignworksUSA Inc 2201 Corporate Ctr Dr *Web:* designworksusa.com	Newbury Park	CA	91320	805-499-9590	
Deteq Services 1771 Westborough Dr *Web:* www.deteqservices.com	Katy	TX	77449	281-828-3030	
Device Engineering Inc 385 E Alamo Dr *Web:* www.deiaz.com	Chandler	AZ	85225	480-303-0822	
Dewalt Corp 1930 22nd St *Web:* dewaltcorp.com	Bakersfield	CA	93301	661-323-4600	
Dewberry & Davis 8401 Arlington Blvd *Web:* www.dewberry.com	Fairfax	VA	22031	703-849-0100	849-0100
Dexter Wilson Engineering 2234 Faraday Ave *Web:* www.dwilsoneng.com	Carlsbad	CA	92008	760-438-4422	
DfR Solutions LLC 5110 Roanoke Pl Ste 101 *Web:* www.dfrsolutions.com	College Park	MD	20740	301-474-0607	
Dfw Consulting Group Inc 1616 Corporate Ct *Web:* dfwcgi.com	Irving	TX	75038	972-929-1199	929-4691
Diamond Z Engineering Inc 5670 State Rd *Web:* diamondzengineering.com	Cleveland	OH	44134	440-842-6501	
Dias, Clifford Pe PC Seven Dey St *Web:* www.diaseng.com	New York	NY	10007	212-608-4811	
Dibble & Associates Consulting 7500 N Dreamy Draw Dr Ste 200 *Web:* www.dibblecorp.com	Phoenix	AZ	85020	602-957-1155	
Dileonardo International Inc 2348 Post Rd *Web:* dileonardo.com	Warwick	RI	02886	401-732-2900	
Dimension Engineering LLC 899 Moe Dr Ste 21 *Web:* dimensionengineering.com	Akron	OH	44310	330-634-1430	
Dimension Group I LP, The 10755 Sandhill Rd *Web:* www.dimensiongrp.com	Dallas	TX	75238	214-343-9400	
Dimitri J Ververelli Inc 211 N 13th St *Web:* djvinc.com	Philadelphia	PA	19107	215-496-0000	
Diversified Technology Consultants Inc (DTC) 2321 Whitney Ave Ste 301 *Web:* www.teamdtc.com	Hamden	CT	06518	203-239-4200	234-7376
Dixon Assoc Engineering LLC 313 E Jimmie Leeds Rd 2nd Fl *Web:* dixonassociates.com	Galloway	NJ	08205	609-652-7131	
DLR Group Inc 6457 Frances Ste 200 *Web:* www.dlrgroup.com	Omaha	NE	68106	402-393-4100	393-8747
DLZ Corp 6121 Huntley Rd *TF:* 800-336-5352 ■ *Web:* www.dlzcorp.com	Columbus	OH	43229	614-888-0040	436-0161
DMK Assoc Inc 435 Commercial Ct	Venice	FL	34292	941-412-1293	
Dobil Laboratories Inc 727 Butler St *Web:* dobil.com	Pittsburgh	PA	15223	412-782-3399	
Doerfer Engineering Corp PO Box 816 *TF:* 877-483-4700 ■ *Web:* www.doerfer.com	Waverly	IA	50677	877-483-4700	
Dominion Engineering Associates Inc 5110 Southpoint Pkwy *Web:* www.dea-inc.net	Fredericksburg	VA	22407	540-710-9339	
Don Ray George & Assoc Inc 1604 Rio Grande St *Web:* drgainc.com	Austin	TX	78701	512-476-1245	476-6025
Donald W Mcintosh Associates 2200 N Park Ave *Web:* dwma.com	Winter Park	FL	32789	407-644-4068	
Donofrio Kottke & Assoc Inc 7530 Wward Way *Web:* donofrio.cc	Madison	WI	53717	608-833-7530	
Doucet & Associates Inc 7401B Hwy 71 W Ste 160 *Web:* www.doucetengineers.com	Austin	TX	78735	512-583-2600	
Dowl LLC 4041 B St *Web:* www.dowlhkm.com/	Anchorage	AK	99503	907-562-2000	
Downes Associates Inc 2129 Northwood Dr *Web:* www.downesassociates.com	Salisbury	MD	21801	410-546-4422	
DPIS Engineering LLC 1600 E Hufsmith Rd *Web:* www.dpis.ws	Tomball	TX	77375	281-351-0048	
Dubois & King Inc 28 N Main St *Web:* www.dubois-king.com	Randolph	VT	05060	802-728-3376	
Dudek 605 Third St *Web:* dudek.com	Encinitas	CA	92024	760-942-5147	
Duffner Engineering 50 W Summit Dr *Web:* duffnerengineering.com	Emerald Hills	CA	94062	650-701-1055	
Dyer Riddle Mills & Precourt Inc (DRMP) 941 Lk Baldwin Ln *TF:* 800-375-3767 ■ *Web:* www.drmp.com	Orlando	FL	32814	407-896-0594	896-4836
Dynamic Civil Solutions Inc 2210 Second Ave N Ste 1010 *Web:* dcseng.com	Birmingham	AL	35203	205-358-7256	
Dynamic Research Inc 355 Van Ness Ave Ste 200 *Web:* www.dynres.com	Torrance	CA	90501	310-212-5211	
Dynamix Engineering Ltd 855 Grandview Ave *Web:* dynamix-ltd.com	Columbus	OH	43215	614-443-1178	
DynaTen Corp 4375 Diplomacy Rd *Web:* www.dynaten.com	Fort Worth	TX	76155	817-616-2200	
E. L. Robinson Engineering Co 5088 Washington St W *Web:* www.elrobinson.com	Charleston	WV	25313	304-776-7473	
E.S. Fox Ltd 9127 Montrose Rd *Web:* www.esfox.com	Niagara Falls	ON	L2E7J9	905-354-3700	
E2 Consulting Engineers Inc 450 E 17th Ave Ste 200 *TF:* 888-772-9773 ■ *Web:* www.e2.com	Denver	CO	80203	303-232-9800	238-8972
EADS Group 1126 Eigth Ave *TF:* 800-626-0904 ■ *Web:* www.eadsgroup.com	Altoona	PA	16602	814-944-5035	944-4862
Eagle Engineering Inc 2013 Van Bruen Ave *Web:* www.eagleonline.net	Indian Trail	NC	28079	704-882-4222	
EarthRes Group Inc 6912 Old Easton Rd PO Box 468 *Web:* www.earthres.com	Pipersville	PA	18947	215-766-1211	
EBA Engineering Inc 4813 Seton Dr *Web:* ebaengineering.com	Baltimore	MD	21215	410-358-7171	
Ecm International 404 Executive Ctr Blvd *Web:* ecmintl.com	El Paso	TX	79902	915-351-1900	351-1908
Eco Engineering LLC 11815 Hwy Dr Ste 600 *Web:* www.ecoengineering.com	Cincinnati	OH	45241	513-985-8300	

	City	State	Zip	Phone	Fax
ECS Corporate Services LLC 14026 Thunderbolt Pl Ste 300 *Fax Area Code: 541 ■ *Web:* www.ecslimited.com	Chantilly	VA	20151	571-299-6000	474-2479*
Edm Services Inc 4100 Guardian St. *Web:* edmsvc.com	Simi Valley	CA	93063	805-527-3300	
EI Assoc Eight Ridgedale Ave *Web:* www.eiassociates.com	Cedar Knolls	NJ	07927	973-775-7777	775-7770
Eichleay Engineers Inc of California 1390 Willow Pass Rd Ste 600 *Web:* www.eichleay.com	Concord	CA	94520	925-689-7000	689-7006
Einhorn Yaffee Prescott Architecture & Engineering PC NanoFab E 257 Fuller Rd First Fl *Web:* www.eypaedesign.com	Albany	NY	12203	518-795-3800	
Eisman & Russo Inc 6455 Powers Ave *Web:* eismanandrusso.com	Jacksonville	FL	32217	904-733-1478	636-8828
EJM Engineering Inc 411 S Wells St Ste 800 *Web:* www.ejmengineering.com	Chicago	IL	60607	312-922-1700	
Electric Power Systems Inc 3305 Arctic Blvd Ste 201 *Web:* www.epsinc.com	Anchorage	AK	99503	907-522-1953	
Elite Electronic Engineering Inc 1516 Centre Cir *Web:* www.elitetest.com	Downers Grove	IL	60515	630-495-9770	
Ellicom Inc 905 Rue De Nemours *Web:* ellicom.com	Quebec	QC	G1H6Z5	418-623-8804	
ELM Engineering Inc 900 Center Pk Dr *Web:* elmengr.com	Charlotte	NC	28217	704-335-0396	
Elwer Engineering Services 11033 Aurora Ave *Web:* www.eescompanies.com	Urbandale	IA	50322	515-276-2588	
Emats Inc 480 Claypool Hill Mall Rd *Web:* www.emats-inc.com	Cedar Bluff	VA	24609	276-963-8888	
Emc-tempest Technical Support Services 2190 E Winston Rd *Web:* www.emctempest.com	Anaheim	CA	92806	714-778-1726	
EMCOR Services Betlem 704 Clinton Ave South *Web:* www.emcorbetlem.com	Rochester	NY	14620	585-271-5500	
Emjay Engineering & Construction Company Inc 1706 Whitehead Rd *Web:* emjaycons.com	Baltimore	MD	21207	410-298-2000	
EMK Consultants of Florida Inc 7815 N Dale Mabry Hwy *Web:* www.emkfla.com	Tampa	FL	33614	813-931-8900	
Emprise Corp 3900 Kennesaw 75 Pkwy N W Ste 125 *Web:* www.emprise-usa.com	Kennesaw	GA	30144	770-425-1420	
Emtec Consultants, Professional Engineers PLLC 3555 Veterans Memorial Hw *Web:* www.emtec-engineers.com	Ronkonkoma	NY	11779	631-981-3990	
EN Engineering 28100 Torch Pkwy Ste 400 *Web:* www.enengineering.com/	Warrenville	IL	60517	630-353-4000	353-7777
Encon International 7307 Remcon Cir 101 *Web:* www.enconinternational.com	El Paso	TX	79912	915-833-3740	
Encotech Engineering Cnsltnts 8500 Bluffstone Cv *Web:* www.encotechengineering.com	Austin	TX	78759	512-338-1101	
Encur Inc 200 Division St *Web:* encur.com	Keyport	NJ	07735	732-264-2098	
EnerCom Inc 800 18th St Ste 200 *Web:* www.enercominc.com	Denver	CO	80264	303-296-8834	
Enercon Services Inc 5100 E Skelly Dr Ste 450 *Web:* www.enercon.com	Tulsa	OK	74135	918-665-7693	665-7232
Energy Engineering Assoc Inc 6615 Vaught Ranch Rd Ste 200	Austin	TX	78730	512-744-4400	
ENERGYneering Solutions Inc 15820 Barclay Dr *Web:* energyneeringsolutions.com	Sisters	OR	97759	541-549-8766	
Enertech Consultants Inc 494 Salmar Ave 200 *Web:* enertech.net	Campbell	CA	95008	408-866-7266	
Engeo Inc 2010 Crow Canyon Pl Ste 250 *Web:* engeo.com	San Ramon	CA	94583	925-866-9000	
Engineering & Environmental Consultants Inc 4625 E Ft Lowell Rd *Web:* www.eec-info.com	Tucson	AZ	85712	520-321-4625	321-0333
Engineering Planning & Management Inc 959 Concord St *Web:* www.epm-inc.com	Framingham	MA	01701	508-875-2121	879-3291
Ennead Architects 320 W 13 St *Web:* www.ennead.com	New York	NY	10014	212-807-7171	807-5917
Enovity Inc 100 Montgomery St *Web:* enovity.com	San Francisco	CA	94104	415-974-0390	
Enroute Computer Solutions Inc 2511 Fire Rd Ste A4 *Web:* enroute-computer.com	Egg Harbor Township	NJ	08234	609-569-9255	
ENSCO Inc 3110 Fairview Pk Dr Ste 300 *TF:* 800-367-2682 ■ *Web:* www.ensco.com	Falls Church	VA	22042	703-321-9000	321-7863
Envar Services Inc 505 Milltown Rd *Web:* www.envarservices.com	North Brunswick	NJ	08902	732-296-9601	
Envieta LLC 7175 Columbia Gateway Dr Ste D *Web:* envieta.com	Columbia	MD	21046	410-290-1136	
Envirocon Inc 101 International Dr *Web:* www.envirocon.com	Missoula	MT	59808	406-523-1150	
Envisioneering Inc 5904 Richmond Hwy Ste 300 *Fax Area Code: 703 ■ *Web:* www.envisioneeringinc.com	Alexandria	VA	22303	571-483-4100	317-1970*
Eoa Inc 1410 Jackson St *Web:* eoainc.com	Oakland	CA	94612	510-832-2852	
Epiphany Productions Inc 104 Hume Ave *Web:* www.epiphanyproductions.com	Alexandria	VA	22301	703-683-7500	
Eps Group, Inc Engineers, Planners & Surveyors 2045 S Vineyard Ste 101 *Web:* www.epsgroupinc.com	Mesa	AZ	85210	480-503-2250	
Erdman Anthony 145 Culver Rd Ste 200 *Web:* erdmananthony.com	Rochester	NY	14620	585-427-8888	
Erica Lane Enterprises Inc 2905 Wcorp Blvd Ste 114 *Web:* eleinc.com	Huntsville	AL	35805	256-536-7117	536-7133
eSentio Technologies 700 12Th St NW Ste 700 *Web:* www.esentio.com	Washington	DC	20005	202-628-6010	
ESI Inc of Tennessee 1250 Roberts Blvd *Web:* esitenn.com	Kennesaw	GA	30144	770-427-6200	
Espa Corp Inc 7120 Grand Blvd Ste 100 *Web:* kci.com	Houston	TX	77054	713-680-0080	
Estes Mcclure & Assoc Inc 3608 Wway St *Web:* estesmcclure.com	Tyler	TX	75703	903-581-2677	
Etalex Inc 8501 Jarry St E *Web:* www.etalex.net	Montreal	QC	H1J1H7	514-351-2000	
Etc Group Inc 1997 South 1100 East *Web:* www.etcgrp.com	Salt Lake City	UT	84106	801-278-1927	
Etegent Technologies Ltd 1775 Mentor Ave *Web:* www.sdltd.com	Cincinnati	OH	45212	513-631-0579	
Evans Mechwart Hambleton & Tilton Inc (EMHT) 5500 New Albany Rd *Web:* www.emht.com	Columbus	OH	43054	614-775-4500	775-4800
Ewing Cole 100 N Sixth St *Web:* ewingcole.com	Philadelphia	PA	19106	215-923-2020	574-9163
Exceletech Coating & Applications LLC 901 12th St *Web:* www.excelcoatings.com	Clermont	FL	34711	352-394-2155	
Exodyne Inc 8433 N Black Canyon Hwy *Web:* www.exodyne.com	Phoenix	AZ	85021	602-995-3700	995-4091
Experts-conseils Cep Inc 1345 Boul Louis-xiv *Web:* www.expcep.com	Quebec	QC	G2L1M4	418-622-4480	
Exponential Engineering Co 328 Air Park Dr *Web:* www.exponentialengineering.com	Fort Collins	CO	80524	970-207-9648	
Extreme Engineering Solutions Inc 3225 Deming Way Ste 120 *Web:* xes-inc.com	Middleton	WI	53562	608-833-1155	
F & ME Consultants 3112 Devine St *Web:* fandme.com	Columbia	SC	29205	803-254-4540	
Fabre Engineering Inc 119 Gregory Sq *Web:* www.fabreinc.com	Pensacola	FL	32502	850-433-6438	
Facility Dynamics Engineering 6760 Alexander Bell Dr *Web:* facilitydynamics.com	Columbia	MD	21046	410-290-0900	
Facility Group Inc 2233 Lake Pk Dr Ste 100 *Web:* fdgatlanta.com	Smyrna	GA	30080	770-437-2700	437-3900
Fairwinds International Inc 128 Northpark Blvd *Web:* www.fairwindsintl.com	Covington	LA	70433	985-809-3808	
Fakouri Electrical Engineering Inc 30001 Comercio *Web:* www.fee-ups.com	Rancho Santa Margarita	CA	92688	949-888-2400	
Fanning/Howey Assoc Inc 1200 Irmscher Blvd *TF:* 888-499-2292 ■ *Web:* www.fhai.com	Celina	OH	45822	419-586-2292	586-3393
Farner, Barley & Associates Inc 4450 NE 83rd Rd *Web:* www.farnerbarley.com	Wildwood	FL	34785	352-748-3126	
Farnsworth Group Inc 2709 McGraw Dr *Web:* www.f-w.com	Bloomington	IL	61704	309-663-8435	
Farwest Corrosion Control Co 1480 W Artesia Blvd *TF:* 888-532-7937 ■ *Web:* www.farwestcorrosion.com	Gardena	CA	90248	310-532-9524	532-3934
Fastek International Ltd 1425 60th St Ne *Web:* www.fastekintl.com	Cedar Rapids	IA	52402	319-294-6664	
FATA Hunter Inc 1040 Iowa Ave Ste 100 *TF:* 800-248-6837 ■ *Web:* www.fatahunter.com	Riverside	CA	92507	951-328-0200	328-9205
Fay Spofford & Thorndike LLC 5 Burlington Woods *TF:* 800-835-8666 ■ *Web:* www.fstinc.com	Burlington	MA	01803	781-221-1000	229-1115
FDH Inc 6521 Meridien Dr *Web:* www.fdh-inc.com	Raleigh	NC	27616	919-755-1012	
Feed Forward Inc 1834 W Oak Pkwy *Web:* feedforward.com	Marietta	GA	30062	770-426-4422	
Fehr-Graham & Assoc LLC 221 E Main St Ste 200 *Web:* fehr-graham.com	Freeport	IL	61032	815-235-7643	
Fentress Bradburn Architects Ltd 421 Broadway *Web:* www.fentressarchitects.com	Denver	CO	80203	303-722-5000	722-5080
FEV Inc 4554 Glenmeade Ln *Web:* fev.com	Auburn Hills	MI	48326	248-373-6000	
Fiore Industries Inc 8601 Washington St NE Ste B *Web:* fiore-ind.com	Albuquerque	NM	87113	505-255-9797	
Firepoint Technologies Inc 27-180 Wilkinson Rd *Web:* www.firepoint.ca	Brampton	ON	L6T4W8	905-874-9400	
First Plastics Corp 22 Jytek Rd *Web:* firstplastics.com	Leominster	MA	01453	978-537-0367	
Fishbeck Thompson Carr & Huber Inc 1515 Arboretum Dr SE *Web:* www.ftch.com	Grand Rapids	MI	49546	616-575-3824	464-3993
Fitzpatrick Engineering Group PLLC 19520 W Catawba Ave Ste 311 *Web:* www.fegstructural.com	Cornelius	NC	28031	704-987-9114	
Flad & Assoc 644 Science Dr *Web:* www.flad.com	Madison	WI	53711	608-238-2661	238-6727
Flatter & Associates Inc 16 Ctr St Ste 201 *Web:* www.flatterassociates.com	Stafford	VA	22556	540-658-1922	
Fleet-Fisher Engineering Inc 4250 E Camelback Rd Ste 410K *Web:* www.ffeng.com	Phoenix	AZ	85018	602-264-3335	

Company	City	State	Zip	Phone	Fax
Fleetway Inc 155 Chain Lk Dr Ste 200 *Web:* www.fleetway.ca	Halifax	NS	B3S1B3	902-494-5700	
Fletcher-Thompson Inc Three Corporate Dr Ste 500 *Web:* www.fletcherthompson.com	Shelton	CT	06484	203-225-6500	225-6800
Flexicell Inc 10463 Wilden Dr *Web:* flexicell.com	Ashland	VA	23005	804-550-7300	
Flint Surveying & Engineering Company Inc 5370 Miller Rd *Web:* fse.us	Swartz Creek	MI	48473	810-230-1333	
Florida Turbine Technologies Inc 1701 Military Trl Ste 110 *Web:* www.fttinc.com	Jupiter	FL	33458	561-427-6400	
Fluor Daniel Inc Three Polaris Way *Web:* www.fluor.com	Aliso Viejo	CA	92698	949-349-2000	349-2585
Fluoresco Lighting & Sign Corp 5505 S Nogales Hwy PO Box 27042 *Web:* www.fluoresco.com	Tucson	AZ	85726	520-623-7953	884-0161
Foit-Albert Associates 763 Main St *Web:* www.foit-albert.com	Buffalo	NY	14203	716-856-3933	
Food Perspectives Inc 13755 First Ave N Ste 500 *Web:* foodperspectives.com	Plymouth	MN	55441	763-553-7787	
Ford Bacon & Davis 12021 Lakeland Pk Blvd *Web:* www.fbd.com	Baton Rouge	LA	70809	225-292-0050	257-3752
Forell-Elsesser Engineers Inc 160 Pine St Fl 6 *Web:* www.forell.com	San Francisco	CA	94111	415-837-0700	
Foresite Group Inc 5185 Peachtree Pkwy *Web:* fg-inc.net	Norcross	GA	30092	770-368-1399	
Forsythe & Long Engineering 4560 Helton Dr *Web:* www.forsytheandlong.com	Florence	AL	35630	256-760-0000	
Forte & Tablada Inc 9107 Interline Ave *Web:* forteandtablada.com	Baton Rouge	LA	70809	225-927-9321	
Fortis Construction Inc 1705 SW Taylor St Ste 200 *Web:* fortisconstruction.com	Portland	OR	97205	503-459-4477	
Fosdick & Hilmer Inc 309 Vine St *Web:* www.fosdickandhilmer.com	Cincinnati	OH	45202	513-241-5640	
Foster Wheeler AG 53 Frontage Rd PO Box 9000 *NYSE: LSE* ■ *TF:* 888-288-1464 ■ *Web:* www.fwc.com	Hampton	NJ	08827	908-730-4000	
Foster Wheeler USA Corp Perryville Corporate Pk *Web:* www.fwc.com	Clinton	NJ	08809	908-730-4000	730-5315
Foth & Van Dyke & Assoc Inc 2121 Innovation Ct PO Box 5095 *Web:* www.foth.com	Green Bay	WI	54115	920-497-2500	497-8516
FOX Engineering Associates Inc 414 S 17th St Ste 107 *Web:* www.foxeng.com	Ames	IA	50010	515-233-0000	
Fpm Group Ltd 909 Marconi Ave *Web:* www.fpm-group.com	Ronkonkoma	NY	11779	631-737-6200	
Fralinger Engineering PA 629 Shiloh Pk *Web:* fralinger.com	Bridgeton	NJ	08302	856-451-2990	
Fred Porter & Assoc Inc Dba Porter & Assoc Inc 1200 21st St	Bakersfield	CA	93301	661-327-0362	
Fredrick, Fredrick & Heller Engineers Inc 672 E Royalton Rd *Web:* www.ffhengineers.com	Broadview Heights	OH	44147	440-546-9696	
Freese & Nichols Inc 4055 International Plz Ste 200 *Web:* www.freese.com	Fort Worth	TX	76109	817-735-7300	735-7491
French-Reneker Assoc Inc 1501 S Main St PO Box 135 *Web:* frenchrenekerassociates.com	Fairfield	IA	52556	641-472-5145	
Freyer & Laureta Inc 144 N San Mateo Dr *Web:* freyerlaureta.com	San Mateo	CA	94401	650-344-9901	344-9920
Freyssinet Inc 44880 Falcon Pl Ste 100 *Web:* www.freyssinetusa.com	Sterling	VA	20166	703-378-2500	
Frymire Engineering Company Inc 2818 Satsuma Dr *Web:* www.frymire.com	Dallas	TX	75229	972-620-3500	
FTF Engineering Inc 1916 Mcallister St *Web:* ftfengineering.com	San Francisco	CA	94115	415-931-8460	
Fugro Consultants LP 6100 Hillcroft Ave *Web:* www.fugroconsultants.com	Houston	TX	77081	713-369-5400	369-5518
Fulghum Macindoe & Associates Inc 10330 Hardin Vly Rd Ste 201 *Web:* www.fulghummacindoe.com	Knoxville	TN	37932	865-690-6419	
Function Engineering Inc 163 Everett Ave *Web:* function.com	Palo Alto	CA	94301	650-326-8834	
Fuss & O'Neill Consulting Engineers Inc 146 Hartford Rd *TF:* 800-286-2469 ■ *Web:* www.fando.com	Manchester	CT	06040	860-646-2469	533-5143
Future Research Corp 675 Discovery Dr Bldg 2 Ste 102 *Web:* www.future-research.com	Huntsville	AL	35806	256-430-4304	
Future Technologies Inc 3877 Fairfax Ridge Rd *Web:* www.ftechi.com	Fairfax	VA	22030	703-278-0199	385-0886
G & m Compliance Inc 154 S Cypress St *Web:* www.gmcompliance.com	Orange	CA	92866	714-628-1020	
G & W Engineering Corp 138 Weldon Pkwy *Web:* gandwengineering.com	Maryland Heights	MO	63043	314-469-3737	
G Systems LP 1240 Campbell Rd Ste 100 *Web:* www.gsystems.com	Richardson	TX	75081	972-234-6000	
G3 Technologies Inc 10280 Old Columbia Rd Ste 260 *Web:* www.g3ti.net	Columbia	MD	21046	410-290-8110	
Gables Search Group Inc 37721 Vine St Ste 1 *Web:* www.gablessearch.com	Willoughby	OH	44094	440-951-9990	
GAI Consultants Inc 385 E Waterfront Dr *Web:* www.gaiconsultants.com	Homestead	PA	15120	412-476-2000	
Gannett Fleming Inc 207 Senate Ave *TF:* 800-233-1055 ■ *Web:* www.gannettfleming.com	Camp Hill	PA	17011	717-763-7211	763-8150
Gap Engineering Inc 802 Dominion Dr *Web:* www.gap-eng.com	Katy	TX	77450	281-578-0500	
Garcia Galuska & De Sousa Inc 370 Faunce Corner Rd *Web:* www.g-g-d.com	North Dartmouth	MA	02747	508-998-5700	
Garing Taylor & Assoc Inc 141 S Elm St	Arroyo Grande	CA	93420	805-489-1321	
Garver Engineers 4701 Northshore Dr *TF:* 800-264-3633 ■ *Web:* www.garverusa.com	North Little Rock	AR	72118	501-376-3633	760-3743
Gaskins Surveying Company Inc 1266 Powder Springs Rd *Web:* www.gscsurvey.com	Marietta	GA	30064	770-424-7168	
Gaussian Inc 340 Quinnipiac St Bldg 40 *Web:* www.gaussian.com	Wallingford	CT	06492	203-284-2501	
GDA Technologies Inc 1010 Rincon Cir *Web:* www.gdatech.com	San Jose	CA	95131	408-432-3090	432-3091
GDS Associates Inc 1850 Pkwy Pl Ste 800 *Web:* www.gdsassociates.com	Marietta	GA	30067	770-425-8100	
GEI Consultants Inc 400 Unicorn Pk Dr *TF:* 888-434-9679 ■ *Web:* www.geiconsultants.com	Woburn	MA	01801	781-721-4000	721-4073
Gekko Engineering Inc 1210 E 223rd St *Web:* gckkocng.com	Carson	CA	90745	310-513-0000	
Gem Engineering Inc 1762 Watterson Trl *Web:* www.gemeng.com	Louisville	KY	40299	502-493-7100	
Genesis Engineers Inc 1850 Gravers Rd *Web:* www.geieng.com	Plymouth Meeting	PA	19462	610-592-0280	
Gensler Two Harrison St Ste 400 *Web:* gensler.com/	San Francisco	CA	94105	415-433-3700	836-4599
Geo-Marine Inc 2201 Ave K Ste A2 *Web:* www.geo-marine.com	Plano	TX	75074	972-423-5480	422-2736
Geo-slope International Ltd 633 6 Ave Sw Ste 1400 *Web:* www.geo-slope.com	Calgary	AB	T2P2Y5	403-269-2002	
Geoconcepts Engineering 19955 Highland Vista Dr *Web:* geoconcepts-eng.com	Ashburn	VA	20147	703-726-8030	
GeoEngineers Inc 8410 154th Ave NE *TF:* 888-624-8373 ■ *Web:* www.geoengineers.com	Redmond	WA	98052	425-861-6000	861-6050
Geometric Americas Inc 50 Kirts Blvd Ste A *Web:* geometricglobal.com	Troy	MI	48084	248-404-3500	
Geopentech 525 N Cabrillo Park Dr *Web:* geopentech.com	Santa Ana	CA	92701	714-796-9100	
George Butler Assoc Inc 9801 Renner Blvd *Web:* www.gbateam.com	Lenexa	KS	66219	913-492-0400	577-8200
George G Sharp Inc 22 Cortlandt St Ste 10 *Web:* www.georgesharp.com	New York	NY	10007	212-732-2800	732-2809
George Reed Inc 140 Empire Ave *Web:* www.georgereed.com	Modesto	CA	95352	209-523-0734	
George, Miles & Buhr LLC 206 W Main St *Web:* www.gmbnet.com	Salisbury	MD	21801	410-742-3115	
Geosol Inc 5795 Nw 151st St # A *Web:* www.geographicsolutions.com	Miami Lakes	FL	33014	305-828-4367	
GeoSyntec Consultants Inc 5901 Broken Sound Pkwy NW Ste 300 *TF:* 866-676-1101 ■ *Web:* www.geosyntec.com	Boca Raton	FL	33487	561-995-0900	995-0925
Geotechnical Services Inc 9312 G Ct *Web:* gsinetwork.com	Omaha	NE	68127	402-339-6104	
Geotechnologies Inc 3200 Wellington Court Ste G *Web:* www.geotechpa.com	Raleigh	NC	27615	919-954-1514	
Geotest Engineering Inc 5600 Bintliff Dr *Web:* geotesteng.com	Houston	TX	77036	713-266-0588	266-2977
GGC Engineers Inc 148 N High St *Web:* ggcengineers.com	Gahanna	OH	43230	614-471-7310	
Ghafari Assoc Inc 17101 Michigan Ave **Fax:* Hum Res ■ *TF:* 800-289-7822 ■ *Web:* www.ghafari.com	Dearborn	MI	48126	313-441-3000	441-1545*
GHD Inc 2235 Mercury Way Ste 150 *Web:* www.ghd.com	Santa Rosa	CA	95407	707-523-1010	527-8679
GHR Engineers & Assoc Inc 1615 S Neil St *Web:* ghrinc.com	Champaign	IL	61820	217-356-0536	
Gibson-Thomas Engineering Company Inc 1004 Ligonier St *Web:* www.gibson-thomas.com	Latrobe	PA	15650	724-539-8562	
Giffels-Webster Engineers Inc 28 W Adams Ste 1200 *Web:* giffelswebster.com	Detroit	MI	48226	313-962-4442	
Gillespie, Prudhon & Associates Inc 16111 Se 106th Ave Ste 100 *Web:* www.gpatelecom.com	Clackamas	OR	97015	503-657-0424	
Gilsanz, Murray, Steficek LLP 129 W 27th St Fl 5 *Web:* www.gmsllp.com	New York	NY	10001	212-254-0030	
Gipe Assoc Inc 8719 Brooks Dr *Web:* gipe.net	Easton	MD	21601	410-822-8688	
Glassfab Tempering Services Inc 1448 Mariani Ct *Web:* www.glassfabtempering.com	Tracy	CA	95376	209-229-1060	
Gleason Research Associates Inc 5030 Bradford Dr NW Bldg One Ste 220 *Web:* www.grainc.net	Huntsville	AL	35805	256-883-7000	
Glenmount Global Solutions 5960 Southport Rd *Web:* www.glenmountglobal.com	Portage	IN	46368	219-762-0700	762-1636
Glex Inc 12900 Fm 529 Rd *Web:* www.glexinc.com	Houston	TX	77041	713-849-4985	

Phone | Fax

Glhn Architects & Engineers Inc
2939 E Broadway Blvd ... Tucson AZ 85716 520-881-4546
Web: glhn.com

GLJ Petroleum Consultants Ltd
400 - Third Ave SW Ste 4100 ... Calgary AB T2P4H2 403-266-9500
Web: www.gljpc.com

Global Design Alliance Inc (GDA)
26 Grammercy Pk S 4B ... New York NY 10003 917-887-3860
Web: www.globalda.com

Globetrotters Engineering Corp
300 S Wacker Dr Ste 400 ... Chicago IL 60606 312-922-6400
Web: www.gec-group.com

Golder Assoc Inc 3730 Chamblee Tucker Rd ... Atlanta GA 30341 770-496-1893 934-9476
Web: www.golder.com

Gomez & Sullivan PC 288 Genesee St ... Utica NY 13502 315-724-4860
Web: gomezandsullivan.com

Gonzalez Design Group
29401 Stevenson Hwy ... Madison Heights MI 48071 248-548-6010 548-3160
Web: www.gonzalez-group.com

Gonzalez Strength & Assoc 2176 Pkwy Lk Dr ... Hoover AL 35244 205-942-2486
Web: www.gonzalez-strength.com

Goodgame Company Inc 2311 Third Ave South ... Pell City AL 35128 205-338-2551
Web: www.goodgamecompany.com

Gould Evans International 4041 Mill St ... Kansas City MO 64111 816-931-6655 931-9640
Web: www.gouldevans.com

GPD Group 520 S Main St Ste 2531 ... Akron OH 44311 330-572-2100
Web: www.gpdco.com

GRAEF-USA Inc
One Honey Creek Corporate Ctr 125 S 84th St
Ste 401 ... Milwaukee WI 53214 414-259-1500 259-0037
Web: graef-usa.com

Gravitec Systems Inc
9453 Coppertop Loop NE ... Bainbridge Island WA 98110 206-780-2898
Web: www.gravitec.com

Greeley & Hansen 100 S Wacker Dr Ste 1400 ... Chicago IL 60606 312-558-9000 558-1006
TF: 800-837-9779 ■ *Web:* www.greeley-hansen.com

Greenberg Farrow 44 W 28th St 16th Fl ... New York NY 10001 212-725-9530
Web: www.greenbergfarrow.com

Greenman-Pedersen Inc 325 W Main St ... Babylon NY 11702 631-587-5060 587-5029
Web: www.gpinet.com

Gresham Smith & Partners
511 Union St 1400 Nashville City Ctr ... Nashville TN 37219 615-770-8100 227-4013
Web: www.gspnet.com

Grossman & Keith Engineering Co
10408 Greenbriar Pl ... Oklahoma City OK 73159 405-691-3213
Web: grossman-keith.com

Groupe Stavibel Inc 532 7e Rue Ouest bureau 101 ... Amos QC J9T3W7 819-732-8355
Web: www.stavibel.qc.ca

Gruzen Samton LLC 320 W 13th St Ninth Fl ... New York NY 10014 212-477-0900 477-1257
Web: www.gruzensamton.com

GRW Engineers Inc 801 Corporate Dr ... Lexington KY 40503 859-223-3999 223-8917
TF: 800-432-9537 ■ *Web:* www.grwinc.com

GS Engineering Inc 47500 Us Hwy 41 ... Houghton MI 49931 906-482-1235

Gstek Inc 1100 Madison Plz Ste A ... Chesapeake VA 23320 757-548-1597
Web: www.gstekinc.com

Gts Technologies Inc 441 Friendship Rd ... Harrisburg PA 17111 717-236-3006
Web: gtstech.com

Guerin & Vreeland Engineering Inc
272 Rt 206 ... Flanders NJ 07836 973-252-9340

Guido Perla & Associates Inc
701 Fifth Ave Ste 1200 ... Seattle WA 98104 206-768-1515
Web: www.gpai.com

Gulf Interstate Engineering Co
16010 Barkers Pt Ln Ste 600 ... Houston TX 77079 713-850-3400 850-3579
Web: www.gie.com

Gulf Regional Planning Commission
1232 Pass Rd ... Gulfport MS 39501 228-864-1167
Web: grpc.com

Gwa Electrical Engineers Inc
168 Laurelhurst Ave ... Columbia SC 29210 803-252-6919
Web: www.gwainc.net

Gwin Dobson & Foreman Inc 3121 Fairway Dr ... Altoona PA 16602 814-943-5214
Web: www.gdfengineers.com

H E Bergeron Engineers Inc
2605 White Mtn Hwy ... North Conway NH 03860 603-356-6936
Web: hebengineers.com

H. T. Lyons Inc 7165 Ambassador Dr ... Allentown PA 18106 610-530-2600
Web: m.htlyons.com

Haag Engineering Co 4949 W Royal Ln ... Irving TX 75063 214-614-6500
Web: haagengineering.com

Hahn Engineering Inc 3060 S Dale Mabry Hwy ... Tampa FL 33629 813-831-8599
Web: www.hahneng.com

Hakanson Anderson Assoc Inc 3601 Thurston Ave ... Anoka MN 55303 763-427-5860
Web: hakanson-anderson.com

HAKS Engineers PC 40 Wall St ... New York NY 10005 212-747-1997
Web: www.haks.net

Halcrow Yolles
207 Queens Quay W Ste 550 PO Box 132 ... Toronto ON M5J1A7 416-363-8123 363-0341
Web: ch2m.com/corporate/about_us/halcrow.asp

Haley & Aldrich Inc 465 Medford St Ste 2200 ... Boston MA 02129 617-886-7400 886-7600
Web: www.haleyaldrich.com

Halff Assoc Inc 1201 N Bowser Rd ... Richardson TX 75081 214-346-6200 739-0095
Web: www.halff.com

Hall & Foreman Inc 17782 E 17th St Ste 200 ... Tustin CA 92780 714-665-4500
Web: www.hfinc.com

Hamilton Engineering & Surveyi
311 N Newport Ave ... Tampa FL 33606 813-250-3535
Web: hamiltontampa.com

Hammel Green & Abrahamson Inc
701 Washington Ave N ... Minneapolis MN 55401 612-758-4000 758-4199
TF: 888-442-8255 ■ *Web:* www.hga.com

Hampton, Lenzini & Renwick Inc 380 Shepard Dr ... Elgin IL 60123 847-697-6700
Web: www.hlrengineering.com

Hanson Professional Services Inc
1525 S Sixth St ... Springfield IL 62703 217-788-2450 788-2503
Web: www.hanson-inc.com

Hardesty & Havover LLP 1501 Broadway Ste 310 ... New York NY 10036 212-944-1150 391-0297
Web: www.hardesty-hanover.com

Harris & Assoc Inc 1401 Willow Pass Rd ... Concord CA 94520 925-827-4900 356-0998*
**Fax Area Code:* 866 ■ *Web:* www.harris-assoc.com

Harris Civil Engineers LLC 1200 Hillcrest St ... Orlando FL 32803 407-629-4777
Web: www.harriscivilengineers.com

Harris Group Inc 300 Elliott Ave W ... Seattle WA 98119 206-494-9400 494-9500
TF: 800-488-7410 ■ *Web:* www.harrisgroup.com

Harris Smariga & Assoc Inc
125 S Carroll St Ste 100 ... Frederick MD 21701 301-662-4488

Hart Crowser Inc 1700 Westlake Ave N Ste 200 ... Seattle WA 98109 206-324-9530 328-5581
Web: www.hartcrowser.com

Hatch Mott Macdonald Group 27 Bleeker St ... Millburn NJ 07041 973-379-3400 376-1072
Web: www.hatchmott.com

Hatfield & Dawson 9500 Greenwood Ave N ... Seattle WA 98103 206-783-9151
Web: hatdaw.com

Hawk Technology Ltd 8080 Centennial Expy ... Rock Island IL 61201 309-787-6200
Web: www.hawktechnology.com

Hawkins & Associates Engineering Inc
436 Mitchell Rd ... Modesto CA 95354 209-575-4295
Web: www.hawkins-eng.com

Hayden Consulting Engineers In
12480 SW 68th Ave ... Tigard OR 97223 503-968-9994
Web: hayden-engineers.com

Hayes James & Associates Inc
3005 Breckinridge Blvd ... Duluth GA 30096 770-923-1600
Web: www.hayesjames.com

Hazen & Sawyer PC 498 Seventh Ave 11th Fl ... New York NY 10018 212-777-8400 614-9049
TF: 800-858-9876 ■ *Web:* www.hazenandsawyer.com

HC Nutting Co
Terracon Co 611 Lunken Pk Dr ... Cincinnati OH 45226 513-321-5816 321-0294
Web: www.terracon.com

Hcs Group Inc 1030 First St E Ste B ... Humble TX 77338 281-540-4838
Web: hcsgroup.com

HDR Engineering Inc 8404 Indian Hills Dr ... Omaha NE 68114 402-399-1000 548-5015*
**Fax:* Hum Res ■ *TF:* 800-366-4411 ■ *Web:* www.hdrinc.com

Heapy Engineering Inc 1400 W Dorothy Ln ... Dayton OH 45409 937-224-0861
Web: heapy.com

Heatwave Labs Inc
195 Aviation Way Ste 100 ... Watsonville CA 95076 831-722-9081
Web: www.cathode.com

Heberly & Associates 615 First W ... Havre MT 59501 406-265-6741
Web: www.heberlyeng.com

Hedges Engineering & Consulting Inc
913 Kincaid Ave ... Sumner WA 98390 253-891-9365

Heery International Inc 999 Peachtree St NE ... Atlanta GA 30309 404-881-9880 875-1283
TF: 866-840-3940 ■ *Web:* www.heery.com

Hef Usa Corp 2015 Progress Rd ... Springfield OH 45505 937-323-2556
Web: www.hefusa.net

Hegemony Inc 520 W Roosevelt Rd ... Wheaton IL 60187 630-690-5200
Web: hegemony.com

Henderson Paddon & Associates Ltd
945 Third Ave E Ste 212 ... Owen Sound ON N4K2K8 519-376-7612
Web: www.hp.on.ca

Henman Engineering & Machine Inc
3301 W Mt Pleasant Blvd ... Muncie IN 47302 765-288-8098
Web: henmaneng.com

Henneman Engineering 1605 S State St ... Champaign IL 61820 217-359-1514
Web: henneman.com

Herbert Rowland & Grubic Inc (HRG)
369 E Pk Dr ... Harrisburg PA 17111 717-564-1121 564-1158
Web: www.hrg-inc.com

Hethcoat & Davis Inc
278 Franklin Rd Ste 200 ... Brentwood TN 37027 615-577-4300
Web: www.hdengr.com

HF Lenz Co 1407 Scalp Ave ... Johnstown PA 15904 814-269-9300 269-9301
Web: www.hflenz.com

HGM Associates Inc 640 Fifth Ave ... Council Bluffs IA 51502 712-323-0530
Web: www.hgmonline.com

HGS Engineering Inc 1121 Noble St ... Anniston AL 36201 256-236-1848
Web: hgsengineeringinc.com

Hi-Tec Industries Inc
1000 Sixth Ave NE ... Portage La Prairie MB R1N3C5 204-239-4270
Web: www.hitecindustries.ca

Hi-tech Machining & Engineering LLC
1075 E Wieding Rd ... Tucson AZ 85706 520-889-8325
Web: www.hi-techmachining.net

Hi-Tech Systems Engineering Co
2700 Old Centre Rd ... Portage MI 49024 269-488-7788
Web: www.htse.com

Hi-Test Laboratories Inc 1104 Arvon Rd ... Arvonia VA 23004 434-581-3204
Web: hitestlabs.com

High Mesa Consulting Group Inc
6010 Midway Park Blvd Ne Ste B ... Albuquerque NM 87109 505-345-4250
Web: highmesacg.com

Hill International Inc 303 Lippincott Ctr ... Marlton NJ 08053 856-810-6200 810-1309
NYSE: HIL ■ *Web:* www.hillintl.com

HJ Foundation Inc 8275 N W 80 St ... Miami FL 33166 305-592-8181
Web: www.hjfoundation.com

HKS Inc 1919 McKinney Ave ... Dallas TX 75201 214-969-5599 969-3397
Web: www.hksinc.com

HL Turner Group Inc, The 27 Locke Rd ... Concord NH 03301 603-228-1122
Web: hlturner.com

Hla Engineers Inc 7267 Envoy Ct ... Dallas TX 75247 214-267-0930 267-0970
Web: hlaengineers.com

HLW International 115 Fifth Ave Fifth Fl ... New York NY 10003 212-353-4600 353-4666
Web: www.hlw.com

HMC Archiect 3546 Councours St ... Ontario CA 91764 909-989-9979 483-1400
TF: 800-350-9979 ■ *Web:* www.hmcarchitects.com

Company	City	State	ZIP	Phone	Fax
Hn Burns Engineering Corp 3275 Progress Dr Ste A — *Web:* www.hnbec.com	Orlando	FL	32826	407-273-3770	
HNTB Corp 715 Kirk Dr — *Web:* www.hntb.com	Kansas City	MO	64105	816-472-1201	472-4060
Hodge Engineering Inc 2615 Jahn Ave Nw Ste E5 — *Web:* hodgeengineering.squarespace.com	Gig Harbor	WA	98335	253-857-7055	
Hodges Harbin Newberry & Tribble 3920 Arkwright Rd — *Web:* hhnt.com	Macon	GA	31210	478-743-7175	
Hoffmann & Feige Inc Three Fallsview Ln — *Web:* hoffmann-feige.com	Brewster	NY	10509	845-277-4401	
Hogle-Ireland Inc 2860 Michelle Dr Ste 100 — *Web:* hogleireland.com	Irvine	CA	92606	949-553-1427	
Holdrege & Kull Consulting Engineers & Geologists 792 Searls Ave — *Web:* holdregeandkull.com	Nevada City	CA	95959	530-478-1305	
Horizon Environmental Corp 4771 50th St Se — *Web:* horizonenv.com	Grand Rapids	MI	49512	616-554-3210	
Howard R Green Co 8710 Earhart Ln SW — *TF:* 800-728-7805 ■ *Web:* www.hrgreen.com	Cedar Rapids	IA	52404	319-841-4000	841-4012
HPD, LLC 23563 W Main St — *TF:* 866-362-0993 ■ *Web:* veoliawatertechnologies.com/	Plainfield	IL	60544	815-609-2000	
Hrl Laboratories LLC 3011 Malibu Canyon Rd — *Web:* www.hrl.com	Malibu	CA	90265	310-317-5000	317-5483
HRP Associates Inc 197 Scott Swamp Rd — *TF:* 800-246-9021 ■ *Web:* www.hrpassociates.com	Farmington	CT	06032	800-246-9021	
HSA Engineering Consulting Services Inc 5701 Euper Ln Ste A — *Web:* hsaconsultants.com	Fort Smith	AR	72903	479-452-8922	
Hubbell Roth & Clark Inc 555 Hulet Dr PO Box 824 — *Web:* www.hrc-engr.com	Bloomfield Hills	MI	48303	248-454-6300	338-2592
Huitt-Zollars Inc 1717 McKinney Ave Ste 1400 — *TF:* 866-667-6572 ■ *Web:* www.huitt-zollars.com	Dallas	TX	75202	214-871-3311	871-0757
Hull & Assoc Inc 6397 Emerald Pkwy Ste 200 — *Web:* hullinc.com	Dublin	OH	43016	614-793-8777	
Humantech Inc 1161 Oak Vly Dr — *Web:* www.humantech.com	Ann Arbor	MI	48108	734-663-6707	
Hunsaker & Assoc Irvine Inc Three Hughes — *Web:* www.hunsaker.com	Irvine	CA	92618	949-583-1010	583-0759
Hussey Gay Bell (HGBD) 329 Commercial Dr Ste 200 — *Web:* www.husseygaybell.com	Savannah	GA	31406	912-354-4626	
Hydromantis Environmental Software Solutions Inc One James St S Ste 1601 — *Web:* www.hydromantis.com	Hamilton	ON	L8P4R5	905-522-0012	
Hygun Group Inc 4180 Providence Rd Ste 109 — *Web:* www.hygun.com	Marietta	GA	30062	770-973-0838	
I E T Inc 3539 Glendale Ave — *Web:* www.ieteng.com	Toledo	OH	43614	419-385-1233	
I&S Group Inc 115 E Hickory St Ste 300 — *Web:* is-grp.com	Mankato	MN	56001	507-387-6651	
IC Thomasson Assoc Inc 2950 Kraft Dr Ste 500 — *Web:* icthomasson.com	Nashville	TN	37204	615-346-3400	
ICF International Inc 9300 Lee Hwy — *NASDAQ: ICFI* ■ *Web:* www.icfi.com	Fairfax	VA	22031	703-934-3000	934-3740
iCyt Visionary Bioscience Inc 2100 S Oak St — *Web:* www.i-cyt.com	Champaign	IL	61820	217-328-9396	
IDD Process & Packaging 5450 Tech Cir — *Web:* www.iddeas.com	Moorpark	CA	93021	805-529-9890	
IDEO 100 Forest Ave — *TF:* 866-369-9888 ■ *Web:* www.ideo.com	Palo Alto	CA	94301	650-289-3400	289-3707
IDS Group Inc One Peters Canyon Rd — *Web:* idsgi.com	Irvine	CA	92606	949-387-8500	
IHI Southwest Technologies Inc 6766 Culebra Rd — *Web:* www.ihiswt.com	San Antonio	TX	78238	210-256-4100	
Image Custom Engineering 1304 Langham Creek Dr Ste 170A — *Web:* www.image-ces.com	Houston	TX	77084	713-206-8899	
Image Engineering Group Ltd 635 Westport Pkwy — *Web:* www.iegltd.com	Grapevine	TX	76051	817-410-2858	
Imagine One Technology & Management Ltd 416 Colonial Ave — *Web:* www.imagine-one.com	Colonial Beach	VA	22443	804-224-1555	
Imata & Assoc Inc 171 Kapiolani St	Hilo	HI	96720	808-935-6827	
Impelsys Inc Broad St 16th Fl Ste 55 — *Web:* www.impelsys.com	New York	NY	10004	212-239-4138	
Imperial Electronic Assembly Inc 1000 Federal Rd — *Web:* www.impea.com	Brookfield	CT	06804	203-740-8425	740-8450
Indus Technology Inc 2243 San Diego Ave — *Web:* www.industechnology.com	San Diego	CA	92110	619-299-2555	299-2444
Infomagnetics Technologies Corp 330 Saint Mary Ave — *Web:* www.imt.ca	Winnipeg	MB	R3C3Z5	204-989-4630	
InForm Product Development Inc 700 Wilburn Rd — *Web:* www.in-form.com	Sun Prairie	WI	53590	608-825-4700	
Infrastructure Alternatives 7888 Childsdale Ne — *Web:* infrastructurealternatives.com	Rockford	MI	49341	616-866-1600	
Inhand Electronics 30 W Gude Dr — *Web:* inhand.com	Rockville	MD	20850	240-558-2014	
Innova Technologies Inc 1432 S Jones Blvd — *Web:* www.innovanv.com	Las Vegas	NV	89146	702-220-6640	
Innovation Genesis LLC The Old Corner Bookstore 3 School St — *Web:* www.productgenesis.com	Cambridge	MA	02108	617-234-0070	337-9544
Insitu Inc 118 E Columbia River Way — *Web:* insitu.com	Bingen	WA	98605	509-493-8600	
INSPEC-SOL Inc 4600 De la Cote-Vertu Blvd Saint-Laurent — *Web:* inspecsol.com	Montreal	QC	H4S1C7	514-333-5151	
Intech Inc 2802 Belle Arbor Ave — *Web:* www.intech-intl.com	Chattanooga	TN	37406	423-622-3700	
Integrity Applications Inc (IAI) 15020 Conference Ctr Dr Ste 100 — *Web:* www.integrity-apps.com	Chantilly	VA	20151	703-378-8672	378-8978
Intelitech Group Inc, The 12009 Ne 99th St Ste 1480 — *Web:* www.intelitechgroup.com	Vancouver	WA	98682	360-260-9780	
Intelligent Automation Inc 15400 Calhoun Dr Ste 400 — *Web:* www.i-a-i.com	Rockville	MD	20855	301-294-5200	294-5201
INTERA Inc 1812 Centre Creek Dr Ste 300 — *Web:* www.intera.com	Austin	TX	78754	512-425-2000	
International Electronic Machines Corp (IEM) 850 River St — *Web:* www.iem.net	Troy	NY	12180	518-268-1636	268-1639
Intertek Group PLC 801 Travis St Ste 1500 — *TF:* 800-967-5352 ■ *Web:* www.intertek.com	Houston	TX	77002	713-407-3500	407-3697
Intrinsix Corp 100 Campus Dr — *TF:* 800-783-0330 ■ *Web:* www.intrinsix.com	Marlborough	MA	01752	508-658-7600	
Isani Consultants 3143 Yellowstone Blvd — *Web:* www.isaniconsultants.com	Houston	TX	77054	713-747-2399	
iSense Acquisition LLC 27700 SW 95th Ave — *Web:* www.isensecgm.com	Wilsonville	OR	97070	503-783-5050	
Isine Inc 4155 Veterans Memorial Hwy — *Web:* isine.com	Ronkonkoma	NY	11779	631-913-4400	
J r d Systems Inc 42450 Hayes Rd Ste 3 — *Web:* www.jrdsi.com	Clinton Township	MI	48038	586-416-1500	
J-U-B Engineers Inc 250 S Beechwood Ave Ste 201 — *Web:* jub.com	Boise	ID	83709	208-376-7330	
J.V. Driver Installations Ltd 212- 3601 82 Ave — *Web:* www.jvdriver.com	Leduc	AB	T9E0H7	780-980-5837	
Jacobs Engineering Group Inc 155 N Lake Ave PO Box 7084 — *NYSE: JEC* ■ **Fax:* Hum Res ■ *Web:* www.jacobs.com	Pasadena	CA	91101	626-578-3500	*
Jacobs Technology Inc 600 William Northern Blvd — *Web:* www.jacobstechnology.com	Tullahoma	TN	37388	931-455-6400	
James C Hailey & Co 7518 Hwy 70 S Ste 100 — *Web:* jchengr.com	Nashville	TN	37221	615-883-4933	883-4937
James Machine Works LLC 1521 Adams St — *TF:* 800-259-6104 ■ *Web:* www.jmwinc.net	Monroe	LA	71201	318-322-6104	388-4245
Javan Engineering Inc 465 Maryland Dr Ste 100 — *Web:* javanengineering.com	Ft Washington	PA	19034	215-654-7890	
JBA Consulting Engineers 5155 W Patrick Ln Ste 100 — *Web:* www.jbace.com	Las Vegas	NV	89118	702-362-9200	
Jenike & Johanson Inc 400 Business Park Dr — *Web:* jenike.com	Tyngsboro	MA	01879	978-649-3300	
Jeter Cook & Jepson Architects Inc (JCJ) 38 Prospect St — *Web:* www.jcj.com	Hartford	CT	06103	860-247-9226	
Jewell Assoc Engineers Inc 560 Sunrise Dr — *Web:* jewellassoc.com	Spring Green	WI	53588	608-588-7484	
JF Taylor Inc 21610 S Essex Dr — *Web:* jfti.com	Lexington Park	MD	20653	301-862-3939	
JMP Engineering Inc 4026 Meadowbrook Dr Unit 143 — *Web:* www.jmpeng.com	London	ON	N6L1C9	519-652-2741	
John A Martin & Association Inc 950 S Grand Ave Fourth Fl — *Web:* www.johnmartin.com	Los Angeles	CA	90015	213-483-6490	483-3084
John M. Campbell & Co 1215 Crossroads Blvd — *TF:* 800-821-5933 ■ *Web:* www.jmcampbell.com	Norman	OK	73072	405-321-1383	321-4533
Johnson & Pace Inc 1201 W Loop 281 Lb1 — *Web:* www.johnsonpace.com	Longview	TX	75604	903-753-0663	
Johnson Fain 1201 N Broadway — *Web:* www.johnsonfain.com	Los Angeles	CA	90012	323-224-6000	224-6030
Johnson Mirmiran & Thompson (JMT) 72 Loveton Cir — *TF:* 800-472-2310 ■ *Web:* www.jmt.com	Sparks	MD	21152	410-329-3100	472-2200
Johnson Spellman & Assoc Inc 6991 Peachtree Industrial Blvd — *Web:* jsace.com	Norcross	GA	30092	770-447-4555	
Jones & Henry Engineers Ltd 3103 Executive Pkwy — *Web:* jheng.com	Toledo	OH	43606	419-473-9611	
Jones Edmunds & Assoc Inc 730 NE Waldo Rd — *Web:* www.jonesedmunds.com	Gainesville	FL	32641	352-377-5821	377-3166
Jp Harvey Engineering Solutions 29 Kings Way — *Web:* www.jphes.com	Hampton	VA	23669	757-722-7074	
Jr Gales & Assoc Inc 2704 Brownsville Rd	Pittsburgh	PA	15227	412-885-8885	
Juneau Assoc Inc PC 2100 State St — *Web:* jaipc.com	Granite City	IL	62040	618-877-1400	
JVA Inc 1319 Spruce St — *Web:* www.jvajva.com	Boulder	CO	80302	303-444-1951	
Jviation Inc 35 S 400 W Ste 200 — *Web:* creamerandnoble.com	St George	UT	84770	435-673-4677	
K2 Engineering Services Inc 85 Rangeway Rd — *Web:* k2-eng.com	North Billerica	MA	01862	978-600-1333	600-1331

Company / Address	City	State	Zip	Phone	Fax
Kanata Energy Group Ltd 1900 112 - Fourth Ave SW Sun Life Plz III - E Twr. *Web:* www.kanataenergy.com	Calgary	AB	T2P0H3	587-774-7000	
Kanawha Stone Company Inc 401 Jacobson Dr PO Box 503 *Web:* www.kanawhastone.com	Poca	WV	25159	304-755-8271	755-8274
Kap Medical 1395 Pico St *Web:* www.kapmedical.com	Corona	CA	92881	951-340-4360	
Kaplan McLaughlin Diaz 222 Vallejo St *Web:* www.kmdarchitects.com	San Francisco	CA	94111	415-398-5191	394-7158
Kappes, Cassiday & Associates Inc 7950 Security Cir *Web:* kcareno.com	Reno	NV	89506	775-972-7575	
Karges-Faulconbridge Inc 670 County Rd B W *Web:* www.kaa-eng.com	Saint Paul	MN	55113	651-771-0880	
Kavanagh Associates McDonald Bldg 74 O'Leary Ave *Web:* www.kavanaghandassociates.ca	St. John's	NL	A1B3V8	709-722-0024	
KBA Inc 11000 Main St *Web:* kbacm.com	Bellevue	WA	98004	425-455-9720	
KBR Inc 601 Jefferson St *TF:* 866-313-3046 ■ *Web:* www.kbr.com	Houston	TX	77002	713-753-2000	753-2762
KCF Technologies Inc 336 S Fraser St *Web:* www.kcftech.com	State College	PA	16801	814-867-4097	
KCI Technologies Inc 936 Ridgebrook Rd *TF:* 800-572-7496 ■ *Web:* kci.com	Sparks	MD	21152	410-316-7800	316-7817
Kebs Inc 2116 Haslett Rd *Web:* www.kebs.com	Haslett	MI	48840	517-339-1014	
Kec Engineering 200 N Sherman Ave *Web:* www.kecengineering.com	Corona	CA	92882	951-734-3010	
Keith & Schnars PA 6500 N Andrews Ave *Web:* www.keithandschnars.com	Fort Lauderdale	FL	33309	954-776-1616	771-7690
Kellam Berg Engineering & Surveys Ltd 5800 1a St Sw *Web:* www.kellamberg.com	Calgary	AB	T2H0G1	403-640-0900	
Ken Garner Manufacturing - Rho Inc 1201 E 28th St # B *Web:* www.kgarnermfg.com	Chattanooga	TN	37404	423-698-6200	
Kennedy Consulting Ltd 205 E University Ave *Web:* kci-ltd.com	Georgetown	TX	78626	512-864-2833	
Kennedy/Jenks Consultants 303 Second St Ste 300 S *Web:* www.kennedyjenks.com	San Francisco	CA	94107	415-243-2150	896-0999
Kenvirons Inc 452 Versailles Rd *Web:* www.kenvirons.com	Frankfort	KY	40601	502-695-4357	695-4363
Ketchmark & Assoc Inc 145 Tower Dr *Web:* ketchmark.com	Burr Ridge	IL	60527	630-850-7774	
Kier & Wright Civil Engineers 2850 Collier Canyon Rd *Web:* kierwright.com	Livermore	CA	94551	925-245-8788	
Kinectrics Inc 800 Kipling Ave *Web:* www.kinectrics.com	Toronto	ON	M8Z6C4	416-207-6000	
King Engineering Assoc Inc 4921 Memorial Hwy Ste 300 *TF:* 800-723-1403 ■ *Web:* www.kingengineering.com	Tampa	FL	33634	813-880-8881	
Kirkham Michael Inc 12700 W Dodge Rd PO Box 542030 *Web:* www.kirkham.com	Omaha	NE	68154	402-393-5630	255-3850
Kirksey 6909 Portwest Dr *Web:* www.kirksey.com	Houston	TX	77024	713-850-9600	850-7308
Kisinger Campo & Assoc Corp 201 N Franklin St Ste 400 *Web:* kisingercampo.com	Tampa	FL	33602	813-871-5331	871-5135
Kittelson & Associates Inc 610 SW Alder Ste 700 *Web:* www.kittelson.com	Portland	OR	97205	503-228-5230	
KJWW Engineering Consultants PC 623 26th Ave *Web:* www.kjww.com	Rock Island	IL	61201	309-788-0673	786-5967
KKE Architects Inc 300 First Ave N	Minneapolis	MN	55401	612-339-4200	
Klein & Hoffman Inc 150 S Wacker Dr *Web:* kleinandhoffman.com	Chicago	IL	60606	312-251-1900	
Kleingers Group Inc, The 6305 Centre Park Dr *Web:* kleingers.com	West Chester	OH	45069	513-779-7851	
Klotz Assoc Inc 1160 Dairy Ashford St *Web:* www.klotz.com	Houston	TX	77079	281-589-7257	
KM Ng Assoc Inc 6243 Ih 10 W	San Antonio	TX	78201	210-736-6623	
Kmj Consulting Inc 120 E Lancaster Ave Ste 105 *Web:* www.kmjinc.com	Ardmore	PA	19003	610-896-1996	
Kmm Technologies Inc 2525 Emerson Dr Ste 101 *Web:* kmmtechnologies.com	Frederick	MD	21702	240-286-2321	
Kmn Structural Engineering Inc 321 N Rampart St Ste 145	Orange	CA	92868	714-937-9060	
KMS Solutions LLC 205 S Whiting St Ste 400 *Web:* www.kmssol.com	Alexandria	VA	22304	703-823-8405	
Kna Consulting Engineers Inc 9931 Muirlands Blvd *Web:* www.knaconsulting.com	Irvine	CA	92618	949-462-3200	
Knott Laboratory LLC 7185 S Tucson Way *Web:* www.knottlab.com	Englewood	CO	80112	303-925-1900	
Kohli & Kaliher Assoc Inc 2244 Baton Rouge Ave *Web:* kohlikaliher.com	Lima	OH	45805	419-227-1135	
Kohn Pedersen Fox Assoc PC 111 W 57th St *Web:* www.kpf.com	New York	NY	10019	212-977-6500	956-2526
Kohrs Lonnemann Heil Engineers Psc 1538 Alexandria Pk	Ft Thomas	KY	41075	859-442-8050	
Kolar Corp 412 S Washington Ste 200 *Web:* kolarcorp.com	Royal Oak	MI	48067	248-543-0500	
Koops Inc 987 Productions Ct *Web:* koops.com	Holland	MI	49423	616-395-0230	
KPFF Consulting Engineers Inc 1601 Fifth Ave Ste 1600 *Web:* www.kpff.com	Seattle	WA	98101	206-622-5822	622-8130
Kramer Gehlen & Associates Inc 400 Columbia St Ste 240 *Web:* www.kga.cc	Vancouver	WA	98660	360-693-1621	
Kratos Defense & Security Solutions Inc 4820 Eastgate Mall Ste 200 *TF:* 877-548-7911 ■ *Web:* www.kratosdefense.com	San Diego	CA	92121	858-332-3700	812-7301
Krazan & Assoc Inc 215 W Dakota Ave *Web:* www.krazan.com	Clovis	CA	93612	559-348-2200	348-2201
Kroeschell Inc 3222 N Kennicott Ave *Web:* www.kroeschell.com	Arlington Heights	IL	60004	312-649-7980	649-3654
KS Energy Services LLC 19705 W Lincoln Ave *Web:* www.ksenergyservices.com	New Berlin	WI	53146	262-574-5100	
KSA Engineers Inc 140 E Tyler St Ste 600 Ste 600 *TF:* 877-572-3647 ■ *Web:* www.ksaeng.com	Longview	TX	75601	903-236-7700	236-7779
Kta-Tator Inc 115 Technology Dr *TF:* 800-582-4243 ■ *Web:* ktagage.com	Pittsburgh	PA	15275	412-788-1300	788-1306
Kuhlmann Design Group Inc (KDGI) 66 Progress Pkwy *Web:* www.kdginc.com	Maryland Heights	MO	63043	314-434-8898	434-8280
Kuljian Corp 1880 JF Kennedy Blvd *Web:* www.kuljian.com	Philadelphia	PA	19103	215-243-1900	243-1942
Kumar & Assoc Inc 2390 S Lipan St *Web:* kumarusa.com	Denver	CO	80223	303-742-9700	
L m Engineering Inc 2720 Intertech Dr *Web:* cybozone.com	Youngstown	OH	44509	330-270-2400	
La Jolla Bioengineering Institute 505 Coast Blvd S Ste 406 *Web:* www.ljbi.org	La Jolla	CA	92037	858-456-7500	
LaBella Associates PC 300 State St Ste 201 *Web:* www.labellapc.com	Rochester	NY	14614	585-454-6110	
Lacasse & Weston Inc 203 Anderson St Ste 201 *Web:* lacasseandweston.com	Portland	ME	04101	207-839-3650	
Land Design Consultants Inc 2700 E Foothill Blvd *Web:* ldcla.com	Pasadena	CA	91107	626-578-7000	
Land Development Consultants Inc 14201 NE 200th St Ste 100 *Web:* ldccorp.com	Woodinville	WA	98072	425-806-1869	
Landis Corp 6446 Fairway Ave Se *Web:* landisconsulting.com	Salem	OR	97306	503-584-1576	
Landmark Consultants Inc 141 Ninth St *Web:* www.landmark-co.com	Steamboat Springs	CO	80477	970-871-9494	
Landmark Testing & Engineering 795 E Factory Dr *Web:* landmarktesting.com	St George	UT	84790	435-986-0566	
Lane Engineering LLC 117 Bay St *Web:* www.leinc.com	Easton	MD	21601	410-822-8003	
Langan Engineering & Environmental Services Inc 619 River Dr Ctr 1 *Web:* www.langan.com	Elmwood Park	NJ	07407	201-794-6900	794-7501
Langdon Wilson Architecture Planning Interiors 1055 Wilshire Blvd Ste 1500 *Web:* www.langdonwilson.com	Los Angeles	CA	90017	213-250-1186	482-4654
Lanier & Assoc Consulting Engi Neers Inc 4101 Magazine St *Web:* lanier-engineers.com	New Orleans	LA	70115	504-895-0368	
LaPrairie Crane 235 Front St Ste 209 *Web:* www.laprairiegroup.com	Tumbler Ridge	BC	V0C2W0	250-242-5561	
Larry M Jacobs & Assoc Inc 328 E Gadsden *Web:* lmj-a.com	Pensacola	FL	32501	850-434-0846	
Larry Snyder & Company Inc 4820 N Towne Centre Dr *Web:* lscinc.com	Ozark	MO	65721	417-887-6897	
Larson Design Group Inc 1000 Commerce Pk Dr Ste 201 PO Box 487 *TF:* 877-323-6603 ■ *Web:* www.larsondesigngroup.com	Williamsport	PA	17701	570-323-6603	323-9902
Larson Engineering Inc 3524 Labore Rd *Web:* larsonengr.com	White Bear Lake	MN	55110	651-481-9120	
Lathrop Engineering Inc 1101 S Winchester Blvd *Web:* www.lathropeng.com	San Jose	CA	95128	408-260-2111	
Lauren Engineers & Constructors Inc PO Box 1761 *TF:* 800-433-7300 ■ *Web:* www.laurenec.com	Abilene	TX	79604	325-670-9660	670-9663
Lawson-fisher Associates Pc 525 W Washington St Ste 200 *Web:* lawson-fisher.com	South Bend	IN	46601	574-234-3167	
LBA Group Inc 3400 Tupper Dr *TF:* 800-522-4464 ■ *Web:* www.lbagroup.com	Greenville	NC	27834	252-757-0279	752-9155
Lc Engineers Inc 1471 Pinewood St Bldg 3 *Web:* www.lcengineers.com	Rahway	NJ	07065	732-340-9190	
Lee Burkhart Liu Inc 13335 Maxella Ave	Marina del Rey	CA	90292	310-829-2249	829-1736
Leedy & Petzold Assoc LLC 12970 W Bluemound Rd	Elm Grove	WI	53122	262-860-1544	
Lefler Engineering Inc 1651 Second St *Web:* leflerengineering.com	San Rafael	CA	94901	415-456-4220	
Leighton Group Inc 17781 Cowan St *Web:* leightongeo.com	Irvine	CA	92614	949-250-1421	250-1114

				Phone	Fax

LeMessurier Consultants
1380 Soldiers Field Rd ... Boston MA 02135 617-868-1200 661-7520
Web: www.lemessurier.com

Leo A Daly 8600 Indian Hills Dr ... Omaha NE 68114 402-391-8111 391-8111
Web: www.leoadaly.com

Lerch Bates Inc 8089 S Lincoln St Ste 300 ... Littleton CO 80122 303-795-7956
Web: www.lerchbates.com

Lesco Design & Mfg Company Inc
1120 Ft Pickens Rd ... Lagrange KY 40031 502-222-7101
Web: lescodesign.com

Lewis Innovative Technologies Inc
534 Lawrence St ... Moulton AL 35650 256-905-0775
Web: lewisinnovative.com

Lexington Technologies in 99 Rome St ... Farmingdale NY 11735 631-755-8660
Web: lexingtontech.net

LHB Inc 21 W Superior St Ste 500 ... Duluth MN 55802 218-727-8446
Web: www.lhbcorp.com

Life Cycle Engineering Inc
4360 Corporate Rd ... N Charleston SC 29405 843-744-7110
Web: lce.com

Lilker Associates Consulting Engineers PC
1001 Ave of the Americas Fl 9 ... New York NY 10018 212-695-1000
Web: www.lilker.com

Lincus Inc 8727 S Priest Dr ... Tempe AZ 85284 480-598-8431
Web: lincusenergy.com

Linebach - Funkhouser Inc 114 Fairfax Ave ... Louisville KY 40207 502-895-5009
Web: linebachfunkhouser.com

Linfield Hunter & Junius 3608 18th St 200 ... Metairie LA 70002 504-833-5300
Web: www.lhjunius.com

Link Technologies 9500 Hillwood Dr Ste 112 ... Las Vegas NV 89134 702-233-8703
Web: www.linktechconsulting.com

Lionakis Beaumont Design Group Inc
1919 19th St ... Sacramento CA 95811 916-558-1900 558-1919
Web: lionakis.com

LiRo Group Three Aerial Way ... Syosset NY 11791 516-938-5476 937-5421
Web: www.liro.com

LJB Inc 2500 Newmark Dr PO Box 20246 ... Miamisburg OH 45342 937-259-5000 259-5100
TF: 866-552-3536 ■ *Web:* www.ljbinc.com

Ljm Engineering Group Inc 439 Us Hwy 46 ... Rockaway NJ 07866 973-586-3004
Web: www.ljmengineering.com

LMN Architects 801 Second Ave Ste 501 ... Seattle WA 98104 206-682-3460 343-9388
Web: www.lmnarchitects.com

Lmw Engineering Group LLC 2539 Brunswick Ave ... Linden NJ 07036 908-862-7600
Web: www.ftcny.com

Locating Inc 2575 Westside Pkwy Ste 100 ... Alpharetta GA 30004 678-461-3900 461-3902
Web: www.locatinginc.com

Lochsa Engineering Inc
6345 S Jones Blvd Ste 100 ... Las Vegas NV 89118 702-365-9312
Web: www.lochsa.com

Lockwood Andrews & Newnam Inc
2925 Briar Pk Dr ... Houston TX 77042 713-266-6900 266-2089
Web: www.lan-inc.com

Lockwood Kessler & Bartlett Inc
One Aerial Way ... Syosset NY 11791 516-938-0600 931-6344
Web: www.lkbinc.com

Logistics Value Integrations Inc
3828 Farr Oak Cir ... Fairfax VA 22030 703-934-4218
Web: www.logvalu.com

Lohan Caprile Goettsch Architects
Goettsch Partners 224 S Michigan Ave 17th Fl ... Chicago IL 60604 312-356-0600 356-0601
Web: www.gpchicago.com

Long Engineering Inc
2550 Heritage Court Ste 100 ... Atlanta GA 30339 770-951-2495
Web: www.longeng.com

Looney Ricks Kiss Architects
175 Toyota Plz Ste 600 ... Memphis TN 38103 901-521-1440 525-2760
Web: www.lrk.com

LORE Product Design Engineering & Development Inc
36 Eglinton Ave W Ste 707 ... Toronto ON M4R1A1 416-489-9008
Web: www.designlore.com

Louis Berger Group Inc 412 Mt Kemble Ave ... Morristown NJ 07960 973-407-1000
Web: www.louisberger.com

Loyola Enterprises Inc
2984 S Lynnhaven Rd Ste 101 ... Virginia Beach VA 23452 757-498-6118
Web: www.loyola.com

LPA Inc 5161 California Ave Ste 100 ... Irvine CA 92617 949-261-1001 260-1190
Web: www.lpainc.com

Lps Integration Inc
230 Great Cir Rd Ste 218 ... Nashville TN 37228 615-254-0581
Web: www.lpsintegration.com

LRL Associates Ltd 5430 Canotek Rd ... Ottawa ON K1J9G2 613-842-3434
Web: www.lrl.ca

LS3P Assoc Ltd 205 1/2 King St ... Charleston SC 29401 843-577-4444 722-4789
Web: www.ls3p.com

LTL Consultants Ltd One Town Ctr Dr ... Oley PA 19547 610-987-9290
Web: www.ltlconsultants.com

Lumos & Assoc Inc 800 E College Pkwy ... Carson City NV 89706 775-883-7077 883-7114
TF: 800-621-7155 ■ *Web:* www.lumosinc.com

Lutz, Daily & Brain LLC
6400 Glenwood St ... Shawnee Mission KS 66202 913-831-0833
Web: www.ldbeng.com

LVM-JEGEL 1821 Albion Rd Unit 7 ... Toronto ON M9W5W8 416-213-1060
Web: fr.lvm.ca

M & H Enterprises Inc 19450 Hwy 249 Ste 600 ... Houston TX 77070 281-664-7222
Web: mhes.com

M Gingerich Gereaux & Assoc
240 N Industrial Dr ... Bradley IL 60915 815-939-4921

M K Technical Services Inc
4349 San Felipe Rd ... San Jose CA 95135 408-528-0401
Web: www.mktech.com

M Neils Engineering Inc 100 Howe Ave ... Sacramento CA 95825 916-923-4400
Web: mneilsengineering.com

M S Benbow & Associates Professional Engineering Corp
2450 Severn Ave ... Metairie LA 70001 504-832-2000
Web: www.msbenbow.com

M Squared Engineering LLC
W62n215 Washington Ave ... Cedarburg WI 53012 262-376-4246
Web: msquaredengineering.com

M W Consulting Engineers LLC
222 N Wall St Ste 200 ... Spokane WA 99201 509-838-9020
Web: www.mwengineers.com

M-E Engineers Inc 10055 W 43rd Ave ... Wheat Ridge CO 80033 303-421-6655 421-0331
Web: www.me-engineers.com

M/E Engineering PC 150 N Chestnut St ... Rochester NY 14604 585-288-5590 288-0233
Web: www.meengineering.com

M3 Engineering & Technology Corp
2051 W Sunset Rd ... Tucson AZ 85704 520-293-1488
Web: m3eng.com

Ma Engineers Inc
5160 Carroll Canyon Rd Ste 200 ... San Diego CA 92121 858-200-0030
Web: www.ma-engr.com

Macarthur Associated Consultants LLC
3033 Nw 63rd St Ste 250E ... Oklahoma City OK 73116 405-848-2471
Web: www.macokc.com

Macaulay-Brown Inc 4021 Executive Dr ... Dayton OH 45430 937-426-3421 426-5364
TF: 800-669-4000 ■ *Web:* www.macb.com

Macina Bose Copeland & Assoc Inc
1035 Central Pkwy N ... San Antonio TX 78232 210-545-1122

Macintosh Engineering
300 Delaware Ave Ste 820 ... Wilmington DE 19801 302-252-9200
Web: macintosheng.com

MacKay & Somps (MSCE) 5142 Franklin Dr Ste B ... Pleasanton CA 94588 925-225-0690 225-0698
Web: www.msce.com

Macritchie Engineering Inc 197 Quincy Ave ... Braintree MA 02184 781-848-4464
Web: macritchie.net

Madsen Kneppers & Assoc Inc
100 Pringle Ave Ste 340 ... Walnut Creek CA 94596 925-934-3235
Web: mkainc.com

Magnusson Klemencic Assoc Inc
1301 Fifth Ave Ste 3200 ... Seattle WA 98101 206-292-1200 292-1201
Web: www.mka.com

Mahlum Architects Inc 71 Columbia St 4Fl ... Seattle WA 98104 206-441-4151 441-0478
Web: www.mahlum.com

Mainelli Wagner & Associates Inc
6920 Van Dorn St Ste A ... Lincoln NE 68506 402-421-1717
Web: www.mwaeng.com

Malouf Engineering International Inc
17950 Preston Rd Ste 720 ... Dallas TX 75252 972-783-2578 783-2583
Web: www.maloufengineering.com

Management Consulting Inc
1961 Diamond Springs Rd ... Virginia Beach VA 23455 757-460-0879 457-9337
TF: 877-624-8090 ■ *Web:* www.manconinc.com

Manders Merighi Portadin Farrell Architects LLC
1138 E Chestnut Ave Bldg 4 ... Vineland NJ 08360 856-696-9155

Mannik & Smith Group Inc 1800 Indian Wood Cir ... Maumee OH 43537 419-891-2222
Web: manniksmithgroup.com

Map Assoc Inc Dba North Star Engineering
111 Mission Ranch Blvd ... Chico CA 95926 530-893-1600

MAR Inc 1803 Research Blvd Ste 204 ... Rockville MD 20850 301-231-0100 453-9871*
**Fax Area Code: 240* ■ *Web:* www.marinc.com

March Consulting Associates Inc
200 201 21st St E ... Saskatoon SK S7K0B8 306-651-6330
Web: www.marchconsulting.com

Maren Engineering 111 W Taft Dr ... South Holland IL 60473 708-333-6250
Web: marenengineering.com

Marine Innovation & Technology
2610 Marin Ave ... Berkeley CA 94708 510-931-6135
Web: www.marineitech.com

Marine Systems Corp 70 Fargo St Seaport Ctr ... Boston MA 02210 617-542-3345 542-2461
TF: 800-559-9293 ■ *Web:* www.mscorp.net

Mark Thomas & Company Inc 1960 Zanker Rd ... San Jose CA 95112 408-453-5373 453-5390
Web: www.markthomas.com

MarketCounsel LLC 61 W Palisade Ave ... Englewood NJ 07631 201-705-1200
Web: www.marketcounsel.com

Marshall Miller & Assoc
5415 SW Westgate Dr Ste 100 ... Portland VA 97221 503-419-2500 419-2600
Web: cardno.com

Martenson & Eisele Inc 1377 Midway Rd ... Menasha WI 54952 920-731-0381
Web: www.martenson-eisele.com

Martin Mechanical Design Inc
702 28th Ave N Ste 200 ... Fargo ND 58102 701-293-7957

Martronic Engineering Inc
80 W Cochran St Ste B ... Simi Valley CA 93065 805-583-0808
Web: meilaser.com

Marx | Okubo Associates Inc
455 Sherman St Ste 200 ... Denver CO 80203 303-861-0300
Web: www.marxokubo.com

Maser Consulting PA
331 Newman Springs Rd Ste203 ... Red Bank NJ 07701 732-383-1950 383-1984
Web: www.maserconsulting.com

Matis Warfield Inc 10540 York Rd Ste M ... Cockeysville MD 21030 410-683-7004
Web: matiswarfield.com

Matrix Computer Solutions Inc
3001 Bridgeway Ste K314 ... Sausalito CA 94965 415-331-3600
Web: www.matrixcomp.net

Matrix Design Group Inc 1601 Blake St Ste 200 ... Denver CO 80202 303-572-0200
Web: www.matrixdesigngroup.com

Matrix Engineering Pllc
112 Walter Jetton Blvd ... Paducah KY 42001 270-442-5600
Web: matrixengineer.com

Mattern & Craig Inc 701 First St SW ... Roanoke VA 24016 540-345-9342
Web: matternandcraig.com

MBH Architects 2470 Mariner Sq Loop ... Alameda CA 94501 510-865-8663 865-1611
Web: www.mbharch.com

Company / Address	City	State	Zip	Phone	Fax
MBS Assoc Inc 10148 Commerce Pk Dr *TF:* 888-469-9301 ■ *Web:* www.mbsassociates.com	Cincinnati	OH	45246	513-645-1600	680-4587
Mc Donough Engineering Corp 5625 Schumacher Ln *Web:* www.mectx.com	Houston	TX	77057	713-975-9990	
MC Squared Inc 17 Harbourton Ridge Dr *Web:* www.mcsqd.com	Pennington	NJ	08534	609-474-8100	
McClure Engineering Associates Inc 4700 Kennedy Dr *Web:* www.mcclureengineering.com	East Moline	IL	61244	309-792-9305	
Mccool Carlson Green Inc 421 W First Ave Ste 300 *Web:* mcgalaska.com	Anchorage	AK	99501	907-563-8474	
McCormick Taylor & Assoc Inc Two Commerce Sq 10th Fl *Web:* www.mccormicktaylor.com	Philadelphia	PA	19103	215-592-4200	592-0682
McCrone Inc 20 Ridgely Ave Second Fl *Web:* www.mccrone-inc.com	Annapolis	MD	21401	410-267-8621	
Mcdaniel Tech Services Inc 2009 N Willow Ave *Web:* www.mcdanieltsi.com	Broken Arrow	OK	74012	918-294-1628	
McDonough Bolyard Peck Inc (MBP) 3040 Williams Dr Williams Plz 1 Ste 300 *TF:* 800-898-9088 ■ *Web:* www.mbpce.com	Fairfax	VA	22031	703-641-9088	641-8965
MCG Architecture 111 Pacifica Ste 280 *Web:* www.mcgarchitecture.com	Irvine	CA	92618	949-553-1117	
McGill Smith Punshon Inc 3700 Park 42 Dr Ste 190B *Web:* www.mcgillsmithpunshon.com	Cincinnati	OH	45241	513-759-0004	
Mcgoodwin Williams & Yates Inc (MWY) 302 E Millsap Rd *Web:* www.mwyusa.com	Fayetteville	AR	72703	479-443-3404	443-4340
McKim & Creed PA 243 N Front St *Web:* www.mckimcreed.com	Wilmington	NC	28401	910-343-1048	251-8282
Mckinney & Company Inc 100 S Railroad Ave *Web:* mckinney-usa.com	Ashland	VA	23005	804-798-1451	
McLaren Performance Technologies Inc 32233 W Eight Mile Rd *Web:* www.linamar.com	Livonia	MI	48152	248-477-6240	477-3349
McLaughlin Research Corp 132 Johnnycake Hill Rd *TF:* 800-556-7154 ■ *Web:* www.mrcds.com	Middletown	RI	02842	401-849-4010	847-9716
Mcmahon Assoc Inc 425 Commerce Dr Ste 200 *Web:* mcmahonassociates.com	Fort Washington	PA	19034	215-283-9444	
McMahon Group 1445 McMahon Dr *Web:* www.mcmgrp.com	Neenah	WI	54956	920-751-4200	751-4284
Mcmillen Engineering Inc 115 Wayland Smith Dr *Web:* mcmilleng.com	Uniontown	PA	15401	724-439-8110	
MCR LLC 2010 Corporate Ridge Ste 350 *Web:* www.mcri.com	McLean	VA	22102	703-506-4600	506-8601
Mcs Advertising 4110 Progress Blvd Ste 1c *Web:* www.mcsadv.com	Peru	IL	61354	815-224-3011	
Mctish Kunkel & Assoc 3500 Winchester Rd *Web:* mctish.com	Allentown	PA	18104	610-841-2700	
Mcveigh & Mangum Engineering Inc 9133 Rg Skinner Pkwy *Web:* mcveighmangum.com	Jacksonville	FL	32256	904-483-5200	
MDA Engineering Inc 1415 Holland Rd	Maumee	OH	43537	419-893-3141	
MDA Information Systems Inc 6011 Executive Blvd *TF:* 800-642-1687 ■ *Web:* www.mdafederal.com	Rockville	MD	20852	240-833-8200	833-8201
Mead & Hunt Inc 6501 Watts Rd *Web:* www.meadhunt.com	Madison	WI	53719	608-273-6380	273-6391
Mecanica Solutions Inc 6300 Cote-de-Liesse Ste 200 *Web:* www.mecanicasolutions.com	Saint-laurent	QC	H4T1E3	514-340-1818	
Meers Engineering Inc 209 S Danville Dr Ste B 200 *Web:* www.meersengineering.com/	Abilene	TX	79605	325-691-1200	691-1206
MEI Technologies Inc 18050 Saturn Ln Ste 300 *Web:* www.meitechinc.com	Houston	TX	77058	281-283-6200	
Meier Enterprises Inc 8697 W Gage Blvd *Web:* meierinc.com	Kennewick	WA	99336	509-735-1589	
Melick-Tully & Assoc PC 117 Canal Rd *Web:* melick-tully.com	South Bound Brook	NJ	08880	732-356-3400	
Mellor Engineering Inc 887 North 100 East Ste 1 *Web:* mellorengineering.com	Lehi	UT	84043	801-768-0658	
Mendoza Ribas Farinas & Assoc 6265 Executive Blvd *Web:* www.mrf-a.com	Rockville	MD	20852	301-468-8882	
Meridian West Consultants LLC 7603 S Main St *Web:* www.meridian-west.com	Midvale	UT	84047	801-542-7082	
Merrick & Co 2450 S Peoria St *TF:* 800-544-1714 ■ *Web:* www.merrick.com	Aurora	CO	80014	303-751-0741	751-2581
Merritt Environmental Consulting Corp 77 Arkay Dr *Web:* merrittec.com	Hauppauge	NY	11788	631-617-6200	
Mesa Assoc Inc PO Box 196 *Web:* www.mesainc.com	Madison	AL	35758	256-258-2100	258-2103
Met-Chem Canada Inc 555, Blvd Rene-Levesque Ouest 3e etage *Web:* www.met-chem.com	Montreal	QC	H2Z1B1	514-288-5211	
Met-scan Canada Ltd 30 Kern Rd *Web:* www.met-scan.com	North York	ON	M3B1T1	416-391-2200	
Meta Environmental Inc 49 Clarendon St *Web:* metaenv.com	Watertown	MA	02472	617-923-4662	
Methane Specialists 621 Via Alondra Ste 610 *Web:* methanespecialists.com	Camarillo	CA	93012	805-987-5356	
Metro-Can Construction Ltd 10470 152 St Ste 520 *Web:* www.metrocanconstruction.com	Surrey	BC	V3R0Y3	604-583-1174	
Mge Engineering Inc 7415 Greenhaven Dr *Web:* www.mgeeng.com	Sacramento	CA	95831	916-421-1000	
MHC Engineers Inc 150 Eighth St *Web:* mhcengr.com	San Francisco	CA	94103	415-512-7141	
Michael Baker Corp 100 Airsite Dr Airsite Business Pk *NYSE: BKR* ■ **Fax Area Code: 757* ■ *TF:* 800-553-1153 ■ *Web:* www.mbakercorp.com	Moon Township	PA	15108	412-269-6300	463-0503*
Michaud Cooley Erickson & Assoc Inc 1200 Metropolitan Ctr Ste 1200 *Web:* www.michaudcooley.com	Minneapolis	MN	55402	612-339-4941	339-8354
Mickle Wagner Coleman Inc 3434 Country Club Ave *Web:* www.mwc-engr.com	Fort Smith	AR	72903	479-649-8484	
Microlynx Systems Ltd 1925 18 Ave Ne Ste 107 *Web:* www.microlynxsystems.com	Calgary	AB	T2E7T8	403-275-7346	
Middough Assoc Inc 1901 E 13th St **Fax:* Hum Res ■ *Web:* www.middough.com	Cleveland	OH	44114	216-367-6000	367-6020*
Mide Technology Corp 200 Boston Ave *Web:* mide.com	Medford	MA	02155	781-306-0609	
Midrex Technologies 2725 Water Ridge Pkwy Ste 100 *Web:* www.midrex.com	Charlotte	NC	28217	704-373-1600	373-1611
Mikro Systems Inc 1180 Seminole Trl Ste 220 *Web:* www.mikrosystems.com	Charlottesville	VA	22901	434-244-6480	
Mikros Engineering Inc 8755 Wyoming Ave N *Web:* www.mikros.com	Minneapolis	MN	55445	763-424-4642	
Milhouse Engineering & Construction Inc 60 E Van Buren St Ste 1501 *Web:* milhouseinc.com	Chicago	IL	60605	312-987-0061	
Milian & Swain Associates Inc 2025 SW 32nd Ave *Web:* www.milianswain.com	Miami	FL	33145	305-441-0123	
Miller Engineers & Scientists 5308 S 12th St *Web:* www.startwithmiller.com	Sheboygan	WI	53081	920-458-6164	
Miller Pacific Engineering Group 504 Redwood Blvd Ste 220 *Web:* www.millerpac.com	Novato	CA	94947	415-382-3444	
Millogic Ltd 89 Cambridge St *Web:* millogic.com	Burlington	MA	01803	339-234-5700	
Mills & Assoc Inc 3242 Henderson Blvd	Tampa	FL	33609	813-876-5869	
Mine Development Assoc 210 S Rock Blvd *Web:* www.mda.com	Reno	NV	89502	775-856-5700	
Minnetronix Inc 1635 Energy Park Dr *Web:* minnetronix.com	St Paul	MN	55108	651-917-4060	
Missman Inc 1011 27th Ave PO Box 6040 *TF:* 800-969-3029 ■ *Web:* missman.com	Rock Island	IL	61201	309-788-7644	788-7691
Mkec Engineering Consultants Inc 411 N Webb Rd *Web:* mkec.com	Wichita	KS	67206	316-684-9600	
Modern Process Equipment Inc 3125 S Kolin Ave *Web:* mpechicago.com	Chicago	IL	60623	773-254-3929	
Modern Technology Solutions Inc (MTSI) 5285 Shawnee Rd Ste 400 *Web:* www.mtsi-va.com	Alexandria	VA	22312	703-564-3800	
Modjeski & Masters Inc 100 Sterling Pkwy Ste 302 *Web:* www.modjeski.com	Mechanicsburg	PA	17050	717-790-9565	790-9564
Moffatt & Nichol Engineers 3780 Kilroy Airport Way # 750 *TF:* 888-399-6609 ■ *Web:* www.moffattnichol.com	Long Beach	CA	90806	562-590-6500	590-6512
Mohr & Assoc Inc 6025 Buncombe Rd *Web:* www.mohrandassoc.com	Shreveport	LA	71129	318-686-7190	
Monte R Lee & Co 100 NW 63rd St Ste 100 *Web:* www.mrleng.com	Oklahoma City	OK	73116	405-842-2405	848-8018
Moody Nolan Inc 300 Spruce St Ste 300 *TF:* 877-530-4984 ■ *Web:* www.moodynolan.com	Columbus	OH	43215	614-461-4664	280-8881
Moon-matz Ltd 1435 Hurontario St *Web:* moon-matz.com	Mississauga	ON	L5G3H5	905-274-7556	
Moore Bass Consulting Inc 805 N Gadsden St *Web:* moorebass.com	Tallahassee	FL	32303	850-222-5678	
Moreland & Altobelli Assoc Inc 2211 Beaver Ruin Rd Ste 190 *Web:* www.maai.net	Norcross	GA	30071	770-263-5945	263-0166
Morell Engineering & Development LLC 112 N Marion St *Web:* www.morellengineering.com	Athens	AL	35611	256-867-4957	
Morgan-Keller Inc 70 Thomas Johnson Dr Ste 200 *Web:* www.morgankeller.com	Frederick	MD	21702	301-663-0626	
Morley & Assoc Inc 4800 Rosebud Ln *Web:* www.morleyandassociates.com/	Newburgh	IN	47630	812-464-9585	464-2514
Morris Architects 1001 Fannin St Ste 300 *Web:* www.morrisarchitects.com	Houston	TX	77002	713-622-1180	622-7021
Morrison Hershfield Group Inc 235 Yorkland Blvd Ste 600 *Web:* www.morrisonhershfield.com	Toronto	ON	M2J1T1	416-499-3110	
Morrison-Maierle Inc 1 Engineering Pl *Web:* www.m-m.net	Helena	MT	59604	406-442-3050	
Moseley Technical Services Inc 7500 S Memorial Pkwy Ste 220-131 *Web:* www.moseleytechnical.com	Huntsville	AL	35802	256-880-0446	
Mpe Engineering Ltd Ste 260 E Atrium 2635 37 Ave NE *Web:* www.mpe.ab.ca	Calgary	AB	T1Y5Z6	403-329-3442	
MS Consultants Inc 333 E Federal St *Web:* www.msconsultants.com	Youngstown	OH	44503	330-744-5321	744-5256

	City	State	Zip	Phone	Fax
MS Technology Inc 137 Union Vly Rd	Oak Ridge	TN	37830	865-483-0895	
Web: mstechnology.com					
MSA Consulting Inc 34200 Bob Hope Dr	Rancho Mirage	CA	92270	760-320-9811	
Web: www.msaconsultinginc.com					
MSA Professional Services Inc 1230 South Blvd.	Baraboo	WI	53913	608-356-2771	
Web: msa-ps.com					
MSE Power Systems Inc 403 New Karner Rd	Albany	NY	12205	518-452-7718	452-7716
Web: www.msepower.com					
Muermann Engineering LLC 116 Fremont St	Kiel	WI	53042	920-894-7800	
Web: www.me-pe.com					
Mueser Rutledge Consulting Engineers (MRCE) 14 Penn Plaza 225 W 34th St 6th Fl	New York	NY	10122	917-339-9300	339-9400
Web: www.mrce.com					
Muller Engineering Company Inc 777 S Wadsworth Blvd	Lakewood	CO	80226	303-988-4939	
Web: www.mullereng.com					
Multax Systems Inc 505 N Sepulveda Blvd Ste 7	Manhattan Beach	CA	90266	310-379-8398	379-1142
TF: 800-888-0199 ■ *Web:* www.multax.net					
Municipal Infrastructure Group Ltd, The 2300 Steeles Ave W Ste 120	Vaughan	ON	L4K5X6	905-738-5700	
Web: www.tmig.ca					
Mustang Engineering LP 16001 Pk Ten Pl.	Houston	TX	77084	713-215-8000	215-8506
TF: 866-313-0052 ■ *Web:* www.mustangeng.com					
Mustang Technology Group Lp 6900 K Ave	Plano	TX	75074	972-747-0707	
Web: mustangtechnology.com					
Mw Davis Dumas & Associates Inc 2720 Third Ave S	Birmingham	AL	35233	205-252-0246	
Web: www.mwdda.com					
MWH Americas Inc 370 Interlocken Blvd.	Broomfield	CO	80021	303-410-4000	
Web: mwhglobal.com					
Mwl Engineering Corp 6825 Sw 81st St	Miami	FL	33143	305-661-3357	
Web: mwleng.com					
N K Bhandari, Consulting Engineers PC 1005 W Fayette St Ste 4A	Syracuse	NY	13204	315-428-1177	
Web: nkbpc.com					
Nadel Architects 1990 S Bundy Dr Ste 400	Los Angeles	CA	90025	310-826-2100	826-0182
Web: www.nadelarc.com					
Nadine International Inc 2570 Matheson Blvd E Ste 110	Mississauga	ON	L4W4Z3	905-602-1850	
Web: www.nadineintl.on.ca					
Naik Consulting Group p C 200 Metroplex Dr Ste 403	Edison	NJ	08817	732-777-0030	
Web: www.naikgroup.com					
Nalpro Business Solutions LLC Brier Hill Ct Bldg C	East Brunswick	NJ	08816	732-390-1400	
Web: www.nalpro.com					
Nanohmics Inc 6201 E Oltorf St	Austin	TX	78741	512-389-9990	
Web: nanohmics.com					
Nasland Engineering 4740 Rufner St	San Diego	CA	92111	858-292-7770	
Web: www.nasland.com					
Nathan D. Maier Consulting Engineers Inc 8080 Park Ln Two NorthPark Ste 600	Dallas	TX	75231	214-739-4741	
Web: www.ndmce.com					
National Security Technologies LLC 2621 Losee Rd	Las Vegas	NV	89030	702-295-1000	295-2448
Web: www.nstec.com					
NBBJ 223 Yale Ave N	Seattle	WA	98109	206-223-5555	621-2300
Web: www.nbbj.com					
NCA Architects PA 1306 Rio Grande Blvd NW	Albuquerque	NM	87104	505-255-6400	
Neel-Schaffer Inc 125 S Congress St Ste 1100	Jackson	MS	39201	601-948-3178	948-3071
TF: 800-264-6335 ■ *Web:* www.neel-schaffer.com					
Neff Engineering Co 7114 Innovation Blvd	Fort Wayne	IN	46818	260-489-6007	489-6204
Web: www.neffengineering.com					
Neil O. Anderson & Associates Inc 902 Industrial Way	Lodi	CA	95240	209-367-3701	
Web: noanderson.com					
Nesbitt Engineering Inc (NEI) 227 N Upper St	Lexington	KY	40507	859-233-3111	259-2717
Web: www.nei-ky.com					
Neundorfer Inc 4590 Hamann Pkwy	Willoughby	OH	44094	440-942-8990	
Web: www.neundorfer.com					
New England Construction Company Inc 293 Bourne Ave	Rumford	RI	02916	401-434-0112	
Web: www.neconstruction.com					
New Holland Engineering 43 E Front St	New Holland	OH	43145	740-495-5200	
Web: gutterhangers.net					
New Tech Global (NTG) 1030 Regional Pk Dr	Houston	TX	77060	281-951-4330	951-8719
Web: www.newtechengineering.com					
Newcomb & Boyd 303 Peachtree Ctr Ave NE Ste 525	Atlanta	GA	30303	404-730-8400	730-8401
Web: www.newcomb-boyd.com					
Nextgen Networks Inc 200 Katonah Ave Ste A	Katonah	NY	10536	914-232-8300	
Web: www.nninet.com					
Nfra Inc 77 E Thomas Rd Ste 200	Phoenix	AZ	85012	602-277-0967	
Web: www.nfrainc.us					
Niles Bolton Assoc Inc (NBA) 3060 Peachtree Rd NW Ste 600	Atlanta	GA	30305	404-365-7600	365-7610
Web: www.nilesbolton.com					
Ninyo & Moore 5710 Ruffin Rd.	San Diego	CA	92123	858-576-1000	576-9600
TF: 800-427-0401 ■ *Web:* www.ninyoandmoore.com					
Nobis Engineering Inc 18 Chenell Dr	Concord	NH	03301	603-224-4182	
Web: nobiseng.com					
Noble Technologies Corp 2255 Gateway Dr	Wooster	OH	44691	330-287-1500	
Web: www.nobletek.com					
NORAM Engineering & Constructors Ltd 200 Granville St Ste 1800	Vancouver	BC	V6C1S4	604-681-2030	
Web: www.noram-eng.com					
Nordmin Engineering Ltd 160 Logan Ave	Thunder Bay	ON	P7A6R1	807-683-1730	
Web: nordmin.com					
NorTech Energy Enterprise 737 Bolivar Rd Ste 1000	Cleveland	OH	44115	216-363-6883	
Web: nortech.org					
Northern Digital 5555 Business Pk	Bakersfield	CA	93309	661-322-6044	
Web: ndi.us					
Northwest Hydraulic Consultants 16300 Christensen Rd Ste 350	Tukwila	WA	98188	206-241-6000	
Web: nhcweb.com					
Northwestern Engineering Co PO Box 2624	Rapid City	SD	57709	605-394-3310	341-2558
Web: www.nwemanagement.com					
Notkin Hawaii Inc 738 Kaheka St Ste 301	Honolulu	HI	96814	808-941-6600	
Web: www.notkinhi.com					
Nova Group Inc 185 Devlin Rd	Napa	CA	94558	707-257-3200	257-2774
Web: www.novagrp.com					
Nova Pole International Inc 19433 96th Ave Ste 102	Surrey	BC	V4N4C4	604-881-0090	
Web: www.novapole.com					
Novariant Inc 45700 Northport Loop E	Fremont	CA	94538	510-933-4800	933-4801
Web: www.gpsfarm.com					
NTB Assoc Inc 525 Louisiana Ave.	Shreveport	LA	71101	318-226-9199	
Web: ntbainc.com					
Nuclear Logistics Inc 7410 Pebble Dr	Fort Worth	TX	76118	817-284-0077	
Web: nuclearlogistics.com					
Nuezra 2155 Amethyst Dr.	Santa Clara	CA	95051	408-832-2371	
Web: www.nuezra.com					
Nussbaumer & Clarke Inc 3556 Lk Shore Rd Ste 500	Buffalo	NY	14219	716-827-8000	
Web: www.nussclarke.com					
NV5 2525 Natomas Pk Dr Ste 300	Sacramento	CA	95833	916-641-9100	641-9222
TF: 877-941-2068 ■ *Web:* www.nolte.com					
O'Brien & Gere Engineers Inc 333 W Washington St	East Syracuse	NY	13202	315-956-6100	463-7554
Web: www.obg.com					
O'Connell Robertson & Associates Inc 811 Barton Springs Rd Ste 900	Austin	TX	78704	512-478-7286	
Web: www.oconnellrobertson.com					
O'day Consultants Inc 2710 Loker Ave W Ste 100	Carlsbad	CA	92010	760-931-7700	
Web: www.odayconsultants.com					
O'kane Consultants Inc 112 Research Dr	Saskatoon	SK	S7N3R3	306-955-0702	
Web: www.okc-sk.com					
O'Neal Inc 10 Falcon Crest Dr.	Greenville	SC	29607	864-298-2000	298-2200
Web: www.onealinc.com					
O'Reilly Talbot & Okun Assoc Inc 293 Bridge St	Springfield	MA	01103	413-788-6222	
Web: oto-env.com					
OASIS Alignment Services Inc 255 Pickering Rd	Rochester	NH	03867	603-332-9641	
Web: www.oasisalignment.com					
Ocean Tug & Barge Engineering Corp 258 E Main St Ste 401	Milford	MA	01757	508-473-0545	
Web: www.articulatedtugbarge.com					
Odell Assoc Inc 800 W Hill St Third Fl.	Charlotte	NC	28208	704-414-1000	414-1111
Web: www.odell.com					
Offshore Process Services Inc 1206 Park Dr	Mandeville	LA	70471	985-727-2900	
Web: www.opsincusa.com					
Oil Field Development Engineering LLC 12121 Wickchester Ln	Houston	TX	77079	281-679-9060	
Web: ofdeng.com					
Olson Engineering Inc 365 W Round Bunch Rd	Bridge City	TX	77611	409-697-3333	
Web: www.olsonengineering.com					
Olsson Assoc 1111 Lincoln Mall Ste 111	Lincoln	NE	68508	402-474-6311	474-5160
TF: 877-831-6389 ■ *Web:* www.oaconsulting.com					
Omni Link Corp 12000 Ford Rd Ste 235	Dallas	TX	75234	972-620-9000	
Web: www.omnilinkcorp.com					
Omni-Means Ltd 943 Reserve Dr Ste 100	Roseville	CA	95678	916-782-8688	782-8689
Web: www.omnimeans.com					
Omnni Associates Inc One Systems Dr	Appleton	WI	54914	920-735-6900	
Web: omnni.com					
Ontario Society of Professional Engineers 4950 Yonge St Ste 2200	North York	ON	M2N6K1	416-223-9961	
Web: www.students.ospe.on.ca					
Operational Technologies Corp 4100 NW Loop 410 Ste 230	San Antonio	TX	78229	210-731-0000	731-0008
TF: 855-276-6136 ■ *Web:* www.otcorp.com					
Optimized Process Designs Inc 25610 Clay Rd.	Katy	TX	77493	281-371-7500	
Web: www.opd-inc.com					
Orbital Engineering Inc 1344 Fifth Ave	Pittsburgh	PA	15219	412-261-9100	261-2308
Web: www.orbitalengr.com					
Orchard Hiltz & McCliment Inc (OHM) 34000 Plymouth Rd	Livonia	MI	48150	734-522-6711	522-6427
TF: 888-522-6711 ■ *Web:* www.ohm-advisors.com					
ORI Services Corp 4565 Ruffner St Ste 201	San Diego	CA	92111	858-576-4422	576-4475
Web: www.oriservices.com					
Ortloff Engineers Ltd 415 W Wall Ave Ste 2000	Midland	TX	79701	432-685-0277	685-0258
Web: www.ortloff.com					
Overlook Systems Technologies Inc 1950 Old Gallows Rd Ste 400	Vienna	VA	22182	703-893-1411	356-9029
Web: www.overlooksys.com					
Owen Group Inc 20 Morgan	Irvine	CA	92618	949-860-4800	860-4810
Web: www.owengroup.com					
P K Electrical 681 Sierra Rose Dr Ste B	Reno	NV	89511	775-826-9010	
Web: pkelectrical.com					
P T Systems Inc 1980 Olivera Rd Ste A	Concord	CA	94520	925-676-0709	
Web: www.ptsystemsinc.com					
P2S Engineering Inc 5000 E Spring St Eighth Fl	Long Beach	CA	90815	562-497-2999	
Web: www.p2seng.com					
Pacific Surveying & Engineering Services Inc 1812 Cornwall Ave	Bellingham	WA	98225	360-671-7387	
Web: www.psesurvey.com					

Phone *Fax*

Pacifica Services Inc
106 S Mentor Ave Ste 200 Pasadena CA 91106 626-405-0131 405-0059
Web: www.pacificaservices.com

Padre Associates Inc 1861 Knoll Dr Ventura CA 93003 805-644-2220
Web: www.padreinc.com

Pageau Morel et Associes Inc
365 Boul Greber Gatineau QC J8T5R3 819-776-4665
Web: www.pageaumorel.com

PageSoutherlandPage (PSPAEC)
1100 Louisiana St Ste 1 Houston TX 77002 713-871-8484 871-8440
Web: pagethink.com/

PAL General Engineering Inc
5374 Eastgate Mall San Diego CA 92121 858-638-7100
Web: www.palsd.com

Pape-Dawson Engineers Inc 555 E Ramsey San Antonio TX 78216 210-375-9000 375-9010
Web: www.pape-dawson.com

Paragon Engineering Services Inc
2201 S Queen St York PA 17402 717-854-7374 854-5533
Web: www.peservices.org

Parametrix Inc 1002 15th St SW Ste 220 Auburn WA 98001 253-269-1330 269-6899
Web: www.parametrix.com

Pare Corp Eight Blackstone Vly Pl Lincoln RI 02865 401-334-4100
Web: parecorp.com

Parker Development Company Inc
4525 Serrano Pkwy El Dorado Hills CA 95762 916-939-4060
Web: www.parkerdevco.com

Parkhill Smith & Cooper Inc 4222 85th St Lubbock TX 79423 806-473-2200 473-3500
TF: 800-400-6646 ■ *Web:* www.team-psc.com

Parsons Brinckerhoff Inc
One Penn Plz Second Fl New York NY 10119 212-465-5000 465-5096
Web: www.pbworld.com

Parsons Corp 100 W Walnut St Pasadena CA 91124 626-440-2000 440-2630
TF All: 800-883-7300 ■ *Web:* www.parsons.com

Parsons Harland Bartholomew & Assoc Inc
400 S Woods Mill Rd Chesterfield MO 63017 314-434-2900
Web: www.parsons.com

Parsons Infrastructure & Technology
100 W Walnut St Pasadena CA 91124 626-440-4000 830-0287*
**Fax Area Code:* 256 ■ *TF:* 800-300-0287 ■ *Web:* www.parsons.com

Passero Associates 242 W Main St Ste 100 Rochester NY 14614 585-325-1000
Web: www.passero.com

Patel Burica & Assoc Inc 9283 Research Dr Irvine CA 92618 949-943-8080 352-2209*
**Fax Area Code:* 714 ■ *Web:* www.pbastructural.com

Patrick Engineering Inc 4970 Varsity Dr Lisle IL 60532 630-795-7200
TF: 800-799-7050 ■ *Web:* www.patrickengineering.com

Patriot Engineering & Environmental Inc
6330 E 75th St Ste 216 Indianapolis IN 46250 317-576-8058
Web: patrioteng.com

Patti Engineering Inc
2110 E Walton Blvd Ste A Auburn Hills MI 48326 248-364-3200
Web: pattiengineering.com

Paul C Rizzo Assoc Inc 500 Penn Ctr Blvd Pittsburgh PA 15235 412-856-9700
Web: www.rizzoassoc.com

Paulus Engineering Inc 2871 E Coronado St Anaheim CA 92806 714-632-3975
Web: www.paulusengineering.com

Paulus Sokolowski & Sartor LLC
67 Mountain Blvd Ste B Warren NJ 07059 732-560-9700
Web: www.psands.com

Payette Assoc Inc 290 Congress St Fifth Fl Boston MA 02210 617-895-1000 895-1002
Web: www.payette.com

Payne-huber Engineering Inc
7060 S Yale Ave Ste 600 Tulsa OK 74136 918-492-0975
Web: payne-huber.com

PBS Engineering & Environmenal Inc
4412 SW Corbett Ave Portland OR 97239 503-248-1939
Web: pbsenv.com

PCA Engineering Inc
57 Cannonball Rd PO Box 196 Pompton Lakes NJ 07442 973-616-4501 616-4451
TF: 800-666-7221 ■ *Web:* pcaengineering.com/default.asp

Pearl Engineering Corp
110 E Grand Ave Wisconsin Rapids WI 54494 715-424-4008
Web: www.pearlengineering.com

Pearson Engineering Associates Inc
8825 N 23rd Ave Ste 11 Phoenix AZ 85021 602-264-0807
Web: www.peaeng.com

PEDCo E & A Services Inc
11499 Chester Rd Ste 301 Cincinnati OH 45246 513-782-4920
Web: www.pedcoea.com

Pegasus Engineering Inc
301 W State Rd 434 Ste 309 Winter Springs FL 32708 407-992-9160
Web: www.pegasusengineering.net

PegasusTSI Inc 5310 Cypress Ctr Dr Ste 200 Tampa FL 33609 813-876-2424
Web: www.pegasustsi.com

Pei Cobb Freed & Partners Architects LLP
88 Pine St New York NY 10005 212-751-3122 872-5443
Web: www.pcfandp.com

Penn Pro Inc 4000 Hwy 60 E Mulberry FL 33860 863-648-9990
Web: www.pennpro.net

Pennterra Engineering Inc
3075 Enterprise Dr State College PA 16801 814-231-8285
Web: www.pennterra.com

Penta Engineering PA 13835 S Lakes Dr Charlotte NC 28273 704-588-8877
Web: pentaengr.com

PeopleTec Inc 4901-I Corporate Dr NW Huntsville AL 35805 256-319-3800
Web: www.people-tec.com

Pepg LLC 8805 S Sandy Pkwy Sandy UT 84070 801-562-2521 562-2551
Web: pepg.net

Perkins & Will 330 N Wabash Ave Ste 3600 Chicago IL 60611 312-755-0770 755-0775
Web: www.perkinswill.com

Perkowitz + Ruth Architects
111 W Ocean Blvd 21st Fl Long Beach CA 90802 562-628-8000 628-8001
Web: www.prarchitects.com

Phone *Fax*

Perry & Associates LLC
221 N La Salle St Ste 3100 Chicago IL 60601 312-364-9112
Web: www.perryllc.com

Perteet Inc 2707 Colby Ave Ste 900 Ste900 Everett WA 98201 425-252-7700 339-6018
TF: 800-615-9900 ■ *Web:* www.perteet.com

Pes Environmental Inc 1682 Novato Blvd Ste 100 Novato CA 94947 415-899-1600
Web: www.pesenv.com

Peter Basso Associates Inc
5145 Livernois Ste 100 Troy MI 48098 248-879-5666
Web: www.peterbassoassociates.com

Peterson Structural Engineers Inc
5319 Sw Westgate Dr Ste 215 Portland OR 97221 503-292-1635
Web: psengineers.com

Petitt Barraza LLC 300 Municipal Dr Richardson TX 75080 214-221-9955
Web: www.petittbarraza.com

Peto MacCallum Ltd 165 Cartwright Ave Toronto ON M6A1V5 416-785-5110
Web: www.petomaccallum.com

Pettigrew & Assoc PA 100 E Navajo Hobbs NM 88240 575-393-9827
Web: pettigrew.us

Pfeiler & Assoc Engineers Inc 14181 Fern Ave Chino CA 91710 909-993-5800
Web: pfeilerassociates.com

Phoenix Analysis & Design Inc
7755 S Research Dr Ste 110 Tempe AZ 85284 480-813-4884
Web: padtinc.com

Physical Resource Engineering Inc
4655 N Flowing Wells Rd Tucson AZ 85705 520-690-1669
Web: www.prengr.com

Picco Engineering 350 Caldari Rd Concord ON L4K4J4 905-760-9688
Web: www.picco-engineering.com

Pie Consulting & Engineering Inc
6275 Joyce Dr Ste 200 Arvada CO 80403 303-552-0177
Web: www.callpie.com

Pieper O'Brien Herr Architects Ltd
3000 Royal Blvd South Alpharetta GA 30022 770-569-1706
Web: www.poharchitects.com

Piercon Solutions LLC
63 Beaverbrook Rd Ste 201 Lincoln Park NJ 07035 973-628-9330
Web: piercon.net

Pincock Allen & Holt A Div of Runge Inc
165 S Union Blvd Ste 950 Lakewood CO 80228 303-986-6950 987-8907
Web: www.rpmglobal.com

PINNACLE Converting Equipment 1720 Toal St Charlotte NC 28206 704-376-3855
Web: www.pinnacleconverting.com

Pinnacle Engineering Inc
7660 Woodway Dr Ste 350 Houston TX 77063 713-784-1005
Web: www.pinnacleengr.com

Piping Systems Engineering 1905 S Lindsay Rd Mesa AZ 85204 480-345-0052
Web: piping-systems.com

Pittsburgh Design Services Inc PO Box 469 Carnegie PA 15106 412-276-3000 276-1216
Web: www.pittsdesign.com

Plateau Excavation Inc
375 Lee Industrial Blvd Austell GA 30168 770-948-2600
Web: plateauexcavation.com

Pliteq Inc 1370 Don Mills Rd Unit 300 Toronto ON M3B3N7 416-449-0049
Web: pliteq.com

Poggemeyer Design Group Inc
1168 N Main St Bowling Green OH 43402 419-352-7537 353-0187
Web: www.poggemeyer.com

Polaris Consulting Engineers
214 W Main St 208 Moorestown NJ 08057 856-778-5400
Web: www.polarisce.com

Polarity Inc 11294 Sunrise Park Dr Rancho Cordova CA 95742 916-635-3050
Web: www.polarity.net

Poly Plant Project Inc 3099 N Lima St Burbank CA 91504 818-848-2111
Web: www.polyplantproject.com

Polyengineering Inc 1935 Headland Ave Dothan AL 36303 334-793-4700
Web: www.polyengineering.com

Pond & Co 3500 Pkwy Ln Ste 600 Norcross GA 30092 678-336-7740
Web: pondco.com

Porter Consulting Engineers PC
814 N Main St Meadville PA 16335 814-337-4447
Web: www.pceengineers.com

Portfolio Defense
Seven Mount Lassen Dr Ste D150 San Rafael CA 94903 415-492-8262
Web: portfoliodefense.com

Power & Control Engineering Solutions LLC
10810 E 45th St Ste 200 Tulsa OK 74146 918-627-7237
Web: www.pcescorp.com

Power Engineering Corp PO Box 766 Wilkes-Barre PA 18703 570-823-8822 823-8143
TF: 800-626-0903 ■ *Web:* www.powerengineeringcorp.com

Power Engineers Inc
3940 Glenbrook Dr PO Box 1066 Hailey ID 83333 208-788-3456 788-2082
Web: www.powereng.com

Power Equipment Maintenance Inc
110 Prosperity Blvd Piedmont SC 29673 864-375-9030
Web: www.peminc.net

Powercast Corp 566 Alpha Dr Pittsburgh PA 15238 724-238-3700
Web: www.powercastco.com

PPM Consultants Inc 2508 Ticheli Rd Monroe LA 71202 318-323-7270 323-6593
TF: 800-761-8675 ■ *Web:* www.ppmco.com

Prater Engineering Associates Inc
6130 Wilcox Rd Dublin OH 43016 614-766-4896
Web: praterengr.com

Prefix Corp 1300 W Hamlin Rd Rochester Hills MI 48309 248-650-1330
Web: www.prefix.com

Prein & Newhof Inc 3355 Evergreen Dr NE Grand Rapids MI 49525 616-364-8491 364-6955
Web: www.preinnewhof.com

Premier Civil Engineering LLC
1302 Calle Del Norte Ste 2 Laredo TX 78041 956-717-1199
Web: premier-ce.com

Prestige Technicall Services
7908 Cincinnati Dayton Rd Ste T West Chester OH 45069 513-779-6800
Web: www.prestigetechnical.com

	City	State	ZIP	Phone	Fax
Preston Partnership 115 Perimeter Ctr Pl Ste 950	Atlanta	GA	30346	770-396-7248	396-2945
Web: www.theprestonpartnership.com					
Pribuss Engineering Inc 523 Mayfair Ave	South San Francisco	CA	94080	650-588-0447	
Web: www.pribuss.com					
Pride Signs Ltd 255 Pinebush Rd	Cambridge	ON	N1T1B9	519-622-4040	
Web: www.pridesigns.com					
Principle Engineering Group Inc 833 E Plaza Cir Ste 100	Yuma	AZ	85365	928-782-5700	
Priority Designs Inc 501 Morrison Rd	Columbus	OH	43230	614-337-9979	337-9499
Web: www.prioritydesigns.com					
Prism Maritime LLC 1416 Kelland Dr Ste B	Chesapeake	VA	23320	757-460-8800	
Web: prismmaritime.com					
Pro Star Aviation LLC Five Industrial Dr	Londonderry	NH	03053	603-627-7827	
Web: www.prostaraviation.com					
Proctor Engineering Group Ltd 418 Mission Ave	San Rafael	CA	94901	415-451-2480	
Web: www.proctoreng.com					
Product Development Technologies Inc One Corporate Dr	Lake Zurich	IL	60047	847-821-3000	821-3020
Web: www.pdt.com					
Professional Engineering Consultants PA 303 S Topeka St	Wichita	KS	67202	316-262-2691	262-3003
Web: www.pec1.com					
Professional Service Industries Inc (PSI) 1901 S Meyers Rd Ste 400	Oakbrook Terrace	IL	60181	630-691-1490	691-1587
TF: 800-548-7901 ■ *Web:* www.psiusa.com					
Project Resources Inc 3760 Convoy St Ste 230	San Diego	CA	92111	858-505-1000	505-1010
Web: www.priworld.com					
ProjectDesign Consultants 701 B St Ste 800	San Diego	CA	92101	619-235-6471	234-0349
Web: www.projectdesign.com					
PROJECTXYZ Inc 1500 Perimeter Pkwy Ste 426	Huntsville	AL	35806	256-721-9001	
Web: projectxyz.com					
Prolitec Inc 1235 W Canal St	Milwaukee	WI	53233	414-615-4630	
Web: www.prolitec.com					
Promation Engineering Inc 16138 Flight Path Dr	Brooksville	FL	34604	352-544-8436	
Web: promationei.com					
Propak Systems Ltd 440 East Lk Rd NE	Airdrie	AB	T4A2J8	403-912-7000	
Web: www.propaksystems.com					
Protean Design Group Inc 100 E Pine St	Orlando	FL	32801	407-246-0044	
Web: www.proteandg.com					
Protection Engineering Consultants LLC 14144 Trautwein Rd	Austin	TX	78737	512-380-1988	
Web: www.protection-consultants.com					
Protostatix Engineering Consultants 10117 Jasper Ave Nw	Edmonton	AB	T5J1W8	780-423-5855	
Web: protostatix.com					
Provenance Consulting 301 W Sixth St Ste 200	Borger	TX	79007	806-273-5100	
Web: www.provenanceconsulting.com					
Pruitt Eberly & Stone Inc 1852 Century Pl Ne	Atlanta	GA	30345	770-457-5923	
Web: www.pesengineers.com					
Pryde Schropp McComb Inc 311 Goderich St	Port Elgin	ON	N0H2C0	519-389-4343	
Web: www.psmi.ca					
PSARA Technologies Inc 10925 Reed Hartman Hwy Ste 220	Cincinnati	OH	45242	513-791-4418	
Web: psara.com					
Psomas 555 S Flower St Ste 4300	Los Angeles	CA	90071	213-223-1400	
Web: www.psomas.com					
PTI Engineered Plastics Inc 50900 Corporate Dr	Macomb	MI	48044	586-263-5100	263-6680
Web: www.teampti.com					
Purdy-McGuire Inc 17300 Dallas Pkwy Ste 3000	Dallas	TX	75248	972-239-5357	
Web: www.purdy-mcguire.com					
Q. Grady Minor & Associates PA 3800 Via Del Rey	Bonita Springs	FL	34134	239-947-1144	
Web: www.gradyminor.com					
QCA Systems Ltd #16 7355 72 St	Delta	BC	V4G1L5	604-940-0868	
Web: www.qcasystems.com					
Quad Three Group Inc 37 N Washington St	Wilkes Barre	PA	18701	570-829-4200	
Web: www.quad3.com					
Qualis Corp 689 Discovery Dr NW Ste 400	Huntsville	AL	35806	256-971-1707	
Web: www.qualis-corp.com					
Quality Solutions Inc 128 N First St	Colwich	KS	67030	316-721-3656	
Web: www.qsifacilities.com					
Qualortran Inc 236 Carpenter Rd Ne	Calhoun	GA	30701	706-295-4510	
Web: qualortran.com					
Quantum Marine Engineering of Florida Inc 3790 Sw 30th Ave	Fort Lauderdale	FL	33312	954-587-4205	
Web: www.quantumhydraulic.com					
Quantum Signal LLC 200 N Ann Arbor St	Saline	MI	48176	734-429-9100	
Web: quantumsignal.com					
Quantum Technology Sciences Inc 1980 N Atlantic Ave Ste 201	Cocoa Beach	FL	32931	321-868-0288	
Web: www.qtsi.com					
Quest Construction Data Network LLC Po Box 412	Spring Park	MN	55384	952-474-8345	
Web: www.questcdn.com					
Quest Convergence Systems Inc 43 Metcalf Dr	Belleville	IL	62223	618-398-3311	
Web: questai.com					
Quorum Consulting Inc 180 Sansome St Tenth Fl	San Francisco	CA	94104	415-835-0190	
Web: quorumconsulting.com					
R & a Tool & Engineering Co 39127 Ford Rd	Westland	MI	48185	734-981-2000	
Web: www.randatool.com					
R & D Consulting 9448 Brookline Ave	Baton Rouge	LA	70809	225-926-1665	
Web: www.rdcon.com					
R e Dimond & Associates Inc 732 N Capitol Ave	Indianapolis	IN	46204	317-634-4672	
Web: www.redimond.com					
R G Engineering Inc 505 London Bridge Rd Unit 101	Virginia Beach	VA	23454	757-463-3045	
Web: www.rgengineering.com					
R J Wood & Co 652 Arlington Pl	Macon	GA	31201	478-741-7044	
R T Patterson Company Inc 230 Third Ave Second Fl	Pittsburgh	PA	15222	412-227-6600	227-6672
Web: www.rtpatterson.com					
R-S-H Engineering Inc 909 N 18th St Ste 200	Monroe	LA	71201	318-323-4009	
Web: www.rsh.com					
R.M.Thornton Inc 120 Westhampton Ave	Capitol Heights	MD	20743	301-350-5000	
Web: www.rmthornton.com					
R.O. Anderson Engineering Inc 1603 Esmeralda	Minden	NV	89423	775-782-2322	
Web: www.roanderson.com					
R2t Inc 580 W Crssvlle Rd	Roswell	GA	30075	770-569-7038	
Web: www.r2tinc.com					
Rae Engineering & Inspection Ltd 4810 93 St Nw	Edmonton	AB	T6E5M4	780-469-2401	
Web: www.raeengineering.ca					
Railplan International Inc 1200 Bernard Dr	Baltimore	MD	21223	410-947-5900	
Web: www.railplan.com					
Ramaker & Assoc Inc 1120 Dallas St	Sauk City	WI	53583	608-643-4100	
Web: ramaker.com					
Ramey Kemp & Assoc Inc 5808 Faringdon Pl Ste 100	Raleigh	NC	27609	919-872-5115	
Web: rameykemp.com					
Rangaswamy & Assoc Inc 304 W Liberty St	Louisville	KY	40202	502-589-2212	
Web: rangaswamy.com					
Rapid Global Business Solutions Inc 31791 Sherman Dr	Madison Heights	MI	48071	248-589-1135	
Web: www.rgbsi.com					
Rathgeber Goss Associates PC 15871 Crabbs Branch Way	Rockville	MD	20855	301-590-0071	
Web: www.rath-goss.com					
Ravi Engineering & Land Surveying PC 2110 S Clinton Ave Ste 1	Rochester	NY	14618	585-223-3660	
Web: www.ravieng.com					
Raymond L Goodson Jr Inc 5445 La Sierra Ste 300 LB 17	Dallas	TX	75231	214-739-8100	739-6354
Web: rlginc.com					
RBA Group Inc, The Seven Campus Dr Ste 300	Parsippany	NJ	07054	973-946-5600	984-5421
Web: www.rbagroup.com					
RBC Inc 100 N Pitt St Ste 300	Alexandria	VA	22314	703-549-6921	549-6926
Web: www.rbcinc.com					
RBF Consulting 14725 Alton Pkwy	Irvine	CA	92618	949-472-3505	472-8373
TF: 800-479-3808 ■ *Web:* www.rbf.com					
RCM Technologies Inc 2500 McClellan Ave Ste 350	Pennsauken	NJ	08109	856-356-4500	356-4600
NASDAQ: RCMT ■ *TF:* 800-322-2885 ■ *Web:* www.rcmt.com					
Rcr Technology Corp 251 N Illinois St	Indianapolis	IN	46204	317-624-9500	
Web: www.rcrtechnology.com					
Reaction Engineering International Inc 77 West 200 South Ste 210	Salt Lake City	UT	84101	801-364-6925	
Web: www.reaction-eng.com					
Ready Technologies Ohio Inc 101 Capitol Way N Ste 301	Olympia	WA	98501	360-413-9800	
Web: www.readyengineering.com					
Realtime Technologies Inc 1523 N Main St	Royal Oak	MI	48067	248-548-4876	
Web: www.simcreator.com					
Rec Consulting Inc 2442 Second Ave	San Diego	CA	92101	619-232-9200	
Web: rec-consultants.com					
Reese Engineering Inc 2021 Pine Hall Rd	State College	PA	16801	814-234-2548	
Web: www.reeseinc.com/					
Rega Engineering 1620 S 70th St Ste 103	Lincoln	NE	68506	402-484-7342	
Web: regaengineering.com					
Regulus 238 N Main St	Woodstock	VA	22664	540-459-2142	
Web: regulus-group.com					
Reid Middleton Inc 728 134th St SW Ste 200	Everett	WA	98204	425-741-3800	
Web: www.reidmiddleton.com					
Reigstad & Associates Inc 192 Ninth St W Ste 200	Saint Paul	MN	55102	651-292-1123	
Web: www.reigstad.com					
Reliability Center 501 Westover Ave	Hopewell	VA	23860	804-458-0645	
Web: www.reliability.com					
Remington & Vernick Engineers Inc 232 Kings Hwy E	Haddonfield	NJ	08033	856-795-9595	795-1882
Web: www.rve.com					
Rentenbach Engineering Co 2400 Sutherland Ave	Knoxville	TN	37919	865-546-2440	546-3414
TF: 877-546-2440 ■ *Web:* www.rentenbach.com					
Research & Development Solutions Inc 7921 Jones Branch Dr	Mclean	VA	22102	703-893-9533	
Web: rdsi.com					
Research Management Consultants Inc 816 Camarillo Springs Rd Ste J	Camarillo	CA	93012	805-987-5538	987-2868
Web: www.rmci.com					
Resources Applications Designs & Controls Inc 3220 E 59th St	Long Beach	CA	90805	562-272-7231	
Respec Inc 3824 Jet Dr	Rapid City	SD	57703	605-394-6400	394-6456
TF: 877-737-7321 ■ *Web:* www.respec.com					
Rettew Assoc Inc 3020 Columbia Ave	Lancaster	PA	17603	717-394-3721	394-1063
TF: 800-738-8395 ■ *Web:* www.rettew.com					
Revolutionary Engineering Inc 36865 Schoolcraft Rd	Livonia	MI	48150	734-432-9334	
Web: www.revoleng.com					
Reynolds Smith & Hills Inc 10748 Deerwood Pk Blvd	Jacksonville	FL	32256	904-256-2500	256-2501
TF: 800-741-2014 ■ *Web:* www.rsandh.com					
RGA Environmental Inc 1466 66th St	Emeryville	CA	94608	510-547-7771	
Web: www.rgaenv.com					
RHP Mechanical Systems Inc 1008 E Fourth St	Reno	NV	89512	775-322-9434	
Web: www.rhpinc.net					

	City	State	Zip	Phone	Fax
Ribbeck Engineering Inc					
14335 Sw 120th St Ste 205	Miami	FL	33186	305-383-5909	
Web: ribbeck.co					
Richard Brady & Associates 3710 Ruffin Rd	San Diego	CA	92123	858-496-0500	
Web: www.richardbrady.com					
Richardson Smith Gardner & Associates					
14 N Boylan Ave	Raleigh	NC	27603	919-828-0577	
Web: www.smithgardnerinc.com					
Ricker, Atkinson, Mcbee & Associates Inc					
2105 S Hardy Dr Ste 13	Tempe	AZ	85282	480-921-8100	
Web: www.rammeng.com					
Rindt-McDuff Associates Inc					
334 Cherokee St NE	Marietta	GA	30060	770-427-8123	
Web: www.rindt-mcduff.com					
Rio Technical Services LLC 4200 S Hulen	Fort Worth	TX	76109	817-735-8264	
Ripa Engineering Corp					
9555 Owensmouth Ave Nbr 8	Chatsworth	CA	91311	818-773-8722	
Web: ripaeng.com					
Risk Integrated LLC 37 Main St	Cold Spring	NY	10516	845-598-1620	
Web: www.riskintegrated.com					
Rist-Frost-Shumway Engineering PC					
71 Water St	Laconia	NH	03246	603-524-4647	
Web: www.rfsengineering.com					
Rivermoor Engineering LLC 146 Front St	Scituate	MA	02066	781-545-2848	
Web: rivermoorengineering.com					
RK Engineering Group Inc					
4000 Werly Pl Ste 280	Newport Beach	CA	92660	949-474-0809	
Web: rkengineer.com					
RK&K 81 Mosher St	Baltimore	MD	21217	410-728-2900	728-0282
Web: www.rkk.com					
RKR Hess Assoc Inc					
112 N Courtland St	East Stroudsburg	PA	18301	570-421-1550	
Web: rkrhess.com					
RM Towill Corp 2024 N King St Ste 200	Honolulu	HI	96819	808-842-1133	842-1937
Web: www.rmtowill.com					
RMA Group Inc					
12130 Santa Margarita Ct	Rancho Cucamonga	CA	91730	909-989-1751	
Web: www.rmacompanies.com					
RMC Water & Environment Inc					
2175 N California Blvd Ste 315	Walnut Creek	CA	94596	925-627-4100	
Web: www.rmcwater.com					
RMF Engineering Inc					
5520 Research Pk Dr Third Fl	Baltimore	MD	21228	410-576-0505	385-0327
TF: 800-938-5760 ■ *Web:* www.rmf.com					
RNL Design 1050 17th St Ste A200	Denver	CO	80265	303-295-1717	292-0845
Web: www.rnldesign.com					
Roake & Assoc Inc 1684 Quincy Ave	Naperville	IL	60540	630-355-3232	
Web: roake.com					
Roald Haestad Inc 37 Brookside Rd	Waterbury	CT	06708	203-753-9800	
Web: rhiengineering.com					
Robert Allan Ltd 1639 Second Ave W Ste 230	Vancouver	BC	V6J1H3	604-736-9466	
Web: www.ral.ca					
Robert E. Lee & Associates Inc					
1250 Centennial Centre Blvd	Hobart	WI	54155	920-662-9641	
Web: www.releeinc.com					
Roberts & Schaefer Co					
222 S Riverside Plz Ste 1800	Chicago	IL	60606	312-236-7292	726-2872
Web: www.r-s.com					
Robson Technologies Inc 135 E Main Ave	Morgan Hill	CA	95037	408-779-8008	
Web: www.testfixtures.com					
Roche Ltd - Consulting Group					
Centre d'affaires Henri-IV 1015 Wilfrid-Pelletier Ave	Quebec City	QC	G1W0C4	418-654-9600	
Web: www.roche.ca					
Rocscience 31 Balsam Ave	Toronto	ON	M4E3B5	416-698-8217	
Web: www.rocscience.com					
Roddey Engineering Services Inc					
10100 Woolworth Rd	Keithville	LA	71047	318-221-1996	
Web: roddey-engr.com					
Rodeberg & Berryman Inc 119 S First St	Montevideo	MN	56265	320-269-7695	
Rogers Engineering & Manufacturing Inc					
112 S Center St	Cambridge City	IN	47327	765-478-5444	
Web: rogersengineering.net					
Rolls Anderson & Rolls 115 Yellowstone Dr	Chico	CA	95973	530-895-1422	
Web: rarcivil.com					
Roma Design Group 1527 Stockton St	San Francisco	CA	94133	415-616-9900	
Web: roma.com					
Ronald T Jepson & Assoc Ps 222 Grand Ave	Bellingham	WA	98225	360-733-5760	
Web: jepsonengineering.com					
Rosenwasser Grossman Consulting					
132 W 36th St Frnt 2	New York	NY	10018	212-564-2424	
Web: www.rosenwassergrossman.com					
Roshanian & Associates Inc					
6404 Wilshire Blvd	Los Angeles	CA	90048	323-933-5252	
Web: www.roshanian.com					
Ross & Baruzzini Six S Old Orchard	Saint Louis	MO	63119	314-918-8383	918-1766
Web: www.rossbar.com					
Rotating Machinery Services Inc					
2760 Baglyos Cir	Bethlehem	PA	18020	484-821-0702	
Web: www.rotatingmachinery.com					
Rothenbuhler Engineering					
524 Rhodes Rd PO Box 708	Sedro Woolley	WA	98284	360-856-0836	856-2183
Web: www.rothenbuhlereng.com					
Rowan Williams Davies & Irwin Inc					
650 Woodlawn Rd W	Guelph	ON	N1K1B8	519-823-1311	
Web: www.rwdi.com					
Royal Engineering Inc 34450 Commerce Rd	Fraser	MI	48026	586-294-9400	
Web: royalinc.com					
RSA Engineering Inc					
2522 Arctic Blvd Ste 200	Anchorage	AK	99503	907-276-0521	
RSP Architects 1220 Marshall St NE	Minneapolis	MN	55413	612-677-7100	677-7499
Web: www.rsparch.com					
RT Tanaka Engineers Inc 871 Kolu St Ste 201	Wailuku	HI	96793	808-242-6861	
RTKL Assoc Inc 901 S Bond St	Baltimore	MD	21231	410-537-6000	276-2136
Web: www.rtkl.com					
Ruekert & Mielke Inc					
W233 N2080 Ridgeview Pkwy	Waukesha	WI	53188	262-542-5733	542-5631
Web: www.ruekert-mielke.com					
Runtime Design Automation					
2560 Mission College Blvd Ste 130	Santa Clara	CA	95054	408-492-0940	
Web: rtda.com					
RW Engineering & Surveying Inc 6225 N 89th Cir	Omaha	NE	68134	402-573-2205	
Web: rwomaha.com					
Ryan-Biggs Assoc PC 257 Ushers Rd	Clifton Park	NY	12065	518-406-5506	
Web: ryanbiggs.com					
S & B Engineers & Constructors Ltd					
7825 Pk Pl Blvd	Houston	TX	77087	713-645-4141	643-8029
Web: www.sbec.com					
S E A Consultants Inc 215 First St Ste 320	Cambridge	MA	02142	617-497-7800	498-4630
TF: 855-746-4849 ■ *Web:* www.kleinfelder.com					
S Systems Corp					
5777 W Century Blvd Ste 520	Los Angeles	CA	90045	310-215-0248	642-3738
Web: www.s-sc.com					
S.S. Mechanical Corp					
17631 Metzler Ln	Huntington Beach	CA	92647	714-847-1317	
Web: www.ssmechanical.biz					
S/L/A/M Collaborative					
80 Glastonbury Blvd	Glastonbury	CT	06033	860-657-8077	657-3141
Web: www.slamcoll.com					
S2L Inc 531 Versailles Dr Ste 202	Maitland	FL	32751	407-475-9163	
Web: s2li.com					
SA Healy Co 1910 S Highland Ave Ste 300	Lombard	IL	60148	630-678-3110	754-6450*
**Fax Area Code:* 702 ■ *TF:* 888-724-3259 ■ *Web:* www.sahealy.com					
Sabre Industries Inc 8653 E Hwy 67	Alvarado	TX	76009	817-852-1700	852-1703
TF: 866-254-3707 ■ *Web:* www.sabreindustriesinc.com					
Sadat Associates Inc 1545 Lamberton Rd	Trenton	NJ	08611	609-826-9600	
Web: www.sadat.com					
Sage Consulting Group 1623 Blake St Ste 400	Denver	CO	80202	303-571-0237	
Web: www.sageconsulting.com					
SAI Consulting Engineers Inc					
1350 Penn Ave Ste 300	Pittsburgh	PA	15222	412-392-8750	392-8785
Web: www.saiengr.com					
Sam Zax Assoc 14 Wood Rd	Braintree	MA	02184	781-303-1700	
Samuel Engineering Inc					
8450 E Crescent Pkwy	Greenwood Village	CO	80111	303-714-4840	
Web: www.samuelengineering.com					
San Jose Redevelopment Agency					
200 E Santa Clara St 14th Fl	San Jose	CA	95113	408-535-8500	
Web: www.sjredevelopment.org					
Sanborn Head & Assoc Inc 20 Foundry St	Concord	NH	03301	603-229-1900	
Web: sanbornhead.com					
Sarafinchin Associates Ltd 238 Galaxy Blvd	Toronto	ON	M9W5R8	416-674-1770	
Web: www.sarafinchin.com					
Sargent & Lundy LLC 55 E Monroe St	Chicago	IL	60603	312-269-2000	269-3454
Web: www.sargentlundy.com					
Sasaki Assoc Inc 64 Pleasant St	Watertown	MA	02472	617-926-3300	924-2748
Web: www.sasaki.com					
Sathre Bergquist Inc 150 Broadway Ave S	Wayzata	MN	55391	952-476-6000	
Web: sathre.com					
Savin Engineers PC Three Campus Dr	Pleasantville	NY	10570	914-769-3200	747-6686
Web: www.savinengineers.com					
SC Engineers Inc					
17075 Via Del Campo First Fl	San Diego	CA	92127	858-946-0333	
Web: scengineers.net					
Scale Models Unlimited 400 S Front St Ste 300	Memphis	TN	38103	901-577-5155	577-5157
Web: www.smu.com					
Schaeffer & Associates Ltd Six Ronrose Dr	Concord	ON	L4K4R3	905-738-6100	
Web: www.schaeffers.com					
Schaeffer Nassar Schneidegg Consulting Engineers LLC					
1425 Cantillon Blvd	Mays Landing	NJ	08330	609-625-7400	
Web: www.snsce.com					
Schafer Corp 321 Billerica Rd	Chelmsford	MA	01824	978-256-2070	256-1404*
**Fax:* Hum Res ■ *Web:* www.schafercorp.com					
Scheeser Buckley Mayfield Inc					
1540 Corporate Woods Pkwy	Uniontown	OH	44685	330-896-4664	
Web: www.sbmce.com					
Schemmer Assoc Inc, The 1044 N 115th St	Omaha	NE	68154	402-493-4800	
SchenkelShultz Architects					
200 E Robinson St Ste 300	Orlando	FL	32801	407-872-3322	872-3303
Web: www.schenkelshultz.com					
Schnabel Engineering Inc					
9800 JEB Stuart Pkwy Ste 200	Glen Allen	VA	23059	804-264-3222	264-3244
Web: www.schnabel-eng.com					
Schneider Corp 8901 Otis Ave	Indianapolis	IN	46216	317-826-7100	826-7200
TF: 866-973-7100 ■ *Web:* schneidercorp.com					
Schofield Brothers of New England Inc					
1071 Worcester Rd	Framingham	MA	01701	508-879-0030	
Web: www.schofieldbros.com					
Scientech Inc 200 S Woodruff Ave	Idaho Falls	ID	83401	208-524-9200	
Web: scientech.cwfc.com					
SCS Engineers					
3900 Kilroy Airport Way Ste 100	Long Beach	CA	90806	562-426-9544	427-0805
TF: 800-326-9544 ■ *Web:* www.scsengineers.com					
SE Technologies LLC 98 Vanadium Rd Bldg D	Bridgeville	PA	15017	412-221-1100	257-6103
Web: www.se-env.com					
Sea Engineering Inc 863 N Nimitz	Honolulu	HI	96817	808-536-3603	
Web: seaengineering.com					
Sea-Land Chemical Co 821 Wpoint Pkwy	Westlake	OH	44145	440-871-7887	
Web: sealandchem.com					
Seacon Engineering Associates Inc					
716B Lakeside Dr W	Mobile	AL	36693	251-662-0300	
Web: www.seaconeng.com					
Sebago Technics Inc					
75 John Roberts Rd Ste 1A	South Portland	ME	04106	207-200-2100	
Web: sebagotechnics.com					

Phone Fax

Sebesta Blomberg & Assoc Inc
1450 Energy Park Dr Ste 300 St Paul MN 55108 651-634-0775 522-8070*
*Fax Area Code: 703 ■ TF: 877-706-6858 ■ Web: www.sebesta.com

SEI Group Inc 689 Discovery Dr Ste 310 Huntsville AL 35806 256-533-0500 533-5516
Web: www.seigroupinc.com

Senga Engineering 1525 E Warner Ave Santa Ana CA 92705 714-549-8011
Web: senga-eng.com

Sensorwise Inc 2908 Rogerdale Rd Houston TX 77042 713-952-3350
Web: www.sensorwise.com

SENTEL Corp 1101 King St Ste 550 Alexandria VA 22314 703-739-0084 739-6028
Web: www.sentel.com

SGS Architects Engineers Inc One Tyler Ct Carlisle PA 17015 717-249-4569
Web: www.sgsarchitects.com

Shah & Associates Inc
416 N Frederick Ave Gaithersburg MD 20877 301-926-2797
Web: www.shahpe.com

Shah Smith & Assoc Inc 2825 Wilcrest Ste 350 Houston TX 77042 713-780-7563
Web: shahsmith.com

Sheladia Assoc Inc
15825 Shady Grove Rd Ste 100 Rockville MD 20850 301-590-3939 948-7174
Web: www.sheladia.com

Shelby Engineering Ltd 9632 54 Ave Nw Edmonton AB T6E5V1 780-438-2540
Web: www.shelbyengineering.ca

Shepley Bulfinch Two Seaport Ln Boston MA 02210 617-423-1700 451-2420
Web: shepleybulfinch.com

Shermco Industries Inc 2425 E Pioneer Dr Irving TX 75061 972-793-5523
Web: www.shermco.com

Sherwood Design Engineers
One Union St Fl 2 San Francisco CA 94111 415-677-7300
Web: www.sherwoodengineers.com

Sherwood-Logan & Assoc Inc 2140 Renard Ct Annapolis MD 21401 410-841-6810
Web: sherwoodlogan.com

Shield Engineering Inc
4301 Taggart Creek Rd Charlotte NC 28208 704-394-6913
Web: www.shieldengineering.com

Shive-Hattery Inc (SH)
316 Second St SE Ste 500 PO Box 1599 Cedar Rapids IA 52406 319-362-0313 362-2883
TF: 800-798-0227 ■ Web: www.shive-hattery.com

SHN Consulting Engineers & Geologists Inc
812 W Wabash Eureka CA 95501 707-441-8855
Web: www.shn-engr.com

Short-Elliott-Hendrickson Inc
3535 Vadnais Ctr Dr Saint Paul MN 55110 651-490-2000 490-2150
TF: 800-325-2055 ■ Web: www.sehinc.com

Shumaker Consulting Engineer PC
143 Court St Binghamton NY 13901 607-798-8081
Web: www.shumakerengineering.com

Shutler Consulting Engineers Inc
12503 Bel Red Rd Bellevue WA 98005 425-450-4075
Web: shutler.com

SI Organization Inc, The
15052 Conference Ctr Dr Chantilly VA 20151 571-313-6000
Web: www.vencore.com

Sid Goldstien - Civil Engineer
650 Alamo Pintado Rd Ste 302 Solvang CA 93463 805-688-1526
Web: sjgce.com

Sierra Pacific West 2125 La Mirada Dr Vista CA 92081 760-599-0755
Web: sierrapacificwest.com

Sigit Automation Inc 734 7 Ave Sw Calgary AB T2P3P8 403-723-4256
Web: www.sigit.com

Signa Engineering Corp
Two Northpoint Dr Ste 700 Houston TX 77060 281-774-1000
Web: www.signaengineering.com

Silver Engineering Inc 255 E Dr Ste A Melbourne FL 32904 321-676-7596
Web: silvereng.com

Silverman & Light Inc
1201 Park Ave Ste 100 Emeryville CA 94608 510-655-1200
Web: www.silvermanlight.com

Simbex LLC 10 Water St Ste 410 Lebanon NH 03766 603-448-2367
Web: www.simbex.com

Simmons Engineering Corp 1200 Willis Ave Wheeling IL 60090 847-419-9800
Web: simcut.com

Simon & Assoc Inc 3200 Commerce St Blacksburg VA 24060 540-951-4234
Web: simonassoc.com

SimPhonics Inc 3226 N Falkenburg Rd Tampa FL 33619 813-623-9917
Web: www.simphonics.com

Simpson Gumpertz & Heger Inc
41 Seyon St Bldg 1 Ste 500 Waltham MA 02453 781-907-9000 907-9009
TF: 800-729-7429 ■ Web: www.sgh.com

Simulent Inc 203 College St Ste 302 Toronto ON M5T1P9 416-979-5544
Web: www.simulent.com

Sinclair Pratt Cameron PC
1630 Donna Dr Ste 103 Virginia Bch VA 23451 757-417-0565
Web: spc-eng.com

Site Design Concepts Inc 127 W Market St Ste 200 York PA 17401 717-757-9414
Web: sitedc.com

SJB Group Inc 5745 Essen Ln Ste 200 Baton Rouge LA 70810 225-769-3400 769-3596
Web: www.sjbgroup.com

SKA Consulting Engineers Inc
300 Pomona Dr Greensboro NC 27407 336-855-0993
Web: skaeng.com

Skelton, Brumwell & Associates Inc
93 Bell Farm Rd Ste 107 Barrie ON L4M5G1 705-726-1141
Web: www.skeltonbrumwell.ca

Skidmore Owings & Merrill
224 S Michigan Ave Ste 1000 Chicago IL 60604 312-554-9090 360-4545
Web: www.som.com

SM Engineering Co Nine Ninth Ave N Hopkins MN 55343 952-938-7407
Web: www.smeng.com

Smallwood Reynolds Stewart Stewart & Assoc Inc (SRSSA)
One Piedmont Ctr 3565 Piedmont Rd Ste 303 Atlanta GA 30305 404-233-5453 264-0929
Web: www.srssa.com

Phone Fax

Smith Engineering Co
2201 San Pedro Dr NE 4-200 Albuquerque NM 87110 505-884-0700
Web: www.smithengineering.pro

Smith Seckman Reid Inc 2995 Sidco Dr Nashville TN 37204 615-383-1113
Web: ssr-inc.com

SmithGroup Inc 500 Griswold St Ste 1700 Detroit MI 48226 313-983-3600 983-3636
Web: www.smithgroupjjr.com

SMS Concast America Inc 100 Sandusky St Pittsburgh PA 15212 412-237-8950 237-8951
Web: www.sms-concast.ch

SMS Demag Inc 100 Sandusky St Pittsburgh PA 15212 412-231-1200 231-3995
Web: sms-millcraft.us

SNC Lavalin Group Inc
455 Rene-Levesque Blvd W Montreal QC H2Z1Z3 514-393-1000 866-0795
TSE: SNC ■ Web: www.snclavalin.com

Snowline Engineering 4261 Business Dr Cameron Park CA 95682 530-677-2675
Web: www.snowlineengineering.com

Snyder & Assoc Inc PO Box 1159 Ankeny IA 50023 515-964-2020 964-7938
TF General: 888-964-2020 ■ Web: www.snyder-associates.com

Sofec Inc 14741 Yorktown Plaza Houston TX 77040 713-510-6600 510-6601
Web: www.sofec.com

Software Synergy Inc 151 Hwy 33 E Manalapan NJ 07726 732-617-9300
Web: ssi-corp.com

Soil & Materials Engineers Inc
43980 Plymouth Oaks Blvd Plymouth MI 48170 734-454-9900 454-0629
Web: sme-usa.com

Soil Consultant Engineering (SCE) 9303 Ctr St Manassas VA 20110 703-366-3000 366-3400
Web: www.soilconsultants.net

Solekai Systems Corp 3398 Carmel Mtn Rd San Diego CA 92121 858-436-2040 436-2041
Web: www.solekai.com

Somat Engineering Inc
660 Woodward Ave Ste 2430 Detroit MI 48226 313-963-2721
Web: www.somateng.com

Sonalysts Inc 215 Waterford Pkwy N Waterford CT 06385 860-442-4355 447-8883
TF: 800-526-8091 ■ Web: www.sonalysts.com

Sonometrics Corp 500 Nottinghill Rd London ON N6K3P1 519-474-6464
Web: www.sonometrics.com

Southern Company Services Inc
42 Inverness Ctr Pkwy Birmingham AL 35242 205-992-6011
Web: www.southerncompany.com

SPACECO Inc 9575 W Higgins Rd Ste 700 Rosemont IL 60018 847-696-4060 696-4065
TF: 888-772-2326 ■ Web: www.spacecoinc.com

Spagnuolo & Assoc LLC
3057 W Market St Ste 201 Fairlawn OH 44333 330-836-6661
Web: spagnuoloassoc.com

Spalding Dedecker Assoc Inc
905 S Blvd E Rochester Hills MI 48307 248-844-5400
Web: sda-eng.com

Spears-Votta & Assoc Inc 7526 Harford Rd Baltimore MD 21234 410-254-5800
Web: www.spearsvotta.com

Spec Ops Inc 319 Business Ln Ashland VA 23005 804-752-4790
Web: www.specopsinc.com

SPEC Services Inc 10540 Talbert Ave Fountain Valley CA 92708 714-963-8077 963-0364
Web: www.specservices.com

Spectrum Solutions Inc 114 Castle Dr Madison AL 35758 256-830-9759
Web: spectrumsi.com

SPI/Mobile Pulley Works Inc 905 S Ann St Mobile AL 36605 251-653-0606 653-0668
TF: 866-334-6325 ■ Web: www.spimpw.com

Spitzer Engineering LLC
730 Fifth Ave Ste 2202 New York NY 10019 212-765-5170

Sponseller Group Inc 1600 Timber Wolf Dr Holland OH 43528 419-861-3000
Web: www.sponsellergroup.com

Sproule Associates Ltd
900 N Tower Sun Life Plz 140 Fourth Ave SW Calgary AB T2P3N3 403-294-5500
Web: www.sproule.com

SRF Consulting Group Inc
1 Carlson Pkwy N Ste 150 Minneapolis MN 55447 763-475-0010 475-2429
Web: www.srfconsulting.com

SRK Consulting Inc
7175 W Jefferson Ave Ste 3000 Lakewood CO 80235 303-985-1333 985-9947
Web: www.na.srk.com

SSOE Inc 1001 Madison Ave Toledo OH 43624 419-255-3830 255-6101
Web: www.ssoe.com

Staggs & Fisher Consulting Engineers Inc
3264 Lochness Dr Lexington KY 40517 859-271-3246
Web: sfengineering.com

Stanley Consultants Inc 225 Iowa Ave Muscatine IA 52761 563-264-6600 264-6658
TF: 800-553-9694 ■ Web: www.stanleyconsultants.com

Stantec 3200 Bailey Ln Ste 200 Naples FL 34105 239-649-4040
Web: www.stantec.com

Stantec Inc 10160-112 St Edmonton AB T5K2L6 780-917-7000 917-7330
NYSE: STN ■ Web: www.stantec.com

Steger & Bizzell Engineering Inc
1978 S Austin Ave Georgetown TX 78626 512-930-9412
Web: stegerbizzell.com

Stellar Engineering Inc
2899 E Coronado St Unit E Anaheim CA 92806 714-632-0040

Stellar Solutions Inc
250 Cambridge Ave Ste 204 Palo Alto CA 94306 650-473-9866
Web: stellarsolutions.com

Stem Engineering Group
875 Queen St E Sault Ste. Marie ON P6A2B3 705-942-6628
Web: stemeng.ca

Steven Schaefer Associates Inc
10411 Medallion Dr Cincinnati OH 45241 513-542-3300
Web: schaefer-inc.com

Stimmel Associates PA
601 N Trade St Ste 200 Winston-Salem NC 27101 336-723-1067
Web: www.stimmelpa.com

Strand Assoc Inc 910 W Wingra Dr Madison WI 53715 608-251-4843 251-8655
Web: www.strand.com

Strata Inc 8653 W Hackamore Dr Boise ID 83709 208-376-8200
Web: stratageotech.com

Company	City	State	Zip	Phone	Fax
Stratasys Inc 7665 Commerce Way *NASDAQ: SSYS* ■ *TF:* 800-937-3010 ■ *Web:* www.stratasys.com	Eden Prairie	MN	55344	952-937-3000	937-0070
Stray Light Optical Technologies Inc 821 S Lk Rd South *Web:* straylightoptical.com	Scottsburg	IN	47170	812-752-9104	
STRONE Inc 2717 Coventry Rd *Web:* www.strone.ca	Oakville	ON	L6H5V9	905-829-5707	
Studio Red Inc 115 Independence Dr. *Web:* www.studiored.com	Menlo Park	CA	94025	650-324-2244	
STV Group Inc 205 W Welsh Dr *Web:* www.stvinc.com	Douglassville	PA	19518	610-385-8200	385-8500
STV Inc 225 Pk Ave S 5th Fl. *Web:* www.stvinc.com	New York	NY	10003	212-777-4400	529-5237
Subcoe 117 Pembina Rd *Web:* www.subcoe.com	Sherwood Park	AB	T8H0J4	780-467-3477	
SUBNET Solutions Inc 4639 Manhattan Rd SE Ste 100 *Web:* www.subnet.com	Calgary	AB	T2G4B3	403-270-8885	
Subsea 7 (Us) LLC 10787 Clay Rd *Web:* subsea7.com	Houston	TX	77041	713-430-1100	
Suburban Electrical Engineers/ Contractors Inc 709 Hickory Farm Ln *Web:* suburbanelectric.com	Appleton	WI	54914	920-739-5156	
Sullivan International Group Inc 2750 Womble Rd *TF:* 888-744-1432 ■ *Web:* www.onesullivan.com	San Diego	CA	92106	619-260-1432	260-1421
Sun Engineering Services Inc 5405 Garden Grove Blvd. *Web:* www.sunengr.net	Westminster	CA	92683	714-379-2300	
Sunland Group Inc 1033 La Posada Dr Ste 370 *TF:* 866-732-8500 ■ *Web:* www.sunlandgrp.com	Austin	TX	78752	512-494-0208	494-0406
Sunrise Engineering Inc 25 East 500 North *Web:* sunrise-eng.com	Fillmore	UT	84631	435-743-6151	
Sunstone Projects Ltd 540 - Fifth Ave SW Ste 400 *Web:* www.sunstone.ab.ca	Calgary	AB	T2P0M2	403-262-3030	
Support Systems Assoc Inc (SSAI) 709 S Harbor City Blvd Ste 350 *TF:* 877-234-7724 ■ *Web:* www.ssai.org	Melbourne	FL	32901	321-724-5566	724-6673
Sur-Flo Plastics & Engineering Inc 24358 Groesbeck Hwy *Web:* www.sur-flo.com	Warren	MI	48089	586-773-0400	773-8946
Swanson Rink Inc 1120 Lincoln St 1200 *Web:* www.swansonrink.com	Denver	CO	80203	303-832-2666	
Swat Energy Inc 3220 Blume Dr Ste 118	Richmond	CA	94806	510-758-1568	
Symmes Maini & McKee Assoc (SMMA) 1000 Massachusetts Ave **Fax Area Code:* 800 ■ *Web:* www.smma.com	Cambridge	MA	02138	617-547-5400	648-4920*
Synchrony Inc 4655 Technology Dr. *Web:* www.synchrony.com	Salem	VA	24153	540-444-4200	444-4201
Synesis International Inc 30 Creekview Ct *Web:* www.synesisintl.com	Greenville	SC	29615	864-288-1550	
Syska & Hennessy Group 11 W 42nd St. *TF:* 800-328-1600 ■ *Web:* www.syska.com	New York	NY	10036	212-921-2300	556-3333
System Dynamics International Inc (SDI) 560 Discovery Dr NW *Web:* www.sdi-inc.com	Huntsville	AL	35806	256-895-9000	895-9443
Systems & Processes Engineering Corp (SPEC) 6800 Burleson Rd Ste 320 *Web:* www.spec.com	Austin	TX	78744	512-479-7732	494-0756
Systems Planning & Analysis Inc (SPA) 2001 N Beauregard St. *Web:* www.spa.com	Alexandria	VA	22311	703-399-7550	399-7555
Systems Technologies Inc 185 Rt 36 *Web:* www.systek.com	West Long Branch	NJ	07764	732-571-6400	571-6401
T Bailey Inc 12441 Bartholomew Rd *Web:* www.tbailey.com	Anacortes	WA	98221	360-293-0682	
T-solutions Inc 100 Bruton Ct Ste B *Web:* www.tsoln-inc.com	Chesapeake	VA	23322	757-410-9450	
TABCON Engineering 494 McNicoll Ave Ste 201 *Web:* www.tabcon.com	Toronto	ON	M2H2E1	416-491-7006	
Taber Consultants 3911 W Capitol Ave. *Web:* www.taberconsultants.com	West Sacramento	CA	95691	916-371-1690	
Tait & Assoc Inc 701 N Parkcenter Dr *Web:* tait.com	Santa Ana	CA	92705	714-560-8200	
Talascend LLC 5700 Crooks Rd Ste 450 *Web:* talascend.com	Troy	MI	48098	248-537-1300	
Talbert & Bright Inc 4810 Shelley Dr *Web:* talbertandbright.com	Wilmington	NC	28405	910-763-5350	
Talon Energy Services Inc 215 Water St Atlantic Pl Ste 301 *Web:* talonenergyservices.ca	St. John's	NL	A1C6C9	709-739-8450	
Tanco Engineering Inc 1400 Taurus Ct. *Web:* tancoeng.com	Loveland	CO	80537	970-776-4200	
Tandel Systems Inc 3982 Tampa Rd *Web:* www.tandelsystems.com	Oldsmar	FL	34677	727-530-1110	
Tangent Design Engineering 2719 7 Ave Ne. *Web:* www.tangentservices.com	Calgary	AB	T2A2L9	403-274-4647	
Tank Industry Consultants Inc 7740 W New York St. *Web:* tankindustry.com	Indianapolis	IN	46214	317-271-3100	
Taylor & Syfan Consulting Engineers Inc 684 Clarion Ct *Web:* www.taylorsyfan.com	San Luis Obispo	CA	93401	805-547-2000	
Taylor Wiseman & Taylor (TWT) 124 Gaither Dr Ste 150 *Web:* www.taylorwiseman.com	Mount Laurel	NJ	08054	856-235-7200	722-9250
Tdm Technical Services 3924 Chesswood Dr *Web:* www.tdm.ca	North York	ON	M3J2W6	416-777-0007	
TeamLogic IT Inc 26722 Plz Dr. *Web:* www.teamlogicit.com	Mission Viejo	CA	92691	949-582-6300	
Tech 4 3547 French Rd. *Web:* tech4.com	De Pere	WI	54115	920-532-0480	
Tech Conveyor Inc 195 Strykers Rd. *Web:* www.techconveyor.com	Phillipsburg	NJ	08865	908-454-1515	
Techni Core Professionals Inc 4681 Research Park Blvd *Web:* www.techni-core.com	Huntsville	AL	35806	256-704-0234	
Technical Field Engineering Inc 1114 Ridgecrest Ave	North Augusta	SC	29841	803-279-0331	
Tectonic Engineering & Surveying Consultants PC 70 Pleasant Hill Rd *Web:* tectonicengineering.com	Mountainville	NY	10953	845-534-5959	
TEECOM Design Group 1333 Broadway Ste 601 *Web:* teecom.com	Oakland	CA	94612	510-337-2800	
Tejas Research & Engineering LP 9185 Six Pines Dr. *Web:* www.tejasre.com	The Woodlands	TX	77380	281-466-8700	
Telamon Engineering Consultant 855 Folsom St *Web:* zentec.com	San Francisco	CA	94107	415-837-1336	
Teledyne Brown Engineering Inc 300 Sparkman Dr PO Box 070007 **Fax:* Hum Res ■ *TF:* 800-933-2091 ■ *Web:* www.tbe.com	Huntsville	AL	35807	256-726-1000	726-5556*
Tepa LLC 5045 List Dr *Web:* tepa.com	Colorado Springs	CO	80919	719-596-8114	
Terracon 18001 W 106th St *TF:* 800-593-7777 ■ *Web:* www.terracon.com	Olathe	KS	66061	913-599-6886	599-0574
Terracon Geotechnique Ltd 800 734 - Seventh Ave SW *Web:* www.terracon.ca	Calgary	AB	T2P3P8	403-266-1150	
Terragon Environmental Technologies Inc 651 rue Bridge *Web:* terragon.net	Montreal	QC	H3K2C8	514-938-3772	
Test Connection Inc, The 11400 Cronridge Dr Ste H *Web:* www.ttci.info	Owings Mills	MD	21117	410-526-2800	
Testing Engineers & Consultants Inc 1343 Rochester Rd *Web:* www.tectest.com	Troy	MI	48083	248-588-6200	
Testwell Laboratories Inc 47 Hudson St.	Ossining	NY	10562	914-762-9004	
Tetra Tech EC Inc 1000 the American Rd. **Fax Area Code:* 303 ■ *TF:* 800-580-3765 ■ *Web:* www.tteci.com	Morris Plains	NJ	07950	973-630-8000	980-3539*
Tetra Tech Inc 3475 E Foothill Blvd *NASDAQ: TTEK* ■ *Web:* www.tetratech.com	Pasadena	CA	91107	626-351-4664	351-5291
Tetra Tech WEI Inc 330 Bay St Ste 900. *Web:* www.wardrop.com	Toronto	ON	M5H2S8	416-368-9080	
Tetra Tech/KCM 3475 E Foothill Blvd. *NASDAQ: TTEK* ■ *TF:* 888-288-8288 ■ *Web:* www.tetratech.com	Pasadena	CA	91107	626-351-4664	351-5291
Texas Design Interests LLC 6001 W William Cannon Dr Ste 203C *Web:* tdi-llc.net	Austin	TX	78749	512-301-3389	
Thacher Associates LLC 330 W 42nd St 23rd Fl *Web:* thacherassociates.com	New York	NY	10036	212-845-7500	
Thelen Assoc Inc 1398 Cox Ave *Web:* www.thelenassoc.com	Erlanger	KY	41018	859-746-9400	746-9408
Thermal Tech 5141 Forsyth Commerce Rd Ste 1 *Web:* tti-fl.com	Orlando	FL	32807	407-373-0042	
Thermasource LLC 3883 Airway Dr Ste 340 *Web:* thermasource.com	Santa Rosa	CA	95403	707-523-2960	
Thermo Design Engineering Ltd 1424 - 70th Ave *Web:* www.thermodesign.com	Edmonton	AB	T6P1P5	780-440-6064	
Thielsch Engineering Inc 195 Frances Ave *Web:* thielsch.com	Cranston	RI	02910	401-467-6454	
Think-A-Move Ltd 23307 Commerce Park *Web:* www.think-a-move.com	Beachwood	OH	44122	216-765-8875	
Thomas F Moran Inc 48 Constitution Dr.	Bedford	NH	03110	603-472-4488	
Thomas Russell LLC 7050 S Yale Ave Ste 210 *Web:* www.thomasrussellco.com	Tulsa	OK	74136	918-481-5682	
Thompson & Litton Inc 103 E Main St. *Web:* t-l.com	Wise	VA	24293	276-328-2161	
Thorburn Assoc Inc 20880 Baker Rd *Web:* ta-inc.com	Castro Valley	CA	94546	510-886-7826	
Thornton-Tomasetti Group Inc (TTINC) 2000 L St NW Ste 840 *Web:* www.thorntontomasetti.com	Washington	DC	20036	202-580-6300	580-6301
Three Streams Engineering Ltd Ste 401 1925-18th Ave NE *Web:* www.threestreams.com	Calgary	AB	T2E7T8	403-536-5000	
Tighe & Bond Inc 53 Southampton Rd. *Web:* www.tighebond.com	Westfield	MA	01085	413-562-1600	562-5317
Timmons Group Inc 1001 Boulders Pkwy Ste 300 *Web:* www.timmons.com	Richmond	VA	23225	804-200-6500	
Tindale Oliver & Associates Inc 1000 N Ashley Dr *Web:* www.tindaleoliver.com	Tampa	FL	33602	813-224-8862	
Tipping Mar & Assoc 1906 Shattuck Ave *Web:* tippingmar.com	Berkeley	CA	94704	510-549-1906	
Tj Cross Engineers Inc 200 New Stine Rd Ste 270 *Web:* tjcrossengineers.com	Bakersfield	CA	93309	661-831-8782	831-5019
TL Industries Inc 2541 Tracy Rd. *Web:* www.tlindustries.com	Northwood	OH	43619	419-666-8144	666-6534
TLC Engineering for Architecture 255 S Orange Ave # 1600 *TF:* 800-835-9926 ■ *Web:* www.tlc-engineers.com	Orlando	FL	32801	407-841-9050	317-7182
TLM Associates Inc 117 E Lafayette St *Web:* www.tlmassociates.com	Jackson	TN	38301	731-988-9840	
TMAD Taylor & Gaines (TTG) 300 N Lake Ave 14th Fl. *Web:* www.tmadengineers.com	Pasadena	CA	91101	626-463-2711	
TMP Architecture 1191 W Sq Lk Rd PO Box 289 *Web:* www.tmp-architecture.com	Bloomfield Hills	MI	48302	248-338-4561	338-0223

Company / Address	City	State	ZIP	Phone	Fax
TMP Consulting Engineers Inc 52 Temple Pl *Web:* www.tmpeng.com	Boston	MA	02211	617-357-6060	
Toledo Engineering Company Inc 3400 Executive Pkwy PO Box 2927 *Web:* www.teco.com	Toledo	OH	43606	419-537-9711	537-1369
Tolunay-Wong Engineers Inc 10710 S Sam Houston Pkwy W *Web:* tweinc.com	Houston	TX	77031	713-722-7064	722-0319
Traffic Engineering Consultants Inc 6000 S Western Ste 300 *Web:* tecokc.com	Oklahoma City	OK	73139	405-720-7721	
Traffic Planning & Design Inc 2500 E High St Ste 650 *Web:* www.trafficpd.com	Pottstown	PA	19464	610-326-3100	
Trandes Corp 4601 Presidents Dr Ste 360 *Web:* www.trandes.com	Lanham	MD	20706	301-459-0200	459-1069
TransCore Holdings Inc 8158 Adams Dr *TF:* 800-923-4824 ■ *Web:* www.transcore.com	Hummelstown	PA	17036	717-561-2400	564-8439
Transmission Engineering Company Inc 1851 N Penn Rd *Web:* www.tecoinc.com	Hatfield	PA	19440	215-822-6737	
TranSystems Corp 2400 Pershing Rd Ste 400 *Web:* www.transystems.com	Kansas City	MO	64108	816-329-8700	329-8703
Trayer Engineering Corp 898 Pennsylvania Ave *Web:* trayer.com	San Francisco	CA	94107	415-285-7770	
TRC Worldwide Engineering Inc (TRCWW) 217 Ward Cir *Web:* www.trcww.com	Brentwood	TN	37027	615-661-7979	661-0644
Trenton Engineering Company Inc 2193 Spruce St *Web:* trentoneng.com	Trenton	NJ	08638	609-882-0616	
Tri Star Engineering Inc 3000 16th St *Web:* www.star3.com	Bedford	IN	47421	812-277-0208	277-0219
Tri Tech Surveying Company LP 10401 Westoffice Dr *Web:* www.surveyingcompany.com	Houston	TX	77042	713-667-0800	
Triad Consulting Engineers Inc 2740 State Rt 10 Ste 2 *Web:* www.triadcei.com	Morris Plains	NJ	07950	973-984-1919	
Triaxis Engineering Inc 1600 Sw Western Blvd *Web:* www.triaxiseng.com	Corvallis	OR	97333	541-766-4600	
Trident Environmental & Engineeri 110 L St Ste 1 *Web:* tridenteng.com	Antioch	CA	94509	925-706-6931	
Trihydro Corp 1252 Commerce Dr *Web:* trihydro.com	Laramie	WY	82070	307-745-7474	
TriLeaf Inc 10845 Olive Blvd Ste 310 *Web:* www.trileaf.com	Saint Louis	MO	63141	314-997-6111	997-8066
Triodyne Inc 666 Dundee Rd Ste 103 *Web:* www.triodyne.com	Northbrook	IL	60062	847-677-4730	647-2047
Truevance Management Inc 7666 Blanding Blvd PO Box 440879 *TF:* 800-285-2028 ■ *Web:* www.truenetcommunications.com	Jacksonville	FL	32244	904-777-9052	777-9553
Trussell Technologies Inc 232 N Lk Ave Ste 300 *Web:* www.trusselltech.com	Pasadena	CA	91101	626-486-0560	
TS Civil Engineering Inc 1776 Technology Dr *Web:* tscivileng.com	San Jose	CA	95110	408-452-9300	
TSM Corp 7622 Bartlett Corporate Dr *Web:* tsmcorporation.com	Bartlett	TN	38133	901-373-0300	
Tsoi/Kobus & Assoc Inc (TKA) One Brattle Sq PO Box 9114 *Web:* www.tka-architects.com	Cambridge	MA	02238	617-475-4000	475-4445
Turner EnviroLogic Inc 1140 SW 34 Ave *Web:* www.tenviro.com	Deerfield Beach	FL	33442	954-422-9787	
TVT Video Technologies Inc 2056 NW Alocleck Dr Ste 313 *Web:* www.tvti.net	Hillsboro	OR	97124	503-466-1446	
Tysinger Hampton & Partners Inc 3428 Bristol Hwy *Web:* tysinger-engineering.com	Johnson City	TN	37601	423-282-2687	
UELS LLC 85 South 200 East *Web:* www.uintahgroup.com	Vernal	UT	84078	435-789-1017	
Ulteig Engineers Inc 3350 38th Ave S PO Box 9615 *TF:* 888-858-3441 ■ *Web:* www.ulteig.com	Fargo	ND	58104	701-280-8500	237-3191
UNI Engineering Inc 156 Stockton St *Web:* uni-engineering.com	Hightstown	NJ	08520	609-448-4633	
Unicon Inc 1760 E Pecos Rd Ste 432 *Web:* www.unicon.net	Gilbert	AZ	85295	480-558-2400	
Unified Industries Inc 6551 Loisdale Ct Ste 400 *TF:* 800-666-1642 ■ *Web:* www.uii.com	Springfield	VA	22150	703-922-9800	971-5892
United States Steel Corp 600 Grant St *NYSE: X* ■ *TF:* 866-433-4801 ■ *Web:* www.ussteel.com	Pittsburgh	PA	15219	412-433-1121	
Universal Technical Resource Services Inc (UERS) 950 Kings Hwy N Ste 208 *Web:* www.utrs.com	Cherry Hill	NJ	08034	856-667-6770	667-7586
Universal Technology Corp (UTC) 1270 N Fairfield Rd *Web:* www.utcdayton.com	Dayton	OH	45432	937-426-2808	426-0839
UniversalPegasus International Inc 4848 Loop Central Dr *TF General:* 800-966-1811 ■ *Web:* www.universalpegasus.com	Houston	TX	77081	713-977-7770	977-1047
Urbahn Architects 49 W 37th St Sixth Fl *Web:* www.urbahn.com	New York	NY	10018	212-239-0220	563-5621
Urban Engineers Inc 530 Walnut St 14th Fl *Web:* www.urbanengineers.com	Philadelphia	PA	19106	215-922-8080	922-8082
Urban Robotics Inc 33 NW First Ave Ste 200 *Web:* www.urbanrobotics.net	Portland	OR	97209	503-224-9239	
URS Corp 600 Montgomery St 26th Fl *NYSE: URS* ■ *TF:* 877-877-8970 ■ *Web:* www.urscorp.com	San Francisco	CA	94111	415-774-2700	398-1905
Ursa Navigation Solutions Inc 616 Innovation Dr *Web:* ursanav.com	Chesapeake	VA	23320	757-312-0790	
Urwiler & Walter Inc 3126 Main St *Web:* urwilerwalter.com	Sumneytown	PA	18084	215-234-4562	
US Infrastructure Group Inc 774 Second St	Helena	AL	35080	205-358-3070	
US Trackworks LLC 1165 142nd Ave *Web:* ustrackworks.com	Wayland	MI	49348	616-877-4284	
USM Business Systems Inc 14175 Sullyfield Cir *Web:* usmsystems.com	Chantilly	VA	20151	703-263-0855	
Utility Engineering Park Central Bldg 1515 Arapahoe St Twr 1 Ste 800 *Web:* www.ue-corp.com	Denver	CO	80202	303-928-4400	928-4368
V. B. Cook Company Ltd 740 S Syndicate Ave *Web:* www.cookeng.com	Thunder Bay	ON	P7E1E9	807-625-6700	
V3 Cos Ltd 7325 Janes Ave *Web:* v3co.com	Woodridge	IL	60517	630-724-9200	
Vadum Inc 601 Hutton St Ste 109 *Web:* www.vaduminc.com	Raleigh	NC	27606	919-341-8241	
Valcom Consulting Group Inc 85 Albert St *Web:* www.valcom.ca	Ottawa	ON	K1P6A4	613-594-5200	
Valsamis Inc 5814 Northdale St *Web:* valsamis.com	Houston	TX	77087	713-640-1500	
Van Dijk Westlake Reed Leskosky (WRL) 1422 Euclid Ave Ste 300 *Web:* www.wrldesign.com	Cleveland	OH	44115	216-522-1350	522-1357
Vanadium Group Corp 134 Three Degree Rd *TF:* 800-685-0354 ■ *Web:* zoominfo.com	Pittsburgh	PA	15237	412-367-6060	630-8430
Vanasse Hangen Brustlin Inc (VHB) 101 Walnut St PO Box 9151 *Web:* www.vhb.com	Watertown	MA	02472	617-924-1770	924-2286
VanDemark & Lynch Inc 4305 Miller Rd *Web:* www.vandemarklynch.com	Wilmington	DE	19802	302-764-7635	
Vanderweil Engineers 274 Summer St *Web:* www.vanderweil.com	Boston	MA	02210	617-423-7423	423-7401
Vanteon Corp 250 Cross Keys Office Pk Bldg 250 *TF:* 888-506-5677 ■ *Web:* www.vanteon.com	Fairport	NY	14450	585-419-9555	248-0537
Vaughn Coast & Vaughn Inc 154 S Marietta St *Web:* vaughncoastvaughn.com	St Clairsville	OH	43950	740-695-7256	
Vectech Pharmaceutical Consultants Inc 12501 E Grand River Ave *TF:* 800-966-8832 ■ *Web:* www.vectech.com	Brighton	MI	48116	248-478-5820	442-0060
Veenstra & Kimm Inc 3000 Westown Pkwy *TF:* 800-241-8000 ■ *Web:* www.v-k.net	West Des Moines	IA	50266	515-225-8000	225-7848
Vektrel LLC 9988 Hibert St Ste 104 *Web:* www.vektrel.com	San Diego	CA	92131	858-564-0301	
Verdant Power LLC 888 Main St The Octagon Ste 1 *Web:* www.verdantpower.com	New York	NY	10044	212-888-8887	
Verifact Corp 11220 W Loop 1604 N *Web:* verifactcorp.com	San Antonio	TX	78254	210-523-5696	
Versar Inc 6850 Versar Ctr *NYSE: VSR* ■ *TF Cust Svc:* 800-283-7727 ■ *Web:* www.versar.com	Springfield	VA	22151	703-750-3000	642-6825
Vigen Construction Inc PO Box 6109 *Web:* www.vigenconstruction.com	Grand Forks	ND	58206	218-773-1159	773-3454
Villaverd Inc 1218 E Yandell Dr Ste 201 *Web:* villaverdeinc.com	El Paso	TX	79902	915-351-8822	
Virent Energy Systems Inc 3571 Anderson St *Web:* www.virent.com	Madison	WI	53704	608-663-0228	
Vista Engineering Corp 1030 Pleasantview Terr *Web:* vistaengineeringcorp.com	Ridgefield	NJ	07657	201-945-9434	
Visual Engineering Inc 164 Main St Second Fl *Web:* www.ve.com	Los Altos	CA	94022	650-949-5410	
Vitetta Two International Pl *Web:* www.vitetta.com	Philadelphia	PA	19113	215-218-4747	405-2729
Vizient Ii LLC 3129 State St Unit 2 *Web:* vizient.com	Bettendorf	IA	52722	563-355-4812	
VOA Assoc Inc 224 S Michigan Ave Ste 1400 *Web:* www.voa.com	Chicago	IL	60604	312-554-1400	554-1412
Volkert & Assoc Inc 3809 Moffett Rd *Web:* www.volkert.com	Mobile	AL	36618	251-342-1070	342-7962
Vollmer Inc 3822 Sandwich St *Web:* www.vollmer.ca	Windsor	ON	N9C1C1	519-966-6100	
VSE Corp 2550 Huntington Ave *NASDAQ: VSEC* ■ *TF:* 800-455-4873 ■ *Web:* www.vsecorp.com	Alexandria	VA	22303	703-960-4600	329-4623
W & H Pacific 12100 NE 195th St Ste 300 *Web:* www.whpacific.com	Bothell	WA	98011	425-951-4800	951-4808
W R Chesnut Engineering Inc 14 Spielman Rd *Web:* chesnuteng.com	Fairfield	NJ	07004	973-227-6995	
W R Systems Ltd 11351 Random Hills Rd Ste 400 *Web:* wrsystems.com	Fairfax	VA	22030	703-934-0200	
Wade-Trim Group Inc 500 Griswold Ave Ste 2500 *TF:* 800-482-2864 ■ *Web:* www.wadetrim.com	Detroit	MI	48226	313-961-3650	961-0898
Waldemar S Nelson & Company Inc 1200 St Charles Ave *Web:* www.wsnelson.com	New Orleans	LA	70130	504-523-5281	523-4587
Waldron Engineering & Construction Inc 37 Industrial Dr *Web:* www.waldron.com	Exeter	NH	03833	603-772-7153	

Phone *Fax*

Walker Parking Consultants/Restoration Engineers Inc
2121 Hudson Ave. Kalamazoo MI 49008 269-381-6080 343-5811
Web: www.walkerparking.com

Wallace Engineering Structural Consultants Inc
200 E Brady. Tulsa OK 74103 918-584-5858
Web: www.wallacesc.com

Wallace Roberts & Todd LLC
1700 Market St 28th Fl. Philadelphia PA 19103 215-732-5215 732-2551
TF: 800-978-4450 ■ *Web:* www.wrtdesign.com

Walter P Moore 1301 Mckinney St Ste 1100. Houston TX 77010 713-630-7300 630-7396
TF: 800-364-7300 ■ *Web:* www.walterpmoore.com

Ware Malcomb 10 Edelman. Irvine CA 92618 949-660-9128 863-1581
Web: www.waremalcomb.com

Warren Group Inc, The 7805 Saint Andrews Rd. Irmo SC 29063 803-732-6600
Web: warren-group.com

Washington Corp PO Box 16630. Missoula MT 59808 406-523-1300 523-1799
TF: 800-832-7329 ■ *Web:* www.washcorp.com

Wastech Controls & Engineering Inc
21201 Itasca St. Chatsworth CA 91311 818-998-3500
Web: www.wastechengineering.com

Water Technology Inc 100 Park Ave. Beaver Dam WI 53916 920-887-7375
Web: www.watertechnologyinc.com

Watermark Environmental Inc 175 Cabot St. Lowell MA 01854 978-452-9696
Web: www.watermarkenv.com

Watkins Hamilton Ross Architects Inc
1111 Louisiana St Fl 26. Houston TX 77002 713-665-5665 665-6213
Web: www.whrarchitects.com

Watson Engineering Inc 16445 Racho Rd. Taylor MI 48180 734-285-2200
Web: watsoneng.com

Wavetronix LLC 78 East 1700 South. Provo UT 84606 801-734-7200
Web: www.wavetronix.com

WC Cammett Engineering Inc 297 Elm St. Amesbury MA 01913 978-388-2157
Web: www.cammett.com

WD Partners 7007 Discovery Blvd. Dublin OH 43017 614-634-7000
Web: www.wdpartners.com

Weidlinger Assoc 375 Hudson St 12th Fl. New York NY 10014 212-367-3000 367-3030
Web: www.wai.com

Weir International Inc
1431 Opus Pl Executive Towers W I
Ste 210. Downers Grove IL 60515 630-968-5400
Web: www.weirintl.com

Welkin Sciences LLC
102 S Tejon St Ste 200. Colorado Springs CO 80903 719-520-5115
Web: www.welkinsciences.com

Wenck Assoc Inc PO Box 249. Maple Plain MN 55359 763-479-4200 479-4242
Web: www.wenck.com

West Consultants Pllc 405 S Sterling St. Morganton NC 28655 828-433-5661
Web: west-consultants.com

Westech International Inc
2500 Louisiana Blvd NE Ste 325. Albuquerque NM 87110 505-888-6666 837-9424
Web: www.westech-intl.com

Westermeyer Industries Inc 1441 State Rt 100. Bluffs IL 62621 217-754-3277
Web: www.westermeyerind.com

Western Engineering Contractors Inc
3171 Rippey Rd. Loomis CA 95650 916-652-3990 652-3995
Web: www.westeng.com/

Westfall Engineers Inc 14583 Big Basin Way. Saratoga CA 95070 408-867-0244
Web: westf.com

Westinghouse Electric Co
1000 Westinghouse Dr Ste 572A. Cranberry Township PA 16066 412-374-4111
Web: www.westinghousenuclear.com

Weston & Sampson Inc Five Centennial Dr. Peabody MA 01960 978-532-1900 977-0100
TF: 800-726-7766 ■ *Web:* www.westonandsampson.com

Weston Solutions Inc
1400 Weston Way PO Box 2653. West Chester PA 19380 610-701-3000 701-3186
Web: www.westonsolutions.com

Wetland Studies & Solutions Inc
5300 Wellington Branch Dr. Gainesville VA 20155 703-679-5600
Web: www.wetlandstudies.com

Wheaton & Sprague Engineering Inc
1100 Campus Dr Ste 200. Stow OH 44224 330-923-5560
Web: www.wheatonsprague.com

Whipsaw Inc 434 S First St. San Jose CA 95113 408-297-9771
Web: www.whipsaw.com

Whitlock & Weinberger
490 Mendocino Ave Ste 201. Santa Rosa CA 95401 707-542-9500
Web: w-trans.com

Whitman Requardt & Assoc 801 S Caroline St. Baltimore MD 21231 410-235-3450 243-5716
Web: www.wrallp.com

Whitney Bailey Cox & Magnani LLC
849 Fairmount Ave Ste 100. Baltimore MD 21286 410-512-4500 324-4100
Web: www.wbcm.com

Wight & Co 2500 N Frontage Rd. Darien IL 60561 630-969-7000 969-7979
Web: wightco75.com/

Wiley & Wilson Inc 127 Nationwide Dr. Lynchburg VA 24502 434-947-1901
Web: wileywilson.com

Willbros Downstream LLC 1900 N 161st E Ave. Tulsa OK 74116 918-556-3600 879-2730
Web: www.willbros.com

Willbros Engineers Inc 2087 E 71st St. Tulsa OK 74136 918-496-0400 491-9436
Web: www.willbros.com

Willdan 2401 E Katella Ave Ste 300. Anaheim CA 92806 714-940-6300 940-4920
TF: 800-424-9144 ■ *Web:* www.willdan.com

Williams & Works Inc 549 Ottawa NW. Grand Rapids MI 49503 616-224-1500
Web: williams-works.com

Williams Notaro & Assoc LLC
3928 Pender Dr Ste 220. Fairfax VA 22030 703-563-0381
Web: wnainc.com

Wilson & Company Engineers & Arch
4900 Lang Ave Ne. Albuquerque NM 87109 505-348-4000
Web: wilsonco.com

Wilson T Ballard Co 17 Gwynns Mill Ct. Owings Mills MD 21117 410-363-0150
Web: www.wtbco.com

Phone *Fax*

Wimberly Allison Tong & Goo
700 Bishop St Ste 1800. Honolulu HI 96813 808-521-8888 521-3888
Web: www.watg.com

Wink Inc 8641 United Plaza Blvd. Baton Rouge LA 70809 225-932-6000 932-9035
Web: www.willbros.com

Wiss Janney Elstner Assoc Inc
330 Pfingsten Rd. Northbrook IL 60062 847-272-7400 291-9599
TF: 800-345-3199 ■ *Web:* www.wje.com

Wke Inc 400 N Tustin Ave Ste 285. Santa Ana CA 92705 714-953-2665
Web: www.wke-inc.com

WMA Consulting Engineers Ltd
815 S Wabash Ave. Chicago IL 60605 312-786-4310
Web: www.wmace.com

Wolfberg Alvarez & Partners
3225 Aviation Ave Ste 400. Miami FL 33133 305-666-5474 666-4994
Web: www.wolfbergalvarez.com

Wong Engineers Inc
4578 Feather River Dr Ste A. Stockton CA 95219 209-476-0011

Wood Consulting Services Inc
8161 Maple Lawn Blvd Ste 375. Fulton MD 20759 301-377-5300
Web: woodcons.com

Wood Patel & Assoc Inc
2051 W Northern Ave Ste 100. Phoenix AZ 85021 602-335-8500 335-8580
Web: www.woodpatel.com

Woodard & Curran 41 Hutchins Dr. Portland ME 04102 207-774-2112
TF: 800-426-4262 ■ *Web:* www.woodardcurran.com

Woolpert Inc 4454 Idea Ctr Blvd. Dayton OH 45430 937-461-5660 461-0743
Web: www.woolpert.com

Workforce Insight Inc 1600 Wynkoop Ste 5B. Denver CO 80202 303-309-4006
Web: www.workforceinsight.com

Wright Water Engineers Inc
2490 W 26th Ave Ste 100a. Denver CO 80211 303-480-1700 480-1020
Web: www.wrightwater.com

Wright-Pierce 99 Main St. Topsham ME 04086 207-725-8721
Web: www.wright-pierce.com

Wunderlich-Malec Engineering Inc
5501 Feltl Rd. Minnetonka MN 55343 952-933-3222
Web: www.wmeng.com

Yoder 4899 Commerce Pkwy. Cleveland OH 44128 216-292-4460 831-7948
TF: 800-631-0520 ■ *Web:* yodermfg.com

Zapata Inc 6302 Fairview Rd Ste 600. Charlotte NC 28210 704-358-8240
Web: zapatainc.com

Zephyr Environmental Corp
2600 Via Fortuna Ste 450. Austin TX 78746 512-329-5544 329-8253
TF: 800-452-5558 ■ *Web:* www.zephyrenv.com

Zeton Inc 740 Oval Ct. Burlington ON L7L6A9 905-632-3123
Web: www.zeton.com

ZFA Structural Engineers
1212 Fourth St Ste Z. Santa Rosa CA 95404 707-526-0992
Web: www.zfa.com

265 ENGINES & TURBINES

SEE ALSO Aircraft Engines & Engine Parts p. 1731; Motors (Electric) & Generators p. 2776; Automotive Parts & Supplies - Mfr p. 1839

Phone *Fax*

Alturdyne Inc 660 Steele St. El Cajon CA 92020 619-440-5531 442-0481
Web: www.alturdyne.com

Anatech Electronics Inc 70 Outwater Ln. Garfield NJ 07026 973-772-4242
Web: www.anatechelectronics.com

Arrow Engine Co 2301 E Independence St. Tulsa OK 74110 918-583-5711 592-1481
TF: 800-331-3662 ■ *Web:* www.arrowengines.com

Briggs & Stratton Corp 12301 W Wirth St. Milwaukee WI 53222 414-259-5333 259-5338
NYSE: BGG ■ *TF:* 800-444-7774 ■ *Web:* www.briggsandstratton.com

Brunswick Corp One N Field Ct. Lake Forest IL 60045 847-735-4700 735-4765
NYSE: BC ■ *Web:* www.brunswick.com

Brunswick Corp Mercury Marine Div
W 6250 Pioneer Rd. Fond du Lac WI 54935 920-929-5040 929-5893
Web: www.mercurymarine.com

Capstone Turbine Corp 21211 Nordhoff St. Chatsworth CA 91311 818-734-5300 734-5320
NASDAQ: CPST ■ *TF:* 866-422-7786 ■ *Web:* www.capstoneturbine.com

Caterpillar Inc 100 NE Adams St. Peoria IL 61629 309-675-1000 675-4332*
NYSE: CAT ■ **Fax:* PR ■ *Web:* www.cat.com

Caterpillar Remanufacturing
751 International Dr. Franklin IN 46131 317-738-2117

Chromium Corp 14911 Quorum Dr Ste 600. Dallas TX 75254 216-271-4910
Web: www.chromcorp.com

Clayton Industries 17477 Hurley St. City of Industry CA 91744 626-435-1200 435-0180
TF: 800-423-4585 ■ *Web:* www.claytonindustries.com

Cummins Inc 500 Jackson St PO Box 3005. Columbus IN 47201 812-377-5000 377-3334
NYSE: CMI ■ *TF:* 800-343-7357 ■ *Web:* www.cummins.com

Delaware Mfg Industries Corp
3776 Commerce Ct. Wheatfield NY 14120 716-743-4360 743-4370
TF: 800-248-3642 ■ *Web:* www.dmic.com

Detroit Diesel Corp 13400 Outer Dr. Detroit MI 48239 313-592-5000 592-7288
Web: www.demanddetroit.com

Dresser Inc Waukesha Engine Div
1101 W St Paul Ave. Waukesha WI 53188 262-547-3311 549-2795
Web: www.ge-energy.com

Dresser-Rand Control Systems
1202 W Sam Houston Pkwy N. Houston TX 77043 713-365-2630
Web: www.dresser-rand.com/products/controls

Dresser-Rand Steam Turbines
10205 Westheimer Rd. Houston TX 77042 713-354-6100 354-6110
Web: www.dresser-rand.com

Electro Steam Generator Corp
50 Indel Ave PO Box 438. Rancocas NJ 08073 609-288-9071 288-9078
TF: 866-617-0764 ■ *Web:* www.electrosteam.com

EnPro Industries Inc
5605 Carnegie Blvd Ste 500. Charlotte NC 28209 704-731-1500 731-1511
NYSE: NPO ■ *TF:* 800-356-6955 ■ *Web:* www.enproindustries.com

Phone Fax

EnPro Industries Inc Fairbanks Morse Engine
701 White Ave. . . . . Beloit WI 53511 800-356-6955 364-8302*
*Fax Area Code: 608 ■ *Fax: Mktg ■ TF: 800-356-6955 ■ Web: www.fairbanksmorse.com

Exergonix Inc 101 SE 30th St . . . . . Lee'S Summit MO 64082 816-875-4790
Web: www.exergonix.com

GE Aviation One Neumann Way. . . . . Cincinnati OH 45215 513-243-2000
Web: www.geaviation.com

GE Energy 4200 Wildwood Pkwy . . . . . Atlanta GA 30339 203-373-2211 368-1317*
*Fax Area Code: 800 ■ TF: 800-368-1316 ■ Web: www.ge-energy.com

Globe Turbocharger Specialties Inc
201 Edison Way . . . . . Reno NV 89502 775-856-7337 856-7367
Web: www.globeturbocharger.com

H & H Mfg Company Inc Two Horne Dr. . . . . Folcroft PA 19032 610-532-8100 461-4620

Hatch & Kirk Inc 5111 Leary Ave NW . . . . . Seattle WA 98107 206-783-2766 782-6482
TF: 800-426-2818 ■ Web: www.hatchkirk.com

HDM Hydraulics LLC 125 Fire Tower Dr. . . . . Tonawanda NY 14150 716-694-8004 694-4164
Web: www.hdmhydraulics.com

Hercules Engine Components Co
2770 S Erie St. . . . . Massillon OH 44646 330-830-2498 830-4081
TF: 800-345-0662 ■ Web: www.herculesengine.com

Industrial Parts Depot LLC
23231 Normandie Ave . . . . . Torrance CA 90501 310-530-1900
Web: www.ipdparts.com

INI Power Systems Inc
175 Southport Dr Ste 100. . . . . Morrisville NC 27560 919-677-7112
Web: inipowersystems.com/

JASPER Engines & Transmissions
815 Wernsing Rd PO Box 650 . . . . . Jasper IN 47547 812-482-1041 634-1820
TF: 800-827-7455 ■ Web: www.jasperengines.com

John Deere Power Systems
3801 W Ridgeway Ave PO Box 5100 . . . . . Waterloo IA 50704 800-533-6446 292-5075*
*Fax Area Code: 319 ■ TF: 800-533-6446 ■ Web: www.deere.com

KMS Ventures Inc 1301 W 25th St Ste 300. . . . . Austin TX 78705 512-474-6312
TF: 844-282-7433

Kohler Engines 444 Highland Dr . . . . . Kohler WI 53044 920-457-4441 459-1570*
*Fax: Sales ■ TF: 800-544-2444 ■ Web: www.kohlerengines.com

Marine Power Holding LLC
17506 Marine Power Industrial Pk . . . . . Ponchatoula LA 70454 985-386-2081 386-4010
Web: www.marinepowerusa.com

NREC Power Systems 5222 Hwy 311 . . . . . Houma LA 70360 985-872-5480 872-0611
TF: 800-851-6732 ■ Web: www.nrecps.com

Pratt & Whitney Canada Inc
1000 Marie-Victorin Blvd. . . . . Longueuil QC J4G1A1 450-677-9411 647-3620
TF: 800-268-8000 ■ Web: www.pwc.ca

Solar Turbines Inc 2200 Pacific Hwy. . . . . San Diego CA 92101 619-544-5000 544-5825*
*Fax: Sales ■ Web: mysolar.cat.com

Springfield ReManufacturing Corp
650 N Broadview Pl . . . . . Springfield MO 65802 417-862-3501
TF: 800-772-7733 ■ Web: www.srcreman.com

SRC Holdings Corp 531 S Union Ave. . . . . Springfield MO 65802 417-862-2337
Web: www.srcholdings.com

Voith Siemens Hydro Power 760 E Berlin Rd . . . . . York PA 17408 717-792-7000 792-7263
Web: www.voith.com

Volvo Penta of the Americas Inc
1300 Volvo Penta Dr. . . . . Chesapeake VA 23320 757-436-2800 436-5150
TF: 800-522-1959 ■ Web: www.volvopenta.com

Wartsila North America Inc
16330 Air Ctr Blvd . . . . . Houston TX 77032 281-233-6200 233-6233
TF: 877-927-8745 ■ Web: www.wartsila.com

Westerbeke Corp
150 John Hancock Rd
Miles Standish Industrial Pk. . . . . Taunton MA 02780 508-823-7677 884-9688
TF: 800-582-7846 ■ Web: www.westerbeke.com

Western Diesel Services Inc
1100 Research Blvd . . . . . Saint Louis MO 63132 314-868-8620 868-9314
TF: 855-257-6937

266 ENVELOPES

Phone Fax

ADM Corp 100 Lincoln Blvd. . . . . Middlesex NJ 08846 732-469-0900 469-0785
TF: 800-327-0718 ■ Web: www.admcorporation.com

Alvah Bushnell Co 519 E Chelten Ave . . . . . Philadelphia PA 19144 215-842-9520 843-7725
TF: 800-255-7434 ■ Web: www.bushnellco.com

AmericanChurch Inc
525 McClurg Rd PO Box 3120. . . . . Youngstown OH 44513 330-758-4545 758-4363
TF: 800-446-3035 ■ Web: www.americanchurch.com

B & W Press Inc 401 E Main St . . . . . Georgetown MA 01833 978-352-6100 352-5955
TF: 877-246-3467 ■ Web: www.bwpress.com

Bowers Envelope Co 5331 N Tacoma Ave. . . . . Indianapolis IN 46220 317-253-4321 254-2239
Web: www.bowersenvelope.com

Cenveo Inc 201 Broad St 1 Canterberry Green . . . . . Stamford CT 06901 203-595-3000 595-3070
NYSE: CVO ■ Web: www.cenveo.com

Curtis 1000 Inc 1725 Breckinridge Pkwy Ste 500 . . . . . Duluth GA 30096 678-380-9095 944-8817*
*Fax Area Code: 800 ■ TF: 877-287-8715 ■ Web: www.curtis1000.com

Federal Envelope Co 608 Country Club Dr. . . . . Bensenville IL 60106 630-595-2000 595-1212
Web: www.federalenvelope.com

Heinrich Envelope Corp 925 Zane Ave N. . . . . Minneapolis MN 55422 763-544-3571 544-6287
TF: 800-346-7957 ■ Web: www.heinrichenvelope.com

Love Envelopes Inc 10733 E Ute St. . . . . Tulsa OK 74116 918-836-3535 832-9978
TF: 800-532-9747 ■ Web: www.loveenvelopes.com

Mackay Envelope Corp 2100 Elm St SE. . . . . Minneapolis MN 55414 800-622-5299
TF: 800-622-5299 ■ Web: mackaymitchell.com

Motion Envelope Inc 1455 Terre Colony Ct . . . . . Dallas TX 75212 214-634-2131 634-2132
Web: i3plasticcards.com

National Church Supply Co, The PO Box 269 . . . . . Chester WV 26034 304-387-5200 387-5266
TF: 800-627-9900 ■ Web: www.envelopeservice.com

Papercone Corp 3200 Fern Vly Rd . . . . . Louisville KY 40213 502-961-9493 961-9346
TF: 800-626-5308 ■ Web: papercone.com

Poly-Pak Industries Inc 125 Spagnoli Rd. . . . . Melville NY 11747 800-969-1993 454-6366*
*Fax Area Code: 631 ■ TF: 800-969-1993 ■ Web: www.poly-pak.com

Phone Fax

Response Envelope Inc 1340 S Baker Ave. . . . . Ontario CA 91761 909-923-5855 923-3639
TF: 800-750-0046 ■ Web: www.response-envelope.com

Royal Envelope Co 4114 S Peoria St. . . . . Chicago IL 60609 773-376-1212 376-0011
Web: royalenv.com

Tension Envelope Corp 819 E 19th St . . . . . Kansas City MO 64108 800-388-5122 283-1498*
*Fax Area Code: 816 ■ TF: 800-388-5122 ■ Web: tensionenvelope.com

Top Flight Inc 1300 Central Ave. . . . . Chattanooga TN 37408 423-266-8171 266-6857
TF: 800-777-3740 ■ Web: www.topflightpaper.com

Western States Envelope & Label Co
4480 N 132nd St . . . . . Butler WI 53007 262-781-5540 781-5791
TF: 800-558-0514 ■ Web: www.wsel.com

Worcester Envelope Co
22 Millbury St PO Box 406. . . . . Auburn MA 01501 508-832-5394 832-3796*
*Fax: Sales ■ TF: 800-343-1398 ■ Web: www.worcesterenvelope.com

267 EQUIPMENT RENTAL & LEASING

SEE ALSO Credit & Financing - Commercial p. 2177; Credit & Financing - Consumer p. 2178; Fleet Leasing & Management p. 2291

267-1 Computer Equipment Leasing

Phone Fax

Data Sales Company Inc
3450 W Burnsville Pkwy. . . . . Burnsville MN 55337 952-890-8838 895-3369
TF: 800-328-2730 ■ Web: www.datasales.com

Electro Rent Corp 6060 Sepulveda Blvd . . . . . Van Nuys CA 91411 818-787-2100 786-4354
NASDAQ: ELRC ■ TF Sales: 800-688-1111 ■ Web: www.electrorent.com

First Equipment Co PO Box 2129 . . . . . Addison TX 75001 972-380-2300 380-8350
TF: 888-780-8631 ■ Web: www.firstequipment.com

Hitachi Credit America Ltd
800 Connecticut Ave Ste 4n01 . . . . . Norwalk CT 06854 866-718-4222
Web: hitachicapitalamerica.com

LaSalle Systems Leasing Inc 6111 N River Rd. . . . . Rosemont IL 60018 847-823-9600 823-1646
Web: www.elasalle.com

Leasing Technologies International Inc
221 Danbury Rd . . . . . Wilton CT 06897 203-563-1100 563-1112
Web: www.ltileasing.com

Manufacturers' Lease Plans Inc
818 E Osborn Rd Ste 200. . . . . Phoenix AZ 85014 602-944-4411 944-4417
Web: www.leaseplans.com

Newport Leasing Inc
4750 Von Karman Ave . . . . . Newport Beach CA 92660 949-476-8476
TF Cust Svc: 800-274-0042 ■ Web: www.newportleasing.com

Rent-A-PC Inc 265 Oser Ave . . . . . Hauppauge NY 11788 631-273-8888 582-9806*
*Fax Area Code: 407 ■ TF: 800-800-8686 ■ Web: www.smartsourcerentals.com

Summit Funding Group Inc
4680 Parkway Dr Ste 300. . . . . Mason OH 45040 513-489-1222 489-1490
Web: www.summit-funding.com

Vicom Computer Services Inc
400 Broadhollow Rd. . . . . Farmingdale NY 11735 631-694-3900 694-2640
Web: www.vicomnet.com

267-2 Home & Office Equipment Rental (General)

Phone Fax

Bakercorp 3020 Old Ranch Pkwy Ste 220 . . . . . Seal Beach CA 90740 562-430-6262 430-4865
Web: www.bakercorp.com

Bestway Inc 12400 Coit Rd Ste 950. . . . . Dallas TX 75251 214-630-6655 630-8404
TF: 800-316-4567 ■ Web: www.bestwayrto.com

Brook Furniture Rental Inc
100 N Field Dr Ste 220. . . . . Lake Forest IL 60045 847-810-4000 283-0478
TF: 877-285-7368 ■ Web: www.bfr.com

Buddy's Home Furnishings 6608 E Adamo Dr. . . . . Tampa FL 33619 866-779-5085 626-8195*
*Fax Area Code: 813 ■ TF: 866-779-5085 ■ Web: www.buddyrents.com

Celtic Commercial Finance 4 Pk Plz Ste 300 . . . . . Irvine CA 92614 949-263-3880 263-1331
Web: www.celticfinance.com

Classic Party Rentals
11766 Wilshire Blvd Ste 350 . . . . . Los Angeles CA 90025 310-535-3660
TF: 800-678-3854 ■ Web: www.classicpartyrentals.com

Exhibitors Carpet Service Inc
6112 W 73rd St . . . . . Bedford Park IL 60638 773-247-0604
Web: www.ecscarpet.com

GFC Leasing Co 2675 Research Pk Dr . . . . . Madison WI 53711 800-677-7877 271-9703*
*Fax Area Code: 608 ■ TF: 800-333-5905 ■ Web: gfcleasing.com

Independent Rental Inc 2020 S Cushman St . . . . . Fairbanks AK 99701 888-456-6595 456-2927*
*Fax Area Code: 907 ■ Web: www.independentrentalinc.com

LMG Inc PO Box 770429 . . . . . Orlando FL 32877 407-850-0505 438-8422
TF: 888-226-3100 ■ Web: www.lmg.net

Marlin Business Services Inc
300 Fellowship Rd Ste 170. . . . . Mount Laurel NJ 08054 888-479-9111 479-1100
NASDAQ: MRLN ■ TF: 888-479-9111 ■ Web: www.marlinfinance.com

Party Rental Ltd 275 N St . . . . . Teterboro NJ 07608 201-727-4700 727-4701
Web: www.partyrentalltd.com

Projection Presentation Technology
5803 Rolling Rd . . . . . Springfield VA 22152 703-912-1334 912-1350
TF: 800-377-7650 ■ Web: projection.com

Rent Rite 1260 E Higgins Rd. . . . . Elk Grovevillage IL 60007 847-640-8860 437-4402
Web: www.rentriteequipment.com

Rent-A-Center Inc 5501 Headquarters Dr . . . . . Plano TX 75024 800-422-8186 943-0113*
NASDAQ: RCII ■ *Fax Area Code: 972 ■ *Fax: Cust Svc ■ TF: 800-422-8186 ■ Web: www6.rentacenter.com

Rug Doctor LP 4701 Old Shepard Pl. . . . . Plano TX 75093 972-673-1400 261-6602*
*Fax Area Code: 888 ■ TF: 800-784-3628 ■ Web: www.rugdoctor.com

Somerset Capital Group Ltd
612 Wheelers Farms Rd . . . . . Milford CT 06461 203-701-5100 301-3253
TF: 877-282-9922 ■ Web: www.somersetcapital.com

Taylor Rental 1547 Brandy Pkwy . . . . . Streamwood IL 60107 630-289-2550
Web: www.taylorrental.com

267-3 Industrial & Heavy Equipment Rental

Phone *Fax*

Aggreko 4607 W Admiral Doyle Dr .... New Iberia LA 70560 337-367-7884 367-0870
Web: www.aggreko.com

AH Harris & Son Inc 367 Alumni Rd .... Newington CT 06111 860-665-9494 665-9444
TF: 800-382-6555 ■ *Web:* www.ahharris.com

Ahern Rentals Inc 4241 Arville St .... Las Vegas NV 89103 702-362-0623 362-9316
TF: 800-589-6797 ■ *Web:* www.ahern.com

Allied Steel Construction Co Inc
2211 NW First Terr PO Box 1111 .... Oklahoma City OK 73107 405-232-7531 236-3705
TF: 800-522-4658 ■ *Web:* www.alliedsteelerectors.com

American Equipment Co 2106 Anderson Rd .... Greenville SC 29611 864-295-7800 295-7843
Web: www.ameco.com

APi Supply Inc 624 Arthur St NE .... Minneapolis MN 55413 612-379-8000 379-8038
Web: www.apisupplyinc.com

Beco Equipment Co 5555 Dahlia St .... Commerce City CO 80022 303-288-2613 288-5776
Web: www.becoequipment.com

Broussard Bros Inc 25817 Louisiana Hwy 333 .... Abbeville LA 70510 337-893-5303 893-7148
TF: 800-299-5303 ■ *Web:* www.broussardbrothers.com

Buck & Knobby Equipment Co
6220 Sterns Rd .... Ottawa Lake MI 49267 734-856-2811 856-2709
TF: 855-213-2825 ■ *Web:* www.buckandknobby.com

Cloverdale Equipment Co 13133 Cloverdale St .... Oak Park MI 48237 248-399-6600 399-7730
TF: 888-388-9182 ■ *Web:* www.cloverdale-equip.com

Cornell & Co Inc 224 Cornell Ln PO Box 807 .... Westville NJ 08093 856-742-1900 742-8186
Web: www.cornellcraneandsteel.com

D & D Equipment Rental Inc
10936 Shoemaker Ave .... Santa Fe Springs CA 90670 562-595-4555 903-8881
Web: www.ddrental.com

Equipment Technology LLC
341 NW 122nd St .... Oklahoma City OK 73114 888-748-3841 755-6829*
**Fax Area Code:* 405 ■ *TF:* 888-748-3841 ■ *Web:* etiequipment.com

Ervin Leasing Co 3893 Research Pk Dr .... Ann Arbor MI 48108 800-748-0015 968-2808
TF: 800-748-0015 ■ *Web:* www.ervinleasing.com

Essex Crane Rental Corp
1110 Lake Cook Rd Ste 220 .... Buffalo Grove IL 60089 847-215-6500 215-6535
Web: www.essexcrane.com

Force Construction Company Inc
990 N National Rd .... Columbus IN 47201 812-372-8441 372-5424
Web: www.forceco.com

G & C Equipment Corp
1875 W Redondo Beach Blvd Ste 102 .... Gardena CA 90247 310-515-6715 515-5046
Web: www.gandccorp.com

H & E Equipment Services Inc
11100 Mead Rd .... Baton Rouge LA 70809 225-298-5200
NASDAQ: HEES ■ *TF:* 866-467-3682 ■ *Web:* www.he-equipment.com

Hawthorne Machinery Co
16945 Camino San Bernardo .... San Diego CA 92127 858-674-7000 674-7155
TF: 800-437-4228 ■ *Web:* www.hawthornecat.com

HB Rentals LC 5813 Hwy 90 E .... Broussard LA 70518 337-839-1641 839-1628
TF: 800-262-6790 ■ *Web:* hbrentals.com/

Hertz equipment rental
5500 Commerce Blvd .... Rohnert Park CA 94928 707-586-4444 586-4421
Web: www.hertzequip.com

Hertz Equipment Rental Corp 225 Brae Blvd .... Park Ridge NJ 07656 201-307-2000 817-7694*
**Fax Area Code:* 888 ■ *TF:* 800-654-3131 ■ *Web:* www.hertzequip.com

Independent Rental Inc 2020 S Cushman St .... Fairbanks AK 99701 888-456-6595 456-2927*
**Fax Area Code:* 907 ■ *Web:* www.independentrentalinc.com

Klochko Equipment Rental Company Inc
2782 Corbin Ave .... Melvindale MI 48122 313-386-7220 386-2530
TF: 800-783-7368 ■ *Web:* www.klochko.com

Leppo Inc PO Box 154 .... Tallmadge OH 44278 330-633-3999 630-1599
TF: 800-453-7762 ■ *Web:* www.leppos.com

Marco Crane & Rigging Co 221 S 35th Ave .... Phoenix AZ 85009 602-272-2671 352-0413
TF: 800-668-2671 ■ *Web:* www.marcocrane.com

Maxim Crane Works 1225 Washington Pk .... Bridgeville PA 15017 412-504-0200 504-0126
TF: 877-629-5438 ■ *Web:* www.maximcrane.com

Medico Industries Inc 1500 Hwy 315 .... Wilkes-Barre PA 18711 570-825-7711 824-1169
TF: 800-633-0027 ■ *Web:* medicoind.com

Mitcham Industries Inc (MII)
8141 Hwy 75 S PO Box 1175 .... Huntsville TX 77340 936-291-2277 295-1922*
NASDAQ: MIND ■ **Fax:* Sales ■ *Web:* www.mitchamindustries.com

Modern Group 2501 Durham Rd .... Bristol PA 19007 877-879-4188 943-4978*
**Fax Area Code:* 215 ■ *TF:* 877-879-4188 ■ *Web:* www.moderngroup.com

Morrow Equipment Company LLC
3218 Pringle Rd SE PO Box 3306 .... Salem OR 97302 503-585-5721 363-1172
Web: www.morrow.com

Mustang Rental Services Inc 15907 E Fwy .... Channelview TX 77530 281-452-7368
Web: www.mustangcat.com

National Construction Rentals Inc
15319 Chatsworth St .... Mission Hills CA 91345 818-221-6000 896-8411*
**Fax Area Code:* 800 ■ *TF:* 800-352-5675 ■ *Web:* www.rentnational.com

Norcal Rental Group LLC 318 Stealth Ct .... Livermore CA 94551 925-961-0130 456-9760
TF: 800-649-6629 ■ *Web:* www.crescorent.com

Quantum Analytics 3400 East Third Ave .... Foster City CA 94404 650-312-0900
TF: 800-992-4199 ■ *Web:* www.lqa.com

Raymond Handling Concepts Corp
41400 Boyce Rd .... Fremont CA 94538 510-745-7500 745-7686
TF: 800-675-2500 ■ *Web:* www.raymondhandling.com

Rush Enterprises Inc
555 IH 35 S Ste 500 .... New Braunfels TX 78130 830-626-5200 626-5310
NASDAQ: RUSHA ■ *TF:* 800-973-7874 ■ *Web:* www.rushenterprises.com

Safway Services Inc
N 19 W 24200 Riverwood Dr .... Waukesha WI 53188 262-523-6500 523-9808
TF: 800-558-4772 ■ *Web:* www.safway.com

Skyworks LLC 100 Thielman Dr .... Buffalo NY 14206 716-822-5438
TF: 866-983-1184 ■ *Web:* www.skyworksllc.com

Stanley W Bowles Corp
3375 Joseph Martin Hwy PO Box 4706 .... Martinsville VA 24115 276-956-3442 956-7038
Web: www.bowlesproperties.com

Phone *Fax*

Star Rentals Inc 1919 Fourth Ave S .... Seattle WA 98134 206-622-7880
TF: 800-825-7880 ■ *Web:* www.starrentals.com

Stephenson Equipment Inc (SEI)
7201 Paxton St .... Harrisburg PA 17111 717-564-3434 564-7580
TF: 800-325-6455 ■ *Web:* www.stephensonequipment.com

Sunbelt Rentals Inc 2341 Deerfield Dr .... Fort Mill SC 29715 704-348-2676
TF General: 800-667-9328 ■ *Web:* www.sunbeltrentals.com

T & T Truck & Crane Service Inc
1375 N Olive St .... Ventura CA 93001 805-648-3348
Web: www.truckandcrane.com

Tetra Corporate Services LLC
6995 Union Park Ctr Suite 360 .... Salt Lake City UT 84047 801-566-2600 365-6263
TF: 800-417-0548 ■ *Web:* www.tetracsi.com

Thomas Instrument & Machine Company Inc
3440 First St .... Brookshire TX 77423 281-375-6300 375-5264
Web: www.thomasinstrument.com

Timco Services Inc 1724 E Milton Rd .... Lafayette LA 70508 337-233-5185 856-8158
TF: 800-749-2054 ■ *Web:* www.timcoservices.com

Traffic Control Service Inc
2435 Lemon Ave .... Signal Hill CA 90755 800-763-3999 424-0266*
**Fax Area Code:* 562 ■ *TF:* 800-763-3999 ■ *Web:* www.trafficmanagement.com

United Crane Rentals Inc
111 N Michigan Ave .... Kenilworth NJ 07033 908-245-6260 245-1708

United Rentals 3266 E Washington St .... Phoenix AZ 85233 602-267-3898
TF: 800-624-1808 ■ *Web:* www.unitedrentals.com

United Rentals Inc 224 Selleck St .... Stamford CT 06902 203-622-3131 622-6080
NYSE: URI ■ *TF:* 800-877-3687 ■ *Web:* www.unitedrentals.com

Western Oilfields Supply Co
3404 State Rd .... Bakersfield CA 93308 661-399-9124 392-9427*
**Fax:* Acctg ■ *TF:* 800-350-7246 ■ *Web:* www.rainforrent.com

267-4 Medical Equipment Rental

Phone *Fax*

American Shared Hospital Services
Four Embarcadero Ctr Ste 3700 .... San Francisco CA 94111 415-788-5300 788-5660
NYSE: AMS ■ *TF:* 800-735-0641 ■ *Web:* www.ashs.com

Dynasplint Systems Inc
770 Ritchie Hwy Ste W21 .... Severna Park MD 21146 410-544-9530 380-3784*
**Fax Area Code:* 800 ■ *TF:* 800-638-6771 ■ *Web:* www.dynasplint.com

First Lease Inc
1300 Virginia Dr Ste 450 .... Fort Washington PA 19034 866-493-4778 283-9870*
**Fax Area Code:* 215 ■ *TF:* 866-493-4778 ■ *Web:* www.firstleaseonline.com

Freedom Medical Inc 219 Welsh Pool Rd .... Exton PA 19341 610-903-0200 903-0180
TF: 800-784-8849 ■ *Web:* www.freedommedical.com

King's Medical Co 1894 Georgetown Rd .... Hudson OH 44236 330-653-3968 656-0600
Web: www.kingsmedical.com

Modern Medical Modalities Corp 439 Chestnut St ...... Union NJ 07083 908-933-0216
NYSE: MODM

Universal Hospital Services Inc
7700 France Ave S Ste 275 .... Minneapolis MN 55435 952-893-3200 893-0704
TF: 800-847-7368 ■ *Web:* www.uhs.com

267-5 Transport Equipment Rental

Phone *Fax*

Andersons Inc Rail Group
480 W Dussel Dr PO Box 119 .... Maumee OH 43537 419-893-5050 891-2749
TF General: 800-537-3370 ■ *Web:* www.andersonsinc.com

Cronos Containers Inc
1 Front St Ste 925 .... San Francisco CA 94111 415-677-8990 677-9396
TF: 866-275-3711 ■ *Web:* www.cronos.com

Eurotainer Inc 5810 Wilson Rd Ste 200 .... Humble TX 77396 832-300-5001 300-5050
Web: www.eurotainer.com

EXSIF Worldwide Inc
2700 Westchester Ave Ste 400 .... Purchase NY 10577 914-848-4200 848-4201
Web: www.exsif.com

Flexi-Van Leasing Inc 251 Monroe Ave .... Kenilworth NJ 07033 908-276-8000 276-7666
TF: 866-965-9288 ■ *Web:* www.flexi-van.com

GATX Rail Canada
1801 Magill College Ave Ste 1475 .... Montreal QC H3A2N4 514-931-7343 931-5534
Web: www.cgtx.com

GE Rail Car Services 161 N Clark St 7th Fl .... Chicago IL 60601 312-853-5000
TF: 800-626-2000 ■ *Web:* www.ge.com/capital/rail

GLNX Corp
10077 Grogan's Mill Rd Ste 450 .... The Woodlands TX 77380 281-363-7053 363-7060
Web: www.glnx.com

Greenbrier Co One Centerpointe Dr Ste 200 .... Lake Oswego OR 97035 503-684-7000 684-7553
NYSE: GBX ■ *TF:* 800-343-7188 ■ *Web:* www.gbrx.com

Procor Ltd 2001 Speers Rd .... Oakville ON L6L2X9 905-827-4111
Web: www.procor.com

Railserve Inc 1691 Phoenix Blvd Ste 110 .... Atlanta GA 30349 770-996-6838 996-6830
TF: 800-345-7245 ■ *Web:* www.railserveinc.com

TAL International Group Inc
100 Manhattanville Rd .... Purchase NY 10577 914-251-9000 697-2549
NYSE: TAL ■ *Web:* www.talinternational.com

TTX Co 101 N Wacker Dr .... Chicago IL 60606 312-853-3223 984-3790
TF: 800-889-4357 ■ *Web:* www.ttx.com

268 ETHICS COMMISSIONS

Phone *Fax*

Federal Election Commission 999 E St NW .... Washington DC 20463 202-694-1100
TF: 800-424-9530 ■ *Web:* www.fec.gov

US Office of Government Ethics
1201 New York Ave NW Ste 500 .... Washington DC 20005 202-482-9300 482-9237
Web: www.oge.gov

				Phone	Fax
Alabama Ethics Commission 100 N Union St Ste 104 *Web:* www.ethics.alabama.gov	Montgomery	AL	36104	334-242-2997	242-0248
Alaska Legislative Ethics Committee 716 W 4th Ave Ste 230 *Web:* anchorage.akleg.gov	Anchorage	AK	99501	907-269-0111	269-0229
Arakansas Ethics Commission PO Box 1917 *TF:* 800-422-7773 ■ *Web:* www.arkansasethics.com	Little Rock	AR	72203	501-324-9600	324-9606
California Fair Political Practices Commission 428 J St Ste 620 *TF:* 866-275-3772 ■ *Web:* www.fppc.ca.gov	Sacramento	CA	95814	916-322-5660	322-0886
Connecticut Ethics Commission 18-20 Trinity St Ste 205 *Web:* www.ct.gov/ethics/site/default.asp	Hartford	CT	06106	860-263-2400	263-2402
Delaware Public Integrity Commission 410 Federal St Margaret O'Neill Bldg Ste 3 *Web:* www.depic.delaware.gov	Dover	DE	19901	302-739-2399	739-2398
Florida Ethics Commission 3600 Maclay Blvd S Ste 201 *Web:* www.ethics.state.fl.us	Tallahassee	FL	32312	850-488-7864	488-3077
Georgia Transparency & Campaign Finance Commission 200 Piedmont Ave SE Ste 1402 *TF:* 866-589-7327 ■ *Web:* www.ethics.state.ga.us	Atlanta	GA	30334	404-463-1980	
Indiana State Ethics Commission (OIG) 315 W Ohio St Rm 104 *Web:* www.in.gov/ig	Indianapolis	IN	46202	317-232-3850	232-0707
Iowa Ethics & Campaign Disclosure Board 510 E 12th St Ste 1-A *Web:* www.state.ia.us	Des Moines	IA	50319	515-281-4028	281-3701
Kansas Governmental Ethics Commission 109 W Ninth St Ste 504 *Web:* www.kansas.gov	Topeka	KS	66612	785-296-4219	296-2548
Kentucky Legislative Ethics Commission 22 Mill Creek Pk *Web:* www.klec.ky.gov	Frankfort	KY	40601	502-573-2863	573-2929
Louisiana Ethics Board 617 N Third St LaSalle Bldg Ste 10-36 *TF:* 800-842-6630 ■ *Web:* www.ethics.state.la.us	Baton Rouge	LA	70802	225-219-5600	381-7271
Maine Governmental Ethics & Election Practices Commission 45 Memorial Cir *Web:* www.maine.gov	Augusta	ME	04330	207-287-4179	287-6775
Maryland Ethics Commission 45 Calvert St 3rd Fl *TF:* 877-669-6085 ■ *Web:* ethics.maryland.gov	Annapolis	MD	21401	410-260-7770	260-7746
Massachusetts State Ethics Commission 1 Ashburton Pl Rm 619 *Web:* www.mass.gov/ethics	Boston	MA	02108	617-371-9500	723-5851
Minnesota Campaign Finance & Public Disclosure Board 658 Cedar St Ste 190 *TF:* 800-657-3889 ■ *Web:* www.cfboard.state.mn.us	Saint Paul	MN	55155	651-296-5148	296-1722
Mississippi Ethics Commission 146 E Amite St Ste 103 *Web:* www.ethics.state.ms.us	Jackson	MS	39201	601-359-1285	354-6253
Montana Commissioner of Political Practices 1205 Eigth Ave PO Box 202401 *Web:* www.politicalpractices.mt.gov	Helena	MT	59620	406-444-2942	444-1643
Nebraska Accountability & Disclosure Commission PO Box 95086 *Web:* nadc.nebraska.gov	Lincoln	NE	68509	402-471-2522	471-6599
Nevada Commission on Ethics 704 W Nye Ln Ste 204 *Web:* www.ethics.nv.gov	Carson City	NV	89703	775-687-5469	687-1279
New Jersey Ethical Standards Commission 28 W State St Rm 1407 PO Box 082 *Web:* www.state.nj.us/lps/ethics	Trenton	NJ	08625	609-292-1892	633-9252
New Mexico Ethics Administration 325 Don Gaspar St Ste 300 *TF:* 800-477-3632 ■ *Web:* www.sos.state.nm.us	Santa Fe	NM	87501	505-827-3600	
North Carolina Ethics Board 424 N Blount St *Web:* www.ethicscommission.nc.gov	Raleigh	NC	27601	919-715-2071	715-1644
Ohio Ethics Commission 30 W Spring St L3 *Web:* www.ethics.ohio.gov	Columbus	OH	43215	614-466-7090	466-8368
Oklahoma Ethics Commission 2300 N Lincoln Blvd Rm B5 *Web:* www.ok.gov	Oklahoma City	OK	73105	405-521-3451	521-4905
Oregon Government Standards & Practices Commission 3218 Pringle Rd SE Ste 220 *Web:* www.oregon.gov	Salem	OR	97302	503-378-5105	373-1456
Pennsylvania State Ethics Commission 309 Finance Bldg PO Box 11470 *TF:* 800-932-0936 ■ *Web:* www.ethics.state.pa.us	Harrisburg	PA	17108	717-783-1610	787-0806
Rhode Island Ethics Commission 40 Fountain St *Web:* www.ethics.ri.gov	Providence	RI	02903	401-222-3790	222-3382
South Carolina Ethics Commission 5000 Thurmond Mall Ste 250 *Web:* www.state.sc.us	Columbia	SC	29201	803-253-4192	253-7539
Texas Ethics Commission 201 E 14th St 10th Fl *Web:* www.ethics.state.tx.us	Austin	TX	78701	512-463-5800	463-5777
Washington Public Disclosure Commission PO Box 40908 *Web:* www.pdc.wa.gov	Olympia	WA	98504	360-753-1111	753-1112
West Virginia Ethics Commission 210 Brooks St Ste 300 *TF:* 866-558-0664 ■ *Web:* www.ethics.wv.gov	Charleston	WV	25301	304-558-0664	558-2169
Wisconsin Ethics Board 212 E Washington Ave 3rd Fl *Web:* www.gab.wi.gov	Madison	WI	53703	608-266-8123	264-9319

269 EXECUTIVE RECRUITING FIRMS

				Phone	Fax
Accretive Solutions Inc 1 S Wacker Dr Ste 950 *Web:* www.accretivesolutions.com	Chicago	IL	60606	312-994-4600	994-4638
Barton Assoc Inc 701 Richmond Ave *Web:* www.bartona.com	Houston	TX	77006	713-961-9111	
Battalia Winston International 555 Madison Ave 19th Fl *Web:* www.battaliawinston.com	New York	NY	10022	212-308-8080	308-1309
Bishop Partners Ltd 28 W 44th St #1120 *Web:* www.bishoppartners.com	New York	NY	10036	212-986-3419	575-1050
Boyden World Corp 50 Broadway *TF:* 877-226-9336 ■ *Web:* www.boyden.com	Hawthorne	NY	10532	914-747-0093	747-0108
Canny Bowen Inc 400 Madison Ave Ste 11-D *Web:* www.cannybowen.com	New York	NY	10017	212-949-6611	949-5191
Chadick Ellig Inc 300 Pk Ave 25th Fl *Web:* www.chadickellig.com	New York	NY	10022	212-688-8671	308-4510
Chicago Legal Search Ltd 180 N LaSalle St *Web:* www.chicagolegalsearch.com	Chicago	IL	60601	312-251-2580	251-0223
Choi & Burns LLC 156 W 56th St 18th Fl *Web:* www.choiburns.com	New York	NY	10019	212-755-7051	355-2610
Christian & Timbers 25825 Science Pk Dr *TF:* 800-299-9630 ■ *Web:* www.ctnet.com	Cleveland	OH	44122	216-464-8710	
Cole Warren & Long Inc Two Penn Ctr Ste 312 *TF:* 800-394-8517 ■ *Web:* www.cwl-inc.com	Philadelphia	PA	19102	215-563-0701	563-2907
Compass Group Ltd 401 S Old Woodward Ave Ste 460	Birmingham	MI	48009	248-540-9110	
Cook Assoc Inc 212 W Kinzie St *Web:* www.cookassociates.com	Chicago	IL	60654	312-329-0900	329-1528
Dahl Morrow International 11260 Roger Bacon St Ste 204 *Web:* www.dahl-morrowintl.com	Reston	VA	20190	703-787-8117	787-8114
Daniel & Yeager (D&Y) 6767 Old Madison Pk Ste 690 *Fax Area Code: 256 ■ *TF:* 800-955-1919 ■ *Web:* www.dystaffing.com	Huntsville	AL	35806	800-955-1919	551-1075*
DHR International 10 S Riverside Plz Ste 2220 *Web:* www.dhrinternational.com	Chicago	IL	60606	312-782-1581	782-2096
Dieckmann & Assoc 500 N Michigan Ave	Chicago	IL	60611	312-819-5900	
Diversified Search Cos 2005 Market St 33rd Fl *TF:* 800-423-3932 ■ *Web:* www.divsearch.com	Philadelphia	PA	19103	215-732-6666	568-8399
Early Cochran & Olson LLC One E Upper Wacker Dr Ste 2510 *Web:* www.ecollc.com	Chicago	IL	60601	312-595-4200	595-4209
Eastman & Beaudine Inc 7201 Bishop Rd Ste 220 *Web:* www.eastman-beaudine.com	Plano	TX	75024	972-312-1012	312-1020
Egon Zehnder International Inc 1 N Wacker Dr Ste 2300 *TF:* 800-367-3989 ■ *Web:* www.egonzehnder.com	Chicago	IL	60606	312-260-8800	782-2846
Fergus Partnership Consulting Inc 14 Wall St # 3C *Web:* www.ferguslex.com	New York	NY	10005	212-767-1775	315-0351
Halbrecht Lieberman Assoc Inc 32 Surf Rd *Web:* www.hlassoc.com	Westport	CT	06880	203-222-4890	222-4895
Heath/Norton Assoc 301 Crocus Ct Ste L-7	Dayton	NJ	08810	732-329-4663	
Heidrick & Struggles International Inc 233 S Wacker Dr Ste 4900 *NASDAQ: HSII* ■ *Web:* www.heidrick.com	Chicago	IL	60606	312-496-1000	496-1048
Herbert Mines Assoc Inc 375 Pk Ave *Web:* www.herbertmines.com	New York	NY	10152	212-355-0909	223-2186
Horton International LLC 29 S Main St *Web:* www.hortoninternational.com	West Hartford	CT	06107	860-521-0101	521-0140
Howard Fischer Assoc International 1800 Kennedy Blvd Ste 700 *Web:* www.hfischer.com	Philadelphia	PA	19103	215-568-8363	568-4815
Hughes & Sloan Inc 1360 Peachtree St NE *Web:* hughesandsloan.com	Atlanta	GA	30309	404-873-3421	
IMC Group of Cos 120 White Plains Rd Ste 405 *Web:* www.the-imc.com	Tarrytown	NY	10591	914-468-7050	468-7051
Kenzer Group LLC One Penn Plz *Fax Area Code: 917 ■ *Web:* www.kenzer.com	New York	NY	10119	212-308-4300	534-6280*
Korn/Ferry International 1900 Ave of the Stars Ste 2600 *NYSE: KFY* ■ *TF:* 877-345-3610 ■ *Web:* www.kornferry.com	Los Angeles	CA	90067	310-552-1834	553-6452
Kovensky Daniels 1250 Connecticut Ave NW Ste 200 *Fax Area Code: 413 ■ *Web:* www.kovdan.com	Washington	DC	20036	202-261-3555	832-1838*
Major Lindsey & Africa 555 Montgomery St Ste 1500 *Web:* www.mlaglobal.com	San Francisco	CA	94111	415-956-1010	398-2425
Management Recruiters International Worldwide Inc 1717 Arch St 36th Fl *TF:* 800-875-4000 ■ *Web:* www.mrinetwork.com	Philadelphia	PA	19103	800-875-4000	
Mestel & Company Inc 575 Madison Ave Ste 3000 *Web:* www.mestel.com	New York	NY	10022	646-356-0500	356-0545
MSI International Inc 650 Pk Ave *Web:* www.msimsi.com	King of Prussia	PA	19406	610-265-2000	265-2213
National Search Assoc 2035 Corte del Nogal Ste 100 *Web:* www.nsasearch.com	Carlsbad	CA	92011	760-431-1115	683-3044
Nordeman Grimm 65 E 55th St 33rd Fl *Web:* www.nordemangrimm.com	New York	NY	10022	212-935-1000	980-1443
Pittleman & Assoc 336 E 43rd St *Web:* www.pittlemanassociates.com	New York	NY	10017	212-370-9600	370-9608
Rice Cohen International 301 Oxford Vly Rd Ste 1506A *Web:* ricecoheninternational.com	Yardley	PA	19067	215-321-4100	

Phone Fax

Rusher Loscavio & LoPresto
369 Pine St Ste 221 San Francisco CA 94104 415-765-6583
Web: www.rll.com

Russell Reynolds Assoc Inc
200 Pk Ave 23rd Fl New York NY 10166 212-351-2000 370-0896
TF: 800-259-0470 ■ *Web:* www.russellreynolds.com

Skott/Edwards Consultants Seven Royal Dr Cherry Quay NJ 08723 732-920-1883 477-1541
Web: www.skottedwards.com

Spencer Reed Group Inc
6900 College Blvd Ste 1 Overland Park KS 66211 913-663-4400 663-4464
TF: 800-477-5035 ■ *Web:* www.spencerreed.com

Stanton Chase International
400 E Pratt St Ste 420 Baltimore MD 21202 410-528-8400 528-8409
Web: www.stantonchase.com

Swan Legal Search
11400 Olympic Blvd Ste 200 Los Angeles CA 90064 310-201-2500
Web: www.swanlegal.com

Tyler & Co 400 Northridge Rd Ste 1250 Atlanta GA 30350 770-396-3939 396-6693
TF: 800-989-6789 ■ *Web:* www.tylerandco.com

Whitney Partners 747 Third Ave 17th Fl New York NY 10017 212-508-3500 508-3540
Web: www.whitneypartners.net

Witt/Kieffer Ford Hadelman & Lloyd
2015 Spring Rd Ste 510 Oak Brook IL 60523 630-990-1370 990-1382
TF: 888-281-1370 ■ *Web:* www.wittkieffer.com

Wyatt & Jaffe 4999 France Ave S Ste 260 Minneapolis MN 55410 612-285-2858 285-2786
Web: www.wyattjaffe.com

XEC Solutions Inc
5655 Lindero Canyon Rd Ste 521 Westlake Village CA 91362 818-991-1400 575-8099
Web: xecsolutions.com

270 EXERCISE & FITNESS EQUIPMENT

SEE ALSO Sporting Goods p. 3182

Phone Fax

Body-Solid Inc 1900 Des Plaines Ave Forest Park IL 60130 708-427-3500 427-3556
TF: 800-833-1227 ■ *Web:* www.bodysolid.com

Cybex International Inc 10 Trotter Dr Medway MA 02053 508-533-4300 533-5500
NASDAQ: CYBI ■ *TF:* 888-462-9239 ■ *Web:* www.cybexintl.com

Heartline Fitness Products Inc
8041 Cessna Ave Ste 200 Gaithersburg MD 20879 301-921-0661 330-5479
TF: 800-262-3348 ■ *Web:* www.heartlinefitness.com

Hoggan Health Industries Inc
8020 South 1300 West West Jordan UT 84088 801-572-6500 572-6514
TF: 800-678-7888 ■ *Web:* hogganhealth.net

Hoist Fitness Systems Inc
9990 Empire St Ste 130 San Diego CA 92126 858-578-7676 578-9558
TF: 800-548-5438 ■ *Web:* www.hoistfitness.com

HYDRO-FIT Inc 160 Madison St Eugene OR 97402 541-484-4361 484-1443
TF Cust Svc: 800-346-7295 ■ *Web:* www.hydrofit.com

ICON Health & Fitness Inc 1500 South 1000 West Logan UT 84321 435-750-5000
TF: 800-999-3756 ■ *Web:* www.iconfitness.com

IronMaster LLC 14562 167th Ave SE Ste E Monroe WA 98272 360-217-7780 217-8415
TF: 800-533-3339 ■ *Web:* www.ironmaster.com

Nautilus Inc 16400 SE Nautilus Dr Vancouver WA 98684 360-694-7722 694-7755
NYSE: NLS ■ *TF:* 800-628-8458 ■ *Web:* nautilusinc.com/

New York Barbells 160 Home St Elmira NY 14904 607-733-8038 733-1010
TF: 800-446-1833 ■ *Web:* www.newyorkbarbells.com

Paramount Fitness Corp
6450 E Bandini Blvd Los Angeles CA 90040 323-721-2121 724-2000
TF: 800-721-2121 ■ *Web:* www.paramountfitness.com

Precor Inc 20031 142nd Ave NE Woodinville WA 98072 425-486-9292 486-3856
TF: 800-786-8404 ■ *Web:* www.precor.com

Pro Star Sports Inc 1133 Winchester Ave Kansas City MO 64126 816-241-9737 241-2459
TF: 800-821-8482 ■ *Web:* www.prostarsports.com

Soloflex Inc 22590 NW Badertscher Rd Hillsboro OR 97124 800-547-8802
TF: 800-547-8802 ■ *Web:* www.soloflex.com

Spirit Manufacturing Inc 2601 Commerce Dr Jonesboro AR 72402 870-935-1107 935-7611
TF: 800-258-4555 ■ *Web:* www.spiritfitness.com

Star Trac by Unisen Inc 14410 Myford Rd Irvine CA 92606 714-669-1660 838-6286
TF: 800-228-6635 ■ *Web:* www.startrac.com

True Fitness Technology Inc 865 Hoff Rd O'Fallon MO 63366 636-272-7100 272-7148
TF: 800-426-6570 ■ *Web:* www.truefitness.com

Vectra Fitness Inc 7901 S 190th St Kent WA 98032 425-291-9550 291-9650
TF: 800-283-2872 ■ *Web:* www.vectrafitness.com

Woodway USA W229 N591 Foster Ct Waukesha WI 53186 262-548-6235 522-6235
TF: 800-966-3929 ■ *Web:* www.woodway.com

York Barbell Co Inc 3300 BoaRd Rd York PA 17406 717-767-6481 764-0044
TF Cust Svc: 800-358-9675 ■ *Web:* www.yorkbarbell.com

271 EXPLOSIVES

Phone Fax

Accurate Energetics Systems LLC
5891 Hwy 230 W McEwen TN 37101 931-729-4207 729-4214
Web: www.aesys.biz

Action Manufacturing Co 100 E Erie Ave Philadelphia PA 19134 215-739-6400
Web: www.action-mfg.com

Alliant Powder 2299 Snake River Ave PO Box 6 Lewiston ID 83501 800-379-1732
TF: 800-276-9337 ■ *Web:* www.alliantpowder.com

Austin Powder Co
25800 Science Pk Dr Ste 300 Cleveland OH 44122 216-464-2400 464-4418
TF: 800-321-0752 ■ *Web:* www.austinpowder.com

Buckley Powder Co 42 Inverness Dr E Englewood CO 80112 303-790-7007 790-7033
TF: 800-333-2266 ■ *Web:* www.buckleypowder.com

Can-Blast Inc 755 Wallace Rd Unit 3 North Bay ON P1B8K4 705-474-3431 476-7643
Web: www.can-blast.com

Cartridge Actuated Devices Inc (CAD)
51 Dwight Pl Fairfield NJ 07004 973-575-1312 575-6039
Web: cartactdev.com

Phone Fax

Combined Systems Inc 388 Kinsman Rd Jamestown PA 16134 724-932-2177
Web: www.combinedsystems.com

Dyno Nobel Inc
2795 E Cottonwood Pkwy Ste 500 Salt Lake City UT 84121 801-364-4800 328-6452
TF: 800-473-2675 ■ *Web:* www.dynonobel.com

Ensign-Bickford Aerospace & Defense Co
640 Hopmeadow St PO Box 429 Simsbury CT 06070 860-843-2289
Web: www.ebaerospaceanddefense.com

General Dynamics Ordnance & Tactical Systems Inc
11399 16th Court N Ste 200 Saint Petersburg FL 33716 727-578-8100
Web: www.gd-ots.com

Hanley Industries Inc
3640 Seminary Rd PO Box 1058 Alton IL 62002 618-465-8892
Web: www.hanleyindustries.com

Hodgdon Powder Company Inc
6231 Robinson St Shawnee Mission KS 66202 913-362-9455 362-1307
Web: www.hodgdon.com

Nammo Inc 2000 N 14th St Ste 250 Arlington VA 22201 703-524-6100
Web: www.nammoinc.com

Orica USA Inc 33101 E Quincy Ave Watkins CO 80137 303-268-5000 268-5250
Web: www.oricaminingservices.com

Pyrotechnic Specialties Inc
1661 Juniper Creek Rd Byron GA 31008 478-956-5400 956-5108
Web: www.pyrotechonline.com

Schaefer Pyrotechnics Inc
376 Hartman Bridge Rd Ronks PA 17572 717-687-0647 687-8982
TF: 877-598-2264 ■ *Web:* www.schaeferfireworks.com

Senex Explosives Inc 710 Millers Run Rd Cuddy PA 15031 412-221-3218 221-6032

Special Devices Inc 14370 White Sage Rd Moorpark CA 93021 805-553-1200 387-1001
TF: 888-782-0082 ■ *Web:* www.specialdevices.com

Stresau Laboratory Inc N8265 Medley Rd Spooner WI 54801 715-635-2777 635-7979
Web: www.stresau.com

Teledyne Reynolds Inc 5005 McConnell Ave Los Angeles CA 90066 310-823-5491 822-8046
Web: www.teledynereynolds.com

272 EYE BANKS

SEE ALSO Organ & Tissue Banks p. 2848; Transplant Centers - Blood Stem Cell p. 3250

Eye banks listed here are members of the Eye Bank Association of America (EBAA), an accrediting body for eye banks. The EBAA medical standards for member eye banks are endorsed by the American Academy of Ophthalmology.

Phone Fax

Alabama Eye Bank 500 Robert Jemison Rd Birmingham AL 35209 800-423-7811 942-2129*
**Fax Area Code:* 205 ■ *TF:* 800-423-7811 ■ *Web:* www.alabamaeyebank.org

Alcon Laboratories Inc 6201 S Fwy Fort Worth TX 76134 817-293-0450 568-7128
TF: 800-862-5266 ■ *Web:* www.alcon.com

Arkansas Lions Eye Bank & Laboratory
4301 W Markham St Slot 523-1 Little Rock AR 72205 501-686-5822 686-7037
Web: eye.uams.edu

Baton Rouge Regional Eye Bank
7777 Hennessy Blvd Ste 207 Baton Rouge LA 70808 225-766-8996 765-4366
Web: www.eyebankbr.org

Center for Organ Recovery & Education (CORE)
204 Sigma Dr RIDC Pk Pittsburgh PA 15238 412-963-3550 963-3596
TF: 800-366-6777 ■ *Web:* www.core.org

Central Ohio Lions Eye Bank
262 Neil Ave Ste 140 Columbus OH 43215 614-545-2057
Web: www.coleb.org

Cincinnati Eye Bank for Sight Restoration Inc
4015 Executive Pk Dr Ste 330 Cincinnati OH 45241 513-861-3716 483-3984
Web: www.cintieb.org

Donor Network of Arizona 201 W Coolidge St Phoenix AZ 85013 602-222-2200 222-2202
TF: 800-447-9477 ■ *Web:* www.dnaz.org

Donor Network West 1000 Broadway Ste 600 Oakland CA 94607 510-444-8500 444-8501
Web: www.donornetworkwest.org

Eye Bank Assn of America (EBAA)
1015 18th St NW Ste 1010 Washington DC 20036 202-775-4999 429-6036
TF: 888-491-8833 ■ *Web:* www.restoresight.org

Eye Bank for Sight Restoration Inc
120 Wall St 3rd Fl New York NY 10005 212-742-9000 269-3139
TF: 866-287-3937 ■ *Web:* www.eyedonation.org

Eye Bank of British Columbia
2550 Willow St Eye Care Ctr Third Fl Vancouver BC V5Z3N9 604-875-4567 875-5316
Web: www.eyebankofbc.ca

Eye Bank of Canada Ontario Div
1929 Bayview Ave Toronto ON M5T3A9 416-978-7355 978-1522
Web: www.eyebank.utoronto.ca

Great Plains Lions Eye Bank
Texas Tech University Health Sciences Ctr
3601 Fourth St Ste BAB104-HSC Lubbock TX 79430 806-743-2242 743-1431
Web: www.ttuhsc.edu/eye

Hawaii Lions Eye Bank & Makana Foundation
405 N Kuakini St Ste 801 Honolulu HI 96817 808-536-7416
Web: www.hlebmf.org

Heartland Lions Eye Bank
10100 N Ambassador Dr Ste 200 Kansas City MO 64153 816-454-5454 727-3843*
**Fax Area Code:* 410 ■ *TF:* 800-756-4824

Idaho Lions Eye Bank 1090 N Cole Rd Boise ID 83704 208-338-5466 338-6543
TF: 800-546-6889 ■ *Web:* www.idaholions.org

International Cornea Project
9246 Lightwave Ave Ste 120 San Diego CA 92123 858-694-0400 565-7368
TF: 800-393-2265 ■ *Web:* www.sdeb.org

International Sight Restoration Inc
3808 Gunn Hwy Ste B Tampa FL 33618 813-264-6003 264-6007
TF: 877-477-3210 ■ *Web:* www.internationalsight.com

LABS Inc 6933 S Revere Pkwy Centennial CO 80112 720-528-4750 528-4786
TF: 866-393-2244 ■ *Web:* www.labs-inc.org

LifePoint Inc 3950 Faber Pl Dr Charleston SC 29405 843-763-7755 763-6393
TF: 800-462-0755 ■ *Web:* www.lifepoint-sc.org

Phone Fax

LifeShare of the Carolinas
1200 Ridgefield Blvd Ste 150 ....Asheville NC 28806 828-665-0107 665-4729
TF: 800-932-4483 ■ *Web:* www.lifesharecarolinas.org

Lions Eye Bank Alberta Society
7007 14th St SW ....Calgary AB T2V1P9 403-943-3406
Web: www.act4sight.com

Lions Eye Bank for Long Island
North Shore University Hospital
350 Community Dr ....Manhasset NY 11030 516-465-8430 465-8434
Web: www.northshorelij.com

Lions Eye Bank of Lexington
3290 Blazer Pkwy Ste 201 ....Lexington KY 40509 859-323-6740 323-5927
Web: www.mc.uky.edu

Lions Eye Bank of Manitoba & Northwest Ontario Inc
691 Wolseley Ave..............................Winnipeg MB R3G1C3 204-788-8507 983-6823
TF: 800-552-6820 ■ *Web:* www.eyebankmanitoba.com

Lions Eye Bank of Nebraska Inc
University of Nebraska Medical Ctr UNMC 985541... Omaha NE 68198 402-559-4039 559-7705
TF: 800-225-7244 ■ *Web:* www.eyebanknebraska.org

Lions Eye Bank of North Dakota
410 E Thayer Ave Ste 201..........................Bismarck ND 58501 701-250-9390 250-1880
TF: 800-372-3751 ■ *Web:* lebnd.org/

Lions Eye Bank of Northwest Pennsylvania Inc
5105 Richmond St ....Erie PA 16509 814-866-3545 864-1875

Lions Eye Bank of Texas at Baylor College of Medicine
Dept of Opthalmology 6565 Fannin St NC-205 ..... Houston TX 77030 713-798-4714 798-4645
Web: www.bcm.edu

Lions Eye Bank of Wisconsin 2401 American Ln ...... Madison WI 53704 608-233-2354 233-2895
TF: 877 233 2354 ■ *Web:* lcbw.org

Lions Medical Eye Bank & Research Ctr of Eastern Virginia Inc
600 Gresham Dr.................................. Norfolk VA 23507 800-453-6059 388-3744*
**Fax Area Code: 757* ■ *TF:* 800-453-6059 ■ *Web:* www.lionseyebank.org

Lone Star Lions Eye Bank
102 E Wheeler St PO Box 347 .... Manor TX 78653 512-457-0638 457-0658
TF: 800-977-3937 ■ *Web:* www.lsleb.org

Medical Eye Bank of Florida
2902 N Orange Ave................................Orlando FL 32804 407-422-2020
Web: tbionline.org

Medical Eye Bank of Maryland 815 Pk Ave..........Baltimore MD 21201 410-752-2020 783-0183
TF: 800-756-4824 ■ *Web:* www.tbionline.org

Medical Eye Bank of West Virginia
Three Courtney Dr ....Charleston WV 25304 304-926-9200 926-6779

Midwest Eye Banks 4889 Venture Dr .... Ann Arbor MI 48108 734-780-2100 780-2143
TF: 800-247-7250 ■ *Web:* www.midwesteyebanks.org

Minnesota Lions Eye Bank
1000 Westgate Dr Ste 260 .... Saint paul MN 55114 612-625-5159 626-1192
TF Cust Svc: 866-887-4448 ■ *Web:* www.mnlionseyebank.org

Mississippi Lions Eye Bank 431 Katherine Dr .... Flowood MS 39232 601-420-5739 420-5743
Web: www.mslionseyebank.org

National Disease Research Interchange (NDRI)
1628 John F Kennedy Blvd
8 Penn Ctr 8th Fl .... Philadelphia PA 19103 215-557-7361 557-7154
TF: 800-222-6374 ■ *Web:* www.ndriresource.org

New Mexico Lions Eye Bank
2501 Yale Blvd SE Ste 100...................... Albuquerque NM 87106 505-266-3937
TF: 888-616-3937 ■ *Web:* www.nmleb.org

North Carolina Eye Bank Inc
3900 Westpoint Blvd Ste F ....Winston-Salem NC 27103 336-765-0932 765-8803
TF: 800-552-9956 ■ *Web:* miraclesinsight.org/

Northeast Pennsylvania Lions Eye Bank Inc
Lehigh Valley Hospital
2346 Jacksonville Rd..........................Bethlehem PA 18017 610-625-3800
Web: www.paeyebank.org

Northwest La Lions Eye Bank 721 Blvd St..........Shreveport LA 71104 318-222-7999 222-8779

Oklahoma Lions Eye Bank
3840 N Lincoln Blvd..........................Oklahoma City OK 73105 405-557-1393

Old Dominion Eye Bank (ODEF)
9200 Arboretum Pkwy Ste 104.................... Richmond VA 23236 804-560-7540 560-4752
Web: www.odef.org

Oregon Lions Sight & Hearing Foundation
1010 NW 22nd Ave Ste 144 ....Portland OR 97210 503-413-7399 413-7522
TF: 800-635-4667 ■ *Web:* www.olshf.org

Regional Tissue Bank QEII Health Sciences Centre
5788 University Ave Rm 431 MacKenzie Bldg ....Halifax NS B3H1V7 902-473-4171 473-2170
TF: 800-314-6515 ■ *Web:* www.cdha.nshealth.ca/regional-tissue-bank

Rochester Eye & Tissue Bank
524 White Spruce Blvd........................... Rochester NY 14623 585-272-7890 272-7897
TF: 800-568-4321 ■ *Web:* www.rehpb.org

Rocky Mountain Lions Eye Bank (RMLEB)
1675 Aurora Crt Ste EI2049 PO Box 6026 .... Aurora CO 80045 720-848-3937 848-3938
TF: 800-444-7479 ■ *Web:* www.corneas.org

San Antonio Eye Bank
8122 Datapoint Dr Ste 325.......................San Antonio TX 78229 210-614-1209 614-1422
Web: www.tbionline.org

San Diego Eye Bank (SDEB)
9246 Lightwave Ave Ste 120...................... San Diego CA 92123 858-694-0400 565-7368
TF: 800-393-2265 ■ *Web:* www.sdeb.org

Sight Society of Northeastern New York Inc
Lions Eye Bank at Albany 6 Executive Pk Dr ....Albany NY 12203 518-489-7606 489-7607
TF: 888-615-3937 ■ *Web:* www.lionseyebankalbany.org

SightLife 221 Yale Ave N Ste 450.......................... Seattle WA 98109 206-682-8500 682-4666
TF: 800-847-5786 ■ *Web:* www.sightlife.org

South Dakota Lions Eye Bank
4501 W 61st St N................................ Sioux Falls SD 57107 605-373-1008 373-1261
TF: 800-245-7846 ■ *Web:* www.sdletb.org

Southern Eye Bank 2701 Kingman St Ste 200 ....Metairie LA 70006 504-891-3937 891-2401
Web: www.southerneyebank.com

Tennessee District 12-0 Lions Eye Bank
979 E Third St Ste A250.......................... Chattanooga TN 37403 423-778-4000 778-4050
Web: www.tennesseelions.com

University of Louisville Lions Eye Bank
301 E Muhammad Ali Blvd.........................Louisville KY 40202 502-852-5457 852-5471
Web: www.ulleb.org

Upstate New York Transplant Services Inc
110 Broadway.......................................Buffalo NY 14203 716-853-6667 853-6674
TF: 800-227-4771 ■ *Web:* www.unyts.org

Utah Lions Eye Bank
John A Moran Eye Ctr
65 Mario Capecchi Dr .... Salt Lake City UT 84132 801-581-2039 585-5703
Web: www.utaheyebank.org

Western Texas Lions Eye Bank Alliance
2030 Pullman St Ste 4 .... San Angelo TX 76902 325-653-8666 655-2847
TF: 866-226-7632 ■ *Web:* www.wtleb.org

273 FABRIC STORES

SEE ALSO Patterns - Sewing p. 2899

Phone Fax

Britex Fabrics LLC 146 Geary St ....San Francisco CA 94108 415-392-2910 392-3906
Web: www.britexfabrics.com

Everfast Inc 203 Gale Ln .... Kennett Square PA 19348 610-444-9700 444-1221
TF Cust Svc: 800-213-6366 ■ *Web:* www.calicocorners.com

Fishman's Fabrics Inc 1101 S Des Plaines St..........Chicago IL 60607 312-922-7250 922-7402
Web: www.fishmansfabrics.com

Hancock Fabrics Inc One Fashion Way ....Baldwyn MS 38824 662-365-6000
Web: hancockfabrics.com

Jo-Ann Fabrics & Crafts 5555 Darrow Rd .... Hudson OH 44236 330-656-2600 463-6760
TF: 888-739-4120 ■ *Web:* www.joann.com

Jo-Ann Stores Inc (JAS) 5555 Darrow Rd............. Hudson OH 44236 330-656-2600 463-6760
TF: 888-739-4120 ■ *Web:* www.joann.com

Mary Maxim Inc
2001 Holland Ave PO Box 5019....................Port Huron MI 48061 810-987-2000 987-5056
TF: 800-962-9504 ■ *Web:* www.marymaxim.com

Scrapbook Factory Inc 2004 W Hwy 50 Ste D ....Ofallon IL 62269 618-628-8877
Web: scrapbookfactory.net

Vogue Fabrics 718 Main St .... Evanston IL 60202 847-864-9600 475-8958
Web: www.voguefabricsstore.com

274 FACILITIES MANAGEMENT SERVICES

SEE ALSO Correctional & Detention Management (Privatized) p. 2167

Phone Fax

ABM Industries Inc 8020 W Doe Ste C .... Visalia SC 93291 559-651-1612 579-9578*
**Fax Area Code: 864* ■ *Web:* www.abm.com

Agracel Inc 2201 Willenborg Ave................... Effingham IL 62401 217-342-4443
Web: agracel.com

Alexander Company Inc, The
145 E Badger Rd Ste 200 .... Madison WI 53713 608-258-5580 258-5599
Web: www.alexandercompany.com

American Pool Enterprises Inc
11515 Cronridge Dr # Q........................Owings Mills MD 21117 443-471-1190 471-1189
Web: www.americanpool.com

Apparatus Inc 1401 N Meridian St ....Indianapolis IN 46202 317-254-8488
Web: apparatus.net

ARAMARK Uniform & Career Apparel LLC
1101 Market St.............................. Philadelphia PA 19107 800-272-6275
TF: 800-272-6275 ■ *Web:* www.aramarkuniform.com

Bechta Group Ltd 1780 S Bellaire St Ste 100 ....Denver CO 80222 303-860-0990
Web: bechtagroup.com

Big Horn Energy 376 33rd St .... Cody WY 82414 307-587-5613
Web: bighornenergyinc.com

Brookfield Global Integrated Solutions
7400 Birchmount Rd.............................Markham ON L3R4E6 905-475-7610
Web: www.brookfieldgis.com

Creative Dining Services
One Royal Pk Dr Ste 3 .... Zeeland MI 49464 616-748-1700 748-1900
Web: www.creativedining.com

Delaware North Cos Gaming & Entertainment
40 Fountain Plz...................................Buffalo NY 14202 716-858-5000 858-5926
TF: 800-828-7240 ■ *Web:* www.delawarenorth.com

Delaware North Cos Parks & Resorts
40 Fountain Plz...................................Buffalo NY 14202 716-858-5000 858-5882
TF: 800-828-7240 ■ *Web:* delawarenorth.com

Elite Show Services Inc
2878 Camino Del Rio S Ste 260.................... San Diego CA 92108 619-574-1589 574-1588
Web: www.eliteservicesusa.com

Financial & Realty Services LLC
1110 Bonifant St Ste 301 .... Silver Spring MD 20910 301-650-9112
Web: frsllc.com

FLIK Hotels & Conference Centers
Three International Dr Second Fl .... Rye Brook NY 10573 914-935-5394
Web: www.flikccm.compass-usa.com

Harrison Senior Living Inc
300 Strode Ave............................East Fallowfield PA 19320 610-384-6310 383-3945
Web: harrisonseniorliving.com

IAP Worldwide Services Inc
7315 N Atlantic Ave ....Cape Canaveral FL 32920 321-784-7100
TF: 877-296-8010 ■ *Web:* www.iapws.com

Kansas Turnpike Authority (KTA)
9401 E Kellogg PO Box 780007...................... Wichita KS 67207 316-682-4537 651-0864
Web: www.ksturnpike.com

L & M Technologies Inc
4209 Balloon Pk Rd NE .... Albuquerque NM 87109 505-343-0200 343-0300
Web: www.lmtechnologies.com

Lasalle Management Company LLC
192 Bastille Ln.....................................Ruston LA 71270 318-232-1500
Web: lasallecorrections.com

Logistics Applications
2760 Eisenhower Ave ....Alexandria VA 22314 703-317-9800
Web: logapp.com

Mainthia Technologies Inc
7055 Engle Rd Ste 502.......................... Cleveland OH 44130 440-816-0202 816-1121
Web: www.mainthia.com

Phone *Fax*

Marenzana Group Inc 780 Third Ave .... New York NY 10017 212-735-0011 230-1119
Web: www.marenzana.com

New York State Bridge Authority PO Box 1010 .... Highland NY 12528 845-691-7245 691-3560
TF: 800-333-8655 ■ *Web:* www.nysba.state.ny.us

Olympia Entertainment Inc 2211 Woodward Ave .... Detroit MI 48201 313-471-3200 471-3595
Web: www.olympiaentertainment.com

OMNIPLEX World Services Corp
14151 Pk Meadow Dr Ste 300 .... Chantilly VA 20151 703-652-3100 652-3101
TF: 800-356-3406 ■ *Web:* www.omniplex.com

Penguin Logistics LLC 4500 Brooktree Rd .... Wexford PA 15090 724-772-9800
Web: mhfservices.com

Philotechnics Ltd 201 Renovare Blvd .... Oak Ridge TN 37830 865-483-1551
TF: 888-723-9278 ■ *Web:* www.philotechnics.com

Phoenix Park 'n Swap 3801 E Washington St .... Phoenix AZ 85034 602-273-1250 273-7375
TF: 800-772-0852 ■ *Web:* www.americanparknswap.com

Sarakem Corp 15 Buell St .... Hanover NH 03755 603-643-5720
Web: sarakem.com

Serco Group Inc 1818 Library St Ste 1000. .... Reston VA 20190 703-939-6000 939-6001
Web: www.serco.com

Summit Aerospace 1260 NW 57th Ave .... Miami FL 33126 305-267-6400
Web: summitmro.com

Terranear PMC LLC 5005 W Royal Ln Ste 216 .... Irving TX 75063 972-929-1095
Web: www.terranear.com

United Space Alliance (USA) 600 Gemini Ave. .... Houston TX 77058 281-212-6200 212-6177
TF: 800-367-5690 ■ *Web:* unitedspacealliance.com

Vinnell Corp 12150 E Monument Dr. .... Fairfax VA 22033 703-385-4544

Viox Services Inc 15 W Voorhees St .... Cincinnati OH 45215 513-948-8469
TF: 888-846-9462 ■ *Web:* www.viox-services.com

Wastren Advantage Inc 1571 Shyville Rd .... Piketon OH 45661 740-443-7924
Web: www.wastrenadvantage.com

Xanterra Parks & Resorts
6312 S Fiddlers Green Cir
Ste 600-N .... Greenwood Village CO 80111 303-600-3400 600-3600
TF: 800-236-7916 ■ *Web:* www.xanterra.com

275 FACTORS

Factors are companies that buy accounts receivable (invoices) from other businesses at a discount.

Phone *Fax*

Accounts Receivable Funding Corp (ARFC)
PO Box 35750 .... Houston TX 77235 800-992-1717 999-3384
TF: 800-992-1717 ■ *Web:* www.arfc.com

Action Capital Corp 230 Peachtree St Ste 910 .... Atlanta GA 30343 404-524-3181 577-4880
TF: 800-525-7767 ■ *Web:* www.actioncapital.com

Advantage Funding Corp 1000 Parkwood Cir SE .... Atlanta GA 30339 770-955-2274
TF: 800-241-2274 ■ *Web:* www.advantagefunding.com

AmeriFactors 215 Celebration Pl Ste 340 .... Celebration FL 34747 407-566-1150 566-1250
TF: 800-884-3863 ■ *Web:* www.amerifactors.com

Applied Capital Inc
3700 Rio Grande Blvd NW Ste 4 .... Albuquerque NM 87107 505-342-1840 342-2246
Web: www.appliedcapital.net

Asta Funding Inc 210 Sylvan Ave .... Englewood Cliffs NJ 07632 201-567-5648
NASDAQ: ASFI ■ *TF:* 866-389-7627 ■ *Web:* www.astafunding.com

Bibby Financial Services
1901 South Congress ave Ste 150 .... Boynton Beach, FL 33426 877-882-4229
TF: 877-882-4229 ■ *Web:* www.bibbyusa.com

Capital-Plus Inc (CPI)
3250 W Henderson Rd Ste 201. .... Columbus OH 43220 614-848-7620
Web: www.capitalplusfactoring.com

Crestmark Bank 5480 Corporate Dr Ste 350 .... Troy MI 48098 888-999-8050 641-5101*
**Fax Area Code:* 248 ■ *TF:* 888-999-8050 ■ *Web:* www.crestmark.com

Diversified Funding Services Inc
255 N Main St Ste 873 .... Jonesboro GA 30237 770-603-0055
TF: 888-603-0055 ■ *Web:* www.divfunding.com

DSA Factors 3126 N Lincoln Ave PO Box 577520 .... Chicago IL 60657 773-248-9000 248-9005
Web: www.dsafactors.com

Goodman Factors 3010 LBJ Fwy Ste 140 .... Dallas TX 75234 972-241-3297 243-6285
TF: 877-446-6362 ■ *Web:* www.goodmanfactors.com

Hamilton Group 100 Elwood Davis Rd .... North Syracuse NY 13212 315-413-0086 413-0087
TF: 800-351-3066 ■ *Web:* www.hamiltongroup.net

LSQ Funding Group LC 2600 Lucien Way Ste 100 .... Maitland FL 32751 800-474-7606
TF: 800-474-7606 ■ *Web:* www.lsqgroup.com

Magnolia Financial Inc 187 W Broad St .... Spartanburg SC 29306 864-573-9900 573-9912
TF: 866-573-0611 ■ *Web:* www.magfinancial.com

Mazon Assoc Inc 800 W Airport Fwy Ste 900 .... Irving TX 75062 972-554-6967 554-0951
TF: 800-442-2740 ■ *Web:* www.mazon.com

Merchant Factors Corp 1441 Broadway 22nd Fl .... New York NY 10018 212-840-7575 869-1752
TF All: 800-929-3293 ■ *Web:* www.merchantfactors.com

Performance Funding 11022 N 28th Dr .... Phoenix AZ 85029 602-912-0200 912-0480
Web: www.performancefunding.com

Porter Capital Corp 2112 First Ave N .... Birmingham AL 35203 205-322-5442 322-7719
TF: 800-737-7344 ■ *Web:* www.portercap.net

Prestige Capital Corp 400 Kelby St 14th Fl .... Fort Lee NJ 07024 201-944-4455 944-9477
Web: www.pcc-cash.com

Quantum Corporate Funding Ltd
1140 Ave of the Americas 16th Fl .... New York NY 10036 212-768-1200 944-8216
TF: 800-352-2535 ■ *Web:* www.quantumfunding.com

Riviera Finance 220 Ave I .... Redondo Beach CA 90277 800-872-7484 454-8122*
**Fax Area Code:* 651 ■ *TF:* 800-872-7484 ■ *Web:* www.rivierafinance.com

Rosenthal & Rosenthal Inc 1370 Broadway .... New York NY 10018 212-356-1400 356-0910
TF: 800-999-4800 ■ *Web:* www.rosenthalinc.com

RTS Financial Service 8601 Monrovia .... Lenexa KS 66215 877-242-4390 492-1998*
**Fax Area Code:* 913 ■ *TF:* 877-242-4390 ■ *Web:* www.rtsfinancial.com

Seven Oaks Capital Assoc LLC
7854 Anselmo Ln PO Box 82360 .... Baton Rouge LA 70810 225-757-1919 757-1916
TF: 800-511-4588 ■ *Web:* www.sevenoakscapital.com

TCE Capital Corp 505 Consumers Rd Ste 707 .... Toronto ON M2J4V8 416-497-7400 497-3139
TF: 800-465-0400 ■ *Web:* www.tcecapital.com

Phone *Fax*

Transport Clearings East Inc
210 E Woodlawn Rd .... Charlotte NC 28217 704-527-1820 527-1851
Web: www.tceast.com

United Capital Funding Corp
146 Second St N Ste 200 .... Saint Petersburg FL 33701 727-894-8232 898-4205
Web: www.ucfunding.com

276 FARM MACHINERY & EQUIPMENT - MFR

SEE ALSO Lawn & Garden Equipment p. 2639

Phone *Fax*

ADM Alliance Nutrition Inc 1000 N 30th St. .... Quincy IL 62301 217-222-7100
TF: 800-292-3333 ■ *Web:* www.admani.com

AGCO Corp (AGCO) 4205 River Green Pkwy .... Duluth GA 30096 770-813-9200 813-6140
NYSE: AGCO ■ *TF:* 877-525-4384 ■ *Web:* www.agcocorp.com

Agile Manufacturing Inc
720 Industrial Pk Rd .... Anderson MO 64831 417-845-6065 845-6069
Web: roxell.com/en/

Alamo Group Inc 1627 E Walnut .... Seguin TX 78155 830-379-1480 372-9683
NYSE: ALG ■ *TF Cust Svc:* 800-788-6066 ■ *Web:* www.alamo-group.com

All-American Co-op PO Box 125 .... Stewartville MN 55976 507-533-4222 280-0066
TF: 888-354-4058 ■ *Web:* www.allamericancoop.com

Allied Systems Co 21433 SW Oregon St. .... Sherwood OR 97140 503-625-2560 625-7269
TF: 800-285-7000 ■ *Web:* www.alliedsystems.com

Amadas Industries Inc 1100 Holland Rd .... Suffolk VA 23434 757-539-0231 934-3264
Web: www.amadas.com

Amarillo Wind Machine Co 20513 Ave 256 .... Exeter CA 93221 559-592-4256 592-4194
TF: 800-311-4498 ■ *Web:* www.amarillowind.com

Amerequip Corp 1015 Calumet Ave. .... Kiel WI 53042 920-894-2000 894-3799
Web: www.amerequip.com

Anholt Technologies Inc 440 Church Rd. .... Avondale PA 19311 610-268-2758
Web: anholt.com

Applegate Livestock Equipment Inc
902 S State Rd 32 .... Union City IN 47390 765-964-4631
Web: www.applegatelivestock.com

Arts-Way Mfg Co Inc 5556 Hwy 9 PO Box 288 .... Armstrong IA 50514 712-864-3131 864-3154
NASDAQ: ARTW ■ *TF:* 800-535-4517 ■ *Web:* www.artsway-mfg.com

Atom-Jet Industries Ltd 2110 Park Ave. .... Brandon MB R7B0R9 204-728-8590 726-5734
Web: atomjet.com

Automatic Equipment Manufacturing Co
One Mill Rd Industrial Pk .... Pender NE 68047 402-385-3051 385-3360
TF: 800-228-9289 ■ *Web:* www.aemfg.com

B & H Manufacturing Inc 141 County Rd 34 E .... Jackson MN 56143 507-847-2802 847-4655
TF: 800-240-3288 ■ *Web:* www.bhmfg.com

Berg Equipment Co 2700 W Veterans Pkwy. .... Marshfield WI 54449 715-384-2151 387-6777
TF: 800-494-1738 ■ *Web:* www.bergequipment.com

Big Dutchman Inc 3900 John F Donnelly Dr .... Holland MI 49424 616-392-5981 392-6188
Web: www.bigdutchmanusa.com

Bigham Brothers Inc 705 E Slaton Rd .... Lubbock TX 79452 806-745-0384
Web: www.bighambrothers.com

Bou-Matic PO Box 8050. .... Madison WI 53708 608-222-3484
Web: www.boumatic.com

Bourgault Industries Ltd
One mile NE side Hwy 368 .... St. Brieux SK S0K3V0 306-275-2300
Web: www.bourgault.com

Bowie Industries Inc 1004 E Wise St .... Bowie TX 76230 940-872-1106 872-4792
TF: 800-433-0934 ■ *Web:* www.bowieindustries.com

Brillion Iron Works Inc
200 Pk Ave PO Box 127 .... Brillion WI 54110 920-756-2121 756-3062
TF: 855-320-0373 ■
Web: landoll.com/content/index.php/products/farm_equipment/

Brock Grain Systems
611 N Higbee St P.O. Box 2000 .... Milford IN 46542 574-658-4191 658-4133
TF: 800-541-7900 ■ *Web:* www.brockgrain.com

Brown Mfg Corp 6001 E Hwy 27 .... Ozark AL 36360 800-633-8909 795-3029*
**Fax Area Code:* 334 ■ *TF:* 800-633-8909 ■ *Web:* www.brownmfgcorp.com

Broyhill Co One N Market Sq .... Dakota City NE 68731 402-987-3412 987-3601
TF: 800-228-1003 ■ *Web:* www.broyhill.com

Bucklin Tractor & Implement Co
115 W Railroad PO Box 127 .... Bucklin KS 67834 620-826-3271 826-3760
TF: 800-334-4823 ■ *Web:* www.btiequip.com

Buhler Versatile Inc 1260 Clarence Ave .... Winnipeg MB R3T1T2 204-661-8711 654-2503
TF: 888-524-1003 ■ *Web:* www.buhlerindustries.com

Bushnell Illinois Tank Co 650 W Davis St .... Bushnell IL 61422 309-772-3106 772-2045
Web: www.schuldbushnell.com

Cal-Coast Dairy Systems Inc 424 S Tegner Rd .... Turlock CA 95380 209-634-9026 634-3458
TF Cust Svc: 800-732-6826 ■ *Web:* www.calcoastinc.com

Carter Day International Inc
500 73rd Ave NE. .... Minneapolis MN 55432 763-571-1000 571-3012
Web: www.carterday.com

Chick Master Incubator Co
945 Lafayette Rd PO Box 704 .... Medina OH 44258 330-722-5591 723-0233
TF: 800-727-8726 ■ *Web:* www.chickmaster.com

CLAAS of America Inc 8401 S 132nd St. .... Omaha NE 68145 402-861-1000
Web: www.claasofamerica.com

Conrad-American Inc PO Box 2000 .... Houghton IA 52631 800-553-1791 469-4402*
**Fax Area Code:* 319 ■ *TF General:* 800-553-1791 ■ *Web:* www.conradamerican.com

Covington Planter Co 410 Hodges Ave .... Albany GA 31701 229-888-2032 888-0448
Web: www.covingtonplanter.com

CTAQ 1000 rue Raoul-Charette .... Joliette QC J6E8S6 450-755-4122
Web: www.intelia.com

CTB Inc 611 N Higbee St PO Box 2000 .... Milford IN 46542 574-658-4191 658-3471
TF: 800-261-8651 ■ *Web:* www.ctbinc.com

Custom Products of Litchfield Inc
1715 S Sibley Ave. .... Litchfield MN 55355 320-693-3221 693-7252
TF: 800-222-5463 ■ *Web:* www.800cabline.com

Daco Inc 609 Airport Rd .... North Aurora IL 60542 630-897-8797 897-4076
Web: www.dacoinc.com

Danuser Machine Co 500 E Third St. .... Fulton MO 65251 573-642-2246 642-2240
Web: www.danuser.com

Company	City	State	Zip	Phone	Fax
Dig Corp 1210 Activity Dr. TF: 800-322-9146 ■ Web: www.digcorp.com	Vista	CA	92081	760-727-0914	
Driptech Inc 2580 Wyandotte St Ste B Web: www.driptech.com	Mountain View	CA	94043	415-793-6735	
DuraTech Industries International Inc PO Box 1940 TF: 800-243-4601 ■ Web: www.duratechindustries.net	Jamestown	ND	58401	701-252-4601	252-0502
Egging Co, The 12145 Rd 38 Web: www.egging.com	Gurley	NE	69141	308-884-2233	
EGM LLC 3748 Industrial Park Dr Web: www.egm-llc.com	Mobile	AL	36693	251-662-1250	
Empire Plow Company Inc 3140 E 65th St Web: www.mckayempire.com	Cleveland	OH	44127	216-641-2290	441-4709
EVH Mfg Company LLC 4895 Red Bluff Rd TF: 888-990-2555 ■ Web: hardeebyevh.com	Loris	SC	29569	843-756-2555	756-4436
EZ Trail Inc 1050 E Columbia St PO Box 168 TF: 800-677-2802 ■ Web: www.e-ztrail.com	Arthur	IL	61911	217-543-3471	543-3473
Fabrication JR Tardif Inc 62 Blvd Cartier TF: 877-962-7273 ■ Web: www.jrtardif.com	Rivi Re-Du-Loup	QC	G5R6B2	418-862-7273	
Finn Corp 9281 Le St Dr TF: 800-543-7166 ■ Web: www.finncorp.com	Fairfield	OH	45014	513-874-2818	874-2914
Flint Cliffs Manufacturing Co 1600 Bluff Rd	Burlington	IA	52601	319-752-2781	752-5538
Forsbergs Inc 1210 Pennington Ave PO Box 510 TF Cust Svc: 800-654-1927 ■ Web: www.forsbergs.com	Thief River Falls	MN	56701	218-681-1927	681-2037
Gandy Co 528 Gandrud Rd. TF: 800-443-2476 ■ Web: www.gandy.net	Owatonna	MN	55060	507-451-5430	451-2857
GMP Metal Products Inc 3883 Delor St. TF: 800-325-9808 ■ Web: www.gmpmetal.com	Saint Louis	MO	63116	314-481-0300	481-1379
GSI Group Inc 1004 E Illinois St PO Box 20 Web: www.grainsystems.com	Assumption	IL	62510	217-226-4421	226-4420
Hagie Manufacturing Co PO Box 273 TF: 800-247-4885 ■ Web: www.hagie.com	Clarion	IA	50525	515-532-2861	532-3553
Hanson Silo Co 11587 County Rd 8 SE Web: www.hansonsilo.com	Lake Lillian	MN	56253	320-664-4171	664-4140
Hardi Inc 1500 W 76th St TF: 866-770-7063 ■ Web: www.hardi-us.com	Davenport	IA	52806	563-386-1730	386-1280
Harsh International Inc 600 Oak Ave Web: www.harshenviro.com	Eaton	CO	80615	970-454-2291	
Hastings Equity Grain Bin Mfg Co 1900 Summit Ave TF: 888-883-2189 ■ Web: www.hastingstanks.com	Hastings	NE	68901	402-462-2189	462-2900
HCC Inc 1501 First Ave. TF: 800-548-6633 ■ Web: www.hccincorporated.com	Mendota	IL	61342	815-539-9371	539-3135
HD Hudson Manufacturing Co 500 N Michigan Ave Ste 2300 TF: 800-977-7293 ■ Web: www.hdhudson.com	Chicago	IL	60611	312-644-2830	644-7989
Heartland Equipment Inc 2100 N Falls Blvd *Fax Area Code: 870 ■ TF: 800-530-7617 ■ Web: www.tractorscraper.com	Wynne	AR	72396	800-530-7617	238-8545*
Henderson Manufacturing Inc 1085 S Third St TF: 800-359-4970 ■ Web: www.henderson-mfg.com	Manchester	IA	52057	563-927-2828	927-2521
Herschel-Adams Inc 1301 N 14th St TF: 800-247-2167 ■ Web: www.alamo-group.com	Indianola	IA	50125	800-247-2167	
Hiniker Co 58766 240th St *Fax: Sales ■ TF: 800-433-5620 ■ Web: www.hiniker.com	Mankato	MN	56002	507-625-6621	625-5883*
Honiron Corp 400 Canal St. Web: www.honiron.com	Jeanerette	LA	70544	337-276-6314	276-3614
Howse Implement Company Inc 2013 Hwy 184 E PO Box 86 Web: howseimplement.com/	Laurel	MS	39441	601-428-0841	425-4900
Hutchinson/Mayrath/TerraTrack Industries 514 W Crawford PO Box 629 TF: 800-523-6993 ■ Web: www.hutchinson-mayrath.com	Clay Center	KS	67432	785-632-2161	632-5964
Irridelco International Corp 440 Sylvan Ave	Englewood Cliffs	NJ	07632	201-569-3030	
ISS LLC 820 E 20th St Web: www.sproutnet.com	Cookeville	TN	38501	931-526-1106	
Jamesway Incubator Co Inc 30 High Ridge Ct TF: 800-438-8077 ■ Web: www.jamesway.com	Cambridge	ON	N1R7L3	519-624-4646	
Johnson Farm Machinery Company Inc 152 W Kentucky Ave Web: www.jfmco.com	Woodland	CA	95695	530-662-1788	666-5585
KBH Corp, The 395 Anderson Blvd TF: 800-843-5241 ■ Web: www.kbhequipment.com	Clarksdale	MS	38614	662-624-5471	
Kelley Manufacturing Co 80 Vernon Dr PO Box 1467 TF: 800-444-5449 ■ Web: www.kelleymfg.com	Tifton	GA	31793	229-382-9393	382-5259
Kelly Ryan Equipment Co 900 Kelly Ryan Dr TF: 800-640-6967 ■ Web: www.kryan.com	Blair	NE	68008	402-426-2151	426-2186
Kinze Manufacturing Inc 2172 M Ave Web: kinze.com	Williamsburg	IA	52361	319-668-1300	
Kirby Mfg Inc 484 S Hwy 59 Web: www.kirbymfg.com	Merced	CA	95341	209-723-0778	723-3941
KMW Ltd PO Box 327 TF: 800-445-7388 ■ Web: www.kmwloaders.com	Sterling	KS	67579	620-278-3641	278-2388
Krone North America 3363 Miac Cove Web: www.krone-northamerica.com	Memphis	TN	38118	901-842-6011	
Kubota Tractor Corp 3401 Del Amo Blvd TF: 888-458-2682 ■ Web: www.kubota.com	Torrance	CA	90503	310-370-3370	370-3166
Kuhn Knight Inc 1501 W Seventh Ave PO Box 0167 Web: www.kuhnnorthamerica.com	Brodhead	WI	53520	608-897-2131	897-2561
Lindsay Corp 2222 N 111th St NYSE: LNN ■ TF: 866-404-5049 ■ Web: www.lindsay.com	Omaha	NE	68164	402-829-6800	829-6834
Loftness Specialized Farm Equipment Inc 650 S Main St PO Box 337 TF: 800-828-7624 ■ Web: www.loftness.com	Hector	MN	55342	320-848-6266	848-6269
LS Tractor USA LLC 6900 Corporation Pkwy Web: www.lstractorusa.com	Battleboro	NC	27809	252-984-0700	
Lund Industrial Group 400 E Industrial Pk Rd Web: www.lundonline.com	Holly Springs	MS	38635	662-252-2340	252-3352
MacDon Industries Ltd 680 Moray St Web: www.macdon.com	Winnipeg	MB	R3J3S3	204-885-5590	832-7749
Mathews Co 500 Industrial Ave TF: 800-323-7045 ■ Web: www.mathewscompany.com	Crystal Lake	IL	60012	815-459-2210	459-5889
Mertz Mfg LLC 1701 N Waverly St TF: 800-654-6433 ■ Web: www.mertzok.com	Ponca City	OK	74601	580-762-5646	767-8411
Meyer Manufacturing Corp County Hwy A W 574 W Ctr Ave PO Box 405 Web: www.meyermfg.com	Dorchester	WI	54425	715-654-5132	
Miller Saint Nazianz Inc 511 E Main St TF: 800-247-5557 ■ Web: www.millerstn.com	Saint Nazianz	WI	54232	920-773-2121	773-1200
Montgomery Industries International Inc 2017 Thelma St Web: www.montgomeryindustries.com	Jacksonville	FL	32206	904-355-4055	355-0401
Moorfeed Corp 1445 Brookville Way Ste R Web: www.moorfeed.com	Indianapolis	IN	46239	317-545-7171	542-7317
Orchard Machinery Corp 2700 Colusa Hwy Web: www.shakermaker.com	Yuba City	CA	95993	530-673-2822	673-0296
Orthman Manufacturing Inc 75765 Rd 435 PO Box 638 TF: 800-658-3270 ■ Web: www.orthman.com	Lexington	NE	68850	308-324-4654	324-5001
Osborne Industries Inc 120 N Industrial Ave TF: 800-255-0316 ■ Web: www.osborneindustries.com	Osborne	KS	67473	785-346-2192	346-2194
Oxbo International Corp 7275 Batavia Byron Rd Web: www.oxbocorp.com	Byron	NY	14422	585-548-2665	548-2599
P & H Manufacturing Co 604 S Lodge St Web: www.phmfg.com	Shelbyville	IL	62565	217-774-2123	774-5341
Performance Feeders Inc 251 Dunbar Web: www.performancefeeders.com	Oldsmar	FL	34677	813-855-2685	855-4296
Precision Tank & Equipment Company Inc 3503 Conover Rd TF: 800-258-4197 ■ Web: www.precisiontank.com	Virginia	IL	62691	217-452-7228	452-3956
Rainbow Manufacturing Co PO Box 70 *Fax: Cust Svc ■ Web: www.rainbowirrigation.com	Fitzgerald	GA	31750	229-423-4341	423-4645*
Rayne Plane Inc 9107 Grand Prairie Hwy *Fax Area Code: 713 ■ Web: www.rayneplane.com	Church Point	LA	70525	337-334-2101	634-2813*
Reinke Mfg Co Inc 5325 Reinke Rd. TF: 866-365-7381 ■ Web: www.reinke.com	Deshler	NE	68340	402-365-7251	365-4370
Root-Lowell Manufacturing Co 1000 Foreman Rd PO Box 289 TF: 800-748-0098 ■ Web: www.rlflomaster.com	Lowell	MI	49331	616-897-9211	897-8223
Schlagel Inc 491 N Emerson Web: www.schlagel.com	Cambridge	MN	55008	763-689-5991	
Schuette Mfg & Steel Sales Inc 5028 Hwy 42 Web: www.schuettemfg.com	Manitowoc	WI	54220	920-758-2491	758-2599
Scranton Mfg Company Inc 101 State St PO Box 336 TF: 800-831-1858 ■ Web: www.scrantonmfg.com	Scranton	IA	51462	712-652-3396	652-3399
Seed Hawk Inc Hwy 9 Web: www.seedhawk.com	Langbank	SK	S0G2X0	306-538-2221	
Shivvers Inc 614 W English St TF: 800-245-9093 ■ Web: www.shivvers.com	Corydon	IA	50060	641-872-1005	872-1593
Simonsen Industries Inc 500 Iowa 31 TF: 800-831-4860 ■ Web: www.simonsen-industries.com	Quimby	IA	51049	712-445-2211	445-2626
Sioux Steel Co 196 1/2 E Sixth St TF: 800-557-4689 ■ Web: www.siouxsteel.com	Sioux Falls	SD	57104	605-336-1750	336-2528
Spudnik Equipment Co 584 W 100 N Rd Web: www.spudnik.us	Blackfoot	ID	83221	208-785-0480	785-1497
Star Forge Inc 1801 S Ihm Blvd Web: www.starmfg.com	Freeport	IL	61032	815-235-7750	235-4813
Stock Equipment Co 16490 Chillicothe Rd TF: 888-742-1249 ■ Web: www.stockequipment.com	Chagrin Falls	OH	44023	440-543-6000	543-5944
Sudenga Industries Inc 2002 Kingbird Ave TF: 888-783-3642 ■ Web: www.sudenga.com	George	IA	51237	712-475-3301	475-3320
Sukup Manufacturing Co 1555 255th St PO Box 677 Web: www.sukup.com	Sheffield	IA	50475	641-892-4222	892-4629
Sun Circle Inc 286 S G St TF: 800-458-6543 ■ Web: www.amhydro.com	Arcata	CA	95521	707-822-5777	
T-l Irrigation Co 151 E Hwy 6 AB Rd PO Box 1047 *Fax Area Code: 800 ■ TF: 800-330-4264 ■ Web: www.tlirr.com	Hastings	NE	68902	402-462-4128	330-4268*
Taylor Pittsburgh Mfg Seven Rocky Mt Rd Web: taylorpittsburgh.com	Athens	TN	37303	423-745-3110	744-9662
Tigercat Industries Inc 54 Morton Ave E Web: www.tigercat.com	Brantford	ON	N3R7J7	519-753-2000	
Top Air Sprayers 601 S Broad St TF: 800-322-6301 ■ Web: www.topairequip.com	Kalida	OH	45853	419-532-3121	532-2468
Toro Co Irrigation Div 5825 Jasmine St TF: 800-654-1882 ■ Web: www.toro.com	Riverside	CA	92504	800-654-1882	451-1390
Unverferth Mfg Company Inc 601 S Broad St TF: 800-322-6301 ■ Web: www.unverferth.com	Kalida	OH	45853	419-532-3121	532-2468
Valmont Industries Inc One Valmont Plz NYSE: VMI ■ TF: 800-825-6668 ■ Web: www.valmont.com	Omaha	NE	68154	402-963-1000	
Vermeer Corp 1210 Vermeer Rd E PO Box 200 Web: www2.vermeer.com	Pella	IA	50219	641-628-3141	621-7773
Westfield Industries Ltd 74 Hwy 205 E Web: www.grainaugers.com	Rosenort	MB	R0G1W0	204-746-2396	
Wiese Industries Inc 1501 Fifth St PO Box 39 TF: 800-568-4391 ■ Web: www.wiesecorp.com	Perry	IA	50220	515-465-9854	465-9858
Woods Equipment Co 2606 S Illinois Rt 2 PO Box 1000 *Fax: Sales ■ TF: 800-319-6637 ■ Web: www.woodsequipment.com	Oregon	IL	61061	815-732-2141	732-7580*
Worksaver Inc Nine Worksaver Trl. Web: www.worksaver.com	Litchfield	IL	62056	217-324-5973	
Wylie Spray Center 702 E 40th St TF: 888-249-5162 ■ Web: www.wyliesprayers.com	Lubbock	TX	79404	806-763-1335	763-1092

Phone *Fax*

Yargus Manufacturing Inc PO Box 238 .... Marshall IL 62441 217-826-6352
Web: yargus.com

Yetter Manufacturing Inc
109 S McDonough St PO Box 358 .... Colchester IL 62326 309-776-4111 776-3222
TF: 800-447-5777 ■ *Web:* yetterco.com

277 FARM MACHINERY & EQUIPMENT - WHOL

Phone *Fax*

Abilene Machine Inc PO Box 129 .... Abilene KS 67410 785-655-9455 655-3838
TF: 800-255-0337 ■ *Web:* www.abilenemachine.com

Ag West Supply Inc 9055 Rickreall Rd. .... Rickreall OR 97371 503-363-2332 363-5662
TF: 800-842-2224 ■ *Web:* www.agwestsupply.com

Ag-Land Implement Inc Hwy 63 N PO Box 31 ..... New Hampton IA 50659 641-394-4226 394-3936
Web: www.aglandimplement.com

Ag-Pro Companies US 84 .... Dixie GA 31629 229-263-4133
Web: www.agprocompanies.com/en/boston.html

Agri-Service 3204 Kimberly Rd E .... Twin Falls ID 83301 208-734-7772 734-7775
TF: 800-388-3599 ■ *Web:* www.agri-service.com

Apple Farm Service Inc
10120 W Versailles Rd .... Covington OH 45318 937-526-4851
Web: www.applefarmservice.com

Arends & Sons Inc 715 S Sangamon Ave .... Gibson City IL 60936 217-784-4241 784-8749
TF: 800-637-6052 ■ *Web:* www.arends-sons.com

Arends Bros Inc 1190 E 1200N Rd. .... Melvin IL 60952 217-388-7717 388-2882
TF: 800-356-6811 ■ *Web:* www.arendshoganwalker.com

Baker Implement Co 421 E Main St .... Portageville MO 63873 573-379-5455 379-5313
Web: www.bakerimplement.com

Barnett Implement Co Inc 4220 Old Hwy 99 S ...... Snohomish WA 98273 425-334-4048 296-830*
*Fax Area Code: 587 ■ *TF:* 800-453-9274 ■ *Web:* www.barnettimplement.com

BE Implement Co 1645 FM 403 PO Box 752 .... Brownfield TX 79316 806-637-3594 637-8992
TF: 800-725-5435 ■ *Web:* www.beimplement.com

Beard Implement Co 216 Frederick St .... Arenzville IL 62611 217-997-5514
Web: www.beardimplement.com

Belarus Tractor International Inc
7842 N Faulkner Rd .... Milwaukee WI 53224 800-356-2336 355-6903*
*Fax Area Code: 414 ■ *Fax: Sales ■ *TF:* 800-356-2336 ■ *Web:* www.belarus.com

Bell Equipment Inc 511 Fourth St .... Nezperce ID 83543 208-937-2402 937-2118
TF: 800-343-2355 ■ *Web:* belleq.com

Berchtold Equipment Co Inc 330 E 19th St .... Bakersfield CA 93305 661-323-7817 325-4059
TF: 800-691-7817 ■ *Web:* www.berchtold.com

Big W Sales 1040 W Charter Way .... Stockton CA 95206 209-464-9493
Web: www.bigwsales.com

Blain Supply Inc 3507 E Racine St .... Janesville WI 53547 608-754-2821
Web: www.farmandfleet.com

Blanchard Compact Equipment
1410 Ashville Hwy .... Spartanburg SC 29303 864-582-1245 582-7121
TF: 888-799-3606 ■ *Web:* www.blanchardmachinery.com

Browning Equipment Inc 800 E Main St .... Purcellville VA 20132 540-338-7123 338-5835
Web: www.browningequipment.com

Burks Tractor Co Inc 3140 Kimberly Rd .... Twin Falls ID 83301 208-733-5543 734-9852
TF: 800-247-7419 ■ *Web:* www.burkstractor.com

Carco International Inc 2721 Midland Blvd. .... Fort Smith AR 72904 479-441-3270 441-3273
TF: 800-824-3215 ■ *Web:* www.carcoint.com

Carrico Implement Company Inc 3160 US 24 Hwy .... Beloit KS 67420 785-738-5744 738-2648
TF: 877-542-4099 ■ *Web:* www.carricoimplement.com

Coleman Equipment Inc 24000 W 43rd St. ...... Bonner Springs KS 66012 913-422-3040 422-3044
Web: www.colemanequip.com

Delta Implement Co Inc 3180 U.S. 82 .... Greenville MS 38703 662-332-2683
TF: 800-264-2741 ■ *Web:* www.deltagrp.com

Delta Ridge Implement Inc 1150 US Hwy 425 .... Rayville LA 71269 318-728-6423 728-6426
Web: stihldealer.net

Ernie Williams Ltd 2613 Hwy 18 E .... Algona IA 50511 515-295-3561 295-3419
Web: www.erniewilliamsltd.com

Farm Implement & Supply Company Inc
1200 S Washington Hwy 183 .... Plainville KS 67663 785-434-4824 434-7390
TF: 888-589-6029 ■ *Web:* www.farmimp.com

Farmer Boy Ag Systems Inc PO Box 435 .... Myerstown PA 17067 800-845-3374 866-6233*
*Fax Area Code: 717 ■ *TF:* 800-845-3374 ■ *Web:* www.farmerboyag.com

Farmers Supply Sales Inc 1409 E Ave. .... Kalona IA 52247 319-656-2291
TF: 800-493-4917 ■ *Web:* www.farmers.com

Fruit Growers Supply Company Inc
14130 Riverside Dr. .... Sherman Oaks CA 91423 818-986-6480 783-1941
Web: www.fruitgrowers.com

Gardner Inc 3641 Interchange Rd .... Columbus OH 43204 614-456-4000 456-4001
TF: 800-848-8946 ■ *Web:* www.gardnerinc.com

Garton Tractor Inc 2400 N Golden State Blvd .... Turlock CA 95382 209-632-3931 632-8006
TF: 877-872-2767 ■ *Web:* www.garton-tractor.com

Giles & Ransome Inc Ransome Engine Power Div
2975 Galloway Rd. .... Bensalem PA 19020 215-639-4300 245-2830
TF: 877-726-7663 ■ *Web:* www.ransome.com

Glade & Grove Supply Inc
1006 State Rd 80 PO Box 760 .... Belle Glade FL 33430 561-996-3095 996-2048
Web: www.gladeandgrove.com

Golden Spike Equipment Co
1352 W Main St PO Box 70 .... Tremonton UT 84337 435-257-5346 257-5719
TF: 800-821-4474 ■ *Web:* www.gspike.com

Greenline Equipment
14750 S Pony Express Rd .... Bluffdale UT 84065 801-966-4231 966-4313
TF: 888-201-5500 ■ *Web:* stotzequipment.com/

Grossenburg Implement Inc 31341 US Hwy 18 .... Winner SD 57580 605-842-2040 842-3485
TF: 800-658-3440 ■ *Web:* www.grossenburg.com

Hamilton Equipment Inc
567 S Reading Rd PO Box 478 .... Ephrata PA 17522 717-733-7951 733-1783
Web: www.haminc.com

Harcourt Equipment 313 Hwy 169 & 175 E .... Harcourt IA 50544 515-354-5332 354-5328
TF: 800-445-5646 ■ *Web:* www.kcnielsen.com

Harry J Whelchel Co 1332 Stuart St .... Chattanooga TN 37406 423-698-4415

HB Duvall Inc 901 E Patrick St PO Box 70. .... Frederick MD 21701 301-662-1125 695-0265
TF: 800-325-2252 ■ *Web:* www.hbduvall.com

Phone *Fax*

HH Halferty & Sons Inc 1300 S US Hwy 169 .... Smithville MO 64089 816-532-0221
Web: www.halfertyandsons.com

Hillsboro Equipment Inc E18898 Hwy 33 .... Hillsboro WI 54634 608-489-2275 489-2717
TF: 800-521-5133 ■ *Web:* www.hillsboroequipment.com

Hollingsworth Inc 1775 SW 30th St. .... Ontario OR 97914 541-889-7254 889-8364
TF: 800-541-1612 ■ *Web:* www.hollingsworthsinc.com

HOLT Texas Ltd 3302 S WW White Rd .... San Antonio TX 78222 210-648-1111 648-0079
TF: 800-275-4658 ■ *Web:* www.holtcat.com

Hoober Inc
3452 Old Philadelphia Pk PO Box 518 .... Intercourse PA 17534 717-768-8231 768-3005
TF: 800-732-0017 ■ *Web:* www.hoober.com

Horizon Equipment 402 Sixth St .... Manning IA 51455 712-653-2574
Web: horizonequip.com

Hoxie Implement Co Inc 933 Oak Ave Hwy 23&24 .... Hoxie KS 67740 785-675-3201 675-3438
Web: www.hoxieimplement.com

Hultgren Implements Inc 5698 State Hwy 175 .... Ida Grove IA 51445 712-364-3105
TF: 800-827-1650 ■ *Web:* hultgrenimplement.com

Hurst Farm Supply Inc 105 Ave D .... Abernathy TX 79311 806-298-2541 298-2936
TF: 800-535-8903 ■ *Web:* www.hurstfs.com

Implement Sales Company LLC
1574 Stone Ridge Dr .... Stone Mountain GA 30083 770-908-9439 908-8123
Web: implementsalesga.com

Jacobi Sales Inc 425 Main St NE PO Box 67 .... Palmyra IN 47164 812-364-6141 364-6157
Web: www.jacobisales.com

James River Equipment 11047 Leadbetter Rd .... Ashland VA 23005 804-798-6001
Web: jamesriverequipment.com

JD Equipment Inc 1660 US 42 NE .... London OH 43140 614-879-6620 879-5767
TF: 800-659-5646 ■ *Web:* www.jdequipment.com

Jerry Pate Turf & Irrigation Inc
301 Schubert Dr .... Pensacola FL 32504 850-479-4653 484-8596
TF: 800-700-7004 ■ *Web:* www.jerrypate.com

JJ Nichting Co Inc 1342 Pilot Grove Rd. .... Pilot Grove IA 52648 319-469-4461 469-4703
Web: jjnichting.com

John Day Co 6263 Abbott Dr .... Omaha NE 68110 402-455-8000 457-3812
TF: 800-767-2273 ■ *Web:* www.johnday.com

JS Woodhouse Company Inc
1314 Union St .... West Springfield MA 01090 413-736-5462 732-3786
Web: www.jswoodhouse.com

Kelly Sauder Rupiper Equipment LLC
805 E Howard St .... Pontiac IL 61764 815-842-1149
Web: www.ksrequipment.com

Lansdowne-Moody Company LP 8445 E Fwy .... Houston TX 77029 713-672-8366 672-8173
Web: www.lmtractor.com

Larchmont Engineering & Irrigation Co
11 Larchmont Ln PO Box 66 .... Lexington MA 02420 781-862-2550 862-0173
TF: 877-862-2550 ■ *Web:* www.larchmont-eng.com

Lawrence Tractor Company Inc 2530 E Main St .... Visalia CA 93292 559-734-7406 734-8325
Web: www.lawrencetractor.com

Liechty Farm Equipment Inc
1701 S Defiance St .... Archbold OH 43502 419-445-1565 445-1779
TF: 800-272-5898 ■ *Web:* www.kennfeldgroup.com

Linder Equipment Co 311 E Kern St .... Tulare CA 93274 559-685-5000 685-0452
Web: www.linderequipment.com

Littau Harvester Inc 855 Rogue Ave .... Stayton OR 97383 503-769-5953
TF: 866-262-2495 ■ *Web:* www.littauharvester.com

Maine Potato Growers Inc 56 Parsons St .... Presque Isle ME 04769 207-764-2471 764-8450
Web: www.mpgco-op.com

MDMA Equipment Dealers Inc N6291 State Hwy 25 ..... Durand WI 54736 715-672-8915 672-4112
Web: tractorcentral.com/

Mid-State Equipment Inc W 1115 Bristol Rd .... Columbus WI 53925 920-623-4020 623-4500
TF: 877-677-4020 ■ *Web:* www.midstateequipment.com

Miller Machinery & Supply Co 127 NE 27th St. .... Miami FL 33137 305-573-1300

Monroe Tractor & Implement Company Inc
1001 Lehigh Stn Rd .... Henrietta NY 14467 585-334-3867 334-0001
Web: www.monroetractor.com

N & S Tractor Co 600 S Hwy 59 .... Merced CA 95340 209-383-5888
Web: www.nstractor.com

Nueces Farm Center Inc
7510 IH 37 Exit 6 Southern Minerals Rd
.... Corpus Christi TX 78469 361-289-0066
Web: www.nuecespower.com

Peterson Tractor Co 955 Marina Blvd .... San Leandro CA 94577 510-357-6200 352-4570
TF: 800-590-5945 ■ *Web:* www.petersoncat.com

Pioneer Equipment Co 21276 Lassen Ave .... Five Points CA 93624 559-884-2431 884-2805
Web: www.pioneercvcsouth.com

Premier Equipment LLC 2025 US Hwy 14 W .... Huron SD 57350 605-352-7100 352-7071
TF: 800-627-5469 ■ *Web:* www.premiereqhuron.com

Price Bros Equipment Co 619 S Washington St. .... Wichita KS 67211 316-265-9577 265-1062
Web: www.pricebroseq.com

RDO Equipment Co 3401 38th St S .... Fargo ND 58104 701-282-5400 282-8220
TF: 800-342-4643 ■ *Web:* www.rdoequipment.com

Revels Tractor Company Inc
2217 N Main St .... Fuquay-Varina NC 27526 919-552-5697
TF: 800-849-5469 ■ *Web:* www.revelstractor.com

Riesterer & Schnell Inc N2909 Hwy 32. .... Pulaski WI 54162 920-822-3077
Web: www.riesterandschnell.com

RN Johnson Inc (RNJ) 269 Main St PO Box 448 .... Walpole NH 03608 603-756-3321 756-3452
Web: www.rnjohnsoninc.com

Rockingham New Holland Inc
600 W Market St. .... Harrisonburg VA 22802 540-434-6791 434-6780
TF: 888-864-5503 ■ *Web:* rockinghamnh.com

Roeder Implement Inc 2550 Rockdale Rd .... Dubuque IA 52003 563-557-1184 583-1821
TF: 800-557-1184 ■ *Web:* www.roederimplement.com

Rose Bros Inc 302 Main St. .... Lingle WY 82223 307-837-2261 837-2922
Web: rosebrosinc.com

Ryan Lawn & Tree Inc 9120 Barton St .... Overland Park KS 66214 913-381-1505
Web: ryanlawn.com

Schilling Bros Inc 5400 US Hwy 45 .... Mattoon IL 61938 217-234-6478 235-3991
Web: www.schillingbros.com

Schmidt Machine Co 7013 Ohio 199 .... Upper Sandusky OH 43351 419-294-3814 294-2607
Web: www.schmidtmachine.com

Company	City	State	Zip	Phone	Fax
SEMA Equipment Inc 11555 Hwy 60 Blvd. *TF:* 800-569-1377 ■ *Web:* www.semaequip.com	Wanamingo	MN	55983	507-824-2256	824-2668
Simpson Norton Corp 4144 S Bullard Ave *TF:* 877-859-8676 ■ *Web:* www.simpsonnorton.com	Goodyear	AZ	85338	623-932-5116	932-5299
Sioux Automation Ctr Inc 877 First Ave NW *TF:* 866-722-1488 ■ *Web:* www.siouxautomation.com	Sioux Center	IA	51250	712-722-1488	722-1487
Sloan Implement Co 120 N Business 51 *TF:* 800-745-4020 ■ *Web:* www.sloans.com	Assumption	IL	62510	217-226-4411	226-3351
Spartan Distributors Inc 487 W Div St *TF:* 800-822-2216 ■ *Web:* www.spartandistributors.com	Sparta	MI	49345	616-887-7301	
Stoller International Inc 15521 E 1830 N Rd *Web:* www.stollerih.com	Pontiac	IL	61764	815-844-6197	842-3213
Straub International Inc 214 SW 40th Ave PO Box 1606 *TF:* 800-658-1706 ■ *Web:* www.straubint.com	Great Bend	KS	67530	620-792-5256	793-5167
Studer Super Service Inc 1703-6th St	Monroe	WI	53566	608-328-8331	
Teeter Irrigation Inc 2729 W Oklahoma *TF:* 800-524-5497 ■ *Web:* www.teeterirrigation.com	Ulysses	KS	67880	620-353-1111	
Texas Timberjack Inc 6004 S First St *Web:* www.texastimberjack.com	Lufkin	TX	75901	936-634-3365	639-3673
Thomas Equipment Inc 204 Upper Kent Rd *Web:* www.thomasloaders.com	Upper Kent	NB	E7J2E4	506-278-5695	
Titan Machinery Inc 7955 179th Ave SE *NASDAQ: TITN* ■ *Web:* www.titanmachinery.com	Wahpeton	ND	58075	701-642-8424	642-9514
Tom Hassenfritz Equipment Co 1300 W Washington St *TF:* 800-634-4885 ■ *Web:* www.the-co.com	Mount Pleasant	IA	52641	319-385-3114	385-3731
Torrence's Farm Implement Inc 190 E Hwy 86 PO Box C *Web:* www.torrencesfarmimplements.com	Heber	CA	92249	760-352-5355	352-8707
Tractor Supply Co 200 Powell Pl *NASDAQ: TSCO* ■ *TF:* 877-718-6750 ■ *Web:* www.tractorsupply.com	Brentwood	TN	37027	877-718-6750	
Valley Truck & Tractor Company Inc 793 N First St *Web:* www.valleytruckandtractor.com	Dixon	CA	95620	707-678-2395	
Van-Wall Equipment Inc 22728 141st Dr PO Box 575 *TF:* 800-568-2381 ■ *Web:* www.vanwall.com	Perry	IA	50220	515-465-5681	
Wade Inc 1505 Hwy 82 W *Web:* www.wadeincorporated.com	Greenwood	MS	38930	662-453-6312	455-3287
Washington County Tractor Inc PO Box 1619 *TF:* 800-256-5655 ■ *Web:* www.wctractor.com	Brenham	TX	77834	979-836-4591	836-7446
West Central Coop 406 First St *Web:* www.west-central.com	Ralston	IA	51459	712-667-3200	
Western Equipment Distributors Inc 20224 80th Ave S *Web:* www.western-equip.com	Kent	WA	98032	253-872-8858	872-6942
Western Implement Co Inc 2919 N Ave *Web:* www.westernimplement.com	Grand Junction	CO	81504	970-242-7960	242-5241
WG Leffelman & Sons Inc 340 N Metcalf Ave	Amboy	IL	61310	815-857-2513	857-3105
White's Inc 4614 Navigation Blvd PO Box 2344 **Fax Area Code: 888* ■ *TF:* 800-231-9559 ■ *Web:* www.whitesinc.com	Houston	TX	77011	713-928-2632	944-8373*
Witmer's Inc 39821 SR 14 *TF:* 888-427-6025 ■ *Web:* www.witmersinc.com	Salem	OH	44460	330-427-2147	427-2611
Wyandot Tractor & Implement Co 10264 County Hwy 121 *Web:* www.findlay-imp.com/wyandot/default.asp	Upper Sandusky	OH	43351	419-294-2349	294-5200
Wyatt-Quarles Seed Co 730 US Hwy 70 W *TF:* 800-662-7591 ■ *Web:* www.wqseeds.com	Garner	NC	27529	919-772-4243	772-4278

278 FARM PRODUCT RAW MATERIALS

Company	City	State	Zip	Phone	Fax
ADM Corn Processing 4666 Faries Pkwy *Web:* www.adm.com	Decatur	IL	62526	217-424-5200	451-4122
ADM Grain Co 4666 E Faries Pkwy *Web:* www.admworld.com	Decatur	IL	62526	217-424-5200	
Agri Co-op 310 Logan St *Web:* www.agrico-op.com	Holdrege	NE	68949	308-995-8626	995-5779
Allenberg Cotton Co 7255 Goodlett Farms Pkwy *Web:* www.ldcom.com	Cordova	TN	38016	901-383-5000	383-5010
Alliance Grain Co 1306 W Eigth St *TF:* 800-222-2451 ■ *Web:* www.alliance-grain.com	Gibson City	IL	60936	217-784-4284	784-8949
Apache Farmers Co-op 201 W Floyd PO Box 332 *Web:* www.apachecoop.com	Apache	OK	73006	580-588-3351	588-9277
Aurora Co-op Elevator Co 605 12th St PO Box 209 *TF:* 800-642-6795 ■ *Web:* www.auroracoop.com	Aurora	NE	68818	402-694-2106	694-6943
Birdsong Corp 612 Madison Ave *Web:* www.birdsong-peanuts.com	Suffolk	VA	23434	757-539-3456	
Bunge Ltd 50 Main St Sixth Fl *NYSE: BG* ■ *Web:* www.bunge.com	White Plains	NY	10606	914-684-2800	684-3499
C & F Foods Inc 15620 E Valley Blvd *Web:* www.cnf-foods.com	City of Industry	CA	91744	626-723-1000	723-1212
Calcot Ltd 1900 E Brundage Ln *Web:* www.calcot.net	Bakersfield	CA	93307	661-327-5961	
Cargill Inc 15407 McGinty Rd W **Fax:* Cust Svc ■ *TF:* 800-227-4455 ■ *Web:* www.cargill.com	Wayzata	MN	55391	952-742-7575	742-7209*
Cargill Ltd 300-240 Graham Ave PO Box 5900 *Web:* www.cargill.ca	Winnipeg	MB	R3C4C5	204-947-0141	947-6444
Central Connecticut Co-op Farmers Assn 10 Apel Pl PO Box 8500 *TF:* 800-640-4523 ■ *Web:* www.cccfeeds.com	Manchester	CT	06042	860-649-4523	643-5305
Central Iowa Co-op 2829 Westown Pkwy Ste 350 *TF:* 800-513-3938 ■ *Web:* www.heartlandcoop.com	West Des Moines	IA	50266	515-225-1334	225-8511
Ceres Solutions LLP 2112 Indianapolis Rd PO Box 432 *TF General:* 800-878-0952 ■ *Web:* cereslip.com	Crawfordsville	IN	47933	765-362-6700	362-7010
Co-Alliance LLP 5250 E US Hwy 36 Bldg 1000 *TF:* 800-525-0272 ■ *Web:* www.co-alliance.com	Avon	IN	46123	317-745-4491	718-1850
Co-op Elevator Co 7211 E Michigan Ave *TF:* 800-968-0601 ■ *Web:* www.coopelev.com	Pigeon	MI	48755	989-453-4500	453-3942
Effingham Equity Inc 201 W Roadway Ave *TF:* 800-223-1337 ■ *Web:* www.effinghamequity.com	Effingham	IL	62401	217-342-4101	347-7601
Farmers Co-op Co 2321 N Loop Dr Ste 220 *Web:* www.fccoop.com	Ames	IA	50010	515-817-2100	
Federated Co-operatives Ltd 401 22nd St E PO Box 1050 *Web:* www.coopconnection.ca	Saskatoon	SK	S7K0H2	306-244-3311	244-3403
Frick Services Inc 570 E Boundary Rd *Web:* www.frickservices.com	Portage	IN	46368	219-787-8548	787-8101
Frontier Co-op 211 S Lincoln PO Box 37 *TF:* 800-869-0379 ■ *Web:* www.frontiercooperative.com	Brainard	NE	68626	402-545-2811	545-2821
Heartland Co-op 2829 Westown Pkwy Ste 350 *TF:* 800-513-3938 ■ *Web:* www.heartlandcoop.com	West Des Moines	IA	50266	515-225-1334	225-8511
Italgrani USA Inc 7900 Van Buren St *TF:* 800-274-1274 ■ *Web:* italgraniusa.com	Saint Louis	MO	63111	314-638-1447	752-7621
James Richardson International (JRI) 2800 One Lombard Pl *Web:* www.richardson.ca	Winnipeg	MB	R3B0X8	204-934-5961	947-2647
Joy Dog Food PO Box 305 **Fax Area Code: 618* ■ *TF:* 800-245-4125 ■ *Web:* www.joypetfood.com	Pinckneyville	IL	62274	800-245-4125	357-3651*
Kelley Bean Company Inc 2407 Cir Dr *Web:* www.kelleybean.com	Scottsbluff	NE	69361	308-635-6438	635-7345
MaxYield Co-op 313 Third Ave NE PO Box 49 *TF:* 800-383-0003 ■ *Web:* www.maxyieldcooperative.com	West Bend	IA	50597	515-887-7211	887-7291
Mont Eagle Mills Inc 804 W Main St *Web:* monteaglemills.com	Oblong	IL	62449	618-592-4211	
NEW Co-op Inc 2626 First Ave S *TF:* 800-362-2233 ■ *Web:* www.newcoop.com	Fort Dodge	IA	50501	515-955-2040	955-5565
NF Davis Drier & Elevator Inc 9421 N Dos Palos Ave	Firebaugh	CA	93622	559-659-3035	659-2275
Northwest Grain Growers Inc 850 N Fourth Ave *TF:* 800-994-4290 ■ *Web:* www.nwgrgr.com	Walla Walla	WA	99362	509-525-6510	529-6050
Parrish & Heimbecker Ltd (P&H) 201 Portage Ave Ste 1400 *TF:* 800-665-8937 ■ *Web:* www.parrishandheimbecker.com	Winnipeg	MB	R3B3K6	204-956-2030	943-8233
Pendleton Grain Growers Inc 1000 SW Dorian St PO Box 1248 *TF:* 800-422-7611 ■ *Web:* www.pggcountry.com	Pendleton	OR	97801	541-276-7611	276-4839
Plains Cotton Co-op Assn 3301 E 50th St PO Box 2827 *TF:* 800-333-8011 ■ *Web:* www.pcca.com	Lubbock	TX	79408	806-763-8011	762-7335
PremierCo-op Inc 2104 W Pk Ct *Web:* www.grandprairiecoop.com	Champaign	IL	61821	217-355-1983	355-3478
Rockingham Co-Operative 101 W Grace St *Web:* www.rockinghamcoop.com	Harrisonburg	VA	22801	540-434-3856	434-6890
Scoular Co 2027 Dodge St *TF:* 800-488-3500 ■ *Web:* www.scoular.com	Omaha	NE	68102	402-342-3500	342-5568
South Dakota Wheat Growers Assn 908 Lamont St SE *TF:* 888-429-4902 ■ *Web:* www.wheatgrowers.com	Aberdeen	SD	57401	605-225-5500	225-0859
Staplcotn Co-op Assn Inc 214 W Market St *TF:* 800-293-6231 ■ *Web:* www.staplcotn.com	Greenwood	MS	38930	662-453-6231	453-6274
Stratton Equity Co-op Co Inc 98 Colorado Ave PO Box 25 *TF:* 800-438-7070 ■ *Web:* www.strattoncoop.com	Stratton	CO	80836	719-348-5326	
Virginia Diner Inc, The 322 W Main St *Web:* www.vadiner.com	Wakefield	VA	23888	757-899-6213	
Watonwan Farm Service 233 W Ciro St *TF:* 800-657-3282 ■ *Web:* www.wfsag.com	Truman	MN	56088	507-776-2831	776-2871
Western Iowa Co-op 3330 Moville St PO Box 106 *TF:* 800-488-3201 ■ *Web:* www.westerniowacoop.com	Hornick	IA	51026	712-874-3211	874-3230

279 FARM SUPPLIES

Company	City	State	Zip	Phone	Fax
Abilene Ag Service & Supply Inc 303 S 14th St	Abilene	TX	79602	325-677-4371	
Ag-Land FS Inc 1505 Valle Vista Blvd *Web:* www.aglandfs.com	Pekin	IL	61554	309-346-4145	
Agfinity 260 Factory Rd *TF:* 800-433-4688 ■ *Web:* www.aglandinc.com	Eaton	CO	80615	970-454-4000	
Agri Producers Inc 205 Main St *Web:* www.api.coop	Tampa	KS	67483	785-965-2221	965-2263
AgVantage FS Inc 1600 Eigth St SW *TF:* 800-346-0058 ■ *Web:* www.agvantagefs.com	Waverly	IA	50677	319-483-4900	483-4992
Alforex Seeds 38001 County Rd 27 *TF:* 877-560-5181 ■ *Web:* www.calwestseeds.com	Woodland	CA	95695	530-666-3331	666-5317
Allied Seed LLC 9311 Hwy 45 *Web:* www.alliedseed.com	Nampa	ID	83686	208-466-6700	466-9074
American Pride Co-Op 55 W Bromley Ln *TF:* 800-332-6478 ■ *Web:* www.americanpridecoop.com	Brighton	CO	80601	303-659-1230	659-7650
Battle Creek Farmers Co-op 83755 S Hwy 121 PO Box 10 *Web:* www.bccoop.com	Battle Creek	NE	68715	402-675-2375	675-1645
BFG Supply Co LLC PO Box 479 *Web:* www.bfgsupply.com	Burton	OH	44021	440-834-1883	834-1885
BinghamCo-op Inc PO Box 887 *Web:* www.binghamcoop.com	Blackfoot	ID	83221	208-785-3440	785-3444
Bleyhl Farm Service Inc 940 E Wine Country Rd *TF Cust Svc:* 800-862-6806 ■ *Web:* www.bleyhl.com	Grandview	WA	98930	509-882-2248	882-4208
Bradley Caldwell Inc 200 Kiwanis Blvd **Fax:* Cust Svc ■ *TF Cust Svc:* 800-257-9100 ■ *Web:* www.bradleycaldwell.com	Hazleton	PA	18202	570-455-7511	455-0385*
Carroll Service Co 505 W Illinois Rt 64 *Web:* carrollsvc.com	Lanark	IL	61046	815-493-2181	493-6173

	City	State	ZIP	Phone	Fax
Central Valley Co-op 900 30th Pl NW *TF:* 800-270-2339 ■ *Web:* centralvalleycoop.com	Owatonna	MN	55060	507-451-1230	451-7579
Chem Nut Inc 800 Business Pk Dr	Leesburg	GA	31763	229-883-7050	439-0842
Co-op Feed Dealers Inc 380 Broome Corporate Pkwy PO Box 670 *TF Cust Svc:* 800-333-0895 ■ *Web:* www.cfd.coop	Conklin	NY	13748	607-651-9078	651-9078
Countryside Co-op 514 E Main St *TF:* 800-236-7585 ■ *Web:* www.countrysidecoop.com	Durand	WI	54736	715-672-8947	672-5131
CropKing Inc 134 W Dr *TF:* 800-321-5656 ■ *Web:* www.cropking.com	Lodi	OH	44254	330-302-4203	302-4204
Crystal Valley Coop 721 W Humphrey PO 210 *TF:* 800-622-2910 ■ *Web:* www.crystalvalley.coop	Lake Crystal	MN	56055	507-726-6455	726-6901
Dragon Claw USA Inc 16033 Arrow Hwy *TF:* 800-238-5296 ■ *Web:* www.dcamerica.net	Irwindale	CA	91706	626-480-0068	480-0018
Edon Farmers Co-op Assn Inc 205 S Michigan PO Box 308 *TF:* 800-878-4093 ■ *Web:* www.edonfarmerscoop.com	Edon	OH	43518	419-272-2121	485-4509
Evergreen FS Inc 402 N Hershey Rd *TF:* 877-963-2392 ■ *Web:* www.evergreen-fs.com	Bloomington	IL	61704	309-663-2392	663-0494
Farm Service Co-op 2308 Pine St *TF:* 800-452-4372 ■ *Web:* www.fscoop.com	Harlan	IA	51537	712-755-3185	755-7098
Farmers Co-op Assn 105 Jackson St *TF:* 800-864-3847 ■ *Web:* www.fcajackson.com	Jackson	MN	56143	507-847-4160	847-2521
Farmers Feed & Grain Company Inc 306 Birch St PO Box 291 *Web:* www.ffgcoinc.com	Riceville	IA	50466	641-985-2147	985-4000
Farmway Inc 204 E Ct St PO Box 568 *Web:* www.farmwaycoop.com	Beloit	KS	67420	785-738-2241	738-9659
Federation Co-op 108 N Water St *TF:* 800-944-1784 ■ *Web:* www.fedcoop.com	Black River Falls	WI	54615	715-284-5354	284-9672
Fifield Land Co 4307 Fifield Rd *TF:* 800-536-6395 ■ *Web:* www.kfseeds.com	Brawley	CA	92227	760-344-6391	344-6394
Florida Fertilizer Company Inc PO Box 1087 *Web:* www.floridafertilizer.com	Wauchula	FL	33873	863-773-4159	
Frenchman Valley Farmers Co-op Exchange 202 Broadway *TF:* 800-538-2667 ■ *Web:* www.fvcoop.com	Imperial	NE	69033	308-882-3200	882-3242
Gold Star FS Inc 101 NE St PO Box 79 *TF:* 800-443-8497 ■ *Web:* www.goldstarfs.com	Cambridge	IL	61238	309-937-3369	937-5465
Gowan Company LLC PO Box 5569 *TF:* 800-883-1844 ■ *Web:* www.gowanco.com	Yuma	AZ	85366	928-783-8844	343-9255
Grangetto's Farm & Garden Supply Co 1105 W Mission Ave *TF:* 800-536-4671 ■ *Web:* www.grangettos.com	Escondido	CA	92025	760-745-4671	745-5111
GROWMARK Inc 1701 Towanda Ave *Web:* www.growmark.com	Bloomington	IL	61701	309-557-6000	829-8530
Growth Products Ltd 80 Lafayette Ave *TF:* 800-648-7626 ■ *Web:* www.growthproducts.com	White Plains	NY	10603	914-428-1316	
Hummert International Inc 4500 Earth City Expy *TF:* 800-325-3055 ■ *Web:* www.hummert.com	Earth City	MO	63045	314-506-4500	506-4510
Hutchinson Co-Op PO Box 158 *TF:* 800-795-1299 ■ *Web:* www.hutchcoop.com	Hutchinson	MN	55350	320-587-4647	587-6964
Intermountain Farmers Assn 1147 West 2100 South *Web:* www.ifa-coop.com	Salt Lake City	UT	84119	801-972-2122	972-2186
Keller Grain & Feed Inc 7977 Main St *Web:* www.kellergrain.com	Greenville	OH	45331	937-448-2284	448-2102
Kreamer Feed Inc PO Box 38 *TF:* 800-767-4537 ■ *Web:* www.kreamerfeed.com	Kreamer	PA	17833	570-374-8148	374-2007
Kugler Co 209 W Third St PO Box 1748 *TF:* 800-445-9116 ■ *Web:* www.kuglercompany.com	McCook	NE	69001	308-345-2280	345-7756
Lakes Area Co-op 459 Third Ave SE PO Box 247 *Web:* lakesareacoop.com	Perham	MN	56573	218-346-6240	346-6241
Legend Seeds Inc PO Box 241 *Web:* www.legendseeds.net	De Smet	SD	57231	605-854-3346	854-3135
Luckey Farmers Inc 1200 W Main St PO Box 217 *Web:* www.luckeyfarmers.com	Woodville	OH	43469	419-849-2711	849-2720
Martrex Inc 1107 Hazeltine Blvd Ste 535 *TF:* 800-328-3627 ■ *Web:* www.martrexinc.com	Minnetonka	MN	55345	952-933-5000	933-1889
McFarlane Mfg Company Inc 1259 Water St PO Box 100 *TF:* 800-627-8569 ■ *Web:* www.mcfarlanes.net	Sauk City	WI	53583	608-643-3321	643-2309
Meherrin Agricultural & Chemical Co Inc 413 Main St *TF:* 800-775-0333 ■ *Web:* fda.gov	Severn	NC	27877	252-585-1744	585-1718
MFA Inc 201 Ray Young Dr *Web:* www.mfaincorporated.com	Columbia	MO	65201	573-874-5111	876-5505
New Alliance FS Inc 802 W N St *Web:* agrilandfs.com	Moravia	IA	52571	641-724-3233	
NEW Co-op Inc 2626 First Ave S *TF:* 800-362-2233 ■ *Web:* www.newcoop.com	Fort Dodge	IA	50501	515-955-2040	955-5565
Northwest Wholesale Inc 1567 N Wenatchee Ave *TF:* 800-874-6607 ■ *Web:* www.nwwinc.com	Wenatchee	WA	98801	509-662-2141	663-4540
Nu Way Co-op Inc PO Box Q *TF:* 800-445-4118 ■ *Web:* www.nuwaycoop.com	Trimont	MN	56176	507-639-2311	639-4006
Orange Belt Supply Co 25244 Rd 204	Lindsay	CA	93221	559-562-2574	732-7029
Orangeburg Pecan Company Inc 761 Russell St *TF:* 800-845-6970 ■ *Web:* www.uspecans.com	Orangeburg	SC	29115	803-534-4277	534-4279
Orscheln Farm & Home LLC 1800 Overcenter Dr PO Box 698 *TF:* 800-498-5090 ■ *Web:* www.orscheln.com	Moberly	MO	65270	660-263-4377	269-3500
Pacific Coast Chemical Co 2424 Fourth St *Web:* www.pcchem.com	Berkeley	CA	94710	510-549-3535	549-0890
Panhandle Co-op Assn 401 S Beltline Hwy W *TF Cust Svc:* 800-732-4546 ■ *Web:* www.panhandlecoop.com	Scottsbluff	NE	69361	308-632-5301	632-5375
Paris Farmers' Union PO Box D *TF:* 800-639-3603 ■ *Web:* www.parisfarmersunion.net	South Paris	ME	04281	207-743-8976	743-8564
Pickseed West Disc Inc 33149 Hwy 99 E *Web:* www.pickseed.com	Tangent	OR	97389	541-926-8886	926-1599
ProVision Partners Coop PO Box 14 *Web:* www.cwco-op.com	Stratford	WI	54484	715-687-4443	
Quality Liquid Feeds Inc PO Box 240 *TF:* 800-236-2345 ■ *Web:* www.qlf.com	Dodgeville	WI	53533	608-935-2345	935-3198
Red River Specialties Inc PO Box 7241 *TF:* 800-256-3344 ■ *Web:* www.rrsi.com	Shreveport	LA	71137	318-425-5944	424-6562
Reedsville Co-op Assn Inc PO Box 460 *TF:* 800-236-4047 ■ *Web:* www.countryvisionscoop.com	Reedsville	WI	54230	920-754-4321	754-4536
Richardson Seeds Inc PO Box 60 *Web:* www.richardsonseeds.com	Vega	TX	79092	806-267-2379	267-2820
S R C Corp PO Box 30676 *TF:* 800-888-4545 ■ *Web:* www.steveregan.com	Salt Lake City	UT	84130	801-268-4500	268-4596
Siegers Seed Co 13031 Reflections Dr *TF:* 800-962-4999 ■ *Web:* www.siegers.com	Holland	MI	49424	616-786-4999	994-0333
Silver Edge Co-op 39999 Hilton Rd *TF:* 800-632-5953 ■ *Web:* www.silveredgecoop.com	Edgewood	IA	52042	563-928-6419	
Southern FS Inc 2002 E Main St PO Box 728 *TF:* 800-492-7684 ■ *Web:* southernfs.com	Marion	IL	62959	618-993-2833	997-2526
Southern States Co-op Inc 6606 W Broad St *TF:* 866-372-8272 ■ *Web:* www.southernstates.com	Richmond	VA	23230	804-281-1000	281-1141
Southern States Frederick Co-op Inc 500 E South St *TF:* 866-633-5747 ■ *Web:* www.southernstates.com	Frederick	MD	21705	301-663-6164	663-8173
Stanislaus Farm Supply Co 624 E Service Rd *TF:* 800-323-0725 ■ *Web:* www.stanislausfarmsupply.com	Modesto	CA	95358	209-538-7070	541-3191
Tennessee Farmers Co-op 180 Old Nashville Hwy *TF:* 800-366-2667 ■ *Web:* www.ourcoop.com	La Vergne	TN	37086	615-793-8011	793-8343
TriOak Foods Inc 103 W Railroad St PO Box 68 *Web:* www.trioak.com	Oakville	IA	52646	319-766-2230	
United Suppliers Inc 30473 260th St PO Box 538 *TF:* 800-782-5123 ■ *Web:* www.unitedsuppliers.com	Eldora	IA	50627	641-858-2341	858-5493
Universal Co-ops Inc (UCOOP) 1300 Corporate Ctr Curve *Web:* www.ucoop.com	Eagan	MN	55121	651-239-1000	
Van Horn Inc PO Box 380 *TF:* 800-252-1615 ■ *Web:* www.vanhorninc.com	Cerro Gordo	IL	61818	217-677-2131	677-2134
Virginia Fork Produce Company Inc 719 Virginia Rd	Edenton	NC	27932	252-482-2165	
Wabash Valley Service Company Inc 909 N Ct St *TF:* 888-869-8127 ■ *Web:* www.wabashvalleyfs.com	Grayville	IL	62844	618-375-2311	375-5351
West Agro Inc 11100 N Congress Ave *Web:* www.delavalcleaningsolutions.com	Kansas City	MO	64153	816-891-1600	891-1595
Western Consolidated Co-op 520 Co Rd 9 PO Box 78 *TF:* 800-368-3310 ■ *Web:* www.west-con.com	Holloway	MN	56249	320-394-2171	394-2180
Western Reserve Farm Co-op Inc 14961 S State Ave PO Box 339 *TF:* 888-427-6672 ■ *Web:* www.wrfc.com	Middlefield	OH	44062	440-632-1192	632-1258
Wilbur-Ellis Co 345 California St 27th Fl *Web:* www.wilburellis.com/pages/home.aspx	San Francisco	CA	94104	415-772-4000	772-4011
Wilco Farmers 200 Industrial Way *TF:* 800-382-5339 ■ *Web:* www.wilco.coop	Mount Angel	OR	97362	503-845-6122	845-9310
Yankton Ag Service 114 Mulberry St *Web:* yanktonag.com	Yankton	SD	57078	605-665-3691	

280 FASHION DESIGN HOUSES

SEE ALSO Clothing & Accessories - Mfr p. 1952

	City	State	ZIP	Phone	Fax
Armani Exchange 568 Broadway *TF:* 800-717-2929 ■ *Web:* www.armaniexchange.com	New York	NY	10012	212-431-6000	431-4669
BCBG Max Azria 2761 Fruitland Ave *Web:* www.bcbg.com	Vernon	CA	90058	323-589-2224	277-5461
Carolina Herrera Ltd 501 Seventh Ave 17th Fl *Web:* www.carolinaherrera.com	New York	NY	10018	212-944-5757	944-7996
Christian Dior 712 Fifth Ave 37th Fl *TF:* 800-929-3467 ■ *Web:* dior.com	New York	NY	10019	212-582-0500	582-1063
Cynthia Rowley 376 Bleecker St *Web:* www.cynthiarowley.com	New York	NY	10014	212-242-0847	242-4136
Diane Von Furstenberg 440 W 14th St *TF:* 888-472-2383 ■ *Web:* world.dvf.com	New York	NY	10014	212-741-6607	753-1180
Donna Karan International Inc 550 Seventh Ave 15th Fl *TF General:* 888-737-5743 ■ *Web:* www.donnakaran.com	New York	NY	10018	212-789-1500	789-1820
Evy of California Inc 810A S Flower St *Web:* www.evy.com	Los Angeles	CA	90017	213-746-4647	746-9788
Kay Green Design Inc 859 Outer Rd *TF:* 800-226-5186 ■ *Web:* www.kaygreendesign.com	Orlando	FL	32814	407-246-7155	426-7873
Marc Bouwer 413 W 14th St Ste 402 *Web:* www.marcbouwer.com	New York	NY	10014	212-242-7510	
Marc Jacobs International 72 Spring St *Web:* www.marcjacobs.com	New York	NY	10012	212-965-5523	965-5510
Max Mara USA Inc 530 Seventh Ave	New York	NY	10018	212-536-6200	302-1134
Michael Kors 11 W 42nd St 21st Fl *Web:* www.michaelkors.com	New York	NY	10036	212-201-8100	
Norma Kamali 11 W 56th St *Web:* shop.normakamali.com	New York	NY	10019	212-957-9797	956-1060
Oscar De La Renta Ltd 11 W. 42nd St 8th Fl *Web:* www.oscardelarenta.com	New York	NY	10036	212-282-0500	768-9110
Prada 610 W 52nd St *Web:* www.prada.com	New York	NY	10019	212-974-2555	246-3653
Vivienne Tam 40 Mercer St At Grand *Web:* viviennetam.com	New York	NY	10013	212-966-2398	

281 FASTENERS & FASTENING SYSTEMS

SEE ALSO Hardware - Mfr p. 2444; Precision Machined Products p. 2957

				Phone	Fax
Air Industries Corp 12570 Knott St *Web:* www.air-industries.com	Garden Grove	CA	92841	714-892-5571	892-7904
Allfast Fastening Systems Inc 15200 Don Julian Rd *Web:* www.allfastinc.com	City of Industry	CA	91745	626-968-9388	968-9393
Atlas Bolt & Screw Co 1628 Troy Rd *TF:* 800-321-6977 ■ *Web:* www.atlasfasteners.com	Ashland	OH	44805	419-289-6171	289-2564
Avibank Manufacturing Inc 11500 Sherman Way *Web:* www.avibank.com	North Hollywood	CA	91605	818-392-2100	255-2094
B & G Mfg Company Inc 3067 Unionville Pk **Fax:* Sales ■ *TF:* 800-366-3067 ■ *Web:* www.bgmfg.com	Hatfield	PA	19440	215-822-1925	822-1006*
Bristol Industries 630 E Lambert Rd **Fax:* Sales ■ *Web:* www.bristol-ind.com	Brea	CA	92821	714-990-4121	529-6726*
Captive Fastener Corp 19 Thornton Rd *TF:* 800-526-4430 ■ *Web:* www.captive-fastener.com	Oakland	NJ	07436	201-337-6800	337-1012
Chicago Rivet & Machine Co 901 Frontenac Rd *AMEX: CVR* ■ *Web:* www.chicagorivet.com	Naperville	IL	60563	630-357-8500	983-9314
Cold Heading Co 21777 Hoover Rd *Web:* www.coldheading.com	Warren	MI	48089	586-497-7000	497-7007
CONTMID Group 24000 Western Ave *Web:* www.contmid.com	Park Forest	IL	60466	708-747-1200	747-9373
Decker Manufacturing Corp 703 N Clark St *Web:* www.deckernut.com	Albion	MI	49224	517-629-3955	629-3535
ELF Fastening Systems Inc 29019 Solon Rd *TF:* 800-248-2376 ■ *Web:* www.etf-fastening.com	Solon	OH	44139	440-248-8655	248-0423
Elgin Fastener Group 4 S Pk Ave ste203 *Web:* www.elginfasteners.com	Batesville	IN	47006	812-689-8917	689-6635
Fastco Industries Inc PO Box 141427 *Web:* www.fastcoind.com	Grand Rapids	MI	49514	616-453-5428	453-2490
Ford Fasteners Inc 110 S Newman St *TF:* 800-272-3673 ■ *Web:* www.fordfasteners.com	Hackensack	NJ	07601	201-487-3151	487-1919
Hohmann & Barnard Inc 30 Rasons Ct *TF:* 800-645-0616 ■ *Web:* www.h-b.com	Hauppauge	NY	11788	631-234-0600	234-0683
Indiana Automotive Fasteners Inc 1300 Anderson Blvd *Web:* www.iafi.com	Greenfield	IN	46140	317-467-0100	467-2782
ITW Brands 955 National Pkwy Ste 95500 *TF:* 877-489-2726 ■ *Web:* www.itwbrands.com	Schaumburg	IL	60173	847-944-2260	619-8344
ITW Buildex 1349 W Bryn Mawr *TF:* 800-284-5339 ■ *Web:* www.itwbuildex.com	Itasca	IL	60143	630-595-3500	595-3549
Lawrence Screw Products Inc 7230 W Wilson Ave *Web:* www.lawrencescrew.com	Harwood Heights	IL	60706	708-867-5150	867-7052
Mid-States Bolt & Screw Co 4126 Somers Dr *TF:* 800-482-0867 ■ *Web:* www.midstatesbolt.com	Burton	MI	48529	810-744-0123	744-3798
Mid-States Screw Corp 1817 18th Ave *Web:* www.midstatesscrew.com	Rockford	IL	61104	815-397-2440	398-1047
Monogram Aerospace Fasteners 3423 S Garfield Ave *Web:* www.monogramaerospace.com	Los Angeles	CA	90040	323-722-4760	721-1851
Ms Aerospace Inc 13928 Balboa Blvd *TF:* 866-487-2365 ■ *Web:* www.msaerospace.com	Sylmar	CA	91342	818-833-9095	833-9525
National Rivet & Manufacturing Co 21 E Jefferson St *TF:* 888-324-5511 ■ *Web:* www.nationalrivet.com	Waupun	WI	53963	920-324-5511	324-3388
Ohio Nut & Bolt Co 5250 W 164th St *TF:* 800-362-0291 ■ *Web:* www.on-b.com	Brook Park	OH	44142	216-267-2240	267-3228
Pan American Screw Inc 630 Reese Dr SW *TF Cust Svc:* 800-951-2222 ■ *Web:* www.panamericanscrew.com	Conover	NC	28613	828-466-0060	466-0070
PennEngineering & Manufacturing Corp 5190 Old Easton Rd *TF:* 800-237-4736 ■ *Web:* www.penn-eng.com	Danboro	PA	18916	215-766-8853	766-3680
Robertson Inc 97 Bronte St N *TF:* 800-268-5090 ■ *Web:* www.robertsonscrew.com	Milton	ON	L9T2N8	905-878-2861	878-2867
Scovill Fasteners Inc 1802 Scovill Dr **Fax:* Cust Svc ■ *TF Cust Svc:* 888-726-8455 ■ *Web:* www.scovill.com	Clarkesville	GA	30523	706-754-1000	754-4000*
Southern Fastening Systems Inc 635 Fairgrounds Rd *Web:* www.southernfastening.com	Muscle Shoals	AL	35661	256-381-3628	381-3631
SPS Technologies Inc 301 Highland Ave *Web:* www.spstech.com	Jenkintown	PA	19046	215-572-3000	572-3790
Stafast Products Inc 505 Lk Shore Blvd *TF:* 800-782-3278 ■ *Web:* shop.stafast.com	Painesville	OH	44077	440-357-5546	357-7137
TriMas Corp 39400 Woodward Ave Ste 130 *Web:* www.trimascorp.com	Bloomfield Hills	MI	48304	248-631-5450	631-5455
Vertex Distribution 523 Pleasant St Bldg 10 *Web:* www.vertexdistribution.com	Attleboro	MA	02703	508-431-1120	431-1114

282 FENCES - MFR

SEE ALSO Recycled Plastics Products p. 3046

				Phone	Fax
Accu-Systems Inc 1810 West 5000 South *TF:* 800-369-5746 ■ *Web:* www.accu-systems.com	Salt Lake City	UT	84118	800-369-5746	
Acorn Wire & Iron Works Inc 2035 S Racine Ave *TF:* 800-552-2676 ■ *Web:* www.acornwire.com	Chicago	IL	60608	773-585-0600	585-2403
Boulanger, Roland & Cie Ltd 235 rue St-Louis *Web:* www.boulanger.qc.ca	Warwick	QC	J0A1M0	819-358-4100	
Cherry Tree Design 320 Pronghorn Trl *Web:* www.cherrytreedesign.com	Bozeman	MT	59718	406-582-8800	
Conifex Timber Inc 980 700 W Georgia St PO Box 10070 *Web:* www.conifex.com	Vancouver	BC	V7Y1B6	604-216-2949	
Dare Products Inc 860 Betterly Rd PO Box 157 *TF:* 800-922-3273 ■ *Web:* www.dareproducts.com	Battle Creek	MI	49015	269-965-2307	965-3261
Easy Drive Stake Inc 4111 Todd Ln *Web:* www.ieasydrive.com	Austin	TX	78744	512-447-9879	
Epicurean Cutting Surfaces Inc 1325 N 59th Ave W *Web:* www.epicureancs.com	Duluth	MN	55807	218-740-3500	
Federal Program Integrators LLC 12 Wabanaki Way *Web:* www.fedintegrators.com	Indian Island	ME	04468	207-817-7334	
Gizmo Art Production Inc 1315 Egbert Ave *Web:* www.gizmosf.com	San Francisco	CA	94124	415-222-6181	
Holland Bowl Mill 120 James St *Web:* www.hollandbowlmill.com	Holland	MI	49424	616-396-6513	
Kalinich Fence Company Inc 12223 Prospect Rd *Web:* www.kalinichfenceco.com	Strongsville	OH	44149	440-238-6127	238-2178
Lafitte Cork & Capsule Inc 45 Executive Ct *Web:* www.lafitte-usa.com	Napa	CA	94558	707-258-2675	
Master Halco Inc 1321 Greenway Dr **Fax Area Code:* 800 ■ **Fax:* Cust Svc ■ *TF:* 800-883-8384 ■ *Web:* www.masterhalco.com	Irving	TX	75038	972-714-7300	542-8488*
Matelski Lumber Co 2617 M 75 S *Web:* matelskilumber.com	Boyne Falls	MI	49713	231-549-2780	
Merchants Metals Inc 900 Ashwood Pkwy Ste 600 *TF:* 866-888-5611 ■ *Web:* www.merchantsmetals.com	Atlanta	GA	30338	678-731-8077	
Paddle Tramps Manufacturing Co 1317 University Ave *Web:* www.paddletramps.com	Lubbock	TX	79401	806-765-9901	
Peavey Performance Systems 10749 W 84th Ter *Web:* www.safetyjackpot.com	Lenexa	KS	66214	913-888-0600	
Riverdale Mills Corp 130 Riverdale St PO Box 200 *TF:* 800-762-6374 ■ *Web:* www.riverdale.com	Northbridge	MA	01534	508-234-8715	234-9593
Sauk Technologies 300 N Dekora Woods Blvd *Web:* www.customtank.com	Saukville	WI	53080	262-268-3800	
Taiga Building Products Ltd 4710 Kingsway Ste 800 *Web:* www.taigabuilding.com	Burnaby	BC	V5H4M2	604-438-1471	
Tru-Link Fence Co 5440 Touhy Ave *TF:* 800-568-9300 ■ *Web:* www.tru-link.com	Skokie	IL	60077	847-568-9300	568-9600
Walnut Hollow Farm Inc 1409 State Rd 23 *Web:* www.walnuthollow.com	Dodgeville	WI	53533	608-935-2341	
Western Bee Supplies Inc Five Ninth Ave E *Web:* www.westernbee.com	Polson	MT	59860	406-883-2918	

283 FERTILIZERS & PESTICIDES

SEE ALSO Farm Supplies p. 2285

				Phone	Fax
Abell Corp 2500 Sterlington Rd *TF:* 800-325-7204 ■ *Web:* www.ouachitafertilizer.com	Monroe	LA	71203	800-325-7204	
Agricultural Commodities Inc 2224 Oxford Rd	New Oxford	PA	17350	717-624-8249	
Agrium Inc 13131 Lk Fraser Dr SE *NYSE: AGU* ■ **Fax:* PR ■ *TF:* 877-247-4861 ■ *Web:* www.agrium.com	Calgary	AB	T2J7E8	403-225-7000	225-7609*
Airgas Specialty Products 2530 Sever Rd Ste 300 **Fax Area Code:* 770 ■ *TF:* 800-295-2225 ■ *Web:* www.airgasspecialtyproducts.com	Lawrenceville	GA	30043	800-295-2225	717-2222*
Alabama Farmers Co-op Inc PO Box 2227 *TF:* 888-255-2667 ■ *Web:* www.alafarm.com	Decatur	AL	35601	256-353-6843	350-1770
Alco Industries Inc 820 Adams Ave Ste 130 *Web:* www.alcoind.com	Norristown	PA	19403	610-666-0930	666-0752
Amvac Chemical Corp 4100 E Washington Blvd *TF:* 800-424-9300 ■ *Web:* www.amvac-chemical.com	Los Angeles	CA	90023	323-264-3910	268-1028
Apache Nitrogen Products Inc 1436 S Apache Powder Rd PO Box 700 *Web:* apachenitrogen.com	Benson	AZ	85602	520-720-2217	720-4158
Brandt Consolidated Inc 211 W Rt 125 PO Box 350 *Web:* www.brandt.co	Pleasant Plains	IL	62677	217-476-3438	
California Ammonia Co (CALAMCO) 1776 W March Ln Ste 420 *TF:* 800-624-4200 ■ *Web:* www.calamco.com	Stockton	CA	95207	209-982-1000	983-0822
Cargill Inc North America 15407 McGinty Rd *Web:* cargill.com	Wayzata	MN	55391	952-742-7575	
Certis USA LLC 9145 Guilford Rd Ste 175 **Fax Area Code:* 301 ■ *TF:* 800-250-5024 ■ *Web:* www.certisusa.com	Columbia	MD	21046	800-250-5024	604-7015*
CF Industries Inc Four Pkwy N Ste 400 *Web:* www.cfindustries.com	Deerfield	IL	60015	847-405-2400	405-2711
CFC Farm & Home Ctr 15172 Brandy Rd PO Box 2002 *TF:* 800-284-2667 ■ *Web:* www.cfcfarmhome.net	Culpeper	VA	22701	540-825-2200	825-2200
Coastal Agrobusiness Inc 3702 Evans St PO Box 856 *TF:* 800-758-1828 ■ *Web:* www.coastalagro.com	Greenville	NC	27835	252-756-1126	756-3282
Coffeyville Resources LLC 10 E Cambridge Cir Dr *Web:* www.coffeyvillegroup.com	Kansas City	KS	66103	913-982-0500	982-0505
Degesch America Inc PO Box 116 *TF:* 800-330-2525 ■ *Web:* www.degeschamerica.com	Weyers Cave	VA	24486	540-234-9281	234-8225
Dow AgroSciences LLC 9330 Zionsville Rd **Fax Area Code:* 800 ■ *TF:* 800-258-1470 ■ *Web:* www.dowagro.com	Indianapolis	IN	46268	317-337-3000	905-7326*
Dow Chemical Co, The 100 Independence Mall W *Web:* www.dow.com	Philadelphia	PA	19106	215-592-3000	

Company	City	State	Zip	Phone	Fax
Drexel Chemical Co 1700 Ch Ave PO Box 13327 *Web:* www.drexchem.com	Memphis	TN	38113	901-774-4370	774-4666
DuPont Crop Protection PO Box 80705 *TF:* 888-638-7668 ■ *Web:* www.dupont.com	Wilmington	DE	19880	302-774-1000	999-4399
Enforcer Products Inc PO Box 1060 **Fax Area Code:* 770 ■ *TF:* 888-805-4357 ■ *Web:* www.enforcer.com	Cartersville	GA	30120	888-805-4357	386-1659*
FMC Corp 1735 Market St *NYSE:* FMC ■ *TF:* 888-548-4486 ■ *Web:* www.fmc.com	Philadelphia	PA	19103	215-299-6000	299-5998
FMC Corp Agricultural Products Group 1735 Market St *Web:* www.fmccrop.com	Philadelphia	PA	19103	215-299-6000	299-5999
Frit Industries Inc 1792 Jodie Parker Rd *TF:* 800-633-7685 ■ *Web:* www.fritind.com	Ozark	AL	36360	334-774-2515	774-9306
Good Earth Inc PO Box 290 *Web:* www.goodearth.org	Lancaster	NY	14086	716-684-8111	684-3722
Helena Chemical Co 225 Schilling Blvd Ste 300 *Web:* www.helenachemical.com	Collierville	TN	38017	901-761-0050	821-5455
Hillshire Brands PO Box 3901 *TF:* 800-323-7117 ■ *Web:* www.hillshirebrands.com	Peoria	IL	61612	800-323-7117	
Hintzsche Fertilizer Inc 2 S 181 County Line Rd	Maple Park	IL	60151	630-557-2406	557-2557
HJ Baker & Bros Inc 228 Saugatuck Ave *Web:* hjbaker.com	Westport	CT	06880	203-682-9200	227-8351
Ibe Trade Corp 950 Third Ave 3rd Fl *Web:* www.ibetrade.com	New York	NY	10022	212-593-3255	308-3642
Intrepid Potash Inc 700 17th St Ste 1700 *NYSE:* IPI ■ *TF:* 800-451-2888 ■ *Web:* www.intrepidpotash.com	Denver	CO	80202	303-296-3006	298-7502
JR Simplot Co 999 W Main St Ste 1300 *TF:* 800-832-8893 ■ *Web:* www.simplot.com	Boise	ID	83702	208-336-2110	389-7515
Kellogg Garden Products 350 W Sepulveda Blvd **Fax Area Code:* 310 ■ *Web:* www.kellogggarden.com	Carson	CA	90745	800-232-2322	835-6174*
Kirby Agri Inc 500 Running Pump Rd PO Box 6277 *TF:* 800-745-7524 ■ *Web:* www.kirbyagri.com	Lancaster	PA	17607	717-299-2541	293-9306
Koch Nitrogen Co 4111 E 37th St N *Web:* www.kochind.com	Wichita	KS	67220	316-828-8441	829-7618
Kronos Micronutrients 213 W Moxee Ave PO Box 1167 *TF:* 800-541-4086 ■ *Web:* www.kronoslp.com	Moxee	WA	98936	509-248-4911	248-4916
Landec Ag LLC 201 N Michigan St *TF:* 800-241-7252 ■ *Web:* incotec.com	Oxford	IN	47971	765-385-1000	
Lebanon Seaboard Corp 1600 E Cumberland St *TF:* 800-233-0628 ■ *Web:* www.lebsea.com	Lebanon	PA	17042	717-273-1685	273-9466
Living Earth Technology Co 1901 California Crossing *Web:* www.livingearth.net	Dallas	TX	75220	972-506-8575	
MFA Inc 201 Ray Young Dr *Web:* www.mfaincorporated.com	Columbia	MO	65201	573-874-5111	876-5505
Miller Chemical & Fertilizer Corp 120 Radio Rd PO Box 333 *TF:* 800-233-2040 ■ *Web:* www.millerchemical.com	Hanover	PA	17331	717-632-8921	632-4581
Na-Churs/Alpine Solutions 421 Leader St *TF:* 800-622-4877 ■ *Web:* www.nachurs.com	Marion	OH	43302	740-382-5701	383-2615
PBI/Gordon Corp 1217 W 12th St PO Box 014090 *TF:* 800-821-7925 ■ *Web:* www.pbigordon.com	Kansas City	MO	64101	816-421-4070	474-0462
Potash Corp 1101 Skokie Blvd *TF:* 800-667-0403 ■ *Web:* www.potashcorp.com	Northbrook	IL	60062	847-849-4200	849-4695
Potash Corp of Saskatchewan Inc 122 First Ave S Ste 500 *NYSE:* POT ■ *TF:* 800-667-3930 ■ *Web:* www.potashcorp.com	Saskatoon	SK	S7K7G3	306-933-8500	652-2699
Safeguard Chemical Corp 411 Wales Ave *TF:* 800-536-3170 ■ *Web:* www.safeguardchemical.com	Bronx	NY	10454	718-585-3170	585-3657
SC Johnson & Son Inc 1525 Howe St *TF:* 800-494-4855 ■ *Web:* www.scjohnson.com	Racine	WI	53403	262-260-2154	260-6004
Scotts Miracle Gro Products Inc 14111 Scottslawn Rd *TF:* 888-270-3714 ■ *Web:* www.scotts.com/smg	Marysville	OH	43041	937-644-0011	644-7600
Scotts Miracle-Gro Co 14111 Scottslawn Rd *NYSE:* SMG ■ *TF Cust Svc:* 800-543-8873 ■ *Web:* www.scotts.com	Marysville	OH	43041	937-644-0011	644-7600
Share Corp 7821 N Faulkner Rd *TF:* 800-776-7192 ■ *Web:* www.sharecorp.com	Milwaukee	WI	53224	414-355-4000	355-0516
Southern States Chemical Co 1600 E President St *TF:* 888-337-8922 ■ *Web:* www.sschemical.com	Savannah	GA	31404	912-232-1101	232-1103
Spectrum Brands 3001 Deming Way **Fax Area Code:* 888 ■ *TF:* 800-566-7899 ■ *Web:* www.spectrumbrands.com	Middleton	WI	53711	608-275-3340	677-4770*
Stoller USA 4001 W Sam Houston Pkwy N Ste 100 *TF:* 800-539-5283 ■ *Web:* www.stollerusa.com	Houston	TX	77043	713-461-1493	461-4467
Summit Chemical Co 235 S Kresson St *TF:* 800-227-8664 ■ *Web:* www.summitchemical.com	Baltimore	MD	21224	410-522-0661	522-0833
Syngenta Corp 3411 Silverside Rd Ste 100 *TF:* 800-555-2470 ■ *Web:* www.syngenta.com	Wilmington	DE	19810	302-425-2000	425-2001
Syngenta Crop Protection Inc 410 Swing Rd PO Box 18300 **Fax:* Sales ■ *TF:* 800-797-5040 ■ *Web:* www.syngenta.com	Greensboro	NC	27409	336-632-6000	632-7353*
Tender Corp 106 Burndy Rd *TF:* 800-258-4696 ■ *Web:* www.tendercorp.com	Littleton	NH	03561	603-444-5464	444-6735
Trans-Resources Inc 200 W 57th St	New York	NY	10019	212-515-4100	515-4111
Valley Fertilizer & Chemical Company Inc 201 Valley Rd PO Box 816	Mount Jackson	VA	22842	540-477-3121	477-3123
Van Diest Supply Co 1434 220th St PO Box 610 *TF:* 800-779-2424 ■ *Web:* www.vdsc.com	Webster City	IA	50595	515-832-2366	832-2955
Woodstream Corp 69 N Locust St *TF All:* 800-800-1819 ■ *Web:* www.woodstreamcorp.com	Lititz	PA	17543	717-626-2125	626-1912
Y-Tex Corp 1825 Big Horn Ave PO Box 1450 *TF:* 800-443-6401 ■ *Web:* www.y-tex.com	Cody	WY	82414	307-587-5515	527-6433

284 FESTIVALS - BOOK

Festival	City	State	Zip	Phone	Fax
Amelia Island Book Festival PO Box 15286 *Web:* www.ameliaislandbookfestival.com	Fernandina Beach	FL	32035	904-624-1665	
Baltimore Book Festival Baltimore Office of Promotion 7 E Redwood St Ste 500 *Web:* baltimorebookfestival.com	Baltimore	MD	21202	410-752-8632	385-0361
Banff Mountain Book Festival The Banff Ctr PO Box 1020 Stn 38 *Web:* www.banffcentre.ca	Banff	AB	T1L1H5	403-762-6675	762-6277
Boston Globe Book Festival PO Box 55819 PO Box 2378 **Fax Area Code:* 617 ■ *Web:* www.bostonglobe.com	Boston	MA	02205	888-694-5623	929-2606*
Buckeye Book Fair 205 W Liberty St *Web:* www.buckeyebookfair.com	Wooster	OH	44691	330-262-3244	
Great Salt Lake Book Festival Utah Humanities Council 202 W 300 N *TF:* 877-786-7598 ■ *Web:* www.utahhumanities.org	Salt Lake City	UT	84103	801-359-9670	531-7869
Latino Book & Family Festival (LBFF) 3445 Catalina Dr *Web:* www.lbff.us	Carlsbad	CA	92010	858-603-8680	
Los Angeles Times Festival of Books Los Angeles Times 202 W First St *TF:* 800-528-4637 ■ *Web:* events.latimes.com	Los Angeles	CA	90012	213-237-2335	237-2335
Miami Book Fair International (MBFI) 401 NE Second Ave Ste 4102 *Web:* www.miamibookfair.com	Miami	FL	33132	305-237-3258	237-3978
National Book Festival Library of Congress 101 Independence Ave SE *TF:* 888-714-4696 ■ *Web:* www.loc.gov/bookfest	Washington	DC	20540	202-707-2777	707-9199
NOVELLO Festival of Reading Public Library of Charlotte & Mecklenburg County 310 N Tryon St *Web:* www.cmlibrary.org	Charlotte	NC	28202	704-416-0100	
South Carolina Book Festival PO Box 5287 *Web:* www.schumanities.org	Columbia	SC	29250	803-771-2477	771-2487
Southern Festival of Books Humanities Tennessee 306 Gay St Ste 306 *Web:* www.humanitiestennessee.org	Nashville	TN	37201	615-770-0006	770-0007
Southern Kentucky Book Fest Western Kentucky University Libraries & Museum Cravens Library Rm 106 *Web:* www.sokybookfest.org	Bowling Green	KY	42101	270-745-5016	745-6422
Texas Book Festival 610 Brazos St Ste 200 *TF:* 800-222-8733 ■ *Web:* www.texasbookfestival.org	Austin	TX	78701	512-477-4055	322-0722
Virginia Festival of the Book Virginia Foundation for the Humanities 145 Ednam Dr *Web:* virginiahumanities.org	Charlottesville	VA	22903	434-924-3296	296-4714

285 FESTIVALS - FILM

Festival	City	State	Zip	Phone	Fax
AFI Fest 2021 N Western Ave *Web:* www.afi.com	Los Angeles	CA	90027	323-856-7600	467-4578
Anchorage Film Festival 111 W Ninth Ave *Web:* www.anchoragefilmfestival.org	Anchorage	AK	99501	907-338-3761	786-4981
Ann Arbor Film Festival 217 N First St ?PO Box 8232? *Web:* www.aafilmfest.org	Ann Arbor	MI	48104	734-995-5356	995-5396
Arpa International Film Festival 2919 Maxwell St *Web:* www.affma.org	Los Angeles	CA	90027	323-663-1882	663-1882
Austin Film Festival 1801 Salina St Ste 210 *TF:* 800-310-3378 ■ *Web:* www.austinfilmfestival.com	Austin	TX	78702	512-478-4795	478-6205
Beverly Hills Film Festival 9663 Santa Monica Blvd Ste 777 *Web:* www.beverlyhillsfilmfestival.com	Beverly Hills	CA	90210	310-779-1206	
Boston Film Festival 126 S St *Web:* www.bostonfilmfestival.org	Rockport	MA	01966	617-523-8388	
Brooklyn International Film Festival 180 S Fourth St Ste 2S *Web:* www.brooklynfilmfestival.org	Brooklyn	NY	11211	718-486-8181	599-5039
Chicago International Film Festival Cinema Chicago 30 E Adams St Ste 800 *TF:* 800-982-2787 ■ *Web:* www.chicagofilmfestival.com	Chicago	IL	60603	312-683-0121	683-0122
Cleveland International Film Festival 2510 Market Ave *Web:* www.clevelandfilm.org	Cleveland	OH	44113	216-623-3456	623-0103
DC Independent Film Festival (DCIFF) 701 Pennsylvania Ave NW *Web:* dciff-indie.org	Washington	DC	20004	202-737-2300	
Denver International Film Festival 1510 York 3rd Fl *TF:* 800-228-5838 ■ *Web:* www.denverfilm.org	Denver	CO	80206	303-595-3456	595-0956
Fort Lauderdale International Film Festival 503 SE Sixth St *Web:* www.fliff.com	Fort Lauderdale	FL	33301	954-760-9898	760-9099
Full Frame Documentary Film Festival 320 Blackwell St Ste 101 *Web:* www.fullframefest.org	Durham	NC	27701	919-687-4100	687-4200
Heartland Film Festival 1043 Virginia Ave Ste 2 *Web:* heartlandfilm.org/	Indianapolis	IN	46203	317-464-9405	464-9409
High Falls Film Festival 45 E Ave Ste 400 *Web:* www.highfallsfilmfestival.com	Rochester	NY	14604	585-279-8312	232-4822

Phone Fax

Hot Springs Documentary Film Festival (HSDFF)
659 Ouachita Ave PO Box 6450 .... Hot Springs AR 71901 501-538-2290 321-0211
Web: www.hsdfi.org

Los Angeles International Short Film Festival
1610 Argyle Ave Ste 113 .... Hollywood CA 90028 323-461-4400
Web: www.lashortsfest.com

Maryland Film Festival 107 E Read St. .... Baltimore MD 21202 410-752-8083 752-8273
Web: www.mdfilmfest.com

Miami International Film Festival
Miami Dade College 25 NE Second St
Bldg 5 Rm 5501 .... Miami FL 33132 305-237-3456 237-7344
Web: www.miamifilmfestival.com

Mill Valley Film Festival (MVFF)
1001 Lootens Pl Ste 220 .... San Rafael CA 94901 415-383-5256 383-8606
Web: www.mvff.com

Minneapolis/St Paul International Film Festival
Minnesota Film Arts 309 Oak St SE .... Minneapolis MN 55414 612-331-7563 378-7750
Web: www.mnfilmarts.org

Montreal World Film Festival
1432 Rue de Bleury .... Montreal QC H3A2J1 514-848-3883 848-3886
Web: www.ffm-montreal.org

Nashville Film Festival 161 Rains Ave .... Nashville TN 37203 615-742-2500 742-1004
Web: www.nashvillefilmfestival.org

New Hampshire Film Festival
28 Chestnut St .... Portsmouth NH 03801 603-436-2400
Web: www.nhfilmfestival.com

New Orleans Film Festival 900 Camp St.......... New Orleans LA 70130 504-309-6633 309-0923
Web: neworleansfilmsociety.org

New York Film Festival 70 Lincoln Ctr Plaza .... New York NY 10023 212-875-5610 875-5636
Web: www.filmlinc.com

Outfest-Los Angeles Gay & Lesbian Film Festival
3470 Wilshire Blvd Ste 935 .... Los Angeles CA 90010 213-480-7088 480-7099
Web: www.outfest.org

Phoenix Film Festival
7000 E Mayo Blvd Ste 1059......................... Phoenix AZ 85054 602-955-6444 955-0966
Web: www.phoenixfilmfestival.com

Portland International Film Festival
1219 SW Pk Ave................................. Portland OR 97205 503-221-1156 294-0874
Web: www.nwfilm.org

Riverrun International Film Festival
305 W Fourth St Ste 1A .... Winston-Salem NC 27101 336-724-1502 724-1112
Web: www.riverrunfilm.com

Rochester International Film Festival
PO Box 17746 .... Rochester NY 14617 585-234-7411
Web: www.rochesterfilmfest.org

San Diego Film Festival
2683 Via de la Valle Ste G210 .... Del Mar CA 92014 619-818-2221
Web: www.sdfilmfest.com

San Francisco Film Society
39 Mesa St Ste 110 .... San Francisco CA 94129 415-561-5000 440-1760
Web: www.sfiff.org

San Jose Film Festival - CineQuest
PO Box 720040 .... San Jose CA 95172 408-995-5033 995-5713
Web: www.cinequest.org

Santa Barbara International Film Festival
1528 Chapala St Ste 203 .... Santa Barbara CA 93101 805-963-0023 962-2524
Web: sbiff.org

Sarasota Film Festival 332 Cocoanut Ave............ Sarasota FL 34236 941-364-9514 364-8411
TF: 866-575-3456 ■ *Web:* www.sarasotafilmfestival.com

Seattle International Film Festival
305 Harrison St .... Seattle WA 98109 206-464-5830 264-7919
Web: www.siff.net

Sidewalk Moving Picture Festival
310 18th St N................................ Birmingham AL 35203 205-324-0888
Web: www.sidewalkfest.com

Sonoma Valley Film Festival 103A E Napa St.......... Sonoma CA 95476 707-933-2600 933-2602
Web: www.sonomafilmfest.org

South by Southwest Film Festival
500 E Cesar Chavez St .... Austin TX 78701 512-467-7979 451-0754
Web: www.sxsw.com

Sundance Film Festival 1895 Sidewinder Dr.......... Park City UT 84060 801-328-3456 575-5175
Web: www.sundance.org/festival

Telluride Film Festival 800 Jones St................. Berkeley CA 94710 510-665-9494 665-9589
Web: www.telluridefilmfestival.org

Toronto International Film Festival Inc
Reitman Sq 350 King St W.......................... Toronto ON M5V3X5 888-599-8433
TF: 888-599-8433 ■ *Web:* www.tiff.net

Worldfest Houston International Film Festival
PO Box 56566 .... Houston TX 77256 713-629-3700 965-9960
TF: 866-965-9955 ■ *Web:* www.houstontheatre.com

286 FIRE PROTECTION SYSTEMS

SEE ALSO Personal Protective Equipment & Clothing p. 2914; Safety Equipment - Mfr p. 3130; Security Products & Services p. 3160

Phone Fax

BRK Brands Inc 3901 Liberty St Rd .... Aurora IL 60504 630-851-7330 851-7452
TF: 800-323-9005 ■ *Web:* www.firstalert.com

Chemetron Fire Systems
16 W 361 S Frontage Rd Ste 125 .... Burr Ridge IL 60527 708-748-1503 748-2847
TF Cust Svc: 800-878-5631 ■ *Web:* www.chemetron.com

Fike Corp 704 SW Tenth St .... Blue Springs MO 64015 816-229-3405 228-9277
TF: 877-342-3453 ■ *Web:* www.fike.com

Fire & Life Safety America
3017 Vernon Rd Ste 100.......................... Richmond VA 23228 804-222-1381 222-4393
TF: 800-252-5069 ■ *Web:* flsamerica.com

Fire Systems West Inc 206 Frontage Rd N Ste C .... Pacific WA 98047 253-833-1248 735-0113
Web: www.firesystemswest.com

Firecom Inc 39-27 59th St........................ Woodside NY 11377 718-899-6100 899-1932
TF: 888-347-3269 ■ *Web:* firecominc.com

Phone Fax

First Alert Inc 3901 Liberty St Rd...................... Aurora IL 60504 630-851-7330 851-9254
TF: 800-323-9005 ■ *Web:* www.firstalert.com

Gamewell FCI 12 Clintonville Rd .... Northford CT 06472 203-484-7161 484-7118
TF: 800-606-1983 ■ *Web:* www.gamewell-fci.com

General Monitors Inc 26776 Simpatica Cir .... Lake Forest CA 92630 949-581-4464 581-1151
TF: 866-686-0741 ■ *Web:* www.generalmonitors.com

Harrington Signal Co 2519 Fourth Ave................ Moline IL 61265 309-762-0731 762-8215
Web: www.harringtonsignal.com

Honeywell Fire Solutions One Fire-Lite Pl .... Northford CT 06472 203-484-7161 484-7118
TF: 800-627-3473 ■ *Web:* www.firelite.com

Kidde Aerospace 4200 Airport Dr NW.................. Wilson NC 27896 252-237-7004 246-7181*
**Fax:* Hum Res ■ *Web:* utcaerospacesystems.com

Meggitt Safety Systems Inc
1915 Voyager Ave............................. Simi Valley CA 93063 805-584-4100 578-3400
Web: www.meggitt.com

Potter Electric Signal Company Inc
5757 Phantom Dr Ste 125 .... Hazelwood MO 63042 314-878-4321 595-6999
TF: 800-325-3936 ■ *Web:* www.pottersignal.com

Siemens Bldg Technologies Inc Fire Safety Div
8 Fernwood Rd................................ Florham Park NJ 07932 973-593-2600 593-6670
TF: 888-303-3353 ■ *Web:* usa.siemens.com/infrastructure-cities/us/en/

Silent Knight 7550 Meridian Cir Ste 100 .... Maple Grove MN 55369 763-493-6400 493-6475
TF: 800-328-0103 ■ *Web:* www.silentknight.com

Smeal Fire Apparatus Co
610 W Fourth St PO Box 8 .... Snyder NE 68664 402-568-2224 568-2346
Web: www.smeal.com

Task Force Tips Inc 3701 Innovation Way............ Valparaiso IN 46383 219-462-6161 464-7155
TF: 800-348-2686 ■ *Web:* www.tft.com

Tyco SimplexGrinnell 50 Technology Dr........... Westminster MA 01441 978-731-2500
TF: 800-746-7539 ■ *Web:* www.simplexgrinnell.com

Viking Corp 210 N Industrial Pk Dr.................. Hastings MI 49058 269-945-9501 945-9599
TF: 800-968-9501 ■ *Web:* www.vikingcorp.com

287 FIREARMS & AMMUNITION (NON-MILITARY)

SEE ALSO Sporting Goods p. 3182; Weapons & Ordnance (Military) p. 3295

Phone Fax

American Derringer Corp 127 N Lacy Dr................ Waco TX 76705 254-799-9111 799-7935
Web: www.amderringer.com

Beretta USA Corp 17601 Beretta Dr.................. Accokeek MD 20607 301-283-2191 283-0189
TF: 800-237-3882 ■ *Web:* www.berettausa.com

Connecticut Valley Arms (CVA)
1685 Boggs Rd Ste 300 .... Duluth GA 30096 770-449-4687 242-8546
TF: 800-320-8767 ■ *Web:* www.cva.com

Crosman Corp 7629 Rt 5 & 20..................... Bloomfield NY 14469 585-657-6161 657-5405
TF: 800-724-7486 ■ *Web:* www.crosman.com

Defense Technology/Federal Laboratories
1855 S Loop PO Box 248............................. Casper WY 82601 307-235-2136 473-2713
TF: 877-248-3835 ■ *Web:* www.defense-technology.com

Federal Cartridge Co 900 Ehlen Dr .... Anoka MN 55303 800-379-1732 323-2506*
**Fax Area Code:* 763 ■ **Fax:* Hum Res ■ *TF:* 800-379-1732 ■ *Web:* www.federalpremium.com

Freedom Arms Inc 314 Wyoming 239................ Freedom WY 83120 307-883-2468 883-2005
Web: www.freedomarms.com

Galion LLC 515 NE St PO Box 447 .... Galion OH 44833 419-468-5214 468-1661
Web: www.galionllc.com

Glock Inc 6000 Highlands Pkwy .... Smyrna GA 30082 770-432-1202 433-8719
Web: www.glock.com

Green Mountain Rifle Barrel Co
153 W Main St PO Box 2670 .... Conway NH 03818 603-447-1095 447-1099
Web: www.gmriflebarrel.com

Gun Parts Corp 226 Williams Ln .... Kingston NY 12401 845-679-4867 486-7278*
**Fax Area Code:* 877 ■ *TF:* 866-686-7424 ■ *Web:* www.gunpartscorp.com

H & R 1871 60 Industrial Rowe .... Gardner MA 01440 866-776-9292 548-7801*
**Fax Area Code:* 336 ■ *TF:* 866-776-9292 ■ *Web:* www.hr1871.com

Heckler & Koch Inc 5675 Transport Blvd .... Columbus GA 31907 706-568-1906 568-9151
Web: www.hk-usa.com

Heritage Mfg Inc 16175 NW 49th Ave................. Hialeah FL 33014 305-685-5966 687-6721
Web: www.heritagemfg.com

Hornady Manufacturing Co
3625 W Old Potash Hwy........................ Grand Island NE 68803 308-382-1390 382-5761
TF: 800-338-3220 ■ *Web:* www.hornady.com

Knight Rifles 213 Dennis st Athens .... Athens TN 37303 866-518-4181
TF: 866-518-4181 ■ *Web:* www.knightrifles.com

Lyman Products Corp 475 Smith St .... Middletown CT 06457 860-632-2020 632-1699
TF: 800-225-9626 ■ *Web:* www.lymanproducts.com

Marlin Firearms Co PO Box 1871.................... Madison NC 27025 800-544-8892 548-7801*
**Fax Area Code:* 336 ■ *TF Cust Svc:* 800-544-8892 ■ *Web:* www.marlinfirearms.com

OF Mossberg & Sons Inc Seven Grasso Ave........ North Haven CT 06473 203-230-5300 230-5420*
**Fax:* Mktg ■ *TF:* 800-363-3555 ■ *Web:* www.mossberg.com

Olin Corp Winchester Div
427 N Shamrock St............................. East Alton IL 62024 618-258-2000 258-3084
TF: 800-356-2666 ■ *Web:* www.winchester.com

Remington Arms Company Inc
870 Remington Dr PO Box 700..................... Madison NC 27025 336-548-8700 548-7801
TF: 800-243-9700 ■ *Web:* www.remington.com

Savage Arms Inc 100 Springdale Rd................. Westfield MA 01085 413-568-7001 378-4688*
**Fax Area Code:* 714 ■ *TF:* 800-243-3220 ■ *Web:* www.savagearms.com

SIG SAUER Inc 18 Industrial Dr....................... Exeter NH 03833 603-772-2302 772-9082
TF: 866-345-6744 ■ *Web:* www.sigsauer.com

Smith & Wesson Corp 2100 Roosevelt Ave........... Springfield MA 01104 413-781-8300 747-3317
TF Cust Svc: 800-331-0852 ■ *Web:* www.smith-wesson.com

Smith & Wesson Holding Corp
2100 Roosevelt Ave .... Springfield MA 01104 413-781-8300 747-3317
NASDAQ: SWHC ■ *TF:* 800-372-6454 ■ *Web:* www.smith-wesson.com

Springfield Armory 420 W Main St................... Geneseo IL 61254 309-944-5631 944-3676
TF: 800-680-6866 ■ *Web:* www.springfield-armory.com

Taurus International Mfg Inc 16175 NW 49th Ave....... Miami FL 33014 305-624-1115 624-1126
TF: 800-327-3776 ■ *Web:* www.taurususa.com

Weatherby Inc 1605 Commerce Way .... Paso Robles CA 93446 805-227-2600 237-0427
TF: 800-227-2016 ■ *Web:* www.weatherby.com

				Phone	Fax
Williams Gun Sight Co 7389 Lapeer Rd *TF:* 800-530-9028 ■ *Web:* www.williamsgunsight.com	Davison	MI	48423	810-653-2131	658-2140

288 FISHING - COMMERCIAL

				Phone	Fax
American Seafoods Holdings LLC 2025 First Ave Ste 900 *Web:* www.americanseafoods.com	Seattle	WA	98121	206-374-1515	374-1516
Arctic Storm Management Group LLC 2727 Alaskan Way Pier 69 *TF:* 800-929-0908 ■ *Web:* www.arcticstorm.com	Seattle	WA	98121	206-547-6557	547-3165
Blue North Fisheries Inc 2930 Westlake Ave N Ste 300 *TF:* 877-878-3263 ■ *Web:* bluenorth.com/	Seattle	WA	98109	206-352-9252	352-9380
Bon Secour Fisheries Inc 17449 County Rd 49 S *TF:* 800-633-6854 ■ *Web:* www.bonsecourfisheries.com	Bon Secour	AL	36511	251-949-7411	949-6478
Canadian Fishing Co Foot of Gore Ave *TF:* 877-506-1294 ■ *Web:* www.canfisco.com	Vancouver	BC	V6A2Y7	604-681-0211	681-3277
JH Miles & Co Inc 902 S Hampton Ave	Norfolk	VA	23510	757-622-9264	622-9261
Lund's Fisheries Inc 997 Ocean Dr PO Box 830 *Web:* www.lundsfish.com	Cape May	NJ	08204	609-884-7600	884-0664
North Pacific Corp 5612 Lake Washington Blvd NE *Web:* www.npc-usa.com	Kirkland	WA	98033	425-822-1001	822-1004
Nova Fisheries 2532 Yale Ave E *TF:* 888-458-6682 ■ *Web:* www.novafish.com	Seattle	WA	98102	206-781-2000	781-9011
Ocean Beauty Seafoods Inc 1100 W Ewing St *TF:* 800-365-8950 ■ *Web:* www.oceanbeauty.com	Seattle	WA	98119	206-285-6800	
Raffield Fisheries Inc 1624 Grouper Ave PO Box 309 *Web:* www.raffieldfisheries.com	Port Saint Joe	FL	32456	850-229-8229	229-8782
Sahlman Seafoods Inc 1601 Sahlman Dr PO Box 5009 *Web:* www.sahlmanseafood.com	Tampa	FL	33605	813-248-5726	247-5787
Trident Seafood Corp 5303 Shilshole Ave NW *TF:* 800-426-5490 ■ *Web:* www.tridentseafoods.com	Seattle	WA	98107	206-783-3818	782-7195
Wanchese Fish Co 2000 Northgate Commerce Pkwy *Web:* www.wanchese.com	Suffolk	VA	23435	757-673-4500	673-4550

289 FIXTURES - OFFICE & STORE

SEE ALSO Commercial & Industrial Furniture p. 2344

				Phone	Fax
Able Steel Equipment Co Inc 50-02 23rd St *TF:* 800-428-8722 ■ *Web:* www.ablesteelequipment.com	Long Island City	NY	11101	718-361-9240	937-5742
Advanced Equipment Corp 2401 W Commonwealth Ave *Web:* www.advancedequipment.com	Fullerton	CA	92833	714-635-5350	525-6083
American Sanitary Partition Corp 300 Enterprise St PO Box 99 *Web:* www.am-sanitary-partition.com	Ocoee	FL	34761	407-656-0611	656-8189
Ampco Products Inc 11400 NW 36th Ave **Fax Area Code:* 866 ■ *Web:* www.ampco.com	Miami	FL	33167	305-821-5700	642-5300*
Angola Wire Products Inc 803 Wohlert St *TF:* 800-800-7225 ■ *Web:* www.angolawire.com	Angola	IN	46703	260-665-9447	665-6182
Architectural Bronze Aluminum Corp 655 Deerfield Rd Ste 100 **Fax Area Code:* 847 ■ *TF:* 800-339-6581 ■ *Web:* www.architecturalbronze.com	Deerfield	IL	60015	800-339-6581	266-7301*
Aspects Inc 9441 Opal Ave	Mentone	CA	92359	909-794-7722	794-6996
Bel-Mar Wire Products Inc 2343 N Damen Ave *Web:* www.belmarwire.net	Chicago	IL	60647	773-342-3800	342-0038
Benner-Nawman Inc 3450 Sabin Brown Rd *TF:* 800-992-3833 ■ *Web:* www.bnproducts.com	Wickenburg	AZ	85390	928-684-2813	684-7041
Bennett Mfg Company Inc 13315 Railroad St *Web:* www.bennettmfg.com	Alden	NY	14004	716-937-9161	937-3137
Best-Rite Mfg 2885 Lorraine Ave PO Box D *TF:* 800-749-2258 ■ *Web:* www.moorecoinc.com	Temple	TX	76501	800-749-2258	697-6258
Bob-Leon Plastics Inc 5151 Franklin Blvd *Web:* www.bob-leon.com	Sacramento	CA	95820	916-452-4063	452-3759
Borroughs Corp 3002 N Burdick St *TF:* 800-748-0227 ■ *Web:* www.borroughs.com	Kalamazoo	MI	49004	269-342-0161	342-4161
Boston Group 400 Riverside Ave **Fax Area Code:* 781 ■ *TF:* 800-225-1633 ■ *Web:* www.bostonretail.com	Medford	MA	02155	800-225-1633	391-5766*
Cal-Partitions Inc 23814 President Ave *Web:* www.calpartitions.com	Harbor City	CA	90710	310-539-1911	
Cano Corp 225 Industrial Rd *Web:* www.canocorp.com	Fitchburg	MA	01420	978-342-0953	342-5082
Carolina Cabinet Co 3363 Hwy 301 N *Web:* www.3c-inc.net	Wilson	NC	27893	252-291-5181	291-8039
Churchill Cabinet Co 4616 W 19th St *TF Sales:* 800-379-9776 ■ *Web:* www.chicago-gaming.com	Cicero	IL	60804	708-780-0070	780-9762
Consolidated Storage Cos 225 Main St **Fax Area Code:* 888 ■ *TF Cust Svc:* 800-323-0801 ■ *Web:* www.equipto.com	Tatamy	PA	18085	610-253-2775	859-2121*
Cres-Cor 5925 Heisley Rd *TF:* 877-273-7267 ■ *Web:* www.crescor.com	Mentor	OH	44060	440-350-1100	350-7267
Crown Metal Manufacturing Co 765 S SR 83 *Web:* www.crownmetal.com	Elmhurst	IL	60126	630-279-9800	279-9807
Datum Filing Systems Inc 89 Church Rd *TF:* 800-828-8018 ■ *Web:* datumstorage.com/	Emigsville	PA	17318	717-764-6350	764-6656
DeBourgh Manufacturing Co 27505 Otero Ave PO Box 981 **Fax Area Code:* 719 ■ *TF:* 800-328-8829 ■ *Web:* www.debourgh.com	La Junta	CO	81050	800-328-8829	384-8161*
Design Workshops 486 Lesser St *Web:* www.design-workshops.com	Oakland	CA	94601	510-434-0727	434-0727
Dixie Store Fixtures & Sales Company Inc 2425 First Ave N *TF:* 800-323-4943 ■ *Web:* www.dixiestorefixtures.com	Birmingham	AL	35203	205-322-2442	322-2445
Durham Manufacturing Co 201 Main St *TF:* 800-243-3774 ■ *Web:* www.durhammfg.com	Durham	CT	06422	860-349-3427	349-8235
Econoco Corp 300 Karin Ln **Fax Area Code:* 800 ■ *TF:* 800-645-7032 ■ *Web:* www.econoco.com	Hicksville	NY	11801	516-935-7700	505-8300*
Edsal Mfg Company Inc 4400 S Packers Ave *Web:* www.edsal.com	Chicago	IL	60609	773-254-0600	
EQUIPTO 225 Main St **Fax Area Code:* 888 ■ *TF:* 800-323-0801 ■ *Web:* www.equipto.com	Tatamy	PA	18085	610-253-2775	859-2121*
Ex-Cell Metal Products Inc 11240 Melrose St *TF:* 800-392-3557 ■ *Web:* www.ex-cell.com	Franklin Park	IL	60131	847-451-0451	261-9448
Eyelematic Mfg Company Inc One Seemar Rd	Watertown	CT	06795	860-274-6791	
Farmington Displays Inc 21 Hyde Rd *Web:* www.fdi-group.com	Farmington	CT	06032	860-677-2497	677-1418
Ferrante Manufacturing Co 6626 Gratiot Ave *Web:* ferrantemfg.com	Detroit	MI	48207	313-571-1111	571-0325
Frazier Industrial Co 91 Fairview Ave *TF:* 800-859-1342 ■ *Web:* www.frazier.com	Long Valley	NJ	07853	908-876-3001	876-3615
General Partitions Manufacturing Corp 1702 Peninsula Dr PO Box 8370 *Web:* generalpartitions.com	Erie	PA	16505	814-833-1154	838-3473
Giannelli Cabinets 19443 Londelius St	Northridge	CA	91324	818-882-9787	
Giffin Interior & Fixture Inc 500 Scotti Dr *Web:* giffininterior.com	Bridgeville	PA	15017	412-221-1166	221-3745
Goebel Fixture Co 528 Dale St *TF:* 800-727-4646 ■ *Web:* www.gf.com	Hutchinson	MN	55350	320-587-2112	587-2378
Hamilton Sorter Co Inc 3158 Production Dr **Fax Area Code:* 800 ■ *TF:* 800-503-9966 ■ *Web:* www.hamiltonsorter.com	Fairfield	OH	45014	513-870-4400	503-9963*
Handy Store Fixtures Inc 337 Sherman Ave *TF:* 800-631-4280 ■ *Web:* www.handystorefixtures.com	Newark	NJ	07114	973-242-1600	642-6222
Harbor Industries Inc 14130 172nd Ave *TF:* 800-968-6993 ■ *Web:* www.harbor-ind.com	Grand Haven	MI	49417	616-842-5330	842-1385
Holcomb & Hoke Mfg Company Inc 1545 Van Buren St *Web:* www.foldoor.com	Indianapolis	IN	46203	317-784-2448	781-9164
Hoosier Co 5421 W 86th St PO Box 681064 *TF:* 800-521-4184 ■ *Web:* www.hoosierco.com	Indianapolis	IN	46268	317-872-8125	872-7183
Hufcor Inc 2101 Kennedy Rd *TF:* 800-356-6968 ■ *Web:* www.hufcor.com	Janesville	WI	53545	608-756-1241	756-1246
Hurco Design & Mfg 200 W 33rd St	Ogden	UT	84401	801-394-9471	394-8218
IDX Corp One Rider Trail Plaza Dr Ste 400 *Web:* www.idxcorporation.com	Earth City	MO	63045	314-739-4120	739-4129
Imperial Counters Inc 725 Spiral Blvd *Web:* www.imperialcounters.com	Hastings	MN	55033	651-437-3903	438-3855
InterMetro Industries Corp 651 N Washington St **Fax:* Hum Res ■ *TF Cust Svc:* 800-992-1776 ■ *Web:* www.metro.com	Wilkes-Barre	PA	18705	570-825-2741	823-2852*
International Visual Corp (IVC) 11839 Rodolphe Forget *TF:* 866-643-0570 ■ *Web:* www.ivcweb.com	Montreal	QC	H1E7J8	514-643-0570	643-4867
Jaken Company Inc 6842 Walker St *Web:* www.jaken.com	La Palma	CA	90623	714-522-1700	522-1788
Jesco-Wipco Industries Inc 950 Anderson Rd PO Box 388 *TF:* 800-455-0019 ■ *Web:* www.jescoonline.com	Litchfield	MI	49252	517-542-2903	542-2501
JL Industries Inc 4450 W 78th St Cir *TF:* 800-554-6077 ■ *Web:* www.activarcpg.com	Bloomington	MN	55435	952-835-6850	835-2218
John Boos & Co 3601 S Banker St PO Box 609 *TF:* 888-431-2667 ■ *Web:* www.johnboos.com	Effingham	IL	62401	217-347-7701	347-7705
JR Jones Fixture Co 3216 Winnetka Ave N *Web:* jonesfixture.com	Minneapolis	MN	55427	763-544-4239	544-3106
Kardex Systems Inc 114 Westview Ave PO Box 171 **Fax:* Mktg ■ *TF:* 800-639-5805 ■ *Web:* www.kardex.com	Marietta	OH	45750	740-374-9300	374-9953*
Karges Furniture Company Inc 1501 W Maryland St *TF:* 800-252-7437 ■ *Web:* www.karges.com	Evansville	IN	47710	812-425-2291	425-4016
Kawneer Company Inc 555 Guthridge Ct *Web:* www.kawneer.com	Norcross	GA	30092	770-449-5555	734-1560
Kent Corp 4446 Pinson Valley Pkwy *TF:* 800-252-5368 ■ *Web:* www.kentcorp.com	Birmingham	AL	35215	205-853-3420	856-3622
Killion Industries Inc 1380 Poinsettia Ave *TF:* 800-421-5352 ■ *Web:* www.killionindustries.com	Vista	CA	92081	760-727-5102	727-5108
Knickerbocker Partition Corp 193 Hanse Ave PO Box 690 *Web:* www.knickerbockerpartition.com	Freeport	NY	11520	516-546-0550	546-0549
Kwik-Wall Co 1010 E Edwards St *TF:* 800-280-5945 ■ *Web:* www.kwik-wall.com	Springfield	IL	62703	217-522-5553	522-1170
LA Darling Co 1401 Hwy 49B *TF:* 800-643-3499 ■ *Web:* www.ladarling.com	Paragould	AR	72450	870-239-9564	239-6427
Lista International Corp 106 Lowland St *TF Cust Svc:* 800-722-3020 ■ *Web:* www.listaintl.com	Holliston	MA	01746	508-429-1350	429-0711
Lozier Corp 6336 John J Pershing Dr **Fax:* Cust Svc ■ *TF:* 800-228-9882 ■ *Web:* www.lozier.com	Omaha	NE	68110	402-457-8000	457-8297*
Lyon Work Space Products 420 N Main St *TF:* 800-433-8488 ■ *Web:* www.lyonworkspace.com	Montgomery	IL	60538	630-892-8941	892-8966
M.E.G. LLC 502 S Green St PO Box 240 **Fax Area Code:* 765 ■ *TF Cust Svc:* 800-645-3315 ■ *Web:* www.megfixtures.com	Cambridge City	IN	47327	800-645-3315	478-4439*
Metpar Corp 95 State St *Web:* www.metpar.com	Westbury	NY	11590	516-333-2600	333-2618
Miller/Zell Inc 4715 Frederick Dr SW *Web:* www.millerzell.com	Atlanta	GA	30336	404-691-7400	699-2189
Millrock *RiverRun Commercial* 4660 Early Rd *Web:* www.riverruncommercial.com	Mt. Crawford	VA	22841	540-437-3458	
Modern Woodcrafts LLC 72 NW Dr Farmington Industrial Pk *Web:* www.modernwoodcrafts.com	Plainville	CT	06062	860-677-7371	676-8381

Phone Fax

Modernfold Inc 215 W New Rd Greenfield IN 46140 800-869-9685 410-5016*
*Fax Area Code: 866 ■ TF: 800-869-9685 ■ Web: www.modernfold.com

Modular Systems Inc 169 Pk St Fruitport MI 49415 231-865-3167 865-6101
Web: www.mod-eez.com

Monarch Industries Inc 99 Main St Warren RI 02885 401-247-5200
Web: www.monarchinc.com

National Partitions 10300 Goldenfern Ln Knoxville TN 37931 865-670-2100
TF: 888-818-5749 ■ Web: www.n-p.com

NNM Peterson Manufacturing Co
24133 W 143rd St Plainfield IL 60544 815-436-9201 436-2863
TF: 800-826-9086 ■ Web: www.peterson-mfg.com

Northway Industries Inc
434 Paxtonville Rd PO Box 277 Middleburg PA 17842 570-837-1564 837-1575
Web: www.northwayind.com

Oak & More Ltd 4949 SE 25th Ave Portland OR 97202 503-245-4522 245-4503

Pacific Fixture Company Inc
12860 San Fernando Rd Unit B Sylmar CA 91342 818-362-2130 367-8968
TF: 800-272-2349 ■ Web: www.pacificfixture.com

Packard Industries Inc 1515 US 31 N Niles MI 49120 269-684-2550 684-2422
TF: 800-253-0866 ■ Web: www.packardindustries.com

Pan-Osten Co 6944 Louisville Rd Bowling Green KY 42101 270-783-3900 783-3911
TF: 800-472-6678 ■ Web: www.panoston.com

Panelfold Inc 10700 NW 36th Ave Miami FL 33167 305-688-3501 688-0185
TF: 800-433-3222 ■ Web: www.panelfold.com

Pentwater Wire Products Inc (PWP)
474 Carroll St PO Box 947 Pentwater MI 49449 231-869-6911 869-4020
TF: 877-869-6911 ■ Web: www.pentwaterwire.com

Plasticrest Products Inc 4519 W Harrison St Chicago IL 60624 773-826-2163 826-4227
TF: 800-828-2163 ■ Web: signaturejewelrypackaging.com

Racks Inc PO Box 530840 San Diego CA 92153 619-661-0987
TF: 877-920-7225 ■ Web: www.racksinc.com

RC Smith Co 14200 Southcross Dr W Burnsville MN 55306 952-854-0711 854-8160
TF: 800-747-7648 ■ Web: www.rcsmith.com

Reeve Store Equipment Co
9131 Bermudez St PO Box 276 Pico Rivera CA 90660 562-949-2535 949-3862
TF: 800-927-3383 ■ Web: www.reeveco.com

Republic Storage Systems LLC
1038 Belden Ave NE Canton OH 44705 330-438-5800 454-7772
TF Sales: 800-477-1255 ■ Web: www.republicstorage.com

Ridg-U-Rak Inc 120 S Lake St PO Box 150 North East PA 16428 814-725-8751 725-5659
TF: 866-479-7225 ■ Web: www.ridgurak.com

Russ Bassett Co 8189 Byron Rd Whittier CA 90606 562-945-2445 698-8972
TF: 800-350-2445 ■ Web: www.russbassett.com

Salsbury Industries Inc 1010 E 62nd St Los Angeles CA 90001 323-846-6700 846-6800
TF: 800-624-5299 ■ Web: www.mailboxes.com

Sandusky Cabinets Inc
16125 Widmere Rd PO Box 517 Arvin CA 93203 661-854-5551 854-2003
TF Cust Svc: 800-886-8688 ■ Web: www.sanduskycabinets.com

Semasys Inc 702 Ashland St Houston TX 77007 713-869-8331 869-5077
TF Cust Svc: 800-231-1425 ■ Web: www.semasys.com

Showbest Fixture Corp 4112 Sarellen Rd Richmond VA 23231 804-222-5535 222-7220
Web: www.showbest.com

Southern Imperial Inc 1400 Eddy Ave Rockford IL 61103 815-877-7041
TF Cust Svc: 800-747-4665 ■ Web: www.southernimperial.com

SpaceGuard Products Inc 711 S Commerce Dr Seymour IN 47274 812-523-3044 428-5758*
*Fax Area Code: 800 ■ TF: 800-841-0680 ■ Web: www.spaceguardproducts.com

Spacesaver Corp 1450 Janesville Ave Fort Atkinson WI 53538 800-255-8170 563-2702*
*Fax Area Code: 920 ■ TF: 800-492-3434 ■ Web: www.spacesaver.com

Sparks Marketing Group Inc
2828 Charter Rd Philadelphia PA 19154 215-676-1100
TF: 800-925-7727 ■ Web: www.sparksonline.com

Spectrum Industries Inc 925 First Ave Chippewa Falls WI 54729 715-723-6750 335-0473*
*Fax Area Code: 800 ■ TF: 800-235-1262 ■ Web: www.spectrumfurniture.com

SPG International 11230 Harland Dr Covington GA 30014 877-503-4774 577-2210*
*Fax Area Code: 800 ■ TF: 877-503-4774 ■ Web: www.spgusa.com

Stanley Vidmar Storage Technologies
11 Grammes Rd Allentown PA 18103 800-523-9462 523-9934
TF: 800-523-9462 ■ Web: www.stanleyvidmar.com

Stanly Fixtures Company Inc
11635 NC 138 Hwy PO Box 616 Norwood NC 28128 704-474-3184 474-3011
Web: www.stanlyfixtures.com

Stevens Industries Inc 704 W Main St Teutopolis IL 62467 217-540-3100 857-7101
Web: www.stevensind.com

Stevens Wire Products Inc
351 NW 'F' St PO Box 1146 Richmond IN 47374 765-966-5534 962-3586
Web: www.stevenswire.com

Store Kraft Mfg Co 500 Irving St Beatrice NE 68310 402-223-2348 223-1268
Web: www.storekraft.com

Streater Inc 411 S First Ave Albert Lea MN 56007 800-527-4197 373-7630*
*Fax Area Code: 507 ■ TF: 800-527-4197 ■ Web: www.streater.com

Structural Concepts Corp 888 Porter Rd Muskegon MI 49441 231-798-8888 798-4960
TF: 800-433-9489 ■ Web: www.structuralconcepts.com

Stylmark Inc PO Box 32008 Minneapolis MN 55432 763-574-7474 574-1415
TF: 800-328-2495 ■ Web: www.stylmark.com

Sumner Group Inc 2121 Hampton Ave Saint Louis MO 63139 314-633-8000 633-8002
Web: www.sumner-group.com

Tarrant Interiors Inc 5000 S Fwy Fort Worth TX 76115 817-922-5000 922-5015

Tesko Welding & Manufacturing Co
7350 W Montrose Ave Norridge IL 60706 708-452-0045 452-0112
TF: 800-621-4514 ■ Web: teskoenterprises.com

Timely Inc 10241 Norris Ave Pacoima CA 91331 818-492-3500 899-2677
TF: 800-247-6242 ■ Web: www.timelyframes.com

TJ Hale Co
W 139 N 9499 Hwy 145 PO Box 250 Menomonee Falls WI 53051 262-255-5555 255-5678
TF: 800-236-4253 ■ Web: www.tjhale.com

Trendway Corp 13467 Quincy St PO Box 9016 Holland MI 49422 616-399-3900 399-2231
TF: 800-968-5344 ■ Web: www.trendway.com

Trion Industries Inc 297 Laird St Wilkes-Barre PA 18702 570-824-1000 824-0802
TF: 800-444-4665 ■ Web: www.triononline.com

Unarco Material Handling Inc
701 16th Ave E Springfield TN 37172 800-862-7261 382-2777*
*Fax Area Code: 615 ■ TF: 800-862-7261 ■ Web: www.unarcorack.com

Viking Metal Cabinet Co
24047 W Lockport St Ste 209 Plainfield IL 60544 800-776-7767 863-7065*
*Fax Area Code: 630 ■ TF: 800-776-7767 ■ Web: www.vikingmetal.com

VIRA Insight LLC 1 Buckingham Ave Perth Amboy NJ 08861 732-442-8472 442-8464
Web: www.viranet.com

W/M Display Group 1040 W 40th St Chicago IL 60609 773-254-3700 254-3188
TF: 800-443-2000 ■ Web: www.wmdisplay.com

Weis/Robart Partitions Inc
3501 E La Palma Ave Anaheim CA 92806 714-666-0108 666-0110
Web: www.weisrobart.com

Western Pacific Storage Systems Inc
300 E Arrow Hwy San Dimas CA 91773 800-732-9777 451-0311*
*Fax Area Code: 909 ■ TF: 800-732-9777 ■ Web: www.wpss.com

WJ Egli Company Inc 205 E Columbia St Alliance OH 44601 330-823-3666 823-0011
Web: www.wjegli.com

290 FLAGS, BANNERS, PENNANTS

Phone Fax

Aaa Flag & Banner Manufacturing Co
8955 National Blvd Los Angeles CA 90034 800-266-4222 836-7253*
*Fax Area Code: 310 ■ TF: 800-266-4222 ■ Web: www.aaaflag.com

Annin & Co 105 Eisenhower Pkwy Roseland NJ 07068 973-228-9400 228-4905
TF: 800-534-5611 ■ Web: www.annin.com

Eder Flag Mfg Company Inc
1000 W Rawson Ave Oak Creek WI 53154 414-764-3522 333-7329*
*Fax Area Code: 800 ■ *Fax: Orders ■ TF: 800-558-6044 ■ Web: www.ederflagnews.com

Metro Flag 353 Richard Mine Rd Ste 100 Wharton NJ 07885 973-366-1776 366-0956
Web: nationalflag.com

National Banner Co 11938 Harry Hines Blvd Dallas TX 75234 972-241-2131 468-0700*
*Fax Area Code: 800 ■ TF: 800-527-0860

Olympus Flag & Banner 9000 W Heather Ave Milwaukee WI 53224 414-355-2010 355-1931
TF: 800-558-9620 ■ Web: olympusgrp.com

291 FLASH MEMORY DEVICES

Phone Fax

Advanced Micro Devices Inc (AMD)
One AMD Pl PO Box 3453 Sunnyvale CA 94088 408-749-4000
NYSE: AMD ■ TF: 800-538-8450 ■ Web: www.amd.com

Kingston Technology Co
17600 Newhope St Fountain Valley CA 92708 714-435-2600 435-2699
TF: 800-835-6575 ■ Web: www.kingston.com

Lexar Media Inc 47300 Bayside Pkwy Fremont CA 94538 510-413-1200 440-3499
TF: 877-747-4031 ■ Web: www.lexar.com

Micron Technology Inc 8000 S Federal Way Boise ID 83707 208-368-4000 368-4617
NASDAQ: MU ■ TF: 888-363-2589 ■ Web: www.micron.com

PNY Technologies Inc 299 Webro Rd Parsippany NJ 07054 973-515-9700 560-5590*
*Fax: Sales ■ TF: 800-769-7079 ■ Web: www3.pny.com

SanDisk Corp 601 McCarthy Blvd Milpitas CA 95035 408-801-1000 801-8657
NASDAQ: SNDK ■ Web: www.sandisk.com

Sharp Microelectronics of the Americas
5700 NW Pacific Rim Blvd Camas WA 98607 360-834-2500 834-8903
Web: www.sharpsma.com

Sony Electronics Inc One Sony Dr Park Ridge NJ 07656 201-930-1000 358-4058*
*Fax: Hum Res ■ TF Cust Svc: 800-222-7669 ■ Web: www.sony.com

Spansion Inc 915 DeGuigne Dr Sunnyvale CA 94085 408-962-2500
NYSE: CODE ■ TF: 866-772-6746 ■ Web: www.spansion.com

292 FLEET LEASING & MANAGEMENT

Phone Fax

Allstate Leasing Inc One Olympic Pl Towson MD 21204 410-363-6500 363-1784
TF: 800-223-4885 ■ Web: www.allstateleasing.com

Automotive Resources International
4001 Leadenhall Rd Mount Laurel NJ 08054 856-778-1500 778-6200
Web: www.arifleet.com

Donlen Corp 2315 Sanders Rd Northbrook IL 60062 847-714-1400 714-1500
TF: 800-323-1483 ■ Web: www.donlen.com

Emkay Inc 805 W Thorndale Ave Itasca IL 60143 630-250-7400 250-7400
TF: 800-621-2001 ■ Web: www.emkay.com

Executive Car Leasing Inc
7807 Santa Monica Blvd Los Angeles CA 90046 323-654-5000 848-9015
TF: 800-994-2277 ■ Web: www.executivecarleasing.com

GE Capital Fleet Services
Three Capital Dr Eden Prairie MN 55344 800-469-0044 828-1040*
*Fax Area Code: 952 ■ *Fax: Hum Res ■ TF: 800-469-0044 ■ Web: www.gefleet.com/fleet

GE Equipment Services 120 Long Ridge Rd Stamford CT 06902 203-357-4000

Lease Plan USA 1165 Sanctuary Pkwy Alpharetta GA 30004 770-933-9090 202-8700*
*Fax Area Code: 678 ■ TF: 800-457-8721 ■ Web: www.leaseplan.com

Leasing Assoc Inc
12600 N Featherwood Dr Ste 400 Houston TX 77034 832-300-1300 300-1317
TF: 800-449-4807 ■ Web: www.theleasingcompany.com

Lily Transportation Corp 145 Rosemary St Needham MA 02494 781-449-8811 449-7128
Web: www.lily.com

Motorlease Corp 1506 New Britain Ave Farmington CT 06032 860-677-9711 674-8677
TF: 800-243-0182 ■ Web: www.motorleasecorp.com

Park Avenue Auto Group 250 W Passaic St Maywood NJ 07607 201-843-7900 843-4941
TF General: 800-269-2891 ■ Web: www.parkavemotors.com

RUAN Transportation Management Systems
666 Grand Ave 3200 Ruan Ctr Des Moines IA 50309 515-245-2500 245-2611
TF: 866-782-6669 ■ Web: www.ruan.com

Wheels Inc 666 Garland Pl Des Plaines IL 60016 847-699-7000 699-4047*
*Fax: Mail Rm ■ Web: www.wheels.com

FLOOR COVERINGS - MFR

SEE Tile - Ceramic (Wall & Floor) p. 3236; Flooring - Resilient p. 2292; Carpets & Rugs p. 1903

293 FLOOR COVERINGS STORES

Company	City	State	Zip	Phone	Fax
Action Floor Systems LLC 4781 N US Hwy 51 *Web:* www.actionfloors.com	Mercer	WI	54547	715-476-3512	
Air Base Carpet Mart Inc 230 N Dupont Hwy *Web:* airbasecarpetandtile.com	New Castle	DE	19720	302-328-1597	
Allied Property Services LLC Dba Cmq Floor Covering 2524 Ford Rd	Bristol	PA	19007	215-785-5900	
Architectural Surfaces Inc 5801 Midway Park NE *Web:* www.architectstudio.com	Albuquerque	NM	87109	505-889-0124	
Augusta Flooring Inc 202 Bobby Jones Expy *Web:* augustafloor.com	Martinez	GA	30907	706-650-0400	650-2167
Award Hardwood Floors LLP 401 N 72nd Ave	Wausau	WI	54401	715-849-8080	849-8181
Big d Floor Covering Supplies 7412 Anaconda Ave *Web:* www.bigdfloorcovering.com	Garden Grove	CA	92841	714-894-2443	
Blue Ridge Builders Supply Inc 5221 Rockfish Gap Tpke *Web:* www.brbs.net	Charlottesville	VA	22903	434-823-1387	
Boa-Franc Inc 1255-98th St *Web:* www.boa-franc.com	Saint-georges	QC	G5Y8J5	418-227-1181	
Bois BSL Energie Inc 1081 Rue Industrielle CP4 *Web:* www.smartlog.ca	Mont-joli	QC	G5H3T9	418-775-5360	
Butler Carpet Mart Inc Dba Bob'S Carpet Mart 10815 Us Hwy 19 N	Clearwater	FL	33764	727-571-9998	
Carol'S Carpet Inc 1640 NE Blvd *Web:* carolscarpetmontgomery.com	Montgomery	AL	36117	334-603-8713	
Carpet House 1320 Woodlawn	Lincoln	IL	62656	217-735-2531	
Carpet King Inc 1815 W River Rd N *Web:* www.carpet-king.com	Minneapolis	MN	55411	612-588-7600	588-2401
Carpet Tech 6613 19th St **Fax Area Code:* 972 ■ *Web:* www.callcarpettech.com	Lubbock	TX	79407	806-795-5142	795-2916*
Carpetile Co Eight W Main St	Plano	IL	60545	630-552-3400	
Century Tile Supply Co 747 E Roosevelt Rd **Fax Area Code:* 773 ■ *TF:* 888-845-3968 ■ *Web:* www.century-tile.com	Lombard	IL	60148	630-495-2300	237-8257*
Circle Floors Inc 1911 Revere Beach Pkwy *Web:* circlefloors.com	Everett	MA	02149	617-381-6600	
Clark-Dunbar Carpets 3232 Empire Dr *Web:* www.clarkdunbarsuperstore.com	Alexandria	LA	71301	318-445-0262	
Clayton Tile Distributing Company Inc 535 Woodruff Rd *Web:* claytontileco.com	Greenville	SC	29607	864-288-6290	
Coleman Floor Company Inc 1930 N Thoreau Dr Ste 100 *Web:* www.colemanfloor.com	Schaumburg	IL	60173	847-259-6100	
Commercial Contractors Inc 4900 Fairbanks St *Web:* www.aphome.com	Anchorage	AK	99503	907-563-1911	
Commercial Interior Resources Inc 1761 Reynolds Ave *Web:* www.cir-resource.com	Irvine	CA	92614	949-752-1470	
Contract Furnishings Mart 14160 Sw 72nd Ave Ste 110 *Web:* www.cfmfloors.com	Portland	OR	97224	503-542-8900	
Coyle Carpet One Inc 250 W Beltline Hwy *Web:* www.coylecarpet.com	Madison	WI	53713	608-257-0291	258-7248
Dean Hardwoods Inc 9244 Industrial Blvd *Web:* www.deanwood.com	Leland	NC	28451	910-763-5409	
Designer Floors of Texas 3841 Ranch Rd 620 S *Web:* designerfloorsoftexas.com	Austin	TX	78738	512-263-3333	
Dolphin Carpet & Tile 3550 NW 77th Ct *TF:* 800-639-3566 ■ *Web:* www.dolphincarpet.com	Miami	FL	33122	305-591-4141	378-1700
Eckards Home Improvement 2402 N Belt Hwy *Web:* eckardsflooring.com	Saint Joseph	MO	64506	816-279-4522	
EG Penner Building Centres 200 Park Rd W *Web:* www.egpenner.com	Steinbach	MB	R5G1A1	204-326-1325	
Elias Wilf Corp 10234 S Dolfield Rd *Web:* www.flooryou.com	Owings Mills	MD	21117	410-363-2400	
Elkton Supply Company Inc 202 W Main St *Web:* www.elktonsupply.com	Elkton	MD	21921	410-398-1900	
Elte 80 Ronald Ave *Web:* www.elte.com	Toronto	ON	M6E5A2	416-785-7885	
Essis & Sons Inc 6220 Carlisle Pk *Web:* carpetmechanicsburg.com	Mechanicsburg	PA	17050	717-697-9423	
Everett Carpet Co 318 Ashman St *Web:* everettcarpet.com	Midland	MI	48640	989-835-7191	
Farrell Distributing 19 Delaware Ave *Web:* www.farrelldistributing.com	Endicott	NY	13760	607-754-0707	
Faus Group Inc 100 Marine Dr SE *Web:* www.fausinc.com	Calhoun	GA	30701	706-879-4120	
Feizy Import & Export Co Ltd 1949 Stemmons Fwy *Web:* feizy.com	Dallas	TX	75207	214-747-6000	760-0521
Floor Coverings International 5250 Triangle Pwy Ste 100 *TF Sales:* 800-955-4324 ■ *Web:* www.floorcoveringsinternational.com	Norcross	GA	30092	770-874-7600	
Floor King Inc 10961 Research Blvd *Web:* floorking.net	Austin	TX	78759	512-346-7034	
Flooring Sales Group 1251 First Ave S *TF:* 877-478-3577 ■ *Web:* www.greatfloors.com	Seattle	WA	98134	206-624-7800	622-8407
Furniture Outlets USA Inc 140 E Hinks Ln *TF:* 877-395-8998 ■ *Web:* www.thefurnituremart.com	Sioux Falls	SD	57104	605-336-5000	336-5010
G & W Commercial Flooring Inc 6407 S 211th St *Web:* gwcfloor.com	Kent	WA	98032	253-479-1760	
Great Floors LLC 524 E Sherman Ave *Web:* greatfloors.com	Coeur D Alene	ID	83814	208-664-5405	
Harry L Murphy Inc 42 Bonaventura Dr *Web:* harrylmurphyinc.com	San Jose	CA	95134	408-955-1100	955-1111
Hi Tech Data Floors Inc 1885 Swarthmore Ave *Web:* hitechdatafloors.com	Lakewood	NJ	08701	732-905-1799	
Holmes Tile & Marble Company Inc 1202 Falls St *Web:* holmestile.com	Jonesboro	AR	72401	870-932-8011	
JJJ Floor Covering Inc 4831 Passons Blvd Ste A *Web:* www.jjjfloorcovering.com	Pico Rivera	CA	90660	562-692-9008	
Landers Premier Flooring Inc 2601 Mchale Ct Ste 140 *Web:* landerspremierflooring.com	Austin	TX	78758	512-873-9470	
Lumber Liquidators Inc 1455 VFW Pkwy **Fax Area Code:* 978 ■ *TF:* 800-227-0332 ■ *Web:* www.lumberliquidators.com	West Roxbury	MA	02132	617-327-1222	750-7802*
Mccabes Quality Carpet & Linoleum Inc 101 Genesee St *Web:* mccabesflooring.com	Marquette	MI	49855	906-228-8821	
MCI Inc 26 First Ave N *Web:* mcicarpetone.com	Waite Park	MN	56387	320-253-5078	
Mill Creek Carpet & Tile Co 6845 E 41st St *Web:* www.millcreekcarpet.com	Tulsa	OK	74145	918-621-4000	
Miller's Carpet One 15615 Hwy 99 *Web:* www.carpetone.com	Lynnwood	WA	98087	425-742-4141	
Narita Trading Company Inc 154 Morgan Ave Ste 6 *Web:* www.naritatrading.com	Brooklyn	NY	11237	718-628-4382	
Pyramid Floor Covering Inc 38 Harbor Park Dr *Web:* www.pyramidfloors.com	Port Washington	NY	11050	516-932-7200	
Quality Craft Ltd 17750-65A Ave Ste 301 *Web:* www.qualitycraft.com	Surrey	BC	V3S5N4	604-575-5550	
Redi-Carpet Inc 10225 Mula Rd Ste 120 *Web:* www.redicarpet.com	Stafford	TX	77477	832-310-2000	310-2001
Roysons Corp 40 Vanderhoof Ave *TF:* 888-769-7667 ■ *Web:* www.roysons.com	Rockaway	NJ	07866	973-625-7923	625-5917
Saint Paul Linoleum & Carpet Co 2956 Ctr Ct *Web:* www.stpaullinocpt.com	Eagan	MN	55121	651-686-7770	686-6660
Sergenian's Residential Flooring 2805 W Beltline Hwy *Web:* sergenians.com	Madison	WI	53713	608-271-1111	
Spraggins Flooring Inc 3815 Silver Star Rd *Web:* www.spragginsflooring.com	Orlando	FL	32808	407-295-4150	
Starline Associates Inc 3901 Sw 47th Ave Ste 410 *Web:* www.starlineusa.com	Davie	FL	33314	954-792-1965	
Teragren Fine Bamboo Flooring Panels & Veneer 12715 Miller Rd Ne Ste 301 *Web:* www.teragren.com	Bainbridge Is	WA	98110	206-842-9477	
Third Floor Inc, The 5410 Wilshire Blvd Ste 1000 *Web:* www.thethirdfloorinc.com	Los Angeles	CA	90036	323-931-6633	
Tom Duffy Co 5200 Watt Ct Ste B *TF:* 800-479-5671 ■ *Web:* www.tomduffy.com	Fairfield	CA	94534	800-479-5671	
Total Kitchen & Bath Inc 155 S Rohlwing Rd *Web:* www.totalstonesolutions.com	Addison	IL	60101	630-847-6805	
Weisshouse 324 S Highland Ave *Web:* weisshouse.com	Pittsburgh	PA	15206	412-441-8888	

294 FLOORING - RESILIENT

SEE ALSO Recycled Plastics Products p. 3046

Company	City	State	Zip	Phone	Fax
American Biltrite Inc 57 River St *OTC:* ABLT ■ *Web:* www.ambilt.com	Wellesley Hills	MA	02481	781-237-6655	237-6880
American Floor Products Company Inc 7977 Cessna Ave **Fax Area Code:* 301 ■ *TF:* 800-342-0424 ■ *Web:* www.afco-usa.com	Gaithersburg	MD	20879	800-342-0424	987-0422*
Ari Products Inc 102 Gaither Dr Ste 3 *Web:* www.ariproducts.com	Mount Laurel	NJ	08054	856-234-0757	
Armstrong World Industries Inc 2500 Columbia Ave *NYSE:* AWI ■ **Fax:* Hum Res ■ *TF Cust Svc:* 800-233-3823 ■ *Web:* www.armstrong.com	Lancaster	PA	17603	717-397-0611	396-6133*
Buchanan Hardwoods Inc 600 Baptist Line Rd *Web:* www.buchananhardwoods.com	Aliceville	AL	35442	205-373-8710	
Chiro Inc 2260 S Vista Ave *Web:* www.mrcleansystems.com	Bloomington	CA	92316	909-879-1160	
Classic Floors Inc 13725 S Mur Len Rd *Web:* www.classicfloors.com	Olathe	KS	66062	913-780-2171	
Columbia Forest Products Inc 7900 Triad Ctr Dr Ste 200 *TF:* 800-637-1609 ■ *Web:* www.columbiaforestproducts.com	Greensboro	NC	27409	336-291-5905	
Congoleum Corp 3500 Quakerridge Rd PO Box 3127 *TF:* 800-274-3266 ■ *Web:* www.congoleum.com	Mercerville	NJ	08619	609-584-3000	584-3521
Country Floors Inc 15 E 16th St *Web:* www.countryfloors.com	New York	NY	10003	212-627-8300	242-1604
De Ruijter int Usa 120 Harvest Dr *Web:* www.deruijterusa.com	Coldwater	OH	45828	419-678-3909	
DFS Flooring Inc 15651 Saticoy St *Web:* www.dfsflooring.com	Van Nuys	CA	91406	818-374-5200	
Expanko Inc 180 Gordon Dr Ste 113 **Fax Area Code:* 610 ■ *TF:* 800-345-6202 ■ *Web:* www.expanko.com	Exton	PA	19341	800-345-6202	363-0735*
Floor Seal Technology Inc 1005 Ames Ave *Web:* www.floorseal.com	Milpitas	CA	95035	408-436-8181	
Florida Brick & Clay Company Inc (FBC) 1708 Turkey Creek Rd *Web:* www.floridabrickandclay.com	Plant City	FL	33567	813-754-1521	754-5469
Forbo Flooring Systems Eight Maplewood Dr Humboldt Industrial Pk **Fax Area Code:* 570 ■ **Fax:* Cust Svc ■ *TF Cust Svc:* 800-842-7839 ■ *Web:* www.forboflooringna.com	Hazleton	PA	18202	800-842-7839	450-0258*

Company / Address	City	State	Zip	Phone	Fax
Formica Corp 10155 Reading Rd	Cincinnati	OH	45241	513-786-3400	
TF: 800-367-6422 ■ *Web:* www.formica.com					
Fryer-Knowles Inc 205 S Dawson St	Seattle	WA	98108	206-767-7710	
Web: www.fryerk.com					
Hambro Forest Products Inc 445 Elk Valley Rd	Crescent City	CA	95531	707-464-6131	464-9375
Interior Specialists Inc 1630 Faraday Ave	Carlsbad	CA	92008	760-929-6700	
Web: www.isidc.com					
JTJ Commercial Interiors Inc 200 Shady Grove Rd	Nashville	TN	37214	615-872-9363	
Web: jtjcommercialinteriors.com					
Leewens Corp 630 Seventh Ave	Kirkland	WA	98033	425-827-7667	
Web: www.leewens.com					
Mannington Mills Inc 75 Mannington Mills Rd	Salem	NJ	08079	856-935-3000	339-6124
TF Cust Svc: 800-356-6787 ■ *Web:* www.mannington.com					
Natco Products Corp 155 Brookside Ave	West Warwick	RI	02893	401-828-0300	823-7670
Pergo Inc 3128 Highwoods Blvd Ste 100	Raleigh	NC	27604	919-773-6000	
TF: 800-337-3746 ■ *Web:* na.pergo.com					
Pionite Decorative Surfaces One Pionite Rd	Auburn	ME	04210	207-784-9111	784-0392
Web: www.pionite.com					
RCA Rubber Co 1833 E Market St	Akron	OH	44305	330-784-1291	794-6446
TF: 800-321-2340 ■ *Web:* www.rcarubber.com					
Regupol America 33 Keystone Dr	Lebanon	PA	17042	800-537-8737	675-2199*
**Fax Area Code:* 717 ■ *TF:* 800-537-8737 ■ *Web:* www.regupol.com					
Roppe Corp 1602 N Union St	Fostoria	OH	44830	419-435-8546	435-1056
TF: 800-537-9527 ■ *Web:* www.roppe.com					
Stonhard Inc 1000 E Pk Ave	Maple Shade	NJ	08052	856-779-7500	321-7510
TF Cust Svc: 800 854 0310 ■ *Web:* www.stonhard.com					
Sun Interiors Ltd 2329 Severn Ave	Metairie	LA	70001	504-833-8104	
Web: suninteriors.com					
Superior Mfg Group 5655 W 73rd St	Chicago	IL	60638	708-458-4600	458-4730
TF: 800-621-2802 ■ *Web:* www.notrax.com					
Surface Shields Inc 10457 163rd Pl	Orland Park	IL	60467	708-226-9810	226-9817
TF: 800-913-5667 ■ *Web:* www.surfaceshields.com					
Synthetic Turf Resources 809 Kenner St	Dalton	GA	30721	706-272-4200	
Web: synthecticturfresources.com					
Tarkett Inc 1001 Yamaska St E	Farnham	QC	J2N1J7	450-293-3173	293-8489
TF: 800-363-9276 ■ *Web:* www.tarkettna.com					

295 FLORISTS

SEE ALSO Flowers-by-Wire Services p. 2295; Garden Centers p. 2353

Company / Address	City	State	Zip	Phone	Fax
1-800-Flowers.com Inc One Old Country Rd Ste 500	Carle Place	NY	11514	516-237-6000	
NASDAQ: FLWS ■ *TF:* 800-356-9377 ■ *Web:* ww30.1800flowers.com					
A Few of My Favorite Things 108 N Sixth St	Wyoming	IL	61491	309-695-9966	
Web: afewofmyfavoritethingsflowershop.com					
Abbey Party Rents 411 Allan St	Daly City	CA	94014	415-715-6900	
Web: www.abbeyrentssf.com					
Alaska Experience Theater & Gift Shop 333 W Fourth Ave	Anchorage	AK	99501	907-272-9076	
Web: alaskaexperiencetheatre.com					
Angel Plants Inc 560 W Deer Park Ave	Dix Hills	NY	11746	631-242-7788	
Web: www.angelplants.com					
Annieglass Retail Stores 110 Cooper St Ste F	Santa Cruz	CA	95060	831-427-4260	
Web: www.annieglass.com					
Arrow Florist & Park Avenue Greenhouses Inc 757 Pk Ave	Cranston	RI	02910	401-785-1900	785-4120
TF: 800-556-7097 ■ *Web:* www.arrowflorist.net					
Artistic Ribbon & Novelty Company Inc 22 W 21st St Fl 3	New York	NY	10010	212-255-4224	
Web: www.artisticribbon.com					
Ashland Addison Florist Co 1640 W Fulton St	Chicago	IL	60612	312-432-1800	432-9813
Web: www.ashaddflorist.com					
Astoria-Pacific Inc 15130 SE 82nd Dr	Clackamas	OR	97015	503-657-3010	
TF: 800-536-3111 ■ *Web:* www.astoria-pacific.com					
Avila Retail Development & Management LLC 5001 Ellison St NE	Albuquerque	NM	87109	505-341-3753	
Web: www.avilaretail.com					
Bachman's Inc 6010 Lyndale Ave S	Minneapolis	MN	55419	612-861-7311	861-7748
TF: 888-222-4626 ■ *Web:* www.bachmans.com					
Baisch & Skinner Inc 2721 Lasalle St	Saint Louis	MO	63104	314-664-1212	
TF: 800-523-0013 ■ *Web:* www.baischandskinner.com					
Barry-owen Co Inc 5625 Smithway St	Los Angeles	CA	90040	323-724-4800	724-4996
TF: 800-682-6682 ■ *Web:* www.barryowen.com					
Bert R Hybels Inc 3322 Grand Prairie Rd	Kalamazoo	MI	49006	269-382-4921	
Web: www.hybels.com					
Billy Heroman's Flowerland 10812 N Harrell'S Ferry Rd	Baton Rouge	LA	70816	225-272-7673	
Web: www.billyheromans.com					
Birthday Direct 120 Commerce St	Muscle Shoals	AL	35661	256-381-0310	
Web: www.birthdaydirect.com					
BloomNation LLC 8889 W Olympic Blvd	Beverly Hills	CA	90211	877-702-5666	
TF: 877-702-5666 ■ *Web:* www.bloomnation.com					
Blossom Bucket, The 13305 Wooster St NW	North Lawrence	OH	44666	330-834-2551	
Boesen the Florist 3422 Beaver Ave	Des Moines	IA	50310	515-274-4761	274-6369
TF: 800-274-4761 ■ *Web:* www.boesen.com					
Boite a Fleur De Laval Inc La 3266 Boul Sainte-Rose	Laval	QC	H7P4K8	450-622-0341	
Web: alaboiteafleurs.com					
Bonnett Wholesale Florists 119 Eigth St E	Milan	IL	61264	309-787-4401	
Web: www.bonnettwholesale.com					
Booman Floral 2302 Bautista Ave	Vista	CA	92084	760-630-4170	
Web: www.boomanfloral.com					
Brian's Toys W730 State Rd 35	Fountain City	WI	54629	608-687-7572	
Web: www.brianstoys.com					
Bunches 14 1/2 N Santa Cruz Ave	Los Gatos	CA	95030	408-395-5451	
Web: buncheslosgatos.com					
Burchell Nursery Inc, The 12000 Hwy 120	Oakdale	CA	95361	209-845-8733	847-0284
TF: 800-828-8733 ■ *Web:* www.burchellnursery.com					
Cactus Flower Florists 10822 N Scottsdale Rd	Scottsdale	AZ	85254	480-483-9200	483-9200*
**Fax:* Sales ■ *TF:* 800-922-2887 ■ *Web:* www.cactusflower.com					
Calendarscom LLC 6411 Burleson Rd	Austin	TX	78744	512-386-7220	
Web: www.calendars.com					
Callaway Partners LLC 100 Glenridge Point Pkwy Ste 200	Atlanta	GA	30342	404-496-5230	
Web: www.warbirdconsulting.com					
Calyx Flowers 6655 Shelburne Rd	Shelburne	VT	05482	802-985-3001	985-1304
Web: www.calyxflowers.com					
Canada Flowers 4073 Longhurst Ave	Niagara Falls	ON	L2E6G5	905-354-2713	
TF: 888-705-9999 ■ *Web:* www.canadaflowers.ca					
Cathy's Concepts Inc 6900 E 30th St	Indianapolis	IN	46219	317-860-1700	
Web: www.cathysconcepts.com					
Century City Flower Mart 9551 W Pico Blvd	Los Angeles	CA	90035	310-277-6737	
Web: www.centurycityflowermarket.com					
City Florist of Redlands 122 Cajon St	Redlands	CA	92373	909-793-4141	
Web: cityfloristofredlands.com					
Collectors Alliance Inc 1942 Swarthmore Ave	Lakewood	NJ	08701	732-730-3580	
Web: www.collectorsalliance.com					
Colwell Flower Shop & Wedding Boutique 2448 Brightwood Rd Se	New Philadelphia	OH	44663	330-339-1661	
Web: www.colwellflowershop.com					
Connell's Map Lee Flowers & Gifts 2408 E Main St	Bexley	OH	43209	614-237-8653	
TF: 800-790-8980 ■ *Web:* www.cmlflowers.com					
Continental Flowers Inc 8175 Nw 31st St	Doral	FL	33122	305-594-4214	
Web: www.continentalflowers.com					
Country Lane Flower Shop 729 S Michigan Ave	Howell	MI	48843	517-546-1111	546-5168
TF: 800-764-7673 ■ *Web:* www.countrylaneflowers.com					
Danson Decor Inc 3425 Douglas B Floreani	St Laurent	QC	H4S1Y6	514-335-2435	
Web: www.dansondecor.com					
Dead Ringer Putter Co 228 W Baltimore Ave	Clifton Heights	PA	19018	610-284-4653	
Dejuan Stroud Inc 530 Prospect Ave Ste 1	Little Silver	NJ	07739	732-224-8333	
Web: www.dejuanstroud.com					
DeLoache Flowers 2927 Millwood Ave	Columbia	SC	29205	803-256-1681	
Web: deloacheflowershop.com					
Dr Delphinium Designs & Events 5806 W Lovers Ln & Tollway	Dallas	TX	75225	214-522-9911	525-1240
TF: 800-783-8790 ■ *Web:* www.drdelphinium.com					
Eastern Floral & Gift Shop 818 Butterworth St SW	Grand Rapids	MI	49504	616-949-2200	949-9009
TF: 800-494-2202 ■ *Web:* www.easternfloral.com					
Eufloria Flowers 885 Mesa Rd	Nipomo	CA	93444	805-929-4683	
Web: www.eufloriaflowers.com					
Everbloom Growers Inc 20450 SW 248th St	Homestead	FL	33031	305-248-1478	
Felly's Flowers Inc PO Box 6620	Madison	WI	53716	800-993-7673	
TF: 800-993-7673 ■ *Web:* www.fellys.net					
Flower City Communications LLC 1848 Lyell Ave	Rochester	NY	14606	585-458-5350	
Web: www.fccomm.com					
Flower Factory Inc 5655 Whipple Ave NW	North Canton	OH	44720	330-494-0010	
Web: www.flowerfactory.com					
Flower Patch Inc 4370 S 300 W	Murray	UT	84107	801-747-2824	263-7896
TF General: 888-865-6858 ■ *Web:* www.flowerpatch.com					
Flower Pot Florists 2314 N Broadway St	Knoxville	TN	37917	865-523-5121	524-8654
TF: 800-824-7792 ■ *Web:* www.knoxvilleflowerpot.com					
Flowerbud.com 155 B Ave Ste 110	Lake Oswego	OR	97034	503-697-1790	
Web: www.flowerbud.com					
FlowerClub PO Box 60910	Los Angeles	CA	90060	310-966-8644	
TF: 800-493-5610 ■ *Web:* www.teleflora.com					
Flowers & Fancies-greenlea 11404 Cronridge Dr	Owings Mills	MD	21117	410-653-0600	
Web: www.flowersandfancies.com					
Flowers by Anthony Inc 3300 SW Ninth St Ste 1	Des Moines	IA	50315	515-288-6789	
Web: flowersbyanthony.com					
Flowers By Burton Inc 426 Old Walt Whitman Rd	Melville	NY	11747	631-424-3377	
Web: flowersbyburton.com					
Flowers by Sleeman for All Seasons & Reasons Ltd 1201 Memorial Rd	Houghton	MI	49931	906-482-4023	
Web: flowersbysleeman.com					
Flowers Chemical Laboratories Inc 481 Newburyport Ave	Altamonte Springs	FL	32701	407-339-5984	
Web: www.flowerslabs.com					
Formaggio Kitchen on Line LLC 244 Huron Ave	Cambridge	MA	02138	617-354-4750	
Web: www.formaggiokitchen.com					
Fossil Creek Nursery Inc 7029 S College Ave	Fort Collins	CO	80525	970-226-4924	
Web: www.fossilcreek.com					
Foster City Flowers & Gifts 1160 Chess Dr Ste 1	Foster City	CA	94404	650-573-6607	578-6756
TF: 800-970-7673 ■ *Web:* www.fostercity-flowers.com					
Frantz Wholesale Nursery LLC 12161 Delaware Rd	Hickman	CA	95323	209-874-1459	
Web: frantznursery.com					
Freeman's Flowers & Event Consultants 2934 Duniven Cir	Amarillo	TX	79109	806-355-4451	
Web: www.freemansflowers.com					
Fruit Co, The 2900 Van Horn Dr	Hood River	OR	97031	541-387-3100	
TF: 800-387-3100 ■ *Web:* www.thefruitcompany.com					
FTD Inc 3113 Woodcreek Dr	Downers Grove	IL	60515	800-736-3383	719-6170*
**Fax Area Code:* 630 ■ *TF Cust Svc:* 800-736-3383 ■ *Web:* www.ftd.com					

Name / Address	City	State	Zip	Phone	Fax
Gainans Flowers 1211 24th St W Ste 3 *Web:* www.gainans.com	Billings	MT	59102	406-652-1650	
Galaxy Glass 208 N W Blvd	Newfield	NJ	08344	856-697-3934	
Gift of Life Foundation 3861 Research Park Dr *Web:* giftoflifemichigan.org	Ann Arbor	MI	48108	734-973-1577	
Gifts for You LLC 2425 Curtiss St *Web:* www.giftsforyounow.com	Downers Grove	IL	60515	630-771-0095	
Giftwares Co 436 First Ave *Web:* www.giftwaresco.com	Royersford	PA	19468	610-792-8177	
Golden Flowers 2600 NW 79th Ave *Web:* terrafloristvancouver.com/	Doral	FL	33122	305-599-0193	
Goldin & Company Ltd 263 Stanley St	Winnipeg	MB	R3A0W8	204-982-1188	
Greeters of Hawaii Ltd 300 Rodgers Blvd Ste 266 *TF:* 800-366-8559 ■ *Web:* www.greetersofhawaii.com	Honolulu	HI	96819	808-836-0161	833-7756
Grower Direct Fresh Cut Flowers 9613 41 Ave Ste 201 *TF:* 877-277-4787 ■ *Web:* www.growerdirect.com	Edmonton	AB	T6E5X7	780-436-7774	436-3336
Guggisberg Cheese Inc 5060 SR- 557 *Web:* www.babyswiss.com/	Millersburg	OH	44654	330-893-2500	
H & P Sales Inc 2022 Victory Dr *Web:* www.handpsalesinc.com	Vista	CA	92084	760-727-2614	
Hardin's Florist Supply 329 W Bowman Ave *Web:* www.hardins.com	Liberty	NC	27298	336-622-3035	
Higdon Florist 201 E 32nd St *TF:* 800-641-4726 ■ *Web:* www.higdonflorist.com	Joplin	MO	64804	417-624-7171	624-7244
Hillcrest Garden 95 W Century Rd *Web:* hillcrestgarden.com	Paramus	NJ	07652	201-599-3030	
Howard Bros Florists 8700 S Pennsylvania Ave *TF:* 800-648-0524 ■ *Web:* www.howardbrothersflorist.com	Oklahoma City	OK	73159	405-632-4747	632-1672
Jacobson Floral Supply Inc 500 Albany St *Web:* www.jacobsonfloral.com	Boston	MA	02118	617-426-4287	
John Wolf Florist 6228 Waters Ave *TF:* 800-944-6435 ■ *Web:* www.johnwolfflorist.com	Savannah	GA	31406	912-352-9843	353-8843
Johns Greenhouse & Florist Shop 517 Copeland St *Web:* johnsgreenhouses-florist.com	Brockton	MA	02301	508-588-0955	
Johnston the Florist Inc 14179 Lincoln Way *TF:* 800-356-9371 ■ *Web:* www.johnstontheflorist.com	North Huntingdon	PA	15642	412-751-2821	
Jon's Nursery Inc 24546 Nursery Way *Web:* jonsnursery.com	Eustis	FL	32736	352-357-4289	
Jonathan Club Charitable Fund 545 S Figueroa St *Web:* www.jc.org	Los Angeles	CA	90071	213-624-0881	
Joyce Florist 2729 S Hampton Rd *TF:* 800-527-1520 ■ *Web:* www.joyceflorist.com	Dallas	TX	75224	214-942-1776	331-6272
KaBloomcom Ltd 305 Harvard St *Web:* www.kabloom.com	Brookline	MA	02446	617-730-9966	
Ken's Flower Shop 140 W S Boundary St *TF:* 800-253-0100 ■ *Web:* www.kensflowers.com	Perrysburg	OH	43551	419-874-1333	874-3441
KITSON 115 S Robertson Blvd *Web:* www.shopkitson.com	Los Angeles	CA	90048	310-859-2652	
Krueger Wholesale Florist Inc 10706 Tesch Ln *Web:* kruegerwholesale.com	Rothschild	WI	54474	715-359-7202	
Kuhn Flowers Inc 3802 Beach Blvd *TF:* 800-458-5846 ■ *Web:* kuhnflowers.com	Jacksonville	FL	32207	904-398-8601	
La Canada Flowers 5971 University Ave Ste 312 *Web:* www.lacanadaflowers.com	San Diego	CA	92115	619-582-5021	
Las Vegas Floral & Plant Wholesale 2404 We Ste A *Web:* floral2000.com	Las Vegas	NV	89102	702-383-0603	
Lester's Florist Inc 2100 Bull St *TF:* 800-841-1103 ■ *Web:* www.lestersflorist.com	Savannah	GA	31401	912-233-6066	233-3654
Lewistown Florist Store 129 S Main St Ste 200 *Web:* www.lewistownflorist.com	Lewistown	PA	17044	717-248-9683	
Lloyd's Florist 9216 Preston Hwy *TF:* 800-264-1825 ■ *Web:* www.lloydsflorist.net	Louisville	KY	40229	502-968-5428	964-5696
Locker's Florist 1640 S 83rd St *Web:* www.lockersflorist.com	West Allis	WI	53214	414-276-7673	
Luurtsema Sales Inc 6672 Ctr Industrial Dr *Web:* luurtsema.com	Jenison	MI	49428	616-669-9301	
Martina's Flowers & Gifts 3830 Washington Rd *TF:* 800-927-1204 ■ *Web:* www.martinas.com	Martinez	GA	30907	706-863-7172	863-1234
Mayesh Wholesale Florist Inc 5401 W 104th St *TF:* 888-462-9374 ■ *Web:* www.mayesh.com	Los Angeles	CA	90045	310-348-4921	
Mellano & Co 766 Wall St *TF:* 888-635-5266 ■ *Web:* www.mellano.com	Los Angeles	CA	90014	213-622-0796	
Metropolitan Plant & Flower Exchange 2125 Fletcher Ave *TF:* 800-638-7613 ■ *Web:* www.metroplantexchange.com	Fort Lee	NJ	07024	201-944-1050	944-7970
Midwest Trading Horticultural Supplies Inc 48w805 Il Rt 64 *Web:* www.midwest-trading.com	Maple Park	IL	60151	630-365-1990	
Milgro Nursery LLC 1085 Victoria Ave	Oxnard	CA	93030	805-985-0855	
Misco Home and Garden 100 S Washington Ave *Web:* www.miscohomeandgarden.com/	Dunellen	NJ	08812	732-752-7500	752-6305
Missouri Office Systems & Supplies 941 W 141st Terrace Ste D *Web:* www.8asupplier.com	Kansas City	MO	64145	816-761-5152	761-5170
Nakase Bros Wholesale Nursery 9441 Krepp Dr *TF:* 800-747-4388 ■ *Web:* www.nakasebros.com	Huntington Beach	CA	92646	714-962-6604	
Nanz & Kraft Florists Inc 141 Breckenridge Ln *TF:* 800-897-6551 ■ *Web:* www.nanzandkraft.com	Louisville	KY	40207	502-897-6551	897-2082
National Floral Supply Inc 3825 LeonaRdtown Rd Ste 4 *TF:* 800-932-2772 ■ *Web:* www.flowersonbase.com	Waldorf	MD	20601	301-932-7600	
Niagara Helicopters Ltd 3731 Victoria Ave *Web:* www.niagarahelicopters.com	Niagara Falls	ON	L2E6V5	905-357-5672	
Norton's Flowers & Gifts 2900 Washtenaw Ave *TF:* 800-682-8667 ■ *Web:* www.nortonsflowers.com	Ypsilanti	MI	48197	734-434-2700	434-1140
Nottawaseppi Huron Band of Potawatomi's FireKeepers Development Authority 11177 E Michigan Ave *Web:* www.firekeeperscasino.com	Battle Creek	MI	49014	877-353-8777	
Office Playground Inc 83 Hamilton Dr Ste 100 *Web:* www.officeplayground.com	Novato	CA	94949	415-883-6920	
Performance Plants Inc 700 Gardiners Rd *Web:* www.performanceplants.com	Kingston	ON	K7M3X9	613-545-0390	
Phillip's Flower Shops Inc 524 N Cass Ave *TF:* 800-356-7257 ■ *Web:* www.800florals.com	Westmont	IL	60559	630-719-5200	719-2292
Phoenix Flower Shops 5733 E Thomas Rd Ste 4 *TF:* 888-311-0404 ■ *Web:* www.phoenixflowershops.com	Scottsdale	AZ	85251	480-289-4000	
Plant Interscapes Inc 6436 Babcock Rd *Web:* www.plantinterscapes.com	San Antonio	TX	78249	281-304-7190	
Platon Craft & Floral Inc 1327 N Carolan Ave	Burlingame	CA	94010	650-373-7888	
Pleasant Nursery Inc 4234 W Wabash *Web:* pleasant-nursery.com	Springfield	IL	62711	217-522-2222	
Pope Scientific Inc 351 N Dekora Woods Blvd *Web:* www.popeinc.com	Saukville	WI	53080	262-268-9300	
Primitives by Kathy Inc 1817 William Penn Way *Web:* www.primitivesbykathy.com	Lancaster	PA	17601	866-295-2849	
Proflowers.com 4840 Eastgate Mall **Fax Area Code: 858* ■ *TF:* 800-580-2913 ■ *Web:* www.proflowers.com	San Diego	CA	92121	800-580-2913	638-4725*
Provide Commerce Inc 4840 Eastgate Mall *TF Cust Svc:* 800-776-3569 ■ *Web:* www.providecommerce.com	San Diego	CA	92121	858-638-4900	909-4201
Royal Expressions Flowers & Gifts 131 S Ln St	Blissfield	MI	49228	517-486-4351	
Royer's Flowers Inc 201 Rohrerstown Rd *Web:* www.royers.com	Lancaster	PA	17603	717-397-0376	
Russell Florist Inc 5001 Gravois Ave *TF:* 800-351-9003 ■ *Web:* www.russellflorist.com	Saint Louis	MO	63116	314-351-4676	351-6842
Sawyer Nursery Inc 5401 Port Sheldon St *Web:* www.sawyernursery.com	Hudsonville	MI	49426	616-669-9094	
Schroeder's Flowerland Inc 1530 S Webster Ave *TF:* 800-236-4769 ■ *Web:* www.schroederflowers.com	Green Bay	WI	54301	920-436-6363	433-9685
Schubert Nursery Inc 7715 Gorman Dr	Browns Summit	NC	27214	336-656-1981	
Shibata Floral Company Supplies 620 Brannan St *Web:* www.shibatafc.com	San Francisco	CA	94107	415-495-8611	
Shirl K Floral Designs 2701 Pontoon Rd *Web:* www.shirlkfloral.com	Granite City	IL	62040	618-797-6210	
Smith Southwestern Inc 1850 N Rosemont *Web:* www.smith-southwestern.com	Mesa	AZ	85205	480-854-9545	
Strange's Florist Inc 3313 Mechanicsville Pk *TF:* 800-421-4070 ■ *Web:* stranges.com	Richmond	VA	23223	804-321-2200	
Success Promotions 14304 S Outer 40 Rd *Web:* www.successpromo.com	Chesterfield	MO	63017	314-878-1999	
Sunwest Silver Company Inc 324 Lomas Blvd NW *TF:* 800-771-3781 ■ *Web:* www.sunwestsilver.com	Albuquerque	NM	87102	505-243-3781	
Swenson & Silacci Flowers 110 John St *Web:* www.onlineflowers.com	Salinas	CA	93901	831-424-2725	
Technical Glass Products Inc 881 Callendar Blvd *Web:* www.technicalglass.com	Painesville	OH	44077	440-639-6399	
Thirstystone Resources Inc 1304 Corporate Dr *TF:* 800-829-6888 ■ *Web:* www.thirstystone.com	Gainesville	TX	76240	940-668-6793	668-6207
Thurbers of Richmond Inc 7324 Port Side Dr	Midlothian	VA	23112	804-639-5770	
Tipton & Hurst Inc 1801 N Grant St *Web:* www.tiptonhurst.com	Little Rock	AR	72207	501-666-3333	
Triple Oaks Nursery & Herb Garden 2359 Delsea Dr *Web:* www.tripleoaks.com	Franklinville	NJ	08322	856-694-4272	
United Nations Assoc Information & Un Icef Center 1403B Addison St *Web:* unausaeastbay.org	Berkeley	CA	94704	510-849-1752	
US Retail Flowers Inc 810 S 12th St PO Box 330 *Web:* royers.com	Lebanon	PA	17042	717-273-4090	
USA Bouquet Company Inc, The 1500 NW 95 Ave *Web:* www.usabq.com	Miami	FL	33172	786-437-6500	
Valley Flowers Inc 3675 Foothill Rd *Web:* valleyflowers.com	Carpinteria	CA	93013	805-684-6651	
Van Belle Nursery Inc 34825 Hallert Rd *Web:* www.vanbelle.com	Abbotsford	BC	V3G1R3	604-853-3415	
Veldkamp's Flowers 9501 W Colfax Ave *TF:* 800-247-3730 ■ *Web:* www.veldkampsflowers.com	Lakewood	CO	80215	303-232-2673	234-5686
Villere's Florist 750 Martin Behrman Ave *TF:* 800-845-5373 ■ *Web:* www.villeresflowers.com	Metairie	LA	70005	504-833-3716	
Viviano Flower Shop 32050 Harper Ave *Web:* viviano.com	Saint Clair Shores	MI	48082	586-293-0227	
Vogue Flowers & Gifts Ltd 1114 N Blvd *Web:* www.vogueflowers.com	Richmond	VA	23230	804-353-9600	
Warners Florist 179 S Montgomery St	Hollidaysburg	PA	16648	814-695-9431	
Washington Floral Service Inc 2701 S 35th St *Web:* www.washingtonfloral.com	Tacoma	WA	98409	253-472-8343	

	City	State	Zip	Phone	Fax
Watanabe Floral Inc 1607 Hart St *Web:* www.watanabefloral.com	Honolulu	HI	96817	808-832-9360	
Westbrook Floral Ltd 109 Av Lindsay *Web:* westbrookfloral.com	Dorval	QC	H9P2S6	514-636-1255	
Winston Bros Inc 131 Newbury St *TF:* 800-457-4901 ■ *Web:* www.winstonflowers.com	Boston	MA	02116	617-541-1100	541-1126
Winward International Inc 3089 Whipple Rd *TF:* 800-888-8898 ■ *Web:* www.winwardsilks.com	Union City	CA	94587	510-487-8686	
Wondertreats Inc 2200 Lapham Dr *Web:* www.wondertreats.com	Modesto	CA	95354	209-521-8881	
Worrell Corp 305 S Post Rd *Web:* worrellcorp.com	Indianapolis	IN	46219	317-895-9708	

296 FLOWERS & NURSERY STOCK - WHOL

SEE ALSO Horticultural Products Growers p. 2478

	City	State	Zip	Phone	Fax
Allstate Floral & Craft Inc 14038 Park Pl *TF:* 800-433-4056 ■ *Web:* allstatefloral.com	Cerritos	CA	90703	562-926-2302	926-8613
Arazoza Brothers Corp 15901 SW 242nd St *Web:* www.arazozabrothers.com	Homestead	FL	33031	305-246-3223	
Atwoods Distributing Inc 5400 Owen K Garriott *Web:* www.atwoods.com	Enid	OK	73703	580-233-3702	
Ball Horticultural Co 622 Town Rd *TF:* 800-879-2255 ■ *Web:* www.ballhort.com	West Chicago	IL	60185	630-231-3600	231-3605
Blumen Gardens Inc 403 Edward St *Web:* blumengardens.com	Sycamore	IL	60178	815-895-3737	
Central Garden & Pet Co 1340 Treat Blvd Ste 600 *NASDAQ: CENT* ■ *Web:* www.central.com	Walnut Creek	CA	94597	925-948-4000	287-0601
Claymore C Sieck Wholesale Florist 311 E Chase St *TF:* 800-624-7134 ■ *Web:* www.sieck.com	Baltimore	MD	21202	410-685-4660	685-1547
Cleveland Plant & Flower Co 12920 Corporate Dr *TF:* 800-688-8012 ■ *Web:* www.cpfco.com	Cleveland	OH	44130	216-898-3500	898-1075
Country Silk Inc 100 S Washington Ave *Web:* www.countrysilk.com	Dunellen	NJ	08812	732-752-5556	752-7550
Cut Flower Wholesale Inc 2122 Faulkner Rd NE *TF:* 888-997-8367 ■ *Web:* www.cutflower.com	Atlanta	GA	30324	404-320-1619	634-7922
Delaware Valley Wholesale Florist Inc (DVWF) 520 Mantua Blvd N *TF:* 800-676-1212 ■ *Web:* www.dvwf.com	Sewell	NJ	08080	856-468-7000	464-2772
Denver Wholesale Florists Co 4800 Dahlia St *TF:* 800-829-8280 ■ *Web:* www.dwfwholesale.com	Denver	CO	80216	303-399-0970	376-3123
Distinctive Designs International Inc 120 Sibley Dr *TF:* 800-243-4787 ■ *Web:* www.distinctivedesigns.com	Russellville	AL	35654	256-332-7390	332-7890
Dodds & Eder Inc 221 S St *Web:* doddsandeder.com	Oyster Bay	NY	11771	516-922-4412	
Esprit Miami 3043 NW 107th Ave *TF:* 800-327-2320 ■ *Web:* www.espritmiami.com	Miami	FL	33172	305-591-2244	591-2603
Florist Distributing Inc 2403 Bell Ave *TF:* 800-373-3741 ■ *Web:* www.fdionline.net	Des Moines	IA	50321	515-243-5228	282-9241
Holmberg Farms Inc 13430 Hobson Simmons Rd *TF:* 800-282-3562 ■ *Web:* www.holmbergfarms.com	Lithia	FL	33547	800-282-3562	
Johnson Nursery Corp 985 Johnson Nursery Rd *Web:* www.johnson-nursery.com	Willard	NC	28478	910-285-7861	
Karthauser & Sons Inc W 147 N 11100 Fond du Lac Ave *TF:* 800-338-8620 ■ *Web:* www.karthauser.net	Germantown	WI	53022	262-255-7815	255-6920
Kennicott Bros 452 N Ashland Ave *TF:* 866-346-2826 ■ *Web:* www.kennicott.com	Chicago	IL	60622	312-492-8200	492-8202
L & L Nursery Supply Co Inc 2552 Shenandoah Way *TF:* 800-624-2517 ■ *Web:* www.llsupply.net	San Bernardino	CA	92407	909-591-0461	
Magnetecs Corp 10524 La Cienega Blvd *Web:* www.magnetecs.com	Inglewood	CA	90304	310-670-7700	
Monterey Bay Nursery Inc 748 San Miguel Canyon Rd *Web:* www.montereybaynsy.com	Watsonville	CA	95077	831-724-6361	
Norben Import Corp 99 S Newman St *TF General:* 800-526-4652 ■ *Web:* www.larksilk.com	Hackensack	NJ	07601	201-487-0855	487-0787
Oklahoma Flower Market Inc, The 36 N Broadway Cir	Oklahoma City	OK	73103	405-232-3143	
Pennock Co 7135 Colonial Ln *Web:* www.pennock.com	Pennsauken	NJ	08109	215-492-7900	951-6498
Pittsburgh Cut Flower Co 1901 Liberty Ave *TF:* 800-837-2837 ■ *Web:* www.pittsburghcutflower.com	Pittsburgh	PA	15222	412-355-7000	391-0649
Rexius Forest By-Products Inc 1275 Bailey Hill Rd *Web:* www.rexius.com	Eugene	OR	97402	541-342-1835	343-4802
Roman J Claprood Co 242 N Grant Ave *Web:* rjclaprood.com	Columbus	OH	43215	614-221-5515	
Roy Houff Co, The 6200 S Oak Pk Ave *Web:* royhouff.com/	Chicago	IL	60638	773-586-8666	586-8790
Shemin Nurseries 1081 King St *Web:* www.shemin.net	Greenwich	CT	06831	203-207-5000	531-7393
Sylvan Nursery Inc 1028 Horseneck Rd *Web:* sylvannursery.com	Westport	MA	02790	508-636-4573	
Tapscott's 1403 E 18th St *TF:* 800-626-1922 ■ *Web:* www.tapfloral.com	Owensboro	KY	42303	270-684-2308	683-3702
Teters Floral Products Inc 1425 S Lillian Ave *TF:* 800-999-5996 ■ *Web:* www.teters.com	Bolivar	MO	65613	417-326-7654	326-8061
Teufel Nursery Inc 3431 NW John Olsen Pl *TF:* 800-483-8335 ■ *Web:* www.teufellandscape.com	Hillsboro	OR	97124	503-646-1111	646-1112
Van Well Nursery 2821 Grant Rd *TF:* 800-572-1553 ■ *Web:* www.vanwell.net	East Wenatchee	WA	98802	509-886-8189	886-0294
Van Zyverden Inc 8079 Van Zyverden Rd *TF:* 800-332-2852 ■ *Web:* www.vanzyverden.com	Meridian	MS	39305	601-679-8274	679-8039

	City	State	Zip	Phone	Fax
W & E Radtke Inc W168 N12276 Century Ln *Web:* weradtke.com	Germantown	WI	53022	262-253-1412	
Zieger & Sons Inc 6215 Ardleigh St *TF:* 800-752-2003 ■ *Web:* www.zieger.com	Philadelphia	PA	19138	215-438-7060	438-8729

297 FLOWERS-BY-WIRE SERVICES

	City	State	Zip	Phone	Fax
Teleflora Inc 11444 Olympic Blvd *Web:* www.teleflora.com	Los Angeles	CA	90064	310-966-5700	966-3612

298 FOIL & LEAF - METAL

	City	State	Zip	Phone	Fax
Accurate Metal Fabricating 1657 N Kostner Ave *Web:* www.accuratemetalfab.com	Chicago	IL	60639	773-235-0400	
Action SuperAbrasive Products Inc 945 Greenbriar Pkwy *Web:* www.actionsuper.com	Brimfield	OH	44240	330-673-7333	
Ad-vance Magnetics Inc 625 Monroe St *Web:* www.advancemag.com	Rochester	IN	46975	574-223-3158	
Adamson Industries Corp 45 Research Dr *Web:* www.adamsonindustries.com	Haverhill	MA	01832	978-681-0370	
Advex Corp 121 Floyd Thompson Dr *Web:* www.advex.net	Hampton	VA	23666	757-865-0920	
AFC Finishing Systems Inc 250 Airport Pkwy *Web:* www.afc-ca.com	Oroville	CA	95965	530-533-8907	
Air Cycle Corp 2200 Ogden Ave Ste 100 *TF:* 800-909-9709 ■ *Web:* www.aircycle.com	Lisle	IL	60532	800-909-9709	
Alamo Industrial Inc 1502 East Walnut St **Fax Area Code:* 830 ■ *TF:* 800-356-6286 ■ *Web:* www.alamo-industrial.com	Seguin	TX	78155	800-356-6286	379-0864*
Alphi Manufacturing Inc 576 Beck St *Web:* www.alphimfg.com	Jonesville	MI	49250	517-849-9945	
American Alloy Fabrication Inc 2842 Jordan Ln Nw *Web:* www.americanalloy.com	Huntsville	AL	35816	256-837-6369	837-6090
American Products Inc (API) 12157 W LinebaughAve Ste 335 *Web:* www.americanprod.com	Tampa	FL	33626	813-925-0144	
American Ramp Sales Co 601 S Mckinley Ave *Web:* www.americanrampcompany.com	Joplin	MO	64801	417-206-6816	
Analytical Industries Inc 2855 Metropolitan Pl *Web:* www.aii1.com	Pomona	CA	91767	909-392-6900	
API Foils Inc 329 New Brunswick Ave *Web:* www.apigroup.com	Rahway	NJ	07065	732-382-6800	
ARC Technology Solutions LLC 165 Ledge St Ste 4 *Web:* www.arcserv.com	Nashua	NH	03060	603-883-3027	
Architectural Brass Co 1130 Donald Lee Hollowell Pkwy Nw *Web:* www.architecturalbrass.com	Atlanta	GA	30318	404-351-0594	
Astro Manufacturing & Design Corp 34459 Curtis Blvd *Web:* www.astromfg.com	Eastlake	OH	44095	440-946-8171	
Automated Precision Inc 15000 Johns Hopkins Dr *Web:* www.apisensor.com	Rockville	MD	20850	240-268-0400	
Automotive Resources Inc 12775 Randolph Ridge Ln *Web:* www.ari-hetra.com	Manassas	VA	20109	703-359-6265	
Axton Inc 441 Derwent Pl Annacis Business Park *Web:* www.axton.ca	Delta	BC	V3M5Y9	604-522-2731	
B&G Equipment Company Inc 135 Region S Dr *Web:* www.bgequip.com	Jackson	GA	30233	678-688-5601	
Begneaud Manufacturing Inc 306 E Amedee Dr *Web:* www.begno.com	Scott	LA	70583	337-237-5069	
Ben O'neal Company Inc 3003 Tenth Ave *Web:* www.bonealco.com	Chattanooga	TN	37407	423-624-3359	
Bergen-Power Pipe Supports Inc 225 Merrimac St *Web:* www.bergenpower.com	Woburn	MA	01801	781-935-9550	
Binder Metal Products Inc 14909 S Broadway *Web:* www.bindermetal.com	Gardena	CA	90248	323-321-4835	
Bob's Barricades Inc 921 Shotgun Rd *Web:* www.bobsbarricades.com	Sunrise	FL	33326	954-423-2627	
Boston Barricade Company Inc 1151 19th St *Web:* www.bostonbarricade.com	Vero Beach	FL	32960	772-569-7202	
Brinkman International Group Inc 167 Ames St *Web:* www.brinkmanig.com	Rochester	NY	14611	585-235-4545	
Bromma Inc 2285 Durham Rd *Web:* www.bromma.com	Roxboro	NC	27573	919-471-4000	
Brudi Bolzoni Auramo Inc 17635 Hoffman Way *Web:* www.bolzoni-auramo.com	Homewood	IL	60430	708-957-8809	
Buff & Shine Manufacturing Inc 2139 E Del Amo Blvd *Web:* www.buffandshine.com	Compton	CA	90220	310-886-5111	
Buffalo Abrasives Inc 960 Erie Ave *Web:* www.buffaloabrasives.com	North Tonawanda	NY	14120	716-693-3856	
Busche Enterprise Division Inc 1563 E State Rd 8 *Web:* www.busche-cnc.com	Albion	IN	46701	260-636-7030	
BW Rogers Co 380 Water St PO Box 1030 *Web:* www.bwrogers.com	Akron	OH	44308	330-315-3100	
C&C Metal Products Corp 456 Nordhoff Pl *Web:* www.ccmetal.com	Englewood	NJ	07631	201-569-7300	
CAM Innovation Inc 215 Philadelphia St *Web:* www.caminnovation.com	Hanover	PA	17331	717-637-5988	

Company	City	State	Zip	Phone	Fax
Carter Enterprises Inc 119 W Main St *Web:* www.carterent.com	Arcadia	IN	46030	317-984-1497	
Catlow Inc 2750 US Rt 40 *Web:* catlow.com	Tipp City	OH	45371	937-898-3236	
CBR Laser Inc 340 Rt 116 W *Web:* www.cbrlaser.com	Plessisville	QC	G6L2Y2	819-362-9339	
Century 3-Plus LLC 2410 W Aero Park Ct *Web:* www.centinc.com	Traverse City	MI	49686	231-946-7500	
Chem-pak Inc 242 Corning Way *Web:* www.chem-pak.com	Martinsburg	WV	25405	304-262-1880	
Chemetal 39 O'Neil St *TF:* 800-807-7341 ■ *Web:* www.chmetal.com	EastHampton	MA	01027	413-529-0718	529-9898
Chicago Powdered Metal Products Co 9700 Waveland Ave *Web:* www.chipm.com	Franklin Park	IL	60131	847-678-2836	
Clark Technology Systems Inc 159 Harveys Ln *Web:* www.clarkts.com	Milton	PA	17847	570-742-1819	
Colliflower Inc 9320 Pulaski Hwy *Web:* www.colliflower.com	Baltimore	MD	21220	410-686-1200	
Columbiana Hi Tech LLC 1802 Fairfax Rd *Web:* www.chtnuclear.com	Greensboro	NC	27407	336-852-5679	
Compx Security Products Inc 200 Old Mill Rd *Web:* www.compxnet.com	Mauldin	SC	29662	864-297-6655	
Comtec Manufacturing Inc 1012 Delaum Rd *Web:* www.comtecmfg.com	Saint Marys	PA	15857	814-834-9300	
Concast Metal Products Co 131 Myoma Rd PO Box 816 *Web:* www.concast.com	Mars	PA	16046	724-538-4000	
Concord Steel Centre Ltd 147 Ashbridge Cir *Web:* www.concordsteel.com	Woodbridge	ON	L4L3R5	905-856-1717	
Creamer Metal Products Inc 77 S Madison Rd *Web:* creamermetal.com	London	OH	43140	740-852-1752	
Crown Roll Leaf Inc 91 Illinois Ave *TF:* 800-631-3831 ■ *Web:* www.crownrollleaf.com	Paterson	NJ	07503	973-742-4000	742-0219
Cryomagnetics Inc 1006 Alvin Weinberg Dr *Web:* www.cryomagnetics.com	Oak Ridge	TN	37830	865-482-9551	
Curtiss-Wright Flow Control Corp 13925 Ballantyne Corporate Pl Ste 400 *Web:* www.cwfc.com	Charlotte	NC	28277	704-869-4602	
Dalco Metals Inc 857 Walworth St *Web:* www.dalcometals.com	Walworth	WI	53184	262-275-6175	
Dalmec Inc 469 Fox Ct *Web:* www.dalmec.com	Bloomingdale	IL	60108	630-307-8426	
Detroit Tool Metal Products Inc 949 Bethel Rd *Web:* www.dtmp.com	Lebanon	MO	65536	417-532-2142	
Dexmet Corp 22 Barnes Industrial Rd S *Web:* www.dexmet.com	Wallingford	CT	06492	203-294-4440	
Diamond Z Manufacturing 11299 Bass Ln *Web:* www.diamondz.com	Caldwell	ID	83605	208-585-2929	
DiSanto Technology Inc 10 Constitution Blvd S *Web:* www.disanto.com	Shelton	CT	06484	203-712-1030	
Diversified Metal Products Inc 3710 N Yellowstone Hwy *Web:* www.diversifiedmetal.com	Idaho Falls	ID	83401	208-529-9655	
Dixie Metal Products Inc 442 Sw 54th Ct *Web:* www.dixiemetals.com	Ocala	FL	34474	352-873-2554	
Durable Packaging International Inc 750 Northgate Pkwy *Web:* www.durablepackaging.com	Wheeling	IL	60090	847-541-4400	
Edmonton Exchanger Group of Cos 5545-89 St *Web:* www.edmontonexchanger.com	Edmonton	AB	T6E5W9	780-468-6722	
Electro Prime Group LLC 4510 Lint Ave Ste B *Web:* www.electroprime.com	Toledo	OH	43612	419-476-0100	
Executive Safe & Security Corp 1480 S Carlos Ave *Web:* www.amphion.biz	Ontario	CA	91761	909-947-7020	
FBN Metal Products 5020 S Nathaniel Lyon St *Web:* fbnmetal.com	Battlefield	MO	65619	417-882-2830	
Ferragon Corp 11103 Memphis Ave *Web:* www.ferragon.com	Cleveland	OH	44144	216-671-6161	
Ferrell-Ross Roll Manufacturing Inc 102 FM 2856 (Holly Sugar Rd) *Web:* www.ferrellross.com	Hereford	TX	79045	806-364-9051	
Ferrousouth 38 County Rd 370 *Web:* www.ferrousmetalprocessing.com	Iuka	MS	38852	662-424-0115	
Formco Metal Products Inc 556 Clayton Ct *Web:* www.formcometal.com	Wood Dale	IL	60191	630-766-4441	
Fort Wayne Metals Inc 9609 Ardmore Ave *Web:* www.fwmetals.com	Fort Wayne	IN	46809	260-747-4154	
Freeman Metal Products Inc 2124 US Hwy 13 S *Web:* www.freemanmetal.com	Ahoskie	NC	27910	252-332-5390	
Fulton Bellows LLC 2801 Red Dog Ln *Web:* www.fultonbellows.com	Knoxville	TN	37914	865-546-0550	
Gamber-Johnson Inc 3001 Borham Ave *Web:* www.gamberjohnson.com	Stevens Point	WI	54481	715-344-3482	
GH Metal Solutions Inc 2890 Airport Rd NW *Web:* www.ghmetalsolutions.com	Fort Payne	AL	35968	256-845-5411	
Glendo Corp PO Box 1153 *Web:* www.glendo.com	Emporia	KS	66801	620-343-1084	
Global Gear & Machining LLC 2500 Curtiss St *Web:* www.globalgearllc.com	Downers Grove	IL	60515	630-969-9400	
Golberg Companies Inc 4179 County Rd 40 Nw *Web:* www.gcilift.com	Garfield	MN	56332	320-834-2211	
Gould Electronics Inc 2929 W Chandler Blvd *Web:* www.gould.com	Chandler	AZ	85224	480-899-0343	
Grace Manufacturing Inc 614 Sr 247 *Web:* www.gracemfg.com	Russellville	AR	72802	479-968-5455	
Gray Metal Products Inc 495 Rochester St *Web:* www.graymetal.com	Avon	NY	14414	585-226-8660	
Handi-Foil Corp 135 E Hintz Rd *Web:* www.handi-foil.com	Wheeling	IL	60090	847-520-1000	
Harbor Manufacturing Inc 8300 W 185th St *Web:* www.harbormfg.com	Tinley Park	IL	60487	708-614-6400	
Herr-Voss Corp 130 Main St *Web:* www.herr-voss.com	Callery	PA	16024	724-538-3180	
Hodge Products Inc 1410 Hill St *TF:* 800-778-2217 ■ *Web:* www.hpionline.com	El Cajon	CA	92020	800-778-2217	
Hoover Materials Handling Group Inc 2135 Hwy Six S *Web:* www.hooversolutions.com	Houston	TX	77077	281-870-8402	
HW Metal Products Inc 19480 SW 118th Ave *Web:* www.hwmetals.com	Tualatin	OR	97062	503-692-1690	
HyPro Inc 600 S Jefferson St PO Box 370 *Web:* www.hypro.com	Waterford	WI	53185	262-534-5141	
Ideal Shield LLC 2525 Clark St *TF:* 866-825-8659 ■ *Web:* www.idealshield.com	Detroit	MI	48209	313-842-7290	
J L Manufacturing Inc 12310 Hwy 99 Ste 131 *Web:* www.jlmfg.com	Everett	WA	98204	425-355-3330	
Jireh Metal Inc 3635 Nardin St *Web:* www.jirehmetal.com	Grandville	MI	49418	616-531-7581	
John R Wald Company Inc 10576 Fairgrounds Rd *Web:* www.jrwald.com	Huntingdon	PA	16652	814-643-3908	
Johnson Screens Inc 1950 Old Hwy 8 NW *Web:* www.water.bilfinger.com/	New Brighton	MN	55112	651-636-3900	
JW Winco Inc 2815 S Calhoun Rd *Web:* www.jwwinco.com	New Berlin	WI	53151	262-786-8227	
King Machine & Tool Co 1237 Sanders Ave Sw *Web:* www.kmtco.com	Massillon	OH	44647	330-833-7217	
KrisDee & Associates Inc 755 Schneider Dr *Web:* www.krisdee.com	South Elgin	IL	60177	847-608-8300	
Lisega Inc 375 Lisega Blvd *Web:* www.lisega.de	Newport	TN	37821	423-625-2000	
Mancor Industries Inc 2485 Speers Rd *Web:* www.mancor.com	Oakville	ON	L6L2X9	905-827-3737	844-0999
Manncorp Inc 1610 Republic Rd *Web:* www.manncorp.com	Huntingdon Valley	PA	19006	215-830-1200	
Master Magnetics Inc 747 S Gilbert St *Web:* www.magnetsource.com	Castle Rock	CO	80104	303-688-3966	
Matandy Steel & Metal Products LLC 1200 Central Ave *Web:* www.matandy.com	Hamilton	OH	45011	513-844-2277	
Meridian Lightweight Technologies Inc 25 MacNab Ave *Web:* www.meridian-mag.com	Strathroy	ON	N7G4H6	519-246-9600	245-6605
Metal Culverts Inc 2107 Rear Missouri Blvd *Web:* www.metalculverts.com	Jefferson City	MO	65109	573-636-7312	
Microflex Inc 1800 N US Hwy 1 *Web:* www.microflexinc.com	Ormond Beach	FL	32174	386-677-8100	
Mid-State Machine & Fabricating Corp 2730 Mine and Mill Rd *Web:* www.midstatefl.com	Lakeland	FL	33801	863-665-6233	
MPI Group LLC, The 319 N Hills Rd *Web:* www.metalproductsinc.com	Corbin	KY	40701	606-523-0461	
Newman Brothers Inc 5609 Ctr Hill Ave *Web:* www.newmanbrothers.com	Cincinnati	OH	45216	513-242-0011	
Northshore Manufacturing Inc 530 Recycle Ctr Dr *Web:* www.builtritehandlers.com	Two Harbors	MN	55616	218-834-5555	
Oak-Mitsui Inc 80 First St *TF:* 800-424-8802 ■ *Web:* www.oakmitsui.com	Hoosick Falls	NY	12090	518-686-4961	686-8080
October Company Inc 51 Ferry St *TF:* 800-628-9346 ■ *Web:* octobercompany.com	EastHampton	MA	01027	413-527-9380	527-0091
Pasco 2600 S Hanley Rd Ste 450 *Web:* pascosystems.com	Saint Louis	MO	63144	314-781-2212	
Pauli Systems Inc 1820 Walters Ct *Web:* www.paulisystems.com	Fairfield	CA	94533	707-429-2434	
Pearlman Industries Inc 6210 S Garfield Ave *Web:* www.pearlabrasive.com	Commerce	CA	90040	562-927-5561	
Penn Engineering Components 29045 Ave Penn *Web:* www.pemnet.com	Valencia	CA	91355	818-503-1511	
Perfection Metal Products Inc 3393 De La Cruz Blvd *Web:* www.pmp-inc.com	Santa Clara	CA	95054	408-496-2950	
Precision Hose 2200 Centre Park Ct *Web:* www.precisionhose.com	Stone Mountain	GA	30087	770-413-5680	
Precision Manufacturing Group LLC 501 Little Falls Rd *Web:* www.servometer.com	Cedar Grove	NJ	07009	973-785-4630	
Prentex Alloy Fabricators Inc 3108 Sylvan Ave *Fax Area Code: 972 ■ *Web:* www.prentex.com	Dallas	TX	75212	214-748-7837	748-7850*
ProSteel Security Products Inc 1400 S State St *Web:* www.prosteel.us	Provo	UT	84603	801-373-2385	
PSM Industries Inc 14000 Avalon Blvd *Web:* www.psmindustries.com	Los Angeles	CA	90061	310-715-9800	
Quickparts.com Inc 301 Perimeter Ctr N Ste 400 *Web:* www.quickparts.com	Atlanta	GA	30346	770-901-3200	
Reel-Neat Systems Inc 6408 S Eastern Ave *Web:* www.reelomatic.com	Oklahoma City	OK	73149	405-672-0000	
Regal Metal Products Co 3615 Union Ave Se *Web:* www.regalmetalproducts.com	Minerva	OH	44657	330-868-6343	
Reo Hydraulics & Manufacturing 18475 Sherwood St *Web:* www.regroup.com	Detroit	MI	48234	313-891-2244	

Company	City	State	Zip	Phone	Fax
River City Metal Products Inc 655 Godfrey Ave SW *Web:* www.rcmpinc.com	Grand Rapids	MI	49503	616-235-3746	
Riverhawk Company LP 215 Clinton Rd *Web:* www.riverhawk.com	New Hartford	NY	13413	315-768-4855	
Rivers Metal Products Inc 3100 N 38th St *Web:* www.riversmetal.com	Lincoln	NE	68504	402-466-2329	
Robinson Fin Machines Inc 13670 Us Hwy 68 *Web:* www.robfin.com	Kenton	OH	43326	419-674-4152	
Rochester Metal Products Corp 616 Indiana Ave PO Box 488 *Web:* www.rochestermetals.com	Rochester	IN	46975	574-223-3164	
Sandbox Industries Inc 213 N Racine Ave Ste 213 *Web:* www.sandboxindustries.com	Chicago	IL	60607	312-243-4100	
Screen Tech Inc 470 Needles Dr *Web:* www.screentechinc.com	San Jose	CA	95112	408-885-8750	
Selig Group Inc 342 E Wabash Ave *Web:* www.seligsealing.com	Forrest	IL	61741	815-785-2100	
Shade Systems Inc 4150 Sw 19th St *Web:* www.shadesystemsinc.com	Ocala	FL	34474	352-237-0135	
Smart Machine Technologies Inc 650 Frith Dr *Web:* www.smartmachine.com	Ridgeway	VA	24148	276-632-9853	
Spartan Light Metal Products Inc 3668 S Geyer Rd Ste 210 *Web:* www.spartanlmp.com	St. Louis	MO	63127	314-620-2500	
Spinco Metal Products Inc One Country Club Dr *Web:* www.spincometal.com	Newark	NY	14513	315-331-6285	
Steel Craft Technologies Inc 8057 Graphic Dr NE *Web:* www.steelcrafttech.com	Belmont	MI	49306	616-866-4400	
Suhm Spring Works Inc 2710 McKinney *Web:* www.suhm.net	Houston	TX	77003	713-224-9293	
Superior Metal Products Inc 2463 Hwy 107 *Web:* www.superiormetal.com	Chuckey	TN	37641	423-257-2154	257-3617
Superior Metal Technologies LLC 9850 E 30th St *Web:* www.superiormetals.us	Indianapolis	IN	46229	317-897-9850	
Tam Metal Products Inc 55 Whitney Rd *Web:* www.tam-ind.com	Mahwah	NJ	07430	201-848-7800	
Topcraft Metal Products Inc 5112 40th Ave *Web:* www.topcraftmetal.com	Hudsonville	MI	49426	616-669-1790	
TrafFix Devices Inc 160 Avenida La Pata *Web:* www.traffixdevices.com	San Clemente	CA	92673	949-361-5663	
Tricor Metals Inc 3225 W Old Lincoln Way *Web:* www.tricormetals.com	Wooster	OH	44691	330-264-3299	
Trulock Tool Co 113 Drayton St *Web:* trulockchokes.com	Whigham	GA	39897	229-762-4678	
Turbotec Products Inc 651 Day Hill Rd *Web:* turbotecproducts.com	Windsor	CT	06095	860-731-4200	
United Metal Products Inc 1920 E Encanto Dr *Web:* www.unitedmetal.com	Tempe	AZ	85281	480-968-9550	
USM Aerostructures Corp 74 W Sixth St *Web:* www.usmaero.net	Wyoming	PA	18644	570-613-1234	
Utica Metal Products Inc 1526 Lincoln Ave *Web:* www.uticametals.com	Utica	NY	13502	315-732-6163	
V&M Precision Machining & Grinding 1130 Columbia St *Web:* www.vm-machining.com	Brea	CA	92821	714-257-4850	
Valco Manufacturing Company Inc 925 Boren Rd *Web:* www.valcomfg.com	Duncan	OK	73533	580-255-4300	
Vooner Flogard Corp 4729 Stockholm Ct *Web:* www.vooner.com	Charlotte	NC	28273	704-552-9314	
Wagman Metal Products Inc 400 S Albemarle St *Web:* www.wagmanmetal.com	York	PA	17403	717-854-2120	
Warren Co, The 2201 Loveland Ave *TF:* 800-562-0357 ■ *Web:* www.thewarrencompany.com	Erie	PA	16506	800-562-0357	
Wayne Metal Products Inc 5461 Benchmark Ln *Web:* www.waynemetalproductsinc.com	Sanford	FL	32773	407-321-7168	
Weiser Metal Products 34311 E M72 PO Box 370 *Web:* www.weisermetal.com	Lincoln	MI	48742	989-736-6055	736-6717
Welded Ring Products Company Inc 2180 W 114th St *Web:* www.weldedring.com	Cleveland	OH	44102	216-961-3800	
Weldship Corp 225 W Second St *Web:* www.weldship.com	Bethlehem	PA	18015	610-861-7330	

299 FOOD PRODUCTS - MFR

SEE ALSO Agricultural Products p. 1721; Ice - Manufactured p. 2550; Livestock & Poultry Feeds - Prepared p. 2672; Meat Packing Plants p. 2723; Pet Products p. 2916; Poultry Processing p. 2955; Bakeries p. 1847; Salt p. 3131; Beverages - Mfr p. 1865

Company	City	State	Zip	Phone	Fax
AlturnaMATS Inc 701 E Spring St Mailbox #9 *Web:* www.alturnamats.com	Titusville	PA	16354	814-827-8884	
Broaster Company LLC, The 2855 Cranston Rd *Web:* www.broaster.com	Beloit	WI	53511	608-365-0193	
Brown International Corporation LLC 333 Ave M NW *Web:* www.brown-intl.com	Winter Haven	FL	33881	863-299-2111	
Cantrell Machine Company Inc 1400 S Bradford St *Web:* www.cantrell.com	Gainesville	GA	30503	770-536-3611	
Computerway Food Systems 635 Southwest St *Web:* www.mycfs.com	High Point	NC	27260	336-841-7289	
Conchita Foods Inc 10051 NW 99th Ave Ste 3 *Web:* www.conchita-foods.com	Miami	FL	33178	305-888-9703	888-1020
Contemar Silo Systems Inc 30 Pennsylvania Ave Unit 8 *Web:* www.contemar.com	Concord	ON	L4K4A5	905-669-3604	
Fetco 600 Rose Rd *Web:* www.fetco.com	Lake Zurich	IL	60047	847-821-1177	
Flatout Inc 1422 Woodland Dr *TF:* 866-944-5445 ■ *Web:* www.flatoutbread.com	Saline	MI	48176	734-944-4262	
Graybill Machines Inc 221 W Lexington Rd *Web:* www.graybillmachines.com	Lititz	PA	17543	717-626-5221	
John Bean Technologies Corp 70 W Madison Ste 4400 *Web:* www.jbtcorporation.com	Chicago	IL	60602	312-861-5900	
Koss Industrial Inc 1943 Commercial Way *Web:* www.kossindustrial.com	Green Bay	WI	54311	920-469-5300	
Nemco Food Equipment Ltd 301 Meuse Argonne *Web:* www.nemcofoodequip.com	Hicksville	OH	43526	419-542-7751	
NuTEC Manufacturing 908 Garnet Ct *Web:* nutecmfg.com	New Lenox	IL	60451	815-722-2800	
Prime Equipment Group Inc 2000 E Fulton St *Web:* www.primeequipmentgroup.com	Columbus	OH	43205	614-253-8590	
Qualtech Inc 1880 Leon-Harmel St *Web:* www.qualtech.ca	Quebec City	QC	G1N4K3	418-686-3802	
Remco Products Corp 4735 W 106th St *Web:* remcoproducts.com	Zionsville	IN	46077	317-876-9856	
Revent Inc 100 Ethel Rd W *Web:* www.revent.com	Piscataway	NJ	08854	732-777-9433	
Rhee Bros Inc 7461 Coca Cola Dr *Web:* www.rheebros.com	Hanover	MD	21076	410-381-9000	381-4989
Starflex Corp 204 Turner Rd *Web:* www.starflexcorp.com	Jonesboro	GA	30236	770-471-2111	
Sunny Dell Foods Inc 135 N Fifth St *Web:* www.sunnydell.com	Oxford	PA	19363	610-932-5164	932-9479
Thomsen Group LLC 1303 43rd St *TF:* 800-558-4018 ■ *Web:* www.lcthomsen.com	Kenosha	WI	53140	800-558-4018	
Wixon Inc 1390 E Bolivar Ave *TF:* 800-841-5304 ■ *Web:* www.wixon.com	Saint Francis	WI	53235	414-769-3000	769-3024
Wolf-tec Inc 20 Kieffer Ln *Web:* www.wolf-tec.com	Kingston	NY	12401	845-340-9727	

299-1 Bakery Products - Fresh

Company	City	State	Zip	Phone	Fax
Alessi Bakeries Inc 2909 W Cypress St *Web:* www.alessibakeries.com	Tampa	FL	33609	813-879-4544	872-9103
Alfred Nickles Bakery Inc 26 N Main St *TF:* 800-635-1110 ■ *Web:* www.nicklesbakery.com	Navarre	OH	44662	330-879-5635	879-5896
Amoroso's Baking Co 845 S 55th St *TF:* 800-377-6557 ■ *Web:* www.amorosobaking.com	Philadelphia	PA	19143	215-471-4740	471-5323
Arnie's Inc 722 Leonard St NW *Web:* www.arniesrestaurants.com	Grand Rapids	MI	49503	616-454-3098	
Bakewise Brands Inc 1688 N Wayneport Rd	Macedon	NY	14502	315-986-9999	
Bama Pie Ltd 5377 E 66th St N *Web:* bama.com	Tulsa	OK	74117	918-592-0778	
Barker Specialty Products LLC 703 Franklin St PO Box 478 *Web:* www.barkercompany.com	Keosauqua	IA	52565	319-293-3777	
Bays Corp PO Box 1455 **Fax Area Code:* 312 ■ *Web:* www.bays.com	Chicago	IL	60690	800-367-2297	226-3435*
Better Baked Foods Inc 56 Smedley St *Web:* www.betterbaked.com	North East	PA	16428	814-725-8778	725-8785
Bimbo Bakeries USA PO Box 976 **Fax Area Code:* 610 ■ *TF:* 800-984-0989 ■ *Web:* www.bimbobakeriesusa.com	Horsham	PA	19044	800-984-0989	320-9286*
Brown's Bakery 1226 Versailles Rd *Web:* www.brownbakery.com	Lexington	KY	40508	859-225-8400	
Byrnes & Kiefer Coompany 131 Kline Ave *Web:* www.bkcompany.com	Callery	PA	16024	724-538-5200	538-9292
Calise & Sons Bakery Inc Two Quality Dr *TF:* 800-225-4737 ■ *Web:* www.calisebakery.com	Lincoln	RI	02865	401-334-3444	334-0938
Carolina Foods Inc 1807 S Tryon St *Web:* carolinafoodsinc.com	Charlotte	NC	28203	704-333-9812	
Cloverhill Bakery Inc 2035 N Narragansett Ave *Web:* www.cloverhill.com	Chicago	IL	60639	773-745-9800	745-1647
Colchester Bakery 96 Lebanon Ave *Web:* colchester.areaconnect.com	Colchester	CT	06415	860-537-2415	
Country Oven Bakery Inc 2840 Pioneer Dr	Bowling Green	KY	42101	270-782-3200	782-7170
Dakota Brands International Inc 2121 13th St NE *Web:* www.dakotabrands.com	Jamestown	ND	58401	701-252-5073	251-1047
De Wafelbakkers LLC 10000 Crystal Hill Rd *TF:* 800-924-3391 ■ *Web:* www.dewafelbakkers.com	North Little Rock	AR	72113	501-791-3320	791-0309
Delight Grecian Foods Inc 1201 Tonne Rd *TF:* 800-621-4387 ■ *Web:* www.greciandelight.com	Elk Grove Village	IL	60007	847-364-1010	364-1077
Dinkel's Bakery 3329 N Lincoln Ave *TF Orders:* 800-822-8817 ■ *Web:* www.dinkels.com	Chicago	IL	60657	773-281-7300	281-6169
Ellison Bakery 4108 W Ferguson Rd *Web:* www.ebakery.com	Fort Wayne	IN	46809	260-747-6136	747-1954
Fantini Baking Company Inc 375 Washington St *TF:* 800-223-9037 ■ *Web:* www.fantinibakery.com	Haverhill	MA	01832	978-373-1273	373-6250
Flowers Foods Inc 1919 Flowers Cir *NYSE:* FLO ■ **Fax:* Mktg ■ *Web:* www.flowersfoods.com	Thomasville	GA	31757	229-226-9110	226-1318*
Franz Family Bakeries 2006 S Weller St *Web:* franzbakery.com	Seattle	WA	98144	206-726-7535	
Franz Family Bakeries William's Div 690 Biddle Rd *Web:* franzbakery.com	Medford	OR	97504	541-772-5816	

Company	City	State	Zip	Phone	Fax
Fresh Start Bakeries 145 S State College Blvd Ste 200 *Web:* www.freshstartbakeries.com	Brea	CA	92821	714-256-8900	256-8916
Greyston Bakery Inc 104 Alexander St *TF:* 800-289-2253 ■ *Web:* greyston.com	Yonkers	NY	10701	914-375-1510	375-1514
H & S Bakery Inc 601 S Caroline St *TF:* 800-959-7655 ■ *Web:* www.hsbakery.com	Baltimore	MD	21231	410-276-7254	558-3096
Heinemann's Bakeries LLC PO Box 558265 *Web:* www.heinemanns.com	Chicago	IL	60655	616-885-9094	885-9031
Heiners Bakery Inc 1300 Adams Ave *TF:* 800-776-8411 ■ *Web:* heinersbakery.com	Huntington	WV	25704	304-523-8411	525-9268
Herman Seekamp Inc 1120 W Fullerton Ave *Web:* www.clydesdonuts.com	Addison	IL	60101	630-628-6555	628-6838
JTM Foods Inc 2126 E 33rd St *Web:* www.jjsbakery.net	Erie	PA	16510	814-899-0886	899-9862
Klosterman Baking Company Inc 4760 Paddock Rd *TF:* 877-301-1004 ■ *Web:* www.klostermanbakery.com	Cincinnati	OH	45229	513-242-1004	242-8257
Lawler Foods Ltd Inc PO Box 2558 *TF:* 800-541-8285 ■ *Web:* www.lawlers.com	Humble	TX	77347	281-446-0059	446-3806
Leidenheimer Baking Co 1501 Simon Bolivar Ave *TF:* 800-259-9099 ■ *Web:* www.leidenheimer.com	New Orleans	LA	70113	504-525-1575	525-1596
Lepage Bakeries Inc 1919 Flowers Cir *Web:* www.flowersfoods.com	Thomasville	GA	31757	229-226-9110	
Lewis Bakeries Inc 500 N Fulton Ave *TF:* 800-365-2812 ■ *Web:* lewisbakeries.net	Evansville	IN	47710	812-425-4642	425-7609
Little Dutch Boy Bakery Inc 12349 South 970 East	Draper	UT	84020	801-571-3800	571-3802
Martin's Famous Pastry Shoppe Inc 1000 Potato Roll Ln *TF Cust Svc:* 800-548-1200 ■ *Web:* potatorolls.com	Chambersburg	PA	17201	717-263-9580	263-6687
Mary Ann's Baking Co 8371 Carbide Ct *Web:* maryannsbaking.com	Sacramento	CA	95828	916-681-7444	681-7470
McKee Foods Corp PO Box 750 **Fax:* Hum Res ■ *TF Cust Svc:* 800-522-4499 ■ *Web:* www.mckeefoods.com	Collegedale	TN	37315	423-238-7111	238-7127*
Morabito Baking Company Inc 757 Kohn St *TF:* 800-525-7747 ■ *Web:* www.morabito.com	Norristown	PA	19401	610-275-5419	275-0358
Oak State Products Inc PO Box 549 *Web:* www.oakstate.com	Wenona	IL	61377	815-853-4348	853-4625
Omni Baking Co 2621 Freddy Ln Bldg 7 *Web:* www.omnibaking.com	Vineland	NJ	08360	856-205-1485	
Orlando Baking Company Inc 7777 Grand Ave *TF:* 800-362-5504 ■ *Web:* www.orlandobaking.com	Cleveland	OH	44104	216-361-1872	391-3469
Pan-O-Gold Baking Co 444 E St Germain *TF:* 800-444-7005 ■ *Web:* www.panogold.com	Saint Cloud	MN	56304	320-251-9361	
Pechters Baking 840 Jersey St *Web:* pechters.com	Harrison	NJ	07029	973-483-3374	
Pepperidge Farm Inc 595 Westport Ave *TF PR:* 888-737-7374 ■ *Web:* www.pepperidgefarm.com	Norwalk	CT	06851	203-846-7000	846-7145
Piantedosi Baking Company Inc 240 Commercial St *TF:* 800-339-0080 ■ *Web:* www.piantedosi.com	Malden	MA	02148	781-321-3400	324-5647
Quinzani's Bakery 380 Harrison Ave *Web:* www.quinzanisbakery.com	Boston	MA	02118	617-426-2114	451-8075
Ralcorp Frozen Bakery Products 3250 Lacey Rd Ste 600 *Web:* www.ralcorpfrozen.com	Downers Grove	IL	60515	630-455-5200	920-8945
Richmond Baking Co 520 N Sixth St *Web:* www.richmondbaking.com	Richmond	IN	47374	765-962-8535	962-2253
Rockland Bakery Inc 94 Demarest Mill Rd W *Web:* www.rocklandbakery.com	Nanuet	NY	10954	845-623-5800	623-6921
Rothbury Farms PO Box 202 *TF:* 877-684-2879 ■ *Web:* rothburyfarms.com	Grand Rapids	MI	49501	877-684-2879	
Schmidt Baking Company Inc 7801 Fitch Ln *TF:* 800-456-2253 ■ *Web:* www.schmidtbaking.com	Baltimore	MD	21236	410-668-8200	882-2051
Schwebel Baking Co PO Box 6018 *TF:* 800-860-2867 ■ *Web:* www.schwebels.com	Youngstown	OH	44501	330-783-2860	782-1774
Signature Breads Inc 100 Justin Dr *TF:* 888-602-6533 ■ *Web:* www.signaturebreads.com	Chelsea	MA	02150	888-602-6533	
Sokol & Co 5315 Dansher Rd *TF Cust Svc:* 800-328-7656 ■ *Web:* www.solofoods.com	Countryside	IL	60525	708-482-8250	482-9750
Specialty Bakers Inc 450 S State Rd *Web:* www.sbiladyfingers.com	Marysville	PA	17053	717-957-2131	
Svenhard's Swedish Bakery Inc 335 Adeline St *TF:* 800-705-3379 ■ *Web:* www.svenhards.com	Oakland	CA	94607	510-834-5035	839-6797
Table Talk Pies Inc 120 Washington St *Web:* www.tabletalkpie.com	Worcester	MA	01610	508-798-8811	798-0848
Tasty Baking Co 4300 S 26th St Ste 200 *TF:* 800-248-2789 ■ *Web:* www.tastykake.com	Philadelphia	PA	19112	215-221-8500	
Turano Baking Co 6501 Roosevelt Rd *Web:* www.turano.com	Berwyn	IL	60402	708-788-9220	788-3075
Wenner Bread Products Inc 33 Rajon Rd *TF:* 800-869-6262 ■ *Web:* www.wenner-bread.com	Bayport	NY	11705	631-563-6262	
Wolferman's 2500 S Pacific Hwy PO Box 9100 *TF:* 800-999-0169 ■ *Web:* www.wolfermans.com	Medford	OR	97501	800-999-0169	999-7548

299-2 Bakery Products - Frozen

Company	City	State	Zip	Phone	Fax
Athens Pastries & Frozen Foods Inc 13600 Snow Rd **Fax Area Code:* 210 ■ *TF:* 800-837-5683 ■ *Web:* www.athens.com	Brookpark	OH	44142	216-676-8500	324-1875*
Bridgford Foods Corp 1308 N Patt St *NASDAQ: BRID* ■ *TF:* 800-854-3255 ■ *Web:* www.bridgford.com	Anaheim	CA	92801	714-526-5533	526-4360
Country Oven Bakery Inc 2840 Pioneer Dr	Bowling Green	KY	42101	270-782-3200	782-7170
Dessert Innovations Inc 25-B Enterprise Blvd *TF:* 800-359-7351 ■ *Web:* www.dessertinnovations.com	Atlanta	GA	30336	404-691-5000	691-5001
Don Lee Farms 200 E Beach Ave *Web:* donleefarms.com	Inglewood	CA	90302	310-674-3180	673-7008
Eli's Cheesecake Co 6701 W Forest Preserve Dr *TF:* 800-999-8300 ■ *Web:* www.elicheesecake.com	Chicago	IL	60634	773-736-3417	205-3801
Guttenplans Frozen Dough 100 Hwy 36 *TF General:* 888-422-4357 ■ *Web:* www.guttenplan.com	Middletown	NJ	07748	732-495-9480	
James Skinner Baking Co 4657 G St *TF:* 800-358-7428 ■ *Web:* www.skinnerbaking.com	Omaha	NE	68117	402-734-1672	734-0516
Main Street Gourmet Inc 170 Muffin Ln *TF:* 800-678-6246 ■ *Web:* www.mainstreetgourmet.com	Cuyahoga Falls	OH	44223	330-929-0000	920-8329
Maplehurst Inc 50 Maplehurst Dr *TF:* 800-344-4235 ■ *Web:* www.maplehurstbakeries.com	Brownsburg	IN	46112	317-858-9000	
Rhino Foods Inc 79 Industrial Pkwy *TF:* 800-542-3463 ■ *Web:* www.rhinofoods.com	Burlington	VT	05401	802-862-0252	865-4145
Vie de France Yamazaki Inc 2070 Chain Bridge Rd Ste 500 *TF General:* 800-446-4404 ■ *Web:* www.vdfy.com	Vienna	VA	22182	703-442-9205	821-2695

299-3 Butter (Creamery)

Company	City	State	Zip	Phone	Fax
AMPI 315 N Broadway *TF:* 800-533-3580 ■ *Web:* www.ampi.com	New Ulm	MN	56073	507-354-8295	
Cabot Creamery One Home Farm Way *TF:* 888-792-2268 ■ *Web:* www.cabotcheese.coop	Montpelier	VT	05602	802-229-9361	
California Dairies Inc 2000 N Plz Dr *Web:* www.californiadairies.com	Visalia	CA	93291	559-625-2200	625-5433
Challenge Dairy Products Inc 11875 Dublin Blvd Ste B230 *Web:* www.challengedairy.com	Dublin	CA	94568	925-828-6160	551-7591
Farmers Co-op Creamery Inc (FCC) 700 N Hwy 99 W *Web:* www.farmerscoop.org	McMinnville	OR	97128	503-472-2157	472-3821
Grassland Dairy Products Company Inc N 8790 Fairgrounds Ave PO Box 160 *TF:* 800-428-8837 ■ *Web:* www.grassland.com	Greenwood	WI	54437	715-267-6182	267-6044
Land O'Lakes Inc 4001 Lexington Ave N **Fax:* Hum Res ■ *TF:* 800-328-9680 ■ *Web:* www.landolakesinc.com	Arden Hills	MN	55126	651-481-2222	481-2022*
O-AT-KA Milk Products Co-op Inc 700 Ellicott St *TF:* 800-828-8152 ■ *Web:* www.oatkamilk.com	Batavia	NY	14020	585-343-0536	343-4473
Plainview Milk Products Co-Op 130 Second St SW *TF:* 800-356-5606 ■ *Web:* www.plainviewmilk.com	Plainview	MN	55964	507-534-3872	534-3992
Schreiber Foods Inc 425 Pine St *Web:* www.schreiberfoods.com	Green Bay	WI	54301	920-437-7601	437-1617
Sommermaid Creamery Inc PO Box 350 *Web:* www.sommermaid.com	Doylestown	PA	18901	215-345-6160	345-4945

299-4 Cereals (Breakfast)

Company	City	State	Zip	Phone	Fax
Big G Cereals PO Box 9452 PO Box 9452 **Fax Area Code:* 763 ■ **Fax:* PR ■ *TF:* 800-248-7310 ■ *Web:* www.generalmills.com	Minneapolis	MN	55440	800-248-7310	764-8330*
Bob's Red Mill Natural Foods Inc 13521 SE Pheasant Ct *TF:* 800-553-2258 ■ *Web:* www.bobsredmill.com	Milwaukie	OR	97222	503-654-3215	653-1339
Gilster-Mary Lee Corp 1037 State St PO Box 227 *Web:* gilstermarylee.com	Chester	IL	62233	618-826-2361	826-2973
Homestead Mills 221 N River St PO Box 1115 *TF:* 800-652-5233 ■ *Web:* www.homesteadmills.com	Cook	MN	55723	218-666-5233	666-5236
Honeyville Grain Inc 11600 Dayton Dr *TF:* 888-810-3212 ■ *Web:* www.honeyville.com	Rancho Cucamonga	CA	91730	909-980-9500	980-6503
Hyde & Hyde Inc 300 El Sobrante Rd *Web:* www.hydeandhyde.com	Corona	CA	92879	951-817-2300	270-3526
Kellogg Co One Kellogg Sq PO Box 3599 *NYSE: K* ■ *TF Cust Svc:* 800-962-1413 ■ *Web:* www.kelloggs.com	Battle Creek	MI	49016	269-961-2000	961-2871
Lundberg Family Farms 5370 Church St PO Box 369 *Web:* www.lundberg.com	Richvale	CA	95974	530-882-4551	882-4500
New England Natural Bakers 74 Fairview St E *TF:* 800-910-2884 ■ *Web:* www.newenglandnaturalbakers.com	Greenfield	MA	01301	413-772-2239	772-2936
Organic Milling Co 505 W Allen Ave *TF:* 800-638-8686 ■ *Web:* www.organicmilling.com/contact.html	San Dimas	CA	91773	909-599-0961	599-5180
Quaker Oats Co 555 W Monroe St *TF:* 800-367-6287 ■ *Web:* www.quakeroats.com	Chicago	IL	60661	312-821-1000	
Weetabix Co Inc 300 Nickerson Rd *TF:* 800-343-0590 ■ *Web:* www.weetabixusa.com	Marlborough	MA	01752	978-368-0991	

299-5 Cheeses - Natural, Processed, Imitation

Company	City	State	Zip	Phone	Fax
AMPI 315 N Broadway *TF:* 800-533-3580 ■ *Web:* www.ampi.com	New Ulm	MN	56073	507-354-8295	
Barker Specialty Products LLC 703 Franklin St PO Box 478 *Web:* www.barkercompany.com	Keosauqua	IA	52565	319-293-3777	
Bel/Kaukauna USA 1500 E N Ave *Web:* www.kaukaunacheese.com	Little Chute	WI	54140	920-788-3524	
Berner Foods Inc 2034 E Factory Rd *TF:* 800-819-8199 ■ *Web:* www.bernerfoods.com	Dakota	IL	61018	815-563-4222	563-4017
Biery Cheese Co 6544 Paris Ave *TF:* 800-243-3731 ■ *Web:* www.bierycheese.com	Louisville	OH	44641	330-875-3381	875-5896
Boar's Head Provisions Co Inc 1819 Main St Ste 800 *Web:* www.boarshead.com	Sarasota	FL	34236	941-955-0994	366-0354

Company	City	State	Zip	Phone	Fax
Bongards' Creameries 13200 County Rd 51 *Web:* www.bongards.com	Norwood	MN	55368	952-466-5521	466-5556
Burnett Dairy Co-op 11631 SR- 70 *TF:* 800-854-2716 ■ *Web:* www.burnettdairy.com	Grantsburg	WI	54840	715-689-2468	689-2135
Cabot Creamery One Home Farm Way *TF:* 888-792-2268 ■ *Web:* www.cabotcheese.coop	Montpelier	VT	05602	802-229-9361	
Cacique Inc 14923 Procter Ave **Fax:* Sales ■ *TF:* 800-521-6987 ■ *Web:* caciqueinc.com	La Puente	CA	91746	626-961-3399	369-8083*
Calabro Cheese Corp 580 Coe Ave PO Box 120186 *TF:* 800-969-1311 ■ *Web:* www.calabrocheese.com	East Haven	CT	06512	203-469-1311	469-6929
California Dairies Inc 2000 N Plz Dr *Web:* www.californiadairies.com	Visalia	CA	93291	559-625-2200	625-5433
Colonna Bros Inc PO Box 808 *Web:* www.colonnabrothers.com	North Bergen	NJ	07047	201-864-1115	
ConAgra Foods Retail Products Co Deli Foods Group 215 W Field Rd *TF:* 877-266-2472 ■ *Web:* www.conagrafoods.com	Naperville	IL	60563	630-857-1000	
Dairiconcepts LP 3253 E Chestnut Expy *TF:* 877-596-4374 ■ *Web:* www.dairiconcepts.com	Springfield	MO	65802	417-829-3400	829-3401
Dairy Farmers of America Inc 10220 N Ambassador Dr Northpointe Tower *TF:* 888-332-6455 ■ *Web:* www.dfamilk.com	Kansas City	MO	64153	816-801-6455	801-6456
Dairy Food USA Inc 2819 County Rd F *Web:* www.dairyfoodusa.com	Blue Mounds	WI	53517	608-437-5598	437-8850
Ellsworth Co-op Creamery Inc 232 N Wallace St *Web:* ellsworthcheesecurds.com	Ellsworth	WI	54011	715-273-4311	273-5318
Empire Cheese Inc 4520 County Rd 6 *Web:* greatlakescheese.com	Cuba	NY	14727	585-968-1552	968-2660
F & A Dairy Products Inc 212 State Rd 35 S *Web:* www.fadairy.com	Dresser	WI	54009	715-755-3485	755-3480
Farmdale Creamery Inc 1049 W Baseline St *Web:* farmdale.net	San Bernardino	CA	92411	909-889-3002	888-2541
First District Assn (FDA) 101 S Swift Ave *Web:* www.firstdistrict.com	Litchfield	MN	55355	320-693-3236	693-6243
Fleur De Lait Foods Inc 400 S Custer Ave	New Holland	PA	17557	717-355-8580	355-8546
Galaxy Nutritional Foods Inc 66 Whitecap Dr *TF:* 800-441-9419 ■ *Web:* goveggiefoods.com/	North Kingstown	RI	02852	401-667-5000	
Golden Cheese Company of California 1138 W Rincon St *Web:* waterboards.ca.gov	Corona	CA	92880	951-493-4700	
Gossner Foods Inc 1051 N 1000 W *TF:* 800-944-0454 ■ *Web:* www.gossner.com	Logan	UT	84321	435-713-6100	713-6200
Grande Cheese Co 301 E Main St **Fax Area Code:* 920 ■ *TF:* 800-772-3210 ■ *Web:* www.grandecig.com	Lomira	WI	53048	800-772-3210	269-1445*
Great Lakes Cheese Company Inc 17825 Great Lakes Pkwy *Web:* www.greatlakescheese.com	Hiram	OH	44234	440-834-2500	834-1002
Hilmar Cheese Company Inc PO Box 910 *TF:* 888-300-4465 ■ *Web:* www.hilmarcheese.com	Hilmar	CA	95324	209-667-6076	634-1408
Holmes Cheese Co 9444 SR-39	Millersburg	OH	44654	330-674-6451	674-6673
Jerome Cheese Co 547 W Nez Perce *TF:* 800-757-7611 ■ *Web:* daviscofoods.com	Jerome	ID	83338	208-324-8806	324-8892
Klondike Cheese Co W7839 Hwy 81 *Web:* www.klondikecheese.com	Monroe	WI	53566	608-325-3021	325-3027
Kraft Foods North America Inc 3 Lakes Dr *NASDAQ: KHC* ■ *Web:* www.kraftfoodsgroup.com	Northfield	IL	60093	847-646-2000	
Land O'Lakes Inc 4001 Lexington Ave N **Fax:* Hum Res ■ *TF:* 800-328-9680 ■ *Web:* www.landolakesinc.com	Arden Hills	MN	55126	651-481-2222	481-2022*
Le Sueur Cheese Company Inc 719 N Main St *TF:* 800-247-0871 ■ *Web:* daviscofoods.com	Le Sueur	MN	56058	507-665-3353	665-2820
Leprino Foods Co 1830 W 38th Ave *TF:* 800-537-7466 ■ *Web:* www.leprinofoods.com	Denver	CO	80211	303-480-2600	480-2605
Los Altos Food Products Inc 15130 Nelson Ave *Web:* www.losaltosfoods.com	City of Industry	CA	91744	626-330-6555	330-6755
Mancuso Cheese Co 612 Mills Rd *Web:* mancusocheese.com	Joliet	IL	60433	815-722-2475	722-1302
Marathon Cheese Corp 304 E St PO Box 185 *Web:* www.mcheese.com	Marathon	WI	54448	715-443-2211	443-3843
Miceli Dairy Products 2721 E 90th St *Web:* www.miceli-dairy.com	Cleveland	OH	44104	216-791-6222	
Pace Dairy Foods Co 2700 Vly High Dr NW	Rochester	MN	55901	507-288-6315	
Saputo Inc 6869 boul Metropolitain *NYSE: SAP* ■ *Web:* www.saputo.com	Saint-Leonard	QC	H1P1X8	514-328-6662	328-3364
Sargento Foods Inc 1 Persnickety Pl *TF:* 800-243-3737 ■ *Web:* www.sargento.com	Plymouth	WI	53073	920-893-8484	892-5390
Sartori Food Corp 107 Pleasant View Rd *TF Cust Svc:* 800-558-5888 ■ *Web:* www.sartoricheese.com	Plymouth	WI	53073	920-893-6061	892-2732
Schreiber Foods Inc 425 Pine St *Web:* www.schreiberfoods.com	Green Bay	WI	54301	920-437-7601	437-1617
Sun-Re Cheese Corp 178 Lenker Ave	Sunbury	PA	17801	570-286-1511	286-5123
Swiss Valley Farms 247 Research Pkwy PO Box 4493 *TF:* 800-747-6113 ■ *Web:* www.swissvalley.com	Davenport	IA	52808	563-468-6600	468-6613
Tillamook County Creamery Assn Inc 4185 Hwy 101 N *Web:* www.tillamook.com	Tillamook	OR	97141	503-815-1300	842-6039
Tropical Cheese Industries Inc 450 Fayette St PO Box 1357 *TF:* 888-874-4928 ■ *Web:* www.tropicalcheese.com	Perth Amboy	NJ	08861	732-442-4898	442-8227
Valley Queen Cheese Factory Inc 200 E Railway Ave *Web:* www.vqcheese.com	Milbank	SD	57252	605-432-4563	432-9383
Wapsie Valley Creamery Inc 300 Tenth St NE	Independence	IA	50644	319-334-7193	

299-6 Chewing Gum

Company	City	State	Zip	Phone	Fax
Concord Confections Ltd 345 Courtland Ave *TF:* 800-267-0037 ■ *Web:* ic.gc.ca/eic/site/icgc.nsf/eng/home	Concord	ON	L4K5A6	905-660-8989	660-8979
Ford Gum & Machine Company Inc 18 Newton Ave *Web:* www.fordgum.com	Akron	NY	14001	716-542-4561	542-4610
Lotte USA Inc 5243 Wayne Rd *Web:* koalasmarch-usa.com	Battle Creek	MI	49037	269-963-6664	963-6695
Topps Company Inc One Whitehall St *TF:* 800-489-9149 ■ *Web:* www.topps.com	New York	NY	10004	212-376-0300	376-0573
Wrigley Co, The 410 N Michigan Ave *TF:* 888-985-2064 ■ *Web:* www.wrigley.com	Chicago	IL	60611	312-644-2121	

299-7 Coffee - Roasted (Ground, Instant, Freeze-Dried)

Company	City	State	Zip	Phone	Fax
Allegro Coffee Co 12799 Claude Ct *TF:* 800-530-3995 ■ *Web:* www.allegro-coffee.com	Thornton	CO	80241	303-444-4844	920-5468
ARCO Coffee Company 2206 Winter St *TF:* 800-283-2726 ■ *Web:* www.arcocoffee.com/	Superior	WI	54880	715-392-4771	392-4776
Autocrat Coffee Inc 10 Blackstone Vly Pl *TF:* 800-288-6272 ■ *Web:* www.autocrat.com	Lincoln	RI	02865	401-333-3300	333-3719
Bargreen Coffee Co 2821 Rucker Ave *Web:* bargreenscoffee.com	Everett	WA	98201	425-252-3161	259-4673
Boyd Coffee Co 19730 NE Sandy Blvd *TF Cust Svc:* 800-545-4077 ■ *Web:* www.boyds.com	Portland	OR	97230	503-666-4545	669-2223
Cadillac Coffee Co 194 E Maple Rd *TF:* 800-438-6900 ■ *Web:* www.cadillaccoffee.com	Troy	MI	48083	248-545-2266	545-2011
Coffee Holding Company Inc 3475 Victory Blvd *NASDAQ: JVA* ■ *TF:* 800-458-2233 ■ *Web:* www.coffeeholding.com	Staten Island	NY	10314	718-832-0800	832-0892
Community Coffee Co PO Box 2311 *TF:* 800-688-0990 ■ *Web:* www.communitycoffee.com	Baton Rouge	LA	70821	800-884-5282	643-8199
DeCoty Coffee Company Inc 1920 Austin St **Fax Area Code:* 325 ■ *TF:* 800-588-8001 ■ *Web:* www.decoty.com	San Angelo	TX	76903	800-588-8001	655-6837*
Excellent Coffee Company Inc 259 E Ave *Web:* excellentcoffee.com	Pawtucket	RI	02860	401-724-6393	724-0560
Farmer Bros Co 20333 S Normandie Ave *NASDAQ: FARM* ■ *TF:* 800-735-2878 ■ *Web:* www.farmerbrosco.com	Torrance	CA	90502	310-787-5200	
Frontier Natural Products Co-op 3021 78th St PO Box 299 *TF:* 800-669-3275 ■ *Web:* www.frontiercoop.com	Norway	IA	52318	319-227-7996	227-7966
Hawaiian Isles Kona Coffee Co 2839 Mokumoa St *TF Orders:* 800-657-7716 ■ *Web:* www.hawaiianisles.com	Honolulu	HI	96819	808-839-3255	
Keurig Green Mountain Inc 33 Coffee Ln *NASDAQ: GMCR* ■ *TF Cust Svc:* 888-879-4627 ■ *Web:* www.greenmountaincoffee.com	Waterbury	VT	05676	888-879-4627	
McCullagh Coffee 245 Swan St *TF:* 800-753-3473 ■ *Web:* www.mccullaghcoffee.com	Buffalo	NY	14204	800-753-3473	856-3486
Melitta Canada Inc 10-6201 Hwy Ste 7 *TF:* 800-565-4882 ■ *Web:* www.melitta.ca	Vaughan	ON	L4H0K7	905-851-9375	851-8042
Nestle USA Inc 800 N Brand Blvd **Fax:* Sales ■ *Web:* www.nestle.com	Glendale	CA	91203	818-549-6000	553-3547*
New England Coffee Co 100 Charles St **Fax Area Code:* 781 ■ *TF:* 800-225-3537 ■ *Web:* www.newenglandcoffee.com	Malden	MA	02148	800-225-3537	388-2838*
Old Mansion Foods 3811 Corporate Rd PO Box 1838 *TF:* 800-476-1877 ■ *Web:* www.oldmansionfoods.com	Petersburg	VA	23805	804-862-9889	861-8816
Paul deLima Co Inc 7546 Morgan Rd *TF:* 800-962-8864 ■ *Web:* www.delimacoffee.com	Liverpool	NY	13090	315-457-3725	457-3730
Port City Java Inc 101 Portwatch Way PO Box 785 *Web:* www.portcityjava.com	Wilmington	NC	28412	910-796-6646	
Red Diamond Inc 400 Park Ave *TF:* 800-292-4651 ■ *Web:* www.reddiamond.com	Moody	AL	35004	205-577-4000	
Reily Foods Co 640 Magazine St *TF:* 800-535-1961 ■ *Web:* www.frenchmarketcoffee.com	New Orleans	LA	70130	504-524-6131	539-5427
Royal Cup Coffee 160 Cleage Dr **Fax Area Code:* 205 ■ *TF Cust Svc:* 800-366-5836 ■ *Web:* www.royalcupcoffee.com	Birmingham	AL	35217	800-366-5836	271-6071*
S & D Coffee Inc 300 Concord Pkwy PO Box 1628 *TF Cust Svc:* 800-933-2210 ■ *Web:* www.sdcoffeetea.com	Concord	NC	28026	704-782-3121	721-5792
Stewarts Private Blend Food Inc 4110 W Wrightwood Ave *Web:* www.stewarts.com	Chicago	IL	60639	773-489-2500	489-2148
Texas Coffee Co Inc 3297 S M L King Jr Pkwy *TF:* 800-259-3400 ■ *Web:* www.texjoy.com	Beaumont	TX	77705	409-835-3434	835-4248
Torke Coffee Roasting Company Inc 3455 Paine Ave PO Box 694 *TF:* 800-242-7671 ■ *Web:* www.torkecoffee.com	Sheboygan	WI	53081	920-458-4114	458-0488
Van Roy Coffee Co, The 4569 Spring Rd *TF:* 877-826-7669 ■ *Web:* www.vanroycoffee.com	Cleveland	OH	44131	216-749-7069	749-7039
White Coffee Corp 18-35 Steinway Pl *TF:* 800-221-0140 ■ *Web:* www.whitecoffee.com	Astoria	NY	11105	718-204-7900	956-8504

299-8 Confectionery Products

Company	City	State	Zip	Phone	Fax
Adams & Brooks Inc 1915 S Hoover St PO Box 7303 *TF Orders:* 800-999-9808 ■ *Web:* www.adams-brooks.com	Los Angeles	CA	90007	213-749-3226	746-7614
ADM Cocoa Div 12500 W Carmen Ave *TF:* 800-637-5843 ■ *Web:* www.adm.com	Milwaukee	WI	53225	217-424-5200	
Andes Candies Inc 1400 E Wisconsin St	Delavan	WI	53115	262-728-9121	728-6794
Anthony-Thomas Candy Co 1777 Arlingate Ln *TF:* 877-226-3921 ■ *Web:* www.anthony-thomas.com	Columbus	OH	43228	614-274-8405	
Asher's Chocolates 80 Wambold Rd *TF:* 800-223-4420 ■ *Web:* www.ashers.com	Souderton	PA	18964	215-721-3000	721-3265

	City	State	Zip	Phone	Fax
Atkinson Candy Co 1608 W Frank Ave *TF:* 800-231-1203 ■ *Web:* www.atkinsoncandy.com	Lufkin	TX	75904	936-639-2333	639-2337
Barry Callebaut USA LLC 400 Industrial Pk Rd *TF:* 800-556-8845 ■ *Web:* www.barry-callebaut.com	Saint Albans	VT	05478	802-524-9711	524-5148
Best Sweet Inc 288 Mazeppa Rd **Fax:* Mktg ■ *TF:* 888-211-5530 ■ *Web:* www.bestco.com	Mooresville	NC	28115	704-664-4300	664-9640*
Blommer Chocolate Co 600 W Kinzie St *TF:* 800-621-1606 ■ *Web:* www.blommer.com	Chicago	IL	60654	312-226-7700	226-4141
Boyer Candy Inc 821 17th St *Web:* www.boyercandies.com	Altoona	PA	16602	814-944-9401	943-2354
Brown & Haley PO Box 1596 *TF:* 800-426-8400 ■ *Web:* www.brown-haley.com	Tacoma	WA	98401	253-620-3085	274-0628
Cargill Inc North America 15407 McGinty Rd *Web:* cargill.com	Wayzata	MN	55391	952-742-7575	
Ce De Candy Inc 1091 Lousons Rd *Web:* www.smarties.com	Union	NJ	07083	908-964-0660	
Charms Co 7401 S Cicero Ave **Fax Area Code:* 415 ■ *Web:* tootsie.com	Chicago	IL	60629	773-838-3400	401-0087*
Cherrydale Farms Fundraising 707 N Vly Forge Rd *TF:* 877-619-4822 ■ *Web:* www.cherrydale.com	Lansdale	PA	19446	877-619-4822	
Chocolates a la Carte Inc 28455 Livingston Ave **Fax Area Code:* 661 ■ **Fax:* Sales ■ *TF Cust Svc:* 800-818-2462 ■ *Web:* www.chocolatesalacarte.com	Valencia	CA	91355	800-818-2462	257-4999*
Decko Products Inc 2105 Superior St *TF General:* 800-537-4487 ■ *Web:* www.decko.com	Sandusky	OH	44870	419-626-5757	626-3135
Eaton Farm Confectioners Inc 30 Burbank Rd *TF:* 800-343-9300 ■ *Web:* www.eatonfarmcandies.com	Sutton	MA	01590	508-865-5235	865-7087
Elmer Candy Corp 401 N Fifth St *Web:* elmerchocolate.com	Ponchatoula	LA	70454	985-386-6166	
Esther Price Candies Inc 1709 Wayne Ave *TF:* 800-782-0326 ■ *Web:* www.estherprice.com	Dayton	OH	45410	937-253-2121	253-3294
Farley's & Sathers Candy Company Inc One Sather Plz *Web:* www.ferrarausa.com	Round Lake	MN	56167	507-945-8181	
FB Washburn Candy Corp 137 Perkins Ave *Web:* www.fbwashburncandy.com	Brockton	MA	02302	508-588-0820	588-2205
Ferrara Cafe 195 Grand St *TF:* 800-871-6068 ■ *Web:* www.ferraracafe.com	New York	NY	10013	212-226-6150	226-0667
Ferrara Pan Candy Co 7301 Harrison St *Web:* www.ferrarausa.com	Forest Park	IL	60130	708-366-0500	366-5921
Ferrero USA Inc 600 Cottontail Ln *Web:* www.ferrerousa.com	Somerset	NJ	08873	732-764-9300	764-9300
Fowler's Chocolate Co 100 River Rock Dr Ste 102 *TF:* 800-824-2263 ■ *Web:* www.fowlerschocolates.com	Buffalo	NY	14207	716-877-9983	877-9959
Frankford Candy & Chocolate Co Inc 9300 Ashton Rd *Web:* www.frankfordcandy.com	Philadelphia	PA	19114	215-735-5200	735-0721
Ganong Bros Ltd One Chocolate Dr *Web:* www.ganong.com	Saint Stephen	NB	E3L2X5	506-465-5600	465-5610
Gayle's Chocolates 417 S Washington Ave *Web:* www.gayleschocolates.com	Royal Oak	MI	48067	248-398-0001	
Gertrude Hawk Chocolates Inc 9 Keystone Pk **Fax Area Code:* 570 ■ *TF:* 866-932-4295 ■ *Web:* www.gertrudehawkchocolates.com	Dunmore	PA	18512	800-822-2032	338-0947*
Ghirardelli Chocolate Co 1111 139th Ave *TF:* 800-877-9338 ■ *Web:* www.ghirardelli.com	San Leandro	CA	94578	800-877-9338	
Goetze's Candy Company Inc 3900 E Monument St *TF Orders:* 800-295-8058 ■ *Web:* www.goetzecandy.com	Baltimore	MD	21205	410-342-2010	522-7681
Guittard Chocolate Co 10 GuittaRd Rd *TF:* 800-468-2462 ■ *Web:* www.guittard.com	Burlingame	CA	94010	650-697-4427	692-2761
Harry London Candies Inc 5353 Lauby Rd *TF Cust Svc:* 800-333-3629 ■ *Web:* www.fanniemay.com	North Canton	OH	44720	330-494-0833	499-6902
Hershey Co 100 Crystal A Dr *NYSE:* HSY ■ *TF Cust Svc:* 800-468-1714 ■ *Web:* www.thehersheycompany.com	Hershey	PA	17033	800-468-1714	
Hillside Candy Co 35 Hillside Ave *TF:* 800-524-1304 ■ *Web:* www.hillsidecandy.com	Hillside	NJ	07205	973-926-2300	926-4440
James Candy Co 1519 Boardwalk *TF Orders:* 800-441-1404 ■ *Web:* www.jamescandy.com	Atlantic City	NJ	08401	609-344-1519	344-0246
Jelly Belly Candy Co 1 Jelly Belly Ln **Fax:* Cust Svc ■ *TF:* 800-323-9380 ■ *Web:* www.jellybelly.com	Fairfield	CA	94533	707-428-2800	423-4436*
Joyva Corp 53 Varick Ave *Web:* www.joyva.com	Brooklyn	NY	11237	718-497-0170	366-8504
Just Born Inc 1300 Stefko Blvd *TF:* 800-445-5787 ■ *Web:* www.justborn.com	Bethlehem	PA	18017	610-867-7568	867-3983
Katharine Beecher Candies 1250 Slate Hill Rd *TF:* 800-233-7082 ■ *Web:* www.padutchcandies.com	Camp Hill	PA	17011	717-761-5440	761-5702
Koeze Co PO Box 9470 **Fax Area Code:* 866 ■ *TF:* 800-555-9688 ■ *Web:* www.koeze.com	Grand Rapids	MI	49509	800-555-9688	817-0147*
Lammes Candies Since 1885 Inc PO Box 1885 *TF:* 800-252-1885 ■ *Web:* www.lammes.com	Austin	TX	78767	512-310-2223	238-2019
Lincoln Snacks Co 5020 S 19th St *TF:* 800-228-2478 ■ *Web:* www.lincolnsnacks.com	Lincoln	NE	68512	402-328-9345	
Lindt & Sprungli USA 1 Fine Chocolate Pl *TF:* 877-695-4638 ■ *Web:* www.lindtusa.com	Stratham	NH	03885	603-778-8100	778-3102
Lucks Co, The 3003 S Pine St **Fax:* Orders ■ *TF:* 800-426-9778 ■ *Web:* www.lucks.com	Tacoma	WA	98409	253-383-4815	383-0071*
Madelaine Chocolate Novelties Inc 9603 Beach Ch Dr *TF:* 800-322-1505 ■ *Web:* www.madelainechocolate.com	Rockaway Beach	NY	11693	718-945-1500	318-4607
Malleys Chocolates 13400 Brookpark Rd **Fax Area Code:* 800 ■ *TF:* 800-835-5684 ■ *Web:* www.malleys.com	Cleveland	OH	44135	216-362-8700	211-0567*
Mars Snack Food 800 High St *TF:* 800-551-0895 ■ *Web:* www.mars.com	Hackettstown	NJ	07840	908-852-1000	850-2734
Masterson Company Inc 4023 W National Ave *Web:* www.mastersoncompany.com	Milwaukee	WI	53215	414-647-1132	647-1170
Moonstruck Chocolate Co 6600 N Baltimore Ave *TF:* 800-557-6666 ■ *Web:* www.moonstruckchocolate.com	Portland	OR	97203	503-247-3448	247-3450
Morley Candy Makers Inc 23770 Hall Rd *TF:* 800-651-7263 ■ *Web:* www.sanderscandy.com	Clinton Township	MI	48036	586-468-4300	468-9407
Munson's Candy Kitchen Inc 174 Hop River Rd *TF:* 888-686-7667 ■ *Web:* www.munsonschocolates.com	Bolton	CT	06043	860-649-4332	649-7209
Nestle USA Inc 800 N Brand Blvd **Fax:* Sales ■ *Web:* www.nestle.com	Glendale	CA	91203	818-549-6000	553-3547*
Palmer Candy Co 2600 Hwy 75 N PO Box 326 *Web:* www.palmercandy.com	Sioux City	IA	51102	712-258-5543	258-3224
Paradise Inc 1200 W MLK Blvd PO Box Y *OTC:* PARF ■ **Fax Area Code:* 813 ■ *TF:* 800-330-8952 ■ *Web:* www.paradisefruitco.com	Plant City	FL	33563	800-330-8952	754-3168*
Pearson's Candy Co 2140 W Seventh St *TF Cust Svc:* 800-328-6507 ■ *Web:* www.pearsoncandy.com	Saint Paul	MN	55116	651-698-0356	696-2222
Pennsylvania Dutch Candies 1250 Slate Hill Rd *TF:* 800-233-7082 ■ *Web:* www.padutchcandies.com	Camp Hill	PA	17011	717-761-5440	761-5702
Pez Candy Inc 35 Prindle Hill Rd *Web:* www.pez.com	Orange	CT	06477	203-795-0531	799-1679
PLB Sports Inc Penn Ctr W Bldg 3 Ste 411 *TF:* 877-752-7778 ■ *Web:* www.plbsports.com	Pittsburgh	PA	15276	412-787-8800	787-8745
Primrose Candy Co 4111 W Parker Ave *Web:* www.primrosecandy.com	Chicago	IL	60639	773-276-9522	
RM Palmer Co 77 S Second Ave *Web:* www.rmpalmer.com	West Reading	PA	19611	610-372-8971	378-5208
Russell Stover Candies Inc 4900 Oak St *TF:* 800-477-8683 ■ *Web:* www.russellstover.com	Kansas City	MO	64112	816-842-9240	
Santa Cruz Nutritionals 2200 Delaware Ave **Fax:* Sales ■ *Web:* www.santacruznutritionals.com	Santa Cruz	CA	95060	831-457-3200	454-0915*
Sconza Candy Co One Sconza Candy Ln *Web:* www.sconzacandy.com	Oakdale	CA	95361	209-845-3700	845-3737
See's Candies Inc 210 El Camino Real *TF Cust Svc:* 800-877-7337 ■ *Web:* www.sees.com	South San Francisco	CA	94080	650-761-2490	
Sorbee International Ltd 9990 Global Rd *TF:* 800-654-3997 ■ *Web:* www.sorbee.com	Philadelphia	PA	19115	215-645-1111	677-7736
Spangler Candy Co 400 N Portland St PO Box 71 *TF Sales:* 888-636-4221 ■ *Web:* www.spanglercandy.com	Bryan	OH	43506	419-636-4221	636-3695
Standard Candy Company Inc 715 Massman Dr *Web:* www.googoo.com	Nashville	TN	37210	615-889-6360	889-7775
Storck USA LP 325 N LaSalle St Ste 400 *TF:* 800-852-5542 ■ *Web:* www.storck.com	Chicago	IL	60654	312-467-5700	467-9722
Supreme Chocolatier LLC 1150 S Ave *Web:* www.supremechocolatier.com	Staten Island	NY	10314	718-698-3300	
Sweet Candy Co Inc 3780 W Directors Row *TF:* 800-669-8669 ■ *Web:* www.sweetcandy.com	Salt Lake City	UT	84104	801-886-1444	886-1404
T R Toppers Inc 320 Fairchild *TF:* 800-748-4635 ■ *Web:* www.trtoppers.com	Pueblo	CO	81001	719-948-4902	948-4908
Tootsie Roll Industries Inc 7401 S Cicero Ave *NYSE:* TR ■ *TF:* 866-972-6879 ■ *Web:* www.tootsie.com	Chicago	IL	60629	773-838-3400	838-3534
Vitasoy USA Inc 1 New England Way **Fax Area Code:* 978 ■ *TF:* 800-848-2769 ■ *Web:* www.nasoya.com	Ayer	MA	01432	800-462-7692	772-6881*
Waymouth Farms Inc 5300 Boone Ave *TF:* 800-527-0094 ■ *Web:* www.goodsensesnacks.com	New Hope	MN	55428	763-533-5300	533-9890
Wolfgang Candy Co 50 E Fourth Ave *TF:* 800-248-4273 ■ *Web:* www.wolfgangcandy.com	York	PA	17404	717-843-5536	845-2881
World's Finest Chocolate Inc 4801 S Lawndale **Fax Area Code:* 877 ■ *TF:* 888-821-8452 ■ *Web:* www.worldsfinestchocolate.com	Chicago	IL	60632	888-821-8452	256-2685*
Y & S Candies 400 Running Pump Rd	Lancaster	PA	17603	717-299-1261	394-9109
Zachary Confections Inc 2130 IN-28 **Fax Area Code:* 765 ■ *TF Cust Svc:* 800-445-4222 ■ *Web:* www.zacharyconfections.com	Frankfort	IN	46041	800-445-4222	659-1491*

299-9 Cookies & Crackers

	City	State	Zip	Phone	Fax
Benzel's Pretzel Bakery Inc 5200 Sixth Ave *TF:* 800-344-4438 ■ *Web:* www.benzels.com	Altoona	PA	16602	814-942-5062	942-4133
Bremner Biscuit Co 4600 Joliet St *TF:* 866-972-6879 ■ *Web:* www.bremnerbiscuitco.com	Denver	CO	80239	303-371-8180	371-8185
Buckeye Snack Food Co 11677 Chesterdale Rd	Cincinnati	OH	45246	513-458-6200	
Christie Cookie Co 1205 Third Ave N *TF:* 800-458-2447 ■ *Web:* www.christiecookies.com	Nashville	TN	37208	615-242-3817	242-5572
Deep Foods Inc 1090 Springfield Rd *Web:* www.deepfoods.com	Union	NJ	07083	908-810-7500	810-8482
Delyse Inc 505 Reactor Way *TF:* 800-441-6887 ■ *Web:* www.delyse.com	Reno	NV	89502	775-857-1811	857-4722
Ellison Bakery 4108 W Ferguson Rd *Web:* www.ebakery.com	Fort Wayne	IN	46809	260-747-6136	747-1954
Fehr Foods Inc 5425 N First St *Web:* www.fehrfoods.com	Abilene	TX	79603	325-691-5425	
Ferrara Cafe 195 Grand St *TF:* 800-871-6068 ■ *Web:* www.ferraracafe.com	New York	NY	10013	212-226-6150	226-0667
Gurley's Foods 1118 E Hwy 12 *Web:* www.gurleysfoods.com	Willmar	MN	56201	320-235-0600	235-0659
J & J Snack Foods Corp 6000 Central Hwy *NASDAQ:* JJSF ■ *TF:* 800-486-9533 ■ *Web:* www.jjsnack.com	Pennsauken	NJ	08109	856-665-9533	665-6718
Joy Cone Co 3435 Lamor Rd *TF:* 800-242-2663 ■ *Web:* www.joycone.com	Hermitage	PA	16148	724-962-5747	962-3470
Keystone Pretzels 124 W Airport Rd **Fax Area Code:* 717 ■ *TF:* 888-572-4500 ■ *Web:* www.keystonepretzels.com	Lititz	PA	17543	888-572-4500	560-2241*
Little Dutch Boy Bakery Inc 12349 South 970 East	Draper	UT	84020	801-571-3800	571-3802
Norse Dairy Systems 1740 Joyce Ave *TF:* 800-637-2663 ■ *Web:* www.norse.com	Columbus	OH	43219	614-294-4931	
Pretzels Inc 123 Harvest Rd PO Box 503 *TF:* 800-456-4838 ■ *Web:* www.pretzels-inc.com	Bluffton	IN	46714	260-824-4838	824-0895
Richmond Baking Co 520 N Sixth St *Web:* www.richmondbaking.com	Richmond	IN	47374	765-962-8535	962-2253

Phone Fax

Rudolph Foods Company Inc 6575 Bellefontaine Rd....... Lima OH 45804 419-648-3611 648-4087
TF: 800-241-7675 ■ Web: www.rudolphfoods.com

Silver Lake Cookie Company Inc 141 Freeman Ave........ Islip NY 11751 631-581-4000 581-4510
TF: 800-645-9048 ■ Web: www.silverlakecookie.com

Snyder's of Hanover 1250 York St PO Box 6917 .... Hanover PA 17331 717-632-4477 632-7207
TF: 800-233-7125 ■ Web: snyderslance.com

T. Marzetti Company. P.O. Box 29163............... Columbus OH 43229 800-999-1835
TF: 800-999-1835 ■ Web: www.marzetti.com

Tom Sturgis Pretzels Inc 2267 Lancaster Pk .... Reading PA 19607 610-775-0335 796-1418*
*Fax: Sales ■ TF: 800-817-3834 ■ Web: www.tomsturgispretzels.com

Venus Wafers Inc 100 Research Rd.................. Hingham MA 02043 781-740-1002 740-0791
TF: 800-545-4538 ■ Web: www.venuswafers.com

Wege Pretzel Co PO Box 334......................... Hanover PA 17331 717-843-0738 632-4190
TF: 800-888-4646 ■ Web: www.wege.com

299-10 Dairy Products - Dry, Condensed, Evaporated

Phone Fax

Abbott Laboratories Ross Products Div
625 Cleveland Ave .... Columbus OH 43215 614-624-7485 624-7616*
*Fax: PR ■ TF PR: 800-227-5767 ■ Web: abbottnutrition.com

American Casein Co 109 Elbow Ln .... Burlington NJ 08016 609-387-3130 387-7204
Web: www.americancasein.com

AMPI 315 N Broadway .... New Ulm MN 56073 507-354-8295
TF: 800-533-3580 ■ Web: www.ampi.com

California Dairies Inc 2000 N Plz Dr.................. Visalia CA 93291 559-625-2200 625-5433
Web: www.californiadairies.com

Dairy Farmers of America Inc
10220 N Ambassador Dr Northpointe Tower.......... Kansas City MO 64153 816-801-6455 801-6456
TF: 888-332-6455 ■ Web: www.dfamilk.com

Davisco International Inc 719 N Main St .... Le Sueur MN 56058 507-665-8811 665-3701
TF: 800-757-7611 ■ Web: www.daviscofoods.com

Erie Foods International Inc
401 Seventh Ave PO Box 648........................... Erie IL 61250 309-659-2233 659-2822
TF: 800-447-1887 ■ Web: www.eriefoods.com

Farmers Co-op Creamery Inc (FCC)
700 N Hwy 99 W.............................. McMinnville OR 97128 503-472-2157 472-3821
Web: www.farmerscoop.org

Foremost Farms USA E10889A Penny Ln............. Baraboo WI 53913 608-355-8700 355-8699
TF: 800-362-9196 ■ Web: www.foremostfarms.com

Galloway Company Inc 601 S Commercial St .... Neenah WI 54956 920-722-7741 722-1927
Web: www.gallowaycompany.com

Gehl's Guernsey Farms Inc
N116 W15970 Main St......................... Germantown WI 53022 262-251-8572 251-8744
TF: 800-521-2873 ■ Web: www.gehls.com

Instantwhip Foods Inc 2200 Cardigan Ave .... Columbus OH 43215 614-488-2536 488-0307*
*Fax: Sales ■ TF Cust Svc: 800-544-9447 ■ Web: www.instantwhip.com

Jackson-Mitchell Inc PO Box 934 .... Turlock CA 95381 209-667-2019
Web: meyenberg.com

John Volpi & Company Inc 5263 Northrup Ave .... St Louis MO 63110 314-772-8550
TF: 800-288-3439 ■ Web: www.volpifoods.com

Land O'Lakes Inc 4001 Lexington Ave N .... Arden Hills MN 55126 651-481-2222 481-2022*
*Fax: Hum Res ■ TF: 800-328-9680 ■ Web: www.landolakesinc.com

Maple Island Inc
2497 Seventh Ave E Ste 105.................. North Saint Paul MN 55109 651-773-1000 773-2155
TF: 800-369-1022 ■ Web: www.maple-island.com

Mead Johnson Nutritionals
2701 Patriot Blvd Fourth Fl......................... Glenview IL 60026 847-832-2420
Web: www.meadjohnson.com

Milk Products LLC PO Box 150...................... Chilton WI 53014 920-849-2348 849-9014
TF: 800-657-0793 ■ Web: www.milkproductsinc.com

Nestle USA Inc 800 N Brand Blvd.................... Glendale CA 91203 818-549-6000 553-3547*
*Fax: Sales ■ Web: www.nestle.com

O-AT-KA Milk Products Co-op Inc
700 Ellicott St...................................... Batavia NY 14020 585-343-0536 343-4473
TF: 800-828-8152 ■ Web: www.oatkamilk.com

Ohio Processors Inc 244 E First St .... London OH 43140 740-852-9243
Web: www.instantwhip.com/home.html

Penn Maid Foods Inc 10975 Dutton Rd .... Philadelphia PA 19154 215-824-2800
Web: www.pennmaid.com

Sinton Dairy Foods Co LLC
3801 Sinton Rd.......................... Colorado Springs CO 80907 719-633-3821 667-7470
TF: 800-388-4970 ■ Web: www.sintondairy.com

Valentine Enterprises Inc
1291 Progress Ctr Ave .... Lawrenceville GA 30043 770-995-0661 995-0725
Web: www.veiusa.com

Vern Dale Products Inc 8445 Lyndon St .... Detroit MI 48238 313-834-4190 834-6280
Web: www.verndaleproducts.com

299-11 Diet & Health Foods

Phone Fax

Alle Processing Corp 56-20 59th St................. Maspeth NY 11378 718-894-2000 326-4642
Web: alleprocessing.com

AMS Health Sciences Inc 4000 N Lindsay........ Oklahoma City OK 73105 405-842-0131 843-4935
TF: 800-426-4267 ■ Web: www.amsonline.com

BAZI Inc 1730 Blake St Ste 305 .... Denver CO 80202 303-316-8577
Web: www.drinkbazi.com

Eden Foods Inc 701 Tecumseh Rd .... Clinton MI 49236 517-456-7424 456-6075
TF Cust Svc: 800-248-0320 ■ Web: www.edenfoods.com

Grow Company Inc 55 Railroad Ave.................. Richfield NJ 07657 201-941-8777 941-1881
Web: www.growco.us

Health Hut 1512 First Ave NE .... Cedar Rapids IA 52402 319-362-7345 369-0440
Web: healthhutcr.com

Isagenix International LLC 2225 S Price Rd.......... Chandler AZ 85286 480-889-5747 636-5386
TF: 877-877-8111 ■ Web: isagenix.com/

Medifast Inc 11445 Cronhill Dr................. Owings Mills MD 21117 800-209-0878 581-8070*
NYSE: MED ■ *Fax Area Code: 410 ■ TF: 800-209-0878 ■ Web: www.medifast1.com

Nutrition 21 Inc Three Manhattanville Rd .... Purchase NY 10577 914-701-4500 696-0860
Web: www.nutrition21.com

Phone Fax

RC Fine Foods PO Box 236....................... Belle Mead NJ 08502 908-359-5500 359-6957
TF: 800-526-3953 ■ Web: www.rcfinefoods.com

Seasons' Enterprises Ltd
1790 W Cortland Ct Ste B PO Box 965................. Addison IL 60101 630-628-0211 628-0385
Web: www.seasonssnacks.com

Tahitian Noni International 333 W Riverpark Dr.......... Provo UT 84604 801-234-1000 234-1001
TF Cust Svc: 800-445-2969 ■ Web: morinda.com

TreeHouse Foods Inc 2021 Spring Rd Ste 600........ Oak Brook IL 60523 708-483-1300 409-1062
NYSE: THS ■ Web: www.treehousefoods.com

Vitaminerals Inc 1815 Flower St .... Glendale CA 91201 800-432-1856 240-2785*
*Fax Area Code: 818 ■ TF: 800-432-1856 ■ Web: www.cryogel.tv

299-12 Fats & Oils - Animal or Marine

Phone Fax

Baker Commodities Inc 4020 Bandini Blvd .... Vernon CA 90058 323-268-2801 268-5166
Web: www.bakercommodities.com

Coast Packing Co 3275 E Vernon Ave.................. Vernon CA 90058 323-277-7700 277-7712

Darling International Inc
251 O'Connor Ridge Blvd Ste 300 .... Irving TX 75038 972-717-0300 717-1588
NYSE: DAR ■ TF: 855-327-7761 ■ Web: www.darlingii.com

GA Wintzer & Son Co 204 W Auglaize St............ Wapakoneta OH 45895 419-739-4900 738-9058
TF: 800-331-1801 ■ Web: www.gawintzer.com

Griffin Industries Inc
4413 Tanner Church Rd .... Ellenwood GA 30294 404-363-1320 363-1335
Web: griffinind.com

Harbinger Group Inc 450 Pk Ave 27th Fl .... New York NY 10022 212-906-8555
NYSE: HRG ■ Web: www.harbingergroupinc.com

Jacob Stern & Sons Inc
1464 E Valley Rd.............................. Santa Barbara CA 93108 805-565-1411 565-1415
TF Cust Svc: 800-223-7054 ■ Web: www.jacobstern.com

Kaluzny Bros Inc 1528 Mound Rd................... Rockdale IL 60436 815-744-1453 729-5069

Omega Protein Corp 2105 City W Blvd Ste 500 .... Houston TX 77042 713-623-0060 940-6122
Web: www.omegaprotein.com

San Luis Tallow Co 445 Prado Rd .... San Luis Obispo CA 93401 805-543-8660

Werner G Smith Inc 1730 Train Ave................. Cleveland OH 44113 216-861-3676 861-3680
TF General: 800-535-8343 ■ Web: www.wernergsmithinc.com

299-13 Fish & Seafood - Canned

Phone Fax

Acme Smoked Fish Corp 30 Gem St................. Brooklyn NY 11222 718-383-8585
Web: www.acmesmokedfish.com

Beaver Street Fisheries Inc
1741 W Beaver St............................. Jacksonville FL 32209 904-354-8533
TF: 800-874-6426 ■ Web: beaverstreetfisheries.com

Bumble Bee Seafoods Inc
9655 Granite Ridge Dr Ste 100..................... San Diego CA 92123 858-715-4000
TF: 800-800-8572 ■ Web: www.bumblebee.com

High Liner Foods Inc (HLF) One Highliner Ave....... Portsmouth NH 03801 603-431-6865
NYSE: HLF ■ Web: www.highlinerfoods.com

Icicle Seafoods Inc 4019 21st Ave W.................. Seattle WA 98199 206-282-0988 282-7222
Web: www.icicleseafoods.com

Inlet Fish Producers Inc PO Box 114.................. Kenai AK 99611 907-283-9275 283-4097
Web: www.inletfish.com

Los Angeles Smoking & Curing Co (LASCCO)
1100 W Ewing St .... Seattle WA 98119 206-285-6800
Web: www.oceanbeauty.com

Nelson Crab Inc 3088 Kindred Ave .... Tokeland WA 98590 360-267-2911
TF: 800-262-0069 ■ Web: seatreats.stores.yahoo.net

Noon Hour Food Products Inc
215 N Des Plaines .... Chicago IL 60661 312-596-4225
TF Cust Svc: 888-463-6332 ■ Web: fda.gov

Overwaitea Food Group 19855 92A Ave .... Langley BC V1M3B6 604-888-1213
TF: 800-242-9229 ■ Web: www.owfg.com

Pacific Choice Seafoods Co One Commercial St .... Eureka CA 95501 707-442-2981 442-2985
Web: www.pacseafood.com

Peter Pan Seafoods Inc
2200 Sixth Ave Ste 1000 .... Seattle WA 98121 206-728-6000 441-9090
TF: 800-331-3522 ■ Web: www.ppsf.com

Petersburg Fisheries PO Box 1147 .... Petersburg AK 99833 907-772-4294 772-4472
TF: 877-772-4294 ■ Web: www.hookedonfish.com

RJ Peacock Canning Co 72 Water St .... Lubec ME 04652 207-733-5556 733-0936

Snow's/Doxsee Inc 994 Ocean Dr .... Cape May NJ 08204 609-884-0440

Vita Food Products Inc 2222 W Lake St................ Chicago IL 60612 312-738-4500 738-3215
TF: 800-989-8482 ■ Web: www.vitafoodproducts.com

Westward Seafoods 2101 Fourth Ave Ste 1700.......... Seattle WA 98121 206-682-5949 682-1825
Web: www.westwardseafoods.com

299-14 Fish & Seafood - Fresh or Frozen

Phone Fax

Bama Sea Products 756 28th St S .... Saint Petersburg FL 33712 727-327-3474 322-0580
Web: www.bamasea.com

Blount Seafood Corp 630 Currant Rd................ Fall River MA 02720 774-888-1300 888-1399
TF Hotline: 800-274-2526 ■ Web: www.blountseafood.com

Bon Secour Fisheries Inc
17449 County Rd 49 S .... Bon Secour AL 36511 251-949-7411 949-6478
TF: 800-633-6854 ■ Web: www.bonsecourfisheries.com

Camanchaca Inc 7200 NW 19th St Ste 410 .... Miami FL 33126 305-406-9560
TF: 800-335-7553 ■ Web: www.camanchacainc.com

Chef John Folse & Company Inc
2517 S Philippe Ave............................. Gonzales LA 70737 225-644-6000
Web: www.jfolse.com

Chesapeake Bay Packing LLC
800 Terminal Ave .... Newport News VA 23607 757-244-8440 244-8500
Web: www.chesapeakebaypacking.com

Company	City	State	ZIP	Phone	Fax
Coast Seafoods Co 14711 NE 29th Pl Ste 111 *Web:* coastseafoods.com	Bellevue	WA	98007	425-702-8800	
Consolidated Catfish Cos LLC 299 S St PO Box 271 *TF:* 800-228-3474 ■ *Web:* countryselect.com	Isola	MS	38754	662-962-3101	962-0114
Crocker & Winsor Seafoods Inc PO Box 51905 *TF:* 800-225-1597 ■ *Web:* www.crockerwinsor.com	Boston	MA	02205	617-269-3100	269-3376
Eastern Fisheries Inc 14 Hervey Tichon Ave *Web:* easternfisheries.com	New Bedford	MA	02740	508-993-5300	991-2226
Eastern Shore Foods LLC 13249 Lankford Hwy	Mappsville	VA	23407	757-824-5651	
Fishermen's Pride Processors 4510 S Alameda St *Web:* www.neptunefoods.com	Vernon	CA	90058	323-232-8300	232-8833
Freshwater Farm Products LLC 4554 State Hwy 12 E PO Box 850 *TF:* 800-748-9338 ■ *Web:* www.freshwatercatfish.com	Belzoni	MS	39038	662-247-4205	247-4442
Gorton's Inc 128 Rogers St *TF:* 800-222-6846 ■ *Web:* www.gortons.com	Gloucester	MA	01930	978-283-3000	281-8295
Great Northern Products Ltd 2700 Plainfield Pk *Web:* northernproducts.com	Cranston	RI	02921	401-490-4590	490-5595
King & Prince Seafood Corp One King & Prince Blvd *TF:* 800-841-0205 ■ *Web:* www.kpseafood.com	Brunswick	GA	31520	912-265-5155	
Luther L Smith & Son Inc PO Box 67 *TF:* 800-328-8313 ■ *Web:* www.ncagr.gov	Atlantic	NC	28511	252-225-3341	225-6391
Metompkin Bay Oyster Co 101 N 11th St Ste 105 *Web:* www.metompkinseafood.com	Crisfield	MD	21817	410-968-0660	968-0670
Morey's Seafood International LLC 1218 Hwy 10 S *TF:* 800-808-3474 ■ *Web:* www.moreys.com	Motley	MN	56466	218-352-6345	
Netuno USA Inc 18501 Pines Blvd Ste 206 *Web:* www.netunousa.com	Pembroke Pines	FL	33029	305-513-0904	513-3904
Ocean Beauty Seafoods Inc 1100 W Ewing St *TF:* 800-365-8950 ■ *Web:* www.oceanbeauty.com	Seattle	WA	98119	206-285-6800	
Orca Bay Seafoods Inc 900 Powell Ave SW *Web:* orcabayseafoods.com	Renton	WA	98057	425-204-9100	
Overwaitea Food Group 19855 92A Ave *TF:* 800-242-9229 ■ *Web:* www.owfg.com	Langley	BC	V1M3B6	604-888-1213	
Pinnacle Foods Corp 399 Jefferson Rd *TF:* 866-266-7596 ■ *Web:* www.pinnaclefoodscorp.com	Parsippany	NJ	07054	973-541-6620	
Riverside Foods Inc 2520 Wilson St *TF:* 800-678-4511 ■ *Web:* riversidefoods.com	Two Rivers	WI	54241	920-793-4511	794-7332
Sea Fresh USA Inc 45 All American Way *Web:* seafreshusa.com	North Kingstown	RI	02852	401-583-0200	
Sea Harvest Packing Co PO Box 818 *TF:* 800-627-4300 ■ *Web:* www.seaharvest.com	Brunswick	GA	31521	912-264-3212	264-2749
Sea Watch International Ltd 8978 Glebe Pk Dr *Web:* www.seawatch.com	Easton	MD	21601	410-822-7500	822-1266
Seafood Producers Co-op 2875 Roeder Ave *Web:* www.spcsales.com	Bellingham	WA	98225	360-733-0120	733-0513
Simmons Farm Raised Catfish Inc 2628 Erickson Rd *Web:* www.simmonscatfish.com	Yazoo City	MS	39194	662-746-5687	746-8625
Stoller Fisheries 1301 18th St PO Box B *TF:* 800-831-5174 ■ *Web:* www.stollerfisheries.com	Spirit Lake	IA	51360	712-336-1750	336-4681
Sugiyo USA Inc PO Box 468 *Web:* www.sugiyo.com	Anacortes	WA	98221	360-293-0180	293-6964
Tampa Bay Fisheries Inc 3060 Gallagher Rd *TF:* 800-732-3663 ■ *Web:* www.tbfish.com	Dover	FL	33527	813-752-8883	
Texas Pack Inc 508 Port Rd	Port Isabel	TX	78578	956-943-5461	943-6630
Thomas Seafood of Carteret Inc 421 Merrimon Rd	Beaufort	NC	28516	252-728-2391	
Tichon Seafood Corp Seven Conway St *Web:* tichonseafood.com	New Bedford	MA	02740	508-999-5607	990-8271
Trident Seafood Corp 5303 Shilshole Ave NW *TF:* 800-426-5490 ■ *Web:* www.tridentseafoods.com	Seattle	WA	98107	206-783-3818	782-7195
UniSea Inc 15400 NE 90th St PO Box 97019 *TF:* 800-535-8509 ■ *Web:* www.unisea.com	Redmond	WA	98073	425-881-8181	
Wanchese Fish Co 2000 Northgate Commerce Pkwy *Web:* www.wanchese.com	Suffolk	VA	23435	757-673-4500	673-4550

299-15 Flavoring Extracts & Syrups

Company	City	State	ZIP	Phone	Fax
Brady Enterprises Inc 167 Moore Rd *TF:* 800-225-5126 ■ *Web:* bradyenterprises.com/	East Weymouth	MA	02189	781-337-5000	337-9338
David Michael & Co Inc 10801 Decatur Rd **Fax Area Code:* 909 ■ *TF:* 800-363-5286 ■ *Web:* www.dmflavors.com	Philadelphia	PA	19154	215-632-3100	887-3339*
DD Williamson & Company Inc 100 S Spring St *TF:* 800-227-2635 ■ *Web:* www.ddwcolor.com	Louisville	KY	40206	502-895-2438	
Dr Pepper Snapple Group Inc 5301 Legacy Dr *NYSE: DPS* ■ *TF:* 800-686-7398 ■ *Web:* www.drpeppersnapplegroup.com	Plano	TX	75024	972-673-7000	673-7980
Emerald Kalama Chemical LLC 1296 Third St NW *TF:* 877-300-9545 ■ *Web:* www.emeraldmaterials.com	Kalama	WA	98625	360-673-2550	673-3564
Firmenich Inc 250 Plainsvoro *Web:* www.firmenich.com	Plainsboro	NJ	08536	609-452-1000	452-6077
Frutarom Corp 9500 Railroad Ave **Fax:* Cust Svc ■ *TF:* 866-229-7198 ■ *Web:* www.frutarom.com	North Bergen	NJ	07047	201-861-9500	861-9267*
Givaudan Flavors Corp 1199 Edison Dr *Web:* www.givaudan.com	Cincinnati	OH	45216	513-948-8000	
I Rice & Company Inc 11500 Roosevelt Blvd Bldg D *TF:* 800-232-6022 ■ *Web:* www.iriceco.com	Philadelphia	PA	19116	215-673-7423	673-2616
Jel Sert Co Rt 59 & Conde St *TF:* 800-323-2592 ■ *Web:* www.jelsert.com	West Chicago	IL	60185	630-876-4838	
Kalsec Inc 3713 W Main St *TF:* 800-323-9320 ■ *Web:* www.kalsec.com	Kalamazoo	MI	49006	269-349-9711	382-3060
Limpert Bros Inc 202 NW Blvd PO Box 1480 *TF:* 800-691-1353 ■ *Web:* www.limpertbrothers.com	Vineland	NJ	08362	856-691-1353	794-8968
Lyons Magnus Inc 3158 E Hamilton Ave **Fax Area Code:* 559 ■ *TF:* 800-344-7130 ■ *Web:* www.lyonsmagnus.com	Fresno	CA	93702	800-344-7130	233-8249*
M & F Worldwide Corp 35 E 62nd St *NYSE: MFW* ■ *Web:* www.mandfworldwide.com	New York	NY	10021	212-572-8600	572-8400
Mother Murphy's Labs Inc 2826 S Elm St PO Box 16846 *TF:* 800-849-1277 ■ *Web:* www.mothermurphys.com	Greensboro	NC	27416	336-273-1737	273-2615
Nielsen-Massey Vanillas Inc 1550 S Shields Dr *TF:* 800-525-7873 ■ *Web:* www.nielsenmassey.com	Waukegan	IL	60085	847-578-1550	578-1570
Northwestern Flavors Inc 120 N Aurora St	West Chicago	IL	60185	630-231-0489	
Ottens Flavors 7800 Holstein Ave *TF:* 800-523-0767 ■ *Web:* www.ottensflavors.com	Philadelphia	PA	19153	215-365-7800	365-7801
Phillips Syrup Corp 28025 Ranney Pkwy *Web:* www.phillipssyrup.com	Westlake	OH	44145	440-835-8001	835-1148
Sea Breeze Inc 441 Rt 202 *TF:* 800-732-2733 ■ *Web:* www.seabreezesyrups.com	Towaco	NJ	07082	973-334-7777	334-2617
Sensient Technologies Corp 777 E Wisconsin Ave 11th Fl *NYSE: SXT* ■ *TF:* 800-558-9892 ■ *Web:* www.sensient-tech.com	Milwaukee	WI	53202	414-271-6755	347-3785
Sethness Products Co 3422 W Touhy Ave *TF:* 888-772-1880 ■ *Web:* www.sethness.com	Lincolnwood	IL	60712	847-329-2080	329-2090
Symrise Inc 300 N St *TF General:* 800-422-1559 ■ *Web:* www.symrise.com	Teterboro	NJ	07608	201-288-3200	462-2200
T Hasegawa USA Inc 14017 183rd St *Web:* www.thasegawa.com	Cerritos	CA	90703	714-522-1900	522-6800
Virginia Dare Extract Company Inc 882 Third Ave *Web:* www.virginiadare.com	Brooklyn	NY	11232	718-788-1776	768-3978
Western Syrup Co 13766 Milroy Pl *TF:* 800-521-3888 ■ *Web:* www.jogue.com	Santa Fe Springs	CA	90670	562-921-4485	
Wild Flavors Inc 1261 Pacific Ave **Fax:* Sales ■ *TF:* 800-263-5286 ■ *Web:* www.wildflavors.com	Erlanger	KY	41018	859-342-3600	342-3610*
Zink & Triest Company Inc 200 Highpoint Dr *Web:* bizapedia.com	Chalfont	PA	18914	215-469-1950	469-1951

299-16 Flour Mixes & Doughs

Company	City	State	ZIP	Phone	Fax
Abitec Corp Inc PO Box 569 *TF Sales:* 800-555-1255 ■ *Web:* www.abiteccorp.com	Columbus	OH	43215	614-429-6464	299-8279
Bake'n Joy Foods Inc 351 Willow St *TF:* 800-666-4937 ■ *Web:* www.bakenjoy.com	North Andover	MA	01845	978-683-1414	683-1713
Caravan Products Company Inc 100 Adams Dr *TF:* 800-526-5261 ■ *Web:* caravaningredients.com	Totowa	NJ	07512	973-256-8886	256-8395
Cereal Food Processors Inc 2001 Shawnee Mission Pkwy *Web:* www.cerealfood.com	Mission Woods	KS	66205	913-890-6300	
Dawn Food Products Inc 3333 Sargent Rd *TF Cust Svc:* 800-292-1362 ■ *Web:* www.dawnfoods.com	Jackson	MI	49201	517-789-4400	789-4465
Gilster-Mary Lee Corp 1037 State St PO Box 227 *Web:* gilstermarylee.com	Chester	IL	62233	618-826-2361	826-2973
Langlois Co 10810 San Sevaine Way *TF:* 800-962-5993 ■ *Web:* www.langloiscompany.com	Mira Loma	CA	91752	951-360-3900	
Pinnacle Foods Corp 399 Jefferson Rd *TF:* 866-266-7596 ■ *Web:* www.pinnaclefoodscorp.com	Parsippany	NJ	07054	973-541-6620	
Puratos Corp 1941 Old Cuthbert Rd *TF All:* 800-654-0036 ■ *Web:* www.puratos.com	Cherry Hill	NJ	08034	856-428-4300	428-2939
Rhodes International Inc PO Box 25487 *TF Cust Svc:* 800-876-7333 ■ *Web:* www.rhodesbread.com	Salt Lake City	UT	84125	801-972-0122	972-0286
Southern Maid Donut Flour Co 3615 Cavalier Dr *Web:* www.southernmaiddonuts.com	Garland	TX	75042	972-272-6425	276-3549
Subco Foods Inc 4350 S Taylor Dr *TF:* 800-473-0757 ■ *Web:* www.subcofoods.com	Sheboygan	WI	53081	920-457-7761	457-3899
Watson Foods Company Inc 301 Heffernan Dr *TF:* 800-388-3481 ■ *Web:* www.watson-inc.com	West Haven	CT	06516	203-932-3000	932-8266

299-17 Food Emulsifiers

Company	City	State	ZIP	Phone	Fax
ADM Specialty Food Ingredients Div 4666 E Faries Pkwy *TF:* 800-637-5843 ■ *Web:* www.adm.com	Decatur	IL	62526	217-424-5200	
American Lecithin Company Inc 115 Hurley Rd Unit 2B *TF:* 800-364-4416 ■ *Web:* www.americanlecithin.com	Oxford	CT	06478	203-262-7100	262-7101
Bunge Ltd 50 Main St Sixth Fl *NYSE: BG* ■ *Web:* www.bunge.com	White Plains	NY	10606	914-684-2800	684-3499
Crest Foods Company Inc 905 Main St *Web:* www.crestfoods.com	Ashton	IL	61006	815-453-7411	453-7744
Frutarom Corp 9500 Railroad Ave **Fax:* Cust Svc ■ *TF:* 866-229-7198 ■ *Web:* www.frutarom.com	North Bergen	NJ	07047	201-861-9500	861-9267*

299-18 Fruits & Vegetables - Dried or Dehydrated

Company	City	State	ZIP	Phone	Fax
Basic American Foods 2185 N California Blvd Ste 215 *TF:* 800-227-4050 ■ *Web:* www.baf.com	Walnut Creek	CA	94596	925-472-4000	472-4314

Phone Fax

Bernard Food Industries Inc
1125 Hartrey Ave ... Evanston IL 60204 847-869-5222 869-5315
TF: 800-323-3663 ■ *Web:* www.bernardfoods.com

Concord Foods Inc 10 Minuteman Way ... Brockton MA 02301 508-580-1700 584-9425
Web: www.concordfoods.com

Custom Culinary 2505 S Finley Rd ... Lombard IL 60148 630-928-4898
TF Cust Svc: 800-621-8827 ■ *Web:* www.customculinary.com

Del Monte Foods Co 1 Maritime Plaza ... San Francisco CA 94111 415-247-3000 247-3311
TF Cust Svc: 800-543-3090 ■ *Web:* www.delmonte.com

Derco Foods 2670 W Shaw Ln ... Fresno CA 93711 559-435-2664 435-8520
Web: www.dercofoods.com

Freskeeto Frozen Foods Inc 8019 Rt 209 ... Ellenville NY 12428 845-647-5111
TF: 800-356-3663

Garry Packing Inc
11272 E Central Ave PO Box 249 ... Del Rey CA 93616 559-888-2126 888-2848
TF: 800-248-2126 ■ *Web:* www.garrypacking.com

Graceland Fruit Inc 1123 Main St ... Frankfort MI 49635 231-352-7181 352-4711
TF: 800-352-7181 ■ *Web:* www.gracelandfruit.com

Idaho Supreme Potatoes Inc
614 E 800 N PO Box 246 ... Firth ID 83236 208-346-6841 346-4104
Web: idahosupreme.com

Idaho-Pacific Corp 4723 E 100 N PO Box 478 ... Ririe ID 83443 208-538-6971 538-5082
TF Sales: 800-238-5503 ■ *Web:* www.idahopacific.com

Larsen Farms 2650 N 2375 E ... Hamer ID 83425 208-662-5501 662-5568
TF Sales: 800-767-6104 ■ *Web:* www.larsenfarms.com

Meridian Foods 201 E Babb Rd ... Eaton IN 47338 765-396-3344 396-3430

National Raisin Co PO Box 219 ... Fowler CA 93625 559-834-5981 834-1055
Web: www.nationalraisin.com

Nonpareil Corp 40 N 400 W ... Blackfoot ID 83221 208-785-5880 785-3656
TF: 800-522-2223 ■ *Web:* nonpareilfarms.com

Northwest Pea & Bean Company Inc
6109 E Desmet Ave ... Spokane WA 99212 509-534-3821 534-4350
Web: co-ag.com

Oregon Freeze Dry Inc PO Box 1048 ... Albany OR 97321 541-926-6001
TF: 800-547-4060 ■ *Web:* www.ofd.com

Oregon Potato Co PO Box 3110 ... Pasco WA 99302 509-545-4545
TF: 800-336-6311 ■ *Web:* www.oregonpotato.com

Small Planet Foods Inc
106 Woodworth St ... Sedro Woolley WA 98284 360-855-0100
TF: 800-624-4123 ■ *Web:* www.smallplanetfoods.com

Stapleton-Spence Packing Co
1530 The Alameda Ste 320 ... San Jose CA 95126 408-297-8815 297-0611
TF: 800-297-8815 ■ *Web:* www.stapleton-spence.com

Sun-Maid Growers of California
13525 S Bethel Ave ... Kingsburg CA 93631 559-896-8000 897-6209
Web: sunmaid.com

Sunsweet Growers Inc 901 N Walton Ave ... Yuba City CA 95993 530-674-5010 751-5238
TF: 800-417-2253 ■ *Web:* www.sunsweet.com

Tree Top Inc 220 E Second Ave ... Selah WA 98942 509-697-7251 698-1421
TF: 800-237-0515 ■ *Web:* www.treetop.com

Tule River Co-op Dryer Inc
16548 Rd 168 PO Box 4477 ... ÿPorterville CA 93257 559-784-3396

299-19 Fruits & Vegetables - Pickled

Phone Fax

B & G Foods Inc Four Gatehall Dr Ste 110 ... Parsippany NJ 07054 973-401-6500 630-6553
NYSE: BGS ■ *Web:* www.bgfoods.com

Bay View Food Products Inc
2606 N Huron Rd ... Pinconning MI 48650 989-879-3555 879-2659
Web: www.bayviewfoods.com

Beaverton Foods Inc 7100 NW Century Blvd ... Hillsboro OR 97124 503-646-8138 644-9204
TF: 800-223-8076 ■ *Web:* www.beavertonfoods.com

Best Maid Products Inc PO Box 1809 ... Fort Worth TX 76101 817-335-5494
TF: 800-447-3581 ■ *Web:* www.bestmaidproducts.com

Cain's Foods Inc 114 E Main St ... Ayer MA 01432 978-772-0300 772-0200
TF: 800-225-0601 ■ *Web:* www.cainsfoods.com

Cajun Chef Products Inc
519 Joseph Rd ... Saint Martinville LA 70582 337-394-7112 394-7115

Clorox Co 1221 Broadway ... Oakland CA 94612 510-271-7000 832-1463
NYSE: CLX ■ *TF Cust Svc:* 800-424-9300 ■ *Web:* www.thecloroxcompany.com

Conway Import Co Inc
11051 W Addison St ... Franklin Park IL 60131 847-455-5600 304-4021*
**Fax Area Code:* 800 ■ *TF:* 800-323-8801 ■ *Web:* conwaydressings.com

Eastern Foods Inc 1000 Naturally Fresh Blvd ... Atlanta GA 30349 800-765-1950 765-9016*
**Fax Area Code:* 404 ■ **Fax:* Hum Res ■ *TF:* 800-765-1950 ■ *Web:* www.naturallyfresh.com

GLK Foods LLC 11 Clark St ... Shortsville NY 14548 585-289-4414
Web: www.greatlakeskraut.com

Gold Pure Food Products Inc
One Brooklyn Rd ... Hempstead NY 11550 516-483-5600 483-5798
Web: www.goldshorseradish.com

Henri's Food Products Company Inc
8622 N 87th St ... Milwaukee WI 53224 414-365-5720

HV Food Products Co 1221 Broadway ... Oakland CA 94612 510-271-7000 832-1463
Web: www.hiddenvalley.com

JG Van Holten & Son Inc
703 W Madison St PO Box 66 ... Waterloo WI 53594 920-478-2144 478-2316
Web: www.vanholtenpickles.com

Kaplan & Zubrin Inc 146 Kaighns Ave ... Camden NJ 08103 856-964-1083
TF: 800-248-1736

Ken's Foods Inc 1 D'Angelo Dr ... Marlborough MA 01752 508-229-1100 229-1146
TF General: 800-633-5800 ■ *Web:* www.kensfoods.com

Kikkoman Foods Inc N 1365 Six Corners Rd ... Walworth WI 53184 262-275-6181 275-9452
Web: www.kikkoman.com

KT's Kitchens Inc 1065 E Walnut St Ste C ... Carson CA 90746 310-764-0850 764-0855
Web: www.ktskitchens.com

Langlois Co 10810 San Sevaine Way ... Mira Loma CA 91752 951-360-3900
TF: 800-962-5993 ■ *Web:* www.langloiscompany.com

Lee Kum Kee Inc 14841 Don Julian Rd ... City of Industry CA 91746 626-709-1888 709-1899
TF Orders: 800-654-5082 ■ *Web:* lkk.com

Phone Fax

Litehouse Inc 1109 N Ella Ave ... Sandpoint ID 83864 208-263-7569 263-7821
TF: 800-669-3169 ■ *Web:* www.litehousefoods.com

MA Gedney Co 2100 Stoughton Ave ... Chaska MN 55318 952-448-2612 448-1790
TF: 888-244-0653 ■ *Web:* www.gedneyfoods.com

Maurice's Gourmet Barbeque PO Box 6847 ... West Columbia SC 29171 803-791-5887 791-8707
TF: 800-628-7423 ■ *Web:* www.piggiepark.com

McIlhenny Co Hwy 329 ... Avery Island LA 70513 337-365-8173 596-6444*
**Fax Area Code:* 504 ■ *TF Orders:* 800-634-9599 ■ *Web:* www.tabasco.com

Meduri Farms Inc PO Box 636 ... Dallas OR 97338 503-623-0308
Web: www.medurifarms.com

Moody Dunbar Inc
2000 Waters Edge Dr Ste 21 ... Johnson City TN 37604 423-952-0100 952-0289
TF: 800-251-8202 ■ *Web:* moodydunbar.com

Morehouse Foods Inc 760 Epperson Dr ... City of Industry CA 91748 626-854-1655 854-1656
Web: www.morehousefoods.com

Mullins Food Products Inc 2200 S 25th Ave ... Broadview IL 60155 708-344-3224 344-0153
Web: www.mullinsfood.com

Newman's Own Inc 246 Post Rd E ... Westport CT 06880 203-222-0136 227-5630
Web: www.newmansown.com

NewStar Fresh Foods LLC 900 Work St ... Salinas CA 93901 831-758-7800 758-7869
TF: 888-782-7220 ■ *Web:* www.newstarfresh.com

Old Dutch Mustard Co 98 Cutter Mill Rd ... Great Neck NY 11021 516-466-0522 466-0762
Web: pilgrimfoods.net

Olds Products Co 10700 88th Ave ... Pleasant Prairie WI 53158 262-947-3500 947-3517
TF: 800-233-8064 ■ *Web:* www.oldsproducts.com

Pacific Choice Brands Inc 4667 E Date Ave ... Fresno CA 93725 559-237-5583 237-2078

Plochman Inc 1333 N Boudreau Rd ... Manteno IL 60950 815-468-3434 468-8755
Web: www.plochman.com

Portion Pac Inc 7325 Snider Rd ... Mason OH 45040 513-398-0400 459-5300
Web: heinz.com

Spring Glen Fresh Foods Inc
314 Spring Glen Dr PO Box 518 ... Ephrata PA 17522 717-733-2201 721-6720
TF: 800-641-2853 ■ *Web:* www.springglen.com

Swanson Pickle Company Inc
11561 Heights Ravenna Rd ... Ravenna MI 49451 231-853-2289 853-6281

T Marzetti Co 1105 Schrock Rd ... Columbus OH 43229 614-846-2232 848-8330
TF: 800-999-1835 ■ *Web:* www.marzetti.com

Walden Farms 1209 W St Georges Ave ... Linden NJ 07036 800-229-1706 925-9537*
**Fax Area Code:* 908 ■ *TF:* 800-229-1706 ■ *Web:* www.waldenfarms.com

Yamasa Corp USA 3500 Fairview Industrial Dr SE ... Salem OR 97302 503-363-8550 363-8710
Web: www.yamasausa.com

299-20 Fruits, Vegetables, Juices - Canned or Preserved

Phone Fax

American Spoon Foods Inc 1668 Clarion Ave ... Petoskey MI 49770 231-347-9030 347-2512
TF: 800-222-5886 ■ *Web:* www.spoon.com

Apple & Eve Inc 2 Seaview Blvd ... Port Washington NY 11050 516-621-1122 621-2164
TF: 800-969-8018 ■ *Web:* www.appleandeve.com

Ardmore Farms Inc 1915 N Woodland Blvd ... DeLand FL 32724 330-753-2293 848-4287
Web: www.juice4u.com

B & G Foods Inc Four Gatehall Dr Ste 110 ... Parsippany NJ 07054 973-401-6500 630-6553
NYSE: BGS ■ *Web:* www.bgfoods.com

Baumer Foods Inc 2424 Edenborn Ave Ste 510 ... Metairie LA 70001 504-482-5761 483-2425
Web: www.baumerfoods.com

Beckman & Gast Company Inc
282 W Kremer-Hoying Rd PO Box 307 ... Saint Henry OH 45883 419-678-4195
Web: www.beckmangast.com

Braswell Food Co 226 N Zetterower Ave ... Statesboro GA 30458 912-764-6191 489-1572
TF: 800-673-9388 ■ *Web:* www.braswells.com/

Brooklyn Bottling Co 643 S Rd ... Milton NY 12547 845-795-2171 649-2596*
**Fax Area Code:* 718

Bruce Foods Corp PO Drawer 1030 ... New Iberia LA 70561 337-365-8101 369-9026
TF: 800-299-9082 ■ *Web:* www.brucefoods.com

Burnette Foods Inc 701 US Hwy 31 ... Elk Rapids MI 49629 231-264-8116 264-9597
Web: www.burnettefoods.com

Bush Bros & Co 1016 E Weisgarber Rd ... Knoxville TN 37909 865-588-7685 584-8157
Web: www.bushbeans.com

Campbell Soup Co One Campbell Pl ... Camden NJ 08103 856-342-4800 342-3878
NYSE: CPB ■ *TF:* 800-257-8443 ■ *Web:* www.campbellsoupcompany.com

Cargill Inc North America 15407 McGinty Rd ... Wayzata MN 55391 952-742-7575
Web: cargill.com

Carriage House Cos Inc, The 196 Newton St ... Fredonia NY 14063 716-673-1000 673-8443*
**Fax:* Sales ■ *TF:* 800-828-8915

Cherry Growers Inc 6331 US Hwy 31 ... Grawn MI 49637 231-276-9241 276-7075
Web: www.cherrygrowers.net

Cincinnati Preserving Company Inc
3015 E Kemper Rd ... Cincinnati OH 45241 513-771-2000 771-8381
TF Cust Svc: 800-222-9966 ■ *Web:* www.clearbrookfarms.com

Citrus Systems Inc 125 Jackson Ave N ... Hopkins MN 55343 952-935-0410
Web: www.citrussystems.com

Clement Pappas & Company Inc
One Colons Dr Ste 200 ... Carneyspoint NJ 08069 856-455-1000 455-8746
TF: 800-257-7019 ■ *Web:* www.clementpappas.com

Cornelius Seed Corn Co 14760 317th Ave ... Bellevue IA 52031 563-672-3463 672-3521
TF: 800-218-1862 ■ *Web:* www.corneliusseed.com

Country Pure Foods Inc 681 W Waterloo Rd ... Akron OH 44314 330-753-2293 848-4287
Web: www.countrypurefoods.com

Crookham Company Inc PO Box 520 ... Caldwell ID 83606 208-459-7451 454-2108
Web: www.crookham.com

Daily Juice Products One Daily Way ... Verona PA 15147 412-828-9020
Web: www.dailyscocktails.com

Del Monte Foods Co 1 Maritime Plaza ... San Francisco CA 94111 415-247-3000 247-3311
TF Cust Svc: 800-543-3090 ■ *Web:* www.delmonte.com

Del Monte Fresh Produce Co
241 Sevilla Ave ... Coral Gables FL 33134 305-520-8400 567-0320
TF Cust Svc: 800-950-3683 ■ *Web:* www.freshdelmonte.com

Diana Fruit Company Inc 651 Mathew St ... Santa Clara CA 95050 408-727-9631 727-9890
Web: www.dianafruit.com

Dole Packaged Foods Co One Dole Dr ... Westlake Village CA 91362 818-874-4000 874-4893
Web: dole.com

Phone Fax

Don Pepino Sales Co 123 Railroad Ave........... Williamstown NJ 08094 856-629-7429 629-6340
TF: 888-281-6400 ■ *Web:* www.donpepino.com

Escalon Premier Brands 1905 McHenry Ave........... Escalon CA 95320 209-838-7341
TF: 800-255-5750 ■ *Web:* www.escalon.net

Faribault Foods Inc
Campbell Mithun Tower Ste 3380................ Minneapolis MN 55402 612-333-6461
Web: www.faribaultfoods.com

Fremont Co 802 N Front St......................... Fremont OH 43420 419-334-8995 334-8120

Furmano Foods Inc
770 Cannery Rd PO Box 500 .... Northumberland PA 17857 570-473-3516 473-7367
TF: 877-877-6032 ■ *Web:* www.furmanos.com

Giorgio Foods Inc PO Box 96 .... Temple PA 19560 610-926-2139 926-7012
TF: 800-220-2139 ■ *Web:* www.giorgiofoods.com

Gray & Co 5520 SW Macadam Ave Ste 230............. Portland OR 97239 503-248-4729 248-4729
Web: www.cherryman.com

Growers Co-op Grape Juice Company Inc
112 N Portage St PO Box 399....................... Westfield NY 14787 716-326-3161 326-6566
Web: www.concordgrapejuice.com

Hanover Foods Corp 1550 York St PO Box 334 .... Hanover PA 17331 717-632-6000 632-6681
OTC: HNFSA ■ *TF:* 800-888-4646 ■ *Web:* www.hanoverfoods.com

Hawaiian Sun Products Inc
259 Sand Island Access Rd .... Honolulu HI 96819 808-845-3211 842-0532
Web: www.hawaiiansunproducts.com

Hirzel Canning Company & Farms
411 Lemoyne Rd.............................. Northwood OH 43619 419-693-0531 693-4859
TF: 800-837-1631 ■ *Web:* www.deifratelli.com

HJ Heinz Co One PPG Pl Ste 3100.................. Pittsburgh PA 15230 412-456-5700
TF: 800-255-5750 ■ *Web:* www.heinz.com

House Foods America Corp
7351 Orangewood Ave .... Garden Grove CA 92841 714-901-4350 901-4235
TF: 877-333-7077 ■ *Web:* www.house-foods.com

Indian Summer Co-op 3958 W Chauvez Rd .... Ludington MI 49431 231-845-6248 843-9453*

Ingomar Packing Co
9950 S Ingomar Grade PO Box 1448 .... Los Banos CA 93635 209-826-9494 854-6292
Web: www.ingomarpacking.com

J. Lieb Foods Inc PO Box 389 .... Forest Grove OR 97116 503-359-9279
Web: www.jliebfoods.com

Jasper Wyman & Son PO Box 100 .... Milbridge ME 04658 800-341-1758
TF Sales: 800-341-1758 ■ *Web:* www.wymans.com

JM Smucker Co One Strawberry Ln .... Orrville OH 44667 330-682-3000 684-6410
NYSE: SJM ■ *TF:* 888-550-9555 ■ *Web:* www.smuckers.com

JM Smucker Pennsylvania Inc
300 Keck Ave .... New Bethlehem PA 16242 814-275-1323 275-1340

Johanna Foods Inc
20 Johanna Farm Rd PO Box 272.................. Flemington NJ 08822 908-788-2200
TF: 800-727-6700 ■ *Web:* www.johannafoods.com

Juice Bowl Products Inc 2090 Bartow Rd .... Lakeland FL 33801 863-665-5515 667-7116

Knouse Foods Co-op Inc
800 Peach Glen-Idaville Rd .... Peach Glen PA 17375 717-677-8181 677-7069
Web: www.knouse.com

Lakeside Foods Inc 808 Hamilton St .... Manitowoc WI 54220 920-684-3356 686-4033
TF: 800-466-3834 ■ *Web:* www.lakesidefoods.com

Langers Juice Company Inc
16195 Stephens St.......................... City of Industry CA 91745 626-336-1666 961-2021
Web: www.langers.com

Lawrence Foods Inc 2200 Lunt Ave........... Elk Grove Village IL 60007 847-437-2400 437-2567
Web: www.lawrencefoods.com

Leelanau Fruit Co 2900 SW Bay Shore Dr .... Suttons Bay MI 49682 231-271-3514 271-4367
TF: 800-431-0718 ■ *Web:* www.leelanaufruit.com

LiDestri Foods Inc 815 Whitney Rd W................. Fairport NY 14450 585-377-7700 377-8150
Web: www.lidestrifoods.com

Louis Maull Co, The 219 N Market St............. Saint Louis MO 63102 314-241-8410
Web: www.maull.com

Lyons Magnus Inc 3158 E Hamilton Ave .... Fresno CA 93702 800-344-7130 233-8249*
**Fax Area Code:* 559 ■ *TF:* 800-344-7130 ■ *Web:* www.lyonsmagnus.com

Maui Land & Pineapple Company Inc
120 Kane St PO Box 187 .... Kahului HI 96733 808-877-3351 871-0953
Web: www.mauiland.com

Mayer Bros Apple Products Inc
3300 Transit Rd........................... West Seneca NY 14224 716-668-1787 668-2437
Web: www.mayerbrothers.com

Moody Dunbar Inc
2000 Waters Edge Dr Ste 21.................... Johnson City TN 37604 423-952-0100 952-0289
TF: 800-251-8202 ■ *Web:* moodydunbar.com

Morgan Foods Inc 90 W Morgan St.................... Austin IN 47102 812-794-1170 794-1211
TF: 888-430-1780 ■ *Web:* www.morganfoods.com

Mott's LLP PO Box 869077............................ Plano TX 75086 800-426-4891
TF Consumer Info: 800-426-4891 ■ *Web:* www.motts.com

Mrs Clark's Foods 740 SE Dalbey Dr.................. Ankeny IA 50021 515-299-6400
Web: www.mrsclarks.com

Muir Glen Organic Tomato Products
PO Box 18932 .... Denver CO 80218 800-248-7310
TF: 800-832-6345 ■ *Web:* www.muirglen.com

Mullins Food Products Inc 2200 S 25th Ave......... Broadview IL 60155 708-344-3224 344-0153
Web: www.mullinsfood.com

Mushroom Co, The 902 Woods Rd.................. Cambridge MD 21613 410-221-8971 221-8952
Web: www.themushroomcompany.com

National Fruit Product Co Inc
701 Fairmont Ave PO Box 2040 .... Winchester VA 22601 540-723-9614 665-4671*
**Fax:* Sales ■ *TF:* 800-655-4022 ■ *Web:* www.whitehousefoods.com

Ocean Spray Cranberries Inc
1 Ocean Spray Dr .... Lakeville-Middleboro MA 02349 508-946-1000 946-4594
TF: 800-662-3263 ■ *Web:* www.oceanspray.com

Odwalla Inc 1625 North Market Blvd .... Sacramento CA 95834 800-952-5210
Web: www.odwalla.com

Pacific Coast Producers 631 N Cluff Ave .... Lodi CA 95240 209-367-8800 367-1084
TF: 877-618-4776 ■ *Web:* canned-fresh.com

Pastorelli Food Products Inc
162 N Sangamon St................................ Chicago IL 60607 312-666-2041 666-2415
TF: 800-767-2829 ■ *Web:* www.pastorelli.com

President Global Corp 6965 Aragon Cir............ Buena Park CA 90620 714-994-2990 523-3142

Phone Fax

Ray Bros & Noble Canning Company Inc
3720 E 150 S PO Box 314 .... Hobbs IN 46047 765-675-7451 675-7400
Web: www.tiptonguide.com

Red Gold Inc 120 E Oak St .... Orestes IN 46063 765-754-7527
Web: www.redgold.com

Ryan Trading Corp
2500 Westchester Ave Ste 102 .... Purchase NY 10577 914-253-6767 253-6722
Web: www.ryantrading.com

Seneca Foods Corp 3736 S Main St.................. Marion NY 14505 315-926-8100 926-8300
NASDAQ: SENEA ■ *Web:* www.senecafoods.com

Simply Orange Juice Co 2659 Orange Ave............. Apopka FL 32703 800-871-2653
TF: 800-871-2653 ■ *Web:* www.simplyorangejuice.com

Southern Gardens Citrus
1820 Country Rd 833 .... Clewiston FL 33440 863-983-3030 983-3060
Web: southerngardens.com

Stanislaus Food Products Co 1202 D St .... Modesto CA 95354 800-327-7201 521-4014*
**Fax Area Code:* 209 ■ *TF:* 800-327-7201 ■ *Web:* www.stanislausfoodproducts.com

Stapleton-Spence Packing Co
1530 The Alameda Ste 320......................... San Jose CA 95126 408-297-8815 297-0611
TF: 800-297-8815 ■ *Web:* www.stapleton-spence.com

Sun Orchard Inc 1198 W Fairmont Dr .... Tempe AZ 85282 800-505-8423
TF: 800-505-8423 ■ *Web:* www.sunorchard.com

Talk O'Texas Brands Inc 1610 Roosevelt St......... San Angelo TX 76905 325-655-6077 655-7967
TF: 800-749-6572 ■ *Web:* www.talkotexas.com

Texas Citrus Exchange 702 E Expy 83 .... Mission TX 78572 956-585-8321 585-1655
Web: www.texascitrusexchange.com

Tip Top Canning Co
505 S Second St PO Box 126....................... Tipp City OH 45371 937-667-3713 667-3802
TF: 800-352-2635 ■ *Web:* www.tiptopcanning.com

Tree Top Inc 220 E Second Ave........................... Selah WA 98942 509-697-7251 698-1421
TF: 800-237-0515 ■ *Web:* www.treetop.com

Truitt Bros Inc 1105 Front St NE .... Salem OR 97301 503-362-3674 588-2868*
**Fax:* Sales ■ *TF:* 800-547-8712 ■ *Web:* www.truittbros.com

TW Garner Food Co
4045 Indiana Ave PO Box 4239 .... Winston-Salem NC 27105 336-661-1550 661-1901
Web: www.texaspete.com

Valley Processing Inc
108 E Blaine Ave PO Box 246...................... Sunnyside WA 98944 509-837-8084 837-3481
Web: valleyprocessing.com

Vegetable Juices Inc 7400 S Narragansett Ave......... Chicago IL 60638 708-924-9500 924-9510
TF General: 888-776-9752 ■ *Web:* www.vegetablejuices.com

Vita-Pakt Citrus Products 707 N Barranca Ave.......... Covina CA 91723 626-332-1101 966-8196
Web: www.vita-pakt.com

Welch's Inc 300 Baker Ave Ste 101 .... Concord MA 01742 978-371-1000
Web: www.welchs.com

Whitlock Packaging Corp 1701 S Lee St .... Fort Gibson OK 74434 918-478-4300 478-7362
TF: 800-833-9382 ■ *Web:* whitlockpkg.com

Zeigler Beverage Co 1513 N Broad St .... Lansdale PA 19446 215-855-5161 855-4548
TF Sales: 800-854-6123 ■ *Web:* www.zeiglers.com

299-21 Fruits, Vegetables, Juices - Frozen

Phone Fax

American Fruit Processors 10725 Sutter Ave......... Pacoima CA 91331 818-899-9574 899-6042*
**Fax:* Sales ■ *Web:* www.americanfruit.com

Apio Inc PO Box 727 .... Guadalupe CA 93434 805-343-2835 343-2849
TF Sales: 800-454-1355 ■ *Web:* www.apioinc.com

Ardmore Farms Inc 1915 N Woodland Blvd .... DeLand FL 32724 330-753-2293 848-4287
Web: www.juice4u.com

Bernatello's PO Box 729......................... Maple Lake MN 55358 952-831-6622 831-6606
TF: 800-622-6935 ■ *Web:* www.bernatellos.com

Capitol City Produce
16550 Commercial Ave.......................... Baton Rouge LA 70816 225-272-8153 272-8152
TF: 800-349-1583 ■ *Web:* www.capitolcityproduce.com

Cherry Growers Inc 6331 US Hwy 31 .... Grawn MI 49637 231-276-9241 276-7075
Web: www.cherrygrowers.net

Coloma Frozen Foods Inc 4145 Coloma Rd............ Coloma MI 49038 269-849-0500 849-0886
TF: 800-642-2723 ■ *Web:* www.colomafrozen.com

Del Mar Food Products Corp 1720 Beach Rd .... Watsonville CA 95076 831-722-3516 722-7690
Web: delmarfoods.com

Dole Food Company Inc One Dole Dr.......... Westlake Village CA 91362 818-879-6600 874-4893*
NYSE: DOLE ■ **Fax:* Hum Res ■ *TF:* 800-232-8888 ■ *Web:* www.dole.com

Fresh Frozen Foods LLC
1814 Washington St PO Box 215.................... Jefferson GA 30549 706-367-9851 367-4646
TF: 800-277-9851 ■ *Web:* www.freshfrozenfoods.com

Frozsun Inc 701 W Kimberly Ave Ste 210............. Placentia CA 92870 714-630-6292
Web: sunrisegrowers.com

Giorgio Foods Inc PO Box 96 .... Temple PA 19560 610-926-2139 926-7012
TF: 800-220-2139 ■ *Web:* www.giorgiofoods.com

Graceland Fruit Inc 1123 Main St .... Frankfort MI 49635 231-352-7181 352-4711
TF: 800-352-7181 ■ *Web:* www.gracelandfruit.com

HJ Heinz Co One PPG Pl Ste 3100.................. Pittsburgh PA 15230 412-456-5700
TF: 800-255-5750 ■ *Web:* www.heinz.com

HPC Foods Ltd 288 Libby St........................ Honolulu HI 96819 808-848-2431 841-4398
TF: 877-370-0919 ■ *Web:* hpcfoods.com

JR Simplot Co 999 W Main St Ste 1300 .... Boise ID 83702 208-336-2110 389-7515
TF: 800-832-8893 ■ *Web:* www.simplot.com

Lakeside Foods Inc 808 Hamilton St .... Manitowoc WI 54220 920-684-3356 686-4033
TF: 800-466-3834 ■ *Web:* www.lakesidefoods.com

Lamb Weston Inc 8701 W Gage Blvd............... Kennewick WA 99336 509-735-4651 736-0395*
**Fax:* Sales ■ *Web:* www.lambweston.com

Leelanau Fruit Co 2900 SW Bay Shore Dr .... Suttons Bay MI 49682 231-271-3514 271-4367
TF: 800-431-0718 ■ *Web:* www.leelanaufruit.com

Lewis Dreyfus Citrus Inc (LDCI)
355 S Ninth St .... Winter Garden FL 34787 407-656-1000 656-1229

McCain Foods Ltd 181 Bay St Ste 3600 .... Toronto ON M5J2T3 416-955-1700
TF: 800-938-7799 ■ *Web:* www.mccain.com

McCain Foods USA Inc 2275 Cabot Dr.................. Lisle IL 60532 800-938-7799 857-4560*
**Fax Area Code:* 630 ■ *TF:* 800-938-7799 ■ *Web:* www.mccainusa.com

Milne Fruit Products Inc 804 Bennett Ave............ Prosser WA 99350 509-786-2611 786-4915
Web: www.milnefruit.com

Company	City	State	ZIP	Phone	Fax
Mrs Clark's Foods 740 SE Dalbey Dr *Web:* www.mrsclarks.com	Ankeny	IA	50021	515-299-6400	
National Frozen Foods Corp 1600 Fairview Ave E Ste 200 *Web:* www.nffc.com	Seattle	WA	98102	206-322-8900	322-4458
NORPAC Foods Inc 930 W Washington St *TF:* 800-733-9311 ■ *Web:* www.norpac.com	Stayton	OR	97383	503-769-2101	769-1273
Patterson Frozen Foods Inc 100 W Las Palmas Ave *Web:* www.pattersonfrozenfoods.com	Patterson	CA	95363	209-892-2611	892-2582
Penobscot McCrum LLC 28 Pierce St *TF:* 800-435-4456 ■ *Web:* www.penobscotmccrum.com	Belfast	ME	04915	207-338-4360	338-5742
Peterson Farms Inc 3104 W Baseline Rd PO Box 115 *Web:* www.petersonfarmsinc.com	Shelby	MI	49455	231-861-7101	
Pictsweet Co, The 10 Pictsweet Dr **Fax Area Code:* 888 ■ *Web:* www.pictsweet.com	Bells	TN	38006	731-663-7600	662-7651*
Seabrook Bros & Sons Inc 85 Finley Rd *Web:* www.seabrookfarms.com	Bridgeton	NJ	08302	856-455-8080	455-9282
Seneca Foods Corp 3736 S Main St *NASDAQ: SENEA* ■ *Web:* www.senecafoods.com	Marion	NY	14505	315-926-8100	926-8300
Smith Frozen Foods Inc 101 Depot St *Web:* www.smithfrozenfoods.com	Weston	OR	97886	541-566-3515	566-3772
Sweet Ovations 1741 Tomlinson Rd *TF:* 800-280-9387 ■ *Web:* www.sweetovations.com	Philadelphia	PA	19116	215-676-3900	613-2115
Sysco Seattle Inc 22820 54th Ave S *Web:* seattle.sysco.com	Kent	WA	98032	206-622-2261	721-2787
Townsend Farms Inc 23400 NE Townsend Way *Web:* www.townsendfarms.com	Fairview	OR	97024	503-666-1780	
Tree Top Inc 220 E Second Ave *TF:* 800-237-0515 ■ *Web:* www.treetop.com	Selah	WA	98942	509-697-7251	698-1421
Twin City Foods Inc 10120 269th Pl NW *Web:* twincityfoods.com	Stanwood	WA	98292	206-515-2400	515-2499
Vita-Pakt Citrus Products 707 N Barranca Ave *Web:* www.vita-pakt.com	Covina	CA	91723	626-332-1101	966-8196
Wawona Frozen Foods Inc 100 W Alluvial Ave *Web:* www.wawona.com	Clovis	CA	93611	559-299-2901	299-1921

299-22 Gelatin

Company	City	State	ZIP	Phone	Fax
Gelita USA Inc PO Box 927 *Web:* www.gelita.com	Sioux City	IA	51102	712-943-5516	943-3372
Langlois Co 10810 San Sevaine Way *TF:* 800-962-5993 ■ *Web:* www.langloiscompany.com	Mira Loma	CA	91752	951-360-3900	
Milligan & Higgins Maple Ave PO Box 506 *Web:* www.milligan1868.com	Johnstown	NY	12095	518-762-4638	762-7039
Nitta Gelatin Inc 598 Airport Blvd Ste 900 *TF:* 888-648-8287 ■ *Web:* www.nitta-gelatin.com	Morrisville	NC	27560	919-238-3300	238-3222
Subco Foods Inc 4350 S Taylor Dr *TF:* 800-473-0757 ■ *Web:* www.subcofoods.com	Sheboygan	WI	53081	920-457-7761	457-3899
Swagger Foods Corp 900 Corporate Woods Pkwy *Web:* www.swaggerfoods.com	Vernon Hills	IL	60061	847-913-1200	913-1263

299-23 Grain Mill Products

Company	City	State	ZIP	Phone	Fax
ACH Food Cos Inc 7171 Goodlet Farms Pkwy *TF:* 800-691-1106 ■ *Web:* www.achfood.com	Cordova	TN	38016	901-381-3000	381-2968
ADM Corn Processing Div 4666 E Faries Pkwy *TF:* 800-637-5843 ■ *Web:* www.adm.com	Decatur	IL	62526	217-424-5200	424-5978
ADM Milling Co (ADM) 8000 W 110th St *TF:* 800-422-1688 ■ *Web:* www.adm.com	Overland Park	KS	66210	913-491-9400	
Ag Processing Inc 12700 W Dodge Rd PO Box 2047 *TF:* 800-247-1345 ■ *Web:* www.agp.com	Omaha	NE	68103	402-496-7809	498-2215
American Rice Inc 10700 N Fwy Ste 800 *Web:* www.amrice.com	Houston	TX	77037	281-272-8800	272-8782
Bay State Milling Co 100 Congress St **Fax Area Code:* 617 ■ *TF:* 800-553-5687 ■ *Web:* www.baystatemilling.com	Quincy	MA	02169	800-553-5687	479-8910*
Beaumont Rice Mills Inc 1800 Pecos St *Web:* bmtricemills.com	Beaumont	TX	77701	409-832-2521	832-6927
Blendex Company Inc 11208 Electron Dr *TF:* 800-626-6325 ■ *Web:* www.blendex.com	Louisville	KY	40299	502-267-1003	267-1024
Cargill Inc North America 15407 McGinty Rd *Web:* cargill.com	Wayzata	MN	55391	952-742-7575	
Cereal Food Processors Inc 2001 Shawnee Mission Pkwy *Web:* www.cerealfood.com	Mission Woods	KS	66205	913-890-6300	
Chelsea Milling Co 201 W N St PO Box 460 *TF:* 800-727-2460 ■ *Web:* www.jiffymix.com	Chelsea	MI	48118	734-475-1361	475-4630
Cormier Rice Milling Co Inc 501 W Third St	De Witt	AR	72042	870-946-3561	
Farmers Rice Co-op PO Box 15223 *TF:* 800-326-2799 ■ *Web:* www.farmersrice.com	Sacramento	CA	95851	916-923-5100	920-3321
Farmers Rice Milling Co 3211 Hwy 397 S *Web:* www.frmco.com	Lake Charles	LA	70615	337-433-5205	433-1735
Florida Crystals Corp 1 N Clematis St Ste 200 *Web:* www.floridacrystals.com	West Palm Beach	FL	33401	561-366-5100	366-5158
Gold Medal PO Box 9452 **Fax Area Code:* 763 ■ *TF:* 800-248-7310 ■ *Web:* www.generalmills.com	Minneapolis	MN	55440	800-248-7310	764-8330*
Grain Processing Corp 1600 Oregon St *Web:* www.grainprocessing.com	Muscatine	IA	52761	563-264-4265	264-4289
Hodgson Mill Inc 1100 Stevens Ave *TF:* 800-347-0105 ■ *Web:* www.hodgsonmill.com	Effingham	IL	62401	217-347-0105	347-0198
Hopkinsville Milling Co P.O. Box 669 *Web:* sunflourflour.com	Hopkinsville	KY	42240	270-886-1231	886-6407
House-Autry Mills Inc 7000 US Hwy 301 S **Fax Area Code:* 919 ■ *TF:* 800-849-0802 ■ *Web:* www.house-autry.com	Four Oaks	NC	27524	800-849-0802	963-6458*
HR Wentzel Sons Inc 5521 Waggoners Gap Rd PO Box 125	Landisburg	PA	17040	717-789-3306	789-0128
Indian Harvest Specialtifoods Inc 1012 Paul Bunyan Dr SE **Fax Area Code:* 218 ■ *TF Orders:* 800-346-7032 ■ *Web:* inharvest.com/	Bemidji	MN	56601	800-346-7032	751-8519*
King Milling Co 115 S Broadway St *Web:* www.kingmilling.com	Lowell	MI	49331	616-897-9264	897-4350
Knappen Milling Co 110 S Water St *TF:* 800-562-7736 ■ *Web:* www.knappen.com	Augusta	MI	49012	269-731-4141	731-5441
Lacey Milling Co 217 W Fifth St	Hanford	CA	93230	559-584-6634	
Mallet & Company Inc 51 Arch St Ext *TF:* 800-245-2757 ■ *Web:* www.malletoil.com	Carnegie	PA	15106	412-276-9000	276-9002
Manildra Group USA 4210 Shawnee Mission Pkwy Ste 312A *TF:* 800-323-8435 ■ *Web:* manildrausa.com/	Shawnee Mission	KS	66205	913-362-0777	362-0052
Mars Snack Food 800 High St *TF:* 800-551-0895 ■ *Web:* www.mars.com	Hackettstown	NJ	07840	908-852-1000	850-2734
McShares Inc PO Box 1460 *TF:* 800-234-7174 ■ *Web:* www.researchprod.com	Salina	KS	67402	785-825-2181	825-8908
Mennel Milling Co 128 W Crocker St *TF:* 800-688-8151 ■ *Web:* www.mennel.com	Fostoria	OH	44830	419-435-8151	436-5150
MGP Ingredients Inc 100 Commercial St PO Box 130 *NASDAQ: MGPI* ■ *TF:* 800-255-0302 ■ *Web:* www.mgpingredients.com	Atchison	KS	66002	913-367-1480	367-0192
Minn-Dak Growers Ltd 4034 40th Ave N *Web:* www.minndak.com	Grand Forks	ND	58203	701-746-7453	780-9050
Morrison Milling Co 319 E Prairie St *TF:* 800-531-7912 ■ *Web:* morrisonmilling.com	Denton	TX	76201	940-387-6111	566-5992
North Dakota Mill & Elevator 1823 Mill Rd *TF:* 800-538-7721 ■ *Web:* www.ndmill.com	Grand Forks	ND	58203	701-795-7000	795-7272
Pacific Grain Products International Inc 351 Hanson Way PO Box 2060 *TF Cust Svc:* 800-333-0110	Woodland	CA	95776	530-662-5056	662-6074
Pacific International Rice Mills Inc 845 Kentucky Ave *TF:* 800-747-4764 ■ *Web:* www.pirmirice.com	Woodland	CA	95695	530-661-6028	661-6028
Producers Rice Mill Inc PO Box 1248 *TF:* 800-369-7675 ■ *Web:* www.producersrice.com	Stuttgart	AR	72160	870-673-4444	673-8131
Riceland Foods Inc PO Box 927 *Web:* www.riceland.com	Stuttgart	AR	72160	870-673-5500	673-3366
RiceTec Inc 1925 FM 2917 PO Box 1305 *TF:* 877-580-7423 ■ *Web:* www.ricetec.com	Alvin	TX	77511	281-393-3502	393-3532
Riviana Foods Inc PO Box 2636 *Web:* www.riviana.com	Houston	TX	77252	713-529-3251	529-1866
Rock River Lumber & Grain Co 5502 Lyndon Rd PO Box 68 *TF:* 800-605-4333 ■ *Web:* www.rockriverag.com	Prophetstown	IL	61277	815-537-5131	
Roquette America 1417 Exchange St PO Box 6647 *Web:* www.roquette.com	Keokuk	IA	52632	319-524-5757	
Shawnee Milling Company Inc 201 S Broadway PO Box 1567 *TF:* 800-654-2600 ■ *Web:* www.shawneemilling.com	Shawnee	OK	74802	405-273-7000	273-7333
Siemer Milling Co 111 W Main St PO Box 670 *TF:* 800-826-1065 ■ *Web:* www.siemermilling.com	Teutopolis	IL	62467	217-857-3131	857-3092
SunOpta Inc 2838 Bovaird Dr W *TSE: SOY* ■ *Web:* www.sunopta.com	Brampton	ON	L7A0H2	905-455-2528	455-2529
Wilkins-Rogers Inc 27 Frederick Rd *TF Cust Svc:* 877-438-4338 ■ *Web:* wrmills.com	Ellicott City	MD	21043	410-465-5800	

299-24 Honey

Company	City	State	ZIP	Phone	Fax
Barkman Honey 120 Santa Fe St *Web:* barkmanhoney.com/	Hillsboro	KS	67063	620-947-3173	947-3640
Dutch Gold Honey Inc 2220 Dutch Gold Dr *TF:* 800-846-2753 ■ *Web:* www.dutchgoldhoney.com	Lancaster	PA	17601	717-393-1716	393-8687
Fisher Honey Co One Belle Ave Bldg 21 *Web:* www.fisherhoney.com	Lewistown	PA	17044	717-242-4373	242-3978
Glorybee Foods Inc 120 N Seneca Rd *TF:* 800-456-7923 ■ *Web:* www.glorybee.com	Eugene	OR	97402	541-689-0913	689-9692
Honey Acres 1557 Hwy 67 N **Fax Area Code:* 920 ■ *TF:* 800-558-7745 ■ *Web:* www.honeyacres.com	Ashippun	WI	53003	800-558-7745	474-4018*
Honeytree Inc 8570 M 50 *TF:* 800-968-1889 ■ *Web:* honeytreehoney.com	Onsted	MI	49265	517-467-2482	467-2056
Miller's Honey Co Inc 3000 SW Temple *Web:* www.millerhoney.com	Salt Lake City	UT	84115	801-486-8479	486-8494
Pure Sweet Honey Farm Inc 514 Commerce Pkwy *Web:* puresweethoney.com	Verona	WI	53593	608-845-9601	
Silverbow Honey Company Inc 1120 E Wheeler Rd *Web:* www.silverbowhoney.com	Moses Lake	WA	98837	509-765-6616	765-6549
Sioux Honey Assn Co-op 301 Lewis Blvd *TF:* 888-270-6956 ■ *Web:* www.suebee.com	Sioux City	IA	51101	712-258-0638	258-1332
TW Burleson & Son Inc 301 Peters St *Web:* www.burlesons-honey.com	Waxahachie	TX	75165	972-937-4810	937-8711
Wixson Honey Inc 4937 Lakemont-Himrod Rd *Web:* wixsonhoney.com	Dundee	NY	14837	607-243-7301	243-7143

299-25 Ice Cream & Frozen Desserts

Company	City	State	ZIP	Phone	Fax
Anderson Erickson Dairy Co 2420 E University Ave *TF:* 800-234-7257 ■ *Web:* www.aedairy.com	Des Moines	IA	50317	515-265-2521	263-6301
Arista Industries Inc 557 Danbury Rd *Web:* www.aristaindustries.com	Wilton	CT	06897	203-761-1009	

Phone *Fax*

Attune Foods Inc 900 Kearny St Ste 600 .... San Francisco CA 94133 415-486-2101
Web: www.attunefoods.com

Aurora Organic Dairy Corp
1919 14th St Ste 300 .... Boulder CO 80302 720-564-6296
Web: www.auroraorganic.com

Baldwin Richardson Foods Company Inc
20201 S La Grange Rd Ste 200 .... Frankfort IL 60423 815-464-9994 464-9995
TF Cust Svc: 866-644-2732 ■ *Web:* www.brfoods.com

Barber Dairies Inc 36 Barber Ct .... Birmingham AL 35209 205-942-2351 943-0297
Web: www.barbersdairy.com

Ben & Jerry's Homemade Inc
30 Community Dr .... South Burlington VT 05403 802-846-1500 846-1538
Web: www.benjerry.com

Berkeley Farms Inc 25500 Clawiter Rd .... Hayward CA 94545 510-265-8600 265-8754*
*Fax: Sales ■ *Web:* www.berkeleyfarms.com

Blue Bell Creameries Inc PO Box 1807 .... Brenham TX 77834 979-836-7977 830-7398
Web: www.bluebell.com

Borden Dairy Co 8750 N Central Expy Ste 400 .... Dallas TX 75231 214-459-1100 526-5425
Web: www.lalafoods.com

Broughton Foods Co 1701 Green St .... Marietta OH 45750 740-373-4121 373-2861
TF: 800-283-2479 ■ *Web:* www.broughtonfoods.com

Butterball Farms Inc
1435 Buchanan Ave SW .... Grand Rapids MI 49507 616-243-0105
Web: www.butterballfarms.com

Cedar Crest Specialties Inc
7269 Hwy 60 PO Box 260 .... Cedarburg WI 53012 262-377-7252 377-5554
TF Hotline: 800-877-8341 ■ *Web:* www.cedarcresticecream.com

Cento Fine Foods Inc 100 Cento Blvd .... West Deptford NJ 08086 856-853-5445
Web: www.cento.com

Coleman Dairy Inc 6901 I-30 .... Little Rock AR 72209 501-748-1700 748-1710
TF: 800-365-1551 ■ *Web:* hilanddairy.com

Creamland Dairies Inc
10 Indian School Rd NW .... Albuquerque NM 87105 505-247-0721 246-9696
TF: 800-334-3865 ■ *Web:* www.creamland.com

Crossroad Farms Dairy
400 S Shortridge Rd .... Indianapolis IN 46219 317-229-7600 229-7676

Dean Foods 400 S Chamber Dr .... Decatur IN 46733 260-724-2136 724-2136

Dreyer's Grand Ice Cream Inc
5929 College Ave .... Oakland CA 94618 510-652-8187
Web: dreyers.com

Farrs Better Foods
2575 South 300 West .... South Salt lake City UT 84115 801-484-8724 484-8768
TF: 877-553-2777 ■ *Web:* www.farrsicecream.com

Galliker Dairy Company Inc 143 Donald Ln .... Johnstown PA 15907 814-266-8702
TF: 800-477-6455 ■ *Web:* www.gallikers.com

Gandy's Dairies Inc 201 University Blvd .... Lubbock TX 79415 806-765-8833
TF: 877-382-4357 ■ *Web:* search.lubbockonline.com

Graeter's Inc 2145 Reading Rd .... Cincinnati OH 45202 513-721-3323
TF: 800-721-3323 ■ *Web:* www.graeters.com

Green Foods Corp 2220 Camino Del Sol .... Oxnard CA 93030 805-983-7470
TF: 800-777-4430 ■ *Web:* www.greenfoods.com

Heisler's Cloverleaf Dairy 743 Catawissa Rd .... Tamaqua PA 18252 570-668-3399 668-3041
Web: www.heislersdairy.com

Hershey Creamery Co 301 S Cameron St .... Harrisburg PA 17101 717-238-8134 233-7195
TF: 888-240-1905 ■ *Web:* www.hersheyicecream.com

High Road Craft Ice Cream Inc
1730 W Oak Commons Ct Ste B .... Atlanta GA 30062 678-701-7623
Web: www.highroadcraft.com

Hiland Dairy Co PO Box 2270 .... Springfield MO 65801 417-862-9311
TF: 800-641-4022 ■ *Web:* www.hilanddairy.com

Ice Cream Specialties
8419 Hanley Industrial Ct .... Saint Louis MO 63144 314-962-2550
TF: 800-662-7550 ■ *Web:* www.northstarfrozentreats.com

J & J Snack Foods Corp 6000 Central Hwy .... Pennsauken NJ 08109 856-665-9533 665-6718
NASDAQ: JJSF ■ *TF:* 800-486-9533 ■ *Web:* www.jjsnack.com

Klinke Bros Ice Cream Co 2450 Scaper Cove .... Memphis TN 38114 901-743-8250 743-8254

Newport Creamery Inc
35 Stockanosset Cross Rd PO Box 8819 .... Cranston RI 02920 401-946-4000 946-4392
Web: www.newportcreamery.com

Perry's Ice Cream Company Inc
One Ice Cream Plz .... Akron NY 14001 716-542-5492 542-2544
TF: 800-873-7797 ■ *Web:* www.perrysicecream.com

Pet Dairy 2900 Bristol Hwy .... Johnson City TN 37601 423-283-5700 283-5716
Web: petdairy.com

Royal Ice Cream Co 6200 Euclid Ave .... Cleveland OH 44103 216-432-1144 432-0433
TF: 888-645-6606 ■ *Web:* www.pierres.com

Schwan Food Co 115 W College Dr .... Marshall MN 56258 507-532-3274
TF: 800-533-5290 ■ *Web:* www.theschwanfoodcompany.com

Southwest Cheese Company LLC
1141 Curry County Rd Ste 4 .... Clovis NM 88101 575-742-9200
Web: www.southwestcheese.com

Stonyfield Farm Inc 10 Burton Dr .... Londonderry NH 03053 603-437-4040 437-7594
TF: 800-776-2697 ■ *Web:* www.stonyfield.com

Sugar Creek Foods International
301 N El Paso St .... Russellville AR 72801 800-445-2715
TF: 800-445-2715 ■ *Web:* sugarcreekfoodsinc.com

Tofutti Brands Inc 50 Jackson Dr .... Cranford NJ 07016 908-272-2400 272-9492
NYSE: TOF ■ *Web:* www.tofutti.com

Turkey Hill Dairy Inc 2601 River Rd .... Conestoga PA 17516 717-872-5461 872-0602
TF: 800-693-2479 ■ *Web:* www.turkeyhill.com

Turner Dairy Farms Inc 1049 Jefferson Rd .... Pittsburgh PA 15235 412-372-2211
TF: 800-892-1039 ■ *Web:* www.turnerdairy.net

Umpqua Dairy Products Co
333 SE Sykes Ave PO Box 1306 .... Roseburg OR 97470 541-672-2638 673-0256
TF: 888-672-6455 ■ *Web:* www.umpquadairy.com

Wells Enterprises Inc 1 Blue Bunny Dr .... Le Mars IA 51031 712-546-4000 548-3008
TF All: 888-309-1742 ■ *Web:* www.wellsenterprisesinc.com

Yarnell Ice Cream Co 205 S Spring St .... Searcy AR 72143 501-268-6355
Web: www.yarnells.com

YoCream International Inc 5858 NE 87th Ave .... Portland OR 97220 503-256-3754 256-3976
TF: 800-962-7326 ■ *Web:* www.yocream.com

299-26 Meat Products - Prepared

Phone *Fax*

Advance Brands LLC 3540 S Blvd Ste 225 .... Edmond OK 73013 405-562-1500
Web: www.advancedbrands.com

Aidells Sausage Co 1625 Alvarado St .... San Leandro CA 94577 510-614-5450 614-2287
TF: 877-243-3557 ■ *Web:* www.aidells.com

Albertville Quality Foods Inc
130 Quality Dr PO Box 756 .... Albertville AL 35950 256-840-9923 840-9906
TF: 800-353-2806 ■ *Web:* www.albertvillequalityfoods.com

Alderfer Inc 382 Main St PO Box 2 .... Harleysville PA 19438 215-256-8818 256-6120
TF Sales: 800-341-1121 ■ *Web:* www.alderfermeats.com

Aliments Asta Inc
511 Ave De La Gare .... St Alexandre-De-Kamouraska QC G0L2G0 418-495-2728 495-2879
TF: 800-463-1355 ■ *Web:* alimentsasta.com

American Foods Group Inc 544 Acme St .... Green Bay WI 54302 920-437-6330 436-6510
TF: 800-345-0293 ■ *Web:* www.americanfoodsgroup.com

Ballard's Farm Sausage Inc
2131 Right Fork Wilson Creek Rd PO Box 699 .... Wayne WV 25570 304-272-5147 272-5336
TF General: 800-346-7675 ■ *Web:* www.ballardsfarm.com

Bar-S Foods Co PO Box 29049 .... Phoenix AZ 85038 800-699-4115
TF: 800-699-4115 ■ *Web:* www.bar-s.com

Beef Products Inc 891 Two Rivers Dr .... Dakota Dunes SD 57049 605-217-8000 217-8001
Web: www.beefproducts.com

Berks Packing Company Inc
307-323 Bingaman St PO Box 5919 .... Reading PA 19610 610-376-7291 378-1210
TF: 800-882-3757 ■ *Web:* www.berksfoods.com

Best Provision Company Inc 144 Avon Ave .... Newark NJ 07108 973-242-5000 648-0041
TF: 800-631-4466 ■ *Web:* www.bestprovision.com

Bi-county Scale & Equipment Co
75 Kean St .... West Babylon NY 11704 631-643-2300
Web: www.bicountyscale.com

Blue Grass Quality Meats
2645 Commerce Dr .... Crescent Springs KY 41017 859-331-7100 331-4273
Web: www.bluegrassqualitymeats.com

Blue Ribbon Meats Inc 3316 W 67th Pl .... Cleveland OH 44102 216-631-8850
Web: blueribbonmeatco.com

Boar's Head Provisions Co Inc
1819 Main St Ste 800 .... Sarasota FL 34236 941-955-0994 366-0354
Web: www.boarshead.com

Bobak Sausage Co 5275 S Archer Ave .... Chicago IL 60632 773-735-5334 735-8605
Web: www.bobak.com

Bridgford Foods Corp 1308 N Patt St .... Anaheim CA 92801 714-526-5533 526-4360
NASDAQ: BRID ■ *TF:* 800-854-3255 ■ *Web:* www.bridgford.com

Brown Packing Company Inc 116 Willis St .... Gaffney SC 29341 864-489-5723

Burger's Ozark Country Cured Hams Inc
32819 hwy 87 .... California MO 65018 573-796-3134 796-3137
TF: 800-203-4424 ■ *Web:* www.smokehouse.com

Busseto Foods Inc 1351 N Crystal Ave .... Fresno CA 93728 559-485-9882
Web: www.busseto.com

Carando Inc 20 Carando Dr .... Springfield MA 01104 413-781-5620 737-7314
Web: carando.com

Cargill Inc North America 15407 McGinty Rd .... Wayzata MN 55391 952-742-7575
Web: cargill.com

Caribbean Products Ltd 3624 Falls Rd .... Baltimore MD 21211 410-235-7700
TF: 888-689-5068

Carl Buddig & Co 950 175th St .... Homewood IL 60430 708-798-0900 798-1284
TF: 888-633-5684 ■ *Web:* www.buddig.com

Carlton Foods Corp 880 Texas 46 .... New Braunfels TX 78130 830-625-7583
TF: 800-628-9849 ■ *Web:* www.carltonfoods.com

Carolina Pride Foods Inc One Packer Ave .... Greenwood SC 29646 864-229-5611
Web: carolinapride.publishpath.com/

Cattaneo Bros Inc 769 Caudill St .... San Luis Obispo CA 93401 805-543-7188 543-4698
TF: 800-243-8537 ■ *Web:* www.cattaneobros.com

Cher-Make Sausage Co 2915 Calumet Ave .... Manitowoc WI 54220 920-683-5980 682-2588
TF: 800-242-7679 ■ *Web:* www.cher-make.com

Chicago Meat Authority Inc (CMA) 1120 W 47th Pl .... Chicago IL 60609 773-254-3811 254-5851
TF: 800-383-3811 ■ *Web:* www.chicagomeat.com

Chicopee Provision Co Inc 19 Sitarz St .... Chicopee MA 01013 413-594-4765
TF: 800-924-6328 ■ *Web:* www.bluesealkielbasa.com

Citterio USA Corp 2008 SR 940 .... Freeland PA 18224 570-636-3171 636-5340
TF: 800-435-8888 ■ *Web:* www.citteriousa.com

Cloverdale Foods Co 3015 34th St NW .... Mandan ND 58554 800-669-9511 663-0690*
*Fax Area Code: 701 ■ *TF:* 800-669-9511 ■ *Web:* www.cloverdalefoods.com

Continental-Capri Inc 250 Jackson St .... Englewood NJ 07631 201-568-7100 568-7180

Cook's Ham Inc 200 S Second St .... Lincoln NE 68508 402-475-6700
TF: 800-332-8400 ■ *Web:* www.mycooksham.com

Counts Sausage Company Inc 222 Church St .... Prosperity SC 29127 803-364-2392

D'Artagnan Inc 280 Wilson Ave Ste 1 .... Newark NJ 07105 973-344-0565
Web: www.dartagnan.com

Daniele Inc PO Box 106 .... Pascoag RI 02859 401-568-6228 568-4788
TF: 800-451-2535 ■ *Web:* www.danielefoods.com

Dean Sausage Company Inc
3750 Pleasant Vly Rd PO Box 750 .... Attalla AL 35954 256-538-6082 538-2584
Web: www.deansausage.com

Dearborn Sausage Co Inc 2450 Wyoming Ave .... Dearborn MI 48120 313-842-2375 842-2640
Web: www.dearbornsausage.com

Dewied International Inc 5010 IH- 10 E .... San Antonio TX 78219 210-661-6161 662-6112
TF: 800-992-5600 ■ *Web:* www.dewied.com

Dietz & Watson Inc 5701 Tacony St .... Philadelphia PA 19135 215-831-9000 831-1044
TF: 800-333-1974 ■ *Web:* www.dietzandwatson.com

Fabbri Sausage Manufacturing Co
166 N Aberdeen St .... Chicago IL 60607 312-829-6363
Web: www.fabbrisausage.com

Family Brands International LLC
1001 Elm Hill Rd PO Box 429 .... Lenoir City TN 37771 800-356-4455 986-7171*
*Fax Area Code: 865 ■ *TF:* 800-356-4455 ■ *Web:* www.fbico.com

Fargo Packing & Sausage Co 307 E Main Ave .... West Fargo ND 58078 701-282-3211 282-0325
Web: qualitymeats.com

Farmington Foods Inc 7419 W Franklin St .... Forest Park IL 60130 708-771-3600
Web: www.farmingtonfoods.com

	City	State	Zip	Phone	Fax
Fisher Meats Inc 85 Front St N *Web:* fischermeatsnw.com	Issaquah	WA	98027	425-392-3131	392-0168
Frank Wardynski & Sons Inc 336 Peckham St *Web:* www.wardynski.com	Buffalo	NY	14206	716-854-6083	854-4887
Fred Usinger Inc 1030 N Old World Third St *TF:* 800-558-9998 ■ *Web:* www.usinger.com	Milwaukee	WI	53203	414-276-9100	291-5277
Freedom Sausage Inc 4155 E 1650th Rd	Earlville	IL	60518	815-792-8276	792-8283
Fremont Beef Co 960 S Schneider St *Web:* www.fremontbeef.com	Fremont	NE	68025	402-727-7200	
G & G Supermarket Inc 1211 W College Ave *Web:* www.gandgmarket.com	Santa Rosa	CA	95401	707-546-6877	575-5921
Gallo Salame 2411 Baumann Ave *Web:* gallosalame.com	San Lorenzo	CA	94580	800-988-6464	
Garcia Foods Inc PO Box 13280 *Web:* www.garciafoods.com	San Antonio	TX	78213	210-349-6262	
Gaytan Foods 15430 Proctor Ave *TF:* 800-242-9826 ■ *Web:* www.gaytanfoods.com	City Of Industry	CA	91745	626-330-4553	
Gold Star Sausage Co 2800 Walnut St *Web:* ww.goldstarsausage.com	Denver	CO	80205	303-295-6400	294-0495
Golden State Foods 18301 Von Karman Ave Ste 1100 *Web:* www.goldenstatefoods.com	Irvine	CA	92612	949-252-2000	252-2080
Great Lakes Packing Co 1535 W 43rd St *Web:* glpacking.com	Chicago	IL	60609	773-927-6660	927-8587
Green Tree Packing Co 65 Central Ave *TF:* 800-562-6934 ■ *Web:* www.greentreepacking.com	Passaic	NJ	07055	973-473-1305	473-7975
Grote & Weigel Inc 76 Granby St *TF:* 800-943-6376 ■ *Web:* www.groteandweigel.com	Bloomfield	CT	06002	860-242-8528	242-4162
Habbersett Scrapple Inc 103 S Railroad Ave *TF:* 800-338-4727 ■ *Web:* www.habbersettscrapple.com	Bridgeville	DE	19933	800-338-4727	
Hatfield Quality Meats Inc 2700 Clemens Rd *TF:* 800-743-1191 ■ *Web:* www.hatfieldqualitymeats.com	Hatfield	PA	19440	215-368-2500	
Hazle Park Packing Co 260 Washington Ave Hazle Pk *TF:* 800-238-4331 ■ *Web:* hazlepark.com	Hazletownship	PA	18202	570-455-7571	455-6030
Hormel Foods Corp 1 Hormel Pl *NYSE:* HRL ■ **Fax:* Sales ■ *TF:* 800-523-4635 ■ *Web:* www.hormel.com	Austin	MN	55912	507-437-5611	437-5129*
Hummel Bros Inc 180 Sargent Dr *Web:* hummelbros.3dcartstores.com/	New Haven	CT	06511	203-787-4113	
Interstate Meat Distributors Inc 9550 SE Last Rd	Clackamas	OR	97015	503-656-0633	
John Hofmeister & Son Inc 2386 S Blue Island Ave *Web:* www.hofhaus.com	Chicago	IL	60608	773-847-0700	847-6624
John Morrell & Co 805 E Kemper Rd **Fax Area Code:* 408 ■ **Fax:* Cust Svc ■ *TF:* 800-722-1127 ■ *Web:* www.johnmorrell.com	Cincinnati	OH	45246	513-346-3540	220-9679*
Johnsonville Sausage LLC PO Box 906 *TF:* 888-556-2728 ■ *Web:* www.johnsonville.com	Sheboygan Falls	WI	53085	888-556-2728	
Jones Dairy Farm 800 Jones Ave *TF:* 800-635-6637 ■ *Web:* www.jonesdairyfarm.com	Fort Atkinson	WI	53538	920-563-2431	563-6801
Karl Ehmer Inc 48 S Ocean Ave *TF:* 800-487-5275 ■ *Web:* www.karlehmer.com	Patchogue	NY	11772	631-289-3448	
Kayem Foods Inc 75 Arlington St *TF:* 800-426-6100 ■ *Web:* www.kayem.com	Chelsea	MA	02150	617-889-1600	889-5478
Kent Quality Foods Inc 703 Leonard St NW *TF:* 800-748-0141 ■ *Web:* www.kentqualityfoods.com	Grand Rapids	MI	49504	800-748-0141	
Kessler's Inc 1201 Hummel Ave *TF:* 800-382-1328 ■ *Web:* www.kesslerfoods.com	Lemoyne	PA	17043	717-763-7162	763-4982
Keystone Foods LLC 300 Bar Harbor Dr Ste 600 5 Tower Bridge *Web:* www.keystonefoods.com	West Conshohocken	PA	19428	610-667-6700	667-1460
King's Command Foods Inc 7622 S 188th St *Web:* www.kingscommand.com	Kent	WA	98032	425-251-6788	251-0523
Kiolbassa Provision Co 1325 S Brazos St *Web:* www.kiolbassa.com	San Antonio	TX	78207	210-226-8127	226-7464
Klement Sausage Co Inc 207 E Lincoln Ave *TF:* 800-553-6368 ■ *Web:* www.klements.com	Milwaukee	WI	53207	414-744-2330	744-2438
Koegel Meats Inc 3400 W Bristol Rd *Web:* www.koegelmeats.com	Flint	MI	48507	810-238-3685	238-2467
Kowalski Sausage Company Inc 2270 Holbrook Ave *Web:* kowality.com	Hamtramck	MI	48212	313-873-8200	873-4220
Kraft Foods Inc Oscar Mayer Foods Div 910 Mayer Ave **Fax Area Code:* 973 ■ *Web:* www.kraftbrands.com	Madison	WI	53704	608-241-3311	503-4483*
Kronos Products Inc One Kronos Dr *TF:* 800-621-0099 ■ *Web:* www.kronosproducts.com	Glendale Heights	IL	60139	800-621-0099	
Land O'Frost Inc 16850 Chicago Ave *TF:* 800-323-3308 ■ *Web:* www.landofrost.com	Lansing	IL	60438	708-474-7100	
Les Trois Petits Cochons Inc 4223 First Ave Second Fl *TF General:* 800-537-7283 ■ *Web:* www.3pigs.com	Brooklyn	NY	11232	212-219-1230	941-9726
Lopez Foods Inc 6016 NW 120th Ct *Web:* www.lopezfoods.com	Oklahoma City	OK	73162	405-603-7500	
Louie's Finer Meats Inc PO Box 774 *TF:* 800-270-4297 ■ *Web:* www.louiesfinermeats.com	Cumberland	WI	54829	715-822-4728	822-3150
Maid-Rite Steak Company Inc 105 Keystone Industrial Pk *TF:* 800-233-4259 ■ *Web:* maidritesteak.com	Dunmore	PA	18512	570-343-4748	969-2878
Makowski's Real Sausage Co 2710 S Poplar Ave *Web:* realsausage.com	Chicago	IL	60608	312-842-5330	842-5414
Maple Leaf Foods Inc 30 St Clair Ave W Ste 1500 *TSE:* MFI ■ *Web:* www.mapleleaf.ca	Toronto	ON	M4V3A1	416-926-2000	
Marathon Enterprises Inc Nine Smith St *TF:* 800-722-7388 ■ *Web:* sabrett.com	Englewood	NJ	07631	201-935-3330	935-5693
Marfood USA Inc 21655 Trolley Industrial Dr *Web:* marfoodusa.com	Taylor	MI	48180	313-292-4100	
Martin Rosol Inc 45 Grove St *Web:* martinrosolsinc.com	New Britain	CT	06053	860-223-2707	
Martin`s Abattoir & Wholesale Meats Inc 1600 Martin Rd *Web:* www.martinmeats.com	Godwin	NC	28344	910-567-6102	
Meadow Farms Sausage Co 6215 S Western Ave *Web:* meadowfarmssausage.com	Los Angeles	CA	90047	323-752-2300	
Milan Salami Company Inc 1155 67th St	Oakland	CA	94608	510-654-7055	
Miller Packing Co 1122 Industrial Way PO Box 1390 *TF:* 800-624-2328 ■ *Web:* www.millerhotdogs.com	Lodi	CA	95241	209-339-2310	334-0848
Mims Meat Company Inc 12634 E Farway	Houston	TX	77015	713-453-0151	
Mongolia Casing Corp 4706 Grand Ave *TF:* 800-472-2197 ■ *Web:* industrynet.com	Maspeth	NY	11378	718-628-3800	
Mrs Ressler's Food Products Co 5501 Tabor Ave PO Box 5717 *Web:* www.ressler.com	Philadelphia	PA	19120	215-744-4700	744-4750
National Steak Processors Inc 301 E Fifth Ave *Web:* www.nationalsteak.com	Owasso	OK	74055	918-274-8787	
Natural Casing Co 410 E Railroad St PO Box A **Fax Area Code:* 715 ■ *TF:* 877-515-0270 ■ *Web:* www.naturalcasingco.com	Peshtigo	WI	54157	877-515-0270	582-3931*
Neto Sausage Co Inc 1313 Franklin St *TF:* 888-482-6386 ■ *Web:* www.netosausage.com	Santa Clara	CA	95050	408-296-0818	296-0538
Nossack Fine Meats Ltd 7240 Johnstone Dr Ste 100 *Web:* www.nossack.com	Red Deer	AB	T4P3Y6	403-346-5006	
Oberto Sausage Co 7060 S 238th St *TF:* 877-453-7591 ■ *Web:* www.oberto.com	Kent	WA	98032	253-854-7056	437-6151
Odom's Tennessee Pride Sausage Inc 1201 Neelys Bend Rd *TF:* 866-484-8641 ■ *Web:* www.tnpride.com	Madison	TN	37115	615-868-1360	860-4703
Old Wisconsin Sausage Co 5030 PlaybiRd Rd **Fax Area Code:* 708 ■ *TF:* 877-451-7988 ■ *Web:* www.oldwisconsin.com	Sheboygan	WI	53083	877-451-7988	798-1284*
Omni Custom Meats Inc 151 Vanderbilt Ct *Web:* omnimeats.com	Bowling Green	KY	42103	270-796-6664	
OSI Industries LLC 1225 Corporate Blvd *Web:* www.osigroup.com	Aurora	IL	60505	630-851-6600	692-2340
Palama Meat Company Inc 2029 Lauwiliwili St *Web:* sbcontract.com	Kapolei	HI	96707	808-682-8305	834-8895
Palmyra Bologna Company Inc 230 N College St *TF:* 800-282-6336 ■ *Web:* www.seltzerslebanon.com	Palmyra	PA	17078	717-838-6336	
Park 100 Foods Inc 326 E Adams St *TF:* 800-854-6504 ■ *Web:* www.park100foods.com	Tipton	IN	46072	765-675-3480	675-3474
Peer Foods Group Inc 1200 W 35th St Ste 5E *TF:* 800-365-5644 ■ *Web:* www.peerfoods.com	Chicago	IL	60609	773-927-1440	927-9859
Pine Ridge Farms 1800 SE Maury St *Web:* www.pineridgefarmspork.com	Des Moines	IA	50317	515-266-4100	
Plumrose USA Inc 1901 Butterfield Rd Ste 305 *TF:* 800-526-4909 ■ *Web:* www.plumroseusa.com	Downers Grove	IL	60515	732-624-4040	257-6644
Pocino Foods Co 14250 Lomitas Ave *TF:* 800-345-0150 ■ *Web:* www.pocinofoods.com	City of Industry	CA	91746	626-968-8000	968-0196
Premio Foods Inc 50 Utter Ave *TF:* 800-864-7622 ■ *Web:* www.premiofoods.com	Hawthorne	NJ	07506	973-427-1106	427-1140
Quality Sausage Company Ltd 1925 Lone Star Dr *Web:* www.qualitysausage.com	Dallas	TX	75212	214-634-3400	634-2296
Quantum Foods LLC 750 S Schmidt Rd *Web:* www.quantumfoods.com	Bolingbrook	IL	60440	630-679-2300	
R Torre & Company Inc 233 E Harris Ave *Web:* www.perfectpalate.com	South San Francisco	CA	94080	650-875-1200	
Randolph Packing Co 275 Roma Jean Pkwy *TF:* 800-451-1607 ■ *Web:* www.randolphpacking.com	Streamwood	IL	60107	630-830-3100	
Reser's Fine Foods Inc 15570 SW Jenkins Rd *TF:* 800-333-6431 ■ *Web:* www.resers.com	Beaverton	OR	97006	503-643-6431	
Richwood Meat Company Inc 2751 N Santa Fe Ave *Web:* www.richwoodmeat.com	Merced	CA	95348	209-722-8171	
Rosina Food Products Inc 170 French Rd *Web:* www.rosina.com	Buffalo	NY	14227	716-668-0123	
Ruprecht Co 1301 Allanson Rd *Web:* www.ruprechtcompany.com	Mundelein	IL	60060	312-829-4100	
Saags Products Inc 1799 Factor Ave *TF:* 800-352-7224 ■ *Web:* www.saags.com	San Leandro	CA	94577	510-352-8000	
Sadler's Smokehouse Ltd PO Box 1088 *TF:* 800-777-5581 ■ *Web:* www.sadlerssmokehouse.com	Henderson	TX	75653	903-655-7262	
Sahlen Packing Company Inc 318 Howard St *TF:* 800-466-8165 ■ *Web:* www.sahlen.com	Buffalo	NY	14206	716-852-8677	
Schaller & Weber Inc 22-35 46th St *TF Orders:* 800-847-4115 ■ *Web:* www.schallerweber.com	Astoria	NY	11105	718-721-5480	956-9157
Silver Star Meats Inc 1720 Middletown Rd PO Box 393 *TF:* 800-548-1321 ■ *Web:* www.silverstarmeats.com	McKees Rocks	PA	15136	412-771-5539	
Smith Packing Company Inc 105-125 Washington St *Web:* www.smithpacking.com	Utica	NY	13503	315-732-5125	732-5129
Smithfield Foods Inc 200 Commerce St *NYSE:* SFD ■ *TF:* 800-276-6158 ■ *Web:* www.smithfieldfoods.com	Smithfield	VA	23430	757-365-3000	365-3017
Specialty Foods Group Inc 21 Enterprise Pkwy Fourth Fl *Web:* www.specialtyfoodsgroup.com	Hampton	VA	23666	757-952-1200	952-1201
Stampede Meat Inc 7351 S 78th Ave *TF:* 800-353-0933 ■ *Web:* www.stampedemeat.com	Bridgeview	IL	60455	800-353-0933	
Standard Casing Company Inc, The 165 Chubb Ave *Web:* www.standardcasing.com	Lyndhurst	NJ	07071	201-434-6300	434-1508
Standard Meat Company LP 5105 Investment Dr *TF:* 866-859-6313 ■ *Web:* www.standardmeat.com	Dallas	TX	75236	214-561-0561	561-0560
Stevison Ham Co 125 Stevison Ham Rd *Web:* www.tennesseetraditions.com	Portland	TN	37148	615-325-4161	325-5914

				Phone	Fax
Stock Yards Packing Co Inc					
2457 W North Ave	Melrose Park	IL	60160	877-785-9273	
TF: 877-785-9273 ■ *Web:* www.stockyards.com					
Storer Meats Company Inc 3007 Clinton Ave	Cleveland	OH	44113	216-621-7538	361-0622
Web: fivestarbrandmeats.com					
Sugar Creek Packing Co					
2101 Kenskill Ave	Washington Court House	OH	43160	740-335-7440	551-5263*
**Fax Area Code:* 513 ■ *TF:* 800-848-8205 ■ *Web:* www.sugarcreek.com					
Suzanna's Kitchen Inc 4025 Buford Hwy	Duluth	GA	30096	770-476-9900	476-8899
Web: www.suzannaskitchen.com					
Sysco Kansas City Inc 1915 E Kansas City Rd	Olathe	KS	66061	913-829-5555	780-8625
TF: 800-735-3341 ■ *Web:* www.kc.sysco.com					
Sysco Newport Meat Company Inc 16691 Hale Ave	Irvine	CA	92606	949-474-4040	
Web: www.newportmeat.com					
TF Kinnealey & Company Inc 1100 Pearl St	Brockton	MA	02301	508-638-7700	
TF: 800-225-4950 ■ *Web:* www.kinnealey.com					
Tyson Prepared Foods Inc 5701 McNutt Rd	Santa Teresa	NM	88008	575-589-0100	
TF: 888-301-7304 ■ *Web:* www.tyson.com					
US Premium Beef LLC (USPB)					
12200 N Ambassador Dr PO Box 20103	Kansas City	MO	64163	816-713-8800	713-8810
TF: 866-877-2525 ■ *Web:* www.uspremiumbeef.com					
Vienna Sausage Manufacturing Co					
2501 N Damen Ave	Chicago	IL	60647	773-278-7800	
TF: 800-366-3647 ■ *Web:* www.viennabeef.com					
Vincent Giordano Corp					
2600 Washington Ave	Philadelphia	PA	19146	215-467-6629	467-6339
Web: www.vgiordano.com					
Vista International Packaging LLC					
1126 88th Pl	Kenosha	WI	53143	262-694-2276	694-4824
Vollwerth & Co 200 Hancock St PO Box 239	Hancock	MI	49930	906-482-1550	482-0842
TF: 800-562-7620 ■ *Web:* www.vollwerth.com					
Wimmer's Meat Products Inc 126 W Grant St	West Point	NE	68788	402-372-2437	372-5659
TF Cust Svc: 800-762-9865 ■ *Web:* www.wimmersmeats.com					
Wolfson Casing Corp 700 S Fulton Ave	Mount Vernon	NY	10550	914-668-9000	668-5744
TF: 800-221-8042 ■ *Web:* www.wolfsoncasing.com					
Zweigles Inc 651 Plymouth Ave N	Rochester	NY	14608	585-546-1740	546-8721
Web: www.zweigles.com					

299-27 Milk & Cream Products

				Phone	Fax
Agri-Mark Inc PO Box 5800	Lawrence	MA	01842	978-689-4442	794-8304
Web: agrimark.coop/					
Alta Dena Dairy 17851 E Railrd	City of Industry	CA	91748	800-535-1369	
TF Orders: 800-535-1369 ■ *Web:* www.altadenadairy.com					
AMPI 315 N Broadway	New Ulm	MN	56073	507-354-8295	
TF: 800-533-3580 ■ *Web:* www.ampi.com					
Anderson Dairy Inc 801 Searles Ave	Las Vegas	NV	89101	702-642-7507	642-3480
Web: www.andersondairy.com					
Anderson Erickson Dairy Co					
2420 E University Ave	Des Moines	IA	50317	515-265-2521	263-6301
TF: 800-234-7257 ■ *Web:* www.aedairy.com					
Barber Dairies Inc 36 Barber Ct	Birmingham	AL	35209	205-942-2351	943-0297
Web: www.barbersdairy.com					
Bartlett Dairy Inc 105-03 150th St	Jamaica	NY	11435	718-658-2299	725-2527
Web: www.bartlettny.com					
Berkeley Farms Inc 25500 Clawiter Rd	Hayward	CA	94545	510-265-8600	265-8754*
**Fax:* Sales ■ *Web:* www.berkeleyfarms.com					
Broughton Foods Co 1701 Green St	Marietta	OH	45750	740-373-4121	373-2861
TF: 800-283-2479 ■ *Web:* www.broughtonfoods.com					
California Dairies Inc 2000 N Plz Dr	Visalia	CA	93291	559-625-2200	625-5433
Web: www.californiadairies.com					
Century Foods International					
400 Century Ct PO Box 257	Sparta	WI	54656	608-269-1900	269-1910
Web: www.centuryfoods.com					
Clover Farms Dairy PO Box 14627	Reading	PA	19612	610-921-9111	
TF: 800-323-0123 ■ *Web:* www.farmersdairy.com					
Cloverland Green Spring Dairy Inc					
2701 Loch Raven Rd	Baltimore	MD	21218	410-235-4477	
TF Orders: 800-492-0094 ■ *Web:* www.cloverlanddairy.com					
Coleman Dairy Inc 6901 I-30	Little Rock	AR	72209	501-748-1700	748-1710
TF: 800-365-1551 ■ *Web:* hilanddairy.com					
Crossroad Farms Dairy					
400 S Shortridge Rd	Indianapolis	IN	46219	317-229-7600	229-7676
Dannon Co 100 Hillside Ave	White Plains	NY	10603	914-872-8400	872-1565*
**Fax:* Hum Res ■ *Web:* www.dannon.com					
Darigold Inc 1130 Rainier Ave S	Seattle	WA	98144	206-284-7220	
Web: darigold.com					
Dean Foods Co 2711 N Haskell Ave Ste 3400	Dallas	TX	75204	214-303-3400	303-3499
NYSE: DF ■ *TF:* 800-395-7004 ■ *Web:* www.deanfoods.com					
Eagle Family Foods Inc One Strawberry Ln	Orrville	OH	44667	888-656-3245	684-6410*
**Fax Area Code:* 330 ■ *TF:* 888-656-3245 ■ *Web:* www.eaglebrand.com					
Farmers Select LLC 7321 N Loop Rd	El Paso	TX	79915	915-772-2736	772-0907
Farmland Dairies LLC 520 Main Ave	Wallington	NJ	07057	973-777-2500	249-3849*
**Fax:* Sales ■ *Web:* www.skimplus.com					
Galliker Dairy Company Inc 143 Donald Ln	Johnstown	PA	15907	814-266-8702	
TF: 800-477-6455 ■ *Web:* www.gallikers.com					
Guida-Seibert Dairy Co 433 Pk St	New Britain	CT	06051	860-224-2404	225-0035
TF: 800-832-8929 ■ *Web:* www.supercow.com					
Harrisburg Dairies Inc 2001 Herr St	Harrisburg	PA	17105	717-233-8701	231-4584
TF: 800-692-7429 ■ *Web:* www.harrisburgdairies.com					
Heritage Foods LLC 4002 Westminster Ave	Santa Ana	CA	92703	714-775-5000	775-7677
TF Orders: 800-321-5960 ■ *Web:* stremicksheritagefoods.com					
Hiland Dairy Co PO Box 2270	Springfield	MO	65801	417-862-9311	
TF: 800-641-4022 ■ *Web:* www.hilanddairy.com					
Kemps LLC 1270 Energy Ln	Saint Paul	MN	55108	651-379-6500	
TF: 800-322-9566 ■ *Web:* kemps.com					
Kleinpeter Farms Dairy LLC					
14444 Airline Hwy	Baton Rouge	LA	70817	225-753-2121	752-8964
Web: www.kleinpeterdairy.com					
Land O'Lakes Inc 4001 Lexington Ave N	Arden Hills	MN	55126	651-481-2222	481-2022*
**Fax:* Hum Res ■ *TF:* 800-328-9680 ■ *Web:* www.landolakesinc.com					
Land O'Lakes Inc Dairyman's Div 400 S 'M' St	Tulare	CA	93274	559-687-8287	481-2000*
**Fax Area Code:* 651 ■ **Fax:* Sales ■ *TF:* 800-328-4155 ■ *Web:* landolakesinc.com					
Lehigh Valley Dairies Inc 880 Allentown Rd	Lansdale	PA	19446	215-855-8205	855-9834
Web: www.lehighvalleydairyfarms.com					
Lifeway Foods Inc 6431 W Oakton St	Morton Grove	IL	60053	847-967-1010	967-6558
NASDAQ: LWAY ■ *TF:* 877-281-3874 ■ *Web:* www.lifeway.net					
Maple Hill Farms Inc 12 Burr Rd PO Box 767	Bloomfield	CT	06002	860-242-9689	243-2490
Web: mhfct.com					
Marcus Dairy Inc Four Eagle Rd	Danbury	CT	06810	203-748-5611	791-2759
TF: 800-243-2511 ■ *Web:* www.marcusdairy.com					
McArthur Dairy 456 Flamingo Dr	West Palm Beach	FL	33401	561-659-4811	659-1763
TF: 800-432-4872 ■ *Web:* www.mcarthurdairy.com					
Meadow Brook Dairy 2365 Buffalo Rd	Erie	PA	16510	814-899-3191	464-9152
TF: 800-352-4010 ■ *Web:* www.meadowbrookdairy.com					
Michigan Milk Producers Assn 41310 Bridge St	Novi	MI	48375	248-474-6672	474-0924
Web: www.mimilk.com					
Milkco Inc 220 Deaverview Rd	Asheville	NC	28806	828-254-9560	
TF: 800-842-8021 ■ *Web:* www.milkco.com					
Oakhurst Dairy 364 Forest Ave	Portland	ME	04101	207-772-7468	874-0714
TF: 800-482-0718 ■ *Web:* www.oakhurstdairy.com					
Parmalat Canada Ltd 405 the W Mall 10th Fl	Toronto	ON	M9C5J1	800-563-1515	
TF: 800-563-1515 ■ *Web:* www.parmalat.ca					
Penn Maid Foods Inc 10975 Dutton Rd	Philadelphia	PA	19154	215-824-2800	
Web: www.pennmaid.com					
Prairie Farms Dairy Inc					
1100 N Broadway St	Carlinville	IL	62626	217-854-2547	854-6426
TF: 800-654-2547 ■ *Web:* www.prairiefarms.com					
Pride of Main Street Dairy 214 Main St S	Sauk Centre	MN	56378	320-351-8300	351-8500
Producers Dairy Foods Inc 250 E Belmont Ave	Fresno	CA	93701	559-264-6583	
TF: 800-660-1171 ■ *Web:* www.producersdairy.com					
Purity Dairies Inc 360 Murfreesboro Rd	Nashville	TN	37210	615-244-1970	242-8547
Web: www.puritydairies.com					
Readington Farms Inc 12 Mill Rd	Whitehouse Station	NJ	08889	908-534-2121	534-5235
Royal Crest Dairy Inc 350 S Pearl St	Denver	CO	80209	303-777-2227	744-9173
TF: 888-226-6455 ■ *Web:* www.royalcrestdairy.com					
Rutter Dairy Inc 2100 N George St	York	PA	17404	717-848-9827	845-8751
Web: www.rutters.com					
Schneider Valley Farms Dairy					
1860 E Third St	State College	PA	17701	814-237-3426	564-5519*
**Fax Area Code:* 502 ■ *TF:* 800-516-1750 ■ *Web:* schneidersdairypgh.com					
Schneider's Dairy Inc 726 Frank St	Pittsburgh	PA	15227	412-881-3525	881-7722
Web: schneidersdairy.com					
Shamrock Foods 3900 E Camelback Rd Ste 300	Phoenix	AZ	85018	602-477-2500	477-2533
TF: 800-289-3663 ■ *Web:* www.shamrockfoods.com					
Smith Dairy 1381 Dairy Ln	Orrville	OH	44667	330-683-8710	684-6728
TF: 800-776-7076 ■ *Web:* www.smithdairy.com					
Southeast Milk Inc					
1950 SE Hwy 484 PO Box 3790	Belleview	FL	34420	800-598-7866	245-9434*
**Fax Area Code:* 352 ■ *TF:* 800-598-7866 ■ *Web:* www.southeastmilk.org					
Springfield Creamery Inc 29440 Airport Rd	Eugene	OR	97402	541-689-2911	689-2915
Web: www.nancysyogurt.com					
Stonyfield Farm Inc 10 Burton Dr	Londonderry	NH	03053	603-437-4040	437-7594
TF: 800-776-2697 ■ *Web:* www.stonyfield.com					
Superior Dairy Inc 4719 Navarre Rd SW	Canton	OH	44706	330-477-4515	
TF: 800-597-5460 ■ *Web:* reliableplant.com					
T Marzetti Company Allen Milk Div					
1709 Frank Rd	Columbus	OH	43223	614-279-8673	279-5674
Web: marzetti.com					
Umpqua Dairy Products Co					
333 SE Sykes Ave PO Box 1306	Roseburg	OR	97470	541-672-2638	673-0256
TF: 888-672-6455 ■ *Web:* www.umpquadairy.com					
United Dairy Farmers 3955 Montgomery Rd	Cincinnati	OH	45212	513-396-8700	396-8736
TF General: 800-654-2809 ■ *Web:* www.udfinc.com					
United Dairy Inc 300 N Fifth St	Martins Ferry	OH	43935	740-633-1451	633-6759
TF: 800-252-1542 ■ *Web:* www.uniteddairy.com					
WhiteWave Foods Co 12002 Airport Way	Broomfield	CO	80021	303-635-4000	
Web: www.whitewave.com					
Whittier Farms Inc 90 Douglas Rd PO Box 455	Sutton	MA	01590	508-865-0640	865-1096
Web: www.whittierfarms.com					
Wilcox Farms Inc 40400 Harts Lake Valley Rd	Roy	WA	98580	360-458-7774	458-3995
Web: www.wilcoxfarms.com					

299-28 Nuts - Edible

				Phone	Fax
Azar Nut Co 1800 NW Dr	El Paso	TX	79912	915-877-4079	877-1198
TF: 800-351-8178					
Beer Nuts Inc 103 N Robinson St	Bloomington	IL	61701	309-827-8580	827-0914
Web: www.beernuts.com					
Dahlgren & Co Inc 1220 Sunflower St	Crookston	MN	56716	218-281-2985	281-7350
TF: 877-312-9198 ■ *Web:* www.sunflowerseed.com					
Diamond Foods Inc 1050 S Diamond St	Stockton	CA	95205	209-467-6000	461-7309
NASDAQ: DMND ■ *Web:* www.diamondfoods.com					
Gurley's Foods 1118 E Hwy 12	Willmar	MN	56201	320-235-0600	235-0659
Web: www.gurleysfoods.com					
Hines Nut Co Inc 990 S St Paul St	Dallas	TX	75201	214-939-0253	
TF: 800-561-6374 ■ *Web:* www.hinesnut.com					
John B Sanfilippo & Son Inc 1703 N Randall Rd	Elgin	IL	60123	847-289-1800	289-1843
NASDAQ: JBSS ■ *TF:* 800-874-8734 ■ *Web:* www.jbssinc.com					
Kar's Nuts 1200 E 14 Mile Rd	Madison Heights	MI	48071	248-588-1903	588-1902
TF: 800-527-6887 ■ *Web:* www.karsnuts.com					
King Nut Co 31900 Solon Rd	Solon	OH	44139	440-248-8484	248-0153
TF: 800-860-5464 ■ *Web:* www.kingnut.com					
Koinonia Partners 1324 Georgia Hwy 49 S	Americus	GA	31719	229-924-0391	924-6504
TF: 877-738-1741 ■ *Web:* www.koinoniapartners.org					
Leavitt Corp 100 Santilli Hwy	Everett	MA	02149	617-389-2600	387-9085
Web: teddie.com					
Pippin Snack Pecan Co 1332 Old Pretoria Rd	Albany	GA	31721	229-432-9316	
Web: georgiapecan.org					

Company	City	State	ZIP	Phone	Fax
Priester Pecan Company Inc PO Box 381 *TF:* 800-277-3226 ■ *Web:* www.priesters.com	Fort Deposit	AL	36032	334-227-4301	227-4294
South Georgia Pecan Co 309 S Lee St *TF:* 800-627-6630 ■ *Web:* georgiapecan.com	Valdosta	GA	31601	229-244-1321	247-6361
Superior Nut Co Inc 225 Monsignor O'Brien Hwy *Web:* www.superiornut.com	Cambridge	MA	02141	617-876-3808	876-8225
Trophy Nut Company Inc 320 N Second St *TF:* 800-729-6887 ■ *Web:* www.trophynut.com	Tipp City	OH	45371	937-667-8478	667-4656
Wricley Nut Products Co 480 Pattison Ave *Web:* wricleynutproductsco.com	Philadelphia	PA	19148	215-467-1106	467-4127
Young Pecan Co 1831 W Evans St Ste 200 *TF All:* 800-829-6864 ■ *Web:* www.youngpecan.com	Florence	SC	29501	843-662-8591	664-2344

299-29 Oil Mills - Cottonseed, Soybean, Other Vegetable Oils

Company	City	State	ZIP	Phone	Fax
Abitec Corp Inc PO Box 569 *TF Sales:* 800-555-1255 ■ *Web:* www.abiteccorp.com	Columbus	OH	43215	614-429-6464	299-8279
Ag Processing Inc 12700 W Dodge Rd PO Box 2047 *TF:* 800-247-1345 ■ *Web:* www.agp.com	Omaha	NE	68103	402-496-7809	498-2215
American Lecithin Company Inc 115 Hurley Rd Unit 2B *TF:* 800-364-4416 ■ *Web:* www.americanlecithin.com	Oxford	CT	06478	203-262-7100	262-7101
Bunge Ltd 50 Main St Sixth Fl *NYSE:* BG ■ *Web:* www.bunge.com	White Plains	NY	10606	914-684-2800	684-3499
Cargill Inc 15407 McGinty Rd W **Fax:* Cust Svc ■ *TF:* 800-227-4455 ■ *Web:* www.cargill.com	Wayzata	MN	55391	952-742-7575	742-7209*
Cargill Inc North America 15407 McGinty Rd *Web:* cargill.com	Wayzata	MN	55391	952-742-7575	
Delta Oil Mill PO Box 29 *Web:* www.deltaoilmill.com	Jonestown	MS	38639	662-358-4481	358-4629
Hartsville Oil Mill 311 Washington St	Darlington	SC	29532	843-393-2855	
Owensboro Grain Co 822 E Second St *TF:* 800-874-0305 ■ *Web:* www.owensborograin.com	Owensboro	KY	42303	270-926-2032	686-6509
Planters Cotton Oil Mill Inc 2901 Planters Dr *TF:* 800-264-7070 ■ *Web:* www.plantersoil.com	Pine Bluff	AR	71601	870-534-3631	534-1421
Producers Co-op Oil Mill Six SE Fourth St *Web:* www.producerscoop.net	Oklahoma City	OK	73129	405-232-7555	236-4887
Pyco Industries Inc PO Box 841 *Web:* www.pycoindustriesinc.com	Lubbock	TX	79404	806-747-3434	744-3221
Valley Co-op Oil Mill 1910 N Expwy 77 PO Box 533609 *Web:* valleycoopoilmill.com	Harlingen	TX	78553	956-425-4545	425-4264

299-30 Oils - Edible (Margarine, Shortening, Table Oils, etc)

Company	City	State	ZIP	Phone	Fax
Aarhuskarlshamn USA Inc 131 Marsh St *Web:* www.aak.com	Newark	NJ	07114	973-741-5049	344-6638
ACH Food Cos Inc 7171 Goodlet Farms Pkwy *TF:* 800-691-1106 ■ *Web:* www.achfood.com	Cordova	TN	38016	901-381-3000	381-2968
Fuji Vegetable Oil Inc One Barker Ave *Web:* www.fujioilusa.com	White Plains	NY	10601	914-761-7900	
Golden Foods/Golden Brands LLC 2520 Seventh St Rd *TF:* 800-622-3055 ■ *Web:* www.gfgb.com	Louisville	KY	40208	502-636-3712	636-3904
Kagome Creative Foods LLC 710 N Pearl St *TF:* 800-643-0006 ■ *Web:* www.kagomeusa.com	Osceola	AR	72370	870-563-2601	563-3824
Par-Way Tryson Co 107 Bolte Ln *TF:* 800-844-4554 ■ *Web:* parway.com/	Saint Clair	MO	63077	636-629-4545	629-1330
Star Fine Foods 2680 W Shaw Ln *Web:* www.starfinefoods.com	Fresno	CA	93711	559-498-2900	
Ventura Foods LLC 40 Pt Dr *TF:* 800-421-6257 ■ *Web:* www.venturafoods.com	Brea	CA	92821	714-257-3700	257-3702
Veronica Foods Co 1991 Dennison St *TF:* 800-370-5554 ■ *Web:* www.evoliveoil.com	Oakland	CA	94606	510-535-6833	532-2837

299-31 Pasta

Company	City	State	ZIP	Phone	Fax
A Zerega's Sons Inc PO Box 241 *Web:* www.zerega.com	Fair Lawn	NJ	07410	201-797-1400	797-0148
American Italian Pasta Co (AIPC) 1251 NW Briarcliff Pkwy Ste 500 *Web:* makesameal.com	Kansas City	MO	64116	816-584-5000	
Carla's Pasta Inc 50 Talbot Ln *Web:* www.carlaspasta.com	South Windsor	CT	06074	860-436-4042	436-4073
Dakota Growers Pasta Company Inc One Pasta Ave *TF:* 800-543-5561 ■ *Web:* www.viterra.com	Carrington	ND	58421	701-652-2855	652-3552
Everfresh Food Corp 501 Huron Blvd SE	Minneapolis	MN	55414	612-331-6393	331-1172
Foulds Inc 520 E Church St *Web:* fouldspasta.com	Libertyville	IL	60048	847-362-3062	362-6658
Gilster-Mary Lee Corp 1037 State St PO Box 227 *Web:* gilstermarylee.com	Chester	IL	62233	618-826-2361	826-2973
Monterey Pasta Co 2315 Moore Ave **Fax Area Code:* 831 ■ *TF:* 800-588-7782 ■ *Web:* www.montereygourmetfoods.com	Fullerton	CA	92833	800-588-7782	753-6255*
Nanka Seimen Co 3030 Leonis Blvd	Vernon	CA	90058	323-585-9967	
New World Pasta Co 85 Shannon Rd **Fax:* Sales ■ *TF Sales:* 800-730-5957 ■ *Web:* www.newworldpasta.com	Harrisburg	PA	17112	717-526-2200	526-2468*
Nissin Foods USA Company Inc 2001 W Rosecrans Ave **Fax Area Code:* 310 ■ **Fax:* Sales ■ *Web:* www.nissinfoods.com	Gardena	CA	90249	323-321-6453	515-3751*
OB Macaroni Co PO Box 53 *TF Orders:* 800-553-4336 ■ *Web:* www.obmacaroni.com	Fort Worth	TX	76101	817-335-4629	335-4726
Peking Noodle Co Inc 1514 N San Fernando Rd **Fax:* Sales ■ *TF:* 877-735-4648 ■ *Web:* www.pekingnoodle.com	Los Angeles	CA	90065	323-223-2023	223-3211*
Philadelphia Macaroni Co 760 S 11th St *Web:* www.philamacaroni.com	Philadelphia	PA	19147	215-923-3141	925-4298

299-32 Peanut Butter

Company	City	State	ZIP	Phone	Fax
Algood Food Co 7401 Trade Port Dr *Web:* www.algoodfood.com	Louisville	KY	40258	502-637-3631	637-1502
Carriage House Cos Inc, The 196 Newton St **Fax:* Sales ■ *TF:* 800-828-8915	Fredonia	NY	14063	716-673-1000	673-8443*
Edwards-Freeman Inc 441 E Hector St **Fax Area Code:* 610 ■ *TF:* 877-448-6887 ■ *Web:* www.edwardsfreeman.com	Conshohocken	PA	19428	877-448-6887	832-0126*
Jimbo's Jumbos Inc 185 Peanut Dr PO Box 465 *TF General:* 800-334-4771 ■ *Web:* www.jimbosjumbos.com	Edenton	NC	27932	800-334-4771	
JM Smucker Co One Strawberry Ln *NYSE:* SJM ■ *TF:* 888-550-9555 ■ *Web:* www.smuckers.com	Orrville	OH	44667	330-682-3000	684-6410
John B Sanfilippo & Son Inc 1703 N Randall Rd *NASDAQ:* JBSS ■ *TF:* 800-874-8734 ■ *Web:* www.jbssinc.com	Elgin	IL	60123	847-289-1800	289-1843
Leavitt Corp 100 Santilli Hwy *Web:* teddie.com	Everett	MA	02149	617-389-2600	387-9085
Producers Peanut Company Inc PO Box 250 *TF:* 800-847-5491 ■ *Web:* www.producerspeanut.com	Suffolk	VA	23434	757-539-7496	934-7730

299-33 Salads - Prepared

Company	City	State	ZIP	Phone	Fax
Chelten House Products Inc 607 Heron Dr *Web:* www.cheltenhouse.com	Bridgeport	NJ	08014	856-467-1600	467-4769
D'Arrigo Bros Company of California Inc PO Box 850 *TF Cust Svc:* 800-995-5939 ■ *Web:* www.andyboy.com	Salinas	CA	93902	831-455-4500	455-4445
Earth Island 9201 Owensmouth Ave *Web:* followyourheart.com	Chatsworth	CA	91311	818-725-2820	725-2812
Herold's Salads Inc 17512 Miles Ave *TF:* 800-427-2523 ■ *Web:* www.heroldssalads.com	Cleveland	OH	44128	216-991-7500	991-9565
Home Made Brand Foods Inc Two Opportunity Way	Newburyport	MA	01950	978-462-3663	462-7117
Kayem Foods Inc 75 Arlington St *TF:* 800-426-6100 ■ *Web:* www.kayem.com	Chelsea	MA	02150	617-889-1600	889-5478
Ready Pac Produce Inc 4401 Foxdale Ave **Fax Area Code:* 626 ■ *TF:* 800-800-7822 ■ *Web:* www.readypac.com	Irwindale	CA	91706	800-800-7822	856-0088*
Reser's Fine Foods Inc 15570 SW Jenkins Rd *TF:* 800-333-6431 ■ *Web:* www.resers.com	Beaverton	OR	97006	503-643-6431	
Sandridge Food Corp (SFC) 133 Commerce Dr *TF:* 800-672-2523 ■ *Web:* www.sandridge.com	Medina	OH	44256	330-725-2348	722-3998
Suter Company Inc 258 May St *TF:* 800-435-6942 ■ *Web:* www.suterco.com	Sycamore	IL	60178	815-895-9186	895-4814

299-34 Sandwiches - Prepared

Company	City	State	ZIP	Phone	Fax
Bridgford Foods Corp 1308 N Patt St *NASDAQ:* BRID ■ *TF:* 800-854-3255 ■ *Web:* www.bridgford.com	Anaheim	CA	92801	714-526-5533	526-4360
Cloverdale Foods Co 3015 34th St NW **Fax Area Code:* 701 ■ *TF:* 800-669-9511 ■ *Web:* www.cloverdalefoods.com	Mandan	ND	58554	800-669-9511	663-0690*
Hormel Foods Corp 1 Hormel Pl *NYSE:* HRL ■ **Fax:* Sales ■ *TF:* 800-523-4635 ■ *Web:* www.hormel.com	Austin	MN	55912	507-437-5611	437-5129*
Konop Cos 1725 Industrial Dr *TF:* 800-770-0477 ■ *Web:* www.konopcompanies.com	Green Bay	WI	54302	920-468-8517	468-1190
Landshire Inc 12 Tucker Dr **Fax Area Code:* 314 ■ *TF:* 800-468-3354 ■ *Web:* www.landshire.com	Caseyville	IL	62232	618-293-6525	925-4099*
Lloyd's Barbecue Co 1455 Mendota Heights Rd *Web:* hormel.com/brands/hormel-lloyds	Mendota Heights	MN	55120	651-688-6000	681-1430
Sunburst Foods Inc 1002 Sunburst Dr *Web:* www.sunburstfoods.net	Goldsboro	NC	27534	919-778-2151	778-9203

299-35 Snack Foods

Company	City	State	ZIP	Phone	Fax
Azteca Foods Inc PO Box 427 *Web:* www.aztecafoods.com	Summit-Argo	IL	60501	708-563-6600	
Better Made Snack Foods Inc 10148 Gratiot Ave *TF:* 800-332-2394 ■ *Web:* www.bmchips.com	Detroit	MI	48213	313-925-4774	925-6028
Bickel's Snack Foods 1120 Zinns Quarry Rd **Fax:* Cust Svc ■ *TF:* 800-233-1933 ■ *Web:* www.bickelssnacks.com	York	PA	17404	717-843-0738	843-4569*
Cape Cod Potato Chip Co 100 Breed's Hill Rd *TF:* 888-881-2447 ■ *Web:* www.capecodchips.com	Hyannis	MA	02601	508-775-3358	775-2808
Chester Inc 555 Eastport Ctr Dr *TF:* 800-778-1131 ■ *Web:* chesterinc.com	Valparaiso	IN	46383	219-465-7555	
CJ Vitner & Co 4202 W 45th St *TF General:* 800-523-7900 ■ *Web:* www.vitners.com	Chicago	IL	60632	773-523-7900	523-9143
Evans Food Group Ltd 4118 S Halsted St *TF:* 866-254-7400 ■ *Web:* www.evansfood.com	Chicago	IL	60609	773-254-7400	254-7791
Frito-Lay North America 7701 Legacy Dr *TF:* 800-352-4477 ■ *Web:* www.fritolay.com	Plano	TX	75024	972-334-7000	334-2019
Golden Flake Snack Foods Inc One Golden Flake Dr *TF:* 800-239-2447 ■ *Web:* www.goldenflake.com	Birmingham	AL	35205	205-323-6161	458-7121
Herr Foods Inc 20 Herr Dr PO Box 300 *TF:* 800-344-3777 ■ *Web:* www.herrs.com	Nottingham	PA	19362	610-932-9330	932-1190

Company	City	State	Zip	Phone	Fax
Ideal Snacks Corp 89 Mill St. *Web:* www.idealsnacks.com	Liberty	NY	12754	845-292-7000	292-7000
Keystone Food Products Inc PO Box 326 *Web:* www.keystonesnacks.com	Easton	PA	18044	610-258-0888	250-0721
Martin's Potato Chips Inc 5847 Lincoln Hwy W PO Box 28 *TF:* 800-272-4477 ■ *Web:* www.martinschips.com	Thomasville	PA	17364	717-792-3565	792-4906
Mike-Sell's Potato Chip Co 333 Leo St PO Box 115 *TF:* 800-257-4742 ■ *Web:* www.mike-sells.com	Dayton	OH	45404	937-228-9400	461-5707
Mission Foods 1159 Cottonwood Ln Ste 200 *TF:* 800-443-7994 ■ *Web:* missionmenus.com	Irving	TX	75038	972-232-5200	232-5167
Old Dutch Foods Inc 2375 Terminal Rd *TF:* 800-989-2447 ■ *Web:* www.olddutchfoods.com	Roseville	MN	55113	651-633-8810	633-8894
Smith Bros Co 3501 W 48th Pl *TF:* 800-621-0225 ■ *Web:* www.thesmithbrothers.com	Chicago	IL	60632	773-927-3737	
Snacks Unlimited One General Mills Blvd. **Fax:* PR ■ *TF:* 800-248-7310 ■ *Web:* www.generalmills.com	Minneapolis	MN	55426	763-764-7600	764-3232*
Snyder of Berlin 1313 Stadium Dr *TF:* 800-374-7949 ■ *Web:* www.snyderofberlin.com	Berlin	PA	15530	814-267-4641	267-3582
Tim's Cascade Snacks 1150 Industry Dr N **Fax:* Cust Svc ■ *TF:* 800-533-8467 ■ *Web:* www.timschips.com	Algona	WA	98001	253-833-0255	939-9411*
Uncle Ray's LLC 14245 Birwood St *TF:* 800-800-3286 ■ *Web:* www.unclerays.com	Detroit	MI	48238	313-834-0800	834-0443
UTZ Quality Foods Co 900 High St *TF:* 800-367-7629 ■ *Web:* www.utzsnacks.com	Hanover	PA	17331	717-637-6644	633-5102
Wise Foods Inc 245 Townpark Dr Ste 75 *TF:* 888-759-4401 ■ *Web:* www.wisesnacks.com	Kennesaw	GA	30144	770-426-5821	
Wyandot Inc 135 Wyandot Ave. **Fax:* Cust Svc ■ *TF:* 800-992-6368 ■ *Web:* www.wyandotsnacks.com	Marion	OH	43302	740-383-4031	382-0115*

299-36 Specialty Foods

Company	City	State	Zip	Phone	Fax
AFP Advanced Food Products LLC 402 S Custer Ave *Web:* www.afpllc.com	New Holland	PA	17557	717-355-8667	355-8848
Alphin Bros Inc 2302 US 301 S *TF:* 800-672-4502 ■ *Web:* alphinbrothers.com	Dunn	NC	28334	910-892-8751	892-2709
Ameriqual Group LLC 18200 Hwy 41 N *Web:* www.ameriqual.com	Evansville	IN	47725	812-867-1444	867-0278
Amy's Kitchen Inc PO Box 449 *Web:* www.amyskitchen.com	Petaluma	CA	94953	707-568-4500	
Armanino Foods of Distinction Inc 30588 San Antonio St *OTC: AMNF* ■ *TF:* 800-255-5855 ■ *Web:* www.armaninofoods.com	Hayward	CA	94544	510-441-9300	441-0101
Ateeco Inc 600 E Ctr St PO Box 606 *TF:* 800-233-3170 ■ *Web:* www.pierogy.com	Shenandoah	PA	17976	570-462-2745	462-1392
Avanti Foods 109 Depot St *TF:* 800-243-3739 ■ *Web:* www.avantifoods.com	Walnut	IL	61376	815-379-2155	379-9357
Beech-Nut Nutrition Corp One Nutritious Pl *TF:* 800-233-2468 ■ *Web:* www.beechnut.com	Amsterdam	NY	12010	800-233-2468	
Bellisio Foods Inc 1201 Harman Pl Ste 302 *TF:* 800-368-7337 ■ *Web:* www.bellisiofoods.com	Minneapolis	MN	55403	612-371-8222	337-8427
Border Foods Inc 4065 J St SE **Fax Area Code:* 575 ■ *Web:* www.borderfoodsinc.com	Deming	NM	88030	800-323-4358	546-8676*
Bruce Foods Corp PO Drawer 1030 *TF:* 800-299-9082 ■ *Web:* www.brucefoods.com	New Iberia	LA	70561	337-365-8101	369-9026
Buddy's Kitchen Inc 12105 Nicollet Ave. *Web:* www.buddyskitchen.com	Burnsville	MN	55337	952-894-2540	895-1664
Camino Real Foods Inc 2638 E Vernon Ave *TF:* 800-421-6201 ■ *Web:* www.caminorealkitchens.com	Vernon	CA	90058	323-585-6599	585-5420
Campbell Soup Co One Campbell Pl *NYSE: CPB* ■ *TF:* 800-257-8443 ■ *Web:* www.campbellsoupcompany.com	Camden	NJ	08103	856-342-4800	342-3878
Champion Foods LLC 23900 Bell Rd. *Web:* www.championfoods.com	New Boston	MI	48164	734-753-3663	753-5366
Chungs Gourmet Foods 3907 Dennis St. *TF:* 800-824-8640 ■ *Web:* www.chungsfoods.com	Houston	TX	77004	713-741-2118	741-2330
Cromers Inc 1700 Huger St **Fax Area Code:* 803 ■ *TF:* 800-322-7688 ■ *Web:* www.cromers.com	Columbia	SC	29201	800-322-7688	779-0731*
Cuisine Solutions Inc 4106 Wheeler Ave Ste 450 *OTC: CUSI* ■ *TF:* 888-285-4679 ■ *Web:* www.cuisinesolutions.com	Alexandria	VA	22304	703-270-2900	270-2994
D & D Foods Inc 9425 N 48th St *TF:* 800-208-0364 ■ *Web:* hy-vee.com	Omaha	NE	68152	402-571-4113	
Del Monte Foods Co 1 Maritime Plaza *TF Cust Svc:* 800-543-3090 ■ *Web:* www.delmonte.com	San Francisco	CA	94111	415-247-3000	247-3311
Deli Express 16101 W 78th St *TF:* 800-328-8184 ■ *Web:* www.deliexpress.com	Eden Prairie	MN	55344	800-328-8184	
Don Miguel Mexican Foods Inc One Hormel Pl *TF:* 800-725-7212 ■ *Web:* www.donmiguel.com	Austin	MN	55912	800-725-7212	
Durrset Amigos Ltd 4669 Hwy 90 W *TF:* 800-580-3477 ■ *Web:* www.amigosfoods.com	San Antonio	TX	78237	210-798-5360	798-5365
Ebro Foods Inc 1330 W 43rd St *Web:* www.ebrofoods.com	Chicago	IL	60609	773-696-0150	696-0151
Eden Foods Inc 701 Tecumseh Rd *TF Cust Svc:* 800-248-0320 ■ *Web:* www.edenfoods.com	Clinton	MI	49236	517-456-7424	456-6075
El Encanto Inc 2001 Fourth St SW PO Box 293 *TF:* 800-888-7336 ■ *Web:* www.buenofoods.com	Albuquerque	NM	87103	505-243-2722	242-1680
Ener-G Foods Inc 5960 First Ave S PO Box 84487 *TF:* 800-331-5222 ■ *Web:* www.ener-g.com	Seattle	WA	98124	206-767-3928	764-3398
Fairmont Foods of Minnesota 905 E Fourth St *Web:* www.fairmontfoods.com	Fairmont	MN	56031	507-238-9001	238-9560
Fiesta Canning Co Inc 1480 E Bethany Home Ste 110 *Web:* www.fiestacan.com	Phoenix	AZ	85014	602-212-2424	274-7233
Frozen Specialties Inc 8600 S Wilkinson Wy Ste G *Web:* www.frozenspecialties.com	Perrysburg	OH	43551	419-867-2005	
Gerber Products Co 445 State St. **Fax Area Code:* 231 ■ *TF:* 800-284-9488 ■ *Web:* www.gerber.com	Fremont	MI	49413	800-284-9488	928-2723*
Grandma Brown's Beans Inc 5837 Scenic Ave	Mexico	NY	13114	315-963-7221	963-4072
Hain Celestial Group Inc 4600 Sleepytime Dr Ste 250 *NASDAQ: HAIN* ■ **Fax Area Code:* 631 ■ *TF:* 800-434-4246 ■ *Web:* www.hain-celestial.com	Boulder	CO	80301	800-434-4246	730-2550*
Hanover Foods Corp 1550 York St PO Box 334 *OTC: HNFSA* ■ *TF:* 800-888-4646 ■ *Web:* www.hanoverfoods.com	Hanover	PA	17331	717-632-6000	632-6681
HJ Heinz Co One PPG Pl Ste 3100 *TF:* 800-255-5750 ■ *Web:* www.heinz.com	Pittsburgh	PA	15230	412-456-5700	
Home Market Foods Inc 140 Morgan Dr *TF:* 800-367-8325 ■ *Web:* www.homemarketfoods.com	Norwood	MA	02062	781-948-1500	702-6171
Home Run Inn Frozen Foods Corp 1300 International Pkwy *Web:* www.homeruninnpizza.com	Woodridge	IL	60517	630-783-9696	783-0069
Homestead Pasta Co 315 S Maple Ave Bldg 106 *Web:* www.homesteadpasta.com	South San Francisco	CA	94080	650-615-0750	615-0764
Hormel Foods Corp 1 Hormel Pl *NYSE: HRL* ■ **Fax:* Sales ■ *TF:* 800-523-4635 ■ *Web:* www.hormel.com	Austin	MN	55912	507-437-5611	437-5129*
J & B Sausage Company Inc 100 Main St *Web:* www.jbfoods.com	Waelder	TX	78959	830-788-7511	788-7279
JM Smucker Co One Strawberry Ln *NYSE: SJM* ■ *TF:* 888-550-9555 ■ *Web:* www.smuckers.com	Orrville	OH	44667	330-682-3000	684-6410
Juanita's Foods Inc P.O. Box 847 PO Box 847 **Fax Area Code:* 310 ■ *TF:* 800-303-2965 ■ *Web:* www.juanitasfoods.com	Wilmington	CA	90748	800-303-2965	835-6516*
Kahiki Foods Inc 1100 Morrison Rd *TF:* 855-524-4540 ■ *Web:* www.kahiki.com	Columbus	OH	43230	614-322-3180	751-0039
La Reina Inc 316 N Ford Blvd *TF:* 800-367-7522 ■ *Web:* www.lareinainc.com	Los Angeles	CA	90022	323-268-2791	265-4295
La Tapatia Tortilleria Inc 104 E Belmont Ave *Web:* www.tortillas4u.com	Fresno	CA	93701	559-441-1030	441-1712
Lamb Weston Inc 8701 W Gage Blvd. **Fax:* Sales ■ *Web:* www.lambweston.com	Kennewick	WA	99336	509-735-4651	736-0395*
Leon's Texas Cuisine Co 2100 Redbud Blvd *Web:* www.texascuisine.com	McKinney	TX	75069	972-529-5050	
Little Lady Foods Inc 2323 Pratt Blvd *TF:* 800-439-1440 ■ *Web:* www.littleladyfoods.com	Elk Grove Village	IL	60007	847-631-3500	806-0026
Mancini Foods PO Box 157 **Fax Area Code:* 863 ■ *Web:* www.mancinifoods.com	Zolfo Springs	FL	33890	800-741-1778	735-1172*
Manischewitz Company, The 80 Ave K *Web:* www.rabfoodgroup.com	Newark	NJ	07105	201-553-1100	
McCain Foods Ltd 181 Bay St Ste 3600 *TF:* 800-938-7799 ■ *Web:* www.mccain.com	Toronto	ON	M5J2T3	416-955-1700	
McCain Foods USA Inc 2275 Cabot Dr. **Fax Area Code:* 630 ■ *TF:* 800-938-7799 ■ *Web:* www.mccainusa.com	Lisle	IL	60532	800-938-7799	857-4560*
Michael Angelo's Gourmet Foods Inc 200 Michael Angelo Way *TF:* 877-482-5426 ■ *Web:* www.michaelangelos.com	Austin	TX	78728	512-218-3500	218-3600
Morgan Foods Inc 90 W Morgan St *TF:* 888-430-1780 ■ *Web:* www.morganfoods.com	Austin	IN	47102	812-794-1170	794-1211
Mott's LLP PO Box 869077 *TF Consumer Info:* 800-426-4891 ■ *Web:* www.motts.com	Plano	TX	75086	800-426-4891	
Nardone Bros Baking Company Inc 420 New Commerce Blvd *TF:* 800-822-5320 ■ *Web:* www.nardonebros.com	Wilkes-Barre	PA	18706	570-823-0141	823-2581
Ole Mexican Foods Inc 6585 Crescent Dr *Web:* www.olemexicanfoods.com	Norcross	GA	30071	770-582-9200	582-9400
Overhill Farms Inc 2727 E Vernon Ave *NYSE: OFI* ■ *TF:* 800-859-6406 ■ *Web:* www.overhillfarms.com	Vernon	CA	90058	323-582-9977	582-6122
Panhandle Foods Inc 1980 Smith Township SR *Web:* panhandlefoodsales.com	Burgettstown	PA	15021	724-947-2216	947-4940
Papa John's International Inc PO Box 99900 *NASDAQ: PZZA* ■ *TF:* 877-547-7272 ■ *Web:* www.papajohns.com	Louisville	KY	40269	877-547-7272	
Pastorelli Food Products Inc 162 N Sangamon St *TF:* 800-767-2829 ■ *Web:* www.pastorelli.com	Chicago	IL	60607	312-666-2041	666-2415
Pinnacle Foods Corp 399 Jefferson Rd *TF:* 866-266-7596 ■ *Web:* www.pinnaclefoodscorp.com	Parsippany	NJ	07054	973-541-6620	
Preferred Meal Systems Inc 5240 St Charles Rd *TF Cust Svc:* 800-886-6325 ■ *Web:* preferredmeals.com	Berkeley	IL	60163	708-318-2500	493-2690
Quaker Oats Co 555 W Monroe St *TF:* 800-367-6287 ■ *Web:* www.quakeroats.com	Chicago	IL	60661	312-821-1000	
Request Foods Inc PO Box 2577 *TF Sales:* 800-748-0378 ■ *Web:* www.requestfoods.com	Holland	MI	49422	616-786-0900	786-9180
Reynaldo's Mexican Food Company Inc 3301 E Vernon Ave *Web:* www.rmfood.com	Vernon	CA	90058	562-803-3188	803-3196
Ruiz Foods Inc PO Box 37 *TF:* 800-477-6474 ■ *Web:* www.elmonterey.com	Dinuba	CA	93618	559-591-5510	591-1968
Schwan Food Co 115 W College Dr. *TF:* 800-533-5290 ■ *Web:* www.theschwanfoodcompany.com	Marshall	MN	56258	507-532-3274	
Seviroli Foods 601 Brook St. *Web:* www.seviroli.com	Garden City	NY	11530	516-222-6220	222-0534
Small Planet Foods Inc 106 Woodworth St *TF:* 800-624-4123 ■ *Web:* www.smallplanetfoods.com	Sedro Woolley	WA	98284	360-855-0100	
Suter Company Inc 258 May St. *TF:* 800-435-6942 ■ *Web:* www.suterco.com	Sycamore	IL	60178	815-895-9186	895-4814
Tastefully Simple Inc 1920 Turning Leaf Ln SW PO Box 3006 *Web:* www.tastefullysimple.com	Alexandria	MN	56308	320-763-0695	763-2458
Vanee Foods Company Inc 5418 McDermott Dr *TF Cust Svc:* 800-654-6647 ■ *Web:* vaneefoodservice.com	Berkeley	IL	60163	708-449-7300	449-2558
Windsor Foods 3355 W Alabama St Ste 730 *TF:* 800-458-4054 ■ *Web:* www.windsorfoods.com	Houston	TX	77098	713-843-5200	960-9709

Phone | Fax

Winter Gardens Quality Foods Inc
304 Commerce St PO Box 339 . . . New Oxford PA 17350 717-624-4911 624-7729
TF: 800-242-7637 ■ *Web:* www.wintergardens.com

299-37 Spices, Seasonings, Herbs

Phone | Fax

Abco Laboratories Inc 2450 S Watney Way . . . Fairfield CA 94533 707-432-2200 432-2240
TF: 800-678-2226 ■ *Web:* www.abcolabs.com

Ajinomoto Food Ingredients LLC
8430 W Bryn Mawr Ave Ste 635 . . . Chicago IL 60631 773-714-1436
Web: www.ajiusafood.com

Aliments Ouimet-Cordon Bleu Inc
8383 Rue J-Ren Ouimet . . . Anjou QC H1J2P8 514-352-3000
Web: www.cordonbleu.ca

All American Seasonings 10600 E 54th Ave . . . Denver CO 80239 303-623-2320 623-1920
Web: www.allamericanseasonings.com

American Outdoor Products Inc
6350 Gunpark Dr . . . Boulder CO 80301 303-581-0518
TF: 800-641-0500 ■ *Web:* www.backpackerspantry.com

Basic American Foods
2185 N California Blvd Ste 215 . . . Walnut Creek CA 94596 925-472-4000 472-4314
TF: 800-227-4050 ■ *Web:* www.baf.com

Benson's Gourmet Seasonings PO Box 638 . . . Azusa CA 91702 626-969-4443 969-2912
TF: 800-325-5619 ■ *Web:* www.bensonsgourmetseasonings.com

Blendex Company Inc 11208 Electron Dr . . . Louisville KY 40299 502-267-1003 267-1024
TF: 800-626-6325 ■ *Web:* www.blendex.com

Cedarome Canada Inc 3650 Matte Blvd Ste E-22 . . . Brossard QC J4Y2Z2 450-659-8000 659-8010
Web: www.cedarome.com

Celtrade Canada Inc 7566 Bath Rd . . . Mississauga ON L4T1L2 905-678-1322
Web: www.celtradecanada.ca

Circle Foods LLC 8411 Siempre Viva Rd . . . San Diego CA 92154 619-671-3900
Web: www.circlefoods.com

Flavurence Corp
1916 Tubeway Ave Commerce . . . Commerce City CA 90040 323-727-1957

Frontier Natural Products Co-op
3021 78th St PO Box 299 . . . Norway IA 52318 319-227-7996 227-7966
TF: 800-669-3275 ■ *Web:* www.frontiercoop.com

Fuchs North America
9740 Reisterstown Rd . . . Owings Mills MD 21117 410-363-1700 363-6619
TF: 800-365-3229 ■ *Web:* www.fuchsnorthamerica.com

Golden Specialty Foods LLC 14605 Best Ave . . . Norwalk CA 90650 562-802-2537
Web: www.goldenspecialtyfoods.com

Griffith Laboratories Worldwide Inc
1 Griffith Ctr . . . Alsip IL 60803 708-371-0900 371-4783
TF Cust Svc: 800-346-9494 ■ *Web:* www.griffithlaboratories.com

Harris Freeman & Company LP
3110 E Miraloma Ave . . . Anaheim CA 92806 714-765-1190
Web: www.harrisfreeman.com

Johnny's Fine Foods Inc 319 E 25th St . . . Tacoma WA 98421 253-383-4597
TF General: 855-654-9590 ■ *Web:* www.johnnysfinefoods.com

Lucile's Famous Creole Seasonings
2124 14th St . . . Boulder CO 80302 303-442-4743 939-9848
Web: www.luciles.com

McCormick & Co Inc 18 Loveton Cir . . . Sparks MD 21152 410-771-7244
NYSE: MKC ■ *TF:* 800-632-5847 ■ *Web:* www.mccormickcorporation.com

McCormick & Company Inc Food Service Div
226 Schilling Cir . . . Hunt Valley MD 21031 410-771-7500 771-1111
TF: 800-322-7742 ■ *Web:* www.mccormickforchefs.com

McCormick & Company Inc McCormick Flavor Div
226 Schilling Cir . . . Hunt Valley MD 21031 410-771-7500 771-1111
TF: 800-322-7742 ■ *Web:* www.mccormickforchefs.com

McCormick & Company Inc US Consumer Products Div
211 Schilling Cir . . . Hunt Valley MD 21031 410-527-6000
Web: www.mccormick.com

McCormick Ingredients 18 Loveton Cir . . . Sparks MD 21152 410-771-7301
TF: 800-632-5847 ■ *Web:* www.mccormick.com

Newly Weds Foods Inc 4140 W Fullerton Ave . . . Chicago IL 60639 773-489-7000 292-3809
TF: 800-621-7521 ■ *Web:* www.newlywedsfoods.com

Pepsi Bottling Ventures LLC
4141 Parklake Ave Ste 600 . . . Raleigh NC 27612 919-865-2300
TF: 800-662-8792 ■ *Web:* www.pepsibottlingventures.com

Precision Foods Inc
11457 Olde Cabin Rd Ste 100 . . . Saint Louis MO 63141 314-567-7400 567-5402
TF: 800-442-5242 ■ *Web:* www.precisionfoods.com

Produits Alimentaires Berthelet Inc
1805 Berlier St . . . Laval QC H7L3S4 514-334-5503 334-3584
Web: www.berthelet.com

Pyure Brands 2277 Trade Ctr Way . . . Naples FL 34109 305-509-5096
Web: www.pyuresweet.com

Rex Fine Foods Inc 1536 River Oaks Rd W . . . Harahan LA 70123 504-602-9487
Web: www.rexfoods.com

Royal Food Products LLC
2322 E Minnesota St . . . Indianapolis IN 46203 317-782-2660
Web: www.royalfp.com

Sabra Dipping Co LLC 2420 49th St . . . Astoria NY 11103 888-957-2272
Web: www.sabra.com

SensoryEffects Flavor Co
231 Rock Industrial Park Dr . . . Bridgeton MO 63044 314-291-5444
TF: 800-422-5444 ■ *Web:* www.sensoryeffects.com

Soy Vay Enterprises Inc 5969 Hillside Dr . . . Felton CA 95018 831-335-3824
Web: www.soyvay.com

Specialty Commodities Inc 1530 47th St NW . . . Fargo ND 58102 701-282-8222
Web: www.scifargo.com

Spice Hunter Inc
184 Suburban Rd PO Box 8110 . . . San Luis Obispo CA 93403 800-444-3061 544-9046*
**Fax Area Code: 805* ■ **Fax:* Cust Svc ■ *TF:* 800-444-3061 ■ *Web:* www.spicehunter.com

Spice World Inc 8101 Presidents Dr . . . Orlando FL 32809 800-433-4979 857-7171*
**Fax Area Code: 407* ■ *TF:* 800-433-4979 ■ *Web:* www.spiceworldinc.com

Tampico Spice Company Inc
5941 S Central Ave . . . Los Angeles CA 90001 323-235-3154 232-8686
Web: www.tampicospice.com

TC Heartland LLC 14300 Clay Terr Blvd Ste 249 . . . Carmel IN 46032 317-566-9750
Web: www.hsweet.com

Tulocay & Company Inc 388 Devlin Rd Napa Valley . . . Napa CA 94558 707-253-7655
Web: www.madeinnapavalley.com

Wizard's Cauldron Inc 878 Firetower Rd . . . Yanceyville NC 27379 336-694-5665
Web: www.wizardscauldron.com

World Spice Inc 223 E Highland Pkwy . . . Roselle NJ 07203 908-245-0600 245-0696
TF: 800-234-1060 ■ *Web:* www.wsispice.com

Zatarain's Inc 82 First St . . . Gretna LA 70053 504-367-2950 362-2004
Web: mccormick.com/zatarains

299-38 Sugar & Sweeteners

Phone | Fax

Alma Plantation Ltd 4612 Alma Rd . . . Lakeland LA 70752 225-627-6666

Amalgamated Sugar Co LLC
1951 S Saturn Way Ste 100 . . . Boise ID 83709 208-383-6500 242-3108*
**Fax Area Code: 800*

American Crystal Sugar Co 101 Third St N . . . Moorhead MN 56560 218-236-4400 236-4702
Web: www.crystalsugar.com

C & H Sugar Co Inc 850 Loring Ave . . . Crockett CA 94525 800-773-1803 787-3196*
**Fax Area Code: 510* ■ *TF:* 800-773-1803 ■ *Web:* www.chsugar.com

Cajun Sugar Co-op Inc 2711 Northside Rd . . . New Iberia LA 70563 337-365-3401 365-7820
Web: amscl.org

Cora-Texas Mfg Company Inc
32505 Louisiana 1 PO Box 280 . . . White Castle LA 70788 225-545-3679 545-8360
Web: www.coratexas.com

Cumberland Packing Corp 2 Cumberland St . . . Brooklyn NY 11205 718-858-4200 260-9017
Web: www.sweetnlow.com

Florida Crystals Corp
1 N Clematis St Ste 200 . . . West Palm Beach FL 33401 561-366-5100 366-5158
Web: www.floridacrystals.com

Hawaiian Commercial & Sugar Co 1 Hansen St . . . Puunene HI 96784 808-877-0081 871-7663
Web: www.hcsugar.com

Lafourche Sugars Corp
141 Lk Leighton Quarters Rd . . . Thibodaux LA 70301 985-447-3210 447-8728

Lantic Sugar Ltd 4026 Notre-Dame St NE . . . Montreal QC H1W2K3 514-527-8686 527-8406
Web: www.lantic.ca

Lula Westfield LLC
451 Hwy 1005 PO Box 10 . . . Paincourtville LA 70391 985-369-6450 369-6139

MA Patout & Son Ltd
3512 J Patout Burns Rd . . . Jeanerette LA 70544 337-276-4592 276-4247
Web: www.mapatout.com

Merisant Worldwide Inc
33 N Dearborn St Ste 200 . . . Chicago IL 60602 312-840-6000 840-5146
Web: www.merisant.com

Michigan Sugar Company Inc
2600 S Euclid Ave . . . Bay City MI 48706 989-686-0161 671-3695
Web: www.michigansugar.com

Minn-Dak Farmers Co-op 7525 Red River Rd . . . Wahpeton ND 58075 701-642-8411 642-6814
Web: www.mdfarmerscoop.com

Rio Grande Valley Sugar Growers
PO Box 459 . . . Santa Rosa TX 78593 956-636-1411 636-1046
Web: www.rgvsugar.com

Southern Minnesota Beet Sugar Co-op
83550 CR 21 PO Box 500 . . . Renville MN 56284 320-329-8305 329-3252
Web: www.smbsc.com

Sterling Sugars Inc 611 Irish Bend Rd . . . Franklin LA 70538 337-828-0620 828-1757
Web: amscl.org

Sugar Cane Growers Co-op of Florida
PO Box 666 . . . Belle Glade FL 33430 561-996-5556 996-4747
Web: www.scgc.org

US Sugar Corp 111 Ponce de Leon Ave . . . Clewiston FL 33440 863-983-8121 983-9827
Web: www.ussugar.com

Western Sugar Co-op 7555 E Hampden Ave Ste 600 . . . Denver CO 80231 303-830-3939 830-3941
TF: 800-523-7497 ■ *Web:* www.westernsugar.com

299-39 Syrup - Maple

Phone | Fax

Carriage House Cos Inc, The 196 Newton St . . . Fredonia NY 14063 716-673-1000 673-8443*
**Fax:* Sales ■ *TF:* 800-828-8915

Golden Eagle Syrup Company Inc
205 First Ave SE . . . Fayette AL 35555 205-932-5294 932-5296
Web: www.goldeneaglesyrup.com

H Fox & Company Inc 416 Thatford Ave . . . Brooklyn NY 11212 718-385-4600 345-4283
Web: www.foxs-syrups.com

Maple Grove Farms of Vermont
1052 Portland St . . . Saint Johnsbury VT 05819 802-748-5141 748-9647
TF: 800-525-2540 ■ *Web:* www.maplegrove.com

Pinnacle Foods Corp 399 Jefferson Rd . . . Parsippany NJ 07054 973-541-6620
TF: 866-266-7596 ■ *Web:* www.pinnaclefoodscorp.com

Richards Maple Products Inc 545 Water St . . . Chardon OH 44024 800-352-4052 286-7203*
**Fax Area Code: 440* ■ *TF:* 800-352-4052 ■ *Web:* www.richardsmapleproducts.com

Sea Breeze Inc 441 Rt 202 . . . Towaco NJ 07082 973-334-7777 334-2617
TF: 800-732-2733 ■ *Web:* www.seabreezesyrups.com

299-40 Tea

Phone | Fax

4C Foods Corp 580 Fountain Ave . . . Brooklyn NY 11208 718-272-4242 272-2899
Web: www.4c.com

Bigelow Tea 201 Black Rock Tpke . . . Fairfield CT 06825 888-244-3569
TF: 888-244-3569 ■ *Web:* www.bigelowtea.com

Celestial Seasonings Inc 4600 Sleepytime Dr . . . Boulder CO 80301 303-530-5300 581-1332*
**Fax:* Cust Svc ■ *TF:* 800-351-8175 ■ *Web:* www.celestialseasonings.com

Eastern Tea Corp One Engelhard Dr . . . Monroe Township NJ 08831 609-860-1100 860-1105
Web: www.easterntea.com

				Phone	Fax
Fee Bros Inc 453 Portland Ave *Web:* www.feebrothers.com	Rochester	NY	14605	585-544-9530	
Redco Foods Inc One Hansen Island *TF:* 800-556-6674 ■ *Web:* www.redrosetea.com	Little Falls	NY	13365	315-823-1300	823-0578
S & D Coffee Inc 300 Concord Pkwy PO Box 1628 *TF Cust Svc:* 800-933-2210 ■ *Web:* www.sdcoffeetea.com	Concord	NC	28026	704-782-3121	721-5792

299-41 Vinegar & Cider

				Phone	Fax
Boyajian Inc 144 Will Dr *TF General:* 800-965-0665 ■ *Web:* www.boyajianinc.com	Canton	MA	02021	781-828-9966	828-9922
Consumers Vinegar & Spice Company Inc 4723 S Washtenaw Ave *Web:* cvsco.com	Chicago	IL	60632	773-376-4100	376-6224
Creole Fermentation Industries Inc 7331 Den Frederick Rd	Abbeville	LA	70510	337-898-9377	898-9376
Gold Pure Food Products Inc One Brooklyn Rd *Web:* www.goldshorseradish.com	Hempstead	NY	11550	516-483-5600	483-5798
Heintz & Weber Co Inc 150 Reading Ave *TF:* 800-438-6878 ■ *Web:* www.webersmustard.com	Buffalo	NY	14220	716-852-7171	852-7173
Knouse Foods Co-op Inc 800 Peach Glen-Idaville Rd *Web:* www.knouse.com	Peach Glen	PA	17375	717-677-8181	677-7069
MA Gedney Co 2100 Stoughton Ave *TF:* 888-244-0653 ■ *Web:* www.gedneyfoods.com	Chaska	MN	55318	952-448-2612	448-1790
Mizkan Americas Inc 1661 Feehanville Dr Ste 300 *TF:* 800-323-4358 ■ *Web:* www.mizkan.com	Mount Prospect	IL	60056	847-590-0059	590-0405
National Fruit Product Co Inc 701 Fairmont Ave PO Box 2040 **Fax:* Sales ■ *TF:* 800-655-4022 ■ *Web:* www.whitehousefoods.com	Winchester	VA	22601	540-723-9614	665-4671*
Pastorelli Food Products Inc 162 N Sangamon St *TF:* 800-767-2829 ■ *Web:* www.pastorelli.com	Chicago	IL	60607	312-666-2041	666-2415
Rex Wine Vinegar Co 828-30 Raymond Blvd	Newark	NJ	07105	973-589-6911	
Silver Palate 211 Knickerbocker Rd PO Box 512 *Web:* silverpalate.com	Dumont	NJ	07628	201-568-0110	568-8844

299-42 Yeast

				Phone	Fax
Brolite Products Inc 1900 S Pk Ave *TF:* 888-276-5483 ■ *Web:* www.bakewithbrolite.com	Streamwood	IL	60107	630-830-0340	830-0356
DSM Food Specialties Inc 45 Waterview Blvd *TF:* 800-526-0189 ■ *Web:* www.dsm.com	Parsippany	NJ	07054	973-257-1063	257-8420
Lesaffre Yeast Corp 7475 W Main St *TF Cust Svc:* 877-677-7000 ■ *Web:* www.lesaffreyeastcorp.com	Milwaukee	WI	53214	877-677-7000	
Minn-Dak Yeast Company Inc 18175 Red River Rd W *TF:* 800-348-0991 ■ *Web:* www.dakotayeast.com/home.html	Wahpeton	ND	58075	701-642-3300	642-1908
Ohly Americas 3388 Bacon St *TF:* 800-321-2689 ■ *Web:* www.ohly.com	Rhinelander	WI	54501	320-587-2481	587-8617

300 FOOD PRODUCTS - WHOL

SEE ALSO Beverages - Whol p. 1866

				Phone	Fax
Carlsen & Associates 1439 Grove St *Web:* carlsenassociates.com	Healdsburg	CA	95448	707-431-2000	
Chocolate Factory Theater 549 49th Ave *Web:* chocolatefactorytheater.org	Long Island City	NY	11101	718-482-7069	
Lassen's Health Food 2857 E Thousand Oaks Blvd *Web:* laddassociates.com	Thousand Oaks	CA	91362	805-495-2609	
Mayway Corp 1338 Mandela Pkwy *Web:* mayway.com	Oakland	CA	94607	510-208-3113	
Quantum Inc 754 Washington St *Web:* www.quantumhealth.com	Eugene	OR	97401	541-345-5556	
Saladino's Inc 3325 W Figarden Dr PO Box 12266 *Web:* www.saladinos.com	Fresno	CA	93777	559-271-3700	271-3701

300-1 Baked Goods - Whol

				Phone	Fax
Fresh Start Bakeries 145 S State College Blvd Ste 200 *Web:* www.freshstartbakeries.com	Brea	CA	92821	714-256-8900	256-8916
Tri-State Baking Co 6800 S Washington St *Web:* afiama.com	Amarillo	TX	79118	806-373-6696	
Turano Baking Co 6501 Roosevelt Rd *Web:* www.turano.com	Berwyn	IL	60402	708-788-9220	788-3075
Wheat Montana Farms Inc 10778 US Hwy 287 *TF:* 800-535-2798 ■ *Web:* www.wheatmontana.com	Three Forks	MT	59752	406-285-3614	285-3749

300-2 Coffee & Tea - Whol

				Phone	Fax
Barrie House Coffee Company Inc Four Warehouse In *TF:* 800-876-2233 ■ *Web:* www.barriehouse.com	Elmsford	NY	10523	800-876-2233	
Becharas Bros Coffee Co Inc 14501 Hamilton Ave *TF:* 800-944-9675 ■ *Web:* www.becharas.com	Highland Park	MI	48203	313-869-4700	869-7940
Capricorn Coffees Inc 353 Tenth St *TF:* 800-541-0758 ■ *Web:* www.capricorncoffees.com	San Francisco	CA	94103	415-621-8500	621-9875
Coffee Bean International 9120 NE Alderwood Rd *TF:* 800-877-0474 ■ *Web:* www.coffeebeanintl.com	Portland	OR	97220	503-227-4490	225-9604
Coffee Masters Inc 7606 Industrial Ct *TF:* 800-334-6485 ■ *Web:* www.coffeemasters.com	Spring Grove	IL	60081	815-675-0088	675-3166
Red Diamond Inc 400 Park Ave *TF:* 800-292-4651 ■ *Web:* www.reddiamond.com	Moody	AL	35004	205-577-4000	
Royal Cup Coffee 160 Cleage Dr **Fax Area Code:* 205 ■ *TF Cust Svc:* 800-366-5836 ■ *Web:* www.royalcupcoffee.com	Birmingham	AL	35217	800-366-5836	271-6071*

300-3 Confectionery & Snack Foods - Whol

				Phone	Fax
AMCON Distributing Co 7405 Irvington Rd *NYSE:* DIT ■ *TF:* 888-201-5997 ■ *Web:* www.amcon.com	Omaha	NE	68122	402-331-3727	331-4834
Annabelle Candy Company Inc 27211 Industrial Blvd *Web:* annabellecandy.com/	Hayward	CA	94545	510-783-2900	785-7675
Brown & Haley PO Box 1596 *TF:* 800-426-8400 ■ *Web:* www.brown-haley.com	Tacoma	WA	98401	253-620-3085	274-0628
Burklund Distributors Inc 2500 N Main St Ste 3 *TF:* 800-322-2876 ■ *Web:* www.burklund.com	East Peoria	IL	61611	309-694-1900	694-6788
Continental Concession Supplies Inc 575 Jericho Turnpike Ste 300 *TF:* 800-516-0090 ■ *Web:* www.ccsicandy.com	Jericho	NY	11753	516-739-8777	739-8750
Diamond Bakery Co 756 Moowaa St *Web:* www.diamondbakery.com	Honolulu	HI	96817	808-847-3551	847-7482
Eby-Brown Co 280 W Shuman Blvd Ste 280 *TF:* 800-553-8249 ■ *Web:* www.eby-brown.com	Naperville	IL	60563	630-778-2800	778-2830
Edward A. Berg & Sons Inc (EAB) 75 W Century Rd *Web:* www.eaberg.com	Paramus	NJ	07652	201-845-8200	845-8201
Foreign Candy Company Inc One Foreign Candy Dr *TF:* 800-831-8541 ■ *Web:* www.foreigncandy.com	Hull	IA	51239	712-439-1496	439-3207
Frito-Lay North America 7701 Legacy Dr *TF:* 800-352-4477 ■ *Web:* www.fritolay.com	Plano	TX	75024	972-334-7000	334-2019
Hammons Products Co 105 Hammons Dr PO Box 140 **Fax Area Code:* 417 ■ *TF:* 888-429-6887 ■ *Web:* www.hammonsproducts.com	Stockton	MO	65785	888-429-6887	276-5187*
Harold Levinson Assoc (HLA) 21 Banfi Plz *TF:* 800-325-2512 ■ *Web:* www.hlacigars.com	Farmingdale	NY	11735	631-962-2400	962-9000
Hines Nut Co Inc 990 S St Paul St *TF:* 800-561-6374 ■ *Web:* www.hinesnut.com	Dallas	TX	75201	214-939-0253	
Keilson-Dayton Co 107 Commerce Pk Dr *TF:* 800-759-3174 ■ *Web:* keilsondayton.com	Dayton	OH	45404	937-236-1070	236-2124
Kennedy Wholesale Inc 16014 Adelante St *TF:* 877-292-2639 ■ *Web:* www.kennedywholesale.com	Irwindale	CA	91706	818-241-9977	241-3046
McDonald Wholesale Co 2350 W Broadway St *TF:* 877-722-5503 ■ *Web:* www.mcdonaldwhsl.com	Eugene	OR	97402	541-345-8421	345-7146
Old Dutch Foods Inc 2375 Terminal Rd *TF:* 800-989-2447 ■ *Web:* www.olddutchfoods.com	Roseville	MN	55113	651-633-8810	633-8894
Showtime Concession Supply Inc 200 SE 19th St *Web:* www.showplacemarket.com/showtimeconcessionsupply	Moore	OK	73160	405-895-9902	
Sultana Distribution Services Inc 600 Food Ctr Dr *TF:* 877-617-5500 ■ *Web:* www.sultanadist.com	Bronx	NY	10474	718-617-5500	617-5225
Superior Nut & Candy Company Inc 1111 W 40th St *Web:* www.superiornutandcandy.com	Chicago	IL	60609	773-254-7900	254-9171
Superior Nut Co Inc 225 Monsignor O'Brien Hwy *Web:* www.superiornut.com	Cambridge	MA	02141	617-876-3808	876-8225
Taste of Nature Inc 2828 Donald Douglas Loop N Ste A *Web:* www.candyasap.com	Santa Monica	CA	90405	310-396-4433	396-4432
Thayer Distribution Inc 333 Swedesboro Ave *Web:* www.thayerdist.com	Gibbstown	NJ	08027	856-687-0000	224-7129
Torn & Glasser Inc 1622 E Olympic Blvd PO Box 21823 *Web:* www.tornandglasser.com	Los Angeles	CA	90021	213-627-6496	688-0941
Trophy Nut Company Inc 320 N Second St *TF:* 800-729-6887 ■ *Web:* www.trophynut.com	Tipp City	OH	45371	937-667-8478	667-4656

300-4 Dairy Products - Whol

				Phone	Fax
Ambriola Company Inc Seven Patton Dr *TF:* 800-962-8224 ■ *Web:* www.ambriola.com	West Caldwell	NJ	07006	800-962-8224	
AMPI 315 N Broadway *TF:* 800-533-3580 ■ *Web:* www.ampi.com	New Ulm	MN	56073	507-354-8295	
Broughton Foods Co 1701 Green St *TF:* 800-283-2479 ■ *Web:* www.broughtonfoods.com	Marietta	OH	45750	740-373-4121	373-2861
Clofine Dairy Products Inc 1407 New Rd *TF:* 800-441-1001 ■ *Web:* www.clofinedairy.com	Linwood	NJ	08221	609-653-1000	653-0127
Clover-Stornetta Farms Inc PO Box 750369 *TF:* 800-237-3315 ■ *Web:* www.cloverstornetta.com	Petaluma	CA	94975	707-769-3235	778-9166
Cream-O-Land Dairy Inc 529 Cedar Ln PO Box 146 *TF:* 800-220-6455 ■ *Web:* www.creamoland.com	Florence	NJ	08518	609-499-3601	499-3896
Erie Foods International Inc 401 Seventh Ave PO Box 648 *TF:* 800-447-1887 ■ *Web:* www.eriefoods.com	Erie	IL	61250	309-659-2233	659-2822
Hautly Cheese Company Inc 251 Axminister Dr *Web:* www.hautly.com	Fenton	MO	63026	636-533-4400	533-4401

Phone Fax

Hillcrest Foods 2695 E 40th St .... Cleveland OH 44115 216-361-4625 361-0764
TF: 800-952-4344 ■ *Web:* www.hillcrestfoods.com

Lowville Producers Dairy Co-op
7396 Utica Blvd ....Lowville NY 13367 315-376-3921 376-3442
Web: www.gotgoodcheese.com

Luberski Inc 310 N Harbor Blvd Ste 205 .... Fullerton CA 92832 714-680-3447 680-3380
TF: 800-326-3220 ■ *Web:* www.hiddenvilla.com

Maryland & Virginia Milk Producers Co-op Assn Inc
1985 Isaac Newton Sq W ....Reston VA 20190 703-742-6800 742-7459
TF: 800-552-1976 ■ *Web:* www.mdvamilk.com

Masters Gallery Foods Inc
328 County Hwy PP PO Box 170 ....Plymouth WI 53073 920-893-8431
TF General: 800-236-8431 ■ *Web:* www.mastersgalleryfoods.com

Plains Dairy Products 300 N Taylor St ....Amarillo TX 79107 806-374-0385
TF: 800-365-5608 ■ *Web:* www.plainsdairy.com

Prairie Farms Dairy Inc
1100 N Broadway St .... Carlinville IL 62626 217-854-2547 854-6426
TF: 800-654-2547 ■ *Web:* www.prairiefarms.com

Purity Dairies Inc 360 Murfreesboro Rd .... Nashville TN 37210 615-244-1970 242-8547
Web: www.puritydairies.com

Queensboro Farm Products Inc
156-02 Liberty Ave Ste 1 ....Jamaica NY 11433 718-658-5000

Roberts Dairy Co 2901 Cuming St......................Omaha NE 68131 402-344-4321 346-0277
TF: 800-779-4321 ■ *Web:* hilanddairy.com

Rockview Dairies Inc 7011 Stewart & Gray Rd .... Downey CA 90241 562-927-5511 928-9866
TF: 800-423-2479 ■ *Web:* www.rockviewfarms.com

Schenkel's All-Star Dairy LLC
1019 Flax Mill Rd.............................. Huntington IN 46750 260-356-4225

Schneider's Dairy Inc 726 Frank St................ Pittsburgh PA 15227 412-881-3525 881-7722
Web: schneidersdairy.com

Simco Sales Service of Pennsylvania Inc
101 Commerce Dr .... Moorestown NJ 08057 856-813-2300
Web: www.jackjillicecream.com

Sunshine Dairy Foods Inc 801 NE 21st Ave............Portland OR 97232 503-234-7526 233-9441
TF: 800-544-0554 ■ *Web:* www.sunshinedairyfoods.com

Sure Winner Foods Inc Two Lehner Rd.................. Saco ME 04072 207-282-1258 286-1410
TF: 800-640-6447 ■ *Web:* www.swfoods.com

Umpqua Dairy Products Co
333 SE Sykes Ave PO Box 1306....................Roseburg OR 97470 541-672-2638 673-0256
TF: 888-672-6455 ■ *Web:* www.umpquadairy.com

300-5 Fish & Seafood - Whol

Phone Fax

Arrowac Fisheries Inc
4039 21st Ave W
Ste 200 Fisherman's Commerce Bldg..................Seattle WA 98199 206-282-5655 282-9329
Web: www.arrowac-merco.com

Beaver Street Fisheries Inc
1741 W Beaver St............................Jacksonville FL 32209 904-354-8533
TF: 800-874-6426 ■ *Web:* beaverstreetfisheries.com

Blount Seafood Corp 630 Currant Rd ....Fall River MA 02720 774-888-1300 888-1399
TF Hotline: 800-274-2526 ■ *Web:* www.blountseafood.com

Bon Secour Fisheries Inc
17449 County Rd 49 S.........................Bon Secour AL 36511 251-949-7411 949-6478
TF: 800-633-6854 ■ *Web:* www.bonsecourfisheries.com

California Shellfish Co
505 Beach St Ste 200......................... San Francisco CA 94133 415-923-7400

Cassidy Fine Foods 3657 Old Getwell Rd............Memphis TN 38118 901-542-5100 542-5150

ConAgra Foods Foodservice Co 1 ConAgra Dr ....Omaha NE 68102 800-357-6543
Web: www.conagrafoodservice.com

Del Mar Seafoods Inc 331 Ford St .... Watsonville CA 95076 831-763-3000 763-2444
Web: www.delmarseafoods.com

Golden-Tech International Inc
2461 152nd Ave NE ....Redmond WA 98052 425-869-1461 867-1368
TF: 800-311-8090 ■ *Web:* www.gtiinc.com

Inland Seafood Corp 1651 Montreal Cir................ Tucker GA 30084 404-350-5850 350-5871
TF: 800-883-3474 ■ *Web:* www.inlandseafood.com

Interamerican Trading & Products Corp
1800 Purdy Ave .... Miami Beach FL 33139 305-885-9666

Ipswich Shellfish Co Inc 8 Hayward St .... Ipswich MA 01938 978-356-6800 356-9235
TF: 800-477-9424 ■ *Web:* www.ipswichshellfish.com

LD Amory & Co Inc 101 S King St .... Hampton VA 23669 757-722-1915 723-1184
TF: 800-552-9963 ■ *Web:* virginiaseafood.org

Maine Lobster Direct 48 Union Wharf ....Portland ME 04101 800-556-2783 772-0169*
**Fax Area Code:* 207 ■ *TF:* 800-556-2783 ■ *Web:* www.mainelobsterdirect.com

Mazzetta Co 1990 St Johns Ave................. Highland Park IL 60035 847-433-1150 433-8973
Web: www.mazzetta.com

Metropolitan Poultry & Seafood Co
1920 Stanford Ct .... Landover MD 20785 301-772-0060 772-1013
TF: 800-522-0060 ■ *Web:* www.metropoultry.com

Morey's Seafood International LLC
1218 Hwy 10 S.......................................Motley MN 56466 218-352-6345
TF: 800-808-3474 ■ *Web:* www.moreys.com

Morley Sales Company Inc 119 N Second St .... Geneva IL 60134 630-845-8750 845-8749
Web: www.morleysales.com

Oceanpro Industries Ltd
1900 Fenwick St NE ....Washington DC 20002 202-529-3003
Web: www.profish.com

Pacific Giant Inc 4625 District Blvd ....Vernon CA 90058 323-587-5000 587-5050
Web: www.pacificgiant.com

Premier Pacific Seafoods Inc
111 W Harrison St ....Seattle WA 98119 206-286-8584 286-8810
Web: prempac.com

Quirch Foods Co 7600 NW 82nd Pl.................... Miami FL 33166 305-691-3535 593-0272
TF: 800-458-5252 ■ *Web:* www.quirchfoods.com

Red Chamber Co 1912 E Vernon Ave ....Vernon CA 90058 323-234-9000 231-8888
Web: www.redchamber.com

Sager's Seafood Plus Inc
4802 Bridal Wreath Dr .... Richmond TX 77406 281-342-8833 583-7674*
**Fax Area Code:* 713 ■ *Web:* sagersseafoodplus.com

Phone Fax

Slade Gorton Company Inc 225 Southampton St.........Boston MA 02118 617-442-5800 442-9090
TF: 800-225-1573 ■ *Web:* www.sladegorton.com

Southern Foods Inc
3500 Old Battleground Rd .... Greensboro NC 27410 336-545-3800 545-5281
Web: www.southernfoods.com

Stavis Seafoods Inc 212 Northern Ave Ste 305...........Boston MA 02210 617-482-6349 482-1340
TF: 800-390-5103 ■ *Web:* www.stavis.com

Tri Marine Fish Co 220 Cannery St .... San Pedro CA 90731 310-547-1144 547-1166
Web: www.trimarinegroup.com

Troyer Foods Inc 17141 State Rd 4 .... Goshen IN 46528 574-533-0302 533-3851
TF: 800-876-9377 ■ *Web:* www.troyers.com

Val's Distributing Co
6124 E 30th St N PO Box 581583....................... Tulsa OK 74115 918-835-9987 835-3808

300-6 Frozen Foods (Packaged) - Whol

Phone Fax

Advantage Sales & Marketing
18100 Von Karman Ave Ste 1000.......................Irvine CA 92612 949-797-2900 797-9112
Web: www.asmnet.com

Baja Foods LLC 636 W Root St......................Chicago IL 60609 773-376-9030 376-9245
Web: www.bajafoodsllc.com

Cedar Farms 2100 Hornig Rd.................... Philadelphia PA 19116 215-934-7100 934-5851
Web: www.cedarfarms.com

ConAgra Foods Foodservice Co 1 ConAgra Dr ....Omaha NE 68102 800-357-6543
Web: www.conagrafoodservice.com

Dot Foods Inc One Dot Way PO Box 192 .... Mount Sterling IL 62353 217-773-4411 773-3321
TF: 800-366-3687 ■ *Web:* www.dotfoods.com

Happy & Healthy Products Inc
1600 S Dixie Hwy Ste 200 .... Boca Raton FL 33432 561-367-0739 368-5267
Web: www.fruitfull.com

Paris Foods Corp 3965 Ocean Gateway PO Box 121....... Trappe MD 21673 410-200-9595
Web: www.parisfoods.com

Quality Frozen Foods Inc 1663 62nd St............. Brooklyn NY 11204 718-256-9100 234-3755
Web: www.qualityfrozenfoods.com

Sun Belt Food Company Inc
4755 Technology Way Ste 209 .... Boca Raton FL 33431 561-995-9100 997-5664
Web: www.sunbeltfoods.com

Trudeau Distributing Co
25 Cliff Rd W Ste 115........................... Burnsville MN 55337 952-882-8295 882-4703
Web: www.trudeaudistributing.com

Wilcox Frozen Foods Inc
2200 Oakdale Ave........................... San Francisco CA 94124 415-282-4116 282-3044

300-7 Fruits & Vegetables - Fresh - Whol

Phone Fax

Albert's Organics Inc 3268 E Vernon Ave...............Vernon CA 90058 800-899-5944
TF: 800-899-5944 ■ *Web:* www.albertsorganics.com

Alpine Fresh Inc 9300 NW 58th St Ste 201............. Miami FL 33178 305-594-9117 594-8506
TF: 800-292-8777 ■ *Web:* www.alpinefresh.com

Anthony Marano Company Inc
3000 S Ashland Ave ....Chicago IL 60608 773-321-7500 321-7800
Web: www.anthonymarano.com

Banacol Marketing Corp
355 Alhambra Cir Ste 1510 .... Coral Gables FL 33134 305-441-9036 446-4291
TF: 877-324-7619 ■ *Web:* www.banacol.com

Belair Produce Company Inc 7226 Pkwy Dr...........Hanover MD 21076 410-782-8000 782-8009
TF: 888-782-8008 ■ *Web:* www.belairproduce.com

Bernard Zell Anshe Emet Day School
3751 N Broadway St...............................Chicago IL 60613 773-281-1858 281-4709
Web: www.bzaeds.org

Bix Produce Co 1415 L'Orient St................. Saint Paul MN 55117 651-487-8000 487-1314
TF: 800-642-9514 ■ *Web:* www.bixproduce.com

Bland Farms Inc 1126 Raymond Bland Rd............ Glennville GA 30427 912-654-1330 654-3532
Web: www.blandfarms.com

Bouten Construction Co
627 N Napa St PO Box 3507........................ Spokane WA 99220 509-535-3531 535-6047
Web: www.boutenconstruction.com

Brothers Produce Inc 3173 Produce Row ....Houston TX 77023 713-924-4196 921-3060
Web: www.brothersproduce.com

Calavo Growers Inc 1141-A Cummings Rd.......... Santa Paula CA 93060 805-525-1245 921-3287
NASDAQ: CVGW ■ *TF:* 800-654-8758 ■ *Web:* www.calavo.com

Caro Foods Inc 2324 Bayou Blue Rd ....Houma LA 70364 985-872-1483 876-0825
TF: 800-395-2276 ■ *Web:* www.performancefoodservice.com/Caro

Community Suffolk Inc 304 Second St .... Everett MA 02149 617-389-5200 389-6680
TF: 800-225-4470 ■ *Web:* community-suffolk.com

Consumers Produce Co One 21st St .... Pittsburgh PA 15222 412-281-0722 281-6541
Web: www.consumersproduce.com

Costa Fruit & Produce
18 Bunker Hill Industrial Pk PO Box 290754 ....Boston MA 02129 617-241-8007 241-8007
TF: 800-322-1374 ■ *Web:* www.freshideas.com

Country Fresh Mushroom Co
289 Chambers Rd P.O. Box 490 .... Toughkenamon PA 19374 610-268-3043 268-0479
Web: www.countryfreshmushrooms.com

Crosset Company Inc 10295 Toebben Dr......... Independence KY 41051 859-283-5830 817-7634
TF: 800-347-4902 ■ *Web:* crosset.com

D'Arrigo Bros Company of New York Inc
315 Hunts Pt Terminal Market...........................Bronx NY 10474 718-991-5900 960-0544
Web: www.darrigony.com

Del Monte Fresh Produce Co
241 Sevilla Ave............................... Coral Gables FL 33134 305-520-8400 567-0320
TF Cust Svc: 800-950-3683 ■ *Web:* www.freshdelmonte.com

DiMare Bros/New England Farms Packing Co
84 New England Produce Ctr ....Chelsea MA 02150 617-889-3800
Web: dimarefresh.com

DiMare Fresh Inc 1049 Ave H E.................... Arlington TX 76011 817-385-3000 385-3015
TF General: 800-322-2184 ■ *Web:* www.dimarefresh.com

Dole Food Company Hawaii 802 Mapunapuna St ...... Honolulu HI 96819 808-861-8015 861-8020
TF: 800-697-9100 ■ *Web:* www.dolefruithawaii.com

Phone Fax

Egan Bernard & Co 1900 Old Dixie Hwy . . . . Fort Pierce FL 34946 800-327-6676 465-1181*
*Fax Area Code: 772 ■ TF: 800-327-6676 ■ Web: www.dneworld.com

Federal Fruit & Produce Co 1890 E 58th Ave . . . . Denver CO 80216 303-292-1303 292-1303
Web: www.fedfruit.com

FreshPoint Inc 1390 Enclave Pkwy . . . . Houston TX 77077 281-899-4242 899-4231
Web: www.freshpoint.com

Freshway Foods 601 Stolle Ave . . . . Sidney OH 45365 937-498-4664 498-4124
Web: www.freshwayfoods.com

Frieda's Inc 4465 Corporate Ctr Dr . . . . Los Alamitos CA 90720 714-826-6100 816-0273*
*Fax: Sales ■ TF: 800-241-1771 ■ Web: www.friedas.com

General Produce Co 1330 N 'B' St . . . . Sacramento CA 95814 916-441-6431 441-2483
TF: 800-366-4991 ■ Web: www.generalproduce.com

Giumarra Bros Fruit Company Inc
1601 E Olympic Blvd Bldg 400 Ste 408 . . . . Los Angeles CA 90021 213-627-2900 628-4878
Web: www.giumarra.com

Gold Harbor Commodities Inc
9750 Third Ave NE . . . . Seattle WA 98115 206-527-3494
Web: www.goldharbor.com

Graves Menu Maker Foods Inc
913 Big Horn Dr . . . . Jefferson City MO 65109 573-893-3000 893-2172
Web: www.menumakerfoods.com

H Smith Packing Corp 99 Ft Fairfield Rd . . . . Presque Isle ME 04769 207-764-4540 764-2816
Web: www.smithsfarm.com

Hearn Kirkwood 7251 Standard Dr . . . . Hanover MD 21076 410-712-6000 712-0020
TF General: 800-777-9489 ■ Web: www.hearnkirkwood.com

Heeren Bros Inc 1060 Hall St SW . . . . Grand Rapids MI 49503 616-452-8641 243-7070
TF: 800-733-5466 ■ Web: www.heerenbros.com

Hollar & Greene Produce Co Inc
230 Cabbage Rd PO Box 3500 . . . . Boone NC 28607 828-264-2177 264-4413
TF: 800-222-1077 ■ Web: www.hollarandgreene.com

Indianapolis Fruit Company Inc
4501 Massachusetts Ave . . . . Indianapolis IN 46218 317-546-2425 543-0521
TF: 800-377-2425 ■ Web: www.indyfruit.com

Kegel's Produce Inc 2851 Old Tree Dr . . . . Lancaster PA 17603 717-392-6612 392-6482
TF: 800-535-3435 ■ Web: kegels.com

Melissa's/World Variety Produce Inc
5325 S Soto St . . . . Vernon CA 90058 800-588-0151 588-1768*
*Fax Area Code: 323 ■ TF: 800-588-0151 ■ Web: www.melissas.com

Mission Produce Inc 2500 Vineyard Ave Ste 300 . . . . Oxnard CA 93036 805-981-3650 981-3660
TF: 800-549-3420 ■ Web: www.missionpro.com

Moore Food Distributors Co 9910 Page Ave . . . . Saint Louis MO 63132 314-426-1300 426-6690
TF: 800-467-7878 ■ Web: www.moorefooddist.com

Muir Enterprises Inc
3575 West 900 South PO Box 26775 . . . . Salt Lake City UT 84104 801-363-7695 322-1640*
*Fax: Sales ■ TF: 877-268-2002 ■ Web: www.coppercanyonfarms.com

North Bay Produce Inc PO Box 988 . . . . Traverse City MI 49685 800-678-1941 946-1902*
*Fax Area Code: 231 ■ TF: 800-678-1941 ■ Web: www.northbayproduce.com

Oneonta Trading Corp 1 Oneonta Way . . . . Wenatchee WA 98801 509-663-2191 663-6333
TF: 800-688-2191 ■ Web: www.oneonta.com

Organic Valley Family of Farms
One Organic Way . . . . LaFarge WI 54639 888-444-6455 625-3025*
*Fax Area Code: 608 ■ TF: 888-444-6455 ■ Web: www.organicvalley.coop

Pacific Coast Fruit Co
201 NE Second Ave Ste 100 . . . . Portland OR 97232 503-234-6411 963-5435
TF: 800-423-4945 ■ Web: www.pcfruit.com

Pandol Bros Inc 401 Rd 192 . . . . Delano CA 93215 661-725-3755 725-4741
Web: www.pandol.com

Paramount Export Co 175 Filbert St Ste 201 . . . . Oakland CA 94607 510-839-0150 839-1002
Web: www.paramountexport.net

Peak of the Market 1200 King Edward St . . . . Winnipeg MB R3H0R5 204-632-7325 774-7325
TF: 888-289-7325 ■ Web: www.peakmarket.com

Peirone Produce Co 9818 W Hallett Rd . . . . Spokane WA 99224 509-838-3515 838-3916
Web: urmstores.com

Procacci Bros Sales Corp
3333 S Front St . . . . Philadelphia PA 19148 215-463-8000 467-1144
Web: www.procaccibrothers.com

Produce Source Partners 13167 Telcourt Rd . . . . Ashland VA 23005 804-262-8300 264-2313
TF: 800-344-4728 ■ Web: www.producesourcepartners.com

Progressive Produce Co 5790 Peachtree St . . . . Los Angeles CA 90040 323-890-8100 890-8113
TF: 800-900-0757 ■ Web: www.progressiveproduce.com

ProPacificfresh 70 Pepsi Way PO Box 1069 . . . . Durham CA 95938 530-893-0596 893-5973
TF: 888-232-0908 ■ Web: www.propacificfresh.com

Sambazon Inc 1160 Calle Cordillera . . . . San Clemente CA 92673 949-498-8618 498-8619
TF: 877-726-2296 ■ Web: www.sambazon.com

Sandridge Food Corp (SFC) 133 Commerce Dr . . . . Medina OH 44256 330-725-2348 722-3998
TF: 800-672-2523 ■ Web: www.sandridge.com

Simonian Fruit Co 511 N Seventh St PO Box 340 . . . . Fowler CA 93625 559-834-5921 834-2363
Web: www.simonianfruit.com

Strobe Celery & Vegetable Co
2404 S Wolcott Ave . . . . Chicago IL 60608 773-446-4000 226-7644*
*Fax Area Code: 312 ■ Web: www.strube.com

Sunkist Growers Inc 14130 Riverside Dr . . . . Sherman Oaks CA 91423 818-986-4800 379-7511*
*Fax: PR ■ Web: www.sunkist.com

Sunnyridge Farm Inc
1900 Fifth St NW PO Box 3036 . . . . Winter Haven FL 33881 863-294-8856 595-4095
Web: www.sunnyridge.com

Superior Foods Inc 275 Westgate Dr . . . . Watsonville CA 95076 831-728-3691 722-0926
Web: www.superiorfoods.com

Taylor Farms Inc PO Box 1649 . . . . Salinas CA 93902 831-676-9765 676-9751
TF: 866-675-6120 ■ Web: www.taylorfarms.com

W. R. Vernon Produce Co PO Box 4054 . . . . Winston Salem NC 27101 336-725-9741 761-1841
TF: 800-222-6406 ■ Web: www.vernonproduce.com

300-8 Groceries - General Line

Phone Fax

ACE Bakery Ltd One Hafis Rd . . . . Toronto ON M6M2V6 416-241-3600
Web: www.acebakery.com

Acme Food Sales Inc 5940 1st Ave S . . . . Seattle WA 98108 206-762-5150
TF: 800-777-2263 ■ Web: www.acmefood.com

Active Organics Inc 1097 Yates St . . . . Lewisville TX 75057 972-221-7500
TF: 800-541-1478 ■ Web: www.activeorganics.com

Adams Extract & Spice LLC 3217 Johnston Rd . . . . Gonzales TX 78629 830-672-1850 672-8100
Web: www.adamsextract.com

ADM Agri-Industries Co 5550 Maplewood Dr . . . . Windsor ON N9C0B9 519-972-8100
Web: adm.com

Advantage Sales & Marketing
18100 Von Karman Ave Ste 1000 . . . . Irvine CA 92612 949-797-2900 797-9112
Web: www.asmnet.com

Affiliated Foods Inc 1401 W Farmers Ave . . . . Amarillo TX 79118 806-372-3851
TF: 800-234-3661 ■ Web: www.afiama.com

Affiliated Foods Midwest 1301 W Omaha Ave . . . . Norfolk NE 68701 402-371-0555 371-1884
Web: www.afmidwest.com

AJC International 5188 Roswell Rd NW . . . . Atlanta GA 30342 404-252-6750 252-9340
Web: www.ajcfood.com

Aladdin Bakers Inc 240 25th St . . . . Brooklyn NY 11232 718-499-1818
Web: www.aladdinbakersinc.com

Albert Guarnieri Co 1133 E Market St . . . . Warren OH 44483 330-394-5636 394-4982
TF: 800-686-2639 ■ Web: www.albertguarnieri.com

Albertsons LLC 250 E Parkcenter . . . . Boise ID 83706 208-395-6200
Web: www.albertsons.com

Ale-8-one Bottling Co 25 Carol Rd . . . . Winchester KY 40391 859-744-3484
Web: ale8one.com

Aliments Novali Foods Inc
3080 Rue St-Prosper . . . . St Hyacinthe QC J2S2A4 450-773-9944

Allann Bros Coffee Co 1852 Fescue St SE . . . . Albany OR 97322 541-812-8000
Web: allannbroscoffee.com

Allen Flavors Inc 23 Progress St . . . . Edison NJ 08820 908-561-5995
Web: www.allenflavors.com

Aloft Charlotte Uptown at the EpiCentre
210 E Trade St . . . . Charlotte NC 28202 704-333-1999
Web: www.aloftcharlotteuptown.com

AMCON Distributing Co 7405 Irvington Rd . . . . Omaha NE 68122 402-331-3727 331-4834
NYSE: DIT ■ TF: 888-201-5997 ■ Web: www.amcon.com

American Seaway Foods Inc
5300 Richmond Rd . . . . Bedford Heights OH 44146 216-292-7000 968-1618*
*Fax Area Code: 412

Amster-Kirtz Co 2830 Cleveland Ave NW . . . . Canton OH 44709 330-535-6021
TF: 800-257-9338 ■ Web: www.amsterkirtz.com

Anderson-DuBose Co 5300 Tod Ave SW . . . . Lordstown OH 44481 440-248-8800 824-2256*
*Fax Area Code: 330 ■ TF: 800-248-1080 ■ Web: anderson-dubose.com

Animal Supply Company LLC
32001 32nd Ave S Ste 420 . . . . Federal Way WA 98001 253-237-0400
TF: 800-323-2963 ■ Web: www.animalsupplycompany.com

Apetito Canada Ltd 12 Indell Ln . . . . Brampton ON L6T3Y3 905-799-1022
Web: apetito.ca

Arcobasso Foods Inc 8850 Pershall Rd . . . . Hazelwood MO 63042 314-381-8083
Web: www.arcobasso.com

Armelle Supermarket
140 W Boynton Beach Blvd . . . . Boynton Beach FL 33435 561-739-6543

Asiana Cuisine Enterprises Inc
1447 W 178th St . . . . Gardena CA 90248 310-327-2233
Web: acesushi.com

Associated Food Stores Inc
1850 West 2100 South . . . . Salt Lake City UT 84119 801-973-4400 978-8551
TF Cust Svc: 888-574-7100 ■ Web: www.afstores.com

Associated Grocers Inc 8600 Anselmo Ln . . . . Baton Rouge LA 70810 225-444-1000 763-6194
TF: 800-637-2021 ■ Web: www.agbr.com

Associated Grocers of Florida Inc
1141 SW 12th Ave . . . . Pompano Beach FL 33069 954-876-3000 876-3003
Web: www.agfla.com

Associated Grocers of New England Inc
11 Co-op Way . . . . Pembroke NH 03275 603-223-6710 223-5672
TF: 800-242-2248 ■ Web: www.agne.com

Associated Grocers of the South
3600 Vanderbilt Rd . . . . Birmingham AL 35217 205-841-6781 808-4920
TF: 800-695-6051 ■ Web: www.agsouth.com

Associated Wholesale Grocers Inc
5000 Kansas Ave . . . . Kansas City KS 66106 913-288-1000 288-1587
Web: www.awginc.com

Associated Wholesalers Inc PO Box 67 . . . . Robesonia PA 19551 610-693-3161 693-3171*
*Fax: Orders ■ TF: 800-927-7771 ■ Web: www.awiweb.com

Astra Foods Inc 6430 Market St . . . . Upper Darby PA 19082 610-352-4400
Web: www.astrafoods.com

Atalanta Corp 1 Atalanta Plaza . . . . Elizabeth NJ 07206 908-351-8000 351-1693
Web: www.atalanta1.com

Au Ptit Marche De Notre Dame
552 Rue Notre Dame . . . . Bon-Conseil QC J0C1A0 819-336-2686

Bakery Barn Inc 111 Terence Dr . . . . Pittsburgh PA 15236 412-655-1113
Web: www.bakery-barn.com

Barbara Timken Ccna 304 Timberwood Cir . . . . Lafayette LA 70508 337-989-2653

Baron Spices Inc 1440 Kentucky Ave . . . . Saint Louis MO 63110 314-535-9020
Web: www.baronspices.com

Bartush-Schnitzius Foods Co
1137 N Kealy St . . . . Lewisville TX 75057 972-219-1270
Web: www.bartushfoods.com

Bassham Wholesale Egg Company Inc
5409 Hemphill St . . . . Fort Worth TX 76115 817-921-1600
Web: www.basshamfoods.com

Bay Bread LLC 2325 Pine St . . . . San Francisco CA 94115 415-440-0356
Web: laboulangebakery.com

Berry Coffee Co 14825 Martin Dr . . . . Eden Prairie MN 55344 952-937-8697
Web: www.berrycoffee.com

Bill & Ralphs Inc 118 B & R Dr . . . . Sarepta LA 71071 318-539-2071

Bill's Distributing Ltd 5900 Packer Dr Ne . . . . Menomonie WI 54751 715-235-5820

Boston Organics 50 Terminal St . . . . Charlestown MA 02129 617-242-1700
Web: bostonorganics.com

Bozzuto's Inc 275 School House Rd . . . . Cheshire CT 06410 203-272-3511 250-2880*
OTC: BOZZ ■ *Fax: Sales ■ Web: www.bozzutos.com

Bragg Live Food Products Inc PO Box 7 . . . . Santa Barbara CA 93102 805-968-1020
Web: bragg.com

Company	City	State	ZIP	Phone	Fax
Brenham Wholesale Grocery Co 602 W First St *TF:* 800-392-4869 ■ *Web:* www.bwgroc.com	Brenham	TX	77833	979-836-7925	830-0346
Bridge City Food Mktg Inc 110 SE Second Ave.	Portland	OR	97214	503-239-8024	
Brim's Snack Foods 3045 Bartlett Corporate Dr Ste 101 *Web:* www.brimsnacks.com	Bartlett	TN	38133	901-377-9016	
Brownie Baker, The 4870 W Jacquelyn Ave *Web:* www.browniebaker.com	Fresno	CA	93722	559-277-7070	
Browns Corner Short Stop 5550 Auburn Way S. *Web:* 76.com	Auburn	WA	98092	253-833-7185	
Bruceton Farm Service Inc 1768 Mileground Rd. *Web:* www.bfscompanies.com	Morgantown	WV	26505	304-291-6980	
Bryant Convenience Inc 510 Bryant St	Denver	CO	80204	303-534-1379	
Bud's Best Cookies Inc 2070 Pkwy Office Cir *Web:* www.budsbestcookies.com	Hoover	AL	35244	205-987-4840	
Buona Vita Inc One S Industrial Blvd. *Web:* www.buonavitainc.com	Bridgeton	NJ	08302	856-453-7972	
C & S Wholesale Grocers Inc 47 Old Ferry Rd PO Box 821 *Web:* www.cswg.com	Brattleboro	VT	05301	802-464-6333	257-6613
Cambrooke Foods Inc Four Copeland Dr. *TF:* 866-456-9776 ■ *Web:* www.cambrookefoods.com	Ayer	MA	01432	508-782-2300	
Camp Olympia 723 Olympia Dr. *TF:* 800-735-6190 ■ *Web:* www.campolympia.com	Trinity	TX	75862	936-594-2541	594-8143
Canton Food Co 750 S Alameda St *Web:* www.cantonfoodco.com	Los Angeles	CA	90021	213-688-7707	
Canyon Specialty Foods Inc 11035 Switzer Ave	Dallas	TX	75238	214-352-1771	
Captain Kens Foods Inc 344 Robert St S. *Web:* www.captainkens.com	Saint Paul	MN	55107	651-298-0071	
Carlie C's IGA Inc 10 Carlie C'S Dr *Web:* www.carliecs.com	Dunn	NC	28334	910-892-4124	
Carnicerias Jimenez 4204 W N Ave. *Web:* www.carniceriasjimenez.com	Chicago	IL	60639	773-486-5805	
Carrington Foods Company Inc 200 Jacintoport Blvd # D *Web:* www.carringtonfoods.com	Saraland	AL	36571	251-675-9700	
Caruthers Raisin Packing Company Inc 12797 S Elm Ave	Caruthers	CA	93609	559-864-9448	
Cash-Wa Distributing Co 401 W Fourth St *TF:* 800-652-0010 ■ *Web:* www.cashwa.com	Kearney	NE	68845	308-237-3151	234-6018
Catania-Spagna Corp One Nemco Way. *Web:* www.cataniausa.com	Ayer	MA	01432	978-772-7900	
CB Ragland Co 2720 Eugenia Ave. **Fax:* Hum Res ■ *TF:* 866-770-5263 ■ *Web:* www.cbragland.com	Nashville	TN	37211	615-254-2841	254-2842*
CD Hartnett Co 302 N Main St *Web:* esite.cd-hartnett.com	Weatherford	TX	76086	817-594-3813	594-9714
Central Grocers Co-op Inc 2600 W Haven Ave **Fax Area Code:* 847 ■ *Web:* www.central-grocers.com	Joliet	IL	60433	815-553-8800	288-8710*
Chef's Requested Foods Inc 2600 Exchange Ave. *Web:* www.chefsrequested.com	Oklahoma City	OK	73108	405-239-2610	
Ciranda Inc 221 Vine St *Web:* www.ciranda.com	Hudson	WI	54016	715-386-1737	
Citarella 2135 Broadway. *Web:* www.citarella.com	New York	NY	10023	212-874-0383	
Clean Foods Inc 760 E Santa Maria St. *Web:* cafealtura.com	Santa Paula	CA	93060	805-933-3027	
Coastal Foods Inc 14212 Interdr W. *Web:* coastalfoodsinc.net	Houston	TX	77032	281-987-8985	987-8988
Coastal Pacific Food Distributors Inc (CPFD) 1015 Performance Dr **Fax:* Cust Svc ■ *TF:* 800-500-2611 ■ *Web:* www.cpfd.com	Stockton	CA	95206	209-983-2454	983-8009*
Convenience Retailers LLC 80980 Us Hwy 111	Indio	CA	92201	760-347-2900	
Core-Mark International 395 Oyster Pt Blvd Ste 415 *TF:* 800-622-1713 ■ *Web:* www.coremark.com	South San Francisco	CA	94080	650-589-9445	
County Beverage Company Inc 1290 SE Hamblen Rd *Web:* www.countybev.com	Lee'S Summit	MO	64081	816-525-4550	
Cracker Box, The 6682 Hwy 7	Bismarck	AR	71929	501-865-2249	
Create a Pack Foods Inc W1344 Industrial Dr. *Web:* create-a-pack.com	Ixonia	WI	53066	262-567-6069	
Creme Curls Bakery Inc 5292 Lawndale Ave *Web:* www.cremecurls.com	Hudsonville	MI	49426	616-669-2468	
Dallo Enterprises 5075 Federal Blvd *Web:* www.harvestranchmarkets.com	San Diego	CA	92102	619-527-3385	
Dara's Fast Lane Store 1709 Ft Riley Blvd *Web:* darascornermarket.com	Manhattan	KS	66502	785-537-2150	
Deb-El Food Products LLC 2 Papetti Plaza *TF:* 800-421-0330 ■ *Web:* www.debelfoods.com	Elizabeth	NJ	07206	908-351-0330	
Devault Packing Company Inc One Devault Ln *Web:* www.devaultfoods.com	Devault	PA	19432	610-644-2536	
DiCarlo Distributors Inc 1630 N Ocean Ave *TF:* 800-342-2756 ■ *Web:* www.dicarlofood.com	Holtsville	NY	11742	631-758-6000	758-6096
Dinovite Inc 101 Miller Dr *Web:* www.dinovite.com	Crittenden	KY	41030	859-428-1000	
Dipasa USA Inc 6600 Fm 802 Ste B *Web:* dipasausa.com	Brownsville	TX	78526	956-831-4072	831-5893
Dismex Food Inc 12255 SW 133rd Ct *Web:* www.dismexfood.com	Miami	FL	33186	305-238-6146	238-4032
Divvies LLC 700 Oakridge Common *Web:* www.divvies.com	South Salem	NY	10590	914-533-0333	
Dolce Europa 7520 Fullerton Rd.	Springfield	VA	22153	703-451-9501	
Doublebees 111 Bill Foster Memorial Hwy *Web:* www.doublebees.com	Cabot	AR	72023	501-605-8989	
Dutch Maid Bakery Inc 50 Park St. *Web:* www.dutchmaidbakery.com	Dorchester	MA	02122	617-265-5417	
Dutch Valley Bulk Food Distributors Inc 7615 Lancaster Ave. *TF:* 800-733-4191 ■ *Web:* www.dutchvalleyfoods.com	Myerstown	PA	17067	717-933-4191	933-5466
E. G. Ayers Distributing Inc 5819 S Broadway St *Web:* www.ayersdistributing.com	Eureka	CA	95503	707-445-2077	445-5719
Eagle Beverage Corp 1043 County Rt 25 *Web:* www.eaglebev.com	Oswego	NY	13126	315-343-5221	
Eastland Food Corp 8305 Stayton Dr *Web:* www.eastlandfood.com	Jessup	MD	20794	301-621-8140	
El Rancho Supermercado 22291 Redwood Rd	Castro Valley	CA	94546	510-728-1945	
El Tapatio Markets Inc 13635 Fwy Dr *Web:* www.eltapatiomarkets.com	Santa Fe Springs	CA	90670	562-293-4200	
Ellwood Thompson 10 S Thompson St *Web:* www.ellwoodthompsons.com	Richmond	VA	23221	804-359-7525	
Empire Food Brokers of Ohio Inc 11243 Cornell Pk Dr. *Web:* www.empirefoods.com	Cincinnati	OH	45242	513-793-6241	
Ettline Foods Corp 525 N State St. *Web:* www.ettline.com	York	PA	17403	717-848-1564	
Europa Market Company Inc, The 8100 Water St. *Web:* www.europa-market.com	Saint Louis	MO	63111	314-631-7288	
F Mcconnell & Sons Inc 11102 Lincoln Hwy E. *TF:* 800-552-0835 ■ *Web:* www.fmcconnell.com/	New Haven	IN	46774	260-493-6607	749-6116
Farm Stores Corp 16777 Old Cutler Rd *Web:* www.farmstores.com	Palmetto Bay	FL	33157	305-677-0645	
Farner-Bocken Co 1751 US Hwy 30 E PO Box 368 *TF:* 800-274-8692 ■ *Web:* farner-bocken.com	Carroll	IA	51401	712-792-3503	792-3503
Feesers Inc 5561 Grayson Rd *TF:* 800-326-2828 ■ *Web:* www.feesers.com	Harrisburg	PA	17111	717-564-4636	558-7445
Felbro Food Products Inc 5700 W Adams Blvd *Web:* www.employeepraise.com	Los Angeles	CA	90016	323-936-5266	
Field Trip Factory 2211 N Elston Ave Ste 304 *Web:* www.fieldtripfactory.com	Chicago	IL	60614	773-577-8800	
Fill in Foods 10554 Scott Hwy	Helenwood	TN	37755	423-663-2749	
Fiorucci Foods Inc 1800 Ruffin Mill Rd *Web:* www.fioruccifoods.com	Colonial Heights	VA	23834	804-520-7775	
Fisher Foods Mktg Inc 5215 Fulton Dr NW *Web:* www.fishersfoods.com	Canton	OH	44718	330-497-3000	
Flash Foods Inc 215 Pendleton St. *Web:* www.flashfoods.com	Waycross	GA	31501	912-285-4011	
Flavor Dynamics Inc 640 Montrose Ave. *TF:* 888-271-8424 ■ *Web:* www.flavordynamics.com	South Plainfield	NJ	07080	908-822-8855	
Flavorchem Corp 1525 Brook Dr *Web:* www.flavorchem.com	Downers Grove	IL	60515	630-932-8100	
Flavour Tech International LLC 66 Industrial Ave.	Little Ferry	NJ	07643	201-440-3281	
Food 4 Less 8014 Lower Sacramento Rd Ste I *Web:* food-4-less.com	Stockton	CA	95210	209-956-8594	
Food Services of America Inc 16100 N 71st St Ste 400. *TF:* 800-528-9346 ■ *Web:* www.fsafood.com	Scottsdale	AZ	85254	480-927-4000	927-4299
Franklin Supply Inc 75 Lee St. *Web:* franklinsupplyinc.com	Franklin	LA	70538	337-828-3208	
Fresh Food Concepts Inc 6535 Caballero Blvd Bldg C *Web:* www.ffci.us	Buena Park	CA	90620	714-562-5000	562-5002
Fresh Foods Corp of America PO Box 19225 *Web:* www.cyruspies.com	Spokane	WA	99219	509-624-5000	
Fresh Grocer at Chester Avenue, The 5406 Chester Ave *Web:* thefreshgrocer.com	Philadelphia	PA	19143	215-730-0881	
Fuji Health Science Inc Three Terri Ln Ste 12 *TF:* 877-385-4777 ■ *Web:* www.fujihealthscience.com	Burlington	NJ	08016	609-386-3030	
G r Manufacturing Inc 4800 Commerce Dr. *TF:* 800-841-8001 ■ *Web:* www.grtractors.com	Trussville	AL	35173	205-655-8001	
George E DeLallo Co Inc 6390 Rt 30 *TF:* 877-335-2556 ■ *Web:* www.delallo.com	Jeannette	PA	15644	724-523-6577	523-0981
Get & Go Market 10950 Beech Daly Rd.	Taylor	MI	48180	313-295-3434	
Giardoni Foods Inc 44 W Jefryn Blvd Ste R *Web:* giardonifoods.com	Deer Park	NY	11729	631-586-2331	
Glazier Foods Co 11303 Antoine Dr. *TF General:* 800-989-6411 ■ *Web:* www.glazierfoods.com	Houston	TX	77066	832-375-6300	375-6394
Glory Foods Inc 901 Oak St *Web:* www.gloryfoods.com	Columbus	OH	43205	614-252-2042	
Glover Foods Inc 119 Old Anderson Ville Rd.	Americus	GA	31719	229-924-2974	
Gold Coast Ingredients Inc 2429 Yates Ave. *TF:* 800-352-8673 ■ *Web:* www.goldcoastinc.com	Commerce	CA	90040	323-724-8935	
Golden Platter Foods Inc 37 Tompkins Point Rd. *Web:* goldenplatter.com	Newark	NJ	07114	973-242-0290	
Granite Falls Energy LLC 15045 Hwy 23 SE. *TF:* 877-485-8595 ■ *Web:* www.granitefallsenergy.com	Granite Falls	MN	56241	320-564-3100	
Grocers Supply International Inc 3131 E Holcombe Blvd PO Box 14200 **Fax:* Acctg ■ *TF:* 800-352-8003 ■ *Web:* www.grocerssupply.com	Houston	TX	77021	713-747-5000	*
Grocery People Ltd, The 14505 Yellowhead Trl *Web:* www.tgp.ca	Edmonton	AB	T5L3C4	780-447-5700	
Grocery Supply Co 130 Hillcrest Dr. *TF:* 800-231-1938 ■ *Web:* www.grocerysupply.com	Sulphur Springs	TX	75482	903-885-7621	439-3249
Hagelin & Co Inc 200 Meister Ave. *Web:* www.hagelin.com	Branchburg	NJ	08876	800-229-2112	
Hannaford Bros Co 145 Pleasant Hill Rd *Web:* www.hannaford.com	Scarborough	ME	04074	800-213-9040	
Hansen Beverage Co One Monster Way *TF:* 800-426-7367 ■ *Web:* www.hansens.com	Corona	CA	92879	800-426-7367	
Hardings Market-West Inc 211 Bannister *Web:* www.hardings.com	Plainwell	MI	49080	269-685-9807	

			Phone	Fax
Harold L King & Company Inc 1420 Stafford St Ste 3 ... Redwood City *Web:* king-coffee.com	CA	94063	650-368-2233	
Harris Soup Co, The 17711 NE Riverside Pkwy ... Portland *TF:* 800-307-7687 ■ *Web:* www.harrysfresh.com	OR	97230	503-257-7687	
Harvest Health Foods 1944 Eastern Ave SE ... Grand Rapids *Web:* www.harvesthealthfoods.com	MI	49507	616-245-6268	
Harvey Alpert & Company Inc 2014 S Sepulveda Blvd Ste 200 ... Los Angeles	CA	90025	310-689-6000	
Henry's Foods Inc 104 Mckay Ave N ... Alexandria *Web:* www.henrysfoods.com	MN	56308	320-763-3194	
High Country Beverage Corp 5706 Wright Dr ... Loveland *Web:* www.highcountrybeverage.com	CO	80538	970-622-8444	
Highway 11 Food Mart 322 Chesnee Hwy ... Gaffney	SC	29341	864-489-4958	
Holsum of Fort Wayne Inc 136 Murray St ... Fort Wayne *Web:* www.holsum.com	IN	46803	260-456-2130	
Honey Farms Inc 505 Pleasant St ... Worcester *Web:* www.myhoneyfarms.com	MA	01609	508-753-7678	
Honor Foods 1801 N Fifth St ... Philadelphia *Web:* honorfoods.com	PA	19122	215-236-1700	
Huy Fong Foods Inc 5001 Earle Ave ... Rosemead *Web:* www.huyfong.com	CA	91770	626-286-8328	
Imperial Trading Co Inc 701 Edwards Ave PO Box 23508 ... Elmwood **Fax Area Code:* 877 ■ *TF Cust Svc:* 800-775-4504 ■ *Web:* www.imperialtrading.com	LA	70123	504-733-1400	855-1416*
Inderbitzin Distributors Inc 901 Valley Ave NW ... Puyallup *Web:* www.inderbitzin.com	WA	98371	253-922-2592	
Institution Food House Inc (IFH) 543 12th St Dr NW ... Hickory **Fax Area Code:* 828 ■ *TF:* 800-800-0434 ■ *Web:* ifh.com	NC	28601	800-800-0434	725-4500*
J&J Foods Inc 1075 Jesse Jewell Pkwy SW ... Gainesville *Web:* www.jandjfoods.com	GA	30501	770-287-7217	
Jace Holdings Ltd 6649 Butler Crescent ... Saanichton *TF:* 800-667-8280 ■ *Web:* www.thriftyfoods.com	BC	V8M1Z7	250-483-1715	
Jana Foods LLC 100 Wood Ave S Ste 206 ... Iselin *Web:* www.janafoods.com	NJ	08830	201-866-5001	
JM Swank Co 395 Herky St ... North Liberty *TF:* 800-593-6333 ■ *Web:* www.jmswank.com	IA	52317	319-626-3683	
Johnny's Stop n Shop 505 S Commercial St ... Emporia	KS	66801	620-343-3803	
Johnson Bros Bakery Supply 10731 N Interstate 35 ... San Antonio **Fax Area Code:* 210 ■ *TF:* 877-446-2767 ■ *Web:* www.jbrosbakerysupply.com	TX	78233	800-590-2575	599-3102*
Johnson O'hare Company Inc One Progress Rd ... Billerica *Web:* www.johare.com	MA	01821	978-663-9000	262-2200
Jonathan Lord Corp 87 Carlough Rd Ste A ... Bohemia *Web:* jonathanlord.com	NY	11716	631-563-4445	
Jordano's Inc 550 S Patterson Ave ... Santa Barbara *TF:* 800-325-2278 ■ *Web:* www.jordanos.com	CA	93111	805-964-0611	964-3821
JTM Provisions Company Inc 200 Sales Dr ... Harrison *Web:* www.jtmfoodgroup.com	OH	45030	513-367-4900	
Just Bagels Manufacturing Inc 527 Casanova St ... Bronx *Web:* www.justbagels.com	NY	10474	718-328-9700	328-9997
Kelley Foods of Alabama Inc 1697 Lower Curtis Rd ... Elba *Web:* www.kelleyfoods.com	AL	36323	334-897-5761	
Key Food Stores Co-op Inc 1200 S Ave ... Staten Island *Web:* keyfood.com	NY	10314	718-370-4200	
King's County Market 13735 Roundlake Blvd ... Andover *Web:* kingscountymarket.com	MN	55304	763-422-1768	
Kings Super Markets Inc 700 Lanidex Plaza ... Parsippany *Web:* kingsfoodmarkets.com	NJ	07054	800-325-4647	
Koa Trading Co 2975 Aukele St ... Lihue *Web:* www.koatradingcoinc.com	HI	96766	808-245-6961	245-8036
KVMart Co 1245 E Watson Ctr Rd ... Carson *Web:* kvmart.com	CA	90745	310-816-0200	
L & W Group Inc 30845 Huntwood Ave ... Hayward *Web:* lwgroupinc.com	CA	94544	510-475-0111	
La Petite Bretonne Inc 1210 Boul Mich Le-Bohec ... Blainville *TF:* 800-361-3381 ■ *Web:* www.petitebretonne.com	QC	J7C5S4	450-435-3381	435-0944
La Preferida Inc 3400 W 35th St ... Chicago *Web:* www.lapreferida.com/	IL	60632	773-254-7200	
Labatt Food Service 4500 Industry Pk Dr ... San Antonio *Web:* www.labattfood.com	TX	78218	210-661-4216	661-0973
Lang Naturals Inc 20 Silva Ln ... Middletown *Web:* www.langnaturals.com	RI	02842	401-848-7700	
Larue Coffee 2631 S 156th Cir ... Omaha *TF:* 800-658-4498 ■ *Web:* www.laruecoffee.com	NE	68130	402-333-9099	
Lasco Foods Inc 4553 Gustine Ave ... St Louis *Web:* www.lascofoods.com	MO	63116	314-832-1906	
Laurel Grocery Co Inc 129 Barbourville Rd ... London **Fax Area Code:* 606 ■ *TF:* 800-467-6601 ■ *Web:* laurelgrocery.com	KY	40744	800-467-6601	878-9361*
Lee's Marketplace Inc 555 East 1400 North ... Logan *Web:* www.leesmarketplace.com	UT	84341	435-755-5100	
LFI Inc 271 Us Hwy 46 Ste C101 ... Fairfield *Web:* lfiincorporated.com	NJ	07004	973-882-0550	
Liberty Vegetable Oil Co 15306 S Carmenita Rd ... Santa Fe Springs *Web:* www.libertyvegetableoil.com	CA	90670	562-921-3567	
Lifetech Resources LLC 9540 Cozycroft Ave ... Chatsworth *Web:* www.lifetechresources.com	CA	91311	818-885-1199	
Limra Trading 30 Mall Dr W ... Jersey City	NJ	07310	201-792-7003	
Long Wholesale Distributors Inc 5173 Pioneer Rd ... Meridian *Web:* www.longwholesale.com	MS	39301	601-482-3144	
Longo Bros Fruit Markets Inc 8800 Huntington Rd ... Vaughan *Web:* www.longos.com	ON	L4H3M6	905-264-4100	
Lowes Wilshire Market 301 N Richman Ave ... Fullerton	CA	92832	714-870-7310	
Luke Soules Acosta 2003 Rickety Ln Ste D ... Tyler	TX	75703	903-561-4241	

			Phone	Fax
Magnetic Springs Water Co 1917 Joyce Ave ... Columbus *Web:* www.magneticsprings.com	OH	43219	614-421-1780	
Maines Paper & Food Service Co 101 Broome Corporate Pkwy ... Conklin **Fax:* Cust Svc ■ *TF:* 800-366-3669 ■ *Web:* www.maines.net	NY	13748	607-779-1200	723-3245*
Maple Ridge Farms Inc 975 S Park View Cir ... Mosinee *Web:* www.mapleridge.com	WI	54455	715-693-4346	
Maramor Chocolates 1855 E 17th Ave ... Columbus *Web:* www.maramor.com	OH	43219	614-291-2244	
Marche Akhavan 6170 Rue Sherbrooke O ... Montreal *Web:* akhavanfood.com	QC	H4B1L8	514-485-4744	
Market of Choice 1475 Siskiyou Blvd ... Ashland *Web:* www.marketofchoice.com	OR	97520	541-488-2773	
Market Semiotics PO Box 1457 ... Castleton *Web:* www.marketsemiotics.com	VT	05735	802-273-3800	
Marquez Bros International Inc 5801 Rue Ferrari ... San Jose *TF:* 800-858-1119 ■ *Web:* www.marquezbrothers.com	CA	95138	408-960-2700	
Maverick Enterprises Inc 751 E Gobbi St ... Ukiah *Web:* www.maverickcaps.com	CA	95482	707-463-5591	
Maxi Foods LLC 8616 California Ave ... Riverside *Web:* www.maxifoods.com	CA	92504	951-688-0538	
Maya Overseas Foods Inc 48-85 Maspeth Ave ... Maspeth *Web:* www.mayafoods.com	NY	11378	718-894-5145	894-5178
McLane Company Inc 4747 McLane Pkwy ... Temple *TF:* 800-299-1401 ■ *Web:* www.mclaneco.com	TX	76504	254-771-7500	771-7244
McLane Foodservice Inc 2085 Midway Rd ... Carrollton **Fax Area Code:* 254 ■ *TF:* 800-299-1401 ■ *Web:* www.mclaneco.com	TX	75006	972-364-2000	771-7244*
Merchants Co 1100 Edwards St ... Hattiesburg *TF:* 800-451-8346 ■ *Web:* www.themerchantscompany.com	MS	39401	601-583-4351	582-5333
Metro Supermarkets 156 Main St S ... Brampton *Web:* metro.ca	ON	L6W2C9	905-459-6212	
Metropolis Coffee Company LLC 1039 W Granville Ave Ste 1041 ... Chicago *Web:* metropoliscoffee.com	IL	60660	773-764-0400	
Mineral Resources International 1990 W 3300 S ... Ogden *TF:* 800-731-7866 ■ *Web:* www.mineralresourcesint.com	UT	84401	801-731-7040	731-7985
Mockler Beverage Co 11811 Reiger Rd ... Baton Rouge *Web:* mocklerbeverage.com	LA	70809	225-408-4283	
Monin Inc 2100 Range Rd ... Clearwater *Web:* www.monin.com	FL	33765	727-461-3033	
Mrs Stratton's Salads Inc 380 Industrial Ln ... Birmingham *Web:* www.mrsstrattons.com	AL	35211	205-940-9640	
MWS Enterprises Inc 5701 Transit Rd ... East Amherst *Web:* www.arrowmart.com	NY	14051	716-689-0600	
Nash Finch Co 7600 France Ave S ... Minneapolis *NASDAQ: NAFC* ■ *Web:* spartannash.com	MN	55440	952-832-0534	844-1237
National Flavors Inc 1206 E Crosstown ... Kalamazoo *Web:* www.nationalflavors.com	MI	49001	269-344-3640	
New Century Snacks 5560 E Slauson Ave ... Commerce *Web:* www.newcenturysnacks.com	CA	90040	323-278-9578	
Nice N Easy Grocery Shoppes Inc 7840 Oxbow Rd ... Canastota *Web:* www.niceneasy.com	NY	13032	315-697-2287	
North Coast Co-op Inc 811 I St ... Arcata	CA	95521	707-822-5947	
Northern Eagle Beverage Co 600 16th St ... Carlstadt *Web:* www.northerneaglebeverage.com	NJ	07072	201-531-7100	
nuherbs co 3820 Penniman Ave ... Oakland *TF:* 800-233-4307 ■ *Web:* www.nuherbs.com	CA	94619	510-534-4372	
Nutramed Inc 13840 Magnolia Ave ... Chino *Web:* www.nutramedinc.com	CA	91710	909-902-5005	
Olean Wholesale Grocery Co-op Inc 1587 Haskell Rd PO Box 1070 ... Olean *TF:* 866-774-9751 ■ *Web:* www.oleanwholesale.com	NY	14760	716-372-2020	
Omega Alpha Pharmaceuticals Inc 795 Pharmacy Ave ... Scarborough *Web:* omegaalpha.ca	ON	M1L3K2	416-297-6900	
Oppenheimer Cos Inc 877 W Main Ste 700 ... Boise *TF:* 800-727-9939 ■ *Web:* www.oppcos.com	ID	83702	208-343-4883	
P J Noyes Company Inc 89 Bridge St ... Lancaster *TF:* 800-522-2469 ■ *Web:* www.pjnoyes.com	NH	03584	603-788-4952	
Paint Sundries Solutions Inc 930 Seventh Ave ... Kirkland *Web:* www.paintsundries.com	WA	98033	425-827-9200	
Par Mar Stores 101 Alta St ... Marietta *Web:* www.parmarstores.com	OH	45750	304-572-3500	
Paris Gourmet of New York Inc 145 Grand St ... Carlstadt **Fax Area Code:* 201 ■ *TF:* 800-727-8791 ■ *Web:* www.parisgourmet.com	NJ	07072	800-727-8791	939-5613*
Pasco Corp of America 6500 N Marine Dr ... Portland *Web:* www.pascoamerica.com	OR	97203	503-289-6500	
Patty Palace Ltd 595 Middlefield Rd ... Scarborough *Web:* pattypalace.net	ON	M1V3S2	416-297-0510	
Pearson Foods Corp 1024 Ken O Sha Ind Park Dr SE Ste A ... Grand Rapids *Web:* www.pearsonfoods.com	MI	49508	616-245-5053	
Peppers Unlimited of Louisiana Inc 602 W Bridge St ... St Martinville *Web:* www.peppersunlimitedofla.com	LA	70582	337-394-8035	
Performance Food Group Co 12500 W Creek Pkwy ... Richmond *Web:* www.pfgc.com	VA	23238	804-484-7700	484-7701
Performance Foodservice 12500 W Creek Pkwy ... Richmond *Web:* performancefoodservice.com	VA	23238	804-484-7700	
Perishable Distributors of Iowa Ltd 2741 SE PDI Pl ... Ankeny *Web:* www.contactpdi.com	IA	50021	515-965-6300	965-1105
Peter Gillhams Natural Vitality 4879 Fountain Ave ... Los Angeles *TF:* 888-324-9904 ■ *Web:* www.vites.com	CA	90029	888-324-9904	
Pharmore Ingredients Inc 12569 South 2700 West Ste 201 ... Riverton *Web:* pharmore.com/	UT	84065	801-446-8188	

Company / Address	City	State	Zip	Phone	Fax
Piggly Wiggly 2400 J Terrell Wooten Dr *Web:* www.pwadc.com	Bessemer	AL	35021	205-481-2300	
Piggly Wiggly Carolina Company Inc PO Box 118047 *TF:* 800-243-9880 ■ *Web:* thepig.net	Charleston	SC	29423	843-554-9880	745-2730
Pittsville Pdq Inc 549 NW SR- 131 *Web:* shell.com	Holden	MO	64040	816-850-6915	
Power Buying Dealers Exxonmobil Convenience Stores 2459 W 208th St Ste 100 *Web:* www.vitalife.com	Torrance	CA	90501	310-212-9999	
Pure Express Mart 4002 Knight Arnold Rd	Memphis	TN	38118	901-794-3100	
Purity Wholesale Grocers Inc 5400 Broken Sound Blvd NW *TF:* 800-323-6838 ■ *Web:* www.pwg-inc.com	Boca Raton	FL	33487	561-994-9360	
Red Lodge Beverages Seven Pepsi Dr	Red Lodge	MT	59068	406-446-2040	
Riba Foods Inc 3735 Arc St *Web:* www.ribafoods.com	Houston	TX	77063	713-975-7001	975-7036
Ricker Oil Company Inc 30 W 11th St *Web:* rickersrewards.com/	Anderson	IN	46016	765-643-3016	
Rigsby Food Mart 5602 Us Hwy 87 E *Web:* texaco.com	San Antonio	TX	78222	210-648-0093	
Rishi Tea LLC 427 E Stewart St S- 5 *Web:* rishi-tea.com	Milwaukee	WI	53207	414-747-4001	
Ritt-beyer & Weir Inc 9900 S Franklin Dr *Web:* www.rbwinc.com	Franklin	WI	53132	414-421-9505	
RL Jordan Oil Co 1451 Fernwood Glendale Rd *Web:* www.hotspotcstore.com	Spartanburg	SC	29307	864-585-2784	
Roman Meal Company Inc 2101 S Tacoma Way *Web:* www.romanmeal.com	Tacoma	WA	98411	253-475-0964	
Rutan Poly Industries Inc 39 Siding Pl *Web:* www.rutanpoly.com	Mahwah	NJ	07430	201-529-1474	
S Abraham & Sons Inc PO Box 1768 *TF General:* 866-248-3163 ■ *Web:* www.sasinc.com	Grand Rapids	MI	49501	616-453-6358	453-9259
Sac n Pac 1405 United Dr Ste 115 *Web:* www.sacnpac.com	San Marcos	TX	78666	512-392-6484	
Safeway Foods Inc 2435 N Sherman Dr Ste O1a *Web:* safeway.com	Indianapolis	IN	46218	317-547-8528	
Sahadi Fine Foods Inc 4215 First Ave *Web:* www.sahadifinefoods.com	Brooklyn	NY	11232	718-369-0100	
Sams Discount Food Mart 5703 Timuquana Rd	Jacksonville	FL	32210	904-573-8899	
Santini Foods Inc 16505 Worthley Dr *Web:* www.santinifoods.com	San Lorenzo	CA	94580	510-317-8888	
Satin Fine Foods Inc 32 Leone Ln Ste 1 *Web:* satinice.com/	Chester	NY	10918	845-469-1034	
Saver Systems Inc 95 London Dr *Web:* www.savergroup.com	Campbellsville	KY	42718	270-465-8675	
Schiff's Restaurant Service Inc 3410 N Main Ave *Web:* www.myschiffs.com	Scranton	PA	18508	570-343-1294	969-6255
Schuette Stores Inc 17919 Saint Rose Rd *Web:* www.onlinegrocer.com	Breese	IL	62230	618-526-7203	
Shah Distributors Inc 540 Patrice Pl *Web:* shahdistributors.com	Gardena	CA	90248	310-719-1011	
Shaheen Bros Inc PO Box 897 *Web:* www.shaheenbros.com	Amesbury	MA	01913	978-388-6776	388-6617
Shamrock Foods 3900 E Camelback Rd Ste 300 *TF:* 800-289-3663 ■ *Web:* www.shamrockfoods.com	Phoenix	AZ	85018	602-477-2500	477-2533
Shanks Extracts Inc 350 Richardson Dr *TF:* 800-346-3135 ■ *Web:* www.shanks.com	Lancaster	PA	17603	717-393-4441	
Soderholm Wholesale Foods 1100 Wilburn Rd *Web:* www.soderholmfoods.com	Sun Prairie	WI	53590	608-834-9850	
Southco Distributing Co 2201 S John St *TF:* 800-969-3172 ■ *Web:* www.southcodistributing.com	Goldsboro	NC	27530	919-735-8012	735-0097
Spartan Stores Inc 850 76th St SW PO Box 8700 *NASDAQ: SPTN* ■ *Web:* spartannash.com/	Grand Rapids	MI	49518	616-878-2000	
Specialty Brands Of America Inc 1400 Old Country Rd *TF:* 877-795-3599 ■ *Web:* bgfoods.com/	Westbury	NY	11590	516-997-6969	
Speedee Mart Inc 3670 Paradise Rd	Las Vegas	NV	89169	702-733-7950	
St Clair Foods Inc 3100 Bellbrook Dr *Web:* www.stclair.com	Memphis	TN	38116	901-396-8680	
St Joe Petroleum Co 2520 S Second St *Web:* www.stjoepetroleum.com	Saint Joseph	MO	64501	816-279-0770	
Star Market Inc 702 Pratt Ave NW *Web:* www.huntsvillestarmarket.com	Huntsville	AL	35801	256-534-4509	
Steins Thriftway Foods Inc 135 Central Ave N	Watkins	MN	55389	320-764-2980	
Sukhi's Gourmet Indian Foods 23682 Clawiter Rd *Web:* sukhis.com	Hayward	CA	94545	510-264-9265	
Sunny Morning 5330 NW 35th Ave *Web:* www.sunnymorning.com	Fort Lauderdale	FL	33309	954-735-3447	
Sunshine Foods Partners 1115 Main St *Web:* www.sunshinefoodstores.com	Saint Helena	CA	94574	707-963-7070	
Super Store Industries 16888 McKinley Ave PO Box 549 *TF:* 888-292-8004 ■ *Web:* ssica.com	Lathrop	CA	95330	209-858-2010	858-5674
SUPERVALU Inc 7075 Flying Cloud Dr *NYSE: SVU* ■ *TF Cust Svc:* 877-322-8228 ■ *Web:* www.supervalu.com	Eden Prairie	MN	55344	952-828-4000	
SUPERVALU International 495 E 19th St *Web:* www.supervaluinternational.com	Tacoma	WA	98421	253-593-3198	593-7828
SYGMA Network Inc 5550 Blazer Pkwy Ste 300 **Fax Area Code:* 614 ■ *TF:* 877-441-1144 ■ *Web:* www.sygmanetwork.com	Dublin	OH	43017	877-441-1144	734-2550*
Sysco Central Ohio Inc 2400 Harrison Rd **Fax Area Code:* 907 ■ *TF:* 800-735-3341 ■ *Web:* sysco.com	Columbus	OH	43204	614-272-0655	565-5627*
SYSCO Corp 1390 Enclave Pkwy *NYSE: SYY* ■ **Fax:* PR ■ *Web:* www.sysco.com	Houston	TX	77077	281-584-1390	584-1737*
Sysco Denver Inc 5000 Beeler St *TF:* 800-366-6696 ■ *Web:* www.syscodenver.com	Denver	CO	80238	303-585-2000	
Sysco Food Services of Idaho Inc 5710 Pan Am Ave *TF:* 800-747-9726 ■ *Web:* www.syscoidaho.com	Boise	ID	83716	208-345-9500	387-2598
Sysco Grand Rapids 3700 Sysco Ct SE *TF:* 800-669-6967 ■ *Web:* www.syscogr.com	Grand Rapids	MI	49512	616-949-3700	977-4510
Sysco Hampton Roads Inc 7000 Harbour View Blvd *TF:* 800-234-2451 ■ *Web:* www.syscohamptonroads.com	Suffolk	VA	23435	757-673-4000	673-4148
Tarrier Foods Corp 3915 Zane Trace Dr *Web:* www.tarrierfoods.com	Columbus	OH	43228	614-876-8595	
Taste Maker Foods LLC 1415 E Mclemore Ave # 1425 *Web:* www.tomlinsonassociates.com	Memphis	TN	38106	901-274-4407	
Thomas & Howard Wholesale Grocers Inc 209 Flintlake Rd PO Box 23659	Columbia	SC	29223	803-788-5520	699-9097
Thoms Proestler Co 8001 TPC Rd *TF:* 800-747-1234 ■ *Web:* www.performancefoodservice.com	Rock Island	IL	61204	309-787-1234	787-1254
Thor Inc 1280 W 2550 S St *TF:* 888-846-7462 ■ *Web:* www.thor.com	Ogden	UT	84401	801-393-3312	621-3298
Tom Cat Bakery Inc 43-05 Tenth St *Web:* www.tomcatbakery.com	Long Island City	NY	11101	718-786-7659	
Tony's Meats & Specialty Foods 874 W Happy Canyon Rd *Web:* tonysmarket.com	Castle Rock	CO	80108	303-814-3888	
Topco Assoc LLC 7711 Gross Pt Rd *TF:* 888-423-0139 ■ *Web:* www.topco.com	Skokie	IL	60077	847-676-3030	676-4949
Tower Isles Frozen Foods Ltd 2025 Atlantic Ave *Web:* www.towerislespatties.com	Brooklyn	NY	11233	718-495-2626	
Treatt USA Inc 4900 Lakeland Commerce Pkwy *Web:* www.treattusa.com	Lakeland	FL	33805	863-668-9500	
Tri Venture Mktg Inc 2525 Drane Field Rd Ste 1	Lakeland	FL	33811	863-648-1881	
Tri-cities Beverage Corp 612 Industrial Park Dr *Web:* tricitiesbeverage.com	Newport News	VA	23608	757-874-6600	
Tripifoods Inc 1427 William St *Web:* www.tripifoods.com	Buffalo	NY	14206	716-853-7400	852-7400
Truco Enterprises LP 10515 King William Dr *Web:* ontheborderproducts.com	Dallas	TX	75367	972-869-4600	869-8050
Uncle Giuseppe's of Smithtown 95 Rt 111 *Web:* www.uncleg.com	Smithtown	NY	11787	631-863-0900	
UNFI Specialty Distribution Services 88 Huntoon Memorial Hwy *TF:* 877-476-8749 ■ *Web:* unfi.com	Leicester	MA	01524	508-892-8171	892-4827
Unified Grocers Inc 5200 Sheila St *TF:* 800-724-7762 ■ *Web:* www.unifiedgrocers.com	Commerce	CA	90040	323-264-5200	729-6610
UniPro Foodservice Inc 2500 Cumberland Pkwy Ste 600 *Web:* www.uniprofoodservice.com	Atlanta	GA	30339	770-952-0871	
United Natural Foods Inc (UNFI) 313 Iron Horse Way *NASDAQ: UNFI* ■ *Web:* www.unfi.com	Providence	RI	02908	401-528-8634	
Valley Fine Foods Company Inc 3909 Park Rd Ste H *Web:* www.cafferata.com	Benicia	CA	94510	707-746-6888	
Valley Natural Foods 13750 County Rd 11 *Web:* www.valleynaturalfoods.com	Burnsville	MN	55337	952-891-1212	
Vantage General Store 551 Main St	Vantage	WA	98950	509-856-2803	
Vend Mart Inc 1950 Williams St *Web:* www.vendmart.com	San Leandro	CA	94577	510-297-5132	352-8363
Venda Ravioli Inc 265 Atwells Ave *Web:* www.vendaravioli.com	Providence	RI	02903	401-421-9105	
Vistar/VSA Corp 12650 E Arapahoe Rd Bldg D *TF:* 800-880-9900 ■ *Web:* www.vistar.com	Centennial	CO	80112	303-662-7100	662-7565
W L Halsey Grocery Company Inc PO Box 6485 *TF:* 800-621-0240 ■ *Web:* www.halseyfoodservice.com	Huntsville	AL	35824	256-772-9691	461-8386
Wakefern Food Corp 600 York St *TF:* 800-746-7748 ■ *Web:* www.shoprite.com	Elizabeth	NJ	07207	908-527-3300	527-3397
Wellington Foods Inc 1930 California Ave *Web:* www.wellingtonfoods.com	Corona	CA	92881	951-547-7000	
White Rose Inc 380 Middlesex Ave *Web:* www.whiterose.com	Carteret	NJ	07008	732-541-5555	541-3730
Williamson Street Grocery Company Op 1221 Williamson St *Web:* www.willystreet.coop	Madison	WI	53703	608-251-0884	
Wind River Petroleum Inc 2046 E Murray Holladay Rd Ste 200	Salt Lake City	UT	84117	801-272-9229	
Wing's Food Products 50 Torlake Cres *Web:* www.wings.ca	Toronto	ON	M8Z1B8	416-259-2662	259-3414
Winkler Inc 535 E Medcalf St *TF:* 800-621-3843 ■ *Web:* www.winklerinc.com	Dale	IN	47523	812-937-4421	937-2044
Woeber Mustard Mfg Company Inc 1966 Commerce Cir PO Box 388 *Web:* www.woebermustard.com	Springfield	OH	45501	937-323-6281	
Wood-Fruitticher Grocery Company Inc 2900 Alton Rd *TF:* 800-328-0026 ■ *Web:* www.woodfruitticher.com	Birmingham	AL	35210	205-836-9663	836-9681
Woolco Foods Inc 135 Amity St *Web:* woolcofoods.net	Jersey City	NJ	07304	201-716-2700	
World Nutrition Inc 7001 N Scottsdale Rd Ste 2000 *Web:* www.bodylabs.net	Scottsdale	AZ	85253	480-921-1188	
Wynn Starr Foods of Kentucky Inc 4820 Allmond Ave	Louisville	KY	40214	502-368-6345	
Zausner Foods Corp 400 S Custer Ave	New Holland	PA	17557	717-355-8505	

300-9 Meats & Meat Products - Whol

Phone | Fax

Agar Supply Company Inc 225 John Hancock Rd .... Taunton MA 02780 508-821-2060 880-5113*
Fax Area Code: 617 ■ **Fax:* Sales ■ *TF:* 800-669-6040 ■ *Web:* www.agarsupply.com

Allied Specialty Foods Inc 313 Hickory Pl .... Vineland NJ 08360 856-507-1100
Web: www.alliedsteaks.com

Amigos Meat Distributors-East LP
611 Crosstimber .... Houston TX 77022 713-928-3111 694-0610
Web: www.amigosfoods.biz

Aurora Packing Company Inc
125 S Grant St .... North Aurora IL 60542 630-897-0551 897-0647
Web: aurorabeef.com

Ava Pork Products Inc
383 W John St Hicksville .... Hicksville NY 11802 516-750-1500 750-1501
Web: www.avapork.com

Bruss Co 3548 N Kostner Ave .... Chicago IL 60641 773-282-2900 282-6966
TF: 800-621-3882 ■ *Web:* bruss.com

Buckhead Beef of Florida 355 Progress Rd .... Auburndale FL 33823 863-508-1050
Web: buckheadbeef.com

Calumet Diversified Meats Inc
10000 80th Ave. .... Pleasant Prairie WI 53158 262-947-7200 947-7209
TF: 800-752-7427 ■ *Web:* www.porkchops.com

Cambridge Packing Co Inc 41-43 Foodmart Rd .... Boston MA 02118 617-269-6700 889-9898*
Fax Area Code: 800 ■ *TF:* 800-722-6726 ■ *Web:* www.cambridgepacking.com

Cardinal Meat Specialists Ltd
155 Hedgedale Rd .... Brampton ON L6T5P3 905-459-4436
TF: 800-363-1439 ■ *Web:* www.cardinalmeats.com

Cell Response Formulation LLC 4115 S Pub Pl .... Jackson WY 83002 307-734-7839
TF: 888-364-7839 ■ *Web:* www.mulliganstewpetfood.com

Colorado Boxed Beef Co 302 Progress Rd .... Auburndale FL 33823 863-967-0636
Web: www.coloradoboxedbeef.com

ConAgra Foods Foodservice Co 1 ConAgra Dr .... Omaha NE 68102 800-357-6543
Web: www.conagrafoodservice.com

Cusack Wholesale Meat Inc
301 SW 12th St .... Oklahoma City OK 73109 405-232-2114 232-2127
TF: 800-241-6328 ■ *Web:* www.cusackmeats.com

Cypress Food Distributors Inc
3111 N University Dr Ste 612 .... Coral Springs FL 33065 954-344-2900 344-3607
Web: www.cypressfood.com

Dairyland Corp 1300 Viele Ave .... Bronx NY 10474 718-842-8700 378-2234

Day-Lee Foods Inc 13055 Molette St .... Santa Fe Springs CA 90670 562-802-6800
Web: www.day-lee.com

Deen Meats PO Box 4155 PO Box 4155 .... Fort Worth TX 76164 817-335-2257 338-9256
TF: 800-333-3953 ■ *Web:* www.deenmeat.com

Ditta Meat Co PO Box 5623 .... Pasadena TX 77508 281-487-2010
Web: www.dittameat.com

Flanders Provision Company LLC
1104 Gilmore St .... Waycross GA 31501 912-283-5191
Web: www.flandersprovision.com

Freshwater Fish Mktg Corp 1199 Plessis Rd .... Winnipeg MB R2C3L4 204-983-6601
Web: www.freshwaterfish.com

Green Tree Packing Co 65 Central Ave. .... Passaic NJ 07055 973-473-1305 473-7975
TF: 800-562-6934 ■ *Web:* www.greentreepacking.com

Heartland Meat Company Inc 3461 Main St .... Chula Vista CA 91911 619-407-3668 407-3678
TF: 888-407-3668 ■ *Web:* www.heartlandmeat.com

Holten Meat Inc 1682 Sauget Business Blvd. .... Sauget IL 62206 618-337-8400 337-3292
TF: 800-851-4684 ■ *Web:* www.holtenmeat.com

Huisken Meats Co 245 Industrial Blvd .... Sauk Rapids MN 56379 320-259-0305
Web: www.huiskenmeats.com

Jensen Meat Company Inc 2525 Birch St. .... Vista CA 92081 760-727-6700 727-8598
Web: www.jensenmeat.com

Keystone Foods LLC
300 Bar Harbor Dr
Ste 600 5 Tower Bridge .... West Conshohocken PA 19428 610-667-6700 667-1460
Web: www.keystonefoods.com

Manda Fine Meats 2445 Sorrel Ave .... Baton Rouge LA 70802 225-344-7636 344-7647
TF: 800-343-2642 ■ *Web:* www.mandafinemeats.com

Michael's Finer Meats & Seafoods
3775 Zane Trace Dr. .... Columbus OH 43228 614-527-4900 527-4520
TF: 800-282-0518 ■ *Web:* www.michaelsmeats.com

Midamar Corp PO Box 218 .... Cedar Rapids IA 52406 319-362-3711 362-4111
TF: 800-362-3711 ■ *Web:* www.midamar.com

Northwestern Meat Inc 2100 NW 23rd St. .... Miami FL 33142 305-633-8112 633-6907
Web: www.numeat.com

Orrell's Food Service 9827 S NC Hwy 150 .... Linwood NC 27299 336-752-2114 752-2060
Web: www.orrellsfoodservice.com

Paper Pak Industries (PPI) 1941 N White Ave. .... La Verne CA 91750 909-392-1750 392-1760
TF: 888-293-6529 ■ *Web:* www.paperpakindustries.com

Porky Products Corp 400 Port Carteret Dr .... Carteret NJ 07008 732-541-0200 969-6110
TF General: 800-952-0265 ■ *Web:* www.porkyproducts.com

Pucci Foods 25447 Industrial Blvd. .... Hayward CA 94545 510-300-6800 300-6805
Web: www.puccifoods.com

Quality Meats & Seafoods 700 Ctr St .... West Fargo ND 58078 701-282-0202
TF: 800-342-4250 ■ *Web:* www.qualitymeats.com

Quirch Foods Co 7600 NW 82nd Pl .... Miami FL 33166 305-691-3535 593-0272
TF: 800-458-5252 ■ *Web:* www.quirchfoods.com

Sampco Inc 651 W Washington Blvd Ste 300. .... Chicago IL 60661 312-346-1506 346-8302
TF: 800-767-0689 ■ *Web:* www.sampcoinc.com

Southern Foods Inc
3500 Old Battleground Rd .... Greensboro NC 27410 336-545-3800 545-5281
Web: www.southernfoods.com

Tapia Bros Co 6067 District Blvd .... Maywood CA 90270 323-560-7415 560-8924
Web: www.tapiabrothers.com

Thumann Inc 670 Dell Rd. .... Carlstadt NJ 07072 201-935-3636 935-2226
Web: www.thumanns.com

Tri-City Meats Inc 1346 N Hickory Ave. .... Meridian ID 83642 208-884-2600
TF: 800-747-9726 ■ *Web:* www.tricitymeats.com

Phone | Fax

Trim-Rite Food Corp
801 Commerce Pkwy .... Carpentersville IL 60110 847-649-3400 649-3420
TF: 800-626-9442 ■ *Web:* www.trim-rite.com

Troyer Foods Inc 17141 State Rd 4 .... Goshen IN 46528 574-533-0302 533-3851
TF: 800-876-9377 ■ *Web:* www.troyers.com

U W Provision Company Inc PO Box 620038 .... Middleton WI 53562 608-836-7421 836-6328
TF: 800-832-0517 ■ *Web:* www.uwprovision.com

Williams Sausage Company Inc
5132 Old Troy Hickman Rd .... Union City TN 38261 731-885-5841 885-5884
TF: 800-844-4242 ■ *Web:* www.williams-sausage.com

300-10 Poultry, Eggs, Poultry Products - Whol

Phone | Fax

Acme Farms Inc 1024 S King St .... Seattle WA 98104 206-323-4300

Agar Supply Company Inc 225 John Hancock Rd .... Taunton MA 02780 508-821-2060 880-5113*
Fax Area Code: 617 ■ **Fax:* Sales ■ *TF:* 800-669-6040 ■ *Web:* www.agarsupply.com

Butts Foods Inc 432 N Royal St PO Box 2466 .... Jackson TN 38301 731-423-3456 423-4566
TF: 800-962-8570 ■ *Web:* www.buttsfoods.com

Chino Valley Ranchers 5611 Peck Rd .... Arcadia CA 91006 800-354-4503 652-0893*
Fax Area Code: 626 ■ *TF:* 800-354-4503 ■ *Web:* www.chinovalleyranchers.com

Dutt & Wagner of Virginia Inc
1142 W Main St .... Abingdon VA 24210 276-628-2116 628-4619
TF: 800-688-2116 ■ *Web:* duttandwagner.com

Harker's Distribution Inc 801 Sixth St SW .... Le Mars IA 51031 712-546-8171
Web: lemarssentinel.com

Hemmelgarn & Sons Inc 3763 Philothea Rd .... Coldwater OH 45828 419-678-2351 678-4922

House of Raeford Farms Inc 520 E Central Ave .... Raeford NC 28376 910-875-5161 875-8300
TF: 800-888-7539 ■ *Web:* www.houseofraeford.com

Metropolitan Poultry & Seafood Co
1920 Stanford Ct .... Landover MD 20785 301-772-0060 772-1013
TF: 800-522-0060 ■ *Web:* www.metropoultry.com

Norbest Inc PO Box 890 .... Moroni UT 84646 800-453-5327 597-5416*
Fax Area Code: 888 ■ *TF:* 800-453-5327 ■ *Web:* www.norbest.com

Nulaid Foods Inc 200 W Fifth St .... Ripon CA 95366 209-599-2121 599-5220
Web: www.nulaid.com

Quirch Foods Co 7600 NW 82nd Pl .... Miami FL 33166 305-691-3535 593-0272
TF: 800-458-5252 ■ *Web:* www.quirchfoods.com

RW Sauder Inc 570 Furnace Hills Pk .... Lititz PA 17543 717-626-2074 626-0493
Web: www.saudereggs.com

Troyer Foods Inc 17141 State Rd 4 .... Goshen IN 46528 574-533-0302 533-3851
TF: 800-876-9377 ■ *Web:* www.troyers.com

Zacky Farms
13200 Crossroads Pkwy N Ste 250 .... City of Industry CA 91746 562-641-2020 641-2040
TF: 800-888-0235 ■ *Web:* www.zacky.com

300-11 Specialty Foods - Whol

Phone | Fax

Camerican International Inc 45 Eisenhower Dr. ...... Paramus NJ 07652 201-587-0101 587-2040*
**Fax:* Hum Res ■ *Web:* camerican.com

Charles C. Parks Co 500 Belvedere Dr .... Gallatin TN 37066 615-452-2406 451-4212
TF: 800-873-2406 ■ *Web:* www.charlescparks.com

ConAgra Foods Foodservice Co 1 ConAgra Dr .... Omaha NE 68102 800-357-6543
Web: www.conagrafoodservice.com

Condal Distributors 531 Dupont St. .... Bronx NY 10474 718-589-1100 589-9200

Conway Import Co Inc
11051 W Addison St. .... Franklin Park IL 60131 847-455-5600 304-4021*
Fax Area Code: 800 ■ *TF:* 800-323-8801 ■ *Web:* conwaydressings.com

CRS Onesource 2803 Tamarack Rd PO Box 1984 ...... Owensboro KY 42302 270-684-1469 685-5696
TF: 800-264-0710 ■ *Web:* www.crsonesource.com

Diaz Wholesale & Mfg Co Inc
5501 Fulton Industrial Blvd .... Atlanta GA 30336 404-344-5421 344-3003
TF: 800-394-4639 ■ *Web:* www.diazfoods.com

Ellis Coffee Co 2835 Bridge St. .... Philadelphia PA 19137 215-537-9500 535-5311
TF: 800-822-3984 ■ *Web:* www.elliscoffee.com

Essex Grain Products Nine Lee Blvd. .... Frazer PA 19355 610-647-3800 647-4990
TF: 800-441-1017 ■ *Web:* www.essexgrain.com

Garden Spot Distributors Inc
191 Commerce Dr .... New Holland PA 17557 717-354-4936 829-5100*
Fax Area Code: 877 ■ *Web:* www.gardenspotdist.com

Ginsburg Bakery Inc
300 N Tennessee Ave .... Atlantic City NJ 08401 609-345-2265 345-2268
Web: www.ginsburgbakery.com

Gregory's Foods Inc 1301 Trapp Rd .... Eagan MN 55121 651-454-0277 454-2254
Web: www.gregorysfoods.com

Hain Celestial Group Inc
4600 Sleepytime Dr Ste 250 .... Boulder CO 80301 800-434-4246 730-2550*
NASDAQ: HAIN ■ **Fax Area Code:* 631 ■ *TF:* 800-434-4246 ■ *Web:* www.hain-celestial.com

Harlan Bakeries-Avon LLC 7597 E US Hwy 36 .... Avon IN 46123 317-272-3600 272-1110
Web: www.harlanbakeries.com

Indiana Sugars Inc 911 Virginia St .... Gary IN 46402 219-886-9151 886-5124
Web: www.sugars.com

Industrial Commodities Inc PO Box 4380 .... Glen Allen VA 23060 800-523-7902
Web: www.industrialcommodities.com

J Sosnick & Sons Inc
258 Littlefield Ave. .... South San Francisco CA 94080 650-952-2226 952-2439
TF: 800-443-6737 ■ *Web:* www.sosnick.com

JFC International Inc 7101 E Slauson Ave .... Los Angeles CA 90040 323-721-6100 721-6133
TF: 800-633-1004 ■ *Web:* www.jfc.com

Joffrey's Coffee & Tea Co 3803 Corporex Pk Dr. .... Tampa FL 33619 813-250-0404 250-0303
TF: 800-458-5282 ■ *Web:* www.joffreys.com

John E Koerner & Company Inc
4820 Jefferson Hwy .... New Orleans LA 70121 800-333-1913 734-0630*
Fax Area Code: 504 ■ *TF:* 800-333-1913 ■ *Web:* www.koerner-co.com

King Milling Co 115 S Broadway St .... Lowell MI 49331 616-897-9264 897-4350
Web: www.kingmilling.com

Lecoq Cuisine Corp 35 Union Ave. .... Bridgeport CT 06607 203-334-1010 334-1800
Web: www.lecoqcuisine.com

Phone Fax

Lipari Foods LLC 26661 Bunert Rd. Warren MI 48089 586-447-3500 447-3524
Web: liparifoods.com/
Lomar Distributing 2500 Dixon St. Des Moines IA 50316 515-244-3105 244-0515
Losurdo Foods Inc 20 Owens Rd. Hackensack NJ 07601 201-343-6680 343-8078
Web: www.losurdofoods.com
Love & Quiches Desserts 178 Hanse Ave. Freeport NY 11520 516-623-8800 623-8817
TF: 800-525-5251 ■ *Web:* www.loveandquiches.com
Mitsui Foods International 35 Maple St. Norwood NJ 07648 201-750-0500 750-0150
Web: www.mitsuifoods.com
Morris J Golombeck Inc 960 Franklin Ave. Brooklyn NY 11225 718-284-3505 693-1941
Web: www.golombeckspice.com
Mutual Trading Company Ltd
431 Crocker St. Los Angeles CA 90013 213-626-9458 626-5130
Web: www.lamtc.com
Nantze Springs Inc 156 W Carroll St. Dothan AL 36301 334-794-4218
TF: 800-239-7873 ■ *Web:* www.nantzesprings.com
Neiman Bros Company Inc 3322 W Newport Ave Chicago IL 60618 773-463-3000 463-3181
Web: www.neimanbrothers.com
O S F Flavors Inc 40 Baker Hollow Rd Windsor CT 06095 860-298-8350 298-8363
TF: 800-466-6015 ■ *Web:* www.osfflavors.com
Otis McAllister Inc 160 Pine St Ste 350 San Francisco CA 94111 415-421-6010 421-6016
Web: www.otismac.com
Otto Brehm Inc PO Box 249 Yonkers NY 10710 914-968-6100 968-8926
TF: 800-272-6886 ■ *Web:* www.ottobrehm.com
Producers Rice Mill Inc PO Box 1248. Stuttgart AR 72160 870-673-4444 673-8131
TF: 800-369-7675 ■ *Web:* www.producersrice.com
Rain Creek Baking Co, The 2401 W Almond Ave Madera CA 93637 559-674-4445 674-4466
TF: 800-530-0505 ■ *Web:* www.raincreekbaking.com
ReNew Life Formulas Inc
2076 Sunnydale Blvd Clearwater FL 33765 727-450-1061 594-5468*
**Fax Area Code:* 866 ■ *TF:* 800-830-1800 ■ *Web:* www.renewlife.com
Riceland Foods Inc PO Box 927. Stuttgart AR 72160 870-673-5500 673-3366
Web: www.riceland.com
Ron-Son Foods Inc PO Box 38 Swedesboro NJ 08085 856-241-7333 241-7338
Web: www.ronsonfoods.com
Roxy Trading Inc 389 Humane Way Pomona CA 91768 626-610-1388 610-1339
Web: www.roxytrading.com
Royal Pacific Tea Company Inc, The
PO Box 6277 Scottsdale AZ 85261 480-951-8251 951-0092
Web: www.royalpacificintl.com
Schreiber Foods International Inc
600 E Crescent Ave Ste 103 Upper Saddle River NJ 07458 201-327-3535 327-2812
TF: 800-631-7070 ■ *Web:* www.ambrosia-foods.com
Setton Pistachio of Terra Bella Inc
9370 Rd 234 PO Box 11089. Terra Bella CA 93270 559-535-6050 535-6089
Web: www.settonfarms.com
Silver Springs Bottled Water Company Inc
PO Box 926 Silver Springs FL 34489 800-556-0334 368-2374*
**Fax Area Code:* 352 ■ *TF:* 800-556-0334 ■ *Web:* www.ssbwc.com
SK Food International Inc 4666 Amber Vly Pkwy. Fargo ND 58104 701-356-4106 356-4102
Web: www.skfood.com
Sturm Foods Inc PO Box 287. Manawa WI 54949 920-596-2511 596-3040
TF: 800-347-8876 ■ *Web:* www.sturmfoods.com
Sugar Foods Corp 950 Third Ave 21st Fl New York NY 10022 212-753-6900 753-6988
TF: 800-732-8963 ■ *Web:* www.sugarfoods.com
Sunsweet Growers Inc 901 N Walton Ave Yuba City CA 95993 530-674-5010 751-5238
TF: 800-417-2253 ■ *Web:* www.sunsweet.com
Sysco Indianapolis LLC 4000 W 62nd St Indianapolis IN 46268 317-291-2020 717-4561*
**Fax Area Code:* 877 ■ *TF:* 800-347-3920 ■ *Web:* www.syscoindy.com
SYSCO Philadelphia LLC 600 Packer Ave. Philadelphia PA 19148 215-463-8200 218-1618
Web: www.syscophilly.com/ordereze/1000/Page.aspx
T. J. Harkins Co 279 Beaudin Blvd Bolingbrook IL 60440 630-427-3400 783-1806*
**Fax Area Code:* 603
United Sugars Corp
7803 Glenroy Rd Ste 300 Bloomington MN 55439 952-896-0131 896-0400
TF: 800-984-3585 ■ *Web:* www.unitedsugars.com
Westway Trading Corp
365 Canal St Ste 2929 New Orleans LA 70130 504-581-1620 522-1638
Web: www.westwaytrading.com
Wildflower Bread Co 7755 E Gray Rd Ste 101 Scottsdale AZ 85260 480-951-9453 951-9464
Web: www.wildflowerbread.com
William George Co Inc 1002 Mize Ave. Lufkin TX 75904 936-634-7738 634-7794
Web: www.williamgeorgeinc.com
Woodland Foods Inc 3751 Sunset Ave. Waukegan IL 60087 847-625-8600 625-5050
Web: www.woodlandfoods.com
Yamamoto of Orient Inc 122 Voyager St. Pomona CA 91768 909-594-7356 595-5849
Web: www.yamamotoyama.com

301 FOOD PRODUCTS MACHINERY

SEE ALSO Food Service Equipment & Supplies p. 2321

Phone Fax

Abec Inc 3998 Schelden Cir Bethlehem PA 18017 610-861-4666 861-2636
Web: www.abec.com
Acme Pizza & Bakery Equipment Inc
7039 E Slauson Blvd Commerce CA 90040 323-722-7900 726-4700
TF: 800-428-2263 ■ *Web:* www.acmepbe.com
Adamatic Equipment Corp
607 Industrial Way W Eatontown NJ 07724 732-544-8400 544-0735
TF: 800-526-2807 ■ *Web:* www.belshaw-adamatic.com
Alto-Shaam Inc
W 164 N 9221 Water St PO Box 450 Menomonee Falls WI 53052 262-251-3800 251-7067
TF: 800-329-8744 ■ *Web:* www.alto-shaam.com
American Permanent Ware Inc 729 Third Ave. Dallas TX 75226 214-421-7366 565-0976
TF: 800-527-2100 ■ *Web:* www.apwwyott.com
Anderson International Corp
6200 Harvard Ave. Cleveland OH 44105 216-641-1112 641-0709
TF: 800-336-4730 ■ *Web:* www.andersonintl.net
APV 1415 California Ave. Brockville ON K6V7H7 613-345-2280 760-1865*
**Fax Area Code:* 905 ■ *TF:* 800-263-3958 ■ *Web:* www.spx.com

Phone Fax

Atlas Metal Industries 1135 NW 159th Dr. Miami FL 33169 305-625-2451 623-0475
TF Cust Svc: 800-762-7565 ■ *Web:* www.atlasfoodserv.com
Atlas Pacific Engineering Co 1 Atlas Ave Pueblo CO 81001 719-948-3040 948-3058
TF: 800-588-5438 ■ *Web:* www.atlaspacific.com
Baader-Johnson 2955 Fairfax Trafficway Kansas City KS 66115 913-621-3366
Web: www.baader.com
Baker Perkins Inc 3223 Kraft Ave SE Grand Rapids MI 49512 616-784-3111 784-0973
Web: bakerperkins.com/
Belshaw Bros Inc 1750 22nd Ave S Seattle WA 98144 206-322-5474 322-5425
TF: 800-578-2547 ■ *Web:* www.belshaw-adamatic.com
Bepex International LLC 333 Taft St NE Minneapolis MN 55413 612-331-4370 627-1444
Web: www.bepex.com
Bettcher Industries Inc PO Box 336 Vermilion OH 44089 440-965-4422 967-6166
TF: 800-321-8763 ■ *Web:* www.bettcher.com
BIRO Mfg Co 1114 W Main St. Marblehead OH 43440 419-798-4451 798-9106
Web: www.birosaw.com
Brewmatic Co
20333 S Normandie Ave PO Box 2959 Torrance CA 90509 310-787-5444 787-5412
TF: 800-421-6860 ■ *Web:* www.brewmatic.com
C Cretors & Co 3243 N California Ave. Chicago IL 60618 773-588-1690 588-7141
TF: 800-228-1885 ■ *Web:* www.cretors.com
Carlisle Cos Inc
13925 Ballantyne Corporate Pl Ste 400 Charlotte NC 28277 704-501-1100 501-1190
NYSE: CSL ■ *TF:* 800-248-5995 ■ *Web:* www.carlisle.com
Casa Herrerra Inc 2655 N Pine St Pomona CA 91767 909-392-3930 392-0231
TF: 800-624-3916 ■ *Web:* www.casaherrera.com
CE Rogers Co 1895 Frontage Rd Mora MN 55051 320-679-2172 679-2180
TF: 800-279-8081 ■ *Web:* www.cerogers.com
Chester-Jensen Company Inc PO Box 908 Chester PA 19016 610-876-6276 876-0485
TF: 800-685-3750 ■ *Web:* www.chester-jensen.com
Cleveland Range Co 1333 E 179th St. Cleveland OH 44110 216-481-4900 481-3782
TF: 800-338-2204 ■ *Web:* www.clevelandrange.com
Colborne Corp 28495 N Ballard Dr. Lake Forest IL 60045 847-371-0101 371-0101
Web: www.colbornefoodbotics.com
CPM Wolverine Proctor LLC 251 Gibraltar Rd. Horsham PA 19044 215-443-5200 443-5206
TF: 800-428-0846 ■ *Web:* www.cpm.net
Delfield Co 980 S Isabella Rd Mount Pleasant MI 48858 989-773-7981 773-3210
TF: 800-733-8821 ■ *Web:* www.delfield.com
Duke Manufacturing Co 2305 N Broadway Saint Louis MO 63102 314-231-1130 231-5074
TF: 800-735-3853 ■ *Web:* www.dukemfg.com
Dunkley International Inc 1910 Lake St Kalamazoo MI 49001 269-343-5583 343-5614
TF: 800-666-1264 ■ *Web:* www.dunkleyintl.com
Dupps Co 548 N Cherry St. Germantown OH 45327 937-855-6555 855-6554
Web: www.dupps.com
Edlund Company Inc 159 Industrial Pkwy. Burlington VT 05401 802-862-9661 862-4822
TF: 800-772-2126 ■ *Web:* www.edlundco.com
Feldmeier Equipment Inc 6800 Townline Rd. Syracuse NY 13211 315-454-8608 454-3701
TF: 800-258-0118 ■ *Web:* www.feldmeier.com
Fish Oven & Equipment Corp 120 W Kent Ave Wauconda IL 60084 847-526-8686
TF: 877-526-8720 ■ *Web:* www.fishoven.com
Fitzpatrick Co 832 Industrial Dr Elmhurst IL 60126 630-530-3333 530-0832
Web: www.fitzmill.com
Food Warming Equipment Company Inc
7900 S Rt 31. Crystal Lake IL 60014 815-459-7500 459-7989
TF Sales: 800-222-4393 ■ *Web:* www.fwe.com
Frymaster LLC 8700 Line Ave Shreveport LA 71106 318-865-1711 868-5987
TF Cust Svc: 800-221-4583 ■ *Web:* www.frymaster.com
Fulton Iron & Mfg LLC 3844 Walsh St Saint Louis MO 63116 314-752-2400 353-2987
Web: www.fultoniron.net
Garland Commercial Industries 185 S St. Freeland PA 18224 570-636-1000 624-0218*
**Fax Area Code:* 800 ■ *TF:* 800-424-2411 ■ *Web:* www.garland-group.com
Gem Equipment of Oregon Inc PO Box 359 Woodburn OR 97071 503-982-9902 981-6316
Web: www.gemequipment.com
Globe Food Equipment Co 2153 Dryden Rd. Dayton OH 45439 937-299-5493 299-8623
TF: 800-347-5423 ■ *Web:* www.globeslicers.com
Great Western Mfg Co Inc
2017 S Fourth St PO Box 149. Leavenworth KS 66048 913-682-2291 682-1431
TF: 800-682-3121 ■ *Web:* www.gwmfg.com
Grindmaster Crathco Systems Inc
4003 Collins Ln Louisville KY 40245 502-425-4776 425-4664
TF: 800-695-4500 ■ *Web:* www.grindmaster.com
GS Blodgett Corp 44 Lakeside Ave Burlington VT 05401 802-658-6600 864-0183
TF: 800-331-5842 ■ *Web:* www.blodgett.com
Hayes & Stolz Industrial Manufacturing Co
3521 Hemphill St PO Box 11217 Fort Worth TX 76110 817-926-3391 926-4133
TF: 800-725-7272 ■ *Web:* www.hayes-stolz.com
Heat & Control Inc 21121 Cabot Blvd. Hayward CA 94545 510-259-0500 259-0600
TF: 800-227-5980 ■ *Web:* www.heatandcontrol.com
Henny Penny Corp 1219 US 35 W PO Box 60. Eaton OH 45320 937-456-8400 417-8402*
**Fax Area Code:* 800 ■ *TF:* 800-417-8417 ■ *Web:* www.hennypenny.com
Hobart Corp 701 S Ridge Ave Troy OH 45374 937-332-3000 332-2852
TF Cust Svc: 800-333-7447 ■ *Web:* www.hobartcorp.com
Hollymatic Corp 600 E Plainfield Rd Countryside IL 60525 708-579-3700 579-1057
Web: www.hollymatic.com
Horix Manufacturing Co 1384 Island Ave. McKees Rocks PA 15136 412-771-1111 331-8599
Idaho Steel Products Co
255 E Anderson St Idaho Falls ID 83401 208-522-1275 522-6041
Web: www.idahosteel.com
Insinger Machine Co 6245 State Rd. Philadelphia PA 19135 215-624-4800 624-6966
Web: insingermachine.com
ITW Food Equipment Group 701 S Ridge Ave Troy OH 45374 937-332-3000 332-2852
Web: www.hobartcorp.com
Jarvis Products Corp 33 Anderson Rd Middletown CT 06457 860-347-7271 347-6978
Web: www.jarvisproducts.com
Key Technology Inc 150 Avery St Walla Walla WA 99362 509-529-2161 527-1331
NASDAQ: KTEC ■ *TF:* 877-341-5668 ■ *Web:* www.key.net
Kuhl Corp 39 Kuhl Rd PO Box 26 Flemington NJ 08822 908-782-5696 782-2751
Web: www.kuhlcorp.com
Kwik Lok Corp 2712 S 16th Ave PO Box 9548 Yakima WA 98909 509-248-4770 457-6531
TF: 800-688-5945 ■ *Web:* www.kwiklok.com
Lawrence Equipment Inc 2034 Peck Rd El Monte CA 91733 626-442-2894 350-5181
TF: 800-423-4500 ■ *Web:* www.lawrenceequipment.com

Company	City	State	ZIP	*Phone*	*Fax*
Lewis M Carter Mfg Co PO Box 428 *TF:* 800-332-8232 ■ *Web:* www.lmcarter.com	Donalsonville	GA	39845	229-524-2197	524-2531
LK Industries 1357 W Beaver St *TF:* 800-531-4975 ■ *Web:* www.loadking.com	Jacksonville	FL	32209	904-354-8882	353-1984
Lucks Co, The 3003 S Pine St **Fax:* Orders ■ *TF:* 800-426-9778 ■ *Web:* www.lucks.com	Tacoma	WA	98409	253-383-4815	383-0071*
Luthi Machinery Co Inc 1 Magnuson Ave *TF:* 800-227-0682 ■ *Web:* www.luthi.com	Pueblo	CO	81003	719-948-1110	948-4273
M-E-C Co 1400 W Main St *Web:* www.m-e-c.com	Neodesha	KS	66757	620-325-2673	325-2678
Manitowoc Beverage Equipment 2100 Future Dr *TF:* 800-367-4233 ■ *Web:* www.manitowocbeverage.com	Sellersburg	IN	47172	812-246-7000	246-9922
Manitowoc Company Inc 2400 S 44th St *NYSE: MTW* ■ *Web:* www.manitowoc.com	Manitowoc	WI	54220	920-684-4410	652-9778
Market Forge Industries Inc 35 Garvey St **Fax Area Code:* 800 ■ *TF:* 866-698-3188 ■ *Web:* www.mfii.com	Everett	MA	02149	617-387-4100	227-2659*
Marlen International Inc 9202 Barton St **Fax Area Code:* 913 ■ *TF:* 800-862-7536 ■ *Web:* www.marlen.com	Overland Park	KS	66214	800-862-7536	888-6440*
Merco-Savory Inc 1111 N Hadley Rd *TF Cust Svc:* 888-417-5462 ■ *Web:* www.mercoproducts.com	Fort Wayne	IN	46804	260-459-8200	436-0735
Meyer Machine Company Inc 3528 Fredericksburg Rd PO Box 5460 *Web:* www.meyer-industries.com	San Antonio	TX	78201	210-736-1811	736-9452
Microfluidics International Corp 30 Ossipee Rd PO Box 9101 *TF:* 800-370-5452 ■ *Web:* www.microfluidicscorp.com	Newton	MA	02464	617-969-5452	965-1213
Middleby Corp 1400 Toastmaster Dr *NASDAQ: MIDD* ■ *TF:* 800-331-5842 ■ *Web:* www.middleby.com	Elgin	IL	60120	847-741-3300	741-0015
Myers Engineering Inc 8376 Salt Lk Ave *Web:* www.myersmixer.com	Bell	CA	90201	323-560-4723	771-7789
Nitta Casings Inc 141 Southside Ave PO Box 858 *TF Cust Svc:* 800-526-3970 ■ *Web:* www.nittacasings.com	Bridgewater	NJ	08807	908-218-4400	725-2835
Oliver Products Co 445 Sixth St NW *TF:* 800-253-3893 ■ *Web:* www.oliverproducts.com	Grand Rapids	MI	49504	616-456-7711	456-5820
Peerless Food Equipment 500 S Vandemark Rd *TF:* 800-999-3327 ■ *Web:* www.peerlessfood.com/	Sidney	OH	45365	937-492-4158	492-3688
Peerless Machinery Corp 500 S Vandenmark Rd PO Box 769 *TF:* 877-795-7377 ■ *Web:* www.peerlessfood.com	Sidney	OH	45365	937-492-4158	492-3688
Philadelphia Mixing Solutions, Ltd 1221 E Main St *TF:* 800-956-4937 ■ *Web:* www.philamixers.com	Palmyra	PA	17078	717-832-2800	832-1740
Piper Products Inc 300 S 84th Ave *TF:* 800-544-3057 ■ *Web:* www.piperonline.net	Wausau	WI	54401	715-842-2724	842-3125
Pitco Frialator Inc PO Box 501 *TF:* 800-258-3708 ■ *Web:* pitco.com	Concord	NH	03302	603-225-6684	225-8472
Planet Products Corp 4200 Malsbary Rd *Web:* www.planet-products.com	Cincinnati	OH	45242	513-984-5544	984-5580
Prince Castle Inc 355 E Kehoe Blvd *TF:* 800-722-7853 ■ *Web:* www.princecastle.com	Carol Stream	IL	60188	630-462-8800	462-1460
Resina West Inc 27455 Bostik Ct *Web:* www.resina.com	Temecula	CA	92590	951-296-6585	296-5018
RMF Steel Products Co 4417 E 119th St *Web:* www.rmfsteel.com	Grandview	MO	64030	816-765-4101	765-0067
Ross Industries Inc 5321 Midland Rd *TF:* 800-336-6010 ■ *Web:* www.rossindinc.com	Midland	VA	22728	540-439-3271	439-2740
S Howes Company Inc 25 Howard St *TF:* 888-255-2611 ■ *Web:* www.showes.com	Silver Creek	NY	14136	716-934-2611	934-2081
SaniServ Inc 451 E County Line Rd *TF:* 800-733-8073 ■ *Web:* www.saniserv.com	Mooresville	IN	46158	317-831-7030	831-7036
Schlueter Co 310 N Main St *TF:* 800-359-1700 ■ *Web:* www.schlueterco.com	Janesville	WI	53545	608-755-5444	755-5440
Server Products Inc 3601 Pleasant Hill Rd PO Box 98 *TF:* 800-558-8722 ■ *Web:* www.server-products.com	Richfield	WI	53076	262-628-5600	628-5110
Southbend Inc 1100 Old Honeycutt Rd *TF:* 800-755-4777 ■ *Web:* www.southbendnc.com	Fuquay-Varina	NC	27526	919-762-1000	762-1121
Stoelting LLC 502 Hwy 67 *TF:* 800-558-5807 ■ *Web:* www.stoelting.com	Kiel	WI	53042	920-894-2293	894-7029
Stolle Machinery Co LLC 6949 S Potomac St *TF:* 800-433-8333 ■ *Web:* www.stollemachinery.com	Centennial	CO	80112	303-708-9044	708-9045
Taylor 750 N Blackhawk Blvd *TF:* 800-255-0626 ■ *Web:* www.taylor-company.com	Rockton	IL	61072	815-624-8333	624-8000
Tomlinson Industries 13700 Broadway Ave **Fax Area Code:* 604 ■ *TF:* 800-945-4589 ■ *Web:* www.tomlinsonind.com	Cleveland	OH	44125	216-587-3400	939-7598*
Town Food Service Equipment Co 72 Beadel St *TF:* 800-221-5032 ■ *Web:* www.townfood.com	Brooklyn	NY	11222	718-388-5650	388-5860
Ultrafryer Systems Inc 302 Spencer Ln *Web:* www.ultrafryer.com	San Antonio	TX	78201	210-731-5000	731-5099
Union Standard Equipment Co 801 E 141st St *TF:* 877-282-7333 ■ *Web:* www.unionmachinery.com	Bronx	NY	10454	718-585-0200	993-2650
United Bakery Equipment Co Inc 15815 W 110th St *TF:* 888-823-2253 ■ *Web:* www.ubeusa.com	Lenexa	KS	66219	913-541-8700	541-0781
Univex Corp Three Old Rockingham Rd *TF:* 800-258-6358 ■ *Web:* www.univexcorp.com	Salem	NH	03079	603-893-6191	893-1249
Urschel Laboratories Inc 2503 Calumet Ave PO Box 2200 *TF:* 844-877-2435 ■ *Web:* www.urschel.com	Valparaiso	IN	46384	219-464-4811	462-3879
Van Doren Sales Inc 10 NE Cascade Ave *TF:* 866-886-1837 ■ *Web:* www.vandorensales.com	East Wenatchee	WA	98802	509-886-1837	886-2837
Vendome Copper & Brass Works Inc 729 Franklin St *Web:* www.vendomecopper.com	Louisville	KY	40202	502-587-1930	589-0639
Viking Range Corp 111 Front St *TF:* 888-845-4641 ■ *Web:* www.vikingrange.com	Greenwood	MS	38930	662-455-1200	455-3127
Volckening Inc 6700 Third Ave *Web:* www.volckening.com	Brooklyn	NY	11220	718-836-4000	748-2811
Walker Stainless Equipment Co LLC 625 W State St *TF:* 800-356-5734 ■ *Web:* www.walkerstainless.com	New Lisbon	WI	53950	608-562-7500	562-7549
Wells Bloomfield Industries 10 Sunnen Dr **Fax Area Code:* 800 ■ *TF:* 888-356-5362 ■ *Web:* www.wellsbloomfield.com	Saint Louis	MO	63143	888-356-5362	264-6666*
Wenger Manufacturing Inc 714 Main St *Web:* www.wenger.com	Sabetha	KS	66534	785-284-2133	284-3771
Wilbur Curtis Company Inc 6913 Acco St *TF:* 800-421-6150 ■ *Web:* www.wilburcurtis.com	Montebello	CA	90640	323-837-2300	837-2406
Winston Industries LLC 2345 Carton Dr *TF:* 800-234-5286 ■ *Web:* www.winstonind.com	Louisville	KY	40299	502-495-5400	495-5458
Witte Company Inc 507 Rt 31 S PO Box 47 *Web:* www.witte.com	Washington	NJ	07882	908-689-6500	537-6806

302 FOOD SERVICE

SEE ALSO Restaurant Companies p. 3069

Company	City	State	ZIP	*Phone*	*Fax*
A'viands LLC 1751 County Rd B W Ste 300 *Web:* www.aviands.com	Roseville	MN	55113	651-631-0940	
Advance Food Company Inc 9987 Carver Rd Ste 500 **Fax Area Code:* 580 ■ *TF:* 800-969-2747 ■ *Web:* www.advancepierre.com	Cincinnati	OH	45242	800-969-2747	213-4707*
Aircraft Service International Group 201 S Orange Ave Ste 1100 *Web:* www.asig.com	Orlando	FL	32801	407-648-7373	206-5391
American Food & Vending Corp 124 Metropolitan Pk Dr *TF:* 800-466-9261 ■ *Web:* www.afvusa.com	Syracuse	NY	13088	315-457-9950	457-9103
ARAMARK Food & Support Services 1101 Market St *TF:* 800-388-3300 ■ *Web:* www.aramark.com	Philadelphia	PA	19107	215-238-3000	238-3333
Atlas Food Systems & Services Inc 205 Woods Lk Rd *TF:* 800-476-1123 ■ *Web:* www.atlasfoods.com	Greenville	SC	29607	864-232-1885	232-1671
Blue Line Foodservice Distribution 24120 Haggerty Rd **Fax Area Code:* 248 ■ *TF General:* 800-892-8272 ■ *Web:* www.bluelinedist.com	Farmington Hills	MI	48335	800-892-8272	442-4570*
Bon Appetit Management Co 100 Hamilton Ave Ste 400 *Web:* www.bamco.com	Palo Alto	CA	94301	650-798-8000	798-8090
Bran-Zan Holdings Inc 1548 Barclay Blvd *TF:* 866-266-9670 ■ *Web:* www.branzan.com	Buffalo Grove	IL	60089	866-266-9670	
Canteen Service Co 712 Industrial Dr *TF:* 800-467-2471 ■ *Web:* www.canteenatyourservice.com	Owensboro	KY	42301	270-683-2471	
Canteen Vending Services *Compass Group* 2400 Yorkmont Rd *TF:* 800-357-0012 ■ *Web:* www.compass-usa.com	Charlotte	NC	28217	704-328-4000	
Cara Operations Ltd 199 Four Valley Dr *TF:* 800-860-4082 ■ *Web:* www.cara.com	Vaughan	ON	L4K0B8	905-760-2244	
Centerplate 2187 Atlantic St *TF:* 800-698-6992 ■ *Web:* www.centerplate.com	Stamford	CT	06902	203-975-5900	
Chefs' Warehouse Holdings LLC 100 E Ridge Rd *Web:* www.chefswarehouse.com	Ridgefield	CT	06877	718-842-8700	
CL Swanson Corp 4501 Femrite Dr *Web:* www.swansons.net	Madison	WI	53716	608-221-7640	221-7648
Compass Group North American Div (CGNAD) 2400 Yorkmont Rd *TF:* 800-357-0012 ■ *Web:* www.compass-usa.com	Charlotte	NC	28217	704-328-4000	
Culinaire International 2100 Ross Ave Ste 3100 *Web:* www.culinaireintl.com	Dallas	TX	75201	214-754-1880	754-1891
Edsung Foodservice 1337 Mookaula St *Web:* edsung.com	Honolulu	HI	96817	808-845-3931	
Excelsior Grand 2380 Hylan Blvd *TF:* 888-233-6743 ■ *Web:* www.excelsiorgrand.com	Staten Island	NY	10306	718-987-4800	987-4803
Five Star Food Service Inc 6005 Century Oaks Dr Ste 100 *TF:* 800-327-0043 ■ *Web:* www.fivestar-food.com	Chattanooga	TN	37416	423-643-2600	
Flying Food Group 212 N Sangamon St Ste 1-A *Web:* www.flyingfood.com	Chicago	IL	60607	312-243-2122	264-2490
Food Bank For New York City 39 Broadway 10th Fl *TF:* 866-692-3663 ■ *Web:* www.foodbanknyc.org	New York	NY	10006	212-566-7855	566-1463
Garb-ko Inc 3925 Fortune Blvd *Web:* 7-eleven.com	Saginaw	MI	48603	989-799-6937	
GC Partners Inc 3816 Forrestgate Dr *Web:* www.gcpartners.com	Winston Salem	NC	27103	336-767-1600	744-2610
General Mills Inc One General Mills Blvd *NYSE: GIS* ■ **Fax Area Code:* 763 ■ **Fax:* PR ■ *TF:* 800-248-7310 ■ *Web:* www.generalmills.com	Minneapolis	MN	55426	800-248-7310	764-8330*
Guest Services Inc 3055 Prosperity Ave *TF:* 800-345-7534 ■ *Web:* www.guestservices.com	Fairfax	VA	22031	703-849-9300	641-4690
HMSHost Corp 6905 Rockledge Dr # 1 *Web:* www.hmshost.com	Bethesda	MD	20817	240-694-4100	694-4790
Host America Corporate Dining Inc One Leonardo Dr	North Haven	CT	06473	203-239-4678	234-1503
Institution Food House Inc (IFH) 543 12th St Dr NW **Fax Area Code:* 828 ■ *TF:* 800-800-0434 ■ *Web:* ifh.com	Hickory	NC	28601	800-800-0434	725-4500*
Institutional Wholesale Co 535 Dry Vly Rd **Fax:* Cust Svc ■ *TF:* 800-239-9588 ■ *Web:* goiwc.com	Cookeville	TN	38506	931-537-4000	537-4017*
Island Oasis 141 Norfolk St PO Box 769 *TF:* 800-777-4752 ■ *Web:* www.islandoasis.com	Walpole	MA	02081	508-660-1176	
Lackmann Culinary Services 303 Crossways Pk Dr *Web:* www.lackmann.com	Woodbury	NY	11797	516-364-2300	364-9788
Lee Bros Foodservice Inc 660 E Gish Rd *Web:* www.leebros.com	San Jose	CA	95112	408-275-0700	275-0416
Love & Quiches Desserts 178 Hanse Ave *TF:* 800-525-5251 ■ *Web:* www.loveandquiches.com	Freeport	NY	11520	516-623-8800	623-8817

Phone Fax

Maximum Quality Foods Inc 3351 Tremley Pt Rd........Linden NJ 07036 908-474-0003 474-1320
Web: www.maximumqualityfoods.com

Morrison Management Specialists Inc
5801 Peachtree Dunwoody Rd........Atlanta GA 30342 800-225-4368 845-3333*
**Fax Area Code:* 404 ■ *TF General:* 800-367-5690 ■ *Web:* www.iammorrison.com

Nantze Springs Inc 156 W Carroll St........Dothan AL 36301 334-794-4218
TF: 800-239-7873 ■ *Web:* www.nantzesprings.com

Open Kitchen Inc 1161 W 21st St........Chicago IL 60608 312-666-5335 666-9242
TF: 800-339-5334 ■ *Web:* www.openkitchens.com

Port City Java Inc
101 Portwatch Way PO Box 785........Wilmington NC 28412 910-796-6646
Web: www.portcityjava.com

Rodrigo's Online Store 1320 N Manzanita........Orange CA 92867 714-633-7844
Web: www.rodrigos-shop.com

Romeo & Sons Inc 100 Romeo Ln........Uniontown PA 15401 724-438-5561 438-1149
Web: www.romeofoods.com

Sanese Services Inc 6465 Busch Blvd........Columbus OH 43229 614-436-1234
Web: avifoodsystems.com

SeamlessWeb Professional Solutions LLC
232 Madison Ave Ste 1409........New York NY 10016 212-944-7755
Web: www.seamless.com

Signature Services Corp
2705 Hawes Ave PO Box 35885........Dallas TX 75235 214-353-2661 353-4843
TF: 800-929-5519 ■ *Web:* www.signatureservices.com

Sodexo Inc 9801 Washingtonian Blvd........Gaithersburg MD 20878 800-763-3946 987-4438*
**Fax Area Code:* 301 ■ *TF:* 800-763-3946 ■ *Web:* www.sodexousa.com

Spartan Foods of America Inc PO Box 1003........Fairforest SC 29336 864-595-6262 576-5972
Web: www.mamamarys.com

Sportservice Corp 40 Fountain Plz........Buffalo NY 14202 716-858-5000 858-5424
TF: 800-828-7240 ■ *Web:* delawarenorth.com

Summit Food Service Distributors Inc
580 Industrial Rd........London ON N5V1V1 519-453-3410 453-5148
TF: 800-265-9267 ■ *Web:* summit.colabor.com

Sysco Jacksonville Inc
1501 Lewis Industrial Dr PO Box 37045........Jacksonville FL 32254 904-786-2600 695-8135
TF General: 800-786-2611 ■ *Web:* www.sysco-jax.com

SYSCO Philadelphia LLC 600 Packer Ave........Philadelphia PA 19148 215-463-8200 218-1618
Web: www.syscophilly.com/ordereze/1000/Page.aspx

Sysco Portland Inc 26250 SW Pkwy Ctr Dr........Wilsonville OR 97070 503-682-8700 682-6699
Web: www.syscoportland.com

Taher Inc 5570 Smetana Dr........Minnetonka MN 55343 952-945-0505 945-0444
Web: www.taher.com

Trujillo & Sons Inc 3325 NW 62nd ST........Miami FL 33147 305-696-8701 696-4510
Web: www.trujilloandsons.com

Universal Sodexho 5749 Susitna Dr........Harahan LA 70123 301-987-4000
TF: 888-763-3967 ■ *Web:* sodexousa.com/usen/default.aspx

Value Creation Partners Inc
445 Hutchinson Ave........Columbus OH 43235 614-515-5515

Zaugs Inc 4100 W Wisconsin Ave........Appleton WI 54913 920-734-9881 734-4322

303 FOOD SERVICE EQUIPMENT & SUPPLIES

SEE ALSO Food Products Machinery p. 2319

Phone Fax

Adams-Burch Inc 1901 Stanford Ct........Landover MD 20785 301-276-2000 341-5114
TF Cust Svc: 800-347-8093 ■ *Web:* www.adams-burch.com

Advance Tabco 200 Heartland Blvd........Edgewood NY 11717 631-242-4800 242-6900
TF: 800-645-3166 ■ *Web:* www.advancetabco.com

Anderson-DuBose Co 5300 Tod Ave SW........Lordstown OH 44481 440-248-8800 824-2256*
**Fax Area Code:* 330 ■ *TF:* 800-248-1080 ■ *Web:* anderson-dubose.com

Atlanta Fixture & Sales Co 3185 NE Expy........Atlanta GA 30341 770-455-8844 986-9202
TF: 800-282-1977 ■ *Web:* www.atlantafixture.com

Bargreen Ellingson Inc 2925 70th Ave E........Fife WA 98424 253-722-2600 896-3620
TF: 866-722-2665 ■ *Web:* www.bargreen.com

Boelter Cos Inc
N22W23685 Ridgeview Pkwy W........West Waukesha WI 53188 262-523-6200 523-6003
TF: 800-263-5837 ■ *Web:* www.boelter.com

Bolton & Hay Inc 2701 Delaware Ave........Des Moines IA 50317 515-265-2554 265-6090
TF: 800-362-1861 ■ *Web:* www.boltonhay.com

Browne & Co 100 Esna Pk Dr........Markham ON L3R1E3 905-475-6104 475-5843
TF: 866-306-3672 ■ *Web:* www.browneco.com

Browne-Halco Inc 2840 Morris Ave........Union NJ 07083 973-232-1065 964-6677*
**Fax Area Code:* 908 ■ *TF:* 888-289-1005 ■ *Web:* www.halco.com

Buffalo Hotel Supply Company Inc
375 Commerce Dr........Amherst NY 14228 716-691-8080
TF: 800-333-1678 ■ *Web:* www.buffalohotelsupply.com

Cambro Manufacturing Co
5801 Skylab Rd........Huntington Beach CA 92647 714-848-1555 842-3430*
**Fax:* Cust Svc ■ *TF:* 800-833-3003 ■ *Web:* www.cambro.com

Carlisle FoodService Products Inc
4711 E Hefner Rd........Oklahoma City OK 73131 405-475-5600 475-5607
TF: 800-654-8210 ■ *Web:* www.carlislefsp.com

CHUDNOW Mfg Company Inc
3055 New St PO Box 10........Oceanside NY 11572 516-593-4222 593-4156
Web: www.chudnowmfg.com

Curtis Restaurant Supply & Equipment Co
6577 E 40th St........Tulsa OK 74145 918-622-7390 665-0990
TF: 800-766-2878 ■ *Web:* www.curtisequipment.com

Eagle Group Inc 100 Industrial Blvd........Clayton DE 19938 302-653-3000 653-2065
TF: 800-441-8440 ■ *Web:* www.eaglegrp.com

Edsung Foodservice 1337 Mookaula St........Honolulu HI 96817 808-845-3931
Web: edsung.com

Edward Don & Co 2500 S Harlem Ave........North Riverside IL 60546 800-777-4366 883-8676*
**Fax Area Code:* 708 ■ *TF Cust Svc:* 800-777-4366 ■ *Web:* www.don.com

Genpak Carthage 505 E Cotton St........Carthage TX 75633 903-693-7151 932-5222*
**Fax Area Code:* 800 ■ *TF:* 800-626-6695 ■ *Web:* www.genpak.com

HB Hunter Co 1512 Brown Ave PO Box 1599........Norfolk VA 23504 757-664-5200 664-2372

Hotel & Restaurant Supply Inc
5020 Arundel Rd PO Box 6........Meridian MS 39302 601-482-7127 482-7170
TF: 800-782-6651 ■ *Web:* www.hnrsupply.com

Phone Fax

Intedge Mfg 1875 Chumley Rd........Woodruff SC 29388 864-969-9601 969-9604
TF: 866-969-9605 ■ *Web:* www.intedge.com

InterMetro Industries Corp
651 N Washington St........Wilkes-Barre PA 18705 570-825-2741 823-2852*
**Fax:* Hum Res ■ *TF Cust Svc:* 800-992-1776 ■ *Web:* www.metro.com

Kittredge Equipment Co Inc 100 Bowles Rd........Agawam MA 01001 413-304-4100 786-7086
TF: 800-423-7082 ■ *Web:* www.kittredgeequipment.com

Lakeside Manufacturing Inc
4900 W Electric Ave........West Milwaukee WI 53219 414-902-6400 902-6446
TF: 800-558-8565 ■ *Web:* www.elakeside.com

Lancaster Colony Commercial Products Inc
3902 Indianola Ave........Columbus OH 43214 614-263-2850 263-2857
TF: 800-292-7260 ■ *Web:* www.lccpinc.com

Maines Paper & Food Service Co
101 Broome Corporate Pkwy........Conklin NY 13748 607-779-1200 723-3245*
**Fax:* Cust Svc ■ *TF:* 800-366-3669 ■ *Web:* www.maines.net

Manitowoc Foodservice
2227 Welbilt Blvd........New Port Richey FL 34655 727-375-7010
Web: www.manitowocfoodservice.com

McLane Foodservice Inc 2085 Midway Rd........Carrollton TX 75006 972-364-2000 771-7244*
**Fax Area Code:* 254 ■ *TF:* 800-299-1401 ■ *Web:* www.mclaneco.com

N Wasserstrom & Sons Inc 2300 Lockbourne Rd........Columbus OH 43207 614-228-5550 737-8501
TF: 800-444-4697 ■ *Web:* www.wasserstrom.com

PBI Market Equipment Inc 2667 Gundry Ave........Signal Hill CA 90755 562-595-4785 426-2262
TF: 800-421-3753 ■ *Web:* www.pbimarketing.com

Perkins Equipment Div 630 John Hancock Rd........Taunton MA 02780 508-824-2800 821-2670
TF: 800-733-5708 ■ *Web:* www.perkins1.com

RAPIDS Wholesale Equipment Co
6201 S Gateway Dr........Marion IA 52302 319-447-1670 447-1680
TF: 800-472-7431 ■ *Web:* rapidswholesale.com

Regal Ware Inc 1675 Reigle Dr........Kewaskum WI 53040 262-626-2121 626-8565
Web: www.regalware.com

Reinhart Food Service
7735 Westside Industrial Dr........Jacksonville FL 32219 904-781-9888 786-7035
TF: 888-781-5464 ■ *Web:* www.rfsdelivers.com

Restaurant & Stores Equipment Co
230 West 700 South........Salt Lake City UT 84101 801-364-1981 355-2029
TF: 800-877-0087 ■ *Web:* rescoslc.com

Restaurant Technologies Inc
2250 Pilot Knob Rd Ste 100........Mendota Heights MN 55120 651-796-1600 379-4082
TF: 888-796-4997 ■ *Web:* www.rti-inc.com

Ricos Products Company Inc
830 S Presa St........San Antonio TX 78210 210-222-1415 226-6453
Web: www.ricos.com

Service Ideas Inc 2354 Ventura Dr........Woodbury MN 55125 651-730-8800 730-8880
TF: 800-328-4493 ■ *Web:* www.serviceideas.com

Smith & Greene Co 19015 66th Ave S........Kent WA 98032 425-656-8000 656-8075
TF: 800-232-8050 ■ *Web:* www.smithandgreene.com

Southern Foods Inc
3500 Old Battleground Rd........Greensboro NC 27410 336-545-3800 545-5281
Web: www.southernfoods.com

Standex International Corp Food Service Equipment Group
11 Keewaydin Dr........Salem NH 03079 603-893-9701 893-7324
NYSE: SXI ■ *TF:* 800-647-1284 ■ *Web:* www.standex.com

SYSCO Corp 1390 Enclave Pkwy........Houston TX 77077 281-584-1390 584-1737*
NYSE: SYY ■ **Fax:* PR ■ *Web:* www.sysco.com

TriMark USA Inc 505 Collins St........South Attleboro MA 02703 508-399-2400 761-3605
TF: 800-755-5580 ■ *Web:* www.trimarkusa.com

United Restaurant Equipment Company Inc
One Executive Park Dr........North Billerica MA 01862 978-439-5500 262-9999
Web: www.unitedrestaurant.com

US Foods Culinary Equipment & Supplies
2621 Fairview Ave N Ste 2........Roseville MN 55113 651-638-8993
TF: 866-636-2338 ■ *Web:* www.usfoodsculinaryequipmentandsupplies.com

Vollrath Co LLC, The 1236 N 18th St........Sheboygan WI 53081 920-457-4851 459-6570
TF: 800-624-2051 ■ *Web:* vollrath.com

Wasserstrom Co 477 S Front St........Columbus OH 43215 614-228-6525 737-8911
TF: 866-634-8927 ■ *Web:* www.wasserstrom.com

Western Pioneer Sales Co 406 E Colorado St........Glendale CA 91205 818-244-1466 245-7285*
**Fax Area Code:* 323 ■ *Web:* westernpioneersales.com

304 FOOTWEAR

Phone Fax

Acor Orthopaedic Inc 18530 S Miles Pkwy........Cleveland OH 44128 216-662-4500 662-4547
TF: 800-237-2267 ■ *Web:* www.acor.com

Acushnet Co 333 Bridge St........Fairhaven MA 02719 508-979-2000 979-3927*
**Fax:* Hum Res ■ *TF:* 800-225-8500 ■ *Web:* www.acushnetcompany.com

Aerosoles Inc 201 Meadow Rd........Edison NJ 08817 732-985-6900 985-1332
TF: 800-798-9478 ■ *Web:* www.aerosoles.com

Aldo Shoes 2300 Emile Belanger........Montreal QC H4R3J4 514-747-2536
TF: 888-818-2536 ■ *Web:* www.aldoshoes.com

Allen-Edmonds Shoe Corp
201 E Seven Hills Rd........Port Washington WI 53074 262-235-6512 235-6265
TF Cust Svc: 800-235-2348 ■ *Web:* www.allenedmonds.com

Ariat International Inc 3242 Whipple Rd........Union City CA 94587 510-477-7000
Web: ariat.com

Asics America Corp 29 Parker Ste 100........Irvine CA 92618 949-453-8888 453-0292
TF: 800-333-8404 ■ *Web:* www.asicsamerica.com

ATP-USA Mfg LLC 600 Putnam Pike Suite 8........Greenville RI 02858 401-757-3910 766-5327
Web: www.atp-usa.com

Badorf Shoe Co Inc
1958 Auction Road PO Box 367........Manheim PA 17545 717-653-0155 627-4952
TF: 800-325-1545 ■ *Web:* www.badorfshoe.com

Barbour Welting Company Div Barbour Corp
1001 N Montello St........Brockton MA 02301 508-583-8200 583-4113
TF: 800-955-9649 ■ *Web:* www.barbourcorp.com

Belleville Shoe Manufacturing Co
100 Premier Dr........Belleville IL 62220 618-233-5600 257-1112
Web: www.bellevilleboot.com

Company	City	State	Zip	Phone	Fax
Benchmark Brands Inc 5250 Triangle Pkwy Ste 200 *Web:* www.benchmarkbrands.com	Norcross	GA	30092	770-242-1254	242-1962
Brooks Sports Inc 19910 N Creek Pkwy Ste 200 **Fax Area Code:* 425 ■ *TF:* 800-227-6657 ■ *Web:* www.brooksrunning.com	Bothell	WA	98011	800-227-6657	489-1975*
Capezio/Ballet Makers Inc One Campus Rd *TF Acctg:* 800-533-1887 ■ *Web:* www.capezio.com	Totowa	NJ	07512	973-595-9000	595-9120
Cardinal Shoe Corp 468 Canal St *Web:* cardinalshoe.com	Lawrence	MA	01840	978-686-9706	686-9707
Cels Enterprises Inc 3485 S La Cienega Blvd *Web:* www.chineselaundry.com	Los Angeles	CA	90016	310-838-2103	838-8732
Charles David of California 5731 Buckingham Pkwy	Culver City	CA	90230	310-348-5050	348-5041
Cherokee Inc 5990 Sepulveda Blvd Ste 600 *NASDAQ: CHKE* ■ *Web:* www.thecherokeegroup.com	Sherman Oaks	CA	91411	818-908-9868	
Chinese Laundry Shoes 3485 S La Cienega Blvd *TF:* 888-935-8825 ■ *Web:* www.chineselaundry.com	Los Angeles	CA	90016	310-838-2103	838-8732
Clark Cos NA 156 Oak St *TF Cust Svc:* 800-211-5461 ■ *Web:* www.clarksusa.com	Newton Upper Falls	MA	02464	617-964-1222	243-4213
Cole-Haan 8701 Keystone Crossing *TF:* 800-695-8945 ■ *Web:* www.colehaan.com	Indianapolis	IN	46240	317-810-0160	
Connors Footwear 20 Whitcher St	Lisbon	NH	03585	603-838-6694	
Consolidated Shoe Company Inc 22290 Timberlake Rd **Fax:* Sales ■ *TF:* 800-368-7463 ■ *Web:* www.consolidatedshoe.com/	Lynchburg	VA	24502	434-239-0391	582-5631*
Cowtown Boots 11401 Gateway Blvd W *TF:* 800-580-2698 ■ *Web:* store.cowtownboots.com	El Paso	TX	79936	915-593-2709	593-2249
Crocs Inc 6328 Monarch Pk Pl *NASDAQ: CROX* ■ *TF:* 866-306-3179 ■ *Web:* www.crocs.com	Niwot	CO	80503	303-848-7000	468-4266
Dan Post Boot Co 1751 Alpine Dr *Web:* www.danpostboots.com	Clarksville	TN	37040	931-645-1626	
Danner Shoe Manufacturing Co 17634 NE Airport *TF Cust Svc:* 800-345-0430 ■ *Web:* www.danner.com	Portland	OR	97230	503-251-1100	251-1119
Deckers Outdoor Corp 495-A S Fairview Ave *NYSE: DECK* ■ *TF:* 877-337-8333 ■ *Web:* www.deckers.com	Goleta	CA	93117	805-967-7611	967-9722
Drew Shoe Corp 252 Quarry Rd *TF:* 800-837-3739 ■ *Web:* www.drewshoe.com	Lancaster	OH	43130	740-653-4271	654-4979
East Lion Corp 318 Brea Canyon Rd *TF:* 877-939-1818 ■ *Web:* www.eastlioncorp.com	City of Industry	CA	91789	626-912-1818	935-5858
Eastland Shoe Mfg Corp 4 Meeting House Rd *TF:* 888-988-1998 ■ *Web:* www.eastlandshoe.com	Freeport	ME	04032	207-865-6314	865-9261
ES Originals Inc 440 9th Ave 7th Fl *TF General:* 800-677-6577 ■ *Web:* www.esoriginals.com	New York	NY	10001	212-736-8124	736-8366
Famous Footwear 7010 Mineral Pt Rd *TF Cust Svc:* 800-888-7198 ■ *Web:* www.famousfootwear.com	Madison	WI	53717	608-833-3340	
Fancy Feet Inc 26650 Harding St	Oak Park	MI	48237	248-398-8460	398-5650
Finish Line Inc, The 3308 N Mitthoeffer Rd *NASDAQ: FINL* ■ *TF:* 888-777-3949 ■ *Web:* www.finishline.com	Indianapolis	IN	46235	317-899-1022	899-0237
Florsheim Inc 333 W Estabrook Blvd **Fax Area Code:* 414 ■ *TF:* 866-454-0449 ■ *Web:* www.florsheim.com	Glendale	WI	53212	866-454-0449	908-1601*
Foot Locker Inc 112 W 34th St *NYSE: FL* ■ *TF:* 800-952-5210 ■ *Web:* www.footlocker-inc.com	New York	NY	10120	212-720-3700	720-4460
Foot Solutions Inc 2359 Windy Hill Rd Ste 400 **Fax Area Code:* 602 ■ *TF General:* 888-358-3668 ■ *Web:* footsolutions.com	Marietta	GA	30067	770-984-0844	298-1823*
Foot-So-Port Shoe Corp 405 E Forest St PO Box 247 *Web:* www.footsoport.com	Oconomowoc	WI	53066	262-567-4416	567-5323
Footaction Inc 112 W 34th St *TF:* 800-863-8932 ■ *Web:* www.footaction.com	New York	NY	10120	715-261-9588	
Footstar Inc 933 MacArthur Blvd *TF:* 800-322-2885 ■ *Web:* www.footstar.com	Mahwah	NJ	07430	201-934-2000	
Gateway Shoe Co 910 Kehro Mill Rd Ste 112 *TF:* 800-539-6063 ■ *Web:* www.gatewayshoes.com	Ballwin	MO	63011	636-256-7050	527-3797
Genesco Inc 1415 Murfreesboro Rd *NYSE: GCO* ■ *Web:* www.genesco.com	Nashville	TN	37217	615-367-7000	
Georgia Boot Inc 39 E Canal St *TF:* 877-795-2410 ■ *Web:* www.georgiaboot.com	Nelsonville	OH	45764	740-753-1951	
HH Brown Shoe Company Inc 124 W Putnam Ave *TF:* 888-444-2769 ■ *Web:* www.hhbrown.com	Greenwich	CT	06830	203-661-2424	661-1818
Hush Puppies Co 9341 Courtland Dr NE **Fax:* Acctg ■ *TF:* 866-699-7365 ■ *Web:* www.hushpuppies.com	Rockford	MI	49351	616-866-5500	866-5625*
Ilani Shoes Ltd 1350 Broadway	New York	NY	10018	212-947-5830	
Impo International Inc PO Box 639 *TF:* 800-367-4676 ■ *Web:* www.impo.com	Santa Maria	CA	93456	805-922-7753	
Inter-Pacific Corp 2257 Colby Ave *TF:* 877-605-8414	Los Angeles	CA	90064	310-473-7591	
International Marketing Assn (IMA) 3509 Virginia Beach Blvd *Web:* www.imacorporate.com	Virginia Beach	VA	23452	757-490-9860	490-0716
Jack Schwartz Shoes Inc 155 Ave of the Americas *Web:* www.lugz.com	New York	NY	10013	212-691-4700	
John Reyer Shoe Store 40 S Water Ave **Fax Area Code:* 724 ■ *TF Cust Svc:* 800-245-1550 ■ *Web:* www.reyers.com	Sharon	PA	16146	800-245-1550	983-8269*
Johnston & Murphy Inc 1415 Murfreesboro Rd *TF:* 800-424-2854 ■ *Web:* www.johnstonmurphy.com	Nashville	TN	37217	615-367-7168	367-7139
Justin Boot Co Inc 610 W Daggett St **Fax Area Code:* 405 ■ **Fax:* Cust Svc ■ *TF Cust Svc:* 866-240-8853 ■ *Web:* www.justinboots.com	Fort Worth	TX	76104	817-332-7797	521-9801*
K-Swiss Inc 31248 Oak Crest Dr *NASDAQ: KSWS* ■ *TF:* 800-938-8000 ■ *Web:* www.kswiss.com	Westlake Village	CA	91361	818-706-5100	706-5390
Kaepa USA Inc 9050 Autobahn Dr Ste 500 *Web:* www.kaepa.com	Dallas	TX	75237	972-296-7300	
Keds Corp 1400 Industries Rd *TF:* 800-680-0966 ■ *Web:* www.keds.com	Richmond	IN	47374	800-680-0966	446-1339
Kenneth Cole Productions Inc 603 W 50th St *NYSE: KCP* ■ **Fax:* Cust Svc ■ *TF:* 800-536-2653 ■ *Web:* www.kennethcole.com	New York	NY	10019	212-265-1500	315-8279*
L A Gear Inc 844 Moraga Dr *Web:* www.lagear.com	Los Angeles	CA	90049	310-889-3499	
La Sportiva North America Inc 3850 Frontier Ave Ste 100 *Web:* www.sportiva.com	Boulder	CO	80301	303-443-8710	442-7541
LaCrosse Footwear Inc 17634 NE Airport **Fax Area Code:* 503 ■ *TF Cust Svc:* 800-323-2668 ■ *Web:* lacrossefootwear.com/	Portland	OR	97230	800-323-2668	766-1015*
Lady Foot Locker (LFL) 112 W 34th St *TF:* 800-991-6686 ■ *Web:* www.ladyfootlocker.com	New York	NY	10120	800-991-6686	
Lake Catherine Footwear 3770 Malvern Rd PO Box 6048 *Web:* munroshoes.com/	Hot Springs	AR	71901	800-819-1901	
Lamey-Wellehan Inc 940 Turner St *TF:* 800-370-6900 ■ *Web:* www.lwshoes.com	Auburn	ME	04210	207-784-6595	784-9650
Lucchese Boot Co 20 ZANE GREY *TF:* 800-637-6888 ■ *Web:* www.lucchese.com	El Paso	TX	79906	888-582-1883	
Lyn-Flex West Inc 405 Red Oak Rd PO Box 570 *Web:* www.lynflex.com	Owensville	MO	65066	573-437-4125	437-2350
Marty's Shoe Outlet Inc 121 Carver Ave *TF General:* 888-662-7897 ■ *Web:* www.martyshoes.com	Westwood	NJ	07675	201-497-6637	497-6639
Meramec Group Inc 338 Ramsey St *Web:* www.meramec.com	Sullivan	MO	63080	573-468-3101	860-3101
Mercury International 20 Alice Agnew Dr *Web:* mercuryfootwear.com	North Attleboro	MA	02763	508-699-9000	699-9099
Merrell Footwear 9341 Courtland Dr NE *TF Cust Svc:* 800-288-3124 ■ *Web:* www.merrell.com/us/en	Rockford	MI	49351	616-866-5500	866-5625
Mizuno USA 4925 Avalon Ridge Pkwy *TF:* 800-966-1211 ■ *Web:* www.mizunousa.com	Norcross	GA	30071	770-441-5553	448-3234
Montello Heel Mfg Inc 13 Emerson Ave *Web:* www.montelloheel.com	Brockton	MA	02301	508-586-0603	
Munro & Co Inc 3770 Malvern Rd 71901 PO Box 6048 *TF:* 800-819-1901 ■ *Web:* munroshoes.com/	Hot Springs	AR	71902	501-262-6000	262-6165
New Balance Athletic Shoe Inc 20 Guest St Brighton Landing *TF:* 800-595-9138 ■ *Web:* www.newbalance.com	Brighton	MA	02135	617-783-4000	787-9355
Nike Inc One Bowerman Dr *NYSE: NKE* ■ *TF Cust Svc:* 800-344-6453 ■ *Web:* www.nike.com	Beaverton	OR	97005	503-671-6453	646-6926
Novus Inc 655 Calle Cubitas *TF:* 888-530-4546 ■ *Web:* www.novushoes.com	Guaynabo	PR	00969	787-272-4546	272-4500
Nunn-Bush Shoe Co Inc 333 W Estabrook Blvd *Web:* nunnbush.com	Glendale	WI	53212	414-908-1600	908-1605
ONGUARD Industries 1850 Clark Rd *TF:* 800-365-2282 ■ *Web:* www.onguardindustries.com	Havre de Grace	MD	21078	410-272-2000	272-3346
Otomix Inc 747 Glasgow Ave *TF:* 800-701-7867 ■ *Web:* www.otomix.com	Inglewood	CA	90301	310-215-6100	
Payless ShoeSource Inc 3231 SE Sixth Ave *TF:* 877-452-7500 ■ *Web:* www.collectivebrands.com	Topeka	KS	66607	785-233-5171	368-7519
Pentland USA Inc 3333 New Hyde Pk Rd Ste 200 *Web:* www.pentland.com	New Hyde Park	NY	11042	516-365-1333	365-2333
Phoenix Footwear Group Inc 5937 Darwin Ct Ste 109 *OTC: PXFG* ■ *TF:* 888-218-7275 ■ *Web:* www.phoenixfootwear.com	Carlsbad	CA	92008	760-602-9688	602-0152
Propet USA Inc 2415 W Valley Hwy N *TF:* 800-877-6738 ■ *Web:* www.propetusa.com	Auburn	WA	98001	253-854-7600	854-7607
Puma North America Inc 10 Lyberty Way *TF General:* 888-565-7862 ■ *Web:* www.puma.com	Westford	MA	01886	978-698-1000	968-1150
PW Minor & Son Inc 3 Tread Easy Ave PO Box 678 *TF:* 800-333-4067 ■ *Web:* www.pwminor.com	Batavia	NY	14020	585-343-1500	343-1514
Quabaug Corp 18 School St *Web:* www.vibram.com	North Brookfield	MA	01535	508-867-7731	
Rack Room Shoes 8310 Technology Dr *Web:* www.rackroomshoes.com	Charlotte	NC	28262	704-501-4674	547-8153
Red Wing Shoe Company Inc 314 Main St *TF Cust Svc:* 800-733-9464 ■ *Web:* www.redwingshoes.com	Red Wing	MN	55066	651-388-8211	388-7415
Reebok International Ltd 1895 JW Foster Blvd **Fax:* Cust Svc ■ *TF:* 866-870-1743 ■ *Web:* www.reebok.com	Canton	MA	02021	781-401-5000	401-7402*
RG Barry Corp 13405 Yarmouth Dr NW *NASDAQ: DFZ* ■ *TF:* 800-848-7560 ■ *Web:* www.rgbarry.com	Pickerington	OH	43147	614-864-6400	866-9787
Rockport Company Inc 1895 JW Foster Blvd **Fax:* Cust Svc ■ *TF:* 800-828-0545 ■ *Web:* www.rockport.com	Canton	MA	02021	781-401-5000	401-5230*
Rocky Shoes & Boots Inc 39 E Canal St *NASDAQ: RCKY* ■ *TF:* 877-795-2410 ■ *Web:* www.rockyboots.com	Nelsonville	OH	45764	740-753-3130	
Romika USA LLC 3405 Del Webb Ave NE *TF:* 888-777-4174 ■ *Web:* www.romikausa.com	Salem	OR	97301	503-485-1848	
Safety Shoe Distributors of Oki 10156 Reading Rd *Web:* safetyshoedistributors.com	Cincinnati	OH	45241	513-563-4220	
SAS Shoemakers 1717 SAS Dr **Fax Area Code:* 210 ■ *TF:* 877-782-7463 ■ *Web:* www.sasshoes.com	San Antonio	TX	78224	877-782-7463	921-7896*
Saucony Inc 191 Spring St *TF:* 800-282-6575 ■ *Web:* www.saucony.com	Lexington	MA	02420	800-282-6575	
Saxon Shoes Inc 11800 W Broad St Ste 2750 *TF General:* 800-686-5616 ■ *Web:* shop.saxonshoes.com	Richmond	VA	23233	804-285-3473	285-8526
Schwartz & Benjamin Inc 20 W 57th St Fourth Fl	New York	NY	10019	212-541-9092	974-0609
Sebago Inc 9341 Courtland Dr *TF:* 866-699-7367 ■ *Web:* www.sebago.com	Rockford	MI	49351	616-866-5500	866-5625
SG Footwear Inc 3 University Plaza Ste 400 *Web:* www.sgfootwear.com	Hackensack	NJ	07601	201-342-1200	342-4405
Shoe Carnival Inc 7500 E Columbia St *NASDAQ: SCVL* ■ *TF Cust Svc:* 800-430-7463 ■ *Web:* www.shoecarnival.com	Evansville	IN	47715	812-867-6471	
Shoe Sensation Inc 253 America Pl *Web:* www.shoesensation.com	Jeffersonville	IN	47130	812-288-7659	288-7747
Shoe Show of Rocky Mountain Inc 2201 Trinity Church Rd *TF Cust Svc:* 888-557-4637 ■ *Web:* www.shoeshow.com	Concord	NC	28027	704-782-4143	782-3411
Shtofman Co 1905 W Gentry Pkwy	Tyler	TX	75702	903-592-0861	592-8380

Phone Fax

Skechers USA Inc
228 Manhattan Beach Blvd Ste 200 Manhattan Beach CA 90266 310-318-3100 318-5019
NYSE: SKX ■ *TF Cust Svc:* 800-746-3411 ■ *Web:* www.skechers.com

Spalding PO Box 90015 Bowling Green KY 42103 855-253-4533 729-4800*
**Fax Area Code:* 877 ■ *TF:* 855-253-4533 ■ *Web:* www.spalding.com

Stanbee Company Inc 70 Broad St Carlstadt NJ 07072 201-933-9666 933-7985
Web: www.stanbee.com

Stride Rite Corp 191 Spring St Lexington MA 02420 617-824-6000 824-6969
TF Cust Svc: 800-299-6575 ■ *Web:* www.striderite.com

Super Shoe Stores Inc 601 Dual Hwy Hagerstown MD 21740 866-842-7510
Web: www.supershoes.com

Teva Sport Sandals 123 N Leroux St Flagstaff AZ 86001 928-779-5938
TF General: 800-367-8382 ■ *Web:* www.teva.com

Timberland Co, The 200 Domain Dr Stratham NH 03885 603-772-9500
NYSE: VFC ■ *TF:* 800-258-0855 ■ *Web:* shop.timberland.com

Tony Lama Boot Company Inc 1137 Tony Lama St El Paso TX 79915 915-778-8311
Web: www.tonylama.com

Topline Corp 13150 SE 32nd St Bellevue WA 98005 425-643-3003 643-3846
Web: www.toplinecorp.com

Trimfoot Co LLC 115 Trimfoot Terr Farmington MO 63640 800-325-6116 756-8482*
**Fax Area Code:* 573 ■ *TF:* 800-325-6116 ■ *Web:* www.trimfootco.com

TT Group Inc 702 Carnation Dr Aurora MO 65605 417-678-2181 678-6901
TF General: 800-445-0886 ■ *Web:* www.tt-group.com

Vans Inc 15700 Shoemaker Ave Santa Fe Springs CA 90670 562-565-8267
TF: 855-909-8267 ■ *Web:* www.vans.com

Weinbrenner Shoe Co Inc 108 S Polk St Merrill WI 54452 715-536-5521 536-1172
TF General: 800-569-6817 ■ *Web:* www.weinbrennerusa.com

West Coast Shoe Co
52828 NW Shoe Factory Ln PO Box 607 Scappoose OR 97056 503-543-7114 543-7110
TF: 800-326-2711 ■ *Web:* www.westcoastshoe.com

Weyco Group Inc 333 W Estabrook Blvd Glendale WI 53212 414-908-1880 908-1603
NASDAQ: WEYS ■ *Web:* www.weycogroup.com

Wolverine World Wide Inc
9341 Courtland Dr NE Rockford MI 49351 616-866-5500 866-5658
Web: wolverineworldwide.com

305 FORESTRY SERVICES

SEE ALSO Timber Tracts p. 3236

Phone Fax

American Forest Management Inc
407 N Pike Rd E PO Box 1919 Sumter SC 29151 803-773-5461 773-4248
Web: www.americanforestmanagement.com

Baldwin Aviation Safety & Compliance
19 Shelter Cove Ln Ste 101 Hilton Head Island SC 29928 843-342-5434
Web: www.baldwinaviation.com

Bioforest Technologies Inc
105 Bruce St Sault Ste Marie ON P6A2X6 705-942-5824 942-8829
Web: bioforest.ca

Boundary County School District
6577 Main St Ste 101 Bonners Ferry ID 83805 208-267-3146
Web: bcsd101.com

Cascade Timber Consulting Inc 3210 Hwy 20 Sweet Home OR 97386 541-367-2111 367-2117
Web: cascadetimber.com

Central Yavapai Fire District
8555 E Yavapai Rd Prescott Valley AZ 86314 928-772-7711
Web: centralyavapaifire.org

CH Fenstermaker & Associates LLC
135 Regency Sq Lafayette LA 70508 337-237-2200
Web: www.fenstermaker.com

Columbia River Log Scaling & Grading Bureau
260 Oakway Ctr Eugene OR 97401 541-342-6007 485-3086
Web: www.crls.com

Continental Design & Engineering Inc
1524 Jackson St Anderson IN 46016 765-778-9999
Web: continental-design.com

Cooperative Forestiere Des Hautes-Laurentides
395 Boul Des Ruisseaux Des Ruisseaux QC J9L1R6 819-623-4422
Web: www.cfhl.qc.ca

Curtis Contracting Inc 7481 Theron Rd West Point VA 23181 804-843-4633
Web: www.curtiscontracting.net

Environmental Consultants Inc
295 Buck Rd Ste 203 SouthHampton PA 18966 215-322-4040 322-9404
Web: www.eci-consulting.com

F & W Forestry Services Inc
1310 W Oakridge Dr Albany GA 31707 229-883-0505
Web: www.fwforestry.com

Faller Davis & Assoc in 5525 W Cypress St Tampa FL 33607 813-261-5136
Web: www.fallerdavis.com

Firezat 5173 Waring Rd Ste 158 San Diego CA 92120 619-955-6788
Web: www.firezat.com

Fountains America Inc
175 Barnstead Rd Ste 4 Pittsfield NH 03263 603-435-8234
Web: www.fountainsamerica.com

Fountains Forestry Inc 175 Barnstead Rd Pittsfield NH 03263 603-435-8234 435-7274
Web: www.fountainforestry.com

Georgia Timberlands Inc 3250 Waterville Rd Macon GA 31206 478-788-4660
Web: gatimberlands.com

Green Diamond Resource Co
1301 Fifth Ave Ste 2700 Seattle WA 98101 206-224-5800
Web: www.greendiamond.com

Hal Hays Construction Inc 4181 Latham St Riverside CA 92501 951-788-0703 275-0752
TF: 888-425-4297 ■ *Web:* www.halhays.com

International Air Response Inc
6250 S Taxiway Cir Mesa AZ 85212 480-840-9860 840-9866
Web: www.internationalairresponse.com

Lake County Forest Preserve District
2000 N Milwaukee Ave Libertyville IL 60048 847-367-6640 367-6649
Web: www.lcfpd.org

Pro-west & Associates Inc 8239 State 371 Nw Walker MN 56484 218-547-3374
Web: www.prowestgis.com

Phone Fax

Resource Management Service LLC
31 Inverness Ctr Pkwy Ste 360 Birmingham AL 35242 800-995-9516 991-2807*
**Fax Area Code:* 205 ■ *TF:* 800-995-9516 ■ *Web:* www.resourcemgt.com

Sealaska Corp One Sealaska Plz Ste 400 Juneau AK 99801 907-586-1512 586-2304
Web: www.sealaska.com

Southwest Conservation Corps
701 Camino Del Rio Ste 101 Durango CO 81301 970-259-8607
Web: sccorps.org

Summit Engineering Inc 131 Summit Dr Pikeville KY 41501 606-432-1447
Web: www.summit-engr.com

US Underwater Services LP 123 Sentry Dr Mansfield TX 76063 817-447-7321
Web: www.neptunems.com

Vestra Resources Inc 5300 Aviation Dr Redding CA 96002 530-223-2585
TF: 877-983-7872 ■ *Web:* www.vestra.com

306 FOUNDATIONS - COMMUNITY

SEE ALSO Charitable & Humanitarian Organizations p. 1761

Phone Fax

Adelphoi Village Inc 1119 Village Way Latrobe PA 15650 724-520-1111 520-1878
Web: www.adelphoivillage.org

Arizona Community Foundation
2201 E Camelback Rd Ste 405B Phoenix AZ 85016 602-381-1400 381-1575
TF: 800-222-8221 ■ *Web:* www.azfoundation.org

Boston Foundation 75 Arlington St 10th Fl Boston MA 02116 617-338-1700 338-1604
Web: www.tbf.org

California Community Foundation
445 S Figueroa St Ste 3400 Los Angeles CA 90071 213-413-4130 383-2046
Web: www.calfund.org

California Wellness Foundation (CWF)
6320 Canoga Ave Ste 1700 Woodland Hills CA 91367 818-702-1900 702-1999
Web: www.calwellness.org

Chicago Community Trust & Affiliates
111 E Wacker Dr Ste 1400 Chicago IL 60601 312-616-8000 616-7955
Web: www.cct.org

Cleveland Foundation
1422 Euclid Ave Ste 1300 Cleveland OH 44115 216-861-3810 861-1729
Web: www.clevelandfoundation.org

Colorado Trust 1600 Sherman St Denver CO 80203 303-837-1200 839-9034
TF: 888-847-9140 ■ *Web:* www.coloradotrust.org

Columbus Foundation, The 1234 E Broad St Columbus OH 43205 614-251-4000 251-4009
Web: www.columbusfoundation.org

Communities Foundation of Texas Inc
5500 Caruth Haven Ln Dallas TX 75225 214-750-4222 750-4210
Web: www.cftexas.org

Community Foundation for Greater Atlanta Inc
50 Hurt Plz Ste 449 Atlanta GA 30303 404-688-5525 688-3060
Web: www.cfgreateratlanta.org

Community Foundation for Greater New Haven
70 Audubon St New Haven CT 06510 203-777-2386 787-6584
TF: 877-829-5500 ■ *Web:* www.cfgnh.org

Community Foundation for the National Capital Region
1201 15th St NW Ste 420 Washington DC 20005 202-955-5890 955-8084
Web: www.thecommunityfoundation.org

Community Foundation of Greater Memphis
1900 Union Ave Memphis TN 38104 901-728-4600 722-0010
Web: www.cfgm.org

Community Foundation Serving Richmond & Central Virginia, The
7501 Boulders View Dr Ste 110 Richmond VA 23225 804-330-7400 330-5992
Web: www.tcfrichmond.org

Community Foundation Silicon Valley
60 S Market St Ste 1000 San Jose CA 95113 408-278-2200
Web: www.siliconvalleycf.org

Dayton Foundation 40 N Main St Ste 500 Dayton OH 45423 937-222-0410 222-0636
TF: 877-222-0410 ■ *Web:* www.daytonfoundation.org

Foundation for the Carolinas
217 S Tryon St Charlotte NC 28202 704-973-4500 973-4599
TF: 800-973-7244 ■ *Web:* www.fftc.org

Greater Cincinnati Foundation
200 W Fourth St Cincinnati OH 45202 513-241-2880 852-6886
Web: www.gcfdn.org

Greater Kansas City Community Foundation & Affiliated Trusts (GKCCF)
1055 Broadway Ste 130 Kansas City MO 64105 816-842-0944 842-8079
Web: www.gkccf.org

Greater Milwaukee Foundation
101 W Pleasant St Ste 210 Milwaukee WI 53212 414-272-5805 272-6235
Web: www.greatermilwaukeefoundation.org

Hartford Foundation for Public Giving
10 Columbus Blvd Hartford CT 06106 860-548-1888 524-8346
Web: www.hfpg.org

Hawaii Community Foundation
65-1279 Kawaihae Rd Ste 203 Kamuela HI 96743 808-537-6333 521-6286
TF: 888-731-3863 ■ *Web:* www.hawaiicommunityfoundation.org

Houston Endowment Inc 600 Travis St Ste 6400 Houston TX 77002 713-238-8100 238-8101
Web: www.houstonendowment.org

Marin Community Foundation
Five Hamilton Landing Ste 200 Novato CA 94949 415-464-2500 464-2555
Web: www.marincf.org

Minneapolis Foundation
80 S Eigth St 800 IDS Ctr Minneapolis MN 55402 612-672-3878 672-3846
TF: 866-305-0543 ■ *Web:* www.minneapolisfoundation.org

New York Community Trust
909 Third Ave 22nd Fl New York NY 10022 212-686-0010 532-8528
TF: 877-829-5500 ■ *Web:* www.nycommunitytrust.org

Northwest Area Foundation
60 Plato Blvd E Ste 400 Saint Paul MN 55107 651-224-9635 225-7701
Web: www.nwaf.org

Omaha Community Foundation (OCF)
302 S 36th St Ste 100 Omaha NE 68131 402-342-3458 342-3582
TF: 800-794-3458 ■ *Web:* www.omahafoundation.org

				Phone	Fax
Oregon Community Foundation, The 1221 SW Yamhill St Ste 100 *Web:* www.oregoncf.org	Portland	OR	97205	503-227-6846	274-7771
Peninsula Community Foundation 19101 Peninsula Club Dr *Web:* www.thepeninsulacommunityfoundation.org	Cornelius	NC	28031	704-237-0630	
Pittsburgh Foundation Five PPG Pl Ste 250 *Web:* www.pittsburghfoundation.org	Pittsburgh	PA	15222	412-391-5122	391-7259
Rhode Island Foundation One Union Stn. *Web:* www.rifoundation.org	Providence	RI	02903	401-274-4564	331-8085
Saint Paul Foundation 55 E Fifth St Ste 600 *TF:* 800-875-6167 ■ *Web:* www.saintpaulfoundation.org	Saint Paul	MN	55101	651-224-5463	224-8123
San Diego Foundation, The 2508 Historic Decatur Rd Ste 200 *Web:* www.sdfoundation.org	San Diego	CA	92106	619-235-2300	239-1710
San Francisco Foundation 225 Bush St Ste 500 *Web:* www.sff.org	San Francisco	CA	94104	415-733-8500	477-2783
Seattle Foundation 1200 Fifth Ave Ste 1300 *Web:* www.seattlefoundation.org	Seattle	WA	98101	206-622-2294	622-7673

307 FOUNDATIONS - CORPORATE

SEE ALSO Charitable & Humanitarian Organizations p. 1761

				Phone	Fax
Abbott Laboratories Fund 100 Abbott Pk Rd *NYSE: ABT* ■ *Web:* abbott.com	Abbott Park	IL	60064	847-937-6100	
Aetna Foundation Inc 151 Farmington Ave *Web:* www.aetna.com	Hartford	CT	06156	860-273-6382	273-4764
Allstate Insurance Co 2775 Sanders Rd *NYSE: ALL* ■ *Web:* www.allstate.com	Northbrook	IL	60062	847-402-5000	326-7517
Baxter International Foundation One Baxter Pkwy **Fax Area Code:* 800 ■ *Web:* www.baxter.com	Deerfield	IL	60015	847-948-4605	568-5020*
Burroughs Wellcome Fund 21 TW Alexander Dr PO Box 13901 *Web:* www.bwfund.org	Research Triangle Park	NC	27709	919-991-5100	991-5160
Cargill Foundation 15407 McGinty Rd W Ste 46 **Fax Area Code:* 952 ■ *TF:* 800-227-4455 ■ *Web:* www.cargill.com	Wayzata	MN	55391	877-765-8867	742-1087*
Caterpillar Foundation 100 NE Adams St *Web:* www.caterpillar.com	Peoria	IL	61629	309-675-1000	675-4332
CIGNA Foundation 900 Cottage Grove Rd *NYSE: CI* ■ *TF:* 866-438-2446 ■ *Web:* cigna.com/index.html	Bloomfield	CT	06002	866-438-2446	
Cisco Systems Foundation 170 W Tasman Dr. *TF:* 800-553-6387 ■ *Web:* www.cisco.com	San Jose	CA	95134	408-527-3040	
Coca-Cola Foundation Inc PO Box 1734 **Fax Area Code:* 404 ■ *TF:* 800-438-2653 ■ *Web:* www.coca-colacompany.com	Atlanta	GA	30301	800-306-2653	676-8804*
Dow Chemical Company Foundation 2030 Dow Ctr *TF:* 800-331-6451 ■ *Web:* www.dow.com/about/corp/social/social.htm	Midland	MI	48674	989-636-1000	636-4460
Eli Lilly & Co Foundation Lilly Corporate Ctr *TF:* 800-545-5979 ■ *Web:* www.lilly.com	Indianapolis	IN	46285	317-276-2000	276-3492
ExxonMobil Foundation Inc 5959 Las Colinas Blvd *Web:* exxonmobil.com	Irving	TX	75039	972-444-1000	444-1405
Freddie Mac Foundation 8250 Jones Branch Dr. *TF:* 800-424-5401 ■ *Web:* www.freddiemacfoundation.org	McLean	VA	22102	703-918-5000	
GE Foundation 3135 Easton Tpke *Web:* www.ge.com	Fairfield	CT	06828	203-373-3216	373-3029
General Mills Foundation PO Box 9452 **Fax Area Code:* 763 ■ *TF:* 800-248-7310 ■ *Web:* www.generalmills.com	Minneapolis	MN	55440	800-248-7310	764-8330*
General Motors Foundation Inc PO Box 33170 *TF:* 800-222-1020 ■ *Web:* www.gm.com	Detroit	MI	48232	800-222-1020	
Georgia Power Foundation Inc 96 Annex *Web:* www.southerncompany.com	Atlanta	GA	30396	404-506-5000	506-1485
Hallmark Corp Foundation 2501 McGee St. **Fax Area Code:* 816 ■ *Web:* corporate.hallmark.com	Kansas City	MO	64108	800-425-5627	274-5061*
Hess Corp 1185 Ave of the Americas *Web:* www.hess.com	New York	NY	10036	212-997-8500	536-8390
HJ Heinz Company Foundation 600 Grant St. *Web:* www.heinz.com	Pittsburgh	PA	15219	412-456-5773	442-3227
Humana Foundation Inc 500 W Main St Ste 208 *TF:* 888-431-4748 ■ *Web:* www.humanafoundation.org	Louisville	KY	40202	502-580-4140	580-1256
IBM International Foundation One New OrchaRd Rd *Web:* www.ibm.com	Armonk	NY	10504	914-499-1900	499-7684
Koch Foundation Inc 4421 NW 39th Ave Bldg 1 Ste 1 *Web:* www.thekochfoundation.org	Gainesville	FL	32606	352-373-7491	
Levi Strauss Foundation 1155 Battery St. *TF:* 866-290-6064 ■ *Web:* levistrauss.com/levi-strauss-foundation/	San Francisco	CA	94111	415-501-6000	501-7112
Lutheran Community Foundation 625 Fourth Ave S Ste 200 *TF:* 800-365-4172 ■ *Web:* infaithfound.org/	Minneapolis	MN	55415	612-340-4110	340-4109
Mead Westvaco Office Products Group 4751 Hempstead Station Dr	Dayton	OH	45429	937-495-6323	
MetLife Foundation 2701 Queens Plz N 1 MetLife Plz *Web:* www.metlife.com	Long Island City	NY	11101	212-578-2555	
Motorola Foundation 1303 E Algonquin Rd. *Web:* motorola.com	Schaumburg	IL	60196	847-576-5000	
New York Life Foundation 51 Madison Ave Ste 1600 *Web:* www.newyorklife.com	New York	NY	10010	212-576-7341	
New York Times Co Foundation Inc 229 W 43rd St *Web:* crainsnewyork.com	New York	NY	10036	212-210-0100	556-4450
Pfizer Foundation Inc 235 E 42nd St *Web:* www.pfizer.com	New York	NY	10017	212-733-2323	
Playboy Foundation 680 N Lake Shore Dr *Web:* www.playboyenterprises.com/foundation	Chicago	IL	60611	310-315-8361	264-1944
Principal Financial Group Foundation Inc 711 High St *TF:* 800-986-3343 ■ *Web:* www.principal.com/about/giving	Des Moines	IA	50392	515-247-7227	246-5475
Revlon Foundation Inc 237 Pk Ave *TF Cust Svc:* 800-473-8566 ■ *Web:* www.revlon.com	New York	NY	10017	800-473-8566	
SBC Foundation 130 E Travis St Ste 350 *TF:* 800-591-9663 ■ *Web:* www.att.com	San Antonio	TX	78205	800-591-9663	
Scripps Howard Foundation 312 Walnut St PO Box 5380 *TF:* 800-888-3000 ■ *Web:* www.scripps.com/foundation	Cincinnati	OH	45201	513-977-3035	977-3800
Siemens Foundation 170 Wood Ave S **Fax Area Code:* 732 ■ *TF:* 877-822-5233 ■ *Web:* www.siemens-foundation.org	Iselin	NJ	08830	877-822-5233	603-5890*
Union Pacific Foundation 1400 Douglas St MS 1560 *Web:* up.com/aboutup/community/foundation/index.htm	Omaha	NE	68179	402-544-5600	
UPS Foundation 55 Glenlake Pkwy NE *Web:* sustainability.ups.com/	Atlanta	GA	30328	404-828-7123	
Wal-Mart Foundation 702 SW Eigth St *NYSE: WMT* ■ *TF:* 800-438-6278 ■ *Web:* www.foundation.walmart.com	Bentonville	AR	72716	479-273-4000	273-6850
Whirlpool Foundation 2000 N M-63 *TF:* 800-952-9245 ■ *Web:* www.whirlpoolcorp.com	Benton Harbor	MI	49022	269-923-5000	925-0154
Xerox Foundation 45 Glover Ave *TF:* 800-275-9376 ■ *Web:* www.xerox.com	Norwalk	CT	06856	800-275-9376	

308 FOUNDATIONS - PRIVATE

SEE ALSO Charitable & Humanitarian Organizations p. 1761

				Phone	Fax
A Glimmer of Hope Foundation 3600 N Capital of Texas Hwy Bldg B Ste 330 *Web:* www.aglimmerofhope.org	Austin	TX	78746	512-328-9944	
Adolph Coors Foundation 4100 E Mississippi Ave Ste 1850	Denver	CO	80246	303-388-1636	388-1684
Ahmanson Foundation 9215 Wilshire Blvd *Web:* www.theahmansonfoundation.org	Beverly Hills	CA	90210	310-278-0770	
Aid Matrix Foundation, The 11701 Luna Rd *Web:* www.aidmatrix.org	Dallas	TX	75234	469-357-6209	
AIDS Foundation of Chicago 200 W Jackson Blvd Ste 2200 *Web:* www.aidschicago.org	Chicago	IL	60606	312-922-2322	
AIDS Healthcare Foundation 6255 W Sunset Blvd 21st Fl *Web:* www.aidshealth.org	Los Angeles	CA	90028	323-860-5200	
AKRON COMMUNITY FOUNDATION 345 W Cedar St *Web:* akroncommunityfdn.org	Akron	OH	44307	330-376-8522	
Alberta Cancer Foundation 1331 29 St Nw *Web:* www.donate.albertacancer.ca	Calgary	AB	T2N4N2	403-521-3433	
Alfred P Sloan Foundation 630 Fifth Ave Ste 2550 *Web:* www.sloan.org	New York	NY	10111	212-649-1649	757-5117
Amity Foundation of California 2260 Watson Way *Web:* amityfdn.org	Vista	CA	92083	760-599-1882	
Amon G Carter Foundation 201 Main St Ste 1945 *Web:* www.agcf.org	Fort Worth	TX	76102	817-332-2783	332-2787
Andrew W Mellon Foundation 140 E 62nd St. *Web:* www.mellon.org	New York	NY	10021	212-838-8400	888-4172
Andy Warhol Foundation For The Visual Arts Inc 65 Bleecker St Seventh Fl *Web:* www.warholfoundation.org	New York	NY	10012	212-242-2524	
Animal Protection of New Mexico Inc Foundation Po Box 11395 *Web:* apnm.org	Albuquerque	NM	87192	505-265-2322	
Annenberg Foundation 150 N Radnor-Chester Rd Ste 200 *Web:* www.annenbergfoundation.org	Radnor	PA	19087	610-341-9066	964-8688
Annie E Casey Foundation 701 St Paul St. *TF:* 800-222-1099 ■ *Web:* www.aecf.org	Baltimore	MD	21202	410-547-6600	547-6624
Anschutz Family foundation, The 555 Seventeenth St Ste 2400 *Web:* www.anschutzfamilyfoundation.org	Denver	CO	80202	303-293-2338	
Archibald Bush Foundation 332 Minnesota St Ste E-900 *Web:* www.bushfoundation.org	Saint Paul	MN	55101	651-227-0891	297-6485
Arizona Scholarship Fund 4850 E Baseline Rd Ste 112 *Web:* www.azscholarships.org	Mesa	AZ	85206	480-497-4564	
Arnold & Mabel Beckman Foundation 100 Academy Dr. *Web:* www.beckman-foundation.com	Irvine	CA	92617	949-721-2222	
Art Gallery of Ontario 317 Dundas St W *Web:* www.ago.net	Toronto	ON	M5T1G4	416-979-6660	
Arthur Vining Davis Foundations 225 Water St. *TF:* 800-222-3448 ■ *Web:* www.avdf.org	Jacksonville	FL	32202	904-359-0670	359-0675
Arts Foundation of Cape Cod, The Three Shootflying Hill Rd *Web:* www.artsfoundation.org	Centerville	MA	02632	508-362-0066	
Ayn Rand Institute, Endowment 2121 Alton Pkwy Ste 250 *Web:* www.aynrand.org	Irvine	CA	92608	949-222-6550	
Barr Foundation 136 NE Olive Way *Web:* www.oandp.com	Boca Raton	FL	33432	561-394-6514	391-7601
Benton Foundation 1625 K St NW 11th Fl *Web:* www.benton.org	Washington	DC	20006	202-638-5770	638-5771
Bill & Melinda Gates Foundation PO Box 23350 *TF:* 800-728-3843 ■ *Web:* www.gatesfoundation.org	Seattle	WA	98102	206-709-3100	709-3180

Organization / Address	City	State	ZIP	Phone	Fax
Bluebonnet Trail Elementary 11316 Farmhaven Rd *Web:* www.manorisd.net	Austin	TX	78754	512-468-9375	
Breakeven Inc 7100 Woodbine Ave Ste 313 *Web:* www.causeview.com	Markham	ON	L3R5J2	905-752-1500	
Brown Foundation Inc 2217 Welch St *Web:* www.brownfoundation.org	Houston	TX	77019	713-523-6867	523-2917
Canada-Israel Industrial Research & Development Foundation 371A Richmond Rd *Web:* www.ciirdf.ca	Ottawa	ON	K2A0E7	613-724-1284	
Careers The Next Generation Foundation 10470 176 St Nw *Web:* nextgen.org	Edmonton	AB	T5S1L3	780-426-3414	
Carnegie Corp of New York 437 Madison Ave 26th Fl *TF:* 800-336-7323 ■ *Web:* www.carnegie.org	New York	NY	10022	212-371-3200	754-4073
Center Township Trustee of Marion Company Indiana 863 Massachusetts Ave *Web:* www.centergov.org	Indianapolis	IN	46204	317-633-3610	920-4726
Centre for Addiction & Mental Health Foundation 901 King St W Ste 502 *Web:* www.supportcamh.ca	Toronto	ON	M5V3H5	416-979-6909	
Challenged Athletes Foundation 9591 Waples St *Web:* www.challengedathletes.org	San Diego	CA	92121	858-866-0959	
Champlin Foundations, The 300 Centerville Rd **Fax Area Code:* 401 ■ *Web:* foundationcenter.org	Warwick	RI	02886	212-620-4230	736-7248*
Charles & Helen Schwab Foundation 1650 S Amphlett Blvd Ste 300 *Web:* www.schwabfoundation.org	San Mateo	CA	94402	650-655-2410	655-2411
Charles Hayden Foundation 140 Broadway 51st Fl *Web:* foundationcenter.org	New York	NY	10005	212-785-3677	785-3689
Charles Stewart Mott Foundation 503 S Saginaw St Ste 1200 *Web:* www.mott.org	Flint	MI	48502	810-238-5651	766-1753
Chatlos Foundation PO Box 915048 *Web:* www.chatlos.org	Longwood	FL	32791	407-862-5077	
Chautauqua Region Community Foundation Inc 418 Spring St *Web:* crcfonline.org	Jamestown	NY	14701	716-661-3390	
Cicatelli Associates Inc-ccd 100 Edgewood Ave Ne Ste 900 *Web:* cicatelli.org	Atlanta	GA	30303	404-521-2153	
Colonial Williamsburg Foundation PO Box 1776 **Fax:* Hum Res ■ *TF:* 800-447-8679 ■ *Web:* www.history.org	Williamsburg	VA	23187	757-229-1000	565-8796*
Colorado School of Mines Foundation Inc, The 923 16th St *Web:* giving.mines.edu	Golden	CO	80401	303-273-3275	
Columbus Jewish Foundation 1175 College Ave *Web:* www.jewishcolumbus.org	Columbus	OH	43209	614-338-2365	
Commonwealth Fund One E 75th St *Web:* www.commonwealthfund.org	New York	NY	10021	212-606-3800	606-3500
Community College Foundation, The 1901 Royal Oaks Dr Ste 100 *Web:* www.communitycollege.org	Sacramento	CA	95815	916-418-5100	
ConnectEd 2150 Shattuck Ste 1200 *Web:* www.connectedcalifornia.org	Berkeley	CA	94704	510-849-4945	
Conrad N Hilton Foundation 100 W Liberty St Ste 840 *Web:* www.hiltonfoundation.org	Reno	NV	89501	775-323-4221	323-4150
Corporation for Public Broadcasting (CPB) 401 Ninth St NW *TF:* 800-272-2190 ■ *Web:* www.cpb.org	Washington	DC	20004	202-879-9600	879-9700
Dave Thomas Foundation for Adoption 716 Mt Airyshire Blvd Ste 100 *TF:* 800-275-3832 ■ *Web:* www.davethomasfoundation.org	Columbus	OH	43235	800-275-3832	
David Bohnett Foundation 245 S Beverly Dr *Web:* www.bohnettfoundation.org	Beverly Hills	CA	90212	310-276-0001	
David Suzuki Foundation 2211 Fourth Ave W *Web:* www.davidsuzuki.org	Vancouver	BC	V6K4S2	604-732-4228	
Donald W Reynolds Foundation 1701 Village Ctr Cir *Web:* www.dwreynolds.org	Las Vegas	NV	89134	702-804-6000	804-6099
Doris Duke Charitable Foundation (DDCF) 650 Fifth Ave 19th Fl *Web:* www.ddcf.org	New York	NY	10019	212-974-7000	974-7590
Duke Endowment 100 N Tryon St Ste 3500 *Web:* www.dukeendowment.org	Charlotte	NC	28202	704-376-0291	376-9336
Edna McConnell Clark Foundation 415 Madison Ave 10th Fl *Web:* www.emcf.org	New York	NY	10017	212-551-9100	421-9325
Elfenworks Foundation 20 park rd *Web:* elfenworks.org	Burlingame	CA	94010	650-347-9700	
Ellison Medical Foundation 104 E Ridgeville Blvd *Web:* www.ellisonfoundation.org	Mount Airy	MD	21771	301-829-6410	657-1828
Energy Foundation, The Fifth Fl 301 Battery St *Web:* www.ef.org	San Francisco	CA	94111	415-561-6700	
Evangelical Lutheran Good Samaritan Foundation, The 4800 W 57th St *Web:* www.good-sam.com	Sioux Falls	SD	57108	605-362-3100	
Evelyn & Walter Haas Jr Fund 114 Sansome St Ste 600 *Web:* www.haasjr.org	San Francisco	CA	94104	415-856-1400	856-1500
Ewing Marion Kauffman Foundation (EMKF) 4801 Rockhill Rd *TF:* 800-385-1607 ■ *Web:* www.kauffman.org	Kansas City	MO	64110	816-932-1000	932-1484
Facey Medical Group & Foundation 11211 Sepulveda Blvd *Web:* www.facey.com	Mission Hills	CA	91345	818-365-9531	
Fannie & John Hertz Foundation 2300 First St Ste 250 *Web:* www.hertzfoundation.org	Livermore	CA	94550	925-373-1642	
FJC 520 Eighth Ave 20th Fl *Web:* www.fjc.org	New York	NY	10018	212-714-0001	
Flinn Foundation, The 1802 N Central Ave *Web:* www.flinn.org	Phoenix	AZ	85004	602-744-6800	
Flintridge Operating Foundation 1040 Lincoln Ave Ste 100 *Web:* www.flintridge.org	Pasadena	CA	91103	626-449-0839	
Flora Family Foundation, The 2121 Sand Hill Rd Ste 123 *Web:* www.florafamily.org	Menlo Park	CA	94025	650-233-1335	
Florida School Choice Fund Inc PO Box 1670 *Web:* www.stepupforstudents.org	Tampa	FL	33601	813-318-0995	
Food & Water Watch 1616 P St Nw Ste 300 *Web:* www.foodandwaterwatch.org	Washington	DC	20036	202-683-2500	
Food Corps 281 Park Ave South *Web:* foodcorps.org	New York	NY	10010	212-596-7045	
Ford Family Foundation 1600 NW Stewart Pkwy *Web:* www.tfff.org	Roseburg	OR	97471	541-957-5574	957-5720
Ford Foundation 320 E 43rd St *Web:* www.fordfoundation.org	New York	NY	10017	212-573-5000	351-3677
Free Methodist Foundation, The 8050 Spring Arbor Rd *Web:* fmfoundation.org	Spring Arbor	MI	49283	517-750-2727	
Fremont Area Community Foundation 4424 W 48th St *Web:* facommunityfoundation.org	Fremont	MI	49412	231-924-5350	
GAR Foundation Andrew Jackson House 277 E Mill St *Web:* www.garfdn.org	Akron	OH	44308	330-576-2926	
Gates Family Foundation 1390 Lawrence Street *TF:* 866-590-4377 ■ *Web:* www.gatesfamilyfoundation.org	Denver	CO	80204	303-722-1881	316-3038
George Kaiser Family Foundation 7030 S Yale Ave Ste 600 *Web:* www.gkff.org	Tulsa	OK	74136	918-392-1612	
George S & Dolores Dore Eccles Foundation 79 S Main St 14th Fl *Web:* www.gsecclesfoundation.org	Salt Lake City	UT	84111	801-246-5340	350-3510
Georgia Northwestern Technical College Foundation Inc One Maurice Culberson Dr Sw *Web:* www.coosavalleytech.edu	Rome	GA	30161	706-295-6842	
Geraldine R Dodge Foundation 14 Maple Ave *Web:* www.grdodge.org	Morristown	NJ	07962	973-540-8442	540-1211
Gleaner's Food Bank of Indianapolis 3737 Waldemere Ave *Web:* www.gleaners.org	Indianapolis	IN	46241	317-925-0191	
Global Citizen Year Inc 1625 Clay St Ste 400 *Web:* globalcitizenyear.org	Oakland	CA	94612	415-963-9293	
GlobalGiving Foundation Inc 1816 12th St N W Third Fl *Web:* www.globalgiving.org	Washington	DC	20009	202-232-6212	
Goizueta Foundation 4401 Northside Pkwy Ste 520 *Web:* www.goizuetafoundation.org	Atlanta	GA	30327	404-239-0390	239-0018
Goodcity 5049 W Harrison St *Web:* www.goodcitychicago.org	Chicago	IL	60644	773-473-4790	
Gordon & Betty Moore Foundation PO Box 29910 *Web:* www.moore.org	San Francisco	CA	94129	415-561-7700	
Granite State Independent Living Foundation 21 Chenell Dr *Web:* www.gsil.org	Concord	NH	03301	603-228-9680	
Greater Texas Foundation 6100 Foundation Pl Dr *Web:* greatertexasfoundation.org	Bryan	TX	77807	979-779-6100	
Hall Family Foundation PO Box 419580 MD 323 *Web:* www.hallfamilyfoundation.org	Kansas City	MO	64141	816-274-8516	274-8547
Harry & Jeanette Weinberg Foundation Inc, The Seven Park Ctr Ct *Web:* hjweinbergfoundation.org	Owings Mills	MD	21117	410-654-8500	
Hearst Foundation, The 300 W 57th St 26th Fl *TF:* 800-841-7048 ■ *Web:* hearstfdn.org	New York	NY	10019	212-649-3750	586-1917
Help Foundation Inc 3622 Prospect Ave E *Web:* www.helpfoundationinc.org	Cleveland	OH	44115	216-432-4810	
Henry J Kaiser Family Foundation 2400 Sand Hill Rd *Web:* www.kff.org	Menlo Park	CA	94025	650-854-9400	854-4800
Henry Luce Foundation Inc 51 Madison Ave 30th Fl *Web:* www.hluce.org	New York	NY	10010	212-489-7700	581-9541
Henry M. Jackson Foundation For the Advancement of Military Medicine Inc 6720-A Rockledge Dr Ste 100 *Web:* www.hjf.org	Bethesda	MD	20817	240-694-2000	
Herbert H & Grace A Dow Foundation 1018 W Main St *TF:* 800-362-4874 ■ *Web:* www.hhdowfoundation.org	Midland	MI	48640	989-631-3699	631-0675
Hispanics in Philanthropy 414 13th St Ste 200 *Web:* www.hiponline.org	Oakland	CA	94612	415-837-0427	
Horace W Goldsmith Foundation 375 Pk Ave Rm 1602 *Web:* akfengyo.com.tr	New York	NY	10152	212-319-8700	319-2881
Hudson-Webber Foundation 333 W Ft St Ste 1310 *Web:* www.hudson-webber.org	Detroit	MI	48226	313-963-7777	963-2818
Human Development Foundation 1350 Remington Rd Ste W *Web:* www.hdf.com	Schaumburg	IL	60173	847-490-0100	
Idaho Community Foundation Inc 210 W State St *Web:* www.idcomfdn.org	Boise	ID	83702	208-342-3535	

Name / Address	City	State	Zip	*Phone*	*Fax*
Incentive Research Foundation 100 Chesterfield Business Pkwy Ste 200 *Web:* theirf.org	St. Louis	MO	63005	314-473-5601	
IU School of Medicine - Office of Gift Development 1110 W Michigan St Lo 506 *Web:* medgifts.iu.edu	Indianapolis	IN	46202	317-274-3270	
J Bulow Campbell Foundation 3050 Peachtree Rd NW *Web:* www.jbcf.org	Atlanta	GA	30305	404-658-9066	659-4802
J Paul Getty Trust 1200 Getty Ctr Dr Ste 403 *Web:* www.getty.edu	Los Angeles	CA	90049	310-440-7300	440-7722
JA & Kathryn Albertson Foundation PO Box 70002 *Web:* www.jkaf.org	Boise	ID	83707	208-424-2600	
James Irvine Foundation One Market Plz *Web:* www.irvine.org	San Francisco	CA	94105	415-777-2244	777-0869
JE & LE Mabee Foundation Inc 401 S Boston Ave Ste 3001 *Web:* www.mabeefoundation.com	Tulsa	OK	74103	918-584-4286	
John D & Catherine T MacArthur Foundation 140 S Dearborn St *Web:* www.macfound.org	Chicago	IL	60603	312-726-8000	920-6258
John S & James L Knight Foundation 200 S Biscayne Blvd Ste 3300 *Web:* www.knightfoundation.org	Miami	FL	33131	305-908-2600	908-2698
John Simon Guggenheim Memorial Foundation 90 Pk Ave 33rd Fl *Web:* www.gf.org	New York	NY	10016	212-687-4470	697-3248
John Templeton Foundation 300 Conshohocken State Rd Ste 500 *Web:* www.templeton.org	West Conshohocken	PA	19428	610-941-2828	825-1730
Jones Family Foundation 31021 Lakeview Ave *Web:* www.jonesfamilyfoundation.org	Red Wing	MN	55066	651-388-7941	
Joyce Foundation 70 W Madison St Ste 2750 *Web:* www.joycefdn.org	Chicago	IL	60602	312-782-2464	782-4160
Joyce Theatre Foundation 175 Eighth Ave *Web:* www.joyce.org	New York	NY	10011	212-691-9740	
Kakkis Everylife Foundation 77 Digital Dr Ste 210 *Web:* everylifefoundation.org	Novato	CA	94949	415-884-0223	
Kansas Health Foundation 309 E Douglas *Web:* www.kansashealth.org	Wichita	KS	67202	316-262-7676	
Kate B Reynolds Charitable Trust 128 Reynolda Village *Web:* www.kbr.org	Winston-Salem	NC	27106	336-397-5500	723-7765
Kidango Inc 44000 Old Warm Springs Blvd *Web:* www.kidango.org	Fremont	CA	94538	408-258-3710	
Kids Cancer Care Foundation of Alberta 609 14 St Nw *Web:* www.kidscancercare.ab.ca	Calgary	AB	T2N2A1	403-216-9210	
Kiwanis International Foundation 3636 Woodview Trace *TF:* 800-549-2647 ■ *Web:* www.kiwanis.org	Indianapolis	IN	46268	317-875-8755	879-0204
Kresge Foundation 3215 W Big Beaver Rd *Web:* www.kresge.org	Troy	MI	48007	248-643-9630	
Krishnamurti Foundation of America 134 Besant Rd *Web:* kfa.org	Ojai	CA	93023	805-646-2726	
Krochet Kids International 1630 Superior Ave Unit C *Web:* www.krochetkids.org	Costa Mesa	CA	92627	949-791-2560	
Lake Avenue Community Foundation Inc 712 E Villa St *Web:* www.lakeavefoundation.org	Pasadena	CA	91101	626-449-4960	
Landesa 1424 Fourth Ave Ste 300 *Web:* www.landesa.org	Seattle	WA	98101	206-528-5880	
Lasalle College High School Endowment 8605 Cheltenham Ave *Web:* www.lschs.org	Wyndmoor	PA	19038	215-233-2911	
Liberty Fund Inc 8335 Allison Pt Trial Ste 300 *TF:* 800-955-8335 ■ *Web:* www.libertyfund.org	Indianapolis	IN	46250	317-842-0880	579-6060
Liliuokalani Trust 1300 Halona St *Web:* www.onipaa.org	Honolulu	HI	96817	808-847-1302	
Lilly Endowment Inc 2801 N Meridian St *Web:* www.lillyendowment.org	Indianapolis	IN	46208	317-924-5471	926-4431
Lois Pope LIFE Foundation 6274 Linton Blvd Ste 103 *Web:* www.life-edu.org	Delray Beach	FL	33484	561-865-0955	865-0938
Los Altos Community Foundation 183 Hillview Ave *Web:* www.losaltoscf.org	Los Altos	CA	94022	650-949-5908	
Lown Cardiovascular Research Foundation 21 Longwood Ave *Web:* lowninstitute.org	Brookline	MA	02446	617-732-1318	
Lumina Foundation for Education 30 S Meridian St Ste 700 *TF:* 800-834-5756 ■ *Web:* www.luminafoundation.org	Indianapolis	IN	46204	317-951-5300	951-5063
Lyndhurst Foundation 517 E Fifth St *Web:* www.lyndhurstfoundation.org	Chattanooga	TN	37403	423-756-0767	756-0770
Magic Johnson Foundation Inc 9100 Wilshire Blvd *Web:* magicjohnson.org	Beverly Hills	CA	90212	310-247-2033	786-8796
Maravilla Foundation 5723 Union Pacific Ave *Web:* www.maravilla.org	Commerce	CA	90022	323-721-4162	
Marbridge Foundation Inc 2310 Bliss Spillar Rd *Web:* marbridge.org	Manchaca	TX	78652	512-282-1144	
McCune Foundation Six PPG Pl Ste 750 *Web:* www.mccune.org	Pittsburgh	PA	15222	412-644-8779	644-8059
McKnight Foundation 710 Second St S Ste 400 *Web:* www.mcknight.org	Minneapolis	MN	55401	612-333-4220	332-3833
Meadows Foundation Inc 3003 Swiss Ave *TF:* 800-826-9431 ■ *Web:* www.mfi.org	Dallas	TX	75204	214-826-9431	827-7042
Meals on Wheels Inc of Tarrant County Endowment Fund 320 S Fwy *Web:* mealsonwheels.org	Fort Worth	TX	76104	817-336-0912	
Meyer Memorial Trust 425 NW Tenth Ave Ste 400 *Web:* www.mmt.org	Portland	OR	97209	503-228-5512	228-5840
Michael J Fox Foundation for Parkinson's Research Grand Central Stn PO Box 4777 *TF:* 800-708-7644 ■ *Web:* www.michaeljfox.org	New York	NY	10163	800-708-7644	
Midland Area Community Foundation 76 Ashman Cir *Web:* www.midlandfoundation.org	Midland	MI	48640	989-839-9661	
Milken Family Foundation 1250 Fourth St *Web:* www.mff.org	Santa Monica	CA	90401	310-570-4800	570-4801
MJ Murdock Charitable Trust 703 Broadway St Ste 710 *Web:* www.murdock-trust.org	Vancouver	WA	98660	360-694-8415	694-1819
Mobile Area Education Foundation 605 Bel Air Blvd Ste 400 *Web:* maef.net	Mobile	AL	36606	251-476-0002	
Moody Foundation 2302 Post Office St Ste 704 *Web:* www.moodyf.org	Galveston	TX	77550	409-797-1500	763-5564
Morris & Gwendolyn Cafritz Foundation 1825 K St NW Ste 1400 *Web:* www.cafritzfoundation.org	Washington	DC	20006	202-223-3100	296-7567
Mosaic Foundation 4980 S 118th St Ste A *Web:* www.mosaicinfo.org	Omaha	NE	68137	402-896-3884	
Narrow Gate Foundation 242 Dry Prong Rd *Web:* narrowgatefoundation.org	Williamsport	TN	38487	931-583-0633	
Nathan Cummings Foundation 475 Tenth Ave 14th Fl *Web:* www.nathancummings.org	New York	NY	10018	212-787-7300	
National Foundation for Cancer Research (NFCR) 4600 E W Hwy Ste 525 *TF:* 800-321-2873 ■ *Web:* www.nfcr.org	Bethesda	MD	20814	301-654-1250	654-5824
National PTA 1250 N Pitt St *Web:* pta.org	Alexandria	VA	22314	703-518-1200	
Nebraska Humane Society Foundation 8929 Ft St *Web:* www.nehumanesociety.org	Omaha	NE	68134	402-444-7800	
Nellie Mae Education Foundation 1250 Hancock St Ste 205N *TF:* 877-635-5436 ■ *Web:* www.nmefoundation.org	Quincy	MA	02169	781-348-4200	348-4299
New Leaders for New Schools 30 W 26th St Second Fl *Web:* www.nlns.org	New York	NY	10010	646-792-1070	
New York Road Runners Club Nine E 89th St *Web:* www.nyrr.org	New York	NY	10128	212-860-4455	
Noyce Foundation 419 S San Antonio Rd Ste 213 *Web:* www.noycefdn.org	Los Altos	CA	94022	650-856-2600	
NYU Alumni Association 25 W Fourth St Fourth Fl *Web:* www.alumni.nyu.edu	New York	NY	10012	212-998-6912	
Ogden-weber Applied Technology College Foundation 200 N Washington Blvd *Web:* www.owatc.com	Ogden	UT	84404	801-627-8300	
Olmsted Center for Sight 1170 Main St *Web:* www.olmstedcenter.org	Buffalo	NY	14209	716-882-1025	
Open Society Institute 400 W 59th St *Web:* www.opensocietyfoundations.org	New York	NY	10019	212-548-0600	548-4679
Orfalea Family Foundation 1283 Coast Village Cir Ste 2 *Web:* www.orfaleafoundation.org	Santa Barbara	CA	93108	805-565-7550	
Ottawa Regional Cancer Foundation The 1500 Alta Vista Dr *Web:* www.ottawacancer.ca	Ottawa	ON	K1G3Y9	613-247-3527	
Otto Bremer Foundation 445 Minnesota St Ste 2000 *Web:* www.ottobremer.org	Saint Paul	MN	55101	651-227-8036	
Pacific Legal Foundation 930 G St *Web:* www.pacificlegal.org	Sacramento	CA	95814	916-419-7111	
Packard Humanities Institute, The (PHI) 300 Second St *Web:* www.packhum.org	Los Altos	CA	94022	650-948-0150	
Padre Pio Foundation of America Inc 463 Main St *Web:* padrepio.com	Cromwell	CT	06416	860-635-4996	
Pangaea Global AIDS Foundation 436 14th St Ste 920 *Web:* www.pgaf.org	Oakland	CA	94612	510-379-4003	
Patient Advocate Foundation Inc 700 Thimble Shoals Blvd Ste 200 *TF:* 800-532-5274 ■ *Web:* www.patientadvocate.org	Newport News	VA	23606	800-532-5274	
Paul G Allen Family Foundation 505 Fifth Ave S Ste 900 *Web:* www.pgafamilyfoundation.org	Seattle	WA	98104	206-342-2030	342-3000
Pew Charitable Trusts 2005 Market St 1 Commerce Sq Ste 1700 *TF:* 800-595-4889 ■ *Web:* www.pewtrusts.org	Philadelphia	PA	19103	215-575-9050	575-4939
Phi Kappa Phi Foundation 7576 Goodwood Blvd *Web:* www.phikappaphi.org	Baton Rouge	LA	70806	225-388-4917	
Phillips Brooks School Endowment 2245 Avy Ave *Web:* www.phillipsbrooks.org	Menlo Park	CA	94025	650-854-4545	
Princeton Public Library 65 Witherspoon St *Web:* www.princeton.lib.nj.us	Princeton	NJ	08542	609-924-9529	
Public Interest Network 1543 Wazee St Fourth Fl *Web:* www.publicinterestnetwork.org	Denver	CO	80202	303-573-5995	

	City	State	Zip	Phone	Fax
Public Welfare Foundation 1200 U St NW *TF:* 800-275-7934 ■ *Web:* www.publicwelfare.org	Washington	DC	20009	202-965-1800	265-8851
Research Corp 4703 E Camp Lowell Dr Ste 201 *Web:* www.rescorp.org	Tucson	AZ	85712	520-571-1111	571-1119
Retirement Research Foundation 8765 W Higgins Rd Ste 430 *Web:* www.rrf.org	Chicago	IL	60631	773-714-8080	714-8089
Richard King Mellon Foundation 500 Grant St Ste 4106 *TF:* 800-424-9836 ■ *Web:* foundationcenter.org	Pittsburgh	PA	15219	412-392-2800	392-2837
Robert A Welch Foundation 5555 San Felipe St Ste 1900 *Web:* www.welch1.org	Houston	TX	77056	713-961-9884	961-5168
Robert R McCormick Tribune Foundation 205 N Michigan Ave Ste 4300 *TF:* 800-435-7352 ■ *Web:* www.mccormickfoundation.org	Chicago	IL	60611	312-445-5000	445-5001
Robert W Woodruff Foundation Inc 50 Hurt Plz Ste 1200 *Web:* www.woodruff.org	Atlanta	GA	30303	404-522-6755	522-7026
Robert Wood Johnson Foundation PO Box 2316 *Web:* www.rwjf.org	Princeton	NJ	08543	877-843-7953	
Rockefeller Bros Fund 475 Riverside Dr Ste 900 *Web:* www.rbf.org	New York	NY	10115	212-812-4200	812-4299
Rockefeller Foundation 420 Fifth Ave **Fax:* Mail Rm ■ *Web:* www.rockefellerfoundation.org	New York	NY	10018	212-869-8500	764-3468*
Rose & Sherle Wagner Foundation 224 W 29th St Fl 12 *Web:* yayanetwork.org	New York	NY	10001	212-239-0022	
Roy J Carver Charitable Trust 202 Iowa Ave *Web:* www.carvertrust.org	Muscatine	IA	52761	563-263-4010	263-1547
Saint Luke Institute Foundation Inc 8901 New Hampshire Ave *Web:* sli.org	Silver Spring	MD	20903	301-445-7970	
Salesforce.Com Foundation The Landmark @ One Market Ste 300 *TF:* 800-667-6389 ■ *Web:* www.salesforcefoundation.org	San Francisco	CA	94105	800-667-6389	
San Diego Yacht Club Sailing Foundation 1011 Anchorage Ln *Web:* sdycsf.org	San Diego	CA	92106	619-221-8400	
Sarcoma Foundation of America Inc, The 9899 Main St Ste 204 *Web:* www.curesarcoma.org	Damascus	MD	20872	301-253-8687	
Scholarship Foundation of Santa Barbara 2253 Las Positas Rd *Web:* www.sbscholarship.org	Santa Barbara	CA	93105	805-687-6065	
Sen. George J Mitchell Scholarship Resea 22 Monument Sq Ste 200 *Web:* mitchellinstitute.org	Portland	ME	04101	207-773-7700	
Seniors First Foundation Inc 5395 L B Mcleod Rd *Web:* www.seniorsfirstinc.org	Orlando	FL	32811	407-292-0177	
Seva Foundation 1786 Fifth St *Web:* www.seva.org	Berkeley	CA	94710	510-845-7382	
Shubert Foundation Inc, The 234 W 44th St *Web:* www.shubertfoundation.org	New York	NY	10036	212-944-3777	
Sierra Health Foundation 1321 Garden Hwy *Web:* www.sierrahealth.org	Sacramento	CA	95833	916-922-4755	
Smith Richardson Foundation Inc 60 Jesup Rd *Web:* www.srf.org	Westport	CT	06880	203-222-6222	222-6282
Spencer Foundation 625 N Michigan Ave Ste 1600 *Web:* www.spencer.org	Chicago	IL	60611	312-337-7000	337-0282
St. Croix Valley Foundation 516 Second St Ste 214 *Web:* www.scvfoundation.org	Hudson	WI	54016	715-386-9490	
St. Hope Foundation 6800 W Loop S Ste 560 *Web:* www.offeringhope.org	Bellaire	TX	77401	713-839-7111	
Starr Foundation 399 Pk Ave 17th Fl *Web:* www.starrfoundation.org	New York	NY	10022	212-909-3600	750-3536
StayClassy Productions Inc 533 F St Ste 300 *Web:* www.stayclassy.org	San Diego	CA	92101	619-961-1892	
Stowers Institute For Medical Research 1000 E 50th St *Web:* www.stowers.org	Kansas City	MO	64110	816-926-4000	926-2000
Student Agencies Foundation Inc 409 College Ave *Web:* www.studentagencies.com	Ithaca	NY	14850	607-272-2000	
Student Veterans of America PO Box 77673 *Web:* www.studentveterans.org	Washington	DC	20013	202-223-4710	
Sunlight Foundation 1818 N St NW Ste 410 *Web:* www.sunlightfoundation.com	Washington	DC	20036	202-742-1520	
Sunrise Children Foundation 2795 E Desert Inn Rd Ste 100 *Web:* www.sunrisechildren.org	Las Vegas	NV	89121	702-731-8373	
Sunrise House Foundation Inc 37 Sunset Inn Rd PO Box 600 *Web:* www.sunrisehouse.com	Lafayette	NJ	07848	973-383-6300	
Surdna Foundation Inc 330 Madison Ave 30th Fl *Web:* www.surdna.org	New York	NY	10017	212-557-0010	557-0003
Sutter East Bay Medical Foundation 3687 Mt Diablo Blvd Ste 200 *Web:* www.sebmf.org	Lafayette	CA	94549	925-962-6600	
T Buck Suzuki Environmental Foundation 326 Twelfth St *Web:* www.bucksuzuki.org	New Westminster	BC	V3M4H6	604-519-3635	
T4 Global Inc PO Box 130266 *Web:* t4global.org	Dallas	TX	75313	214-205-4245	
Temple Kol Ami Emanu-el Foundation Inc 8200 Peters Rd *Web:* tkae.org	Plantation	FL	33324	954-472-1988	
Terra Foundation for American Art 120 E Erie St Ste 1315 *Web:* terraamericanart.org	Chicago	IL	60611	312-664-3939	664-2052
Texas Methodist Foundation 11709 Boulder Ln Ste 100 *Web:* www.tmf-fdn.org	Austin	TX	78726	512-331-9971	
Thomas Jefferson Foundation PO Box 316 *Web:* www.monticello.org	Charlottesville	VA	22902	434-984-9808	977-7757
Tides Canada Foundation 400-163 W Hastings St *Web:* tidescanada.org	Vancouver	BC	V6B1H5	604-647-6611	
Tides Foundation Po Box 29903 *Web:* www.tides.org	San Francisco	CA	94129	415-561-6400	
Toledo Community Foundation 300 Madison Ave Ste 1300 *Web:* www.toledocf.org	Toledo	OH	43604	419-241-5049	
Tuality Healthcare Foundation Inc 335 SE Eighth Ave *Web:* tualityfoundation.org	Hillsboro	OR	97123	503-681-1170	
Turner Foundation Inc 133 Luckie St Second Fl *Web:* www.turnerfoundation.org	Atlanta	GA	30303	404-681-9900	681-0172
UCF Foundation Inc 12424 Research Pkwy Ste 250 *Web:* ucffoundation.org	Orlando	FL	32826	407-882-1220	
UCLA Foundation, The 10920 Wilshire Blvd Ste 900 *Web:* www.uclafoundation.org	Los Angeles	CA	90024	310-794-3193	
Universitas Foundation of Canada 3005 Ave Maricourt *Web:* www.universitas.ca	Quebec	QC	G1W4T8	418-651-8975	
Utility Notification Center of Colorado 16361 Table Mtn Pkwy *Web:* colorado811.org	Golden	CO	80403	303-232-1991	
Van Andel Institute 333 Bostwick Ave NE *Web:* www.vai.org	Grand Rapids	MI	49503	616-234-5000	234-5001
Verland Foundation Inc, The 212 Iris Rd *Web:* verland.org	Sewickley	PA	15143	412-741-2375	
Vira I Heinz Endowment 625 Liberty Ave 30 Dominion Twr *Web:* www.heinz.org	Pittsburgh	PA	15222	412-281-5777	281-5788
Wallace Foundation, The Five Penn Plz Seventh Fl *Web:* www.wallacefoundation.org/pages/default.aspx	New York	NY	10001	212-251-9700	679-6990
Walter & Elise Haas Fund One Lombard St Ste 305 *Web:*	San Francisco	CA	94111	415-398-4474	
Walton Family Foundation Inc (WFF) PO Box 2030 *Web:* www.waltonfamilyfoundation.org	Bentonville	AR	72712	479-464-1570	464-1580
Way to Happiness Foundation International, The 201 E Broadway *Web:* www.thewaytohappiness.org	Glendale	CA	91205	818-254-0600	
Wayne & Gladys Valley Foundation 1939 Harrison St Ste 510 *Web:* foundationcenter.org	Oakland	CA	94612	510-466-6060	466-6067
Weingart Foundation 1055 W Seventh St Ste 3050 *Web:* www.weingartfnd.org	Los Angeles	CA	90017	213-688-7799	688-1515
Wesley Foundation-msu 3625 Midland Ave *Web:* rivers-edge.org	Memphis	TN	38111	901-458-5808	
Whitehall Foundation Inc 125 Worth Ave *Web:* www.whitehall.org	Palm Beach	FL	33480	561-655-4474	659-4978
William & Flora Hewlett Foundation 2121 Sand Hill Rd *Web:* www.hewlett.org	Menlo Park	CA	94025	650-234-4500	234-4501
William Penn Foundation 100 N 18th St 2 Logan Sq 11th Fl *Web:* www.wpennfdn.org	Philadelphia	PA	19103	215-988-1830	988-1823
Wisconsin Alumni Research Foundation 614 Walnut St 13th Fl *Web:* www.warf.org	Madison	WI	53726	608-263-2500	
WK Kellogg Foundation One Michigan Ave E *Web:* www.wkkf.org	Battle Creek	MI	49017	269-968-1611	968-0413
WM Keck Foundation 550 S Hope St Ste 2500 *Web:* www.wmkeck.org	Los Angeles	CA	90071	213-680-3833	
Women's Foundation of Colorado, The The Chambers Ctr 1901 E Asbury Ave *Web:* www.wfco.org	Denver	CO	80208	303-285-2960	
Women's Independence Scholarship Program Inc (WISP) 4900 Randall Pkwy Ste H *TF:* 866-255-7742 ■ *Web:* www.wispinc.org	Wilmington	NC	28403	910-397-7742	397-0023
XanGo Goodness 2889 Ashton Blvd *Web:* www.xango.com	Lehi	UT	84043	801-816-8000	

309 FOUNDRIES - INVESTMENT

	City	State	Zip	Phone	Fax
Aero Metals Inc 1201 E Lincoln Way *Web:* www.aerometals.com	La Porte	IN	46350	219-326-1976	326-1972
Bescast Inc 4600 E 355th St *Web:* www.bescast.com	Willoughby	OH	44094	440-946-5300	946-8437
Bimac Corp 3034 Dryden Rd *Web:* www.bimac.com	Dayton	OH	45439	937-299-7333	299-7367
Consolidated Casting Corp 1501 S I-45 *TF:* 800-649-5289 ■ *Web:* www.consolicast.com	Hutchins	TX	75141	972-225-7305	225-2970
Dolphin Inc 740 S 59th Ave *Web:* www.dolphincasting.com	Phoenix	AZ	85043	602-272-6747	233-9570
Engineered Precision Casting Company Inc 952 Palmer Ave *Web:* www.epcast.com	Middletown	NJ	07748	732-671-2424	671-8615

				Phone	Fax
FS Precision Tech Co LLC 3025 E Victoria St. *Web:* www.fs-precision.com	Rancho Dominguez	CA	90221	310-638-0595	631-1664
Hitchiner Mfg Company Inc 594 Elm St *Web:* www.hitchiner.com	Milford	NH	03055	603-673-1100	673-7960
Houser & Plessl Wealth Management Group 5100 W Tilghman St Ste 240 *Web:* houserplessl.com	Allentown	PA	18104	610-530-0700	
Northern Precision Casting Co 300 Interchange N PO Box 580 *TF:* 800-934-4903 ■ *Web:* www.northernprecision.com	Lake Geneva	WI	53147	262-248-4461	248-1796
PCC Structurals Inc 4600 SE Harney Dr *Web:* www.pccstructurals.com	Portland	OR	97206	503-777-3881	652-3593
Pennsylvania Precision Cast Parts Inc 521 N Third Ave PO Box 1429 *Web:* www.ppcpinc.com	Lebanon	PA	17042	717-273-3338	273-2662
Post Precision Castings Inc 21 Walnut St. *Web:* www.postprecision.com	Strausstown	PA	19559	610-488-1011	488-6928
Precision Metalsmiths Inc 1081 E 200th St. *Web:* avalon-castings.com/	Cleveland	OH	44117	216-481-8900	
Remet Corp 210 Commons Rd *TF:* 877-939-0171 ■ *Web:* www.remet.com	Utica	NY	13502	315-797-8700	787-4848
Stainless Foundry & Engineering Inc 5110 N 35th St *Web:* www.stainlessfoundry.com	Milwaukee	WI	53209	414-462-7400	462-7303
Waltek Inc 14310 Sunfish Lk Blvd *TF:* 800-937-9496 ■ *Web:* www.waltekinc.com	Ramsey	MN	55303	763-427-3181	427-3216

310 FOUNDRIES - IRON & STEEL

SEE ALSO Foundries - Nonferrous (Castings) p. 2329

				Phone	Fax
Aarrowcast Inc 2900 E Richmond St *Web:* www.aarrowcast.com	Shawano	WI	54166	715-526-3600	526-9758
Allegheny Technologies Inc 1000 Six PPG Pl *NYSE:* ATI ■ **Fax:* Hum Res ■ *TF Sales:* 800-258-3586 ■ *Web:* www.atimetals.com	Pittsburgh	PA	15222	412-394-2800	394-3034*
Alloy Engineering & Casting Co 1700 W Washington St. **Fax Area Code:* 260 ■ *TF:* 866-352-8001 ■ *Web:* www.wirco.com	Champaign	IL	61821	217-398-3200	897-2525*
American Cast Iron Pipe Co (ACIPCO) 1501 31st Ave N *TF:* 800-442-2347 ■ *Web:* www.american-usa.com	Birmingham	AL	35207	205-325-7701	
AMSTED Industries Inc 180 N Stetson St Ste 1800 **Fax:* Hum Res ■ *Web:* www.amsted.com	Chicago	IL	60601	312-645-1700	819-8494*
Atlantic States Cast Iron Pipe Co 183 Sitgreaves St *TF:* 800-634-4746 ■ *Web:* www.atlanticstates.com	Phillipsburg	NJ	08865	908-454-1161	454-1026
Atlas Foundry Company Inc 601 N Henderson Ave *Web:* www.atlasfdry.com	Marion	IN	46952	765-662-2525	662-2902
Badger Foundry Co 1058 E Mark St *Web:* www.badgerfoundry.com	Winona	MN	55987	507-452-5760	452-6469
Bailey Metal Products Ltd One Caldari Rd *Web:* www.bmp-group.com	Concord	ON	L4K3Z9	905-738-6738	
Bay Cast Inc 2611 Ctr Ave *Web:* www.baycast.com	Bay City	MI	48708	989-892-0511	892-0599
Benton Foundry Inc 5297 SR 487 *Web:* www.bentonfoundry.com	Benton	PA	17814	570-925-6711	925-6929
Bremen Castings Inc 500 N Baltimore St **Fax Area Code:* 574 ■ *TF:* 800-837-2411 ■ *Web:* www.bremencastings.com	Bremen	IN	46506	800-837-2411	546-5016*
Buck Company Inc 897 Lancaster Pk *Web:* www.buckcompany.com	Quarryville	PA	17566	717-284-4114	284-3737
Campbell Foundry Co 800 Bergen St *Web:* www.campbellfoundry.com	Harrison	NJ	07029	973-483-5480	483-1843
Canada Alloy Casting Co 529 Manitou Dr *Web:* www.cac.ca	Kitchener	ON	N2C1S2	519-895-1161	895-1169
Cast-Fab Technologies Inc 3040 Forrer St *Web:* www.cast-fab.com	Cincinnati	OH	45209	513-758-1000	758-1002
Castalloy Inc 1701 Industrial Ln PO Box 827 *TF:* 800-211-0900 ■ *Web:* www.castalloycorp.com	Waukesha	WI	53189	262-547-0070	547-2215
Casting Service 300 Philadelphia St *Web:* www.atimetals.com	La Porte	IN	46350	219-362-1000	
Casting Solutions LLC 2345 Licking Rd *Web:* www.burnhamfoundry.com	Zanesville	OH	43701	740-452-9371	
Charter Dura-Bar 2100 W Lake Shore Dr *TF:* 800-227-6455 ■ *Web:* charterdura-bar.com/	Woodstock	IL	60098	815-338-3900	
Columbia Steel Casting Co Inc 10425 N Bloss Ave *TF:* 800-547-9471 ■ *Web:* www.columbiasteel.com	Portland	OR	97203	503-286-0685	286-1743
Columbus Castings 2211 Parsons Ave *Web:* www.columbuscastings.com	Columbus	OH	43207	614-444-2121	445-2084
Complex Steel & Wire Corp 36254 Annapolis St *TF:* 800-521-0666 ■ *Web:* www.complexsteel.com	Wayne	MI	48184	734-326-1600	326-7421
Delta Centrifugal Corp PO Box 1043 *TF Sales:* 888-433-3100 ■ *Web:* www.deltacentrifugal.com	Temple	TX	76503	254-773-9055	773-8988
Dixie Southern Industrial Inc 1060 N Commonwealth Ave *Web:* www.dsisteel.com	Polk City	FL	33868	863-984-1900	984-1825
Donsco Inc 124 N Front St *Web:* www.donsco.com	Wrightsville	PA	17368	717-252-1561	252-4530
Dotson Company Inc 200 W Rock St *Web:* www.dotson.com	Mankato	MN	56001	507-345-5018	345-1270
Douglas Steel Fabricating Corp 1312 S Waverly Rd *Web:* www.douglassteel.com	Lansing	MI	48917	517-322-2050	322-0050
Duraloy Technologies Inc 120 Bridge St **Fax:* Sales ■ *Web:* www.duraloy.com	Scottdale	PA	15683	724-887-5100	887-5224*
Eagle Foundry Co Inc PO Box 250 *Web:* www.eaglefoundryco.com	Eagle Creek	OR	97022	503-637-3048	637-3091
EJ Group Inc 301 Spring St *TF:* 800-874-4100 ■ *Web:* americas.ejco.com	East Jordan	MI	49727	231-536-2261	536-4458
Elyria Foundry Co 120 Filbert St *Web:* www.elyriafoundry.com	Elyria	OH	44036	440-322-4657	323-1101
Eureka Foundry Co 1601 Reggie White Blvd *Web:* www.eurekafoundryco.com	Chattanooga	TN	37402	423-267-3328	756-2607
Farrar Corp 142 W Burns St *Web:* www.farrarusa.com	Norwich	KS	67118	620-478-2212	478-2200
Frazier & Frazier Industries Inc 817 S First St PO Box 279 *Web:* www.ffcastings.com	Coolidge	TX	76635	254-786-2293	786-2284
Frog Switch & Mfg Co 600 E High St *TF:* 800-233-7194 ■ *Web:* www.frogswitch.com	Carlisle	PA	17013	717-243-2454	243-7768
Gartland Foundry Company Inc 330 Grant St *Web:* www.gartlandfoundry.com	Terre Haute	IN	47802	812-232-0226	232-7569
Goldens' Foundry & Machine Co (GFMCO) 600 12th St PO Box 96 *Web:* www.gfmco.com	Columbus	GA	31902	706-323-0471	596-2850
Great Lakes Castings LLC 800 N Washington Ave *Web:* www.greatlakescastings.com	Ludington	MI	49431	231-843-2501	845-1534
Grede Holdings LLC 4000 Town Ctr Ste 500 *Web:* www.grede.com	Southfield	MI	48075	248-440-9500	440-9577
Harrison Steel Castings Co Inc 900 S Mound St *TF:* 888-782-7937 ■ *Web:* www.hscast.com	Attica	IN	47918	765-762-2481	762-2487
Hensley Industries Inc 2108 Joe Field Rd PO Box 29779 **Fax:* Cust Svc ■ *TF:* 888-406-6262 ■ *Web:* www.hensleyind.com	Dallas	TX	75229	972-241-2321	241-0915*
Hitachi Metals America Ltd 2 Manhattanville Rd Ste 301 *TF:* 800-777-5757 ■ *Web:* www.hitachimetals.com	Purchase	NY	10577	914-694-9200	694-9279
Howco Metals Management 9611 Telge Rd *TF:* 800-392-7720 ■ *Web:* www.howcogroup.com	Houston	TX	77095	281-649-8800	649-8900
Huron Casting Inc 7050 Hartley St PO Box 679 *Web:* www.huroncasting.com	Pigeon	MI	48755	989-453-3933	453-3319
Intat Precision Inc 2148 N State Rd 3 PO Box 488 *Web:* www.intat.com	Rushville	IN	46173	765-932-5323	932-3032
Interstate Castings Co 3823 Massachusetts Ave *Web:* www.interstatecastings.com	Indianapolis	IN	46218	317-546-2427	546-4004
Jencast PO Box 1509 *TF:* 800-331-2662 ■ *Web:* www.jencast.com	Coffeyville	KS	67337	620-251-5700	251-3622
Johnson Brass & Machine Foundry Inc 270 N Mill St PO Box 219 *Web:* www.johnsoncentrifugal.com	Saukville	WI	53080	262-377-9440	284-7066
Johnstown Specialty Castings Inc 545 Central Ave **Fax:* Sales ■ *Web:* whemco.com	Johnstown	PA	15902	814-535-9000	536-0868*
Lufkin Industries Inc 601 S Raguet St *NASDAQ:* LUFK ■ *Web:* www.lufkin.com	Lufkin	TX	75902	936-634-2211	637-5474
Maddox Foundry & Machine Works Inc 13370 SW 170th St *Web:* www.maddoxfoundry.com	Archer	FL	32618	352-495-2121	495-3962
Maynard Steel Casting Co 2856 S 27th St *Web:* www.maynardsteel.com	Milwaukee	WI	53215	414-645-0440	645-7378
McWane Cast Iron Pipe Co 1201 Vanderbilt Rd *Web:* www.mcwanepipe.com	Birmingham	AL	35234	205-322-3521	241-4243
McWane Inc 2900 Hwy 280 Ste 300 *TF:* 877-231-0904 ■ *Web:* www.mcwane.com	Birmingham	AL	35223	205-414-3100	414-3170
Milwaukee Malleable & Grey Iron Works 2773 S 29th St *Web:* milwtool.com	Milwaukee	WI	53201	414-645-0200	
Minnotte Corp Minnotte Sq *Web:* www.minnotte.com	Pittsburgh	PA	15220	412-922-1633	922-5051
Motor Castings Co 1323 S 65th St *Web:* www.motorcastings.com	Milwaukee	WI	53214	414-476-1434	476-2845
Neenah Foundry Co 2121 Brooks Ave *TF:* 800-558-5075 ■ *Web:* www.nfco.com	Neenah	WI	54956	920-725-7000	729-3661
Northern Iron & Machine 867 Forest St *Web:* www.northernim.com	Saint Paul	MN	55106	651-778-3300	778-1321
Omaha Steel Castings Co 4601 Farnam St *Web:* www.omahasteel.com/contact-us.html	Omaha	NE	68132	402-558-6000	558-0327
Osco Industries Inc PO Box 1388 *Web:* www.oscoind.com	Portsmouth	OH	45662	740-354-3183	353-1504
Pacific States Cast Iron Pipe Co 1401 East 2000 South PO Box 1219 *Web:* www.pscipco.com	Provo	UT	84603	801-373-6910	377-0338
Pacific Steel Casting Company Inc 1333 Second St *Web:* www.pacificsteel.com	Berkeley	CA	94710	510-525-9200	524-4673
Paxton-Mitchell Co 108 S 12th St *Web:* www.paxton-mitchell.com	Blair	NE	68008	402-426-3131	345-6772
Prospect Foundry LLC 1225 Winter St NE *Web:* www.prospectfdry.com	Minneapolis	MN	55413	612-331-9282	331-4122
Quaker City Castings Inc 310 E Euclid Ave *Web:* www.qccast.com	Salem	OH	44460	330-332-1566	332-1159
Quality Castings Co 1200 N Main St *Web:* www.qcfoundry.com	Orrville	OH	44667	330-682-6010	683-3153
Richmond Foundry 126 Collins Rd *Web:* www.matrixmetalsllc.com	Richmond	TX	77469	281-342-5511	
Rodney Hunt Co 46 Mill St *TF:* 800-448-8860 ■ *Web:* www.rodneyhunt.com	Orange	MA	01364	978-544-2511	544-7204
Samuel Steel Pickling Co 1400 Enterprise Pkwy *Web:* www.samuelsteel.com	Twinsburg	OH	44087	330-963-3777	963-0770
Sawbrook Steel Castings Co 425 Shepherd Ave *Web:* www.sawbrooksteel.com	Cincinnati	OH	45215	513-554-1700	554-0092

	City	State	Zip	Phone	Fax
Sentinel Bldg Systems Inc 237 S Fourth St PO Box 348 *Web:* www.sentinelbuildings.com	Albion	NE	68620	402-395-5076	395-6369
Sharon Coating LLC 277 Sharpsville Ave *TF:* 800-456-1794 ■ *Web:* www.us.nlmk.com	Sharon	PA	16146	724-981-3545	981-3009
Sioux City Foundry Co 801 Div St *TF:* 800-831-0874 ■ *Web:* www.siouxcityfoundry.com	Sioux City	IA	51102	712-252-4181	252-4197
Sivyer Steel Corp 225 S 33rd St *Web:* www.sivyersteel.com	Bettendorf	IA	52722	563-355-1811	355-3946
Smith Foundry Co 1855 E 28th St *Web:* www.smithfoundry.com	Minneapolis	MN	55407	612-729-9395	729-2519
Spokane Steel Foundry Co 3808 N Sullivan Rd Bldg 1 *Web:* spokaneindustries.com	Spokane	WA	99216	509-924-0440	924-9448
Standard Alloys & Mfg PO Box 969 *TF:* 800-231-8240 ■ *Web:* www.standardalloys.com	Port Arthur	TX	77640	409-983-3201	983-7837
Steel Service Corp 2260 Flowood Dr PO Box 321425 *TF:* 800-844-9222 ■ *Web:* www.steelservicecorp.com	Jackson	MS	39232	601-939-9222	939-9359
T & B Foundry Co 2469 E 71st St	Cleveland	OH	44104	216-391-4200	
Talladega Castings & Machine Co Inc 228 N Ct St *TF:* 800-766-6708 ■ *Web:* www.tmsco.com	Talladega	AL	35160	256-362-5550	362-1321
Talladega Machinery & Supply Co Inc 301 N Johnson Ave PO Box 736 *TF Cust Svc:* 800-289-8672 ■ *Web:* www.tmsco.com	Talladega	AL	35161	256-362-4124	761-2579
Taylor & Fenn Co 22 Deerfield Rd *Web:* www.taylorfenn.com	Windsor	CT	06095	860-249-7531	525-2961
Tyler Pipe Co 11910 CR 492 **Fax Area Code:* 800 ■ *TF:* 800-527-8478 ■ *Web:* www.tylerpipe.com	Tyler	TX	75706	903-882-5511	248-9537*
Unicast Co 241 N Washington St *Web:* www.unicastco.com	Boyertown	PA	19512	610-367-0155	367-2787
Union Electric Steel Corp 726 Bell Ave *Web:* www.uniones.com	Carnegie	PA	15106	412-429-7655	276-1711
Urick Foundry Co 1501 Cherry St *Web:* www.urick.net	Erie	PA	16502	814-454-2461	454-1397
US Pipe & Foundry Co Two Chase Corporate Drive Suite 200 **Fax Area Code:* 205 ■ *TF:* 866-347-7473 ■ *Web:* www.uspipe.com	Birmingham	AL	35244	866-347-7473	417-8411*
Walker Machine & Foundry Corp PO Box 4587 *Web:* www.walkerfoundry.com	Roanoke	VA	24015	540-344-6265	342-2278
Waukesha Foundry Company Inc 1300 Lincoln Ave **Fax:* Sales ■ *TF:* 800-727-0741 ■ *Web:* www.waukeshafoundry.com	Waukesha	WI	53186	262-542-0741	549-8440*
Waupaca Foundry 1955 Brunner Dr PO Box 249 *TF:* 800-669-6820 ■ *Web:* www.waupacafoundry.com	Waupaca	WI	54981	715-258-6611	258-9268
Wheeling-Nisshin Inc 400 Penn St *Web:* www.wheeling-nisshin.com	Follansbee	WV	26037	304-527-2800	527-0985
Willman Industries Inc 338 S Main St *Web:* www.willmanind.com	Cedar Grove	WI	53013	920-668-8526	668-8998
Winsert Inc 2645 Industrial Pkwy S PO Box 0198 *Web:* www.winsert.com	Marinette	WI	54143	715-732-1703	732-2824
Wollaston Alloys Inc 205 Wood Rd *Web:* www.wollastonalloys.com	Braintree	MA	02184	781-848-3333	848-3993

311 FOUNDRIES - NONFERROUS (CASTINGS)

SEE ALSO Foundries - Iron & Steel p. 2328

	City	State	Zip	Phone	Fax
Advance Die Casting Co 3760 N Holton St *Web:* www.advancediecasting.com	Milwaukee	WI	53212	414-964-0284	964-8092
Ahresty Wilmington Corp 2627 S South St *Web:* www.ahresty.com	Wilmington	OH	45177	937-382-6112	382-5871
Akron Foundry Co 2728 Wingate Ave *Web:* www.akronfoundry.com	Akron	OH	44314	330-745-3101	745-7999
Alloy Die Casting Co 6550 Caballero Blvd **Fax:* Sales ■ *Web:* alloydie.com	Buena Park	CA	90620	714-521-9800	521-5510*
Aurora Metals Divison LLC 1995 Greenfield Ave *Web:* www.aurorametals.com	Montgomery	IL	60538	630-844-4900	844-6839
Bardane Mfg PO Box 70 *Web:* www.bardane.com	Jermyn	PA	18433	570-876-4844	876-1938
Basic Aluminum Castings Co 1325 E 168th St *Web:* www.basicaluminum.com	Cleveland	OH	44110	216-481-5606	481-7031
Blaser Die Casting Co 5700 Third Ave S	Seattle	WA	98108	206-767-7800	767-7055
Brillcast Inc 3400 Wentworth Dr SW *Web:* www.brillcast.com	Grand Rapids	MI	49519	616-534-4977	534-0880
Buck Company Inc 897 Lancaster Pk *Web:* www.buckcompany.com	Quarryville	PA	17566	717-284-4114	284-3737
Bunting Bearings Corp 1001 Holland Pk Blvd *TF:* 888-286-8464 ■ *Web:* www.buntingbearings.com	Holland	OH	43528	419-866-7000	866-0653
Cast Technologies Inc 1100 SW Washington St *Web:* casttechnologies.net	Peoria	IL	61602	309-676-2157	676-2167
Cast-Rite Corp 515 E Airline Way *Web:* www.cast-rite.com	Gardena	CA	90248	310-532-2080	532-0605
Chicago White Metal Casting Inc 649 N Rt 83 *Web:* www.cwmdiecast.com	Bensenville	IL	60106	630-595-4424	595-4474
Consolidated Metco Inc 13940 N Rivergate Blvd **Fax Area Code:* 503 ■ **Fax:* Sales ■ *TF Sales:* 800-547-9473 ■ *Web:* www.conmet.com	Portland	OR	97203	800-547-9473	240-5488*
Consolidated Precision Products 8333 Wilcox Ave *Web:* cppcorp.com	Cudahy	CA	90201	323-773-2363	562-3174
Deco Products Co 506 Sanford St *TF:* 800-327-9751 ■ *Web:* www.decoprod.com	Decorah	IA	52101	563-382-4264	382-9845
Del Mar Die Casting Co 12901 S Western Ave **Fax Area Code:* 310 ■ *TF:* 800-624-7468 ■ *Web:* www.delmarindustries.com	Gardena	CA	90249	323-321-0600	327-1951*
Denison Industries (DI) 22 Fielder Dr *Web:* www.denisonindustries.com	Denison	TX	75020	903-786-6500	786-6575
Dynacast Inc 14045 Ballantyne Corporate Pl *TF:* 866-662-2750 ■ *Web:* www.dynacast.com	Charlotte	NC	28277	704-927-2790	927-2791
Eck Industries Inc 1602 N Eigth St PO Box 967 *Web:* www.eckindustries.com	Manitowoc	WI	54221	920-682-4618	682-9298
Electric Materials Co 50 S Washington St *TF:* 800-356-2211 ■ *Web:* www.elecmat.com	North East	PA	16428	814-725-9621	725-3620
Empire Die Casting Co Inc 635 Highland Rd E *Web:* www.empiredie.com	Macedonia	OH	44056	330-467-0750	467-9118
Falcon Foundry Co 96 Sixth St *TF:* 800-253-8624 ■ *Web:* www.falconfoundry.com	Lowellville	OH	44436	330-536-6221	536-6371
Fall River Group 670 S Main *Web:* www.fallrivergroup.com	Fall River	WI	53932	920-484-3311	
General Die Casters Inc 2150 Highland Rd *TF:* 800-332-2278 ■ *Web:* www.generaldie.com	Twinsburg	OH	44087	330-657-2300	657-2192
Gibbs Die Casting Corp 369 Community Dr *Web:* www.gibbsdc.com	Henderson	KY	42420	270-827-1801	827-7840
Globalfoundries Inc 2600 Great America Way *Web:* www.globalfoundries.com	Santa Clara	CA	95054	408-462-3900	
H-J Enterprises Inc 3010 High Ridge Blvd *Web:* www.h-jenterprises.com	High Ridge	MO	63049	636-677-3421	376-1915
Halex Co 23901 Aurora Rd *TF:* 800-749-3261 ■ *Web:* www.halexco.com	Bedford Heights	OH	44146	440-439-1616	439-1792
Harmony Castings LLC 251 Perry Hwy *Web:* www.harmonycastings.com	Harmony	PA	16037	724-452-5811	452-0118
Hoffmann Die Cast Corp 229 Kerth St *Web:* www.hoffmanndc.com	Saint Joseph	MI	49085	269-983-1102	983-2928
Howmet Castings One Misco Dr *Web:* www.alcoa.com	Whitehall	MI	49461	231-894-5686	894-7607
ICG Castings Inc 9864 Church St	Bridgman	MI	49106	269-782-2108	783-3104
Imperial Die Casting Co 2249 Old Liberty Rd *Web:* www.rcmindustries.com	Liberty	SC	29657	864-859-0202	855-1597
Johnson Brass & Machine Foundry Inc 270 N Mill St PO Box 219 *Web:* www.johnsoncentrifugal.com	Saukville	WI	53080	262-377-9440	284-7066
Kitchen-Quip Inc 405 E Marion St *Web:* www.kqcasting.com	Waterloo	IN	46793	260-837-8311	837-7919
Lee Brass Co 1800 Golden Springs Rd *TF General:* 800-876-1811 ■ *Web:* www.leebrass.com	Anniston	AL	36207	800-876-1811	876-1800
Littlestown Foundry Inc 150 Charles St PO Box 69 *TF:* 800-471-0844 ■ *Web:* www.littlestownfoundry.com	Littlestown	PA	17340	717-359-4141	359-5010
Madison Precision Products Inc 94 E 400 N *Web:* www.madisonprecision.com	Madison	IN	47250	812-273-4702	273-2451
Madison-Kipp Corp 201 Waubesa St *TF:* 800-356-6148 ■ *Web:* www.madison-kipp.com	Madison	WI	53704	800-356-6148	
Magnolia Metal Corp 10675 Bedford Ave Ste 200 *TF:* 800-228-4043 ■ *Web:* www.magnoliabronze.com	Omaha	NE	68134	402-455-8760	455-8762
New Products Corp 448 N Shore Dr *Web:* www.npc.com	Benton Harbor	MI	49022	269-925-2161	934-6180
NGK Metals Corp 917 Hwy 11 S **Fax Area Code:* 877 ■ *TF:* 800-523-8268 ■ *Web:* www.ngkmetals.com	Sweetwater	TN	37874	423-337-5500	645-2328*
Ohio Decorative Products Inc 220 S Elizabeth St *Web:* www.ohiodec.com	Spencerville	OH	45887	419-647-4191	647-4202
Pacific Die Casting Corp 6155 S Eastern Ave *Web:* www.pacdiecast.com	Commerce	CA	90040	323-725-1332	728-1115
Park-Ohio Holdings Corp (PKOH) 6065 Parkland Blvd *NASDAQ: PKOH* ■ *Web:* www.pkoh.com	Cleveland	OH	44124	440-947-2000	947-2099
PHB Inc 7900 W Ridge Rd *Web:* www.phbcorp.com	Fairview	PA	16415	814-474-5511	474-3091
Piad Precision Casting Corp 112 Industrial Pk Rd *TF:* 800-441-9858 ■ *Web:* www.piad.com	Greensburg	PA	15601	724-838-5500	838-5520
Premier Die Casting Co 1177 Rahway Ave *TF:* 800-394-3006 ■ *Web:* www.diecasting.com	Avenel	NJ	07001	732-634-3000	634-0590
Premier Tool & Die Cast Corp 9886 N Tudor Rd *TF:* 800-417-8717 ■ *Web:* www.premierdiecast.com	Berrien Springs	MI	49103	269-471-7715	471-3855
Reliable Castings Corp 3530 Spring Grove Ave *TF:* 866-722-2278 ■ *Web:* www.reliablecastings.com	Cincinnati	OH	45223	513-541-2627	541-5696
Ridco Casting Co 6 Beverage Hill Ave *Web:* www.ridco.com	Pawtucket	RI	02860	401-724-0400	724-6320
Selmet Inc 33992 SE 7 Mile Ln PO Box 689 *Web:* www.selmetinc.com	Albany	OR	97322	541-926-7731	928-9346
Southern Centrifugal Inc 4180 S Creek Rd *TF:* 800-634-8176 ■ *Web:* www.metaltek.com	Chattanooga	TN	37406	423-622-4131	622-2227
Stahl Specialty Co 11 E Pacific PO Box 6 *TF:* 800-821-7852 ■ *Web:* www.stahlspecialty.com	Kingsville	MO	64061	816-597-3322	597-3485
Talladega Castings & Machine Co Inc 228 N Ct St *TF:* 800-766-6708 ■ *Web:* www.tmsco.com	Talladega	AL	35160	256-362-5550	362-1321
Tampa Brass & Aluminum 8511 Florida Mining Blvd *Web:* www.tampabrass.com	Tampa	FL	33634	813-885-6064	882-3271
Techni-Cast Corp 11220 Garfield Ave **Fax:* Sales ■ *TF:* 800-923-4585 ■ *Web:* www.techni-cast.com	South Gate	CA	90280	562-923-4585	861-4259*
Texas Die Casting Inc 600 S Loop 485 *Web:* www.texasdiecasting.com	Gladewater	TX	75647	903-845-2224	845-6155
Top Die Casting Co 13910 Dearborn Ave *Web:* www.topdie.com	South Beloit	IL	61080	815-389-2599	389-3057
Travis Pattern & Foundry Inc 1413 E Hawthorne Rd *Web:* www.pduinc.com	Spokane	WA	99218	509-466-3545	467-6465
Twin City Die Castings Co 1070 33rd Ave SE *Web:* www.tcdcinc.com	Minneapolis	MN	55414	651-645-3611	645-0724
United Titanium Inc 3450 Old Airport Rd *TF:* 800-321-4938 ■ *Web:* www.unitedtitanium.com	Wooster	OH	44691	330-264-2111	263-1336

Phone Fax

Walker Die Casting Inc
1125 Higgs Rd PO Box 1189 .... Lewisburg TN 37091 931-359-6206 359-8030
Web: www.walkerdiecasting.com

Ward Aluminum Casting Co 642 Growth Ave........ Fort Wayne IN 46808 260-426-8700 420-1919
Web: www.wardcorp.com

Watry Industries Inc 3312 Lakeshore Dr .... Sheboygan WI 53081 920-457-4886 457-5241
Web: www.watry.com

Wisconsin Aluminum Foundry Company Inc
838 S 16th St ....Manitowoc WI 54220 920-682-8286 682-7285
Web: www.wafco.com

Wollaston Alloys Inc 205 Wood Rd .... Braintree MA 02184 781-848-3333 848-3993
Web: www.wollastonalloys.com

Wolverine Bronze Co 28178 Hayes Rd............... Roseville MI 48066 586-776-8180 776-4510*
**Fax:* Sales ■ *Web:* www.wolverinebronze.com

Yoder Industries Inc 2520 Needmore Rd ....Dayton OH 45414 937-278-5769 278-6321
Web: www.yoderindustries.com

312 FRAMES & MOULDINGS

Phone Fax

Alexander Moulding Mill Co 250 US 281........... Hamilton TX 76531 254-386-3187

Alexandria Moulding 20352 Powerdam Rd.......... Alexandria ON K0C1A0 613-525-2784 265-8746*
**Fax Area Code:* 800 ■ *TF:* 866-377-2539 ■ *Web:* www.alexmo.com

ELSAL Inc 800 A St .... San Rafael CA 94901 415-472-8388 472-8389
Web: www2.elsal.com

Groovfold Inc 1050 W State St................ Newcomerstown OH 43832 740-498-8363 498-8782
TF: 800-367-1133 ■ *Web:* www.groovfold.com

Larson-Juhl 3900 Steve Reynolds Blvd .... Norcross GA 30093 800-221-4123 279-5297*
**Fax Area Code:* 770 ■ **Fax:* Hum Res ■ *TF:* 800-221-4123 ■ *Web:* www.larsonjuhl.com

Monarch Industries Inc 99 Main St...................Warren RI 02885 401-247-5200
Web: www.monarchinc.com

North American Enclosures Inc
65 Jetson Ln.....................................Central Islip NY 11722 631-234-9500 234-9504
TF: 800-645-9209 ■ *Web:* www.naeframes.com

PB & H Moulding Corp 124 Pickard Dr E............. Syracuse NY 13211 315-455-5602 455-8748
TF: 800-746-9724 ■ *Web:* www.pbhmoulding.com

Peterson Picture Frame Company Inc
2720 W Belmont Ave ....Chicago IL 60618 773-463-8888 463-4603
Web: www.peterson-picture.com

Quanex Building Products 2270 Woodale Dr ..... Mounds View MN 55112 763-231-4000
TF: 800-233-4383 ■ *Web:* www.quanex.com

Royal Mouldings Ltd
135 Bearcreek Rd PO Box 610 ....Marion VA 24354 276-783-8161 782-3285
TF: 800-368-3117 ■ *Web:* www.royalbuildingproducts.com

Sunset Moulding Company Inc 2231 Paseo Ave ...... Live Oak CA 95953 530-695-1000 695-2560
Web: www.sunsetmoulding.com

Uniek Inc 805 Uniek Dr.......................... Waunakee WI 53597 608-849-9999 849-9799*
**Fax:* Mktg ■ *TF:* 800-248-6435 ■ *Web:* www.uniekinc.com

Woodgrain Distribution 80 Shelby St .... Montevallo AL 35115 205-665-2546 665-3432
TF: 800-756-0199 ■ *Web:* www.woodgraindistribution.com

FRAMES & MOULDINGS - METAL

SEE Doors & Windows - Metal p. 2203

313 FRANCHISES

SEE ALSO Business Service Centers p. 1895; Candles p. 1900; Car Rental Agencies p. 1901; Children's Learning Centers p. 1948; Cleaning Services p. 1951; Remodeling, Refinishing, Resurfacing Contractors p. 2102; Convenience Stores p. 2152; Health Food Stores p. 2453; Home Inspection Services p. 2476; Hotels & Hotel Companies p. 2530; Ice Cream & Dairy Stores p. 2550; Laundry & Drycleaning Services p. 2621; Auto Supply Stores p. 1827; Optical Goods Stores p. 2846; Pest Control Services p. 2915; Automotive Services p. 1843; Printing Companies - Commercial Printers p. 2965; Real Estate Agents & Brokers p. 3030; Restaurant Companies p. 3069; Bakeries p. 1847; Staffing Services p. 3195; Beauty Salons p. 1861; Travel Agency Networks p. 3255; Weight Loss Centers & Services p. 3296
Please see the category on Hotel & Resort Operation & Management for listings of hotel franchises.

Phone Fax

1-800-Got-Junk
301 - 887 Great Northern Way 3rd Fl ....Vancouver BC V5T4T5 800-468-5865
TF: 800-468-5865 ■ *Web:* www.1800gotjunk.com

1-800-Water Damage 1167 Mercer St.................Seattle WA 98109 206-381-3041 381-3052
TF: 800-928-3732 ■ *Web:* www.1800waterdamage.com

A-Ok Rentals Inc 950 Bloomfield Ave .... West Caldwell NJ 07006 973-575-7900 575-7847
Web: www.affiliatedcarrental.com

ABC Seamless 3001 Fiechtner Dr.......................Fargo ND 58103 701-293-5952 293-3107
TF: 800-732-6577 ■ *Web:* www.abcseamless.com

Abrakadoodle Inc 46030 Manekin Pl Ste 110 .... Sterling VA 20166 703-860-6570 860-6574
Web: www.abrakadoodle.com

ActionCOACH 5781 S Ft Apache Rd................. Las Vegas NV 89148 702-795-3188 795-3183
TF: 888-483-2828 ■ *Web:* www.actioncoach.com

Aire Serv Heating & Air Conditioning Inc
5387 Texas 6 Fwy Ste 101 ....Woodway TX 76712 254-523-3600 782-2013*
**Fax Area Code:* 716 ■ *TF:* 855-983-0630 ■ *Web:* www.aireserv.com

Aire-Master of America Inc 1821 N State Hwy Cc.........Nixa MO 65714 417-725-2691 725-5737
TF: 800-525-0957 ■ *Web:* www.airemaster.com

All Tune & Lube Brakes & More Inc
8334 Veteran's Hwy.............................. Millersville MD 21108 410-987-1011 987-7273
TF: 877-978-1758 ■ *Web:* www.alltuneandlube.com

AmeriSpec Inc 889 Ridge Lk Blvd..................Memphis TN 38120 901-820-8500
TF: 800-426-2270 ■ *Web:* www.amerispec.com

Phone Fax

Arby's Restaurant Group Inc
1155 Perimeter Ctr W.................................Atlanta GA 30338 678-514-4100
Web: www.arbys.com

Archadeck 2924 Emerywood Pkwy Ste 101........... Richmond VA 23294 804-353-6999 353-2364
TF: 800-722-4668 ■ *Web:* www.archadeck.com

Bad Ass Coffee Co of Hawaii Inc
3530 S State St.................................Salt Lake City UT 84115 801-265-1182 463-2606
Web: www.badasscoffee.com

Baskin-Robbins Inc 130 Royall St......................Canton MA 02021 781-737-3000
TF: 800-859-5339 ■ *Web:* www.baskinrobbins.com

Beef O'Bradys Inc 5660 W Cypress St Ste A............. Tampa FL 33607 813-226-2333 226-0030
TF: 800-728-8878 ■ *Web:* www.beefobradys.com

Bellacino's Corp 10096 Shaver Rd.................. Portage MI 49024 269-329-0782 329-0930
TF: 877-379-0700 ■ *Web:* bellacinos.com

Ben & Jerry's Homemade Inc
30 Community Dr..........................South Burlington VT 05403 802-846-1500 846-1538
Web: www.benjerry.com

Benjamin Franklin Plumbing
50 Central Ave Ste 920............................ Sarasota FL 34236 941-366-9692 951-0942
TF: 800-471-0809 ■ *Web:* www.benjaminfranklinplumbing.com

Big Apple Bagels 500 Lk Cook Rd Ste 475 .... Deerfield IL 60015 847-948-7520 405-8140
TF: 800-251-6101 ■ *Web:* www.babcorp.com

Big Boy Restaurants International LLC
4199 Marcy St ....Warren MI 48091 586-759-6000
Web: www.bigboy.com

Bojangles' Restaurants Inc
9432 Southern Pine Blvd .... Charlotte NC 28273 704-335-1804 523-6676
TF: 800-366-9921 ■ *Web:* www.bojangles.com

Boston Pizza Restaurants LP
1501 LBJ Fwy Ste 450 .... Dallas TX 75234 972-484-9022 484-7630
TF: 866-277-8721 ■ *Web:* www.bostons.com

BrickKicker Inc 849 N Ellsworth St................. Naperville IL 60563 630-420-9900 420-2270
TF: 800-821-1820 ■ *Web:* www.brickkicker.com

Bruegger's Enterprises 159 Bank St .... Burlington VT 05401 802-660-4020 652-9293
Web: www.brueggers.com

BuildingStars Inc
33 Worthington Access Dr .... Maryland Heights MO 63043 314-991-3356 991-3198
Web: www.buildingstars.com

Candy Bouquet International Inc
510 Mclean St .... Little Rock AR 72202 501-375-9990 375-9998
TF: 877-226-3901 ■ *Web:* www.candybouquet.com

Captain D's LLC
624 Grassmere Park Dr Ste 30 .... Nashville TN 37211 615-391-5461
TF: 800-314-4819 ■ *Web:* www.captainds.com

Car-X Assoc Corp
1375 E Woodfield Rd Ste 500.................... Schaumburg IL 60173 847-273-8920 619-3310
TF: 800-359-2359 ■ *Web:* www.carx.com

CardSmart Retail Corp 11 Executive Ave.............. Edison NJ 08817 888-782-7050 726-2384*
**Fax Area Code:* 401 ■ *TF:* 888-782-7050 ■ *Web:* www.cardsmart.com

Carlson Wagonlit Travel Inc
701 Carlson Pkwy.............................. Minnetonka MN 55305 800-213-7295 212-2409*
**Fax Area Code:* 763 ■ *TF:* 800-213-7295 ■ *Web:* www.carlsonwagonlit.com

Carvel Express 200 Glenridge Pt Pkwy Ste 200........... Atlanta GA 30342 800-322-4848 255-4978*
**Fax Area Code:* 404 ■ *TF:* 800-322-4848 ■ *Web:* www.carvel.com

CertaPro Painters Ltd 150 Green Tree Rd Ste 1003........ Oaks PA 19456 800-689-7271 650-9997*
**Fax Area Code:* 610 ■ *TF:* 800-689-7271 ■ *Web:* www.certapro.com

Certified Restoration DryCleaning Network LLC
2060 Coolidge Hwy .... Berkley MI 48072 800-963-2736 246-7868*
**Fax Area Code:* 248 ■ *TF:* 800-963-2736 ■ *Web:* www.restorationdrycleaning.com

Charley's Grilled Subs
2500 Farmers Dr Ste 140 .... Columbus OH 43235 614-923-4700 923-4701
TF: 800-437-8325 ■ *Web:* www.charleys.com

Checkers Drive-In Restaurants Inc
4300 W Cypress St Ste 600 .... Tampa FL 33607 813-283-7000 283-7208
TF: 800-800-8072 ■ *Web:* www.checkers.com

Chester's International LLC
3500 Colonnade Pkwy Ste 325.....................Birmingham AL 35243 205-949-4690 298-0332
TF: 800-554-4537 ■ *Web:* www.chestersinternational.com

Christmas Decor Inc 709 E 44th St .... Lubbock TX 79404 806-722-1225 722-9627
Web: www.christmasdecor.net

CiCi Enterprises LP 1080 W Bethel Rd .... Coppell TX 75019 972-745-4200 745-4204
Web: www.cicispizza.com

Cleaning Authority
7230 Lee DeForest Dr Ste 200 ....Columbia MD 21046 410-740-1900 740-1906
TF: 888-658-0659 ■ *Web:* www.thecleaningauthority.com

Closet Factory 12800 S Broadway................Los Angeles CA 90061 310-516-7000 516-8065
TF: 800-838-7995 ■ *Web:* www.closetfactory.com

Coffee Beanery Ltd, The 3429 Pierson Pl............ Flushing MI 48433 800-441-2255 733-1536*
**Fax Area Code:* 810 ■ *TF:* 800-441-2255 ■ *Web:* www.coffeebeanery.com

Cold Stone Creamery Inc
9311 E Via De Ventura .... Scottsdale AZ 85258 480-362-4800 362-4812
TF Cust Svc: 866-452-4252 ■ *Web:* www.coldstonecreamery.com

Color Me Mine Enterprises Inc
3722 San Fernando Rd.............................. Glendale CA 91204 818-291-5900 312-5501*
**Fax Area Code:* 858 ■ *TF:* 888-265-6764 ■ *Web:* www.colormemine.com

Color-Glo International 7111 Ohms Ln........... Minneapolis MN 55439 952-835-1338 835-1395
TF: 800-333-8523 ■ *Web:* colorglo.com

ComForcare Senior Services Inc
2520 Telegraph Rd Ste 100....................Bloomfield Hills MI 48302 248-745-9700 745-9763
TF: 800-886-4044 ■ *Web:* www.comforcare.com

Computer Explorers 12715 Telge Rd ....Cypress TX 77429 800-531-5053 373-4450*
**Fax Area Code:* 281 ■ *TF:* 800-531-5053 ■ *Web:* www.computerexplorers.com

Computer Troubleshooters USA
755 Commerce Dr Ste 605........................... Decatur GA 30030 404-477-1302
TF: 877-704-1702 ■ *Web:* www.comptroub.com

Contours Express Inc 156 Imperial Way........... Nicholasville KY 40356 855-589-9662 241-2234*
**Fax Area Code:* 859 ■ *TF:* 855-589-9662 ■ *Web:* www.contoursexpress.com

Cookies By Design Inc 1865 Summit Ave Ste 605.........Plano TX 75074 972-398-9536 398-9542
TF: 800-945-2665 ■ *Web:* www.cookiesbydesign.com

Coverall Cleaning Concepts
5201 Congress Ave Ste 275 .... Boca Raton FL 33487 866-296-8944 922-2423*
**Fax Area Code:* 561 ■ *TF:* 800-537-3371 ■ *Web:* www.coverall.com

Phone Fax

Craters & Freighters 331 Corporate Cir Ste J .... Golden CO 80401 800-736-3335 399-9964*
Fax Area Code: 303 ■ *TF:* 800-736-3335 ■ *Web:* www.cratersandfreighters.com

Creative Colors International Inc
19015 S Jodi Rd Ste E .... Mokena IL 60448 708-478-1437 478-1636
TF: 800-933-2656 ■ *Web:* www.wecanfixthat.com

Crest Foods Inc 101 W Renner Rd Ste 240 .... Richardson TX 75082 214-495-9533 853-5347
Web: www.nestlecafe.com

Crestcom International Ltd
6900 E Belleview Ave .... Greenwood Village CO 80111 303-267-8200
Web: www.crestcomleadership.com

Critter Control Inc
9435 E Cherry Bend Rd .... Traverse City MI 49684 231-947-2400 947-9440
TF: 800-451-6544 ■ *Web:* www.crittercontrol.com

Crown Trophy 529 N State Rd .... Briarcliff NY 10510 914-941-0020 941-3039
Web: www.crowntrophy.com

CruiseOne Inc
1201 W Cypress Creek Rd Ste 100 .... Fort Lauderdale FL 33309 800-278-4731
TF: 800-278-4731 ■ *Web:* www.cruiseone.com

Culver Franchising System Inc
1240 Water St .... Prairie du Sac WI 53578 608-643-7980 643-7982
Web: www.culvers.com

D'Angelo Sandwich Shops 600 Providence Hwy .... Dedham MA 02026 781-461-1200 461-1896
TF: 800-727-2446 ■ *Web:* www.dangelos.com

Dairy Queen 7505 Metro Blvd .... Minneapolis MN 55439 952-830-0200 830-0227
TF: 800-883-4279 ■ *Web:* www.dairyqueen.com

Decor & You Inc 900 Main St S .... Southbury CT 06488 203-264-3500 264-5095
TF: 800-477-3326 ■ *Web:* www.decorandyou.com

Decorating Den Systems Inc 8659 Commerce Dr .... Easton MD 21601 410-822-9001
TF: 800-332-3367 ■ *Web:* www.decoratingden.com

Denny's Inc 203 E Main St .... Spartanburg SC 29319 864-597-8000 597-7708*
Fax: Mktg ■ *Web:* www.dennys.com

DirectBuy Inc 8450 Broadway .... Merrillville IN 46410 219-736-1100 755-6279
TF: 800-320-3462 ■ *Web:* www.directbuy.com

Domino's Pizza Inc
30 Frank Lloyd Wright Dr .... Ann Arbor MI 48106 734-930-3030 930-3580*
NYSE: DPZ ■ *Fax:* Mail Rm ■ *Web:* dominos.com

Dr Vinyl & Assoc Ltd 1350 SE Hamblen Rd .... Lees Summit MO 64081 816-525-6060
TF General: 800-531-6600 ■ *Web:* www.drvinyl.com

DreamMaker Bath & Kitchen by Worldwide
510 N Valley Mills Dr Ste 304 .... Waco TX 76710 800-583-2133
TF: 800-583-2133 ■ *Web:* www.dreammaker-remodel.com

Dunkin' Donuts 130 Royall St .... Canton MA 02021 781-737-3000 737-4000
TF Cust Svc: 800-859-5339 ■ *Web:* www.dunkindonuts.com

Duraclean International Inc
220 W Campus Dr .... Arlington Heights IL 60004 847-704-7100 704-7101
TF: 800-862-5326 ■ *Web:* www.duraclean.com

Edible Arrangements LLC 95 Barnes Rd .... Wallingford CT 06492 304-894-8901 774-0531*
Fax Area Code: 203 ■ *TF Cust Svc:* 877-363-7848 ■ *Web:* www.ediblearrangements.com

EmbroidMe Inc 2121 Vista Pkwy .... West Palm Beach FL 33411 561-640-7367 640-6062
TF: 877-877-0234 ■ *Web:* www.embroidme.com

Emerging Vision Inc 520 Eigth Ave 23rd Fl .... New York NY 10018 646-737-1500
Web: www.emergingvision.com

Express Employment Professionals
8516 NW Expy .... Oklahoma City OK 73162 405-840-5000 717-5665
TF: 800-222-4057 ■ *Web:* www.expresspros.com

Express Oil Change 1880 S Pk Dr .... Hoover AL 35244 205-945-1771 413-8732
TF: 888-945-1771 ■ *Web:* www.expressoil.com

Extreme Pita 2187 Dunwin Dr .... Mississauga ON L5L1X2 905-820-7887 820-8448
TF: 888-729-7482 ■ *Web:* www.extremepita.com

Famous Dave's of America Inc
12701 Whitewater Dr Ste 200 .... Minnetonka MN 55343 952-294-1300 822-9921*
NASDAQ: DAVE ■ *Fax Area Code:* 612 ■ *TF:* 800-929-4040 ■ *Web:* www.famousdaves.com

Fantastic Sams Inc 50 Dunham Rd 3rd Fl .... Beverly MA 01915 651-770-1449 232-5601*
Fax Area Code: 978 ■ *Web:* www.fantasticsams.com

Fast-Fix Jewelry & Watch Repairs
451 Altamonte Ave .... Altamonte Springs FL 32701 407-261-1595 261-1595
TF: 800-359-0407 ■ *Web:* www.fastfix.com

FasTracKids International Ltd
6900 E Belleview Ave Ste 100 .... Greenwood Village CO 80111 303-224-0200 224-0222
TF: 888-576-6888 ■ *Web:* fastrackids.com

Figaro's Italian Pizza Inc
1500 Liberty St SE Ste 160 .... Salem OR 97302 503-371-9318 363-5364
TF: 888-344-2767 ■ *Web:* www.figaros.com

Firehouse Restaurant Group Inc
3400 Kori Rd Ste 8 .... Jacksonville FL 32257 904-886-8300 886-2111
TF: 877-309-7332 ■ *Web:* www.firehousesubs.com

Fish Window Cleaning Services Inc
200 Enchanted Pkwy .... Manchester MO 63021 636-779-1500 530-7856
TF: 877-707-3474 ■ *Web:* www.fishwindowcleaning.com

Floor Coverings International
5250 Triangle Pwy Ste 100 .... Norcross GA 30092 770-874-7600
TF Sales: 800-955-4324 ■ *Web:* www.floorcoveringsinternational.com

Foot Solutions Inc
2359 Windy Hill Rd Ste 400 .... Marietta GA 30067 770-984-0844 298-1823*
Fax Area Code: 602 ■ *TF General:* 888-358-3668 ■ *Web:* footsolutions.com

Fox's Pizza Den Inc
4425 Willaim Penn Hwy .... Murrysville PA 15668 724-733-7888 325-5479
TF: 800-899-3697 ■ *Web:* www.foxspizza.com

Furniture Medic 3839 S Forest Hill Irene Rd .... Memphis TN 38125 800-877-9933
TF: 800-877-9933 ■ *Web:* www.furnituremedic.com

GNC Inc 300 Sixth Ave 14th Fl .... Pittsburgh PA 15222 877-462-4700
NYSE: GNC ■ *TF:* 877-462-4700 ■ *Web:* www.gnc.com

Goddard Systems Inc 1016 W Ninth Ave .... King of Prussia PA 19406 610-265-8510 265-8867
TF: 800-463-3273 ■ *Web:* www.goddardschool.com

Golden Chick 1131 Rockingham Dr .... Richardson TX 75080 972-831-0911 831-0401
Web: www.goldenchick.com

Golden Corral Corp 5151 Glenwood Ave .... Raleigh NC 27612 919-781-9310 881-4654
Web: goldencorral.com

Golden Krust Carribean Bakery & Grill
3958 Pk Ave .... Bronx NY 10457 718-655-7878 583-1883
Web: www.goldenkrustbakery.com

Phone Fax

Grease Monkey International
7450 E Progress Pl .... Greenwood Village CO 80111 303-308-1660 308-5908
TF: 800-822-7706 ■ *Web:* www.greasemonkeyintl.com

Great American Cookie Company Inc
1346 Oakbrook Dr Ste 170 .... Norcross GA 30093 877-639-2361
TF: 877-639-2361 ■ *Web:* www.greatamericancookies.com

Great Clips Inc 7700 France Ave S Ste 425 .... Minneapolis MN 55435 952-893-9088 844-3444
TF: 800-999-5959 ■ *Web:* www.greatclips.com

Great Harvest Bread Co 28 S Montana St .... Dillon MT 59725 406-683-6842 683-5537
TF: 800-442-0424 ■ *Web:* www.greatharvest.com

Great Steak & Potato Co
9311 E Via de Ventura .... Scottsdale AZ 85258 480-362-4800 362-4812
TF: 866-452-4252 ■ *Web:* www.thegreatsteak.com

Griswold Special Care Inc
717 Bethlehem Pike Ste 300 .... Erdenheim PA 19038 215-402-0200 277-3820*
Fax Area Code: 469 ■ *TF:* 855-303-9470 ■ *Web:* www.griswoldhomecare.com

Growth Coach, The
10700 Montgomery Rd Ste 300 .... Cincinnati OH 45242 888-292-7992 563-2691*
Fax Area Code: 513 ■ *TF:* 888-292-7992 ■ *Web:* www.thegrowthcoach.com

Gymboree Corp 500 Howard St .... San Francisco CA 94105 415-278-7000 278-7100
NASDAQ: GYMB ■ *TF:* 877-449-6932 ■ *Web:* www.gymboree.com

Gymboree Corp Play & Music Program
500 Howard St .... San Francisco CA 94105 415-278-7000 278-7100
TF Cust Svc: 877-449-6932 ■ *Web:* www.gymboree.com

Handyman Matters Inc
12567 W Cedar Dr Ste 250 .... Lakewood CO 80228 303-984-0177 984-0133
TF: 866-349-6946 ■ *Web:* www.handymanmatters.com

Happy & Healthy Products Inc
1600 S Dixie Hwy Ste 200 .... Boca Raton FL 33432 561-367-0739 368-5267
Web: www.fruitfull.com

Hayes Handpiece Franchises Inc
5375 Avenida Encinas Ste C .... Carlsbad CA 92008 760-602-0521 602-0505
TF: 800-228-0521 ■ *Web:* www.hayeshandpiece.com

Hobbytown USA 1233 Libra Dr .... Lincoln NE 68512 402-434-5050
Web: www.hobbytown.com

Hollywood Tans 588 N Main St .... Manahawkin NJ 08050 609-698-6400
Web: www.hollywoodtans.com

Homes & Land Magazine Affiliates LLC
1830 E Pk Ave .... Tallahassee FL 32301 850-575-0189 574-2525
TF: 800-277-7800 ■ *Web:* www.homesandland.com

HomeTeam Inspection Service Inc
575 Chamber Dr .... Milford OH 45150 800-598-5297 831-6010*
Fax Area Code: 513 ■ *TF:* 800-598-5297 ■ *Web:* www.hometeaminspection.com

HomeVestors of America Inc
6500 Greenville Ave Ste 400 .... Dallas TX 75206 972-761-0046 761-9022
TF: 800-442-8937 ■ *Web:* www.homevestors.com

HouseMaster 850 Bear Tavern RD Ste 303 .... Ewing NJ 08628 732-469-6565 469-7405
TF: 800-526-3939 ■ *Web:* www.housemaster.com

Hungry Howie's Pizza & Subs Inc
30300 Stephenson Hwy Ste 200 .... Madison Heights MI 48071 248-414-3300 414-3301
Web: www.hungryhowies.com

Ident-A-Kid Services of America
1780 102nd Ave N Ste 100 .... Saint Petersburg FL 33716 727-577-4646 576-8258
TF: 800-890-1000 ■ *Web:* www.identakid.com

IHOP Corp 450 N Brand Blvd .... Glendale CA 91203 818-240-6055 637-4730
TF: 800-901-5248 ■ *Web:* www.ihop.com

Inspiring Wellness LLC
665 S Orange Ave Ste 7 .... Sarasota FL 34236 941-953-5000
Web: www.babybootcamp.com

Instant Imprints 5897 Oberlin Dr Ste 200 .... San Diego CA 92121 858-642-4848 453-6513
TF: 800-542-3437 ■ *Web:* www.instantimprints.com

Interim HealthCare Inc
1601 Sawgrass Corporate Pkwy .... Sunrise FL 33323 954-858-6000 858-2720
TF: 800-338-7786 ■ *Web:* www.interimhealthcare.com

iSold It 1106 E Colorado Ave .... Pasadena CA 91106 626-584-0844
Web: www.i-soldit.com

Jackson Hewitt Inc
Three Sylvan Way Ste 301 .... Parsippany NJ 07054 800-234-1040
OTC: JHTXQ ■ *TF:* 800-234-1040 ■ *Web:* www.jacksonhewitt.com

Jazzercise Inc 2460 Impala Dr .... Carlsbad CA 92010 760-476-1750 602-7180
TF Cust Svc: 800-348-4748 ■ *Web:* www.jazzercise.com

Jenny Craig International Inc 5770 Fleet St .... Carlsbad CA 92008 760-696-4000 696-4506
TF: 800-443-2331 ■ *Web:* www.jennycraig.com

Jet's America Inc 37501 Mound Rd .... Sterling Heights MI 48310 586-268-5870 268-6762
Web: www.jetspizza.com

Juice It Up! Franchise Corp
17915 Sky Pk Cir Ste J .... Irvine CA 92614 949-475-0146 475-0137
Web: www.juiceitup.com

Keller Williams Realty Inc
807 Las Cimas Pkwy Ste 200 .... Austin TX 78746 512-327-3070 328-1433
Web: www.kw.com

KFC Corp 1441 Gardiner Ln .... Louisville KY 40213 818-780-6990
TF: 800-225-5532 ■ *Web:* www.kfc.com

Kid to Kid 1244 Township Line Rd .... Drexel Hill PA 19026 610-446-2544
Web: www.kidtokid.com

Kinderdance International Inc
1333 Gateway Dr Ste 1033 .... Melbourne FL 32901 321-984-4448 984-4490
TF: 800-554-2334 ■ *Web:* www.kinderdance.com

Kitchen Tune-Up Inc 813 Cir Dr .... Aberdeen SD 57401 605-225-4049
TF: 800-333-6385 ■ *Web:* www.kitchentuneup.com

Lady of America Franchise Corp
159 Weston RD Ste 1650 .... Weston FL 33326 954-217-8660
TF: 800-833-5239 ■ *Web:* www.ladyofamerica.com

Lawn Doctor Inc 142 SR 34 .... Holmdel NJ 07733 800-631-5660
TF: 800-631-5660 ■ *Web:* www.lawndoctor.com

Learning Express Inc 29 Buena Vista St .... Devens MA 01434 978-889-1000 889-1010
TF: 800-924-2296 ■ *Web:* www.learningexpress.com

Liberty Tax Service Inc
1716 Corporate Landing Pkwy .... Virginia Beach VA 23454 757-493-8855 493-0169
TF Cust Svc: 800-790-3863 ■ *Web:* www.libertytax.com

Lil' Angels Photography
6831 Crumpler Blvd Ste 101 .... Olive Branch MS 38654 662-890-9103 890-9104
Web: lilangels.photogra.com

				Phone	Fax

Little Caesars Inc 2211 Woodward Ave. Detroit MI 48201 313-983-6409
TF: 800-722-3727 ■ *Web:* www.littlecaesars.com

Little Gym International Inc
7001 N Scottsdale Rd Paradise Valley AZ 85253 888-228-2878
TF General: 888-228-2878 ■ *Web:* www.thelittlegym.com

Living Assistance Services Inc
937 Haverford Rd Ste 200 Bryn Mawr PA 19010 610-924-0630 924-9690
TF: 800-365-4189 ■ *Web:* www.livingassistance.com

Long John Silver's Restaurants Inc
9505 Williamsburg Plaza Louisville KY 40222 502-815-6100
Web: www.ljsilvers.com

Mad Science Group
8360 Bougainville St Ste 201 Montreal QC H4P2G1 514-344-4181 344-6695
TF: 800-586-5231 ■ *Web:* www.madscience.org

MaggieMoo's International LLC
1346 Oakbrook Dr Ste 170 Norcross GA 30093 877-639-2361 514-4903*
**Fax Area Code:* 770 ■ *TF:* 877-639-2361 ■ *Web:* www.maggiemoos.com

Magnetsigns Adv Inc 4225 38th St Camrose AB T4V3Z3 780-672-8720 672-8716
TF: 800-219-8977 ■ *Web:* www.magnetsigns.com

Maid Brigade USA/Minimaid Canada
Four Concourse Pkwy Ste 200 Atlanta GA 30328 770-551-9630 391-9092
TF: 800-722-6243 ■ *Web:* www.maidbrigade.com

MaidPro Corp 180 Canal St Boston MA 02114 617-742-8787 720-0700
TF: 888-624-3776 ■ *Web:* www.maidpro.com

Mail Boxes Etc 6060 Cornerstone Ct W San Diego CA 92121 858-455-8800 546-7493
TF: 800-789-4623 ■ *Web:* www.mbe.com

Manhattan Bagel Co Inc 555 Zang St Ste 300 Lakewood CO 80228 303-568-8000
TF: 800-224-3563 ■ *Web:* www.manhattanbagel.com

Martinizing Dry Cleaning
8944 Columbia Rd Ste J Loveland OH 45140 800-827-0207 731-0818*
**Fax Area Code:* 513 ■ *TF:* 800-827-0207 ■ *Web:* www.martinizing.com

Mathnasium LLC
5120 W Goldleaf Cir Ste 300 Los Angeles CA 90056 323-421-8000 943-2111*
**Fax Area Code:* 310 ■ *TF:* 877-601-6284 ■ *Web:* www.mathnasium.com

Maui Wowi Inc 1509 York St Ste 300 Denver CO 80206 303-781-7800 781-2438
Web: www.mauiwowi.com

McDonald's Corp One McDonald's Plz Oak Brook IL 60523 630-623-3000 623-5500
NYSE: MCD ■ *TF:* 800-244-6227 ■ *Web:* www.mcdonalds.com

Medicap Pharmacies Inc
1 Rider Trail Plaza Dr Earth City MO 63045 314-993-6000
TF: 800-407-8055 ■ *Web:* www.medicap.com

Merle Norman Cosmetics Inc
9130 Bellanca Ave Los Angeles CA 90045 310-641-3000 641-7144
TF: 800-421-6648 ■ *Web:* www.merlenorman.com

Merlin Corp 3815 E Main St Ste D Saint Charles IL 60174 630-513-8200 513-1388
TF: 800-652-9910 ■ *Web:* www.merlins.com

Midas International Corp
1300 Arlington Heights Rd Itasca IL 60143 630-438-3000 438-3700
TF: 800-621-8545 ■ *Web:* www.midas.com

Minuteman Press International Inc
61 Executive Blvd Farmingdale NY 11735 631-249-1370 249-5618
TF: 800-645-3006 ■ *Web:* www.minutemanpress.com

Money Mailer LLC 12131 Western Ave Garden Grove CA 92841 714-889-3800 265-7624*
**Fax Area Code:* 847 ■ *TF:* 800-468-5865 ■ *Web:* www.moneymailer.com

Mr Appliance Corp 1020 N University Parks Dr Waco TX 76707 256-415-5069 537-0745*
**Fax Area Code:* 254 ■ *TF:* 888-998-2011 ■ *Web:* www.mrappliance.com

Mr Handyman International LLC
3796 Plz Dr Ste 1C Ann Arbor MI 48108 800-289-4600 822-6888*
**Fax Area Code:* 734 ■ *TF Cust Svc:* 800-289-4600 ■ *Web:* www.mrhandyman.com

Mr Hero Restaurants
7010 Engle Rd Ste 100 Middleburg Heights OH 44130 440-625-3080 625-3081
TF: 888-860-5082 ■ *Web:* www.mrhero.com

My Favorite Muffin 500 Lk Cook Rd Ste 475 Deerfield IL 60015 847-948-7520 405-8140
TF: 800-251-6101 ■ *Web:* www.babcorp.com

Nathan's Famous Inc One Jericho Plz Second Fl Jericho NY 11753 516-338-8500 338-7220
NASDAQ: NATH ■ *TF:* 800-628-4267 ■ *Web:* www.nathansfamous.com

National Property Inspections Inc (NPI)
9375 Burt St Ste 201 Omaha NE 68114 402-333-9807 933-2508*
**Fax Area Code:* 800 ■ *TF:* 800-333-9807

Navis Pack & Ship Centers
6551 S Revere Pkwy Ste 250 Centennial CO 80111 800-344-3528 741-6653*
**Fax Area Code:* 303 ■ *TF:* 800-344-3528 ■ *Web:* www.gonavis.com

NOVUS Auto Glass 12800 Hwy 13 S Ste 500 Savage MN 55378 952-736-7843
TF: 800-776-6887 ■ *Web:* www.novusglass.com

Nutrilawn Inc 25-1040 Martin Grove Rd Toronto ON M9W4W4 416-620-7100 620-7771
Web: www.nutrilawn.com

OctoClean Franchising Systems
3357 Chicago Ave Riverside CA 92507 951-683-5859 779-0270
Web: www.octoclean.com

OpenWorks 4742 N 24th St Ste 450 Phoenix AZ 85016 602-224-0440 468-3788
TF: 800-777-6736 ■ *Web:* www.openworksweb.com

Orange Julius of America 7505 Metro Blvd Minneapolis MN 55439 952-830-0200 *
**Fax:* Mktg ■ *TF:* 866-793-7582 ■ *Web:* www.dairyqueen.com

Outdoor Connection Inc 424 Neosho Burlington KS 66839 620-364-5500 364-5563
Web: www.outdoor-connection.com

Padgett Business Services 160 Hawthorne Pk Athens GA 30606 800-723-4388 543-8537*
**Fax Area Code:* 706 ■ *TF:* 800-723-4388 ■ *Web:* www.padgettbusinessservices.com

Pak Mail Centers of America Inc
7173 S Havana St Ste 600 Centennial CO 80112 303-957-1000 957-1015
TF Cust Svc: 800-778-6665 ■ *Web:* www.pakmail.com

Palm Beach Tan Inc
633 E State Hwy 121 Ste 500 Coppell TX 75019 972-966-5300 406-2508
Web: www.palmbeachtan.com

Papa Murphy's International Inc
8000 NE Pkwy Dr Ste 350 Vancouver WA 98662 360-260-7272 260-0500
TF: 800-778-7879 ■ *Web:* www.papamurphys.com

Party City Corp 25 Green Pond Rd Ste 1 Rockaway NJ 07866 973-453-8600
TF: 800-727-8924 ■ *Web:* www.partycity.com

Pearle Vision Inc 4000 Luxottica Pl Mason OH 45040 513-765-4321 765-6388
Web: www.pearlevision.com

Perkins Restaurant & Bakery
6075 Poplar Ave Ste 800 Memphis TN 38119 901-766-6400 766-6482
TF: 800-877-7375 ■ *Web:* www.perkinsrestaurants.com

				Phone	Fax

Perma-Glaze Inc 1638 Research Loop Rd Ste 160 Tucson AZ 85710 520-722-9718 296-4393
TF: 800-332-7397 ■ *Web:* www.permaglaze.com

Pet Supplies "Plus" Inc
17197 N Laurel Prk Dre Ste 402 Livonia MI 48152 734-793-6600 374-7900*
**Fax Area Code:* 248 ■ *Web:* www.petsuppliesplus.com

Petland Inc 250 Riverside St Chillicothe OH 45601 740-775-2464 775-2575
TF: 800-221-5935 ■ *Web:* petland.com

Physicians Weight Loss Centers of America Inc
395 Springside Dr Akron OH 44333 330-666-7952 666-2197
TF: 800-205-7887 ■ *Web:* www.pwlc.com

PIP Printing & Document Services Inc
26722 Plaza Dr Ste 200 Mission Viejo CA 92691 949-348-5000 348-5066
Web: www.pip.com

Pizza Inn Inc 3551 Plano Pkwy The Colony TX 75056 469-384-5000 384-5058
NASDAQ: RAVE ■ *TF:* 800-880-9955 ■ *Web:* www.pizzainn.com

Pizza Ranch Inc 204 19th St SE Orange City IA 51041 800-321-3401
TF: 800-321-3401 ■ *Web:* www.pizzaranch.com

Plato's Closet 23021 Outer Dr Allen Park MI 48101 313-278-2300
TF: 800-592-8049 ■ *Web:* www.platoscloset.com

Postal Connections of America
6136 Frisco Sq Blvd Ste 400 Frisco TX 75034 800-767-8257 294-4550*
**Fax Area Code:* 619 ■ *TF:* 800-767-8257 ■ *Web:* www.postalconnections.com

PostalAnnex+ Inc
7580 Metropolitan Dr Ste 200 San Diego CA 92108 619-563-4800 563-9850
TF: 800-456-1525 ■ *Web:* www.postalannex.com

PostNet International Franchise Corp
1819 Wazee St Denver CO 80202 303-771-7100 771-7133
TF: 800-841-7171 ■ *Web:* www.postnet.com

Powerhouse Gym International
355 S Old Woodward Ste 150 Birmingham MI 48009 248-476-2888 530-9816*
**Fax Area Code:* 249 ■ *Web:* www.powerhousegym.com

Precision Auto Care Inc 748 Miller Dr SE Leesburg VA 20175 703-777-9095 771-7108
OTC: PACI ■ *TF:* 800-438-8863 ■ *Web:* www.precisiontune.com

PremierGarage Systems LLC 21405 N 15th Ln Phoenix AZ 85027 480-483-3030 340-2665*
**Fax Area Code:* 778 ■ *TF:* 866-590-9411 ■ *Web:* www.premiergarage.com

Pressed4Time Inc Eight Clock Tower Pl Ste 110 Maynard MA 01754 800-423-8711 823-8301*
**Fax Area Code:* 978 ■ *TF:* 800-423-8711 ■ *Web:* www.pressed4time.com

Primrose School Franchising Co
3660 Cedarcrest Rd Acworth GA 30101 770-529-4100 529-1551
TF: 800-745-0677 ■ *Web:* www.primroseschools.com

Priority Management Systems Inc
11160 Silversmith Pl Richmond BC V7A5E4 604-214-7772 214-7773
Web: www.prioritymanagement.com

Pro Image Sports 233 N 1250 W Ste 200 Centerville UT 84014 801-296-9999 296-1319
Web: www.proimagesports.com

ProForma 8800 E Pleasant Vly Rd Independence OH 44131 216-520-8400 520-8444
TF: 800-825-1525 ■ *Web:* www.proforma.com

Property Damage Appraisers Inc (PDA)
6100 SW Blvd Ste 200 Fort Worth TX 76109 800-749-7324 866-4732
TF: 800-749-7324 ■ *Web:* www.pdacorporation.com

Qdoba Restaurant Corp
4865 WaRd Rd Ste 500 Wheat Ridge CO 80033 720-898-2300 898-2396
Web: www.qdoba.com

RadioShack Corp 300 RadioShack Cir Fort Worth TX 76102 800-442-7221 415-2303*
NYSE: RSH ■ **Fax Area Code:* 817 ■ *TF:* 800-843-7422 ■ *Web:* www.radioshack.com

Rainbow International 1010 N University Pk Dr Waco TX 76707 254-756-5463 745-2592
TF: 855-724-6269 ■ *Web:* www.rainbowintl.com

Re-Bath LLC 16879 N 75th Ave Ste 101 Peoria AZ 85382 800-426-4573
TF: 800-426-4573 ■ *Web:* rebath.com

RE/MAX International Inc 5075 S Syracuse St Denver CO 80237 303-770-5531 796-3599
TF Cust Svc: 800-525-7452 ■ *Web:* www.remax.com

Real Living Inc 77 E Nationwide Blvd Columbus OH 43215 614-459-7400 457-6807
TF: 800-848-7400 ■ *Web:* www.realliving.com

Realty Executives International Inc
7600 N 16th St Ste 100 Phoenix AZ 85020 602-957-0747 224-5542
TF: 800-252-3366 ■ *Web:* www.realtyexecutives.com

Red Robin Gourmet Burgers Inc
6312 S Fiddlers Green Cir
Ste 200-N Greenwood Village CO 80111 303-846-6000 846-6013
NASDAQ: RRGB ■ *TF:* 877-733-6543 ■ *Web:* www.redrobin.com

Rescuecom Corp 2560 Burnet Ave Syracuse NY 13206 800-737-2837 433-5228*
**Fax Area Code:* 315 ■ *TF:* 800-737-2837 ■ *Web:* www.rescuecom.com

Results Travel 701 Carlson Pkwy Minnetonka MN 55305 763-212-5000
TF: 800-456-4000 ■ *Web:* www.carlson.com

Right at Home Inc 6464 Crt St Ste 150 Omaha NE 68106 402-697-7537 697-0289
TF: 877-697-7537 ■ *Web:* www.rightathome.net

Rita's Water Ice Franchise Co LLC
1401 Bridgetown Pike Feasterville PA 19053 215-322-8774
Web: www.ritasice.com

RSVP Publications 6730 W Linebaugh Ave Ste 201 Tampa FL 33625 813-960-7787 549-3306
TF: 800-360-7787 ■ *Web:* www.rsvppublications.com

Ruby Tuesday Inc 150 W Church Ave Maryville TN 37801 865-379-5700 380-7639*
NYSE: RT ■ **Fax:* Mktg ■ *TF:* 800-325-0755 ■ *Web:* www.rubytuesday.com

Sandler Sales Institute 10411 Stevenson Rd Stevenson MD 21153 410-653-1993 358-7858
TF: 800-669-3537 ■ *Web:* www.sandler.com

Screenmobile 72-050A Corporate Way Thousand Palms CA 92276 760-343-3500 343-7543
Web: www.screenmobile.com

Sea Tow Services International Inc
1560 Youngs Ave PO Box 1178 Southold NY 11971 631-765-3660
TF: 800-473-2869 ■ *Web:* www.seatow.com

Second Cup Ltd 6303 Airport Rd Mississauga ON L4V1R8 877-212-1818
TF: 877-212-1818 ■ *Web:* www.secondcup.com

Shefield Group 2265 W Railway St Abbotsford BC V2S2E3 604-859-1014 859-1711
Web: www.shefield.com

Signs by Tomorrow USA Inc
8681 Robert Fulton Dr Columbia MD 21046 410-312-3600 312-3520
TF: 800-765-7446 ■ *Web:* www.signsbytomorrow.com

Sir Speedy Inc 26722 Plaza Dr Mission Viejo CA 92691 949-348-5000 348-5066
TF: 800-854-8297 ■ *Web:* www.sirspeedy.com

Snap-on Inc 2801 80th St Kenosha WI 53143 262-656-5200 656-5577
NYSE: SNA ■ *TF:* 877-762-7664 ■ *Web:* www.snapon.com

Phone Fax

Sonny's Franchise Co
2605 Maitland Ctr Pkwy Ste C Maitland FL 32751 407-660-8888 660-9050
Web: www.sonnysbbq.com

Sport Clips Inc 110 Briarwood Dr. Georgetown TX 78628 512-869-1201
TF: 800-872-4247 ■ *Web:* www.sportclips.com

Spring-Green Lawn Care Corp
11909 Spaulding School Dr Plainfield IL 60585 815-436-8777 436-9056
TF: 800-435-4051 ■ *Web:* www.spring-green.com

Stork News of America Inc
1305 Hope Mills Rd Ste A Fayetteville NC 28304 910-429-2229 426-2473
TF: 800-633-6395 ■ *Web:* www.storknews.com

Stretch-N-Grow International Inc
PO Box 7599 Seminole FL 33775 800-348-0166
TF: 800-348-0166 ■ *Web:* www.stretch-n-grow.com

Successories Inc 1040 Holland Dr. Boca Raton FL 33487 800-535-2773 952-4097*
**Fax Area Code:* 561 ■ *TF:* 800-535-2773 ■ *Web:* www.successories.com

Super Wash Inc 707 W Lincolnway PO Box 188 Morrison IL 61270 815-772-2111 772-7160
Web: www.superwash.com

SuperCoups 350 Revolutionary Dr East Taunton MA 02718 508-977-2000 977-0644
TF: 800-626-2620 ■ *Web:* www.supercoups.com

Supercuts 7201 Metro Blvd Minneapolis MN 55439 877-857-2070 947-7300*
**Fax Area Code:* 952 ■ *TF:* 877-857-2070 ■ *Web:* www.supercuts.com

SuperShuttle International Inc
14500 N Northsight Blvd Ste 329 Scottsdale AZ 85260 480-609-3000 607-9317
Web: www.supershuttle.com

Terminix International Company LP
860 Ridge Lk Blvd Memphis TN 38120 866-399-0453 363-8541*
**Fax Area Code:* 901 ■ **Fax:* Mktg ■ *TF:* 866-399-0453 ■ *Web:* www.terminix.com

Treats International Franchise Corp
1550-A Laperriere Ave Ste 201 Ottawa ON K1Z7T2 613-563-4073 563-1982
TF: 800-461-4003 ■ *Web:* www.treats.com

Truly Nolen of America Inc
3636 E Speedway Blvd Tucson AZ 85716 800-528-3442 322-4002*
**Fax Area Code:* 520 ■ *TF:* 800-468-7859 ■ *Web:* www.trulynolen.com

Tuffy Assoc Corp 7150 Granite Cir. Toledo OH 43617 419-865-6900 865-7343
TF: 800-228-8339 ■ *Web:* www.tuffy.com

United Financial Services Group
325 Chestnut St Ste 3000 Philadelphia PA 19106 215-238-0300 238-9056
Web: www.unitedfsg.com

United Shipping Solutions
6985 Union Pk Ctr Ste 565 Midvale UT 84047 801-352-0012 352-0339
Web: www.usshipit.com

UPS Store, The 6060 Cornerstone Ct W San Diego CA 92121 858-455-8800 546-7492
TF: 800-789-4623 ■ *Web:* www.theupsstore.com

Valpak Direct Marketing Systems Inc
8605 Largo Lakes Dr Largo FL 33773 800-237-6266
TF: 800-237-6266 ■ *Web:* www.valpak.com

Weed Man 2399 Royal Windsor Dr Mississauga ON L5J1K9 905-823-8300
Web: www.weedmancanada.com

Wetzel's Pretzels LLC 35 Hugus Alley Ste 300 Pasadena CA 91103 626-432-6900 432-6904
Web: www.wetzels.com

Wild Birds Unlimited Inc
11711 N College Ave Ste 146 Carmel IN 46032 317-571-7100 571-7110
TF: 800-326-4928 ■ *Web:* www.wbu.com

WineStyles Inc
5515 Mills Civic Pkwy Ste 110 West Des Moines IA 50266 866-424-9463 984-0074*
**Fax Area Code:* 954 ■ *TF:* 866-424-9463 ■ *Web:* www.winestyles.com

Wing Zone Franchise Corp
900 Cir 75 Pkwy Ste 930 Atlanta GA 30339 404-875-5045 875-6631
TF: 877-946-4966 ■ *Web:* wingzonefranchise.com

Wingstop Restaurants Inc
1101 E Arapaho Rd Ste 150 Richardson TX 75081 972-686-6500 686-6502
Web: www.wingstop.com

Wireless Toyz Ltd 29155 NW Hwy. Southfield MI 48034 248-426-8200
TF: 866-237-2624 ■ *Web:* www.wirelesstoyz.com

Wireless Zone 34 Industrial Pk Pl Middletown CT 06457 860-632-9494 652-0520*
**Fax Area Code:* 989 ■ *TF:* 888-881-2622 ■ *Web:* www.wirelesszone.com

Woodcraft Supply LLC
1177 Rosemar Rd PO Box 1686 Parkersburg WV 26105 800-535-4482 428-8271*
**Fax Area Code:* 304 ■ *TF:* 800-535-4482 ■ *Web:* www.woodcraft.com

World Inspection Network International Inc
12345 Lk City Way NE Ste 365 Seattle WA 98125 800-309-6753
TF: 800-309-6753 ■ *Web:* www.wini.com

Worldwide Express 2828 Routh St Ste 400 Dallas TX 75201 214-720-2400 720-2446
TF: 800-758-7447 ■ *Web:* www.wwex.com

WSI Internet 5580 Explorer Dr Ste 600 Mississauga ON L4W4Y1 905-678-7588 678-7242
TF: 888-678-7588 ■ *Web:* www.wsicorporate.com

Yogen Fruz 210 Shields Ct Markham ON L3R8V2 905-479-8762 479-5235
Web: www.yogenfruz.com

Young Rembrandts 23 N Union St. Elgin IL 60123 847-742-6966 742-7197
Web: www.youngrembrandts.com

Ziebart International Corp 1290 E Maple Rd Troy MI 48083 248-588-4100 588-0431*
**Fax:* Orders ■ *TF:* 800-877-1312 ■ *Web:* www.ziebart.com

314 FREIGHT FORWARDERS

SEE ALSO Logistics Services (Transportation & Warehousing) p. 2673

Phone Fax

A & S Services Group LLC 310 N Zarfoss Dr. York PA 17404 717-759-3017 235-2456
TF: 800-227-6782 ■ *Web:* askinard.com

A Pm Systems Inc 1440 21st St Ste 101 Rockford IL 61108 815-229-1440
Web: apmsystems.com

Advance Transportation Systems Inc
1125 Glendale Milford Rd. Cincinnati OH 45215 513-771-4848
Web: www.atslogistics.com

Aeropost International Services Inc
6703 NW Seventh St Ste 4567 Miami FL 33126 305-592-5534
Web: www.aeropost.com

Air Courier Dispatch 12333 S Van Ness Ave. Hawthorne CA 90250 310-419-1230
Web: www.aics.com

Phone Fax

Airways Freight Corp
3849 W Wedington Dr Fayetteville AR 72704 479-442-6301 442-6522
TF: 800-643-3525 ■ *Web:* www.airwaysfreight.com

AIT Worldwide Logistics 701 N Rohlwing Rd. Itasca IL 60143 630-766-8300
Web: aitworldwide.com

Alaska Tanker Company LLC
15400 NW Greenbrier Pkwy Parkside Bldg
Ste A400 Beaverton OR 97006 503-207-0046
Web: www.aktanker.com

Alba Wheels Up International Inc
525 Washington Blvd Jersey City NJ 07310 201-435-7050 435-5650
TF: 888-720-9917 ■ *Web:* www.albawheelsup.com

Alliance International Forwarders Inc
7155 Old Katy Rd Houston TX 77024 713-428-3100

Alliance Shippers Inc
516 Sylvan Ave Englewood Cliffs NJ 07632 201-227-0400
Web: alliance.com

Aloha Freight Forwarders Inc
1800 S Anderson Ave Compton CA 90220 310-631-6116
Web: www.alohafreight.com

Apex Maritime Ord 1900 E Golf Rd Schaumburg IL 60173 630-227-9818
Web: apexshipping.com

Arrow Freight Management Inc PO Box 371974 El Paso TX 79937 915-778-3999 590-1953
TF: 888-598-9891 ■ *Web:* www.arrowelp.com

Autobahn Freight Lines Ltd 27 Automatic Rd Brampton ON L6S5N8 416-741-5454
Web: www.autobahnfreight.com

Axsun Inc 4900 Armand Frappier St Hubert QC J3Z1G5 450-445-3003
Web: www.axsungroup.com

Barthco International Inc
5101 S Broad St Philadelphia PA 19112 215-238-8600 592-1254
TF General: 877-401-6400 ■ *Web:* www.ohl.com

Bassler Energy Services Inc 8050 Hwy 21 W Caldwell TX 77836 979-535-4593
Web: www.basslerenergyservices.com

Big Daddy Drayage Inc 575 Ave P Newark NJ 07105 973-522-1717
Web: www.bigdaddydrayage.com

Big Freight Systems Inc 360 Hwy 12 N Steinbach MB R5G1A6 204-326-3434
Web: www.bigfreight.com

Blue-Grace Logistics LLC
2846 S Falkenburg Rd Riverview FL 33578 813-641-0357
TF: 800-697-4477 ■ *Web:* www.mybluegrace.com

BNX Shipping Inc 910 E 236th St Carson CA 90745 310-764-0999
Web: www.bnxinc.com

Bolanos & Company Inc 8708 Killam Indus Blvd Laredo TX 78045 956-722-0976
Web: www.bolanos.com

Bongo International LLC
10040 18th St Ste 1 St Petersburg FL 33716 203-683-4894
Web: www.bongous.com

Bulk Connection Inc 15 Allen St Mystic CT 06355 860-572-9111
Web: www.bulkconnection.com

Buscemi Co, International LLC
317 Isis Ave Ste 201 Inglewood CA 90301 310-568-1011
Web: buscemico.com

C W s Inc 411 Blaine St Gary IN 46406 219-944-5315
Web: www.cws-boco.com

Capital Transportation Solutions LLC
1915 Vaughn Rd Kennesaw GA 30144 770-690-8684
Web: shipwithcts.com

Carbon Resources of Florida Inc
11023 Gatewood Dr Ste 103 Bradenton FL 34211 941-747-2630
Web: www.carbonresourcesofflorida.com

Casas International Brokerage Inc
9355 Airway Rd Ste 4 San Diego CA 92154 619-661-6162 661-6800
Web: www.casasinternational.com

CBSL Transportation Services Inc
4750 S Merrimac Ave Chicago IL 60638 708-496-1100
Web: www.cbsltrans.com

CDA 8500 S Tryon St Charlotte NC 28273 704-504-1877
Web: www.oemdisc.com

CDS Logistics Management Inc
1225 Bengies Rd Ste A Baltimore MD 21220 410-314-8000
TF: 866-649-9559 ■ *Web:* www.cdslogistics.net

Certified Freight Logistics Inc
1344 White Ct Santa Maria CA 93458 805-925-9900
Web: www.cflrecruiting.com

CEVA Ground US LP 15390 Vickery Dr Ste B Houston TX 77032 281-227-5000
Web: www.selectscg.com

Ceva Logistics US Holdings Inc
10751 Deerwood Park Blvd 201 Jacksonville FL 32256 904-928-1400 928-1550
Web: cevalogistics.com

CH Powell Co 75 Shawmut Rd Canton MA 02021 781-302-7300
Web: chpowell.com

Cold Star Freight Systems Inc
1015 Henry Eng Pl Victoria BC V9B6B2 250-381-3399
Web: www.coldstarfreight.com

Coldiron Companies Inc 200 N Sooner Rd Edmond OK 73034 405-562-2910
Web: www.coldironcompanies.com

Combined Express Inc 3685 Marshall Ln. Bensalem PA 19020 215-633-1535
Web: www.combinedexpress.com

Concordia International Forwarding Inc
70 E Sunrise Hwy Ste 605 Valley Stream NY 11581 516-561-1100 561-1323
Web: www.concordiafreight.com

ContainerWorld Forwarding Services Inc
16133 Blundell Rd Richmond BC V6W0A3 604-276-1300
TF: 877-838-8880 ■ *Web:* www.containerworld.com

Continental Traffic Service Inc (CTSI)
5100 Poplar Ave 15th Fl Memphis TN 38137 901-766-1500 766-1520
TF: 888-836-5135 ■ *Web:* www.ctsi-global.com

Corporate Traffic Inc
2002 Southside Blvd Jacksonville FL 32216 904-727-0051 727-6804
Web: www.corporate-traffic.com

D & B Logistics 720 Washington St Hanover MA 02339 781-829-4500
Web: www.dblinc.net

				Phone	Fax
D J Powers Company Inc 5000 Business Ctr Dr Ste 1000 *Web:* www.djpowers.com	Savannah	GA	31405	912-234-7241	
Daybreak Express Inc 500 Ave P *Web:* www.dbke.com	Newark	NJ	07105	973-589-5931	
DHL Global Forwarding (Canada) Inc 6200 Edwards Blvd **Fax Area Code:* 905 ■ *Web:* international.dhl.ca	Mississauga	ON	L5T2V7	289-405-9300	405-9301*
Dimerco Express (USA) Corp 955 Dillon Dr *Web:* dimerco.com	Wood Dale	IL	60191	630-595-7310	
DJS International Services Inc 4215 Gateway Dr Ste 100 *Web:* www.djsintl.com	Colleyville	TX	76034	972-929-8433	
Dupre' Transport LLC 201 Energy Pkwy *Web:* www.duprelogistics.com	Lafayette	LA	70508	337-237-8471	
Evans Delivery Company Inc PO Box 268 *TF:* 800-666-7885 ■ *Web:* www.evansdelivery.com	Pottsville	PA	17901	570-385-9048	385-9058
Excel Transportation Inc 333 Ongman Rd *Web:* exceltransportation.ca	Prince George	BC	V2K4K9	250-563-7356	
Faye Stewart Transportation Service LLC 3056 N 33rd Ave *Web:* www.fayestewarttrans.com	Phoenix	AZ	85017	602-233-3500	
FESCO Agencies NA Inc 1000 Second Ave Ste 1310 *TF:* 800-275-3372 ■ *Web:* www.fesco-na.com	Seattle	WA	98104	206-583-0860	583-0889
Fetch Logistics Inc 25 Northpointe Pkwy Ste 200 *TF:* 800-964-4940 ■ *Web:* www.fetchlogistics.com	Amherst	NY	14228	716-689-4556	689-9676
First Coast Logistics Services Inc 11460 Boote Blvd Ste 1 *Web:* www.firstcoast.net	Jacksonville	FL	32218	904-757-6008	
Fleetgistics Holdings Inc 2251 Lynx Ln Ste 7 *Web:* www.fleetgistics.com	Orlando	FL	32804	407-843-6505	
Foreign Trade Export Packing Co 1350 Lathrop St *Web:* www.ftep.com	Houston	TX	77020	713-672-8211	
FPA Customs Brokers Inc 152-31 134th Ave *Web:* www.fpajfk.com	Jamaica	NY	11434	718-527-2280	
Freight Logistics Inc PO Box 1712 *TF:* 800-866-7882 ■ *Web:* www.shipfli.com	Medford	OR	97501	541-734-5617	
Frontier Logistics LP 1806 S 16th St **Fax Area Code:* 281 ■ *TF:* 800-610-6808 ■ *Web:* www.frontierlogistics.com	La Porte	TX	77571	800-610-6808	307-2399*
FTS International Express Inc 400 Country Club Dr *Web:* www.fts.com	Bensenville	IL	60106	630-694-0644	694-0778
Garcia Express LLC 639 S 54th Ave *Web:* www.garciaexpress.com	Phoenix	AZ	85043	602-352-0150	
Gateway Logistics Group Inc, The 18201 Viscount Rd *Web:* www.gateway-group.com	Houston	TX	77032	281-443-7447	
Gazelle Transportation Inc 34915 Gazelle Ct *Web:* www.gazelletrans.com	Bakersfield	CA	93308	661-322-8868	
Geodis Wilson Canada Ltd 3061 Orlando Dr *Web:* www.geodiswilson.com	Mississauga	ON	L4V1R4	905-677-5266	
Gif Services Inc 2525 Brunswick Ave Ste 204 *Web:* www.gifservices.com	Linden	NJ	07036	908-474-1270	
Gold Coast Freightways Inc 12250 NW 28th Ave *TF:* 877-465-3585 ■ *Web:* www.gcfreight.com	Miami	FL	33167	305-687-3560	685-8056
GoodShip International Inc 699 Lively Blvd *Web:* www.goodship.com	Elk Grove Village	IL	60007	847-621-1444	
Graulich International Inc 6411 NW 35th Ave *Web:* www.graulichinternational.com	Miami	FL	33147	305-836-1700	836-1763
Gravy Train Express LLC 65 Gravy Train Ln *Web:* gravytrainllc.com	Lewistown	PA	17044	717-242-8515	
Group Transportation Services Inc 5876 Darrow Rd	Hudson	OH	44236	330-342-8700	
GTO 2000 Inc 2555 Flintridge Rd *Web:* www.gto2000.com	Gainesville	GA	30501	770-287-9233	
HA Logistics Inc 5175 Johnson Dr *TF:* 800-449-5778 ■ *Web:* www.halogistics.com	Pleasanton	CA	94588	925-251-9300	251-9333
Hancock International Corp 351 Main Pl Ste 220 *Web:* hancock-international.com	Carol Stream	IL	60188	630-510-7697	
Harbor Freight Transport Corp 301 Craneway St *Web:* www.harborfrt.com	Newark	NJ	07114	973-589-6700	589-6677
Hassett Air Express 877 S Rt 83 *TF:* 800-323-9422 ■ *Web:* hassettexpress.com/	Elmhurst	IL	60126	630-530-6524	530-6539
Hawaiian Express Service Inc 3623 Munster Ave PO Box 57136 *Web:* www.hawaiianexpressinc.com	Hayward	CA	94545	510-783-6100	782-5794
Holland Transportation Management Inc 305 N Center St *Web:* www.hollandtms.com	Statesville	NC	28677	704-872-4269	
Hubtrucker Inc 315 Freeport St Ste B *Web:* hubtrucker.com	Houston	TX	77015	713-547-5482	
I. C. S. Customs Service Inc 1099 Morse Ave *Web:* www.icscustoms.com	Elk Grove Village	IL	60007	847-718-9998	718-9987
ICAT Logistics Inc 6805 Douglas Legum Dr Third Fl *Web:* www.icatlogistics.com	Elkridge	MD	21075	443-459-8070	
IntegraCore LLC 6077 W Wells Park Rd *Web:* www.integracore.com	West Jordan	UT	84081	801-975-9411	
Interdom LLC 11800 S 75th Ave Ste 2N *TF:* 800-935-0851 ■ *Web:* www.interdompartners.com	Palos Heights	IL	60463	800-935-0851	
J & A Freight Systems Inc 4704 Irving Park Rd Ste 8 **Fax Area Code:* 773 ■ *TF:* 877-668-3378 ■ *Web:* jandafreight.com	Chicago	IL	60641	877-668-3378	205-7725*
Jan Packaging Inc 100 Harrison St *Web:* www.janpackaging.com	Dover	NJ	07801	973-361-7200	

				Phone	Fax
Jas Forwarding USA Inc 6165 Barfield Rd *Web:* jas.com	Atlanta	GA	30328	770-688-1206	
JD & Billy Hines Trucking Inc 407 Hines Blvd *Web:* www.hinestrucking.com	Prescott	AZ	71857	870-887-9400	
Jefferson Forwarding 2222 Jefferson St *Web:* gomsa.com	Laredo	TX	78040	956-723-0111	
JHOC Inc 323 Cash Memorial Blvd	Forest Park	GA	30297	404-675-1950	
Johanson Transportation Service Inc 5583 E Olive Ave *Web:* www.johansontrans.com	Fresno	CA	93727	559-458-2200	
JW Hampton Jr & Company Inc 161-15 Rockaway Blvd *Web:* jwhampton.com	Jamaica	NY	11434	718-276-0301	
K&L Freight Management Inc 745 S Rohlwing Rd *Web:* www.kandlfreight.com	Addison	IL	60101	630-607-1500	
KCC Transport Systems Inc 311 W Artesia Blvd *Web:* www.kccusa.com	Compton	CA	90220	310-764-5933	
Knichel Logistics LP 5347 William Flynn Hwy Second Fl *Web:* www.knichellogistics.com	Gibsonia	PA	15044	724-449-3300	
Knitney Lines Inc PO Box 350 *TF General:* 800-266-7883 ■ *Web:* www.knitneylines.com	Scranton	PA	18501	570-457-5060	457-6725
KW International Inc 18655 S Bishop Ave *Web:* www.kwinternational.com	Carson	CA	90746	310-354-6944	
Kyfi Inc 4300 Fern Vly Rd *Web:* www.kyfi.com	Louisville	KY	40219	502-810-9800	
L E Coppersmith Inc 525 S Douglas St *TF:* 888-827-4388 ■ *Web:* www.coppersmith.com	El Segundo	CA	90245	310-607-8000	607-8001
L. H. P. Transportation Services Inc 2032 E Kearney Ste 213 *Web:* www.lhp-transport.com	Springfield	MO	65803	417-865-7577	
L. J. Rogers Inc 170 Cherry & Webb Ln *Web:* www.ljrogers.com	Westport	MA	02791	508-636-6658	
LeanLogistics Inc 1351 S Waverly Rd *TF:* 866-584-7280 ■ *Web:* www.leanlogistics.com	Holland	MI	49423	616-738-6400	738-6462
Leman USA Inc 1860 Renaissance Blvd *Web:* www.lemanusa.com	Sturtevant	WI	53177	262-884-4700	884-4690
Linkex Inc 2230 Lyndon B Johnson Fwy Ste 300 *Web:* www.linkex.us	Dallas	TX	75234	972-481-9900	
Logfret Inc 6801 W Side Ave Ste 1 *Web:* www.logfret.com	North Bergen	NJ	07047	201-817-1140	656-7876
Logistics Plus Inc 1406 Peach St *TF:* 866-564-7587 ■ *Web:* www.logisticsplus.net	Erie	PA	16501	814-461-7600	461-7635
Longhorn Imports Inc 2202 E Union Bower *Web:* longhornimports.com	Irving	TX	75061	972-721-9102	579-4890
Lynden Inc 18000 International Blvd Ste 800 *TF:* 888-596-3361 ■ *Web:* www.lynden.com	Seattle	WA	98188	206-241-8778	243-8415
M&M Transport Services Inc 21 Mcgrath Hwy Ste 204 *Web:* www.mmtransport.com	Quincy	MA	02169	617-769-9370	
Marinsa Miami Corp 14250 SW 136 St Ste 4 *Web:* marinsa.com	Miami	FL	33186	305-252-0118	
Maritime Company For Navigation, The 249 Shipyard Blvd *Web:* themaritimecompany.com	Wilmington	NC	28412	910-343-8900	
Masterpiece International Ltd 39 Broadway 14th Fl *Web:* www.masterpieceintl.com	New York	NY	10006	212-825-4800	825-7010
Metro Express Transportation Services Inc 875 Fee Fee Rd *Web:* www.metroexpressinc.com	St. Louis	MO	63043	314-993-1511	
MHF Inc 2328 Evans City Rd *Web:* mhftrans.com	Zelienople	PA	16063	724-452-3900	
Mihlfeld & Assoc Inc 2841 E Division St *Web:* www.mihlfeld.com	Springfield	MO	65803	417-831-6727	
MLS Freight Logistics (MLS) 1802 S Expy 281 *Web:* mlsfreight.com	Edinburg	TX	78542	956-292-2700	292-2755
Modaexpress of USA Inc 900 Secaucus Rd Unit A *Web:* www.modaexpress.com	Secaucus	NJ	07094	201-325-8808	
Morrison Express Corp USA 2000 S Hughes Way *Web:* www.morrisonexpress.com	El Segundo	CA	90245	310-322-8999	322-6688
MSE Express America Inc 2700 Delta Ln *Web:* www.tasexpress.com	Elk Grove Village	IL	60007	847-238-2600	
MSM Transportation Inc 124 Commercial Rd *TF:* 800-667-4175 ■ *Web:* wheelsgroup.com/	Bolton	ON	L7E1K4	905-951-6800	
MVP Global Logistics LLC 580 Chelsea St Ste 212 *Web:* mvpgloballogistics.com	East Boston	MA	02128	617-569-6300	
N2it Containers LP 6012 Murphy St *Web:* clsmith.com/n2it_containers.asp	Houston	TX	77033	713-644-5055	
Nippon Express USA Inc 590 Madison Ave Ste 2401 *Web:* www.nipponexpressusa.com	New York	NY	10022	212-405-1650	758-2595
Noble Logistic Services Inc 11335 Clay Rd Ste 100 *Web:* www.noblelogistics.com	Houston	TX	77041	713-690-0200	
Norvanco International Inc 4301 W Vly Hwy Ste 100 *Web:* www.norvanco.com	Sumner	WA	98390	253-987-4031	987-4015
NVC Logistics Group Inc One Pond Rd *Web:* www.nvclogistics.com	Rockleigh	NJ	07647	201-767-0911	
OCEANAIR Inc 186A Lee Burbank Hwy *Web:* www.oceanair.net	Revere	MA	02151	781-286-2700	
Oceane Marine Shipping Inc 407 E Maple St *Web:* oceanems.com	Cumming	GA	30040	770-888-5941	
OIA Global Logistics Inc 17230 NE Sacramento St *Web:* oiaglobal.com	Portland	OR	97230	503-736-5900	

				Phone	Fax
Ontario Northland Transportation Commission 555 Oak St E. *Web:* www.ontarionorthland.ca	North Bay	ON	P1B8L3	705-472-4500	
OTS Astracon LLC 3115 Beam Rd PO Box 19413 *Web:* otsusa.org	Charlotte	NC	28217	704-424-5522	424-5622
Pac Marine Express Inc 19401 S Main St Ste 102 *Web:* www.gopacmarine.com	Gardena	CA	90248	310-329-2478	
Pacific Alaska Freightways Inc 2812 70th Ave E *TF:* 800-426-9940 ■ *Web:* www.pafak.com	Fife	WA	98424	253-926-3292	926-3161
Page & Jones Inc 52 N Jackson St 36602 PO Box 2167 *Web:* www.pageandjones.com	Mobile	AL	36652	251-432-1646	
Pan Pacific Express Corp 19481 Harborgate Way *Web:* www.panpacificusa.com	Torrance	CA	90501	310-638-3887	
Pan Star Express Corp 1134 Tower Ln *Web:* www.panstarexpress.com	Bensenville	IL	60106	630-787-1672	
Phoenix International Freight Services Ltd 14701 Charlson Road **Fax Area Code:* 630 ■ *TF:* 855-229-6128 ■ *Web:* www.chrobinson.com	Eden Prairie	MN	55347	952-937-6761	766-6395*
Pioneer Transfer LLC 2034 S St Aubin St PO Box 2567 **Fax Area Code:* 712 ■ *TF:* 800-325-4650 ■ *Web:* www.pioneertransfer.com	Sioux City	IA	51106	800-325-4650	274-2946*
Poten & Partners Inc 805 Third Ave 19th Fl *Web:* www.poten.com	New York	NY	10022	212-230-2000	355-0295
Priefert Manufacturing Company Inc 2630 S Jefferson Ave PO box 1540 *Web:* www.priefert.com	Mount Pleasant	TX	75456	903-572-1741	
Primary Freight Services Inc 6545 Caballero Blvd *Web:* www.primaryfreight.com	Buena Park	CA	90620	310-635-3000	
Priority Distribution Inc 330 Milltown Rd Ste W31 *Web:* www.pdi3pl.com	East Brunswick	NJ	08816	732-234-1919	
ProTrans International Inc 8311 N Perimeter Rd *Web:* www.protrans.com	Indianapolis	IN	46241	317-240-4100	
Pulau Electronics Corp 12633 Challenger Pkwy *Web:* www.pulau.com	Orlando	FL	32826	407-380-9191	380-9786
Quality Customs Broker Inc 4464 S Whitnall Ave *TF:* 888-813-4647 ■ *Web:* www.qualitybrokers.com	Saint Francis	WI	53235	414-482-9447	482-9448
Quality Transportation 36-40 37th St Ste 201 *TF:* 800-677-2838 ■ *Web:* www.qualityca.com	Long Island City	NY	11101	212-308-6333	308-6595
R & D Transportation Services Inc 4036 Adolfo Rd *Web:* rdtsi.com	Camarillo	CA	93012	805-529-7511	
Raymond Express International (REI) 320 Harbor Way *Web:* www.reiexpress.com	South San Francisco	CA	94080	650-871-8560	952-3288
Ready Auto Transport LLC 1030 N Colorado St Ste 109 *Web:* www.readyautotransport.com	Gilbert	AZ	85233	480-558-3200	
Recon Logistics LLC 10205 Queens Way Ste 5 *Web:* reconlogistics.com	Chagrin Falls	OH	44023	440-708-2306	
Rmx Global Logistics 35715 US Hwy 40 Bldg B **Fax Area Code:* 303 ■ *TF:* 888-824-7365 ■ *Web:* www.rmxglobal.com	Evergreen	CO	80439	888-824-7365	674-3803*
Rock-It Cargo USA Inc 5438 W 104th St PO Box 90519 *TF:* 800-973-1727 ■ *Web:* www.rockitcargo.com	Los Angeles	CA	90045	310-410-0935	410-0628
Rogers & Brown Custom Brokers Inc Two Cumberland St *Web:* www.rogers-brown.com	Charleston	SC	29401	843-577-3630	
Romar Transportation Systems Inc 3500 S Kedzie Ave *TF:* 800-621-5416 ■ *Web:* www.romartrans.com	Chicago	IL	60632	773-376-8800	650-1644
Rpl Associates Inc 21650 W 11 Mile Rd *Web:* www.rplassociates.com	Southfield	MI	48076	248-353-0011	
RTL Robinson Enterprises Ltd 350 Old Airport Rd *Web:* westcanbulk.ca/rtl	Yellowknife	NT	X1A2P4	867-873-6271	
Ryder CRSA Logistics 1275 Kingsway Ave *Web:* www.crsalog.com	Port Coquitlam	BC	V3C1S2	604-941-8228	
Samuel Shapiro & Company Inc 100 N Charles St One Charles Ctr Ste 1200 *Web:* www.shapiro.com	Baltimore	MD	21201	410-539-0540	
Satellite Logistics Group Inc 12621 Featherwood Ste 390 *TF:* 877-795-7540 ■ *Web:* www.slg.com	Houston	TX	77034	281-902-5500	902-5501
Saturn Freight Systems Inc 561 Village Trace Ste 13A *Web:* www.saturnfreight.com	Marietta	GA	30067	770-952-3490	
Scarbrough International Ltd 10841 Ambassador Dr *Web:* www.scarbrough-intl.com	Kansas City	MO	64153	816-891-2400	
Schenker Inc 150 Albany Ave *Web:* www.dbschenkerusa.com	Freeport	NY	11520	516-377-3000	
Schenker of Canada Ltd 5935 Airport Rd 10th Fl *Web:* www.dbschenker.ca	Mississauga	ON	L4V1W5	905-676-0676	
Scott Logistics Corp PO Box 391 *TF:* 800-893-6689 ■ *Web:* www.scottlogistics.com	Rome	GA	30162	706-234-1184	234-1184
Senderex Cargo Inc 5451 104th St *TF:* 800-421-5846 ■ *Web:* www.senderex.com	Los Angeles	CA	90045	310-342-2900	642-0427
Senvoy LLC 115 SE Yamhill St *Web:* www.senvoy.com	Portland	OR	97214	503-234-7722	
Serra International Inc 75 Montgomery St Ste 300 *Web:* www.serraintl.com	Jersey City	NJ	07302	201-860-9600	
Seven R Transportation Inc 2818 Queen City Dr *Web:* www.sevenr.com	Charlotte	NC	28208	704-391-0694	
Sho-Air International 5401 Argosy Ave *TF:* 800-227-9111 ■ *Web:* www.shoair.com	Huntington Beach	CA	92649	949-476-9111	476-9991
Simcoe Parts Service Inc 6795 Industrial Pkwy *Web:* www.simcoeparts.com	Alliston	ON	L9R1W1	705-435-7814	
Smith Systems Transportation Inc 417 Ninth Ave *Web:* smithsystemsus.weebly.com/	Scottsbluff	NE	69361	308-632-5148	
Sos Global Express Inc 2803 Trent Rd *Web:* sosglobal.com	New Bern	NC	28562	252-635-1400	
Sotech Nitram Inc 1695 Boul Laval *Web:* www.sotechnitram.com	Laval	QC	H7S2M2	450-975-2100	
Sound Brokerage International LLC 3600 Port Of Tacoma Rd Ste 301 *Web:* soundbrokerage.com	Fife	WA	98424	253-922-7718	
Star Asia International Inc 208 Church St *Web:* www.star-asia.com	Decatur	GA	30030	404-761-6900	
Stone Transport Inc 3495 Hack Rd *Web:* www.stonetransport.com	Saginaw	MI	48601	989-754-4788	
Sunset Transportation Inc 11325 Concord Village Ave *TF:* 800-849-6540 ■ *Web:* www.sunsettrans.com	St Louis	MO	63123	800-849-6540	
Suntrans International Inc 1550 W Glenlake Ave *Web:* www.suntrans.com	Itasca	IL	60143	630-285-9900	
Superior Freight Services Inc 1230 Trapp Rd *Web:* www.supfrt.com	Saint Paul	MN	55121	952-854-5053	
Team Drive-Away Inc 23712 W 83rd Ter *Web:* www.teamdriveaway.com	Shawnee	KS	66227	913-825-4776	
Tech Transport Inc PO Box 431 *Web:* www.techtransport.com	Milford	NH	03055	603-673-0898	
Technical Traffic Consultants Corp 30 Hemlock Dr *Web:* www.technicaltraffic.com	Congers	NY	10920	845-623-6144	
Terminal Corp, The 1657 S Highland Ave Ste A **Fax Area Code:* 410 ■ *TF:* 800-560-7207 ■ *Web:* www.termcorp.com	Baltimore	MD	21224	800-560-7207	246-0519*
Thill Logistics Inc 355 Byrd Ave *Web:* www.thilllogistics.com	Neenah	WI	54956	920-967-8000	
Thompson, Ahern & Company Ltd 6299 Airport Rd Ste 506 *Web:* www.taco.ca	Mississauga	ON	L4V1N3	905-677-3471	
Time Definite Services Inc 1360 Madeline Ln Ste 300 *TF:* 800-466-8040 ■ *Web:* timedefinite.com	Elgin	IL	60124	800-466-8040	
Total Quality Logistics Inc (TQL) 4289 Ivy Pointe Blvd *TF:* 800-580-3101 ■ *Web:* www.tql.com	Cincinnati	OH	45245	513-831-2600	965-7630
Total Transportation Concept 8728 Avaition Blvd *Web:* www.totaltrans.com	Inglewood	CA	90301	310-337-0515	
Towne Air Freight 24805 US 20 W *TF:* 800-468-6963 ■ *Web:* www.towneair.com	South Bend	IN	46628	574-233-3183	
Trademark Transportation Inc 739 Vandalia St *Web:* www.trademarktrans.com	Saint Paul	MN	55114	651-646-2500	
Trancy Logistics America Corp 1670 Dolwick Rd Ste 8 *Web:* trancyamerica.com	Erlanger	KY	41018	859-282-7780	
Trans-Border Global Freight Systems Inc 2103 Route 9 *TF:* 800-493-9444 ■ *Web:* www.tbgfs.com	Round Lake	NY	12151	518-785-6000	785-6239
TransGroup Express Inc 18850 Eighth Ave S Ste 100 *Web:* www.transgroup.com	Seattle	WA	98148	206-244-0330	
TransGuardian Inc International Jewelry Ctr 550 S Hill St Lobby 103 *Web:* www.transguardian.com	Los Angeles	CA	90013	213-622-5877	
TRANSInternational System Inc 130 E Wilson Bridge Rd Ste 150 Ste 150 *TF:* 800-340-7540 ■ *Web:* www.trnj.com	Worthington	OH	43085	614-891-4942	891-4929
Transit Systems Inc 999 Old Eagle School Rd Ste 114 *Web:* www.transitsystems.com	Wayne	PA	19087	610-971-1830	
Transmaritime Central Inc 14213 Transportation Ave *Web:* www.globalpc.net	Laredo	TX	78045	956-724-8417	
Transmodal Corp 48 S Franklin Tpke *Web:* www.transmodal.net	Ramsey	NJ	07446	201-316-1600	
Transportation Management Assoc Inc 344 Oak Grove Church Rd *TF:* 800-745-8292 ■ *Web:* www.tmaco.com	Mocksville	NC	27028	800-745-8292	
TransportGistics Inc 4170 Veterans Memorial Hwy Ste 202 *Web:* www.transportgistics.com	Bohemia	NY	11716	631-567-4100	
TransX Group of Cos 2595 Inkster Blvd *Web:* www.transx.com	Winnipeg	MB	R3C2E6	204-632-6694	
TranzAct Technologies Inc 360 W Butterfield Rd 4th Fl *Web:* www.tranzact.com	Elmhurst	IL	60126	630-833-0890	833-8538
Travelers Transportation Services Inc 195 Heart Lk Rd South *Web:* www.travelers.ca	Brampton	ON	L6W3N6	905-457-8789	
Tricor America Inc 717 Airport Blvd *TF:* 800-669-7874 ■ *Web:* www.tricor.com	South San Francisco	CA	94080	650-877-3650	583-3197

				Phone	Fax
Triple B Forwarders Inc 1511 Glen Curtis St *Web:* www.tripleb.com	Carson	CA	90746	310-604-5840	
Tucker Company Worldwide Inc 900 Dudley Ave. *Web:* tuckerco.com	Cherry Hill	NJ	08002	856-317-9600	
U-Freight America Inc 320 Corey Way PO Box 1890 *Web:* www.ufreight.com	South San Francisco	CA	94080	650-583-6527	583-8122
Updike Distribution Logistics LLC 4411 W Roosevelt St *Web:* www.updikedl.com	Phoenix	AZ	85043	602-682-1800	
UTXL Inc 10771 NW Ambassador Dr *Web:* www.utxl.com	Kansas City	MO	64153	816-891-7770	
Vascor Ltd 100 Farmers Bank Dr Ste 300 *Web:* www.vascorlogistics.com	Georgetown	KY	40324	502-570-2020	
Veeco Holdings LLC 6801 W Side Ave *Web:* www.veeco1.com	North Bergen	NJ	07047	201-865-6200	
Victory Transportation Systems Inc 9009 N Loop E Ste 135 *Web:* www.victorytrucks.com	Houston	TX	77029	713-682-8900	
Ware Pak Inc 2427 Bond St *Web:* www.ware-pak.com	University Park	IL	60466	708-534-2600	
Wellcorp Express Inc 8616 La Tijera Blvd Ste 310 *Web:* welltonexpress.com.hk	Los Angeles	CA	90045	310-645-6410	645-3874
Wider Consolidated Inc 175-35 148th Rd Second Fl *Web:* widerlogistics.com	Jamica	NY	11434	718-244-8800	
Wilk Forwarding Company Inc 2900 Emerson Expy	Jacksonville	FL	32207	904-346-3550	
Worldtrans Services Inc 7130 Miramar Rd Ste 100a *Web:* www.worldtransinc.com	San Diego	CA	92121	858-536-7900	
WR Zanes & Company of Louisiana Inc 223 Tchoupitoulas St *Web:* www.wrzanes.com	New Orleans	LA	70130	504-524-1301	524-1309
Yusen Logistics (Americas) Inc 300 Lighting Way *Web:* www.us.yusen-logistics.com	Secaucus	NJ	07094	201-553-3800	

315 FREIGHT TRANSPORT - DEEP SEA (DOMESTIC PORTS)

				Phone	Fax
Alaska Marine Lines Inc 5615 W Marginal Way SW *TF Cust Svc:* 800-326-8346 ■ *Web:* www.lynden.com	Seattle	WA	98106	206-763-4244	764-5782
Algoma Central Corp 63 Church St Ste 600 *Web:* www.algonet.com	St. Catharines	ON	L2R3C4	905-687-7888	
Berman Moving & Storage Inc 23800 Corbin Dr. *Web:* www.bermanmovers.com	Cleveland	OH	44128	216-663-8816	
Coastal Transportation Inc 4025 13th Ave W *TF:* 800-544-2580 ■ *Web:* www.coastaltransportation.com	Seattle	WA	98119	206-282-9979	283-9121
Crowley Maritime Corp 9487 Regency Square Blvd Ste 2130 *TF:* 800-276-9539 ■ *Web:* www.crowley.com	Jacksonville	FL	32225	904-727-2200	727-2501
Econocaribe Consolidators Inc 2401 NW 69th St. *Web:* www.econocaribe.com	Miami	FL	33147	305-693-5133	696-9350
Express Marine Inc PO Box 329 *Web:* www.expressmarine.com	Pennsauken	NJ	08110	856-541-4600	541-0338
Freightquote.com Inc 16025 W 113th St *TF:* 800-323-5441 ■ *Web:* www.freightquote.com	Lenexa	KS	66219	913-642-4700	642-6773
Hapag-Lloyd America Inc 401 E Jackson St *TF:* 800-282-8977 ■ *Web:* www.hapag-lloyd.com/en	Tampa	FL	33602	813-276-4600	
Horizon Lines Inc 4064 Colony Rd Ste 200 *TF Cust Svc:* 877-678-7447 ■ *Web:* www.horizonlines.com	Charlotte	NC	28211	704-973-7000	973-7075
Inchcape Shipping Services Inc 11 N Water St Ste 9290 *Web:* www.iss-shipping.com	Mobile	AL	36602	251-461-2747	
Intermarine LLC 365 Canal St One Canal Pl Ste 2400 *Web:* www.intelifuse.com	New Orleans	LA	70130	504-529-2100	
International Shipholding Corp 11 N Water Ste 18290 *NYSE: ISH* ■ **Fax Area Code:* 504 ■ *TF:* 800-826-3513 ■ *Web:* www.intship.com	Mobile	AL	36602	251-243-9100	529-5745*
Keystone Shipping Co One Bala Plz E Ste 600 *Web:* www.keyship.com	Bala Cynwyd	PA	19004	610-617-6800	617-6899
Loveland SC & Co 127 W Supawna Rd	Pennsville Township	NJ	08070	856-935-8100	
Matson Navigation Co 555 12th St *TF Cust Svc:* 800-462-8766 ■ *Web:* www.matson.com	Oakland	CA	94607	510-628-4000	628-7380
Mormac Marine Group Inc One Landmark Sq Ste 710	Stamford	CT	06901	203-977-8900	977-8933
Northland Services Inc 6700 W Marginal Way SW *TF:* 800-426-3113 ■ *Web:* www.northlandservices.com	Seattle	WA	98106	206-763-3000	767-5579
Overseas Shipholding Group Inc 666 Third Ave *TF:* 800-851-9677 ■ *Web:* www.osg.com	New York	NY	10017	212-953-4100	578-1832
Sea Star Line LLC 10550 Deerwood Pk Blvd Ste 509 *TF:* 877-775-7447 ■ *Web:* www.seastarline.com	Jacksonville	FL	32256	904-855-1260	724-3011
Seaboard Marine 8001 NW 79th Ave *TF:* 866-676-8886 ■ *Web:* www.seaboardmarine.com	Miami	FL	33166	305-863-4444	863-4400
Totem Ocean Trailer Express Inc 32001 32nd Ave S Ste 200 *TF:* 800-426-0074 ■ *Web:* www.totemocean.com	Federal Way	WA	98001	253-449-8100	449-8225
Trailer Bridge Inc 10405 New Berlin Rd E *OTC: TRBRQ* ■ *TF:* 800-554-1589 ■ *Web:* www.trailerbridge.com	Jacksonville	FL	32226	904-751-7100	751-7444

				Phone	Fax
US Shipping Corp 399 Thornall St 8th Fl *TF:* 866-942-6592 ■ *Web:* www.usslp.com	Edison	NJ	08837	732-635-1500	635-1918
Western Pioneer Inc 4601 Shilshole Ave NW *TF:* 800-426-6783 ■ *Web:* www.wpioneer.com	Seattle	WA	98107	206-789-1930	781-2486
Young Bros Ltd PO Box 3288 *TF:* 800-572-2743 ■ *Web:* www.htbyb.com	Honolulu	HI	96801	808-543-9311	

316 FREIGHT TRANSPORT - DEEP SEA (FOREIGN PORTS)

				Phone	Fax
Alter Barge Line Inc 2117 State St *Web:* www.alterlogistics.com	Bettendorf	IA	52722	563-344-5100	
American Overseas Marine Corp 100 Newport Ave Ext. *Web:* gdamsea.com	Quincy	MA	02171	617-786-8300	472-4925
Antillean Marine Shipping Corp 3038 NW N River Dr *Web:* www.antillean.com	Miami	FL	33142	305-633-6361	
Artemus Group 4456 Corporation Ln Ste 200 *Web:* www.artemus.us	Virginia Bch	VA	23462	757-201-6811	
Atlantic Container Line (ACL) 50 Cardinal Dr. *TF:* 800-225-1235 ■ *Web:* www.aclcargo.com	Westfield	NJ	07090	908-518-5300	518-7321
Bisso Marine Company Inc 11311 Neeshaw Dr. *Web:* www.bissomarine.com	Houston	TX	77065	281-897-1500	
Ceres Consulting LLC 3808 Cookson Rd E St Louis *Web:* www.ceresbarge.com	St Louis	IL	62201	618-271-7903	
CSL International Inc 152 Conant St *Web:* www.cslships.com	Beverly	MA	01915	978-922-1300	922-1772
Dura Freight Inc 20405 E Business Pkwy *Web:* www.durafreight.com	Walnut	CA	91789	909-595-8100	
Eagle Bulk Shipping Inc 477 MADISON Ave Ste 1405 *Web:* www.eagleships.com	New York	NY	10022	212-785-2500	
Eagle Maritime Consultants Inc 1600 Space Park Dr *Web:* www.eaglemaritime.com	Houston	TX	77058	281-333-9880	333-9885
Eagle Van Lines Inc 5041 Beech Pl. *Web:* www.eaglevanlines.com	Temple Hills	MD	20748	301-899-2022	
Fednav Ltd 1000 Rue de la GauchetiFre O Bureau 3500 *TF General:* 800-678-4842 ■ *Web:* www.fednav.com	Montreal	QC	H3B4W5	514-878-6500	878-6642
GDB International Inc One Home News Row *Web:* www.gdbinternational.com	New Brunswick	NJ	08901	732-246-3001	246-3004
Genco Shipping & Trading Ltd 299 Pk Ave 12th Fl *NYSE: GNK* ■ *Web:* www.gencoshipping.com	New York	NY	10171	646-443-8550	
General Maritime Corp 299 Pk Ave Second Fl. *Web:* www.generalmaritimecorp.com	New York	NY	10171	212-763-5600	763-5603
Grand Power Logistics Group Inc Ste 2806 505 - Sixth St SW *Web:* www.grandpowerlogistics.com	Calgary	AB	T2P1X5	403-237-8211	
Groupe Desgagnes Inc 21 March-Champlain St *Web:* www.groupedesgagnes.com	Quebec	QC	G1K8Z8	418-692-1000	
Hamburg Sud North America Inc 465 S St. **Fax Area Code:* 770 ■ *TF:* 888-228-8241 ■ *Web:* www.hamburgsud.com	Morristown	NJ	07960	973-775-5300	916-5901*
Hapag-Lloyd America Inc 401 E Jackson St *TF:* 800-282-8977 ■ *Web:* www.hapag-lloyd.com/en	Tampa	FL	33602	813-276-4600	
Inchcape Shipping Services Inc 11 N Water St Ste 9290 *Web:* www.iss-shipping.com	Mobile	AL	36602	251-461-2747	
Interlake Steamship Co, The 7300 Engle Rd *Web:* www.interlake-steamship.com	Middleburg Heights	OH	44130	440-260-6900	
Interlog USA Inc 2818A Anthony Ln S. *TF:* 800-603-6030 ■ *Web:* www.interlogusa.com	Minneapolis	MN	55418	612-789-3456	789-2118
International Shipholding Corp 11 N Water Ste 18290 *NYSE: ISH* ■ **Fax Area Code:* 504 ■ *TF:* 800-826-3513 ■ *Web:* www.intship.com	Mobile	AL	36602	251-243-9100	529-5745*
K Line America Inc 8730 Stony Pt Pkwy Ste 400 *TF:* 800-609-3221 ■ *Web:* www.k-line.com	Richmond	VA	23235	804-560-3600	560-3463
Liberty Maritime Corp 1979 Marcus Ave Ste 200 *Web:* libertygl.com	Lake Success	NY	11042	516-488-8800	488-8806
Maersk Inc Two Giralda Farms *Web:* maerskline.com	Madison	NJ	07940	973-514-5000	
Maersk Line Ltd One Commercial Pl 20th Fl. *Web:* www.maersklinelimited.com	Norfolk	VA	23510	757-857-4800	
Main Industries Inc 107 E St. *Web:* www.mainindustries.com	Hampton	VA	23661	757-380-0180	
Maritime Helicopters 3520 Faa Rd *Web:* www.maritimehelicopters.com	Homer	AK	99603	907-235-7771	
Mckeil Marine Ltd 208 Hillyard St *Web:* www.mckeil.com	Hamilton	ON	L8L6B6	905-528-4780	
North America Cosco Inc 100 Lighting Way Ste 1 *Web:* www.coscoamericas.com	Secaucus	NJ	07094	201-422-0500	
Northern Transportation Co Ltd 42003 Mackenzie Hwy *TF:* 866-935-6825 ■ *Web:* www.ntcl.com	Hay River	NT	X0E0R9	867-587-2442	
Ocean Flow International LLC 2100 W Loop S Ste 500 *Web:* www.oceanflowinternational.com	Houston	TX	77027	281-358-5885	
Overseas Shipholding Group Inc 666 Third Ave *TF:* 800-851-9677 ■ *Web:* www.osg.com	New York	NY	10017	212-953-4100	578-1832
Pasha Group Inc 5725 Paradise Dr Ste 1000 *Web:* www.pashagroup.com	Corte Madera	CA	94925	415-927-6400	924-5672

	City	State	ZIP	Phone	Fax
Rand Logistics Inc 500 Fifth Ave 50th Fl. *Web:* www.randlogisticsinc.com	New York	NY	10110	212-644-3450	
Seaboard Marine 8001 NW 79th Ave *TF:* 866-676-8886 ■ *Web:* www.seaboardmarine.com	Miami	FL	33166	305-863-4444	863-4400
Sealift Inc 68 W Main St. *Web:* www.sealiftinc.com	Oyster Bay	NY	11771	516-922-1000	
Stevens Towing Company Inc 4170 Hwy 165 *Web:* www.stevens-towing.com	Yonges Island	SC	29449	843-889-2254	
Stolt-Nielsen Transportation Group 800 Connecticut Ave Fourth Fl E *Web:* www.stolt-nielsen.com	Norwalk	CT	06854	203-838-7100	299-0067
Teras Cargo Transport (America) LLC 5358 33rd Ave NW Ste 302 *Web:* www.terasamerica.com	Gig Harbor	WA	98335	253-857-9209	
Tidewater Inc 601 Poydras St Ste 1900 *NYSE: TDW* ■ *TF:* 800-678-8433 ■ *Web:* www.tdw.com	New Orleans	LA	70130	504-568-1010	566-4580
Tropical Shipping Five E 11th St. *TF:* 800-367-6200 ■ *Web:* tropical.com	Riviera Beach	FL	33404	561-881-3900	
UTC Overseas Inc 370 W Passaic St Ste 3000. *Web:* www.utcoverseas.com	Rochelle Park	NJ	07662	201-270-4600	
Wallenius Wilhelmsen Lines Americas 188 Broadway PO Box 1232 *Web:* www.2wglobal.com	Woodcliff Lake	NJ	07677	201-307-0069	
Wallenius Wilhelmsen Logistics PO Box 1232 **Fax:* Cust Svc ■ *Web:* www.2wglobal.com	Woodcliff Lake	NJ	07677	201-307-1300	307-0069*

317 FREIGHT TRANSPORT - INLAND WATERWAYS

	City	State	ZIP	Phone	Fax
A & B Freight Line Inc 4805 Sandy Hollow Rd *Web:* www.aandbfreight.com	Rockford	IL	61125	815-874-4700	
American Commercial Barge Lines Inc 1701 E Market St *TF:* 800-457-6377 ■ *Web:* www2.aclines.com	Jeffersonville	IN	47130	812-288-0100	288-1664
American Commercial Lines Inc 1701 E Market St *TF:* 800-899-7195 ■ *Web:* www.aclines.com	Jeffersonville	IN	47130	812-288-0100	288-1664
American Steamship Co 500 Essjay Rd Centerpointe Corporate Pk *Web:* www.americansteamship.com	Williamsville	NY	14221	716-635-0222	635-0220
AMJ Campbell International 1445 Courtneypark Dr E *Web:* www.amj-international.com	Mississauga	ON	L5T2E3	905-670-6683	
Andrie Inc 561 E Western Ave *TF:* 800-722-2421 ■ *Web:* www.andrie.com	Muskegon	MI	49442	231-728-2226	726-6747
Bear Cartage & Intermodal Inc 8600 Joliet Rd. *Web:* www.bearcartage.com	Mccook	IL	60525	708-924-9093	
Becker Transportation Inc 1501 S Bulington Ave *Web:* www.beckertrans.com	Hastings	NE	68901	402-461-4454	
Best Way Logistics 14004 Century Ln *Web:* bestwaylogistics.com	Grandview	MO	64030	816-767-8008	
Big Apple Car Inc 169 Bay 17th St. *Web:* www.bigapplecar.com	Brooklyn	NY	11214	718-331-9500	
Big Dog Logistics LLP 1235 N Loop W *Web:* www.bigdoglogistics.com	Houston	TX	77008	713-996-8171	
Bouchard Transportation Company Inc 58 S Service Rd Ste 150 *Web:* www.bouchardtransport.com	Melville	NY	11747	631-390-4900	390-4905
Brighton Cromwell LLC 111 Canfield Ave Bldg C 1-10 *Web:* www.brightoncromwell.com	Randolph	NJ	07869	973-252-4100	
Budway Enterprises Inc 13600 Napa St. *Web:* www.budway.net	Fontana	CA	92335	909-463-0500	
Calyx Transportation Group Inc 107 Alfred Kuehne Blvd *Web:* www.calyxinc.com	Brampton	ON	L6T4K3	905-494-4747	
Canal Barge Company Inc 835 Union St *Web:* www.canalbarge.com	New Orleans	LA	70112	504-581-2424	584-1505
CareGo Holdings Inc 400 Longwood Rd South *Web:* carego.com	Hamilton	ON	L8P4Z3	905-529-7656	
Cargo Pacific Logistics 800 Mark St *Web:* www.cargopacificlogistics.com	Elk Grove Village	IL	60007	847-750-1230	
Celtic Marine Corp 3888 S Sherwood Forest Blvd Celtic Ctr Bldg 1 *Web:* www.celticmarine.com	Baton Rouge	LA	70816	225-752-2490	752-2582
Clark Freight Lines Inc 5129 Pine Ave. *Web:* www.clarkfreight.com	Pasadena	TX	77503	281-487-3160	
Cline Design Assoc of Wilmington Pllc 125 N Harrington St *Web:* www.clinedesignassoc.com	Raleigh	NC	27603	919-833-6413	
Cole International Inc 3033 - 34th Ave NE. *Web:* www.cole.ca	Calgary	AB	T1Y6X2	403-262-2771	
Crounse Corp 400 Marine Way *Web:* www.crounse.com	Paducah	KY	42003	270-444-9611	444-9615
Crowley Maritime Corp 9487 Regency Square Blvd Ste 2130 *TF:* 800-276-9539 ■ *Web:* www.crowley.com	Jacksonville	FL	32225	904-727-2200	727-2501
Custom Global Logistics LLC 317 W Lk St *TF:* 800-446-8336 ■ *Web:* www.customgl.com	Northlake	IL	60164	800-446-8336	
Dayton Freight Lines Inc 6450 Poe Ave. *Web:* www.daytonfreight.com	Dayton	OH	45414	937-264-4060	
De Well Container Shipping Corp One Cross Island Plz Ste 302 *Web:* www.dewellusa.com	Rosedale	NY	11422	718-528-1888	
Delmar International Inc 10636 Cote de Liesse *Web:* www.delmarcargo.com	Montreal	QC	H8T1A5	514-636-8800	
Falcon Express Transportation Inc 6804 Virginia Manor Rd *Web:* www.fxtran.com	Beltsville	MD	20705	240-264-1215	
FastAsset Inc 170 W Rd Ste 15 *Web:* www.fastasset.com	Portsmouth	NH	03801	603-559-9900	
FDSI Logistics Inc 5703 Corsa Ave *Web:* www.fdsi.com	Westlake Village	CA	91362	818-971-3300	
Fednav Ltd 1000 Rue de la GauchetiFre O Bureau 3500 *TF General:* 800-678-4842 ■ *Web:* www.fednav.com	Montreal	QC	H3B4W5	514-878-6500	878-6642
Focus Logistics Inc 1311 Howard Dr *Web:* focuslogisticsinc.com	West Chicago	IL	60185	630-231-8200	
Fraser Direct Distribution Services Ltd 100 Armstrong Ave *Web:* www.fraserdirect.ca	Georgetown	ON	L7G5S4	905-877-4411	
Freight Handlers Inc 310 N Judd Pkwy NE *Web:* www.freighthandlers.com	Fuquay Varina	NC	27526	919-552-3157	
Frontline Logistics Inc 9555 Main St *Web:* www.frontlinelogistics.com	Whitmore Lake	MI	48189	734-449-9474	
Hackbarth Delivery Service Inc 3504 Brookdale Dr N *TF:* 800-277-3322 ■ *Web:* www.hackbarthdelivery.com	Mobile	AL	36618	251-478-1401	
Horizon Freight Lines Inc 6579 S Us Hwy 31 *Web:* www.horizonfreightlines.com	Edinburgh	IN	46124	812-526-3380	526-3390
Hunter Marine Transport Inc 6615 Robertson Ave *Web:* www.huntermarine.net	Nashville	TN	37209	615-352-6935	
I C C Logistics Services Inc 960 S Broadway Ste 110 *Web:* www.icclogistics.com	Hicksville	NY	11801	516-822-1183	
ICECORP Logistics Inc 1600 Courtneypark Dr E *Web:* icecorp.ca	Mississauga	ON	L5T2W8	905-672-7400	
Ingram Barge Co 4400 HaRding Rd *Web:* www.ingrambarge.com	Nashville	TN	37205	615-298-8200	298-8213
Integral Transportation Networks Corp 6975 D Pacific Cir *Web:* www.itn-logistics.com	Mississauga	ON	L5T2H3	905-362-1111	
Itochu Logistics (USA) Corp 1830 W 205th St. *Web:* www.ilogi.co.jp	Torrance	CA	90501	310-787-6500	
ITS Logistics LLC 620 Spice Island Dr *Web:* www.its4logistics.com	Sparks	NV	89431	775-358-5300	
J s Logistics 4550 Gustine Ave *TF:* 800-814-2634 ■ *Web:* www.jslogistics.com	Saint Louis	MO	63116	314-832-6008	
J.M. Rodgers Company Inc 1975 Linden Blvd *Web:* www.jmrodgers.com	Elmont	NY	11003	516-872-5570	
Keltic Transportation Inc 90 MacNaughton Ave Caledonia Industrial Park *Web:* www.keltictransportation.com	Moncton	NB	E1H3L9	506-854-1233	
L & M Botruc Rental Inc 18692 W Main St. *Web:* www.botruc.com	Galliano	LA	70354	985-475-5733	475-5669
La Corporation D'urgences-Sant, 3232 Rue Belanger *Web:* www.urgences-sante.qc.ca	Montreal	QC	H1Y3H5	514-723-5600	
Laidlaw Carriers Bulk LP 240 Universal Rd. *Web:* www.laidlaw.ca	Woodstock	ON	N4S0A9	519-539-0471	
Lawndale Logistics 1239 12th Ave. *Web:* www.lawndalelogistics.com	Grafton	WI	53024	262-375-3684	
Lipsey Logistics Worldwide LLC 1701 Oakbrook Dr Ste D *Web:* www.lipseylogistics.com	Norcross	GA	30093	678-336-1180	
LoadMatch Logistics Inc 1013 Ashes Dr Ste 200 *Web:* www.loadmatch123.com	Wilmington	NC	28405	910-344-0700	
Logistic Dynamics Inc 1140 Wehrle Dr *Web:* www.logisticdynamics.com	Amherst	NY	14221	716-250-3477	
Logistics Store, The 26 Westwoods Dr *Web:* www.thelogisticsstore.com	Liberty	MO	64068	816-781-0450	
LTI Trucking Services Inc 411 N 10th St Ste 500 *TF:* 800-642-7222 ■ *Web:* www.ltitrucking.com	St. Louis	MO	63101	800-642-7222	
Lykes Cartage Company Inc 8606 Wall St Bldg 19 *Web:* www.lykescartage.com	Austin	TX	78754	512-933-9060	
Lynnco Supply Chain Solutions Inc 2448 E 81St St Ste 2600 *Web:* lynnco-scs.com	Tulsa	OK	74137	918-664-5540	
Mackie Group 933 Bloor St W *Web:* www.mackiegroup.com	Oshawa	ON	L1J5Y7	905-728-2400	
Magellan Transport Logistics 2511 St Johns Bluff Rd Ste 107 *Web:* www.magellantransportlogistics.com	Jacksonville	FL	32246	904-620-0311	
Mammoet USA Inc 20525 Farm-to-Market Rd 521 *Web:* www.mammoet.com	Rosharon	TX	77583	281-369-2200	
MG Maher & Company Inc 365 Canal St Ste 1600 *Web:* www.mgmaher.com	New Orleans	LA	70130	504-581-3320	
Midwest Energy Resources Co 2400 W Winter St PO Box 787 *Web:* www.midwestenergy.com	Superior	WI	54880	715-392-9807	392-9137
Milgram & Company Ltd 400 - 645 Wellington *Web:* www.milgram.com	Montreal	QC	H3C0L1	514-288-2161	
Mobile One Courier Services Inc 1457 Miller Store Rd Ste 101 *Web:* www.mobileonecourier.com	Virginia Bch	VA	23455	757-622-9500	
Muir's Cartage Ltd 205 Doney Crescent *Web:* www.muirscartage.com	Concord	ON	L4K1P6	905-761-8251	

	City	State	ZIP	Phone	Fax
NEPW Logistics Inc 55 Logistics Dr *Web:* www.nepw.com	Auburn	ME	04210	207-333-3345	
Nex Transport Inc 13900 SR- 287 *Web:* nextransportinc.com	East Liberty	OH	43319	937-645-3761	642-3032
Oak Harbor Freight Lines Inc 1339 W Valley Hwy N PO Box 1469 *Web:* www.oakh.com	Auburn	WA	98071	253-288-8300	
OATS Inc 2501 Maguire Blvd Ste 101 *Web:* www.oatstransit.org	Columbia	MO	65201	573-443-4516	
Overseas Express Consolidators (Canada) Inc 725 Montee De Liesse *Web:* www.oecgroup.ca	Saint Laurent	QC	H4T1P5	514-905-1246	
Ozark Trucking Inc 4916 Dudley Blvd *Web:* www.ozarktruckinginc.com	Mcclellan	CA	95652	916-561-5400	
Paul's Hauling Ltd 250 Oak Point Hwy *Web:* www.paulshauling.com	Winnipeg	MB	R2R1V1	204-633-4330	
R d s Delivery Service Company Inc 436 E 11th St Frnt A *Web:* www.rdsdelivery.com	New York	NY	10009	212-260-5800	
RBS Bulk Systems Inc 610 Moraine Rd NE *Web:* www.rbsbulk.com	Calgary	AB	T2A2P3	403-248-1530	
Rigel Shipping Canada Inc 3521 Rt 134 *Web:* www.rigelcanada.com	Shediac Cape	NB	E4P3G6	506-533-9000	
Rockpoint Logistics LLC 901 Bilter Rd *Web:* www.rockpointlogistics.com	Aurora	IL	60502	630-801-2900	
Rowland Transportation Inc 40824 Messick Rd *Web:* www.rowlandtransportation.com	Dade City	FL	33525	352-567-2002	
Roy Miller Freight Lines LLC 3165 E Coronado St *Web:* www.roymiller.com	Anaheim	CA	92806	714-632-5511	
Scanwell Logistics (NYC) Inc 1995 Linden Blvd *Web:* www.scanwell.com	Elmont	NY	11003	516-285-8100	
SCI Logistics Ltd 180 Attwell Dr Ste 600 *Web:* www.scilogistics.com	Toronto	ON	M9W6A9	416-401-3011	
St Lawrence Seaway Management Corp 202 Pitt St *Web:* www.seaway.ca	Cornwall	ON	K6J3P7	613-932-5170	
Stone Belt Freight Lines Inc 101 W Dillman Rd *Web:* www.stonebeltfreight.com	Bloomington	IN	47403	812-824-6741	
Summit Travel Group 830 Menlo Ave Ste 110 *Web:* www.summittravelgroup.com	Menlo Park	CA	94025	650-373-4400	
Tidewater Barge Lines Inc 6305 NW Old Lower River Rd *TF:* 800-562-1607 ■ *Web:* www.tidewater.com	Vancouver	WA	98660	360-693-1491	694-8981
Transports J.M. Bernier Inc 75 rue des Erables *Web:* www.jmbernier.qc.ca	Metabetchouan-lac-a-la-croix	QC	G8G1P9	418-349-3496	
Tri-line Carriers L.p 235185 Ryan Rd *TF:* 800-661-9191 ■ *Web:* www.triline.ca	Rocky View	AB	T1X0K1	800-661-9191	
TST Solutions Inc 5200 Maingate Dr *Web:* www.tstoverland.com	Mississauga	ON	L4W1G5	905-625-7500	
Van-Kam Freightways Ltd 10155 Grace Rd *Web:* www.vankam.com	Surrey	BC	V3V3V7	604-582-7451	
Versacold International Corp 2115 Commissioner St *Web:* www.versacold.com	Vancouver	BC	V5L1A6	604-255-4656	
Warrior & Gulf Navigation LLC (WGN) 50 Viaduct Rd *Web:* www.tstarinc.com	Mobile	AL	36611	251-452-6000	
Wheels Group Inc 5090 Orbitor Dr *Web:* www.thewheelsgroup.com	Mississauga	ON	L4W5B5	905-602-2700	
Zenith Freight Lines LLC 210 Dehart Motor Terminal Rd SW *Web:* www.zenithcompanies.com	Conover	NC	28613	828-465-7036	

318 FRUIT GROWERS

SEE ALSO Crop Preparation Services p. 1724; Wines - Mfr p. 1865

318-1 Berry Growers

	City	State	ZIP	Phone	Fax
AD Makepeace Company Inc 158 Tihonet Rd *Web:* www.admakepeace.com	Wareham	MA	02571	508-295-1000	291-7453
Atlantic Blueberry Co 7201 Weymouth Rd *Web:* www.atlanticblueberry.com	Hammonton	NJ	08037	609-561-8600	561-5033
Brady Farms Inc 14786 Winans St	West Olive	MI	49460	616-842-3916	842-8357
California Giant Inc 75 Sakata Ln *Web:* www.calgiant.com	Watsonville	CA	95076	831-728-1773	728-0613
Cherryfield Foods Inc 320 Ridge Rd PO Box 128 *Web:* www.oxfordfrozenfoods.com	Cherryfield	ME	04622	207-546-7573	546-2713
Driscoll Strawberry Assoc Inc 345 Westridge Dr *TF:* 800-871-3333 ■ *Web:* www.driscolls.com	Watsonville	CA	95077	800-871-3333	
Fujii Farms Inc 2511 S Troutdale Rd PO Box 188 *Web:* fujiifarms.com	Troutdale	OR	97060	503-665-6659	661-2799
Habelman Bros Co Inc 10688 Estate Rd *Web:* www.habelmancranberries.com	Tomah	WI	54660	608-372-5353	
Jasper Wyman & Son PO Box 100 *TF Sales:* 800-341-1758 ■ *Web:* www.wymans.com	Milbridge	ME	04658	800-341-1758	
Michigan Blueberry Growers Assn 4726 County Rd 215 *Web:* www.blueberries.com	Grand Junction	MI	49056	269-434-6791	434-6997
Naturipe Berry Growers PO Box 4280 *Web:* www.naturipeberrygrowers.com	Salinas	CA	93912	831-722-2430	728-9398
Reenders Blueberries Farms 14079 168th Ave *Web:* www.reendersblueberryfarms.com	Grand Haven	MI	49417	616-842-5238	842-0890
Reiter Affiliated Cos 1767 San Juan Rd *Web:* berry.net	Aromas	CA	93030	805-483-1000	
Sandy Farms 34500 SE Hwy 211	Boring	OR	97009	503-668-4525	668-8813
Sunrise Growers 701 W Kimberly St Ste 210 *Web:* www.sunrisegrowers.com	Placentia	CA	92870	714-630-2050	630-0215

318-2 Citrus Growers

	City	State	ZIP	Phone	Fax
A Duda & Sons Inc 1200 Duda Trail *Web:* www.duda.com	Oviedo	FL	32765	407-365-2111	365-2147
Alico Inc (ALCO) 10070 Daniels Interstate Ct Ste 100 *NASDAQ: ALCO* ■ *Web:* www.alicoinc.com	Fort Myers	FL	33913	863-675-2966	
Ben Hill Griffin Inc 700 S SR 17 PO Box 127	Frostproof	FL	33843	863-635-2251	635-7333
Blue Banner Company Inc 2601 Third St *Web:* pe.com	Riverside	CA	92502	951-686-2422	
Corona College Heights Orange & Lemon Assn 8000 Lincoln Ave *Web:* www.cchcitrus.com	Riverside	CA	92504	951-688-1811	689-5115
ECA Edinburg Citrus Association 401 W Chapin St *Web:* edinburgcitrus.com	Edinburg	TX	78541	956-383-2743	
Egan Bernard & Co 1900 Old Dixie Hwy **Fax Area Code:* 772 ■ *TF:* 800-327-6676 ■ *Web:* www.dneworld.com	Fort Pierce	FL	34946	800-327-6676	465-1181*
G & S Packing 16600 Florida 25	Weirsdale	FL	32195	352-821-2251	
Graves Bros Co 2770 Indian River Blvd Ste 201 *Web:* www.gravesbrotherscompany.com	Vero Beach	FL	32960	772-562-3886	562-3565
Highland Exchange Service Co-op 5916 Waverly Rd	Waverly	FL	33877	863-439-3661	439-5383
Leroy E Smith's Sons Inc 4776 Old Dixie Hwy **Fax:* Orders ■ *Web:* leroysmith.com	Vero Beach	FL	32967	772-567-3421	567-8428*
Limoneira Co 1141 Cummings Rd *NASDAQ: LMNR* ■ *TF:* 866-321-8953 ■ *Web:* www.limoneira.com	Santa Paula	CA	93060	805-525-5541	525-8211
Nelson & Co Inc 110 E Broadway	Oviedo	FL	32765	407-365-6631	
Paramount Citrus Assn 1901 S Lexington St *Web:* www.paramountcitrus.com	Delano	CA	93215	661-720-2400	720-2403
Saticoy Lemon Assn 7560 E Bristol Rd *Web:* www.saticoylemon.com	Ventura	CA	93003	805-654-6500	654-6587
Silver Springs Citrus Inc 25411 N Mare Ave *TF:* 800-940-2277 ■ *Web:* silverspringscitrus.com	Howey in the Hills	FL	34737	352-324-2101	324-2033
Southern Gardens Citrus 1820 Country Rd 833 *Web:* southerngardens.com	Clewiston	FL	33440	863-983-3030	983-3060
Sunkist Growers Inc 14130 Riverside Dr **Fax:* PR ■ *Web:* www.sunkist.com	Sherman Oaks	CA	91423	818-986-4800	379-7511*
Villa Park Orchards Assn 960 Third St *Web:* vpoa.net	Fillmore	CA	93016	805-524-0411	524-4286

318-3 Deciduous Tree Fruit Growers

	City	State	ZIP	Phone	Fax
Auvil Fruit Co Inc 21902 SR 97 *Web:* www.auvilfruit.com	Orondo	WA	98843	509-784-1033	784-1712
Bertuccio Farms 2410 Airline Hwy *Web:* www.thefarmbertuccios.com	Hollister	CA	95023	831-636-0821	
Big Six Farms 5575 Zenith Mill Rd	Fort Valley	GA	31030	478-825-7504	825-1194
Blue Bird Inc 10135 Mill Rd *Web:* bluebirdpears.net	Peshastin	WA	98847	509-548-1700	548-0288
Blue Mountain Growers Inc 231 E Broadway Ave	Milton-Freewater	OR	97862	541-938-3391	938-5304
Blue Star Growers Inc 200 Blue Star Rd	Cashmere	WA	98815	509-782-2922	
Borton & Sons Inc 2550 Borton Rd *Web:* www.bortonfruit.com	Yakima	WA	98903	509-966-3905	966-5131
Broetje Orchards 1111 Fishhook Pk Rd *Web:* broetjeorchards.com	Prescott	WA	99348	509-749-2217	749-2354
Capital Agricultural Property Services Inc 801 Warrenville Rd Ste 150 *TF:* 800-243-2060 ■ *Web:* www.capitalag.com	Lisle	IL	60532	630-434-9150	434-9343
Chappell Farms Inc 166 Boiling Springs Rd *Web:* www.chappellfarms.com	Barnwell	SC	29812	803-584-2565	584-3676
Chelan Fruit Marketing 5 Howser Rd *Web:* www.chelanfresh.com	Chelan	WA	98816	509-682-4252	682-2651
Cowiche Growers Inc 251 Cowiche City Rd *Web:* www.cowichegrowers.com	Cowiche	WA	98923	509-678-4168	678-5678
Evans Fruit Farm 200 Cowiche City Rd PO Box 70 *Web:* www.evansfruitco.com	Cowiche	WA	98923	509-678-4127	678-5450
EW Brandt & Sons Inc (EWB) 561 Ragan Rd *Web:* rembrandtfruit.com/	Wapato	WA	98951	509-877-3193	877-2737
Fagundes Agribusiness 8700 Fargo Ave *Web:* fagundes.net	Hanford	CA	93230	559-582-2000	582-0683
Fowler Packing Company Inc 8570 S Cedar Ave *Web:* fowlerpacking.com	Fresno	CA	93725	559-834-5911	834-5272
Henggeler Packing Company Inc 6730 Elmore Rd PO Box 313	Fruitland	ID	83619	208-452-4212	452-5416
Highland Fruit Growers Inc 8304 Wide Hollow Rd	Yakima	WA	98908	509-966-3990	966-3992
Hudson River Fruit Distributors 65 Old Indian Rd *Web:* hudsonriverfruit.com	Milton	NY	12547	800-640-2774	

Company	City	State	Zip	Phone	Fax
Ito Packing Company Inc 707 W S Ave PO Box 707 *Web:* itopack.com	Reedley	CA	93654	559-638-2531	
McDougal & Sons 305 Olds Stn Rd	Wenatchee	WA	98801	509-662-2136	
Mt Konocti Growers Inc 2550 Big Vly Rd PO Box 365 *Web:* mtkonoctiwines.com	Kelseyville	CA	95451	707-279-4213	
National Fruit Product Co Inc 701 Fairmont Ave PO Box 2040 **Fax:* Sales ■ *TF:* 800-655-4022 ■ *Web:* www.whitehousefoods.com	Winchester	VA	22601	540-723-9614	665-4671*
Orchard View Farms Inc 4055 Skyline Rd *Web:* www.orchardviewfarms.com	The Dalles	OR	97058	541-298-4496	298-1808
Oregon Cherry Growers Inc 1520 Woodrow NE *TF:* 800-367-2536 ■ *Web:* www.orcherry.com	Salem	OR	97301	503-364-8421	362-2647
P-R Farms Inc 2917 E Shepherd Ave *Web:* www.prfarms.com	Clovis	CA	93619	559-299-0201	299-7292
Rice Fruit Co 2760 Carlisle Rd PO Box 66 *TF:* 800-627-3359 ■ *Web:* www.ricefruit.com	Gardners	PA	17324	717-677-8131	677-9842
Stadelman Fruit LLC 111 Meade St PO BOX 445 *Web:* www.stadelmanfruit.com	Zillah	WA	98953	509-829-5145	
Stemilt Growers Inc PO Box 2779 *Web:* www.stemilt.com	Wenatchee	WA	98807	509-663-1451	665-4376
Sun Valley Packing Co 7381 Ave 432 PO Box 351	Reedley	CA	93654	559-591-1515	591-1616
Sun World International Inc 16350 Drive Rd *Web:* www.sun-world.com	Bakersfield	CA	93308	661-392-5000	
Symms Fruit Ranch Inc 14068 Sunny Slope Rd *Web:* symmsfruit.com	Caldwell	ID	83607	208-459-4821	459-6932
Thiara Bros Orchards 1205 Kibby Rd	Merced	CA	95340	209-383-6126	383-1012
Titan Farms Five RW Du Bose Rd *Web:* www.titanfarms.com	Ridge Spring	SC	29129	803-685-5381	685-5885
Twin Hill Ranch 1689 Pleasant Hill Rd *Web:* www.twinhillranch.com	Sebastopol	CA	95472	707-823-2815	823-6268
Valley View Packing Company Inc 7547 Sawtelle Ave *Web:* www.valleyviewpacking.com	Yuba City	CA	95991	530-673-7356	673-9432

318-4 Fruit Growers (Misc)

Company	City	State	Zip	Phone	Fax
Brooks Tropicals Inc 18400 SW 256th St PO Box 900160 **Fax:* Sales ■ *TF:* 800-327-4833 ■ *Web:* www.brookstropicals.com	Homestead	FL	33090	305-247-3544	246-5827*
Calavo Growers Inc 1141-A Cummings Rd *NASDAQ: CVGW* ■ *TF:* 800-654-8758 ■ *Web:* www.calavo.com	Santa Paula	CA	93060	805-525-1245	921-3287
Chiquita Brands International Inc 250 E Fifth St *NYSE: CQB* ■ *Web:* chiquita.com	Cincinnati	OH	45202	513-784-8000	784-8030
Del Monte Fresh Produce Co 241 Sevilla Ave *TF Cust Svc:* 800-950-3683 ■ *Web:* www.freshdelmonte.com	Coral Gables	FL	33134	305-520-8400	567-0320
Dole Food Company Inc One Dole Dr *NYSE: DOLE* ■ **Fax:* Hum Res ■ *TF:* 800-232-8888 ■ *Web:* www.dole.com	Westlake Village	CA	91362	818-879-6600	874-4893*
Growers Express LLC 1219 Abbott St PO Box 948 **Fax:* Sales ■ *Web:* www.growersexpress.com	Salinas	CA	93901	831-757-9700	422-4246*
Jewel Date Co 84675 60th Ave *Web:* www.shieldsdategarden.com	Thermal	CA	92274	760-399-4474	399-4476
Martori Farms 7332 E Butherus Dr *Web:* www.martorifarms.com	Scottsdale	AZ	85260	480-998-1444	
Maui Land & Pineapple Company Inc 120 Kane St PO Box 187 *Web:* www.mauiland.com	Kahului	HI	96733	808-877-3351	871-0953
Mission Produce Inc 2500 Vineyard Ave Ste 300 *TF:* 800-549-3420 ■ *Web:* www.missionpro.com	Oxnard	CA	93036	805-981-3650	981-3660
Mount Dora Farms 16398 Jacinto Ft Blvd *Web:* www.mountdorafarms.com	Houston	TX	77015	713-821-7439	821-7342
Valley Fig Growers 2028 S Third St *Web:* www.valleyfig.com	Fresno	CA	93702	559-237-3893	237-3898
Van Drunen Farms 300 W Sixth St *Web:* www.vandrunenfarms.com	Momence	IL	60954	815-472-3100	472-3850

318-5 Grape Vineyards

Company	City	State	Zip	Phone	Fax
Del Rey Packing 5287 S Del Rey Ave *Web:* delreypacking.com	Del Rey	CA	93616	559-888-2031	888-2715
Giumarra Vineyards Corp 1601 E Olympic Blvd Bldg 400 *Web:* giumarra.com	Los Angeles	CA	93220	213-627-2900	628-4878
John Kautz Farms 5490 E Bear Oak Rd	Lodi	CA	95240	209-334-4786	
Lion Raisins 9500 S De Wols Ave PO Box 1350 *Web:* www.lionraisins.com	Selma	CA	93662	559-834-6677	834-6622
National Grape Co-op Assn Inc Two S Portage St	Westfield	NY	14787	716-326-5200	326-5494
National Raisin Co PO Box 219 *Web:* www.nationalraisin.com	Fowler	CA	93625	559-834-5981	834-1055
Niven Family Wine Estates 4915 Orcutt Rd *Web:* www.baileyana.com	San Luis Obispo	CA	93401	805-597-8200	781-3635
Pacific Agri Lands Inc 5206 Hammett Rd	Modesto	CA	95358	209-545-1623	
Scheid Vineyards Inc 305 Hilltown Rd *Web:* www.scheidvineyards.com	Salinas	CA	93908	831-455-9990	455-9998
Spring Mountain Vineyards 2805 Spring Mtn Rd *TF:* 877-769-4637 ■ *Web:* www.springmtn.com	Saint Helena	CA	94574	707-967-4188	963-2753
Sun Valley Packing Co 7381 Ave 432 PO Box 351	Reedley	CA	93654	559-591-1515	591-1616
Sun World International Inc 16350 Drive Rd *Web:* www.sun-world.com	Bakersfield	CA	93308	661-392-5000	
Symms Fruit Ranch Inc 14068 Sunny Slope Rd *Web:* symmsfruit.com	Caldwell	ID	83607	208-459-4821	459-6932
Vino Farms Inc 1377 E Lodi Ave	Lodi	CA	95240	209-334-6975	369-8765
Windsor Vineyards 205 Concourse Blvd *TF:* 800-289-9463 ■ *Web:* www.windsorvineyards.com	Santa Rosa	CA	95403	800-289-9463	

319 FUEL DEALERS

Company	City	State	Zip	Phone	Fax
AC & T Company Inc 11535 Hopewell Rd *TF:* 800-458-3835 ■ *Web:* www.acandt.com	Hagerstown	MD	21740	301-582-2700	582-2719
Aero ALL-GAS Company Inc, The 3150 Main St *Web:* www.allgas.com	Hartford	CT	06120	860-278-2376	
Alvin Hollis & Co One Hollis St *TF:* 800-649-5090 ■ *Web:* www.alvinhollis.com	South Weymouth	MA	02190	781-335-2100	335-6134
AmeriGas Inc 460 N Gulph Rd *Web:* www.amerigas.com	King of Prussia	PA	19406	610-337-7000	768-7647
AmeriGas Partners LP 460 N Gulph Rd *NYSE: APU* ■ *TF:* 800-427-4968 ■ *Web:* www.amerigas.com	King of Prussia	PA	19406	610-337-7000	992-3259
AOC Holding Company Inc 4506 State 359 and Loop 20 *Web:* www.argpetro.com	Laredo	TX	78042	956-722-5251	
Apollo Oil LLC 1175 Early Dr *TF:* 800-473-5823 ■ *Web:* www.apollooil.com	Winchester	KY	40391	859-744-5444	745-5823
Atlanta Fuel Co 2324 Donald Lee Hollowell Pkwy *Web:* atlantafuel.com	Atlanta	GA	30318	404-792-9888	
Automotive Service Inc 910 Mtn Home Rd PO Box 2157 *TF:* 800-383-3421 ■ *Web:* berkspottstownheatingoil.com	Sinking Spring	PA	19608	610-678-3421	678-3515
Axmen 7655 Us Hwy 10 W *Web:* www.axmen.com	Missoula	MT	59808	406-728-7020	
Barrett Oil Inc 2126 W Bay St *Web:* www.barrettoil.com	Savannah	GA	31415	912-234-7231	
Berico Fuels Inc 2200 E Bessemer Ave *Web:* berico.com	Greensboro	NC	27405	336-273-8663	
Best Aire LLC 3648 Rockland Cir *Web:* www.best-aire.com	Millbury	OH	43447	419-726-0055	
Blossman Gas Inc 809 Washington Ave **Fax Area Code:* 228 ■ *TF:* 800-256-7762 ■ *Web:* www.blossmangas.com	Ocean Springs	MS	39564	888-256-7762	875-9307*
Bowden Oil Company Inc PO Box 145 *TF:* 800-280-0393 ■ *Web:* www.bowdenoil.com	Sylacauga	AL	35150	256-245-5611	249-2975
Bowers & Burrows Oil Co 213 Young St *Web:* bbfuels.net	Henderson	NC	27536	252-492-0181	
Burns & McBride Inc 240 S DuPont Hwy *Web:* www.burnsandmcbride.com	New Castle	DE	19720	302-656-5110	
Carroll Independent Fuel Co 2700 Loch Raven Rd *TF:* 800-834-8590 ■ *Web:* www.carrollhomeservices.com	Baltimore	MD	21218	410-235-1070	235-3842
Cheshire Oil Company Inc 678 Marlborough St PO Box 586 *Web:* www.cheshireoil.com	Keene	NH	03431	603-352-0001	
Columbia Utilities Heating Corp 1350 60 St *Web:* www.columbiautilities.com	Brooklyn	NY	11219	718-851-6655	
Consumer Oil & Supply Co 100 Railroad St	Braymer	MO	64624	660-645-2721	
Cota & Cota Inc Four Green St *Web:* www.cotaoil.com	Bellows Falls	VT	05101	802-463-0000	
Crus Oil Inc 2260 SW Temple *Web:* crusoil.com	Salt Lake City	UT	84101	801-466-8783	
D F Richard Inc 124 Broadway *Web:* www.dfrichard.com	Dover	NH	03821	603-742-2020	
Davis Oil Co 904 Jernigan St *Web:* www.davis-company.com	Perry	GA	31069	478-987-2443	
DDLC Energy 410 Bank St *Web:* ddlcenergy.com	New London	CT	06320	860-271-2020	271-2050
Delta Western Inc 420 L St Ste 101 *Web:* www.deltawestern.com	Anchorage	AK	99501	907-276-2688	
District Petroleum Products Inc 1814 River Rd Ste 100 *Web:* hymiler.com	Huron	OH	44839	419-433-8373	433-9646
E E Wine Inc 9108 Centreville Rd *Web:* www.eewine.com	Manassas	VA	20110	703-368-6568	
Ed Staub & Sons Petroleum Inc 1301 Esplanade Ave *TF:* 800-435-3835 ■ *Web:* www.edstaub.com	Klamath Falls	OR	97601	800-435-3835	
Energy Petroleum Co 2130 Kienlen Ave *Web:* www.energypetroleum.com	St. Louis	MO	63121	314-383-3700	
Energy Transfer Equity LP 3738 Oak Lawn Ave *NYSE: ETE* ■ *Web:* www.energytransfer.com	Dallas	TX	75219	214-981-0700	981-0703
Energy Transfer Partners LP 3738 Oak Lawn Ave *NYSE: ETP* ■ *Web:* www.energytransfer.com	Dallas	TX	75219	214-981-0700	981-0703
Essex Oil Co 2174 Springfield Ave *Web:* essexoil.com	Vauxhall	NJ	07088	973-372-7700	
Farm & Home Oil Co 3115 State Rd *Web:* www.suburbanpropane.com	Telford	PA	18969	800-776-7263	
Farmers Union Oil Co of Southern Valley (FUOSV) 204 S Front St *Web:* www.fuosv.com	Fairmount	ND	58030	701-474-5440	474-5445
FC Haab Company Inc 2314 Market St *TF:* 800-486-5663 ■ *Web:* www.fchaab.com	Philadelphia	PA	19103	215-563-0800	563-9448
Felicia Oil Company Inc R78 Commercial St	Gloucester	MA	01930	978-283-3808	
Ferrellgas Partners LP 1 Liberty Plaza *NYSE: FGP* ■ *TF:* 888-337-7355 ■ *Web:* www.ferrellgas.com	Liberty	MO	64068	816-792-1600	792-7985
First Corporate Sedans Inc 60 E 42nd St Ste 2424 *TF:* 800-473-8876 ■ *Web:* www.fcsny.com	New York	NY	10165	212-972-2282	286-9130
Fred M Schildwachter & Sons Inc 1400 Ferris Pl *TF:* 800-642-3646 ■ *Web:* www.schildwachteroil.com	Bronx	NY	10461	718-828-2500	828-3661

				Phone	Fax
G. A. Bove & Sons Inc 76 Railroad St *Web:* www.bovefuels.com	Mechanicville	NY	12118	518-664-5111	
Gary Jet Center Inc 5401 Industrial Hwy *Web:* www.garyjetcenter.com	Gary	IN	46406	219-944-1210	
Gas Inc 77 Jefferson Pkwy *Web:* www.gasinc.net	Newnan	GA	30263	770-502-8800	502-8833
Gateway Energy Services Corp 400 Rella Blvd Ste 300 *Web:* www.gesc.com	Montebello	NY	10901	845-503-5100	
Glassmere Fuel Service Inc 1967 Saxonburg Blvd *TF:* 800-235-9054 ■ *Web:* www.glassmerefuel.com	Tarentum	PA	15084	724-265-4646	265-3588
Heritagenergy Inc 625 Sawkill Rd *Web:* www.heritagenergy.com	Kingston	NY	12401	845-336-2000	
Kingston Oil Supply Corp 2926 Rt 32 N *TF:* 800-755-6726 ■ *Web:* www.koscocomfort.com	Saugerties	NY	12477	845-247-2200	246-0207
Kolkhorst Petroleum Co 1685 E Washington PO Box 410 *TF:* 800-548-6671 ■ *Web:* www.kolkhorst.com	Navasota	TX	77868	936-825-6868	870-3355
Landmark Industries Ltd 11111 Wilcrest Green Dr Ste 100 PO Box 42374 *Web:* www.landmarkindustries.com	Houston	TX	77042	713-789-0310	789-2907
Lansing Ice & Fuel Co 911 Ctr St *Web:* propanefuellansing.com	Lansing	MI	48906	517-372-3850	485-9482
Lawes Coal Company Inc Sycamore Ave PO Box 258 *Web:* www.lawescompany.com	Shrewsbury	NJ	07702	732-741-6300	
Lazzari Fuel Company LLC 11 Industrial Way *Web:* www.lazzari.com	Brisbane	CA	94005	415-467-2970	
Lewis & Raulerson Inc 1759 State St PO Box 289 *Web:* www.lewisandraulerson.com	Waycross	GA	31501	912-283-5951	283-8281
Lincoln Land Oil Co PO Box 4307 *TF:* 800-238-4912 ■ *Web:* www.lincolnlandoil.com	Springfield	IL	62708	217-523-5050	523-5001
Manitoba Agricultural Services Corp Unit 100 - 1525 First St S *Web:* www.masc.mb.ca	Brandon	MB	R7A7A1	204-726-6850	
Martin Resource Management Corp (MRMC) PO Box 191 *TF:* 888-334-7473 ■ *Web:* www.martinmidstream.com	Kilgore	TX	75663	903-983-6200	983-6271
Metro Energy Group 1011 Hudson Ave *TF:* 800-951-2941 ■ *Web:* www.metroenergynj.com	Ridgefield	NJ	07657	201-941-3470	941-6854
Mirabito Fuel Group Inc 49 Ct St PO Box 5306 *TF:* 800-934-9480 ■ *Web:* mirabito.com	Binghamton	NY	13902	607-352-2800	584-5130
Mitchell Fuel Company Inc 1209 Sullivan Ave *Web:* www.mitchellfuel.com	South Windsor	CT	06074	860-644-2561	
Mitchell Supreme Fuel Co 532 Freeman St *TF:* 800-832-7090 ■ *Web:* www.supremeenergyinc.com	Orange	NJ	07050	973-678-1800	672-0148
Mutual Liquid Gas & Equipment Co Inc 17117 S Broadway St **Fax Area Code:* 310 ■ *TF:* 800-633-3574 ■ *Web:* www.mutualpropane.com	Gardena	CA	90248	323-321-3771	515-2633*
Nebraska Iowa Supply Company Inc 1160 Lincoln St PO Box 368 *Web:* www.neiasupply.com	Blair	NJ	68008	402-426-2171	
Noonan Energy Corp 86 Robbins Rd *Web:* www.noonanenergy.com	Springfield	MA	01104	413-734-7396	
O'Rourke Petroleum Inc 223 McCarty Dr *Web:* www.orpp.com	Houston	TX	77029	713-672-4500	
Osage Exploration & Development Inc 2445 Fifth Ave Ste 310 *Web:* www.osageexploration.com	San Diego	CA	92101	619-677-3956	
Palmer Gas Company Inc 13 Hall Farm Rd *Web:* www.palmergasco.com	Atkinson	NH	03811	603-898-7986	
Parman Energy Corp 7101 Cockrill Bend Blvd *Web:* www.parmanenergy.com	Nashville	TN	37209	615-350-7920	
Petroleum Marketers Inc 3000 Ogden Rd *Web:* www.petroleummarketers.com	Roanoke	VA	24014	540-772-4900	772-6900
Phelps Sungas Inc 224 Cross Rd *Web:* sungas.com	Geneva	NY	14456	315-789-3285	
Planters Oil Inc 217 S Main St	Fitzgerald	GA	31750	229-423-2231	
Polsinello Fuels Inc 41 Riverside Ave *TF:* 800-334-5823 ■ *Web:* www.polsinello.com	Rensselaer	NY	12144	518-463-0084	463-4086
Prairie Pride Co-op 1100 E Main St *Web:* www.prairiepridecoop.com	Marshall	MN	56258	507-532-9686	
Range LP Gas 1613 E Camp St *Web:* rangelp.com	Ely	MN	55731	218-365-8888	
Rawhide Chemoil Inc 2650 N Rawhide Dr *Web:* www.rawhidechemoil.com	Fremont	NE	68025	402-721-7601	
Reinhardt Corp 3919 State Hwy 23 *Web:* www.reinhardthomeheating.com	West Oneonta	NY	13861	607-432-6633	
Ricochet Fuel Distributors Inc 1201 Royal Pkwy *Web:* www.ricochetfuel.com	Euless	TX	76040	817-268-5910	
River Bend Business Products 304 Downtown Plz *Web:* www.riverbendbusiness.com	Fairmont	MN	56031	507-235-3800	
Robison Oil Corp 500 Executive Blvd *Web:* www.robisonoil.com	Elmsford	NY	10523	914-345-5700	345-5792
Rose Brick & Materials Inc 918 Oliver Plow Ct *Web:* www.rosebrick.com	South Bend	IN	46601	574-234-2133	
Santoro Oil Company Inc 101 Corliss St *Web:* www.santorooil.com	Providence	RI	02904	401-942-5000	
Sharp Energy Inc 648 Ocean Hwy **Fax Area Code:* 410 ■ *Web:* www.sharpenergy.com	Pocomoke City	MD	21851	888-742-7740	957-0716*
Shipley Energy 415 Norway St **Fax Area Code:* 800 ■ *TF:* 800-839-1849 ■ *Web:* www.shipleyenergy.com	York	PA	17403	717-848-4100	839-1849*
Southeast Fuels Inc 604 Green Vly Rd Ste 207 *Web:* www.southeastfuels.com	Greensboro	NC	27408	336-854-1106	547-8720
Spencer Oil Company Inc 16410 Common Rd *Web:* spenceroilcompany.com	Roseville	MI	48066	586-775-5022	776-8264
Star Gas Partners LP 2187 Atlantic St *NYSE:* SGU ■ *TF:* 877-237-3063 ■ *Web:* www.Star-Gas.com	Stamford	CT	06902	203-328-7310	328-7470
Stripes Convenience Stores 4525 Ayers St *NYSE:* SUSS ■ *TF:* 800-569-3585 ■ *Web:* www.susser.com	Corpus Christi	TX	78415	361-884-2464	884-2494
Suburban Propane LP One Suburban Plz 240 Rt 10 W PO Box 206 *TF:* 800-776-7263 ■ *Web:* www.suburbanpropane.com	Whippany	NJ	07981	973-887-5300	
Super Save Group 19395 Langley By-pass *Web:* www.supersave.ca	Surrey	BC	V3S6K1	604-533-4423	
Tiger Fuel Company Inc 200 Carlton Rd PO Box 1607 *Web:* www.tigerfuel.com	Charlottesville	VA	22902	434-293-6157	
Tropigas De Puerto Rico Inc Urb Industrial Luchetti Calle C Lote 30 *Web:* www.tropigasprogas.com	Bayamon	PR	00961	787-641-8002	
Western Natural Gas Co 2960 Strickland St *Web:* www.westernnaturalgas.com	Jacksonville	FL	32254	904-387-3511	387-6034
Wever Petroleum Inc 100 S Hudson St *Web:* www.weverpetroleum.com	Mechanicville	NY	12118	518-664-7331	
WH Riley & Son Inc 35 Chestnut St *Web:* www.whriley.com	North Attleboro	MA	02760	508-699-4651	699-7712
William G. Satterlee & Sons Inc 12475 Route 119 Hwy N *Web:* www.satterleefuel.com	Rochester Mills	PA	15771	724-397-2400	
William R Peterson Oil Co 12 W Rd PO Box 31 *Web:* portland.ct.phonepagesinc.com	Marlborough	CT	06480	860-295-9200	
Wilson of Wallingford Inc 221 Rogers Ln PO Box 185 *TF:* 888-607-2621 ■ *Web:* www.wilsonoilandpropane.com	Wallingford	PA	19086	610-566-7600	566-7608
Wo Stinson & Son Ltd 4726 Bank St *Web:* www.wostinson.com	Ottawa	ON	K1T3W7	613-822-7400	
Woodford Oil Company Inc 13th St PO Box 567 *Web:* www.woodfordoil.com	Elkins	WV	26241	304-636-2688	
Woodruff Energy 73 Water St PO Box 777 *TF:* 800-557-1121 ■ *Web:* www.woodruffenergy.com	Bridgeton	NJ	08302	856-455-1111	455-4085
Worley & Obetz Inc 85 White Oak Rd PO Box 429 *TF:* 800-697-6891 ■ *Web:* www.worleyobetz.com	Manheim	PA	17545	717-665-6891	665-2867

320 FUND-RAISING SERVICES

				Phone	Fax
1-Stop Translation USA LLC 3700 Wilshire Blvd Ste 630 *Web:* www.1stoptr.com	Los Angeles	CA	90010	213-480-0011	
A All Languages Ltd 421 Bloor St E Ste 306 *Web:* www.alllanguages.com	Toronto	ON	M4W3T1	647-427-8308	
ABS Direct Inc 4724 Enterprise Way *Web:* www.absdirectinc.com	Modesto	CA	95356	209-545-6090	
ACCU Translations Three Mays Crescent *Web:* www.accutranslation.com	Waterdown	ON	L0R2H4	905-639-0323	
Accuimage LLC 2807 Biloxi Ave *Web:* www.accuimagellc.com	Nashville	TN	37204	615-242-7226	
Ackroo Inc 436 Hazeldean Rd Ste 202 *Web:* ackroo.com	Kanata	ON	K2L1T9	613-599-2396	
Active Concepts Inc 389 Fifth Ave Ste 506 *Web:* www.activeconceptsinc.com	New York	NY	10016	212-679-4994	
Advantage Fund Raising Consulting Inc 208 Passaic Ave *Web:* sos.wa.gov	Fairfield	NJ	07004	973-575-9196	575-5614
Air Compressor Solutions 3001 Kermit Hwy *Web:* acsir.com	Odessa	TX	79764	432-335-5900	
Alqimi Technology Solutions Inc 9210 Corporate Blvd Ste 150 *Web:* www.absicorp.com	Rockville	MD	20850	301-337-0100	
Amerilist Inc 978 Route 45 Ste L2 *Web:* www.amerilist.com	Pomona	NY	10970	845-362-6737	
APC Integrated Services Inc 770 SPIRIT OF SAINT LOUIS Blvd *TF:* 888-294-7886 ■ *Web:* www.apcisg.com	CHESTERFIELD	MO	63005	888-294-7886	
Apelles LLC 3700 Corporate Dr Ste 240 *Web:* www.apellesnow.com	Columbus	OH	43231	614-899-7322	
Aq Technologies 10 W Elm St Apt 1302 *Web:* www.aqtechnologies.com	Chicago	IL	60610	312-867-5400	
Artex Risk Solutions Inc Two Pierce Pl *Web:* www.artexrisk.com	Itasca	IL	60143	630-694-5050	
Assured Document Destruction Inc 8050 Arville St Ste 105 *Web:* shreddinglv.com	Las Vegas	NV	89139	702-614-0001	
Avantpage Translations 1138 Villaverde Ln *Web:* www.avantpage.com	Davis	CA	95618	530-750-2040	
Barchart.com Inc 330 S Wells Ste 618 *Web:* www.barchart.com	Chicago	IL	60606	312-554-8122	
Barkley Kalpak Associates Inc 315 W 39th St Rm 608 *Web:* www.bka.net	New York	NY	10018	212-947-1502	
Barnet Associates LLC Two Round Lk Rd *TF:* 888-827-7070 ■ *Web:* www.barnetassociates.com	Ridgefield	CT	06877	888-827-7070	
Barton Cotton Inc 3030 Waterview Ave **Fax Area Code:* 410 ■ *TF:* 800-638-4652 ■ *Web:* www.bartoncotton.com	Baltimore	MD	21230	800-348-1102	536-0491*
Bayaud Industries Inc 333 W Bayaud Ave *Web:* www.bayaudenterprises.org	Denver	CO	80223	303-830-6885	
BBH Consulting Inc 1669 East 1400 South Ste 110 *Web:* www.bbhconsulting.com	Clearfield	UT	84015	801-779-4405	
Be Media 655 Hawaii St *Web:* bemedia.com	El Segundo	CA	90245	310-725-8500	

Phone Fax

BeenVerified Inc 307 Fifth Ave 16th Fl .... New York NY 10016 888-579-5910
TF: 888-579-5910 ■ *Web:* www.beenverified.com

Bentz Whaley Flessner 7251 Ohms Ln .... Minneapolis MN 55439 952-921-0111 921-0109
TF: 800-921-0111 ■ *Web:* www.bwf.com

Bold Ideas 645 N Michigan Ave Ste 800 .... Chicago IL 60611 312-280-0440
Web: bold-ideas.com

Brakeley Briscoe Inc
322 W Bellevue Ave Ste 204 .... San Mateo CA 94402 650-344-8883
TF: 800-416-3086 ■ *Web:* www.brakeleybriscoe.com

C12 Group LLC, The 4101 Piedmont Pkwy .... Greensboro NC 27410 336-841-7100
Web: www.c12group.com

Cargill Assoc Inc 4701 Altamesa Blvd .... Fort Worth TX 76133 817-292-9374
TF: 800-433-2233 ■ *Web:* www.cargillassociates.com

Carver & Associates Inc 4177 Northeast Expy .... Atlanta GA 30340 770-446-2677
Web: www.carverassoc.com

Center Partners Inc 4401 Innovation Dr .... Fort Collins CO 80525 970-206-9000
Web: www.qualfon.com

Central Ontario Healthcare Procurement Alliance
95 Mural St .... Richmond Hill ON L4B3G2 905-886-5319
Web: www.cohpa.ca

Changing Our World Inc
220 E 42nd St Fifth Fl .... New York NY 10017 212-499-0866
Web: www.changingourworld.com

Chapman Cubine Adams + Hussey
2000 15th St N Ste 550 .... Arlington VA 22201 703-248-0025 248-0029
Web: www.ccah.com

Chapter IV Investors
301 S Tryon St Ste 1850 .... Charlotte NC 28202 704-644-4070
Web: www.chapterivinvestors.com

Clayton Capital Partners
8112 Maryland Ave Ste 250 .... St. Louis MO 63105 314-725-9939
Web: claytoncapitalpartners.com

Cohen Group, The 1200 19th St Nw Ste 400 .... Washington DC 20036 202-863-7200
Web: www.cohengroup.net

Compass iTech LLC
4800 N Federal Hwy Ste A306 .... Boca Raton FL 33431 561-756-8285
Web: www.compassprofusion.com

ConsultKAP Inc
3115 Woodchuck Way SW Dept 101 .... Conyers GA 30094 770-918-9390
Web: www.consultkap.com

Content Solutions 1413 E Mckinney St .... Denton TX 76209 940-384-9407
Web: www.yourcontentsolutions.com

Cox North America Inc 8181 Coleman Rd .... Haslett MI 48840 517-339-3330
Web: www.cox-applicators.com

Cramer & Assoc
Hodge Cramer & Assoc 555 Metro Pl N Ste 500 ...... Dublin OH 43017 614-766-4483 568-7685
Web: www.cramerfundraising.com

Creative Sign Designs
12801 Commodity Pl Ste 200 .... Tampa FL 33626 813-818-7100
Web: www.creativesigndesigns.com

Crosbie & Company Inc
150 King St W Sun Life Financial Tower
15th Fl .... Toronto ON M5H1J9 416-362-7726
Web: www.crosbieco.com

CrowdFlower Inc 2111 Mission St Ste 302 .... San Francisco CA 94110 415-471-1920
Web: www.crowdflower.com

Crown Consulting Inc 1400 Key Blvd Ste 1100 .... Arlington VA 22209 703-650-0663
Web: www.crownci.com

CSA Group 178 Rexdale Blvd .... Toronto ON M9W1R3 416-747-4000
Web: www.csagroup.org

Cull Martin & Assoc Inc 320 N Jensen Rd .... Vestal NY 13850 607-722-3884 722-4264
Web: www.cullmartin.com

Cummings Co Inc 3500 Fairmount St Ste 504 .... Dallas TX 75219 214-526-1772 665-9590
Web: www.cummingsco.com

Customer Value Partners Inc
3701 Pender Dr Ste 200 .... Fairfax VA 22030 703-345-9100
Web: www.cvpcorp.com

Cygnus Expositions 801 Cliff Rd E Ste 201 .... Burnsville MN 55337 952-894-8007
Web: www.cygnusexpos.com

Data Guardian 9136 Portage Industrial Dr .... Portage MI 49024 269-327-6296
Web: www.kalamazooxray.com

Diamond Energy Services Inc
1521 N Service Rd W .... Swift Current SK S9H3S9 306-778-6682
Web: www.diamondenergy.ca

Diversitec LLC 14321 Sommerville Ct .... Midlothian VA 23113 804-379-6772
Web: www.diversitec.com

DM Contact Management 100-645 Tyee Rd .... Victoria BC V9A6X5 250-383-8267
Web: www.dmcontact.com

eCoast Marketing Services
35E Industrial Way Ste 201 .... Rochester NH 03867 603-516-7450
Web: www.ecoastsales.com

Economic Opportunity Board Of Clark County
330 W Washington Ave Ste 7 .... Las Vegas NV 89106 702-647-3307 647-3125
Web: www.eobccnv.org

Eggleston Services 6431 Tidewater Dr .... Norfolk VA 23509 757-625-2311
Web: egglestonservices.org

Eichelbergers Inc 107 Texaco Rd .... Mechanicsburg PA 17050 717-766-4800
Web: www.eichelbergers.com

eLawMarketing 25 Robert Pitt Dr Ste 209G .... Monsey NY 10952 866-833-6245
TF: 866-833-6245 ■ *Web:* www.elawmarketing.com

EMI Network Inc 312 Elm St Ste 1150 .... Cincinnati OH 45202 513-579-1950
Web: www.eminetwork.com

Employers Association, The
3020 W Arrowood Rd .... Charlotte NC 28273 704-522-8011
Web: www.employersassoc.com

Encoll Corp. Inc 4576 Enterprise St .... Fremont CA 94538 510-795-8581
Web: www.encoll.com

Endurant Business Solutions
12100 Singletree Ln Ste 165 .... Eden Prairie MN 55344 952-746-1373
Web: www.endurant.com

Equi Tax Inc 17111 Rolling Creek Dr Ste 200 .... Houston TX 77090 281-444-4866
Web: www.equitaxinc.com

Phone Fax

Extended Presence 3570 E 12th Ave Ste 200 .... Denver CO 80206 303-325-8600
Web: www.extendedpresence.com

Fam Funds 384 N Grand St PO Box 310 .... Cobleskill NY 12043 518-234-4393 234-4473
TF: 800-721-5391 ■ *Web:* www.famfunds.com

Field Nation LLC
310 Fourth Ave S Ste 8100 .... Minneapolis MN 55415 877-573-4353
TF: 877-573-4353 ■ *Web:* www.fieldnation.com

FilterBoxx Water & Environmental Corp
5716 Burbank Rd SE .... Calgary AB T2H1Z4 403-203-4747
Web: filterboxx.com

FinTrack Systems 194 Calyer St .... Brooklyn NY 11222 212-742-1800
Web: www.fintrack.com

Format International Inc
10715 Kahlmeyer Dr .... Saint Louis MO 63132 314-428-2671
Web: www.format-international.com

Fort Docs 975 Corporate Cntr Pkwy .... Santa Rosa CA 95407 707-571-8313
Web: www.rmscd.com

Fulco Fulfillment Inc 26 Richboynton Rd .... Dover NJ 07801 973-361-1700
Web: www.fulcofulfillment.com

Gale Force Petroleum Inc
Ste 5700 100 King St W .... Toronto ON M5X1C7 888-440-3411
TF: 888-440-3411 ■ *Web:* www.galeforcepetroleum.com

Galveston Central Appraisal District
9850 Emmett F Lowry Expy Ste A .... Texas City TX 77591 409-935-1980
Web: www.galvestoncad.org

Georgia Duplicating Products Inc
1180 Eisenhower Pkwy .... Macon GA 31206 478-781-8991
Web: www.gadup.com

Gift Planning Assoc 4417 11th St NW .... Albuquerque NM 87107 415-970-2380
Web: www.giftplanner1.com

Gilligan & Ferneman LLC
1754 Business Ctr Ln .... Kissimmee FL 34758 800-720-4152
TF: 800-720-4152 ■ *Web:* gilliganandferneman.com

Gis Assocs Inc 806a Nw 16th Ave .... Gainesville FL 32601 352-384-1465
Web: gis-associates.com

Global Corporate College
6001 Cochran Rd Ste 305 .... Solon OH 44139 440-793-0202
Web: corporatecollege.com

Global Pacific Financial Services Ltd
10430 144 St .... Surrey BC V3T4V5 800-561-1177
TF: 800-561-1177 ■ *Web:* www.globalpacific.com

Gonser Gerber 400 E Diehl Rd Ste 380 .... Naperville IL 60563 630-505-1433 505-7710
Web: www.gonsergerber.com

Greater Giving Inc
1920 N W Amberglen Pkwy Ste 140 .... Beaverton OR 97006 503-597-0378
Web: greatergiving.com

Grenzebach Glier & Assoc Inc
401 N Michigan Ave Ste 2800 .... Chicago IL 60611 312-372-4040 589-6358
Web: www.grenzebachglier.com

GroveWare Technologies Ltd
Ste 411 90 Eglinton Ave E .... Toronto ON M4P2Y3 877-701-9378
TF: 877-701-9378 ■ *Web:* www.groveware.com

GTS Consultants Two Monmouth Ave .... Freehold NJ 07728 732-409-0900
Web: gtsconsultants.com

Hardline Installation Inc
1759 Green Cove Rd St B .... Brasstown NC 28902 828-835-8209
Web: www.hardlineinstallation.com

Health Revenue Assurance Holdings Inc
Ste 304 8551 W Sunrise Blvd .... Plantation FL 33322 954-472-2340
Web: www.healthrevenue.com

High Tech Design Safety LLC
15304 Rainbow One St Ste 101 .... Austin TX 78734 512-266-0222
Web: hightechdesignsafety.com

Ho-Chunk Inc One Mission Dr PO Box 390 .... Winnebago NE 68071 402-878-2809
Web: www.hochunkinc.com

hrQ Inc 2859 Umatilla St .... Denver CO 80211 303-455-1118
Web: www.hrqinc.com

ICX Group Inc
SunTrust Tower 76 S Laura St Ste 1700 .... Jacksonville FL 32202 904-208-2200
Web: www.icxgroup.com

IFS Financial Services Inc
250 Brownlow Ave Ste 1 .... Dartmouth NS B3B1W9 902-481-6106
Web: www.ifs-finance.com

Iknow LLC 100 Overlook Ctr Second Fl .... Princeton NJ 08540 609-419-0500
Web: www.iknow.us

Info Cubic LLC
9250 E Costilla Ave Ste 525 .... Greenwood Village CO 80112 303-220-0170
Web: www.infocubic.net

Infoshred LLC Three Craftsman Rd .... East Windsor CT 06088 860-627-5800
Web: www.infoshred.com

Inline Packaging LLC 1205 18th Ave S .... Princeton MN 55371 763-631-1555
Web: www.inlinepkg.com

Insight Resource Group
Three Altarinda Rd Ste 301 .... Orinda CA 94563 925-254-4114
Web: www.insightresourcegroup.com

Institutional Advancement Programs Inc
65 Main St Ste 208 .... Tuckahoe NY 10707 914-779-4092 961-3114

InteliSpend Prepaid Solutions LLC
1400 S Hwy Dr .... Fenton MO 63099 636-226-2000
Web: www.intelispend.com

Intellimeter Canada Inc
1125 Squires Beach Rd .... Pickering ON L1W3T9 905-426-3837
Web: intellimeter.on.ca

Interuniversity Services Inc
1550 Bedford Hwy .... Bedford NS B4A1E6 902-453-2470
Web: www.interuniversity.ns.ca

Intronix Technologies Inc
26 McEwan Dr West Unit 15 .... Bolton ON L7E1E6 905-951-3361
Web: www.intronixtech.com

Issuer Direct Corp
500 Perimeter Park Dr Ste D .... Morrisville NC 27560 919-461-1600
Web: www.issuerdirect.com

Phone | Fax

Itco Solutions Inc 1003 Whitehall Ln ... Redwood City CA 94061 650-367-0514
Web: www.itcosolutions.com

Itgroove Professional Services Ltd
1035 Nakini Pl ... Brentwood Bay BC V8M1A3 250-220-4575
Web: itgroove.net

ITR of Georgia Inc 3346 Montreal ... Tucker GA 30084 770-496-0366
Web: www.itrofgeorgia.com

J M Field Marketing Inc
3570 NW 53rd Ct ... Fort Lauderdale FL 33309 954-523-1957
Web: www.jmfield.com

John Brown Ltd Inc
46 Grove St PO Box 296 ... Peterborough NH 03458 603-924-3834 924-7998
Web: www.johnbrownlimited.com

Jopari Solutions Inc
1855 Gateway Blvd Ste 500 ... Concord CA 94520 925-459-5200
Web: www.jopari.com

Joseph C. Sansone Co 18040 Edison Ave ... Chesterfield MO 63005 636-537-2700
Web: www.jcsco.com

Jumpstart Automotive Group
747 Front St Ste 400 ... San Francisco CA 94111 415-738-3400
Web: www.jumpstartautomotivegroup.com

K3 Enterprises Inc 225 Ray Ave Ste 300 ... Fayetteville NC 28301 910-307-3017
Web: www.k3-enterprises.com

KCI Aviation 2100 Aviation Way ... Bridgeport WV 26330 304-842-3591
Web: www.kciaviation.com

King Business Interiors Inc
6155 Huntley Rd Ste D ... Columbus OH 43229 614-430-0020
Web: www.kbiinc.com

Las Vegas Events
770 E Warm Springs Rd Ste 140 ... Las Vegas NV 89119 702-260-8605
Web: lasvegasevents.com

Las Vegas Presort LLC
3655 E Patrick Ln Ste 300 ... Las Vegas NV 89120 702-320-0450
Web: lasvegaspresort.net

LeadSwell PO Box 170432 ... San Francisco CA 94117 415-518-6701
Web: www.leadswell.com

Leapset Inc 2010 Broadway St ... Redwood City CA 94063 650-215-7777
Web: www.leapset.com

Leigh Bureau Inc 92 E Main St Ste 200 ... Somerville NJ 08876 908-253-8600
Web: www.leighbureau.com

Levy Diamond Bello & Associates LLC
497 Bic Dr ... Milford CT 06461 203-876-1000
Web: www.ldbassociates.com

Lipman Hearne Inc 200 S Michigan Ave Ste 1600 ... Chicago IL 60604 312-356-8000 356-4005
Web: www.lipmanhearne.com

Live Auctioneers LLC 220 12th Ave Second Fl ... New York NY 10001 212-947-4428
Web: www.liveauctioneers.com

Locordia Inc 16600 Sherman Way Ste 170 ... Van Nuys CA 91406 818-827-1328
Web: www.locordia.com

London Economics International LLC
717 Atlantic Ave Ste 1A ... Boston MA 02111 617-933-7200
Web: www.londoneconomics.com

LW Robbins Assoc 201 Summer St ... Holliston MA 01746 800-229-5972 893-0212*
**Fax Area Code:* 508 ■ *TF:* 800-229-5972 ■ *Web:* www.lwra.com

MacIntyre Assoc Inc 106 W State St ... Kennett Square PA 19348 610-925-5925
Web: www.macintyreassociates.com

Mail Dispatch LLC 9710 Distribution Ave ... San Diego CA 92121 858-444-2350
Web: www.maildispatch.com

marketRx Inc 1200 US Route 22 E ... Bridgewater NJ 08807 908-541-0045
Web: www.marketrx.com

MCMC LLC 300 Crown Colony Dr Ste 203 ... Quincy MA 02169 617-375-7700
Web: www.mcmcllc.com

MD&E Inc 3201 Peachtree Corners Cir ... Norcross GA 30092 678-291-9690
Web: www.mdeclarity.com

Medbuy Corp 4056 Meadowbrook Dr Unit 135 ... London ON N6L1E4 519-652-1688
Web: www.medbuy.ca

Miami Direct Inc 8200 NW 41 St Ste 225 ... Miami FL 33166 305-597-3998
Web: www.gbm.net

Milieu Design Corp 48 E Hintz Rd ... Wheeling IL 60090 847-465-1160
Web: www.milieudesignllc.com

Minnesuing Acres
8084 E Minnesuing Acres Dr ... Lake Nebagamon WI 54849 715-374-2262
Web: www.minnesuingacres.com

Mirifex Systems LLC
1383 Sharon Copley Rd PO Box 328 ... Sharon Center OH 44274 440-891-1210
Web: www.mirifex.com

MSDSonline Inc 350 N Orleans Ste 950 ... Chicago IL 60654 312-881-2000
Web: www.msdsonline.com

MyUSACorporation.com Inc
One Radisson Plz Ste 800 ... New Rochelle NY 10801 877-330-2677
TF: 877-330-2677 ■ *Web:* myusacorporation.com

National Franchise Sales
1601 Dove St Ste 150 ... Newport Beach CA 92660 949-428-0480
Web: www.nationalfranchisesales.com

Netzel Grigsby Assoc Inc
9696 Culver Blvd Ste 105 ... Culver City CA 90232 310-836-7624 836-9357
Web: www.netzelgrigsby.com

New Age Industrial Corporation Inc
16788 E Hwy 36 PO Box 520 ... Norton KS 67654 785-877-5121
Web: www.newageindustrial.com

Nomadic Display Capitol Inc
5617 Industrial Dr ... Springfield VA 22151 703-912-4700
Web: www.nomadicdisplay.com

NorAm Capital Holdings Inc
15303 N Dallas Pkwy Ste 1030 ... Addison TX 75001 888-886-6726
TF: 888-886-6726 ■ *Web:* noramcapitalholdings.com

Nova Corp Inc 74 W Sheffield Ave ... Englewood NJ 07631 201-567-4404
Web: nova-corp.com

Nova Express Millennium Inc
105 - 14271 Knox Way ... Richmond BC V6V2Z4 604-278-8044
Web: www.novex.ca

oberoSPM 7560 Airport Rd Unit 12 ... Mississauga ON L4T4H4 888-815-2996
TF: 888-815-2996 ■ *Web:* oberosolutions.com

Phone | Fax

Odesia Group Inc
1010 Ste-Catherine West Ste 560 ... Montreal QC H3B1G4 514-876-1155
Web: www.odesia.com

Office Liquidators Inc
11111 W Sixth Ave Unit A ... Denver CO 80215 303-759-3375
Web: m.officeliquidators.com

Omni Workspace Co
1300 N Washington Ave Ste 200 ... Minneapolis MN 55411 612-627-1700
Web: www.omniworkspace.com

Omnilingua Worldwide LLC
306 Sixth Ave SE ... Cedar Rapids IA 52401 319-365-8565
Web: www.omnilingua.com

On 3 Promotional Partners 1543 Sheridan Rd ... Kenosha WI 53140 262-551-8715
Web: www.on3promopartners.com

OnCorp Direct Inc 1033 Bay St Ste 313 ... Toronto ON M5S3A5 416-964-2677
Web: www.oncorp.com

Optimum Card Solution LLC 855 S Fiene Dr ... Addison IL 60101 630-458-0077
Web: optimumcard.com

Ounce of Prevention Fund of Florida Inc, The
111 N Gadsden St Ste 200 ... Tallahassee FL 32301 850-921-4494
Web: www.ounce.org

PakCom Inc 196 Newton St ... Waltham MA 02453 781-890-3888
Web: www.pakcominc.com

Palmer Temps The Palmer Group
4302 Roosevelt Blvd ... Middletown OH 45044 513-422-1126
Web: www.palmergroup.com

Parallon Business Solutions LLC
6640 Carothers Pkwy ... Franklin TN 37067 615-807-8000
Web: parallon.com

Parenty Reitmeier Inc 605 Des Meurons St ... Winnipeg MB R2H2R1 204-237-3737
Web: www.parentyreitmeier.com

Parsec Inc 1100 Gest St ... Cincinnati OH 45203 513-621-6111
Web: www.parsecinc.com

Patented Acquisition Corp
2490 CrossPointe Dr ... Miamisburg OH 45342 937-353-2299
Web: thinkpatented.com

Payment Services Corp Inc
360 Albert St Ste 1220 ... Ottawa ON K1R7X7 866-972-0616
TF: 866-972-0616 ■ *Web:* www.paymentservicescorp.com

PEP Direct Inc 19 Stoney Brook Dr ... Wilton NH 03086 603-654-6141 654-2159

Phillips & Assoc PO Box 241040 ... Los Angeles CA 90024 310-247-0963 247-0966
Web: www.phillipsontheweb.com

Phone Ware Inc 8902 Activity Rd ... San Diego CA 92126 858-459-3000
Web: www.phonewareinc.com

Polymer Solutions Inc 2903-C Commerce St ... Blacksburg VA 24060 540-961-4300
Web: www.polymersolutions.com

Practice Concepts 2706 Harbor Blvd ... Costa Mesa CA 92626 714-545-5110
Web: www.practiceconcepts.com

Premier Courier Service Inc 410 Eighth Ave ... New York NY 10001 212-684-0901
Web: www.premier-nyc.com

Product Support Solutions Inc
7172 Regional St Ste 431 ... Dublin CA 94568 925-208-2450
Web: www.psshelp.com

Pursuant 5151 Belt Line Rd Ste 900 ... Dallas TX 75254 214-866-7700
Web: www.pursuant.com

QCSS Inc 21925 Field Pkwy Ste 210 ... Deer Park IL 60010 847-229-7046
Web: www.qcssinc.com

R d d Associates LLC 930 Riverview Dr Ste 400 ... Totowa NJ 07512 973-812-8070
Web: www.rddassociates.com

R G s Financial Corp
3333 Earhart Dr Ste 150 ... Carrollton TX 75006 469-791-4700
Web: www.rgsfinancial.com

Radish Tools 12 Mckendree Ave ... Annapolis MD 21401 443-321-2732
Web: www.radishtools.com

Reed Brennan Media Associates Inc
628 Virginia Dr ... Orlando FL 32803 407-894-7300
Web: www.rbma.com

Rethink Innovations 118 Burrs Rd Ste C1 ... Westampton NJ 08060 609-784-8427
Web: www.myrethink.com

RGIS LLC 2000 E Taylor Rd ... Auburn Hills MI 48326 248-651-2511
Web: www.rgis.com

Rival Capital Management Inc
160 - 99 Scurfield Bvld ... Winnipeg MB R3Y1Y1 204-992-6210
Web: rivalcapital.ca

Robbinex Inc 80 Bancroft St ... Hamilton ON L8E2W5 905-523-7510
Web: www.robbinex.com

Roger Black Studio Inc
245 Fifth Ave Rm 2345 ... New York NY 10016 212-481-9800
Web: rogerblack.com

RuffaloCODY LLC 65 Kirkwood N Rd SW ... Cedar Rapids IA 52404 319-362-7483
Web: www.ruffalocody.com

Ruotolo Assoc Inc (RA) 29 Broadway Ste 210 ... Cresskill NJ 07626 201-568-3898 568-8783
TF: 800-786-8656 ■ *Web:* www.ruotoloassociates.com

Sageworks Inc 5565 Centerview Dr ... Raleigh NC 27606 919-851-7474
Web: www.sageworks.com

Sanky Perlowin Assoc Inc
Sanky Communications Inc
599 11th Ave Sixth Fl ... New York NY 10036 212-868-4300 868-4310
Web: www.sankyinc.com

SDG Corp 55 N Water St ... Norwalk CT 06854 203-866-8886
Web: www.sdgc.com

Ship-Right Solutions LLC
165 Pleasant Ave ... South Portland ME 04106 207-321-3500
Web: www.shiprightsolutions.com

Show Management Services Inc
1963 University Ln ... Lisle IL 60532 630-271-8210
Web: www.rocexhibitions.com

Shred Works Inc 1601 Bayshore Hwy Ste 211 ... Burlingame CA 94010 510-729-7110
Web: www.shredworks.com

Skystone Ryan
Skystone Partners LLC
635 W Seventh St Ste 107 ... Cincinnati OH 45203 513-241-6778 241-0551
TF: 800-883-0801 ■ *Web:* www.skystoneryan.com

Phone Fax

SMARTLogix Inc 10306 Barberville Rd . . . . .Ft. Mill SC 29715 803-547-8265
Web: www.smartlogixinc.com

SMI Companies Inc 1456 Hwy 317 South . . . . .Franklin LA 70538 337-836-9894
Web: www.smicompanies.com

South Atlantic Packaging Corp
3946 Westpoint Blvd. . . . . Winston Salem NC 27103 336-774-3122
Web: southatlanticpackaging.com

Special Journeys LLC 422 S 153rd Cir. . . . . .Omaha NE 68154 402-991-5520
Web: www.specializedeng.com

Stirling Mercantile Corp
450 - 400 Burrard St. . . . . .Vancouver BC V6C3A6 604-484-0070
Web: www.stirlingmercantile.com

Sureshred Security 3166 Diablo Ave . . . . Hayward CA 94545 510-784-1150
Web: www.sureshred.com

SWOT Management Group Inc
105 Raider Blvd Ste 201. . . . . .Hillsborough NJ 08844 908-359-7968
Web: www.swotmg.com

Synergent Two Ledgeview Dr . . . . .Westbrook ME 04092 207-773-5671
Web: www.synergentcorp.com

TeamBonding 298 Tosca Dr. . . . . Stoughton MA 02072 781-793-9700
Web: www.www.teambonding.com

TechTrans International Inc
2200 Space Park Ste 410 . . . . .Houston TX 77058 281-335-8000
Web: www.tti-corp.com

Telematic Controls Inc 3364 114 Ave Se . . . . Calgary AB T2Z3V6 403-253-7939
Web: www.telematic.ca

Ter Molen Watkins & Brandt LLC
Two N Riverside Plz Ste 1030. . . . . .Chicago IL 60606 312-222-0560 222-0565
Web: www.twbfundraising.com

TharpeRobbins Company Inc, The
149 Crawford Rd. . . . . Statesville NC 28625 704-872-5231
Web: www.tharperobbins.com

Thermosoft International Corp
310 Lexington Dr . . . . .Buffalo Grove IL 60089 847-279-3800
Web: www.thermosoft.com

Thetubestore Inc 120 Lancing Dr. . . . . Hamilton ON L8W3A1 905-570-0979
Web: www.thetubestore.com

Ti Squared Technologies Inc
1305 Clark Mill Rd . . . . Sweet Home OR 97386 541-367-2929
Web: ramcast.com

TIS Group 100 Village Ctr Dr Ste 260. . . . . North Oaks MN 55127 651-379-5070
Web: theinstitutionalstrategist.com

Total Parts Plus Inc
709 Anchors St NW . . . . .Fort Walton Beach FL 32548 850-244-7293
Web: www.totalpartsplus.com

Townsend Oil Company Inc
27 Cherry St PO Box 90. . . . . .Danvers MA 01923 978-777-0700
Web: www.townsendoil.com

Trade Technologies Inc
3939 Bee Cave Rd Ste B-22 . . . . Austin TX 78746 512-327-9996
Web: www.tradetechnologies.com

Transcepta LLC 135 Columbia Ste 202. . . . . .Aliso Viejo CA 92656 949-382-2840
Web: www.trancascapital.com

Travelink Inc 404 BNA Dr #650. . . . . .Nashville TN 37217 615-367-4900
Web: www.travelink.com

TRSB Inc 276 Saint-Jacques St Ste 900. . . . . Montreal QC H2Y1N3 514-844-4682
Web: www.trsb.com

Txi Network Systems Inc 12868 Kingsbridge Ln . . . . .Houston TX 77077 281-293-9422
Web: www.txi.net

Ultraex Inc 2633 Barrington Ct. . . . . Hayward CA 94545 510-786-3499
Web: www.ultraex.com

Van Groesbeck & Co 2124 Hanovar Ave. . . . . Richmond VA 23220 804-285-3176 359-7271
Web: www.vangroesbeckco.com

Vision Offices Executive Suites Lp
14362 N Frank Lloyd Wright Blvd Ste 1000 . . . . Scottsdale AZ 85260 480-477-7777
Web: visionoffices.com

Vitech Business Group Inc 1776 Iowa St . . . . Bellingham WA 98229 360-647-1622
Web: www.vitechgroup.com

W Squared.com 5500 Maryland Way Ste 200. . . . . .Brentwood TN 37027 615-577-4927
Web: www.wsquared.com

Whitney Jones Inc
119 Brookstown Ave Ste PH2. . . . . .Winston-Salem NC 27101 336-722-2371
Web: www.whitneyjonesinc.com

World Services LLC 1954 Airport Rd Ste 201 . . . . Chamblee GA 30341 404-486-5986
Web: worldservicesusa.com

Xerox Mortgage Services Inc
9040 Roswell Rd Ste 700 . . . . .Sandy Springs GA 30350 678-460-2460
Web: www.advectis.com

Youth Consultation Service (Inc) 284 Broadway . . . . Newark NJ 07104 973-482-8411
Web: www.ycs.org

321 FURNACES & OVENS - INDUSTRIAL PROCESS

Phone Fax

AFC Holcroft LLC 49630 Pontiac Trl. . . . . .Wixom MI 48393 248-624-8191 624-3710
Web: www.afc-holcroft.com

AGF Burner Inc 1955 Swarthmore Ave Unit 2. . . . . Lakewood NJ 08701 732-730-8090 730-8060
Web: www.agfburner.com

AJAX Electric Co 60 Tomlinson Rd . . . . .Huntingdon Valley PA 19006 215-947-8500 947-6757
Web: www.ajaxelectric.com

Ajax Tocco Magnethermic Corp
1745 Overland Ave NE . . . . .Warren OH 44483 330-372-8511 372-8608
TF: 800-547-1527 ■ *Web:* www.ajaxtocco.com

Alabama Specialty Products Inc
152 Metal Samples Rd PO Box 8 . . . . Munford AL 36268 256-358-5200 358-4515
TF: 888-388-1006 ■ *Web:* www.alspi.com

Alpha 1 Induction Service Ctr Inc
1525 Old Alum Creek Dr. . . . . Columbus OH 43209 614-253-8900 253-8981
TF: 800-991-2599 ■ *Web:* www.alpha1induction.com

Armor Group Inc, The
4600 N Mason-Montgomery Rd. . . . . .Mason OH 45040 800-255-0393 923-5694*
**Fax Area Code:* 513 ■ **Fax:* Sales ■ *TF:* 800-255-0393 ■ *Web:* www.thearmorgroup.com

Phone Fax

AVS Inc 60 Fitchburg Rd. . . . . Ayer MA 01432 978-772-0710 772-6462
TF: 800-772-0710 ■ *Web:* www.avsinc.com

Belco Industries Inc 9138 W Belding Rd . . . . Belding MI 48809 616-794-0410 794-3424
Web: www.belcoind.com

Bloom Engineering Co Inc 5460 Curry Rd. . . . . Pittsburgh PA 15236 412-653-3500 653-2253
TF: 800-451-5491 ■ *Web:* www.bloomeng.com

BriskHeat Corp 1055 Gibbard Ave. . . . . Columbus OH 43201 614-294-3376 294-3807
TF: 800-848-7673 ■ *Web:* www.bhthermal.com

Callidus Technologies Inc
7130 S Lewis St Ste 335. . . . . Tulsa OK 74136 918-496-7599 488-9450
Web: www.callidus.com

Cambridge Engineering Inc PO Box 1010 . . . . .Chesterfield MO 63006 636-532-2233 530-6133
TF: 800-899-1989 ■ *Web:* www.cambridge-eng.com

CCI Thermal Technologies Inc 5918 Roper Rd . . . . Edmonton AB T6B3E1 780-466-3178 468-5904
TF Cust Svc: 800-661-8529 ■ *Web:* www.ccithermal.com

CI Hayes 33 Fwy Dr . . . . Cranston RI 02920 401-467-5200 467-2108
Web: www.cihayes.com

CMI EFCO Inc 435 W Wilson St . . . . Salem OH 44460 330-332-4661 332-4661
TF: 877-225-2674 ■ *Web:* www.cmigroupe.com

Consarc Corp 100 Indel Ave. . . . . .Rancocas NJ 08073 609-267-8000 267-1366*
**Fax:* Sales ■ *Web:* www.consarc.com

Consutech Systems LLC PO Box 15119 . . . . Richmond VA 23227 804-746-4120 730-9056
Web: www.consutech.com

Despatch Industries Inc 8860 207th St W. . . . . Lakeville MN 55044 952-469-5424 469-4513
TF: 800-726-0110 ■ *Web:* www.despatch.com

Detroit Radiant Product Co 21400 Hoover Rd . . . . .Warren MI 48089 586-756-0950 756-2626
TF: 800-222-1100 ■ *Web:* www.reverberray.com

Detroit Stoker Co 1510 E First St . . . . Monroe MI 48161 734-241-9500 241-7126
TF: 800-786-5374 ■ *Web:* www.detroitstoker.com

Eclipse Inc 1665 Elmwood Rd . . . . Rockford IL 61103 815-877-3031 877-3336*
**Fax:* Cust Svc ■ *TF:* 888-826-3473 ■ *Web:* www.eclipsenet.com

Eisenmann Corp 150 E Dartmoor Dr . . . . .Crystal Lake IL 60014 815-455-4100 455-1018
Web: www.eisenmann.com

Electric Heating Equipment Co
1240 Oronoque Rd . . . . Milford CT 06461 203-882-0199

Fast Heat Inc 776 Oaklawn Ave . . . . Elmhurst IL 60126 630-833-5400 833-2040
TF: 877-747-8575 ■ *Web:* www.fastheat.com

Gas-Fired Products Inc 305 Doggett St. . . . . Charlotte NC 28203 704-372-3485 332-5843
TF: 800-830-3983 ■ *Web:* www.gasfiredproducts.com

GC Broach Co 7667 E 46th Pl . . . . Tulsa OK 74145 918-664-7420 627-4083
Web: www.broach.com

Glenro Inc 39 McBride Ave . . . . Paterson NJ 07501 973-279-5900 279-9103
TF: 888-453-6761 ■ *Web:* www.glenro.com

Glo-Quartz Electric Heater Company Inc
7084 Maple St . . . . .Mentor OH 44060 440-255-9701 255-7852
TF Sales: 800-321-3574 ■ *Web:* www.gloquartz.com

Hauck Manufacturing Co 100 N Harris St. . . . . .Cleona PA 17042 717-272-3051 273-9882
Web: www.hauckburner.com

Heatrex Inc PO Box 515 . . . . .Meadville PA 16335 814-724-1800 333-6580
TF: 800-394-6589 ■ *Web:* www.heatrex.com

Henry F Teichmann Inc 3009 Washington Rd. . . . . McMurray PA 15317 724-941-9550 941-3479
Web: www.hft.com

Hotwatt Inc 128 Maple St. . . . . .Danvers MA 01923 978-777-0070 774-2409*
**Fax:* Sales ■ *Web:* www.hotwatt.com

Huppert Industries Inc 16808 S Lathrop Ave. . . . . .Harvey IL 60426 708-339-2020 339-2225
Web: www.huppert.com

Inductoheat Inc 32251 N Avis Dr. . . . . .Madison Heights MI 48071 248-585-9393 589-1062
TF: 800-624-6297 ■ *Web:* www.inductoheat.com

Inductotherm Group 10 Indel Ave PO Box 157 . . . . .Rancocas NJ 08073 609-267-9000
TF: 800-257-9527 ■ *Web:* www.inductotherm.com

Industrial Combustion Inc 351 21st St. . . . . Monroe WI 53566 608-325-3141 325-4379
Web: www.ind-comb.com

Industrial Heater Corp 30 Knotter Dr. . . . . Cheshire CT 06410 203-250-0500 250-0599
Web: www.industrialheater.com

Industronics Service Co
489 Sullivan Ave PO Box 649. . . . . South Windsor CT 06074 860-289-1551 289-3526
TF: 800-878-1551 ■ *Web:* www.industronics.com

International Thermal Systems LLC (ITS)
4697 W Greenfield Ave. . . . . .Milwaukee WI 53214 414-672-7700 672-8800
Web: internationalthermalsystems.com

IntriCon Corp 1260 Red Fox Rd . . . . Arden Hills MN 55112 651-636-9770 636-9503
NASDAQ: IIN ■ *Web:* www.intricon.com

Ipsen Inc PO Box 6266 . . . . Rockford IL 61125 815-332-4941 332-4995
TF: 800-727-7625 ■ *Web:* www.ipsenusa.com

John Zink Company LLC 11920 E Apache St. . . . . Tulsa OK 74116 918-234-1800 234-2700
TF: 800-421-9242 ■ *Web:* www.johnzink.com

Johnson Gas Appliance Co 520 E Ave NW . . . . .Cedar Rapids IA 52405 319-365-5267 365-6282
TF: 800-553-5422 ■ *Web:* www.johnsongas.com

JT Thorpe & Son Inc 1060 Hensley St. . . . . Richmond CA 94801 510-233-2500 233-2901
Web: www.jtthorpe.com

Koch Chemical Technology Group LLC
4111 E 37th St N PO Box 2256. . . . . Wichita KS 67220 316-828-8441 829-7618
Web: www.kochind.com/IndustryAreas/process.aspx

Lanly Co, The 26201 Tungsten Rd . . . . Cleveland OH 44132 216-731-1115 731-7900
TF: 800-327-8064 ■ *Web:* www.lanly.com

Lepel Corp 200-G Executive Dr . . . . Edgewood NY 11717 631-586-3300 586-3232
Web: lepel.com

Marathon Heater Inc 808 Hackberry Ln. . . . . Del Rio TX 78840 830-775-1417 775-4379
Web: www.marathonheater.com

Novatec Inc 222 Thomas Ave. . . . . .Baltimore MD 21225 410-789-4811 789-4638
TF: 800-237-8379 ■ *Web:* www.novatec.com

Paragon Industries Inc 2011 S Town E Blvd . . . . Mesquite TX 75149 972-288-7557 222-0646
TF: 800-876-4328 ■ *Web:* www.paragonweb.com

Phoenix Solutions Co
5480 Nathan Ln N Ste 110 . . . . .Plymouth MN 55442 763-544-2721 546-5617
Web: www.phoenixsolutionsco.com

Pillar Induction Co 21905 Gateway Rd . . . . Brookfield WI 53045 262-317-5300 317-5353
TF: 800-558-7733 ■ *Web:* www.pillar.com

Procedyne Corp 11 Industrial Dr. . . . . New Brunswick NJ 08901 732-249-8347 249-7220
Web: www.procedyne.com

Process Combustion Corp 5460 Curry Rd. . . . . Pittsburgh PA 15236 412-655-0955 650-5569
Web: www.pcc-sterling.com

Phone Fax

Pyronics Inc 17700 Miles Rd...................... Cleveland OH 44128 216-662-8800 663-8954
Web: www.selas.com

Radio Frequency Company Inc 150 Dover Rd ....Millis MA 02054 508-376-9555 376-9944
Web: www.radiofrequency.com

Radyne Corp 211 W Boden St......................Milwaukee WI 53207 414-481-8360 481-8303
TF: 800-236-8360 ■ *Web:* www.radyne.com

Rapid Engineering Inc
1100 7-Mile Rd NW .... Comstock Park MI 49321 616-784-0500 784-1910
TF: 800-536-3461 ■ *Web:* www.rapidengineering.com

Red-Ray Mfg Co Inc 10-22 County Line Rd .... Branchburg NJ 08876 908-722-0040 722-2535
TF: 800-883-9218 ■ *Web:* www.selas.com

SECO/Warwick Corp 180 Mercer St................Meadville PA 16335 814-332-8400 724-1407
Web: www.secowarwick.com

Selas Heat Technology Company LLC
130 Keystone Dr.........................Montgomeryville PA 18936 215-646-6600 646-3536
TF: 800-523-6500 ■ *Web:* www.selas.com

ST Johnson Co 925 Stanford Ave ....Oakland CA 94608 510-652-6000 652-4302
TF: 800-225-1348 ■ *Web:* www.stjohnson.com

Steelman Industries Inc
2800 Hwy 135 N PO Box 1461.............................Kilgore TX 75662 903-984-3061 984-1384
TF: 800-287-6633 ■ *Web:* www.steelman.com

StrikoDynarad 501 E Roosevelt Ave .... Zeeland MI 49464 616-772-3705 772-5271
TF: 855-787-4561 ■ *Web:* www.strikodynarad.com

Surface Combustion Inc 1700 Indian Wood Cir .... Maumee OH 43537 419-891-7150 891-7151
TF: 800-537-8980 ■ *Web:* www.surfacecombustion.com

Swindell Dressler International Co
5100 Casteel Dr ....Coraopolis PA 15108 412-788-7100
Web: www.swindelldressler.com

T-M Vacuum Products Inc
630 S Warrington Ave..........................Cinnaminson NJ 08077 856-829-2000 829-0990
Web: www.tmvacuum.com

Tempco Electric Heater Corp
607 N Central Ave..................................Wood Dale IL 60191 630-350-2252 350-0232
TF: 888-268-6396 ■ *Web:* www.tempco.com

Tenova Core 100 Corporate Ctr Dr ....Coraopolis PA 15108 412-262-2240 262-2055
Web: www.corefurnace.com

Thermal Circuits Inc One Technology Way............. Salem MA 01970 978-745-1162 741-3420
TF: 800-808-4328 ■ *Web:* www.thermalcircuits.com

Thermal Engineering Corp 2741 The Blvd...........Columbia SC 29209 803-783-0750 783-0756
TF: 800-331-0097 ■ *Web:* www.tecinfrared.com

Thermal Equipment Corp
2030 E University Dr..................... Rancho Dominguez CA 90220 310-328-6600 603-9625
Web: www.thermalequipment.com

Thermal Product Solutions
3827 Riverside Rd ....Riverside MI 49084 269-849-2700 849-3021
TF: 800-873-4468 ■ *Web:* www.thermalproductsolutions.com

Thermcraft Inc PO Box 12037 .... Winston Salem NC 27117 336-784-4800 784-0634
Web: www.thermcraftinc.com

Trent Inc 201 Leverington Ave.................... Philadelphia PA 19127 215-482-5000 482-9389
TF: 800-544-8736 ■ *Web:* www.trentheat.com

Truheat Inc 700 Grand St .... Allegan MI 49010 269-673-2145 673-7219
TF: 800-879-6199 ■ *Web:* www.ddrheating.com

Webster Engineering & Mfg Company LLC
619 Industrial Rd ....Winfield KS 67156 620-221-7464 221-9447
Web: www.webster-engineering.com

Wisconsin Oven Corp 2675 Main St................. East Troy WI 53120 262-642-3938 363-4018
Web: www.wisoven.com

322 FURNITURE - MFR

SEE ALSO Cabinets - Wood p. 1896; Fixtures - Office & Store p. 2290; Mattresses & Adjustable Beds p. 2722; Baby Products p. 1846; Recycled Plastics Products p. 3046

Phone Fax

Unisource Solutions Inc 8350 Rex Rd............. Pico Rivera CA 90660 562-949-1111 949-7110
Web: www.unisourceit.com

322-1 Commercial & Industrial Furniture

Phone Fax

Abco Office Furniture 4121 Rushton St .... Florence AL 35630 256-767-4100 760-1247
TF: 800-336-0070 ■ *Web:* www.abcofurniture.com

Adelphia Steel Equipment Co
7372 State Rd.......................................Philadelphia PA 19136 215-333-6300 331-6090
TF: 800-865-8211 ■ *Web:* www.adelphiafurniture.com

Allied Plastics Company Inc
2001 Walnut St...................................Jacksonville FL 32206 904-359-0386 353-4746
TF Cust Svc: 800-999-0386 ■ *Web:* www.alliedplasticsco.com

Allsteel Inc 2210 Second Ave....................... Muscatine IA 52761 563-272-4800 272-4887
TF Cust Svc: 888-255-7833 ■ *Web:* www.allsteeloffice.com

American of Martinsville
128 E Church St..................................Martinsville VA 24112 276-632-2061 632-4707
Web: www.americanofmartinsville.com

Anthro Corp 10450 SW Manhasset Dr .... Tualatin OR 97062 503-691-2556 325-0045*
*Fax Area Code: 800 ■ *TF:* 800-325-3841 ■ *Web:* www.anthro.com

Artistic Frame Corp 979 Third Ave 17th Fl............New York NY 10022 212-289-2100 289-2101
Web: www.artisticframe.com

Bernhardt Furniture Company Inc
1839 Morganton Blvd..................................... Lenoir NC 28645 828-758-9811
Web: www.bernhardt.com

Bestar Inc 4220 Villeneuve St.................. Lac-Megantic QC G6B2C3 819-583-1017 583-5370
TF: 888-823-7827 ■ *Web:* www.bestar.ca

Bevco Precision Manufacturing Co
21320 Doral Rd .... Waukesha WI 53186 262-798-9200 798-9201
TF: 800-864-2991 ■ *Web:* www.bevco.com

BGD Cos Inc 5323 Lakeland Ave N .... Minneapolis MN 55429 612-338-6804 338-4942
TF: 800-699-3537 ■ *Web:* www.bgdcompanies.com

Biofit Engineered Products
15500 Biofit Way ....Bowling Green OH 43402 419-823-1089 823-1342
TF: 800-597-0246 ■ *Web:* www.biofit.com

Phone Fax

Boling Furniture Co 311 NE Church Rd ....Mount Olive NC 28365 919-635-2400 635-4845
Web: bolingfurniture.com

Borroughs Corp 3002 N Burdick St.................Kalamazoo MI 49004 269-342-0161 342-4161
TF: 800-748-0227 ■ *Web:* www.borroughs.com

Bright Chair Co 51 Railroad Ave PO Box 269......... Middletown NY 10940 845-343-2196 343-4958
TF: 888-524-5997 ■ *Web:* www.brightchair.com

CabotWrenn 405 Rink Dam Rd PO Box 1767........... Hickory NC 28603 828-495-4607 495-1294
Web: www.cabotwrenn.com

Carolina Business Furniture LLC
535 Archdale Blvd .... Archdale NC 27263 336-431-9400 431-9511
TF: 800-763-0212 ■ *Web:* www.carolinabusinessfurniture.com

Carson's Inc PO Box 14186....................... Archdale NC 27263 336-431-1101 431-0677
Web: www.carsonsofhp.com

Cramer Inc 1222 Quebec St .... North Kansas City MO 64116 800-366-6700 471-7188*
*Fax Area Code: 816 ■ *TF:* 800-366-6700 ■ *Web:* www.cramerinc.com

CTB Corp 26327 Fallbrook Ave ....Wyoming MN 55092 651-462-3550 462-8806
Web: www.ctbcorp.com

Danver One Grand St.............................. Wallingford CT 06492 203-269-2300 265-6190
TF: 888-441-0537 ■ *Web:* www.danver.com

Dar-Ran Furniture Industries
2402 Shore St...................................High Point NC 27263 336-861-2400 861-6485
TF: 800-334-7891 ■ *Web:* www.darran.com

Dauphin North America 300 Myrtle Ave..............Boonton NJ 07005 973-263-1100 220-3844*
*Fax Area Code: 800 ■ *TF Cust Svc:* 800-631-1186 ■ *Web:* www.dauphin.com

Davis Furniture Industries Inc
2401 S College Dr ....High Point NC 27261 336-889-2009 889-0031
Web: www.davis-furniture.com

Delco Office Systems Div Delco Assoc Inc
55 Old Field Pt Rd ....Greenwich CT 06830 203-661-5101
Web: radarfrog.gatehousemedia.com

Emeco 805 W Elm Ave PO Box 179....................Hanover PA 17331 717-637-5951 633-6018
TF: 800-366-5951 ■ *Web:* www.emeco.net

Ergotron Inc 1181 Trapp Rd...................... Saint Paul MN 55121 651-681-7600 681-7710
TF Sales: 800-888-8458 ■ *Web:* www.ergotron.com

Executive Office Concepts Inc
1705 S Anderson Ave............................... Compton CA 90220 310-537-1657 603-9100
TF: 800-421-5927 ■ *Web:* www.eoccorp.com

Fillip Metal Cabinet Co 4500 W 47th St ....Chicago IL 60632 773-733-7527 376-7507
TF: 800-535-0733 ■ *Web:* www.fillipmetal.com

First Office 1204 E Sixth St.................... Huntingburg IN 47542 800-983-4415 683-7155*
*Fax Area Code: 812 ■ *Fax: Cust Svc ■ *TF:* 800-983-4415 ■ *Web:* www.firstoffice.com

Flex-Y-Plan Industries Inc 6960 W Ridge Rd..........Fairview PA 16415 814-474-1565 474-2129
TF Cust Svc: 800-458-0552 ■ *Web:* www.fyp.com

Flexible-Montisa 323 Acorn St .... Plainwell MI 49080 269-924-0730 685-9195
TF Cust Svc: 800-875-6836 ■ *Web:* www.flexiblemontisa.com

Flexsteel Industries Inc 3400 Jackson St............ Dubuque IA 52001 563-556-7730 556-8345*
NASDAQ: FLXS ■ *Fax: Cust Svc ■ *Web:* www.flexsteel.com

Foldcraft Co 615 Centennial Dr .... Kenyon MN 55946 507-789-5111 544-0480*
*Fax Area Code: 800 ■ *TF:* 800-759-6653 ■ *Web:* www.plymold.com

Furniture Values International LLC
601 N 75 Th Ave.................................Phoenix AZ 85043 602-442-5600 278-0103
Web: www.aspenhome.net

Geiger International Inc
6095 Fulton Industrial Blvd SW ....Atlanta GA 30336 404-344-1100 836-7519
TF: 800-456-6452 ■ *Web:* www.geigerintl.com

Global Industries Inc 17 W Stow Rd................. Marlton NJ 08053 856-596-3390 596-5684
TF: 800-220-1900 ■ *Web:* www.globaltotaloffice.com

Groupe Lacasse LLC 99 St-Pierre St............... Sainte-Pie QC J0H1W0 450-772-2495 248-1865*
*Fax Area Code: 888 ■ *Fax: Cust Svc ■ *TF:* 888-522-2773 ■ *Web:* www.groupelacasse.com

Gunlocke Company LLC One Gunlocke Dr............Wayland NY 14572 585-728-5111 728-8334*
*Fax: Hum Res ■ *TF Cust Svc:* 800-828-6300 ■ *Web:* www.gunlocke.com

H Wilson Co 2245 Delany Rd...................... Waukegan IL 60087 800-245-7224 327-1698
TF: 800-245-7224 ■ *Web:* www.hwilson.com

Hausmann Industries Inc 130 Union St ....Northvale NJ 07647 201-767-0255 767-1369
TF: 888-428-7626 ■ *Web:* www.hausmann.com

Haworth Inc One Haworth Ctr....................... Holland MI 49423 616-393-3000 393-1570
TF: 800-344-2600 ■ *Web:* www.haworth.com

Herman Miller Inc 855 E Main Ave .... Zeeland MI 49464 616-654-3000 654-5385
NASDAQ: MLHR ■ *TF:* 888-443-4357 ■ *Web:* www.hermanmiller.com

High Point Furniture Industries Inc
1104 Bedford St PO Box 2063 ....High Point NC 27261 336-431-7101 434-1964
TF: 800-447-3462 ■ *Web:* www.hpfi.com

Hirsh Industries Inc
3636 Westown Pkwy Ste 100............... West Des Moines IA 50266 515-299-3200 299-3300
TF: 800-383-7414 ■ *Web:* www.hirshindustries.com

HON Co 200 Oak St............................... Muscatine IA 52761 563-272-7100 328-7257*
*Fax Area Code: 800 ■ *TF:* 800-553-8230 ■ *Web:* www.hon.com

Huot Manufacturing Co 550 Wheeler St N........... Saint Paul MN 55104 651-646-1869 646-0457
TF: 800-832-3838 ■ *Web:* www.huot.com

IAC Industries 895 Beacon St............................Brea CA 92821 714-990-8997 990-0557
TF: 800-989-1422 ■ *Web:* www.iacindustries.com

Indiana Furniture 1224 Mill St .... Jasper IN 47546 812-482-5727 482-9035
TF: 800-422-5727 ■ *Web:* www.indianafurniture.com

Interior Crafts Inc 2513 W Cullerton Ave ....Chicago IL 60608 773-376-8160 376-9578
Web: interiorcraftsinc.com

Invincible Office Furniture Co
842 S 26th St PO Box 1117 ....Manitowoc WI 54220 920-682-4601 683-2970
TF: 877-682-4601 ■ *Web:* www.invinciblefurniture.com

Inwood Office Invironments
1108 E 15th St PO Box 646 .... Jasper IN 47547 812-482-6121 482-9732
Web: www.inwood.net

izzydesign 17237 Van Wagoner Rd.................Spring Lake MI 49456 616-916-9369 847-7000
Web: www.izzyplus.com

Jasper Desk Co 415 E Sixth St......................... Jasper IN 47546 812-482-4132 482-9552
TF Cust Svc: 800-365-7994 ■ *Web:* www.jasperdesk.com

Jasper Seating Company Inc
Jasper Group 225 Clay St ....Jasper IN 47546 812-482-3204 482-1548
TF: 800-622-5661 ■ *Web:* www.jaspergroup.us.com

JOFCO PO Box 71.................................... Jasper IN 47547 812-482-5154 634-2392
TF: 800-235-6326 ■ *Web:* www.jofco.com

JSJ Corp 700 Robbins Rd....................... Grand Haven MI 49417 616-842-6350 847-3112
Web: www.jsjcorp.com

Company	City	State	Zip	Phone	Fax
Khoury Inc 1129 Webster Ave PO Box 1746 — *TF:* 800-725-6765 ■ *Web:* www.khouryinc.com	Waco	TX	76703	254-754-5481	754-1606
KI 1330 Bellevue St — *TF:* 800-424-2432 ■ *Web:* ki.com	Green Bay	WI	54302	920-468-8100	468-0280
Kimball Hospitality 1180 E 16th St — **Fax Area Code:* 812 ■ *TF:* 800-634-9510 ■ *Web:* www.kimballhospitality.com	Jasper	IN	47549	276-666-8933	634-4324*
Kimball Office Furniture Co 1600 Royal St — **Fax Area Code:* 812 ■ *TF:* 800-482-1818 ■ *Web:* www.kimballoffice.com	Jasper	IN	47549	800-482-1818	482-8300*
Knoll Inc 1235 Water St — *NYSE:* KNL ■ *TF Cust Svc:* 800-343-5665 ■ *Web:* www.knoll.com	East Greenville	PA	18041	215-679-7991	679-1755
Lakeside Manufacturing Inc 4900 W Electric Ave — *TF:* 800-558-8565 ■ *Web:* www.elakeside.com	West Milwaukee	WI	53219	414-902-6400	902-6446
LB Furniture Industries LLC 99 S Third St — **Fax Area Code:* 800 ■ *TF:* 800-221-8752 ■ *Web:* www.lbempire.com	Hudson	NY	12534	518-828-1501	969-9009*
Liberty Furniture Industries 6195 Purdue Dr SW — **Fax:* Cust Svc ■ *Web:* www.mylibertyfurniture.com	Atlanta	GA	30336	404-629-1003	629-0717*
Luxor Div EBSCO Industries Inc 2245 Delany Rd — **Fax Area Code:* 800 ■ *TF:* 800-323-4656 ■ *Web:* www.luxorfurn.com	Waukegan	IL	60087	847-244-1800	327-1698*
Magna Design Inc 26246 Twelve Trees Ln NW — *TF:* 800-426-1202 ■ *Web:* www.magnadesign.com	Poulsbo	WA	98370	360-394-1300	394-1321
Martin Furniture 2345 Britannia Blvd — **Fax Area Code:* 619 ■ *TF Cust Svc:* 800-268-5669 ■ *Web:* www.martinfurniture.com	San Diego	CA	92154	800-268-5669	671-5199*
Marvel Group Inc 3843 W 43rd St — **Fax:* Cust Svc ■ *TF Cust Svc:* 800-621-8846 ■ *Web:* www.marvelgroup.com	Chicago	IL	60632	800-621-8846	237-0358*
Maxon Furniture Inc 660 SW 39th St Ste 150 — *TF Cust Svc:* 800-876-4274 ■ *Web:* www.maxonfurniture.com	Renton	WA	98057	800-876-4274	257-2635
Mayline Group 619 N Commerce St PO Box 728 — *TF:* 800-822-8037 ■ *Web:* www.mayline.com	Sheboygan	WI	53082	920-457-5537	457-7388
McDowell-Craig Office Furniture 13146 Firestone Blvd — *TF:* 877-921-2100 ■ *Web:* www.mcdowellcraig.com	Norwalk	CA	90650	562-921-4441	921-9638
Midwest Commercial Interiors 987 SW Temple — *Web:* www.midwestcommercialinteriors.com	Salt Lake City	UT	84101	801-505-4288	355-2713
MLP Seating Corp 2125 Lively Blvd — *TF:* 800-723-3030 ■ *Web:* www.mlpseating.com	Elk Grove Village	IL	60007	847-956-1700	956-1776
MTS Seating Inc 7100 Industrial Dr — **Fax Area Code:* 800 ■ *Web:* www.mtsseating.com	Temperance	MI	48182	734-847-3875	329-0687*
National Business Services 1601 Magoffin Ave — *TF Sales:* 800-777-7807 ■ *Web:* www.nbsinc.com	El Paso	TX	79901	915-544-1271	544-0325
National Office Furniture 1205 Kimball Blvd — **Fax Area Code:* 812 ■ *TF:* 800-482-1717 ■ *Web:* www.nationalofficefurniture.com	Jasper	IN	47549	800-482-1717	482-8800*
NER Data Products Inc 307 S Delsea Dr — **Fax Area Code:* 856 ■ *TF:* 888-637-3282 ■ *Web:* www.nerdata.com	Glassboro	NJ	08028	888-637-3282	881-5524*
Neutral Posture Inc 3904 N Texas Ave — *TF:* 800-446-3746 ■ *Web:* www.igoergo.com	Bryan	TX	77803	979-778-0502	778-0408
Nomanco Inc 501 Nmc Dr — *TF:* 800-345-7279 ■ *Web:* www.nomaco.com	Zebulon	NC	27597	919-269-6500	269-7936
Nova Solutions Inc 421 Industrial Ave — **Fax Area Code:* 800 ■ *TF:* 800-730-6682 ■ *Web:* www.novadesk.com	Effingham	IL	62401	217-342-7070	940-6682*
Office Chairs Inc 14815 Radburn Ave — *TF:* 866-624-4968 ■ *Web:* ocicontract.com	Santa Fe Springs	CA	90670	562-802-0464	926-5561
Omni International Inc 435 12th St SW PO Box 1409 — *TF:* 800-844-6664 ■ *Web:* www.omniinternational.com	Vernon	AL	35592	205-695-9173	695-6465
Open Plan Systems Inc 4700 Deepwater Terminal Rd — *TF:* 888-869-4681 ■ *Web:* www.openplan.com	Richmond	VA	23234	804-275-2468	275-2329
Paoli Inc 201 E Martin St — **Fax Area Code:* 812 ■ *TF:* 800-472-8669 ■ *Web:* www.paoli.com	Orleans	IN	47452	800-472-8669	865-1516*
Penco Products Inc 99 Brower Ave — *TF:* 800-562-1000 ■ *Web:* www.pencoproducts.com	Oaks	PA	19456	610-666-0500	666-7561
Reconditioned Systems Inc (RSI) 2636 S Wilson St Ste 105 — *TF:* 800-280-5000 ■ *Web:* www.rsisystemsfurniture.com	Tempe	AZ	85282	480-968-1772	894-1907
Robertson Furniture Company Inc 890 Elberton St — *TF:* 800-241-0713 ■ *Web:* www.robertson-furniture.com	Toccoa	GA	30577	706-886-1494	886-8998
Rush Industries Inc 118 N Wrenn St — *TF:* 800-524-0258 ■ *Web:* www.rushfurniture.com	High Point	NC	27260	336-886-7700	886-2227
Safco Products Co 9300 W Research Ctr Rd — *TF Cust Svc:* 800-328-3020 ■ *Web:* www.safcoproducts.com	New Hope	MN	55428	763-536-6700	536-6784
Sedgewick Industries 667 W Ward Ave — *Web:* www.sedgewick.com	High Point	NC	27260	336-885-9300	885-9174
Shafer Commercial Seating 4101 E 48th Ave — *Web:* www.shafer.com	Denver	CO	80216	303-322-7792	393-1836
Shure Manufacturing Corp 1901 W Main St — *TF:* 800-227-4873 ■ *Web:* www.shureusa.com	Washington	MO	63090	636-390-7100	390-7171
Southwood Furniture Corp 2860 Nathan St — *Web:* www.southwoodfurn.com	Hickory	NC	28602	828-465-1776	465-0858
Spectrum Industries Inc 925 First Ave — **Fax Area Code:* 800 ■ *TF:* 800-235-1262 ■ *Web:* www.spectrumfurniture.com	Chippewa Falls	WI	54729	715-723-6750	335-0473*
Statton Furniture Mfg Company Inc 504 E First St — *Web:* www.statton.com	Hagerstown	MD	21740	301-739-0360	739-8421
Steelcase Inc 801 44th St SE PO Box 1967 — *NYSE:* SCS ■ **Fax:* Mail Rm ■ *TF:* 888-783-3522 ■ *Web:* www.steelcase.asia	Grand Rapids	MI	49501	616-247-2710	247-2256*
Stevens Industries Inc 704 W Main St — *Web:* www.stevensind.com	Teutopolis	IL	62467	217-540-3100	857-7101
Stylex PO Box 5038 — **Fax Area Code:* 856 ■ *TF:* 800-257-5742 ■ *Web:* www.stylexseating.com	Delanco	NJ	08075	800-257-5742	461-5574*
TAB Products Co 605 Fourth St — **Fax Area Code:* 800 ■ *TF:* 888-466-8228 ■ *Web:* www.tab.com	Mayville	WI	53050	888-466-8228	304-4947*
Techline USA LLC 500 S Div St — **Fax Area Code:* 608 ■ *TF:* 800-356-8400 ■ *Web:* www.techlineusa.com	Waunakee	WI	53597	800-356-8400	850-2379*
Teknion Corp 1150 Flint Rd — *Web:* www.teknion.com	Toronto	ON	M3J2J5	416-661-3370	661-4586
Tennsco Corp 201 Tennsco Dr PO Box 1888 — **Fax Area Code:* 800 ■ *TF Cust Svc:* 866-446-8686 ■ *Web:* www.tennsco.com	Dickson	TN	37056	615-446-8000	722-0134*
Trendway Corp 13467 Quincy St PO Box 9016 — *TF:* 800-968-5344 ■ *Web:* www.trendway.com	Holland	MI	49422	616-399-3900	399-2231
Tuohy Furniture Corp 42 St Albans Pl — *TF Cust Svc:* 800-533-1696 ■ *Web:* www.tuohyfurniture.com	Chatfield	MN	55923	507-867-4280	867-3374
Ulrich Planfiling Equipment Corp 2120 Fourth Ave PO Box 135 — *Web:* www.ulrichcorp.com	Lakewood	NY	14750	716-763-1815	763-1818
Viking Acoustical Corp 21480 Heath Ave — *TF:* 800-328-8385 ■ *Web:* www.vikingusa.com	Lakeville	MN	55044	952-469-3405	469-4503
Vitro Seating Products Inc 201 Madison St — *TF Cust Svc:* 800-325-7093 ■ *Web:* www.vitroseating.com	Saint Louis	MO	63102	314-241-2265	241-8723
Watson Furniture Group Inc 26246 Twelve Trees Ln NW — *TF:* 800-426-1202 ■ *Web:* www.watsonfurniture.com	Poulsbo	WA	98370	360-394-1300	394-1322
West Coast Industries Inc 10 Jackson St — *TF:* 800-243-3150 ■ *Web:* www.westcoastindustries.com	San Francisco	CA	94111	415-621-6656	552-5368
Workplace Systems Inc 562 Mammoth Rd — *TF:* 800-258-9700 ■ *Web:* www.workplacesystemsinc.com	Londonderry	NH	03053	603-622-3727	622-0174
Wright Line LLC 160 Gold Star Blvd — *TF:* 800-225-7348 ■ *Web:* www.wrightline.com	Worcester	MA	01606	508-852-4300	853-8904

322-2 Household Furniture

Company	City	State	Zip	Phone	Fax
Acacia Home & Garden Inc 101 McLin Creek Rd N PO Box 426 — *Web:* www.acaciahomeandgarden.com	Conover	NC	28613	828-465-1700	465-4205
Alan White Co 506 Thomas St — *Web:* www.alanwhiteco.com	Stamps	AR	71860	870-533-4471	
Albany Industries Inc 504 N Glenfield Rd — *TF:* 877-534-9804 ■ *Web:* www.albanyindustries.com	New Albany	MS	38652	662-534-9800	534-9805
Ameriwood Industries Inc 410 E S First St — *TF General:* 800-489-3351 ■ *Web:* www.ameriwood.com	Wright City	MO	63390	636-745-3351	
Ashley Furniture Industries Inc One Ashley Way — *TF:* 800-477-2222 ■ *Web:* www.ashleyfurniture.com	Arcadia	WI	54612	608-323-6225	323-6008
Baby's Dream Furniture Inc 411 Industrial Blvd PO Box 579 — *TF:* 800-835-2742 ■ *Web:* www.babysdream.com	Buena Vista	GA	31803	229-649-4404	649-2007
Bassett Furniture Industries Inc 3525 Fairystone Pk Hwy PO Box 626 — *NASDAQ:* BSET ■ *TF:* 877-525-7070 ■ *Web:* www.bassettfurniture.com	Bassett	VA	24055	714-222-1010	
Bauhaus USA Inc One Bauhaus Dr — *Web:* www.bauhaususa.com	Saltillo	MS	38866	662-869-2664	869-5910
Bellini 495 Central Ave — *Web:* www.bellini.com	Scarsdale	NY	10583	914-472-7336	
Berg Furniture 120 E Gloucester Pike — *Web:* www.bergfurniture.com	Barrington	NJ	08007	856-310-0511	310-0512
Bielecky Bros Inc 979 Third Ave — *Web:* www.bieleckybrothers.com	New York	NY	10022	212-753-2355	751-9369
Bradington-Young 1340 14th Ave Ct SW — *Web:* www.bradington-young.com	Hickory	NC	28602	704-435-5881	435-4276
Broyhill Furniture Industries Inc 3483 Hickory Blvd — *TF Cust Svc:* 800-327-6944 ■ *Web:* www.broyhillfurniture.com	Hudson	NC	28638	828-396-2361	
Brueton Industries Inc 146 Hanse Ave — *TF Cust Svc:* 800-221-6783 ■ *Web:* www.brueton.com	Freeport	NY	11520	516-379-3400	543-4520
Bush Industries Inc 1 Mason Dr — *TF:* 800-950-4782 ■ *Web:* www.bushfurniture.com	Jamestown	NY	14701	716-665-2000	665-2074
Bushline Inc 707 Industrial Pk Rd — *Web:* bushline.com	New Tazewell	TN	37825	423-626-5246	
Canadel Furniture Inc 700 Canadel Ave — *Web:* www.canadel.com	Louiseville	QC	J5V2L6	819-228-8471	228-8389
Capris Furniture Industries Inc 1401 NW 27th Ave — *Web:* www.caprisfurniture.com	Ocala	FL	34475	352-629-8889	732-7310
Carrom 218 E Dowland St — *TF:* 800-223-6047 ■ *Web:* www.carrom.com	Ludington	MI	49431	231-845-1263	843-9276
Carson's Inc PO Box 14186 — *Web:* www.carsonsofhp.com	Archdale	NC	27263	336-431-1101	431-0677
Century Furniture LLC 401 11th St NW — *TF:* 800-852-5552 ■ *Web:* www.centuryfurniture.com	Hickory	NC	28601	828-328-1851	328-2176
Chromcraft Revington Inc 1330 Win Hentschel Blvd — *OTC:* CRCV ■ *Web:* www.chromcraft-revington.com	West Lafayette	IN	47906	765-807-2640	807-2660
Classic Leather Inc PO Box 2404 — *Web:* www.classic-leather.com	Hickory	NC	28603	828-328-2046	324-6212
Craftmaster Furniture Corp 221 Craftmaster Rd — *Web:* www.cmfurniture.com	Hiddenite	NC	28636	828-632-9786	632-0301
Cresent Fine Furniture PO Box 1438 — *Web:* www.cresent.com	Gallatin	TN	37066	615-452-1671	452-0098
DeFehr Furniture Ltd 125 Furniture Pk — *TF:* 877-333-3471 ■ *Web:* www.defehr.com	Winnipeg	MB	R2G1B9	204-988-5630	663-4458
DMI Furniture Inc 9780 Ormsby Stn Rd Ste 2000 — *TF:* 888-750-5834 ■ *Web:* www.dmifurniture.com	Louisville	KY	40223	502-426-4351	429-6285
Dorel Industries Inc 1255 Greene Ave Ste 300 — *TSE:* DII.B ■ *Web:* www.dorel.com	Montreal	QC	H3Z2A4	514-934-3034	934-9379
Durham Furniture Inc 450 Lambton St W — *Web:* www.durhamfurnitures.com	Durham	ON	N0G1R0	519-369-2345	369-6515
Dutailier Group Inc 299 Rue Chaput — *TF:* 800-363-9817 ■ *Web:* www.dutailier.com	Sainte-Pie	QC	J0H1W0	450-772-2403	772-5055
El Ran Furniture Ltd 2751 Transcanada Hwy — *TF:* 800-361-6546 ■ *Web:* www.elran.com	Pointe-Claire	QC	H9R1B4	514-630-5656	630-9150
Ethan Allen Interiors Inc Ethan Allen Dr — *NYSE:* ETH ■ **Fax Area Code:* 203 ■ *Web:* www.ethanallen.com	Danbury	CT	06811	888-324-3571	743-8298*

Phone *Fax*

Evenflo Company Inc 1801 Commerce Dr Piqua OH 45356 800-233-5921 415-3112*
*Fax Area Code: 937 ■ *Fax: Hum Res ■ TF: 800-233-5921 ■ Web: www.evenflo.com

Fairfield Chair Co PO Box 1710 Lenoir NC 28645 828-758-5571 758-0211
Web: www.fairfieldchair.com

Finnleo Sauna 575 Cokato St E Cokato MN 55321 800-346-6536 286-2224*
*Fax Area Code: 320 ■ TF: 800-346-6536 ■ Web: www.finnleo.com

Flexsteel Industries Inc 3400 Jackson St Dubuque IA 52001 563-556-7730 556-8345*
NASDAQ: FLXS ■ *Fax: Cust Svc ■ Web: www.flexsteel.com

Franklin Corp 600 Franklin Dr Houston MS 38851 662-456-4286 456-0008
Web: franklincorp.com/

Furniture Brands International Inc
One N Brentwood Blvd 15th Fl Saint Louis MO 63105 314-863-1100 863-5306
NYSE: FBN ■ Web: www.furniturebrands.com

Furniture Values International LLC
601 N 75 Th Ave Phoenix AZ 85043 602-442-5600 278-0103
Web: www.aspenhome.net

Hancock & Moore PO Box 3444 Hickory NC 28603 828-495-8235 495-3021
Web: www.hancockandmoore.com

Harden Furniture Inc
8550 Mill Pond Way McConnellsville NY 13401 315-245-1000 245-2884
Web: www.hardenfurniture.com

Hekman 860 E Main Ave Zeeland MI 49464 616-748-2660 748-2645
Web: www.hekman.com

Henkel Harris Company Inc
2983 S Pleasant Vly Rd PO Box 2170 Winchester VA 22601 540-667-4900 667-8261
Web: www.henkelharris.com

Hooker Furniture Corp
440 E Commonwealth Blvd Martinsville VA 24112 276-632-0459 388-2289*
NASDAQ: HOFT ■ *Fax Area Code: 800 ■ *Fax: Cust Svc ■ TF Cust Svc: 800-422-1511 ■ Web: www.hookerfurniture.com

Hughes Furniture Industries Inc
952 S Stout Rd Randleman NC 27317 336-498-8700 498-8750
Web: www.hughesfurniture.com

Human Touch 3030 Walnut Ave Long Beach CA 90807 562-426-8700 426-9690
TF: 800-742-5493 ■ Web: www.humantouch.com

Interior Crafts Inc 2513 W Cullerton Ave Chicago IL 60608 773-376-8160 376-9578
Web: interiorcraftsinc.com

J-Art Iron Co 9435 Jefferson Blvd Culver City CA 90232 310-202-1126 202-1642
Web: www.jartiron.com

Kessler Industries 8600 Gateway Blvd E El Paso TX 79907 915-591-8161 598-7353
Web: www.kesslerind.com

King Hickory Furniture Co 1820 Main Ave SE Hickory NC 28602 828-322-6025 328-2159
Web: www.kinghickory.com

Klaussner Home Furnishings 405 Lewallen Rd Asheboro NC 27205 336-625-6174 625-5584
TF: 888-732-5948 ■ Web: www.klaussner.com

La-Z-Boy Inc 1284 N Telegraph Rd Monroe MI 48162 734-242-1444 457-2005*
NYSE: LZB ■ *Fax: Sales ■ TF: 800-375-6890 ■ Web: www.la-z-boy.com

Lamont Ltd 1530 Bluff Rd Burlington IA 52601 319-753-5131 753-0946
TF: 800-553-5621 ■ Web: www.lamontlimited.com

Leathercraft 102 Section House Rd Hickory NC 28601 800-627-1561 627-1562
TF: 800-627-1561 ■ Web: www.leathercraft-furniture.com

Lexington Home Brands 1300 National Hwy Thomasville NC 27360 336-474-5300
TF: 800-952-5210 ■ Web: www.lexington.com

Little Tikes Co, The 2180 Barlow Rd Hudson OH 44236 800-321-0183
TF Cust Svc: 800-321-0183 ■ Web: www.littletikes.com

Mantua Mfg Co 7900 Northfield Rd Walton Hills OH 44146 800-333-8333 929-8014
TF Orders: 800-333-8333 ■ Web: www.bedframes.com

Marge Carson Inc 9056 Garvey Ave Rosemead CA 91770 626-571-1111 571-0924
Web: margecarson.com

McGuire Furniture Co 1201 Bryant St San Francisco CA 94103 415-626-1414 864-8593
TF: 800-662-4847 ■ Web: www.mcguirefurniture.com

Michael Thomas Furniture Inc
100 E Newberry Ave Liberty NC 27298 336-622-3075
Web: themtcompany.com/

Million Dollar Baby 841 Washington Blvd Montebello CA 90640 323-728-9988 722-8866
Web: www.milliondollarbaby.com

Mitchell Gold & Bob Williams Co (MGBW)
135 One Comfortable Pl Taylorsville NC 28681 828-632-9200 632-2693
TF: 800-789-5401 ■ Web: www.mgbwhome.com

New England Woodcraft Inc PO Box 165 Forest Dale VT 05745 802-247-8211 247-8042
Web: www.newoodcraft.com

Nichols & Stone One Stickley Dr PO Box 480 Manlius NY 13104 315-682-1554
Web: www.nichols-stone.com

Norwalk Furniture Corp 100 Furniture Pkwy Norwalk OH 44857 419-744-3200 668-6223
TF Orders: 800-837-2565 ■ Web: www.norwalkfurniture.com

Pearson Co 1420 Progress Ave High Point NC 27260 336-882-8135
TF: 800-225-0265 ■ Web: www.pearsonco.com

Perdue Woodworks Inc 2415 Creek Dr Rapid City SD 57703 605-341-2101 341-1565
Web: www.perduesinc.com

Progressive Furniture Inc PO Box 308 Archbold OH 43502 828-459-2151 459-9702
Web: www.progressivefurniture.com

Riverside Furniture Corp 1400 S Sixth St Fort Smith AR 72901 479-785-8100 785-6009
Web: www.riverside-furniture.com

Robern Inc 701 N Wilson Ave Bristol PA 19007 215-826-9800 826-9633
TF: 800-877-2376 ■ Web: www.robern.com

Room & Board Inc
4600 Olson Memorial Hwy Golden Valley MN 55422 763-521-4431 520-0811
TF: 800-301-9720 ■ Web: www.roomandboard.com

Rumble Tuff Inc 865 North 1430 West Orem UT 84057 801-609-8168 796-2688
TF: 855-228-8388 ■ Web: www.rumbletuff.com

Rush Industries Inc 118 N Wrenn St High Point NC 27260 336-886-7700 886-2227
TF: 800-524-0258 ■ Web: www.rushfurniture.com

Sam Moore Furniture Industries 1556 Dawn Dr Bedford VA 24523 540-586-8253 586-8497
Web: www.sammoore.com

Sauder Woodworking Co
502 Middle St PO Box 156 Archbold OH 43502 419-446-2711 446-3692
TF Cust Svc: 800-523-3987 ■ Web: www.sauder.com

Schnadig International Corp 4200 Tudor Ln Greensboro NC 27410 800-468-8730
TF: 800-468-8730 ■ Web: www.schnadig.com

Shermag Inc 3035 Boul Industriel Sherbrooke QC J1L2T9 819-566-1515 566-7323
Web: www.shermag.com

Sherrill Furniture Co 2405 Highland Ave NE Hickory NC 28601 828-322-2640
Web: www.sherrillfurniture.com

Sico North America Inc 7525 Cahill Rd Minneapolis MN 55439 952-941-1700 941-6737
TF: 800-328-6138 ■ Web: www.sicoinc.com

Southern Motion Inc PO Box 1064 Pontotoc MS 38863 662-488-9301
Web: www.southernmotion.com

Southwood Furniture Corp 2860 Nathan St Hickory NC 28602 828-465-1776 465-0858
Web: www.southwoodfurn.com

Standard Furniture Mfg Company Inc
801 Hwy 31 S Bay Minette AL 36507 251-937-6741 937-1178*
*Fax: Cust Svc ■ TF General: 877-788-1899 ■ Web: www.standard-furniture.com

Stanley Furniture Co Inc
1641 Fairystone Pk Hwy Stanleytown VA 24168 877-772-4858
NASDAQ: STLY ■ Web: www.stanleyfurniture.com

Statton Furniture Mfg Company Inc
504 E First St Hagerstown MD 21740 301-739-0360 739-8421
Web: www.statton.com

Storkcraft Baby 7433 Nelson Rd Richmond BC V6W1G3 604-274-5121 274-9727
TF: 877-274-0277 ■ Web: www.storkcraftdirect.com

Style Line Furniture Inc 116 Godfrey Rd Verona MS 38879 662-566-1113 566-7657
Web: styleline.us

Suncast Corp 701 N Kirk Rd Batavia IL 60510 630-879-2050 879-6112
TF: 800-444-3310 ■ Web: suncast.com

Swaim Inc 1801 S College Dr High Point NC 27260 336-885-6131 885-6227
Web: www.swaim-inc.com

Techline USA LLC 500 S Div St Waunakee WI 53597 800-356-8400 850-2379*
*Fax Area Code: 608 ■ TF: 800-356-8400 ■ Web: www.techlineusa.com

Thomasville Furniture Industries Inc
401 E Main St PO Box 339 Thomasville NC 27361 336-472-4000 472-4085
Web: www.thomasville.com

Vanguard Furniture Co Inc 109 Simpson St Conover NC 28613 828-328-5601
Web: www.vanguardfurniture.com

Walter E Smithe Furniture Inc
1251 W Thorndale Ave Itasca IL 60143 630-285-8000 620-1552
TF: 800-948-4263 ■ Web: www.smithe.com

Whittier Wood Products
3787 W First Ave PO Box 2827 Eugene OR 97402 541-687-0213 687-2060
TF: 800-653-3336 ■ Web: www.whittierwood.com

Winners Only Inc 1365 Pk Ctr Dr Vista CA 92081 760-599-0300
Web: www.winnersonly.com

Woodland Furniture 4475 S 15th W Idaho Falls ID 83402 208-523-9006
Web: www.woodlandfurniture.com

Zenith Products Corp 400 Lukens Dr New Castle DE 19720 800-892-3986 326-8400*
*Fax Area Code: 302 ■ *Fax: Cust Svc ■ TF: 800-892-3986 ■ Web: zenith-products.com/

322-3 Institutional & Other Public Buildings Furniture

Phone *Fax*

Achieva Inc 197 Funder Dr PO Box 729 Mocksville NC 27028 336-751-7104 751-5623
TF: 800-788-7213 ■ Web: www.achievaweb.com

Adden Furniture Inc 710 Chelmsford St Lowell MA 01851 978-454-7848 453-1449
TF: 800-625-3876 ■ Web: www.addenfurniture.com

American Desk 1302 Industrial Blvd Temple TX 76504 800-433-3142 773-7370*
*Fax Area Code: 254 ■ TF: 800-433-3142 ■ Web: americandesk.com

American of Martinsville
128 E Church St Martinsville VA 24112 276-632-2061 632-4707
Web: www.americanofmartinsville.com

American Seating Co
401 American Seating Ctr NW Grand Rapids MI 49504 616-732-6600 732-6401
TF Cust Svc: 800-748-0268 ■ Web: www.americanseating.com

Artco-Bell Corp 1302 Industrial Blvd Temple TX 76504 254-778-1811 771-0827
TF: 877-778-1811 ■ Web: www.artcobell.com

Bay Concepts Inc (BCI) 1036-47th Ave PO Box 7229 Oakland CA 94601 510-534-4511 534-4515

Bretford Manufacturing Inc
11000 Seymour Ave Franklin Park IL 60131 847-678-2545 343-1779*
*Fax Area Code: 800 ■ TF: 800-521-9614 ■ Web: www.bretford.com

Brodart Co 500 Arch St Williamsport PA 17701 570-326-2461
TF: 800-233-8467 ■ Web: www.brodart.com

Columbia Mfg Inc 1 Cycle St Westfield MA 01085 413-562-3664 568-5345
Web: www.columbiamfginc.com

ENOCHS Examining Room Furniture
PO Box 50559 Indianapolis IN 46250 800-428-2305 580-2944*
*Fax Area Code: 317 ■ *Fax: Cust Svc ■ TF Cust Svc: 800-428-2305 ■ Web: www.enochsmed.com

ErgoGenesis LLC One BodyBilt Pl Navasota TX 77868 936-825-1700 825-1725
TF: 800-364-5299 ■ Web: www.ergogenesis.com

Fleetwood Group Inc 11832 James St Holland MI 49424 616-396-1142 396-8022
TF: 800-257-6390 ■ Web: www.fleetwoodgroup.com

Fordham Equipment Co
1204 Village Market Place Suite 262 Morrisville NC 27560 919-467-0708
TF: 866-467-0708 ■ Web: www.fordhamplastics.com

Furniture by Thurston 12250 Charles Dr Grass Valley CA 95945 530-272-4331 272-4962
Web: thurstonmfg.net

Gaylord Bros 7282 William Barry Blvd Syracuse NY 13212 315-457-5070 453-5030
TF: 800-345-5330 ■ Web: www.gaylord.com

Gunlocke Company LLC One Gunlocke Dr Wayland NY 14572 585-728-5111 728-8334*
*Fax: Hum Res ■ TF Cust Svc: 800-828-6300 ■ Web: www.gunlocke.com

HAECO Americas 10262 Norris Ave Pacoima CA 91331 818-896-2938
Web: www.timco.aero

Hard Mfg Company Inc 230 Grider St Buffalo NY 14215 800-873-4273 896-2579*
*Fax Area Code: 716 ■ TF: 800-873-4273 ■ Web: www.hardmfg.com

Herman Miller for Health Care
855 E Main Ave PO Box 302 Zeeland MI 49464 616-654-3000
TF: 888-443-4357 ■ Web: www.hermanmiller.com/healthcare

Hill-Rom Services Inc 1069 SR 46 E Batesville IN 47006 812-934-7777 934-8189
TF: 800-267-2337 ■ Web: www.hill-rom.com

Hussey Seating Co 38 Dyer St Ext North Berwick ME 03906 207-676-2271 676-2222*
*Fax: Sales ■ TF: 800-341-0401 ■ Web: www.husseyseating.com

Imperial Woodworks Inc 7201 Mars Dr PO Box 7835 Waco TX 76714 800-234-6624 741-0736*
*Fax Area Code: 254 ■ TF: 800-234-6624 ■ Web: www.pews.com

Interkal Inc 5981 E Cork St Kalamazoo MI 49048 269-349-1521 349-6530
Web: www.interkal.com

	Phone	Fax
Inwood Office Invironments 1108 E 15th St PO Box 646 .... Jasper IN 47547 *Web:* www.inwood.net	812-482-6121	482-9732
Irwin Seating Company Inc 3251 Fruit Ridge NW .... Grand Rapids MI 49544 *TF:* 866-464-7946 ■ *Web:* www.irwinseating.com	616-574-7400	574-7411
Joerns Healthcare 5001 Joerns Dr .... Stevens Point WI 54481 **Fax Area Code:* 800 ■ *TF:* 800-826-0270	715-341-3600	457-8827*
Kimball Hospitality 1180 E 16th St .... Jasper IN 47549 **Fax Area Code:* 812 ■ *TF:* 800-634-9510 ■ *Web:* www.kimballhospitality.com	276-666-8933	634-4324*
KLN Steel Products Co Two Winnco Dr .... San Antonio TX 78218 *TF:* 800-624-9101 ■ *Web:* www.kln.com	210-227-4747	227-4047
LB Furniture Industries LLC 99 S Third St .... Hudson NY 12534 **Fax Area Code:* 800 ■ *TF:* 800-221-8752 ■ *Web:* www.lbempire.com	518-828-1501	969-9009*
List Industries Inc 401 Jim Moran Blvd .... Deerfield Beach FL 33442 *TF:* 800-776-1342 ■ *Web:* www.listindustries.com	954-429-9155	428-3843
Luxor Div EBSCO Industries Inc 2245 Delany Rd .... Waukegan IL 60087 **Fax Area Code:* 800 ■ *TF:* 800-323-4656 ■ *Web:* www.luxorfurn.com	847-244-1800	327-1698*
Meadows Office Furniture Co 71 W 23rd St .... New York NY 10010 *Web:* www.meadowsoffice.com	212-741-0333	741-0303
Meco Corp 1500 Industrial Rd .... Greeneville TN 37745 **Fax Area Code:* 423 ■ *TF:* 800-251-7558 ■ *Web:* www.meco.net	800-251-7558	639-1055*
Midwest Folding Products Inc 1414 S Western Ave .... Chicago IL 60608 *TF:* 800-621-4716 ■ *Web:* www.midwestfolding.com	312-666-3366	666-2606
Mitchell Furniture Systems Inc 1700 W St Paul Ave .... Milwaukee WI 53201 *TF:* 800-290-5960 ■ *Web:* www.mitchell-tables.com	414-342-3111	342-4239
Mity-Lite Inc 1301 West 400 North .... Orem UT 84057 *TF:* 800-909-8034 ■ *Web:* www.mitylite.com	801-224-0589	224-6191
MLP Seating Corp 2125 Lively Blvd .... Elk Grove Village IL 60007 *TF:* 800-723-3030 ■ *Web:* www.mlpseating.com	847-956-1700	956-1776
Monroe Table Co 316 N Walnut St .... Colfax IA 50054	515-674-3511	674-3513
Nemschoff Healthcare Furniture and Clinic Furniture 909 N Eigth St .... Sheboygan WI 53081 **Fax Area Code:* 920 ■ *TF Cust Svc:* 800-203-8916 ■ *Web:* www.nemschoff.com	800-203-8916	459-1234*
New Holland Church Furniture 313 Prospect St PO Box 217 .... New Holland PA 17557 **Fax Area Code:* 717 ■ *TF:* 800-648-9663 ■ *Web:* www.newhollandwood.com	800-648-9663	354-2481*
Omni International Inc 435 12th St SW PO Box 1409 .... Vernon AL 35592 *TF:* 800-844-6664 ■ *Web:* www.omniinternational.com	205-695-9173	695-6465
Parisi Royal Inc 305 Pheasant Run .... Newtown PA 18940 *Web:* www.parisi-royal.com	215-968-6677	968-3580
Royal Seating Ltd 1110 Industrial Blvd .... Cameron TX 76520 **Fax Area Code:* 920 ■ *TF Cust Svc:* 888-388-3224 ■ *Web:* www.royalseating.com	254-605-5500	725-0998*
Scholarcraft Inc PO Box 170748 .... Birmingham AL 35217 *Web:* www.scholarcraft.com	205-841-1922	841-1992
Shelby Williams Industries Inc 810 W Hwy 25/70 .... Newport TN 37821 **Fax Area Code:* 866 ■ *TF General:* 800-873-3252 ■ *Web:* shelbywilliams.com	423-623-0031	319-9371*
Sico North America Inc 7525 Cahill Rd .... Minneapolis MN 55439 *TF:* 800-328-6138 ■ *Web:* www.sicoinc.com	952-941-1700	941-6737
Spectrum Industries Inc 925 First Ave .... Chippewa Falls WI 54729 **Fax Area Code:* 800 ■ *TF:* 800-235-1262 ■ *Web:* www.spectrumfurniture.com	715-723-6750	335-0473*
Sturdisteel Co PO Box 2655 .... Waco TX 76702 **Fax Area Code:* 254 ■ *TF:* 800-433-3116 ■ *Web:* www.sturdisteel.com	800-433-3116	666-4472*
Tesco Industries LP 1035 E Hacienda .... Bellville TX 77418 **Fax Area Code:* 979 ■ *TF:* 800-699-5824 ■ *Web:* www.tesco-ind.com	800-699-5824	865-9074*
TMI Systems Design Corp 50 S Third Ave W .... Dickinson ND 58601 *TF:* 800-456-6716 ■ *Web:* www.tmisystems.com	701-456-6716	456-6700
UMF Medical 1316 Eisenhower Blvd .... Johnstown PA 15904 *TF:* 800-638-5322 ■ *Web:* www.umfmedical.com	814-266-8726	266-1870
Valley City Mfg Co Ltd, The 64 Hatt St .... Dundas ON L9H2G3 *TF:* 800-306-3319 ■ *Web:* www.valleycity.com	905-628-2253	628-0753
Virco Manufacturing Corp 2027 Harpers Way .... Torrance CA 90501 *NASDAQ: VIRC* ■ **Fax Area Code:* 800 ■ *TF Cust Svc:* 800-448-4726 ■ *Web:* www.virco.com	310-533-0474	258-7367*
Wieland 13737 Main St PO Box 1000 .... Grabill IN 46741 *TF:* 888-943-5263 ■ *Web:* www.wielandhealthcare.com	260-627-3686	627-6496
Winco Inc 5516 SW First Ln .... Ocala FL 34474 *TF:* 800-237-3377 ■ *Web:* www.wincomfg.com	352-854-2929	854-9544
Worden Company Inc 199 E 17th St .... Holland MI 49423 *TF:* 800-748-0561 ■ *Web:* www.wordencompany.com	616-392-1848	392-2542

322-4 Outdoor Furniture

	Phone	Fax
A Homecrest Outdoor Living LLC 1250 Homecrest Ave .... Wadena MN 56482 *TF:* 888-346-4852 ■ *Web:* www.homecrest.com	218-631-1000	
Belson Outdoors Inc 111 N River Rd .... North Aurora IL 60542 *TF:* 800-323-5664 ■ *Web:* www.belson.com	630-897-8489	897-0573
Bemis Manufacturing Co 300 Mill St .... Sheboygan Falls WI 53085 *TF:* 800-558-7651 ■ *Web:* www.bemismfg.com	920-467-4621	467-8573
Brown Jordan Co 9860 Gidley St .... El Monte CA 91731 *TF:* 800-743-4252 ■ *Web:* www.brownjordan.com	800-743-4252	
CFI Manufacturing Inc 2150 Whitfield Ave .... Sarasota FL 34243	941-751-1000	
Cox Industries Inc 860 Cannon Bridge Rd PO Box 1124 .... Orangeburg SC 29116 *TF:* 800-476-4401 ■ *Web:* www.coxwood.com	803-534-7467	534-1410
DuMor Inc PO Box 142 .... Mifflintown PA 17059 *TF:* 800-598-4018 ■ *Web:* www.dumor.com	717-436-2106	436-9839
Gardenside Ltd 808 Anthony St Ste 140 .... Berkeley CA 94710 *TF:* 888-999-8325 ■ *Web:* www.gardenside.com	415-455-4500	455-4505
Hatteras Hammocks Inc 305 Industrial Blvd .... Greenville NC 27834 *TF:* 800-643-3522 ■ *Web:* www.hatterashammocks.com	252-758-0641	758-0375
Hill Co 8040 Germantown Ave .... Philadelphia PA 19118 *Web:* www.hill-company.com	215-247-7600	247-7603
J Robert Scott Inc 500 N Oak St .... Inglewood CA 90302 *TF:* 877-207-5130 ■ *Web:* www.jrobertscott.com	310-680-4300	672-3710
Kay Park Recreation Corp 1301 Pine St .... Janesville IA 50647 **Fax Area Code:* 319 ■ **Fax:* Cust Svc ■ *TF Cust Svc:* 800-553-2476 ■ *Web:* www.kaypark.com	800-553-2476	987-2900*
Kessler Industries 8600 Gateway Blvd E .... El Paso TX 79907 *Web:* www.kesslerind.com	915-591-8161	598-7353
Kingsley-Bate Ltd 7200 Gateway Ct .... Manassas VA 20109 *Web:* www.kingsleybate.com	703-361-7000	361-7001
Mallin Casual Furniture One Minson Way .... Montebello CA 90640 **Fax Area Code:* 323 ■ *TF:* 800-251-6537 ■ *Web:* www.mallinfurniture.com	800-251-6537	513-1047*
Minson Corp 1 Minson Way .... Montebello CA 90640 *TF:* 800-251-6537 ■ *Web:* www.minson.com	323-513-1041	513-1047
OW Lee Company Inc 1822 E Francis St .... Ontario CA 91761 *TF:* 800-776-9533 ■ *Web:* www.owlee.com	909-947-3771	947-6614
RIO Brands 10981 Decatur Rd .... Philadelphia PA 19154 *Web:* riobrands.com	215-632-2800	824-1172
RJ Thomas Mfg Company Inc PO Box 946 .... Cherokee IA 51012 *Web:* www.pilotrock.com	712-225-5115	225-5796
Telescope Casual Furniture Inc 82 Church St .... Granville NY 12832 *Web:* telescopecasual.com	518-642-1100	642-2536
Tropitone Furniture Co Inc 5 Marconi .... Irvine CA 92618 **Fax Area Code:* 800 ■ **Fax:* Cust Svc ■ *TF All:* 800-654-7000 ■ *Web:* www.tropitone.com	949-951-2010	972-5714*
Twin Oaks Hammocks 138 Twin Oaks Rd .... Louisa VA 23093 *TF:* 800-688-8946 ■ *Web:* www.twinoakshammocks.com	540-894-5125	894-4112
Wabash Valley Manufacturing Inc 505 E Main St .... Silver Lake IN 46982 *TF:* 800-253-8619 ■ *Web:* www.wabashvalley.com	260-352-2102	352-2160
Walpole Woodworkers Inc 767 E St Rt 7 .... Walpole MA 02081 *TF Cust Svc:* 800-343-6948 ■ *Web:* www.walpolewoodworkers.com	508-668-2800	668-7301
Winston Furniture 540 Dolphin Rd .... Haleyville AL 35565 *Web:* www.winstonfurniture.com	205-486-9211	

323 FURNITURE - WHOL

	Phone	Fax
A Lava & Son Co 4800 S Kilbourn Ave .... Chicago IL 60632 *Web:* www.alavason.com	773-254-2800	
Adirondack Direct 3040 48th Ave .... Long Island City NY 11101 *TF:* 800-221-2444 ■ *Web:* www.adirondack.com	718-204-4500	204-4537
AFD Contract Furniture Inc 810 Seventh Ave # 2 .... New York NY 10019 *Web:* www.afd-inc.com	212-721-7100	721-7175
All Purpose Manufacturing Inc 614 Airport Rd .... Oceanside CA 92058 *Web:* www.apmfg.net	760-967-8464	
Amini Innovation Corp 8725 Rex Rd .... Pico Rivera CA 90660 *Web:* www.amini.com	562-222-2500	222-2525
ATD-American Co 135 Greenwood Ave .... Wyncote PA 19095 **Fax Area Code:* 800 ■ *TF:* 866-283-9327 ■ *Web:* www.atdamerican.com	215-576-1380	523-2300*
BCinteriors 3390 Valmont Rd .... Boulder CO 80301 *Web:* www.bcinteriors.com	303-443-3666	443-0406
Bellia Office Furniture Inc 1047 N Broad St Ste 2 .... Woodbury NJ 08096 *Web:* www.bellia.net	856-845-2234	
Berco Inc 1120 Montrose Ave .... Saint Louis MO 63104 *Web:* www.bercoinc.com	314-772-4700	
BIF New York Inc 465 Barell Ave .... Carlstadt NJ 07072 *Web:* www.bifnewyork.com	201-933-7777	
Borden Office Equipment Co 141 N Fifth St .... Steubenville OH 43952 *Web:* www.bordenofficeequipment.com	740-283-3321	
Brown & Saenger 711 W Russell St PO Box 84040 .... Sioux Falls SD 57118 *TF:* 800-952-3509 ■ *Web:* www.brown-saenger.com	605-336-1960	332-0963
Business Furniture Corp 6102 Victory Way .... Indianapolis IN 46278 *TF:* 800-774-5544 ■ *Web:* businessfurniture.net	317-216-1600	216-1602
Business Furniture Inc 10 Lanidex Ctr W .... Parsippany NJ 07054 *Web:* www.bfionline.com	973-503-0730	503-1565
California Office Furniture 1724 Tenth St .... Sacramento CA 95811 *TF:* 877-442-6959 ■ *Web:* caloffice.com	916-442-6959	442-3480
Carithers Wallace Courtenay Co 4343 NE Expy .... Atlanta GA 30340 *TF:* 800-292-8220 ■ *Web:* www.c-w-c.com	770-493-8200	491-6374
Carolina Wholesale Office Machine Company Inc 425 E Arrowhead Dr .... Charlotte NC 28213 *Web:* www.cwholesale.com	704-598-8101	
Carroll Seating Company Inc 10 Lincoln St .... Kansas City KS 66103 *TF:* 800-972-3779 ■ *Web:* www.carrollseating.com	816-471-2929	471-3001
Champion Industries Inc PO Box 2968 PO Box 2968 .... Huntington WV 25728 *OTC: CHMP* ■ *TF:* 800-624-3431 ■ *Web:* champion-industries.com	304-528-2791	528-2746
COECO Office Systems Co 2521 N Church St PO Box 2088 .... Rocky Mount NC 27804 *TF:* 800-682-6844 ■ *Web:* www.coeco.com	252-977-1121	985-1566
Commercial Furniture Interiors Inc 1154 Rt 22 W .... Mountainside NJ 07092 *Web:* www.cfioffice.com	908-518-1670	654-8436
Conklin Office Furniture 56 N Canal St .... Holyoke MA 01040 *Web:* www.conklinoffice.com	413-315-6777	
Corporate Environments 1636 NE Expwy .... Atlanta GA 30329 *Web:* www.corporateenvironments.com	404-492-8775	679-8950
Corry Contract Inc 21 Maple Ave .... Corry PA 16407 *Web:* www.corrycontract.com	814-665-8221	
Cubicles Office Environments Inc 2560 Fortune Way .... Vista CA 92081 *Web:* www.sandiegocubicles.com	760-560-5800	
Culver-newlin Inc Schl Furn 840 S Wanamaker Ave .... Ontario CA 91761 *Web:* www.culver-newlin.com	909-390-3715	

Company	City	State	Zip	Phone	Fax
Dancker Sellew & Douglas 291 Evans Way *TF:* 800-326-2537 ■ *Web:* www.dancker.com	Somerville	NJ	08876	908-231-1600	231-0469
Egan Visual Inc 300 Hanlan Rd *Web:* www.egan.com	Woodbridge	ON	L4L3P6	905-851-2826	851-3426
Elrod's Cost Plus #2 2025 Ft Worth Ave *Web:* www.elrodscostplus.com	Dallas	TX	75208	214-942-1104	
Empire Office Inc 105 Madison Ave Ste 15 *TF:* 877-533-6747 ■ *Web:* www.empireoffice.com	New York	NY	10016	212-607-5500	607-5650
Enriching Spaces 1360 Kemper Meadow Dr *Web:* www.enrichingspaces.com	Cincinnati	OH	45240	513-851-0933	742-6415
Evergreen Enterprises Inc 5915 Midlothian Trnpk *TF:* 877-558-1511 ■ *Web:* www.myevergreen.com	Richmond	VA	23225	804-231-1800	231-2888
EVS Ltd 3702 W Sample St Ste 1119 *Web:* www.evsltd.com	South Bend	IN	46619	574-233-5707	
Facilitec Inc 4501 E McDowell Rd *Web:* www.facilitec-inc.com	Phoenix	AZ	85008	602-275-0101	
Facilitech Inc 1111 Vly View Ln *Web:* www.businessinteriors.com	Irving	TX	75061	817-858-2000	
Fournitures De Bureau Denis Inc 2990 boul Le Corbusier *Web:* www.denis.ca	Laval	QC	H7L3M2	450-687-3110	
Furniture Consultants Inc 641 Ave of the Americas Second Fl *Web:* www.e-fci.com	New York	NY	10011	212-229-4500	807-0036
Furniture Source Inc, The 6813 Shady Oak Rd *Web:* www.thefsi.com	Eden Prairie	MN	55344	952-829-7100	
General Office Products Co 4521 Hwy 7 *Web:* www.gopco.com	Minneapolis	MN	55416	952-925-7500	925-7531
GL Seaman & Co 4201 International Pkwy *Web:* www.glseamancompany.com	Carrollton	TX	75007	214-764-6400	764-6420
Glover Sales Group LLC 221 Cockeysville Rd *TF:* 800-966-9016 ■ *Web:* www.gloverequipment.com	Cockeysville	MD	21030	410-771-8000	771-8010
GT Grandstands Inc 2810 Sydney Rd *Web:* www.gtgrandstands.com	Plant City	FL	33566	813-305-1415	
Haldeman-Homme Inc 430 Industrial Blvd NE *TF:* 800-795-0696 ■ *Web:* www.haldemanhomme.com	Minneapolis	MN	55413	612-331-4880	378-2236
Hangman Products Inc 6400 Variel Ave *Web:* www.hangmanproducts.com	Woodland Hills	CA	91367	818-610-0487	
Hart Furniture Company Inc 12 Harold Hart Rd *Web:* www.hartfurnitureco.com	Siler City	NC	27344	919-742-4141	663-2925
Henricksen & Co 1101 W River Pkwy Ste 100 *Web:* www.henricksen.com	Minneapolis	MN	55415	612-455-2200	877-3300
Heritage Office Furnishings 807 Powell St *Web:* www.heritageoffice.com	Vancouver	BC	V6A1H7	604-688-2381	
Hudson Seating & Mobility 151 Rockwell Rd *TF:* 800-321-4442 ■ *Web:* www.hudsonhhc.com	Newington	CT	06111	860-666-7500	666-7501
Hummels Office Equipment Co 25 Canal St *Web:* www.hummelsop.com	Mohawk	NY	13407	315-866-3860	
Intereum 845 Berkshire Ln N *Web:* www.intereum.com	Plymouth	MN	55441	763-417-3300	417-3309
Interiors Inc 1325 N Dutton Ave *Web:* interiorsincorporated.com	Santa Rosa	CA	95401	707-544-4770	544-0722
J L Business Interiors Inc 515 Schoenhaar Dr PO Box 303 *TF:* 866-338-5524 ■ *Web:* www.jlbusinessinteriors.com	West Bend	WI	53090	262-338-2221	338-2269
Jules Seltzer Assoc 9020 W Olympic Blvd *Web:* www.julesseltzer.com	Beverly Hills	CA	90211	310-274-7243	274-7243
Kayhan International Ltd 1475 E Woodfield Rd Ste 104 *Web:* www.kayhan.com	Schaumburg	IL	60173	847-843-5060	
KBM Workspace 160 w santa clara st Ste 102 *Web:* www.kbmworkspace.com	San Jose	CA	95113	408-351-7100	938-0699
Kentwood Office Furniture Inc 3063 Breton Rd SE *TF:* 877-698-6250 ■ *Web:* www.kentwoodoffice.com	Grand Rapids	MI	49512	616-957-2320	957-2361
Lee Company Inc 27 S 12th St *Web:* leecompanyinc.com	Terre Haute	IN	47807	812-235-8155	235-3587
Lenoir Empire Furniture 1625 Cherokee Rd *Web:* lenoirempirefurniture.com	Johnson City	TN	37604	423-929-7283	929-7040
Loth Inc 3574 E Kemper Rd *Web:* www.lothexperts.com	Cincinnati	OH	45241	513-554-4900	554-8700
Magnussen Home Furnishings Ltd 66 Hincks St *Web:* www.magnussen.com	New Hamburg	ON	N3A2A3	519-662-3040	662-3733
Mazany Office Interiors 428 Livingston Ave *Web:* www.mazanyoffice.com	Jamestown	NY	14701	716-487-1617	
MISSCO Contract Sales 2510 Lakeland Terr Ste 100 *Web:* www.missco.com	Jackson	MS	39216	601-987-8600	987-3038
Najarian Furniture Company Inc 17560 Rowland St *TF:* 888-781-3088 ■ *Web:* www.najarianfurniture.com	City of Industry	CA	91748	626-839-8700	839-8707
National Business Furniture Inc 735 N Water St Ste 440 *TF Sales:* 800-558-1010 ■ *Web:* www.nationalbusinessfurniture.com	Milwaukee	WI	53202	414-276-8511	276-8371
Nevers Industries Inc 14125 21st Ave N *Web:* www.nevers.com	Minneapolis	MN	55447	763-210-4206	
Nickerson Corp PO Box 5751 *Web:* www.nickersoncorp.com	Bay Shore	NY	11706	631-666-0200	666-2667
North Country Business Products Inc 1112 S Railroad St SE *TF:* 800-937-4140 ■ *Web:* www.ncbpinc.com	Bemidji	MN	56619	218-751-4140	755-6039
Office Environments Inc 11407 Granite St *TF:* 888-861-2525 ■ *Web:* www.office-environments.com	Charlotte	NC	28273	704-714-7200	714-7400
Office Furniture Team 4204 Lindbergh Dr *Web:* www.oftoffice.com	Addison	TX	75001	972-503-8326	503-8327
Office Pavilion 10030 Bent Oak Dr *Web:* www.ophouston.com	Houston	TX	77040	713-803-0000	803-0001
Office Plus of Lake County 1428 Glen Flora Ave PO Box 8758 *Web:* www.getofficeplus.com	Waukegan	IL	60085	847-662-5393	662-8761
Office Star Products 1901 S Archibald PO Box 3520 *TF:* 800-950-7262 ■ *Web:* www.officestar.net	Ontario	CA	91761	909-930-2000	930-5419
Ohio Desk Co 1122 Prospect Ave E *TF:* 800-334-4922 ■ *Web:* www.ohiodesk.com	Cleveland	OH	44115	216-623-0600	623-0611
OMED of Nevada LLC 800 Stillwell Ave Ste 80 *Web:* www.omednevada.com	Reno	NV	89512	775-857-3008	
OneWorkplace 475 Brannan St Ste 210 *Web:* oneworkplace.com	San Francisco	CA	94107	415-357-2200	357-2201
Pacific Design Ctr 8687 Melrose Ave *Web:* www.pacificdesigncenter.com	West Hollywood	CA	90069	310-657-0800	652-8576
Paragon Furniture Management Inc 2224 E Randol Mill Rd *Web:* www.paragoninc.com	Arlington	TX	76011	817-633-3242	
Patton Sales Corp 1095 E California St *Web:* www.pattonscorp.com	Ontario	CA	91761	909-988-0661	
Peabody Office Furniture Corp 234 Congress St *Web:* www.peabodyoffice.com	Boston	MA	02110	617-542-1902	542-1609
Pear Commercial Interiors Inc 1515 Arapahoe St Ste 100 *Web:* www.pearcom.com	Denver	CO	80202	303-824-2000	824-2001
Pigott Inc 3815 Ingersoll Ave *Web:* www.pigottnet.com	Des Moines	IA	50312	515-279-8879	279-7338
Pivot Interiors 2740 Zanker Rd Ste 100 *Web:* www.pivotinteriors.com	San Jose	CA	95134	408-432-5600	432-5601
Planned Furniture Promotions Inc Nine Moody Rd Bldg D Ste 18 *Web:* www.pfpnow.com	Enfield	CT	06082	860-749-1472	
Quality Enclosures Inc 2025 Porter Lk Dr *Web:* www.qualityenclosures.com	Sarasota	FL	34240	941-378-0051	
R & M Office Furniture 9615 Oates Dr *TF:* 800-660-1756 ■ *Web:* www.randmoffice.com	Sacramento	CA	95827	916-362-1756	362-1086
Red Thread 300 E River Dr *TF:* 800-334-4922 ■ *Web:* www.red-thread.com	East Hartford	CT	06108	860-528-9981	528-1843
RH Kyle Furniture Co 1352 Hansford St	Charleston	WV	25301	304-346-0671	
Rieke Office Interiors 2000 Fox Ln *Web:* www.rieke.com	Elgin	IL	60123	847-622-9711	
Sarreid Ltd 3905 Airport Dr NW *Web:* www.sarreid.com	Wilson	NC	27896	252-291-1414	237-1592
Saxton Inc Design Group 600 Third St Se Ste 300 *Web:* www.saxtoninc.com	Cedar Rapids	IA	52401	319-365-6967	
Southern Office Furniture Distributors Inc 7820 Thorndike Rd	Greensboro	NC	27409	336-668-4192	668-2076
Sterling Collection Inc, The 1730 First St *Web:* www.sterling-collection.com	San Fernando	CA	91340	818-837-4680	361-2250
Superior Medical Supply Inc 11005 Dover St Unit 1100 *TF:* 877-460-1411 ■ *Web:* superiormedicalsupply.com	Broomfield	CO	80021	877-460-1411	
Systechs Inc 249 W Baywood Ave Ste B *Web:* www.systechs.com	Orange	CA	92865	714-283-2890	
Tangram Interiors Inc 9200 Sorensen Ave *Web:* www.tangraminteriors.com	Santa Fe Springs	CA	90670	562-365-5000	365-5399
Teammates Commercial Interiors 320 S Teller St Ste 250 *Web:* www.team-mates.com	Lakewood	CO	80226	303-639-5885	
Tolar Manufacturing Company Inc 258 Mariah Cir *Web:* www.tolarmfg.com	Corona	CA	92879	951-808-0081	
Trade Products Corp 12124 Popes Head Rd *TF:* 888-352-3580 ■ *Web:* www.tradeproductscorp.com	Fairfax	VA	22030	703-502-9000	502-9399
Treasure Garden Inc 13401 Brooks Dr Ste A *Web:* treasuregarden.com	Baldwin Park	CA	91706	626-814-0168	
Trinity Hardwood Distributors Inc 110 East Oregon *TF:* 800-492-9856 ■ *Web:* www.trinityhardwood.net	Dallas	TX	75203	214-948-3001	946-1219
UCC Totalhome 8450 Broadway *Web:* www.ucctops.com	Merrillville	IN	46411	219-736-1100	
Waldner's Business Environment 125 Rt 110 *Web:* www.waldners.com	Farmingdale	NY	11735	631-844-9300	694-3503
Wasserstrom Co 477 S Front St *TF:* 866-634-8927 ■ *Web:* www.wasserstrom.com	Columbus	OH	43215	614-228-6525	737-8911
Wholesale Interiors Inc 794 Golf Ln *Web:* www.interiorexpressoutlet.com	Bensenville	IL	60106	630-238-8877	
Winners Only Inc 1365 Pk Ctr Dr *Web:* www.winnersonly.com	Vista	CA	92081	760-599-0300	
Workplace Solutions 30800 Telegraph Rd Ste 2985 *Web:* www.myworkplacesolutions.com	Bingham Farms	MI	48025	248-430-2500	
Workscapes Inc 1173 N Orange Ave *Web:* www.workscapes.com	Orlando	FL	32804	407-599-6770	599-6780

324 FURNITURE STORES

SEE ALSO Department Stores p. 2197

Company	City	State	Zip	Phone	Fax
A A Office Equipment & Furniture 2140 American Ave *Web:* www.aaoffice.com	Hayward	CA	94545	510-782-6110	
A D Wynne Co Inc 710 Baronne St *Web:* www.adwynne.com	New Orleans	LA	70113	504-585-0800	522-7070

				Phone	Fax
A Diamond Production Inc 2150 Cesar Chavez St. *Web:* www.thefutonshop.com	San Francisco	CA	94124	415-920-6800	
Activeforevercom 10799 N 90th St. *TF:* 800-377-8033 ■ *Web:* www.activeforever.com	Scottsdale	AZ	85260	480-459-3202	
Addison House Interiors Inc 5201 Nw 77th Ave Ste 400 *Web:* www.addisonhouse.com	Doral	FL	33166	305-640-2400	
Afinety Inc 1956 Cotner Ave. *TF:* 877-423-4638 ■ *Web:* www.afinety.com	Los Angeles	CA	90025	310-996-2700	
Agati Inc 1219 W Lake St *Web:* www.agati.com	Chicago	IL	60607	312-829-1977	
Albany Bedding LLC 3900 Pecan Grove Ct	Albany	GA	31701	229-420-7399	
All Makes Office Equipment Co 2558 Farnam St *TF:* 800-341-2413 ■ *Web:* www.allmakes.com	Omaha	NE	68131	402-341-2413	
Allen Furniture City Inc 7808 L St. *Web:* allenshome.com	Omaha	NE	68127	402-331-8480	
Ambella Home Collection Corporate Office 4910 Lakawana St.	Dallas	TX	75247	214-631-8901	
AMC Industries LLC 1120 N 28th St *Web:* www.amcind.com	Tampa	FL	33605	813-989-9663	
America The Beautiful Dreamer Inc 9700 Ne 126th Ave. *Web:* www.atbd.com	Vancouver	WA	98682	360-816-0167	
American Factory Direct Furniture Outlets Inc 210 New Camellia Blvd. *Web:* www.afd-furniture.com	Covington	LA	70433	985-845-2465	
American Freight Ohio Inc 2770 Lexington Ave *Web:* www.americanfreight.us	Mansfield	OH	44904	419-884-2224	
American Furniture Warehouse Co 8501 Grant St. *TF:* 888-615-9415 ■ *Web:* www.afwonline.com	Thornton	CO	80229	303-289-3300	288-1726
American Home Furnishings 3535 Menaul Blvd NE. *TF:* 800-854-6755 ■ *Web:* www.americanhome.com	Albuquerque	NM	87107	505-883-2211	816-6521
American Office Equipment Company Inc 309 N Calvert St. *Web:* www.americanoffice.com	Baltimore	MD	21202	410-539-7529	
American Surplus Inc One Noyes Ave Bldg B *Web:* www.americansurplus.com	Rumford	RI	02916	401-434-4355	
Ameublements Tanguay Inc 7200 Rue Armand-Viau *Web:* www.tanguay.ca	Quebec	QC	G2C2A7	418-847-4411	847-4848
Andreas Furniture Company Inc 114 Dover Rd Ne *Web:* www.andreasfurniture.com	Sugarcreek	OH	44681	330-852-2494	
APG Office Furnishings Inc 12075 Northwest Blvd Ste 100 *Web:* www.apgof.com	Cincinnati	OH	45246	513-621-9111	
Applied Knowledge Group Inc 2100 Reston Pkwy Ste 400 *Web:* www.akgroup.com	Reston	VA	20191	703-860-1145	
Arcadia Chair Co 5692 Fresca Dr *Web:* www.encoreseating.com	La Palma	CA	90623	714-562-8200	
Arenson Office Furnishings Inc 1115 Broadway Sixth Fl *Web:* www.aof.com	New York	NY	10010	646-395-3563	
Arenson Office Furniture 8185 Camino Santa Fe *Web:* www.arensonof.com	San Diego	CA	92121	858-453-2411	
Arizona Leather Company Inc 4235 Schaefer Ave *TF:* 888-669-5328 ■ *Web:* www.arizonaleather.com	Chino	CA	91710	909-993-5101	
ART Furniture Inc 1165 Auto Ctr Dr. *Web:* www.arthomefurnishings.com	Ontario	CA	91761	909-390-1039	
Atlantic Corporate Interiors Inc (ACI) 7001 Muirkirk Meadows Dr Ste A. *Web:* www.aciinc.com	Beltsville	MD	20705	301-931-3600	931-3601
August Inc 354 Congress Park Dr. *Web:* www.augustinc.com	Centerville	OH	45459	937-434-2520	
Avis Furniture Co 1410 Union Ave. *Web:* www.avisfurniture.com	Kansas City	MO	64101	816-421-5939	
Back To Bed Inc 700 Hill Top Dr *Web:* www.backtobed.com	Itasca	IL	60143	630-931-4602	
Bad Boy Furniture Warehouse Ltd 500 Fenmar Dr. *Web:* www.badboy.ca	Weston	ON	M9L2V5	416-667-7546	
Badcock's Economy Furniture Store Inc 3931 RCA Blvd. *Web:* www.badcockinc.com	Palm Beach Gardens	FL	33410	561-694-8588	
Baer's Furniture Co Inc 1589 Northwest 12th Ave *Web:* baers.com	Pompano Beach	FL	33069	954-582-4200	
Baileys Furniture Outlet Inc 350 W Intl Airport Rd Ste 100. *Web:* www.baileysfurniture.com	Anchorage	AK	99518	907-563-4083	
Bar Productscom Inc 1990 Lake Ave SE. *TF:* 800-256-6396 ■ *Web:* www.barproducts.com	Largo	FL	33771	727-584-2093	
Barn Furniture Mart Inc 6206 N Sepulveda Blvd *TF:* 888-302-2276 ■ *Web:* www.barnfurnituremart.com	Van Nuys	CA	91411	818-780-4070	780-4749
Bay View Plaza Furniture Inc 2181 E Pass Rd *Web:* bayviewfurniture.com	Gulfport	MS	39507	228-896-4400	
Beaufurn LLC 5269 US Hwy 158 *TF:* 888-766-7706 ■ *Web:* www.beaufurn.com	Advance	NC	27006	888-766-7706	
Becks Furniture Inc 11840 Folsom Blvd *Web:* www.becksfurniture.com	Rancho Cordova	CA	95742	916-353-5000	
Bedroom Store Inc 2440 Adie Rd *Web:* www.thebedroomstore.com	Maryland Heights	MO	63043	314-569-0259	
Beiter's Inc 560 Montgomery Pk *Web:* www.beiters.com	South Williamsport	PA	17702	570-326-2073	
Belfort Furniture Inc 22250 and 22267 Shaw Rd. *Web:* www.belfortfurniture.com	Dulles	VA	20166	703-406-7600	
Bernie & Phyl's Furniture 308 E Main St. *Web:* www.bernieandphyls.com	Norton	MA	02766	508-286-4000	
Best Material Handling Inc 4754 N Chestnut St *TF:* 800-933-5270 ■ *Web:* www.best-materials.com	Colorado Springs	CO	80907	719-599-9191	
bkm Officeworks 9201 Spectrum Ctr Blvd Ste 100 *Web:* www.bkmofficeworks.com	San Diego	CA	92123	858-569-4700	
Blackledge Furniture 233 Sw Second St. *Web:* www.blackledgefurniture.com	Corvallis	OR	97333	541-753-4851	
Blacklion International Inc 10605 Park Rd *Web:* www.blacklion.com	Charlotte	NC	28210	704-541-1148	
Bmea Enterprises Inc 13370 Kirkham Way.	Poway	CA	92064	858-513-6584	
Bob Mills Furniture Company LLC 3600 W Reno Ave *Web:* bobmillsfurniture.com	Oklahoma City	OK	73107	405-947-6500	
Bob's Discount Furniture Inc 428 Tolland Tpke *Web:* www.mybobs.com	Manchester	CT	06042	860-645-3208	
Boss Chair Inc 5353 Jillson St *TF:* 800-593-1888 ■ *Web:* www.bosschair.com	Commerce	CA	90040	323-262-1919	262-2300
Boston Bed Company Inc, The 1113 Commonwealth Ave.	Boston	MA	02215	617-782-3830	
Boston Inc 2917 Business Park Dr *Web:* www.furnitureappliancemart.com	Stevens Point	WI	54482	715-344-7700	
Bratt Decor Inc Five N Haven St. *Web:* www.brattdecor.com	Baltimore	MD	21224	703-448-6833	
Bridgeport Inc 1432 Old W Main St *Web:* www.bridgeport.com	Red Wing	MN	55066	651-388-1264	
Brownstone Furniture 3435 Regatta Blvd *Web.* brownstonefurniture.com	Richmond	CA	94804	510-236-0762	
Bunch/Shoemaker Inc 7026 Old Katy Rd No 152 *Web:* bunchshoemaker.com	Houston	TX	77024	713-426-2850	
Cabinet Discounters Inc 9500 Berger Rd *Web:* www.cabinetdiscounters.com	Columbia	MD	21046	410-793-1265	
Cabot House Inc 10 Industrial Way *Web:* www.cabothouse.com	Amesbury	MA	01913	978-834-9280	373-8058
Capital Office Systems 3201 Industrial Ave. *Web:* www.capital-office.com	Fairbanks	AK	99701	907-777-1500	
Cardi's Furniture One Furniture Way. *Web:* www.cardis.com	Swansea	MA	02777	508-379-7510	
Carol House Furniture Co 2332 Millpark Dr *Web:* www.carolhouse.com	Maryland Heights	MO	63043	314-427-4200	427-8176
Carolina Mattress Guild Inc 385 N Dr # Business	Thomasville	NC	27360	336-476-1333	
Carr & Co 2556 Piney Rd. *Web:* www.carr.com	Morganton	NC	28655	828-433-5200	
Casa Linda Furniture Inc 4815 Whittier Blvd *Web:* www.furniturecasalinda.com	Los Angeles	CA	90022	888-783-0632	
Caseys Furniture Inc 11 S Second St. *Web:* www.caseysfurnitureinc.com	Temple	TX	76501	254-773-5555	
Casual Designs Furniture Inc 36523 Lighthouse Rd *Web:* www.casualdesignsfurniture.com	Selbyville	DE	19975	302-436-8224	
Cemco Partitions Inc 5340 Us Hwy 220 N. *Web:* www.cemcopartitions.com	Summerfield	NC	27358	336-643-6316	
CG Sparks World Furniture LLC 454 South 500 West. *Web:* www.cgsparks.com	Salt Lake City	UT	84101	801-519-6900	
Chair King Inc, The 5405 W Sam Houston Pkwy N *Web:* www.chairking.com	Houston	TX	77041	713-690-1919	
Chairish 1657 Defoor Ave NW. *Web:* chairish.drewchan1881.com	Atlanta	GA	30318	404-351-5717	
Charles Eisen & Assoc Inc 595 S Broadway Ste 110E. *Web:* www.egg-and-dart.com	Denver	CO	80209	303-744-3200	
Charlotte Appliances Inc 3200 Lake Ave *Web:* www.charlotteappliance.com	Rochester	NY	14612	585-663-5050	
Cherryman Industries 5690 Lindbergh Ln. *Web:* cherrymanindustries.com	Bell	CA	90201	323-780-0859	
Cholla Custom Cabinets Inc 1727 E Deer Vly Rd.	Phoenix	AZ	85024	623-322-9949	
Circle Furniture Inc 19 Craig Rd. *Web:* outlet.circlefurniture.com	Acton	MA	01720	978-263-4509	
City Furniture Inc 6701 N Hiatus Rd *TF:* 866-930-4233 ■ *Web:* www.cityfurniture.com	Tamarac	FL	33321	954-597-2200	718-3360
City Mattress Inc 12660 Bonita Beach Rd *Web:* www.citymattress.com	Bonita Springs	FL	34135	239-908-2700	
CJ & Associates Inc 16915 W Victor Rd *Web:* www.cjassociatesinc.com	New Berlin	WI	53151	262-786-1772	
CoCaLo Inc 2920 Red Hill Ave *Web:* www.cocalo.com	Costa Mesa	CA	92626	714-434-7200	
Colder's Inc 333 S 108th St *Web:* www.colders.com	West Allis	WI	53214	414-476-1574	
Compass Office Solutions LLC 3320 Enterprise Way. *Web:* www.compass-office.com	Miramar	FL	33025	954-430-4590	
Conlin's Furniture Inc 739 S 20th St W *Web:* www.conlins.com	Billings	MT	59102	406-656-4900	
Container Mktg Inc 110 Matthews Dr. *Web:* www.iwantcmi.com	Americus	GA	31709	229-924-5622	
Contract Office Group Inc 1731 Technology Dr *Web:* www.cog.com	San Jose	CA	95110	408-213-1790	
Contract Resource Group LLC 7108 Old Katy Rd Ste 150. *Web:* www.crgoffice.com	Houston	TX	77024	713-803-0100	
Cook Brothers Inc 1740 N Kostner Ave *Web:* www.cookbrothers.com	Chicago	IL	60639	773-770-1200	
Copenhagen 1701 E Camelback Rd. *Web:* www.copenhagenliving.com	Phoenix	AZ	85016	602-266-8060	

Company	City	State	Zip	Phone	Fax
Copper Creek Canyon 3953 E 82nd St *Web:* www.coppercreekcanyon.com	Indianapolis	IN	46240	317-577-2990	
Corporate Facilities Inc 2129 Chestnut St *Web:* www.cfi-knoll.com	Philadelphia	PA	19103	215-279-9999	
Corporate Interior Systems 3311 E Broadway Rd Ste A *Web:* www.cisinphx.com	Phoenix	AZ	85040	602-304-0100	
Coulter's Furniture 1324 Windsor Ave *Web:* www.coulters.com	Windsor	ON	N8X3L9	519-253-7422	253-3744
Country Home Furniture LLC 1352 Main St *Web:* www.chfs1.com	East Earl	PA	17519	717-354-2329	
CS Wo & Sons Ltd 702 S Beretenia St *Web:* www.cswo.com	Honolulu	HI	96813	808-545-5966	543-5366
Cumberland Furniture 321 Terminal St Sw *Web:* www.cumberlandfurniture.com	Grand Rapids	MI	49548	800-401-7877	
Dallas Desk Inc 15207 Midway Rd *Web:* dallasdesk.com	Addison	TX	75001	972-788-1802	
Daniels Home Center 255 S Euclid St *Web:* www.danielshomecenter.com	Anaheim	CA	92802	714-999-1285	
Darvin Furniture 15400 S La Grange Rd **Fax Area Code:* 662 ■ *TF:* 800-232-7846 ■ *Web:* darvin.com	Orland Park	IL	60462	708-460-4100	869-5910*
Dates Weiser Furniture Corp 1700 Broadway St *Web:* www.datesweiser.com	Buffalo	NY	14212	716-891-1700	
Dearden's Furniture Co 700 S Main St *Web:* www.deardens.com	Los Angeles	CA	90014	213-362-9600	627-9600
Deco Designs Systems Furniture Inc 1435 Koll Cir Ste 106 *Web:* www.decodesigns.com	San Jose	CA	95112	408-919-0234	
Decor Rest Furniture Ltd 208 Jacobs Pl	High Point	NC	27260	336-884-3420	
Designed Business Interiors of Topeka Inc 107 W Sixth St *Web:* dbi-topeka.com	Topeka	KS	66603	785-233-2078	
Desks Inc Business Furniture 445 Bryant St Unit 8 *Web:* www.desks-incorporated.com	Denver	CO	80204	303-777-7778	
DFW Furniture Warehouse 2500 Fairmont Ave	Fairmont	WV	26554	304-367-8980	
Dillmeier Enterprises Inc 2903 Industrial Park Rd *Web:* www.dillmeierglass.com	Van Buren	AR	72956	479-474-7733	
Dixie Furniture Co 282 Richmond Hill	West Helena	AR	72390	870-572-3493	
Docuforce 8343 E 32nd St N *Web:* www.docuforce.biz	Wichita	KS	67226	316-636-5400	
Dufresne Furniture Ltd 116 Nature Pk Way *Web:* www.dufresne.ca	Winnipeg	MB	R3P0X8	204-989-9898	989-9885
E S Kluft & Company LLC 11096 Jersey Blvd Ste 101 *Web:* www.kluftmattress.com	Rancho Cucamonga	CA	91730	909-373-4211	
Easylife Furniture Inc 6101 Knott Ave	Buena Park	CA	90620	714-367-1640	
Eaton Clothing & Furniture Center 116 E Lovett St *Web:* www.eatoncounty.org	Charlotte	MI	48813	517-543-4334	
EC Power International Inc 5120 Woodway Ste 5005 *Web:* www.ec-power.com	Houston	TX	77056	713-626-8700	
El Dorado Furniture Corp 4200 NW 167th St *TF:* 888-451-7800 ■ *Web:* www.eldoradofurniture.com	Miami	FL	33054	305-624-2400	
Empresas Berrios Inc PO Box 674	Cidra	PR	00739	787-653-9393	
Epoch Design 17617 Ne 65th St Ste 2 *Web:* www.epochbydesign.com	Redmond	WA	98052	425-284-0880	
Ethan Allen Interiors Inc Ethan Allen Dr *NYSE:* ETH ■ **Fax Area Code:* 203 ■ *Web:* www.ethanallen.com	Danbury	CT	06811	888-324-3571	743-8298*
Factory Direct Furniture & Mattress 2330 Freedom Dr *Web:* www.fdf.com	Charlotte	NC	28208	704-393-2750	
Family Furniture Centers Inc 7870 Central Ave *Web:* www.familyfurniture.com	Landover	MD	20785	301-499-4300	
Famous Tate Electric Co 8317 N Armenia Ave *Web:* www.famoustate.com	Tampa	FL	33604	813-935-3151	
Fastfurnishings.com 340 S Lemon Ave Ste 6043 *TF:* 877-404-6072 ■ *Web:* www.fastfurnishings.com	Walnut	CA	91789	443-371-3278	
FCC Commercial Furniture Inc 8452 Old Hwy 99 N *Web:* www.fccfurn.com	Roseburg	OR	97470	541-673-3351	
Fisher Home Furnishings 2175 N Main St *Web:* www.fisherhf.com	Logan	UT	84341	435-753-1018	
Flegels Home Furnishings 870 Santa Cruz Ave *Web:* www.flegels.com	Menlo Park	CA	94025	650-326-9661	
Florida Business Interiors 767 Stirling Ctr Pl *Web:* www.4fbi.com	Lake Mary	FL	32746	407-805-9911	
Forum Manufacturing Inc 77 Brown St *Web:* www.forummfg.com	Milford Center	OH	43045	937-349-8685	
Franklin Interiors Inc 2740 Smallman St Ste 600 *Web:* www.franklininteriors.com	Pittsburgh	PA	15222	412-261-2525	255-4089
Fredrick Furniture Inc 703 G Ave *Web:* frederickfurnitureinc.com	Grundy Center	IA	50638	319-824-5235	
Freed's Fine Furnishings Inc 3645 Sturgis Rd *Web:* freedsfurniture.com	Rapid City	SD	57702	605-343-2538	343-3662
Fulkerson Services Inc 111 Parce Rd *Web:* fulkersonservices.com	Fairport	NY	14450	585-223-2541	
Furniture Buy Consignment Inc 1348 W Main St *Web:* furniturebuyconsignment.com	Lewisville	TX	75067	972-436-4389	
Furniture Factory Outlet LLC 901 Industrial Park Rd *Web:* www.furniturefactoryoutlet.com	Muldrow	OK	74948	918-427-0241	
Furniture Fair 7200 Dixie Hwy *Web:* www.furniturefair.com	Fairfield	OH	45014	513-874-5553	
Furniture Mall of Kansas 1901 SW Wanamaker Rd *Web:* www.furnituremallofkansas.com	Topeka	KS	66604	785-271-0684	
Gabberts Inc 3501 Galleria *Web:* www.gabberts.com	Minneapolis	MN	55435	952-927-1500	
Gallery Model Homes Inc 6006 N Fwy *Web:* www.galleryfurniture.com	Houston	TX	77076	713-694-5570	
Gardiners Home Furnishing Center 4241 Brookhill Rd *Web:* www.gardiners.com	Baltimore	MD	21215	410-358-1730	
Gardner Mattress Corp 254 Canal St *TF:* 800-564-2736 ■ *Web:* www.gardnermattress.com	Salem	MA	01970	978-744-1810	
Gardner White Furniture Company Inc 21001 Groesbeck Hwy *Web:* www.gardner-white.com	Warren	MI	48089	586-774-8853	
GCI Outdoor Inc 66 Killingworth Rd *Web:* www.gcioutdoor.com	Higganum	CT	06441	860-345-9595	
Gibraltar Steel Furniture Inc 9976 Westwanda Dr *Web:* www.gibraltarfurniture.com	Beverly Hills	CA	90210	310-276-8889	
Globe Business Interiors 6454 Centre Park Dr *Web:* www.g-b-i.com	West Chester	OH	45069	513-771-5550	
Golden Chair Inc 958 Washington Rd *Web:* www.goldenchair.com	Houlka	MS	38850	662-568-7830	
Gorman's 29145 Telegraph Rd *Web:* www.gormans.com	Southfield	MI	48034	248-353-9880	
Gothic Cabinet Craft Inc 5877 57th St *Web:* www.gothiccabinetcraft.com	Maspeth	NY	11378	347-881-1458	
Gracious Living Corp 7200 Martin Grove Rd *Web:* www.graciousliving.com	Woodbridge	ON	L4L9J3	905-264-5660	
Grand Furniture Discount Store 836 E Little Creek Rd *Web:* www.grandfurniture.com	Norfolk	VA	23518	757-588-1331	583-9075
Grand Home Furnishings 4235 Electric Rd SW Ste 100 *Web:* www.grandhomefurnishings.com	Roanoke	VA	24018	540-776-7000	776-5528
Great American Home Store 5295 Pepper Chase Dr *TF:* 877-303-1964 ■ *Web:* www.greatamericanhomestore.com	Southaven	MS	38671	662-996-1000	
Gressco Ltd 328 Moravian Vly Rd *Web:* gresscoltd.com	Waunakee	WI	53597	608-849-6300	
Groupe Ameublement Focus Inc 1310 Rue Nobel *Web:* www.groupefocus.com	Boucherville	QC	J4B5H3	514-644-5551	644-5555
Hampton Office Products Inc 248 Donohoe Rd *Web:* www.hamptonoffice.com	Greensburg	PA	15601	724-836-6430	
Harden House, The 626 Grand Central St	Clearwater	FL	33756	727-442-7546	
Hart Furniture Company Inc 12 Harold Hart Rd *Web:* www.hartfurnitureco.com	Siler City	NC	27344	919-742-4141	663-2925
Haverty Furniture Cos Inc 780 Johnson Ferry Rd NE Ste 800 *NYSE:* HVT ■ *TF:* 888-428-3789 ■ *Web:* www.havertys.com	Atlanta	GA	30342	404-443-2900	443-4169
Haynes Furniture Company Inc 5324 Virginia Beach Blvd *Web:* www.haynesfurniture.com	Virginia Beach	VA	23462	757-497-9681	552-1545
Healthy Back Store LLC 11714 Baltimore Ave *Web:* www.healthyback.com	Beltsville	MD	20705	703-339-7100	
Heliodyne Corp 4910 Seaport Ave *Web:* www.heliodyne.com	Richmond	CA	94804	510-237-9614	
Heliotrope 248 W Ponce De Leon Ave *Web:* heliotropehome.com	Decatur	GA	30030	404-371-0100	
Heritage Office Furnishings Victoria Ltd 555 Ardersier Rd *Web:* www.heritagevictoria.com	Victoria	BC	V8Z1C8	250-386-5121	
Hernandez Office Supply 119 N 17th St *Web:* www.hernandezsupply.com	Nederland	TX	77627	409-724-0135	724-0210
Heuristic Workshop Inc 203 W Jackson Ave *Web:* www.heuristicworkshop.com	Knoxville	TN	37902	865-523-9867	
Hill Country Furniture Partners Ltd 1431 Fm 1101 *Web:* www.hillcountryholdings.com	New Braunfels	TX	78130	830-515-1400	
Hill Home Furnishings Inc 116 N Fifth St *Web:* hillhomefurnishings.com	Beatrice	NE	68310	402-228-4085	
HM Richards Inc 414 Rd 2790 *Web:* www.hmrichards.com	Guntown	MS	38849	662-365-9485	
Hollywood Bed & Spring Manufacturing Co 5959 Corvette St *Web:* www.hollywoodbed.com	Commerce	CA	90040	323-887-9500	
Home & Hearth 2090 E Main St *Web:* www.homeandhearth-mainst.com	Cortlandt Manor	NY	10567	914-734-9773	
Home Comfort Furniture & Mattress Center Inc 7016 Glenwood Ave *Web:* www.homecomfortfurniture.com	Raleigh	NC	27612	919-781-3900	
Home Gallery 12777 Perris Blvd *Web:* hgmags.com	Moreno Valley	CA	92553	951-485-6478	
Homelegance Inc 3129 Corp Pl *Web:* www.homelegance.com	Hayward	CA	94545	510-783-8010	
Howell Furniture Galleries Inc 6095 Folsom Dr *Web:* howellfurniture.com	Beaumont	TX	77706	409-832-2544	
Hudson's Furniture Showroom Inc 3290 W State Rd 46 *Web:* www.hudsonsfurniture.com	Sanford	FL	32771	407-708-5635	
Huggy Bear's Cupboards Inc 2731 N Hayden Island Dr *Web:* www.huggybear.com	Portland	OR	97217	503-289-5541	
Hurwitz-Mintz Furniture Co 1751 Airline Dr *Web:* www.hurwitzmintz.com	Metairie	LA	70001	504-378-1000	523-7273
IcwUSACom Inc 1487 Kingsley Dr *Web:* icwusa.com	Medford	OR	97504	541-608-2824	

Name / Address	City	State	Zip	Phone	Fax
IKEA 420 Alan Wood Rd *TF:* 800-434-4532 ■ *Web:* www.ikea.com	Conshohocken	PA	19428	610-834-0180	
Imperial Hardware Company Inc 355 Olive Ave P O Box 3010 *Web:* www.imperialstores.com	El Centro	CA	92244	760-353-1120	
Innovative Mattress Solutions LLC 2982 Winfield Rd *Web:* www.innovativemattresssolutions.com	Winfield	WV	25213	304-586-2863	
Inside Source Inc 985 Industrial Rd Ste 101 *Web:* www.insidesource.com	San Carlos	CA	94070	650-508-9101	
Intelligent Interiors Inc 16837 Addison Rd Ste 500 *Web:* www.intelligentinteriors.net	Addison	TX	75001	972-716-9979	
Interior Design Services Inc 209 Powell Pl *TF:* 800-433-7446 ■ *Web:* www.ids-tn.com	Brentwood	TN	37027	615-376-1200	
Interior Office Solutions Inc 17800 Mitchell N *Web:* www.interiorofficesolutions.com	Irvine	CA	92614	949-724-9444	
International Contract Furnishings Inc (ICF) 19 Ohio Ave **Fax Area Code:* 888 ■ *TF:* 800-237-1625 ■ *Web:* www.icfsource.com	Norwich	CT	06360	860-886-1700	784-8209*
International Market Centers 209 S Main St *Web:* www.imchighpointmarket.com	High Point	NC	27260	336-888-3700	
Inviting Home.com 4700 SW 51st St Unit 219 **Fax Area Code:* 954 ■ *TF:* 866-751-6606 ■ *Web:* www.invitinghome.com	Davie	FL	33314	781-444-8001	616-8037*
IO Metro LLC 12911 Cantrell Rd *Web:* www.iometro.com	Little Rock	AR	72223	501-217-0300	
Irpinia Kitchens 278 Newkirk Rd *Web:* www.irpinia.com	Richmond Hill	ON	L4C3G7	905-780-7722	
J P Kane's Town & Country Furniture 641 Missouri Ave N *Web:* jpkfurniture.com	Largo	FL	33770	727-584-2121	
Jayson Home & Garden 1885 N Clybourn Ave *Web:* jaysonhome.com	Chicago	IL	60614	773-248-8180	
Jerome's Furniture Warehouse 16960 Mesamint St **Fax Area Code:* 858 ■ *TF:* 866-633-4094 ■ *Web:* www.jeromes.com	San Diego	CA	92127	866-633-4094	753-0826*
Joe Tahan's Furniture Liquidation Centers Inc 131 Henry St *Web:* www.joetahan.com	Rome	NY	13440	315-339-2330	
John Portman & Assoc Inc 303 Peachtree Ctr Ave Ste 575 *Web:* www.portmanusa.com	Atlanta	GA	30303	404-614-5555	
Johnny Janosik Inc 11151 Trussum Pond Rd *Web:* www.johnnyjanosik.com	Laurel	DE	19956	302-875-5955	
Jonathan Louis International Ltd 544 W 130th St *Web:* www.jonathanlouis.net	Gardena	CA	90248	323-770-3330	
Jordan'S Furniture Company Inc 450 Revolutionary Dr *Web:* jordans.com	E Taunton	MA	02718	508-828-4000	
K b L Design Center 6710 N Big Hollow Rd *Web:* www.kbldesign.com	Peoria	IL	61615	309-692-8700	
Kane Furniture Corp 5700 70th Ave N *Web:* www.kanesfurniture.com	Pinellas Park	FL	33781	727-545-9555	541-6960
Kegworkscom 1460 Military Rd *Web:* www.kegworks.com	Buffalo	NY	14217	716-856-9675	
Kehoe Custom Wood Designs Inc 1320 N Miller St Ste D *Web:* kehoecustomwood.com	Anaheim	CA	92806	714-993-0444	
Ken Ton Fabricators Inc 2505 Main St *Web:* www.kentonfab.com	Buffalo	NY	14214	716-832-1200	
Kensington Furniture & Mattress 200 Tilton Rd *Web:* www.kensingtonfurniture.com	Northfield	NJ	08225	609-241-9102	
Kittle's Home Furnishings Center Inc 8600 Allisonville Rd *Web:* www.kittles.com	Indianapolis	IN	46250	317-849-5300	
Knoxville Wholesale Furniture Co Inc 410 North Peters Rd *Web:* www.knoxvillewholesalefurniture.com	Knoxville	TN	37922	865-671-5300	671-5301
Kookoo Bear Baby & Kids 12060 Etris Rd *Web:* www.kookoobearkids.com	Roswell	GA	30075	770-771-5665	
Kravet Fabrics Inc 8687 Melrose Ave *Web:* www.kravetcanada.com	West Hollywood	CA	90069	310-659-7100	
L & M Office Furniture Inc 4444 S 91st E Ave *Web:* www.l-mofficefurn.com	Tulsa	OK	74145	918-664-1010	
Lack's Valley Stores Ltd 1300 San Patricia St *TF:* 800-870-6999 ■ *Web:* www.lacksvalley.com	Pharr	TX	78577	956-702-3361	782-5740
Lastick Furniture Inc 269 E High St *Web:* www.lastickfurniture.com	Pottstown	PA	19464	610-323-4000	
Leaders Casual Furniture 6303 126th Ave *Web:* www.leadersfurniture.com	Largo	FL	33773	727-538-5577	
Leath Furniture LLC 4370 Peachtree Rd *Web:* www.leathfurniture.com	Atlanta	GA	30319	404-848-0880	
Leather Creations Inc 2692 Peachtree Sq *Web:* leathercreationsfurniture.com	Atlanta	GA	30360	678-584-1000	
Legacy Classic Furniture Inc 2575 Penny Rd *Web:* www.legacyclassic.com	High Point	NC	27265	336-885-9946	
Legends Furniture Inc 10300 W Buckeye Rd *Web:* legendsfurniture.com	Tolleson	AZ	85353	623-931-6500	
Leick Furniture Inc 2219 S 19th St	Sheboygan	WI	53081	920-451-4060	
Levin Furniture Co 5280 Rt 30 *Web:* www.levinfurniture.com	Greensburg	PA	15601	724-834-3550	
Lexington Furniture Company Inc, The 3024 Blake James Dr	Lexington	KY	40509	859-254-4412	
Lifestyle Enterprises Inc 529 Townsend Ave *Web:* www.lifestyle-datong.com	High Point	NC	27263	336-882-7900	882-9122
Lindsey Office Furnishings 2223 First Ave N *Web:* www.lindseyof.com	Birmingham	AL	35203	205-251-9088	
Living Spaces Furniture LLC 14501 Artesia Blvd *TF:* 877-266-7300 ■ *Web:* www.livingspaces.com	La Mirada	CA	90638	877-266-7300	
Logo Inc 117 SE Pkwy *Web:* www.logochairs.com	Franklin	TN	37064	615-261-2100	
London Luxury Bedding Inc 271 N Ave Ste 412 *Web:* www.londonlux.com	New Rochelle	NY	10801	914-636-2100	
Louis Shanks of Texas 2930 W Anderson Ln *Web:* www.louisshanksfurniture.com	Austin	TX	78757	512-451-6501	451-6520
Lozano Caseworks Inc 242 W Hanna St	Colton	CA	92324	909-783-7530	
Luminaire (Miami) Inc 8950 NW 33rd St *Web:* www.luminaire.com	Miami	FL	33172	305-437-7975	
MacKenzie-Childs LLC 3260 SR- 90 *TF:* 888-665-1999 ■ *Web:* www.mackenzie-childs.com	Aurora	NY	13152	315-364-7123	
Marlo Furniture Company Inc 3300 Marlo Ln *Web:* www.marlofurniture.com	Forestville	MD	20747	301-735-2000	
Marmol Radziner & Associates AIA 12210 Nebraska Ave *Web:* www.marmol-radziner.com	Los Angeles	CA	90025	310-826-6222	
Marshall Furniture Inc 999 Anita Ave *Web:* www.marshallfurniture.com	Antioch	IL	60002	847-395-9350	
Mash Studios Inc 12705 Venice Blvd *Web:* mashstudios.com	Los Angeles	CA	90066	310-313-4700	
Massoud Furniture Manufacturing Inc 8351 Moberly Ln *Web:* www.massoudfurniture.com	Dallas	TX	75227	214-388-8655	
Mathis Bros Furniture Inc 6611 S 101 St E Ave *TF Cust Svc:* 800-329-3434 ■ *Web:* www.mathisbrothers.com	Tulsa	OK	74133	918-461-7785	
Maurice Vaughan Furniture Co 610 E Stuart Dr *Web:* www.mauricevaughaninc.com	Galax	VA	24333	276-236-9781	
Maynard Furniture Company Inc 725 Anderson St *Web:* www.maynardshomefurnishings.com	Belton	SC	29627	864-338-7751	
Mayo Manufacturing Corp 4101 Terry St *Web:* www.mayofurniture.com	Texarkana	TX	75501	903-838-0518	838-4531
Mcneills Furniture & Appliance of Denton Inc 104 W Oak *Web:* mcneillsappliance.com	Denton	TX	76201	940-382-6932	
Mealey's Furniture Inc 908 W St Rd *Web:* www.mealeysfurniture.com	Warminster	PA	18974	215-672-1333	
Meredith O'Donnell Inc 1751 Post Oak Blvd *Web:* www.meredithodonnell.com	Houston	TX	77056	713-526-7332	
Michael Taylor Designs Inc 155 Rhode Island St *Web:* www.michaeltaylordesigns.com	San Francisco	CA	94103	415-558-9940	
Miskelly Furniture 101 Airport Rd *Web:* www.miskellys.com	Jackson	MS	39208	601-939-6288	933-5950
Morris Furniture Co Inc 2377 Commerce Ctr Dr *Web:* morrisathome.com	Fairborn	OH	45324	937-874-7130	
Moser Corp 601 N 13th St *TF:* 800-632-4564 ■ *Web:* www.mosercorporation.com	Rogers	AR	72756	479-636-3481	
N o a Medical Industries Inc 801 Terry Ln *Web:* www.noamedical.com	Washington	MO	63090	636-239-7600	
N Tepperman Ltd 2595 Ouellette Ave *TF:* 800-265-5062 ■ *Web:* www.teppermans.com	Windsor	ON	N8X4V8	519-969-9700	
Nashville Office Interiors 1621 Church St *TF:* 877-342-0294 ■ *Web:* www.noifurniture.com	Nashville	TN	37203	615-329-1811	
National Furniture Liquidators I LLC 2870 Plant Atkinson Rd Se *Web:* www.nflinc.com	Smyrna	GA	30080	404-603-9714	
NB Liebman & Company Inc 4705 Carlisle Pk *Web:* www.nbliebman.com	Mechanicsburg	PA	17050	717-761-4550	
Near North Business Machines 86 W Rd *Web:* nearnorthbusiness.com	Huntsville	ON	P1H1M1	705-787-0517	
Nebraska Furniture Mart Inc 700 S 72nd St *TF:* 800-336-9136 ■ *Web:* www.nfm.com	Omaha	NE	68114	402-397-6100	
Niche Modern Home 1901 Hwy 190 *Web:* www.nichemodernhome.com	Mandeville	LA	70448	985-624-4045	
Nickerson Business Supplies 876A Lebanon St *Web:* nickbiz.com	Monroe	OH	45050	513-539-6600	
Norco Products Furniture Mfrs 4985 Blue Mtn Rd *Web:* www.norcoproducts.com	Missoula	MT	59804	406-251-3800	
Norcon Industries Inc 5412 E Calle Cerrito *Web:* www.norconindustries.net	Guadalupe	AZ	85283	480-839-2324	
Northland Furniture Co 681 Se Glenwood Dr *Web:* www.northlandfurniture.com	Bend	OR	97702	541-389-3600	
Norwood Furniture 216 N Gilbert Rd *Web:* www.norwoodfurniture.com	Gilbert	AZ	85234	480-892-0174	
Nucraft Furniture Co 5151 W River Dr *TF:* 877-682-7238 ■ *Web:* www.nucraft.com	Comstock Park	MI	49321	616-784-6016	
Office Express Supply Inc 8005 W 20th Ave *Web:* www.xpressbuy.com	Hialeah	FL	33014	305-557-1667	
Office Furniture Installers Inc 3167 Spaulding St *Web:* www.ofi-usa.com	Omaha	NE	68111	402-451-8009	
Office Furniture Partnership Inc, The 67 E Pk Pl *Web:* www.officefurniturepartnership.com	Morristown	NJ	07960	973-267-6966	
OFIS LP, The 7110 Old Katy Rd *Web:* theofis.com	Houston	TX	77024	713-629-5599	
Olinde's Furniture 9536 Airline Hwy *Web:* www.olindes.com	Baton Rouge	LA	70815	225-926-3380	924-2063
Olum's of Binghamton Inc 3701 Vestal Pkwy E *TF Cust Svc:* 855-264-8674 ■ *Web:* www.olums.com	Vestal	NY	13850	607-729-5775	729-6166
Osborne Wood Products Inc 4618 Hwy 123 *Web:* www.osbornewood.com	Toccoa	GA	30577	706-886-1065	

Phone Fax

Ostermancron Inc 10830 Millington Ct............Cincinnati OH 45242 513-771-3377
Web: www.ostermancron.com

Otterbine Barebo Inc 3840 Main Rd E...............Emmaus PA 18049 610-965-6018
TF: 800-237-8837 ■ *Web:* www.otterbine.com

Paris Kitchens 245 W Beaver Creek Rd..........Richmond Hill ON L4B1L1 905-886-5751
Web: pariskitchens.com

Parker Furniture
10375 SW Beaverton-Hillsdale Hwy.................Beaverton OR 97005 503-644-0155 275-1087*
**Fax Area Code:* 971 ■ *TF:* 866-515-9673 ■ *Web:* www.parker-furniture.com

Patioshoppers Inc 41188 Sandalwood Cir............Murrieta CA 92562 951-696-1700
TF: 800-940-6123 ■ *Web:* www.patioshoppers.com

Pier 1 Kids 100 Pier 1 Pl..........................Fort Worth TX 76102 817-252-8000 252-8995
TF: 800-433-4035 ■ *Web:* www.pier1.com

Porters of Racine 301 Sixth St......................Racine WI 53403 262-633-6363 633-5011
TF: 800-558-3245 ■ *Web:* www.portersofracine.com

Preservation Technologies LP
111 Thomson Park Dr...................Cranberry Township PA 16066 724-779-2111
Web: www.ptlp.com

Privilege International Inc
2419 Firestone Blvd............................South Gate CA 90280 323-585-0777
Web: www.privilegeinc.com

R C Furniture Inc 1111 S Jellick Ave..................Industry CA 91748 626-964-4100
Web: www.rcfurniture.com

Ravensberg Inc 1338 Strassner Dr................Saint Louis MO 63144 314-968-4020
Web: www.ravensberg.com

Raymour & Flanigan Furniture PO Box 220.........Liverpool NY 13088 315-453-2500 453-2551*
**Fax:* Mktg ■ *Web:* www.raymourflanigan.com

Reborn Cabinets 2981 E La Palma Ave...............Anaheim CA 92806 714-630-2220
Web: www.reborncabinets.com

Refurbished Office Furniture
1212 N 39th St Ste 200.............................Tampa FL 33605 813-241-4515
Web: www.rofinc.net

Regency Furniture Inc 7900 Cedarville Rd.........Brandywine MD 20613 301-782-3800
Web: www.regencyfurniture.com

Regency Seating Inc 2375 Romig Rd..................Akron OH 44320 330-848-3700
Web: regencyof.com

Robb & Stucky International
13170 S Cleveland Ave..........................Fort Myers FL 33907 239-415-2800
Web: robbstuckyintl.com

Roche Bobios 200 Madison St......................New York NY 10016 212-889-0700
Web: www.roche-bobois.com

Rocky Top Furniture Inc 8957 Lexington Rd..........Lancaster KY 40444 859-548-2828
Web: www.rockytoplogfurniture.com

Romar Cabinet & Top Company Inc
23949 S Northern Illinois Dr.....................Channahon IL 60410 815-467-9900
Web: www.romarcabinet.com

Roomplace, The 1000-46 Rohlwing Rd..............Lombard IL 60148 630-261-3900
Web: www.theroomplace.com

Roomstores of Phoenix LLC, The
3011 E Broadway Rd Ste 100........................Phoenix AZ 85040 602-268-1111
Web: arizonaroomstore.com

Roost Home Furnishings
200 Gate Five Rd Number 116......................Sausalito CA 94965 415-339-9500
Web: www.roostco.com

Rosewood Industries Inc 1203 E Central Ter...........Stigler OK 74462 800-228-3306
Web: www.rosewood.net

Rothman Furniture Stores Inc
2101 E Terra Ln.................................O'Fallon MO 63366 636-978-3500 696-4300
Web: www.rothmanfurniture.com

Rotmans Furniture & Carpet
725 Southbridge St...............................Worcester MA 01610 508-755-5276 752-4258
TF: 800-768-6267 ■ *Web:* www.rotmans.com

Royal Discount Furniture Company Inc
122 S Main St...................................Memphis TN 38103 901-527-6407 527-8166
Web: www.royalfurniture.com

Royals Inc 324 SW 16th St.......................Belle Glade FL 33430 561-996-7646 996-4480
Web: royalsfurnitureinc.com

RTA Furniture Corporation
5500 Linglestown Rd..........................Harrisburg PA 17112 717-540-5500
Web: www.justcabinets.com/

S Rose Inc 1213 Prospect Ave E...................Cleveland OH 44115 216-781-8200

Sam Clar Office Furniture Inc
1221 Diamond Way..............................Concord CA 94520 925-602-3900
TF: 800-726-2527 ■ *Web:* www.samclar.com

Sam Levitz Furniture 3430 E 36th St..................Tucson AZ 85713 520-624-7443 628-4175
Web: www.samlevitz.com

Sam's Appliance & Television Rental Inc
5050 E Belknap St.............................Fort Worth TX 76117 817-665-5050
Web: www.samsfurniture.com

San Francisco Design Ctr
Two Henry Adams St Ste 450...................San Francisco CA 94103 415-490-5800 490-5885
Web: www.sfdesigncenter.com

Sawbridge Studios 1015 Tower Ct.................Winnetka IL 60093 847-441-2441
Web: sawbridge.com

Schewel Furniture Company Inc 1031 Main St......Lynchburg VA 24504 434-522-0200 522-0207
Web: schewels.com

Schmidt-Goodman Office Products
1920 N Broadway..............................Rochester MN 55906 507-282-3870 282-7355*
**Fax Area Code:* 517 ■ *TF:* 800-247-0663 ■ *Web:* www.schmidtgoodman.com

Scott Rice Office Works 14720 W 105th St............Lenexa KS 66215 913-888-7600 227-7793
Web: www.scottrice.com

Sedlak Interiors Inc 34300 Solon Rd..................Solon OH 44139 440-248-2424 349-8724
TF: 800-260-2949 ■ *Web:* www.sedlakinteriors.com

Sei/Aarons Inc 3108 Piedmont Rd Ne Ste 202..........Atlanta GA 30305 404-495-9707
Web: seiaarons.com

Selden's Home Furnishings 1802 62nd Ave E..........Tacoma WA 98424 253-922-5700 620-6341
TF: 800-870-7880 ■ *Web:* seldens.com

Senator International Inc 1630 Holland Rd..........Maumee OH 43537 419-887-5805
Web: www.allermuir.com

Sheely's Furniture & Appliance Company Inc
11450 S Ave....................................North Lima OH 44452 330-549-3901
Web: www.sheelys.com

Shenandoah Furniture Inc
225 Beaver Creek Dr............................Martinsville VA 24112 276-632-0502
Web: www.shenandoahfurniture.com

Sheridan Group Inc, The 2045 Pontius Ave.........Los Angeles CA 90025 310-575-0664
Web: www.sheridaninc.com

Shofer'S Furniture Company LLC
930 S Charles St...............................Baltimore MD 21230 410-752-4212
Web: shofers.com

Shops at Carolina Furniture of Williamsburg
5425 Richmond Rd.............................Williamsburg VA 23188 757-565-3000 565-4476
TF: 800-582-8916 ■ *Web:* www.carolina-furniture.com

Sit 'n Sleep 14300 S Main St.......................Gardena CA 90248 310-604-8903 604-8903
Web: www.sitnsleep.com

Sitonit Seating 6415 Katella Ave.....................Cypress CA 90630 714-995-4800
Web: www.sitonit.net

Sleep America Inc 1202 N 54th Ave Ste 111...........Phoenix AZ 85043 602-269-7000

Slumberland Inc 3060 Centerville Rd............Little Canada MN 55117 651-482-7500
Web: www.slumberland.com

Smart Furniture Inc 430 Market St..............Chattanooga TN 37402 423-267-7007
TF: 888-467-6278 ■ *Web:* www.smartfurniture.com

Smith Village Home Furnishings 34 N Main St........Jacobus PA 17407 717-428-1921
Web: smithvillage.com

Smulekoff's Fine Home Furnishings
PO Box 74090..................................Cedar Rapids IA 52407 319-362-2181 362-2180
TF: 888-384-6995 ■ *Web:* www.smulekoffs.com

Snuggle Bugz 3245 Fairview St...................Burlington ON L7N3L1 905-631-0005
Web: snugglebugz.ca

Southern Finishing 801 E Church St..............Martinsville VA 24112 276-632-4901
Web: www.southernfinishing.com

Southern Furniture Company of Conover Inc
1099 Second Ave Pl SE...........................Conover NC 28613 828-464-0311
Web: www.southernfurniture.net

Spears Furniture Co 7004 Salem Ave...............Lubbock TX 79424 806-747-3401
Web: spearsfurniture.com

Specified Woodworking Corp
9327 Washington Blvd N Ste A........................Laurel MD 20723 301-598-8200
Web: www.specifiedwoodworking.com

Spiller Furniture 5605 Mcfarland Blvd..............Northport AL 35476 205-333-2030
Web: www.spillerfurniture.com

Spine Align Inc 741 Chicago Dr.....................Holland MI 49423 616-392-4565
Web: www.chirobed.com

Sprintz Furniture Showroom Inc
6205 Cockrill Bend Cir...........................Nashville TN 37209 615-234-3200
Web: sprintz.com

Stacy Furniture 1900 S Main St Ste 200............Grapevine TX 76051 817-424-8800
Web: www.stacyfurniture.com

Stageright Corp 495 Pioneer Pkwy......................Clare MI 48617 989-386-7393
Web: www.stageright.com

Standard Office Supply 35 Sheridan St Nw.........Washington DC 20011 202-829-4820
Web: www.standardofficesupply.com

Star Furniture Company Inc
16666 Barker Springs Rd..........................Houston TX 77084 281-492-6661 579-5900
TF: 800-364-6661 ■ *Web:* www.starfurniture.com

Stein World Inc 5800 Challenge Dr.................Memphis TN 38115 901-261-3050
Web: www.steinworld.com

Steinhafels W 231 N 1013 County Hwy F...........Waukesha WI 53186 262-436-4600 436-4601
TF Cust Svc: 866-351-4600 ■ *Web:* www.steinhafels.com

Sterling Furniture Co
2051 South 1100 East.........................Salt Lake City UT 84106 801-467-1579

Stone County Ironworks
408 Ironworks Dr..............................Mountain View AR 72560 870-269-8108
Web: www.stoneiron.com

Sunnyland Outdoor & Casual Furniture
7879 Spring Vly Rd Ste 125..........................Dallas TX 75254 972-239-3716
Web: www.sunnylandfurniture.com

Superior Woodcraft Inc 160 N Hamilton St.........Doylestown PA 18901 215-348-9942
Web: www.superiorwoodcraft.com

Swartz Kitchens & Baths
5550 Allentown Blvd (Route 22)....................Harrisburg PA 17112 717-652-7111
Web: www.swartzsupply.com

SWC Office Furniture Outlet
375 Fairfield Ave...............................Stamford CT 06902 203-967-8367
Web: swcoffice.com

Symar Installations Inc 1960 Foxridge Dr..........Kansas City KS 66106 913-236-4441
Web: symarinstallations.com

TC Mill Work Inc 3433 Marshall Ln.................Bensalem PA 19020 215-245-4210
Web: www.tcmillwork.com

Techline Bozeman-mcphie Cabinetry
435 E Main St...................................Bozeman MT 59715 406-586-1708
Web: www.mcphiecabinetry.com

Terra Furniture Inc
14819 Salt Lk Ave...........................City Of Industry CA 91746 626-912-8523
Web: www.terrafurniture.com

Thomas-Hines Co 3027 W Cary St.................Richmond VA 23221 804-355-2782
Web: thomashinesinc.com

Thrifty Office Furniture 1023 S Miami Blvd............Durham NC 27703 919-598-8454
Web: www.thriftyofficefurniture.com

Toms-price Co 303 E Front St......................Wheaton IL 60187 630-668-7878
Web: www.tomsprice.com

Town & Country Furniture
6545 Airline Hwy..............................Baton Rouge LA 70805 225-355-6666 355-7459
Web: www.tcfurniture.com

trade associates group Ltd
1730 W Wrightwood Ave..........................Chicago IL 60614 773-871-1300
Web: www.tagltd.com

Tri-boro Shelving & Partition Corp
300 Dominion Dr...............................Farmville VA 23901 434-315-5600
Web: www.triboroshelving.com

Trinity Business Furniture 6089 Kennedy Rd...........Trinity NC 27370 336-472-6660
Web: www.trinityfurniture.com

Trivest Partners LP
550 S Dixie Hwy Ste 300.........................Coral Gables FL 33146 305-858-2200
Web: www.trivest.com

Company	City	State	Zip	Phone	Fax
Troy Wesnidge Inc 2024 S Main St *Web:* www.wesnidge.com	Newcastle	OK	73065	405-387-4720	
True North America Inc 2052 Alton Pkwy *Web:* trueinnovations.com	Irvine	CA	92606	714-368-7464	
TUFF SHED Inc 1777 S Harrison St Ste 600 *Web:* www.tuffshed.com	Denver	CO	80210	303-753-8833	
Tupelo Furniture Market Inc 1879 N Coley Rd *Web:* www.tupelofurnituremarket.com	Tupelo	MS	38801	662-842-4442	
Turners Fine Furniture Co 707 Second St W *Web:* turnerfurniture.com	Tifton	GA	31794	229-382-3266	
Twentieth Modern 7470 Beverly Blvd *Web:* www.twentieth.net	Los Angeles	CA	90036	323-904-1200	
U.S. Quality Furniture Services Inc 8920 Winkler Dr Ste 100 *Web:* www.usqfs.com	Houston	TX	77017	713-943-7016	
Unger Furniture Company of Sauk Centre Inc 516 Sinclair Lewis Ave *Web:* ungerfurniture.com	Sauk Centre	MN	56378	320-352-2247	
United Corporate Furnishings Inc 1780 N Market Blvd	Sacramento	CA	95834	916-553-5900	
Universal Business Supply Inc 4344 Rider Trl N *Web:* www.universalbusinesssupply.com	Earth City	MO	63045	314-298-0153	
Urban Barn Ltd 4085 Marine Way Ste 1 *Web:* www.urbanbarn.com	Burnaby	BC	V5J5E2	604-456-2200	
USA Baby 793 Springer Dr *TF:* 800-767-9464 ■ *Web:* www.usababy.com	Lombard	IL	60148	630-652-0600	
Usine Rotec Inc 125 Rue De L'eglise Rr 1 *Web:* www.rotecbeds.com	Baie-du-febvre	QC	J0G1A0	450-783-6444	783-6446
Value City Furniture 40 East 53rd St *Web:* www.valuecitynj.com	Bayonne	NJ	07002	201-436-2000	
Victory Furniture 9040 W Pico Blvd *Web:* www.victoryfurniture.com	Los Angeles	CA	90035	310-276-4272	
W H Cress Company Inc 9966 Sw Katherine St *Web:* www.whcress.com	Tigard	OR	97223	503-620-1664	
Walker Furniture 301 S Martin L King Blvd *Web:* www.walkerfurniture.com	Las Vegas	NV	89106	702-384-9300	
Walker's Furniture Inc 2611 N Woodruff Rd *TF:* 866-667-6655 ■ *Web:* www.walkersfurniture.com	Spokane	WA	99206	509-535-1995	534-0013
Warehouse Home Furnishings Distributors Inc 1851 Telfair St PO Box 1140 **Fax Area Code:* 478 ■ *TF:* 800-456-0424 ■ *Web:* farmershomefurniture.com	Dublin	GA	31021	800-456-0424	275-6276*
Waterbeds n Stuff Inc 3933 Brookham Dr *Web:* www.bedsnstuff.com	Grove City	OH	43123	614-871-1171	
Wayneco Inc 800 Hanover Rd *Web:* www.waynecoinc.com	York	PA	17408	717-225-4413	
Wayside Furniture Inc 1367 Canton Rd *TF:* 877-499-3968 ■ *Web:* www.wayside-furniture.com	Akron	OH	44312	330-733-6221	733-6420
WB Mason Company Inc 59 Centre St *Web:* www.wbmason.com	Brockton	MA	02303	508-586-3434	
Weekends Only Inc 349 Marshall Ave 3rd Fl *Web:* www.weekendsonly.com	Saint Louis	MO	63119	314-447-1500	447-1591
Weir's Furniture Village Inc 3219 Knox St *Web:* www.weirsfurniture.com	Dallas	TX	75205	214-528-0321	
Wells Home Furnishings 101 Bowers Rd *Web:* www.wellshome.com	Charleston	WV	25314	304-343-3600	
Wenger Furniture Appliance & Electronics 4552 Whittier Blvd *Web:* www.wengerfurniture.com	Los Angeles	CA	90022	323-261-1136	261-0968
Westco Home Furnishings Inc 400 NW Veterans Blvd *Web:* www.westcohomefurnishings.com	Miami	OK	74354	918-540-2464	540-1186
Western Contract 11455 Folsom Blvd *Web:* www.westerncontract.com	Rancho Cordova	CA	95742	916-638-3338	638-2698
WG&R Furniture Co 900 Challenger Dr *TF:* 888-947-7782 ■ *Web:* www.wgrfurniture.com	Green Bay	WI	54311	920-469-4880	
Whalen Furniture Manufacturing Inc 1578 Air Wing Rd *Web:* www.whalenfurniture.com	San Diego	CA	92154	619-423-9948	
Wieser & Cawley Furniture 1301 Colegate Dr *TF:* 800-339-0094 ■ *Web:* wieserandcawleyfurniture.com/	Marietta	OH	45750	740-373-1676	373-9336
William M Bloomfield Inc 170 Barnard Ave	San Jose	CA	95125	408-998-2995	
Willis Furniture Company Inc 4220 Virginia Beach Blvd *Web:* willisfurniture.com	Virginia Beach	VA	23452	757-340-2112	
Wine Appreciation Guild 360 Swift Ave Ste 34 *Web:* wineappreciation.com	South San Francisco	CA	94080	650-866-3020	
Wittigs Office Interiors Ltd 2013 Broadway St *Web:* www.wittigs.com	San Antonio	TX	78215	210-270-0100	
WL Rubottom Company Inc 320 W Lewis St *Web:* wlrubottom.com	Ventura	CA	93001	805-648-6943	
Wolf Furniture Inc 1620 N Tuckahoe St *Web:* www.wolffurniture.com	Bellwood	PA	16617	814-742-4380	
Wood You Furniture 11700 San Jose Blvd *Web:* www.woodyou.com	Jacksonville	FL	32223	904-370-1333	
Woodley'S Fine Furniture Inc 320 S Sunset St *Web:* woodleys.com	Longmont	CO	80501	303-443-5692	
Woodstock Furniture Outlet 100 Robin Rd Ext *Web:* www.woodstockoutlet.com	Acworth	GA	30102	678-255-1000	
Workplace Resource LLC 4400 NE Loop 410 Ste 130 *TF:* 800-580-3000 ■ *Web:* www.hmwrasa.com	San Antonio	TX	78218	512-472-7300	
WS Badcock Corp (WSBC) PO Box 497 *TF:* 800-223-2625 ■ *Web:* www.badcock.com	Mulberry	FL	33860	800-223-2625	
Yamada Enterprises 16552 Burke Ln *Web:* www.yamadaenterprises.com	Huntington Beach	CA	92647	714-843-9882	
Zuri Furniture 4880 Alpha Rd *Web:* zurifurniture.com	Dallas	TX	75244	972-716-9874	716-9877

325 GAMES & GAMING

SEE ALSO Casino Companies p. 1904; Casinos p. 1904; Lotteries, Games, Sweepstakes p. 2679; Toys, Games, Hobbies p. 3246

Company	City	State	Zip	Phone	Fax
Ac Coin & Slot 201 W Decatur Ave *TF:* 800-284-7568	Pleasantville	NJ	08232	609-641-7811	383-2758
American Gaming & Electronics 9500 W 55th St Ste A *TF:* 800-336-6630 ■ *Web:* www.agegaming.com	Countryside	IL	60525	708-290-2100	290-2200
Amtote International Inc 11200 Pepper Rd **Fax:* Acctg ■ *TF:* 800-345-1566 ■ *Web:* www.amtote.com	Hunt Valley	MD	21031	410-771-8700	785-5299*
Arachnid Inc 6212 Material Ave *TF:* 800-435-8319 ■ *Web:* www.bullshooter.com	Loves Park	IL	61111	815-654-0212	654-0447
Aristocrat Technologies 7230 Amigo St *TF:* 800-748-4156 ■ *Web:* aristocrattechnologies.com	Las Vegas	NV	89119	702-270-1000	270-1001
Bmi Gaming Inc 3500 NW Boca Raton Blvd Ste 721 *Web:* www.bmigaming.com	Boca Raton	FL	33431	561-391-7200	892-2268
Douglas Press Inc 2810 Madison St *TF:* 800-323-0705 ■ *Web:* www.douglaspress.com	Bellwood	IL	60104	708-547-8400	
eLottery Inc 46 Southfield Ave 3 Stamford Landing Ste 370 *Web:* www.elottery.com	Stamford	CT	06902	203-388-1808	388-1808
FortuNet Inc 2950 S Highland Dr Ste C *Web:* www.fortunet.com	Las Vegas	NV	89109	702-796-9090	796-9069
Gaming Partners International Corp 1700 Industrial Rd *NASDAQ: GPIC* ■ *TF:* 800-728-5766 ■ *Web:* gpigaming.com	Las Vegas	NV	89102	702-384-2425	
GTECH Corp GTECH Ctr 10 Memorial Blvd *Web:* www.gtech.com	Providence	RI	02903	401-392-1000	392-1234
International Game Technology (IGT) 9295 Prototype Dr *NYSE: IGT* ■ *TF:* 800-522-4700 ■ *Web:* www.igt.com	Reno	NV	89521	775-448-7777	
Jacobs Entertainment Inc 17301 W Colfax Ave Ste 250 *Web:* jacobsentertainmentinc.com	Golden	CO	80401	303-215-5200	
Konami Gaming Inc 585 Trade Ctr Dr *TF:* 866-544-7568 ■ *Web:* www.gaming.konami.com/corporate/home.aspx	Las Vegas	NV	89119	702-616-1400	367-0007
Littlefield Corp 2501 N Lamar Blvd *OTC: LTFD* ■ *Web:* www.littlefield.com	Austin	TX	78705	512-476-5141	476-5680
Mondial International Corp 101 Secor Ln PO Box 889 *Web:* mondialgroup.com	Pelham Manor	NY	10803	914-738-7411	738-7521
Monolith Productions Inc 12131 113th Ave NE Ste 300 *Web:* www.lith.com	Kirkland	WA	98034	425-739-1500	
Multimedia Games Inc 206 Wild Basin Rd Bldg B 4th Fl *NASDAQ: MGAM* ■ *TF:* 800-833-7110 ■ *Web:* www.multimediagames.com	Austin	TX	78746	512-334-7500	334-7695
Newport Diversified Inc 2301 Dupont Dr Ste 500 *Web:* www.nd-inc.com	Irvine	CA	92612	949-851-1355	851-6304
Nickels & Dimes Inc 4534 Old Denton Rd *Web:* www.tilt.com	Carrollton	TX	75010	972-939-4200	492-5705
PokerTek Inc 1150 Crews Rd Ste F *NASDAQ: PTEK* ■ *Web:* www.pokertek.com	Matthews	NC	28105	704-849-0860	
Scientific Games Corp 750 Lexington Ave 25th Fl *NASDAQ: SGMS* ■ *TF:* 800-827-2946 ■ *Web:* www.scientificgames.com	New York	NY	10022	212-754-2233	
Skee-Ball Amusement Games 121 Liberty Ln *Web:* www.skeeball.com	Chalfont	PA	18914	215-997-8900	997-8982
Smart Industries Corp 1626 Delaware Ave *TF:* 800-553-2442 ■ *Web:* www.smartind.com	Des Moines	IA	50317	515-265-9900	265-3148
Valley-Dynamo 7224 Burns Rd *TF:* 800-826-7856 ■ *Web:* www.vdlp.net	Richland Hills	TX	76118	972-595-5365	595-5380
Video King Gaming Systems (VKGS LLC) 2717 N 118 Cir Ste 210 *TF:* 800-635-9912 ■ *Web:* www.videokingnetwork.com	Omaha	NE	68164	402-951-2970	951-2990
Western Regional Off-Track Betting Corp 8315 Park Rd *Web:* www.westernotb.com	Batavia	NY	14020	585-343-1423	343-6873
WMS Gaming Inc 800 S Northpoint Blvd *TF:* 800-522-4700 ■ *Web:* www.wms.com	Waukegan	IL	60085	847-785-3000	785-3058

326 GARDEN CENTERS

SEE ALSO Horticultural Products Growers p. 2478; Seed Companies p. 3165

Company	City	State	Zip	Phone	Fax
Armstrong Garden Centers Inc (AGC) 2200 E Rt 66 Ste 200 *Web:* www.armstronggarden.com	Glendora	CA	91740	626-914-1091	335-0257
Behnke Nurseries Co 11300 Baltimore Ave *Web:* www.behnkes.com	Beltsville	MD	20705	301-937-1100	937-8034
Breck's PO Box 65 *Web:* www.brecks.com	Guilford	IN	47022	513-354-1511	354-1505
Cal Herbold Nursery 9403 E Ave	Hesperia	CA	92345	760-244-6125	
Calloway's Nursery Inc 4200 Airport Fwy Ste 200 *OTC: CLWY* ■ *Web:* www.calloways.com	Fort Worth	TX	76117	817-222-1122	302-0031
Champlain Valley Equipment Inc 453 Exchange St *Web:* www.champlainvalleyequipment.com	Middlebury	VT	05753	802-388-4967	
DA Hoerr & Sons Inc 8020 N Shadetree Dr *Web:* www.hoerrnursery.com	Peoria	IL	61615	309-691-4561	691-1834
Earl May Seed & Nursery 208 N Elm St *TF:* 877-800-5556 ■ *Web:* www.earlmay.com	Shenandoah	IA	51603	712-246-1020	246-2210

	City	State	Zip	Phone	Fax
Farmers Market Garden Ctr Inc 4110 N Elston Ave *Web:* www.gardenchicago.com	Chicago	IL	60618	773-539-1200	539-1482
Flowerwood Garden Ctr 7625 Us Hwy 14 *Web:* www.flowerwoodgardencenter.net	Crystal Lake	IL	60012	815-459-6200	
Fruit Basket Flowerland 765 28th St SW *Web:* www.myflowerland.com	Wyoming	MI	49509	616-532-7404	531-7858
Gardener's Supply Co 128 Intervale Rd *TF:* 800-863-1700 ■ *Web:* www.gardeners.com	Burlington	VT	05401	802-660-3500	660-3501
Green Thumb International Inc 21812 Sherman Way *Web:* www.supergarden.com	Canoga Park	CA	91303	818-340-6400	340-8598
Greenbrier Farms Inc 225 Sign Pine Rd *TF:* 800-829-2141 ■ *Web:* www.historicgreenbrierfarms.com	Chesapeake	VA	23322	757-421-2141	
Home & Garden Showplace 8600 W Bryn Mawr *TF:* 877-502-4641 ■ *Web:* truevaluecompany.com/gardencenters	Chicago	IL	60631	773-695-5000	
Home Depot Inc 2455 Paces Ferry Rd NW *NYSE: HD* ■ *TF Cust Svc:* 800-553-3199 ■ *Web:* www.homedepot.com	Atlanta	GA	30339	770-433-8211	384-2356
Johnson's Garden Centers 2707 W 13th St *TF:* 888-542-8463 ■ *Web:* www.johnsonsgarden.com	Wichita	KS	67203	316-942-1443	
Johnson's Nursery Inc W180 N 6275 Marcy Rd *Web:* www.johnsonsnursery.com	Menomonee Falls	WI	53051	262-252-4988	252-4495
JW Jung Seed Co 335 S High St *TF:* 800-297-3123 ■ *Web:* www.jungseed.com	Randolph	WI	53956	800-297-3123	692-5864
L. J. Thalmann Co 3132 Lake Ave *Web:* www.chaletnursery.com	Wilmette	IL	60091	847-256-0561	256-4978
Lowe's Cos Inc 1000 Lowe's Blvd *NYSE: LOW* ■ **Fax Area Code:* 336 ■ *TF:* 800-445-6937 ■ *Web:* www.lowes.com	Mooresville	NC	28117	704-758-1000	658-4766*
Mahoney's Garden Ctr 242 Cambridge St *Web:* www.mahoneysgarden.com	Winchester	MA	01890	781-729-5900	721-1277
McKay Nursery Company Inc 750 S Monroe St PO Box 185 *TF:* 800-236-4242 ■ *Web:* www.mckaynursery.com	Waterloo	WI	53594	920-478-2121	478-3615
Meadows Farms Inc 43054 John Mosby Hwy *Web:* www.meadowsfarms.com	Chantilly	VA	20152	703-327-3940	
Michigan Bulb Co PO Box 4180 *Web:* www.michiganbulb.com	Lawrenceburg	IN	47025	513-354-1498	354-1499
Milaeger's Inc 4838 Douglas Ave *TF:* 800-669-1229 ■ *Web:* www.milaegers.com	Racine	WI	53402	262-639-2040	681-6192
North Haven Gardens Inc 7700 Northaven Rd *Web:* www.nhg.com	Dallas	TX	75230	214-363-6715	987-1511
Oakland Nursery Inc 1156 Oakland Pk Ave *Web:* www.oaklandnursery.com	Columbus	OH	43224	614-268-3511	
Panhandle Co-op Assn 401 S Beltline Hwy W *TF Cust Svc:* 800-732-4546 ■ *Web:* www.panhandlecoop.com	Scottsbluff	NE	69361	308-632-5301	632-5375
Pike Nurseries Holding LLC 2675 Breckinridge Blvd Ste 300 *Web:* www.pikenursery.com	Duluth	GA	30096	770-921-1022	638-6941
Plant Delights Nursery Inc 9241 Sauls Rd *Web:* www.plantdelights.com	Raleigh	NC	27603	919-772-4794	662-0370
Plants of the Southwest 3095 Agua Fria Rd *TF:* 800-788-7333 ■ *Web:* www.plantsofthesouthwest.com	Santa Fe	NM	87507	505-438-8888	438-8800
Pleasant View Gardens Inc 7316 Pleasant St *TF:* 866-862-2974 ■ *Web:* www.pvg.com	Loudon	NH	03307	603-435-8361	435-6849
Por La Mar Nursery Inc 905 S Patterson Ave *Web:* www.porlamarnursery.com	Santa Barbara	CA	93160	805-699-4500	
Ritchie Tractor 1746 W Lmar Alxander Pkwy *TF:* 888-319-0282 ■ *Web:* www.ritchietractor.com	Maryville	TN	37801	865-981-3199	981-1740
Round Butte Seed Growers Inc 505 C St *TF:* 866-385-7001 ■ *Web:* helenaculver.com	Culver	OR	97734	541-546-5222	546-2237
San Gabriel Nursery & Florist 632 S San Gabriel Blvd *Web:* www.sgnurserynews.com/site	San Gabriel	CA	91776	626-286-3782	
Shanti Bithi Nursery 3047 High Ridge Rd *Web:* www.shantibithi.com	Stamford	CT	06903	203-329-0768	
Siebenthaler Co 3001 Catalpa Dr *Web:* www.siebenthaler.com	Dayton	OH	45405	937-274-1154	274-9448
Sloat Garden Ctr Inc 420 Coloma St *Web:* www.sloatgardens.com	Sausalito	CA	94965	415-332-0657	332-1009
Stein Garden & Gift Centers Inc 5400 S 27th St *Web:* www.steingg.com	Milwaukee	WI	53221	414-761-5400	761-8812
Summerwinds Nursery 17826 N Tatum Blvd *Web:* www.summerwindsnursery.com	Phoenix	AZ	85032	602-867-1822	
TLC Florist & Greenhouse Inc 105 W Memorial Rd *Web:* www.tlcgarden.com	Oklahoma City	OK	73114	405-751-0630	751-1300
Treelands Inc 1000 Huntington Tpke *Web:* treelandgardencenter.com	Bridgeport	CT	06610	203-372-3511	371-6023
Twombly Nursery 163 Barn Hill Rd *Web:* www.twomblynursery.com	Monroe	CT	06468	203-261-2133	261-9230
Village Nurseries 1589 N Main St **Fax Area Code:* 714 ■ *TF:* 800-542-0209 ■ *Web:* www.villagenurseries.com	Orange	CA	92867	800-542-0209	279-3199*
Wal-Mart Stores Inc 702 SW Eigth St *NYSE: WMT* ■ *TF Cust Svc:* 800-925-6278 ■ *Web:* corporate.walmart.com	Bentonville	AR	72716	479-273-4000	
Walker Nursery Co 3809 Manchester Hwy *Web:* walkernurseryco.com	Mcminnville	TN	37110	931-668-4622	
Waterloo Gardens Inc 200 N Whitford Rd *Web:* www.waterloogardens.com	Exton	PA	19341	610-363-0800	363-6416
Weingartz Supply Co 46061 Van Dyke Ave *TF:* 855-669-7278 ■ *Web:* weingartz.com	Utica	MI	48317	586-731-7240	731-9319
White Flower Farm Inc 30 Irene St *TF Cust Svc:* 800-411-6159 ■ *Web:* www.whiteflowerfarm.com	Torrington	CT	06790	860-496-9624	496-1418
Zamzows Inc 1201 N Franklin Blvd *Web:* www.zamzows.com	Nampa	ID	83687	208-465-3630	465-3468

327 GAS STATIONS

SEE ALSO Convenience Stores p. 2152

	City	State	Zip	Phone	Fax
Addington Oil Corp 2154 US Hwy 23 N Ste 102 *Web:* www.addingtonoil.com	Weber City	VA	24290	276-386-3961	
Alpena Oil Co Inc 235 Water St *TF:* 800-968-1098 ■ *Web:* www.alpenaoil.net	Alpena	MI	49707	989-356-1098	356-9486
AMBEST Inc 5115 Maryland Way *TF:* 800-910-7220 ■ *Web:* www.am-best.com	Brentwood	TN	37027	615-371-5187	371-5186
Arfa Enterprises Inc 4300 Haddonfield Rd	Pennsauken Township	NJ	08109	856-486-0550	
B&t Service Station Contractors 630 S Frontage Rd *Web:* btssc.com	Nipomo	CA	93444	805-929-8944	
Bi-Mor Stations Inc 1890 S Pacific Hwy PO Box 1220	Medford	OR	97501	541-772-2061	779-2602
Blossman Oil Company Inc PO Box 89 *Web:* www.blossmanoil.com	Covington	LA	70434	985-898-2663	
BP PLC 28100 Torch Pkwy *NYSE: BP* ■ *TF:* 877-638-5672 ■ *Web:* www.bp.com	Warrenville	IL	60555	630-420-5111	
Busler Enterprises Inc 2601 N St Joseph Ave *TF:* 800-457-3232 ■ *Web:* buslerinc.com	Evansville	IN	47720	812-424-7511	429-0669
Chevron Corp 6001 Bollinger Canyon Rd *NYSE: CVX* ■ **Fax Area Code:* 866 ■ *TF Cust Svc:* 800-243-8766 ■ *Web:* www.chevron.com	San Ramon	CA	94583	925-842-1000	420-0335*
Colonial Group Inc 101 N Lathrop Ave *Web:* colonialgroupinc.com	Savannah	GA	31415	912-236-1331	235-3881
Cone Solvents, Inc. 6185 Cockrill Bend Cir *Web:* conesolvents.com	Nashville	TN	37209	615-350-6166	
Dakota Plains Co-op 151 Ninth Ave NW *TF:* 800-288-7922 ■ *Web:* www.dakotaplains.coop	Valley City	ND	58072	701-845-0812	845-2680
Dunlap Oil Company Inc 759 S Haskell Ave *TF:* 800-854-1646 ■ *Web:* www.dunlapoil.com	Willcox	AZ	85643	520-384-2248	384-5159
Englefield Oil Co 447 James Pkwy *TF Cust Svc:* 800-837-4458 ■ *Web:* www.englefieldoil.com	Heath	OH	43056	740-928-8215	928-1531
Erickson Oil Products Inc 1231 Industrial St *TF:* 800-521-0104 ■ *Web:* www.freedomvalu.com	Hudson	WI	54016	715-386-8241	386-2022
Exxon Mobil Corp 5959 Las Colinas Blvd *NYSE: XOM* ■ *TF:* 800-252-1800 ■ *Web:* www.exxonmobil.com	Irving	TX	75039	972-444-1000	444-1433
Fabian Oil Inc 20 Oak St PO Box 99 *Web:* www.fabianoil.com	Oakland	ME	04963	207-465-2000	
FL Roberts & Company Inc 93 W Broad St *Web:* www.flroberts.com	Springfield	MA	01105	413-781-7444	781-4328
Forward Corp 219 N Front St *TF:* 800-664-4501 ■ *Web:* www.forwardcorp.com	Standish	MI	48658	989-846-4501	
Freedom Oil Co 814 W Chestnut St *Web:* www.freedomoil.com	Bloomington	IL	61701	309-828-7750	
Gallagher Lieb Moroni & Assoc 200 W Higgins Rd Ste 326 *Web:* glmfinancial.com	Schaumburg	IL	60195	847-884-1781	
Gas 'n' Shop Inc 701 Marina Bay Pl *Web:* gitnsplit.com	Lincoln	NE	68528	402-475-1101	475-0976
Gas Depot Oil Company Inc 8700 N Waukegan Rd Ste 200 *Web:* www.gasdepot.com	Morton Grove	IL	60053	847-581-0303	
GasAmerica Services Inc 2700 W Main St **Fax Area Code:* 937 ■ *TF:* 800-643-1948 ■ *Web:* www.speedway.com	Greenfield	IN	46140	317-468-2515	864-3091*
Gate Petroleum Co 9540 San Jose Blvd PO Box 23627 *TF:* 866-571-1982 ■ *Web:* www.gatepetro.com	Jacksonville	FL	32241	904-737-7220	732-7660
Gawfco Enterprises Inc 587 Ygnacio Vly Rd *Web:* www.gawfco.com	Walnut Creek	CA	94596	925-979-0560	
Getty Realty Corp 125 Jericho Tpke Ste 103 *NYSE: GTY* ■ *TF:* 866-399-4335 ■ *Web:* www.gettyrealty.com	Jericho	NY	11753	516-478-5400	478-5490
Graham Enterprise Inc 446 Morris Ave *Web:* www.grahamei.com	Mundelein	IL	60060	847-837-0777	837-0778
Greystone Oil & Gas LLP 1616 S Voss Rd Ste 400 *Web:* www.greystone.biz	Houston	TX	77057	832-333-4000	
Houston Food Bank, The 535 Portwall St *TF:* 866-384-4277 ■ *Web:* www.houstonfoodbank.org	Houston	TX	77029	713-223-3700	
Hunt & Sons Inc 5750 S Watt Ave *TF:* 800-734-2999 ■ *Web:* www.huntnsons.com	Sacramento	CA	95829	916-383-4868	383-1005
Imperial Oil Resources Ltd 237 Fourth Ave SW PO Box 2480 Stn M **Fax Area Code:* 403 ■ *TF:* 800-567-3776 ■ *Web:* www.imperialoil.ca	Calgary	AB	T2P3M9	800-567-3776	237-2072*
Iowa 80 Group Inc 515 Sterling Dr PO Box 639 *TF:* 800-336-9889 ■ *Web:* www.iowa80group.com	Walcott	IA	52773	563-284-6965	
J & H Oil Co 2696 Chicago Dr SW *TF:* 800-442-9110 ■ *Web:* www.jhoil.com	Wyoming	MI	49519	616-534-2181	245-0618
Jubitz Corp 33 NE Middlefield Rd *TF:* 800-523-0600 ■ *Web:* www.jubitz.com	Portland	OR	97211	503-283-1111	240-5834
Lassus Bros Oil Inc 1800 Magnavox Way *TF:* 800-686-2836 ■ *Web:* lassus.com	Fort Wayne	IN	46804	260-436-1415	436-0340
Mid-Atlantic Convenience Stores LLC 1011 Boulder Springs Dr Ste 100 *TF:* 877-468-7797 ■ *Web:* www.midatlanticcstores.com	Richmond	VA	23225	804-706-4702	
Midtex Oil LP 3455 IH 35 South *Web:* midtexoil.com	New Braunfels	TX	78132	830-625-4214	
MM Fowler Inc 4220 Neal Rd *Web:* familyfareconveniencestores.com	Durham	NC	27705	919-309-2925	309-9924
Monroe Oil Co 519 E Franklin St PO Box 1109 *TF General:* 800-452-2717 ■ *Web:* www.monroeoilco.com	Monroe	NC	28111	704-289-5438	
Moto Mart 3301 hiawatha ave *Web:* www.fkgoil.com	Minneapolis	MN	55406	612-722-9665	
NELLA Oil Co 2360 Lindbergh St *TF:* 800-995-0401 ■ *Web:* nellaoil.com	Auburn	CA	95602	530-885-0401	885-5851

Company	City	State	Zip	Phone	Fax
Ney Oil Company Inc 145 S Water St PO Box 155 *TF:* 800-962-9839 ■ *Web:* www.neyoil.com	Ney	OH	43549	419-658-2324	658-2723
O'Connell Oil Assoc Inc 545 Merrill Rd *TF:* 800-464-4894 ■ *Web:* www.oconnelloil.com	Pittsfield	MA	01201	413-499-4800	499-6072
Olds-olympic Inc PO Box 180 *Web:* www.olds-olympic.com	Lynnwood	WA	98046	425-778-1000	771-4346
PDQ Food Stores Inc 2002 Parmenter St *Web:* www.pdqstores.com	Middleton	WI	53562	608-831-6600	
Pilot Travel Centers LLC PO Box 10146 **Fax:* Cust Svc ■ *TF:* 800-562-6210 ■ *Web:* www.pilotflyingj.com	Knoxville	TN	37939	865-938-1439	450-2800*
Ports Petroleum Company Inc 1337 Blachleyville Rd *Web:* www.portspetroleum.com	Wooster	OH	44691	330-264-1885	
Quality Oil Company LLC 1540 Silas Creek Pkwy *Web:* www.qualityoilnc.com	Winston-Salem	NC	27127	336-722-3441	721-9520
RaceTrac Petroleum Inc 3225 Cumberland Blvd Ste 100 *TF:* 888-636-5589 ■ *Web:* www.racetrac.com	Atlanta	GA	30339	770-431-7600	319-7944
Riiser Energy 709 S 20th Ave *Web:* www.riiser.com	Wausau	WI	54401	715-845-7272	
Rip Griffin Truck Travel Ctr Inc 4710 Fourth St *TF:* 800-333-9330 ■ *Web:* www.ripgriffin.com	Lubbock	TX	79416	806-795-8785	795-6574
Sampson-Bladen Oil Co Inc 510 Commerce St PO Box 469 *TF:* 800-849-4177 ■ *Web:* www.sboil.com	Clinton	NC	28329	910-592-4177	299-0866
Sapp Bros Truck Stops Inc 9915 S 148th St *Web:* sappbros.net/travel-centers/	Omaha	NE	68138	402-895-7038	895-1957
Sayle Oil Company Inc 410 W Main *Web:* www.sayleoil.com	Charleston	MS	38921	662-647-5802	
Schmuckal Oil Co 1516 Barlow St *Web:* www.schmuckaloil.com	Traverse City	MI	49686	231-946-2800	941-7435
Scott-Gross Company Inc 664 Magnolia Ave **Fax Area Code:* 859 ■ *TF:* 800-967-6874 ■ *Web:* www.scottgross.com	Lexington	KY	40505	800-967-6874	737-5452*
Service Oil Inc 1718 E Main Ave *Web:* www.stamart.com	West Fargo	ND	58078	701-277-1050	277-1723
Shepherd Oil Company LP 1831 S Main *Web:* www.shepherdoil.com	Blackwell	OK	74631	580-363-4280	
Shirtcliff Oil Co PO Box 6003 *TF:* 800-422-0536 ■ *Web:* www.shirtcliffoil.com	Myrtle Creek	OR	97457	541-863-5268	863-5144
Speedway LLC 500 Speedway Dr *TF Cust Svc:* 800-643-1948 ■ *Web:* www.speedway.com	Enon	OH	45323	937-864-3001	
Spencer Cos Inc 120 Woodson St PO Box 18128 *TF:* 800-633-2910 ■ *Web:* www.spencercos.com	Huntsville	AL	35801	256-533-1150	535-2910
Super Quik Inc 2000 Ashland Dr Ste 105 *Web:* www.superquik.net	Ashland	KY	41101	606-836-9641	
Swifty Oil Company Inc 1515 W Tipton St	Seymour	IN	47274	812-522-1640	
Thornton Oil Corp 10101 Linn Stn Rd Ste 200 *TF:* 800-928-8022 ■ *Web:* www.thorntonsinc.com	Louisville	KY	40223	502-425-8022	327-9026
Town Pump Inc 600 S Main St *TF:* 800-823-4931 ■ *Web:* www.townpump.com	Butte	MT	59701	406-497-6700	497-6060
TravelCenters of America 24601 Ctr Ridge Rd Ste 200 **Fax:* Mktg ■ *TF:* 800-632-9240 ■ *Web:* www.tatravelcenters.com	Westlake	OH	44145	440-808-9100	808-3301*
Triple A Oil 12342 Inwood Rd	Dallas	TX	75244	972-503-3333	392-7502
True North Energy LLC 5565 Airport Hwy *Web:* www.truenorth.org	Toledo	OH	43615	419-868-6800	868-1458
UPI Energy LP 105 Silvercreek Pkwy N Ste 200 *Web:* www.upienergylp.com	Guelph	ON	N1H8M1	519-821-2667	
Van De Pol Enterprises Inc 4895 S Airport Way *Web:* www.vandepol.us	Stockton	CA	95206	209-465-3421	
Vermont Gas Systems Inc 85 Swift St *TF:* 800-639-8081 ■ *Web:* www.vermontgas.com	South Burlington	VT	05403	802-863-4511	863-8872
W & H Co-op Oil Co 407 13th St N *TF:* 800-392-3816 ■ *Web:* whcoop.com	Humboldt	IA	50548	515-332-2782	332-1559
Wallace Oil Co-Voco 5370 Oakdale Rd	Smyrna	GA	30082	404-799-9400	799-0322
Wallis Oil Co 106 E Washington St *TF:* 800-467-6652 ■ *Web:* www.wallisco.com	Cuba	MO	65453	573-885-2277	885-4760
Wesco Inc 1460 Whitehall Rd **Fax Area Code:* 231 ■ *TF:* 800-968-0200 ■ *Web:* www.gowesco.com	Muskegon	MI	49445	800-968-0200	719-4301*
Wills Group Inc, The 6355 Crain Hwy *Web:* www.willsgroup.com	La Plata	MD	20646	301-932-3600	
Wilson Oil Inc 95 Panel Way *Web:* www.wilcoxandflegel.com	Longview	WA	98632	360-575-9222	

328 GAS TRANSMISSION - NATURAL GAS

Companies that transmit or store natural gas but do not distribute it.

Company	City	State	Zip	Phone	Fax
Aka Energy Group LLC 65 Mercado St Ste 250 *Web:* www.akaenergy.com	Durango	CO	81301	970-764-6650	375-2216
ANR Pipeline Co 717 Texas St *TF:* 800-827-5267 ■ *Web:* www.anrpl.com/company_info/	Houston	TX	77002	832-320-5230	
Atlas Pipeline Partners LP 110 W 7th Ste 2300 *TF:* 877-950-7473 ■ *Web:* www.atlaspipeline.com	Tulsa	OK	74119	918-574-3500	
Boardwalk Pipeline Partners LP 3800 Frederica St *NYSE: BWP* ■ *TF:* 866-913-2122 ■ *Web:* bwpmlp.com	Owensboro	KY	42301	270-686-3620	688-5872
Boardwalk Pipeline Partners, LP 9 Greenway Plaza Suite 2800 *Web:* www.gulfsouthpl.com	Houston	TX	77046	866-913-2122	
British Gas Services Inc (BG) 811 Main St *Web:* www.bg-group.com	Houston	TX	77002	713-599-4000	599-4250
Cheniere Energy Inc 700 Milam St Ste 800 *NYSE: LNG* ■ *TF:* 877-375-5002 ■ *Web:* www.cheniere.com	Houston	TX	77002	713-375-5000	375-6000
Colorado Interstate Gas Co PO Box 1087 *Web:* www.cigco.com	Colorado Springs	CO	80944	719-520-4245	473-2300
Columbia Gulf Transmission Co 5151 San Felipe St *Web:* columbiapipelinegroup.com	Houston	TX	77056	713-386-3400	267-4110
ConocoPhillips Alaska Inc 700 G St	Anchorage	AK	99501	907-276-1215	263-4731
DCP Midstream Partners LP 370 17th St Ste 2775 *NYSE: DPM* ■ *Web:* dcppartners.com	Denver	CO	80202	303-633-2900	605-2225
Enterprise Products Partners LP 1100 Louisiana St 10th Fl *NYSE: EPD* ■ *Web:* www.enterpriseproducts.com	Houston	TX	77002	713-381-6500	
Gas Transmission-Northwest 1400 SW Fifth Ave Ste 900 *Web:* www.gastransmissionnw.com	Portland	OR	97201	888-750-6275	
Iroquois Gas Transmission System LP 1 Corporate Dr Ste 600 *TF:* 800-888-3982 ■ *Web:* www.iroquois.com	Shelton	CT	06484	203-925-7200	929-9501
Kern River Gas Transmission Co 2755 E Cottonwood Pkwy Ste 300 *TF:* 800-420-7500 ■ *Web:* www.kernrivergas.com	Salt Lake City	UT	84121	801-937-6000	
Kinder Morgan 1001 Louisiana St Ste 1000 *NYSE: KMI* ■ *TF:* 800-247-4122 ■ *Web:* www.kindermorgan.com	Houston	TX	77002	713-369-9000	230-5675
Kinder Morgan Energy Partners LP 500 Dallas St Ste 1000 *NYSE: KMI* ■ **Fax Area Code:* 403 ■ **Fax:* Hum Res ■ *TF:* 866-208-3372 ■ *Web:* www.kindermorgan.com	Houston	TX	77002	713-369-9000	514-6401*
Kinder Morgan Inc 1001 Louisiana St Ste 1000 *NYSE: KMI* ■ *Web:* www.kindermorgan.com	Houston	TX	77002	713-369-9000	369-9100
Kinder Morgan Management LLC 500 Dallas St 1 Allen Ctr Ste 1000 *NYSE: KMI* ■ *TF:* 800-781-4152 ■ *Web:* www.kindermorgan.com	Houston	TX	77002	713-369-9000	
Kinder Morgan Texas Pipeline LLC 500 Dallas St Ste 1000 *TF:* 800-324-2900 ■ *Web:* www.kindermorgan.com	Houston	TX	77002	713-369-9000	
NiSource 1700 MacCorkle Ave SE	Charleston	WV	25314	304-357-2000	357-2000
Northern Natural Gas Co 1111 S 103rd St *TF:* 877-654-0646 ■ *Web:* northernnaturalgas.com	Omaha	NE	68124	402-398-7000	398-7006
Northwest Pipeline LLC 295 Chipeta Way *Web:* www.northwest.williams.com	Salt Lake City	UT	84108	801-583-8800	
Paiute Pipeline Co 5241 W Spring Mtn Rd *Web:* www.paiutepipeline.com	Las Vegas	NV	89146	702-876-7178	873-3820
Questar Gas Management Co PO Box 45360 *TF:* 800-323-5517 ■ *Web:* questargas.com	Salt Lake City	UT	84145	801-324-5111	
Questar Pipeline Co PO Box 45360 **Fax:* Cust Svc ■ *Web:* www.questarpipeline.com	Salt Lake City	UT	84145	801-324-5604	324-2684*
Regency Energy Partners LP 2001 Bryan St Ste 3700 *NASDAQ: RGNC* ■ *Web:* regencygasservices.com	Dallas	TX	75201	214-750-1771	750-1749
SemGroup LP 6120 S Yale Ave Ste 700 *Web:* www.semgroupcorp.com	Tulsa	OK	74136	918-524-8100	388-8290
Seminole Energy Services LLC 1323 E 71st St Ste 300 *Web:* www.seminoleenergy.com	Tulsa	OK	74136	918-492-2840	492-3075
Spark Energy Gas LP 2105 Citywest Blvd *TF:* 877-547-7275 ■ *Web:* www.sparkenergy.com	Houston	TX	77042	877-547-7275	374-8007
Trailblazer Pipeline Co 2442 P Rd	Heartwell	NE	68945	308-563-3221	
TransCanada Pipelines Ltd 450 First St SW *TF:* 800-661-3805 ■ *Web:* www.transcanada.com	Calgary	AB	T2P5H1	403-920-2000	920-2200
Tri-Gas & Oil Company Inc 3941 Federalsburg Hwy PO Box 465 *TF:* 800-638-7802 ■ *Web:* www.trigas-oil.com	Federalsburg	MD	21632	410-754-8184	754-9158
Veresen Inc 222 Third Ave SW *TSE: VSN* ■ *Web:* www.veresninc.com	Calgary	AB	T2P0B4	403-296-0140	213-3648
WBI Energy 1250 W Century Ave *TF:* 877-924-4677 ■ *Web:* www.wbienergy.com	Bismarck	ND	58503	701-530-1064	
WBI Holdings Inc 1250 W Century Ave *TF General:* 877-924-4677 ■ *Web:* www.wbienergy.com	Bismarck	ND	58503	877-924-4677	
Williams Gas Pipeline Gulfstream 1905 Intermodal Cir Ste 310 *TF:* 800-440-8475 ■ *Web:* co.williams.com	Palmetto	FL	34221	800-440-8475	
Williams Partners LP One Williams Ctr *NYSE: WPZ* ■ *TF:* 800-600-3782 ■ *Web:* www.williamslp.com	Tulsa	OK	74172	918-573-2000	573-8805

329 GASKETS, PACKING, SEALING DEVICES

SEE ALSO Automotive Parts & Supplies - Mfr p. 1839

Company	City	State	Zip	Phone	Fax
A f a Industries 140 E Pond Dr *Web:* www.afaindustries.com	Romeo	MI	48065	586-752-2900	
Abric (North America) Inc 220 Barren Springs Dr Ste 1 *TF:* 888-922-7429 ■ *Web:* www.abric.com	Houston	TX	77090	281-569-7100	
Accratronics Seals Corp 2211 Kenmere Ave *Web:* www.accratronics.com	Burbank	CA	91504	818-843-1500	841-2117
Accro Gasket Inc 511 Princeland Ct	Corona	CA	92879	951-340-1562	340-1604
Aesseal Inc 355 Dunavant Dr *Web:* www.aesseal.com	Rockford	TN	37853	865-531-0192	
AGIS LLC 16 Poplar St *Web:* www.agismfg.com	Ambler	PA	19002	215-646-8010	
Akron Gasket & Packing Enterprises Inc 445 NE Ave *TF:* 800-888-2088 ■ *Web:* www.akrongasket.com	Tallmadge	OH	44278	330-633-3742	
All Custom Gasket & Materials 355 Watline Ave *Web:* www.allcustomgasket.com	Mississauga	ON	L4Z1P3	905-507-4580	507-4589
American Casting & Manufacturing Corp 51 Commercial St *TF:* 800-342-0333 ■ *Web:* www.americancasting.com	Plainview	NY	11803	516-349-7010	349-8389

	City	State	Zip	Phone	Fax
American Gasket & Rubber Co 119 E Commerce Dr	Schaumburg	IL	60173	847-882-8333	882-9333
Web: agr.tekni-plex.com					
American Packing & Gasket Co (APG) 6039 Armour Dr PO Box 213	Houston	TX	77020	713-675-5271	675-2730
TF: 800-888-5223 ■ *Web:* callapg.com					
Amesbury Group Inc 57 S Hunt Rd	Amesbury	MA	01913	978-834-3262	289-6699*
**Fax Area Code:* 800 ■ *Web:* www.amesbury.com					
APM Hexseal Corp 44 Honeck St	Englewood	NJ	07631	201-569-5700	569-4106
TF: 800-498-9034 ■ *Web:* www.apmhexseal.com					
Apple Rubber Products Inc 310 Erie St	Lancaster	NY	14086	716-684-6560	684-8302
TF Cust Svc: 800-828-7745 ■ *Web:* www.applerubber.com					
AR Thomson Group 7930 130th St	Surrey	BC	V3W0H7	604-507-6050	507-6098
TF: 800-410-9116 ■ *Web:* www.arthomson.com					
Archer Advanced Rubber Components Inc 2860 Lowery St	Winston Salem	NC	27101	336-996-7776	
Web: www.archerseal.com					
Artus Corp PO Box 511	Englewood	NJ	07631	201-568-1000	568-8865
Web: www.artuscorp.com					
Atlantic Gasket Corp 3908 Frankford Ave	Philadelphia	PA	19124	215-533-6400	533-4130
TF: 800-229-8881 ■ *Web:* www.atlanticgasket.com					
Auburn Manufacturing Co 29 Stack St	Middletown	CT	06457	860-346-6677	346-1334
TF: 800-427-5387 ■ *Web:* www.auburn-mfg.com					
AW Chesterton Co 500 Unicorn Pk Dr	Woburn	MA	01801	781-438-7000	438-8971
Web: www.chesterton.com					
Bal Seal Engineering Company Inc 19650 Pauling	Foothill Ranch	CA	92610	949-460-2100	460-2300
TF: 800-366-1006 ■ *Web:* www.balseal.com					
Basic Rubber & Plastics Co 8700 Boulder Ct	Walled Lake	MI	48390	248-360-7400	360-7101
Web: www.basicrubber.com					
Bentley Mfg Company Inc 520 Pk Industrial Dr	La Habra	CA	90631	562-501-2955	697-5319
Web: www.gasketsonline.com					
California Gasket & Rubber Corp 533 W Collins Ave	Orange	CA	92867	310-323-4250	639-0586*
**Fax Area Code:* 714 ■ *TF:* 800-635-7084 ■ *Web:* www.calgasket.com					
Calpico Inc 1387 San Mateo Ave	South San Francisco	CA	94080	650-588-2241	872-7325*
**Fax Area Code:* 800 ■ *TF:* 800-998-9115 ■ *Web:* www.calpicoinc.com					
Cascade Rubber Products Inc 1828 Nw Quimby St	Portland	OR	97209	503-248-1998	
Web: cascaderubber.com					
CE Conover & Company Inc 4106 Blanche Rd	Bensalem	PA	19020	215-639-6666	639-1799
TF: 800-266-6837 ■ *Web:* conoverseals.com					
CGR Products Inc 4655 US Hwy 29 N	Greensboro	NC	27405	336-621-4568	375-5324
TF: 877-313-6785 ■ *Web:* www.cgrproducts.com					
Chambers Gasket & Manufacturing Co 4701 W Rice St	Chicago	IL	60651	773-626-8800	626-1430
Web: www.chambersgasket.com					
Chicago Gasket Co 1285 W N Ave	Chicago	IL	60622	773-486-3060	486-3784
TF: 800-833-5666 ■ *Web:* www.chicagogasket.com					
Chicago-Wilcox Mfg Co 16928 State St PO Box 126	South Holland	IL	60473	800-323-5282	339-9876*
**Fax Area Code:* 708 ■ *TF:* 800-323-5282 ■ *Web:* www.chicagowilcox.com					
Cinchseal Associates Inc 731 Hylton Rd	Pennsauken	NJ	08110	856-662-5162	
Web: www.cinchseal.com					
Cincinnati Gasket Packing & Manufacturing Inc 40 Illinois Ave	Cincinnati	OH	45215	513-761-3458	761-2994
Web: www.cgindustrialglass.com					
Cometic Gasket Inc 8090 Auburn Rd	Concord	OH	44077	440-354-0777	354-0350
TF: 800-752-9850 ■ *Web:* www.cometic.com					
Conservco Water Conservation Products LLC 550 W Plumb Ln Ste B-147	Reno	NV	89509	775-747-3333	
Web: www.dripstop.com					
Corpus Christi Gasket & Fastener Inc PO Box 4074	Corpus Christi	TX	78469	361-884-6366	884-0695
TF: 800-460-6366 ■ *Web:* www.ccgasket.com					
Ct Gasket & Polymer Company Inc 12308 Cutten Rd	Houston	TX	77066	800-299-1685	
TF: 800-299-1685 ■ *Web:* www.ctgasket.com					
DAR Industrial Products Inc Two Union Hill Bldg 1	West Conshohocken	PA	19428	610-825-4900	825-4901
Web: www.darindustrial.com					
Delta Rubber Co 39 Wauregan Rd PO Box 300	Danielson	CT	06239	860-779-0300	774-0402
Web: nninc.com					
Eagle Burgmann Industries LP 10035 Brookriver Dr	Houston	TX	77040	800-303-7735	
TF General: 800-303-7735 ■ *Web:* www.eagleburgmann.com					
EnPro Industries Inc 5605 Carnegie Blvd Ste 500	Charlotte	NC	28209	704-731-1500	731-1511
NYSE: NPO ■ *TF:* 800-356-6955 ■ *Web:* www.enproindustries.com					
Eriks Seals & Plastics Inc 15600 Trinity Blvd Ste 100	Fort Worth	TX	76155	682-292-5060	
Web: www.eriksusa.com					
Fast Group Houston Inc 8103 Rankin Rd	Humble	TX	77396	281-446-6662	446-7034
Web: www.fast-houston.com					
FB Wright Company Inc 9999 Mercier Ave PO Box 770	Dearborn	MI	48121	313-843-8250	
Web: www.fbwright.com					
Fibreflex Packing & Manufacturing Company Inc 5101 Umbria St	Philadelphia	PA	19128	215-482-1490	
Web: www.fibreflex.com					
Flexitallic Ltd 6915 Hwy 225	Deer Park	TX	77536	281-604-2400	
Web: www.flexitallic.com					
Flow Dry Technology Inc 379 Albert Rd PO Box 190	Brookville	OH	45309	937-833-2161	833-3208
TF: 800-533-0077 ■ *Web:* flowdry.com/					
Flowserve Corp 5215 N O'Connor Blvd Ste 2300	Irving	TX	75039	972-443-6500	443-6800
NYSE: FLS ■ *TF:* 800-350-1082 ■ *Web:* www.flowserve.com					
Forest City Technologies Inc 299 Clay St	Wellington	OH	44090	440-647-2115	647-2644
Web: www.forestcitytech.com					
Freudenberg-NOK General Partnership 47690 E Anchor Ct	Plymouth	MI	48170	734-451-0020	451-0043
Web: www.fst.com					
Gasket & Seal Fabricators Inc 1640 Sauget Industrial Pkwy	East Saint Louis	IL	62206	618-332-0425	
Web: www.gasketandseal.com					
Gasket Engineering Company Inc 4500 E 75th Terr	Kansas City	MO	64132	816-363-8333	363-3558
Web: www.gasketeng.com					
Gasket Manufacturing Co 18001 Main St	Gardena	CA	90248	310-217-5600	217-5608
TF: 800-442-7538 ■ *Web:* www.gasketmfg.com					
Gaskets Inc 301 W Hwy 16	Rio	WI	53960	920-992-3137	992-3124
TF: 800-558-1833 ■ *Web:* www.gasketsinc.com					
Greene Tweed & Co 2075 Detwiler Rd	Kulpsville	PA	19443	215-256-9521	256-0189
Web: www.gtweed.com					
Gunite Supply & Equipment Company - West 1726 S Magnolia Ave	Monrovia	CA	91016	626-358-0143	359-7985
TF: 888-393-8635 ■ *Web:* www.gunitesupply.com					
Higbee Inc 6741 Thompson Rd	Syracuse	NY	13211	315-432-8021	432-0227
Web: www.higbee-inc.com					
Hoosier Gasket Corp 2400 Enterprise Pk Pl	Indianapolis	IN	46218	317-545-2000	545-5500
Web: www.hoosiergasket.com					
Houston Mfg Specialty Company Inc 9909 Wallisville Rd	Houston	TX	77013	713-675-7400	
TF: 800-231-6030 ■ *Web:* www.houmfg.com					
IG Inc 720 S Sara Rd	Mustang	OK	73137	405-376-9393	376-3933
TF: 800-654-8433 ■ *Web:* www.igok.com					
Ilene Industries Inc 301 Stanley Blvd	Shelbyville	TN	37160	931-684-8731	684-8735
TF: 800-251-1602 ■ *Web:* www.ileneindustries.com					
Indian Springs Mfg Company Inc 2095 W Genesse Rd PO Box 469	Baldwinsville	NY	13027	315-635-6101	635-7473
Web: www.indiansprings.com					
Industrial Custom Products Inc 2801 37th Ave NE	Minneapolis	MN	55421	612-781-2255	781-1144
TF: 800-654-0886 ■ *Web:* www.industrialcustom.com					
Industrial Gasket & Shim Company Inc (IGS) 200 Country Club Rd	Meadow Lands	PA	15347	724-222-5800	222-5898
TF: 800-229-1447 ■ *Web:* www.igsind.com					
Inertech Supply Inc 641 Monterey Pass Rd	Monterey Park	CA	91754	626-282-2000	
Web: inertech.com					
Intek Plastic Inc 1000 Spiral Blvd	Hastings	MN	55033	888-468-3531	437-3805*
**Fax Area Code:* 651 ■ *TF:* 888-468-3531 ■ *Web:* www.intekplastics.com					
Interface Solutions Inc 216 Wohlsen Way	Lancaster	PA	17603	717-207-6000	207-6080
TF: 800-942-7538 ■ *Web:* www.sealinfo.com					
Jade Engineered Plastic Inc 121 Broadcommon Rd	Bristol	RI	02809	401-253-4440	253-1605
TF: 800-557-9155 ■ *Web:* www.jadeplastics.com					
James Walker Manufacturing Co 511 W 195th St	Glenwood	IL	60425	708-754-4020	
Web: www.jameswalker.biz					
John Crane Canada Inc 423 Green Rd N	Stoney Creek	ON	L8E3A1	905-662-6191	662-1564
Web: www.johncrane.com					
John Crane Inc 6400 W Oakton St	Morton Grove	IL	60053	847-967-2400	967-2400
TF: 800-732-5464 ■ *Web:* www.johncrane.com					
Kaydon Ring & Seal Inc 1600 Wicomico St PO Box 626	Baltimore	MD	21230	410-547-7700	576-9059
Web: www.kaydonringandseal.com					
Kimber Manufacturing Inc 555 Taxter Rd Ste 235	Elmsford	NY	10523	406-758-2222	
Web: www.kimberamerica.com					
Lamons Gasket Co 7300 Airport Blvd	Houston	TX	77061	713-222-0284	547-9502
TF: 800-231-6906 ■ *Web:* www.lamonsgasket.com					
Leader Global Technologies Inc 905 W 13th St	Deer Park	TX	77536	281-542-0600	
Web: www.leadergt.com					
LGS Technologies LP 2950 W Wintergreen Rd	Lancaster	TX	75134	972-224-9201	
Web: www.lgstechnologies.com					
Marco Rubber 35 Woodworkers Way	Seabrook	NH	03874	603-468-3600	
TF: 800-775-6525 ■ *Web:* www.marcorubber.com					
Marsh Industries Inc 49680 Leona Dr	Chesterfield	MI	48051	586-949-9300	949-1290
Web: www.marshindustries.com					
Melrath Gasket 1500 John F Kennedy Blvd Ste 200	Philadelphia	PA	19102	215-223-6000	
Mesa Industries Inc 1726 S Magnolia Ave	Monrovia	CA	91016	626-359-9361	359-7985
Web: www.mesaetp.com					
Mr Gasket Inc 10601 Memphis Ave Bldg 12-A	Cleveland	OH	44144	216-688-8300	688-8305
Web: mr-gasket.com					
Netherland Rubber Co 2931 Exon Ave	Cincinnati	OH	45241	513-733-0883	733-1096
TF: 800-582-1877 ■ *Web:* www.netherlandrubber.com					
Novagard Solutions Inc 5109 Hamilton Ave	Cleveland	OH	44114	216-881-8111	881-6977
TF: 800-380-0138 ■ *Web:* www.novagard.com					
Ohio Gasket & Shim Company Inc 976 Evans Ave	Akron	OH	44305	330-630-2030	630-2075
TF: 800-321-2438 ■ *Web:* www.ogsindustries.com					
Omega Shielding Products Inc 1384 Pompton Ave	Cedar Grove	NJ	07009	973-890-7455	
TF: 800-828-5784 ■ *Web:* www.omegashielding.com					
Pacific States Felt & Mfg Company Inc 23850 Clawiter Rd	Hayward	CA	94545	510-783-0277	783-4725
TF: 800-566-8866 ■ *Web:* www.pacificstatesfelt.net					
Parco Inc 1801 S Archibald Ave	Ontario	CA	91761	909-947-2200	923-0288
Web: www.parcoinc.com					
Parker Hannifin Corp TechSeal Div 3025 W Croft Cir	Spartanburg	SC	29302	864-573-7332	583-4299
Web: www.parker.com					
Peck B G Company Inc 50 Shepard St	Lawrence	MA	01843	978-686-4181	
Web: www.bgpeck.com					
Pemko Mfg Company Inc 4226 Transport St	Ventura	CA	93003	805-642-2600	642-4109
TF: 800-283-9988 ■ *Web:* www.pemko.com					
Performance Polymer Technologies Co 8801 Washington Blvd Ste 109	Roseville	CA	95678	916-677-1414	677-1474
Web: www.pptech.com					

Phone Fax

PPC Mechanical Seals 2769 Mission Dr .... Baton Rouge LA 70805 225-356-4333 355-2126
TF: 800-731-7325 ■ *Web:* www.ppcmechanicalseals.com

Precision Gasket Co (PGC) 5732 Lincoln Dr............. Edina MN 55436 952-942-6711
Web: www.pgc-solutions.com

Presray Corp 32 Nelson Hill Rd PO Box 200 .... Wassaic NY 12592 845-373-9300 855-8034
Web: www.presray.com

Press-Seal Gasket Corp 2424 W State Blvd .... Fort Wayne IN 46808 260-436-0521 436-1908
TF: 800-348-7325 ■ *Web:* www.press-seal.com

Presscut Industries Inc
1730 Briercroft Ct.............................. Carrollton TX 75006 972-389-0615 245-2488
TF: 800-442-4924 ■ *Web:* www.presscut.com

Pureflex Inc 4855 Broadmoor Ave .... Kentwood MI 49512 616-554-1100 554-3633
Web: www.pureflex.com

Rotor Clip Company Inc 187 Davidson Ave .... Somerset NJ 08873 732-469-7333 469-7898
TF Cust Svc: 800-557-6867 ■ *Web:* www.rotorclip.com

Rubbercraft Corp of California
15627 S Broadway .... Gardena CA 90248 310-328-5402 618-1832
Web: www.rubbercraft.com

Santa Fe Rubber Products Inc
12306 E Washington Blvd............................ Whittier CA 90606 562-693-2776 693-4936
Web: www.santaferubber.com

Schlegel Systems Inc 1555 Jefferson Rd............ Rochester NY 14623 585-427-7200
TF: 888-924-7694 ■ *Web:* www.schlegel.com

Seal Methods Inc
11915 Shoemaker Ave .... Santa Fe Springs CA 90670 562-944-0291 946-9439
TF: 800-423-4777 ■ *Web:* www.sealmethodsinc.com

Sealing Devices Inc 4400 Walden Ave .... Lancaster NY 14086 716-684-7600 684-0760
TF Cust Svc: 800-727-3257 ■ *Web:* www.sealingdevices.com

Sealing Equipment Products Co Inc
123 Airpark Industrial Rd .... Alabaster AL 35007 800-633-4770
TF Cust Svc: 800-633-4770 ■ *Web:* www.sepcousa.com

Seals-Eastern Inc 134 Pearl St..................... Red Bank NJ 07701 732-747-9200
Web: www.sealseastern.com

Secon Rubber & Plastics Inc 240 Kaskaskia Dr........ Red Bud IL 62278 618-282-7700
Web: www.seconrubber.com

Sorbothane Inc 2144 State Rt 59......................... Kent OH 44240 330-678-9444
Web: www.sorbothane.com

Southern Rubber Company Inc
2209 Patterson St.............................. Greensboro NC 27407 336-299-2456 294-4970
Web: southernrubber.com

Specification Rubber Products Inc
1568 First St N................................. Alabaster AL 35007 205-663-2521 663-1875
TF: 800-633-3415 ■ *Web:* www.specrubber.com

Stein Seal Company Inc
1500 Industrial Blvd............................. Kulpsville PA 19443 215-256-0201 256-4818
Web: www.steinseal.com

Sur-Seal Gasket & Packing Inc
6156 Wesselman Rd.............................. Cincinnati OH 45248 800-345-8966 574-2220*
**Fax Area Code:* 513 ■ *TF:* 800-345-8966 ■ *Web:* www.sur-seal.com

T & E Industries Inc 215 Watchung Ave................. Orange NJ 07050 973-672-5454 672-0180
TF Sales: 800-245-7080 ■ *Web:* www.teindustries.com

Thermoseal 2350 Campbell Rd .... Sidney OH 45365 937-498-2222
Web: www.thermosealinc.com

Trelleborg Sealing Solutions
5503 Distribution Dr............................ Fort Wayne IN 46825 260-749-2709
Web: www.trelleborg.com

Triseal Corp 11920 Price Rd......................... Hebron IL 60034 815-648-2473
Web: www.triseal.com

Trostel Ltd 901 Maxwell St...................... Lake Geneva WI 53147 262-248-4481 248-6406
Web: www.trostel.com

United Gasket Corp 1633 55th Ave.................... Cicero IL 60804 708-656-3700 656-6292
Web: www.unitedgasket.com

UTEX Industries Inc 10810 Katy Fwy Ste 100........... Houston TX 77043 713-467-1000 467-3602
TF: 800-359-9230 ■ *Web:* www.utexind.com

Vellumoid Inc 54 Rockdale St .... Worcester MA 01606 508-853-2500 852-0741
TF: 800-609-5558 ■ *Web:* www.vellumoid.com

William H Harvey 4334 S 67th St .... Omaha NE 68117 402-331-1175 321-9532*
**Fax Area Code:* 800 ■ *TF:* 800-321-9532 ■ *Web:* www.oatey.com

Zero International Inc 415 Concord Ave .... Bronx NY 10455 718-585-3230 292-2243
TF: 800-635-5335 ■ *Web:* www.zerointernational.com

330 GIFT SHOPS

SEE ALSO Card Shops p. 1902; Duty-Free Shops p. 2210; Home Furnishings Stores p. 2470

Phone Fax

Arribas Bros Inc 1500 Live Oak Ln .... Orlando FL 32830 407-828-4840 828-8019
Web: www.arribas.com

Atkinson Trading Co 3911 W Saragosa St .... Chandler AZ 85226 480-899-9597

Atlantic Center For The Arts Inc
1414 Art Ctr Ave......................... New Smyrna Beach FL 32168 386-427-6975
Web: atlanticcenterforthearts.org

Brookstone Inc 1 Innovation Way .... Merrimack NH 03054 603-880-9500 577-8004
TF Cust Svc: 800-846-3000 ■ *Web:* www.brookstone.com

CM Paula Co 6049 Hi-Tek Ct.......................... Mason OH 45040 800-543-4464 293-8471
TF: 800-543-4464 ■ *Web:* www.cmpaula.com

Colors of The West LLC 201 W Rt 66................ Williams AZ 86046 928-635-9559
Web: colorsofthewestusa.com

Disney Consumer Products
500 S Buena Vista St .... Burbank CA 91521 818-560-1000 553-5402*
**Fax Area Code:* 215 ■ **Fax:* Cust Svc ■ *TF PR:* 877-282-8322 ■ *Web:* thewaltdisneycompany.com

EBSCO Industries Inc Military Service Company Div
PO Box 1943 .... Birmingham AL 35201 205-991-6600
Web: www.ebscoind.com

Evelyn Hill Inc 1 Liberty Island.................... New York NY 10004 212-363-3180
Web: www.thestatueofliberty.com

Friendly Gift Shop Inc 1812 Marsh Rd............ Wilmington DE 19810 302-475-6560 475-4605
Web: facebook.com

GiftCertificates.com 11510 Blondo St............... Omaha NE 68164 800-773-7368 445-0075*
**Fax Area Code:* 402 ■ *TF:* 800-773-7368 ■ *Web:* www.giftcertificates.com

Phone Fax

Hazelwood Enterprises Inc 402 N 32nd St............ Phoenix AZ 85008 602-275-7709
Web: hazelwoods.com

Historical Research Ctr Inc
2107 Corporate Dr .... Boynton Beach FL 33426 561-732-5263
TF: 800-985-9956 ■ *Web:* www.names.com

Hummel Gift Shop 1656 Garfield Rd .... New Springfield OH 44443 330-549-3728

Kirlins Inc 532 Maine St............................ Quincy IL 62301 217-222-0813 224-9400
Web: www.kirlins.com

Mathews Jewelers 126 Strickland Dr................. Orange TX 77630 409-886-7233
Web: mathewsjewelers.com

Mole Hollow Candles Ltd
208 Charlton Rd Rt 20 PO Box 223 .... Sturbridge MA 01566 800-445-6653 998-9292*
**Fax Area Code:* 888 ■ *TF Cust Svc:* 800-445-6653 ■ *Web:* www.moleholIowcandles.com

New Seasons Market 7300 SW Beaverton Hwy .... Portland OR 97225 503-292-6838 292-2349
Web: www.newseasonsmarket.com

Olympia Promotions & Distribution
226 E Jericho Tpke............................... Mineola NY 11501 516-775-4500
Web: olympiapromo.com

Only in San Francisco Pier 39................. San Francisco CA 94133 415-397-0143 956-8124
Web: www.onlyinsanfrancisco.net

Oregon Connection 1125 S First St................. Coos Bay OR 97420 541-267-7804 267-6497
TF: 800-255-5318 ■ *Web:* www.oregonconnection.com

Pacific Trade International Inc
5515 Security Ln Ste 1100........................ Rockville MD 20852 301-816-4200 816-4220
Web: chesapeakebaycandle.com

Paradies Shops 2849 Paces Ferry Rd .... Atlanta GA 30339 404-344-7905 349-3226
Web: www.theparadiesshops.com

PM Parties Inc
701 Matthews Mint Hill Rd Ste C.................... Matthews NC 28105 704 841 1370

Red Rocket Fireworks Company Inc
1166 Porter Rd .... Rock Hill SC 29730 803-329-2577
Web: blackcatfireworks.com

Rockstar Industries LLP 6012 12th Ave S.............. Seattle WA 98108 206-297-8330

San Francisco Music Box Co
5370 W 95th St.............................. Prairie Village KS 66207 800-227-2190 481-4677*
**Fax Area Code:* 888 ■ *TF:* 800-227-2190 ■ *Web:* www.sanfranciscomusicbox.com

Sanrio Inc 570 Eccles Ave................. South San Francisco CA 94080 650-952-2880 872-1077
TF: 800-759-6454 ■ *Web:* www.sanrio.com

Silver Towne LP
120 E Union City Pike PO Box 424................. Winchester IN 47394 765-584-7481 584-1246
TF: 800-788-7481 ■ *Web:* www.silvertowne.com

Soap Plant 4633 Hollywood Blvd .... Los Angeles CA 90027 323-663-0122 663-0243
Web: www.soapplant.com

Spencer Gifts LLC
6826 Black Horse Pk .... Egg Harbor Township NJ 08234 609-645-3300
Web: spencersonline.com

Tuesday Morning Corp 6250 LBJ Fwy .... Dallas TX 75240 972-387-3562 387-2344
NASDAQ: TUES ■ *TF:* 800-457-0099 ■ *Web:* www.tuesdaymorning.com

Wall Drug Store Inc PO Box 401........................ Wall SD 57790 605-279-2175 279-2699
Web: www.walldrug.com

Wendell August Forge Inc
2074 Leesburg-Grove City Rd .... Mercer PA 16137 724-748-9501 458-0906
TF: 866-354-5192 ■ *Web:* www.wendellaugust.com

Yankee Candle Company Inc PO Box 110 ...... South Deerfield MA 01373 413-665-8306 665-4815
TF: 877-803-6890 ■ *Web:* www.yankeecandle.com

331 GIFTS & NOVELTIES - WHOL

Phone Fax

Accoutrements 10915 47th Ave W.................. Mukilteo WA 98275 425-349-3838 349-5188
TF: 800-886-2221 ■ *Web:* www.accoutrements.com

Admiral Exchange Company Inc 1443 Union St ..... San Diego CA 92101 619-239-2165

Aerial Photography Services Inc (APS)
2511 S Tryon St .... Charlotte NC 28203 704-333-5143 333-4911
Web: www.aps-1.com

Angel Sales Inc 4147 N Ravenswood Ave .... Chicago IL 60613 773-883-8858 883-8889
Web: www.angelsales.com

Blair Cedar & Novelty Works Inc
680 W US Hwy 54 .... Camdenton MO 65020 573-346-2235 346-5534
TF: 800-325-3943 ■ *Web:* www.blaircedar.com

Boyds Collection Ltd 300 Frederick St .... Hanover PA 17331 717-633-9898 633-5511
TF: 800-436-3726 ■ *Web:* www.boydsstuff.com

Bright Ideas in Broad Ripple Inc
7425 Westfield Blvd .... Indianapolis IN 46240 317-257-4111 257-4174
Web: www.bright-ideas.org

Drysdales Inc 3220 S Memorial Dr .... Tulsa OK 74145 918-664-6481 832-8900
TF: 800-444-6481 ■ *Web:* www.drysdales.com

Fridgedoor.com 65 School St........................ Quincy MA 02169 617-770-7913 801-8026
TF: 800-955-3741 ■ *Web:* www.fridgedoor.com

Hayes Specialties Corp 1761 E Genesee .... Saginaw MI 48601 989-755-6541 755-2341
TF: 800-248-3603 ■ *Web:* www.ehayes.com

Hollywood Ribbon Industries Inc
9000 Rochester Ave .... Rancho Cucamonga CA 91730 323-266-0670 266-6709
TF: 800-457-7652 ■ *Web:* www.hollywoodribbon.com

Hornung's Golf Products Inc
815 Morris St .... Fond du Lac WI 54935 920-922-2640 922-4986
TF: 800-323-3569 ■ *Web:* www.hornungs.com

Kurt S Adler Inc Seven W 34th St.................... New York NY 10001 212-924-0900 807-0575
TF: 866-919-9757 ■ *Web:* www.kurtadler.com

Morrow Enterprises 350 130th Ave .... Vero Beach FL 32968 772-257-3300 770-9175
Web: morrowent.com

Northwestern Products Inc
721 Industrial Pk Rd................................ Ashland WI 54806 715-685-9500

Sanrio Inc 570 Eccles Ave................. South San Francisco CA 94080 650-952-2880 872-1077
TF: 800-759-6454 ■ *Web:* www.sanrio.com

Service Systems Assoc Inc 4699 Marion St............ Denver CO 80216 303-322-3031 815-1698
Web: www.kmssa.com

Star Sales Company Inc 1803 N Central St .... Knoxville TN 37917 865-524-0771 524-4889
TF: 800-347-9494 ■ *Web:* www.starsalescompany.com

Trends International LLC 5188 W 74th St .... Indianapolis IN 46268 317-388-1212 388-1414
TF: 866-406-7771 ■ *Web:* www.trendsinternational.com

Company	City	State	ZIP	Phone	Fax
Unique Industries Inc 4750 League Island Blvd **Fax Area Code:* 800 ■ *TF:* 800-888-0559 ■ *Web:* www.favors.com	Philadelphia	PA	19112	215-336-4300	888-1490*
US Balloon Mfg Company Inc 140 58th St. *TF:* 800-285-4000 ■ *Web:* www.usballoon.com	Brooklyn	NY	11220	800-285-4000	832-9872
Variety Distributors Inc 609 Seventh St. *TF:* 800-274-1095 ■ *Web:* www.varietydistributors.com	Harlan	IA	51537	712-755-2184	755-5041
WinCraft Inc 1124 W Fifth St *TF:* 800-533-8006 ■ *Web:* www.wincraft.com	Winona	MN	55987	507-454-5510	453-0690

332 GLASS - FLAT, PLATE, TEMPERED

Company	City	State	ZIP	Phone	Fax
ABC Window Company Inc 621 S Bon View Ave	Ontario	CA	91761	909-391-6491	
Abrisa Industrial Glass Inc 200 S Hallock Dr *Web:* www.abrisa.com	Santa Paula	CA	93060	805-525-4902	
AGC Flat Galss North America Inc 11175 Cicero Dr Ste 400 *TF:* 800-251-0441 ■ *Web:* us.agc.com	Alpharetta	GA	30022	404-446-4200	446-4221
Anthony International 12391 Montera Ave *TF:* 800-772-0900 ■ *Web:* www.anthonyintl.com	Sylmar	CA	91342	818-365-9451	361-9611
Apogee Enterprises Inc 4400 W 78th St Ste 520 *NASDAQ: APOG* ■ *TF:* 877-752-3432 ■ *Web:* www.apog.com	Minneapolis	MN	55435	952-835-1874	
Basco Shower Enclosures 7201 Snider Rd *TF:* 800-543-1938 ■ *Web:* www.bascoshowerdoor.com	Mason	OH	45040	513-573-1900	573-1919
Binswanger Glass 965 Ridge Lk Blvd Ste 305 **Fax Area Code:* 901 ■ *TF:* 800-365-9922 ■ *Web:* www.binswangerglass.com	Memphis	TN	38120	800-365-9922	683-9351*
Bullseye Glass Co 3722 SE 21st Ave. *TF:* 888-220-3002 ■ *Web:* www.bullseyeglass.com	Portland	OR	97202	503-232-8887	238-9963
Cameron Glass Inc 3550 W Tacoma St *Web:* www.camglass.com	Broken Arrow	OK	74012	918-254-6000	252-4665
Cardinal Glass Industries 775 Prairie Center Dr *Web:* www.cardinalcorp.com	Eden Prairie	MN	55344	952-229-2600	935-5538
City Glass Co 8037 H St *Web:* www.cityglasscompany.com	Omaha	NE	68127	402-593-1242	
Core Six Precision Glass 1737 Endeavor Dr *Web:* www.coresix.com	Williamsburg	VA	23185	757-888-1361	
Corning Display Technologies One Riverfront Plz *Web:* www.corning.com/displaytechnologies	Corning	NY	14831	607-974-9000	974-7097
D & W Inc 941 Oak St. *TF:* 800-255-0829 ■ *Web:* www.dwincorp.com	Elkhart	IN	46514	574-264-9674	264-9859
Gentex Corp 600 N Centennial St *NASDAQ: GNTX* ■ *Web:* www.gentex.com	Zeeland	MI	49464	616-772-1800	772-7348
Glaz-Tech Industries Inc 2207 E Elvira Rd *TF:* 800-755-8062 ■ *Web:* www.glaztech.com	Tucson	AZ	85756	520-629-0268	629-8811
Gray Glass Co 217-44 98th Ave *TF:* 800-523-3320 ■ *Web:* www.grayglass.net	Queens Village	NY	11429	718-217-2943	217-0280
Guardian Industries Corp 2300 Harmon Rd *TF:* 800-822-5599 ■ *Web:* www.guardian.com	Auburn Hills	MI	48326	248-340-1800	340-9988
Hartung Agalite Glass Co 17830 W Valley Hwy. *TF:* 800-552-2227 ■ *Web:* www.hartung-glass.com	Seattle	WA	98188	425-656-2626	656-2601
Hartung Glass Industries 10450 SW Ridder Rd *TF:* 800-552-2227 ■ *Web:* hartung-glass.com	Wilsonville	OR	97070	503-682-3846	
Hehr International Inc 3333 Casitas Ave *Web:* www.hehrintl.com	Los Angeles	CA	90039	323-663-1261	666-2372
JNL Glass Inc 417 Santa Barbara St Ste B1 *Web:* jnlglass.com	Santa Barbara	CA	93101	805-957-1685	
Kokomo Opalescent Glass Co 1310 S Market St *TF:* 877-475-6329 ■ *Web:* www.kog.com	Kokomo	IN	46902	765-457-8136	459-5177
Northwestern Industries Inc 2500 W Jameson St *TF:* 800-426-2771 ■ *Web:* www.nwiglass.com	Seattle	WA	98199	206-285-3140	285-3603
Obrien Glass Co 4916 W SR- 97	Springfield	IL	62707	217-522-5660	
ODL Inc 215 E Roosevelt Ave **Fax:* Cust Svc ■ *TF:* 800-253-3900 ■ *Web:* www.odl.com	Zeeland	MI	49464	616-772-9111	772-9110*
Oldcastle BuildingEnvelope 4161 S Morgan St *TF:* 866-653-2278 ■ *Web:* www.oldcastlebe.com	Chicago	IL	60609	773-523-8400	
Oran Safety Glass Inc 48 Industrial Pkwy	Emporia	VA	23847	434-336-1620	
Paul Wissmach Glass Company Inc 420 Stephen St PO Box 228 *Web:* www.wissmachglass.com	Paden City	WV	26159	304-337-2253	337-8800
Pilkington Holdings Inc 811 Madison Ave PO Box 0799 *Web:* www.pilkington.com	Toledo	OH	43697	419-247-3731	247-3821
Prelco Inc 94 Blvd Cartier *Web:* www.prelco.ca	Rivi Re-Du-Loup	QC	G5R2M9	418-862-2274	
Rainbow Art Glass Inc 1761 Rt 34 S *TF:* 800-526-2356 ■ *Web:* www.rainbowartglass.com	Farmingdale	NJ	07727	732-681-6003	681-4984
Rambusch Decorating Co 160 Cornelison Ave *Web:* www.rambusch.com	Jersey City	NJ	07304	201-333-2525	433-3355
Royal Glass Company Inc 3200 De La Cruz Blvd	Santa Clara	CA	95054	408-969-0444	
Saint-Gobain Corp 750 E Swedesford Rd *TF:* 800-506-7427 ■ *Web:* saint-gobain-northamerica.com	Valley Forge	PA	19482	610-341-7000	341-7777
Schott North America Inc 555 Taxter Rd *TF:* 877-261-2100 ■ *Web:* www.us.schott.com	Elmsford	NY	10523	914-831-2200	831-2201
SCHOTT North America, Inc. 615 Hwy 68 *Web:* gemtron.net	Sweetwater	TN	37874	423-337-3522	337-7979
Spectrum Glass Co PO Box 646 *TF:* 800-426-3120 ■ *Web:* www.spectrumglass.com	Woodinville	WA	98072	425-483-6699	483-9007
Thermoseal Glass Corp 400 Water St *Web:* www.thermoseal.com	Gloucester City	NJ	08030	856-456-3109	456-0989
Torstenson Glass Co 3233 N Sheffield Ave. *Web:* www.tglass.com	Chicago	IL	60657	773-525-0435	525-0009
Tru Vue Inc 9400 W 55th St. *TF:* 800-621-8339 ■ *Web:* www.tru-vue.com	McCook	IL	60525	708-485-5080	485-5980
Viracon Inc 800 Pk Dr *TF:* 800-533-2080 ■ *Web:* www.viracon.com	Owatonna	MN	55060	507-451-9555	444-3555
Virginia Mirror Co Inc 300 Moss St S *TF:* 800-368-3011 ■ *Web:* va-glass.com	Martinsville	VA	24112	276-632-9816	956-3020
Wasco Products Inc 22 Pioneer Ave PO Box 351 *TF:* 800-388-0293 ■ *Web:* www.wascoskylights.com	Sanford	ME	04073	207-324-8060	490-1218

333 GLASS FIBERS

Company	City	State	ZIP	Phone	Fax
Advanced Glazings Ltd 870 King's Rd Sta A *Web:* www.advancedglazings.com	Sydney	NS	B1P6R7	902-794-2899	
Anchor Glass Container Corp 401 E Jackson St Ste 2800 *Web:* www.anchorglass.com	Tampa	FL	33607	813-884-0000	
Armour Group Inc 350 E Las Olas Blvd Ste 800 *Web:* www.thearmourgroup.com	Fort Lauderdale	FL	33301	954-767-2030	
Capitol Aluminum & Glass Corp 1276 W Main St *Web:* www.capitol-windows.com	Bellevue	OH	44811	419-483-7050	
Carlex Glass Co 77 Excellence Way *Web:* www.carlex.com	Vonore	TN	37885	423-884-1105	
City Glass Company of Colorado Springs 414 W Colorado Ave *Web:* www.cityglasscompany.net	Colorado Springs	CO	80905	719-634-2891	
Corning Inc One Riverfront Plz *NYSE: GLW* ■ *Web:* www.corning.com	Corning	NY	14831	607-974-9000	
Culver Glass Co 2619 Nw Industrial St. *Web:* www.culver-glass.com	Portland	OR	97210	503-226-2520	
Evanite Fiber Corp 1115 SE Crystal Lake Dr. *Web:* hollingsworth-vose.com	Corvallis	OR	97333	541-753-1211	753-0388
Fiberoptics Technology Inc One Quassett Rd. *TF Cust Svc:* 800-433-5248 ■ *Web:* www.fiberopticstech.com	Pomfret	CT	06258	860-928-0443	928-7664
Giant Glass Company Inc 1000 Osgood St *Web:* www.giantglass.com	North Andover	MA	01845	978-688-8211	
Gordon Glass Co 5116 Warrensville Center Rd *Web:* www.technologylk.com	Maple Heights	OH	44137	757-366-9900	
Ibis Tek LLC 220 S Noah Dr. *Web:* www.ibistek.com	Saxonburg	PA	16056	724-586-6005	
Incom USA Inc 294 Southbridge Rd *Web:* www.incomusa.com	Charlton	MA	01507	508-765-9151	765-0041
JN Phillips Glass Company Inc 11 Wheeling Ave *Web:* www.jnphillips.com	Woburn	MA	01801	781-939-3400	
Magnatex Inc 2520 Ridgemar Ct	Louisville	KY	40207	502-493-0558	
Mesko Glass & Mirror Company Inc 801 Wyoming Ave. *Web:* www.mesko.com	Scranton	PA	18509	570-346-0777	
Moderne Glass Company Inc 1000 Industrial Blvd *Web:* www.glassamerica.com	Aliquippa	PA	15001	724-857-5700	
Nashville Tempered Glass Corp 1860 Air Ln Dr *Web:* www.egpglass.com	Nashville	TN	37210	615-889-6350	
Novatech Group Inc 160 Murano St *Web:* www.novatechgroup.com	Sainte-julie	QC	J3E0C6	450-922-1045	
Sentinel Process 3265 Sunset Ln *TF:* 800-345-3569 ■ *Web:* www.sentinelprocess.com	Hatboro	PA	19040	919-462-7108	
Shaw Glass Company Inc 55 Bristol Dr *Web:* www.solarseal.com	South Easton	MA	02375	508-238-0112	
Syracuse Glass Company Inc One General Motors Dr Ste 4 *Web:* www.syracuseglass.com	Syracuse	NY	13206	315-437-9971	
Tec5USA Inc 80 Skyline Dr. *Web:* www.tec5usa.com	Plainview	NY	11803	516-653-2000	
Vitrum Industries Ltd 9739 201 St	Langley	BC	V1M3E7	604-882-3513	
Western States Glass Corp 43443 Osgood Rd Ste 6058 *Web:* www.westernstatesglass.com	Fremont	CA	94538	510-623-5000	

334 GLASS JARS & BOTTLES

Company	City	State	ZIP	Phone	Fax
Jarden Corp 555 Theodore Fremd Ave Ste B-302 *NYSE: JAH* ■ *Web:* jarden.com	Rye	NY	10580	914-967-9400	
Leone Industries Co 443 SE Ave. *Web:* www.leonebottles.us	Bridgeton	NJ	08302	856-455-2000	
New High Glass Inc 12713 SW 125th Ave *Web:* www.newhighglass.net	Miami	FL	33186	305-232-0840	251-7622
Owens-Illinois Inc One Michael Owens Way *NYSE: OI* ■ **Fax Area Code:* 419 ■ *Web:* www.o-i.com	Perrysburg	OH	43551	567-336-5000	247-1082*

335 GLASS PRODUCTS - INDUSTRIAL (CUSTOM)

Company	City	State	ZIP	Phone	Fax
Abrisa Technologies 200 S Hallock Dr **Fax Area Code:* 805 ■ *TF:* 877-622-7472 ■ *Web:* www.abrisatechnologies.com	Santa Paula	CA	93060	877-622-7472	525-8604*
Bassett Mirror Company Inc PO Box 627 *Web:* www.bassettmirror.com	Bassett	VA	24055	276-629-3341	
Elan Technology 169 Elan Ct *Web:* www.elantechnology.com	Midway	GA	31320	912-880-3526	
Flex-O-Lite Inc 50 Crestwood Executive Ctr Ste 522 *TF:* 800-325-9525 ■ *Web:* www.flexolite.com	Saint Louis	MO	63126	800-325-9525	541-3193

Company / Address	City	State	Zip	Phone	Fax
Fredericks Co, The 2400 Philmont Ave PO Box 67 *Web:* www.fredericks.com	Huntingdon Valley	PA	19006	215-947-2500	947-7464
Headwest Inc 15650 S Avalon Blvd *Web:* www.headwestinc.com	Compton	CA	90220	310-532-5420	532-5920
Henderson Glass Inc 715 S Blvd E **Fax Area Code:* 248 ■ *TF:* 800-694-0672 ■ *Web:* www.hendersonglass.com	Rochester Hills	MI	48307	855-543-8663	829-4799*
King Precision Glass Inc 177 S Indian Hill Blvd *TF:* 866-554-2773 ■ *Web:* www.kingprecisionglass.com	Claremont	CA	91711	909-626-3526	625-0173
Lang-Mekra North America LLC 101 Tillessen Blvd *Web:* www.lang-mekra.com	Ridgeway	SC	29130	803-337-5264	337-5265
Lenoir Mirror Company Inc 401 Kincaid St *TF:* 800-438-8204 ■ *Web:* www.lenoirmirror.com	Lenoir	NC	28645	828-728-3271	728-5010
North American Specialty Glass 2175 Kumry Rd PO Box 70 *TF:* 888-785-5962 ■ *Web:* www.naspecialtyglass.com	Trumbauersville	PA	18970	215-536-0333	536-6872
Precision Electronic Glass Inc 1013 Hendee Rd *TF:* 800-982-4734 ■ *Web:* www.pegglass.com	Vineland	NJ	08360	856-691-2234	691-3090
Richland Glass Company Inc 1640 SW Blvd *TF:* 800-959-0312 ■ *Web:* www.richlandglass.com	Vineland	NJ	08360	856-691-1697	691-4525
Swift Glass Company Inc 131 W 22nd St *TF:* 800-537-9438 ■ *Web:* www.swiftglass.com	Elmira Heights	NY	14903	607-733-7166	732-5829

336 GLASSWARE - LABORATORY & SCIENTIFIC

Company / Address	City	State	Zip	Phone	Fax
Ace Glass Inc 1430 NW Blvd PO Box 688 **Fax Area Code:* 800 ■ *TF:* 800-223-4524 ■ *Web:* www.aceglass.com	Vineland	NJ	08360	856-692-3333	543-6752*
Altira Inc 3225 NW 112th St *Web:* www.altira.com	Miami	FL	33167	305-687-8074	
Bellco Glass Inc 340 Edrudo Rd *TF:* 800-257-7043 ■ *Web:* www.bellcoglass.com	Vineland	NJ	08360	856-691-1075	691-3247
Bioscreen Testing Services Inc 3904 Del AMO Blvd Ste 801 *Web:* www.bioscreen.com	Torrance	CA	90503	310-214-0043	370-3642
Bottlemate Inc 2095 Leo Ave *Web:* www.bottlemate.com	Commerce	CA	90040	323-887-9009	
Container Manufacturing Inc 50 Baekeland Ave *Web:* www.containermanufacturing.com	Middlesex	NJ	08846	732-563-0100	
Corning Inc One Riverfront Plz *NYSE: GLW* ■ *Web:* www.corning.com	Corning	NY	14831	607-974-9000	
Eden Labs LLC 1601 W Fifth St Ste 240 **Fax Area Code:* 801 ■ *Web:* edenlabs.com	Columbus	OH	43212	614-374-2455	469-0148*
Gerresheimer Glass Inc 537 Crystal Ave *Web:* www.gerresheimer.com	Vineland	NJ	08360	856-692-3600	
Industrial Container & Supply Company Inc 1845 South 5200 West *Web:* www.industrialcontainer.com	Salt Lake City	UT	84104	801-972-1561	
Quadrex Corp PO Box 3881 *TF Sales:* 800-275-7033 ■ *Web:* www.quadrexcorp.com	Woodbridge	CT	06525	203-393-3112	393-0391
Schott North America Inc 555 Taxter Rd *TF:* 877-261-2100 ■ *Web:* www.us.schott.com	Elmsford	NY	10523	914-831-2200	831-2201
Wale Apparatus Co Inc 400 Front St *TF:* 800-334-9253 ■ *Web:* www.waleapparatus.com	Hellertown	PA	18055	610-838-7047	838-7440
WB Bottle Supply Company Inc 3400 S Clement Ave *Web:* www.wbbottle.com	Milwaukee	WI	53207	414-482-4300	

337 GLASSWARE & POTTERY - HOUSEHOLD

SEE ALSO Table & Kitchen Supplies - China & Earthenware p. 3203

Company / Address	City	State	Zip	Phone	Fax
Anchor Hocking Co 519 Pierce Ave **Fax Area Code:* 800 ■ *Web:* www.anchorhocking.com	Lancaster	OH	43130	740-681-6478	848-0082*
Berney-Karp Inc 3350 E 26th St *TF:* 800-237-6395 ■ *Web:* www.ceramic-source.com	Los Angeles	CA	90058	323-260-7122	260-7245
Blenko Glass Co PO Box 67 *TF:* 877-425-3656 ■ *Web:* www.blenko.com	Milton	WV	25541	304-743-9081	
Ceramo Company Inc 681 Kasten Dr *TF:* 800-325-8303 ■ *Web:* www.ceramousa.com	Jackson	MO	63755	573-243-3138	243-3130
Enesco LLC 225 Windsor Dr *TF:* 800-436-3726 ■ *Web:* www.enesco.com	Itasca	IL	60143	630-875-5300	875-5350
Fenton Art Glass Co 700 Elizabeth St *TF Cust Svc:* 800-933-6766 ■ *Web:* www.fentonartglass.com	Williamstown	WV	26187	304-375-6122	375-6459
Friedman Bros Decorative Arts 9015 NW 105th Way *TF:* 800-327-1065 ■ *Web:* www.friedmanmirrors.com	Medley	FL	33178	305-887-3170	885-5331
Gainey Ceramics Inc 1200 Arrow Hwy *TF Cust Svc:* 800-451-8155 ■ *Web:* www.gaineyceramics.com	La Verne	CA	91750	909-593-3533	596-9337
Gardner Glass Products Inc 301 Elkin Hwy PO Box 1570 *TF:* 800-334-7267 ■ *Web:* www.gardnerglass.com	North Wilkesboro	NC	28659	800-334-7267	
Haeger Industries Inc Seven Maiden Ln *TF Cust Svc:* 800-288-2529 ■ *Web:* www.haegerpotteries.com	Dundee	IL	60118	847-426-3441	426-0017
Haggerty Enterprises Inc 370 Kimberly Dr *TF:* 800-336-5282 ■ *Web:* www.lavalamp.com	Carol Stream	IL	60188	630-315-3300	315-3392
Libbey Inc 300 Madison Ave PO Box 10060 *NYSE: LBY* ■ *TF:* 888-794-8469 ■ *Web:* www.libbey.com	Toledo	OH	43699	419-325-2100	325-2369
Marshall Pottery 4901 Elysian Fields Rd *TF:* 888-768-8721 ■ *Web:* marshallpotterystore.com/	Marshall	TX	75672	903-927-5400	938-8222
Pfaltzgraff Co PO Box 21769 **Fax:* Cust Svc ■ *TF:* 800-999-2811 ■ *Web:* www.pfaltzgraff.com	York	PA	17402	800-999-2811	717-2481*
Rauch Industries Inc 2408 Forbes Rd	Gastonia	NC	28056	704-867-5333	
Swarovski North America Ltd One Kenney Dr **Fax Area Code:* 800 ■ *TF:* 800-289-4900 ■ *Web:* www.swarovski.com	Cranston	RI	02920	401-463-6400	870-5660*

Company / Address	City	State	Zip	Phone	Fax
Waterford Wedgwood USA Inc 1330 Campus Pkwy *Web:* wedgwood.com/	Wall	NJ	07753	732-938-5800	

338 GLOBAL DISTRIBUTION SYSTEMS (GDSS)

A global distribution system (GDS) is a computer reservations system that includes reservations databases of air travel suppliers in many countries. GDSs typically are owned jointly by airlines operating in different countries.

Company / Address	City	State	Zip	Phone	Fax
Amadeus North America Inc 3470 NW 82nd Ave Ste 1000 *TF:* 888-262-3387 ■ *Web:* www.amadeus.com	Miami	FL	33122	305-499-6000	499-6889
American Sales Company Inc 4201 Walden Ave *Web:* www.americansalescompany.net	Lancaster	NY	14086	716-686-7000	685-6144
Century Distributors Inc 15710 Crabbs Branch Way *Web:* www.centurydist.com	Rockville	MD	20855	301-212-9100	212-9681
Pegasus Solutions Inc 5430 LBJ Fwy Ste 1100 *TF:* 800-843-4343 ■ *Web:* www.pegs.com	Dallas	TX	75240	214-234-4000	234-4040
Sabre Inc 3150 Sabre Dr *Web:* www.sabre.com	Southlake	TX	76092	682-605-1000	

339 GOURMET SPECIALTY SHOPS

Company / Address	City	State	Zip	Phone	Fax
Graber Olive House Inc 315 E Fourth St **Fax Area Code:* 909 ■ *TF:* 800-996-5483 ■ *Web:* www.graberolives.com	Ontario	CA	91764	800-996-5483	984-2180*
Harry & David Holdings Inc 2500 S Pacific Hwy *TF Cust Svc:* 877-322-1200 ■ *Web:* www.harryanddavid.com	Medford	OR	97501	877-322-1200	233-2300
Hickory Farms Inc 811 Madison Ave **Fax Area Code:* 419 ■ *TF:* 800-753-8558 ■ *Web:* www.hickoryfarms.com	Toledo	OH	43604	800-753-8558	893-0164*
Logan Farms Honey Glazed Hams 10560 Westheimer Rd *TF:* 800-833-4267 ■ *Web:* www.loganfarmsinc.com	Houston	TX	77042	713-781-4335	977-0532
M&M Meat Shops 640 Trillium Dr PO Box 2488 *Web:* www.mmmeatshops.com	Kitchener	ON	N2H6M3	519-895-1075	895-0762
Stew Leonard's 100 Westport Ave *Web:* stewleonards.com	Norwalk	CT	06851	203-847-7214	

340 GOVERNMENT - CITY

Name / Address	City	State	Zip	Phone	Fax
Abilene City Hall 555 Walnut St *Web:* www.abilenetx.com	Abilene	TX	79601	325-676-6200	676-6229
Akron City Hall 166 S High St Rm 202 *Web:* www.akronohio.gov	Akron	OH	44308	330-375-2133	375-2468
Albany City Hall 24 Eagle St *Web:* www.albanyny.org	Albany	NY	12207	518-434-5100	434-5013
Alexandria City Hall 301 King St *Web:* www.alexandriava.gov	Alexandria	VA	22314	703-838-4000	838-6433
Allentown City Hall 435 Hamilton St *Web:* www.allentownpa.gov	Allentown	PA	18101	610-437-7539	437-7554
Amarillo City Hall 509 E Seventh Ave *Web:* www.ci.amarillo.tx.us	Amarillo	TX	79101	806-378-3000	378-9394
Anaheim City Hall 200 S Anaheim Blvd *Web:* www.anaheim.net	Anaheim	CA	92805	714-765-5162	765-5164
Anchorage City Hall 632 Sixth Ave Second Fl Ste 250 PO Box 196650 *Web:* www.muni.org	Anchorage	AK	99519	907-343-4431	
Ann Arbor City Hall 301 E Huron St *Web:* www.a2gov.org	Ann Arbor	MI	48104	734-994-2700	994-1765
Annapolis City Hall 160 Duke of Gloucester St *Web:* www.ci.annapolis.md.us	Annapolis	MD	21401	410-263-7997	216-9284
Arlington (TX) City Hall 101 W Abram St *Web:* www.arlingtontx.gov	Arlington	TX	76010	817-275-3271	459-6116
Asheville City Hall 70 Ct Plaza PO Box 7148 *Web:* www.ashevillenc.gov	Asheville	NC	28802	828-259-5600	259-5499
Atlanta City Hall 55 Trinity Ave SW Ste 2500 *Web:* www.atlantaga.gov	Atlanta	GA	30303	404-330-6004	658-6893
Atlantic City City Hall 1301 Bacharach Blvd *Web:* www.cityofatlanticcity.org	Atlantic City	NJ	08401	609-347-5300	347-6408
Augusta (GA) Municipal Hall 535 Telfair St *Web:* www.augustaga.gov	Augusta	GA	30901	706-821-2300	826-4790
Aurora City Hall 15151 E Alameda Pkwy *Web:* www.auroragov.org	Aurora	CO	80012	303-739-7015	739-7594
Austin City Hall PO Box 1088 *Web:* www.cityofaustin.org	Austin	TX	78767	512-974-2000	974-2337
Bakersfield City Hall 1600 Truxtun Ave # 300 *Web:* bakersfieldcity.us	Bakersfield	CA	93301	661-326-3751	324-1850
Bangor City Hall 73 Harlow St *Web:* www.bangormaine.gov	Bangor	ME	04401	207-992-4200	945-4449
Bar Harbor Town Hall 93 Cottage St *Web:* www.barharbormaine.gov	Bar Harbor	ME	04609	207-288-4098	288-4461
Baton Rouge City Hall 222 St Louis St Ste 301 *Web:* www.brgov.com	Baton Rouge	LA	70802	225-389-3100	389-5203
Billings City Hall 210 N 27th St *Web:* www.ci.billings.mt.us	Billings	MT	59101	406-657-8210	657-8390
Biloxi City Hall PO Box 429 *Web:* www.biloxi.ms.us	Biloxi	MS	39533	228-435-6254	435-6129
Birmingham City Hall 710 N 20th St *Web:* www.birminghamal.gov	Birmingham	AL	35203	205-254-2000	254-2926
Bismarck City Hall 500 E Front St *Web:* www.bismarcknd.gov	Bismarck	ND	58504	701-355-1540	221-6883

Name / Address	City	State	Zip	Phone	Fax
Bloomington City Hall 401 N Morton St *Web:* www.bloomington.in.gov	Bloomington	IN	47404	812-339-2261	349-3570
Boise City Hall 150 N Capitol Blvd. *Web:* www.cityofboise.org	Boise	ID	83702	208-384-4422	384-4420
Boston City Hall 1 City Hall Plaza *Web:* www.cityofboston.gov	Boston	MA	02201	617-635-4601	248-1937
Boulder City Hall PO Box 791 *Web:* bouldercolorado.gov	Boulder	CO	80306	303-441-3388	441-4478
Branson City Hall 110 W Maddux St Ste 205 *Web:* www.cityofbranson.org	Branson	MO	65616	417-334-3345	335-4354
Bridgeport City Hall 999 Broad St *Web:* bridgeportct.gov	Bridgeport	CT	06604	203-576-7201	576-3913
Brownsville City Hall 1001 E Elizabeth St *Web:* www.cob.us	Brownsville	TX	78520	956-548-6000	546-4021
Buffalo City Hall 65 Niagara Sq. *Web:* www.ci.buffalo.ny.us	Buffalo	NY	14202	716-851-4200	851-4360
Burlington City Hall 149 Church St *Web:* www.burlingtonvt.gov	Burlington	VT	05401	802-865-7000	865-7014
Calgary City Hall 800 Macleod Trail SE PO Box 2100 *Web:* www.calgary.ca	Calgary	AB	T2P2M5	403-268-2489	538-6111
Carson City City Hall 201 N Carson St *Web:* carson.org	Carson City	NV	89701	775-887-2100	887-2139
Casper City Hall 200 N David St *Web:* www.casperwy.gov	Casper	WY	82601	307-235-8400	235-7575
Cedar Rapids City Hall 3851 River Ridge Dr NE *Web:* www.cedar-rapids.org	Cedar Rapids	IA	52402	319-286-5670	286-5130
Champaign City Hall 102 N Neil St *Web:* www.ci.champaign.il.us	Champaign	IL	61820	217-403-8700	403-8980
Charleston (SC) City Hall 50 Broad St *Web:* www.charleston-sc.gov	Charleston	SC	29401	843-577-6970	720-3959
Charleston (WV) City Hall 200 Civic Ctr Dr *Web:* www.cityofcharleston.org	Charleston	WV	25301	304-348-8000	348-8157
Charlotte City Hall Charlotte-Mecklenburg Government Ctr 600 E 4th St *Web:* charmeck.org	Charlotte	NC	28202	704-336-2241	336-6644
Chattanooga City Hall 101 E 11th St Ste 100 *Web:* www.chattanooga.gov	Chattanooga	TN	37402	423-757-5152	
Chesapeake City Hall 306 Cedar Rd *Web:* www.cityofchesapeake.net	Chesapeake	VA	23322	757-382-2489	
Cheyenne City Hall 2101 O'Neil Ave *Web:* www.cheyennecity.org	Cheyenne	WY	82001	307-637-6200	637-6454
Chicago City Hall 121 N La Salle St *Web:* cityofchicago.org	Chicago	IL	60602	312-744-4000	
Chula Vista City Hall 276 Fourth Ave *Web:* www.ci.chula-vista.ca.us	Chula Vista	CA	91910	619-691-5044	476-5379
Cincinnati City Hall 801 Plum St *Web:* www.cincinnati-oh.gov	Cincinnati	OH	45202	513-352-3000	
Cleveland City Hall 601 Lakeside Ave *Web:* www.cleveland-oh.gov	Cleveland	OH	44114	216-664-2000	
Colorado Springs City Hall 107 N Nevada Ave Ste 205 *Web:* www.springsgov.com	Colorado Springs	CO	80903	719-385-5900	385-5488
Columbia (MO) City Hall 701 E Broadway PO Box 6015 *Web:* www.gocolumbiamo.com	Columbia	MO	65205	573-874-7111	
Columbus Consolidated Government Ctr 100 Tenth St *Web:* www.columbusga.org	Columbus	GA	31901	706-653-4000	653-4970
Concord City Hall 41 Green St. *Web:* www.concordnh.gov	Concord	NH	03301	603-225-8500	225-8592
Corpus Christi City Hall 1201 Leopard St PO Box 9277 *Web:* www.cctexas.com	Corpus Christi	TX	78469	361-826-2489	880-3839
Dallas City Hall 1500 Marilla St. *Web:* www.dallascityhall.com	Dallas	TX	75201	214-670-4538	670-3946
Dayton City Hall 101 W Third St P.O. Box 22 *Web:* www.daytonohio.gov	Dayton	OH	45401	937-333-3636	333-4297
Daytona Beach City Hall 301 S Ridgewood Ave Rm 210 PO Box 2451 *Web:* www.codb.us	Daytona Beach	FL	32114	386-671-8100	671-8115
Denver City Hall 201 W Colfax Ave 1st Fl *Web:* www.denvergov.org	Denver	CO	80202	720-865-8400	865-8580
Des Moines City Hall 400 Robert D Ray Dr *Web:* www.dmgov.org	Des Moines	IA	50309	515-283-4500	237-1645
Detroit City Hall 2 Woodward Ave Ste 200 *Web:* detroitmi.gov	Detroit	MI	48226	313-224-3270	224-1466
Dover City Hall 15 ELoockerman St *Web:* www.cityofdover.com	Dover	DE	19901	302-736-7008	736-7177
Dubuque City Hall 50 W 13th St *Web:* www.cityofdubuque.org	Dubuque	IA	52001	563-589-4100	589-0890
Duluth City Hall 411 W First St *Web:* www.duluthmn.gov	Duluth	MN	55802	218-730-5500	730-5923
Durham City Hall 101 City Hall Plaza *Web:* www.durhamnc.gov	Durham	NC	27701	919-560-1200	560-4835
Edmonton City Hall 1 Sir Winston Churchill Sq 3rd Fl. *Web:* www.edmonton.ca	Edmonton	AB	T5J2R7	780-442-5311	496-8210
El Paso City Hall 2 Civic Ctr Plaza *Web:* home.elpasotexas.gov	El Paso	TX	79901	915-541-4000	541-4501
Erie City Hall 626 State St. *Web:* www.erie.pa.us	Erie	PA	16501	814-870-1234	870-1296
Eugene City Hall 777 Pearl St Rm 105 *Web:* www.eugene-or.gov	Eugene	OR	97401	541-682-5010	682-5414
Evansville City Hall 1 NW ML King Jr Blvd *Web:* www.evansvillegov.org	Evansville	IN	47708	812-436-4992	436-4999
Fairbanks City Hall 800 Cushman St *Web:* www.fairbanksalaska.us	Fairbanks	AK	99701	907-459-6771	452-5913
Fargo City Hall 200 N Third St *Web:* www.cityoffargo.com	Fargo	ND	58102	701-241-1310	476-4136
Flagstaff City Hall 211 W Aspen Ave *Web:* www.flagstaff.az.gov	Flagstaff	AZ	86001	928-774-5281	779-7696
Flint City Hall 1101 S Saginaw St Rm 101 *Web:* www.cityofflint.com	Flint	MI	48502	810-766-7346	766-7218
Fort Collins City Hall 300 Laporte Ave *Web:* www.fcgov.com	Fort Collins	CO	80521	970-221-6505	224-6107
Fort Lauderdale City Hall 100 N Andrews Ave. *Web:* www.fortlauderdale.gov	Fort Lauderdale	FL	33301	954-828-5000	828-5017
Fort Wayne City Hall 1 Main St. *Web:* www.cityoffortwayne.org	Fort Wayne	IN	46802	260-427-1221	427-1371
Fort Worth City Hall 1000 Throckmorton St *Web:* fortworthtexas.gov	Fort Worth	TX	76102	817-392-2255	392-6187
Frankfort City Hall PO Box 697 *Web:* frankfort.ky.gov	Frankfort	KY	40602	502-875-8523	
Fremont City Hall PO Box 5006 *Web:* www.fremont.gov	Fremont	CA	94537	510-284-4000	284-4001
Fresno City Hall 2600 Fresno St Rm 2064 *Web:* www.fresno.gov	Fresno	CA	93721	559-621-7770	621-7776
Garden Grove City Hall 11222 Acacia Pkwy. *Web:* www.ci.garden-grove.ca.us	Garden Grove	CA	92840	714-741-5000	741-5044
Garland City Hall 200 N Fifth St *Web:* www.ci.garland.tx.us	Garland	TX	75040	972-205-2000	205-2504
Gettysburg Borough Hall 59 E High St *Web:* www.gettysburg-pa.gov	Gettysburg	PA	17325	717-334-1160	334-7258
Glendale (AZ) City Hall 5850 W Glendale Ave *Web:* www.glendaleaz.com	Glendale	AZ	85301	623-930-2000	930-2690
Glendale (CA) City Hall 613 E Broadway Rm 110 *Web:* glendaleca.gov/	Glendale	CA	91206	818-548-2090	241-5386
Grand Forks City Hall 255 N Fourth St *Web:* www.grandforksgov.com	Grand Forks	ND	58203	701-746-2626	787-3740
Grand Rapids City Hall 300 Monroe Ave NW *Web:* grcity.us	Grand Rapids	MI	49503	616-456-3010	456-4607
Great Falls City Hall 2 Pk Dr S *Web:* greatfallsmt.net	Great Falls	MT	59401	406-771-1180	727-0005
Green Bay City Hall 100 N Jefferson St Rm 106 *Web:* www.ci.green-bay.wi.us	Green Bay	WI	54301	920-448-3010	448-3016
Greensboro City Hall 300 W Washington St PO Box 3136 *Web:* www.greensboro-nc.gov	Greensboro	NC	27401	336-373-2489	373-2117
Greenville City Hall 206 S Main St. *TF:* 800-829-4477 ■ *Web:* www.greenvillesc.gov	Greenville	SC	29601	864-232-2273	467-5725
Gulfport City Hall 2309 15th St. *Web:* gulfport-ms.gov	Gulfport	MS	39501	228-868-5700	868-5800
Harrisburg City Hall 10 N Second St *Web:* www.harrisburgpa.gov	Harrisburg	PA	17101	717-255-3060	255-3081
Hartford City Hall 550 Main St *Web:* www.hartford.gov	Hartford	CT	06103	860-522-4888	
Hattiesburg City Hall 200 Forest St PO Box 1898 *Web:* www.hattiesburgms.com	Hattiesburg	MS	39401	601-545-4500	
Helena City Hall 316 N Pk Ave. *Web:* www.helenamt.gov	Helena	MT	59623	406-447-8410	447-8434
Hialeah City Hall 501 Palm Ave Ste 310 *Web:* hialeahfl.gov	Hialeah	FL	33010	305-883-5820	883-5814
Hilton Head Island Town Hall 1 Town Ctr Ct *Web:* www.hiltonheadislandsc.gov	Hilton Head Island	SC	29928	843-341-4600	842-7728
Honolulu City Hall 530 S King St *Web:* www.honolulu.gov	Honolulu	HI	96813	808-768-4141	768-5552
Hot Springs City Hall 133 Convention Blvd *Web:* www.cityhs.net	Hot Springs	AR	71901	501-321-6800	321-6809
Houston City Hall 901 Bagby St *Web:* www.houstontx.gov	Houston	TX	77002	713-247-1000	247-2355
Huntington Beach City Hall 2000 Main St *Web:* www.ci.huntington-beach.ca.us	Huntington Beach	CA	92648	714-536-5511	374-1557
Huntsville City Hall PO Box 308 *Web:* www.hsvcity.com	Huntsville	AL	35804	256-427-5240	427-5257
Independence City Hall 111 E Maple Ave *Web:* www.ci.independence.mo.us	Independence	MO	64050	816-325-7000	325-7012
Indianapolis City Hall 200 E Washington St Ste 2501 *Web:* www.indy.gov	Indianapolis	IN	46204	317-327-3601	327-3980
Irving City Hall 825 W Irving Blvd *Web:* www.ci.irving.tx.us	Irving	TX	75060	972-721-2600	721-2420
Jackson (MS) City Hall 219 S President St *Web:* www.city.jackson.ms.us	Jackson	MS	39201	601-960-1084	960-2193
Jackson (WY) Town Hall 150 E Pearl Ave. *Web:* townofjackson.com	Jackson	WY	83001	307-733-3932	739-0919
Jacksonville City Hall 117 W Duval St Ste 400 *Web:* www.coj.net	Jacksonville	FL	32202	904-630-1776	630-2391
Jefferson City City Hall 320 E McCarty St *Web:* www.jeffcitymo.org	Jefferson City	MO	65101	573-634-6304	634-6329
Jersey City City Hall 280 Grove St *Web:* www.cityofjerseycity.com	Jersey City	NJ	07302	201-547-5000	547-5461
Johnson City City Hall 601 E Main St *Web:* www.johnsoncitytn.com	Johnson City	TN	37601	423-434-6000	434-6295
Juneau City Hall 155 S Seward St *Web:* www.juneau.org	Juneau	AK	99801	907-586-5278	586-2536
Kansas City (KS) City Hall 701 N Seventh St *Web:* www.wycokck.org	Kansas City	KS	66101	913-573-5000	573-5210

Name / Address	City	State	Zip	Phone	Fax
Kansas City (MO) City Hall 414 E 12th St 25th Fl *Web:* www.kcmo.org	Kansas City	MO	64106	816-513-3360	513-3353
Key West City Hall 3132 Flagler Ave *Web:* www.keywestcity.com	Key West	FL	33040	305-809-3700	809-3833
Knoxville City Hall 400 W Main St *Web:* www.cityofknoxville.org	Knoxville	TN	37902	865-215-2000	215-2085
Lafayette City Hall 705 W University Ave *Web:* www.lafayettegov.org	Lafayette	LA	70506	337-291-8200	
Lansing City Hall 124 W Michigan Ave 9th Fl *Web:* www.lansingmi.gov	Lansing	MI	48933	517-483-4131	377-0068
Las Cruces City Hall 200 N Church St *Web:* www.las-cruces.org	Las Cruces	NM	88001	575-541-2000	541-2117
Las Vegas City Hall 495 S. Main St *Web:* www.lasvegasnevada.gov	Las Vegas	NV	89101	702-229-6011	386-9108
Lincoln City Hall 555 S Tenth St *Web:* www.lincoln.ne.gov	Lincoln	NE	68508	402-441-7515	441-6533
Little Rock City Hall 500 W Markham St *Web:* www.littlerock.org	Little Rock	AR	72201	501-371-4500	371-4498
Long Beach City Hall 333 W Ocean Blvd *Web:* www.longbeach.gov	Long Beach	CA	90802	562-570-6101	570-6789
Los Angeles City Hall 200 N Spring St Rm 360 *Web:* www.lacity.org	Los Angeles	CA	90012	213-473-3231	978-1027
Louisville City Hall 601 W Jefferson St *Web:* www.louisvilleky.gov	Louisville	KY	40202	502-574-1100	574-4420
Lubbock City Hall 1625 13th St *Web:* www.ci.lubbock.tx.us	Lubbock	TX	79401	806-775-3000	775-3002
Macon City Hall 700 Poplar St *Web:* www.maconbibb.us	Macon	GA	31201	478-751-7400	
Madison City Hall 210 Martin Luther King Jr Blvd Rm 403 *Web:* www.cityofmadison.com	Madison	WI	53703	608-266-4611	267-8671
Manchester City Hall 1 City Hall Plaza *Web:* www.manchesternh.gov	Manchester	NH	03101	603-624-6455	624-6481
Memphis City Hall 125 N Main St *Web:* www.cityofmemphis.org	Memphis	TN	38103	901-576-6500	
Mesa City Hall PO Box 1466 *Web:* www.mesaaz.gov	Mesa	AZ	85211	480-644-2011	644-2821
Miami City Hall 3500 Pan American Dr *Web:* www.ci.miami.fl.us	Miami	FL	33133	305-250-5400	250-5410
Milwaukee City Hall 200 E Wells St *Web:* www.city.milwaukee.gov	Milwaukee	WI	53202	414-286-2200	286-3191
Minneapolis City Hall 350 S Fifth St *Web:* www.ci.minneapolis.mn.us	Minneapolis	MN	55415	612-673-3000	673-3812
Mobile City Hall 205 Government St *Web:* www.cityofmobile.org	Mobile	AL	36602	251-208-7411	208-7576
Modesto City Hall PO Box 642 *Web:* www.modestogov.com	Modesto	CA	95353	209-577-5200	571-5152
Monterey City Hall 580 Pacific St *Web:* www.monterey.org	Monterey	CA	93940	831-646-3935	646-3702
Montgomery City Hall 103 N Perry St *Web:* www.montgomeryal.gov	Montgomery	AL	36104	334-241-4400	
Montpelier City Hall 39 Main St *Web:* montpelier-vt.org	Montpelier	VT	05602	802-223-9502	223-9519
Morgantown City Hall 389 Spruce St *Web:* www.morgantownwv.gov	Morgantown	WV	26505	304-284-7439	
Myrtle Beach City Hall 937 Broadway St *Web:* www.cityofmyrtlebeach.com	Myrtle Beach	SC	29577	843-918-1000	918-1028
Naples City Hall 735 Eigth St S *Web:* www.naplesgov.com	Naples	FL	34102	239-213-1015	213-1025
Nashville & Davidson County Metropolitan City Hall 100 Metropolitan Courthouse *Web:* www.nashville.gov	Nashville	TN	37201	615-862-6000	862-6040
New Haven City Hall 165 Church St *Web:* www.cityofnewhaven.com	New Haven	CT	06510	203-946-8200	946-7683
New Orleans City Hall 1300 Perdido St *Web:* www.nola.gov	New Orleans	LA	70112	504-658-4000	658-4938
New York City Hall Broadway & Murray Sts *Web:* www.nyc.gov	New York	NY	10007	212-788-2656	
Newark City Hall 920 Broad St *Web:* www.ci.newark.nj.us	Newark	NJ	07102	973-733-8004	733-5352
Newport City Hall 43 Broadway *Web:* www.cityofnewport.com	Newport	RI	02840	401-846-9600	845-2510
Newport News City Hall 2400 Washington Ave *Web:* www.ci.newport-news.va.us	Newport News	VA	23607	757-926-8000	926-3503
Norfolk City Hall 810 Union St *Web:* www.norfolk.gov	Norfolk	VA	23510	757-664-4000	664-4226
Oakland City Hall 1 Frank H Ogawa Plaza *Web:* www.oaklandnet.com	Oakland	CA	94612	510-444-2489	
Ocean City City Hall 301 Baltimore Ave *TF:* 800-626-2326 ■ *Web:* www.oceancitymd.gov	Ocean City	MD	21842	410-289-8931	289-7385
Ogden City Hall 2549 Washington Blvd *Web:* www.ogdencity.com	Ogden	UT	84401	801-629-8150	629-8154
Oklahoma City City Hall 200 N Walker Ave *Web:* www.okc.gov	Oklahoma City	OK	73102	405-297-2578	297-3124
Olympia City Hall PO Box 1967 *Web:* olympiawa.gov	Olympia	WA	98507	360-753-8447	709-2791
Omaha City Hall 1819 Farnam St Ste LC1 *Web:* www.ci.omaha.ne.us	Omaha	NE	68183	402-444-5550	444-5263
Orlando City Hall 400 S Orange Ave *Web:* www.cityoforlando.net	Orlando	FL	32801	407-246-2221	246-2842
Ottawa City Hall 110 Laurier Ave W *TF:* 866-261-9799 ■ *Web:* www.ottawa.ca/city_hall/index_en.html	Ottawa	ON	K1P1J1	613-580-2400	580-2495
Oxnard City Hall 300 W 3rd St *Web:* www.ci.oxnard.ca.us	Oxnard	CA	93030	805-385-7803	
Palm Springs City Hall 3200 E Tahquitz Canyon Way *Web:* www.ci.palm-springs.ca.us	Palm Springs	CA	92262	760-323-8299	322-8332
Paterson City Hall 155 Market St *Web:* www.patersonnj.gov	Paterson	NJ	07505	973-321-1500	
Pensacola City Hall 180 Governmental Ctr *Web:* www.cityofpensacola.com	Pensacola	FL	32521	850-435-1626	
Peoria City Hall 419 Fulton St Ste 401 *Web:* www.peoriagov.org	Peoria	IL	61602	309-494-8565	494-8574
Philadelphia City Hall 1234 Market St 17th Fl *Web:* philafound.org	Philadelphia	PA	19107	215-686-9749	
Phoenix City Hall 200 W Washington St 11th Fl *Web:* www.phoenix.gov	Phoenix	AZ	85003	602-262-7111	495-5583
Pierre City Hall 222 E Dakota Ave *Web:* ci.pierre.sd.us	Pierre	SD	57501	605-773-7407	773-7406
Pittsburgh City Hall 414 Grant St City-County Bldg *Web:* pittsburghpa.gov	Pittsburgh	PA	15219	412-255-2883	255-2821
Plano City Hall 1520 Ave K *Web:* www.plano.gov	Plano	TX	75074	972-941-7000	423-9587
Pocatello City Hall 911 N Seventh Ave *Web:* www.pocatello.us	Pocatello	ID	83201	208-234-6163	234-6297
Portland (ME) City Hall 389 Congress St *Web:* www.portlandmaine.gov	Portland	ME	04101	207-874-8610	874-8612
Portland (OR) City Hall 1221 SW Fourth Ave *Web:* portlandoregon.gov/	Portland	OR	97204	503-823-4000	823-3588
Providence City Hall 25 Dorrance St *Web:* providenceri.com	Providence	RI	02903	401-421-7740	
Provo City Hall 351 W Ctr St *Web:* provo.org	Provo	UT	84601	801-852-6100	852-6107
Quebec City Hall 2 Rue des Jardins *Web:* www.ville.quebec.qc.ca	Quebec	QC	G1R4S9	418-641-6651	
Rapid City City Hall 300 Sixth St *Web:* www.rcgov.org	Rapid City	SD	57701	605-394-4110	394-6793
Rehoboth Beach City Hall 229 Rehoboth Ave *Web:* www.cityofrehoboth.com	Rehoboth Beach	DE	19971	302-227-6181	227-4643
Reno City Hall PO Box 1900 *Web:* www.reno.gov	Reno	NV	89505	775-334-2030	334-2432
Richmond City Hall 900 E Broad St Rm 201 *Web:* www.richmondgov.com	Richmond	VA	23219	804-646-7000	
Riverside City Hall 3900 Main St *Web:* www.riversideca.gov	Riverside	CA	92522	951-826-5312	826-5470
Roanoke City Hall 215 Church Ave SW *Web:* roanokeva.gov	Roanoke	VA	24011	540-853-2000	853-1145
Rochester Mayor's 201 Fourth St SE *Web:* rochestermn.gov	Rochester	MN	55904	507-328-2700	287-7979
Rochester (NY) City Hall 30 Church St *Web:* cityofrochester.gov	Rochester	NY	14614	585-428-7045	428-6059
Rockford City Hall 425 E State St *Web:* www.ci.rockford.il.us	Rockford	IL	61104	815-987-5590	967-6952
Sacramento City Hall 915 'I' St *Web:* portal.cityofsacramento.org	Sacramento	CA	95814	916-808-7200	808-7672
Saint Augustine City Hall PO Box 210 *Web:* www.staugustinegovernment.com	Saint Augustine	FL	32085	904-825-1040	209-4286
Saint Louis City Hall 1200 Market St *Web:* stlouis-mo.gov	Saint Louis	MO	63103	314-622-3201	622-4061
Saint Paul City Hall 15 W Kellogg Blvd 390 City Hall *Web:* www.stpaul.gov	Saint Paul	MN	55102	651-266-8510	266-8521
Saint Petersburg City Hall PO Box 2842 *Web:* www.stpete.org	Saint Petersburg	FL	33731	727-893-7111	892-5102
Salem City Hall 555 Liberty St SE Rm 220 *Web:* www.cityofsalem.net	Salem	OR	97301	503-588-6255	588-6354
Salt Lake City City Hall 451 S State St *Web:* www.slcgov.com	Salt Lake City	UT	84111	801-535-7704	535-6331
San Antonio City Hall PO Box 839966 *Web:* www.sanantonio.gov	San Antonio	TX	78283	210-207-7040	207-7027
San Bernardino City Hall 300 N 'D' St *Web:* www.ci.san-bernardino.ca.us	San Bernardino	CA	92418	909-384-5211	384-5158
San Diego City Hall 202 C St *Web:* www.sandiego.gov	San Diego	CA	92101	619-533-4000	533-4045
San Jose City Hall 200 Santa Clara St *Web:* www.sanjoseca.gov	San Jose	CA	95113	408-535-3500	292-6731
Santa Ana City Hall 20 Civic Ctr Plaza *Web:* www.ci.santa-ana.ca.us	Santa Ana	CA	92701	714-647-6900	647-6954
Santa Fe City Hall 200 Lincoln Ave *Web:* www.santafenm.gov	Santa Fe	NM	87501	505-955-6520	
Savannah City Hall PO Box 1027 *Web:* savannahga.gov	Savannah	GA	31402	912-651-6441	651-4260
Scottsdale City Hall 7447 E Indian School Rd *Web:* www.scottsdaleaz.gov	Scottsdale	AZ	85251	480-312-3111	312-2888
Scranton City Hall 340 N Washington Ave *Web:* www.scrantonpa.gov	Scranton	PA	18503	570-348-4100	348-4207
Seattle City Hall 600 Fourth Ave 2nd Fl *Web:* www.seattle.gov	Seattle	WA	98104	206-684-8888	684-8587
Shreveport City Hall PO Box 31109 *Web:* www.shreveportla.gov	Shreveport	LA	71130	318-673-5370	673-5099
Sioux Falls City Hall 224 W 9th St *Web:* siouxfalls.org	Sioux Falls	SD	57104	605-367-8000	367-7801
South Bend City Hall 227 W Jefferson Blvd 455 County-City Bldg *Web:* www.ci.south-bend.in.us	South Bend	IN	46601	574-235-9221	235-9173
Spokane City Hall 808 W Spokane Falls Blvd *Web:* www.spokanecity.org	Spokane	WA	99201	509-625-6250	
Springfield (IL) City Hall 800 E Monroe St Rm 300 *Web:* www.springfield.il.us	Springfield	IL	62701	217-789-2200	789-2109
Springfield (MA) City Hall 36 Ct St *Web:* www3.springfield-ma.gov	Springfield	MA	01103	413-787-6000	

Phone Fax

Springfield (MO) City Hall
840 Boonville Ave. Springfield MO 65802 417-864-1000 864-1649
Web: www.springfieldmo.gov/home

Stamford City Hall
888 Washington Blvd 10th Fl Stamford CT 06901 203-977-4150 977-5845
Web: www.stamfordct.gov

Stockton City Hall 425 N El Dorado St Stockton CA 95202 209-937-8212 937-7149
Web: www.stocktongov.com

Tacoma City Hall 747 Market St Tacoma WA 98402 253-591-5000 591-5300
Web: www.cityoftacoma.org

Tallahassee City Hall 300 S Adams St. Tallahassee FL 32301 850-891-0000
Web: talgov.com

Tampa City Hall 306 E Jackson St Tampa FL 33602 813-274-8251 274-7050
Web: www.tampagov.net

Tempe City Hall 31 E Fifth St Tempe AZ 85281 480-350-8221 350-8930
Web: www.tempe.gov

Toledo City Hall 1 Government Ctr Ste 2120 Toledo OH 43604 419-245-1050 245-1072
Web: toledo.oh.gov

Topeka City Hall 215 SE 7th St Topeka KS 66603 785-368-3754 368-3966
Web: www.topeka.org

Toronto City Hall 100 Queen St W Toronto ON M5H2N2 416-392-8016 392-2980
Web: www.toronto.ca

Trenton City Hall 319 E State St Trenton NJ 08608 609-989-3185 989-3190
Web: www.trentonnj.org

Tucson City Hall 255 W Alameda St. Tucson AZ 85701 520-791-4204 791-5198
Web: tucsonaz.gov/

Tulsa City Hall 175 E 2nd St Fl 14 Tulsa OK 74103 918-596-2100 596-9010
Web: www.cityoftulsa.org

Tupelo City Hall 71 E Troy St Tupelo MS 38804 662-841-6513 840-2075
Web: www.tupeloms.gov

Tuscaloosa City Hall 2201 University Blvd Tuscaloosa AL 35401 205-349-2010 349-0147
Web: www.ci.tuscaloosa.al.us

Vancouver (BC) City Hall
453 W 12th Ave PO Box 7747 Vancouver BC V5Y1V4 604-873-7000 873-7051
Web: vancouver.ca

Vancouver (WA) City Hall PO Box 1995 Vancouver WA 98668 360-487-8000 274-8049
Web: www.cityofvancouver.us

Virginia Beach City Hall
2401 Courthouse Dr
Municipal Ctr Bldg 1 Virginia Beach VA 23456 757-385-3111
Web: www.vbgov.com

Washington (DC) City Hall
1350 Pennsylvania Ave NW Washington DC 20004 202-727-1000 727-0505
Web: www.dc.gov

West Palm Beach City Hall
200 Second St West Palm Beach FL 33401 561-822-1200 822-1424
Web: wpb.org

Wheeling City Council Chambers
1500 Chapline St Wheeling WV 26003 304-234-3694
Web: www.wheelingchamber.com

Wichita City Hall 455 N Main St 1st Fl Wichita KS 67202 316-268-4331
Web: www.wichita.gov

Williamsburg City Hall 401 Lafayette St Williamsburg VA 23185 757-220-6100 220-6107
Web: www.williamsburgva.gov

Winston-Salem City Hall
101 N Main St PO Box 2511 Winston-Salem NC 27101 336-727-8000 748-3060
Web: www.cityofws.org

Yonkers City Hall 40 S Broadway Yonkers NY 10701 914-377-6000
Web: www.cityofyonkers.com

Youngstown City Hall 26 S Phelps St 6th Fl Youngstown OH 44503 330-742-8859
Web: youngstownmuniclerk.com

341 GOVERNMENT - COUNTY

Phone Fax

Abbeville County 102 Ct Sq Abbeville SC 29620 864-366-5312
Web: www.sccounties.org

Accomack County 23296 Courthouse Ave Ste 203 Accomac VA 23301 757-787-5700 787-2468
Web: www.co.accomack.va.us

Ada County 200 W Front St Ste 3255 Boise ID 83702 208-287-7000 287-7009
Web: adacounty.id.gov/

Adair County 424 Public Sq Columbia KY 42728 270-384-2801
Web: www.columbia-adaircounty.com

Adams County 450 S Fourth Ave Brighton CO 80601 303-654-6100
Web: www.co.adams.co.us

Addison County 7 Mahady Ct Middlebury VT 05753 802-388-7741 388-8066
Web: www.addisoncounty.com

Aiken County 828 Richland Ave W Aiken SC 29801 803-642-2012
TF: 866-876-7074 ■ *Web:* www.aikencountysc.gov

Alachua County 12 SE First St Gainesville FL 32601 352-374-5204
Web: www.alachuacounty.us

Alamance County 124 W Elm St Graham NC 27253 336-228-1312 570-6788
Web: www.alamance-nc.com

Alameda County 1221 Oak St Ste 555 Oakland CA 94612 510-272-6984 272-3784
Web: www.acgov.org

Alamosa County 8900 Independence Way Alamosa CO 81101 719-589-4848 589-1900
Web: www.alamosacounty.org

Albany County 112 State St Rm 200 Albany NY 12207 518-447-7040 447-5589
Web: www.albanycounty.com

Albemarle County 401 McIntire Rd Charlottesville VA 22902 434-296-5841 296-5800
Web: www.albemarle.org

Alcorn County 600 Waldron St PO Box 179 Corinth MS 38834 662-286-7733 286-2548
Web: www.alcorncounty.org

Aleutians East Borough 3380 C St Ste 205 Anchorage AK 99503 907-274-7555 276-7569
TF: 888-383-2699 ■ *Web:* www.aleutianseast.org

Alexander County 2000 Washington Ave Cairo IL 62914 8-7-34--0107 -73-4-7003*
**Fax Area Code:* 618 ■
Web: www.illinoiscourts.gov/circuitcourt/CircuitCourtJudges/CCC_County.asp#Alexander

Phone Fax

Alexandria (Independent City)
301 King St Ste 2300 Alexandria VA 22314 703-838-4500
Web: alexandriava.gov

Alfalfa County 300 S Grand Ave Cherokee OK 73728 405-596-2392 596-2254

Alger County 100 Ct St Munising MI 49862 906-387-2076 387-2156
Web: algercourthouse.com

Allamakee County 110 Allamakee St Waukon IA 52172 563-864-7454
Web: www.allamakeecounty.com

Allegany County 7 Ct St County Courthouse Belmont NY 14813 585-268-9270 268-5881
Web: www.alleganyco.com

Allen County
715 S Calhoun St County Courthouse Rm 201 Fort Wayne IN 46802 260-449-7245 449-7658
Web: www.allencounty.us

Allen Parish PO Box 1280 Oberlin LA 70655 337-639-4868 639-4911
TF: 888-639-4868 ■ *Web:* www.allenparish.com

Allendale County 526 Memorial Ave. Allendale SC 29810 803-584-3438 584-7042
Web: www.allendalecounty.com

Alpena County 720 W Chisholm St Alpena MI 49707 989-354-9500 354-9648
Web: www.alpenacounty.org

Alpine County 99 Waters St PO Box 158 Markleeville CA 96120 530-694-2281 694-2491
Web: www.alpinecountyca.gov

Amador County 810 Ct St. Jackson CA 95642 209-223-6470 257-0619
Web: www.co.amador.ca.us

Amelia County 16360 Dunn St Ste 101 Amelia Courthouse VA 23002 804-561-3039 561-6039
Web: www.ameliacova.com

Amherst County 153 Washington St Amherst VA 24521 434-946-9400 946-9370
Web: www.countyofamherst.com

Amite County PO Box 680 Liberty MS 39645 601-657-8022 657-8288
Web: www.amitecounty.ms

Anaconda-Deer Lodge County 800 S Main Anaconda MT 59711 406-563-4000 563-4001
Web: anacondadeerlodge.mt.gov

Anchorage Municipality
632 W Sixth Ave # 250 Anchorage AK 99501 907-343-4311 343-4313
Web: www.muni.org

Anderson County 100 N Main St Rm 111 Clinton TN 37716 865-457-5400
Web: www.andersoncountychamber.org

Andrew County PO Box 206 Savannah MO 64485 816-324-3624 324-6154
Web: www.andrewcounty.org

Andrews County 215 NW First St Annex Bldg Andrews TX 79714 432-524-1426
Web: www.co.andrews.tx.us

Androscoggin County 2 Turner St Unit 2 Auburn ME 04210 207-784-8390
Web: www.androscoggincounty.com

Anne Arundel County 44 Calvert St Annapolis MD 21401 410-222-7000
Web: clerkannearundel.org

Anoka County 325 E Main St Anoka MN 55303 763-422-7350 422-6919
Web: anokacounty.us/

Anson County 101 S Greene St Wadesboro NC 28170 704-994-3201
Web: www.co.anson.nc.us

Antelope County 501 Main St Neligh NE 68756 402-887-4410 887-4719
Web: www.co.antelope.ne.us

Antrim County 203 E Cayuga St Bellaire MI 49615 231-533-6353 533-6935
Web: www.antrimcounty.org

Apache County 75 W Cleveland St Saint Johns AZ 85936 928-337-4364 337-2771
Web: www.co.apache.az.us

Appling County 69 Tippins St Baxley GA 31513 912-367-8100 367-8161
Web: www.baxley.org

Aransas County 301 N Live Oak St Rockport TX 78382 361-790-0122 790-0119
Web: www.aransascounty.org

Arenac County PO Box 747 Standish MI 48658 989-846-4626
Web: www.arenaccountygov.com

Arkansas County 302 S College St Stuttgart AR 72160 870-673-6586

Arlington County
2100 Clarendon Blvd Ste 300 Arlington VA 22201 703-228-3130 228-7430
Web: www.arlingtonva.us

Armstrong County 100 Trice St PO Box 189 Claude TX 79019 806-226-3221
Web: www.co.armstrong.tx.us

Arthur County 205 Fir St Arthur NE 69121 308-764-2201
Web: www.arthurcounty.ne.gov

Ascension Parish 208 E Railroad St Gonzales LA 70737 225-621-5709 621-5704
Web: www.ascensionparish.net

Ashe County Chamber of Commerce
1 N Jefferson Ave Ste C West Jefferson NC 28694 336-846-9550 846-8671
TF: 888-343-2743 ■ *Web:* ashechamber.com

Ashland County 142 W Second St Ashland OH 44805 419-282-4242
Web: www.ashlandcounty.org

Ashley County 215 E Jefferson St Hamburg AR 71646 870-853-2000
Web: local.arkansas.gov/local.php?agency=Ashley%20County

Asotin County 135 Second St Asotin WA 99402 509-243-2016 243-4978
Web: www.co.asotin.wa.us

Assumption Parish 4813 Hwy 1 PO Box 520 Napoleonville LA 70390 985-369-7435 369-2972
Web: www.assumptionla.com

Atascosa County
1 Courthouse Cir Dr Ste 102 Jourdanton TX 78026 830-767-2511 769-1021
Web: www.co.atascosa.tx.us

Atchison County 423 N Fifth St Atchison KS 66002 913-367-1653 367-0227
Web: www.atchisoncountyks.org

Athens County Board of Developmental Disabilities
801 W Union St Athens OH 45701 740-594-3539
Web: athenscbdd.org

Athens-Clarke County
325 E Washington St Rm 200 PO Box 1868 Athens GA 30601 706-613-3031 613-3033
Web: www.athensclarkecounty.com

Atkinson County PO Box 518 Pearson GA 31642 912-422-3391 422-3429
Web: atkinsoncounty.georgia.gov

Atlantic County 5901 E Main St Mays Landing NJ 08330 609-641-7867 625-4738
Web: www.aclink.org

Atoka County PO Box 900 Atoka OK 74525 580-889-3341 889-7584
Web: atokaok.org

Attala County 230 W Washington St Kosciusko MS 39090 662-289-2921 289-7662
Web: attalacounty.net

Audrain County 101 N Jefferson St Rm 101 Mexico MO 65265 573-473-5820 581-2380
Web: www.audraincounty.org

				Phone	Fax
Audubon County 318 Leroy St Ste 6 *Web:* www.auduboncounty.org	Audubon	IA	50025	712-563-4275	
Auglaize County 209 S Blackhoof St Ste 201 *Web:* www.auglaizecounty.org	Wapakoneta	OH	45895	419-739-6710	
Augusta County 18 Government Ctr Ln *Web:* www.co.augusta.va.us	Verona	VA	24482	540-245-5600	245-5621
Augusta-Richmond County 535 Telfair St *Web:* www.augustaga.gov	Augusta	GA	30901	706-821-2300	826-4790
Aurora County 401 N Main St P.O. Box 366 *Web:* ujs.sd.gov/	Plankinton	SD	57368	605-942-7165	942-7170
Austin County 1 E Main St *Web:* www.austincounty.com	Bellville	TX	77418	979-865-5911	865-8786
Avery County PO Box 115 *Web:* www.averycounty.com	Newland	NC	28657	828-733-2910	
Avoyelles Parish 675 Government St *Web:* avoyellesso.org	Marksville	LA	71351	318-253-8085	253-4061
Baca County 741 Main St *Web:* www.springfieldcolorado.com	Springfield	CO	81073	719-523-4372	523-4881
Bacon County 504 N Pierce St PO Box 450 *Web:* www.almaone.com	Alma	GA	31510	912-632-5859	632-7710
Bailey County 300 S First St *Web:* www.co.bailey.tx.us	Muleshoe	TX	79347	806-272-3044	272-3538
Baker County 1995 Third St Ste 150 *Web:* www.bakercounty.org	Baker City	OR	97814	541-523-8207	523-8240
Baldwin County 322 Courthouse Sq *Web:* www.baldwincountyal.gov	Bay Minette	AL	36507	251-937-9561	580-2500
Baltimore County 401 Bosley Ave *Web:* baltimorecountymd.gov	Towson	MD	21204	410-887-2139	
Bamberg County 2340 Main Hwy *Web:* www.bambergsc.com	Bamberg	SC	29003	803-245-5128	245-5156
Banks County 106 Yonah Homer Rd PO Box 57 *Web:* www.bankscountychamber.com	Homer	GA	30547	706-677-2108	677-2109
Banner County 206 State St *Web:* bannercounty-gov.us	Harrisburg	NE	69345	308-436-5265	436-4180
Bannock County PO Box 4016 *Web:* www.co.bannock.id.us	Pocatello	ID	83205	208-236-7211	236-7363
Baraga County 16 N Third St *Web:* www.baragacounty.org/contactlocation	L'Anse	MI	49946	906-524-6183	
Barber County Development Inc PO Box 4 *Web:* www.barbercounty.net	Medicine Lodge	KS	67104	620-886-3988	
Barbour County 8 N Main St *Web:* barbourcounty.wv.gov	Philippi	WV	26416	304-457-3454	457-5983
Barnes County 230 Fourth St NW Rm 202 *Web:* www.co.barnes.nd.us	Valley City	ND	58072	701-845-8500	
Barnstable County PO Box 427 *Web:* www.barnstablecounty.org	Barnstable	MA	02630	508-362-2511	
Barnwell County 141 Main St *Web:* barnwellcounty.sc.gov	Barnwell	SC	29812	803-541-1020	
Barren County 117-1A N Public Sq	Glasgow	KY	42141	270-651-3783	651-1083
Barron County 330 E LaSalle Ave Rm 210 *Web:* www.co.barron.wi.us	Barron	WI	54812	715-537-6200	537-6277
Barrow County 233 E Broad St *Web:* www.barrowga.org	Winder	GA	30680	770-307-3005	307-3141
Barry County 220 W State St *Web:* barrycounty.org	Hastings	MI	49058	269-945-1290	945-0209
Barry County Clerk 700 Main St Ste 2 *Web:* barrycountycollector.com	Cassville	MO	65625	417-847-2561	
Bartholomew County 234 Washington St *Web:* www.bartholomewco.com	Columbus	IN	47201	812-379-1600	379-1675
Barton County 1400 Main St Ste 202 *Web:* www.bartoncounty.org	Great Bend	KS	67530	620-793-1835	793-1990
Bartow County 135 W Cherokee Ave Ste 251 *Web:* www.bartowga.org	Cartersville	GA	30120	770-387-5030	387-5023
Bastrop County 804 Pecan St *Web:* www.co.bastrop.tx.us	Bastrop	TX	78602	512-581-4000	
Bates County 1 N Delaware St *Web:* www.batescounty.net	Butler	MO	64730	660-679-3371	679-9922
Bath County 17 W Main St *Web:* www.bath.clerkinfo.net	Owingsville	KY	40360	606-674-2613	674-9526
Baxter County 1 E Seventh St Fl 1 Baxter County Courthouse *Web:* www.baxtercounty.org	Mountain Home	AR	72653	870-425-3475	
Bay County 515 Ctr Ave Ste 101 *Web:* www.baycounty-mi.gov	Bay City	MI	48708	989-895-4280	895-4284
Bayfield County PO Box 878 *Web:* www.bayfieldcounty.org	Washburn	WI	54891	715-373-6100	373-6153
Baylor County 301 N Washington PO Box 31 *Web:* www.cityofseymour.org	Seymour	TX	76380	940-889-3148	889-8882
Beadle County 450 3rd St SW *Web:* beadle.sdcounties.org	Huron	SD	57350	605-353-7161	
Bear Lake County 7 E Ctr St PO Box 190 *Web:* www.bearlakecounty.info	Paris	ID	83261	208-945-2212	
Beaufort County 102 Ribaut Rd *Web:* www.co.beaufort.sc.us	Beaufort	SC	29902	843-255-5050	
Beauregard Parish PO Box 100 *Web:* beauregardclerk.org	DeRidder	LA	70634	337-463-8595	462-3916
Beaver County PO Box 338 *Web:* www.okcounties.org	Beaver	OK	73932	580-625-3151	
Beaverhead County 2 S Pacific St Ste 16 *Web:* www.beaverheadcounty.org	Dillon	MT	59725	406-683-3700	683-3728
Becker County 915 Lake Ave *Fax: Acctg ■ *Web:* www.co.becker.mn.us	Detroit Lakes	MN	56501	218-846-7311	846-7257*
Beckham County PO Box 67 *Web:* beckham.okcounties.org	Sayre	OK	73662	580-928-2457	928-2467
Bedford County 200 S Juliana St *Web:* www.bedford.sapdc.org	Bedford	PA	15522	814-623-4807	623-4831
Bedford (Independent City) 215 E Main St *Web:* bedfordva.gov	Bedford	VA	24523	540-587-6001	
Bee County 105 W Corpus Christi St Rm 103 *Web:* www.co.bee.tx.us	Beeville	TX	78102	361-362-3245	362-3247
Belknap County 34 County Dr *Web:* www.belknapcounty.org	Laconia	NH	03246	603-527-5400	527-5409
Bell County 101 E Central Ave PO Box 480 *TF:* 800-460-2355 ■ *Web:* www.bellcountytx.com	Belton	TX	76513	254-933-5160	933-5176
Belmont County 101 W Main St Courthouse *Web:* www.belmontcountyohio.org/county-departments	Saint Clairsville	OH	43950	740-695-2121	
Beltrami County 619 Beltrami Ave NW Courthouse *Web:* www.co.beltrami.mn.us	Bemidji	MN	56601	218-333-4120	333-4209
Ben Hill County 402A E Pine St *Web:* www.benhillcounty.com	Fitzgerald	GA	31750	229-426-5100	426-5630
Benewah County 701 College Ave *Web:* www.idaho.gov	Saint Maries	ID	83861	208-245-3212	245-9152
Bennett County 201 State St *Web:* www.bennettcosheriff.org/deputies.html	Martin	SD	57551	605-685-6516	685-2255
Bennington County 100 Veterans Memorial Dr *TF:* 800-229-0252 ■ *Web:* www.bennington.com	Bennington	VT	05201	802-447-3311	447-1163
Benson County PO Box 213 *Web:* www.bensoncountynd.com/contact.htm	Minnewaukan	ND	58351	701-473-5345	473-5571
Bent County 725 Bent Ave *Web:* www.bentcounty.org	Las Animas	CO	81054	719-456-1600	456-0375
Benton County 408 SW Monroe Ave Ste 111 *Web:* www.co.benton.or.us	Corvallis	OR	97339	541-766-6800	766-6893
Benzie County 448 Ct Pl *Web:* www.benzieco.net	Beulah	MI	49617	231-882-9671	882-5941
Bergen County 1 Bergen County Plaza Rm 580 *Web:* www.co.bergen.nj.us	Hackensack	NJ	07601	201-336-7300	336-7304
Berkeley County 1003 Hwy 52 PO Box 6122 *Web:* www.berkeleycountysc.gov	Moncks Corner	SC	29461	843-719-4234	
Berkeley County Council 400 W Stephen St Ste 201 *Web:* www.berkeleycountycomm.org	Martinsburg	WV	25401	304-264-1923	267-1794
Berks County *Law Library* 633 Ct St 4th Fl *Web:* www.co.berks.pa.us	Reading	PA	19601	610-478-3370	478-6375
Berkshire County 66 Allen St *Web:* www.berkshirechamber.com	Pittsfield	MA	01201	413-499-4000	447-9641
Bernalillo County 1 Civic Plaza NW 10th Fl *Web:* www.bernco.gov	Albuquerque	NM	87102	505-468-7000	768-4329
Berrien County 201 N Davis St Ste 105 *Web:* www.berriencountygeorgia.com	Nashville	GA	31639	229-686-7461	686-7819
Bertie County 106 Dundee St PO Box 530 *Web:* www.co.bertie.nc.us	Windsor	NC	27983	252-794-5300	794-5327
Bexar County 100 Dolorosa St *Web:* www.bexar.org	San Antonio	TX	78205	210-335-2011	335-2252
Bibb County 157 SW Davidson Dr *Web:* www.bibbal.com	Centreville	AL	35042	205-926-3114	
Bienville Parish 100 Courthouse Dr Rm 100 *Web:* www.bienvilleparish.org	Arcadia	LA	71001	318-263-2123	
Big Horn County 420 W C St *Web:* www.bighorncountywy.gov	Basin	WY	82410	307-568-2357	568-9375
Big Stone County 20 SE Second St *Web:* www.bigstonecounty.org	Ortonville	MN	56278	320-839-6376	
Billings County 495 Fourth St PO Box 168 *Web:* www.billingscountynd.gov	Medora	ND	58645	701-623-4377	623-4761
Bingham County 501 N Maple St Ste 205 *Web:* www.co.bingham.id.us	Blackfoot	ID	83221	208-782-3013	
Black Hawk County 316 E Fifth St *Web:* www.co.black-hawk.ia.us	Waterloo	IA	50703	319-833-3012	
Blackford County 110 W Washington St *Web:* gov.blackfordcounty.org	Hartford City	IN	47348	765-348-1620	348-7222
Bladen County 166 E Broad St Rm 105 *Web:* www.bladennc.govoffice3.com	Elizabethtown	NC	28337	910-862-6700	862-6767
Blaine County 145 Lincoln Ave *Web:* www.blainecounty.ne.gov	Brewster	NE	68821	308-547-2222	547-2228
Blair County 423 Allegheny St *Web:* www.blairco.org	Hollidaysburg	PA	16648	814-693-3000	693-3033
Blanco County 101 E Pecan Dr PO Box 65 *Web:* www.co.blanco.tx.us	Johnson City	TX	78636	830-868-0973	868-2084
Bland County 612 Main St Ste 104 *Web:* www.bland.org	Bland	VA	24315	276-688-4622	688-9758
Bleckley County 306 SE Second St *Web:* www.bleckley.org	Cochran	GA	31014	478-934-3200	
Bledsoe County PO Box 205 *Web:* www.pikeville-bledsoe.com	Pikeville	TN	37367	423-447-2791	
Blount County 341 Ct St *Web:* www.blounttn.org	Maryville	TN	37804	865-273-5700	273-5705
Blue Earth County 204 S Fifth St *Web:* www.co.blue-earth.mn.us	Mankato	MN	56001	507-304-4000	
Board of Supervisors 201 State St	Boone	IA	50036	515-433-0500	432-8102
Boise County 420 Main St PO Box 1300 *Web:* www.boisecounty.us	Idaho City	ID	83631	208-392-4431	392-4473
Bolivar County 200 S Ct St *Web:* www.co.bolivar.ms.us	Cleveland	MS	38732	662-846-5877	846-5880
Bollinger County 207 Mayfield Dr *Web:* bcmnh.org	Marble Hill	MO	63764	573-238-1174	
Bon Homme County 300 W 18th Ave P.O. Box 6 *Web:* ujs.sd.gov/	Tyndall	SD	57066	605-589-4215	589-4245
Bond County 203 W College Ave *Web:* www.bondcountyil.com/circuitclerk/circuitclerk.html	Greenville	IL	62246	618-664-3208	664-2257
Bonner County 215 S First Ave *Web:* bonnercounty.us/	Sandpoint	ID	83864	208-265-1432	
Bonneville County 605 N Capital Ave *Web:* www.co.bonneville.id.us	Idaho Falls	ID	83402	208-529-1350	
Boone County 801 E Walnut St *Web:* www.showmeboone.com	Columbia	MO	65201	573-886-4270	886-4254
Bosque County PO Box 617 *Web:* www.bosquecounty.us/	Meridian	TX	76665	254-435-2382	435-2152

Name / Address	City	State	Zip	Phone	Fax
Botetourt County 1 W Main St 1st Fl *Web:* www.co.botetourt.va.us	Fincastle	VA	24090	540-473-8220	
Bottineau County 314 W 5th St *Web:* www.bottineau.com	Bottineau	ND	58318	701-228-3983	
Boulder County 1750 33rd St Ste 201 *Web:* www.bouldercounty.org	Boulder	CO	80301	303-413-7770	413-7775
Boundary County PO Box 419 *Web:* www.boundarycountyid.org	Bonners Ferry	ID	83805	208-267-5504	267-7814
Bourbon County 210 S National Ave *Web:* bourboncountyks.org	Fort Scott	KS	66701	620-223-3800	223-5832
Bowie County 710 James Bowie Dr *Web:* www.co.bowie.tx.us	New Boston	TX	75570	903-628-2571	628-6729
Bowman County 104 First St NW Ste 3 *Web:* www.bowmannd.com	Bowman	ND	58623	701-523-3450	523-5443
Box Butte County 7006 Otoe Rd PO Box 802 *Web:* www.co.box-butte.ne.us	Alliance	NE	69301	308-762-4607	762-2867
Box Elder County 01 S Main St *Web:* www.boxeldercounty.org	Brigham City	UT	84302	435-734-3300	723-7562
Boyd County PO Box 26 *Web:* boydcounty.ne.gov	Butte	NE	68722	402-775-2391	775-2146
Boyle County 321 W Main St *Web:* www.boyleky.com	Danville	KY	40422	859-238-1110	238-1108
Bracken County 116 W Miami St PO Box 264 *Web:* www.brackencounty.ky.gov	Brooksville	KY	41004	606-735-2300	735-2615
Bradford County 945 N Temple Ave PO Box B *Web:* www.bradford-co-fla.org	Starke	FL	32091	904-966-6280	964-4454
Bradley County 155 N Ocoee St *Web:* www.bradleyco.net	Cleveland	TN	37311	423-728-7226	478-8845
Branch County 31 Div St *Web:* www.co.branch.mi.us	Coldwater	MI	49036	517-279-4301	278-4130
Brantley County 33 Allen Rd *Fax Area Code: 916	Nahunta	GA	31553	912-462-5256	462-5648*
Braxton County 300 Main St PO Box 486 *Web:* www.braxtoncounty.wv.gov	Sutton	WV	26601	304-765-2833	765-2947
Brazoria County 111 E Locust St Ste 200 *Web:* www.brazoria-county.com	Angleton	TX	77515	979-849-5711	
Brazos County 300 E 26th St Ste 120 *Web:* www.brazoscountytx.gov	Bryan	TX	77803	979-361-4135	
Breathitt County PO Box 227 *Web:* www.breathittcounty.com	Jackson	KY	41339	606-666-5060	666-7018
Breckinridge County PO Box 227 *Web:* www.breckinridgecountyky.com	Hardinsburg	KY	40143	270-756-2269	756-2364
Bremer County 415 E Bremer Ave *Web:* www.co.bremer.ia.us	Waverly	IA	50677	319-352-0130	
Brevard County 400 S St Ste 1-A *Web:* www.brevardcounty.us	Titusville	FL	32780	321-264-6750	264-6751
Brewster County 201 W Ave E *Web:* brewstercountytx.com	Alpine	TX	79830	432-837-3366	837-6217
Briscoe County PO Box 555 *Web:* www.co.briscoe.tx.us	Silverton	TX	79257	806-823-2134	823-2359
Bristol Bay Borough PO Box 189 *Web:* www.bristolbayboroughak.us	Naknek	AK	99633	907-246-4224	246-6633
Bristol County 9 Ct St *Web:* www.countyofbristol.net	Taunton	MA	02780	508-824-9681	821-3101
Bristol (Independent City) 497 Cumberland St Rm 210 *Web:* www.bristolva.org	Bristol	VA	24201	276-645-7321	821-6097
Broadwater County 515 Broadway *Web:* broadwater.countycriminal.com	Townsend	MT	59644	406-266-3443	
Bronx County 851 Grand Concourse Ste 301 *Web:* www.nyc.gov	Bronx	NY	10451	718-590-3500	590-3537
Brooke County 632 Main St *Web:* www.brookewv.org	Wellsburg	WV	26070	304-737-3661	
Brookings County 314 Sixth Ave *Web:* www.brookingscountysd.gov	Brookings	SD	57006	605-696-8205	696-8211
Brooks County 100 E Miller St *Web:* co.brooks.tx.us	Falfurrias	TX	78355	361-325-5604	325-4944
Broome County 44 Hawley St *Web:* www.gobroomecounty.com	Binghamton	NY	13901	607-778-2451	778-2243
Broomfield City & County 1 DesCombes Dr *Web:* www.ci.broomfield.co.us	Broomfield	CO	80020	303-469-3301	438-6296
Broward County 115 S Andrews Ave Rm 409 *Web:* www.broward.org	Fort Lauderdale	FL	33301	954-357-7000	
Brown County 200 Ct St Rm 4 *Fax Area Code: 217 ■ *Web:* www.illinoiscourts.gov/circuitcourt/CircuitCourtJudges/CCC_County.asp#Brown	Mount Sterling	IL	62353	7-7-73--2713	-77-3-3648*
Brule County 300 S Courtland St Ste 111 *Web:* brulecounty.org	Chamberlain	SD	57325	605-734-4580	
Brunswick County 250 Grey Water Rd *Web:* www.brunsco.net	Bolivia	NC	28422	910-253-2657	253-2022
Bryan County PO Box 1789 *Web:* www.ok.gov	Durant	OK	74702	580-924-2202	
Buchanan County 1012 Walnut St PO Box 950 *Web:* www.buchanancountyonline.com	Grundy	VA	24614	276-935-6503	935-4479
Buckingham County 13360 W James Anderson Hwy *Web:* buckinghamcountyva.org	Buckingham	VA	23921	434-969-4242	969-1638
Bucks County 55 E Ct St *Web:* www.buckscounty.org	Doylestown	PA	18901	215-348-6000	
Buena Vista County 215 E Fifth St *Web:* www.co.buena-vista.ia.us	Storm Lake	IA	50588	712-749-2545	749-2703
Buffalo County 407 S Second St *Web:* www.buffalocounty.com	Alma	WI	54610	608-685-6209	685-6213
Bullitt County 300 S Buckman St *Web:* www.bullittcounty.org	Shepherdsville	KY	40165	502-543-2262	
Bulloch County 115 N Main St *Web:* www.bullochcounty.net	Statesboro	GA	30458	912-764-6245	764-8634
Bullock County 106 Conecuh Ave PO Box 87 *Web:* www.bullockcountyal.com	Union Springs	AL	36089	334-738-5411	

Name / Address	City	State	Zip	Phone	Fax
Buncombe County 205 College St Ste 300 *Web:* www.buncombecounty.org	Asheville	NC	28801	828-250-4100	250-6077
Bureau County 700 S Main St *Web:* www.bureaucounty-il.com	Princeton	IL	61356	815-879-0113	
Burke County PO Box 89 *Web:* www.burkecounty-ga.gov	Waynesboro	GA	30830	706-554-2324	554-0350
Burleigh County 514 E Thayer Ave PO Box 1055 *Web:* www.ndcourts.gov	Bismarck	ND	58502	701-222-6690	222-6758
Burleson County 100 W Buck St Ste 203 *Web:* www.co.burleson.tx.us	Caldwell	TX	77836	979-567-2329	567-2376
Burlington County 49 Rancocas Rd *Web:* www.co.burlington.nj.us	Mount Holly	NJ	08060	609-265-5122	265-0696
Burnet County 220 S Pierce St *Web:* www.burnetcountytexas.org	Burnet	TX	78611	512-756-5420	756-5410
Burnett County 7410 County Rd K *Web:* www.burnettcounty.com/gov	Siren	WI	54872	715-349-2181	349-2830
Burt County 111 N 13th St PO Box 8787 *Web:* www.burtcounty.ne.gov	Tekamah	NE	68061	402-374-2955	374-2956
Butler County 428 Sixth St *Web:* www.butlercoiowa.org	Allison	IA	50602	319-267-2487	267-2488
Butler County Revenue Commission 700 Ct Sq *Web:* butlercountyal.com	Greenville	AL	36037	334-382-3221	382-0385
Butte County 248 W Grand *Fax Area Code: 208 ■ *Web:* local.dmv.org/idaho/butte-county/arco/248-w-grand/dmv-office-locations.php	Arco	ID	83213	8-5-27--8288	-52-7-3916*
Butte County Extension Office 849 Fifth Ave *Web:* butte.sdcounties.org	Belle Fourche	SD	57717	605-892-3371	892-9064
Butte-Silver Bow County 155 W Granite St *Web:* www.co.silverbow.mt.us	Butte	MT	59703	406-497-6200	497-6328
Butts County 625 W 3rd St # 4 *Web:* buttscountyga.com	Jackson	GA	30233	770-775-8200	775-8211
Cabarrus County 65 Church St S *Web:* www.cabarruscounty.us	Concord	NC	28025	704-920-2100	920-2820
Cabell County 750 Fifth Ave Ste 108 *Web:* www.cabellcounty.org	Huntington	WV	25701	304-526-8625	526-8632
Caddo County PO Box 68 *Web:* www.ok.gov	Anadarko	OK	73005	405-247-6609	
Caddo Parish 505 Travis St 8th Fl *Web:* www.caddo.org	Shreveport	LA	71101	318-226-6900	429-7630
Calaveras County 891 Mountain Ranch Rd *Web:* calaverasgov.us	San Andreas	CA	95249	209-754-6370	754-6733
Calcasieu Parish 1000 Ryan St Ste 5 *Web:* www.cppj.net	Lake Charles	LA	70601	337-437-3550	
Caldwell County 49 E Main St *Web:* caldwellcountymo.org	Kingston	MO	64650	816-586-2571	
Caldwell Parish PO Box 1737 *Web:* lpgov.org	Columbia	LA	71418	318-649-2681	649-5930
Caledonia County 1126 Main St	Saint Johnsbury	VT	05819	802-748-6600	748-1972
Calhoun County 1702 Noble St Ste 103 *Web:* www.calhounchamber.com	Anniston	AL	36201	256-241-2800	231-1744
Callahan County 100 W 4th St *Web:* www.co.callahan.tx.us	Baird	TX	79504	325-854-1155	854-1227
Callaway County 10 E Fifth St *Web:* callawaycountyclerk.com	Fulton	MO	65251	573-642-0730	642-7181
Calloway County 101 S Fifth St 2nd Fl *Web:* calloway.clerkinfo.net	Murray	KY	42071	270-753-3923	759-9611
Calumet County 206 Ct St *Web:* www.co.calumet.wi.us	Chilton	WI	53014	920-849-2361	849-1469
Calvert County 175 Main St *Web:* www.co.cal.md.us	Prince Frederick	MD	20678	410-535-1600	
Camas County 501 Soldier Rd *Web:* www.idaho.gov/aboutidaho/county/camas.html	Fairfield	ID	83327	208-764-2242	764-2349
Cambria County 200 S Ctr St *Web:* www.cambriacountypa.gov	Ebensburg	PA	15931	814-472-1540	472-0761
Camden County 117 N NC 343 PO Box 190 *Web:* camdencountync.gov	Camden	NC	27921	252-338-1919	333-1603
Cameron County 964 E Harrison St *Web:* www.co.cameron.tx.us	Brownsville	TX	78520	956-544-0815	544-0813
Cameron Parish 148 Smith Cir PO Box 1280 *Web:* www.parishofcameron.net	Cameron	LA	70631	337-775-5718	775-5567
Camp County 126 Church St *Web:* www.co.camp.tx.us	Pittsburg	TX	75686	903-856-2731	856-2309
Campbell County 1635 Reata Dr *Web:* www.ccgov.net	Gillette	WY	82718	307-682-0552	682-8418
Canadian County 201 N Choctaw St *Web:* www.canadiancounty.org	El Reno	OK	73036	405-262-1070	422-2411
Candler County 500 Ave K PO Box 1527 *Web:* www.myglades.com	Moore Haven	FL	33471	863-946-6000	946-2860
Cannon County 200 W Main St *Web:* www.cannontn.com	Woodbury	TN	37190	615-563-4278	
Canyon County 1115 Albany St *Web:* www.canyoncounty.org	Caldwell	ID	83605	208-454-7458	454-7525
Cape Girardeau County 1 Barton Sq Ste 301 *Web:* www.capecounty.us	Jackson	MO	63755	573-243-3547	204-2418
Cape May County 7 N Main St PO Box 5000 *Web:* capemaycountynj.gov	Cape May Court House	NJ	08210	609-465-1010	465-8625
Carbon County 2 Hazard Sq PO Box 129 *Web:* www.carboncounty.com	Jim Thorpe	PA	18229	570-325-3611	325-3622
Caribou County 159 S Main *TF:* 800-972-7660 ■ *Web:* www.cariboucounty.us/	Soda Springs	ID	83276	208-547-4324	547-4759
Carlisle County PO Box 176 *Web:* carlislecountyclerk.com/printable-forms	Bardwell	KY	42023	270-628-3233	628-0191
Carlton County PO Box 130 *Web:* www.co.carlton.mn.us	Carlton	MN	55718	218-384-9166	384-9182
Caroline County 117 Ennis St *Web:* www.co.caroline.va.us	Bowling Green	VA	22427	804-633-5380	633-4970
Carroll County 114 E Sixth St *Web:* www.co.carroll.ia.us	Carroll	IA	51401	712-792-4923	

Name / Address	City	State	Zip	Phone	Fax
Carroll County Sheriff's Office 95 Water Village Rd PO Box 190 *Web:* carrollcountynh.net	Ossipee	NH	03864	603-539-2284	
Carroll CountyClerk 210 W Church St	Berryville	AR	72616	870-423-2022	
Carson City (Independent City) 201 N Carson St *Web:* carson.org	Carson City	NV	89701	775-887-2100	887-2286
Carson County PO Box 487 *Web:* www.co.carson.tx.us	Panhandle	TX	79068	806-537-3873	537-3623
Carter County 300 W Main St Rm 232 *Web:* www.cartercountyclerksoffice.com	Grayson	KY	41143	606-474-5188	
Carteret County Courthouse Sq *Web:* carteretcountync.gov	Beaufort	NC	28516	252-728-8450	728-2092
Carver County 606 E Fourth St *Web:* www.co.carver.mn.us	Chaska	MN	55318	952-361-1500	361-1491
Cascade County 325 Second Ave N # 100 *Web:* www.co.cascade.mt.us	Great Falls	MT	59401	406-454-6800	454-6703
Cass County 5 W Seventh St *Web:* www.casscountyiowa.us	Atlantic	IA	50022	712-243-5503	
Cassia County 1459 Overland Ave *Web:* www.cassiacounty.org	Burley	ID	83318	208-878-7302	878-9109
Castro County 100 E Bedford St *Web:* www.co.castro.tx.us	Dimmitt	TX	79027	806-647-3338	647-5438
Caswell County 139 Church St *Web:* www.caswellcountync.gov	Yanceyville	NC	27379	336-694-4010	
Catahoula Parish 301 Bushley St PO Box 654 *Web:* www.laclerksofcourt.org	Harrisonburg	LA	71340	318-744-5497	744-5488
Catawba County PO Box 389 *Web:* www.co.catawba.nc.us	Newton	NC	28658	828-465-8201	465-8392
Catoosa County 875 Lafayette St *Web:* www.catoosa.com	Ringgold	GA	30736	706-935-4231	
Cattaraugus County 303 Ct St *Web:* www.cattco.org	Little Valley	NY	14755	716-938-9111	
Cavalier County 901 Third St Ste 15 *Web:* www.ccjda.org	Langdon	ND	58249	701-256-3475	256-3536
Cayuga County 160 Genesee St *Web:* www.cayugacounty.us	Auburn	NY	13021	315-253-1271	
Cecil County 129 E Main St Rm 108 *Web:* www.ccgov.org	Elkton	MD	21921	410-996-5375	
Cedar County 101 S Broadway *Web:* www.co.cedar.ne.us	Hartington	NE	68739	402-254-7411	254-7410
Centre County 420 Holmes St Willowbank Office Bldg *Web:* centrecountypa.gov	Bellefonte	PA	16823	814-355-6700	355-6980
Cerro Gordo County 220 N Washington Ave *Web:* co.cerro-gordo.ia.us	Mason City	IA	50401	641-421-3065	421-3072
Chaffee County 104 Crestone Ave *Web:* www.chaffeecounty.org	Salida	CO	81201	719-539-4004	539-8588
Chambers County 404 Washington Ave *Web:* www.co.chambers.tx.us	Anahuac	TX	77514	409-267-8309	267-8315
Champaign County 1512 S US Hwy 68 Ste A100 *Web:* www.co.champaign.oh.us	Urbana	OH	43078	937-484-1611	484-1609
Chariton County 306 S Cherry St *Web:* www.rootsweb.ancestry.com/	Keytesville	MO	65261	660-288-3273	
Charles County 200 Baltimore St *Web:* www.charlescountymd.gov	La Plata	MD	20646	301-645-0600	645-0560
Charles Mix County PO Box 490 *Web:* charlesmix.sdcounties.org	Lake Andes	SD	57356	605-487-7131	487-7221
Charleston County 4045 Bridge View *Web:* www.charlestoncounty.org	Charleston	SC	29405	843-958-4030	958-4035
Charlevoix County 203 Antrim St *Web:* www.charlevoixcounty.org	Charlevoix	MI	49720	231-547-7200	547-7217
Charlotte County 250 LeGrande Ave Ste A PO Box 608 *Web:* www.charlotteva.com	Charlotte Court House	VA	23923	434-542-5117	542-5248
Charlottesville (Independent City) 605 E Main St *Web:* www.charlottesville.org	Charlottesville	VA	22902	434-970-3101	970-3890
Charlton County 68 Kingsland Ste B *Web:* georgia.gov/cities-counties/charlton-county	Folkston	GA	31537	912-496-2549	496-7792
Chase County 300 Pearl St *Web:* chasecountychamber.org/county-government/	Cottonwood Falls	KS	66845	620-273-6423	
Chatham County 124 Bull St *Web:* www.chathamcounty.org	Savannah	GA	31401	912-652-7869	652-7874
Chattooga County 10102 Commerce St *Web:* www.chattoogacountyga.org	Summerville	GA	30747	706-857-0700	857-0742
Chautauqua County 3 N Erie St *Web:* www.co.chautauqua.ny.us	Mayville	NY	14757	716-753-4211	753-4756
Cheatham County 100 Public Sq *Web:* www.cheathamcountytn.gov	Ashland City	TN	37015	615-792-4316	
Cheboygan County 870 S Main St *Web:* www.cheboygancounty.net	Cheboygan	MI	49721	231-627-8808	
Chelan County 350 Orondo Ave *Web:* www.co.chelan.wa.us	Wenatchee	WA	98801	509-667-6380	667-6611
Chemung County 210 Lake St PO Box 588 *Web:* www.chemungcounty.com	Elmira	NY	14902	607-737-2920	
Chenango County 5 Ct St *Web:* www.co.chenango.ny.us	Norwich	NY	13815	607-337-1700	337-1455
Cherokee County 90 N St Ste 310 *Web:* www.cherokeega.com	Canton	GA	30114	678-493-6511	493-6013
Cherry County PO Box 120 *Web:* www.co.cherry.ne.us	Valentine	NE	69201	402-376-2771	376-3095
Cheshire County 12 Ct St *Web:* www.co.cheshire.nh.us	Keene	NH	03431	603-352-6902	
Chester County 140 Main St PO Box 580 *Web:* www.chestercounty.org	Chester	SC	29706	803-385-2605	581-7975
Chesterfield County 200 W Main St Ste K *Web:* www.chesterfield.k12.sc.us	Chesterfield	SC	29709	843-792-2536	623-6944
Cheyenne County PO Box 567 *Web:* www.co.cheyenne.co.us	Cheyenne Wells	CO	80810	719-767-5685	767-8730
Chickasaw County 797 S Jackson St *Web:* chickasaw.msghn.org	Houston	MS	38851	662-456-2513	
Chickasaw Voting Information 8 E Prospect St *Web:* www.chickasawcoia.org	New Hampton	IA	50659	641-394-2100	394-5541
Chicot County 108 Main St County Courthouse *Web:* chicotcounty.arkansas.gov	Lake Village	AR	71653	870-265-8040	265-8018
Childress County 100 Ave E NW PO Box 1 *Web:* www.childresscad.org/	Childress	TX	79201	940-937-6062	937-3386
Chilton County PO Box 1948 *Web:* www.chiltoncounty.org	Clanton	AL	35046	205-755-1551	280-7204
Chippewa County 711 N Bridge St *Web:* www.co.chippewa.wi.us	Chippewa Falls	WI	54729	715-726-7980	726-7987
Chisago County 313 N Main St *TF:* 888-234-1246 ■ *Web:* www.co.chisago.mn.us	Center City	MN	55012	651-257-1300	213-8876
Chittenden County 175 Main St *Web:* www.ccrpcvt.org	Burlington	VT	05401	802-863-3467	
Choctaw County 55 E Quinn St PO Box 737 *Web:* choctawcountyms.com	Ackerman	MS	39735	662-285-3778	285-2440
Chouteau County 1308 Franklin St *Web:* www.co.chouteau.mt.us	Fort Benton	MT	59442	406-622-5151	622-3012
Chowan County 113 E King St *Web:* www.chowancounty-nc.gov	Edenton	NC	27932	252-482-8431	
Christian County 511 S Main St *Web:* www.christiancounty.org	Hopkinsville	KY	42240	270-887-4105	
Churchill County 155 N Taylor St Ste 110 *Web:* www.churchillcounty.org	Fallon	NV	89406	775-423-6028	
Cibola County 515 W High Ave *Web:* www.co.cibola.nm.us	Grants	NM	87020	505-285-2510	
Cimarron County PO Box 145 *Web:* www.tax.ok.gov	Boise City	OK	73933	580-544-2251	
Citrus County 110 N Apopka Ave *Web:* www.clerk.citrus.fl.us	Inverness	FL	34450	352-341-6400	341-6491
City of Buena Vista 2039 Sycamore Ave *Web:* www.bvcity.org	Buena Vista	VA	24416	540-261-6121	
City of Clinton Sheriff Department 184 Detention Dr PO Box 451 *Web:* www.vbcso.com/	Clinton	AR	72031	501-745-2112	
Clackamas County 2051 Kaen Rd *Web:* www.clackamas.us	Oregon City	OR	97045	503-655-8551	650-5688
Claiborne County 404 Market St *Web:* www.claiborne.k12.ms.us/	Port Gibson	MS	39150	601-437-4232	437-4409
Claiborne Parish 512 E Main St PO Box 330 *Web:* www.claiborneone.org	Homer	LA	71040	318-927-9601	927-2345
Clallam County 223 E Fourth St Ste 2 *Web:* www.clallam.net	Port Angeles	WA	98362	360-417-2318	417-2493
Clare County 225 W Main PO Box 438 *Web:* www.clareco.net	Harrison	MI	48625	989-539-2510	539-6616
Clarendon County 19 N Brooks St *Web:* www.clarendoncounty.com	Manning	SC	29102	803-435-4405	
Clarion County 421 Main St Courthouse *Web:* www.co.clarion.pa.us	Clarion	PA	16214	814-226-4000	227-2501
Clark County 320 W Main St *Web:* www.idaho.gov	Grangeville	ID	83530	208-983-2751	983-1428
Clarke County 101 N Church Ct Ste B *Web:* www.clarkecounty.gov	Berryville	VA	22611	540-955-5100	
Clatsop County 820 Exchange St 2nd Fl *Web:* www.co.clatsop.or.us	Astoria	OR	97103	503-325-8511	325-9307
Clay County 609 E National Ave Rm 213	Brazil	IN	47834	812-448-9036	
Clayton County 111 High St NE *Web:* www.claytoncountyiowa.net	Elkader	IA	52043	563-245-2204	245-1175
Clear Creek County PO Box 2000 *Web:* www.co.clear-creek.co.us	Georgetown	CO	80444	303-679-2312	679-2440
Clearfield County 230 E Market St *Web:* www.clearfieldco.org	Clearfield	PA	16830	814-765-2641	765-2640
Clearwater County 213 Main Ave N **Fax:* Acctg ■ *Web:* www.co.clearwater.mn.us	Bagley	MN	56621	218-694-6520	694-6244*
Cleburne County 300 W Main St *Web:* www.cleburnecountyar.com	Heber Springs	AR	72543	501-362-8402	362-4605
Clermont County 101 E Main St Rm 322 *Web:* www.clermontcountyohio.gov	Batavia	OH	45103	513-732-7300	732-7826
Cleveland County 2550 W Franklin Rd *Web:* www.clevelandcountyok.com	Norman	OK	73069	405-701-8888	366-0234
Clinch County 46 S College St *Web:* www.clinchcounty.com	Homerville	GA	31634	912-487-5321	487-5068
Clinton County 46 S S St 2nd Fl Courthouse *Web:* www.co.clinton.oh.us	Wilmington	OH	45177	937-382-2316	383-3455
Fiscal Court 100 S Cross St *Web:* www.clintoncounty.ky.gov	Albany	KY	42602	606-387-5234	387-7651
Cloud County 811 Washington St *Web:* www.cloudcountyks.org	Concordia	KS	66901	785-243-8110	
Coahoma County PO Box 98 *Web:* www.coahomacounty.net	Clarksdale	MS	38614	662-624-3000	624-3040
Coal County 4 N Main St	Coalgate	OK	74538	580-927-2103	927-4003
Cobb County 100 Cherokee St Ste 300 *Web:* www.cobbcounty.org	Marietta	GA	30090	770-528-1000	528-2606
Cochise County 1415 W Melody Ln Bldg G *Web:* cochise.az.gov	Bisbee	AZ	85603	520-432-9200	432-5016
Cochran County 100 N Main St *Web:* www.co.cochran.tx.us	Morton	TX	79346	806-266-5508	266-9027
Cocke County Tourism 433 B Prospect Ave *Web:* www.cockecounty.com	Newport	TN	37821	423-625-9675	
Coconino County 219 E Cherry Ave *TF:* 800-559-9289 ■ *Web:* www.coconino.az.gov	Flagstaff	AZ	86001	928-774-5011	
Codington County 14 First Ave SE *Web:* www.codington.org	Watertown	SD	57201	605-882-6288	
Coffee County 101 S Peterson Ave *Web:* www.coffeecountygov.com	Douglas	GA	31533	912-384-4799	384-0291
Coffey County 110 S Sixth St *Web:* www.coffeycountyks.org	Burlington	KS	66839	620-364-2191	364-8975

Phone | Fax

Coke County PO Box 150 Robert Lee TX 76945 325-453-2631 453-2650
Web: co.coke.tx.us
Colbert County 201 N Main St Tuscumbia AL 35674 256-386-8500 386-8510
Web: www.colbertcounty.org
Cole County 301 E High St Ste 100 Jefferson City MO 65101 573-634-9100 634-8031
Web: www.colecounty.org
Coleman County 100 W Live Oak Coleman TX 76834 325-625-2889
Web: www.co.coleman.tx.us
Coles County 651 Jackson Ave Rm 122 Charleston IL 61920 217-348-0501 348-7337
Web: www.co.coles.il.us
Colfax County 230 N Third St PO Box 1498 Raton NM 87740 575-445-9661 445-2902
Web: www.co.colfax.nm.us
Colleton County 31 Klein St Walterboro SC 29488 843-549-1725 549-7215
Web: www.colletoncounty.org
Collier County 3301 Tamiami Trail E Naples FL 34112 239-252-8383 252-4010
Web: www.colliergov.net
Collin County 200 S McDonald St Ste 120 McKinney TX 75069 800-336-5996 547-5731*
**Fax Area Code:* 972 ■ *TF:* 800-336-5996 ■ *Web:* www.co.collin.tx.us
Collingsworth County 800 W Ave 2nd Fl Rm 1 Wellington TX 79095 806-447-5408 447-5418
Web: co.collingsworth.tx.us
Colonial Heights (Independent City)
201 James Ave PO Box 3401 Colonial Heights VA 23834 804-520-9265 520-9207
Web: www.colonialheightsva.gov
Colorado County 318 Springs St Ste 103 Columbus TX 78934 979-732-2155 732-8852
Web: www.co.colorado.tx.us
Colquitt County PO Box 517 Moultrie GA 31776 229-616-7056 616-7498
Web: www.ccboc.com
Columbia County 35 W Main St Bloomsburg PA 17815 570-389-5600 784-0257
Web: www.columbiapa.org
Columbiana County 105 S Market St Lisbon OH 44432 330-424-7777
Web: www.columbianacounty.org
Columbus County PO Box 1587 Whiteville NC 28472 910-641-3000
Web: www.columbusco.org
Columbus-Muscogee County PO Box 1340 Columbus GA 31902 6-6-53--4000
Web: georgia.gov/cities-counties/columbus-muscogee-county
Colusa County 546 Jay St Colusa CA 95932 530-458-0500 458-0512
Web: countyofcolusa.org
Comal County 199 Main Plaza New Braunfels TX 78130 830-221-1100 620-5506
TF: 877-724-9475 ■ *Web:* www.co.comal.tx.us
Comanche County 201 S New York PO Box 268 Coldwater KS 67029 620-582-2993
Web: www.comanchecounty.com
Concho County PO Box 98 Paint Rock TX 76866 325-732-4322 732-2040
Web: www.co.concho.tx.us
Concordia Parish PO Box 790 Vidalia LA 71373 318-336-4204 336-8777
Web: www.concordiaclerk.org
Conecuh County PO Box 347 Evergreen AL 36401 251-578-2095
Web: www.alabama.gov
Conejos County 6683 County Rd 13 Conejos CO 81129 719-376-2014 376-6769
Web: www.conejoscounty.org
Contra Costa County 651 Pine St 3rd Fl Martinez CA 94553 925-335-1080 335-1098
Web: www.co.contra-costa.ca.us
Converse County 107 N Fifth St Ste 114 Douglas WY 82633 307-358-2244 770-3590*
**Fax Area Code:* 866 ■ *Web:* www.conversecounty.org
Conway County 117 S Moose St Morrilton AR 72110 501-354-9621
Web: prsearch.com
Cook County 69 W Washington Ste 500 Chicago IL 60602 312-603-5656 603-0902
Web: www.co.cook.il.us
Cooke County 101S Dixon Gainesville TX 76240 940-668-5420 668-5522
Web: www.co.cooke.tx.us
Cooper County 200 Main St Boonville MO 65233 660-882-2114 882-5645
Web: coopercountymo.org
Coos County 250 N Baxter St Coquille OR 97423 541-396-3121 396-4861
Web: www.co.coos.or.us
Coosa County PO Box 10 Rockford AL 35136 256-377-1350 377-2524
Web: www.coosacountyal.com
Copiah County 122 S Lowe St PO Box 507 Hazlehurst MS 39083 601-894-3021 894-4081
Web: www.copiahcounty.org
Corson County 242 Second Ave E PO Box 317 McIntosh SD 57641 605-273-4481 273-4481
Web: corson.sdcounties.org
Cortland County 46 Greenbush St Ste 101 Cortland NY 13045 607-753-5021 753-5378
Web: www.cortland-co.org
Coryell County 620 E Main St PO Box 237 Gatesville TX 76528 254-865-5911 865-8631
Web: www.co.coryell.tx.us
Coshocton County 401 1/2 Main St Coshocton OH 43812 740-622-1753 622-4917
Web: coshoctoncounty.net
Costilla County 233 Main St Ste C PO Box 99 San Luis CO 81152 719-672-3681 672-3856
Web: www.colorado.gov
Cottle County PO Box 717 Paducah TX 79248 806-492-3823 492-2625
Web: www.co.cottle.tx.us
Cotton County 301 N Broadway Walters OK 73572 580-875-3029
Cottonwood County 900 Third Ave Windom MN 56101 507-831-1905 831-4553
Web: www.co.cottonwood.mn.us
County & Circuit Clerk 206 W 3rd St Fordyce AR 71742 870-352-2307
County of Greene 93 E High St Waynesburg PA 15370 724-852-5210 852-5327
TF: 888-852-5399 ■ *Web:* www.co.greene.pa.us
Covington County
260 Hillcrest Dr PO Box 188 Andalusia AL 36420 334-428-2540 428-2606
Web: www.covcounty.com
Covington (Independent City)
333 W Locust St Covington VA 24426 540-965-6300 965-6303
Web: www.covington.va.us
Coweta County 22 E Broad St Newnan GA 30263 770-254-2601 254-2606
Web: www.coweta.ga.us
Cowley County 311 E Ninth Ave Winfield KS 67156 620-221-5400 221-5498
Web: www.cowleycounty.org
Cowlitz County 312 SW First Ave Kelso WA 98626 360-577-3016
Web: www.co.cowlitz.wa.us
Craig County PO Box 308 New Castle VA 24127 540-864-5010 864-5590
Web: www.craigcountyva.gov
Craighead County 511 S Main St Ste 202 Jonesboro AR 72401 870-933-4520 933-4514
Web: www.craigheadcounty.org

Phone | Fax

Crane County 201 W Sixth St Crane TX 79731 432-558-3581 558-1185
Web: www.co.crane.tx.us
Craven County 406 Craven St New Bern NC 28560 252-636-6600 637-0526
Web: www.cravencountync.gov
Crawford County 225 N Beaumont Rd Prairie du Chien WI 53821 608-326-0200
Web: www.crawfordcountywi.org
Creek County 317 E Lee St Rm 100 Sapulpa OK 74066 918-224-4084
Web: www.okcountyrecords.com
Crenshaw County PO Box 167 Luverne AL 36049 334-335-6575
Web: www.sos.alabama.gov
Crisp County 210 S Seventh St Cordele GA 31015 229-276-2672 276-2675
Web: www.crispcounty.com
Crittenden County 100 Ct St County Courthouse Marion AR 72364 870-739-3200
Web: crittendencounty.arkansas.gov
Crockett County PO Box C Ozona TX 76943 325-392-2022 392-3742
Web: www.co.crockett.tx.us
Crook County 300 NE Third St Rm 23 Prineville OR 97754 541-447-6553 416-2145
Web: www.co.crook.or.us
Crosby County 201 W Aspen St Ste 102 Crosbyton TX 79322 806-675-2334
Web: www.co.crosby.tx.us
Cross County 705 E Union St Rm 8 Wynne AR 72396 870-238-5735 238-5739
Web: crosscountyar.org
Crow Wing County 326 Laurel St Brainerd MN 56401 218-824-1067 824-1054
TF: 888-829-6680 ■ *Web:* crowwing.us
Crowley County 631 Main St Ste 102 Ordway CO 81063 719-267-5225 267-4608
Web: www.colorado.gov
Culberson County PO Box 158 Van Horn TX 79855 432-283-2058 283-9234
Web: www.co.culberson.tx.us
Cullman County 500 Second Ave SW Cullman AL 35055 256-739-3530
Web: www.co.cullman.al.us
Culpeper County 151 N Main St # 201 Culpeper VA 22701 540-727-3427 727-3460
Web: web.culpepercounty.gov
Cumberland County 27 Fayette St Bridgeton NJ 08302 856-451-8000 455-1410
Web: www.co.cumberland.nj.us
Cuming County 200 S Lincoln St PO Box 290 West Point NE 68788 402-372-6002
Web: cuming.unl.edu
Currituck County
153 Courthouse Rd Ste 204 PO Box 39 Currituck NC 27929 252-232-2075 232-3551
Web: www.co.currituck.nc.us
Curry County
29821 Ellensburg Ave PO Box 746 Gold Beach OR 97444 541-247-3296 247-6440
Web: www.co.curry.or.us
Cusseta-Chattahoochee County
Courthouse Annex 377 Broad St PO Box 299 Cusseta GA 31805 706-989-3602 989-2005
Web: www.ugoccc.us
Custer County PO Box 300 Arapaho OK 73620 405-522-0018 331-1131*
**Fax Area Code:* 580 ■ *Web:* custer.okcounties.org
Cuyahoga County 1219 Ontario St Cleveland OH 44113 216-443-7010 443-5091
Web: www.cuyahogacounty.us
Dade County 71 Case Ave Trenton GA 30752 706-657-4625 657-8284
Web: www.dadecounty-ga.gov
Daggett County 95 N First W Manila UT 84046 435-784-3154 784-3335
Web: www.daggettcounty.org
Dakota County 1601 Broadway Dakota City NE 68731 402-987-2126 987-2186
Web: www.dakotacountyne.org
Dale County 202 Hwy 123 S Ste C Ozark AL 36360 334-774-6025 774-1841
Web: dalecountyal.org
Dallam County PO Box 1352 Dalhart TX 79022 806-244-4751 244-3751
Web: www.dallam.org
Dallas County 801 Ct St Adel IA 50003 515-993-5814
Web: www.co.dallas.ia.us
Dane County 210 ML King Jr Blvd Rm 106 Madison WI 53703 608-266-4121
Web: www.countyofdane.com
Daniels County 120 Main St PO Box 91 Scobey MT 59263 406-487-2061 487-5583
Web: scobeymt.com
Danville (Independent City)
401 Patton St PO Box 3300 Danville VA 24543 434-799-5168 799-6502
Web: www.danville-va.gov
Dare County 954 Marshall Collins Dr Manteo NC 27954 252-475-5800 473-1817
Web: www.co.dare.nc.us
Darke County 520 S Broadway St Greenville OH 45331 937-547-7300 547-7367
Web: www.co.darke.oh.us
Darlington County 1 Public Sq Darlington SC 29532 843-398-4100 393-8539
Web: www.darcosc.com
Dauphin County 2 S Second St 3rd Fl Harrisburg PA 17101 717-780-6636 780-6468
TF: 800-328-0058 ■ *Web:* www.dauphincounty.org
Davidson County
913 Greensboro St PO Box 1067 Lexington NC 27293 336-242-2000 248-8440
Web: www.co.davidson.nc.us
Davie County 123 S Main St Mocksville NC 27028 336-753-6040 751-7408
Web: www.daviecountync.gov
Daviess County 212 St Ann St Ste 104 Owensboro KY 42303 270-685-8434
Web: www.daviessky.org
Daviess County Clerk 102 N Main St Gallatin MO 64640 660-663-2641
Web: daviesscountysheriff.com
Davis County 28 E State St PO Box 618 Farmington UT 84025 801-451-3324 451-3421
Web: www.co.davis.ut.us
Davis County Clerk of Courts
100 Courthouse Sq Bloomfield IA 52537 641-664-2011 664-2041
Web: www.daviscountyiowa.org
Davison County Auditor 200 E Fourth Ave Mitchell SD 57301 605-995-8608 995-8618
Web: www.davisoncounty.org
Dawes County 451 Main St Chadron NE 69337 308-432-0100 432-5179
Web: www.co.dawes.ne.us
Dawson County 25 Justice Way Ste 2214 Dawsonville GA 30534 706-344-3501 344-3504
Web: www.dawsoncounty.org
Day County 711 W First St Webster SD 57274 605-345-3771 345-3818
Web: ujs.sd.gov/
Deaf Smith County 136 E Third St Hereford TX 79045 806-364-0625 364-6895
Web: deafsmithcad.org
Dearborn County 215 W High St Lawrenceburg IN 47025 812-537-8877 532-2021
Web: dearborncounty.org

				Phone	Fax
Decatur County 120 E Hall St *Web:* www.oberlinkansas.org	Oberlin	KS	67749	785-475-8102	
Defiance County 500 Ct St Ste A *Web:* www.defiance-county.com	Defiance	OH	43512	419-782-4761	782-8449
DeKalb County 556 N McDonough St *Web:* www.co.dekalb.ga.us	Decatur	GA	30030	404-371-2000	
Del Norte County 981 H St Ste 200 *Web:* www.co.del-norte.ca.us	Crescent City	CA	95531	707-464-7204	464-1165
Delaware County 101 N Sandusky St *Web:* www.co.delaware.oh.us	Delaware	OH	43015	740-833-2100	833-2099
Delta County 90 Texas Hwy 24 S *Web:* delta-cad.org	Cooper	TX	75432	903-395-4118	395-4455
Denali Borough PO Box 480 *Web:* www.denaliborough.govoffice.com	Healy	AK	99743	907-683-1330	683-1340
Dent County 400 N Main St *Web:* salemmo.com	Salem	MO	65560	573-729-4144	
Denton County 1450 E McKinney *Web:* dentoncounty.com/	Denton	TX	76209	940-349-2012	349-2019
Denver City & County 201 W Colfax Ave 1st Fl *Web:* www.denvergov.org	Denver	CO	80202	720-865-8400	
Des Moines County 513 N Main St *Web:* www.dmcounty.com	Burlington	IA	52601	319-753-8232	
Deschutes County 1300 NW Wall St Ste 200 *Web:* www.deschutes.org	Bend	OR	97701	541-330-4631	385-3202
Desha County 608 Robert S Moore Ave PO Box 188 *Web:* deshacounty.arkansas.gov	Arkansas City	AR	71630	870-877-2426	
DeSoto County 201 E Oak St *Web:* desotobocc.com	Arcadia	FL	34266	863-993-4800	993-4809
DeSoto Parish 101 Texas St PO Box 1206 *Web:* desotoparishclerk.org	Mansfield	LA	71052	318-872-3110	872-4202
Deuel County 718 Third St PO Box 327 *Web:* www.co.deuel.ne.us	Chappell	NE	69129	308-874-3308	874-3472
Dewey County PO Box 368 *Web:* www.okgenweb.org/~okdewey	Taloga	OK	73667	580-328-5521	
Dewey County Clerk of Courts PO Box 96 *Web:* ujs.sd.gov	Timber Lake	SD	57656	605-865-3566	865-3641
DeWitt County 201 W Washington St PO Box 439 *Web:* www.dewittcountyill.com	Clinton	IL	61727	217-935-7780	
Dickens County 512 Montgomery St PO Box 120 *Web:* co.dickens.tx.us	Dickens	TX	79229	806-623-5531	623-5240
Dickenson County 293 Main St PO Box 1098 *Web:* www.dickensonva.org	Clintwood	VA	24228	276-926-1676	926-1649
Dickey County 205 15th St N PO Box 238 *Web:* www.dickeynd.com	Ellendale	ND	58436	701-349-4348	349-3277
Dickinson County PO Box 248 *Web:* www.dkcoks.org	Abilene	KS	67410	785-263-3774	263-2045
Dickson County PO Box 267 *Web:* www.dicksoncountytn.gov	Charlotte	TN	37036	615-789-7003	789-6075
Dillon County 109 S Third Ave PO Box 449 *Web:* dilloncounty.sc.gov	Dillon	SC	29536	843-774-1400	774-1443
Dimmit County 103 N Fifth St *Web:* www.dimmitcounty.org	Carrizo Springs	TX	78834	830-876-2323	
Dinwiddie County 14016 Boydton Plank Rd *Web:* www.dinwiddieva.us	Dinwiddie	VA	23841	804-469-4500	469-4503
Divide County 300 N Main *Web:* www.ndaco.org	Crosby	ND	58730	701-834-2451	
Dixie County 214 NE 351 Hwy PO Box 2600 *Web:* dixie.fl.gov	Cross City	FL	32628	352-498-1206	498-1207
Dixon County PO Box 395 *Web:* www.co.dixon.ne.us	Ponca	NE	68770	402-755-5604	755-5651
Doddridge County 118 E Ct St Rm 102 *Web:* doddridgecounty.wv.gov	West Union	WV	26456	304-873-2631	873-1840
Dodge County PO Box 818 *Web:* www.dodgecountyga.com	Eastman	GA	31023	478-374-4361	374-8121
Dolores County 409 N Main St *Web:* www.dolorescounty.org	Dove Creek	CO	81324	970-677-2383	677-2815
Dona Ana County 845 N Motel Blvd *Web:* donaanacounty.org	Las Cruces	NM	88007	575-647-7200	585-5538
Doniphan County PO Box 278 *Web:* www.dpcountyks.com	Troy	KS	66087	785-985-3513	985-3723
Donley County 300 S Sully St PO Box 909 *Web:* www.co.donley.tx.us	Clarendon	TX	79226	806-874-3625	874-1181
Dooly County 110 E Union St PO Box 308 *Web:* www.doolychamber.com	Vienna	GA	31092	229-268-8275	268-8200
Door County 421 Nebraska St *Web:* www.co.door.wi.gov	Sturgeon Bay	WI	54235	920-746-2200	746-2330
Dorchester County 501 Ct Ln *Web:* www.docogonet.com	Cambridge	MD	21613	410-228-1700	228-9641
Dougherty County 222 Pine Ave *Web:* www.albany.ga.us	Albany	GA	31701	229-431-2121	438-3967
Douglas County 305 Eigth Ave W *Web:* www.co.douglas.mn.us	Alexandria	MN	56308	320-762-3877	762-2389
Drew County 210 S Main St	Monticello	AR	71655	870-460-6260	
Dubuque County 720 Central Ave *Web:* www.dubuquecounty.org	Dubuque	IA	52001	563-589-4432	
Duchesne County 734 N Ctr St *Web:* www.duchesne.utah.gov	Duchesne	UT	84021	435-738-1100	738-5522
Dukes County PO Box 190 *Web:* www.dukescounty.org	Edgartown	MA	02539	508-696-3840	696-3841
Dundy County PO Box 506 *Web:* www.co.dundy.ne.us	Benkelman	NE	69021	308-423-2058	
Dunklin County P.O. Box 567 *Web:* www.courts.mo.gov	Kennett	MO	63857	573-888-2456	888-0319
Dunn County 800 Wilson Ave *Web:* co.dunn.wi.us/	Menomonie	WI	54751	715-232-1677	232-2534
DuPage County 421 N County Farm Rd *Web:* www.dupageco.org	Wheaton	IL	60187	630-407-5500	407-5501
Duplin County 112 Duplin St Ste 101 *Web:* www.duplincountync.com	Kenansville	NC	28349	910-296-2150	296-2156
Durham County 200 E Main St *Web:* dconc.gov	Durham	NC	27701	919-560-0000	560-0020
Dutchess County 22 Market St *Web:* www.co.dutchess.ny.us	Poughkeepsie	NY	12601	845-486-2120	
Duval County 117 W Duval St *Web:* www.coj.net	Jacksonville	FL	32202	904-630-2489	630-2906
Dyer County 115 Market St PO Box 1360 *Web:* tn.gov	Dyersburg	TN	38025	731-286-7814	288-7719
Eagle County PO Box 850 *Web:* www.eaglecounty.us	Eagle	CO	81631	970-328-8600	328-8716
Early County PO Box 693 *Web:* georgia.gov/cities-counties/early-county	Blakely	GA	39823	229-723-4304	723-8684
East Baton Rouge Parish 1755 Florida St *Web:* www.brgov.com	Baton Rouge	LA	70802	225-389-3129	389-3118
East Carroll Parish 400 First St PO Box 246 *Web:* www.ecsheriff.com	Lake Providence	LA	71254	318-559-2800	559-2567
East Feliciana Parish 12305 St. Helena St. PO Box 599 *Web:* www.felicianatourism.org	Clinton	LA	70722	225-683-5145	683-3556
Eastland County 100 W Main PO Box 110 *Web:* www.eastlandcountytexas.com	Eastland	TX	76448	254-629-1583	629-8125
Eaton County 1045 Independence Blvd *Web:* eatoncounty.org	Charlotte	MI	48813	517-543-7500	541-0666
Eau Claire County 721 Oxford Ave *Web:* co.eau-claire.wi.us	Eau Claire	WI	54703	715-839-4801	839-4854
Echols County 110 General Beloach St *Web:* echolscountyga.com	Statenville	GA	31648	229-559-6538	
Ector County 300 N Grant Ave Rm 111 *Web:* www.co.ector.tx.us	Odessa	TX	79761	432-498-4130	498-4177
Eddy County 101 W Greene St Ste 110 *Fax Area Code: 575 ■ *Web:* www.co.eddy.nm.us	Carlsbad	NM	88220	505-887-9511	234-1835*
Edgar County 115 W Ct St Rm J *Web:* edgarcountyillinois.com	Paris	IL	61944	217-466-7433	466-7430
Edgecombe County 201 St Andrew St PO Box 10 *Web:* www.edgecombecountync.gov	Tarboro	NC	27886	252-641-7852	641-0456
Edgefield County 129 Courthouse Sq PO Box 34 *Web:* www.edgefieldcounty.sc.gov	Edgefield	SC	29824	803-637-4080	
Edmonson County PO Box 830 *Web:* edmonsoncountyclerk.com	Brownsville	KY	42210	270-597-2624	597-9714
Edmunds County PO Box 384 *Web:* www.edmunds.sdcounties.org	Ipswich	SD	57451	605-426-6671	426-6323
Edwards County 50 E Main St *Web:* edwards.countycriminal.com	Albion	IL	62806	618-445-2115	
Effingham County 101 N Fourth St PO Box 628 *Web:* www.co.effingham.il.us	Effingham	IL	62401	217-342-6535	342-3577
El Dorado County 360 Fair Ln Bldg B *Web:* edcgov.us	Placerville	CA	95667	530-621-5490	621-2147
El Paso County 200 S Cascade Ave *Web:* www.elpasoco.com	Colorado Springs	CO	80903	719-520-6200	520-6212
Elbert County 215 Comanche St PO Box 7 *Web:* www.elbertcounty-co.gov	Kiowa	CO	80117	303-621-2131	621-2343
Elbert County Chamber Of Commerce 104 Heard St *Web:* www.elbertga.com	Elberton	GA	30635	706-283-5651	283-5722
Elk County PO Box 606 *Web:* elkcountyks.org	Howard	KS	67349	620-374-2490	374-2771
Elkhart County 117 N Second St *Web:* www.elkhartcountyindiana.com	Goshen	IN	46526	574-535-6743	
Elko County 569 Ct St *Web:* www.elkocountynv.net	Elko	NV	89801	775-738-5398	753-8535
Elliott County PO Box 710 *Web:* www.elliottcounty.ky.gov	Sandy Hook	KY	41171	606-738-5826	738-5627
Ellis County PO Box 176 *Web:* www.ellis.oklahoma.usassessor.com	Arnett	OK	73832	580-885-7975	885-7258
Ellsworth County 210 N Kansas St *Web:* www.ellsworthcounty.org	Ellsworth	KS	67439	785-472-4161	472-3818
Elmore County 150 S Fourth E St Ste 5 *Web:* www.elmorecounty.org	Mountain Home	ID	83647	208-587-2129	587-2134
Emanuel County 101 N Main St *Web:* emanuelchamber.org	Swainsboro	GA	30401	478-237-3881	
Emery County 75 E Main PO Box 907 *Web:* www.emerycounty.com	Castle Dale	UT	84513	435-381-5106	381-5183
Emmet County 609 First Ave N *Web:* www.emmetcountyia.com	Estherville	IA	51334	712-362-4261	362-7454
Emmons County 100 NW Fourth St PO Box 272 *Web:* emmonscounty.tripod.com	Linton	ND	58552	701-254-5410	
Emporia (Independent City) 201 S Main St *Web:* www.ci.emporia.va.us	Emporia	VA	23847	434-634-3332	634-0003
Erath County 100 W Washington *Web:* www.co.erath.tx.us	Stephenville	TX	76401	254-965-1452	965-5732
Erie County 92 Franklin St *Web:* www.erie.gov	Buffalo	NY	14202	716-858-8785	858-6550
Escambia County 314 Belleville Ave *Web:* www.co.escambia.al.us	Brewton	AL	36426	251-867-0300	
Esmeralda County PO Box 547 *TF:* 800-884-4072 ■ *Web:* www.accessesmeralda.com	Goldfield	NV	89013	775-485-6309	485-6376
Essex County 7559 Ct St PO Box 247	Elizabethtown	NY	12932	518-873-3370	451-8738
Estill County 130 Main St Rm 102 *Web:* www.estillky.com	Irvine	KY	40336	606-723-5156	723-5108
Etowah County 800 Forrest Ave *Web:* www.etowahcounty.org	Gadsden	AL	35901	256-549-5300	549-5400
Eureka County 10 S Main St *Web:* www.co.eureka.nv.us	Eureka	NV	89316	775-237-5262	237-6015
Evangeline Parish 200 Ct St Ste 104 *Web:* evangelineparishclerkofcourt.com/contact.aspx	Ville Platte	LA	70586	337-363-5671	363-5780
Evans County 3 Freeman St *Web:* www.claxtonevanschamber.com	Claxton	GA	30417	912-739-1141	
Fairbanks North Star Borough 809 Pioneer Rd *Web:* www.co.fairbanks.ak.us	Fairbanks	AK	99701	907-459-1000	459-1224
Fairfax County 12000 Government Ctr Pkwy *Web:* fairfaxcounty.gov/	Fairfax	VA	22035	703-324-2531	324-3956

Phone Fax

Fairfax (Independent City)
10455 Armstrong St .... Fairfax VA 22030 703-324-7329 385-7811
Web: fairfaxcounty.gov/

Fairfield County 210 E Main St .... Lancaster OH 43130 740-687-7090 687-6048
Web: www.co.fairfield.oh.us

Fall River County 906 N River St .... Hot Springs SD 57747 605-745-5131 745-6835
Web: ujs.sd.gov

Fallon County 10 W Fallon St .... Baker MT 59313 406-778-7114
Web: www.falloncounty.net

Falls Church (Independent City)
300 Pk Ave .... Falls Church VA 22046 703-248-5001 248-5146
Web: www.fallschurchva.gov

Falls County 125 Bridge St Ste 202 .... Marlin TX 76661 254-883-1408
Web: falls.countycriminal.com

Fannin County 400 W Main St Ste 100 .... Blue Ridge GA 30513 706-632-2203 632-2507
Web: fannincountyga.org

Faribault County 415 N Main St .... Blue Earth MN 56013 507-526-6221
Web: faribaultcountyrecorder.com

Faulkner County 801 Locust St .... Conway AR 72034 501-450-4909 450-4938
Web: www.faulknercounty.org

Fauquier County 10 Hotel St Ste 204 .... Warrenton VA 20186 540-422-8001 422-8022
Web: www.fauquiercounty.gov

Fayette County 401 N Central Ave # 6 .... Connersville IN 47331 765-825-1813 827-4902

Fayette County Goverment
221 S Seventh St Ste 106 .... Vandalia IL 62471 618-283-5000 283-5004
Web: www.fayettecountyillinois.org

Fentress County 101 S Main St .... Jamestown TN 38556 931-879-8014
Web: www.jamestowntn.org

Fergus County 712 W Main St .... Lewistown MT 59457 406-535-5026 535-6076
Web: www.co.fergus.mt.us

Ferry County 290 E Tessie Ave .... Republic WA 99166 509-775-5229 775-5230
Web: www.ferry-county.com

Fillmore County 900 G St .... Geneva NE 68361 402-759-4931 759-4307
Web: www.fillmorecounty.org

Finney County 311 N Ninth St PO Box M .... Garden City KS 67846 620-272-3542 272-3599
Web: www.finneycounty.org

Fisher County PO Box 368 .... Roby TX 79543 325-776-2401 776-3274
Web: www.co.fisher.tx.us

Flagler County 1769 E Moody Blvd Bldg 2 .... Bunnell FL 32110 386-313-4000
Web: www.flaglercounty.org

Flathead County 800 S Main St .... Kalispell MT 59901 406-758-5503 758-5861
Web: flathead.mt.gov

Florence County 180 N Irby St .... Florence SC 29501 843-665-3035 665-3070
Web: www.florenceco.org

Floyd County 101 S Main St .... Charles City IA 50616 641-228-7777 228-7772
Web: www.floydcoia.org

Fluvanna County 132 Main St .... Palmyra VA 22963 434-591-1910 591-1911
Web: www.fluvannacounty.org

Foard County 101 S Main St .... Crowell TX 79227 940-684-1919

Fond du Lac County PO Box 1557 .... Fond du Lac WI 54936 920-929-3000 929-3293
Web: www.fdlco.wi.gov

Ford County 100 Gunsmoke St 4th Fl .... Dodge City KS 67801 620-227-4670 227-4699
Web: www.fordcounty.net

Forest County 200 E Madison St .... Crandon WI 54520 715-478-2422
Web: www.forestcountywi.com

Forrest County 641 Main St .... Hattiesburg MS 39401 601-545-6000
Web: www.co.forrest.ms.us

Forsyth County 100 Courthouse Sq Ste 010 .... Cumming GA 30040 770-781-2120 886-2858
Web: forsythco.com

Fort Bend County 301 Jackson St Ste 101 .... Richmond TX 77469 281-342-3411 341-8669
Web: www.fortbendcountytx.gov

Foster County PO Box 257 .... Carrington ND 58421 701-652-1001 652-2173
Web: www.fostercounty.com

Fountain County
301 4th St County Courthouse .... Covington IN 47932 765-793-2411
Web: www.in.gov/judiciary/2948.htm

Franklin County 855 Dinah Shore Blvd Ste 3 .... Winchester TN 37398 931-967-2905
Web: www.franklincotn.us

Franklin (Independent City) 1020 Pretlow St .... Franklin VA 23851 757-562-8550 562-1156
Web: www.courts.state.va.us

Franklin Parish 6550 Main St .... Winnsboro LA 71295 318-435-5133
Web: laclerksofcourt.org

Frederick County 107 N Kent St .... Winchester VA 22601 540-665-5600 667-0370
Web: www.co.frederick.va.us

Fredericksburg (Independent City)
715 Princess Ann St .... Fredericksburg VA 22401 540-372-1010 372-1201
Web: www.fredericksburgva.gov

Freeborn County 411 S Broadway .... Albert Lea MN 56007 507-377-5116 377-5109
Web: www.co.freeborn.mn.us

Freestone County 103 E Main PO Box 1010 .... Fairfield TX 75840 903-389-2635
Web: www.co.freestone.tx.us

Fremont County 615 Macon Ave Rm 102 .... Canon City CO 81212 719-276-7330 276-7338
Web: www.fremontco.com

Fresno County 1100 Van Ness Ave .... Fresno CA 93721 559-488-1710 488-1830
Web: www.co.fresno.ca.us

Frio County 500 E San Antonio St PO Box 9 .... Pearsall TX 78061 830-334-3668
Web: www.co.frio.tx.us

Frontier County PO Box 40 .... Stockville NE 69042 308-367-8641 367-8730
Web: www.co.frontier.ne.us

Fulton County 100 N Main St .... Lewistown IL 61542 309-547-3041 547-3326
Web: www.fultonco.org

Furnas County PO Box 387 .... Beaver City NE 68926 308-268-4145 268-3205
Web: furnascounty.ne.gov

Gadsden County 10 E Jefferson St .... Quincy FL 32351 850-875-8601 875-8612
Web: www.gadsdengov.net

Gage County 612 Grant St Rm 21 .... Beatrice NE 68310 402-223-1344 223-1380
Web: www.gagecountynebraska.us

Gaines County 101 S Main St PO Box 847 .... Seminole TX 79360 432-758-5411 758-4031
Web: co.gaines.tx.us

Galax (Independent City) 111 E Grayson St .... Galax VA 24333 276-236-5773 236-2889
Web: www.galaxva.com

Phone Fax

Gallatin County 311 W Main St .... Bozeman MT 59715 406-582-3050 582-3068
Web: www.gallatin.mt.gov

Gallia County 18 Locust St .... Gallipolis OH 45631 740-446-4612 446-4804
Web: www.galliacounty.org

Galveston County
600 59th St Second Fl Ste 2001
PO Box 17253 .... Galveston TX 77550 409-766-2200 770-5133
Web: www.galvestoncountytx.gov

Garden County 611 Main St .... Oshkosh NE 69154 308-772-3924 772-0124
Web: www.co.garden.ne.us

Garfield County 250 S 8th PO Box 218 .... Burwell NE 68823 308-346-4161
Web: www.garfieldcounty.ne.gov

Garland County 501 Ouachita Ave .... Hot Springs AR 71901 501-622-3610 624-0665
Web: www.garlandcounty.org

Garrard County 15 Public Sq Ste 3 .... Lancaster KY 40444 859-792-3531 792-2010
Web: www.garrardcounty.ky.gov

Garrett County 203 S Fourth St Rm 207 .... Oakland MD 21550 301-334-8970 334-5000
Web: www.garrettcounty.org

Garvin County 201 W Grant St .... Pauls Valley OK 73075 405-238-2772
Web: okcountyrecords.com

Garza County PO Box 366 .... Post TX 79356 806-495-4430 495-4431
Web: www.garzacounty.net

Gasconade County 119 E First St Rm 23 .... Hermann MO 65041 573-486-3100 486-3693
Web: www.gasconadecountyassessor.com/

Gaston County 128 W Main Ave PO Box 1578 .... Gastonia NC 28053 704-866-3111 866-3147
Web: www.gastongov.com

Gates County 200 Ct St .... Gatesville NC 27938 252-357-2411 357-0073*
**Fax:* Financial ■ *TF:* 800-272-9829 ■ *Web:* www.gatescounty.govoffice2.com

Geary County 200 E 8th .... Junction City KS 66441 785-238-3912 238-5419
Web: ks-geary.manatron.com

Geauga County 470 Ctr St Bldg 4 .... Chardon OH 44024 440-285-2222
Web: www.co.geauga.oh.us

Gem County 415 E Main St .... Emmett ID 83617 208-365-4561 365-7795
Web: www.co.gem.id.us

Genesee County 15 Main St Ste 1 .... Batavia NY 14020 585-344-2550 344-8582
Web: www.co.genesee.ny.us

Geneva County 123 Main St .... Geneva AL 36340 800-123-4567
Web: www.genevacounty.us

Gentry County 200 W Clay St .... Albany MO 64402 660-726-3618 726-4102
Web: www.gentrycounty.net

Georgetown County 715 Prince St .... Georgetown SC 29440 843-545-3063 545-3292
Web: www.georgetowncountysc.org

Gibson County 101 N Main .... Princeton IN 47670 812-385-4885 385-3089
Web: gibsoncounty-in.gov

Gila County 1400 E Ash St .... Globe AZ 85501 928-425-3231
TF: 800-304-4452 ■ *Web:* co.gila.az.us

Gilchrist County 112 S Main St .... Trenton FL 32693 352-463-3170 463-3166
Web: gilchrist.fl.us

Giles County 501 Wenonah Ave .... Pearisburg VA 24134 540-921-1722 921-3825
Web: www.gilescounty.org

Gillespie County 101 W Main St Unit 13 .... Fredericksburg TX 78624 830-997-6515 997-9958
Web: www.gillespiecounty.org

Gilmer County 368 Craig St PO Box 505 .... Ellijay GA 30540 706-635-7400 635-7410
Web: www.gilmerchamber.com

Gilpin County 203 Eureka St .... Central City CO 80427 303-582-5321 582-3086
Web: www.co.gilpin.co.us

Glacier County 512 E Main St .... Cut Bank MT 59427 406-873-2711 873-4218
Web: www.glaciercountygov.com

Gladwin County 401 W Cedar Ave .... Gladwin MI 48624 989-426-7351 426-6917
Web: www.gladwinco.com

Glascock County PO Box 66 .... Gibson GA 30810 706-598-2671 598-0124
Web: www.glascockcountyga.com

Glasscock County 117 E Currie St .... Garden City TX 79739 432-354-2371
Web: www.co.glasscock.tx.us

Glenn County 526 W Sycamore St Ste B1 .... Willows CA 95988 530-934-6400 934-6419
Web: www.countyofglenn.net

Gloucester County 6467 Main St .... Gloucester VA 23061 804-693-4042 693-6004
Web: www.co.gloucester.va.us

Glynn County 701 G St .... Brunswick GA 31520 912-554-7400 554-7596
Web: www.glynncounty.org

Gogebic County 200 N Moore St .... Bessemer MI 49911 906-663-4518 663-4660
Web: www.gogebic.org

Golden Valley County 150 First Ave SE .... Beach ND 58621 701-872-3713
Web: www.beachnd.com

Goliad County 127 N Courthouse Sq PO Box 50 .... Goliad TX 77963 361-645-3294 645-3858
Web: www.co.goliad.tx.us

Gonzales County 1709 Sarah Dewitt Dr .... Gonzales TX 78629 830-672-2801 672-2636
Web: co.gonzales.tx.us

Goochland County 1800 Sandy Hook Rd .... Goochland VA 23063 804-556-5800 556-4617
Web: www.co.goochland.va.us

Goodhue County 454 W Sixth St .... Red Wing MN 55066 651-267-4800
Web: www.co.goodhue.mn.us

Gooding County 145 Seventh Ave E PO Box 417 .... Gooding ID 83330 208-934-4841 934-5085
Web: goodingcounty.org

Gordon County 201 N Wall St .... Calhoun GA 30701 706-629-3795 629-9516
Web: www.gordoncounty.org

Goshen County 2125 E 'A' St PO Box 160 .... Torrington WY 82240 307-532-4051 532-7375
Web: www.goshencounty.org

Gosper County 507 Smith Ave PO Box 136 .... Elwood NE 68937 308-785-2611 785-2300
Web: www.co.gosper.ne.us

Gove County 520 Washington St Ste 105 PO Box 128 .... Gove KS 67736 785-938-2300 938-4486
Web: www.govecountyks.com/county-clerk

Grady County 250 N Broad St .... Cairo GA 39828 229-377-1512 377-1039
Web: www.gradycountyga.gov

Grafton County
3855 Dartmouth College Hwy PO Box 4 .... North Haverhill NH 03774 603-787-6921 787-2363
Web: www.graftoncountynh.us

Graham County 34 Wall St Suite 407 .... Asheville NC 28801 828-255-0182 254-2286
TF: 866-962-6246 ■ *Web:* www.main.nc.us

Grainger County PO Box 101 .... Rutledge TN 37861 865-828-4222
Web: www.graingertn.com

Phone Fax

Grand County 308 W Byers Ave .... Hot Sulphur Springs CO 80451 970-725-3347 725-0100
Web: www.co.grand.co.us

Grand Forks County 124 S Fourth St............... Grand Forks ND 58206 701-787-2733
Web: www.gfcounty.nd.gov

Grand Isle County 9 Hyde Rd PO Box 49............. Grand Isle VT 05458 802-372-8830 372-8815
Web: www.grandislevt.org

Grand Traverse County 400 Boardman Ave .... Traverse City MI 49684 231-922-4760 922-4658
Web: www.co.grand-traverse.mi.us

Granite County
220 N Sansome St PO Box 925 .... Philipsburg MT 59858 406-859-3771 859-3817
Web: www.co.granite.mt.us

Grant County 105 E Harrison St .... Hyannis NE 69350 308-458-2422 471-4020*
**Fax Area Code: 402* ■ *Web:* local.dmv.org/

Grant Parish 512 Main St PO Box 208 .... Colfax LA 71417 318-627-3274 627-5931
Web: www.gpsb.org

Granville County
141 Williamsboro St PO Box 906...................... Oxford NC 27565 919-693-4761 690-1766
Web: www.granvillecounty.org

Gratiot County
County Courthouse 214 E Ctr St PO Box 437............. Ithaca MI 48847 989-875-5215 875-5254
Web: www.gratiotmi.com

Graves County 101 E S St .... Mayfield KY 42066 270-247-3626 247-1274
Web: gravescounty.ky.gov

Gray County PO Box 487........................... Cimarron KS 67835 620-855-3618 855-3107
Web: www.grayco.org

Grays Harbor County
102 W Broadway St Rm 203...................... Montesano WA 98563 360-249-3842 249-6381
Web: www.co.grays-harbor.wa.us

Grayson County 129 Davis St PO Box 130......... Independence VA 24348 276-773-2231 773-3338
Web: www.courts.state.va.us

Grayson County Chamber of Commerce
425 S Main St................................. Leitchfield KY 42754 270-259-5587
Web: www.graysoncountychamber.com

Greeley County PO Box 287.......................... Greeley NE 68842 308-428-3625 428-3022
Web: greeleycounty.ne.gov

Green County 203 W Ct St .... Greensburg KY 42743 270-932-4024 932-3635
Web: www.greencounty.ky.gov

Green Lake County 492 Hill St .... Green Lake WI 54941 920-294-4005 294-4009
Web: www.co.green-lake.wi.us

Greenbrier County 200 W Washington St........... Lewisburg WV 24901 304-647-6602
TF: 800-833-2068 ■ *Web:* www.greenbrierwv.com

Greene County 450 High St .... Jackson MS 39201 601-359-3694 359-2407
Web: mssc.state.ms.us

Greenlee County 223 Fifth St .... Clifton AZ 85533 928-865-2072 865-4417
Web: www.co.greenlee.az.us

Greensville County 337 S Main St................... Emporia VA 23847 434-348-4215 348-4020
Web: www.greensvillecountyva.gov

Greenup County 301 Main St....................... Greenup KY 41144 606-473-7394 473-5354
Web: greenupcountyclerk.com

Greenville County 305 E N St.................... Greenville SC 29601 864-467-8551 467-8540
Web: www.greenvillecounty.org

Greenwood County 311 N Main St.................... Eureka KS 67045 620-583-8121 583-8124
Web: www.greenwoodcounty.org

Greer County 119 E Jefferson St.................... Mangum OK 73554 580-782-2444 782-2229
Web: www.greercountychamber.com

Gregg County 101 E Methvin Ste 200................ Longview TX 75601 903-236-8430 237-2574
Web: www.co.gregg.tx.us

Grenada County 59 Green St Ste 8 .... Grenada MS 38902 662-226-1941 227-2865
Web: www.grenadamississippi.com

Griggs County 808 Rollin Ave SW .... Cooperstown ND 58425 701-797-3613
Web: www.cooperstownnd.com

Grundy County 68 Cumberland St PO Box 177 .... Altamont TN 37301 931-692-3721 692-3718
Web: www.grundycountytn.net

Guadalupe County 211 W Ct St .... Seguin TX 78155 830-303-4188 401-0300
Web: www.co.guadalupe.tx.us

Guernsey County 627 Wheeling Ave Ste 300 .... Cambridge OH 43725 740-432-9200 432-9359
Web: www.guernseycounty.org

Guilford County PO Box 3427 .... Greensboro NC 27402 336-641-3383
Web: www.co.guilford.nc.us

Gulf County
1000 Cecil Costin Sr Blvd Rm 148............... Port Saint Joe FL 32456 850-229-6112 229-6174
Web: www.gulfcounty-fl.gov

Gunnison County 221 N Wisconsin St Ste C........... Gunnison CO 81230 970-641-1516 641-7956
Web: gunnisoncounty.org

Guthrie County 200 N Fifth St .... Guthrie Center IA 50115 641-747-3415
Web: guthriecounty.org

Gwinnett County
75 Langley Dr
Gwinnett Justice & Administration Ctr .... Lawrenceville GA 30045 770-822-8000 822-7097
Web: www.gwinnettcounty.com

Haakon County 140 Howard Ave P.O. Box 70............. Philip SD 57567 605-859-2627 859-2257
Web: ujs.sd.gov/County_Information/haakon.aspx

Habersham County 555 Monroe St Ste 20 .... Clarkesville GA 30523 706-839-0200 839-0219
Web: www.habershamga.com

Haines Borough 103 Third Ave S PO Box 1209 .... Haines AK 99827 907-766-2231 766-2716
Web: www.hainesalaska.gov

Hale County 500 Broadway Rm 140 .... Plainview TX 79072 806-291-5261 291-9810
Web: whc.net/

Halifax County 33 S Granville St .... Halifax NC 27839 252-583-1131 583-9921
Web: www.halifaxnc.com

Hall County 225 Green St SE....................... Gainesville GA 30501 770-531-7025 531-7070
Web: www.hallcounty.org
County Courthouse 512 Main St .... Memphis TX 79245 806-259-2627 259-5078
Web: www.texasfile.com/

Hamblen County 511 W Second N St .... Morristown TN 37814 423-586-1993 318-2508
Web: www.hamblencountytn.gov/

Hamilton County 1111 13th St Ste 1.................. Aurora NE 68818 402-694-3443
Web: www.co.hamilton.ne.us

Hamlin County 300 Fourth St PO Box 208................ Hayti SD 57241 605-783-3232 783-1330
Web: hamlincountysheriff.com

Hampden County 50 State St...................... Springfield MA 01102 413-748-8600
Web: hcbar.org

Hampshire County 99 Main St .... NorthHampton MA 01060 413-584-1300 584-1465
Web: www.hampshirecog.org

Hampton County
201 Jackson Ave W
B T Deloach Administrative Bldg .... Hampton SC 29924 803-914-2103 914-2107
Web: www.hamptoncountysc.org

Hampton (Independent City) 22 Lincoln St........... Hampton VA 23669 757-727-8311
Web: hampton.gov

Hancock County 854 Highway 90 Ste A .... Bay Saint Louis MS 39520 228-467-2100 467-2503
Web: www.hancockcounty.ms.gov/

Hand County 415 W First Ave .... Miller SD 57362 605-853-3337 853-3779
Web: ujs.sd.gov

Hanover County 7497 County Complex Rd .... Hanover VA 23069 804-365-6000 365-6234
Web: hanovercounty.gov/

Hansford County 15 NW Ct...................... Spearman TX 79081 806-659-4110 659-4168
Web: www.co.hansford.tx.us

Hanson County 720 5th St PO Box 127 .... Alexandria SD 57311 605-239-4446 239-9446
Web: ujs.sd.gov/

Haralson County 70 Murphy Campus Blvd .... Waco GA 30182 770-537-5594 537-5873
Web: www.haralson.org

Hardee County 412 W Orange St Rm A-203 .... Wauchula FL 33873 863-773-6952 773-0958
Web: www.hardeecounty.net

Hardeman County PO Box 30 .... Quanah TX 79252 940-663-2911 663-6302
Web: hardemantx.com

Hardin County
1215 Edgington Ave County Courthouse .... Eldora IA 50627 641-939-8109 939-8245
Web: www.co.hardin.ia.us

Harding County 410 Ramsland St PO Box 534 .... Buffalo SD 57720 605-375-3351 375-3432
Web: ujs.sd.gov/

Hardy County 204 Washington St Rm 111 .... Moorefield WV 26836 304-530-0250 530-0251
TF: 800-222-1222 ■ *Web:* hardycounty.com

Harlan County 311 Main St .... Alma NE 68920 800-762-5498
TF: 800-762-5498 ■ *Web:* www.harlantourism.org

Harmon County 114 W Hollis St.......................... Hollis OK 73550 580-688-3617
Web: harmon.countycriminal.com

Harnett County PO Box 759....................... Lillington NC 27546 910-893-7555 814-2662
Web: www.harnett.org

Harney County 450 N Buena Vista Ste 14 .... Burns OR 97720 541-573-6641 573-8370
Web: www.co.harney.or.us

Harper County 201 N Jennings Ave .... Anthony KS 67003 620-842-5555 842-3455
TF: 877-537-2110 ■ *Web:* www.harpercountyks.gov

Harris County 112 S College St PO Box 426 .... Hamilton GA 31811 706-628-0010 628-4429
TF: 888-478-0010 ■ *Web:* www.harriscountychamber.org

Harrison County 1501 Main St PO Box 169............ Bethany MO 64424 660-425-3199
Web: harrisoncountysheriffmo.org/

Harrisonburg (Independent City)
345 S Main St................................. Harrisonburg VA 22801 540-432-7701 432-7778
Web: www.harrisonburgva.gov

Hart County 800 Chandler St......................... Hartwell GA 30643 706-376-2024 376-9477
Web: www.hartcountyga.org

Hartley County 900 Main St........................ Channing TX 79018 806-235-3582 235-2316
Web: www.co.hartley.tx.us

Harvey County 800 N Main PO Box 687 .... Newton KS 67114 316-284-6840 284-6856
Web: www.harveycounty.com

Haskell County 1 Ave D .... Haskell TX 79521 940-864-3448
Web: www.co.haskell.tx.us

Hawaii County 1055 Kinoole St Ste 101.................. Hilo HI 96720 808-961-8255 961-8603
Web: www.hawaiicounty.gov

Hawkins County 110 E Main St.................. Rogersville TN 37857 423-272-7002
Web: www.hawkinscountytn.gov

Hayes County 505 Troth St PO Box 370 .... Hayes Center NE 69032 308-286-3413 286-3208
Web: www.hayescounty.ne.gov

Hays County 110 E Martin Luther King St............ San Marcos TX 78666 512-393-7738 393-7735
Web: www.co.hays.tx.us

Haywood County 1 N Washington St............... Brownsville TN 38012 731-772-1432 772-3864
Web: www.haywoodcountybrownsville.com

Heard County PO Box 40 .... Franklin GA 30217 706-675-3821 675-2493
Web: www.heardcountyga.com

Hemphill County 400 Main St Ste 200 .... Canadian TX 79014 806-323-6521 323-5260
Web: co.hemphill.tx.us

Hempstead County 400 S Washington Hope .... Hope AR 71801 870-777-6164
Web: www.hempsteadcountyar.com

Henderson County 17 Monroe Ave Ste 2 .... Lexington TN 38351 731-968-2856 968-6644
Web: hendersoncountytn.gov

Hendricks County 1 Courthouse Sq .... Danville IN 46122 317-745-9231 745-9306
Web: www.co.hendricks.in.us

Hendry County PO Box 1760 .... LaBelle FL 33975 863-675-5217
Web: www.hendryfla.net

Hennepin County 300 S Sixth St................ Minneapolis MN 55487 612-348-3081 348-8701
Web: hennepin.us/

Henrico County 4301 E Parham Rd .... Henrico VA 23228 804-501-4000 501-5214
Web: henrico.us

Henry County 307 W Ctr St......................... Cambridge IL 61238 309-937-3578
Web: www.henrycty.com

Herkimer County 109 Mary St Ste 1111 .... Herkimer NY 13350 315-867-1129 867-1349
Web: www.herkimercounty.org

Hernando County 16110 Aviation Loop Dr .... Brooksville FL 34604 352-754-4000 754-4477
Web: www.co.hernando.fl.us

Hettinger County 336 Pacific Ave......................... Mott ND 58646 701-824-4227
Web: www.hettingercounty.net

Hickman County 114 N Central Ave # 202........... Centerville TN 37033 931-729-2621 729-9951
Web: www.hickmanco.com

Hickory County 100 New Hermitage Dr .... Hermitage MO 65668 417-745-6939 745-2132
Web: www.hickorylibrary.org

Hidalgo County PO Box 58......................... Edinburg TX 78540 956-318-2100 318-2105
TF: 888-318-2811 ■ *Web:* www.co.hidalgo.tx.us

Highland County 119 Governor Foraker Pl .... Hillsboro OH 45133 937-393-1911 393-5850
Web: www.co.highland.oh.us

Highlands County 430 S Commerce Ave............... Sebring FL 33870 863-402-6500 402-6507
Web: www.hcbcc.net

Hill County 315 Fourth St .... Havre MT 59501 406-265-5481 265-3693
Web: www.hillcounty.us

Name / Address	City	State	ZIP	Phone	Fax
Hillsborough County 329 Mast Rd *Web:* www.hillsboroughcountynh.org	Goffstown	NH	03045	603-627-5600	627-5603
Hillsdale County 29 N Howell St *Web:* www.co.hillsdale.mi.us	Hillsdale	MI	49242	517-437-3391	437-3392
Hinds County 316 S President St *Web:* www.co.hinds.ms.us	Jackson	MS	39205	601-968-6501	968-6794
Hinsdale County 311 N Henson St *Web:* www.hinsdalecountycolorado.us	Lake City	CO	81235	970-944-2225	944-2630
Hitchcock County 229 E D St *Web:* hitchcockcounty.ne.gov	Trenton	NE	69044	308-334-5646	334-5398
Hocking County 1 E Main St *Web:* www.co.hocking.oh.us	Logan	OH	43138	740-385-3000	385-7413
Hockley County 802 Houston St Ste 213 *Web:* www.co.hockley.tx.us	Levelland	TX	79336	806-894-4404	
Hodgeman County PO Box 247 *Web:* www.hodgemancountyks.com	Jetmore	KS	67854	620-357-6421	357-6313
Hoke County 227 N Main St *TF:* 888-302-9793 ■ *Web:* www.hoke-raeford.com	Raeford	NC	28376	910-875-8751	875-9222
Holmes County 106 E Byrd Ave *Web:* www.holmescountyonline.com	Bonifay	FL	32425	850-547-6153	
Holt County 204 N Fourth St PO Box 329 *Web:* www.co.holt.ne.us	O'Neill	NE	68763	402-336-1762	336-1762
Honolulu City & County 530 S King St Rm 100 *Web:* www.honolulu.gov	Honolulu	HI	96813	808-768-3810	768-3835
Hood County 100 E Pearl St Ste 5 *Web:* www.co.hood.tx.us	Granbury	TX	76048	817-579-3222	579-3227
Hood River County 601 State St *Web:* www.co.hood-river.or.us	Hood River	OR	97031	541-386-3970	386-9392
Hooker County PO Box 184 *Web:* www.co.hooker.ne.us	Mullen	NE	69152	308-546-2244	546-2490
Hopewell (Independent City) 300 N Main St Rm 217 *Web:* www.hopewellva.gov	Hopewell	VA	23860	804-541-2243	541-2248
Hopkins County 24 Union St *Web:* www.hopkinscounty.net	Madisonville	KY	42431	270-821-7361	
Horry County 1301 Second Ave *Web:* www.horrycounty.org	Conway	SC	29526	843-915-5080	915-6081
Hot Spring County 210 Locust St	Malvern	AR	72104	501-332-2291	
Hot Springs County 415 Arapahoe St *Web:* www.hscounty.com	Thermopolis	WY	82443	307-864-3515	864-3333
Houghton County 401 E Houghton Ave *Web:* www.houghtoncounty.net	Houghton	MI	49931	906-482-1150	483-0364
Houston County 200 Carl Vinson Pkwy *Web:* www.houstoncountyga.com	Warner Robins	GA	31088	478-542-2115	923-5697
Howard County 300 Main St *Web:* www.co.howard.tx.us	Big Spring	TX	79720	432-264-2213	264-2215
Howell County 35 Court Sq *Web:* www.howellcounty.net	West Plains	MO	65775	417-256-2591	
Hubbard County 301 Ct Ave County Courthouse **Fax:* Acctg ■ *Web:* www.co.hubbard.mn.us	Park Rapids	MN	56470	218-732-2300	732-3645*
Hudson County 257 Cornelison Ave 4th Fl *Web:* www.hudsoncountyclerk.org	Jersey City	NJ	07302	201-369-3470	369-3478
Hudspeth County 109 Brown St *TF:* 888-368-4689 ■ *Web:* www.txdmv.gov/	Sierra Blanca	TX	79851	915-369-2331	369-3005
Huerfano County 401 Main St Ste 201 *Web:* www.huerfano.us	Walsenburg	CO	81089	719-738-2370	738-3996
Hughes County 200 N Broadway St	Holdenville	OK	74848	405-379-2746	
Humboldt County 203 Main St *Web:* www.humboldtcountyia.org	Dakota City	IA	50529	515-332-1571	
Humphreys County 102 Thompson St *Web:* www.humphreystn.com	Waverly	TN	37185	931-296-7795	
Hunt County PO Box 1316 *Web:* www.huntcounty.net	Greenville	TX	75403	903-408-4130	408-4287
Hunterdon County 71 Main St *Web:* www.co.hunterdon.nj.us	Flemington	NJ	08822	908-788-1221	782-4068
Huntingdon County 223 Penn St County Courthouse *Web:* www.huntingdoncounty.net	Huntingdon	PA	16652	814-643-3091	643-8152
Huntington County 201 N Jefferson St County Courthouse Rm 103 *Web:* www.huntington.in.us	Huntington	IN	46750	260-358-4804	358-4823
Huron County 250 E Huron Ave Rm 305 *Web:* www.huroncounty.com	Bad Axe	MI	48413	989-269-8242	269-6152
Hutchinson County PO Box 1186 *Web:* www.co.hutchinson.tx.us	Stinnett	TX	79083	806-878-4002	
Hyde County 30 Oyster Creek Rd *Web:* hydecountync.gov	Swanquarter	NC	27885	252-926-4178	926-3701
Iberia Parish 300 Iberia St Ste 400 *Web:* www.iberiaparishgovernment.com	New Iberia	LA	70560	337-365-8246	369-4470
Iberville Parish 58050 Meriam St *Web:* www.ibervilleparish.com	Plaquemine	LA	70764	225-687-5160	
Ida County 401 Moorehead St *Web:* idacounty.org	Ida Grove	IA	51445	712-364-2626	
Idaho County 320 W Main St Rm 5 *Web:* www.idahocounty.org	Grangeville	ID	83530	208-983-2751	
Imperial County 940 W Main St Rm 202 *Web:* www.co.imperial.ca.us	El Centro	CA	92243	760-482-4427	482-4271
Independence County 192 E Main St *Web:* www.independencecounty.com	Batesville	AR	72501	870-793-8800	793-8803
Indian River County 1801 27th St *Web:* www.ircgov.com	Vero Beach	FL	32960	772-567-8000	978-1822
Indiana County 350 N Fourth St *TF:* 888-559-6355 ■ *Web:* www.countyofindiana.org	Indiana	PA	15701	724-465-3805	465-3179
Ingham County 315 S Jefferson St PO Box 179 *Web:* www.ingham.org	Mason	MI	48854	517-676-7201	676-7254
Inyo County PO Drawer N *Web:* www.inyocounty.us	Independence	CA	93526	760-878-0292	878-2241
Ionia County 100 W Main St *Web:* www.ioniacounty.org	Ionia	MI	48846	616-527-5322	527-8201
Iosco County 422 W Lake St *Web:* iosco.m33access.com	Tawas City	MI	48763	989-362-3485	
Iowa County 222 N Iowa St Ste 102 *Web:* www.iowacounty.org	Dodgeville	WI	53533	608-935-0318	935-3024
Iredell County 200 S Ctr St PO Box 788 *Web:* www.co.iredell.nc.us	Statesville	NC	28687	704-878-3000	878-5355
Irion County PO Box 736 *Web:* www.co.irion.tx.us	Mertzon	TX	76941	325-835-2421	835-2008
Iron County 2 S Sixth St *Web:* www.iron.org	Crystal Falls	MI	49920	906-875-3221	875-6775
Iroquois County 1001 E Grant St Rm 106 *Web:* www.co.iroquois.il.us	Watseka	IL	60970	815-432-6978	432-6999
Irwin County 301 E 1st St *Web:* irwincountyrealty.com	Ocilla	GA	31774	229-468-0050	
Isabella County 200 N Main St *Web:* www.isabellacounty.org	Mount Pleasant	MI	48858	989-772-0911	773-7431
Isanti County 555 18th Ave SW *Web:* www.co.isanti.mn.us	Cambridge	MN	55008	763-689-3859	689-8226
Island County 1 NE Seventh St Ste 214 *Web:* www.islandcounty.net	Coupeville	WA	98239	360-679-7354	679-7381
Isle of Wight County 17090 Monument Cir # 123 *Web:* www.co.isle-of-wight.va.us	Isle of Wight	VA	23397	757-365-6204	357-9171
Itasca County 123 NE Fourth St *Web:* www.co.itasca.mn.us	Grand Rapids	MN	55744	218-327-2847	327-2848
Itawamba County PO Box 776 *Web:* www.itawamba.com	Fulton	MS	38843	662-862-3421	862-3421
Izard County 400 Ct St *Web:* izardcountyar.org	Melbourne	AR	72556	870-368-4316	
Jack County 100 Main St *Web:* jackcounty.org	Jacksboro	TX	76458	940-567-2111	
Jackson County 700 S Main *Web:* ujs.sd.gov/County_Information/jackson.aspx	Kadoka	SD	57543	605-837-2122	837-2120
Jackson County Courthouse, The 101 N Main St *Web:* jackson.okcounties.org	Altus	OK	73521	580-482-2370	
Jackson Parish 500 E Ct St Ste 103 *Web:* www.jacksonparishpolicejury.org	Jonesboro	LA	71251	318-259-2424	
James City County PO Box 8784 *Web:* www.jamescitycountyva.gov	Williamsburg	VA	23187	757-253-6728	253-6833
Jasper County PO Box 611 *Web:* www.co.jasper.ms.us	Bay Springs	MS	39422	601-764-2700	764-3999
Jay County 504 W Arch St *Web:* www.co.jay.in.us	Portland	IN	47371	260-726-8080	726-2220
Jeff Davis County 100 Ct Ave *Web:* www.co.jeff-davis.tx.us	Fort Davis	TX	79734	432-426-3251	
Jefferson County 100 Jefferson County Pkwy *Web:* www.jeffco.us	Golden	CO	80419	303-279-6511	271-8197
Jefferson Davis County 1025 Third St PO Box 342 *Web:* www.jeffdavisms.com	Prentiss	MS	39474	601-792-5903	792-0291
Jefferson Parish 200 Derbigny St Ste 3100 *Web:* www.jeffparish.net	Gretna	LA	70053	504-364-2600	
Jenkins County 548 Cotton Ave *Web:* www.jenkinscountyga.com	Millen	GA	30442	478-982-5595	
Jennings County 25 N Pike St *Web:* jenningscounty-in.gov	Vernon	IN	47282	812-352-3070	
Jerauld County 205 S Wallace *Web:* ujs.sd.gov/County_Information/jerauld.aspx	Wessington Springs	SD	57382	605-539-1202	539-1203
Jerome County 300 N Lincoln Ave *Web:* jeromecountyid.us	Jerome	ID	83338	208-644-2715	
Jersey County 209 N State St *Web:* www.jerseycounty.org	Jerseyville	IL	62052	618-498-5571	
Jessamine County 101 N Main St *Web:* www.jessamineco.com	Nicholasville	KY	40356	859-885-4161	885-5837
Jim Hogg County 102 E Tilley St *Web:* jimhoggcounty.net	Hebbronville	TX	78361	361-527-4031	
Jim Wells County PO Box 1459 *Web:* www.co.jim-wells.tx.us	Alice	TX	78333	361-668-5702	
Jo Daviess County 330 N Bench St *Web:* www.jodaviess.org	Galena	IL	61036	815-777-0161	777-3688
Johnson County 76 N Main St *Web:* www.johnsoncountywyoming.org	Buffalo	WY	82834	307-684-7272	684-2708
Johnson County Clerk 230 Ct St *Web:* johnsoncountyclerkky.com	Paintsville	KY	41240	606-789-2557	789-2559
Johnston County 207 E Johnston St PO Box 1049 *Web:* www.johnstonnc.com	Smithfield	NC	27577	919-989-5100	989-5179
Jones County 500 W Main St *Web:* www.jonescountyiowa.org	Anamosa	IA	52205	319-462-2282	
Josephine County 500 NW Sixth St *Web:* www.co.josephine.or.us	Grants Pass	OR	97526	541-474-5240	474-5246
Juab County 160 N Main St *Web:* www.co.juab.ut.us	Nephi	UT	84648	435-623-3410	
Judith Basin County 91 Third St N PO Box 339 *Web:* co.judith-basin.mt.us	Stanford	MT	59479	406-566-2277	
Juneau City & Borough 155 S Seward St *Web:* www.juneau.org	Juneau	AK	99801	907-586-5278	586-5385
Juneau County 220 Wisconsin 82 Trunk *Web:* www.juneaucounty.com	Mauston	WI	53948	608-847-9300	
Juniata County 498 Jefferson St *Web:* www.co.juniata.pa.us	Mifflintown	PA	17059	717-436-5152	436-7734
Kalamazoo County 201 W Kalamazoo Ave *Web:* www.kalcounty.com	Kalamazoo	MI	49007	269-383-8840	384-8143
Kalkaska County 605 N Birch St *Web:* www.tcchamber.org	Kalkaska	MI	49646	231-258-3336	
Kanabec County 18 N Vine St *Web:* www.kanabeccounty.org	Mora	MN	55051	320-679-6466	679-6431
Kanawha County 409 Virginia St E *Web:* www.kanawha.us	Charleston	WV	25301	304-357-0130	357-0585
Kandiyohi County PO Box 936 *Web:* www.co.kandiyohi.mn.us	Willmar	MN	56201	320-231-6202	231-6263

Phone | Fax

Kane County 719 Batavia Ave Bldg A ... Geneva IL 60134 630-232-5930 232-9188
Web: www.countyofkane.org

Kankakee County 189 E Ct St ... Kankakee IL 60901 815-937-2990 939-8831
Web: www.co.kankakee.il.us

Karnes County 101 N Panna Maria Ave Ste 9 ... Karnes City TX 78118 830-780-3938 780-4576
Web: www.co.karnes.tx.us

Kauai County 4386 Rice St Ste 101 ... Lihue HI 96766 808-241-4800 241-6207
Web: www.kauai.gov

Kaufman County 100 W Mulberry St ... Kaufman TX 75142 972-932-4331 932-7628
Web: www.kaufmancounty.net

Kay County 201 S Main St ... Newkirk OK 74647 580-362-2565 362-3668
Web: www.courthouse.kay.ok.us

Kearney County 424 N Colorado Ave ... Minden NE 68959 308-832-2723 832-2729
Web: www.kearneycounty.ne.gov

Kearny County PO Box 86 ... Lakin KS 67860 620-355-6422 355-7382
Web: www.kearnycountykansas.com

Keith County 511 N Spruce St Ste 102 ... Ogallala NE 69153 308-284-4726 284-6277
Web: www.co.keith.ne.us

Kemper County 14062 Hwy 16 W ... De Kalb MS 39328 601-743-2754 743-2760
Web: countycriminal.com/court-records

Kenai Peninsula Borough 144 N Binkley St ... Soldotna AK 99669 907-262-4441 262-8615
Web: www.borough.kenai.ak.us

Kendall County 201 E San Antonio St ... Boerne TX 78006 830-249-9343 249-1763
Web: www.co.kendall.tx.us

Kenedy County 139 N Main ... Sarita TX 78385 361-294-5785 294-5788
Web: www.co.kenedy.tx.us

Kennebec County 125 State St ... Augusta ME 04330 207-622-0971 623-4083
Web: www.kennebeccounty.org

Kenosha County 1010 56th St ... Kenosha WI 53140 262-653-2552 653-2564
Web: www.co.kenosha.wi.us

Kent County 400 High St ... Chestertown MD 21620 410-778-7435 778-7482
Web: www.kentcounty.com

Kenton County 303 Ct St ... Covington KY 41011 859-392-1600
Web: www.kentoncounty.org

Keokuk County 101 S Main St ... Sigourney IA 52591 641-622-2210 622-2171
Web: www.keokukcountyia.com

Kern County 1115 Truxtun Ave 5th Fl ... Bakersfield CA 93301 661-868-3198 868-3190
Web: www.co.kern.ca.us

Kerr County 700 Main St Rm 122 ... Kerrville TX 78028 830-792-2255 895-1861
Web: www.co.kerr.tx.us

Kershaw County 1121 Broad St Rm 202 ... Camden SC 29020 803-425-7226 425-6044
Web: www.kershaw.sc.gov

Ketchikan Gateway Borough
1900 First Ave Ste 115 ... Ketchikan AK 99901 907-228-6604 247-8439
Web: www.borough.ketchikan.ak.us

Kewaunee County 613 Dodge St ... Kewaunee WI 54216 920-388-7144
Web: www.kewauneeco.org

Keweenaw County 902 College Ave ... Houghton MI 49931 906-482-5240
Web: www.keweenaw.org

Keya Paha County PO Box 349 ... Springview NE 68778 402-497-3791 497-3799
Web: www.co.keya-paha.ne.us

Kidder County
120 E Broadway Kidder County Courthouse ... Steele ND 58482 701-475-2632 475-2202
Web: ndcourts.gov

Kimball County 114 E Third St ... Kimball NE 69145 308-235-2241 235-3654
Web: www.co.kimball.ne.us

Kimble County 501 Main St Courthouse ... Junction TX 76849 325-446-3353 446-2986
Web: www.co.kimble.tx.us

King & Queen County
242 Allens Cir Ste L
PO Box 177 ... King & Queen Court House VA 23085 804-785-5975 785-5999
Web: www.kingandqueenco.net

King County PO Box 66 ... Guthrie TX 79236 806-596-4470
Web: www.tdcj.state.tx.us

King George County 9483 Kings Hwy Ste 3 ... King George VA 22485 540-775-3322 775-5466
Web: www.king-george.va.us

King William County
351 Courthouse Ln PO Box 215 ... King William VA 23086 804-769-4938
Web: www.kingwilliamcounty.us

Kingfisher County 101 S Main St ... Kingfisher OK 73750 405-375-3887

Kingman County 130 N Spruce St ... Kingman KS 67068 620-532-2521
Web: kingmancoks.com

Kings County 360 Adams St Rm 189 ... Brooklyn NY 11201 347-404-9772
Web: www.nycourts.gov/courts/2jd/kingsclerk

Kingsbury County 202 2nd St SE ... De Smet SD 57231 605-854-3811 854-9080
Web: ujs.sd.gov

Kinney County 501 S Ann St ... Brackettville TX 78832 830-563-2521 563-2644
Web: www.co.kinney.tx.us

Kiowa County 211 E Florida Ave ... Greensburg KS 67054 620-723-3366 723-3234
Web: kiowacountyks.org

Kit Carson County 251 16th St # 103 ... Burlington CO 80807 719-346-8638 346-7242
Web: www.kitcarsoncounty.org

Kitsap County 614 Div St MS 4 ... Port Orchard WA 98366 360-337-7146 337-4632
Web: www.kitsapgov.com

Kittitas County 205 W Fifth Ave Ste 108 ... Ellensburg WA 98926 509-962-7508 962-7679
Web: www.co.kittitas.wa.us

Kittson County 410 Fifth St SE Ste 214 ... Hallock MN 56728 218-843-2655
Web: www.visitnwminnesota.com

Klamath County 305 Main St ... Klamath Falls OR 97601 541-883-5134 883-5165
TF: 800-377-6094 ■ *Web:* www.klamathcounty.org

Kleberg County PO Box 1327 ... Kingsville TX 78364 361-595-8548 593-1355
Web: www.co.kleberg.tx.us

Klickitat County
205 S Columbus Ave Rm 204 MS CH3 ... Goldendale WA 98620 509-773-5744 773-4559
Web: www.klickitatcounty.org

Knox County PO Box 196 ... Benjamin TX 79505 940-459-2441 459-2005
Web: www.knoxcountytexas.org

Kodiak Island Borough 710 Mill Bay Rd ... Kodiak AK 99615 907-486-9300
Web: www.kodiakak.us

Koochiching County 715 Fourth St ... International Falls MN 56649 218-283-1152 283-1151
Web: www.co.koochiching.mn.us

Phone | Fax

Kootenai County 451 N Government Way ... Coeur d'Alene ID 83814 208-446-1000 446-1188
Web: www.co.kootenai.id.us

Kosciusko County 121 N Lake St ... Warsaw IN 46580 574-372-2331 372-2338
Web: www.kcgov.com

Kossuth County 114 W State St ... Algona IA 50511 515-295-2718 295-3071
Web: www.co.kossuth.ia.us

La Crosse County 400 N Fourth St Rm 1210 ... La Crosse WI 54601 608-785-9581 785-9741
Web: www.co.la-crosse.wi.us

La Paz County 1108 S Joshua Ave ... Parker AZ 85344 928-669-6115 669-9709
Web: www.co.la-paz.az.us

La Plata County 1060 E Second Ave Ste 134 ... Durango CO 81301 970-382-6280 382-6285
Web: www.co.laplata.co.us

La Porte County 813 Lincolnway ... La Porte IN 46350 219-326-6808
Web: www.laportecounty.org

La Salle County 101 Courthouse Sq Ste 107 ... Cotulla TX 78014 830-879-4432 483-5101
Web: www.co.la-salle.tx.us

Labette County 501 Merchant St ... Oswego KS 67356 620-795-2138 795-2928
Web: www.labettecounty.com

Lac qui Parle County (LQP) 600 Sixth St ... Madison MN 56256 320-598-7444 598-3125
Web: www.lqpco.com

Lackawanna County 436 Spruce St ... Scranton PA 18503 570-963-6723 963-6387
Web: www.lackawannacounty.org

Laclede County 200 N Adams Ave ... Lebanon MO 65536 417-532-5471 588-9288
Web: www.lacledecountymissouri.org

Lafayette Consolidated Government
705 W University Ave PO Box 4017-C ... Lafayette LA 70506 337-291-8200
Web: www.lafayettegov.org

Lafayette County 626 Main St PO Box 40 ... Darlington WI 53530 608-776-4850 776-8893
Web: www.co.lafayette.wi.gov

Lafourche Parish 402 Green St PO Box 5548 ... Thibodaux LA 70302 985-446-8427 446-8459
TF: 800-834-8832 ■ *Web:* www.lafourchegov.org

LaGrange County 114 W Michigan St ... LaGrange IN 46761 260-499-6300
Web: lagrangecounty.org

Lake County 200 E Ctr St ... Madison SD 57042 605-256-5644 256-5080
Web: ujs.sd.gov/County_Information/lake.aspx

Lake of the Woods County 206 Eigth Ave SE ... Baudette MN 56623 218-634-2836 634-2509
Web: www.co.lake-of-the-woods.mn.us

Lamar County 408 Thomaston St Ste E ... Barnesville GA 30204 770-358-5146 358-5149
Web: www.lamarcountyga.com

Lamb County 100 6th St Rm 103 ... Littlefield TX 79339 806-385-4222 385-6485

Lamoille County PO Box 455 ... Morrisville VT 05661 802-888-5640 851-1136
Web: www.lamoilleeconomy.org

LaMoure County PO Box 217 ... La Moure ND 58458 701-883-5987
Web: www.lamourend.com

Lampasas County 409 Pecan St PO Box 347 ... Lampasas TX 76550 512-556-8271 556-8270
Web: www.co.lampasas.tx.us

Lancaster County 50 N Duke St ... Lancaster PA 17602 717-299-8000 293-7208
Web: www.co.lancaster.pa.us

Lander County 315 S Humboldt St ... Battle Mountain NV 89820 775-635-5738
Web: landercountynv.org

Lane County PO Box 290 ... Dighton KS 67839 620-397-2802 397-2802
Web: www.kansastreasurers.org

Langlade County 800 Clermont St ... Antigo WI 54409 715-627-6200 627-6303
Web: www.co.langlade.wi.us

Lanier County 56 W Main St Ste 9 ... Lakeland GA 31635 229-482-2088
Web: www.laniercountyboc.com

Lapeer County 255 Clay St ... Lapeer MI 48446 810-667-0356
Web: lapeercountyweb.org

Laramie County 309 W 20th St ... Cheyenne WY 82001 307-633-4264 633-4240
Web: laramiecountyclerk.com

Larimer County 1 Old Town Sq ... Fort Collins CO 80524 970-498-7860 498-7906
Web: www.larimer.org

LaRue County 209 W High St ... Hodgenville KY 42748 270-358-3544 358-4528
Web: www.laruecounty.org

Las Animas County 200 E First St Rm 204 ... Trinidad CO 81082 719-846-2981 845-2591
Web: lasanimascounty.org

LaSalle County 707 E Etna Rd ... Ottawa IL 61350 815-433-3366 433-9522
TF: 800-247-5243 ■ *Web:* www.lasallecounty.org

LaSalle Parish PO Box 1288 ... Jena LA 71342 318-992-2101 992-2103
Web: www.lpgov.org

Lassen County 220 S Lassen St Ste 5 ... Susanville CA 96130 530-251-8217 257-3480
Web: www.co.lassen.ca.us

Latah County 522 S Adams St PO Box 8068 ... Moscow ID 83843 208-882-8580 883-7203
Web: www.latah.id.us

Latimer County 109 N Central St ... Wilburton OK 74578 918-465-3450 465-4005
Web: www.latimer.okcountytreasurers.com

Lauderdale County PO Box 1059 ... Florence AL 35631 256-760-5750
Web: www.lauderdalecountyonline.com

Laurel County 101 S Main St Rm 203 ... London KY 40741 606-864-5158 864-7369
Web: laurelcountyclerk.com

Laurens County 117 E Jackson St ... Dublin GA 31040 478-272-4755 272-3895
Web: www.laurenscoga.org

Lavaca County 412 N Texana ... Hallettsville TX 77964 361-798-3612 798-1610
Web: www.co.lavaca.tx.us

Lawrence County 111 S Fourth St Ste 11 ... Ironton OH 45638 740-533-4355
Web: www.lawrencecountyohio.org

Le Sueur County 88 S Pk Ave ... Le Center MN 56057 507-357-2251 357-6433
Web: www.co.le-sueur.mn.us

Lea County 100 N Main St Ste 11 ... Lovington NM 88260 575-396-8619 396-3293
Web: www.leacounty.net

Leake County 103 N Pearl St ... Carthage MS 39051 601-267-9231
Web: www.leakems.com

Leavenworth County 300 Walnut St ... Leavenworth KS 66048 913-684-0421
Web: www.leavenworthcounty.org

Lebanon County
400 S Eigth St Rms 102 Municipal Bldg ... Lebanon PA 17042 717-228-4419
Web: www.lebcounty.org

Lee County PO Box G ... Beattyville KY 41311 606-464-4100 464-4145
Web: www.leecounty.ky.gov
Lee County Courthouse PO Box 367 Rm 111 ... Jonesville VA 24263 276-346-7714 346-7712
Web: www.leecountyvachamber.org

Name / Address	City	State	Zip	Phone	Fax
Leelanau County 8527 E Government Ctr Dr	Suttons Bay	MI	49682	231-256-9824	256-0174
TF: 866-256-9711 ■ Web: www.leelanau.cc					
LeFlore County 100 S Broadway PO Box 100	Poteau	OK	74953	918-647-3525	647-7122
Web: leflore.okcountytreasurers.com					
Lehigh County 455 W Hamilton St Rm 132	Allentown	PA	18101	610-782-3148	
Web: www.lehighcounty.org					
Lemhi County 206 Courthouse Dr	Salmon	ID	83467	208-756-2815	756-8424
Web: www.lemhicountyidaho.org					
Lenawee County 425 N Main St Third Fl Judicial Bldg	Adrian	MI	49221	517-264-4599	264-4790
Web: www.lenawee.mi.us					
Lenoir County 130 S Queen St PO Box 3289	Kinston	NC	28502	252-559-6450	559-6454
Web: www.co.lenoir.nc.us					
Leon County PO Box 98	Centerville	TX	75833	903-536-2352	
Web: www.co.leon.tx.us					
Leslie County PO Box 619	Hyden	KY	41749	606-672-3200	672-7373
Web: www.lesliecounty.ky.gov					
Letcher County 156 Main St Ste 102	Whitesburg	KY	41858	606-633-2129	633-7105
Web: letchercounty.ky.gov					
Levy County 355 S Ct St PO Box 310	Bronson	FL	32621	352-486-5218	486-5167
Web: www.levycounty.org					
Lewis & Clark County 316 N Pk Ave	Helena	MT	59623	406-447-8200	447-8370
Web: www.lccountymt.gov					
Lewis County 351 NW North St	Chehalis	WA	98532	360-740-1192	
Web: lewiscountywa.gov					
Economic Development 106 N Ct St PO Box 10	Hohenwald	TN	38462	931-796-6012	796-6020
Web: middletndevelopmentalliance.com/					
Lexington (Independent City) 300 E Washington St	Lexington	VA	24450	540-462-3700	463-5310
Web: lexingtonva.gov					
Lexington-Fayette County 162 E Main St	Lexington	KY	40507	859-253-3344	231-9619
Web: local.dmv.org					
Liberty County PO Box 523	Bristol	FL	32321	850-643-2359	
Web: www.libertycountyflorida.com					
Licking County 20 S Second St	Newark	OH	43055	740-670-5110	670-5119
Web: www.lcounty.com					
Limestone County 310 W Washington St	Athens	AL	35611	256-233-6400	
Web: limestonecounty.net					
Lincoln County 300 Central Ave	Carrizozo	NM	88301	575-648-2385	648-2381
TF: 800-687-2705 ■ Web: www.lincolncountynm.net					
Lincoln Parish 100 W Texas Ave	Ruston	LA	71270	318-251-5150	
Web: www.lincolnparish.org					
Linn County 300 Fourth Ave SW	Albany	OR	97321	541-967-3831	926-5109
Web: www.co.linn.or.us					
Lipscomb County PO Box 70	Lipscomb	TX	79056	806-862-3091	862-3004
Web: www.co.lipscomb.tx.us					
Litchfield County 6 Titus Rd PO Box 396	Litchfield	CT	06759	860-868-7313	
Web: www.litchfieldcty.com					
Little River County 351 N Second St	Ashdown	AR	71822	870-898-7211	
Web: www.littlerivercounty.org/					
Live Oak County PO Box 280	George West	TX	78022	361-449-2733	
Web: www.co.live-oak.tx.us					
Livingston County 6 Ct St Rm 201	Geneseo	NY	14454	585-243-7010	
Web: www.co.livingston.state.ny.us					
Livingston Parish 20399 Government Blvd	Livingston	LA	70754	225-686-4400	
Web: www.livingstonparishla.gov					
Llano County PO Box 40	Llano	TX	78643	325-247-4455	247-2406
Web: www.co.llano.tx.us					
Logan County 117 E Columbus St	Bellefontaine	OH	43311	937-599-7283	599-7268
Web: www.co.logan.oh.us					
Long County 459 S McDonald St	Ludowici	GA	31316	912-545-2143	545-2150
Web: longcountyboc.com					
Lonoke County 301 N Ctr St	Lonoke	AR	72086	501-676-2368	
Web: www.lonokecircuitclerk.com					
Lorain County 225 Ct St	Elyria	OH	44035	440-329-5536	329-5404
Web: www.loraincounty.us					
Los Angeles County 500 W Temple St	Los Angeles	CA	90012	213-974-1311	680-1122
Web: www.lacounty.info					
Loudon County 100 River Road	Loudon	TN	37774	865-458-5411	
Web: www.loudoncounty.org					
Loudoun County 1 Harrison St SE PO Box 7000	Leesburg	VA	20177	703-777-0200	777-0325
Web: www.loudoun.gov					
Louisa County 1 Woolfolk Ave	Louisa	VA	23093	540-967-0401	967-3411
Web: www.louisacounty.com					
Louisville-Jefferson County 527 W Jefferson St	Louisville	KY	40202	502-574-5700	
Web: www.louisvilleky.gov					
Loup County 408 Fourth St PO Box 187	Taylor	NE	68879	308-942-6146	942-3103
Web: www.co.loup.ne.us					
Love County 405 W Main St Ste 203	Marietta	OK	73448	580-276-3059	
Web: love.okcounties.org					
Loving County 100 Bell St PO Box 194	Mentone	TX	79754	806-775-1338	
Lowndes County 505 Second Ave N	North Columbus	MS	39701	662-329-5884	
Lubbock County 904 Broadway St Rm 207	Lubbock	TX	79401	806-775-1000	775-7950
Web: www.co.lubbock.tx.us					
Lucas County 1 Government Ctr Ste 800	Toledo	OH	43604	419-213-4500	213-4532
Web: www.co.lucas.oh.us					
Luce County 407 W Harrie St	Newberry	MI	49868	906-293-5521	
Web: www.lucecountymi.org/clerk					
Lumpkin County 99 Courthouse Hill Ste A	Dahlonega	GA	30533	706-864-3742	864-4760
Web: www.lumpkincounty.gov					
Lunenburg County 11413 Courthouse Rd	Lunenburg	VA	23952	434-696-2142	
Web: www.lunenburgva.org					
Luzerne County 200 N River St	Wilkes-Barre	PA	18711	570-825-1500	825-9343
Web: www.luzernecounty.org					
Lyman County PO Box 38	Kennebec	SD	57544	605-869-2247	869-2203*
*Fax: Acctg ■ Web: www.lymancounty.org					
Lynchburg (Independent City) 900 Church St	Lynchburg	VA	24504	434-856-2489	847-1536
Web: www.lynchburgva.gov					
Lynn County PO Box 937	Tahoka	TX	79373	806-561-4750	561-4988
Web: www.co.lynn.tx.us					
Lyon County PO Box 310	Eddyville	KY	42038	270-388-2331	388-0634
Web: www.lyoncounty.ky.gov					
Mackinac County 100 S Marley St	Saint Ignace	MI	49781	906-643-7300	643-7302
Web: www.mackinaccounty.net					
Macomb County 40 N Main St 1st Fl	Mount Clemens	MI	48043	586-469-5120	
Web: www.macombcountymi.gov					
Macon County 101 E Northside St Courthouse	Tuskegee	AL	36083	334-727-5120	
Web: alabama.travel					
Macoupin County 201 E Main	Carlinville	IL	62626	217-854-3214	854-7361
Web: www.macoupincountyil.gov					
Madera County 200 W Fourth St	Madera	CA	93637	559-675-7703	673-3302
Web: www.madera-county.com					
Madison County 201 Main St	Huntsville	AR	72740	479-738-2747	
Web: madisoncogov.com					
Madison Parish 102 Burnside Dr	Tallulah	LA	71282	318-574-2206	
Web: louisiana.gov/government/parish_madison					
Magoffin County 249 Mountain Pkwy Dr PO Box 430	Salyersville	KY	41465	606-349-2313	
Web: magoffincounty.ky.gov					
Mahaska County 106 S First St Mahaska Courthouse 2nd Fl	Oskaloosa	IA	52577	641-673-7786	
Web: www.mahaskacounty.org					
Mahoning County 120 Market St	Youngstown	OH	44503	330-740-2104	740-2105
Web: www.mahoningcountyoh.gov					
Major County 500 E Broadway	Fairview	OK	73737	580-227-4665	227-3243
Malheur County 251 B St W	Vale	OR	97918	541-473-5151	473-5523
Web: www.malheurco.org					
Manassas (Independent City) 9027 Ctr St	Manassas	VA	20110	703-257-8200	335-0042
Web: www.manassascity.org					
Manassas Park (Independent City) 1 Pk Ctr Ct	Manassas Park	VA	20111	703-335-8800	335-0053
Web: www.cityofmanassaspark.us					
Manatee County 1112 Manatee Ave W	Bradenton	FL	34205	941-748-4501	
Web: www.mymanatee.org					
Manitowoc County PO Box 2000	Manitowoc	WI	54221	920-683-4030	683-2733
Web: www.co.manitowoc.wi.us					
Marathon County 500 Forest St	Wausau	WI	54403	715-261-1500	261-1515
Web: www.co.marathon.wi.us					
Marengo County County Courthouse PO Box 480715	Linden	AL	36748	334-295-2200	
Web: www.marengocountyal.com					
Maricopa County 301 W Jefferson St 10th Fl	Phoenix	AZ	85003	602-506-3415	506-6402
Web: www.maricopa.gov					
Maries County 211 Fourth St	Vienna	MO	65582	573-422-3388	
Web: mariesco.org					
Marin County 3501 Civic Ctr Dr	San Rafael	CA	94903	415-499-6450	
Web: www.marin.org					
Marinette County 1926 Hall Ave	Marinette	WI	54143	715-732-7406	732-7532
Web: www.marinettecounty.com					
Marion County 1 Courthouse Sq	Jasper	TN	37347	423-942-2552	
Web: www.marioncountychamber.com					
Mariposa County 5100 Bullion St PO Box 784	Mariposa	CA	95338	209-966-3222	966-5147
Web: www.mariposacounty.org					
Marlboro County PO Box 419	Bennettsville	SC	29512	843-479-5600	479-5639
Web: www.marlborocounty.sc.gov					
Marquette County 234 W Baraga Ave	Marquette	MI	49855	906-225-8151	225-8155
Web: www.co.marquette.mi.us					
Marshall County 520 J M Ash Dr	Holly Springs	MS	38635	662-252-3916	252-7168
Web: marshallcoms.com					
Martin County 201 Lake Ave Ste 201	Fairmont	MN	56031	507-238-3211	238-3259*
*Fax: Acctg ■ Web: co.martin.mn.us					
Martinsville (Independent City) PO Box 1112	Martinsville	VA	24114	276-403-5106	403-5280
Web: www.martinsville-va.gov					
Mason County 125 N Plum PO Box 77	Havana	IL	62644	309-543-6661	543-2085
Web: www.masoncountyil.org					
Massac County 1 Superman Sq	Metropolis	IL	62960	618-524-9359	
Web: www.state.il.us/court/circuitcourt/circuitmap/1st.asp					
Matagorda County 1700 Seventh St Rm 202	Bay City	TX	77414	979-244-7680	244-7688
Web: www.co.matagorda.tx.us					
Matanuska-Susitna Borough 350 E Dahlia Ave	Palmer	AK	99645	907-745-4801	745-9845
Web: matsugov.us					
Mathews County PO Box 463	Mathews	VA	23109	804-725-2550	725-7456
Web: co.mathews.va.us					
Maui County 200 S High St	Wailuku	HI	96793	808-270-7748	270-7171
Web: www.co.maui.hi.us					
Maury County 106 W 6th St PO Box 1076	Columbia	TN	38402	931-388-2155	
Web: www.mauryalliance.com					
Maverick County Rt 3 US Hwy 57 N PO Box 1033	Eagle Pass	TX	78852	830-773-2321	
Web: www.co.maverick.tx.us					
Mayes County 1 Ct Pl Ste 120	Pryor	OK	74361	918-825-2426	
Web: mayes.okcounties.org					
McClain County 121 N Second St PO Box 629	Purcell	OK	73080	405-527-3360	
Web: www.mcclain-co-ok.us					
McCone County 1004 C Ave PO Box 199	Circle	MT	59215	406-485-3505	485-2689
Web: www.mccone.mt.gov					
McCook County 130 W Essex PO Box 504	Salem	SD	57058	605-425-2781	425-3144
Web: www.mccookcountysd.com					
McCormick County 133 S Mine St Rm 102	McCormick	SC	29835	864-852-2231	
Web: www.mccormickcountysc.org					
McCracken County PO Box 609	Paducah	KY	42002	270-444-4700	444-4704
Web: www.countyclerk.mccrackencounty.ky.gov					
McCreary County PO Box 699	Whitley City	KY	42653	606-376-2411	376-3898
Web: www.mccrearycounty.com					
McCulloch County 199 Courthouse Sq Rm 103	Brady	TX	76825	325-597-0733	597-0606
Web: co.mcculloch.tx.us					
McCurtain County 108 N Central St	Idabel	OK	74745	580-286-2370	
Web: okcountyrecords.com					
McDonald County 602 Main St P.O. Box 606	Pineville	MO	64856	417-223-7523	223-2881
Web: www.mcdonaldcountygov.com					
McDowell County 60 E Court St	Marion	NC	28752	828-652-7121	
Web: www.mcdowellgov.com					

	City	State	ZIP	Phone	Fax
McDuffie County PO Box 158 *Web:* www.dca.state.ga.us	Thomson	GA	30824	404-679-4940	
McHenry County 407 Main St S Rm 201 *Web:* www.mchenrycountynd.com	Towner	ND	58788	701-537-5724	
McIntosh County PO Box 584 *Web:* georgia.gov	Darien	GA	31305	912-437-6671	437-6416
McKean County 500 W Main St *TF:* 800-482-1280 ■ *Web:* www.mckeancountypa.org	Smethport	PA	16749	814-887-5571	887-2242
McKenzie County PO Box 699 *TF:* 800-701-2804 ■ *Web:* county.mckenziecounty.net	Watford City	ND	58854	701-444-2804	444-3916
McKinley County 207 W Hill Ave *Web:* www.co.mckinley.nm.us	Gallup	NM	87301	505-863-6866	863-1419
McLean County 115 E Washington St Rm 102 *Web:* www.co.mclean.il.us	Bloomington	IL	61701	309-888-5190	888-5932
McLennan County 215 N Fifth St Ste 223B *Web:* www.co.mclennan.tx.us	Waco	TX	76701	254-757-5078	757-5146
McLeod County 830 11th St *Web:* www.co.mcleod.mn.us	Glencoe	MN	55336	320-864-5551	
McMinn County 5 S Hill St Ste A *Web:* mcminncountytn.gov	Athens	TN	37303	423-745-4440	744-1657
McNairy County County Courthouse 170 W Ct Ave Rm 104 *Web:* www.mcnairycountytn.com	Selmer	TN	38375	731-645-3511	646-1414
McPherson County 117 N Maple Courthouse PO Box 425 *Web:* www.mcphersoncountyks.us	McPherson	KS	67460	620-241-3656	241-1168
Meade County 516 Hillcrest Dr PO Box 614 *Web:* countyclerk.meadecounty.ky.gov	Brandenburg	KY	40108	270-422-2152	422-2158
Meagher County 15 W Main St *Web:* meaghercounty.mt.gov	White Sulphur Springs	MT	59645	406-547-3612	547-3388
Mecklenburg County 393 Washington St PO Box 307 *Web:* www.mecklenburgva.com	Boydton	VA	23917	434-738-6191	738-6861
Mecosta County 400 Elm St *Web:* www.co.mecosta.mi.us	Big Rapids	MI	49307	231-796-2505	592-0121
Medina County 1100 16th St Rm 109 *Web:* www.medinacountytexas.org	Hondo	TX	78861	830-741-6000	741-6015
Meeker County 325 N Sibley Ave *Web:* www.co.meeker.mn.us	Litchfield	MN	55355	320-693-5200	
Meigs County *Economic Development Office* 238 W Main St *Web:* www.meigscountyohio.com	Pomeroy	OH	45769	740-992-3034	992-7942
Mellette County S First & McKinley St P.O. Box 257 *Web:* ujs.sd.gov/County_Information/mellette.aspx	White River	SD	57579	605-259-3230	259-3030
Menard County 102 S Seventh St PO Box 465 *Web:* www.menardcountyil.com	Petersburg	IL	62675	217-632-2415	632-4301
Menard County Texas PO Box 1038 *Web:* www.menardtexas.com	Menard	TX	76859	325-396-4682	396-2047
Mendocino County 501 Low Gap Rd Rm 1020 *Web:* www.co.mendocino.ca.us	Ukiah	CA	95482	707-463-4376	463-4257
Menifee County Clerk PO Box 123 *Web:* www.menifeecountyclerk.com	Frenchburg	KY	40322	606-768-3512	768-6738
Menominee County PO Box 279 *Web:* www.wisconline.com/counties/menominee	Keshena	WI	54135	715-799-3311	
Merced County 2222 M St *Web:* www.co.merced.ca.us	Merced	CA	95340	209-385-7637	385-7375
Mercer County 109 Courthouse *Web:* www.mcc.co.mercer.pa.us	Mercer	PA	16137	724-662-7548	
Meriwether County PO Box 428 *Web:* meriwethercountyga.gov	Greenville	GA	30222	706-672-1314	
Merrick County PO Box 27 *Web:* www.merrickcounty.ne.gov	Central City	NE	68826	308-946-2881	946-2332
Mesa County PO Box 20000 *Web:* www.mesacounty.us	Grand Junction	CO	81502	970-244-1800	256-1588
Metcalfe County 100 E Stockton Ste 1 *Web:* www.metcalfecountyclerk.com	Edmonton	KY	42129	270-432-4821	
Miami County 201 S Pearl St Ste 102 *Web:* www.miamicountyks.org	Paola	KS	66071	913-294-3976	294-9544
Miami-Dade County 111 NW First St Ste 220 *Web:* www.miamidade.gov	Miami	FL	33128	305-375-5924	
Middlesex County 56 Paterson St *Web:* www.judiciary.state.nj.us	New Brunswick	NJ	08901	732-519-3200	
Judicial Department Small Claims 1 Ct St *Web:* www.jud.ct.gov/	Middletown	CT	06457	860-756-7800	343-6423
Midland County 220 W Ellsworth St *Web:* www.co.midland.mi.us	Midland	MI	48640	989-832-6739	832-6680
Mifflin County 20 N Wayne St *Web:* www.co.mifflin.pa.us	Lewistown	PA	17044	717-248-6733	248-3695
Milam County 107 W Main St *Web:* www.milamcounty.net	Cameron	TX	76520	254-697-7049	697-7055
Millard County 765 S Hwy 99 Ste 6 *Web:* www.millardcounty.com	Fillmore	UT	84631	435-743-5227	743-6923
Mille Lacs County 635 Second St SE *Web:* www.co.mille-lacs.mn.us	Milaca	MN	56353	320-983-8313	983-8384
Miller County 400 Laurel St Rm 105 *Web:* www.millercountyar.org	Texarkana	AR	71854	870-774-1501	
Mills County 418 Sharp St County Courthouse *Web:* www.millscoia.us	Glenwood	IA	51534	712-527-4880	
Milwaukee County 901 N Ninth St *Web:* county.milwaukee.gov	Milwaukee	WI	53233	414-278-4067	223-1379
Miner County 217 S Main St PO Box 129 *Web:* www.minercountybank.com	Howard	SD	57349	605-772-4561	
Mineral County 1201 N Main St PO Box 70 *Web:* www.mineralcountycolorado.com	Creede	CO	81130	719-658-2575	658-2764
Mingo County 75 E 2nd Ave *Web:* mingocountywv.com	Williamson	WV	25661	304-235-0378	
Minidoka County 715 G St PO Box 368 *Web:* www.minidoka.id.us	Rupert	ID	83350	208-436-7111	436-0737
Minnehaha County 415 N Dakota Ave *Web:* www.minnehahacounty.org	Sioux Falls	SD	57104	605-367-4206	367-8314
Missaukee County 111 S Canal PO Box 800 *Web:* www.missaukee.org	Lake City	MI	49651	231-839-4967	839-3684
Mississippi County 200 W Walnut St Rm 204 *Web:* www.mcagov.com/	Blytheville	AR	72315	870-763-3212	838-7784
Missoula County 200 W Broadway St *Web:* www.co.missoula.mt.us	Missoula	MT	59802	406-721-5700	258-4899
Mitchell County 26 Crimson Laurel Cir # 5 *Web:* www.mitchellcounty.org	Bakersville	NC	28705	828-688-2139	688-4443
Mobile County 205 Government St *Web:* www.mobilecountyal.gov	Mobile	AL	36644	251-574-5077	
Modoc County 204 S Ct St PO Box 131 *Web:* www.co.modoc.ca.us	Alturas	CA	96101	530-233-6201	233-2434
Moffat County 221 W Victory Way *Web:* colorado.gov/cs/satellite/cnty-moffat/cbon/1251574649345	Craig	CO	81625	970-824-9104	824-0351
Mohave County PO Box 7000 *Web:* www.mohavecounty.us	Kingman	AZ	86402	928-753-0729	753-5103
Moniteau County 200 E Main St *Web:* moniteau.countycriminal.com	California	MO	65018	573-796-4661	
Monmouth County 1 E Main St *Web:* www.visitmonmouth.com	Freehold	NJ	07728	732-431-7324	409-7566
Mono County PO Box 237 *Web:* www.monocounty.ca.gov	Bridgeport	CA	93517	760-932-5530	932-5531
Monona County 610 Iowa Ave *Web:* www.mononacounty.org/	Onawa	IA	51040	712-423-2491	423-2744
Monongalia County 243 High St Rm 123 *Web:* www.co.monongalia.wv.us	Morgantown	WV	26505	304-291-7230	
Monroe County 124 W Commerce St *Web:* www.gomonroe.org	Aberdeen	MS	39730	662-369-6488	369-6489
Montague County PO Box 77 *Web:* www.co.montague.tx.us	Montague	TX	76251	940-894-2461	894-3110
Montcalm County PO Box 368 *Web:* montcalm.org	Stanton	MI	48888	989-831-7339	831-7474
Monterey County 168 W Alisal St *Web:* www.co.monterey.ca.us	Salinas	CA	93901	831-755-5115	757-5792
Montezuma County 601 N Mildred Rd *Web:* www.co.montezuma.co.us	Cortez	CO	81321	970-565-8317	565-3420
Montgomery County 755 Roanoke St Ste 2E *Web:* www.montva.com	Christiansburg	VA	24073	540-382-6954	382-6943
Montmorency County PO Box 789 *Web:* montmorencycountymichigan.us	Atlanta	MI	49709	989-785-8013	785-8014
Montour County 29 Mill St *Web:* www.montourco.org	Danville	PA	17821	570-271-3010	271-3089
Montrose County 161 S Townsend *Web:* www.co.montrose.co.us	Montrose	CO	81401	970-249-3362	249-7761
Moody County 101 E Pipestone Ave *Web:* moodycounty.net	Flandreau	SD	57028	605-997-3181	
Moore County PO Box 905 *Web:* www.co.moore.nc.us	Carthage	NC	28327	910-947-6363	947-1874
Morehouse Parish 100 E Madison Ave *Web:* 4jdc.com	Bastrop	LA	71221	318-281-3343	281-3775
Morgan County 77 Fairfax St Rm 102 *Web:* www.morgancountywv.gov	Berkeley Springs	WV	25411	304-258-8547	258-8545
Morrill County 606 L St *Web:* www.co.morrill.ne.us	Bridgeport	NE	69336	308-262-0860	262-1469
Morris County 501 W Main St	Council Grove	KS	66846	620-767-5518	
Morrison County 213 SE First Ave *TF:* 866-401-1111 ■ *Web:* www.co.morrison.mn.us	Little Falls	MN	56345	320-632-2941	
Morrow County 100 Ct St PO Box 788 *Web:* morrowcountyoregon.com	Heppner	OR	97836	541-676-9061	676-9876
Morton County PO Box 1116 *Web:* www.mtcoks.com	Elkhart	KS	67950	620-697-2157	697-2159
Motley County *Judges Office* 701 Dundee Ave	Matador	TX	79244	806-347-2334	347-2072
Moultrie County County Courthouse 10 S Main St, Ste 6 *Web:* moultriecountyil.com	Sullivan	IL	61951	217-728-4389	728-8178
Mountrail County 101 N Main St *Web:* www.co.mountrail.nd.us	Stanley	ND	58784	701-627-4835	
Mower County 201 First St NE *Web:* www.co.mower.mn.us	Austin	MN	55912	507-437-9535	437-9471
Muhlenberg County PO Box 137 *Web:* www.muhlenbergcounty.ky.gov	Greenville	KY	42345	270-338-2520	338-6116
Multnomah County 1221 SW Fourth Ave *Web:* multco.us/	Portland	OR	97204	503-823-4000	
Murray County PO Box 1129 *Web:* www.murraycountyga.org	Chatsworth	GA	30705	706-695-2413	695-8721
Muscatine County 401 E Third St *Web:* www.co.muscatine.ia.us	Muscatine	IA	52761	563-263-5821	263-7248
Muskegon County 990 Terrace St *Web:* www.co.muskegon.mi.us	Muskegon	MI	49442	231-724-6520	724-6673
Muskingum County 401 Main St *Web:* www.muskingumcounty.org	Zanesville	OH	43701	740-455-7104	
Muskogee County 229 W Okmulgee Ave *Web:* www.cityofmuskogee.com	Muskogee	OK	74401	918-682-6602	
Musselshell County 506 Main St *Web:* musselshellcounty.org/	Roundup	MT	59072	406-323-1104	
Nacogdoches County 101 W Main St Rm 205 *Web:* co.nacogdoches.tx.us	Nacogdoches	TX	75961	936-560-7733	559-5926
Nance County 209 Esther St PO Box 338 *Web:* www.co.nance.ne.us	Fullerton	NE	68638	308-536-2331	536-2742
Nantucket County 16 Broad St *Web:* www.nantucket-ma.gov	Nantucket	MA	02554	508-228-7216	325-5313
Napa County 1195 Third St Ste 310 *Web:* www.countyofnapa.org	Napa	CA	94559	707-253-4421	253-4176
Nash County 120 W Washington St Ste 3072 *Web:* www.co.nash.nc.us	Nashville	NC	27856	252-459-9800	459-9817
Nassau County PO Box 870 *TF:* 888-615-4398 ■ *Web:* www.nassauflpa.com	Fernandina Beach	FL	32035	904-491-7300	491-3629

Phone Fax

Natchitoches Parish
200 Church St Ste 210 ... Natchitoches LA 71457 318-352-2714
Web: www.nppj.org

Natrona County 200 N Ctr St ... Casper WY 82601 307-235-9200
Web: www.natronacounty-wy.gov

Navajo County
100 E Code Talkers Dr PO Box 668 ... Holbrook AZ 86025 928-524-4000 524-4261
Web: www.navajocountyaz.gov

Navarro County PO Box 423 ... Corsicana TX 75151 903-654-3040 654-3097
Web: www.co.navarro.tx.us

Nelson County 210 B Ave W Ste 203 ... Lakota ND 58344 701-247-2462
Web: nelsonco.org

Nemaha County 607 Nemaha ... Seneca KS 66538 5-3-36--3502 -33-6-3765*
**Fax Area Code: 785* ■ *Web:* ks-nemaha.manatron.com

Neosho County 100S Main St Rm 104 PO Box 138 ... Erie KS 66733 620-244-3858 244-3860
Web: www.neoshocountyks.org

Neshoba County 401 Beacon St Ste 107 ... Philadelphia MS 39350 601-656-3581 656-5915
Web: www.neshoba.org

Ness County 102 W Main PO Box 262 ... Ness City KS 67560 785-798-2413
Web: www.nesscountychamber.com

Nevada County 950 Maidu Ave ... Nevada City CA 95959 530-265-1218
Web: www.mynevadacounty.com

Nevada County Depot & Museum
403 W First St S PO Box 592 ... Prescott AR 71857 870-887-5821
Web: www.depotmuseum.org

New Kent County
12001 Courthouse Cir PO Box 98 ... New Kent VA 23124 804-966-9520 966-9528
Web: www.co.new-kent.va.us

New York County 60 Centre St ... New York NY 10007 646-386-5955 374-5790*
**Fax Area Code: 212* ■ *Web:* www.nyc.gov

Newaygo County 1087 Newell St ... White Cloud MI 49349 231-689-7200 689-7205
Web: www.countyofnewaygo.com

Newberry County 1226 College St PO Box 10 ... Newberry SC 29108 803-321-2110 321-2111
Web: www.newberrycounty.net

Newport County 45 Washington Sq ... Newport RI 02840 401-841-8330 846-1673
Web: www.courts.ri.gov

Newport News (Independent City)
2400 Washington Ave ... Newport News VA 23607 757-926-8411 926-3503
Web: nngov.com

Newton County 1124 Clark St ... Covington GA 30014 678-625-1202
Web: www.co.newton.ga.us

Nez Perce County 1230 Main St PO Box 896 ... Lewiston ID 83501 208-799-3020 799-3070
Web: www.co.nezperce.id.us

Niagara County PO Box 461 ... Lockport NY 14095 716-439-7022 439-7066
Web: www.niagaracounty.com

Nicholas County PO Box 227 ... Carlisle KY 40311 859-289-3730
Web: www.carlisle-nicholascounty.org
Commission 700 Main St Suite 1 ... Summersville WV 26651 304-872-7830 872-7863
Web: www.nicholascountywv.org

Nicollet County 501 S Minnesota Ave ... Saint Peter MN 56082 507-931-6800 931-9220
Web: www.co.nicollet.mn.us

Niobrara County PO Box 420 ... Lusk WY 82225 307-334-2211 334-3013
Web: www.county-clerk.net/countyclerk.asp?state=Wyoming&county=Niobrara

Noble County 101 N Orange St ... Albion IN 46701 260-636-2736 636-4000
Web: www.nobleco.org

Nobles County 1530 Airport Rd ... Worthington MN 56187 507-372-8263 372-4994
Web: www.co.nobles.mn.us

Nodaway County 403 N Market PO Box 218 ... Maryville MO 64468 660-582-2251 582-5282
Web: nodawaycountymo.com

Nolan County 100 E Third St Ste 108 ... Sweetwater TX 79556 325-235-2462 236-9416
Web: www.co.nolan.tx.us

Norfolk County 614 High St ... Dedham MA 02026 781-461-6105 326-6480
Web: www.norfolkcounty.org

Norfolk (Independent City)
810 Union St Rm 1101 ... Norfolk VA 23510 757-664-4242 664-4239
Web: www.norfolk.gov

Norman County 16 Third Ave E PO Box 146 ... Ada MN 56510 218-784-5473 784-4531
Web: www.co.norman.mn.us

North Slope Borough PO Box 69 ... Barrow AK 99723 907-852-2611 852-0229
Web: www.co.north-slope.ak.us

Northampton County 669 Washington St ... Easton PA 18042 610-559-6700
Web: www.northamptoncounty.org

Northumberland County PO Box 217 ... Heathsville VA 22473 804-580-3700 580-2261
Web: www.co.northumberland.va.us

Northwest Arctic Borough PO Box 1110 ... Kotzebue AK 99752 907-442-2500 442-2930
Web: www.nwabor.org

Norton County 105 S Kansas PO Box 70 ... Norton KS 67654 785-877-5710 877-5794
Web: www.nortoncounty.net

Norton (Independent City)
618 Virginia Ave PO Box 618 ... Norton VA 24273 276-679-1160 679-3510
Web: www.nortonva.org

Nottoway County 344 W Ct House Rd PO Box 92 ... Nottoway VA 23955 434-645-8696 645-8667
Web: www.nottoway.org

Nowata County 229 N Maple St ... Nowata OK 74048 918-273-0175 273-1936

Noxubee County 503 S Washington St PO Box 308 ... Macon MS 39341 800-487-0165
TF: 800-487-0165 ■ *Web:* noxubeecountyms.com

Nuckolls County PO Box 366 ... Nelson NE 68961 402-225-4361 225-4301
Web: www.nuckollscounty.ne.gov

Nueces County 901 Leopard St Ste 201 ... Corpus Christi TX 78401 361-888-0459 888-0329
Web: www.co.nueces.tx.us

Nye County PO Box 1031 ... Tonopah NV 89049 775-482-8127 482-8133
Web: www.co.nye.nv.us

O'Brien County PO Box 340 ... Primghar IA 51245 712-957-3045 957-3046
Web: www.obriencounty.com

Obion County 1604B W Reelfoot Ave ... Union City TN 38261 731-884-2133 884-2719
Web: www.tn.gov

Ocean County 118 Washington St ... Toms River NJ 08753 732-929-2018 349-4336
Web: www.co.ocean.nj.us

Oceana County 100 State St Ste 1 ... Hart MI 49420 231-873-4328 873-1391
Web: www.oceana.mi.us

Phone Fax

Ochiltree County 511 S Main St ... Perryton TX 79070 806-435-8039 435-2081
Web: www.co.ochiltree.tx.us

Oconee County 415 S Pine St PO Box 678 ... Walhalla SC 29691 864-638-4280 638-4280
Web: www.oconeesc.com

Oconto County 301 Washington St ... Oconto WI 54153 920-834-6800 834-6867
Web: www.co.oconto.wi.us

Ogemaw County 806 W Houghton Ave ... West Branch MI 48661 989-345-0215 345-7223
Web: www.ogemawcountymi.gov/hours.php

Ogle County 105 S 5th St ... Oregon IL 61061 815-732-3201 732-6273
Web: www.oglecounty.org

Oglethorpe County 341 W Main St ... Lexington GA 30648 706-743-5270 743-8371
Web: onlineoglethorpe.com

Ohio County 413 Main St PO Box 185 ... Rising Sun IN 47040 812-438-2610 438-1215

Okaloosa County 101 E James Lee Blvd ... Crestview FL 32536 850-689-5000 689-5818
Web: www.co.okaloosa.fl.us

Okanogan County 149 N Third Ave PO Box 980 ... Okanogan WA 98840 509-422-7170 422-7174
Web: www.okanogancounty.org

Okeechobee County 304 NW Second St ... Okeechobee FL 34972 863-763-6441 763-9529
Web: www.co.okeechobee.fl.us

Oklahoma County 320 Robert S Kerr Ave ... Oklahoma City OK 73102 405-270-0082
Web: www.oklahomacounty.org

Okmulgee County 314 W Seventh St ... Okmulgee OK 74447 918-756-3042
Web: www.okgenweb.org/~okokmulg

Oktibbeha County 101 E Main St ... Starkville MS 39759 662-323-5834
Web: www.gtpdd.com/counties/oktibbeha

Oldham County 100 W Jefferson St ... LaGrange KY 40031 502-222-1476 222-3210
Web: www.oldhamcounty.net

Oliver County 115 W Main ... Center ND 58530 701-794-8777 794-3476
Web: ndcourts.gov

Oneida County 800 Pk Ave ... Utica NY 13501 315-798-5054
Web: kidsoneida.org

Onondaga County 401 Montgomery St ... Syracuse NY 13202 315-435-2226 435-3455
Web: www.ongov.net

Onslow County 4024 Richland Hwy ... Jacksonville NC 28540 910-347-4717 455-7878
Web: onslowcountync.gov

Ontario County 20 Ontario St ... Canandaigua NY 14424 585-396-4200 393-2951
Web: www.co.ontario.ny.us

Ontonagon County 725 Greenland Rd ... Ontonagon MI 49953 906-884-4155 884-2916

Orange County 5 Ct St ... Chelsea VT 05038 802-685-4610 685-3246
Web: orange.countycriminal.com

Orangeburg County 1406 Amelia St ... Orangeburg SC 29118 803-533-6263 534-3848
Web: www.orangeburgcounty.org

Oregon County PO Box 324 ... Alton MO 65606 417-778-7475

Orleans County 247 Main St ... Newport VT 05855 802-334-3344 334-3385
Web: orleans.countycriminal.com/

Orleans Parish 839 St Charles Ave Ste 305 ... New Orleans LA 70130 504-309-1004
Web: www.neworleans.com

Osage County 205 E Main St ... Linn MO 65051 573-897-2139
Web: www.osagecountyhd.org

Osborne County PO Box 160 ... Osborne KS 67473 785-346-2431 346-5252
Web: www.osbornecounty.org

Osceola County 1 Courthouse Sq ... Kissimmee FL 34741 407-343-3500
Web: www.osceola.org

Oscoda County PO Box 399 ... Mio MI 48647 989-826-1109 826-1136
Web: www.oscodacountymi.com

Oswego County 46 E Bridge St ... Oswego NY 13126 315-349-8235 349-8237
Web: www.co.oswego.ny.us

Otero County 1000 New York Ave Ste 109 ... Alamogordo NM 88310 575-434-8849 443-2941
Web: www.co.otero.nm.us

Otoe County PO Box 726 ... Nebraska City NE 68410 402-873-9500
Web: www.co.otoe.ne.us

Otsego County 197 Main St ... Cooperstown NY 13326 607-547-4202 547-4260
Web: www.otsegocounty.com

Ottawa County 102 E Central Ave Ste 203 ... Miami OK 74354 918-673-1100

Otter Tail County 520 Fir Ave W ... Fergus Falls MN 56537 218-998-8000 998-8438
Web: www.co.ottertail.mn.us

Ouachita County 109 Goodgame St ... Camden AR 71701 870-231-5300 231-4329
Web: www.ouachitacountysheriff.org

Ouachita Parish 301 South Grand St Ste 104 ... Monroe LA 71201 318-327-1444 327-1462
Web: www.opclerkofcourt.com

Ouray County 541 Fourth St PO Box C ... Ouray CO 81427 970-325-4961 325-0452
Web: www.ouraycountyco.gov

Outagamie County 410 S Walnut St ... Appleton WI 54911 920-832-5077 832-2200
Web: www.outagamie.org

Overton County 317 E University St Rm 22 ... Livingston TN 38570 931-823-2631 823-2696
Web: www.overtoncountytn.com

Owen County
60 S Main St County Courthouse Fl 1 Rm 100 ... Spencer IN 47460 812-829-5030
Web: www.owencounty.in.gov

Owsley County PO Box 500 ... Booneville KY 41314 606-593-5735 593-5737
Web: www.owsleycountykentucky.org

Owyhee County PO Box 128 ... Murphy ID 83650 208-495-2421 495-1173
Web: www.owyheecounty.net

Oxford County 26 Western Ave PO Box 179 ... South Paris ME 04281 207-743-6359 743-1545
Web: www.oxfordcounty.org

Ozark County 361 Main St PO Box 605 ... Gainesville MO 65655 417-679-4913
Web: www.ozarkcounty.net/

Ozaukee County PO Box 994 ... Port Washington WI 53074 262-284-8110 284-8100
Web: www.co.ozaukee.wi.us

Pacific County PO Box 67 ... South Bend WA 98586 360-875-9300
Web: www.co.pacific.wa.us

Page County 112 E Main St ... Clarinda IA 51632 712-542-2516 542-6005
Web: www.co.page.ia.us

Palm Beach County 301 N Olive Ave ... West Palm Beach FL 33401 561-355-2001 355-3990
Web: www.co.palm-beach.fl.us

Palo Pinto County PO Box 219 ... Palo Pinto TX 76484 940-659-1277
Web: www.co.palo-pinto.tx.us

Pamlico County PO Box 776 ... Bayboro NC 28515 252-745-3133 745-5514
Web: www.co.pamlico.nc.us

Panola County 110 Sycamore St Rm 201 ... Carthage TX 75633 903-693-0302
Web: www.carthagetexas.com

				Phone	Fax
Park County 1002 Sheridan Ave *TF:* 800-786-2844 ■ *Web:* www.parkcounty.us	Cody	WY	82414	307-527-8510	527-8515
Parke County 116 W High St Rm 204 *Web:* www.parkecounty-in.gov	Rockville	IN	47872	765-569-5132	
Parker County 1112 Santa Fe Dr *Web:* parkercountytx.com/	Weatherford	TX	76086	817-594-7461	
Parmer County 401 3rd Street *Web:* www.co.parmer.tx.us	Farwell	TX	79325	806-481-3691	481-9548
Pasco County 7530 Little Rd *Web:* www.pascocountyfl.net	New Port Richey	FL	34654	727-847-2411	847-8969
Pasquotank County PO Box 39 *Web:* www.co.pasquotank.nc.us	Elizabeth City	NC	27907	252-335-0865	335-0866
Passaic County 401 Grand St *Web:* www.passaiccountynj.org	Paterson	NJ	07505	973-225-3632	754-1920
Patrick County 106 Rucker Street PO Box 466 *Web:* www.co.patrick.va.us	Stuart	VA	24171	276-694-6094	694-2160
Paulding County 240 Constitution Blvd. *Web:* www.paulding.gov	Dallas	GA	30132	770-443-7550	443-7537
Pawnee County 715 Broadway *Web:* www.pawneecountykansas.com	Larned	KS	67550	620-285-3721	285-2559
Payette County 1130 Third Ave N Rm 104 *Web:* www.payettecounty.org	Payette	ID	83661	208-642-6000	642-6011
Payne County 315 W Sixth St Ste 202 *Web:* www.paynecounty.org	Stillwater	OK	74074	405-747-8310	747-8304
Peach County 205 W Church St *Web:* www.peachcounty.net	Fort Valley	GA	31030	478-825-2535	825-2678
Pearl River County 200 S Main St PO Box 431 *Web:* www.pearlrivercounty.net	Poplarville	MS	39470	601-403-2300	
Pecos County 103 W Callaghan St *Web:* www.co.pecos.tx.us	Fort Stockton	TX	79735	432-336-7555	336-7557
Pembina County 301 Dakota St W Ste 1 *Web:* www.pembinacountynd.gov	Cavalier	ND	58220	701-265-4231	265-4876
Pemiscot County 610 Ward Ave *Web:* www.courts.mo.gov	Caruthersville	MO	63830	573-333-0187	333-4157
Pend Oreille County 229 S Garden Ave *Web:* www.pendoreilleco.org	Newport	WA	99156	509-447-2435	447-2734
Pender County PO Box 5 *Web:* www.pendercountync.gov	Burgaw	NC	28425	910-259-1200	259-1402
Pendleton County 233 Main St *Web:* pendletoncounty.ky.gov	Falmouth	KY	41040	859-654-4321	654-5047
Pennington County 315 St Joseph St *Web:* pennco.org/	Rapid City	SD	57701	605-394-2171	
Penobscot County 97 Hammond St *Web:* www.penobscot-county.net	Bangor	ME	04401	207-942-8535	
Peoria County 324 Main St Rm 101 *Web:* www.co.peoria.il.us	Peoria	IL	61602	309-672-6059	672-6054
Pepin County 740 Seventh Ave W *Web:* www.co.pepin.wi.us	Durand	WI	54736	715-672-8857	672-8677
Perkins County 100 E Main St P.O. Box 426 *Web:* ujs.sd.gov/County_Information/perkins.aspx	Bison	SD	57620	605-244-5626	244-7110
Perquimans County PO Box 45 *Web:* www.co.perquimans.nc.us	Hertford	NC	27944	252-426-8484	426-4034
Perry County 333 7th St *TF:* 888-343-6262 ■ *Web:* www.perrycountyindiana.org	Tell City	IN	47586	812-547-7933	547-8378
Pershing County 398 Main St PO Box 820 *Web:* www.pershingcounty.net	Lovelock	NV	89419	775-273-2208	273-3015
Person County 304 S Morgan St Rm 212 *Web:* www.personcounty.net	Roxboro	NC	27573	336-597-1720	599-1609
Petersburg (Independent City) 135 N Union St Ste 202 *Web:* www.petersburg-va.org	Petersburg	VA	23803	804-733-2301	
Petroleum County 302 E Main PO Box 226 *Web:* www.petroleumcountymt.com	Winnett	MT	59087	406-429-5311	429-6328
Pettis County 415 S Ohio *Web:* www.pettiscomo.com	Sedalia	MO	65301	660-826-5000	
Phelps County PO Box 404 *Web:* www.phelpsgov.org	Holdrege	NE	68949	308-995-4469	995-4368
Philadelphia County City Hall Broad & Market St *Web:* phila.gov	Philadelphia	PA	19107	215-686-1776	567-7380
Phillips County 101/2 S 4th E PO Box 1637 *Web:* www.maltachamber.com/	Malta	MT	59538	406-654-1776	654-1776
Piatt County 101 W Washington St *Web:* www.piattcounty.org	Monticello	IL	61856	217-762-9487	762-7563
Pickaway County 139 W Franklin St *Web:* www.pickaway.org	Circleville	OH	43113	740-474-6093	474-8988
Pickens County 1266 E Church St *Web:* pickenscountyga.gov	Jasper	GA	30143	706-253-8809	
Pickett County 1 Courthouse Sq Ste 200 *TF:* 888-406-4704 ■ *Web:* dalehollow.com/info-resources/government	Byrdstown	TN	38549	931-864-3798	864-6615
Pierce County PO Box 679 *Web:* www.piercecountyga.org	Blackshear	GA	31516	912-449-2022	449-2024
Pike County PO Box 219	Murfreesboro	AR	71958	870-285-2231	
Pima County 130 W Congress St 10th Fl *Web:* webcms.pima.gov	Tucson	AZ	85701	520-740-8661	740-8171
Pinal County 31 N Pinal St *Web:* pinalcountyaz.gov	Florence	AZ	85232	520-866-6000	866-6512
Pine County 635 Northridge Dr NW *TF:* 800-450-7463 ■ *Web:* www.co.pine.mn.us	Pine City	MN	55063	320-591-1400	
Pinellas County 315 Ct St Rm 601 *Web:* www.pinellascounty.org	Clearwater	FL	33756	727-464-3485	464-4384
Pipestone County 416 S Hiawatha Ave *Fax: Acctg ■ *Web:* www.mncounties.org	Pipestone	MN	56164	507-825-6740	*
Piscataquis County 50 Mayo St *Web:* www.pcedc.org	Dover-Foxcroft	ME	04426	207-564-3638	
Pitkin County 530 E Main St Ste 101 *Web:* pitkinclerk.org	Aspen	CO	81611	970-920-5180	
Pitt County 1717 W Fifth St *Web:* www.pittcountync.gov	Greenville	NC	27834	252-902-2950	830-6311
Pittsburg County 115 E Carl Albert Pkwy *Web:* pittsburg.okcountytreasurers.com	McAlester	OK	74501	918-423-6895	423-7379
Pittsylvania County 1 Center St PO Box 426 *Web:* www.pittgov.org	Chatham	VA	24531	434-432-7700	
Piute County 550 N Main *Web:* www.piute.org	Junction	UT	84740	435-577-2840	577-2433
Placer County 2954 Richardson Dr *Web:* www.placer.ca.gov	Auburn	CA	95603	530-886-5600	886-5687
Plaquemines Parish 301 Main St *Web:* www.plaqueminesparish.com	Belle Chasse	LA	70037	504-391-1878	
Platte County 2610 14th St *Web:* www.plattecounty.net	Columbus	NE	68601	402-563-4904	564-4164
Pleasants County 301 Ct Ln	Saint Marys	WV	26170	304-684-7882	
Plumas County 520 Main St Rm 104 *Web:* www.countyofplumas.com	Quincy	CA	95971	530-283-6155	283-6415
Plymouth County 215 Fourth Ave SE *Fax: Acctg ■ *Web:* www.co.plymouth.ia.us	Le Mars	IA	51031	712-546-6100	546-5784*
Pocahontas County PO Box 275 *TF:* 800-336-7009 ■ *Web:* www.pocahontascountywv.com	Marlinton	WV	24954	800-336-7009	
Poinsett County 1500 Justice Dr *Web:* www.poinsettcountysheriff.org	Harrisburg	AR	72432	870-578-5411	578-4417
Pointe Coupee Parish 201 E Main St *Web:* laclerksofcourt.org	New Roads	LA	70760	225-638-9596	
Polk County 100 Polk County Plaza Ste 110 *Web:* www.co.polk.wi.us	Balsam Lake	WI	54810	715-485-9226	485-9104
Pondera County 20 Fourth Ave SW *Web:* www.ponderacountymontana.org	Conrad	MT	59425	406-271-4000	271-4070
Pontotoc County 301 S Broadway Ave	Ada	OK	74820	580-332-1425	
Pope County 130 E Minnesota Ave *Fax: Acctg ■ *Web:* www.mncounties.org	Glenwood	MN	56334	320-634-5727	*
Poquoson (Independent City) 500 City Hall Ave *Web:* www.ci.poquoson.va.us	Poquoson	VA	23662	757-868-3000	868-3101
Portage County 449 S Meridian St 7th Fl *TF:* 800-772-3799 ■ *Web:* www.co.portage.oh.us	Ravenna	OH	44266	330-297-3600	297-3610
Porter County 155 Indiana Ave *Web:* porterco.org	Valparaiso	IN	46383	219-465-3445	465-3592
Posey County 126 E Third St Rm 132 *Fax Area Code: 812	Mount Vernon	IN	47620	2-8-38--1300	-83-8-1344*
Pottawatomie County 325 N Broadway *Web:* www.pottcoso.com	Shawnee	OK	74801	405-273-1727	
Potter County 900 S Polk St Rm 418 PO Box 9638 *Web:* www.co.potter.tx.us	Amarillo	TX	79105	806-379-2275	379-2296
Powder River County PO Box 270 *Web:* prco.mt.gov/	Broadus	MT	59317	406-436-2361	436-2151
Powell County 409 Missouri Ave *Web:* www.powellcountymontana.com	Deer Lodge	MT	59722	406-846-3680	
Power County 543 Bannock Ave *Web:* www.co.power.id.us	American Falls	ID	83211	208-226-7610	
Poweshiek County PO Box 218 *Web:* www.poweshiekcounty.org	Montezuma	IA	50171	641-623-5644	
Powhatan County 3880 Old Buckingham Rd Ste C PO Box 37 *Web:* www.powhatanva.com	Powhatan	VA	23139	804-598-5660	598-5608
Prairie County 200 Ct House Sq Ste 101 Ste 101 *Web:* prairiecountysheriff.org	Des Arc	AR	72040	870-256-4137	
Pratt County *Pratt County Court House* 300 S Ninnescah *Web:* www.prattcounty.org	Pratt	KS	67124	620-672-4112	672-9541
Preble County 101 E Main St *Web:* www.prebco.org	Eaton	OH	45320	937-456-8143	456-8114
Prentiss County 1901-B E Chambers *Web:* prentisscountysheriff.com	Booneville	MS	38829	662-728-6232	
Presidio County 301 Highland St *Web:* www.txdmv.gov/	Marfa	TX	79843	432-729-4081	729-4920
Presque Isle County PO Box 110 *Web:* www.presqueislecounty.org	Rogers City	MI	49779	989-734-3810	734-7635
Price County 126 Cherry St *Web:* www.co.price.wi.us	Phillips	WI	54555	715-339-3325	339-3089
Prince Edward County 111 S St Second Fl PO Box 304 *Web:* www.co.prince-edward.va.us	Farmville	VA	23901	434-392-5145	392-3913
Prince George County 6602 Courts Dr PO Box 68 *Web:* www.princegeorgeva.org/	Prince George	VA	23875	804-722-8669	732-1967
Prince George's County 14741 Governor Oden Bowie Dr *Web:* www.princegeorgescountymd.gov	Upper Marlboro	MD	20772	301-952-3600	
Prince William County 1 County Complex Ct	Woodbridge	VA	22192	703-792-6000	
Providence County 1 Dorrance Plaza *Web:* www.courts.ri.gov	Providence	RI	02903	401-458-5400	
Pueblo County 215 W Tenth St *Web:* pueblo.org	Pueblo	CO	81003	719-583-6000	583-4894
Pulaski County 112 E Main St Rm 230	Winamac	IN	46996	4-9-46--3561	
Pushmataha County 302 SW B St *Web:* www.usgennet.org	Antlers	OK	74523	580-298-2512	
Putnam County 40 Gleneida Ave Rm 100 *Web:* www.putnamcountyny.com	Carmel	NY	10512	845-225-3641	228-0231
Putnam County Commissioners 245 E Main St Ste 101 *Web:* www.putnamcountyohio.com	Ottawa	OH	45875	419-523-3656	
Quay County PO Box 1246 *Fax Area Code: 505 ■ *Web:* www.quaycounty-nm.gov	Tucumcari	NM	88401	575-461-2112	461-6208*
Queen Anne's County 107 N Liberty St *Web:* www.qactv.com	Centreville	MD	21617	410-758-4098	758-1170
Queens County 120-55 Queens Blvd *Web:* www.queensda.org	Kew Gardens	NY	11415	718-286-6000	
Quitman County PO Box 582 *Web:* www.qpublic.net	Georgetown	GA	39854	229-334-2159	334-2158
Rabun County 25 Courthouse Sq Ste 201 *Web:* www.gamountains.com	Clayton	GA	30525	706-782-5271	

Phone | Fax

Racine County 730 Wisconsin Ave — Racine WI 53403 — 262-636-3121 636-3491
Web: www.racineco.com
Radford (Independent City) 619 Second St. — Radford VA 24141 — 540-731-3603 731-3699
Web: www.radford.va.us
Raleigh County 215 Main St — Beckley WV 25801 — 304-255-9178 255-9111
Web: raleighcountyassessor.com
Ralls County 311 S Main St PO Box 466 — New London MO 63459 — 573-985-5633 985-3446
Web: www.courts.mo.gov/
Ramsey County 524 Fourth Ave Rm 4 — Devils Lake ND 58301 — 701-662-7001
Web: www.co.ramsey.nd.us
Randall County PO Box 660 — Canyon TX 79015 — 806-468-5505
Web: www.randallcounty.org
Randolph County 1 Taylor St — Chester IL 62233 — 8-8-26--5000 -82-6-3761*
*Fax Area Code: 618 ■ *Web:* randolphcountyclerk.com
Rankin County 211 E Government St Ste A — Brandon MS 39042 — 601-825-1475 825-9600
Web: business.rankinchamber.com
Ransom County 204 5th Ave W PO Box 626 — Lisbon ND 58054 — 701-683-6120 683-5826
Web: ransomcountynd.com
Rapides Parish PO Box 952 — Alexandria LA 71309 — 318-473-8153 473-4667
Web: rapidesclerk.org
Rappahannock County 290 Gay St PO Box 519 — Washington VA 22747 — 540-675-5330 675-5331
Web: www.rappahannockcountyva.gov
Ravalli County 215 S Fourth St Ste C — Hamilton MT 59840 — 406-375-6212 375-6595
Web: ravalli.us
Rawlins County 607 Main St — Atwood KS 67730 — 785-626-3351
Web: www.rawlinscounty.info
Ray County 100 W Main St County Courthouse — Richmond MO 64085 — 816-776-4502 776-4512
Web: raycountycourthouse.com
Reagan County 3rd St — Big Lake TX 76932 — 325-884-2442
Real County PO Box 750 — Leakey TX 78873 — 830-232-5202 232-6888
Web: www.co.real.tx.us
Red Lake County 124 Langevin Ave — Red Lake Falls MN 56750 — 218-253-2996
Web: www.redlakecounty.org
Red River County 200 N Walnut St — Clarksville TX 75426 — 903-427-2401 427-5510
Web: www.co.red-river.tx.us
Red River Parish Clerk of Court's Office
PO Box 485 — Coushatta LA 71019 — 318-932-6741 932-3126
Web: www.redriverclerk.com
Red Willow County 502 Norris Ave — McCook NE 69001 — 308-345-1552 345-4460
Web: www.co.red-willow.ne.us
Redwood County 403 S Mill St PO Box 130 — Redwood Falls MN 56283 — 507-637-4016 637-4017
Web: www.co.redwood.mn.us
Reeves County 100 E Fourth St — Pecos TX 79772 — 432-445-5467 445-3997
Web: reevescountytexas.net
Refugio County 808 Commerce St PO Box 704 — Refugio TX 78377 — 361-526-2233 526-1325
Web: www.co.refugio.tx.us
Reno County 206 W First St — Hutchinson KS 67501 — 620-694-2934 694-2534
Web: renogov.org
Rensselaer County 1600 Seventh Ave — Troy NY 12180 — 518-270-2900 270-2961
Web: www.rensco.com
Renville County PO Box 68 — Mohall ND 58761 — 701-756-6398 756-6494
Web: www.ndcourts.gov
Republic County 1815 M St — Belleville KS 66935 — 785-527-7231
Web: www.republiccounty.org
Reynolds County 2323 Green St — Centerville MO 63633 — 573-648-2491
Web: reynoldsso.org
Rhea County 444 2nd Ave — Dayton TN 37321 — 423-775-7832
Web: www.rheacountytn.gov
Rice County 320 NW Third St — Faribault MN 55021 — 507-332-6101 332-5999
Web: www.co.rice.mn.us
Rich County 20 S Main St — Randolph UT 84064 — 435-793-2415
Web: www.utahreach.org
Richardson County 1700 Stone St — Falls City NE 68355 — 402-245-2911 245-2946
Web: www.co.richardson.ne.us
Richland County 103 W Main St — Olney IL 62450 — 618-392-3111 393-4005
Web: ci.olney.il.us
Richland Parish 708 Julia St — Rayville LA 71269 — 318-728-2061 728-7004
Web: lpgov.org
Richmond County 130 Stuyvesant Pl — Staten Island NY 10301 — 718-556-7240 390-5269
Web: www.nyc.gov
Riley County 110 Courthouse Plaza — Manhattan KS 66502 — 785-537-6300 537-6394
Web: rileycountyks.gov
Ringgold County 109 W Madison St — Mount Ayr IA 50854 — 641-464-3234
Rio Blanco County 555 Main St PO Box 1067 — Meeker CO 81641 — 970-878-9460 878-3587
Web: www.co.rio-blanco.co.us
Rio Grande County 965 Sixth St PO Box 160 — Del Norte CO 81132 — 719-657-3334 657-2621
Web: www.riograndecounty.org
Ripley County 209 W Highway St — Doniphan MO 63935 — 573-996-2212
Web: www.ripleycountymissouri.org
Ritchie County 115 E Main St — Harrisville WV 26362 — 304-643-2164 643-2906
Web: www.ritchiecounty.wv.gov
Riverside County 4080 Lemon St 4th Fl — Riverside CA 92501 — 951-955-1100 955-1105
Web: countyofriverside.us
Roane County 200 E Race St — Kingston TN 37763 — 865-376-5556
Web: www.roanealliance.org
Roanoke County 5204 Bernard Dr — Roanoke VA 24018 — 540-772-2004 561-2884
Web: roanokecountyva.gov
Roanoke (Independent City)
210 Reserve Ave SW — Roanoke VA 24016 — 540-853-2000 853-1138
Web: www.roanokeva.gov
Roberts County 122 E Water St PO Box 458 — Miami TX 79059 — 806-868-2341 868-3381
Web: www.uccsource.com/
Robertson County PO Box 1029 — Franklin TX 77856 — 979-828-4130 828-1260
Web: www.co.robertson.tx.us
Robeson County 701 N Elm St — Lumberton NC 28358 — 910-671-3000 671-3010
Web: www.co.robeson.nc.us
Rock County 204 E Brown St — Luverne MN 56156 — 507-283-5020
Web: www.co.rock.mn.us
Rock Island County 1504 Third Ave — Rock Island IL 61201 — 309-786-4451
Web: www.rockislandcounty.org

Rockbridge County 150 S Main St — Lexington VA 24450 — 540-463-4361 463-5981
Web: www.co.rockbridge.va.us
Rockcastle County 205 E Main St Rm 102 — Mount Vernon KY 40456 — 606-256-2831
Web: www.rockcastlecountyky.com
Rockdale County 922 Ct St — Conyers GA 30012 — 770-278-7900 278-7921
Web: rockdaleclerk.com
Rockingham County 10 Rt 125 — Brentwood NH 03833 — 603-642-5526 642-5930
Web: www.nhdeeds.com
Rockland County 11 New Hempstead Rd — New City NY 10956 — 845-638-5100 638-5675
Web: rocklandgov.com
Roger Mills County 500 E Broadway PO Box 708 — Cheyenne OK 73628 — 580-497-3350
Web: www.rogermills.org
Rogers County 219 S Missouri St — Claremore OK 74017 — 918-341-3159 341-4529
Web: www.rogerscounty.org
Rolette County PO Box 276 — Rolla ND 58367 — 701-477-3816
Web: www.rolettecounty.com
Rooks County 115 N Walnut St — Stockton KS 67669 — 785-425-6391 425-6015
Web: www.rookscounty.net
Roosevelt County
109 W First St
4th Fl of the Roosevelt County Courthouse — Portales NM 88130 — 575-356-4990 356-8307
Web: www.rooseveltcounty.com
Roscommon County 500 Lake St — Roscommon MI 48653 — 989-275-5923 275-8640
Web: www.roscommoncounty.net
Roseau County 606 Fifth Ave SW Rm 20 — Roseau MN 56751 — 218-463-2541
Web: www.visitnwminnesota.com/Roseau.htm
Rosebud County 1200 Main St — Forsyth MT 59327 — 406-356-7318
Web: www.rosebudmontana.com/
Ross County 2 N Paint St Ste B — Chillicothe OH 45601 — 740-702-3010 702-3018
Web: www.co.ross.oh.us
Routt County
136 Sixth St PO Box 775227 — Steamboat Springs CO 80477 — 970-870-5405 871-8140
Web: www.co.routt.co.us
Rowan County 130 W Innes St — Salisbury NC 28144 — 704-636-0361 638-3092
Web: rowancountync.gov
Court house 627 E Main St 2nd Fl — Morehead KY 40351 — 606-784-5212 784-2923
Web: rowancountyclerk.com
Runnels County 613 Hutchings Ave Rm 303 — Ballinger TX 76821 — 325-365-2137 365-4823
Web: www.co.runnels.tx.us
Rush County
101 E Second St County Courthouse — Rushville IN 46173 — 765-932-2077 938-1163*
*Fax: Acctg ■ *Web:* www.rushcounty.in.gov
Rusk County 115 N Main St Ste 206 — Henderson TX 75652 — 903-657-0330 657-0062
Web: www.co.rusk.tx.us
Russell County 410 Monument Sq PO Box 397 — Jamestown KY 42629 — 270-343-2112 343-2134
Web: rckygov.com
Rutherford County 319 N Maple St Ste 121 — Murfreesboro TN 37130 — 615-898-7800 898-7830
Web: rutherfordcountytn.gov
Rutland Region Chamber of Commerce
50 Merchants Row — Rutland VT 05701 — 802-773-2747 773-2772
TF: 800-756-8880 ■ *Web:* www.rutlandvermont.com
Sabine County 1555 Worth St PO Box 717 — Hemphill TX 75948 — 409-787-2732 787-2158
Web: www.sabinecountytexas.com
Sabine Parish 400 S Capitol St PO Box 419 — Many LA 71449 — 318-256-6223
Web: www.sabineparishclerk.com
Sac County 100 NW State St — Sac City IA 50583 — 712-662-4492 662-7358
Web: www.saccounty.org
Sacramento County 700 H St Rm 7650 — Sacramento CA 95814 — 916-874-5833 874-5885
Web: www.saccounty.net
Sagadahoc County 752 High St — Bath ME 04530 — 207-443-8200 443-8213
Web: www.sagcounty.com
Saginaw County 111 S Michigan Ave — Saginaw MI 48602 — 989-790-5251
Web: www.saginawcounty.com
Saguache County 501 Fourth St PO Box 176 — Saguache CO 81149 — 719-655-2512 655-2730
Web: www.saguachecounty.net
Saint Charles County 201 N 2nd St — St. Charles MO 63301 — 636-949-7900 822-4012*
*Fax Area Code: 800
Saint Charles Parish
15045 River Rd PO Box 302 — Hahnville LA 70057 — 985-783-5000 783-2067
Web: www.stcharlesgov.net
Saint Clair County 165 Fifth Ave Ste 100 — Ashville AL 35953 — 205-594-2100 594-2110
Web: www.stclairco.com
Saint Croix County 1101 Carmichael Rd — Hudson WI 54016 — 715-386-4600 381-4400
Web: www.co.saint-croix.wi.us
Saint Francis County
313 S Izard St Ste 10 PO Box 1817 — Forrest City AR 72335 — 870-261-1700
Web: stfranciscountyar.org
Saint Francois County 1 W Liberty St — Farmington MO 63640 — 573-756-3623 431-6967
Web: www.sfcgov.org
Saint James Parish 5800 Hwy 44 PO Box 106 — Convent LA 70723 — 225-562-2286 562-2279
Web: www.stjamesla.com
Saint John the Baptist Parish
1801 W Airline Hwy — LaPlace LA 70068 — 985-652-9569 652-4131
Web: www.sjbparish.com
Saint Johns County
4010 Lewis Speedway — Saint Augustine FL 32084 — 904-819-3600 819-3661
Web: www.co.st-johns.fl.us
Saint Joseph County
125 W Main St PO Box 189 — Centreville MI 49032 — 269-467-5500 467-5628
Web: www.stjosephcountymi.org
Saint Landry Parish 118 S Ct St PO Box 750 — Opelousas LA 70571 — 337-942-5606 948-7265
Web: www.stlandry.org
Saint Lawrence County 48 Ct St Bldg 2 — Canton NY 13617 — 315-379-2237 379-2302
Web: www.co.st-lawrence.ny.us
Saint Louis County 41 S Central Ave — Clayton MO 63105 — 314-615-5000 615-7890
Web: www.stlouisco.com
Saint Mary's County
41770 Baldridge St PO Box 653 — Leonardtown MD 20650 — 301-475-4200 475-4935
Web: www.co.saint-marys.md.us
Sainte Genevieve County 55 S 3rd St — Sainte Genevieve MO 63670 — 573-883-5589 883-5312
Salem County 94 Market St — Salem NJ 08079 — 856-935-7510 935-6725
Web: www.salemcountynj.gov/cmssite

	City	State	Zip	Phone	Fax
Salem (Independent City) 114 N Broad St PO Box 869 *Web:* salemva.gov	Salem	VA	24153	540-375-3000	
Saline County 215 N Main St Ste 9 *Web:* www.salinecounty.org	Benton	AR	72015	501-303-5630	776-2412
Salt Lake County 2001 S State St Ste S2200 *Web:* slco.org	Salt Lake City	UT	84190	801-468-3000	468-3440
Sampson County 435 Rowan Rd *Web:* www.sampsonnc.com	Clinton	NC	28328	910-592-6308	592-1945
San Augustine County 223 N Harrison *Web:* www.co.san-augustine.tx.us	San Augustine	TX	75972	936-275-2452	275-2263
San Benito County 440 Fifth St Rm 206 *Web:* www.cosb.us	Hollister	CA	95023	831-636-4029	636-2939
San Bernardino County 385 N Arrowhead Ave Fl 5 *TF:* 888-818-8988 ■ *Web:* sbcounty.gov	San Bernardino	CA	92415	909-387-8306	
San Diego County 1600 Pacific Hwy Rm 166 *Web:* www.sandiegocounty.gov	San Diego	CA	92101	619-531-5413	531-5219
San Francisco City & County 1 Dr Carlton B Goodlett Pl City Hall Rm 168 *Web:* sfgsa.org	San Francisco	CA	94102	415-554-4950	554-4951
San Jacinto County 1 State Hwy 150 Rm 2 *Web:* www.co.san-jacinto.tx.us	Coldspring	TX	77331	936-653-2324	653-5604
San Joaquin County 222 E Weber Ave Second Fl Rm 202 PO Box 990 *Web:* www.sjgov.org	Stockton	CA	95201	209-468-2400	468-0371
San Juan County 100 S Oliver Dr *Web:* www.sjcounty.net	Aztec	NM	87410	505-334-9481	334-3168
San Luis Obispo County 1055 Monterey St **Fax Area Code:* 800 ■ *Web:* www.slocounty.ca.gov	San Luis Obispo	CA	93408	805-781-5000	834-4636*
San Mateo County 455 County Ctr 4th Fl *Web:* www.smcgov.org	Redwood City	CA	94063	650-599-1388	
San Miguel County 500 W National St Ste 200 *Web:* www.smcounty.net	Las Vegas	NM	87701	505-425-9333	425-7019
San Saba County 500 E Wallace St County Courthouse *Web:* www.co.san-saba.tx.us	San Saba	TX	76877	325-372-3614	372-6484
Sanborn County 604 W Sixth St *Web:* ujs.sd.gov	Woonsocket	SD	57385	605-796-4515	
Sanders County 111 Main St PO Box 519 *Web:* co.sanders.mt.us	Thompson Falls	MT	59873	406-827-6942	827-4388
Sandoval County 1500 Idalia Rd Bldg D *Web:* www.sandovalcounty.com	Bernalillo	NM	87004	505-867-7500	
Sandusky County 622 Croghan St *Web:* www.sandusky-county.com	Fremont	OH	43420	419-334-6100	334-6104
Sangamon County 200 S Ninth St Rm 201 *Web:* www.co.sangamon.il.us	Springfield	IL	62701	217-753-6700	
Sanilac County 60 W Sanilac Ave Rm 203 *Web:* www.sanilaccounty.net	Sandusky	MI	48471	810-648-3212	648-5466
Sanpete County 160 N Main St *Web:* www.utahreach.org	Manti	UT	84642	435-835-2101	
Santa Barbara County PO Box 159 *Web:* www.countyofsb.org	Santa Barbara	CA	93102	805-568-2550	568-3247
Santa Clara County 70 W Hedding St 11th Fl E Wing *Web:* www.sccgov.org	San Jose	CA	95110	408-299-5105	295-2192
Santa Cruz County 2150 N Congress Dr *Web:* www.co.santa-cruz.az.us	Nogales	AZ	85621	520-761-7800	
Santa Fe County 102 Grant Ave *TF:* 877-607-0741 ■ *Web:* www.co.santa-fe.nm.us	Santa Fe	NM	87504	505-986-6200	995-2740
Santa Rosa County 6495 Caroline St Ste F *Web:* data2.santarosa.fl.gov	Milton	FL	32570	850-983-1900	983-1829
Saratoga County 40 McMaster St *Web:* www.saratogacountyny.gov	Ballston Spa	NY	12020	518-885-5381	884-4726
Sargent County 355 Main St Ste 2 *Web:* sargentnd.com/	Forman	ND	58032	701-724-6241	724-6244
Sarpy County 1210 Golden Gate Dr Ste 1118 *Web:* www.co.sarpy.ne.us	Papillion	NE	68046	402-593-2100	593-4360
Sauk County 505 S Broadway St *Web:* www.co.sauk.wi.us	Baraboo	WI	53913	608-355-3286	355-3522
Saunders County PO Box 61 *Web:* www.saunderscounty.ne.gov	Wahoo	NE	68066	402-443-8101	443-8174
Sawyer County 10610 Main St Ste 10 *TF:* 877-699-4110 ■ *Web:* www.sawyercountygov.org	Hayward	WI	54843	715-634-4866	634-3666
Schenectady County 620 State St *Web:* www.schenectadycounty.com	Schenectady	NY	12305	518-285-8435	388-4224
Schleicher County 164 US 190	Eldorado	TX	76936	325-853-2593	
Schley County 49 Pecan St	Ellaville	GA	31806	229-937-2609	
Schoharie County 284 Main St PO Box 429 *Web:* www.schohariecounty-ny.gov	Schoharie	NY	12157	518-295-8347	295-8482
Schoolcraft County 300 Walnut St Rm 135 *Web:* www.schoolcraftcounty.net	Manistique	MI	49854	906-341-3630	
Schuyler County Hwy 136 E *Web:* www.courts.mo.gov	Lancaster	MO	63548	660-457-3784	457-3016
Schuylkill County 401 N Second St *Web:* www.co.schuylkill.pa.us	Pottsville	PA	17901	570-622-5570	628-1210
Scioto County 602 Seventh St Rm 205 *Web:* www.sciotocountyohio.com	Portsmouth	OH	45662	740-355-8313	354-2057
Scotland County PO Box 489 *Web:* www.scotlandcounty.org	Laurinburg	NC	28353	910-277-2406	277-2411
Scott County 131 S Winchester St PO Box 188 *Web:* www.scottcountymo.com	Benton	MO	63736	573-545-3549	545-3540
Scotts Bluff County 1825 Tenth St *Web:* www.scottsbluffcounty.org	Gering	NE	69341	308-436-6600	436-3178
Screven County 101 S Main St *Web:* www.screvencounty.com	Sylvania	GA	30467	912-564-7878	
Scurry County 1806 25th St Ste 300 *Web:* www.co.scurry.tx.us	Snyder	TX	79549	325-573-5332	573-7396
Searcy County PO Box 1385 *Web:* searcycountyarkansas.org	Marshall	AR	72650	870-448-2557	
Sebastian County 35 S Sixth St Rm 102 *Web:* sebastiancountyar.gov	Fort Smith	AR	72901	479-782-5065	784-1567
Sedgwick County 315 Cedar St Ste 200 *Web:* sedgwickcountygov.net	Julesburg	CO	80737	970-474-2531	474-3507
Seminole County 200 S Knox Ave *Web:* www.seminolecountyga.com	Donalsonville	GA	39845	229-524-2878	
Seneca County 111 Madison St *Web:* www.seneca-county.com	Tiffin	OH	44883	419-447-4550	
Sequatchie County 22 Cherry St PO Box 595 *Web:* www.sequatchiecounty-tn.gov	Dunlap	TN	37327	423-949-2522	
Sequoyah County 120 E Chickasaw Ave	Sallisaw	OK	74955	918-775-9321	775-7861
Sevier County 115 N 3rd St Rm 102 *Web:* www.seviercountyar.com	De Queen	AR	71832	870-642-2852	642-3896
Seward County 1801 N Kansas PO Box 1137 **Fax Area Code:* 620 ■ *Web:* www.sccc.edu/	Liberal	KS	67901	0-3-73--9951	-41-7-1079*
Shackelford County 225 S Main St *Web:* shackelfordcountytexas.com	Albany	TX	76430	325-762-2232	762-2830
Shannon County PO Box 148,	Eminence	MO	65466	573-226-3315	226-5321
Sharkey County PO Box 218 *Web:* sharkey.msghn.org/addresses.html	Rolling Fork	MS	39159	662-873-2755	
Sharp County 718 Ash Flat Dr *Web:* www.sharpcounty.org/	Ash Flat	AR	72513	870-994-3286	
Shasta County 1643 Market St *Web:* www.co.shasta.ca.us	Redding	CA	96099	530-225-5730	225-5454
Shawano County 311 N Main St *Web:* www.co.shawano.wi.us	Shawano	WI	54166	715-526-9150	524-5157
Shawnee County 200 SE Seventh St *Web:* www.snco.us	Topeka	KS	66603	785-233-8200	291-4912
Sheboygan County 615 N 6th St *Web:* www.co.sheboygan.wi.us	Sheboygan	WI	53081	920-459-3003	459-0304
Shelby County 100 Hurst St *Web:* www.co.shelby.tx.us	Center	TX	75935	936-598-5600	598-3701
Shenandoah County 600 N Main St Ste 102 *Web:* shenandoahcountyva.us	Woodstock	VA	22664	540-459-6167	459-6192
Sheridan County 925 Ninth St *Web:* www.kansas.gov/sheridan/	Hoxie	KS	67740	785-675-3361	
Sherman County 813 Broadway Rm 102 *Web:* ks-sherman.manatron.com	Goodland	KS	67735	785-890-4825	
Shiawassee County 208 N Shiawassee St *Web:* www.shiawassee.net	Corunna	MI	48817	989-743-2242	743-2241
Shoshone County 700 Bank St *Web:* www.shoshonecounty.org	Wallace	ID	83873	208-752-3331	752-4304
Sibley County 400 Ct St *Web:* www.co.sibley.mn.us	Gaylord	MN	55334	507-237-4051	237-4062
Sierra County 100 Courthouse Sq Ste 11 PO Box D *Web:* www.sierracounty.ca.gov	Downieville	CA	95936	530-289-3295	289-2830
Simpson County 103 W Cedar St *Web:* www.simpsoncountyclerk.ky.gov	Franklin	KY	42134	270-586-8161	586-6464
Sioux County PO Box 158 *Web:* www.co.sioux.ne.us	Harrison	NE	69346	308-668-2443	668-2443
Siskiyou County 201 Fourth St *Web:* www.co.siskiyou.ca.us	Yreka	CA	96097	530-842-8005	842-8013
Sitka City & Borough 100 Lincoln St *Web:* www.cityofsitka.com	Sitka	AK	99835	907-747-3294	747-7403
Skagit County 205 W Kincaid St Rm 103 *Web:* www.skagitcounty.net	Mount Vernon	WA	98273	360-336-9440	
Skamania County 240 Vancouver Ave PO Box 790 *Web:* www.skamaniacounty.org	Stevenson	WA	98648	509-427-3770	427-3777
Slope County 206 S Main St	Amidon	ND	58620	701-879-6272	879-4392
Smith County 122 Turner High Cir *Web:* www.smithcountychamber.org	Carthage	TN	37030	615-735-9833	
Smyth County 109 W Main St Rm 144 *Web:* www.smythcounty.org	Marion	VA	24354	276-782-4044	782-4045
Snohomish County 3000 Rockefeller Ave *Web:* snohomishcountywa.gov	Everett	WA	98201	425-388-3411	
Snyder County 9 W Market St *Web:* www.snydercounty.org	Middleburg	PA	17842	570-837-4207	837-4282
Socorro County 101 Plaza St PO Box 743 *Web:* www.socorro-nm.com	Socorro	NM	87801	575-835-0424	
Solano County 675 Texas St Ste 1900	Fairfield	CA	94533	707-784-7485	784-6311
Somerset County 11916 Somerset Ave Rm 111 *Web:* www.visitsomerset.com	Princess Anne	MD	21853	410-651-0320	
Sonoma County 575 Admin Dr Ste 104A *Web:* sonomacounty.ca.gov/	Santa Rosa	CA	95403	707-565-2431	565-3778
Southampton County 22350 Main St *Web:* www.southamptoncounty.org	Courtland	VA	23837	757-653-2200	653-2547
Spalding County PO Box 1087 *Web:* www.spaldingcounty.com	Griffin	GA	30224	770-467-4200	
Spartanburg County 180 Magnolia St *Web:* www.spartanburgcounty.org	Spartanburg	SC	29306	864-596-2591	
Spencer County 200 Main St PO Box 12 *Web:* spencercounty.in.gov	Rockport	IN	47635	812-649-6028	649-6030
Spokane County 1116 W Broadway Ave *Web:* www.spokanecounty.org	Spokane	WA	99260	509-477-2265	477-2274
Spotsylvania County 1905 Courthouse Rd PO Box 99 *Web:* www.spotsylvania.va.us	Spotsylvania	VA	22553	540-507-7010	507-7019
Stafford County 209 N Broadway St *Web:* www.staffordcounty.org	Saint John	KS	67576	620-549-3295	549-3298
Stanislaus County 1021 I St Ste 101 *Web:* www.stancounty.com	Modesto	CA	95354	209-525-5250	525-5804
Stanley County Auditor 8 E Second Ave *Web:* stanleycounty.org	Fort Pierre	SD	57532	605-223-7780	223-7791
Stanly County 201 S Second St PO Box 668 *Web:* www.co.stanly.nc.us	Albemarle	NC	28001	704-986-3600	

Name / Address	City	State	ZIP	Phone	Fax
Stanton County PO Box 190 *Web:* stantoncountyks.com	Johnson	KS	67855	620-492-2140	492-2688
Stark County PO Box 130 **Fax:* Acctg ■ *Web:* starkcountynd.gov	Dickinson	ND	58602	701-456-7630	456-7634*
Starke County 53 E Washington St County Courthouse *Web:* co.starke.in.us	Knox	IN	46534	574-772-9128	772-9169
Starr County Industrial Foundation 601 E Main St Rm 201 *Web:* www.starrcounty.org	Rio Grande City	TX	78582	956-487-2709	716-8560
Staunton (Independent City) 113 E Beverley St *Web:* www.staunton.va.us	Staunton	VA	24401	540-332-3874	332-3970
Stearns County 705 Courthouse Sq Rm 121 *Web:* www.co.stearns.mn.us	Saint Cloud	MN	56303	320-656-3601	656-6393
Steele County PO Box 296 *Web:* www.co.steele.nd.us	Finley	ND	58230	701-524-2152	
Stephens County 200 W Walker St *Web:* www.co.stephens.tx.us	Breckenridge	TX	76424	254-559-3700	559-9645
Stephenson County 50 W Douglas St Ste 500 *Web:* www.co.stephenson.il.us	Freeport	IL	61032	815-235-8289	235-8378
Steuben County 206 E Gale St *Web:* www.co.steuben.in.us	Angola	IN	46703	260-668-1000	668-3702
Stevens County 215 S Oak St *Web:* www.co.stevens.wa.us	Colville	WA	99114	509-684-3751	684-8310
Stewart County 225 Donelson Pkwy PO Box 67 *Web:* www.stewartcogov.com	Dover	TN	37058	931-232-7616	232-4934
Stewart County Commissioner 552 Martin Luther King Junior Dr *Web:* www.stewartcountyga.gov	Lumpkin	GA	31815	229-838-6769	
Stillwater County 400 Third Ave N PO Box 149 *Web:* www.stillwater.mt.gov	Columbus	MT	59019	406-322-8000	322-8007
Stoddard County 106 S Prairie St *Web:* idasc.org	Bloomfield	MO	63825	573-568-4640	568-2271
Stokes County 1012 Main St PO Box 250 *Web:* www.co.stokes.nc.us	Danbury	NC	27016	336-593-4400	593-4401
Stone County HC 71 Box 1427 *Web:* www.arkansasties.com	Mountain View	AR	72560	870-269-5550	
Stonewall County PO Box P *Web:* www.stonewallcountytexas.us	Aspermont	TX	79502	940-989-2272	989-2715
Storey County 26 S B St *Web:* storeycounty.org	Virginia City	NV	89440	775-847-0968	847-0949
Story County 1315 S B Ave *Web:* www.storycountyiowa.gov	Nevada	IA	50201	515-382-7410	
Strafford County 259 County Farm Rd *Web:* www.co.strafford.nh.us	Dover	NH	03820	603-742-1458	743-4407
Stutsman County 511 Second Ave SE *Web:* www.co.stutsman.nd.us	Jamestown	ND	58401	701-252-9035	251-6325
Sublette County PO Box 250 *Web:* www.sublettewyo.com	Pinedale	WY	82941	307-367-4372	367-6396
Suffolk County County Rd 51 *Web:* www.suffolkcountyny.gov	Riverhead	NY	11901	631-852-1400	
Suffolk (Independent City) 441 Market St *Web:* www.suffolkva.us	Suffolk	VA	23434	757-514-4000	
Sullivan County 109 N Main St *Web:* sullivan.countycriminal.com	Milan	MO	63556	660-265-3786	
Sully County PO Box 265 *Web:* www.sullycounty.net	Onida	SD	57564	605-258-2541	258-2884
Summers County 120 Ballengee St *Web:* www.summerscountywv.org	Hinton	WV	25951	304-466-7104	
Summit County 175 S Main St *Web:* co.summitoh.net	Akron	OH	44308	330-643-2500	643-2507
Sumner County 101 Public Sq PO Box 549 *Web:* www.sumnertn.org	Gallatin	TN	37066	615-452-4367	451-6027
Sumter County 500 W Lamar St PO Box 295 *Web:* sumtercountyga.us	Americus	GA	31709	229-928-4500	928-4503
Sunflower County 200 Main St	Indianola	MS	38751	662-887-1252	
Superior Court Clerk Office 4800 Tower Hill Rd *Web:* www.courts.ri.gov	Wakefield	RI	02879	401-782-4121	782-4190
Surry County 118 Hamby Rd *Web:* www.co.surry.nc.us	Dobson	NC	27017	336-386-3700	
Susquehanna County 75 Public Ave *Web:* www.susqco.com	Montrose	PA	18801	570-278-4600	278-9268
Sussex County 2 The Cr PO Box 589 *Web:* www.sussexcountyde.gov	Georgetown	DE	19947	302-855-7743	855-7749
Sutter County 433 Second St *Web:* www.co.sutter.ca.us	Yuba City	CA	95991	530-822-7134	822-7214
Sutton County 300 E Oak St *Web:* co.sutton.tx.us	Sonora	TX	76950	325-387-3815	
Suwannee County 212 N Ohio Ave *Web:* www.suwanneechamber.com	Live Oak	FL	32064	386-362-3071	362-4758
Swain County 101 Mitchell St PO Box 2321 *Web:* www.swaincountync.gov	Bryson City	NC	28713	828-488-9273	
Sweet Grass County 115 W Fifth Ave PO Box 888 *Web:* sweetgrasscountygov.com/	Big Timber	MT	59011	406-932-5152	932-3026
Sweetwater County 80 W Flaming Gorge Way *Web:* www.sweet.wy.us	Green River	WY	82935	307-872-3732	
Swift County PO Box 288 *Web:* www.swiftcounty.com	Benson	MN	56215	320-843-2744	
Swisher County 119 S Maxwell St *Web:* www.co.swisher.tx.us	Tulia	TX	79088	806-995-3294	995-4121
Switzerland County 212 W Main St County Courthouse *Web:* switzerland-county.com	Vevay	IN	47043	812-427-3302	427-3179
Talbot County 11 N Washington St County Courthouse *Web:* talbotcountymd.gov	Easton	MD	21601	410-770-8010	770-8007
Taliaferro County PO Box 114 *Web:* taliaferrocountyga.org	Crawfordville	GA	30631	706-456-2229	456-2904
Talladega County PO Box 6170 *Web:* www.talladegacountyal.org	Talladega	AL	35161	256-362-1357	761-2147
Tallapoosa County 125 N Broadnax St Rm 131 *Web:* tallaco.com	Dadeville	AL	36853	256-825-4268	
Tama County 104 W State St PO Box 61 *Web:* www.tamacounty.org	Toledo	IA	52342	641-484-3980	484-5127
Taney County 132 David St PO Box 156 *Web:* www.co.taney.mo.us	Forsyth	MO	65653	417-546-7200	546-2519
Tangipahoa Parish 206 E Mulberry St *Web:* www.tangipahoa.org	Amite	LA	70422	985-748-3211	748-7576
Taos County 105 Albright St Ste A *Web:* www.taoscounty.org	Taos	NM	87571	575-737-6300	737-6314
Tarrant County 100 E Weatherford St *Web:* www.tarrantcounty.com	Fort Worth	TX	76196	817-884-1195	884-3295
Tattnall County PO Box 759 *Web:* www.tattnall.com	Reidsville	GA	30453	912-557-6323	557-3046
Taylor County 300 Oak St *Web:* www.taylorcountytexas.org	Abilene	TX	79602	325-674-1202	674-1279
Tazewell County 11 S Fourth St Fl 2 Ste 203 *Web:* www.tazewell.com	Pekin	IL	61554	309-477-2264	477-2244
Tehama County 633 Washington St Rm 11 *Web:* www.co.tehama.ca.us	Red Bluff	CA	96080	530-527-3350	527-1745
Telfair County 91 Telfair Ave *Web:* georgia.gov/cities-counties/telfair-county	McRae	GA	31055	229-868-5688	868-7950
Teller County PO Box 959 *Web:* www.co.teller.co.us	Cripple Creek	CO	80813	719-689-2988	686-7900
Tensas Parish 201 Hancock St PO Box 78 *Web:* www.laclerksofcourt.org	Saint Joseph	LA	71366	318-766-3921	766-3926
Terrebonne Parish PO Box 1569 *Web:* terrebonneclerk.org	Houma	LA	70361	985-868-5660	868-5143
Terrell County 105 E Hackberry *Web:* www.co.terrell.tx.us	Sanderson	TX	79848	432-345-2391	345-2740
Terry County 500 W Main St Rm 105 *Web:* www.co.terry.tx.us	Brownfield	TX	79316	806-637-8551	637-4874
Teton County PO Box 610 *Web:* www.tetoncomt.org	Choteau	MT	59422	406-466-2151	466-2151
Texas County PO Box 197 *Web:* www.txcountyok.com	Guymon	OK	73942	580-338-3141	338-4311
Thayer County 225 N Fourth St Rm 201 PO Box 208 *Web:* www.thayercounty.ne.gov	Hebron	NE	68370	402-768-6126	768-2129
Thomas County 110 N Crawford St PO Box 920 *Web:* www.thomascountyboc.org	Thomasville	GA	31799	229-225-4100	226-3430
Thomas County Clerk 503 Main St *Web:* thomascountynebraska.us	Thedford	NE	69166	308-645-2261	645-2623
Throckmorton County PO Box 309	Throckmorton	TX	76483	940-849-2501	849-3032
Thurston County 2000 Lakeridge Dr SW Bldg 2 *Web:* www.co.thurston.wa.us	Olympia	WA	98502	360-786-5430	753-4033
Tift County 225 N Tift Ave *Web:* www.tiftcounty.org	Tifton	GA	31794	229-386-7850	
Tillamook County 201 Laurel Ave *Web:* www.co.tillamook.or.us	Tillamook	OR	97141	503-842-3403	842-1384
Tioga County Clerk 16 Ct St PO Box 307 *Web:* www.tiogacountyny.com	Owego	NY	13827	607-687-8660	687-8686
Tippah County 212 E Jefferson St *Web:* www.tippahcounty.ripley.ms	Ripley	MS	38663	662-837-3353	837-3006
Tippecanoe County 20 N Third St *Web:* www.tippecanoe.in.gov	Lafayette	IN	47901	765-463-2306	423-9196
Tipton County 220 Highway 51 N Ste 2 *Web:* www.tiptonco.com	Covington	TN	38019	901-476-0207	476-0297
Titus County 100 W 1st Ste 204 *Web:* www.co.titus.tx.us	Mount Pleasant	TX	75455	903-577-6796	572-5078
Todd County 221 First Ave S Ste 200 **Fax:* Acctg ■ *Web:* www.co.todd.mn.us	Long Prairie	MN	56347	320-732-6447	732-4001*
Tolland County 69 Brooklyn St *Web:* tolland.countycriminal.com	Rockville	CT	06066	860-875-6294	
Tom Green County 122 W Harris Ave *Web:* www.co.tom-green.tx.us	San Angelo	TX	76903	325-659-6444	659-6459
Tompkins County 320 N Tioga St *Web:* www.nycourts.gov	Ithaca	NY	14850	607-274-5431	274-5445
Tooele County 47 S Main St *Web:* www.co.tooele.ut.us	Tooele	UT	84074	435-843-3140	882-7317
Toole County 226 First St S *Web:* toolecountymt.gov	Shelby	MT	59474	406-424-8310	424-8301
Toombs County 100 Courthouse Sq PO Box 112 *Web:* www.toombscountyga.gov	Lyons	GA	30436	912-526-3311	526-1004
Torrance County 205 Ninth St PO Box 48 *Web:* www.torrancecountynm.org	Estancia	NM	87016	505-246-4725	384-5294
Towns County 1411 Jack Dayton Cir *TF:* 800-984-1543 ■ *Web:* www.mountaintopga.com	Young Harris	GA	30582	706-896-4966	
Travis County PO Box 1748	Austin	TX	78767	512-854-9244	854-4464
Treasure County PO Box 392	Hysham	MT	59038	406-342-5547	
Trego County 18001 283 Hwy *TF:* 877-962-7248 ■ *Web:* www.wakeeney.org	WaKeeney	KS	67672	785-743-6385	
Trempealeau County 36245 Main St *Web:* www.tremplocounty.com	Whitehall	WI	54773	715-538-2311	538-4210
Treutlen County PO Box 229 *Web:* soperton-treutlen.org	Soperton	GA	30457	912-529-6173	529-6996
Trigg County PO Box 672 *Web:* www.triggcounty.ky.gov	Cadiz	KY	42211	270-522-8459	522-9489
Trimble County 4874 Hwy 421 N PO Box 312 *Web:* www.trimblecounty.com	Bedford	KY	40006	502-255-0062	255-0063
Trinity County PO Box 456 *Web:* www.co.trinity.tx.us	Groveton	TX	75845	936-642-1208	642-3004
Tripp County Historical Society 200 E Third St *Web:* ujs.sd.gov	Winner	SD	57580	605-842-2266	842-2267

				Phone	Fax
Troup County PO Box 866 *Web:* www.troupcountyga.org	LaGrange	GA	30241	706-883-1740	883-1724
Trousdale County 240 Broadway Rm 2 *Web:* hartsvilletrousdale.com	Hartsville	TN	37074	615-374-9243	374-9243
Trumbull County 160 High St NW	Warren	OH	44481	330-675-2451	675-2462
Tucker County 215 First St Ste 201 *Web:* www.tuckercounty.wv.gov	Parsons	WV	26287	304-478-2414	478-2217
Tulare County 2800 W Burrel Ave *Web:* www.tularecounty.ca.gov	Visalia	CA	93291	559-636-5005	733-6318
Tulsa County 500 S Denver Ave Ste 120 *Web:* www.tulsacounty.org	Tulsa	OK	74103	918-596-5801	596-5819
Tunica County 1058 S Ct St *Web:* tunicacounty.com	Tunica	MS	38676	662-363-1465	
Tunica County Admnistrators Department 1058 S Ct St *Web:* www.tunicacounty.com	Tunica	MS	38676	662-363-1465	
Tuolumne County 2 S Green St *Web:* www.co.tuolumne.ca.us	Sonora	CA	95370	209-533-5511	533-5510
Turner County PO Box 191 *TF:* 800-436-7442 ■ *Web:* georgia.gov	Ashburn	GA	31714	229-567-2011	567-4794
Tuscaloosa County 714 Greensboro Ave *Web:* www.tuscco.com	Tuscaloosa	AL	35401	205-349-3870	
Tuscarawas County 125 E High Ave Rm 230 *Web:* www.co.tuscarawas.oh.us	New Philadelphia	OH	44663	330-365-3243	343-4682
Twiggs County Commissioners 425 N Railroad St *Web:* www.twiggscounty.us	Jeffersonville	GA	31044	478-945-3629	
Twin Falls County 630 Addison Ave W 2nd Fl *Web:* www.twinfallscounty.org	Twin Falls	ID	83301	208-736-4004	736-4155
Tyler County 100 Bluff St Rm 110 *Web:* www.co.tyler.tx.us	Woodville	TX	75979	409-283-2281	283-6305
Tyler County Assessor 121 Main St *Web:* www.tylercountywv.com	Middlebourne	WV	26149	304-758-4781	758-2126
Tyrrell County 108 S Water St PO Box 449 *Fax: Acctg ■ *Web:* www.visittyrrellcounty.com	Columbia	NC	27925	252-796-1371	796-1188*
Uinta County 225 Ninth St PO Box 810 *Web:* www.uintacounty.com	Evanston	WY	82931	307-783-0306	783-0376
Uintah County 147 E Main St *TF:* 800-966-4680 ■ *Web:* www.co.uintah.ut.us	Vernal	UT	84078	435-781-0770	781-6701
Ulster County 240 Fair St *Web:* ulstercountyny.gov/	Kingston	NY	12401	845-340-3288	340-3299
Umatilla County 216 SE Fourth St *Web:* www.co.umatilla.or.us	Pendleton	OR	97801	541-278-6236	278-6345
Unicoi County 100 Main St PO Box 713 *Web:* www.unicoicounty.org	Erwin	TN	37650	423-743-3000	
Unified Government of Wyandotte County/Kansas City 701 N Seventh St Ste 323 *Web:* www.wycokck.org	Kansas City	KS	66101	913-573-5260	573-5005
Union County 65 Courthouse St PO Box 1 *Web:* unioncountyga.gov	Blairsville	GA	30512	706-439-6000	439-6004
Union County Clerk 215 W 6th St *Web:* co.union.oh.us	Marysville	OH	43040	937-645-3006	
Union Parish 100 E Bayou St Ste 105 *Web:* upclerk.com	Farmerville	LA	71241	318-368-3055	368-3861
Upshur County 40 W Main St Rm 101 *Web:* www.buchamber.com	Buckhannon	WV	26201	304-472-1068	
Upson County 106 E Lee St Ste 110 *Web:* upsoncountyga.org	Thomaston	GA	30286	706-647-3293	647-7030
Upton County 205 E 10th St *Web:* co.upton.tx.us	Rankin	TX	79778	432-693-2861	693-2129
Utah County 100 E Ctr St Ste 2200 *Web:* www.co.utah.ut.us	Provo	UT	84606	801-851-8000	
Uvalde County PO Box 284 *Web:* www.uvaldecounty.com	Uvalde	TX	78802	830-278-6614	278-8692
Val Verde County PO Box 1267 *Web:* valverdecounty.org	Del Rio	TX	78841	830-774-7564	774-7608
Valencia County 444 Luna Ave *Web:* www.co.valencia.nm.us	Los Lunas	NM	87031	505-866-2014	866-2023
Valley County 219 N Main St *Web:* www.co.valley.id.us	Cascade	ID	83611	208-382-7150	382-7107
Van Buren County PO Box 475 *Web:* vanburencoia.org	Keosauqua	IA	52565	319-293-3129	293-6404
Van Wert County 114 E Main St *Web:* www.vanwertcounty.org	Van Wert	OH	45891	419-238-6159	238-4528
Van Zandt County 121 E Dallas St Rm 202 *Web:* www.vanzandtcounty.org	Canton	TX	75103	903-567-6503	567-6722
Vance County 122 Young St Ste E *Web:* www.vancecounty.org	Henderson	NC	27536	252-738-2040	
Vanderburgh County 1 NW ML King Jr Blvd *Web:* www.vanderburghgov.org	Evansville	IN	47708	812-435-5241	435-5963
Venango County Courthouse Annex 1174 Elk St *Web:* www.co.venango.pa.us	Franklin	PA	16323	814-432-9500	432-3149
Ventura County 800 S Victoria Ave *Web:* www.countyofventura.org	Ventura	CA	93009	805-289-8900	
Vermilion County 6 N Vermilion St Fl 1 Courthouse Annex *Web:* www.co.vermilion.il.us	Danville	IL	61832	217-554-1900	554-1914
Vermilion Parish 100 N State St Suite 101 *Web:* www.vermilionparishclerkofcourt.com	Abbeville	LA	70510	337-898-1992	898-9803
Vermillion County 255 S Main St *TF:* 800-340-8155 ■ *Web:* www.vermilliongov.us	Newport	IN	47966	765-492-5345	
Vernon County 100 W Cherry St *Web:* www.vernoncountymo.org	Nevada	MO	64772	417-448-2500	667-6035
Victoria County 115 N Bridge St Ste 103 *Web:* www.victoriacountytx.org	Victoria	TX	77901	361-575-1478	575-6276
Vigo County 121 Oak St *Web:* www.vigocounty.in.gov	Terre Haute	IN	47807	812-462-3367	
Vilas County 330 Ct St *Web:* www.co.vilas.wi.us	Eagle River	WI	54521	715-479-3600	479-3605
Vinton County 100 E Main St County Courthouse *Web:* www.vintoncounty.com	McArthur	OH	45651	740-596-4571	596-4571
Virginia Beach (Independent City) 2401 Courthouse Dr Municipal Ctr Bldg 1 *Web:* www.vbgov.com	Virginia Beach	VA	23456	757-385-4242	427-5626
Volusia County 123 W Indiana Ave *Web:* volusia.org	DeLand	FL	32720	386-736-5920	822-5707
Wabash County 221 S Miami St Ste 101 *Web:* www.wabashcountycvb.com	Wabash	IN	46992	260-563-7171	563-3451
Wabash County Clerk 401 N Market St *Web:* state.il.us	Mount Carmel	IL	62863	618-262-4561	
Wabasha County 625 Jefferson Ave	Wabasha	MN	55981	651-565-3096	565-3159*
Wabaunsee County 215 Kansas Ave PO Box 278 *Web:* ks-wabaunsee.manatron.com	Alma	KS	66401	785-863-2461	765-3704
Wadena County 415 S Jefferson St *Web:* www.co.wadena.mn.us	Wadena	MN	56482	218-631-7650	631-7635
Wagoner County 307 E Cherokee St *Web:* www.ok.gov/wagonercounty	Wagoner	OK	74467	918-485-2367	485-8033
Wahkiakum County 64 Main St *Web:* www.co.wahkiakum.wa.us	Cathlamet	WA	98612	360-795-3558	795-8813
Wake County 336 Fayetteville St *Web:* www.wakegov.com	Raleigh	NC	27601	919-856-6160	856-6168
Wakulla County 3056 Crawfordville Hwy *Web:* www.wakullaclerk.com	Crawfordville	FL	32327	850-926-0905	926-0938
Waldo County PO Box D *Web:* www.waldocountyme.gov	Belfast	ME	04915	207-338-1710	338-6360
Walker County PO Box 1207 *Web:* www.co.walker.tx.us	Huntsville	TX	77342	936-436-4933	436-4920
Walla Walla County 315 W Main St *Web:* www.co.walla-walla.wa.us	Walla Walla	WA	99362	509-527-3200	527-3235
Wallace County 313 N Main St *Web:* www.wallacecounty.net/government/localgov.php	Sharon Springs	KS	67758	785-852-4282	
Waller County 836 Austin St *Web:* www.wallercounty.org	Hempstead	TX	77445	979-826-3357	
Wallowa County 101 S River St Rm 100 *Web:* www.co.wallowa.or.us	Enterprise	OR	97828	541-426-4543	426-5901
Walsh County 600 Cooper Ave *Web:* www.co.walsh.nd.us	Grafton	ND	58237	701-352-1300	352-1104
Walthall County PO Box 227 *Web:* www.walthallcountychamber.org	Tylertown	MS	39667	601-876-2680	
Walton County PO Box 1260 *Web:* www.co.walton.fl.us	DeFuniak Springs	FL	32435	850-892-8115	
Walton County Board-Commissioner 303 S Hammond Dr Ste 330 *Web:* www.waltoncountyga.org	Monroe	GA	30655	770-267-1301	
Walworth County 100 W Walworth St PO Box 1001 *Web:* www.co.walworth.wi.us	Elkhorn	WI	53121	262-741-4241	741-4287
Wapello County 101 W Fourth St *Web:* www.wapellocounty.org	Ottumwa	IA	52501	641-683-0060	683-0053
Ward County County Courthouse 400 S Allen St Ste 101 *Web:* www.co.ward.tx.us	Monahans	TX	79756	432-943-3294	943-6054
Ware County 800 Church St *Web:* www.warecounty.com	Waycross	GA	31501	912-287-4300	287-4301
Warren County 100 W Broadway *Web:* www.warrencountyil.com	Monmouth	IL	61462	309-734-8592	734-7406
Warrick County 107 W Locust St Ste 301 *Web:* www.warrickcounty.gov	Boonville	IN	47601	812-897-6120	897-6189
Wasatch County 25 N Main St *Web:* www.co.wasatch.ut.us	Heber City	UT	84032	435-657-3221	654-5048
Wasco County 511 Washington St *Web:* www.co.wasco.or.us	The Dalles	OR	97058	541-506-2530	298-3607
Waseca County 307 N State St *Fax: Acctg ■ *Web:* www.co.waseca.mn.us	Waseca	MN	56093	507-835-0610	835-0633*
Washakie County PO Box 260 *Web:* www.washakiecounty.net	Worland	WY	82401	307-347-3131	347-9366
Washburn County PO Box 639 *Web:* www.co.washburn.wi.us	Shell Lake	WI	54871	715-468-4600	468-4725
Washington County 205 Academy Dr *Web:* www.washcova.com	Abingdon	VA	24210	276-525-1300	525-1309
Washington Parish 909 Pearl St *Web:* www.washingtonparishalerts.org	Franklinton	LA	70438	985-839-7825	839-7827
Washita County 111 E Main Rm 6 *Web:* washita.oklahoma.usassessor.com	Cordell	OK	73632	580-832-2468	832-4110
Washoe County 1001 E. Ninth St *Web:* www.washoecounty.us	Reno	NV	89512	775-328-2000	
Washtenaw County PO Box 8645 *Web:* www.ewashtenaw.org	Ann Arbor	MI	48107	734-222-6850	222-6715
Watauga County 842 W King St Courthouse *Web:* www.wataugacounty.org	Boone	NC	28607	828-265-8000	264-3230
Watonwan County 710 Seventh Ave S PO Box 518 *Web:* www.co.watonwan.mn.us	Saint James	MN	56081	507-375-1236	375-5010
Waukesha County 515 W Moreland Blvd Rm 120 *Web:* www.waukeshacounty.gov	Waukesha	WI	53188	262-548-7010	548-7722
Waupaca County 811 Harding St *Web:* www.co.waupaca.wi.us	Waupaca	WI	54981	715-258-6200	258-6212
Waushara County 209 S St Marie St PO Box 300 *Web:* www.co.waushara.wi.us	Wautoma	WI	54982	920-787-0431	
Wayne County PO Box 435 *Web:* www.waynecountyiowa.com	Corydon	IA	50060	641-872-1536	872-2843
Wayne County Clerk 700 Hendricks St *Web:* waynecountywv.org	Wayne	WV	25570	304-272-6365	
Waynesboro (Independent City) 503 W Main St *Web:* www.waynesboro.va.us	Waynesboro	VA	22980	540-942-6600	942-6671

	City	State	Zip	Phone	Fax
Weakley County 116 W Main St Rm 104 Room G01 *Web:* www.weakleycountytn.gov	Dresden	TN	38225	731-364-3643	364-9577
Webb County 1110 Washington St *Web:* www.webbcounty.com	Laredo	TX	78040	956-523-4143	523-5012
Weber County 2380 Washington Blvd Ste 350 *Web:* www.co.weber.ut.us	Ogden	UT	84401	801-399-8454	399-8314
Webster County 25 Us Hwy 41A S PO Box 19 *Web:* webstercountyclerk.ky.gov	Dixon	KY	42409	270-639-7006	639-7029
Weld County PO Box 758 *Web:* www.co.weld.co.us	Greeley	CO	80632	970-336-7204	352-0242
Wells County 102 W Market St Ste 201 *Web:* www.wellscounty.org	Bluffton	IN	46714	260-824-6479	824-6559
West Baton Rouge Parish PO Box 757 *Web:* www.wbrcouncil.org	Port Allen	LA	70767	225-383-4755	387-0218
West Carroll Parish PO Box 1078 *Web:* www.laclerksofcourt.org	Oak Grove	LA	71263	318-428-3281	428-9896
West Feliciana Parish PO Box 1921 *Web:* www.lpgov.org	Saint Francisville	LA	70775	225-635-3864	635-3705
Westchester County 110 Dr Martin Luther King Jr Blvd 3rd Fl *Web:* www.westchesterclerk.com	White Plains	NY	10601	914-995-3080	995-4030
Westmoreland County 2 N Main St Courthouse Sq Ste 101 *Web:* www.co.westmoreland.pa.us	Greensburg	PA	15601	724-830-3100	830-3029
Weston County 400 Stampede St PO Box 130 *Web:* www.westongov.com	Newcastle	WY	82701	307-746-4775	
Wetzel County PO Box 156 *Web:* www.wetzelcounty.wv.gov	New Martinsville	WV	26155	304-455-8217	455-5256
Wexford County 437 E Div St *Web:* www.wexfordcounty.org	Cadillac	MI	49601	231-779-9453	779-9745
Wharton County PO Box 69 *Web:* www.co.wharton.tx.us	Wharton	TX	77488	979-532-2381	532-8426
Whatcom County 311 Grand Ave Rm 301 *Web:* www.co.whatcom.wa.us	Bellingham	WA	98225	360-676-6777	676-6693
Wheatland County 201 A Ave NW *Web:* mbcc.mt.gov	Harlowton	MT	59036	406-632-4891	632-4880
Wheeler County 701 Adams St PO Box 447 *Web:* wheelercounty-oregon.com	Fossil	OR	97830	541-763-2911	763-2026
White County 301 E Main St PO Box 339 *Web:* www.whitecounty-il.gov	Carmi	IL	62821	618-382-7211	382-2322
White Pine County 801 Clark St Ste 4 *Web:* www.whitepinecounty.net	Ely	NV	89301	775-289-2341	289-2544
Whiteside County 200 E Knox St *Web:* www.whiteside.org	Morrison	IL	61270	815-772-5100	772-7673
Whitfield County PO Box 248 *Web:* www.whitfieldcountyga.com	Dalton	GA	30722	706-876-2559	275-7540
Whitley County 101 W Van Buren St *Web:* whitleygov.com	Columbia City	IN	46725	260-248-3102	248-3137
Whitley County Court Clerk 200 Main St Ste 2 *Web:* whitleycountyfiscalcourt.com	Williamsburg	KY	40769	606-549-6002	549-2790
Whitman County 400 N Main St *Web:* www.co.whitman.wa.us	Colfax	WA	99111	509-397-6240	397-3546
Wibaux County PO Box 199 *Web:* wibauxco.com/	Wibaux	MT	59353	406-796-2481	
Wichita County 206 S Fourth St *Web:* wichita.ksu.edu	Leoti	KS	67861	620-375-2731	
Wicomico County 125 N Div St *Web:* www.wicomicocounty.org	Salisbury	MD	21803	410-548-4801	548-4803
Wilbarger County 1700 Wilbarger St County Courthouse Rm 15 *Web:* www.co.wilbarger.tx.us	Vernon	TX	76384	940-552-5486	553-1202
Wilcox County 103 N Broad St *Web:* wilcoxcountygeorgia.com	Abbeville	GA	31001	229-467-2737	467-2000
Wilkes County 22 W Robert Toombs Ave PO Box 661 *Web:* www.washingtonwilkes.org	Washington	GA	30673	706-678-2511	
Wilkin County PO Box 219 *Web:* www.co.wilkin.mn.us	Breckenridge	MN	56520	218-643-7172	643-7167
Wilkinson County 100 Bacon St *Web:* wilkinsoncounty.net	Irwinton	GA	31042	478-946-2236	946-3767
Will County 302 N Chicago St *Web:* www.willcountyillinois.com	Joliet	IL	60432	815-740-4615	740-4699
Willacy County 576 W Main St 1st Fl *Web:* co.willacy.tx.us	Raymondville	TX	78580	956-689-2710	689-9849
Williams County 1 Courthouse Sq *Web:* www.co.williams.oh.us	Bryan	OH	43506	419-636-2059	636-0643
Williamsburg County 201 W Main St *Web:* www.williamsburgcounty.sc.gov	Kingstree	SC	29556	843-355-9321	355-1587
Williamsburg (Independent City) 401 Lafayette St *Web:* www.williamsburgva.gov	Williamsburg	VA	23185	757-220-6100	220-6107
Williamson County 1320 W Main St PO Box 624 *Web:* www.williamsoncounty-tn.gov/	Franklin	TN	37064	615-790-5712	790-5610
Wilson County 1103 Fourth St Ste 2 *Web:* co.wilson.tx.us	Floresville	TX	78114	830-393-7346	393-7345
Register of Deeds 101 N Goldsboro St PO Box 1728 *Web:* www.wilson-co.com	Wilson	NC	27894	252-399-2935	237-4341
Winchester (Independent City) 5 N Kent St *Web:* www.winchesterva.gov	Winchester	VA	22601	540-667-5770	
Windham County 11 Jail St *Web:* www.windhamsheriff.com	Newfane	VT	05345	802-365-4942	365-4945
Winkler County 100 E Winkler St *Web:* www.co.winkler.tx.us	Kermit	TX	79745	432-586-3161	586-3535
Winn Parish Police Jury 119 W Main St Ste 102	Winnfield	LA	71483	318-628-5824	
Winnebago County PO Box 2808 *Web:* www.co.winnebago.wi.us	Oshkosh	WI	54903	920-236-4800	303-3025
Winneshiek County 201 W Main St *Web:* winneshiekcounty.org	Decorah	IA	52101	563-382-0603	
Winona County 177 Main St *Web:* www.co.winona.mn.us	Winona	MN	55987	507-457-6350	454-9365
Winston County 311 W Park St *Web:* www.winstoncountyms.com	Louisville	MS	39339	662-773-8719	773-8909
Wirt County PO Box 53 *Web:* www.wirtcounty.wv.gov	Elizabeth	WV	26143	304-275-4271	275-3418
Wise County 200 N Trinity St *Web:* www.co.wise.tx.us	Decatur	TX	76234	940-627-3351	627-2138
Wolfe County 10 Ct St *Web:* kentuckycountyclerks.com	Campton	KY	41301	606-668-3515	
Wood County 1 Courthouse Sq *TF:* 866-860-4140 ■ *Web:* www.co.wood.oh.us	Bowling Green	OH	43402	419-354-9000	
Woodbury County 620 Douglas St *Web:* www.woodburyiowa.com	Sioux City	IA	51101	712-279-6611	
Woodford County 190 N Main St County Courthouse **Fax Area Code: 877* ■ *Web:* kwib.ky.gov	Versailles	KY	40383	859-873-5122	817-6585*
Woodruff County 500 N Third St *Web:* www.prsearch.com/arkansas/	Augusta	AR	72006	870-347-2391	
Woods County 407 Government St PO Box 431 *Web:* woods.oklahoma.usassessor.com	Alva	OK	73717	580-327-3118	327-6230
Woodson County 105 W Rutledge St Rm 103 *Web:* www.woodsoncounty.net	Yates Center	KS	66783	620-625-8605	625-8670
Woodward County 1600 Main St Ste 9 *Web:* woodwardcounty.org	Woodward	OK	73801	580-256-8097	254-6840
Worcester County 1 W Market St Rm 1103 *Web:* www.co.worcester.md.us	Snow Hill	MD	21863	410-632-1194	632-3131
Worcester District Registry of Deeds 90 Front St	Worcester	MA	01608	508-798-7717	
Worth County PO Box 450 *Web:* worthcounty.us	Grant City	MO	64456	660-564-2219	564-2432
Wright County 10 Second St NW Rm 201 *Web:* www.co.wright.mn.us	Buffalo	MN	55313	763-682-7539	682-7300
Wyandot County 109 S Sandusky Ave County Courthouse *Web:* www.co.wyandot.oh.us	Upper Sandusky	OH	43351	419-294-1432	294-6414
Wyoming County PO Box 309 *Web:* wyomingcounty.com	Pineville	WV	24874	304-732-8000	732-9659
Wythe County 340 S Sixth St *Web:* www.wytheco.org	Wytheville	VA	24382	276-223-6020	223-6030
Yadkin County 217 E Willow St *Web:* yadkincountync.gov	Yadkinville	NC	27055	336-679-4200	679-6005
Yakima County 128 N Second St Rm 323 *Web:* www.yakimacounty.us	Yakima	WA	98901	509-574-1430	
Yamhill County 414 NE Evans St *Web:* co.yamhill.or.us	McMinnville	OR	97128	503-434-7518	434-7520
Yancey County 110 Town Sq Ste 11 *Web:* www.yanceycountync.gov	Burnsville	NC	28714	828-682-3819	682-4301
Yankton County 410 Walnut St Ste 205 *Web:* ujs.sd.gov	Yankton	SD	57078	605-668-3080	668-5411
Yates County 417 Liberty St *Web:* www.yatescounty.org	Penn Yan	NY	14527	315-536-5120	536-5545
Yavapai County 1015 Fair St Rm 310 *Web:* www.yavapai.us	Prescott	AZ	86305	928-771-3200	771-3257
Yazoo County PO Box 186 *Web:* visityazoo.org/	Yazoo City	MS	39194	662-746-1815	746-1816
Yell County PO Box 219 *Web:* yellcounty.net	Danville	AR	72833	479-495-4850	229-5634
Yellow Medicine County 415 9th Ave *Web:* mncourts.gov	Granite Falls	MN	56241	320-564-3325	564-4435
Yellowstone County 217 N 27th St *Web:* co.yellowstone.mt.gov	Billings	MT	59101	406-256-2720	
Yoakum County PO Box 309 *Web:* www.co.yoakum.tx.us	Plains	TX	79355	806-456-2721	456-2258
Yolo County 625 Ct St Ste 202 *Web:* yolocounty.org	Woodland	CA	95695	530-666-8150	668-4029
York County 45 Kennebunk Rd PO Box 399 *Web:* www.yorkcountyme.gov	Alfred	ME	04002	207-324-1577	490-6990
Young County 516 Fourth St Rm 104 *Web:* co.young.tx.us	Graham	TX	76450	940-549-8432	521-0305
Yuba County 915 Eigth St Ste 115 *Web:* www.co.yuba.ca.us	Marysville	CA	95901	530-749-7575	749-7312
Yuma County 310 Ash St Ste F *Web:* www.yumacounty.net	Wray	CO	80758	970-332-5809	332-5919
Zapata County 200 E Seventh St Ste 115 *Web:* www.co.zapata.tx.us	Zapata	TX	78076	956-765-9920	765-9926
Zavala County 200 E Uvalde St County Courthouse *Web:* www.co.zavala.tx.us	Crystal City	TX	78839	830-374-2331	374-5955

342 GOVERNMENT - STATE

SEE ALSO Correctional Facilities - State p. 2168; Employment Offices - Government p. 2250; Ethics Commissions p. 2278; Governors - State p. 2437; Legislation Hotlines p. 2641; Lotteries, Games, Sweepstakes p. 2679; Parks - State p. 2865; Sports Commissions & Regulatory Agencies - State p. 3189; Student Assistance Programs p. 3199; Veterans Nursing Homes - State p. 3282

342-1 Alabama

	City	State	Zip	Phone	Fax
Administrative Office of Alabama Courts 300 Dexter Ave *TF:* 866-954-9411 ■ *Web:* www.alacourt.gov	Montgomery	AL	36104	334-954-5000	

	City	State	Zip	Phone	Fax
Agriculture & Industries Dept 1445 Federal Dr PO Box 3336 *Web:* agi.alabama.gov	Montgomery	AL	36109	334-240-7171	240-7190
Archives & History Dept 624 Washington Ave *Web:* www.archives.state.al.us	Montgomery	AL	36130	334-242-4435	240-3433
Arts Council 201 Monroe St Ste 110 *Web:* www.arts.alabama.gov	Montgomery	AL	36130	334-242-4076	240-3269
Attorney General 501 Washington Ave	Montgomery	AL	36130	334-242-7300	
Banking Dept 401 Adams Ave Ste 680 *Web:* www.bank.state.al.us	Montgomery	AL	36130	334-242-3452	242-3500
Child Support Enforcement Div 50 N Ripley St *Web:* www.dhr.state.al.us	Montgomery	AL	36130	334-242-9300	
Commission on Higher Education 100 N Union St PO Box 302000 *Web:* ache.alabama.gov	Montgomery	AL	36104	334-242-1998	242-0268
Conservation & Natural Resources Dept 64 N Union St PO Box 301450 *TF:* 800-262-3151 ■ *Web:* www.outdooralabama.com	Montgomery	AL	36130	334-242-3486	
Consumer Affairs Office 11 S Union St *Web:* www.aldoi.gov	Montgomery	AL	36130	334-242-7334	
Corrections Dept 301 S Ripley St *Web:* www.doc.state.al.us	Montgomery	AL	36104	334-353-3883	353-3891
Crime Victims Compensation Commission 5845 Carmichael Rd *TF:* 800-541-9388 ■ *Web:* acvcc.alabama.gov	Montgomery	AL	36117	334-290-4420	290-4455
Economic & Community Affairs Dept PO Box 5690 *Web:* adeca.alabama.gov	Montgomery	AL	36103	334-242-5100	242-5099
Education Dept 50 N Ripley St PO Box 302101 *Web:* www.alsde.edu	Montgomery	AL	36104	334-242-9700	242-9708
Emergency Management Agency 5898 County Rd 41 PO Box 2160 *TF:* 800-843-0699 ■ *Web:* www.ema.alabama.gov	Clanton	AL	35046	205-280-2200	280-2410
Environmental Management Dept 1400 Coliseum Blvd *Web:* www.adem.state.al.us	Montgomery	AL	36110	334-271-7700	271-7950
Ethics Commission 100 N Union St Ste 104 *Web:* www.ethics.alabama.gov	Montgomery	AL	36104	334-242-2997	242-0248
Finance Dept 600 Dexter Ave Ste N-105 *Web:* www.finance.state.al.us	Montgomery	AL	36130	334-242-7160	353-3300
Forensic Sciences Dept 525 Carter Hill Rd *Web:* www.adfs.alabama.gov	Montgomery	AL	36106	334-242-2938	240-3284
Higher Education Commission 100 N Union St PO Box 302000 *Web:* www.ache.state.al.us	Montgomery	AL	36130	334-242-1998	242-0268
Highway Patrol Div 301 S Ripley St PO Box 1511 *Web:* www.dps.alabama.gov	Montgomery	AL	36102	334-242-4395	277-3285
Historical Commission 468 S Perry St *Web:* www.preserveala.org	Montgomery	AL	36104	334-242-3184	240-3477
Homeland Security Dept PO Box 304115	Montgomery	AL	36130	334-956-7250	223-1120
Housing Finance Authority PO Box 242967 *Web:* www.ahfa.com	Montgomery	AL	36124	334-244-9200	244-9214
Human Resources Dept Gordon Persons Bldg 50 N Ripley St Ste 2104 *Web:* www.dhr.state.al.us	Montgomery	AL	36130	334-242-1310	353-1115
Industrial Relations Dept 649 Monroe St *Web:* labor.alabama.gov/	Montgomery	AL	36131	334-242-8005	242-3960
Information Services Div 64 N Union St Ste 200 *Web:* www.isd.state.al.us	Montgomery	AL	36130	334-242-8600	
Insurance Dept 201 Monroe St Ste 502 PO Box 303351 *Web:* www.aldoi.gov	Montgomery	AL	36104	334-269-3550	241-4192
Labor Dept 649 Monroe St *Web:* www.labor.alabama.gov	Montgomery	AL	36131	334-242-8620	242-0539
Legislature 11 S Union St *Web:* www.legislature.state.al.us	Montgomery	AL	36130	334-242-7800	
Lieutenant Governor 11 S Union St Ste 725 *Web:* www.ltgov.state.al.us	Montgomery	AL	36130	334-242-7900	242-4661
Mental Health & Mental Retardation Dept 100 N Union St PO Box 301410 *TF:* 800-367-0955 ■ *Web:* mh.alabama.gov	Montgomery	AL	36130	334-242-3454	
Motor Vehicle Div 50 N Ripley St *Web:* revenue.alabama.gov	Montgomery	AL	36104	334-242-9000	
National Guard PO Box 3711 *Web:* www.alguard.state.al.us	Montgomery	AL	36109	334-271-7200	
Pardons & Paroles Board 301 S Ripley St PO Box 302405 *Web:* www.pardons.state.al.us	Montgomery	AL	36130	334-353-7771	242-1809
Prepaid Affordable College Tuition (PACT) Program 100 N Union St Ste 660 *TF:* 800-252-7228 ■ *Web:* www.treasury.state.al.us	Montgomery	AL	36130	334-242-7514	
Public Health Dept 201 Monroe St *TF:* 800-252-1818 ■ *Web:* www.adph.org	Montgomery	AL	36104	334-206-5300	206-5534
Public Safety Dept 502 Washington Ave *Web:* dps.alabama.gov	Montgomery	AL	36104	334-242-4259	
Public Service Commission 100 N Union St RSA Union PO Box 304260 *TF:* 800-392-8050 ■ *Web:* www.psc.state.al.us	Montgomery	AL	36130	334-242-5218	242-0509
Rehabilitation Services Dept 602 S Lawrence St *TF:* 800-441-7607 ■ *Web:* www.rehab.alabama.gov	Montgomery	AL	36104	334-293-7500	293-7383
Revenue Dept 50 N Ripley St *Web:* www.revenue.alabama.gov	Montgomery	AL	36132	334-242-1170	
Robert Bentley Governor 600 Dexter Ave *Web:* www.governor.alabama.gov	Montgomery	AL	36130	334-242-7100	353-0004
Secretary of State PO Box 5616 *Web:* www.sos.state.al.us	Montgomery	AL	36103	334-242-7200	242-4993
Securities Commission 770 Washington Ave Ste 570 *TF:* 800-222-1253 ■ *Web:* www.asc.state.al.us	Montgomery	AL	36130	334-242-2984	242-0240
Senior Services Dept 201 Monroe Ste 350 *Web:* alabamaageline.gov	Montgomery	AL	36104	334-242-5743	
State Legislature State House 11 S Union St *TF:* 800-499-3051 ■ *Web:* www.legislature.state.al.us/senate/senate.html	Montgomery	AL	36130	334-242-7600	
State Parks Div 64 N Union St *TF:* 800-252-7275 ■ *Web:* www.alapark.com	Montgomery	AL	36130	800-252-7275	
State Port Authority PO Box 1588 *Web:* www.asdd.com	Mobile	AL	36633	251-441-7200	441-7216
Tourism Department 401 Adams Ave PO Box 4927 *TF:* 800-252-2262 ■ *Web:* www.tourism.alabama.gov	Montgomery	AL	36104	334-242-4169	242-4554
Transportation Dept 1409 Coliseum Blvd *Web:* www.dot.state.al.us	Montgomery	AL	36130	334-242-6207	353-6530
Treasury Dept 600 Dexter Ave Ste S-106 *Web:* www.treasury.state.al.us	Montgomery	AL	36104	334-242-7500	242-7592
Veterans Affairs Dept 770 Washington Ave # 530 *Web:* www.va.state.al.us	Montgomery	AL	36104	334-242-5077	242-5102
Vital Records PO Box 5625 *Web:* www.adph.org	Montgomery	AL	36103	334-206-5418	
Weights & Measures Div 1445 Federal Dr	Montgomery	AL	36107	334-240-7133	
Workers Compensation Div 649 Monroe St *Web:* labor.alabama.gov/wc	Montgomery	AL	36131	334-353-0990	353-8262

342-2 Alaska

	City	State	Zip	Phone	Fax
Administration, Personnel Div & Labor Relations Dept 10th Fl State Office Building PO Box 110201 *Web:* opd.doa.alaska.gov	Juneau	AK	99811	907-465-4430	465-2576
Aging Commission 150 Third St PO Box 116093 *Web:* dhss.alaska.gov	Juneau	AK	99801	907-465-3250	465-1398
Arts Council 411 W Fourth Ave Ste 1E *Web:* www.eed.state.ak.us	Anchorage	AK	99501	907-269-6610	269-6601
Attorney General PO Box 110300 *Web:* www.law.state.ak.us	Juneau	AK	99811	907-465-3600	465-2075
Banking Securities & Corporations Div 333 Willoughby Ave Fl 9 PO Box 110807 *TF:* 888-925-2521 ■ *Web:* www.commerce.alaska.gov	Juneau	AK	99801	907-465-2521	465-1230
Behavioral Health Div PO Box 110620 *Web:* www.hss.state.ak.us/dbh	Juneau	AK	99811	907-465-3370	465-2668
Child Support Enforcement Div 550 W Seventh Ave Ste 310 *Web:* www.csed.state.ak.us	Anchorage	AK	99501	907-269-6900	269-6650
Children's Services Office PO Box 110630 *Web:* www.hss.state.ak.us/ocs	Juneau	AK	99811	907-465-3191	465-3397
Commerce Community & Economic Development Dept 333 Willoughby Ave PO Box 11080 *Web:* www.commerce.state.ak.us	Juneau	AK	99811	907-465-2500	465-5442
Commission on Postsecondary Education PO Box 110510 *TF:* 800-441-2962 ■ *Web:* acpe.alaska.gov	Juneau	AK	99811	907-465-2962	465-5316
Corrections Dept PO Box 112000 *Web:* www.correct.state.ak.us	Juneau	AK	99811	907-465-3399	465-3390
Court System 303 K St *Web:* www.courts.alaska.gov	Anchorage	AK	99501	907-264-0547	264-0585
Education & Early Development Dept 801 W Tenth St Ste 200 PO Box 110500 *Web:* www.eed.state.ak.us	Juneau	AK	99811	907-465-2800	465-4156
Employment Security Div PO Box 115509 *Web:* www.labor.state.ak.us/esd/home.htm	Juneau	AK	99811	907-465-2712	465-4537
Enterprise Technology Services Div PO Box 110206 *Fax Area Code: 907 ■ *TF:* 888-565-8680 ■ *Web:* www.alaska.gov	Juneau	AK	99811	888-565-8680	465-3450*
Environmental Conservation Dept 410 Willoughby Ave Ste 303 *Web:* www.alaska.gov	Juneau	AK	99801	907-465-5066	465-5070
Fish & Game Dept 1255 W Eigth St PO Box 25526 *Web:* www.adfg.alaska.gov	Juneau	AK	99802	907-465-4100	465-2332
Health & Social Services Dept PO Box 110601 *Web:* www.hss.state.ak.us	Juneau	AK	99811	907-465-3030	465-3068
History & Archeology Office 550 W Seventh Ave Ste 1310 *Web:* dnr.alaska.gov/parks/oha	Anchorage	AK	99501	907-269-8721	269-8908
Homeland Security & Emergency Services Div PO Box 5750 *Web:* www.ak-prepared.com	Fort Richardson	AK	99505	907-428-7000	428-7009
Housing Finance Corp 4300 Boniface Pkwy 99504 PO Box 101020 *TF:* 800-478-2432 ■ *Web:* www.ahfc.us	Anchorage	AK	99504	907-338-6100	338-9218
Insurance Div PO Box 110805 *Web:* www.commerce.alaska.gov	Juneau	AK	99811	907-465-2515	465-3422
Labor & Workforce Development Dept 111 W Eigth St PO Box 21149 *Web:* www.labor.state.ak.us	Juneau	AK	99802	907-465-2700	465-2784
Legislative Ethics Committee 716 W 4th Ave Ste 230 *Web:* anchorage.akleg.gov	Anchorage	AK	99501	907-269-0111	269-0229
Lieutenant Governor PO Box 110001 *Web:* www.gov.state.ak.us	Juneau	AK	99811	907-465-3500	465-3532

	City	State	Zip	Phone	Fax
Measurement Standards Div 12050 Industry Way Bldg O Ste 6 *Web:* www.dot.state.ak.us	Anchorage	AK	99515	907-222-0900	222-1011
Military & Veterans Affairs Dept (DMVA) PO Box 5800 *TF:* 888-248-3682 ■ *Web:* dmva.alaska.gov	Fort Richardson	AK	99505	907-428-6896	
Motor Vehicles Div 3300 B Fairbanks St *Web:* www.alaska.gov	Anchorage	AK	99503	907-269-5559	269-6084
Natural Resources Dept 550 W. 7th Ave Ste 1100 *Web:* dnr.alaska.gov	Anchorage	AK	99501	907-269-8667	269-8917
Occupational Licensing Div 333 Willoughby Ave # 9 *Web:* www.commerce.state.ak.us	Juneau	AK	99801	907-465-2534	465-2974
Parks & Outdoor Recreation Div 550 W Seventh Ave Ste 1260 *Web:* dnr.alaska.gov/parks	Anchorage	AK	99501	907-269-8400	269-8901
Parole Board 550 W Seventh Ave Ste 601 *Web:* www.correct.state.ak.us/parole-board	Anchorage	AK	99501	907-269-4642	269-4697
Permanent Fund Dividend Div 333 Willoughby Ave 11th Fl *Web:* www.pfd.alaska.gov	Juneau	AK	99811	907-465-2326	465-3470
Postsecondary Education Commission 3030 Vintage Blvd PO Box 110510 *TF:* 800-441-2962 ■ *Web:* acpe.alaska.gov	Juneau	AK	99801	907-465-2962	465-5316
Public Assistance Div 350 Main St Rm 304 PO Box 110640 *Web:* dhss.alaska.gov	Juneau	AK	99811	907-465-3347	465-5154
Real Estate Commission 550 W Seventh Ave Ste 1500 *Web:* www.commerce.alaska.gov	Anchorage	AK	99501	907-269-8162	269-8156
Regulatory Commission 550 W Eigth Ave Ste 300 *Web:* www.alaska.gov	Anchorage	AK	99501	907-276-6222	276-0160
Revenue Dept P.O. Box 110400 Ste 1820 PO Box 110400 *Web:* www.revenue.state.ak.us	Juneau	AK	99811	907-465-2300	465-2389
State Legislature State Capitol *Web:* w3.legis.state.ak.us	Juneau	AK	99801	907-465-4648	465-2864
State Libraries Archives & Museums Div 333 Willoughby Ave PO Box 110571 *Web:* www.eed.state.ak.us/lam	Juneau	AK	99811	907-465-2910	465-2151
State Medical Examiner 5455 Dr Martin Luther King Jr Ave *Web:* www.hss.state.ak.us/dph/sme	Anchorage	AK	99507	907-334-2200	334-2216
State Troopers Div 5700 E Tudor Rd *Web:* www.dps.state.ak.us	Anchorage	AK	99507	907-269-5511	337-2059
Supreme Court 303 K St *Web:* courts.alaska.gov/ctinfo.htm	Anchorage	AK	99501	907-264-0612	264-0878
Tourism Development Office PO Box 118004 *Web:* www.commerce.alaska.gov	Juneau	AK	99811	907-465-2510	465-3767
Transportation & Public Facilities Dept 3132 Ch Dr *Web:* www.dot.state.ak.us	Juneau	AK	99811	907-465-3900	586-8365
Violent Crimes Compensation Board 333 Willoughby Ave State Office Bldg Fl 10 *Web:* doa.alaska.gov	Juneau	AK	99801	907-465-3040	465-2379
Vital Statistics Bureau 5441 Commercial Blvd *Web:* dhss.alaska.gov/dph/vitalstats/pages/default.aspx	Juneau	AK	99801	907-465-3391	465-3618
Vocational Rehabilitation Div 801 W Tenth St Ste 200 *TF:* 800-478-2815 ■ *Web:* www.labor.state.ak.us	Juneau	AK	99801	907-465-2814	465-2856
Workers Compensation Div 1111 W Eigth St Rm 305 PO Box 115512 *Web:* www.labor.state.ak.us/wc	Juneau	AK	99801	907-465-2790	465-2797

342-3 Arizona

	City	State	Zip	Phone	Fax
Administrative Office of the Courts 1501 W Washington St *Web:* www.azcourts.gov	Phoenix	AZ	85007	602-542-9301	542-9484
Agriculture Dept 1688 W Adams St *Web:* agriculture.az.gov/	Phoenix	AZ	85007	602-542-4373	542-5420
Arts Commission 417 W Roosevelt St *Web:* azarts.gov	Phoenix	AZ	85003	602-255-5882	256-0282
Attorney General 1275 W Washington St *TF:* 888-377-6108 ■ *Web:* www.azag.gov	Phoenix	AZ	85007	602-542-5025	542-4085
Boxing Commission 1110 W Washington St Ste 260 *Web:* azboxingandmma.gov	Phoenix	AZ	85007	602-364-1700	364-1703
Children Youth & Families Div 1789 W Jefferson St *TF:* 866-229-5553 ■ *Web:* www.azdes.gov	Phoenix	AZ	85007	602-542-0419	542-3330
Commerce Dept 1700 W Washington St Ste 600 *Web:* www.azcommerce.com	Phoenix	AZ	85007	602-771-1100	771-1200
Consumer Protection & Antitrust Unit 1275 W Washington St *Web:* www.azag.gov	Phoenix	AZ	85007	602-542-5763	542-4579
Corrections Dept 1601 W Jefferson St *Web:* corrections.az.gov	Phoenix	AZ	85007	602-542-5497	542-2859
Criminal Justice Commission 1110 W Washington St Ste 230 *Web:* www.azcjc.gov	Phoenix	AZ	85007	602-364-1146	364-1175
Education Dept 1535 W Jefferson St *Web:* www.azed.gov	Phoenix	AZ	85007	602-542-4361	542-5440
Emergency & Military Affairs Dept 5636 E McDowell Rd *Web:* www.azdema.gov	Phoenix	AZ	85008	602-267-2700	267-2954
Employment Administration PO Box 6123 *Web:* www.azdes.gov	Phoenix	AZ	85005	602-542-3957	542-2491
Executive Clemency Board 1645 W Jefferson St Rm 101 *Web:* boec.az.gov/	Phoenix	AZ	85007	602-542-5656	542-5680
Financial Institutions 2910 N 44th St Ste 310 *Web:* www.azdfi.gov	Phoenix	AZ	85018	602-771-2800	381-1225
Game & Fish Dept 5000 W Carefree Hwy *Web:* www.azgfd.com	Phoenix	AZ	85086	602-942-3000	
Government Information Technology Agency 100 N 15th Ave Ste 440 *Web:* www.azdfi.gov	Phoenix	AZ	85007	602-364-4482	364-4799
Health Services Dept 150 N 18th Ave *Web:* www.azdhs.gov	Phoenix	AZ	85007	602-364-3150	542-1062
Highway Patrol Div PO Box 6638 *Web:* www.azdps.gov	Phoenix	AZ	85005	602-223-2000	223-2928
Historic Preservation Office 1300 W Washington St *TF:* 800-285-3703 ■ *Web:* www.azstateparks.com	Phoenix	AZ	85007	602-542-4174	542-4180
Housing Dept 1110 W Washington St Ste 310 *Web:* azhousing.gov	Phoenix	AZ	85007	602-771-1000	771-1002
Industrial Commission 800 W Washington St *Web:* www.ica.state.az.us	Phoenix	AZ	85007	602-542-4411	542-3373
Insurance Dept 2910 N 44th St 2nd Fl *Web:* azinsurance.gov	Phoenix	AZ	85018	602-912-8400	912-8452
Land Dept 1616 W Adams St *Web:* land.az.gov/	Phoenix	AZ	85007	602-542-4602	
Legislature Capitol Complex 1700 W Washington St *TF:* 800-352-8404 ■ *Web:* www.azleg.state.az.us	Phoenix	AZ	85007	602-926-3559	926-3429
Lottery 4740 E University Dr *Web:* arizonalottery.com	Phoenix	AZ	85034	480-921-4400	
Medical Board 9545 Doubletree Ranch Rd *Web:* www.azmd.gov	Scottsdale	AZ	85258	480-551-2700	551-2704
Motor Vehicle Div PO Box 2100 *TF:* 800-251-5866 ■ *Web:* www.azdot.gov/mvd	Phoenix	AZ	85001	602-255-0072	
Nursing Board 4747 N Seventh St Ste 200 *Web:* www.azbn.gov	Phoenix	AZ	85014	602-771-7800	771-7888
Office of the Governor 1700 W Washington St *Web:* www.governor.state.az.us	Phoenix	AZ	85007	602-542-4331	542-7601
Postsecondary Education Commission 2020 N Central Ave Ste 550 *Web:* highered.az.gov	Phoenix	AZ	85004	602-258-2435	258-2483
Racing Dept 1110 W Washington St Ste 260 *Web:* racing.az.gov/	Phoenix	AZ	85007	602-364-1700	364-1703
Real Estate Dept 2910 N 44th St Ste 100 *Web:* www.re.state.az.us	Phoenix	AZ	85018	602-771-7799	468-0562
Rehabilitation Services Admin 1789 W Jefferson St 2nd Fl NW *TF:* 800-563-1221 ■ *Web:* www.azdes.gov	Phoenix	AZ	85007	602-542-3332	542-3778
Revenue Dept 1600 W Monroe St *Web:* www.azdor.gov	Phoenix	AZ	85007	602-716-6090	542-4772
Secretary of State 1700 W Washington St W Wing 7th Fl *Web:* www.azsos.gov	Phoenix	AZ	85007	602-542-4285	542-1575
Securities Div 1300 W Washington St 3rd Fl *Web:* www.azinvestor.gov	Phoenix	AZ	85007	602-542-4242	594-7470
State Boards Office 1400 W Washington St Ste 230 *Web:* ppse.az.gov	Phoenix	AZ	85007	602-542-5709	542-1253
State Compensation Fund 3030 N Third St *Web:* www.nvfc.org	Phoenix	AZ	85012	602-631-2000	631-2213
State Parks 1300 W Washington St *Web:* www.azstateparks.com	Phoenix	AZ	85007	602-542-4174	542-4188
Supreme Court 1501 W Washington St *Web:* azcourts.gov	Phoenix	AZ	85007	602-542-9300	542-9480
Tourism Office 1110 W Washington St Ste 155 *TF:* 888-520-3434 ■ *Web:* visitarizona.com/	Phoenix	AZ	85007	602-364-3700	364-3701
Treasurer 1700 W Washington St 1st Fl *TF:* 877-365-8310 ■ *Web:* www.aztreasury.gov	Phoenix	AZ	85007	602-542-7800	542-7176
Veterans Service Dept 3839 N Third St Ste 200 *Web:* www.azdvs.gov	Phoenix	AZ	85012	602-255-3373	255-1038
Vital Records Office 1818 W Adams St *Web:* www.azdhs.gov	Phoenix	AZ	85007	602-364-1300	364-1257
Weights & Measures Dept 4425 W Olive Ave Ste 134 **Fax Area Code:* 623 ■ *TF:* 800-277-6675 ■ *Web:* www.azdwm.gov	Glendale	AZ	85302	602-771-4920	939-8586*

342-4 Arkansas

	City	State	Zip	Phone	Fax
Administrative Office of the Courts 625 Marshall St *Web:* courts.arkansas.gov	Little Rock	AR	72201	501-682-9400	682-9410
Aging & Adult Services Div PO Box 1437 *Web:* www.daas.ar.gov	Little Rock	AR	72203	501-682-2441	682-8155
Arts Council 323 Ctr St Ste 1500 *Web:* www.arkansasarts.org	Little Rock	AR	72201	501-324-9766	324-9207
Attorney General 323 Ctr St Ste 200 *TF Consumer Info:* 800-482-8982 ■ *Web:* www.ag.state.ar.us	Little Rock	AR	72201	501-682-2007	682-8084
Bank Dept 400 HaRdin Rd Ste 100	Little Rock	AR	72211	501-324-9019	324-9028
Bill Status-Senate State Capitol Rm 320 *Web:* www.arkleg.state.ar.us	Little Rock	AR	72201	501-682-5951	
Bureau of Standards 4608 W 61st St *Web:* plantboard.arkansas.gov/Standards	Little Rock	AR	72209	501-570-1159	562-7605
Child Support Enforcement Office 1509 W Seventh St *TF:* 800-264-2445 ■ *Web:* dfa.arkansas.gov	Little Rock	AR	72201	501-682-8398	

Name / Address	City	State	Zip	Phone	Fax
Children & Family Services Div Slot S560 PO Box 1437 *Web:* humanservices.arkansas.gov	Little Rock	AR	72203	501-682-8772	682-6968
Consumer Protection Div 323 Ctr St Ste 200 *Web:* arkansasag.gov	Little Rock	AR	72201	501-682-2007	
Contractors Licensing Board 4100 RichaRds Rd *Web:* aclb.arkansas.gov	North Little Rock	AR	72117	501-372-4661	372-2247
Correction Dept PO Box 8707 *Web:* www.ark.org	Pine Bluff	AR	71611	870-267-6999	
Cosmetology Board 101 E Capitol Ave Ste 108 *Web:* www.accessarkansas.org	Little Rock	AR	72201	501-682-2168	682-5640
Crime Victims Reparations Board 323 Ctr St Ste 200 *TF:* 800-448-3014 ■ *Web:* arkansasag.gov	Little Rock	AR	72201	501-682-1020	
Development Finance Authority 423 Main St Ste 500 *Web:* www.arkansas.gov	Little Rock	AR	72201	501-682-5900	682-5859
Education Dept 4 Capitol Mall *Web:* arkansased.org	Little Rock	AR	72201	501-682-4475	682-1079
Environmental Quality Dept 5301 Northshore Dr *Web:* www.adeq.state.ar.us	Little Rock	AR	72118	501-682-0744	682-0798
Ethics Commission PO Box 1917 *TF:* 800-422-7773 ■ *Web:* www.arkansasethics.com	Little Rock	AR	72203	501-324-9600	324-9606
Finance & Administration Dept 1509 W Seventh St *Web:* dfa.arkansas.gov	Little Rock	AR	72201	501-682-2242	682-1029
Financial Aid Office 114 Silas Hunt Hall *TF:* 800-547-8839 ■ *Web:* finaid.uark.edu	Fayetteville	AR	72701	479-575-3806	575-7790
Game & Fish Commission 2 Natural Resource Dr. *TF:* 800-364-4263 ■ *Web:* www.agfc.com	Little Rock	AR	72205	501-223-6300	
General Assembly State Capitol Bldg *Web:* www.arkleg.state.ar.us	Little Rock	AR	72201	501-682-6107	682-2917
Governor State Capitol Bldg *Web:* www.arkansas.gov	Little Rock	AR	72201	501-682-2345	682-1382
Health & Human Services Dept 4815 W Markham St *Web:* www.healthy.arkansas.gov	Little Rock	AR	72205	501-661-2000	671-1450
Heritage Dept 323 Ctr St Ste 1500 *Web:* www.arkansasheritage.com	Little Rock	AR	72201	501-324-9150	324-9154
Higher Education Dept 423 Main St Ste 400 *Web:* www.adhe.edu	Little Rock	AR	72201	501-371-2000	371-2001
Highway & Transportation Dept 10324 I- 30 *TF:* 800-245-1672 ■ *Web:* www.arkansashighways.com	Little Rock	AR	72209	501-569-2000	569-2400
Human Services Dept PO Box 1437 *Web:* humanservices.arkansas.gov	Little Rock	AR	72203	501-682-1001	
Information Systems Dept (DIS) 1 Capitol Mall PO Box 3155 *Web:* www.dis.arkansas.gov	Little Rock	AR	72201	501-682-9990	682-4310
Insurance Dept 1200 W Third St *TF:* 800-282-9134 ■ *Web:* insurance.arkansas.gov	Little Rock	AR	72201	501-371-2600	371-2618
Labor Dept 10421 W Markham St *Web:* www.labor.ar.gov	Little Rock	AR	72205	501-682-4500	682-4506
Lieutenant Governor 500 Woodlane St Ste 270 State Capitol *Web:* www.ltgovernor.arkansas.gov	Little Rock	AR	72201	501-682-2144	
Motor Vehicle Office 1900 W Seventh St Rm 2030 *Web:* www.dfa.arkansas.gov	Little Rock	AR	72203	501-682-4630	682-1116
Natural Resources Commission 101 E Capitol Ste 350 *Web:* www.anrc.arkansas.gov	Little Rock	AR	72201	501-682-1611	682-3991
Parks & Tourism Dept 1 Capitol Mall *TF:* 800-628-8725 ■ *Web:* www.arkansas.com	Little Rock	AR	72201	501-682-7777	682-1364
Public Accountancy Board 101 E Capitol Ave Ste 450 *Web:* www.arkansas.gov	Little Rock	AR	72201	501-682-1520	682-5538
Public Service Commission 1000 Center St (PSC Bldg) *Web:* www.arkansas.gov	Little Rock	AR	72201	501-682-2051	682-1717
Racing Commission 1515 W Seventh St Rm 505 *Web:* www.dfa.arkansas.gov	Little Rock	AR	72203	501-682-1467	682-5273
Real Estate Commission 612 S Summit St *Web:* arec.arkansas.gov	Little Rock	AR	72201	501-683-8010	683-8020
Rehabilitation Services 525 W Capitol Ave *TF:* 800-330-0632 ■ *Web:* ace.arkansas.gov	Little Rock	AR	72201	501-296-1600	296-1655
Revenue Div PO Box 1272 *Web:* www.dfa.arkansas.gov	Little Rock	AR	72203	501-682-7025	682-7900
Secretary of State 500 Woodlane Ave Ste 256 *Web:* www.sos.arkansas.gov	Little Rock	AR	72201	501-682-1010	682-3510
Securities Dept 201 E Markham St Rm 300 *TF:* 800-981-4429 ■ *Web:* securities.arkansas.gov/	Little Rock	AR	72201	501-324-9260	324-9268
State Medical Board 2100 Riverfront Dr. *Web:* www.armedicalboard.org	Little Rock	AR	72202	501-296-1802	296-1805
State Police 1 State Police Plaza Dr *Web:* www.asp.state.ar.us	Little Rock	AR	72209	501-618-8000	
Supreme Court 625 Marshall St 1320 Justice Bldg. *Web:* courts.arkansas.gov/cotc	Little Rock	AR	72201	501-682-6849	682-6877
Treasurer 500 Woodlane State Capitol Ste 220 *Web:* www.artreasury.gov	Little Rock	AR	72201	501-682-5888	682-9692
Veterans Affairs Dept 2200 Fort Roots Dr Bldg 65 Rm 119 *Web:* www.veterans.arkansas.gov	North Little Rock	AR	72114	501-370-3820	370-3829
Vital Records Div 4815 W Markham St Slot 44 *TF:* 800-637-9314 ■ *Web:* www.healthy.arkansas.gov	Little Rock	AR	72205	501-661-2000	
Worker's Compensation Commission PO Box 950 *TF:* 800-622-4472 ■ *Web:* www.awcc.state.ar.us	Little Rock	AR	72203	501-682-3930	682-2777
Workforce Services Dept 2 Capitol Mall *Web:* www.arkansas.gov	North Little Rock	AR	72201	501-682-2121	682-2273

342-5 California

Name / Address	City	State	Zip	Phone	Fax
Administrative Office of the Courts 455 Golden Gate Ave 3rd Fl *Web:* www.courtinfo.ca.gov	San Francisco	CA	94102	415-865-4200	865-4205
Aging Dept 1300 National Dr Ste 200 *Web:* www.aging.ca.gov	Sacramento	CA	95834	916-419-7500	928-2267
Arts Council 1300 'I' St Ste 930 *TF:* 800-201-6201 ■ *Web:* www.cac.ca.gov	Sacramento	CA	95814	916-322-6555	322-6575
Athletic Commission 1430 Howe Ave. *Web:* www.dca.ca.gov	Sacramento	CA	95825	916-263-2195	263-2197
Attorney General PO Box 944255 *Web:* oag.ca.gov	Sacramento	CA	94244	916-445-9555	324-5341
Bill Status-Assembly State Capitol Rm 3196 *Web:* www.leginfo.ca.gov/bilinfo.html	Sacramento	CA	95814	916-445-2323	
Bureau of Real Estate 2201 Broadway PO Box 187000 *Web:* www.dre.ca.gov	Sacramento	CA	95818	916-227-0782	227-0777
Child Support Services Dept PO Box 419064 *TF:* 866-901-3212 ■ *Web:* www.childsup.ca.gov	Sacramento	CA	95741	916-464-5000	464-5211
Conservation Dept 801 K St MS 24-01 *Web:* www.conservation.ca.gov	Sacramento	CA	95814	916-322-1080	445-0732
Consumer Affairs Dept 400 R St *Web:* www.dca.ca.gov	Sacramento	CA	95814	916-445-1254	445-3755
Corporations Dept 1515 K St Ste 200 *TF:* 866-275-2677	Sacramento	CA	95814	916-445-7205	
Corrections Dept PO Box 942883 *TF:* 877-256-6877 ■ *Web:* www.cdcr.ca.gov	Sacramento	CA	94283	877-256-6877	
Economic Development Dept 915 I St 3rd Fl *Web:* portal.cityofsacramento.org	Sacramento	CA	95814	916-808-7223	
Education Dept 1430 N St Ste 5602 *Web:* www.cde.ca.gov	Sacramento	CA	95812	916-319-0800	319-0100
Emergency Services Office 3650 Schriever Ave. *Web:* www.caloes.ca.gov	Mather	CA	95655	916-845-8510	
Employment Development Dept 800 Capitol Mall MIC 83 *Web:* www.edd.ca.gov	Sacramento	CA	95814	916-654-8210	657-5294
Energy Commission 1516 Ninth St *Web:* www.energy.ca.gov	Sacramento	CA	95814	916-654-4287	
Environmental Protection Agency 555 Capitol Mall *Web:* www.calepa.ca.gov	Sacramento	CA	95814	916-445-3846	445-6401
Fair Political Practices Commission 428 J St Ste 620 *TF:* 866-275-3772 ■ *Web:* www.fppc.ca.gov	Sacramento	CA	95814	916-322-5660	322-0886
Finance Dept State Capitol Rm 1145 *Web:* www.dof.ca.gov	Sacramento	CA	95814	916-445-3878	
Fish & Game Dept 1416 Ninth St 12th Fl *TF:* 888-334-2258 ■ *Web:* www.dfg.ca.gov	Sacramento	CA	95814	916-445-0411	653-7387
Food & Agriculture Dept 1220 N St *Web:* www.cdfa.ca.gov	Sacramento	CA	95814	916-654-0433	654-0403
Health Care Services Dept PO Box 997413 MS 8502 *TF:* 800-735-2929 ■ *Web:* www.dhcs.ca.gov	Sacramento	CA	95899	800-735-2929	
Historic Preservation Office PO Box 942896 *Web:* www.ohp.parks.ca.gov	Sacramento	CA	94296	916-653-6624	653-9824
Horse Racing Board 1010 Hurley Way Rm 300 *Web:* www.chrb.ca.gov	Sacramento	CA	95825	916-263-6000	263-6042
Housing Finance Agency 500 Capitol Mall Ste 1400 *TF:* 877-922-5432 ■ *Web:* www.calhfa.ca.gov	Sacramento	CA	95814	916-322-3991	
Industrial Relations Dept 455 Golden Gate Ave *Web:* www.dir.ca.gov	San Francisco	CA	94102	415-703-5050	703-5058
Insurance Dept 300 Capitol Mall Ste 1700 *Web:* www.insurance.ca.gov	Sacramento	CA	95814	916-492-3500	445-5280
Lieutenant Governor State Capitol Rm 1114 *Web:* www.ltg.ca.gov	Sacramento	CA	95814	916-445-8994	323-4998
Medical Board 2005 Evergreen St Ste 1200 *Web:* www.mbc.ca.gov	Sacramento	CA	95815	916-263-2382	263-2944
Mental Health Dept 1600 Ninth St PO Box 944202 *Web:* www.dds.ca.gov	Sacramento	CA	94244	916-654-1690	
Military Dept 9800 Goethe Rd *Web:* www.calguard.ca.gov	Sacramento	CA	95827	916-854-3000	
Motor Vehicles Dept PO Box 942869 *Web:* www.dmv.ca.gov	Sacramento	CA	95818	916-657-6437	657-5716
Office of the Governor State Capitol Ste 1173 *Web:* www.gov.ca.gov	Sacramento	CA	95814	916-445-2841	558-3160
Office of Vital Records PO Box 997410 **Fax Area Code:* 800 ■	Sacramento	CA	95899	916-445-2684	858-5553*
Parks & Recreation Dept PO Box 942896 *TF:* 800-777-0369 ■ *Web:* www.parks.ca.gov	Sacramento	CA	94296	916-653-6995	657-3903

				Phone	Fax
Postsecondary Education Commission 1303 J St Ste 500 *Web:* www.cpec.ca.gov	Sacramento	CA	95814	916-445-7933	327-4417
Prison Terms Board 1515 K St Ste 600 *Web:* www.cold.ca.gov	Sacramento	CA	95814	916-445-4071	
Public Utilities Commission 505 Van Ness Ave *TF:* 800-848-5580 ■ *Web:* www.cpuc.ca.gov	San Francisco	CA	94102	415-703-2782	703-1758
Rehabilitation Dept 721 Capitol Mall *Web:* www.rehab.cahwnet.gov	Sacramento	CA	95814	916-324-1313	
Secretary of State 1500 11th St *Web:* www.sos.ca.gov	Sacramento	CA	95814	916-653-6814	653-4620
State Legislature State Capitol *Web:* www.leginfo.ca.gov	Sacramento	CA	95814	916-324-4676	445-1830
Student Aid Commission PO Box 419027 *TF:* 888-224-7268 ■ *Web:* www.csac.ca.gov	Rancho Cordova	CA	95741	916-526-8999	526-8002
Supreme Court 333 W Santa Clara St Ste 1060 *Web:* www.courts.ca.gov	San Jose	CA	95113	408-277-1004	
Teacher Credentialing Commission 1900 Capitol Ave *TF:* 888-921-2682 ■ *Web:* www.ctc.ca.gov	Sacramento	CA	95814	916-445-7254	
Transportation Dept 1120 N St *Web:* www.dot.ca.gov	Sacramento	CA	95814	916-654-5266	654-6608
Treasurer PO Box 942809 *Web:* www.treasurer.ca.gov	Sacramento	CA	94209	916-653-2995	653-3125
Veterans Affairs Dept 1227 'O' St *TF:* 800-221-8998 ■ *Web:* www.calvet.ca.gov/	Sacramento	CA	95814	916-653-2158	653-2456
Victim Compensation Program PO Box 3036 **Fax Area Code:* 866 ■ *TF:* 800-777-9229 ■ *Web:* www.vcgcb.ca.gov/victims	Sacramento	CA	95812	800-777-9229	902-8669*
Workers Compensation Div PO Box 420603 *Web:* www.dir.ca.gov/dwc	San Francisco	CA	94142	415-703-4600	703-4664

342-6 Colorado

				Phone	Fax
State Government Information 1525 Sherman St *Web:* www.colorado.gov	Denver	CO	80203	303-866-5000	
Aging & Adult Services Div 1575 Sherman St Ground Fl *TF:* 800-773-1366 ■ *Web:* www.colorado.gov	Denver	CO	80203	303-866-2636	866-2696
Agriculture Dept 700 Kipling St Ste 4000 *Web:* www.colorado.gov/ag	Lakewood	CO	80215	303-239-4100	239-4125
Arts Council 1625 Broadway Ste 2700 *Web:* www.coloradocreativeindustries.org	Denver	CO	80202	303-892-3840	892-3848
Attorney General 1525 Sherman St 5th Fl *Web:* www.coloradoattorneygeneral.gov	Denver	CO	80203	303-866-4494	866-5691
Banking Div 1560 Broadway St Ste 975 *Web:* colorado.gov/cs	Denver	CO	80202	303-894-7575	894-7570
Child Support Enforcement Div 1575 Sherman St 5th Fl *Web:* www.childsupport.state.co.us	Denver	CO	80203	303-866-4300	866-4360
Children Youth & Families Office 1575 Sherman St *Web:* www.colorado.gov	Denver	CO	80203	303-866-5700	866-2214
CollegeInvest 1560 Broadway Ste 1700 *TF:* 800-448-2424 ■ *Web:* collegeinvest.org	Denver	CO	80202	303-376-8800	296-4811
Corrections Dept 2862 S Cir Dr *Web:* www.doc.state.co.us	Colorado Springs	CO	80906	719-579-9580	
Economic Development Commission 1625 Broadway Ste 2700 *Web:* www.advancecolorado.com	Denver	CO	80202	303-892-3840	892-3848
Education Dept 201 E Colfax Ave *Web:* www.cde.state.co.us	Denver	CO	80203	303-866-6600	830-0793
Educator Licensing Unit 201 E Colfax Ave *Web:* www.cde.state.co.us	Denver	CO	80203	303-866-6628	866-6866
Emergency Management Office 9195 E Mineral Ave Ste 200 *Web:* www.colorado.gov	Centennial	CO	80112	720-852-6600	852-6750
General Assembly 200 E Colfax Ave *Web:* www.leg.state.co.us	Denver	CO	80203	303-866-3521	
Governor 136 State Capitol Bldg *Web:* www.colorado.gov/governor	Denver	CO	30203	303-866-2471	866-2003
Higher Education Commission 1380 Lawrence St Ste 1200 *Web:* www.state.co.us	Denver	CO	80203	303-866-2723	866-4266
Historical Society 1300 Broadway *Web:* www.historycolorado.org	Denver	CO	80203	303-866-3682	
Housing & Finance Authority 1981 Blake St *TF:* 800-877-2432 ■ *Web:* www.chfainfo.com	Denver	CO	80202	303-297-2432	297-2615
Human Services Dept 1200 Federal Blvd **Fax Area Code:* 720 ■ *Web:* www.colorado.gov	Denver	CO	80204	303-866-5700	944-3019*
Insurance Div 1560 Broadway Ste 850 *Web:* www.colorado.gov	Denver	CO	80202	303-894-7499	894-7455
Labor & Employment Dept 633 17th St Ste 201 *TF:* 800-390-7936 ■ *Web:* www.coworkforce.com	Denver	CO	80203	303-318-8000	
Lieutenant Governor 130 State Capitol Bldg *Web:* colorado.gov	Denver	CO	80203	303-866-2087	866-5469
Lottery 212 W Third St Ste 210 *TF:* 800-999-2959 ■ *Web:* www.coloradolottery.com	Pueblo	CO	81003	719-546-2400	546-5208
Measurements Standards Section 3125 Wyandot St *Web:* www.colorado.gov/ag	Denver	CO	80211	303-867-9217	477-4248
Medical Examiners Board 1560 Broadway Ste 1350 *Web:* colorado.gov/cs	Denver	CO	80202	303-894-7690	894-7692
Motor Vehicle Div 1881 Pierce St *Web:* www.colorado.gov/revenue/dmv	Lakewood	CO	80214	303-205-5600	205-5940
Natural Resources Dept 1313 Sherman St Rm 718 *TF:* 800-536-5308 ■ *Web:* www.dnr.state.co.us	Denver	CO	80203	303-866-3311	866-2115
Office of Information Technology 601 E 18th Ave Ste 250	Denver	CO	80203	303-764-7700	764-7725
Parks & Outdoor Recreation Div 1313 Sherman St Rm 618 *TF Campground Resv:* 800-678-2267 ■ *Web:* cpw.state.co.us	Denver	CO	80203	303-866-3437	866-3206
Parole Board 1600 W 24th St Bldg 54 *Web:* www.ccjrc.org/resources.shtml	Pueblo	CO	81003	719-583-5800	583-5805
Public Health & Environment Dept (CDPHE) 4300 Cherry Creek Dr S *TF:* 800-886-7689 ■ *Web:* www.colorado.gov	Denver	CO	80246	303-692-2000	782-0095
Public Utilities Commission 1560 Broadway Ste 250 *TF:* 800-888-0170 ■ *Web:* advancecolorado.com	Denver	CO	80203	303-894-2000	894-2071
Real Estate Commission 1560 Bdwy Ste 925 *Web:* www.dora.state.co.us/real-estate	Denver	CO	80202	303-894-2166	894-2683
Regulatory Agencies Dept 1560 Broadway Ste 1550 *TF:* 800-886-7675 ■ *Web:* cdn.colorado.gov	Denver	CO	80202	303-894-7855	894-7885
Secretary of State 1700 Broadway 2nd Fl *Web:* www.sos.state.co.us	Denver	CO	80290	303-894-2200	869-4860
Securities Div 1560 Broadway Ste 900 *Web:* cdn.colorado.gov	Denver	CO	80202	303-894-2320	
State Court Administrator 1301 Pennsylvania St Ste 300 *TF:* 800-888-0001 ■ *Web:* www.courts.state.co.us	Denver	CO	80203	303-837-3668	837-2340
State Patrol 700 Kipling St *Web:* www.colorado.gov	Lakewood	CO	80215	303-239-4500	239-4485
Supreme Court 1560 Broadway Ste 1800 *TF:* 877-888-1370 ■ *Web:* www.coloradosupremecourt.com	Denver	CO	80202	303-866-6400	
Tourism Office 1625 Broadway Ste 2700 *Web:* www.colorado.com	Denver	CO	80202	303-892-3840	892-3848
Transportation Dept 4201 E Arkansas Ave *Web:* www.coloradodot.info	Denver	CO	80222	303-757-9228	757-9153
Treasurer 200 E Colfax Ave State Capitol Ste 140 *Web:* www.colorado.gov	Denver	CO	80203	303-866-2441	866-2123
Victims Programs Office 700 Kipling St Ste 1000 *TF:* 888-282-1080 ■ *Web:* dcj.state.co.us/ovp	Lakewood	CO	80215	303-239-5719	239-4491
Vital Records Section 4300 Cherry Creek Dr S *Web:* www.cdc.gov/nchs/w2w.htm	Denver	CO	80246	303-692-2200	
Vocational Rehabilitation Div 1575 Sherman St 4th Fl *TF:* 866-870-4595 ■ *Web:* www.dvrcolorado.com	Denver	CO	80203	303-866-4150	866-4905
Wildlife Div 6060 Broadway *Web:* cpw.state.co.us	Denver	CO	80216	303-297-1192	
Workers Compensation Div 633 17th St Ste 400 *TF:* 888-390-7936 ■ *Web:* www.colorado.gov	Denver	CO	80202	303-318-8700	318-8710

342-7 Connecticut

				Phone	Fax
State Government Information 101 E River Dr *Web:* www.ct.gov	East Hartford	CT	06108	860-622-2200	
Accountancy Board 30 Trinity St *Web:* www.sots.ct.gov	Hartford	CT	06106	860-509-6179	509-6247
Administrative Services Dept 165 Capitol Ave 4th Fl *Web:* www.das.state.ct.us	Hartford	CT	06106	860-713-5100	713-7459
Aging Commission 210 Capitol Ave Ste 508 *Web:* www.cga.ct.gov	Hartford	CT	06106	860-240-5200	240-5204
Agriculture Dept 165 Capitol Ave *TF:* 860-713-2500 ■ *Web:* www.ct.gov/doag	Hartford	CT	06106	860-713-2500	713-2515
Attorney General 55 Elm St *Web:* www.ct.gov	Hartford	CT	06106	860-808-5318	808-5387
Banking Dept 260 Constitution Plaza *TF:* 800-831-7225 ■ *Web:* www.ct.gov	Hartford	CT	06103	860-240-8299	240-8178
Chief Medical Examiner 11 Shuttle Rd *TF:* 800-842-1508 ■ *Web:* www.ct.gov	Farmington	CT	06032	860-679-3980	679-1257
Child Support Assistance 55 Elm St *Web:* www.ct.gov	Hartford	CT	06106	860-808-5150	
Commission on Culture & Tourism 1 Constitution Plaza *Web:* www.cultureandtourism.org	Hartford	CT	06103	860-256-2800	256-2811
Consumer Protection Dept 165 Capitol Ave *TF:* 800-842-2649 ■ *Web:* www.ct.gov	Hartford	CT	06106	860-713-6100	707-1966
Correction Dept 24 Wolcott Hill Rd *Web:* www.ct.gov/doc	Wethersfield	CT	06109	860-692-7780	692-7783
Economic & Community Development Dept 505 Hudson St *Web:* www.ct.gov	Hartford	CT	06106	860-270-8000	270-8188
Education Dept PO Box 150471 *Web:* www.ct.gov	Hartford	CT	06115	860-713-6969	713-7017
Emergency Management & Homeland Security Div 25 Sigourney St 6th Fl *TF:* 800-397-8876 ■ *Web:* www.ct.gov/hls	Hartford	CT	06106	860-256-0800	256-0815
Environmental & Energy Protection Dept 79 Elm St *Web:* www.ct.gov	Hartford	CT	06106	860-424-3000	424-4051
Ethics Commission 18-20 Trinity St Ste 205 *Web:* www.ct.gov/ethics/site/default.asp	Hartford	CT	06106	860-263-2400	263-2402
General Assembly 300 Capitol Ave Rm 5100 *Web:* www.cga.ct.gov	Hartford	CT	06106	860-240-0100	240-0122
Governor 210 Capitol Ave *Web:* www.ct.gov	Hartford	CT	06106	860-566-4840	524-7395
Higher Education Dept 61 Woodland St *TF:* 800-842-0229 ■ *Web:* www.ctdhe.org	Hartford	CT	06105	860-947-1800	947-1310
Housing Finance Authority 999 W St *Web:* www.chfa.org	Rocky Hill	CT	06067	860-721-9501	571-4367
Information Technology Dept 101 E River Dr *Web:* www.ct.gov	East Hartford	CT	06108	860-622-2200	610-0672

				Phone	Fax
Insurance Dept 153 Market St Ste 7 *Web:* www.ct.gov	Hartford	CT	06103	860-297-3800	566-7410
Judicial Branch 231 Capitol Ave *Web:* www.jud.state.ct.us	Hartford	CT	06106	860-757-2100	757-2130
Labor Dept 200 Folly Brook Blvd *Web:* www.ctdol.state.ct.us	Wethersfield	CT	06109	860-263-6000	263-6699
Lieutenant Governor 210 Capitol Ave Rm 304 *Web:* www.ct.gov	Hartford	CT	06106	860-524-7384	524-7304
Motor Vehicles Dept 60 State St *Web:* www.ct.gov	Wethersfield	CT	06161	860-263-5700	524-4898
Parole Board 55 W Main St Ste 520 *Web:* www.ct.gov	Waterbury	CT	06702	203-805-6605	805-6652
Public Health Dept 410 Capitol Ave *Web:* www.ct.gov	Hartford	CT	06134	860-509-8000	509-7111
Public Utility Control Dept 10 Franklin Sq *TF:* 800-382-4586 ■ *Web:* www.ct.gov	New Britain	CT	06051	860-827-2935	
Real Estate & Professional Trades Div 165 Capitol Ave *TF:* 800-842-2649 ■ *Web:* www.ct.gov	Hartford	CT	06106	860-713-6100	713-7239
Rehabilitation Services Bureau 25 Sigourney St 11th Fl *TF:* 800-537-2549 ■ *Web:* www.ct.gov	Hartford	CT	06106	860-424-4844	424-4850
Secretary of State 30 Trinity St *Web:* www.sots.ct.gov	Hartford	CT	06106	860-509-6200	509-6209
State Parks Div 79 Elm St *TF:* 866-287-2757 ■ *Web:* www.ct.gov	Hartford	CT	06106	860-424-3000	424-4070
State Police Div 1111 Country Club Rd *Web:* ct.gov	Middletown	CT	06457	860-685-8000	685-8354
Supreme Court 231 Capitol Ave *Web:* www.jud.state.ct.us/external/supapp	Hartford	CT	06106	860-757-2200	757-2217
Transportation Dept 2800 Berlin Tpke *Web:* www.ct.gov	Newington	CT	06111	860-594-2000	594-3008
Treasurer 55 Elm St *Web:* www.ct.gov	Hartford	CT	06106	860-702-3000	
Veterans Affairs Dept 287 W St *TF:* 800-447-0961 ■ *Web:* www.ct.gov/ctva	Rocky Hill	CT	06067	860-721-5891	721-5904
Victim Services Office 225 Spring St 4th Fl *TF:* 800-822-8428 ■ *Web:* www.jud.state.ct.us	Wethersfield	CT	06109	800-822-8428	
Weights & Measures Div 165 Capitol Ave *TF:* 800-842-2649 ■ *Web:* www.ct.gov	Hartford	CT	06106	860-713-6100	713-7239
Workers Compensation Commission 21 Oak St 4th Fl *TF:* 800-223-9675 ■ *Web:* www.wcc.state.ct.us	Hartford	CT	06106	860-493-1500	247-1361

342-8 Delaware

				Phone	Fax
Administrative Office of the Courts 500 N King St 11th Fl *Web:* www.courts.delaware.gov	Wilmington	DE	19801	302-255-0090	255-2217
Aging & Adults with Physical Disabilities Services Div 1901 N DuPont Hwy *Web:* www.dhss.delaware.gov	New Castle	DE	19720	302-255-9390	
Agriculture Dept 2320 S DuPont Hwy *TF:* 800-282-8685 ■ *Web:* dda.delaware.gov	Dover	DE	19901	302-739-4811	
Arts Div 820 N French St 4th Fl *Web:* www.artsdel.org	Wilmington	DE	19801	302-577-8278	577-6561
Attorney General 820 N French St *Web:* attorneygeneral.delaware.gov	Wilmington	DE	19801	302-577-8400	577-6630
Bank Commissioner 555 E Loockerman St Ste 210 *Web:* banking.delaware.gov	Dover	DE	19901	302-739-4235	739-3609
Chief Medical Examiner 200 S Adam St *Web:* dhss.delaware.gov/dhss/ocme	Wilmington	DE	19801	302-577-3420	577-3416
Child Support Enforcement Div (DCSE) 84A Christiana Rd *TF:* 800-464-4357 ■ *Web:* www.dhss.delaware.gov/dhss/dcse	New Castle	DE	19720	302-577-7171	395-6734
Consumer Protection Unit 820 N French St 5th Fl *Web:* attorneygeneral.delaware.gov	Wilmington	DE	19801	302-577-8600	577-6499
Correction Dept 245 McKee Rd **Fax:* Mail Rm ■ *Web:* doc.delaware.gov	Dover	DE	19904	302-739-5601	739-8220*
Economic Development Office 99 Kings Hwy *Web:* dedo.delaware.gov	Dover	DE	19901	302-739-4271	739-5749
Education Dept 401 Federal St Ste 2 *Web:* www.doe.state.de.us	Dover	DE	19901	302-735-4035	739-4654
Emergency Management Agency 165 Brick Store Landing Rd *TF:* 877-729-3362 ■ *Web:* dema.delaware.gov	Smyrna	DE	19977	302-659-3362	659-6855
Finance Dept 820 N French St 8th Fl *Web:* finance.delaware.gov	Wilmington	DE	19801	302-577-8979	577-8982
Fish & Wildlife Div 89 Kings Hwy *Web:* www.dnrec.state.de.us/fw	Dover	DE	19901	302-739-9921	739-6157
General Assembly Legislative Hall PO Box 1401 *Web:* www.legis.delaware.gov	Dover	DE	19903	302-744-4162	739-6890
Governor 150 William Penn St 2nd Fl *Web:* governor.delaware.gov	Dover	DE	19901	302-577-3210	739-2775
Harness Racing Commission 2320 S Dupont Hwy *Web:* dda.delaware.gov	Dover	DE	19901	302-698-4599	697-6287
Health & Social Services Dept 1901 N DuPont Hwy *Web:* www.dhss.delaware.gov/dhss	New Castle	DE	19720	302-255-9675	255-4429
Higher Education Commission 401 Federal St Ste 2 *Web:* www.doe.state.de.us	Dover	DE	19901	302-735-4000	
Historical & Cultural Affairs Div 21 The Green *Web:* www.history.delaware.gov/aboutagency.shtml	Dover	DE	19901	302-736-7400	739-5660
Housing Authority 18 The Green *Web:* www.delaware.gov	Dover	DE	19901	302-739-4263	739-6122
Lieutenant Governor 150 William Penn St 3rd Fl *Web:* ltgov.delaware.gov	Dover	DE	19901	302-744-4333	
Motor Vehicles Div 303 Transportation Cir PO Box 698 *Web:* www.dmv.de.gov	Dover	DE	19903	302-744-2500	
Natural Resources & Environmental Control Dept 89 Kings Hwy *Web:* www.dnrec.state.de.us	Dover	DE	19901	302-739-9902	739-6242
Parks & Recreation Div 89 Kings Hwy *TF Campground Resv:* 877-987-2757 ■ *Web:* www.destateparks.com	Dover	DE	19901	302-739-9200	739-3817
Parole Board 820 N French St 5th Fl *Web:* delaware.gov	Wilmington	DE	19801	302-577-5233	577-3501
Professional Regulation Div 861 Silver Lake Blvd Ste 203 *Web:* www.dpr.delaware.gov	Dover	DE	19904	302-744-4500	739-2711
Professional Standards Board 401 Federal St *Web:* www.doe.k12.de.us/csa/profstds/default.shtml	Dover	DE	19901	302-735-4000	739-4654
Public Integrity Commission 410 Federal St Margaret O'Neill Bldg Ste 3 *Web:* www.depic.delaware.gov	Dover	DE	19901	302-739-2399	739-2398
Revenue Div 820 N French St 1st Fl *Web:* revenue.delaware.gov	Wilmington	DE	19801	302-577-8200	577-8202
Secretary of State 401 Federal St Ste 3 *Web:* sos.delaware.gov	Dover	DE	19901	302-739-4111	739-3811
Securities Div 820 N French St 5th Fl *Web:* attorneygeneral.delaware.gov	Wilmington	DE	19801	302-577-8424	577-6987
Services for Children Youth & Their Families Dept 1825 Faulkland Rd *Web:* www.delaware.gov	Wilmington	DE	19805	302-633-2500	995-8290
State Police Div PO Box 430 *Web:* dsp.delaware.gov	Dover	DE	19903	302-739-5901	739-5966
Supreme Court 820 N French St *Web:* www.courts.delaware.gov	Wilmington	DE	19801	302-577-8425	577-3702
Technology & Information Dept 801 Silver Lake Blvd *Web:* dti.delaware.gov	Dover	DE	19904	302-739-9500	739-6251
Thoroughbred Racing Commission 2320 S DuPont Hwy *Web:* dda.delaware.gov	Dover	DE	19901	302-698-4599	
Tourism Office 99 Kings Hwy *TF:* 866-284-7483 ■ *Web:* www.visitdelaware.com	Dover	DE	19901	302-739-4271	739-5749
Treasurer 820 Silver Lake Blvd Ste 100 *Web:* www.treasury.delaware.gov	Dover	DE	19904	302-672-6700	739-5635
Unemployment Insurance Div 4425 N Market St *Web:* uicc.delawareworks.com	Wilmington	DE	19802	302-761-8446	
Veterans Affairs Commission 802 Silverlake Blvd Ste 100 *Web:* veteransaffairs.delaware.gov	Dover	DE	19904	302-739-2792	739-2794
Violent Crimes Compensation Board 240 N James St Ste 203 *Web:* regulations.delaware.gov	Newport	DE	19804	302-995-8383	
Vital Statistics Office PO Box 637 *Web:* www.dhss.delaware.gov	Dover	DE	19903	302-283-7130	283-7131
Vocational Rehabilitation Div (DVR) 4425 N Market St *Web:* dvr.delawareworks.com	Wilmington	DE	19802	302-761-8275	
Weights & Measures Office 2320 S DuPont Hwy *TF:* 800-282-8685 ■ *Web:* dda.delaware.gov	Dover	DE	19901	302-739-4811	697-6287

342-9 District of Columbia

				Phone	Fax
Government Information 920 Varnum St NE *Web:* dc.gov	Washington	DC	20017	202-727-1000	
Aging Office 441 Fourth St NW Ste 900 S *Web:* www.dcoa.dc.gov	Washington	DC	20001	202-724-5622	724-4979
Banking Bureau PO Box 96378 *Web:* disb.dc.gov	Washington	DC	20090	202-727-8000	535-1197
Bill Status 1350 Pennsylvania Ave NW *Web:* dccouncil.us	Washington	DC	20004	202-724-8080	347-3070
Commission on the Arts & Humanities 200 I Street, SE. *Web:* www.dcarts.dc.gov/dcarts	Washington	DC	20003	202-724-5613	727-4135
Consumer & Regulatory Affairs Dept 1100 4th St SW	Washington	DC	20024	202-442-4400	442-9445
Convention & Tourism Corp 901 7th St NW 4th Fl *TF:* 800-422-8644 ■ *Web:* washington.org	Washington	DC	20001	202-789-7000	789-7037
Crime Victims Compensation Program 515 Fifth St NW Rm 109 Court Bldg A *Web:* www.dccourts.gov	Washington	DC	20001	202-879-4216	879-4230
Economic Development 1350 Pennsylvania Ave NW Ste 317 *Web:* dmped.dc.gov	Washington	DC	20004	202-727-6365	727-6703
Historic Preservation Office (HPO) 1100 Fourth St SW Ste E650 *Web:* planning.dc.gov	Washington	DC	20024	202-442-7600	442-7638
Homeland Security & Emergency Management Agency 2720 Martin Luther King Jr Ave SE 8th Fl *Web:* hsema.dc.gov	Washington	DC	20032	202-727-6161	
Housing Finance Agency 815 Florida Ave NW *Web:* www.dchfa.org	Washington	DC	20001	202-777-1600	
Human Services Dept 64 New York Ave NE 6th Fl *Web:* www.dhs.dc.gov	Washington	DC	20002	202-671-4200	
Insurance Securities & Banking Dept 810 First St NE Ste 701 *Web:* disb.dc.gov	Washington	DC	20002	202-727-8000	
Lottery & Charitable Games Control Board 2101 ML King Jr Ave SE *Web:* www.dclottery.com	Washington	DC	20020	202-645-8000	

	City	State	Zip	Phone	Fax
Paternity & Child Support Enforcement Office 441 Fourth St NW Ste 550N *Web:* cssd.dc.gov	Washington	DC	20001	202-442-9900	
Public Service Commission 1333 H St Ste 200 W Tower *Web:* www.dcpsc.org	Washington	DC	20005	202-626-5100	
Rehabilitation Services Administration (RSA) 1125 15th St NW *Web:* dds.dc.gov	Washington	DC	20005	202-730-1700	
Securities Bureau 810 First St NE Ste 701 *Web:* disb.dc.gov	Washington	DC	20002	202-727-8000	535-1196
Tuition Assistance Grant Program 810 First St NE *TF:* 877-485-6751 ■ *Web:* www.osse.dc.gov	Washington	DC	20001	202-727-2824	727-2834
Vital Records Div 825 N Capitol St NE 1st Fl *Web:* doh.dc.gov	Washington	DC	20002	202-671-5000	
Weights & Measures Office 1110 Fourth St SW *Web:* dcra.dc.gov	Washington	DC	20020	202-442-4400	442-9445

342-10 Florida

	City	State	Zip	Phone	Fax
Agriculture & Consumer Services Dept State Capitol PL-10 *Web:* www.freshfromflorida.com	Tallahassee	FL	32399	850-488-3022	
Attorney General State Capitol PL-01 *TF:* 866-966-7226 ■ *Web:* myfloridalegal.com	Tallahassee	FL	32399	850-487-1963	487-2564
Bill Status 111 W Madison St Rm 704 *TF:* 800-342-1827 ■ *Web:* www.leg.state.fl.us	Tallahassee	FL	32399	850-488-4371	
Business & Professional Regulation Dept 1940 N Monroe St *TF:* 866-532-1440 ■ *Web:* www.myfloridalicense.com/dbpr	Tallahassee	FL	32399	850-487-1395	
Chief Financial Officer 200 E Gaines St *Web:* www.myfloridacfo.com	Tallahassee	FL	32399	850-413-3089	
Citrus Dept 605 E Main St PO Box 9010 *Web:* www.floridacitrus.org	Bartow	FL	33830	863-272-8180	
Colleges & Universities Div 325 W Gaines St *Web:* www.fldoe.org	Tallahassee	FL	32399	850-245-0505	245-9667
Consumer Services Div 2005 Apalachee Pkwy *TF:* 800-435-7352 ■ *Web:* www.freshfromflorida.com	Tallahassee	FL	32399	800-435-7352	
Corrections Dept 501 S Calhoun St *Web:* www.dc.state.fl.us	Tallahassee	FL	32399	850-488-5021	
Cultural Affairs Div 329 N Meridian St *Web:* florida-arts.org	Tallahassee	FL	32301	850-254-6470	245-6454
Education Dept 325 W Gaines St Ste 1514 *TF:* 800-445-6739 ■ *Web:* www.fldoe.org	Tallahassee	FL	32399	850-245-0505	245-9667
Elder Affairs Dept 4040 Esplanade Way *Web:* www.elderaffairs.state.fl.us	Tallahassee	FL	32399	850-414-2000	414-2004
Emergency Management Div 2555 Shumard Oak Blvd *Web:* www.floridadisaster.org	Tallahassee	FL	32399	850-413-9900	488-7841
Environmental Protection Dept 3900 Commonwealth Blvd MS 10 *Web:* www.dep.state.fl.us	Tallahassee	FL	32399	850-245-2118	245-2128
Ethics Commission 3600 Maclay Blvd S Ste 201 *Web:* www.ethics.state.fl.us	Tallahassee	FL	32312	850-488-7864	488-3077
Financial Services Dept 200 E Gaines St *TF:* 800-342-2762 ■ *Web:* www.myfloridacfo.com	Tallahassee	FL	32399	850-413-3100	
Fish & Wildlife Conservation Commission 620 S Meridian St *Web:* myfwc.com	Tallahassee	FL	32399	850-488-4676	
Historical Resources Div 500 S Bronough St Ste 305 *Web:* www.flheritage.com	Tallahassee	FL	32399	850-245-6300	245-6435
Housing Finance Corp 227 N Bronough St Ste 5000 *Web:* www.floridahousing.org	Tallahassee	FL	32301	850-488-4197	488-9809
Information Technology Services 644 W Call St *Web:* www.its.fsu.edu	Tallahassee	FL	32306	850-644-4357	644-4554
Insurance Regulation Office 200 E Gaines St *TF:* 800-342-2762 ■ *Web:* floir.com	Tallahassee	FL	32301	850-413-3140	
Law Enforcement Dept 2331 Phillips Rd PO Box 1489 *Web:* www.fdle.state.fl.us	Tallahassee	FL	32302	850-410-7000	
Legislature 111 W Madison St *Web:* www.leg.state.fl.us	Tallahassee	FL	32399	850-488-4371	
Lieutenant Governor State Capitol 400 S Monroe St *Web:* www.flgov.com	Tallahassee	FL	32399	850-488-7146	921-6114
Lottery Dept 250 Marriott Dr **Fax:* Hum Res ■ *Web:* www.flalottery.com	Tallahassee	FL	32301	850-487-7777	*
Medical Quality Assurance Div 4052 Bald Cypress Way *Web:* www.floridahealth.gov	Tallahassee	FL	32399	850-488-0595	
Military Affairs Dept 82 Marine St *Web:* dma.myflorida.com	St. Augustine	FL	32084	904-823-0364	
Office of the Governor State Capitol *Web:* www.myflorida.com	Tallahassee	FL	32399	850-488-7146	487-0801
Parole Commission 4070 Esplanade Way *Web:* www.fcor.state.fl.us/	Tallahassee	FL	32399	850-488-3417	414-1915
Prepaid College Board PO Box 6567 **Fax Area Code:* 850 ■ **Fax:* Cust Svc ■ *Web:* www.myfloridaprepaid.com	Tallahassee	FL	32314	800-552-4723	309-1766*
Public Service Commission 2540 Shumard Oak Blvd *Web:* www.floridapsc.com	Tallahassee	FL	32399	850-413-6042	487-1716
Recreation & Parks Div 3900 Commonwealth Blvd MS 500 *TF Campground Resv:* 800-326-3521 ■ *Web:* www.dep.state.fl.us	Tallahassee	FL	32399	850-245-2157	
Secretary of State RA Gray Bldg 500 S Bronough St *TF:* 800-955-8771 ■ *Web:* dos.myflorida.com	Tallahassee	FL	32399	850-245-6500	245-6125
State Courts Administrator Office 500 S Duval St *Web:* www.flcourts.org	Tallahassee	FL	32399	850-922-5081	488-0156
Student Financial Assistance Office 1940 N Monroe St Ste 70 *TF:* 888-827-2004 ■ *Web:* www.floridastudentfinancialaid.org	Tallahassee	FL	32303	850-410-5200	488-3612
Supreme Court 500 S Duval St *Web:* www.flcourts.org	Tallahassee	FL	32399	850-488-0125	
Transportation Dept 605 Suwannee St *Web:* www.dot.state.fl.us	Tallahassee	FL	32399	850-414-5200	414-5201
Veterans' Affairs Dept 11351 Ulmerton Rd Rm 311-K *Web:* www.floridavets.org	Largo	FL	33778	727-518-3202	
Vital Records Bureau PO Box 210 *Web:* www.floridahealth.gov	Jacksonville	FL	32231	904-359-6900	
Vocational Rehabilitation Services Div 2002 Old St Augustine Rd Bldg A *TF:* 800-451-4327 ■ *Web:* www.rehabworks.org	Tallahassee	FL	32301	850-245-3399	
Workers Compensation Div 200 E Gaines St *Web:* www.myfloridacfo.com	Tallahassee	FL	32399	850-413-3089	
Workforce Florida Inc 1580 Waldo Palmer Ln Ste 1 *Web:* careersourceflorida.com	Tallahassee	FL	32303	850-921-1119	921-1101

342-11 Georgia

	City	State	Zip	Phone	Fax
State Government Information 7 Martin Luther King JrDr Ste 643 *TF:* 800-436-7442 ■ *Web:* www.georgia.gov	Atlanta	GA	30303	678-436-7442	
Administrative Office of the Courts 244 Washington St SW Ste 300 *Web:* www.georgiacourts.org	Atlanta	GA	30334	404-656-5171	651-6449
Aging Services Div 2 Peachtree St NW Fl 33 *Web:* aging.dhs.georgia.gov	Atlanta	GA	30303	404-657-5258	657-5285
Agriculture Dept 19 ML King Jr Dr SW *Web:* www.agr.state.ga.us	Atlanta	GA	30334	404-656-3627	656-9380
Arts Council 260 14th St NW Ste 401 *TF:* 800-222-6006 ■ *Web:* www.gpb.org/education	Atlanta	GA	30318	404-685-2400	
Attorney General 40 Capitol Sq SW *Web:* georgia.gov	Atlanta	GA	30334	404-656-3300	657-8733
Banking & Finance Dept 2990 Brandywine Rd Ste 200 *Web:* www.ganet.org	Atlanta	GA	30341	770-986-1633	
Behavioral Health & Developmental Disabilities Dept 2 Peachtree St NW Ste 22-224 *Web:* dbhdd.georgia.gov	Atlanta	GA	30303	404-657-2252	
Bill Status-House 309 State Capitol *Web:* www.house.ga.gov	Atlanta	GA	30334	404-656-5015	
Child Support Enforcement Office 2 Peachtree St NW *Web:* dcss.dhs.georgia.gov	Atlanta	GA	30303	404-657-3865	
Community Affairs Dept 60 Executive Pk S NE *Web:* www.dca.state.ga.us	Atlanta	GA	30329	404-679-4940	679-0589
Composite Medical Board 2 Peachtree St NW 36th Fl *Web:* medicalboard.georgia.gov	Atlanta	GA	30303	404-656-3913	656-9723
Corrections Dept 300 Patrol Rd Forsyth *TF:* 888-343-5627 ■ *Web:* www.dcor.state.ga.us	Atlanta	GA	31029	404-656-4661	
Driver Services Dept 2206 E View Pkwy *Web:* www.dds.ga.gov	Conyers	GA	30013	678-413-8400	
Economic Development Dept 75 Fifth St NW Ste 1200 *Web:* www.georgia.org	Atlanta	GA	30308	404-962-4000	
Education Dept 205 Jesse Hill Jr Dr SE Ste 2066E *Web:* www.gadoe.org	Atlanta	GA	30334	404-656-2800	651-8737
Emergency Management Agency (GEMA) 935 E Confederate Ave SE PO Box 18055 *TF:* 800-879-4362 ■ *Web:* www.gema.ga.gov	Atlanta	GA	30316	404-635-7000	635-7205
Employment Services Div 148 Andrew Young International Blvd NE *Web:* www.dol.state.ga.us	Atlanta	GA	30303	404-232-3515	
Environmental Protection Div 2 Martin Luther King Jr Dr Ste 1152 E Tower *TF:* 888-373-5947 ■ *Web:* www.georgiaepd.org	Atlanta	GA	30334	404-657-5947	
Family & Children Services Div 2 Peachtree St NW Ste 19-400 *Web:* dfcs.dhs.georgia.gov	Atlanta	GA	30303	404-651-9361	657-5105
General Assembly State Capitol *Web:* www.legis.ga.gov	Atlanta	GA	30334	404-656-5020	651-8086
Governor 203 State Capitol *Web:* www.gov.georgia.gov	Atlanta	GA	30334	404-656-1776	657-7332
Governor's Office of Consumer Protection 2 ML King Jr Dr Ste 356 **Fax Area Code:* 404 ■ *TF:* 800-869-1123 ■ *Web:* consumer.georgia.gov	Atlanta	GA	30334	800-869-1123	651-9018*
Historic Preservation Div 254 Washington St SW *Web:* www.georgiashpo.org	Atlanta	GA	30334	404-656-2840	
Housing Finance Div 60 Executive Pk S NE *Web:* www.dca.state.ga.us	Atlanta	GA	30329	404-679-0607	679-4837
Human Resources Dept 2 Peachtree St NW Ste 29-250 *Web:* dhs.georgia.gov	Atlanta	GA	30303	404-656-5680	651-8669

	City	State	Zip	Phone	Fax
Information Technology Office 258 Fourth St NW Rich Bldg *Web:* www.oit.gatech.edu	Atlanta	GA	30332	404-894-7173	
Insurance Commissioner Two Martin Luther King, Jr. Drive West Tower, Suite 704 *Web:* www.gainsurance.org	Atlanta	GA	30334	404-656-2070	656-4030
Labor Dept 148 Andrew Young International Blvd NE *Web:* www.dol.state.ga.us	Atlanta	GA	30303	404-232-7300	
Lieutenant Governor 240 State Capitol *Web:* ltgov.georgia.gov	Atlanta	GA	30334	404-656-5030	656-6739
Natural Resources Dept 2 ML King Jr Dr SE Ste 1252E *Web:* www.gadnr.org	Atlanta	GA	30334	404-656-3500	656-0770
Ports Authority PO Box 2406 *TF:* 800-342-8012 ■ *Web:* www.gaports.com	Savannah	GA	31402	912-964-3811	964-3921
Professional Licensing Boards Div 237 Coliseum Dr **Fax Area Code:* 866 ■	Macon	GA	31217	478-207-2440	888-8026*
Public Health Div 2 Peachtree St NW Ste 15-470 *Web:* dph.georgia.gov	Atlanta	GA	30303	404-657-2700	657-2715
Public Service Commission 244 Washington St SW Ste 126 *Web:* www.psc.state.ga.us	Atlanta	GA	30334	404-656-4501	656-2341
Rehabilitation Services Div 148 Andrew Young International Blvd NE *Web:* georgia.gov/agencies/georgia-department labor	Atlanta	GA	30303	404-232-7300	
Revenue Dept 1800 Century Ctr Blvd NE *Web:* www.etax.dor.ga.gov	Atlanta	GA	30345	404-417-4477	417-2101
Secretary of State 214 State Capitol *Web:* georgia.gov	Atlanta	GA	30334	404-656-2881	
Securities & Business Regulation Div 2 Martin Luther King Jr Dr W Tower Ste 802 **Fax Area Code:* 404 ■ *TF:* 844-753-7825 ■ *Web:* sos.ga.gov/index.php/?section=securities	Atlanta	GA	30334	478-207-2440	657-8410*
State Patrol PO Box 1456 *Web:* www.dps.georgia.gov	Atlanta	GA	30371	404-624-7000	
Student Finance Commission 2082 E Exchange Pl Ste 200 *TF:* 800-505-4732 ■ *Web:* www.gsfc.org	Tucker	GA	30084	770-724-9000	724-9089
Supreme Court 244 Washington St SW Rm 572 State Office Annex Bldg *Web:* www.gasupreme.us	Atlanta	GA	30334	404-656-3470	656-2253
Tourism Div 75 Fifth St NW Ste 1200 *TF Resv:* 800-255-0056 ■ *Web:* georgia.org/georgia_slide/tourism/	Atlanta	GA	30308	404-962-4000	
Transparency & Campaign Finance Commission 200 Piedmont Ave SE Ste 1402 *TF:* 866-589-7327 ■ *Web:* www.ethics.state.ga.us	Atlanta	GA	30334	404-463-1980	
University System Board of Regents 270 Washington St SW *Web:* www.usg.edu	Atlanta	GA	30334	404-656-2250	651-9301
Veterans Service Dept Floyd Veterans Memorial Bldg Ste 970E *Web:* veterans.georgia.gov	Atlanta	GA	30334	404-656-2300	656-7006
Vital Records Office 2600 Skyland Dr NE *Web:* dph.georgia.gov	Atlanta	GA	30319	404-679-4701	
Wildlife Resources Div 2070 US Hwy 278 SE **Fax Area Code:* 706 ■ *Web:* georgiawildlife.org	Social Circle	GA	30025	770-918-6400	557-3030*
Workers Compensation Board 270 Peachtree St NW *Web:* www.sbwc.georgia.gov	Atlanta	GA	30303	404-656-2048	651-9467

342-12 Hawaii

	City	State	Zip	Phone	Fax
State Government Information 201 Merchant St Ste 1805 *Web:* portal.ehawaii.gov	Honolulu	HI	96813	808-695-4620	695-4618
Accounting & General Services Dept 1151 Punchbowl St *Web:* www.hawaii.gov	Honolulu	HI	96813	808-586-1920	586-1922
Administrative Office of the Courts 417 S King St Rm 206 *Web:* www.courts.state.hi.us	Honolulu	HI	96813	808-539-4900	539-4855
Aging Office (HCOA) 250 S Hotel St Rm 406 *Web:* www.hcoahawaii.org	Honolulu	HI	96813	808-586-0100	
Agriculture Dept 1428 S King St *Web:* hdoa.hawaii.gov	Honolulu	HI	96814	808-973-9560	
Attorney General 425 Queen St *Web:* ag.hawaii.gov	Honolulu	HI	96813	808-586-1500	586-1239
Bill Status 415 S Beretania St Rm 401 *Web:* www.capitol.hawaii.gov	Honolulu	HI	96813	808-587-0478	587-0793
Budget & Finance Dept 201 Merchant St Suite 1805 *Web:* portal.ehawaii.gov	Honolulu	HI	96813	808-695-4620	586-1976
Business Economic Development & Tourism Dept PO Box 2359 *Web:* www.hawaii.gov	Honolulu	HI	96804	808-586-2355	586-2377
Child Support Enforcement Agency 601 Kamokila Blvd Ste 251 *TF:* 888-317-9081 ■ *Web:* ag.hawaii.gov	Kapolei	HI	96707	888-317-9081	
Civil Defense Div 3949 Diamond Head Rd *Web:* scd.hawaii.gov	Honolulu	HI	96816	808-733-4300	733-4287
Commerce & Consumer Affairs Dept 335 Merchant St *Web:* cca.hawaii.gov	Honolulu	HI	96813	808-586-2727	
Consumer Protection Office 235 S Beretania St Ste 801 *Web:* cca.hawaii.gov	Honolulu	HI	96813	808-586-2630	586-2640
Education Dept 1390 Miller St *Web:* www.hawaiipublicschools.org	Honolulu	HI	96813	808-586-3230	586-3234
Forestry & Wildlife Div 1151 Punchbowl St Rm 325 *Web:* hawaii.gov	Honolulu	HI	96813	808-587-0166	587-0160
Governor 415 S Beretania St State Capitol *Web:* governor.hawaii.gov	Honolulu	HI	96813	808-586-0034	586-0006
Historic Preservation Div 601 Kamokila Blvd Rm 555 *Web:* dlnr.hawaii.gov	Kapolei	HI	96707	808-692-8015	692-8020
Human Resources Development Dept 235 S Beretania St Rm 1400 *Web:* dhrd.hawaii.gov	Honolulu	HI	96813	808-587-1100	587-1106
Human Services Dept PO Box 339 *Web:* humanservices.hawaii.gov	Honolulu	HI	96809	808-586-4997	586-4890
Information Consortium 1136 Union Mall Rm 600 *Web:* www.hawaii.gov	Honolulu	HI	96813	808-587-1143	587-1146
Insurance Div 201 Merchant St Ste 1805 *Web:* www.hawaii.gov	Honolulu	HI	96813	808-695-4620	695-4618
Labor & Industrial Relations Dept 830 Punchbowl St *Web:* www.dlir.state.hi.us	Honolulu	HI	96813	808-586-8842	586-9099
Land & Natural Resources Dept 1151 Punchbowl St *Web:* dlnr.hawaii.gov	Honolulu	HI	96813	808-587-0400	587-0390
Legislature 415 S Beretania St *Web:* www.capitol.hawaii.gov	Honolulu	HI	96813	808-587-0478	587-0681
Lieutenant Governor 415 S Beretania St 5th Fl *Web:* ltgov.hawaii.gov	Honolulu	HI	96813	808-586-0255	586-0231
Measurement Standards Branch 1851 Auiki St *Web:* hdoa.hawaii.gov/qad/measurement-standards-branch/	Honolulu	HI	96819	808-832-0690	832-0683
Motor Vehicle Safety Office 601 Kamokila Blvd Rm 511 *Web:* hidot.hawaii.gov	Kapolei	HI	96707	808-692-7650	692-7665
Paroling Authority 1177 Alakea St Ground Fl *Web:* www.hawaii.gov	Honolulu	HI	96813	808-587-1300	
Postsecondary Education Commission 2444 Dole St Bachman Hall Rm 209 *TF:* 877-531-2333 ■ *Web:* hawaii.edu	Honolulu	HI	96822	808-956-8213	956-5156
Professional & Vocational Licensing Div PO Box 3469 *Web:* www.hawaii.gov	Honolulu	HI	96801	808-586-2708	
Public Safety Dept 919 Ala Moana Blvd Fl 4 *Web:* dps.hawaii.gov	Honolulu	HI	96814	808-587-1288	587-1282
Public Utilities Commission 465 S King St Rm 103 *Web:* www.state.hi.us	Honolulu	HI	96813	808-586-2020	
Securities Compliance Div 335 Merchant St *Web:* www.hawaii.gov	Honolulu	HI	96813	808-586-2744	586-3977
Sheriffs Div Pier 20 *Web:* dps.hawaii.gov	Honolulu	HI	96817	808-587-3621	
Social Services Div 810 Richards St Ste 400 *Web:* www.hawaii.gov	Honolulu	HI	96813	808-586-5675	586-5700
State Foundation for Culture & the Arts 250 S Hotel St 2nd Fl *Web:* sfca.hawaii.gov	Honolulu	HI	96813	808-586-0300	586-0308
State Parks Div PO Box 621 *Web:* www.state.hi.us	Honolulu	HI	96809	808-587-0300	587-0311
Supreme Court 417 S King St *Web:* www.courts.state.hi.us	Honolulu	HI	96813	808-539-4919	539-4928
Taxation Dept 830 Punchbowl St Rm 221 *TF:* 800-222-3229 ■ *Web:* tax.hawaii.gov	Honolulu	HI	96813	808-587-4242	587-1488
Teacher Standards Board 650 Iwilei Rd Ste 201 *Web:* www.htsb.org	Honolulu	HI	96817	808-586-2600	586-2606
Tourism Authority 1801 Kalakaua Ave 1st Fl *Web:* www.hawaiitourismauthority.org	Honolulu	HI	96815	808-973-2255	973-2253
Transportation Dept 869 Punchbowl St *Web:* www.hawaii.gov	Honolulu	HI	96813	808-587-2160	587-2313
Veterans Services Office 459 Patterson Rd E-Wing Rm 1-A103 *Web:* dod.hawaii.gov	Honolulu	HI	96819	808-433-0420	433-0385
Vocational Rehabilitation Div 1901 Bachelot St *TF:* 800-316-8005 ■ *Web:* humanservices.hawaii.gov/vocationalrehab/	Honolulu	HI	96817	808-586-9744	586-9755
Workforce Development Div 201 Merchant St Ste 1805 *Web:* www.hawaii.gov	Honolulu	HI	96813	808-695-4620	695-4618

342-13 Idaho

	City	State	Zip	Phone	Fax
Accountancy Board 3101 W Main St Ste 210 *Web:* www.isba.idaho.gov	Boise	ID	83702	208-334-2490	334-2615
Administrative Director of the Courts PO Box 83720 *Web:* www.isc.idaho.gov	Boise	ID	83720	208-334-2246	947-7590
Aging Commission (ICOA) 341 W Washington Fl 3 PO Box 83720 *TF:* 800-926-2588 ■ *Web:* www.idahoaging.com	Boise	ID	83702	208-334-3833	334-3033
Agriculture Dept 2270 Old Penitentiary Rd *Web:* www.agri.state.id.us	Boise	ID	83712	208-332-8500	334-2170
Arts Commission 2410 Old Penitentiary Rd *TF:* 800-278-3863 ■ *Web:* www.arts.idaho.gov	Boise	ID	83712	208-334-2119	334-2488
Attorney General PO Box 83720 *Web:* www.state.id.us	Boise	ID	83720	208-334-2520	

	City	State	Zip	Phone	Fax
Bill Status PO Box 83720 *Web:* www.legislature.idaho.gov	Boise	ID	83720	208-334-2475	334-2125
Board of Medicine 1755 N Westgate Dr Ste 140 PO Box 83720 *TF:* 800-333-0073 ■ *Web:* www.bom.idaho.gov	Boise	ID	83704	208-327-7000	327-7005
Child Support Services Bureau PO Box 83720 *Web:* www.healthandwelfare.idaho.gov	Boise	ID	83720	208-334-2479	334-0666
Commerce Dept 700 W State St PO Box 83720 *TF:* 800-842-5858 ■ *Web:* commerce.idaho.gov	Boise	ID	83720	208-334-2470	334-2631
Consumer Protection Unit PO Box 83720 *Web:* www.state.id.us	Boise	ID	83720	208-332-0102	
Correction Board 1299 N Orchard St Ste 110 *Web:* www.idoc.idaho.gov	Boise	ID	83706	208-658-2000	327-7404
Crime Victims Compensation Program PO Box 83720 *TF:* 800-950-2110 ■ *Web:* www.iic.idaho.gov	Boise	ID	83720	208-334-6000	334-2321
Education Dept 650 W State St PO Box 83720 *Web:* www.sde.idaho.gov	Boise	ID	83720	208-332-6800	334-2228
Finance Dept 800 Pk Blvd Ste 200 PO Box 83720 *Web:* www.finance.idaho.gov	Boise	ID	83712	208-332-8000	332-8096
Fish & Game Dept 600 S Walnut St *Web:* www.fishandgame.idaho.gov	Boise	ID	83712	208-334-3700	334-2114
Health & Welfare Dept 450 W State St Tenth Fl PO Box 83720 **Fax:* PR ■ *Web:* www.healthandwelfare.idaho.gov	Boise	ID	83720	208-334-5500	334-5926*
Historical Society 2205 Old Penitentiary Rd *Web:* history.idaho.gov	Boise	ID	83712	208-334-2682	334-2774
Homeland Security Bureau 4040 W Guard St Bldg 600 *TF:* 800-344-0984 ■ *Web:* www.bhs.idaho.gov	Boise	ID	83705	208-422-3040	422-3044
Housing & Finance Assn 565 W Myrtle Ave *TF:* 800-526-7145 ■ *Web:* www.idahohousing.com	Boise	ID	83702	208-331-4882	331-4804
Insurance Dept 700 W State St PO Box 83720 *Web:* www.doi.idaho.gov	Boise	ID	83720	208-334-4250	334-4398
Lands Dept 300 N Sixth St Ste 103 PO Box 83720 *Web:* www.idl.idaho.gov	Boise	ID	83720	208-334-0200	334-5342
Legislature PO Box 83720 *Web:* www.legislature.idaho.gov	Boise	ID	83720	208-334-2475	334-2125
Lieutenant Governor State Capitol *Web:* www.lgo.idaho.gov	Boise	ID	83720	208-334-2200	334-3259
Lottery 1199 Shoreline Ln Ste 100 *TF:* 800-432-5688 ■ *Web:* www.idaholottery.com	Boise	ID	83702	208-334-2600	334-2610
Motor Vehicles Div 3311 W State St PO Box 7129 *Web:* itd.idaho.gov	Boise	ID	83707	208-334-8000	334-8739
National Board For Professional Teaching Standards PO Box 83720 *Web:* www.sde.idaho.gov	Boise	ID	83720	208-332-6882	334-4664
Occupational Licenses Bureau 700 W State St *Web:* www.ibol.idaho.gov	Boise	ID	83702	208-334-3233	334-3945
Office of the Governor PO 83720 Ste 228 *Web:* www.gov.idaho.gov	Boise	ID	83720	208-334-2100	334-3454
Pardon & Parole Commission PO Box 83720 *Web:* www.state.id.us	Boise	ID	83720	208-334-2520	
Parks & Recreation Dept 5657 Warm Springs Ave *TF:* 855-514-2429 ■ *Web:* www.parksandrecreation.idaho.gov	Boise	ID	83716	855-514-2429	
Public Utilities Commission PO Box 83720 *TF:* 800-432-0369 ■ *Web:* www.puc.idaho.gov	Boise	ID	83720	208-334-0300	334-3762
Racing Commission 700 S Stratford Dr *Web:* isp.idaho.gov	Meridian	ID	83642	208-884-7080	884-7098
Real Estate Commission 575 E Parkcenter Blvd Ste 180 *TF:* 866-447-5411 ■ *Web:* www.irec.idaho.gov	Boise	ID	83706	208-334-3285	334-2050
Secretary of State 700 W Jefferson St Rm 205 *Web:* sos.idaho.gov	Boise	ID	83720	208-334-2100	
Supreme Court PO Box 83720 *Web:* www.isc.idaho.gov	Boise	ID	83720	208-334-2210	334-2616
Tax Commission 800 E Pk Blvd *TF:* 800-972-7660 ■ *Web:* www.tax.idaho.gov	Boise	ID	83712	208-334-7660	334-7844
Tourism Development Div 700 W State St PO Box 83720 *TF General:* 800-847-4843 ■ *Web:* www.visitidaho.org	Boise	ID	83720	208-334-2470	334-2631
Transportation Dept PO Box 7129 *Web:* www.itd.idaho.gov	Boise	ID	83707	208-334-8000	334-3858
Treasurer 700 W Jefferson St Ste 126 PO Box 83720 *Web:* sto.idaho.gov	Boise	ID	83720	208-334-3200	332-2959
Veterans Services Div 351 Collins Rd *Web:* www.veterans.idaho.gov	Boise	ID	83702	208-577-2310	
Vital Records & Health Statistics Bureau PO Box 83720 *Web:* www.healthandwelfare.idaho.gov	Boise	ID	83720	208-334-5988	
Vocational Rehabilitation Div 650 W State St Rm 150 *Web:* www.vr.idaho.gov	Boise	ID	83720	208-334-3390	334-5305
Weights & Measures Bureau 2216 Kellogg Ln *Web:* www.agri.state.id.us	Boise	ID	83712	208-332-8690	334-2378

342-14 Illinois

	City	State	Zip	Phone	Fax
Administrative Office of the Illinois Courts 3101 Old Jacksonville Rd *Web:* www.state.il.us/court	Springfield	IL	62704	217-558-4490	
Aging Dept 421 E Capitol Ave Ste 100 *Web:* illinois.gov/aging	Springfield	IL	62701	217-785-3356	785-4477
Agriculture Dept PO Box 19281 *Web:* www.agr.state.il.us	Springfield	IL	62794	217-782-2172	785-4505
Attorney General 100 W Randolph St 12th Fl *Web:* www.illinoisattorneygeneral.gov	Chicago	IL	60601	312-814-3000	
Attorney General 500 S Second St *Web:* www.illinoisattorneygeneral.gov	Springfield	IL	62706	217-782-1090	
Banks & Real Estate Div 500 E Monroe St 3rd Fl *Web:* www.idfpr.com	Springfield	IL	62701	217-782-3000	
Bill Status 705 Stratton Bldg *Web:* www.ilga.gov/legislation	Springfield	IL	62706	217-782-3944	524-6059
Child Support Enforcement Div 509 S Sixth St *TF:* 800-447-4278 ■ *Web:* www.childsupportillinois.com	Springfield	IL	62701	800-447-4278	
Children & Family Services Dept 406 E Monroe St *Web:* www.state.il.us/dcfs	Springfield	IL	62701	217-785-2509	524-0014
Commerce & Economic Opportunity Dept 620 E Adams St *Web:* illinois.gov/dceo	Springfield	IL	62701	217-782-7500	524-0864
Commerce Commission 527 E Capitol Ave *Web:* www.state.il.us/icc	Springfield	IL	62701	217-785-1407	
Community College Board 401 E Capitol Ave *Web:* www.iccb.state.il.us	Springfield	IL	62701	217-785-0123	524-4981
Crime Victims Services Div 100 W Randolf Rd 13th Fl *TF:* 800-228-3368 ■ *Web:* www.illinoisattorneygeneral.gov	Chicago	IL	60601	312-814-2581	814-7105
Driver Services Office 2701 S Dirksen Pkwy *Web:* www.cyberdriveillinois.com/departments/drivers	Springfield	IL	62723	217-782-6212	
Emergency Management Agency 2200 S Dirksen Pkwy *Web:* www.state.il.us/iema	Springfield	IL	62703	217-782-7860	
Environmental Protection Agency 1021 N Grand Ave E **Fax Area Code:* 217 ■ *Web:* www.epa.state.il.us	Springfield	IL	62794	17--782--3362	782-9039*
General Assembly 705 Stratton Bldg *Web:* www.ilga.gov	Springfield	IL	62706	217-782-2000	
Governor State Capitol Bldg Rm 207 *Web:* www.illinois.gov/gov	Springfield	IL	62706	217-782-6830	524-4049
Healthcare & Family Services Dept 201 S Grand Ave E 3rd Fl *Web:* www.hfs.illinois.gov	Springfield	IL	62763	217-782-1200	524-7979
Higher Education Board 431 E Adams St 2nd Fl *Web:* www.ibhe.org	Springfield	IL	62701	217-782-2551	782-8548
Historic Preservation Agency 1 Old State Capitol Plaza *Web:* www.state.il.us	Springfield	IL	62701	217-785-7930	785-7937
Housing Development Authority 401 N Michigan Ave Ste 900 *Web:* www.ihda.org	Chicago	IL	60611	312-836-5200	
Human Services Dept 100 S Grand Ave E 3rd Fl *TF:* 800-843-6154 ■ *Web:* www.dhs.state.il.us	Springfield	IL	62762	217-557-1601	
Insurance Div 320 W Washington St 4th Fl *Web:* insurance.illinois.gov	Springfield	IL	62767	217-782-4515	782-5020
Labor Dept 160 N LaSalle St Ste C-1300 *Web:* www.illinois.gov	Chicago	IL	60601	312-793-2800	793-5257
Lottery 101 W Jefferson St **Fax Area Code:* 866 ■ *TF:* 800-252-1775 ■ *Web:* www.illinoislottery.com	Springfield	IL	62702	217-524-6435	877-0436*
Mental Health Div 100 W Randolf St Ste 3-400 *TF:* 800-252-2923 ■ *Web:* illinois.gov/dceo	Chicago	IL	60601	312-814-2811	
Military Affairs Dept 1301 N MacArthur Blvd *Web:* www.il.ngb.army.mil	Springfield	IL	62702	217-761-3569	761-3527
Natural Resources Dept 1 Natural Resources Way *Web:* dnr.state.il.us	Springfield	IL	62702	217-782-6302	
Professional Regulation Div 320 W Washington St 3rd Fl *Web:* www.ildpr.com	Springfield	IL	62786	217-785-0820	782-7645
Public Health Dept 535 W Jefferson St *Web:* www.idph.state.il.us	Springfield	IL	62761	217-782-4977	782-3987
Racing Board 100 W Randolph St Ste 5-700 **Fax Area Code:* 866 ■ *Web:* www2.illinois.gov	Chicago	IL	60601	312-814-2600	323-0273*
Revenue Dept 101 W Jefferson St *TF:* 800-732-8866 ■ *Web:* www.revenue.state.il.us	Springfield	IL	62702	217-782-3336	
Secretary of State 213 State Capitol *TF:* 800-252-8980 ■ *Web:* www.cyberdriveillinois.com	Springfield	IL	62756	217-782-2201	
Securities Dept 300 W Jefferson St Ste 300-A *Web:* www.cyberdriveillinois.com	Springfield	IL	62702	217-782-2256	782-8876
State Board of Education 100 N First St *Web:* www.isbe.state.il.us	Springfield	IL	62777	217-782-4321	524-4928
State Police 801 S Seventh St PO Box 19461 *Web:* www.isp.state.il.us	Springfield	IL	62794	217-782-7263	785-2821
Student Assistance Commission 1755 Lake Cook Rd **Fax:* Cust Svc ■ *TF:* 800-899-4722 ■ *Web:* collegeillinois.org/	Deerfield	IL	60015	847-948-8500	831-8549*
Supreme Court 200 E Capitol Ave *Web:* www.state.il.us/court	Springfield	IL	62701	217-782-2035	
Tourism Bureau 100 W Randolph St Ste 3-400 *TF:* 800-226-6632 ■ *Web:* www.enjoyillinois.com	Chicago	IL	60601	312-814-4732	814-6175
Treasurer Capitol Bldg 219 Statehouse *Web:* www.treasurer.il.gov/contact-us.aspx	Springfield	IL	62701	217-782-2211	785-2777
Veterans Affairs Dept James R. Thompson Ctr 100 W Randolph Ste 5-570 **Fax Area Code:* 217 ■ *TF:* 800-437-9824 ■ *Web:* www2.illinois.gov	Chicago	IL	60601	312-814-5391	524-0344*
Vital Records Div 605 W Jefferson St *Web:* www.idph.state.il.us/vitalrecords	Springfield	IL	62702	217-782-6553	
Wildlife Resources Div 1 Natural Resources Way *Web:* www.dnr.state.il.us	Springfield	IL	62702	217-782-6384	

Phone Fax

Workers Compensation Commission
100 W Randolph St 8th Fl. .... Chicago IL 60601 312-814-6611 814-6523
TF: 866-352-3033 ■ *Web:* www.iwcc.il.gov

342-15 Indiana

Phone Fax

State Government Information
402 W Washington St Rm W160A .... Indianapolis IN 46204 317-233-0800
TF: 800-457-8283 ■ *Web:* www.in.gov

Agriculture Dept 101 W Ohio St Ste 1200 .... Indianapolis IN 46204 317-232-8770 232-1362
Web: www.in.gov/isda

Arts Commission 150 W Market St Ste 618 .... Indianapolis IN 46204 317-232-1268 232-5595
Web: www.in.gov/arts

Attorney General
302 W Washington St 5th Fl. .... Indianapolis IN 46204 317-232-6201 232-7979
Web: www.in.gov/attorneygeneral

Bill Status
State House 200 W Washington St Ste 220 .... Indianapolis IN 46204 317-233-5293
Web: www.in.gov/apps/lsa/session/billwatch

Child Support Bureau
402 W Washington St. .... Indianapolis IN 46204 317-232-2350
TF: 800-840-8757 ■ *Web:* www.in.gov/dcs/support

Consumer Protection Div
402 W Washington St 5th Fl. .... Indianapolis IN 46204 317-232-6330 233-4393
TF: 800-382-5516 ■ *Web:* www.in.gov

Correction Dept
302 W Washington St Rm E334 .... Indianapolis IN 46204 317-232-5715 232-6798
Web: in.gov/idoc/

Disability Aging & Rehabilitative Services Div
402 W Washington St Rm W451 .... Indianapolis IN 46204 317-232-1147 232-1240
TF: 800-545-7763 ■ *Web:* www.in.gov

Economic Development Corp
1 N Capitol Ave Ste 700 .... Indianapolis IN 46204 317-232-8800 232-4146
Web: www.iedc.in.gov

Education Dept
115 W Washington St Rm 229 .... Indianapolis IN 46204 317-232-6610 232-9121

Environmental Management Dept
100 N Senate Ave Rm 1301 .... Indianapolis IN 46204 317-232-8611 233-6647
TF: 800-451-6027 ■ *Web:* www.in.gov/idem

Family & Social Services Admin
402 W Washington St Rm W461 PO Box 7083. .... Indianapolis IN 46207 800-545-7763 232-6478*
**Fax Area Code:* 317 ■ *Web:* www.in.gov/fssa

Finance Authority
1 N Capitol Ave Ste 900 .... Indianapolis IN 46204 317-233-4332 232-6786
Web: www.in.gov

Financial Institutions Dept
402 W Washington St. .... Indianapolis IN 46204 317-232-3955 232-7655
Web: www.in.gov

Fish & Wildlife Div
402 W Washington St Rm W273 .... Indianapolis IN 46204 317-232-4080 232-8150
Web: www.in.gov/dnr/fishwild

General Assembly
State House 200 W Washington St. .... Indianapolis IN 46204 317-232-9600 232-2554
TF: 800-382-9842 ■ *Web:* www.in.gov/legislative

Governor
State House 200 W Washington St Rm 206 .... Indianapolis IN 46204 317-232-4567 232-3443
Web: www.in.gov

Health Dept 2 N Meridian St. .... Indianapolis IN 46204 317-233-1325
Web: www.in.gov

Higher Education Commission
101 W Ohio St Ste 550. .... Indianapolis IN 46204 317-464-4400 464-4410
Web: www.in.gov

Historical Bureau
140 N Senate Ave Rm 130 .... Indianapolis IN 46204 317-232-2537 232-3728
Web: www.in.gov/history

Homeland Security Dept
302 W Washington St Rm E208 .... Indianapolis IN 46204 317-232-3980 232-3895
Web: www.in.gov/dhs

Horse Racing Commission
150 W Market St Ste 530 .... Indianapolis IN 46204 317-233-3119 233-4470
Web: www.in.gov

Housing Finance Authority
30 S Meridian St Ste 1000 .... Indianapolis IN 46204 317-232-7777 232-7778
Web: www.in.gov

Insurance Dept
311 W Washington St Ste 300 .... Indianapolis IN 46204 317-232-2385 232-5251
TF Cust Svc: 800-622-4461 ■ *Web:* www.in.gov

Labor Dept 402 W Washington St Rm W195. .... Indianapolis IN 46204 317-232-2655
Web: www.in.gov/labor

Lieutenant Governor
200 W Washington St Ste 230 .... Indianapolis IN 46204 317-232-9856
Web: in.gov/lg

Lottery 201 S Capitol Ave Ste 1100. .... Indianapolis IN 46225 317-264-4800
TF: 800-955-6886 ■ *Web:* www.in.gov

Motor Vehicles Bureau
100 N Senate Ave Rm N440 .... Indianapolis IN 46204 317-233-6000 233-3135
Web: www.in.gov

Natural Resources Dept
402 W Washington St. .... Indianapolis IN 46204 317-232-4200 233-6811
Web: www.in.gov/dnr

Parole Services Div
302 W Washington St Rm E-334 .... Indianapolis IN 46204 317-232-5757
Web: in.gov/ai/errors/idoc_404.html

Port Commission 150 W Market St Ste 100. .... Indianapolis IN 46204 317-232-9200 232-0137
TF: 800-232-7678 ■ *Web:* www.portsofindiana.com

Professional Licensing Agency
302 W Washington St Rm E034 .... Indianapolis IN 46204 317-232-2980 232-2312
Web: www.in.gov/pla

Professional Standards Div
101 W Ohio St Ste 300. .... Indianapolis IN 46204 317-232-9010 232-9023

Phone Fax

Revenue Dept 100 N Senate Ave Rm N128 .... Indianapolis IN 46204 317-232-2240 245-4877*
**Fax Area Code:* 574 ■ *Web:* www.in.gov/dor

Secretary of State
200 W Washington St Rm 201 .... Indianapolis IN 46204 317-232-6531 233-3283
Web: www.in.gov

Securities Div
302 W Washington St Rm E111 .... Indianapolis IN 46204 317-232-6681 233-3675
Web: www.in.gov

State Court Administration Div
30 S Meridian St Ste 500 .... Indianapolis IN 46204 317-232-2542 233-6586
Web: www.in.gov

State Ethics Commission
315 W Ohio St Rm 104. .... Indianapolis IN 46202 317-232-3850 232-0707
Web: www.in.gov/ig

State Parks & Reservoirs Div
402 W Washington St Rm W298 .... Indianapolis IN 46204 317-232-4124 232-4132
TF: 800-622-4931 ■ *Web:* www.in.gov

State Police 100 N Senate Ave 3rd Fl. .... Indianapolis IN 46204 317-232-8248 232-0652
Web: www.in.gov/isp

Students Assistance Commission
150 W Market St Ste 500 .... Indianapolis IN 46204 317-232-2350 232-3260
TF: 888-528-4719 ■ *Web:* www.in.gov

Supreme Court
State House 200 W Washington St Rm 315 .... Indianapolis IN 46204 317-232-2540 232-8372
Web: www.in.gov/judiciary/supreme

Technology Office
100 N Senate Ave Ste N-551 .... Indianapolis IN 46204 317-232-3172 232-0748
Web: www.in.gov

Tourism Development Office
1 N Capitol Ave Ste 100 .... Indianapolis IN 46204 317-232-8860 233-6887
TF: 800-457-8283 ■ *Web:* www.in.gov

Transportation Dept
100 N Senate Ave Rm N755 .... Indianapolis IN 46204 317-232-5533 232-0238
Web: www.in.gov

Treasurer
State House 200 W Washington St Rm 242 .... Indianapolis IN 46204 317-232-6386 233-1780
Web: www.in.gov/tos

Utility Regulatory Commission
302 W Washington St Rm E306 .... Indianapolis IN 46204 317-232-2701 232-6758
Web: www.in.gov/iurc

Veterans' Affairs Dept
302 W Washington St Rm E120 .... Indianapolis IN 46204 317-232-3910 232-7721
Web: www.in.gov

Victims Services Div
101 West Washington Street
Suite 1170 .... East Tower Indianapolis IN 46204 317-232-1233 233-3912
TF: 800-353-1484 ■ *Web:* www.in.gov

Vital Records Office PO Box 7125 .... Indianapolis IN 46206 317-233-2700
Web: www.cdc.gov/nchs/w2w/indiana.htm

Weights & Measures Div
2525 Shadeland Ave Unit D3 .... Indianapolis IN 46219 317-356-7078 351-2877
Web: www.in.gov/isdh/23288.htm

Worker's Compensation Board
402 W Washington St Rm W196 .... Indianapolis IN 46204 317-232-3808
Web: in.gov/wcb/

Workforce Development Dept
10 N Senate Ave .... Indianapolis IN 46204 317-232-7670 233-4793
TF: 800-891-6499 ■ *Web:* www.in.gov

342-16 Iowa

Phone Fax

State Government Information
1305 E Walnut St .... Des Moines IA 50319 515-281-5011
Web: www.iowa.gov

Adult Children & Family Services Div
1305 E Walnut St .... Des Moines IA 50319 515-281-3094 564-4044*
■ *TF:* 800-735-2942 ■ *Web:* www.dhs.state.ia.us

Agriculture & Land Stewardship Dept
502 E Ninth St .... Des Moines IA 50319 515-281-5321 281-6236
Web: www.iowaagriculture.gov

Arts Council 600 E Locust. .... Des Moines IA 50319 515-242-6194 242-6498
Web: www.iowaartscouncil.org

Attorney General 1305 E Walnut St 2nd Fl .... Des Moines IA 50319 515-281-5164 281-4209
Web: www.state.ia.us/government/ag

Banking Div 200 E Grand Ave Ste 300 .... Des Moines IA 50309 15--725--0505

Child Support Recovery Unit PO Box 9125. .... Des Moines IA 50306 888-229-9223
TF: 888-229-9223 ■ *Web:* secureapp.dhs.state.ia.us/childsupport

Commerce Dept 1918 SE Hulsizer Rd. .... Ankeny IA 50021 515-281-7400 281-5329
Web: commerce.iowa.gov

Community Development Div 200 E Grand Ave .... Des Moines IA 50309 515-725-3000 725-3010
Web: www.iowaeconomicdevelopment.com/community

Consumer Protection Div
1305 E Walnut St 2nd Fl. .... Des Moines IA 50319 515-281-5926 281-6771
TF: 888-777-4590 ■ *Web:* www.iowaattorneygeneral.org

Corrections Dept 420 Watson Powell Jr Way .... Des Moines IA 50309 515-242-5702
Web: www.doc.state.ia.us

Economic Development Dept 200 E Grand Ave .... Des Moines IA 50309 515-242-4700
Web: www.state.ia.us/government/ided

Education Dept 400 E 14th St. .... Des Moines IA 50319 515-281-3436 242-5988
Web: www.iowa.gov

Educational Examiners Board
400 E 14th St Grimes State Office Bldg. .... Des Moines IA 50319 515-281-5849 281-7669
Web: www.state.ia.us/boee

Elder Affairs Dept 510 E 12th Street Ste 2. .... Des Moines IA 50309 515-242-3333
TF: 800-532-3213 ■ *Web:* www.iowaaging.gov

Emergency Management Div
7105 NW 70th Ave Camp Dodge Bldg W-4 .... Des Moines IA 50131 515-281-3231 725-3260
Web: homelandsecurity.iowa.gov/

	City	State	Zip	Phone	Fax
Environmental Services Div 11101 Aurora Ave *Web:* www.iesiowa.com	Urbandale	IA	50322	515-279-8042	279-1853
Ethics & Campaign Disclosure Board 510 E 12th St Ste 1-A *Web:* www.state.ia.us	Des Moines	IA	50319	515-281-4028	281-3701
General Assembly State Capitol 1007 E Grand Ave *Web:* www.legis.iowa.gov	Des Moines	IA	50319	515-281-5129	
Governor 1007 East Grand Ave State Capitol *Web:* governor.iowa.gov/	Des Moines	IA	50319	515-281-5211	
Human Services Dept 1305 E Walnut St Fl 5 SE *Web:* www.dhs.state.ia.us	Des Moines	IA	50319	515-669-8002	242-6036
Information Technology Dept 1305 E Walnut St Level B *Web:* www.state.ia.us	Des Moines	IA	50319	515-281-5503	
Insurance Div 330 Maple St *Web:* www.iid.state.ia.us	Des Moines	IA	50319	515-281-5705	281-3059
Lottery 2323 Grand Ave ■ *Web:* www.ialottery.com/	Des Moines	IA	50312	515-323-4633	
Medical Examiners Board 400 SW Eigth St Ste C *Web:* medicalboard.iowa.gov	Des Moines	IA	50309	515-281-5171	242-5908
Motor Vehicle Div 100 Euclid Ave PO Box 9204 *TF:* 800-532-1121 ■ *Web:* www.dmvusa.com	Des Moines	IA	50306	515-244-9124	
Natural Resource Dept 502 E Ninth St *Web:* www.iowadnr.gov	Des Moines	IA	50319	515-281-5918	281-6794
Natural Resources Dept 502 E Ninth St *Web:* www.iowadnr.gov	Des Moines	IA	50319	515-281-5918	281-6794
Office of Governor 1007 E Grand Ave *Web:* www.ltgovernor.iowa.gov	Des Moines	IA	50319	515-281-5211	
Parks & Preserves Bureau 502 E Ninth St *Web:* iowadnr.gov	Des Moines	IA	50319	515-281-5918	
Parole Board 510 E 12th St Ste 3 *Web:* www.bop.state.ia.us	Des Moines	IA	50319	515-725-5757	725-5762
Professional Licensing & Regulation Div 200 E Grand Ave Ste 390 *Web:* www.state.ia.us/government/com/prof	Des Moines	IA	50309	515-243-4723	281-4862
Public Health Dept 321 E 12th St *Web:* www.idph.state.ia.us	Des Moines	IA	50319	515-281-5787	281-4958
Regents Board 11260 Aurora Ave *Web:* regents.iowa.gov	Urbandale	IA	50322	515-281-3934	281-6420
Revenue & Finance Dept 1305 E Walnut *TF:* 800-367-3388 ■ *Web:* www.iowa.gov	Des Moines	IA	50319	515-281-3204	
Secretary of State 321 E 12th St 1st Fl *Web:* sos.iowa.gov	Des Moines	IA	50319	515-281-5204	242-5953
Securities Bureau 340 Maple St *Web:* www.iid.state.ia.us/securities_complaint	Des Moines	IA	50319	515-281-5705	281-3059
State Court Administration 1111 E Ct Ave *Web:* www.iowacourts.gov	Des Moines	IA	50319	515-281-5241	
State Historical Society 600 E Locust St *Web:* www.iowahistory.org	Des Moines	IA	50319	515-281-5111	242-6498
State Patrol Div 215 E Seventh St *Web:* www.dps.state.ia.us/isp	Des Moines	IA	50319	515-725-6090	
Supreme Court 1111 E Ct Ave Iowa Judicial Branch Bldg *Web:* iowautility.org	Des Moines	IA	50319	515-281-5911	
Transportation Dept 800 Lincoln Way *Web:* iowadot.gov	Ames	IA	50010	515-239-1101	
Treasurer State Treasurer's Office Capitol Bldg *Web:* www.treasurer.state.ia.us	Des Moines	IA	50319	515-281-5368	281-7562
Utilities Board 1375 E Ct Ave Rm 69 *TF:* 877-565-4450 ■ *Web:* www.state.ia.us/government/com/util	Des Moines	IA	50319	515-725-7300	
Veterans Affairs Dept 7105 NW 70th Ave Camp Dodge Bldg A6A *Web:* va.iowa.gov	Johnston	IA	50131	515-242-5331	242-5659
Vital Records Bureau 321 E 12th St Lucas State Office Bldg 1st Fl *Web:* www.idph.state.ia.us	Des Moines	IA	50319	515-281-4944	281-0479
Vocational Rehabilitation Services Div 510 E 12th St *Web:* www.ivrs.iowa.gov	Des Moines	IA	50319	515-281-4311	281-7645
Weights & Measures Bureau 502 E Ninth St *Web:* www.iowaagriculture.gov/weightsandmeasures.asp	Des Moines	IA	50319	515-725-1492	
Workforce Development 1000 E Grand Ave *TF:* 800-562-4692 ■ *Web:* www.iowaworkforce.org	Des Moines	IA	50319	515-281-5387	281-4698

342-17 Kansas

	City	State	Zip	Phone	Fax
Accountancy Board 900 SW Jackson St Ste 556 *Web:* www.ksboa.org	Topeka	KS	66612	785-296-2162	291-3501
Aging Dept 503 S Kansas Ave *Web:* www.kdads.ks.gov	Topeka	KS	66603	785-296-4986	296-0256
Agriculture Dept 109 SW Ninth St *Web:* agriculture.ks.gov	Topeka	KS	66612	785-296-3556	296-8389
Attorney General 120 SW Tenth Ave 2nd Fl *Web:* ag.ks.gov	Topeka	KS	66612	785-296-2215	296-6296
Banking Commissioner 700 SW Jackson St Ste 300 *Web:* www.osbckansas.org	Topeka	KS	66603	785-296-2266	296-0168
Bill Status 300 SW Tenth Ave State Capitol Bldg Rm 343N *Web:* www.kslegislature.org	Topeka	KS	66612	785-296-2391	296-1153
Chief Legal Governor's Office 2nd Fl Capitol Bldg *Web:* www.kansas.gov	Topeka	KS	66612	785-368-8767	
Commerce Dept 1000 SW Jackson St Ste 100 *Web:* www.kansascommerce.com	Topeka	KS	66612	785-296-3481	296-5055
Conservation Commission 109 SW Ninth St Ste 500 *Web:* agriculture.ks.gov	Topeka	KS	66612	785-296-3600	296-6172
Consumer Protection Div 534 S Kansas Ave Ste 1210 *TF:* 800-452-6727 ■ *Web:* www.kansas.gov	Topeka	KS	66603	785-296-5059	296-5563
Corp Commission 1500 SW Arrowhead Rd *Web:* www.kcc.state.ks.us	Topeka	KS	66604	785-271-3220	271-3354
Corrections Dept 900 SW Jackson St Ste 400 *Web:* www.dc.state.ks.us	Topeka	KS	66612	785-296-3317	296-0014
Cosmetology Board 714 SW Jackson St Ste 100 *Web:* www.kansas.gov/kboc	Topeka	KS	66603	785-296-3155	296-3002
Crime Victims Compensation Board 120 SW 10th Ave 2nd Fl *Web:* ag.ks.gov/victim-services/victim-compensation	Topeka	KS	66612	785-296-2359	296-0652
Emergency Management Div 2800 SW Topeka Blvd *Web:* www.kansas.gov	Topeka	KS	66611	785-296-5059	
Governmental Ethics Commission 109 W Ninth St Ste 504 *Web:* www.kansas.gov	Topeka	KS	66612	785-296-4219	296-2548
Healing Arts Board 800 SW Jackson Lower Level Ste A *TF:* 888-886-7205 ■ *Web:* www.ksbha.org	Topeka	KS	66612	785-296-7413	296-0852
Health & Environment Dept 1000 SW Jackson St *Web:* www.kdheks.gov	Topeka	KS	66612	785-296-1500	
Highway Patrol 122 SW Seventh St *Web:* www.kansashighwaypatrol.org	Topeka	KS	66603	785-296-6800	
Historical Society 6425 SW Sixth Ave *Web:* www.kshs.org	Topeka	KS	66615	785-272-8681	272-8682
Housing Resources Corp 611 S Kansas Ave Ste 300 *Web:* www.kshousingcorp.org	Topeka	KS	66603	785-296-5865	296-8985
Information Systems & Communications Div 900 SW Jackson *Web:* da.ks.gov	Topeka	KS	66612	785-296-3343	296-1168
Insurance Dept 420 SW Ninth St *TF:* 800-432-2484 ■ *Web:* www.ksinsurance.org	Topeka	KS	66612	785-296-3071	296-2283
Judicial Administrator 301 W Tenth St Kansas Judicial Ctr *Web:* www.kscourts.org	Topeka	KS	66612	785-296-2256	296-7076
Legislature 300 SW Tenth Ave State Capitol Bldg *Web:* www.kslegislature.org	Topeka	KS	66612	785-296-2391	296-1153
Lieutenant Governor 300 SW Tenth Ave State Capitol Bldg Rm 222 *Web:* kansashighwaypatrol.org	Topeka	KS	66612	785-296-2213	
Lottery 128 N Kansas Ave *TF:* 800-544-9467 ■ *Web:* kslottery.com	Topeka	KS	66603	785-296-5700	
Motor Vehicles Div 915 SW Harrison St Rm 159 *Web:* www.ksrevenue.org	Topeka	KS	66626	785-296-3621	296-3852
Real Estate Commission 120 SE Sixth Ave Ste 200 *Web:* www.accesskansas.org/krec	Topeka	KS	66603	785-296-3411	296-1771
Regents Board 1000 SW Jackson St Ste 520 *Web:* www.kansasregents.org	Topeka	KS	66612	785-296-3421	296-0983
Rehabilitation Services Div 915 SW Harrison Docking State Office Bldg 9th Fl N *Web:* www.dcf.ks.gov	Topeka	KS	66612	785-368-7471	368-7467
Revenue Dept 915 SW Harrison St *Web:* www.ksrevenue.org	Topeka	KS	66612	785-296-3041	368-8392
Secretary of State 120 SW Tenth Ave 1st Fl *Web:* www.kssos.org	Topeka	KS	66612	785-296-4564	296-4570
Securities Commission 618 S Kansas Ave 2nd Fl *Web:* www.securities.state.ks.us	Topeka	KS	66603	785-296-3307	296-6872
Social & Rehabilitation Services Dept 915 SW Harrison St 6th Fl *Web:* dcf.ks.gov	Topeka	KS	66612	785-296-3959	296-2173
Supreme Court 301 SW 10th Ave Rm 374 ■ *Web:* kansas.gov	Topeka	KS	66612	785-296-3229	296-1028
Technical Professions Board 900 SW Jackson St Ste 507 *Web:* www.ksbtp.ks.gov/	Topeka	KS	66612	785-296-3053	
Travel & Tourism Development Div 1020 S Kansas Ave Ste 200 *TF:* 800-252-6727 ■ *Web:* www.travelks.com	Topeka	KS	66612	785-296-2009	296-6988
Treasurer 900 SW Jackson St Ste 201 *TF:* 800-432-0386 ■ *Web:* www.kansasstatetreasurer.com	Topeka	KS	66612	785-296-3171	296-7950
Veterans Affairs Commission 700 SW Jackson St Ste 701 *Web:* kcva.ks.gov	Topeka	KS	66603	785-296-3976	296-1462
Vital Statistics Div 1000 SW Jackson *Web:* www.kdheks.gov/vital	Topeka	KS	66612	785-296-1400	
Weights & Measures Div Forbes Field Bldg 282 PO Box 19282 *Web:* www.kansas.gov	Topeka	KS	66619	785-862-2415	
Wildlife & Parks Dept 1020 S Kansas Ave Ste 200 *Web:* www.kdwpt.state.ks.us	Topeka	KS	66612	785-296-2281	296-6953
Workers Compensation Div 401 SW Topeka Blvd Ste 2 *TF:* 800-332-0353 ■ *Web:* www.dol.ks.gov	Topeka	KS	66603	785-296-4000	

342-18 Kentucky

	City	State	Zip	Phone	Fax
State Government Information 229 W Main St Ste 400 *TF:* 877-855-3573 ■ *Web:* kentucky.gov	Frankfort	KY	40601	502-875-3733	875-3722

	City	State	Zip	Phone	Fax
Accountancy Board 332 W Broadway Ste 310 *Web:* www.cpa.ky.gov	Louisville	KY	40202	502-595-3037	595-4500
Aging Services Office 275 E Main St Ste 3E-E *Web:* www.chfs.ky.gov/dail	Frankfort	KY	40621	502-564-6930	564-4595
Arts Council 500 Mero St 21st Fl Capital Plaza Tower *TF:* 888-833-2787 ■ *Web:* www.artscouncil.ky.gov	Frankfort	KY	40601	502-564-3757	564-2839
Attorney General State Capitol Bldg 700 Capitol Ave Ste 120 *Web:* www.e-archives.ky.gov	Frankfort	KY	40601	502-696-5614	564-2894
Bill Status 702 Capitol Ave Rm 424F *Web:* kentuckyhouserepublicans.org	Frankfort	KY	40601	502-564-8100	
Child Support Div 730 Schenkel Ln *TF:* 800-248-1163 ■ *Web:* www.chfs.ky.gov	Frankfort	KY	40601	502-564-2285	564-5988
Consumer Protection Div 1024 Capital Ctr Dr Ste 200 *TF:* 888-432-9257 ■ *Web:* www.ag.ky.gov	Frankfort	KY	40601	502-696-5389	573-8317
Corrections Dept 275 E Main St Rm G-41 PO Box 2400 *Web:* www.corrections.ky.gov	Frankfort	KY	40602	502-564-4726	564-5037
Crime Victims Compensation Board 130 Brighton Pk Blvd *TF:* 800-469-2120 ■ *Web:* www. cvcb.ky.gov	Frankfort	KY	40601	502-573-2290	573-4817
Economic Development Cabinet 500 Mero St *Web:* www.thinkkentucky.com	Frankfort	KY	40601	502-564-7670	564-3256
Education Dept 500 Mero St *Web:* www.education.ky.gov/KDE	Frankfort	KY	40601	502-564-4770	564-5680
Education Professional Standards Board 100 Airport Dr 3rd Fl *TF:* 888-598-7667 ■ *Web:* www.kyepsb.net	Frankfort	KY	40601	502-564-4606	564-7080
Emergency Management Div 100 Minuteman Pkwy *Web:* www.kyem.ky.gov	Frankfort	KY	40601	502-607-5721	607-1614
Energy & Environment Cabinet 500 Mero St Ste 5 *Web:* www.eec.ky.gov	Frankfort	KY	40601	502-564-3350	564-3969
Environmental Protection Dept 200 Fair Oaks Ln *Web:* www.dep.ky.gov	Frankfort	KY	40601	502-564-2150	564-4245
Finance & Administration Cabinet Capitol Annex Rm 383 *Web:* www.finance.ky.gov	Frankfort	KY	40601	502-564-4240	564-6785
Financial Institutions Dept 1025 Capital Ctr Dr Ste 200 *TF:* 800-223-2579 ■ *Web:* www.kfi.ky.gov	Frankfort	KY	40601	502-573-3390	573-2182
Fish & Wildlife Resources Dept 1 Game Farm Rd *TF:* 800-858-1549 ■ *Web:* fw.ky.gov/	Frankfort	KY	40601	502-564-3400	564-6508
General Assembly 700 Capitol Ave State Capitol Bldg *TF:* 800-372-7181 ■ *Web:* www.lrc.state.ky.us	Frankfort	KY	40601	502-564-8100	564-6543
Governor State Capitol Bldg 700 Capitol Ave Rm 100 *Web:* www.governor.ky.gov	Frankfort	KY	40601	502-564-2611	564-2517
Governor's Office for Technology 101 Cold Harbor Dr *Web:* www.got.state.ky.us	Frankfort	KY	40601	502-564-1201	
Hairdressers & Cosmetologists Board 111 St James Ct Ste A	Frankfort	KY	40601	502-564-4262	564-0481
Health & Family Services Cabinet 275 E Main St 5th Fl W *Web:* www.chfs.ky.gov	Frankfort	KY	40621	502-564-7042	564-7091
Higher Education Assistance Authority 100 Airport Rd *TF:* 800-928-8926 ■ *Web:* www.kheaa.com	Frankfort	KY	40602	800-928-8926	
Historical Society 100 W Broadway *TF:* 877-444-7867 ■ *Web:* www.history.ky.gov	Frankfort	KY	40601	502-564-1792	
Horse Racing Authority 4063 Iron Works Pkwy Bldg B *Web:* khrc.ky.gov	Lexington	KY	40511	859-246-2040	246-2039
Housing Corp 1231 Louisville Rd *TF:* 800-633-8896 ■ *Web:* www.kyhousing.org	Frankfort	KY	40601	502-564-7630	564-5708
Insurance Dept 215 W Main St *TF:* 800-595-6053	Frankfort	KY	40602	502-564-3630	
Labor Cabinet 1047 US Hwy 127 S Ste 4 *Web:* www.labor.ky.gov	Frankfort	KY	40601	502-564-3070	564-5387
Legislative Ethics Commission 22 Mill Creek Pk *Web:* www.klec.ky.gov	Frankfort	KY	40601	502-573-2863	573-2929
Lieutenant Governor State Capitol Bldg 700 Capitol Ave Ste 142 *Web:* www.ltgovernor.ky.gov	Frankfort	KY	40601	502-564-2611	564-2849
Lottery Corp 1011 W Main St *TF:* 800-937-8946 ■ *Web:* www.kylottery.com	Louisville	KY	40202	502-560-1500	560-1532
Medical Licensure Board 310 Whittington Pkwy Ste 1B *Web:* www.kbml.ky.gov	Louisville	KY	40222	502-429-7150	429-7158
Natural Resources Dept 2 Hudson Hollow *Web:* www.dnr.ky.gov	Frankfort	KY	40601	502-564-6940	564-5698
Parks Dept 500 Mero St *Web:* kentuckytourism.com	Frankfort	KY	40601	502-564-2172	
Parole Board PO Box 2400 *Web:* justice.ky.gov	Frankfort	KY	40602	502-564-3620	564-8995
Postsecondary Education Council 1024 Capital Ctr Dr Ste 320 *Web:* www.cpe.ky.gov	Frankfort	KY	40601	502-573-1555	573-1535
Public Service Commission PO Box 615 *TF:* 800-772-4636 ■ *Web:* www.psc.state.ky.us	Frankfort	KY	40602	502-564-3940	564-3460
Real Estate Commission (KREC) 10200 Linn Stn Rd Ste 201 *TF General:* 888-373-3300 ■ *Web:* www.krec.ky.gov	Louisville	KY	40223	502-429-7250	429-7246
Revenue Dept 501 High St MS 68 *Web:* www.revenue.ky.gov/	Frankfort	KY	40601	502-564-4581	564-3875
Secretary of State The Capitol Bldg 700 Capital Ave Ste 152 *Web:* www.sos.ky.gov	Frankfort	KY	40601	502-564-3490	564-5687
Supreme Court 700 Capitol Ave Rm 235 *Web:* apps.courts.ky.gov	Frankfort	KY	40601	502-564-5444	564-2665
Travel & Tourism Dept 500 Mero St Ste 2200 *TF:* 800-225-8747 ■ *Web:* www.kentuckytourism.com	Frankfort	KY	40601	502-564-4930	564-5695
Treasury 1050 US Hwy 127 S Ste 100 *Web:* www.kytreasury.com	Frankfort	KY	40601	502-564-4722	564-6545
Vehicle Regulation Div 200 Mero St 3rd Fl	Frankfort	KY	40601	502-564-7000	564-6403
Veterans Affairs Dept (KDVA) 1111B Louisville Rd *TF:* 800-572-6245 ■ *Web:* www.veterans.ky.gov	Frankfort	KY	40601	502-564-9203	564-9240
Vital Statistics Div 275 E Main St Ste 1EA *Web:* www.chfs.ky.gov	Frankfort	KY	40621	502-564-4212	227-9849
Vocational Rehabilitation Dept 275 E Main St MS 2E-K *TF:* 800-372-7172 ■ *Web:* ovr.ky.gov	Frankfort	KY	40601	502-564-4440	564-6745
Workers Claims Dept (DWC) 657 Chamberlin Ave *TF:* 800-554-8601 ■ *Web:* www.labor.ky.gov/workersclaims	Frankfort	KY	40601	502-564-5550	564-5732
Workforce Investment Dept 500 Mero St Fl 3 *Web:* www.workforce.ky.gov	Frankfort	KY	40601	502-564-4286	

342-19 Louisiana

	City	State	Zip	Phone	Fax
Agriculture & Forestry Dept 5825 Florida Blvd *Web:* www.ldaf.state.la.us	Baton Rouge	LA	70806	225-922-1234	922-1253
Arts Div PO Box 44247 *Web:* www.crt.state.la.us	Baton Rouge	LA	70804	225-342-8180	342-8173
Attorney General PO Box 94005 *Web:* www.ag.state.la.us	Baton Rouge	LA	70804	225-326-6705	326-6793
Board of Regents PO Box 3677 *Web:* www.regents.state.la.us	Baton Rouge	LA	70821	225-342-4253	342-6926
Certified Public Accountants Board 601 Poydras St Ste 1770 *Web:* www.cpaboard.state.la.us	New Orleans	LA	70130	504-566-1244	566-1252
Community Services Office 627 N 4th St **Fax Area Code:* 225 ■ *TF:* 888-524-3578 ■ *Web:* www.dss.state.la.us	Baton Rouge	LA	70802	888-524-3578	342-2268*
Consumer Protection Office PO Box 94095 **Fax Area Code:* 225 ■ *TF:* 800-351-4889 ■ *Web:* www.ag.state.la.us	Baton Rouge	LA	70804	800-351-4889	326-6499*
Contractors Licensing Board 2525 Quail Dr *Web:* www.lslbc.louisiana.gov	Baton Rouge	LA	70808	225-765-2301	765-2431
Crime Victims Reparations Board 1885 Wooddale Blvd Rm 1230 *Web:* www.lcle.state.la.us	Baton Rouge	LA	70806	225-925-4842	
Culture Recreation & Tourism Dept PO Box 94361 *Web:* www.crt.state.la.us	Baton Rouge	LA	70804	225-342-8115	342-3207
Education Dept PO Box 94064 **Fax Area Code:* 225 ■ *TF:* 877-453-2721 ■ *Web:* www.louisianabelieves.com	Baton Rouge	LA	70804	877-453-2721	342-0193*
Environmental Quality Dept 602 N Fifth St *TF:* 866-896-5337 ■ *Web:* www.deq.louisiana.gov	Baton Rouge	LA	70802	225-219-5337	
Ethics Board 617 N Third St LaSalle Bldg Ste 10-36 *TF:* 800-842-6630 ■ *Web:* www.ethics.state.la.us	Baton Rouge	LA	70802	225-219-5600	381-7271
Financial Institutions Office PO Box 94095 *Web:* www.ofi.state.la.us	Baton Rouge	LA	70804	225-925-4660	925-4548
Health & Hospitals Dept PO Box 629 *Web:* www.dhh.state.la.us	Baton Rouge	LA	70821	225-342-9500	342-5568
Historic Preservation Div Capitol Annex Bldg 1051 N Third St PO Box 44247 *Web:* doa.louisiana.gov	Baton Rouge	LA	70802	225-342-8160	219-9772
Homeland Security & Emergency Preparedness Office 7667 Independence Blvd *Web:* lerc.dps.louisiana.gov	Baton Rouge	LA	70806	225-925-7500	925-7501
Housing Finance Agency 2415 Quail Dr *TF:* 888-454-2001 ■ *Web:* www.lhfa.state.la.us	Baton Rouge	LA	70808	225-763-8700	763-8710
Information Services Office 1201 N Third St *Web:* louisiana.gov	Baton Rouge	LA	70802	225-342-0900	342-0902
Insurance Dept PO Box 94214 *TF:* 800-259-5300 ■ *Web:* www.ldi.state.la.us	Baton Rouge	LA	70804	225-342-5900	
Judicial Administrators Office 400 Royal St Ste 1190 *Web:* www.lasc.org	New Orleans	LA	70130	504-310-2550	
Legislature PO Box 94062 *TF:* 800-256-3793 ■ *Web:* www.legis.state.la.us	Baton Rouge	LA	70804	225-342-2456	
Lieutenant Governor 1051 N Third St *Web:* www.crt.state.la.us	Baton Rouge	LA	70802	225-342-7009	342-1949
Lottery Corp 555 Laurel St *Web:* louisianalottery.com	Baton Rouge	LA	70801	225-297-2000	297-2005
Medical Examiners Board (LSBME) 630 Camp St PO Box 30250 *Web:* www.lsbme.louisiana.gov	New Orleans	LA	70130	504-568-6820	568-8893
Natural Resources Dept PO Box 94396 *Web:* dnr.louisiana.gov	Baton Rouge	LA	70804	225-342-4500	342-5861
Office of Student Financial Assistance 602 N Fifth St PO Box 91202 *TF:* 800-259-5626 ■ *Web:* www.osfa.la.gov	Baton Rouge	LA	70802	225-219-1012	208-1496
Office of the Governor PO Box 94004 *TF:* 866-366-1121 ■ *Web:* www.gov.state.la.us	Baton Rouge	LA	70804	225-342-7015	342-7099

	City	State	Zip	Phone	Fax
Public Safety & Corrections Dept 504 Mayflower St PO Box 94304 *Web:* www.doc.louisiana.gov	Baton Rouge	LA	70804	225-342-6633	342-3095
Public Service Commission PO Box 91154 *TF:* 800-256-2397 ■ *Web:* www.lpsc.org	Baton Rouge	LA	70821	225-342-4404	342-2831
Racing Commission 320 N Carrollton Ave Ste 2-B *Web:* horseracing.louisiana.gov	New Orleans	LA	70119	504-483-4000	483-4898
Real Estate Commission PO Box 14785 *TF:* 800-821-4529 ■ *Web:* www.lrec.state.la.us	Baton Rouge	LA	70898	225-765-0191	765-0637
Rehabilitation Services 627 N Fourth St *Web:* www.dss.louisiana.gov	Baton Rouge	LA	70802	225-686-7257	
Revenue Dept 617 N Third St PO Box 201 *Web:* www.rev.state.la.us	Baton Rouge	LA	70801	855-307-3893	
Secretary of State PO Box 94125 *Web:* www.sos.la.gov	Baton Rouge	LA	70804	225-922-2880	922-2003
Securities Commission 8660 United Plaza Blvd Ste 200 *Web:* gov.louisiana.gov	Baton Rouge	LA	70809	225-925-4660	925-4524
State Parks Office PO Box 44426 *TF:* 888-677-1400 ■ *Web:* www.crt.state.la.us	Baton Rouge	LA	70804	225-342-8111	342-8107
State Police PO Box 66614 *Web:* www.lsp.org	Baton Rouge	LA	70896	225-925-6006	
Supreme Court 400 Royal St *Web:* www.lasc.org	New Orleans	LA	70112	504-310-2300	
Tourism Office 1051 N Third Stt PO Box 94291 *Web:* www.crt.state.la.us	Baton Rouge	LA	70802	225-342-8100	342-1051
Treasurer 900 N Third St Fl 3 PO Box 44154 *Web:* www.treasury.state.la.us/default.aspx	Baton Rouge	LA	70802	225-342-0010	342-0046
Veterans Affairs Dept PO Box 94095 *TF:* 877-432-8982 ■ *Web:* www.vetaffairs.la.gov	Baton Rouge	LA	70804	225-219-5000	219-5590
Weights & Measures Div PO Box 3098 *Web:* vwwwprd.doa.louisiana.gov	Baton Rouge	LA	70821	225-922-1341	923-4877
Wildlife & Fisheries Dept PO Box 98000 *TF:* 800-442-2511 ■ *Web:* www.wlf.louisiana.gov	Baton Rouge	LA	70898	225-765-2800	765-2892
Workers Compensation Office PO Box 94040 *Web:* www.laworks.net/WorkersComp/OWC_MainMenu.asp	Baton Rouge	LA	70804	225-342-8980	342-5665
Workforce Commission 1001 N 23rd St *TF:* 877-529-6757 ■ *Web:* www.laworks.net	Baton Rouge	LA	70802	225-342-3111	342-7960

342-20 Maine

	City	State	Zip	Phone	Fax
State Government Information 26 Edison Dr *TF:* 888-577-6690 ■ *Web:* www.maine.gov	Augusta	ME	04330	207-624-9494	
Administrative Office of the Courts PO Box 4820 *Web:* courts.maine.gov/	Portland	ME	04112	207-822-0792	
Agriculture Dept 28 State House Stn *Web:* www.maine.gov	Augusta	ME	04333	207-287-3871	287-7548
Arts Commission 193 State St *Web:* mainearts.maine.gov	Augusta	ME	04330	207-287-2724	287-2725
Attorney General 6 State House Stn *Web:* www.maine.gov	Augusta	ME	04333	207-626-8800	
Chief Medical Examiner 37 State House Stn *Web:* www.maine.gov	Augusta	ME	04333	207-624-7180	624-7178
Child & Family Services Office 221 State St *Web:* maine.gov/dhhs/ocfs/	Augusta	ME	04333	207-287-5060	287-5031
Conservation Dept 22 State House Stn *Web:* maine.gov/dacf/	Augusta	ME	04333	207-287-2211	287-2400
Consumer Protection Unit 6 State House Stn *TF:* 800-436-2131 ■ *Web:* www.maine.gov	Augusta	ME	04333	207-626-8849	
Corrections Dept 25 Tyson Dr Third Fl 111 State House Stn *Web:* www.maine.gov	Augusta	ME	04333	207-287-2711	287-4370
Economic & Community Development Dept 59 State House Stn *TF:* 800-541-5872 ■ *Web:* www.maine.gov	Augusta	ME	04333	207-624-9800	
Education Dept 23 State House Stn *Web:* www.maine.gov/education	Augusta	ME	04333	207-624-6600	624-6700
Elder Services Office 11 Statehouse Stn *TF:* 800-624-8404 ■ *Web:* maine.gov/dhhs/oes	Augusta	ME	04333	800-624-8404	
Employment Services Bureau 55 State House Station *Web:* www.mainecareercenter.com	Augusta	ME	04330	207-623-7981	287-5933
Environmental Protection Dept 17 State House Stn *TF:* 800-452-1942 ■ *Web:* www.maine.gov	Augusta	ME	04333	207-287-7688	287-7814
Finance Authority 5 Community Dr PO Box 949 *TF:* 800-228-3734 ■ *Web:* www.famemaine.com	Augusta	ME	04332	207-623-3263	623-0095
Financial Institutions Bureau 35 Anthony Ave 11 State House Stn *TF:* 800-452-1926 ■ *Web:* www.maine.gov	Augusta	ME	04333	207-624-8090	624-8124
Governmental Ethics & Election Practices Commission 45 Memorial Cir *Web:* www.maine.gov	Augusta	ME	04330	207-287-4179	287-6775
Governor 1 State House Stn *TF:* 888-577-6690 ■ *Web:* www.maine.gov/governor	Augusta	ME	04333	207-287-3531	287-1034
Health Bureau 11 State House Stn *Web:* www.maine.gov	Augusta	ME	04333	207-287-8016	287-9058
Historic Preservation Commission 65 State House Stn *Web:* www.maine.gov	Augusta	ME	04333	207-287-2132	287-2335
Housing Authority 353 Water St *Web:* www.mainehousing.org	Augusta	ME	04330	207-626-4600	626-4678
Human Services Dept 221 State St *Web:* www.maine.gov	Augusta	ME	04333	207-287-3707	
Information Services Bureau 145 State House Stn *Web:* www.maine.gov	Augusta	ME	04333	207-624-8800	287-4563
Inland Fisheries & Wildlife Dept 41 State House Stn *Web:* www.maine.gov	Augusta	ME	04333	207-287-8000	287-6395
Insurance Bureau 34 State House Stn *TF:* 800-300-5000 ■ *Web:* www.maine.gov/pfr/insurance	Augusta	ME	04333	207-624-8475	624-8599
Labor Dept PO Box 259 *Web:* www.state.me.us/labor	Augusta	ME	04332	207-623-7900	
Legislature 115 State House Stn *Web:* maine.gov/legis/	Augusta	ME	04333	207-287-1615	287-1621
Licensure in Medicine Board 161 Capitol St *Web:* www.docboard.org	Augusta	ME	04330	207-287-3601	287-6590
Motor Vehicles Bureau 29 State House Stn *Web:* www.maine.gov/sos/bmv	Augusta	ME	04333	207-624-9000	624-9013
Parks & Land Bureau 22 State House Stn *Web:* www.maine.gov	Augusta	ME	04333	207-287-3821	287-6170
Parole Board 111 State House Stn *Web:* www.maine.gov	Augusta	ME	04333	207-287-2711	287-4370
Public Utilities Commission 18 State House Stn *Web:* www.maine.gov	Augusta	ME	04333	207-287-3831	287-1039
Quality Assurance & Regulations Div 22 State House Station 18 Elkins Lane *Web:* www.maine.gov	Augusta	ME	04333	207-287-3841	
Rehabilitation Services Bureau 150 State House Stn **Fax Area Code: 207* ■ *TF:* 800-698-4440 ■ *Web:* www.maine.gov/rehab	Augusta	ME	04333	800-698-4440	287-5292*
Revenue Services 24 State House Stn *Web:* www.maine.gov	Augusta	ME	04333	207-287-2076	287-3618
Secretary of State 148 State House Stn *Web:* www.maine.gov/sos	Augusta	ME	04333	207-626-8400	287-8598
Securities Div 76 Northern Ave *Web:* www.maine.gov	Gardiner	ME	04345	207-624-8551	624-8590
State Police 45 Commerce Dr *Web:* www.maine.gov/dps/msp	Augusta	ME	04333	207-624-7200	624-7088
Supreme Court 205 Newbury St Rm 139 *Web:* courts.maine.gov/maine_courts/supreme	Portland	ME	04101	207-822-4146	
Tourism Office 59 State House Stn **Fax Area Code: 877* ■ *Web:* www.visitmaine.com	Augusta	ME	04333	888-624-6345	624-6331*
Transportation Dept 16 State House Stn *Web:* www.maine.gov/mdot	Augusta	ME	04333	207-624-3000	624-3001
University of Maine System Board of Trustees 16 Central St *Web:* www.maine.edu	Bangor	ME	04401	207-973-3211	973-3296
Veterans Services Bureau 117 State House Stn *Web:* www.maine.gov	Augusta	ME	04333	207-430-6035	626-4509
Victims Compensation Program 6 State House Sta *Web:* www.maine.gov	Augusta	ME	04333	207-624-7882	624-7730
Vital Records Office 11 State House Stn *Web:* www.maine.gov/dhhs	Augusta	ME	04333	207-287-3181	287-1093
Workers Compensation Board 27 State House Stn *Web:* www.maine.gov	Augusta	ME	04333	207-287-3751	287-7198

342-21 Maryland

	City	State	Zip	Phone	Fax
State Government Information State House *TF:* 800-811-8336 ■ *Web:* www.maryland.gov	Annapolis	MD	21401	410-974-3901	
Administrative Office of the Courts 580 Taylor Ave *Web:* www.courts.state.md.us	Annapolis	MD	21401	410-260-1400	974-2169
Aging Dept 301 W Preston St Rm 1007 *Web:* www.aging.maryland.gov	Baltimore	MD	21201	410-767-1100	333-7943
Agriculture Dept 50 Harry S Truman Pkwy *Web:* mda.maryland.gov	Annapolis	MD	21401	410-841-5700	841-5914
Assessments & Taxation Dept 301 W Preston St 8th Fl *TF:* 888-246-5941 ■ *Web:* www.dat.state.md.us	Baltimore	MD	21201	410-767-1184	
Attorney General 200 St Paul Pl 16th Fl *Web:* www.oag.state.md.us	Baltimore	MD	21202	410-576-6300	576-7040
Budget & Management Dept 45 Calvert St *TF:* 800-705-3493 ■ *Web:* dbm.maryland.gov	Annapolis	MD	21401	800-705-3493	
Business & Economic Development Dept 217 E Redwood St *Web:* business.maryland.gov/	Baltimore	MD	21202	410-767-6300	333-6911
Chief Medical Examiner 111 Penn St *Web:* dhmh.maryland.gov	Baltimore	MD	21201	410-333-3250	333-3063
Court of Appeals 361 Rowe Blvd 4th Fl *TF:* 800-926-2583 ■ *Web:* www.courts.state.md.us/coappeals	Annapolis	MD	21401	410-260-1500	
Criminal Injuries Compensation Board 6776 Reisterstown Rd Ste 206 *TF:* 888-679-9347 ■ *Web:* msa.maryland.gov	Baltimore	MD	21215	410-585-3010	764-3815
Education Dept 200 W Baltimore St *TF:* 888-246-0016 ■ *Web:* www.marylandpublicschools.org	Baltimore	MD	21201	410-767-0100	333-2226
Emergency Management Agency 5401 Rue St Lo Dr *TF:* 877-636-2872 ■ *Web:* mema.state.md.us	Reisterstown	MD	21136	410-517-3600	517-3610
Environment Dept 1800 Washington Blvd *TF:* 800-633-6101 ■ *Web:* www.mde.state.md.us	Baltimore	MD	21230	410-537-3000	537-3888
Ethics Commission 45 Calvert St 3rd Fl *TF:* 877-669-6085 ■ *Web:* ethics.maryland.gov	Annapolis	MD	21401	410-260-7770	260-7746
Financial Regulation Div 500 N Calvert St Rm 402 *Web:* www.dllr.state.md.us	Baltimore	MD	21202	410-230-6097	
Fisheries Service 580 Taylor Ave *Web:* www.dnr.state.md.us/fisheries	Annapolis	MD	21401	410-260-8281	260-8279

Agency	City	State	ZIP	Phone	Fax
General Assembly 90 State Cir *Web:* www.mlis.state.md.us	Annapolis	MD	21401	410-841-3000	841-3850
Governor State House 100 State Cir *Web:* www.gov.state.md.us	Annapolis	MD	21401	410-974-3901	
Health & Mental Hygiene Dept 201 W Preston St 5th Fl *Web:* dhmh.maryland.gov	Baltimore	MD	21201	410-767-6500	767-6489
Higher Education Commission 839 Bestgate Rd Ste 400 *TF:* 800-974-0203 ■ *Web:* www.mhec.state.md.us	Annapolis	MD	21401	410-260-4500	260-3200
Historical & Cultural Programs Div 100 Community Pl 3rd Fl *Web:* www.marylandhistoricaltrust.net	Crownsville	MD	21032	410-514-7600	514-7678
Housing & Community Development Dept 100 Community Pl **Fax Area Code:* 410 ■ *TF:* 800-756-0119 ■ *Web:* www.dhcd.state.md.us	Crownsville	MD	21032	800-756-0119	987-4070*
Insurance Administration 525 St Paul Pl *TF:* 800-492-6116 ■ *Web:* www.mdinsurance.state.md.us	Baltimore	MD	21202	410-468-2000	468-2020
Labor & Industry Div 1100 N Eutaw St Rm 606 *Web:* www.dllr.state.md.us	Baltimore	MD	21201	410-767-2241	767-2986
Legislative Services Dept 90 State Cir *TF:* 800-492-7122 ■ *Web:* www.mlis.state.md.us	Annapolis	MD	21401	410-946-5400	946-5405
Motor Vehicle Administration 6601 Ritchie Hwy NE *Web:* www.mva.maryland.gov	Glen Burnie	MD	21062	410-768-7000	768-7506
Natural Resources Dept 580 Taylor Ave *TF:* 877-620-8367 ■ *Web:* dnr2.maryland.gov/	Annapolis	MD	21401	410-260-8021	260-8024
Parole & Probation Div 6776 Reisterstown Rd *TF:* 877-227-8031 ■ *Web:* msa.maryland.gov	Baltimore	MD	21215	410-585-3500	
Physician Quality Assurance Board 4201 Patterson Ave *TF:* 800-492-6836	Baltimore	MD	21215	410-764-4777	358-2252
Public Service Commission 6 St Paul St 16th Fl *TF:* 800-492-0474 ■ *Web:* www.psc.state.md.us	Baltimore	MD	21202	410-767-8000	333-6495
Racing Commission 500 N Calvert St Rm 201 *Web:* www.dllr.state.md.us	Baltimore	MD	21202	410-230-6320	
Secretary of State 16 Francis St Jeffery Bldg 1st Fl *Web:* www.sos.state.md.us	Annapolis	MD	21401	410-974-5521	974-5190
Securities Div 200 St Paul Pl 20th Fl *Web:* www.oag.state.md.us/Securities	Baltimore	MD	21202	410-576-6360	576-6532
Social Services Administration 311 W Saratoga St *Web:* www.dhr.state.md.us	Baltimore	MD	21201	410-767-7216	333-0127
State Arts Council 175 W Ostend St Ste E *Web:* www.msac.org	Baltimore	MD	21230	410-767-6555	333-1062
State Athletic Commission 500 N Calvert St Rm 304 *Web:* www.dllr.state.md.us/license/occprof/athlet.html	Baltimore	MD	21202	410-230-6223	333-6314
State Forest & Park Service 580 Taylor Ave Rm E-3 *TF Campground Resv:* 877-620-8367 ■ *Web:* dnr2.maryland.gov/	Annapolis	MD	21401	410-260-8186	260-8191
State Lottery 1800 Washington Blvd Ste 330 *Web:* www.mdlottery.com	Baltimore	MD	21230	410-230-8790	230-8728
State Police 1201 Reisterstown Rd *TF:* 800-525-5555 ■ *Web:* www.mdsp.org	Pikesville	MD	21208	410-653-4200	
Teacher Certification & Accreditation Div 200 W Baltimore St *TF:* 866-772-8922 ■ *Web:* www.marylandpublicschools.org	Baltimore	MD	21201	410-767-0412	
Tourism Development Office 217 E Redwood St 9th Fl *TF:* 800-543-1036 ■ *Web:* visitmaryland.org	Baltimore	MD	21202	410-767-3400	333-6643
Treasurer 80 Calvert St Rm 109 *TF:* 800-974-0468 ■ *Web:* www.treasurer.state.md.us	Annapolis	MD	21401	410-260-7533	974-3530
Veterans Affairs Dept 31 Hopkins Plaza Rm 1231 *TF:* 800-446-4926 ■ *Web:* veterans.maryland.gov	Baltimore	MD	21201	410-230-4444	230-4445
Vital Records Div 6550 Reisterstown Rd *TF:* 800-832-3277 ■ *Web:* www.dhmh.maryland.gov	Baltimore	MD	21215	410-764-3038	
Weights & Measures Section 50 Harry S Truman Pkwy Rm 410 *Web:* mda.maryland.gov	Annapolis	MD	21401	410-841-5700	841-2765
Workers Compensation Commission 10 E Baltimore St *Web:* www.wcc.state.md.us	Baltimore	MD	21202	410-864-5100	
Workforce Development Div 1100 N Eutaw St Rm 616 *Web:* www.dllr.state.md.us/employment	Baltimore	MD	21201	410-767-2400	767-2986

342-22 Massachusetts

Agency	City	State	ZIP	Phone	Fax
Agricultural Resources Dept 251 Cswy St Ste 500 *Web:* www.mass.gov	Boston	MA	02114	617-626-1700	626-1850
Attorney General 1 Ashburton Pl *Web:* www.mass.gov	Boston	MA	02108	617-727-2200	
Banks Div 1000 Washington St Ste 710 *TF:* 800-495-2265 ■ *Web:* www.mass.gov	Boston	MA	02118	617-956-1501	956-1599
Bill Status 1 Ashburton Pl Rm 1611 *TF:* 800-392-6090 ■ *Web:* malegislature.gov	Boston	MA	02108	617-727-7030	742-4528
Business Development Office 10 Pk Plaza Ste 5220 *Web:* www.mass.gov	Boston	MA	02116	617-973-8600	973-8554
Child Support Enforcement Div 51 Sleeper St 4th Fl *TF:* 800-332-2733 ■ *Web:* www.mass.gov	Boston	MA	02205	617-660-1234	626-3894
Correction Dept 50 Maple St *Web:* www.mass.gov	Milford	MA	01757	508-422-3300	422-3386
Cultural Council 10 St James Ave 3rd Fl *Web:* www.massculturalcouncil.org	Boston	MA	02116	617-727-3668	727-0044
Elementary & Secondary Education Dept 350 Main St *Web:* www.doe.mass.edu	Malden	MA	02148	781-338-3300	338-3399
Emergency Management Agency 400 Worcester Rd *Web:* www.mass.gov	Framingham	MA	01702	508-820-2000	820-2030
Environmental Protection Dept 1 Winter St *Web:* mass.gov/eea/agencies/massdep/	Boston	MA	02108	617-292-5500	556-1049
Executive Office of Transportation 10 Pk Plaza Ste 3170 *TF:* 800-219-9936 ■ *Web:* www.massdot.state.ma.us	Boston	MA	02116	617-973-7000	973-8031
Fish & Game Dept 251 Cswy St Ste 400 *Web:* mass.gov/eea/pagenotfound.html	Boston	MA	02114	617-626-1500	626-1505
General Court State House *Web:* malegislature.gov	Boston	MA	02133	617-722-2000	
Governor State House Executive Office Rm 360 *Web:* www.mass.gov	Boston	MA	02133	617-725-4000	727-9725
Higher Education Board 1 Ashburton Pl Rm 1401 *Web:* www.mass.edu	Boston	MA	02108	617-994-6950	727-6397
Historical Commission 220 William T Morrissey Blvd *Web:* www.sec.state.ma.us	Boston	MA	02125	617-727-8470	727-5128
Housing & Community Development Dept 100 Cambridge St Ste 300 *Web:* mass.gov/hed/economic/eohed/dhcd/	Boston	MA	02114	617-573-1100	573-1120
Housing Finance Agency 1 Beacon St *Web:* www.masshousing.com	Boston	MA	02108	617-854-1000	854-1029
Information Technology Div 1 Ashburton Pl Rm 804 *Web:* www.mass.gov	Boston	MA	02108	617-727-2040	727-2779
Insurance Div 1000 Washington St Ste 810 *TF:* 877-563-4467 ■ *Web:* mass.gov/ocabr/government/oca-agencies/doi-lp/	Boston	MA	02118	617-521-7794	521-7490
Medical Examiner 720 Albany St *Web:* www.mass.gov	Boston	MA	02118	617-267-6767	266-6763
Mental Health Dept 25 Staniford St *Web:* www.mass.gov/eohhs/gov/departments/dmh	Boston	MA	02214	617-626-8000	
Parole Board 12 Mercer Rd *TF:* 888-298-6272 ■ *Web:* mass.gov/eopss/agencies/parole-board/	Natick	MA	01760	508-650-4500	650-4599
Professional Licensure Div 1000 Washington St Ste 710 *Web:* mass.gov/ocabr/government/oca-agencies/dpl-lp/	Boston	MA	02118	617-727-3074	727-2197
Public Health Dept 250 Washington St *Web:* mass.gov/eohhs/gov/departments/dph/	Boston	MA	02108	617-624-6000	624-5206
Public Protection & Advocacy Bureau 100 Cambridge St *Web:* www.sec.state.ma.us	Boston	MA	02114	617-727-2200	
Public Utilities Dept 1 S Stn *Web:* www.mass.gov/eea	Boston	MA	02110	617-305-3500	345-9101
Registry of Motor Vehicles PO Box 55891 *Web:* www.massrmv.com	Boston	MA	02205	617-351-4500	
Rehabilitation Commission 27 Wormwood St Ste 600 *Web:* www.mass.gov	Boston	MA	02210	617-204-3600	
Revenue Dept PO Box 7010 *TF:* 800-392-6089 ■ *Web:* www.mass.gov/dor	Boston	MA	02204	617-626-2201	
Secretary of the Commonwealth State House Rm 337 *Web:* www.sec.state.ma.us	Boston	MA	02133	617-727-9180	742-4722
Securities Div 1 Ashburton Pl Rm 1710 *Web:* www.sec.state.ma.us/sct	Boston	MA	02108	617-878-3152	248-0177
Standards Div 1 Ashburton Pl Rm 1301 *Web:* www.mass.gov	Boston	MA	02108	617-727-3480	727-5705
State Boxing Commission 1 Ashburton Pl Rm 1301 *Web:* www.mass.gov/mbc	Boston	MA	02108	617-727-3200	727-5732
State Ethics Commission 1 Ashburton Pl Rm 619 *Web:* www.mass.gov/ethics	Boston	MA	02108	617-371-9500	723-5851
State Lottery Commission 60 Columbian St *Web:* www.masslottery.com	Braintree	MA	02184	781-849-5555	849-5546
State Parks & Recreation Div 251 Cswy St Ste 900 *Web:* mass.gov	Boston	MA	02114	617-626-1250	626-1351
State Police Dept 470 Worcester Rd *Web:* www.mass.gov	Framingham	MA	01702	508-820-2300	820-2211
State Racing Commission 1 Ashburton Pl 11th Fl *Web:* www.mass.gov	Boston	MA	02108	617-727-2581	
Supreme Judicial Ct 1 Pemberton Sq Ste 2500 *Web:* www.mass.gov/courts	Boston	MA	02108	617-557-1000	723-3577
Transitional Assistance Dept 600 Washington St *Web:* www.mass.gov	Boston	MA	02111	617-348-8500	
Travel & Tourism Office 10 Pk Plaza Ste 4510 *TF:* 800-227-6277 ■ *Web:* www.massvacation.com	Boston	MA	02116	617-973-8500	973-8525
Treasurer State House Rm 227 *Web:* mass.gov/treasury/	Boston	MA	02133	617-367-6900	248-0372
Veterans Services Dept 600 Washington St Ste 1100 *Web:* www.mass.gov/veterans	Boston	MA	02111	617-727-3578	727-5903
Victim Compensation & Assistance Div 1 Ashburton Pl 19th Fl *Web:* www.mass.gov	Boston	MA	02108	617-727-2200	
Vital Records & Statistics Registry 150 Mt Vernon St 1st Fl *Web:* www.mass.gov	Dorchester	MA	02125	617-740-2600	

Phone Fax

Workforce Development Dept
1 Ashburton Pl Rm 1301 Boston MA 02108 617-626-7100 727-1090
Web: www.mass.gov

342-23 Michigan

Phone Fax

Aging Services Office
201 N Washington Sq Ste 920 Lansing MI 48933 517-323-3687
Web: leadingagemi.org

Arts & Cultural Affairs Council
300 N Washington Sq Lansing MI 48913 517-241-3972 241-3979
Web: www.michigan.gov

Attorney General 525 W Ottawa St Lansing MI 48933 517-373-1110 373-3042
TF: 877-765-8388 ■ *Web:* www.michigan.gov

Career Education & Workforce Programs
201 N Washington Sq Victor Office Center Lansing MI 48913 517-335-5858 373-0314
TF: 888-253-6855 ■ *Web:* www.michigan.gov/mdcd

Child Support Office
235 S Grand Ave PO Box 30037 Lansing MI 48933 866-661-0005
TF: 866-661-0005 ■ *Web:* www.michigan.gov/dhs

Civil Rights Dept
110 W Michigan Ave Ste 800
Capitol Tower Bldg Lansing MI 48933 517-335-3165 241-0546
Web: www.michigan.gov/mdcr

Civil Service Dept
Capitol Commons Ctr 400 S Pine St Lansing MI 48913 517-373-3030 373-7690
TF: 800-788-1766 ■ *Web:* www.michigan.gov

Community Health Dept
Capitol View Bldg 201 Townsend St Lansing MI 48913 517-373-3740
TF: 800-649-3777 ■ *Web:* www.michigan.gov/mdch

Consumer Protection Div PO Box 30213 Lansing MI 48909 517-373-1140 241-3771
Web: www.michigan.gov/ag

Corrections Dept
206 E Michigan Ave Grandview Plaza
PO Box 30003 Lansing MI 48909 517-335-1426 373-6883
Web: www.michigan.gov/corrections

Crime Victims Services Commission
320 S Walnut St Garden Level Lewis Cass Bldg Lansing MI 48913 877-251-7373 373-2439*
**Fax Area Code:* 517 ■ *TF:* 877-251-7373 ■ *Web:* www.michigan.gov

Driver & Vehicle Bureau 7064 Crowner Dr Lansing MI 48918 517-322-1460 322-5458
Web: www.michigan.gov/sos

Drug Control Policy Office
320 S Walnut St Lewis Cass Bldg 5th Fl Lansing MI 48913 517-373-4700 241-2199
Web: www.michigan.gov/mdch

Economic Development Corp (MEDC)
300 N Washington Sq Lansing MI 48913 517-373-9808 241-3683
TF: 888-522-0103 ■ *Web:* www.michiganbusiness.org

Education Dept 608 W Allegan St PO Box 30008 Lansing MI 48909 517-373-3324
Web: www.michigan.gov

Education Trust PO Box 30198 Lansing MI 48909 517-335-4767 373-6967
TF General: 800-638-4543 ■ *Web:* www.setwithmet.com

eLibrary Information
702 W Kalamazoo St PO Box 30007 Lansing MI 48909 517-373-4331 373-5700
TF: 877-479-0021 ■ *Web:* www.michigan.gov

Emergency Management & Homeland Security Div
PO Box 30636 Lansing MI 48909 517-336-6198 333-4987
Web: michigan.gov

Environmental Quality Dept 3423 N Logan St Lansing MI 48906 517-373-7917
Web: www.michigan.gov

Financial & Insurance Regulation
PO Box 30220 Lansing MI 48909 517-373-0220 335-4978
TF: 877-999-6442 ■ *Web:* www.michigan.gov

Gaming Control Board
3062 West Grand Blvd Suite L-700 Detroit MI 48202 313-456-4100 241-0510*
**Fax Area Code:* 517 ■ *Web:* www.michigan.gov/mgcb

Governor PO Box 30013 Lansing MI 48909 517-373-3400 335-6863
Web: www.michigan.gov/gov

Human Services Dept
235 S Grand Ave PO Box 30037 Lansing MI 48909 517-373-2035 335-6101
Web: www.michigan.gov/dhs

Labor & Economic Growth Dept 611 W Ottawa St Lansing MI 48933 517-373-1820 373-2129
Web: www.michigan.gov

Lieutenant Governor PO Box 30013 Lansing MI 48909 517-373-3400
Web: www.michigan.gov/ltgov

Management & Budget Dept PO Box 30026 Lansing MI 48909 517-373-1004 373-7268
Web: www.michigan.gov/dmb

Military & Veterans Affairs Dept
3411 N ML King Blvd Lansing MI 48906 517-481-8000
Web: www.michigan.gov/dmva

Parks & Recreation Div PO Box 30257 Lansing MI 48909 517-373-9900 373-4625
TF Campground Resv: 800-447-2757 ■ *Web:* www.michigan.gov/dnr

Public Service Commission PO Box 30221 Lansing MI 48909 517-241-6180 241-6181
Web: www.michigan.gov/mpsc

Racing Commissioners Office
525 W Allegan St PO Box 30773 Lansing MI 48909 517-335-1420 241-3018
Web: www.michigan.gov

Rehabilitation Services
201 N Washington Sq 4th Fl Lansing MI 48933 517-373-3390 335-7277
Web: www.michigan.gov

Secretary of State 430 W Allegan St 4th Fl Lansing MI 48918 517-373-2510
Web: www.michigan.gov

State Court Administrator 925 W Ottawa St Lansing MI 48913 517-373-0130 373-7517
Web: courts.mi.gov

State Historic Preservation Office
702 W Kalamazoo St PO Box 30740 Lansing MI 48909 517-373-1630 335-0348
Web: www.michigan.gov

State Housing Development Authority
PO Box 30044 Lansing MI 48909 517-373-8370 335-4797
Web: www.michigan.gov/mshda

State Lottery 101 E Hillsdale St PO Box 30023 Lansing MI 48909 517-335-5600 335-5644
Web: www.michigan.gov/lottery

Phone Fax

State Police Dept 714 S Harrison Rd East Lansing MI 48823 517-332-2521 336-6255
Web: www.michigan.gov/msp

Student Financial Services Bureau
Austin Bldg 430 W Allegan Lansing MI 48922 888-447-2687 335-6792*
**Fax Area Code:* 517 ■ *TF General:* 800-642-5626 ■ *Web:* www.michigan.gov/mistudentaid

Supreme Court PO Box 30052 Lansing MI 48909 517-373-0120
Web: courts.mi.gov

Transportation Dept PO Box 30050 Lansing MI 48909 517-373-2090 373-0167
Web: www.michigan.gov/mdot

Travel Michigan 300 N Washington Sq Lansing MI 48913 517-373-0670 373-0059
TF: 888-784-7328 ■ *Web:* www.michigan.org

Treasurer 430 W Allegan St Lansing MI 48922 517-373-3200 373-4968
Web: www.michigan.gov/treasury

Unemployment Insurance Agency
Cadillac Pl Suite 11-500 Detroit MI 48202 313-456-2400 456-2424
Web: www.michigan.gov/uia

Vital Records Div
201 Townsend St Capitol View Bldg 3rd Fl Lansing MI 48913 517-335-8656
Web: www.michigan.gov/mdch

Wildlife Div PO Box 30444 Lansing MI 48909 517-373-1263 373-6705
Web: www.michigan.gov/dnr

Workers Compensation Agency PO Box 30016 Lansing MI 48909 517-322-1106 322-6689
Web: www.michigan.gov/wca

342-24 Minnesota

Phone Fax

Aging Board 540 Cedar St Saint Paul MN 55155 651-431-2500
TF: 800-882-6262 ■ *Web:* www.mnaging.org

Arts Board 400 Sibley St Ste 200 Saint Paul MN 55101 651-215-1600 215-1602
TF: 800-866-2787 ■ *Web:* www.arts.state.mn.us

Attorney General
1400 Bremer Tower 445 Minnesota St Saint Paul MN 55101 651-296-3353 297-4193
TF: 800-657-3787 ■ *Web:* www.ag.state.mn.us

Attorney General's Office
445 Minnesota St Ste 1400 Saint Paul MN 55101 651-296-3353
TF: 800-657-3787 ■ *Web:* www.ag.state.mn.us

Bill Status-Senate
100 Rev Dr Martin Luther King Junior Blvd
Saint Paul MN 55155 651-296-2146
Web: www.house.leg.state.mn.us

Campaign Finance & Public Disclosure Board
658 Cedar St Ste 190 Saint Paul MN 55155 651-296-5148 296-1722
TF: 800-657-3889 ■ *Web:* www.cfboard.state.mn.us

Child Support Enforcement Div
444 Lafayette Rd Saint Paul MN 55155 651-431-2000 431-7517
Web: mn.gov

Commerce Dept 85 Seventh Pl E Ste 500 Saint Paul MN 55101 651-539-1500 539-1547
Web: mmd.admin.state.mn.us

Corrections Dept 1450 Energy Pk Dr Ste 200 Saint Paul MN 55108 651-361-7200 642-0223
Web: www.corr.state.mn.us

Driver & Vehicle Services Div
445 Minnesota St Ste 190 Town Sq Bldg Saint Paul MN 55101 651-297-3298 296-3141
Web: dps.mn.gov/divisions/dvs/Pages/default.aspx

Education Dept 1500 Hwy 36 W Roseville MN 55113 651-582-8200 582-8202
Web: education.state.mn.us

Employment & Economic Development Dept (DEED)
1st National Bank Bldg 332 Minnesota St
Ste E200 Saint Paul MN 55101 651-259-7114
TF: 800-657-3858 ■ *Web:* mn.gov/deed

Enterprise Technology Office 658 Cedar St Saint Paul MN 55155 651-201-8000
Web: www.mmb.state.mn.us

Finance Dept 658 Cedar St Ste 400 Saint Paul MN 55155 651-201-8000 296-8685
TF: 800-627-3529 ■ *Web:* www.mmb.state.mn.us

Fish & Wildlife Div 500 Lafayette Rd Saint Paul MN 55155 651-259-5180 297-7272
Web: www.dnr.state.mn.us

Governor
130 State Capitol
75 Rev Dr Martin Luther King Jr Blvd Saint Paul MN 55155 651-201-3400 296-2089
TF: 800-657-3717 ■ *Web:* mn.gov

Health Dept PO Box 64975 Saint Paul MN 55164 651-201-5000
TF: 888-345-0823 ■ *Web:* www.health.state.mn.us

Historical Society 345 Kellogg Blvd W Saint Paul MN 55102 651-259-3000
TF: 800-657-3773 ■ *Web:* www.mnhs.org

Homeland Security & Emergency Management Div
445 Minnesota St Ste 223 Saint Paul MN 55101 651-201-7400 296-0459
Web: dps.mn.gov/divisions/hsem

Housing Finance Authority
400 Sibley St Ste 300 Saint Paul MN 55101 651-296-7608 296-8139
TF: 800-657-3769 ■ *Web:* www.mnhousing.gov

Human Services Dept 444 Lafayette Rd Saint Paul MN 55155 651-431-2000 296-6244
Web: mn.gov

Labor & Industry Dept 443 Lafayette Rd N Saint Paul MN 55155 651-284-5005 284-5727
TF: 800-342-5354 ■ *Web:* www.doli.state.mn.us

Legislature
75 Constitution Ave State Capitol Saint Paul MN 55155 651-296-2146
TF: 800-657-3550 ■ *Web:* www.leg.state.mn.us

Medical Practice Board
2829 University Ave SE Ste 500 Minneapolis MN 55414 612-617-2130 617-2166
TF: 800-657-3709 ■ *Web:* mn.gov

Natural Resources Dept 500 Lafayette Rd Saint Paul MN 55155 651-296-6157
TF: 888-646-6367 ■ *Web:* www.dnr.state.mn.us

Office of Higher Education
1450 Energy Pk Dr Ste 350 Saint Paul MN 55108 651-642-0567 642-0675
TF: 800-657-3866 ■ *Web:* www.ohe.state.mn.us

Office of State Registrar
85 E Seventh Pl Third Fl PO Box 64882 Saint Paul MN 55164 651-201-5970
Web: www.health.state.mn.us/divs/chs/osr

Parks & Recreation Div 500 Lafayette Rd Saint Paul MN 55155 651-296-6157
TF: 888-646-6367 ■ *Web:* dnr.state.mn.us/contact/index.html

Public Safety Dept 444 Minnesota St Saint Paul MN 55101 651-201-7100 296-5937
Web: www.dps.mn.gov

	City	State	Zip	Phone	Fax
Public Utilities Commission 121 Seventh Pl E Ste 350 *TF:* 800-657-3782 ■ *Web:* mn.gov/puc/	Saint Paul	MN	55101	651-296-7124	297-7073
Revenue Dept 600 N Roberts St *TF:* 800-652-9094 ■ *Web:* www.revenue.state.mn.us	Saint Paul	MN	55101	651-296-3403	
Secretary of State 60 Empire Dr Ste 100 *Web:* www.sos.state.mn.us	Saint Paul	MN	55103	651-296-2803	215-0682
State Court Administrator 25 Rev Dr Martin Luther King Jr Blvd Rm 135 *Web:* www.mncourts.gov	Saint Paul	MN	55155	651-296-2474	297-5636
State Lottery 2645 Long Lake Rd *Web:* www.mnlottery.com	Saint Paul	MN	55113	651-635-8273	
Supreme Court 25 Rev Dr Martin Luther King Jr Blvd *Web:* www.mncourts.gov	Saint Paul	MN	55155	651-297-7650	
Transportation Dept 395 John Ireland Blvd *TF:* 800-657-3774 ■ *Web:* www.dot.state.mn.us	Saint Paul	MN	55155	651-296-3000	
Veterans Affairs Dept 20 W 12th St Room 206 *Web:* mn.gov	Saint Paul	MN	55155	651-296-2562	296-3954
Weights & Measures Div 14305 Southcross Dr W Ste 150 **Fax Area Code:* 952	Burnsville	MN	55306	651-539-1555	435-4040*
Workers Compensation Div 443 Lafayette Rd *TF:* 800-342-5354 ■ *Web:* www.dli.mn.gov	Saint Paul	MN	55155	651-284-5005	

342-25 Mississippi

	City	State	Zip	Phone	Fax
State Government Information 200 S Lamar Ste 800 *TF:* 877-290-9487 ■ *Web:* www.ms.gov	Jackson	MS	39201	601-351-5023	
Administrative Office of the Courts 450 High St PO Box 117 *Web:* courts.ms.gov	Jackson	MS	39205	601-576-4630	576-4630
Archives & History Dept 200 N St PO Box 571 *Web:* www.mdah.state.ms.us	Jackson	MS	39201	601-576-6850	576-6975
Arts Commission 501 NW St Ste 1101-A *Web:* www.arts.state.ms.us	Jackson	MS	39201	601-359-6030	359-6008
Attorney General PO Box 220 *Web:* www.ago.state.ms.us	Jackson	MS	39205	601-359-3680	
Banking & Consumer Finance Dept PO Box 23729 *TF:* 800-844-2499 ■ *Web:* www.dbcf.state.ms.us	Jackson	MS	39225	601-359-1031	359-3557
Bill Status PO Box 2611 *Web:* billstatus.ls.state.ms.us	Jackson	MS	39215	601-359-2420	
Child Support Enforcement Div 750 N State St *TF:* 800-345-6347	Jackson	MS	39202	601-359-4929	
Consumer Protection Div PO Box 22947 *TF:* 800-281-4418 ■	Jackson	MS	39225	601-359-4230	359-4231
Contractors Board 215 Woodline Dr Ste B *TF:* 800-880-6161 ■ *Web:* msboc.us	Jackson	MS	39232	601-354-6161	354-6715
Corrections Dept 723 N President St *Web:* www.mdoc.state.ms.us	Jackson	MS	39202	601-359-5600	359-5624
Development Authority 501 NW St *Web:* www.mississippi.org	Jackson	MS	39201	601-359-3449	359-2832
Education Dept 359 N West St Ste 270	Jackson	MS	39201	601-359-3768	
Emergency Management Agency PO Box 5644 *TF:* 800-222-6362 ■ *Web:* www.msema.org	Pearl	MS	39288	601-933-6362	933-6800
Employment Security Commission 1235 Echelon Pkwy PO Box 1699 *TF:* 888-844-3577 ■ *Web:* www.mdes.ms.gov	Jackson	MS	39215	601-321-6000	321-6004
Environmental Quality Dept PO Box 20305 *Web:* www.deq.state.ms.us	Jackson	MS	39289	601-961-5611	354-6356
Ethics Commission 146 E Amite St Ste 103 *Web:* www.ethics.state.ms.us	Jackson	MS	39201	601-359-1285	354-6253
Family & Children Services Div 750 N State St *TF:* 800-345-6347	Jackson	MS	39202	601-359-4570	
Finance & Administration Dept 1301 Wolfolk Bldg Ste B *Web:* www.dfa.state.ms.us	Jackson	MS	39201	601-359-3402	359-2405
Governor PO Box 139 *Web:* mississippi.gov	Jackson	MS	39205	601-359-3150	359-3741
Health Dept PO Box 1700 *Web:* www.msdh.state.ms.us	Jackson	MS	39215	601-576-7400	
Higher Learning Institutions Board of Trustees 3825 Ridgewood Rd Ste 915 *TF:* 800-327-2980 ■ *Web:* www.ihl.state.ms.us	Jackson	MS	39211	601-432-6198	432-6972
Historic Preservation Div PO Box 571 *Web:* www.mdah.state.ms.us/hpres	Jackson	MS	39205	601-576-6940	576-6955
Home Corp 735 Riverside Dr *Web:* www.mshomecorp.com	Jackson	MS	39202	601-718-4642	718-4643
Human Services Dept 750 N State St *Web:* www.mdhs.state.ms.us	Jackson	MS	39205	601-359-4500	
Information Technology Services Dept 301 N Lamar St Ste 508 *Web:* www.its.ms.gov	Jackson	MS	39201	601-359-1395	354-6016
Insurance Dept 1001 Woolfolk State Office Bldg 501 NW St PO Box 79 *TF:* 800-562-2957 ■ *Web:* www.mid.ms.gov	Jackson	MS	39201	601-359-3569	
Legislature New Capitol PO Box 1018 *Web:* billstatus.ls.state.ms.us	Jackson	MS	39215	601-359-3770	359-3935
Medical Licensure Board 1867 Crane Ridge Dr Ste 200-B *Web:* www.msbml.ms.gov	Jackson	MS	39216	601-987-3079	987-4159
Motor Vehicle Commission 1755 Lelia Dr *Web:* www.mmvc.state.ms.us	Jackson	MS	39236	601-987-3995	987-3997
Parole Board 660 N St Ste 100 A *Web:* www.mpb.state.ms.us	Jackson	MS	39202	601-576-3520	576-3528
Public Accountancy Board (MSBPA) 5 Old River Pl Ste 104 *Web:* www.msbpa.ms.gov	Jackson	MS	39202	601-354-7320	354-7290
Public Health Statistics Bureau 571 Stadium Dr PO Box 1700 *Web:* www.msdh.state.ms.us/phs	Jackson	MS	39215	601-576-7960	
Public Service Commission PO Box 1174 *Web:* www.psc.state.ms.us	Jackson	MS	39215	601-961-5434	961-5469
Real Estate Commission 2506 Lakeland Dr Ste 300 *Web:* www.mrec.state.ms.us	Flowood	MS	39232	601-932-6770	932-2990
Rehabilitation Services Dept 1281 Highway 51 PO Box 1698 *TF:* 800-443-1000 ■ *Web:* www.mdrs.ms.gov	Madison	MS	39110	800-443-1000	
Securities Div 401 Mississippi St *Web:* www.sos.ms.gov	Jackson	MS	39201	601-359-1350	359-1499
State Medical Examiner PO BOX 958 *Web:* www.dps.state.ms.us	Jackson	MS	39205	601-987-1212	
Student Financial Aid Office 3825 Ridgewood Rd *TF:* 800-327-2980 ■ *Web:* www.ihl.state.ms.us/financialaid	Jackson	MS	39211	601-432-6997	432-6527
Supreme Court PO Box 117 *Web:* courts.ms.gov	Jackson	MS	39205	601-359-3694	359-2407
Tax Commission PO Box 22828 *Web:* www.dor.ms.gov	Jackson	MS	39225	601-923-7000	
Treasury Dept 501 N West St Ste 1101	Jackson	MS	39205	601-359-3600	
Veterans Affairs Board (MSVAB) PO Box 5947 *Web:* www.vab.ms.gov	Pearl	MS	39288	601-576-4850	576-4868
Weights & Measures Div 121 N Jefferson St	Jackson	MS	39201	601-359-1100	
Wildlife Fisheries & Parks Dept 1505 Eastover Dr *Web:* www.mdwfp.com	Jackson	MS	39211	601-432-2400	
Worker's Compensation Commission PO Box 5300 *Web:* www.mwcc.state.ms.us	Jackson	MS	39296	601-987-4200	

342-26 Missouri

	City	State	Zip	Phone	Fax
Revenue Dept 301 W High St *Web:* dor.mo.gov	Jefferson City	MO	65101	573-526-3669	
Agriculture Dept 1616 Missouri Blvd PO Box 630 *Web:* mda.mo.gov	Jefferson City	MO	65102	573-751-4211	751-1784
Arts Council 815 Olive St Ste 16 *Web:* www.missouriartscouncil.org	Saint Louis	MO	63101	314-340-6845	340-7215
Attorney General 207 W High St PO Box 899 *Web:* www.ago.mo.gov	Jefferson City	MO	65102	573-751-3321	751-0774
Child Support Enforcement Div PO Box 109002 *TF:* 800-859-7999 ■ *Web:* www.dss.mo.gov/cse	Jefferson City	MO	65102	800-859-7999	
Conservation Dept 2901 W Truman Blvd *Web:* www.mdc.mo.gov	Jefferson City	MO	65109	573-751-4115	751-4467
Consumer Protection Div 207 W High St PO Box 899 *TF:* 800-392-8222 ■ *Web:* ago.mo.gov/divisions/consumerprotection.htm	Jefferson City	MO	65102	573-751-3321	751-0774
Corrections Dept PO Box 236 *Web:* www.doc.mo.gov	Jefferson City	MO	65102	573-522-1118	
Crime Victims' Compensation Unit PO Box 1589 *Web:* www.dps.mo.gov	Jefferson City	MO	65102	573-526-6006	
Economic Development Dept 301 W High St PO Box 1157 *Web:* www.ded.mo.gov/Ded	Jefferson City	MO	65102	573-751-4962	526-7700
Elementary & Secondary Education Dept 205 Jefferson St PO Box 480 *TF:* 800-735-2966 ■ *Web:* www.dese.mo.gov	Jefferson City	MO	65101	573-751-4212	751-8613
Emergency Management Agency 2302 Militia Dr PO Box 116 *Web:* www.sema.dps.mo.gov	Jefferson City	MO	65102	573-526-9100	634-7966
Family Services Div PO Box 2320 *Web:* www.dss.mo.gov/fsd	Jefferson City	MO	65102	573-751-3221	
Finance Div PO Box 716 *TF:* 888-246-7225 ■ *Web:* www.finance.mo.gov	Jefferson City	MO	65102	573-751-3242	751-9192
General Assembly State Capitol *Web:* www.moga.mo.gov	Jefferson City	MO	65101	573-751-4633	
Governor PO Box 720 *Web:* www.governor.mo.gov	Jefferson City	MO	65102	573-751-3222	
Healing Arts Board 3605 Missouri Blvd PO Box 4 *Web:* www.pr.mo.gov	Jefferson City	MO	65102	573-751-0098	751-3166
Health & Senior Services Dept 912 Wildwood PO Box 570 *Web:* www.health.mo.gov	Jefferson City	MO	65102	573-751-6400	751-6010
Higher Education Dept 3515 Amazonas Dr *TF:* 800-473-6757 ■ *Web:* www.dhe.mo.gov	Jefferson City	MO	65109	573-751-2361	751-6635
Historical Preservation Office 1101 Riverside Dr *Web:* www.dnr.mo.gov	Jefferson City	MO	65101	573-751-7858	522-6262
Housing Development Commission 3435 Broadway *Web:* www.mhdc.com	Kansas City	MO	64111	816-759-6600	759-6828
Insurance Dept 301 W High St Ste 530 *Web:* insurance.mo.gov	Jefferson City	MO	65101	573-751-4126	751-1165
Labor & Industrial Relations Dept 3315 W Truman Blvd Rm 214 PO Box 599 *Web:* www.labor.mo.gov/lirc	Jefferson City	MO	65102	573-751-2461	751-7806
Lieutenant Governor State Capitol Bldg Rm 224 *Web:* ltgov.mo.gov/	Jefferson City	MO	65101	573-751-4727	751-9422

	City	State	ZIP	Phone	Fax
Lottery 1823 Southridge Dr PO Box 1603 — *Web:* www.molottery.com	Jefferson City	MO	65109	573-751-4050	751-5188
Motor Vehicles & Drivers Licensing Div PO Box 500 — *Web:* dor.mo.gov/drivers	Jefferson City	MO	65106	573-751-3505	751-2195
Natural Resources Dept PO Box 176 — *TF Cust Svc:* 800-361-4827 ■ *Web:* www.dnr.mo.gov	Jefferson City	MO	65102	573-751-3443	751-7627
Professional Registration Div 3605 Missouri Blvd PO Box 1335 — *Fax Area Code: 800 ■ *TF:* 800-735-2966 ■ *Web:* www.pr.mo.gov	Jefferson City	MO	65102	573-751-0293	735-2966*
Public Service Commission 200 Madison St PO Box 360 — *TF:* 800-819-3180 ■ *Web:* www.psc.mo.gov	Jefferson City	MO	65102	573-751-3234	
Real Estate Commission 3605 Missouri Blvd PO Box 1339 — *Web:* www.pr.mo.gov/realestate.asp	Jefferson City	MO	65102	573-751-2628	751-2777
Secretary of State PO Box 778 — *Web:* www.sos.mo.gov	Jefferson City	MO	65102	573-751-4936	526-4903
Securities Div 600 W Main St PO Box 1276 — *TF:* 800-721-7996 ■ *Web:* s1.sos.mo.gov/	Jefferson City	MO	65102	573-751-4704	
Social Services Dept PO Box 1527 — *Web:* www.dss.mo.gov	Jefferson City	MO	65102	573-751-4815	751-3203
State Courts Administrator PO Box 104480 — *TF:* 888-541-4894 ■ *Web:* www.courts.mo.gov	Jefferson City	MO	65110	888-541-4894	
State Highway Patrol 1510 E Elm St — *Web:* www.mshp.dps.missouri.gov	Jefferson City	MO	65102	573-751-3313	751-9419
State Parks Div PO Box 176 — *TF:* 800-334-6946 ■ *Web:* www.mostateparks.com	Jefferson City	MO	65102	573-751-2479	
Supreme Court 207 W High St — *TF:* 888-541-4894 ■ *Web:* www.courts.mo.gov/page.jsp?id=27	Jefferson City	MO	65101	573-751-4144	
Tourism Div PO Box 1055 — *TF:* 800-519-2100 ■ *Web:* www.visitmo.com	Jefferson City	MO	65102	573-751-4133	751-5160
Transportation Dept 105 W Capitol Ave — *TF:* 888-275-6636 ■ *Web:* www.modot.org	Jefferson City	MO	65102	573-751-2551	751-6555
Treasurer PO Box 210 — *Web:* www.treasurer.mo.gov	Jefferson City	MO	65102	573-751-8533	751-0343
Veterans Commission 205 Jefferson St Fl 12 — *Web:* mvc.dps.mo.gov	Jefferson City	MO	65102	573-751-3779	
Vital Records Bureau 930 Wildwood PO Box 570 — *Web:* www.sos.mo.gov	Jefferson City	MO	65102	573-751-6400	
Vocational & Adult Education Div 3024 Dupont Cir PO Box 480 — *TF:* 877-222-8963 ■ *Web:* dese.mo.gov/college-career-readiness	Jefferson City	MO	65109	573-751-3251	751-1441
Weights & Measures Div 1616 Missouri Blvd PO Box 630 — *Web:* agriculture.mo.gov/weights	Jefferson City	MO	65102	573-751-4316	
Workers Compensation Div PO Box 58 — *TF:* 800-775-2667 ■ *Web:* www.labor.mo.gov/DWC	Jefferson City	MO	65102	573-751-4231	751-2012

342-27 Montana

	City	State	ZIP	Phone	Fax
State Government Information PO Box 200113 — *Web:* www.mt.gov	Helena	MT	59620	406-444-2511	444-2701
Arts Council PO Box 202201 — *TF:* 800-282-3092 ■ *Web:* www.art.mt.gov	Helena	MT	59620	406-444-6430	444-6548
Attorney General 215 N Sanders St — *Web:* dojmt.gov/	Helena	MT	59601	406-444-2026	444-3549
Banking & Financial Institutions Div Rm 155 Mitchell Bldg 125 N Roberts St PO Box 200101 — *TF:* 800-914-8423 ■ *Web:* www.banking.mt.gov	Helena	MT	59620	406-841-2920	841-2930
Child & Family Services Div PO Box 8005 — *TF:* 866-820-5437 ■ *Web:* dphhs.mt.gov/	Helena	MT	59604	406-841-2400	841-2487
Commerce Dept 301 S Pk Ave PO Box 200501 — *Web:* www.commerce.mt.gov	Helena	MT	59601	406-841-2700	841-2701
Commissioner of Political Practices 1205 Eigth Ave PO Box 202401 — *Web:* www.politicalpractices.mt.gov	Helena	MT	59620	406-444-2942	444-1643
Community Development Div 301 S Pk Ave PO Box 200523 — *Web:* www.comdev.mt.gov	Helena	MT	59601	406-841-2770	841-2771
Consumer Protection Office POBox 200151 — *TF:* 800-481-6896 ■ *Web:* dojmt.gov/	Helena	MT	59620	406-444-4500	442-2174
Corrections Dept 5 S Last Chance Gulch PO Box 201301 — *Web:* www.cor.mt.gov	Helena	MT	59620	406-444-3930	444-4920
Court Administration 215 N Sanders St Rm 315 — *Web:* www.montanacourts.org	Helena	MT	59620	406-444-5490	
Disability Services Div 111 N Sanders St Ste 305	Helena	MT	59601	406-444-2995	
Environmental Quality Dept PO Box 200901 — *Web:* montanatu.org	Helena	MT	59620	406-444-2544	
Forensic Science Div 2679 Palmer St — *Web:* dojmt.gov/crime	Missoula	MT	59808	406-728-4970	549-1067
Healthcare Licensing Bureau 301 S Pk Ave Rm 430 — *Web:* mt.gov	Helena	MT	59620	406-841-2303	841-2305
Higher Education Board of Regents 2500 Broadway St PO Box 203201 — *TF:* 877-501-1722 ■ *Web:* www.mus.edu	Helena	MT	59620	406-444-6570	444-1469
Highway Patrol Div 2550 Prospect Ave PO Box 201419 — *Web:* dojmt.gov/highwaypatrol	Helena	MT	59620	406-444-3780	444-4169
Historical Society 225 N Roberts St — *Web:* helenamt.com	Helena	MT	59601	406-442-4120	
Housing Div PO Box 200528 — *Web:* www.housing.mt.gov	Helena	MT	59620	406-841-2840	841-2841
Information Technology Services Div 125 N Roberts St — *TF:* 800-628-4917 ■ *Web:* www.itsd.mt.gov	Helena	MT	59601	406-444-2700	444-2701
Insurance Div 1315 E Lockey — *Web:* uid.dli.mt.gov/	Helena	MT	59604	406-444-3783	
Labor & Industry - Business Standards Dept 301 S Pk Rm 430 PO Box 200513 — *Web:* www.bsd.dli.mt.gov	Helena	MT	59620	406-841-2300	
Labor & Industry Dept PO Box 1728 — *Web:* www.dli.mt.gov	Helena	MT	59624	406-444-2840	444-1394
Legislative Services 1301 E Sixth Ave PO Box 201706 — *Web:* leg.mt.gov	Helena	MT	59620	406-444-3064	444-3036
Lieutenant Governor PO Box 200801 — *Web:* www.governor.mt.gov	Helena	MT	59620	406-444-3111	444-5529
Motor Vehicle Div 302 N Roberts St, PO Box 201430 — *Web:* dojmt.gov/driving/	Helena	MT	59620	406-444-3933	
Natural Resources & Conservation Dept 1625 11th Ave — *Web:* www.dnrc.mt.gov	Helena	MT	59620	406-444-2074	444-2684
Office of Governor PO Box 200801 — *Web:* www.governor.mt.gov	Helena	MT	59620	406-444-3111	444-5529
Public Education Board 46 N Last Chance Gulch PO Box 200601 — *Web:* bpe.mt.gov/	Helena	MT	59620	406-444-6576	444-0847
Public Health & Human Services Dept 111 N Sanders — *Web:* mt.gov/	Helena	MT	59604	406-444-5622	444-1970
Public Service Commission 1701 Prospect Ave	Helena	MT	59601	406-444-6199	444-7618
Revenue Dept PO Box 5805 — *TF:* 866-859-2254 ■ *Web:* revenue.mt.gov	Helena	MT	59604	406-444-6900	444-3696
Secretary of State 1301 E Sixth Ave PO Box 202801 — *Web:* www.sos.mt.gov	Helena	MT	59601	406-444-2034	444-3976
Securities Dept 840 Helena Ave — *TF:* 800-332-6148 ■ *Web:* www.sao.mt.gov	Helena	MT	59601	406-444-2040	444-3497
State Auditor Office 840 Helena Ave — *Web:* www.sao.mt.gov	Helena	MT	59601	406-444-2040	444-3497
State Legislature 1301 E Sixth Ave — *Web:* www.leg.mt.gov	Helena	MT	59620	406-444-3060	444-3036
Supreme Court 215 N Sanders St Rm 323 — *Web:* courts.mt.gov	Helena	MT	59620	406-444-3858	444-5705
Transportation Dept 2701 Prospect Ave PO Box 201001 — *Web:* www.mdt.mt.gov	Helena	MT	59620	406-444-6200	444-7643
Victim Services Office 2225 11th Ave PO Box 201410 — *TF:* 800-498-6455 ■ *Web:* dojmt.gov/victims	Helena	MT	59620	406-444-1907	444-9680
Vital Records Bureau 111 N Sanders St — *TF:* 888-877-1946 ■ *Web:* montanagenealogy.com	Helena	MT	59604	406-444-4228	444-1803
Weights & Measures Program 301 South Park, Room 430 PO Box 200513 — *Web:* www.bsd.dli.mt.gov/bc/ms_index.asp	Helena	MT	59620	406-443-8065	443-8163
Wildlife & Parks 1420 E Sixth Ave PO Box 200701 — *Web:* www.fwp.mt.gov	Helena	MT	59620	406-444-2535	444-4952
Worker's Compensation Ct 1625 11th Avenue PO Box 537 — *Web:* www.wcc.dli.mt.gov	Helena	MT	59624	406-444-7794	444-7798

342-28 Nebraska

	City	State	ZIP	Phone	Fax
State Electrical Div 521 S 14th St Ste 300 — *Web:* www.electrical.nebraska.gov	Lincoln	NE	68508	402-471-3550	471-4297
Accountability & Disclosure Commission PO Box 95086 — *Web:* nadc.nebraska.gov	Lincoln	NE	68509	402-471-2522	471-6599
Aging Div PO Box 95026 — *Web:* dhhs.ne.gov	Lincoln	NE	68509	402-471-2307	
Agriculture Dept 301 Centennial Mall S — *Web:* www.nda.nebraska.gov	Lincoln	NE	68509	402-471-2341	471-2759
Arts Council 1004 Farnam St — *TF:* 800-341-4067 ■ *Web:* www.nebraskaartscouncil.org	Omaha	NE	68131	402-595-2122	
Attorney General 2115 State Capitol — *Web:* www.ago.ne.gov	Lincoln	NE	68509	402-471-2683	471-3297
Banking & Finance Dept (NDBF) 1230 'O' St Ste 400 PO Box 95006 — *Web:* www.ndbf.ne.gov	Lincoln	NE	68508	402-471-2171	471-3062
Child Support Enforcement Div PO Box 95026 — *TF:* 877-631-9973 ■ *Web:* dhhs.ne.gov	Lincoln	NE	68509	402-471-3121	471-7311
Coordinating Commission for Postsecondary Education 140 N Eigth St Ste 300 PO Box 95005 — *Web:* www.ccpe.state.ne.us	Lincoln	NE	68509	402-471-2847	471-2886
Correctional Services Dept PO Box 94661 — *Web:* www.corrections.state.ne.us	Lincoln	NE	68509	402-471-2654	
Crime Victim Reparations Programs 301 Centennial Mall S PO Box 94946 — *Web:* www.ncc.state.ne.us	Lincoln	NE	68509	402-471-2194	471-2837
Economic Development Dept 301 Centennial Mall S PO Box 94666 — *TF:* 800-426-6505 ■ *Web:* www.neded.org	Lincoln	NE	68509	402-471-3747	471-3778
Education Dept 301 Centennial Mall S — *Web:* www2.ed.gov	Lincoln	NE	68509	402-471-2295	471-4433
Emergency Management Agency 1300 Military Rd — *TF:* 877-297-2368 ■ *Web:* www.nema.ne.gov	Lincoln	NE	68508	402-471-7421	471-7433
Environmental Quality Dept 1200 N St Ste 400 — *TF:* 877-253-2603 ■ *Web:* www.deq.state.ne.us	Lincoln	NE	68508	402-471-2186	471-2909

				Phone	Fax
Game & Parks Commission PO Box 30370 *Web:* outdoornebraska.ne.gov	Lincoln	NE	68503	402-471-0641	471-5528
Governor PO Box 94848 *Web:* www.governor.nebraska.gov	Lincoln	NE	68509	402-471-2244	471-6031
Health & Human Services Dept 301 Centennial Mall S *TF:* 800-430-3244 ■ *Web:* dhhs.ne.gov	Lincoln	NE	68508	402-471-3121	471-9449
Historical Society 1500 R St *TF:* 800-833-6747 ■ *Web:* www.nebraskahistory.org	Lincoln	NE	68501	402-471-3270	471-3100
Insurance Dept 941 O St Ste 400 *TF:* 877-564-7323 ■ *Web:* www.doi.nebraska.gov	Lincoln	NE	68508	402-471-2201	471-4610
Investment Finance Authority 1230 'O' St Ste 200 *TF:* 800-204-6432 ■ *Web:* www.nifa.org	Lincoln	NE	68508	402-434-3900	434-3921
Lieutenant Governor 1445 K St Ste 2315 *Web:* governor.nebraska.gov	Lincoln	NE	68508	402-471-2256	471-6031
Motor Vehicles Dept PO Box 94789 *Web:* www.dmv.state.ne.us	Lincoln	NE	68509	402-471-3918	
Natural Resources Dept 301 Centennial Mall S 4th Fl *Web:* nebraska.gov	Lincoln	NE	68509	402-471-2363	471-2900
Parks Div 2200 N 33rd St *Web:* outdoornebraska.ne.gov	Lincoln	NE	68503	402-471-0641	471-5528
Parole Board PO Box 94754 *Web:* www.parole.state.ne.us	Lincoln	NE	68509	402-471-2156	471-2453
Power Review Board 301 Centennial Mall S *Web:* powerreviewboard.nebraska.gov/	Lincoln	NE	68508	402-471-2301	471-3715
Public Accountancy Board 140 N Eigth St Ste 290 *Web:* www.nbpa.ne.gov	Lincoln	NE	68508	402-471-3595	471-4404
Public Service Commission 1200 N St Ste 300 *TF:* 800-526-0017 ■ *Web:* psc.nebraska.gov/	Lincoln	NE	68508	402-471-3101	471-0254
Real Estate Commission 1200 N St Ste 402 PO Box 94667 *Web:* www.nrec.ne.gov	Lincoln	NE	68509	402-471-2004	471-4492
Revenue Dept 301 Centennial Mall S Second Fl PO Box 94818 *Web:* revenue.nebraska.gov/	Lincoln	NE	68509	402-471-5729	471-5608
Secretary of State 1445 K St Ste 2300 *Web:* sos.ne.gov/	Lincoln	NE	68508	402-471-2554	471-3237
Securities Bureau 1230 'O' St Ste 400 PO Box 95006 *Web:* www.ndbf.ne.gov	Lincoln	NE	68508	402-471-3445	
State Court Administrator 1213 State Capitol PO Box 98910 *Web:* supremecourt.nebraska.gov	Lincoln	NE	68509	402-471-3730	471-2197
State Patrol PO Box 94907 *Web:* statepatrol.nebraska.gov	Lincoln	NE	68509	402-471-4545	
State Racing Commission 5903 Walker Ave *Web:* nebraskaracingcommission.com/	Lincoln	NE	68507	402-471-4155	
Supreme Court State Capitol Bldg *Web:* court.nol.org	Lincoln	NE	68509	402-471-3730	471-3480
Teacher Certification Office PO Box 94987 *Web:* www.teaching-certification.com	Lincoln	NE	68509	402-471-2295	
Travel & Tourism Div PO Box 98907 *TF:* 877-632-7275 ■ *Web:* www.visitnebraska.com	Lincoln	NE	68509	402-471-3796	471-3026
Treasurer PO Box 94788 State Capitol Rm 2005 *Web:* www.treasurer.org/up/	Lincoln	NE	68508	402-471-2455	471-4390
Veterans' Affairs Dept 301 Centennial Mall S Fl 1 PO Box 95083 *Web:* www.vets.state.ne.us	Lincoln	NE	68509	402-471-2458	471-2491
Vital Statistics Div 1033 "O" St Ste 130 PO Box 95065 *Web:* dhhs.ne.gov	Lincoln	NE	68509	402-471-2871	
Vocational Rehabilitation Services Div 3901 N 27th St Ste 6 *TF:* 800-472-3382	Lincoln	NE	68521	402-471-3231	471-6309
Weights & Measures Div 301 Centennial Mall S *Web:* www.nda.nebraska.gov	Lincoln	NE	68508	402-471-4292	471-2759
Workers Compensation Court 1010 Lincoln Mall Ste 100 *TF:* 800-599-5155 ■ *Web:* allworkerscomp.com	Lincoln	NE	68508	402-471-6468	471-2700
Workforce Development - Dept of Labor 550 S 16th St PO Box 94600 *Web:* dol.nebraska.gov	Lincoln	NE	68509	402-471-2600	471-9867

342-29 Nevada

				Phone	Fax
Accountancy Board 1325 Airmotive Way Ste 220 *Web:* www.nvaccountancy.com	Reno	NV	89502	775-786-0231	786-0234
Administrative Office of the Courts 201 S Carson St Ste 250 *Web:* nevadajudiciary.us	Carson City	NV	89701	775-684-1700	684-1723
Aging Services Div 1860 E Sahara Ave *Web:* adsd.nv.gov	Las Vegas	NV	89104	702-486-3545	486-3572
Arts Council 716 N Carson St Ste A *Web:* nac.nevadaculture.org	Carson City	NV	89701	775-687-6680	687-6688
Attorney General 100 N Carson St *Web:* ag.nv.gov	Carson City	NV	89701	775-684-1100	684-1108
Bill Status 401 S Carson St *TF:* 800-978-2878 ■ *Web:* www.leg.state.nv.us	Carson City	NV	89701	775-684-3360	684-3330
Business & Industry Dept 555 E Washington Ave Ste 4900 *Web:* www.business.nv.gov	Las Vegas	NV	89101	702-486-2750	486-2758
Child & Family Services Div 4126 Technology Way 3rd Fl *Web:* www.dcfs.state.nv.us	Carson City	NV	89706	775-684-4400	684-4455
Child Support Enforcement Office 1470 College Pkwy *TF:* 800-992-0900 ■ *Web:* dwss.nv.gov	Carson City	NV	89706	775-684-0500	684-0646
Commission on Ethics 704 W Nye Ln Ste 204 *Web:* www.ethics.nv.gov	Carson City	NV	89703	775-687-5469	687-1279
Conservation & Natural Resources Dept 901 S Stewart St Ste 1003 *Web:* www.dcnr.nv.gov	Carson City	NV	89701	775-684-2700	684-2715
Consumer Affairs Div 555 E Washington Ave Ste 4900 *Web:* www.fightfraud.nv.gov	Las Vegas	NV	89101	702-486-7355	
Corrections Dept PO Box 7011 **Fax Area Code:* 702 ■ *Web:* www.doc.nv.gov	Carson City	NV	89702	775-887-3285	486-9908*
Economic Development Commission 808 W Nye Ln *TF:* 800-336-1600 ■ *Web:* www.diversifynevada.com	Carson City	NV	89703	775-687-9900	687-9924
Education Dept 700 E Fifth St *Web:* www.doe.nv.gov	Carson City	NV	89701	775-687-9200	687-9101
Emergency Management Div 2478 Fairview Dr *Web:* dem.nv.gov	Carson City	NV	89701	775-687-0400	687-0322
Employment Training & Rehabilitation Dept 500 E Third St *Web:* www.nvdetr.org	Carson City	NV	89713	775-684-3911	684-3908
Environmental Protection Div 901 S Stewart St Ste 4001 *Web:* www.ndep.nv.gov	Carson City	NV	89701	775-687-4670	687-5856
Gaming Commission 1919 College Pkwy PO Box 8003 *Web:* gaming.nv.gov	Carson City	NV	89706	775-684-7750	687-5817
Governor 101 N Carson St *Web:* nevadatreasurer.gov	Carson City	NV	89701	775-684-5670	684-5683
Health Div 4150 Technology Way *Web:* www.health.nv.gov	Carson City	NV	89706	775-684-4200	684-4211
Highway Patrol Div 555 Wright Way *Web:* nevadadot.com	Carson City	NV	89711	775-687-5300	
Historic Preservation Office 901 S Stewart St Ste 5004 *Web:* www.nvshpo.org	Carson City	NV	89701	775-684-3448	684-3442
Human Resources Dept 4126 Technology Way Rm 100 *Web:* dhhs.nv.gov	Carson City	NV	89706	775-684-4000	
Information Technology Dept 100 N Stewart St Ste 100 *Web:* it.nv.gov	Carson City	NV	89701	775-684-5800	
Insurance Div 1818 E College Pkwy Ste 103 *Web:* doi.nv.gov	Carson City	NV	89706	775-687-0700	687-0787
Legislature 401 S Carson St *Web:* www.leg.state.nv.us	Carson City	NV	89701	775-684-6800	
Lieutenant Governor 101 N Carson St Ste 2 *Web:* www.ltgov.nv.gov	Carson City	NV	89701	775-684-7111	684-7110
Medical Examiners Board 1105 Terminal Way Ste 301 *Web:* www.medboard.nv.gov	Reno	NV	89502	775-688-2559	688-2321
Motor Vehicles Dept 555 Wright Way *TF:* 877-368-7828 ■ *Web:* www.dmvnv.com	Carson City	NV	89711	775-684-4368	
Parole & Probation Div 1445 Old Hot Springs Rd Ste 104 *Web:* www.dps.nv.gov	Carson City	NV	89706	775-684-2600	
Postsecondary Education Commission 3663 E Sunset Rd Ste 202 *Web:* www.cpe.state.nv.us	Las Vegas	NV	89120	702-486-7330	486-7340
Public Safety Dept 555 Wright Way *Web:* www.nhp.nv.gov	Carson City	NV	89711	775-684-4650	
Public Utilities Commission 1150 E William St *Web:* puc.nv.gov	Carson City	NV	89701	775-684-6101	684-6110
Real Estate Div 2501 E Sahara Ave Ste 102 *Web:* www.red.state.nv.us	Las Vegas	NV	89104	702-486-4033	486-4275
Rehabilitation Div 1370 S Curry St *Web:* detr.state.nv.us	Carson City	NV	89703	775-684-4040	684-4184
Secretary of State 101 N Carson St Ste 3 *TF:* 800-450-8594 ■ *Web:* www.nvsos.gov	Carson City	NV	89701	775-684-5708	684-5725
State Athletic Commission 555 E Washington Ave Ste 3300 *Web:* www.boxing.nv.gov	Las Vegas	NV	89101	702-486-2575	486-2577
State Parks Div 901 S Stewart St 5th Fl *Web:* www.parks.nv.gov	Carson City	NV	89701	775-684-2770	684-2777
Supreme Court 201 S Carson St Ste 250 *Web:* www.nevadajudiciary.us	Carson City	NV	89701	775-684-1600	
System of Higher Education 2601 Enterprise Rd *Web:* www.nevada.edu	Reno	NV	89512	775-784-4901	784-1127
Taxation Dept 1550 E College Pkwy Ste 115 *Web:* tax.nv.gov	Carson City	NV	89706	775-684-2000	684-2020
Teacher Licensure Office 700 E Fifth St *Web:* www.doe.nv.gov	Carson City	NV	89701	775-687-9115	687-9101
Tourism & Cultural Affairs Dept 716 N Carson St Ste A *Web:* www.nevadaculture.org	Carson City	NV	89701	775-687-8393	684-5446
Tourism Commission 401 N Carson St *TF:* 800-237-0774 ■ *Web:* www.travelnevada.com	Carson City	NV	89701	775-687-4322	
Transportation Dept 1263 S Stewart St *Web:* www.nevadadot.com	Carson City	NV	89712	775-888-7000	888-7115
Treasurer 101 N Carson St Ste 4 *Web:* nevadatreasurer.gov	Carson City	NV	89701	775-684-5600	684-5781
Veterans Services Office 5460 Reno Corporate Dr *Web:* www.veterans.nv.gov	Reno	NV	89511	775-688-1653	688-1656
Vital Statistics Office 4150 Technology Way Ste 104	Carson City	NV	89706	775-684-4242	684-4156
Weights & Measures Bureau 2150 Frazier Ave *Web:* agri.nv.gov	Sparks	NV	89431	775-353-3782	688-2533

	City	State	Zip	Phone	Fax
Welfare Div 1470 College Pkwy *TF:* 800-992-0900 ■ *Web:* carson.org	Carson City	NV	89706	775-684-0500	

342-30 New Hampshire

	City	State	Zip	Phone	Fax
State Government Information 64 S St *Web:* www.nh.gov	Concord	NH	03301	603-271-1110	
Accountancy Board 78 Regional Dr Bldg 2 *Web:* www.nh.gov	Concord	NH	03301	603-271-3286	271-8702
Administrative Office of the Courts 2 Charles Doe Dr *Web:* www.courts.state.nh.us/aoc	Concord	NH	03301	603-271-2521	513-5454
Agriculture Markets & Food Dept PO Box 2042 *Web:* agriculture.nh.gov	Concord	NH	03302	603-271-3551	271-1109
Arts Council 2 1/2 Beacon St 2nd Fl *Web:* www.nh.gov/nharts	Concord	NH	03301	603-271-2789	271-3584
Attorney General 33 Capitol St *Web:* www.nh.gov	Concord	NH	03301	603-271-3658	271-2110
Banking Dept 53 Regional Dr Ste 200 *TF:* 800-437-5991 ■ *Web:* www.nh.gov	Concord	NH	03301	603-271-3561	271-1090
Board of Medicine 2 Industrial Pk Dr Ste 8 *Web:* www.nh.gov	Concord	NH	03301	603-271-1203	271-6702
Bureau of Elderly & Adult Services (BEAS) 129 Pleasant St *Web:* www.dhhs.nh.gov	Concord	NH	03301	603-271-4680	271-4643
Chief Medical Examiner 246 Pleasant St Ste 218 *Web:* doj.nh.gov/medical-examiner/	Concord	NH	03301	603-271-1235	271-6308
Child Support Services 129 Pleasant St *TF:* 800-852-3345 ■ *Web:* www.dhhs.nh.gov/dcss	Concord	NH	03301	603-271-4427	271-4787
Children Youth & Families Div 129 Pleasant St 4th Fl *Web:* www.dhhs.state.nh.us	Concord	NH	03301	603-271-4451	271-4729
Consumer Protection & Antitrust Bureau 33 Capitol St *Web:* www.doj.nh.gov	Concord	NH	03301	603-271-3641	271-2110
Corrections Dept PO Box 1806 *Web:* www.nh.gov	Concord	NH	03302	603-271-5600	271-5643
Education Dept 101 Pleasant St *Web:* www.education.nh.gov	Concord	NH	03301	603-271-3494	271-1953
Emergency Management Office 33 Hazen Dr *Web:* www.nh.gov	Concord	NH	03305	603-271-2231	225-7341
Employment Security 32 S Main St *TF:* 800-852-3400 ■ *Web:* www.nh.gov	Concord	NH	03301	603-224-3311	228-4145
Environmental Services Dept 29 Hazen Dr PO Box 95 *TF:* 800-735-2964 ■ *Web:* des.nh.gov	Concord	NH	03301	603-271-3503	271-2867
Fish & Game Dept 11 Hazen Dr *Web:* www.wildlife.state.nh.us	Concord	NH	03301	603-271-3511	271-1438
General Court 107 N Main St *Web:* gencourt.state.nh.us	Concord	NH	03301	603-271-2154	
Governor State House 107 N Main St Rm 208 *Web:* www.nh.gov	Concord	NH	03301	603-271-2121	271-7680
Historical Resources Div 19 Pillsbury St *Web:* www.nh.gov/nhdhr	Concord	NH	03301	603-271-3483	271-3433
Housing Finance Authority PO Box 5087 *TF:* 800-439-7247 ■ *Web:* www.nhhfa.org	Manchester	NH	03108	603-472-8623	472-8501
Insurance Dept 21 S Fruit St Ste 14 *Web:* www.nh.gov	Concord	NH	03301	603-271-2261	271-1406
Joint Board of Licensure & Certification 57 Regional Dr *Web:* www.nh.gov	Concord	NH	03301	603-271-2219	271-6990
Lottery Commission 14 Integra Dr *TF:* 800-852-3324 ■ *Web:* www.nhlottery.com	Concord	NH	03301	603-271-3391	271-1160
Motor Vehicles Div 23 Hazen Dr *Web:* nh.gov/safety/divisions/dmv/	Concord	NH	03305	603-227-4000	
Parks & Recreation Div 172 Pembroke Rd *Web:* www.nhstateparks.org	Concord	NH	03301	603-271-3556	271-3553
Postsecondary Education Commission 64 South Street Ste 300 *TF:* 800-735-2964 ■ *Web:* www.nh.gov	Concord	NH	03301	603-271-2555	271-2696
Public Utilities Commission 21 S Fruit St Ste 10 *TF Consumer Assistance:* 800-852-3793 ■ *Web:* www.puc.state.nh.us	Concord	NH	03301	603-271-2431	271-3878
Real Estate Commission 25 Capitol St Rm 434 *Web:* www.nh.gov/nhrec	Concord	NH	03301	603-271-2701	271-1039
Resources & Economic Development Dept PO Box 1856 *Web:* www.dred.state.nh.us	Concord	NH	03302	603-271-2411	271-2629
Revenue Administration Dept 45 Chenell Dr *Web:* www.revenue.nh.gov	Concord	NH	03301	603-271-2191	
Secretary of State 107 N Main St State House Rm 204 *Web:* www.sos.nh.gov	Concord	NH	03301	603-271-3242	271-6316
State Office of Veterans Services 275 Chestnut St Rm 517 *Web:* www.nh.gov	Manchester	NH	03101	603-624-9230	624-9236
State Police Div 33 Hazen Dr *Web:* nh.gov/safety/divisions/nhsp	Concord	NH	03305	603-223-8813	271-6497
Supreme Court 1 Charles Doe Dr *Web:* www.courts.state.nh.us	Concord	NH	03301	603-271-2646	
Teacher Credentialing Bureau 101 Pleasant St *Web:* www.education.nh.gov	Concord	NH	03301	603-271-3494	
Transportation Dept PO Box 483 *Web:* www.nh.gov/dot	Concord	NH	03301	603-271-3734	271-3914
Travel & Tourism Development Office PO Box 1856 *TF:* 800-262-6660 ■ *Web:* www.visitnh.gov	Concord	NH	03302	603-271-2665	271-6870
Treasury Dept 25 Capitol St Rm 121 *Web:* www.nh.gov/treasury	Concord	NH	03301	603-271-2621	271-3922
Victims Assistance Commission 33 Capitol St *TF:* 800-300-4500 ■ *Web:* www.nh.gov	Concord	NH	03301	603-271-1284	223-6291
Vital Records Administration Div 71 S Fruit St *TF:* 800-735-2964 ■ *Web:* www.sos.nh.gov/vitalrecords	Concord	NH	03301	603-271-4650	271-3447
Vocational Rehabilitation Office 21 S Fruit St Ste 20 *TF:* 800-299-1647 ■ *Web:* www.education.nh.gov	Concord	NH	03301	603-271-3471	271-7095
Weights & Measures Bureau PO Box 2042 *Web:* agriculture.nh.gov	Concord	NH	03302	603-271-3685	271-1109

342-31 New Jersey

	City	State	Zip	Phone	Fax
Administrative Office of the Courts 25 Market St PO Box 037 *Web:* www.judiciary.state.nj.us	Trenton	NJ	08625	609-984-0275	984-6968
Agriculture Dept PO Box 330 *Web:* www.state.nj.us/agriculture	Trenton	NJ	08625	609-292-3976	292-3978
Arts Council 225 W State St PO Box 306 *Web:* nj.gov	Trenton	NJ	08625	609-292-6130	989-1440
Attorney General 25 Market St PO Box 080 *Web:* www.state.nj.us	Trenton	NJ	08625	609-292-4925	292-3508
Banking & Insurance Dept 20 W State St PO Box 325 *TF:* 800-446-7467 ■ *Web:* www.state.nj.us/dobi	Trenton	NJ	08625	609-292-7272	984-5273
Bill Status State House Annex PO Box 068 *TF:* 800-792-8630 ■ *Web:* www.njleg.state.nj.us	Trenton	NJ	08625	609-292-4840	777-2440
Board of Public Utilities 2 Gateway Ctr *Web:* www.state.nj.us/bpu	Newark	NJ	07102	973-648-2013	648-4195
Child Support Office 175 S Broad St PO Box 8068 *TF:* 877-655-4371 ■ *Web:* www.njchildsupport.org	Trenton	NJ	08650	877-655-4371	
Commerce Economic Growth & Tourism Commission 20 W State St PO Box 820 *Web:* www.state.nj.us/commerce	Trenton	NJ	08625	609-777-0885	777-4097
Community Affairs Dept 101 S Broad St PO Box 204 *Web:* www.nj.gov/dca	Trenton	NJ	08625	609-777-3474	292-3292
Consumer Affairs Div 124 Halsey St *Web:* www.state.nj.us	Newark	NJ	07102	973-504-6200	648-3538
Corrections Dept PO Box 863 *Web:* www.state.nj.us	Trenton	NJ	08625	609-292-4036	292-9083
Economic Development Authority PO Box 990 **Fax:* PR ■ *Web:* www.njeda.com	Trenton	NJ	08625	609-292-1800	292-5722*
Education Dept PO Box 500 *Web:* www.state.nj.us/education	Trenton	NJ	08625	609-292-4450	777-4099
Emergency Management Office PO Box 7068 *Web:* www.njsp.org/feedback.html	West Trenton	NJ	08628	609-882-2000	
Environmental Protection Dept 401 E State St PO Box 402 *Web:* www.state.nj.us/dep	Trenton	NJ	08625	609-292-2885	292-1921
Ethical Standards Commission 28 W State St Rm 1407 PO Box 082 *Web:* www.state.nj.us/lps/ethics	Trenton	NJ	08625	609-292-1892	633-9252
Fish Game & Wildlife Div PO Box 400 *Web:* www.state.nj.us/dep/fgw	Trenton	NJ	08625	609-292-9410	984-1414
Governor 125 W State St PO Box 001 *Web:* www.state.nj.us/governor	Trenton	NJ	08625	609-292-6000	292-3454
Health & Senior Services Dept PO Box 360 *Web:* www.state.nj.us/health	Trenton	NJ	08625	609-292-7837	984-5474
Higher Education Commission 20 W State St PO Box 542 *Web:* www.state.nj.us	Trenton	NJ	08625	609-292-4310	292-7225
Higher Education Student Assistance Authority 4 Quakerbridge Plaza PO Box 540 *TF:* 800-792-8670 ■ *Web:* www.hesaa.org	Trenton	NJ	08625	609-584-4480	588-7389
Historical Commission 225 W State St PO Box 305 *Web:* www.state.nj.us	Trenton	NJ	08625	609-292-6062	633-8168
Housing & Mortgage Finance Agency 637 S Clinton Ave PO Box 18550 *Web:* www.state.nj.us/dca/hmfa	Trenton	NJ	08650	609-278-7400	278-1754
Human Services Dept 240 W State St PO Box 700 *Web:* www.state.nj.us/humanservices	Trenton	NJ	08625	609-292-3717	292-3824
Information Technology Office PO Box 212 *Web:* www.nj.gov/it/oit	Trenton	NJ	08625	609-633-8975	633-8888
Labor & Workforce Development Dept PO Box 110 *Web:* lwd.state.nj.us	Trenton	NJ	08625	609-659-9045	633-9271
Lottery PO Box 041 *Web:* www.state.nj.us	Trenton	NJ	08625	609-599-5800	599-5935
Mental Health Services Div PO Box 272 *TF:* 800-382-6717 ■ *Web:* www.state.nj.us/humanservices/dmhs	Trenton	NJ	08625	609-777-0700	777-0662
Military & Veterans Affairs Dept 101 Eggert Crossing Rd *TF:* 800-624-0508 ■ *Web:* www.state.nj.us	Lawrenceville	NJ	08648	609-530-4600	530-7100
Motor Vehicle Commission 225 E State St PO Box 160 *TF:* 888-486-3339 ■ *Web:* www.state.nj.us/mvc	Trenton	NJ	08666	609-292-6500	
Parks & Forestry Div PO Box 404 *Web:* www.state.nj.us/dep/parksandforests	Trenton	NJ	08625	609-292-2733	984-0503
Parole Board PO Box 862 *Web:* www.state.nj.us/parole	Trenton	NJ	08625	609-292-4257	943-4769
Personnel Dept 44 S Clinton Ave PO Box 317 *Web:* www.nj.gov	Trenton	NJ	08625	609-292-4145	984-1064
Racing Commission 140 E Front St *Web:* www.njpublicsafety.org	Trenton	NJ	08625	609-292-0613	599-1785
Secretary of State 125 W State St PO Box 300 *Web:* www.state.nj.us	Trenton	NJ	08625	609-984-1900	292-7665

Phone | Fax

Securities Bureau
153 Halsey St Sixth Fl PO Box 47029 ... Newark NJ 07101 973-504-3600
TF: 866-446-8378 ■ *Web:* www.state.nj.us/lps/ca/bos

State Athletic Control Board
25 Market Street 1st Fl W Wing ... Trenton NJ 08625 609-292-0317 292-3756
Web: www.state.nj.us/lps/sacb

State Legislature
State House Annex PO Box 068 ... Trenton NJ 08625 609-292-4840 777-2440
Web: www.njleg.state.nj.us

State Medical Examiner PO Box 360 ... Trenton NJ 08608 609-826-7100
Web: www.nj.gov

State Police PO Box 7068 ... West Trenton NJ 08628 609-882-2000 882-6920
Web: www.state.nj.us/lps/njsp

Supreme Court PO Box 970 ... Trenton NJ 08625 609-292-4837 396-9056
Web: www.judiciary.state.nj.us/supreme

Transportation Dept 1035 PkwyAve PO Box 600 ... Trenton NJ 08625 609-530-2000
Web: www.state.nj.us/transportation

Travel & Tourism Div
225 W State St PO Box 460 ... Trenton NJ 08625 609-599-6540
TF: 800-847-4865 ■ *Web:* www.visitnj.org

Treasurer PO Box 002 ... Trenton NJ 08625 609-292-6748 984-3888
Web: www.state.nj.us/treasury

Victims of Crime Compensation Board 50 Pk Pl ... Newark NJ 07102 973-648-2107 648-3937
TF: 877-658-2221 ■ *Web:* www.nj.gov/oag/njvictims

Vital Statistics Bureau 140 E Front St ... Trenton NJ 8625 609-292-4087
Web: www.state.nj.us

Vocational Rehabilitation Services Div (DVRS)
One John Fitch Way PO Box 110 ... Trenton NJ 08625 609-292-5987 292-8347
Web: jobs4jersey.com

Weights & Measures Office 1261 US Hwy 1 Ste 9 ... Avenel NJ 07001 732-815-4840 382-5298
Web: www.state.nj.us

Workers Compensation Div PO Box 381 ... Trenton NJ 08625 609-292-2515 984-2515
Web: lwd.dol.state.nj.us/labor/wc

Workforce 1 John Fitch Plz Fl 3 ... Trenton NJ 08611 609-292-2305 695-1174
Web: lwd.dol.state.nj.us

342-32 New Mexico

Phone | Fax

Administrative Office of the Courts
237 Don Gaspar St Rm 25 ... Santa Fe NM 87501 505-827-4800
Web: www.nmcourts.com

Adult Parole Board 4337 NM 14 PO Box 27116 ... Santa Fe NM 87502 505-827-8645 827-8533
Web: www.corrections.state.nm.us

Aging Agency 2550 Cerrillos Rd ... Santa Fe NM 87505 505-476-4799 476-4836
Web: www.nmaging.state.nm.us

Agriculture Dept
3190 S Espina PO Box 30005 ... Las Cruces NM 88003 575-646-3007
Web: www.nmda.nmsu.edu

Arts Div 407 Galisteo St Ste 270 ... Santa Fe NM 87501 505-827-6490 827-6043
Web: www.nmarts.org

Attorney General PO Drawer 1508 ... Santa Fe NM 87504 505-827-6000 827-5826
Web: www.nmag.gov

Child Support Enforcement Div PO Box 25110 ... Santa Fe NM 87504 505-476-7207 476-7045
Web: www.hsd.state.nm.us/csed

Children Youth & Families Dept
PO Drawer 5160 ... Santa Fe NM 87502 800-432-2075 827-9978*
**Fax Area Code:* 505 ■ *TF:* 800-610-7610 ■ *Web:* www.cyfd.org

Consumer Protection Div
408 Galisteo St Villagra Bldg PO Box 1508 ... Santa Fe NM 87501 505-827-6000 827-5826
Web: www.nmag.gov/consumer

Corrections Dept (NMCD)
4337 NM 14 PO Box 27116 ... Santa Fe NM 87502 505-827-8645 827-8533
Web: www.corrections.state.nm.us

Crime Victims Reparation Commission
8100 Mountain Rd NE Ste 106 ... Albuquerque NM 87110 505-841-9432 841-9437
TF: 800-306-6262 ■ *Web:* www.cvrc.state.nm.us

Economic Development Dept PO Box 20003 ... Santa Fe NM 87504 505-827-0300 827-0328
TF: 800-374-3061 ■ *Web:* www.gonm.biz

Education Dept 300 Don Gaspar St ... Santa Fe NM 87501 505-827-5800 827-6696
Web: www.sde.state.nm.us

Energy Minerals & Natural Resources Dept
1220 S St Francis Dr ... Santa Fe NM 87505 505-476-3200 476-3220

Environment Dept 1190 St Francis Dr Ste 4050 ... Santa Fe NM 87502 505-827-2855 827-2836
TF: 800-219-6157 ■ *Web:* www.nmenv.state.nm.us

Ethics Administration
325 Don Gaspar St Ste 300 ... Santa Fe NM 87501 505-827-3600
TF: 800-477-3632 ■ *Web:* www.sos.state.nm.us

Finance & Administration Dept
407 Galisteo St Ste 166 ... Santa Fe NM 87501 505-827-4985 827-4984
Web: www.newmexico.gov

Financial Aid & Student Services Unit
2048 Galisteo St ... Santa Fe NM 87505 505-476-8400 476-8453
TF: 800-279-9777 ■ *Web:* www.hed.state.nm.us

Financial Institutions Div
2550 Cerrillos Rd ... Santa Fe NM 87505 505-476-4885 476-4670
Web: www.rld.state.nm.us

Game & Fish Dept 1 Wildlife Way ... Santa Fe NM 87507 505-476-8000 476-8116
Web: www.wildlife.state.nm.us

Governor
State Capitol Bldg
490 Santa Fe Trail Rm 400 ... Santa Fe NM 87501 505-827-3000 476-2226
Web: www.governor.state.nm.us

Health Dept 1190 S St Francis Dr Ste N-4100 ... Santa Fe NM 87505 505-827-2613 827-2530
Web: nmhealth.org/

Higher Education Dept 2048 Galisteo St ... Santa Fe NM 87505 505-476-8400 476-8453
TF: 800-279-9777 ■ *Web:* www.hed.state.nm.us

Highway & Transportation Dept (NMDOT)
1120 Cerrillos Rd PO Box 1149 ... Santa Fe NM 87504 505-827-5100
TF General: 800-432-4269 ■ *Web:* www.dot.state.nm.us

Historic Preservation Div
407 Galisteo St Ste 236 ... Santa Fe NM 87501 505-827-6320 827-6338
Web: www.nmhistoricpreservation.org

Human Services Dept (NMHSD) PO Box 2348 ... Santa Fe NM 87504 505-827-7750 827-6286
Web: www.hsd.state.nm.us

Information Technology Dept
715 Alta Vista St PO Box 22550 ... Santa Fe NM 87505 505-827-0000
Web: www.doit.state.nm.us

Legislative Council Services
625 Don Gaspar Ave ... Santa Fe NM 87501 505-986-4600
Web: www.nmlegis.gov

Lieutenant Governor
490 Old Santa Fe Trail Rm 417 ... Santa Fe NM 87501 505-476-2250 476-2257
TF: 800-432-4406 ■ *Web:* www.ltgov.state.nm.us

Lottery 4511 Osuna Rd NE PO Box 93190 ... Albuquerque NM 87199 505-342-7600 342-7511
Web: www.nmlottery.com

Medical Board 2055 S Pacheco Bldg 400 ... Santa Fe NM 87505 505-476-7220 476-7237
Web: www.nmmb.state.nm.us

Mortgage Finance Authority
344 Fourth St SW ... Albuquerque NM 87102 505-843-6880 243-3289
TF: 800-444-6880 ■ *Web:* www.nmmfa.org

Professional (Educator) Licensure Unit
300 Don Gaspar St ... Santa Fe NM 87501 505-827-6581 827-4148
Web: www.ped.state.nm.us

Public Accountancy Board
5200 Oakland Ave NE # C ... Albuquerque NM 87113 505-222-9800
Web: www.rld.state.nm.us

Public Regulation Commission PO Box 1269 ... Santa Fe NM 87504 505-827-4500 827-4747
Web: www.nmprc.state.nm.us

Public Safety Dept PO Box 1628 ... Santa Fe NM 87504 505-827-9000
Web: www.dps.nm.org

Racing Commission 4900 Alameda NE ... Albuquerque NM 87113 505-222-0700 222-0713
Web: www.nmrc.state.nm.us

Regulation & Licensing Dept
2550 Cerrillos Rd ... Santa Fe NM 87505 505-476-4500 476-4511
Web: www.rld.state.nm.us

Secretary of State
325 Don Gaspar Ave Ste 300 ... Santa Fe NM 87503 505-827-3600 827-8081
TF: 800-477-3632 ■ *Web:* www.sos.state.nm.us

Securities Div 2550 Cerrillos Rd ... Santa Fe NM 87505 505-476-4580 984-0617
Web: www.rld.state.nm.us/Securities

Standards & Consumers Services Div
MSC 3170 PO Box 30005 ... Las Cruces NM 88003 575-646-1616 646-2361
Web: www.nmda.nmsu.edu

State Legislature State Capitol Rm 100 ... Santa Fe NM 87501 505-986-4751 986-4680
Web: www.nmlegis.gov

State Parks Div 1220 S St Francis Dr ... Santa Fe NM 87505 505-476-3355

State Police Div
4491 Cerrillos Rd PO Box 1628 ... Santa Fe NM 87507 505-827-9300 827-3394
Web: www.nmsp.dps.state.nm.us

Supreme Court 237 Don Gaspar Ave ... Santa Fe NM 87501 505-827-4860 827-4837
Web: nmsupremecourt.nmcourts.gov

Taxation & Revenue Dept
1100 S St Francis Dr ... Santa Fe NM 87504 505-827-0700
Web: www.tax.newmexico.gov

Tourism Dept 491 Old Santa Fe Trail ... Santa Fe NM 87503 800-545-2070
TF: 800-545-2070 ■ *Web:* www.newmexico.org

Treasurer 2055 S Pacheco St ... Santa Fe NM 87505 505-995-1120 995-1195
Web: www.nmsto.gov

Veterans Services Dept 490 Old SF Trail ... Santa Fe NM 87504 505-827-6300 827-6372
TF: 866-433-8387 ■ *Web:* www.dvs.state.nm.us/

Vital Records & Health Statistics Bureau
1105 S St Francis Dr ... Santa Fe NM 87502 505-827-0121
TF: 866-534-0051 ■ *Web:* nmhealth.org/about/erd/bvrhs/vrp/

Vocational Rehabilitation Div
435 St Michaels Dr Bldg D ... Santa Fe NM 87505 505-954-8500 954-8562
TF: 800-224-7005 ■ *Web:* www.dvrgetsjobs.com

Workers Compensation Admin
2410 Ctr Ave SE PO Box 27198 ... Albuquerque NM 87125 505-841-6000
TF: 800-255-7965 ■ *Web:* www.workerscomp.state.nm.us

Workforce Solutions Dept 301 W DeVargas ... Santa Fe NM 87501 505-827-7434 827-7346
Web: www.dws.state.nm.us

Workforce Solutions Dept
401 Broadway NE PO Box 1928 ... Albuquerque NM 87103 505-841-8576 841-8491
Web: www.dws.state.nm.us

342-33 New York

Phone | Fax

State Government Information
NYS State Capitol Bldg ... Albany NY 12224 518-474-8390
Web: www.ny.gov

Aging Office 2 Empire State Plaza ... Albany NY 12223 800-342-9871
TF: 800-342-9871 ■ *Web:* www.aging.ny.gov

Arts Council 175 Varick St 3rd Fl ... New York NY 10014 212-627-4455
Web: www.nysca.org

Athletic Commission 123 William St 20th Fl ... New York NY 10038 212-417-5700 417-4987
TF: 866-269-3769 ■ *Web:* www.dos.ny.gov

Attorney General State Capitol ... Albany NY 12224 518-474-7330 474-5481
Web: www.oag.state.ny.us

Banking Dept 1 State St ... New York NY 10004 800-342-3736 709-3582*
**Fax Area Code:* 212 ■ **Fax:* Hum Res ■ *TF:* 877-226-5697 ■ *Web:* www.dfs.ny.gov

Bill Status 202 Legislative Office Bldg ... Albany NY 12248 518-455-4218
TF: 800-342-9860 ■ *Web:* www.assembly.state.ny.us

Child Support Enforcement Div 40 N Pearl St ... Albany NY 12243 518-474-9081
Web: www.childsupport.ny.gov

Children & Family Services Office
52 Washington St ... Rensselaer NY 12144 518-473-7793 486-7550
Web: ocfs.ny.gov/main/

	City	State	Zip	Phone	Fax
Consumer Protection Div 5 Empire State Plaza Ste 2101 *TF:* 800-697-1220 ■ *Web:* www.dos.ny.gov	Albany	NY	12223	518-474-3514	474-2474
Correctional Services Dept 1220 Washington Ave Bldg 2 *Web:* www.doccs.ny.gov	Albany	NY	12226	518-457-8126	457-7070
Court of Appeals 20 Eagle St *Web:* www.nycourts.gov	Albany	NY	12207	518-455-7700	
Crime Victims Board 845 Central Ave *Web:* www.ovs.ny.gov	Albany	NY	12206	518-457-8727	457-8658
Education Dept 89 Washington Ave **Fax:* Hum Res ■ *Web:* www.nysed.gov	Albany	NY	12234	518-474-3852	*
Emergency Management Office (OEM) 1220 Washington Ave Bldg 22 Ste 101 *Web:* www.dhses.ny.gov/oem	Albany	NY	12226	518-292-2200	322-4985
Empire State Development 30 S Pearl St *TF:* 800-782-8369 ■ *Web:* www.empire.state.ny.us	Albany	NY	12245	518-292-5100	292-5812
Environmental Conservation Dept 625 Broadway 14th Fl *Web:* www.dec.ny.gov	Albany	NY	12233	518-891-0235	402-9016
Fish Wildlife & Marine Resources Div 50 Wolf Rd Rm 290 *Web:* www.dec.ny.gov	Albany	NY	12233	518-457-3682	
Governor State Capitol Executive Chamber *Web:* www.ny.gov	Albany	NY	12224	518-474-8390	474-1513
Health Dept Empire State Plaza Corning II Tower **Fax Area Code:* 518 ■ *TF:* 866-881-2809 ■ *Web:* www.health.ny.gov	Albany	NY	12237	866-881-2809	473-7071*
Higher Education Services Corp 99 Washington Ave *TF:* 888-697-4372 ■ *Web:* www.hesc.ny.gov	Albany	NY	12255	518-473-1574	473-3749
Historic Preservation Div PO Box 189 *TF:* 800-456-2267 ■ *Web:* www.nysparks.com	Waterford	NY	12188	518-237-8643	
Housing Finance Agency 641 Lexington Ave *Web:* www.nyshcr.org	New York	NY	10022	212-688-4000	872-0789
Insurance Dept 1 Commerce Plaza *Web:* www.dfs.ny.gov	Albany	NY	12260	518-474-6600	
Investor Protection & Securities Bureau 120 Broadway 23rd Fl *Web:* www.ag.ny.gov	New York	NY	10271	212-416-8200	416-8816
Labor Dept WA Harriman Campus Bldg 12 *TF:* 888-469-7365 ■ *Web:* www.labor.ny.gov	Albany	NY	12240	518-457-9000	457-6908
Lieutenant Governor NYS State Capitol Bldg *Web:* www.governor.ny.gov	Albany	NY	12224	518-474-8390	
Lower Manhattan Development Corp 1 Liberty Plaza 20th Fl *Web:* www.renewnyc.com	New York	NY	10006	212-962-2300	962-2431
Mental Health Office 44 Holland Ave *TF:* 800-597-8481 ■ *Web:* www.omh.ny.gov	Albany	NY	12229	518-474-4403	474-2149
Military & Naval Affairs Div 330 Old Niskayuna Rd *Web:* dmna.ny.gov	Latham	NY	12110	518-786-4786	786-4785
Motor Vehicles Dept 6 Empire State Plaza *TF:* 800-368-1186 ■ *Web:* www.dmv.ny.gov	Albany	NY	12228	518-473-5595	
Office of Court Admin 25 Beaver St Rm 852 *TF:* 800-268-7869 ■ *Web:* www.courts.state.ny.us/admin	New York	NY	10004	212-428-2100	428-2188
Office of the Professions 89 Washington Ave 2nd Fl *Web:* www.op.nysed.gov	Albany	NY	12234	518-474-3817	474-1449
Parks Recreation & Historic Preservation Office 1 Empire State Plaza *TF Campground Resv:* 800-456-2267 ■ *Web:* www.nysparks.com	Albany	NY	12238	518-474-0456	486-2924
Parole Div 97 Central Ave *Web:* www.parole.ny.gov	Albany	NY	12206	518-473-9400	473-6037
Power Authority 30 S Pearl St 10th Fl *Web:* www.nypa.gov	Albany	NY	12207	518-433-6700	
Public Service Commission 90 Church St *Web:* www.dps.ny.gov	New York	NY	12223	518-474-7080	473-2838
Secretary of State 41 State St *Web:* www.dos.ny.gov	Albany	NY	12231	518-473-2492	474-4765
State Comptroller 110 State St 15th Fl *Web:* www.osc.state.ny.us	Albany	NY	12236	518-474-4044	473-3004
State Education Dept 89 Washington Ave 5N EB *Web:* www.highered.nysed.gov	Albany	NY	12234	518-474-3901	
State Legislature Nys Senate Ste 321 *Web:* www.nysenate.gov	Albany	NY	12247	518-455-2800	
State Police Div 1220 Washington Ave Bldg 22 *Web:* nytrooper.com	Albany	NY	12226	518-457-6811	
Taxation & Finance Dept WA Harriman Campus Bldg 9 *TF:* 800-225-5829 ■ *Web:* www.tax.ny.gov	Albany	NY	12227	518-457-5149	
Technology Office 255 Greenwich Fl 9 *Web:* www.nyc.gov	Albany	NY	12220	212-788-5889	
Temporary & Disability Assistance Office 40 N Pearl St 16th Fl *TF:* 800-342-3009 ■ *Web:* www.otda.ny.gov	Albany	NY	12243	518-473-1090	
Tourism Div PO Box 2603 *TF:* 800-225-5697 ■ *Web:* www.iloveny.com	Albany	NY	12223	518-473-1064	
Transportation Dept 50 Wolf Rd *Web:* www.dot.ny.gov	Albany	NY	12205	518-457-7082	485-5217
Veterans' Affairs Div 333 E Washington St Ste 430 *TF:* 888-838-7697 ■ *Web:* www.veterans.ny.gov	Albany	NY	12223	315-428-4046	
Vital Records Office PO Box 2602 *TF:* 877-854-4481 ■ *Web:* www.health.ny.gov	Albany	NY	12220	518-474-3077	474-9168
Vocational & Educational Services for Individuals 1 Commerce Plaza Rm 1606 *Web:* www.acces.nysed.gov	Albany	NY	12234	518-474-2714	474-8802
Workers Compensation Board 328 State St *TF:* 877-632-4996 ■ *Web:* www.wcb.ny.gov	Schenectady	NY	12305	518-462-8880	

342-34 North Carolina

	City	State	Zip	Phone	Fax
Administrative Office of the Courts PO Box 2448 *Web:* www.nccourts.org	Raleigh	NC	27602	919-733-7107	715-5779
Aging & Adult Service Div 693 Palmer Dr *Web:* www.ncdhhs.gov	Raleigh	NC	27603	919-733-3983	733-0443
Agriculture Dept 2 W Edenton St 1001 MSC *Web:* www.ncagr.gov	Raleigh	NC	27699	919-733-7125	733-1141
Arts Council MSC 4632 Dept of Cultural Resources *Web:* www.ncarts.org	Raleigh	NC	27699	919-807-6500	807-6532
Attorney General 114 W Edenton St *Web:* www.ncdoj.com	Raleigh	NC	27603	919-716-6400	716-6750
Banking Commission 316 W Edenton St *Web:* www.nccob.org	Raleigh	NC	27603	919-733-3016	733-6918
Bill Status 16 W Jones St *Web:* www.ncleg.net	Raleigh	NC	27601	919-733-4111	
Child Support Enforcement Section PO Box 20800 *Web:* www.ncdhhs.gov	Raleigh	NC	27619	252-789-5225	
Commerce Dept 301 N Wilmington St *Web:* www.nccommerce.com	Raleigh	NC	27699	919-733-4151	733-9299
Community College System 200 W Jones St *Web:* nccommunitycolleges.edu	Raleigh	NC	27603	919-807-7100	807-7164
Consumer Protection Div 114 W Edenton St *Web:* www.ncdoj.com	Raleigh	NC	27603	919-716-6000	716-6050
Correction Dept 214 W Jones St 4201 MSC *Web:* www.doc.state.nc.us	Raleigh	NC	27699	919-716-3700	716-3794
Cultural Resources Dept 109 E Jones St *Web:* www.ncdcr.gov	Raleigh	NC	27601	919-807-7385	733-1620
Employment Security Commission 700 Wade Ave PO Box 25903 *Web:* desncc.com/deshome	Raleigh	NC	27605	919-707-1010	733-9420
Ethics Board 424 N Blount St *Web:* www.ethicscommission.nc.gov	Raleigh	NC	27601	919-715-2071	715-1644
General Assembly 16 W Jones St *Web:* www.ncleg.net	Raleigh	NC	27601	919-733-7928	715-2880
Governor 116 W Jones St *Web:* www.governor.state.nc.us	Raleigh	NC	27603	919-733-5811	733-2120
Health & Human Services Dept 2001 MSC *Web:* www.ncdhhs.gov	Raleigh	NC	27699	919-733-4534	715-4645
Housing Finance Agency 3508 Bush St *Web:* www.nchfa.com	Raleigh	NC	27609	919-877-5700	877-5701
Information Technology Services Office (ITS) PO Box 17209 *Web:* www.its.nc.gov	Raleigh	NC	27619	919-981-5555	
Insurance Dept 1201 MSC *Web:* www.ncdoi.com	Raleigh	NC	27699	919-807-6750	733-0085
Labor Dept 4 W Edenton St *Web:* www.nclabor.com	Raleigh	NC	27601	919-733-7166	733-6197
Lieutenant Governor 310 N Blount St *Web:* ltgov.nc.gov/	Raleigh	NC	27601	919-733-7350	733-6595
Marine Fisheries Div PO Box 769 *TF:* 800-682-2632 ■ *Web:* www.ncfisheries.net	Morehead City	NC	28557	252-726-7021	
Mental Health Developmental Disabilities & Substance 2001 Mail Service Center *Web:* www.ncdhhs.gov/mhddsas	Raleigh	NC	27699	919-855-4800	733-4962
Motor Vehicles Div 1100 New Bern Ave *Web:* local.dmv.org	Raleigh	NC	27699	919-715-7000	
Parks & Recreation Div 217 W Jones St 1615 MSC *TF:* 877-722-6762 ■ *Web:* www.ncparks.gov	Raleigh	NC	27604	919-707-9300	
Parole Commission 4222 MSC *Web:* www.ncdps.gov	Raleigh	NC	27699	919-716-3010	716-3987
Public Instruction Dept 301 N Wilmington St *Web:* www.ncpublicschools.org	Raleigh	NC	27601	919-807-3300	807-3445
Public Safety Dept 4201 Mail Service Ctr *Web:* www.ncem.org	Raleigh	NC	27699	919-716-3100	733-5406
Real Estate Commission 1313 Navajo Dr *Web:* ncrec.gov/	Raleigh	NC	27609	919-875-3700	877-4221
Revenue Dept 4701 Atlantic Ave Ste 118 *Web:* www.dor.state.nc.us	Raleigh	NC	27604	919-707-0880	
Secretary of State PO Box 29622 *Web:* www.secstate.state.nc.us	Raleigh	NC	27699	919-807-2005	807-2010
Securities Div PO Box 29622 *Web:* www.secretary.state.nc.us	Raleigh	NC	27626	919-733-3924	821-0818
Social Services Div 2401 MSC *Web:* www.ncdhhs.gov	Raleigh	NC	27699	919-733-3055	733-9386
Standards Div 2 W Edenton St 1050 MSC *Web:* www.ncagr.gov	Raleigh	NC	27699	919-733-3313	715-0524
State Highway Patrol 512 N Salisbury St *Web:* www.nccrimecontrol.org	Raleigh	NC	27699	919-716-4080	716-3923
State Personnel Office 116 W Jones St *Web:* www.oshr.nc.gov	Raleigh	NC	27603	919-807-4800	733-0653
State Ports Authority 2202 Burnett Blvd PO Box 9002 *TF:* 800-334-0682 ■ *Web:* www.ncports.com	Wilmington	NC	28402	910-763-1621	
State Treasurer 325 N Salisbury St *Web:* www.nctreasurer.com	Raleigh	NC	27603	919-508-5176	508-5167
Supreme Court 2 E Morgan St PO Box 2170 *Web:* www.nccourts.org	Raleigh	NC	27602	919-831-5700	
Tourism Div 301 N Wilmington St *TF:* 800-847-4862 ■ *Web:* www.visitnc.com	Raleigh	NC	27601	919-733-4171	733-8582
Transportation Dept 1 S Wilmington St *TF:* 877-368-4968 ■ *Web:* www.ncdot.gov	Raleigh	NC	27611	877-368-4968	

	City	State	Zip	Phone	Fax
Utilities Commission 4325 Mail Service Ctr. *TF:* 866-380-9816 ■ *Web:* www.ncuc.commerce.state.nc.us	Raleigh	NC	27699	919-733-7328	733-7300
Veterans Affairs Div 1315 Mail Service Ctr *Web:* www.doa.nc.gov	Raleigh	NC	27699	919-733-3851	
Victims Compensation Services Div 4232 Mail Service Ctr. *TF:* 800-826-6200 ■ *Web:* www.nccrimecontrol.org	Raleigh	NC	27699	919-733-7974	
Vital Records Unit 225 N McDowell St *Web:* www.vitalrecords.nc.gov	Raleigh	NC	27601	919-733-3000	733-1511
Vocational Rehabilitation Services Div 2801 MSC *Web:* www.ncdhhs.gov	Raleigh	NC	27699	919-855-3500	733-7968

342-35 North Dakota

	City	State	Zip	Phone	Fax
State Government Information 600 E Blvd Ave Dept 130 *Web:* www.nd.gov	Bismarck	ND	58505	701-328-2471	328-3230
Accountancy Board 2701 S Columbia Rd *TF:* 800-532-5904 ■ *Web:* www.nd.gov	Grand Forks	ND	58201	701-775-7100	775-7430
Aging Services Div 1237 W Divide Ave Ste 6 *Web:* www.nd.gov	Bismarck	ND	58501	701-328-4601	328-8744
Agriculture Dept 600 E Blvd Ave Dept 602 *TF:* 800-242-7535 ■ *Web:* www.nd.gov	Bismarck	ND	58505	701-328-2231	328-4567
Attorney General 600 E Blvd Ave Dept 125 *TF:* 800-366-6888 ■ *Web:* www.ag.nd.gov	Bismarck	ND	58505	701-328-2210	
Child Support Enforcement Div 1600 E Century Ave Ste 7 *TF:* 800-231-4255 ■ *Web:* www.nd.gov/dhs/services/childsupport	Bismarck	ND	58501	701-328-3582	328-6575
Children & Family Services Div 600 E Blvd Ave *Web:* www.nd.gov	Bismarck	ND	58505	701-328-2316	328-3538
Consumer Protection Div 1050 E Interstate Ave Ste 200 *TF:* 800-472-2600 ■ *Web:* www.ag.state.nd.us	Bismarck	ND	58503	701-328-3404	
Corrections & Rehabilitation Dept 3100 Railroad Ave. *Web:* www.nd.gov	Bismarck	ND	58501	701-328-6390	328-6651
Court Administrator Office 600 E Blvd Ave Dept 180 *Web:* www.ndcourts.gov	Bismarck	ND	58505	701-328-4216	328-2092
Crime Victims Compensation Program PO Box 5521 *TF:* 800-445-2322 ■ *Web:* www.ndcrimevictims.org	Bismarck	ND	58506	701-328-6195	
Drivers License & Traffic Safety Div 608 E Blvd Ave *Web:* www.dot.nd.gov/public/divdist/dlts.htm	Bismarck	ND	58505	701-328-2600	328-2435
Economic Development & Finance Div 1600 E Century Ave Ste 200-B *TF:* 866-432-5682 ■ *Web:* www.business.nd.gov	Bismarck	ND	58503	701-328-5300	328-5320
Education Standards & Practices Board 2718 Gateway Ave Dept 303 *Web:* www.nd.gov	Bismarck	ND	58503	701-328-9641	328-9647
Emergency Management Div PO Box 5511 *Web:* www.nd.gov/des	Bismarck	ND	58506	701-328-8100	328-8181
Financial Institutions Dept 2000 Schafer St Ste G *TF:* 800-366-6888 ■ *Web:* www.nd.gov/dfi	Bismarck	ND	58501	701-328-9933	328-0290
Game & Fish Dept 100 N Bismarck Expy *Web:* www.gf.nd.gov	Bismarck	ND	58501	701-328-6300	328-6352
Governor 600 E Blvd Ave Dept 101 *Web:* www.governor.nd.gov	Bismarck	ND	58505	701-328-2200	328-2205
Health Dept 600 E Blvd Ave Dept 301 *Web:* www.ndhealth.gov	Bismarck	ND	58505	701-328-2372	328-4727
Highway Patrol 600 E Blvd Ave Dept 504 *Web:* www.nd.gov	Bismarck	ND	58505	701-328-2455	328-1717
Historical Society 612 E Blvd Ave *Web:* www.nd.gov	Bismarck	ND	58505	701-328-2666	328-3710
Housing Finance Agency PO Box 1535 *TF:* 800-292-8621 ■ *Web:* www.ndhfa.org	Bismarck	ND	58502	701-328-8080	328-8090
Indian Affairs Commission 600 E Blvd Ave Rm 117 *Web:* www.nd.gov	Bismarck	ND	58505	701-328-2428	328-1537
Information Technology Dept 600 E Blvd Ave Dept 112 *Web:* www.nd.gov/itd	Bismarck	ND	58505	701-328-3190	328-3000
Insurance Dept 600 E Blvd Ave Dept 401 *TF:* 800-247-0560 ■ *Web:* www.nd.gov	Bismarck	ND	58505	701-328-2440	328-4880
Labor & Human Rights Dept 600 E Blvd Ave Dept 406 *Web:* www.nd.gov/labor	Bismarck	ND	58505	701-328-2660	328-2031
Legislative Assembly State Capitol 600 E Blvd Ave *Web:* www.legis.nd.gov	Bismarck	ND	58505	701-328-2916	328-3615
Medical Examiners Board 418 E Broadway Ste 12 *Web:* www.ndbomex.org	Bismarck	ND	58501	701-328-6500	328-6505
Office of Governor 600 E Blvd Ave *Web:* governor.nd.gov	Bismarck	ND	58505	701-328-2200	328-2205
Parks & Recreation Dept 1600 E Century Ave Ste 3 *TF:* 800-807-4723 ■ *Web:* www.parkrec.nd.gov	Bismarck	ND	58503	701-328-5357	328-5363
Parole & Probation Div 3100 E Railroad Ave *Web:* www.nd.gov/docr	Bismarck	ND	58501	701-328-6190	328-6651
Public Instruction Dept 600 E Blvd Ave Dept 201 *Web:* www.dpi.state.nd.us	Bismarck	ND	58505	701-328-2260	328-2461
Public Service Commission 600 E Blvd Ave Dept 408 *Web:* www.psc.nd.gov	Bismarck	ND	58505	701-328-2400	328-2410
Racing Commission 500 N Ninth St *Web:* www.ndracingcommission.com	Bismarck	ND	58501	701-328-4290	
Real Estate Commission 200 E Main Ave Ste 204 *Web:* www.realestatend.org	Bismarck	ND	58501	701-328-9749	328-9750
Secretary of State 600 E Blvd Ave Dept 108 *TF:* 800-352-0867 ■ *Web:* www.nd.gov/sos	Bismarck	ND	58505	701-328-2900	328-2992
Securities Dept 600 E Blvd Ave Dept 414 *Web:* www.nd.gov	Bismarck	ND	58505	701-328-2910	328-2946
Student Financial Assistance Program 600 E Blvd Ave 10th Fl Dept 215 *Web:* www.ndus.nodak.edu	Bismarck	ND	58505	701-328-2960	328-2961
Supreme Court 600 E Blvd Ave Dept 180 *Web:* www.ndcourts.gov	Bismarck	ND	58505	701-328-2221	328-4480
Tax Dept 600 E Blvd Ave *Web:* www.nd.gov	Bismarck	ND	58505	701-328-2770	328-3700
Testing & Safety Div 600 E Blvd Ave *Web:* www.psc.nd.gov	Bismarck	ND	58505	701-328-2400	328-2410
Tourism Div 1600 Eentury Ave Ste 200S *TF:* 800-435-5663 ■ *Web:* www.ndtourism.com	Bismarck	ND	58502	701-328-2525	328-4878
Transportation Dept 608 E Blvd Ave *Web:* www.dot.nd.gov	Bismarck	ND	58505	701-328-2500	328-1420
Treasurer 600 E Blvd Ave Dept 120 *Web:* www.nd.gov/ndtreas	Bismarck	ND	58505	701-328-2643	328-3002
University System 600 E Blvd Ave Dept 215 *Web:* www.ndus.edu	Bismarck	ND	58505	701-328-2960	328-2961
Veterans Affairs Dept 4201 38th St S Ste 104 *TF:* 866-634-8387 ■ *Web:* www.nd.gov	Fargo	ND	58104	701-239-7165	239-7166
Vocational Rehabilitation Div 1237 W Divide Ave Ste 2 *TF:* 800-755-2745 ■ *Web:* www.nd.gov	Bismarck	ND	58501	701-328-8800	328-8969
Workers Compensation 1600 E Century Ave Ste 1000 *TF:* 800-777-5033 ■ *Web:* www.workforcesafety.com	Bismarck	ND	58503	701-328-3800	328-3820

342-36 Ohio

	City	State	Zip	Phone	Fax
Adjutant's General Dept 2825 W Dublin Granville Rd *Web:* www.ong.ohio.gov	Columbus	OH	43235	614-336-7324	
Administrative Director of the Supreme Court 65 S Front St Fl 5 *Web:* www.supremecourt.ohio.gov	Columbus	OH	43215	614-387-9340	387-9349
Aging Dept 50 W Broad St 9th Fl *Web:* aging.ohio.gov	Columbus	OH	43215	614-466-5500	466-5741
Agriculture Dept 8995 E Main St *TF:* 800-282-1955 ■ *Web:* www.agri.ohio.gov	Reynoldsburg	OH	43068	614-728-6201	728-6310
Arts Council 30 E Broad St Ste 33 *Web:* www.oac.state.oh.us	Columbus	OH	43215	614-466-2613	466-4494
Commerce Dept 77 S High St 23rd Fl *Web:* www.com.state.oh.us	Columbus	OH	43215	614-466-3636	
Consumer Protection Section 30 E Broad St 14th Fl *TF:* 800-282-0515 ■ *Web:* www.ohioattorneygeneral.gov	Columbus	OH	43215	614-466-8831	
Education Dept 25 S Front St *TF:* 877-644-6338 ■ *Web:* education.ohio.gov	Columbus	OH	43215	614-995-1545	
Emergency Management Agency 2855 W Dublin-Granville Rd *Web:* www.ema.ohio.gov	Columbus	OH	43235	614-889-7150	889-7183
Environmental Protection Agency 122 S Front St PO Box 1049 *Web:* www.epa.state.oh.us	Columbus	OH	43216	614-644-3020	644-3184
Ethics Commission 30 W Spring St L3 *Web:* www.ethics.ohio.gov	Columbus	OH	43215	614-466-7090	466-8368
Financial Institutions Div 77 S High St 21st Fl *TF:* 866-278-0003 ■ *Web:* com.ohio.gov/fiin	Columbus	OH	43266	614-728-8400	728-0380
Governor 77 S High St 30th Fl *Web:* www.governor.ohio.gov	Columbus	OH	43215	614-466-3555	466-9354
Health Dept 246 N High St *Web:* www.odh.ohio.gov	Columbus	OH	43215	614-466-3543	644-0085
Highway Patrol (OSHP) 1970 W Broad St PO Box 182074 *TF:* 877-772-8765 ■ *Web:* statepatrol.ohio.gov	Columbus	OH	43223	614-466-2660	
Historical Society 1982 Velma Ave *Web:* www.ohiohistory.org	Columbus	OH	43211	614-297-2300	297-2411
Housing Finance Agency 57 E Main St *Web:* www.ohiohome.org	Columbus	OH	43215	614-466-7970	644-5393
Information Technology 30 E Broad St Ste 4040	Columbus	OH	43215	614-466-6930	644-8151
Insurance Dept 50 W Town St Third Fl Ste 300 *TF:* 800-686-1526 ■ *Web:* www.insurance.ohio.gov	Columbus	OH	43215	614-644-2658	
Job & Family Services Dept 30 E Broad St 32nd Fl *Web:* www.jfs.ohio.gov	Columbus	OH	43215	614-466-6282	466-2815
Legislative Information Office 77 S High St *Web:* www.lis.state.oh.us/	Columbus	OH	43215	614-728-0711	
Mental Health Dept 30 E Broad St 8th Fl *TF:* 888-636-4889 ■ *Web:* mha.ohio.gov	Columbus	OH	43215	614-466-2596	752-9453
Motor Vehicles Bureau 1970 W Broad St PO Box 16520 *Web:* www.bmv.ohio.gov	Columbus	OH	43216	614-752-7500	
Natural Resources Dept 2045 Morse Rd *Web:* www.ohiodnr.com	Columbus	OH	43229	614-265-6565	
Office of Governor 77 S High St 30th Fl *Web:* governor.ohio.gov	Columbus	OH	43215	614-466-3396	
Parks & Recreation Div 2045 Morse Rd Bldg C-3 *TF:* 800-282-7275 ■ *Web:* www.ohiodnr.com	Columbus	OH	43229	614-265-6561	261-8407

	City	State	Zip	Phone	Fax
Parole Board 1050 Fwy Dr N *Web:* www.drc.state.oh.us	Columbus	OH	43229	614-752-1200	752-1251
Public Utilities Commission 180 E Broad St *Web:* www.puco.ohio.gov	Columbus	OH	43215	614-466-3016	
Racing Commission 77 S High St 18th Fl *Web:* www.racing.ohio.gov	Columbus	OH	43215	614-466-2757	466-1900
Regents Board 30 E Broad St 36th Fl *Web:* www.ohiohighered.org	Columbus	OH	43215	614-466-6000	466-5866
Rehabilitation & Correction Dept 770 W Broad St *Web:* www.drc.state.oh.us	Columbus	OH	43222	614-752-1159	
Secretary of State 180 E Broad St 16th Fl *Web:* www.sos.state.oh.us	Columbus	OH	43215	614-466-2655	644-0649
Securities Div 77 S High St Ste 22 *Web:* www.com.ohio.gov	Columbus	OH	43215	614-644-7381	
Supreme Court 65 S Front St *Web:* www.sconet.state.oh.us	Columbus	OH	43215	614-387-9530	387-9539
Taxation Dept 30 E Broad St 22nd Fl PO Box 530 *TF:* 888-405-4089 ■ *Web:* tax.ohio.gov	Columbus	OH	43215	614-466-2166	466-6401
Transportation Dept 1980 W Broad St *Web:* dot.state.oh.us	Columbus	OH	43223	614-466-7170	
Travel & Tourism Div PO Box 1001 *TF:* 800-282-5393 ■ *Web:* consumer.discoverohio.com	Columbus	OH	43216	614-466-8844	
Treasurer 30 E Broad St 9th Fl *Web:* www.tos.ohio.gov	Columbus	OH	43215	614-466-2160	
Tuition Trust Authority 580 S High St Ste 208 *TF Cust Svc:* 800-233-6734 ■ *Web:* www.collegeadvantage.com	Columbus	OH	43215	614-752-9400	
Veterans Services Dept 77 S High St 7th Fl *Web:* dvs.ohio.gov	Columbus	OH	43215	614-644-0898	
Vital Statistics Unit 246 N High St PO Box 15098 *Web:* www.odh.ohio.gov	Columbus	OH	43215	614-466-2531	
Wildlife Div 2045 Morse Rd Bldg G *TF:* 800-945-3543 ■ *Web:* www.ohiodnr.com/wildlife	Columbus	OH	43229	614-265-6300	
Workers Compensation Bureau 30 W Spring St *TF:* 800-644-6292 ■ *Web:* www.bwc.ohio.gov	Columbus	OH	43215	614-644-6292	
Workforce Development Office 4020 E Fifth Ave PO Box 1618 **Fax Area Code:* 614 ■ *TF:* 888-296-7541 ■ *Web:* www.jfs.ohio.gov/owd	Columbus	OH	43219	888-296-7541	644-7102*
Youth Services Dept 51 N High St *Web:* www.dys.ohio.gov	Columbus	OH	43215	614-466-4314	752-9859

342-37 Oklahoma

	City	State	Zip	Phone	Fax
Administrative Office of the Courts 2100 N Lincoln Blvd Ste 3 *Web:* www.ok.gov	Oklahoma City	OK	73105	405-556-9300	
Aging Services Div 312 NE 28th St *Web:* www.okdhs.org/aging	Oklahoma City	OK	73105	405-521-2327	
Agriculture Food & Forestry Dept 2800 N Lincoln Blvd *Web:* www.oda.state.ok.us	Oklahoma City	OK	73105	405-521-3864	
Arts Council 2101 N Lincoln Blvd Ste 640 *Web:* arts.ok.gov	Oklahoma City	OK	73152	405-521-2931	521-6418
Attorney General 313 NE 21st St *Web:* ok.gov/oag	Oklahoma City	OK	73105	405-521-3921	521-6246
Banking Dept 4545 N Lincoln Blvd Ste 164 *Web:* www.ok.gov	Oklahoma City	OK	73105	405-521-2782	522-2993
Chief Medical Examiner 901 N Stonewall Ave *Web:* www.state.ok.us	Oklahoma City	OK	73117	405-239-7141	239-2430
Child Support Enforcement Div PO Box 248822 *TF:* 800-522-2922 ■ *Web:* www.okdhs.org	Oklahoma City	OK	73124	405-522-2273	
Commerce Dept 900 N Stiles Ave *TF:* 800-879-6552 ■ *Web:* www.okcommerce.gov	Oklahoma City	OK	73104	405-815-6552	815-5199
Conservation Commission 2800 N Lincoln Blvd Ste 160 *Web:* www.okcc.state.ok.us	Oklahoma City	OK	73105	405-521-2384	521-6686
Consumer Protection Div 313 NE 21st St	Oklahoma City	OK	73105	405-521-4274	528-1867
Corporation Commission (OCC) 2101 N Lincoln PO Box 52000 *Web:* www.occeweb.com	Oklahoma City	OK	73152	405-521-2211	522-1623
Corrections Dept 3400 N Martin Luther King Ave *Web:* www.ok.gov	Oklahoma City	OK	73111	405-425-2500	425-2886
Development Finance Authority 5900 N Classen Ct *Web:* www.ok.gov	Oklahoma City	OK	73118	405-842-1145	848-3314
Education Dept 2500 N Lincoln Blvd *Web:* www.ok.gov	Oklahoma City	OK	73105	405-521-3301	521-6205
Emergency Management Dept 4600 N Martin Luther King Ave *Web:* www.ok.gov	Oklahoma City	OK	73111	405-521-2481	521-4053
Employment Security Commission PO Box 52003 *Web:* www.ok.gov	Oklahoma City	OK	73152	405-557-5400	557-5355
Environmental Quality Dept 707 N Robinson Ave PO Box 1677 *TF:* 800-869-1400 ■ *Web:* www.deq.state.ok.us	Oklahoma City	OK	73101	405-702-1000	702-7101
Ethics Commission 2300 N Lincoln Blvd Rm B5 *Web:* www.ok.gov	Oklahoma City	OK	73105	405-521-3451	521-4905
Health Dept 1000 NE Tenth St *Web:* www.health.state.ok.us	Oklahoma City	OK	73117	405-271-4200	271-3431
Highway Patrol PO Box 11415 *Web:* www.dps.state.ok.us	Oklahoma City	OK	73136	405-425-2424	
Historical Society 800 Nahzi Zuhzi Dr *Web:* www.okhistory.org	Oklahoma City	OK	73105	405-521-2491	521-2492
Housing Finance Agency 100 NW 63rd St Ste 200 *TF:* 800-256-1489 ■ *Web:* www.ohfa.org	Oklahoma City	OK	73116	405-848-1144	
Human Services Dept 2400 N Lincoln Blvd *Web:* www.okdhs.org	Oklahoma City	OK	73105	405-521-3646	521-6458
Indian Affairs Commission 4545 Lincoln Blvd Ste 282 *Web:* www.ok.gov	Oklahoma City	OK	73105	405-521-3828	522-4427
Insurance Dept (OID) 3625 NW 56th Ste 100 *TF:* 800-522-0071 ■ *Web:* www.ok.gov/oid	Oklahoma City	OK	73152	405-521-2828	521-6635
Labor Dept 4001 N Lincoln Blvd *Web:* www.ok.gov	Oklahoma City	OK	73105	405-528-1500	528-5751
Legislation Service Bureau 2300 N Lincoln Blvd *Web:* www.oklegislature.gov	State Capitol Bldg	OK	73105	405-521-4081	521-5507
Lieutenant Governor 2300 N Lincoln Blvd Ste 211 *Web:* www.ok.gov	Oklahoma City	OK	73105	405-521-2161	522-8694
Mental Health & Substance Abuse Services Dept 1200 NE 13th St PO Box 53277 *Web:* www.odmhsas.org	Oklahoma City	OK	73152	405-522-3908	522-3650
Motor Vehicle Commission 4334 NW Expy Ste 183 *Web:* www.ok.gov	Oklahoma City	OK	73116	405-607-8227	607-8909
National Guard 3501 Military Cir *Web:* www.ok.ngb.army.mil	Oklahoma City	OK	73111	405-228-5000	228-5524
Pardon & Parole Board 120 N Robinson Ave Ste 900W *Web:* www.ok.gov	Oklahoma City	OK	73102	405-521-6600	602-6437
Parks Div PO Box 52002 *TF:* 800-654-8240 ■ *Web:* www.travelok.com	Oklahoma City	OK	73152	405-230-8300	
Personnel Management Office 2101 N Lincoln Blvd Ste G-80 *Web:* www.ok.gov	Oklahoma City	OK	73105	405-521-2177	524-6942
Real Estate Commission 2401 NW 23rd St Ste 18 *Web:* www.ok.gov	Oklahoma City	OK	73107	405-521-3387	521-2189
Rehabilitative Services Dept 5501 N Portland Ave *TF:* 800-845-8476 ■ *Web:* www.okrehab.org	Oklahoma City	OK	73112	405-951-3400	951-3529
Secretary of State 2300 N Lincoln Blvd Ste 101 *Web:* www.sos.ok.gov	Oklahoma City	OK	73105	405-521-3912	521-3771
Securities Dept 204 N Robinson Ave Ste 400 *Web:* www.securities.ok.gov	Oklahoma City	OK	73102	405-280-7700	280-7742
State Regents for Higher Education 655 Research Pkwy Ste 200 *Web:* www.okhighered.org	Oklahoma City	OK	73104	405-225-9100	225-9235
Supreme Court 2100 N Lincoln Blvd Ste 3 *Web:* www.ok.gov	Oklahoma City	OK	73105	405-556-9300	
Tax Commission 2501 N Lincoln Blvd *Web:* www.oktax.state.ok.us	Oklahoma City	OK	73194	405-521-3160	521-3826
Treasurer 2300 N Lincoln Rd Rm 217 *Web:* www.ok.gov	Oklahoma City	OK	73105	405-521-3191	521-4994
Veterans Affairs Dept 2311 N Central Ave *Web:* www.ok.gov	Oklahoma City	OK	73105	405-521-3684	521-6533
Victim Services Unit 313 NE 21st St *Web:* www.oag.ok.gov/oagweb.nsf/vservices.html	Oklahoma City	OK	73105	405-521-3921	521-6246
Vital Records Div 1000 NE 10th St *Web:* www.ok.gov	Oklahoma City	OK	73117	405-271-4040	
Weights & Measures 2800 N Lincoln Blvd *Web:* www.ok.gov	Oklahoma City	OK	73105	405-521-3864	
Wildlife Conservation Dept (ODWC) PO Box 53465 *TF:* 800-522-8039 ■ *Web:* www.wildlifedepartment.com	Oklahoma City	OK	73152	405-521-4660	

342-38 Oregon

	City	State	Zip	Phone	Fax
Arts Commission 775 Summer St NE Ste 200 *Web:* www.oregonartscommission.org	Salem	OR	97301	503-986-0082	986-0260
Attorney General 1162 Ct St NE Justice Bldg *Web:* www.doj.state.or.us	Salem	OR	97301	503-378-4400	378-4017
Business Development Dept 775 Summer St NE Ste 200 *TF General:* 800-735-2900 ■ *Web:* www.oregon4biz.com	Salem	OR	97301	503-986-0123	581-5115
Child Support Div 494 State St Ste 300 *Web:* oregonchildsupport.gov	Salem	OR	97301	503-986-6166	986-6158
Children Adults & Families Div (CAF) 500 Summer St NE E62 *Web:* www.oregon.gov	Salem	OR	97301	503-945-5600	373-7032
Community Colleges & Workforce Development Dept 255 Capitol St NE *Web:* www.worksourceoregon.org	Salem	OR	97310	503-378-8648	
Consumer & Business Services Dept 350 Winter St NE PO Box 14480 *Web:* www.oregon.gov	Salem	OR	97309	503-378-4100	378-6444
Corrections Dept (DOC) 2575 Ctr St NE *Web:* www.oregon.gov/DOC	Salem	OR	97301	503-945-9090	373-1173
Crime Victims Service Div 1162 Ct St NE *TF:* 877-877-9392 ■ *Web:* www.doj.state.or.us/crimev/welcome1.htm	Salem	OR	97301	503-378-4400	378-5738
Driver & Motor Vehicle Services Div 1905 Lana Ave NE *Web:* www.oregon.gov/ODOT/DMV	Salem	OR	97314	503-945-5000	945-5254

Phone Fax

Education Dept 255 Capitol St NE. Salem OR 97310 503-947-5600

Emergency Management 3225 State St Ste 115. . . . . Salem OR 97301 503-378-2911 373-7933
Web: www.oregon.gov

Energy Dept 625 Marion St NE. . . . . Salem OR 97301 503-378-4040 373-7806
Web: oregon.gov

Environmental Quality Dept 811 SW Sixth Ave . . . . .Portland OR 97204 503-229-5696 229-6124
Web: www.oregon.gov

Finance & Corporate Securities Div
350 Winter St NE Rm 410 PO Box 14480. . . . . Salem OR 97309 503-378-4140 947-7862
Web: www.oregon.gov

Financial Fraud/Consumer Protection Section
1162 Ct St NE. . . . . Salem OR 97301 503-378-4400 373-7067
TF: 877-877-9392 ■ *Web:* www.doj.state.or.us

Fish & Wildlife Dept (ODFW) 3406 Cherry Ave NE . . . . Salem OR 97303 503-947-6000 947-6042
TF: 800-720-6339 ■ *Web:* www.dfw.state.or.us

Forestry Dept 2600 State St Ste 110 . . . . Salem OR 97310 503-945-7200 945-7212
Web: www.oregon.gov

Government Standards & Practices Commission
3218 Pringle Rd SE Ste 220. . . . . Salem OR 97302 503-378-5105 373-1456
Web: www.oregon.gov

Governor 900 Ct St NE Ste 160. . . . . Salem OR 97310 503-378-3111 378-6827
Web: www.oregon.gov/gov

Housing & Community Services Dept
725 Summer St NE Ste B . . . . Salem OR 97301 503-986-2000 986-2020
Web: www.oregon.gov/OHCS

Human Services Dept 500 Summer St NE . . . . Salem OR 97301 503-945-5944 378-2897
Web: www.oregon.gov/DHS

Insurance Div 350 Winter St NE Rm 440. . . . . Salem OR 97301 503-947-7980 378-4351
Web: www.cbs.state.or.us

Labor & Industries Bureau
800 NE Oregon St Ste 1045 . . . . .Portland OR 97232 503-731-4200 731-4103
Web: oregon.gov/boli/pages/index.aspx

Land Conservation & Development Dept
635 Capitol St NE Ste 150 . . . . Salem OR 97301 503-373-0050 378-5518
Web: www.oregon.gov

Legislative Assembly 900 Ct St NE. . . . . Salem OR 97301 800-332-2313 373-1527*
**Fax Area Code:* 503 ■ *TF:* 800-332-2313 ■ *Web:* www.leg.state.or.us

Lottery 500 Airport Rd SE . . . . Salem OR 97301 503-540-1000 540-1001
Web: oregonlottery.org

Measurement Standards Div 635 Capitol St NE . . . . Salem OR 97301 503-986-4670 986-4784
Web: www.oregon.gov

Military Dept 1776 Militia Way SE PO Box 14350. . . . . Salem OR 97309 503-584-3980 584-3987
Web: www.oregon.gov

Parks & Recreation Dept (OPRD)
725 Summer St NE Ste C . . . . Salem OR 97301 503-986-0707 986-0794
TF: 800-551-6949 ■ *Web:* www.oregon.gov/OPRD

Parole & Post-Prison Supervision Board
2575 Ctr St NE Ste 100. . . . . Salem OR 97301 503-945-0900 373-7558
Web: www.oregon.gov/BOPPPS

Public Health Div 800 NE Oregon St Ste 465-B . . . . .Portland OR 97232 971-673-1222 731-4031*
**Fax Area Code:* 503 ■ *Web:* public.health.oregon.gov/PHD

Publication & Distribution Services
900 Ct St NE Rm 49 . . . . Salem OR 97310 503-986-1360 373-1527
Web: Www.oregonlegislature.gov

Racing Commission 800 NE Oregon St Ste 310 . . . . .Portland OR 97232 971-673-1555 673-0213
Web: www.oregon.gov

Revenue Dept 955 Ctr St NE . . . . Salem OR 97301 503-378-4988 945-8738
Web: www.oregon.gov

Secretary of State 136 State Capitol . . . . Salem OR 97310 503-986-1523 986-1616
Web: sos.oregon.gov

Seniors & People with Disabilities Div
500 Summer St NE. . . . . Salem OR 97301 503-945-5944 581-6198
Web: www.oregon.gov

State Court Administrator Office 1163 State St. . . . . Salem OR 97301 503-986-5500 986-5503
Web: courts.oregon.gov/ojd/osca

State Police Dept 255 Capitol St NE 4th Fl. . . . . Salem OR 97310 503-378-3720 378-8282
Web: www.oregon.gov

Student Assistance Commission
1500 Valley River Dr Ste 100 . . . . Eugene OR 97401 541-687-7400
Web: oregonstudentaid.gov

Supreme Court 1163 State St. . . . . Salem OR 97301 503-986-5550 986-5503
Web: courts.oregon.gov

Transportation Dept
355 Capitol St NE Ste 135 Rm 222. . . . . Salem OR 97301 503-986-4000 986-3432
TF: 888-275-6368 ■ *Web:* www.oregon.gov/ODOT

Treasurer 350 Winter St NE Ste 100. Salem OR 97301 503-378-4000 373-7051
Web: www.oregon.gov

Veterans' Affairs Dept 700 Summer St NE . . . . Salem OR 97301 503-373-2000 373-2362
Web: www.oregon.gov

Vital Records Unit
800 NE Oregon St Ste 225 PO Box 14050 . . . . .Portland OR 97232 971-673-1180 673-1201
Web: public.health.oregon.gov

Vocational Rehabilitation Services Office (OVRS)
700 Summer St NE E-87. . . . . Salem OR 97301 800-692-9666 947-5010*
**Fax Area Code:* 503 ■ *TF:* 877-277-0513 ■ *Web:* www.oregon.gov

Workers Compensation Board
2601 SE 25th St Ste 150. . . . . Salem OR 97302 503-378-3308 373-1684
Web: www.cbs.state.or.us/wcb

342-39 Pennsylvania

Phone Fax

Administrative Office of the Courts (AOPC)
1515 Market St Ste 1414 . . . . Philadelphia PA 19102 215-560-6300 560-6315
Web: www.pacourts.us/T/AOPC

Aging Dept 555 Walnut St 5th Fl. .Harrisburg PA 17101 717-787-7313 783-6842
Web: www.aging.state.pa.us

Agriculture Dept 2301 N Cameron St. . . . . .Harrisburg PA 17110 717-772-2853 705-8402
Web: www.agriculture.state.pa.us

Attorney General Strawberry Sq 16th Fl . . . . .Harrisburg PA 17120 717-787-3391
Web: www.attorneygeneral.gov

Banking Dept
17 N Second St Market Square Plz. . . . . .Harrisburg PA 17101 717-783-4721
TF: 800-722-2657 ■ *Web:* www.banking.state.pa.us

Bill Status 462 Main Capitol Bldg. . . . . .Harrisburg PA 17120 717-787-5920
Web: www.legis.state.pa.us

Child Support Enforcement Bureau
PO Box 8018 . . . . .Harrisburg PA 17105 717-787-2600 787-9706
Web: www.dpw.state.pa.us

Community & Economic Development Dept
400 N St 4th Fl. . . . . .Harrisburg PA 17120 717-787-3003 787-6866
Web: www.newpa.com

Conservation & Natural Resources Dept
400 Market St Ste 7 . . . . .Harrisburg PA 17120 717-787-2869 705-2832
Web: www.dcnr.state.pa.us

Consumer Advocate 555 Walnut St 5th Fl . . . . .Harrisburg PA 17101 717-783-5048 783-7152
Web: www.oca.state.pa.us

Corrections Dept PO Box 598. . . . . Camp Hill PA 17001 717-728-2573 787-0132
Web: www.cor.state.pa.us

Driver & Vehicle Services Bureau
1101 S Front St . . . . .Harrisburg PA 17104 717-787-2977 705-1046
Web: www.dmv.state.pa.us

Education Dept 333 Market St. .Harrisburg PA 17126 717-783-6788 783-4517
Web: www.pde.state.pa.us

Emergency Management Agency 2605 I- Dr . . . . . . .Harrisburg PA 17110 717-651-2001 651-2021
Web: pema.pa.gov

Environmental Protection Dept PO Box 2063. . . . . . .Harrisburg PA 17105 717-783-2300 783-8926
Web: www.dep.state.pa.us

Fish & Boat Commission 1601 Elmerton Ave. . . . . .Harrisburg PA 17110 717-705-7800 705-7802
Web: www.fish.state.pa.us

Game Commission 2001 Elmerton Ave . . . . .Harrisburg PA 17110 717-787-4250 772-2411
Web: www.pgc.state.pa.us

General Assembly Capitol Bldg. . . . . .Harrisburg PA 17120 717-787-5920 772-2344
Web: www.legis.state.pa.us

Governor 508 Main Capitol Bldg. . . . . .Harrisburg PA 17120 717-787-2500 772-8284
Web: www.governor.state.pa.us

Health Dept
Health & Welfare Bldg PO Box 90. . . . . .Harrisburg PA 17108 717-787-6436 772-6959
Web: www.portal.health.state.pa.us

Higher Education Assistance Agency
1200 N Seventh St . . . . .Harrisburg PA 17102 800-233-0557 720-3901*
**Fax Area Code:* 717 ■ *TF:* 800-233-0557 ■ *Web:* www.pheaa.org

Historical & Museum Commission 300 N St. . . . . . . .Harrisburg PA 17120 717-787-3362 783-9924
Web: www.phmc.state.pa.us

Homeland Security Office
1800 Elmerton Ave . . . . .Harrisburg PA 17110 717-346-4460
Web: homelandsecurity.pa.gov

Housing Finance Agency 211 N Front St. . . . . .Harrisburg PA 17101 717-780-3800
Web: www.phfa.org

Information Technology Office
209 Finance Bldg . . . . .Harrisburg PA 17120 717-787-5440 787-4523
Web: www.oit.state.pa.us

Insurance Dept 1326 Strawberry Sq . . . . .Harrisburg PA 17120 877-881-6388 783-3898*
**Fax Area Code:* 717 ■ *TF:* 877-881-6388 ■ *Web:* www.ins.state.pa.us

Mental Health & Substance Abuse Office
PO Box 2675 . . . . .Harrisburg PA 17105 717-787-6443
Web: www.dpw.state.pa.us

Military & Veterans Affairs Dept
Fort Indiantown Gap Bldg S-0-47. .Annville PA 17003 717-861-8500 861-8314
Web: www.dmva.state.pa.us

Office of Governor
200 Capitol Bldg 501 N 3rd St . . . . .Harrisburg PA 17120 717-787-3300
Web: www.governor.state.pa.us

Probation & Parole Board
1101 S Front St Ste 5100. . . . . .Harrisburg PA 17104 717-787-5699 705-1774
Web: www.pbpp.state.pa.us

Public Utility Commission
400 N St Keystone Bldg PO Box 3265 . . . . .Harrisburg PA 17120 717-783-1740 787-6641
TF: 800-692-7380 ■ *Web:* www.puc.state.pa.us

Public Welfare Dept PO Box 2675 . . . . .Harrisburg PA 17105 717-787-2600 772-2062
Web: www.dpw.state.pa.us

Revenue Dept Strawberry Sq 11th Fl. . . . . .Harrisburg PA 17128 717-783-3680 787-3990
Web: www.revenue.state.pa.us

Secretary of the Commonwealth
210 N Office Bldg . . . . .Harrisburg PA 17120 717-787-5280 787-1734
Web: www.dos.state.pa.us

Securities Commission 17 N Second St . . . . .Harrisburg PA 17101 717-787-2665
Web: www.pa.gov/

State Ethics Commission
309 Finance Bldg PO Box 11470 .Harrisburg PA 17108 717-783-1610 787-0806
TF: 800-932-0936 ■ *Web:* www.ethics.state.pa.us

State Parks Bureau PO Box 8551. . . . . .Harrisburg PA 17105 717-787-6640 787-8817
TF: 888-727-2757 ■ *Web:* www.dcnr.state.pa.us

State Police 1800 Elmerton Ave. . . . . .Harrisburg PA 17110 717-783-5599
Web: psp.pa.gov

State System of Higher Education
2986 N Second St. . . . . .Harrisburg PA 17110 717-720-4000 720-4011
TF: 800-732-0999 ■ *Web:* www.passhe.edu

Supreme Court 468 City Hall. Philadelphia PA 19107 215-560-6370
Web: www.pacourts.us

Transportation Dept 400 N St . . . . .Harrisburg PA 17120 717-787-2838
TF: 800-932-4600 ■ *Web:* www.dot.state.pa.us

Treasury Dept 129 Finance Bldg . . . . .Harrisburg PA 17120 717-787-2465
Web: www.patreasury.gov

Victims Compensation Assistance Program
PO Box 1167 . . . . .Harrisburg PA 17101 717-783-5153 787-4306
Web: pccd.pa.gov/pages/default.aspx

Vital Records Div
101 S Mercer St PO Box 1528 . . . . New Castle PA 16103 724-656-3100 652-8951
Web: www.portal.health.state.pa.us

Vocational Rehabilitation Office (OVR)
1521 N Sixth St . . . . .Harrisburg PA 17102 717-787-5244 783-5221
TF: 800-442-6351 ■ *Web:* www.portal.state.pa.us

				Phone	Fax
Workers Compensation Bureau 1171 S Cameron St Rm 324 *TF:* 800-482-2383 ■ *Web:* www.portal.state.pa.u	Harrisburg	PA	17104	717-783-5421	

342-40 Rhode Island

				Phone	Fax
State Government Information 40 Fountain St *Web:* www.ri.gov	Providence	RI	02903	401-222-2000	
Adjutant General's Office 645 New London Ave *Web:* Www.sos.ri.gov	Cranston	RI	02920	401-946-9996	944-1891
Agriculture & Resource Marketing Div 235 Promenade St Rm 370 *Web:* www.dem.ri.gov	Providence	RI	02908	401-222-2781	222-6047
Arts Council 1 Capitol Hill 3rd Fl *Web:* arts.ri.gov	Providence	RI	02908	401-222-3880	222-3018
Attorney General 150 S Main St *Web:* www.riag.state.ri.us/contact/	Providence	RI	02903	401-274-4400	222-1331
Bill Status 82 Smith St Rm 217 *Web:* www.rilin.state.ri.us	Providence	RI	02903	401-222-3580	
Board of Governors for Higher Education (RIBGHE) 80 Washington St Shepard Bldg *Web:* www.ribghe.org	Providence	RI	02903	401-456-6000	456-6028
Child Support Services 77 Dorrance St *Web:* www.cse.ri.gov/	Providence	RI	02906	401-458-4400	
Children Youth & Families Dept 101 Friendship St *Web:* www.dcyf.state.ri.us	Providence	RI	02903	401-528-3575	528-3590
Consumer Protection Unit 150 S Main St *Web:* www.riag.ri.gov	Providence	RI	02903	401-274-4400	222-5110
Corrections Dept 40 Howard Ave *Web:* www.doc.state.ri.us	Cranston	RI	02920	401-462-1000	
Court Administrators Office 250 Benefit St *Web:* www.courts.ri.gov	Providence	RI	02903	401-222-3215	
Crime Victim Compensation Program 50 Service Ave *Web:* www.treasury.ri.gov	Warwick	RI	02886	401-462-7650	222-6140
Economic Development Corp 315 Iron Horse Way Ste 101 *Web:* commerceri.com	Providence	RI	02908	401-278-9100	
Elderly Affairs Dept 74 W Rd Hazard Bldg 2nd fl *Web:* www.google.co.in	Cranston	RI	02920	401-462-3000	
Elementary & Secondary Education Dept 255 Westminster St *Web:* www.ride.ri.gov	Providence	RI	02903	401-222-4600	222-6178
Emergency Management Agency 645 New London Ave *Web:* www.riema.ri.gov	Cranston	RI	02920	401-946-9996	944-1891
Environmental Management Dept 235 Promenade St *Web:* www.dem.ri.gov/	Providence	RI	02908	401-222-6800	222-6802
Ethics Commission 40 Fountain St *Web:* www.ethics.ri.gov	Providence	RI	02903	401-222-3790	222-3382
General Assembly 82 Smith St *Web:* www.rilin.state.ri.us	Providence	RI	02903	401-222-2466	
Health Dept 3 Capitol Hill *Web:* www.health.ri.gov	Providence	RI	02908	401-222-2231	222-6548
Higher Education Assistance Authority (RIHEAA) 560 Jefferson Blvd *TF:* 800-922-9855 ■ *Web:* www.riheaa.org	Warwick	RI	02886	401-736-1100	732-3541
Historical Preservation & Heritage Commission 150 Benefit St *Web:* eisenhowerhouse.com	Providence	RI	02903	401-222-2678	222-2968
Housing & Mortgage Finance Corp 44 Washington St *Web:* www.rhodeislandhousing.org	Providence	RI	02903	401-751-5566	
Human Services Dept 600 New London Ave Louis Pasteur Bldg, Ste 57 *Web:* www.dhs.ri.gov	Cranston	RI	02920	401-462-5300	
Labor & Training Dept 1511 Pontiac Ave *Web:* www.dlt.state.ri.us	Cranston	RI	02920	401-462-8000	462-8872
Library & Information Services Office One Capitol Hil 4th fl *Web:* www.olis.ri.gov	Providence	RI	02908	401-574-9300	574-9320
Lieutenant Governor 82 Smith St Rm 116 *Web:* www.ltgov.ri.gov	Providence	RI	02903	401-222-2371	222-2012
Lottery 1425 Pontiac Ave *Web:* www.rilot.com	Cranston	RI	02920	401-463-6500	
Medical Examiner 48 Orms St *Web:* www.health.ri.gov	Providence	RI	02908	401-222-5500	222-5517
Office of the Governor State House *Web:* www.governor.state.ri.us	Providence	RI	02903	401-222-2080	
Parks & Recreation Div 2321 Hartford Ave *Web:* www.riparks.com	Johnston	RI	02919	401-222-2632	
Professional Regulation Div 1511 Pontiac Ave Howard Ctr Bldg 70 *Web:* www.dlt.ri.gov/profregs	Cranston	RI	02920	401-462-8580	
Public Utilities Commission 89 Jefferson Blvd *Web:* www.ripuc.org	Warwick	RI	02888	401-941-4500	
Rehabilitation Services Office 40 Fountain St *Web:* www.ors.state.ri.us	Providence	RI	02903	401-421-7005	222-3574
State Police 311 Danielson Pike *Web:* risp.ri.gov	North Scituate	RI	02857	401-444-1000	444-1105
Supreme Court 250 Benefit St *Web:* www.courts.ri.gov	Providence	RI	02903	401-222-3272	222-3599
Tourism Div 315 Iron Horse Way Ste 101 **Fax Area Code:* 401 ■ *TF:* 800-556-2484 ■ *Web:* www.visitrhodeisland.com	Providence	RI	02908	800-556-2484	273-8270*
Transportation Dept 2 Capitol Hill *Web:* rhodeislandbids.com	Providence	RI	02903	401-222-2481	222-2086
Treasurer 82 Smith St Rm 102 *Web:* www.treasury.ri.gov/	Providence	RI	02903	401-222-2397	222-6140
Veterans Affairs Div 480 Metacom Ave *Web:* www.vets.ri.gov	Bristol	RI	2809	401-253-8000	254-2320
Weights & Measures Office 1511 Pontiac Ave *Web:* www.dlt.ri.gov/occusafe/weightsmeasures.htm	Cranston	RI	02920	401-462-8570	462-8576
Worker's Compensation Div 1511 Pontiac Ave Bldg 69 2nd Fl *Web:* www.dlt.ri.gov/wc	Cranston	RI	02920	401-462-8100	462-8105

342-41 South Carolina

				Phone	Fax
State Government Information 1301 Gervais St Ste 710 *TF:* 866-340-7105 ■ *Web:* sc.gov	Columbia	SC	29201	803-771-0131	771-0131
Adoption Services Div PO Box 1520 *Web:* dss.sc.gov	Columbia	SC	29202	803-898-7561	898-7641
Agriculture Dept 1200 Senate St PO Box 11280 *Web:* agriculture.sc.gov	Columbia	SC	29211	803-734-2190	734-2192
Arts Commission 1800 Gervais St *Web:* www.state.sc.us	Columbia	SC	29201	803-734-8696	734-8526
Attorney General 1000 Assembly St	Columbia	SC	29201	803-734-3970	253-6283
Business Carolina Inc (BCI) 1523 Huger St Ste A *Web:* www.bcilending.com	Columbia	SC	29201	803-461-3801	
Child Support Enforcement Office 3150 Harden St Ext *TF:* 800-768-5858 ■ *Web:* www.sc.gov	Columbia	SC	29203	803-898-9210	
Commerce Dept 1201 Main St Ste 1600 *TF:* 800-868-7232 ■ *Web:* www.sccommerce.com	Columbia	SC	29201	803-737-0400	737-0418
Commission on Higher Education 1122 Lady St Ste 300 *Web:* www.che.sc.gov	Columbia	SC	29201	803-737-2260	737-2297
Corrections Dept 4444 Broad River Rd *Web:* www.doc.sc.gov	Columbia	SC	29210	803-896-8500	896-3972
Court Administration 1015 Sumter St 2nd Fl *Web:* www.judicial.state.sc.us	Columbia	SC	29201	803-734-1800	734-1821
Education Lottery 1333 Main St 4th Fl *Web:* www.sceducationlottery.com	Columbia	SC	29201	803-737-2002	737-2005
Emergency Management Div (SCEMD) 2779 Fish Hatchery Rd *Web:* scemd.org	West Columbia	SC	29172	803-737-8500	737-8570
Ethics Commission 5000 Thurmond Mall Ste 250 *Web:* www.state.sc.us	Columbia	SC	29201	803-253-4192	253-7539
Health & Environmental Control Dept 2600 Bull St *Web:* www.scdhec.gov	Columbia	SC	29201	803-898-3432	
Health & Human Services Dept 1801 Main St	Columbia	SC	29201	803-898-2500	
Higher Education Tuition Grants Commission 115 Atrium Wy Ste 102 *TF:* 877-382-4357 ■ *Web:* www.sctuitiongrants.com	Columbia	SC	29203	803-896-1120	896-1126
Highway Patrol 5400 Broad River Rd bldg 12 *Web:* www.scdps.gov	Columbia	SC	29212	803-896-7920	896-7922
Historic Preservation Office 8301 Parklane Rd *Web:* scdah.sc.gov	Columbia	SC	29223	803-896-6100	896-6167
Insurance Dept (SCDOI) 1201 Main St Ste 1000 PO Box 100105 *Web:* www.doi.sc.gov	Columbia	SC	29201	803-737-6160	737-6205
Labor Licensing & Regulation Dept 110 Centerview Dr *Web:* www.llr.state.sc.us	Columbia	SC	29210	803-896-4300	896-4393
Law Enforcement Div 4400 Broad River Rd PO Box 21398 *Web:* www.sled.sc.gov	Columbia	SC	29210	803-896-7001	896-7041
Legislature State House PO Box 142 *Web:* www.scstatehouse.gov	Columbia	SC	29202	803-212-6200	212-6299
Medical Examiners Board 110 Centerview Dr Ste 202 *Web:* www.llr.state.sc.us	Columbia	SC	29210	803-896-4500	896-4515
Mental Health Dept 2414 Bull St PO Box 485 *Web:* www.state.sc.us/dmh/	Columbia	SC	29202	803-898-8581	898-8316
Motor Vehicles Div PO Box 1498 *Web:* www.scdps.gov	Blythewood	SC	29016	803-896-5442	
Natural Resources Dept PO Box 167 *Web:* www.dnr.sc.gov	Columbia	SC	29202	803-734-4007	734-4300
Office of Governor 1205 Pendleton St *Web:* governor.sc.gov	Columbia	SC	29201	803-734-2100	734-5167
Parks Recreation & Tourism Dept 1205 Pendleton St *Web:* www.southcarolinaparks.com	Columbia	SC	29201	803-734-0156	
Probation Parole & Pardon Services Dept 2221 Devine St Ste 600 PO Box 50666 *Web:* www.dppps.sc.gov	Columbia	SC	29250	803-734-9220	734-9440
Professional & Occupational Licensing Boards 110 Centerview Dr *Web:* www.llr.state.sc.us/pol.asp	Columbia	SC	29210	803-896-4300	896-4310
Secretary of State 1205 Pendleton St Ste 525 *Web:* www.scsos.com	Columbia	SC	29201	803-734-2170	734-1661
Securities Div 1000 Assembly St PO Box 11549 *Web:* www.scag.gov/scsecurities	Columbia	SC	29211	803-734-3970	253-6283
Social Services Dept PO Box 1520 *Web:* dss.sc.gov	Columbia	SC	29202	803-898-7601	898-7277
State Housing Finance & Development Authority 300 Outlet Pointe Blvd Ste C *Web:* www.sha.state.sc.us	Columbia	SC	29210	803-896-9001	

				Phone	Fax
State Ports Authority 176 Concord St *TF:* 800-845-7106 ■ *Web:* www.scspa.com	Charleston	SC	29401	843-723-8651	577-8710
Supreme Court 1231 Gervais St Supreme Court Bldg *Web:* dss.sc.gov	Columbia	SC	29201	803-734-1080	734-1499
Transportation Dept 955 Pk St PO Box 191 *Web:* www.scdot.org	Columbia	SC	29202	803-737-1302	737-2038
Treasurer PO Box 11778 *Web:* www.state.sc.us/treas	Columbia	SC	29211	803-734-2101	734-2690
Veterans Affairs Div 1205 Pendleton St Ste 463 *TF:* 800-827-1000 ■ *Web:* va.sc.gov/	Columbia	SC	29201	803-734-0200	734-4014
Victim Assistance Div 1205 Pendleton St *Web:* www.sova.sc.gov	Columbia	SC	29201	803-734-1900	734-1708
Vocational Rehabilitation Dept 1410 Boston Ave PO Box 15 *TF:* 800-832-7526 ■ *Web:* www.scvrd.net	West Columbia	SC	29171	803-896-6500	
Wildlife & Freshwater Fisheries Div 1000 Assembly St PO Box 167 *Web:* www.dnr.sc.gov/divisions/wildlife.html	Columbia	SC	29202	803-734-3886	734-6020
Workers Compensation Commission 1333 Main St # 500 *Web:* wcc.sc.gov	Columbia	SC	29201	803-737-5700	737-5764

342-42 South Dakota

				Phone	Fax
State Government Information 500 E Capitol Ave *Web:* www.sd.gov	Pierre	SD	57501	605-773-3011	
Adult Services & Aging Office 700 Governors Dr *Web:* sd.gov	Pierre	SD	57501	605-773-3656	773-6834
Agriculture Dept 523 E Capitol Ave *Web:* sd.gov	Pierre	SD	57501	605-773-3375	773-5926
Arts Council 800 Governors Dr *Web:* www.artscouncil.sd.gov	Pierre	SD	57501	605-773-3131	773-6962
Attorney General 1302 E Hwy 14 *Web:* sd.gov	Pierre	SD	57501	605-773-3215	773-4106
Banking Div 1601 N Harrison Ave Ste 1 *Web:* dlr.sd.gov/banking/default.aspx	Pierre	SD	57501	605-773-3421	773-5367
Bill Status 500 E Capitol *Web:* legis.sd.gov	Pierre	SD	57501	605-773-3251	
Career Center Div 116 W Missouri Ave *Web:* www.sdjobs.org	Pierre	SD	57501	605-773-3372	773-6680
Child Protection Services 700 Governors Dr *Web:* dss.sd.gov	Pierre	SD	57501	605-773-3227	773-6834
Child Support Div 700 Governors Dr *TF:* 800-286-9145 ■ *Web:* dss.sd.gov	Pierre	SD	57501	605-773-3641	773-7295
Consumer Protection Div 500 E Capitol Ave *Web:* sd.gov	Pierre	SD	57501	605-773-4400	773-4344
Corrections Dept 500 E Capital Ave *Web:* doc.sd.gov	Pierre	SD	57501	605-773-3478	773-3194
Crime Victims' Compensation Program 700 Governors Dr *TF:* 800-696-9476 ■ *Web:* sd.gov	Pierre	SD	57501	605-773-6317	773-6834
Economic Development Office 711 E Wells Ave *TF:* 800-872-6190 ■ *Web:* www.sdreadytowork.com	Pierre	SD	57501	605-773-3301	
Education Dept 700 Governors Dr *Web:* www.doe.sd.gov	Pierre	SD	57501	605-773-3134	773-6139
Emergency Management Office 118 W Capitol Ave *Web:* dps.sd.gov	Pierre	SD	57501	605-773-3231	773-5380
Environment & Natural Resources Dept 523 E Capitol Ave *Web:* sd.gov	Pierre	SD	57501	605-773-3151	773-6035
Finance & Management Bureau 500 E Capitol Ave Rm A-216	Pierre	SD	57501	605-773-3411	773-4711
Gaming Commission 221 W Capitol Ave Ste 101 *Web:* sd.gov	Pierre	SD	57501	605-773-6050	773-6053
Governor 500 E Capitol Ave *Web:* sd.gov	Pierre	SD	57501	605-773-3212	773-6873
Health Dept 600 E Capitol Ave *TF:* 800-738-2301 ■ *Web:* sd.gov	Pierre	SD	57501	605-773-4961	773-5683
Highway Patrol Div 118 W Capitol Ave *Web:* dps.sd.gov	Pierre	SD	57501	605-773-3105	773-3018
Housing Development Authority PO Box 1237 *Web:* www.sdhda.org	Pierre	SD	57501	605-773-3181	773-5154
Information & Telecommunications Bureau 700 Governors Dr *Web:* sd.gov	Pierre	SD	57501	605-773-3165	
Insurance Div 445 E Capitol Ave *Web:* dlr.sd.gov	Pierre	SD	57501	605-773-3563	773-5369
Labor Dept 447 Crook St *Web:* www.sdjobs.org	Pierre	SD	57730	605-673-4488	773-4211
Legislature Capitol Bldg 500 E Capitol Ave 3rd Fl *Web:* legis.sd.gov	Pierre	SD	57501	605-773-3251	773-4576
Lieutenant Governor 500 E Capitol Ave *Web:* sd.gov	Pierre	SD	57501	605-773-3661	773-4711
Military & Veterans Affairs Dept 2823 W Main St *Web:* bhr.sd.gov/	Rapid City	SD	57702	605-737-6721	737-6677
Motor Vehicle Div 445 E Capital Ave *Web:* dor.sd.gov	Pierre	SD	57501	605-773-3541	773-5129
Pardons & Parole Board 1600 N Dr PO Box 5911 *Web:* doc.sd.gov	Sioux Falls	SD	57117	605-367-5040	
Parks & Recreation Div 523 E Capitol Ave *TF Campground Resv:* 800-710-2267 ■ *Web:* gfp.sd.gov/	Pierre	SD	57501	605-773-3391	773-6245
Personnel Bureau 500 E Capitol Ave *Web:* bhr.sd.gov	Pierre	SD	57501	605-773-3148	773-4344
Public Utilities Commission 500 E Capitol Ave *Web:* sd.gov	Pierre	SD	57501	605-773-3201	
Real Estate Commission 221 W Capitol Ave Ste 101 *Web:* sd.gov	Pierre	SD	57501	605-773-3600	773-4356
Regents Board 306 E Capitol Ave Ste 200 *Web:* www.sdbor.edu	Pierre	SD	57501	605-773-3455	
Rehabilitation Services Div 500 E Capitol Ave *TF:* 800-265-9684 ■ *Web:* sd.gov	Pierre	SD	57501	605-773-3195	773-5483
Revenue 445 E Capitol Ave *Web:* dor.sd.gov	Pierre	SD	57501	605-773-3311	773-5129
Secretary of State 500 E Capitol Ave Ste 204 *Web:* www.sdsos.gov	Pierre	SD	57501	605-773-3537	773-6580
Securities Div 445 E Capitol Ave *Web:* sd.gov	Pierre	SD	57501	605-773-4823	773-5953
Social Services Dept 700 Governors Dr *Web:* dss.sd.gov	Pierre	SD	57501	605-773-3165	773-4855
State Court Administrator 500 E Capitol Ave *Web:* ujs.sd.gov	Pierre	SD	57501	605-773-8459	773-8437
State Historical Society 900 Governors Dr *Web:* www.history.sd.gov	Pierre	SD	57501	605-773-3458	773-6041
Supreme Court 500 E Capitol Ave *Web:* ujs.sd.gov	Pierre	SD	57501	605-773-3511	773-6128
Tourism Office 711 E Wells Ave *TF:* 800-952-3625 ■ *Web:* www.travelsd.com	Pierre	SD	57501	605-773-3301	
Treasurer 500 E Capitol Ave Ste 212 *Web:* sdtreasurer.gov	Pierre	SD	57501	605-773-3378	773-3115
Tribal Relations Dept 302 E Dakota *Web:* www.sdtribalrelations.com	Pierre	SD	57501	605-773-3415	773-6592
Weights & Measures Office 118 W Capitol Ave *Web:* dps.sd.gov	Pierre	SD	57501	605-773-3697	773-6631

342-43 Tennessee

				Phone	Fax
Administrative Office of the Courts 511 Union St Ste 600 *Web:* www.tsc.state.tn.us	Nashville	TN	37219	615-741-2687	741-6285
Aging & Disability Commission 500 Deaderick St 8th Fl *Web:* www.state.tn.us/comaging	Nashville	TN	37243	615-741-2056	741-3309
Agriculture Dept 440 Hogan Rd PO Box 40627 *Web:* www.state.tn.us/agriculture	Nashville	TN	37204	615-837-5100	837-5333
Arts Commission 401 Charlotte Ave *Web:* www.tn.gov	Nashville	TN	37243	615-741-1701	741-8559
Attorney General PO Box 20207 *Web:* www.tn.gov	Nashville	TN	37202	615-741-3491	741-2009
Bill Status 320 Sixth Ave N 1st Fl *Web:* www.tn.gov/directory	Nashville	TN	37243	615-741-1000	
Child Support Services Div 400 Deaderick St 12th Fl *TF:* 800-838-6911 ■ *Web:* www.tn.gov	Nashville	TN	37248	615-313-4880	532-2791
Children's Services Dept 436 Sixth Ave N 7th Fl *Web:* www.state.tn.us	Nashville	TN	37243	615-741-9699	
Claims Administration Div 502 Deaderick St *Web:* treasury.tn.gov	Nashville	TN	37243	615-741-2734	532-4979
Commerce & Insurance Dept 500 James Robertson Pkwy 5th Fl *Web:* www.state.tn.us/commerce	Nashville	TN	37243	615-741-6007	
Consumer Affairs Div 500 James Robertson Pkwy 5th Fl *Web:* www.state.tn.us	Nashville	TN	37243	615-741-4737	532-4994
Correction Dept 320 Sixth Ave N 4th Fl *Web:* www.state.tn.us	Nashville	TN	37243	615-741-1000	741-4605
Economic & Community Development Dept (ECD) 312 Eigth Ave N 11th Fl *TF:* 877-768-6374 ■ *Web:* www.tn.gov/ecd	Nashville	TN	37243	615-741-1888	741-7306
Education Dept 710 James Robertson Pkwy 6th Fl *Web:* www.state.tn.us	Nashville	TN	37243	615-741-2731	532-4791
Emergency Management Agency 3041 Sidco Dr *Web:* www.tn.gov/tema/	Nashville	TN	37204	615-741-0001	242-9635
Environment & Conservation Dept 312 Rosa L Parks Ave *Web:* www.state.tn.us/environment	Nashville	TN	37243	615-532-0109	532-0120
Finance & Administration Dept 312 Rosa L Parks Ave *Web:* www.state.tn.us/finance	Nashville	TN	37243	615-741-0320	
Financial Institutions Dept 414 Union St Ste 1000 *Web:* www.tn.gov	Nashville	TN	37219	615-741-2236	
General Assembly 320 Sixth Ave N *Web:* www.legislature.state.tn.us	Nashville	TN	37243	615-741-1000	
Governor State Capitol 1st Fl *Web:* www.tennessee.gov	Nashville	TN	37243	615-741-2001	
Health Dept 425 Fifth Ave N 3rd Fl *Web:* www.state.tn.us	Nashville	TN	37247	615-741-3111	741-2491
Higher Education Commission 404 James Robertson Pkwy Ste 1900 *Web:* www.state.tn.us	Nashville	TN	37243	615-741-3605	741-6230
Highway Patrol 1150 Foster Ave *Web:* www.state.tn.us	Nashville	TN	37249	615-251-5175	532-1051
Historical Commission 2941 Lebanon Rd *Web:* www.state.tn.us	Nashville	TN	37214	615-532-1550	532-1549
Homeland Security Office 312 Rosa L Parks Ave *Web:* www.tennessee.gov	Nashville	TN	37243	615-532-7825	253-5379
Housing Development Agency 404 James Robertson Pkwy Ste 1114 *Web:* thda.org	Nashville	TN	37243	615-741-2400	

	City	State	Zip	Phone	Fax
Human Resources Dept 505 Deaderick St	Nashville	TN	37243	615-741-2958	532-0728
Web: www.state.tn.us					
Human Services Dept 400 Deaderick St	Nashville	TN	37248	615-313-4700	741-4165
Web: www.state.tn.us					
Information Resources Office 312 Rosa L Parks Ave	Nashville	TN	37243	615-741-3700	532-0471
Web: www.state.tn.us					
Insurance Div 500 James Robertson Pkwy	Nashville	TN	37243	615-741-2176	532-2788
Web: www.tn.gov					
Labor & Workforce Development Dept 220 French Landing Dr	Nashville	TN	37243	615-741-6642	741-5078
Web: www.state.tn.us					
Lottery 200 Athens Way Ste 200	Nashville	TN	37228	615-324-6500	*
**Fax:* Hum Res ■ *Web:* www.tnlottery.com/					
Mental Health & Developmental Disabilities Dept 425 Fifth Ave N 3rd Fl	Nashville	TN	37243	615-532-6500	532-6514
TF: 800-669-1851 ■ *Web:* www.state.tn.us					
Military Dept 3041 Sidco Dr	Nashville	TN	37204	615-313-0633	313-3129
Web: www.tnmilitary.org					
Probation & Parole Board 404 James Robertson Pkwy Ste 1300	Nashville	TN	37243	615-741-1673	
Web: www.tennessee.gov/bopp					
Real Estate Commission 500 James Robertson Pkwy Ste 180	Nashville	TN	37243	615-741-2273	741-0313
TF: 800-342-4031 ■ *Web:* www.tn.gov					
Regulatory Authority 460 James Robertson Pkwy	Nashville	TN	37243	615-741-2904	
Web: www.state.tn.us/tra					
Regulatory Boards Div 500 James Robertson Pkwy	Nashville	TN	37243	615-741-3449	741-6470
Web: www.tn.gov					
Rehabilitation Services Div 400 Deaderick St 11th Fl	Nashville	TN	37248	615-313-4700	741-4165
Web: www.tn.gov					
Revenue Dept 500 Deaderick St	Nashville	TN	37242	615-741-2461	741-0682
Web: www.state.tn.us/revenue					
Secretary of State State Capitol 1st Fl	Nashville	TN	37243	615-741-2819	
Web: www.state.tn.us/sos					
Securities Div 500 James Robertson Pkwy Ste 680	Nashville	TN	37243	615-741-2947	532-8375
TF: 800-863-9117 ■ *Web:* www.tennessee.gov					
State Parks Div 401 Church St 7th Fl	Nashville	TN	37243	615-532-0001	
TF: 888-867-2757 ■ *Web:* tnstateparks.com					
Student Assistance Corp 404 James Robertson Pkwy Ste 1510	Nashville	TN	37243	615-741-1346	741-6101
Web: www.state.tn.us/tsac					
Supreme Court 511 Union St Nashville City Ctr Ste 600	Nashville	TN	37219	615-741-2687	
TF: 800-448-7970 ■ *Web:* www.tsc.state.tn.us					
Title & Registration Div 44 Vantage Way Ste 160	Nashville	TN	37243	615-741-3101	
Web: www.tn.gov/revenue/vehicle					
Tourist Development Dept 312 Eigth Ave N 25th Fl	Nashville	TN	37243	615-741-2159	741-7225
Web: www.state.tn.us/tourdev					
Transportation Dept 505 Deaderick St Ste 700	Nashville	TN	37243	615-741-2848	741-2508
Web: www.tdot.state.tn.us					
Treasurer Tennessee State Capitol 1st Fl 600 Charlotte Ave	Nashville	TN	37243	615-741-2956	
Web: www.treasury.state.tn.us					
Treasury Dept 600 Charlotte Ave	Nashville	TN	37243	615-741-2956	
Web: www.treasury.state.tn.us					
Veterans Affairs Dept 312 Rosa L Parks Ave 13th Fl	Nashville	TN	37243	615-741-2931	
Web: www.state.tn.us/veteran					
Vital Records Div 421 Fifth Ave N 1st Fl	Nashville	TN	37247	615-741-1763	741-9860
Web: www.tn.gov					
Wildlife Resources Agency PO Box 40747	Nashville	TN	37204	615-781-6500	741-4606
Web: www.state.tn.us/twra					
Workers Compensation Div 220 French Landing Dr	Nashville	TN	37243	615-741-6642	
Web: tn.gov/maint/tngov/notfound.shtml					

342-44 Texas

	City	State	Zip	Phone	Fax
State Government Information 1501 N Congress Ste 4224	Austin	TX	78711	512-936-9500	936-9400
TF: 877-452-9060 ■ *Web:* www.texas.gov					
Aging & Disability Services 701 W 51st St Ste W253	Austin	TX	78751	512-438-3011	438-5885
TF: 888-388-6332					
Agriculture Dept PO Box 12847	Austin	TX	78711	512-463-7476	223-8861*
**Fax Area Code:* 888 ■ *TF Cust Svc:* 800-835-5832 ■ *Web:* texasagriculture.gov					
Arts Commission 920 Colorado Ste 501 PO Box 13406	Austin	TX	78701	512-463-5535	475-2699
TF: 800-252-9415 ■ *Web:* www.arts.texas.gov					
Assistive & Rehabilitation Services Dept 4800 N Lamar Blvd 3rd Fl	Austin	TX	78756	512-706-7288	407-3251
Web: www.sorm.state.tx.us					
Attorney General PO Box 12548	Austin	TX	78711	512-463-2191	
Web: www.texasattorneygeneral.gov/					
Banking Dept 2601 N Lamar Blvd	Austin	TX	78705	512-475-1300	475-1313
TF: 877-276-5554 ■ *Web:* dob.texas.gov					
Child Support Div 300 W 15th St	Austin	TX	78701	512-460-6000	475-2994
TF: 800-252-8014 ■ *Web:* www.texasattorneygeneral.gov/					
Comptroller of Public Accounts 111 E 17th St	Austin	TX	78774	512-463-4600	475-0352
TF: 800-531-5441 ■ *Web:* www.cpa.state.tx.us					
Consumer Protection Div PO Box 12548	Austin	TX	78711	800-621-0508	
TF General: 800-621-0508 ■ *Web:* www.texasattorneygeneral.gov/consumer					
Crime Victims Services Div PO Box 12198	Austin	TX	78711	512-936-1200	320-8270
TF: 800-983-9933 ■ *Web:* www.texasattorneygeneral.gov/					
Criminal Justice Dept PO Box 13084	Austin	TX	78711	512-475-3250	305-9398
Web: www.tdcj.state.tx.us					
Economic Development PO Box 12428	Austin	TX	78711	512-936-0100	936-0080
Web: www.texaswideopenforbusiness.com					
Education Agency 1701 N Congress Ave	Austin	TX	78701	512-463-9734	463-9838
Web: www.tea.state.tx.us					
Emergency Management Div PO Box 4087	Austin	TX	78773	512-424-2138	424-2444
Web: dps.texas.gov					
Environmental Quality Commission (TCEQ) 12100 Pk 35 Cir PO Box 13087	Austin	TX	78711	512-239-1000	
TF: 800-735-2989 ■ *Web:* www.tceq.state.tx.us					
Ethics Commission 201 E 14th St 10th Fl	Austin	TX	78701	512-463-5800	463-5777
Web: www.ethics.state.tx.us					
Family & Protective Services Dept 701 W 51st St PO Box 149030	Austin	TX	78752	512-438-4800	438-3525
Web: www.dfps.state.tx.us					
General Land Office 1700 N Congress Ave Ste 935	Austin	TX	78701	512-463-5001	475-1558
TF: 800-998-4456 ■ *Web:* www.glo.texas.gov					
Governor PO Box 12428	Austin	TX	78711	512-463-2000	463-1849
TF: 800-843-5789 ■ *Web:* www.governor.state.tx.us					
Higher Education Coordinating Board 1200 E Anderson Ln	Austin	TX	78752	512-427-6101	427-6169
Web: www.thecb.state.tx.us					
Historical Commission 108 W 16th St	Austin	TX	78701	512-463-6100	463-8222
Web: www.thc.state.tx.us					
Housing & Community Affairs Dept 507 Sabine St PO Box 13941	Austin	TX	78711	512-475-3800	472-8526
Web: www.tdhca.state.tx.us					
Information Resources Dept 300 W 15th St Ste 1300	Austin	TX	78701	512-475-4700	475-4759
Web: www.dir.state.tx.us					
Insurance Dept 333 Guadalupe St PO Box 149104	Austin	TX	78714	512-463-6169	475-2005
TF: 800-252-3439 ■ *Web:* www.tdi.texas.gov					
Legislature State Capitol	Austin	TX	78711	512-463-0124	463-0694
Web: www.capitol.state.tx.us					
Licensing & Regulation Dept PO Box 12157	Austin	TX	78711	512-463-6599	475-2874
Web: tdlr.texas.gov/					
Lieutenant Governor David Dewhurst PO Box 12068	Austin	TX	78711	512-463-0001	463-0677
Web: www.ltgov.state.tx.us					
Medical Board PO Box 2018	Austin	TX	78768	512-305-7010	305-7008
TF Cust Svc: 800-248-4062 ■ *Web:* www.tmb.state.tx.us					
Motor Vehicle Div 4000 Jackson Ave PO Box 2293	Austin	TX	78731	888-368-4689	
TF: 888-368-4689 ■ *Web:* www.txdmv.gov					
Office of Court Administration 205 W 14th St Ste 600	Austin	TX	78711	512-463-1625	463-1648
Web: www.courts.state.tx.us					
Pardons & Parole Board PO Box 13401	Austin	TX	78701	512-936-6351	463-8120
Web: www.tdcj.state.tx.us/bpp					
Parks & Wildlife Dept 4200 Smith School Rd	Austin	TX	78744	512-389-4800	389-4814
TF: 800-792-1112 ■ *Web:* www.tpwd.state.tx.us					
Public Safety Dept 5805 N Lamar Blvd	Austin	TX	78752	512-424-2000	424-5708
Web: txdps.state.tx.us					
Public Utility Commission PO Box 13326	Austin	TX	78711	512-936-7000	936-7003
TF: 888-782-8477 ■ *Web:* www.puc.texas.gov					
Racing Commission 8505 Cross Pk Dr Ste 110	Austin	TX	78754	512-833-6699	833-6907
Web: txrc.state.tx.us					
Railroad Commission PO Box 12967	Austin	TX	78711	512-463-7131	463-7161
TF: 877-228-5740 ■ *Web:* www.rrc.state.tx.us					
Secretary of State PO Box 12887	Austin	TX	78711	512-463-5770	475-2761
Web: www.sos.state.tx.us					
State Securities Board 208 E Tenth St Fl 5	Austin	TX	78701	512-305-8300	305-8310
Web: www.ssb.state.tx.us					
Supreme Court 201 W 14th St Rm 104 PO Box 12248	Austin	TX	78711	512-463-1312	463-1365
Web: www.supreme.courts.state.tx.us					
Transportation Dept 125 E 11th St	Austin	TX	78701	512-463-8585	463-9896
Web: txdot.gov/					
Valadez Adolfo M MD 1100 W 49th St	Austin	TX	78756	512-458-7111	458-7750
Veterans Commission PO Box 12277	Austin	TX	78711	512-463-5538	475-2395
TF: 800-252-8387 ■ *Web:* www.tvc.state.tx.us					
Vital Statistics Bureau 1100 W 49th St PO Box 12040	Austin	TX	78756	888-963-7111	458-7111*
**Fax Area Code:* 512 ■ *TF:* 888-963-7111 ■ *Web:* www.dshs.state.tx.us/VS					
Workers Compensation Commission 7551 Metro Ctr Dr	Austin	TX	78744	512-804-4000	804-4001
TF Cust Svc: 800-252-7031 ■ *Web:* tdi.texas.gov					
Workforce Commission 101 E 15th St	Austin	TX	78778	512-463-2222	
Web: twc.state.tx.us					

342-45 Utah

	City	State	Zip	Phone	Fax
Administrative Office of the Courts PO Box 140241	Salt Lake City	UT	84114	801-578-3800	578-3843
Web: www.utcourts.gov					
Aging & Adult Services Div 195 N 1950 W Rm 325	Salt Lake City	UT	84116	801-538-3910	538-4395
TF: 877-424-4640 ■ *Web:* www.hsdaas.utah.gov					
Agriculture & Food Dept 350 N Redwood Rd	Salt Lake City	UT	84116	801-538-7100	538-7126
Web: www.ag.utah.gov					
Arts Council 617 E S Temple	Salt Lake City	UT	84102	801-236-7555	236-7556
Web: heritage.utah.gov					

				Phone	Fax
Attorney General PO Box 142320 *Web:* www.attorneygeneral.utah.gov	Salt Lake City	UT	84114	801-538-9600	538-1121
Child & Family Services Div 195 N 1950 W Rm 225 *TF:* 855-323-3237 ■ *Web:* dcfs.utah.gov/	Salt Lake City	UT	84116	801-538-4100	538-3993
Child Support Div 515 E 100 S 8th Fl *Web:* attorneygeneral.utah.gov/childsupport.html	Salt Lake City	UT	84102	801-536-8300	536-8315
Commerce Dept 160 E Broadway Ste 4 *Web:* www.commerce.utah.gov	Salt Lake City	UT	84111	801-530-6701	530-6446
Community & Economic Development Dept 60 E S Temple 3rd Fl *TF:* 855-204-9046 ■ *Web:* business.utah.gov	Salt Lake City	UT	84111	801-538-8680	538-8888
Consumer Protection Div 160 E Broadway *Web:* www.commerce.utah.gov	Salt Lake City	UT	84111	801-530-6601	530-6001
Corrections Dept 14717 S Minuteman Dr. *Web:* www.corrections.utah.gov	Draper	UT	84020	801-545-5500	
Crime Victim Reparations Office 350 E 500 S Ste 200 *Web:* www.crimevictim.utah.gov	Salt Lake City	UT	84111	801-238-2360	533-4127
Education Office 250 E 500 S *Web:* schools.utah.gov	Salt Lake City	UT	84111	801-538-7500	538-7521
Emergency Services & Homeland Security Div 1110 State Office Bldg *Web:* publicsafety.utah.gov	Salt Lake City	UT	84114	801-538-3400	538-3770
Environmental Quality Dept 195 N 1950 W *TF:* 800-458-0145 ■ *Web:* www.deq.utah.gov	Salt Lake City	UT	84116	801-536-4400	536-0061
Financial Institutions Dept PO Box 146800 *Web:* www.dfi.utah.gov	Salt Lake City	UT	84111	801-538-8830	538-8894
Governor 350 N State St Ste 200 PO Box 142220 *TF:* 800-705-2464 ■ *Web:* www.utah.gov/governor	Salt Lake City	UT	84114	801-538-1000	538-1528
Health Dept PO Box 141010 *Web:* www.health.utah.gov	Salt Lake City	UT	84114	801-538-6003	
Higher Education Assistance Authority PO Box 145112 *TF:* 877-336-7378 ■ *Web:* www.uheaa.org	Salt Lake City	UT	84114	801-321-7294	366-8431
Higher Education System 60 S 400 W *Web:* www.utahsbr.edu	Salt Lake City	UT	84101	801-321-7101	321-7199
Highway Patrol 4501 S 2700 W *Web:* www.utah.gov	Salt Lake City	UT	84119	801-965-4518	
Housing Corp 2479 Lake Pk Blvd *Web:* www.utahhousingcorp.org	West Valley City	UT	84120	801-902-8200	
Human Resource Management Dept State Office Bldg Ste 2120 *Web:* www.dhrm.utah.gov	Salt Lake City	UT	84114	801-538-3025	538-3403
Human Services Dept 195 N 1950 W *Web:* hs.utah.gov/	Salt Lake City	UT	84116	801-538-4171	538-4016
Insurance Dept 3110 State Office Bldg *Web:* www.insurance.utah.gov	Salt Lake City	UT	84114	801-538-3800	538-3829
Labor Commission PO Box 146600 *TF:* 800-530-5090 ■ *Web:* www.laborcommission.utah.gov	Salt Lake City	UT	84114	801-530-6800	530-6390
Legislature State Capitol Complex W Bldg *Web:* www.le.utah.gov	Salt Lake City	UT	84114	801-538-1029	538-1908
Lieutenant Governor PO Box 142325 **Fax Area Code:* 801 ■ *TF:* 800-705-2464 ■ *Web:* www.utah.gov/ltgovernor	Salt Lake City	UT	84114	800-705-2464	538-1133*
Medical Examiner's Office (OME) 48 Medical Dr *Web:* health.utah.gov/ome	Salt Lake City	UT	84113	801-584-8410	584-8435
Motor Vehicle Div PO Box 30412 *TF:* 800-368-8824 ■ *Web:* dmv.utah.gov	Salt Lake City	UT	84130	801-297-7780	297-3570
Natural Resources Dept 1594 W N Temple Ste 3710 *Web:* seis.utah.edu	Salt Lake City	UT	84116	801-538-7200	538-7315
Occupational & Professional Licensing Div PO Box 146741 *TF:* 866-275-3675 ■ *Web:* www.dopl.utah.gov	Salt Lake City	UT	84111	801-530-6628	530-6511
Office of Tourism 300 N State St *TF:* 800-200-1160 ■ *Web:* www.travel.utah.gov	Salt Lake City	UT	84114	801-538-1900	538-1399
Pardons & Parole Board 448 E Winchester St Ste 300 *Web:* bop.utah.gov	Murray	UT	84107	801-261-6464	261-6481
Parks & Recreation Div 1594 W N Temple Ste 116 *TF:* 800-322-3770 ■ *Web:* www.stateparks.utah.gov	Salt Lake City	UT	84116	801-538-7220	538-7378
Public Service Commission 160 E 300 S PO Box 45585 *Web:* www.psc.state.ut.us	Salt Lake City	UT	84114	801-530-6716	530-6796
Real Estate Div PO Box 146711 *Web:* realestate.utah.gov	Salt Lake City	UT	84114	801-530-6747	526-4387
Rehabilitation Office 250 E 500 S *TF:* 800-473-7530 ■ *Web:* www.usor.utah.gov	Salt Lake City	UT	84111	801-538-7530	538-7522
Securities Div 160 E Broadway Ste 2 *Web:* securities.utah.gov	Salt Lake City	UT	84111	801-530-6600	530-6980
Sports Commission 201 S Main St Ste 2002 *Web:* www.utahsportscommission.com	Salt Lake City	UT	84111	801-328-2372	328-2389
State Treasurer 315 State Capitol Bldg Ste E *Web:* www.utah.gov	Salt Lake City	UT	84114	801-538-1042	538-1465
Supreme Court 450 S State St *Web:* www.utcourts.gov/courts/sup	Salt Lake City	UT	84114	801-238-7967	
Tax Commission 210 N 1950 W *Web:* www.tax.utah.gov	Salt Lake City	UT	84134	801-297-2200	297-3891
Technology Services Dept 1 State Office Bldg Fl 6 *Web:* www.dts.utah.gov	Salt Lake City	UT	84114	801-537-9000	538-3622
Transportation Dept 4501 S 2700 W PO Box 141265 *Web:* www.udot.utah.gov	Salt Lake City	UT	84119	801-965-4000	965-4338
Veterans' Affairs Office 550 Foothills Blvd Ste 206 *Web:* veterans.utah.gov	Salt Lake City	UT	84108	801-326-2372	326-2369
Vital Records & Statistics Office 288 N 1460 W PO Box 141012 *Web:* www.health.utah.gov/vitalrecords	Salt Lake City	UT	84114	801-538-6105	
Wildlife Resources Div 1594 W N Temple *Web:* wildlife.utah.gov	Salt Lake City	UT	84116	801-538-4700	
Workers Compensation Fund 100 W Towne Ridge Pkwy *TF:* 800-446-2667 ■ *Web:* www.wcfgroup.com	Sandy	UT	84070	385-351-8000	351-8372

342-46 Vermont

				Phone	Fax
State Government Information 535 Stone Cutters Way Fl 3 Ste 2 *Web:* www.vermont.gov	Montpelier	VT	05602	802-828-1110	
Aging & Disabilities Dept 103 S Main St *Web:* www.dail.vermont.gov	Waterbury	VT	05671	802-241-2401	241-2325
Agriculture Food & Markets Dept 116 State St *Web:* agriculture.vermont.gov	Montpelier	VT	05620	802-828-2430	828-2361
Arts Council 136 State St *Web:* www.vermontartscouncil.org	Montpelier	VT	05633	802-828-3291	828-3363
Attorney General 109 State St *Web:* www.state.vt.us	Montpelier	VT	05609	802-828-3171	828-2154
Banking Div 89 Main St *Web:* www.dfr.vermont.gov	Montpelier	VT	05620	802-828-3307	828-1477
Bill Status 115 State St State House *Web:* www.leg.state.vt.us	Montpelier	VT	05633	802-828-2231	828-2424
Board of Medical Practice 108 Cherry St PO Box 70 *Web:* healthvermont.gov	Burlington	VT	05402	802-657-4220	657-4227
Chief Medical Examiner 111 Colchester Ave *Web:* healthvermont.gov/hc/med_exam/med_index.aspx	Burlington	VT	05401	802-863-7320	
Children & Families Dept 103 S Main St 2nd Fl 5 N *TF:* 800-786-3214 ■ *Web:* dcf.vermont.gov	Waterbury	VT	05671	802-241-2100	241-2407
Consumer Assistance Program 146 University Pl *TF:* 800-649-2424 ■ *Web:* www.atg.state.vt.us	Burlington	VT	05405	802-656-3183	656-1423
Corrections Dept 103 S Main St *Web:* www.doc.state.vt.us	Waterbury	VT	05671	802-241-2442	241-2565
Court Administrator 111 State St *Web:* www.vermontjudiciary.org	Montpelier	VT	05609	802-828-3278	828-3457
Crime Victim Services Ctr 58 S Main St *Web:* www.ccvs.state.vt.us	Waterbury	VT	05676	802-241-1250	241-4337
Economic Development Dept PO Box 20 *Web:* accd.vermont.gov	Montpelier	VT	05601	802-828-3080	828-3258
Education Dept 120 State St *Web:* www.state.vt.us	Montpelier	VT	05620	802-828-3135	828-3140
Educator Licensing Div 120 State St *Web:* education.vermont.gov	Montpelier	VT	05620	802-828-2445	828-5107
Emergency Management Office 103 S Main St *TF:* 800-347-0488 ■ *Web:* dps.vermont.gov	Waterbury	VT	05671	802-241-5000	241-5556
Environmental Conservation Dept 1 National Life Drive Main 2 *Web:* www.anr.state.vt.us/dec/dec.htm	Montpelier	VT	05620	802-828-1556	244-5141
Fish & Wildlife Dept 103 S Main St Bldg 10S *Web:* www.anr.state.vt.us	Waterbury	VT	05671	802-241-3700	241-3295
General Assembly 115 State St *Web:* www.leg.state.vt.us	Montpelier	VT	05633	802-828-2228	828-2424
Governor 109 State St 5th Fl *Web:* www.vermont.gov	Montpelier	VT	05609	802-828-3333	828-3339
Health Dept 108 Cherry St *Web:* www.healthvermont.gov	Burlington	VT	05402	802-863-7200	865-7754
Historic Preservation Div National Life Bldg 6th Fl *TF:* 800-639-1522 ■ *Web:* accd.vermont.gov	Montpelier	VT	05620	802-828-3213	828-3206
Insurance Div 89 Main St *Web:* www.dfr.vermont.gov	Montpelier	VT	05620	802-828-3301	
Labor Dept 5 Green Mountain Dr PO Box 488 *Web:* www.labor.vermont.gov	Montpelier	VT	05601	802-828-4000	828-4022
Licensing & Professional Regulation Office National Life Bldg N 2nd Fl *Web:* www.vtprofessionals.org	Montpelier	VT	05620	802-828-2367	828-2368
Lieutenant Governor State House *Web:* www.ltgov.vermont.gov	Montpelier	VT	05633	802-828-2226	828-3198
Lottery Commission 1311 US Rt 302 Ste 100 *Web:* wherezit.com	Barre	VT	05641	802-479-5686	479-4294
Motor Vehicles Dept 120 State St *Web:* dmv.vermont.gov	Montpelier	VT	05603	802-828-2000	828-2098
Natural Resources Agency 103 S Main St *Web:* www.anr.state.vt.us	Waterbury	VT	05671	802-241-3600	244-1102
Public Service Board 112 State St 4th Fl *Web:* www.state.vt.us/psb	Montpelier	VT	05620	802-828-2358	828-3351
Secretary of State 128 State St Drawer 9 **Fax Area Code:* 800 ■ *Web:* www.sec.state.vt.us	Montpelier	VT	05633	802-828-2363	439-8683*
Securities Div 89 Main St *Web:* www.dfr.vermont.gov	Montpelier	VT	05620	802-828-3420	828-2896
State Police 103 S Main St *Web:* vsp.vermont.gov	Waterbury	VT	05671	802-241-5000	241-5551
Supreme Court 111 State St *Web:* www.vermontjudiciary.org	Montpelier	VT	05609	802-828-3278	828-3457

Phone Fax

Taxes Dept 133 State St ..... Montpelier VT 05609 802-828-2505 828-2701
Web: www.state.vt.us/tax

Tourism & Marketing Dept
6 Baldwin St PO Box 22 ..... Montpelier VT 05633 802-828-3168 828-3163
Web: www.vermontvacation.com

Transportation Agency 1 National Life Dr ..... Montpelier VT 05633 802-828-2657 828-2024
Web: vtrans.vermont.gov

Treasurer 109 State St 4th Fl ..... Montpelier VT 05609 802-828-2301 828-2772
Web: www.vermonttreasurer.gov

Veterans Affairs Office 118 State St ..... Montpelier VT 05602 802-828-3379 828-5932
TF: 888-666-9844 ■ *Web:* www.veterans.vermont.gov/ova

Vital Records Section PO Box 70 ..... Burlington VT 05402 802-863-7275 651-1787
Web: www.healthvermont.gov

Vocational Rehabilitation Div
103 S Main St ..... Waterbury VT 05671 802-241-2186 241-3359
TF: 866-879-6757 ■ *Web:* www.vocrehab.vermont.gov

Workers Compensation Div
5 Green Mountain Dr ..... Montpelier VT 05601 802-828-2286 828-2195
Web: www.labor.vermont.gov

342-47 Virginia

Phone Fax

Aging & Rehabilitative Services Dept
8004 Franklin Farms Dr ..... Richmond VA 23229 804-662-7000 662-9532
TF: 800-552-5019 ■ *Web:* www.vadrs.org

Aging Dept 1610 Forest Ave # 100 ..... Richmond VA 23229 804-662-9333 662-9354
Web: www.vda.virginia.gov

Agriculture & Consumer Services Dept
1100 Bank St Ste 210 ..... Richmond VA 23219 804-786-3501 371-2945
Web: www.vdacs.virginia.gov

Arts Commission 223 Governor St 2nd Fl ..... Richmond VA 23219 804-225-3132 225-4327
Web: arts.virginia.gov

Attorney General 900 E Main St ..... Richmond VA 23219 804-786-2071 786-1991
Web: www.oag.state.va.us

Chief Medical Examiner 400 E Jackson St ..... Richmond VA 23219 804-786-3174 371-8595
Web: www.vdh.virginia.gov/medexam

Child Support Enforcement Div
730 E Broad St ..... Richmond VA 23219 800-468-8894
TF: 800-468-8894 ■ *Web:* www.dss.state.va.us

Community College System
101 N 14th St 15th Fl ..... Richmond VA 23219 804-819-4901 819-4766
Web: www.vccs.edu

Corrections Dept 6900 Atmore Dr ..... Richmond VA 23225 804-674-3000 674-3509
Web: vadoc.virginia.gov

Criminal Injuries Compensation Fund (CICF)
PO Box 26927 ..... Richmond VA 23261 800-552-4007 367-1021*
**Fax Area Code:* 804 ■ *TF:* 800-552-4007 ■ *Web:* www.cicf.state.va.us

Economic Development Partnership
901 E Byrd St ..... Richmond VA 23219 804-371-8100 371-8112
Web: www.yesvirginia.org

Education Dept PO Box 2120 ..... Richmond VA 23218 804-225-2020 371-2099
Web: www.pen.k12.va.us

Emergency Management Dept 10501 Trade Ct ..... Richmond VA 23236 804-897-6500 897-6506
Web: vaemergency.gov

Employment Commission 703 E Main St ..... Richmond VA 23219 804-786-1485 225-3923
Web: www.vec.virginia.gov

Environmental Quality Dept 629 E Main St ..... Richmond VA 23240 804-698-4000 698-4500
Web: www.deq.state.va.us

Financial Institutions Bureau
1300 E Main St Ste 800 PO Box 640 ..... Richmond VA 23218 804-371-9657 371-9416
Web: www.scc.virginia.gov

Game & Inland Fisheries Dept
4010 W Broad St ..... Richmond VA 23230 804-367-1000 367-0405
Web: www.dgif.virginia.gov

General Assembly
General Assembly Bldg 1000 Bank St ..... Richmond VA 23219 804-698-1788
Web: virginiageneralassembly.gov

Governor 1111 E Broad St PO Box 1475 ..... Richmond VA 23219 804-786-2211 371-6351
TF: 800-828-1120 ■ *Web:* www.governor.virginia.gov

Health Dept 109 Governor St Ste 13 ..... Richmond VA 23219 804-864-7001 864-7022
Web: www.vdh.virginia.gov

Health Professions Dept
9960 Mayland Dr Ste 300 ..... Henrico VA 23233 804-367-4400 527-4475
TF: 800-533-1560 ■ *Web:* www.dhp.virginia.gov

Historic Resources Dept 2801 Kensington Ave ..... Richmond VA 23221 804-367-2323 367-2391
Web: www.dhr.virginia.gov

Housing Development Authority
601 S Belvidere St ..... Richmond VA 23220 804-782-1986
TF: 800-968-7837 ■ *Web:* www.vhda.com

Human Resource Management Dept
101 N 14th St 12th Fl ..... Richmond VA 23219 804-225-2131 371-7401
Web: www.dhrm.virginia.gov

Information Technologies Agency (VITA)
11751 Meadowville Ln ..... Chester VA 23836 866-637-8482 416-6355*
**Fax Area Code:* 804 ■ *TF:* 866-637-8482 ■ *Web:* www.vita.virginia.gov

Labor & Industry Dept
Main St Centre Bldg 600 E Main St Ste 207 ..... Richmond VA 23219 804-371-2327 371-6524
Web: www.doli.virginia.gov

Lieutenant Governor 102 Governor St 1st Fl W ..... Richmond VA 23219 804-786-2078 786-7514
Web: www.ltgov.virginia.gov

Lottery 900 E Main St ..... Richmond VA 23219 804-692-7777 692-7775
Web: www.valottery.com

Mental Health Mental Retardation & Substance Abuse Services Dept
1220 Bank St ..... Richmond VA 23219 804-786-3921 371-6638
Web: www.dbhds.virginia.gov

Parole Board 6900 Atmore Dr ..... Richmond VA 23225 804-674-3081 674-3284
Web: vpb.virginia.gov

Port Authority 101 W Main St ..... Norfolk VA 23510 757-683-8000 683-8500
Web: www.portofvirginia.com

Professional & Occupational Regulation Dept
9960 Mayland Dr # 400 ..... Richmond VA 23233 804-367-8500
Web: www.dpor.virginia.gov

Racing Commission 10700 Horsemen's Rd ..... New Kent VA 23124 804-966-7400 966-7418
Web: www.vrc.virginia.gov

Secretary of Commerce & Trade
1111 E Broad St PO Box 1475 ..... Richmond VA 23219 804-786-7831 371-0250
Web: www.commerce.virginia.gov

Secretary of the Commonwealth
830 E Main St 14th Fl ..... Richmond VA 23219 804-786-2441 371-0017
Web: commonwealth.virginia.gov

Social Services Dept 801 E Main St ..... Richmond VA 23219 804-726-7000
Web: www.dss.state.va.us

State Corp Commission
1300 E Main St PO Box 1197 ..... Richmond VA 23218 804-371-9967 371-9836
Web: www.scc.virginia.gov

State Council of Higher Education
101 N 14th St 9th Fl ..... Richmond VA 23219 804-225-2600 225-2604
Web: www.schev.edu

State Parks Div 203 Governor St Ste 306 ..... Richmond VA 23219 800-933-7275
TF Resv: 800-933-7275 ■ *Web:* dcr.virginia.gov/state-parks

State Police 7700 Midlothian Tpke ..... Richmond VA 23235 804-674-2000 674-2936
Web: www.vsp.state.va.us

Supreme Court 100 N Ninth St ..... Richmond VA 23219 804-786-2251 786-6249
Web: vcsc.virginia.gov

Taxation Dept 3610 W Broad St Ste 101 ..... Richmond VA 23230 804-367-8031 786-3536
Web: www.tax.virginia.gov

Treasury Dept 101 N 14th St Ste 4th ..... Richmond VA 23219 804-225-2142 225-3187
Web: www.trs.virginia.gov

Vital Records Div
2001 Maywill St PO Box 1000 ..... Richmond VA 23230 804-662-6200 644-2550
TF: 877-572-6333 ■ *Web:* www.vdh.virginia.gov/vitalrec

Workers Compensation Commission 1000 DMV Dr ..... Richmond VA 23220 804-205-3603 367-9740
Web: www.vwc.state.va.us

342-48 Washington

Phone Fax

Administrative Office of the Courts
1112 Quince St SE PO Box 41174 ..... Olympia WA 98501 360-753-3365

Aging & Disability Services Administration
PO Box 45600 ..... Olympia WA 98504 360-725-2300 407-0369
Web: www.altsa.dshs.wa.gov

Agriculture Dept PO Box 42560 ..... Olympia WA 98504 360-902-1800 902-2092
Web: www.agr.wa.gov

Arts Commission 711 Capitol Way S Ste 600 ..... Olympia WA 98504 360-753-3860 586-5351
Web: www.arts.wa.gov

Attorney General PO Box 40100 ..... Olympia WA 98504 360-753-6200 664-0228
Web: www.atg.wa.gov

Bill Status PO Box 40600 ..... Olympia WA 98504 360-786-7573
TF: 800-562-6000 ■ *Web:* www.leg.wa.gov

Child Support Div PO Box 11520 ..... Olympia WA 98411 800-442-5437 586-3274*
**Fax Area Code:* 360 ■ *Web:* www.dshs.wa.gov

Consumer Protection Div
1125 Washington St SE PO Box 40100 ..... Olympia WA 98504 360-753-6200
Web: www.atg.wa.gov/page.aspx?id=1792

Corrections Dept PO Box 41100 ..... Olympia WA 98504 360-725-8213 664-4056
Web: www.doc.wa.gov

Ecology Dept PO Box 47600 ..... Olympia WA 98504 360-407-6000 407-6989
Web: www.ecy.wa.gov

Emergency Management Div
20 Aviation Dr Bldg 20 TA-20 ..... Camp Murray WA 98430 253-512-7000
Web: mil.wa.gov

Employment Security Dept 212 Maple Pk Ave SE ..... Olympia WA 98504 360-902-9500
Web: www.esd.wa.gov

Financial Institutions Dept PO Box 41200 ..... Olympia WA 98504 360-902-8703
TF: 877-746-4334 ■ *Web:* www.dfi.wa.gov/cs

Fish & Wildlife Dept 600 Capitol Way N ..... Olympia WA 98501 360-902-2200 902-2156
Web: www.wdfw.wa.gov

Governor PO Box 40002 ..... Olympia WA 98504 360-902-4111 753-4110
Web: www.governor.wa.gov

Health Dept PO Box 47890 ..... Olympia WA 98504 360-236-4501 586-7424
TF: 800-525-0127 ■ *Web:* www.doh.wa.gov

Higher Education Coordinating Board
917 Lakeridge Way PO Box 43430 ..... Olympia WA 98504 360-753-7800 753-7808
Web: www.wsac.wa.gov

Historical Society 1911 Pacific Ave ..... Tacoma WA 98402 253-272-3500 272-9518
TF: 888-238-4373 ■ *Web:* www.washingtonhistory.org

Horse Racing Commission
6326 Martin Way Ste 209 ..... Olympia WA 98516 360-459-6462 459-6461
Web: www.whrc.wa.gov

Housing Finance Commission
1000 Second Ave Ste 2700 ..... Seattle WA 98104 206-464-7139 587-5113
TF: 800-767-4663 ■ *Web:* www.wshfc.org

Indeterminate Sentence Review Board
PO Box 40907 ..... Olympia WA 98504 360-493-9266 493-9287
Web: www.doc.wa.gov

Information Services Dept PO Box 42445 ..... Olympia WA 98504 360-902-3550
Web: www.governor.wa.gov

Insurance Commissioner PO Box 40255 ..... Olympia WA 98504 360-725-7000 586-3535
Web: www.insurance.wa.gov

Labor & Industries Dept PO Box 44000 ..... Olympia WA 98504 360-902-5800 902-4202
Web: www.lni.wa.gov

Legislature 106 Legislative Bldg ..... Olympia WA 98504 360-786-7550 786-7520
Web: www.leg.wa.gov

Licensing Dept PO Box 9020 ..... Olympia WA 98504 360-902-3600 902-4042
Web: www.dol.wa.gov

Agency / Address	City	State	ZIP	Phone	Fax
Lieutenant Governor 416 Sid Snyder Ave SW *Web:* www.ltgov.wa.gov	Olympia	WA	98501	360-786-7700	786-7749
Natural Resources Dept 1111 Washington St SE PO Box 47000 *TF:* 800-258-5990 ■ *Web:* www.dnr.wa.gov	Olympia	WA	98504	360-902-1000	
Office of Superintendent Public Instruction Dept 600 Washington St SE PO Box 47200 *Web:* www.k12.wa.us	Olympia	WA	98504	360-725-6000	753-6712
Personnel Dept 1500 Jefferson St S PO Box 44530 *Web:* www.hr.wa.gov	Olympia	WA	98504	360-407-9100	407-9178
Professional Educator Standards Board PO Box 47236 *Web:* www.pesb.wa.gov	Olympia	WA	98504	360-725-6275	586-4548
Public Disclosure Commission PO Box 40908 *Web:* www.pdc.wa.gov	Olympia	WA	98504	360-753-1111	753-1112
Revenue Dept PO Box 47478 *TF:* 800-647-7706 ■ *Web:* dor.wa.gov	Olympia	WA	98504	360-705-6714	705-6655
Secretary of State PO Box 40220 *Web:* www.sos.wa.gov	Olympia	WA	98504	360-902-4151	586-5629
Securities Div PO Box 9033 *Web:* www.dfi.wa.gov/sd	Olympia	WA	98507	360-902-8760	902-0524
Social & Health Services Dept PO Box 45130 *TF:* 800-737-0617 ■ *Web:* www.wa.gov/dshs	Olympia	WA	98504	360-902-8400	902-7848
State Lottery PO Box 43000 *TF:* 800-732-5101 ■ *Web:* www.walottery.com	Olympia	WA	98504	360-664-4720	664-2630
State Parks & Recreation Commission 1111 Israel Rd SW *TF Campground Resv:* 888-226-7688 ■ *Web:* www.parks.wa.gov	Olympia	WA	98504	360-902-8500	
State Patrol PO Box 42600 **Fax:* Hum Res ■ *Web:* www.wsp.wa.gov	Olympia	WA	98504	360-753-6540	704-2297*
Supreme Court 415 12th Ave SW *Web:* www.courts.wa.gov	Olympia	WA	98501	360-357-2077	
Transportation Dept PO Box 47300 *Web:* www.wsdot.wa.gov	Olympia	WA	98504	360-705-7000	705-6800
Treasurer 416 Sid Snyder Ave SW Rm 230 PO Box 40200 *Web:* www.tre.wa.gov	Olympia	WA	98504	360-902-9000	902-9044
Utilities & Transportation Commission 1300 S Evergreen Pk Dr SW PO Box 47250 *TF:* 888-333-9882 ■ *Web:* www.utc.wa.gov	Olympia	WA	98504	360-664-1160	664-1150
Veterans Affairs Dept PO Box 41150 *TF:* 800-562-2308 ■ *Web:* www.dva.wa.gov	Olympia	WA	98504	360-753-5586	725-2197
Vital Records Div PO Box 47814 *Web:* www.cdc.gov/nchs/w2w.htm	Olympia	WA	98504	360-236-4300	
Vocational Rehabilitation Div PO Box 45340 *TF:* 800-637-5627 ■ *Web:* www.dshs.wa.gov	Olympia	WA	98504	360-438-8000	438-8007

342-49 West Virginia

Agency / Address	City	State	ZIP	Phone	Fax
State Government Information 100 Dee Dr *Web:* www.wv.gov	Charleston	WV	25311	304-558-3456	
Accountancy Board 405 Capitol St Ste 908 *Web:* www.boa.wv.gov	Charleston	WV	25301	304-558-3557	558-1325
Administrative Office of the Courts 1900 Kanawha Blvd E Bldg 1 Rm E-100 *Web:* www.state.wv.us	Charleston	WV	25305	304-558-0145	558-1212
Agriculture Dept 1900 Kanawha Blvd E Bldg 1 Rm E-28 *Web:* www.wvagriculture.org	Charleston	WV	25305	304-558-2201	558-2203
Arts Commission 1900 Kanawha Blvd E Cultural Ctr *Web:* www.wvculture.org/arts	Charleston	WV	25305	304-558-0220	558-2779
Attorney General 1900 Kanawha Blvd E Bldg 1 Rm 26-E *Web:* ago.wv.gov	Charleston	WV	25305	304-558-2021	558-0140
Bill Status State Capitol Complex Rm MB27 Bldg 1 *TF:* 877-565-3447 ■ *Web:* www.legis.state.wv.us	Charleston	WV	25305	304-347-4836	347-4901
Board of Medicine 101 Dee Dr Ste 103 *Web:* www.wvdhhr.org	Charleston	WV	25311	304-558-2921	558-2084
Bureau for Public Health 350 Capitol St Rm 702 *Web:* www.wvdhhr.org/bph	Charleston	WV	25301	304-558-2971	558-1035
Child Support Enforcement Bureau 231 Capitol St Ste 111 *TF:* 800-571-4864 ■ *Web:* www.wv-childsupport.com	Charleston	WV	25301	304-347-8688	720-9666
Children & Families Bureau 350 Capitol St Rm R-730 *TF:* 800-642-8589 ■ *Web:* www.wvdhhr.org/bcf	Charleston	WV	25301	304-558-0628	558-4194
Community Development Div 1900 Kanawha Blvd E *TF:* 800-982-3386 ■ *Web:* www.wvcommerce.org	Charleston	WV	25311	304-558-2234	
Consumer Protection Div 812 Quarrier St 1st Fl *TF:* 800-368-8808 ■ *Web:* www.ago.wv.gov	Charleston	WV	25301	304-558-8986	558-0184
Corrections Div 112 California Ave Bldg 4 Rm 300 *Web:* www.wvdoc.com	Charleston	WV	25305	304-558-2036	558-5367
Crime Victims Compensation Fund 1900 Kanawha Blvd E Rm W-334 *TF:* 877-562-6878 ■ *Web:* www.legis.state.wv.us	Charleston	WV	25305	304-347-4850	347-4915
Development Office 1900 Kanawah Blvd E Bldg 6 Rm 525B *TF:* 800-982-3386 ■ *Web:* www.wvcommerce.org	Charleston	WV	25305	304-558-2234	558-1189
Education Dept 1900 Kanawha Blvd E Bldg 6 Rm 358	Charleston	WV	25305	304-558-2681	558-0048
Emergency Services Office 1900 Kanawha Blvd E	Charleston	WV	25305	304-558-5380	
Environmental Protection Dept 601 57th St SE *Web:* www.dep.wv.gov	Charleston	WV	25304	304-926-0440	926-0446
Ethics Commission 210 Brooks St Ste 300 *TF:* 866-558-0664 ■ *Web:* www.ethics.wv.gov	Charleston	WV	25301	304-558-0664	558-2169
Higher Education Policy Commission 1018 Kanawha Blvd E Ste 700 *TF:* 888-825-5707 ■ *Web:* wvhepc.com	Charleston	WV	25301	304-558-2101	
Historic Preservation Unit 1900 Kanawha Blvd E *Web:* www.wvculture.org/shpo	Charleston	WV	25305	304-558-0220	558-2779
Housing Development Fund 814 Virginia St E *TF:* 800-933-9843 ■ *Web:* www.wvhdf.com	Charleston	WV	25301	304-345-6475	
Insurance Commission PO Box 50540 *TF:* 888-879-9842 ■ *Web:* www.wvinsurance.gov	Charleston	WV	25305	304-558-3354	558-0412
Labor Div Capitol Complex 749 B Bldg 6 *Web:* wvlabor.com	Charleston	WV	25305	304-558-7890	558-2415
Lottery 900 Pennsylvania Ave *Web:* www.wvlottery.com/	Charleston	WV	25302	304-558-0500	
Motor Vehicles Div 5707 Maccorkle Ave SE Ste 400 *TF:* 800-642-9066 ■ *Web:* www.transportation.wv.gov	Charleston	WV	25304	304-558-3900	
Natural Resources Div 324 Fourth Ave Bldg 74 *Web:* www.wvdnr.gov	South Charleston	WV	25303	304-558-2754	558-2768
Office of Governor State Capitol Bldg 1900 Kanawha Blvd E *Web:* www.governor.wv.gov	Charleston	WV	25305	304-558-2000	558-1558
Office of Technology 321-323 Capitol St *Web:* www.technology.wv.gov	Charleston	WV	25304	304-558-5472	
Probation & Parole Board 1409 Greenbrier Ste 220 *Web:* paroleboard.wv.gov	Charleston	WV	25311	304-558-6366	558-5678
Public Service Commission 208 Brooke St PO Box 812 *TF:* 800-344-5113 ■ *Web:* www.psc.state.wv.us	Charleston	WV	25301	304-340-0300	340-0325
Racing Commission 900 Pennsylvania Ave Ste 533 *Web:* www.racing.wv.gov	Charleston	WV	25302	304-558-2150	558-6319
Real Estate Commission 300 Capitol St Ste 400 *Web:* www.wvrec.org	Charleston	WV	25301	304-558-3555	558-6442
Rehabilitation Services Div 107 Capitol St *TF:* 800-642-8207 ■ *Web:* www.wvdrs.org	Charleston	WV	25301	800-642-8207	642-3021
Revenue Dept State Capitol Bldg 1 Rm W-300 *Web:* www.revenue.wv.gov	Charleston	WV	25305	304-558-1017	558-2324
Secretary of State 1900 Kanawha Blvd E Bldg 1 Ste 157K *TF:* 866-767-8683 ■ *Web:* www.sos.wv.gov	Charleston	WV	25305	304-558-6000	558-0900
Securities Div 1900 Kanawha Blvd E Bldg 1 Rm W-100 *TF:* 877-982-9148 ■ *Web:* www.wvsao.gov	Charleston	WV	25305	304-558-2257	558-4211
State Legislature State Capitol Complex Rm MB-27 Bldg 1 *Web:* www.legis.state.wv.us	Charleston	WV	25305	304-347-4836	347-4901
State Parks & Forests 324 4th Ave *TF:* 800-225-5982 ■ *Web:* www.wvstateparks.com	Charleston	WV	25305	304-558-2764	558-0077
State Police 725 Jefferson Rd *Web:* www.wvsp.gov	South Charleston	WV	25309	304-746-2100	
Supreme Court of Appeals 1900 Kanawha Blvd E Bldg 1 Rm E-317 *Web:* www.courtswv.gov	Charleston	WV	25305	304-558-2601	558-3815
Tourism Div 90 MacCorkle Ave SW *TF:* 800-225-5982 ■ *Web:* www.wvtourism.com	Charleston	WV	25303	800-225-5982	
Transportation Dept 1900 Kanawha Blvd E Bldg 5 Rm A-109 *Web:* www.wv.gov/	Charleston	WV	25305	304-558-0444	558-1004
Treasurer 1900 Kanawha Blvd E Bldg 1 Ste E-145 *TF:* 800-422-7498 ■ *Web:* www.wvsto.com	Charleston	WV	25305	304-558-5000	558-4097
Veterans Affairs Div 1321 Plaza E Ste 101 *TF:* 888-838-2332 ■ *Web:* www.veterans.idaho.gov	Charleston	WV	25301	304-558-3661	558-3662
Vital Statistics 350 Capitol St Rm 165 *Web:* www.wvdhhr.org/bph/oehp/hsc/vr/birtcert.htm	Charleston	WV	25301	304-558-2931	558-1051
Weights & Measures Div 570 W MacCorkle Ave	Saint Albans	WV	25177	304-722-0602	722-0605

342-50 Wisconsin

Agency / Address	City	State	ZIP	Phone	Fax
Aging & Long Term Care Resources Bureau PO Box 7851 *Web:* www.dhs.wisconsin.gov	Madison	WI	53707	608-266-2536	267-3203
Agriculture Trade & Consumer Protection Dept PO Box 8911 *Web:* datcp.wi.gov	Madison	WI	53708	608-224-4889	
Attorney General PO Box 7857 *Web:* www.doj.state.wi.us	Madison	WI	53707	608-266-1221	267-2779
Bill Status 1 E Main St *TF:* 800-362-9472 ■ *Web:* legis.wisconsin.gov	Madison	WI	53708	608-266-9960	
Board of Regents 1220 Linden Dr 1860 Van Hise Hall *Web:* www.wisconsin.edu/bor	Madison	WI	53706	608-262-2324	262-5739
Child Support Bureau 201 E Washington Ave *Web:* dcf.wisconsin.gov/bcs	Madison	WI	53703	608-266-9909	267-2824

				Phone	Fax
Children & Family Services Div 201 E Washington Ave Second Fl PO Box 8916 *Web:* www.dcf.wi.gov	Madison	WI	53708	608-267-3905	266-6836
Consumer Protection Office 2811 Agriculture Dr PO Box 8911 *Web:* datcp.wi.gov	Madison	WI	53708	608-224-5012	
Corrections Dept PO Box 7925 *Web:* doc.wi.gov	Madison	WI	53707	608-240-5000	240-3300
Crime Victims Services Office PO Box 7951 *TF:* 800-446-6564 ■ *Web:* www.doj.state.wi.us	Madison	WI	53707	608-264-9497	264-6368
Director of State Courts 16E Capitol Bldg PO Box 1688 *Web:* www.wicourts.gov	Madison	WI	53701	608-266-6828	267-0980
Economic Development Div 201 W Washington Ave *Web:* inwisconsin.com	Madison	WI	53703	608-210-6700	
Emergency Management Div PO Box 7865 *Web:* www.emergencymanagement.wi.gov	Madison	WI	53707	608-242-3232	242-3247
Ethics Board 212 E Washington Ave 3rd Fl *Web:* www.gab.wi.gov	Madison	WI	53703	608-266-8123	264-9319
Fisheries Management PO Box 7921 *Web:* dnr.wi.gov/topic/Fishing	Madison	WI	53707	608-267-7498	266-2244
Health Professions Bureau Dept of Regulation & Licensing PO Box 8935 *Web:* dsps.wi.gov	Madison	WI	53708	608-266-2112	261-7083
Health Services Dept PO Box 7850 *Web:* www.dhs.wisconsin.gov	Madison	WI	53707	608-266-1865	266-7882
Historical Society 816 State St *Web:* www.wisconsinhistory.org	Madison	WI	53706	608-264-6400	
Housing & Economic Development Authority 201 W Washington Ave Ste 700 *TF:* 800-334-6873 ■ *Web:* www.wheda.com	Madison	WI	53703	608-266-7884	267-1099
Insurance Commission PO Box 7873 *TF:* 800-236-8517 ■ *Web:* www.oci.wi.gov	Madison	WI	53707	608-266-3585	266-9935
Legislature State Capitol *TF:* 800-362-9472 ■ *Web:* legis.wisconsin.gov	Madison	WI	53702	608-266-9960	
Lieutenant Governor 19 E State Capitol *Web:* legis.wisconsin.gov	Madison	WI	53702	608-266-3516	267-3571
Lottery PO Box 8941 *Web:* www.wilottery.com	Madison	WI	53708	608-261-4916	264-6644
Motor Vehicles Div 4802 Sheboygan Ave *Web:* www.dot.wisconsin.gov/drivers	Madison	WI	53707	608-266-2233	
Natural Resources Dept 101 S Webster St PO Box 7921 *Web:* dnr.wi.gov	Madison	WI	53707	608-266-2621	261-4380
Office of Governor PO Box 7863 *Web:* walker.wi.gov	Madison	WI	53707	608-266-1212	267-8983
Parks & Recreation Bureau 101 S Webster St PO Box 7921 *TF:* 888-936-7463 ■ *Web:* dnr.wi.gov	Madison	WI	53707	608-266-2621	261-4380
Public Instruction Dept 125 S Webster St PO Box 7841 *TF:* 800-441-4563 ■ *Web:* www.dpi.state.wi.us	Madison	WI	53707	608-266-3390	
Public Service Commission PO Box 610 N Whitney Way *Web:* psc.wi.gov	Madison	WI	53707	608-266-5481	266-3957
Revenue Dept 2135 Rimrock Rd PO Box 8933 *Web:* www.dor.state.wi.us	Madison	WI	53708	608-266-6466	266-5718
Safety & Professional Services Dept PO Box 8935 *Web:* dsps.wi.gov	Madison	WI	53708	608-266-2112	267-0644
Secretary of State 30 W Mifflin Fl 10 *Web:* www.sos.state.wi.us	Madison	WI	53703	608-266-8888	266-3159
Securities Div 201 W Washington Ave	Madison	WI	53703	608-266-1064	
State Patrol Div PO Box 7912 *Web:* www.dot.wisconsin.gov/statepatrol	Madison	WI	53707	608-266-3212	267-4495
Supreme Court 110 E Main St Ste 215 PO Box 1688 *Web:* www.wicourts.gov	Madison	WI	53701	608-266-1880	267-0640
Teacher Education & Licensing Bureau 125 S Webster St *TF:* 800-441-4563 ■ *Web:* www.dpi.state.wi.us	Madison	WI	53703	608-266-3390	264-9558
Treasurer PO Box 2114 **Fax Area Code:* 608 ■ *TF:* 855-375-2274 ■ *Web:* www.ost.state.wi.us	Madison	WI	53707	855-375-2274	261-6799*
Veterans Affairs Dept 201 W Washington Ave PO Box 7843 *TF:* 800-947-8387 ■ *Web:* www.dva.state.wi.us	Madison	WI	53703	608-266-1311	267-0403
Vital Records Office PO Box 309 *Web:* www.dhs.wisconsin.gov	Madison	WI	53701	608-266-1373	255-2035
Vocational Rehabilitation Div 201 East Washington Avenue PO Box 7852 *TF:* 800-442-3477 ■ *Web:* dwd.wisconsin.gov/	Madison	WI	53707	608-261-0050	266-1133
Worker's Compensation Div PO Box 7901 *Web:* dwd.wisconsin.gov	Madison	WI	53707	608-266-1340	267-0394
Workforce Development Dept 201 E Washington Ave *Web:* dwd.wisconsin.gov	Madison	WI	53702	608-266-3131	266-1784

342-51 Wyoming

				Phone	Fax
State Government Information State Capitol Bldg 200 W 24th St *Web:* ag.wyo.gov	Cheyenne	WY	82002	307-777-7841	777-6869
Aging Div 6101 Yellowstone Rd N Rm 259B *TF:* 800-442-2766 ■ *Web:* health.wyo.gov	Cheyenne	WY	82002	307-777-7986	777-5340
Agriculture Dept (WDA) 2219 Carey Ave *Web:* wyagric.state.wy.us	Cheyenne	WY	82002	307-777-7321	777-6593
Arts Council 2320 Capitol Ave *Web:* wyoarts.state.wy.us	Cheyenne	WY	82002	307-777-7742	777-5499
Banking Div 122 W 25th St Herschler Bldg 3rd Fl E *Web:* audit.wyo.gov	Cheyenne	WY	82002	307-777-7797	777-3555
Board of Medicine 130 Hobbs Ave Ste A *Web:* wyomedboard.state.wy.us	Cheyenne	WY	82001	307-778-7053	778-2069
Business Council 214 W 15th St *Web:* www.wyomingbusiness.org	Cheyenne	WY	82002	307-777-2800	777-2838
Certified Public Accountants Board 325 W 18th St Ste 4	Cheyenne	WY	82002	307-777-7551	777-3796
Community College Commission 2300 Capitol Ave Fl 5 Ste B *Web:* communitycolleges.wy.edu	Cheyenne	WY	82002	307-777-7763	777-6567
Community Development Authority PO Box 634 *Web:* www.wyomingcda.com	Casper	WY	82602	307-265-0603	266-5414
Consumer Protection Unit 122 W 25th St *Web:* ag.wyo.gov	Cheyenne	WY	82001	307-777-7874	777-7956
Corrections Dept 1934 Wyott Dr Ste 100 *Web:* corrections.wy.gov	Cheyenne	WY	82002	307-777-7208	777-7846
Education Dept 2300 Capitol Ave 2nd Fl *Web:* www.edu.wyoming.gov	Cheyenne	WY	82002	307-777-7675	777-6234
Environmental Quality Dept 122 W 25th St Herschler Bldg *Web:* deq.state.wy.us	Cheyenne	WY	82002	307-777-7937	777-7682
Family Services Dept 2300 Capitol Ave 3rd Fl Hathaway Bldg *Web:* dfsweb.wyo.gov	Cheyenne	WY	82002	307-777-7561	777-7747
Game & Fish Dept 5400 Bishop Blvd *Web:* wgfd.wyo.gov	Cheyenne	WY	82006	307-777-4600	777-4610
Governor State Capitol 200 W 24th St Rm 124 *Web:* governor.wyo.gov	Cheyenne	WY	82002	307-777-7434	632-3909
Health Dept 2300 Capitol Ave Ste 401 *Web:* health.wyo.gov	Cheyenne	WY	82002	307-777-7656	777-7439
Highway Patrol (WHP) 5300 Bishop Blvd *TF:* 800-442-9090 ■ *Web:* www.whp.dot.state.wy.us	Cheyenne	WY	82009	307-777-4301	777-3897
Historic Preservation Office 2301 Central Ave 3rd Fl *Web:* wyoshpo.state.wy.us	Cheyenne	WY	82002	307-777-7697	777-6421
Homeland Security Office 5500 Bishop Blvd E Door *Web:* wyohomelandsecurity.state.wy.us	Cheyenne	WY	82002	307-777-4663	635-6017
Information Technology Div 2001 Capitol Ave	Cheyenne	WY	82001	307-777-5003	
Insurance Dept 106 E Sixth Ave *Web:* doi.wyo.gov	Cheyenne	WY	82001	307-777-7401	777-2446
Legislative Service Office 3001 E Pershing Blvd *TF:* 800-342-9570 ■ *Web:* legisweb.state.wy.us	Cheyenne	WY	82002	307-777-7881	777-5466
Legislature 213 State Capitol *Web:* legisweb.state.wy.us	Cheyenne	WY	82002	307-777-7881	777-5466
Motor Vehicles Services Div 5300 Bishop Blvd *Web:* www.dot.state.wy.us	Cheyenne	WY	82009	307-777-4375	777-4772
Probation & Parole Div 700 W 21st St Ste 200	Cheyenne	WY	82001	307-777-7208	
Professional Teaching Standards Board 1920 Thomes Ave Ste 400 *Web:* uwyo.edu	Cheyenne	WY	82002	307-777-7291	
Public Service Commission 2515 Warren Ave Ste 300 *Web:* psc.state.wy.us	Cheyenne	WY	82002	307-777-7427	777-5700
Real Estate Commission 2020 Carey Ave Ste 702 *Web:* www.wyoming.gov	Cheyenne	WY	82002	307-777-7141	777-3796
Revenue Dept Herschler Bldg 2nd Fl W *Web:* revenue.wyo.gov	Cheyenne	WY	82002	307-777-7961	777-7722
Secretary of State 200 W 24th St *Web:* soswy.state.wy.us	Cheyenne	WY	82002	307-777-7378	777-6217
Securities Div 200 W 24th St *Web:* soswy.state.wy.us	Cheyenne	WY	82002	307-777-7370	777-7640
State Parks & Historical Sites Div 2301 Central Ave *TF:* 877-996-7275 ■ *Web:* wyoparks.state.wy.us	Cheyenne	WY	82002	307-777-6323	
Supreme Court 2301 Capitol Ave *Web:* courts.state.wy.us	Cheyenne	WY	82002	307-777-7316	777-6129
Technical Services Div 2219 Carey Ave *Web:* wyagric.state.wy.us	Cheyenne	WY	82001	307-777-7324	777-6593
Tourism Div 1520 Etchepare Cir *TF:* 800-225-5996 ■ *Web:* www.wyomingtourism.org	Cheyenne	WY	82007	307-777-7777	777-2877
Transportation Dept 5300 Bishop Blvd *Web:* www.dot.state.wy.us	Cheyenne	WY	82009	307-777-4375	777-4163
Treasurer 200 W 24th St *Web:* treasurer.state.wy.us	Cheyenne	WY	82002	307-777-7408	
Victims Services Div 200 W 24th St Ste 110 *Web:* ag.wyo.gov	Cheyenne	WY	82001	307-777-7200	
Vital Records Services Hathaway Bldg *Web:* health.wyo.gov	Cheyenne	WY	82002	307-777-7591	
Vocational Rehabilitation Div 1510 East Pershing Blvd Ste 1100 *Web:* www.wyomingworkforce.org	Cheyenne	WY	82002	307-777-3700	777-5939
Workers Safety & Compensation Div 1510 E Pershing Blvd *Web:* wyomingsafety.org	Cheyenne	WY	82002	307-777-7159	
Workforce Services Dept 122 W 25th St 2nd Fl E *Web:* www.wyomingworkforce.org	Cheyenne	WY	82002	307-777-8650	777-7106

343 GOVERNMENT - US - EXECUTIVE BRANCH

SEE ALSO Cemeteries - National p. 1908; Coast Guard Installations p. 1958; Correctional Facilities - Federal p. 2167; Military Bases p. 2758; Parks - National - US p. 2859

				Phone	Fax
Office of the President 1600 Pennsylvania Ave NW *Web:* www.whitehouse.gov	Washington	DC	20500	202-456-1414	456-2461

Phone | Fax

Office of the Vice President
1650 Pennsylvania Ave NW . . . Washington DC 20501 202-456-4444
Web: whitehouse.gov/administration/vice-president-biden

Council of Economic Advisers
732 N Capitol St NW 8th Fl . . . Washington DC 20401 202-512-1800
Web: www.whitehouse.gov

Council on Environmental Quality
722 Jackson Pl NW . . . Washington DC 20506 202-395-5750 456-0753
Web: www.whitehouse.gov/ceq

Domestic Policy Council
1600 Pennsylvania Ave NW . . . Washington DC 20500 202-456-1111
Web: whitehouse.gov/administration/eop/dpc/

National Economic Council
1600 Pennsylvania Ave NW . . . Washington DC 20500 202-456-1111
Web: www.whitehouse.gov/nec

National Security Council (NSC)
1600 Pennsylvania Ave NW . . . Washington DC 20500 202-456-1414
Web: www.whitehouse.gov/nsc

Office of Management & Budget (OMB)
725 17th St NW . . . Washington DC 20503 202-395-3080 395-3888
Web: www.whitehouse.gov/omb

Office of National AIDS Policy (ONAP)
The White House . . . Washington DC 20502 202-456-4533
Web: www.whitehouse.gov/onap/aids.html

Office of National Drug Control Policy
PO Box 6000 . . . Rockville MD 20849 800-666-3332 519-5212*
**Fax Area Code:* 301 ■ *TF:* 800-666-3332 ■ *Web:* whitehouse.gov/ondcp

Office of Science & Technology Policy
1650 Pennsylvania Ave . . . Washington DC 20504 202-456-4444
Web: www.whitehouse.gov

Office of the US Trade Representative
600 17th St NW . . . Washington DC 20508 202-395-7360
Web: www.ustr.gov

President's Foreign Intelligence Advisory Board (PIAB)
White House 1600 Pennsylvania Ave . . . Washington DC 20500 202-456-1414 456-2461
Web: www.whitehouse.gov/administration/eop/piab

USA Freedom Corps 1201 New York Ave NW . . . Washington DC 20005 202-606-5000
TF: 800-833-3722 ■ *Web:* www.nationalservice.gov

White House Office
1600 Pennsylvania Ave NW . . . Washington DC 20500 202-456-1414
Web: www.whitehouse.gov

White House Press Secretary
1600 Pennsylvania Ave NW . . . Washington DC 20500 202-456-1111 456-2461
Web: www.whitehouse.gov

343-1 US Department of Agriculture

Phone | Fax

Department of Agriculture (USDA)
1400 Independence Ave SW . . . Washington DC 20250 202-720-3631 720-2166
Web: www.usda.gov

Agricultural Marketing Service
1400 Independence Ave SW . . . Washington DC 20250 202-720-5115 720-8477
Web: www.ams.usda.gov

Agricultural Research Service
US Dept of Agriculture
1400 Independence Ave SW . . . Washington DC 20250 202-720-3656 720-5427
Web: www.ars.usda.gov

Animal & Plant Health Inspection Service (APHIS)
National Veterinary Services Laboratories
2300 Dayton Ave . . . Ames IA 50010 515-663-7200
Web: www.aphis.usda.gov

Center for Nutrition Policy & Promotion (CNPP)
3101 Pk Ctr Dr 10th Fl . . . Alexandria VA 22302 703-305-7600 305-3300
TF: 888-779-7264 ■ *Web:* www.cnpp.usda.gov

Co-op State Research Education & Extension Service
1400 Independence Ave SW Ste 2220 . . . Washington DC 20250 202-401-4952 720-6486
Web: nifa.usda.gov

Commodity Credit Corp, The (CCC)
1400 Independence Ave SW . . . Washington DC 20250 202-720-3111
Web: fsa.usda.gov/fsa/webapp?area=about&subject=landing&topic=sao-cc

Economic Research Service (ERS)
US Dept of Agriculture 1800 M St NW . . . Washington DC 20036 202-694-5050 694-5757
Web: www.ers.usda.gov

Farm Service Agency
1400 Independence Ave SW . . . Washington DC 20250 202-720-3865
Web: www.fsa.usda.gov

Food & Nutrition Service
Food Stamp Program 3101 Pk Ctr Dr . . . Alexandria VA 22302 703-305-2022 305-2454
TF: 800-221-5689 ■ *Web:* www.fns.usda.gov
Mid-Atlantic Region 300 Corporate Blvd . . . Robbinsville NJ 08691 609-259-5025 259-5185
Web: fns.usda.gov/
Midwest Region 77 W Jackson Blvd 20th Fl . . . Chicago IL 60604 312-353-6664 886-2475
Web: www.fns.usda.gov
Mountain Plains Region 1244 Speer Blvd Ste 903 . . . Denver CO 80204 303-844-0300 844-2160
Web: www.fns.usda.gov
Northeast Region
10 Cswy St Rm 501 Federal Bldg . . . Boston MA 02222 617-565-6370 565-6473
Web: www.fns.usda.gov
Southeast Region 61 Forsyth St SW Ste 8T36 . . . Atlanta GA 30303 404-562-1801 562-1807
Web: www.fns.usda.gov

Food & Nutrition Service Regional Offices
Southwest Region 1100 Commerce St Rm 522 . . . Dallas TX 75242 214-290-9800 767-0271
Web: www.fns.usda.gov
Western Region 90 7th St Ste 10-100 . . . San Francisco CA 94103 415-705-1310 705-1364
Web: www.fns.usda.gov

Food Safety & Inspection Service
1400 Independence Ave SW Rm 331E . . . Washington DC 20250 202-720-7025 205-0158
Web: www.fsis.usda.gov

Foreign Agricultural Service
1400 Independence Ave SW . . . Washington DC 20250 202-720-3935 690-2159
Web: www.fas.usda.gov

Phone | Fax

Forest Service (USFS)
1400 Independence Ave SW . . . Washington DC 20050 202-205-8333
TF: 800-832-1355 ■ *Web:* www.fs.fed.us
Region 1 (Northern Region) PO Box 7669 . . . Missoula MT 59807 406-329-3511 329-3347
Web: www.fs.fed.us

Forest Service Regional Offices
Region 10 (Alaska Region) PO Box 21628 . . . Juneau AK 99802 907-586-8806 586-7876
Web: www.fs.fed.us
Region 2 (Rocky Mountain Region) 740 Simms St . . . Golden CO 80401 303-275-5350 275-5366
Web: www.fs.fed.us
Region 3 (Southwestern Region)
333 Broadway Blvd SE . . . Albuquerque NM 87102 505-842-3292
Web: www.fs.fed.us
Region 4 (Intermountain Region) 324 25th St . . . Ogden UT 84401 801-625-5306 625-5127
Web: fs.fed.us
Region 5 (Pacific Southwest Region)
1323 Club Dr . . . Vallejo CA 94592 707-562-8737
Web: fs.fed.us
Region 6 (Pacific Northwest Region)
333 SW First Ave PO Box 3623 . . . Portland OR 97208 503-808-2468 808-2469
Web: fs.fed.us
Region 8 (Southern Region)
1720 Peachtree St Ste 760S . . . Atlanta GA 30309 404-347-4177 347-4821
TF: 877-372-7248 ■ *Web:* www.fs.fed.us
Region 9 (Eastern Region)
626 E Wisconsin Ave . . . Milwaukee WI 53202 414-297-3600 297-3808
Web: www.fs.fed.us

Grain Inspection Packers & Stockyards Administration
1400 Independence Ave SW Rm 2055-S Bldg . . . Washington DC 20250 202-720-0219
Web: www.gipsa.usda.gov

National Agricultural Library
10301 Baltimore Ave Abraham Lincoln Bldg . . . Beltsville MD 20705 301-504-5755
Web: www.nal.usda.gov

National Agricultural Statistics Service (NASS)
1400 Independence Ave SW . . . Washington DC 20250 202-720-2707 720-9013
TF: 800-727-9540 ■ *Web:* www.nass.usda.gov

Natural Resources Conservation Service
1400 Independence Ave SW Rm 5105A . . . Washington DC 20250 202-720-7246 720-7690
Web: www.nrcs.usda.gov

Risk Management Agency
1400 Independence Ave SW MS 0801 . . . Washington DC 20250 202-690-2803 690-2818
Web: www.rma.usda.gov

Rural Business-Co-op Service
1400 Independence Ave SW Ste 1510 Rm 5135 . . . Washington DC 20250 202-720-9540 720-1725
Web: www.rd.usda.gov

Rural Development
1400 Independence Ave SW . . . Washington DC 20250 202-720-9540 720-1725
Web: www.rurdev.usda.gov

Rural Housing Service
1400 Independence Ave SW Rm 5014 . . . Washington DC 20250 202-690-1533
TF: 800-414-1226 ■ *Web:* www.rurdev.usda.gov/rhs

Rural Utilities Service
1400 Independence Ave SW . . . Washington DC 20250 202-720-9545
Web: rurdev.usda.gov

Secretary of Agriculture
1400 Independence Ave SW Rm 200A . . . Washington DC 20250 202-720-3631 720-2166
Web: www.usda.gov

USDA Graduate School 600 Maryland Ave SW . . . Washington DC 20024 202-314-3600
Web: cicorp.com

World Agricultural Outlook Board
1400 Independence Ave SW . . . Washington DC 20250 202-720-6030 720-4043
Web: www.usda.gov/oce/commodity

343-2 US Department of Commerce

Phone | Fax

Department of Commerce
1401 Constitution Ave NW Hoover Bldg . . . Washington DC 20230 202-482-4883 482-5168
Web: www.commerce.gov

Bureau of Economic Analysis (BEA)
1441 L St NW . . . Washington DC 20005 202-606-9900 606-5311
Web: www.bea.gov

Bureau of Industry & Security
1401 Constitution Ave NW Rm 4620 . . . Washington DC 20230 202-622-2480
Web: www.bis.doc.gov

Economic Development Administration
1401 Constitution Ave NW . . . Washington DC 20230 202-482-2900
Web: www.eda.gov

Economic Development Administration Regional Offices
Atlanta 401 W Peachtree St NW Ste 1820 . . . Atlanta GA 30308 404-730-3002 730-3025
Web: www.eda.gov
Austin 504 Lavaca St Ste 1100 . . . Austin TX 78701 512-381-8144 381-8177
Web: www.eda.gov
Chicago 111 N Canal St Ste 855 . . . Chicago IL 60606 312-353-8143 353-8575
Web: www.eda.gov
Denver 410 17th St Ste 250 . . . Denver CO 80202 303-844-4715 844-3968
Web: www.eda.gov/contacts.htm
Philadelphia
Curtis Ctr 601 Walnut St Ste 140-S . . . Philadelphia PA 19106 215-597-4603 597-1063
Web: www.eda.gov
Seattle 915 Second Ave Rm 1890 . . . Seattle WA 98174 206-220-7660 220-7669
Web: www.eda.gov

Economics & Statistics Administration
1401 Constitution Ave NW . . . Washington DC 20230 202-482-0436 482-2552
Web: www.esa.doc.gov

International Trade Administration
1401 Constitution Ave NW . . . Washington DC 20230 202-482-3809 482-5819
Web: www.ita.doc.gov

Minority Business Development Agency (MBDA)
1401 Constitution Ave NW . . . Washington DC 20230 202-482-1940
Web: www.mbda.gov

Phone Fax

Minority Business Development Agency Regional Offices
Atlanta Region 75 5th St NW Ste 300 .... Atlanta GA 30308 404-894-2096
Web: www.mbda.gov
Chicago Region 105 W Adams St Ste 2300 .... Chicago IL 60603 312-353-0182
TF: 888-324-1551 ■ *Web:* www.mbda.gov
Dallas Region 1100 Commerce St Rm 726 .... Dallas TX 75242 214-767-8001 767-0613
Web: www.mbda.gov
New York Region 26 Federal Plaza Ste 3720 .... New York NY 10278 212-264-3262
Web: www.mbda.gov
San Francisco Region
1401 Constitution Ave .... Washington DC 20230 202-482-1960
Web: www.mbda.gov

National Environmental Satellite Data & Information Service
1335 East-West Hwy SSMC1 8th Fl .... Silver Spring MD 20910 301-713-3578 713-1249
Web: www.nesdis.noaa.gov
National Climatic Data Ctr
151 Patton Ave Rm 120 .... Asheville NC 28801 828-271-4800 271-4876
Web: www.ncdc.noaa.gov
National Coastal Data Development Ctr
Bldg 1100 Ste 101 .... Stennis Space Center MS 39529 228-688-2936 688-2010
TF: 866-732-2382 ■ *Web:* www.ncddc.noaa.gov
National Geophysical Data Ctr
E/GC 325 Broadway .... Boulder CO 80305 303-497-6826 497-6513
Web: www.ngdc.noaa.gov
National Oceanographic Data Ctr
1315 East-West Hwy 4th Fl .... Silver Spring MD 20910 301-713-3277 713-3302
Web: www.nodc.noaa.gov

National Institute of Standards & Technology (NIST)
100 Bureau Dr Sp 1070 .... Gaithersburg MD 20899 301-975-6478 926-1630
TF: 800-877-8339 ■ *Web:* www.nist.gov

National Marine Fisheries Service Regional Offices
Alaska Region PO Box 21668 .... Juneau AK 99802 907-586-7221 586-7249
Web: alaskafisheries.noaa.gov
NortheastRegion 1 Blackburn Dr .... Gloucester MA 01930 978-281-9300 281-9333
Web: greateratlantic.fisheries.noaa.gov/
Northwest Region 7600 Sand Pt Way NE .... Seattle WA 98115 206-526-6150 526-6426
Web: westcoast.fisheries.noaa.gov/#moved
Pacific Islands Region
1601 Kapiolani Blvd Rm 1110 .... Honolulu HI 96814 808-944-2200 973-2906
TF: 888-674-7411 ■ *Web:* www.fpir.noaa.gov
Southwest Region 501 W Ocean Blvd Ste 4200 ... Long Beach CA 90802 562-980-4000 980-4018
Web: nmfs.noaa.gov

National Ocean Service
1305 East-West Hwy .... Silver Spring MD 20910 301-713-3074 713-4269
Web: oceanservice.noaa.gov

National Oceanic & Atmospheric Administration (NOAA)
1401 Constitution Ave NW .... Washington DC 20230 202-482-6090 482-3154
Web: www.noaa.gov

National Sea Grant Program
1315 East-West Hwy SSMC-3 11th Fl .... Silver Spring MD 20910 301-734-1066 713-0799
Web: www.seagrant.noaa.gov

National Technical Information Service (NTIS)
5285 Port Royal Rd .... Springfield VA 22161 703-605-6000 605-6900
TF Orders: 800-553-6847 ■ *Web:* www.ntis.gov

National Telecommunications & Information Administration (NTIA)
1401 Constitution Ave NW Hoover Bldg .... Washington DC 20230 202-482-7002
Web: www.ntia.doc.gov

National Weather Service (NWS)
1325 East-West Hwy .... Silver Spring MD 20910 301-713-0689 713-0662
Web: www.weather.gov
National Hurricane Ctr 11691 SW 17th St .... Miami FL 33165 305-229-4470 553-1901
Web: www.nhc.noaa.gov

National Weather Service Regional Offices
Alaska Region
222 W Seventh Ave Ste 23 Rm 517 .... Anchorage AK 99513 907-271-5088 271-3711
Web: www.arh.noaa.gov
Central Region 7220 NW 101st Terr .... Kansas City MO 64153 816-891-7734
Web: www.crh.noaa.gov
Eastern Region 630 Johnson Ave .... Bohemia NY 11716 631-244-0100
Web: weather.gov/erh/
Pacific Region 2525 Correa Rd Ste 250 .... Honolulu HI 96822 808-973-5286
Web: www.prh.noaa.gov/pr
Southern Region 819 Taylor St Rm 10A06 .... Fort Worth TX 76102 817-978-1000
Web: www.srh.noaa.gov
Western Region 125 S State St .... Salt Lake City UT 84138 801-524-5133 524-5270
Web: www.wrh.noaa.gov

North American Industry Classification System (NAICS)
US Census Bureau 4600 Silver Hill Rd .... Washington DC 20233 301-763-4636
TF: 800-923-8282 ■ *Web:* www.census.gov/eos/www/naics

Secretary of Commerce
1401 Constitution Ave NW .... Washington DC 20230 202-482-2000 482-2741
Web: www.commerce.gov

US Census Bureau 4600 Silver Hill Rd .... Washington DC 20233 301-763-6460
Web: www.census.gov

US Census Bureau Regional Offices
Atlanta 101 Marietta St NW Ste 3200 .... Atlanta GA 30303 404-730-3832 730-3835
TF: 800-424-6974 ■ *Web:* www.census.gov
Boston 4 Copley Pl Ste 301 .... Boston MA 02117 617-424-4501 424-0547
TF: 800-562-5721 ■ *Web:* www.census.gov
Chicago 1111 W 22nd St Ste 400 .... Oak Brook IL 60523 630-288-9200 288-9288
TF: 800-865-6384 ■ *Web:* www.census.gov
Denver 6900 W Jefferson Ave Ste 100 .... Denver CO 80235 303-264-0202 969-6777
TF: 800-852-6159 ■ *Web:* www.census.gov
Los Angeles 15350 Sherman Way Ste 300 .... Van Nuys CA 91406 818-267-1700 904-6429
TF: 800-992-3530 ■ *Web:* www.census.gov/rolax/www
New York 395 Hudson St Ste 800 .... New York NY 10014 212-584-3400 478-4800
TF: 800-991-2520 ■ *Web:* www.census.gov/regions
Philadelphia 833 Chestnut St Ste 504 .... Philadelphia PA 19107 215-717-1800 717-0755
TF: 800-262-4236 ■ *Web:* www.census.gov

Phone Fax

US Patent & Trademark Office PO Box 1450 .... Alexandria VA 22313 571-272-1000 273-8300
TF: 800-786-9199 ■ *Web:* www.uspto.gov

343-3 US Department of Defense

Phone Fax

Department of Defense (DOD) The Pentagon .... Washington DC 20301 703-545-6700
Web: www.defense.gov

American Forces Information Service (AFIS)
601 N Fairfax St .... Alexandria VA 22314 703-571-3343
Web: www.defense.gov

Defense Commissary Agency 1300 E Ave .... Fort Lee VA 23801 804-734-8000 734-8009
Web: www.commissaries.com

Defense Contract Audit Agency
8725 John J Kingman Rd Ste 2135 .... Fort Belvoir VA 22060 703-767-3265
Web: www.dcaa.mil

Defense Contract Management Agency
6350 Walker Ln Ste 300 .... Alexandria VA 22310 888-576-3262
Web: www.dcma.mil

Defense Hotline for Fraud Waste & Abuse
The Pentagon .... Washington DC 20301 703-604-8799 604-8567
TF: 800-424-9098 ■ *Web:* dodig.mil/errorpages/index.html

Defense Information Systems Agency
PO Box 4502 .... Arlington VA 22204 703-607-6515 607-4344
Web: www.disa.mil

Defense Intelligence Agency
200 MacDill Blvd .... Washington DC 20340 301-394-5587 394-5356
Web: www.dia.mil

Defense Logistics Agency (DLA)
8725 John J Kingman Rd Ste 1644 .... Fort Belvoir VA 22060 703-767-5200 767-6091
Web: www.dla.mil/Pages/default.aspx

Defense Office of Economic Adjustment
400 Army-Navy Dr Ste 200 .... Arlington VA 22202 703-604-6020
Web: www.oea.gov

Defense Prisoner of War/Missing Personnel Office (DPMO)
2600 Defense Pentagon .... Washington DC 20301 703-699-1169 602-4375
Web: www.dpaa.mil

Defense Security Cooperation Agency
201 12th St S Ste 402 .... Washington DC 20301 703-604-6566
Web: www.dsca.mil

Defense Security Service 27130 Telegraph Rd .... Quantico VA 22314 571-305-6562
Web: www.dss.mil

Defense Technical Information Ctr (DTIC)
8725 John J Kingman Rd Ste 0944 .... Fort Belvoir VA 22060 703-767-9100 767-9183
TF: 800-225-3842 ■ *Web:* www.dtic.mil

Defense Threat Reduction Agency
8725 John T Kingman Rd MS 6201 .... Fort Belvoir VA 22060 703-767-5870 767-4450
TF: 800-701-5096 ■ *Web:* www.dtra.mil

Joint Chiefs of Staff
Chairman
9999 Joint Chiefs of Staff Pentagon .... Washington DC 20318 703-767-8267
Web: www.dtic.mil

Missile Defense Agency
7100 Defense Pentagon .... Washington DC 20301 703-693-7100
Web: www.mda.mil

National Defense University
Fort McNair 300 5th Ave SW .... Washington DC 20319 202-685-4700
Web: ndu.edu

National Security Agency 9800 Savage Rd .... Fort Meade MD 20755 301-688-6524 688-6198
Web: www.nsa.gov

343-4 US Department of Defense - Department of the Air Force

Phone Fax

Department of the Air Force
1670 Air Force Pentagon .... Washington DC 20330 703-695-9664 693-9601
Web: www.af.mil
North American Aerospace Defense Command
250 Vandenberg St Ste B-016 .... Peterson AFB CO 80914 719-554-6889 554-3165
Web: www.norad.mil

Air Combat Command 205 Dodd Blvd Ste 101 ...... Langley AFB VA 23665 757-764-8346
Web: www.acc.af.mil

Air Education & Training Command (AETC)
100 H St Ste 4 .... Randolph AFB TX 78150 210-652-6564 652-2027
Web: www.aetc.af.mil

Air Force Chief of Staff
1670 Air Force Pentagon .... Washington DC 20330 703-697-9225
Web: www.defense.gov

Air Force Materiel Command
4375 Chidlaw Rd Rm N-152 .... Wright-Patterson AFB OH 45433 937-257-1110
Web: www.afmc.af.mil

Air Force Reserve Command
155 Richard Ray Blvd .... Robins AFB GA 31098 478-327-1753 327-0625
Web: www.afrc.af.mil

Air Force Space Command
150 Vandenberg St .... Peterson AFB CO 80914 719-554-3731 554-6013
Web: www.afspc.af.mil

Air Force Special Operations Command
229 Cody Ave Ste 103 .... Hurlburt Field FL 32544 850-884-5515
Web: www.afsoc.af.mil

Air Mobility Command 503 Ward Dr Ste 214 .... Scott AFB IL 62225 8-2-29--7821
Web: www.amc.af.mil

343-5 US Department of Defense - Department of the Army

	City	State	ZIP	Phone	Fax
Department of the Army 1500 Army Pentagon *Web:* www.army.mil	Washington	DC	20310	703-697-5131	
US Army Center of Military History 103 Third Ave SW Fort McNair Bldg 35 *Web:* www.history.army.mil	Washington	DC	20319	202-685-2727	512-2104
Army National Guard Army National Guard Readiness Ctr 111 S George Mason Dr *TF:* 800-404-8273 ■ *Web:* www.nationalguard.com	Arlington	VA	22204	703-607-2584	
US Army Corps of Engineers 441 G St NW *Web:* www.usace.army.mil	Washington	DC	20314	202-761-0010	761-1803
Great Lakes & Ohio River Div 550 Main St *Web:* www.lrd.usace.army.mil	Cincinnati	OH	45202	513-684-3010	684-3755
Mississippi Valley Div 1400 Walnut St *Web:* www.mvd.usace.army.mil	Vicksburg	MS	39180	601-634-7783	
North Atlantic Div 302 General Lee Ave Fort Hamilton *Web:* www.nad.usace.army.mil	Brooklyn	NY	11252	347-370-4550	
US Army Corps of Engineers Regional Offices					
Northwestern Div PO Box 2870 *Web:* www.nwd.usace.army.mil	Portland	OR	97208	503-808-3700	808-3706
Pacific Ocean Div Fort Shafter Bldg 525 *Web:* www.pod.usace.army.mil	Honolulu	HI	96858	808-438-8319	438-2656
South Atlantic Div 60 Forsyth St SW Rm 9M15 *Web:* www.sad.usace.army.mil	Atlanta	GA	30303	404-562-5011	
South Pacific Div 1455 Market St *Web:* www.spd.usace.army.mil	San Francisco	CA	94103	415-503-6514	
Southwestern Div 1100 Commerce St *Web:* www.swd.usace.army.mil	Dallas	TX	75242	469-487-7007	
US Army Criminal Investigation Command Public Affairs Office 6010 6th St *Web:* www.cid.army.mil	Fort Belvoir	VA	22060	703-806-0372	
US Army Forces Command 1777 Hardee Ave SW *Web:* www.forscom.army.mil	Fort McPherson	GA	30330	404-464-7276	464-5628
US Army Intelligence & Security Command 8825 Beulah St *Web:* www.inscom.army.mil	Fort Belvoir	VA	22060	703-428-4965	
US Army Special Operations Command (USASOC) 2929 Desert Storm Dr *Web:* www.soc.mil	Fort Bragg	NC	28310	910-432-6005	432-1046
US Army War College 122 Forbes Ave *TF:* 800-453-0992 ■ *Web:* www.carlisle.army.mil	Carlisle	PA	17013	717-245-3131	245-4224

343-6 US Department of Defense - Department of the Navy

	City	State	ZIP	Phone	Fax
Department of the Navy 1000 Navy Pentagon *Web:* www.navy.mil	Washington	DC	20350	703-695-8400	
Judge Advocate General's Corps 1322 Patterson Ave Ste 3000 *Web:* www.jag.navy.mil	Washington Navy Yard	DC	20374	202-685-5275	
Medicine & Surgery Bureau 2300 E St NW *Web:* www.nlm.nih.gov	Washington	DC	20372	202-762-3211	
Office of Naval Intelligence 4251 Suitland Rd *Web:* www.oni.navy.mil	Washington	DC	20395	301-669-3001	
Office of Naval Research 1 Liberty Ctr 875 N Randolph St Ste 1425 *Web:* www.onr.navy.mil	Arlington	VA	22203	703-696-5031	696-5940
Military Sealift Command 914 Charles Morris Ct SE Washington Navy Yard	Washington	DC	20398	800-793-5784	
Naval Air Systems Command 47123 Buse Rd Bldg 2272, Ste 075 *Web:* www.navair.navy.mil	Patuxent River	MD	20670	301-757-1487	
Naval Education & Training Command (NETC) 250 Dallas St *Web:* www.netc.navy.mil	Pensacola	FL	32508	850-452-4858	
Naval Sea Systems Command 1333 Isaac Hull Ave SE Washington Navy Yard *Web:* www.navsea.navy.mil	Washington	DC	20376	202-781-4123	
Naval Special Warfare Command 2000 Trident Way *Web:* www.public.navy.mil	San Diego	CA	92155	619-537-1133	537-1986
Navy Personnel Command (NPC) 5720 Integrity Dr *TF:* 866-827-5672 ■ *Web:* www.public.navy.mil	Millington	TN	38055	901-874-3165	874-2615

343-7 US Department of Defense - US Marine Corps

	City	State	ZIP	Phone	Fax
Commandant 3000 Marine Corps Pentagon Rm 4C645 *Web:* usmcbirthdayball.com	Washington	DC	20350	703-614-4851	693-4414
US Marine Corps					
Public Affairs Div 3000 Marine Corps Pentagon Rm 2B253 *Web:* www.hqmc.marines.mil	Washington	DC	20350	703-693-3088	614-6539
Marine Corps Recruiting Station 3280 Russell Rd *Web:* www.marines.com	Quantico	VA	22134	703-784-9454	

343-8 US Department of Education

	City	State	ZIP	Phone	Fax
Department of Education 400 Maryland Ave SW *TF:* 800-872-5327 ■ *Web:* www.ed.gov	Washington	DC	20202	202-401-2000	401-0689
Inspector General's Fraud & Abuse Hotline 400 Maryland Ave SW *TF:* 800-647-8733 ■ *Web:* www.ed.gov/about/offices/list/oig/hotline.html	Washington	DC	20202	800-647-8733	
Office of Elementary & Secondary Education 400 Maryland Ave SW *TF:* 800-872-5327 ■ *Web:* www.ed.gov	Washington	DC	20202	800-872-5327	
Office of English Language Acquisition (OELA) 400 Maryland Ave SW *Web:* www.ed.gov/oela	Washington	DC	20202	202-401-4300	205-1229
Office of Innovation & Improvement 400 Maryland Ave SW *Web:* www.ed.gov	Washington	DC	20202	202-205-4500	401-4123
Office of Safe & Drug-Free Schools 400 Maryland Ave SW *Web:* www.ed.gov/about/offices/list/osdfs	Washington	DC	20202	202-260-3954	260-7767
Office of Vocational & Adult Education 400 Maryland Ave SW Room 4W116 *TF:* 800-872-5327 ■ *Web:* www.ed.gov/ovae	Washington	DC	20202	800-872-5327	
Region 1 5 Post Office Sq Ninth Fl Rm 24 POCH Bldg *Web:* www.ed.gov	Boston	MA	02110	617-289-0100	
Department of Education Regional Offices					
Region 10 400 Maryland Ave SW Jackson Federal Bldg **Fax Area Code:* 800 ■ *Web:* www.ed.gov	Washington	DC	20202	202-401-2000	872-5327*
Region 2 Financial Sq 32 Old Slip 25th Fl *Web:* www.ed.gov	New York	NY	10005	646-428-3906	428-3904
Region 3 100 Penn Sq E Ste 505 *Web:* www.ed.gov	Philadelphia	PA	19107	215-656-6010	656-6020
Region 4 Federal Ctr 61 Forsyth St SW Ste 19T40 *Web:* www.ed.gov	Atlanta	GA	30303	404-974-9450	974-9459
Region 5 500 W Madison St Ste 1427 *Web:* www.ed.gov	Chicago	IL	60661	312-730-1700	730-1704
Region 7 8930 Ward Pkwy Ste 2043 *Web:* www.ed.gov	Kansas City	MO	64114	816-268-0400	268-0407
Region 8 Federal Bldg 1244 Speer Blvd Ste 615 *Web:* www.ed.gov	Denver	CO	80204	303-844-3544	844-2524
Office of Special Education & Rehabilitation Services (OSERS) 400 Maryland Ave SW **Fax Area Code:* 800 ■ *Web:* www2.ed.gov	Washington	DC	20202	202-401-0418	872-5327*
US Dept of Education					
Region 6 1999 Bryan St Ste 1620 *TF:* 877-521-2172 ■ *Web:* www.ed.gov	Dallas	TX	75201	214-661-9600	661-9587
National Ctr for Education Statistics 1990 K St NW *Web:* nces.ed.gov	Washington	DC	20006	202-502-7300	502-7466
National Institute for Literacy (NIFL) 1775 'I' St NW Ste 730 *TF:* 800-228-8813 ■ *Web:* www.lincs.ed.gov	Washington	DC	20006	202-233-2025	233-2050
Secretary of Education 400 Maryland Ave SW *TF:* 800-872-5327 ■ *Web:* www.ed.gov/news/staff/bios/spellings.html	Washington	DC	20202	202-401-3000	

343-9 US Department of Energy

	City	State	ZIP	Phone	Fax
Office of Civilian Radioactive Waste Management 1000 Independence Ave SW *TF:* 888-363-7289 ■ *Web:* www.ocrwm.doe.gov	Washington	DC	20585	202-586-4940	586-4403
Department of Energy					
Office of Electricity Delivery & Energy Reliability 1000 Independence Ave SW *Web:* www.energy.gov/oe	Washington	DC	20585	202-586-1411	
Office of Energy Efficiency & Renewable Energy 1000 Independence Ave SW *TF:* 877-337-3463 ■ *Web:* energy.gov	Washington	DC	20585	202-586-9171	586-9260
Office of Environmental Management 1000 Independence Ave SW *Web:* energy.gov	Washington	DC	20585	202-586-7709	586-7757
Office of Fossil Energy 1000 Independence Ave SW *Web:* energy.gov	Washington	DC	20585	202-586-6660	586-7847
Office of Legacy Management Office of Stakeholder Relations LM-5 *Web:* energy.gov	Washington	DC	20585	202-586-3559	586-1540
Office of Nuclear Energy 1000 Independence Ave SW **Fax Area Code:* 202 ■ *TF:* 800-342-5363 ■ *Web:* energy.gov	Washington	DC	20585	800-342-5363	586-0544*
Energy Information Administration 1000 Independence Ave SW *Web:* www.eia.gov	Washington	DC	20585	202-586-8800	586-0727
Federal Energy Regulatory Commission 888 First St NE *TF:* 866-208-3372 ■ *Web:* www.ferc.gov	Washington	DC	20426	202-502-8004	208-2106
Federal Energy Regulatory Commission Regional Offices					
Atlanta 3700 Crestwood Pkwy NW 9th Fl *Web:* www.ferc.gov/contact-us/tel-num/regional/atlanta.asp	Atlanta	GA	30096	678-245-3075	245-3010
Chicago 230 S Dearborn St Rm 3130 *Web:* www.ferc.gov/contact-us/tel-num/regional/chicago.asp	Chicago	IL	60604	312-596-4437	596-4460
New York 19 W 34th St Ste 400 *Web:* www.ferc.gov/contact-us/tel-num/regional/newyork.asp	New York	NY	10001	212-273-5911	631-8124
Portland 888 First St NE Fox Tower Ste 550 **Fax Area Code:* 503 ■ *Web:* www.ferc.gov/contact-us/tel-num/regional.asp	Washington	DC	20426	202-502-6088	552-2799*

Phone Fax

San Francisco 100 First St Ste 2300 ....San Francisco CA 94105 415-369-3318 369-3322
Web: www.ferc.gov

National Nuclear Security Administration (NNSA)
1000 Independence Ave SW......................Washington DC 20585 202-586-5000 586-4892
Web: www.nnsa.energy.gov

Power Marketing Administrations
Bonneville Power Administration
905 NE 11th Ave ....Portland OR 97232 503-230-3000
Web: www.bpa.gov
Southeastern Power Administration
1166 Athens Tech Rd...........................Elberton GA 30635 706-213-3800 213-3884
Web: energy.gov

Secretary of Energy
1000 Independence Ave SW......................Washington DC 20585 202-586-6210 586-4403
Web: energy.gov/about-us

343-10 US Department of Health & Human Services

Phone Fax

Department of Health & Human Services (HHS)
330 Independence Ave SW.......................Washington DC 20201 202-619-0150
TF: 877-696-6775 ■ *Web:* www.hhs.gov
Region 10 701 5th Ave Ste 1600..................Seattle WA 98121 206-615-2010 615-2087
Web: hhs.gov
Region 2 26 Federal Plaza Rm 3835 ....New York NY 10278 212-264-4600 264-3620
Web: hhs.gov

Department of Health & Human Services Regional Offices
Region 4 1301 61 Forsyth St SW Ste 5B95..........Atlanta GA 30303 404-562-7889 562-7899
Web: www.hhs.gov
Region 5 233 N Michigan Ave Ste 1300 .... Chicago IL 60601 2-3-53--1385 -35-3-0718*
**Fax Area Code:* 312
Region 6 1301 Young St Ste 1124.................Dallas TX 75202 214-767-3879 767-3209
Web: www.hhs.gov/
Region 7 601 E 12th St ....Kansas City MO 64106 816-426-2821 426-2178
Web: hhs.gov

US Health & Human Services Department
Region 1 15 Sudbury St Ste 2100 .... Boston MA 02203 617-565-1500 565-1491
Web: www.sots.ct.gov
Region 8 999 18th St S Terr Ste 410 .... Denver CO 80202 303-844-6163 844-2019
Web: www.hhs.gov
Region 9 90 7th St Ste 4-100..............San Francisco CA 94103 800-368-1019 437-8329*
**Fax Area Code:* 415 ■ *TF:* 800-368-1019 ■ *Web:* www.hhs.gov

Administration for Children & Families (ACF)
370 L'Enfant Promenade SW......................Washington DC 20447 202-401-9215 401-5450
Web: www.acf.hhs.gov
Atlanta 61 Forsyth St Ste 4M60..................Atlanta GA 30303 404-562-2800 562-2981
Web: www.acf.hhs.gov/programs/region4

Administration for Children & Families Regional Offices
Boston JFK Federal Bldg Rm 2000 .... Boston MA 02203 617-565-1020 565-2493
Web: www.acf.hhs.gov
Chicago 233 N Michigan Ave Ste 400........... Chicago IL 60601 312-353-4237 353-2204
Web: www.acf.hhs.gov/programs/region5
Dallas 1301 Young St Ste 914....................Dallas TX 75202 214-767-9648 767-3743
Web: www.acf.hhs.gov/programs/region6
New York 26 Federal Plaza Rm 4114............New York NY 10278 212-264-2890 264-4881
Web: www.acf.hhs.gov/programs/region2
Philadelphia
150 S Independence Mall W Ste 864........... Philadelphia PA 19106 215-861-4000 861-4070
Web: www.acf.hhs.gov/programs/region3
San Francisco 90 Seventh St 9th Fl..........San Francisco CA 94103 415-437-8400 437-8444
Web: www.acf.hhs.gov/programs/region9

Administration on Aging (AoA)
1 Massachusetts Ave NW.........................Washington DC 20201 202-619-0724 357-3555
Web: www.aoa.gov

Administration on Aging Regional Offices (AOA)
Region I JFK Federal Bldg Rm 2075 .... Boston MA 02203 617-565-1158 565-4511
Web: www.aoa.gov
Region V 233 N Michigan Ave Ste 1300 .... Chicago IL 60601 2-3-53--5160 -35-3-4144*
**Fax Area Code:* 312 ■
Web: www.hhs.gov/about/agencies/staff-divisions/iea/regional-offices/region-5/index.html
Region VIII 999 18th St S Terr Ste 496............ Denver CO 80202 303-844-2951 844-2943
Web: www.aoa.gov
Regions II & III 26 Federal Plaza Rm 38-102.......New York NY 10278 212-264-2976 264-0114
Web: www.aoa.gov/AoARoot/About/Organization/index.aspx

Agency for Healthcare Research & Quality
540 Gaither Rd.................................Rockville MD 20850 301-427-1200
TF: 800-358-9295 ■ *Web:* www.ahrq.gov

Agency for Toxic Substances & Disease Registry
4770 Buford Hwy NE ....Atlanta GA 30341 800-232-4636
TF: 800-232-4636 ■ *Web:* www.atsdr.cdc.gov

AIDSinfo PO Box 6303.............................Rockville MD 20849 301-519-0459 519-6616
TF: 800-448-0440 ■ *Web:* www.aidsinfo.nih.gov
National Center for Chronic Disease Prevention & Health Promotion (NCCDPHP)
4770 Buford Hwy NE............................Atlanta GA 30341 800-232-4636
TF: 800-232-4636 ■ *Web:* www.cdc.gov/nccdphp
National Center for Emerging & Zoonotic Infectious Diseases
1600 Clifton Rd.................................Atlanta GA 30333 404-639-3311
TF: 800-232-4636 ■ *Web:* cdc.gov
National Center for Environmental Health
4770 Buford Hwy Bldg 101........................Atlanta GA 30341 404-639-3311
TF: 800-232-4636 ■ *Web:* www.cdc.gov
National Center for Health Marketing
1600 Clifton Rd NE..............................Atlanta GA 30333 404-498-1515
TF: 800-311-3435 ■ *Web:* cdc.gov/healthcommunication
National Center for Health Statistics
6525 Belcrest Rd............................Hyattsville MD 20782 301-458-4000
Web: www.cdc.gov

Phone Fax

National Center for HIV/AIDS Viral Hepatitis STD & TB Prevention
1600 Clifton Rd.................................Atlanta GA 30333 800-232-4636
TF: 800-232-4636 ■ *Web:* www.cdc.gov/NCHHSTP
National Center for Immunization & Respiratory Diseases
1600 Clifton Rd NE MS E-05......................Atlanta GA 30333 800-232-4636
TF: 800-232-4636 ■ *Web:* www.cdc.gov/vaccines
National Center for Injury Prevention & Control (NCIPC)
4770 Buford Hwy NE............................Atlanta GA 30341 800-232-4636
TF: 800-232-4636 ■ *Web:* www.cdc.gov/injury
National Center for Public Health Informatics
1600 Clifton Rd NE MS E-78......................Atlanta GA 30333 800-232-4636 718-2093*
**Fax Area Code:* 404 ■ *TF:* 800-232-4636 ■ *Web:* www.cdc.gov/ncphi
National Center on Birth Defects & Developmental Disabilities
1600 Clifton Rd.................................Atlanta GA 30329 770-498-3800 498-3550
TF: 800-232-4636 ■ *Web:* www.cdc.gov/ncbddd
National Institute for Occupational Safety & Health
200 Independence Ave SW...................Washington DC 20201 404-639-3286
TF: 800-356-4674 ■ *Web:* www.cdc.gov/niosh
National Office of Public Health Genomics
4770 Buford Hwy MS K-89........................Atlanta GA 30341 770-488-8510 488-8355
Web: www.cdc.gov/genomics

Centers for Disease Control & Prevention
Travelers Health 1600 Clifton Rd NE ....Atlanta GA 30333 800-232-4636 232-3299*
**Fax Area Code:* 888 ■ *TF:* 800-232-4636 ■ *Web:* wwwnc.cdc.gov/travel

Centers for Medicare & Medicaid Services (CMS)
7500 Security Blvd..............................Baltimore MD 21244 800-633-4227
TF: 800-633-4227 ■ *Web:* www.cms.gov
Medicare Hotline 7500 Security Blvd............ Baltimore MD 21244 800-633-4227
TF: 800-633-4227 ■ *Web:* www.medicare.gov
Region I JFK Federal Bldg Rm 2325 .... Boston MA 02203 617-565-1188 565-1339
Web: www.cms.gov

Centers for Medicare & Medicaid Services Regional Offices
Region II 26 Federal Plaza.....................New York NY 10278 212-616-2439 380-8855*
**Fax Area Code:* 443 ■ *Web:* cms.gov/regionaloffices
Region III
150 S Independence Mall W Ste 216............Philadelphia PA 19106 215-861-4140 861-4240
Web: www.cms.gov
Region IV 61 Forsyth St SW Ste 4T20.............Atlanta GA 30303 404-562-1738 380-8945*
**Fax Area Code:* 443 ■ *Web:* www.cms.gov
Region IX 90 Seventh St Ste 5-300 ....San Francisco CA 94105 415-744-3502 744-3517
Web: www.cms.gov
Region V 233 N Michigan Ave Ste 600 .... Chicago IL 60601 312-353-9866 353-0252
Web: cms.gov/regionaloffices
Region VI 1301 Young St Ste 714 .... Dallas TX 75202 214-767-6427
Web: www.cms.gov
Region VII
Federal Bldg 601 E 12th St Ste 235.............Kansas City MO 64106 303-844-7481
Web: www.cms.gov
Region VIII 1600 Broadway Ste 700............... Denver CO 80202 303-844-7035 844-3753
Web: www.cms.gov
Region X 2201 Sixth Ave Ste 801 ....Seattle WA 98121 206-615-2306
Web: www.cms.gov

Child Welfare Information Gateway
1250 Maryland Ave SW 8th Fl ....Washington DC 20024 703-385-7565 385-3206
TF: 800-394-3366 ■ *Web:* www.childwelfare.gov
Center for Biologics Evaluation & Research
1401 Rockville Pike Ste 200N MS HFM-4...........Rockville MD 20852 301-827-0372
Web: www.fda.gov/cber
Center for Devices & Radiological Health (CDRH)
10903 New Hampshire Ave WO66-5429.........Silver Spring MD 20993 301-796-7100 847-8149
TF: 800-638-2041 ■ *Web:* www.fda.gov
Center for Drug Evaluation & Research
Hillandale Bldg 4th Fl ....Silver Spring MD 20993 301-796-3400
TF: 855-543-3784 ■ *Web:* www.fda.gov
Center for Food Safety & Applied Nutrition
5100 Paint Branch Pkwy ....College Park MD 20740 888-723-3366
TF: 888-723-3366 ■ *Web:* www.fda.gov
Center for Veterinary Medicine
7519 Standish Pl...............................Rockville MD 20855 240-276-9000 276-9115
Web: www.fda.gov/cvm

Food & Drug Administration
National Center for Toxicological Research
3900 N Ctr Rd ....Jefferson AR 72079 870-543-7000 543-7576
TF: 800-638-3321 ■ *Web:* www.fda.gov/nctr
Central Region 200 Chestnut St Rm 900....... Philadelphia PA 19106 215-597-4390 597-4660
Web: www.fda.gov
Northeast Region 158-15 Liberty Ave..............Jamaica NY 11433 718-662-5416 662-5434
Web: www.fda.gov
Pacific Region 1301 Clay St Ste 1180N............Oakland CA 94612 510-287-2700 287-2739
Web: www.hhs.gov

Food & Drug Administration Regional Offices
Southwest Region 4040 N Central Expwy Ste 900..... Dallas TX 75204 214-253-4901 253-4960
Web: www.fda.gov

Health Resources & Services Administration (HRSA)
5600 Fishers Ln.................................Rockville MD 20857 301-443-2216
TF: 888-275-4772 ■ *Web:* hrsa.gov

Indian Health Service (IHS)
801 Thompson Ave Ste 400........................Rockville MD 20852 301-443-1083 443-4794

National Child Care Information & Technical Assistance Ctr (NCCIC)
9300 Lee Hwy.....................................Fairfax VA 22031 877-296-2250
TF: 877-296-2250 ■ *Web:* acf.hhs.gov/programs/occ

National Clearinghouse for Alcohol & Drug Information
11426 Rockville Pk PO Box 2345..................Rockville MD 20847 800-729-6686
TF: 800-729-6686 ■ *Web:* samhsa.gov

National Hansen's Disease Program (NHDP)
1770 Physicians Pk Dr.........................Baton Rouge LA 70816 225-756-3700
TF: 800-642-2477 ■ *Web:* hrsa.gov

National Institutes of Biomedical Imaging & Bioengineering
National Institute of Biomedical Imaging & Bioengineering (NIBIB)
6707 Democracy Blvd..........................Bethesda MD 20892 301-496-8859 480-0679
Web: www.nibib.nih.gov

	City	State	Zip	Phone	Fax
Center for Scientific Review 6701 Rockledge Dr MSC 7950	Bethesda	MD	20892	301-435-1115	
Web: www.nih.gov/					
Clinical Ctr 10 Ctr Dr Bldg 10	Bethesda	MD	20892	301-496-2563	402-2984
Web: www.cc.nih.gov					
National Cancer Institute Public Inquiries Office 6116 Executive Blvd Rm 3036A	Bethesda	MD	20892	301-435-3848	
TF: 800-422-6237 ■ *Web:* www.cancer.gov					
National Center for Complementary & Alternative Medicine 31 Ctr Dr Bldg 31	Bethesda	MD	20892	301-594-7103	
TF: 888-644-6226 ■ *Web:* www.nccam.nih.gov					
National Institutes of Health					
National Center on Minority Health & Health Disparities 6707 Democracy Blvd Ste 800 Ste 800	Bethesda	MD	20892	301-402-1366	480-4049
Web: www.nimhd.nih.gov					
National Eye Institute 2020 Vision Pl	Bethesda	MD	20892	301-496-5248	402-1065
Web: www.nei.nih.gov					
National Heart Lung & Blood Institute (NHLBI) 31 Ctr Dr Bldg 31 Rm 5A52 MSC 2486	Bethesda	MD	20892	301-496-5166	402-0818
Web: www.nhlbi.nih.gov					
National Human Genome Research Institute 31 Ctr Dr Bldg 31 Rm 4B09	Bethesda	MD	20892	301-402-0911	402-2218
Web: www.genome.gov					
National Institute of Arthritis & Musculoskeletal & Skin Diseases 31 Ctr Dr MSC 2350 Bldg 31 Rm 4C02	Bethesda	MD	20892	301-496-8190	480-2814
Web: www.niams.nih.gov					
National Institute of Dental & Craniofacial Research 31 Ctr Dr	Bethesda	MD	20892	301-496-3571	402-2185
Web: www.nidcr.nih.gov					
National Institute of Diabetes & Digestive & Kidney Diseases 31 Ctr Dr MSC 2560	Bethesda	MD	20892	301-496-3583	496-7422
Web: www.niddk.nih.gov					
National Institute of Environmental Health Sciences PO Box 12233	Research Triangle Park	NC	27709	919-541-3201	541-2260
Web: www.niehs.nih.gov					
National Institute of General Medical Sciences 45 Ctr Dr MSC 6200	Bethesda	MD	20892	301-496-7301	
Web: www.nigms.nih.gov					
National Institute of Mental Health 6001 Executive Blvd Rm 8184 MSC 9663	Bethesda	MD	20892	301-443-4513	443-4279
TF: 866-615-6464 ■ *Web:* www.nimh.nih.gov					
National Institute of Neurological Disorders & Stroke PO Box 5801	Bethesda	MD	20824	301-496-5751	
TF: 800-352-9424 ■ *Web:* www.ninds.nih.gov					
National Institute of Nursing Research 31 Ctr Dr Bldg 31 Rm 5B10	Bethesda	MD	20892	301-496-8230	594-3405
Web: www.ninr.nih.gov					
National Institute on Aging 31 Ctr Dr Bldg 31 Rm 5C27 MSC 2292	Bethesda	MD	20892	301-496-1752	496-1072
Web: www.nia.nih.gov					
National Institute on Alcohol Abuse & Alcoholism 5635 Fishers Ln MSC 9304	Bethesda	MD	20892	301-443-3885	443-7043
Web: www.niaaa.nih.gov					
National Institute on Deafness & Other Communication Disorders 31 Ctr Dr Bldg 31 Rm 3C35	Bethesda	MD	20892	301-496-7243	402-0018
TF: 800-241-1044 ■ *Web:* www.nidcd.nih.gov					
National Institute on Drug Abuse 6001 Executive Blvd Rm 4123	Bethesda	MD	20892	301-443-6480	
Web: www.drugabuse.gov					
National Library of Medicine 8600 Rockville Pike Bldg 38	Bethesda	MD	20894	301-594-5983	402-1384
TF: 888-346-3656 ■ *Web:* www.nlm.nih.gov					
Office of Communications & Public Liason 31 Ctr Dr Bldg 1 Rm 344	Bethesda	MD	20892	301-496-4461	496-0017
Web: www.nih.gov					
Office of Dietary Supplements 6100 Executive Blvd Ste 3B01	Bethesda	MD	20892	301-435-2920	480-1845
Web: www.ods.od.nih.gov					
Office of Rare Diseases 6701 Democracy Blvd Ste 1001	Bethesda	MD	20892	301-402-4336	480-9655
Web: www.rarediseases.info.nih.gov					
National Library of Medicine					
Lister Hill National Center for Biomedical Communications 8600 Rockville Pike Bldg 38A 7th Fl	Bethesda	MD	20894	301-496-4441	480-3035
Web: www.lhncbc.nlm.nih.gov					
National Mental Health Information Ctr PO Box 42557	Washington	DC	20015	800-487-4889	747-5470*
**Fax Area Code:* 240 ■ *TF:* 800-487-4889 ■ *Web:* www.samhsa.gov					
National Women's Health Information Ctr 200 Independence Ave S.W	Washington	DC	20201	800-994-9662	
TF: 800-994-9662 ■ *Web:* www.womenshealth.gov					
NIH Osteoporosis & Related Bone Diseases-National Resource Ctr 2 AMS Cir	Bethesda	MD	20892	202-223-0344	293-2356
TF: 800-624-2663 ■ *Web:* niams.nih.gov/health_info/bone/default.asp					
Office of Intergovernmental and External Affairs					
Region II 26 Federal Plaza Ste 3835	New York	NY	10278	212-264-4600	264-1324
Web: www.hhs.gov/ophs/rha					
Office of Public Health & Science 200 Independence Ave SW Rm 716G	Washington	DC	20201	202-690-7694	690-6960
Web: www.hhs.gov/ophs					
Region I John F Kennedy Federal Bldg Rm 2100	Boston	MA	02203	617-565-1491	
Web: www.hhs.gov					
Office of Public Health & Science Regional Offices					
Region III 150 S Independence Mall W Ste 436	Philadelphia	PA	19106	215-861-4639	861-4617
Web: www.hhs.gov/ash/rha					
Region IV 1301 61 Forsyth St SW Ste 5B95	Atlanta	GA	30303	404-562-7888	562-7899
Web: www.hhs.gov/ash/rha					
Region IX 90 Seventh St Ste 5-100	San Francisco	CA	94103	415-437-8096	437-8004
Web: www.hhs.gov/ash/rha					
Region VI 1301 Young St Ste 1124	Dallas	TX	75202	214-767-3879	767-3209
Web: www.hhs.gov/ash/rha					
Region VII 601 E 12th St Rm S-1801	Kansas City	MO	64106	816-426-3291	426-2178
Web: www.hhs.gov					
Region X 2201 Sixth Ave MS 20	Seattle	WA	98121	206-615-2469	615-2481
Web: www.hhs.gov/ash/rha					
Office of the Assistant Secretary for Health					
Region VIII 999 18th St South Terrace	Denver	CO	80202	303-844-6163	844-2019
Web: www.hhs.gov/ash/rha					
President's Council on Physical Fitness Sports & Nutrition 1101 Wootton Pkwy	Rockville	MD	20852	240-276-9567	276-9860
Web: www.fitness.gov					
Secretary of Health & Human Services 200 Independence Ave SW	Washington	DC	20201	202-690-7000	690-7755
Web: www.hhs.gov/about					
Substance Abuse & Mental Health Services Administration (SAMHSA) 1 Choke Cherry Rd	Rockville	MD	20857	240-276-2000	276-2010
TF: 877-726-4727 ■ *Web:* www.samhsa.gov					
Center for Mental Health Services 1 Choke Cherry Ln	Rockville	MD	20857	877-726-4727	221-4292*
**Fax Area Code:* 240 ■ *TF:* 877-726-4727 ■ *Web:* www.samhsa.gov					
Center for Substance Abuse Prevention 1 Choke Cherry Rd	Rockville	MD	20857	240-276-2420	276-2430
TF: 877-726-4727 ■ *Web:* www.samhsa.gov					
Center for Substance Abuse Treatment 1 Choke Cherry Rd PO Box 2345	Rockville	MD	20857	240-276-2130	221-4292
TF: 877-726-4727 ■ *Web:* www.samhsa.gov					
US Surgeon General 1101 Wootton Pkwy Rm 100	Rockville	MD	20857	240-276-8853	453-6141
Web: www.surgeongeneral.gov					

343-11 US Department of Homeland Security

	City	State	Zip	Phone	Fax
Department of Homeland Security					
Ready Campaign 500 C St SW Ste 714	Washington	DC	20472	800-621-3362	621-3362
Web: www.ready.gov					
Federal Emergency Management Agency					
FEMA for Kids 500 C St SW Ste 714	Washington	DC	20472	800-621-3362	
TF: 800-621-3362 ■ *Web:* www.ready.gov					
National Flood Insurance Program 500 C St SW	Washington	DC	20472	888-379-9531	646-2818*
**Fax Area Code:* 202 ■ *TF:* 888-379-9531 ■ *Web:* www.floodsmart.gov					
US Fire Administration 16825 S Seton Ave	Emmitsburg	MD	21727	301-447-1000	447-1346
Web: www.usfa.fema.gov					
Region 1 99 High St	Boston	MA	02110	617-956-7551	
TF: 877-336-2734 ■ *Web:* www.fema.gov/region-i					
Region 10 Federal Regional Ctr 130 228th St SW	Bothell	WA	98021	425-487-4600	487-4622
TF General: 800-772-1252 ■ *Web:* www.fema.gov					
Region 2 26 Federal Plaza	New York	NY	10278	212-680-3600	
Web: www.fema.gov					
Region 3 1 Independence Mall 615 Chestnut St 6th Fl	Philadelphia	PA	19106	215-931-5500	931-5621
TF: 800-621-3362 ■ *Web:* www.fema.gov					
Region 4 3003 Chamblee-Tucker Rd	Atlanta	GA	30341	770-220-5200	220-5230
Web: www.fema.gov					
Region 5 536 S Clark St 6th Fl	Chicago	IL	60605	312-408-5500	408-5234
TF: 877-336-2627 ■ *Web:* www.fema.gov					
Region 6 800 N Loop 288	Denton	TX	76209	940-898-5399	898-5325
TF: 800-426-5460 ■ *Web:* www.fema.gov					
Region 7 9221 Ward Pkwy	Kansas City	MO	64114	816-283-7061	
Web: www.fema.gov					
Region 8 Denver Federal Ctr Bldg 710 PO Box 25267	Denver	CO	80225	303-235-4900	235-4976
Web: www.fema.gov					
Federal Emergency Management Agency Regional Offices					
Region 9 1111 Broadway Ste 1200	Oakland	CA	94607	510-627-7100	
TF: 877-336-2627 ■ *Web:* www.fema.gov					
Federal Law Enforcement Training Ctr 1131 Chapel Crossing Rd	Glynco	GA	31524	912-267-2100	
Web: www.fletc.gov					
Secretary of Homeland Security Naval Security Stn	Washington	DC	20528	202-282-8000	
Web: www.dhs.gov/dhspublic					
Transportation Security Administration (TSA) 601 S 12th St	Arlington	VA	22202	202-282-8000	
TF: 866-289-9673 ■ *Web:* www.tsa.gov					
Federal Air Marshal Service 601 S 12th St	Arlington	VA	22202	866-289-9673	
TF: 866-289-9673 ■ *Web:* www.tsa.gov					
Central Region 7701 N Stemmons Fwy	Dallas	TX	75247	214-905-5430	905-5435
Web: uscis.gov					
US Citizenship & Immigration Services Regional Offices					
Eastern Region 70 Kimball Ave	South Burlington	VT	05403	800-767-1833	
TF: 800-767-1833 ■ *Web:* www.uscis.gov					
Western Region 24000 Avila Rd 2nd Fl PO Box 10526	Laguna Niguel	CA	92677	800-375-5283	
Web: www.uscis.gov					
Boating Safety Office 2703 Martin Luther King Jr Ave SE Ste 7501	Washington	DC	20593	202-372-1062	
Web: www.uscgboating.org					
Law Enforcement Office 2100 Second St SW	Washington	DC	20593	202-372-2183	
Web: www.uscg.mil/hq/cg5/cg531					
National Maritime Ctr 100 Forbes Dr	Martinsburg	WV	25404	304-433-3400	
TF: 888-427-5662 ■ *Web:* www.uscg.mil					
US Coast Guard					
National Pollution Funds Ctr 4200 Wilson Blvd Ste 1000	Arlington	VA	20598	202-493-6700	493-6900
Web: uscg.mil/ccs/npfc					
Navigation Ctr 7323 Telegraph Rd	Alexandria	VA	22315	703-313-5900	313-5920
Web: www.navcen.uscg.gov					
Search & Rescue Office 2100 Second St SW	Washington	DC	20593	202-372-2090	372-2912
Web: uscg.mil/hq/cg5/cg534					

				Phone	Fax
US Coast Guard Academy 15 Mohegan Ave	New London	CT	06320	860-444-8500	701-6700
TF: 800-883-8724 ■ *Web:* www.cga.edu					
US Customs & Border Protection					
1300 Pennsylvania Ave NW	Washington	DC	20229	703-526-4200	
TF: 877-227-5511 ■ *Web:* www.cbp.gov					
US Immigration & Customs Enforcement (ICE)					
425 'I' St NW	Washington	DC	20536	202-514-1900	
TF: 866-347-2423 ■ *Web:* www.ice.gov					
US Secret Service 245 Murray Dr Bldg 410	Washington	DC	20223	202-406-5830	
Web: www.secretservice.gov					

343-12 US Department of Housing & Urban Development

				Phone	Fax
Department of Housing & Urban Development (HUD)					
451 Seventh St SW	Washington	DC	20410	202-708-0685	619-8153
TF: 800-569-4287 ■ *Web:* www.hud.gov					
Public Affairs Office 451 Seventh St SW	Washington	DC	20410	202-708-0980	
TF: 800-333-4636 ■ *Web:* www.hud.gov					
Boston 10 Cswy St 3rd Fl	Boston	MA	02222	617-994-8200	565-6558
TF: 800-225-5342 ■ *Web:* portal.hud.gov/hudportal/hud					
Great Plains Region 400 State Ave	Kansas City	KS	66101	913-551-6857	551-5469
Web: portal.hud.gov					
Mid-Atlantic Region 100 Penn Sq E	Philadelphia	PA	19107	215-656-0500	656-3445
TF: 800-225-5342 ■ *Web:* www.hud.gov					
New York City Regional Office					
26 Federal Plaza Ste 3541	New York	NY	10278	212-264-8000	264-3068
TF: 800-496-4294 ■ *Web:* portal.hud.gov					
Pacific/Hawaii Region					
600 Harrison St 3rd Fl	San Francisco	CA	94107	415-489-6572	436-8412
TF: 800-347-3739 ■ *Web:* portal.hud.gov					
Region 5 - Chicago					
Federal Bldg 77 W Jackson Blvd	Chicago	IL	60604	312-353-6236	353-5417
Web: portal.hud.gov					
Rocky Mountain Region 1670 Bdwy 25th Fl	Denver	CO	80202	303-672-5440	672-5004
TF: 800-955-2232 ■ *Web:* portal.hud.gov					
Seattle Federal Bldg 909 1st Ave Ste 200	Seattle	WA	98104	509-368-3200	
Web: portal.hud.gov					
Department of Housing & Urban Development Regional Offices					
Southeast/Caribbean Region					
5 Points Plaza Bldg 40 Marietta St	Atlanta	GA	30303	404-331-5136	730-2392
Web: www.hud.gov					
Southwest Region					
801 N Cherry St Unit 45 Ste 2500	Fort Worth	TX	76102	817-978-5965	978-5569
Web: www.hud.gov					
Government National Mortgage Assn					
451 Seventh St SW Ste B-133	Washington	DC	20410	202-708-1535	
Web: www.ginniemae.gov					
HUD Office of Community Planning & Development					
Affordable Housing Programs Office					
451 Seventh St SW	Washington	DC	20410	202-708-1112	
Web: portal.hud.gov					
Block Grant Assistance Office					
451 Seventh St SW	Washington	DC	20410	202-708-1112	708-1455
Web: portal.hud.gov					
HIV/AIDS Housing Office 451 7th St SW	Washington	DC	20410	202-708-1112	
Web: portal.hud.gov					
Special Needs Assistance Programs Office					
451 Seventh St SW	Washington	DC	20410	202-708-1112	
Web: portal.hud.gov					
HUD Office of Fair Housing & Equal Opportunity					
Housing Discrimination Hotline					
451 Seventh St SW	Washington	DC	20410	202-708-1112	
TF: 800-333-4636 ■ *Web:* portal.hud.gov					
HUD Office of Healthy Homes & Lead Hazard Control					
451 Seventh St SW	Washington	DC	20410	202-708-1112	
Web: portal.hud.gov					
HUD Office of Housing and Urban Development (FHA)					
451 Seventh St SW Ste 9100	Washington	DC	20410	202-708-1112	
TF: 800-767-7468 ■ *Web:* portal.hud.gov					
HUD Office of Policy Development & Research					
451 Seventh St SW MC R	Washington	DC	20410	202-708-3178	
Web: www.huduser.org					
HUD Office of Public & Indian Housing					
451 Seventh St SW Rm 4100	Washington	DC	20410	202-708-0950	619-8478
TF: 800-955-2232 ■ *Web:* portal.hud.gov					
Real Estate Assessment Ctr					
550 12th St SW Ste 100	Washington	DC	20410	202-708-1112	
TF: 888-245-4860 ■ *Web:* portal.hud.gov					
Secretary of Housing & Urban Development					
451 Seventh St SW	Washington	DC	20410	202-708-0417	619-8365
Web: portal.hud.gov					

343-13 US Department of the Interior

				Phone	Fax
Department of the Interior (DOI)					
1849 C St NW	Washington	DC	20240	202-208-3100	
Web: www.doi.gov					
Bureau of Indian Affairs (BIA)					
1849 C St NW MS 4141 MIB	Washington	DC	20240	202-208-7163	208-5320
Web: www.bia.gov					
Alaska Region 3601 C St Ste 1100	Anchorage	AK	99503	907-271-1536	271-1349
TF: 800-645-8397 ■ *Web:* www.bia.gov					
Eastern Oklahoma Region					
3100 W Peak Blvd PO Box 8002	Muskogee	OK	74402	918-781-4600	781-4604
Web: www.bia.gov					
Eastern Region 545 Marriott Dr Ste 700	Nashville	TN	37214	615-564-6700	564-6701
Web: www.bia.gov					
Bureau of Indian Affairs Regional Offices					
Great Plains Region 115 Fourth Ave SE	Aberdeen	SD	57401	605-226-7343	226-7446
Web: www.bia.gov					
Midwest Region					
Norman Pointe II Bldg					
5600 W American Blvd Ste 500	Bloomington	MN	55347	612-713-4400	713-4401
Web: www.bia.gov					
Navajo Region 301 W Hill St PO Box 1060	Gallup	NM	87305	505-863-8314	863-8324
Web: www.bia.gov					
Northwest Region 911 NE 11th Ave	Portland	OR	97232	503-231-6702	231-2201
Web: www.bia.gov					
Pacific Region 2800 Cottage Way	Sacramento	CA	95825	916-978-6000	978-6099
Web: www.bia.gov					
Rocky Mountain Region 316 N 26th St	Billings	MT	59101	406-247-7943	247-7976
Web: www.bia.gov					
Southern Plains Region PO Box 368	Anadarko	OK	73005	405-247-6673	247-5611
Web: www.indianaffairs.gov					
Southwest Region					
1001 Indian School Rd NW	Albuquerque	NM	87104	505-563-3103	563-3101
Web: www.bia.gov					
Western Region					
2600 N Central Ave FL 8 Ste 310	Phoenix	AZ	85008	602-379-6600	379-4413
Web: www.bia.gov					
Bureau of Land Management (BLM)					
1849 C St NW Rm 5665	Washington	DC	20240	202-208-3801	208-5242
Web: www.blm.gov					
National Wild Horse & Burro Program					
1849 C Street NW Rm. 5665	Washington	DC	20240	202-208-3801	
TF: 866-468-7826 ■ *Web:* www.blm.gov					
Alaska State Office					
222 W Seventh Ave Ste 13	Anchorage	AK	99513	907-271-5960	271-3684
Web: www.blm.gov					
Bureau of Land Management Regional Offices					
Arizona State Office 1 N Central Ave Ste 800	Phoenix	AZ	85004	602-417-9200	417-9556
Web: www.blm.gov					
California State Office					
2800 Cottage Way Ste W-1834	Sacramento	CA	95825	916-978-4400	978-4416
Web: www.blm.gov					
Colorado State Office 2850 Youngfield St	Lakewood	CO	80215	303-239-3600	239-3933
Web: www.blm.gov					
Eastern States Office 7450 Boston Blvd	Springfield	VA	22153	703-440-1600	
Web: www.blm.gov					
Idaho State Office 1387 S Vinnell Way	Boise	ID	83709	208-373-4000	373-3899
Web: www.blm.gov					
Montana State Office 5001 Southgate Dr	Billings	MT	59101	406-896-5000	
Web: www.blm.gov					
Nevada State Office 1340 Financial Blvd	Reno	NV	89502	775-861-6400	861-6606
Web: www.blm.gov					
Oregon/Washington State Office					
333 SW First Ave	Portland	OR	97204	503-808-6001	808-6422
Web: www.blm.gov					
Wyoming State Office					
5353 Yellowstone Rd PO Box 1828	Cheyenne	WY	82003	307-775-6256	775-6129
Web: www.blm.gov					
Bureau of Reclamation 1849 C St NW	Washington	DC	20240	202-513-0501	
Web: www.usbr.gov					
Bureau of Reclamation Regional Offices					
Great Plains Region PO Box 36900	Billings	MT	59107	406-247-7600	247-7604
Web: www.usbr.gov					
Lower Colorado Region PO Box 61470	Boulder City	NV	89006	702-293-8411	293-8333
Web: www.usbr.gov					
Mid-Pacific Region					
2800 Cottage Way Federal Bldg.	Sacramento	CA	95825	916-978-5000	978-5005
Web: www.usbr.gov					
Pacific Northwest Region					
1150 N Curtis Rd Ste 100	Boise	ID	83706	208-378-5012	378-5019
Web: www.usbr.gov					
Upper Colorado Region					
125 S State St Rm 6107	Salt Lake City	UT	84138	801-524-3600	524-5499
Web: www.usbr.gov/uc					
Minerals Management Service					
1849 C St NW Ste 4210	Washington	DC	20240	202-208-3985	208-7242
Web: www.doi.gov					
National Interagency Fire Ctr					
3833 S Development Ave	Boise	ID	83705	208-387-5512	
Web: www.nifc.gov					
Conservation & Outdoor Recreation Programs					
1849 C St NW Org Code 2220	Washington	DC	20240	202-354-6900	371-5179
Web: www.nps.gov/ncrc					
National Park Service					
National Register of Historic Places					
1201 Eye St NW FL 8	Washington	DC	20005	202-354-2201	371-5197
Web: www.cr.nps.gov					
National Park Service Regional Offices					
Alaska Region 240 W Fifth Ave Ste 114	Anchorage	AK	99501	907-644-3510	644-3816
Web: nps.gov					
National Park Service Regional Offices Intermountain Region					
12795 W Alameda Pkwy	Denver	CO	80225	303-969-2500	
Web: www.nps.gov					
National Park Service Regional Offices National Capital Region					
1100 Ohio Dr SW	Washington	DC	20242	202-619-7000	619-7220
Web: www.nps.gov/ncro					
National Park Service Regional Offices NortheastRegion					
200 Chestnut St Ste 3	Philadelphia	PA	19106	215-597-7013	597-0815
Web: www.nps.gov					
National Park Service Regional Offices Southeast Region					
100 Alabama St SW 1924 Bldg.	Atlanta	GA	30303	404-507-5600	562-3201
Web: www.nps.gov					
Office of Surface Mining Reclamation & Enforcement					
1951 Constitution Ave NW					
S Interior Bldg Rm 233	Washington	DC	20240	202-208-4006	
Web: www.osmre.gov					
Secretary of the Interior 1849 C St NW	Washington	DC	20240	202-208-3100	
Web: www.doi.gov					

	City	State	Zip	Phone	Fax
US Board on Geographic Names					
12201 Sunrise Valley Dr	Reston	VA	20192	703-648-4552	648-4549
Web: geonames.usgs.gov					
US Fish & Wildlife Service (USFWS)					
1849 C St NW	Washington	DC	20240	202-208-4717	208-6965
TF: 800-344-9453 ■ *Web:* www.fws.gov					
Alaska Region 1011 E Tudor Rd	Anchorage	AK	99503	907-786-3309	786-3495
Web: www.fws.gov					
California & Nevada Region					
2800 Cottage Way	Sacramento	CA	95825	916-414-6464	414-6486
Web: www.fws.gov					
Great Lakes/Big Rivers Region					
5600 American Blvd W Ste 900	Bloomington	MN	55437	612-713-5360	713-5280
TF: 800-877-8339 ■ *Web:* www.fws.gov/midwest					
Mountain-Prairie Region 134 Union Blvd	Lakewood	CO	80228	303-236-7905	236-8295
Web: www.fws.gov/mountain-prairie					
NortheastRegion 300 Westgate Ctr Dr	Hadley	MA	01035	413-253-8200	253-8308
Web: www.fws.gov					
US Fish & Wildlife Service Regional Offices					
Pacific Region					
Eastside Federal Complex 911 NE 11th Ave	Portland	OR	97232	503-231-6838	231-6161
Web: www.fws.gov/pacific					
Southeast Region 1875 Century Blvd Ste 400	Atlanta	GA	30345	404-679-4000	679-4006
Web: www.fws.gov/southeast					
Southwest Region					
500 Gold Ave SW PO Box 1306	Albuquerque	NM	87102	505-248-6911	248-6910
Web: www.fws.gov/southwest					
US Geological Survey					
Ask USGS 12201 Sunrise Valley Dr	Reston	VA	20192	703-648-5953	
TF: 888-275-8747 ■ *Web:* usgs.gov					

343-14 US Department of Justice

	City	State	Zip	Phone	Fax
Department of Justice (DOJ)					
950 Pennsylvania Ave NW	Washington	DC	20530	202-514-2007	514-5331
Web: www.justice.gov					
Antitrust Div 950 Pennsylvania Ave NW	Washington	DC	20530	202-514-2401	616-2645
Web: www.justice.gov					
Civil Div 950 Pennsylvania Ave NW	Washington	DC	20530	202-514-3301	514-8071
Web: www.justice.gov					
Civil Rights Div 950 Pennsylvania Ave NW	Washington	DC	20530	202-514-4609	
Web: www.justice.gov					
Community Relations Service 600 E St NW	Washington	DC	20530	202-305-2935	305-3009
Web: www.justice.gov					
Criminal Div 601 D St NW	Washington	DC	20530	202-514-0296	
Web: www.justice.gov					
Environment & Natural Resources Div					
950 Pennsylvania Ave NW	Washington	DC	20530	202-514-2701	514-0557
Web: www.justice.gov					
National Security Div					
950 Pennsylvania Ave NW	Washington	DC	20530	202-514-1057	
Web: www.justice.gov					
Office of Information & Privacy					
1425 New York Ave NW Ste 11050	Washington	DC	20530	202-514-3642	514-1009
Web: www.justice.gov					
Public Affairs Office					
950 Pennsylvania Ave NW	Washington	DC	20530	202-514-2000	
Web: www.justice.gov					
Tax Div 950 Pennsylvania Ave NW 4th Fl	Washington	DC	20530	202-514-2901	514-5479
Web: www.justice.gov					
Department of Justice Antitrust Div Regional Office					
Dallas Field Office 1601 Elm St Ste 4950	Dallas	TX	75201	214-880-9401	353-8856*
**Fax Area Code:* 202 ■ *Web:* www.justice.gov					
Department of Justice Antitrust Div Regional Offices					
Atlanta Field Office					
Federal Bldg 75 Spring St SW Ste 1176	Atlanta	GA	30303	404-331-7100	331-7110
Web: www.justice.gov/atr					
Chicago Field Office 209 S LaSalle St Ste 600	Chicago	IL	60604	312-353-5559	353-1046
Web: www.justice.gov					
Cleveland Field Office					
55 Erieview Plaza Ste 700	Cleveland	OH	44114	216-522-4070	522-8332
Web: www.justice.gov					
New York Field Office					
26 Federal Plaza Rm 3630	New York	NY	10278	212-264-0383	264-0678
Web: www.justice.gov/atr					
Philadelphia Field Office					
7th & Walnut St Ste 650	Philadelphia	PA	19106	215-597-7405	597-8838
Web: www.justice.gov					
San Francisco Field Office					
PO Box 36046	San Francisco	CA	94102	415-436-6660	436-6687
Web: www.justice.gov/atr					
Bureau of Alcohol Tobacco Firearms & Explosives (ATF)					
650 Massachusetts Ave NW	Washington	DC	20226	202-927-8210	
Web: www.atf.gov					
Atlanta Field Div 2600 Century Pkwy NE	Atlanta	GA	30345	404-417-2600	417-2601
Web: www.atf.gov					
Baltimore Field Div 31 Hopkins Plaza 5th Fl	Baltimore	MD	21201	410-779-1700	
Web: www.atf.gov/field/baltimore					
Boston Field Div 10 Cswy St Ste 791	Boston	MA	02222	617-557-1200	
Charlotte Field Div 6701 Carmel Rd Ste 200	Charlotte	NC	28226	704-716-1800	716-1801
Web: www.atf.gov					
Bureau of Alcohol Tobacco Firearms & Explosives Regional Offices					
Chicago Field Div 525 W Van Buren St Ste 600	Chicago	IL	60607	312-846-7200	846-7201
Web: atf.gov					
Columbus Field Div 37 W Broad St Ste 200	Columbus	OH	43215	614-827-8400	827-8401
Web: www.atf.gov					
Dallas Field Div 1114 Commerce St Rm 303	Dallas	TX	75242	469-227-4300	227-4330
Web: www.atf.gov					
Denver Field Div 950 17th St Ste 1800	Denver	CO	80202	303-575-7600	575-7601
Web: www.atf.gov					
Detroit Field Div					
1155 Brewery Pk Blvd Ste 300	Detroit	MI	48207	313-202-3400	202-3445
Web: www.atf.gov					
Houston Field Div 333 W Loop N # 111	Houston	TX	77024	713-220-2157	
Web: www.atf.gov					
Kansas City Field Div					
2600 Grand Ave Ste 280	Kansas City	MO	64108	816-559-0850	559-0831
Louisville Field Div					
600 Martin Luther King Pl #322	Louisville	KY	40202	502-753-3400	753-3401
Web: www.atf.gov					
Miami Field Div 11410 NW 20 St Ste 201	Miami	FL	33172	305-597-4800	597-4801
Web: www.atf.gov					
Nashville Field Div					
5300 Maryland Way Ste 200	Brentwood	TN	37027	615-565-1400	565-1401
Web: www.atf.gov/field/nashville					
New Orleans Field Div					
1 Galleria Blvd Ste 1700	Metairie	LA	70001	504-841-7120	841-7159
Philadelphia Field Div 601 Walnut St	Philadelphia	PA	19106	215-446-7800	446-7811
Web: www.atf.gov					
Phoenix Field Div 201 E Washington St Ste 940	Phoenix	AZ	85004	602-776-5400	776-5429
Web: www.atf.gov					
Saint Paul Field Div					
30 E Seventh St Ste 1900	Saint Paul	MN	55101	651-726-0200	726-0201
Web: www.atf.gov					
Tampa Field Div 400 N Tampa St Ste 2100	Tampa	FL	33602	813-202-7300	202-7301
Web: www.atf.gov					
Washington (DC) Field Div					
1401 H St NW Ste 900	Washington	DC	20226	202-648-8010	648-8001
Web: www.atf.gov/field/washington					
Community Oriented Policing Services (COPS)					
1100 Vermont Ave NW 10th Fl	Washington	DC	20530	202-616-2888	
TF: 800-421-6770 ■ *Web:* www.cops.usdoj.gov					
Drug Enforcement Administration (DEA)					
700 Army-Navy Dr	Arlington	VA	22202	202-307-7596	
Web: www.justice.gov					
DEA Training Academy PO Box 1475	Quantico	VA	22134	703-632-5000	
Web: justice.gov/					
El Paso Intelligence Ctr 11339 Simms St	El Paso	TX	79908	202-307-1000	
Web: www.justice.gov					
Atlanta Div Federal Bldg 75 Spring St SW	Atlanta	GA	30303	404-893-7000	
Web: www.justice.gov					
Boston Div 15 New Sudbury St Rm E400	Boston	MA	02203	617-557-2100	
Web: www.justice.gov					
Chicago Div Federal Bldg 230 S Dearborn St	Chicago	IL	60604	312-353-7875	
Web: www.justice.gov					
Dallas Div 10160 Technology Blvd E	Dallas	TX	75220	214-366-6900	
Web: www.justice.gov					
Detroit Div 431 Howard St	Detroit	MI	48226	313-234-4000	
Web: www.justice.gov					
Drug Enforcement Administration Regional Offices					
El Paso Div 660 S Mesa Hills Ste 2000	El Paso	TX	79912	915-832-6000	
Web: www.justice.gov/dea/divisions/elp/elp.shtml					
Houston Div 1433 W Loop S Ste 600	Houston	TX	77027	713-693-3000	
Web: www.justice.gov					
Los Angeles Div					
Federal Bldg 255 E Temple St 20th Fl	Los Angeles	CA	90012	213-621-6700	
Web: www.justice.gov					
Miami Div 8400 NW 53rd St	Miami	FL	33166	305-994-4870	
Web: www.justice.gov					
New Orleans Div 3838 N Cswy Blvd Ste 1800	Metairie	LA	70002	504-840-1100	
Web: www.justice.gov					
New York Div 99 Tenth Ave	New York	NY	10011	212-337-3900	
Web: www.justice.gov					
Philadelphia Div					
Federal Bldg 600 Arch St Rm 10224	Philadelphia	PA	19106	215-861-3474	
Web: www.justice.gov					
Phoenix Div 3010 N Second St Ste 301	Phoenix	AZ	85012	602-664-5600	
Web: www.justice.gov					
Saint Louis Div 317 S 16th St	Saint Louis	MO	63103	314-538-4600	
Web: www.justice.gov					
San Diego Div 4560 Viewridge Ave	San Diego	CA	92123	858-616-4100	
Web: www.justice.gov					
San Francisco Div 450 Golden Gate Ave	San Francisco	CA	94102	415-436-7900	
Web: www.justice.gov					
Seattle Div 400 Second Ave W	Seattle	WA	98119	206-553-5443	
Web: www.justice.gov					
Washington DC Div 800 K St NW Ste 500	Washington	DC	20001	202-305-8500	514-1009
Web: www.justice.gov					
Executive Office for Immigration Review					
5107 Leesburg Pike	Falls Church	VA	22041	703-305-0289	605-0365
Web: www.justice.gov					
Executive Office for US Trustees					
441 G St NW Ste 6150	Washington	DC	20530	202-307-1399	307-2397
Federal Bureau of Investigation (FBI)					
935 Pennsylvania Ave NW	Washington	DC	20535	202-324-3000	
Web: www.fbi.gov					
Criminal Justice Information Services					
1000 Custer Hollow Rd	Clarksburg	WV	26306	304-625-4995	
Web: fbi.gov/about-us/cjis/cjis					
FBI Laboratory 1970 E Parham Rd	Richmond	VA	23228	804-261-1044	627-4494
Web: www.fbi.gov					
Management & Specialty Training Ctr					
791 Chambers Rd	Aurora	CO	80011	303-340-7800	
Web: www.bop.gov/about/train					
Federal Bureau of Prisons					
National Institute of Corrections					
320 First St NW	Washington	DC	20534	202-307-3106	
TF: 800-995-6423 ■ *Web:* nicic.gov					
National Institute of Corrections Information Cent					
11900 E Cornell Ave Unit C	Aurora	CO	80014	800-877-1461	
TF: 800-877-1461 ■ *Web:* nicic.gov					

Phone Fax

Federal Bureau of Prisons Regional Offices
Mid-Atlantic Region
302 Sentinel Dr Ste 200................. Annapolis Junction MD 20701 301-317-3100
Web: www.bop.gov
North Central Region
400 State Ave Ste 800........................ Kansas City KS 66101 913-621-3939
Web: www.bop.gov/about/ro/ncr
Northeast Region
2nd & Chestnut St 7th Fl..................... Philadelphia PA 19106 215-521-7301
Web: www.bop.gov
South Central Region 4211 Cedar Springs Rd........ Dallas TX 75219 214-224-3389
Web: www.bop.gov
Southeast Region
3800 Camp Creek Pk SW Bldg 2000................. Atlanta GA 30331 678-686-1200
Web: www.bop.gov
Foreign Claims Settlement Commission of the US
600 E St NW.................................. Washington DC 20579 202-616-6975 616-6993
Web: www.justice.gov
National Criminal Justice Reference Service
PO Box 6000.................................. Rockville MD 20849 301-240-7760 240-5830
Web: www.ncjrs.gov
National Drug Intelligence Ctr
319 Washington St 5th Fl......................... Johnstown PA 15901 814-532-4601 532-4690
Web: www.justice.gov
Office of Justice Programs (OJP)
810 Seventh St NW............................. Washington DC 20531 202-307-0703
Web: ojp.gov/
Bureau of Justice Assistance
810 Seventh St NW.......................... Washington DC 20531 202-616-6500 305-1367
Web: www.bja.gov
Bureau of Justice Statistics
810 Seventh St NW.......................... Washington DC 20531 202-307-0765 307-5846
TF: 800-851-3420 ■ *Web:* www.bjs.gov
Community Capacity Development Office
810 Seventh St NW.......................... Washington DC 20531 202-307-5933
Web: www.ojp.usdoj.gov/ccdo
National Institute of Justice
810 Seventh St NW.......................... Washington DC 20531 202-307-2942
Web: www.nij.gov
Office for Victims of Crime
810 Seventh St NW 8th Fl.................... Washington DC 20531 202-307-5983 514-6383
Web: ojp.gov/ovc
Office of Juvenile Justice & Delinquency Prevention (OJJDP)
810 Seventh St NW.......................... Washington DC 20531 202-307-5911 307-2093
Web: www.ojjdp.gov
Office of Special Counsel for Immigration-Related Unfair Employment Practices
950 Pennsylvania Ave NW....................... Washington DC 20038 202-616-5594 616-5509
TF: 800-255-7688 ■ *Web:* www.justice.gov
Office of the Pardon Attorney
145 N St NE Rm 5E............................ Washington DC 20530 202-616-6070 616-6069
Web: www.justice.gov
Office of Tribal Justice
950 Pennsylvania Ave NW....................... Washington DC 20530 202-514-2000
Web: www.justice.gov
Office on Violence Against Women
145 N St Ste 10W 121.......................... Washington DC 20530 202-307-6026 307-2277
Web: justice.gov/ovw/
US Marshals Service 401 Courthouse Square......... Alexandria VA 22314 202-307-9100
TF General: 800-336-0102 ■ *Web:* www.usmarshals.gov
US National Central Bureau of INTERPOL (INTERPOL)
600 E St NW Ste 600........................... Washington DC 20530 202-616-9000 616-8400
Web: www.justice.gov
US Parole Commission
5550 Friendship Blvd Rm 420................... Chevy Chase MD 20815 301-492-5990
TF: 888-585-9103 ■ *Web:* www.justice.gov

343-15 US Department of Labor

Phone Fax

Job Corps
200 Constitution Ave NW Ste N4463............ Washington DC 20210 202-693-3000 693-2767
TF: 800-733-5627 ■ *Web:* www.jobcorps.gov
Office of Administrative Law Judges
200 Constitution Ave NW Ste 400 N............ Washington DC 20210 202-693-7300 693-7365
TF: 877-889-5627 ■ *Web:* www.oalj.dol.gov
Department of Labor
Public Affairs Office
200 Constitution Ave NW...................... Washington DC 20210 202-693-4650 693-5057
TF: 866-487-2365 ■ *Web:* www.dol.gov
Region 1 - Boston JFK Federal Bldg Ste 525........ Boston MA 02203 617-565-2072
Web: www.dol.gov
Region 10-Seattle 300 Fifth Ave Ste 1280.......... Seattle WA 98104 206-757-6700 757-6705
Web: www.osha.gov
Region 2 - New York 201 Varick St Rm 983....... New York NY 10014 646-264-3650
Web: www.dol.gov
Department of Labor Regional Offices
Region 3 - Philadelphia
170 S Independence Mall W Ste 631E West...... Philadelphia PA 19106 215-861-4860 861-4867
Web: www.dol.gov
Region 3 Atlanta 400 W Bay St Rm 939....... Jacksonville FL 32202 904-351-0551 351-0560
Web: www.dol.gov
Region 5 - Chicago 230 S Dearborn St.......... Chicago IL 60604 312-596-5400 596-5401
Web: www.doleta.gov
Region 6 Dallas
Federal Bldg 525 S Griffin St Rm 407.............. Dallas TX 75202 972-850-2409 850-2401
Web: www.dol.gov/owcp/contacts/dallas/arf.htm
Region 8 - Denver 1999 Broadway Ste 1620........ Denver CO 80202 303-844-1286 844-1283
Web: www.dol.gov
Employment & Training Administration
200 Constitution Ave NW....................... Washington DC 20210 866-487-2365
Web: www.doleta.gov

Phone Fax

US Dept of Labor 200 Constitution Ave NW.......... Washington DC 20210 202-693-4700 693-4754
Web: www.dol.gov/vets
Bureau of International Labor Affairs
200 Constitution Ave NW........................ Washington DC 20210 202-693-4770 693-4780
Web: www.dol.gov/ilab
Bureau of Labor Statistics
Consumer Price Index
2 Massachusetts Ave NE...................... Washington DC 20212 202-691-5200 691-6325
Web: www.bls.gov/cpi
Mid-Atlantic Information Office
170 S Independence Mall W Ste 610 E.......... Philadelphia PA 19106 215-597-3282 861-5720
Web: www.bls.gov/ro3
Midwest Information Office
230 S Dearborn St Ste 960....................... Chicago IL 60604 312-353-1880 353-1886
Web: www.bls.gov
Mountain-Plains Information Office
2300 Main St Ste 1190....................... Kansas City MO 64108 816-285-7000 285-7009
Web: www.bls.gov/ro7
New England Information Office
JFK Federal Bldg Rm E-310........................ Boston MA 02203 617-565-2327 565-4182
Web: www.bls.gov/ro1
New York-New Jersey Information Office
201 Varick St Rm 808.......................... New York NY 10014 646-264-3600 337-2532*
**Fax Area Code:* 212 ■ *Web:* www.bls.gov/ro2
Bureau of Labor Statistics Regional Offices
Southeast Information Office 61 Forsyth St.......... Atlanta GA 30303 404-893-4222 893-4221
Web: www.bls.gov
Southwest Information Office
Federal Bldg 525 Griffin St Rm 221.................. Dallas TX 75202 972-850-4800 767-8881*
**Fax Area Code:* 214 ■ *Web:* www.bls.gov/ro6
Western Information Office
PO Box 193766........................... San Francisco CA 94119 415-625-2270 625-2351
Web: www.bls.gov
Employee Benefits Security Administration
200 Constitution Ave NW Rm S2524............... Washington DC 20210 202-693-8300 219-5526
Web: www.dol.gov/ebsa
Region I - Boston 25 New Sudbury St Rm E-350..... Boston MA 02203 617-788-0170 788-0101
Web: www.doleta.gov/regions/reg01bos
Region II-Philadelphia
170 S Independence Mall W Ste 825 E.......... Philadelphia PA 19106 215-861-5200 861-5260
Web: www.doleta.gov
Employment & Training Administration Regional Offices
Region III - Atlanta
Federal Ctr 61 Forsyth St SW Rm 6M12.............. Atlanta GA 20210 877-872-5627 302-5382*
**Fax Area Code:* 404 ■ *TF:* 877-872-5627 ■ *Web:* www.doleta.gov/regions/reg03
Region IV - Dallas
Federal Bldg 525 Griffin St Rm 317.................. Dallas TX 75202 972-850-4600 850-4605
Web: www.doleta.gov/regions/reg04
Region V - Chicago
Federal Bldg 230 S Dearborn St 6th Fl.............. Chicago IL 60604 312-596-5400 596-5401
Web: www.doleta.gov/regions/reg05
Office of Labor-Management Standards (OLMS)
200 Constitution Ave NW Rm N-1519............ Washington DC 20210 866-487-2365
Web: www.dol.gov/olms
Employment Standards Administration
Office of Workers" Compensation Programs
200 Constitution Ave Ste S3524................ Washington DC 20210 866-487-2365
Wage & Hour Div 200 Constitution Ave NW..... Washington DC 20210 202-693-0051
Web: doleta.gov
Labor Racketeering & Fraud Investigations Office
200 Constitution Ave NW Rm S5014............... Washington DC 20210 202-693-5100
Web: www.oig.dol.gov/olrfi.htm
Mine Safety & Health Administration (MSHA)
1100 Wilson Blvd................................ Arlington VA 22209 202-693-9400 693-9401
TF: 800-746-1553 ■ *Web:* www.msha.gov
Coal Mine Safety & Health Office
1100 Wilson Blvd............................ Arlington VA 22209 202-693-9500 693-9501
Web: www.msha.gov/programs/coal.htm
Metal & Non-Metal Mine Safety & Health Office
1100 Wilson Blvd............................ Arlington VA 22209 202-693-9600 693-9601
Web: www.msha.gov/programs/metal.htm
National Mine Health & Safety Academy
1301 Airport Rd................................. Beaver WV 25813 304-256-3100 256-3324
Web: www.msha.gov
Occupational Safety & Health Administration (OSHA)
200 Constitution Ave NW......................... Washington DC 20210 202-693-1999 693-1659
TF: 800-321-6742 ■ *Web:* www.osha.gov
Region 1 JFK Federal Bldg Rm E-340............. Boston MA 02203 617-565-9860 565-9827
TF: 800-321-6742 ■ *Web:* www.osha.gov/oshdir/r01.html
Region 10 300 Fifth Ave Ste 1280................. Seattle WA 98104 206-757-6700 757-6705
TF Help Line: 800-321-6742 ■ *Web:* www.osha.gov/oshdir
Region 2 201 Varick St Ste 670................. New York NY 10014 212-337-2378 337-2371
TF: 800-321-6742 ■ *Web:* www.osha.gov/oshdir/r02.html
Region 3
Curtis Ctr 170 S Independence Mall W
Ste 740W.................................. Philadelphia PA 19106 215-861-4900 861-4904
TF: 800-321-6742 ■ *Web:* www.osha.gov
Occupational Safety & Health Administration Regional Offices
Region 4 61 Forsyth St SW Rm 6T50................ Atlanta GA 30303 678-237-0400 562-2295*
**Fax Area Code:* 404 ■ *Web:* www.osha.gov/oshdir/r04.html
Region 5 230 S Dearborn St Rm 3244............ Chicago IL 60604 312-353-2220 353-7774
Web: www.osha.gov/oshdir/r05.html
Region 6 525 Griffin Street Suite 602............... Dallas TX 75202 972-850-4145 850-4149
Web: www.osha.gov/oshdir/r06.html
Region 7
2300 Main St
Suite 1010 Two Pershing Square Building......... Kansas City MO 64108 816-283-8745 283-0547
Web: www.osha.gov/oshdir/r07.html
Region 8
1244 Speer Blvd
Suite 551 Cesar Chavez Memorial Building............ Denver CO 80204 720-264-6550 264-6585
Web: www.osha.gov/oshdir/r08.html
Region 9 90 Seventh St Ste 18100........... San Francisco CA 94103 415-625-2547 625-2534
Web: www.osha.gov/oshdir/r09.html

Phone Fax

Office of Disability Employment Policy
200 Constitution Ave NW Ste S1303 .... Washington DC 20210 202-693-7880 693-7888
TF: 866-633-7365 ■ *Web:* www.dol.gov/odep

Secretary of Labor
200 Constitution Ave NW Rm S2018 .... Washington DC 20210 202-693-6000 693-6111
TF: 866-487-2365 ■ *Web:* www.dol.gov

Women's Bureau
200 Constitution Ave NW Rm S3002 .... Washington DC 20210 202-693-6710 693-6746
TF: 800-827-5335 ■ *Web:* www.dol.gov/wb

Women's Bureau Regional Offices
Region 1 JFK Federal Bldg Rm 525-A .... Boston MA 02203 617-565-1988 565-1986
Web: www.dol.gov/wb
Region 10 1111 Third Ave Rm 925 .... Seattle WA 98101 206-553-1534 553-5085
TF: 800-827-5335 ■ *Web:* www.dol.gov
Region 2 201 Varick St Rm 602 .... New York NY 10014 212-337-2389 337-2394
TF: 800-827-5335 ■ *Web:* www.dol.gov/wb
Region 3 200 Constitution Ave NW Ste 631E..... Washington DC 20210 866-487-2365 861-4867*
**Fax Area Code:* 215 ■ *TF:* 800-827-5335 ■ *Web:* www.dol.gov/wb
Region 4
Sam Nunn Federal Ctr
61 Forsyth St SW Ste 6B75 .... Atlanta GA 30303 404-562-2336 562-2413
TF: 800-827-5335 ■ *Web:* www.dol.gov
Region 5
Federal Bldg 230 S Dearborn St Rm 1022 .... Chicago IL 60604 312-353-6985 353-6986
TF: 800-827-5335 ■ *Web:* www.dol.gov
Region 6 Federal Bldg 525 Griffin St Ste 735......... Dallas TX 75202 972-850-4700 850-4706
TF: 800-827-5335 ■ *Web:* www.dol.gov/wb
Region 7 2300 Main St Ste 1050 .... Kansas City MO 64108 816-285-7233 285-7237
TF: 800-827-5335 ■ *Web:* www.dol.gov
Region 8 1999 Broadway Ste 1620 PO Box 46550 ... Denver CO 80201 303-844-1286 844-1283
TF: 800-827-5335 ■ *Web:* www.dol.gov/wb
Region 9 90 Seventh St Ste 2650............ San Francisco CA 94103 415-625-2638 625-2641
TF: 800-827-5335 ■ *Web:* www.dol.gov

343-16 US Department of State

Phone Fax

Department of State 2201 C St NW.............. Washington DC 20520 202-647-4000 647-3344
Web: www.state.gov

Bureau of Consular Affairs
2201 C St NW SA-29 .... Washington DC 20520 202-501-4444
TF: 888-407-4747 ■ *Web:* travel.state.gov
Office of Children's Issues SA-17 9th Fl......... Washington DC 20522 202-501-4444 485-6221
TF: 888-407-4747 ■ *Web:* www.travel.state.gov
Passport Services 1111 19th St NW Ste 500..... Washington DC 20524 877-487-2778
TF: 888-874-7793 ■ *Web:* travel.state.gov

Bureau of Diplomatic Security
DS Public Affairs 2201 C St NW.................. Washington DC 20522 571-345-2502
Web: www.state.gov

Bureau of East Asian & Pacific Affairs
2201 C St NW Rm 2236 .... Washington DC 20520 202-895-3500
Web: www.state.gov/p/eap

Colorado Passport Agency
Colorado Agency 3151 S Vaughn Way Ste 600 .... Aurora CO 80014 877-487-2778
TF: 888-874-7793 ■ *Web:* travel.state.gov

Foreign Service Institute
4000 Arlington Blvd Rt 50 .... Arlington VA 22204 703-302-6703
Web: www.state.gov/m/fsi

International Boundary & Water Commission - US & Mexico
4171 N Mesa Ste C-100............................ El Paso TX 79902 915-832-4101 832-4190
TF: 800-262-8857 ■ *Web:* www.ibwc.state.gov

International Boundary Commission - US & Canada
2000 L St NW Ste 615 .... Washington DC 20036 202-736-9102 632-2008
Web: www.internationalboundarycommission.org
Boston Agency
10 Cswy St Rm 247 Tip O'Neill Federal Bldg.......... Boston MA 02222 877-487-2778
TF: 877-487-2778 ■ *Web:* www.travel.state.gov
Chicago Agency
Kluczynski Federal Bldg
230 S Dearborn St 18th Fl .... Chicago IL 60604 877-487-2778 874-7793*
**Fax Area Code:* 888 ■ *Web:* www.travel.state.gov
Connecticut Agency 850 Canal Street .... Stamford CT 06902 877-487-2778
TF: 877-487-2778 ■ *Web:* www.travel.state.gov
Honolulu Agency 300 Ala Moana Bldg Ste 1-330 ... Honolulu HI 96850 877-487-2778
TF: 877-487-2778 ■ *Web:* www.travel.state.gov
Los Angeles Agency
11000 Wilshire Blvd Ste 1000.................. Los Angeles CA 90024 877-487-2778
TF: 877-487-2778 ■ *Web:* www.travel.state.gov
New Orleans Agency 365 Canal St Ste 1300 .... New Orleans LA 70130 877-487-2778
TF: 877-487-2778 ■
Web: travel.state.gov/content/travel/english/404.html
New York Agency 376 Hudson St 10th Fl.......... New York NY 10014 877-487-2778
TF: 877-487-2778 ■ *Web:* www.travel.state.gov
Philadelphia Agency
US Custom House 200 Chesnut St Rm 103....... Philadelphia PA 19106 877-487-2778
TF: 877-487-2778 ■ *Web:* www.travel.state.gov
San Francisco Agency
95 Hawthorne St 5th Fl .... San Francisco CA 94105 877-487-2778
TF: 877-487-2778 ■ *Web:* www.travel.state.gov

Passport Services Regional Offices
Seattle Agency 300 Fifth Ave Ste 800............... Seattle WA 98104 206-393-0740 393-0739
Web: www.state.gov/m/ds/rls/rpt/18892.htm
Washington (DC) Agency
600 19th St NW First Floor Sidewalk Level .... Washington DC 20006 877-487-2778
TF: 877-487-2778 ■ *Web:* www.travel.state.gov

Secretary of State 2201 C St NW................ Washington DC 20520 202-647-4000
Web: www.state.gov
Bureau of Intelligence & Research
2201 C St NW Rm 6531 .... Washington DC 20520 202-895-3500 736-4688
Web: www.state.gov/s/inr

Phone Fax

Office of the Chief of Protocol
2201 C St NW Rm 1238 .... Washington DC 20520 202-647-1735
Web: www.state.gov/s/cpr
Office of the Coordinator for Counterterrorism
2201 C St NW Rm 2507 .... Washington DC 20520 202-895-3500
Web: www.state.gov/s/ct

U.S Department of State Diplomacy in action
Houston Agency
Federal Bldg 1919 Smith St Ste 1100 .... Houston TX 77002 713-654-0401 209-3470
Web: www.state.gov/m/ds/rls/rpt/18892.htm

Under Secretary for Arms Control & International Security
Bureau of International Security & Nonproliferatio
2201 C St NW Rm 2236 .... Washington DC 20520 202-647-5116
Web: www.state.gov
Bureau of Verification Compliance & Implementation
2201 C St NW Rm 2236 .... Washington DC 20520 202-647-5116
Web: www.state.gov

Under Secretary for Democracy & Global Affairs
Bureau of Democracy Human Rights & Labor
2201 C St NW Rm 7802 .... Washington DC 20520 202-647-5116
Web: www.state.gov
Bureau of African Affairs 2201 C St NW......... Washington DC 20520 202-647-4000 222-6301*
**Fax Area Code:* 312 ■ *Web:* www.state.gov/p/af

Under Secretary for Political Affairs
Bureau of European & Eurasian Affairs
2201 C St NW Rm 2236 .... Washington DC 20520 202-647-5116
Web: www.state.gov/p/eur
Bureau of International Narcotics & Law Enforcement Affairs
2201 C St NW .... Washington DC 20520 202-647-4000
Web: www.state.gov/j/inl
Bureau of International Organization Affairs
2201 C St NW .... Washington DC 20520 202-647-9600
Web: www.state.gov/p/io
Bureau of Near Eastern Affairs
2201 C St NW Rm 2236 .... Washington DC 20520 202-647-7209
Web: www.state.gov/p/nea
Bureau of South & Central Asian Affairs
2201 C St NW .... Washington DC 20520 202-647-4000
TF: 800-877-8339 ■ *Web:* www.state.gov/p/sca
Bureau of Western Hemisphere Affairs
2201 C St NW .... Washington DC 20520 202-647-4000
Web: www.state.gov/p/wha
Bureau of Educational & Cultural Affairs
301 Fourth St SW Ste 334..................... Washington DC 20547 202-453-8800
Web: eca.state.gov

Under Secretary for Public Diplomacy & Public Affairs
Bureau of Public Affairs
2201 C St NW Rm 2206 .... Washington DC 20520 202-647-8411 647-3344
Web: www.state.gov

343-17 US Department of Transportation

Phone Fax

Department of Transportation (DOT)
1200 New Jersey Ave SE......................... Washington DC 20590 202-366-4000
Web: www.dot.gov
Accident Investigation Office
800 Independence Ave SW Rm 840............. Washington DC 20591 202-267-9612
Web: www.faa.gov/about/office_org/headquarters_offices/avs
Aircraft Certification Service
800 Independence Ave SW Ste 800 E .... Washington DC 20591 202-267-8235 267-5364
Web: www.faa.gov/about/office_org/headquarters_offices/avs/offices/air
Commercial Space Transportation Office
800 Independence Ave SW .... Washington DC 20591 202-267-7793 267-5450
Web: www.faa.gov

Federal Aviation Administration
FAA Academy
Mike Monroney Aeronautical Ctr
6500 S MacArthur Blvd .... Oklahoma City OK 73169 405-954-6900 954-3018
Web: www.faa.gov
Flight Standards Service
800 Independence Ave SW Rm 821............. Washington DC 20591 202-267-8237 267-5230
Web: www.faa.gov/about/office_org/headquarters_offices/avs
Great Lakes Region 2300 E Devon Ave .... Des Plaines IL 60018 847-294-7272 294-7036
Web: www.faa.gov
International Aviation Office
800 Independence Ave SW .... Washington DC 20591 202-385-8900 267-7198
Web: www.faa.gov
Mike Monroney Aeronautical Ctr
6500 S MacArthur Blvd .... Oklahoma City OK 73125 405-954-4821
Web: www.faa.gov/about/office_org
Safety Hotline 800 Independence Ave SW .... Washington DC 20591 800-255-1111
TF: 800-255-1111 ■ *Web:* www.faa.gov
William J Hughes Technical Ctr
Bldg 300 4th Fl G34.......................... Atlantic City NJ 08405 609-485-6675 485-4667
Web: www.faa.gov/about/office_org/tc

Federal Aviation Administration Northwest Mountain Region
1601 Lind Ave SW .... Renton WA 98057 425-227-2001
TF: 800-220-5715 ■ *Web:* www.faa.gov
Alaskan Region 222 W Seventh Ave Ste 14 .... Anchorage AK 99513 907-271-5438 271-2851
Web: www.faa.gov
Central Region Federal Bldg 901 Locust St...... Kansas City MO 64106 816-329-3050
Web: www.faa.gov
Eastern Region 159-30 Rockaway Blvd .... Jamaica NY 11434 718-553-3001
Web: www.faa.gov

Federal Aviation Administration Regional Offices
New England Region
12 New England Executive Pk .... Burlington MA 01803 781-238-7020 238-7608
Web: www.faa.gov/airports/new_england
Western Pacific Region 15000 Aviation Blvd .... Lawndale CA 90261 310-725-7800 725-6811
Web: www.faa.gov/airports/western_pacific

	City	State	Zip	Phone	Fax
Federal Aviation Administration Southern Region					
1701 Columbia Ave	College Park	GA	30337	404-305-5000	
Web: www.faa.gov					
Federal Highway Administration (FHWA)					
400 Seventh St SW	Washington	DC	20590	202-366-0660	
Web: www.fhwa.dot.gov					
National Highway Institute					
4600 Fairfax Dr Ste 800	Arlington	VA	22203	703-235-0500	235-0593
TF: 877-558-6873 ■ *Web:* www.nhi.fhwa.dot.gov					
Federal Motor Carrier Safety Administration (FMCSA)					
1200 New Jersey Ave SE	Washington	DC	20590	800-832-5660	
TF: 800-832-5660 ■ *Web:* www.fmcsa.dot.gov					
Federal Railroad Administration					
1200 New Jersey Ave Se	Washington	DC	20590	202-493-6014	
Web: www.fra.dot.gov					
Federal Railroad Administration Regional Offices (FRA)					
Region 1 55 Broadway Room 1077	Cambridge	MA	02142	617-494-2302	494-2967
TF: 800-724-5991 ■ *Web:* www.fra.dot.gov					
Region 2					
Baldwin Tower Ste 660 1510 Chester Pike	Crum Lynne	PA	19022	610-521-8200	521-8225
TF: 800-724-5992 ■ *Web:* www.fra.dot.gov					
Region 3 61 Forsyth St SW Ste 16T20	Atlanta	GA	30303	404-562-3800	562-3830
TF: 800-724-5993 ■ *Web:* www.fra.dot.gov					
Region 4 200 W Adams St	Chicago	IL	60606	312-353-6203	886-9634
TF: 800-724-5040 ■ *Web:* www.fra.dot.gov					
Region 5 4100 International Plaza Ste 450	Fort Worth	TX	76109	817-862-2200	862-2204
Web: www.fra.dot.gov					
Region 6 901 Locust St Ste 464	Kansas City	MO	64106	816-329-3840	329-3867
TF: 800-724-5996 ■ *Web:* www.fra.dot.gov					
Region 7 801 'I' St Ste 466	Sacramento	CA	95814	916-498-6540	498-6546
Web: www.fra.dot.gov					
Region 8 703 Broadway St Ste 650	Vancouver	WA	98660	360-696-7536	696-7548
TF: 800-724-5998 ■ *Web:* www.fra.dot.gov					
Federal Transit Administration					
1200 New Jersey Ave SE	Washington	DC	20590	202-366-4043	366-9854
Web: www.fta.dot.gov					
Federal Transit Administration Regional Offices					
Region 1 55 Broadway Ste 920	Cambridge	MA	02142	617-494-2055	494-2865
Web: www.fta.dot.gov					
Region 10 Federal Bldg 915 2nd Ave Ste 3142	Seattle	WA	98174	206-220-7954	220-7959
Web: www.fta.dot.gov					
Region 2 1 Bowling Green Ste 429	New York	NY	10004	212-668-2170	668-2136
Web: www.fta.dot.gov					
Region 3 1760 Market St Ste 500	Philadelphia	PA	19103	215-656-7100	656-7260
Web: www.fta.dot.gov					
Region 4 230 Peachtree St NW Ste 800	Atlanta	GA	30303	404-865-5600	865-5605
Web: www.fta.dot.gov					
Region 5 200 W Adams St Ste 320	Chicago	IL	60606	312-353-2789	886-0351
Web: www.fta.dot.gov					
Region 6 819 Taylor St Rm 8A36	Fort Worth	TX	76102	817-978-0550	978-0575
Web: www.fta.dot.gov					
Region 7 901 Locust St Ste 404	Kansas City	MO	64106	816-329-3920	329-3921
Web: www.fta.dot.gov					
Region 8 12300 W Dakota Ave Ste 310	Lakewood	CO	80228	720-963-3300	963-3333
Web: www.fta.dot.gov					
Region 9 201 Mission St Ste 1650	San Francisco	CA	94105	415-744-3133	744-2726
Web: www.fta.dot.gov					
Div of Gulf Operations					
500 Poydras St Ste 1223	New Orleans	LA	70130	504-589-2000	589-6559
Web: www.marad.dot.gov					
Maritime Administration					
National Maritime Resource & Education Ctr (NMREC)					
1200 New Jersey Ave SE	Washington	DC	20590	202-366-9595	
Web: www.marad.dot.gov					
US Merchant Marine Academy					
300 Steamboat Rd	Kings Point	NY	11024	516-773-5387	773-5509
Web: www.usmma.edu					
Maritime Administration Regional Offices					
Great Lakes Region 500 W Madison St Ste 1110	Chicago	IL	60661	2-3-53--1032	-35-3-1036*
**Fax Area Code:* 312 ■					
Web: www.marad.dot.gov/about-us/gateway-offices/great-lakes-gateway-office/					
North Atlantic Region 1 Bowling Green Rm 418	New York	NY	10004	212-668-3330	
Web: www.marad.dot.gov					
Western Region 201 Mission St Ste 2200	San Francisco	CA	94105	415-744-3125	744-2576
Web: marad.dot.gov					
National Center for Statistics & Analysis					
1200 New Jersey Ave SE	Washington	DC	20590	202-366-1503	366-7078
TF: 800-934-8517 ■ *Web:* www.nhtsa.gov					
National Highway Traffic Safety Administration					
Vehicle Research & Test Ctr					
10820 SR 347 PO Box B37	East Liberty	OH	43319	937-666-4511	666-3590
TF: 800-262-8309 ■ *Web:* www.nhtsa.gov					
NHTSA Region 1 Volpe Ctr Kendall Sq MS 903	Cambridge	MA	02142	617-494-3427	494-3646
Web: www.nhtsa.gov					
NHTSA Region 10 915 Second Ave Ste 3140	Seattle	WA	98174	206-220-7640	220-7651
Web: www.nhtsa.gov					
National Highway Traffic Safety Administration Regional Offices					
NHTSA Region 2					
222 Mamaroneck Ave Ste 204	White Plains	NY	10605	914-682-6162	682-6239
Web: www.nhtsa.gov					
NHTSA Region 3					
1200 New Jersey Ave Ste 6700	Washington	DC	20590	888-327-4236	962-2770*
**Fax Area Code:* 410 ■ *TF:* 888-327-4236 ■ *Web:* www.nhtsa.gov					
NHTSA Region 4 61 Forsyth St SW	Atlanta	GA	30303	404-562-3739	562-3763
Web: www.nhtsa.gov					
NHTSA Region 5 4749 Lincoln Mall Dr Ste 300B	Matteson	IL	60443	708-503-8822	503-8991
Web: www.nhtsa.gov					
NHTSA Region 6 819 Taylor St Rm 8A38	Fort Worth	TX	76102	817-978-3653	978-8339
Web: www.nhtsa.gov					
NHTSA Region 7 901 Locust St Rm 466	Kansas City	MO	64106	816-329-3900	329-3910
Web: www.nhtsa.gov					
NHTSA Region 8 12300 W Dakota Ave Ste 140	Lakewood	CO	80228	720-963-3100	963-3124
Web: www.nhtsa.gov					
NHTSA Region 9 201 Mission St Ste 2230	San Francisco	CA	94105	415-744-3089	744-2532
Web: www.nhtsa.gov					
Office of Hazardous Materials Safety					
1200 New Jersey Ave SE	Washington	DC	20590	202-366-4433	366-5713
TF: 800-467-4922 ■ *Web:* phmsa.dot.gov					
Pipeline & Hazardous Materials Safety Administration					
Office of Pipeline Safety					
1200 New Jersey Ave SE E Bldg 2nd Fl	Washington	DC	20590	202-366-4595	366-4566
Web: phmsa.dot.gov					
Pipeline & Hazardous Materials Safety Administration Regional Offices (PHMSA)					
Central Region (Pipeline)					
901 Locust St Rm 462	Kansas City	MO	64106	816-329-3800	329-3831
Web: www.phmsa.dot.gov/about/region.html					
Eastern Region (Pipeline)					
820 Bear Tavern Rd Ste 103	West Trenton	NJ	08628	609-989-2256	882-1209
Web: www.phmsa.dot.gov/about/region.html					
Southern Region 233 Peachtree St NE Ste 602	Atlanta	GA	30303	404-832-1140	832-1168
Web: www.phmsa.dot.gov/about/region.html					
Southwest Region 8701 S Gessner Rd Ste 900	Houston	TX	77074	713-272-2820	272-2821
Web: www.phmsa.dot.gov					
Western Region (Pipeline)					
12300 W Dakota Ave Ste 110	Lakewood	CO	80228	720-963-3160	963-3161
Web: www.phmsa.dot.gov/about/region.html					
Research & Innovative Technology Administration					
Bureau of Transportation Statistics					
1200 New Jersey Ave SE	Washington	DC	20590	202-366-1270	
TF: 800-853-1351 ■ *Web:* www.rita.dot.gov					
Office of Research Development & Technology					
1200 New Jersey Ave SE	Washington	DC	20590	800-853-1351	366-3759*
**Fax Area Code:* 202 ■ *TF:* 800-853-1351 ■ *Web:* www.rita.dot.gov/rdt					
Volpe National Transportation Systems Ctr					
55 Broadway	Cambridge	MA	02142	617-494-2000	
Web: www.volpe.dot.gov					
Saint Lawrence Seaway Development Corp					
1200 New Jersey Ave SE	Washington	DC	20590	202-366-0091	366-7147
TF: 800-785-2779 ■ *Web:* www.seaway.dot.gov					
Secretary of Transportation					
1200 New Jersey Ave SE	Washington	DC	20590	855-368-4200	
Web: www.transportation.gov					
Surface Transportation Board 395 E St SW	Washington	DC	20423	202-245-0245	245-0461
Web: www.stb.dot.gov					

343-18 US Department of the Treasury

	City	State	Zip	Phone	Fax
Department of the Treasury					
1500 Pennsylvania Ave NW	Washington	DC	20220	202-622-2000	622-6415
Web: www.treasury.gov					
Treasurer of the US					
1500 Pennsylvania Ave NW Rm 2134	Washington	DC	20220	202-622-2000	622-6464
Web: www.treasury.gov					
Alcohol & Tobacco Tax & Trade Bureau					
1310 G St NW Ste 300	Washington	DC	20220	202-453-2000	
TF: 877-882-3277 ■ *Web:* www.ttb.gov					
Bureau of Engraving & Printing					
14th & C Sts SW	Washington	DC	20228	877-874-4114	874-3177*
**Fax Area Code:* 202 ■ *TF:* 877-874-4114 ■ *Web:* www.moneyfactory.gov					
Bureau of the Public Debt 799 Ninth St NW	Washington	DC	20239	202-504-3500	
Web: www.publicdebt.treas.gov					
TreasuryDirect PO Box 7015	Parkersburg	WV	26106	304-480-7711	
TF: 800-722-2678 ■ *Web:* www.savingsbonds.gov					
Comptroller of the Currency 250 E St SW	Washington	DC	20219	202-874-5000	874-5221
TF Cust Svc: 800-613-6743 ■ *Web:* www.occ.treas.gov					
Financial Crimes Enforcement Network					
2070 Chain Bridge Rd PO Box 39	Vienna	VA	22182	703-905-3591	905-3690
Web: www.fincen.gov					
Financial Management Service					
401 14th St SW	Washington	DC	20227	202-874-6950	
Web: www.fms.treas.gov					
Internal Revenue Service (IRS)					
1111 Constitution Ave NW	Washington	DC	20224	202-622-9511	
TF: 800-829-1040 ■ *Web:* www.irs.gov					
Appeals Office 77 K St NE	Washington	DC	20002	202-803-9000	
Web: www.irs.gov					
Taxpayer Advocate Service					
77 K St NE Ste 1500	Washington	DC	20002	202-803-9000	810-2125*
**Fax Area Code:* 855 ■ *TF:* 877-777-4778 ■ *Web:* www.irs.gov/advocate					
Wage & Investment Div 401 W Peachtree St NW	Atlanta	GA	30308	404-338-7060	338-7054
Web: www.irs.gov					
Secretary of the Treasury					
1500 Pennsylvania Ave NW	Washington	DC	20220	202-622-2000	622-6415
Web: www.treasury.gov					
US Mint 801 Ninth St NW	Washington	DC	20220	202-756-6468	
TF Cust Svc: 800-872-6468 ■ *Web:* www.usmint.gov					
Denver 320 W Colfax Ave	Denver	CO	80204	303-405-4761	
Web: www.usmint.gov					
Philadelphia 151 N Independence Mall E	Philadelphia	PA	19106	215-408-0112	
Web: www.usmint.gov					
San Francisco 155 Hermann St	San Francisco	CA	94102	415-575-8000	
TF: 800-872-6468 ■ *Web:* www.usmint.gov					
West Point (NY) PO Box 37	West Point	NY	10996	845-446-6270	
Web: usmint.gov					

343-19 US Department of Veterans Affairs

Name / Address	City	State	Zip	Phone	Fax
Department of Veterans Affairs (VA) 810 Vermont Ave NW *TF Cust Svc:* 800-827-1000 ■ *Web:* www.va.gov	Washington	DC	20420	202-461-7600	
Public & Intergovernmental Affairs Office 810 Vermont Ave NW **Fax Area Code:* 202 ■ *TF:* 800-273-8255 ■ *Web:* www1.va.gov/opa	Washington	DC	20420	800-273-8255	273-7635*
National Center for Post-Traumatic Stress Disorder 215 N Main St *Web:* www.ptsd.va.gov	White River Junction	VT	05009	802-296-5132	296-5135
National Cemetery Administration 810 Vermont Ave NW *Web:* www.cem.va.gov	Washington	DC	20420	202-565-4964	
Secretary of Veterans Affairs 810 Vermont Ave NW *Web:* www1.va.gov/opa/bios	Washington	DC	20420	202-461-7600	
Board of Veterans' Appeals 810 Vermont Ave NW **Fax Area Code:* 202 ■ *TF:* 800-923-8387 ■ *Web:* www.bva.va.gov	Washington	DC	20420	800-923-8387	343-1889*
Center for Minority Veterans 441 Fourth St NW Ste 570 *Web:* ova.dc.gov	Washington	DC	20001	202-273-6708	724-7117
Center for Veterans Enterprise 810 Vermont Ave *TF:* 800-273-8255 ■ *Web:* vba.va.gov	Washington	DC	20420	800-827-1000	
Center for Women Veterans 810 Vermont Ave NW **Fax Area Code:* 202 ■ *TF:* 800-827-1000 ■ *Web:* www1.va.gov/womenvet	Washington	DC	20420	800-827-1000	273-7092*
Veterans Benefits Administration 810 Vermont Ave NW **Fax Area Code:* 202 ■ *TF:* 800-827-1000 ■ *Web:* www.vba.va.gov	Washington	DC	20420	800-827-1000	275-5947*
Veterans Canteen Service 1 Jefferson Barracks Rd Bldg 25 *Web:* www.va.gov	Saint Louis	MO	63125	314-652-4100	845-1201
Veterans Health Administration 810 Vermont Ave NW *Web:* www2.va.gov	Washington	DC	20420	202-273-5400	
Gulf War Veterans Information 50 Irving St NW *Web:* gulfwarvets.com	Washington	DC	20422	202-745-8000	
Office of Research & Development 810 Vermont Ave NW MC 12 **Fax Area Code:* 202 ■ *TF:* 800-827-1000 ■ *Web:* www.research.va.gov	Washington	DC	20420	800-827-1000	254-0460*

343-20 US Independent Agencies Government Corporations & Quasi-Official Agencies

Included also among these listings are selected Federal Boards, Committees, and Commissions.

Name / Address	City	State	Zip	Phone	Fax
Federal Election Commission 999 E St NW *TF:* 800-424-9530 ■ *Web:* www.fec.gov	Washington	DC	20463	202-694-1100	
US Office of Government Ethics 1201 New York Ave NW Ste 500 *Web:* www.oge.gov	Washington	DC	20005	202-482-9300	482-9237
Advisory Council on Historic Preservation 1100 Pennsylvania Ave NW Rm 803 *Web:* www.achp.gov	Washington	DC	20004	202-606-8503	606-8647
African Development Foundation 1400 'I' St NW 10th Fl *Web:* www.adf.gov	Washington	DC	20005	202-673-3916	673-3810
American Battle Monuments Commission Courthouse Plaza II Ste 500 2300 Clarendon Blvd *Web:* www.abmc.gov	Arlington	VA	22201	703-696-6900	696-6666
Architectural & Transportation Barriers Compliance Board 1331 F St NW Ste 1000 *TF:* 800-872-2253 ■ *Web:* www.access-board.gov	Washington	DC	20004	202-272-0080	272-0081
International Broadcasting Bureau 330 Independence Ave SW *Web:* www.bbg.gov	Washington	DC	20237	202-203-4000	
Broadcasting Board of Governors *Voice of America* 330 Independence Ave SW *Web:* www.voanews.com	Washington	DC	20237	202-203-4959	
Central Intelligence Agency (CIA) Office of Public Affairs *Web:* www.cia.gov	Washington	DC	20505	703-482-0623	482-1739
Commission of Fine Arts 401 F St NW Ste 312 *Web:* www.cfa.gov	Washington	DC	20001	202-504-2200	504-2195
Commission on Presidential Scholars Dept of Education *Web:* www.ed.gov/programs/psp/commission.html	Washington	DC	20202	202-401-0961	260-7464
Commission on Security & Cooperation in Europe 234 Ford House Office Bldg 3rd & D Sts SW *Web:* www.csce.gov	Washington	DC	20515	202-225-1901	226-4199
Committee for Purchase from People Who Are Blind or Severely Disabled 1421 Jefferson Davis Hwy Jefferson Plaza 2 Ste 10800 *Web:* www.abilityone.gov	Arlington	VA	22202	703-603-7740	603-0655
Committee on Foreign Investments in the US *Dept of the Treasury Office of International Investment* 1500 Pennsylvania Ave NW Rm 5221 *Web:* www.treasury.gov	Washington	DC	20220	202-622-2000	622-2000
Commodity Futures Trading Commission 3 Lafayette Ctr 1155 21 St NW *TF:* 866-366-2382 ■ *Web:* www.cftc.gov	Washington	DC	20581	202-418-5000	418-5521
Commodity Futures Trading Commission Regional Offices *Central Region* 525 W Monroe St *Web:* www.cftc.gov	Chicago	IL	60661	312-596-0700	596-0713
Eastern Region 140 Broadway 19th Fl *Web:* www.cftc.gov	New York	NY	10005	646-746-9700	746-9938
Southwestern Region 2 Emanuel Cleaver II Blvd Ste 300 *Web:* www.cftc.gov	Kansas City	MO	64112	816-960-7700	960-7750
Consumer Product Safety Commission (CPSC) 4340 E W Hwy Ste 502 *TF:* 800-638-2772 ■ *Web:* www.cpsc.gov	Bethesda	MD	20814	301-504-7923	504-0051
Coordinating Council on Juvenile Justice & Delinquency Prevention 810 Seventh St NW *Web:* www.juvenilecouncil.gov	Washington	DC	20531	202-307-5911	307-2093
Corp for National & Community Service *AmeriCorps USA* 1201 New York Ave NW *TF:* 800-833-3722 ■ *Web:* www.nationalservice.gov	Washington	DC	20525	202-606-5000	
Learn & Serve America 1201 New York Ave NW *TF:* 800-833-3722 ■ *Web:* www.nationalservice.gov	Washington	DC	20525	202-606-5000	
Senior Corps 1201 New York Ave NW *TF:* 800-833-3722 ■ *Web:* www.nationalservice.gov	Washington	DC	20525	202-606-5000	
Court Services & Offender Supervision Agency for the District of Columbia 633 Indiana Ave NW *Web:* www.csosa.gov	Washington	DC	20004	202-220-5300	220-5350
Defense Nuclear Facilities Safety Board 625 Indiana Ave NW Ste 700 *TF:* 800-788-4016 ■ *Web:* www.dnfsb.gov	Washington	DC	20004	202-694-7000	
Denali Commission 510 L St Ste 410 *TF:* 888-480-4321 ■ *Web:* www.denali.gov	Anchorage	AK	99501	907-271-1414	271-1415
Environmental Protection Agency (EPA) 1200 Pennsylvania Ave NW *TF:* 888-372-8255 ■ *Web:* www.epa.gov	Washington	DC	20460	202-564-4700	501-1450
US National Response Team 1200 Pennsylvania Ave NW *TF:* 800-424-9346 ■ *Web:* www.nrt.org	Washington	DC	20593	202-267-2675	564-6392
Region 1 1 Congress St Ste 1100 *TF:* 888-372-7341 ■ *Web:* www.epa.gov	Boston	MA	02114	617-918-1111	918-0101
Region 10 1200 Sixth Ave Ste 900 *TF:* 800-424-4372 ■ *Web:* www.epa.gov	Seattle	WA	98101	206-553-1200	553-0059
Region 2 290 Broadway *Web:* www.epa.gov	New York	NY	10007	212-637-3000	
Region 3 1650 Arch St *TF:* 800-438-2474 ■ *Web:* www.epa.gov	Philadelphia	PA	19103	215-814-5000	
Environmental Protection Agency Regional Offices *Region 4* Federal Ctr 61 Forsyth St SW *TF:* 800-241-1754 ■ *Web:* www.epa.gov	Atlanta	GA	30303	404-562-9900	562-8174
Region 5 77 W Jackson Blvd *Web:* www.epa.gov	Chicago	IL	60604	312-353-2000	
Region 6 1445 Ross Ave Ste 1200 *TF:* 800-887-6063 ■ *Web:* www.epa.gov	Dallas	TX	75202	214-665-2200	665-2182
Region 7 901 N Fifth St *Web:* www.epa.gov	Kansas City	KS	66101	913-551-7003	
Region 8 1595 Wynkoop St *TF:* 800-227-8917 ■ *Web:* www.epa.gov	Denver	CO	80202	303-312-6312	
Region 9 75 Hawthorne St *TF:* 866-372-9378 ■ *Web:* www.epa.gov	San Francisco	CA	94105	415-947-8000	947-3598
Equal Employment Opportunity Commission (EEOC) 1801 L St NW *TF:* 800-669-4000 ■ *Web:* www.eeoc.gov	Washington	DC	20507	202-663-4191	
Equal Employment Opportunity Commission Regional Offices *Atlanta District* 100 Alabama St SW Ste 4R30 **Fax Area Code:* 404 ■ *TF:* 800-669-6820 ■ *Web:* www.eeoc.gov	Atlanta	GA	30303	800-669-6820	562-6909*
Birmingham District 1130 22nd St S Ste 2000 *TF:* 800-669-4000 ■ *Web:* www.eeoc.gov	Birmingham	AL	35205	205-212-2100	212-2105
Charlotte District 129 W Trade St Ste 400 *TF:* 800-669-4000 ■ *Web:* www.eeoc.gov	Charlotte	NC	28202	704-344-6682	344-6734
Chicago District 500 W Madison St Ste 2800 *Web:* www.eeoc.gov	Chicago	IL	60661	312-353-2713	353-4041
Dallas District 207 S Houston St 3rd Fl *TF:* 800-669-4000 ■ *Web:* www.eeoc.gov	Dallas	TX	75202	214-253-2700	253-2720
Houston District 1201 Louisiana St 6th Fl **Fax Area Code:* 713 ■ *TF:* 800-669-4000 ■ *Web:* www.eeoc.gov	Houston	TX	77002	800-669-4000	651-4987*
Indianapolis District 101 W Ohio St Ste 1900 *Web:* www.eeoc.gov	Indianapolis	IN	46204	317-226-7212	226-7953
Los Angeles District 255 E Temple St 4th Fl **Fax Area Code:* 213 ■ *TF:* 800-669-4000 ■ *Web:* www.eeoc.gov	Los Angeles	CA	90012	800-669-4000	894-1118*
Miami District 2 S Biscayne Blvd Ste 2700 *Web:* www.eeoc.gov	Miami	FL	33131	305-808-1740	808-1834
New York District 33 Whitehall St 5th Fl *TF:* 866-408-8075 ■ *Web:* www.eeoc.gov	New York	NY	10004	212-336-3620	336-3790
Philadelphia District 801 Market St Ste 1300 **Fax Area Code:* 215 ■ *Web:* www.eeoc.gov/field/philadelphia/	Philadelphia	PA	19107	800-669-4000	440-2606*
Phoenix District 3300 N Central Ave Ste 690 *Web:* www.eeoc.gov	Phoenix	AZ	85012	602-640-5000	640-5071
Saint Louis District 1222 Spruce St Rm 8.100 *TF:* 800-669-4000 ■ *Web:* www.eeoc.gov	Saint Louis	MO	63103	314-539-7800	539-7894
San Francisco District 450 Golden Gate Ave 5 W PO Box 36025 **Fax Area Code:* 415 ■ *TF:* 800-669-4000 ■ *Web:* www.eeoc.gov	San Francisco	CA	94102	800-669-4000	522-3415*
Export-Import Bank of the US 811 Vermont Ave NW *TF:* 800-565-3946 ■ *Web:* www.exim.gov	Washington	DC	20571	202-565-3946	
Farm Credit Administration 1501 Farm Credit Dr *Web:* www.fca.gov	McLean	VA	22102	703-883-4000	734-5784

Phone Fax

Bloomington (MN) Field Office
2051 Killebrew Dr Ste 610 ... Minneapolis MN 55425 952-854-7151
Web: www.fca.gov
Dallas Field Office
511 E Carpenter Fwy Ste 650 ... Irving TX 75062 972-869-0550
Web: fca.gov
Denver Field Office 3131 S Vaughn Way Ste 250 ... Aurora CO 80014 303-696-9737
Web: www.fca.gov

Farm Credit Administration Regional Offices
McLean Field Office 1501 Farm Credit Dr ... McLean VA 22102 703-883-4056 883-4056
Web: www.fca.gov
Sacramento Field Office
2180 Harvard St Ste 300 ... Sacramento CA 95815 916-648-1118
Web: www.fca.gov

Federal Acctg Standards Advisory Board
441 G St NW Ste 6814 ... Washington DC 20548 202-512-7350 512-7366
Web: www.fasab.gov

Federal Communications Commission (FCC)
445 12th St SW ... Washington DC 20554 888-225-5322 418-0232*
**Fax Area Code:* 202 ■ *TF:* 888-225-5322 ■ *Web:* www.fcc.gov

Federal Deposit Insurance Corp
550 17th St NW ... Washington DC 20429 202-898-7192
TF: 877-275-3342 ■ *Web:* www.fdic.gov

Federal Deposit Insurance Corp Regional Offices
Atlanta Area Office 10 Tenth St NW Ste 800 ... Atlanta GA 30309 678-916-2200
TF: 800-765-3342 ■ *Web:* www.fdic.gov
Boston Area Office
15 Braintree Hill Office Pk Ste 300 ... Braintree MA 02184 781-794-5500
TF: 866-728-9953 ■ *Web:* www.fdic.gov
Chicago Area Office
300 S Riverside Plaza Ste 1700 ... Chicago IL 60606 312-382-6000
TF: 800-944-5343 ■ *Web:* www.fdic.gov
Dallas Area Office 1601 Bryan St ... Dallas TX 75201 214-754-0098
TF: 800-568-9161 ■ *Web:* www.fdic.gov
Kansas City Area Office
2345 Grand Blvd Ste 1200 ... Kansas City MO 64108 816-234-8000
TF: 800-209-7459 ■ *Web:* www.fdic.gov
Memphis Area Office 5100 Poplar Ave Ste 1900 ... Memphis TN 38137 901-685-1603
TF: 800-210-6354 ■ *Web:* www.fdic.gov
New York Area Office 350 5th Ave Ste 1200 ... New York NY 11215 917-320-2500
TF: 800-334-9593 ■ *Web:* fdic.gov
San Francisco Area Office
25 Jessie St at Ecker Sq Ste 2300 ... San Francisco CA 94105 415-546-0160
TF: 800-756-3558 ■ *Web:* www.fdic.gov

Federal Financing Bank
Dept of the Treasury
1500 Pennsylvania Ave NW ... Washington DC 20220 202-622-2470 622-0707
Web: www.treasury.gov

Federal Housing Finance Board
400 7th St SW ... Washington DC 20024 202-649-3800 649-1071
Web: www.fhfa.gov

Federal Labor Relations Authority
1400 K St NW ... Washington DC 20424 202-357-6029 482-6724
Web: www.flra.gov

Federal Labor Relations Authority Regional Offices
Atlanta Region 225 Peachtree St NE ... Atlanta GA 30303 404-331-5300 331-5280
Web: www.flra.gov
Boston Region Federal Bldg 10 Cswy St Ste 472 ... Boston MA 02222 617-565-5100 565-6262
Web: www.flra.gov
Chicago Region 55 W Monroe St Ste 1150 ... Chicago IL 60603 312-886-3465 886-5977
Web: www.flra.gov
Dallas Region 525 S Griffin St Ste 926 LB-107 ... Dallas TX 75202 214-767-6266 767-0156
Web: www.flra.gov
Denver Region 1391 Speer Blvd # 300 ... Denver CO 80204 303-844-5224 844-2774
Web: flra.gov
San Francisco Region
901 Market St Ste 470 ... San Francisco CA 94103 202-418-5000 356-5017*
**Fax Area Code:* 415 ■ *Web:* www.flra.gov/ogc_ro_sf
Washington (DC) Region 1400 K St NW 2nd Fl ... Washington DC 20424 202-357-6029 482-6724
Web: www.flra.gov

Federal Laboratory Consortium for Technology Transfer
950 Kings Hwy N Ste 208 ... Cherry Hill NJ 08034 856-667-7727 667-8009
Web: www.federallabs.org

Federal Maritime Commission
800 N Capitol St NW ... Washington DC 20573 202-523-5725 523-0014
Web: www.fmc.gov

Federal Maritime Commission Regional Offices
Los Angeles Area 839 S Beacon St Rm 320 ... San Pedro CA 90733 310-514-4905 514-3931
Web: www.fmc.gov
New Orleans Area 1515 Poydras St ... New Orleans LA 70112 504-589-6662 589-6663
Web: www.fmc.gov
South Florida Area PO Box 813609 ... Hollywood FL 33081 954-963-5362 963-5630
Web: www.fmc.gov

Federal Mediation & Conciliation Service
2100 K St NW ... Washington DC 20427 202-606-8100 606-4251
Web: www.fmcs.gov

Federal Mediation & Conciliation Service Regional Offices
Eastern Region
6161 Oak Tree Blvd Ste 120 ... Independence OH 44131 216-520-4800 520-4819
Web: www.fmcs.gov/internet
Western Region 1300 Godward St Ste 3950 ... Minneapolis MN 55413 612-331-6670 331-5272
Web: www.fmcs.gov

Federal Mine Safety & Health Review Commission
601 New Jersey Ave NW ... Washington DC 20001 202-434-9900 434-9944
Web: www.fmshrc.gov

Federal Retirement Thrift Investment Board
1250 H St NW ... Washington DC 20005 202-942-1600 942-1674
Web: www.frtib.gov

Federal Trade Commission (FTC)
600 Pennsylvania Ave NW ... Washington DC 20580 202-326-2222
TF: 877-382-4357 ■ *Web:* www.ftc.gov

Phone Fax

National Do Not Call Registry
600 Pennsylvania Ave NW ... Washington DC 20580 888-382-1222
TF: 888-382-1222 ■ *Web:* www.ftc.gov
East Central Region
1111 Superior Ave Ste 200 ... Cleveland OH 44114 216-263-3455 263-3426
TF: 877-382-4357 ■ *Web:* www.ftc.gov
Midwest Region 55 W Monroe St Ste 1825 ... Chicago IL 60603 312-960-5634 960-5600
TF: 877-382-4357 ■
Web: www.ftc.gov/about-ftc/bureaus-offices/regional-offices/midwest-region
NortheastRegion 1 Bowling Green Ste 318 ... New York NY 10004 212-607-2829 607-2822
Web: www.ftc.gov
Northwest Region 915 Second Ave Rm 2896 ... Seattle WA 98174 877-382-4357
TF: 877-382-4357 ■ *Web:* www.ftc.gov

Federal Trade Commission Regional Offices
Southeast Region 60 Forsyth St SW ... Atlanta GA 30303 404-656-1390 656-1379
TF: 877-282-4357 ■ *Web:* www.ftc.gov
Southwest Region 1999 Bryan St Ste 2150 ... Dallas TX 75201 877-382-4357
TF: 877-382-4357 ■ *Web:* www.ftc.gov/
Western Region
901 Market Street Ste 570 ... San Francisco CA 94103 877-382-4357 824-4380*
**Fax Area Code:* 310 ■ *TF:* 877-382-4357 ■
Web: ftc.gov/about-ftc/bureaus-offices/regional-offices/western-region

General Services Administration (GSA)
1275 F St NE ... Washington DC 20417 202-501-0800
Web: www.gsa.gov
FCIC National Contact Ctr PO Box 100 ... Pueblo CO 81009 888-878-3256
TF: 888-878-3256 ■ *Web:* publications.usa.gov
Regulatory Information Service Ctr
1800 F St NW Rm 3039 ... Washington DC 20405 202-482-7340
Web: www.gsa.gov
Region 1 - New England
10 Cswy St Rm 1010
Thomas P O'Neill Federal Bldg ... Boston MA 02222 617-565-5860
TF: 866-734-1727 ■ *Web:* www.gsa.gov
Region 10 - Northwest/Arctic 400 15th St SW ... Auburn WA 98001 253-931-7000
Web: www.gsa.gov
Region 11 - National Capital Region
301 Seventh St SW ... Washington DC 20407 202-708-9100
Web: www.gsa.gov
Region 2 - Northeast & Caribbean
26 Federal Plaza ... New York NY 10278 212-264-2600
Web: www.gsa.gov
Region 3 - Mid-Atlantic
Strawbridge Bldg 20 N 8th St ... Philadelphia PA 19107 215-446-5100
TF: 800-333-4636 ■ *Web:* www.gsa.gov
Region 4 - Southeast Sunbelt
1800 F St NW Ste 600 ... Washington DC 20405 800-333-4636 331-0931*
**Fax Area Code:* 404 ■ *TF:* 800-333-4636 ■ *Web:* www.gsa.gov
Region 5 - Great Lakes 230 S Dearborn St ... Chicago IL 60604 312-886-8900 886-8901
Web: www.gsa.gov
Region 6 - Heartland 1800 F St NW ... Washington DC 20405 816-823-5320 926-7513
Web: www.gsa.gov
Region 7 - Greater Southwest
819 Taylor St ... Fort Worth TX 76102 817-978-2321
Web: www.gsa.gov

General Services Administration Regional Offices
Region 8 - Rocky Mountain
Denver Federal Ctr Bldg 41 ... Denver CO 80225 303-236-7329
TF: 888-999-4777 ■ *Web:* www.gsa.gov
Region 9 - Pacific Rim
450 Golden Gate Ave ... San Francisco CA 94102 530-756-3082
Web: www.gsa.gov

Harry S Truman Scholarship Foundation
712 Jackson Pl NW ... Washington DC 20006 202-395-4831 395-6995
Web: www.truman.gov

Indian Arts & Crafts Board
Dept of the Interior 1849 C St NW
MS 2528-MIB ... Washington DC 20240 202-208-3773 208-5196
TF: 888-278-3253 ■ *Web:* www.iacb.doi.gov

Inter-American Foundation (IAF)
901 N Stuart St 10th Fl ... Arlington VA 22203 703-306-4301 306-4365
Web: www.iaf.gov

Interagency Council on Homelessness
409 Third St SW Ste 310 ... Washington DC 20024 202-708-4663
Web: www.usich.gov

Japan-US Friendship Commission
1201 15th St NW Ste 330 ... Washington DC 20005 202-653-9800 653-9802
Web: www.jusfc.gov

Joint Board for the Enrollment of Actuaries
Internal Revenue Service SE:OPR
1111 Constitution Ave NW ... Washington DC 20224 202-622-8229 622-8300
Web: www.irs.gov

Legal Services Corp 3333 K St NW 3rd Fl ... Washington DC 20007 202-295-1500 337-6797
Web: www.lsc.gov

Marine Mammal Commission 4340 E W Hwy Rm 700 ... Bethesda MD 20814 301-504-0087 504-0099
Web: www.mmc.gov

Merit Systems Protection Board (MSPB)
1615 M St NW ... Washington DC 20419 202-653-7200 653-7130
TF: 800-209-8960 ■ *Web:* www.mspb.gov
Atlanta Region 401 W Peachtree St NW 10th Fl ... Atlanta GA 30308 404-730-2755 730-2767
TF: 800-209-8960 ■ *Web:* www.mspb.gov
Central Region 230 S Dearborn St 31st Fl ... Chicago IL 60604 312-353-2923 886-4231
Web: www.mspb.gov
Denver Field Office 165 S Union Blvd Ste 318 ... Lakewood CO 80228 303-969-5101 969-5109
Web: www.mspb.gov
New York Field Office
26 Federal Plaza Rm 3137-A ... New York NY 10278 212-264-9372 264-1417
Web: www.mspb.gov

Merit Systems Protection Board Regional Offices
Northeastern Region
1601 Market St Ste 1700 ... Philadelphia PA 19103 215-597-9960 597-3456
Web: mspb.gov

				Phone	Fax
Washington (DC) Region					
1800 Diagonal Rd Ste 205	Alexandria	VA	22314	703-756-6250	756-7112
Web: www.mspb.gov					
Western Region 201 Mission St Ste 2310	San Francisco	CA	94105	415-904-6772	904-0580
Web: www.mspb.gov					
Migratory Bird Conservation Commission					
5275 Leesburg Pike	Falls Church	VA	22203	703-358-1716	
Web: www.fws.gov					
Millenium Challenge Corp 875 15th St NW	Washington	DC	20005	202-521-3600	
Web: www.mcc.gov					
Morris K Udall Foundation 130 S Scott Ave	Tucson	AZ	85709	520-901-8500	670-5530
Web: www.udall.gov					
National Aeronautics & Space Administration (NASA)					
300 E St SW	Washington	DC	20546	202-358-0001	358-3469
Web: www.nasa.gov					
National Archives & Records Administration (NARA)					
8601 Adelphi Rd	College Park	MD	20740	866-272-6272	837-0483*
**Fax Area Code:* 301 ■ *TF:* 866-272-6272 ■ *Web:* www.archives.gov					
Archival Research Catalog					
8601 Adelphi Rd	College Park	MD	20740	866-272-6272	
TF: 866-272-6272 ■ *Web:* archives.gov/research/search/					
Office of Presidential Libraries					
8601 Adelphi Rd Rm 2200	College Park	MD	20740	301-837-3250	837-3199
Web: www.archives.gov					
Office of the Federal Register					
800 N Capitol St NW Ste 700-K	Washington	DC	20002	202-741-6000	741-6012
Web: www.archives.gov/federal-register					
Central Plains Region 400 W Pershing Rd	Kansas City	MO	64108	816-268-8000	
Web: www.archives.gov					
National Archives & Records Administration Regional Offices					
Great Lakes Region 7358 S Pulaski Rd	Chicago	IL	60629	773-948-9001	948-9050
Web: www.archives.gov/great-lakes					
Mid Atlantic Region 900 Market St	Philadelphia	PA	19107	215-606-0100	606-0116
Web: www.archives.gov/midatlantic					
Northeast Region 380 Trapelo Rd	Waltham	MA	02452	781-663-0130	663-0154
TF: 866-406-2379 ■ *Web:* www.archives.gov					
Pacific Alaska Region 6125 Sand Pt Way NE	Seattle	WA	98115	206-336-5115	336-5112
TF: 866-325-7208 ■ *Web:* www.archives.gov					
Pacific Region 1000 Commodore Dr	San Bruno	CA	94066	650-238-3500	238-3507
Web: www.archives.gov					
Southeast Region 5780 Jonesboro Rd	Morrow	GA	30260	770-968-2100	968-2547
Web: www.archives.gov/southeast					
Southwest Region					
501 W Felix St Bldg 1 PO Box 6216	Fort Worth	TX	76115	817-551-2051	334-5621
Web: www.archives.gov/southwest					
National Capital Planning Commission					
401 Ninth St NW N Lobby Ste 500	Washington	DC	20004	202-482-7200	482-7272
Web: www.ncpc.gov					
National Council on Disability (NCD)					
1331 F St NW Ste 850	Washington	DC	20004	202-272-2004	272-2022
Web: www.ncd.gov					
National Credit Union Administration					
1775 Duke St	Alexandria	VA	22314	703-518-6300	518-6319
TF Fraud Hotline: 800-827-9650 ■ *Web:* ncua.gov					
National Credit Union Administration Regional Offices					
Region 1 9 Washington Sq Washington Ave Ext	Albany	NY	12205	518-862-7400	862-7420
Web: ncua.gov					
Region 2 1775 Duke St Ste 4206	Alexandria	VA	22314	703-518-6300	519-4620
Web: www.ncua.gov/					
Region 3 7000 Central Pkwy Ste 1600	Atlanta	GA	30328	678-443-3000	443-3020
Web: ncua.gov					
Region 4 4807 Spicewood Springs Rd Ste 5200	Austin	TX	78759	512-342-5600	342-5620
Web: ncua.gov					
Region 5 1230 W Washington St Ste 301	Tempe	AZ	85281	602-302-6000	302-6024
Web: ncua.gov					
National Endowment for the Arts (NEA)					
1100 Pennsylvania Ave NW	Washington	DC	20506	202-682-5400	
Web: www.arts.gov					
National Endowment for the Humanities (NEH)					
400 7th St SW	Washington	DC	20506	202-606-8400	606-8282
TF: 800-634-1121 ■ *Web:* www.neh.gov					
National Indian Gaming Commission					
1441 L St NW Ste 9100	Washington	DC	20005	202-632-7003	632-7066
Web: www.nigc.gov					
National Labor Relations Board (NLRB)					
1099 14th St NW	Washington	DC	20570	202-273-1991	
TF: 866-667-6572 ■ *Web:* www.nlrb.gov					
National Labor Relations Board Regional Offices					
Region 1 10 Cswy St 6th Fl	Boston	MA	02222	617-565-6700	565-6725
TF: 866-667-6572 ■ *Web:* www.nlrb.gov					
Region 10 233 Peachtree St NE Ste 1000	Atlanta	GA	30303	404-331-2896	331-2858
Web: www.nlrb.gov					
Region 11 4035 University Pkwy Ste 200	Winston-Salem	NC	27106	336-631-5201	631-5210
TF: 866-667-6572 ■ *Web:* www.nlrb.gov					
Region 12 201 E Kennedy Blvd Ste 530	Tampa	FL	33602	813-228-2641	228-2874
Web: www.nlrb.gov					
Region 13 200 W Adams St	Chicago	IL	60606	312-353-7570	886-1341
Web: www.nlrb.gov					
Region 14 1222 Spruce St Rm 8.302	Saint Louis	MO	63103	314-539-7770	539-7794
TF: 866-667-6572 ■ *Web:* www.nlrb.gov					
Region 15 1515 Poydras St Rm 610	New Orleans	LA	70112	504-589-6361	589-4069
Web: www.nlrb.gov					
Region 16					
Federal Bldg 819 Taylor St Rm 8A24	Fort Worth	TX	76102	817-978-2921	978-2928
TF: 866-667-6572 ■ *Web:* www.nlrb.gov					
Region 17 8600 Farley St Ste 100	Overland Park	KS	66212	913-967-3000	967-3010
Web: www.nlrb.gov					
Region 18 330 Second Ave S Ste 790	Minneapolis	MN	55401	612-348-1757	348-1785
TF: 866-667-6572 ■ *Web:* www.nlrb.gov					
Region 19 915 Second Ave # 2948	Seattle	WA	98174	206-220-6300	220-6305
Web: www.nlrb.gov					
Region 2 26 Federal Plaza Rm 3614	New York	NY	10278	212-264-0300	264-2450
Web: www.nlrb.gov					
Region 20 901 Market St Ste 400	San Francisco	CA	94103	415-356-5130	356-5156
TF: 866-667-6572 ■ *Web:* www.nlrb.gov					
Region 21 888 S Figueroa St 9th Fl	Los Angeles	CA	90017	213-894-5200	894-2778
Web: www.nlrb.gov					
Region 22 20 Washington Pl 5th Fl	Newark	NJ	07102	973-645-2100	645-3852
Web: www.nlrb.gov					
Region 24 525 FD Roosevelt Ave Ste 1002	San Juan	PR	00918	787-766-5347	766-5478
Web: www.nlrb.gov					
Region 25 575 N Pennsylvania St Ste 238	Indianapolis	IN	46204	317-226-7381	226-5103
TF: 866-667-6572 ■ *Web:* www.nlrb.gov					
Region 26 80 Monroe Ave Ste 350	Memphis	TN	38103	901-544-0018	544-0008
Web: www.nlrb.gov					
Region 27 600 17th St 7th Fl N Tower	Denver	CO	80202	303-844-3551	844-6249
Web: www.nlrb.gov					
Region 28 2600 N Central Ave Ste 1800	Phoenix	AZ	85004	602-640-2160	640-2178
Web: www.nlrb.gov					
Region 29 1 Metrotech Ctr N # A	Brooklyn	NY	11201	718-330-7713	330-7579
Web: www.nlrb.gov					
Region 3					
Niagara Ctr Bldg 130 S Elmwood Ave Ste 630	Buffalo	NY	14202	716-551-4931	551-4972
TF: 866-667-6572 ■ *Web:* www.nlrb.gov					
Region 30 310 W Wisconsin Ave Ste 700	Milwaukee	WI	53203	414-297-3861	297-3880
Web: www.nlrb.gov					
Region 31 11150 W Olympic Blvd Ste 700	Los Angeles	CA	90064	310-235-7352	235-7420
TF: 866-667-6572 ■ *Web:* www.nlrb.gov					
Region 32 1301 Clay St Rm 300N	Oakland	CA	94612	510-637-3300	637-3315
Web: www.nlrb.gov					
Region 34 450 Main St	Hartford	CT	06103	860-240-3522	240-3564
Web: nlrb.gov					
Region 4 615 Chestnut St 7th Fl	Philadelphia	PA	19106	215-597-7601	597-7658
Web: www.nlrb.gov					
Region 5 103 S Gay St 8th Fl	Baltimore	MD	21202	410-962-2822	962-2198
Web: www.nlrb.gov					
Region 6 1000 Liberty Ave Rm 904	Pittsburgh	PA	15222	412-395-4400	395-5986
Web: www.nlrb.gov					
Region 7 477 Michigan Ave Rm 300	Detroit	MI	48226	313-226-3200	226-2090
Web: www.nlrb.gov					
Region 8 1240 E Ninth St Rm 1695	Cleveland	OH	44199	216-522-3715	522-2418
TF: 866-667-6572 ■ *Web:* www.nlrb.gov					
Region 9 550 Main St Rm 3003	Cincinnati	OH	45202	513-684-3686	684-3946
TF: 866-667-6572 ■ *Web:* www.nlrb.gov					
National Mediation Board					
1301 K St NW Ste 250E	Washington	DC	20005	202-692-5000	
Web: www.nmb.gov					
National Railroad Passenger Corp					
60 Massachusetts Ave NE	Washington	DC	20002	202-906-3741	906-3285
TF: 800-872-7245 ■ *Web:* www.amtrak.com					
National Science Foundation (NSF)					
4201 Wilson Blvd	Arlington	VA	22230	703-292-5111	292-9232
TF: 800-877-8339 ■ *Web:* www.nsf.gov					
National Transportation Safety Board (NTSB)					
490 L'Enfant Plaza SW	Washington	DC	20594	202-314-6000	314-6293
Web: www.ntsb.gov					
Nuclear Regulatory Commission Regional Offices					
Region 1 2100 Renaissance Blvd	King of Prussia	PA	19406	610-337-5000	
TF: 800-432-1156 ■ *Web:* www.nrc.gov					
Region 2 61 Forsyth St SW Ste 23T85	Atlanta	GA	30303	404-562-4400	562-4900
TF: 800-577-8510 ■ *Web:* www.nrc.gov					
Region 3 2443 Warrenville Rd Ste 210	Lisle	IL	60532	630-829-9500	515-1078
TF: 800-522-3025 ■ *Web:* www.nrc.gov					
Region 4 1600 E Lamar Blvd	Arlington	TX	76011	817-860-8100	
TF: 800-952-9677 ■ *Web:* www.nrc.gov					
Nuclear Waste Technical Review Board (NWTRB)					
2300 Clarendon Blvd Ste 1300	Arlington	VA	22201	703-235-4473	235-4495
Web: www.nwtrb.gov					
Occupational Safety & Health Review Commission					
1120 20th St NW 9th Fl	Washington	DC	20036	202-606-5400	606-5050
Web: www.oshrc.gov					
Occupational Safety & Health Review Commission Regional Offices					
Atlanta Region 100 Alabama St SW Rm 2R90	Atlanta	GA	30303	404-562-1640	562-1650
TF: 800-321-6742 ■ *Web:* www.oshrc.gov					
Office of Compliance					
110 Second St SE Rm LA 200	Washington	DC	20540	202-724-9250	426-1913
Web: www.compliance.gov					
Office of Personnel Management (OPM)					
1900 E St NW	Washington	DC	20415	202-606-1800	
Web: www.opm.gov					
Office of Special Counsel					
1730 M St NW Ste 218	Washington	DC	20036	202-254-3600	653-5151
TF: 800-872-9855 ■ *Web:* www.osc.gov					
Office of Special Counsel Regional Offices					
Dallas Field Office					
525 Griffin St Rm 824 PO Box 103	Dallas	TX	75202	214-747-1519	767-2764
TF: 800-872-9855 ■ *Web:* www.osc.gov					
San Francisco Bay Area Field Office					
Federal Bldg 1301 Clay St Ste 1220-N	Oakland	CA	94612	510-637-3460	637-3474
TF: 800-872-9855 ■ *Web:* www.osc.gov					
Office of the National Counterintelligence Executive (ONCIX)					
LX/ICC-B	Washington	DC	20511	571-204-6537	874-8910*
**Fax Area Code:* 703 ■ *Web:* ncsc.gov					
Overseas Private Investment Corp (OPIC)					
1100 New York Ave NW	Washington	DC	20527	202-336-8400	408-9859
Web: www.opic.gov					
Peace Corps 1111 20th St NW	Washington	DC	20526	202-692-1040	
TF: 800-424-8580 ■ *Web:* www.peacecorps.gov					
Atlanta Regional Office					
1111 20th Street NW	Washington	DC	20526	404-562-3456	562-3455
TF: 855-855-1961 ■ *Web:* www.peacecorps.gov					
Chicago Regional Office					
55 W Monroe St Ste 450	Chicago	IL	60603	312-353-4990	353-4192
TF: 800-424-8580 ■ *Web:* www.peacecorps.gov					

Phone | Fax

Dallas Regional Office
1100 Commerce St Ste 427 . . . Dallas TX 75242 855-855-1961 253-5401*
*Fax Area Code: 214 ■ TF: 855-855-1961 ■ Web: www.peacecorps.gov

Peace Corps Regional Offices
Denver Regional Office 1999 Broadway Ste 2205 . . . Denver CO 80202 855-855-1961
Web: www.peacecorps.gov
Los Angeles Regional Office
2361 Rosecrans Ave Ste 155 . . . El Segundo CA 90245 310-356-1100 356-1125
TF: 800-424-8580 ■ Web: www.peacecorps.gov
Mid-Atlantic Regional Office
1525 Wilson Blvd Ste 100 . . . Arlington VA 22209 202-692-1040
TF: 800-424-8580 ■ Web: www.peacecorps.gov
New York Regional Office
201 Varick St Ste 1025 . . . New York NY 10014 212-352-5440 352-5441
TF: 800-424-8580 ■ Web: www.peacecorps.gov
Northwest Regional Office
1601 Fifth Ave Ste 605 . . . Seattle WA 98101 206-553-5490 553-2343
TF: 800-424-8580 ■ Web: www.peacecorps.gov
San Francisco Regional Office
1301 Clay St Ste 620-N . . . Oakland CA 94610 510-452-8444 452-8441
TF: 800-424-8580 ■ Web: www.peacecorps.gov

Pension Benefit Guaranty Corp
1200 K St NW . . . Washington DC 20005 202-326-4000 326-4047
TF Cust Svc: 800-400-7242 ■ Web: www.pbgc.gov

Postal Regulatory Commission
901 New York Ave NW Ste 200 . . . Washington DC 20268 202-789-6800 789-6891
Web: www.prc.gov

Presidio Trust
103 Montgomery Street PO Box 29052 . . . San Francisco CA 94129 415-561-5300 561-5315
Web: www.presidio.gov

Railroad Retirement Board 844 N Rush St . . . Chicago IL 60611 312-751-4300 -75-1-7136
TF: 877-772-5772 ■ Web: www.rrb.gov/general/contact_us.asp

Securities & Exchange Commission (SEC)
100 F St NE . . . Washington DC 20549 202-942-8088 772-9295
TF: 800-732-0330 ■ Web: www.sec.gov
Office of Investor Education & Advocacy
100 F St NE . . . Washington DC 20549 202-942-8088 772-9295
Web: sec.gov/servlet/sec/investor
Atlanta Regional Office
3475 Lenox Rd NE Ste 1000 . . . Atlanta GA 30326 404-842-7600
Web: www.sec.gov
Boston Regional Office 33 Arch St 23rd Fl . . . Boston MA 02110 617-573-8900
Web: www.sec.gov/contact/addresses.htm
Chicago Regional Office
175 W Jackson Blvd Ste 900 . . . Chicago IL 60604 312-353-7390 353-7398
Web: www.sec.gov
Denver Regional Office
1801 California St Ste 1500 . . . Denver CO 80202 303-844-1000 844-1010
Web: www.sec.gov

Securities & Exchange Commission Regional Offices
Fort Worth Regional Office
801 Cherry St, Unit 18 . . . Fort Worth TX 76102 817-978-3821
Web: sec.gov
Los Angeles Regional Office
5670 Wilshire Blvd 11th Fl . . . Los Angeles CA 90036 323-965-3998 965-3815
Web: www.sec.gov
Miami Regional Office 801 Brickell Ave Ste 1800 . . . Miami FL 33131 305-982-6300
Web: www.sec.gov
New York Regional Office
3 World Financial Ctr Ste 400 . . . New York NY 10281 212-336-1100
Web: www.sec.gov
Philadelphia Regional Office
Mellon Independence Ctr 701 Market St . . . Philadelphia PA 19106 215-597-3100
Web: www.sec.gov
Salt Lake Regional Office
15 W S Temple St Ste 1800 . . . Salt Lake City UT 84101 801-524-5796
Web: sec.gov
San Francisco Regional Office
44 Montgomery St Ste 2600 . . . San Francisco CA 94104 415-705-2500
Web: sec.gov

Selective Service System 1515 Wilson Blvd . . . Arlington VA 22209 847-688-6888
Web: www.sss.gov
Region 1 PO Box 94638 . . . Palatine IL 60094 847-688-6888
TF: 888-655-1825 ■ Web: www.sss.gov

Selective Service System Regional Offices
Region 2 PO Box 94638 . . . Palatine IL 60094 847-688-6888
TF: 888-655-1825 ■ Web: www.sss.gov

Small Business Administration (SBA)
409 Third St SW . . . Washington DC 20416 202-205-6600 205-6802
TF: 800-827-5722 ■ Web: www.sba.gov
National Women's Business Council
409 Third St SW Ste 210 . . . Washington DC 20024 202-205-3850 205-6825
Web: www.nwbc.gov

Small Business Administration Regional Offices (SBA)
Region 1 10 Cswy St Ste 265A . . . Boston MA 02222 617-565-8416 565-8420
Web: www.sba.gov/about-offices-list/3
Region 10 2401 Fourth Ave Ste 400 . . . Seattle WA 98121 206-553-5676 553-4155
Web: www.sba.gov
Region 10 701 Fifth Ave Ste 2900 . . . Seattle WA 98104 206-615-2236
TF: 800-772-1213 ■ Web: www.ssa.gov
Region 3 1150 First Ave Ste 1001 . . . King Of Prussia PA 19406 610-382-3092
Web: www.sba.gov/about-offices-list/3
Region 4 233 Peachtree St NE Ste 1800 . . . Atlanta GA 30303 404-331-4999 331-2354
Web: www.sba.gov/about-offices-list/3
Region 5 500 W Madison St Ste 1150 . . . Chicago IL 60661 312-353-0357 353-3426
Web: www.sba.gov/about-offices-list/3
Region 6 4300 Amon Carter Blvd Ste 108 . . . Fort Worth TX 76155 817-684-5581 684-5588
Web: www.sba.gov
Region 6 1301 Young St . . . Dallas TX 75202 214-767-9401 767-8986
TF: 800-772-1213 ■ Web: www.ssa.gov/dallas
Region 7 100 Walnut Ste 530 . . . Kansas City MO 64106 816-426-4840 426-4848
Web: www.sba.gov
Region 8 721 19th St Ste 426 . . . Denver CO 80202 303-844-2607 292-3582*
*Fax Area Code: 202 ■ Web: sba.gov
Region 9 330 N Brand Blvd Ste 1200 . . . Glendale CA 91203 818-552-3437 481-0344*
*Fax Area Code: 202 ■ Web: www.sba.gov

Social Security Administration (SSA)
6401 Security Blvd . . . Baltimore MD 21235 410-965-8904
TF: 800-772-1213 ■ Web: www.ssa.gov

Social Security Administration Regional Offices
Region 1 JFK Federal Bldg Rm 1900 . . . Boston MA 02203 617-565-2870 565-2143
Web: www.ssa.gov/boston
Region 2 26 Federal Plaza Rm 40-102 . . . New York NY 10278 212-264-4036
TF: 800-772-1213 ■ Web: www.ssa.gov/ny
Region 4 61 Forsyth St SW Ste 23T30 . . . Atlanta GA 30303 800-772-1213
TF: 800-772-1213 ■ Web: www.ssa.gov/atlanta
Region 5 600 W Madison St PO Box 8280 . . . Chicago IL 60680 312-575-4050
TF: 800-772-1213 ■ Web: www.ssa.gov

Social Security Advisory Board
400 Virginia Ave SW Ste 625 . . . Washington DC 20024 202-475-7700 475-7715
Web: www.ssab.gov

State Justice Institute (SJI)
11951 Freedom Drive Suite 1020 . . . Reston VA 20190 571-313-8843 313-1173
Web: www.sji.gov/

Susquehanna River Basin Commission
1721 N Front St . . . Harrisburg PA 17102 717-238-0423 238-2436
Web: www.srbc.net

Tennessee Valley Authority (TVA)
400 W Summit Hill Dr . . . Knoxville TN 37902 865-632-2101
Web: www.tva.gov

US Agency for International Development (USAID)
1300 Pennsylvania Ave NW . . . Washington DC 20523 202-712-0000 216-3524
Web: www.usaid.gov

US Arctic Research Commission
4350 N Fairfax Dr Ste 510 . . . Arlington VA 22203 703-525-0111 525-0114
Web: www.arctic.gov

US Chemical Safety & Hazard Investigation Board
2175 K St NW Ste 400 . . . Washington DC 20037 202-261-7600 261-7650
Web: csb.gov

US Commission on Civil Rights
624 Ninth St NW . . . Washington DC 20425 202-376-7700 376-7672
Web: www.usccr.gov

US Commission on Civil Rights Regional Offices
Central Regional Office
400 State Ave Ste 908 . . . Kansas City KS 66101 913-551-1400 551-1413
Web: www.usccr.gov
Eastern Regional Office
624 Ninth St NW Ste 700 . . . Washington DC 20425 202-376-7700 376-7672
Web: www.usccr.gov
Midwestern Regional Office
55 W Monroe St Ste 410 . . . Chicago IL 60603 312-353-8311 353-8324
TF: 800-552-6843 ■ Web: www.usccr.gov
Rocky Mountain Regional Office 1700 Broadway . . . Denver CO 80290 303-866-1040 866-1050
Web: www.usccr.gov
Southern Regional Office
61 Forsyth St SW Ste 1840 T . . . Atlanta GA 30303 404-562-7000 562-7004
Web: www.usccr.gov
Western Regional Office
300 N Los Angeles St Ste 2010 . . . Los Angeles CA 90012 213-894-3437 894-0508
Web: www.usccr.gov

US Commission on International Religious Freedom (USCIRF)
800 N Capitol St NW Ste 790 . . . Washington DC 20002 202-523-3240 523-5020
Web: www.uscirf.gov

US Election Assistance Commission
1201 New York Ave NW Ste 300 . . . Washington DC 20005 202-566-3100 566-3127
TF: 866-747-1471 ■ Web: www.eac.gov

US General Services Administration (GSA)
1275 First St NW . . . Washington DC 20405 202-208-7642
Web: www.gsa.gov/portal/category/100000

US Institute of Peace
2301 Constitution Ave NW . . . Washington DC 20037 202-457-1700 429-6063
Web: www.usip.org

US International Trade Commission
500 E St SW . . . Washington DC 20436 202-205-2000
Web: www.usitc.gov

US Postal Service (USPS)
475 L'Enfant Plaza W SW . . . Washington DC 20260 202-268-2000
TF Cust Svc: 800-275-8777 ■ Web: www.usps.com

US Trade & Development Agency
1000 Wilson Blvd Ste 1600 . . . Arlington VA 22209 703-875-4357 875-4009
Web: www.ustda.gov

Vietnam Education Foundation (VEF)
2111 Wilson Blvd Ste 700 . . . Arlington VA 22201 703-351-5053 351-1423
Web: home.vef.gov

White House Commission on Remembrance
1750 New York Ave NW . . . Washington DC 20006 202-783-4665

344 GOVERNMENT - US - JUDICIAL BRANCH

Phone | Fax

Federal Judicial Ctr 1 Columbus Cir NE . . . Washington DC 20544 202-502-4000
Web: www.fjc.gov

Judicial Conference of the US
1 Columbus Cir NE . . . Washington DC 20544 202-502-2600
Web: www.uscourts.gov/judconf.html

Judicial Panel on Multidistrict Litigation
Thurgood Marshall Federal Judiciary Bldg
1 Columbus Cir NE Rm G-255 N Lobby . . . Washington DC 20544 202-502-2800 502-2888
Web: www.jpml.uscourts.gov

Supreme Court of the US
US Supreme Ct Bldg 1 1st St NE . . . Washington DC 20543 202-479-3000 479-3472
Web: www.supremecourt.gov

US Court of Appeals for the Armed Forces
450 E St NW . . . Washington DC 20442 202-761-1448 761-4672

	City	State	Zip	Phone	Fax
US Court of Appeals for Veterans Claims					
625 Indiana Ave NW Ste 900	Washington	DC	20004	202-501-5970	501-5848
Web: www.uscourts.cavc.gov					
US Court of Federal Claims					
717 Madison Pl NW	Washington	DC	20005	202-357-6400	
Web: www.uscfc.uscourts.gov					
US Court of International Trade					
1 Federal Plaza	New York	NY	10278	212-264-2800	264-1085
Web: www.cit.uscourts.gov					
US Sentencing Commission					
Thurgood Marshall Federal Judiciary Bldg					
1 Columbus Cir NE S Lobby	Washington	DC	20002	202-502-4500	
Web: www.ussc.gov					
US Tax Court 400 Second St NW	Washington	DC	20217	202-521-0700	
Web: www.ustaxcourt.gov					

344-1 US Appeals Courts

	City	State	Zip	Phone	Fax
Federal Circuit 717 Madison Pl NW	Washington	DC	20439	202-275-8000	
Web: www.cafc.uscourts.gov					
Circuit 1 1 Courthouse Way Ste 2500	Boston	MA	02210	617-748-9057	
Web: www.ca1.uscourts.gov					
Circuit 10 1823 Stout St	Denver	CO	80202	303-844-3157	
Web: www.ca10.uscourts.gov					
Circuit 11 56 Forsyth St NW	Atlanta	GA	30303	404-335-6100	335-6270
Web: www.ca11.uscourts.gov					
Circuit 2 US Courthouse 40 Foley Sq	New York	NY	10007	212-857-8500	
Web: www.ca2.uscourts.gov					
Circuit 3 US Courthouse 601 Market St	Philadelphia	PA	19106	215-597-2995	
Web: www.ca3.uscourts.gov					
Circuit 4 US Courthouse Annex 1100 E Main St	Richmond	VA	23219	804-916-2700	
Web: www.ca4.uscourts.gov					
Circuit 5 600 Camp St	New Orleans	LA	70130	504-310-7700	
Web: www.ca5.uscourts.gov					
Circuit 6 100 E Fifth St Ste 532	Cincinnati	OH	45202	513-564-7000	
Web: www.ca6.uscourts.gov					
Circuit 7 219 S Dearborn St Ste 2722	Chicago	IL	60604	312-435-5850	
Web: www.ca7.uscourts.gov					
Circuit 8 111 S Tenth St Rm 22.329	Saint Louis	MO	63102	314-244-2400	244-2780
Web: www.ca8.uscourts.gov					
US Court of Appeals					
Circuit 9 PO Box 193939 PO Box 193939	San Francisco	CA	94119	415-355-8000	
Web: www.ca9.uscourts.gov					
District of Columbia Circuit					
333 Constitution Ave NW US Courthouse	Washington	DC	20001	202-216-7000	
Web: www.cadc.uscourts.gov					

344-2 US Bankruptcy Courts

	City	State	Zip	Phone	Fax
Alabama Middle 1 Church St	Montgomery	AL	36104	334-954-3800	954-3819
Web: www.almb.uscourts.gov					
Alabama Northern 1800 Fifth Ave N Rm 120	Birmingham	AL	35203	205-714-4000	
Web: www.alnb.uscourts.gov					
Alabama Southern 201 St Louis St	Mobile	AL	36602	251-441-5391	441-6286
Web: www.alsb.uscourts.gov					
Alaska 605 W Fourth Ave Ste 138	Anchorage	AK	99501	907-271-2655	
TF: 800-859-8059 ■ *Web:* www.akb.uscourts.gov					
Arizona 230 N First Ave Ste 101	Phoenix	AZ	85003	602-682-4000	
Web: www.azb.uscourts.gov					
Arkansas 300 W Second St	Little Rock	AR	72201	501-918-5500	918-5520
Web: www.arb.uscourts.gov					
California Central 255 E Temple St	Los Angeles	CA	90012	213-894-3118	
Web: www.cacb.uscourts.gov					
California Eastern 501 'I' St Ste 3-200	Sacramento	CA	95814	916-930-4400	
Web: www.caeb.uscourts.gov					
California Northern 235 Pine St Ste 19	San Francisco	CA	94120	415-268-2300	
Web: www.canb.uscourts.gov					
California Southern 325 W F St	San Diego	CA	92101	619-557-5620	
Web: www.casb.uscourts.gov					
Central District of Illinois					
600 E Monroe St 2nd Fl Rm 226	Springfield	IL	62701	217-492-4551	
Web: www.ilcb.uscourts.gov					
Colorado US Custom House 721 19th St	Denver	CO	80202	720-904-7300	
Web: www.cob.uscourts.gov					
Connecticut 450 Main St 7th Fl	Hartford	CT	06103	860-240-3675	
Web: www.ctb.uscourts.gov					
Delaware 824 N Market St 3rd Fl	Wilmington	DE	19801	302-252-2900	
Web: www.deb.uscourts.gov					
District of Columbia					
333 Constitution Ave NW	Washington	DC	20001	202-354-3280	
Web: www.dcb.uscourts.gov					
Eastern District of Texas					
110 N College Ave 9th Fl	Tyler	TX	75702	903-590-3200	
Web: www.txeb.uscourts.gov					
Florida Middle 801 N Florida Ave Ste 727	Tampa	FL	33602	813-301-5162	
Web: www.flmb.uscourts.gov					
Florida Northern 110 E Pk Ave Ste 100	Tallahassee	FL	32301	850-521-5001	
Web: www.flnb.uscourts.gov					
Florida Southern 51 SW First Ave	Miami	FL	33130	305-714-1800	
Web: www.flsb.uscourts.gov					
Georgia Middle 433 Cherry St PO Box 1957	Macon	GA	31202	478-752-3506	
Web: www.gamb.uscourts.gov					
Georgia Northern 75 Spring St SW	Atlanta	GA	30303	404-215-1000	
Web: www.ganb.uscourts.gov					
Georgia Southern 125 Bull St	Savannah	GA	31401	912-650-4100	
Web: www.gasb.uscourts.gov					
Hawaii 1132 Bishop St	Honolulu	HI	96813	808-522-8100	522-8120
Web: www.hib.uscourts.gov					
Idaho 550 W Fort St	Boise	ID	83724	208-334-1074	
Web: www.id.uscourts.gov					
Illinois Northern 219 S Dearborn St Rm 713	Chicago	IL	60604	312-435-5694	
Web: www.ilnb.uscourts.gov					
Illinois Southern 750 Missouri Ave	East Saint Louis	IL	62201	618-482-9400	
Web: www.ilsb.uscourts.gov					
Indiana Northern 401 S Michigan St	South Bend	IN	46601	574-968-2100	
Web: www.innb.uscourts.gov					
Indiana Southern 46 E Ohio St	Indianapolis	IN	46204	317-229-3800	229-3801
Web: www.insb.uscourts.gov					
Iowa Northern 425 Second St SE Ste 800	Cedar Rapids	IA	52401	319-286-2200	286-2280
Web: www.ianb.uscourts.gov					
Iowa Southern 110 E Ct Ave PO Box 9264	Des Moines	IA	50306	515-284-6230	284-6303
Web: www.iasb.uscourts.gov					
Kansas 401 N Market St Rm 167	Wichita	KS	67202	316-269-6486	
Web: www.ksb.uscourts.gov					
Kentucky Eastern 100 E Vine St Ste 200	Lexington	KY	40507	859-233-2608	
Web: www.kyeb.uscourts.gov					
Kentucky Western 601 W Broadway Ste 450	Louisville	KY	40202	502-627-5700	
Web: www.kywb.uscourts.gov					
Louisiana Eastern					
500 Poydras St Ste B-601	New Orleans	LA	70130	504-589-7878	
Web: www.laeb.uscourts.gov					
Louisiana Middle 707 Florida St Ste 119	Baton Rouge	LA	70801	225-389-0211	
Web: www.lamb.uscourts.gov					
Louisiana Western 300 Fannin St Ste 2201	Shreveport	LA	71101	318-676-4267	
Web: www.lawb.uscourts.gov					
Maine 537 Congress St 2nd Fl	Portland	ME	04101	207-780-3482	780-3679
Web: www.meb.uscourts.gov					
Massachusetts 5 Post Office Sq	Boston	MA	02109	617-748-5300	
Web: www.mab.uscourts.gov/mab					
Michigan Eastern 211 W Fort St Ste 2100	Detroit	MI	48226	313-234-0065	
Web: www.mieb.uscourts.gov					
Michigan Western 1 Div Ave N Rm 200	Grand Rapids	MI	49503	616-456-2693	
Web: www.miwb.uscourts.gov					
Minnesota					
300 S Fourth St 7W US Courthouse	Minneapolis	MN	55415	612-664-5260	
TF: 866-260-7337 ■ *Web:* www.mnb.uscourts.gov					
Mississippi Northern 703 Hwy 145 N	Aberdeen	MS	39730	662-369-2596	
Web: www.msnb.uscourts.gov					
Mississippi Southern PO Box 2448	Jackson	MS	39225	601-965-5301	
Web: www.mssb.uscourts.gov					
Missouri Eastern 111 S Tenth St 4th Fl	Saint Louis	MO	63102	314-244-4500	244-4990
TF: 866-803-9517 ■ *Web:* www.moeb.uscourts.gov					
Missouri Western 400 E Ninth St Rm1510	Kansas City	MO	64106	816-512-1800	
Web: www.mow.uscourts.gov					
Montana 400 N Main St	Butte	MT	59701	406-497-1240	
Web: www.mtb.uscourts.gov					
Nebraska 111 S 18th Plaza Ste 1125	Omaha	NE	68102	402-661-7444	
Web: www.neb.uscourts.gov					
Nevada 300 Las Vegas Blvd S	Las Vegas	NV	89101	702-388-6257	
Web: www.nvb.uscourts.gov					
New Hampshire 1000 Elm St 10th Fl	Manchester	NH	03101	603-222-2600	222-2697
Web: www.nhb.uscourts.gov					
New Jersey PO Box 1352	Newark	NJ	07102	973-645-4764	
Web: www.njb.uscourts.gov					
New Mexico 333 Lomas Blvd N.W.	Albuquerque	NM	87102	505-348-2000	348-2028
Web: www.nmd.uscourts.gov					
New York Eastern 271 Cadman Plaza E	Brooklyn	NY	11201	347-394-1700	
Web: www.nyeb.uscourts.gov					
North Carolina Eastern 1760-A Parkwood Blvd	Wilson	NC	27893	252-237-0248	
Web: www.nceb.uscourts.gov					
North Carolina Middle					
101 S Edgeworth St Fl 1	Greensboro	NC	27401	336-358-4000	
Web: www.ncmb.uscourts.gov					
North Carolina Western					
401 W Trade St PO Box 34189	Charlotte	NC	28234	704-350-7500	
Web: www.ncwb.uscourts.gov					
North Dakota 655 First Ave N Ste 210	Fargo	ND	58102	701-297-7100	
Web: www.ndb.uscourts.gov					
Northern District of New York					
445 Broadway Ste 330	Albany	NY	12207	518-257-1661	
Web: www.nynb.uscourts.gov					
Ohio Northern 201 Superior Ave	Cleveland	OH	44114	216-615-4300	
Web: www.ohnb.uscourts.gov					
Ohio Southern 120 W Third St	Dayton	OH	45402	937-225-2516	
Web: www.ohsb.uscourts.gov					
Oklahoma Eastern 111 W Fourth St PO Box 1347	Okmulgee	OK	74447	918-758-0126	756-9248
Web: www.okeb.uscourts.gov					
Oklahoma Northern 224 S Boulder Ave Rm 105	Tulsa	OK	74103	918-699-4000	
Web: www.oknb.uscourts.gov					
Oklahoma Western 215 Dean A McGee Ave	Oklahoma City	OK	73102	405-609-5700	
Web: www.okwb.uscourts.gov					
Oregon 1001 SW Fifth Ave Rm 700	Portland	OR	97204	503-326-1500	
Web: www.orb.uscourts.gov					
Pennsylvania Eastern					
900 Market St Ste 400	Philadelphia	PA	19107	215-408-2800	
Web: www.paeb.uscourts.gov					
Pennsylvania Middle 197 S Main St	Wilkes-Barre	PA	18701	570-831-2500	829-0249
TF: 877-298-2053 ■ *Web:* www.pamb.uscourts.gov					
Pennsylvania Western					
5414 US Steel Tower 600 Grant St	Pittsburgh	PA	15219	412-644-2700	644-6512
Web: www.pawb.uscourts.gov					
Puerto Rico 300 Calle Del Recinto Sur	San Juan	PR	00901	787-977-6000	977-6008
Web: www.prb.uscourts.gov					
Rhode Island					
The Federal Ctr					
380 Westminster Mall 6th Fl	Providence	RI	02903	401-626-3100	626-3150
Web: www.rib.uscourts.gov					
South Carolina 1100 Laurel St	Columbia	SC	29201	803-765-5436	
Web: www.scb.uscourts.gov					

	City	State	ZIP	Phone	Fax
South Dakota 400 S Phillips Ave Rm 104 *Web:* www.sdb.uscourts.gov	Sioux Falls	SD	57104	605-357-2430	357-2401
Southern District of New York US Custom House 1 Bowling Green *Web:* www.nysb.uscourts.gov	New York	NY	10004	212-668-2870	668-2878
Tennessee Eastern 800 Market St Ste 330 *Web:* www.tneb.uscourts.gov	Knoxville	TN	37902	865-545-4279	
Tennessee Middle 701 Broadway Rm 170 *Web:* www.tnmb.uscourts.gov	Nashville	TN	37203	615-736-5584	736-2305
Tennessee Western 200 Jefferson Ave Ste 413 *Web:* www.tnwb.uscourts.gov	Memphis	TN	38103	901-328-3500	
Texas Northern 1100 Commerce St Rm 1254 *TF:* 800-442-6850 ■ *Web:* www.txnb.uscourts.gov	Dallas	TX	75242	214-753-2000	
Texas Southern PO Box 61010 *Web:* www.txs.uscourts.gov	Houston	TX	77208	713-250-5500	
Texas Western 615 E Houston St Rm 597 PO Box 1439 *Web:* www.txwb.uscourts.gov	San Antonio	TX	78205	210-472-6720	472-5196
US Virgin Islands US Courthouse 5500 Veterans Dr Rm 310 *Web:* www.vid.uscourts.gov	Saint Thomas	VI	00802	340-774-0640	775-8075
Utah 350 S Main St Rm 301 *Web:* www.utb.uscourts.gov	Salt Lake City	UT	84101	801-524-6687	524-4409
Vermont 67 Merchants Row PO Box 6648 *Web:* www.vtb.uscourts.gov	Rutland	VT	05702	802-776-2000	776-2020
Virginia Eastern 200 S Washington St *Web:* www.vaeb.uscourts.gov	Alexandria	VA	23219	804-916-2400	
Virginia Western 210 Church Ave SW Rm 200 *Web:* www.vawb.uscourts.gov	Roanoke	VA	24011	540-857-2391	857-2873
Washington Eastern 904 W Riverside Ave Ste 304 *TF:* 800-519-2549 ■ *Web:* www.waeb.uscourts.gov	Spokane	WA	99201	509-353-2404	
Washington Western 700 Stewart St Ste 6301 *Web:* www.wawb.uscourts.gov	Seattle	WA	98101	206-370-5200	
West Virginia Northern 1125 Chapline St Third Fl PO Box 70 *Web:* www.wvnb.uscourts.gov	Wheeling	WV	26003	304-233-1655	233-0185
West Virginia Southern 300 Virginia St E Rm 3200 *Web:* www.wvsb.uscourts.gov	Charleston	WV	25301	304-347-3003	
Western District of New York 100 State St Rm 1220 *Web:* www.nywb.uscourts.gov	Rochester	NY	14614	585-613-4200	
Wisconsin Eastern US Courthouse 517 E Wisconsin Ave Rm 126 *TF:* 877-781-7277 ■ *Web:* www.wieb.uscourts.gov	Milwaukee	WI	53202	414-297-3291	
Wisconsin Western 120 N Henry St Rm 340 PO Box 548 *Web:* www.wiwb.uscourts.gov	Madison	WI	53701	608-264-5178	
US Bankruptcy Court *Wyoming* 2120 Capitol Ave Ste 6004 *Web:* www.wyb.uscourts.gov	Cheyenne	WY	82001	307-433-2200	

344-3 US District Courts

	City	State	ZIP	Phone	Fax
United States District Court, Central District 312 N Spring St *Web:* www.cacd.uscourts.gov	Los Angeles	CA	90012	213-894-1565	
US District Court Alabama Northern 1729 Fifth Ave N *Web:* www.alnd.uscourts.gov	Birmingham	AL	35203	205-278-1700	
US District Court Arizona 401 W Washington St Ste 130 *Web:* www.azd.uscourts.gov	Phoenix	AZ	85003	602-322-7200	
US District Court Arkansas Western 30 S Sixth St *Web:* www.arwd.uscourts.gov	Fort Smith	AR	72901	479-783-6833	783-6308
US District Court California Eastern 501 I St *Web:* www.caed.uscourts.gov	Sacramento	CA	95814	916-930-4000	
US District Court California Northern 450 Golden Gate Ave PO Box 36060 *Web:* www.cand.uscourts.gov	San Francisco	CA	94102	415-522-2000	
US District Court California Southern 880 Front St Rm 4290 *Web:* www.casd.uscourts.gov	San Diego	CA	92101	619-557-6348	702-9900
US District Court Colorado 901 19th St *TF:* 800-359-8699 ■ *Web:* www.cod.uscourts.gov/Home.aspx	Denver	CO	80294	303-844-3433	335-2040
US District Court Connecticut 141 Church St *Web:* www.ctd.uscourts.gov	New Haven	CT	06510	203-773-2140	773-2334
US District Court Delaware 844 N King St Ste 18 *Web:* www.ded.uscourts.gov	Wilmington	DE	19801	302-573-6170	
US District Court District of Columbia 333 Constitution Ave NW # 6822 *Web:* www.dcd.uscourts.gov	Washington	DC	20001	202-354-3000	
US District Court Florida Middle 401 W Central Blvd Ste 1200 *Web:* www.flmd.uscourts.gov	Orlando	FL	32801	407-835-4200	
US District Court Florida Southern 301 N Miami Ave *Web:* www.flsd.uscourts.gov	Miami	FL	33128	305-523-5100	
US District Court for the District of Alaska 222 W Seventh Ave Ste 4 *TF:* 866-243-3814 ■ *Web:* www.akd.uscourts.gov	Anchorage	AK	99513	907-677-6100	
US District Court Georgia Middle 475 Mulberry St PO Box 128 *Web:* www.gamd.uscourts.gov	Macon	GA	31202	478-752-3497	752-3496
US District Court Georgia Northern 75 Spring St SW Rm 2211 *Web:* www.gand.uscourts.gov	Atlanta	GA	30303	404-215-1600	
US District Court Georgia Southern PO Box 8286 *Web:* www.gasd.uscourts.gov	Savannah	GA	31412	912-650-4020	
US District Court Guam 520 W Soledad Ave 4th Fl *Web:* www.gud.uscourts.gov	Hagatna	GU	96910	671-473-9100	
US District Court Hawaii 300 Ala Moana Blvd Rm C-338 *Web:* www.hid.uscourts.gov	Honolulu	HI	96850	808-541-1300	
US District Court Idaho 550 W Fort St *Web:* www.id.uscourts.gov	Boise	ID	83724	208-334-1361	
US District Court Illinois Central 600 E Monroe St *Web:* www.ilcd.uscourts.gov	Springfield	IL	62701	217-492-4020	492-4028
US District Court Illinois Northern 219 S Dearborn St 20th Fl *Web:* www.ilnd.uscourts.gov	Chicago	IL	60604	312-435-5670	
US District Court Illinois Southern 750 Missouri Ave *Web:* www.ilsd.uscourts.gov	East Saint Louis	IL	62201	618-482-9371	482-9383
US District Court Indiana Northern 204 S Main St *Web:* www.innd.uscourts.gov	South Bend	IN	46601	574-246-8000	
US District Court Indiana Southern 46 E Ohio St *Web:* www.insd.uscourts.gov	Indianapolis	IN	46204	317-229-3700	229-3959
US District Court Iowa Northern 101 First St SE *Web:* www.iand.uscourts.gov	Cedar Rapids	IA	52401	319-286-2300	286-2301
US District Court Iowa Southern PO Box 9344 *Web:* www.iasd.uscourts.gov	Des Moines	IA	50306	515-284-6248	284-6418
US District Court Kansas 500 State Ave *Web:* www.ksd.uscourts.gov	Kansas City	KS	66101	913-735-2200	551-6942
US District Court Kentucky Eastern 101 Barr St *Web:* www.kyed.uscourts.gov	Lexington	KY	40507	859-233-2503	
US District Court Kentucky Western 601 W Broadway Rm 106 *Web:* www.kywd.uscourts.gov	Louisville	KY	40202	502-625-3500	625-3880
US District Court Louisiana Eastern 500 Poydras St Rm C-151 *Web:* www.laed.uscourts.gov	New Orleans	LA	70130	504-589-7650	589-7697
US District Court Louisiana Middle 777 Florida St Ste 139 *Web:* www.lamd.uscourts.gov	Baton Rouge	LA	70801	225-389-3500	389-3501
US District Court Louisiana Western 300 Fannin St Ste 1167 *Web:* www.lawd.uscourts.gov	Shreveport	LA	71101	318-676-4273	676-3962
US District Court Maine 156 Federal St *Web:* www.med.uscourts.gov	Portland	ME	04101	207-780-3356	
US District Court Maryland 101 W Lombard St *Web:* www.mdd.uscourts.gov	Baltimore	MD	21201	410-962-2600	
US District Court Massachusetts 1 Courthouse Way Ste 2300 *Web:* www.mad.uscourts.gov	Boston	MA	02210	617-748-9152	
US District Court Michigan Eastern 231 W Lafayette Blvd *Web:* www.mied.uscourts.gov	Detroit	MI	48226	313-234-5005	
US District Court Michigan Western 110 Michigan St NW Rm 399 *Web:* www.miwd.uscourts.gov	Grand Rapids	MI	49503	616-456-2381	
US District Court Minnesota 300 S Fourth St Ste 202 *Web:* www.mnd.uscourts.gov	Minneapolis	MN	55415	612-664-5000	664-5033
US District Court Mississippi Northern 911 Jackson Ave E Rm 369 *Web:* www.msnd.uscourts.gov	Oxford	MS	38655	662-234-1971	236-5210
US District Court Mississippi Southern PO Box 23552 *TF:* 866-517-7682 ■ *Web:* www.mssd.uscourts.gov	Jackson	MS	39225	601-965-4439	
US District Court Missouri Eastern 111 S Tenth St Ste 3.300 *Web:* www.moed.uscourts.gov	Saint Louis	MO	63102	314-244-7900	244-7909
US District Court Missouri Western 400 E Ninth St *Web:* www.mow.uscourts.gov	Kansas City	MO	64106	816-512-5000	
US District Court Montana PO Box 8537 *Web:* www.mtd.uscourts.gov	Missoula	MT	59807	406-542-7260	542-7272
US District Court Nebraska 111 S 18th Plaza Ste 1152 *TF:* 866-220-4381 ■ *Web:* www.ned.uscourts.gov	Omaha	NE	68102	402-661-7350	661-7387
US District Court Nevada 333 Las Vegas Blvd S 1st Fl *Web:* www.nvd.uscourts.gov	Las Vegas	NV	89101	702-464-5400	
US District Court New Hampshire 55 Pleasant St Rm 110 *Web:* www.nhd.uscourts.gov	Concord	NH	03301	603-225-1423	
US District Court New Jersey 50 Walnut St *Web:* www.njd.uscourts.gov	Newark	NJ	07101	973-645-3730	
US District Court New Mexico 333 Lomas Blvd NW *Web:* www.nmcourt.fed.us	Albuquerque	NM	87102	505-348-2000	
US District Court New York Northern 100 S Clinton St PO Box 7367 *Web:* www.nynd.uscourts.gov	Syracuse	NY	13261	315-234-8500	
US District Court New York Southern 500 Pearl St *Web:* www.nysd.uscourts.gov	New York	NY	10007	212-805-0136	

				Phone	Fax
US District Court New York Western					
2 Niagara Sq	Buffalo	NY	14202	716-551-4211	551-4850
Web: www.nywd.uscourts.gov					
US District Court North Carolina Eastern					
PO Box 25670	Raleigh	NC	27611	919-645-1700	645-1750
Web: www.nced.uscourts.gov					
US District Court North Carolina Middle					
324 W Market St 4th Fl	Greensboro	NC	27401	336-332-6000	332-6060
Web: www.ncmd.uscourts.gov					
US District Court North Carolina Western					
401 W Trade St	Charlotte	NC	28202	704-350-7400	
TF: 866-851-1605 ■ *Web:* www.ncwd.uscourts.gov					
US District Court North Dakota PO Box 1193	Bismarck	ND	58502	701-530-2300	530-2312
Web: www.ndd.uscourts.gov					
US District Court Northern District Of Florida					
111 N Adams St	Tallahassee	FL	32301	850-521-3501	521-3656
Web: www.flnd.uscourts.gov					
US District Court Ohio Northern					
801 W Superior Ave	Cleveland	OH	44113	216-357-7000	357-7040
Web: www.ohnd.uscourts.gov					
US District Court Ohio Southern					
85 Marconi Blvd	Columbus	OH	43215	614-719-3000	
Web: www.ohsd.uscourts.gov					
US District Court Oklahoma Eastern					
PO Box 607	Muskogee	OK	74402	918-684-7920	684-7902
Web: www.oked.uscourts.gov					
US District Court Oklahoma Northern					
333 W Fourth St	Tulsa	OK	74103	918-699-4700	
TF: 866 213 1957 ■ *Web:* www.oknd.uscourts.gov					
US District Court Oklahoma Western					
200 NW Fourth St Rm 1210	Oklahoma City	OK	73102	405-609-5000	609-5099
Web: www.okwd.uscourts.gov					
US District Court Oregon					
1000 SW Third Ave Ste 740	Portland	OR	97204	503-326-8000	
Web: www.ord.uscourts.gov					
US District Court Pennsylvania Eastern					
601 Market St	Philadelphia	PA	19106	215-597-7704	597-6390
Web: www.paed.uscourts.gov					
US District Court Pennsylvania Middle					
235 N Washington Ave PO Box 1148	Scranton	PA	18501	570-207-5600	207-5650
Web: www.pamd.uscourts.gov					
US District Court Pennsylvania Western					
700 Grant St	Pittsburgh	PA	15219	412-208-7500	
Web: www.pawd.uscourts.gov					
US District Court Puerto Rico					
150 Carlos Chardon Ave Rm 150 Federal Bldg	San Juan	PR	00918	787-772-3000	766-5693
Web: www.prd.uscourts.gov					
US District Court South Carolina					
1845 Assembly St	Columbia	SC	29201	803-765-5816	
Web: www.scd.uscourts.gov					
US District Court South Dakota					
400 S Phillips Ave Rm 128	Sioux Falls	SD	57104	605-330-6600	330-6601
Web: www.sdd.uscourts.gov					
US District Court Tennessee Eastern					
800 Market St Ste 130	Knoxville	TN	37902	865-545-4228	545-4247
Web: www.tned.uscourts.gov					
US District Court Tennessee Middle					
801 Broadway Rm 800	Nashville	TN	37203	615-736-5498	736-7488
Web: www.tnmd.uscourts.gov					
US District Court Tennessee Western					
167 N Main St Rm 242	Memphis	TN	38103	901-495-1200	495-1250
Web: www.tnwd.uscourts.gov					
US District Court Texas Eastern					
211 W Ferguson St	Tyler	TX	75702	903-590-1000	
Web: www.txed.uscourts.gov					
US District Court Texas Northern					
1100 Commerce St Rm 1452	Dallas	TX	75242	214-753-2200	753-2266
Web: www.txnd.uscourts.gov					
US District Court Texas Southern					
PO Box 61010	Houston	TX	77208	713-250-5500	
Web: www.txs.uscourts.gov					
US District Court Texas Western					
655 E Durango Blvd Rm G65	San Antonio	TX	78206	210-472-6550	
TF: 800-659-2497 ■ *Web:* www.txwd.uscourts.gov					
US District Court US Virgin Islands					
3013 Estate Golden Rock	Saint Croix	VI	00820	340-773-1130	773-1563
Web: www.vid.uscourts.gov					
US District Court Utah					
350 S Main St Rm 150	Salt Lake City	UT	84101	801-524-6100	526-1175
Web: www.utd.uscourts.gov					
US District Court Vermont					
11 Elmwood Ave Rm 506 PO Box 945	Burlington	VT	05402	802-951-6301	
TF: 800-837-8718 ■ *Web:* www.vtd.uscourts.gov					
US District Court Virginia Eastern					
401 Courthouse Sq 2nd Fl	Alexandria	VA	22314	703-299-2100	
Web: www.vaed.uscourts.gov					
US District Court Virginia Western					
180 W. Main St Rm 104	Abingdon	VA	24210	540-857-5100	857-5110
Web: www.vawd.uscourts.gov					
US District Court Washington Eastern					
920 W Riverside Ave Ste 840	Spokane	WA	99201	509-458-3400	458-3420
Web: www.waed.uscourts.gov					
US District Court Washington Western					
700 Stewart St	Seattle	WA	98101	206-370-8400	
Web: www.wawd.uscourts.gov					
US District Court West Virginia Northern					
300 Third St PO Box 1518	Elkins	WV	26241	304-636-1445	636-5746
Web: www.wvnd.uscourts.gov					
US District Court West Virginia Southern					
300 Virginia St E Ste 2400	Charleston	WV	25301	304-347-3000	
Web: www.wvsd.uscourts.gov					
US District Court Wisconsin Eastern					
517 E Wisconsin Ave	Milwaukee	WI	53202	414-297-3372	
Web: www.wied.uscourts.gov					
US District Court Wisconsin Western					
120 N Henry St Rm 320 PO Box 432	Madison	WI	53701	608-264-5156	264-5925
Web: www.wiwd.uscourts.gov					
US District Court Wyoming					
2120 Capitol Ave 2nd Fl	Cheyenne	WY	82001	307-433-2120	433-2152
Web: www.wyd.uscourts.gov					

344-4 US Supreme Court

				Phone	Fax
Roberts John G Jr					
US Supreme Ct Bldg 1 1st St NE	Washington	DC	20543	202-479-3000	479-3472
Web: www.supremecourt.gov					
Alito Samuel A Jr 1 1st St NE	Washington	DC	20543	202-479-3000	479-3472
Web: www.supremecourt.gov					
Breyer Stephen G					
US Supreme Ct Bldg 1 1st St NE	Washington	DC	20543	202-479-3000	
Web: www.supremecourt.gov					
Ginsburg Ruth Bader					
US Supreme Ct Bldg 1 1st St NE	Washington	DC	20543	202-479-3000	
Web: www.supremecourt.gov					
Kennedy Anthony M					
US Supreme Ct Bldg 1 1st St NE	Washington	DC	20543	202-479-3000	479-3472
Web: www.supremecourt.gov					
Scalia Antonin					
US Supreme Ct Bldg 1 1st St NE	Washington	DC	20543	202-479-3000	479-3472
Web: www.supremecourt.gov					
Stevens John Paul					
US Supreme Ct Bldg 1 1st St NE	Washington	DC	20543	202-479-3000	479-3472
Web: www.supremecourt.gov					
Thomas Clarence					
US Supreme Ct Bldg 1 1st St NE	Washington	DC	20543	202-479-3000	
Web: www.supremecourt.gov					

345 GOVERNMENT - US - LEGISLATIVE BRANCH

SEE ALSO Legislation Hotlines p. 2641

				Phone	Fax
Aleph Institute Inc, The 9540 Collins Ave	Surfside	FL	33154	305-864-5553	
Web: www.aleph-institute.org					
Brant County Power Inc 65 Dundas St E	Paris	ON	N3L3H1	519-442-2215	
Web: www.brantcountypower.com					
Calgary Economic Development 731 First St SE	Calgary	AB	T2G2G9	403-221-7831	
Web: www.calgaryeconomicdevelopment.com					
Coast Mountain Bus Company Ltd					
13401 108th Ave	Surrey	BC	V3T5T4	604-953-3000	
Web: www.coastmountainbus.com					
Congressional Budget Office					
Ford House Office Bldg 4th Fl	Washington	DC	20515	202-226-2602	
Web: www.cbo.gov					
E.L.K. Energy Inc 172 Forest Ave	Essex	ON	N8M3E4	519-776-5291	
Web: www.elkenergy.com					
Fermi Research Alliance LLC					
Wilson and Kirk Roads MS Ste 105	Batavia	IL	60510	630-840-3211	
Web: www.fra-hq.org					
Atlanta Office 2635 Century Pkwy Ste 700	Atlanta	GA	30345	404-679-1900	679-1819
Web: www.gao.gov					
Boston Office 10 Cswy St Rm 575	Boston	MA	02222	617-788-0500	788-0505
Web: www.gao.gov					
Dallas Office 1999 Bryan St Ste 2200	Dallas	TX	75201	214-777-5600	777-5758
Web: www.gao.gov					
Dayton Office					
2196 D St Area B Bldg 39	Wright-Patterson AFB	OH	45433	937-258-7900	258-7118
Web: www.gao.gov					
Denver Office 1244 Speer Blvd Ste 800	Denver	CO	80204	303-572-7306	572-7433
Web: www.gao.gov					
Government Accountability Office					
Huntsville Office					
6767 Old Madison Pike Bldg 5 Ste 520	Huntsville	AL	35806	256-922-7500	971-9240
Web: www.gao.gov					
Los Angeles Office					
350 S Figueroa St Ste 1010	Los Angeles	CA	90071	213-830-1000	830-1180
Web: www.gao.gov					
Norfolk Office					
5029 Corporate Woods Dr Ste 300	Virginia Beach	VA	23462	757-552-8100	552-8197
Web: www.gao.gov					
San Francisco Office					
301 Howard St Ste 1200	San Francisco	CA	94105	415-904-2000	904-2111
Web: www.gao.gov					
Seattle Office 701 Fifth Ave Ste 2700	Seattle	WA	98104	206-287-4800	287-4872
Web: www.gao.gov					
American Folklife Ctr					
101 Independence Ave SE	Washington	DC	20540	202-707-5510	707-2076
Web: www.loc.gov/folklife					
Congressional Research Service					
101 Independence Ave SE	Washington	DC	20540	202-707-5507	707-5643
Web: www.loc.gov/crsinfo					
Law Library of Congress					
101 Independence Ave SE	Washington	DC	20540	202-707-5079	707-1820
Web: loc.gov/law/index.html					
National Library Service for the Blind & Physically Handicapped					
1291 Taylor St NW	Washington	DC	20011	202-707-5100	707-0712
TF: 888-657-7323 ■ *Web:* www.loc.gov/nls					
THOMAS: Legislative Information on the Internet					
101 Independence Ave SE	Washington	DC	20540	202-707-5000	
Web: loc.gov					
Library of Congress					
US Copyright Office					
101 Independence Ave SE	Washington	DC	20559	202-707-3000	
Web: www.copyright.gov					

Phone Fax

Port of Belledune 112 Shannon Dr ... Belledune NB E8G2W2 506-522-1200
Web: www.portofbelledune.ca

Thomas Edison & Henry Ford Winter Estates Inc
2350 Mcgregor Blvd ... Fort Myers FL 33901 239-334-7419
Web: www.edisonfordwinterestates.org

Thunder Bay Hydro Corp
34 Cumberland St N ... Thunder Bay ON P7A4L4 807-343-1111
Web: www.tbhydro.com

Tourism Abbotsford Society
34561 Delair Rd ... Abbotsford BC V2S2E1 604-859-1721
Web: www.tourismabbotsford.ca

US Government Accountability Office (US GAO)
Chicago Office 200 W Adams St Ste 700 ... Chicago IL 60606 312-220-7600 220-7726
Web: www.gao.gov

US Government Printing Office Bookstore (GPO)
732 N Capitol St NW ... Washington DC 20401 202-512-1800 512-2104
TF: 866-512-1800 ■ *Web:* bookstore.gpo.gov

Veridian Corp 55 Taunton Rd E ... Ajax ON L1T3V3 905-427-9870
Web: www.veridiancorporation.ca

Victoria Conference Centre 720 Douglas St ... Victoria BC V8W3M7 250-361-1000
Web: victoriaconference.com

345-1 US Congressional Committees

Phone Fax

Select Committee on Ethics 220 Hart Bldg. ... Washington DC 20510 202-224-2981 224-7416
Web: ethics.senate.gov

United States Senate Special Committee on Aging
G31 Dirksen Senate Office Bldg ... Washington DC 20510 202-224-5364 224-9926
Web: aging.senate.gov
Joint Committee on Printing
1309 Longworth House Office Building ... Washington DC 20515 202-225-8281
Web: cha.house.gov

US Congress
Joint Committee on Taxation, The
H2-502 Ford House Office Bldg. ... Washington DC 20515 202-225-3621
Web: www.jct.gov
Joint Economic Committee
G-01 Dirksen Bldg. ... Washington DC 20510 202-224-5171 224-0240
Web: www.jec.senate.gov
Agriculture Committee 1301 Longworth Bldg ... Washington DC 20515 202-225-2171 225-0917
Web: www.agriculture.house.gov
Armed Services Committee
2120 Rayburn House Office Bldg. ... Washington DC 20515 202-225-4151 225-0858
Web: www.armedservices.house.gov
Budget Committee
207 Cannon House Office Bldg ... Washington DC 20515 202-226-7270
Web: www.budget.house.gov
Committee on Education & Labor
2181 Rayburn Bldg ... Washington DC 20515 202-225-4527
Web: edworkforce.house.gov
Committee on Natural Resources
1324 Longworth Bldg ... Washington DC 20515 202-225-6065 225-1031
Web: naturalresources.house.gov
Energy & Commerce Committee
2125 Rayburn Bldg ... Washington DC 20515 202-225-2927
Web: www.energycommerce.house.gov

US House of Representatives
Government Reform Committee
2157 Rayburn House Office Bldg. ... Washington DC 20515 202-225-5074 225-3974
Web: oversight.house.gov
Homeland Security Committee
176 Ford House Office Bldg Ste H2 ... Washington DC 20515 202-226-8417 226-3399
Web: homeland.house.gov
House Administration Committee
1309 Longworth Bldg ... Washington DC 20515 202-225-2061 226-2774
Web: cha.house.gov
House Committee on Foreign Affairs
2170 Rayburn Bldg ... Washington DC 20515 202-225-5021 225-2035
Web: foreignaffairs.house.gov
Judiciary Committee 2138 Rayburn Bldg. ... Washington DC 20515 202-225-3951 225-7680
Web: www.judiciary.house.gov
Permanent Select Committee on Intelligence
US Capitol Bldg. ... Washington DC 20515 202-225-4121 225-1991
TF: 877-858-9040 ■ *Web:* www.intelligence.house.gov
Rules Committee H-312 Capitol Bldg ... Washington DC 20515 202-225-9191 225-1061
Web: www.rules.house.gov
Small Business Committee
2361 Rayburn Bldg ... Washington DC 20515 202-225-5821
Web: www.smallbusiness.house.gov
Transportation & Infrastructure Committee
2165 Rayburn Bldg ... Washington DC 20515 202-225-9446
Web: transportation.house.gov
Veterans Affairs Committee
335 Cannon Bldg. ... Washington DC 20515 202-225-3527
Web: veterans.house.gov
Ways & Means Committee
1102 Longworth Bldg ... Washington DC 20515 202-225-3625 225-2610
Web: www.waysandmeans.house.gov
Agriculture Nutrition & Forestry Committee
328A Russell Senate Office Building ... Washington DC 20510 202-224-2035 228-2125
Web: agriculture.senate.gov
Budget Committee 624 Drksen Senate Bldg. ... Washington DC 20510 202-224-0642
Web: budget.senate.gov
Commerce Science & Transportation Committee
Dirksen Senate Office Bldg SD-508 ... Washington DC 20510 202-224-5115
Web: www.commerce.senate.gov
Committee on Health, Education, Labor and Pensions
428 Dirksen Bldg. ... Washington DC 20510 202-224-5375
Web: www.help.senate.gov
Committee on Small Business & Entrepreneurship
428A Russell Senate Office Bldg ... Washington DC 20510 202-224-5175 224-5619
Web: www.sbc.senate.gov
Energy & Natural Resources Committee
304 Dirksen Senate Office Bldg ... Washington DC 20510 202-224-4971 224-6163
Web: energy.senate.gov
Environment & Public Works Committee
410 Dirksen Senate Office Bldg ... Washington DC 20510 202-224-8832
Web: epw.senate.gov
Finance Committee
219 Dirksen Senate Office Bldg ... Washington DC 20510 202-224-4515 228-0554
Web: finance.senate.gov
Foreign Relations Committee
446 Dirksen Senate Office Bldg ... Washington DC 20510 202-224-4651
Web: foreign.senate.gov
Homeland Security & Governmental Affairs Committee
340 Dirksen Senate Office Bldg ... Washington DC 20510 202-224-2627
Web: www.hsgac.senate.gov
Judiciary Committee
224 Dirksen Senate Office Bldg ... Washington DC 20510 202-224-5225
Web: www.judiciary.senate.gov
Rules & Administration Committee
305 Russell Senate Office Bldg ... Washington DC 20510 202-224-6352
Web: www.rules.senate.gov

US Senate
Veterans Affairs Committee
412 Russell Bldg ... Washington DC 20510 202-224-9126
Web: veterans.senate.gov

US Senate Committee on Indian Affairs
838 Hart Bldg ... Washington DC 20510 202-224-2251 228-2589
Web: indian.senate.gov

US Senate Select Committee on Intelligence
211 Hart Senate Office Bldg ... Washington DC 20510 202-224-1700 224-1772
Web: intelligence.senate.gov

345-2 US Senators, Representatives, Delegates

The circled letter S denotes that a listing is for a senator.

Alabama

Phone Fax

Aderholt Robert (Rep R - AL)
235 Cannon House Office Bldg. ... Washington DC 20515 202-225-4876
Web: aderholt.house.gov

Brooks Mo (Rep R - AL)
1230 Longworth Bldg ... Washington DC 20515 202-225-4801 225-4392
Web: brooks.house.gov

Byrne Bradley (Rep R - AL)
2236 Rayburn HOB ... Washington DC 20515 202-225-4931 225-0562
Web: byrne.house.gov

Palmer Gary (Rep R - AL)
206 Cannon House Office Bldg. ... Washington DC 20515 202-225-4912 225-2082
Web: palmer.house.gov

Roby Martha (Rep R - AL) 428 Cannon Bldg ... Washington DC 20515 202-225-2901 225-8913
Web: roby.house.gov

Rogers Mike (Rep R - AL) 324 Cannon Bldg ... Washington DC 20515 202-225-3261 226-8485
Web: mikerogers.house.gov

ⓈSessions Jeff (Sen R - AL)
326 Russell Bldg ... Washington DC 20510 202-224-4124 224-3149
Web: www.sessions.senate.gov

Sewell Terri A (Rep D - AL)
1133 Longworth Bldg ... Washington DC 20515 202-225-2665 226-9567
Web: sewell.house.gov

ⓈShelby Richard C (Sen R - AL)
304 Russell Bldg ... Washington DC 20510 202-224-5744 224-3416
Web: www.shelby.senate.gov

Alaska

Phone Fax

ⓈMurkowski Lisa (Sen R - AK) 709 Hart Bldg. ... Washington DC 20510 202-224-6665 224-5301
Web: www.murkowski.senate.gov

ⓈSullivan Daniel (Sen R - AK)
702 Hart Senate Office Bldg ... Washington DC 20510 202-224-3004 224-6501
Web: www.sullivan.senate.gov

Young Don (Rep R - AK) 2314 Rayburn Bldg. ... Washington DC 20515 202-225-5765 225-0425
Web: donyoung.house.gov

American Samoa

Phone Fax

Radewagen Amata(Rep R - AS)
1339 Longworth House Office Bldg ... Washington DC 20515 202-225-8577 225-8757
Web: radewagen.house.gov

Arizona

Phone Fax

Franks Trent (Rep R - AZ)
2435 Rayburn Bldg. ... Washington DC 20515 202-225-4576 225-6328
Web: franks.house.gov

Gallego, Ruben(Rep D - AZ)
1218 Longworth House Office Bldg ... Washington DC 20515 202-225-4065
Web: rubengallego.house.gov

Gosar Paul A (Rep R - AZ) 504 Cannon Bldg ... Washington DC 20515 202-225-2315 226-9739
Web: gosar.house.gov

Grijalva Raul (Rep D - AZ)
1511 Longworth Bldg. ... Washington DC 20515 202-225-2435 225-1541
Web: grijalva.house.gov

Name / Address	City	State	ZIP	Phone	Fax
ⓈJeff Flake (Sen R - AZ) 368 Russell Senate Office Building *Web:* www.flake.senate.gov	Washington	DC	20510	202-224-4521	228-0515
Kirkpatrick, Ann (Rep D AZ) 201 Cannon HOB *Web:* kirkpatrick.house.gov/	Washington	DC	20515	202-225-3361	225-3462
ⓈMcCain John (Sen R - AZ) 218 Russell Senate Office Bldg *Web:* www.mccain.senate.gov	Washington	DC	20510	202-224-2235	228-2862
McSally, Martha(Rep R - AZ) 1029 Longworth House Office Bldg *Web:* mcsally.house.gov	Washington	DC	20515	202-225-2542	225-0378
Salmon Matt (Rep R - AZ) 2349 Rayburn Bldg *Web:* salmon.house.gov	Washington	DC	20515	202-225-2635	226-4386
Schweikert David (Rep R - AZ) 409 Cannon House Office Bldg *Web:* schweikert.house.gov	Washington	DC	20515	202-225-2190	225-0096
Sinema Krysten (Rep D - AZ) 1237 Longworth Bldg *Web:* sinema.house.gov	Washington	DC	20515	202-225-9888	225-9731

Arkansas

Name / Address	City	State	ZIP	Phone	Fax
ⓈBoozman John (Sen R - AR) 141 Hart Senate Office Bldg *Web:* www.boozman.senate.gov	Washington	DC	20510	202-224-4843	228-1371
ⓈCotton Tom (Sen R - AR) 124 Russell Senate Office Bldg *Web:* www.cotton.senate.gov	Washington	DC	20510	202-224-2353	
Crawford Rick (Rep R - AR) 1711 Longworth Bldg *Web:* crawford.house.gov	Washington	DC	20515	202-225-4076	225-5602
Hill French(Rep R - AR) 1229 Longworth House Office Bldg *Web:* hill.house.gov	Washington	DC	20515	202-225-2506	225-5903
Westerman Bruce(Rep R - AR) 130 Cannon House Office Bldg *Web:* westerman.house.gov	Washington	DC	20515	202-225-3772	225-1314
Womack Steve (Rep R - AR) 1508 Longworth Bldg *Web:* womack.house.gov	Washington	DC	20515	202-225-4301	225-5713

California

Name / Address	City	State	ZIP	Phone	Fax
Aguilar Pete(Rep D - CA) 1223 Longworth HOB *Web:* aguilar.house.gov	Washington	DC	20515	202-225-3201	226-6962
Bass Karen (Rep D - CA) 408 Cannon Bldg *Web:* bass.house.gov	Washington	DC	20515	202-225-7084	225-2422
Becerra Xavier (Rep D - CA) 1226 Longworth Bldg *Web:* becerra.house.gov	Washington	DC	20515	202-225-6235	225-2202
Bera Ami (Rep D - CA) 1535 Longworth Bldg *Web:* bera.house.gov	Washington	DC	20515	202-225-5716	226-1298
ⓈBoxer Barbara (Sen D - CA) 112 Hart Bldg. *Web:* www.boxer.senate.gov	Washington	DC	20510	202-224-3553	
Brownley Julia (Rep D - CA) 1019 Longworth Bldg *Web:* juliabrownley.house.gov	Washington	DC	20515	202-225-5811	225-1100
Calvert Ken (Rep R - CA) 2205 Rayburn Bldg *Web:* calvert.house.gov	Washington	DC	20515	202-225-1986	225-2004
Capps Lois (Rep D - CA) 2231 Rayburn Bldg *Web:* capps.house.gov	Washington	DC	20515	202-225-3601	225-5632
Cardenas Tony (Rep D - CA) 1508 Longworth Bldg *Web:* cardenas.house.gov	Washington	DC	20515	202-225-6131	225-0819
Chu Judy (Rep D - CA) 2423 Rayburn HOB *Web:* chu.house.gov	Washington	DC	20515	202-225-5464	225-5467
Cook Paul (Rep R - CA) 1222 Longworth Bldg *Web:* cook.house.gov	Washington	DC	20515	202-225-5861	
Costa Jim (Rep D - CA) 1314 Longworth Bldg *Web:* costa.house.gov	Washington	DC	20515	202-225-3341	225-9308
Davis Susan (Rep D - CA) 1526 Longworth Bldg *Web:* www.house.gov/susandavis	Washington	DC	20515	202-225-2040	225-2948
Denham Jeff (Rep R - CA) 1730 Longworth Bldg *Web:* denham.house.gov	Washington	DC	20515	202-225-4540	225-3402
DeSaulnier Mark(Rep D - CA) 327 Cannon HOB *Web:* desaulnier.house.gov	Washington	DC	20515	202-225-2095	225-5609
Eshoo Anna G (Rep D - CA) 241 Cannon Bldg *Web:* eshoo.house.gov	Washington	DC	20515	202-225-8104	225-8890
Farr Sam (Rep D - CA) 1126 Longworth Bldg *Web:* www.farr.house.gov	Washington	DC	20515	202-225-2861	225-6791
ⓈFeinstein Dianne (Sen D - CA) 331 Hart Bldg *Web:* www.feinstein.senate.gov	Washington	DC	20510	202-224-3841	228-3954
Garamendi John (Rep D - CA) 2438 Rayburn Bldg *Web:* garamendi.house.gov	Washington	DC	20515	202-225-1880	225-5914
Hahn Janice (Rep D - CA) 404 Cannon Bldg *Web:* hahn.house.gov	Washington	DC	20515	202-225-8220	226-7290
Honda Mike (Rep D - CA) 1713 Longworth Bldg *Web:* honda.house.gov	Washington	DC	20515	202-225-2631	225-2699
Huffman Jared (Rep D - CA) 1630 Longworth Bldg *Web:* huffman.house.gov	Washington	DC	20515	202-225-5161	225-5163
Hunter Duncan D (Rep R - CA) 2429 Rayburn HOB *Web:* hunter.house.gov	Washington	DC	20515	202-225-5672	225-0235
Issa Darrell (Rep R - CA) 2269 Rayburn HOB *Web:* issa.house.gov	Washington	DC	20515	202-225-3906	225-3303
Knight Steve(Rep R - CA) 1023 Longworth HOB *Web:* knight.house.gov	Washington	DC	20515	202-225-1956	
LaMalfa Doug (Rep R - CA) 506 Cannon Bldg *Web:* lamalfa.house.gov	Washington	DC	20515	202-225-3076	
Lee Barbara (Rep D - CA) 2267 Rayburn Bldg *Web:* lee.house.gov	Washington	DC	20515	202-225-2661	225-9817
Lieu Ted(Rep D - CA) 415 Cannon HOB *Web:* lieu.house.gov	Washington	DC	20515	202-225-3976	
Lofgren Zoe (Rep D - CA) 1401 Longworth Bldg *Web:* lofgren.house.gov	Washington	DC	20515	202-225-3072	
Lowenthal Alan (Rep D - CA) 108 Cannon HOB *Web:* lowenthal.house.gov	Washington	DC	20515	202-225-7924	225-7926
Matsui Doris O (Rep D - CA) 2331 Rayburn HOB *Web:* matsui.house.gov	Washington	DC	20515	202-225-7163	225-0566
McCarthy Kevin (Rep R - CA) 2421 Rayburn Bldg *Web:* kevinmccarthy.house.gov	Washington	DC	20515	202-225-2915	225-2908
McClintock Tom (Rep R - CA) 2331 Rayburn HOB *Web:* mcclintock.house.gov	Washington	DC	20515	202-225-2511	225-5444
McNerney Jerry (Rep D - CA) 1210 Longworth Bldg *Web:* mcnerney.house.gov	Washington	DC	20515	202-225-1947	225-4060
Napolitano Grace (Rep D - CA) 1610 Longworth *Web:* napolitano.house.gov	Washington	DC	20515	202-225-5256	225-0027
Nunes Devin (Rep R - CA) 1013 Longworth Bldg *Web:* nunes.house.gov	Washington	DC	20515	202-225-2523	225-3404
Pelosi Nancy (Rep D - CA) 235 Cannon Bldg *Web:* pelosi.house.gov	Washington	DC	20515	202-225-4965	225-4188
Peters Scott (Rep D - CA) 1122 Longworth HOB *Web:* scottpeters.house.gov	Washington	DC	20515	202-225-0508	225-2558
Rohrabacher Dana (Rep R - CA) 2300 Rayburn Bldg *Web:* rohrabacher.house.gov	Washington	DC	20515	202-225-2415	225-0145
Roybal-Allard Lucille (Rep D - CA) 2330 Rayburn Bldg *Web:* roybal-allard.house.gov	Washington	DC	20515	202-225-1766	226-0350
Royce Ed (Rep R - CA) 2310 Rayburn HOB *Web:* www.royce.house.gov	Washington	DC	20515	202-225-4111	226-0335
Ruiz Raul (Rep D - CA) 1319 Longworth Bldg *Web:* ruiz.house.gov	Washington	DC	20515	202-225-5330	225-1238
Sanchez Linda (Rep D - CA) 2329 Rayburn HOB *Web:* lindasanchez.house.gov	Washington	DC	20515	202-225-6676	226-1012
Sanchez Loretta (Rep D - CA) 1114 Longworth Bldg *Web:* www.lorettasanchez.house.gov	Washington	DC	20515	202-225-2965	225-5859
Schiff Adam (Rep D - CA) 2411 Rayburn Bldg *Web:* schiff.house.gov	Washington	DC	20515	202-225-4176	225-5828
Sherman Brad (Rep D - CA) 2242 Rayburn Bldg *Web:* sherman.house.gov/	Washington	DC	20515	202-225-5911	225-5879
Speier Jackie (Rep D - CA) 2465 Rayburn HOB *Web:* speier.house.gov	Washington	DC	20515	202-225-3531	226-4183
Swalwell Eric (Rep D - CA) 129 Cannon HOB *Web:* swalwell.house.gov	Washington	DC	20515	202-225-5065	
Takano Mark (Rep D - CA) 1507 Longworth Bldg *Web:* takano.house.gov	Washington	DC	20515	202-225-2305	225-7018
Thompson Mike (Rep D - CA) 231 Cannon Bldg *Web:* mikethompson.house.gov	Washington	DC	20515	202-225-3311	225-4335
Torres Norma(Rep D - CA) 516 Cannon HOB *Web:* torres.house.gov	Washington	DC	20515	202-225-6161	225-8671
Valadao David (Rep R - CA) 1004 Longworth Bldg *Web:* valadao.house.gov	Washington	DC	20515	202-225-4695	
Vargas Juan (Rep D - CA) 1605 Longworth Bldg *Web:* vargas.house.gov	Washington	DC	20515	202-225-8045	225-9073
Walters Mimi(Rep R - CA) 236 Cannon HOB *Web:* walters.house.gov	Washington	DC	20515	202-225-5611	225-9177
Waters Maxine (Rep D - CA) 2221 Rayburn Bldg *Web:* waters.house.gov	Washington	DC	20515	202-225-2201	225-7854

Colorado

Name / Address	City	State	ZIP	Phone	Fax
ⓈBennet Michael F (Sen D - CO) 717 Hart Senate Office Bldg *Web:* www.baldwin.senate.gov	Washington	DC	20510	202-224-5653	224-9787

Name / Address	City	State	Zip	Phone	Fax
Buck Ken(Rep R - CO) 416 Cannon HOB *Web:* buck.house.gov	Washington	DC	20515	202-225-4676	225-5870
Coffman Mike (Rep R - CO) 2443 Rayburn Bldg *Web:* coffman.house.gov	Washington	DC	20515	202-225-7882	226-4623
DeGette Diana (Rep D - CO) 2368 Rayburn Bldg *Web:* degette.house.gov	Washington	DC	20515	202-225-4431	225-5657
ⓈGardner Cory (Sen R - CO) 354 Russell Senate Office Bldg *Web:* www.gardner.senate.gov	Washington	DC	20510	202-224-5941	224-6524
Lamborn Doug (Rep R - CO) 2402 Rayburn Bldg *Web:* lamborn.house.gov	Washington	DC	20515	202-225-4422	226-2638
Perlmutter Ed (Rep D - CO) 1410 Longworth Bldg *Web:* perlmutter.house.gov	Washington	DC	20515	202-225-2645	225-5278
Polis Jared (Rep D - CO) 1433 Longworth Bldg *Web:* polis.house.gov	Washington	DC	20515	202-225-2161	226-7840
Tipton Scott (Rep R - CO) 218 Cannon Bldg *Web:* tipton.house.gov	Washington	DC	20515	202-225-4761	226-9669

Connecticut

Name / Address	City	State	Zip	Phone	Fax
ⓈBlumenthal Richard (Sen D - CT) 706 Hart Senate Office Bldg *Web:* www.blumenthal.senate.gov	Washington	DC	20510	202-224-2823	224-9673
Courtney Joe (Rep D - CT) 2348 Rayburn Bldg *Web:* courtney.house.gov	Washington	DC	20515	202-225-2076	225-4977
DeLauro Rosa L (Rep D - CT) 2413 Rayburn Bldg *Web:* delauro.house.gov	Washington	DC	20515	202-225-3661	225-4890
Esty Elizabeth (Rep D - CT) 405 Cannon HOB **Fax Area Code:* 860 ■ *Web:* esty.house.gov	Washington	DC	20515	202-225-4476	225-7289*
Himes Jim (Rep D - CT) 1227 Longworth HOB *Web:* himes.house.gov	Washington	DC	20515	202-225-5541	225-9629
Larson John B (Rep D - CT) 1501 Longworth Bldg *Web:* www.larson.house.gov	Washington	DC	20515	202-225-2265	225-1031
ⓈMurphy Christopher (Sen D - CT) 136 Hart Senate Office Bldg *Web:* www.murphy.senate.gov	Washington	DC	20510	202-224-4041	224-9750

Delaware

Name / Address	City	State	Zip	Phone	Fax
Carney John (Rep D - DE) 1406 Longworth Bldg *Web:* johncarney.house.gov	Washington	DC	20515	202-225-4165	
ⓈCarper Thomas R (Sen D - DE) 513 Hart Bldg *Web:* www.carper.senate.gov	Washington	DC	20510	202-224-2441	228-2190
ⓈCoons Christopher A (Sen D - DE) 127A Russell Bldg *Web:* www.coons.senate.gov	Washington	DC	20510	202-224-5042	

District of Columbia

Name / Address	City	State	Zip	Phone	Fax
Norton Eleanor Holmes (Rep D - DC) 2136 Rayburn Bldg *Web:* www.norton.house.gov	Washington	DC	20515	202-225-8050	225-3002

Florida

Name / Address	City	State	Zip	Phone	Fax
Bilirakis Gus M (Rep R - FL) 2112 Rayburn HOB *Web:* bilirakis.house.gov	Washington	DC	20515	202-225-5755	225-4085
Buchanan Vern (Rep R - FL) 2104 Rayburn Bldg *Web:* buchanan.house.gov	Washington	DC	20515	202-225-5015	226-0828
Castor Kathy (Rep D - FL) 205 Cannon Bldg *Web:* castor.house.gov	Washington	DC	20515	202-225-3376	225-5652
Clawson Curt (Rep R - FL) 228 Cannon House Office Bldg *Web:* clawson.house.gov	Washington	DC	20515	202-225-2536	226-0439
Crenshaw Ander (Rep R - FL) 440 Cannon Bldg *Web:* crenshaw.house.gov	Washington	DC	20515	202-225-2501	225-2504
Curbelo Carlos(Rep R - FL) 1429 Longworth HOB *Web:* curbelo.house.gov	Washington	DC	20515	202-225-2778	
DeSantis Ron (Rep R - FL) 427 Cannon Bldg *Web:* desantis.house.gov	Washington	DC	20515	202-225-2706	226-6299
Deutch Ted (Rep D - FL) 2447 Rayburn Bldg *Web:* teddeutch.house.gov	Washington	DC	20515	202-225-3001	225-5974
Diaz-Balart Mario (Rep R - FL) 440 Cannon HOB *Web:* mariodiazbalart.house.gov	Washington	DC	20515	202-225-4211	225-8576
Frankel Lois (Rep D - FL) 1037 Longworth Bldg *TF:* 866-264-0957 ■ *Web:* frankel.house.gov	Washington	DC	20515	202-225-9890	
Graham Gwen(Rep D - FL) 1213 Longworth HOB *Web:* graham.house.gov	Washington	DC	20515	202-225-5235	225-5615
Grayson Alan (Rep D - FL) 430 Cannon Bldg *Web:* grayson.house.gov	Washington	DC	20515	202-225-9889	225-9742
Hastings Alcee L (Rep D - FL) 2353 Rayburn Bldg *Web:* www.alceehastings.house.gov	Washington	DC	20515	202-225-1313	225-1171
Jolly David (Rep R - FL) 2407 Rayburn HOB *Web:* jolly.house.gov	Washington	DC	20515	202-225-5961	225-9764
Mica John (Rep R - FL) 2187 Rayburn Bldg *Web:* mica.house.gov	Washington	DC	20515	202-225-4035	226-0821
Miller Jeff (Rep R - FL) 336 Cannon Bldg *Web:* jeffmiller.house.gov	Washington	DC	20515	202-225-4136	225-3414
Murphy Patrick (Rep D - FL) 211 Cannon HOB *Web:* patrickmurphy.house.gov	Washington	DC	20515	202-225-3026	225-8398
ⓈNelson Bill (Sen D - FL) 716 Hart Bldg *Web:* www.billnelson.senate.gov	Washington	DC	20510	202-224-5274	228-2183
Nugent Richard (Rep R - FL) 1727 Longworth Bldg *Web:* nugent.house.gov	Washington	DC	20515	202-225-1002	226-6559
Posey Bill (Rep R - FL) 120 Cannon Bldg *Web:* posey.house.gov	Washington	DC	20515	202-225-3671	225-3516
Radel Trey (Rep R - FL) 1123 Longworth Bldg *TF:* 866-264-0957 ■ *Web:* wilson.house.gov	Washington	DC	20515	202-225-2536	
Rooney Tom (Rep R - FL) 2160 Rayburn HOB *Web:* rooney.house.gov	Washington	DC	20515	202-225-5792	225-3132
Ros-Lehtinen Ileana (Rep R - FL) 2206 Rayburn Bldg *Web:* ros-lehtinen.house.gov	Washington	DC	20515	202-225-3931	225-5620
Ross Dennis (Rep R - FL) 229 Cannon Bldg *Web:* dennisross.house.gov	Washington	DC	20515	202-225-1252	226-0585
ⓈRubio Marco (Sen R - FL) 284 Russell Bldg *Web:* www.rubio.senate.gov	Washington	DC	20510	202-224-3041	
Wasserman Schultz Debbie (Rep D - FL) 1114 Longworth HOB *Web:* wassermanschultz.house.gov	Washington	DC	20515	202-225-7931	226-2052
Webster Daniel (Rep R - FL) 1039 Longworth Bldg *Web:* webster.house.gov	Washington	DC	20515	202-225-2176	225-0999
Wilson Frederica (Rep D - FL) 208 Cannon Bldg *Web:* wilson.house.gov	Washington	DC	20515	202-225-4506	226-0777
Yoho Ted (Rep R - FL) 511 Cannon Bldg *Web:* yoho.house.gov	Washington	DC	20515	202-225-5744	

Georgia

Name / Address	City	State	Zip	Phone	Fax
Allen Rick(Rep R - GA) 513 Cannon HOB *Web:* allen.house.gov	Washington	DC	20515	202-225-2823	225-3377
Bishop Sanford D Jr (Rep D - GA) 2407 Rayburn HOB *Web:* bishop.house.gov	Washington	DC	20515	202-225-3631	225-2203
Carter Buddy(Rep R - GA) 432 Cannon HOB *Web:* buddycarter.house.gov	Washington	DC	20515	202-225-5831	226-2269
Collins Doug (Rep R - GA) 513 Cannon Bldg *Web:* dougcollins.house.gov	Washington	DC	20515	202-225-9893	226-1224
Graves Tom (Rep R - GA) 2442 Rayburn HOB *Web:* tomgraves.house.gov	Washington	DC	20515	202-225-5211	225-8272
Hice Jody(Rep R - GA) 1516 Longworth HOB *Web:* hice.house.gov	Washington	DC	20515	202-225-4101	225-0776
ⓈIsakson Johnny (Sen R - GA) 131 Russell Bldg *Web:* www.isakson.senate.gov	Washington	DC	20510	202-224-3643	228-0724
Johnson Henry C "Hank" Jr (Rep D - GA) 2240 Rayburn Bldg *Web:* hankjohnson.house.gov	Washington	DC	20515	202-225-1605	226-0691
Lewis John (Rep D - GA) 343 Cannon Bldg *Web:* johnlewis.house.gov	Washington	DC	20515	202-225-3801	225-0351
Loudermilk Barry(Rep R - GA) 238 Cannon HOB *Web:* loudermilk.house.gov	Washington	DC	20515	202-225-2931	225-2944
ⓈPerdue David (Sen R - GA) 383 Russell Senate Office Bldg *Web:* www.perdue.senate.gov	Washington	DC	20510	202-224-3521	228-1031
Price Tom (Rep R - GA) 100 Cannon Bldg *Web:* tomprice.house.gov	Washington	DC	20515	202-225-4501	225-4656
Scott Austin (Rep R - GA) 2417 Rayburn HOB *Web:* austinscott.house.gov	Washington	DC	20515	202-225-6531	225-3013
Scott David (Rep D - GA) 225 Cannon Bldg *Web:* davidscott.house.gov	Washington	DC	20515	202-225-2939	225-4628
Westmoreland Lynn A (Rep R - GA) 2433 Rayburn Bldg *Web:* westmoreland.house.gov	Washington	DC	20515	202-225-5901	225-2515
Woodall Robert (Rep R - GA) 1724 Longworth HOB *Web:* woodall.house.gov	Washington	DC	20515	202-225-4272	225-4696

Guam

Name / Address	City	State	Zip	Phone	Fax
Bordallo Madeleine (Rep D - GU) 2441 Rayburn Bldg *Web:* bordallo.house.gov	Washington	DC	20515	202-225-1188	226-0341

Hawaii

Name / Address	City	State	Zip	Phone	Fax
Gabbard Tulsi (Rep D - HI) 1609 Longworth HOB *Web:* gabbard.house.gov	Washington	DC	20515	202-225-4906	
ⓈHirono Mazie K (Sen D - HI) 330 Hart Bldg *Web:* www.hirono.senate.gov	Washington	DC	20510	202-224-6361	224-2126

Name	City	State	Zip	Phone	Fax
Ⓢ**Schatz Brian (Sen D - HI)** 722 Hart Bldg *Web:* www.schatz.senate.gov	Washington	DC	20510	202-224-3934	228-1153
Takai Mark (Rep D - HI) 422 Cannon HOB *Web:* takai.house.gov	Washington	DC	20515	202-225-2726	225-0688

Idaho

Name	City	State	Zip	Phone	Fax
Ⓢ**Crapo Mike (Sen R - ID)** 239 Dirksen Bldg *Web:* www.crapo.senate.gov	Washington	DC	20510	202-224-6142	228-1375
Labrador Raul R (Rep R - ID) 1523 Longworth Bldg *Web:* labrador.house.gov	Washington	DC	20515	202-225-6611	225-3029
Ⓢ**Risch James E (Sen R - ID)** 483 Russell Bldg *Web:* www.risch.senate.gov	Washington	DC	20510	202-224-2752	224-2573
Simpson Mike (Rep R - ID) 2312 Rayburn Bldg *Web:* simpson.house.gov	Washington	DC	20515	202-225-5531	225-8216

Illinois

Name	City	State	Zip	Phone	Fax
Bost Mike (Rep R - IL) 1440 Longworth HOB *Web:* bost.house.gov	Washington	DC	20515	202-225-5661	225-0285
Bustos Cheri (Rep D - IL) 1009 Longworth Bldg *Web:* bustos.house.gov	Washington	DC	20515	202-225-5905	
Davis Danny K (Rep D - IL) 2159 Rayburn Bldg *Web:* www.davis.house.gov	Washington	DC	20515	202-225-5006	225-5641
Davis Rodney (Rep R - IL) 1740 Longworth Bldg *Web:* rodneydavis.house.gov	Washington	DC	20515	202-225-2371	226-0791
Dold Bob (Rep R - IL) 221 Cannon HOB *Web:* dold.house.gov	Washington	DC	20515	202-225-4835	225-0837
Duckworth Tammy (Rep D - IL) 104 Cannon Bldg *Web:* duckworth.house.gov	Washington	DC	20515	202-225-3711	
Ⓢ**Durbin Richard J (Sen D - IL)** 711 Hart Bldg *Web:* www.durbin.senate.gov	Washington	DC	20510	202-224-2152	228-0400
Foster Bill (Rep D - IL) 1224 Longworth Bldg *Web:* foster.house.gov	Washington	DC	20515	202-225-3515	225-9420
Gutierrez Luis (Rep D - IL) 2408 Rayburn Bldg *Web:* gutierrez.house.gov	Washington	DC	20515	202-225-8203	225-7810
Hultgren Randy (Rep R - IL) 2455 Rayburn HOB *Web:* hultgren.house.gov	Washington	DC	20515	202-225-2976	225-0697
Kelly Robin (Rep D - IL) 2419 Rayburn Bldg *Web:* robinkelly.house.gov	Washington	DC	20515	202-225-0773	225-4583
Kinzinger Adam (Rep R - IL) 1221 Longworth Bldg *Web:* kinzinger.house.gov	Washington	DC	20515	202-225-3635	225-3521
Ⓢ**Kirk Mark (Sen R - IL)** 524 Hart Bldg *Web:* www.kirk.senate.gov	Washington	DC	20510	202-224-2854	228-4611
Lipinski Daniel (Rep D - IL) 1717 Longworth Bldg *Web:* www.lipinski.house.gov	Washington	DC	20515	202-225-5701	225-1012
Quigley Mike (Rep D - IL) 2458 Rayburn HOB *Web:* quigley.house.gov	Washington	DC	20515	202-225-4061	225-5603
Roskam Peter J (Rep R - IL) 2246 Rayburn HOB *Web:* roskam.house.gov	Washington	DC	20515	202-225-4561	225-1166
Rush Bobby L (Rep D - IL) 2268 Rayburn Bldg *Web:* rush.house.gov	Washington	DC	20515	202-225-4372	226-0333
Schakowsky Jan (Rep D - IL) 2367 Rayburn Bldg *Web:* schakowsky.house.gov	Washington	DC	20515	202-225-2111	226-6890
Shimkus John (Rep R - IL) 2452 Rayburn Bldg *Web:* shimkus.house.gov	Washington	DC	20515	202-225-5271	225-5880

Indiana

Name	City	State	Zip	Phone	Fax
Brooks Susan W (Rep R - IN) 1505 Longworth Bldg *Web:* susanwbrooks.house.gov	Washington	DC	20515	202-225-2276	225-0016
Bucshon Larry (Rep R - IN) 1005 Longworth Bldg *Web:* bucshon.house.gov	Washington	DC	20515	202-225-4636	225-3284
Carson Andre (Rep D - IN) 2453 Rayburn Bldg *Web:* carson.house.gov	Washington	DC	20515	202-225-4011	225-5633
Ⓢ**Coats Daniel (Sen R - IN)** 493 Russell Bldg *Web:* www.coats.senate.gov	Washington	DC	20510	202-224-5623	228-1820
Ⓢ**Donnelly Joe (Sen D - IN)** 720 Hart Bldg *Web:* www.donnelly.senate.gov	Washington	DC	20510	202-224-4814	224-4814
Messer Luke (Rep R - IN) 508 Cannon Bldg *Web:* messer.house.gov	Washington	DC	20515	202-225-3021	
Rokita Todd (Rep R - IN) 236 Cannon Bldg *Web:* rokita.house.gov	Washington	DC	20515	202-225-5037	226-0544
Stutzman Marlin (Rep R - IN) 2418 Rayburn HOB *Web:* stutzman.house.gov	Washington	DC	20515	202-225-4436	226-9870
Visclosky Peter (Rep D - IN) 2328 Rayburn Bldg *Web:* visclosky.house.gov	Washington	DC	20515	202-225-2461	225-2493
Walorski Jackie (Rep R - IN) 419 Cannon Bldg *Web:* walorski.house.gov	Washington	DC	20515	202-225-3915	225-6798
Young Todd (Rep R - IN) 1007 Longworth Bldg *Web:* toddyoung.house.gov	Washington	DC	20515	202-225-5315	226-6866

Iowa

Name	City	State	Zip	Phone	Fax
Blum Rod (Rep R - IA) 213 Cannon HOB *Web:* blum.house.gov	Washington	DC	20515	202-225-2911	
Ⓢ**Ernst Joni (Sen R - IA)** 111 Russell Senate Office Bldg *Web:* www.ernst.senate.gov	Washington	DC	20510	202-224-3254	224-9369
Ⓢ**Grassley Chuck (Sen R - IA)** 135 Hart Bldg *Web:* www.grassley.senate.gov	Washington	DC	20510	202-224-3744	224-6020
King Steve (Rep R - IA) 2210 Rayburn Bldg *Web:* steveking.house.gov	Washington	DC	20515	202-225-4426	225-3193
Loebsack David (Rep D - IA) 1527 Longworth Bldg *Web:* loebsack.house.gov	Washington	DC	20515	202-225-6576	226-0757
Young David (Rep R - IA) 515 Cannon HOB *Web:* davidyoung.house.gov	Washington	DC	20515	202-225-5476	

Kansas

Name	City	State	Zip	Phone	Fax
Huelskamp Tim (Rep R - KS) 1110 Longworth HOB *Web:* huelskamp.house.gov	Washington	DC	20515	202-225-2715	225-5124
Jenkins Lynn (Rep R - KS) 1526 Longworth HOB *Web:* lynnjenkins.house.gov	Washington	DC	20515	202-225-6601	225-7986
Ⓢ**Moran Jerry (Sen R - KS)** 521 Dirksen Senate Office Bldg *Web:* www.moran.senate.gov	Washington	DC	20510	202-224-6521	228-6966
Pompeo Mike (Rep R - KS) 436 Cannon HOB *Web:* pompeo.house.gov	Washington	DC	20515	202-225-6216	225-3489
Ⓢ**Roberts Pat (Sen R - KS)** 109 Hart Bldg *Web:* www.roberts.senate.gov	Washington	DC	20510	202-224-4774	224-3514
Yoder Kevin (Rep R - KS) 215 Cannon Bldg *Web:* yoder.house.gov	Washington	DC	20515	202-225-2865	

Kentucky

Name	City	State	Zip	Phone	Fax
Barr Andy (Rep R - KY) 1432 Longworth Bldg *Web:* barr.house.gov	Washington	DC	20515	202-225-4706	
Guthrie S Brett (Rep R - KY) 2434 Rayburn HOB *Web:* guthrie.house.gov	Washington	DC	20515	202-225-3501	226-2019
Massie Thomas (Rep R - KY) 314 Cannon Bldg *Web:* massie.house.gov	Washington	DC	20515	202-225-3465	225-0003
Ⓢ**McConnell Mitch (Sen R - KY)** 317 Russell Bldg *Web:* www.mcconnell.senate.gov	Washington	DC	20510	202-224-2541	
Ⓢ**Paul Rand (Sen R - KY)** 167 Russell Senate Office Bldg *Web:* www.paul.senate.gov	Washington	DC	20510	202-224-4343	228-6917
Rogers Harold (Rep R - KY) 2406 Rayburn Bldg *Web:* halrogers.house.gov	Washington	DC	20515	202-225-4601	225-0940
Whitfield Ed (Rep R - KY) 2184 Rayburn Bldg *Web:* whitfield.house.gov	Washington	DC	20515	202-225-3115	225-3547
Yarmuth John A (Rep D - KY) 403 Cannon Bldg *Web:* yarmuth.house.gov	Washington	DC	20515	202-225-5401	225-5776

Louisiana

Name	City	State	Zip	Phone	Fax
Abraham Ralph (Rep R - LA) 417 Cannon HOB *Web:* abraham.house.gov	Washington	DC	20515	202-225-8490	225-5639
Boustany Charles W Jr (Rep R - LA) 1431 Longworth Bldg *Web:* boustany.house.gov	Washington	DC	20515	202-225-2031	225-5724
Ⓢ**Cassidy Bill (Sen R - LA)** 703 Hart Senate Office Bldg *Web:* www.cassidy.senate.gov	Washington	DC	20510	202-224-5824	224-9735
Fleming John (Rep R - LA) 2182 Rayburn HOB *Web:* fleming.house.gov	Washington	DC	20515	202-225-2777	225-8039
Graves Garret (Rep R - LA) 204 Cannon HOB *Web:* garretgraves.house.gov	Washington	DC	20515	202-225-3901	225-7313
Richmond Cedric (Rep D - LA) 240 Cannon Bldg *Web:* richmond.house.gov	Washington	DC	20515	202-225-6636	225-1988
Scalise Steve (Rep R - LA) 2338 Rayburn Bldg *Web:* scalise.house.gov	Washington	DC	20515	202-225-3015	226-0386

Name	Address	City	State	Zip	Phone	Fax
Ⓢ Vitter David (Sen R - LA)	516 Hart Bldg	Washington	DC	20510	202-224-4623	228-5061
Web: www.vitter.senate.gov						

Maine

Name	Address	City	State	Zip	Phone	Fax
Ⓢ Collins Susan M (Sen R - ME)	413 Dirksen Bldg	Washington	DC	20510	202-224-2523	224-2693
Web: www.collins.senate.gov						
Ⓢ King Angus S Jr (Sen I - ME)	133 Hart Senate Office Bldg	Washington	DC	20510	202-224-5344	
Web: www.king.senate.gov						
Pingree Chellie (Rep D - ME)	1318 Longworth Bldg	Washington	DC	20515	202-225-6116	225-5590
Web: pingree.house.gov						
Poliquin Bruce (Rep R - ME)	426 Cannon HOB	Washington	DC	20515	202-225-6306	225-2943
Web: poliquin.house.gov						

Maryland

Name	Address	City	State	Zip	Phone	Fax
Ⓢ Cardin Benjamin L (Sen D - MD)	509 Hart Bldg	Washington	DC	20510	202-224-4524	224-1651
Web: www.cardin.senate.gov						
Cummings Elijah (Rep D - MD)	2230 Rayburn HOB	Washington	DC	20515	202-225-4741	225-3178
Web: cummings.house.gov						
Delaney John (Rep D - MD)	1632 Longworth Bldg	Washington	DC	20515	202-225-2721	
Web: delaney.house.gov						
Edwards Donna F (Rep D - MD)	2445 Rayburn Bldg	Washington	DC	20515	202-225-8699	225-8714
Web: donnaedwards.house.gov						
Harris Andy (Rep R - MD)	1533 Longworth Bldg	Washington	DC	20515	202-225-5311	225-0254
Web: harris.house.gov						
Hoyer Steny H (Rep D - MD)	1705 Longworth Bldg	Washington	DC	20515	202-225-4131	225-4300
Web: hoyer.house.gov						
Ⓢ Mikulski Barbara A (Sen D - MD)	503 Hart Bldg	Washington	DC	20510	202-224-4654	224-8858
Web: www.mikulski.senate.gov						
Ruppersberger Dutch (Rep D - MD)	2416 Rayburn Bldg	Washington	DC	20515	202-225-3061	225-3094
Web: ruppersberger.house.gov						
Sarbanes John P (Rep D - MD)	2444 Rayburn Bldg	Washington	DC	20515	202-225-4016	225-9219
Web: sarbanes.house.gov						
Van Hollen Chris (Rep D - MD)	1707 Longworth Bldg	Washington	DC	20515	202-225-5341	225-0375
Web: vanhollen.house.gov						

Massachusetts

Name	Address	City	State	Zip	Phone	Fax
Capuano Michael E (Rep D - MA)	1414 Longworth Bldg	Washington	DC	20515	202-225-5111	225-9322
Web: www.house.gov/capuano						
Clark Katherine (Rep D - MA)	1721 Longworth HOB	Washington	DC	20515	202-225-2836	
Web: katherineclark.house.gov						
Keating William (Rep D - MA)	315 Cannon Bldg	Washington	DC	20515	202-225-3111	225-5658
Web: keating.house.gov						
Kennedy III Joseph P (Rep D - MA)	306 Cannon HOB	Washington	DC	20515	202-225-5931	225-0182
Web: kennedy.house.gov						
Lynch Stephen F (Rep D - MA)	2369 Rayburn HOB	Washington	DC	20515	202-225-8273	225-3984
Web: lynch.house.gov						
Ⓢ Markey Edward J (Sen D - MA)	255 Dirksen Senate Office Bldg	Washington	DC	20510	202-224-2742	
Web: www.markey.senate.gov						
McGovern James (Rep D - MA)	438 Cannon Bldg	Washington	DC	20515	202-225-6101	225-5759
Web: mcgovern.house.gov						
Moulton Seth (Rep D - MA)	1408 Longworth HOB	Washington	DC	20515	202-225-8020	225-5915
Web: moulton.house.gov						
Neal Richard E (Rep D - MA)	341 Cannon HOB	Washington	DC	20515	202-225-5601	225-8112
Web: neal.house.gov						
Tsongas Niki (Rep D - MA)	1714 Longworth HOB	Washington	DC	20515	202-225-3411	226-0771
Web: tsongas.house.gov						
Ⓢ Warren Elizabeth (Sen D - MA)	317 Hart Bldg	Washington	DC	20510	202-224-4543	
Web: www.warren.senate.gov						

Michigan

Name	Address	City	State	Zip	Phone	Fax
Amash Justin (Rep R - MI)	114 Cannon Bldg	Washington	DC	20515	202-225-3831	225-5144
Web: amash.house.gov						
Benishek Dan (Rep R - MI)	514 Cannon Bldg	Washington	DC	20515	202-225-4735	225-4710
Web: benishek.house.gov						
Bishop Mike (Rep R - MI)	428 Cannon HOB	Washington	DC	20515	202-225-4872	225-5820
Web: mikebishop.house.gov						
Conyers Jr John (Rep D - MI)	2426 Rayburn Bldg	Washington	DC	20515	202-225-5126	225-0072
Web: conyers.house.gov						
Dingell Debbie (Rep D - MI)	116 Cannon HOB	Washington	DC	20515	202-225-4071	226-0371
Web: debbiedingell.house.gov						
Huizenga Bill (Rep R - MI)	1217 Longworth Bldg	Washington	DC	20515	202-225-4401	226-0779
Web: huizenga.house.gov						
Kildee Daniel (Rep D - MI)	227 Cannon Bldg	Washington	DC	20515	202-225-3611	
Web: dankildee.house.gov						
Lawrence Brenda (Rep D - MI)	1237 Longworth HOB	Washington	DC	20515	202-225-5802	226-2356
Web: lawrence.house.gov						
Levin Sander (Rep D - MI)	1236 Longworth Bldg	Washington	DC	20515	202-225-4961	226-1033
Web: levin.house.gov						
Moolenaar John (Rep R - MI)	117 Cannon HOB	Washington	DC	20515	202-225-3561	225-9679
Web: moolenaar.house.gov						
Ⓢ Peters Gary (Sen D - MI)	Hart Senate Office Bldg Ste 724	Washington	DC	20510	202-224-6221	
Web: www.peters.senate.gov						
Ⓢ Stabenow Debbie (Sen D - MI)	731 Hart Senate Office Bldg	Washington	DC	20510	202-224-4822	228-0325
Web: www.stabenow.senate.gov						
Trott, Dave (Rep R - MI)	1722 Longworth HOB	Washington	DC	20515	202-225-8171	225-2667
Web: trott.house.gov						
Upton Fred (Rep R - MI)	2183 Rayburn Bldg	Washington	DC	20515	202-225-3761	225-4986
Web: upton.house.gov						
Walberg Tim (Rep R - MI)	2436 Rayburn Bldg	Washington	DC	20515	202-225-6276	225-6281
Web: walberg.house.gov						

Minnesota

Name	Address	City	State	Zip	Phone	Fax
Ellison Keith (Rep D - MN)	2263 Rayburn Bldg	Washington	DC	20515	202-225-4755	225-4886
Web: ellison.house.gov						
Emmer Tom (Rep R - MN)	503 Cannon HOB	Washington	DC	20515	202-225-2331	225-6475
Web: emmer.house.gov						
Ⓢ Franken Al (Sen D - MN)	309 Hart Bldg	Washington	DC	20510	202-224-5641	
Web: www.franken.senate.gov						
Kline John (Rep R - MN)	2439 Rayburn Bldg	Washington	DC	20515	202-225-2271	225-2595
Web: kline.house.gov						
Ⓢ Klobuchar Amy (Sen D - MN)	302 Hart Bldg	Washington	DC	20510	202-224-3244	228-2186
Web: www.klobuchar.senate.gov						
McCollum Betty (Rep D - MN)	2256 Rayburn HOB	Washington	DC	20515	202-225-6631	225-1968
Web: mccollum.house.gov						
Nolan Rick (Rep D - MN)	2366 Rayburn HOB	Washington	DC	20515	202-225-6211	225-0699
Web: nolan.house.gov						
Paulsen Erik (Rep R - MN)	127 Cannon Bldg	Washington	DC	20515	202-225-2871	225-6351
Web: paulsen.house.gov						
Peterson Collin C (Rep D - MN)	2204 Rayburn HOB	Washington	DC	20515	202-225-2165	225-1593
Web: collinpeterson.house.gov						
Walz Timothy J (Rep D - MN)	1034 Longworth Bldg	Washington	DC	20515	202-225-2472	225-6351
Web: walz.house.gov						

Mississippi

Name	Address	City	State	Zip	Phone	Fax
Ⓢ Cochran Thad (Sen R - MS)	113 Dirksen Bldg	Washington	DC	20510	202-224-5054	
Web: www.cochran.senate.gov						
Harper Gregg (Rep R - MS)	307 Cannon Bldg	Washington	DC	20515	202-225-5031	225-5797
Web: harper.house.gov						
Kelly Trent (Rep R - MS)	1427 Longworth HOB	Washington	DC	20515	202-225-4306	225-3549
Web: trentkelly.house.gov						
Palazzo Steven (Rep R - MS)	331 Cannon Bldg	Washington	DC	20515	202-225-5772	225-7074
Web: palazzo.house.gov						
Thompson Bennie G (Rep D - MS)	2466 Rayburn Bldg	Washington	DC	20515	202-225-5876	225-5898
Web: benniethompson.house.gov						
Ⓢ Wicker Roger F (Sen R - MS)	555 Dirksen Bldg	Washington	DC	20510	202-224-6253	228-0378
Web: www.wicker.senate.gov						

Missouri

Name	Address	City	State	Zip	Phone	Fax
Ⓢ Blunt Roy (Sen R - MO)	260 Russell Bldg	Washington	DC	20510	202-224-5721	224-8149
Web: www.blunt.senate.gov						
Clay William "Lacy" Jr (Rep D - MO)	2428 Rayburn HOB	Washington	DC	20515	202-225-2406	226-3717
Web: lacyclay.house.gov						
Cleaver Emanuel (Rep D - MO)	2335 Rayburn Bldg	Washington	DC	20515	202-225-4535	225-4403
Web: cleaver.house.gov						
Graves Sam (Rep R - MO)	1415 Longworth Bldg	Washington	DC	20515	202-225-7041	225-8221
Web: graves.house.gov						

Name / Address	City	State	Zip	Phone	Fax
Hartzler Vicky (Rep R - MO) 2235 Rayburn HOB *Web:* hartzler.house.gov	Washington	DC	20515	202-225-2876	225-0148
Long Billy (Rep R - MO) 1541 Longworth Bldg *Web:* long.house.gov	Washington	DC	20515	202-225-6536	225-5604
Luetkemeyer Blaine (Rep R - MO) 2440 Rayburn Bldg *Web:* luetkemeyer.house.gov	Washington	DC	20515	202-225-2956	225-5712
Ⓢ**McCaskill Claire (Sen D - MO)** 730 Hart Senate Office Bldg *Web:* www.mccaskill.senate.gov	Washington	DC	20510	202-224-6154	228-6326
Smith Jason (Rep R - MO) 1118 Longworth HOB *Web:* jasonsmith.house.gov	Washington	DC	20515	202-225-4404	226-0326
Wagner Ann (Rep R - MO) 435 Cannon Bldg *Web:* wagner.house.gov	Washington	DC	20515	202-225-1621	

Montana

Name / Address	City	State	Zip	Phone	Fax
Ⓢ**Daines Steve (Sen R - MT)** 320 Hart Senate Office Bldg *Web:* www.daines.senate.gov	Washington	DC	20510	202-224-2651	
Ⓢ**Tester Jon (Sen D - MT)** 311 Hart Senate Office Bldg *Web:* www.tester.senate.gov	Washington	DC	20510	202-224-2644	224-8594
Zinke, Ryan (Rep R - MT) 113 Cannon House Office Bldg. *Web:* zinke.house.gov	Washington	DC	20515	202-225-3211	225-5687

Nebraska

Name / Address	City	State	Zip	Phone	Fax
Ashford Brad (Rep D - NE) 107 Cannon HOB *Web:* ashford.house.gov	Washington	DC	20515	202-225-4155	226-5452
Ⓢ**Fischer Deb (Sen R - NE)** 454 Russell Senate Office Bldg *Web:* www.fischer.senate.gov	Washington	DC	20510	202-224-6551	228-1325
Fortenberry Jeff (Rep R - NE) 1514 Longworth Bldg *Web:* fortenberry.house.gov	Washington	DC	20515	202-225-4806	225-5686
Ⓢ**Sasse Ben (Sen R - NE)** 386A Russell Senate Office Bldg. *Web:* www.sasse.senate.gov	Washington	DC	20510	202-224-4224	
Smith Adrian (Rep R - NE) 2241 Rayburn Bldg *Web:* adriansmith.house.gov	Washington	DC	20515	202-225-6435	225-0207

Nevada

Name / Address	City	State	Zip	Phone	Fax
Amodei Mark (Rep R - NV) 332 Cannon HOB *Web:* amodei.house.gov	Washington	DC	20515	202-225-6155	225-5679
Hardy Cresent (Rep R - NV) 430 Cannon HOB *Web:* hardy.house.gov	Washington	DC	20515	202-225-9894	225-9783
Heck Joe (Rep R - NV) 132 Cannon Bldg *Web:* heck.house.gov	Washington	DC	20515	202-225-3252	225-2185
Ⓢ**Heller Dean (Sen R - NV)** 324 Hart Bldg *Web:* www.heller.senate.gov	Washington	DC	20510	202-224-6244	228-6753
Ⓢ**Reid Harry (Sen D - NV)** 522 Hart Bldg *Web:* www.reid.senate.gov	Washington	DC	20510	202-224-3542	224-7327
Titus Dina (Rep D - NV) 401 Cannon Bldg *Web:* titus.house.gov	Washington	DC	20515	202-225-5965	

New Hampshire

Name / Address	City	State	Zip	Phone	Fax
Ⓢ**Ayotte Kelly (Sen R - NH)** 144 Russell Bldg *Web:* www.ayotte.senate.gov	Washington	DC	20510	202-224-3324	224-4952
Guinta Frank (Rep R - NH) 326 Cannon HOB *Web:* guinta.house.gov	Washington	DC	20515	202-225-5456	225-5822
Kuster Ann (Rep D - NH) 137 Cannon Bldg. *Web:* kuster.house.gov	Washington	DC	20515	202-225-5206	225-2946
Ⓢ**Shaheen Jeanne (Sen D - NH)** 506 Hart Senate Office Bldg *Web:* www.shaheen.senate.gov	Washington	DC	20510	202-224-2841	228-3194

New Jersey

Name / Address	City	State	Zip	Phone	Fax
Ⓢ**Booker Cory A (Sen D - NJ)** 359 Dirksen Senate Office Bldg *Web:* www.booker.senate.gov/?p=contact	Washington	DC	20510	202-224-3224	224-8378
Frelinghuysen Rodney (Rep R - NJ) 2369 Rayburn Bldg *Web:* frelinghuysen.house.gov	Washington	DC	20515	202-225-5034	
Garrett Scott (Rep R - NJ) 2232 Rayburn Bldg *Web:* garrett.house.gov	Washington	DC	20515	202-225-4465	225-9048
Lance Leonard (Rep R - NJ) 2352 Rayburn HOB *Web:* lance.house.gov	Washington	DC	20515	202-225-5361	225-9460
LoBiondo Frank (Rep R - NJ) 2427 Rayburn Bldg *Web:* lobiondo.house.gov	Washington	DC	20515	202-225-6572	225-3318
MacArthur Tom (Rep R - NJ) 506 Cannon HOB *Web:* macarthur.house.gov	Washington	DC	20515	202-225-4765	225-0778
Ⓢ**Menendez Robert (Sen D - NJ)** 528 Hart Bldg *Web:* menendez.senate.gov	Washington	DC	20510	202-224-4744	
Norcross Donald (Rep D - NJ) 1531 Longworth HOB *Web:* norcross.house.gov	Washington	DC	20515	202-225-6501	225-6583
Pallone Frank Jr (Rep D - NJ) 237 Cannon Bldg *Web:* pallone.house.gov	Washington	DC	20515	202-225-4671	225-9665
Pascrell Bill Jr (Rep D - NJ) 2370 Rayburn Bldg *Web:* pascrell.house.gov	Washington	DC	20515	202-225-5751	225-5782
Payne Jr Donald (Rep D - NJ) 103 Cannon Bldg *Web:* payne.house.gov	Washington	DC	20515	202-225-3436	225-4160
Sires Albio (Rep D - NJ) 2342 Rayburn Bldg *Web:* sires.house.gov	Washington	DC	20515	202-225-7919	226-0792
Smith Chris (Rep R - NJ) 2373 Rayburn Bldg *Web:* chrissmith.house.gov	Washington	DC	20515	202-225-3765	225-7768
Watson Coleman Bonnie (Rep D - NJ) 126 Cannon HOB *Web:* watsoncoleman.house.gov	Washington	DC	20515	202-225-5801	225-6025

New Mexico

Name / Address	City	State	Zip	Phone	Fax
Ⓢ**Heinrich Martin (Sen D - NM)** 303 Hart Senate Office Bldg *Web:* www.heinrich.senate.gov	Washington	DC	20510	202-224-5521	228-2841
Lujan Ben R (Rep D - NM) 2446 Rayburn Bldg *Web:* lujan.house.gov	Washington	DC	20515	202-225-6190	226-1528
Lujan Grisham Michelle (Rep D - NM) 214 Cannon Bldg *Web:* lujangrisham.house.gov	Washington	DC	20515	202-225-6316	225-4975
Pearce Steve (Rep R - NM) 2432 Rayburn Bldg *Web:* pearce.house.gov	Washington	DC	20515	202-225-2365	225-9599
Ⓢ**Udall Tom (Sen D - NM)** 531 Hart Senate Office Bldg *Web:* www.tomudall.senate.gov	Washington	DC	20510	202-224-6621	

New York

Name / Address	City	State	Zip	Phone	Fax
Clarke Yvette D (Rep D - NY) 2351 Rayburn Bldg *Web:* clarke.house.gov	Washington	DC	20515	202-225-6231	226-0112
Collins Chris (Rep R - NY) 1117 Longworth Bldg *Web:* chriscollins.house.gov	Washington	DC	20515	202-225-5265	225-5910
Crowley Joseph (Rep D - NY) 1436 Longworth Bldg *Web:* crowley.house.gov	Washington	DC	20515	202-225-3965	
Donovan Daniel (Rep R - NY) 1725 Longworth HOB *Web:* donovan.house.gov	Washington	DC	20515	202-225-3371	
Engel Eliot (Rep D - NY) 2462 Rayburn HOB *Web:* engel.house.gov	Washington	DC	20515	202-225-2464	225-5513
Gibson Chris (Rep R - NY) 1708 Longworth Bldg *Web:* gibson.house.gov	Washington	DC	20515	202-225-5614	225-1168
Ⓢ**Gillibrand Kirsten E (Sen D - NY)** 478 Russell Bldg *Web:* www.gillibrand.senate.gov	Washington	DC	20510	202-224-4451	228-0282
Hanna Richard (Rep R - NY) 319 Cannon Bldg *Web:* hanna.house.gov	Washington	DC	20515	202-225-3665	225-1891
Higgins Brian (Rep D - NY) 2459 Rayburn Bldg *Web:* higgins.house.gov	Washington	DC	20515	202-225-3306	226-0347
Israel Steve (Rep D - NY) 2457 Rayburn Bldg *Web:* israel.house.gov	Washington	DC	20515	202-225-3335	225-4669
Jeffries Hakeem (Rep D - NY) 1339 Longworth Bldg *Web:* jeffries.house.gov	Washington	DC	20515	202-225-5936	
Katko John (Rep R - NY) 1123 Longworth HOB *Web:* katko.house.gov	Washington	DC	20515	202-225-3701	225-4042
King Pete (Rep R - NY) 339 Cannon Bldg *Web:* peteking.house.gov	Washington	DC	20515	202-225-7896	226-2279
Lowey Nita (Rep D - NY) 2365 Rayburn Bldg *Web:* lowey.house.gov	Washington	DC	20515	202-225-6506	225-0546
Maloney Carolyn (Rep D - NY) 2308 Rayburn Bldg *Web:* maloney.house.gov	Washington	DC	20515	202-225-7944	225-4709
Maloney Sean Patrick (Rep D - NY) 1529 Longworth Bldg *Web:* seanmaloney.house.gov	Washington	DC	20515	202-225-5441	225-3289
Meeks Gregory W (Rep D - NY) 2234 Rayburn Bldg *Web:* meeks.house.gov	Washington	DC	20515	202-225-3461	226-4169
Meng Grace (Rep D - NY) 1317 Longworth Bldg *Web:* meng.house.gov	Washington	DC	20515	202-225-2601	225-1589
Nadler Jerrold (Rep D - NY) 2109 Rayburn HOB *Web:* nadler.house.gov	Washington	DC	20515	202-225-5635	225-6923

				Phone	Fax
Rangel Charles B (Rep D - NY) 2354 Rayburn Bldg *Web:* rangel.house.gov	Washington	DC	20515	202-225-4365	225-0816
Reed Tom (Rep R - NY) 2437 Rayburn HOB *Web:* reed.house.gov	Washington	DC	20515	202-225-3161	226-6599
Rice Kathleen (Rep D - NY) 1508 Longworth HOB *Web:* kathleenrice.house.gov	Washington	DC	20515	202-225-5516	225-5758
ⓈSchumer Charles E (Sen D - NY) 322 Hart Bldg *Web:* www.schumer.senate.gov	Washington	DC	20510	202-224-6542	228-3027
Serrano Jose E (Rep D - NY) 2227 Rayburn Bldg *Web:* serrano.house.gov	Washington	DC	20515	202-225-4361	225-6001
Slaughter Louise (Rep D - NY) 2469 Rayburn Bldg *Web:* www.louise.house.gov	Washington	DC	20515	202-225-3615	225-7822
Stefanik Elise (Rep R - NY) 512 Cannon HOB *Web:* stefanik.house.gov	Washington	DC	20515	202-225-4611	
Tonko Paul D (Rep D - NY) 2463 Rayburn Bldg *Web:* tonko.house.gov	Washington	DC	20515	202-225-5076	225-5077
Velazquez Nydia M (Rep D - NY) 2302 Rayburn Bldg *Web:* velazquez.house.gov	Washington	DC	20515	202-225-2361	226-0327
Zeldin Lee (Rep R - NY) 1517 Longworth HOB *Web:* zeldin.house.gov	Washington	DC	20515	202-225-3826	225-3143

North Carolina

				Phone	Fax
Adams Alma (Rep D - NC) 222 Cannon HOB *Web:* adams.house.gov	Washington	DC	20515	202-225-1510	225-1512
ⓈBurr Richard (Sen R - NC) 217 Russell Senate Office Bldg *Web:* www.burr.senate.gov	Washington	DC	20510	202-224-3154	
Butterfield GK (Rep D - NC) 2305 Rayburn Bldg *Web:* butterfield.house.gov	Washington	DC	20515	202-225-3101	225-3354
Ellmers Renee (Rep R - NC) 1210 Longworth HOB *Web:* ellmers.house.gov	Washington	DC	20515	202-225-4531	225-5662
Foxx Virginia (Rep R - NC) 2350 Rayburn Bldg *Web:* foxx.house.gov	Washington	DC	20515	202-225-2071	225-2995
Holding George (Rep R - NC) 507 Cannon Bldg *Web:* holding.house.gov	Washington	DC	20515	202-225-3032	
Hudson Richard (Rep R - NC) 429 Cannon Bldg *Web:* hudson.house.gov	Washington	DC	20515	202-225-3715	
Jones Walter B (Rep R - NC) 2333 Rayburn Bldg *Web:* jones.house.gov	Washington	DC	20515	202-225-3415	225-3286
McHenry Patrick T (Rep R - NC) 2334 Rayburn Bldg *Web:* mchenry.house.gov	Washington	DC	20515	202-225-2576	225-0316
Meadows Mark (Rep R - NC) 1024 Longworth HOB *Web:* meadows.house.gov	Washington	DC	20515	202-225-6401	226-6422
Pittenger Robert (Rep R - NC) 224 Cannon Bldg *Web:* pittenger.house.gov	Washington	DC	20515	202-225-1976	225-3389
Price David (Rep D - NC) 2108 Rayburn Bldg *Web:* price.house.gov	Washington	DC	20515	202-225-1784	225-2014
Rouzer David (Rep R - NC) 424 Cannon HOB *Web:* rouzer.house.gov	Washington	DC	20515	202-225-2731	225-5773
ⓈTillis Thom (Sen R - NC) 185 Dirksen Senate Office Bldg *Web:* www.tillis.senate.gov	Washington	DC	20510	202-224-6342	228-2563
Walker Mark (Rep R - NC) 312 Cannon HOB *Web:* walker.house.gov	Washington	DC	20515	202-225-3065	225-8611

North Dakota

				Phone	Fax
Cramer Kevin (Rep R - ND) 1032 Longworth Bldg *Web:* cramer.house.gov	Washington	DC	20515	202-225-2611	226-0893
ⓈHeitkamp Heidi (Sen D - ND) SH-110 Hart Senate Office Bldg *Web:* www.heitkamp.senate.gov	Washington	DC	20510	202-224-2043	224-7776
ⓈHoeven John (Sen R - ND) 338 Russell Bldg *Web:* www.hoeven.senate.gov	Washington	DC	20510	202-224-2551	224-7999

Northern Mariana Islands

				Phone	Fax
Sablan Gregorio (Rep D - MP) 423 Cannon Bldg *Web:* sablan.house.gov	Washington	DC	20515	202-225-2646	226-4249

Ohio

				Phone	Fax
Beatty Joyce (Rep D - OH) 133 Cannon HOB *Web:* beatty.house.gov	Washington	DC	20515	202-225-4324	225-1984
Boehner John A (Rep R - OH) 1011 Longworth Bldg *Web:* boehner.house.gov	Washington	DC	20515	202-225-6205	225-0704
ⓈBrown Sherrod (Sen D - OH) 713 Hart Bldg *Web:* www.brown.senate.gov	Washington	DC	20510	202-224-2315	228-6321
Chabot Steve (Rep R - OH) 2371 Rayburn Bldg *Web:* chabot.house.gov	Washington	DC	20515	202-225-2216	225-3012
Fudge Marcia L (Rep D - OH) 2344 Rayburn Bldg *Web:* fudge.house.gov	Washington	DC	20515	202-225-7032	225-1339
Gibbs Bob (Rep R - OH) 329 Cannon Bldg. *Web:* gibbs.house.gov	Washington	DC	20515	202-225-6265	225-3394
Johnson Bill (Rep R - OH) 1710 Longworth Bldg *Web:* billjohnson.house.gov	Washington	DC	20515	202-225-5705	225-5907
Jordan Jim (Rep R - OH) 1524 Longworth Bldg *Web:* jordan.house.gov	Washington	DC	20515	202-225-2676	226-0577
Joyce David (Rep R - OH) 1535 Longworth Bldg *Web:* joyce.house.gov	Washington	DC	20515	202-225-5731	225-3307
Kaptur Marcy (Rep D - OH) 2186 Rayburn Bldg *Web:* www.kaptur.house.gov	Washington	DC	20515	202-225-4146	225-7711
Latta Robert E (Rep R - OH) 2448 Rayburn Bldg *Web:* latta.house.gov	Washington	DC	20515	202-225-6405	225-1985
ⓈPortman Rob (Sen R - OH) 448 Russell Bldg *Web:* www.portman.senate.gov	Washington	DC	20510	202-224-3353	224-9075
Renacci Jim (Rep R - OH) 328 Cannon HOB *Web:* renacci.house.gov	Washington	DC	20515	202-225-3876	225-3059
Ryan Tim (Rep D - OH) 1421 Longworth Bldg *Web:* timryan.house.gov	Washington	DC	20515	202-225-5261	225-3719
Stivers Steve (Rep R - OH) 1022 Longworth Bldg *Web:* stivers.house.gov	Washington	DC	20515	202-225-2015	225-3529
Tiberi Pat (Rep R - OH) 1203 Longworth HOB *Web:* tiberi.house.gov	Washington	DC	20515	202-225-5355	226-4523
Turner Michael (Rep R - OH) 2239 Rayburn Bldg *Web:* turner.house.gov	Washington	DC	20515	202-225-6465	225-6754
Wenstrup Brad (Rep R - OH) 1318 Longworth HOB *Web:* wenstrup.house.gov	Washington	DC	20515	202-225-3164	225-1992

Oklahoma

				Phone	Fax
Bridenstine Jim (Rep R - OK) 216 Cannon Bldg *Web:* bridenstine.house.gov	Washington	DC	20515	202-225-2211	
Cole Tom (Rep R - OK) 2467 Rayburn HOB *Web:* cole.house.gov	Washington	DC	20515	202-225-6165	225-3512
ⓈInhofe James M (Sen R - OK) 205 Russell Bldg *Web:* www.inhofe.senate.gov	Washington	DC	20510	202-224-4721	228-0380
ⓈLankford James (Sen R - OK) 316 Hart Senate Office Bldg *Web:* www.lankford.senate.gov	Washington	DC	20510	202-224-5754	
Lucas Frank (Rep R - OK) 2405 Rayburn HOB *Web:* lucas.house.gov	Washington	DC	20515	202-225-5565	225-8698
Mullin Markwayne (Rep R - OK) 1113 Longworth Bldg *Web:* mullin.house.gov	Washington	DC	20515	202-225-2701	225-3038
Russell Steve (Rep R - OK) 128 Cannon HOB *Web:* russell.house.gov	Washington	DC	20515	202-225-2132	226-1463

Oregon

				Phone	Fax
Blumenauer Earl (Rep D - OR) 1111 Longworth Bldg *Web:* blumenauer.house.gov	Washington	DC	20515	202-225-4811	225-8941
Bonamici Suzanne (Rep D - OR) 439 Cannon Bldg *Web:* bonamici.house.gov	Washington	DC	20515	202-225-0855	225-9497
DeFazio Peter (Rep D - OR) 2134 Rayburn Bldg *Web:* www.defazio.house.gov	Washington	DC	20515	202-225-6416	
ⓈMerkley Jeff (Sen D - OR) 313 Hart Bldg *Web:* www.merkley.senate.gov	Washington	DC	20510	202-224-3753	228-3997
Schrader Kurt (Rep D - OR) 2431 Rayburn HOB *Web:* schrader.house.gov	Washington	DC	20515	202-225-5711	225-5699
Walden Greg (Rep R - OR) 2185 Rayburn Bldg *Web:* walden.house.gov	Washington	DC	20515	202-225-6730	225-5774
ⓈWyden Ron (Sen D - OR) 221 Dirksen Bldg. *Web:* www.wyden.senate.gov	Washington	DC	20510	202-224-5244	228-2717

Pennsylvania

				Phone	Fax
Barletta Lou (Rep R - PA) 115 Cannon Bldg *Web:* barletta.house.gov	Washington	DC	20515	202-225-6511	226-6250
Boyle Brendan (Rep D - PA) 118 Cannon HOB *Web:* boyle.house.gov	Washington	DC	20515	202-225-6111	226-0611
Brady Robert (Rep D - PA) 102 Cannon Bldg *Web:* www.brady.house.gov	Washington	DC	20515	202-225-4731	225-0088

Phone Fax

Cartwright Matthew (Rep D - PA)
1419 Longworth Bldg .... Washington DC 20515 202-225-5546
Web: cartwright.house.gov

ⓈCasey Robert P Jr (Sen D - PA)
393 Russell Bldg .... Washington DC 20510 202-224-6324 228-0604
Web: www.casey.senate.gov

Costello Ryan (Rep R - PA) 427 Cannon HOB .... Washington DC 20515 202-225-4315
Web: costello.house.gov

Dent Charles W (Rep R - PA)
2211 Rayburn HOB .... Washington DC 20515 202-225-6411 226-0778
Web: dent.house.gov

Doyle Mike (Rep D - PA) 239 Cannon Bldg .... Washington DC 20515 202-225-2135 225-3084
Web: doyle.house.gov

Fattah Chaka (Rep D - PA)
2301 Rayburn Bldg .... Washington DC 20515 202-225-4001 225-5392
Web: fattah.house.gov

Fitzpatrick Michael G (Rep R - PA)
2400 Rayburn Bldg .... Washington DC 20515 202-225-4276 225-9511
Web: fitzpatrick.house.gov

Kelly Mike (Rep R - PA)
1519 Longworth Bldg .... Washington DC 20515 202-225-5406 225-3103
Web: kelly.house.gov

Marino Tom (Rep R - PA) 410 Cannon Bldg .... Washington DC 20515 202-225-3731 225-9594
Web: marino.house.gov

Meehan Pat (Rep R - PA) 434 Cannon HOB .... Washington DC 20515 202-225-2011 226-0280
Web: meehan.house.gov

Murphy Tim (Rep R - PA) 2332 Rayburn Bldg .... Washington DC 20515 202-225-2301 225-1844
Web: murphy.house.gov

Perry Scott (Rep R - PA)
1207 Longworth HOB .... Washington DC 20515 202-225-5836 226-1000
Web: perry.house.gov

Pitts Joseph R (Rep R - PA)
420 Cannon Bldg .... Washington DC 20515 202-225-2411 225-2013
Web: pitts.house.gov

Rothfus Keith (Rep R - PA)
1205 Longworth HOB .... Washington DC 20515 202-225-2065 225-5709
Web: rothfus.house.gov

Shuster Bill (Rep R - PA)
2268 Rayburn HOB .... Washington DC 20515 202-225-2431 225-2486
Web: shuster.house.gov

Thompson Glenn W (Rep R - PA)
124 Cannon Bldg .... Washington DC 20515 202-225-5121 225-5796
Web: thompson.house.gov

ⓈToomey Patrick J (Sen R - PA)
248 Hart Bldg .... Washington DC 20510 202-224-4254 228-0284
Web: www.toomey.senate.gov

Puerto Rico

Phone Fax

Pierluisi Pedro (Rep D - PR)
2410 Rayburn HOB .... Washington DC 20515 202-225-2615 225-2154
Web: pierluisi.house.gov

Rhode Island

Phone Fax

Cicilline David (Rep D - RI)
2244 Rayburn HOB .... Washington DC 20515 202-225-4911 225-3290
Web: cicilline.house.gov

Langevin Jim (Rep D - RI) 109 Cannon Bldg .... Washington DC 20515 202-225-2735 225-5976
Web: langevin.house.gov

ⓈReed Jack (Sen D - RI) 728 Hart Bldg .... Washington DC 20510 202-224-4642 224-4680
Web: www.reed.senate.gov

ⓈWhitehouse Sheldon (Sen D - RI)
530 Hart Bldg .... Washington DC 20510 202-224-2921 228-6362
Web: www.whitehouse.senate.gov

South Carolina

Phone Fax

Clyburn James E (Rep D - SC)
242 Cannon House Office Bldg .... Washington DC 20515 202-225-3315 225-2313
Web: clyburn.house.gov

Duncan Jeff (Rep R - SC) 106 Cannon HOB .... Washington DC 20515 202-225-5301 225-3216
Web: jeffduncan.house.gov

Gowdy Trey (Rep R - SC)
1404 Longworth Bldg .... Washington DC 20515 202-225-6030 226-1177
Web: gowdy.house.gov

ⓈGraham Lindsey (Sen R - SC)
290 Russell Bldg .... Washington DC 20510 202-224-5972 224-3808
Web: www.lgraham.senate.gov

Mulvaney Mick (Rep R - SC)
2419 Rayburn HOB .... Washington DC 20515 202-225-5501 225-0464
Web: mulvaney.house.gov

Rice Tom (Rep R - SC) 223 Cannon HOB .... Washington DC 20515 202-225-9895 225-9690
Web: rice.house.gov

Sanford Mark R(Rep R - SC)
2201 Rayburn HOB .... Washington DC 20515 202-225-3176
Web: sanford.house.gov

ⓈScott Tim (Sen R - SC)
520 Hart Senate Office Bldg .... Washington DC 20510 202-224-6121 228-5143
TF: 855-425-6324 ■ *Web:* www.scott.senate.gov

Wilson Joe (Rep R - SC) 2229 Rayburn Bldg .... Washington DC 20515 202-225-2452 225-2455
Web: joewilson.house.gov

South Dakota

Phone Fax

Noem Kristi (Rep R - SD) 2422 Rayburn HOB .... Washington DC 20515 202-225-2801 225-5823
Web: noem.house.gov

ⓈRounds Mike (Sen R - SD)
502 Hart Senate Office Bldg .... Washington DC 20510 202-224-5842
Web: www.rounds.senate.gov

ⓈThune John (Sen R - SD) 511 Dirksen Bldg .... Washington DC 20510 202-224-2321 228-5429
Web: www.thune.senate.gov

Tennessee

Phone Fax

ⓈAlexander Lamar (Sen R - TN)
455 Dirksen Bldg .... Washington DC 20510 202-224-4944 228-3398
Web: www.alexander.senate.gov

Black Diane (Rep R - TN)
1131 Longworth HOB .... Washington DC 20515 202-225-4231 225-6887
Web: black.house.gov

Blackburn Marsha (Rep R - TN)
2266 Rayburn Bldg .... Washington DC 20515 202-225-2811 225-3004
Web: blackburn.house.gov

Cohen Steve (Rep D - TN)
2404 Rayburn Bldg .... Washington DC 20515 202-225-3265 225-5663
Web: cohen.house.gov

Cooper Jim (Rep D - TN)
1536 Longworth Bldg .... Washington DC 20515 202-225-4311 226-1035
Web: www.cooper.house.gov

ⓈCorker Bob (Sen R - TN) 425 Dirksen Bldg .... Washington DC 20510 202-224-3344 228-0566
Web: www.corker.senate.gov

DesJarlais Scott (Rep R - TN)
413 Cannon Bldg .... Washington DC 20515 202-225-6831 226-5172
Web: desjarlais.house.gov

Duncan John J Jr (Rep R - TN)
2207 Rayburn Bldg .... Washington DC 20515 202-225-5435 225-6440
Web: duncan.house.gov

Fincher Stephen (Rep R - TN)
2452 Rayburn HOB .... Washington DC 20515 202-225-4714 225-1765
Web: fincher.house.gov

Fleischmann Chuck (Rep R - TN)
230 Cannon HOB .... Washington DC 20515 202-225-3271 225-3494
Web: fleischmann.house.gov

Roe Phil (Rep R - TN) 407 Cannon Bldg .... Washington DC 20515 202-225-6356 225-5714
Web: roe.house.gov

Texas

Phone Fax

Babin Brian (Rep R - TX) 316 Cannon HOB .... Washington DC 20515 202-225-1555 226-0396
Web: babin.house.gov

Barton Joe (Rep R - TX) 2107 Rayburn Bldg .... Washington DC 20515 202-225-2002 225-3052
Web: joebarton.house.gov

Brady Kevin (Rep R - TX) 301 Cannon Bldg .... Washington DC 20515 202-225-4901 225-5524
Web: kevinbrady.house.gov

Burgess Michael (Rep R - TX)
2336 Rayburn Bldg .... Washington DC 20515 202-225-7772 225-2919
Web: burgess.house.gov

Carter John (Rep R - TX)
2110 Rayburn Bldg .... Washington DC 20515 202-225-3864 225-5866
Web: carter.house.gov

Castro Joaquin (Rep D - TX)
212 Cannon HOB .... Washington DC 20515 202-225-3236 225-1915
Web: castro.house.gov

Conaway K Michael (Rep R - TX)
2430 Rayburn Bldg .... Washington DC 20515 202-225-3605 225-1783
Web: conaway.house.gov

ⓈCornyn John (Sen R - TX) 517 Hart Bldg .... Washington DC 20510 202-224-2934 228-2856
Web: www.cornyn.senate.gov

ⓈCruz Ted (Sen R - TX) 404 Russell Bldg .... Washington DC 20510 202-224-5922
Web: www.cruz.senate.gov

Cuellar Henry (Rep D - TX)
2209 Rayburn Bldg .... Washington DC 20515 202-225-1640 225-1641
Web: cuellar.house.gov

Culberson John (Rep R - TX)
2372 Rayburn Bldg .... Washington DC 20515 202-225-2571 225-4381
Web: culberson.house.gov

Doggett Lloyd (Rep D - TX)
2307 Rayburn HOB .... Washington DC 20515 202-225-4865
Web: doggett.house.gov

Farenthold Blake (Rep R - TX)
1027 Longworth HOB .... Washington DC 20515 202-225-7742 226-1134
Web: farenthold.house.gov

Flores Bill (Rep R - TX)
1030 Longworth HOB .... Washington DC 20515 202-225-6105 225-0350
Web: flores.house.gov

Gohmert Louie (Rep R - TX)
2243 Rayburn Bldg .... Washington DC 20515 202-225-3035 226-1230
Web: gohmert.house.gov

Granger Kay (Rep R - TX)
1026 Longworth HOB .... Washington DC 20515 202-225-5071 225-5683
Web: kaygranger.house.gov

Green Al (Rep D - TX) 2347 Rayburn Bldg .... Washington DC 20515 202-225-7508 225-2947
Web: algreen.house.gov

Green Gene (Rep D - TX) 2470 Rayburn Bldg .... Washington DC 20515 202-225-1688 225-9903
Web: green.house.gov

Hensarling Jeb (Rep R - TX)
2228 Rayburn Bldg .... Washington DC 20515 202-225-3484 226-4888
Web: hensarling.house.gov

Hinojosa, Ruben (Rep D - TX)
2262 Rayburn Bldg .... Washington DC 20515 202-225-2531 225-5688
Web: hinojosa.house.gov

Hurd Will (Rep R - TX) 317 Cannon HOB .... Washington DC 20515 202-225-4511
Web: hurd.house.gov

				Phone	Fax
Jackson Lee Sheila (Rep D - TX) 2252 Rayburn Bldg *Web:* jacksonlee.house.gov	Washington	DC	20515	202-225-3816	225-3317
Johnson Eddie Bernice (Rep D - TX) 2468 Rayburn Bldg *Web:* ebjohnson.house.gov	Washington	DC	20515	202-225-8885	226-1477
Johnson Sam (Rep R - TX) 2304 Rayburn HOB *Web:* samjohnson.house.gov	Washington	DC	20515	202-225-4201	225-1485
Marchant Kenny (Rep R - TX) 1110 Longworth Bldg *Web:* marchant.house.gov	Washington	DC	20515	202-225-6605	225-0074
McCaul Michael T (Rep R - TX) 131 Cannon Bldg *Web:* mccaul.house.gov	Washington	DC	20515	202-225-2401	225-5955
Neugebauer Randy (Rep R - TX) 1424 Longworth Bldg *Web:* randy.house.gov	Washington	DC	20515	202-225-4005	225-9615
O'Rourke Beto (Rep D - TX) 1330 Longworth Bldg *Web:* orourke.house.gov	Washington	DC	20515	202-225-4831	
Olson Pete (Rep R - TX) 2133 Cannon Bldg *Web:* olson.house.gov	Washington	DC	20515	202-225-5951	225-5241
Poe Ted (Rep R - TX) 2412 Rayburn Bldg *Web:* poe.house.gov	Washington	DC	20515	202-225-6565	225-5547
Ratcliffe John (Rep - TX) 325 Cannon HOB *Web:* ratcliffe.house.gov	Washington	DC	20515	202-225-6673	225-3332
Sessions Pete (Rep R - TX) 2233 Rayburn Bldg *Web:* sessions.house.gov	Washington	DC	20515	202-225-2231	225-5878
Smith Lamar (Rep R - TX) 2409 Rayburn Bldg *Web:* lamarsmith.house.gov	Washington	DC	20515	202-225-4236	225-8628
Thornberry Mac (Rep R - TX) 2208 Rayburn Bldg *Web:* thornberry.house.gov	Washington	DC	20515	202-225-3706	225-3486
Veasey Marc (Rep D - TX) 414 Cannon Bldg *Web:* veasey.house.gov	Washington	DC	20515	202-225-9897	225-9702
Vela Filemon (Rep D - TX) 437 Cannon Bldg *Web:* vela.house.gov	Washington	DC	20515	202-225-9901	225-9770
Weber Randy (Rep R - TX) 510 Cannon Bldg *Web:* weber.house.gov	Washington	DC	20515	202-225-2831	225-0271
Williams Roger (Rep R - TX) 1323 Longworth Bldg *Web:* williams.house.gov	Washington	DC	20515	202-225-9896	

Utah

				Phone	Fax
Bishop Rob (Rep R - UT) 123 Cannon Bldg *Web:* robbishop.house.gov	Washington	DC	20515	202-225-0453	225-5857
Chaffetz Jason (Rep R - UT) 2236 Rayburn Bldg *Web:* chaffetz.house.gov	Washington	DC	20515	202-225-7751	225-5629
ⓈHatch Orrin G (Sen R - UT) 104 Hart Bldg *Web:* www.hatch.senate.gov	Washington	DC	20510	202-224-5251	224-6331
ⓈLee Mike (Sen R - UT) 361A Russell Senate Office Bldg *Web:* www.lee.senate.gov	Washington	DC	20510	202-224-5444	228-1168
Love Mia (Rep R - UT) 217 Cannon HOB *Web:* love.house.gov	Washington	DC	20515	202-225-3011	225-5638
Stewart Chris (Rep R - UT) 323 Cannon Bldg *Web:* stewart.house.gov	Washington	DC	20515	202-225-9730	

Vermont

				Phone	Fax
ⓈLeahy Patrick J (Sen D - VT) 437 Russell Bldg *Web:* www.leahy.senate.gov	Washington	DC	20510	202-224-4242	224-3479
ⓈSanders Bernard (Sen I - VT) 332 Dirksen Bldg *Web:* www.sanders.senate.gov	Washington	DC	20510	202-224-5141	228-0776
Welch Peter (Rep D - VT) 2303 Rayburn House Office Bldg *Web:* www.welch.house.gov	Washington	DC	20515	202-225-4115	225-6790

Virgin Islands

				Phone	Fax
Plaskett Stacey (Rep D - VI) 509 Cannon HOB *Web:* plaskett.house.gov	Washington	DC	20515	202-225-1790	225-5517

Virginia

				Phone	Fax
Beyer Don (Rep D - VA) 431 Cannon HOB *Web:* beyer.house.gov	Washington	DC	20515	202-225-4376	225-0017
Brat Dave (Rep R - VA) 330 Cannon HOB *Web:* brat.house.gov	Washington	DC	20515	202-225-2815	225-0011
Comstock Barbara (Rep R - VA) 226 Cannon HOB *Web:* comstock.house.gov	Washington	DC	20515	202-225-5136	225-0437
Connolly Gerald E "Gerry" (Rep D - VA) 2238 Rayburn HOB *Web:* connolly.house.gov	Washington	DC	20515	202-225-1492	225-3071
Forbes J Randy (Rep R - VA) 2135 Rayburn Bldg *Web:* forbes.house.gov	Washington	DC	20515	202-225-6365	226-1170
Goodlatte Bob (Rep R - VA) 2309 Rayburn Bldg *Web:* goodlatte.house.gov	Washington	DC	20515	202-225-5431	225-9681
Griffith Morgan (Rep R - VA) 1108 Longworth Bldg *Web:* morgangriffith.house.gov	Washington	DC	20515	202-225-3861	225-0076
Hurt Robert (Rep R - VA) 125 Cannon HOB *Web:* hurt.house.gov	Washington	DC	20515	202-225-4711	225-5681
ⓈKaine Tim (Sen D - VA) 231 Russell Senate Office Bldg *Web:* www.kaine.Senate.gov	Washington	DC	20510	202-224-4024	228-6363
Rigell Scott (Rep R - VA) 418 Cannon Bldg *Web:* rigell.house.gov	Washington	DC	20515	202-225-4215	225-4218
Scott Robert C (Rep D - VA) 1201 Longworth Bldg *Web:* www.bobbyscott.house.gov	Washington	DC	20515	202-225-8351	225-8354
ⓈWarner Mark R (Sen D - VA) 475 Russell Bldg *Web:* www.warner.senate.gov	Washington	DC	20510	202-224-2023	
Wittman Robert J (Rep R - VA) 2454 Rayburn Bldg *Web:* www.wittman.house.gov	Washington	DC	20515	202-225-4261	225-4382

Washington

				Phone	Fax
ⓈCantwell Maria (Sen D - WA) 511 Hart Senate Office Bldg *Web:* www.cantwell.senate.gov	Washington	DC	20510	202-224-3441	228-0514
DelBene Suzan (Rep D - WA) 318 cannon Bldg *Web:* delbene.house.gov	Washington	DC	20515	202-225-6311	226-1606
Heck Denny (Rep D - WA) 425 Cannon Bldg *Web:* dennyheck.house.gov	Washington	DC	20515	202-225-9740	225-0129
Herrera Beutler Jaime (Rep R - WA) 1130 Longworth Bldg *Web:* herrerabeutler.house.gov	Washington	DC	20515	202-225-3536	225-3478
Kilmer Derek (Rep D - WA) 1520 Longworth HOB *Web:* kilmer.house.gov	Washington	DC	20515	202-225-5916	
Larsen Rick (Rep D - WA) 2113 Rayburn HOB *Web:* larsen.house.gov	Washington	DC	20515	202-225-2605	225-4420
McDermott Jim (Rep D - WA) 1035 Longworth Bldg *Web:* mcdermott.house.gov	Washington	DC	20515	202-225-3106	225-6197
McMorris Rodgers Cathy (Rep R - WA) 203 Cannon Bldg *Web:* mcmorris.house.gov	Washington	DC	20515	202-225-2006	225-3392
ⓈMurray Patty (Sen D - WA) 154 Russell Bldg *Web:* www.murray.senate.gov	Washington	DC	20510	202-224-2621	224-0238
Newhouse Dan (Rep R - WA) 1641 Longworth HOB *Web:* newhouse.house.gov	Washington	DC	20515	202-225-5816	225-3251
Reichert David G (Rep R - WA) 1127 Longworth Bldg *Web:* reichert.house.gov	Washington	DC	20515	202-225-7761	225-4282
Smith Adam (Rep D - WA) 2264 Rayburn HOB *Web:* adamsmith.house.gov	Washington	DC	20515	202-225-8901	225-5893

West Virginia

				Phone	Fax
ⓈCapito Shelley Moore (R - WV) 172 Russell Senate Office Bldg *Web:* www.capito.senate.gov	Washington	DC	20510	202-224-6472	
Jenkins Evan (Rep R - WV) 502 Cannon HOB *Web:* evanjenkins.house.gov	Washington	DC	20515	202-225-3452	225-9061
ⓈManchin Joe III (Sen D - WV) 306 Hart Bldg *Web:* www.manchin.senate.gov	Washington	DC	20510	202-224-3954	228-0002
McKinley David (Rep R - WV) 412 Cannon Bldg *Web:* mckinley.house.gov	Washington	DC	20515	202-225-4172	225-7564
Mooney Alex (Rep R - WV) 1232 Longworth HOB *Web:* mooney.house.gov	Washington	DC	20515	202-225-2711	225-7856

Wisconsin

				Phone	Fax
ⓈBladwin Tammy (Sen D - WI) 717 Hart Bldg *Web:* www.baldwin.senate.gov	Washington	DC	20510	202-224-5653	224-9787
Duffy Sean P (Rep R - WI) 1208 Longworth Bldg *Web:* duffy.house.gov	Washington	DC	20515	202-225-3365	225-3240
Grothman Glenn (Rep R - WI) 501 Cannon HOB *Web:* grothman.house.gov	Washington	DC	20515	202-225-2476	225-2356
ⓈJohnson Ron (Sen R - WI) 328 Russell Bldg *Web:* www.ronjohnson.senate.gov	Washington	DC	20510	202-224-5323	228-6965
Kind Ron (Rep D - WI) 1502 Longworth Bldg *Web:* kind.house.gov	Washington	DC	20515	202-225-5506	225-5739
Moore Gwen (Rep D - WI) 2245 Rayburn Bldg *Web:* gwenmoore.house.gov	Washington	DC	20515	202-225-4572	225-8135
Petri Thomas (Rep R - WI) 2462 Rayburn Bldg	Washington	DC	20515	202-225-2476	225-2356

Name / Address	City	State	ZIP	Phone	Fax
Pocan Mark (Rep D - WI) 313 Cannon Bldg *Web:* pocan.house.gov	Washington	DC	20515	202-225-2906	225-6942
Ribble Reid (Rep R - WI) 1513 Longworth Bldg *Web:* ribble.house.gov	Washington	DC	20515	202-225-5665	225-5729
Ryan Paul (Rep R - WI) 1233 Longworth Bldg *Web:* paulryan.house.gov	Washington	DC	20515	202-225-3031	225-3393
Sensenbrenner F James (Rep R - WI) 2449 Rayburn Bldg *Web:* sensenbrenner.house.gov	Washington	DC	20515	202-225-5101	225-3190

Wyoming

Name / Address	City	State	ZIP	Phone	Fax
❸Barrasso John (Sen R - WY) 307 Dirksen Bldg *Web:* www.barrasso.senate.gov	Washington	DC	20510	202-224-6441	224-1724
❸Enzi Michael B (Sen R - WY) 379A Russell Bldg *Web:* www.enzi.senate.gov	Washington	DC	20510	202-224-3424	228-0359
Lummis Cynthia M (Rep R - WY) 2433 Rayburn HOB *Web:* lummis.house.gov	Washington	DC	20515	202-225-2311	225-3057

346 GOVERNORS - STATE

Listings for governors are organized by state names.

Name / Address	City	State	ZIP	Phone	Fax
City Hall 801 Washington St *Web:* www.ci.northfield.mn.us	Northfield	MN	55057	507-645-8831	
Clean Water Services Inc 2550 SW Hillsboro Hwy *Web:* www.cleanwaterservices.org	Hillsboro	OR	97123	503-681-3600	
Brown Edmund Gerald (D) State Capitol Bldg Suite 1173 *Web:* gov.ca.gov	Sacramento	CA	95814	916-445-2841	558-3160

347 GRAPHIC DESIGN

SEE ALSO Typesetting & Related Services p. 3265

Name / Address	City	State	ZIP	Phone	Fax
1 Stop Design Shop Inc 25 Hart Pl *Web:* www.1stopdesign.com	Woburn	MA	01801	781-938-3866	
1185 Design Inc 941Emerson St *Web:* www.1185design.com	Palo Alto	CA	94301	650-325-4804	
1K Studios LLC 3400 W Olive Ave Ste 300 *Web:* weareonek.com/	Burbank	CA	91505	818-531-3800	
24 Hour Co 6521 Arlington Blvd *Web:* www.24hrco.com	Falls Church	VA	22042	703-533-7209	
3 Strikes Inc 1905 Elizabeth Ave *Web:* www.3strikes.com	Rahway	NJ	07065	732-382-3820	
300 Feet Out 292 Ivy St *Web:* www.300feetout.com	San Francisco	CA	94102	415-551-2377	
ABBTECH Professional Resources Inc 45625 Willow Pond Plz *Web:* www.abbtech.com	Sterling	VA	20164	703-450-5252	
Accent Imaging Inc 8121 Brownleigh Dr *Web:* www.accentimaging.com	Raleigh	NC	27617	919-782-3332	
Adcetera Design Studio Inc 3000 Louisiana St *Web:* www.adcetera.com	Houston	TX	77006	713-522-8006	
Adcolor Inc 950 Brookstown Ave *Web:* www.adcolornc.com	Winston Salem	NC	27101	336-727-0309	
Adrenalin Inc 54 W 11th Ave *Web:* www.goadrenalin.com	Denver	CO	80204	303-454-8888	
Aesthetic Visual Solutions Inc 7565 Commercial Way	Henderson	NV	89011	702-248-7122	
Akoya 2325 E Carson St *Web:* www.akoyaonline.com	Pittsburgh	PA	15203	412-481-3958	
Albarella Design Inc 100 Bridgepoint Dr *Web:* www.albarella.com	South Saint Paul	MN	55075	651-552-8966	
Aljon Graphics 1721 E Lambert Rd C *Web:* www.aljongraphics.com	La Habra	CA	90631	562-694-3144	
American Fleet & Retail Graphics Inc 780 S Milliken Ave Ste G *Web:* www.amgraph.biz	Ontario	CA	91761	909-937-7570	
Anabliss Inc 3195 Blake St Apt 106 *Web:* anabliss.com	Denver	CO	80205	303-825-4441	
Anfield Inc 5625 Dillard Dr Ste 217 *Web:* www.anfield-information.com	Cary	NC	27518	919-851-8681	
Anthem 537 E Pete Rose Way Ste 100 *Web:* www.anthemww.com/	Cincinnati	OH	45202	513-784-0066	784-0986
Armada Group Inc, The 325 Soquel Ave Ste A *TF:* 800-408-2120 ■ *Web:* www.thearmadagroup.com	Santa Cruz	CA	95062	800-408-2120	
Art4Orm Inc 1933 NW Quimby St *Web:* www.art4orm.com	Portland	OR	97209	503-228-1399	
B&B Image Group 1712 Marshall St NE *TF:* 888-788-9461 ■ *Web:* www.bbimagegroup.com	Minneapolis	MN	55413	612-788-9461	788-3253
Basicgrey LLC 377 Marshall Way *Web:* www.basicgrey.com	Layton	UT	84041	801-544-1116	
Bbr Creative Inc 300 Rue Beauregard *Web:* www.bbrcreative.com	Lafayette	LA	70508	337-233-1515	
Be Original 1520 Lk Louella Rd *Web:* beoriginal.com	Suwanee	GA	30024	770-813-9933	
Bendsen Signs & Graphics Inc 2901 N Woodford St *Web:* www.bendsensigns.com	Decatur	IL	62526	217-877-2345	877-2347
BrandEquity International 2330 Washington St *Fax Area Code: 617 ■ *TF:* 800-969-3150 ■ *Web:* www.brandequity.com	Newton	MA	02462	800-969-3150	969-1944*
Brandscope 700 N Sacramento Blvd *Web:* www.thinkkaleidoscope.com	Chicago	IL	60612	773-533-4488	
Bruce Mau Design Inc 469C King St W *Web:* www.brucemaudesign.com	Toronto	ON	M5V3M4	416-306-6401	
C & K Commercial Development LLC 76 Eastern Blvd *Web:* www.cashman-katz.com	Glastonbury	CT	06033	860-652-0300	
Candid Litho Printing Ltd 25-11 Hunters Point *Web:* www.candidlitho.com	Long Island City	NY	11101	212-431-3800	
Cg Design Concepts 1150 N Highland Ave Ste 3 *Web:* www.cgdesignconcepts.com	Fullerton	CA	92835	714-871-7342	
Champion Awards Inc 3649 Winplace Rd *Web:* www.gochampion.net	Memphis	TN	38118	901-365-4830	
Corporate Visions Inc 1020 19th St NW Ste LL20 *Web:* www.corpvisions.com	Washington	DC	20036	202-833-4333	833-4332
Cosgrove Associates Inc 747 Third Ave Fl 16 *Web:* www.cosgroveny.com	New York	NY	10017	212-888-7202	
Cottonimages.Com Inc 10481 Nw 28th St *Web:* www.cottonimages.com	Miami	FL	33172	305-251-2560	
Creative Assoc One Snoopy Pl	Santa Rosa	CA	95403	707-546-7121	526-7361
Curran & Connors Inc 40 Adams Ave Ste 20 C *Web:* www.curran-connors.com	Hauppauge	NY	11788	631-435-0400	435-0422
Cyclone Interactive Multimedia Group Inc 535 Albany St Ste 402-A *Web:* www.cycloneinteractive.com	Boston	MA	02118	617-350-8834	
David Berman Developments 340 Selby Ave *Web:* www.davidberman.com	Ottawa	ON	K2A3X6	613-728-6777	
Del Tec Packaging Inc 4020 Pelham Ct *Web:* www.del-tec.com	Greenville	SC	29606	864-288-7390	
Democrat Printing & Lithographing Company Inc 6401 Lindsey Rd *Web:* www.democratprinting.com	Little Rock	AR	72206	501-374-0271	
Direct Edge Media Inc 430 W Collins Ave *Web:* directedgemedia.com	Orange	CA	92867	714-221-8686	
Donaldson Group Inc, The 88 Hopmeadow St *Web:* www.donaldson-group.com	Simsbury	CT	06089	860-658-9777	
Drum Creative 35 Cessna Ct *Web:* drumcreative.com	Greenville	SC	29607	864-254-6096	
Duggal Visual Solutions Inc 29 W 23th St *Web:* m.duggal.com	New York	NY	10010	212-924-8100	
Envision Media Inc 331 Soquel Ave Ste 100 *Web:* www.envisionmedia.com	Santa Cruz	CA	95062	831-429-5400	
envisionit media Inc 153 W Ohio St *Web:* www.envisionitmedia.com	Chicago	IL	60654	312-236-2000	
Falk Harrison Creative Inc 1300 Baur Blvd *Web:* falkharrison.com	St. Louis	MO	63132	314-531-1410	
Firstbase Services Ltd 34609 Delair Rd *Web:* www.firstbase.ca	Abbotsford	BC	V2S2E1	604-850-5334	
Flexy Foam 12315 Colony Ave *Web:* www.flexy-foam.com	Chino	CA	91710	909-465-5555	
Focal Point LLC, The 501 14th St Ste 200 *Web:* www.thefocalpoint.com	Oakland	CA	94612	510-208-1760	
GANCOM Inc 209 Senate Ave *Web:* www.gancom.com	Camp Hill	PA	17011	717-763-7387	
General Theming Contractors LLC 3750 Courtright Ct	Columbus	OH	43227	614-252-6342	
Genesys Creative Inc 500 Queens Quay W Ste 103e *Web:* www.genesisxd.com	Toronto	ON	M5V3K8	416-595-9823	
Gerard Design 28371 Davis Pkwy Ste 100 *Web:* www.gerarddesign.com	Warrenville	IL	60555	630-355-0775	
Girvin Inc 121 Stewart St Ste 212 *Web:* www.girvin.com	Seattle	WA	98101	206-674-7808	674-7909
Glad Works 545 Pawtucket Ave *Web:* www.gladworks.com	Pawtucket	RI	02860	401-724-4523	
Goldmark Group Inc, The 1155 Bloomfield Ave *Web:* www.goldmarkgroup.com	Clifton	NJ	07012	973-777-5720	
Graphic Reproduction 1381 Franquette Ave Bldg B1 *TF:* 800-498-9939 ■ *Web:* www.graphic4u.com	Concord	CA	94520	925-674-0900	
Graphics Service Bureau 370 Park Ave S *Web:* www.gsbinc.net	New York	NY	10010	212-684-3600	
Gravity Switch Inc 89 Market St *Web:* www.gravityswitch.com	Northampton	MA	01060	413-586-9596	
Group 22 Inc 1205 E Grand Ave *Web:* www.group22.com	El Segundo	CA	90245	310-322-2210	
GSP Marketing Technologies Inc 14055 46th St N Ste 1112 *Web:* www.gspretail.com	Clearwater	FL	33760	727-532-0647	
H & H Graphics Inc 854 N Prince St *Web:* www.hhgraphicsgroup.com	Lancaster	PA	17603	717-393-3941	
Handelan-pedersen 1453 N Ashland Ave *Web:* www.hpdesign.net	Chicago	IL	60622	773-634-8181	
Holiday Image Inc 135 W Commercial Ave *Web:* www.holidayimageinc.com	Moonachie	NJ	07074	718-369-3212	
Homer Group, The 2605 Egypt Rd *Web:* www.homergroup.com	Trooper	PA	19403	610-539-8400	
Hudson Printing & Graphic Design 611 S Mobberly Ave *Web:* www.hudsonprint.com	Longview	TX	75602	903-758-1773	
Hunt Design Assoc Inc 25 N Mentor Ave *Web:* www.huntdesign.com	Pasadena	CA	91106	626-793-7847	
Idamerica 941 Corporate Ln *Web:* idamerica.com	Chesapeake	VA	23320	757-549-2300	
Imprimis Group Inc 4835 Lyndon B Johnson Fwy *TF:* 888-772-9682 ■ *Web:* www.imprimis.com	Dallas	TX	75244	972-419-1700	419-1799

				Phone	Fax
Internet Exposure Inc 1101 Washington Ave S *Web:* www.iexposure.com	Minneapolis	MN	55415	612-333-2606	
J Allan Writing & Design Studios LLC 115 12th Ave Ne *Web:* www.jallanstudios.com	Saint Petersburg	FL	33701	727-822-2526	
Jaguar Design Studio Inc 9039 Soquel Dr. *Web:* www.jaguardesignstudio.com	Aptos	CA	95003	831-662-9991	
Jarrett Industries of The Carolinas Inc 11511 Cronridge Dr *Web:* www.jarrettindustries.com	Owings Mills	MD	21117	410-581-0303	
JK Design Inc 465 Amwell Rd *Web:* www.jkdesign.com	Hillsborough	NJ	08844	908-428-4700	
Kane Graphical Corp 2255 W Logan Blvd. *TF:* 800-992-2921 ■ *Web:* www.kanegraphical.com	Chicago	IL	60647	773-384-1200	384-1207
Kathoderay Media Inc 20 Country Estates Rd *Web:* www.kathoderay.com	Greenville	NY	12083	518-966-5600	
Kmt Creative Group Inc 402 Riverside Ave. *Web:* www.kmtcreative.com	Chattanooga	TN	37405	423-634-9070	
LAM Design Associates Inc 409 Manville Rd *Web:* www.lamdesign.com	Pleasantville	NY	10570	914-773-7600	
Lansmont Corp Ryan Ranch Research Pk 17 Mandeville Ct. *TF:* 800-526-7666 ■ *Web:* www.lansmont.com	Monterey	CA	93940	831-655-6600	
Lautze & Lautze Cpas & Financial Consult 303 Second St *Web:* www.lautze.com	San Francisco	CA	94107	415-543-6900	
Leroy & Clarkson 211 Centre St Rm 5l *Web:* www.leroyandclarkson.com	New York	NY	10013	212-431-9291	
Lucas Color Card 4900 N Santa Fe Ave *Web:* lucascolorcard.com	Oklahoma City	OK	73118	405-524-1811	
Matrix 2 Inc 1903 NW 97th Ave *Web:* www.matrix2advertising.com	Miami	FL	33172	305-591-7672	
McClung Cos Inc 550 Commerce Ave *Web:* www.mcclungco.com	Waynesboro	VA	22980	540-949-8139	
McDill Design 626 N Water St *Web:* www.waterworksalliance.org	Milwaukee	WI	53202	414-277-8111	
Mentus 6755 Mira Mesa Blvd Ste 123-137 *Web:* www.mentus.com	San Diego	CA	92121	858-455-5500	455-6872
Mercury Mambo 1107 S Eighth St. *Web:* www.mercurymambo.com	Austin	TX	78704	512-447-4440	
Metro Creative Graphics Inc 519 Eigth Ave *TF:* 800-223-1600 ■ *Web:* www.metrocreativegraphics.com	New York	NY	10018	212-947-5100	714-9139
Mike Davis & Associates Inc 15505 Long Vista Dr # 200 *Web:* www.imagecraftexhibits.com	Austin	TX	78728	512-836-8442	
Newhall Klein Inc 6109 W Kl Ave *Web:* www.newhallklein.com	Kalamazoo	MI	49009	269-544-0844	
Object Design Comms Inc 8212 Old Courthouse Rd Ste A *Web:* www.objectdc.com	Vienna	VA	22182	703-917-0023	
Oden & Associates Inc 119 S Main St Ste 300 *Web:* www.oden.com	Memphis	TN	38103	901-578-8055	
Odopod Inc 385 Grove St *Web:* www.odopod.com	San Francisco	CA	94102	415-436-9980	
Off The Wall Company Inc 4814 Bethlehem Pk *Web:* www.offthewall.net	Telford	PA	18969	215-453-9400	
Offwhite 521 Ft St *Web:* www.offwhite.com	Marietta	OH	45750	740-373-9010	
Optima Graphics Inc 1540 Fencorp Ct *Web:* www.optimagfx.com	Fenton	MO	63026	636-349-3396	
Otherwise Inc 1144 W Randolph St. *Web:* otherwiseinc.com	Chicago	IL	60607	312-226-1144	
Outside Source Inc 7202 E 71st St *Web:* outsidesource.com	Indianapolis	IN	46256	317-842-4853	
Par-Tech Inc 139 Premier Dr *Web:* www.partechgss.com	Lake Orion	MI	48359	248-276-0213	
Phase 3 Marketing & Communications 3560 Atlanta Industrial Dr *Web:* www.phase3media.com	Atlanta	GA	30331	404-367-9898	
Phoenix Creative Services Inc 611 N 10th St Ste 700 *Web:* www.phoenixcreative.com	Saint Louis	MO	63101	314-421-5646	
Plastic Package Inc 4600 Beloit Dr *Web:* www.plasticpack.com	Sacramento	CA	95838	916-921-3399	
Premedia Group LLC 1185 Revolution Mill Dr Ste 1 *Web:* www.premediagroup.com	Greensboro	NC	27405	336-274-2421	
Primary Color Systems Corp 265 Briggs Ave *Web:* www.primarycolor.com	Costa Mesa	CA	92626	949-660-7080	975-1557
Printing House Ltd, The 1403 Bathurst St *TF:* 800-874-0870 ■ *Web:* www.tph.ca	Toronto	ON	M5R3H8	416-536-6113	
Psyop Inc 124 Rivington St Ground Fl *Web:* www.psyop.tv	New York	NY	10002	212-533-9055	
Pudik Graphics Inc 111 Oakwood Rd *Web:* www.pudik.com	East Peoria	IL	61611	309-694-2900	
Q Prime Inc 729 Seventh Ave Lbby *Web:* www.qprime.com	New York	NY	10019	212-302-9790	
Rage Unlimited Inc 1715 Pearl St *Web:* www.rageco.com	Boulder	CO	80302	303-444-6506	
Red Hill Studios 1017 E St Ste C *Web:* www.redhillstudios.com	San Rafael	CA	94901	415-457-0440	
Rgi Inc 2245 Gilbert Ave Ste 103 *Web:* rgidesign.com	Cincinnati	OH	45206	513-221-2121	
Sametz Blackstone Assoc 40 W Newton St. *Web:* www.sametz.com	Boston	MA	02118	617-266-8577	
Sanger & Eby Design LLC 501 Chestnut St *Web:* www.sangereby.com	Cincinnati	OH	45203	513-784-9046	
Screen Works Inc 3970 Image Dr *Web:* screenworksinc.com	Dayton	OH	45414	937-264-9111	
Selbert Perkins Design 432 Culver Blvd *Web:* www.selbertperkins.com	Playa Del Rey	CA	90293	310-822-5223	
Sequel Studio LLC 12 W 27th St *Web:* sequelstudio.com	New York	NY	10001	212-994-4320	
Signature Graphics Inc 1000 Signature Dr *TF:* 800-356-3235 ■ *Web:* www.signaturegraphicsinc.com	Porter	IN	46304	219-926-4994	926-7231
Silver Oaks Communications 824 17th St. *Web:* www.silveroaks.com	Moline	IL	61265	309-797-9898	
Snavely Associates Ltd 300 S Allen St *Web:* www.snavelyassociates.com	State College	PA	16801	814-234-3672	
Solid Light Inc 438 S Third St *Web:* www.solidlight-inc.com	Louisville	KY	40202	502-562-0060	
Sonjara Inc 8215 Briar Creek Dr *Web:* www.sonjara.com	Annandale	VA	22003	703-425-1907	
Spire Inc 65 Bay St *TF:* 877-350-8837 ■ *Web:* www.spire.net	Boston	MA	02125	617-350-8837	350-9951
Spyglass Creative Inc 1639 Hennepin Ave 100 *Web:* www.spyglasscreative.com	Minneapolis	MN	55403	612-486-5959	
Store Decor Co, The 5050 Boyd Blvd *Web:* www.thestoredecor.com	Rowlett	TX	75088	972-475-4404	
Studio One Digital Inc 180 N Wabash Ave Ste 300 *Web:* studio1digital.com	Chicago	IL	60601	312-376-3300	
Subia Corp 6612 Gulton Ct NE *TF:* 800-275-2636 ■ *Web:* www.brilliantdigitalprinting.com	Albuquerque	NM	87109	505-345-2636	344-9177
Susan Davis International 1101 K St Nw Ste 400 *Web:* www.susandavis.com	Washington	DC	20005	202-408-0808	
SW!TCH Studio Inc 1835 E Sixth St Ste 18 *Web:* www.switchstudio.com	Tempe	AZ	85281	480-966-2211	
Tailored Marketing 401 Wood St Ste 902 *Web:* www.tailoredmarketing.com	Pittsburgh	PA	15222	412-281-1442	
Terrapin Systems LLC 1201 Seven Locks Rd Ste 300 *Web:* www.terpsys.com	Rockville	MD	20854	301-530-9106	
theprinters.com 3500 E College Ave *Web:* www.theprinters.com	State College	PA	16801	814-237-7600	
Think Big Solutions LLC 4995 Monaco St *Web:* thinkbigsolutions.com	Commerce City	CO	80022	303-286-7200	
Toky Branding & Design 3139 Olive St. *Web:* toky.com	Saint Louis	MO	63103	314-534-2000	
Tolleson Design Inc 560 Pacific Ave. *Web:* tolleson.com	San Francisco	CA	94133	415-626-7796	
Toolbox Studios Inc 454 Soledad St *Web:* www.toolbox.net	San Antonio	TX	78205	210-225-8269	
Tribe Design LLC 1420 Mcilhenny St *Web:* www.tribedesign.com	Houston	TX	77004	713-523-5119	
Unimac Graphics 350 Michele Pl *Web:* www.unimacgraphics.com	Carlstadt	NJ	07072	201-372-1000	372-0699
Vango Graphics Inc 1371 S Inca St. *Web:* vango-graphics.com	Denver	CO	80223	303-722-6109	
Vista Color Lab Inc 2048 Fulton Rd *TF:* 800-890-0062 ■ *Web:* www.vistacolorimaging.com	Cleveland	OH	44113	216-651-2830	651-5004
Vista Graphics Inc 1264 Perimeter Pkwy *Web:* www.vgnet.com	Virginia Beach	VA	23454	757-422-8979	
Visual Citi Inc 770 Railroad Ave. *Web:* visualciti.com	West Babylon	NY	11704	631-482-3030	
Wallace Church Inc 330 E 48th St *Web:* www.wallacechurch.net	New York	NY	10017	212-755-2903	
Wesco Graphics Inc 410 E Grant Line Rd Ste B *Web:* www.wescographics.com	Tracy	CA	95376	209-832-1000	832-7800
West Canadian Digital Imaging Inc 200 - 1601 Ninth Ave SE *TF:* 800-267-2555 ■ *Web:* www.westcanadian.com	Calgary	AB	T2G0H4	403-245-2555	
Weymouth Design 332 Congress St *Web:* www.weymouthdesign.com	Boston	MA	02210	617-542-2647	
William Fox Munroe Inc Three E Lancaster Ave *Web:* wfoxm.com	Reading	PA	19607	610-775-4521	
Zamboo LLC 4079A Redwood Ave. *Web:* zamboo.com	Los Angeles	CA	90066	310-822-4643	
Zebra Studios Inc 152 Ave Rd *Web:* www.zebrastudios.com	Toronto	ON	M5R2H8	416-293-3134	
Zen Design Group Ltd 2850 Coolidge Hwy *Web:* www.zendesigngroup.com	Berkley	MI	48072	248-398-5209	

348 GROCERY STORES

SEE ALSO Convenience Stores p. 2152; Gourmet Specialty Shops p. 2359; Health Food Stores p. 2453; Ice Cream & Dairy Stores p. 2550; Bakeries p. 1847; Wholesale Clubs p. 3297

				Phone	Fax
85C Bakery Caf 2700 Alton Pkwy *Web:* www.85cafe.us	Irvine	CA	92606	949-553-8585	
A-Pac Manufacturing Company Inc 2719 Courier NW *Web:* www.polybags.com	Grand Rapids	MI	49534	616-791-7222	
A.g. Ferrari Foods 14234 Catalina St *TF:* 877-878-2783 ■ *Web:* www.agferrari.com	San Leandro	CA	94577	510-346-2100	351-2672
Acme Markets Inc 75 Valley Stream Pkwy *TF:* 877-932-7948 ■ *Web:* www.acmemarkets.com	Malvern	PA	19355	610-889-4000	

Company	City	State	Zip	Phone	Fax
Adam Matthews Inc 2104 Plantside Dr	Louisville	KY	40299	502-499-2253	
Web: www.adammatthews.com					
Advanced Orthomolecular Research Inc 3900 - 12 St Ne	Calgary	AB	T2E8H9	403-250-9997	
Web: www.aor.ca					
Akins Harvest Foods 106 F St Sw	Quincy	WA	98848	509-787-4421	
Web: www.harvestfoodsnw.com					
Alameda Natural Grocery 1650 Park St Unit L	Alameda	CA	94501	510-865-1500	
Web: www.alamedanaturalgrocery.com					
Alaska Commercial Co 550 W 64th Ave Ste 200	Anchorage	AK	99518	907-273-4600	
TF: 800-563-0002 ■ *Web:* acvaluecenter.com					
ALDI Inc 1200 N Kirk Rd	Batavia	IL	60510	630-879-8100	879-8114
TF: 800-388-2534 ■ *Web:* www.aldi.us					
Allen's of Hastings Inc 1115 W Second St	Hastings	NE	68901	402-463-5633	463-5730
Web: www.allensuperstore.com					
Alliance Foods Inc 605 W Chicago Rd	Coldwater	MI	49036	517-278-2396	278-7936
TF: 800-388-4158 ■ *Web:* www.alliance-foods.com					
Amax Nutrasource Inc 14291 E Don Julian Rd	City Of Industry	CA	91746	626-961-6600	
TF: 800-893-5306 ■ *Web:* www.amaxnutrasource.com					
American Consumers Inc 55 Hannah Way	Rossville	GA	30741	706-861-3347	861-3364
Web: shoprite-ga.com					
American Metal Market LLC 225 Park Ave S Sixth Fl	New York	NY	10003	212-213-6202	
Web: www.amm.com					
Andersen Bakery Inc 30703 San Clemente St	Hayward	CA	94544	510-429-7100	
Web: www.andersenbakery.com					
Archon Group LP 6011 Connection Dr	Irving	TX	75039	972-368-2200	
Web: www.archon.com					
Arkansas Poly Inc 1248 S 28th St	Van Buren	AR	72956	479-474-5036	
Web: www.arkpoly.com					
Arlans Market Inc 6500 Fm 2100	Crosby	TX	77532	281-328-4868	
Web: www.arlansmarket.com					
Ascenta Health Ltd 4-15 Garland Ave	Dartmouth	NS	B3B0A6	902-435-7329	435-3513
Web: www.ascentahealth.com					
Autry Greer & Sons Inc 2850 W Main St	Mobile	AL	36612	251-457-8655	456-3744
TF: 800-999-7750 ■ *Web:* www.greers.com					
B&R Stores Inc 4554 W St	Lincoln	NE	68503	402-464-6297	
Web: www.russmarket.com					
B. Green & Co 1300 S Monroe St	Baltimore	MD	21230	410-539-6134	
Web: www.bgreenco.com					
Balls Food Stores Inc 5300 Speaker Rd	Kansas City	KS	66106	913-321-4223	551-8500
Web: www.henhouse.com					
Banner Wholesale Grocers Inc 3000 S Ashland Ave Ste 300	Chicago	IL	60608	312-421-2650	
Web: www.bannerwholesale.com					
Bashas Inc 22402 S Bashas Rd	Chandler	AZ	85248	480-895-9350	895-5371*
**Fax:* PR ■ *TF:* 800-755-7292 ■ *Web:* www.bashas.com					
Beckmann's Old World Bakery Ltd 104 Bronson St Ste 6	Santa Cruz	CA	95062	831-423-9242	
Web: www.beckmannsbakery.com					
Belmont Village LP 8554 Katy Fwy Ste 200	Houston	TX	77024	713-463-1700	
Web: www.belmontvillage.com					
Berkot Super Foods 20005 Wolf Rd	Mokena	IL	60448	708-479-7411	
Web: www.berkotfoods.com					
Best Yet Market Inc One Lexington Ave	Bethpage	NY	11714	516-570-5300	
Web: bestmarket.com					
BI-LO LLC PO Box 99	Mauldin	SC	29662	800-862-9293	
TF: 800-862-9293 ■ *Web:* www.bi-lo.com					
Big Saver Foods Inc 4260 Charter St	Vernon	CA	90058	323-582-7222	582-2331
Web: www.bigsaverfoods.com					
Big Y Foods Inc 2145 Roosevelt Ave	Springfield	MA	01102	413-784-0600	
TF Cust Svc: 800-828-2688 ■ *Web:* www.bigy.com					
BioCell Technology LLC 4695 Macarthur Ct 11th Fl	Newport Beach	CA	92660	714-632-1231	
Web: www.biocelltechnology.com					
Biotab Nutraceuticals Inc 401 E Huntington Dr	Monrovia	CA	91016	626-775-6334	
Web: www.biotab.com					
Bloomfield Bakers 16100 Foothill Blvd	Azusa	CA	91702	626-610-2253	
Bodega Latina Corp 14601B Lakewood Blvd Bldg B	Paramount	CA	90723	562-616-8800	
Web: elsupermarkets.com					
Body By Jake Global LLC 11611 San Vicente Blvd Ste 515	Los Angeles	CA	90049	310-571-7101	
Bordner PJ Company Inc 2100 Wales Rd NE	Massillon	OH	44646	330-832-7522	
Bosselman Inc 3123 W Stolley Park Rd Ste A	Grand Island	NE	68801	308-381-2800	
Web: www.bosselman.com					
Boyer's Food Markets Inc 301 S Warren St	Orwigsburg	PA	17961	570-366-1477	
Web: www.boyersfood.com					
Breadbox Food Stores Inc 10636 HaRdin Vly Rd	Knoxville	TN	37932	865-531-3299	777-2167
Web: conocophillips.com					
Bristol Farms 915 E 230th St	Carson	CA	90745	310-233-4700	233-4701
Web: www.bristolfarms.com					
Brookshire Bros Ltd 1201 Ellen Trout Dr	Lufkin	TX	75904	936-634-8155	279-3374*
**Fax Area Code:* 979 ■ *TF:* 855-467-7837 ■ *Web:* www.brookshirebrothers.com					
Brookshire Grocery Co 1600 W SW Loop 323	Tyler	TX	75701	903-534-3000	534-2240
Web: brookshires.com					
Buds Salads 2428 Harrison Ave	Dallas	TX	75215	214-428-1200	
Web: www.buds-salads.com					
Buehler Food Markets Inc 1401 Old Mansfield Rd	Wooster	OH	44691	330-264-4355	
Web: www.buehlers.com					
Buffalo Services Inc 2100 Veterans Blvd	Mccomb	MS	39648	601-249-3013	
Web: www.buffaloservices.com					

Company	City	State	Zip	Phone	Fax
Bulk Foods.com 3040 Hill Ave	Toledo	OH	43607	419-531-6887	
Web: www.bulkfoods.com					
Busch's Inc 2240 S Main St	Ann Arbor	MI	48103	734-214-8088	
Web: www.buschs.com					
Byrd Cookie Company Inc 6700 Waters Ave	Savannah	GA	31406	912-355-1716	
TF: 800-291-2973 ■ *Web:* www.byrdcookiecompany.com					
C & K Markets Inc 615 Fifth St	Brookings	OR	97415	541-469-3113	469-6717
Web: www.ckmarket.com					
Cache Creek Foods LLC 411 Pioneer Ave	Woodland	CA	95776	530-662-1764	
Web: www.cachecreekfoods.com					
Cajun Kettle Foods 698 Saint George Ave	New Orleans	LA	70121	504-733-8800	
Web: www.kajunkettle.com					
Calhoun Enterprises 4155 Lomac St Ste G	Montgomery	AL	36106	334-272-4400	272-7799
Web: calhounent.com					
Camellia Foods 1300 Diamond Springs Rd	Virginia Beach	VA	23455	757-855-3371	855-3423
Capital Markets Advisors LLC One Great Neck Rd Ste 1	Great Neck	NY	11021	516-487-9815	
Web: www.capmark.org					
Capital Markets Cooperative LLC 814 A1A N Ste 303	Ponte Vedra Beach	FL	32082	904-543-0052	
Web: www.capmkts.org					
Capitol Distributing Inc 3500 E Commercial Ct	Meridian	ID	83642	208-888-5112	888-5989
TF: 800-769-5659 ■ *Web:* www.capitoldist.com					
Capri IGA Foodliner 224 E Harris Ave	Greenville	IL	62246	618-664-0022	664-4629
Caramagno Foods Co 14255 Dequindre St	Detroit	MI	48212	313-869-8200	
Web: www.caramagnofoods.com					
Cardenas Markets Inc 2501 E Guasti Rd	Ontario	CA	91761	909-923-7426	
Web: cardenasmarkets.com					
Carmines Gourmet Market 2401 Pga Blvd	Palm Beach Gardens	FL	33410	561-775-0105	
Web: www.carmines.com					
Casey's Foods Inc 130 Holly Hills Mall Rd	Hindman	KY	41822	630-369-1686	
Web: www.caseysfoods.com					
Cefco Convenience Stores Inc 6261 Central Pointe Pkwy PO Box 1287	Temple	TX	76504	254-791-0009	791-0018
Web: www.cefcostores.com					
Chief Super Market Inc 1340 W High St Ste E	Defiance	OH	43512	419-782-0950	782-6047
Web: chiefmarkets.com					
City Market 555 Sandhill Ln	Grand Junction	CO	81505	970-241-0750	255-0941
Web: www.citymarket.com					
ClearFreight Inc 880 Apollo St Ste 101	El Segundo	CA	90245	310-726-0400	
Web: clearfreight.com					
Clements Marketplace Inc 2575 E Main Rd	Portsmouth	RI	02871	401-683-0180	
Web: www.clementsmarket.com					
Coborn's Inc 1445 E Hwy 23	Saint Cloud	MN	56304	320-252-4222	252-0014
Web: www.cobornsinc.com					
Cogo's Co 2589 Boyce Plz Rd	Pittsburgh	PA	15241	412-257-1550	
Web: www.cogos.com					
Cohn Wholesale Fruit & Grocery 3511 Camino Del Rio S Ste 306	San Diego	CA	92108	619-528-1113	
Community Food Coop 908 W Main St	Bozeman	MT	59715	406-587-4039	
Web: www.bozo.coop					
Compare Plaza 1050 E Main St	Bridgeport	CT	06608	203-366-9060	
Web: www.comparesupermarkets.com					
Convenient Food Mart 123 Gateway Blvd N	Elyria	OH	44035	440-322-6301	
Web: myconvenient.com					
Covington Foods Inc 419 Fourth St PO Box 206	Covington	IN	47932	765-793-2470	793-0209
Cracker Barrel 12221 Industriplex Blvd	Baton Rouge	LA	70809	225-753-3200	
Web: www.crackerbarrelcstores.com					
Creative Foods Corp 200 Garden City Plz Ste 505	Garden City	NY	11530	516-746-6800	
Web: www.creativefoodscorp.com					
Creditera 5300 Richmond Rd	Bedford	OH	44146	216-763-3200	
Web: www.davesmarkets.com					
Crosbys Markets Inc 125 Canal St	Salem	MA	01970	978-745-3571	
Web: www.crosbysmarkets.com					
Cub Foods 2612 S Broadway St	Alexandria	MN	56308	320-762-1158	
Web: www.petescountymarket.com					
Cub Foods Stores 421 S Third St	Stillwater	MN	55082	651-439-7200	439-7200
Web: www.cub.com					
Cubby's Inc 9230 Mormon Bridge Rd	Omaha	NE	68152	402-453-2468	453-4513
Web: www.cubbys.com					
Culpepper & Company Inc 201 Haley Rd	Ashland	VA	23005	804-752-7171	
Web: www.rrsfoodservice.com					
Custom Poly Bag Inc 9465 Edison St NE	Alliance	OH	44601	330-935-2408	
Web: www.custompolybag.com					
CW Brower Inc 413 S Riverside Dr	Modesto	CA	95354	209-523-5447	
D'Agostino Supermarkets Inc 1385 Boston Post Rd	Larchmont	NY	10538	914-833-4000	
Web: www.dagnyc.com					
Dan's Supermarket Inc 835 S Washington St Ste 4	Bismarck	ND	58504	701-258-2127	
Web: www.dansupermarket.com					
Dari-Mart Stores Inc 125 E Sixth Ave	Junction City	OR	97448	541-998-2388	
Web: www.darimart.com					
Dean & DeLuca Brands Inc 560 Broadway	New York	NY	10012	212-226-6800	
Web: www.deandeluca.com					
Del Real Foods LLC 11041 Inland Ave	Mira Loma	CA	91752	951-681-0395	
Web: delrealfoods.com					
Delaware Supermarkets Inc 1600 W Newport Pk	Wilmington	DE	19804	302-999-1801	
Web: www.wsfs.net					
Delsea Shop Rite 215 N Delsea Dr	Vineland	NJ	08360	856-691-9395	713-4176*
**Fax Area Code:* 518 ■ *Web:* www.shoprite.com					
DeMoulas Super Markets Inc 875 E St	Tewksbury	MA	01876	978-851-8000	640-8390
Web: mydemoulas.net					
Derico of East Amherst Corp 18 Limestone Dr Ste 4	Williamsville	NY	14221	716-810-0400	

Company / Address	City	State	Zip	Phone	Fax
Dierbergs Markets Inc 16690 Swingley Ridge Rd *Web:* www.dierbergs.com	Chesterfield	MO	63017	636-532-8884	532-8759
Donelans Super Mkt 248 Great Rd *Web:* www.donelans.com	Acton	MA	01720	978-635-9893	
Dorignac's Food Ctr 725 Focis St *Web:* dorignacs.com	Metairie	LA	70005	504-837-4650	832-8944
Dorothy Lane Market Inc 2710 Far Hills Ave *Web:* www.dorothylane.com	Dayton	OH	45419	937-299-3561	299-3568
Double 8 Foods Inc 2201 E 46th St *Web:* www.double8foods.com	Indianapolis	IN	46205	317-253-3417	257-0209
Doug's Supermarket Inc 310 Main Ave NE *Web:* www.dougssupermarket.com	Warroad	MN	56763	218-386-1246	
Downs Tony Food Co 418 Benzel Ave Sw *Web:* tonydownsfoods.com	Madelia	MN	56062	507-642-3203	
Draeger's Super Markets Inc 222 E Fourth Ave *Web:* www.draegers.com	San Mateo	CA	94401	650-685-3715	244-6548
Easy Way Food Stores Inc 4545 S Mendenhall Rd *Web:* www.easywayproduce.com	Memphis	TN	38141	901-527-6256	462-3965
Econo Foods 1600 Stephenson PO Box 1107 *TF:* 877-295-4558 ■ *Web:* www.econotnc.com	Iron Mountain	MI	49801	906-774-1911	774-1915
El Matador Foods Inc 7201 Bayway Dr *Web:* www.elmatadorfoods.com	Baytown	TX	77520	281-424-4555	
El Metate Mercado 125 N Rancho Santiago Blvd *Web:* www.elmetate.com	Orange	CA	92869	714-771-5527	
El Rancho Inc 2600 McCree Rd Ste 100 *Web:* www.elranchoinc.com	Garland	TX	75041	972-526-7300	
Erla Foods Inc 6233 Church St *Web:* www.erlafoods.com	Cass City	MI	48726	989-872-5100	
Essential Baking Co, The 5601 First Ave S *Web:* www.essentialbaking.com	Seattle	WA	98108	206-545-3804	876-3768
EuroPharma Inc 955 Challenger Dr *TF:* 866-598-5487 ■ *Web:* www.europharmausa.com	Green Bay	WI	54311	920-406-6500	
EW James & Sons Inc 1308-14 Nailling Dr *Web:* www.ewjames.com	Union City	TN	38261	731-885-0601	
Fairplay Inc 4640 S Halsted St *Web:* www.fairplayfoods.com	Chicago	IL	60609	773-247-3077	
Fancy Foods Inc Bldg B-12 Hunts Point Cooperative Market *Web:* www.fancyfoodsinc.com	Bronx	NY	10474	718-617-3000	
Father's Table LLC, The 2100 Country Club Rd *Web:* www.thefatherstable.com	Sanford	FL	32771	407-324-1200	
FBC Industries Inc 110 E Ave H *Web:* www.fbcindustries.com	Rochelle	IL	61068	815-562-8169	
Federated Group Inc 3025 W Salt Creek Ln *TF:* 800-234-0011 ■ *Web:* www.fedgroup.com	Arlington Heights	IL	60005	847-577-1200	632-8302
Field Fresh Foods Inc 14805 S San Pedro St *Web:* www.fieldfresh.com	Gardena	CA	90248	310-719-8422	
Fiesta Mart Inc 5235 Katy Fwy *Web:* www.fiestamart.com	Houston	TX	77007	713-869-5060	869-6197
Finagle-a-Bagel Inc 77 Rowe St *Web:* www.finagleabagel.com	Auburndale	MA	02466	617-213-8400	
First Coast Energy LLP 7014 A C Skinner Pkwy Ste 290 *Web:* www.dailysstores.com	Jacksonville	FL	32256	904-596-3200	596-8550
Fluid Market Strategies Inc 625 SW Broadway Ste 300 *Web:* www.fluidms.com	Portland	OR	97205	503-808-9003	
Food City 1005 N Arizona Ave *TF:* 800-755-7292 ■ *Web:* www.myfoodcity.com	Chandler	AZ	85224	480-857-2198	
Food Country USA 566 E Main St *Web:* foodcountryusainc.com	Abingdon	VA	24210	276-628-3332	628-4613
Food for Thought Inc 10704 Oviatt Rd *Web:* www.foodforthought.net	Honor	MI	49640	231-326-5444	
Food Giant Supermarkets 120 Industrial Dr *Web:* foodgiant.com	Sikeston	MO	63801	573-471-3500	472-3135
Foodland Super Market Ltd 3536 Harding Ave *Web:* www.foodland.com	Honolulu	HI	96816	808-732-0791	737-6952
Foods of All Nations 2121 Ivy Rd *Web:* www.foodsofallnations.com	Charlottesville	VA	22903	434-296-6131	
Fowler Foods Inc 139 Southwest Dr *Web:* www.wfowler.com	Jonesboro	AR	72401	870-935-6032	
Freed'S Super Markets Inc 2024 Swamp Pk *Web:* freedsmarket.com	Gilbertsville	PA	19525	610-326-4189	
Fresh Encounter Inc 317 W Main Cross St *Web:* www.freshencounter.com	Findlay	OH	45840	419-422-8090	424-3932
FreshDirect Inc 23-30 Borden Ave *TF:* 866-511-1240 ■ *Web:* www.freshdirect.com	Long Island City	NY	11101	718-928-1000	
Frontera Foods Inc 449 N Clark St Ste 205 *TF:* 800-509-4441 ■ *Web:* www.fronterafiesta.com	Chicago	IL	60654	312-595-1624	
Fry's Food Stores of Arizona Inc 500 S 99th Ave **Fax Area Code:* 623 ■ *TF:* 866-221-4141 ■ *Web:* www.frysfood.com	Tolleson	AZ	85353	866-221-4141	907-4966*
Fuel South Inc 3020 Harris Rd	Waycross	GA	31503	912-284-0264	
G & J Land & Marine Food Distributors 506 Front St *Web:* www.gjfood.com	Morgan City	LA	70380	985-385-2620	
G & W Foods Inc 2041 Railroad Dr *Web:* gwfoodsinc.com	Willow Springs	MO	65793	417-469-4000	
Gary & Leos Inc 730 First St *Web:* garyandleos.com	Havre	MT	59501	406-265-1404	
GE Foodland Inc 1105 E Beltline Rd *Web:* elrodscostplus.com	Carrollton	TX	75006	972-245-0470	
Gelson's Markets 2020 S Central Ave *Web:* www.gelsons.com	Compton	CA	90220	310-638-2842	631-0950
Gerland Corp 3131 Pawnee St *Web:* www.gerlands.com	Houston	TX	77054	713-746-3600	746-3621
GermanDeli.com 601 Westport Pkwy, Ste 100 *Web:* www.germandeli.com	Grapevine	TX	76051	817-410-9955	421-5617
Gerrity's Supermarket Inc 950 N S Rd *Web:* www.gerritys.com	Scranton	PA	18504	570-342-4144	
Giant Eagle Inc 101 Kappa Dr *TF Cust Svc:* 800-553-2324 ■ *Web:* www.gianteagle.com	Pittsburgh	PA	15238	412-963-6200	968-1615
Giant Food Inc 8301 Professional Pl Ste 115 **Fax Area Code:* 301 ■ **Fax:* Cust Svc ■ *TF:* 888-469-4426 ■ *Web:* www.giantfood.com	Landover	MD	20785	888-469-4426	618-4998*
Giant Food Stores Inc 1149 Harrisburg Pike **Fax:* Mail Rm ■ *TF:* 888-814-4268 ■ *Web:* www.giantfoodstores.com	Carlisle	PA	17013	717-249-4000	960-1356*
Gold Standard Baking Inc 3700 S Kedzie Ave Ste A *Web:* www.gsbaking.com	Chicago	IL	60632	773-523-2333	
Golub Corp 461 Nott St **Fax Area Code:* 518 ■ *TF:* 800-666-7667 ■ *Web:* pricechopper.com	Schenectady	NY	12308	800-666-7667	379-3515*
Goodsons' Supermarkets Inc US Rt 52	Welch	WV	24801	304-436-8481	
Gordys County Market Downtown 212 Bay St *Web:* www.gordysinc.com	Chippewa Falls	WI	54729	715-726-2500	
GPM Investments LLC 8565 Magellan Pkwy Ste 400 *Web:* www.fasmart.com	Richmond	VA	23227	804-730-1568	
Grade A Markets Inc 563 Newfield Ave *Web:* shoprite.com	Stamford	CT	06905	203-356-1662	961-8135
Grandma's Bakery Inc 1765 Buerkle Rd *Web:* www.grandmasbakery.com	White Bear Lake	MN	55110	651-779-0707	
Greenleaf Inc 1955 Jerrold Ave *Web:* www.greenleafsf.com	San Francisco	CA	94124	415-647-2991	
GreenLine Foods Inc 4575 W Main St PO Box 727 *Web:* www.greenlinefoods.com	Guadalupe	CA	93434	419-353-2326	
Groupon Inc 600 W Chicago Ave Ste 620 *Web:* www.groupon.com	Chicago	IL	60654	312-676-5773	676-2728
Gs Foods Inc 5925 S Alcoa Ave *TF:* 800-273-6637 ■ *Web:* www.gsfoods.com	Vernon	CA	90058	323-581-6161	589-2106
Haggen Inc 2900 Woburn St *Web:* www.haggen.com	Bellingham	WA	98226	360-676-5300	
Hancock County Co-op Oil Assn 245 State St *TF:* 800-924-2667 ■ *Web:* www.hancockcountycoop.com	Garner	IA	50438	641-923-2635	
Harmons Grocery 3540 South 4000 West *Web:* www.harmonsgrocery.com	West Valley City	UT	84120	801-969-8261	964-1299
Harps Food Stores Inc 918 S Gutensohn Rd *TF:* 877-772-8193 ■ *Web:* www.harpsfood.com	Springdale	AR	72762	479-751-7601	751-3625
Harris Teeter Inc 701 Crestdale Rd PO Box 10100 *TF Cust Svc:* 800-432-6111 ■ *Web:* www.harristeeter.com	Matthews	NC	28105	704-844-3100	
Hastings Co-op Creamery Co 1701 Vermillion St PO Box 217 *Web:* www.hastingscreamery.com	Hastings	MN	55033	651-437-9414	437-3547
Heinen's Inc 4540 Richmond Rd **Fax Area Code:* 216 ■ *Web:* www.heinens.com	Cleveland	OH	44128	855-475-2300	514-4788*
Hennings Super Market Inc 290 Main St *Web:* henningsmarket.com	Harleysville	PA	19438	215-256-9533	
Herb Pharm LLC 20260 Williams Hwy *Web:* www.herb-pharm.com	Williams	OR	97544	541-846-6262	
Hi Nabor Supermarket Inc 7201 Winbourne Ave *Web:* hinabor.com	Baton Rouge	LA	70805	225-357-1448	
Highland Park Market of Farmington LLC 317 Highland St *Web:* www.highlandparkmarket.com	Manchester	CT	06040	860-646-4277	
Holly Poultry Inc 2221 Berlin St *TF:* 800-342-9464 ■ *Web:* www.hollypoultry.com	Baltimore	MD	21230	410-727-6210	
Hollywood Super Market Inc 2670 W Maple Rd PO Box 1286 *Web:* hollywoodmarkets.com	Troy	MI	48084	248-643-6770	643-0309
Homeland Stores 5857 Northwest Expy *Web:* www.homelandstores.com	Oklahoma City	OK	73132	405-721-6721	
Honey Baked Ham Company of Ohio 11935 Mason Montgomery Rd *Web:* www.honeybaked.com	Cincinnati	OH	45249	513-583-9700	
Hornbacher's 2510 N Broadway *Web:* www.hornbachers.com	Fargo	ND	58102	701-293-5444	293-8770
Houchens Industries Inc 700 Church St *Web:* houchensindustries.com	Bowling Green	KY	42101	270-843-3252	
House of Webster Inc, The 1013 N Second St *Web:* www.houseofwebster.com	Rogers	AR	72756	479-636-4640	
Hyatts Market Inc 70 Mchann Rd	Addison	AL	35540	256-747-6005	
IGA Inc 8725 W Higgins Rd Ste 350 *TF:* 800-321-5442 ■ *Web:* www.iga.com	Chicago	IL	60631	773-693-4520	693-4533
Ingles Markets Inc 2913 US Hwy 70 W *NASDAQ: IMKTA* ■ *TF:* 800-635-5066 ■ *Web:* www.ingles-markets.com	Black Mountain	NC	28711	828-669-2941	669-3536
International Bakers Service Inc 1902 N Sheridan St *Web:* www.internationalbakers.com	South Bend	IN	46628	574-287-7111	
International Gourmet Foods Inc 7520 Fullerton Rd *Web:* www.igf-inc.com	Springfield	VA	22153	703-569-4520	
International Plastics Inc 185 Commerce Ctr *Web:* interplas.com	Greenville	SC	29615	864-297-8000	

Company	City	State	Zip	Phone	Fax
InVite Health Inc One Garden State Plz *TF:* 800-349-0929 ■ *Web:* www.invitehealth.com	Paramus	NJ	07652	201-587-2222	
Ira Higdon 150 IGA WAY PO Box 488 *Web:* irahigdongc.com	Cairo	GA	39828	229-377-1272	377-8756
JA Mktg Inc 18160 Cottonwood Rd.	Sun River	OR	97707	541-593-8113	
Jafco Foods 820 Turnpike St *Web:* www.jafcofoods.com	North Andover	MA	01845	978-989-0012	
Jamac Frozen Foods 570 Grand St. *Web:* www.jamacfrozenfoods.com	Jersey City	NJ	07302	201-333-6200	
Jamba Juice Co 6475 Christie Ave Ste 150 *Web:* www.jambajuice.com	Emeryville	CA	94608	510-596-0100	
Jerry's Foods 5125 Vernon Ave S. *Web:* www.jerrysfoods.com	Edina	MN	55436	952-929-2685	
Jerry's Supermarkets Inc 532 W Jefferson Blvd *Web:* www.supermarket.com	Dallas	TX	75208	214-941-8110	948-1360
JJ Cassone Bakery Inc 202 S Regent St. *Web:* www.jjcassonebakery.com	Port Chester	NY	10573	914-939-1568	
Joe Caputo & Sons Inc 959 E Oakton St. *Web:* www.joecaputoandsons.com	Des Plaines	IL	60018	847-827-6700	
Jons International Market Place 5315 Santa Monica Blvd. *Web:* www.jonsmarketplace.com	Los Angeles	CA	90029	323-460-4646	
JSB Industries Inc 130 Crescent Ave. *TF:* 800-554-2887 ■ *Web:* www.muffintown.com	Chelsea	MA	02150	617-846-1565	
K-VA-T Food Stores Inc PO Box 1158 *TF:* 800-826-8451 ■ *Web:* www.foodcity.com	Abingdon	VA	24212	276-623-5100	623-5441
Karns Quality Foods Ltd 6001 Allentown Blvd. *Web:* www.karns.com	Harrisburg	PA	17112	717-545-4731	
Kennies Market Inc 217 W Middle St. *Web:* www.kenniesmarket.com	Gettysburg	PA	17325	717-334-2179	
Kessler's Food & Liquor 621 Sixth Ave SE *Web:* kesslersgrocery.com	Aberdeen	SD	57401	605-225-1692	
King Kullen Grocery Company Inc 185 Central Ave *Web:* www.kingkullen.com	Bethpage	NY	11714	516-733-7100	827-6325
Kirby Foods Inc 4102-B Fieldstone Rd PO Box 6268 *Web:* www.kirbyfoods.com	Champaign	IL	61826	217-352-2600	352-9394
Klass Ingredients Inc 3885 N Buffalo St. *Web:* www.klassingredients.com	Orchard Park	NY	14127	716-662-6665	662-0285
KM Supermarkets Inc 851 Marketplace Dr *Web:* www.mackenthuns.com	Waconia	MN	55387	952-442-2512	
Kobayashi Travel Service 650 Iwilei Road *Web:* www.kobay.com	Honolulu	HI	96817	808-593-9387	
Kowalski Companies Inc 1261 Grand Ave. *Web:* www.kowalskis.com	St. Paul	MN	55105	651-698-3366	
Krist Oil Co 303 Selden Rd *Web:* www.kristoil.com	Iron River	MI	49935	906-265-6144	
Kroger Co 1014 Vine St. *NYSE: KR* ■ *TF:* 800-576-4377 ■ *Web:* www.kroger.com	Cincinnati	OH	45202	513-762-4000	
KTA Super Stores 321 Keawe St. *Web:* ktastores.com	Hilo	HI	96720	808-935-3751	
Kuukpik Corp PO Box 89187 *TF:* 866-480-6220 ■ *Web:* www.kuukpik.com	Nuiqsut	AK	99789	907-480-6220	
La Cena Fine Foods Ltd Four Rosol Ln. *Web:* www.lacenafoods.com	Saddle Brook	NJ	07663	201-797-4600	
La Fortaleza Inc 501 N Ford Blvd. *Web:* www.la-fortaleza.com	Los Angeles	CA	90022	323-261-1211	
La Michoacana Meat Market Inc 4717 Telephone Rd. *Web:* www.lamichoacanameatmarket.com	Houston	TX	77087	713-645-4202	
La Valle Food Co 10 Henry St Ste 1 *Web:* www.lavallefoodsusa.com	Teterboro	NJ	07608	201-462-0300	
Lake Erie Frozen Foods Co 1830 Orange Rd *Web:* www.leffco.net	Ashland	OH	44805	419-289-9204	
Landis Supermarket Inc 2685 County Line Rd. *Web:* www.landismarket.com	Telford	PA	18969	215-723-1157	
Leevers Foods 501 Main St *Web:* www.leeversfoods.com	Cavalier	ND	58220	701-265-4011	
Leevers Supermarkets Inc 2195 N Hwy 83 Unit AA *Web:* www.leevers.com	Franktown	CO	80116	303-814-8646	814-8645
Life Force International Corp 495 Raleigh Ave *TF:* 800-531-4877 ■ *Web:* lifeforce.net	El Cajon	CA	92064	858-218-3200	
Lion Supermarket 1710 Tully Rd *Web:* www.lionsupermarket.com	San Jose	CA	95122	408-238-4451	
Loblaw Cos Ltd One President's Choice Cir *TF:* 888-495-5111 ■ *Web:* www.loblaw.com	Brampton	ON	L6Y5S5	905-459-2500	861-2387
Loblaws Inc 12 St Clair Ave E Ste 1901 *Web:* www.loblaws.ca	Toronto	ON	M4T1L7	416-960-8108	
Lorann Oils 4518 Aurelius Rd *Web:* www.lorannoils.com	Lansing	MI	48910	517-882-0215	
Lowe's 1804 Hall Ave PO Box 1430 *Web:* www.lowesmarket.com	Littlefield	TX	79339	806-385-3366	385-8629
Lowes Food Stores Inc 1381 Old Mill Cir Ste 200 *TF:* 800-669-5693 ■ *Web:* www.lowesfoods.com	Winston-Salem	NC	27103	336-659-0180	768-4702
Lund Food Holdings Inc 4100 W 50th St	Edina	MN	55424	952-927-3663	
Marjon Specialty Foods Inc 3508 Sydney Rd. *Web:* www.marjonspecialtyfoods.com	Plant City	FL	33567	813-752-3482	

Company	City	State	Zip	Phone	Fax
Market Basket Inc, The 813 Franklin Lakes Rd *Web:* www.marketbasket.com	Franklin Lakes	NJ	07417	201-891-2000	
Market Day Corp 555 W Pierce Rd Ste 200 *TF:* 877-632-7753 ■ *Web:* www.marketday.com	Itasca	IL	60143	630-285-1470	285-3340
Market Grocery Co 16 Forest Pkwy Bldg K. *Web:* www.marketgrocery.com	Forest Park	GA	30297	404-361-8620	361-3773
Market Hall Foods 5655 College Ave Ste 201 *Web:* www.rockridgemarkethall.com	Oakland	CA	94618	510-250-6000	
Mars Supermarkets Inc 9627 Philadelphia Rd *Web:* www.marsfood.com	Rosedale	MD	21237	410-590-0500	
Martin & Bayley Inc 1311 A W Main *TF:* 800-876-2511 ■ *Web:* www.martinandbayley.com	Carmi	IL	62821	618-382-2334	382-8956
Martin's Marketplace 130 Tichenal Way *Web:* martinsmarketplace.com	Cashmere	WA	98815	509-782-3801	782-2212
McClancy Seasoning Co One Spice Rd *TF:* 800-843-1968 ■ *Web:* www.mcclancy.com	Fort Mill	SC	29707	803-548-2366	
McFarling Foods Inc 333 W 14th St *Web:* www.mcfarling.com	Indianapolis	IN	46202	317-635-2633	
Mckeever Enterprises Inc 4216 S Hocker Dr	Independence	MO	64055	816-478-3095	
Meijer Inc 2929 Walker Ave NW *TF:* 800-543-3704 ■ *Web:* www.meijer.com	Grand Rapids	MI	49544	616-453-6711	791-2572
Meijer Stores Inc 2929 Walker Ave NW *TF:* 800-543-3704 ■ *Web:* www.meijer.com	Grand Rapids	MI	49544	616-453-6711	791-5131
Merchants Grocery Co 800 Maddox Dr PO Box 1268 *TF:* 877-897-9893 ■ *Web:* www.merchants-grocery.com	Culpeper	VA	22701	540-825-0786	825-9016
Metabolic Maintenance Products Inc 68994 N Pine St *Web:* www.metabolicmaintenance.com	Sisters	OR	97759	541-549-7800	
Milam's Market 11 N Royal Poinciana Blvd Ste 100 *Web:* www.milamsmarkets.com	Miami Springs	FL	33166	305-884-4870	
Milford Markets Inc Dba Shoprite of Milford 155 Cherry St	Milford	CT	06460	203-882-5280	
Miner'S Inc 5065 Miller Trunk Hwy *Web:* superonefoods.com	Hermantown	MN	55811	218-729-5882	
Mississippi Market Natural Foods Coop 1500 W Seventh St *Web:* www.msmarket.coop	Saint Paul	MN	55102	651-690-0507	
Montalvan Sales Inc 2225 S Castle Harbour Pl *Web:* www.montalvans.com	Ontario	CA	91761	909-930-5670	
Morasch Meats Inc 4050 NE 158th Ave *Web:* moraschmeats.com	Portland	OR	97230	503-257-9821	
Mother's Market & Kitchen 1890 Newport Blvd *Web:* www.mothersmarket.com	Costa Mesa	CA	92627	949-631-4741	
Mountain Fresh Supermarket 2203 SR- 118	Hunlock Creek	PA	18621	570-477-2988	
National Fruit Flavor Company Inc 935 Edwards Ave *Web:* www.nationalfruitflavor.com	New Orleans	LA	70123	504-733-6757	
Natural Healthy Concepts 310 N Westhill Blvd *Web:* www.naturalhealthyconcepts.com	Appleton	WI	54914	920-968-2350	
Nature's Best 6 Pt Dr Ste 300 *TF:* 800-800-7799 ■ *Web:* www.naturesbest.net	Brea	CA	92821	714-255-4600	255-4691
New French Bakery Inc, The 828 Kasota Ave SE *Web:* www.newfrenchbakery.com	Minneapolis	MN	55414	612-455-7500	
New Leaf Community Markets Inc 1101 Pacific Ave. *Web:* www.newleaf.com	Santa Cruz	CA	95060	831-466-9060	
Newport Avenue Market 1121 Nw Newport Ave *Web:* www.newportavemarket.com	Bend	OR	97701	541-382-3940	
Nino Salvaggio International Marketplace 27900 Harper Ave. *Web:* www.ninosalvaggio.com	St Clair Shores	MI	48081	586-778-3650	
Norman Bros Produce Inc 7621 SW 87th Ave *Web:* www.normanbrothers.com	Miami	FL	33173	305-274-9363	596-4541
Norrenberns Foods Inc 205 E Harnett St	Mascoutah	IL	62258	618-566-7010	566-2366
Northgate Gonzalez Inc 1201 N Magnolia Ave *Web:* www.northgatemarkets.com	Anaheim	CA	92801	714-778-3784	778-3295
Nova Produce LP 3380 Woods Edge Cir Ste 102 *Web:* www.novaproduce.com	Bonita Springs	FL	34134	239-444-1140	
Novelty Inc 351 W Muskegon Dr *Web:* www.noveltyinc.com	Greenfield	IN	46140	317-462-3121	
Nugget Markets 157 Main St. *Web:* www.nuggetmarket.com	Woodland	CA	95695	530-662-5479	668-1246
Nutrition Formulators Inc 10407 N Commerce Pkwy *Web:* www.nutritionformulators.com	Miramar	FL	33025	954-272-2220	
Oasis Foods Inc 2222 Kirkman St	Lake Charles	LA	70601	337-439-5262	
Oceana Natural Foods Coop 159 Se Second St *Web:* www.oceanafoods.org	Newport	OR	97365	541-265-8285	
Oleson's Foods Inc 3850 N Long Lk Rd Ste A *Web:* www.olesonsfoods.com	Traverse City	MI	49684	231-947-6510	
Orange Street Food Farm 701 S Orange St *Web:* orangestreetfoodfarm.com	Missoula	MT	59801	406-543-3188	
Orcas International Inc Nine Lenel Rd *Web:* www.orcas-intl.com	Landing	NJ	07850	973-448-2801	
Organic Avenue LLC 116 Suffolk St *Web:* www.organicavenue.com	New York	NY	10002	212-358-0500	
Osborne Bros 201 Eddings Ln *Web:* osbornefoods.com	Nashville	TN	37214	615-885-7338	

Company	City	State	ZIP	Phone	Fax
Our Time Ltd 2100 Dorr St *Web:* www.ourtime.com	Toledo	OH	43607	419-537-1666	
Overwaitea Food Group 19855 92A Ave *TF:* 800-242-9229 ■ *Web:* www.owfg.com	Langley	BC	V1M3B6	604-888-1213	
Pacific Supermarket Inc 1420 Southgate Ave *Web:* www.pacificsuper.com	Daly City	CA	94015	650-994-1688	
Peapod LLC 9933 Woods Dr *TF:* 800-573-2763 ■ *Web:* www.peapod.com	Skokie	IL	60077	847-583-9400	583-9494
Penn Dutch Foods 3201 N State Rd 7 *Web:* www.penn-dutch.com	Margate	FL	33063	954-974-3900	
People's Food Co-op 315 Fifth Ave S *Web:* www.peoplesfoodcoop.com	La Crosse	WI	54601	608-784-5798	
Perlmart Inc 954 Rt 166 *Web:* shoprite.com	Toms River	NJ	08753	732-341-0700	240-9291
Petrey W L Wholesale Company Inc 10345 Petrey Hwy *Web:* www.petrey.com	Luverne	AL	36049	334-230-5674	335-2422
Pick N Save 6950 W State St *Web:* www.picknsave.com	Wauwatosa	WI	53213	414-475-7181	
Piggly Wiggly Carolina Company Inc PO Box 118047 *TF:* 800-243-9880 ■ *Web:* thepig.net	Charleston	SC	29423	843-554-9880	745-2730
Piggly Wiggly Midwest LLC 2215 Union Ave *Web:* pigglywiggly.com	Sheboygan	WI	53081	920-457-4433	
Plum Market Corp 30777 Northwestern Hwy Ste 301 *Web:* www.plummarket.com	Farmington Hills	MI	48334	248-706-1600	
Pressed Juicery LLC 1550 17Th St *Web:* www.pressedjuicery.com	Santa Monica	CA	90404	310-477-7171	
Provigo Inc 400 Ave Suite Croix *Web:* www.provigo.ca	Saint-laurent	QC	H4L5P3	514-383-3000	
Public Market of Newington LLC 437 New Britain Ave *Web:* publicmarketnewington.com	Newington	CT	06111	860-667-1454	
Publix Super Markets Inc 3300 Publix Corporate Pkwy **Fax:* Hum Res ■ *TF PR:* 800-242-1227 ■ *Web:* www.publix.com	Lakeland	FL	33811	863-688-1188	284-5532*
Pumper's Premium Stores Inc 4931 Earle Morris Hwy *Web:* www.pumperspremium.com	Easley	SC	29642	864-306-2999	
Pure Essence Laboratories Inc 6155 S Sandhill Rd Ste 200 *Web:* www.pureessencelabs.com	Las Vegas	NV	89120	702-990-7400	
Rainbow Grocery Co-op Inc 1745 Folsom St *Web:* rainbow.coop	San Francisco	CA	94103	415-863-0620	
Raley's 500 W Capitol Ave PO Box 15618 **Fax:* Cust Svc ■ *TF:* 800-925-9989 ■ *Web:* www.raleys.com	Sacramento	CA	95852	916-373-3333	373-0881*
Ralphs Grocery Co 1014 Vine Street **Fax Area Code:* 310 ■ *TF Cust Svc:* 800-576-4377 ■ *Web:* www.ralphs.com	Cincinnati,	OH	45202	800-576-4377	884-2648*
Real Food Company Inc 3060 Fillmore St *Web:* www.realfoodco.com	San Francisco	CA	94123	415-567-6900	
Redner's Markets Inc 3 Quarry Rd *TF:* 888-673-4663 ■ *Web:* www.rednersmarkets.com	Reading	PA	19605	610-926-3700	926-6327
Reliable Self-Service Market 36 Circuit Av PO Box 542 *Web:* thereliablemarket.com	Oak Bluffs	MA	02557	508-693-1102	
Remke Markets Inc 1299 Cox Ave *Web:* www.remkes.com	Erlanger	KY	41018	859-594-3400	594-3488
Resource Plus 9636 Heckscher Dr *TF:* 888-678-8966 ■ *Web:* www.resourcep.com	Jacksonville	FL	32226	888-678-8966	
RF Owens Company Inc 1062 Broadway *Web:* www.trucchis.com	Raynham	MA	02767	508-824-7514	824-7576
Rhema Health Products Ltd 1751 Brigantine Dr *Web:* www.rhemahealthproducts.com	Coquitlam	BC	V3K7B4	604-516-0199	
Rice Epicurean Markets Inc 5333 Gulfton St *Web:* www.riceepicurean.com	Houston	TX	77081	713-662-7700	662-7757
Rico Foods Inc 578 E 19th St *Web:* www.ricofood.com	Paterson	NJ	07514	973-278-0589	
Riedel Marketing Group 5327 E Pinchot Ave *Web:* 4rmg.com	Phoenix	AZ	85018	602-840-4948	
Riesbeck Food Markets Inc 48661 National Rd *Web:* www.riesbeckfoods.com	Saint Clairsville	OH	43950	740-695-7050	695-7555
Road Ranger LLC 4930 E State St PO Box 4745 *Web:* www.roadrangerusa.com	Rockford	IL	61108	815-387-1700	387-7884
Roasterie Inc, The 1204 W 27th St *TF:* 800-376-0245 ■ *Web:* www.theroasterie.com	Kansas City	MO	64108	816-931-4000	
Roche Bros Supermarkets Inc 70 Hastings St *Web:* rochebros.com	Wellesley Hills	MA	02481	781-235-9400	235-3153
Rochester Meat Co 1825 Seventh St NW *Web:* www.rochestermeat.com	Rochester	MN	55901	507-529-4700	
Rock Cave IGA Junction of Rt 4 and Rt 20 *Web:* www.rockcaveiga.com	Rock Cave	WV	26234	304-924-5296	
Rockdale Grocery Inc 994 Institute St NW *Web:* www.pigglywiggly-atl.com	Conyers	GA	30012	770-922-9209	
Ronetco Supermarkets Inc Morris Canal Plz - 1070 Rt 46	Ledgewood	NJ	07852	973-927-8300	
Rosauers Super Markets Inc 1815 W Garland Ave *Web:* www.rosauers.com	Spokane	WA	99205	509-326-8900	328-2483
Rouse's Enterprises LLC 1301 Saint Mary St *Web:* www.rouses.com	Thibodaux	LA	70301	985-447-5998	
Royals Food Town 135 South Main *Web:* royalsfoodtown.com	Loa	UT	84747	435-836-2841	
Sacramento Natural Foods Cooperative Inc 1900 Alhambra Blvd *Web:* www.sacfoodcoop.com	Sacramento	CA	95816	916-455-2667	
Safeway Inc 5918 Stoneridge Mall Rd *NYSE:* SWY ■ *Web:* www.safeway.com	Pleasanton	CA	94588	925-467-3000	467-3323
Sage V Foods LLC 12100 Wilshire Blvd Ste 605 *Web:* www.sagevfoods.com	Los Angeles	CA	90025	310-820-4496	
Santos Enterprises 5400 Alameda Ave *Web:* www.foodcityep.com	El Paso	TX	79905	915-779-3641	
Save Mart Supermarkets Inc PO Box 4278 *Web:* www.savemart.com	Modesto	CA	95352	209-577-1600	
Save-A-Lot Ltd 100 Corporate Office Dr *TF General:* 800-346-3808 ■ *Web:* www.save-a-lot.com	Earth City	MO	63045	314-592-9100	592-9619
Schnuck Markets Inc 11420 Lackland Rd *TF:* 800-264-4400 ■ *Web:* www.schnucks.com	Saint Louis	MO	63146	314-994-9900	994-4465
Scolari's Food & Drug Co 950 Holman Way *TF:* 800-219-7401 ■ *Web:* www.scolaristores.com	Sparks	NV	89431	775-575-1381	
Seashore Food Distributors Inc One Satt Blvd *Web:* www.seashorefood.com	Rio Grande	NJ	08242	609-886-3100	
Sedano's Supermarkets 3140 W 76 St *Web:* www.sedanos.com	Hialeah	FL	33018	305-824-1034	556-6981
Shady Maple Farm Market Inc 1324 Main St *Web:* www.shady-maple.com	East Earl	PA	17519	717-354-4981	
Sharp Shopper 2475 S Main St Ste A *Web:* www.sharpshopper.net	Harrisonburg	VA	22801	540-434-8848	
Sharp Shopper Inc 1100 Sharp Ave *Web:* sharpshopper.net	Ephrata	PA	17522	717-733-9555	
Shop 'n Save 10461 Manchester Rd **Fax:* Hum Res ■ *TF:* 800-428-6974 ■ *Web:* www.shopnsave.com	Kirkwood	MO	63122	314-984-0900	984-1350*
Shoppers Food & Pharmacy 10501 Martin Luther King Jr Hwy *TF:* 800-866-0514 ■ *Web:* www.shoppersfood.com	Bowie	MD	20720	240-544-0180	544-0187
ShopRite PO Box 7812 **Fax Area Code:* 732 ■ *TF:* 800-746-7748 ■ *Web:* www.shoprite.com	Edison	NJ	08818	800-746-7748	251-9519*
ShopRite Supermarkets Inc 600 York St *TF:* 800-746-7748 ■ *Web:* www.shoprite.com	Elizabeth	NJ	07207	908-527-3300	
Shun Fat Supermarket Inc 421 N Atlantic Blvd *Web:* www.shunfatsupermarket.com	Monterey Park	CA	91754	626-308-3998	
Silva International Inc 523 N Ash St *Web:* silva-intl.com	Momence	IL	60954	815-472-3535	
Simek's Inc 940 Hastings Ave *Web:* www.simeks.com	Saint Paul Park	MN	55071	651-459-5578	
Skogens Foodliner Inc 237 Second Ave S *Web:* www.fastfoods.com	Onalaska	WI	54650	608-783-5500	
Smart & Final Inc 600 Citadel Dr *TF:* 800-894-0511 ■ *Web:* www.smartandfinal.com	Commerce	CA	90040	323-869-7500	869-7865
Sobeys Inc 115 King St *Web:* www.sobeys.com	Stellarton	NS	B0K1S0	902-752-8371	
Speedee Mart 8011 Mission Gorge Rd Ste A *Web:* www.speedeemart.net	Santee	CA	92071	619-448-1036	
Spivey Enterprises Inc 6148 Brookshire Blvd *Web:* www.quikshoppe.com	Charlotte	NC	28216	704-399-4802	393-1940
Starco Impex Inc 2710 S 11th St **Fax Area Code:* 888 ■ *TF:* 866-740-9601 ■ *Web:* www.starcoimpex.com	Beaumont	TX	77701	866-740-9601	842-5650*
Stater Bros Markets Inc 301 S Tippecanoe Ave *Web:* www.staterbros.com	San Bernardino	CA	92408	909-733-5000	
Sterling Extract Company Inc 10929 Franklin Ave Ste V *Web:* www.sterlingextractcompany.com	Franklin Park	IL	60131	847-451-9728	
Stop & Shop Supermarket Co 1385 Hancock St **Fax Area Code:* 617 ■ **Fax:* Hum Res ■ *Web:* www.stopandshop.com	Quincy	MA	02169	781-397-0006	770-8190*
Strack & Van Til Super Market Inc 9632 Cline Ave *Web:* www.strackandvantil.com	Highland	IN	46322	219-924-6932	
Sullivan's Foods 425 First St *Web:* www.sullivansfoods.net	Savanna	IL	61074	815-273-4511	
Sunnyway Foods Inc 212 N Antrim Way *Web:* www.sunnywayfoods.com	Greencastle	PA	17225	717-597-7121	
Sunset Food Mart Inc 1812 Green Bay Rd *Web:* sunsetfoods.com	Highland Park	IL	60035	847-432-5500	432-9335
Sunshine Market Inc 2901 Campbell Ave *Web:* sunshinemarket.com	Lynchburg	VA	24501	434-846-7862	
Sunterra Quality Food Markets Inc 1851 Sirocco Dr SW Ste 200 *Web:* www.sunterramarket.com	Calgary	AB	T3H4R5	403-266-2820	
Super A Foods 7200 Dominion Cir *Web:* www.superafoods.com	Commerce	CA	90040	323-869-0600	722-0911
Super H Mart Inc 2550 Pleasant Hill Rd *TF:* 877-427-7386 ■ *Web:* www.hmart.com	Duluth	GA	30096	678-543-4000	
Super King Market 2 2716 N San Fernando Rd *Web:* www.superkingmarkets.com	Los Angeles	CA	90065	323-225-0044	
Supermercado Mi Tierra LLC 9520 International Blvd *Web:* supermercadomitierra.com	Oakland	CA	94603	510-567-8617	
Supermercados Selectos Inc HC 80 Box 7305 *Web:* www.selectospr.com	Dorado	PR	00646	787-275-2165	
SUPERVALU Inc 7075 Flying Cloud Dr *NYSE:* SVU ■ *TF Cust Svc:* 877-322-8228 ■ *Web:* www.supervalu.com	Eden Prairie	MN	55344	952-828-4000	
Supreme Mfg Company Inc Five Connerty Ct *TF:* 800-772-7632 ■ *Web:* www.supreme-mfg.com	East Brunswick	NJ	08816	732-254-0087	
Sure Save Supermarkets Ltd 16-128 Orchid Land Dr *Web:* www.suresave.com	Keaau	HI	96749	808-966-9009	966-6200
Synergy Worldwide Inc 2162 W Grove Pkwy Ste 100 *Web:* us.synergyworldwide.com	Pleasant Grove	UT	84062	801-769-7800	

	City	State	ZIP	Phone	Fax
Tamura Superette Inc 86-032 Farrington Hwy *Web:* tamurasupermarket.com	Waianae	HI	96792	808-696-3321	696-8127
Tate's Bake Shop Inc 43 N Sea Rd *Web:* www.tatesbakeshop.com	Southampton	NY	11968	631-283-9830	
Tates Supermarket Inc 120 Fourth St *Web:* tatesmarket.com	Clymer	PA	15728	724-254-4420	
Theodoro Baking Company Inc 6038 N Lindbergh Blvd *Web:* www.theodorobaking.com	Hazelwood	MO	63042	314-731-3777	
Thruway Food Market & Shopping Ctr 78 Oak St *Web:* www.shopthruway.com	Walden	NY	12586	845-778-3535	
Thurland Reay Family Investment Co 2100 N Kolb Rd *Web:* www.reaysranchinvestors.com	Tucson	AZ	85715	520-298-2391	
Tilton Market Inc 1524 Tilton Rd *Web:* tiltonmarket.com	Northfield	NJ	08225	609-641-5118	
Titan Foods Incorporated Supermarket 2556 31st St Ste 1 *Web:* www.titanfood.com	Astoria	NY	11102	718-626-7771	
Tom's Food Markets 738 Munson Ave *Web:* www.toms-foodmarkets.com	Traverse City	MI	49686	231-947-7175	
Tony's Finer Foods Inc 3607 W Fullerton Ave *Web:* www.tonysfinerfood.com	Chicago	IL	60647	773-278-8355	
Tops Industries Inc 797 Twin View Blvd	Redding	CA	96003	530-242-0200	
Total Wine & More 11325 Seven Locks Rd Ste 214 *Web:* www.totalwine.com	Potomac	MD	20854	301-795-1000	
Town & Country Markets Inc 20148 Tenth Ave NE *Web:* central-market.com	Poulsbo	WA	98370	360-779-1881	
Trader Joe's Co 800 S Shamrock Ave *Web:* www.traderjoes.com	Monrovia	CA	91016	626-599-3700	
Treasure Island Foods Inc 3460 N Broadway *Web:* www.tifoods.com	Chicago	IL	60657	773-327-4265	
Tribeca Oven Inc 447 Gotham Pkwy *Web:* tribecaoven.com	Carlstadt	NJ	07072	201-935-8800	
Ukrop's Super Markets Inc 2001 Maywill St Ste 100 *Web:* www.ukropshomestylefoods.com	Richmond	VA	23230	804-340-3000	
United Coop N7160 Raceway Rd *Web:* www.unitedcooperative.com	Beaver Dam	WI	53916	920-887-1756	
United Supermarkets Ltd 7830 Orlando Ave *Web:* www.unitedtexas.com	Lubbock	TX	79423	806-791-0220	791-7476
United Supermarkets of Oklahoma Inc 600 E Broadway St *Web:* www.unitedok.com	Altus	OK	73521	580-482-1184	
Uwajimaya Inc 600 Fifth Ave S *Web:* www.uwajimaya.com	Seattle	WA	98104	206-624-6248	405-2996
Value Added Products Coop 2101 College Blvd *Web:* www.vapcoop.com	Alva	OK	73717	580-327-0400	
Village Pantry LLC 9800 Crosspoint Blvd *Web:* www.marsh.net	Indianapolis	IN	46256	317-594-2100	
Village Super Market Inc 733 Mountain Ave *NASDAQ: VLGEA* ■ *TF:* 800-746-7748 ■ *Web:* www.shoprite.com	Springfield	NJ	07081	973-467-2200	467-6582
Vita Coco 38 W 21St St *Web:* www.vitacoco.com	New York	NY	10010	212-206-0763	
Vita Health Products Inc 150 Beghin Ave *Web:* www.vitahealth.ca	Winnipeg	MB	R2J3W2	204-661-8386	663-8386
VitaDigest.com 20687-2 Amar Rd Ste 258 *TF:* 877-848-2168 ■ *Web:* www.vitadigest.com	Walnut	CA	91789	877-848-2168	
Vyse Gelatin Co 5010 Rose St *Web:* www.vyse.com	Schiller Park	IL	60176	847-678-4780	
Waldbaums Two Paragon Dr *TF:* 866-443-7374 ■ *Web:* waldbaums.apsupermarket.com	Montvale	NJ	07645	866-443-7374	
Walts Food Centers 16145 S State St *Web:* www.waltsfoods.com	South Holland	IL	60473	708-333-5500	
Warrenton Oil Co 2299 S Spoede *Web:* www.fastlane-cstore.com	Truesdale	MO	63383	636-456-3346	
Wedge Community Co-Op Inc 2105 Lyndale Ave S *TF:* 800-535-4555 ■ *Web:* www.wedge.coop	Minneapolis	MN	55405	612-871-3993	871-0734
Wegmans Food Markets Inc 1500 Brooks Ave PO Box 30844 **Fax:* Mail Rm ■ *TF:* 800-934-6267 ■ *Web:* www.wegmans.com	Rochester	NY	14603	585-328-2550	464-4626*
Weis Markets 1000 S Second St PO Box 471 *NYSE: WMK* ■ *TF:* 866-999-9347 ■ *Web:* www.weismarkets.com	Sunbury	PA	17801	866-999-9347	
Westborn Inc 21755 Michigan Ave *Web:* www.westbornmarket.com	Dearborn	MI	48124	313-274-6100	
Western Bagel Baking Corp 7814 Sepulveda Blvd *TF:* 800-555-0882 ■ *Web:* www.westernbagel.com	Van Nuys	CA	91405	818-786-5847	787-3221
Western Beef Inc 47-05 Metropolitan Ave *Web:* www.westernbeef.com	Ridgewood	NY	11385	718-417-3770	
Western Supermarkets 2614 19th St S *Web:* www.westernsupermarkets.com	Birmingham	AL	35209	205-879-3471	879-3476
Whittle & Mutch Inc 712 Fellowship Rd *Web:* www.wamiflavor.com	Mount Laurel	NJ	08054	856-235-1165	
Wickens Herzer Panza Cook & Batista Co 35765 Chester Rd *Web:* www.wickenslaw.com	Avon	OH	44011	440-930-8000	
WinCo Foods Inc PO Box 5756 *TF:* 888-674-6854 ■ *Web:* www.wincofoods.com	Boise	ID	83705	208-377-0110	377-0474
Wing Hing Foods Inc 2539 E Philadelphia St *TF:* 855-734-2742 ■ *Web:* www.winghing.com	Ontario	CA	91761	855-734-2742	
Winn-Dixie Stores Inc 5050 Edgewood Ct *Web:* www.winndixie.com	Jacksonville	FL	32254	904-783-5000	783-5294
Woodman'S Food Market Inc 2631 Liberty Ln *Web:* woodmans-food.com	Janesville	WI	53545	608-754-8382	
Woods Supermarkets Inc 703 E College Ave *Web:* www.woodssupermarket.com	Bolivar	MO	65613	417-326-7601	
Zallie Supermarkets 1230 Blackwood-Clementon Rd	Clementon	NJ	08021	856-627-6501	627-8650
ZeaVision LLC Spirit Business Ctr Ii 680F Crown Industrial Ct *TF:* 866-833-2800 ■ *Web:* www.zeavision.com	Chesterfield	MO	63005	314-628-1000	
Zija International Inc 3300 N Ashton Blvd *Web:* www.drinklifein.com	Lehi	UT	84043	801-494-2300	
Zups Food Market 303 E Sheridan St *Web:* www.zups.com	Ely	MN	55731	218-365-3188	

349 GYM & PLAYGROUND EQUIPMENT

	City	State	ZIP	Phone	Fax
American Athletic Inc (AAI) 200 American Ave *TF:* 800-247-3978 ■ *Web:* www.americanathletic.com	Jefferson	IA	50129	515-386-3125	386-4566
American Playground Corp 505 E 31st St Ste X *TF:* 800-541-1602 ■ *Web:* american-playground.net	Anderson	IN	46016	765-642-0288	649-7162
BCI Burke Company Inc 660 Van Dyne Rd *TF:* 800-356-2070 ■ *Web:* www.bciburke.com	Fond du Lac	WI	54937	920-921-9220	921-9566
Columbia Cascade Co 1300 SW Sixth Ave Ste 310 *TF:* 800-547-1940 ■ *Web:* www.timberform.com	Portland	OR	97201	503-223-1157	223-4530
Grounds For Play Inc 1401 E Dallas St *TF:* 800-552-7529 ■ *Web:* www.groundsforplay.com	Mansfield	TX	76063	817-453-5703	477-1140
Jaypro Sports Inc 976 Hartford Tpke *TF Cust Svc:* 800-243-0533 ■ *Web:* www.jaypro.com	Waterford	CT	06385	860-447-3001	444-1779
Landscape Structures Inc 601 Seventh St S *TF:* 800-328-0035 ■ *Web:* www.playlsi.com	Delano	MN	55328	763-972-3391	972-3185
Miracle Recreation Equipment Co 878 Hwy 60 *TF:* 800-523-4202 ■ *Web:* miracle-recreation.com	Monett	MO	65708	417-235-6917	235-6816
PlayCore Inc 401 Chestnut St Ste 410 **Fax Area Code:* 423 ■ *TF:* 877-762-7563 ■ *Web:* www.playcore.com	Chattanooga	TN	37402	877-762-7563	425-3124*
Playworld Systems Inc 1000 Buffalo Rd *TF:* 800-233-8404 ■ *Web:* www.playworldsystems.com	Lewisburg	PA	17837	570-522-9800	522-3030
School-Tech Inc 745 State Cir PO Box 1941 *TF:* 800-521-2832 ■ *Web:* www.school-tech.com	Ann Arbor	MI	48106	800-521-2832	654-4321
SportsPlay Equipment Inc 5642 Natural Bridge Ave *TF:* 800-727-8180 ■ *Web:* www.sportsplayinc.com	Saint Louis	MO	63120	314-389-4140	389-9034

350 GYPSUM PRODUCTS

	City	State	ZIP	Phone	Fax
American Gypsum Co 3811 Turtle Creek Blvd Ste 1200 *TF:* 866-439-5800 ■ *Web:* www.americangypsum.com	Dallas	TX	75219	214-530-5500	530-5635
Canadian Gypsum Company Inc 350 Burnhamthorpe Rd W Fifth Fl *TF:* 800-565-6607 ■ *Web:* www.usg.com	Mississauga	ON	L5B3J1	905-803-5600	803-5688
CertainTeed Gypsum 2424 Lakeshore Rd W *TF:* 800-233-8990 ■ *Web:* www.certainteed.com	Mississauga	ON	L5J1K4	905-823-9881	823-4860
Eagle Materials Inc 3811 Turtle Creek Blvd Ste 1100 *NYSE: EXP* ■ *Web:* www.eaglematerials.com	Dallas	TX	75219	214-432-2000	432-2100
KCG Inc 15720 W 108th St Ste 100 *Web:* www.rewmaterials.com	Lenexa	KS	66219	913-438-4142	
Lafarge North America Inc 12950 Worldgate Dr Ste 600 *Web:* www.lafarge-na.com	Herndon	VA	20170	703-480-3600	480-3899
National Gypsum Co 2001 Rexford Rd **Fax Area Code:* 800 ■ *TF:* 800-628-4662 ■ *Web:* nationalgypsum.com	Charlotte	NC	28211	704-365-7300	329-6421*
PABCO Gypsum 37851 Cherry St *TF:* 877-449-7786 ■ *Web:* www.pabcogypsum.com	Newark	CA	94560	510-792-9555	794-8725
Southern Wall Products Inc 1827 Fellowship Rd *Web:* www.ruco.com	Tucker	GA	30084	770-938-0121	
USG Corp 550 W Adams St *NYSE: USG* ■ *TF:* 800-874-4968 ■ *Web:* www.usg.com	Chicago	IL	60661	312-436-4000	672-4093

351 HAIRPIECES, WIGS, TOUPEES

	City	State	ZIP	Phone	Fax
Aderans Hair Goods Inc *Simplicity Hair Extensions* 5130 N State Rd Seven ft Ninth Fl *TF Sales:* 877-413-5225 ■ *Web:* www.simplicityhair.com	Lauderdale	FL	33319	877-413-5225	
Afro World Hair Goods Inc 7276 Natural Bridge Rd *Web:* www.afroworld.com	Saint Louis	MO	63121	314-389-5194	389-8508
Alkinco PO Box 278 *TF:* 800-424-7118 ■ *Web:* www.alkincohair.com	New York	NY	10116	212-719-3070	764-7804
Eva Gabor International Ltd 5900 Equitable Rd *Web:* virtualrealityhair.com	Kansas City	MO	64120	816-231-3700	
Freeda Wigs 779 E Newyork Ave *Web:* www.freeda.com	Brooklyn	NY	11203	718-771-2000	756-1503
Headcovers Unlimited 35 Tiffany Plz *Web:* www.headcovers.com	Ardmore	OK	73401	580-226-5871	
Headstart Hair For Men Inc 3395 Cypress Gardens Rd *TF:* 800-645-6525 ■ *Web:* www.headstarthairformen.com	Winter Haven	FL	33884	863-324-5559	324-5673
Henry Margu Inc 540 Commerce Dr *TF:* 800-345-8284 ■ *Web:* www.henrymargu.com	Yeadon	PA	19050	610-622-0515	
HPH Corp 1529 SE 47th Terr *TF:* 800-654-9884 ■ *Web:* www.discounthairpiece.com	Cape Coral	FL	33904	239-540-0085	540-0892
Jacquelyn Wigs 15 W 37th St Fourth Fl *TF:* 800-272-2424 ■ *Web:* www.jacquelynwigs.com	New York	NY	10018	212-302-2266	302-0991

Phone *Fax*

Jean Paree Weegs Inc
4041 South 700 East Ste 2 .... Salt Lake City UT 84107 800-422-9447 747-2509*
Fax Area Code: 801 ■ *TF Orders:* 800-422-9447 ■ *Web:* www.jeanparee.com
Jon Renau Collection 2510 Island View Way .... Vista CA 92081 760-598-0067 598-1205
TF: 800-462-9447 ■ *Web:* www.jonrenau.com
Louis Ferre Inc 302 Fifth Ave Ste 10 .... New York NY 10001 212-239-1600 239-1601
TF: 800-695-1061 ■ *Web:* www.louisferre.com
National Fiber Technology LLC 300 Canal St. .... Lawrence MA 01840 978-686-2964
TF Cust Svc: 800-842-2751 ■ *Web:* www.nftech.com
Peggy Knight Solutions Inc 1750 Bridgeway .... Sausalito CA 94965 415-289-1777
TF: 800-997-7753 ■ *Web:* www.peggyknight.com
Rene Of Paris
9100 Wilshire Blvd E Tower 9th Fl .... Beverly Hills CA 90212 800-353-7363 988-2496*
Fax Area Code: 818 ■ **Fax:* Sales ■ *Web:* www.reneofparis.com
Wig America Co 27317 Industrial Blvd. .... Hayward CA 94545 510-887-9579 887-9574
TF: 800-338-7600 ■ *Web:* www.wigamerica.com
World of Wigs 2305 E 17th St. .... Santa Ana CA 92705 714-547-4461 547-6063
TF: 800-794-5572 ■ *Web:* www.worldofwigs.com
YK International Co 3246 W Montrose Ave. .... Chicago IL 60618 773-583-5270
TF: 800-266-5254 ■ *Web:* chicago.enquira.com

352 HANDBAGS, TOTES, BACKPACKS

SEE ALSO Leather Goods - Personal p. 2640; Luggage, Bags, Cases p. 2680; Sporting Goods p. 3182; Tarps, Tents, Covers p. 3204

Phone *Fax*

Accurate Flannel Bag Co 468 Totowa Ave. .... Paterson NJ 07522 973-720-1800 689-6774
Dow Cover Co Inc 373 Lexington Ave .... New Haven CT 06513 203-469-5394 469-5394
TF: 800-735-8877 ■ *Web:* www.dowcover.com
Kate Spade 135 5th Ave Set 7 .... New York NY 10010 212-358-0420
TF: 866-999-5283 ■ *Web:* www.katespade.com
LBU Inc 217 Brook Ave. .... Passaic NJ 07055 973-773-4800 773-6005
TF: 800-678-4528 ■ *Web:* www.lbuinc.com
Ohio Bag Corp 6044 Rossmoor Lakes Ct .... Boynton Beach FL 33437 561-736-3131 735-0150
Web: www.ohiobag.com
Vera Bradley Designs 2208 Production Rd. .... Fort Wayne IN 46808 260-482-4673 484-2278
TF: 800-975-8372 ■ *Web:* www.verabradley.com

353 HARDWARE - MFR

Phone *Fax*

A-jax Company Inc 1500 E Eighth St. .... Jacksonville FL 32206 904-353-4783
Web: www.ajaxco.com
Ababa Bolt 1466 - 1 Pioneer Way .... El Cajon CA 92020 619-440-1781
Aceco 4419 Federal Way .... Boise ID 83716 208-343-7712
TF: 800-359-7012 ■ *Web:* www.aceco.com
Acorn Manufacturing Company Inc
457 School St. .... Mansfield MA 02048 800-835-0121
TF: 800-835-0121 ■ *Web:* www.acornmfg.com
Acryline USA Inc 2015 Becancour .... Lyster QC G0S1V0 800-567-0920
TF: 800-567-0920 ■ *Web:* www.acryline.ca
Adams Rite Manufacturing Co 260 W Santa Fe St. ..... Pomona CA 91767 909-632-2300 632-2370
TF: 800-872-3267 ■ *Web:* www.adamsrite.com
Advanced Integration LLC
4601 Hilton Corporate Dr .... Columbus OH 43232 614-863-2433
Web: www.advint.com
AEHI Inc 14586 Central Ave .... Chino CA 91710 909-606-6998 606-6885
Web: www.aehiinc.com
AGM Container Controls Inc PO Box 40020 .... Tucson AZ 85717 520-881-2130 881-4983
TF: 800-995-5590 ■ *Web:* www.agmcontainer.com
Airtronics Inc 1822 S Research Loop .... Tucson AZ 85710 520-881-3982
Web: www.airtronicsinc.com
Akron Hardware 170 Main Ave .... Akron CO 80720 970-345-6600
AL Hansen Manufacturing Co 701 Pershing Rd ...... Waukegan IL 60085 847-244-8900 244-7222
Web: www.alhansen.com
Albion Industries Inc 800 N Clark St .... Albion MI 49224 517-629-9441
Web: albioncasters.com/
Allied Fastener & Tool Inc 1130 Ng St .... Lake Worth FL 33460 561-585-2113
Web: alliedfastener.com
AluminArt Products Ltd One Summerlea Rd .... Brampton ON L6T4V2 905-791-7521
Web: www.aluminart.com
American Bolt & Screw Manufacturing Corp
601 Kettering Dr .... Ontario CA 91761 909-390-0522
TF: 800-325-0844 ■ *Web:* www.absfasteners.com
AmerTac One Rt 17 S .... Saddle River NJ 07458 201-934-3224 934-3224
Web: www.amertac.com
Anderson Electrical Products Inc
1615 Moores St PO Box 455 .... Leeds AL 35094 573-682-5521 682-8714
TF: 800-423-0730 ■ *Web:* www.hubbell.com
Antenna Factory Inc 931 Albion Ave .... Schaumburg IL 60193 312-242-1727
Web: www.antennafactory.com
AO Precision Mfg LLC 1870 Mason Ave .... Daytona Beach FL 32117 386-274-5882
Web: www.aopmfg.com
Architectural Builders Hardware Manufacturing
1222 Ardmore Ave Apt W .... Itasca IL 60143 630-875-9900
Web: www.abhmfg.com
Architectural Building Supply Co
2965 S Main St. .... Salt Lake City UT 84115 801-486-3481
Web: www.absdoors.com
Aretech LLC 21730 Red Rum Dr Ste 112 .... Ashburn VA 20147 571-292-8889
Web: www.aretechllc.com
Arrow Lock Co 100 Arrow Dr .... New Haven CT 06511 800-839-3157 421-6615
TF: 800-839-3157 ■ *Web:* www.arrowlock.com
ASCO Sintering Co 2750 Garfield Ave .... Commerce CA 90040 323-725-3550
Web: www.ascosintering.com
Asi Technologies 209 Progress Dr. .... Montgomeryville PA 18936 215-661-1002
Web: www.asidrives.com

Phone *Fax*

Assa Abloy of Canada Ltd 160 Four Vly Dr .... Vaughan ON L4K4T9 905-738-2466
Web: www.assaabloy.ca
ASSA Inc 110 Sargent Dr .... New Haven CT 06511 203-624-5225 892-3256*
Fax Area Code: 800 ■ *TF:* 800-235-7482 ■ *Web:* www.assalock.com
ATCO Products Inc 189-V Frelinghuysen Ave .... Newark NJ 07114 973-242-5757 242-0131
Web: www.atcoproducts.com
Attwood Corp 1016 N Monroe St. .... Lowell MI 49331 616-897-9241 897-8358
TF: 844-808-5704 ■ *Web:* www.attwoodmarine.com
Automotive Racing Products Inc
1863 Eastman Ave .... Ventura CA 93003 805-339-2200 650-0742
TF: 800-826-3045 ■ *Web:* www.arp-bolts.com
AWNEX Inc 260 Valley St Ste 100 .... Ball Ground GA 30107 770-704-7140
Web: www.awnexinc.com
Bad Dog Tools 24 Broadcommon Rd. .... Bristol RI 02809 401-253-1330
Web: baddogtools.com
Baden Steelbar & Bolt Corp
852 Big Sewickly Crk Rd R .... Sewickley PA 15143 724-266-3003 266-1619
Web: www.badensteel.com
Baier Marine Company Inc 2920 Airway Ave. .... Costa Mesa CA 92626 800-455-3917
TF: 800-455-3917 ■ *Web:* www.baiermarine.com
Baklund R&D LLC 13835 200th St. .... Hutchinson MN 55350 320-587-0743
Web: www.baklund.com
Baldwin Hardware Corp 841 E Wyomissing Blvd. .... Reading PA 19611 610-777-7811 796-4601
TF: 800-566-1986 ■ *Web:* www.baldwinhardware.com
Band-It-IDEX Inc 4799 Dahlia St. .... Denver CO 80216 303-320-4555 333-6549
TF: 800-525-0758 ■ *Web:* www.band-it-idex.com
Barnhill Bolt Company Inc
2500 Princeton Dr Ne .... Albuquerque NM 87107 505-884-1808
TF: 800-472-3900 ■ *Web:* www.barnhillbolt.com
Baron Mfg Company LLC 1200 Capitol Dr .... Addison IL 60101 630-628-9110 628-9141
TF: 800-368-8585 ■ *Web:* www.baronsnaps.com
Bay Standard Manufacturing Inc
24485 Marsh Creek Rd. .... Brentwood CA 94513 925-634-1181
Web: www.baystandard.com
Beacon Fasteners & Components
198 W Carpenter Ave .... Wheeling IL 60090 847-541-0404
Web: www.beaconfasteners.com
Becknell Wholesale I LP 504 E 44th St. .... Lubbock TX 79404 806-747-3201
Web: www.becknell.com
Belwith International Ltd
3100 Broadway Ave .... Grandville MI 49418 800-235-9484 858-2119
TF: 800-235-9484 ■ *Web:* www.belwith.com
Berenson Corp 2495 Main St. .... Buffalo NY 14214 716-833-2402
Web: www.berensonhardware.com
Best Access Systems 6161 E 75th St .... Indianapolis IN 46250 317-849-2250
TF: 855-365-2407 ■ *Web:* www.bestaccess.com
Bete Fog Nozzle Inc 50 Greenfield St .... Greenfield MA 01301 413-772-0846 772-6729
TF: 800-235-0049 ■ *Web:* www.bete.com
Blum Inc 7733 Old Plank Rd .... Stanley NC 28164 704-827-1345 827-0799
TF: 800-438-6788 ■ *Web:* www.blum.com
Bomar Inc PO Box 1200 .... Charlestown NH 03603 603-826-5791 826-4125
Web: www.pompanette.com/bomar
Bommer Industries Inc PO Box 187 .... Landrum SC 29356 864-457-3301 457-2487
TF: 800-334-1654 ■ *Web:* www.bommer.com
Bostwick-Braun Co, The 7349 Crossleigh Ct. .... Toledo OH 43617 419-259-3600
Web: www.bostwick-braun.com
Bourdon Forge Company Inc 99 Tuttle Rd. .... Middletown CT 06457 860-632-2740 632-7247
Web: www.bourdonforge.com
Brainerd Mfg Company Inc
140 Business Pk Dr .... Winston-Salem NC 27107 336-769-4077 771-6077*
**Fax:* Cust Svc ■ *TF:* 800-652-7277 ■ *Web:* www.libertyhardware.com
Bronze Craft Corp 37 Will St .... Nashua NH 03060 603-883-7747 883-0222
TF: 800-488-7747 ■ *Web:* www.bronzecraft.com
Bud K 475 Us Hwy 319 S .... Moultrie GA 31768 229-985-1667
Web: www.budk.com
Cal Fasteners Inc 4300 E Miraloma Ave .... Anaheim CA 92807 714-854-1715
Web: www.cfi1.com
Cal-Royal Products Inc
6605 Flotilla St. .... City Of Commerce CA 90040 323-888-6601
TF: 800-876-9258 ■ *Web:* www.cal-royal.com
Cassidy-tricker Industrial Sales
1608 Hwy 13 W .... Burnsville MN 55337 952-882-6338
Web: cassidytricker.com
Central Indiana Hardware Company Inc
9190 Corporation Dr. .... Indianapolis IN 46256 317-558-5700
Web: www.cih-indy.com
CH Briggs Hardware Company Inc
2047 Kutztown Rd. .... Reading PA 19605 610-929-6969
Web: www.chbriggs.com
Chamberlain Group 845 Larch Ave. .... Elmhurst IL 60126 630-279-3600 530-6091
TF: 800-528-9131 ■ *Web:* www.chamberlaingroup.com
Charles Leonard Inc 145 Kennedy Dr. .... Hauppauge NY 11788 631-273-6700 273-6777
TF: 800-999-7202 ■ *Web:* www.charlesleonard.com
Charles Leonard Western Inc
235 W 140th St. .... Los Angeles CA 90061 310-715-7464 715-7474
Web: clnational.com
Charles Mcmurray Co 2520 N Argyle Ave .... Fresno CA 93727 559-292-5751
Web: www.charlesmcmurray.com
Chicago Hardware & Fixture Co
9100 Parklane Ave .... Franklin Park IL 60131 847-455-6609 455-0012
Web: www.chicagohardware.com
Chicago Nut & Bolt Inc 150 Covington Dr. .... Bloomingdale IL 60108 630-529-8600
Web: www.cnb-inc.com
Circle Bolt & Nut Company Inc
158 Pringle St. .... Kingston PA 18704 570-718-6001
Web: circlebolt.com
Circor Aerospace Inc 2301 Wardlow Cir .... Corona CA 92880 951-270-6200
Web: www.circoraerospace.com
Clampco Products Inc 1743 Wall Rd. .... Wadsworth OH 44281 330-336-8857
Web: clampco.com
Classic Brass Inc 2051 Stoneman Cir. .... Lakewood NY 14750 716-763-1400
TF: 800-869-3173 ■ *Web:* www.classic-brass.com

	City	State	Zip	Phone	Fax
Cloud-rider Designs Ltd 1260 Eighth Ave *Web:* www.cloud-rider.com	Regina	SK	S4R1C9	306-761-2119	
Coast Tool Co 2099 edison ave. *Web:* www.coasttool.com	San leandro	CA	94577	510-569-1945	
Cobra Anchors Corp 504 Mount-Laurel Ave *Web:* www.cobraanchors.com	Temple	PA	19560	610-929-5764	
Colonial Bronze Co 511 Winsted Rd **Fax Area Code:* 800 ■ *TF All:* 800-355-7903 ■ *Web:* www.colonialbronze.com	Torrington	CT	06790	860-489-9233	355-7903*
Columbia River Knife & Tool Inc 18348 SW 126th Pl *Web:* www.crkt.com	Tualatin	OR	97062	503-685-5015	
Component Hardware Group Inc 1890 Swarthmore Ave. *TF:* 800-526-3694 ■ *Web:* www.componenthardware.com	Lakewood	NJ	08701	732-363-4700	364-8110
CompX International Inc 5430 LBJ Fwy Ste 1700 *NYSE: CIX* ■ *Web:* www.compx.com	Dallas	TX	75240	972-448-1400	448-1408
Controlled Kinematics Inc 46740 Lakeview Blvd *Web:* www.ckinematics.com	Fremont	CA	94538	408-945-1616	
Corbin Russwin Inc 225 Episcopal Rd. *TF:* 800-438-1951 ■ *Web:* www.corbinrusswin.com	Berlin	CT	06037	860-225-7411	
Cordova Bolt Inc 5601 Dolly Ave. *Web:* www.cordovabolt.com	Buena Park	CA	90621	714-739-7500	
Craft Inc 1929 County St PO Box 3049 *TF:* 800-827-2388 ■ *Web:* craft-inc.myshopify.com	South Attleboro	MA	02703	508-761-7917	399-7240
Crown Industrial 213 Michelle Ct *Web:* www.crown-industrial.com	San Francisco	CA	94080	650-952-5150	
Daemar Inc 861 Cranberry Ct *Web:* www.daemar.com	Oakville	ON	L6L6J7	905-847-6500	
Dahl Bros Canada Ltd 2600 S Sheridan Way *Web:* dahlvalve.com	Mississauga	ON	L5J2M4	905-822-2330	
Dayton Superior Corp 1125 Byers Rd *TF:* 800-745-3700 ■ *Web:* www.daytonsuperior.com	Miamisburg	OH	45342	937-866-0711	
DE-STA-CO 1025 Doris Rd **Fax:* Sales ■ *TF:* 888-337-8226 ■ *Web:* www.destaco.com	Auburn Hills	MI	48326	248-836-6700	836-6741*
Detmar Corp 2001 W Alexandrine Ave PO Box 08098 *Web:* www.detmarcorp.com	Detroit	MI	48208	313-831-1155	
Dixie Industries 3510 N Orchard Knob Ave *TF:* 800-933-4943 ■ *Web:* cmforge.com	Chattanooga	TN	37406	423-698-3323	622-3058
Dize Company Inc, The 1512 S Main St *Web:* www.dizeco.com	Winston-salem	NC	27127	336-722-5181	
Dooley Enterprises Inc 1198 N Grove St Ste A *Web:* www.dooleyenterprises.com	Anaheim	CA	92806	714-630-6436	
Door Engineering & Mfg LLC 400 Cherry St *TF:* 800-959-1352 ■ *Web:* www.doorengineering.com	Kasota	MN	56050	507-931-6910	
DORMA Group North America Dorma Dr. *TF:* 800-523-8483 ■ *Web:* www.dorma.com	Reamstown	PA	17567	717-336-3881	336-2106
Dortronics Systems Inc 1668 Sag Harbor Tpke *Web:* www.dortronics.com	Sag Harbor	NY	11963	631-725-0505	
Doug Mockett & Company Inc 1915 Abalone Ave *TF:* 800-523-1269 ■ *Web:* www.mockett.com	Torrance	CA	90501	310-318-2491	
Driv-Lok Inc 1140 Park Ave *Web:* www.driv-lok.com	Sycamore	IL	60178	815-895-8161	
Drivekore Inc 101 Wesley Dr. *Web:* www.drivekore.com	Mechanicsburg	PA	17055	717-697-7440	
Duo Fast Northeast 22 Tolland St *TF:* 888-399-5712 ■ *Web:* www.nailersandstaplers.com	East Hartford	CT	06108	860-289-6861	
Dynamation Research Inc 2301 Pontius Ave *Web:* www.dynamationresearch.com	Los Angeles	CA	90064	310-477-1224	
East Teak Trading Group Inc 1106 Drake Rd **Fax Area Code:* 360 ■ *TF:* 800-338-5636 ■ *Web:* www.eastteak.com	Donalds	SC	29638	864-379-2111	793-7835*
Eastern Co, The 112 Bridge St PO Box 460 *NASDAQ: EML* ■ *Web:* www.easterncompany.com	Naugatuck	CT	06770	203-729-2255	723-8653
Eberhard Hardware Manufacturing Ltd 1523 Bellmill Rd. *Web:* www.eberhardcanada.com	Tillsonburg	ON	N4GOC9	519-688-3443	
Eberhard Mfg Co PO Box 368012 *TF:* 800-334-6706 ■ *Web:* www.eberhard.com	Cleveland	OH	44149	440-238-9720	572-2732
ECA Medical Instruments Inc 1107 Tourmaline Dr *Web:* www.ecamedical.com	Newbury Park	CA	91320	805-376-2509	
Edgewood Building Supply Company Inc 1580 E Epler Ave. *Web:* www.edgewoodbuildingsupply.com	Indianapolis	IN	46227	317-786-9208	
Eklind Tool Comany Inc 11040 King St *Web:* www.eklindtool.net	Franklin Park	IL	60131	847-994-8550	
Emtek Products Inc 15250 Stafford St *TF:* 800-356-2741 ■ *Web:* www.emtek.com	City of Industry	CA	91744	626-961-0413	336-2812
Engineered Products Co (EPCO) 601 Kelso St PO Box 108 *TF:* 888-414-3726 ■ *Web:* www.epcohardware.com	Flint	MI	48506	810-767-2050	767-5084
Entagon Inc 9805 Vly View Rd *Web:* entagon.com	Eden Prairie	MN	55344	952-941-5305	
ER Wagner Mfg Company Inc 4611 N 32nd St *TF:* 800-558-5596 ■ *Web:* www.erwagner.com	Milwaukee	WI	53209	414-871-5080	449-8228
Erie Bolt Corp 1325 Liberty St *Web:* www.ebcind.com	Erie	PA	16502	814-456-4287	
ESPE Mfg Company Inc 9220 Ivanhoe St *TF Cust Svc:* 800-367-3773 ■ *Web:* www.electricalinsulationguys.com	Schiller Park	IL	60176	847-678-8950	678-0253
Fastbolt Corp 200 Louis St *TF:* 800-631-1980 ■ *Web:* www.fastboltcorp.com	South Hackensack	NJ	07606	201-440-9100	
Fastenal Company Caok 5130 N Hwy 167 *Web:* fastenal.com	Catoosa	OK	74015	918-266-8954	
Faultless Caster 3438 Briley Pk Blvd N *TF Cust Svc:* 800-322-7359 ■ *Web:* www.faultlesscaster.com	Nashville	TN	37207	800-322-7359	322-9329
Folger Adam Security Inc 4634 S Presa St *TF:* 888-745-0530 ■ *Web:* www.southernfolger.com	San Antonio	TX	78223	210-533-1231	533-2211
Fortune Brands Home & Hardware Inc 520 Lk Cook Rd *Web:* www.fortunebrands.com	Deerfield	IL	60015	847-484-4400	
Freud America Inc 218 Feld Ave *TF:* 800-334-4107 ■ *Web:* www.freudtools.com	High Point	NC	27263	336-434-3171	
Fulton Corp 303 Eigth Ave **Fax Area Code:* 815 ■ *TF:* 800-252-0002 ■ *Web:* www.fultoncorp.com	Fulton	IL	61252	800-252-0002	589-4433*
G G Schmitt & Sons Inc 2821 Old Tree Dr. *TF:* 866-724-6488 ■ *Web:* www.ggschmitt.com	Lancaster	PA	17603	717-394-3701	291-9739
Garelick Manufacturing Co 644 Second St *Web:* www.garelick.com	Saint Paul Park	MN	55071	651-459-9795	
Genie Co One Door Dr PO Box 67 *TF:* 800-354-3643 ■ *Web:* www.geniecompany.com	Mount Hope	OH	44660	800-354-3643	
Georg Fischer LLC 2882 Dow Ave *Web:* gfps.com/content/gfps/country_us.html	Tustin	CA	92780	714-731-8800	
Grabber Construction Products Inc 20 West Main St Ct Ste 200 *Web:* www.grabberman.com	Alpine	UT	84004	925-680-0777	
Granite Security Products Inc 4801 Esco Dr *Web:* www.winchestersafes.com	Fort Worth	TX	76140	469-735-4901	
Grass America Inc 1202 Hwy 66 S *TF:* 800-334-3512 ■ *Web:* www.grassusa.com	Kernersville	NC	27284	800-334-3512	
Gray Tools Canada Inc 299 Orenda Rd *Web:* www.graytools.com	Brampton	ON	L6T1E8	905-457-3014	457-1050
Great Lakes Power Products Inc 7455 Tyler Blvd. *Web:* www.glpower.com	Mentor	OH	44060	440-951-5111	
H & B Mechanical Inc 111 Cal Ave	Barstow	CA	92311	760-256-8401	
H & C Tool Supply Corp 235 Mount Read Blvd *Web:* www.hctoolsupply.com	Rochester	NY	14611	585-235-5700	
H & G Sales Inc 11635 Lackland Rd *Web:* www.h-gsales.com	St Louis	MO	63146	314-432-8188	
HA Guden Company Inc 99 Raynor Ave. *TF:* 800-344-6437 ■ *Web:* www.guden.com	Ronkonkoma	NY	11779	631-737-2900	737-2933
Hager Co 139 Victor St **Fax Area Code:* 800 ■ **Fax:* Sales ■ *TF:* 800-325-9995 ■ *Web:* www.hagerco.com	Saint Louis	MO	63104	314-772-4400	782-0149*
Halex Corp 750 S Reservoir St *TF:* 800-576-1636 ■ *Web:* www.halexcorp.com	Pomona	CA	91766	909-622-3537	
Hamilton Caster & Manufacturing Co 1637 Dixie Hwy *Web:* www.hamiltoncaster.com	Hamilton	OH	45011	513-863-3300	863-5508
Hampton Products International Corp 50 Icon *TF:* 800-562-5625 ■ *Web:* www.hamptonproducts.com	Foothill Ranch	CA	92610	949-472-4256	
Hardware Sales Inc 2034 James St *Web:* www.hardwaresales.net	Bellingham	WA	98225	360-734-6140	
Hartwell Corp 900 Richfield Rd *Web:* www.hartwellcorp.com	Placentia	CA	92870	714-993-4200	579-4419
Helton Industries Ltd 30840 Peardonville Rd *TF:* 877-300-7412 ■ *Web:* www.heltonindustries.com	Abbotsford	BC	V2T6K2	604-854-3660	
Hi Tech Seals Inc 9211-41 Ave *Web:* www.hitechseals.com	Edmonton	AB	T6E6R5	780-438-6055	434-5866
Highland Threads Inc 11700 Gloger St *Web:* www.highlandthreads.com	Houston	TX	77039	281-986-5100	986-5151
Hindley Mfg Company Inc Nine Havens St *TF:* 800-323-9031 ■ *Web:* www.hindley.com	Cumberland	RI	02864	401-722-2550	722-3083
HL-A Company Inc 902 Ravenwood Dr. *Web:* www.hla.com.my	Selma	AL	36701	334-874-9010	
HMC Holdings LLC 1605 Old Rt 18 Ste 4-36 *Web:* www.homakmfg.com	Wampum	PA	16157	724-535-1080	
Hoppe North America Inc 205 E Blackhawk Dr *Web:* www.us.hoppe.com	Fort Atkinson	WI	53538	920-563-2626	
Hudson Lock Inc 81 Apsley St **Fax Area Code:* 978 ■ *TF:* 800-434-8960 ■ *Web:* www.hudsonlock.com	Hudson	MA	01749	800-434-8960	562-9859*
Hydraflow Inc 1881 W Malvern Ave *Web:* hydraflow.com/	Fullerton	CA	92833	714-773-2600	773-6351
Ideal Clamp 8100 Tridon Dr *TF:* 800-251-3220 ■ *Web:* www.idealclamps.com	Smyrna	TN	37167	615-459-5800	223-1550
Ideal Pipe Ltd 16659 Thorndale Rd *Web:* www.idealpipe.ca	Thorndale	ON	NOM2P0	519-473-2669	
Imperial Carbide Inc 10826 Mercer Pk. *Web:* www.imperialcarbide.com	Meadville	PA	16335	814-724-3732	
Industrial Nut Corp 1425 Tiffin Ave *Web:* www.industrialnut.com	Sandusky	OH	44870	419-625-8543	
Ingenium Aerospace LLC 13979 Willowbrook Rd *Web:* www.ingeniumaerospace.com	Roscoe	IL	61073	815-525-2000	
Inpower LLC 3555 Africa Rd *Web:* www.inpowerdirect.com	Galena	OH	43021	740-548-0965	
Intermotive Inc 986 S Canyon Way *Web:* www.intermotive.net	Colfax	CA	95713	530-346-1801	
Inventory Sales Co 9777 Reavis Rd *TF:* 866-417-3801 ■ *Web:* www.inventorysales.com	St Louis	MO	63123	314-776-6200	
Isoflux Inc 10 Vantage Point Dr Ste 4 *Web:* www.isofluxinc.com	Rochester	NY	14624	585-349-0640	
Jacknob Corp 290 Oser Ave PO Box 18032 *TF:* 800-424-7495 ■ *Web:* www.jacknob.com	Hauppauge	NY	11788	631-546-6560	231-0330
Jacob Holtz Co 10 Industrial Hwy MS-6 Airport Business Complex B *TF:* 800-445-4337 ■ *Web:* www.jacobholtz.com	Lester	PA	19029	215-423-2800	634-7454
James L Howard & Company Inc 10 Britton Dr. *Web:* www.jameslhoward.com	Bloomfield	CT	06002	860-242-3581	
Jarvis Caster Co 881 Lower Brownsville Rd *TF:* 800-995-9876 ■ *Web:* www.jarviscaster.com	Jackson	TN	38301	800-995-9876	881-5701
Jiffy-tite Company Inc 4437 Walden Ave. *Web:* www.jiffy-tite.com	Lancaster	NY	14086	716-681-7200	

				Phone	Fax
Job Shop Managers 28966 Hancock Pkwy	Valencia	CA	91355	661-294-8373	
Web: www.skmindustries.com					
Jonathan Engineered Solutions 410 Exchange St Ste 200	Irvine	CA	92602	714-665-4400	368-7002
Web: www.jonathanengr.com					
Kaba Ilco Corp 400 Jeffreys Rd	Rocky Mount	NC	27804	252-446-3321	446-4702
TF: 800-334-1381 ■ Web: www.kaba-ilco.com					
Kaba Mas 749 W Short St	Lexington	KY	40508	859-253-4744	
Web: www.mas-hamilton.com					
Kanebridge Corp 153 Bauer Dr	Oakland	NJ	07436	201-337-2300	
TF: 888-222-9221 ■ Web: www.kanebridge.com					
Kason Industries Inc 57 Amlajack Blvd	Newnan	GA	30265	770-304-3000	251-4854
TF: 800-935-3550 ■ Web: www.kasonind.com					
Keystone Electronics Corp 31-07 20th Rd	Astoria	NY	11105	718-956-8900	956-9040
TF: 800-221-5510 ■ Web: www.keyelco.com					
Knape & Vogt Manufacturing Co 2700 Oak Industrial Dr NE	Grand Rapids	MI	49505	616-459-3311	459-3290
TF: 800-253-1561 ■ Web: www.knapeandvogt.com					
Kw Automotive North Americainc 1075 N Ave	Sanger	CA	93657	559-875-0222	
Web: kwautomotive.com					
Lane 905 Sw 16th Ave	Portland	OR	97205	503-221-0480	
Web: lanemarketing.com					
Larson Hardware Manufacturing Co PO Box E	Sterling	IL	61081	815-625-0503	625-8786
Web: www.larsonhardware.com					
LE Johnson Products Inc 2100 Sterling Ave	Elkhart	IN	46516	574-293-5664	294-4697
TF: 800-837-5664 ■ Web: www.johnsonhardware.com					
Le Smith Co 1030 E Wilson St	Bryan	OH	43506	419-636-4555	
TF: 888-537-6484 ■ Web: www.lesmith.com					
Liberty Hardware Mfg Corp 140 Business Pk Dr	Winston-Salem	NC	27107	800-542-3789	769-1839*
*Fax Area Code: 336 ■ TF: 800-542-3789 ■ Web: www.libertyhardware.com					
Lockmasters Security Institute 2101 John C Watts Dr	Nicholasville	KY	40356	859-885-6041	
TF: 800-654-0637 ■ Web: www.lockmasters.com					
Magnus Mobility Systems Inc 1912 Wbusiness Ctr Dr	Orange	CA	92867	714-771-2630	
Web: www.magnusinc.com					
Mansfield Industries Inc 1776 Harrington Memorial Rd	Mansfield	OH	44901	419-524-1300	
Web: mansfieldec.com/					
Master Lock Company LLC 137 W Forest Hill Ave PO Box 927	Oak Creek	WI	53154	800-464-2088	308-9245
TF: 800-464-2088 ■ Web: www.masterlock.com					
Medeco Security Locks Inc 3625 Alleghany Dr	Salem	VA	24153	540-380-5000	421-6615*
*Fax Area Code: 800 ■ TF: 800-839-3157 ■ Web: www.medeco.com					
Metabo Corp 1231 Wilson Dr	West Chester	PA	19380	610-436-5900	
Web: metabo.us					
Milan Tool Corp 8989 Brookpark Rd	Cleveland	OH	44129	216-661-1078	
Web: www.milantool.com					
MJL Enterprises LLC 2748 Sonic Dr	Virginia Beach	VA	23453	757-963-8740	
Web: www.mjl-enterprises.com					
Mountz Inc 1080 N 11th St	San Jose	CA	95112	408-292-2214	
TF: 888-925-2763 ■ Web: www.mountztorque.com					
Murray Corp 260 Schilling Cir	Hunt Valley	MD	21031	410-771-0380	771-5576
Web: www.murraycorp.com					
MW Mcwong International Inc 1921 Arena Blvd	West Sacramento	CA	95834	916-371-8080	
Nagel Chase Inc 2323 Delaney Rd	Gurnee	IL	60031	800-323-4552	
TF: 800-323-4552 ■ Web: www.paysoncasters.com					
Newell Rubbermaid Inc Tools & Hardware Group 8935 NorthPointe Executive Dr	Huntersville	NC	28078	704-987-4555	
TF: 800-464-7946 ■ Web: www.newellrubbermaid.com					
Nik-O-Lok Co 3130 N Mitthoeffer Rd	Indianapolis	IN	46235	317-899-6955	899-6977
TF: 800-428-4348 ■ Web: www.nikolok.com					
Norshield Corp 3232 Mobile Hwy	Montgomery	AL	36108	334-551-0650	
Web: www.norshield.net					
Norton Industries Inc 20670 Corsair Blvd	Hayward	CA	94545	510-786-3638	786-3082
Web: nortonclamps.com					
NYC Dot 50 21st St	Brooklyn	NY	11232	718-965-3539	
OceanWorks International Inc 11611 Tanner Rd Ste A	Houston	TX	77041	281-598-3940	
Web: www.oceanworks.com					
OMG Inc 153 Bowles Rd	Agawam	MA	01001	413-789-0252	
Web: www.omgroofing.com					
Omnia Industries Inc Cedar Grove Plant Five Cliffside Dr	Cedar Grove	NJ	07009	973-239-7272	
Web: www.omniaindustries.com					
Otto Dukes Construction Supply Solutions 2556 Agnes St	Corpus Christi	TX	78405	361-883-0921	
Web: www.ottodukestools.com					
P m Industrial Supply Co 9613 Canoga Ave	Chatsworth	CA	91311	818-341-9180	
Web: www.pmindustrial.com					
Paneloc Corp PO Drawer 547	Farmington	CT	06034	860-677-6711	677-8606
TF: 800-394-6711 ■ Web: www.paneloc.com					
ParkDistributors Inc 347 Railroad Ave	Bridgeport	CT	06604	203-366-7200	
Web: www.parkdistributors.com					
Payson Casters Inc 2323 N Delaney Rd	Gurnee	IL	60031	847-336-6200	782-0158
TF: 800-323-4552 ■ Web: www.paysoncasters.com					
PCA Aerospace Inc 17800 Gothard St	Huntington Beach	CA	92647	714-841-1750	
Web: www.pcaaerospace.com					
PDQ Manufacturing 2754 Creek Hill Rd	Leola	PA	17540	717-656-4281	
Web: www.pdqlocks.com					
PE Guerin Inc 23 Jane St	New York	NY	10014	212-243-5270	727-2290
Web: www.peguerin.com					
Peco Fasteners Inc 1218 Six Flags Rd	Austell	GA	30168	770-745-1300	745-1333
Web: www.thesefa.com					
Perko Inc 16490 NW 13th Ave	Miami	FL	33169	305-621-7525	620-9978
Web: www.perko.com					
PL Porter Co 3000 Winona Ave	Burbank	CA	91504	818-526-2600	842-6117
Web: www.craneae.com					
Polar Hardware Manufacturing Co 1813 W Montrose Ave	Chicago	IL	60613	773-935-8600	935-8749
Web: www.polarmfg.com					
PolyPortables Inc 99 Crafton Dr	Dahlonega	GA	30533	706-864-3776	
Web: www.polyportables.com					
Premiere Lock Co 8301 E 81st St	Tulsa	OK	74133	918-294-8179	
TF: 800-575-2658 ■ Web: www.weslock.com					
Prime-Line Products Inc 26950 San Bernardino Ave	Redlands	CA	92374	909-887-8118	
Web: www.prime-line-products.com					
Process Development & Control Inc 1075 Montour W Industrial Park	Coraopolis	PA	15108	724-695-3440	
Web: www.pdcvalve.com					
Prospect Fastener Corp 1295 Kyle Ct	Wauconda	IL	60084	847-526-2950	
Web: www.prospectfastener.com					
Purdy Corp 101 Prospect Ave	Cleveland	OH	44115	800-547-0780	
TF: 800-547-0780 ■ Web: www.purdy.com					
Qual-Craft Industries PO Box 559	Stoughton	MA	02072	781-344-1000	344-0056
TF: 800-231-5647 ■ Web: www.qualcraft.com					
Railway Specialties Corp PO Box 29	Bristol	PA	19007	215-788-9242	788-9244
Web: www.railwayspecialties.com					
Renovator's Supply Inc Renovators Old ML	Millers Falls	MA	01349	413-423-3300	423-3800
TF: 800-659-2211 ■ Web: www.rensup.com					
Riback Supply Co 2412 Business Loop 70 E PO Box 937	Columbia	MO	65205	573-875-3131	449-8738
Web: www.riback.com					
Robert H Peterson Co 14724 Proctor Ave	City Of Industry	CA	91746	626-369-5085	
Web: www.rhpeterson.com					
Rockford Process Control Inc 2020 Seventh St	Rockford	IL	61104	815-966-2000	966-2026
TF: 800-228-3779 ■ Web: rockfordprocess.com					
Rockwood Manufacturing Co 300 Main St	Rockwood	PA	15557	814-926-2026	
Web: www.rockwoodmfg.com					
Rocky Mountain Hardware Inc 1020 Airport Way PO Box 4108	Hailey	ID	83333	208-788-2013	788-2577
TF: 888-788-2013 ■ Web: www.rockymountainhardware.com					
Rohrback Cosasco Systems Inc 11841 E Smith Ave	Santa Fe Springs	CA	90670	562-949-0123	
Web: cosasco.com					
Roll Master 920 Schriewer	Seguin	TX	78155	830-386-0991	836-0995
Web: www.roll-master.com					
Rousseau Metal Inc 105 Ave De Gasp Ouest	St Jean-Port-Joli	QC	G0R3G0	418-598-3381	598-6776
TF: 866-463-4270 ■ Web: www.rousseaumetal.com					
Rutherford Controls Int'l Corp 210 Shearson Crescent	Cambridge	ON	N1T1J6	519-621-7651	
Web: www.rutherfordcontrols.com					
RWM Casters Co PO Box 668	Gastonia	NC	28053	800-634-7704	868-4205*
*Fax Area Code: 704 ■ TF: 800-634-7704 ■ Web: www.rwmcasters.com					
S Parker Hardware Manufacturing Corp PO Box 9882	Englewood	NJ	07631	201-569-1600	569-1082
TF: 800-772-7537 ■ Web: www.sparker.com					
Safemark Systems LP 2101 Park Ctr Dr Ste 125	Orlando	FL	32835	407-299-0044	
Web: www.safemark.com					
Salice America Inc 2123 Crown Centre Dr	Charlotte	NC	28227	704-841-7810	
TF: 800-222-9652 ■ Web: www.saliceamerica.com					
Sandy Valley Fasteners LLC 528 Broadway St	Paintsville	KY	41240	606-788-0222	
Web: www.sandyvalleyfasteners.com					
Sargent & Greenleaf Inc One Security Dr	Nicholasville	KY	40356	859-885-9411	885-3063
TF: 800-826-7652 ■ Web: www.sargentandgreenleaf.com					
Sargent Manufacturing Co 100 Sargent Dr	New Haven	CT	06511	800-727-5477	
TF: 800-727-5477 ■ Web: www.sargentlock.com					
Saturn Fasteners Inc 425 S Varney St	Burbank	CA	91502	818-846-7145	
TF: 800-947-9414 ■ Web: www.saturnfasteners.com					
Savant Manufacturing Inc 2930 Hwy 383 PO Box 520	Kinder	LA	70648	337-738-5896	738-3215
TF: 800-326-6880 ■ Web: www.savantmfg.com					
Seastrom Mfg Company Inc 456 Seastrom St	Twin Falls	ID	83301	208-737-4300	
TF: 800-634-2356 ■ Web: www.seastrom-mfg.com					
Sebewaing Tool & Engineering Co 415 Union St	Sebewaing	MI	48759	989-883-2000	
Web: sebewaingtool.com					
Securitron Magnalock Corp 10027 S 51st St Ste 102	Phoenix	AZ	85044	623-582-4626	582-4641*
*Fax Area Code: 866 ■ TF Sales: 800-624-5625 ■ Web: www.securitron.com					
Security Door Controls Inc 801 Avenida Acaso	Camarillo	CA	93012	805-494-0622	
Web: www.sdcsecurity.com					
Selby Furniture Hardware Company Inc 321 Rider Ave	Bronx	NY	10451	718-993-3700	993-3143
TF: 800-224-0058 ■ Web: www.selbyhardware.com					
Shepherd Caster Corp 203 Kerth St	Saint Joseph	MI	49085	269-983-7351	
Web: www.shepherdcasters.com					
Shepherd's Home Hardware Ltd 3525 Mill St	Armstrong	BC	V0E1B0	250-546-3002	
Web: www.shepherdshardware.com					
Sherwood Windows Ltd 37 Iron St	Toronto	ON	M9W5E3	416-675-3262	
Web: www.sherwoodwindows.com					
Signature Hardware 2700 Crescent Springs Pike	Erlanger	KY	41017	859-647-7564	431-4012
TF: 866-855-2284 ■ Web: www.signaturehardware.com					
Simpson Strong-Tie Company Inc 5956 W Las Positas Blvd	Pleasanton	CA	94588	925-560-9000	847-1597
TF: 800-925-5099 ■ Web: www.strongtie.com					
Smith Fastener Co 3613 Florence Ave	Bell	CA	90201	323-587-0382	
Web: smithfast.com					
Southco Inc 210 N Brinton Lk Rd PO Box 0116	Concordville	PA	19331	610-459-4000	459-4012
Web: www.southco.com					

Phone Fax

Spalding Hardware Ltd 1616 10 Ave SW ... Calgary AB T3C0J5 403-244-5531
Web: spaldinghardware.com
Spokane Hardware Supply Inc 2001 E Trent Ave ... Spokane WA 99202 509-535-1663
TF: 800-888-1663 ■ *Web:* www.spokane-hardware.com
Staples National Advantage
21 S Middlesex Ave ... Monroe Township NJ 08831 609-395-1400
Web: www.staples.com
Starborn Industries Inc 45 Mayfield Ave ... Edison NJ 08837 732-381-9800
Web: www.starbornindustries.com
Storm Industries Inc & Affiliated Co
23223 Normandie Ave ... Torrance CA 90501 310-534-5232
Web: stormind.com
Storms Welding & Manufacturing Inc
513 W Lake St ... Cologne MN 55322 952-466-3343
Web: stormsweldingmfg.com
Suncor Stainless Inc 70 Armstrong Rd ... Plymouth MA 02360 508-732-9191
Web: suncorstainless.com
Sunex International Inc 100 Roe Rd ... Travelers Rest SC 29690 864-834-8759
TF: 800-833-7869 ■ *Web:* www.sunextools.com
Superior Metal Products 713 Maple St ... Wapakoneta OH 45895 419-739-4401
Web: amtrim.com
SW Anderson Co 2425 Wisconsin Ave ... Downers Grove IL 60515 630-964-2600
Web: swaco.com
Swissomation Inc
112 Marschall Creek Rd ... Fredericksburg TX 78624 830-997-6565
Web: www.swissomation.com
Tepro Inc 590 Baxter Ln ... Winchester TN 37398 931-967-5189
Web: www.tepro.com
Tides Marine Inc 3251 SW 13th Dr ... Deerfield Beach FL 33442 954-420-0949
Web: tidesmarine.com
Tiffin Metal Products Co 450 Wall St ... Tiffin OH 44883 800-537-0983
Web: www.tiffinmetal.com
Tompkins Industries Inc 1912 E 123rd St ... Olathe KS 66061 913-764-8088
Web: www.tompkinsind.com
TriLink Saw Chain LLC 4400 Commerce Cir ... Atlanta GA 30336 404-419-2900
Web: www.trilinksawchain.com
Trimark Corp PO Box 350 ... New Hampton IA 50659 641-394-3188
TF: 800-447-0343 ■ *Web:* www.trimarkcorp.com
Trimco/Builders Brass Works
3528 Emery St ... Los Angeles CA 90023 323-262-4191 264-7214
TF: 800-637-8746 ■ *Web:* www.trimcobbw.com
Truth Hardware Inc 700 W Bridge St ... Owatonna MN 55060 507-451-5620 451-5655*
**Fax:* Cust Svc ■ *TF Cust Svc:* 800-866-7884 ■ *Web:* www.truth.com
TS Distributors Inc 4404 Windfern Rd ... Houston TX 77041 832-467-5400 467-5454
Web: www.tsdistributors.com
Unicorp 291 Cleveland St ... Orange NJ 07050 973-674-1700 674-3803
TF: 800-526-1389 ■ *Web:* www.unicorpinc.com
United Rotorcraft Solutions LLC
1942 N Trinity St ... Decatur TX 76234 940-627-0626
Web: www.airmethods.com
Universal Tool Company Inc 33 Rose Pl ... Springfield MA 01104 413-732-4807
Urania Engineering Company Inc
198 S Poplar St ... Hazleton PA 18201 570-455-7531
Web: www.uraniaeng.com
Velko Hinge Inc 9325 Kennedy Ct ... Munster IN 46321 219-924-6363
Web: www.velko.com
Voss Industries Inc 2168 W 25th St ... Cleveland OH 44113 216-771-7655 771-2887
Web: www.vossind.com
Vulcan Threaded Products 10 Crosscreek Trl ... Pelham AL 35124 205-620-5100
Web: vulc.com
Watts Industries (Canada) Inc
5435 N Service Rd ... Burlington ON L7L5H7 905-332-4090
Web: www.wattscanada.ca
Weber-Knapp Co 441 Chandler St ... Jamestown NY 14701 716-484-9135 484-9142
TF: 800-828-9254 ■ *Web:* www.weberknapp.com
Weiser Lock A Masco Co 19701 Da Vinci ... Lake Forest CA 92610 800-677-5625 713-7080
TF: 800-677-5625 ■ *Web:* www.weiserlock.com
Wharton Hardware & Supply
7724 N Crescent Blvd ... Pennsauken NJ 08110 856-662-6935
Web: www.whartonhardware.com
Whiteside Manufacturing Company Inc
309 Hayes St ... Delaware OH 43015 740-363-1179
Web: www.whitesidemfg.com
Wolverine Coil Spring Co
818 Front Ave NW ... Grand Rapids MI 49504 616-459-3504
Web: www.wolverinecoilspring.com
Woodbury Box Company Inc 301 Mcintosh Pkwy ... Thomaston GA 30286 800-722-2061
Web: www.chiefmanufacturing.net
Wright Tool Company Inc One Wright Dr ... Barberton OH 44203 330-848-0600
Web: www.wrighttool.com
Yale Residential Security Products Inc
100 Yale Ave ... Lenoir City TN 37771 800-438-1951 989-8630*
**Fax Area Code:* 865 ■ **Fax:* Cust Svc ■ *TF Cust Svc:* 800-438-1951 ■ *Web:* www.yaleresidential.com
Yale Security Inc.ÿ 1902 Airport Rd ... Monroe NC 28110 800-438-1951 338-0965
TF: 800-438-1951 ■ *Web:* www.yaleresidential.com
Yardley Products Corp 10 W College Ave ... Yardley PA 19067 215-493-2723 493-6796
TF: 800-457-0154 ■ *Web:* www.yardleyproducts.com

354 HARDWARE - WHOL

Phone Fax

Aarch Caster & Equipment 314 Axminister Dr ... Fenton MO 63026 636-349-0220
Web: www.aarchcaster.com
Ace Bolt & Screw Co 200 Brooklyn Ave ... San Antonio TX 78215 210-226-0244
Action Bolt & Tool Co (WURTH)
2051 E Blue Heron Blvd ... Riviera Beach FL 33404 800-423-0700 845-0255*
**Fax Area Code:* 561 ■ *TF:* 800-423-0700 ■ *Web:* www.actionboltandtool.com
Adtec Digital 408 Russell St ... Nashville TN 37206 615-256-6619
Web: www.adtecdigital.com
Aero-Space Southwest Inc 21450 N Third Ave ... Phoenix AZ 85027 623-582-2779
TF: 800-289-2779 ■ *Web:* www.aerospacesw.com

Phone Fax

All State Fastener Corp 15460 E 12 Mile Rd ... Roseville MI 48066 586-773-5400
Web: www.allstatefastener.com
All-Pro Fasteners Inc 1916 Peyco Dr N ... Arlington TX 76001 817-467-5700 467-5365
TF: 800-361-6627 ■ *Web:* www.all-profasteners.com
Allegis Corp
8001 Central Ave NE PO Box 49007 ... Minneapolis MN 55449 763-780-4333
Web: www.allegiscorp.com
Allied International 13207 Bradley Ave ... Sylmar CA 91342 818-364-2333
TF General: 800-533-8333 ■ *Web:* www.alliedtools.com
Associated Steel Corp 18200 Miles Rd ... Cleveland OH 44128 800-321-9300 475-6067*
**Fax Area Code:* 216 ■ *TF:* 800-321-9300 ■ *Web:* www.associatedsteel.com
Baer Supply Co 909 Forest Edge Dr ... Vernon Hills IL 60061 847-913-2237 913-2230
TF: 800-944-2237 ■ *Web:* www.baersupply.com
Bargain Supply Co 844 E Jefferson St ... Louisville KY 40206 502-562-5000 562-5051
TF: 800-322-5226 ■ *Web:* www.bargainsupply.com
Barnett Inc 801 W Bay St ... Jacksonville FL 32204 904-384-6530
TF: 888-803-4467 ■ *Web:* www.e-barnett.com
Bashlin Industries Inc PO Box 867 ... Grove City PA 16127 724-458-8340 458-8342
Web: www.bashlin.com
Behringer Saws Inc 721 Hemlock Rd ... Morgantown PA 19543 610-286-9777
Web: www.behringersaws.com
Better Home Products Ltd
534 Eccles Ave ... South San Francisco CA 94080 650-827-9270
Web: www.betterhomeproducts.com
Blish-Mize Co 223 S Fifth St ... Atchison KS 66002 913-367-1250 367-0667
TF: 800-995-0525 ■ *Web:* www.blishmize.com
Bostwick-Braun Co PO Box 912 ... Toledo OH 43697 419-259-3600 259-3959
TF: 800-777-9640 ■ *Web:* bostwick-braun.com
Buckeye Tools & Supply Company Inc
400 Gargrave Rd ... Dayton OH 45449 937-847-8888
Web: www.buckeyetools.com
Builders Hardware & Supply Company Inc
1516 15th Ave W PO Box C-79005 ... Seattle WA 98119 206-281-3700 281-3747
TF: 800-828-1437 ■ *Web:* www.builders-hardware.com
Bunting Door & Hardware Co
9351G Philadelphia Rd ... Baltimore MD 21237 410-574-8123
Web: www.buntingdoor.com
Burgess Sales & Supply Inc
2121 W Morehead St ... Charlotte NC 28208 704-333-8933
Web: www.burgesssales.com
Carson's Nut-Bolt & Tool Co
301 Hammett St Ext ... Greenville SC 29609 864-242-4720
Web: www.carsons-nbt.com
Cascade Wholesale Hardware Inc 5650 NW ... Hillsboro OR 97124 503-614-2600 629-5793
TF General: 800-877-9987 ■ *Web:* www.cascade.com
Casey Products 11230 Katherine Xing Ste 400 ... Woodridge IL 60517 630-960-3360
Web: www.caseyproducts.com
Caster Technology Corp 11552 Markon Dr ... Garden Grove CA 92841 714-893-6886
Web: www.castertech.com
Charter Industries 2255 29th St S E ... Grand Rapids MI 49508 616-245-3388
Web: www.charterindustries.com
Compatico Inc 4710 44th St SE ... Grand Rapids MI 49512 616-940-1772
Web: www.compatico.com
Concept Electronics Inc 6243 Renoir Ave ... Baton Rouge LA 70806 225-927-8614
Web: www.ceibr.com
Conveyer & Caster Corp 3501 Detroit Ave ... Cleveland OH 44113 216-631-4448
Web: www.cc-efi.com
Custom Stud Inc 8415 220th St W ... Lakeville MN 55044 952-985-7000
Web: www.customstud.com
Delta Fastener Corp 7122 Old Katy Rd ... Houston TX 77024 713-868-2351
Web: www.deltafastener.com
Denver Wire Rope & Supply Inc 4100 Dahlia St ... Denver CO 80216 303-377-5166
Web: denverwirerope.com
Desoto Sales Inc 20945 Osborne St ... Canoga Park CA 91304 818-998-0853 998-7542
TF: 800-826-9779 ■ *Web:* www.desotosales.com
Deutscher & Daughter Inc 10507 150th St ... Jamaica NY 11435 718-291-5600
Web: www.dddoors.com
Digi-Trax Corp 650 Heathrow Dr ... Lincolnshire IL 60069 847-613-2100
Web: www.americanrealtybrokers.com
Dixie Construction Products Inc
970 Huff Rd NW ... Atlanta GA 30318 404-351-1100 350-2359
TF: 800-992-1180 ■ *Web:* www.dixieconstruction.com
Do it Best Corp 6502 Nelson Ave ... Fort Wayne IN 46803 260-748-5300 493-1245
Web: www.doitbest.com
Earnest Machine Products Co 12502 Plz Dr ... Cleveland OH 44130 216-362-1100 362-9970
TF: 800-327-6378 ■ *Web:* www.earnestmachine.com
EB Bradley Co 5080 S Alameda St ... Los Angeles CA 90058 323-585-9201 585-5414
TF: 800-533-3030 ■ *Web:* www.ebbradley.com
Emhart Teknologies Inc
50 Shelton Technology Ctr PO Box 859 ... Shelton CT 06484 203-924-9341 925-3109
Web: www.stanleyengineeredfastening.com
Excelta Corp 60 Easy St ... Buellton CA 93427 805-686-4686
Web: www.excelta.com
Fastec Industrial
2219 Eddie Williams Rd ... Johnson City TN 37601 800-837-2505 975-2544*
**Fax Area Code:* 423 ■ *TF:* 800-837-2505 ■ *Web:* www.fastecindustrial.com
Fastenal Co 2001 Theurer Blvd ... Winona MN 55987 507-454-5374 453-8049
NASDAQ: FAST ■ *TF:* 877-507-7555 ■ *Web:* www.fastenal.com
Faucet Queens Inc 650 Forest Edge Dr ... Vernon Hills IL 60061 847-478-2800 821-0277
Web: faucetqueen.com
Frost Cutlery Company LLC 6861 Mtn View Rd ... Ooltewah TN 37363 423-894-6079
Web: www.frostcutlery.com
Fry Fastening Systems 2150 Waycross Rd ... Cincinnati OH 45240 513-851-2233
Web: artshark.com
General Fasteners Co 37584 Amrhein Rd Ste 150 ... Livonia MI 48150 734-452-2400 452-2257
TF: 800-945-2658 ■ *Web:* www.genfast.com
Handy Hardware Wholesale Inc
8300 Tewantin Dr ... Houston TX 77061 713-644-1495 644-3167
TF: 800-364-3835 ■ *Web:* www.handyhardware.com
Hans Johnsen Co 8901 Chancellor Row ... Dallas TX 75247 214-879-1550 879-1520
TF Sales: 800-879-1515 ■ *Web:* www.hjc.com

Phone | Fax

Harbor Freight Tools
3491 Mission Oaks Blvd. Camarillo CA 93011 805-445-4791
Web: www.harborfreight.com

Hardware Distribution Warehouses Inc (HDW)
6900 Woolworth Rd Shreveport LA 71129 318-686-8527 455-3598*
**Fax Area Code:* 662 ■ *TF Cust Svc:* 800-256-8527 ■ *Web:* www.hdwinc.com

Hardware Suppliers of America Inc (HSI)
1400 E Fire Tower Rd Greenville NC 27858 800-334-5625 334-5635
TF: 800-334-5625 ■ *Web:* www.hardwaresuppliers.com

Hawaii Nut & Bolt Inc 905 Ahua St. Honolulu HI 96819 808-834-1919
Web: www.hawaiinutandbolt.com

Hayes Bolt & Supply Inc 2950 National Ave. San Diego CA 92113 619-231-5966
Web: www.hayesbolt.com

Hillman Group Inc 10590 Hamilton Ave Cincinnati OH 45231 513-851-4900 851-4997
TF: 800-800-4900 ■ *Web:* www.hillmangroup.com

Hodell-natco Industries Inc 7825 Hub Pkwy Cleveland OH 44125 216-447-0165 447-5078
TF: 800-321-4862 ■ *Web:* www.hodell-natco.com

Home Depot Supply
3100 Cumberland Blvd Ste 1480 Atlanta GA 30339 770-852-9000
TF: 855-615-8372 ■ *Web:* www.hdsupply.com

Horizon Distribution Inc PO Box 1021 Yakima WA 98907 509-453-3181 457-5769
Web: www.horizondistribution.com

House-Hasson Hardware Inc
3125 Water Plant Rd Knoxville TN 37914 865-525-0471 525-6178
TF: 800-333-0520 ■ *Web:* www.househasson.com

Industrial Hardware & Specialties Inc
17B Kentucky Ave. Paterson NJ 07503 973-684-4010
Web: www.industrialhardware.com

Interline Brands Inc 801 W Bay St Jacksonville FL 32204 904-421-1400 358-2486
Web: www.interlinebrands.com

J & E Supply & Fastner Company Inc
1903 SE 59th St Oklahoma City OK 73129 405-670-1234
Web: www.jandesupply.com

J.G. Edelen Company Inc 8901 Kelso Dr Baltimore MD 21221 410-918-1200
Web: www.jgedelen.com

Jay Cee Sales & Rivet Inc
32861 Chesley Dr. Farmington MI 48336 248-478-2150
Web: www.rivetsinstock.com

Jensen Distribution Services PO Box 3708 Spokane WA 99220 800-234-1321 838-2432*
**Fax Area Code:* 509 ■ *TF General:* 800-234-1321 ■ *Web:* www.jensenonline.com

JSJ Corp 700 Robbins Rd. Grand Haven MI 49417 616-842-6350 847-3112
Web: www.jsjcorp.com

JSJ Corp Dake Div 724 Robbins Rd Grand Haven MI 49417 616-842-7110 842-0859
TF: 800-846-3253 ■ *Web:* www.dakecorp.com

Karl W Richter Inc 350 Middlefield Rd Scarborough ON M1S5B1 416-757-8951
Web: www.kwrtools.com

Kentec Inc 3250 Centerville Hwy Snellville GA 30039 770-985-1907 985-6989
TF: 800-241-0148 ■ *Web:* www.kentec.com

Key Fasteners Corp 525 Key Way Dr. Berne IN 46711 260-589-2626
Web: adamswells.com

Leight Sales Company Inc 1051 E Artesia Blvd Carson CA 90746 310-223-1000 604-4702
Web: www.leightsales.com

Long-Lewis Hardware Co 430 Ninth St N Birmingham AL 35203 205-322-2561 322-2504
TF: 800-322-0492 ■ *Web:* www.long-lewis.com

Max Tool Inc 119b Citation Ct. Birmingham AL 35209 205-942-2466 942-7144
TF: 800-783-6298 ■ *Web:* www.maxtoolinc.com

MaxTool 1669 Puddingstone Dr La Verne CA 91750 909-568-2800
Web: www.maxtool.com

Mclendon Hardware Inc 440 Rainier Ave S Renton WA 98057 425-235-3555 264-1511
Web: www.mclendons.com

Monroe Hardware Co 101 N Sutherland Ave Monroe NC 28110 704-289-3121 289-2838
TF: 800-222-1974 ■ *Web:* www.monroehardware.com

Nbs Corp 3100 E Slauson Ave Vernon CA 90058 323-923-1627
Web: www.nbsfasteners.com

Norwood Hardware & Supply Company Inc
2906 Glendale Milford Rd. Cincinnati OH 45241 513-733-1175
Web: www.norwoodhardware.com

Oasis Stage Werks Inc
249 S Rio Grande St. Salt Lake City UT 84101 801-363-0364
Web: www.oasis-stage.com

Okee Industries Inc 91 Shield St. West Hartford CT 06110 860-953-1234
Web: www.okee.net

Omaha Wholesale Hardware Co PO Box 3628 Omaha NE 68102 402-444-1673 444-1664
TF: 800-238-4566 ■ *Web:* www.omahawh.com

Onity Inc 2232 Northmont Pkwy Ste 100 Duluth GA 30096 800-424-1433
TF: 800-424-1433 ■ *Web:* region.onity.com

Orgill Inc 3742 Tyndale Dr. Memphis TN 38125 901-754-8850 752-8989
TF: 800-347-2860 ■ *Web:* www.orgill.com

Parts Assoc Inc 12420 Plz Dr Parma OH 44130 216-433-7700 433-9051
TF: 800-321-1128 ■ *Web:* www.pai-net.com

Portland Bolt & Manufacturing Company Inc
3441 NW Guam St Portland OR 97210 503-227-5488
Web: www.portlandbolt.com

Ram Tool & Supply Co 3620 Eigth Ave S. Birmingham AL 35222 205-714-3300 322-6348
Web: www.ram-tool.com

Ram Winch & Hoist Management LLC
14603 Chrisman Rd Houston TX 77039 281-999-8665
Web: www.ramwinch.com

Regitar USA Inc 2575 Container Dr Montgomery AL 36109 334-244-1885 244-1901
TF: 877-734-4827 ■ *Web:* www.regitar.com

Repairclinic.com Inc 48600 Michigan Ave. Canton MI 48188 734-495-3079 495-3842
TF: 800-269-2609 ■ *Web:* www.repairclinic.com

Ryobi Technologies Inc
1428 Pearman Dairy Rd Anderson SC 29625 800-525-2579 261-9435*
**Fax Area Code:* 864 ■ *TF:* 800-525-2579 ■ *Web:* www.ryobitools.com

Serv-a-lite Products Inc 3451 Morton Dr. East Moline IL 61244 800-800-4900 851-4997*
**Fax Area Code:* 513 ■ *TF:* 800-800-4900 ■ *Web:* www.hillmangroup.com

Signal Industrial Products Corp
1601 Cowart St. Chattanooga TN 37408 423-756-4980
Web: www.signalproducts.com

Silicone Specialties Inc 430 S Rockford Ave Tulsa OK 74120 918-587-5567
Web: www.ssicm.com

Phone | Fax

Specialty Bolt & Screw Inc 235 Bowles Rd Agawam MA 01001 413-789-6700 789-9340
TF: 800-322-7878 ■ *Web:* www.specialtybolt.com

Standard Supply & Distributing Co
1431 Regal Row Dallas TX 75247 214-630-7800 630-1894
Web: www.standardsupplyhvac.com

Star Stainless Screw Co 30 W End Rd Totowa NJ 07512 973-256-2300

Supply Technologies LLC 6065 Parkland Blvd. Cleveland OH 44124 440-947-2100 947-2299
TF: 800-695-8650 ■ *Web:* supplytechnologies.com

Techni-Tool Inc
1547 N Trooper Rd PO Box 1117 Worcester PA 19490 610-941-2400 828-5623
TF Cust Svc: 800-832-4866 ■ *Web:* www.techni-tool.com

Thruway Fasteners Inc
2910 Niagara Falls Blvd North Tonawanda NY 14120 716-694-1434 694-3865*
**Fax:* Sales ■ *Web:* www.thruwayfasteners.com

Tomarco Contractor Specialties Inc
14848 Northam St La Mirada CA 90638 714-523-1771 523-1284
Web: www.tomarco.com

Triangle Fastener Corp 1925 Preble Ave Pittsburgh PA 15233 412-321-5000 321-7838
TF General: 800-486-1832 ■ *Web:* www.trianglefastener.com

Tripac Fasteners 475 Klug Cir. Corona CA 92880 951-280-4488
Web: tripaconline.com

United Hardware Distributing Co
5005 Nathan Ln N. Plymouth MN 55442 763-559-1800
Web: www.unitedhardware.com/

Wallace Hardware Company Inc
5050 S Davy Crockett Pkwy PO Box 6004 Morristown TN 37815 423-586-5650 581-0766
TF: 800-776-0976 ■ *Web:* www.wallacehardware.com

Western Tool Supply PO Box 13430 Salem OR 97309 503-588-8222 588-8225
Web: www.westerntool.com

Wurth Revcar Fasteners Inc 3845 Thirlane Rd Roanoke VA 24019 540-561-6565
Web: www.wurthrevcar.com

Wurth Service Supply Inc 4935 W 86th St Indianapolis IN 46268 317-704-1000 668-2264*
**Fax Area Code:* 716 ■ **Fax:* Cust Svc ■ *TF:* 877-999-8784 ■ *Web:* www.servicesupply.com

WW Grainger Inc 100 Grainger Pkwy Lake Forest IL 60045 847-535-1000
NYSE: GWW ■ *TF:* 888-361-8649 ■ *Web:* www.grainger.com

355 HEALTH CARE PROVIDERS - ANCILLARY

SEE ALSO Home Health Services p. 2472; Hospices p. 2479; Vision Correction Centers p. 3286

Phone | Fax

Amedisys Inc
5959 S Sherwood Forest Blvd Ste 300 Baton Rouge LA 70816 225-292-2031 292-8163
NASDAQ: AMED ■ *TF:* 800-464-0020 ■ *Web:* www.amedisys.com

American Family Care
2147 Riverchase Office Rd Birmingham AL 35244 205-403-8902
TF: 800-258-7535 ■ *Web:* www.americanfamilycare.com

American Red Cross In Greater New York (Inc)
520 W 49th St. New York NY 10019 877-733-2767
TF: 877-733-2767 ■ *Web:* www.redcross.org

AmeriHealth Mercy Health Plan
8040 Carlson Rd Ste 500 Harrisburg PA 17112 717-651-3540 937-8776*
**Fax Area Code:* 215 ■ *TF:* 888-991-7200 ■ *Web:* amerihealthcaritaspa.com

AmSurg Corp 1A Burton Hills Blvd 5th Fl Nashville TN 37215 615-665-1283 665-0755
NASDAQ: AMSG ■ *TF:* 800-945-2301 ■ *Web:* www.amsurg.com

Aptium Oncology 8201 Beverly Blvd Los Angeles CA 90048 323-866-3340
Web: www.aptiumoncology.com

CareSource 230 N Main St. Dayton OH 45402 937-224-3300
TF: 800-488-0134 ■ *Web:* www.caresource.com

Central Washington Comprehensive Mental Health
PO Box 959 Yakima WA 98907 509-575-4084
Web: www.cwcmh.org

Children's Bureau of Southern California
1910 Magnolia Ave. Los Angeles CA 90004 213-342-0100 342-0200
TF: 800-730-3933 ■ *Web:* www.all4kids.org

DaVita Inc 1551 Wewatta St Denver CO 80202 303-405-2100
NYSE: DVA ■ *TF:* 800-310-4872 ■ *Web:* www.davita.com

Denver Rescue Mission
3501 E 46th Ave PO Box 5206 Denver CO 80216 303-297-1815 295-1566
Web: www.denverrescuemission.org

Fresenius Medical Care North America
920 Winter St Waltham MA 02451 781-699-9000
TF: 800-662-1237 ■ *Web:* www.fmcna.com

Hanger Orthopedic Group Inc
10910 Domain Dr Ste 300 Austin TX 78758 512-777-3800
TF: 877-442-6437 ■ *Web:* www.hanger.com

HealthDrive Corp 888 Worcester St Wellesley MA 02482 888-964-6681 662-0859
TF: 888-964-6681 ■ *Web:* www.healthdrive.com

HealthSouth Corp
3660 Grandview Pkwy Ste 200 Birmingham AL 35243 205-967-7116 969-4740*
NYSE: HLS ■ **Fax:* Hum Res ■ *TF:* 800-765-4772 ■ *Web:* healthsouth.com

Healthways Inc 701 Cool Springs Blvd Ste 300 Franklin TN 37067 800-327-3822 665-7697*
NASDAQ: HWAY ■ **Fax Area Code:* 615 ■ *TF:* 800-327-3822 ■ *Web:* www.americanhealthways.com

Hooper Holmes Inc 170 Mt Airy Rd. Basking Ridge NJ 07920 908-766-5000
NYSE: HH ■ *Web:* www.hooperholmes.com

Hudson River Healthcare Inc 1037 Main St Peekskill NY 10566 914-734-8800 734-8808
Web: www.hrhcare.org

MedCath Inc 10720 Sikes Pl Ste 300 Charlotte NC 28277 704-708-6600 708-5035
NASDAQ: MDTH ■ *TF:* 800-461-9330 ■ *Web:* www.medcath.com

Miracle-Ear Inc
5000 Cheshire Pkwy N Ste 1 Minneapolis MN 55446 800-464-8002 268-4365*
**Fax Area Code:* 763 ■ *TF:* 800-464-8002 ■ *Web:* www.miracle-ear.com

Open Door Family Medical Ctr Inc
165 Main St Ossining NY 10562 914-941-1263
Web: www.opendoormedical.org

Orion HealthCorp Inc
1805 Old Alabama Rd Ste 350 Roswell GA 30076 678-832-1800 832-1888
OTC: ORNH ■ *Web:* www.orionhealthcorp.com

Radiation Therapy Services Inc
2270 Colonial Blvd. Fort Myers FL 33907 239-931-7275 931-7380
TF: 800-437-1619 ■ *Web:* 21co.com

	Phone	Fax

SCAN Health Plan
3800 Kilroy Airport Way Ste 100 Long Beach CA 90806 562-989-5100 989-5200
TF: 800-247-5091 ■ *Web:* www.scanhealthplan.com

Shapco Inc 1666 20th St Ste 100 Santa Monica CA 90404 310-264-1666 264-1675

Symbion Inc 40 Burton Hills Blvd Ste 500 Nashville TN 37215 615-234-5900 234-5998
Web: www.symbion.com

United Surgical Partners International Inc (USPI)
15305 Dallas Pkwy Addison TX 75001 972-713-3500
Web: www.uspi.com

Unity Physician Group Pc 1155 W Third St Bloomington IN 47404 812-333-2731 331-6585
Web: www.unitypg.com

US Physical Therapy
1300 W Sam Houston Pkwy S Ste 300 Houston TX 77042 713-297-7000 297-7090
NYSE: USPH ■ *TF:* 800-580-6285 ■ *Web:* corporate.usph.com/

356 HEALTH CARE SYSTEMS

SEE ALSO General Hospitals - US p. 2492

Health Care Systems are one or more hospitals owned, leased, sponsored, or managed by a central organization. Single-hospital systems are not included here; however, some large hospital networks or alliances may be listed.

	Phone	Fax

Addus HealthCare Inc 2401 S Plum Grove Rd Palatine IL 60067 847-303-5300 303-5376
NASDAQ: ADUS ■ *TF:* 888-233-8746 ■ *Web:* www.addus.com

Adventist Health 2100 Douglas Blvd Roseville CA 95661 916-781-2000
TF: 877-336-3566 ■ *Web:* www.adventisthealth.org

Albert Einstein Healthcare Network
5501 Old York Rd Philadelphia PA 19141 215-456-7890 456-8539
TF: 800-346-7834 ■ *Web:* www.einstein.edu

Alexian Bros Health System
3040 Salt Creek Ln Arlington Heights IL 60005 847-230-3764 483-7040
Web: www.alexianbrothershealth.org

Allina Health System 710 E 24th St Minneapolis MN 55404 612-813-3600 775-9733
Web: www.allinahealth.org

American Caresource Holdings Inc
5429 LBJ Fwy Ste 850 Dallas TX 75240 800-370-5994 980-2560*
NASDAQ: ANCI ■ **Fax Area Code:* 972

American Kidney Stone Management Ltd (AKSM)
797 Thomas Ln Columbus OH 43214 614-447-0281 447-9374
TF: 800-637-5188 ■ *Web:* www.aksm.com

American Renal Assoc Inc 66 Cherry Hill Dr Beverly MA 01915 978-922-3080
TF: 877-997-3625 ■ *Web:* www.americanrenal.com

AmeriHealth Casualty
1700 Market St Ste 700 Philadelphia PA 19103 215-587-1901 587-1826
Web: www.amerihealthcasualty.com

Amery Regional Medical Ctr 265 Griffin St E Amery WI 54001 715-268-8000 268-0311
TF: 800-424-5273 ■ *Web:* www.amerymedicalcenter.org

Ancilla Systems Inc 1419 S Lk Pk Ave Hobart IN 46342 219-947-8500 947-4037
Web: www.ancilla.org

ApolloMD Inc 5665 New Northside Dr Ste 320 Atlanta GA 30328 770-874-5400 874-5433
Web: www.apollomd.com

Appalachian Regional Healthcare Service (ARH)
2285 Executive Dr PO Box 8086 Lexington KY 40505 859-226-2440 226-2586
TF: 877-243-4782 ■ *Web:* www.arh.org

Ardent Health Services
1 Burton Hills Blvd Ste 250 Nashville TN 37215 615-296-3000 296-6005
Web: www.ardenthealth.com

Ascension Health 4600 Edmundson Rd Saint Louis MO 63134 314-733-8000 733-8000
Web: ascensionhealth.org

Aurora Health Care Inc
750 W Virginia St PO Box 341880 Milwaukee WI 53234 414-647-3000 649-7982
Web: www.aurorahealthcare.org

Avera Health 3900 W Avera Dr Sioux Falls SD 57108 605-322-4700 322-4799
Web: www1.avera.org

Banner Health 1441 N 12th St Phoenix AZ 85006 602-495-4000 495-4728
Web: www.bannerhealth.com

Baptist Health South Florida Inc
6855 Red Rd Ste 600 Coral Gables FL 33143 786-662-7000 662-7334
TF: 800-622-2838 ■ *Web:* www.baptisthealth.net

Baptist Healthcare System 4007 Kresge Way Louisville KY 40207 502-896-5000
Web: www.bhsi.com

Baptist Memorial Health Care Corp
350 N Humphreys Blvd Memphis TN 38120 901-227-5920
TF: 800-422-7847 ■ *Web:* www.baptistonline.org

Baylor Health Care System 3500 Gaston Ave Dallas TX 75246 214-820-0111 820-2594
Web: www.baylorhealth.com

Benedictine Health System
503 E Third St Ste 400 Duluth MN 55805 218-786-2370 786-2373
TF: 800-833-7208 ■ *Web:* www.bhshealth.org

BJC HealthCare 4444 Forest Pk Ave Ste 500 Saint Louis MO 63108 314-286-2000 286-2060
Web: www.bjc.org

Bon Secours Health System Inc
1505 Marriottsville Rd Marriottsville MD 21104 410-442-5511 442-1082
Web: www.bshsi.com

California Family Health Council Inc (CFHC)
3600 Wilshire Blvd Ste 600 Los Angeles CA 90010 213-386-5614 368-4410
Web: www.cfhc.org

CAMC Health System Inc 501 Morris St Charleston WV 25301 304-388-5432
Web: www.camc.org

CareGroup Inc 375 Longwood Ave Boston MA 02215 617-975-5000
Web: www.caregroup.org

Carolinas HealthCare System
1000 Blythe Blvd PO Box 32861 Charlotte NC 28232 704-355-2000
Web: www.carolinashealthcare.org

Catholic Health Initiatives
1999 Broadway Ste 2600 Denver CO 80202 303-298-9100
Web: catholichealthinitiatives.net

Catholic Healthcare Partners
615 Elsinore Pl Cincinnati OH 45202 513-639-2800 639-2700*
**Fax:* Hum Res ■ *TF:* 800-367-9212 ■ *Web:* mercy.com

Catholic Healthcare West
185 Berry St Ste 300 San Francisco CA 94107 415-438-5500 438-5724
Web: www.dignityhealth.org

Centra Health Inc 1920 Atherholt Rd Lynchburg VA 24501 434-947-3000 947-4706
TF: 877-635-4651 ■ *Web:* www.centrahealth.com

Chase Brexton Health Services Inc
1001 Cathedral St Baltimore MD 21201 410-837-2050
Web: www.chasebrexton.org

Chesapeake Medical Systems Inc
118 Cedar St Cambridge MD 21613 410-228-0221 228-4561
Web: chesapeakemedicalsystems.com/

Childhaven 316 Broadway Seattle WA 98122 206-624-6477 621-8374
TF: 877-300-9164 ■ *Web:* www.childhaven.org

Christiana Care Health System
501 W 14th St Wilmington DE 19801 302-366-1929 428-2564
Web: www.christianacare.org

CHRISTUS Health 6363 N Hwy 161 Ste 450 Irving TX 75038 214-492-8500 492-8540
Web: www.christushealth.org

CHRISTUS Schumpert Health System
1 St Mary Pl Shreveport LA 71101 318-681-4500 681-6954
TF: 844-444-8440 ■ *Web:* christushealthsb.org

CHRISTUS Spohn Health System
1702 Santa Fe St Corpus Christi TX 78404 361-881-3000 883-6478
TF: 800-247-6574 ■ *Web:* www.christusspohn.org

Community Health Systems Inc
4000 Meridian Blvd Franklin TN 37067 615-465-7000 370-3548
NYSE: CYH ■ *TF:* 888-373-9600 ■ *Web:* www.chs.net

Community Services Group (CSG)
320 Highland Dr PO Box 597 Mountville PA 17554 717-285-7121 285-2658
TF: 877-907-7970 ■ *Web:* www.csgonline.org

Covenant Health System 3615 19th St Lubbock TX 79410 806-725-0000 725-0324
Web: www.covenanthealth.org

Covenant Health Systems Inc
100 Ames Pond Dr Ste 102 Tewksbury MA 01876 781-861-3535 851-0828*
**Fax Area Code:* 978 ■ *Web:* www.covenanths.org

Crozer-Keystone Health System (CKHS)
190 W Sproul Rd Springfield PA 19064 610-328-8700 328-8725
TF: 800-254-3258 ■ *Web:* www.crozerkeystone.org

DCH Health System 809 University Blvd E Tuscaloosa AL 35401 205-759-7111 750-5541
Web: www.dchsystem.com

Detroit Medical Ctr (DMC) 4707 St Antoine Detroit MI 48201 313-745-6035 966-2040
Web: www.dmc.org

Eastern Maine Healthcare Systems (EMHS)
43 Whiting Hill Rd Brewer ME 04412 207-973-7050 973-7139
Web: www.emhs.org

Edinburg Ctr Inc, The 1040 Waltham St Lexington MA 02421 781-862-3600 863-5903
Web: www.edinburgcenter.org

Fairview Health Services
2450 Riverside Ave Minneapolis MN 55454 612-672-6000 672-6337
TF: 800-824-1953 ■ *Web:* www.fairview.org

Franciscan Missionaries of Our Lady Health System (FMOLHS)
4200 Essen Ln Baton Rouge LA 70809 225-923-2701 926-4846
Web: www.fmolhs.org

General Health System (GHS)
3600 Florida Blvd Baton Rouge LA 70806 225-387-7000 237-1623
Web: www.brgeneral.org

Great Plains Health Alliance Inc
625 Third St Phillipsburg KS 67661 785-543-2111
TF: 800-432-2779 ■ *Web:* www.gpha.com

Greenville Hospital System (GHS)
701 Grove Rd Greenville SC 29605 864-455-8976 455-6218
TF: 877-447-4636 ■ *Web:* www.ghs.org

Guthrie Healthcare System 1 Guthrie Sq Sayre PA 18840 570-887-4401 887-4666
TF: 888-448-8474 ■ *Web:* www.guthrie.org

Hartford Health Care Corp 80 Seymour St Hartford CT 06102 860-545-5000
Web: www.harthosp.com

Harvard Vanguard Medical Assoc Inc
275 Grove St Ste 300 Newton MA 02466 617-559-8444
Web: www.harvardvanguard.org

HCA Holdings Inc One Pk Plz Nashville TN 37203 615-344-9551
NYSE: HCA ■ *Web:* www.hcahealthcare.com

HCA Midwest Health System
903 E 104th St Ste 500 Kansas City MO 64131 816-508-4000 508-4036
TF: 800-386-9355 ■ *Web:* www.hcamidwest.com

Health Net Of Arizona Inc 1230 W Washington St Tempe AZ 85281 602-794-1400
TF: 800-291-6911 ■ *Web:* www.healthnet.com

Healtheast 559 Capitol Blvd Saint Paul MN 55103 651-232-2000 232-2315
Web: www.healtheast.org

Henry Ford Health System One Ford Pl Detroit MI 48202 800-436-7936 874-6380*
**Fax Area Code:* 313 ■ *TF:* 800-436-7936 ■ *Web:* www.henryford.com

Hospital Sisters Health System
4936 Laverna Rd Springfield IL 62707 217-523-4747
Web: www.hshs.org

IASIS Healthcare Corp 117 Seaboard Ln Bldg E Franklin TN 37067 615-844-2747 846-3006
TF: 877-898-6080 ■ *Web:* www.iasishealthcare.com

ICG Link Inc 7003 Chadwick Dr Ste 111 Brentwood TN 37027 615-370-1530 370-9997
Web: www.icglink.net

Infirmary Health System Inc (IHS)
5 Mobile Infirmary Cir Mobile AL 36607 251-435-2400 660-8348
Web: www.mobileinfirmary.org

Inova Health System 8110 Gatehouse Rd Falls Church VA 22042 855-694-6682 504-6607*
**Fax Area Code:* 703 ■ *TF:* 855-694-6682 ■ *Web:* www.inova.org

Integrated Healthcare Holdings Inc
1301 N Tustin Ave Santa Ana CA 92705 714-953-3652 953-3384
OTC: IHCH ■ *Web:* www.ihhioc.com

INTEGRIS Health Inc 3300 NW Expy Oklahoma City OK 73112 405-951-2277 949-3623
Web: www.integrisok.com

Intermountain HealthCare
36 S State St Salt Lake City UT 84111 801-442-2000
TF Hum Res: 800-843-7820 ■ *Web:* www.intermountainhealthcare.org

Iowa Health System 1200 Pleasant St Des Moines IA 50309 515-241-6161 241-5059
Web: www.unitypoint.org

				Phone	Fax
Island Peer Review Organization Inc (IPRO) 1979 Marcus Ave *Web:* www.ipro.org	New Hyde Park	NY	11042	516-326-7767	328-2310
Johns Hopkins Health System (JHH) 600 N Wolfe St *Web:* www.hopkinsmedicine.org	Baltimore	MD	21287	410-955-5000	
Kindred Healthcare Inc 680 S Fourth Ave *NYSE: KND* ■ *TF:* 800-545-0749 ■ *Web:* www.kindredhealthcare.com	Louisville	KY	40202	502-596-7300	596-4052
LifePoint Health 330 Seven Springs Way *NASDAQ: LPNT* ■ *TF:* 888-982-9144 ■ *Web:* www.lifepointhospitals.com	Brentwood	TN	37027	615-920-7000	
Lifespring Inc 460 Spring St *TF:* 800-456-2117 ■ *Web:* lifespringhealthsystems.org	Jeffersonville	IN	47130	812-280-2080	
Loris Community Hospital 3655 Mitchell St PO Box 690001 *Web:* mcleodhealth.org	Loris	SC	29569	843-716-7000	716-7195
Mayo Clinic: Benavente Luis A MD 200 SW First St *Web:* www.mayoclinic.org	Rochester	MN	55905	507-284-2511	284-0161
MedCath Inc 10720 Sikes Pl Ste 300 *NASDAQ: MDTH* ■ *TF:* 800-461-9330 ■ *Web:* www.medcath.com	Charlotte	NC	28277	704-708-6600	708-5035
MedStar Health 5565 Sterrett Pl 5th Fl *TF:* 877-772-6505 ■ *Web:* www.medstarhealth.org	Columbia	MD	21044	410-772-6500	532-5929
Memorial Health Services Inc 7677 Ctr Ave *Web:* www.memorialcare.org	Huntington Beach	CA	92647	562-933-1800	981-1336
Memorial Hermann Healthcare System 7600 Beechnut St **Fax:* Cust Svc ■ *Web:* www.memorialhermann.org	Houston	TX	77074	713-456-4280	776-5144*
Methodist Health Care System 6565 Fannin St **Fax:* Admitting ■ *Web:* www.houstonmethodist.org	Houston	TX	77030	713-790-3311	790-4885*
Methodist Healthcare Inc 1265 Union Ave *Web:* www.methodisthealth.org	Memphis	TN	38104	901-516-7000	516-2394
Methodist Healthcare Ministries of South Texas Inc 4507 Medical Dr *TF:* 800-959-6673 ■ *Web:* www.mhm.org	San Antonio	TX	78229	210-692-0234	614-7563
Methodist Hospitals of Dallas 1441 N Beckley Ave *TF:* 800-725-9664 ■ *Web:* www.methodisthealthsystem.org	Dallas	TX	75203	214-947-8181	947-6501
MultiCare Health System 315 ML King Jr Way PO Box 5299 *Web:* www.multicare.org	Tacoma	WA	98415	253-697-1950	403-1180
New Ctr Community Mental Health Services 2051 W Grand Blvd *Web:* www.newcentercmhs.org	Detroit	MI	48208	313-961-3200	
New York City Health & Hospitals Corp 125 Worth St *Web:* www.nyc.gov/html/hhc/html/home/home.shtml	New York	NY	10013	212-788-3339	788-3348
North Broward Hospital District 303 SE 17th St *Web:* www.browardhealth.org	Fort Lauderdale	FL	33316	954-473-7458	355-4966
North Mississippi Health Services 830 S Gloster St *Web:* www.nmhs.net	Tupelo	MS	38801	662-377-3000	377-2209
Northwestern Counseling Support & Services Inc 107 Fisher Pond Rd *TF:* 800-834-7793 ■ *Web:* www.ncssinc.org	Saint Albans	VT	05478	802-524-6554	527-7801
Novant Health Inc 3333 Silas Creek Pkwy *Web:* www.novanthealth.org	Winston-Salem	NC	27103	336-718-5000	
Oakwood Healthcare Inc 18101 Oakwood Blvd PO Box 2500 *TF:* 800-543-9355 ■ *Web:* www.oakwood.org	Dearborn	MI	48124	313-593-7000	436-2038
OhioHealth Corporate Offices 1087 Dennison Ave 3rd Fl *Web:* www.ohiohealth.com	Columbus	OH	43201	614-484-9700	544-5244
Optimus Health Care Inc 982 E Main St *Web:* www.optimushealthcare.org	Bridgeport	CT	06608	203-696-3260	339-7677
OSF Healthcare System 800 NE Glen Oak Ave *Web:* www.osfhealthcare.org	Peoria	IL	61603	309-655-2850	655-6869
Palomar Pomerado Health 15615 Pomerado Rd *TF:* 800-628-2880 ■ *Web:* www.palomarhealth.org	Poway	CA	92064	858-613-4000	
Partners HealthCare System Inc 800 Boylston St Ste 1150 *Web:* www.partners.org	Boston	MA	02199	617-278-1000	278-1049
Planned Parenthood of Indiana Inc 200 S Meridian St PO Box 397 *Web:* www.ppin.org	Indianapolis	IN	46206	317-637-4343	637-4344
Portland Clinic, The 800 SW 13th Ave *Web:* www.theportlandclinic.com	Portland	OR	97205	503-221-0161	
Premier Inc 12255 El Camino Real *TF:* 877-777-1552 ■ *Web:* www.premierinc.com	San Diego	CA	92130	858-481-2727	481-8919
Provena Health 19065 Hickory Creek Dr Ste 310 *Web:* www.provena.org	Mokena	IL	60448	708-478-7900	
Providence Health & Services 4800 37th Ave SW **Fax Area Code:* 509 ■ *Web:* www2.providence.org	Seattle	WA	98126	206-937-4600	474-4882*
Riverside Health System 701 Town Ctr Dr Ste 1000 *Web:* riversideonline.com	Newport News	VA	23606	757-534-7000	534-7087
Riverside-San Bernardino County Indian Health Inc (RSBCIH) 11555 1/2 Potrero Rd *Web:* www.rsbcihi.org	Banning	CA	92220	951-849-4761	849-5631
Rush System for Health 1653 W Congress Pkwy Kidston Bldg Ste 305 *Web:* www.rush.edu	Chicago	IL	60612	312-942-5000	942-5831
Saint Francis Care 114 Woodland St *Web:* www.stfranciscare.org	Hartford	CT	06105	860-714-4000	714-7809
Schumacher Group 200 Corporate Blvd Ste 201 *TF:* 800-893-9698 ■ *Web:* www.schumachergroup.com	Lafayette	LA	70508	337-354-1332	371-4477
Scottsdale Healthcare 7400 E Osborn Rd *Web:* shc.org	Scottsdale	AZ	85251	480-882-4000	
Scranton Counseling Ctr Inc 326 Adams Ave *Web:* www.scrantonscc.org	Scranton	PA	18503	570-348-6100	
Scripps Health 4275 Campus Pt Ct *TF:* 800-727-4777 ■ *Web:* www.scripps.org	San Diego	CA	92121	800-727-4777	
Sea Mar Community Health Ctr 1040 S Henderson St *TF:* 855-289-4503 ■ *Web:* www.seamar.org	Seattle	WA	98108	206-763-5277	788-3204
Senior Whole Health LLC (SWH) 58 Charles St 2nd Fl *TF:* 888-794-7268 ■ *Web:* www.seniorwholehealth.com	Cambridge	MA	02141	617-494-5353	494-5599
Sentara Healthcare 6015 Poplar Hall Dr **Fax:* Mktg ■ *Web:* www.sentara.com	Norfolk	VA	23502	757-455-7000	455-7964*
Sharp Healthcare 8695 Spectrum Ctr Blvd *Web:* www.sharp.com	San Diego	CA	92123	858-499-4000	499-5237
Shriners Hospitals for Children 2900 N Rocky Pt Dr **Fax:* Hum Res ■ *TF:* 800-237-5055 ■ *Web:* www.shrinershospitalsforchildren.org	Tampa	FL	33607	813-281-0300	281-8174*
Sisters of Charity of Saint Augustine Health System 2475 E 22nd St *Web:* www.sistersofcharityhealth.org	Cleveland	OH	44115	216-696-5560	696-2204
Sisters of Mary of the Presentation Health System 1202 Page Dr SW PO Box 10007 *Web:* www.smphs.org	Fargo	ND	58106	701-237-9290	235-0906
Sisters of Mercy Health System 14528 S Outer Forty Ste 100 *Web:* www.mercy.net	Chesterfield	MO	63017	314-628-3656	628-3723
Sisters of the Holy Family of Nazareth Sacred Heart Province 310 N River Rd	Des Plaines	IL	60016	847-298-6760	803-1941
Southern Illinois Healthcare 1239 E Main St *TF:* 866-744-2468 ■ *Web:* www.sih.net	Carbondale	IL	62902	618-457-5200	
Spartanburg Regional Healthcare System 101 E Wood St **Fax:* Mail Rm ■ *Web:* www.spartanburgregional.com	Spartanburg	SC	29303	864-560-6000	560-6001*
SSM Healthy 1000 N. Lee St **Fax Area Code:* 405 ■ *TF:* 866-203-5846 ■ *Web:* www.smgsi.com	Oklahoma City	OK	73102	618-242-4600	272-6477*
St Elizabeth's Medical Ctr 736 Cambridge St *Web:* steward.org	Brighton	MA	02135	617-789-3000	
St. John Medical Ctr 1923 S Utica Ave *Web:* stjohnhealthsystem.com	Tulsa	OK	74104	918-744-2345	
Summit Medical Group One Diamond Hill Rd *Web:* www.summitmedicalgroup.com	Berkeley Heights	NJ	07922	908-273-4300	790-6593
Suncoast Ctr Inc PO Box 10970 *Web:* www.suncoastcenter.com	Saint Petersburg	FL	33733	727-327-7656	323-8978
SunLink Health Systems Inc 900 Cir 75 Pkwy Ste 1120 *NYSE: SSY* ■ *Web:* www.sunlinkhealth.com	Atlanta	GA	30339	770-933-7000	933-7010
Sutter Health 2200 River Plaza *TF:* 888-888-6044 ■ *Web:* www.sutterhealth.org	Sacramento	CA	95833	916-733-8800	
Tenet Healthcare Corp 1445 Ross Ave *NYSE: THC* ■ *Web:* www.tenethealth.com	Dallas	TX	75202	469-893-2000	893-8600
Terros Inc 3003 N Central Ave Ste 200 *TF:* 800-631-1314 ■ *Web:* www.terros.org	Phoenix	AZ	85012	602-222-9444	
Texas Health Resources 611 Ryan Plz Dr Ste 900 *Web:* www.texashealth.org	Arlington	TX	76011	817-462-7900	
TheraCare 116 W 32nd St 8th Fl *TF:* 800-505-7000 ■ *Web:* www.theracare.com	New York	NY	10001	212-564-2350	564-5896
Trinity Health 27870 Cabot Dr *Web:* www.trinity-health.org	Novi	MI	48377	248-489-6000	489-6075
Trinity Health System 380 Summit Ave *Web:* www.trinityhealth.com	Steubenville	OH	43952	740-283-7000	283-7104
Truman Medical Ctr 2301 Holmes St *Web:* www.trumed.org	Kansas City	MO	64108	816-404-1000	404-2573
United Health Centers of The San Joaquin Valley 650 Zediker Ave PO Box 790 *Web:* www.unitedhealthcenters.org	Parlier	CA	93648	559-646-6618	646-6614
United Health Services Hospitals 10-42 Mitchell Ave *Web:* www.uhs.net	Binghamton	NY	13903	607-762-2200	762-3203
United Medical Corp 603 Main St *Web:* unitedmedical.com	Windermere	FL	34786	407-876-2200	876-3065
Universal Health Services Inc 367 S Gulph Rd *NYSE: UHS* ■ *TF:* 800-347-7750 ■ *Web:* www.uhsinc.com	King of Prussia	PA	19406	610-768-3300	
University Health Network 190 Elizabeth St *Web:* www.uhn.ca	Toronto	ON	M5G2C4	416-340-3388	
University of California Health System 1111 Franklin St **Fax:* Hum Res ■ *Web:* www.universityofcalifornia.edu	Oakland	CA	94607	510-987-9200	987-0894*
University of Maryland Medical System 22 S Greene St *TF:* 800-492-5538 ■ *Web:* www.umm.edu	Baltimore	MD	21201	410-328-8667	
University of Pittsburgh Medical Ctr Health System 200 Lothrop St **Fax:* Hum Res ■ *TF:* 800-533-8762 ■ *Web:* www.upmc.com	Pittsburgh	PA	15213	412-647-2345	647-4522*
University of Texas System Office of Health Affairs 601 Colorado St *Web:* utsystem.edu/offices/health-affairs/	Austin	TX	78701	512-499-4224	499-4313
Valeo Behavioral Health Care Inc 5401 SW Seventh St *Web:* www.valeotopeka.org	Topeka	KS	66606	785-233-1730	
Vanguard Health Systems Inc 20 Burton Hills Blvd Ste 100 *Web:* www.tenethealth.com	Nashville	TN	37215	615-665-6000	665-6059
Vantage Health Plan Inc 130 Desiard St Ste 300 *Web:* www.vantagehealthplan.com/	Monroe	LA	71201	318-361-0900	
Venice Family Clinic 604 Rose Ave *Web:* www.venicefamilyclinic.org	Venice	CA	90291	310-392-8630	392-6642
Verde Valley Medical Ctr (VVMC) 269 S Candy Ln *Web:* www.verdevalleymedicalcenter.com	Cottonwood	AZ	86326	928-634-2251	

Name / Address	City	State	Zip	Phone	Fax
Veterans Health Administration 810 Vermont Ave NW *Web:* www2.va.gov	Washington	DC	20420	202-273-5400	
Vibra Healthcare 4550 Lena Dr *Web:* www.vibrahealthcare.com	Mechanicsburg	PA	17055	717-591-5700	591-5710
Virginia Commonwealth University Medical Ctr (VCU) 1250 E Marshall St *Web:* www.vcuhealth.org	Richmond	VA	23298	804-828-9000	
Virtua Health 401 Rt 73 N 50 Lake Center Dr Ste 401 *Web:* www.virtua.org	Marlton	NJ	08053	856-355-0010	
VistaCare Inc 3350 Riverwood Pkwy Ste 1400 **Fax Area Code:* 480 ■ *Web:* www.gentiva.com	Atlanta	GA	30339	770-951-6450	648-4547*
Washington County Mental Health Services Inc (WCMHS) PO Box 647 *TF:* 800-649-2642 ■ *Web:* www.wcmhs.org	Montpelier	VT	05601	802-229-0591	223-8623
West Oakland Health Council Inc (WOHC) 700 Adeline St *Web:* www.wohc.org	Oakland	CA	94607	510-835-9610	272-0209
West Penn Allegheny Health System 4800 Friendship Ave **Fax Area Code:* 412 ■ *TF:* 800-994-6610 ■ *Web:* ahn.org	Pittsburgh	PA	15224	800-994-6610	359-3933*
West Tennessee Healthcare 620 Skyline Dr *Web:* wth.org/	Jackson	TN	38301	731-541-5000	541-5195
William Beaumont Hospital 3601 W 13-Mile Rd **Fax:* Admitting ■ *Web:* www.beaumont.edu	Royal Oak	MI	48073	248-551-5000	898-0400*
Yakima Neighborhood Health Services (YNHS) 12 S Eigth St PO Box 2605 *Web:* www.ynhs.org	Yakima	WA	98907	509-454-4143	454-3651

357 HEALTH & FITNESS CENTERS

SEE ALSO Spas - Health & Fitness p. 3176; Weight Loss Centers & Services p. 3296

Name / Address	City	State	Zip	Phone	Fax
Ace Golf Inc 820 S Kings Ave *Web:* www.ace-golf.com	Brandon	FL	33511	813-651-4653	
Alaska Club Inc, The 5201 E Tudor Rd *Web:* www.thealaskaclub.com	Anchorage	AK	99507	907-337-9550	
Algoma University College 1520 Queen St E *Web:* algomau.ca	Sault Ste Marie	ON	P6A2G4	705-949-2301	
Any Body Fitness LLC 6513 Kingston Pk Ste 100 *Web:* www.anybodyfit.com	Knoxville	TN	37919	865-247-6705	
Anytime Fitness Inc 12181 Margo Ave S *Web:* www.anytimefitness.com	Hastings	MN	55033	651-438-5000	
Arena Fitness LLC 17200 Ventura Blvd Ste 101 *Web:* www.arenafitness.com	Encino	CA	91316	818-906-3030	
Asheville Racquet Club Inc 200 Racquet Club Rd *Web:* ashevilleracquetclub.com	Asheville	NC	28803	828-274-3361	
Asphalt Green Inc 555 E 90th St *Web:* www.agtri.com	New York	NY	10128	212-369-8890	
Athletic Clubs of America LLC 2920 E Zion Rd *Web:* www.fayac.com	Fayetteville	AR	72703	479-587-0500	
Atlanta Athletic Club 1930 Bobby Jones Dr *Web:* www.atlantaathleticclub.org	Johns Creek	GA	30097	770-448-2166	
Atlantic Club, The 1904 Atlantic Ave *Web:* www.theatlanticclub.com	Manasquan	NJ	08736	732-223-2100	
Auberge et spa Le Nordik Inc 16 ch Nordik *TF:* 866-575-3700 ■ *Web:* www.lenordik.com	Old Chelsea	QC	J9B2P7	819-827-1111	
AXIS Personal Trainers Inc 550 Ravenswood Ave *Web:* www.axispt.com	Menlo Park	CA	94025	650-463-1920	
Balance 2200 California St NW *Web:* www.balancegym.com	Washington	DC	20008	202-797-0021	
Bally Fitness 8700 W Bryn Mawr Ave *Web:* www.ballyfitness.com	Chicago	IL	60631	773-380-3000	
Bar Method, The 3333 Fillmore St *Web:* barmethod.com	San Francisco	CA	94123	415-441-6333	
Barry's Bootcamp 1106 N La Cienega Blvd Ste 104 *Web:* www.barrysbootcamp.com	West Hollywood	CA	90069	310-360-6262	
Bay Club Company, The 150 Greenwich St *Web:* bayclubs.com/sanfrancisco/	San Francisco	CA	94111	415-433-2200	394-5570
Beacon Consulting Group Inc 125 High St 25th Fl *Web:* www.beaconcgi.com	Boston	MA	02110	617-523-4030	
Belle Fourche Area Community Center 1111 National St *Web:* www.bellefourche.org	Belle Fourche	SD	57717	605-892-2467	
Best Fitness Inc 2309 Eggert Rd Ste 3 *Web:* bestfitness.net	Tonawanda	NY	14150	716-832-2378	
Big Fitness 190 Frenchtown Rd *TF:* 800-383-2008 ■ *Web:* www.bigfitness.com	North Kingstown	RI	02852	401-885-5200	
Blast Fitness Group LLC 452 Lexington St *Web:* blastfitness.com	Auburndale	MA	02466	617-916-5683	
Body Logic Fitness Studio 14205 Meridian Ave E Ste A4	Puyallup	WA	98373	253-841-1285	
Body Tech 19815 La Grange Rd *Web:* bodytechtotalfitness.com	Mokena	IL	60448	708-478-5054	
Bosse Sports 141 Boston Post Rd *Web:* bossesports.com	Sudbury	MA	01776	978-443-4613	
Boulevard Club The 1491 Lk Shore Blvd W *Web:* www.boulevardclub.com	Toronto	ON	M6K3C2	416-532-3341	
Boylan Indoor Tennis 4000 Saint Francis Dr *Web:* www.boylan.org	Rockford	IL	61103	815-877-4273	
Brick Bodies Fitness Services Inc 201 Old Padonia Rd *TF:* 866-952-7425 ■ *Web:* www.brickbodies.com	Cockeysville	MD	21030	410-252-8058	560-3299
Broadwater Athletic Clubs & Hot Springs 4920 W Us Hwy 12 *Web:* www.thebroadwater.com	Helena	MT	59601	406-443-5777	
Calgary Winter Club 4611 14 St Nw *Web:* www.calgarywinterclub.com	Calgary	AB	T2K1J7	403-289-5511	
Canlan Ice Sports Corp 6501 Sprott st *Web:* www.icesports.com	Burnaby	BC	V5B3B8	604-736-9152	
Capital City Club Inc Seven John Portman Blvd *Web:* www.capitalcityclub.org	Atlanta	GA	30303	404-523-8221	
Chelsea Piers Sports & Entertainment Complex 23rd St & Hudson River *Web:* www.chelseapiers.com	New York	NY	10011	212-336-6400	336-6130
City of Kamloops 105 Seymour St *Web:* www.city.kamloops.bc.ca	Kamloops	BC	V2C2C6	250-828-3439	
Club Metro Usa LLC 1779 Hooper Ave *Web:* www.clubmetrousa.com	Toms River	NJ	08753	732-864-1999	
Clubsport of San Ramon 350 Bollinger Canyon Ln *Web:* www.clubsportsr.com	San Ramon	CA	94582	925-735-8500	735-7916
Columbia Athletic Clubs 2930 228th Ave SE *Web:* www.columbiaathletic.com	Sammamish	WA	98075	425-313-0123	
Contours Express Inc 156 Imperial Way **Fax Area Code:* 859 ■ *TF:* 855-589-9662 ■ *Web:* www.contoursexpress.com	Nicholasville	KY	40356	855-589-9662	241-2234*
Coop's Health & Fitness Club Inc 19 Gladys Dr *Web:* www.coopsfitness.com	Greenville	SC	29607	864-280-2667	
Core Club, The 66 E 55th St *Web:* www.thecoreclub.com	New York	NY	10022	212-486-6600	
Corporate Fitness Works Inc 1200 16th St N *TF:* 855-417-9697 ■ *Web:* www.corporatefitnessworks.com	St Petersburg	FL	33705	301-417-9697	
Courthouse Fitness 495 State St Sixth Fl Ste 600 *Web:* www.fitfx.com	Salem	OR	97301	503-588-2582	
Crossgates Recreation Inc 200 N Military Rd *Web:* crossgatesclub.com	Slidell	LA	70461	985-643-3500	
Crunch Fitness International 220 W 19th St **Fax Area Code:* 646 ■ *TF:* 888-227-8624 ■ *Web:* www.crunch.com	New York	NY	10011	212-370-0998	217-4163*
D1 Sports Holdings LLC 7115 S Springs Dr *Web:* www.d1sportstraining.com	Franklin	TN	37067	615-778-1893	
Defined Fitness 4930 Mcleod Rd Ne *Web:* www.defined.com	Albuquerque	NM	87109	505-888-7097	
Denver Athletic Club 1325 Glenarm Pl *Web:* www.denverathleticclub.cc	Denver	CO	80204	303-534-1211	534-1125
Detroit Athletic Club 241 Madison St *Web:* www.thedac.com	Detroit	MI	48226	313-963-9200	963-8891
Dumbell Man Fitness Equipment, The 655 Hawaii Ave *TF:* 800-432-6266 ■ *Web:* www.dumbellman.com	Torrance	CA	90503	310-381-2900	
East Bank Club 500 N Kingsbury St *Web:* www.eastbankclub.com	Chicago	IL	60654	312-527-5800	644-3868
Equinox Fitness Holdings Inc 895 Broadway *TF:* 866-332-6549 ■ *Web:* www.equinox.com	New York	NY	10003	212-677-0180	777-9510
Estancia Club 27998 N 99th Pl *Web:* www.brooksidegcc.com	Scottsdale	AZ	85262	480-473-4400	
Fig Garden Swim & Racquet Club 4722 N Maroa Ave *Web:* www.fig-garden.com	Fresno	CA	93704	559-222-4816	
Findlay Country Club Pro. Shop 1500 Country Club Dr *Web:* www.findlaycc.com	Findlay	OH	45840	419-422-9263	
Fitcorp 800 Boylston St *Web:* www.fitcorp.com	Boston	MA	02199	617-262-2050	
Fitness Ctr 1914 Round Barn Rd *Web:* www.fitcen.com	Champaign	IL	61821	217-356-1616	356-7920
Fitness Depot 1808 Lower Roswell Rd *TF:* 800-974-6828 ■ *Web:* www.thefitnessdepot.com	Marietta	GA	30068	770-971-6828	565-7119
Fitness Formula Ltd 619 W Jackson *Web:* www.fitnessformula.com	Chicago	IL	60661	312-648-4666	
Flex Hr 10700 Medlock Bridge Rd Ste 206 *TF:* 877-735-3947 ■ *Web:* www.flexhr.com	Johns Creek	GA	30097	770-814-4225	814-4123
G & G Fitness Equipment Inc 7350 Transit Rd *Web:* www.livefit.com	Williamsville	NY	14221	716-633-2527	
Gaston County Family Ymca 3210 Union Rd *Web:* www.gastonymca.org	Gastonia	NC	28056	704-865-2193	
Gestion Riviere du Diable Inc 4280 Montee Ryan *Web:* www.scandinave.com	Mont Tremblant	QC	J8E1S4	819-425-9595	
Get In Shape For Women 75 Second Ave Ste 220 *Web:* www.getinshapeforwomen.com	Needham	MA	02494	781-444-1913	
Global Fitness Center Inc 215 Hamilton St *Web:* www.globalfitnesscenter.com	Leominster	MA	01453	978-537-2100	
GoodLife Fitness 355 Wellington St PO Box 23091 *Web:* www.goodlifefitness.com	London	ON	N6A3N7	519-433-0601	661-0416
Green Valley Recreation Inc 921 W Via Rio Fuerte *Web:* www.gvrec.org	Green Valley	AZ	85614	520-393-0360	
Greenwood Athletic Club 5801 S Quebec St *Web:* www.greenwoodathleticclub.com	Greenwood Village	CO	80111	303-770-2582	850-9219
Hamilton Area YMCA Inc 1315 Whitehorse-Mercerville Rd *Web:* www.hamiltonymca.org	Hamilton	NJ	08619	609-581-9622	
Harbor Bay Club 200 Packet Landing Rd *Web:* harborbayclub.com	Alameda	CA	94502	510-521-5414	

Name / Address	City	State	Zip	Phone	Fax
Healthridge Fitness Center LLC 17800 W 106th St. *Web:* healthridgefitness.com	Olathe	KS	66061	913-888-0505	
Healthtrax Fitness & Wellness 2345 Main St *TF:* 800-998-0880 ■ *Web:* www.healthtrax.com	Glastonbury	CT	06033	860-652-7066	652-7066
Hiatus Spa & Retreat 5560 W Lovers Ln Ste 250 *Web:* hiatusspa.com	Dallas	TX	75209	214-352-4111	
Ice Specialty Entertainment Inc 409 Santa Monica Blvd Ste E *Web:* www.iceoplex.com	Santa Monica	CA	90401	805-520-7465	
In-Shape Health Clubs 1016 E Bianchi Rd *Web:* www.inshapeclubs.com	Stockton	CA	95210	209-472-2231	
India Community Center Inc 555 Los Coches St *Web:* www.indiacc.org	Milpitas	CA	95035	408-934-1130	
Inspiring Wellness LLC 665 S Orange Ave Ste 7 *Web:* www.babybootcamp.com	Sarasota	FL	34236	941-953-5000	
Iron Tribe Franchise LLC 300 27th St S *TF:* 855-226-8699 ■ *Web:* irontribefitness.com	Birmingham	AL	35233	205-226-8669	
Issaquah Swimming Pool 50 Se Clark St *Web:* ci.issaquah.wa.us	Issaquah	WA	98027	425-837-3350	
It Healthtrack Inc 6500 Main St Ste 3 *Web:* ithealthtrack.com	Williamsville	NY	14221	716-630-0063	
Jonas Fitness Inc 16969 n texas ave *TF:* 800-324-9800 ■ *Web:* www.jonasfitness.com	Webster	TX	77598	800-324-9800	
Jordan Essentials 1106 eaglecrest st *Web:* www.jordanessentials.com	Nixa	MO	65714	417-724-9690	
Kimberly Spa 4130 S 144th St *Web:* kimberlyspaomaha.com	Omaha	NE	68137	402-614-8400	
Kinderdance International Inc 1333 Gateway Dr Ste 1033 *TF:* 800-554-2334 ■ *Web:* www.kinderdance.com	Melbourne	FL	32901	321-984-4448	984-4490
KoKo Fitness Inc 300 Ledgewood Pl Ste 200 *Web:* www.kokofitclub.com	Rockland	MA	02370	781-753-9495	
LA Fitness International 2880 Michelle Dr *Web:* www.lafitness.com	Irvine	CA	92606	714-505-8958	
Lady of America Franchise Corp 159 Weston RD Ste 1650 *TF:* 800-833-5239 ■ *Web:* www.ladyofamerica.com	Weston	FL	33326	954-217-8660	
Lake Hills Golf Club Inc 1930 Clubhouse Way *Web:* www.lakehillsgolf.com	Billings	MT	59105	406-252-9244	
Lake Merced Golf & Country Club 2300 Junipero Serra Blvd *Web:* www.lmgc.org	Daly City	CA	94015	650-755-2233	
Lake Shore Athletic Club Inc 2401 NW 94th St *Web:* www.lsac.com	Vancouver	WA	98665	360-574-1991	574-9233
Landings Club Inc 71 Green Island Rd *Web:* www.landingsclub.com	Savannah	GA	31411	912-598-8050	
Las Vegas 51s, The 850 Las Vegas Blvd N *Web:* lasvegas.51s.milb.com	Las Vegas	NV	89101	702-386-7200	
Las Vegas Athletic Club 2655 S Maryland Pkwy Ste 201 *Web:* www.lvac.com	Las Vegas	NV	89109	702-734-8944	733-7771
Les entreprises energie Cardio 1040 Michele-Bohec Blvd Ste 300 *Web:* www.energiecardio.com	Blainville	QC	J7C5E2	450-979-3613	
Lexington Health Care Ctr 178 Lowell St *Web:* www.healthbridgemanagement.com/lexington	Lexington	MA	02420	781-862-7400	862-7855
Lifecnter Plus Lf. Heath Fitnes 5133 Darrow Rd *Web:* www.lifecenterplus.com	Hudson	OH	44236	330-655-2377	
Litchfield Park Recreation 100 N Old Litchfield Rd *Web:* www.litchfield-park.org	Litchfield Park	AZ	85340	623-935-9040	
Little Gym International Inc 7001 N Scottsdale Rd *TF General:* 888-228-2878 ■ *Web:* www.thelittlegym.com	Paradise Valley	AZ	85253	888-228-2878	
Livermore Valley Tennis Club II 2000 Arroyo Rd *Web:* www.lvtc.com	Livermore	CA	94550	925-443-7700	
Louisville Athletic Club LLC 9565 Taylorsville Rd *Web:* athleticclubs.org	Louisville	KY	40299	502-753-0999	
Lucille Roberts Health Clubs Inc 143 Fulton St *Web:* www.lucilleroberts.com	New York	NY	10038	212-267-3730	734-4151
Makoy Center Inc 5462 Center St *Web:* www.makoy.com	Hilliard	OH	43026	614-777-1211	
Matrix Fitness Systems Corp 1600 Landmark Dr *Web:* www.matrixfitness.com	Cottage Grove	WI	53527	608-839-8686	
Mdr Fitness Corp 14101 Nw Fourth St *Web:* www.mdr.net	Sunrise	FL	33325	954-845-9500	
Merritt Athletic Clubs 2076 Lord Baltimore Dr *Web:* www.merrittclubs.com	Baltimore	MD	21244	410-298-8700	
Milwaukee Athletic Club 758 N Broadway *Web:* www.macwi.org	Milwaukee	WI	53202	414-273-5080	273-4118
Missouri Athletic Club 405 Washington Ave *Web:* www.mac-stl.org	Saint Louis	MO	63102	314-231-7220	
Mountain Empire Family Medicine 31115 Hwy 94 *Web:* wordpress.mtnhealth.org	Campo	CA	91906	619-478-5311	
Mountainside Fitness 9745 W Happy Vly Rd *Web:* www.mountainsidefitness.com	Peoria	AZ	85383	623-561-5525	
Move Your Mind a Fitness First 2100 Tremont Ctr	Columbus	OH	43221	614-486-0575	
Multnomah Athletic Club 1849 SW Salmon St *Web:* www.themac.com	Portland	OR	97205	503-223-6251	525-8998
National Institute for Fitness & Sport Inc, The 250 University Blvd *Web:* www.nifs.org	Indianapolis	IN	46202	317-274-3432	
Naturopathica Spa 74 Montauk Hwy Ste 23 *Web:* www.naturopathica.com	East Hampton	NY	11937	631-329-2525	
Nautilus Entertainment Design Inc 1010 Pearl St Ste Three *Web:* www.n-e-d.com	La Jolla	CA	92037	858-456-6395	
New Castle Community y 20 W Washington St *Web:* www.ncymca.org	New Castle	PA	16101	724-658-4766	
New Orleans Zephyrs, The 6000 Airline Dr *Web:* neworleans.zephyrs.milb.com	Metairie	LA	70003	504-734-5155	
New York Junior Tennis League Inc 5812 Queens Blvd Ste 1 *Web:* www.nyjtl.org	Woodside	NY	11377	718-786-7110	
New York Sports Club 888 Seventh Ave 25th Fl *Web:* www.mysportsclubs.com	New York	NY	10106	212-246-6700	246-8422
Nifty After Fifty LLC 12572 Vly View *Web:* niftyafterfifty.com	Garden Grove	CA	92845	714-823-4400	
Nu Image MedSpa Inc 3753 Howard Hughes Pkwy	Las Vegas	NV	89169	702-784-5922	
Omni Fitness Club 40 E Norton St *Web:* www.omnifitnessclub.com	Muskegon	MI	49444	231-739-3391	
Palisades Tennis Club 1171 Jamboree Rd *Web:* tennisontheweb.com	Newport Beach	CA	92660	949-644-6900	
Peak Physique Inc 50 Holly Hill Ln *Web:* peakphysiqueinc.com	Greenwich	CT	06830	203-625-9595	
Peoplefit Health & Fitness Center 237 Lexington St Ste 110 *Web:* peoplefit.net	Woburn	MA	01801	781-932-9332	
Philadelphia Sports Clubs 888 Seventh Ave *Web:* www.mysportsclubs.com	New York	NY	10106	212-246-6700	246-8422
Pivotal Health & Fitness LLC 1401 Sam Rittenberg Blvd *Web:* www.pivotalfitness.com	Charleston	SC	29845	843-571-5858	
Platte County Community Center North 3101 Running Horse Rd *Web:* www.kansascityymca.org	Platte City	MO	64079	816-858-0114	
Poway Pilates 14053 Midland Rd *Web:* powaypilates.net	Poway	CA	92064	858-748-7864	
Powerhouse Gym International 355 S Old Woodward Ste 150 **Fax Area Code:* 249 ■ *Web:* www.powerhousegym.com	Birmingham	MI	48009	248-476-2888	530-9816*
Prairie Life Fitness 2275 S 132nd St *Web:* www.prairielife.com	Omaha	NE	68144	402-691-8546	
Premier & Curzons Fitness Clubs 5100 Dixie Rd *TF:* 866-371-7307	Mississauga	ON	L4W1C9	905-602-9912	
Ridgewood Racquet Club 249 Ackerman Ave *Web:* ridgewoodracquetclub.com	Ridgewood	NJ	07450	201-652-1991	
River Oaks Country Club Inc 1600 River Oaks Blvd *Web:* www.riveroakscc.net	Houston	TX	77019	713-529-4321	
Rivers Club Inc 301 Grant St *Web:* www.clubcorp.com	Pittsburgh	PA	15219	412-391-5227	391-5016
Riviera Fitness Centers 3908 Veterans Blvd *Web:* www.rivierafitnesscenters.com	Metairie	LA	70002	504-454-5855	454-7717
Rock Sports Complex LLC, The 7900 W Crystal Ridge Dr *Web:* www.skicrystalridge.com	Franklin	WI	53132	414-529-7676	
Royal Fox Country Club 4405 Royal And Ancient Dr *Web:* www.royalfoxcc.com	Saint Charles	IL	60174	630-584-4000	
Sailfish Club of Florida Inc, The 1338 N Lake Way *Web:* www.sailfishclub.com	Palm Beach	FL	33480	561-844-0206	
Scotch Malt Whiskey Society 10210 Nw 50th St *Web:* www.smwsa.com	Sunrise	FL	33351	954-749-2440	
Scripps Ranch Swim & Racquet Club 9875 Aviary Dr *Web:* srsrc.com	San Diego	CA	92131	858-271-6222	
Seahorse Fitness Inc 69 Columbia St *Web:* www.seahorseswimclub.com	New York	NY	10002	212-254-3651	
Seattle Athletic Club 2020 Western Ave *Web:* www.sacdt.com	Seattle	WA	98121	206-443-1111	443-2632
Seattle Tennis Club 922 Mcgilvra Blvd E *Web:* seattletennisclub.org	Seattle	WA	98112	206-324-3200	
Sensor Dynamics Inc 4568 Enterprise St *Web:* sensordynamics.com	Fremont	CA	94538	510-623-1459	
Shockoe Commerce Group LLC 11 S 12th St Fourth Fl *Web:* www.shockoecommerce.com	Richmond	VA	23219	804-343-3441	
Skoah Metrotown Inc 4800 Kingsway *Web:* skoah.com	Burnaby	BC	V5H4J2	604-433-0200	
Somerset Patriots Baseball Club One Patriots Park *Web:* somersetpatriots.com	Bridgewater	NJ	08807	908-252-0700	
Somerset Valley Ymca Two Green St *Web:* ymcasomersetvalley.org	Somerville	NJ	08876	908-722-4567	
Spalon Montage 600 Market St Ste 270 *Web:* www.spalon.com	Chanhassen	MN	55317	952-915-2900	
Sport Fit Bowie Racquet & Fitness Club Inc 100 Whitemarsh Park Dr *Web:* sportfitclubs.com	Bowie	MD	20715	301-262-4553	
Sport&Health Clubs LLC 1800 Old Meadow Rd Ste 300 *Web:* www.sportandhealth.com	Mclean	VA	22102	703-556-6550	
Sportsmen of Stanislaus Club 819 Sunset Ave *Web:* www.sosclub.com	Modesto	CA	95351	209-578-5801	
Talisman Centre 2225 Macleod Trl SE *Web:* www.talismancentre.com	Calgary	AB	T2G5B6	403-233-8393	
Tennis Equities Inc 77 Kensico Dr *Web:* www.sawmillclub.com	Mount Kisco	NY	10549	914-241-0797	

Phone *Fax*

Trail Smoke Eaters Hockey Club
204-1199 Bay Ave . . . Trail BC V1R4A4 250-364-9994
Web: www.trailsmokeeaters.com

Trailhead Athletic Club LLC
7900 E Eagle Crest Dr. . . . Mesa AZ 85207 480-832-6900
Web: www.thetrailhead.org

Transalta Tri Leisure Centre
221 Jennifer Heil Way. . . . Spruce Grove AB T7X4J5 780-960-5080
Web: www.trileisure.com

TuffStuff Fitness Equipment Inc
13971 Norton Ave. . . . Chino CA 91710 909-629-1600
TF: 888-884-8275 ■ *Web:* www.tuffstuffitness.com

Vitense Golfland 5501 Schroeder Rd. . . . Madison WI 53711 608-271-1411
Web: www.vitense.com

Washington Sports Clubs 888 Seventh Ave . . . New York NY 10106 212-246-6700 246-8422
Web: www.mysportsclubs.com

Washington Tennis Services Inc
3200 Tower Oaks Blvd . . . Rockville MD 20852 301-622-7800 622-3373
Web: www.wtsinternational.com

Wellbridge Co
6140 Greenwood Plaza Blvd Ste 200 . . . Greenwood Village CO 80111 303-866-0800 813-4197
TF Acctg: 888-458-0489 ■ *Web:* www.wellbridge.com

Western Athletic Clubs One Lombard St. . . . San Francisco CA 94111 415-781-1874
Web: bayclubs.com/

Whirl Wynn Fitness LLC
36 S Charles St Ste 203 . . . Baltimore MD 21201 410-539-7401
Web: whirl-wynnfitness.com

Winnetka Community House 620 Lincoln Ave . . . Winnetka IL 60093 847-446-0537
Web: winnetkacommunityhouse.org

Work Out World 762 SR- 18. . . . Brunswick NJ 08816 732-390-7390
TF: 888-564-6969 ■ *Web:* www.workoutworld.com

World Health 7222 Edgemont Blvd NW . . . Calgary AB T3A2X7 403-239-4048
TF: 866-278-4131 ■ *Web:* worldhealth.ca

X 3 Sports 2343 Windy Hill Rd Se . . . Marietta GA 30067 678-903-0100
Web: x3sports.com

XSport Fitness Inc 6420 W Fullerton Ave . . . Chicago IL 60707 773-237-5730
Web: www.xsportfitness.com

YMCA of Rock River Valley 200 Y Blvd. . . . Rockford IL 61107 815-987-2252
Web: www.rockfordymca.org

358 HEALTH FOOD STORES

Phone *Fax*

Christopher Enterprises
155 West 2050 North . . . Spanish Fork UT 84660 800-453-1406 794-6801*
**Fax Area Code:* 801 ■ *TF:* 800-453-1406 ■ *Web:* www.drchristopher.com

Ginsberg's Foods Inc 29 Ginsberg Ln PO Box 17 . . . Hudson NY 12534 518-828-4004 828-5653
TF: 800-999-6006 ■ *Web:* www.ginsbergs.com

GNC Inc 300 Sixth Ave 14th Fl . . . Pittsburgh PA 15222 877-462-4700
NYSE: GNC ■ *TF:* 877-462-4700 ■ *Web:* www.gnc.com

Juice It Up! Franchise Corp
17915 Sky Pk Cir Ste J. . . . Irvine CA 92614 949-475-0146 475-0137
Web: www.juiceitup.com

Netrition Inc 25 Corporate Cir Ste 118 . . . Albany NY 12203 518-464-0765 456-9673
TF: 888-817-2411 ■ *Web:* www.netrition.com

Ream's Food Stores
160 E Claybourne Ave. . . . Salt Lake City UT 84115 801-485-8451 485-0845
Web: www.reamsfoods.com

Vincit Group, The 412 Georgia Ave Ste 300 . . . Chattanooga TN 37403 423-265-7090 265-9070
Web: www.vincitgroup.com

Whole Foods Market Inc 550 Bowie St. . . . Austin TX 78703 512-477-4455 482-7000
NASDAQ: WFM ■ *TF:* 888-992-6227 ■ *Web:* www.wholefoodsmarket.com

359 HEALTH & MEDICAL INFORMATION - ONLINE

Phone *Fax*

At Health Inc 7829 Center Blvd SE. . . . Snoqualmie WA 98065 425-292-0329
TF: 888-284-3258 ■ *Web:* www.athealth.com

BabyCenter LLC 163 Freelon St. . . . San Francisco CA 94107 415-537-0900 537-0909
TF: 866-241-2229 ■ *Web:* www.babycenter.com

Body, The 250 W 57th St. . . . New York NY 10107 212-541-8500 541-4911
Web: www.thebody.com

drgreene.com 9000 Crow Canyon Rd Ste S220 . . . Danville CA 94506 925-964-1793 964-1794
Web: www.drgreene.com

eMedicine.com Inc 8420 W Dodge Rd Ste 402 . . . Omaha NE 68114 402-341-3222 341-3336
TF: 866-241-9601 ■ *Web:* emedicine.medscape.com

Medicine Online Inc
18800 Delaware St Ste 650. . . . Huntington Beach CA 92648 714-848-0444 242-1484
Web: www.medicineonline.com

MedlinePlus
National Library of Medicine
8600 Rockville Pk. . . . Bethesda MD 20894 301-594-5983 402-1384
TF: 888-346-3656 ■ *Web:* www.nlm.nih.gov/medlineplus

Pain.com
Dannemiller Memorial Educational Foundation
5711 NW Pkwy Ste 100. . . . San Antonio TX 78246 210-572-2512 641-8329
TF: 800-328-2308 ■ *Web:* www.pain.com

PubMed
US National Library of Medicine
8600 Rockville Pike . . . Bethesda MD 20894 888-346-3656 402-1384*
**Fax Area Code:* 301 ■ *TF:* 888-346-3656 ■ *Web:* www.ncbi.nlm.nih.gov

Scientific Technologies Corp
4400 E Broadway Blvd Ste 705. . . . Tucson AZ 85711 520-202-3333 202-3340
Web: www.stchome.com

WebMD 111 Eigth Ave Ste 7 . . . New York NY 10011 212-624-3700
Web: www.webmd.com

HEATING EQUIPMENT - ELECTRIC

SEE Air Conditioning & Heating Equipment - Residential p. 1728

360 HEATING EQUIPMENT - GAS, OIL, COAL

SEE ALSO Air Conditioning & Heating Equipment - Commercial/Industrial p. 1726; Air Conditioning & Heating Equipment - Residential p. 1728; Furnaces & Ovens - Industrial Process p. 2343; Boiler Shops p. 1875

Phone *Fax*

Aerco International Inc 159 Paris Ave. . . . Northvale NJ 07647 201-768-2400 784-8073
TF: 800-526-0288 ■ *Web:* www.aerco.com

Appalachian Stove & Fabricators Inc
329 Emma Rd. . . . Asheville NC 28806 828-253-0164 254-7803
Web: www.appalachianstove.com

Aquatherm Industries Inc
1940 Rutgers University Blvd . . . Lakewood NJ 08701 800-535-6307 905-9899*
**Fax Area Code:* 732 ■ *TF:* 800-535-6307 ■ *Web:* www.warmwater.com

Atlantis Energy Systems Inc
4517 Industry St. . . . Poughkeepsie NY 12603 916-438-2930
Web: www.atlantisenergy.com

Barnes & Jones Corp 91 Pacella Pk Dr. . . . Randolph MA 02368 781-963-8000 963-3322
Web: www.barnesandjones.com

Besicorp Ltd 1151 Flatbush Rd . . . Kingston NY 12401 845-336-7700 336-7172
Web: www.besicorp.com

BFS Industries LLC 200 Industrial Dr. . . . Butner NC 27509 919-575-6711 575-4275
Web: www.bfs-ind.com

Bosch Thermotechnology 340 Mad River Pk. . . . Waitsfield VT 05673 800-283-3787 496-6924*
**Fax Area Code:* 806 ■ *Web:* www.bosch-climate.us

Burner Systems International Inc (BSI)
3600 Cummings Rd . . . Chattanooga TN 37419 423-822-3600 822-2223
TF: 800-251-6318 ■ *Web:* www.burnersystems.com

Burnham Holdings Inc
1241 Harrisburg Ave PO Box 3205. . . . Lancaster PA 17604 717-390-7800
Web: www.burnhamholdings.com

Charles A Hones Inc
607 Albany Ave PO Box 518. . . . North Amityville NY 11701 631-842-8886 842-9300
Web: www.charlesahones.com

Cool Earth Solar Inc
4659 Las Positas Rd Ste C . . . Livermore CA 94551 925-454-8506
Web: www.coolearthsolar.com

Cool Energy Inc 5541 Central Ave Ste 172. . . . Boulder CO 80301 303-442-2121
Web: coolenergy.com

Cryoquip Inc 25720 Jefferson Ave . . . Murrieta CA 92562 951-677-2060 677-2066
Web: www.cryoquip.com

Ebner Furnaces Inc 224 Quadral Dr . . . Wadsworth OH 44281 330-335-1600 335-1605
Web: ebner.cc/home/

Electro-Flex Heat Inc Five Northwood Rd . . . Bloomfield CT 06002 860-242-6287 242-7298
TF: 800-585-4213 ■ *Web:* www.electroflexheat.com

Embassy Industries Inc 300 Smith St . . . Farmingdale NY 11735 631-694-1800 694-1832
Web: www.embassyind.com

Empire Comfort Systems Inc
918 Freeburg Ave . . . Belleville IL 62222 618-233-7420 233-7097
TF: 800-851-3153 ■ *Web:* www.empirecomfort.com

Freeman Gas Inc
1186 Asheville Hwy PO Box 4366 . . . Spartanburg SC 29303 864-582-5475 582-0937
TF: 800-277-5730 ■ *Web:* www.freemangas.com

Fulton Cos 972 Centerville Rd. . . . Pulaski NY 13142 315-298-5121 298-6390
Web: www.fulton.com

Hago Mfg Company Inc 1120 Globe Ave . . . Mountainside NJ 07092 908-232-8687 232-7246
Web: na.heating.danfoss.com

Hamworthy Peabody Combustion Inc
70 Shelton Technology Ctr . . . Shelton CT 06484 203-922-1199
Web: www.coen.com

Hayward Pool Products Inc 620 Div St. . . . Elizabeth NJ 07207 908-351-5400 351-5675
Web: www.hayward-pool.com

Hearth & Home Technologies Inc
7571 215th St W. . . . Lakeville MN 55044 952-985-6000 985-6005
Web: www.hearthnhome.com

Heat Controller Inc 1900 Wellworth Ave. . . . Jackson MI 49203 517-787-2100 787-9341
Web: www.heatcontroller.com

John Zink Company LLC 11920 E Apache St. . . . Tulsa OK 74116 918-234-1800 234-2700
TF: 800-421-9242 ■ *Web:* www.johnzink.com

Johnston Boiler Co 300 Pine St . . . Ferrysburg MI 49409 616-842-5050 842-1854*
**Fax:* Cust Svc ■ *TF General:* 800-748-0295 ■ *Web:* www.johnstonboiler.com

LB White Company Inc W 6636 LB White Rd . . . Onalaska WI 54650 608-783-5691 783-6115
TF: 800-345-7200 ■ *Web:* www.lbwhite.com

Meeder Equipment Co 12323 Sixth St. . . . Rancho Cucamonga CA 91739 909-463-0600 463-0102
TF: 800-423-3711 ■ *Web:* www.meeder.com

New Buck Corp 8000 Hwy 226 S PO Box 69 . . . Spruce Pine NC 28777 828-765-6144 765-0462
Web: www.buckstove.com

New Yorker Boiler Company Inc PO Box 10. . . . Hatfield PA 19440 215-855-8055 855-8229
TF: 800-535-4679 ■ *Web:* www.newyorkerboiler.com

North American Mfg Company Ltd
4455 E 71st St . . . Cleveland OH 44105 216-271-6000 641-7852
Web: combustion.fivesgroup.com/about-us/about-combustion.html

Parker Boiler Co 5930 Bandini Blvd . . . Los Angeles CA 90040 323-727-9800 722-2848
Web: www.parkerboiler.com

Power Flame Inc 2001 S 21st St PO Box 974. . . . Parsons KS 67357 620-421-0480 421-0948
Web: www.powerflame.com

Powrmatic Inc
2906 Baltimore Blvd PO Box 439. . . . Finksburg MD 21048 410-833-9100 833-7971
TF: 800-966-9100 ■ *Web:* www.powrmatic.com

ProVision solar Inc 69 Railroad Ave Ste A-7 . . . Hilo HI 96720 808-969-3281 934-7462
Web: www.provisiontechnologies.com

Rasmussen Iron Works Inc
12028 E Philadelphia St . . . Whittier CA 90601 562-696-8718 698-3510
TF: 888-301-0440 ■ *Web:* www.rasmussen.biz

Raypak Inc 2151 Eastman Ave . . . Oxnard CA 93030 805-278-5300 278-5468
TF: 800-438-4328 ■ *Web:* www.raypak.com

Reimers Electra Steam Inc
4407 Martinsburg Pk PO Box 37 . . . Clear Brook VA 22624 540-662-3811 726-4215*
**Fax Area Code:* 800 ■ *TF:* 800-872-7562 ■ *Web:* www.reimersinc.com

	City	State	Zip	Phone	Fax
Rite Engineering & Manufacturing Corp 5832 Garfield *Web:* www.riteboiler.com	Commerce	CA	90040	562-862-2135	861-9821
Roberts-Gordon Inc 1250 William St PO Box 44 *TF:* 800-828-7450 ■ *Web:* www.rg-inc.com	Buffalo	NY	14240	716-852-4400	852-0854
RW Beckett Corp PO Box 1289 *TF:* 800-645-2876 ■ *Web:* www.beckettcorp.com	Elyria	OH	44036	440-327-1060	327-1064
Schwank Inc Two Schwank Way at Hwy 56N **Fax Area Code:* 706 ■ *TF:* 877-446-3727 ■ *Web:* www.schwankusa.com	Waynesboro	GA	30830	877-446-3727	554-9390*
Smith Cast Iron Boilers 260 N Elm St *Web:* www.westcastboilers.com	Westfield	MA	01085	413-562-9631	562-3799
Spectrolab Inc 12500 Gladstone Ave *TF:* 800-936-4888 ■ *Web:* www.spectrolab.com	Sylmar	CA	91342	818-365-4611	361-5102
Taco Inc 1160 Cranston St **Fax Area Code:* 905 ■ **Fax:* Cust Svc ■ *TF:* 888-778-2733 ■ *Web:* www.taco-hvac.com	Cranston	RI	02920	401-942-8000	564-9436*
Templeton Coal Co 701 Wabash Ave *Web:* templetoncoal.com	Terre Haute	IN	47807	812-232-7037	232-3752
Thermal Solutions LLC PO Box 3244 **Fax Area Code:* 877 ■ *TF:* 800-860-5726 ■ *Web:* www.thermalsolutions.com	Lancaster	PA	17604	717-239-7642	501-5212*
Utica Boilers Inc PO Box 4729 **Fax Area Code:* 315 ■ *TF:* 800-325-5479 ■ *Web:* www.uticaboilers.com	Utica	NY	13504	866-847-6656	797-3762*
Water Furnace International Inc 9000 Conservation Way **Fax:* Hum Res ■ *TF:* 800-222-5667 ■ *Web:* www.waterfurnace.com	Fort Wayne	IN	46809	260-478-5667	747-5780*
Wayne Combustion Systems 801 Glasgow Ave *TF:* 855-929-6327 ■ *Web:* www.waynecombustion.com	Fort Wayne	IN	46803	260-425-9200	424-0904
Weil-McLain Co 500 Blaine St *Web:* www.weil-mclain.com	Michigan City	IN	46360	219-879-6561	879-4025
Williams Comfort Products 250 W Laurel St *Web:* www.williamscomfortprod.com	Colton	CA	92324	909-825-0993	824-8009
Zeeco Inc 22151 E 91st St S *Web:* www.zeeco.com	Broken Arrow	OK	74014	918-258-8551	251-5519

361 HEAVY EQUIPMENT DISTRIBUTORS

SEE ALSO Farm Machinery & Equipment - Whol p. 2284; Industrial Equipment & Supplies (Misc) - Whol p. 2552

	City	State	Zip	Phone	Fax
4Rivers Equipment 3763 Monarch St *Web:* 4riversequipment.com/	Frederick	CO	80516	303-833-5900	
Able Die Casting Corp 3907 Wesley Ter *Web:* www.ablediecasting.com	Schiller Park	IL	60176	847-678-1991	
Absolute Machine Tools Inc 7420 Industrial Pkwy *Web:* www.absolutemachine.com	Lorain	OH	44053	440-960-6911	
Ace Industries Inc 6295 McDonough Dr *Web:* www.aceindustries.com	Norcross	GA	30093	770-441-0898	
Acer Group 1062 N Kraemer Pl *Web:* acergroup.com	Anaheim	CA	92806	714-632-9701	
ACI Controls Inc 295 Main St *Web:* www.aci-controls.com	West Seneca	NY	14224	716-675-9450	
Action Lift Inc One Memco Dr *Web:* actionliftinc.com	Pittston	PA	18640	570-655-2100	
Adams Air & Hydraulics Inc 7209 E Adamo Dr *Web:* www.adamsair.com	Tampa	FL	33619	813-626-4128	
Adept Corp 4601 N Susquehanna Trl *Web:* adeptcorp.com	York	PA	17406	717-266-3606	
Admar Supply Co Inc 1950 Brighton Henriett *TF:* 800-836-2367 ■ *Web:* www.admarsupply.com	Rochester	NY	14623	585-272-9390	272-9165
Advanced Specialty Products 428 Clough St *Web:* www.aspohio.com	Bowling Green	OH	43402	419-354-2844	352-9663
Advent Electric Inc 301 E Fourth St *Web:* www.advent-elect.com	Bridgeport	PA	19405	610-277-6610	
Aerial Rigging & Leasing Inc 2940 Drane Field Rd *Web:* www.aerialrigging.com	Lakeland	FL	33811	863-607-9100	
Aero Grinding Inc 28300 Groesbeck Hwy *Web:* aerogrinding.com	Roseville	MI	48066	586-774-6450	
Agar Corp Inc 5150 Tacoma Dr *Web:* www.agarcorp.com	Houston	TX	77041	832-476-5100	476-5299
Air Center Inc 2175 Stephenson Hwy *Web:* teamaircenter.com	Troy	MI	48083	248-619-7800	
Air Center Inc, The 270 Monroe Ave *Web:* www.aircenternj.com	Kenilworth	NJ	07033	908-276-1992	
AJ Jersey Inc 125 Saint Nicholas Ave *Web:* www.ajjersey.net	South Plainfield	NJ	07080	908-754-7333	
Ajacs Die Sales Corp 3855 Linden Ave Se *Web:* ajacsdiesales.com	Grand Rapids	MI	49548	616-452-1469	
AKG of America Inc 7315 Oakwood St Ext *Web:* www.akg-america.com	Mebane	NC	27302	919-563-4286	
Akhurst Machinery Ltd 1669 Foster's Way (Annacis Island) *Web:* akhurst.com	Delta	BC	V3M6S7	604-540-1430	
ALBA Enterprises Inc 10260 Indiana Ct *Web:* www.albaent.com	Rancho Cucamonga	CA	91730	909-941-0600	
Alban Tractor Co 8531 Pulaski Hwy **Fax:* Hum Res ■ *TF:* 800-492-6994 ■ *Web:* www.albancat.com	Baltimore	MD	21237	410-686-7777	780-3481*
Allendorph Specialties Inc 201 Stanton St *Web:* www.allendorph.com	Broussard	LA	70518	337-232-0503	
Alta Equipment Co 28775 Beck Rd *Web:* www.altaequipment.com	Wixom	MI	48393	248-449-6700	
Amj Industries Inc 4000 Auburn St Unit 104 *Web:* amjindustries.com	Rockford	IL	61101	815-654-9000	
Amp Machinery Systems Inc 1098 Chetwood Dr *Web:* www.ampmachinery.com	Carol Stream	IL	60188	630-213-8970	
Ams Controls Inc 12180 Prichard Farm Rd *Web:* www.amscontrols.com	Maryland Heights	MO	63043	314-344-3144	
AmTex Machine Products Inc 4517 Brittmoore Rd *Web:* amtexmachine.com	Houston	TX	77041	713-896-4488	896-6363
Anderson America Corp 10710 Southern Loop Blvd *Web:* www.andersonamerica.com	Pineville	NC	28134	704-522-1823	
Anderson Equipment Co 1000 Washington Pk **Fax:* Sales ■ *TF:* 800-414-4554 ■ *Web:* www.andersonequip.com	Bridgeville	PA	15017	412-343-2300	504-4251*
Anderson Machinery Company Inc 6535 Leopard St *Web:* www.andersonmachinerytexas.com	Corpus Christi	TX	78409	361-289-6043	289-6047
Andrews & Hamilton Company Inc 3829 S Miami Blvd *Web:* www.storageequip.com	Durham	NC	27703	919-787-4100	
Aoa Products LLC 3711 King Rd *Web:* www.aoaproductsllc.com	Toledo	OH	43617	419-350-1244	
Apex Packing & Rubbr Co 1855 New Hwy Ste 2 *Web:* apexgaskets.com	Farmingdale	NY	11735	631-420-8150	
Aquatec Inc 1235 Shappert Dr *Web:* www.aquatecinc.com	Machesney Park	IL	61115	815-654-1500	
Arburg Inc 125 Rockwell Rd *Web:* www.arburg.com	Newington	CT	06111	860-667-6500	
Argo Sales Ltd 717-7th Ave SW Ste 1300 *Web:* www.argosales.com	Calgary	AB	T2P0Z3	403-265-6633	
Aring Equipment Company Inc 13001 W Silver Spring Dr *Web:* www.aringequipment.com	Butler	WI	53007	262-781-3770	779-2737
Arnold Machinery Co 2975 West 2100 South *TF Cust Svc:* 800-821-0548 ■ *Web:* www.arnoldmachinery.com	Salt Lake City	UT	84119	801-972-4000	972-4374
Arnold Supply Inc 2409 Pasadena Blvd *Web:* www.arnoldsupply.com	Pasadena	TX	77502	713-477-3333	
ASAP Industries LLC 908 Blimp Rd *Web:* asapind.net	Houma	LA	70363	985-851-7272	
Astro Craft Inc 7509 Spring Grove Rd *Web:* www.astrocraft.com	Spring Grove	IL	60081	815-675-1500	
Attica Hydraulic Exchange Inc 48175 Gratiot Ave *Web:* www.ahx1.com	Chesterfield	MI	48051	586-949-4240	
Avantech Inc 95-A Sunbelt Blvd *Web:* www.avantechinc.com	Columbia	SC	29203	803-407-7171	
Bacon-Universal Company Inc 918 Ahua St *TF:* 800-352-3508 ■ *Web:* www.baconuniversal.com	Honolulu	HI	96819	808-839-7202	834-8110
Bailey Company Inc, The 501 Cowan St *Web:* www.baileycompany.com	Nashville	TN	37207	615-242-0351	
BalTec Corp 121 Hillpointe Dr Ste 900 *Web:* www.baltecorporation.com	Canonsburg	PA	15317	724-873-5757	
Balzer Pacific Equipment Co 2136 SE Eigth Ave *TF:* 800-442-0966 ■ *Web:* www.balzerpacific.com	Portland	OR	97214	503-232-5141	232-9556
Bane Machinery Inc PO Box 541355 *TF:* 800-594-2263 ■ *Web:* www.banemachinery.com	Dallas	TX	75354	214-352-2468	352-2460
Baron Oilfield Supply Ltd 9515-108 St *Web:* www.baronoilfield.ca	Grande Prairie	AB	T8V5R7	780-532-5661	
Belt Tech Industrial Inc 2574 E 700 S *Web:* belttech1.com	Washington	IN	47501	812-644-7623	
Benchmark Automation LLC 380 Commerce Blvd *Web:* www.benchmarkautomation.net	Athens	GA	30606	706-208-0814	
Berco of America Inc W229 N1420 Wwood Dr Ste F *Web:* www.bercoamerica.com	Waukesha	WI	53186	262-524-2222	
Bertelkamp Automation Inc 6321 Baum Dr *Web:* www.bertelkamp.com	Knoxville	TN	37919	865-588-7691	
Best Swivel Joints LP 9298 Baythorne Dr *Web:* www.bestswivel.com	Houston	TX	77041	713-690-4511	
Bevco Sales International Inc 9354 194 St *Web:* bevco.net	Surrey	BC	V4N4E9	604-888-1455	
Bevel Design Company Inc 400 E Joppa Rd Ste 200 *Web:* beveldesign.com	Towson	MD	21286	443-279-9900	
Biar Inc 2506 S Philippe Ave *Web:* www.biar.com	Gonzales	LA	70737	225-647-4300	
Birmingham-Toledo Inc 3620 Vann Rd *Web:* birminghamtoledo.com	Birmingham	AL	35235	205-655-1881	
BLT Enterprises Inc 501 Spectrum Cir *Web:* www.blt-enterprises.com	Oxnard	CA	93030	805-278-8220	
Blue Giant Equipment Corp 85 Heart Lk Rd South *Web:* www.bluegiant.com	Brampton	ON	L6W3K2	905-457-3900	
Boldt Machinery Inc 4803 Pittsburgh Ave *Web:* boldtmachinery.com	Erie	PA	16509	814-833-9836	
Brandeis Machinery & Supply Co 1801 Watterson Trl *Web:* www.brandeismachinery.com	Louisville	KY	40299	502-493-4380	499-3180
Branom Instrument Co 5500 Fourth Ave South *Web:* www.branom.com	Seattle	WA	98108	206-762-6050	
Brenner-Fiedler & Associates Inc 13824 Bentley Pl *Web:* www.brenner-fiedler.com	Cerritos	CA	90703	562-404-2721	
Buckeye Pumps Inc 1311 Freese Works Pl *Web:* www.buckeyepumps.com	Galion	OH	44833	419-468-7866	
Burckhardt Compression (US) Inc 7240 Brittmoore Rd Ste 100 *Web:* www.burckhardtcompression.com	Houston	TX	77041	281-582-1050	
Burns Controls Co 13735 Beta Rd *Web:* www.burnscontrols.com	Dallas	TX	75244	972-233-6712	
Busch LLC 516 Viking Dr *Web:* www.buschusa.com	Virginia Beach	VA	23452	757-463-7800	

				Phone	Fax
C m s North America 4095 Korona Ct Se *Web:* www.cmsna.com	Caledonia	MI	49316	616-698-9970	
C s Precision Manufacturing Inc 140028 Lockwood Rd *Web:* csprecisionmfg.com	Gering	NE	69341	308-436-2099	
Came Americas Automation LLC 11345 Nw 122nd St *Web:* www.came-americas.com	Medley	FL	33178	305-433-3307	
Cameron Instruments Inc 173 Woolwich St *Web:* cameroninstruments.com	Guelph	ON	N1H3V4	519-824-7111	
Canimex Inc 285 Saint-Georges St *Web:* www.canimex.com	Drummondville	QC	J2C4H3	819-477-1335	
Capital Equipment & Handling Inc 1100 Cottonwood Ave *Web:* www.cehnissan.com	Hartland	WI	53029	262-369-5500	
Cardinal Machinery Inc 7535 Appling Ctr Dr *Web:* www.cardinalmachinery.com	Memphis	TN	38133	901-377-3107	
Carotek Inc 700 Sam Newell Rd PO Box 1395 *Web:* www.carotek.com	Matthews	NC	28106	704-844-1100	
Cascade Controls Northwest 19785 NE San Raffael St *Web:* www.cascade-nw.com	Portland	OR	97230	503-252-3116	
Casco Equipment Corp 4141 Flat Rock Dr *Web:* www.cascoequip.com	Riverside	CA	92505	951-324-8500	
Cast Products Inc 4200 N Nordica Ave *Web:* castproducts.com	Norridge	IL	60706	708-457-1500	
Caster Concepts Inc 16000 E Michigan Ave *Web:* www.casterconcepts.com	Albion	MI	49224	517-629-8838	
CFE Equipment Corp 818 Widgeon Rd *Web:* www.cfeequipment.com	Norfolk	VA	23513	757 858 2660	
Chadwick-BaRoss Inc 160 Warren Ave *TF:* 800-804-0775 ■ *Web:* www.chadwick-baross.com	Westbrook	ME	04092	207-854-8411	854-8237
Chandler Instruments Company LLC 2001 N Indianwood Ave *Web:* www.chandlereng.com	Broken Arrow	OK	74012	918-250-7200	
Chase-Logeman Corp 303 Friendship Dr *Web:* www.chaselogeman.com	Greensboro	NC	27409	336-665-0754	
Cherry's Industrial Equipment 600 Morse Ave *TF:* 800-350-0011 ■ *Web:* cherrysind.com	Elk Grove Village	IL	60007	800-350-0011	
Cisco Air Systems Inc 214 27th St *Web:* www.ciscoair.com	Sacramento	CA	95816	916-444-2525	
Clarke Power Services Inc 3133 E Kemper Rd *Web:* www.clarkepowerservices.com	Cincinnati	OH	45241	513-771-2200	
Clausing Industrial Inc 1819 N Pitcher St *Web:* www.clausing-industrial.com	Kalamazoo	MI	49007	269-345-7155	
Cleveland Bros Equipment Company Inc 5300 Paxton St *TF:* 866-551-4602 ■ *Web:* www.clevelandbrothers.com	Harrisburg	PA	17111	717-564-2121	564-6931
Coair Inc 85 Rue Des Buissons *Web:* www.coair.com	Levis	QC	G6V5B6	418-835-0141	
Coast Pneumatics 8055 E Crystal Dr *Web:* www.pneumaticsonly.com	Anaheim	CA	92807	714-921-2255	
Colby Equipment Company Inc 3048 Ridgeview Dr *Web:* www.colbyequipment.com	Indianapolis	IN	46226	317-545-4221	
Coleman Instrument Co 11575 Goldcoast Dr *Web:* www.colemaninstrument.com	Cincinnati	OH	45249	513-489-5745	
Colonial Saw Company Inc 122 Pembroke St *Web:* www.csaw.com	Kingston	NY	02364	781-585-4364	
Colorid LLC 20480 Chartwls Ctr Dr *Web:* www.colorid.com	Cornelius	NC	28031	704-987-2238	
Columbia Specialty Company Inc 5875 Obispo Ave *Web:* www.columbiaspecialty.com	Long Beach	CA	90805	562-634-6425	
Conmaco/Rector LP 1602 Engineers Rd *Web:* www.conmaco.com	Belle Chasse	LA	70037	504-394-7330	393-8715
Contractors Cargo Co 500 S Alameda St *Web:* contractorscargo.com	Compton	CA	90221	310-609-1957	309-1767
Control Southern Inc 3850 Lakefield Dr *Web:* www.controlsouthern.com	Suwanee	GA	30024	770-495-3100	
Conveyor Handling Company Inc 6715 Santa Barbara Ct *Web:* www.conveyorhandling.com	Elkridge	MD	21075	410-379-2700	
Cooke Sales & Service Company Inc 1422 Washington St 	Chillicothe	MO	64601	660-646-1166	646-0381
Copylite Products Corp 4061 SW 47th Ave *Web:* www.copylite.com	Fort Lauderdale	FL	33314	954-581-2470	
Coughlin Equipment Company Inc 2221 E Hwy 66 *Web:* coughlinequipment.com	El Reno	OK	73036	405-262-9101	
Cressman Tubular Products Corp 3939 Beltline Rd Ste 460 *Web:* www.cressmantubular.com	Addison	TX	75001	214-352-5252	
CU ink Inc 612 Swede St *Web:* www.cuink.com	Norristown	PA	19401	484-690-0212	
Cummins Central Power LLC 10088 S 136th St *Web:* www.centralpower.cummins.com	Omaha	NE	68138	402-551-7678	
DC Equipment Inc 57 Old Mill Rd *Web:* www.dcequipmentinc.com	Geraldine	AL	35974	256-659-4707	
Delta Electric Inc 207 Riverview Ave *Web:* www.deltaelectricwv.com	Logan	WV	25601	304-752-4625	
Delta Materials Handling Inc 4676 Clarke Rd *Web:* www.deltamat.com	Memphis	TN	38141	901-795-7230	
Delta t Systems Inc 2171 State Rd 175 *Web:* deltatsys.com	Richfield	WI	53076	262-628-0331	
Den-Con Tool Co 5354 S I-35 *Web:* www.dencon.com	Oklahoma City	OK	73143	405-670-5942	
Diacarb Tools Inc 2525 Rue De Miniac *Web:* www.diacarb.com	Saint-laurent	QC	H4S1E5	514-331-4360	
Diamond Equipment Inc 1060 E Diamond Ave *TF:* 800-258-4428 ■ *Web:* www.diamondequipment.com	Evansville	IN	47711	812-425-4428	421-1036
Diesel Engine & Parts Co 8123 Hillsboro *Web:* www.depco.com	Houston	TX	77029	713-675-6100	
Dixon Group Canada Ltd 2200 Logan Ave *Web:* www.dixongroupcanada.com	Winnipeg	MB	R2R0J2	204-633-5650	
Dove Equipment Company Inc 723 Sabrina Dr *Web:* www.doveequipment.com	East Peoria	IL	61611	309-694-6228	
Doverco Inc 3245 Boul Jean-baptiste-deschamps *Web:* www.doverco.com	Lachine	QC	H8T3E4	514-420-6060	
Durkin Equipment Company Inc 2383 Chaffee Dr *Web:* www.durkininc.com	Saint Louis	MO	63146	314-432-2040	
Dynamic Automation 4525 Runway St *Web:* www.dynamicautomation.com	Simi Valley	CA	93063	805-584-8476	
Eagle Power & Equipment Corp 953 Bethlehem Pk *Web:* www.eaglepowerandequipment.com	Montgomeryville	PA	18936	215-699-5871	
Eagle Scaffolding Services Inc 67 Mill St *Web:* www.eaglescaffolding.com	Amityville	NY	11701	631-842-1700	
Easy Automation Inc 102 Mill St *Web:* www.easy-automation.com	Welcome	MN	56181	507-728-8214	
Ecoa Industrial Products 7700 Nw 74th Ave *TF:* 800-433-3833 ■ *Web:* www.ecoalifts.com	Medley	FL	33166	800-433-3833	
Edm Department Inc 1261 Humbracht Cir Ste A *Web:* edmdept.com	Bartlett	IL	60103	630-736-0531	
Eggelhof Inc 1999 Kolfahl St *Web:* www.eggelhof.com	Houston	TX	77023	713-923-2101	
Electrocut-pacific 993 E San Carlos Ave *Web:* electrocutpacific.com	San Carlos	CA	94070	650-591-8718	
Elliott & Frantz Inc 450 E Church Rd *TF:* 800-220-3025 ■ *Web:* www.elliottfrantz.com	King Of Prussia	PA	19406	610-279-5200	
Ellison Educational Equipment Inc 25862 Commercentre Dr *Web:* www.ellison.com	Lake Forest	CA	92630	949-598-8822	
Empire Southwest Co 1725 S Country Club Dr *TF:* 800-367-4731 ■ *Web:* www.empire-cat.com	Mesa	AZ	85210	480-633-4000	633-4000
Enertechnix Inc 23616 SE 225th St *Web:* www.enertechnix.com	Maple Valley	WA	98038	425-432-1589	
Equipment Depot Ltd 4100 S Interstate 35 *Web:* www.eqdepot.com	Waco	TX	76706	254-662-4322	
EquipNet Inc Five Dan Rd *Web:* www.equipnet.com	Canton	MA	02021	781-821-3482	
Erb Equipment Co Inc 200 Erb Industrial Dr *TF:* 800-634-9661 ■ *Web:* www.erbequipment.com	Fenton	MO	63026	636-349-0200	349-4426
Estes Equipment Company Inc 2007 Polk St *Web:* www.estes-equipment.com	Chattanooga	TN	37407	423-756-0090	
Everyday Technologies Inc 2005 Campbell Rd *Web:* www.everydaytech.com	Sidney	OH	45365	937-492-4171	
Exact Metrology Inc 4766 Interstate Dr *Web:* www.exactmetrology.com	Cincinnati	OH	45246	513-831-6620	
F&H Food Equipment Co 1526 S Enterprise Ave *Web:* www.fhfoodequipment.com	Springfield	MO	65804	417-881-6114	
Fabco Equipment Inc 11200 W Silver Spring Rd *Web:* www.fabco.com	Milwaukee	WI	53225	414-461-9100	461-8899
Falcon Executive Aviation Inc 4766 E Falcon Dr *Web:* www.falconaviation.com	Mesa	AZ	85215	480-832-0704	
Faris Machinery Co 5770 E 77th Ave *Web:* gy.net	Commerce City	CO	80022	303-289-5743	
Feenaughty Machinery Co 4800 NE Columbia Blvd *Web:* www.feenaughty.com	Portland	OR	97218	503-282-2566	
FLAIR Flexible Packaging Corp 4100 72 Ave SE *Web:* www.flairpackaging.com	Calgary	AB	T2C2C1	403-207-3226	
Flint Machine Tools Inc 3710 Hewatt Ct *Web:* www.flintmachine.com	Snellville	GA	30039	770-985-2626	
Flodraulic Group Inc 3539 N 700 W *Web:* www.flodraulicgroup.com	Greenfield	IN	46140	317-890-3700	
Florida Aquastore & Utility Construction Inc 4722 NW Boca Raton Blvd Ste C-102 *Web:* www.florida-aquastore.com	Boca Raton	FL	33431	561-994-2400	
Florida Handling Systems Inc 2651 State Rd 60 W *Web:* www.fhsinc.com	Bartow	FL	33830	863-534-1212	
Flow Dynamics & Automation Inc 1024 11th Ct W *Web:* www.flowdynamics.net	Birmingham	AL	35204	205-581-1200	
Flow Solutions Inc 4401 S Pinemont Ste 208 *Web:* www.flowsolutionsinc.com	Houston	TX	77041	713-939-7000	
Foley Equipment Co 1550 SW St **Fax:* Sales ■ *Web:* www.foleyeq.com	Wichita	KS	67213	316-943-4211	943-0896*
FORCE America Inc 501 E Cliff Rd *Web:* www.forceamerica.com	Burnsville	MN	55337	952-707-1300	
Fordia Inc 2745 de Miniac Ville Saint Laurent *Web:* www.fordia.com	Saint Laurent	QC	H4S1E5	514-336-9211	
Formers by Ernie Inc 7905 Almeda Genoa Rd Ste B *Web:* www.formersbyernie.net	Houston	TX	77075	713-991-3455	
Foxx Equipment Co 421 Southwest Blvd *Web:* foxxequipment.com	Kansas City	MO	64108	816-421-3600	
Franks Supply Company Inc 3311 Stanford Dr NE *TF:* 800-432-5254 ■ *Web:* www.franks-supply.com	Albuquerque	NM	87107	505-884-0000	884-1787
G. & M. Die Consulting Company Inc 284 Richert Rd *Web:* www.gmdiecasting.com	Wood Dale	IL	60191	630-595-2340	
G.N. Plastics Company Ltd 345 Old Trunk 3 *Web:* www.gnplastics.com	Chester	NS	B0J1J0	902-275-3571	
Gammon Technical Products Inc 2300 Hwy 34 *Web:* www.gammontech.com	Manasquan	NJ	08736	732-223-4600	

	City	State	Zip	Phone	Fax
Garden State Engine & Equipment Co 3509 US Hwy 22	Somerville	NJ	08876	908-534-5444	534-5623
TF: 800-479-3857 ■ *Web:* gseecrane.com					
General Equipment & Supplies Inc 4300 Main Ave.	Fargo	ND	58103	701-282-2662	364-2190
TF: 800-437-2924 ■ *Web:* www.genequip.com					
General Oil Equipment Company Inc 60 John Glenn Dr	Amherst	NY	14228	716-691-7012	
Web: www.goe-amhfab.com					
Genesis Automation Inc 3480 Swenson Ave	St. Charles	IL	60174	630-587-0444	
Web: www.genesisautomation.com					
Gil-Mar Manufacturing Company Inc 7925 Ronda Dr	Canton	MI	48187	734-459-4803	
Web: www.gil-mar.com					
Gill Services Inc 650 Aldine Bender Rd	Houston	TX	77060	281-820-5400	
Web: www.gillservicesinc.com					
Gilmore Services Inc 31 E Fairfield Dr	Pensacola	FL	32501	850-434-1054	
Web: www.gilmoreservices.com					
Giuffre Bros Cranes Inc 6635 S 13th St.	Milwaukee	WI	53221	414-764-9200	
Web: www.giuffrebros.com					
Glauber Equipment Corp 1600 Commerce Pkwy	Lancaster	NY	14086	716-681-1234	
Web: www.glauber.com					
Global Equipment Marketing Inc PO Box 810483	Boca Raton	FL	33481	561-750-8662	750-9507
TF: 866-750-8662 ■ *Web:* www.globalmagnetics.com					
Global Oil Tools Inc 5343 Hwy 311	Houma	LA	70360	985-868-3404	
Web: globaloiltools.com					
GMW Associates Inc 955 Industrial Rd.	San Carlos	CA	94070	650-802-8292	
Web: www.gmw.com					
Golden Equipment Co 721 Candelaria NE	Albuquerque	NM	87107	505-345-7811	345-0401
TF: 800-880-8580 ■ *Web:* www.goldenequipment.com					
GPM Inc 4432 Venture Ave.	Duluth	MN	55811	218-722-9904	
Web: virginiachamber.com					
Green Line Hose & Fittings (B.C.) Ltd 1477 Derwent Way	Delta	BC	V3M6N3	604-525-6700	
Web: www.greenlinehose.com					
Grimstad S84w18887 Enterprise Dr	Muskego	WI	53150	414-422-2300	
Web: www.grimstad.com					
Ground Force Manufacturing LLC 5650 E Seltice Way	Post Falls	ID	83854	208-664-9291	
Web: gfmfg.com					
H Gr Industrial Surplus 20001 Euclid Ave	Euclid	OH	44117	216-486-4567	
Web: www.hgrinc.com					
Hales Machine Tool Inc 2730 Niagara Ln N.	Minneapolis	MN	55447	763-553-1711	
Web: halesmachinetool.com					
Hammond Drives & Equipment Inc 8527 Midland Rd	Freeland	MI	48623	989-695-2239	
Web: www.hammondeqp.com					
Handi-Ramp 510 N Ave	Libertyville	IL	60048	847-680-7700	
Web: www.handiramp.com					
Hartwig Inc 10617 Trenton Ave.	Saint Louis	MO	63132	314-426-5300	
Web: www.hartwiginc.com					
Hayes Pump Inc 66 Old Powder Mill Rd I	West Concord	MA	01742	978-369-8800	
Web: www.hayespump.com					
Heavy Machines Inc 3926 E Rains Rd	Memphis	TN	38118	901-260-2200	765-0035*
**Fax Area Code:* 250 ■ *TF:* 888-366-9028 ■ *Web:* www.heavymachinesinc.com					
Hei-Tek Automation LLC 21602 N Second Ave Ste 4	Phoenix	AZ	85027	602-269-7931	
Web: www.heitek.com					
Henderson Sewing Machine Company Inc Waits Dr Industrial Park	Andalusia	AL	36420	334-222-2451	
Web: www.hendersonsewing.com					
Heritage Equipment Co 9000 Heritage Dr	Plain City	OH	43064	614-873-3941	
Web: www.heritage-equipment.com					
Hibon Inc 12055 Cote de Liesse	Dorval	QC	H9P1B4	514-631-3501	
Web: www.hibon.com					
HO Penn Machinery Co Inc 122 Noxon Rd.	Poughkeepsie	NY	12603	845-452-1200	452-3458*
**Fax:* Mktg ■ *Web:* www.hopenn.com					
Hoffman Equipment Inc 300 S Randolphville Rd	Piscataway	NJ	08854	732-752-3600	968-8371
Web: www.hoffmanequip.com					
Hooper Handling Inc 5590 Camp Rd	Hamburg	NY	14075	716-649-5590	
Web: www.hooperhandling.com					
Hydra-Fab Fluid Power Inc 3585 Laird Rd Unit 5	Mississauga	ON	L5L5Z8	905-569-1819	
Web: www.hydrafab.com					
Hydraulic Controls Inc 4700 San Pablo Ave	Emeryville	CA	94608	510-658-8300	
Web: www.hydraulic-controls.com					
Identity Automation LP 8833 N Sam Houston Pkwy W	Houston	TX	77064	281-220-0021	
Web: www.identityautomation.com					
Idesco Corp 37 W 26th St Fl 8	New York	NY	10010	212-889-2530	
Web: www.idesco.com					
ILMO Products Company Inc Seven Eastgate Dr	Jacksonville	IL	62651	217-245-2183	
Web: www.ilmoproducts.com					
Improved Construction Methods 1040 N Redmond Rd	Jacksonville	AR	72076	877-494-5793	
TF: 877-494-5793 ■ *Web:* www.improvedconstructionmethods.com					
Indexing Technologies Inc 37 Orchard St.	Ramsey	NJ	07446	201-934-6333	
Web: www.ititooling.com					
Inline Services Inc 27731 Commercial Park Rd	Tomball	TX	77375	281-401-8142	
Web: www.inlineservices.com					
Innovasys 36735 Metro Ct	Sterling Heights	MI	48312	586-795-3000	
Web: www.innovasys.com					
Innovent Air Handling Equipment 60 28th Ave N	Minneapolis	MN	55411	612-877-4800	
Web: innoventair.com					
J C Bamford Excavators Ltd 2000 Bamford Blvd	Pooler	GA	31322	912-447-2000	447-2299
Web: www.jcbamericas.com					
J.L. Souser & Associates Inc 3495 Industrial Dr	York	PA	17402	717-505-3800	
Web: www.jlsautomation.com					
JACO Environmental Inc PO Box 14307	Mill Creek	WA	98082	425-398-6200	
Web: www.jacoinc.net					
James W Bell Company Inc 1720 I Ave NE	Cedar Rapids	IA	52402	319-362-1151	362-4876
Web: jwbellco.com					
Janell Inc 6130 Cornell Rd	Cincinnati	OH	45242	513-489-9111	
TF: 888-489-9111 ■ *Web:* www.janell.com					
Jasper Engineering & Equipment Co 3800 Fifth Ave W Ste1	Hibbing	MN	55746	218-262-3421	
Web: www.jaspereng.com					
JC Smith Inc 345 Peat St.	Syracuse	NY	13210	315-428-9903	428-9841
Web: www.jcsmithinc.com					
Jobe & Company Inc 7677 Canton Ctr Dr	Baltimore	MD	21224	410-288-0560	
Web: www.jobeandcompany.com					
John Fabick Tractor Co 1 Fabick Dr	Fenton	MO	63026	636-343-5900	343-4910
TF Cust Svc: 800-845-9188 ■ *Web:* www.fabickcat.com					
Kann Enterprises Inc 209 Amendodge Dr.	Shorewood	IL	60404	815-609-7170	
Web: www.kannenterprises.com					
KBC Tools & Machinery Inc 6300 18 Mile Rd.	Sterling Heights	MI	48314	586-979-0500	
Web: www.kbctools.com					
Kc Robotics Inc 9000 Le Saint Dr	Fairfield	OH	45014	513-860-4442	
Web: www.kcrobotics.com					
KDR Supply Inc PO Box 10130	Liberty	TX	77575	936-336-6267	336-1034
Web: www.kdrsupply.com					
Kfm International Industries 14145 Proctor Ave Ste 7	La Puente	CA	91746	626-369-9856	
Web: vip.163.com					
Kibble Equipment 1150 S Victory Dr.	Mankato	MN	56001	507-387-8201	388-3565
TF: 800-624-8983 ■ *Web:* www.kibbleeq.com					
Kraus Global Inc 25 Paquin Rd	Winnipeg	MB	R2J3V9	204-663-3601	
Web: www.krausglobal.com					
Kwm Gutterman 795 S Larkin Ave	Joliet	IL	60436	815-729-4261	
Web: kwmgutterman.com					
Larmar Industries 3700 S County Rd W # 1295	Odessa	TX	79765	432-561-8700	
Web: www.larmarindustries.com					
Leavitt Machinery & Rentals Inc 24389 Fraser Hwy.	Langley	BC	V2Z2L3	604-607-4450	
Web: www.leavittmachinery.com					
Lift Technologies Inc 7040 S Hwy 11	Westminster	SC	29693	864-647-1119	
Web: www.lift-tekelecar.com					
Liftow Ltd 3150 American Dr	Toronto	ON	L4V1B4	905-677-3270	
Web: m.liftow.com					
Lincoln Contractors Supply Inc 11111 W Hayes Ave	Milwaukee	WI	53227	414-541-1327	
Web: www.lincolncontractorssupply.com					
Lumitron Inc 10503 Timberwood Cir Ste 120	Louisville	KY	40223	502-423-7225	
Web: www.lumitron-ir.com					
M G America Inc 31 Kulick Rd	Fairfield	NJ	07004	973-808-8185	
Web: mgamerica.com					
M R L Equipment Company Inc PO Box 31154	Billings	MT	59107	406-869-9900	
TF: 877-788-2907 ■ *Web:* www.markritelines.com					
M&h Plastics Inc 485 Brooke Rd.	Winchester	VA	22603	540-504-0030	
Web: www.mhplastics.com					
M&M Pump & Supply Inc 1125 Olivette Executive Pkwy Ste 110	St. Louis	MO	63132	314-395-8122	
Web: www.mandmpump.com					
M.G. Newell Corp 301 Citation Ct	Greensboro	NC	27409	336-393-0100	
Web: www.mgnewell.com					
M.H. Equipment Co 2001 E Hartman Rd	Chillicothe	IL	61523	309-579-8020	
Web: www.mhequipment.com					
MacAllister Machinery Company Inc 7515 E 30th St	Indianapolis	IN	46219	317-545-2151	860-3310
TF: 800-227-3228 ■ *Web:* www.macallister.com					
Machinery & Equipment Company Inc 3401 Bayshore Blvd	Brisbane	CA	94005	415-467-3400	
Web: www.machineryandequipment.com					
Machinery Values of Nj Inc 401 Supor Blvd Ste 1	Harrison	NJ	07029	973-497-7500	
Web: machineryvalues.com					
Machining Time Savers Inc 1338 S State College Pkwy.	Anaheim	CA	92806	714-635-7373	
Web: www.mtscnc.com					
Mack Pump & Equipment Company Inc 12005 S Spaulding School Dr	Plainfield	IL	60585	815-439-2030	
Web: www.mackpump.com					
Magnus Equipment 4500 Beidler Rd.	Willoughby	OH	44094	440-942-8488	
Web: www.magnusequipment.com					
Main Line Supply Company Inc 300 N Findlay St.	Dayton	OH	45403	937-254-6910	
Web: www.mainlinesupply.com					
Maltz Sales Company Inc 67 Green St.	Foxboro	MA	02035	508-203-2400	
Web: www.maltzsales.com					
Mamata Usa LLC 2275 Cornell Ave	Montgomery	IL	60538	630-801-2320	
Web: www.mamatausa.com					
Mantissa Corp 616 Pressley Rd.	Charlotte	NC	28217	704-525-1749	
Web: www.mantissacorporation.com					
Marco Fluid Power Inc 7902 Hopi Pl	Tampa	FL	33634	813-889-8989	
Web: www.marcofluidpower.com					
Markem-Imaje Inc 5448 Timberlea Blvd	Mississauga	ON	L4W2T7	800-267-5108	
TF: 800-267-5108 ■ *Web:* www.markem-imaje.com					
Mason West Inc 1601 E Miraloma Ave	Placentia	CA	92870	714-630-0701	
Web: www.masonwest.com					
Material Motion Inc 203 Rio Cir	Decatur	GA	30030	404-237-6127	
Web: www.materialmotion.com					
Mbb Enterprises 3352 W Grand Ave	Chicago	IL	60651	773-276-4380	
Web: www.mbbmasonry.com					
Mckinney Petroleum Equipment Inc 3926 Halls Mill Rd	Mobile	AL	36693	251-661-8800	
Web: mckinneypetroleum.com					
McQuade & Bannigan Inc 1300 Stark St.	Utica	NY	13502	315-724-7119	
Web: www.mqb.com					
Mecor Inc 1567 Elmhurst Rd	Elk Grove Village	IL	60007	630-378-4400	
Web: mecor.net					
Medley Material Handling Company Inc 4201 Will Rogers Pkwy.	Oklahoma City	OK	73108	405-946-3453	
Web: www.medleycompany.com					

Company / Address	City	State	Zip	Phone	Fax
Mesa Equipment & Supply Co 7100 Second St NW — *Web:* mesaequipment.com	Albuquerque	NM	87107	505-345-0284	
Methods Machine Tools Inc 65 Union Ave — *Web:* www.methodsmachine.com	Sudbury	MA	01776	978-443-5388	
Metric Equipment Sales Inc 3486 Investment Blvd — *Web:* www.metrictest.com	Hayward	CA	94545	510-264-0887	
Miami Industrial Trucks Inc 2830 E River Rd — *Web:* www.mitlift.com	Dayton	OH	45439	937-293-4194	
Michigan Arc Products Corp 2040 Austin Dr — *Web:* www.micharc.com	Troy	MI	48083	248-740-8066	
Miller-Bradford & Risberg Inc W250 N6851 Hwy 164 — *Web:* www.miller-bradford.com	Sussex	WI	53089	262-246-5700	
Milton CAT 554 Maple St — *Web:* www.miltoncat.com	Hopkinton	NH	03229	603-746-4611	746-8686
Mississippi Valley Equipment Company Inc 1198 Pershall Rd — *TF:* 800-325-8001 ■ *Web:* www.mve-stl.com	Saint Louis	MO	63137	314-869-8600	869-6862
Mister Safety Shoes Inc 6-2300 Finch Ave W — *TF:* 800-707-0051 ■ *Web:* www.mistersafetyshoes.com	Toronto	ON	M9M2Y3	416-746-3000	
Mobile Parts Inc 2472 Evans Rd — *TF:* 800-461-4055 ■ *Web:* www.mobileparts.com	Val Caron	ON	P3N1P5	705-897-4955	
Modern Automation Inc 134 Tennsco Dr — *Web:* www.modernautomation.com	Dickson	TN	37055	615-446-1990	
Monroe Tractor & Implement Company Inc 1001 Lehigh Stn Rd — *Web:* www.monroetractor.com	Henrietta	NY	14467	585-334-3867	334-0001
Moodie Implement Co 80335 US Hwy 87 W — *TF:* 800-823-3373 ■ *Web:* www.moodieimplement.com	Lewistown	MT	59457	406-538-5433	538-2604
Multi-shifter Inc 11110 Park Charlotte Blvd — *Web:* www.multi-shifter.com	Charlotte	NC	28273	704-588-9611	
Mustang Tractor & Equipment Co 12800 NW Fwy — *TF:* 800-256-1001 ■ *Web:* www.mustangcat.com	Houston	TX	77040	713-460-2000	460-8473
Nixon-Egli Equipment Company Inc 2044 S Vineyard Ave — *Web:* www.nixon-egli.com	Ontario	CA	91761	909-930-1822	
Norco Inc 1125 W Amity Rd — *Web:* www.norco-inc.com	Boise	ID	83705	208-336-1643	
Numatic Engineering Inc 7915 Ajay Dr — *Web:* www.numaticengineering.com	Sun Valley	CA	91352	818-768-1200	
O'keefe Elevator Company Inc 1402 Jones St — *Web:* www.okeefe-elevator.com	Omaha	NE	68102	402-345-4056	
Ohio Machinery Co 3993 E Royalton Rd — *TF:* 800-837-6200 ■ *Web:* www.ohiocat.com	Broadview Heights	OH	44147	440-526-6200	526-9513
Ohio Tool Systems Inc 3863 Congress Pkwy — *Web:* www.ohiotool.com	Richfield	OH	44286	330-659-4181	
Oldenburg Group Inc 1717 W Civic Dr — *Web:* www.oldenburggroup.com	Milwaukee	WI	53209	414-977-1717	977-1700
Omnilift Inc Warwick Commons Industrial Park 1938 Stout Dr — *Web:* www.omnilift-inc.com	Warminster	PA	18974	215-443-9090	
Optimal Engineering Systems 6901 Woodley Ave — *Web:* oesincorp.com	Van Nuys	CA	91406	818-222-9200	
Owen Equipment Co 13101 NE Whitaker Way — *Web:* www.owenequipment.com	Portland	OR	97230	503-255-9055	
Oxford Alloys Inc 2632 Tee Dr — *Web:* www.oxfordalloys.com	Baton Rouge	LA	70814	225-273-4800	
P & W Sales Inc 405 N Hwy 135 — *Web:* www.p-wsales.com	Kilgore	TX	75662	903-984-2102	
Pacific Integrated Handling Inc 10215 Portland Ave — *Web:* www.pacificintegrated.com	Tacoma	WA	98445	253-535-5888	
Parlec Inc 101 Perinton Pkwy — *Web:* www.parlec.com	Fairport	NY	14450	585-425-4400	
Patten Industries Inc 635 W Lake St — *TF:* 877-688-2228 ■ *Web:* www.pattencat.com	Elmhurst	IL	60126	630-279-4400	279-7892
PCE Pacific Inc 2525 223rd St SE — *Web:* www.pcepacific.com	Bothell	WA	98021	425-487-9600	
Petersen Inc 1527 North 2000 West — *TF:* 800-410-6789 ■ *Web:* www.peterseninc.com	Ogden	UT	84404	801-732-2000	
Pfeiffer Vacuum Inc 24 Trafalgar Sq — *Web:* www.pfeiffer-vacuum.com	Nashua	NH	03063	603-578-6500	
Pierce Pump Company LP 9010 John W Carpenter Fwy — *Web:* www.piercepump.com	Dallas	TX	75247	214-320-3604	
Pipe Valves Inc 1200 E Fifth Ave — *Web:* www.pipevalves.com	Columbus	OH	43219	614-294-4971	
Piping Resources Inc 4502 F St — *Web:* www.pipingresources.com	Omaha	NE	68117	402-738-8100	
Plasterer Equipment Company Inc 2550 E Cumberland St — *Web:* www.plasterer.com	Lebanon	PA	17042	717-273-2616	
Pme Equip Inc 304 Garden Oaks Blvd — *Web:* www.pmeequip.com	Houston	TX	77018	713-691-3081	
Pneumatic & Hydraulic Systems Company Inc 1338 Petroleum Pkwy — *Web:* pneumaticandhydraulic.com	Broussard	LA	70518	337-839-1999	
Pompaction Inc 119 Blvd Hymus — *Web:* www.pompaction.com	Pointe-claire	QC	H9R1E5	514-697-8600	
Power & Industrial Air Systems 5281 Hamilton Blvd — *Web:* www.pias-usa.com	Allentown	PA	18106	610-395-3242	
Power Motive Corp 5000 Vasquez Blvd — *TF:* 800-627-0087 ■ *Web:* www.powermotivecorp.com	Denver	CO	80216	303-355-5900	388-9328
Precise Printing Equipment 1024 E Arlee Pl — *Web:* preciseequip.com	Anaheim	CA	92805	714-991-0427	
Precision Hydraulic Cylinders Inc 196 N Hwy 41 PO Box 1589 — *Web:* www.phc-global.com	Beulaville	NC	28518	910-298-0100	
Premier Pump & Supply Inc 19 Fruite St — *Web:* www.premierpumpsupply.com	Belmont	NH	03220	603-528-3100	
Primary Flow Signal Inc 800 Wellington Ave — *Web:* www.pfsflowproducts.com	Cranston	RI	02910	401-461-6366	
Proconex Management Group Inc 103 Enterprise Dr — *Web:* www.proconexdirect.com	Royersford	PA	19468	610-495-1835	
Profile Food Ingredients LLC 1151 Timber Dr — *Web:* profilefoodingredients.com	Elgin	IL	60123	847-622-1700	
Pronghorn Controls Ltd 101 4919 72 Ave SE — *Web:* pronghorn.ca	Calgary	AB	T2C3H3	403-720-2526	
Prospec Technologies Inc 3235 Wharton Way — *Web:* prospectech.com	Mississauga	ON	L4X2B6	905-629-3100	
Prosys Industries Inc 47576 Halyard Dr — *Web:* prosys-group.com	Plymouth	MI	48170	734-207-3710	
PV Fluid Products 11245 - Vly Ridge Dr NW Suit 322 — *Web:* www.pvfluid.com	Calgary	AB	T3B5V4	403-640-0331	
Quality Flow Systems Inc 800 Sixth St NW — *Web:* qfsi.net	New Prague	MN	56071	952-758-9445	
Quality Hydraulics & Pneumatics Inc 1415 Wilhelm Rd — *Web:* www.qualityhydraulics.com	Mundelein	IL	60060	847-680-8400	
Quest Engineering Inc 2300 Edgewood Ave South — *Web:* www.questenginc.com	Minneapolis	MN	55426	952-546-4441	
Quickdraft Inc 1525 Perry Dr Sw — *Web:* www.quickdraft.com	Canton	OH	44710	330-477-4574	
R r Floody Co 5065 27th Ave — *Web:* rrfloody.com	Rockford	IL	61109	815-399-1931	
R&M Materials Handling Inc 4501 Gateway Blvd — *Web:* www.rmhoist.com	Springfield	OH	45502	937-328-5100	
Rajason Tools Inc 11664 County Rd 42 — *Web:* www.rajasontools.com	Windsor	ON	N8N2M1	519-979-5320	
Ralph W. Earl Company Inc 5930 E Molloy Rd — *Web:* www.rwearl.com	Syracuse	NY	13211	315-454-4431	
Rasmussen Equipment Co 3333 West 2100 South — *TF:* 800-453-8032 ■ *Web:* www.rasmussenequipment.com	Salt Lake City	UT	84119	801-972-5588	
Raymond of New Jersey LLC 1000 Brighton St — *Web:* www.raymond-nj.com	Union	NJ	07083	908-624-9570	
RBI Corp 10201 Cedar Ridge Dr — *TF:* 800-444-7370 ■ *Web:* www.rbicorp.com	Ashland	VA	23005	800-444-7370	
RDO Equipment Co 3401 38th St S — *TF:* 800-342-4643 ■ *Web:* www.rdoequipment.com	Fargo	ND	58104	701-282-5400	282-8220
Rego-fix Tool Corp 7752 Moller Rd — *Web:* www.cnctoolstore.com	Indianapolis	IN	46268	317-870-5959	
Rencor Controls Inc 21 Sullivan Pkwy — *Web:* rencor.com	Fort Edward	NY	12828	518-747-4171	
Ri-go Lift Truck Ltd 175 Courtland Ave — *Web:* www.rigolift.com	Concord	ON	L4K4T2	905-738-8094	
Rish Equipment Co PO Box 330 — *Web:* www.rish.com	Bluefield	WV	24701	304-327-5124	327-8821
RJM Sales Inc 454 Park Ave — *Web:* rjmsales.com	Scotch Plains	NJ	07076	908-322-7880	
Rk Controls 5901 Corvette St — *Web:* www.rkcontrols.com	Commerce	CA	90040	323-887-7066	
Road Machinery Co 716 S Seventh St — *Web:* www.roadmachinery.com	Phoenix	AZ	85034	602-252-7121	253-9690
Roberts Technology Group Inc 120 New Britain Blvd — *Web:* rtgpkg.com	Chalfont	PA	18914	215-822-0600	
Roland Machinery Co 816 N Dirksen Pkwy — *TF:* 800-252-2926 ■ *Web:* www.rolandmachinery.com	Springfield	IL	62702	217-789-7711	744-7314
Rosenboom Machine & Tool Inc 1530 Western Ave — *Web:* www.rosenboom.com	Sheldon	IA	51201	712-324-4854	
Rowlands Sales Company Inc Butler Industrial Park — *Web:* www.rowlands.com	Hazleton	PA	18201	570-455-5813	
Rudd Equipment Co 4344 Poplar Level Rd — *TF:* 800-527-2282 ■ *Web:* www.ruddequipment.com	Louisville	KY	40213	502-456-4050	459-8695
Ryder Material Handling 210 Annagem Blvd — *Web:* www.jhryder.com	Mississauga	ON	L5T2V5	905-565-2100	
S & s Industrial Equipment & Supply Company Inc Seven Chelten Way — *Web:* www.sandsindustrial.com	Trenton	NJ	08638	609-695-3800	
Sardee Industries Inc 5100 Academy Dr Ste 400 — *Web:* www.sardee.com	Lisle	IL	60532	630-824-4200	
SDT North America Inc PO Box 682 — *Web:* www.sdtnorthamerica.com	Cobourg	ON	K9A4R5	905-377-1313	
Sellers Equipment Inc 400 N Chicago St — *Web:* www.sellersequipment.com	Salina	KS	67401	785-823-6378	823-8083
Sequoia Equipment Company Inc PO Box 2747 — *Web:* www.sequoiaequipment.com	Fresno	CA	93745	559-441-1122	441-0454
Shannahan Crane & Hoist Inc 11695 Wakeside Crossing Ct — *Web:* www.shannahancrane.com	Saint Louis	MO	63146	314-965-2800	
Shredder Company LLC, The 7380 Doniphan Dr — *Web:* www.theshredderco.com	Canutillo	TX	79835	915-877-3814	
Sidel Systems Usa Inc 12500 El Camino Real — *Web:* www.sidelsystems.com	Atascadero	CA	93422	805-462-1250	
Sielc Technologies 65 E Palatine Rd Ste 221 — *Web:* www.sielc.com	Prospect Heights	IL	60070	847-229-2629	
Simark Controls Ltd 10509-46 St S E Ste 10509 — *Web:* www.simarkcontrols.com	Calgary	AB	T2C5C2	403-236-0580	

Company / Address	City	State	Zip	Phone	Fax
Single Source Technologies Inc 2600 Superior Ct *Web:* www.singlesourcetech.com	Auburn Hills	MI	48326	248-232-6232	
SMW Autoblok Corp 285 Egidi Dr *Web:* www.smwautoblok.com	Wheeling	IL	60090	847-215-0591	
Southeastern Equipment Company Inc 10874 E Pike Rd *TF:* 800-798-5438 ■ *Web:* www.southeasternequip.com	Cambridge	OH	43725	740-432-6303	432-3303
Southwest Materials Handling Company Inc 4719 Almond St *Web:* www.swmhc.com	Dallas	TX	75247	214-630-1375	
SpanTech LLC 1115 Cleveland Ave PO Box 369 *Web:* www.spantechllc.com	Glasgow	KY	42141	270-651-9166	
Sparktech Inc 325 Fawnridge St *Web:* sparktechinc.com	Georgetown	TX	78628	512-422-4652	
Spec Inc 1234 Mesa Dr *Web:* www.sanitaryprocess.com	Erlanger	KY	41018	859-342-5419	
Speco Inc 3946 Willow St *Web:* speco.com	Schiller Park	IL	60176	847-678-4240	
SPI Health & Safety inc 60 Rue Gaston-Dumoulin *Web:* www.spi-s.com	Blainville	QC	J7C0A3	450-420-2012	
Spreitzer Inc 3145 16th Ave SW *Web:* localdirectory.kcrg.com	Cedar Rapids	IA	52404	319-365-9155	365-2525
Stamford Scientific International Inc Four Tucker Dr *Web:* www.stamfordscientific.com	Poughkeepsie	NY	12603	845-454-8171	
Stan Houston Equipment Co 501 S Marion Rd *TF:* 800-952-3033 ■ *Web:* www.stanhouston.com	Sioux Falls	SD	57106	605-336-3727	336-7860
Staubli Corp 201 Pkwy W Hillside Park *Web:* www.staubli.com	Duncan	SC	29334	864-433-1980	
Stoffel Equipment Company Inc 7764 N 81st St *Web:* www.stoffelequip.com	Milwaukee	WI	53223	414-354-7500	
Stowers Machinery Corp 6301 Old Rutledge Pike NE *Web:* www.stowerscat.com	Knoxville	TN	37924	865-546-1414	595-1030
Sugino Corp 1380 Hamilton Pkwy *Web:* www.suginocorp.com	Itasca	IL	60143	630-250-8585	
Sun Packaging Technologies Inc 2200 NW 32nd St Ste 1700 *Web:* www.sunpkg.com	Pompano Beach	FL	33069	954-978-3080	
Svf Flow Controls Inc 13560 Larwin Cir *Web:* ezvalve.com	Santa Fe Springs	CA	90670	562-802-2255	
Swift Saw & Tool Supply Company Inc 1200 171st St *Web:* swiftsaw.com	Hazel Crest	IL	60429	708-335-0550	
SYMTECH Inc 100 Sunbeam Rd *Web:* www.symtech-usa.com	Spartanburg	SC	29303	864-578-7101	
Systec Conveyor Corp 10010 Conveyor Dr *Web:* www.systecconveyors.com	Indianapolis	IN	46235	317-890-9230	
Tcm America Inc 107 Mcqueen St *Web:* tcmforklifts.com	West Columbia	SC	29172	803-791-5205	
Technical Packaging Services 319 Lk Hazeltine Dr *Web:* tech-pack.com	Chaska	MN	55318	952-448-1677	
Tecnara Tooling Systems Inc 12535 McCann Dr *Web:* www.tecnaratools.com	Santa Fe Springs	CA	90670	562-941-2000	
Texas Gauge & Control Inc 7575 Dillon St *Web:* www.texasgauge.com	Houston	TX	77061	713-641-2282	
Texas Welders Supply Company Inc 5515 W Richey Rd *Web:* www.twsco.com	Houston	TX	77066	231-880-4200	
Thompson & Johnson Equipment Company Inc 6926 Fly Rd *Web:* www.thompsonandjohnson.com	East Syracuse	NY	13057	315-437-2881	
Tinker Omega Manufacturing LLC 2424 Columbus Rd *Web:* tinkeromega.com	Springfield	OH	45503	937-322-2272	
Tipco Punch Inc One Coventry Rd *Web:* www.tipcopunch.com	Brampton	ON	L6T4B1	905-791-9811	
Tishma Innovations LLC 101 E State Pkwy *Web:* www.tminn.com	Schaumburg	IL	60173	847-884-1805	
Titan Machinery 15125 S Robert Trial *Web:* www.titanmachinery.com	Rosemount	MN	55068	651-423-2222	423-4551
Toll Gas & Welding Supply 3005 Niagara Ln N *Web:* tollgas.com	Plymouth	MN	55447	763-551-5300	
Tool Technology Distributors Inc 3110 Osgood Ct *Web:* www.tooltechnology.com	Fremont	CA	94539	510-656-8220	
Toolmex Corporation Inc 1075 Worcester Rd *Web:* www.eisontmx.com	Natick	MA	01760	508-653-8897	
Toromont Industries Ltd 3131 Hwy 7 W PO Box 5511 *TSE: TIH* ■ *Web:* toromontcat.com	Concord	ON	L4K1B7	416-667-5511	667-5555
Transnorm System Inc 2810 Ave E E *Web:* www.transnorm.com	Arlington	TX	76011	972-606-0303	
TranTek Automation Corp 2470 N Aero Park Ct *Web:* www.trantekautomation.com	Traverse City	MI	49686	231-946-6270	
Tri Star Industrial Co 1645 W Buckeye Rd *Web:* www.tristaraz.com	Phoenix	AZ	85007	602-252-0554	
Triflo International Inc 1000 FM 830 *Web:* www.triflo.com	Willis	TX	77318	936-856-8551	
Trio Pac Inc 386 Rue Mcarthur *Web:* www.triopac.com	Montreal	QC	H4T1X8	514-733-7793	
Turner Designs Hydrocarbon Instruments Inc 2023 N Gateway Ste 101 *Web:* www.oilinwatermonitors.com	Fresno	CA	93727	559-253-1414	
Tuson Corp 475 Bunker Ct *Web:* www.tuson.com	Vernon Hills	IL	60061	847-816-8800	
Tyler Equipment Corp 251 Shaker Rd PO Box 544 *TF:* 800-292-6351 ■ *Web:* www.tylerequipment.com	East Longmeadow	MA	01028	413-525-6351	525-5909
U.S. Materials Handling Corp 2231 State Rt 5 *Web:* www.usmaterialshandling.com	Utica	NY	13502	315-732-4111	
Unisearch Associates Inc 96 Bradwick Dr *Web:* www.unisearch-associates.com	Concord	ON	L4K1K8	905-669-3547	
UPCO Inc 24403 Amah Pkwy	Claremore	OK	74019	918-342-1270	
US Equipment Company Inc 8311 Sorensen Ave *TF:* 800-255-4731 ■ *Web:* www.usequipmentco.com	Santa Fe Springs	CA	90670	800-255-4731	
Valin Corp 555 E California Ave *TF:* 800-774-5630 ■ *Web:* www.valin.com	Sunnyvale	CA	94086	408-730-9850	730-1363
Valley Litho Supply Inc 1047 Haugen Ave *Web:* valleylithosupply.com	Rice Lake	WI	54868	715-234-1525	
VARGO Companies 3709 Pkwy Ln *Web:* www.vmhi.com	Hilliard	OH	43026	614-876-1163	
VBS Inc., Material Handling Equipment 5808 Midlothian Tpke *Web:* www.vbsmhe.com	Richmond	VA	23225	804-232-7816	
Verosonic 590 Telser Rd Ste B *Web:* www.verosonic.com	Lake Zurich	IL	60047	847-540-9257	
Victor L Phillips Co 4100 Gardner Ave *TF:* 800-878-9290 ■ *Web:* www.vlpco.com	Kansas City	MO	64120	816-241-9290	241-1738
Vinson Process Controls Company LP 2747 Highpoint Oaks Dr *Web:* www.vpcco.com	Lewisville	TX	75067	972-459-8200	
Vmc Technologies Inc 1788 Northwood Dr *Web:* www.vmctech.com	Troy	MI	48084	248-786-3000	
W.D. Matthews Machinery Co 901 Center St *Web:* www.wdmatthews.com	Auburn	ME	04210	207-784-9311	
Wajax Corp 3280 Wharton Way *TSE: WJX* ■ *Web:* www.wajax.com	Mississauga	ON	L4X2C5	905-212-3300	624-6020
Wajax Industrial Components LP 2200 52 Nd Ave *Web:* www.wajax-industrial-components.ca	Lachine	QC	H8T2Y3	514-636-3333	
Wallace b e Products Corp 71 N Bacton Hill Rd *Web:* www.wallacecranes.com	Frazer	PA	19355	610-647-1400	
Watts Equipment Co 17547 Comconex Rd *Web:* www.wattsequipment.com	Manteca	CA	95336	209-825-1700	
Weldstar Inc 1750 Mitchell Rd *Web:* www.weldstar.com	Aurora	IL	60505	630-859-3100	
West Side Tractor Sales Co 1400 W Ogden Ave *Web:* www.westsidetractorsales.com	Naperville	IL	60563	630-355-7150	355-7173
Westbrook Engineering 23501 Mound Rd *Web:* www.westbrook-eng.com	Warren	MI	48091	586-759-3100	
Western States Equipment Co 500 E Overland Rd PO Box 38 *TF:* 800-836-4308 ■ *Web:* www.westernstatescat.com	Meridian	ID	83642	208-888-2287	884-2314
White's Farm Supply Inc 4154 State Rt 31 *TF:* 800-633-4443 ■ *Web:* www.whitesfarmsupply.com	Canastota	NY	13032	315-697-2214	697-8024
Winchester Equipment Co 121 Indian Hollow Rd **Fax Area Code: 540* ■ *TF:* 800-323-3581 ■ *Web:* www.winchesterequipment.com	Winchester	VA	22603	800-323-3581	665-3058*
Wisconsin Lift Truck Corp 3125 Intertech Dr *Web:* www.wisconsinlift.com	Brookfield	WI	53045	262-781-8010	
Wojanis Inc 1001 Montour W Ind Park *Web:* www.wojanis.com	Coraopolis	PA	15108	724-695-1415	
WOODCO USA 773 McCarty Dr *Web:* www.woodcousa.com	Houston	TX	77029	713-672-9491	
World Oil Tools Inc 72 Technology Way SE *Web:* www.worldoiltools.com	Calgary	AB	T3S0B9	403-720-5155	
Wynright Corp 2500 York Rd *Web:* www.wynright.com	Elk Grove	IL	60007	847-595-9400	
Wyoming Machinery Co 5300 Old W Yellowstone Hwy *TF:* 800-244-0527 ■ *Web:* www.wyomingcat.com	Casper	WY	82604	307-472-1000	261-4491
Yaro Supply Co 521 Byers Rd Ste 112 *Web:* www.yaro.com	Miamisburg	OH	45342	937-859-6100	

362 HELICOPTER TRANSPORT SERVICES

SEE ALSO Air Charter Services p. 1726; Ambulance Services p. 1740

Company / Address	City	State	Zip	Phone	Fax
Accel Aviation Accessories LLC 11900 Lacy Ln *Web:* www.accelav.com	Fort Myers	FL	33966	239-275-8202	
Aerospace Maintenance Solutions LLC 8759 Mayfield Rd *Web:* aerospacellc.com	Chesterland	OH	44026	440-729-7703	
Air Logistics Inc 4605 Industrial Dr *TF:* 800-365-6771 ■ *Web:* www.bristowgroup.com	New Iberia	LA	70560	337-365-6771	364-8222
Aircoastal Helicopters Inc 2615 Lantana Rd Ste J	Lantana	FL	33462	561-642-6840	642-5393
Bristow Alaska Inc 1915 Donald Ave *TF:* 800-686-4080 ■ *Web:* www.bristowgroup.com	Fairbanks	AK	99701	907-452-1197	452-4539
Carson Helicopters 952 Blooming Glen Rd *TF:* 800-523-2335 ■ *Web:* www.carsonhelicopters.com	Perkasie	PA	18944	215-249-3535	249-1352
CHC Helicopter Corp 4740 Agar Dr *Web:* www.chc.ca	Richmond	BC	V7B1A3	604-276-7500	
Coastal Helicopters Inc 8995 Yandukin Dr *TF:* 800-789-5610 ■ *Web:* www.coastalhelicopters.com	Juneau	AK	99801	907-789-5600	789-7076
Columbia Helicopters Inc 14452 Arndt Rd NE *Web:* www.colheli.com	Aurora	OR	97002	503-678-1222	678-1222

	City	State	Zip	Phone	Fax
Corporate Air Technology 1250 Aviation Ave Ste 125 *Web:* corpairtech.com	San Jose	CA	95110	408-977-0990	
Corporate Helicopters of San Diego 3753 John J Montgomery Dr Ste 2 *TF:* 800-345-6737 ■ *Web:* www.corporatehelicopters.com	San Diego	CA	92123	858-505-5650	874-3038
Cougar Helicopters Inc St John's International Airport 40 Craig Dobbins' Way *Web:* www.cougar.ca	Saint John's	NL	A1A4Y3	709-758-4800	758-4850
Eagle Copters Ltd 823 Mctavish Rd NE *Web:* www.eaglecopters.com	Calgary	AB	T2E7G9	403-250-7370	
Helicopter Transport Services Inc (HTS) 701 Wilson Pt Rd *Web:* www.htshelicopters.com	Baltimore	MD	21220	410-391-7722	686-4507
Helinet Aviation Services LLC 16303 Waterman Dr Hngr 2 *Web:* www.helinet.com	Van Nuys	CA	91406	818-902-0229	902-9278
Highland Helicopters Ltd 4240 Agar Dr *Web:* www.highland.ca	Richmond	BC	V7B1A3	604-273-6161	273-6088
Island Express Helicopter Service 1175 Queens Hwy S *TF Cust Svc:* 800-228-2566 ■ *Web:* www.islandexpress.com	Long Beach	CA	90802	310-510-2525	
Kim Davidson Aviation Inc 2701 Airport Ave *Web:* www.kdasmo.com	Santa Monica	CA	90405	310-391-6293	
Maytag Aircraft Corp 6145 Lehman Dr Ste 300 *Web:* www.maytagaircraft.com	Colorado Springs	CO	80918	719-593-1600	
Midwest Helicopter Airways Inc 525 Executive Dr *TF:* 800-323-7609 ■ *Web:* www.midwesthelicopters.com	Willowbrook	IL	60527	630-325-7860	325-3313
Miraco Inc 102 Maple St *Web:* www.miracoinc.com	Manchester	NH	03103	603-665-9449	
PHI Inc 2001 SE Evangeline Thwy *NASDAQ: PHII* ■ *TF:* 866-815-7101 ■ *Web:* www.phihelico.com	Lafayette	LA	70508	337-235-2452	235-1357
Repairtech International Inc 16134 Saticoy St *Web:* www.repairtechinternational.com	Van Nuys	CA	91406	818-989-2681	
San Joaquin Helicopters 1407 S Lexington *Web:* www.sjhelicopters.com	Delano	CA	93215	661-725-1898	725-5401
Vertical Aviation 15035 N 73rd St Ste B	Scottsdale	AZ	85260	480-991-6558	907-2759
Victoria International Airport 1962 Canso Rd *TF:* 866-844-4354 ■ *Web:* www.vih.com	North Saanich	BC	V8L5V5	250-656-3987	655-6839
VIH Logging Ltd 1962 Canso Rd *Web:* www.vih.com	North Saanich	BC	V8L5V5	250-656-3987	655-6839
Wiggins Airways Inc One Garside Way *Web:* www.wiggins-air.com	Manchester	NH	03103	603-629-9191	665-9644
Yellowhead Helicopters Ltd 3010 Selwyn Rd *TF:* 888-566-4401 ■ *Web:* www.yhl.ca	Valemount	BC	V0E2Z0	250-566-4401	566-4333

363 HOLDING COMPANIES

SEE ALSO Conglomerates p. 2071

A holding company is a company that owns enough voting stock in another firm to control management and operations by influencing or electing its board of directors.

363-1 Airlines Holding Companies

	City	State	Zip	Phone	Fax
Alaska Air Group Inc 19300 International Blvd *NYSE: ALK* ■ *Web:* www.alaskaair.com	Seattle	WA	98188	206-433-3200	392-7825
AMR Corp 4333 Amon Carter Blvd PO Box 619616 *OTC: AAMRQ* ■ *Web:* www.aa.com	Fort Worth	TX	76155	817-963-1234	967-4162
ExpressJet Holdings Inc 990 Toffie Terrac *Web:* www.expressjet.com	Atlanta	GA	30354	404-856-1000	
Frontier Airlines Inc 7001 Tower Rd *TF:* 800-432-1359 ■ *Web:* www.flyfrontier.com	Denver	CO	80249	720-374-4200	374-4621
JetBlue Airways Corp 118-29 Queens Blvd *NASDAQ: JBLU* ■ *TF:* 800-538-2583 ■ *Web:* www.jetblue.com	Forest Hills	NY	11375	718-286-7900	709-3621
Republic Airways Holdings Inc 8909 PuRdue Rd Ste 300 *NASDAQ: RJET* ■ *TF:* 800-433-7300 ■ *Web:* rjet.com	Indianapolis	IN	46268	317-484-6000	484-4524
SkyWest Inc 444 S River Rd *NASDAQ: SKYW* ■ *Web:* www.skywest.com	Saint George	UT	84790	435-634-3000	634-3105
US Airways Group Inc 111 W Rio Salado Pkwy *NYSE: LCC* ■ *TF:* 800-428-4322 ■ *Web:* www.usairways.com	Tempe	AZ	85281	480-693-0800	

363-2 Bank Holding Companies

	City	State	Zip	Phone	Fax
1st Constitution Bancorp 2650 Rt 130 & Dey Rd *NASDAQ: FCCY* ■ *Web:* www.1stconstitution.com	Cranbury	NJ	08512	609-655-4500	655-5653
215 Holding Co 215 S 11th St *Web:* ffmbank.com	Minneapolis	MN	55403	612-332-4732	
Access National Corp 1800 Robert Fulton Dr Ste 310 *NASDAQ: ANCX* ■ *TF:* 800-931-0370 ■ *Web:* www.accessnationalbank.com	Reston	VA	20191	703-871-2100	766-3386
Accuristix 2844 Bristol Cir *TF:* 866-356-6830 ■ *Web:* www.accuristix.com	Oakville	ON	L6H6G4	905-829-9927	491-3001
Activar Inc 7808 Creekridge Cir *Web:* www.activar.com	Minneapolis	MN	55439	952-944-3533	
Allegheny Valley Bank 5137 Butler St *OTC: AVLY* ■ *TF:* 800-889-6440 ■ *Web:* www.avbpgh.com	Pittsburgh	PA	15201	412-781-1464	781-6474
Alpine Bank of Colorado 2200 Grand Ave *TF:* 888-425-7463 ■ *Web:* www.alpinebank.com	Glenwood Springs	CO	81601	970-945-2424	947-1242
AMB Financial Corp 8230 Hohman Ave *OTC: AMFC* ■ *TF:* 800-436-5113 ■ *Web:* www.ambfinancial.com	Munster	IN	46321	219-836-5870	836-5883
Amboy Bancorp 3590 US Hwy 9 S *TF:* 800-942-6269 ■ *Web:* www.amboybank.com	Old Bridge	NJ	08857	732-591-8700	591-0705
Amegy Bancorp Inc 4400 Post Oak Pkwy *Web:* amegybank.com	Houston	TX	77027	713-235-8800	
Ameri-Force Inc 9485 Regency Sq Blvd Ste 300 *Web:* www.ameriforce.com	Jacksonville	FL	32225	904-353-1773	
Ameriana Bancorp 2118 Bundy Ave PO Box H *NASDAQ: ASBI* ■ *TF:* 866-844-7584 ■ *Web:* www.ameriana.com	New Castle	IN	47362	765-529-2230	529-2232
American River Bankshares 3100 Zinfandel Dr Ste 450 *NASDAQ: AMRB* ■ **Fax Area Code:* 916 ■ *TF:* 800-544-0545 ■ *Web:* www.americanriverbank.com	Rancho Cordova	CA	95670	800-544-0545	851-1025*
American State Bank 1401 Ave Q *TF:* 800-531-1401 ■ *Web:* www.prosperitybankusa.com	Lubbock	TX	79401	806-767-7000	
AmericanWest Bancorp 41 W Riverside Ave Ste 100 *TF:* 800-772-5479 ■ *Web:* www.awbank.net	Spokane	WA	99201	509-927-3028	465-9681
Ameris Bancorp 24 Second Ave SE *NASDAQ: ABCB* ■ *TF:* 800-347-9680 ■ *Web:* www.amerisbank.com	Moultrie	GA	31768	229-890-1111	890-2235
Ames National Corp 405 Fifth St PO Box 846 *NASDAQ: ATLO* ■ *Web:* www.amesnational.com	Ames	IA	50010	515-232-6251	663-3033
Anchor BanCorp Wisconsin Inc 25 W Main St *NYSE: ABCW* ■ **Fax:* Hum Res ■ *TF:* 800-252-6246 ■ *Web:* www.anchorbank.com	Madison	WI	53707	608-252-8700	252-1889*
Andrew R Mancini Assoc Inc 129 Odell Ave *Web:* andrewmancini.com	Endicott	NY	13760	607-754-7070	786-0410
Andrus Transportation Services LLC 3185 East Deseret Dr North PO Box 880 *TF:* 800-888-5838 ■ *Web:* www.andrustrans.com	Saint George	UT	84790	435-673-1566	
Annapolis Bancorp Inc 1000 Bestgate Rd *NASDAQ: ANNB* ■ **Fax Area Code:* 800 ■ *TF:* 800-555-5455 ■ *Web:* www.fnb-online.com	Annapolis	MD	21401	410-224-4483	278-6265*
Arrow Financial Corp 250 Glen St *NASDAQ: AROW* ■ *TF:* 800-937-5449 ■ *Web:* www.arrowfinancial.com	Glens Falls	NY	12801	518-745-1000	761-6741
Associated Banc-Corp 1200 Hansen Rd *NYSE: ASB* ■ **Fax:* Hum Res ■ *TF PR:* 800-236-2722 ■ *Web:* www.associatedbank.com	Green Bay	WI	54304	920-491-7000	*
Astoria Financial Corp One Astoria Federal Plz *NYSE: AF* ■ *Web:* astoriafederal.com	Lake Success	NY	11042	516-327-3000	
Atlantic Coast Bank (ACFC) 505 Haines Ave *NASDAQ: ACFC* ■ *TF:* 800-342-2824 ■ *Web:* www.atlanticcoastbank.net/	Waycross	GA	31501	912-283-4711	964-4709
Bancorp Rhode Island 1 Turks Head Pl *NASDAQ: BARI* ■ *Web:* www.bankri.com	Providence	RI	02903	401-456-5000	456-5069
BancorpSouth Inc 2910 W Jackson St *NYSE: BXS* ■ *TF:* 888-797-7711 ■ *Web:* www.bancorpsouthonline.com	Tupelo	MS	38801	662-680-2000	678-7263
Bank Capital Corp 5055 N 32nd St *Web:* biltmorebankaz.com	Phoenix	AZ	85018	602-992-5055	
Bank Independent 710 S Montgomery Ave *TF:* 877-865-5050 ■ *Web:* www.bibank.com	Sheffield	AL	35660	256-386-5000	
Bank Mutual Corp 4949 W Brown Deer Rd *NASDAQ: BKMU* ■ **Fax Area Code:* 608 ■ *TF:* 844-256-8684 ■ *Web:* www.bankmutual.com	Milwaukee	WI	53223	414-354-1500	251-0580*
Bank of Commerce Holdings 1901 Churn Creek Rd *NASDAQ: BOCH* ■ *TF:* 800-421-2575 ■ *Web:* www.reddingbankofcommerce.com	Redding	CA	96002	530-224-3333	224-3337
Bank of Hawaii Corp 130 Merchant St 20th Fl *NYSE: BOH* ■ *TF:* 888-643-3888 ■ *Web:* www.boh.com	Honolulu	HI	96813	888-643-3888	
Bank of New York Mellon Corp, The One Wall St *NYSE: BK* ■ **Fax:* PR ■ *Web:* www.bnymellon.com	New York	NY	10286	212-495-1784	635-1799*
Bank of South Carolina Corp 256 Meeting St *NASDAQ: BKSC* ■ *TF:* 800-523-4175 ■ *Web:* www.banksc.com	Charleston	SC	29401	843-724-1500	723-1513
Bank of the Ozarks Inc 12615 Chenal Pkwy PO Box 8811 *NASDAQ: OZRK* ■ *TF:* 800-628-3552 ■ *Web:* www.bankozarks.com	Little Rock	AR	72211	501-978-2265	
BankAtlantic Bancorp Inc 401 E Las Olas Blvd Ste 800 *Web:* www.bbxcapital.com	Fort Lauderdale	FL	33301	954-940-4000	940-5320
Bar Harbor Bankshares 82 Main St PO Box 400 *NYSE: BHB* ■ *TF:* 888-853-7100 ■ *Web:* www.bhbt.com	Bar Harbor	ME	04609	207-288-3314	288-2626
Barnes Transportation Services Inc 2309 Whitley Rd **Fax Area Code:* 252 ■ *TF:* 800-898-5897 ■ *Web:* www.barnestransport.com	Wilson	NC	27895	800-898-5897	291-2787*
Bay Bank 2328 W Joppa Rd *NASDAQ: BYBK* ■ *TF:* 800-222-6566 ■ *Web:* www.baybankmd.com	Lutherville	MD	21093	410-494-2580	
BB & T Corp 200 W Second St *NYSE: BBT* ■ *TF:* 800-226-5228 ■ *Web:* www.bbt.com	Winston-Salem	NC	27101	336-733-2500	
BBCN Bank 3731 Wilshire Blvd Ste 1000 *NASDAQ: NARA* ■ *TF:* 888-811-6272 ■ *Web:* www.bbcnbank.com	Los Angeles	CA	90010	213-639-1700	235-3033
BCB Bancorp Inc 104-110 Ave C *NASDAQ: BCBP* ■ *Web:* www.bcbbancorp.com	Bayonne	NJ	07002	201-823-0700	339-0403
Beck-ford Construction LP 6750 MayaRd Rd *Web:* www.beck-ford.com	Houston	TX	77041	713-896-7774	937-1942
Benny Whitehead Inc 3265 S Eufaula Ave *TF:* 800-633-7617 ■ *Web:* www.bwitruck.com	Eufaula	AL	36027	334-687-8055	687-1345
Berkshire Bancorp Inc 160 Broadway *NASDAQ: BERK* ■ *Web:* www.berkbank.com	New York	NY	10038	212-791-5362	
Berkshire Hills Bancorp Inc 24 N St *NYSE: BHLB* ■ *TF:* 800-773-5601 ■ *Web:* www.berkshirebank.com	Pittsfield	MA	01201	413-443-5601	443-3587
Big Spring School District 45 Mt Rock Rd *Web:* www.bigspringsd.org	Newville	PA	17241	717-776-2000	
Blackburn Radio Inc 700 Richmond St Ste 102 *Web:* blackburnradio.com	London	ON	N6A5C7	519-679-8680	
Bmo Bankcorp Inc 111 W Monroe St **Fax Area Code:* 312 ■ *TF:* 888-340-2265 ■ *Web:* www.bmoharris.com	Chicago	IL	60603	888-340-2265	765-1208*
BNC Bancorp 1226 Eastchester Dr *NASDAQ: BNCN* ■ *Web:* www.bankofnc.com	High Point	NC	27265	336-476-9200	889-8451
BNCCORP Inc 322 E Main Ave *OTC: BNCC* ■ *Web:* www.bnccorp.com	Bismarck	ND	58501	701-250-3040	222-3653

	City	State	Zip	Phone	Fax
Bomaine Corp 20731 S Fordyce Ave	Carson	CA	90810	310-537-1979	
Boston Private Financial Holdings Inc 10 Post Office Sq	Boston	MA	02109	617-912-1900	912-4511
NASDAQ: BPFH ■ *TF:* 855-738-8916 ■ *Web:* www.bostonprivate.com					
Brannen Banks Of Florida Inc PO Box 1929	Inverness	FL	34451	352-726-1221	726-1156
TF: 866-546-8273 ■ *Web:* www.brannenbanks.com					
Bridge Capital Holdings 55 Almaden Blvd Ste 200	San Jose	CA	95113	408-423-8500	423-8520
NASDAQ: BBNK ■ *TF General:* 866-273-4265 ■ *Web:* www.bridgebank.com					
Bridge Community Bank 200 S Cherry	Mechanicsville	IA	52306	563-432-7291	
Web: bankatbridge.com					
Broadway Financial Corp 4800 Wilshire Blvd	Los Angeles	CA	90010	323-634-1700	634-1728
NASDAQ: BYFC ■ *TF:* 800-227-0845 ■ *Web:* www.broadwayfederalbank.com					
Brookline Bank PO Box 470469	Brookline	MA	02445	617-730-3520	730-3569
NASDAQ: BRKL ■ *TF Cust Svc:* 877-668-2265 ■ *Web:* www.brooklinebank.com					
Brunswick Bank & trust 439 Livingston Ave	New Brunswick	NJ	08901	732-247-5800	247-0292
Web: www.brunswickbank.com					
Bryn Mawr Bank Corp 801 Lancaster Ave	Bryn Mawr	PA	19010	610-525-1700	520-7278*
NASDAQ: BMTC ■ **Fax:* Cust Svc ■ *TF:* 855-381-2631 ■ *Web:* www.bmtc.com					
C & F Financial Corp 802 Main St PO Box 391	West Point	VA	23181	804-843-4584	843-3017
NASDAQ: CFFI ■ *TF:* 800-583-3863 ■ *Web:* cffc.com/					
Camden National Corp Two Elm St	Camden	ME	04843	207-236-8821	236-6256
NYSE: CAC ■ *TF:* 800-860-8821 ■ *Web:* www.camdennational.com					
Capital City Bank Group Inc PO Box 900	Tallahassee	FL	32302	850-402-7500	
NASDAQ: CCBG ■ *TF:* 888-671-0400 ■ *Web:* www.ccbg.com					
Capital Directions Inc 322 S Jefferson St	Mason	MI	48854	517-676-0500	
Capitol Bancorp Ltd 200 N Washington Sq	Lansing	MI	48933	517-487-6555	374-2576
OTC: CBCRQ ■ *Web:* www.capitolbancorp.com					
Capitol City Bancshares Inc 562 Lee St	Atlanta	GA	30310	404-752-6067	
TF: 866-758-6395 ■ *Web:* www.capitolcitybank-atl.com					
Capitol Federal Financial 700 Kansas Ave	Topeka	KS	66603	785-235-1341	231-6216
NASDAQ: CFFN ■ *TF:* 888-822-7333 ■ *Web:* www.capfed.com					
Cardinal Financial Corp 8270 Greensboro Dr Ste 500	McLean	VA	22102	703-584-3400	584-3518*
NASDAQ: CFNL ■ **Fax:* Hum Res ■ *TF:* 800-473-3247 ■ *Web:* www.cardinalbank.com					
Career Path Training Corp 11300 Fourth St N Ste 200	St Petersburg	FL	33716	727-342-6420	
Web: www.careerpathtraining.com					
Carolina Bank Holdings Inc 101 N Spring St	Greensboro	NC	27401	336-288-1898	387-4359
NASDAQ: CLBH ■ *TF:* 800-472-3272 ■ *Web:* www.carolinabank.com					
Caruso Affiliated Holdings LLC 101 The Grove Dr	Los Angeles	CA	90036	323-900-8100	
Web: www.carusoaffiliated.com					
Carver Bancorp Inc 75 W 125th St	New York	NY	10027	718-230-2900	426-6159*
NASDAQ: CARV ■ **Fax Area Code:* 212 ■ *Web:* www.carverbank.com					
Cascade Bancorp 1100 NW Wall St	Bend	OR	97701	541-385-6205	382-8780
NASDAQ: CACB ■ *TF Cust Svc:* 877-617-3400 ■ *Web:* www.botc.com					
Cathay General Bancorp Inc 777 N Broadway	Los Angeles	CA	90012	213-625-4700	625-1368
NASDAQ: CATY ■ *TF:* 800-922-8429 ■ *Web:* www.cathaybank.com					
Center Financial Corp 3435 Wilshire Blvd	Los Angeles	CA	90010	213-365-0114	
Web: taxpayer.net					
Central Bank 101 W Commercial St	Lebanon	MO	65536	417-532-2151	532-2001
Web: www.central-bank.net					
Central Federal Corp 2923 Smith Rd	Fairlawn	OH	44333	330-666-7979	666-7959
NASDAQ: CFBK ■ *TF:* 866-668-4606 ■ *Web:* www.cfbankonline.com					
Central Pacific Financial Corp PO Box 3590	Honolulu	HI	96811	808-544-0500	544-0500
NYSE: CPF ■ *TF:* 800-342-8422 ■ *Web:* www.centralpacificbank.com					
Central Valley Community Bancorp 7100 N Financial Dr Ste 101	Fresno	CA	93720	559-298-1775	298-1483
NASDAQ: CVCY ■ *TF:* 866-294-9588 ■ *Web:* www.cvcb.com					
Century Bancorp Inc 400 Mystic Ave	Medford	MA	02155	781-393-4160	393-4077
NASDAQ: CNBKA ■ *TF:* 866-823-6887 ■ *Web:* www.centurybank.com					
CFS Bancorp Inc 707 Ridge Rd	Munster	IN	46321	219-513-5123	770-7572*
NASDAQ: CITZ ■ **Fax Area Code:* 317 ■ *TF:* 866-622-1370 ■ *Web:* www.firstmerchants.com					
Charter Enterprises LLC 1255 Corporate Ctr Dr Ste PH402	Monterey Park	CA	91754	323-269-6868	
Web: www.charterbbq.com					
Chemical Financial Corp 333 E Main St	Midland	MI	48640	989-839-5350	
NASDAQ: CHFC ■ *TF:* 800-867-9757 ■ *Web:* www.chemicalbankmi.com					
Citizens & Northern Corp 90-92 Main St	Wellsboro	PA	16901	570-724-3411	724-6395
NASDAQ: CZNC ■ *Web:* cnbankpa.com					
Citizens Financial Group Inc One Citizens Dr	Riverside	RI	02915	401-456-7000	
TF: 800-922-9999 ■ *Web:* www.citizensbank.com					
Citizens Holding Co 521 Main St PO Box 209	Philadelphia	MS	39350	601-656-4692	656-4264
NASDAQ: CIZN ■ *Web:* www.thecitizensbankphila.com					
Citizens South Banking Corp 519 S New Hope Rd PO Box 2249	Gastonia	NC	28054	704-868-5200	825-7723*
NASDAQ: CSBC ■ **Fax:* Hum Res ■ *TF:* 877-311-2265 ■ *Web:* www.parksterlingbank.com					
City Holding Co 25 Gatewater Rd	Charleston	WV	25313	304-769-1100	769-1111
NASDAQ: CHCO ■ *Web:* www.bankatcity.com					
Clifton Savings Bancorp Inc 1433 Van Houten Ave 3rd Fl	Clifton	NJ	07015	973-473-2200	
NASDAQ: CSBK ■ *TF:* 888-562-6727 ■ *Web:* www.cliftonsavings.com					
CNB Financial Corp One S Second St PO Box 42	Clearfield	PA	16830	814-765-9621	765-8294
NASDAQ: CCNE ■ *TF:* 800-492-3221 ■ *Web:* www.bankcnb.com					
Colonial Bankshares Inc 85 W Broad St	Bridgeton	NJ	08302	856-451-5800	451-5110
Web: www.colonialbankfsb.com					
Colorado Business Bank 821 17th St	Denver	CO	80202	303-293-2265	312-3476
TF: 800-574-4714 ■ *Web:* cobizbank.com					
Columbia Bank 1301 A St Ste 800	Tacoma	WA	98402	253-305-1900	304-0050
NASDAQ: COLB ■ *TF:* 800-305-1905 ■ *Web:* www.columbiabank.com					
Commercial National Financial Corp 900 Ligonier St	Latrobe	PA	15650	724-539-3501	539-0816*
OTC: CNAF ■ **Fax:* Hum Res ■ *TF:* 800-803-2265 ■ *Web:* www.cnbthebankonline.com					
Community Bank Shares of Indiana Inc 101 W Spring St	New Albany	IN	47150	812-944-2224	
NASDAQ: YCB ■ *TF:* 866-944-2004 ■ *Web:* www.yourcommunitybank.com					
Community Bank System Inc 5790 Widewaters Pkwy	Syracuse	NY	13214	315-445-2282	*
NYSE: CBU ■ **Fax:* Acctg ■ *TF:* 800-847-2911 ■ *Web:* www.communitybankna.com					
Community Bankshares Inc 5570 DTC Pkwy	Greenwood Village	CO	80111	720-529-3336	
Web: www.cobnks.com					
Community First Bank Na PO Box 39	Forest	OH	45843	419-273-2595	273-2598
Web: www.com1stbank.com					
Community Investors Bancorp Inc 119 S Sandusky Ave	Bucyrus	OH	44820	419-562-7055	562-5516
OTC: CIBN ■ *TF:* 800-222-4955 ■ *Web:* www.ffcb.com					
Community Shores Bank Corp 1030 W Norton Ave	Muskegon	MI	49441	231-780-1800	780-3006
OTC: CSHB ■ *TF:* 888-853-6633 ■ *Web:* www.communityshores.com					
Community Trust Bancorp Inc 346 N Mayo Trl	Pikeville	KY	41501	606-432-1414	433-4637*
NASDAQ: CTBI ■ **Fax:* Hum Res ■ *TF:* 800-422-1090 ■ *Web:* www.ctbi.com					
Community West Bancshares 445 Pine Ave	Goleta	CA	93117	805-692-5821	692-8902
NASDAQ: CWBC ■ *Web:* www.communitywest.com					
Compass Bancshares Inc 15 S 20th St	Birmingham	AL	35233	205-297-3584	297-3702
TF: 800-266-7277 ■ *Web:* www.bbvacompass.com					
Connecticut Bank & Trust Co 58 State House Sq	Hartford	CT	06103	860-246-5200	
Web: www.berkshirebank.com					
ConnectOne Bancorp, Inc 2455 Morris Ave	Union	NJ	07083	908-688-9500	
NASDAQ: CNBC					
Contrans Corp 1179 Ridgeway Rd	Woodstock	ON	N4V1E3	519-421-4600	
Web: www.contrans.ca					
Country Club Bank 2310 S Fourth St	Leavenworth	KS	66048	913-682-2300	
Web: www.countryclubbank.com					
Crazy Woman Creek Bancorp Inc PO Box 1020	Buffalo	WY	82834	307-684-5591	684-7854
TF: 877-684-2766 ■ *Web:* www.buffalofed.com					
Crofutt & Smith Moving & Storage One Lenel Rd PO Box 8001	Landing	NJ	07850	973-347-7200	347-8143
Cullen/Frost Bankers Inc 100 W Houston St	San Antonio	TX	78205	210-220-4011	220-4941*
NYSE: CFR ■ **Fax:* Mail Rm ■ *TF:* 800-562-6732 ■ *Web:* www.frostbank.com					
CVB Financial Corp 701 N Haven Ave PO Box 51000	Ontario	CA	91764	909-980-4030	481-2130*
NASDAQ: CVBF ■ **Fax:* Hum Res ■ *TF:* 888-222-5432 ■ *Web:* www.cbbank.com					
Davidson Pipe Supply Company Inc 5002 Second Ave	Brooklyn	NY	11232	718-439-6300	
Web: www.davidsonpipe.com					
Dickinson Financial Corp 1111 Main St Ste 1600	Kansas City	MO	64105	816-472-5244	472-5211
Dime Community Bancshares Inc 209 Havemeyer St	Brooklyn	NY	11211	718-782-6200	486-7535*
NASDAQ: DCOM ■ **Fax:* Hum Res ■ *TF:* 800-321-3463 ■ *Web:* www.dime.com					
Doral Financial Corp 1441 F D Roosevelt Ave	San Juan	PR	00920	787-749-4949	749-4191
NYSE: DRL ■ *TF:* 866-296-3743 ■ *Web:* www.snl.com					
Eagle Bancorp Inc 7815 Woodmont Ave	Bethesda	MD	20814	240-497-2044	986-8529*
NASDAQ: EGBN ■ **Fax Area Code:* 301 ■ *TF:* 800-364-8313 ■ *Web:* www.eaglebankcorp.com					
East West Bancorp Inc 1881 W Main St	Alhambra	CA	91801	626-308-2012	308-2034
NASDAQ: EWBC ■ *TF:* 888-895-5650 ■ *Web:* www.eastwestbank.com					
Eastern Bank Corp 265 Franklin St	Boston	MA	02110	617-897-1008	
TF Cust Svc: 800-327-8376 ■ *Web:* www.easternbank.com					
Eastern Virginia Bankshares Inc 330 Hospital Rd	Tappahannock	VA	22560	804-443-8400	445-1047
NASDAQ: EVBS ■ *TF General:* 866-296-3743 ■ *Web:* www.snl.com					
Enterprise Bancorp Inc 222 Merrimack St	Lowell	MA	01852	978-459-9000	656-5813
NASDAQ: EBTC ■ *Web:* www.enterprisebanking.com					
Enterprise Financial Services Corp 150 N Meramec Ave	Clayton	MO	63105	314-725-5500	721-6793
NASDAQ: EFSG ■ *TF:* 800-396-8141 ■ *Web:* www.enterprisebank.com					
Evanov Communications Inc 5312 Dundas St W	Toronto	ON	M9B1B3	416-213-1035	
Web: www.evanovradio.com					
Evans Bancorp Inc One Grimsby Dr	Hamburg	NY	14075	716-926-2000	926-2005*
NYSE: EVBN ■ **Fax:* Hum Res ■ *TF:* 866-310-0763 ■ *Web:* www.evansbank.com					
Farmer State Bank of Sublette 303 S Pennsylvania Ave PO Box 20	Sublette	IL	61367	815-849-5242	849-5494
TF: 866-269-1722 ■ *Web:* www.sublettebank.com					
Farmers Capital Bank Corp PO Box 309	Frankfort	KY	40602	502-227-1668	227-1692
NASDAQ: FFKT ■ *TF:* 800-776-9437 ■ *Web:* www.farmerscapital.com					
Fauquier Bankshares Inc 10 Courthouse Sq	Warrenton	VA	20186	540-347-2700	349-2093
NASDAQ: FBSS ■ *TF:* 800-638-3798 ■ *Web:* www.fauquierbank.com					
FFD Financial Corp 321 N Wooster Ave	Dover	OH	44622	330-364-7777	364-7779
OTC: FFDF ■ *TF:* 800-558-3424 ■ *Web:* www.onlinefirstfed.com					
FFW Corp 1205 N Cass St	Wabash	IN	46992	260-563-3185	563-4841
OTC: FFWC ■ *TF:* 800-377-4984 ■ *Web:* www.crossroadsbanking.com					
Fidelity Federal Bancorp 18 NW Fourth St	Evansville	IN	47708	812-424-0921	469-2150
OTC: FDLB ■ *Web:* www.unitedfidelity.com					
Fidelity Southern Corp 3490 Piedmont Rd NE	Atlanta	GA	30305	404-814-8114	
Web: www.fidelitysouthern.com					
Financial Institutions Inc 220 Liberty St	Warsaw	NY	14569	585-786-1100	786-5254
NASDAQ: FISI ■ *TF:* 866-296-3743 ■ *Web:* www.snl.com					
First American Bank Corp 1650 Louis Ave	Elk Grove Village	IL	60009	847-952-3700	
Web: www.firstambank.com					
First BanCorp PO Box 9146	San Juan	PR	00908	787-725-2511	
NYSE: FBP ■ *TF:* 866-695-2511 ■ *Web:* www.1firstbank.com/pr/es					
First Bancorp of Indiana Inc 5001 Davis Lant Dr	Evansville	IN	47715	812-492-8100	
OTC: FBPI					
First Bancshares Inc 142 E First St	Mountain Grove	MO	65711	417-926-5151	926-4362
NYSE: FBSI ■ *Web:* firsthomesavingsbank.com					
First Banctrust Corp 101 S Central Ave	Paris	IL	61944	217-465-6381	465-0234
OTC: FIRT ■ *TF:* 800-228-6381 ■ *Web:* www.firstbanktrust.com					
First Banks Inc 135 N Meramec Ave	Clayton	MO	63105	314-854-4600	854-5454
TF: 800-760-2265 ■ *Web:* www.firstbanks.com					
First Busey Corp 100 W University Ave	Champaign	IL	61820	217-365-4516	
NASDAQ: BUSE ■ *TF:* 800-672-8739 ■ *Web:* www.busey.com					

Phone Fax

First Citizens Bancorp Inc PO Box 29 .... Columbia SC 29202 888-612-4444 931-8519*
OTC: FCBN ■ *Fax Area Code: 803 ■ TF: 888-612-4444 ■ Web: www.firstcitizensonline.com

First Citizens BancShares Inc
4300 Six Forks Rd .... Raleigh NC 27609 919-716-7000 716-7074
NASDAQ: FCNCA ■ Web: www.firstcitizens.com

First Citizens Bank
1801 Century Pk E Ste 800 .... Los Angeles CA 90067 888-323-4732 552-1772*
*Fax Area Code: 310 ■ TF: 888-323-4732 ■ Web: www.firstcitizens.com

First Citizens National Bank Charitable Foundation
PO Box 1708 .... Mason City IA 50402 641-423-1600 423-4600
TF: 800-423-1602 ■ Web: www.firstcitizensnb.com

First Commonwealth Financial Corp
601 Philadelphia St .... Indiana PA 15701 724-349-7220 349-7220*
NYSE: FCF ■ *Fax: Hum Res ■ TF: 800-711-2265 ■ Web: www.fcbanking.com

First Community Bank 420 Second Ave SW .... Cullman AL 35055 256-734-4863 737-8900
Web: www.fcbcullman.com

First Community Corp (FCC) 5455 Sunset Blvd .... Lexington SC 29072 803-951-0555 *
NASDAQ: FCCO ■ *Fax: Cust Svc ■ TF: 800-829-6372 ■ Web: www.firstcommunitysc.com

First Defiance Financial Corp
601 Clinton St .... Defiance OH 43512 419-782-5015 784-3467*
NASDAQ: FDEF ■ *Fax: Hum Res ■ TF: 800-472-6292 ■ Web: www.fdef.com

First Federal Bancshares of Arkansas Inc
1401 Hwy 62-65 N .... Harrison AR 72601 870-741-7641 365-8369
NASDAQ: FFBH ■ TF: 866-242-3324 ■ Web: www.ffbh.com

First Financial Bancorp (FFB)
255 E Fifth St Ste 700 .... Cincinnati OH 45202 513-979-5837
NASDAQ: FFBC ■ TF: 877-322-9530 ■ Web: www.bankatfirst.com

First Financial Bankshares Inc PO Box 701 .... Abilene TX 79604 325-627-7155 627-7393
NASDAQ: FFIN ■ TF: 888-588-2623 ■ Web: www.ffin.com

First Financial Corp
One First Financial Plz .... Terre Haute IN 47807 812-238-6000 232-5336
NASDAQ: THFF ■ TF: 800-511-0045 ■ Web: www.first-online.com

First FSB of Frankfort
216 W Main St PO Box 535 .... Frankfort KY 40602 502-223-1638 223-7136
TF: 888-818-3372 ■ Web: www.ffsbfrankfort.com

First Horizon National Corp 165 Madison .... Memphis TN 38103 901-523-4444
NYSE: FHN ■ TF: 800-489-4040 ■ Web: www.firsthorizon.com

First Independence Corp
112 E Myrtle St PO Box 947 .... Independence KS 67301 620-331-1660 331-1600
NYSE: FFSL ■ TF: 800-455-0744 ■ Web: www.firstfederalsl.com

First Interstate Bancsystem Inc
401 N 31st St .... Billings MT 59101 406-255-5000 *
NASDAQ: FIBK ■ *Fax: Hum Res ■ TF: 888-752-3341 ■ Web: www.firstinterstatebank.com

First M & F Corp 221 E Washington St .... Kosciusko MS 39090 662-289-5121
NASDAQ: FMFC

First Merchants Corp 200 E Jackson St .... Muncie IN 47305 765-747-1500 741-7283*
NASDAQ: FRME ■ *Fax: Mktg ■ TF: 800-205-3464 ■ Web: www.firstmerchants.com

First Midwest Bancorp Inc
One Pierce Pl Ste 1500 .... Itasca IL 60143 630-875-7200 875-7396*
NASDAQ: FMBI ■ *Fax: Mktg ■ TF: 800-322-3623 ■ Web: firstmidwest.com

First Mutual Bancshares Inc
400 108th Ave NE PO Box 1647 .... Bellevue WA 98009 425-455-7300 455-7330
TF: 800-735-7303 ■ Web: www.firstmutual.com

First National Bank of Tennessee
214 E Main St .... Livingston TN 38570 931-823-1261
Web: www.fnbotn.com

First National Lincoln Corp
223 Main St PO Box 940 .... Damariscotta ME 04543 207-563-3195 563-3356
TF: 800-564-3195 ■ Web: www.thefirstbancorp.com

First National of Nebraska Inc PO BOX 2490 .... Omaha NE 68197 402-341-0500 938-5302
TF: 800-688-7070 ■ Web: www.firstnational.com

First Niles Financial Inc 55 N Main St .... Niles OH 44446 330-652-2539 652-0911
NYSE: FNFI

First of Long Island Corp 10 Glen Head Ave .... Glen Head NY 11545 516-671-4900 676-7900
NASDAQ: FLIC ■ TF: 800-554-8969 ■ Web: www.fnbli.com

First Security Group Inc 531 Broad St .... Chattanooga TN 37402 423-266-2000 267-3383
NASDAQ: FSGI ■ Web: www.fsgbank.com

First South Bancorp Inc 1311 Carolina Ave .... Washington NC 27889 252-946-4178 946-3873
NASDAQ: FSBK ■ TF: 800-946-4178 ■ Web: www.firstsouthnc.com

First Southern Bank 301 S Ct St .... Florence AL 35630 256-718-4200 718-4296
TF General: 800-625-7131 ■ Web: www.firstsouthern.com

First State Bank 730 Harry Sauner Rd .... Hillsboro OH 45133 937-393-9170 393-3088
TF General: 800-987-2566 ■ Web: www.fsb4me.com

First Trinity Financial Corp
7633 E 63rd Pl Ste 230 .... Tulsa OK 74133 918-249-2438
Web: www.firsttrinityfinancial.com

First United Corp 19 S Second St .... Oakland MD 21550 888-692-2654 334-5784*
NASDAQ: FUNC ■ *Fax Area Code: 301 ■ *Fax: Hum Res ■ TF: 888-692-2654 ■ Web: www.mybank4.com

First West Virginia Bancorp Inc
1701 Warwood Ave .... Wheeling WV 26003 304-277-1100
NYSE: FWV ■ Web: snl.com

Firstbank Corp 311 Woodworth Ave .... Alma MI 48801 989-463-3137
NASDAQ: FBMI ■ Web: www.firstbankmi.com

FirstFed Bancorp Inc
1630 Fourth Ave N PO Box 340 .... Bessemer AL 35020 205-428-8472 428-8652
TF: 800-436-5112 ■ Web: www.firstfedbessemer.com

Flushing Financial Corp
1979 Marcus Ave .... New Hyde Park NY 11042 718-961-5400
NASDAQ: FFIC ■ TF: 800-581-2889 ■ Web: www.flushingbank.com

German American Bancorp 711 Main St .... Jasper IN 47546 812-482-1314 482-0758
NASDAQ: GABC ■ TF: 800-482-1314 ■ Web: www.germanamerican.com

Glacier Bancorp Inc PO Box 27 .... Kalispell MT 59903 406-756-4200
NASDAQ: GBCI ■ TF: 800-735-4371 ■ Web: www.glacierbank.com

Great American Bancorp Inc 1311 S Neil St .... Champaign IL 61820 217-356-2265 356-2502
OTC: GTPS ■ TF: 800-962-4284 ■ Web: www.greatamericanbancorp.com

Greene County Bancorp Inc 302 Main St .... Catskill NY 12414 518-943-2600 943-3756
NASDAQ: GCBC ■ TF: 888-439-4272 ■ Web: thebankofgreenecounty.com

GreenHouse Holdings Inc
5171 Santa Fe St Ste I .... San Diego CA 92109 858-273-2626

Greenwood Racing Inc 3001 St Rd .... Bensalem PA 19020 215-639-9000
TF: 888-238-2946 ■ Web: www.parxracing.com

Guaranty Bancshares Inc
100 W Arkansas St PO Box 1158 .... Mount Pleasant TX 75455 903-572-9881 572-9658
TF: 888-572-9881 ■ Web: www.gnty.com

Hancock Holding Co 2510 14th St .... Gulfport MS 39501 228-822-4371
TF: 800-522-6542 ■ Web: www.hancockbank.com

Hanmi Bank 3660 Wilshire Blvd Ste PH-A .... Los Angeles CA 90010 213-382-2200 384-8608
TF: 877-808-4266 ■ Web: www.hanmi.com

Harleysville Savings Financial Corp
271 Main St .... Harleysville PA 19438 215-256-8828 513-9393
NASDAQ: HARL ■ TF: 888-256-8828 ■ Web: www.harleysvillesavings.com

Harrell Bancshares Inc 1325 Hwy 278 Byp .... Camden AR 71701 870-837-8300

Hawthorn Bancshares Inc
300 SW Longview Blvd .... Lee's Summit MO 64081 816-347-8100
NASDAQ: HWBK ■ TF: 800-761-8362 ■ Web: www.exchangebancshares.com

Heartland Financial USA Inc 1398 Central Ave .... Dubuque IA 52001 563-589-2100 589-2011*
NASDAQ: HTLF ■ *Fax Area Code: 319 ■ TF: 888-739-2100 ■ Web: www.htlf.com

Heritage Bank 201 Fifth Ave SW .... Olympia WA 98501 360-943-1500
TF: 800-455-6126 ■ Web: www.heritagebankwaonline2.com

Heritage Commerce Corp 150 Almaden Blvd .... San Jose CA 95113 408-947-6900 947-6910
NASDAQ: HTBK ■ TF: 800-468-9716 ■ Web: www.heritagecommercecorp.com

Heritage Financial Corp 201 Fifth Ave SW .... Olympia WA 98501 360-943-1500 352-0864
NASDAQ: HFWA ■ TF: 800-962-4284 ■ Web: www.hf-wa.com

HF Financial Corp 225 S Main Ave .... Sioux Falls SD 57104 605-333-7556 333-7621
NASDAQ: HFFC ■ TF: 800-244-2149 ■ Web: www.homefederal.com

High Country Bancorp Inc
7360 W Hwy 50 PO Box 309 .... Salida CO 81201 719-539-2516 530-8881
OTC: HCBC ■ TF: 800-201-0557 ■ Web: www.highcountrybank.net

HMN Financial Inc 1016 Civic Ctr Dr NW .... Rochester MN 55901 507-535-1309 346-7140
NASDAQ: HMNF ■ TF: 888-257-2000 ■ Web: www.hmnf.com/

Home City Financial Corp
2454 N Limestone St PO Box 1288 .... Springfield OH 45503 937-390-0470 390-0876
OTC: HCFL ■ TF: 866-421-2331 ■ Web: www.homecityfederal.com

Home Federal Bank 1602 Cumberland Ave .... Middlesboro KY 40965 606-248-1095 242-1010*
OTC: HFBA ■ *Fax: Hum Res ■ TF: 800-354-0182 ■ Web: www.homefederalbank.com

Home Loan Financial Corp 413 Main St .... Coshocton OH 43812 740-622-0444 623-6000
OTC: HLFN ■ Web: www.homeloansavingsbank.com

Honat Bancorp Inc 733 Main St PO Box 350 .... Honesdale PA 18431 570-253-3355 253-5263
OTC: HONT ■ TF: 800-462-9515 ■ Web: www.hnbbank.com

HopFed Bancorp Inc
2700 Ft Campbell Blvd .... Hopkinsville KY 42240 270-885-1171 889-0313
NASDAQ: HFBC ■ Web: www.bankwithheritage.com

Horizon Bank 515 Franklin Sq .... Michigan City IN 46360 219-879-0211
Web: accesshorizon.com

HSBC North America Holdings Inc
2700 Sanders Rd .... Prospect Heights IL 60070 847-564-5000
TF: 800-975-4722 ■ Web: www.hsbc.com

Hulman & Co 900 Wabash Ave .... Terre Haute IN 47807 812-232-9446
Web: www.clabbergirl.com

Huntington Bancshares Inc 7 Easton Oval .... Columbus OH 43219 800-480-2265
NASDAQ: HBAN ■ TF: 800-480-2265 ■ Web: www.huntington.com

IBERIABANK Corp 200 W Congress St .... Lafayette LA 70501 800-968-0801 364-1171*
NASDAQ: IBKC ■ *Fax Area Code: 337 ■ TF: 800-968-0801 ■ Web: www.iberiabank.com

Independent Bank Corp 230 W Main St PO Box 491 .... Ionia MI 48846 616-527-2400 527-4004
NASDAQ: IBCP ■ TF: 888-300-3193 ■ Web: www.independentbank.com

International Bancshares Corp
1200 San Bernardo Ave .... Laredo TX 78040 956-722-7611 726-6637
NASDAQ: IBOC ■ Web: www.ibc.com

Intervest Bancshares Corp
1 Rockefeller Plaza Ste 400 .... New York NY 10020 212-218-8383 218-8390
NASDAQ: IBCA ■ TF: 877-226-5462 ■ Web: www.intervestnatbank.com

ISCAR Metals 300 Wway Pl .... Arlington TX 76018 817-258-3200 258-3221
Web: www.iscarmetals.com

Jacksonville Bancorp Inc 100 N Laura St .... Jacksonville FL 32202 904-421-3040 421-3050
NASDAQ: JAXB ■ TF: 888-699-5292 ■ Web: www.jaxbank.com

Jeffersonville Bancorp
4866 State Rt 52 PO Box 398 .... Jeffersonville NY 12748 845-482-4000 482-3544
OTC: JFBC ■ Web: www.jeffbank.com

Johnson Financial Group Inc
555 Main St Ste 400 .... Racine WI 53403 262-619-2790
Web: johnsonbank.com

Joy State Bank 101 W Main St .... Joy IL 61260 309-584-4146 584-4148
Web: joystatebank.com

Kearny Financial Corp 120 Passaic Ave .... Fairfield NJ 07004 973-244-4500 439-3985
NASDAQ: KRNY ■ Web: kearnyfederalsavings.com

Keweenaw Financial Corp 235 Quincy St .... Hancock MI 49930 906-482-0404 482-4403
TF: 866-482-0404 ■ Web: www.snb-t.com

KeyCorp 127 Public Sq .... Cleveland OH 44114 216-689-8481 689-3369
NYSE: KEY ■ TF: 800-539-9055 ■ Web: www.key.com

Koss-Winn Bancshares Inc
101 N Main St .... Buffalo Center IA 50424 641-562-2696

Lake Sunapee Bank 9 Main St PO Box 29 .... Newport NH 03773 603-863-5772 863-5025
TF: 800-281-5772 ■ Web: www.lakesunbank.com

Lakeland Bancorp Inc 250 Oak Ridge Rd .... Oak Ridge NJ 07438 973-697-2000 697-8385
NASDAQ: LBAI ■ TF: 866-224-1379 ■ Web: www.lakelandbank.com

Lakeland Financial Corp 202 E Ctr St .... Warsaw IN 46580 574-267-6144 267-9180*
NASDAQ: LKFN ■ *Fax: Hum Res ■ TF: 800-827-4522 ■ Web: www.lakecitybank.com

Lexington B & L Financial Corp
205 S 13th St PO Box 190 .... Lexington MO 64067 660-259-2247 259-2384
Web: www.bl-bank.com

Linkous Construction Company Inc
1661 Aaron Brenner Dr Ste 207 .... Memphis TN 38120 901-754-0700 754-0302
Web: www.linkousconstruction.com

LNB Bancorp Inc 457 Broadway .... Lorain OH 44052 440-989-3348 244-9507
NASDAQ: LNBB ■ TF: 800-860-1007 ■ Web: www.4lnb.com

Logansport Financial Corp
723 E Broadway PO Box 569 .... Logansport IN 46947 574-722-3855 722-3857
OTC: LOGN ■ TF: 800-541-9154 ■ Web: www.logansportsavings.com

Lumber Industries Inc 5809 Kennett Pk .... Wilmington DE 19807 302-655-9651

Macatawa Bank Corp
10753 Macatawa Dr PO Box 3119 .... Holland MI 49424 616-820-1444 494-7644
NASDAQ: MCBC ■ TF: 877-820-2265 ■ Web: www.macatawabank.com

				Phone	Fax
Malaga Financial Corp 2514 Via Tejon *OTC: MLGF* ■ *TF:* 888-562-5242 ■ *Web:* www.malagabank.com	Palos Verdes Estates	CA	90274	310-375-9000	373-3615
Matec Instrument Cos Inc 56 Hudson St *Web:* www.matec.com	Northborough	MA	01532	508-393-0155	
MB Financial Inc 6111 N River Rd *NASDAQ: MBFI* ■ **Fax Area Code:* 773 ■ *TF:* 888-422-6562 ■ *Web:* www.mbfinancial.com	Rosemont	IL	60018	888-422-6562	278-4523*
MBT Financial Corp 102 E Front St *NASDAQ: MBTF* ■ *TF:* 800-321-0032 ■ *Web:* www.mbandt.com	Monroe	MI	48161	734-241-3431	384-8230
Mercantil Commercebank Holding Corp 220 Alhambra Cir **Fax:* Cust Svc ■ *Web:* www.commercebankfl.com	Coral Gables	FL	33134	305-460-8701	460-4010*
Mercantile Bank 200 N 33rd St PO Box 3455 *NYSE: MBCR* ■ *TF:* 800-405-6372 ■ *Web:* www.mercbanx.com	Quincy	IL	62305	217-223-7300	
Mercantile Bank Corp 310 Leonard St NW *NASDAQ: MBWM* ■ *TF:* 888-345-6296 ■ *Web:* www.mercbank.com	Grand Rapids	MI	49504	616-406-3000	454-5807
Merchants Bancshares Inc PO Box 1009 *NASDAQ: MBVT* ■ **Fax:* Cust Svc ■ *TF:* 800-322-5222 ■ *Web:* www.mbvt.com	Burlington	VT	05402	802-658-3400	865-1943*
Mesa Systems Inc 681 Railroad Blvd *TF:* 800-654-3225 ■ *Web:* www.mesasystemsinc.com	Grand Junction	CO	81505	888-229-1409	
Mid Country Financial Corp PO Box 4164 *Web:* www.midcountryfinancial.com	Macon	GA	31208	478-746-8222	746-8005
Mid Penn Bancorp Inc 349 Union St *NASDAQ: MPB* ■ *TF:* 866-642-7736 ■ *Web:* midpennbank.com	Millersburg	PA	17061	717-692-2133	692-4861
MidSouth Bancorp Inc 102 Versailles Blvd *NYSE: MSL* ■ *TF:* 800-213-2265 ■ *Web:* www.midsouthbank.com	Lafayette	LA	70501	337-237-8343	267-4316
MidWestOne Financial Group Inc 102 S Clinton St PO Box 1700 *NASDAQ: MOFG* ■ *TF Cust Svc:* 800-247-4418 ■ *Web:* ir.midwestone.com	Iowa City	IA	52240	319-356-5800	356-5849
Millennium Bankshares Corp 21430 Cedar Dr Ste 200 *OTC: MBVA*	Sterling	VA	20164	703-547-0800	464-0064
Miner-Dederick Construction LLP 1532 Peden *Web:* www.minerdederick.com	Houston	TX	77006	713-529-3001	
MutualFirst Financial Inc 110 E Charles St *NASDAQ: MFSF* ■ *TF:* 800-382-8031 ■ *Web:* bankwithmutual.com	Muncie	IN	47305	765-747-2800	
NASB Financial Inc 12520 S 71 Hwy *NASDAQ: NASB* ■ *TF:* 800-677-6272 ■ *Web:* www.nasb.com	Grandview	MO	64030	816-765-2200	316-4504
National Bankshares Inc 101 Hubbard St *NASDAQ: NKSH* ■ *TF:* 800-552-4123 ■ *Web:* www.nationalbankshares.com	Blacksburg	VA	24060	540-951-6300	951-6324
National Penn Bancshares Inc PO Box 547 *NASDAQ: NPBC* ■ **Fax Area Code:* 610 ■ *TF:* 800-822-3321 ■ *Web:* www.nationalpenn.com	Boyertown	PA	19512	800-822-3321	369-6118*
NBT Bancorp Inc 52 S Broad St *NASDAQ: NBTB* ■ *TF:* 800-628-2265 ■ *Web:* www.nbtbancorp.com	Norwich	NY	13815	607-337-2265	336-7538
New York Community Bancorp Inc 615 Merrick Ave *NYSE: NYCB* ■ *TF:* 877-786-6560 ■ *Web:* www.mynycb.com	Westbury	NY	11590	516-683-4100	
Nico Trading LLC 222 W Adams St Ste 1500 *Web:* www.citigroup.com	Chicago	IL	60606	312-253-8000	
North State Bank Inc 6204 Falls of Neuse Rd *TF:* 877-357-2265 ■ *Web:* www.northstatebank.com	Raleigh	NC	27609	919-787-9696	719-4481
North Valley Bancorp 300 Pk Marina Cir *NASDAQ: NOVB* ■ *Web:* www.novb.com	Redding	CA	96001	530-226-2900	221-4877
Northbridge Financial Corp 105 Adelaide St W Ste 700 *TF:* 855-620-6262 ■ *Web:* www.nbfc.com	Toronto	ON	M5H1P9	416-350-4400	
Northeast Bancorp 500 Canal St *NASDAQ: NBN* ■ *TF:* 800-284-5989 ■ *Web:* www.northeastbank.com	Lewiston	ME	04240	207-786-3245	782-7230
Northeast Indiana Bancorp Inc 648 N Jefferson St *OTC: NIDB* ■ *TF:* 800-550-3372 ■ *Web:* firstfedhuntington.com	Huntington	IN	46750	260-356-3311	358-0036
Northern States Financial Corp 1601 N Lewis Ave *OTC: NSFC* ■ *TF:* 800-339-4432 ■ *Web:* www.norstatesbank.com	Waukegan	IL	60085	847-244-6000	249-9136
Northwest Bancorp Inc PO Box 128 *TF:* 800-859-1000 ■ *Web:* www.northwestsavingsbank.com	Warren	PA	16365	814-728-7263	
Oak Park School District (OPSD) 13900 Granzon *Web:* www.oakparkschools.org	Oak Park	MI	48237	248-336-7700	336-7738
OceanFirst Financial Corp 975 Hooper Ave *NASDAQ: OCFC* ■ *TF:* 888-623-2633 ■ *Web:* www.oceanfirstonline.com	Toms River	NJ	08753	732-240-4500	349-5070
Ocwen Financial Corp 1661 Worthington Rd Ste 100 PO Box 24737 *NYSE: OCN* ■ **Fax:* Hum Res ■ *TF:* 800-746-2936 ■ *Web:* www.ocwen.com	West Palm Beach	FL	33409	561-681-8000	682-8150*
Ohio Valley Banc Corp 420 Third Ave *NASDAQ: OVBC* ■ *TF:* 800-468-6682 ■ *Web:* www.ovbc.com	Gallipolis	OH	45631	740-446-2631	446-4643
Old Point Financial Corp One W Mellen St PO Box 3392 *NASDAQ: OPOF* ■ *TF:* 800-952-0051 ■ *Web:* www.oldpoint.com	Hampton	VA	23663	757-728-1200	728-1279
Old Second Bancorp Inc 37 S River St *NASDAQ: OSBC* ■ **Fax:* Mktg ■ *TF:* 888-892-6565 ■ *Web:* www.oldsecond.com	Aurora	IL	60506	630-892-0202	892-9630*
Oneida Financial Corp 182 Main St *NASDAQ: ONFC* ■ *TF:* 800-211-0564 ■ *Web:* www.oneidabank.com	Oneida	NY	13421	315-363-2000	366-3709
Opus Bank 19900 MacArthur Blvd 12th Fl *TF:* 855-678-7226 ■ *Web:* www.opusbank.com	Irvine	CA	92612	949-250-9800	
Owen Community Bank 279 E Morgan St PO Box 187 *TF:* 800-690-2095 ■ *Web:* owencom.com	Spencer	IN	47460	812-829-2095	829-3069
Pacific & Western Credit Corp 140 Fullarton St Ste 2002 *TSE: PWC* ■ *TF:* 866-979-1919 ■ *Web:* www.pwbank.com	London	ON	N6A5P2	519-645-1919	645-2060
Pacific Mercantile Bancorp 949 S Coast Dr Ste 105 *NASDAQ: PMBC* ■ *TF General:* 877-450-2265 ■ *Web:* www.pmbank.com	Costa Mesa	CA	92626	714-438-2600	438-1088
Pacific Premier Bancorp Inc 1600 Sunflower Ave *NASDAQ: PPBI* ■ *TF:* 888-388-5433 ■ *Web:* www.ppbi.com	Costa Mesa	CA	92626	714-431-4000	433-3000
Pagnotti Enterprises Inc 46 Public Sq Ste 600 *Web:* www.jeddocoal.com	Wilkes-Barre	PA	18701	570-825-8700	
Paradise Ventures Inc 2901 Rigsby Ln *Web:* www.paradisedev.com	Safety Harbor	FL	34695	727-726-1115	
Park Bancorp Inc 5400 S Pulaski Rd *OTC: PFED* ■ *TF:* 888-727-5333 ■ *Web:* www.parkfed.com	Chicago	IL	60632	773-582-8616	434-6043
Park Bank 7540 W Capitol Dr *Web:* www.parkbankonline.com	Milwaukee	WI	53216	414-466-8000	466-7773
Park National Bank 50 N Third St PO Box 3500 *NYSE: PRK* ■ *TF:* 888-791-8633 ■ *Web:* www.parknationalcorp.com	Newark	OH	43058	740-349-8451	
Pathfinder Bancorp Inc 214 W First St *NASDAQ: PBHC* ■ *TF:* 800-811-5620 ■ *Web:* www.pathfinderbank.com	Oswego	NY	13126	315-343-0057	342-9403
Patriot National Bancorp Inc 900 Bedford St *NASDAQ: PNBK* ■ *TF:* 888-728-7468 ■ *Web:* www.pnbk.com	Stamford	CT	06901	203-251-7200	324-8804
Peapack-Gladstone Bank 500 Hills Dr Ste 300 PO Box 700 *NASDAQ: PGC* ■ *TF:* 800-742-7595 ■ *Web:* www.pgbank.com	Bedminster	NJ	07921	908-234-0700	781-2046
People's Mutual Holdings 850 Main St *TF:* 800-392-3009 ■ *Web:* www.peoples.com	Bridgeport	CT	06604	203-338-7171	338-3600
Peoples Bancorp Inc 138 Putnam St *NASDAQ: PEBO* ■ **Fax:* Mail Rm ■ *TF:* 800-374-6123 ■ *Web:* www.peoplesbancorp.com	Marietta	OH	45750	740-373-3155	374-2020*
Peoples Bancorp of North Carolina Inc 518 W 'C' St *NASDAQ: PEBK* ■ *TF:* 800-948-7195 ■ *Web:* www.peoplesbanknc.com	Newton	NC	28658	828-464-5620	466-5043
Pinnacle Bancshares Inc 1811 Second Ave *OTC: PCLB* ■ *Web:* www.pinnaclebancshares.com	Jasper	AL	35501	205-221-4111	221-8860
Placeteco inc 3763 Burrill St *Web:* www.placeteco.com	Shawinigan	QC	G9N6T6	819-539-8808	539-9224
PlainsCapital Corp 2323 Victory Ave Ste 1400 *TF:* 866-762-8392 ■ *Web:* www.plainscapital.com	Dallas	TX	75219	214-252-4100	
PNC Financial Services Group Inc 249 Fifth Ave 1 PNC Plz *NYSE: PNC* ■ **Fax:* Hum Res ■ *TF:* 877-762-2000 ■ *Web:* www.pnc.com	Pittsburgh	PA	15222	412-762-2000	762-3257*
Premier Community Bankshares Inc 4095 Valley Pk *Web:* nasdaq.com	Winchester	VA	22602	540-869-6600	869-4994
Premier Financial Bancorp Inc 2883 Fifth Ave *NASDAQ: PFBI*	Huntington	WV	25702	304-525-1600	
Princeton National Bancorp Inc 606 S Main St *OTC: PNBC* ■ **Fax Area Code:* 815 ■ *TF:* 888-897-2276 ■ *Web:* www.hbtbank.com	Princeton	IL	61356	309-662-4444	872-0247*
PrivateBancorp Inc 120 S LaSalle St *NASDAQ: PVTB* ■ **Fax Area Code:* 312 ■ *TF:* 800-662-7748 ■ *Web:* theprivatebank.com/	Chicago	IL	60603	800-662-7748	683-7111*
Prosperity Bancshares Inc 1301 N Mechanic *NYSE: PB* ■ *TF:* 800-862-9098 ■ *Web:* www.prosperitybankusa.com	El Campo	TX	77437	979-578-8181	543-1906
Provident Bank 3756 Central Ave *NASDAQ: PROV* ■ *TF:* 800-442-5201 ■ *Web:* www.providentbankmortgage.com	Riverside	CA	92506	951-686-6060	
Provident Community Bancshares Inc 2700 Celanese Rd *OTC: PCBS* ■ *TF:* 800-933-3030 ■ *Web:* www.provcombank.com	Rock Hill	SC	29732	803-325-9400	
Pulaski Financial Corp 12300 Olive Blvd *NASDAQ: PULB* ■ *TF:* 888-649-3320 ■ *Web:* www.pulaskibank.com	Saint Louis	MO	63141	314-878-2210	878-7130
Quad City Bank & Trust 3551 Seventh St *NASDAQ: QCRH* ■ *TF:* 866-676-0551 ■ *Web:* www.qcbt.com	Moline	IL	61265	309-736-3580	736-3895
Rabobank International 245 Pk Ave *Web:* rabobank.com	New York	NY	10167	212-916-7800	818-0233
RBC Centura Banks Inc PO Box 1220 *TF:* 800-769-2553 ■ *Web:* www.rbcbankusa.com	Rocky Mount	NC	27802	800-769-2553	
Reece-Campbell Inc 320 S Wayne Ave	Cincinnati	OH	45215	513-542-4600	542-4753
Regions Financial Corp 1900 Fifth Ave N *NYSE: RF* ■ *TF:* 866-688-0658 ■ *Web:* www.regions.com	Birmingham	AL	35203	866-688-0658	
Renasant Corp 209 Troy St PO Box 709 *NASDAQ: RNST* ■ **Fax:* Hum Res ■ *TF Cust Svc:* 800-680-1601 ■ *Web:* www.renasantbank.com	Tupelo	MS	38802	662-680-1001	680-1448*
Republic Bancorp Inc 601 W Market St *NASDAQ: RBCAA* ■ *TF:* 888-540-5363 ■ *Web:* www.republicbank.com	Louisville	KY	40202	502-584-3600	561-7188
Republic First Bancorp Inc 50 S 16th St Ste 2400 *NASDAQ: FRBK* ■ *TF:* 888-875-2265 ■ *Web:* www.myrepublicbank.com	Philadelphia	PA	19102	215-735-4422	
Richline Group Inc 6701 Nob Hill Rd *Web:* www.richlinegroup.com	Tamarac	FL	33321	800-327-1808	
River Valley Bancorp 430 Clifty Dr *NASDAQ: RIVR* ■ **Fax:* Hum Res ■ *TF:* 800-994-4849 ■ *Web:* www.rvfbank.com	Madison	IN	47250	812-273-4949	265-6730*
Riverview Bancorp Inc 900 Washington St Ste 900 *NASDAQ: RVSB* ■ *Web:* www.riverviewbank.com	Vancouver	WA	98660	360-693-6650	693-6275
S&T Bancorp Inc 800 Philadelphia St *NASDAQ: STBA* ■ **Fax:* Cust Svc ■ *TF:* 800-325-2265 ■ *Web:* www.stbank.com	Indiana	PA	15701	724-349-1800	465-6874*
Salisbury Bancorp Inc Five Bissell St PO Box 1868 *NASDAQ: SAL* ■ *TF:* 800-222-9801 ■ *Web:* www.salisburybank.com	Lakeville	CT	06039	860-435-9801	435-0631
Sandy Spring Bancorp Inc 17801 Georgia Ave *NASDAQ: SASR* ■ *TF:* 800-399-5919 ■ *Web:* www.sandyspringbank.com	Olney	MD	20832	301-774-6400	483-6701
Savannah Bancorp Inc 25 Bull St PO Box 188 *NASDAQ: SAVB* ■ *Web:* www.thesavannahbank.com	Savannah	GA	31401	912-629-6486	651-4141
SCBT Financial Corp 950 John C Calhoun Dr *NASDAQ: SCBT* ■ *TF:* 800-277-2175 ■ *Web:* www.southstatebank.com/	Orangeburg	SC	29115	803-534-2175	531-8744
Seacoast Banking Corp of Florida 815 Colorado Ave PO Box 9012 *NASDAQ: SBCF* ■ *TF All:* 800-706-9991 ■ *Web:* www.seacoastbanking.net	Stuart	FL	34994	772-287-4000	288-6012
Shore Bancshares Inc 18 E Dover St *NASDAQ: SHBI* ■ *Web:* www.shorebancshares.com	Easton	MD	21601	410-822-1400	820-4238
Sierra Bancorp 86 N Main St PO Box 1930 *NASDAQ: BSRR* ■ *Web:* bankofthesierra.com	Porterville	CA	93257	559-782-4900	
Simmons First National Corp 501 Main St *NASDAQ: SFNC* ■ **Fax:* Hum Res ■ *TF:* 866-246-2400 ■ *Web:* www.simmonsfirst.com	Pine Bluff	AR	71601	870-541-1000	541-1138*
South Street Financial Corp 103 N Second St PO Box 489 *OTC: SSFC* ■ *Web:* bankofnc.com	Albemarle	NC	28001	704-982-9184	983-1308
Southern Banc Company Inc 221 S Sixth St *OTC: SRNN* ■ *Web:* www.sobanco.com	Gadsden	AL	35901	256-543-3860	543-3864
Southern Missouri Bancorp Inc 531 Vine St *NASDAQ: SMBC* ■ *Web:* www.bankwithsouthern.com	Poplar Bluff	MO	63901	573-778-1800	686-2920
SouthFirst Bancshares Inc 126 N Norton Ave PO Box 167 *OTC: SZBI* ■ *TF:* 800-239-1492 ■ *Web:* www.southfirst.com	Sylacauga	AL	35150	256-245-4365	245-6341

Phone | Fax

Southside Bancshares Inc 1201 S Beckham Ave — Tyler TX 75701 — 903-531-7111 535-4549
NASDAQ: SBSI ■ TF: 877-639-3511 ■ Web: www.southside.com

Southwest Bancorp Inc
608 S Main St PO Box 1988 — Stillwater OK 74076 — 888-762-4762 742-1928*
NASDAQ: OKSB ■ *Fax Area Code: 405 ■ *Fax: Hum Res ■ TF: 888-762-4762 ■ Web: www.banksnb.com

Southwest Georgia Financial Corp
201 First St SE — Moultrie GA 31768 — 229-985-1120 980-2211*
NYSE: SGB ■ *Fax: Hum Res ■ TF: 888-683-2265 ■ Web: www.sgfc.com

Spitzer Management Inc 150 E Bridge St — Elyria OH 44035 — 440-323-4671
Web: www.spitzer.com

SSMB Pacific Holding Company Inc
1755 Adams Ave — San Leandro CA 94577 — 510-836-6100
Web: www.norcalkw.com

Suffolk Bancorp
Four W Second St PO Box 9000 — Riverhead NY 11901 — 631-208-2200 727-3210
NASDAQ: SUBK ■ Web: www.scnb.com

Sun Bancorp Inc (SNBC) 226 Landis Ave — Vineland NJ 08360 — 800-786-9066
NASDAQ: SNBC ■ TF: 800-786-9066 ■ Web: www.sunnationalbank.com

Sunshine Financial Inc 1400 E Park Ave — Tallahassee FL 32301 — 850-219-7200
Web: sunshinesavingsbank.com

Susquehanna Bancshares Inc
26 N Cedar St PO Box 1000 — Lititz PA 17543 — 717-626-4721 626-1874*
NASDAQ: SUSQ ■ *Fax: Edit ■ TF: 800-311-3182 ■ Web: www.susquehanna.net

Sussex Bank 200 Munsonhurst Rd — Franklin NJ 07416 — 973-827-2914 827-2926
NASDAQ: SBBX ■ TF: 800-511-9900 ■ Web: www.sussexbank.com

SVB Financial Group 3005 Tasman Dr — Santa Clara CA 95054 — 408-654-7400 496-2405
NASDAQ: SIVB ■ TF: 800 760 9644 ■ Web: www.svb.com

SY Bancorp Inc 1040 E Main St — Louisville KY 40206 — 502-582-2571 625-2431
NASDAQ: SYBT ■ TF: 800-625-9066 ■ Web: www.syb.com

Synovus Financial Corp
1111 Bay Ave Ste 500 PO Box 120 — Columbus GA 31902 — 706-649-2311 641-6555
NYSE: SNV ■ TF: 888-796-6887 ■ Web: www.synovus.com

Tatum Development Corp 11 Pkwy Blvd — Hattiesburg MS 39401 — 601-544-6043

Taylor Capital Group Inc 9550 W Higgins Rd — Rosemont IL 60018 — 847-653-7978 836-6143*
NASDAQ: TAYC ■ *Fax Area Code: 770 ■ TF: 866-750-9107 ■ Web: coletaylor.com

TCF Financial Corp 801 Marquette Ave — Minneapolis MN 55402 — 612-661-6500 661-8277*
NYSE: TCB ■ *Fax: Hum Res ■ Web: www.tcfbank.com

Teche Holding Co 1120 Jefferson Terr — New Iberia LA 70560 — 337-560-7151 365-7130
NYSE: TSH

Texas Regional Bancshares Inc
3900 N Tenth St 11th Fl PO Box 5910 — McAllen TX 78502 — 956-631-5400 631-5450
Web: www.trbsinc.com

TF Financial Corp 3 Penns Trail — Newtown PA 18940 — 215-579-4000
NASDAQ: THRD ■ TF: 800-822-3321 ■ Web: www.3rdfedbank.com

TIB Financial Corp
121 Alhambra Plz Ste 1601 — Coral Gables FL 33134 — 800-639-5111
NASDAQ: TIBB ■ TF: 800-639-5111 ■ Web: www.capitalbank-us.com

Timberland Bancorp Inc 624 Simpson Ave — Hoquiam WA 98550 — 360-533-4747 533-4743
NASDAQ: TSBK ■ TF: 800-562-8761 ■ Web: www.timberlandbank.com

Titonka Bancshares Inc PO Box 309 — Titonka IA 50480 — 515-928-2142 928-2042
TF: 866-985-3247 ■ Web: www.tsbbank.com

Tower Financial Corp 116 E Berry St — Fort Wayne IN 46802 — 317-706-9500
NASDAQ: TOFC ■ TF: 800-731-2265 ■ Web: oldnational.com

Town Financial Corp 3206 N Walnut St — Hartford City IN 47348 — 765-348-1606
Web: townfin.com

Trenton Bankshares Inc 106 Hamilton — Trenton TX 75490 — 903-989-2235 989-2797
Web: fnbtrenton.com

TriCo Bancshares 63 Constitution Dr — Chico CA 95973 — 530-898-0300 898-0310
NASDAQ: TCBK ■ TF: 800-922-8742 ■ Web: www.tcbk.com

Trustco Bank Corp NY PO Box 1082 — Schenectady NY 12301 — 518-377-3311
NASDAQ: TRST ■ TF: 800-670-3110 ■ Web: www.trustcobank.com

Trustmark National Bank
248 E Capitol St PO Box 291 — Jackson MS 39201 — 601-208-5111
NASDAQ: TRMK ■ TF Cust Svc: 800-243-2524 ■ Web: www.trustmark.com

UBT Bancshares Inc 823 Broadway — Marysville KS 66508 — 785-562-2333

UMB Financial Corp 1010 Grand Blvd — Kansas City MO 64106 — 816-860-7000 860-4952
NASDAQ: UMBF ■ TF: 800-821-2171 ■ Web: www.umb.com

Umpqua Holdings Corp
One SW Columbia St Ste 1200 — Portland OR 97258 — 503-727-4100 544-3250*
NASDAQ: UMPQ ■ *Fax Area Code: 971 ■ TF: 866-486-7782 ■ Web: www.umpquabank.com

Union Bankshares Inc 20 Lower Main St — Morrisville VT 05661 — 802-888-6600 888-4921
NASDAQ: UNB ■ TF: 866-862-1891 ■ Web: www.unionbankvt.com

United Bancorp Inc 201 S Fourth St — Martins Ferry OH 43935 — 740-633-0445 633-1448
NASDAQ: UBCP ■ TF: 888-275-5566 ■ Web: www.unitedbancorp.com

United Bancshares Inc
100 S High St PO Box 67 — Columbus Grove OH 45830 — 419-659-2141 659-2069
NASDAQ: UBOH ■ TF: 800-837-8111 ■ Web: www.theubank.com

United Bankshares Inc 514 Market St — Parkersburg WV 26101 — 304-424-8800 424-8833
NASDAQ: UBSI ■ TF: 800-327-9862 ■ Web: www.unitedbank-wv.com

United Community Banks Inc PO Box 398 — Blairsville GA 30514 — 706-781-2265 745-8960
NASDAQ: UCBI ■ TF: 866-270-7200 ■ Web: www.ucbi.com

United Community Financial Corp
PO Box 1111 — Youngstown OH 44501 — 330-742-0500 742-0532
NASDAQ: UCFC ■ TF: 877-272-7661 ■ Web: ir.ucfconline.com

United Security Bancshares Inc
PO Box 249 — Thomasville AL 36784 — 334-636-5424 636-9606
NASDAQ: USBI ■ TF: 866-546-8273 ■ Web: www.firstusbank.com

Unity Bancorp Inc 64 Old Hwy 22 — Clinton NJ 08809 — 908-730-7630 730-9430
NASDAQ: UNTY ■ TF: 800-618-2265 ■ Web: www.unitybank.com

Universal Enterprises Inc 8030 SW Nimbus — Beaverton OR 97008 — 503-644-8723
TF: 800-547-5740 ■ Web: www.ueitest.com

University Bancorp Inc 2015 Washtenaw Ave — Ann Arbor MI 48104 — 734-741-5858 741-5859
OTC: UNIB ■ Web: www.university-bank.com

Univest Corp of Pennsylvania
14 N Main St PO Box 64197 — Souderton PA 18964 — 877-723-5571 721-2433*
NASDAQ: UVSP ■ *Fax Area Code: 215 ■ TF: 877-723-5571 ■ Web: www.univest.net

US Bancorp 800 Nicollet Mall — Minneapolis MN 55402 — 651-466-3000
NYSE: USB ■ TF Cust Svc: 800-872-2657 ■ Web: www.usbank.com

Valley National Bancorp 1455 Valley Rd — Wayne NJ 07470 — 973-305-8800 686-3491
NYSE: VLY ■ TF: 800-522-4100 ■ Web: valleynationalbank.com

Phone | Fax

Veteran's Truck Line Inc
800 Black Hawk Dr — Burlington WI 53105 — 262-539-3400 539-2720
TF: 800-456-9476 ■ Web: www.vetstruck.com

VIST Financial Corp
PO Box 6219 PO Box 6219 — Wyomissing PA 19610 — 610-926-7632
NASDAQ: VIST ■ TF: 888-238-3330 ■ Web: www.vistbank.com

Washington Federal Inc 425 Pike St — Seattle WA 98101 — 206-624-7930 467-0524
NASDAQ: WAFD ■ TF: 800-324-9375 ■ Web: www.washingtonfederal.com

Washington Trust Bancorp Inc 23 Broad St — Westerly RI 02891 — 401-348-1200 348-1470
NASDAQ: WASH ■ TF: 800-475-2265 ■ Web: www.washtrust.com

Wayne Bank 717 Main St — Honesdale PA 18431 — 570-253-1455 253-3725
TF: 800-598-5002 ■ Web: www.waynebank.com

Wayne Savings Bancshares Inc 151 N Market St — Wooster OH 44691 — 330-264-5767 264-5908
NASDAQ: WAYN ■ TF: 800-414-1103 ■ Web: www.waynesavings.com

Webster City Federal Bancorp
820 Des Moines St — Webster City IA 50595 — 515-832-3071
NYSE: WCFB ■ TF: 866-519-4004 ■ Web: otcmarkets.com

Webster Financial Corp PO Box 10305 — Waterbury CT 06726 — 800-325-2424
NYSE: WBS ■ TF: 800-325-2424 ■ Web: www.websteronline.com

West Bancorp Inc PO Box 65020 — West Des Moines IA 50265 — 515-222-2300 222-2346
NASDAQ: WTBA ■ TF: 800-810-2301 ■ Web: www.westbankstrong.com

West Side Unlimited Corp
4201 16th Ave SW — Cedar Rapids IA 52404 — 319-390-4466
TF: 800-373-2957 ■ Web: www.westsideunlimited.com

Westfield Financial Inc 141 Elm St — Westfield MA 01085 — 413-568-1911 562-7939
NASDAQ: WFD ■ TF: 800-995-5734 ■ Web: www.westfieldbank.com

Westwood Holdings Group Inc
200 Crescent Ct Ste 1200 — Dallas TX 75201 — 214-756-6900 756-6979
NYSE: WHG ■ TF: 800-687-0372 ■ Web: www.westwoodgroup.com

Winona National Bankÿÿÿ PO Box 499 — Winona MN 55987 — 507-454-4320
TF: 800-546-4392 ■ Web: www.winonanationalbank.com

Wintrust Financial Corp
9700 W Higgins Rd Ste 800 — Rosemont IL 60018 — 847-939-9000 480-4435*
NASDAQ: WTFC ■ *Fax Area Code: 212 ■ Web: www.wintrust.com

WSFS Financial Corp 500 Delaware Ave — Wilmington DE 19801 — 302-792-6000 571-6842
NASDAQ: WSFS ■ TF: 888-973-7226 ■ Web: www.wsfsbank.com

WTB Financial Corp PO Box 2127 — Spokane WA 99210 — 800-788-4578
Web: www.watrust.com

WVS Financial Corp 9001 Perry Hwy — Pittsburgh PA 15237 — 412-364-1911 364-4120
NASDAQ: WVFC ■ Web: www.wvsbank.com

363-3 Holding Companies (General)

Phone | Fax

A-Mark Precious Metals Inc
429 Santa Monica Blvd Ste 230 — Santa Monica CA 90401 — 310-587-1485 319-0317
Web: www.amark.com

Access Industries Inc 730 Fifth Ave — New York NY 10019 — 212-247-6400
Web: www.accessindustries.com

Acuity Brands Inc
1170 Peachtree St NE Ste 2400 — Atlanta GA 30309 — 404-853-1400 853-1411
NYSE: AYI ■ Web: www.acuitybrands.com

Adco Holdings Inc
257 Castleberry Industrial Dr — Cumming GA 30040 — 678-867-9600
Web: adco-usa.com

Advanced Disposal Services Inc
90 Fort Wade Rd — Ponte Vedra Beach FL 32081 — 904-737-7900
Web: www.advanceddisposal.com

AeroCare Holdings Inc 3325 Bartlett Blvd — Orlando FL 32811 — 407-206-0040
Web: www.aerocareusa.com

Affiliated Managers Group Inc (AMG)
600 Hale St — Prides Crossing MA 01965 — 617-747-3300 747-3380
NYSE: AMG ■ Web: www.amg.com

Agri-Fab Inc 809 S Hamilton St — Sullivan IL 61951 — 217-728-8388
Web: www.agri-fab.com

Alex Lee Inc PO Box 800 — Hickory NC 28603 — 828-725-4424 323-4435
Web: www.alexlee.com

Alliance Holdings Gp LP
1717 S Boulder Ave Ste 400 — Tulsa OK 74119 — 918-295-1415 295-7361
NASDAQ: AHGP ■ Web: www.ahgp.com

Alliance Holdings Inc
1021 Old York Rd Third Fl — Abington PA 19001 — 215-706-0873
Web: www.allianceholdings.com

Allied Systems Holdings Inc
2302 Parklake Dr NE — Atlanta GA 30345 — 404-373-4285 373-4285
Web: www.alliedholdings.com

Alpine Group Inc One Meadowlands Plz — East Rutherford NJ 07073 — 201-549-4400 549-4428
Web: www.alpine-group.net

Alpine Valley Ski Area
6775 East Highland Rd — White Lake MI 48383 — 248-887-2180
Web: www.skialpinevalley.com

Alutiiq LLC 3909 Arctic Blvd Ste 400 — Anchorage AK 99503 — 907-222-9500 222-9501
TF: 800-829-8547 ■ Web: www.alutiiq.com

American Standard Cos Inc
1 Centennial Ave — Piscataway NJ 08855 — 800-442-1902 980-3335*
*Fax Area Code: 732 ■ TF: 800-442-1902 ■ Web: www.americanstandard-us.com

AMETEK Inc 1100 Cassatt Rd PO Box 1764 — Berwyn PA 19312 — 610-647-2121 323-9337*
NYSE: AME ■ *Fax Area Code: 215 ■ TF: 800-473-1286 ■ Web: www.ametek.com

Amtex Corp 832 East Walnut St — Garland TX 75040 — 972-276-7626 276-5105
Web: www.amtexcorp.com

ANSA McAL (US) Inc 11403 NW 39 th St — Doral FL 33178 — 305-599-8766
Web: www.ansamcal.com

Apollo Athletics Inc 1428 S Central Park Ave — Anaheim CA 92802 — 714-533-8118
Web: www.apolloathletics.com

Arden Group Inc 2020 S Central Ave — Compton CA 90220 — 310-638-2842 735-1123*
NASDAQ: ARDNA ■ *Fax Area Code: 215 ■ *Fax: Hum Res

Arellano Construction Co 7051 SW 12th St — Miami FL 33144 — 305-994-9901
Web: www.arellanogc.com

Arpin International Group Inc
4372 Post Rd — East Greenwich RI 02818 — 401-885-4600
Web: www.arpinintl.com

Company	City	State	Zip	Phone	Fax
Atlas Concrete Inc 335 8 Ave SW Ste 850 *Web:* www.atlasconcrete.com	Calgary	AB	T2P1C9	403-297-0550	
Atlas Copco North America LLC 7 Campus Dr Ste 200 *TF:* 877-342-8527 ■ *Web:* www.atlascopco.com	Parsippany	NJ	07054	973-397-3432	397-3414
Atlas World Group Inc 1212 St George Rd *TF:* 800-252-8885 ■ *Web:* www.atlasvanlines.com	Evansville	IN	47711	812-424-2222	421-7129
Augusta National Inc 2604 Washington Rd *Web:* masters.com	Augusta	GA	30904	706-667-6000	736-2321
AUS Inc 155 Gaither Dr *Web:* ausinc.com	Mount Laurel	NJ	08054	856-234-9200	
Austin Industries Inc 3535 Travis St Ste 300 **Fax:* Acctg ■ *Web:* www.austin-ind.com	Dallas	TX	75204	214-443-5500	443-5581*
Bayer Six W Belt Rd *Web:* www.bayerus.com	Wayne	NJ	07470	973-694-4100	
Benetech Inc 2245 Sequoia Dr *Web:* benetechglobal.com	Aurora	IL	60506	630-844-1300	
Berggruen Holdings Inc 1114 Ave of the Americas 41st Fl *Web:* www.berggruenholdings.com	New York	NY	10036	212-380-2230	
Bertelsmann Inc 1540 Broadway 24th Fl *Web:* www.bertelsmann.com	New York	NY	10036	212-782-1000	782-1010
Biglari Holdings Inc 175 E Houston St Ste 1300 *NYSE: BH* ■ *Web:* www.biglariholdings.com	San Antonio	TX	78205	210-344-3400	344-3411
Block Communications Inc 405 Madison Ave Ste 2100 *Web:* www.blockcommunications.com	Toledo	OH	43604	419-724-6212	724-6167
Blount International Inc 4909 SE International Way **Fax:* Hum Res ■ *Web:* www.blount.com	Portland	OR	97222	503-653-8881	653-4402*
Blue Sky Industries Inc 1230 Monterey Pass Rd *Web:* www.blueskyindustries.com	Monterey Park	CA	91754	213-620-9950	
Blue Tee Corp 250 Park Ave S *Web:* www.bluetee.com	New York	NY	10003	212-598-0880	
Bluestone Industries Inc 100 Cranberry Creek Dr *Web:* www.bluestoneindustries.com	Beckley	WV	25801	304-252-8528	
Boca Resorts 501 E Camino Real *TF:* 888-543-1277 ■ *Web:* www.bocaresort.com	Boca Raton	FL	33432	561-447-3000	447-3183
Boler Co 500 Pk Blvd Ste 450 *Web:* hendrickson-intl.com	Itasca	IL	60143	630-773-9111	773-9121
Boral Industries Inc 200 Mansell Ct E Ste 310 *Web:* boral.com.au	Roswell	GA	30076	770-645-4500	645-2888
Brandt Holdings Co 4650 26th Ave S Ste E *Web:* www.brandtholdings.com	Fargo	ND	58104	701-237-6000	
Brose North America Inc 3933 Automation Ave *Web:* www.brose.com	Auburn Hills	MI	48326	248-339-4000	339-4099
Bruckmann Rosser Sherrill & Company LLC 126 E 56th St 29th Fl *Web:* www.brs.com	New York	NY	10022	212-521-3700	
BT Conferencing Inc 150 Newport Ave. Ext, Ste 300 *TF:* 866-770-8777 ■ *Web:* www.btconferencing.com	North Quincy	MA	02171	866-770-8777	
C D Henderson Construction Services Ltd 1985 Forest Ln *Web:* www.cdhenderson.com	Garland	TX	75042	972-272-5466	
California Sports Inc 555 N Nash St	El Segundo	CA	90245	310-426-6000	426-6115
Cameron Holdings Corp 1200 Prospect St *Web:* www.cameron-holdings.com	La Jolla	CA	92037	858-551-1335	551-1343
Camino Modular Systems Inc 89 Carlingview Dr *Web:* www.caminomodular.com	Toronto	ON	M9W5E4	416-675-2400	675-2424
Campers Inn Inc 35 Robert Milligan Pkwy *Web:* www.campersinn.com	Merrimack	NH	03054	603-883-1082	
Cardinal Health Inc 7000 Cardinal Pl *NYSE: CAH* ■ *Web:* www.cardinal.com	Dublin	OH	43017	614-757-5000	757-6000
Carnival Corp 3655 NW 87th Ave *NYSE: CCL* ■ *TF:* 800-438-6744 ■ *Web:* carnival.com	Miami	FL	33178	305-599-2600	406-4700
CBRL Group Inc PO Box 787 **Fax Area Code:* 888 ■ *TF:* 800-333-9566 ■ *Web:* www.crackerbarrel.com	Lebanon	TN	37088	800-333-9566	263-4304*
CenturyTel Inc 100 Centurylink Dr PO Box 4065 *NYSE: CTL* ■ *TF:* 877-290-5458 ■ *Web:* www.centurylink.com	Monroe	LA	71211	318-388-9000	
CGF Industries Inc 2420 N Woodlawn Bldg 500 *Web:* www.cgcpi.com	Wichita	KS	67220	316-691-4500	691-4545
CIC Group Inc 530 Maryville Centre Dr Ste 100 *Web:* www.cicgroup.com	Saint Louis	MO	63141	314-682-2900	
Citigroup Inc 399 Pk Ave *NYSE: C* ■ **Fax:* Hum Res ■ *Web:* citigroup.com	New York	NY	10043	212-559-1000	559-5138*
Clayton Holdings LLC 100 BeaRd Sawmill Rd Ste 200 *TF:* 877-291-5301 ■ *Web:* www.clayton.com	Shelton	CT	06484	203-926-5600	926-5757
Comcast Corp 1701 JFK Blvd *NASDAQ: CMCSA* ■ *TF:* 800-266-2278 ■ *Web:* www.comcast.com	Philadelphia	PA	19103	215-665-1700	981-7790
ConAgra Foods Inc One ConAgra Dr *NYSE: CAG* ■ **Fax:* Hum Res ■ *TF:* 877-266-2472 ■ *Web:* www.conagrafoods.com	Omaha	NE	68102	402-240-4000	595-4707*
CONSOL Energy Inc 1000 Consol Energy Dr *NYSE: CNX* ■ *TF:* 800-544-8024 ■ *Web:* www.consolenergy.com	Canonsburg	PA	15317	724-485-4000	
Consolidated Communications Holdings Inc 121 S 17th St *NASDAQ: CNSL* ■ *Web:* consolidated.com	Mattoon	IL	61938	217-235-3311	235-3311
Cooper Neff Group Inc 555 Croton Rd Ste 100 *Web:* www.cooperneff.com	King Of Prussia	PA	19406	610-491-1400	
Cortec Group 200 Park Ave 20th Fl *Web:* www.cortecgroup.com	New York	NY	10166	212-370-5600	
Courier-Life Inc One Metrotech Ctr Ste 1001 *Web:* www.brooklyndaily.com	Brooklyn	NY	11201	718-260-2500	
CPI Wire Cloth & Screens Inc 2425 Roy Rd *Web:* cpiwirecloth.com	Pearland	TX	77581	281-485-2300	485-8837
CraftWorks Restaurants & Brewery Inc 201 W Main St Ste 301 *Web:* www.craftworksrestaurants.com	Chattanooga	TN	37408	423-424-2000	
Crestview Partners LP 667 Madison Ave 10th Fl *Web:* www.crestview.com	New York	NY	10065	212-906-0700	
Crown Group Inc, The 2111 Walter Reuther Dr *Web:* www.thecrowngrp.com	Warren	MI	48091	586-575-9800	
CUI Global Inc 20050 SW 112th Ave *NASDAQ: CUI* ■ *Web:* www.cuiglobal.com	Tualatin	OR	97062	503-612-2300	
Dash Multi-Corp Inc 2500 Adie Rd *TF:* 888-889-9655 ■ *Web:* accellacorp.com	Maryland Heights	MO	63043	314-432-3200	
Dectron International Inc 4300 Poirier Blvd *TF:* 888-332-8766 ■ *Web:* www.dectron.com	Montreal	QC	H4R2C5	514-334-9609	334-9184
Del Toro Loan Servicing Inc 2434 Southport Way Ste F *Web:* www.deltoroloanservicing.com	National City	CA	91950	619-474-5400	
Delhaize America Inc 2110 Executive Dr PO Box 1330 **Fax:* Hum Res ■ *Web:* www.delhaizegroup.com	Salisbury	NC	28145	704-633-8250	645-4499*
Deluxe Corp 3680 N Victoria St *NYSE: DLX* ■ *TF:* 800-328-7205 ■ *Web:* ww.deluxe.com	Shoreview	MN	55126	651-483-7111	
Dicke Safety Products 1201 Warren Ave *Web:* www.dicketool.com	Downers Grove	IL	60515	630-969-0050	
DI Rogers Corp 5013 Davis Blvd *Web:* dlrrestaurants.com	North Richland Hills	TX	76180	817-428-2077	
DNP America LLC 335 Madison Ave Third Fl *Web:* www.dnpamerica.com	New York	NY	10017	212-503-1060	
Downing Partners Inc 5150 E Yale Cir	Denver	CO	80222	303-830-6622	
Duchossois Industries Inc 845 Larch Ave *Web:* duch.com	Elmhurst	IL	60126	630-279-3600	
Dundee Bancorp Inc One Adelaide St E Ste 2100 *Web:* www.dundeecorp.com	Toronto	ON	M5C2V9	416-863-6990	363-4536
E & A Industries Inc 101 W Ohio St Ste 1350 *Web:* ea-companies.com	Indianapolis	IN	46204	317-684-3150	681-5068
E Boyd & Associates Inc PO Box 99189 *Web:* www.eboyd.com	Raleigh	NC	27624	919-846-8000	
Edward B Howlin Inc 2880 Dunkirk Way *Web:* ebhowlin.com	Dunkirk	MD	20754	301-855-8900	
Elecsys Corp 846 N Mart-Way Ct *NASDAQ: ESYS* ■ *Web:* www.elecsyscorp.com	Olathe	KS	66061	913-647-0158	647-0132
Elvis Presley Enterprises Inc 3734 Elvis Presley Blvd *TF:* 800-238-2000 ■ *Web:* www.elvis.com	Memphis	TN	38116	901-332-3322	344-3101
EN Engineering LLC 28100 Torch Pkwy Ste 400 *Web:* www.enengineering.com	Warrenville	IL	60555	630-353-4000	
Envision Healthcare 6200 S Syracuse Way Ste 200 *Web:* www.evhc.net	Greenwood Village	CO	80111	303-495-1200	495-1649
EquiLend Holdings LLC 17 State St Ninth Fl *Web:* www.equilend.com	New York	NY	10004	212-901-2200	
ESCO Technologies Inc 9900A Clayton Rd *NYSE: ESE* ■ *TF:* 800-368-5948 ■ *Web:* www.escotechnologies.com	Saint Louis	MO	63124	314-213-7200	213-7250
Esmark Steel Group 2500 Euclid Ave *TF:* 800-323-0340 ■ *Web:* www.esmark.com	Chicago Heights	IL	60411	708-756-0400	756-0099
Evergreen Shipping Agency (America) Corp 1 Evertrust Plz *Web:* www.evergreen-america.com	Jersey City	NJ	07302	201-761-3000	761-3011
Eyak Corp, The 360 W Benson Blvd Ste 210 *Web:* eyakcorporation.com	Anchorage	AK	99503	907-334-6971	
FedEx Corp 3610 Hacks Cross Rd *NYSE: FDX* ■ *TF:* 800-463-3339 ■ *Web:* www.fedex.com	Memphis	TN	38125	901-369-3600	434-9836
Felchar Manufacturing Corp 196 Corporate Dr *Web:* www.felchar.com	Binghamton	NY	13904	607-723-4076	
Ferrara International Logistics Inc 1319 N Broad St *Web:* www.ferrarainternational.com	Hillside	NJ	07205	908-282-9440	
Field & Stream Licenses Company LLC 18 Kings Hwy N	Westport	CT	06880	203-221-0050	
Florens Container Services (USA) Ltd 275 Battery St Ste 800 *Web:* www.florens.com	San Francisco	CA	94111	415-348-2800	
Forge Industries Inc 4450 Market St	Youngstown	OH	44512	330-782-8301	
Fresh Del Monte Produce Co 241 Sevilla Ave PO Box 149222 *NYSE: FDP* ■ *TF Cust Svc:* 800-950-3683 ■ *Web:* www.freshdelmonte.com	Coral Gables	FL	33134	305-520-8400	567-0320
GCI Affiliated Cos 20875 Crossroads Cir Ste 100 *Web:* gcionline.com	Waukesha	WI	53186	262-798-5080	
George Weston Ltd 22 St Clair Ave E *TSE: WN* ■ *TF:* 800-564-6253 ■ *Web:* www.weston.ca	Toronto	ON	M4T2S7	416-922-2500	922-4395
Global Entertainment Corp 6751 N Sunset Blvd Ste 200 *OTC: GNTP* ■ *Web:* www.globalentertainment2000.com	Glendale	AZ	85305	480-994-0772	994-0759
Global Trading & Sourcing Corp 1587 College Park Business Ctr Rd *Web:* www.gtsco.com	Orlando	FL	32804	407-532-7600	
Gower Corp 355 Woodruff Rd *Web:* www.gower.co.uk	Greenville	SC	29607	864-234-4829	
GreenPointe Holdings LLC 7807 Baymeadows Rd E Ste 205 *Web:* www.greenpointellc.com	Jacksonville	FL	32256	904-996-2485	
GSC Enterprises Inc 130 Hillcrest Dr PO Box 638 *Web:* www.grocerysupply.com	Sulphur Springs	TX	75483	903-885-7621	885-6928
Gulf & Ohio Railways Inc 422 W Cumberland Ave PO Box 2408 *Web:* www.gulfandohio.com	Knoxville	TN	37901	865-525-9400	

Phone Fax

GVW Group LLC (GVW)
600 Central Ave Ste 214 .... Highland Park IL 60035 847-681-8417 681-8515
Web: www.gvwholdings.com

H Enterprises International Inc
120 S Sixth St .... Minneapolis MN 55402 612-340-8849

Haram-Christensen Corp 125 Asia Pl .... Carlstadt NJ 07072 201-507-8544
Web: www.haramchris.com

Harold Import Company Inc 747 Vassar Ave .... Lakewood NJ 08701 732-367-2800
Web: www.haroldskitchen.com

Hartz Group Inc, The 667 Madison Ave .... New York NY 10065 201-348-1200 838-8845*
**Fax Area Code:* 212 ■ *Web:* www.hartzmountain.com

Hayman Capital Management LP
2101 Cedar Springs Rd Ste 1400 .... Dallas TX 75201 214-347-8050
Web: www.haymancapitalmanagement.com

Heartland Industrial Partners LP
177 Broad St 10th Fl .... Stamford CT 06901 203-327-1202
Web: www.heartlandpartners.com

Hendricks Holding Company Inc 690 Third St .... Beloit WI 53511 608-362-8000
Web: hendricksholding.com

Hickory Tech Corp
221 E Hickory St PO Box 3248 .... Mankato MN 56002 507-387-1151
NASDAQ: ENVE ■ *TF:* 866-442-5679 ■ *Web:* www.enventis.com

Hines Corp 1218 Pontaluna Rd Ste B .... Spring Lake MI 49456 231-799-6240 799-6298
Web: www.hinescorp.com

Hitch Enterprises Inc
309 Northridge Cir PO Box 1308 .... Guymon OK 73942 580-338-8575 827-6338*
**Fax Area Code:* 407 ■ *TF:* 800-951-2533 ■ *Web:* www.hitchok.com

Home Capital Group Inc 145 King St W Ste 2300 .... Toronto ON M5H1J8 416-360-4663 363-7611
TSE: HCG ■ *TF:* 800-990-7881 ■ *Web:* www.homecapital.com

Horizon Holding Inc 6101 S 58th St Ste B .... Lincoln NE 68516 402-421-6400
Web: www.horizonholding.com

Hunt Consolidated Inc 1900 N Akard St Ste 1500 .... Dallas TX 75201 214-978-8000 978-8888
TF: 800-424-9300 ■ *Web:* www.huntoil.com

Icahn Enterprises LP 767 Fifth Ave 47th Fl .... New York NY 10153 212-702-4300 750-5841
NASDAQ: IEP ■ *TF:* 800-255-2737 ■ *Web:* www.ielp.com

ICD Group International Inc
600 Madison Ave Ste 1800 .... New York NY 10022 212-644-1500
Web: www.icdgroup.com

IG Realty Investments Inc
Two International Blvd .... Toronto ON M9W1A2 416-798-6800
Web: www.igrea.com

InfoPro Inc 8200 Greensboro Dr Ste 1450 .... Mclean VA 22102 703-226-2520
Web: www.infopro.net

InstaMed Communications LLC
1880 John F Kennedy Blvd 12th Fl .... Philadelphia PA 19103 215-789-3680
Web: www.instamed.com

International Textile Group
804 Green Vly Rd Ste 300 .... Greensboro NC 27408 336-379-6220 379-3310*
**Fax:* Hum Res ■ *Web:* www.itg-global.com

Investors Management Corp 5151 Glenwood Ave .... Raleigh NC 27612 919-881-5200
Web: investorsmanagement.com

IsoRay Medical Inc 350 Hills St Ste 106 .... Richland WA 99354 509-375-1202 375-3473
TF: 877-447-6729 ■ *Web:* www.isoray.com

ITC Holding Company LLC
1791 O G Skinner Dr Ste A .... West Point GA 31833 706-645-9482
Web: www.itchold.com

Jacobs Industries Inc 8096 Excelsior Blvd .... Hopkins MN 55343 612-339-9500
Web: www.jacobsinteractive.com

JC Horizon Ltd 825 E State St .... Arcadia CA 91006 626-446-1819
Web: www.jchorizonltd.com

JMK International 4800 Bryant Irvin Ct .... Fort Worth TX 76107 817-737-3703 735-1669
Web: www.jmkint.com

Joseph Cory Holdings LLC
150 Meadowlands Pkwy Third Fl .... Secaucus NJ 07094 201-795-1000
Web: www.corycompanies.com

Kawasaki Heavy Industries USA Inc
60 E 42nd St Ste 2501 .... New York NY 10165 212-759-4950 759-6421
Web: www.khi.co.jp

Keller Group Inc, The
One Northfield Plz Ste 510 .... Northfield IL 60093 847-446-7550
Web: www.kellergroupinc.com

Kingman Group Corp, The
14010 Live Oak Ave .... Baldwin Park CA 91706 626-430-2300
Web: www.kingman.com

Kurt Orban Partners LLC
111 Anza Blvd Ste 350 .... Burlingame CA 94010 650-579-3959
Web: www.kurtorbanpartners.com

Kyocera International Inc 8611 Balboa Ave .... San Diego CA 92123 858-576-2600 569-9412
TF: 877-248-4237 ■ *Web:* global.kyocera.com

Legacy Investments Inc 5910 N Central Expy .... Dallas TX 75206 214-750-1522

Lenny's Franchisor LLC
8295 Tournament Dr Ste 200 .... Memphis TN 38125 901-753-4002
Web: www.lennys.com

Liberty Diversified International Inc
5600 Hwy 169 N .... New Hope MN 55428 763-536-6600 536-6685
TF: 800-421-1270 ■ *Web:* www.libertydiversified.com

Liberty Media Holding Corp
12300 Liberty Blvd .... Englewood CO 80112 720-875-5400
Web: www.libertymedia.com

Lightfoot Capital Partners LP
725 Fifth Ave 19th Fl .... New York NY 10022 212-993-1280
Web: www.lightfootcapital.com

Lincoln Electric Holdings Inc
22801 St Clair Ave .... Cleveland OH 44117 216-481-8100 486-1751
NASDAQ: LECO ■ *TF:* 800-833-9353 ■ *Web:* www.lincolnelectric.com

Louise Paris Ltd 1407 Broadway 14th Fl .... New York NY 10018 212-354-5411
Web: www.louiseparis.com

M Group Inc 187 S Old Woodward Ste 200 .... Birmingham MI 48009 248-540-8843
Web: www.mgroupinc.com

Magnum Hospitality 1515 Cass St Ste D .... Traverse City MI 49684 231-932-1633
Web: www.magnumhospitality.com

Mainsail Partners One Front St Ste 3000 .... San Francisco CA 94111 415-391-3150
Web: www.mainsailpartners.com

Phone Fax

Manifold Capital Corp 140 Broadway 47th Fl .... New York NY 10005 212-375-2000 375-2100
OTC: MANF ■ *Web:* www.aca.com

Marin Investments Ltd
700 W Georgia St Ste 3010 .... Vancouver BC V7Y1B6 604-687-1450
Web: www.marin.ca

Marsh & McLennan Cos Inc
1166 Ave of the Americas .... New York NY 10036 212-345-5000 345-4808
NYSE: MMC ■ *TF:* 866-374-2662 ■ *Web:* www.mmc.com

Maxco Inc 1005 Charlevoix Dr Ste 100 .... Grand Ledge MI 48837 517-627-1734 627-4951

McKesson Corp One Post St .... San Francisco CA 94104 415-983-8300
NYSE: MCK ■ *TF:* 800-482-3784 ■ *Web:* www.mckesson.com

MDC Holdings Inc 4350 S Monaco St Ste 500 .... Denver CO 80237 303-773-1100 771-3461
NYSE: MDC ■ *TF:* 888-500-7060 ■ *Web:* www.richmondamerican.com

MediaTech Capital Partners LLC
70 E 55th St 21st Fl .... New York NY 10022 212-759-3022
Web: www.mediatechcapital.com

MediaTek USA Inc 120 Presidential Way .... Woburn MA 01801 781-503-8000
Web: www.mediatek.com

Medisys Health Network Inc
8900 Van Wyck Expy .... Jamaica NY 11418 718-206-6000
Web: medisyshealth.org

Mel Foster Company Inc
7566 Market Pl Dr .... Eden Prairie MN 55344 952-941-9790
Web: melfoster.com

Merco Group Inc, The 7711 N 81st St .... Milwaukee WI 53223 414-365-2600

Minnwest Corp 14820 Hwy 7 Ste 200 .... Minnetonka MN 55345 952-545-8815
Web: www.minnwest.com

Mitchel Group 1841 Ludlow Ave .... Indianapolis IN 46201 317-639-5331
Web: www.mitchelandscott.com

Mondial International Corp
101 Secor Ln PO Box 889 .... Pelham Manor NY 10803 914-738-7411 738-7521
Web: mondialgroup.com

Moore Tool Company Inc 800 Union Ave .... Bridgeport CT 06607 203-366-3224
Web: www.mooretool.com

Najafi Cos LLC 2525 E Camelback Rd .... Phoenix AZ 85016 602-476-0600
Web: najafi.com

Nanco-Nancy Sales Company Inc 22 Willow St .... Chelsea MA 02150 617-884-1700
Web: www.nancobos.com

Nashville Shores Holdings LLC 4001 Bell Rd .... Hermitage TN 37076 615-889-7050
Web: www.nashvilleshores.com

NBC Universal Inc 30 Rockefeller Plaza .... New York NY 10112 212-664-4444 664-4085
Web: www.nbcuniversal.com

Neenan Company LLP, The
2607 Midpoint Dr .... Fort Collins CO 80525 970-493-8747
Web: www.neenan.com

NewMarket Corp 330 S Fourth St .... Richmond VA 23219 804-788-5000 788-5688
NYSE: NEU ■ *TF:* 800-625-5191 ■ *Web:* www.newmarket.com

NextWave Wireless Inc
10350 Science Ctr Dr Ste 210 .... San Diego CA 92121 858-731-5300 731-5301
OTC: WAVE ■ *TF:* 800-461-9330 ■ *Web:* www.nextwave.com

Nordenia International 14591 State Hwy 177 .... Jackson MO 63755 573-335-4900 335-6172
Web: www.mondigroup.com

North American Stainless Inc 6870 Hwy 42 East .... Ghent KY 41045 502-347-6000 347-6001
TF: 800-499-7833 ■ *Web:* www.northamericanstainless.com

Nustar GP Holdings LLC PO Box 781609 .... San Antonio TX 78248 210-918-2000 345-2646
NYSE: NSH ■ *TF:* 800-866-9060 ■ *Web:* www.nustargpholdings.com

NVE Pharmaceuticals 15 Whitehall Rd .... Andover NJ 07821 973-786-7862
Web: www.stacker2.com

Octal Corp 125 Galway Pl Unit B & C .... Teaneck NJ 07666 201-862-1010
Web: www.octalcorporation.com

OKI Developments Inc 1416 112th Ave NE .... Bellevue WA 98004 425-454-2800 646-6999
TF: 877-465-3654 ■ *Web:* www.okigolf.com

Omega International Inc
1937 NE Loop 410 Ste 200 .... San Antonio TX 78217 210-805-8808
Web: omegaco.com

Omnicom Group Inc 437 Madison Ave .... New York NY 10022 212-415-3600 415-3530*
NYSE: OMC ■ **Fax:* Hum Res ■ *Web:* www.omnicomgroup.com

Orca Bay Sports & Entertainment
800 Griffiths Way .... Vancouver BC V6B6G1 604-899-7400 899-7401
Web: canucks.nhl.com

Orlando Endodontic Specialists
610 N Mills Ave Nbr 210 .... Orlando FL 32803 407-423-7667
Web: orlandorootcanals.com

Otc Global Holdings 5151 San Felipe Ste 2200 .... Houston TX 77056 713-613-0500 365-1866*
**Fax Area Code:* 866 ■ *Web:* www.otcgh.com

Otsuka America Inc
One Embarcadero Ctr Ste 2020 .... San Francisco CA 94111 415-986-5300
Web: otsuka-america.com

Otter Tail Corp 4334 18th Ave SW PO Box 9156 .... Fargo ND 58106 218-739-8479 232-4108*
NASDAQ: OTTR ■ **Fax Area Code:* 701 ■ *TF:* 866-410-8780 ■ *Web:* www.ottertail.com

Owl Cos 2465 Campus Dr .... Irvine CA 92612 949-797-2000 660-4936
Web: www.owlcompanies.com

Pace Resources Inc
445 West Philadelphia St P.O. Box 15040 .... York PA 17405 717-852-1390 852-1391
Web: paceresourcesfcu.virtualcu.net

Pacer International Inc
2300 Clayton Rd Ste 1200 .... Concord CA 94520 925-887-1400
NYSE: XPO ■ *TF:* 877-917-2237 ■ *Web:* www.pacer.com

Pacific Echo Inc 23540 Telo Ave .... Torrance CA 90505 310-539-1822
Web: www.pacificecho.com

Pacific Food Importers Inc
2323 Airport Way S .... Seattle WA 98134 206-682-2740
Web: www.pacificfoodimporters.com

Paragon Gaming Corp
6650 Via Austi Pkwy Ste 150 .... Las Vegas NV 89119 702-631-5161
Web: paragongaming.com

Pearson Inc 1330 Ave of the Americas 7th Fl .... New York NY 10019 212-641-2400 641-2500
Web: www.pearson.com

Penney Group Inc 1309 Topsail Rd Sta A .... St. John's NL A1B3N4 709-782-3404
Web: www.penneygroup.ca

Pennsylvania Macaroni Co
2010 Penn Ave # 12 .... Pittsburgh PA 15222 412-471-8330
Web: www.pennmac.com

Company	City	State	ZIP	Phone	Fax
Petra Industries Inc 2101 S Kelly Ave *Web:* www.petra.com	Edmond	OK	73013	405-216-2100	
Phazar Corp 101 SE 25th Ave *NASDAQ: ANTP* ■ *Web:* www.antennaproducts.com	Mineral Wells	TX	76067	940-325-3301	325-0716
PHC Inc 200 Lake St Ste 102 *Web:* phc-inc.com	Peabody	MA	01960	978-536-2777	
Phillips Service Industries Inc 11878 Hubbard *Web:* www.psi-online.com	Livonia	MI	48150	734-853-5000	853-5032
Phosphate Holdings Inc 100 Web Ste 4 *Web:* www.missphosphates.com	Madison	MS	39110	601-898-9004	
Platinum Group of Cos Inc 9121 Oakdale Ave Sute 201 *Web:* www.platinumgroup.org	Chatsworth	CA	91311	818-721-3800	721-3811
Pro-Dex Inc 2361 McGaw Ave *NASDAQ: PDEX* ■ *TF:* 800-562-6204 ■ *Web:* www.pro-dex.com	Irvine	CA	92614	800-562-6204	
Relco LLC PO Box 1689 *Web:* www.relco.net	Willmar	MN	56201	320-231-2210	231-2282
Rema Foods Inc 140 Sylvan Ave *Web:* www.remafoods.net	Englewood Cliffs	NJ	07632	201-947-1000	
Resource Land Holdings LLC 1530 16th St Ste 300 *Web:* www.rlholdings.com	Denver	CO	80202	720-723-2850	
Revlon Inc 237 Pk Ave *NYSE: REV* ■ *TF:* 800-473-8566 ■ *Web:* www.revlon.com	New York	NY	10017	212-527-4000	527-4995
Reyes Holdings LLC 6250 North River Rd Ste 9000 *Web:* www.reyesholdings.com	Rosemont	IL	60018	847-227-6500	227-6550
Riverstone Holdings LLC 712 Fifth Ave 36th Fl *Web:* www.riverstonellc.com	New York	NY	10019	212-993-0076	
RLJ Companies LLC, The Three Bethesda Metro Ctr Ste 1000 *Web:* www.rljcompanies.com	Bethesda	MD	20814	301-280-7700	
Rock Island Capital LLC 1415 W 22nd St Ste 1250 *Web:* www.rockislandcapital.com	Oak Brook	IL	60523	630-413-9136	
Rosen's Diversified Inc 1120 Lake Ave PO Box 933 *Web:* www.rosensdiversifiedinc.com	Fairmont	MN	56031	507-238-6001	
RSCC Aerospace & Defense 680 Hayward St *Web:* www.rsccaerodefense.com	Manchester	NH	03103	603-622-3500	
Sabre Holdings Corp 3150 Sabre Dr *Web:* www.sabre.com	Southlake	TX	76092	682-605-1000	
Sandstone Group Inc 223 N Water St Ste 500 *Web:* www.diachemix.com	Milwaukee	WI	53202	414-902-6700	
Sandvik Inc 1702 Nevins Rd *TF:* 800-726-3845 ■ *Web:* www.sandvik.com	Fair Lawn	NJ	07410	201-794-5000	794-5165
Saxco International LLC 200 Gibraltar Rd Ste 101 *Web:* www.saxcointl.com	Horsham	PA	19044	215-443-8100	
Sbeeg Holdings LLC 8000 Beverly Blvd *Web:* sbe.com	Los Angeles	CA	90048	323-655-8000	
Schaefer Marine Inc 158 Duchaine Blvd *Web:* schaefermarine.com	New Bedford	MA	02745	508-995-9511	
Schott North America Inc 555 Taxter Rd *TF:* 877-261-2100 ■ *Web:* www.us.schott.com	Elmsford	NY	10523	914-831-2200	831-2201
Schuff International Inc 420 S 19th Ave *OTC: SHFK* ■ *Web:* www.schuff.com	Phoenix	AZ	85009	602-252-7787	452-4468
Sears Holdings Corp 3333 Beverly Rd *NASDAQ: SHLD* ■ *Web:* www.searsholdings.com	Hoffman Estates	IL	60179	847-286-2500	286-7829
SGS North America Inc 201 State Rt 17 N *TF:* 800-645-5227 ■ *Web:* www.sgsgroup.us.com	Rutherford	NJ	07070	201-508-3000	508-3183
Shamrock Cos Inc, The 24090 Detroit Rd *Web:* www.shamrockcompanies.net	Westlake	OH	44145	440-899-9510	250-2180
Shamrock Holdings Inc 3500 W Olive Ave *Web:* www.shamrock.com	Burbank	CA	91505	818-845-4444	
SHC International Inc 1031 Aldridge Rd Ste I *Web:* www.shc-intl.com	Vacaville	CA	95688	707-448-6076	
Shenandoah Telecommunications Co 500 Shentel Way *NASDAQ: SHEN* ■ *TF:* 800-743-6835 ■ *Web:* www.shentel.com	Edinburg	VA	22824	540-984-5224	984-3438
Siebert Financial Corp 885 Third Ave *NASDAQ: SIEB* ■ *TF:* 877-327-8379 ■ *Web:* www.siebertnet.com	New York	NY	10022	212-644-2400	486-2784
Simon Golub & Sons Inc 5506 Sixth Ave S *Web:* www.simongolub.com	Seattle	WA	98108	206-762-4800	
Simpson Investment Co 917 E 11th St *Web:* simpson.com	Tacoma	WA	98421	253-779-6400	280-9000
Sky Holding Company LLC 850 Montgomery St Ste 200 *Web:* www.jacksonsquareaviation.com	San Francisco	CA	94133	415-655-5000	
Solis Capital Partners LLC 23 Corporate Plz Ste 215 *Web:* www.soliscapital.com	Newport Beach	CA	92660	949-296-2440	
Strata Products Worldwide LLC 8995 Roswell Rd Ste 200 *Web:* www.strataworldwide.com	Sandy Springs	GA	30350	770-321-2500	
Sumitomo Canada Ltd (SCL) 150 King St W Ste 2304 *Web:* www.sumitomocanada.com	Toronto	ON	M5H1J9	416-860-3800	365-3141
Sumitomo Corp of America 600 Third Ave 42nd Fl *TF:* 877-980-3283 ■ *Web:* www.sumitomocorp.com	New York	NY	10016	212-207-0700	207-0456
Sunroad Marina Partners LP 955 Harbor Island Dr *Web:* www.sdmarina.com	San Diego	CA	92101	619-574-0736	
Suntory International Corp 600 Third Ave Ste 2101 *Web:* www.suntory.com	New York	NY	10016	212-891-6600	891-6601
Superior Group Inc 100 Front St	West Conshohocken	PA	19428	610-397-2040	397-2041
T Rowe Price Group Inc 100 E Pratt St *NASDAQ: TROW* ■ **Fax:* Hum Res ■ *TF:* 800-638-7890 ■ *Web:* corporate.troweprice.com	Baltimore	MD	21202	410-345-2000	345-2394*
Tabar Inc 251 Greenwood Ave *Web:* www.tabarinc.com	Bethel	CT	06801	203-748-5242	
TAPO Ventures LLC 195 N Harbor Dr Ste 4601 *Web:* www.tapoventures.com	Chicago	IL	60601	312-540-1333	
Taylor Corp 1725 Roe Crest Dr *TF:* 800-545-6620 ■ *Web:* www.taylorcorp.com/Pages/default.aspx	North Mankato	MN	56003	507-625-2828	386-2031
Teijin Holdings USA 600 Lexington Ave 27th Fl *Web:* teijin.com	New York	NY	10022	212-308-8744	308-8902
Telephone & Data Systems Inc 30 N La Salle St Ste 4000 *NYSE: TDS* ■ *TF:* 877-337-1575 ■ *Web:* www.teldta.com	Chicago	IL	60602	312-630-1900	630-9299
Telesystem Ltd 1250 Rene-Levesque Blvd W Ste 3800 *Web:* www.telesystem.ca	Montreal	QC	H3B4W8	514-397-9797	397-1569
Thompson Investment Management Inc 918 Deming Way Third Fl *Web:* www.thompsonim.com	Madison	WI	53717	608-827-5700	
Thought Convergence Inc 11300 W Olympic Blvd Ste 900 *Web:* www.thoughtconvergence.com	Los Angeles	CA	90064	310-909-7891	
Thrall Enterprises Inc 180 N Stetson Ave	Chicago	IL	60601	312-621-8200	
ThyssenKrupp Elevator 9280 Crestwyn Hills Dr *TF:* 877-230-0303 ■ *Web:* www.thyssenkruppelevator.com	Memphis	TN	38125	877-230-0303	
Toma & Assoc Inc 41 Summit St	Jackson	CA	95642	209-223-0156	
Toyota Motor North America Inc 601 Lexington Ave 49th Fl **Fax Area Code:* 212 ■ *TF:* 800-331-4331 ■ *Web:* www.toyota.com	New York	NY	10022	800-331-4331	759-7670*
Transtar Inc 1200 Penn Ave Ste 300 *Web:* www.tstarinc.com	Pittsburgh	PA	15222	412-433-7835	
Tredegar Corp 1100 Boulders Pkwy Ste 200 *NYSE: TG* ■ *TF:* 800-411-7441 ■ *Web:* www.tredegar.com	Richmond	VA	23225	804-330-1000	330-1177
Trian Partners 280 Pk Ave **Fax:* Mail Rm ■ *Web:* www.trianpartners.com	New York	NY	10017	212-451-3000	451-3134*
Trump Organization 725 Fifth Ave 26th Fl *Web:* www.trump.com	New York	NY	10022	212-832-2000	935-0141
TSI Holding Co 999 Executive Pkwy Dr	Saint Louis	MO	63141	314-628-6000	628-6099
Turner Corp 375 Hudson St *Web:* www.turnerconstruction.com	New York	NY	10014	212-229-6000	
Twincorp Inc 316 Marsland Dr *Web:* www.twincorpinc.com	Waterloo	ON	N2J3Z1	519-885-4600	
UM Holding Co 56 N Haddon Ave PO Box 200 *Web:* www.umholdings.com	Haddonfield	NJ	08033	856-354-2200	
Unilever Canada Ltd 160 Bloor St E Ste 1500 *Web:* www.unilever.ca	Toronto	ON	M4W3R2	416-964-1857	964-8831
Union Pacific Corp 1400 Douglas St *NYSE: UNP* ■ *TF:* 888-870-8777 ■ *Web:* www.up.com	Omaha	NE	68179	402-544-5000	
United Co, The 1005 Glenway Ave	Bristol	VA	24201	276-466-3322	
Vector Group Ltd 100 SE Second St 32nd Fl *NYSE: VGR* ■ *Web:* www.vectorgroupltd.com	Miami	FL	33131	305-579-8000	579-8001
VENSURE Employer Services Inc 4140 E Baseline Rd Ste 201 *TF:* 800-409-8958 ■ *Web:* www.vensureinc.com	Mesa	AZ	85206	800-409-8958	
Viking Group Inc 3033 Orchard Vista Dr Se Ste 308 *Web:* vikinggroupinc.com	Grand Rapids	MI	49546	616-831-6448	
VPS Convenience Store Group LLC 1410 Commonwealth Dr Ste 202 *Web:* www.villagepantrystores.com	Wilmington	NC	28403	910-395-5300	
Warnaco Group Inc 501 Seventh Ave *NYSE: WRC* ■ *Web:* www.pvh.com	New York	NY	10018	212-287-8000	
Warren Equities Inc 27 Warren Way *TF:* 877-623-6765 ■ *Web:* www.warreneq.com	Providence	RI	02905	401-781-9900	461-7160
Warren Technology Inc 2050 W 73 St *Web:* www.warrenhvac.com	Hialeah	FL	33016	305-556-6933	
WebMD Health Holdings Inc 111 Eigth Ave Seventh Fl *NASDAQ: WBMD* ■ *Web:* www.webmd.com	New York	NY	10011	212-624-3700	624-3800
WEDGE Group Inc 1415 Louisiana St Ste 3000 *Web:* www.wedgegroup.com	Houston	TX	77002	713-739-6500	
WESCO International Inc 225 W Stn Sq Dr Ste 700 *NYSE: WCC* ■ *Web:* www.wesco.com	Pittsburgh	PA	15219	412-454-2200	454-2505
West Texas Gas Inc 211 N Colorado St *Web:* westtexasgas.com	Midland	TX	79701	432-682-4349	682-4024
Williams Cos Inc 1 Williams Ctr *NYSE: WMB* ■ *TF:* 800-945-5426 ■ *Web:* co.williams.com	Tulsa	OK	74103	918-573-2000	
Wood Resources LLC 100 Northfield St Ste 203 *Web:* www.atlasholdingsllc.com	Greenwich	CT	06830	203-622-9138	622-0151
Worthington Direct Holdings LLC 6301 Gaston Ave Ste 670 *TF:* 800-599-6636 ■ *Web:* www.worthingtondirect.com	Dallas	TX	75214	800-599-6636	
WRB Enterprises 1414 W Swann Ave Ste 201 *Web:* wrbenterprises.com	Tampa	FL	33606	813-251-3737	
YRC Worldwide Inc 10990 Roe Ave *NASDAQ: YRCW* ■ *TF:* 800-846-4300 ■ *Web:* www.yrc.com	Overland Park	KS	66211	913-696-6100	344-4717
Zahava Group Inc 7525 Britannia Park Pl *Web:* www.zahavagroup.com	San Diego	CA	92154	619-671-0001	

363-4 Insurance Holding Companies

Company	City	State	ZIP	Phone	Fax
Affirmative Insurance Holdings Inc 150 Harvester Dr Ste 250 *OTC: AFFM* ■ *TF:* 800-877-0226 ■ *Web:* www.affirmativeholdings.com	Burr Ridge	IL	60527	972-728-6300	728-6491
AFLAC Inc 1932 Wynnton Rd *NYSE: AFL* ■ **Fax:* Mktg ■ *TF:* 800-992-3522 ■ *Web:* www.aflac.com	Columbus	GA	31999	706-323-3431	660-7103*
AIG SunAmerica Inc 21650 Oxnard St *TF:* 800-445-7862 ■ *Web:* www-1000.aig.com/	Woodland Hills	CA	91367	800-445-7862	

Phone Fax

Allstate Corp 2775 Sanders Rd Allstate Plz .... Northbrook IL 60062 847-402-5000 836-3998*
NYSE: ALL ■ **Fax:* Hum Res ■ *TF:* 800-255-7828 ■ *Web:* www.allstate.com

AMBAC Financial Group Inc
One State St Plz 15th Fl .... New York NY 10004 212-668-0340 509-9190
OTC: ABKFQ ■ *TF:* 800-221-1854 ■ *Web:* www.ambac.com

American Equity Investment Life Holding Co
6000 Westown Pkwy Ste 440
PO Box 71216 .... West Des Moines IA 50266 515-221-0002 221-9947
NYSE: AEL ■ *TF:* 888-221-1234 ■ *Web:* www.american-equity.com

American Fidelity Assurance Co
2000 N Classen Blvd .... Oklahoma City OK 73106 405-523-2000 *
**Fax:* Hum Res ■ *TF:* 800-654-8489 ■ *Web:* www.afadvantage.com

American Financial Group Inc
301 E 4th Street .... Cincinnati OH 45202 513-579-2121 579-2580
NYSE: AFG ■ *Web:* www.afginc.com

American Medical Security (AMS)
3100 AMS Blvd PO Box 19032 .... Green Bay WI 54307 800-657-8205
TF: 800-232-5432 ■ *Web:* www.eams.com

American United Mutual Insurance Holding Co (AUMIHC)
One American Sq PO Box 368 .... Indianapolis IN 46206 317-285-1111
Web: www.oneamerica.com

Americo Life Inc 300 W 11th St .... Kansas City MO 64105 816-391-2000 391-2083
TF General: 800-231-0801 ■ *Web:* www.americo.com

Ameritas Holding Co 5900 O St .... Lincoln NE 68510 402-467-1122
TF: 800-311-7871 ■ *Web:* www.ameritas.com

Anthem Insurance Cos Inc
120 Monument Cir Ste 200 .... Indianapolis IN 46204 317-488-6000 488-6028*
**Fax:* Hum Res ■ *TF:* 800-331-1476 ■ *Web:* www.anthem.com

Aon Corp 200 E Randolph St .... Chicago IL 60601 312-381-1000
TF: 877-384-4276 ■ *Web:* www.aon.com

Assicurazioni Generali US Branch
250 Greenwich St 33rd Fl .... New York NY 10007 212-602-7600 587-9537
Web: www.generaliusa.com

Assurant Group 11222 Quail Roost Dr .... Miami FL 33157 305-253-2244 252-7068
TF: 800-852-2244 ■ *Web:* www.assurant.com

Assurant Inc One Chase Manhattan Plz .... New York NY 10005 212-859-7000
NYSE: AIZ ■ *Web:* www.assurant.com

Atlantic American Corp 4370 Peachtree Rd NE .... Atlanta GA 30319 404-266-5500 266-5629*
NASDAQ: AAME ■ **Fax:* Mail Rm ■ *Web:* www.atlam.com

Bexil Corp 11 Hanover Sq .... New York NY 10005 212-785-0400 363-1101
OTC: BXLC ■ *Web:* www.bexil.com

Capitol Transamerica Corp
1600 Aspen Commons .... Middleton WI 53562 608-829-4200 829-7409*
**Fax:* Hum Res ■ *TF:* 800-475-4450 ■ *Web:* www.capspecialty.com/

Chubb Corp 15 Mountain View Rd .... Warren NJ 07059 908-903-2000 903-2027*
NYSE: CB ■ **Fax:* Mail Rm ■ *TF:* 800-252-4670 ■ *Web:* www.chubb.com

CIGNA Corp 1601 Chestnut St .... Philadelphia PA 19192 215-761-1000
NYSE: CI ■ *Web:* www.cigna.com

Cincinnati Financial Corp
6200 S Gilmore Rd .... Fairfield OH 45014 513-870-2000 870-2911
NASDAQ: CINF ■ *Web:* cinfin.com

Citizens Financial Corp
12910 Shelbyville Rd Ste 300 .... Louisville KY 40243 502-244-2420 244-2439
OTC: CFIN ■ *TF:* 800-843-7752 ■ *Web:* www.citizensfinancialcorp.com

Citizens Inc 400 E Anderson Ln .... Austin TX 78752 512-837-7100 836-9785
NYSE: CIA ■ *TF General:* 877-785-9659 ■ *Web:* www.citizensinc.com

CNA Financial Corp 333 S Wabash Ave .... Chicago IL 60604 312-822-5000
NYSE: CNA ■ *TF:* 800-262-4357 ■ *Web:* www.cna.com

Conseco Inc 11825 N Pennsylvania St .... Carmel IN 46032 317-817-3012 817-3773*
NYSE: CNO ■ **Fax:* Hum Res ■ *TF:* 866-595-2255 ■ *Web:* www.conseco.com

CUNA Mutual Group 5910 Mineral Pt Dr .... Madison WI 53705 608-238-5851
TF: 800-937-2644 ■ *Web:* www.cunamutual.com

Delphi Financial Group Inc
1105 N Market St Ste 1230 .... Wilmington DE 19801 302-478-5142
NYSE: DFG ■ *Web:* www.delphifin.com

Deutsche Bank Americas Holding Corp
60 Wall St .... New York NY 10005 212-250-2500
Web: www.db.com

Donegal Group Inc 1195 River Rd .... Marietta PA 17547 717-426-1931 426-7030*
NASDAQ: DGICA ■ **Fax:* Hum Res ■ *TF:* 800-877-0600 ■ *Web:* www.donegalgroup.com

EMC Insurance Group Inc 717 Mulberry St .... Des Moines IA 50309 515-280-2511
NASDAQ: EMCI ■ *TF:* 800-447-2295 ■ *Web:* www.emcins.com

Everest Re Group Ltd
477 Martinsville Rd PO Box 830 .... Liberty Corner NJ 07938 908-604-3000 604-3322
TF: 800-269-6660 ■ *Web:* www.everestre.com

Fairfax Financial Holdings Ltd
95 Wellington St W Ste 800 .... Toronto ON M5J2N7 416-367-4941 367-4946
Web: www.fairfax.ca

Farmers Insurance Group
4680 Wilshire Blvd .... Los Angeles CA 90010 323-932-3200
TF: 800-327-6377 ■ *Web:* farmers.com/

FBL Financial Group Inc
5400 University Ave .... West Des Moines IA 50266 515-225-5400
NYSE: FFG ■ *Web:* www.fblfinancial.com

Federated Insurance Cos
121 E Pk Sq PO Box 328 .... Owatonna MN 55060 507-455-5200 444-6778
TF: 800-533-0472 ■ *Web:* federatedinsurance.com

First Investors Corp 110 Wall St .... New York NY 10005 800-832-7783
TF General: 800-832-7783 ■ *Web:* www.firstinvestors.com

GMAC Insurance Holdings Inc
PO Box 3199 .... Winston-Salem NC 27102 888-293-5108
TF: 888-293-5108 ■ *Web:* nationalgeneral.com

Hallmark Financial Services Inc
777 Main St Ste 1000 .... Fort Worth TX 76102 817-348-1600 348-1815
NASDAQ: HALL ■ *Web:* www.hallmarkgrp.com

Hanover Insurance Group Inc 440 Lincoln St .... Worcester MA 01653 508-855-1000 853-6332
NYSE: THG ■ *TF:* 800-628-0250 ■ *Web:* www.hanover.com

Harleysville Group Inc 355 Maple Ave .... Harleysville PA 19438 215-256-5000 256-5678*
NASDAQ: HGIC ■ **Fax:* Mktg ■ *TF:* 800-523-6344 ■ *Web:* www.harleysvillegroup.com

Hartford Financial Services Group Inc
690 Asylum Ave .... Hartford CT 06115 860-547-5000 547-3799*
NYSE: HIG ■ **Fax:* PR ■ *Web:* www.thehartford.com

HCC Insurance Holdings Inc 13403 NW Fwy .... Houston TX 77040 713-462-1000 462-4210
Web: www.hcc.com

HealthMarkets Inc 9151 Blvd 26 .... North Richland Hills TX 76180 817-255-5200
Web: www.healthmarketsinc.com

Horace Mann Educators Corp
One Horace Mann Plz .... Springfield IL 62715 217-789-2500 788-5161
NYSE: HMN ■ *TF:* 800-999-1030 ■ *Web:* www.horacemann.com

Investors Title Co 121 N Columbia St .... Chapel Hill NC 27514 919-968-2200 690-6105*
NASDAQ: ITIC ■ **Fax Area Code:* 800 ■ *TF:* 800-326-4842 ■ *Web:* invtitle.com

John Hancock Financial Services Inc
601 Congress St .... Boston MA 02210 617-663-3000 663-4790*
**Fax:* PR ■ *Web:* www.johnhancock.com

Kansas City Life Insurance Co
3520 Broadway .... Kansas City MO 64111 816-753-7000 753-4902
NASDAQ: KCLI ■ *TF:* 800-821-6164 ■ *Web:* www.kclife.com

Kingsway America Inc (KAI)
150 NW Pt Blvd .... Elk Grove Village IL 60007 847-700-9100 700-9170
TF: 800-232-0631 ■ *Web:* kaiadvantage.com

Legal & General America Inc
1701 Research Blvd .... Rockville MD 20850 301-279-4800 294-6960*
**Fax:* Cust Svc ■ *TF:* 800-638-8428 ■ *Web:* www.lgamerica.com

Lifetime Healthcare Cos, The 165 Ct St .... Rochester NY 14647 585-454-1700 238-4233
TF: 800-847-1200 ■ *Web:* www.lifethc.com

Lincoln National Corp (LNC)
150 N Radnor-Chester Rd .... Radnor PA 19087 484-583-1400 448-3962*
NYSE: LNC ■ **Fax Area Code:* 215 ■ **Fax:* PR ■ *TF:* 877-275-5462 ■ *Web:* www.lfg.com

Manulife Financial Corp 200 Bloor St E .... Toronto ON M4W1E5 416-926-3000 926-5410
NYSE: MFC ■ *TF:* 800-795-9767 ■ *Web:* www.manulife.com

Markel Corp 4521 Highwoods Pkwy .... Glen Allen VA 23060 800-431-1270 662-7535*
NYSE: MKL ■ **Fax Area Code:* 855 ■ *TF:* 877-566-6323 ■ *Web:* markelinsurance.com

MBIA Inc 113 King St .... Armonk NY 10504 914-273-4545 765-3299*
NYSE: MBI ■ **Fax:* Hum Res ■ *Web:* www.mbia.com

Meadowbrook Insurance Group Inc
26255 American Dr .... Southfield MI 48034 248-358-1100 358-1614
NYSE: MIG ■ *TF:* 800-482-2726 ■ *Web:* www.meadowbrookinsgrp.com

Midland Co 7000 Midland Blvd .... Amelia OH 45102 800-543-2644
TF: 800-759-9008 ■ *Web:* www.amig.com

Munich Reinsurance America Inc
555 College Rd E PO Box 5241 .... Princeton NJ 08543 609-243-4200 243-4257
Web: www.munichre.com/us

Mutual of Omaha Co Mutual of Omaha Plz .... Omaha NE 68175 402-342-7600 351-2775
TF: 800-775-6000 ■ *Web:* www.mutualofomaha.com

Navigators Group Inc One Penn Plz 32nd Fl .... New York NY 10119 212-244-2333 244-4077
NASDAQ: NAVG ■ *TF:* 800-942-6906 ■ *Web:* www.navigators-insurance.com

Pacific Mutual Holding Co
700 Newport Ctr Dr .... Newport Beach CA 92660 949-219-3011 219-7614
TF: 800-347-7787 ■ *Web:* www.pacificlife.com

Patriot Risk Management Inc
401 E Las Olas Blvd Ste 1650 .... Fort Lauderdale FL 33301 954-670-2900 779-3556
Web: www.pnigroup.com

Penn Treaty American Corp 3440 Lehigh St .... Allentown PA 18103 800-362-0700 967-4616*
**Fax Area Code:* 610 ■ *TF:* 800-362-0700 ■ *Web:* www.penntreaty.com

Penn-America Group Inc 420 S York Rd .... Hatboro PA 19040 215-443-3600 443-3604*
**Fax:* Claims ■ *Web:* www.penn-america.com

Phoenix Cos Inc, The
One American Row PO Box 5056 .... Hartford CT 06102 860-403-5000
NYSE: PNX ■ *TF:* 800-628-1936 ■ *Web:* www.phoenixwm.phl.com

PICO Holdings Inc 7979 Ivanhoe Ave Ste 301 .... La Jolla CA 92037 858-456-6022 456-6480
NASDAQ: PICO ■ *TF:* 888-389-3222 ■ *Web:* www.picoholdings.com

PMA Capital Corp 380 Sentry Pkwy .... Blue Bell PA 19422 610-397-5298 397-5422
Web: www.pmacompanies.com

PMI Group Inc 3003 Oak Rd .... Walnut Creek CA 94597 800-288-1970
OTC: PMI ■ *TF:* 800-288-1970 ■ *Web:* www.pmi-us.com

Principal Financial Group Inc 711 High St .... Des Moines IA 50392 515-247-5111 247-5874
NYSE: PFG ■ *TF:* 800-986-3343 ■ *Web:* www.principal.com

ProAssurance Corp 100 Brookwood Pl Ste 300 .... Birmingham AL 35209 205-877-4400 802-4799*
NYSE: PRA ■ **Fax:* Cust Svc ■ *TF:* 800-282-6242 ■ *Web:* www.proassurance.com

Protective Life Corp 2801 Hwy 280 S .... Birmingham AL 35223 205-268-1000 *
NYSE: PL ■ **Fax:* Hum Res ■ *TF:* 800-333-3418 ■ *Web:* www.protective.com

Reinsurance Group of America Inc
1370 Timberlake Manor Pkwy .... Chesterfield MO 63017 636-736-7000 736-7150
NYSE: RGA ■ *TF:* 800-985-4326 ■ *Web:* www.rgare.com

RLI Corp 9025 N Lindbergh Dr .... Peoria IL 61615 309-692-1000 692-1068
NYSE: RLI ■ *TF Cust Svc:* 800-331-4929 ■ *Web:* www.rlicorp.com

Scottish Re Inc
14120 Ballantyne Corporate Pl Ste 300 .... Charlotte NC 28277 704-542-9192 542-5744
Web: www.scottishre.com

Securian Financial Group Inc
400 Robert St N .... Saint Paul MN 55101 651-665-3500 665-4488
Web: www.securian.com

Security Benefit Group of Cos
One Security Benefit Pl .... Topeka KS 66636 785-438-3000 368-1772*
**Fax:* Cust Svc ■ *TF:* 800-888-2461 ■ *Web:* www.securitybenefit.com

Selective Insurance Group Inc
40 Wantage Ave .... Branchville NJ 07890 973-948-3000 948-0292
NASDAQ: SIGI ■ *TF:* 800-777-9656 ■ *Web:* www.selective.com

Sentry Insurance Group 1800 N Pt Dr .... Stevens Point WI 54481 715-346-6000 346-7516
TF: 800-373-6879 ■ *Web:* www.sentry.com

StanCorp Financial Group Inc
1100 SW Sixth Ave .... Portland OR 97204 800-368-1135
NYSE: SFG ■ *Web:* standard.com

Summit Holding Southeast Inc PO Box 600 .... Gainesville GA 30503 678-450-5825
TF: 800-971-2667 ■ *Web:* www.summitholdings.com

Sun Life Financial Inc 150 King St W .... Toronto ON M5H1J9 416-979-9966
TSE: SLF ■ *TF:* 877-786-5433 ■ *Web:* www.sunlife.com

Swiss Re Life & Health America Inc
175 King St .... Armonk NY 10504 914-828-8000 828-7000
TF: 800-937-5449 ■ *Web:* www.swissre.com

Torchmark Corp 3700 S Stonebridge Dr .... McKinney TX 75070 972-569-4000 569-3282
NYSE: TMK ■ *TF:* 877-577-3899 ■ *Web:* www.torchmarkcorp.com

Transatlantic Holdings Inc 80 Pine St .... New York NY 10005 212-365-2200 365-2362*
NYSE: TRH ■ **Fax:* Claims ■ *Web:* www.transre.com

				Phone	Fax
Travelers Cos Inc 385 Washington St	Saint Paul	MN	55102	651-310-7911	310-8204*
NYSE: TRV ■ *Fax: Hum Res ■ TF: 800-328-2189 ■ Web: www.travelers.com					
ULLICO Inc 1625 Eye St NW	Washington	DC	20006	800-431-5425	
TF: 800-431-5425 ■ Web: www.ullico.com					
United Fire Group 118 Second Ave SE PO Box 73909	Cedar Rapids	IA	52407	319-399-5700	399-5499
TF: 800-332-7977 ■ Web: www.unitedfiregroup.com					
United Trust Group Inc (UTGI) 5250 S Sixth St	Springfield	IL	62705	217-241-6410	241-6578
OTC: UTGN ■ TF: 800-323-0050 ■ Web: www.utgins.com					
Universal American Corp (UAFC) 44 S Broadway Ste 1200	White Plains	NY	10601	914-934-5200	934-0700
NYSE: UAM ■ TF: 866-249-8668 ■ Web: www.universalamerican.com					
UnumProvident Corp 1 Fountain Sq	Chattanooga	TN	37402	423-294-1011	872-8999*
*Fax Area Code: 410 ■ TF: 800-262-0018 ■ Web: www.unum.com					
Western & Southern Financial Group 400 Broadway	Cincinnati	OH	45202	513-629-1800	629-1212
TF: 800-333-5222 ■ Web: www.westernsouthern.com					
White Mountains Insurance Group Ltd 80 S Main St	Hanover	NH	03755	603-640-2200	643-4592
NYSE: WTM ■ TF: 866-295-3762 ■ Web: www.whitemountains.com					
WR Berkley Corp 475 Steamboat Rd	Greenwich	CT	06830	203-629-3000	629-3073
NYSE: WRB ■ Web: www.wrbc.com					

363-5 Utilities Holding Companies

				Phone	Fax
AGL Resources Inc 10 Peachtree Pl PO Box 4569	Atlanta	GA	30309	404-584-4000	*
NYSE: GAS ■ *Fax: Hum Res ■ Web: www.aglresources.com					
ALLETE Inc 30 W Superior St	Duluth	MN	55802	218-279-5000	723-3944
NYSE: ALE ■ TF: 800-228-4966 ■ Web: www.allete.com					
Ameren Corp 1901 Chouteau Ave	Saint Louis	MO	63103	314-621-3222	621-2888
NYSE: AEE ■ TF: 800-552-7583 ■ Web: ameren.com					
American Electric Power Company Inc One Riverside Plz	Columbus	OH	43215	614-716-1000	716-1823
NYSE: AEP ■ TF Cust Svc: 800-277-2177 ■ Web: www.aep.com					
American States Water Co 630 E Foothill Blvd	San Dimas	CA	91773	909-394-3600	394-9708
NYSE: AWR ■ TF: 800-999-4033 ■ Web: www.aswater.com					
American Water Works Co Inc 1025 Laurel Oak Rd	Voorhees	NJ	08043	856-346-8200	346-8360
NYSE: AWK ■ TF: 888-282-6816 ■ Web: www.amwater.com					
Artesian Resources Corp 664 Churchmans Rd	Newark	DE	19702	302-453-6900	453-6957
NASDAQ: ARTNA ■ TF: 800-332-5114 ■ Web: www.artesianwater.com					
Atmos Energy Corp 5430 LBJ Fwy Ste 1800	Dallas	TX	75240	972-934-9227	855-3040
NYSE: ATO ■ TF: 888-954-4321 ■ Web: www.atmosenergy.com					
Black Hills Corp 625 Ninth St	Rapid City	SD	57701	605-721-1700	721-2596*
NYSE: BKH ■ *Fax: Hum Res ■ TF: 866-264-8003 ■ Web: www.blackhillscorp.com					
CenterPoint Energy Inc 1111 Louisiana St	Houston	TX	77002	713-207-1111	207-0050*
NYSE: CNP ■ *Fax: Hum Res ■ TF Cust Svc: 800-495-9880 ■ Web: www.centerpointenergy.com					
CH Energy Group Inc 284 S Ave	Poughkeepsie	NY	12601	845-452-2000	486-5415
NYSE: CHG ■ TF: 800-527-2714 ■ Web: www.chenergygroup.com					
CMS Energy Corp One Energy Plz	Jackson	MI	49201	517-788-0550	
NYSE: CMS ■ TF: 800-477-5050 ■ Web: www.cmsenergy.com					
Connecticut Water Service Inc 93 W Main St	Clinton	CT	06413	860-669-8636	664-8081*
NASDAQ: CTWS ■ *Fax: Cust Svc ■ TF: 800-286-5700 ■ Web: www.ctwater.com					
Consolidated Edison Inc Four Irving Pl	New York	NY	10003	212-460-4600	
NYSE: ED ■ TF: 800-752-6633 ■ Web: coned.com					
Dominion Resources Inc 120 Tredegar St	Richmond	VA	23219	804-819-2000	819-2233
NYSE: D ■ TF: 800-552-4034 ■ Web: www.dom.com					
DPL Inc 1065 Woodman Dr	Dayton	OH	45432	800-736-3001	224-6500*
NYSE: DPL ■ *Fax Area Code: 937 ■ TF: 800-433-8500 ■ Web: www.dplinc.com					
DTE Energy Co One Energy Plz	Detroit	MI	48226	313-235-4000	
NYSE: DTE ■ TF: 800-477-4747 ■ Web: www.dteenergy.com					
Duke Energy Corp PO Box 70516	Charlotte	NC	28201	704-594-6200	382-3781*
NYSE: DUK ■ *Fax: Hum Res ■ Web: m.duke-energy.com					
Duquesne Light Holdings Inc 411 Seventh Ave	Pittsburgh	PA	15219	412-393-7000	393-7000
TF: 888-393-7000 ■ Web: www.duquesnelight.com					
Dynegy Inc 601 Travis St Ste 1400	Houston	TX	77002	713-507-6400	
NYSE: DYN ■ TF: 800-633-4704 ■ Web: www.dynegy.com					
Edison International 2244 Walnut Grove Ave	Rosemead	CA	91770	626-302-1212	
NYSE: EIX ■ TF Cust Svc: 800-655-4555 ■ Web: www.edison.com					
Enbridge Energy Management LLC 1100 Louisiana St Ste 3300	Houston	TX	77002	713-821-2000	821-2230
NYSE: EEQ ■ TF: 866-337-4636 ■ Web: www.enbridgemanagement.com					
Energen Corp 605 Richard Arrington Blvd N	Birmingham	AL	35203	205-326-2700	581-1811
NYSE: EGN ■ TF: 800-654-3206 ■ Web: www.energen.com					
Entergy Corp 639 Loyola Ave	New Orleans	LA	70113	504-576-4000	576-4428
NYSE: ETR ■ TF: 800-368-3749 ■ Web: www.entergy.com					
FirstEnergy Corp 76 S Main St	Akron	OH	44308	800-633-4766	384-3866*
NYSE: FE ■ *Fax Area Code: 330 ■ TF: 800-633-4766 ■ Web: www.firstenergycorp.com					
FPL Group Inc NextEra Energy Inc 700 Universe Blvd	Juno Beach	FL	33408	561-694-4000	694-4620
NYSE: NEE ■ TF: 800-979-3967 ■ Web: www.nexteraenergy.com					
Great Plains Energy Inc 1200 Main St PO Box 418679	Kansas City	MO	64106	816-556-2200	556-2884
NYSE: GXP ■ Web: www.greatplainsenergy.com					
Holly Energy Partners LP 100 Crescent Ct Ste 1600	Dallas	TX	75201	214-871-3555	871-3829
TF: 800-642-1687 ■ Web: www.hollyenergy.com					
IDACORP Inc 1221 W Idaho St	Boise	ID	83702	208-388-2200	
NYSE: IDA ■ Web: www.idacorpinc.com					
Integrys Energy Group Inc 130 E Randolph Dr	Chicago	IL	60601	312-228-5400	
TF: 800-699-1269 ■ Web: www.integrysgroup.com					
Laclede Group Inc 720 Olive St Rm 1517	Saint Louis	MO	63101	314-342-0500	
NYSE: LG ■ TF: 800-884-4225 ■ Web: www.thelacledegroup.com					
MidAmerican Energy Holdings Co 666 Grand Ave PO Box 657	Des Moines	IA	50303	800-329-6261	336-3568*
*Fax Area Code: 563 ■ Web: www.midamerican.com					
National Fuel Gas Co 6363 Main St	Williamsville	NY	14221	716-857-7000	857-7206
NYSE: NFG ■ TF Cust Svc: 800-365-3234 ■ Web: nationalfuelgas.com					
National Grid USA Service Company Inc 25 Research Dr	Westborough	MA	01582	508-389-2000	
TF: 800-548-8000 ■ Web: www.nationalgridus.com					
New Jersey Resources Corp 1415 Wyckoff Rd	Wall	NJ	07719	732-938-1000	938-2134*
NYSE: NJR ■ *Fax: Hum Res ■ Web: www.njresources.com					
NSTAR 800 Boylston St	Boston	MA	02199	617-424-2000	441-8886*
NYSE: NST ■ *Fax Area Code: 781 ■ TF: 800-592-2000 ■ Web: nstar.com					
OGE Energy Corp 321 N Harvey St	Oklahoma City	OK	73102	405-553-3000	553-3326
NYSE: OGE ■ TF: 800-272-9741 ■ Web: www.oge.com					
PG & E Corp 77 Beale St 24th Fl	San Francisco	CA	94105	415-267-7000	973-8719*
NYSE: PCG ■ *Fax: Hum Res ■ TF: 800-743-5000 ■ Web: www.pgecorp.com					
Pinnacle West Capital Corp 400 N Fifth St	Phoenix	AZ	85004	602-250-1000	250-2741*
NYSE: PNW ■ *Fax: Investor Rel ■ TF: 800-457-2983 ■ Web: www.pinnaclewest.com					
PNM Resources Inc Alvarado Sq	Albuquerque	NM	87158	505-241-2700	241-4311
NYSE: PNM ■ TF: 888-342-5766 ■ Web: www.pnmresources.com					
PPL Corp Two N Ninth St	Allentown	PA	18101	610-774-5151	774-6043
NYSE: PPL ■ TF: 800-342-5775 ■ Web: www.pplweb.com					
Progress Energy Inc 410 S Wilmington St PO Box 2041	Raleigh	NC	27601	919-546-6111	546-2920
NYSE: PGN ■ TF: 800-452-2777 ■ Web: progress-energy.com					
Public Service Enterprise Group Inc 80 Pk Plz	Newark	NJ	07102	973-430-7000	623-5389
NYSE: PEG ■ TF Cust Svc: 800-436-7734 ■ Web: www.pseg.com					
Puget Energy Inc 10885 NE Fourth St	Bellevue	WA	98004	425-454-6363	
Web: www.pugetenergy.com/pages/terms.html					
Questar Corp 333 S State St PO Box 45433	Salt Lake City	UT	84145	801-324-5000	324-3756
NYSE: STR ■ TF: 800-323-5517 ■ Web: www.questarcorp.com					
RGC Resources Inc 519 Kimball Ave PO Box 13007	Roanoke	VA	24016	540-777-4427	777-3957*
NASDAQ: RGCO ■ *Fax: Hum Res ■ Web: www.rgcresources.com					
SCANA Corp 220 Operation Way	Cayce	SC	29033	803-217-9000	933-8224
NYSE: SCG ■ TF: 800-251-7234 ■ Web: www.scana.com					
Sempra Energy Corp 101 Ash St	San Diego	CA	92101	619-696-2000	696-9202
NYSE: SRE ■ TF: 800-411-7343 ■ Web: www.sempra.com					
SJW Corp 110 W Taylor St	San Jose	CA	95110	408-279-7900	279-7917
NYSE: SJW ■ Web: www.sjwater.com					
Southern Co 30 Ivan Allen Jr Blvd NW	Atlanta	GA	30308	404-506-5000	506-0455
NYSE: SO ■ Web: www.southernco.com					
Tokyo Gas Co Ltd 1540 Broadway Ste 3920	New York	NY	10036	646-865-0577	865-0592
Web: www.tokyo-gas.co.jp					
UGI Corp 460 N Gulph Rd PO Box 858	King Of Prussia	PA	19406	610-337-1000	
NYSE: UGI ■ Web: www.ugicorp.com					
UIL Holdings Corp 157 Church St	New Haven	CT	06506	203-499-2000	499-3664
NYSE: UIL ■ TF: 800-722-5584 ■ Web: www.uil.com					
United Water Resources Inc 200 Old Hook Rd	Harrington Park	NJ	07640	201-767-9300	767-7142*
*Fax: Hum Res ■ Web: www.unitedwater.com					
Unitil Corp Six Liberty Ln W	Hampton	NH	03842	603-772-0775	773-6605
NYSE: UTL ■ TF: 800-852-3339 ■ Web: www.unitil.com					
Vectren Corp 211 NW Riverside Dr PO Box 209	Evansville	IN	47708	812-491-4000	491-4706
NYSE: VVC ■ TF: 800-227-1376 ■ Web: www.vectren.com					
Westar Energy Inc 818 S Kansas Ave	Topeka	KS	66612	785-575-6300	575-6596
NYSE: WR ■ TF: 800-383-1183 ■ Web: www.westarenergy.com					
WGL Holdings Inc 101 Constitution Ave NW	Washington	DC	20080	703-750-2000	664-7317*
NYSE: WGL ■ *Fax Area Code: 301 ■ TF: 800-645-3751 ■ Web: www.wglholdings.com					
Wisconsin Energy Corp 231 W Michigan St	Milwaukee	WI	53203	414-221-2345	
NYSE: WEC ■ TF General: 800-242-9137 ■ Web: www.wisconsinenergy.com					

364 HOME FURNISHINGS - WHOL

				Phone	Fax
A & J Washroom Accessories Inc 509 Temple Hill Rd	New Windsor	NY	12553	845-562-3332	
Web: www.ajwashroom.com					
AA Importing Co Inc 7700 Hall St	Saint Louis	MO	63147	314-383-8800	383-2608
TF Cust Svc: 800-325-0602 ■ Web: www.aaimporting.com					
Abel & Schafer Inc 20 Alexander Ct	Ronkonkoma	NY	11779	631-737-2220	
Web: kompletusa.com					
Adjust-a-brush 10445 49th St N	Clearwater	FL	33762	727-571-1234	
Web: www.adjust-a-brush.com					
Adleta Co 1645 Diplomat Dr Ste 200	Carrollton	TX	75006	972-620-5600	620-5666
TF: 800-423-5382 ■ Web: www.adleta.com					
Aerolite Extrusion Company Inc 4605 Lk Park Rd	Youngstown	OH	44512	330-782-1127	
Web: www.aeroext.com					
Ag Russell Knives Inc 2900 S 26th St	Rogers	AR	72758	479-631-0055	
Web: www.agrussell.com					
Allure Home Creation Co Inc 85 Fulton St	Boonton	NJ	07005	973-402-8888	334-2383
Web: www.allurehome.com					
American Accessories International Inc 550 W Main St Ste 825	Knoxville	TN	37902	865-525-9100	525-0889
Web: americanaccessoriesintl.com					
Amero Foods Manufacturing Corp 9445 Washington Blvd N Ste L	Laurel	MD	20723	301-498-0912	
Web: www.pastryonline.com					
Apn Healthcare Inc 308 Centennial Blvd	Edmond	OK	73013	405-341-6945	
Web: www.apnhealthcare.com					
Architex International 3333 Commercial Ave	Northbrook	IL	60062	847-205-1333	
TF: 800-621-0827 ■ Web: www.architex-ljh.com					
Artistic Stone Kitchen & Bath Inc 2973 Teagarden St	San Leandro	CA	94577	510-483-1298	
Web: www.artisticstoneinc.com					
Ashton Company Inc, The 1510 Primewest Pkwy	Katy	TX	77449	281-578-0165	
Web: www.ashtoncompany.com					
Atlantic Lighting & Supply Company Inc 218 Ottley Dr Ne	Atlanta	GA	30324	404-872-3521	
Web: www.atlanticlightingandsupply.com					

Company / Address	City	State	Zip	Phone	Fax
Atlantic Scale Co Inc 136 Washington Ave *TF:* 888-627-5836 ■ *Web:* atlanticscale.com	Nutley	NJ	07110	973-661-7090	661-3651
B & F System Inc 3920 S Walton Walker *TF:* 877-586-2926 ■ *Web:* www.bnfusa.com	Dallas	TX	75236	214-333-2111	333-1511
Barcalounger Corp 400 W Main St Ste 210 *Web:* www.barcalounger.com	Morristown	TN	37814	423-289-1040	
Beetling Design Corp 2131 Hartley Ave *Web:* www.beetling.com	Coquitlam	BC	V3K6Z3	604-525-6777	
Bellino Fine Linens 18 W Forest Ave *Web:* bellinofinelinens.com	Englewood	NJ	07631	201-568-5255	
Beme International LLC 7333 Ronson Rd *Web:* www.beme.net	San Diego	CA	92111	858-751-0580	
Bettendorf-stanford 1370 W Main St *TF:* 800-548-2253 ■ *Web:* www.bettendorfstanford.com	Salem	IL	62881	618-548-3555	
Bishop Distributing Co 5200 36th St SE **Fax Area Code:* 616 ■ *TF Cust Svc:* 800-748-0363 ■ *Web:* www.bishopdistributing.com	Grand Rapids	MI	49512	800-748-0363	942-6073*
Bisque Imports 406 E Catawba St *TF:* 888-568-5991 ■ *Web:* www.bisqueimports.com	Belmont	NC	28012	704-829-9290	
Blaze Fireplaces of Northern California Inc 101 Cargo Way *Web:* www.blazefireplaces.com	San Francisco	CA	94124	415-495-2002	
Boston Warehouse Trading Corp 59 Davis Ave *TF:* 888-923-2982 ■ *Web:* www.bwtc.com	Norwood	MA	02062	781-769-8550	769-9468
BR Funsten & Co 5200 Watt Ct Ste B *TF:* 888-261-2871 ■ *Web:* www.brfunsten.com	Fairfield	CA	94534	209-825-5375	825-4916
C & F Enterprises Inc 819 Bluecrab Rd *Web:* www.cnfei.com	Newport News	VA	23606	757-310-6100	
C Bennett Building Supply Inc 1700 W Terra Ln *Web:* www.cbennett.net	O'Fallon	MO	63366	636-379-9886	
Caber Sure Fit Inc 35 Valleywood Dr Ste 1 *TF:* 800-520-3152 ■ *Web:* www.caber.ca	Markham	ON	L3R5L9	905-479-5803	
CAC China 30 Camptown Rd *Web:* www.chinacac.com	Maplewood	NJ	07040	973-371-4300	
Cambridge Silversmith Ltd 116 Lehigh Dr *TF:* 800-890-3366 ■ *Web:* www.cambridgesilversmiths.com	Fairfield	NJ	07004	973-227-4400	227-5600
Carlton Group Inc 120 Landmark Dr *TF:* 800-722-7824 ■ *Web:* www.carltonscale.com	Greensboro	NC	27409	336-668-7677	
Carlton Scale 196 Industrial Dr *Web:* carltonscale.com	Roanoke	VA	24019	540-992-6095	
Carnations Home Fashions Inc 53 Jeanne Dr *Web:* www.carnationhomefashions.com	Newburgh	NY	12550	212-679-6017	
Carolina Scales Inc 929 N Lucas St *Web:* www.carolinascales.com	West Columbia	SC	29169	803-739-4360	
Carpentree Inc 2724 N Sheridan Rd *Web:* carpentree.com	Tulsa	OK	74115	918-582-3600	
Casual Cushion Corp 1686 Overview Dr *Web:* www.casualcushion.com	Rock Hill	SC	29730	803-329-2932	
Caye Home Furnishings LLC 1201 W Bankhead St *Web:* www.cayefurniture.com	New Albany	MS	38652	662-534-4762	
CCA Global Partners 4301 Earth City Expy **Fax Area Code:* 603 ■ *TF:* 800-466-6984 ■ *Web:* www.ccaglobalpartners.com	Earth City	MO	63045	314-506-0000	626-3444*
CDC Distributors 10511 Medallion Dr *Web:* cdcdist.com	Cincinnati	OH	45241	513-771-3100	771-2920
Champion Safe Co Inc 2055 S Larsen Pkwy *Web:* www.championsafe.com	Provo	UT	84606	801-377-7199	377-7195
Christopher Guy 12670 World Plz Ln Bldg 62 Ste 2 *Web:* www.christopherguy.com	Fort Myers	FL	33907	239-939-9838	
Classic Blind Ltd 2801 Brasher Ln Ste 100	Bedford	TX	76021	817-540-9300	
Clayworks Ltd 629 Bedford Hwy *Web:* clayworks.ca	Halifax	NS	B3M2L6	902-445-4453	
Clipper Mill Inc 404 Talbert St *Web:* www.clippermill.com	Daly City	CA	94014	415-330-2400	
Company C Inc 102 Old Tpke Rd *Web:* www.companyc.com	Concord	NH	03301	603-226-4460	
Component Design Northwest Inc 2355 NW Vaughn St *Web:* www.cdn-timeandtemp.com	Portland	OR	97210	503-225-0900	
Cook's Corner 19152 Santiago Canyon Rd *Web:* cookscorners.com	Trabuco Canyon	CA	92679	949-858-0266	
Cookshack 2304 N Ash St *Web:* cookshack.com	Ponca City	OK	74601	580-765-3669	
Cool Gear International LLC 10 Cordage Park Cir *TF:* 855-393-2665 ■ *Web:* www.coolgearinc.com	Plymouth	MA	02360	508-830-3440	
Decorative Crafts Inc 50 Chestnut St *TF:* 800-431-4455 ■ *Web:* www.decorativecrafts.com	Greenwich	CT	06830	203-531-1500	531-1590
Delande Lighting 22 New Derby St *Web:* delandelighting.com	Salem	MA	01970	978-744-2609	
Derr Flooring Company Inc 525 Davisville Rd PO Box 912 *TF:* 800-523-3457 ■ *Web:* www.derrflooring.com	Willow Grove	PA	19090	215-657-6300	657-9830
Designer Blinds 4500 S 76th Cir	Omaha	NE	68127	402-331-2283	
Dial Lighting Gallery 2240 Kaluaopalena St Ste C	Honolulu	HI	96819	808-845-7811	
Dimock Gould & Co 190 22nd St	Moline	IL	61265	309-797-0650	
Dormify Inc 10101 Molecular Dr *Web:* www.dormify.com	Rockville	MD	20850	413-367-6439	
Down Under Linen & Bedding Ctr 5170 Dixie Rd *Web:* downunderbedding.com	Mississauga	ON	L4W1E3	905-624-5854	
Down-Lite International Inc 8153 Duke Blvd *Web:* www.downlite.com	Mason	OH	45040	513-229-3696	
Dumdum Nelida 5925 N Sacramento Ave	Chicago	IL	60659	773-561-6776	
EJ Welch Company Inc 13735 Lakefront Dr *Web:* www.ejwelch.com	Earth City	MO	63045	314-739-2273	
Ekornes Inc 615 Pierce St *Web:* www.ekornes.com	Somerset	NJ	08873	732-302-0097	
Erickson's Flooring & Supply Company Inc 1013 Orchard St *Web:* www.ericksonsfloors.com	Ferndale	MI	48220	248-543-9663	
Fabricut Inc 9303 E 46th St *TF:* 800-999-8200 ■ *Web:* www.fabricut.com	Tulsa	OK	74145	918-622-7700	664-8919
Farrey's Wholesale Hardware Company Inc 1850 NE 146th St *TF:* 888-854-5483 ■ *Web:* www.farreys.com	North Miami	FL	33181	305-947-5451	
Finial Company Inc, The 4030 La Reunion Pkwy Ste 100 *Web:* www.thefinialcompany.com	Dallas	TX	75212	214-678-0805	
Fusion Hardware Group 1000 Satellite Blvd NW Ste 103 *Web:* www.fusionhardware.com	Suwanee	GA	30024	678-990-1676	
Galleher Corp 9303 Greenleaf Ave *Web:* www.galleher.com	Santa Fe Springs	CA	90670	562-944-8885	
Gary Draper & Associates of Atlanta Inc 5665 New Northside Dr Nw Ste 100 *Web:* www.draperandassociates.com	Atlanta	GA	30328	404-256-3601	
GBI Tile & Stone Inc 3120 Airway Ave *Web:* www.gbitile.com	Costa Mesa	CA	92626	949-567-1880	
General Floor Industries Inc 190 Benigno Blvd *Web:* www.generalfloor.com	Bellmawr	NJ	08031	856-931-0012	931-0731
Georgia Flooring Outlet 1660 Hwy 155 S *Web:* www.georgiaflooringoutlet.com	Mcdonough	GA	30253	770-474-9270	
Georgian Plantation Shutter Co 455 Wilbanks Dr *TF:* 888-684-0382 ■ *Web:* www.georgianshutters.com	Ball Ground	GA	30107	678-454-1100	
Gina B & Company Inc 23811 Aliso Creek Rd Ste 130 *Web:* www.ginab.com	Laguna Niguel	CA	92677	949-643-1430	
Gourmet Settings Inc 245 W Beaver Creek Rd Ste 10 *Web:* www.gourmetsettings.com	Richmond Hill	ON	L4B1L1	905-707-0336	
Halstead International Inc Halstead Bldg 15 Oakwood Ave Ste 1	Norwalk	CT	06850	203-299-3100	
Heath Ceramics Ltd 400 Gate Five Rd *Web:* www.heathceramics.com	Sausalito	CA	94965	415-332-3732	
Hendee Enterprises Inc 9350 S Point Dr *Web:* www.hendee.com	Houston	TX	77054	713-796-2322	796-0494
Hendrix Batting Co 2310 Surrett Dr *Web:* hendrixbatting.com	High Point	NC	27263	336-431-1181	
Heritage Lace Inc 309 S St *Web:* www.heritagelace.com	Pella	IA	50219	641-628-4949	
Home Design Outlet Center 400 County Ave *Web:* www.homedesignoutletcenter.com	Secaucus	NJ	07094	201-531-0502	
Home Essentials & Beyond Inc 200 Theodore Conrad Dr *TF:* 800-417-6218 ■ *Web:* www.homeessentials.com	Jersey City	NJ	07305	732-590-3600	590-3665
Horizons Window Fashions Inc 1705 Waukegan Rd *TF:* 800-858-2352 ■ *Web:* horizonshades.com	Waukegan	IL	60085	800-858-2352	
Hosley International Inc 20530 Stony Island Ave	Lynwood	IL	60411	708-758-1000	
Innovative Hearth Products 2701 S Harbor Blvd *TF:* 866-328-4537 ■ *Web:* www.fmiproducts.com	Santa Ana	CA	92704	866-328-4537	
Jackson George N Ltd 1139 Mcdermot Ave *Web:* www.jackson.ca	Winnipeg	MB	R3E0V2	204-786-3821	
Jacobs Trading Co 8090 Excelsior Blvd *Web:* www.jacobstrading.com	hopkins	MN	55343	763-843-2000	843-2101
James G Hardy & Co 24919 148th Rd	Jamaica	NY	11422	212-689-6680	
Jay Franco & Sons Inc 295 Fifth Ave Third Fl *Web:* www.jfranco.com	New York	NY	10016	212-679-3022	685-4864
JJ Haines & Company Inc 6950 Aviation Blvd **Fax Area Code:* 410 ■ *TF:* 800-922-9248 ■ *Web:* www.jjhaines.com	Glen Burnie	MD	21061	800-922-9248	760-4045*
John Matouk Company Inc 11 E 26th St *Web:* www.matouk.com	New York	NY	10010	212-683-9242	
Johnson Window Films Inc 20655 Annalee Ave *Web:* www.johnsonwindowfilms.com	Carson	CA	90746	310-631-6672	
JR United Industries Inc 19401 W Dixie Hwy *Web:* www.jrunited.com	Miami	FL	33180	305-933-7100	
Kanawha Scales & Systems Inc Rock Branch Industrial Pk 303 Jacobson Dr *TF:* 800-955-8321 ■ *Web:* www.kanawhascales.com	Poca	WV	25159	304-755-8321	
Kashmir Fabrics + Furnishings 3191 Commonwealth Dr *Web:* www.kasmirfabrics.com	Dallas	TX	75247	214-631-8040	
Keeco LLC 30736 Wiegman Rd Ste 100 *Web:* www.lkeeco.com	Hayward	CA	94544	510-324-8800	
Kiefer Specialty Flooring Inc 2910 Falling Waters Blvd *TF:* 800-322-5448 ■ *Web:* kieferusa.com/	Lindenhurst	IL	60046	847-245-8450	245-8589
Kitchen Art The Store for Cook 1550 Win Hentschel Blvd *Web:* k-art.com	West Lafayette	IN	47906	765-497-3878	
Klaff's Inc 28 Washington St *Web:* www.klaffs.com	South Norwalk	CT	06854	203-866-1603	
KovalWilliamson 11208 47th Ave W *Web:* www.kwawest.com	Mukilteo	WA	98275	425-347-4249	347-2368
Kozy Heat Fireplace 204 Industrial Park Rd	Lakefield	MN	56150	507-662-6641	
Kraus USA Inc 160 Amsler Ave *Web:* www.krausflooring.com	Shippenville	PA	16254	814-226-9300	
L Bornstein & Co Inc 321 Washington St *TF:* 800-842-1111	Somerville	MA	02143	617-776-3555	
Lacera Rajco International 375 County Ave Ste 653	Secaucus	NJ	07094	201-583-0303	
Lambs & Ivy Inc 2040-2042 E Maple Ave *Web:* lambsivy.com	El Segundo	CA	90245	310-322-3800	
Lanz Cabinet Shop Inc 3025 W Seventh Pl *TF:* 800-788-6332 ■ *Web:* www.lanzcabinets.com	Eugene	OR	97402	541-485-4050	

Company	City	State	ZIP	Phone	Fax
Larson Distributing Co Inc 5925 Broadway *TF:* 800-999-8115 ■ *Web:* www.rugbyabp.com	Denver	CO	80216	303-296-7253	
Legendary Whitetails 820 Enterprise Dr *Web:* www.deergear.com	Slinger	WI	53086	262-297-1661	
Legends of England 3520 Roberts Cut Off Rd *TF:* 800-578-1065 ■ *Web:* www.alchemyofengland.com	Fort Worth	TX	76114	817-236-3141	
Leisure World Pool & Hearth Inc 406 E 16th Ave *Web:* www.leisureworldkc.com	Kansas City	MO	64116	816-221-1731	
Les Meubles Saint Damase Inc 246 rue Principale St-Damase Comt *Web:* www.st-damase.com	St-damase	QC	J0H1J0	450-797-3702	
Lighting Unlimited LLC 4211 Richmond Ave *Web:* www.lulighting.com	Houston	TX	77027	713-626-4025	
Lillian August Designs Inc 32 Knight St *Web:* www.lillianaugust.com	Norwalk	CT	06851	203-847-3314	
Longust Distributing Inc 2432 W Birchwood Ave **Fax Area Code:* 800 ■ *TF:* 800-352-0521 ■ *Web:* www.longust.com	Mesa	AZ	85202	480-820-6244	352-0526*
Lonseal Inc 928 E 238th St *TF:* 800-832-7111 ■ *Web:* www.lonseal.com	Carson	CA	90745	310-830-7111	830-9986
Luigi Bormioli Five Walnut Grove Dr *Web:* www.luigibormioli.com	Horsham	PA	19044	215-672-7111	
Lumisolution Inc 162 Av Du Sacre-Coeur *Web:* lumisolution.com	Quebec	QC	G1N2W2	418-522-5693	
M Block & Sons Inc 5020 W 73rd St *TF:* 800-621-8845 ■ *Web:* www.mblock.com	Bedford Park	IL	60638	708-728-8400	728-0022
M Tm Molded Products 3370 Obco Ct *Web:* www.mtmcase-gard.com	Dayton	OH	45414	937-890-7461	
Macy's Home Store 1120 Ave of the Americas *Web:* www.macysinc.com	New York	NY	10036	646-429-4000	
Manduka LLC 345 S Douglas St *Web:* www.manduka.com	El Segundo	CA	90245	310-426-1495	
Mason Mfg LLC 1645 N Railroad Ave *Web:* www.masonmfg.com	Decatur	IL	62524	217-422-2770	
Maxtex Inc 3620 Francis Cir *TF:* 800-241-1836 ■ *Web:* www.maxtexinc.com	Alpharetta	GA	30004	770-772-6757	
Maytex Mills Inc 261 Fifth Ave 17th Fl *Web:* www.maytex.com	New York	NY	10016	212-684-1191	
MDS N30 W22377 Green Rd **Fax Area Code:* 262 ■ *TF:* 888-523-2611 ■ *Web:* www.wiscdrapery.com	Waukesha	WI	53186	888-523-2611	254-1007*
Modus Furniture International 5410 McConnell Ave *Web:* www.modusfurniture.com	Los Angeles	CA	90066	310-827-2129	
More Space Place Inc 5040 140th Ave N *Web:* www.morespaceplace.com	Clearwater	FL	33760	727-539-1611	
Morrison Terrebonne Lumber Center LLC 605 Barataria Ave *Web:* www.lumbercenter.com	Houma	LA	70360	985-879-1597	
National Credit Adjusters LLC 327 W Fourth Ave *Web:* internationalhomescookware.com	Hutchinson	KS	67501	620-665-7708	
National Glass Ltd 5744 198th St *TF:* 800-663-8168 ■ *Web:* www.natglass.com	Langley	BC	V3A7J2	604-530-2311	530-4662
Naturwood Home Furnishings Inc 2711 Mercantile Dr *Web:* www.naturwood.com	Rancho Cordova	CA	95742	916-638-2424	638-7571
New Buffalo Corp 1220 N Price Rd *Web:* www.buffalotools.com	St Louis	MO	63132	636-532-9888	
Northern States Metals Co 3207 Innovation Pl *Web:* extrusions.com	Youngstown	OH	44509	330-799-1855	
O Dell Corp 13833 Indian Mound Rd *Web:* www.odellcorp.com	Ware Shoals	SC	29692	864-861-2222	
Ohio Valley Flooring Inc 5555 Murray Ave *Web:* www.ovf.com	Cincinnati	OH	45227	513-561-3399	
Omega Moulding Company Ltd 1 Sawgrass Dr *Web:* www.omegamoulding.com	Bellport	NY	11713	800-289-6634	
OneCoast Network LLC 230 Spring St Ste 1800 *TF:* 866-592-5514 ■ *Web:* www.onecoast.com	Atlanta	GA	30303	866-592-5514	469-9517
Peking Handicraft Inc 1388 San Mateo Ave *TF:* 800-872-6888 ■ *Web:* www.pkhc.com	South San Francisco	CA	94080	650-871-3788	871-3781
Phoenix AMD International Inc 41 Butler Ct *Web:* www.phoenixamd.com	Bowmanville	ON	L1C4P8	905-427-7440	
Pinnacle Frames & Accents Inc 12201 Technology Blvd Ste 100 *Web:* nielsenbainbridgegroup.com/pinnacle/home	Austin	TX	78727	512-506-3900	506-3933
Pompanoosuc Mills Corp Route 5 PO Box 238 *Web:* www.pompy.com	East Thetford	VT	05043	800-757-4061	
Primelite Manufacturing Corp 407 S Main St *Web:* primelite-mfg.com	Freeport	NY	11520	516-868-4411	
PRO-MART Industries Inc 17421 Von Karman Ave *Web:* www.deltanovaltd.com	Irvine	CA	92614	949-428-7700	
Quiltcraft Industries Inc 1230 E Ledbetter Dr *Web:* quiltcraft.com	Dallas	TX	75216	214-376-1841	376-1852
Regent Products Corp 8999 Palmer St *Web:* www.regentproducts.com	River Grove	IL	60171	708-583-1000	
Revere Mills Inc 2860 S River Rd Ste 250 *TF:* 800-367-8258 ■ *Web:* www.reveremills.com	Des Plaines	IL	60018	847-759-6800	759-6840
Revman International Inc 1211 Ave of the Americas 70th Fl *Web:* www.revman.com	New York	NY	10036	212-278-0300	
RF Supply Inc 3102 63rd Ave E *Web:* www.rfsupply.com	Bradenton	FL	34203	941-755-3622	
Robert Gordon Industries Ltd 1500 Plz Ave *Web:* www.gordonsinclair.com	New Hyde Park	NY	11040	516-354-8888	
Roberts Container Corp, The 20545 Plummer St *Web:* www.robertscontainer.com	Chatsworth	CA	91311	818-727-1700	
Santec Inc 3501 Challenger St *Web:* www.santecfaucet.com	Torrance	CA	90503	310-542-0063	
Scalehouse, The 974 Rd E	Schuyler	NE	68661	402-352-3686	
Scene Weaver 649 Rosewood Dr Ste B *Web:* www.sceneweaver.com	Columbia	SC	29201	803-252-0662	
Selective Enterprises Inc 10701 Texland Blvd *TF:* 800-334-1207 ■ *Web:* www.unitedsupplyco.com	Charlotte	NC	28273	704-588-3310	
Sewing Source Inc, The PO Box 639 *TF:* 800-849-6945 ■ *Web:* www.thesewingsourceinc.com	Spring Hope	NC	27882	252-478-3900	
Shaheen Carpet Mills Inc 3742 US Hwy 41 NW PO Box 167 *Web:* temp.shaheencarpet.com	Resaca	GA	30735	706-629-9544	625-5341
Shavel Assoc 13 Roszel Rd Ste A101 *Web:* www.shavel.com	Princeton	NJ	08540	609-452-1800	
Shelving Inc 32 S Squirrel Rd *TF:* 800-637-9508 ■ *Web:* www.shelving.com	Auburn Hills	MI	48326	248-852-8600	
Sobel Westex Inc 2670 Western Ave **Fax Area Code:* 702 ■ *TF:* 888-887-6235 ■ *Web:* www.sobelwestex.com	Las Vegas	NV	89109	888-887-6235	735-4957*
SOG Specialty Knives & Tools LLC 6521 212th St SW *TF:* 888-405-6433 ■ *Web:* www.sogknives.com	Lynnwood	WA	98036	425-771-6230	
Southern Moulding & Supply Co 7040 Battle Dr Nw *Web:* www.southernmoulding.com	Kennesaw	GA	30152	770-422-3949	
Southern Tile Distributors Inc 4590 Village Ave *TF:* 800-333-8970 ■ *Web:* www.southerntile.com	Norfolk	VA	23502	757-855-8041	
Springs Window Fashions LP 7549 Graber Rd *TF:* 877-792-0002 ■ *Web:* www.springswindowfashions.com	Middleton	WI	53562	608-836-1011	
Star Extruded Shapes Inc 7055 Herbert Rd *Web:* www.starext.com	Canfield	OH	44406	330-533-9863	
Star Tech Glass Inc 1835 N Major Ave *Web:* startechglass.com	Chicago	IL	60639	773-745-0800	
Stephen Miller Gallery 800 Santa Cruz Ave *Web:* www.stephenmillergallery.com	Menlo Park	CA	94025	650-327-5040	
Sterling Cut Glass Company Inc 3233 Mineola Pk *TF:* 800-368-1158 ■ *Web:* www.sterlingcutglass.com	Erlanger	KY	41018	859-283-2333	
Sunshine Drapery & Interior Fashions LLC WorkRm 11800 Adie Rd *Web:* www.sunshinedrapery.com	Maryland Heights	MO	63043	314-569-2980	
Susquehanna Glass 731 Ave H *Web:* www.susquehannaglass.com	Columbia	PA	17512	717-684-2155	
SZCO Supplies Inc 2713 Merchant Dr *Web:* szco.com	Baltimore	MD	21230	410-368-8300	
T & A Supply Company Inc 6821 S 216th St Bldg A PO Box 927 **Fax Area Code:* 206 ■ *TF:* 800-562-2857 ■ *Web:* www.tasupply.com	Kent	WA	98032	253-872-3682	282-3796*
T & L Distributing LP 7350 Langfield Rd *Web:* www.tldistributing.com	Houston	TX	77092	713-461-7802	932-6790
Tailored Living LLC 1927 N Glassell St *TF:* 866-675-8819 ■ *Web:* www.tailoredliving.com	Orange	CA	92865	866-675-8819	
Thomas West Inc 470 Mercury Dr *Web:* www.thomaswest.com	Sunnyvale	CA	94085	408-481-9200	
Thompson Olde Inc 3250 Camino Del Sol *TF:* 800-827-1565 ■ *Web:* www.oldethompson.com	Oxnard	CA	93030	805-983-0388	983-1849
Three Hands Corp 13259 Ralston Ave *TF:* 800-443-5443 ■ *Web:* www.threehands.com	Sylmar	CA	91342	818-833-1200	833-1212
Turf Store.com 237 Boling Industrial Way Se *Web:* www.turfstore.com	Calhoun	GA	30701	706-629-1675	
Twin-Star International Inc 1690 S Congress Ave Ste 210 *Web:* www.twinstarhome.com	Delray Beach	FL	33445	561-330-3201	
Vertex China 131 Brea Canyon Rd *Web:* www.vertexchina.com	Walnut	CA	91789	909-594-4800	
Virginia Tile Co 28320 Plymouth Rd *TF:* 877-356-7461 ■ *Web:* www.virginiatile.com	Livonia	MI	48150	734-762-2400	
Wanke Cascade Co 6330 N Cutter Cir *TF:* 800-365-5053 ■ *Web:* www.wanke.com	Portland	OR	97217	503-289-8609	285-5640
Weightech 1649 Country Elite Dr *TF:* 800-457-3720 ■ *Web:* www.weightechinc.com	Waldron	AR	72958	479-637-4182	
WMF Americas Inc 3512 Faith Church Rd *TF:* 800-966-3009 ■ *Web:* wmfamericas.com/shop/	Indian Trail	NC	28079	704-882-3898	893-2198
WoodCrafters Home Products LLC 3700 Camino de Verdad *Web:* www.woodcrafters-tx.com	Weslaco	TX	78596	956-647-8300	
Woodland Blinds Inc 6120 Griggs Rd *Web:* www.woodlandblinds.com	Houston	TX	77023	713-640-2885	
WOWindows LLC PO Box 581 *Web:* www.wowindows.com	Cranford	NJ	07016	908-272-1011	
Yves Delorme Inc 1725 Broadway St *Web:* www.yvesdelorme.com	Charlottesville	VA	22902	434-979-3911	
Zodax Inc 14040 Arminta St *Web:* www.zodax.com	Panorama City	CA	91402	818-785-5626	

365 HOME FURNISHINGS STORES

SEE ALSO Department Stores p. 2197; Furniture Stores p. 2348

Company	City	State	ZIP	Phone	Fax
A B C Awning & Venetian Blind Corp 858 Saint Andrews Blvd *Web:* www.abcfence.net	Charleston	SC	29407	843-766-6311	
AAA Glass & Mirror Co 3300 McCart *Web:* www.aaa-glass.com	Fort Worth	TX	76110	817-924-4444	
ABL Lights Inc 660 Golf Club Blvd *Web:* abllights.com	Mosinee	WI	54455	715-693-1530	
Able Electric Service 2626 Electronic Ln *Web:* www.ableelectricservice.com	Dallas	TX	75220	214-350-5721	
AC Products Co 4299 S Apple Creek Rd *Web:* www.acproducts.com	Apple Creek	OH	44606	330-698-1105	

Company	City	State	Zip	Phone	Fax
Adco Container Co 9959 Canoga Ave *Web:* www.adcocontainer.com	Chatsworth	CA	91311	818-998-2565	
Alconex Specialty Products Inc 4204 W Ferguson Rd *Web:* www.alconex.com	Fort Wayne	IN	46809	260-744-3446	
Allen & Allen Company Inc 202 Culebra Ave *Web:* www.lumberhardware.com	San Antonio	TX	78201	210-733-9191	
Alliance Scale Inc 1020 Turnpike St Ste 10 *Web:* www.alliancescale.com	Canton	MA	02021	781-828-8507	
Altmeyer Home Stores Inc 6515 Rt 22 *TF:* 800-394-6628 ■ *Web:* www.bedbathhome.com	Delmont	PA	15626	724-468-3434	468-3233
Amcon Block & Precast Inc 2211 Hwy 10 S *Web:* www.amconblock.com	Saint Cloud	MN	56304	320-251-6030	
American Made Cutlery 905 Industrial Rd *Web:* americanmadecutlery.com	Waverly	IA	50677	319-352-2080	
American Scale Service & Supply Co 8590 W 14th Ave *Web:* www.ameriscale.com	Lakewood	CO	80215	303-232-5656	
Ann Clark Ltd 112 Quality Ln *Web:* www.annclark.com	Rutland	VT	05701	802-773-7886	
Anna's Linens Inc 3550 Hyland Ave *TF:* 866-266-2728 ■ *Web:* www.annaslinens.com	Costa Mesa	CA	92626	714-850-0504	
Art Material Services Inc 625 Joyce Kilmer Ave *Web:* www.artmaterialsservice.com	New Brunswick	NJ	08901	732-545-8888	
Associated Energy Systems 8621 S 180th St *Web:* www.aes4home.com	Kent	WA	98032	425-251-9190	
Bath & Beyond, The 77 Connecticut St *Web:* www.bathandbeyond.com	San Francisco	CA	94107	415-552-5001	
Bauerware LLC 3886 17th St *Web:* bauerware.com	San Francisco	CA	94114	415-864-3886	
Beacon Products LLC 2041 58th Ave Cir E *TF:* 800-345-4928 ■ *Web:* www.beaconproducts.com	Bradenton	FL	34203	800-345-4928	
Bed Bath & Beyond Inc 650 Liberty Ave *NASDAQ: BBBY* ■ *TF:* 800-462-3966 ■ *Web:* www.bedbathandbeyond.com	Union	NJ	07083	908-688-0888	688-6483
Belden Brick & Supply Company Inc 620 Leonard St Nw *Web:* www.beldenbrickandsupply.com	Grand Rapids	MI	49504	616-459-8367	
Bergin Glass Impressions Inc 2511 Napa Vly Corporate Dr Ste 111 *Web:* www.berginglass.com	Napa	CA	94558	707-224-0111	
Besco Electric Supply Co 711 S 14th St **Fax Area Code: 352* ■ *TF:* 800-541-6618 ■ *Web:* www.bescoelectric.com	Leesburg	FL	34748	800-541-6618	365-0554*
Bilotta Home Center Inc 564 Mamaroneck Ave *Web:* bilotta.com	Mamaroneck	NY	10543	914-381-7734	
Bishop Hearth & Home Inc 1948 Vanderhorn Dr *Web:* www.bishophome.com	Memphis	TN	38134	901-384-0070	
Bitterman Scales LLC 413 Radcliff Rd *Web:* www.bittermanscales.com	Willow Street	PA	17584	717-464-3009	
Blade HQ 400 South 1000 East Ste E *Web:* www.bladehq.com	Lehi	UT	84043	801-768-0232	
Blanco America Inc 110 Mount Holly By-Pass *TF:* 800-451-5782 ■ *Web:* www.blancoamerica.com	Lumberton	NJ	08048	800-451-5782	
Bridge Kitchenware Inc 711 Third Ave *Web:* www.bridgekitchenware.com	New York	NY	10017	212-688-4220	
Bristol Aluminum 5514 Bristol Emilie Rd *Web:* www.bristolaluminum.com	Levittown	PA	19057	215-946-3160	
Burlington Coat Factory 1830 Rt 130 N *TF:* 855-355-2875 ■ *Web:* burlingtoncoatfactory.com	Burlington	NJ	08016	609-387-7800	
Byers Choice Ltd 4355 County Line Rd *Web:* www.buyerschoiceltd.com	Chalfont	PA	18914	215-822-6700	
Cabinet Outlet Inc 1168 N 50th Pl *Web:* milwaukeecabinetry.com	Milwaukee	WI	53208	414-771-1960	771-3638
Cadco Ltd 145 Colebrook River Rd *Web:* www.cadco-ltd.com	Winsted	CT	06098	860-738-2500	
Calvert Retail LP 100 W Rockland Rd Ste A PO Box 302 *Web:* www.calvertretail.com	Montchanin	DE	19710	302-622-8811	622-8602
Candela Controls Inc 751 Business Park Blvd Ste 101 *Web:* www.candelacontrols.com	Winter Garden	FL	34787	407-654-2420	
Cape & Island Kitchens Inc 99 State Rd *Web:* capekitchens.com	Sagamore Beach	MA	02562	508-888-4762	
Cardinal Scale Manufacturing Company Inc 203 E Daugherty St PO Box 151 *Web:* www.cardinalscale.com	Webb City	MO	64870	417-673-4631	
Carolina Brush Manufacturing Company Inc 3093 Northwest Blvd *Web:* www.carolinabrush.com	Gastonia	NC	28052	704-867-0286	
Carolina Supplyhouse Inc 218 Second Loop Rd *Web:* www.thesupplyhouse.com	Florence	SC	29504	843-662-0702	
Central Boiler Inc 20502 160th St *Web:* www.centralboiler.com	Greenbush	MN	56726	218-782-2575	
Challenger Lighting Company Inc 2475 Alft Ln *Web:* challengerlighting.com	Elgin	IL	60124	847-717-4700	
Chef's Catalog 5070 Centennial Blvd *TF Cust Svc:* 800-541-6390 ■ *Web:* www.chefscatalog.com	Colorado Springs	CO	80919	800-541-6390	967-2433
CHF Home Furnishings 104 S Orchard St *Web:* www.shopchf.com	Boise	ID	83705	208-343-7769	
Chintz & Co 1720 Store St *Web:* www.chintz.com	Victoria	BC	V8W1V5	250-381-2404	
Clarion Bathware Inc 44 Amsler Ave *Web:* www.clarionbathware.com	Shippenville	PA	16254	814-226-5374	
Classic Containers Inc 1700 S Hellman Ave *Web:* www.classiccontainers.com	Ontario	CA	91761	909-930-3610	
Clearlight Glass & Mirror Inc 1318 Shields Rd *Web:* www.clearlightglass.com	Kernersville	NC	27284	336-993-7300	
CMC America Corp 210 S Center St *Web:* cmc-america.com	Joliet	IL	60436	815-726-4336	
COAST Products Inc 8033 NE Holman St *Web:* www.coastportland.com	Portland	OR	97218	503-234-4545	
Container Store, The 500 Freeport Pkwy *TF:* 800-733-3532 ■ *Web:* www.containerstore.com	Coppell	TX	75019	972-538-6000	
Conway Glass Tinting Plus 701 Sixth St *Web:* conwayglasstinting.net	Conway	AR	72032	501-450-7587	
Cooking.com 2850 Ocean Pk Blvd Ste 310 *TF:* 800-663-8810 ■ *Web:* www.cooking.com	Santa Monica	CA	90405	310-450-3270	
Cost Plus Inc 200 Fourth St *NASDAQ: CPWM* ■ *TF:* 877-967-5362 ■ *Web:* www.worldmarket.com	Oakland	CA	94607	510-893-7300	893-3681
Crystal Blanc 225 Gap Way *Web:* www.jcharles.com	Erlanger	KY	41018	859-283-0814	
Cs Illumination Inc 2865 Scott St Ste 101105 *Web:* csillumination.com	Vista	CA	92081	760-477-1244	
Cutlery & More LLC 135 Prairie Lk Rd *TF:* 800-650-9866 ■ *Web:* www.cutleryandmore.com	East Dundee	IL	60118	800-650-9866	
Dacra Glass 3333 N Commerce Dr *Web:* www.dacraglass.com	Muncie	IN	47303	765-286-3855	
Dale Tiffany Inc 14765 Firestone Blvd *Web:* www.daletiffany.com	La Mirada	CA	90638	714-739-2700	
Dcxcavation Inc 10641 Prospect Ave *Web:* dcxcavation.com	Santee	CA	92071	619-312-1550	
DD Traders Inc Dba Demdaco 5000 W 134th St	Leawood	KS	66209	913-402-6800	
Delfin Design & Manufacturing Inc 23301 Antonio Pkwy **Fax Area Code: 800* ■ *Web:* www.delfinfs.com	Rancho Santa Margarita	CA	92688	949-888-4644	354-7919*
Design Specialties Inc 11100 W Heather Ave *Web:* www.glassfireplacedoors.com	Milwaukee	WI	53224	414-371-1200	
Design Within Reach Inc 711 Canal St 3rd fl 3rd Fl *OTC: DWRI* ■ *TF:* 800-944-2233 ■ *Web:* www.dwr.com	Stamford	CT	06902	203-614-0600	614-0845
DirectBuy Inc 8450 Broadway *TF:* 800-320-3462 ■ *Web:* www.directbuy.com	Merrillville	IN	46410	219-736-1100	755-6279
Eagle Microsystems Inc 366 Cir of Progress Dr *Web:* www.eaglemicrosystems.com	Pottstown	PA	19464	610-323-2250	
Edward Joy Electric 905 Canal St *Web:* www.edwardjoyelectric.com	Syracuse	NY	13210	315-474-3361	479-8604
Elite Lighting Company Inc 412 S Cypress St *Web:* www.elitelighting.com	Mullins	SC	29574	843-464-7681	
Eurokera North America Inc 140 Southchase Blvd *Web:* www.eurokera.com	Fountain Inn	SC	29644	864-963-8082	
Euromarket Designs Inc 1250 Techny Rd **Fax Area Code: 630* ■ *Web:* www.crateandbarrel.com	Northbrook	IL	60062	847-272-2888	527-1448*
F M Brush Manufacturing Co 7002 72nd Pl *Web:* www.fmbrush.com	Glendale	NY	11385	718-821-5939	
Fashion Glass & Mirrors 585 S Interstate 35 E *Web:* www.fashionglass.com	Desoto	TX	75115	972-223-8936	
Fireplace & Bar-B-Q Center Inc 10470 Metcalf Ave *Web:* fireplacecenterkc.com	Overland Park	KS	66212	913-383-2286	
Fleetwood Aluminum Products Inc 395 Smitty Way *Web:* www.fleetwoodusa.com	Corona	CA	92879	951-279-1070	
Force Flow Inc 2430 Stanwell Dr *TF:* 800-893-6723 ■ *Web:* www.forceflow.com	Concord	CA	94520	800-893-6723	
Foreston Trends Inc 1483 W Via Plata St *Web:* www.forestontrends.com	Long Beach	CA	90810	310-952-8500	
Gas Turbine Controls Corp 466 Saw Mill River Rd *Web:* www.gasturbinecontrols.com	Ardsley	NY	10502	914-693-0830	
GEARYS Beverly Hills 351 N Beverly Dr *TF:* 800-793-6670 ■ *Web:* www.gearys.com	Beverly Hills	CA	90210	310-273-4741	859-8950
Ginkgo International 8102 Lemont Rd Ste 1100 *Web:* www.ginkgoint.com	Woodridge	IL	60517	630-910-5244	
Glassybaby LLC 3406 E Union St *Web:* www.glassybaby.com	Seattle	WA	98122	206-518-9071	
Gracious Home 1220 Third Ave *TF:* 800-338-7809 ■ *Web:* www.gracioushome.com	New York	NY	10021	212-517-6300	
Grand Rapids Scale Company Inc 4215 Stafford Ave Sw *Web:* www.grmetrology.com	Grand Rapids	MI	49548	616-538-7080	
Grand View Glass & Metal Inc 2134 S Green Privado *Web:* www.grandviewglass.com	Ontario	CA	91761	909-923-9544	
Granite City Electric Supply Co 19 Quincy Ave *TF:* 800-850-9400 ■ *Web:* www.granitecityelectric.com	Quincy	MA	02169	617-472-6500	472-8661
Gump's 135 Post St *TF:* 800-766-7628 ■ *Web:* www.gumps.com	San Francisco	CA	94108	415-982-1616	984-9374
Habitat Housewares 3801 Old Seward Hwy Ste 7 *Web:* www.habitathousewares.com	Anchorage	AK	99503	907-561-1856	563-5863
Halverson Co 235 Paxton Ave *Web:* www.halversoncompany.com	Salt Lake City	UT	84101	801-467-9423	
Hammacher Schlemmer & Co 9307 N Milwaukee Ave **Fax Area Code: 847* ■ *TF:* 800-321-1484 ■ *Web:* www.hammacher.com	Niles	IL	60714	800-321-1484	581-8616*
Home Accents Mart 5521 McFarland Blvd	Northport	AL	35476	205-339-6550	
HomeGoods Inc 770 Cochituate Rd *Web:* www.homegoods.com	Framingham	MA	01701	508-390-1000	
HomePortfolio Inc 288 Walnut St Ste 300 *Web:* www.homeportfolio.com	Newton	MA	02460	617-965-0565	965-4082
Hussong Manufacturing Company Inc 204 Industrial Park Rd *Web:* www.kozyheat.com	Lakefield	MN	56150	507-662-6641	
Hy Cite Corp 333 Holtzman Rd *Web:* www.hycite.com	Madison	WI	53713	608-273-3373	
Interface Logic Systems Inc 3311 E Livingston Ave *Web:* www.interfacelogic.com	Columbus	OH	43227	614-236-8388	

Phone *Fax*

Iron-a-way Inc 220 W Jackson St .... Morton IL 61550 309-266-7232
Web: www.ironaway.com

J & D Interiors Inc 8300 Briarwood St Ste A .... Anchorage AK 99518 907-349-9685
Web: jdinteriors.com

Jackalope Pottery 2820 Cerrillos Rd .... Santa Fe NM 87507 505-471-8539
Web: www.jackalope.com

Jetta Corp 425 Centennial Blvd .... Edmond OK 73013 405-340-6661
Web: www.jettaproducts.com

Kino Flo Inc 2840 N Hollywood Way .... Burbank CA 91505 818-767-6528
Web: www.kinoflo.com

Kirkland's Inc 431 Smith Ln .... Jackson TN 38301 877-541-4855
NASDAQ: KIRK ■ *TF:* 877-541-4855 ■ *Web:* www.kirklands.com

Kitchen & Bath Galleries
914 S Kerr Ave Ste C .... Wilmington NC 28403 910-332-4656
Web: www.kandbgalleries.com

Kitchen & Bath Studios Inc
7001 Wisconsin Ave .... Chevy Chase MD 20815 301-657-1636
Web: kitchenbathstudios.com

Kitchen 24 1608 N Cahuenga Blvd .... Los Angeles CA 90028 323-465-2424
Web: www.kitchen24.info

Kitchen Collection Inc 71 E Water St .... Chillicothe OH 45601 740-773-9150 774-0590
TF General: 888-548-2651 ■ *Web:* www.kitchencollection.com

Kitchen Craft International
4129 United Ave .... Mount Dora FL 32757 352-483-7600
Web: www.cookforlife.com

Kitchen Fantasy 27576 Ynez Rd Ste H9 .... Temecula CA 92591 951-693-4264 693-4265
Web: www.kitchenfantasy.com

Kitchen Supply Co 7540 W Roosevelt Rd .... Forest Park IL 60130 708-383-5990
Web: www.kitchensupply.com

Kiva Kitchen & Bath Holdings LLC
6225 Burnet Rd .... Austin TX 78757 512-454-4526
Web: www.kivahome.com

Kuhn Rikon Corp 46 Digital Dr Ste 5 .... Novato CA 94949 415-883-1101
Web: ch.kuhnrikon.com

Kwik-Covers LLC 811 Ridge Rd .... Webster NY 14580 585-787-9620
Web: kwikcovers.com

Lamps Plus Inc 20250 Plummer St .... Chatsworth CA 91311 818-886-5267
Web: lampsplus.com

LB Sales Assoc LLC 50 Plant St .... New London CT 06320 860-437-3953

LEDdynamics Inc 44 Hull St .... Randolph VT 05060 802-728-4533
Web: www.leddynamics.com

Leed - Himmel Industries Inc
75 Leeder Hill Dr .... Hamden CT 06517 203-287-6662
Web: www.leed-himmel.com

Lematic Inc 2410 W Main St .... Jackson MI 49203 517-787-3301
Web: www.lematic.com

Light Lines Inc 3337 Rauch St .... Houston TX 77029 713-673-7502
Web: lightlines.net

Lighting By Gregory LLC 158 Bowery .... New York NY 10012 212-226-4156
Web: www.lightingbygregory.com

Lighting Zone Inc 17354 Hawthorne Blvd .... Torrance CA 90504 310-921-9495
Web: www.dreamonlighting.com

Lindamar Industries Inc
1603 Commerce Way .... Paso Robles CA 93446 805-237-1910
Web: www.lindamarindustries.com

Linens 'n Things Inc
8674 Pk Meadows Ctr Dr .... Lone Tree CO 80124 303-792-5790
Web: lone-tree-co.opendi.us

Linon Home Dcor Products Inc 22 Jericho Tpke .... Mineola NY 11501 516-699-1000 699-1001
Web: www.linon.com

Litelab Corp 251 Elm St .... Buffalo NY 14203 716-856-4491
Web: www.litelab.com

Los Angeles Lighting Manufacturing Company Inc
10141 Olney St .... El Monte CA 91731 626-454-8300
Web: www.lalighting.com

Luxury Bath Liners Inc
1958 Brandon Ct .... Glendale Heights IL 60139 630-295-9084
Web: www.luxurybath.com

Lynx Grills Inc 5895 Rickenbacker Rd .... Commerce CA 90040 323-838-1770
Web: www.lynxgrills.com

Mason Structural Steel Inc
7500 Northfield Rd .... Walton Hills OH 44146 440-439-1040
TF: 800-686-1223 ■ *Web:* www.masonsteel.com

Mattress Firm Inc 5815 Gulf Fwy .... Houston TX 77023 713-923-1090 923-1096
TF: 800-821-6621 ■ *Web:* www.mattressfirm.com

Measurement Systems International Inc
14240 Interurban Ave S Ste 200 .... Seattle WA 98168 206-433-0199
Web: www.msiscales.com

Michael C Fina Inc 545 Fifth Ave .... New York NY 10022 212-557-2500
TF: 800-289-3462 ■ *Web:* www.michaelcfina.com

Moline Machinery LLC 114 S Central Ave .... Duluth MN 55807 218-624-5734
Web: www.moline.com

Moxie Pictures 18 E 16th St Fl 4 .... New York NY 10003 212-807-6901
Web: www.moxiepictures.com

Nautical Furnishings Inc
60 NW 60th St .... Fort Lauderdale FL 33309 954-771-1100
Web: www.nauticalfurnishings.com

Nevada Contract Carpet 6840 W Patrick Ln .... Las Vegas NV 89118 702-362-3033 362-5455
Web: nevadacontractcarpet.abbeycarpet.com

New Brunswick International Inc
76 Veronica Ave .... Somerset NJ 08873 732-828-3633
Web: www.nbidigi.net

Notoco Industries LLC 10380 Airline Hwy .... Baton Rouge LA 70816 225-292-1303
Web: www.notocoind.com

Nova Lighting Inc 6323 Maywood Ave .... Huntington Park CA 90255 323-277-6266
Web: www.novalamps.com

OCS Checkweighers Inc 2350 Hewatt Rd .... Snellville GA 30039 678-344-8030
Web: www.ocs-cw.com

Ortega Kitchen and Bath 2834 Clovis Rd .... Lubbock TX 79415 806-763-5777
Web: www.ortegakitchenandbath.com

Panaram International 126 Greylock Ave .... Belleville NJ 07109 973-751-1100
Web: www.usatowl.com

Perdue Inc Five W Forsyth St # 100 .... Jacksonville FL 32202 904-737-5858
Web: www.perdueoffice.com

Pier 1 Imports Inc 100 Pier 1 Pl .... Fort Worth TX 76102 817-252-8000 252-8174
NYSE: PIR ■ *TF:* 800-245-4595 ■ *Web:* www.pier1.com

Point Lighting Corp 61 W Dudley Town Rd .... Bloomfield CT 06002 860-243-0600
Web: www.pointlighting.com

Precision Solutions Inc 2525 Tollgate Rd .... Quakertown PA 18951 215-536-4400
Web: www.precisionsolutionsinc.com

Redi Floors Inc 1791 Williams Dr .... Marietta GA 30066 770-590-7334
Web: www.redi-floors.com

Restoration Hardware Inc
2900 N MacArthur Dr Ste 100 .... Tracy CA 95376 800-910-9836
TF: 800-910-9836 ■ *Web:* www.restorationhardware.com

Royal Oak Kitchens & Baths
32790 Woodward Ave .... Royal Oak MI 48073 248-549-2944
Web: www.royaloakkitchen.com

Seattle Lighting Fixture Co
222 Second Ave Ext S .... Seattle WA 98104 206-622-4736 221-1962*
**Fax Area Code: 503* ■ *TF Cust Svc:* 800-689-1000 ■ *Web:* www.seattlelighting.com

Sentran LLC 4355 E Lowell St Ste F .... Ontario CA 91761 909-605-1544
Web: www.sentranllc.com

Shiffler Equipment Sales Inc 745 S St .... Chardon OH 44024 440-285-9175
Web: www.chairglides.com

Smoky Mountain Knife Works Inc
2320 Winfield Dunn Pkwy PO Box 4430 .... Sevierville TN 37864 865-453-5871
Web: www.eknifeworks.com

Soft Tex Manufacturing Co 100 N Mohawk St .... Cohoes NY 12047 518-235-3645
Web: www.bedpillows.com

Southern Wholesale Flooring Company Inc
955B Cobb Pl Blvd PO Box 440069 .... Kennesaw GA 30144 770-514-7110 514-7310
TF: 800-282-7590 ■ *Web:* www.swfloor.com

Springboard Biodiesel LLC 2282 Ivy St .... Chico CA 95928 530-894-1793
Web: www.springboardbiodiesel.com

Sultan & Sons 6601 Lyons Rd Ste E8 .... Coconut Creek FL 33073 954-782-6600
Web: www.sultanandsons.com

Sunteca Systems Inc Two Ave A .... Leetsdale PA 15056 412-749-5200
Web: www.suntecausa.com

Supply New England Inc 123 East St .... Attleboro MA 02703 508-222-5555
Web: www.supplynewengland.com

Sur La Table 5701 Sixth Ave S Ste 486 .... Seattle WA 98108 800-243-0852
TF: 800-243-0852 ■ *Web:* www.surlatable.com

Surrey Satellite Technology US LLC
8310 S Valley Hwy Third Fl .... Englewood CO 80112 303-790-0653
Web: www.sst-us.com

Switch Lighting & Design LLC 1207 Vine St .... Cincinnati OH 45202 513-721-8100
Web: www.switchcollection.com

System Scale Corp 4393 W 96th St .... Indianapolis IN 46268 317-876-9335
Web: www.system-scale.com

Timberlane Inc 150 Domorah Dr .... Montgomeryville PA 18936 215-616-0600
Web: www.timberlane.com

TJX Cos Inc 770 Cochituate Rd .... Framingham MA 01701 508-390-1000 390-2091
NYSE: TJX ■ *TF:* 800-926-6299 ■ *Web:* www.tjx.com

Topaz Lighting Corp 925 Waverly Ave .... Holtsville NY 11742 631-758-5507
Web: www.topaz-usa.com

Totalcomp Scales & Components
13-01 Pollitt Dr Ste 2 .... Fair Lawn NJ 07410 201-797-2718
Web: www.totalcomp.com

Transducer Techniques Inc 42480 Rio Nedo .... Temecula CA 92590 951-719-3965
Web: www.transducertechniques.com

Tri State Distributors Inc 550 E First Ave .... Spokane WA 99202 509-455-8300
Web: www.tristatedistributors.com

Triple Dot Corp 3302 S Susan St .... Santa Ana CA 92704 714-241-0888
Web: www.triple-dot.com

Vaxcel International Co 121 E N Ave .... Carol Stream IL 60188 630-260-0067
Web: www.vaxcelusa.com

Villeroy & Boch Tableware Ltd
Five Vaughn Dr .... Princeton NJ 08540 800-536-2284
TF: 800-536-2284 ■ *Web:* www.villeroy-boch.com

Visionaire Lighting LLC
19645 Rancho Way .... Rancho Dominguez CA 90220 310-512-6480
Web: www.visionairelighting.com

Waterford Wedgwood USA Inc 1330 Campus Pkwy .... Wall NJ 07753 732-938-5800
Web: wedgwood.com/

Wells Rug Service Inc 49 Bank St .... Morristown NJ 07960 973-539-3800
Web: www.wellsrug.com/

Williams-Sonoma Inc 3250 Van Ness Ave .... San Francisco CA 94109 415-421-7900 616-8359
NYSE: WSM ■ *TF:* 800-838-2589 ■ *Web:* www.williams-sonomainc.com

Williamsburg Pottery 6692 Richmond Rd .... Williamsburg VA 23188 757-564-3326
Web: www.williamsburgpottery.com

Winsome Trading Inc
16111 Woodinville Redmo .... Woodinville WA 98072 425-483-8888 483-4141
Web: www.winsomewood.com

World Class Lighting 14350 60th St N .... Clearwater FL 33760 727-524-7661
Web: www.worldclasslighting.com

Z Gallerie Inc 1855 W 139th St .... Gardena CA 90249 310-630-1200 630-1289
TF: 800-358-8288 ■ *Web:* www.zgallerie.com

Zephyr Aluminum LLC
625 Second St PO Box 4906 .... Lancaster PA 17603 717-397-3618
Web: www.zephyraluminum.com

Zimman'S Inc 80 Market St .... Lynn MA 01901 781-598-9432
Web: zimmans.com

366 HOME HEALTH SERVICES

SEE ALSO Hospices p. 2479

Phone *Fax*

A & A Home Health Services
1240 Blalock Rd Ste 210 .... Houston TX 77055 713-783-8803

A Plus Family Care 5835 Callaghan Rd .... San Antonio TX 78228 210-342-2819
Web: aplusfamilycare.net

Name / Address	City	State	ZIP	Phone	Fax
A-1 Action Nursing Care Inc 3508 Greencastle Rd. *Web:* a1actionnursingcare.com	Burtonsville	MD	20866	301-890-7575	
Abarca Health LLC 650 ave munoz rivera *Web:* www.abarcahealth.com	San juan	PR	00918	787-523-1212	
Abbi Home Care Inc 6453 SW Blvd *Web:* abbihomecare.com	Benbrook	TX	76132	817-377-0889	377-0890
AdCare Health Systems Inc 1145 Hembree RD. *NYSE: ADK* ■ *Web:* www.adcarehealth.com	Roswell	GA	30076	678-869-5116	
Advantage Home Health Care Inc 4008 N Wheeling Ave *Web:* www.advantagehhc.com	Muncie	IN	47304	765-284-1211	
Affinity Home Health Care Inc 121 Sandwich St. *Web:* affinityhomehealthcare.com	Plymouth	MA	02360	508-732-8988	
Agape Primary Care 3030 Towne Centre Dr *Web:* www.agapehomehealth.com	Mesquite	TX	75150	972-681-8420	
Alacare Home Health & Hospice 2400 John Hawkins Pkwy *TF:* 800-852-4724 ■ *Web:* www.alacare.com	Birmingham	AL	35244	205-981-8000	981-8743
Alaska Native Tribal Health Consortium Inc 4000 Ambassador Dr *Web:* www.anthctoday.org	Anchorage	AK	99508	907-729-1900	
All About Kids Home Health 2413 Haine Dr. *Web:* allaboutkidshomehealth.com	Harlingen	TX	78550	956-412-3337	
Allcare Medical Inc 125 Newtown Rd Ste 300 *TF:* 800-244-4660 ■ *Web:* allcaremedical.net	Plainview	NY	11803	800-244-4660	
Allied Healthcare International Inc 245 Pk AVe 39th Fl *Web:* www.alliedhealthcare.com	New York	NY	10167	212-750-0064	750-7221
Almost Family Inc 9510 Ormsby Stn Rd Ste 300 *NASDAQ: AFAM* ■ *TF:* 800-828-9769 ■ *Web:* www.almostfamily.com	Louisville	KY	40223	502-891-1000	891-8067
Alphavax Inc Two Triangle Dr. *Web:* www.alphavax.com	Research Triangle Park	NC	27709	919-595-0400	
Altamed Health Services Corp 500 Citadel Dr Ste 490 *TF:* 877-462-2582 ■ *Web:* www.altamed.org	Los Angeles	CA	90040	323-725-8751	889-7399
Alterna-Care 319 E Madison St # 3n. *Web:* alterna-care.com	Springfield	IL	62701	217-525-3733	
Altura Homecare & Rehab 4308 Carlisle Blvd NE Ste 202 *Web:* www.alturahomecare.com	Albuquerque	NM	87107	505-881-0425	
Amedisys Inc 5959 S Sherwood Forest Blvd Ste 300 *NASDAQ: AMED* ■ *TF:* 800-464-0020 ■ *Web:* www.amedisys.com	Baton Rouge	LA	70816	225-292-2031	292-8163
American HomePatient Inc 5200 Maryland Way Ste 400 *TF:* 800-890-7271 ■ *Web:* www.ahom.com	Brentwood	TN	37027	615-221-8884	373-9932
Americare Certified Special Services Inc 5923 Strickland Ave *Web:* www.americareny.com	Brooklyn	NY	11234	718-535-3100	
AmeriCare Medical Inc 1938 Woodslee Dr *Web:* www.americaremedical.com	Troy	MI	48083	248-280-2020	
AMERIS Health Systems LLC 1114 17th Ave S Ste 205 *Web:* www.amerishealth.com	Nashville	TN	37212	615-327-4440	
Amerita Inc 20 Fairbanks Ste 173 *Web:* www.ameritaiv.com	Irvine	CA	92618	949-273-6528	
Androscoggin Home Health Services Inc PO Box 819 *TF:* 800-482-7412 ■ *Web:* www.ahch.org	Lewiston	ME	04243	207-777-7740	777-7748
Angel Healthcare 5828 Balcones Dr Ste 105 *Web:* angelhealthcare.net	Austin	TX	78731	512-453-6449	
Angel Medical Systems Inc 1163 Shrewsbury Ave Ste E *Web:* www.angel-med.com	Shrewsbury	NJ	07702	732-542-5551	
Anthelio Healthcare Solutions Inc 5400 LBJ Fwy Ste 200 *Web:* www.antheliohealth.com	Dallas	TX	75240	214-257-7000	257-7042
Anthem Heatlh Services Inc 57 Karner Rd *Web:* anthemhs.com	Albany	NY	12205	518-862-1247	
Any-Time Home Care Inc 127 S Broadway *Web:* anytimehomecare.com	Nyack	NY	10960	845-353-8280	
Apria Healthcare Group Inc 26220 Enterprise Ct *TF:* 800-277-4288 ■ *Web:* www.apria.com	Lake Forest	CA	92630	949-639-2000	
Arizona Bridge To Independent Living 5025 E Washington St Ste 200 *Web:* abil.org	Phoenix	AZ	85034	602-256-2245	
ARK Diagnostics Inc 48089 Fremont Blvd *TF:* 877-869-2320 ■ *Web:* www.ark-tdm.com	Fremont	CA	94538	510-270-6270	270-6298
Aroostook Home Health Services 658 Main St Ste 2 *TF:* 877-688-9977 ■ *Web:* aroostookhomehealthservices.com	Caribou	ME	04736	207-492-8290	492-8245
Around The Clock Care 5353 Truxtun Ave *Web:* www.bakersfieldcare.com	Bakersfield	CA	93309	661-324-4277	
Back Home Again Inc 291 N State Rd 2	Valparaiso	IN	46383	219-477-4333	
Bayada Nurses Home Care Specialists 290 Chester Ave *Web:* www.bayada.com	Moorestown	NJ	08057	856-231-1000	231-1955
Bios Cos 309 E Dewey *Web:* bioscorp.com	Sapulpa	OK	74066	918-227-8390	
Brandywine Nursing & Rehabilitation Ctr Inc 505 Greenbank Rd *Web:* www.brandywinenursing.org	Wilmington	DE	19808	302-998-0101	998-2922
Bravo Wellness LLC 20445 Emerald Pkwy Dr SW Ste 400 *Web:* www.bravowell.com	Cleveland	OH	44135	440-934-2090	
Cadence Health 25 N Winfield Rd *Web:* www.cadencehealth.org	Winfield	IL	60190	630-315-8000	
Calea Ltd 2785 Skymark Ave Unit 2 *Web:* www.calea.ca	Mississauga	ON	L4W4Y3	905-238-1234	
Calvert Home Health Care Ltd 10207 Indiana Ave *Web:* www.chhci.com	Lubbock	TX	79423	806-747-8972	
CanCare Health Services Inc 45 Sheppard Ave E Ste 204 *Web:* www.cancarehealth.com	Toronto	ON	M2N5W9	416-226-6995	
Care Partners 68 Sweeten Creek Rd *TF:* 800-627-1533 ■ *Web:* www.carepartners.org	Asheville	NC	28803	828-252-2255	252-9355
Carecycle Solutions LLC 3406 Main St. *Web:* carecyclesolutions.net	Dallas	TX	75226	214-698-0600	
Carelinc Medical Equipment & Supply Company LLC 89 - 54th St SW *Web:* www.carelincmed.com	Grand Rapids	MI	49548	616-249-2273	
Carepoint Partners LLC 8280 Montgomery Rd Ste 101 *Web:* carepointpartners.com	Cincinnati	OH	45236	513-891-6666	
Caresource Health Plan 740 SE Seventh St *TF:* 888-460-0185 ■ *Web:* www.mripa.org	Grants Pass	OR	97526	541-471-4106	
Carestar Inc 5566 Cheviot Rd *Web:* carestar.com	Cincinnati	OH	45247	513-618-8300	
Carter Healthcare 3105 S Meridian Ave *TF:* 888-951-1112 ■ *Web:* www.carterhealthcare.com	Oklahoma City	OK	73119	405-947-7700	947-7300
Casepro Inc 21738 Hardy Oak Blvd *Web:* caseproinc.com	San Antonio	TX	78258	210-496-8050	496-8970
Central Home Health Care Inc 20245 W 12 Mile Rd Ste 100 *Web:* centralhomecare.com	Southfield	MI	48076	248-569-5410	
Central Vermont Home Health & Hospice 600 Granger Rd *Web:* www.cvhhh.org	Barre	VT	05641	802-223-1878	
Charity Home Health Services Inc 500 Carson Plz Ste 228 *Web:* charityhhs.com	Carson	CA	90746	310-527-4339	
Cheer Inc 546 S Bedford St *Web:* cheerde.com	Georgetown	DE	19947	302-856-5187	
Christian Homes Inc 200 N Postville Dr *TF:* 800-535-8717 ■ *Web:* www.christianhomes.org	Lincoln	IL	62656	217-732-9651	732-8686
Cole Home Healthcare of Houston Inc 16835 Deer Creek Dr Ste 205 *Web:* colehealthcare.com	Spring	TX	77379	281-379-7052	
ComForcare Senior Services Inc 2520 Telegraph Rd Ste 100 *TF:* 800-886-4044 ■ *Web:* www.comforcare.com	Bloomfield Hills	MI	48302	248-745-9700	745-9763
Comfort Caregivers Inc 6501 E Greenway Pkwy Ste 103 *Web:* www.comfortcaregivers.com	Scottsdale	AZ	85254	602-482-7777	
Commonwealth Health Corporation Inc 800 Park St *Web:* www.chc.net	Bowling Green	KY	42101	270-745-1500	
Comprehensive Wellness 6450 NW Fifth Way *Web:* www.cwshomehealth.com	Fort Lauderdale	FL	33309	954-834-2222	
Confident Care Corp Three University Plz Dr *TF:* 866-839-2273 ■ *Web:* www.confidentcarecorp.com	Hackensack	NJ	07601	201-498-9400	498-1556
Continucare Corp 7200 Corporate Ctr Dr Ste 600 *TF:* 866-312-7154 ■ *Web:* www.continucare.com	Miami	FL	33126	305-500-2000	500-2080
Coon Memorial Home Health 1411 Denver Ave *Web:* www.dhchd.org	Dalhart	TX	79022	806-244-8738	
Coram Healthcare Corp 555 17th St Ste 1500 **Fax Area Code: 303* ■ *TF:* 800-267-2642 ■ *Web:* www.coramhc.com	Denver	CO	80202	800-267-2642	298-0043*
Council of The Community Clinics 7535 Metropolitan Dr *Web:* www.ccc-sd.org	San Diego	CA	92108	619-542-4300	
Creative Family Solutions Inc 180 Teel St *Web:* creativefamilysolutions.net	Christiansburg	VA	24073	540-381-3940	
Delaware Hospice Inc 3515 Silverside Rd *TF:* 800-838-9800 ■ *Web:* www.delawarehospice.org	Wilmington	DE	19810	302-478-5707	479-2586
Dependable Nurses of Phoenix Inc 1120 S Swan Rd *Web:* www.dependablenurses.com	Tucson	AZ	85711	520-721-3822	
Dermatran Health Solutions 1504 market st. *Web:* www.dermatran.com	Redding	CA	96001	530-244-4407	
Divine Healthcare Network 856 Univerity Ave W *Web:* divinecorporation.com	St Paul	MN	55104	651-665-9795	
E-Bizdocs Inc 85 Broadway *Web:* www.ebizdocs.net	Menands	NY	12205	518-456-1011	
Ejq Home Health Care Inc 800 Middle Ave *Web:* ejqhomehealthcare.com	Elyria	OH	44035	440-323-7004	
ELJ Inc D/B/A Millennium Medical Supply 1500 Clarksville St	Paris	TX	75460	903-739-8539	
Episcopal Health Services Inc 327 Beach 19th St *Web:* www.ehs.org	Far Rockaway	NY	11691	718-869-7000	869-8507
Exceptional Home Care LLP 1510 E Grande Blvd. *Web:* ehctx.com	Tyler	TX	75703	903-533-0290	
Fletcher'S Medical Supplies Inc 6851 S Distribution Ave *TF:* 855-541-7809 ■ *Web:* fletchermedical.com	Jacksonville	FL	32256	904-387-4481	389-6965
Gateway to Care 3611 Ennis St. *Web:* gatewaytocare.org	Houston	TX	77004	713-783-4616	
General Healthcare Resources Inc 2250 Hickory Rd Ste 240 *TF:* 800-879-4471 ■ *Web:* www.ghresources.com	Plymouth Meeting	PA	19462	610-834-1122	834-7525
Genesis Home Care Inc 116 E Heritage Dr. *Web:* genesishomecare.net	Tyler	TX	75703	903-509-3374	
Gentiva Health Services Inc 3350 Riverwood Pkwy Ste 1400 *NASDAQ: GTIV* ■ *Web:* www.gentiva.com	Atlanta	GA	30339	770-951-6450	

Phone Fax

Global Medical Solutions Ltd
14140 Ventura Blvd Sherman Oaks CA 91423 818-783-2915
Web: globalmedicalsolutions.com

Griswold Special Care Inc
717 Bethlehem Pike Ste 300 Erdenheim PA 19038 215-402-0200 277-3820*
**Fax Area Code:* 469 ■ *TF:* 855-303-9470 ■ *Web:* www.griswoldhomecare.com

Gurwin Jewish Nursing & Rehabilitation Ctr
68 Hauppauge Rd Commack NY 11725 631-715-2600 715-2940
Web: www.gurwin.org

Halt Medical Inc 131 Sand Creek Rd Ste B Brentwood CA 94513 925-634-7943
TF: 877-412-3828 ■ *Web:* www.haltmedical.com

HCA Gulf Coast 7400 Fannin Ste 650 Houston TX 77054 713-852-1500
Web: hcagulfcoast.com

Health Services of Coshocton County
230 S Fourth St Coshocton OH 43812 740-622-7311
Web: healthservicescoshocton.com

Health Systems 2000 1901 Oak Park Blvd Lake Charles LA 70601 337-562-1140
Web: www.hhc2000.com

Help At Home Inc One N State St Ste 800 Chicago IL 60602 312-762-0900 704-0022
TF: 800-404-3191 ■ *Web:* www.helpathome.com

Helping Hands Home Care
2141 NW Fillmore Ave Corvallis OR 97333 541-757-0214
Web: homecareserv.com

Henry Street Settlement 265 Henry St New York NY 10002 212-766-9200
Web: www.henrystreet.org

Homcare Inc 875 W Summit Ave Muskegon MI 49441 231-755-6951
Web: homcareinc.com

Home Aides of Central New York Inc
723 James St Syracuse NY 13203 315-476-4295
Web: homeaidescny.org

Home Bound Healthcare Inc 1615 Vollmer Rd Flossmoor IL 60422 708-798-0800
TF: 800-444-7028 ■ *Web:* www.homeboundhealth.com

Home Care Network Inc
190A E Spring Vly Rd Centerville OH 45458 937-435-1142
Web: www.hcnmidwest.net

Home Care Partners
1234 Massachusetts Ave NW Ste C-1002 Washington DC 20005 202-638-2382
Web: www.homecarepartners.org

Home Health Corp of America Inc
Healthcare Investment Corp of America
620 Freedom Business Ctr Ste 105 King of Prussia PA 19406 484-690-1200 751-9100
Web: www.healthinvcorp.com

Home Healthcare, Hospice & Community Services Inc
312 Marlboro St Keene NH 03431 603-352-2253
Web: www.hcsservices.org

Home Instead Inc 13330 California St Ste 200 Omaha NE 68154 402-498-4466 498-5757
TF: 888-484-5759 ■ *Web:* www.homeinstead.com

Home IV Care & Nutritional Service
PO Box 700 Stuarts Draft VA 24477 800-552-6576 932-3028*
**Fax Area Code:* 540 ■ *TF:* 800-552-6576 ■ *Web:* www.homeivcare.com

Home Staff Inc 5517 N Cumberland Ave Ste 915 Chicago IL 60656 773-467-6002
Web: homestaffinc.com

Home Staff LLC 40 Millbrook St Worcester MA 01606 508-755-4600
Web: www.homestaffma.com

Homecare Homebase LLC
6688 N Central Expy Ste 1200 Dallas TX 75206 214-239-6700
Web: www.hchb.com

Homecare of Mid Missouri Inc 102 W Reed St Moberly MO 65270 660-263-1517
Web: www.homecaremo.org

Homewatch International Inc
7100 E Belleview Ave Ste 303 Greenwood Village CO 80111 303-758-5111
Web: www.homewatchcaregivers.com

Hosanna Health Care 1001 N Conway Ave Mission TX 78572 956-519-1000

Hospice Atlanta-Visiting Nurse Health System
1244 Pk Vista Dr Atlanta GA 30319 404-869-3000 215-6005
TF: 866-374-4776 ■ *Web:* www.vnhs.org

Hospital Cooperative Laundry Inc
6225 E 38th Ave Denver CO 80207 303-329-6662
Web: hospitalcooperative.com

Inovalon Inc 4321 Collington Rd Bowie MD 20716 301-809-4000
Web: medassurant.com

IntegraCare Holdings Inc
2559 SW Grapevine Pkwy Ste 300 Grapevine TX 76051 817-310-4999
Web: www.integracarehh.com

Intercity Home Care 11 Dartmouth St Malden MA 02148 781-321-6300
Web: intercityhomecare.com

Interim HealthCare Inc
1601 Sawgrass Corporate Pkwy Sunrise FL 33323 954-858-6000 858-2720
TF: 800-338-7786 ■ *Web:* www.interimhealthcare.com

Ira G Steffy & Son Inc 460 Wenger Dr Ephrata PA 17522 717-733-2001 733-0971
Web: www.iragsteffyandson.com

Kelly Home Care Services Inc
999 W Big Beaver Rd Troy MI 48084 248-362-4444
TF: 800-755-8636 ■ *Web:* homehealthcareagencies.com

Knoxville Hospital & Clinics
1002 S Lincoln St Knoxville IA 50138 641-842-2151
Web: www.knoxvillehospital.org

Korman Healthcare LLC 5783 W Erie St Chandler AZ 85226 480-365-0222
Web: www.kormanhealthcare.com

Lakewood Health System 49725 County 83 Staples MN 56479 218-894-1515
Web: lakewoodhealthsystem.com

Lamoille Home Health & Hospice
54 Farr Ave Morrisville VT 05661 802-888-4651
Web: www.lhha.org

LHC Group LLC 420 W Pinhook Rd Lafayette LA 70503 337-289-8188 289-8168
NASDAQ: LHCG ■ *TF:* 866-542-4768 ■ *Web:* www.lhcgroup.com

LHP Hospital Group Inc 2400 Dallas Pkwy Ste 450 Plano TX 75093 972-943-1700
Web: www.lhphospitalgroup.com

Lifecare Alliance 1699 W Mound St Columbus OH 43223 614-278-3130
Web: www.lifecarealliance.org

Lifelink Foundation Inc 409 Bayshore Blvd Tampa FL 33606 813-253-2640
TF: 800-262-5775 ■ *Web:* www.lifelinkfound.org

Phone Fax

Lifetime Care 3111 Winton Rd S Rochester NY 14623 585-214-1000 214-1136
Web: www.lifetimecare.org

Lincare Holdings Inc 19387 US 19 N Clearwater FL 33764 727-530-7700 532-9692
NASDAQ: LNCR ■ *Web:* www.lincare.com

Living Assistance Services Inc
937 Haverford Rd Ste 200 Bryn Mawr PA 19010 610-924-0630 924-9690
TF: 800-365-4189 ■ *Web:* www.livingassistance.com

Long Hill Co, The 580 Long Hill Ave Shelton CT 06484 203-944-8283
Web: www.longhillcompany.com

Long Term Solutions Inc 235 W Central St Natick MA 01760 508-907-6290
Web: www.longtermsol.com

Longwood Management Corp
4032 Wilshire Blvd Ste 600 Los Angeles CA 90010 213-389-6900

Loving Hands Home Care Services Inc
1777 Hamilton Ave San Jose CA 95125 408-266-8331
Web: lovinghandshmcare.com

Mackenzie Eason & Associates
3023 S University Dr Ste 230 Fort Worth TX 76109 817-922-9152
Web: mackenzieeason.com

MaineHealth 110 Free St Portland ME 04101 207-661-7001
Web: www.mainehealth.com

Mains'l Services Inc 200 Hiawatha Ave E Big Lake MN 55309 763-263-3936
Web: mail.google.com

MDX Medical Inc 210 Clay Ave Ste 140 Lyndhurst NJ 07071 201-842-0760
Web: www.vitals.com

Med Team Home Health Care 131 S Beckham Ave Tyler TX 75702 903-592-9747
Web: med-team.com

Med-Staff Oklahoma LLC 8321 E 61st St Ste 221 Tulsa OK 74133 918-317-0270

Medical Ctr at Princeton Home Care
905 Herrontown Rd Princeton NJ 08540 609-497-4900 737-6506
TF: 877-932-8395 ■ *Web:* www.princetonhcs.org

Medical Metrics Inc 2121 Sage Rd Ste 300 Houston TX 77056 713-850-7500
Web: www.medicalmetrics.com

Medical Services of America Inc (MSA)
171 Monroe Ln Lexington SC 29072 803-957-0500 342-6190*
**Fax Area Code:* 888 ■ *TF:* 800-845-5850 ■ *Web:* www.msa-corp.com

Mehling & Associates Inc 9846 Hwy 31 E Tyler TX 75705 903-592-8001
Web: www.athomehealth.org

Mena Hospital Commission 311 Morrow St N Mena AR 71953 479-394-2534
Web: www.menaregional.com

Metro Pavia Health System Inc
MaraMar Plz Bldg Avenida San Patricio
Ste 950-960 Guaynabo PR 00968 888-882-0882
TF: 888-882-0882 ■ *Web:* www.metropavia.com

Millenium Home Health Care Inc
370 Reed Rd Ste 319 Broomall PA 19008 610-543-4126
Web: www.mhomehealth.com

Minnesota Visiting Nurse Agency
3433 Broadway St NE Minneapolis MN 55413 612-617-4600 617-4782
Web: www.mvna.org

Mitchell County Hospital Health Systems
400 W Eighth St P O Box 399 Beloit KS 67420 785-738-9590
Web: www.mchks.com

National Home Health Care Corp
700 White Plains Rd Ste 275 Scarsdale NY 10583 914-722-9000 722-9239
TF: 800-422-4661 ■ *Web:* www.nhhc.net

New Choices Inc 2501 18th St Ste 201 Bettendorf IA 52722 563-355-5502
Web: newchoicesinc.com

New Millenium Home Health
6031 Cleveland Ave Columbus OH 43231 614-882-7782
Web: nmilleniumhomehealth.com

New York Health Care Inc
20 E Sunrise Hwy Ste 201 Valley Stream NY 11581 718-375-6700
OTC: BBAL ■ *TF:* 888-978-6942 ■ *Web:* www.nyhc.com

Nizhoni Health Systems LLC
Five Middlesex Ave Somerville MA 02145 617-623-3211
Web: nizhonihealth.com

North Los Angel County Regional Ctr
15400 Sherman Way Ste 170 Van Nuys CA 91406 818-778-1900 756-6140
TF: 800-430-4263 ■ *Web:* www.nlacrc.org

Nurse On Call Inc 1926 10th Ave N Ste 400 Lake Worth FL 33461 561-586-9148
Web: www.nurseoncallfl.com

NutraBella Inc 1875 S Grant St Ste 305 San Mateo CA 94402 650-212-3559
Web: www.bellybarproducts.com

Ohel Children's Home & Family Services Inc
4510 16th Ave Brooklyn NY 11204 718-851-6300
TF: 800-603-6435 ■ *Web:* www.ohelfamily.org

Olmsted Medical Center 210 Ninth St SE Rochester MN 55904 507-288-3443
Web: www.olmmed.org

Ontario Medical Supply Ltd 1100 Algoma Rd Ottawa ON K1B0A3 613-244-8620
TF: 800-804-1112 ■ *Web:* www.oms.ca

Onyx Capital Holdings Inc
10843 Meadow Garden Ct Las Vegas NV 89135 702-233-8056

Optimae LifeServices Inc
301 W Burlington Ave Fairfield IA 52556 641-472-1684
Web: www.optimaelifeservices.com

Outreach Healthcare Inc 269 W Renner Pkwy Richardson TX 75080 972-840-7360
Web: www.outreachhealth.com

Passport Program-western
925 Euclid Ave Ste 600 Cleveland OH 44115 216-621-0303
Web: www.psa10a.org

Pediatric Home Respiratory Services Inc
2800 Cleveland Ave N Roseville MN 55113 651-642-1825
Web: www.pediatrichomeservice.com

Pediatric Services of America Inc
310 Technology Pkwy Norcross GA 30092 770-441-1580 *
**Fax:* Hum Res ■ *TF:* 800-408-4442 ■ *Web:* www.psahealthcare.com

Pegasus Home Health Care 132 N Maryland Ave Glendale CA 91206 818-551-1932
Web: www.pegasushomecare.com

Pentec Health Inc Four Creek Pkwy Ste A Boothwyn PA 19061 610-494-8700
Web: www.pentechealth.com

People Care Inc 116 W 32nd St 15th Fl New York NY 10001 212-631-7300
Web: www.peoplecare.com

Phone Fax

Personal Care Inc 321 Sycamore St .... Decatur GA 30030 404-373-2727
Web: personalcare.net

Personal-Touch Home Care Inc
186-18 Hillside Ave .... Jamaica NY 11432 718-468-2500 681-2550*
**Fax Area Code: 412 ■ *Fax: Hum Res ■ TF: 888-275-4147 ■ Web:* www.pthomecare.com

Phoenix Home Care Inc 3033 S Kansas Expy .... Springfield MO 65807 417-881-7442
Web: phoenixhomehc.com

Pioneers Medical Center 345 Cleveland St .... Meeker CO 81641 970-878-5047
Web: pioneershospital.org

Pmd Healthcare 6620 grant way .... Allentown PA 18106 610-530-8500
Web: spiropd.com

Preferred Homecare Infusion LLC
4601 E Hilton Ave Ste 100 .... Phoenix AZ 85034 480-446-9010
Web: preferredhomecare.com

Premier Homecare Inc 6123 Montrose Rd. .... Rockville MD 20852 301-984-1742
Web: www.jssa.org

Prevea Health Services Inc
2710 Executive Dr. .... Green Bay WI 54304 920-496-4700
Web: www.prevea.com

Promera Health 61 accord park dr. .... Norwell MA 02061 888-878-9058
TF: 888-878-9058 ■ *Web:* www.promerasports.com

PRS Inc 1761 Old Meadow Rd Ste 100 .... McLean VA 22102 703-536-9000 448-3723
Web: www.prsinc.org

Pulse Home Health Care Inc
2325 Severn Ave Ste 5 .... Metairie LA 70001 504-831-7778
Web: pulsehomehealthcare.com

Qchc Inc 200 narrows pkwy. .... Birmingham AL 35242 205-437-1512
Web: www.qchcweb.com

Qualchoice of Arkansas Inc
12615 Chenal Pkwy Ste 300. .... Little Rock AR 72211 501-228-7111
Web: www.qualchoice.com

Richard A Urbanek Jr DDS Ms Pa
Five Eureka Cir Ste B .... Wichita Falls TX 76308 940-696-2002

Right at Home Inc 6464 Crt St Ste 150 .... Omaha NE 68106 402-697-7537 697-0289
TF: 877-697-7537 ■ *Web:* www.rightathome.net

Scarab Behavioral Health Services LLC
3203 Brick Church Pk. .... Nashville TN 37207 615-262-7822
Web: scarabhealth.com

Selfhelp Community Services Inc
520 Eigth Ave Fifth Fl .... New York NY 10018 866-735-1234 967-4784*
**Fax Area Code: 212 ■ TF: 866-735-1234 ■ Web:* www.selfhelp.net

Sitters & More Inc 125 A Stonebridge Blvd .... Jackson TN 38305 731-660-0001
Web: sittersandmore.com

Society'S Assets Inc
5200 Washington Ave Ste 225 .... Racine WI 53406 262-637-9128
Web: societysassets.org

Solano Coalition for Bett 420 Virginia St .... Vallejo CA 94590 707-643-0145
Web: www.skipperdog.com

Sta-Home Hospice 406 Briarwood Dr Bldg 200 .... Jackson MS 39206 601-956-5100 956-3003
TF: 800-782-4663 ■ *Web:* www.sta-home.com

Star Multi Care Services Inc
115 Broad Hollow Rd Ste 275. .... Melville NY 11747 631-424-7827 427-5466
TF: 877-920-0600 ■ *Web:* www.starmulticare.com

Stowell Associates Select Staff Inc
4485 N Oakland Ave .... Milwaukee WI 53211 414-963-2600
Web: caremanagedhomecare.com

SunCrest Healthcare Inc
510 Hospital Dr Ste 100 .... Madison TN 40223 615-627-9267
Web: www.omnihha.com

Sunrise Home Health Services
3200 Broadway Blvd Ste 260 .... Garland TX 75043 972-278-1414
Web: sunrisehomehealth.com

Texas Visiting Nurse Service Ltd
814 E Tyler .... Harlingen TX 78550 956-412-1401
Web: tvnsltd.com

Todd's Companion Plus Inc
6123 Green Bay Rd Ste 250 .... Kenosha WI 53142 262-605-4700
Web: companionplus.com

Umbrella Medical Systems 505 walnut st. .... Kansas City MO 64106 816-437-7265
Web: www.umbrella-ms.com

Umc Home Health 1301 50th St Ste 9 .... Lubbock TX 79412 806-747-5377
Web: www.teamumc.com

Valley Endodontics Ltd 1100 N Lynndale Dr .... Appleton WI 54914 920-731-4484
Web: valleyendo.com

Verecom Technologies Inc
47 Kearny St Ste 502 .... San Francisco CA 94108 415-234-3018
Web: www.verecom.com

Visiting Nurse Assn of Morris County (Inc)
175 South St. .... Morristown NJ 07960 973-539-1216
TF: 800-938-4748 ■ *Web:* www.vnannj.org

VITAS Healthcare Corp
100 S Biscayne Blvd Ste 400 .... Miami FL 33131 305-374-4143
TF: 866-418-4827 ■ *Web:* www.vitas.com

Vna of Rhode Island 475 Kilvert St .... Warwick RI 02886 401-574-4900 490-8870
TF: 800-638-6274 ■ *Web:* vnari.org

WakeMed Health & Hospitals 3000 New Bern Ave ..... Raleigh NC 27610 919-350-8000
Web: lake-medical.com

We Care Health Services Inc
151 Bloor St W Ste 602 .... Toronto ON M5S1S4 416-922-7601 922-6280
TF: 888-429-3227 ■ *Web:* www.wecare.ca

Whole Health Products LLC
17301 W Colfax Ave Ste 110 .... Golden CO 80401 303-684-9618
Web: www.wholehealth.com

Williamsville Suburban LLC 193 S Union Rd .... Buffalo NY 14221 716-276-1900
Web: www.facebook.com/pages/williamsville-suburban-llc/159706000718409

Wise Regional Health System 2000 S FM 51 .... Decatur TX 76234 940-627-5921
Web: www.wiseregional.com

WorldMed Assist 1230 Mtn Side Ct .... Concord CA 94521 866-999-3848
TF: 866-999-3848 ■ *Web:* www.worldmedassist.com

Phone Fax

367 HOME IMPROVEMENT CENTERS

SEE ALSO Construction Materials p. 2106

Phone Fax

Above Security Inc
955 Michele-Bohec Blvd Ste 244 .... Blainville QC J7C5J6 450-430-8166
Web: www.abovesecurity.com

Ace Hardware Corp 2200 Kensington Ct .... Oak Brook IL 60523 630-990-6600
Web: www.acehardware.com

Ace Hardware Corporation
1056 W Grand Ave .... Grover Beach CA 60523 805-489-0158 489-2971
Web: local.acehardware.com/01751/miners

Al's Garden Art Inc 311 W Citrus .... Colton CA 92324 909-424-0221
Web: www.alsgardenart.com

Alaska Industrial Hardware Inc
2192 Viking Dr .... Anchorage AK 99501 907-276-7201 258-3054
TF: 800-478-7201 ■ *Web:* store.aihalaska.com

Alene Candles LLC 51 Scarborough Ln .... Milford NH 03055 603-673-5050
Web: www.alene.com

Ankmar LLC 4200 Monaco St .... Denver CO 80216 303-321-6051
Web: www.dhpace.com

Arlington Coal & Lumber Company Inc
41 Pk Ave .... Arlington MA 02476 781-643-8100 643-7414
TF: 800-649-8101 ■ *Web:* www.arlcoal.com

Ashland Lumber Company Inc 134 Front St .... Ashland MA 01721 508-881-2660
Web: ashlandlumber.com

Atlanta Hardwood Corp 5596 Riverview Rd SE .... Mableton GA 30126 404-792-2290
TF: 800-476-5393 ■ *Web:* www.hardwoodweb.com

Beisser's Inc 3705 SE Beisser Dr. .... Grimes IA 50111 515-986-4422
Web: www.beisserlumber.com

Belknap White Group Inc, The
111 Plymouth St. .... Mansfield MA 02048 508-337-2700
Web: www.belknapwhite.com

Beronio Lumber Co 2525 Marin St .... San Francisco CA 94124 415-824-4300 824-3706
Web: www.beronio.com

Big B Lumberteria 6600 Brentwood Blvd. .... Brentwood CA 94513 925-634-2442 634-9839
Web: www.bigblumber.com

Big L Corp 620 S Main St P.O. Box 134 .... Sheridan MI 48884 989-291-3232 291-3421
Web: www.big-l-lumber.com

Bloedorn Lumber Company Inc PO Box 1077 .... Torrington WY 82240 307-532-2151 532-3760
Web: www.bloedornlumber.com

BMC West Corp PO Box 70006 .... Boise ID 83707 208-331-4300 331-4366
Web: buildwithbmc.com

Brunsell Bros Ltd 4611 W Beltline Hwy. .... Madison WI 53711 608-275-7171 275-7179
Web: www.brunsell.com

Busy Beaver Bldg Centers 2940 Library Rd. .... Pittsburgh PA 15234 412-882-6633 882-6833
TF: 800-732-0999 ■ *Web:* www.busybeaver.com

CanWel Building Materials Group Ltd
Ste 1100 609 Granville St. .... Vancouver BC V7Y1G6 604-432-1400
Web: www.canwel.com

Cape Cod Lumber Co Inc 225 Groveland St .... Abington MA 02351 781-878-0715 871-6726
TF: 800-368-3117 ■ *Web:* capecodlumber.com

Carlisle Wide Plank Floors Inc 1676 Route 9 .... Stoddard NH 03464 603-446-3937
Web: www.wideplankflooring.com

Carter Lumber Co Inc 601 Tallmadge Rd .... Kent OH 44240 330-673-6100 287-1806*
**Fax Area Code: 765 ■ TF: 877-586-2374 ■ Web:* www.carterlumber.com

Center BMW 5201 Van Nuys Blvd .... Sherman Oaks CA 91401 818-907-9995
Web: centerbmw.com

Chinook Lumber Inc 17606 SR- 9 SE .... Snohomish WA 98296 360-668-8800 863-6498
Web: www.chinooklumber.com

Choo Choo Build-it Mart 325 Commerce Loop .... Vidalia GA 30475 912-537-8964 537-4839
Web: vnscorp.com

City Mill Company Ltd 660 N Nimitz Hwy. .... Honolulu HI 96817 808-533-3811 524-8092
Web: www.citymill.com

Colonial Mills Inc 560 Mineral Spring Ave .... Pawtucket RI 02904 401-724-6279
Web: www.colonialmills.com

Columbia Showcase & Cabinet Co
11034 Sherman Way. .... Sun Valley CA 91352 818-765-9710
Web: www.columbiashowcase.com

CoMc LLC 13423 F St .... Omaha NE 68137 402-505-7627
Web: www.snapstone.com

Dixieline Lumber Company Inc
3250 Sports Arena Blvd .... San Diego CA 92110 619-224-4120 225-8192
Web: www.dixieline.com

Doug Ashy Building Materials Inc
1801 Rees St .... Breaux Bridge LA 70517 337-332-5201 332-5226
Web: www.dougashy.com

Dukes Lumber Company Inc
28504 Dukes Lumber Rd .... Laurel DE 19956 302-875-7551
Web: dukeslumber.com

Economy Lumber 720 Camden Ave. .... Campbell CA 95008 408-378-5231 378-0258
Web: www.economylumber.com

Evanston Lumber Co 1001 Sherman Ave .... Evanston IL 60202 847-864-7700
Web: www.evanstonlumber.com

Evergreen Lumber & Truss Inc
84 Central Industrial Row .... Purvis MS 39475 601-794-8404
Web: www.evergreentruss.com

Fabrica International Inc 3201 S Susan St. .... Santa Ana CA 92704 949-261-7181
Web: www.fabrica.com

Fire Rock Products LLC 3620 Ave C. .... Birmingham AL 35064 205-639-5000
Web: www.firerock.us

Future Home Technology Inc 33 Ralph St. .... Port Jervis NY 12771 845-856-9033
Web: www.futurehometechnology.com

Ganahl Lumber Co 1220 E Ball Rd. .... Anaheim CA 92805 714-772-5444 772-0639
Web: www.ganahl.com

Gemmy Industries Corp 117 Wrangler Dr. .... Coppell TX 75019 972-538-4200
Web: gemmy.com

Grossman's Inc 90 Hawes Way .... Stoughton MA 02072 781-297-3300 297-0180
Web: www.bargain-outlets.com

Phone | Fax

H2O Concepts International Inc 1518 W Knudsen Dr Ste 100 Phoenix AZ 85027 623-582-5222
Web: www.h2oconcepts.com

Hacienda Home Centers Inc 1255 Bosque Farms Blvd Bosque Farms NM 87068 505-869-2637
Web: www.hacienda.doitbest.com

Hayward Lumber Co 429 Front St Salinas CA 93901 831-755-8800 755-8821
Web: www.haywardlumber.com

Herrman Lumber Co 1917 S State Hwy N Springfield MO 65802 417-862-3737 862-8934
TF: 888-238-9778 ■ *Web:* www.herrmanlumber.com

Home Depot Inc 2455 Paces Ferry Rd NW Atlanta GA 30339 770-433-8211 384-2356
NYSE: HD ■ *TF Cust Svc:* 800-553-3199 ■ *Web:* www.homedepot.com

Jackson Lumber & Millwork Company Inc PO Box 449 Lawrence MA 01842 978-686-4141
Web: www.jacksonlumber.com

Jones Cassity Inc 302 Pine Tree Rd Longview TX 75604 903-759-0736 759-1406
Web: www.cassityjones.com

JP Flooring Systems Inc 9097 Union Centre Blvd West Chester OH 45069 513-346-4300
Web: www.jpflooring.com

Junior's Bldg Materials Inc 7574 Battlefield Pkwy Ringgold GA 30736 706-937-3400 937-4100
Web: www.juniorsbuildingmaterials.com

Lampert Yards Inc 1850 Como Ave Saint Paul MN 55108 651-695-3600 695-3601
Web: lampertlumber.com

Len-Co Lumber Corp 1445 Seneca St Buffalo NY 14210 716-822-0243 822-1821
TF: 800-258-4585 ■ *Web:* www.lencobuffalo.com

Liese Lumber Company Inc 319 E Main St Belleville IL 62220 618-234-0105
Web: www.lieselumber.com

Linen Chest Inc 4455 AutoRt Des Laurentides Laval QC H7L5X8 514-341-7077
TF: 800-363-3832 ■ *Web:* www.linenchest.com

Lowe's Cos Inc 1000 Lowe's Blvd Mooresville NC 28117 704-758-1000 658-4766*
NYSE: LOW ■ **Fax Area Code:* 336 ■ *TF:* 800-445-6937 ■ *Web:* www.lowes.com

Lowe's Home Centers Inc PO Box 1111 North Wilkesboro NC 28656 800-445-6937
TF: 800-445-6937 ■ *Web:* www.lowes.com

Manta Group Ltd, The 1300-350 Bay St Toronto ON M5H2S6 416-483-5166
Web: www.mantaconsulting.com

MarJam Supply Co Inc 20 Rewe St Brooklyn NY 11211 718-388-6465 989-0029
TF All: 800-848-8407 ■ *Web:* www.marjam.com

Marson & Marson Lumber Inc PO Box 218 Leavenworth WA 98826 509-548-5829 548-6372
Web: www.marsonandmarson.com

Martin Door Manufacturing Inc 2828 South 900 West Salt Lake City UT 84119 801-973-9310 688-8182
TF: 800-388-9310 ■ *Web:* www.martindoor.com

Matthew Hall Lumber Co 127 Sixth Ave N Saint Cloud MN 56302 320-252-1920
Web: www.mathewhall.com

McCoy's Bldg Supply 1350 IH 35 N San Marcos TX 78666 512-353-5400
Web: www.mccoys.com

Menard Inc 5101 Menard Dr Eau Claire WI 54703 715-876-5911 876-2868
Web: www.menards.com

Montalbano Lumber Company Inc 1309 Houston Ave Houston TX 77007 713-228-9011 228-8222
Web: www.montalbanolumber.com

National Lumber 71 Maple St Mansfield MA 02048 508-339-8020 339-4518
TF: 800-370-9663 ■ *Web:* www.national-lumber.com

Northern Lights Enterprises Inc 3474 Andover Rd Wellsville NY 14895 585-593-1200
Web: www.northernlightscandles.com

Northern Tool & Equipment Co 2800 Southcross Dr W Burnsville MN 55306 952-894-9510 894-1020
TF Cust Svc: 800-222-5381 ■ *Web:* www.northerntool.com

Olshan Lumber Co PO Box 1274 Houston TX 77251 713-225-5551 220-9400
Web: www.olshanlumber.com

Orchard Supply Hardware 6450 Via del Oro San Jose CA 95119 408-281-3500 365-2702
Web: www.osh.com

Pandel Inc 21 River Dr Cartersville GA 30120 770-382-1034
TF: 800-537-3868 ■ *Web:* www.pandel.com

Paramount Builders Inc 501 Central Dr Virginia Beach VA 23454 757-340-9000 431-8200
TF: 888-340-9002 ■ *Web:* www.paramountbuilders.com

Pilgrim Home & Hearth LLC 5600 Imhoff Dr Ste G Concord CA 94520 707-746-1200
Web: www.pilgrimhearth.com

Preston Feather Building Ctr PO Box 637 Petoskey MI 49770 231-347-2501 347-1154
Web: www.prestonfeather.com

Preverco Inc 285 Rue De Rotterdam Saint-augustin-de-desmaures QC G3A2E5 418-878-8930
Web: www.preverco.com

Reisterstown Lumber Co, The PO Box 337 Reisterstown MD 21136 410-833-1300 833-6803
TF: 800-289-8739 ■ *Web:* www.reisterstownlumber.com

Rocky Mountain Prestress 5801 Pecos St Denver CO 80221 303-480-1111
Web: www.rmpprestress.com

RONA Inc 220 Ch du Tremblay Boucherville QC J4B8H7 514-599-5100 599-5137
TSE: RON ■ *TF:* 877-599-5900 ■ *Web:* www.rona.ca

Seigle's 1331 Davis Rd Elgin IL 60123 847-742-2000 697-6521
Web: www.seigles.com

Shane Homes Ltd 5661 Seventh St NE Calgary AB T2E8V3 403-536-2200
Web: www.shanehomes.com

Simonson Properties Co 2455 12th St SE Saint Cloud MN 56304 320-252-9385
Web: www.simonson-lumber.com

Sleep Country Canada LP 140 Wendell Ave Ste 2 North York ON M9N3R2 416-242-4774
Web: www.sleepcountry.ca

Sliters PO Box 130 Somers MT 59932 406-857-3306 857-3369
Web: www.sliters.com

Sneades Ace Home Center Inc 1750 Prosper Ln Owings MD 20736 410-257-2963
Web: acehardware.com

Solutioninc Technologies Ltd 5692 Bloomfield St Halifax NS B3K1T2 902-420-0077
Web: www.solutioninc.com

Stanton Carpet Corp 211 Robbins Ln Syosset NY 11791 516-822-5878
TF: 888-809-2989 ■ *Web:* www.stantoncarpet.com

Star Lumber & Supply 325 S W St Wichita KS 67213 316-942-2221
Web: www.starlumber.com

Stenerson Bros Lumber Co 1702 First Ave N Moorhead MN 56560 218-233-3437 233-2819
Web: www.stenersonlumber.com

Stratford Building Supply Inc 215 Railroad St Stratford WI 54484 715-687-4125
Web: stratfordbuilding.com

Sutherland Lumber Co 4000 Main St Kansas City MO 64111 816-756-3000 360-2195
Web: www.sutherlands.com

Tri Supply Co 7410 Eastex Fwy Beaumont TX 77708 409-835-7966
Web: www.trisupplyhometeam.com

True Value Co 8600 W Bryn Mawr Ave Chicago IL 60631 773-695-5000 695-6516
Web: www.truevaluecompany.com

Viola Bros Inc 180 Washington Ave Nutley NJ 07110 973-667-7000 667-2048
Web: www.violabros.com

WE Aubuchon Company Inc 95 Aubuchon Dr Westminster MA 01473 978-874-0521 874-2096
TF: 800-431-2712 ■ *Web:* www.hardwarestore.com

Wheelwright Lumber Co 3127 S Midland Dr Ogden UT 84401 801-627-0850
Web: www.wheelwrightlumber.com

368 HOME INSPECTION SERVICES

Phone | Fax

A2Z Field Services LLC 7450 Industrial Pkwy Ste 105 Plain City OH 43064 614-873-0211
Web: www.a2zfieldservices.com

AmeriSpec Inc 889 Ridge Lk Blvd Memphis TN 38120 901-820-8500
TF: 800-426-2270 ■ *Web:* www.amerispec.com

BrickKicker Inc 849 N Ellsworth St Naperville IL 60563 630-420-9900 420-2270
TF: 800-821-1820 ■ *Web:* www.brickkicker.com

EVS-US Inc 319 Garlington Rd Ste B4 Greenville SC 29615 864-288-9777
Web: www.evs-sm.com

HomeTeam Inspection Service Inc 575 Chamber Dr Milford OH 45150 800-598-5297 831-6010*
**Fax Area Code:* 513 ■ *TF:* 800-598-5297 ■ *Web:* www.hometeaminspection.com

HouseMaster 850 Bear Tavern RD Ste 303 Ewing NJ 08628 732-469-6565 469-7405
TF: 800-526-3939 ■ *Web:* www.housemaster.com

Infralogix 1315 Jamestown Rd Ste 201 Williamsburg VA 23185 757-229-2965
Web: www.infralogix.com

iv3 Solutions Corp 50 Minthorn Blvd Ste 301 Markham ON L3T7X8 877-995-2651
TF: 877-995-2651 ■ *Web:* www.iv3solutions.com

Metalcare Inspection Services Inc 291 Macalpine Cres Fort Mcmurray AB T9H4Y4 780-715-1889
Web: metalcare.com

Milrose Consultants Inc 498 Seventh Ave New York NY 10018 212-643-4545
Web: www.milrose.com

National Property Inspections Inc (NPI) 9375 Burt St Ste 201 Omaha NE 68114 402-333-9807 933-2508*
**Fax Area Code:* 800 ■ *TF:* 800-333-9807

Parc Environmental 2706 S Railroad Ave Fresno CA 93725 209-233-7156
Web: parcenvironmental.com

PetroChem Inspection Services Inc 1475 E Sam Houston Pkwy S Ste 100 Pasadena TX 77503 281-884-5100
Web: www.petrochemintl.com

Remote Access Technology Inc 61 Atlantic St Dartmouth NS B2Y4P4 902-434-4405
Web: www.rat.ca

TesTex Inc 535 Old Frankstown Rd Pittsburgh PA 15239 412-798-8990
Web: www.testex-ndt.com

World Inspection Network International Inc 12345 Lk City Way NE Ste 365 Seattle WA 98125 800-309-6753
TF: 800-309-6753 ■ *Web:* www.wini.com

369 HOME SALES & OTHER DIRECT SELLING

Phone | Fax

4Life Research 9850 South 300 West Sandy UT 84070 801-256-3102 562-3611
TF Sales: 888-454-3374 ■ *Web:* www.4life.com

Acquireo.com 14584 Baseline Ave Ste 300142 Fontana CA 92336 909-266-0840
Web: www.acquireo.com

Advocare International Lp 2801 Summit Ave Plano TX 75074 972-665-5800
TF: 800-542-4800

Alpine Valley Water Company Inc 10341 Julian Dr Cincinnati OH 45215 513-672-3400
Web: www.alpinevalleydelivers.com

Amway Corp 7575 Fulton St E Ada MI 49355 616-787-4000 787-7550
TF: 800-253-6500 ■ *Web:* www.amway.com

Arrowsight Inc 45 Kensico Dr Second Fl Mount Kisco NY 10549 212-869-8282
Web: arrowsight.com

Ataway Exchange 10474 Armstrong St Fairfax VA 22030 703-934-4700
Web: atawayexchange.com

Audience Partners LLC 414 Commerce Dr Ste 100 Fort Washington PA 19034 484-928-1010
Web: www.audiencepartners.com

Avon Products Inc 1345 Ave of the Americas New York NY 10017 212-282-7000 282-6035
NYSE: AVP ■ *TF Cust Svc:* 800-367-2866 ■ *Web:* www.avon.com

Basch Subscriptions Inc 10 Ferry St Ste 429 Concord NH 03301 603-229-0662
Web: www.basch.com

Beefeaters Inc 885 Progress Ave Ste 318 Scarborough ON M1H3G3 416-438-1108

Chapelwood United Methodist Church 11140 Greenbay St Houston TX 77024 713-465-3467
Web: www.chapelwood.org

Chemready Filter Corp 9594 Velvetleaf Cir San Ramon CA 94582 925-735-0414

Color Me Beautiful 7000 Infantry Ridge Rd Ste 200 Manassas VA 20109 800-265-6763 471-0127*
**Fax Area Code:* 703 ■ *TF:* 800-265-6763 ■ *Web:* www.colormebeautiful.com

Colorado Prime Foods 500 Bi-County Blvd Ste 400 Farmingdale NY 11735 631-694-1111 694-4064*
**Fax:* Cust Svc ■ *TF:* 800-365-2404 ■ *Web:* www.reordermenu.com

Conklin Company Inc 551 Valley Pk Dr Shakopee MN 55379 952-445-6010 496-4281
TF: 800-888-8838 ■ *Web:* www.conklin.com

Company / Address	City	State	Zip	Phone	Fax
Consumer Brands LLC 120 Vantis Ste 570 *Web:* www.consumerbrands.com	Aliso Viejo	CA	92656	949-356-1300	
Corbin Turf & Ornamental Supply 1105 Old Buncombe Rd *Web:* corbinturf.com	Greenville	SC	29617	864-233-2113	
Dew-El Corp 10841 Paw Paw Dr *TF:* 800-443-3935 ■ *Web:* dew-el.com	Holland	MI	49424	616-396-6554	396-6669
Digital Air Strike Co 932 Hamlin Court *Web:* digitalairstrike.com	Sunnyvale	CA	94089	408-220-6500	
Eaccess Solutions Inc 407 N Quentin Rd *Web:* eaccess.com	Palatine	IL	60067	847-991-7190	
Email Co, The 15 Kainona Ave *TF:* 877-933-6245 ■ *Web:* theemailcompany.com	Toronto	ON	M3H3H4	877-933-6245	
Eureka Water Co 729 SW Third St *Web:* ozarkah2o.com	Oklahoma City	OK	73109	405-235-8474	
F G Quality Supply Inc 41 N Hillside Ave	Hillside	IL	60162	708-449-0300	
Fabulous Specialties Inc 600 Livingston Ave	Livingston	NJ	07039	973-535-6300	
Farrar Pump & Machinery Company Inc 1701 S Big Bend Blvd *Web:* farrarpump.com	Saint Louis	MO	63117	314-644-1050	
Fleet Feet Inc 406 E Main St *Web:* fleetfeetsports.com	Carrboro	NC	27510	919-942-3102	
Fosdick Fulfillment Corp 26 Barnes Industrial Park Rd *Web:* www.fosdickfulfillment.com	North Wallingford	CT	06492	203-269-0211	
Getconnect 14114 Dallas Pkwy Ste 430 *TF:* 888-200-1831 ■ *Web:* www.getconnect.com	Dallas	TX	75254	888-200-1831	
Gibraltar Trade Ctr Inc 15525 Racho Blvd *Web:* www.gibraltartrade.com	Taylor	MI	48180	734-287-2000	287-8330
Ginger G 1015 crocker st *Web:* home.mail.nate.com	Los angeles	CA	90021	213-765-8397	
Golden Neo-Life Diamite International 3500 Gateway Blvd **Fax Area Code:* 510 ■ *TF:* 800-432-5842 ■ *Web:* us.gnld.com	Fremont	CA	94538	800-432-5842	657-7563*
Goldshield Elite 1501 Northpoint Pkwy **Fax Area Code:* 800 ■ *TF:* 866-218-8142 ■ *Web:* www.goldenprideonline.com	West Palm Beach	FL	33407	561-615-4701	423-3135*
Hp2 Inc 1630 E Bethany Home Rd *Web:* hp2promo.com	Phoenix	AZ	85016	602-235-9099	
Hunter Events 1686 Union St Ste 305 *Web:* hunterproductionssf.com	San Francisco	CA	94123	415-563-8704	
Ice Mountain Spring Water 4231 C Leap Rd *Web:* www.nestlewatersnorthamerica.com	Hilliard	OH	43026	614-876-0626	
Image Iv Systems Inc 512 S Varney St *Web:* imageiv.com	Burbank	CA	91502	818-841-0756	
Inbox Group LLC 2100 W Northwest Hwy Ste 114-1135 *Web:* www.inboxgroup.com	Grapevine	TX	76051	214-530-5972	
Insight Public Sector Inc 444 Scott Dr *Web:* www.ips.insight.com	Bloomingdale	IL	60108	630-924-6801	
It Fitz Tools Inc 2064 Trlwood Dr W	Burleson	TX	76028	817-295-3093	
Janco Supply Company Inc 723 N Highland Ave	Aurora	IL	60506	630-896-4651	
JAZD Markets Inc Three Dundee Park Ste 102 *Web:* www.jazd.net	Andover	MA	01810	978-470-4620	
JR Watkins Inc 150 Liberty St PO Box 5570 *TF:* 800-243-9423 ■ *Web:* www.jrwatkins.com	Winona	MN	55987	507-457-3300	452-6723
Kabam Inc 795 Folsom St Ste 600 *Web:* kabam.com	San Francisco	CA	94107	415-391-0817	
Kaeser & Blair Inc 4236 Grissom Dr *Web:* kaeser-blair.com	Batavia	OH	45103	800-642-0790	
KMA One 6815 Meadowridge Ct *Web:* www.kmaone.com	Alpharetta	GA	30005	770-886-4000	
Kwik Kafe Company Inc 204 Furnace St *Web:* www.kwikkafeco.com	Bluefield	VA	24605	276-322-4691	
Lonestar Badge & Sign 301 Quail Run *Web:* lonestarbadge.com	San Marcos	TX	78666	512-353-0419	
Magnets.com 51 Pacific Ave Ste 4 *TF:* 866-229-8237 ■ *Web:* www.magnets.com	Jersey City	NJ	07304	866-229-8237	
Mail Shark 4125 New Holland Rd *TF:* 888-457-4275 ■ *Web:* www.themailshark.com	Mohnton	PA	19540	888-457-4275	
Mannatech Inc 600 S Royal Ln Ste 200 *NASDAQ:* MTEX ■ *Web:* us.mannatech.com	Coppell	TX	75019	972-471-7400	471-8191
Mary Kay Inc PO Box 799045 **Fax:* Cust Svc ■ *TF Cust Svc:* 800-627-9529 ■ *Web:* www.marykay.com	Dallas	TX	75379	972-687-6300	687-1608*
MCH Inc 601 E Marshall St *Web:* www.mchdata.com	Sweet Springs	MO	65351	660-335-6373	
Melaleuca Inc 3910 S Yellowstone Hwy **Fax Area Code:* 888 ■ *TF Sales:* 800-282-3000 ■ *Web:* www.melaleuca.com	Idaho Falls	ID	83402	208-522-0700	528-2090*
Mid-West Marketing Inc 239 Hwy 61 PO Box 125 *Web:* mwmktg.espwebsite.com	Bloomsdale	MO	63627	573-483-2577	483-9747
Midwest Railcar Repair Inc 25965 482nd Ave *Web:* www.mwrail.com	Brandon	SD	57005	605-582-8300	
Modern Office Methods Inc 4747 Lk Forest Dr Ste 200 *Web:* momnet.com	Cincinnati	OH	45242	513-791-0909	
Mt Shasta Spring Water Company Inc 1878 Twin View Blvd *Web:* www.mtshastaspringwater.com	Redding	CA	96003	530-246-8800	
Noevir USA Inc 1095 Main St *TF:* 800-872-8817 ■ *Web:* www.noevirusa.com	Irvine	CA	92614	949-660-1111	660-7168
North American Membership Group Inc (NAMG) 12301 Whitewater Dr *Web:* www.namginc.com	Minnetonka	MN	55343	952-936-9333	936-9169
Nutrilite Products Inc 5600 Beach Blvd PO Box 5940 *Web:* www.nutrilite.com	Buena Park	CA	90621	714-562-6200	736-7610
Pampered Chef Ltd 1 Pampered Chef Ln **Fax Area Code:* 630 ■ *TF:* 888-687-2433 ■ *Web:* www.pamperedchef.com	Addison	IL	60101	888-687-2433	261-8522*
Partylite Gifts Inc 59 Armstrong Rd *TF:* 888-999-5706 ■ *Web:* www.partylite.com	Plymouth	MA	02360	508-830-3100	732-5818
Perfect Parties Usa 147 Summit St *Web:* www.perfectpartiesusa.com	Peabody	MA	01960	978-977-0500	
Poly Expert Inc 850 ave Munck *Web:* www.polyexpert.com	Laval	QC	H7S1B1	514-384-5060	
Princess House Inc 470 Miles Standish Blvd *TF Sales:* 800-622-0039 ■ *Web:* www.princesshouse.com	Taunton	MA	02780	508-823-0711	880-1335
Prism Assoc Inc 9747 Business Park Ave Ste 217 *Web:* callprism.com	San Diego	CA	92131	858-695-7099	
Private Party Consignments 11344 Interstate 10 E *Web:* rvconsignment.com	Baytown	TX	77523	281-303-3000	
Rak Medical Inc 340 Duquesne Way *Web:* rakmedical.com	Sewickley	PA	15143	412-741-2880	
Ravenswood Special Events 1100 W Cermak Rd Ste B411 *Web:* www.virtualworld.com	Chicago	IL	60608	312-633-2600	
Razorgator 4094 Glencoe Ave Ste A *Web:* razorgator.com	Marina Del Rey	CA	90292	310-481-3400	
Redi-Direct Marketing Inc Five Audrey Pl *Web:* www.redidirect.com	Fairfield	NJ	07004	973-808-4500	
Reliv International Inc 136 Chesterfield Industrial Blvd *NASDAQ:* RELV ■ *TF:* 800-735-4887 ■ *Web:* www.reliv.com	Chesterfield	MO	63005	636-537-9715	537-9753
Rena Ware International Inc 15885 NE 28th St *Web:* www.renaware.com	Bellevue	WA	98008	425-881-6171	882-7500
Repforce Inc 530 Turner Industrial Way *Web:* repforce.com	Aston	PA	19014	610-485-7800	
Rexair Inc 50 W Big Beaver Rd Ste 350 *Web:* www.rainbowsystem.com	Troy	MI	48084	248-643-7222	643-7676
S Klahr Inc 45 Randolph Dr	Dix Hills	NY	11746	631-462-9630	
Saladmaster Inc 230 Westway Pl Ste 101 *TF:* 800-765-5795 ■ *Web:* www.saladmaster.com	Arlington	TX	76018	817-633-3555	633-5544
Select Publishing Inc 6417 Normandy Ln *Web:* www.selectpublications.ca	Madison	WI	53719	608-277-5787	
Shaklee Corp 4747 Willow Rd *TF:* 800-742-5533 ■ *Web:* www.shaklee.com	Pleasanton	CA	94588	925-924-2000	924-2862
SK Food Group Inc 4600 37th Ave SW *TF:* 800-722-6290 ■ *Web:* skfoodgroup.com	Seattle	WA	98126	206-935-8100	
Smartpak Equine LLC 40 Grissom Rd Ste 500 *TF:* 888-752-5171 ■ *Web:* www.smartpakequine.com	Plymouth	MA	02360	774-773-1000	
Specialty Merchandise Corp 996 Flower Glen St *TF Orders:* 800-345-4762 ■ *Web:* www.smartlivingcompany.com	Simi Valley	CA	93065	805-578-5500	
Stampin Up 12907 South 3600 West *Web:* stampinup.com	Riverton	UT	84065	801-257-5400	
Starfish Junction Productions Llc 226 N Fehr Way *Web:* www.starfishjunction.com	Bay Shore	NY	11706	631-940-7291	
Success Motivation International Inc 4567 Lakeshore Dr *TF Sales:* 888-391-0050 ■ *Web:* www.success-motivation.com	Waco	TX	76710	254-776-9966	776-1230
Sunrider International 1625 Abalone Ave **Fax:* Hum Res ■ *TF Orders:* 888-278-6743 ■ *Web:* www.sunrider.com	Torrance	CA	90501	310-781-3808	222-6329*
Tebons Gas & Auto Service Inc 7415 N Harlem Ave *Web:* tebonsgas.com	Niles	IL	60714	847-647-9800	
Technifax Office Solutions 3220 Keller Springs Rd *Web:* technifaxdfw.com	Carrollton	TX	75006	972-478-2800	478-2812
Terco Supply 12725 Ross Ave	Chino	CA	91710	909-628-4694	
Thirty-One Gifts LLC 3425 Morse Crossing *Web:* thirtyonegifts.com	Columbus	OH	43219	614-414-4300	
Top Dog Express Car Wash 3720 Lake Emma *Web:* lakemarycarwash.com	Lake Mary	FL	32746	407-333-3200	
TouchPoint Technologies LLC 2319 Oak Myrtle Ln Ste 104 *TF:* 877-898-6824 ■ *Web:* www.touchpointtechnologies.com	Wesley Chapel	FL	33544	877-898-6824	
Towsleys Inc 1424 Dewey St *Web:* towsleys.net	Manitowoc	WI	54220	920-683-7400	
Tru-Brew Coffee Service Inc 387 Springdale Ave	Hatboro	PA	19040	215-441-0110	
University Subscription Service 1213 Butterfield Rd	Downers Grove	IL	60515	630-960-3233	960-3246
VC Enterprises Ltd 2025 Olive Ave	Sibley	IA	51249	712-724-6256	
Vector Marketing Co 322 Houghton Ave *TF:* 800-828-0448 ■ *Web:* www.vectoroncampus.com	Olean	NY	14760	800-828-0448	
Verndale Corp, The 28 Damrell St Ste 300 *TF:* 866-942-8376 ■ *Web:* www.verndale.com	Boston	MA	02127	866-942-8376	
Viking Magazine Service Inc PO Box 201059 *TF:* 800-339-9492 ■ *Web:* www.vikingmagazine.com	Bloomington	MN	55420	800-339-9492	
Vita Motivator Company Inc 405 Cedar Ln - Ste 7A	Teaneck	NJ	07666	201-530-0277	
Vorwerk USA Company LP 1964 Corporate Sq *TF:* 800-562-6726 ■ *Web:* www.vorwerk.com	Longwood	FL	32750	407-830-9988	830-9958
We Buy Guitars LLC 705 Bedford Ave Ste A *Web:* webuyguitars.org	Bellmore	NY	11710	516-221-0563	
WEBCARGO Inc 800 Pl Victoria Ste 2603 Tour de la bourse CP 329 *TF:* 866-905-0123 ■ *Web:* www.webcargo.net	Montreal	QC	H4Z1G8	866-905-0123	
WebEyeCare Inc 10 Canal St Ste 302 *TF:* 888-536-7480 ■ *Web:* www.webeyecare.com	Bristol	PA	19007	888-536-7480	
Winfield Micro Systems Inc 2333 Wisconsin Ave *Web:* winfieldmicro.com	Downers Grove	IL	60515	630-960-5515	
Wolper Subscription Services Inc 360 Northampton St *Web:* www.wolper.com	Easton	PA	18042	610-559-9550	
YourAreaCode LLC 6242 28th St Ste B *Web:* www.yourareacode.com	Grand Rapids	MI	49546	616-622-2000	

370 HOME WARRANTY SERVICES

				Phone	Fax
American Home Shield 889 Ridge Lake Blvd PO Box 851	Memphis	TN	38120	901-537-8000	537-8005
TF: 800-776-4663 ■ *Web:* www.ahs.com					
Asset Marketing Systems Insurance Services LLC 15050 Ave of Science	San Diego	CA	92128	888-303-8755	
TF: 888-303-8755 ■ *Web:* amsfmo.com					
Blue Ribbon Home Warranty Inc 95 S Wadsworth Blvd	Lakewood	CO	80226	303-986-3900	986-3152
TF: 800-571-0475 ■ *Web:* blueribbonhomewarranty.com					
Cross Country Home Services 1625 NW 136th Ave Ste 200	Fort Lauderdale	FL	33323	954-845-2468	845-2264
TF Cust Svc: 800-778-8000 ■ *Web:* www.cchs.com					
Cypress Care Inc 2736 Meadow Church Rd Ste 300	Duluth	GA	30097	800-419-7191	
TF: 800-419-7191 ■ *Web:* www.cypresscare.com					
First American Home Buyers Protection Corp 7833 Haskell Ave PO Box 10180	Van Nuys	CA	91410	818-781-5050	772-1151*
**Fax Area Code:* 800 ■ *TF:* 800-444-9030 ■ *Web:* www.homewarranty.firstam.com					
Home Security of America Inc 310 N Midvale Blvd	Madison	WI	53705	800-367-1448	638-1741*
**Fax Area Code:* 877 ■ *TF:* 800-367-1448 ■ *Web:* www.onlinehsa.com					
Warrantech Corp Inc 2200 Hwy 121	Bedford	TX	76021	817-785-6601	
TF: 800-833-8801 ■ *Web:* www.warrantech.com					

371 HORSE BREEDERS

SEE ALSO Livestock Improvement Services p. 1725

				Phone	Fax
Airdrie Stud Inc 2641 Old Frankfort Pk PO Box 487	Midway	KY	40347	859-873-7270	873-6140
Web: www.airdriestud.com					
Ashford Stud 5095 Frankford Rd	Versailles	KY	40383	859-873-7088	879-5756
Web: www.coolmore.com					
Claiborne Farm 703 Winchester Rd	Paris	KY	40361	859-233-4252	987-0008
Web: www.clabornefarm.com					
Country Life Farm 319 Old Joppa Rd	Bel Air	MD	21014	410-879-1952	879-6207
Web: www.countrylifefarm.com					
Darby Dan Farm 3225 Old Frankfort Pk	Lexington	KY	40510	859-254-0424	281-6612
Web: www.darbydan.com					
Gainesway Farm 3750 Paris Pk	Lexington	KY	40511	859-293-2676	299-9371
Web: www.gainesway.com					
Glencrest Farm 1576 Moores Mill Rd PO Box 4468	Midway	KY	40347	859-233-7032	233-9404
TF: 800-903-0136 ■ *Web:* www.glencrest.com					
Grant's Farm 10501 Gravois Rd	Saint Louis	MO	63123	314-843-1700	525-0822
Web: anheuser-busch.com					
Lancaster DHIA 1592 Old Line Rd	Manheim	PA	17545	717-665-5960	
Web: www.lancasterdhia.com					
Lane's End Farm 1500 Midway Rd PO Box 626	Versailles	KY	40383	859-873-7300	873-3746
TF: 800-456-3412 ■ *Web:* www.lanesend.com					
Margaux Farm LLC 596 Moores Mill Rd PO Box 4220	Midway	KY	40347	859-846-4433	846-4486
Web: www.margauxfarm.com					
Mill Ridge Farm 2800 Bowman Mill Rd	Lexington	KY	40513	859-231-0606	255-6010
TF: 800-950-6397 ■ *Web:* www.millridge.com					
Millford Farm 4852 Midway Rd PO Box 4351	Midway	KY	40347	859-846-4705	846-4226
Web: www.millford.com					
Northview Stallion Station 55 Northern Dancer Dr	Chesapeake City	MD	21915	410-885-2855	
Web: www.northviewstallions.com					
Old Frankfort Stud 360 Watts Ferry Rd	Frankfort	KY	40601	859-233-1717	
Pin Oak Stud 830 Grassy Spring Rd PO Box 68	Versailles	KY	40383	859-873-1420	873-2391
Web: www.pinoakstud.com					
Stone Farm 200 Stoney Pt Rd	Paris	KY	40361	859-987-3737	987-1474
Web: www.stonefarm.com					
Sugar Maple Farm Five Sugar Ln	Poughquag	NY	12570	845-221-0575	
Three Chimneys Farm PO Box 114	Midway	KY	40347	859-873-7053	873-5723
Web: www.threechimneys.com					
Vinery Kentucky LLC 4241 Spurr Rd	Lexington	KY	40511	859-455-9388	455-9588
Wimbledon Farm 1725 Walnut Hill Rd	Lexington	KY	40515	859-272-0636	271-1435
Windfall Farms 4710 Flying Paster Ln	Paso Robles	CA	93446	805-239-0711	
Web: www.windfallfarms.net					
Windfields Farm 2525 DeLong Rd	Lexington	KY	40515	859-273-3050	273-3035
WinStar Farm LLC 3001 Pisgah Pk	Versailles	KY	40383	859-873-1717	873-1612
Web: www.winstarfarm.com					

372 HORTICULTURAL PRODUCTS GROWERS

SEE ALSO Garden Centers p. 2353; Seed Companies p. 3161

				Phone	Fax
Ades & Gish Nurseries 2222 N Twin Oaks Vly Rd	San Marcos	CA	92069	760-410-0400	410-0433
Web: www.agnurseries.com					
Aldershot of New Mexico Inc 4884 S Main St	Mesilla Park	NM	88047	575-523-8621	
Alex R Masson Inc 12819 198th St	Linwood	KS	66052	913-301-3281	301-3288
TF General: 800-879-2539 ■ *Web:* www.armasson.com					
Altman Specialty Plants Inc 3742 Blue BiRd Canyon Rd	Vista	CA	92084	760-744-8191	744-8835
TF: 800-773-7667 ■ *Web:* www.altmanplants.com					
Ameri-Cal Floral Inc 94 San Miguel Canyon Rd	Watsonville	CA	95076	831-728-4205	
Web: www.americal.com					
Aris Horticulture Inc 115 Third St SE	Barberton	OH	44203	800-232-9557	745-3098*
**Fax Area Code:* 330 ■ *TF:* 800-232-9557 ■ *Web:* www.arishort.com					
Battlefield Farms Inc 23190 Clarks Mtn Rd	Rapidan	VA	22733	800-722-0744	854-6486*
**Fax Area Code:* 540 ■ *TF:* 800-722-0744 ■ *Web:* www.battlefieldfarms.com					
Bay City Flower Company Inc 2265 Cabrillo Hwy S	Half Moon Bay	CA	94019	650-726-5535	
TF Sales: 800-399-5858 ■ *Web:* www.baycityflower.com					
Bell Nursery Inc 3838 Bell Rd	Burtonsville	MD	20866	301-421-1500	421-4269
Web: www.bellnursery.com					
Bettinger Farms Inc 11602 Frankfort Rd	Swanton	OH	43558	419-829-2771	202-2125*
**Fax Area Code:* 567 ■ *TF:* 855-629-7661 ■ *Web:* bettingersgreenhouse.com					
Blue Ridge Growers Inc 21409 Germanna Hwy	Stevensburg	VA	22741	540-399-1636	
Web: www.blueridgegrowers.com					
Burgett Floral Inc 868 Fuller NE	Grand Rapids	MI	49503	616-456-1999	
TF: 800-404-2999 ■ *Web:* www.burgettflorist.com					
California Pajarosa 133 Hughes Rd PO Box 684	Watsonville	CA	95077	831-722-6374	722-1316
Web: www.pajarosa.com					
CD Ford & Sons Inc PO Box 300	Geneseo	IL	61254	309-944-4661	944-3703
TF: 800-383-4661 ■ *Web:* www.cdford.com					
Color Spot Nurseries Inc 2575 Olive Hill Rd	Fallbrook	CA	92028	760-695-1480	250-5135*
**Fax Area Code:* 800 ■ *TF:* 800-554-4065 ■ *Web:* www.colorspot.com					
Colorama Wholesale Nursery 1025 N Todd Ave	Azusa	CA	91702	626-969-3585	
Web: coloramanursery.com					
Costa Nursery Farms Inc 21800 SW 162nd Ave	Miami	FL	33170	800-327-7074	
TF: 800-327-7074 ■ *Web:* www.costafarms.com					
Cuthbert Greenhouses Inc 4900 Hendron Rd	Groveport	OH	43125	614-836-3866	836-3767
TF: 800-321-1939 ■ *Web:* cuthbertgreenhouse.com					
Dallas Johnson Greenhouse Inc 2802 Twin City Dr	Council Bluffs	IA	51501	712-366-0407	
TF: 800-445-4794 ■ *Web:* www.djgreenhouses.com					
Dan Schantz Farm & Greenhouses LLC 8025 Spinnerstown Rd	Zionsville	PA	18092	610-967-2181	
TF: 800-451-3064 ■ *Web:* www.danschantz.com					
DeLeon's Bromeliads Co 13745 SW 216th St	Miami	FL	33170	305-238-6028	235-2354
TF: 800-448-8649 ■ *Web:* www.deleons4color.com					
Dramm & Echter Inc 1150 Quail Gardens Dr	Encinitas	CA	92024	760-436-0188	436-2974
TF: 800-854-7021 ■ *Web:* www.drammechter.com					
Ever-Bloom Inc 4701 Foothill Rd	Carpinteria	CA	93013	805-684-5566	
Web: www.ever-bloom.com					
Farmers West 5300 Foothill Rd	Carpinteria	CA	93013	805-684-5531	684-1528
TF: 800-549-0085 ■ *Web:* www.farmerswest.com					
Garden State Growers 99 Locust Grove Rd	Pittstown	NJ	08867	908-730-8888	730-6676
TF: 800-288-8484 ■ *Web:* www.gardenstategrowers.com					
Green Circle Growers Inc 51051 US Hwy 20	Oberlin	OH	44074	440-775-1411	774-1465
Web: www.greencirclegrowers.com					
Green Valley Floral Co 24999 Potter Rd	Salinas	CA	93908	831-424-7691	424-4473
TF: 800-228-1255 ■ *Web:* www.greenvalleyfloral.com					
Greenleaf Nursery Co 28406 Hwy 82	Park Hill	OK	74451	918-457-5172	407-5550*
**Fax Area Code:* 800 ■ *TF:* 800-331-2982 ■ *Web:* www.greenleafnursery.com					
Harts Nursery of Jefferson Inc 4049 Jefferson-Scio Rd	Jefferson	OR	97352	541-327-3366	327-1603
TF: 800-356-9335 ■ *Web:* www.hartsnursery.com					
Ingleside Plantation Nurseries 5870 Leedstown Rd	Oak Grove	VA	22443	804-224-7111	224-2032
Web: inglesidenurseries.com					
Johannes Flowers Inc 4990 Foothill Rd	Carpinteria	CA	93013	805-684-5686	566-2199
TF: 800-365-9476 ■ *Web:* www.johannesflowers.com					
Kerry's Nursery Inc 21840 SW 258th St	Homestead	FL	33031	800-331-9127	
TF: 800-331-9127 ■ *Web:* www.kerrys.com					
Knox Nursery Inc 940 Avalon Rd	Winter Garden	FL	34787	800-441-5669	290-1702*
**Fax Area Code:* 407 ■ *TF:* 800-441-5669 ■ *Web:* www.knoxnursery.com					
Kocher Flower Growers 950 Brittany Rd	Encinitas	CA	92024	760-436-1458	
Kurt Weiss Greenhouses Inc 95 Main St	Center Moriches	NY	11934	631-878-2500	878-2553
TF: 800-344-7805 ■ *Web:* www.kurtweiss.com					
Layser's Flowers Inc 501 W Washington Ave	Myerstown	PA	17067	717-866-5746	866-6099
Web: www.laysersflowers.com					
Matsui Nursery Inc 1645 Old Stage Rd	Salinas	CA	93908	831-422-6433	422-2387
TF: 800-793-6433 ■ *Web:* www.matsuinursery.net					
McLellan Botanicals 2352 San Juan Rd	Aromas	CA	95004	800-467-2443	543-6836*
**Fax Area Code:* 415 ■ *TF:* 800-467-2443 ■ *Web:* www.taisucoamerica.com					
Metrolina Greenhouses Inc 16400 Huntersville-Concord Rd	Huntersville	NC	28078	704-875-1371	875-6741
TF: 800-543-3915 ■ *Web:* www.metrolinagreenhouses.com					
Mid American Growers Inc 14240 Greenhouse Ave	Granville	IL	61326	815-339-6831	339-2747
Nurserymen's Exchange 2651 N Cabrillo Hwy	Half Moon Bay	CA	94019	650-712-4195	712-4290
TF General: 800-227-5229 ■ *Web:* www.rocketfarms.com					
Ocean Breeze International (OBI) 3910 Via Real	Carpinteria	CA	93013	805-684-1747	684-0235
TF: 888-715-8888 ■ *Web:* www.oceanbreezeintl.com					
Oglevee Ltd 152 Oglevee Ln	Connellsville	PA	15425	724-628-8360	628-7270
Panzer Nursery Inc 17980 W Baseline Rd	Beaverton	OR	97006	503-645-1185	629-9023
TF: 888-212-5327 ■ *Web:* www.panzernursery.com					
Parks Bros Farm Inc 6733 Parks Rd	Van Buren	AR	72956	479-474-1125	471-7051
TF: 800-334-5770 ■ *Web:* www.parksbrothers.com					
Paul Ecke Ranch Inc 527 Encinitas Ste 104	Encinitas	CA	92024	760-753-1134	
Web: www.ecke.com					
Petitti Garden Centers 24964 Broadway Ave	Oakwood Village	OH	44146	440-439-6511	439-7736
Web: www.petittigardencenter.com					
Post Gardens Inc 21189 Huron River Dr	Rockwood	MI	48173	734-379-9688	
TF: 800-834-4630					
Rockwell Farms Inc 332 Rockwell Farms Rd	Rockwell	NC	28138	800-635-6576	279-8573*
**Fax Area Code:* 704 ■ *TF:* 800-635-6576 ■ *Web:* www.rockwellfarms.com					
Sedan Floral Inc 406 S School St PO Box 339	Sedan	KS	67361	620-725-3111	725-5257
Web: www.sedanfloral.com					
Silver Terrace Nurseries Inc 501 N St	Pescadero	CA	94060	650-879-2110	
Smith Gardens Inc 4164 Meridian St Ste 400	Bellingham	WA	98226	360-733-4671	647-1468
TF: 800-755-6256 ■ *Web:* www.smithgardens.com					

Phone Fax

Speedling Inc 4447 Old 41 Hwy S .... Ruskin FL 33570 800-881-4769 645-8123*
**Fax Area Code:* 813 ■ *TF Cust Svc:* 800-881-4769 ■ *Web:* www.speedling.com

Sun Valley Floral Farms Inc 3160 Upper Bay Rd .... Arcata CA 95521 800-747-0396 826-8708*
**Fax Area Code:* 707 ■ *TF:* 800-747-0396 ■ *Web:* www.sunvalleyfloral.com

Sunshine Foliage World
2060 Steve Roberts Special .... Zolfo Springs FL 33890 863-735-0501
Web: www.sunshinefoliageworld.com

Van Wingerden International Inc
4112 Haywood Rd .... Mills River NC 28759 828-891-4116
TF: 800-226-3597 ■ *Web:* www.natures-heritage.com

Westerlay Orchids 3504 Via Real .... Carpinteria CA 93013 805-684-5411 684-5414
Web: www.westerlayorchids.com

Westland Floral Co 1400 Cravens Ln .... Carpinteria CA 93013 805-684-4011 684-0685
Web: www.westlandfloral.com

White's Nursery & Greenhouses Inc
3133 Old Mill Rd .... Chesapeake VA 23323 757-487-2300 487-7845
TF: 800-966-9969 ■ *Web:* www.whitesnursery.com

Woodburn Nursery & Azaleas
13009 McKee School Rd NE .... Woodburn OR 97071 503-634-2231 634-2238
TF Sales: 888-634-2232 ■ *Web:* www.woodburnnursery.com

Worthington Farms Inc
3661 BallaRds Crossroads Rd .... Greenville NC 27834 252-756-3827 756-9442
Web: www.worthingtonfarms.com

Young's Plant Farm PO Box 3410 .... Auburn AL 36830 800-304-8609
TF: 800-304-8609 ■ *Web:* www.youngsplantfarm.com

373 HOSE & BELTING - RUBBER OR PLASTICS

SEE ALSO Automotive Parts & Supplies - Mfr p. 1839

Phone Fax

ABC Industrie PO Box 77 .... Warsaw IN 46581 574-267-5166 267-2045
TF: 800-426-0921 ■ *Web:* www.abc-industries.net

AdChem Manufacturing Technologies Inc
369 Progress Dr .... Manchester CT 06042 860-645-0592
Web: www.acmtct.com

Advanced Technology Products Inc
12740 State Rt 4 .... Milford Center OH 43045 937-349-4055
Web: atp4pneumatics.com

Aero Rubber Company Inc 8100 W 185th St .... Tinley Park IL 60487 708-430-4900 662-4400*
**Fax Area Code:* 800 ■ *TF:* 800-662-1009 ■ *Web:* www.aerorubber.com

American Hose & Rubber Co 3645 E 44th St .... Tucson AZ 85713 520-514-1666
TF: 800-272-7537 ■ *Web:* amhose.com

Ammeraal Beltech USA 7501 N St Louis Ave .... Skokie IL 60076 847-673-6720 673-6373
TF Cust Svc: 800-323-4170 ■ *Web:* www.ammeraal-beltechusa.com

Apache Hose & Belting Co Inc
4805 Bowling St SW PO Box 1719 .... Cedar Rapids IA 52404 319-365-0471 365-2522
TF Sales: 800-553-5455 ■ *Web:* www.apache-inc.com

Atco Rubber Products Inc 7101 Atco Dr .... Fort Worth TX 76118 817-595-2894 595-5719
TF: 800-877-3828 ■ *Web:* www.atcoflex.com

Atcoflex Inc 14261 172nd Ave .... Grand Haven MI 49417 616-842-4661 842-4623
Web: www.atcoflexinc.com

Belterra Corp 1638 Fosters Way .... Delta BC V3M6S6 604-540-1950
Web: www.belterra.ca

Belting Industries Company Inc
20 Boright Ave .... Kenilworth NJ 07033 908-272-8591 272-3825
TF: 800-843-2358 ■ *Web:* www.beltingindustries.com

Carlstar Group LLC, The
725 Cool Springs Blvd Ste 500 .... Franklin TN 37067 615-503-0220 503-0228
TF: 866-773-2926 ■ *Web:* www.carlisletransportationproducts.com

Chemprene Inc 483 Fishkill Ave PO Box 471 .... Beacon NY 12508 845-831-2800 831-4639
TF: 800-431-9981 ■ *Web:* www.chemprene.com

Cobon Plastics Corporation 90 S St .... Newark NJ 07114 973-344-6330
Web: www.cobonplastics.com

Coilhose Pneumatics Inc
19 Kimberly Rd .... East Brunswick NJ 08816 732-390-8480 390-9693
TF: 800-424-9300 ■ *Web:* www.coilhose.com

Colorite Plastics Co 101 Railroad Ave .... Ridgefield NJ 07657 201-941-2900
Web: tekni-plex.com

Cooper Tire & Rubber Co 701 Lima Ave .... Findlay OH 45840 419-423-1321 424-4108
NYSE: CTB ■ *TF:* 800-854-6288 ■ *Web:* www.coopertire.com

Copper State Rubber of Arizona Inc
750 S 59th Ave .... Phoenix AZ 85043 602-269-5927 269-8106
Web: copperstaterubber.com

Cosmoflex Inc 4142 Industrial Dr .... Hannibal MO 63401 573-221-0242 221-9290

Dormont Manufacturing Co 6015 Enterprise Dr .... Export PA 15632 800-367-6668
TF: 800-367-6668 ■ *Web:* www.dormont.com

Dynacraft Co 650 Milwaukee Ave N .... Algona WA 98001 253-333-3000 333-3041
Web: dynacraftnet.com

Eaton Corp 1111 Superior Ave Eaton Ctr .... Cleveland OH 44114 216-523-5000
Web: www.eaton.com

Fenner Drives 311 W Stiegel St .... Manheim PA 17545 717-665-2421 664-8214
TF Sales: 800-243-3374 ■ *Web:* www.fennerdrives.com

Flexaust Co 1510 Armstrong Rd .... Warsaw IN 46580 574-267-7909 382-8464*
**Fax Area Code:* 800 ■ *TF:* 800-343-0428 ■ *Web:* www.flexaust.com

Flexfab LLC 1699 W M-43 Hwy .... Hastings MI 49058 269-945-2433 945-4802
Web: www.flexfab.com

Freelin-Wade Co 1730 NE Miller St .... McMinnville OR 97128 503-434-5561 472-1989
TF: 888-373-9233 ■ *Web:* www.freelin-wade.com

Gates Corp 1551 Wewatta St .... Denver CO 80202 303-744-1911 744-4000
TF: 800-709-6001 ■ *Web:* www.gates.com

Habasit ABT Inc 150 Industrial Pk Rd .... Middletown CT 06457 860-632-2211 632-1710
TF: 800-522-2358 ■ *Web:* www.habasit.com

Habasit Belting Inc 1400 Clinton St .... Buffalo NY 14206 716-824-8484
TF: 800-325-1585 ■ *Web:* www.habasit.com

HBD/Thermoid Inc 1301 W Sandusky Ave .... Bellefontaine OH 43311 937-593-5010 593-4354
TF: 800-543-8070 ■ *Web:* www.hbdthermoid.com

Industrial Rubber Works
1700 Nicholas Blvd .... Elk Grove Village IL 60007 847-952-1800
Web: www.abbottrubber.com

Jason Industrial Inc 340 Kaplan Dr .... Fairfield NJ 07004 973-227-4904 227-1651
Web: www.jasonindustrial.com

Phone Fax

JGB Enterprises Inc 115 Metropolitan Dr .... Liverpool NY 13088 315-451-2770 451-8503
Web: www.jgbhose.com

Key Fire Hose Corp (KFH) PO Box 7107 .... Dothan AL 36302 334-671-5532 671-5616
TF: 800-447-5666 ■ *Web:* www.keyfire.com

Legg Company Inc 325 E Tenth St .... Halstead KS 67056 800-835-1003 835-3218*
**Fax Area Code:* 316 ■ *TF Sales:* 800-835-1003 ■ *Web:* www.leggbelting.com

Lockwood Products Inc 5615 Willow Ln .... Lake Oswego OR 97035 503-635-8113 635-2844
TF: 800-423-1625 ■ *Web:* www.loc-line.com

Mattracks Systems 202 Cleveland Ave E .... Karlstad MN 56732 218-436-7000
Web: www.mattracks.com

Mercer Rubber Co 350 Rabro Dr .... Hauppauge NY 11788 631-582-1524 348-0279
Web: www.mercer-rubber.com

Mulhern Belting Inc 148 Bauer Dr .... Oakland NJ 07436 201-337-5700 337-6540
TF: 800-253-6300 ■ *Web:* www.mulhernbelting.com

NewAge Industries Inc 145 James Way .... SouthHampton PA 18966 215-526-2300 526-2190
TF: 800-506-3924 ■ *Web:* www.newageindustries.com

Nichirin Tennessee Inc 1620 Old Belfast Rd .... Lewisburg TN 37091 931-359-5709
Web: www.nichirincanada.com

Parker Fluid Connectors Group
6035 Parkland Blvd .... Cleveland OH 44124 216-896-3000 896-4000
TF General: 800-272-7537 ■ *Web:* parker.com

Performance Polymer Technologies Co
8801 Washington Blvd Ste 109 .... Roseville CA 95678 916-677-1414 677-1474
Web: www.pptech.com

Plastiflex Company Inc
601-C E Palomar St Ste 424 .... Chula Vista CA 91911 619-662-8792
Web: www.plastiflex.com

Ro-Lab American Rubber Co Inc 8830 W Linne Rd .... Tracy CA 95304 209-836-0965
TF: 800-678-0726 ■ *Web:* www.rolabamerican.com

Rubber Enterprises Inc 2083 Reek Rd .... Imlay City MI 48444 810-724-2400
Web: www.rubberenterprises.com

Salem-Republic Rubber Co
475 W California Ave .... Sebring OH 44672 330-938-9801 938-9809
TF: 800-686-4199 ■ *Web:* www.salem-republic.com

Shuster Corp Four Wright St .... New Bedford MA 02740 508-999-3261
Web: www.shustercorp.com

Snap-Tite Inc 8325 Hessinger Dr .... Erie PA 16509 814-838-5700 833-0145
Web: www.snap-tite.com

Sparks Belting Co 3800 Stahl Dr SE .... Grand Rapids MI 49546 616-949-2750 949-8518
TF: 800-451-4537 ■ *Web:* www.sparksbelting.com

Swan Hose 1201 Delaware Ave .... Marion OH 43302 800-848-8707
Web: www.swanhose.com

Tigerflex Corp 801 Estes Ave .... Elk Grove Village IL 60007 847-640-8366 640-8372
Web: tiger-poly.com

Titeflex Corp 603 Hendee St .... Springfield MA 01139 413-739-5631 788-7593
TF: 800-765-2525 ■ *Web:* www.titeflex.com

Unaflex LLC 1350 S Dixie Hwy E .... Pompano Beach FL 33064 954-943-5002 946-3583
TF: 800-327-1286 ■ *Web:* www.unaflex.com

US Rubber Corp 211 East Loop 336 .... Conroe TX 77301 936-756-1977 756-1674
Web: www.usrubbercorp.com

Voss Belting & Specialty Co
6965 N Hamlin Ave .... Lincolnwood IL 60712 847-673-8900 673-1408
TF: 800-323-3935 ■ *Web:* www.vossbelting.com

374 HOSPICES

SEE ALSO Specialty Hospitals p. 2522

Phone Fax

AgeCare Ltd 105 20 Sunpark Plz SE .... Calgary AB T2X3T2 403-873-3200
Web: www.agecare.ca

Agemark Corp 2614 Telegraph Ave .... Berkeley CA 94704 510-548-6600
Web: agemark.com

Aliceville Manor 703 17th St Nw .... Aliceville AL 35442 205-373-6307
Web: alicevillemanornursinghome.com

All Saints Health Care
11810 Saticoy St .... North Hollywood CA 91605 818-503-8190
Web: www.allsaints-subacute.com

All Seniors Care Living Centres Ltd
175 Bloor St E Ste 601 .... Toronto ON M4W3R8 416-323-3773
Web: www.allseniorscare.com

Amica at City Centre
380 Princess Royal Dr .... Mississauga ON L5B4M9 905-803-8100
Web: www.amica.ca

Amsterdam Nursing Home Corp
1060 Amsterdam Ave .... New York NY 10025 212-316-7700
Web: www.amsterdamcares.com

Amy Johnson Residence 89 Virginia St .... Saint Paul MN 55102 651-224-3363
Web: www.amyjohnsonresidence.com

Anderson Center For Autism Inc
4885 Route 9 PO Box 367 .... Staatsburg NY 12580 845-889-4034
Web: www.andersoncenterforautism.org

Angels Unaware Inc, The 4918 W Linebaugh Ave .... Tampa FL 33624 813-963-2529
Web: www.angelsunaware.com

Anna Maria of Aurora Inc 889 N Aurora Rd .... Aurora OH 44202 330-562-6171
Web: www.annamariaofaurora.com

Arcadia Convalescent Hospital Inc
1601 S Baldwin Ave .... Arcadia CA 91007 626-445-2170
Web: www.arcadiahealthcarecenter.com

Auburn Manor 501 Oak St N .... Chaska MN 55318 952-448-9303
Web: www.auburnhomes.org

Avante Group Inc
4000 Hollywood Blvd Ste 540N .... Hollywood FL 33021 954-987-7180
Web: www.avantecenters.com

Baptist Housing 6165 Hwy 17 Ste 125 .... Delta BC V4K5B8 604-940-1960
Web: www.baptisthousing.org

Baycrest Centre For Geriatric Care
3560 Bathurst St .... Toronto ON M6A2E1 416-785-2500
Web: www.baycrest.org

Bethesda Home 408 E Main St .... Goessel KS 67053 620-367-2291
Web: www.bethesdahome.org

Name / Address	City	State	Zip	Phone	Fax
Big Meadows 1000 Longmoor Ave *Web:* www.bigmeadows.biz	Savanna	IL	61074	815-273-2238	
Broncus Medical Inc 1400 N Shoreline Blvd Ste A8 *Web:* www.broncus.com	Mountain View	CA	94043	650-428-1600	
Calvert County Nursing Center Inc 85 Hospital Rd *Web:* calvertcountynursingcenter.org	Prince Frederick	MD	20678	410-535-2300	
Carewest 10301 Southport Ln SW Southport Tower *Web:* www.carewest.ca	Calgary	AB	T2W1S7	403-943-8140	
Cartmell Home for Aged Inc 2212 W Reagan St *Web:* cartmellhome.org	Palestine	TX	75801	903-727-8500	
Cedar Lake Nursing Home 1611 W Royall Blvd *Web:* cedarlakenursing.com	Malakoff	TX	75148	903-489-1702	
Chartwell Master Care LP 100 Milverton Dr Ste 700 *Web:* chartwell.com	Mississauga	ON	L5R4H1	905-501-9219	
Clare Oaks 825 Carillon Dr *Web:* www.clareoaks.com	Bartlett	IL	60103	630-372-1983	
Collingswood Nursing Facilities Inc 299 Hurley Ave *Web:* www.collingswoodnursing.com	Rockville	MD	20850	301-762-8900	
Columbus West Park Nursing & Rehabilitation Center 1700 Heinzerling Dr *Web:* columbuswestpark.com	Columbus	OH	43223	614-274-4222	
CommCare Corp 601 Poydras St 2755 Pan American Life Center *Web:* www.commcare.com	New Orleans	LA	70130	504-324-8950	
Compass Health Inc 200 S 13th St Ste 208 *Web:* www.compass-health.com	Grover Beach	CA	93433	805-474-7010	
Concord Care Center of Toledo Inc 3121 Glanzman Rd *Web:* www.concordcarecenters.com	Toledo	OH	43614	419-385-6616	
Convalescent Center of Honolulu 1900 Bachelot St *Web:* ccoh.us	Honolulu	HI	96817	808-531-5302	
Country Court Nursing Center 1076 Coshocton Ave *Web:* countrycourt.com	Mount Vernon	OH	43050	740-397-4125	
Country Hills Health Care Inc 1580 Broadway *Web:* www.countryhills.com	El Cajon	CA	92021	619-441-8745	
Covenant Care Home 600 Mount Moriah Church Rd *Web:* www.covenantcareathome.org	Lumberton	NC	28360	910-738-7777	
Crown Nursing Home Associates Inc 3457 Nostrand Ave *Web:* www.crowncares.com	Brooklyn	NY	11229	718-535-5100	
Davco Rest Home Resident 2526 W 10th St *Web:* www.fernterrace.com	Owensboro	KY	42301	270-684-1705	
Daybreak Venture LLC 401 N Elm St *Web:* www.daybreakventure.com	Denton	TX	76201	940-387-4388	
Diversicare Canada Management Services Inc 2121 Argentia Rd Ste 301 *Web:* www.diversicare.ca	Mississauga	ON	L5N2X4	905-821-1161	
Edgewood Vista 214 Piper St *Web:* www.edgewoodvista.com	Grand Island	NE	68803	308-384-0717	
Eliza Bryant Village 7201 Wade Park Ave *Web:* www.elizabryant.org	Cleveland	OH	44103	216-361-6141	
Elliott Community The 170 Metcalfe St *Web:* www.elliottcommunity.org	Guelph	ON	N1E4Y3	519-822-0491	
English Village Manor Nursing Home 1515 Canterbury Blvd *Web:* englishvillagemanor.com	Altus	OK	73521	580-477-1133	
Enlivant 330 N Wabash Ave Ste 3700 *Web:* www.enlivant.com	Chicago	IL	60611	312-725-7000	
Erwine Home Health & Hospice 270 Pierce St Ste 101 *Web:* erwineshomehealth.com	Kingston	PA	18704	570-288-1013	
Fair View Nursing Home 1714 W 16th St *Web:* fairviewnursinghomesedalia.com	Sedalia	MO	65301	660-827-1594	
Fairview Fellowship Home For Senior Citizens Inc 605 E State Rd *Web:* www.fellowshiphome.com	Fairview	OK	73737	580-227-3783	
Fond Du Lac Lutheran Home Inc 244 N Macy St *Web:* www.fdllutheranhome.org	Fond Du Lac	WI	54935	920-921-9520	
Forest Haven Nursing & Rehabilitation Center LLC 171 Thrasher Dr *Web:* foresthavennh.com	Jonesboro	LA	71251	318-259-2729	
Fox Valley Hospice 200 Whitfield Dr *Web:* www.fvvh.org	Geneva	IL	60134	630-232-2233	
Gatesworth at One Mcknight Place, The One Mcknight Pl *Web:* thegatesworth.com	Saint Louis	MO	63124	314-993-0111	
Gogebic Medical Care Facility 402 N St *Web:* www.gogebicmedicalcare.com	Wakefield	MI	49968	906-224-9811	
Golden Acres 2525 Centerville Rd *Web:* www.goldenacresliving.com	Dallas	TX	75228	214-327-4503	
Golden Hill Nursing Home Inc 520 Friendship St *Web:* goldenhill.com	New Castle	PA	16101	724-654-7791	
Golden State Health Centers Inc 13347 Ventura Blvd *Web:* www.goldenstatehealth.com	Sherman Oaks	CA	91423	818-385-3200	
Grace Hospice 6400 S Lewis Ave Ste 1000 *Web:* www.gracehospice.com	Tulsa	OK	74136	918-744-7223	
Graceworks Lutheran Services 6430 Inner Mission Way *Web:* www.graceworks.org	Dayton	OH	45459	937-433-2140	
Gramercy Park Nursing Center Inc 17475 S Dixie Hwy *Web:* seniorsmanagement.com	Miami	FL	33157	305-255-1045	
Grandvue Medical Care Facility 1728 S Peninsula Rd *Web:* grandvue.org	East Jordan	MI	49727	231-536-2286	
Green Oaks Nursing Homes 500 Valle Vista Dr *Web:* www.swltc.com	Athens	TX	75751	903-677-3434	
Greenhurst Nursing Center 226 Skyler Dr *Web:* greenhurst.net	Charleston	AR	72933	479-965-7373	
Greenwood House 53 Walter St *Web:* www.greenwoodhouse.org	Ewing	NJ	08628	609-883-5391	
Grove Manor Estates Inc 160 Grove St Ste 100 *Web:* www.grovemanorestates.com	Braintree	MA	02184	781-843-3700	
Hamlet Village 200 Hamlet Hills Dr Ofc *Web:* www.hamletretirement.com	Chagrin Falls	OH	44022	440-247-4201	
Hands of Heartland 211 Galvin Rd N *Web:* handsofheartland.com	Bellevue	NE	68005	402-502-1525	
Harbors Home Health & Hospice 201 Seventh St *Web:* myhhhh.org	Hoquiam	WA	98550	360-532-5454	
Harlee Manor Nursing & Rehabilitation Center 463 W Sproul Rd *Web:* harleemanor.com	Springfield	PA	19064	610-544-2200	
Harmony Nursing & Rehabilitation Center Inc 3919 W Foster Ave *Web:* www.harmonychicago.com	Chicago	IL	60625	773-588-9500	
Hayes Convalescent Hospital 1250 Hayes St *Web:* www.hayesconvalescent.com	San Francisco	CA	94117	415-931-8806	
Heath Village 430 Schooley's Mtn Rd *Web:* heathvillage.com	Hackettstown	NJ	07840	908-852-4801	
Highland Nursing Home Inc 182 Highland Rd *Web:* www.highlandnursinghome.com	Massena	NY	13662	315-769-9956	
Hill View Retirement Center 1610 Twenty-Eighth St *Web:* www.hillviewretirement.org	Portsmouth	OH	45662	740-354-3135	
Hilltop Lodge Retirement Community 815 N Independence *Web:* www.hilltoplodgeretirementcomm.org	Beloit	KS	67420	785-738-3516	
Holly Hill Nursing Home 203 Lafayette St *Web:* hollyhill.org	Anna	IL	62906	618-833-3322	
Holy Cross Village At Notre Dame Inc 54515 State Rd 933 N PO Box 303 *Web:* www.holycrossvillage.com	Notre Dame	IN	46556	574-287-1838	
Hospice House Foundation Inc 903 n sam houston ave *Web:* www.homehospicewtx.com	Odessa	TX	79761	432-580-0067	
Hospice of Kankakee Valley Inc 482 Main St Nw *Web:* hkvcares.org	Bourbonnais	IL	60914	815-939-4141	
iCare Management LLC 341 Bidwell St *Web:* www.icaremanagement.com	Manchester	CT	06040	860-570-2140	
Infinity Hospice Care LLC 5110 N 40th St Ste 107 *Web:* www.infinityhospicecare.com	Phoenix	AZ	85018	602-381-0375	
Island Terrace Nursing Home 57 Long Point Rd *Web:* islandterrace.com	Lakeville	MA	02347	508-947-0151	
James L. West Alzheimer Center 1111 Summit Ave *Web:* www.jameslwest.org	Fort Worth	TX	76102	817-877-1199	
Kin On Health Care Center 4416 S Brandon St *Web:* kinon.org	Seattle	WA	98118	206-721-3630	
Lakeshore Estates Inc. Hrtlnd 3025 Fernbrook Ln *Web:* lakeshoreestates.org	Nashville	TN	37214	615-885-2320	
Lakeside Medical Center Inc 129 Sixth Ave SE *Web:* lmc-pcac.com	Pine City	MN	55063	320-629-2542	
Leisure Chateau Care Center Inc 962 River Ave *Web:* leisurechateau.com	Lakewood	NJ	08701	732-370-8600	
Leisure Living Management Inc 3196 Kraft Ave SE Ste 200 *Web:* www.leisure-living.com	Grand Rapids	MI	49512	616-464-1564	
Lincoln Specialty Care Center 1640 S Lincoln Ave *Web:* www.lincolndocs.com	Vineland	NJ	08361	856-692-8080	
Lourdes-Noreen Mckeen Residence For Geriatric Care Inc 315 S Flagler Dr *Web:* www.lourdesmckeen.org	West Palm Beach	FL	33401	561-655-8544	
Lubbock Regional Mental Health Mental Retardation Center 1602 10th St *Web:* www.lubbockmhmr.org	Lubbock	TX	79401	806-766-0310	
Luther Manor 4545 n 92nd st *Web:* www.luthermanor.com	Milwaukee	WI	53225	414-464-5232	
Luther Memorial Home 221 Sixth St SW *Web:* www.luthermemorialhome.org	Madelia	MN	56062	507-642-3271	
Macon County Nursing Home District 701 Sunset Hills Dr *Web:* www.lochhaven.com	Macon	MO	63552	660-385-3113	
Magnolia Estates 1511 Dulles Dr *Web:* www.centralcontrolmgmt.com	Lafayette	LA	70506	337-216-0950	
Mantey Heights Rehabilitation & Care Centre 2825 Patterson Rd *Web:* www.manteyheightsrehabilitationcenter.com	Grand Junction	CO	81506	970-242-7356	
Maple Lawn Homes 700 N Main St Fl 1 *Web:* www.maple-lawn.com	Eureka	IL	61530	309-467-9096	
Maple Lawn Nursing Home 1410 W Line St *Web:* www.maplelawn.org	Palmyra	MO	63461	573-769-2213	
Maplewood Nursing Home Inc 100 Daniel Dr *Web:* m.visitmaplewood.com	Webster	NY	14580	585-872-1800	

Name / Address	City	State	Zip	Phone	Fax
Marina Care Center 5240 Sepulveda Blvd *Web:* www.marinacare.com	Culver City	CA	90230	310-391-7266	
Marrinson Group Inc 1701 NE 26th St *Web:* www.marrinson.com	Fort Lauderdale	FL	33305	954-566-8353	
Marsh's Edge 136 Marsh's Edge Ln *Web:* marshs-edge.com	St. Simons Island	GA	31522	912-291-2000	
MBK Senior Living Ltd Four Park Plz Ste 500 *Web:* www.mbkseniorliving.com	Irvine	CA	92614	949-242-1400	
Meadow View Nursing Center 1404 Hay St *Web:* meadowview.net	Berlin	PA	15530	814-267-4212	
Meadow Wind Health Care Center Inc 300 23rd St NE *Web:* www.meadowwindonline.com	Massillon	OH	44646	330-833-2026	
Medford Care Center 185 Tuckerton Rd *Web:* www.medfordcare.com	Medford	NJ	08055	856-983-8500	
Medicine Lodge Memorial Hospital 710 N Walnut St *Web:* www.mlmh.net	Medicine Lodge	KS	67104	620-886-3771	
Medilodge of Monroe LLC 481 Village Green Ln *Web:* www.medilodge.com	Monroe	MI	48162	734-242-6282	
Methodist Retirement Communities 1440 Lk Front Cir Ste 110 *Web:* www.mrcaff.org	The Woodlands	TX	77380	281-363-2600	
Mid-Delta Health Systems Inc 405 N Hayden St *Web:* www.middelta.com	Belzoni	MS	39038	662-247-1254	
Milestone Retirement Communities LLC 201 NE Park Plz Dr Ste 105 *Web:* www.milestoneretirement.com	Vancouver	WA	98684	360-882-4500	
Milton & Hattie Kutz Home Inc, The 704 River Rd *Web:* kutzhome.org	Wilmington	DE	19809	302-764-7000	
Milwaukee Protestant Home For The Aged 2505 E Bradford Ave *Web:* eastcastleplace.com	Milwaukee	WI	53211	414-963-6151	
Misericordia Nursing & Rehabilitation Center 998 S Russell St *Web:* mn-rc.org	York	PA	17402	717-755-1964	
MorseLife Inc 4847 Fred Gladstone Dr *Web:* www.morselife.org	West Palm Beach	FL	33417	561-471-5111	
Mount Olivet Careview Home 5517 Lyndale Ave S *Web:* mtolivethomes.org	Minneapolis	MN	55419	612-827-5677	
Mountain Manor of Paintsville 1025 Euclid Ave *Web:* www.mountainmanorofpaintsville.com	Paintsville	KY	41240	606-789-5808	
Nathan Littauer Hospital & Nursing Home 99 E State St *Web:* www.nlh.org	Gloversville	NY	12078	518-773-5505	
Nella's Nursing Home Inc 200 Whiteman Ave *Web:* nellasofcrystalsprings.com	Elkins	WV	26241	304-636-2033	
New Dawn Memory Care 2000 S Blackhawk St *Web:* www.newdawnal.com	Aurora	CO	80014	303-997-2929	
Newcastle Place Inc 12600 N Port Washington Rd *Web:* www.newcastleplace.com	Mequon	WI	53092	262-387-8800	
Nexion Health Inc 6937 Warfield Ave *Web:* www.nexion-health.com	Sykesville	MD	21784	410-552-4800	
Northwoods Care Centre 2250 Pearl St *Web:* www.northwoodscare.com	Belvidere	IL	61008	815-544-0358	
Norwell Knoll Nursing Home 329 Washington St *Web:* norwellknoll.com	Norwell	MA	02061	781-659-4901	
Nsa Nursing Solutions America 2055 State St *Web:* nsinursingsolutions.com	East Petersburg	PA	17520	717-560-3863	
Nursing Personnel Homecare Inc 175 S Ninth St *Web:* www.nursingpersonnel.com	Brooklyn	NY	11211	718-218-8991	
Nye Senior Services LLC 2230 N Somers Ave *Web:* nyeseniorservices.com	Fremont	NE	68025	402-753-1400	
Oak Trace 200 Village Dr *Web:* www.oaktracedg.com	Downers Grove	IL	60516	630-769-6100	
Oakland Care Center Inc 20 Breakneck Rd *Web:* www.oaklandcarecenter.com	Oakland	NJ	07436	201-337-3300	
Oakview Manor 929 Mixon School Rd Ofc *Web:* www.oakviewmanor.com	Ozark	AL	36360	334-774-2631	
Obion County Nursing Home 1084 E County Home Rd *Web:* obioncountynursinghome.com	Union City	TN	38261	731-885-9065	
Opis Management Resources 10150 Highlands Manor Dr Ste 300 *Web:* www.opismr.com	Tampa	FL	33610	813-558-6600	
Orchard Manor Inc 600 Bates Rd *Web:* orchardmanor.com	Medina	NY	14103	585-798-4100	
Orem Rehabilitation & Nursing Center 575 East 1400 South *Web:* www.oremrehab.com	Orem	UT	84097	801-225-4741	
Ozark Riverview Manor Inc 1200 W Hall St *Web:* www.ormanor.com	Ozark	MO	65721	417-581-6025	
Park Manor of Quail Valley 2350 Fm 1092 Rd *Web:* parkmanor-quailvalley.com	Missouri City	TX	77459	281-499-4780	
Pathways 200 W Spring St *Web:* www.pathwaysup.org	Marquette	MI	49855	906-225-1181	
Pediatric Special Care Inc 17040 W 12 Mile Rd Ste 200 *Web:* www.pediatricspecialcare.com	Southfield	MI	48076	248-557-4800	
Penacook Place Foundation Inc 150 Water St *Web:* www.penacookplace.org	Haverhill	MA	01830	978-374-0707	
Perley & Rideau Veterans' Health Centre 1750 Russell Rd *Web:* www.perleyrideau.ca	Ottawa	ON	K1G5Z6	613-526-7170	
Perry Green Valley Nursing Home Inc 1103 Birch St *Web:* greenvalleyhealthcare.net	Perry	OK	73077	580-336-2285	
Petersen Health Care Inc 830 W Trlcreek Dr *Web:* www.petersenhealthcare.net	Peoria	IL	61614	309-691-8113	
Pines of Sarasota Inc 1501 N Orange Ave *Web:* pinesofsarasota.com	Sarasota	FL	34236	941-365-0250	
Piqua Manor 1840 W High St *Web:* piquamanor.com	Piqua	OH	45356	937-773-0040	
Port Coquitlam Senior Citizens' Housing Society 2111 Hawthorne Ave *Web:* www.hawthornecare.com	Port Coquitlam	BC	V3C1W3	604-941-4051	
Prestige Care Inc 7700 NE Pkwy Dr Ste 300 *Web:* www.prestigecare.com	Vancouver	WA	98662	360-735-7155	
Quaker Heights Nursing Home Inc 514 High St *Web:* www.quakerheights.org	Waynesville	OH	45068	513-897-6050	
Revera Long Term Care Inc 850 Fourth St E *Web:* www.reveraliving.com	Owen Sound	ON	N4K6A3	519-376-3212	
River Bluff Nursing Home 4401 N Main St *Web:* rbnh.org	Rockford	IL	61103	815-877-8061	
Riverview Estates 303 Bank Ave *Web:* www.riverviewestates.org	Riverton	NJ	08077	856-829-2274	
Schlegel Villages Inc 325 Max Becker Dr Ste 201 *Web:* schlegelvillages.com	Kitchener	ON	N2E4H5	519-571-1873	
Seashore Gardens Living Center 22 W Jimmie Leeds Rd Ste 26 *Web:* www.seashoregardens.org	Galloway	NJ	08205	609-404-4848	
Sensibill 6115 Camp Bowie Blvd Ste 260 *Web:* sensibill.net	Fort Worth	TX	76116	817-731-7771	
Smith Crossing 10501 Emilie Ln Ofc *Web:* smithcrossing.org	Orland Park	IL	60467	708-326-2300	
Southview Acres Health Care Center Inc 2000 Oakdale Ave *Web:* www.southviewacres.com	Saint Paul	MN	55118	651-451-1821	
St Agnes Home 10341 Manchester Rd *Web:* carmelitedcj.org	Saint Louis	MO	63122	314-965-7616	
St James House of Baytown 5800 W Baker Rd *Web:* www.stjameshouse.org	Baytown	TX	77520	281-425-1200	
St Joseph Residence 107 E Beckert Rd *Web:* stjosephresidence.com	New London	WI	54961	920-982-5354	
Sunrise Country Manor 610 224th *Web:* sunrisecountrymanor.com	Milford	NE	68405	402-761-3230	
Sycamores Terrace Retirement 1427 Lebanon Pk *Web:* www.sycamoresterrace.com	Nashville	TN	37210	615-242-2412	
TLC Nursing & Homecare Services Ltd 25 Anderson Ave *Web:* www.tlcnursingandhomecare.com	St. John's	NL	A1B3E4	709-726-3473	
Victorian Village 12600 Renaissance Cir *Web:* www.provinet.com	Homer Glen	IL	60491	708-301-0800	
Vigi Sante Ltee 197 Thornhill *Web:* www.vigisante.com	Dollard-des-ormeaux	QC	H9B3H8	514-684-0930	
Villa Camillus Inc, The 10515 E River Rd *Web:* www.the-villa-camillus.com	Columbia Station	OH	44028	440-236-5091	
Wealshire 150 Jamestown Ln *Web:* www.wealshire.com	Lincolnshire	IL	60069	847-883-9010	
West Anaheim Extended Care 645 S Beach Blvd *Web:* www.westanaheimec.com	Anaheim	CA	92804	714-821-1993	
West Hills Village Senior Residence 5711 Sw Multnomah Blvd *Web:* www.westhillssenior.com	Portland	OR	97219	503-245-7621	
Wexner Heritage Village 1151 College Ave *Web:* www.whv.org	Columbus	OH	43209	614-231-4900	
Willows at Meadow Branch, The 1881 Harvest Dr *Web:* www.thewillows-mb.com	Winchester	VA	22601	540-667-3000	
Woodruff Convalescent 17836 Woodruff Ave *Web:* www.estrella.com	Bellflower	CA	90706	562-925-8457	
York County Cerebral Palsy Home Inc Proj 2050 Barley Rd *Web:* www.margaretemoul.org	York	PA	17408	717-767-6463	

Alabama

Name / Address	City	State	Zip	Phone	Fax
HomeCare of East Alabama Medical Ctr 665 Opelika Rd *TF:* 866-542-4768 ■ *Web:* www.lhcgroup.com	Auburn	AL	36830	334-826-3131	
Hospice of Cullman County 1912 Alabama Hwy 157 *Web:* www.crmchospital.com/our_services/all_services/hospice.aspx	Cullman	AL	35058	256-737-2000	
Hospice of Marshall County 408 Martling Rd *TF:* 888-334-9336 ■ *Web:* www.hospicemc.org	Albertville	AL	35951	256-891-7724	891-7754
Hospice of West Alabama 3851 Loop Rd *TF:* 877-362-7522 ■ *Web:* www.hospiceofwestalabama.com	Tuscaloosa	AL	35404	205-523-0101	523-0102

Alaska

Name / Address	City	State	Zip	Phone	Fax
Hospice of Anchorage 2612 E Northern Lights Blvd *Web:* www.hospiceofanchorage.org	Anchorage	AK	99508	907-561-5322	561-0334

Arizona

	City	State	Zip	Phone	Fax
Hospice of Arizona 19820 N Seventh Ave Ste 130 *TF:* 888-330-8560 ■ *Web:* www.americanhospice.com	Phoenix	AZ	85027	602-678-1313	242-2178

Arkansas

	City	State	Zip	Phone	Fax
Arkansas Hospice 14 Parkstone Cir *TF:* 877-257-3400 ■ *Web:* www.arkansashospice.org	North Little Rock	AR	72116	501-748-3333	748-3334
Hospice Home Care 2200 S Bowman *TF:* 800-479-1219 ■ *Web:* www.hospicehomecare.com	Little Rock	AR	72211	501-296-9043	296-9978
Hospice of the Ozarks 701 Burnett Dr *Web:* www.baxterregional.org	Mountain Home	AR	72653	870-508-1000	

California

	City	State	Zip	Phone	Fax
Citrus Valley Hospice 820 N Phillips Ave. *Web:* www.cvhp.org/our_facilities/hospice_home_health.aspx	West Covina	CA	91791	626-859-2263	
Community Hospice Inc 4368 Spyres Way *TF:* 866-645-4567 ■ *Web:* www.hospiceheart.org	Modesto	CA	95356	209-578-6300	578-6391
Desert Hospital Hospice of the Desert Communities 1150 N Indian Canyon Dr	Palm Springs	CA	92262	760-323-6642	327-8086
Elizabeth Hospice 150 W Crest St *TF:* 800-797-2050 ■ *Web:* www.elizabethhospice.org	Escondido	CA	92025	760-737-2050	796-3781
Hinds Hospice 1616 W Shaw Ste C-1 *TF:* 800-400-4677 ■ *Web:* www.hindshospice.org	Fresno	CA	93711	559-248-8591	222-4782
Hoffmann Hospice of the Valley 8501 Brimhall Rd Bldg 100 *TF:* 888-833-3900 ■ *Web:* www.hoffmannhospice.org	Bakersfield	CA	93312	661-410-1010	410-1110
Hospice By the Bay 17 E Sir Francis Drake Blvd *Web:* www.hospicebythebay.org	Larkspur	CA	94939	415-927-2273	925-1004
Hospice Caring Project of Santa Cruz County 940 Disc Dr *TF:* 877-688-6144 ■ *Web:* www.hospicesantacruz.org	Scotts Valley	CA	95066	831-430-3000	430-9272
Hospice of Redlands Community Hospital 350 Terracina Blvd *Web:* redlandshospital.org	Redlands	CA	92373	909-335-5643	335-5648
Hospice of San Joaquin 3888 Pacific Ave *Web:* www.hospicesj.org	Stockton	CA	95204	209-957-3888	957-3986
Livingston Memorial Visiting Nurse Assn Hospice 1996 Eastman Ave Ste 101 *TF:* 800-830-8881 ■ *Web:* www.lmvna.org	Ventura	CA	93003	805-642-1608	642-2320
Mission Hospice Inc of San Mateo County 1670 S Amphlett Blvd Ste 300 *Web:* www.missionhospice.org	San Mateo	CA	94402	650-554-1000	554-1001
Seasons Hospice & Palliative Care of California-Orange 750 The City Dr *TF:* 877-508-0644 ■ *Web:* www.seasons.org	Orange	CA	92868	714-980-0900	
Torrance Memorial Home Health & Hospice 3330 Lomita Blvd Bldg 1 S *Web:* www.torrancememorial.org	Torrance	CA	90505	310-784-3739	784-3717
Visiting Nurses 222 E Canon Perdido St	Santa Barbara	CA	93101	805-690-6202	568-5178
VITAS Healthcare Corp of California 220 Commerce Ste 100 *Web:* www.vitas.com	Irvine	CA	92602	714-921-2273	734-2780
VITAS Healthcare Corp of San Gabriel Cities 1343 N Grand Ave. *TF:* 800-582-9533 ■ *Web:* www.vitas.com	Covina	CA	91724	626-918-2273	960-8587
VNA & Hospice of Northern California 1900 Powell St Ste 300 *TF:* 800-698-1273 ■ *Web:* www.suttercareathome.org	Emeryville	CA	94608	510-450-8596	347-6874
VNA & Hospice of Southern California 150 W First St Ste 270 *TF:* 888-357-3574 ■ *Web:* www.vnasocal.org	Claremont	CA	91711	909-624-3574	624-1559
VNA California 6235 River Crest Dr Ste L *Web:* vnacalifornia.org	Riverside	CA	92507	951-413-1200	656-0045

Colorado

	City	State	Zip	Phone	Fax
Centura Home Care & Hospice 1391 Speer Blvd Ste 600 *Web:* www.centurahealthathome.org	Denver	CO	80204	303-561-5000	561-5050
Denver Hospice, The 501 S Cherry St Ste 700 *Web:* www.thedenverhospice.org	Denver	CO	80246	303-321-2828	321-7171
Hospice & Palliative Care of Northern Colorado 2726 W 11th St Rd *TF:* 800-564-5563 ■ *Web:* www.hospiceofnortherncolorado.org	Greeley	CO	80634	970-352-8487	475-0037
Hospice & Palliative Care of Western Colorado 2754 Compass Dr Ste 377 *TF:* 866-310-8900 ■ *Web:* www.hopewestco.org	Grand Junction	CO	81506	970-241-2212	257-2400
Hospice of Boulder County 2594 Trlridge Dr E *Web:* www.trucare.org	Lafayette	CO	80026	303-449-7740	449-6961
Sangre de Cristo Hospice 1207 Pueblo Blvd Way *Web:* socohospice.org	Pueblo	CO	81005	719-542-0032	542-1413

Connecticut

	City	State	Zip	Phone	Fax
Abbott Terrace Health Ctr 44 Abbott Terr *Web:* athenahealthcare.com	Waterbury	CT	06702	203-755-4870	755-9016
Connecticut Hospice 100 Double Beach Rd **Fax:* Hum Res ■ *Web:* www.hospice.com	Branford	CT	06405	203-315-7500	315-7561*
Hospice of Southeastern Connecticut Inc 227 Dunham St *TF:* 877-654-4035 ■ *Web:* www.hospicesect.org	Norwich	CT	06360	860-848-5699	848-6898
Regional Hospice of Western Connecticut 30 Milestone Rd *Web:* www.danbury.org/hospice	Danbury	CT	06810	203-702-7400	792-1402
Visiting Nurse & Health Services of Connecticut Inc 8 Keynote Dr *Web:* www.vnhsc.org	Vernon	CT	06066	860-872-9163	872-3030
Visiting Nurse & Hospice Care of Southwestern Connecticut 1266 E Main St *Web:* vnhcsw.org	Stamford	CT	06902	203-276-3000	

Delaware

	City	State	Zip	Phone	Fax
Compassionate Care Hospice of Delaware 702 Wilmington Ave *TF General:* 800-219-0092 ■ *Web:* www.cchnet.net	Wilmington	DE	19805	302-993-9090	993-9094

Florida

	City	State	Zip	Phone	Fax
Avow Hospice Inc 1095 Whippoorwill Ln *Web:* www.avowcares.org	Naples	FL	34105	239-261-4404	
Bigbend Hospice 1723 Mahan Ctr Blvd. *TF:* 800-772-5862 ■ *Web:* www.bigbendhospice.org	Tallahassee	FL	32308	850-878-5310	309-1638
Catholic Hospice Inc 14875 NW 77th Ave Ste 100 *Web:* www.catholichealthservices.org	Miami Lakes	FL	33014	305-822-2380	824-0665
Chapters Health System 12973 Telecom Pkwy Ste 100 *TF:* 866-204-8611 ■ *Web:* www.chaptershealth.org	Temple Terrace	FL	33637	813-871-8111	
Community Hospice of Northeast Florida 4266 Sunbeam Rd *Web:* www.communityhospice.com	Jacksonville	FL	32257	904-268-5200	
Covenant Hospice 5041 N 12th Ave *TF:* 800-541-3072 ■ *Web:* www.covenanthospice.org	Pensacola	FL	32504	850-433-2155	202-5803
Gulfside Hospice Inc 6224 Lafayette St *TF:* 800-561-4883 ■ *Web:* www.gulfsideregionalhospice.org	New Port Richey	FL	34652	727-845-5707	
Hospice & VNA of the Florida Keys 1319 William St *Web:* www.hospicevna.com	Key West	FL	33040	305-294-8812	
Hospice by the Sea 1531 W Palmetto Pk Rd. *TF:* 800-633-2577 ■ *Web:* www.hospice1.org	Boca Raton	FL	33486	561-395-5031	
Hospice Care of South Florida 7270 NW 12th St PH 6	Miami	FL	33126	305-591-1606	591-1618
Hospice of Lake & Sumter Inc 2445 Ln Pk Rd *TF:* 888-728-6234 ■ *Web:* cshospice.org	Tavares	FL	32778	352-343-1341	343-6115
Hospice of Marion County 3231 SW 34th Ave *TF:* 888-482-5018 ■ *Web:* www.hospiceofmarion.com	Ocala	FL	34474	352-873-7400	873-7435
Hospice of Northeast Florida 4266 Sunbeam Rd *TF:* 866-253-6681 ■ *Web:* www.communityhospice.com	Jacksonville	FL	32257	904-268-5200	407-6090
Hospice of Palm Beach County 5300 E Ave *TF:* 800-287-4722 ■ *Web:* www.hpbc.com	West Palm Beach	FL	33407	561-848-5200	863-2955
Hospice of Saint Francis Inc 1250 Grumman Pl Ste B *TF:* 866-269-4240 ■ *Web:* www.hospiceofstfrancis.com	Titusville	FL	32780	321-269-4240	269-5428
Hospice of the Comforter 480 W Central Pkwy **Fax:* Admissions ■ *TF:* 877-696-6775 ■ *Web:* www.hospiceofthecomforter.org	Altamonte Springs	FL	32714	407-682-0808	303-0721*
Hospice of the Florida Suncoast 5771 Roosevelt Blvd *Web:* thehospice.org	Clearwater	FL	33760	727-586-4432	
Hospice of the Treasure Coast 5090 Dunn Rd *TF:* 800-299-4677 ■ *Web:* www.tchospice.org	Fort Pierce	FL	34981	772-462-8900	
Hospice of Volusia/Flagler 3800 Woodbriar Trl *Web:* www.hfch.org	Port Orange	FL	32129	386-322-4701	322-4702
HospiceCare of Southeast Florida Inc 309 SE 18th St Ste 200 *TF:* 866-231-5695 ■ *Web:* www.heartlandhospice.com	Fort Lauderdale	FL	33316	954-467-7423	
Lifepath Hospice 3010 W Azeele St *TF:* 800-209-2200 ■ *Web:* www.chaptershealth.org	Tampa	FL	33609	813-877-2200	872-7037
Tidewell Hospice 5955 Rand Blvd *TF:* 800-959-4291 ■ *Web:* tidewellhospice.org	Sarasota	FL	34238	941-552-7500	925-0969
Treasure Coast Hospice 1201 SE Indian St *TF:* 800-299-4677 ■ *Web:* www.tchospice.org	Stuart	FL	34997	772-403-4500	403-4518
Visiting Nurse Assn of the Treasure Coast 1110 35th Ln *TF:* 800-749-5760 ■ *Web:* www.vnatc.com	Vero Beach	FL	32960	772-567-5551	569-4174
VITAS Healthcare Corp of Central Florida 5151 Adanson St Ste 200 *Web:* www.vitas.com	Orlando	FL	32804	407-875-0028	691-4517
VITAS Hospice Care 100 S Biscayne Blvd Ste 1300 *TF General:* 800-582-9533 ■ *Web:* www.vitas.com	Miami	FL	33131	305-374-4143	

Georgia

	City	State	Zip	Phone	Fax
Columbus Hospice 7020 Moon Rd *Web:* www.columbushospice.com	Columbus	GA	31909	706-569-7992	569-8560
Heyman HospiceCare 420 E Second Ave *TF:* 800-324-1078 ■ *Web:* www.floyd.org	Rome	GA	30161	706-509-3200	509-3201
Hospice Atlanta-Visiting Nurse Health System 1244 Pk Vista Dr. *TF:* 866-374-4776 ■ *Web:* www.vnhs.org	Atlanta	GA	30319	404-869-3000	215-6005

Phone | Fax

Hospice of NE Georgia Medical Ctr
2150 Limestone Pkwy Ste 222 .... Gainesville GA 30501 770-533-8888 219-8887
Web: www.nghs.com

Hospice of Southwest Georgia
114 A Mimosa Dr .... Thomasville GA 31792 229-584-5500
TF: 800-290-6567 ■ *Web:* www.archbold.org

Hospice Savannah Inc PO Box 13190 .... Savannah GA 31416 912-355-2289 355-2376
TF: 888-355-4911 ■ *Web:* www.hospicesavannah.org

Pine Pointe Hospice & Palliative Care
6261 Peak Rd .... Macon GA 31210 478-633-5660 633-6247
TF: 800-211-1084 ■ *Web:* mccg.org

Trinity Hospital of Augusta
2803 Wrightsboro Rd Ste 38 .... Augusta GA 30909 706-729-6000
TF: 800-999-6673 ■ *Web:* www.trinityofaugusta.com

United Hospice of Atlanta 1626 Jeurgens Ct .... Norcross GA 30093 770-279-6200
TF: 800-222-0321 ■ *Web:* pruitthealth.com/

Hawaii

Phone | Fax

Hospice Hawaii 860 Iwilei Rd .... Honolulu HI 96817 808-924-9255 922-9161
Web: www.hospicehawaii.org

Hospice of Hilo 1011 Waianuenue Ave .... Hilo HI 96720 808-969-1733 969-4863
Web: www.hospiceofhilo.org

St. Francis Healthcare Systems
2226 Liliha St PO Box 29700 .... Honolulu HI 96820 808-547-6883
Web: www.stfrancishawaii.org

Idaho

Phone | Fax

Life's Doors Hospice 420 S Orchard St .... Boise ID 83705 208-344-6500 344-6590

Illinois

Phone | Fax

Advocate Hospice
1441 Branding Ave Ste 200 .... Downers Grove IL 60515 630-963-6800 963-6877
Web: www.advocatehealth.com

Blessing Health System PO Box 7005 .... Quincy IL 62305 217-223-1200
Web: www.blessinghospital.org

Carle Hospice 611 W Park St .... Urbana IL 61801 217-383-3311
TF: 800-239-3620 ■ *Web:* www.carle.org

CNS Home Health & Hospice
690 E N Ave Ste 100 .... Carol Stream IL 60188 630-665-7000 665-7371
Web: www.cnshomehealth.org

Family Hospice of Belleville Area
5110 W Main St .... Belleville IL 62226 618-277-1800 277-1074
Web: www.familyhospice.org

Harbor Light Hospice
800 Roosevelt Rd Bldg C Ste 206 .... Glen Ellyn IL 60137 630-942-0100 942-0118
TF: 800-419-0542 ■ *Web:* harborlighthospice.com

Horizon Hospice 833 W Chicago Ave .... Chicago IL 60642 312-733-8900 733-8952
TF: 866-733-6028 ■ *Web:* www.horizonhospice.org

Hospice of Lincolnland 1000 Health Ctr Dr .... Mattoon IL 61938 800-454-4055 347-7197*
**Fax Area Code:* 217 ■ *TF:* 800-454-4055 ■ *Web:* www.sarahbush.org/hospice

Hospice of Northeastern Illinois
405 Lk Zurich Rd .... Barrington IL 60010 847-381-5599 381-1431
Web: www.hospiceanswers.org

Hospice of Southern Illinois
305 S Illinois St .... Belleville IL 62220 618-235-1703 235-2828
TF: 800-233-1708 ■ *Web:* hospice.org

Joliet Area Community Hospice
250 Water Stone Cir .... Joliet IL 60431 815-740-4104 740-4107
TF: 800-360-1817 ■ *Web:* www.joliethospice.org

Little Company of Mary Home Based Services
9800 SW Hwy .... Oak Lawn IL 60453 708-229-4663 499-5975
Web: www.lcmh.org

Methodist Medical Ctr of Illinois Hospice Services
221 NE Glen Oak Ave .... Peoria IL 61636 309-672-5522
Web: unitypoint.org/peoria

Midwest Palliative & Hospice CareCenter
2050 Claire Ct .... Glenview IL 60025 847-467-7423 866-6023
Web: www.carecenter.org

OSF Hospice 2265 W Altorfer Dr .... Peoria IL 61615 800-673-5288 683-7855*
**Fax Area Code:* 309 ■ *TF:* 800-673-5288 ■ *Web:* www.osfhomecare.org

Rainbow Hospice 444 N NW Hwy Ste 145 .... Park Ridge IL 60068 847-685-9900 685-6390
Web: www.rainbowhospice.org

Indiana

Phone | Fax

Center for Hospice Care Inc
111 Sunnybrook Ct .... South Bend IN 46637 574-243-3100 243-3134
TF: 800-413-9083 ■ *Web:* www.centerforhospice.org

Hosparus Inc 624 E Market St .... New Albany IN 47150 812-945-4596 945-4733
TF: 800-895-5633 ■ *Web:* www.hosparus.org

Hospice of the Calumet Area 600 Superior Ave .... Munster IN 46321 219-922-2732 922-1947
TF: 855-225-5344 ■ *Web:* www.hospicecalumet.org

Iowa

Phone | Fax

Cedar Valley Hospice
2101 Kimball Ave Ste 401 .... Waterloo IA 50702 319-272-2002 272-2071
TF: 800-617-1972 ■ *Web:* www.cvhospice.org

Hospice of Central Iowa (HCI)
401 Railroad Pl .... West Des Moines IA 50265 515-333-5810 271-1302
TF: 800-806-9934 ■ *Web:* www.hospiceofcentraliowa.org

Hospice of North Iowa 232 Second St SE .... Mason City IA 50401 641-428-6208
TF: 800-297-4719 ■ *Web:* www.mercynorthiowa.com

Phone | Fax

Hospice of Siouxland 4300 Hamilton Blvd .... Sioux City IA 51104 712-233-4100 233-1123
TF: 800-383-4545 ■ *Web:* www.hospiceofsiouxland.com

Kansas

Phone | Fax

Harry Hynes Memorial Hospice 313 S Market St .... Wichita KS 67202 316-265-9441 265-6066
TF: 800-767-4965 ■ *Web:* www.hynesmemorial.org

Hospice of Reno County 1600 N Lorraine .... Hutchinson KS 67502 620-665-2473 669-5959
TF: 800-267-6891 ■ *Web:* www.hospicerenocounty.com/

Midland Hospice Care 200 SW Frazier Cir .... Topeka KS 66606 785-232-2044 232-5567
TF: 800-491-3691 ■ *Web:* www.midlandcareconnection.org

Kentucky

Phone | Fax

Community Hospice 1480 Carter Ave .... Ashland KY 41101 606-329-1890 329-0018
TF: 800-926-6184 ■ *Web:* www.communityhospicecares.org

Heritage Hospice
120 Enterprise Dr PO Box 1213 .... Danville KY 40423 859-236-2425 236-6152
TF: 800-203-6633 ■ *Web:* www.heritagehospice.com

Hospice of Lake Cumberland 100 Pkwy Dr .... Somerset KY 42503 606-679-4389 678-0191
TF: 800-937-9596 ■ *Web:* www.hospicelc.org

Hospice of Southern Kentucky
5872 Scottsville Rd .... Bowling Green KY 42104 270-782-3402 782-3496
TF: 800-344-9479 ■ *Web:* www.hospicesoky.org

Hospice of the Bluegrass
2312 Alexandria Dr .... Lexington KY 40504 859-276-5344 223-0490
TF: 800-876-6005 ■ *Web:* www.hospicebg.com

Lourdes Homecare & Hospice 2855 Jackson St .... Paducah KY 42003 270-444-2262
TF: 800-870-7460 ■ *Web:* www.elourdes.com

Saint Anthony's Hospice 2410 S Green St .... Henderson KY 42420 270-826-2326 831-2169
TF: 866-380-2326 ■ *Web:* www.stanthonyshospice.org

Louisiana

Phone | Fax

Hospice of Acadiana
2600 Johnston St Ste 200 .... Lafayette LA 70503 337-232-1234 232-1297
TF: 800-738-2226 ■ *Web:* www.hospiceacadiana.com

Hospice of Baton Rouge 9063 Siegen Ln .... Baton Rouge LA 70810 225-767-4673 769-8113
TF: 888-447-0433 ■ *Web:* www.hospicebr.org

Hospice of South Louisiana 6500 W Main St .... Houma LA 70360 985-868-3095 868-3910
Web: www.glendalehealthcare.com

Maryland

Phone | Fax

Carroll Hospice 292 Stoner Ave .... Westminster MD 21157 410-871-8000
TF: 844-211-5403 ■ *Web:* carrollcountytimes.com

Coastal Hospice & Palliative Care
2604 Old Ocean City Rd PO Box 1733 .... Salisbury MD 21804 410-742-8732 548-5669
TF: 800-780-7886 ■ *Web:* www.coastalhospice.org

Gilchrist Hospice Care
11311 McCormick Rd .... Hunt Valley MD 21031 443-849-8200
TF: 800-735-2258 ■ *Web:* www.gilchristhospice.org

Hospice of the Chesapeake 445 Defense Hwy .... Annapolis MD 21401 410-987-2003 837-1505*
**Fax Area Code:* 443 ■ *TF General:* 877-462-1101 ■ *Web:* www.hospicechesapeake.org

Montgomery Hospice 1355 Piccard Dr Ste 100 .... Rockville MD 20850 301-921-4400 921-4433
TF: 800-994-6610 ■ *Web:* www.montgomeryhospice.org

Richey Joseph Hospice 838 N Eutaw St .... Baltimore MD 21201 410-523-2150 523-1146
Web: www.josephricheyhospice.org

Stella Maris Hospice Care Program
2300 Dulaney Vly Rd .... Timonium MD 21093 410-252-4500 560-9693
Web: www.stellamarisinc.com

Massachusetts

Phone | Fax

Baystate Visiting Nurse Assn & Hospice
50 Maple St .... Springfield MA 01103 413-794-6411
TF: 800-249-8298 ■ *Web:* www.baystatehealth.com

Community VNA 10 Emory St .... Attleboro MA 02703 508-222-0118 226-8939
TF: 800-220-0110 ■ *Web:* www.communityvna.com

Hospice & Palliative Care of Cape Cod Inc
765 Attucks Ln .... Hyannis MA 02601 508-957-0200 957-0229
TF: 800-642-2423 ■ *Web:* hopehealthco.org

Hospice Care 100 Sylvan Rd .... Woburn MA 01801 781-569-2888 279-4677
TF: 866-279-7103 ■ *Web:* www.vnahospicecare.org

Hospice Life Care 113 Hampden St .... Holyoke MA 01040 413-533-3923 536-4513
Web: holyokevna.org

Hospice of the North Shore
75 Sylvan St Ste B102 .... Danvers MA 01923 978-774-7566 774-4389
TF: 888-283-1722 ■ *Web:* caredimensions.org/

Merrimack Valley Hospice
360 Merrimack St Bldg 9 .... Lawrence MA 01843 800-933-5593 552-4401*
**Fax Area Code:* 978 ■ *TF:* 800-933-5593 ■ *Web:* www.homehealthfoundation.org

Old Colony Hospice 1 Credit Union Way .... Randolph MA 02368 781-341-4145 297-7345
TF: 800-370-1322 ■ *Web:* www.oldcolonyhospice.org

VNA & Hospice of Cooley Dickinson
168 Industrial Dr .... NorthHampton MA 01060 413-584-1060
Web: www.vnaandhospice.org

Michigan

Phone | Fax

Angela Hospice Home Care 14100 Newburgh Rd .... Livonia MI 48154 734-464-7810 464-6930
TF General: 866-464-7810 ■ *Web:* www.angelahospice.org

Arbor Hospice & Home Care 2366 Oak Vly Dr .... Ann Arbor MI 48103 734-662-5999 662-2330
TF: 888-992-2273 ■ *Web:* www.arborhospice.org

				Phone	Fax
Hospice at Home 4025 Health Pk Ln *TF:* 800-717-3811 ■ *Web:* www.hospiceathomecares.org	Saint Joseph	MI	49085	269-429-7100	428-3499
Hospice Care of Southwest Michigan 222 N Kalamazoo Mall Ste 100 *Web:* www.hospiceswmi.org	Kalamazoo	MI	49007	269-345-0273	345-8522
Hospice of Henry Ford Health System 655 W 13 Mile Rd 1st Fl *TF:* 800-436-7936 ■ *Web:* www.henryford.com	Madison Heights	MI	48071	248-585-5270	585-4210
Hospice of Holland Inc 270 Hoover Blvd *TF:* 800-255-3522 ■ *Web:* www.hollandhospice.org	Holland	MI	49423	616-396-2972	396-2808
Hospice of Lansing 4052 Legacy Pkwy Ste 200 *TF:* 877-882-4500 ■ *Web:* www.lansinghospice.org	Lansing	MI	48911	517-882-4500	882-3010
Hospice of Michigan 400 Mack Ave *TF:* 888-247-5701 ■ *Web:* www.hom.org	Detroit	MI	48201	313-578-5000	578-6380
Hospice of North Ottawa Community 1309 Sheldon Rd *Web:* www.noch.org/main.aspx?id=115	Grand Haven	MI	49417	616-842-3600	
Mercy Hospice 281 Enterprise Ct Ste 200	Bloomfield Hills	MI	48302	248-452-5300	
MidMichigan Home Care 3007 N Saginaw Rd *TF:* 800-852-9350 ■ *Web:* www.midmichigan.org	Midland	MI	48640	989-633-1400	
Munson Healthcare 1105 Sixth St *TF:* 800-468-6766 ■ *Web:* www.munsonhealthcare.org	Traverse City	MI	49684	231-935-5000	
Saint Joseph Mercy Home Care & Hospice 5301 McAuley Dr *TF:* 888-884-6569 ■ *Web:* stjoesannarbor.org	Ypsilanti	MI	48197	734-712-3456	327-3274

Minnesota

				Phone	Fax
Fairview Hospice 2450 26th Ave S *TF:* 800-285-5647 ■ *Web:* www.fairview.org	Minneapolis	MN	55406	612-728-2455	728-2400
Health Partners 8170 33rd Ave S **Fax Area Code:* 320 ■ *Web:* healthpartners.com	Minneapolis	MN	55425	952-883-6877	203-2414*
Mayo Foundation for Medical Education and Research 200 First St SW *TF:* 800-679-9084 ■ *Web:* mayoclinic.org/patient-visitor-guide/minnesota/hospice	Rochester	MN	55902	507-284-4002	538-7802
North Memorial Home Health & Hospice 3500 France Ave N Ste 101 *Web:* northmemorial.com	Robbinsdale	MN	55422	763-520-5200	

Mississippi

				Phone	Fax
Delta Area Hospice Care Ltd 522 Arnold Ave	Greenville	MS	38701	662-335-7040	335-7027
Hospice Ministries 450 Towne Ctr Blvd *TF:* 800-273-7724 ■ *Web:* www.hospiceministries.org	Ridgeland	MS	39157	601-898-1053	898-4320
North Mississippi Medical Ctr Hospice (NMHC) 830 S Gloster St *TF:* 800-882-6274 ■ *Web:* www.nmhs.net	Tupelo	MS	38801	662-377-3000	377-6770

Missouri

				Phone	Fax
Hands of Hope Hospice 137 N Belt Hwy *TF:* 800-443-1143 ■ *Web:* www.mymosaiclifecare.org	Saint Joseph	MO	64506	816-271-7190	271-7672
Kansas City Hospice & Palliative Care 9221 Ward Pkwy Ste 100 *Web:* www.kansascityhospice.org	Kansas City	MO	64114	816-363-2600	523-0068
Odyssey Healthcare of Kansas City 4911 S Arrowhead Dr *TF:* 800-944-4357 ■ *Web:* gentiva.com	Independence	MO	64055	816-795-1333	
Saint Luke's Home Care & Hospice 3100 Broadway St Ste 1000 *Web:* saintlukeshealthsystem.org	Kansas City	MO	64111	816-756-1160	756-0838
SSM Hospice 2 Harbor Bend Ct *TF:* 800-835-1212 ■ *Web:* ssmhealth.com/system	Lake Saint Louis	MO	63367	636-695-2050	695-2060
VNA Hospice Care (VNA) 11440 Olive Blvd Ste 200 *TF:* 800-392-4740 ■ *Web:* www.vnastl.com	Creve Coeur	MO	63141	314-918-7171	918-8054
VNA of Greater St Louis *Hospice Care* 11440 Olive Blvd Ste 200 *TF:* 800-392-4740 ■ *Web:* www.vnastl.com	Creve Coeur	MO	63141	314-918-7171	918-8054

Montana

				Phone	Fax
Peace Hospice of Montana 1101 26th St S	Great Falls	MT	59405	406-455-3040	455-3070

Nebraska

				Phone	Fax
Visiting Nurse Assn 12565 W Ctr Rd Ste 100 *TF:* 800-456-8869 ■ *Web:* www.thevnacares.org	Omaha	NE	68144	402-342-5566	342-5587

Nevada

				Phone	Fax
Family Home Hospice 2724 N Tenaya Way Ste 201 *TF:* 800-748-6773 ■ *Web:* www.uhcnevada.com	Las Vegas	NV	89128	702-242-7000	383-9826
Nathan Adelson Hospice 4141 Swenson St *Web:* www.nah.org	Las Vegas	NV	89119	702-733-0320	
Saint Mary's Hospice of Northern Nevada 3605 Grant Dr	Reno	NV	89509	775-770-3081	

New Hampshire

				Phone	Fax
Concord Regional Visiting Nurse Assoc Hospice Program 30 Pillsbury St *Web:* www.crvna.org	Concord	NH	03301	603-224-4093	227-7525
Home Health & Hospice Care Seven Executive Park Dr *TF:* 800-887-5973 ■ *Web:* www.hhhc.org	Merrimack	NH	03054	603-882-2941	883-1515

New Jersey

				Phone	Fax
Center for Hope Hospice 1900 Raritan Rd *Web:* www.centerforhope.com	Scotch Plains	NJ	07076	908-889-7780	889-5172
Hospice of New Jersey 400 Broadacres Dr 1St Fl *TF:* 800-501-0451 ■ *Web:* www.americanhospice.com	Bloomfield	NJ	07003	973-893-0818	893-0828
Hospice Program of Hackensack University Medical Ctr 25 E Salem St	Hackensack	NJ	07601	201-342-7766	489-7275
Karen Ann Quinlan Hospice 99 Sparta Ave *TF:* 800-882-1117 ■ *Web:* www.karenannquinlanhospice.org	Newton	NJ	07860	973-383-0115	383-6889
Lighthouse Hospice 1040 Kings Hwy N Ste 100 *TF General:* 888-467-7423 ■ *Web:* www.lighthousehospice.net	Cherry Hill	NJ	08034	856-414-1155	414-1313
Saint Barnabas Hospice & Palliative Care Ctr 95 Old Short Hills Rd *Web:* www.barnabashealth.org	West Orange	NJ	07052	973-322-4800	322-4795
Samaritan Hospice Five Eves Dr Ste 300 *TF:* 800-229-8183 ■ *Web:* www.samaritanhealthcarenj.org	Marlton	NJ	08053	856-596-1600	596-7881
South Jersey Healthcare HospiceCare 2848 S Delsea Dr Bldg 1 *TF:* 800-770-7547 ■ *Web:* www.inspirahealthnetwork.org	Vineland	NJ	08360	800-770-7547	
VNA of Central Jersey (VNACJ) 176 Riverside Ave *TF:* 800-862-3330 ■ *Web:* www.vnahg.org	Red Bank	NJ	07701	800-862-3330	

New Mexico

				Phone	Fax
Mesilla Valley Hospice 299 Montana Ave *Web:* www.mvhospice.org	Las Cruces	NM	88005	575-525-5757	527-2204

New York

				Phone	Fax
Catskill Area Hospice & Palliative Care Inc One Birchwood Dr *TF:* 800-306-3870 ■ *Web:* www.cahpc.org	Oneonta	NY	13820	607-432-6773	432-7741
Community Hospice of Albany 445 New Karner Rd *Web:* communityhospice.org	Albany	NY	12205	518-724-0200	724-0299
East End Hospice 481 Westhampton-Riverhead Rd PO Box 1048 *TF:* 877-513-0099 ■ *Web:* www.eeh.org	WestHampton Beach	NY	11978	631-288-8400	288-8492
HomeCare & Hospice 1225 W State St *TF:* 800-339-7011 ■ *Web:* www.homecare-hospice.org	Olean	NY	14760	716-372-5735	372-4635
Hospicare of Tompkins County 172 E King Rd *Web:* www.hospicare.org	Ithaca	NY	14850	607-272-0212	272-0237
Hospice & Palliative Care of Buffalo 225 Como Pk Blvd *Web:* www.hospicebuffalo.com	Cheektowaga	NY	14227	716-686-1900	686-8181
Hospice Care in Westchester & Putnam Inc 540 White Plains Rd Ste 300 *Web:* www.vnahv.org	Tarrytown	NY	10591	914-666-4228	666-0378
Hospice Care Inc 4277 Middle Settlement Rd *TF:* 800-317-5661 ■ *Web:* www.hospicecareinc.org	New Hartford	NY	13413	315-735-6484	793-8852
Hospice Care Network 99 Sunnyside Blvd *TF:* 800-405-6731 ■ *Web:* hospicecarenetwork.org/	Woodbury	NY	11797	516-832-7100	832-7160
Hospice Chautauqua County 20 W Fairmount Ave *Web:* www.hospicechautco.org	Lakewood	NY	14750	716-753-5383	338-1575
Hospice Family Care 550 E Main St *TF:* 800-719-7129 ■ *Web:* www.homecare-hospice.org	Batavia	NY	14020	585-343-7596	343-7629
Hospice of Jefferson County 425 Washington St *Web:* jeffersonhospice.org	Watertown	NY	13601	315-788-7323	788-9653
Hospice of Orange & Sullivan Counties 800 Stony Brook Ct *TF:* 800-924-0157 ■ *Web:* www.hospiceoforange.com	Newburgh	NY	12550	845-561-6111	561-2179
Hospice of Saint Lawrence Valley 6805 State Hwy 11 *Web:* www.seriousillness.org	Potsdam	NY	13676	315-265-3105	265-0323
Hospice of Westchester 311 N St Ste 204 *Web:* www.hospiceofwestchester.com	White Plains	NY	10605	914-682-1484	682-9425
Niagara Hospice 4675 Sunset Dr *TF:* 800-662-1220 ■ *Web:* www.niagarahospice.org	Lockport	NY	14094	716-439-4417	
United Hospice of Rockland 11 Stokum Ln *Web:* www.hospiceofrockland.org	New City	NY	10956	845-634-4974	634-7549
Visiting Nurse Service of New York Hospice Care 1250 Broadway Seventh Fl *Web:* www.vnsny.org	New York	NY	10001	212-609-1900	290-3933
VNS Hospice of Suffolk 505 Main St *Web:* www.visitingnurseservice.org/	Northport	NY	11768	631-261-7200	261-1985

North Carolina

	City	State	Zip	Phone	Fax
Caldwell Hospice & Palliative Care 902 Kirkwood St NW *Web:* www.caldwellhospice.org	Lenoir	NC	28645	828-754-0101	757-3335
CarePartners Mountain Area Hospice PO Box 5779 *TF:* 800-627-1533 ■ *Web:* www.carepartners.org	Asheville	NC	28813	828-255-0231	255-2944
FirstHealth Hospice Five Aviemore Dr *Web:* www.firsthealth.org	Pinehurst	NC	28374	910-715-6000	715-6032
Four Seasons Hospice & Palliative Care 571 S Allen Rd *TF:* 866-466-9734 ■ *Web:* www.fourseasonscfl.org	Flat Rock	NC	28731	828-692-6178	233-0351
Hospice & Palliative Care of Cabarrus County 5003 Hospice Ln *Web:* www.hpccc.org	Kannapolis	NC	28081	704-935-9434	935-9435
Hospice & Palliative CareCenter 101 Hospice Ln *TF:* 888-876-3663 ■ *Web:* www.hospicecarecenter.org	Winston-Salem	NC	27103	336-768-3972	659-0461
Hospice at Charlotte 1420 E Seventh St *Web:* www.hpccr.org	Charlotte	NC	28204	704-375-0100	375-8623
Hospice at Greensboro 2500 Summit Ave *Web:* www.hospicegso.org	Greensboro	NC	27405	336-621-2500	621-4516
Hospice of Alamance Caswell 914 Chapel Hill Rd *TF:* 800-588-8879 ■ *Web:* www.hospiceac.org	Burlington	NC	27215	336-532-0100	532-0060
Hospice of Burke County 1721 Enon Rd *Web:* www.burkehospice.org	Valdese	NC	28690	828-879-1601	879-3500
Hospice of Cleveland County 951 Wendover Heights Dr *Web:* www.hospicecares.cc	Shelby	NC	28150	704-487-4677	481-8050
Hospice of Gaston County 258 E Garrison Blvd PO Box 3984 *Web:* www.gastonhospice.org	Gastonia	NC	28054	704-861-8405	865-0590
Hospice of Randolph County 416 Vision Dr *Web:* www.hospiceofrandolph.org	Asheboro	NC	27203	336-672-9300	672-0868
Hospice of Rockingham County Inc 2150 NC Hwy 65 PO Box 281 *Web:* www.hospiceofrockinghamcounty.com	Wentworth	NC	27375	336-427-9022	427-9030
Hospice of Rowan County Inc 720 Grove St *Web:* hospicecarecenter.org	Salisbury	NC	28144	704-637-7645	
Hospice of Rutherford County 374 Hudlow Rd PO Box 336 *TF:* 800-218-2273 ■ *Web:* www.hospiceofrutherford.org	Forest City	NC	28043	828-245-0095	248-1035
Hospice of Stanly County 960 N First St *TF:* 800-230-4236 ■ *Web:* www.hospiceofstanly.org	Albemarle	NC	28001	704-983-4216	983-6662
Hospice of Union County 700 W Roosevelt Blvd *Web:* www.carolinashealthcare.org	Monroe	NC	28110	704-292-2100	292-2190
Hospice of Wake County Inc 250 Hospice Cir 4th Fl *TF:* 888-900-3959 ■ *Web:* transitionslifecare.org/redirected-from-hospicofwake-org/	Raleigh	NC	27607	919-828-0890	828-0664
Kitty Askins Hospice Ctr 107 Handley Pk Ct *TF:* 800-692-4442 ■ *Web:* www.3hc.org	Goldsboro	NC	27534	919-735-5887	735-5948
Lower Cape Fear Hospice & Life Care 1414 Physicians Dr *TF:* 800-733-1476 ■ *Web:* www.hospiceandlifecarecenter.org	Wilmington	NC	28401	910-796-7900	796-7901
Palliative CareCenter & Hospice of Catawba Valley 3975 Robinson Rd *Web:* www.catawbaregionalhospice.org	Newton	NC	28658	828-466-0466	466-8862
Richmond County Hospice 1119 N US Hwy 1 *TF:* 800-322-2997	Rockingham	NC	28379	910-997-4464	895-7476
University Health Systems Hospice 521 E Myers St	Ahoskie	NC	27910	252-332-3392	

North Dakota

	City	State	Zip	Phone	Fax
Hospice of the Red River Valley 1701 38th St S Ste 101 *TF:* 800-237-4629 ■ *Web:* www.hrrv.org	Fargo	ND	58103	701-356-1500	356-1592

Ohio

	City	State	Zip	Phone	Fax
Bridge Home Health & Hospice 15100 Birchaven Ln *TF:* 800-982-3306 ■ *Web:* www.bvhealthsystem.org	Findlay	OH	45840	419-423-5351	423-8967
Community New Life Hospice 5255 N Abbe Rd *Web:* mercyonline.org	Sheffield Vlg	OH	44035	440-934-1458	
FairHope Hospice & Palliative Care Inc 282 Sells Rd *TF:* 800-994-7077 ■ *Web:* www.fairhopehospice.org	Lancaster	OH	43130	740-654-7077	654-6321
Homereach Hospice 800 McConnell Dr *TF:* 800-837-2455 ■ *Web:* www.ohiohealth.com	Columbus	OH	43214	614-566-5377	338-8063
Hospice of Central Ohio 2269 Cherry Vly Rd *TF:* 800-804-2505 ■ *Web:* www.hospiceofcentralohio.org	Newark	OH	43055	740-344-0311	344-6577
Hospice of Cincinnati 4360 Cooper Rd *TF:* 800-691-7255 ■ *Web:* www.hospiceofcincinnati.org	Cincinnati	OH	45242	513-891-7700	792-6980
Hospice of Dayton 324 Wilmington Ave *TF:* 800-653-4490 ■ *Web:* www.hospiceofdayton.org	Dayton	OH	45420	937-256-4490	256-9802
Hospice of Medina County 5075 Windfall Rd *TF:* 800-700-4771 ■ *Web:* www.hospiceofmedina.org	Medina	OH	44256	330-722-4771	722-5266
Hospice of Miami County 550 Summit Ave Ste 101 *TF:* 800-372-0009 ■ *Web:* www.hospiceofmiamicounty.org	Troy	OH	45373	937-335-5191	335-8841
Hospice of North Central Ohio 1050 Dauch Dr *TF:* 800-952-2207 ■ *Web:* www.hospiceofnorthcentralohio.org	Ashland	OH	44805	419-281-7107	281-8427
Hospice of Northwest Ohio 30000 E River Rd *TF:* 866-661-4001 ■ *Web:* www.hospicenwo.org	Perrysburg	OH	43551	419-661-4001	661-4015
Hospice of the Cleveland Clinic 6801 Brecksville Rd Ste 10 *TF:* 800-263-0403 ■ *Web:* my.clevelandclinic.org	Independence	OH	44131	216-444-9819	520-1973
Hospice of the Valley 5190 Market St *Web:* www.hospiceofthevalley.com	Youngstown	OH	44512	330-788-1992	788-1998
Hospice of the Western Reserve 300 E 185th St *Web:* www.hospicewr.org	Cleveland	OH	44119	216-383-2222	383-3750
Hospice of Visiting Nurse Service 3358 Ridgewood Rd *TF:* 800-335-1455 ■ *Web:* www.vnsa.com	Akron	OH	44333	330-665-1455	668-4680
Mercy Medical Ctr Hospice 7568 Whipple Ave NW *Web:* cantonmercy.org	Canton	OH	44720	330-492-8803	649-4399
State of the Heart Home Health & Hospice 1350 N Broadway *TF:* 800-417-7535 ■ *Web:* www.stateoftheheartcare.org	Greenville	OH	45331	937-548-2999	548-7144
Stein Hospice Service 1912 Hayes Ave Ste 3 *TF:* 800-625-5269 ■ *Web:* www.steinhospice.org	Sandusky	OH	44870	419-625-5269	625-5761
Universal Home Health & Hospice Care 701 S Main St *Web:* www.uhcinc.org	Bellefontaine	OH	43311	937-593-1605	
Valley Hospice Inc 380 Summit Ave *TF:* 877-467-7423 ■ *Web:* www.valleyhospice.org	Steubenville	OH	43952	740-284-4440	284-4478
Visiting Nurse Assn of Ohio 2500 E 22nd St *TF:* 877-698-6264 ■ *Web:* www.vnaohio.org	Cleveland	OH	44115	216-931-1400	694-4182

Oklahoma

	City	State	Zip	Phone	Fax
Good Shepherd Hospice 4350 Will Rogers Pkwy Ste 400 *TF:* 800-687-9808 ■ *Web:* www.goodshepherdhospice.com	Oklahoma City	OK	73108	405-943-0903	943-0950
Hospice of Oklahoma County 4334 NW Expy Ste 106 *Web:* integrisok.com	Oklahoma City	OK	73116	405-848-8884	841-4899

Oregon

	City	State	Zip	Phone	Fax
Hospice of Bend-La Pine 2075 NE Wyatt Ct *Web:* www.partnersbend.org	Bend	OR	97701	541-382-5882	382-2960
Lovejoy Hospice 939 SE Eigth St *TF:* 888-758-8569 ■ *Web:* lovejoyhospice.org	Grants Pass	OR	97526	541-474-1193	474-3035
Willamette Valley Hospice 1015 Third St NW *TF:* 800-555-2431 ■ *Web:* www.wvh.org	Salem	OR	97304	503-588-3600	363-3891

Pennsylvania

	City	State	Zip	Phone	Fax
Berks VNA 1170 Berkshire Blvd **Fax Area Code:* 610 ■ *TF:* 855-843-8627 ■ *Web:* www.berksvna.org/	Wyomissing	PA	19610	855-843-8627	378-9762*
Celtic Healthcare 150 Scharberry Ln *TF:* 800-355-8894 ■ *Web:* www.celtichealthcare.com	Mars	PA	16046	800-355-8894	931-4288
Chandler Hall Hospice 99 Barclay St *TF:* 888-603-1973 ■ *Web:* www.chandlerhall.org	Newtown	PA	18940	215-860-4000	860-3458
Compassionate Care Hospice 3331 St Rd Ste 410 *TF:* 800-584-8165 ■ *Web:* www.cchnet.net	Bensalem	PA	19020	215-245-3525	245-3540
Family Hospice & Palliative Care 50 Moffett St *TF:* 800-513-2148 ■ *Web:* familyhospicepa.org/	Pittsburgh	PA	15243	412-572-8800	572-8827
Forbes Hospice 4800 Friendship Ave *TF:* 800-381-8080 ■ *Web:* ahn.org	Pittsburgh	PA	15224	412-578-5000	
Geisinger Columbia Montour Hospice 410 Glenn Ave *Web:* cmhhs.net	Bloomsburg	PA	17815	570-784-1723	
Heartland Hospice Services 333 N Summit St *TF:* 800-366-1232 ■ *Web:* www.hcr-manorcare.com	Toledo	OH	43604	419-252-5500	252-6404
Holy Redeemer Home Care & Hospice 12265 Townsend Rd Ste 400 **Fax Area Code:* 215 ■ *Web:* www.holyredeemer.com	Philadelphia	PA	19154	888-678-8678	938-0180*
Hospice of Central Pennsylvania 1320 Linglestown Rd *TF:* 866-779-7374 ■ *Web:* www.hospiceofcentralpa.org	Harrisburg	PA	17110	717-732-1000	732-5348
Hospice of Lancaster County 685 Good Dr PO Box 4125 *TF:* 888-236-9563 ■ *Web:* www.hospiceandcommunitycare.org	Lancaster	PA	17604	717-295-3900	391-9582
Lehigh Valley Hospice 2166 S 12th St Ste 401 *TF:* 888-584-2273 ■ *Web:* www.lvhn.org	Allentown	PA	18103	610-969-0300	969-0326
St John Diakon Hospice 1201 N Church St *Web:* diakon.org	Hazleton	PA	18202	570-450-1500	
SUN Home Health Services Inc 61 Duke St PO Box 232 *TF:* 888-478-6227 ■ *Web:* www.sunhomehealth.com	Northumberland	PA	17857	570-473-8320	473-3070
VITAS Healthcare Corp of Pennsylvania 1787 Sentry Pk W Bldg 16 Ste 400 *TF:* 800-582-9533 ■ *Web:* www.vitas.com	Blue Bell	PA	19422	215-542-3000	
VNA 154 Hindman Rd *TF:* 877-862-6659 ■ *Web:* www.vna.com	Butler	PA	16001	724-282-6806	282-7517
VNA Hospice & Home Health of Lackawanna County 301 Delaware Ave *TF:* 800-936-7671 ■ *Web:* www.vnahospice.org	Olyphant	PA	18447	570-383-5180	383-5189

Rhode Island

Phone *Fax*

Home Hospice Care of Rhode Island
1085 N Main St .... Providence RI 02904 401-415-4200
TF: 800-338-6555 ■ *Web:* www.hhcri.org

South Carolina

Phone *Fax*

Hospice Community Care PO Box 993 .... Rock Hill SC 29731 803-329-1500 329-5935
TF: 800-895-2273 ■ *Web:* www.hospicecommunitycare.org

Hospice of the Upstate 1835 Rogers Rd .... Anderson SC 29621 864-224-3358 328-1132
TF: 800-261-8636 ■ *Web:* www.hospicehouse.net

HospiceCare of the Piedmont
408 W Alexander Ave .... Greenwood SC 29646 864-227-9393 227-9377
Web: www.hospicepiedmont.org

McLeod Hospice 1203 E Cheves St................. Florence SC 29506 843-777-2564 777-5135
TF: 800-768-4556 ■ *Web:* www.mcleodhealth.org

Mercy Hospice of Horry County
PO Box 50640 .... Myrtle Beach SC 29579 843-236-2282 347-5535

Open Arms Hospice 1836 W Georgia Rd........... Simpsonville SC 29680 864-688-1700 688-1705
TF: 866-473-6276 ■ *Web:* www.openarmshospice.org

Palmetto Health Home Care & Hospice
1400 Pickens St .... Columbia SC 29202 803-296-3100 296-3320
TF: 800-238-1884 ■ *Web:* www.palmettohealth.org

South Dakota

Phone *Fax*

Dougherty Hospice House
4509 Prince of Peace Pl .... Sioux Falls SD 57103 605-322-7705
Web: www.avera.org/

Tennessee

Phone *Fax*

Alive Hospice Inc 1718 Patterson St................. Nashville TN 37203 615-327-1085 321-8902
TF: 800-327-1085 ■ *Web:* www.alivehospice.org

Amedisys Hospice 1423 W Morris Blvd Ste C .... Morristown TN 37813 423-587-9484 587-9408
TF: 800-659-2633 ■ *Web:* www.amedisys.com

Baptist Trinity Home Care & Hospice
6019 Walnut Grove Rd .... Memphis TN 38120 901-226-5000
TF: 800-422-7847 ■ *Web:* www.baptistonline.org

Hospice of Chattanooga 4411 Oakwood Dr........ Chattanooga TN 37416 423-892-4289 892-8301
TF: 800-267-6828 ■ *Web:* www.hospiceofchattanooga.org

Methodist Alliance Hospice
6400 Shelby View Dr Ste 101....................... Memphis TN 38134 901-516-1999
TF: 800-541-8277 ■ *Web:* www.methodisthealth.org

Texas

Phone *Fax*

AseraCare Hospice of Austin 14205 Burnet Rd .... Austin TX 78728 512-218-9890 218-9288
TF: 800-332-3982 ■ *Web:* www.aseracare.com

CHRISTUS Spohn Hospice
6200 Saratoga Blvd Bldg B Ste 104 .... Corpus Christi TX 78414 361-994-3400 785-5390*
**Fax Area Code:* 210 ■ *TF:* 844-444-8440 ■ *Web:* www.christushomecare.org

CHRISTUS VNA 4241 Woodcock Dr # A100 .... San Antonio TX 78228 210-785-5200 785-5803
Web: www.christushomecare.org

Community Hospice of Texas
6100 Western Pl Ste 500 .... Fort Worth TX 76107 817-870-2795 989-3220
TF: 800-226-0373 ■ *Web:* www.chot.org

Hendrick Hospice Care 1682 Hickory St .... Abilene TX 79601 325-677-8516 675-5031
TF: 800-622-8516 ■ *Web:* www.hendrickhospice.org

Home Hospice of Grayson County 505 W Ctr St ...... Sherman TX 75090 903-868-9315 893-2772
Web: www.homehospice.org

Hope Hospice 611 N Walnut Ave .... New Braunfels TX 78130 830-625-7500 606-1388
TF: 800-499-7501 ■ *Web:* www.hopehospice.net

Hospice at the Texas Medical Ctr
1905 Holcombe Blvd .... Houston TX 77030 713-467-7423
TF: 800-630-7894 ■ *Web:* www.houstonhospice.org/

Hospice Austin
4107 Spicewood Springs Rd Ste 100.................. Austin TX 78759 512-342-4700 795-9053
TF: 800-445-3261 ■ *Web:* www.hospiceaustin.org

Hospice Brazos Valley 502 W 26th St .... Bryan TX 77803 979-821-2266 821-0041
TF: 800-824-2326 ■ *Web:* www.hospicebrazosvalley.org

Hospice Care Team 1708 N Amburn Rd Ste C .... Texas City TX 77591 409-938-0070 938-1509
TF: 800-545-8738 ■ *Web:* www.hospicecareteam.org

Hospice of East Texas 4111 University Blvd .... Tyler TX 75701 903-266-3400 566-0291
TF: 800-777-9860 ■ *Web:* www.hospiceofeasttexas.org

Hospice of El Paso 1440 Miracle Way .... El Paso TX 79925 915-532-5699 532-7822
Web: www.hospiceelpaso.org

Hospice of Midland 911 W Texas Ave................. Midland TX 79701 432-682-2855 682-2989
Web: hospicemidland.org

Hospice of San Angelo
36 E Twohig St PO Box 471 .... San Angelo TX 76903 325-658-6524 658-8895
TF: 800-499-6524 ■ *Web:* www.hospiceofsanangelo.org

Hospice of South Texas 605 E Locust Ave............. Victoria TX 77901 361-572-4300 570-1147
TF: 800-874-6908 ■ *Web:* www.hospiceofsouthtexas.org

Hospice of Wichita Falls
4909 Johnson Rd .... Wichita Falls TX 76310 940-691-0982 691-1608
Web: www.hospiceofwf.org

Virginia

Phone *Fax*

Capital Hospice Inc 2900 Telestar Ct .... Falls Church VA 22042 703-538-2065 538-2165
Web: www.capitalcaring.org

Good Samaritan Hospice 2408 Electric Rd............ Roanoke VA 24018 540-776-0198 776-0841
TF: 888-466-7809 ■ *Web:* www.goodsamhospice.com

Hospice of the Piedmont
675 Peter Jefferson Pkwy Ste 300............... Charlottesville VA 22911 434-817-6900 245-0187
TF: 800-975-5501 ■ *Web:* www.hopva.org

Hospice of the Rapidan
1200 Sunset Ln Ste 2320 .... Culpeper VA 22701 540-825-4840 825-7752
TF: 800-676-2012 ■ *Web:* www.hotr.org

Mary Washington Hospice
5012 Southpoint Pkwy .... Fredericksburg VA 22407 540-741-1667 741-3581
TF: 800-257-1667 ■ *Web:* www.marywashingtonhealthcare.com

Washington

Phone *Fax*

Evergreen Hospice Services
12822 124th Ln NE................................ Kirkland WA 98034 425-899-1070 899-1033
TF: 877-980-7500 ■ *Web:* www.evergreenhealth.com

Hospice of Spokane 121 S Arthur St .... Spokane WA 99202 509-456-0438 458-0359
TF: 888-459-0438 ■ *Web:* www.hospiceofspokane.org

Providence Hospice & Home Care of Snohomish County
2731 Wetmore Ave .... Everett WA 98201 425-261-4800
Web: washington.providence.org

Providence Hospice of Seattle
425 Pontius Ave N Ste 300.......................... Seattle WA 98109 206-320-4000 320-7333
TF: 888-782-4445 ■ *Web:* www2.providence.org

Providence Sound Home Care & Hospice
3432 S Bay Rd NE .... Olympia WA 98506 360-459-8311
TF: 800-869-7062 ■ *Web:* www2.providence.org

Tri-Cities Chaplaincy 2108 W Entiat Ave .... Kennewick WA 99336 509-783-7416 735-7850
TF: 800-783-0544 ■ *Web:* www.tricitieschaplaincy.org

Whatcom Hospice Foundation
2901 Squalicum Pkwy Ste 1C.................... Bellingham WA 98225 360-733-1231 788-6858
Web: www.hospicehelp.org

West Virginia

Phone *Fax*

Hospice of Huntington 1101 Sixth Ave .... Huntington WV 25701 304-529-4217 523-6051
TF: 800-788-5480 ■ *Web:* www.hospiceofhuntington.org

Hospice of the Panhandle
330 Hospice Ln .... Kearneysville WV 25430 304-264-0406 264-0409
TF: 800-345-6538 ■ *Web:* www.hospiceotp.org

Kanawha Hospice Care 1606 Kanawha Blvd W .... Charleston WV 25387 304-768-8523
TF: 800-560-8523 ■ *Web:* www.hospicecarewv.org

Wisconsin

Phone *Fax*

AseraCare Hospice of Milwaukee
7160 Dallas Pkwy Ste 400 .... Plano TX 75024 262-785-1356 607-6196*
**Fax Area Code:* 414 ■ *TF:* 800-598-5132 ■ *Web:* www.aseracare.com

Aurora VNA Zilber Family Hospice
1155 N Honey Creek Pkwy .... Wauwatosa WI 53213 414-615-5900 615-5927
TF: 888-206-6955 ■ *Web:* www.aurorahealthcare.org

Beloit Regional Hospice 655 Third St Ste 200 .... Beloit WI 53511 608-363-7421 363-7426
TF: 877-363-7421 ■ *Web:* www.beloitregionalhospice.com

Gundersen Lutheran at Home HomeCare & Hospice
914 Green Bay St .... La Crosse WI 54601 608-775-8400
TF General: 800-362-9567 ■ *Web:* www.gundersenhealth.org

Horizon Home Care & Hospice
11400 W Lake Park Dr .... Milwaukee WI 53224 414-365-8300 365-8330
TF: 800-468-4660 ■ *Web:* www.horizonhch.com

Hospice Alliance
10220 Prairie Ridge Blvd .... Pleasant Prairie WI 53158 262-652-4400 652-4516
TF: 800-830-8344 ■ *Web:* www.hospicealliance.org

HospiceCare 5395 E Cheryl Pkwy .... Madison WI 53711 608-276-4660 276-4672
TF: 800-553-4289 ■ *Web:* www.agrace.org

Theda Care at Home 3000 E College Ave .... Appleton WI 54915 920-969-0919 969-0020
TF: 800-984-5554 ■ *Web:* www.thedacare.org

Unity Hospice 2366 Oak Ridge Cir .... De Pere WI 54115 920-338-1111 338-8111
TF: 800-990-9249 ■ *Web:* www.unityhospice.org

Wyoming

Phone *Fax*

Central Wyoming Hospice Program
319 S Wilson St .... Casper WY 82601 307-577-4832 577-4841
Web: www.cwhp.org

375 HOSPITAL HOSPITALITY HOUSES

Phone *Fax*

Alegent Creighton Health Hospitality House
7105 Newport Ave.................................. Omaha NE 68122 402-572-2828
Web: alegentcreighton.com

American Cancer Society Hope Lodge of Baltimore
636 W Lexington St .... Baltimore MD 21201 410-547-2522 539-8890
TF: 888-227-6333 ■ *Web:* www.cancer.org

American Cancer Society Hope Lodge of Buffalo
197 Summer St.................................... Buffalo NY 14222 716-882-9244 822-4436
Web: www.cancer.org

Name / Address	City	State	Zip	Phone	Fax
American Cancer Society Hope Lodge of Charleston					
269 Calhoun St	Charleston	SC	29401	843-958-0930	958-9054
TF: 800-227-2345 ■ *Web:* www.cancer.org					
American Cancer Society Hope Lodge of Marshfield					
611 W Doege St	Marshfield	WI	54449	715-486-9100	486-9110
Web: www.cancer.org					
American Cancer Society Hope Lodge of Rochester					
411 Second St NW	Rochester	MN	55901	507-529-4673	529-4666
Web: www.cancer.org					
American Cancer Society Hope Lodge Worcester					
Seven Oak St	Worcester	MA	01609	508-792-2985	753-3986
Web: www.cancer.org					
American Cancer Society Joe Lee Griffin Hope Lodge					
1104 Ireland Way	Birmingham	AL	35205	205-558-7860	558-7862
TF: 888-513-9933 ■ *Web:* www.cancer.org					
American Cancer Society Joseph S. & Jeannette M. Silber Hope Lodge					
11432 Mayfield Rd	Cleveland	OH	44106	216-844-4673	844-2959
Web: www.cancer.org					
American Cancer Society Winn-Dixie Hope Lodge					
1552 Shoup Ct	Atlanta	GA	30033	404-327-9200	327-9808
Web: www.cancer.org					
Arbor House 300 Main St	Lewiston	ME	04240	207-795-0111	795-2303
Web: www.cmmc.org					
Arizona Transplant House 5811 E Mayo Blvd	Phoenix	AZ	85054	480-609-1324	609-7268
Web: www.aztransplanthouse.org					
Atlanta Hospital Hospitality House					
1815 S Ponce De Leon Ave NE	Atlanta	GA	30307	404-377-6333	377-0668
Web: www.atlhhh.org					
Bannister Family House 406 Dickinson St	San Diego	CA	92103	619-543-7977	543-7937
TF: 800-926-8273 ■ *Web:* health.ucsd.edu					
Barnes Lodge 4520 Clayton Ave	Saint Louis	MO	63110	314-652-4319	
TF: 800-551-3492 ■ *Web:* www.barnesjewish.org					
Baylor Plaza Hotel 3600 Gaston Ave	Dallas	TX	75246	800-422-9567	
TF: 800-422-9567 ■ *Web:* www.baylorhealth.com					
Beacon House 1301 N Third St	Marquette	MI	49855	906-225-7100	225-4903
TF: 800-562-9753 ■ *Web:* www.upbeaconhouse.org					
Blount Hospitality House 610 Madison St	Huntsville	AL	35801	256-534-7014	
Web: www.blounthospitalityhouse.org					
Brent's Place 11980 E 16th Ave	Aurora	CO	80010	303-831-4545	831-4567
TF: 800-895-1999 ■ *Web:* www.brentsplace.org					
Caring House Inc 2625 Pickett Rd	Durham	NC	27705	919-490-5449	493-8044
Web: www.caringhouse.com					
Carolyn Scott Rainbow House 7815 Harney St	Omaha	NE	68114	402-955-7815	955-7805
Web: www.childrensomaha.org					
Carpenter Hospitality House 121 Fifth Ave NE	Hickory	NC	28601	828-324-4544	
Casa Esperanza 1005 Yale NE	Albuquerque	NM	87106	505-277-9880	277-9876
TF: 866-654-1338 ■ *Web:* casanm.org/					
Children's Hope House					
7922 W Jefferson Blvd	Fort Wayne	IN	46804	260-459-8550	459-8551
TF: 800-706-9941 ■ *Web:* childrenshopefw.org					
Children's House at Johns Hopkins					
1915 McElderry St	Baltimore	MD	21205	410-614-2560	614-2568
TF: 800-933-5470 ■ *Web:* believeintomorrow.org					
Conine Clubhouse 1005 Joe DiMaggio Dr	Hollywood	FL	33021	954-265-5324	
Web: www.jdch.com/html/at-the-hospital/connie-clubhouse/index.html					
Cynthia C. & William E. Perry Pavilion					
9400 Turkey Lake Rd	Orlando	FL	32819	321-842-8844	842-8871
TF: 800-447-1435 ■ *Web:* www.orlandohealth.com/drpphillipshospital					
Danielle House 160 Riverside Dr	Binghamton	NY	13905	607-724-1540	724-1540
Web: www.daniellehouse.org					
Devon Nicole House 21 Autumn St Fifth Fl	Boston	MA	02215	617-355-8457	
Web: childrenshospital.org					
Doorways, The 612 E Marshall St	Richmond	VA	23219	804-828-6901	827-7213
Web: hhhrichmond.org					
Family House Inc 1509 N Knoxville Ave	Peoria	IL	61603	309-685-5300	685-8122
Web: www.familyhousepeoria.org					
Fisher House Inc 7323 Hwy 90 W Ste 107	San Antonio	TX	78227	210-673-7500	673-7579
Web: www.fisherhouseinc.org					
Francis Cheney Family Place					
2650 Siskiyou Blvd	Medford	OR	97504	541-789-5876	789-5841
Web: www.asante.org					
Gary's House 97 State St	Portland	ME	04101	207-773-9800	
Gift of Life Transplant House					
705 Second St SW	Rochester	MN	55902	507-288-7470	281-9888
TF: 800-479-7824 ■ *Web:* www.gift-of-life.org					
Hanson House 380 E Paseo El Mirador	Palm Springs	CA	92262	760-416-5070	416-5071
Web: www.hansonhouse.org					
Holland's Rose 132 Griegos Rd NW	Albuquerque	NM	87107	505-345-2020	345-5464
Web: www.hollandsrose.com					
Hope Lodge Hershey Pennsylvania					
125 Lucy Ave	Hummelstown	PA	17036	717-533-5111	533-2587
Web: www.cancer.org					
Hospital Hospitality House of Louisville					
120 W Broadway	Louisville	KY	40202	502-625-1360	625-1363
Web: www.hhhlouisville.org					
Hospital Hospitality House of SW Michigan Inc					
527 W S St	Kalamazoo	MI	49007	269-341-7811	341-7817
Web: www.hhhkz.org					
Hospitality House of Charlotte					
1400 Scott Ave	Charlotte	NC	28203	704-376-0060	376-0059
Web: www.hospitalityhouseofcharlotte.org					
Hospitality House of Methodist Hospital Foundation					
990 Oak Ridge Tpke PO Box 2529	Oak Ridge	TN	37830	865-835-5261	481-5403
Web: www.mmcoakridge.com					
Hospitality House of Tulsa 1135 S Victor Ave	Tulsa	OK	74014	918-794-0088	
Web: www.tulsahospitalityhouse.org					
Hubbard House, The 29 W Miller St	Orlando	FL	32806	407-649-6886	849-6447
TF: 800-648-3818 ■ *Web:* www.orlandohealth.com					
Huntington Hospital Hospitality House					
2801 S Staunton Rd	Huntington	WV	25702	304-522-1832	
Inn at Cherry Hill 500 17th Ave	Seattle	WA	98122	206-320-2164	320-3526
Web: www.swedish.org					
Inn at Virginia Mason 1006 Spring St	Seattle	WA	98104	206-583-6453	625-7197
TF: 800-283-6453 ■ *Web:* www.innatvirginiamason.com					
Jenn's House Inc 3250 S Cedar Crest Blvd	Emmaus	PA	18049	610-965-1777	965-1777
Web: www.jennshouse.org					
Kathy's House Inc 600 N 103 St	Milwaukee	WI	53226	414-453-8290	453-8292
Web: www.kathys-house.org					
Kevin Guest House 782 Ellicott St	Buffalo	NY	14203	716-882-1818	882-1291
Web: www.kevinguesthouse.com					
Kohl's House at Children's Memorial Hospital					
225 E Chicago Ave	Chicago	IL	60611	312-227-4000	227-9456
TF: 800-543-7362 ■ *Web:* www.luriechildrens.org					
Mario Pastega Guest House					
3505 NW Samaritan Dr	Corvallis	OR	97330	541-768-4650	768-5124
TF: 888-872-0760 ■ *Web:* www.samhealth.org					
Molly's House 430 SE Osceola St	Stuart	FL	34994	772-223-6659	223-9990
Web: www.mollyshouse.org					
Munson Manor Hospitality House					
1220 Medical Campus Dr	Traverse City	MI	49684	231-935-2300	935-2302
Web: www.munsonhealthcare.org					
Nebraska House 983285 Nebraska Medical Ctr	Omaha	NE	68198	402-559-5000	559-3434
TF: 800-401-4444 ■ *Web:* www.nebraskamed.com/transplant					
Pay It Forward House 719 Somonauk St	Sycamore	IL	60178	815-762-4882	
Web: www.payitforwardhouse.org					
Pete Gross House 525 Minor Ave N	Seattle	WA	98109	206-262-1000	667-6831
TF: 800-331-3131 ■ *Web:* www.fhcrc.org					
Prairie Lakes Caring Club House					
401 9th Ave NW	Watertown	SD	57201	605-882-7000	882-7720
Web: www.prairielakes.com					
Quantum House 901 45th St	West Palm Beach	FL	33407	561-494-0515	494-0522
Web: www.quantumhouse.org					
Quincy Hospitality House 1129 Oak St	Quincy	IL	62301	217-228-3022	223-2569
Web: www.blessinghospital.org					
Rathgeber Hospitality House					
1615 12th St	Wichita Falls	TX	76301	940-764-2400	764-2456
Web: www.rathgeberhospitalityhouse.org					
Rose Hill Hospitality House					
605 26 1/2 Rd	Grand Junction	CO	81506	970-243-7968	
Web: stmarygj.org					
Rosenbaum Family House					
1 Medical Ctr Dr PO Box 8228	Morgantown	WV	26506	304-598-6094	598-6412
TF: 855-988-2273 ■ *Web:* wvuhealthcare.com/wvuh/404					
Sarah House Inc 100 Roberts Ave	Syracuse	NY	13207	315-475-1747	
Web: sarahsguesthouse.org					
Seton Guest Ctr 2131 W Third St	Los Angeles	CA	90057	213-484-7767	207-5816
Web: stvincent.dochs.org					
Seton League House 3207 Medical Pkwy	Austin	TX	78705	512-324-1999	324-1932
Web: www.seton.net					
Stanton Hospitality House					
1617 Roxie Ave	Fayetteville	NC	28304	910-615-4000	
Web: www.capefearvalley.com					
Steven's Hope for Children Inc					
1014 W Foothill Blvd Ste B	Upland	CA	91786	909-373-0678	981-4578
TF: 866-378-3836 ■ *Web:* www.stevenshope.org					
Sumner Foundation Hospitality House					
406 Steam Plant Rd	Gallatin	TN	37066	615-452-4009	
Texoma Medical Center's Reba Ranch House					
5016 S US Hwy 75	Denison	TX	75020	903-416-4000	416-4129
Web: www.texomamedicalcenter.net					
Travis & Beverly Cross Guest Housing Ctr					
9320 SW Barnes Rd	Portland	OR	97225	503-216-1575	216-6283
TF: 888-550-1575 ■ *Web:* www.oregon.providence.org					
University of Virginia Medical Ctr Hospital Hospitality House Inc					
Hospital Box 800703	Charlottesville	VA	22908	434-924-0211	924-1590
Web: www.healthsystem.virginia.edu					
Veterans Guest House 880 Locust St	Reno	NV	89502	775-324-6958	324-6071
Web: www.veteransguesthouse.org					
Zachary & Elizabeth Fisher House					
111 Rockville Pk Ste 420	Rockville	MD	20850	888-294-8560	487-6661*
**Fax Area Code:* 513 ■ *TF:* 888-294-8560 ■ *Web:* www.fisherhouse.org/houses					

376 HOSPITAL HOSPITALITY HOUSES - RONALD MCDONALD HOUSE

Name / Address	City	State	Zip	Phone	Fax
Ronald McDonald House					
Akron 245 Locust St	Akron	OH	44302	330-253-5400	253-5477
TF: 800-262-0333 ■ *Web:* www.akronchildrens.org					
Albany 139 S Lake Ave	Albany	NY	12208	518-438-2655	459-6529
TF: 866-244-8464 ■ *Web:* www.rmhcofalbany.org					
Albuquerque 1011 Yale Ave NE	Albuquerque	NM	87106	505-842-8960	764-0412
TF: 877-842-8960 ■ *Web:* www.rmhc-nm.org					
Amarillo 1501 Streit Dr	Amarillo	TX	79106	806-358-8177	358-8170
Web: rmhc.org					
Ann Arbor 1600 Washington Heights	Ann Arbor	MI	48104	734-994-4442	994-4919
TF: 800-544-8684 ■ *Web:* www.rmh-annarbor.org					
Atlanta 792 Houston Mill Rd NE	Atlanta	GA	30329	404-315-1133	315-7873
Web: www.armhc.org					
Augusta 938 Greene St	Augusta	GA	30901	706-724-5901	722-0884
Web: www.grhealth.org					
Austin 1315 Barbara Jordan Blvd	Austin	TX	78723	512-472-9844	472-5465
Web: www.rmhc-austin.org					
Baltimore 635 W Lexington St	Baltimore	MD	21201	410-528-1010	727-6177
Web: www.rmhcbaltimore.org					
Bangor 654 State St	Bangor	ME	04401	207-942-9003	990-2984
Web: www.rmhbangor.org					
Bend 1700 NE Purcell Blvd	Bend	OR	97701	541-318-4950	318-4994
Web: rmhcofcentraloregon.org					
Billings 1144 N 30th St	Billings	MT	59101	406-256-8006	256-0130
Web: rmhcmontana.org					
Birmingham 1700 Fourth Ave S	Birmingham	AL	35233	205-638-7255	638-7256
Web: www.rmhca.org					

Entry	City	State	Zip	Phone	Fax
Bismarck 609 N Seventh St *Web:* rmhcbismarck.org	Bismarck	ND	58501	701-258-8551	258-5076
Boise 101 Warm Springs Ave. *Web:* www.rmhidaho.org	Boise	ID	83712	208-336-5478	336-0587
Boston 229 Kent St *Web:* www.ronaldmcdonaldhouseboston.org	Brookline	MA	02446	617-734-3333	734-5239
Buffalo 780 W Ferry St. *Web:* www.rmhbuffalo.org	Buffalo	NY	14222	716-883-1177	881-9312
Burlington 16 S Winooski Ave *Web:* www.rmhcvt.org	Burlington	VT	05401	802-862-4943	862-2175
Calgary 111 W Campus Pl NW *Web:* www.ahomeawayfromhome.org	Calgary	AB	T3B2R6	403-240-3000	240-1277
Camden 550 Mickle Blvd. *TF:* 877-858-3539 ■ *Web:* www.ronaldhouse-snj.org	Camden	NJ	08103	856-966-4663	966-1190
Chapel Hill 101 Old Mason Farm Rd *TF:* 800-835-5479 ■ *Web:* www.rmh-chapelhill.org	Chapel Hill	NC	27517	919-913-2040	951-0123
Charleston 81 Gadsden St *Web:* www.rmhcharleston.org	Charleston	SC	29401	843-723-7957	722-2204
Charlottesville 300 Ninth St SW. *Web:* www.rmhcharlottesville.org	Charlottesville	VA	22903	434-295-1885	295-7735
Chattanooga 200 Central Ave. *TF:* 855-670-4787 ■ *Web:* www.rmhchattanooga.com	Chattanooga	TN	37403	423-778-4300	778-4350
Chicago 211 E Grand Ave **Fax Area Code:* 773 ■ *Web:* www.rmhccni.org	Chicago	IL	60611	312-888-2500	348-7619*
Chicago 1301 W 22nd St Ste 905 *Web:* www.rmhccni.org	Oak Brook	IL	60523	630-623-5300	
Chicago Tripp Ave PO Box 7002 *Web:* www.rmhccni.org	Hines	IL	60141	708-327-2273	327-6000
Cleveland 10415 Euclid Ave. *TF:* 800-223-2273 ■ *Web:* www.rmhcleveland.org	Cleveland	OH	44106	216-229-5758	229-0556
Colorado Springs 311 N Logan Ave. *Web:* www.rmhcs.org	Colorado Springs	CO	80909	719-471-1814	471-7147
Columbus 1959 Hamilton Rd. *Web:* www.rmhcwga.org	Columbus	GA	31904	706-321-0033	321-0034
Corpus Christi 3402 Ft Worth St *Web:* www.corpuschristirmhc.org	Corpus Christi	TX	78411	361-854-4073	854-9174
Dallas 4707 Bengal St *Web:* www.rmhdallas.org	Dallas	TX	75235	214-631-7354	631-1527
Danville 100 N Academy Ave PO Box 300 *Web:* www.rmhdanville.org	Danville	PA	17821	570-271-6300	271-8182
Des Moines 1441 Pleasant St *Web:* rmhdesmoines.org	Des Moines	IA	50314	515-243-2111	280-3111
Detroit 3911 Beaubien *TF:* 800-426-7667 ■ *Web:* www.rmhc-detroit.org	Detroit	MI	48201	313-745-5909	993-0399
Durham 506 Alexander Ave *TF:* 866-244-8464 ■ *Web:* rmhdurham.org/	Durham	NC	27705	919-286-9305	286-7307
Edmonton 7726 107 St NW *Web:* www.rmhnorthernalberta.org	Edmonton	AB	T6E4K3	780-439-5437	433-6201
El Paso 300 E California St *Web:* www.rmhc.org	El Paso	TX	79902	915-542-1522	577-0678
Falls Church 3312 Gallows Rd. *TF:* 855-227-7435 ■ *Web:* rmhcdc.org	Falls Church	VA	22042	703-698-7080	698-7745
Fargo 1234 Broadway *Web:* www.rmhcfargo.org	Fargo	ND	58102	701-232-3980	234-9582
Fort Lauderdale 15 SE 15th St *Web:* rmhcsouthflorida.org	Fort Lauderdale	FL	33316	954-828-1822	828-1824
Fort Myers 16100 Roserush Ct *TF:* 800-435-7352 ■ *Web:* www.rmhcswfl.org	Fort Myers	FL	33908	239-437-0202	437-3521
Fort Worth 1004 Seventh Ave. *Web:* www.rmhfw.org	Fort Worth	TX	76104	817-870-4942	870-0254
Galveston 301 14th St *TF:* 800-275-2946 ■ *Web:* www.rmhg.org	Galveston	TX	77550	409-762-8770	762-9902
Grand Rapids 1323 Cedar St NE *Web:* rmhwesternmichigan.org	Grand Rapids	MI	49503	616-776-1300	776-0368
Greater Cincinnati 350 Erkenbrecher Ave. *Web:* www.rmhcincinnati.org	Cincinnati	OH	45229	513-636-7642	636-4887
Greenville 529 Moye Blvd *Web:* www.rmhenc.org	Greenville	NC	27834	252-847-5435	
Halifax 1133 Tower Rd. *Web:* www.rmhatlantic.ca	Halifax	NS	B3H2Y7	902-429-4044	429-8650
Hamilton 1510 Main St W *Web:* www.rmhhamilton.ca	Hamilton	ON	L8S1E3	905-521-9983	521-9515
Hershey 745 W Governor Rd *TF:* 800-732-0999 ■ *Web:* www.rmhc-centralpa.org	Hershey	PA	17033	717-533-4001	533-1299
Honolulu 1970 Judd Hillside Rd *Web:* ronaldhousehawaii.org	Honolulu	HI	96822	808-973-5683	955-8794
Houston 1907 Holcombe Blvd. *Web:* www.ronaldmcdonaldhousehouston.org	Houston	TX	77030	713-795-3500	795-3557
Huntington 1500 17th St *TF:* 855-227-7435 ■ *Web:* www.mchouse.org	Huntington	WV	25701	304-529-1122	529-2970
Indianapolis 435 Limestone St. *Web:* www.rmh-indiana.org	Indianapolis	IN	46202	317-269-2247	267-0606
Iowa City 730 Hawkins Dr *Web:* rmhc-easterniowa.org	Iowa City	IA	52246	319-356-3939	353-6873
Jacksonville 824 Children's Way *Web:* www.rmhjax.org	Jacksonville	FL	32207	904-807-4663	807-4700
Johnson City 418 N State of Franklin Rd *Web:* rmhc.org	Johnson City	TN	37604	423-975-5437	434-8989
Joplin 3402 S Jackson Ave PO Box 2688 *Web:* www.rmhjoplin.org	Joplin	MO	64804	417-624-2273	624-0270
Kansas City 2502 Cherry St. *TF:* 888-353-4537 ■ *Web:* www.rmhckc.org	Kansas City	MO	64108	816-842-8321	842-7033
Knoxville 1705 W Clinch Ave. *Web:* www.knoxrmhc.org	Knoxville	TN	37916	865-637-7475	525-7942
Lansing 121 S Holmes St	Lansing	MI	48912	517-485-9303	349-0850
Las Vegas 2323 Potosi St *TF:* 888-248-1561 ■ *Web:* www.rmhlv.com	Las Vegas	NV	89146	702-252-4663	252-7345
Little Rock 1009 Wolfe St. *Web:* rmhclittlerock.org	Little Rock	AR	72202	501-374-1956	374-2418
Loma Linda 11365 Anderson St. *Web:* www.llrmh.org	Loma Linda	CA	92354	909-558-8300	558-0300
Long Branch 131 Bath Ave. *Web:* www.rmh-cnj.org	Long Branch	NJ	07740	732-222-8755	222-9363
Los Angeles (LARMH) 4560 Fountain Ave. *Web:* www.larmh.org	Los Angeles	CA	90029	323-644-3000	669-0552
Macon 1160 Forsyth St *Web:* www.rmhccga.org	Macon	GA	31201	478-746-4090	746-0580
Madera 9161 Randall Way *Web:* www.rmhccv.org	Madera	CA	93636	559-261-3660	
Madison 2716 Marshall Ct *Web:* www.rmhcmadison.org	Madison	WI	53705	608-232-4660	232-4670
Marshfield 803 W N St. *Web:* www.rmhc-marshfield.org	Marshfield	WI	54449	715-387-5899	389-5991
Memphis 535 Alabama Ave *Web:* rmhc-memphis.org	Memphis	TN	38105	901-529-4055	523-0315
Minneapolis 818 Fulton St SE *Web:* www.rmhc-um.org	Minneapolis	MN	55414	612-331-5752	331-1255
Missoula 3003 Ft Missoula Rd PO Box 1119 *Web:* rmhcmontana.org/	Missoula	MT	59804	406-541-7646	541-7642
Montreal 5800 Hudson Rd. *Web:* www.manoirmontreal.qc.ca	Montreal	QC	H3S2G5	514-731-2871	739-8823
Morgantown 841 Country Club Dr. *Web:* www.rmhcmgtn.org	Morgantown	WV	26505	304-598-0050	599-0780
New Brunswick 145 Somerset St. *Web:* www.rmh-cnj.org	New Brunswick	NJ	08901	732-249-1222	249-1439
New Haven 501 George St. *Web:* www.ronaldmcdonaldhouse-ct.org	New Haven	CT	06511	203-777-5683	777-3082
New Hyde Park 267-07 76th Ave *Web:* www.rmhlongisland.org	New Hyde Park	NY	11040	718-343-5683	343-5798
New Orleans 4403 Canal St **Fax Area Code:* 630	New Orleans	LA	70119	504-486-6668	623-7488*
New York 405 E 73rd St *Web:* www.rmh-newyork.org	New York	NY	10021	212-639-0100	472-0376
Norfolk 404 Colley Ave *Web:* www.rmhcnorfolk.com	Norfolk	VA	23507	757-627-5386	622-0534
Northwest Ohio 3883 Monroe St *Web:* www.rmhctoledo.org	Toledo	OH	43606	419-471-4663	479-6961
Oklahoma City 1301 NE 14th St. *Web:* www.rmhcokc.org	Oklahoma City	OK	73117	405-424-6873	424-0919
Omaha 620 S 38th Ave.	Omaha	NE	68105	402-346-9377	346-9468
Orange 383 S Batavia St *Web:* www.ronaldhouseoc.org	Orange	CA	92868	714-639-3600	516-3697
Orlando 2201 Alden Rd *Web:* www.ronaldmcdonaldhouseorlando.org	Orlando	FL	32803	407-898-6127	896-3562
Orlando 1630 Kuhl Ave *Web:* www.ronaldmcdonaldhouseorlando.org	Orlando	FL	32806	407-581-1289	581-1392
Ottawa 407 Smyth Rd. *Web:* www.rmhottawa.com	Ottawa	ON	K1H8M8	613-737-5523	737-5524
Palo Alto 520 Sand Hill Rd *Web:* www.ronaldhouse.net	Palo Alto	CA	94304	650-470-6000	470-6018
Pasadena 763 S Pasadena Ave *Web:* www.pasadenarmh.org	Pasadena	CA	91105	626-585-1588	585-1688
Pensacola 5200 Bayou Blvd. *Web:* www.rmhpensacola.org	Pensacola	FL	32503	850-477-2273	477-7607
Philadelphia 3925 Chestnut St. *TF:* 800-723-0999 ■ *Web:* www.philarmh.org	Philadelphia	PA	19104	215-387-8406	386-4977
Phoenix 501 E Roanoke Ave. *Web:* www.rmhcphoenix.com	Phoenix	AZ	85004	602-264-2654	264-5670
Pittsburgh 451 44th St. *Web:* www.rmhcpgh.org	Pittsburgh	PA	15201	412-362-3400	362-8540
Portland 250 Brackett St *Web:* www.rmhportlandme.org	Portland	ME	04102	207-780-6282	780-0198
Portland 2115 SW River Pkwy **Fax Area Code:* 503 ■ *Web:* www.rmhcoregon.org	Portland	OR	97201	971-230-0808	243-2969*
Portland 2620 N Commercial Ave *Web:* www.rmhcoregon.org	Portland	OR	97227	971-230-6700	630-6720
Providence 45 Gay St. *TF:* 888-353-4537 ■ *Web:* www.rmhprovidence.org	Providence	RI	02905	401-274-4447	751-3730
Richmond 2330 Monument Ave. *TF:* 800-368-3472 ■ *Web:* www.rmhc-richmond.org	Richmond	VA	23220	804-355-6517	358-3153
Rio Grande Valley, The 1720 Treasure Hills Blvd *Web:* www.rmhcrgv.org	Harlingen	TX	78550	956-412-7200	412-6300
Roanoke 2224 S Jefferson St. *Web:* rmhc-swva.org	Roanoke	VA	24014	540-857-0770	857-9584
Rochester 333 Westmoreland Dr *Web:* www.rmhcrochester.org	Rochester	NY	14620	585-442-5437	442-7330
Sacramento 2555 49th St. *Web:* www.rmhcnc.org	Sacramento	CA	95817	916-734-4230	734-4238
Saint Louis 4381 W Pine Blvd *Web:* www.rmhcstl.com	Saint Louis	MO	63108	314-531-6601	531-6353
Saint Louis 3450 Pk Ave *Web:* www.rmhcstl.com	Saint Louis	MO	63104	314-773-1100	773-2053
Saint Petersburg 401 Seventh Ave S *Web:* rmhctampabay.com	Saint Petersburg	FL	33701	727-821-8961	
San Antonio 227 Lewis St *Web:* ronaldmcdonaldhouse-sa.org	San Antonio	TX	78212	210-223-6014	223-6138
San Antonio 4803 Sid Katz Dr *Web:* www.ronaldmcdonaldhouse-sa.org	San Antonio	TX	78229	210-614-2554	614-2905
San Diego 2929 Children's Way. *Web:* www.rmhcsd.org	San Diego	CA	92123	858-467-4750	467-4757
San Francisco 1640 Scott St *Web:* www.ronaldhouse-sf.org	San Francisco	CA	94115	415-673-0891	673-1335
Saskatoon 1011 University Dr *Web:* www.rmh.sk.ca	Saskatoon	SK	S7N0K4	306-244-5700	244-3099
Scranton 332 Wheeler Ave. *TF:* 800-775-9610 ■ *Web:* rmhscranton.org	Scranton	PA	18510	570-969-8998	969-8991
Seattle 5130 40th Ave NE. *TF:* 866-987-9330 ■ *Web:* www.rmhcseattle.org	Seattle	WA	98105	206-838-0600	838-0650
Spokane 1015 W Fifth Ave *Web:* www.rmhcspokane.org	Spokane	WA	99204	509-624-0500	624-3267
Springfield 34 Chapin Terr. *Web:* www.ronmcdhouse.com	Springfield	MA	01107	413-794-5683	

Phone Fax

Springfield 949 E Primrose St . . . Springfield MO 65807 417-886-0225
Web: www.rmhcozarks.org

Tallahassee 712 E Seventh Ave . . . Tallahassee FL 32303 850-222-0056 222-0086
Web: www.rmhctallahassee.org

Tampa 35 Columbia Dr . . . Tampa FL 33606 813-254-2398 254-8891
Web: www.rmhctampabay.com

Temple 2415 S 47th St. . . . Temple TX 76504 254-770-0910 770-1622
Web: www.rmh-temple.com

Topeka 825 SW Buchanan St. . . . Topeka KS 66606 785-235-6852 235-3170
Web: www.rmhctopeka.org

Toronto 26 Gerrard St E. . . . Toronto ON M5B1G3 416-977-0458 977-8807
Web: www.rmhtoronto.org

Tucson 3838 N Campbell Ave Bldg 6 PO Box 40725. . Tucson AZ 85719 520-326-0060 881-1732
Web: www.rmhctucson.org

Tulsa 6102 S Hudson Ave . . . Tulsa OK 74136 918-496-2727 496-2762
Web: www.rmhtulsa.org

Washington 3727 14th St NE. . . . Washington DC 20017 202-529-8204 635-3578
Web: rmhcdc.org

Wauwatosa 8948 W Watertown Plank Rd. . . . Wauwatosa WI 53226 414-475-5333 475-6342
Web: rmhcmilwaukee.org

Wilmington 1901 Rockland Rd . . . Wilmington DE 19803 302-656-4847 658-6608
TF: 888-656-4847 ■ *Web:* www.rmhde.org

Winnipeg 566 Bannatyne Ave. . . . Winnipeg MB R3A0G7 204-774-4777 774-2160
Web: www.rmhmanitoba.org

Winston-Salem 419 S Hawthorne Rd. . . . Winston-Salem NC 27103 336-723-0228 723-0302
TF: 855-227-7435 ■ *Web:* www.rmhws.org

Ronald McDonald House - Midtown
1110 N Emporia St. . . . Wichita KS 67214 316-269-4420 269-0665
Web: www.rmhcwichita.org

Ronald McDonald House - Sleepy Hollow
520 N Rutan . . . Wichita KS 67208 316-687-2000 687-6654
Web: www.rmhcwichita.org

Ronald McDonald House BC 4116 Angus Dr. . . . Vancouver BC V6J4H9 604-736-2957 736-5974
Web: www.rmhbc.ca

Atlanta 5420 Peachtree Dunwoody Rd . . . Sandy Springs GA 30342 404-847-0760 250-4992
Web: www.armhc.org

Dayton 555 Valley St . . . Dayton OH 45404 937-224-0047 496-2476
Web: rmhc.org

Gainesville 1600 SW 14th St. . . . Gainesville FL 32608 352-374-4404 335-5325
TF: 800-435-7352 ■ *Web:* www.rmhcncf.org

Ronald McDonald House Charities
Reno 323 Maine St . . . Reno NV 89502 775-322-4663 322-8670
Web: www.rmhc-reno.com

Sioux City 2500 Nebraska St. . . . Sioux City IA 51104 712-255-4084 255-4281
Web: rmhc-siouxland.org

Springfield 610 N Seventh St. . . . Springfield IL 62702 217-528-3314 528-6084
Web: www.rmhc-centralillinois.org

Ronald McDonald House Charities of Central Ohio
711 E Livingston Ave . . . Columbus OH 43205 614-227-3700 227-3765
Web: www.rmhc-centralohio.org

Ronald McDonald House Charities of Denver Inc
1300 E 21st Ave . . . Denver CO 80205 303-832-2667 832-3802
Web: www.ronaldhouse.org

Ronald McDonald House Charities of Kentuckiana (RMHC)
550 S First St . . . Louisville KY 40202 502-581-1416 581-0037
Web: www.rmhc-kentuckiana.org

Ronald McDonald House Charities of Nashville
Nashville 2144 Fairfax Ave. . . . Nashville TN 37212 615-343-4000 343-4004
Web: www.rmhcnashville.com

Ronald McDonald House Charities of the Southwest
3413 Tenth St . . . Lubbock TX 79415 806-744-8877 744-3652
Web: www.rmhcsouthwest.com

Ronald McDonald House Charities's
Salt Lake City 935 E Temple. . . . Salt Lake City UT 84102 801-363-4663 363-0092
Web: www.rmhslc.org

Ronald McDonald House of Columbia
2955 Colonial Dr . . . Columbia SC 29203 803-254-3181 254-8688
Web: www.rmhcofcolumbia.org

Ronald McDonald House of Southwestern Ontario
741 Base Line Rd E. . . . London ON N6C2R6 519-685-3232 685-0703
Web: www.rmhlondon.ca

377 HOSPITALS

SEE ALSO Health Care Providers - Ancillary p. 2448; Health Care Systems p. 2449; Hospices p. 2479; Veterans Nursing Homes - State p. 3282

HOSPITALS - DEVELOPMENTAL DISABILITIES

377-1 Children's Hospitals

Phone Fax

Alfred I duPont Hospital for Children
1600 Rockland Rd . . . Wilmington DE 19803 302-651-4000 651-4224*
**Fax:* Admitting ■ *Web:* www.nemours.org

Arkansas Children's Hospital
One Children's Way. . . . Little Rock AR 72202 501-364-1100 364-1452
Web: www.archildrens.org

Arnold Palmer Hospital for Children & Women
92 W Miller St . . . Orlando FL 32806 407-649-9111 649-6926
TF: 800-648-3818 ■ *Web:* www.orlandohealth.com

Bradley Hospital
1011 Veterans Memorial Pkwy . . . East Providence RI 02915 401-432-1000 432-1500
Web: www.bradleyhospital.org

Children's Healthcare of Atlanta at Egleston
1405 Clifton Rd NE. . . . Atlanta GA 30322 404-785-6000 785-6143*
**Fax:* Admitting ■ *TF:* 888-785-7778 ■ *Web:* www.choa.org

Children's Healthcare of Atlanta at Scottish Rite
1001 Johnson Ferry Rd NE. . . . Atlanta GA 30342 404-785-5252 785-4687*
**Fax:* Admitting ■ *TF:* 888-785-7778 ■ *Web:* www.choa.org

Children's Hospital 200 Henry Clay Ave. . . . New Orleans LA 70118 504-899-9511 896-9708*
**Fax:* Admitting ■ *TF:* 800-299-9511 ■ *Web:* www.chnola.org

Children's Hospital & Medical Ctr
8200 Dodge St . . . Omaha NE 68114 402-955-5400 955-4046*
**Fax:* Admitting ■ *Web:* childrensomaha.org

Children's Hospital & Research Ctr at Oakland
747 52nd St . . . Oakland CA 94609 510-428-3000 450-5884*
**Fax:* Admitting ■ *Web:* www.childrenshospitaloakland.org

Children's Hospital Boston 300 Longwood Ave . . . Boston MA 02115 617-355-6000
Web: www.childrenshospital.org

Children's Hospital Central California
9300 Valley Children's Pl . . . Madera CA 93638 559-353-3000 353-8888*
**Fax:* Admitting ■ *TF:* 800-548-5435 ■ *Web:* www.childrenscentralcal.org

Children's Hospital Medical Ctr of Akron
one Perkins Sq . . . Akron OH 44308 330-543-1000 543-3146*
**Fax:* Admitting ■ *TF:* 800-262-0333 ■ *Web:* www.akronchildrens.org

Children's Hospital of Alabama
1600 Seventh Ave S . . . Birmingham AL 35233 205-939-9100
Web: childrensal.org

Children's Hospital of Michigan
3901 Beaubien Blvd . . . Detroit MI 48201 313-745-5437 993-0385*
**Fax:* Admitting ■ *Web:* www.dmc.org

Children's Hospital of Orange County
455 S Main St. . . . Orange CA 92868 714-997-3000
Web: www.choc.org

Children's Hospital of Philadelphia
3400 Civic Ctr Blvd . . . Philadelphia PA 19104 215-590-1000 590-1413*
**Fax:* Admitting ■ *Web:* www.chop.edu

Children's Hospital of Pittsburgh
4401 Penn Ave . . . Pittsburgh PA 15224 412-692-5325
Web: www.chp.edu

Children's Hospital of the King's Daughters
601 Children's Ln . . . Norfolk VA 23507 757-668-7000 668-8050*
**Fax:* Admitting ■ *Web:* www.chkd.org

Children's Hospital of Wisconsin
9000 W Wisconsin Ave. . . . Milwaukee WI 53226 414-266-2000 266-2547*
**Fax:* Admitting ■ *Web:* www.chw.org

Children's Hospitals & Clinics Minneapolis
2525 Chicago Ave. . . . Minneapolis MN 55404 612-813-6000 813-6807
TF: 866-225-3251 ■ *Web:* childrensmn.org/

Children's Institute of Pittsburgh
1405 Shady Ave . . . Pittsburgh PA 15217 412-420-2400 420-2200
TF: 877-433-1109 ■ *Web:* www.amazingkids.org

Children's Medical Ctr one Children's Plaza . . . Dayton OH 45404 937-641-3000 641-3326*
**Fax:* Admitting ■ *TF:* 800-228-4055 ■ *Web:* www.childrensdayton.org

Children's Medical Ctr of Dallas
1935 Medical District Dr. . . . Dallas TX 75235 214-456-7000 456-2197
Web: www.childrens.com

Children's Memorial Hospital
2300 Children's Plz. . . . Chicago IL 60614 773-880-4000
Web: www.luriechildrens.org

Children's Mercy Hospital & Clinics
2401 Gillham Rd. . . . Kansas City MO 64108 816-234-3000
TF: 866-512-2168 ■ *Web:* www.childrensmercy.org

Children's National Medical Ctr (CNMC)
111 Michigan Ave NW . . . Washington DC 20010 202-476-5000
TF: 800-884-5433 ■ *Web:* www.childrensnational.org

Children's Specialized Hospital
150 New Providence Rd . . . Mountainside NJ 07092 908-233-3720 233-4967
Web: www.childrens-specialized.org

Cincinnati Children's Hospital Medical Ctr
3333 Burnet Ave . . . Cincinnati OH 45229 513-636-4200 636-3733*
**Fax:* Admitting ■ *TF:* 800-344-2462 ■ *Web:* www.cincinnatichildrens.org

Connecticut Children's Medical Ctr
282 Washington St . . . Hartford CT 06106 860-545-9000 545-8560
Web: www.connecticutchildrens.org

Cook Children's Medical Ctr
801 Seventh Ave. . . . Fort Worth TX 76104 682-885-4000 885-4229
Web: cookchildrens.org

Copper Hills Youth Ctr 5899 Rivendell Dr . . . West Jordan UT 84081 800-776-7116 569-2959*
**Fax Area Code:* 801 ■ *TF:* 800-776-7116 ■ *Web:* www.copperhillsyouthcenter.com

Covenant Children's Hospital (CCH) 4015 22nd Pl. . . . Lubbock TX 79410 806-725-0000 723-7189
TF: 800-378-4189 ■
Web: covenanthealth.org/about-us/facilities/childrenshospital/default

Crittenton Children's Ctr 10918 Elm Ave . . . Kansas City MO 64134 816-765-6600 767-4101
Web: www.saintlukeshealthsystem.org

CS Mott Children's Hospital
1500 E Medical Ctr Dr . . . Ann Arbor MI 48109 734-936-4000 763-7736
TF: 800-211-8181 ■ *Web:* www.med.umich.edu

Devereux 1291 Stanley Rd NW PO Box 1688. . . . Kennesaw GA 30156 678-303-5233 443-1531*
**Fax Area Code:* 480 ■ *TF:* 800-342-3357 ■ *Web:* www.devereux.org

Devereux Cleo Wallace
8405 Church Ranch Blvd . . . Westminster CO 80021 303-466-7391 466-0904*
**Fax:* Admitting ■ *TF:* 800-456-2536 ■ *Web:* www.devereux.org

Devereux Hospital & Children's Ctr of Florida
8000 Devereux Dr. . . . Melbourne FL 32940 321-242-9100 259-0786
Web: devereux.org

Driscoll Children's Hospital
3533 S Alameda St. . . . Corpus Christi TX 78411 361-694-5000 694-5010
TF: 800-324-5683 ■ *Web:* www.driscollchildrens.org

East Tennessee Children's Hospital
2018 Clinch Ave PO Box 15010. . . . Knoxville TN 37901 865-541-8000
Web: www.etch.com

Franciscan Hospital for Children 30 Warren St . . . Boston MA 02135 617-254-3800 779-1119
Web: franciscanhospital.org

Gillette Children's Specialty Healthcare
200 E University Ave. . . . Saint Paul MN 55101 651-291-2848 229-3999
TF: 800-719-4040 ■ *Web:* www.gillettechildrens.org

Phone *Fax*

Gulf Coast Treatment Ctr
1015 Mar-Walt Dr........................Fort Walton Beach FL 32547 850-863-4160 863-8576
TF: 800-537-5433 ■ *Web:* www.gulfcoastyouthservices.com

Hawthorn Ctr 18471 Haggerty Rd ....Northville MI 48167 248-349-3000 349-8259
TF: 855-444-3911 ■ *Web:* michigan.gov

Helen DeVos Children's Hospital
100 Michigan St NE ....Grand Rapids MI 49503 616-391-9000 391-3105
TF: 800-222-1222 ■ *Web:* www.helendevoschildrens.org

HSC Pediatric Ctr 1731 Bunker Hill Rd NE ....Washington DC 20017 202-832-4400 529-1646
TF: 800-226-4444 ■ *Web:* www.hscpediatriccenter.org

JD McCarty Ctr for Children with Developmental Disabilities
2002 E Robinson St ....Norman OK 73071 405-307-2800 307-2801
TF: 800-777-1272 ■ *Web:* jdmc.org

Kennedy Krieger Institute 707 N Broadway ....Baltimore MD 21205 443-923-9200 923-9425
TF: 800-873-3377 ■ *Web:* www.kennedykrieger.org

KidsPeace Orchard Hills Campus
5300 Kids Peace Dr ....Orefield PA 18069 800-257-3223 799-8900*
**Fax Area Code:* 610 ■ **Fax:* Admitting ■ *TF:* 800-257-3223 ■ *Web:* www.kidspeace.org

Larabida Children's Hospital & Research Ctr
6501 S Promontory Dr
E 65th St at Lk Michigan...........................Chicago IL 60649 773-363-6700
Web: www.larabida.org

Lucile Packard Children's Hospital (LPCH)
725 Welch Rd ....Palo Alto CA 94304 650-497-8000 497-8968*
**Fax:* Admitting ■ *TF:* 800-995-5724 ■ *Web:* stanfordchildrens.org/

Mary Bridge Children's Hospital & Health Ctr
317 Martin Luther King Jr Way....................... Tacoma WA 98405 253-403-1400 403-1247
TF: 800-552-1419 ■ *Web:* www.multicare.org

Massachusetts Hospital School
Three Randolph St ....Canton MA 02021 781-828-2440 821-4086
Web: mhsf.us

Medical University of South Carolina Children's Hospital
165 Ashley Ave.................................Charleston SC 29425 843-792-2300 792-8948
Web: www.musckids.org

Miami Children's Hospital 3100 SW 62nd Ave .... Miami FL 33155 305-666-6511 663-8466
TF: 800-432-6837 ■ *Web:* www.mch.com

Mount Washington Pediatric Hospital
1708 W Rogers Ave ....Baltimore MD 21209 410-578-8600 466-1715
Web: www.mwph.org

New York City Children's Ctr-Queens Campus (NYCCC)
74-03 Commonwealth Blvd ....Bellerose NY 11426 718-264-4500 740-0968
TF: 800-597-8481 ■ *Web:* www.omh.ny.gov

Phoenix Children's Hospital 1919 E Thomas Rd........Phoenix AZ 85016 602-546-1000 933-0628
TF: 888-908-5437 ■ *Web:* www.phoenixchildrens.org

Primary Children's Medical Ctr
100 N Medical Dr............................ Salt Lake City UT 84113 801-662-1000 662-6202*
**Fax:* Admitting ■ *Web:* www.intermountainhealthcare.org

Rady Children's Hospital (RCH)
3020 Children's Way MC 5101..................... San Diego CA 92123 858-576-1700 966-5859*
**Fax:* Library ■ *TF:* 800-788-9029 ■ *Web:* www.rchsd.org

Saint Louis Children's Hospital
One Children's Pl .... Saint Louis MO 63110 314-454-6000 454-2870
TF: 800-427-4626 ■ *Web:* www.stlouischildrens.org

Seattle Children's Hospital
4800 Sand Pt Way NE...............................Seattle WA 98105 206-987-2000 987-5060*
**Fax:* Admitting ■ *TF:* 866-987-2000 ■ *Web:* www.seattlechildrens.org

Shriners Hospitals for Children Boston
51 Blossom St ....Boston MA 02114 617-722-3000 523-1684
TF: 800-255-1916 ■ *Web:* www.shrinershospitalsforchildren.org

Shriners Hospitals for Children Canada
1529 Cedar Ave .... Montreal QC H3G1A6 514-842-4464 842-7553
Web: shrinershospitalsforchildren.org

Shriners Hospitals for Children Chicago
2211 N Oak Pk Ave..................................Chicago IL 60707 773-622-5400 385-5453*
**Fax:* Admitting ■ *Web:* www.shrinershq.org

Shriners Hospitals for Children Cincinnati
3229 Burnet Ave.................................. Cincinnati OH 45229 513-872-6000 872-6999
TF: 800-875-8580 ■ *Web:* shrinershospitalcincinnati.org

Shriners Hospitals for Children Erie
1645 W Eigth St .... Erie PA 16505 814-875-8700 875-8756
TF: 800-873-5437 ■ *Web:* shrinershospitalsforchildren.org

Shriners Hospitals for Children Galveston
2900 Rocky Pt Dr.................................... Tampa Fl 33607 813-281-0300
Web: shrinershospitalsforchildren.org

Shriners Hospitals for Children Greenville
950 W Faris Rd................................ Greenville SC 29605 864-271-3444 271-4471
TF: 800-361-7256 ■ *Web:* www.shrinershospitalsforchildren.org

Shriners Hospitals for Children Honolulu
1310 Punahou St..................................Honolulu HI 96826 808-941-4466 942-8573
TF: 888-888-6314 ■ *Web:* www.shrinershq.org

Shriners Hospitals for Children Houston
6977 Main St......................................Houston TX 77030 713-797-1616 793-3762*
**Fax:* Admitting ■ *Web:* www.shrinershq.org

Shriners Hospitals for Children Lexington
1900 Richmond Rd.................................. Lexington KY 40502 859-266-2101 268-5636
TF: 800-668-4634 ■ *Web:* shrinershospitalsforchildren.org

Shriners Hospitals for Children Los Angeles
3160 Geneva St ....Los Angeles CA 90020 213-388-3151 387-7528*
**Fax:* Admitting ■ *TF:* 888-486-5437 ■ *Web:* losangelesshrinershospital.org

Shriners Hospitals for Children Northern California
2425 Stockton Blvd ....Sacramento CA 95817 916-453-2000 453-2395*
**Fax:* Admitting ■ *Web:* www.shrinershq.org

Shriners Hospitals for Children Philadelphia
3551 N Broad St................................ Philadelphia PA 19140 215-430-4000 430-4079
Web: www.shrinershospitalsforchildren.org

Shriners Hospitals for Children Portland
3101 SW Sam Jackson Pk Rd.........................Portland OR 97239 503-241-5090 221-3475
Web: www.shrinershospitalsforchildren.org

Shriners Hospitals for Children Salt Lake City
Fairfax Rd & Virginia St .... Salt Lake City UT 84103 801-536-3500 536-3782
TF: 800-313-3745 ■ *Web:* www.shrinershospitalsforchildren.org

Shriners Hospitals for Children Shreveport
3100 Samford Ave ....Shreveport LA 71103 318-222-5704 424-7610
Web: www.shrinershospitalsforchildren.org

Shriners Hospitals for Children Spokane
911 W Fifth Ave .... Spokane WA 99204 509-455-7844 623-0474*
**Fax:* Admitting ■ *Web:* www.shrinershq.org

Shriners Hospitals for Children Tampa
12502 N Pine Dr.................................... Tampa FL 33612 813-972-2250 240-3113*
**Fax Area Code:* 864 ■ **Fax:* Admitting ■ *TF:* 800-237-5055 ■ *Web:* shrinershospitalsforchildren.org

Shriners Hospitals for Children Twin Cities
2025 E River Pkwy .... Minneapolis MN 55414 612-596-6100 339-5954
Web: www.shrinershq.org

SSM Cardinal Glennon Children's Hospital
1465 S Grand Blvd .... Saint Louis MO 63104 314-577-5600
Web: www.cardinalglennon.com

Steven & Alexandra Cohen Children's Medical Ctr of New York
269-01 76th Ave............................ New Hyde Park NY 11040 718-470-3000
Web: www.northshorelij.com

Streamwood Behavioral Health Ctr
1400 E Irving Pk Rd .... Streamwood IL 60107 630-837-9000 837-2639
TF: 800-272-7790 ■ *Web:* www.streamwoodhospital.com

Texas Children's Hospital 6621 Fannin St.............Houston TX 77030 832-824-1000 825-3058
TF: 800-364-5437 ■ *Web:* texaschildrens.org

Texas Scottish Rite Hospital for Children
2222 Welborn St...................................... Dallas TX 75219 214-559-5000 559-7447
TF: 800-421-1121 ■ *Web:* www.tsrhc.org

Wolfson Children's Hospital
800 Prudential Dr...............................Jacksonville FL 32207 904-202-8000 202-8173
Web: www.wolfsonchildrens.org

Women's & Children's Hospital of Buffalo
219 Bryant St..Buffalo NY 14222 716-878-7000 888-3979*
**Fax:* Admitting ■ *TF:* 800-462-7653 ■ *Web:* www.kaleidahealth.org

Youth Villages Inner Harbour
4685 Dorsett Shoals Rd .... Douglasville GA 30135 770-852-6333 920-2745
TF: 800-255-8657 ■ *Web:* www.youthvillages.org

377-2 General Hospitals - Canada

Phone *Fax*

Aberdeen Hospital 835 E River Rd ....New Glasgow NS B2H3S6 902-752-7600 755-2356
Web: www.aberdeenhealthfoundation.com

Battlefords Union Hospital
1092 107th St.............................North Battleford SK S9A1Z1 306-446-6600 446-6561
Web: buhfoundation.com

Belleville General Hospital
265 Dundas St E.................................. Belleville ON K8N5A9 613-969-7400 968-8234
TF: 800-483-2811 ■ *Web:* www.qhc.on.ca

Brandon Regional Health Ctr
150 McTavish Ave E................................Brandon MB R7A2B3 204-578-4000 578-4937
Web: www.brandonrha.mb.ca

British Columbia's Women's Hospital & Health Centre
4500 Oak St .... Vancouver BC V6H3N1 604-875-2424 875-3582
TF: 888-300-3088 ■ *Web:* www.bcwomens.ca

Brockville General Hospital 75 Charles St.......... Brockville ON K6V1S8 613-345-5649 345-8336
Web: www.bgh-on.ca

Burnaby Hospital 3935 Kincaid St....................Burnaby BC V5G2X6 604-453-1910 453-1929*
**Fax:* Mail Rm ■ *Web:* www.fraserhealth.ca

Cambridge Memorial Hospital
700 Coronation Blvd.............................Cambridge ON N1R3G2 519-621-2330 740-4938
Web: www.cmh.org

Campbell River Hospital
375 Second Ave .... Campbell River BC V9W3V1 250-850-2141 286-9675
Web: www.viha.ca/

Centre de sant et de services sociaux d'Argenteuil
145 boul Providence................................ Lachute QC J8H4C7 450-562-3761 566-3316
Web: csssargenteuil.qc.ca

Centre de Sante de la MRC de Maskinonge
41 Boul Comtois..................................Louiseville QC J5V2H8 819-228-2731 228-0425
Web: www.csssm.qc.ca

Centre Hospitalier Affilie Universitaire de Quebec-Pavillon Saint-Sacrement
1050 Ch Sainte-Foy .... Quebec QC G1S4L8 418-682-7511 682-7877*
**Fax:* Admissions ■ *Web:* www.cha.quebec.qc.ca

Centre Hospitalier d'Amqui
135 Rue de l'Hopital .... Amqui QC G5J2K5 418-629-2211 629-4498
Web: www.chamqui.com

Centre Hospitalier Hotel-Dieu d'Amos
622 4e Rue O ....Amos QC J9T2S2 819-732-3341 732-7054
Web: csssea.ca

Centre Hospitalier Hotel-Dieu de Roberval
450 Rue Brassard................................ Roberval QC G8H1B9 418-275-0110 275-6202
Web: www.csssdomaineduroy.com

Centre Hospitalier Le Gardeur
911 Montee des Pionniers .... Terrebonne QC J6V2H2 450-654-7525 470-2640
TF: 888-654-7525 ■ *Web:* www.csss.sudlanaudiere.ca

Centre Hospitalier Mount Sinai
5690 Cavendish Blvd .... Montreal QC H4W1S7 514-369-2222 369-2225
Web: sinaimontreal.ca

Centre Hospitalier Pierre Boucher
1333 Boul Jacques-Cartier E .... Longueuil QC J4M2A5 450-468-8111 465-4369
TF: 866-277-3553

Centre Hospitalier Regional du Grand Portage
75 Rue St Henri .... Riviere-du-Loup QC G5R2A4 418-868-1010 868-1035
Web: csssriviereduloup.qc.ca

Centre Hospitalier Regional du Suroit
150 Rue St Thomas .... Salaberry-de-Valleyfield QC J6T6C1 450-371-9920 371-7454
Web: centrejeunessemonteregie.qc.ca

Chatham-Kent Health Alliance
80 Grand Ave W PO Box 2030 .... Chatham ON N7M5L9 519-352-6400 436-2522
Web: www.ckha.on.ca

Children's Hospital of Eastern Ontario
401 Smyth Rd....................................... Ottawa ON K1H8L1 613-737-7600 738-4866
TF: 866-797-0007 ■ *Web:* www.cheo.on.ca

Chilliwack General Hospital
45600 Menholm Rd .... Chilliwack BC V2P1P7 604-795-4141 795-4110
Web: www.fraserhealth.ca

Name / Address	City	Prov	Postal	Phone	Fax
CHU Sainte-Justine 3175 Ch de la Cote-Sainte-Catherine *TF:* 888-235-3667 ■ *Web:* www.chu-sainte-justine.org	Montreal	QC	H3T1C5	514-345-4931	345-4760
Colchester Regional Hospital 207 Willow St *TF:* 800-460-2110 ■ *Web:* www.cehha.nshealth.ca	Truro	NS	B2N5A1	902-893-4321	893-5559
Concordia Hospital 1095 Concordia Ave *TF:* 888-315-9257 ■ *Web:* www.concordiahospital.mb.ca/	Winnipeg	MB	R2K3S8	204-667-1560	667-1049
Cornwall Community Hospital 840 McConnell Ave *Web:* www.cornwallhospital.ca	Cornwall	ON	K6H5S5	613-938-4240	930-4502
Credit Valley Hospital 2200 Eglinton Ave W *TF:* 877-292-4284 ■ *Web:* www.cvh.on.ca	Mississauga	ON	L5M2N1	905-813-2200	813-4444
CSSS du Lac des Deux-Montagnes 520 Boul Sauve *Web:* www.moncsss.com	Saint-Eustache	QC	J7R5B1	450-473-6811	473-6966
Cypress Regional Hospital 2004 Saskatchewan Dr **Fax:* Admitting ■ *Web:* www.cypressrha.ca	Swift Current	SK	S9H5M8	306-778-9400	778-9409*
Dartmouth General Hospital 325 Pleasant St *Web:* www.cdha.nshealth.ca	Dartmouth	NS	B2Y3S3	902-465-8539	
Delta Hospital Foundation 5800 Mtn View Blvd *Web:* www.dhfoundation.ca	Delta	BC	V4K3V6	604-940-9695	940-9670
Dr Georges L Dumont Regional Hospital 330 University Ave *Web:* vitalitenb.ca	Moncton	NB	E1C2Z3	506-862-4000	862-4256
Eagle Ridge Hospital & Health Care Centre 475 Guildford Way *Web:* www.fraserhealth.ca	Port Moody	BC	V3H3W9	604-461-2022	461-9972
Foothills Medical Centre (FMC) 1403 29th St NW **Fax Area Code:* 403 ■ *Web:* www.albertahealthservices.ca	Calgary	AB	T2N2T9	780-342-2000	944-1663*
Glace Bay Healthcare Facility (GBHF) 300 S St *Web:* www.cbdha.nshealth.ca	Glace Bay	NS	B1A1K9	902-849-5511	842-9775
Grace General Hospital 300 Booth Dr *Web:* www.gracehospital.ca	Winnipeg	MB	R3J3M7	204-837-0111	831-0029
Grand River Hospital Kitchener-Waterloo Health Centre 835 King St W PO Box 9056 *Web:* www.grhosp.on.ca	Kitchener	ON	N2G1G3	519-749-4300	749-4208
Greater Niagara General Hospital 5546 Portage Rd *Web:* www.niagarahealth.on.ca	Niagara Falls	ON	L2E6X2	905-378-4647	358-8435
Grey Bruce Health Services 1800 Eigth St E PO Box 1800 *Web:* www.gbhs.on.ca	Owen Sound	ON	N4K6M9	519-376-2121	372-3942
Guelph General Hospital 115 Delhi St *Web:* www.gghorg.ca	Guelph	ON	N1E4J4	519-822-5350	837-6773
Hamilton Health Sciences 1200 Main St W *Web:* www.hamiltonhealthsciences.ca	Hamilton	ON	L8N3Z5	905-521-2100	521-5067
Headwaters Health Care Centre 100 Rolling Hills Dr *Web:* www.headwatershealth.ca	Orangeville	ON	L9W4X9	519-941-2410	942-0483
Health Sciences Centre 820 Sherbrook St *Web:* www.hsc.mb.ca	Winnipeg	MB	R3A1R9	204-787-3661	787-3341
High River Hospital 560 Ninth Ave W *Web:* albertahealthservices.ca	High River	AB	T1V1B3	403-652-2200	652-0199
Hopital Brome Missisquoi-Perkins 950 Rue Principale *Web:* santemonteregie.qc.ca	Cowansville	QC	J2K1K3	450-266-4342	263-8669
Hopital Charles LeMoyne (HCLM) 3120 boul Taschereau *Web:* santemonteregie.qc.ca/champlaincharleslemoyne/index.fr.html	Greenfield Park	QC	J4V2H1	450-466-5000	466-5038
Hopital de Papineau 500 Rue Belanger *Web:* www.csssapapineau.qc.ca	Gatineau	QC	J8L2M4	819-986-3341	
Hopital du Haut-Richelieu 920 Boul du Seminaire N	Saint-Jean-sur-Richelieu	QC	J3A1B7	450-359-5000	359-5251
Hopital Jean-Talon 1385 Jean-Talon St E	Montreal	QC	H2E1S6	514-495-6767	495-6771
Hopital Sainte-Croix 570 Rue Heriot	Drummondville	QC	J2B1C1	819-478-6464	478-6455
Hopital Santa Cabrini 6887 rue Chtelain	Montreal	QC	H1T3X7	514-252-1535	
Hospital Complex Sagamie, The 305 Ave St Vallier CP 5006 *Web:* www.usherbrooke.ca	Chicoutimi	QC	G7H5H6	418-541-1000	541-1168
Hospital Gatineau 909 boul de la Verandrye *Web:* www.csssgatineau.qc.ca	Gatineau	QC	J8P7H2	819-966-6100	
Hotel Dieu Hospital 166 Brock St *Web:* www.hoteldieu.com	Kingston	ON	K7L5G2	613-544-3310	544-9897
Hotel-Dieu d'Arthabaska Five Rue des Hospitalieres *Web:* www.csssae.qc.ca	Victoriaville	QC	G6P6N2	819-357-2030	758-7281
Hotel-Dieu de Sorel 400 Ave Hotel-Dieu *Web:* fondationhoteldieusorel.org	Sorel-Tracy	QC	J3P1N5	450-746-6003	746-6082
Hotel-Dieu Grace Hospital 1030 Ouellette Ave *Web:* www.hdgh.org	Windsor	ON	N9A1E1	519-973-4411	258-5120
James Paton Memorial Hospital 125 Trans Canada Hwy *Web:* centralhealth.nl.ca	Gander	NL	A1V1P7	709-256-2500	256-7800
Jeffrey Hale - St Brigid's Hospital 1250 ch Sainte-Foy *TF:* 888-984-5333 ■ *Web:* jhsb.ca/	Quebec	QC	G1S2M6	418-684-5333	684-5333
Joseph Brant Memorial Hospital (JBMH) 1230 N Shore Blvd *TF:* 800-810-0000 ■ *Web:* www.josephbranthospital.ca	Burlington	ON	L7S1W7	905-632-3730	336-6480
Kelowna General Hospital (KGH) 2268 Pandosy St *TF:* 888-877-4442 ■ *Web:* www.interiorhealth.ca	Kelowna	BC	V1Y1T2	250-862-4000	862-4020
Kootenay Boundary Regional Hospital 1200 Hospital Bench *Web:* www.interiorhealth.ca	Trail	BC	V1R4M1	250-368-3311	364-3422
Lachine General Hospital 650 16th Ave	Lachine	QC	H8S3N5	514-637-2351	*
Lacombe Hospital & Care Centre 5430 47th Ave *Web:* www.albertahealthservices.ca	Lacombe	AB	T4L1G8	403-782-3336	782-2818
Lake of the Woods District Hospital (LWDH) 21 Sylvan St *Web:* www.lwdh.on.ca	Kenora	ON	P9N3W7	807-468-9861	468-3939
Lakeridge Health Bowmanville 47 Liberty St S *Web:* www.lakeridgehealth.on.ca	Bowmanville	ON	L1C2N4	905-623-3331	743-5943
Lakeridge Health Oshawa One Hospital Ct *TF:* 866-338-1778 ■ *Web:* www.lakeridgehealth.on.ca	Oshawa	ON	L1G2B9	905-576-8711	721-4736
Lakeshore General Hospital (LGH) 160 Stillview Ste 5209 *Web:* www.fondationlakeshore.ca	Pointe-Claire	QC	H9R2Y2	514-630-2081	630-2873
Langevin Pierre Dr 2705 Laurier Blvd	Quebec	QC	G1V4G2	418-656-4141	654-2247
Langley Memorial Hospital 22051 Fraser Hwy *Web:* www.fraserhealth.ca	Langley	BC	V3A4H4	604-534-4121	534-8283
Lions Gate Hospital 231 E 15th St *TF:* 800-984-1131 ■ *Web:* www.vch.ca	North Vancouver	BC	V7L2L7	604-988-3131	984-5838
London Health Sciences Centre 800 Commissioners Rd E PO Box 5010 *Web:* www.lhsc.on.ca	London	ON	N6A5W9	519-685-8500	685-8127
London Health Sciences Centre Victoria Campus 800 Commissioners Rd E *Web:* www.lhsc.on.ca	London	ON	N6C6B5	519-685-8500	685-8127
Markham Stouffville Hospital *Markham* 381 Church St PO Box 1800 *Web:* www.msh.on.ca	Markham	ON	L3P7P3	905-472-7000	472-7086
Medical Clinic of North Texas 9003 Airport Fwy Ste 300 *Web:* www.mcnt.com	North Richland	TX	76180	817-514-5200	514-5210
Medicine Hat Regional Hospital 666 Fifth St SW *Web:* albertahealthservices.ca	Medicine Hat	AB	T1A4H6	403-529-8000	529-8998
Misericordia Community Hospital & Health Centre 16940 87th Ave	Edmonton	AB	T5R4H5	780-735-2000	735-2774
Mission Memorial Hospital 7324 Hurd St *Web:* www.fraserhealth.ca	Mission	BC	V2V3H5	604-826-6261	826-9513
Moncton Hospital, The 135 MacBeath Ave *Web:* horizonnb.ca	Moncton	NB	E1C6Z8	506-857-5111	857-5545
Montfort Hospital 713 Montreal Rd *Web:* www.hopitalmontfort.com	Ottawa	ON	K1K0T2	613-746-4621	748-4914
Montreal Heart Institute 5000 Belanger St E *Web:* www.icm-mhi.org	Montreal	QC	H1T1C8	514-376-3330	593-2540
Mount Saint Joseph Hospital 3080 Prince Edward St *Web:* providencehealthcare.org	Vancouver	BC	V5T3N4	604-874-1141	
Mount Sinai Hospital 600 University Ave **Fax:* PR ■ *Web:* www.mountsinai.on.ca	Toronto	ON	M5G1X5	416-596-4200	586-4807*
Nanaimo Regional General Hospital 1200 Dufferin Crescent	Nanaimo	BC	V9S2B7	250-755-7691	
Norfolk General Hospital 365 W St *Web:* www.ngh.on.ca	Simcoe	ON	N3Y1T7	519-426-0750	429-6998
North Bay Regional Health Centre 50 College Dr PO Box 2500 *Web:* www.nbrhc.on.ca	North Bay	ON	P1B5A4	705-474-7525	
North York General Hospital (NYGH) 4001 Leslie St **Fax:* Hum Res ■ *Web:* www.nygh.on.ca	North York	ON	M2K1E1	416-756-6000	756-6738*
Northern Lights Regional Health Centre (NLRHC) Seven Hospital St *Web:* www.albertahealthservices.ca	Fort McMurray	AB	T9H1P2	780-791-6161	791-6029
Oakville-Trafalgar Memorial Hospital 327 Reynolds St *Web:* www.haltonhealthcare.on.ca	Oakville	ON	L6J3L7	905-845-2571	338-4636
Orillia Soldiers' Memorial Hospital (OSMH) 170 Colborne St W **Fax:* Admissions ■ *Web:* www.osmh.on.ca	Orillia	ON	L3V2Z3	705-325-2201	325-7953*
Peace Arch Hospital 15521 Russell Ave *Web:* www.pahfoundation.ca	White Rock	BC	V4B2R4	604-535-4520	541-5820
Peace River Community Health Centre 10101 68th St *Web:* www.albertahealthservices.ca	Peace River	AB	T8S1T6	780-624-7500	
Pembroke Regional Hospital 705 MacKay St *Web:* www.pemreghos.org	Pembroke	ON	K8A1G8	613-732-2811	732-9986
Penticton Regional Hospital (PRH) 550 Carmi Ave *Web:* www.interiorhealth.ca	Penticton	BC	V2A3G6	250-492-4000	492-9068
Perth-Smiths Falls District Hospital 60 Cornelia St W *Web:* www.psfdh.on.ca	Smiths Falls	ON	K7A2H9	613-283-2330	283-8990
Peter Lougheed Centre 3500 26th Ave NE *Web:* www.albertahealthservices.ca	Calgary	AB	T1Y6J4	403-943-4555	943-4878
Peterborough Regional Health Ctr One Hospital Dr *Web:* www.prhc.on.ca	Peterborough	ON	K9J7C6	705-743-2121	876-5107
Powell River General Hospital 5000 Joyce Ave *Web:* www.vch.ca	Powell River	BC	V8A5R3	604-485-3211	485-3243
Prince County Hospital 65 Roy Boapes Ave PO Box 3000 *Web:* www.pchcare.com	Summerside	PE	C1N2A9	902-438-4200	432-2551
Queensway-Carleton Hospital 3045 Baseline Rd *Web:* www.qch.on.ca	Ottawa	ON	K2H8P4	613-721-4700	721-2000
Red Deer Regional Hospital Centre 3942 50th A Ave *Web:* www.albertahealthservices.ca	Red Deer	AB	T4N4E7	403-343-4422	343-4866
Richmond Hospital 7000 Westminster Hwy *Web:* www.vch.ca	Richmond	BC	V6X1A2	604-278-9711	244-5191
Ridge Meadows Hospital 11666 Laity St *Web:* www.fraserhealth.ca	Maple Ridge	BC	V2X7G5	604-463-4111	
Rimbey Hospital & Care Centre 5228 50th Ave PO Box 440 *Web:* albertahealthservices.ca	Rimbey	AB	T0C2J0	403-843-2271	843-2506
Riverside Campus of Ottawa Hospital 1967 Riverside Dr *Web:* www.ottawahospital.on.ca	Ottawa	ON	K1H7W9	613-738-7100	761-5292
Ross Memorial Hospital (RMH) 10 Angeline St N *TF:* 800-510-7365 ■ *Web:* www.rmh.org	Lindsay	ON	K9V4M8	705-324-6111	328-2817

	City	Prov	Postal	Phone	Fax
Rouge Valley Ajax & Pickering 580 Harwood Ave S *Web:* www.rougevalley.ca	Ajax	ON	L1S2J4	905-683-2320	683-8527
Royal Alexandra Hospital 10240 Kingsway Ave. *Web:* www.albertahealthservices.ca	Edmonton	AB	T5H3V9	780-735-4111	
Royal Columbian Hospital 330 E Columbia St *Web:* www.fraserhealth.ca	New Westminster	BC	V3L3W7	604-520-4253	520-4827
Royal Inland Hospital 311 Columbia St *Web:* rihfoundation.ca	Kamloops	BC	V2C2T1	250-374-5111	314-2189
Royal University Hospital 103 Hospital Dr *Web:* saskatoonhealthregion.ca	Saskatoon	SK	S7N0W8	306-655-1000	655-3394
Royal Victoria Hospital 201 Georgian Dr. *Web:* www.rvh.on.ca	Barrie	ON	L4M6M2	705-728-9802	728-0982
Saint Boniface General Hospital (SBGH) 409 Tache Ave Rm D1003 *Fax:* Hum Res ■ *Web:* www.saintboniface.ca	Winnipeg	MB	R2H2A6	204-233-8563	231-0041*
Saint John Regional Hospital 400 University Ave PO Box 2100 *Web:* en.horizonnb.ca	Saint John	NB	E2L4L2	506-648-6000	648-6957
Saint Joseph's General Hospital 2137 Comox Ave *Web:* www.sjghcomox.ca	Comox	BC	V9M1P2	250-339-2242	339-1432
Guelph 100 Westmount Rd *Web:* www.sjhcg.ca	Guelph	ON	N1H5H8	519-824-6000	
Saint Joseph's Health Centre *London* 268 Grosvenor St *Web:* www.sjhc.london.on.ca	London	ON	N6A4V2	519-646-6100	646-6054
Toronto 30 The Queensway *Web:* www.stjoe.on.ca	Toronto	ON	M6R1B5	416-530-6000	530-6243
Saint Joseph's Healthcare Hamilton 50 Charlton Ave E *Web:* stjoes.ca	Hamilton	ON	L8N4A6	905-522-1155	521-6140
Saint Joseph's Lifecare Centre 99 Wayne Gretzky Pkwy *Web:* www.sjlc.ca	Brantford	ON	N3S6T6	519-751-7096	753-7996
Saint Mary's General Hospital 911 Queen's Blvd *Web:* www.smgh.ca	Kitchener	ON	N2M1B2	519-744-3311	749-6426
Saint Mary's Hospital Ctr 3830 Lacombe Ave *Web:* www.smhc.qc.ca	Montreal	QC	H3T1M5	514-345-3511	734-2636
Saint Paul's Hospital 1702 20th St W	Saskatoon	SK	S7M0Z9	306-655-5000	655-5555
Saint Thomas-Elgin General Hospital 189 Elm St *Web:* www.stegh.on.ca	Saint Thomas	ON	N5R5C4	519-631-2020	631-1825
Saskatoon City Hospital 701 Queen St *Web:* www.saskatoonhealthregion.ca	Saskatoon	SK	S7K0M7	306-655-8000	655-8269
Scarborough Hospital Birchmount campus 3030 Birchmount Rd *Web:* www.tsh.to	Scarborough	ON	M1W3W3	416-495-2400	495-2562
Scarborough Hospital General Div 3050 Lawrence Ave E *Web:* www.tsh.to	Scarborough	ON	M1P2V5	416-438-2911	431-8204
Seven Oaks General Hospital 2300 McPhillips St *Web:* sogh.ca	Winnipeg	MB	R2V3M3	204-632-7133	697-2106
Sir Mortimer B Davis Jewish General Hospital 3755 Cote Sainte-Catherine *Web:* www.jgh.ca	Montreal	QC	H3T1E2	514-340-8222	340-7530
Southlake Regional Health Centre 596 Davis Dr. *Web:* www.southlakeregional.org	Newmarket	ON	L3Y2P9	905-895-4521	830-5972
Stanton Territorial Health Authority (S) 550 Byrne Rd PO Box 10 *Web:* stha.hss.gov.nt.ca/	Yellowknife	NT	X1A2N1	867-669-4224	669-4128
Stratford General Hospital 46 General Hospital Dr *Web:* www.hpha.ca	Stratford	ON	N5A2Y6	519-272-8210	271-7137
Sunnybrook Campus 2075 Bayview Ave *Web:* www.sunnybrook.ca	Toronto	ON	M4N3M5	416-480-6100	
Sunnybrook Health Sciences Centre *Women & Babies research program* 76 Grenville St *Web:* www.sunnybrook.ca	Toronto	ON	M5S1B2	416-323-6400	323-6274
Surrey Memorial Hospital 13750 96th Ave *Web:* www.fraserhealth.ca	Surrey	BC	V3V1Z2	604-588-3381	585-5669
Thunder Bay Regional Health Sciences Centre 980 Olvier Rd *Web:* tbrhsc.net/programs_&_services/cancer_care/dap.asp	Thunder Bay	ON	P7B6V4	807-684-6000	684-5890
Timmins & District Hospital 700 Ross Ave E *Web:* www.tadh.com	Timmins	ON	P4N8P2	705-267-2131	267-6311
Toronto General Hospital 200 Elizabeth St *Web:* www.uhn.ca	Toronto	ON	M5G2C4	416-340-3111	340-5191
Toronto Western Hospital 399 Bathurst St *Web:* www.uhn.ca	Toronto	ON	M5T2S8	416-603-2581	603-5434
Trillium Health Centre 100 Queensway W *Web:* www.trilliumhealthcentre.org	Mississauga	ON	L5B1B8	905-848-7100	848-7139
University of Alberta Hospital 8440 112th St *Web:* www.albertahealthservices.ca	Edmonton	AB	T6G2B7	780-407-8822	407-7418
Valley Regional Hospital 150 Exhibition St *Web:* www.avdha.nshealth.ca	Kentville	NS	B4N5E3	902-678-7381	679-1904
Vancouver General Hospital 899 W 12th Ave. *Web:* www.vch.ca	Vancouver	BC	V5Z1M9	604-875-4111	875-5701
Vernon Jubilee Hospital 2101 32nd St *Web:* www.interiorhealth.ca	Vernon	BC	V1T5L2	250-545-2211	545-5602
Victoria General Hospital 2340 Pembina Hwy *Web:* www.vgh.mb.ca	Winnipeg	MB	R3T2E8	204-477-3347	261-0223
Welland County General Hospital 65 Third St *Web:* www.niagarahealth.on.ca	Welland	ON	L3B4W6	905-732-6111	732-3268
West Coast General Hospital 3949 Port Alberni Hwy *Web:* www.viha.ca	Port Alberni	BC	V9Y4S1	250-731-1370	
West Parry Sound Health Centre Six Albert St *Web:* www.wpshc.com	Parry Sound	ON	P2A3A4	705-746-9321	746-7364
Western Memorial Regional Hospital One Brookfield Ave PO Box 2005 *Web:* www.westernhealth.nl.ca	Corner Brook	NL	A2H6J7	709-637-5000	
Windsor Regional Hospital Metropolitan Campus (WRH) 1995 Lens Ave *Web:* www.wrh.on.ca	Windsor	ON	N8W1L9	519-254-5577	254-3458
Windsor Regional Hospital Western Campus (WRHWC) 1453 Prince Rd *Fax:* Acctg ■ *Web:* www.wrh.on.ca	Windsor	ON	N9C3Z4	519-254-5577	254-2317*
Woodstock General Hospital 270 Riddell St *Fax:* Admitting ■ *Web:* www.wgh.on.ca	Woodstock	ON	N4S6N6	519-421-4211	421-4238*
Yarmouth Regional Hospital (YRH) 60 Vancouver St *Fax:* Admitting ■ *Web:* www.swndha.nshealth.ca/pages/yrh.htm	Yarmouth	NS	B5A2P5	902-742-3541	742-0369*
York Central Hospital 10 Trench St *Web:* www.mackenziehealth.ca	Richmond Hill	ON	L4C4Z3	905-883-1212	883-2455

377-3 General Hospitals - US

Alabama

	City	State	Zip	Phone	Fax
Andalusia Regional Hospital (ARH) 849 S Three Notch St PO Box 760 *Web:* www.andalusiaregional.com	Andalusia	AL	36420	334-222-8466	427-0349
Athens-Limestone Hospital 700 W Market St *Web:* www.athenslimestonehospital.com	Athens	AL	35611	256-233-9292	233-9278
Baptist Health System 1000 First St N *Web:* www.bhsala.com	Alabaster	AL	35007	205-620-8100	
Baptist Medical Ctr South 2105 E S Blvd *Fax:* Admitting ■ *Web:* www.baptistfirst.org	Montgomery	AL	36116	334-288-2100	286-3511*
Brookwood Medical Ctr 2010 Brookwood Medical Ctr Dr *Web:* www.bwmc.com	Birmingham	AL	35209	205-877-1000	
Bryan W Whitfield Memorial Hospital 105 Hwy 80 E PO Box 890 *Web:* www.bwwmh.com	Demopolis	AL	36732	334-289-4000	
Citizens Baptist Medical Ctr (CBMC) 604 Stone Ave PO Box 978 *Web:* baptisthealthalabama.org	Talladega	AL	35161	256-362-8111	761-4543
Cooper Green Hospital 1515 Sixth Ave S	Birmingham	AL	35233	205-930-3200	930-3497
Coosa Valley HomeCare 315 W Hickory St *Web:* lhcgroup.com	Sylacauga	AL	35150	256-208-0087	
Crestwood Medical Ctr One Hospital Dr *Web:* www.crestwoodmedcenter.com	Huntsville	AL	35801	256-429-4000	
Cullman Regional Medical Ctr (CRMC) 1912 Alabama Hwy 157 PO Box 1108 *Web:* www.crmchospital.com	Cullman	AL	35058	256-737-2000	737-2005
DCH Regional Medical Ctr 809 University Blvd E *Web:* dchsystem.com/our_facilities/dch_regional_medical_center.aspx	Tuscaloosa	AL	35401	205-759-7111	759-6168
Decatur General Hospital 1201 Seventh St SE *Web:* www.decaturgeneral.org	Decatur	AL	35601	256-341-2000	341-2557
DeKalb Regional Medical Ctr 200 Medical Ctr Dr *Web:* www.dekalbregional.com	Fort Payne	AL	35968	256-845-3150	997-2512
East Alabama Medical Ctr 2000 Pepperell Pkwy *Web:* www.eamc.org	Opelika	AL	36801	334-749-3411	528-1509
Eliza Coffee Memorial Hospital (ECM) 205 Marengo St *Web:* www.chgroup.org/ecm	Florence	AL	35630	256-768-9191	768-9420
Flowers Hospital 4370 W Main St *TF:* 877-456-9617 ■ *Web:* www.flowershospital.com	Dothan	AL	36305	334-793-5000	836-1888
Gadsden Regional Medical Ctr 1007 Goodyear Ave *Web:* www.gadsdenregional.com	Gadsden	AL	35903	256-494-4000	494-4474
Helen Keller Hospital 1300 S Montgomery Ave *Web:* www.helenkeller.com	Sheffield	AL	35660	256-386-4196	386-4469
Highlands Medical Ctr 380 Woods Cove Rd *Web:* www.highlandsmedcenter.com	Scottsboro	AL	35768	256-259-4444	218-3536
Huntsville Hospital 101 Sivley Rd *Web:* hhsys.org	Huntsville	AL	35801	256-265-1000	265-2585
Jackson Hospital 1725 Pine St *Web:* www.jackson.org	Montgomery	AL	36106	334-293-8000	
Lanier Health Services (LHS) 4800 48th St *Fax:* Admissions ■ *Web:* www.lanierhospital.com	Valley	AL	36854	334-756-1400	756-6698*
Marshall Medical Ctr South (MMCS) 2505 US Hwy 431 *Web:* mmcenters.com	Boaz	AL	35957	256-593-8310	840-3647
Medical Ctr Enterprise (MCE) 400 N Edwards St *TF:* 800-994-6610 ■ *Web:* www.mcehospital.com	Enterprise	AL	36330	334-347-0584	347-2080
Mobile Infirmary Medical Ctr (MIMC) Five Mobile Infirmary Cir *Web:* www.mobileinfirmary.org	Mobile	AL	36607	251-435-2400	
Northeast Alabama Regional Medical Ctr 400 E Tenth St *Web:* www.rmccares.org	Anniston	AL	36207	256-235-5121	235-5608
Northport Medical Ctr 2700 Hospital Dr *TF:* 866-840-0750 ■ *Web:* www.dchsystem.com	Northport	AL	35476	205-333-4500	333-4522
Parkway Medical Center Hospital 1874 Beltline Rd *Web:* www.parkwaymedicalcenter.com	Decatur	AL	35601	256-350-2211	
Quality of Life Health Services Inc 1411 Piedmont Cutoff PO Box 97 *Web:* www.qolhs.org	Gadsden	AL	35902	256-492-0131	
Riverview Regional Medical Ctr 600 S Third St *Web:* www.riverviewregional.com	Gadsden	AL	35901	256-543-5200	543-5888

Phone Fax

Saint Vincent's Hospital
810 St Vincent's Dr ... Birmingham AL 35205 205-939-7000 930-2259*
*Fax: Admitting ■ Web: www.stvhs.com

Southeast Alabama Medical Ctr
1108 Ross Clark Cir ... Dothan AL 36301 334-793-8111 677-4901
TF: 800-507-7262 ■ Web: www.samc.org

Springhill Medical Ctr 3719 Dauphin St ... Mobile AL 36608 251-344-9630 461-2439*
*Fax: Admissions ■ Web: www.springhillmedicalcenter.com

Thomas Hospital 750 Morphy Ave ... Fairhope AL 36532 251-928-2375 435-6261
TF: 800-422-2027 ■ Web: www.thomashospital.com

UAB Medical West 995 Ninth Ave SW ... Bessemer AL 35022 205-481-7000 481-7994
TF: 800-994-6610 ■ Web: www.medicalwesthospital.org

University of South Alabama Children & Women's Hospital
1700 Ctr St ... Mobile AL 36604 251-415-1000 415-1002*
*Fax: Admitting ■ Web: www.usahealthsystem.com

University of South Alabama Medical Ctr
2451 Fillingim St ... Mobile AL 36617 251-471-7000
Web: www.usahealthsystem.com

Vaughan Regional Medical Ctr
1015 Medical Ctr Pkwy ... Selma AL 36701 334-418-4100 418-3599
TF: 800-994-6610 ■ Web: www.vaughanregional.com

Walker Baptist Medical Ctr 3400 Hwy 78 E ... Jasper AL 35501 205-387-4000 715-5304
TF: 877-474-4243 ■ Web: bhsala.com

Alaska

Phone Fax

Alaska Native Medical Ctr (ANMC)
4315 Diplomacy Dr ... Anchorage AK 99508 907-563-2662 729-1984
TF Admitting: 800-478-6661 ■ Web: www.anmc.org

Alaska Regional Hospital 2801 Debarr Rd ... Anchorage AK 99508 907-276-1131 264-1179
Web: www.alaskaregional.com

Fairbanks Memorial Hospital 1650 Cowles St ... Fairbanks AK 99701 907-452-8181 458-5324
Web: bannerhealth.com

Providence Alaska Medical Ctr
3200 Providence Dr ... Anchorage AK 99508 907-562-2211
Web: www.providence.org

Arizona

Phone Fax

Banner Baywood Medical Ctr 6644 E Baywood Ave ... Mesa AZ 85206 480-981-2000 981-4198
Web: www.bannerhealth.com

Banner Boswell Medical Ctr
10401 W Thunderbird Blvd ... Sun City AZ 85351 623-977-7211
Web: www.bannerhealth.com

Banner Del E Webb Memorial Hospital
14502 W Meeker Blvd ... Sun City West AZ 85375 623-214-4000 214-4105
TF: 800-254-4357 ■ Web: www.bannerhealth.com

Banner Desert Medical Ctr 1400 S Dobson Rd ... Mesa AZ 85202 480-512-3000 512-8711
Web: www.bannerhealth.com

Banner Good Samaritan Medical Ctr
1111 E McDowell Rd ... Phoenix AZ 85006 602-239-2000 239-5160
Web: www.bannerhealth.com

Banner Thunderbird Medical Ctr (BTMC)
5555 W ThunderbiRd Rd ... Glendale AZ 85306 602-839-2000 865-5930
Web: www.bannerhealth.com

Carondelet Saint Joseph's Hospital
350 N Wilmot Rd ... Tucson AZ 85711 520-873-3968
Web: www.carondelet.org

Carondelet St. Mary's Hospital
1601 W St Mary's Rd ... Tucson AZ 85745 520-872-3000 872-6641
Web: www.carondelet.org/home/hospitals-locations/st.-marys-hospital.aspx

Casa Grande Regional Medical Ctr (CGRMC)
1800 E Florence Blvd ... Casa Grande AZ 85122 520-381-6300 381-6435
Web: bannerhealth.com/casagrande

Chandler Regional Hospital 475 S Dobson Rd ... Chandler AZ 85224 480-728-3000 728-3875
TF: 877-728-5414 ■ Web: hospitals.dignityhealth.org

Flagstaff Medical Ctr 1200 N Beaver St ... Flagstaff AZ 86001 928-779-3366 947-3299
Web: www.flagstaffmedicalcenter.com

Havasu Regional Medical Ctr
101 Civic Ctr Ln ... Lake Havasu City AZ 86403 928-855-8185 505-5744
Web: www.havasuregional.com

HonorHealth John C. Lincoln Medical Center
250 E Dunlap Ave ... Phoenix AZ 85020 602-943-2381
Web: www.jcl.com/hospitals/north-mountain

Kingman Regional Medical Ctr (KRMC)
3269 Stockton Hill Rd ... Kingman AZ 86409 928-757-2101 757-0604
TF: 877-757-2101 ■ Web: www.azkrmc.com

La Paz Regional Hospital Inc 1200 W Mohave Rd ... Parker AZ 85344 928-669-9201
Web: www.lapazhospital.org

Maricopa Medical Ctr 2601 E Roosevelt St ... Phoenix AZ 85008 602-344-5011 344-0719
TF: 866-749-2876 ■ Web: www.mihs.org

Maryvale Hospital 5102 W Campbell Ave ... Phoenix AZ 85031 623-848-5000 848-5553
Web: www.abrazohealth.com

Mayo Clinic Hospital 5777 E Mayo Blvd ... Phoenix AZ 85054 480-515-6296 342-2525
Web: mayoclinic.org/patient-visitor-guide

Paradise Valley Hospital 3929 E Bell Rd ... Phoenix AZ 85032 602-923-5000 923-5657
Web: www.abrazohealth.com

Phoenix Baptist Hospital
2000 W Bethany Home Rd ... Phoenix AZ 85015 602-249-0212 246-5979
Web: www.abrazohealth.com

Saint Luke's Medical Ctr 1800 E Van Buren St ... Phoenix AZ 85006 602-251-8100 251-8207
Web: www.stlukesmedcenter.com

Scottsdale Osborn Medical Center
7400 E Osborn Rd ... Scottsdale AZ 85251 480-882-4000
Web: www.shc.org

Scottsdale Shea Medical Center
9003 E Shea Blvd ... Scottsdale AZ 85260 480-323-3000
Web: www.honorhealth.com

Tempe Saint Luke's Hospital (TSLH)
1500 S Mill Ave ... Tempe AZ 85281 480-784-5500 784-5539
Web: www.tempestlukeshospital.com

Tucson Medical Ctr 5301 E Grant Rd ... Tucson AZ 85712 520-327-5461
TF: 800-526-5353 ■ Web: www.tmcaz.com

University Physicians Healthcare Hospital at Kino Campus (UPH)
2800 E Ajo Way ... Tucson AZ 85713 520-874-2000 874-4042
Web: www.uahealth.com

US Public Health Service Phoenix Indian Medical Ctr
4212 N 16th St ... Phoenix AZ 85016 602-263-1200 263-1618
Web: usphs.gov

Yavapai Regional Medical Ctr
1003 Willow Creek Rd ... Prescott AZ 86301 928-445-2700 771-5509
TF: 877-976-9762 ■ Web: www.yrmc.org

Yuma Regional Medical Ctr 2400 S Ave A ... Yuma AZ 85364 928-344-2000 336-7337
Web: www.yumaregional.org

Arkansas

Phone Fax

Arkansas Methodist Medical Ctr
900 W KingsFwy ... Paragould AR 72451 870-239-7000 239-7202
Web: www.myammc.org

Baptist Health Medical Ctr
3333 Spring Hill Dr ... North Little Rock AR 72117 501-202-3000 202-3813
Web: www.baptist-health.com

Baxter Regional Medical Ctr
624 Hospital Dr ... Mountain Home AR 72653 870-424-1000 424-2444
Web: www.baxterregional.org

Conway Regional Hospital 2302 College Ave ... Conway AR 72032 501-329-3831 450-2283
Web: www.conwayregional.org

Crittenden Regional Hospital
200 Tyler St ... West Memphis AR 72301 870-735-1500 732-7710

Helena Regional Medical Ctr 1801 ML King Dr ... Helena AR 72342 870-338-5800 816-3909
Web: www.helenarmc.com

Jefferson Regional Medical Ctr (JRMC)
1600 W 40th Ave ... Pine Bluff AR 71603 870-541-7100
Web: www.jrmc.org

Medical Ctr of South Arkansas
700 W Grove St ... El Dorado AR 71730 870-863-2000 863-5442
Web: www.themedcenter.net

Mercy Health System of Northwest Arkansas
2710 Rife Medical Ln ... Rogers AR 72758 479-338-8000
Web: www.mercy.net

National Park Medical Ctr
1910 Malvern Ave ... Hot Springs National Park AR 71901 501-321-1000 620-1450
Web: www.nationalparkmedical.com

North Arkansas Regional Medical Ctr
620 N Willow St ... Harrison AR 72601 870-365-2000
Web: www.narmc.com

North metro Medical Ctr 1400 Braden St ... Jacksonville AR 72076 501-985-7000
Web: www.northmetromed.com

Northwest Medical Ctr 609 W Maple Ave ... Springdale AR 72764 479-751-5711 757-2908
Web: www.northwesthealth.com

Ouachita County Medical Ctr (OCMC) PO Box 797 ... Camden AR 71711 870-836-1000 836-1522
TF: 877-836-2472 ■ Web: www.ouachitamedcenter.com

Saint Bernard's Medical Ctr
225 E Jackson Ave ... Jonesboro AR 72401 870-972-4100 974-5112
Web: www.sbrmc.com

Saint Vincent Infirmary Medical Ctr
Two St Vincent Cir ... Little Rock AR 72205 501-552-3000
Web: www.stvincenthealth.com

Saline Memorial Hospital One Medical Pk Dr ... Benton AR 72015 501-776-6000 776-6019
Web: www.salinememorial.org

Sparks Regional Medical Ctr (SRMC)
1001 Towson Ave ... Fort Smith AR 72901 479-441-4000 441-5397
Web: www.sparkshealth.com

UAMS Medical Ctr 4301 W Markham St ... Little Rock AR 72205 501-686-7000 526-4282*
*Fax: Admitting ■ TF: 877-467-6560 ■ Web: www.uams.edu

White County Medical Ctr 3214 E Race Ave ... Searcy AR 72143 501-268-6121 380-1011
TF: 888-562-7520 ■ Web: wcmc.org

White River Medical Ctr 1710 Harrison St ... Batesville AR 72501 870-262-1200 262-1458
Web: www.whiteriverhealthsystem.com

California

Phone Fax

Alameda County Medical Center-Highland Campus
1411 E 31st St ... Oakland CA 94602 510-437-4800 535-7722
Web: www.alamedahealthsystem.org

Alameda County Medical Ctr - Fairmont Hospital
15400 Foothill Blvd ... San Leandro CA 94578 510-895-4200
Web: www.alamedahealthsystem.org

Alhambra Hospital 100 S Raymond Ave ... Alhambra CA 91801 626-570-1606 299-1217
Web: www.alhambrahospital.com

Alta Bates Summit Medical Ctr (ABSMC)
2450 Ashby Ave ... Berkeley CA 94705 510-204-4444 204-1883
Web: www.altabatessummit.org

Alvarado Hospital Medical Ctr
6655 Alvarado Rd ... San Diego CA 92120 619-287-3270 229-7020
Web: www.alvaradohospital.com

Anaheim Memorial Medical Ctr
1111 W La Palma Ave ... Anaheim CA 92801 714-774-1450 999-6027*
*Fax: Admitting ■ Web: www.memorialcare.org

Antelope Valley Hospital 1600 W Ave J ... Lancaster CA 93534 661-949-5000 949-5510
Web: www.avhospital.org

Arrowhead Regional Medical Ctr
400 N Pepper Ave ... Colton CA 92324 909-580-1000 580-6214
TF: 855-422-8029 ■ Web: www.arrowheadmedcenter.org

Bakersfield Memorial Hospital
420 34th St ... Bakersfield CA 93301 661-327-4647 326-0706*
*Fax: Admitting ■ Web: www.bakersfieldmemorial.org

Name / Address	City	State	Zip	Phone	Fax
Baldwin Park Medical Ctr 1011 Baldwin Pk Blvd. *Web:* healthy.kaiserpermanente.org	Baldwin Park	CA	91706	626-851-1011	851-5101
Bellflower Doctors Medical Center 9542 E Artesia Blvd	Bellflower	CA	90706	562-925-8355	925-4413
Beverly Hospital 309 W Beverly Blvd *Web:* www.beverly.org	Montebello	CA	90640	323-726-1222	725-4338
Brotman Medical Ctr 3828 Delmas Terr. *Web:* www.brotmanmedicalcenter.com	Culver City	CA	90231	310-836-7000	202-4141
California Hospital Medical Ctr 1401 S Grand Ave. *Web:* www.chmcla.org	Los Angeles	CA	90015	213-748-2411	765-4078
California Pacific Medical Ctr 3700 California St. **Fax:* Admitting ■ *Web:* www.cpmc.org	San Francisco	CA	94118	415-600-6000	750-5007*
California Pacific Medical Ctr Davies Campus Castro & Duboce Sts *Web:* www.cpmc.org	San Francisco	CA	94114	415-600-6000	565-6223
California Pacific Medical Ctr Pacific Campus 2333 Buchanan St *Web:* www.cpmc.org	San Francisco	CA	94115	415-600-6000	600-3679
Cedars-Sinai Medical Ctr (CSMC) 8700 Beverly Blvd. **Fax:* Admitting ■ *TF:* 800-233-2771 ■ *Web:* cedars-sinai.edu	Los Angeles	CA	90048	310-423-3277	123-0105*
Centinela Hospital Medical Ctr 555 E Hardy St *Web:* www.centinelamed.com	Inglewood	CA	90301	310-673-4660	677-0535
Chapman Medical Center 2601 E Chapman Ave. *Web:* www.chapmanmedicalcenter.com	Orange	CA	92869	714-633-0011	532-4345
Citrus Valley Medical Ctr Inter-Community Campus 210 W San BernaRdino Rd *Web:* www.cvhp.org	Covina	CA	91723	626-331-7331	
City of Hope National Medical Ctr 1500 E Duarte Rd *TF Admissions:* 800-826-4673 ■ *Web:* www.cityofhope.org	Duarte	CA	91010	626-256-4673	
Coast Plaza Doctors Hospital Inc 13100 Studebaker Rd *Web:* avantihospitals.com	Norwalk	CA	90650	562-868-3751	
Coastal Communities Hospital 2701 S Bristol St **Fax Area Code:* 754 ■ *Web:* www.coastalcommhospital.com	Santa Ana	CA	92704	714-754-5454	754-5556*
Community Hospital of Long Beach 1720 Termino Ave. *TF:* 800-994-6610	Long Beach	CA	90804	562-498-1000	498-4434
Community Hospital of San Bernardino (CHSB) 1805 Medical Ctr Dr *Web:* www.chsb.org	San Bernardino	CA	92411	909-887-6333	887-6468
Community Hospital of the Monterey Peninsula (CHOMP) 23625 Holman Hwy *TF:* 888-452-4667 ■ *Web:* www.chomp.org	Monterey	CA	93940	831-624-5311	625-4948
Community Regional Medical Ctr 2823 Fresno St *Web:* www.communitymedical.org	Fresno	CA	93721	559-459-6000	
Contra Costa Health Services 2500 Alhambra Ave. *TF:* 877-661-6230 ■ *Web:* www.cchealth.org/medical_center	Martinez	CA	94553	925-370-5000	370-5138
Dameron Hospital Assn (DHA) 525 W Acacia St *Web:* www.dameronhospital.org	Stockton	CA	95203	209-944-5550	461-3130
Desert Regional Medical Ctr 1150 N Indian Canyon Dr *TF:* 800-491-4990 ■ *Web:* www.desertregional.com	Palm Springs	CA	92262	760-323-6511	864-9577
Doctors Medical Ctr 1441 Florida Ave. *TF:* 800-994-6610 ■ *Web:* www.dmc-modesto.com	Modesto	CA	95350	209-578-1211	576-3680
Dominican Hospital (DH) 1555 Soquel Dr *Web:* www.dominicanhospital.org	Santa Cruz	CA	95065	831-462-7700	462-7761
Downey Regional Medical Ctr 11500 Brookshire Ave. *Web:* pihhealth.org/	Downey	CA	90241	562-904-5000	904-5309
Eden Medical Ctr (EMC) 20103 Lk Chabot Rd *Web:* www.edenmedicalcenter.org	Castro Valley	CA	94546	510-537-1234	889-6506
Eisenhower Medical Ctr 39000 Bob Hope Dr *Web:* www.emc.org	Rancho Mirage	CA	92270	760-340-3911	773-4396
El Centro Regional Medical Ctr 1415 Ross Ave *Web:* www.ecrmc.org	El Centro	CA	92243	760-339-7100	
Emanuel Medical Ctr (EMC) 825 Delbon Ave *Web:* www.emanuelmedicalcenter.org	Turlock	CA	95382	209-667-4200	
Enloe Medical Ctr 1531 Esplanade *TF:* 800-822-8102 ■ *Web:* www.enloe.org	Chico	CA	95926	530-332-7300	899-2067
Family Healthcare Network 305 E Ctr Ave *Web:* www.fhcn.org	Visalia	CA	93291	559-737-4700	
Feather River Hospital (FRH) 5974 Pentz Rd *Web:* www.adventisthealth.org/feather-river/pages/default.aspx	Paradise	CA	95969	530-877-9361	876-2160
Foothill Presbyterian Hospital 250 S Grand Ave. *Web:* www.cvhp.org	Glendora	CA	91741	626-963-8411	857-3274
Fountain Valley Regional Hospital & Medical Ctr 17100 Euclid St *TF:* 866-904-6871 ■ *Web:* www.fountainvalleyhospital.com	Fountain Valley	CA	92708	714-966-7200	966-8039
Fremont Medical Ctr 970 Plumas St *Web:* www.frhg.org	Yuba City	CA	95991	530-751-4000	751-4224
Garden Grove Hospital & Medical Ctr 12601 Garden Grove Blvd. *Web:* www.gardengrovehospital.com	Garden Grove	CA	92843	714-537-5160	741-3322
Garfield Medical Ctr 525 N Garfield Ave *Web:* www.garfieldmedicalcenter.com	Monterey Park	CA	91754	626-573-2222	571-8972
Glendale Adventist Medical Ctr 1509 Wilson Terr *Web:* www.adventisthealth.org/glendale/pages/default.aspx	Glendale	CA	91206	818-409-8000	546-5600
Glendale Memorial Hospital & Health Ctr 1420 S Central Ave. *Web:* www.glendalememorialhospital.org	Glendale	CA	91204	818-502-1900	
Good Samaritan Hospital 2425 Samaritan Dr. **Fax:* Admitting ■ *Web:* www.goodsamsanjose.com	San Jose	CA	95124	408-559-2011	559-2675*
Greater El Monte Community Hospital (GEMCH) 1701 Santa Anita Ave *Web:* www.greaterelmonte.com	South El Monte	CA	91733	626-579-7777	350-0368
Harbor-UCLA Medical Ctr 1000 W Carson St *Web:* www.humc.edu	Torrance	CA	90509	310-222-2345	
Henry Mayo Newhall Memorial Hospital 23845 McBean Pkwy *Web:* www.henrymayo.com	Valencia	CA	91355	661-253-8000	253-8142
Hoag Hospital Irvine (HHI) 16200 Sand Canyon Ave *Web:* www.hoag.org	Irvine	CA	92618	949-764-4624	
Hoag Memorial Hospital Presbyterian One Hoag Dr. *Web:* www.hoag.org	Newport Beach	CA	92658	949-764-4624	
Hollywood Presbyterian Medical Ctr 1300 N Vermont Ave. **Fax Area Code:* 323 ■ *Web:* www.hollywoodpresbyterian.com	Los Angeles	CA	90027	213-413-3000	660-0446*
Huntington Memorial Hospital 100 W California Blvd. *Web:* www.huntingtonhospital.com	Pasadena	CA	91109	626-397-5000	397-2995
John F Kennedy Memorial Hospital 47-111 Monroe St *Web:* www.jfkmemorialhosp.com	Indio	CA	92201	760-347-6191	775-8014
John Muir Medical Ctr (JMMC) 1601 Ygnacio Valley Rd *TF:* 844-398-5376 ■ *Web:* www.johnmuirhealth.com	Walnut Creek	CA	94598	925-939-3000	308-8944
Kaiser Permanente 401 Bicentennial Way *Web:* health.kaiserpermanente.org	Santa Rosa	CA	95403	707-571-4000	571-4556
Kaiser Permanente Fontana Medical Ctr 9961 Sierra Ave *Web:* health.kaiserpermanente.org	Fontana	CA	92335	909-427-5000	
Kaiser Permanente Foundation Hospital 9400 E Rosecrans Ave **Fax Area Code:* 510 ■ *TF:* 866-279-8954	Bellflower	CA	90706	562-461-3000	267-7524*
Kaiser Permanente Harbor City Medical Ctr 25825 S Vermont Ave. *TF:* 800-464-4000 ■ *Web:* healthy.kaiserpermanente.org	Harbor City	CA	90710	310-325-5111	517-2234
Kaiser Permanente Hayward Medical Ctr 27400 Hesperian Blvd *Web:* www.mydoctor.kaiserpermanente.org	Hayward	CA	94545	510-784-4000	784-4722
Kaiser Permanente Hospital 441 N Lakeview Ave *TF:* 800-464-4000 ■ *Web:* healthy.kaiserpermanente.org	Anaheim	CA	92807	714-279-4000	279-5590
Kaiser Permanente Los Angeles Medical Ctr 4867 Sunset Blvd *Web:* healthy.kaiserpermanente.org	Los Angeles	CA	90027	323-783-4011	783-7227
Kaiser Permanente Medical Center-Santa Teresa 250 Hospital Pkwy **Fax:* Cust Svc ■ *Web:* kp.org	San Jose	CA	95119	408-972-7000	972-7156*
Kaiser Permanente Medical Center-South Sacramento 6600 Bruceville Rd *TF:* 800-464-4000 ■ *Web:* mydoctor.kaiserpermanente.org	Sacramento	CA	95823	916-688-2000	688-2978
Kaiser Permanente Medical Center-West Los Angeles 6041 Cadillac Ave. *Web:* kaiserpermanente.org	Los Angeles	CA	90034	323-857-2000	
Kaiser Permanente Medical Ctr San Francisco 2425 Geary Blvd. *Web:* healthy.kaiserpermanente.org	San Francisco	CA	94115	415-833-2000	
Kaiser Permanente Panorama City Medical Ctr 13652 Cantara St *Web:* healthy.kaiserpermanente.org	Panorama City	CA	91402	818-375-2000	
Kaiser Permanente Riverside Medical Ctr 10800 Magnolia Ave. *TF Cust Svc:* 800-464-4000 ■ *Web:* kaiserpermanente.org	Riverside	CA	92505	951-353-2000	353-3055
Kaiser Permanente Vallejo Medical Ctr 975 Sereno Dr *Web:* kaiserpermanente.org	Vallejo	CA	94589	707-651-1000	651-2026
Kaiser Permanente Walnut Creek Medical Ctr 1425 S Main St. *TF:* 800-464-4000 ■ *Web:* mydoctor.kaiserpermanente.org	Walnut Creek	CA	94596	925-295-4000	
Kaweah Delta Hospital 400 W Mineral King Ave. *TF:* 800-717-5670 ■ *Web:* www.kaweahdelta.org	Visalia	CA	93291	559-624-2000	
Kern Medical Ctr 1700 Mt Vernon Ave **Fax:* Admitting ■ *Web:* www.kernmedicalcenter.com	Bakersfield	CA	93306	661-326-2000	326-2969*
La Palma Intercommunity Hospital 7901 Walker St. *Web:* www.lapalmaintercommunityhospital.com	La Palma	CA	90623	714-670-7400	670-6287
Lakewood Regional Medical Ctr 3700 S St. *Web:* www.lakewoodregional.com	Lakewood	CA	90712	562-531-2550	
Lancaster Community Hospital 43830 N 10th St W *Web:* www.lancastergeneralhealth.org	Lancaster	CA	93534	661-948-4781	940-1308
Lifelong Medical Care Inc PO Box 11247 *Web:* www.lifelongmedical.org	Berkeley	CA	94712	510-981-4100	
Lodi Memorial Hospital 975 S Fairmont Ave *TF:* 800-323-3360 ■ *Web:* www.lodihealth.org	Lodi	CA	95240	209-334-3411	274-0634
Loma Linda University Medical Ctr 11234 Anderson St. *TF:* 877-558-6248 ■ *Web:* lomalindahealth.org	Loma Linda	CA	92354	909-558-4000	558-0308
Long Beach Memorial Medical Ctr 2801 Atlantic Ave *Web:* www.memorialcare.org	Long Beach	CA	90806	562-933-2000	933-1336
Los Alamitos Medical Ctr 3751 Katella Ave. *TF:* 800-540-4000 ■ *Web:* www.losalamitosmedctr.com	Los Alamitos	CA	90720	562-598-1311	493-2812
Los Robles Hospital & Medical Ctr (LRHMC) 215 W Janss Rd *Web:* www.losrobleshospital.com	Thousand Oaks	CA	91360	805-497-2727	370-4666
Madera Community Hospital 1250 E Almond Ave *Web:* www.maderahospital.org	Madera	CA	93637	559-675-5555	675-5509
Marian Medical Ctr 1400 E Church St *Web:* www.marianmedicalcenter.org	Santa Maria	CA	93454	805-739-3000	739-3060

Phone Fax

Marin General Hospital 250 Bon Air Rd ... Greenbrae CA 94904 415-925-7000 925-7317
TF: 888-996-9644 ■ *Web:* www.maringeneral.org/

Marina Del Rey Hospital
4650 Lincoln Blvd ... Marina del Rey CA 90292 310-823-8911
Web: www.marinahospital.com

Mendocino Coast District Hospital
700 River Dr ... Fort Bragg CA 95437 707-961-1234 964-1192
TF: 866-767-3224 ■ *Web:* www.mcdh.org

Mercy General Hospital 4001 J St ... Sacramento CA 95819 916-453-4545
Web: hospitals.dignityhealth.org

Mercy Hospitals of Bakersfield Truxtun Campus (MHB)
2215 Truxtun Ave ... Bakersfield CA 93301 661-632-5000 327-2592
Web: www.mercybakersfield.org

Mercy Medical Ctr Merced Community Campus
333 Mercy Ave ... Merced CA 95340 209-564-5000
Web: www.mercymercedcares.org

Mercy Medical Ctr Redding 2175 Rosaline Ave ... Redding CA 96001 530-225-6000 225-6125
TF: 800-521-6377 ■ *Web:* www.mercy.org

Mercy San Juan Medical Ctr 6501 Coyle Ave ... Carmichael CA 95608 916-537-5000 537-5111
Web: hospitals.dignityhealth.org

Mercy Southwest Hospital
400 Old River Rd ... Bakersfield CA 93311 661-663-6000
Web: mercybakersfield.org

Methodist Hospital of Sacramento
7500 Hospital Dr ... Sacramento CA 95823 916-423-3000 423-6045
Web: hospitals.dignityhealth.org

Methodist Hospital of Southern California
300 W Huntington Dr ... Arcadia CA 91007 626-898-8000 462-2688
TF: 888-388-2838 ■ *Web:* www.methodisthospital.org

Mission Hospital Regional Medical Ctr Inc
27700 Medical Ctr Rd ... Mission Viejo CA 92691 949-364-1400
Web: www.mission4health.com

Natividad Medical Ctr (NMC)
1441 Constitution Blvd ... Salinas CA 93906 831-755-4111 755-6254
Web: www.natividad.com

North County Health Services
150 Valpreda Rd ... San Marcos CA 92069 760-736-6767 736-6782
Web: www.nchs-health.org

Northeast Valley Health Corp
1172 N Maclay Ave ... San Fernando CA 91340 818-898-1388 365-4031
Web: www.nevhc.org

Northern Inyo Hospital 150 Pioneer Ln ... Bishop CA 93514 760-873-5811 873-6734
Web: www.nih.org

Northridge Hospital Medical Center-Roscoe Blvd Campus
18300 Roscoe Blvd ... Northridge CA 91328 818-885-8500 885-5321
Web: www.northridgehospital.org

O'Connor Hospital 2105 Forest Ave ... San Jose CA 95128 408-947-2500 947-2887
Web: oconnor.dochs.org

Olive View Medical Ctr (OVMC)
14445 Olive View Dr ... Sylmar CA 91342 818-364-1555 364-3011
Web: uclaoliveview.org

Olympia Medical Ctr 5900 W Olympic Blvd ... Los Angeles CA 90036 310-657-5900 932-5163*
**Fax Area Code:* 323 ■ *TF:* 800-874-4325 ■ *Web:* www.olympiamc.com

Orange Coast Memorial Medical Ctr (OCMMC)
9920 Talbert Ave ... Fountain Valley CA 92708 714-378-7000 229-5399
TF: 877-597-4777 ■ *Web:* www.memorialcare.org

Oroville Hospital (OH) 2767 Olive Hwy ... Oroville CA 95966 530-533-8500
Web: www.orovillehospital.com

Pacific Clinics 800 S Santa Anita Ave ... Arcadia CA 91006 626-254-5000
Web: www.pacificclinics.org

PAMC Ltd 531 W College St ... Los Angeles CA 90012 213-624-8411
Web: www.pamc.net

Parkview Community Hospital Medical Ctr (PCHMC)
3865 Jackson St ... Riverside CA 92503 951-688-2211 352-5484
Web: www.pchmc.org

Physicians For Healthy Hospitals
1117 E Devonshire Ave ... Hemet CA 92543 951-652-2811 929-1653
Web: www.valleyhealthsystem.com

Pioneer Medical Group Inc
17777 Ctr Ct Dr N Ste 400 ... Cerritos CA 90703 562-229-9452
Web: www.pioneermedicalgroup.com

Pioneers Memorial Healthcare District (PMHD)
207 W Legion Rd ... Brawley CA 92227 760-351-3333 344-4401
Web: www.pmhd.org

Placentia-Linda Hospital 1301 N Rose Dr ... Placentia CA 92870 714-993-2000 961-8427
TF: 888-754-9729 ■ *Web:* www.placentialinda.com

Pomerado Hospital 15615 Pomerado Rd ... Poway CA 92064 858-613-4000 613-5678
Web: www.palomarhealth.org

Pomona Valley Hospital Medical Ctr
1798 N Garey Ave ... Pomona CA 91767 909-865-9500 865-9796
Web: www.pvhmc.org

Presbyterian Intercommunity Hospital
12401 Washington Blvd ... Whittier CA 90602 562-698-0811
Web: pihhealth.org

Providence Holy Cross Medical Ctr
15031 Rinaldi St ... Mission Hills CA 91345 818-365-8051 898-4688
Web: providence.org/losangeles/facilities/holycross.htm

Providence Saint Joseph Medical Ctr
501 S Buena Vista St ... Burbank CA 91505 818-843-5111
Web: california.providence.org

Queen of the Valley Medical Ctr 1000 Trancas St ... Napa CA 94558 707-252-4411 257-4032
Web: www.thequeen.org

Redlands Community Hospital Foundation
PO Box 3391 ... Redlands CA 92373 909-335-5500
TF: 888-397-4999 ■ *Web:* www.redlandshospital.org

Regional Medical Ctr of San Jose (RMCSJ)
225 N Jackson Ave ... San Jose CA 95116 408-259-5000 729-2884
Web: www.regionalmedicalsanjose.com

Rideout Memorial Hospital 726 Fourth St ... Marysville CA 95901 530-749-4300 751-4226
TF: 888-923-3800 ■ *Web:* www.frhg.org

Riverside Community Hospital
4445 Magnolia Ave ... Riverside CA 92501 951-788-3000 788-3659
Web: riversidecommunityhospital.com

Riverside County Regional Medical Ctr
26520 Cactus Ave ... Moreno Valley CA 92555 951-486-4000 486-4260
Web: www.rcrmc.org

Ronald Reagan Medical Ctr
757 Westwood Plaza ... Los Angeles CA 90095 310-825-9111 825-7271
Web: www.uclahealth.org

Roseville Medical Ctr One Medical Plz ... Roseville CA 95661 916-781-1000 781-1210
Web: www.sutterroseville.org

Saddleback Memorial Medical Ctr
24451 Health Ctr Dr ... Laguna Hills CA 92653 949-837-4500 452-3467
Web: www.memorialcare.org

Saint Agnes Medical Ctr 1303 E Herndon Ave ... Fresno CA 93720 559-450-3000 450-3990
Web: www.samc.com

Saint Bernardine Medical Ctr
2101 N Waterman Ave ... San Bernardino CA 92404 909-883-8711 881-4546
Web: www.stbernardinemedicalcenter.org

Saint Francis Memorial Hospital
900 Hyde St ... San Francisco CA 94109 415-353-6000 353-6631*
**Fax:* Admitting ■ *Web:* www.saintfrancismemorial.org

Saint Helena Hospital 10 Woodland Rd ... Saint Helena CA 94574 707-963-3611 967-5626*
**Fax:* Hum Res ■ *Web:* www.adventisthealth.org/napa-valley/pages/default.aspx

Saint John's Hospital & Health Ctr
2121 Santa Monica Blvd ... Santa Monica CA 90404 310-829-5511 829-8295
Web: www.stjohns.org

Saint Joseph's Medical Ctr
1800 N California St ... Stockton CA 95204 209-943-2000 461-3299
Web: www.stjosephscares.org

Saint Jude Medical Ctr
101 E Valencia Mesa Dr ... Fullerton CA 92835 714-871-3280 992-3029
Web: www.stjudemedicalcenter.org

Saint Rose Hospital 27200 Calaroga Ave ... Hayward CA 94545 510-264-4000 887-7421
Web: www.strosehospital.org

Saint Vincent Medical Ctr
2131 W Third St ... Los Angeles CA 90057 213-484-7111
Web: stvincent.dochs.org

Salinas Valley Memorial Hospital (SVMH)
450 E Romie Ln ... Salinas CA 93901 831-757-4333
TF: 800-722-4673 ■ *Web:* www.svmh.com

San Antonio Community Hospital
999 San BernaRdino Rd ... Upland CA 91786 909-985-2811 985-7659
Web: www.sach.org

San Dimas Community Hospital
1350 W Covina Blvd ... San Dimas CA 91773 909-599-6811 305-5678
Web: www.sandimashospital.com

San Francisco General Hospital Medical Ctr
1001 Potrero Ave Ste 1E21 ... San Francisco CA 94110 415-206-8426 206-8942
TF: 800-723-7140 ■ *Web:* psych.ucsf.edu/sfgh

San Gabriel Valley Medical Ctr
438 W Las Tunas Dr ... San Gabriel CA 91776 626-289-5454 570-6555
Web: www.sgvmc.com

San Joaquin Community Hospital
2615 Eye St ... Bakersfield CA 93301 661-395-3000 869-6962
Web: sjch.us

San Joaquin General Hospital (SJGH)
500 W Hospital Rd ... French Camp CA 95231 209-468-6000 468-6339*

Santa Barbara Cottage Hospital
PO Box 689 ... Santa Barbara CA 93102 805-682-7111
Web: www.cottagehealthsystem.org

Santa Clara Valley Medical Ctr
751 S Bascom Ave ... San Jose CA 95128 408-885-5000 793-1817
Web: www.scvmc.org

Santa Monica UCLA Medical Ctr
1250 16th St ... Santa Monica CA 90404 310-319-4000 319-4821
Web: www.uclahealth.org/homepage_sanmon.cfm?id=265

Santa Rosa Memorial Hospital (SRMH)
1165 Montgomery Dr ... Santa Rosa CA 95405 707-546-3210
Web: stjosephhealth.org/about-us

Scripps Green Hospital
10666 N Torrey Pines Rd ... La Jolla CA 92037 858-455-9100
TF: 800-727-4777 ■ *Web:* www.scripps.org

Scripps Memorial Hospital-Encinitas
354 Santa Fe Dr ... Encinitas CA 92024 760-753-6501 633-7356
Web: www.scripps.org/locations/hospitals__scripps-memorial-hospital-encinitas

Scripps Memorial Hospital-La Jolla
9888 Genesee Ave ... La Jolla CA 92037 800-727-4777
Web: www.scripps.org/locations/hospitals__scripps-memorial-hospital-la-jolla

Scripps Mercy Hospital 4077 Fifth Ave ... San Diego CA 92103 619-294-8111 686-3530
Web: www.scripps.org

Sequoia Hospital 170 Alameda Ave ... Redwood City CA 94062 650-369-5811 367-5288
Web: www.sequoiahospital.org

Sharp Chula Vista Medical Ctr
751 Medical Ctr Ct ... Chula Vista CA 91911 619-482-5800
Web: www.sharp.com/hospital

Sharp Grossmont Hospital (SGH)
5555 Grossmont Ctr Dr ... La Mesa CA 91942 619-740-6000
TF: 800-827-4277 ■ *Web:* www.sharp.com/grossmont

Sharp Memorial Hospital 7901 Frost St ... San Diego CA 92123 858-939-3400
Web: sharp.com

Shasta Regional Medical Ctr (SRMC)
1100 Butte St ... Redding CA 96001 530-244-5400 244-5119
Web: www.shastaregional.com

Sherman Oaks Hospital & Health Ctr
4929 Van Nuys Blvd ... Sherman Oaks CA 91403 818-981-7111
Web: www.shermanoakshospital.org

Sierra Nevada Memorial Hospital
155 Glasson Way ... Grass Valley CA 95945 530-274-6000 274-6614
Web: www.snmh.org

Sierra View District Hospital (SVDH)
465 W Putnam Ave ... Porterville CA 93257 559-784-1110 788-6135
Web: www.sierra-view.com

Sierra Vista Regional Medical Ctr (SVRMC)
1010 Murray Ave ... San Luis Obispo CA 93405 805-546-7600 546-7892
TF: 866-904-6871 ■ *Web:* www.sierravistaregional.com

Phone *Fax*

Simi Valley Hospital (SVH)
2975 N Sycamore Dr .... Simi Valley CA 93065 805-955-6000 955-6072*
Web: www.adventisthealth.org/simi-valley-hospital/pages/default.aspx

Sonora Regional Medical Ctr (SRMC)
1000 Greenly Rd .... Sonora CA 95370 209-536-5000
TF Compliance: 877-336-3566 ■
Web: www.adventisthealth.org/sonora-regional/pages/default.aspx

Sutter Auburn Faith Community Hospital (SAFH)
11815 Education St .... Auburn CA 95602 530-888-4500 886-6611
TF: 800-478-8837 ■ *Web:* www.sutterauburnfaith.org

Sutter General Hospital 2801 L St .... Sacramento CA 95816 916-454-2222 733-3791
Web: www.sutterhealth.org

Sutter Health Sacramento Sierra Region
2801 L St .... Sacramento CA 95816 916-454-2222 733-8894
Web: www.checksutterfirst.org

Sutter Medical Ctr of Santa Rosa
3325 Chanate Rd .... Santa Rosa CA 95404 707-576-4006
TF: 800-651-5111 ■ *Web:* www.suttersantarosa.org

Sutter Memorial Hospital 5151 F St .... Sacramento CA 95819 916-454-3333 733-8135
Web: www.sutterhealth.org

Sutter Solano Medical Ctr (SSMC)
300 Hospital Dr .... Vallejo CA 94589 707-554-4444 648-3227
Web: www.suttersolano.org

Temple Community Hospital
235 N Hoover St .... Los Angeles CA 90004 213-382-7252 388-1959
Web: www.templecommunityhospital.com

Torrance Memorial Medical Ctr
3330 Lomita Blvd .... Torrance CA 90505 310-325-9110 784-4801
TF: 866-843-2572 ■ *Web:* www.torrancememorial.org

Tri-City Medical Ctr 4002 Vista Way .... Oceanside CA 92056 760-724-8411 940-4050
Web: www.tricitymed.org

Tri-City Regional Medical Ctr
21530 S Pioneer Blvd .... Hawaiian Gardens CA 90716 562-860-0401 924-5871
Web: www.tri-cityrmc.org

Tulare Regional Medical Ctr 869 N Cherry .... Tulare CA 93274 559-688-0821
Web: www.tulareregional.org

UC Irvine Healthcare 101 the City Dr S .... Orange CA 92868 714-456-7890 456-7488
TF: 877-824-3627 ■ *Web:* www.ucirvinehealth.org

UCSF Medical Ctr 505 Parnassus Ave .... San Francisco CA 94143 415-476-1000
Web: www.ucsfhealth.org

Ukiah Valley Medical Ctr 275 Hospital Dr .... Ukiah CA 95482 707-462-3111 463-7384
Web: www.adventisthealth.org/ukiah-valley/

University of California Davis Medical Ctr
2315 Stockton Blvd .... Sacramento CA 95817 916-734-2011 734-8080*
**Fax:* Admitting ■ *Web:* www.ucdmc.ucdavis.edu

University of California San Diego Medical Ctr
200 W Arbor Dr .... San Diego CA 92103 619-543-6222 543-7448
TF: 800-926-8273 ■ *Web:* health.ucsd.edu

Valley Presbyterian Hospital
15107 Vanowen St .... Van Nuys CA 91405 818-782-6600 902-5703
Web: www.valleypres.org

Ventura County Medical Center
3291 Loma Vista Rd .... Ventura CA 93003 805-652-6000
TF: 800-369-7437 ■
Web: www.vchca.org/hospitals/ventura-county-medical-center

Verdugo Hills Hospital 1812 Verdugo Blvd .... Glendale CA 91208 818-790-7100 952-4616
Web: www.uscvhh.org

West Anaheim Medical Ctr (WAMC)
3033 W Orange Ave .... Anaheim CA 92804 714-827-3000 229-6813
Web: westanaheimmedctr.com

West Hills Hospital & Medical Center
7300 Medical Centre Dr .... West Hills CA 91307 818-676-4000
Web: westhillshospital.com

Western Medical Ctr Anaheim (WMCA)
1025 S Anaheim Blvd .... Anaheim CA 92805 714-533-6220
Web: www.westernmedanaheim.com

Western Medical Ctr Santa Ana
1001 N Tustin Ave .... Santa Ana CA 92705 714-953-3500 953-3613
Web: www.westernmedicalcenter.com

White Memorial Medical Ctr
1720 Cesar E Chavez Ave .... Los Angeles CA 90033 323-268-5000 881-8605
Web: www.adventisthealth.org/white-memorial/pages/default.aspx

Whittier Hospital Medical Ctr
9080 Colima Rd .... Whittier CA 90605 562-945-3561 693-6811
TF: 800-613-4291 ■ *Web:* www.whittierhospital.com

Woodland Healthcare 1325 Cottonwood St .... Woodland CA 95695 530-662-3961 666-7948
Web: hospitals.dignityhealth.org

Woodland Hills Medical Center
5601 De Soto Ave .... Woodland Hills CA 91365 818-719-2000
Web: kaiserpermanente.org

Colorado

Phone *Fax*

Arkansas Valley Regional Medical Ctr (AVRMC)
1100 Carson Ave .... La Junta CO 81050 719-384-5412 383-6005
TF: 877-696-6775 ■ *Web:* www.avrmc.org

Avista Adventist Hospital
100 Health Pk Dr .... Louisville CO 80027 303-673-1000 673-1048
Web: avistahospital.org

Boulder Community Hospital (BCH)
1100 Balsam Ave .... Boulder CO 80301 303-440-2273 440-2278*
**Fax:* Admitting ■ *Web:* www.bch.org

Denver Health Medical Ctr (DHMC) 777 Bannock St .... Denver CO 80204 303-436-6000 436-6243
Web: www.denverhealth.org

Exempla Lutheran Medical Ctr
8300 W 38th Ave .... Wheat Ridge CO 80033 303-425-4500 425-8198
Web: sclhealthsystem.org/

Exempla Saint Joseph Hospital
1835 Franklin St .... Denver CO 80218 303-837-7111 837-7123
Web: sclhealthsystem.org/

Phone *Fax*

Littleton Adventist Hospital
7700 S Broadway .... Littleton CO 80122 303-730-8900
Web: www.mylittletonhospital.org

Longmont United Hospital (LUH)
1950 Mountain View Ave .... Longmont CO 80501 303-651-5111 678-4050
Web: www.luhcares.org

McKee Medical Ctr 2000 N Boise Ave .... Loveland CO 80538 970-669-4640 635-4112
Web: www.bannerhealth.com

Medical Ctr of Aurora (MCA) 1501 S Potomac St .... Aurora CO 80012 303-695-2600
Web: www.auroramed.com

Memorial Health System (MHS)
Central 1400 E Boulder St .... Colorado Springs CO 80909 719-365-5000 848-5551*
**Fax Area Code:* 720 ■ **Fax:* Admissions ■ *TF:* 877-422-3648 ■
Web: www.uchealth.org/southerncolorado/pages/default.aspx

North Colorado Medical Ctr 1801 16th St .... Greeley CO 80631 970-352-4121 350-6644
Web: www.bannerhealth.com

North Suburban Medical Ctr (NSMC)
9191 Grant St .... Thornton CO 80229 303-451-7800 450-4458
TF: 877-647-7440 ■ *Web:* www.northsuburban.com

OnCure Medical Corp
188 Inverness Dr W Ste 650 .... Englewood CO 80112 303-643-6500 643-6560
Web: www.oncure.com

Parkview Medical Ctr 400 W 16th St .... Pueblo CO 81003 719-584-4000 584-7376
TF: 800-543-4046 ■ *Web:* www.parkviewmc.com

Penrose Hospital 2222 N Nevada Ave .... Colorado Springs CO 80907 719-776-5000 776-2442*
**Fax:* Admitting ■ *Web:* www.penrosestfrancis.org

Porter Adventist Hospital 2525 S Downing St .... Denver CO 80210 303-778-1955 778-5252
Web: www.porterhospital.org

Poudre Valley Hospital 1024 S Lemay Ave .... Fort Collins CO 80524 970-495-7000 495-7601
TF: 800-994-6610 ■
Web: www.uchealth.org/northerncolorado/pages/default.aspx

Presbyterian-Saint Luke's Medical Ctr
1719 E 19th Ave .... Denver CO 80218 303-839-6000 869-2428
Web: www.pslmc.com

Rose Medical Ctr 4567 E Ninth Ave .... Denver CO 80220 303-320-2121 320-2200
TF: 866-746-4282 ■ *Web:* www.rosemed.com

Saint Anthony Central Hospital
11600 W Second Pl .... Lakewood CO 80228 720-321-0000
Web: www.stanthonyhosp.org

Saint Mary's Hospital & Regional Medical Ctr
2635 N Seventh St .... Grand Junction CO 81502 800-458-3888 244-7510*
**Fax Area Code:* 970 ■ *TF:* 800-458-3888 ■ *Web:* stmarygj.org/

Saint Mary-Corwin Medical Ctr
1008 Minnequa Ave .... Pueblo CO 81004 719-557-4000 557-5529*
**Fax:* Admitting ■ *TF:* 800-228-4039 ■ *Web:* www.stmarycorwin.org

San Luis Valley Regional Medical Ctr
106 Blanca Ave .... Alamosa CO 81101 719-589-2511 587-1372
Web: www.sanluisvalleyhealth.org

Swedish Medical Ctr 501 E Hampden Ave .... Englewood CO 80113 303-788-5000 788-6265
Web: www.swedishhospital.com

University of Colorado Hospital
12605 E 16th Ave .... Aurora CO 80045 720-848-0000
Web: www.uchealth.org/metrodenver/pages/default.aspx

Connecticut

Phone *Fax*

Bridgeport Hospital 267 Grant St .... Bridgeport CT 06610 203-384-3000 384-3046
Web: www.bridgeporthospital.org

Bristol Hospital (BH) 41 Brewster Rd .... Bristol CT 06010 860-585-3000 585-3853
Web: www.bristolhospital.org

Charlotte Hungerford Hospital (CHH)
540 Litchfield St .... Torrington CT 06790 860-496-6666 482-8627
Web: charlottehungerford.org

Danbury Hospital (DH) 24 Hospital Ave .... Danbury CT 06810 203-739-6398
TF: 800-516-3658 ■ *Web:* www.danburyhospital.org

Greenwich Hospital 5 Perryridge Rd .... Greenwich CT 06830 203-863-3000 863-3845
TF: 800-657-8355 ■ *Web:* www.greenhosp.org

Griffin Hospital 130 Div St .... Derby CT 06418 203-735-7421 732-7569
Web: www.griffinhealth.org

Hartford Hospital 80 Seymour St .... Hartford CT 06102 860-545-5000 545-3622
TF: 800-545-7664 ■ *Web:* www.harthosp.org

Hospital of Saint Raphael 1450 Chapel St .... New Haven CT 06511 203-789-3000 867-5235
TF: 888-700-6543 ■ *Web:* www.ynhh.org

Lawrence & Memorial Hospital
365 Montauk Ave .... New London CT 06320 860-442-0711
Web: www.lmhospital.org

Manchester Memorial Hospital 71 Haynes St .... Manchester CT 06040 860-646-1222
Web: townofmanchester.org

Middlesex Hospital 28 Crescent St .... Middletown CT 06457 860-358-6000 358-2626
TF: 800-548-2394 ■ *Web:* www.middlesexhospital.org

Milford Hospital (MH) 300 Seaside Ave .... Milford CT 06460 203-876-4000 876-4220
Web: www.milfordhospital.org

New Britain General Campus 100 Grand St .... New Britain CT 06050 860-224-5011
Web: www.nbgh.org

Norwalk Hospital 34 Maple St .... Norwalk CT 06856 203-852-2000 855-3780
TF: 800-789-4584 ■ *Web:* www.norwalkhospital.org

Rockville General Hospital 31 Union St .... Vernon CT 06066 860-872-0501 872-5393
Web: www.echn.org

Saint Francis Hospital & Medical Ctr
114 Woodland St .... Hartford CT 06105 860-714-4000 714-8038
TF: 800-993-4312 ■ *Web:* www.stfranciscare.org

Saint Vincent's Medical Ctr 2800 Main St .... Bridgeport CT 06606 203-576-6000 576-5345
TF: 877-255-7847 ■ *Web:* www.stvincents.org

Stamford Hospital 30 Shelburne Rd .... Stamford CT 06904 203-276-1000
Web: www.stamfordhospital.org

University of Connecticut Health Ctr
John Dempsey Hospital 263 Farmington Ave .... Farmington CT 06030 860-679-2000 679-1255
TF: 800-535-6232 ■ *Web:* www.uchc.edu

Veterans Admin Medical Center
555 Willard Ave .... Newington CT 06111 860-666-6951 667-6764

				Phone	Fax
Waterbury Hospital 64 Robbins St. *Web:* waterburyhospital.org	Waterbury	CT	06721	203-573-6000	573-6161
William W Backus Hospital 326 Washington St *Web:* backushospital.org	Norwich	CT	06360	860-889-8331	823-1501
Windham Community Memorial Hospital (WCMH) 112 Mansfield Ave *Web:* www.windhamhospital.org	Willimantic	CT	06226	860-456-9116	456-6838
Yale-New Haven Hospital 20 York St. *Web:* www.ynhh.org	New Haven	CT	06504	203-688-4242	

Delaware

				Phone	Fax
Bayhealth Medical Ctr 21 W Clarke Ave **Fax Area Code:* 855 ■ *TF:* 877-453-7107 ■ *Web:* www.bayhealth.org	Milford	DE	19963	302-430-5738	420-6223*
Beebe Medical Ctr 424 Savannah Rd *Web:* beebehealthcare.org/	Lewes	DE	19958	302-645-3300	645-3405
Christiana Hospital 4755 Ogletown-Stanton Rd. **Fax:* Admitting ■ *Web:* www.christianacare.org	Newark	DE	19718	302-733-1000	733-1313*
Kent General Hospital 640 S State St *TF:* 888-761-8300 ■ *Web:* www.bayhealth.org	Dover	DE	19901	302-674-4700	674-2202
Nanticoke Memorial Hospital 801 Middleford Rd *Web:* www.nanticoke.org	Seaford	DE	19973	302-629-6611	629-2493

District of Columbia

				Phone	Fax
George Washington University Hospital 900 23rd St NW *TF:* 888-449-3627 ■ *Web:* www.gwhospital.com	Washington	DC	20037	202-715-4000	
Georgetown University Hospital 3800 Reservoir Rd NW *Web:* www.gumc.georgetown.edu	Washington	DC	20007	202-687-0100	784-2875
Howard University Hospital 2041 Georgia Ave *Web:* huhealthcare.com	Washington	DC	20060	202-865-6100	865-1360
Providence Hospital 1150 Varnum St NE *Web:* www.provhosp.org	Washington	DC	20017	202-269-7000	269-7160
Sibley Memorial Hospital 5255 Loughboro Rd NW **Fax:* Admissions ■ *Web:* www.sibley.org	Washington	DC	20016	202-537-4000	243-2246*
Washington Hospital Ctr 110 Irving St NW *Web:* www.medstarhealth.org	Washington	DC	20010	202-877-7000	877-7826

Florida

				Phone	Fax
Aventura Hospital 20900 Biscayne Blvd *TF:* 800-523-5772 ■ *Web:* www.aventurahospital.com	Aventura	FL	33180	305-682-7000	682-7105
Baptist Hospital 1000 W Moreno St *Web:* www.ebaptisthealthcare.org	Pensacola	FL	32501	850-434-4011	434-4702
Baptist Hospital of Miami 8900 SW 88th St **Fax Area Code:* 305 ■ *TF:* 800-994-6610 ■ *Web:* www.baptisthealth.net	Miami	FL	33176	786-596-1960	598-5910*
Baptist Medical Ctr 800 Prudential Dr *TF:* 800-874-8567 ■ *Web:* www.baptistjax.com	Jacksonville	FL	32207	904-202-2000	
Bay Medical Ctr 615 N Bonita Ave *TF:* 800-222-1222 ■ *Web:* www.baymedical.org	Panama City	FL	32401	850-769-1511	
Blake Medical Ctr 2020 59th St W *Web:* www.blakemedicalcenter.com	Bradenton	FL	34209	941-792-6611	798-6209
Boca Raton Regional Hospital 800 Meadows Rd *Web:* www.brrh.com	Boca Raton	FL	33486	561-395-7100	955-4884
Brandon Regional Hospital 119 Oakfield Dr *Web:* www.brandonhospital.com	Brandon	FL	33511	813-681-5551	654-7203
Brooksville Regional Hospital 17240 Cortez Blvd *TF:* 844-455-8708 ■ *Web:* bayfrontbrooksville.com/	Brooksville	FL	34601	352-796-5111	544-5711
Capital Regional Medical Ctr (CRMC) 2626 Capital Medical Blvd *TF:* 800-994-6610 ■ *Web:* www.capitalregionalmedicalcenter.com	Tallahassee	FL	32308	850-325-5000	325-5198
Central Florida Regional Hospital 1401 W Seminole Blvd *Web:* www.centralfloridaregional.com	Sanford	FL	32771	407-321-4500	
Charlotte Regional Medical Ctr 809 E Marion Ave *Web:* bayfrontcharlotte.com/	Punta Gorda	FL	33950	941-639-3131	637-2579
Citrus Memorial Hospital 502 W Highland Blvd *Web:* www.citrusmh.com	Inverness	FL	34452	352-726-1551	
Cleveland Clinic Hospital 2950 Cleveland Clinic Blvd *TF:* 866-293-7866 ■ *Web:* my.clevelandclinic.org	Weston	FL	33331	954-689-5000	689-5165
Columbia Hospital 2201 45th St *Web:* westpalmhospital.com	West Palm Beach	FL	33407	561-842-6141	881-2650
Community Hospital 5637 Marine Pkwy *Web:* medicalcentertrinity.com	New Port Richey	FL	34652	727-848-1733	
Coral Gables Hospital Inc (CGH) 3100 Douglas Rd *TF:* 866-728-3677 ■ *Web:* www.coralgableshospital.com	Coral Gables	FL	33134	305-445-8461	441-6879
Coral Springs Medical Ctr 3000 Coral Hills Dr *Web:* www.browardhealth.org	Coral Springs	FL	33065	954-344-3000	344-3146
Delray Medical Ctr (DMC) 5352 Linton Blvd *Web:* www.delraymedicalctr.com	Delray Beach	FL	33484	561-498-4440	495-3103
DeSoto Memorial Hospital Inc 900 N Robert Ave *Web:* www.dmh.org	Arcadia	FL	34266	863-494-3535	494-8400
Doctors Hospital Sarasota 5731 Bee Ridge Rd *Web:* www.doctorsofsarasota.com	Sarasota	FL	34233	941-342-1100	
Doctors' Hospital 5000 University Dr *Web:* www.baptisthealth.net	Coral Gables	FL	33146	786-308-3000	308-3402
Edward White Hospital 2323 Ninth Ave N *Web:* www.edwardwhitehospital.com	Saint Petersburg	FL	33713	727-323-1111	328-6226
Fawcett Memorial Hospital 21298 Olean Blvd *Web:* www.fawcetthospital.com	Port Charlotte	FL	33952	941-629-1181	627-6141
Florida Hospital Heartland Medical Ctr 4200 Sun 'n Lake Blvd PO Box 9400 *TF:* 800-756-4447 ■ *Web:* floridahospital.com	Sebring	FL	33871	863-314-4466	402-3415
Florida Hospital North Pinellas 1395 S Pinellas Ave *Web:* www.floridahospital.com	Tarpon Springs	FL	34689	727-942-5000	
Florida Hospital Oceanside 264 S Atlantic Ave *Web:* www.floridahospital.com	Ormond Beach	FL	32176	386-672-4161	231-3323
Florida Hospital Orlando 601 E Rollins St *Web:* www.floridahospital.com	Orlando	FL	32803	407-303-2800	
Florida Hospital Zephyrhills 7050 Gall Blvd *Web:* www.floridahospital.com	Zephyrhills	FL	33541	813-788-0411	783-6196
Fort Walton Beach Medical Ctr (FWBMC) 1000 Mar-Walt Dr *Web:* www.fwbmc.com	Fort Walton Beach	FL	32547	850-862-1111	862-9149
Gulf Coast Medical Ctr 13681 Doctors Way *TF:* 800-809-9906 ■ *Web:* www.leememorial.org/facilities/gcmcenter.asp	Fort Myers	FL	33912	239-343-1000	768-8379
Health First Cape Canaveral Hospital 701 W Cocoa Beach Cswy *Web:* www.health-first.org	Cocoa Beach	FL	32931	321-799-7111	434-6103
Holmes Regional Medical Ctr 1350 Hickory St *TF:* 800-716-7737 ■ *Web:* www.health-first.org	Melbourne	FL	32901	321-434-7000	727-1200
Homestead Hospital 975 Baptist Way *Web:* www.baptisthealth.net	Homestead	FL	33033	786-243-8000	243-8557
Imperial Point Medical Ctr 6401 N Federal Hwy *Web:* www.browardhealth.org	Fort Lauderdale	FL	33308	954-776-8500	776-8520
Indian River Medical Ctr 1000 36th St *Web:* www.indianrivermedicalcenter.com	Vero Beach	FL	32960	772-567-4311	562-5628
Jackson Memorial Hospital 1611 NW 12th Ave *Web:* www.jacksonhealth.org	Miami	FL	33136	305-585-1111	326-9470
Jupiter Medical Ctr 1210 S Old Dixie Hwy *Web:* www.jupitermed.com	Jupiter	FL	33458	561-649-3138	
Kendall Regional Medical Ctr 11750 SW 40th St *Web:* www.kendallmed.com	Miami	FL	33175	305-223-3000	229-2481
Lakeland Regional Health 1324 Lakeland Hills Blvd PO Box 95448 *Web:* www.lrmc.com	Lakeland	FL	33805	863-687-1100	687-1214
Largo Medical Center - Indian Rocks Rd Campus 2025 Indian Rocks Rd	Largo	FL	33774	727-581-9474	586-7106
Lawnwood Regional Medical Ctr (LRMC) 1700 S 23rd St *Web:* www.lawnwoodmed.com	Fort Pierce	FL	34950	772-461-4000	460-1353
Leesburg Regional Medical Ctr (LRMC) 600 E Dixie Ave *Web:* cfhalliance.org	Leesburg	FL	34748	352-323-5762	323-5009
Lower Keys Medical Ctr 5900 College Rd *TF:* 800-355-2470 ■ *Web:* www.lkmc.com	Key West	FL	33040	305-294-5531	294-8065
Manatee County Rural Health Services Inc (MCRHS) 12271 US Hwy 301 PO Box 499 *Web:* www.mcrhs.org	Parrish	FL	34219	941-776-4000	
Manatee Memorial Hospital 206 Second St E *TF:* 844-854-9613 ■ *Web:* www.manateememorial.com	Bradenton	FL	34208	941-746-5111	745-6862
Martin Memorial Health Systems (MMHS) 200 SE Hospital Ave PO Box 9010 *TF:* 800-368-3375 ■ *Web:* www.martinhealth.org	Stuart	FL	34994	772-287-5200	223-5946
Mease Dunedin Hospital 601 Main St	Dunedin	FL	34698	727-733-1111	734-6887
Memorial Hospital of Tampa 2901 W Swann Ave *Web:* www.memorialhospitaltampa.com	Tampa	FL	33609	813-873-6400	874-8685
Memorial Hospital Pembroke (MHP) 7800 Sheridan St *Web:* www.memorialpembroke.com	Pembroke Pines	FL	33024	954-962-9650	
Memorial Hospital West 703 N Flamingo Rd *Web:* www.memorialwest.com	Pembroke Pines	FL	33028	954-436-5000	
Memorial Regional Hospital 3501 Johnson St *Web:* www.memorialregional.com	Hollywood	FL	33021	954-987-2000	985-1428
Mercy Hospital 3663 S Miami Ave *Web:* www.mercymiami.com	Miami	FL	33133	305-854-4400	285-2173
Morton Plant Hospital 300 Pinellas St *Web:* www.baycare.org	Clearwater	FL	33756	727-462-7000	
Mount Sinai Medical Ctr 4300 Alton Rd *Web:* www.msmc.com	Miami Beach	FL	33140	305-674-2121	674-2007
NCH Healthcare System 350 Seventh St N *Web:* www.nchmd.org	Naples	FL	34102	239-436-5000	436-5914
NCH North Naples Hospital 11190 Health Park Blvd *Web:* nchmd.org	Naples	FL	34110	239-552-7000	
North Broward Medical Ctr 201 E Sample Rd *Web:* www.browardhealth.org	Deerfield Beach	FL	33064	954-941-8300	
North Florida Regional Medical Ctr 6500 Newberry Rd *Web:* www.nfrmc.com	Gainesville	FL	32605	352-333-4000	333-4800
North Okaloosa Medical Ctr (NOMC) 151 E Redstone Ave *Web:* www.northokaloosa.com	Crestview	FL	32539	850-689-8100	689-8484
North Shore Medical Ctr 1100 NW 95th St *TF:* 800-984-3434 ■ *Web:* www.northshoremedical.com	Miami	FL	33150	305-835-6000	835-6163
Northside Hospital 6000 49th St N *Web:* www.northsidehospital.com	Saint Petersburg	FL	33709	727-521-4411	521-5007
Oakhill Hospital 11375 Cortez Blvd *Web:* www.oakhillhospital.com	Brooksville	FL	34613	352-596-6632	597-6387

	Phone	Fax

Ocala Regional Medical Ctr (ORMC)
1431 SW First Ave ... Ocala FL 34478 352-401-1000 401-1198
Web: www.ocalahealthsystem.com/about/ocala-regional-medical-center.dot

Orange Park Medical Ctr
2001 Kingsley Ave ... Orange Park FL 32073 904-276-8500
Web: www.orangeparkmedical.com

Orlando Regional Medical Ctr (ORMC)
1414 Kuhl Ave ... Orlando FL 32806 321-841-5111 649-6845*
**Fax Area Code:* 407 ■ *TF:* 800-424-6998 ■ *Web:* www.orlandohealth.com

Orlando Regional South Seminole Hospital
555 W State Rd 434 ... Longwood FL 32750 407-767-1200 767-5801
Web: www.orlandohealth.com/southseminolehospital

Osceola Regional Medical Ctr 700 W Oak St... Kissimmee FL 34741 407-846-2266 518-3616
Web: www.osceolaregional.com

Pacer Corp
14100 Palmetto Frontage Rd Ste 110 ... Miami Lakes FL 33016 305-828-7660 828-2551
Web: www.pacerco.com

Palm Beach Gardens Medical Ctr
3360 Burns Rd ... Palm Beach Gardens FL 33410 561-622-1411 694-7160
Web: www.pbgmc.com

Palm Springs General Hospital 1475 W 49th St... Hialeah FL 33012 305-558-2500 816-1903
Web: psghosp.com

Palms of Pasadena Hospital
1501 Pasadena Ave S ... Saint Petersburg FL 33707 727-381-1000 341-7570
Web: www.palmspasadena.com

Palms West Hospital (PWH)
13001 Southern Blvd ... Loxahatchee FL 33470 561-798-3300 791-2535
TF: 877-549-9337 ■ *Web:* www.palmswesthospital.com

Parrish Medical Ctr 951 N Washington Ave... Titusville FL 32796 321-268-6111 268-6231
Web: www.parrishmed.com

Peace River Regional Medical Ctr
2500 Harbor Blvd ... Port Charlotte FL 33952 941-766-4122 766-4140
TF: 888-941-2495 ■ *Web:* bayfrontcharlotte.com/

Physicians Regional Medical Center
6101 Pine Ridge Rd ... Naples FL 34119 239-348-4000 304-4439
Web: physiciansregional.com

Raulerson Hospital 1796 Hwy 441 N ... Okeechobee FL 34972 863-763-2151 824-2991
TF: 800-449-8642 ■ *Web:* www.raulersonhospital.com

Regional Medical Ctr Bayonet Point
14000 Fivay Rd... Hudson FL 34667 727-819-2929 869-5491
Web: www.rmchealth.com

Sacred Heart Hospital of Pensacola
5151 N Ninth Ave... Pensacola FL 32504 850-416-7000 416-7337
TF: 800-874-1026 ■ *Web:* www.sacred-heart.org

Saint Anthony's Hospital
1200 Seventh Ave N ... Saint Petersburg FL 33705 727-825-1100 825-1230
Web: www.stanthonys.com

Saint Lucie Medical Ctr
1800 SE Tiffany Ave ... Port Saint Lucie FL 34952 772-335-4000 398-3608
Web: www.stluciemed.com

Sarasota Memorial Hospital
1700 S Tamiami Trl... Sarasota FL 34239 941-917-9000 917-1716
TF: 800-764-8255 ■ *Web:* www.smh.com

Sebastian River Medical Ctr 13695 US Hwy 1... Sebastian FL 32976 772-589-3186
Web: www.srmcenter.com

Seven Rivers Regional Medical Ctr (SRRMC)
6201 N Suncoast Blvd ... Crystal River FL 34428 352-795-6560 795-8369
Web: www.sevenriversregional.com

Shands Hospital at the University of Florida
1600 SW Archer Rd ... Gainesville FL 32610 352-265-0111 627-4173
TF: 855-483-7546 ■ *Web:* ufhealth.org

South Bay Hospital
4016 Sun City Ctr Blvd... Sun City Center FL 33573 813-634-3301 634-8712
Web: www.southbayhospital.com

South Florida Baptist Hospital
301 N Alexander St... Plant City FL 33563 813-757-1200 757-8209
Web: www.sjbhealth.org/home_south.cfm?id=587

South Miami Hospital 6200 SW 73rd St... Miami FL 33143 786-662-4000 662-5302
Web: www.baptisthealth.net

Southwest Florida Regional Medical Ctr
2727 Winkler Ave... Fort Myers FL 33901 239-939-8457
Web: www.leememorial.org

St Petersburg General Hospital
6500 38th Ave N... Saint Petersburg FL 33710 727-384-1414 341-4889
TF: 800-733-0610 ■ *Web:* www.stpetegeneral.com

Tampa General Hospital One Tampa General Cir... Tampa FL 33606 813-844-7000 844-4144
Web: www.tgh.org

Town & Country Hospital 6001 Webb Rd... Tampa FL 33615 813-888-7060 887-5112
Web: tampacommunityhospital.com/

UF Health Jacksonville 655 W Eigth St ... Jacksonville FL 32209 904-244-0411 244-2587
Web: ufhealthjax.org/

University Community Hospital
3100 E Fletcher Ave... Tampa FL 33613 813-971-6000 615-8100
Web: www.floridahospital.com

University Community Hospital Carrollwood
7171 N Dale Mabry Hwy... Tampa FL 33614 813-932-2222 558-8011
Web: www.floridahospital.com

University Hospital 7201 N University Dr... Tamarac FL 33321 954-721-2200 724-6575
Web: www.uhmchealth.com

Venice Regional Medical Ctr (VRMC)
540 The Rialto ... Venice FL 34285 941-485-7711 483-7699
Web: www.veniceregional.com

West Boca Medical Ctr (WBMC)
21644 State Rd 7 ... Boca Raton FL 33428 561-488-8000 488-8105
Web: www.westbocamedctr.com

West Florida Hospital 8383 N Davis Hwy... Pensacola FL 32514 850-494-4000
Web: www.westfloridahospital.com

Westside Regional Medical Ctr
8201 W Broward Blvd... Plantation FL 33324 954-473-6600 476-3974
Web: www.westsideregional.com

Winter Haven Hospital 200 Ave F NE... Winter Haven FL 33881 863-293-1121 292-4376
Web: baycare.org/winter-haven-hospital

Wuesthoff Medical Ctr Rockledge
110 Longwood Ave... Rockledge FL 32955 321-636-2211 597-9629*
**Fax Area Code:* 818 ■ *TF:* 800-999-6673 ■ *Web:* www.wuesthoff.com

Georgia

	Phone	Fax

Athens Regional Medical Ctr (ARMC)
1199 Prince Ave... Athens GA 30606 706-475-7000 475-6775
Web: www.athenshealth.org

Atlanta Medical Ctr 303 Pkwy Dr NE... Atlanta GA 30312 404-265-4000 265-3903
Web: www.atlantamedcenter.com

Candler Hospital 5353 Reynolds St... Savannah GA 31405 912-819-6000 819-5887
Web: www.sjchs.org

Coffee Regional Medical Ctr (CRMC)
1101 Ocilla Rd ... Douglas GA 31533 912-384-1900 383-5667
Web: www.coffeeregional.org

Coliseum Medical Ctr 350 Hospital Dr ... Macon GA 31217 478-765-7000 742-1247
Web: www.coliseumhealthsystem.com

Colquitt Regional Medical Ctr (CRMC)
3131 S Main St PO Box 40... Moultrie GA 31768 229-985-3420
TF: 888-262-2762 ■ *Web:* www.colquittregional.com

Dodge County Hospital 901 Griffin Ave ... Eastman GA 31023 478-448-4000
Web: www.dodgecountyhospital.com

East Georgia Regional Medical Ctr (EGRMC)
1499 Fair Rd... Statesboro GA 30458 912-486-1000 871-2354
TF: 844-455-8708 ■ *Web:* www.eastgeorgiaregional.com

Eastside Medical Ctr 1700 Medical Way... Snellville GA 30078 770-979-0200 736-2395
Web: www.eastsidemedical.com

Emory Crawford Long Hospital
550 Peachtree St NE... Atlanta GA 30308 404-686-4411 686-8956
Web: www.emoryhealthcare.org

Emory University Hospital 1364 Clifton Rd... Atlanta GA 30322 404-712-2000 686-8500
Web: www.emoryhealthcare.org

Fairview Park Hospital 200 Industrial Blvd... Dublin GA 31021 478-275-2000 272-0211
Web: www.fairviewparkhospital.com

Floyd Medical Ctr 304 Turner McCall Blvd ... Rome GA 30165 706-509-5000 509-6901
TF: 866-874-2772 ■ *Web:* www.floyd.org

Grady Health System 80 Jesse Hill Jr Dr SE... Atlanta GA 30303 404-616-1000 616-6828
Web: www.gradyhealth.org

Gwinnett Medical Ctr Lawrenceville
1000 Medical Ctr Blvd ... Lawrenceville GA 30046 678-312-1000 682-2257*
**Fax Area Code:* 770 ■ *Web:* www.gwinnettmedicalcenter.org

Hamilton Medical Ctr
1200 Memorial Dr PO Box 1168... Dalton GA 30720 706-272-6000
Web: www.hamiltonhealth.com

Houston Medical Ctr 1601 Watson Blvd... Warner Robins GA 31093 478-922-4281 542-7955
Web: www.hhc.org

Hughes Spalding Children's Hospital
35 Jesse Hill Jr Dr Se... Atlanta GA 30303 404-785-9500 785-6021
Web: www.choa.org/hughesspalding

Hutcheson Medical Ctr (HMC)
100 Gross Crescent Cir ... Fort Oglethorpe GA 30742 706-858-2000 858-2111
Web: www.hutcheson.org

John D Archbold Memorial Hospital
915 Gordon Ave... Thomasville GA 31792 229-228-2000 551-8741
TF: 800-341-1009 ■ *Web:* www.archbold.org

Meadows Regional Medical Ctr (MRMC)
One Meadows Pkwy ... Vidalia GA 30474 912-535-5555
Web: www.meadowsregional.org

Medical College of Georgia Hospital & Clinics
1120 15th St... Augusta GA 30912 706-721-0211
TF: 800-736-2273 ■ *Web:* www.grhealth.org

Memorial Health University Medical Ctr
4700 Waters Ave... Savannah GA 31404 912-350-8000 350-7073
Web: www.memorialhealth.com

Memorial Hospital of Adel 706 N Parrish Ave ... Adel GA 31620 229-896-8000 896-8001
Web: www.memorialofadel.com

Navicent Health 777 Hemlock St... Macon GA 31201 478-633-1000
Web: www.mccg.org

Newton Medical Ctr 5126 Hospital Dr NE ... Covington GA 30014 770-786-7053 385-4256
Web: www.newtonmedical.com

North Fulton Hospital 3000 Hospital Blvd ... Roswell GA 30076 770-751-2500 751-2912
TF: 877-228-3638 ■ *Web:* www.nfultonhospital.com

Northeast Georgia Health System Inc (NGHS)
743 Spring St NE... Gainesville GA 30501 770-535-3553 219-5437
Web: www.nghs.com

Oconee Regional Medical Ctr
821 N Cobb St ... Milledgeville GA 31061 478-454-3505 454-3555
Web: www.oconeeregional.com

Palmyra Medical Centers (PMC) 2000 Palmyra Rd... Albany GA 31701 229-434-2000 434-2563
Web: beta.ehc.com

Phoebe Putney Memorial Hospital
417 W Third Ave... Albany GA 31702 229-312-1000 889-7384
TF: 877-312-1167 ■ *Web:* www.phoebeputney.com

Phoebe Sumter Medical Ctr 1048 E Forsyth St... Americus GA 31709 229-924-6011
Web: www.phoebesumter.org

Piedmont Healthcare
1133 Eagle's Landing Pkwy... Stockbridge GA 30281 678-604-1000 604-5580
Web: www.piedmont.org

Piedmont Hospital 1968 Peachtree Rd NW... Atlanta GA 30309 404-605-5000 609-6661
Web: www.piedmont.org

Piedmont Newnan Hospital (PNH) 60 Hospital Rd... Newnan GA 30263 770-400-1000
Web: www.piedmont.org

Redmond Regional Medical Ctr 501 Redmond Rd ... Rome GA 30165 706-291-0291 291-0971
Web: www.redmondregional.com

Rockdale Medical Ctr (RMC) 1412 Milstead Ave NE ... Conyers GA 30012 770-918-3000 918-3104
Web: www.rockdalemedicalcenter.org

Saint Joseph's Hospital of Atlanta
5665 Peachtree Dunwoody Rd NE ... Atlanta GA 30342 404-851-7001 851-7339
Web: www.emoryhealthcare.org

Hospital	City	State	Zip	Phone	Fax
Saint Mary's Health Care System 1230 Baxter St *TF:* 800-233-7864 ■ *Web:* www.stmarysathens.org	Athens	GA	30606	706-389-3000	
South Georgia Medical Ctr 2501 N Patterson St *Web:* www.sgmc.org	Valdosta	GA	31602	229-333-1000	259-4136
Southeast Georgia Health System Brunswick Campus 2415 Parkwood Dr *TF:* 844-882-7227 ■ *Web:* www.sghs.org	Brunswick	GA	31520	912-466-7000	466-7013
Southern Regional Medical Ctr 11 Upper Riverdale Rd SW *Web:* www.southernregional.org	Riverdale	GA	30274	770-991-8000	
Spalding Regional Medical Ctr 601 S Eigth St *TF:* 866-717-5826 ■ *Web:* www.spaldingregional.com	Griffin	GA	30224	770-228-2721	229-6953
Tanner Medical Ctr 705 Dixie St *Web:* www.tanner.org	Carrollton	GA	30117	770-836-9666	838-8483
Tift Regional Medical Ctr 1641 Madison Ave *TF:* 800-648-1935 ■ *Web:* www.tiftregional.com	Tifton	GA	31794	229-382-7120	353-6192
University Health Care System 1350 Walton Way *TF:* 866-591-2502 ■ *Web:* www.universityhealth.org	Augusta	GA	30901	706-722-9011	774-4500
Upson Regional Medical Ctr 801 W Gordon St *Web:* www.urmc.org	Thomaston	GA	30286	706-647-8111	646-3310
Wayne Memorial Hospital (WMH) 865 S First St *Web:* www.wmhweb.com	Jesup	GA	31545	912-427-6811	530-3495
Wellstar Cobb Hospital 3950 Austell Rd *Web:* www.wellstar.org	Austell	GA	30106	770-732-4000	732-3703
Wellstar Douglas Hospital 8954 Hospital Dr *Web:* www.wellstar.org	Douglasville	GA	30134	770-949-1500	920-6253
Wellstar Kennestone Hospital 677 Church St *Web:* www.wellstar.org	Marietta	GA	30060	770-793-5000	
West Georgia Medical Ctr 1514 Vernon Rd *Web:* www.wghs.org	LaGrange	GA	30240	706-882-1411	

Hawaii

Hospital	City	State	Zip	Phone	Fax
Castle Medical Ctr 640 Ulukahiki St *Web:* www.adventisthealth.org/castle/pages/castle-home.aspx	Kailua	HI	96734	808-263-5500	
Hilo Medical Ctr 1190 Waianuenue Ave *Web:* www.hmc.hhsc.org	Hilo	HI	96720	808-932-3000	974-4746
Kaiser Permanente Medical Ctr 3288 Moanalua Rd *Web:* kaiserpermanente.org	Honolulu	HI	96819	808-432-0000	432-7736
Kuakini Health System 347 N Kuakini St *Web:* www.kuakini.org	Honolulu	HI	96817	808-536-2236	547-9547
Maui Memorial Hospital 221 Mahalani St *TF:* 800-427-5940 ■ *Web:* www.mmmc.hhsc.org	Wailuku	HI	96793	808-244-9056	242-2443
Queen's Medical Ctr, The 1301 Punchbowl St *Web:* www.queensmedicalcenter.org	Honolulu	HI	96813	808-691-7171	
Straub Clinic & Hospital 888 S King St *TF:* 800-232-9491 ■ *Web:* straubhealth.org	Honolulu	HI	96813	808-522-4000	522-4011
Wilcox Memorial Hospital (WMH) 3-3420 Kuhio Hwy *TF:* 877-709-9355 ■ *Web:* www.hawaiipacifichealth.org	Lihue	HI	96766	808-245-1100	

Idaho

Hospital	City	State	Zip	Phone	Fax
Eastern Idaho Regional Medical Ctr (EIRMC) 3100 Channing Way *Web:* www.eirmc.com	Idaho Falls	ID	83404	208-529-6111	529-7021
Portneuf Medical Ctr 651 Memorial Dr *Web:* www.portmed.org	Pocatello	ID	83201	208-239-1000	239-1934
Saint Alphonsus Regional Medical Ctr 1055 N Curtis Rd *TF:* 877-401-3627 ■ *Web:* www.saintalphonsus.org	Boise	ID	83706	208-367-2121	
Saint Joseph Regional Medical Ctr 415 Sixth St *Web:* www.sjrmc.org	Lewiston	ID	83501	208-743-2511	
West Valley Medical Ctr 1717 Arlington Ave *Fax Area Code: 877 ■ *TF:* 866-270-2311 ■ *Web:* www.westvalleymedctr.com	Caldwell	ID	83605	208-459-4641	865-9738*

Illinois

Hospital	City	State	Zip	Phone	Fax
Adventist Hinsdale Hospital 120 N Oak St *Web:* www.keepingyouwell.com/facilities/hinsdale	Hinsdale	IL	60521	630-856-9000	
Adventist La Grange Memorial Hospital (ALMH) 5101 S Willow Springs Rd *Web:* www.keepingyouwell.com/facilities/lagrange	La Grange	IL	60525	708-245-9000	245-5646
Advocate BroMenn Medical Ctr (ABMC) 1304 Franklin Ave *Web:* www.advocatehealth.com/bromenn/default.cfm?id=1	Normal	IL	61761	309-454-1400	454-0103
Advocate Christ Medical Ctr 4440 W 95th St *Web:* www.advocatehealth.com	Oak Lawn	IL	60453	708-684-8000	684-5012
Advocate Condell Medical Ctr (ACMC) 801 S Milwaukee Ave *Web:* www.advocatehealth.com/condell	Libertyville	IL	60048	847-362-2900	362-1721
Advocate Good Samaritan Hospital 3815 Highland Ave *Web:* www.advocatehealth.com	Downers Grove	IL	60515	630-275-5900	963-8605
Advocate Good Shepherd Hospital (AGSH) 450 W Hwy 22 PO Box 70014 *Web:* www.advocatehealth.com/gshp	Barrington	IL	60010	847-381-9600	381-8074
Advocate Illinois Masonic Medical Ctr 836 W Wellington Ave *Web:* www.advocatehealth.com	Chicago	IL	60657	773-975-1600	296-5251
Advocate Lutheran General Hospital 1775 W Dempster St *Web:* www.advocatehealth.com	Park Ridge	IL	60068	847-723-2210	723-2285
Advocate Sherman Hospital 1425 N Randall Rd *TF:* 800-397-9000 ■ *Web:* www.shermanhealth.com	Elgin	IL	60123	847-742-9800	
Advocate South Suburban Hospital (SSUB) 17800 S Kedzie Ave *Web:* www.advocatehealth.com/ssub	Hazel Crest	IL	60429	708-799-8000	213-0100
Advocate Trinity Hospital 2320 E 93rd St *Web:* www.advocatehealth.com/trin	Chicago	IL	60617	773-967-2000	
Alexian Bros Medical Ctr 800 Biesterfield Rd *TF:* 800-432-5005 ■ *Web:* www.alexianbrothershealth.org	Elk Grove Village	IL	60007	847-437-5500	981-5774
Alton Memorial Hospital 1 Memorial Dr *Web:* www.altonmemorialhospital.org	Alton	IL	62002	618-463-7311	463-7290
Anderson Hospital 6800 SR 162 *Web:* www.andersonhospital.org	Maryville	IL	62062	618-288-5711	288-4088
Blessing Hospital Broadway at 11th St *Web:* www.blessinghospital.org	Quincy	IL	62301	217-223-8400	223-6891
Carle Foundation Hospital 611 W Pk St *Web:* www.carle.org	Urbana	IL	61801	217-383-3311	383-3137
Centegra Memorial Medical Ctr 3701 Doty Rd *TF:* 877-236-8347 ■ *Web:* www.centegra.org	Woodstock	IL	60098	815-338-2500	334-3948
Centegra Northern Illinois Medical Ctr 4201 Medical Ctr Dr *Web:* www.centegra.org	McHenry	IL	60050	815-344-5000	759-4387
Central DuPage Hospital 25 N Winfield Rd *TF:* 800-223-9776 ■ *Web:* www.cdh.org	Winfield	IL	60190	630-933-1600	933-1550
CGH Medical Ctr (CGHMC) 100 E LeFevre Rd *TF:* 800-625-4790 ■ *Web:* www.cghmc.com	Sterling	IL	61081	815-625-0400	625-4825
Decatur Memorial Hospital 2300 N Edward St *TF:* 866-364-3600 ■ *Web:* www.dmhcares.org	Decatur	IL	62526	217-876-8121	876-2615
Delnor-Community Hospital (DCH) 300 Randall Rd *TF:* 800-223-9776 ■ *Web:* www.delnor.com	Geneva	IL	60134	630-208-3000	718-2650
Edward Hospital 801 S Washington St *Web:* www.edward.org	Naperville	IL	60540	630-527-3000	
Elmhurst Memorial Hospital 155 E Brushill Rd *Web:* www.emhc.org	Elmhurst	IL	60126	630-833-1400	782-7801
Evanston Hospital 2650 Ridge Ave *TF:* 888-364-6400 ■ *Web:* www.northshore.org/about-us/organization-profile/#EH	Evanston	IL	60201	847-570-2000	570-2940
FHN Memorial Hospital 1045 W Stephenson St *TF:* 800-747-4131 ■ *Web:* www.fhn.org	Freeport	IL	61032	815-599-6000	599-6868
Franciscan St. James Health - Olympia Fields 20201 S Crawford Ave *Web:* franciscanstjames.org	Olympia Fields	IL	60461	708-747-4000	503-3270
Galesburg Cottage Hospital (GCH) 695 N Kellogg St *Web:* www.cottagehospital.com	Galesburg	IL	61401	309-343-8131	
Gateway Regional Medical Ctr (GRMC) 2100 Madison Ave *TF General:* 800-422-6237 ■ *Web:* www.gatewayregional.net	Granite City	IL	62040	618-798-3000	
Genesis Medical Ctr Illini Campus 801 Illini Dr *TF:* 800-250-6020 ■ *Web:* www.genesishealth.com	Silvis	IL	61282	309-792-9363	792-4274
GlenOaks Hospital 701 Winthrop Ave *TF:* 866-751-7127 ■ *Web:* www.keepingyouwell.com	Glendale Heights	IL	60139	630-545-8000	545-3920
Gottlieb Memorial Hospital 701 W N Ave *Web:* www.gottliebhospital.org	Melrose Park	IL	60160	708-681-3200	450-5058
Graham Hospital 210 W Walnut St *Web:* www.grahamhospital.org	Canton	IL	61520	309-647-5240	649-5101
Highland Park Hospital 777 Pk Ave W *Web:* www.northshore.org	Highland Park	IL	60035	847-432-8000	432-9305
Holy Cross Hospital 2701 W 68th St *Web:* www.holycrosshospital.org	Chicago	IL	60629	773-884-9000	884-8001
Holy Family Medical Ctr 100 N River Rd *Web:* www.reshealth.org	Des Plaines	IL	60016	847-297-1800	297-1863
Illinois Valley Community Hospital 925 W St *Web:* www.ivch.org	Peru	IL	61354	815-223-3300	224-6763
Ingalls Memorial Hospital One Ingalls Dr *Web:* www.ingalls.org	Harvey	IL	60426	708-333-2300	915-6136
Katherine Shaw Bethea Hospital 403 E First St *TF:* 800-582-9731 ■ *Web:* www.ksbhospital.com	Dixon	IL	61021	815-288-5531	285-5859
Kishwaukee Community Hospital 1 Kish Hospital Dr *Fax Area Code: 888 ■ *TF:* 800-397-1521 ■ *Web:* www.kishhealth.org	DeKalb	IL	60115	815-756-1521	753-5661*
Lake Forest Hospital 660 N Westmoreland Rd *Web:* www.lakeforesthospital.com	Lake Forest	IL	60045	847-234-5600	234-8056
Lincoln Park Hospital 550 W Webster Ave	Chicago	IL	60614	773-883-2000	883-5168
Little Company of Mary Hospital & Health Care Centers 2800 W 95th St *Web:* www.lcmh.org	Evergreen Park	IL	60805	708-422-6200	425-9756
Loretto Hospital 645 S Central Ave *Web:* www.lorettohospital.org	Chicago	IL	60644	773-626-4300	854-5518
Louis A Weiss Memorial Hospital 4646 N Marine Dr *Web:* weisshospital.com	Chicago	IL	60640	773-878-8700	564-7287
Loyola University Medical Ctr 2160 S First Ave *Fax Area Code: 708 ■ *TF:* 888-584-7888 ■ *Web:* www.luhs.org	Maywood	IL	60153	888-584-7888	216-6791*
MacNeal Hospital 3249 S Oak Pk Ave *TF:* 888-622-6325 ■ *Web:* www.macneal.com	Berwyn	IL	60402	708-783-9100	783-3489
Memorial Hospital of Carbondale 405 W Jackson St *Web:* www.sih.net	Carbondale	IL	62902	618-549-0721	529-0449
Memorial Medical Ctr 701 N First St *Web:* www.memorialmedical.com	Springfield	IL	62781	217-788-3000	788-5591
Mercy Hospital & Medical Ctr (MHMC) 2525 S Michigan Ave *Web:* www.mercy-chicago.org	Chicago	IL	60616	312-567-2000	567-7054
Methodist Hospital of Chicago (MHC) 5025 N Paulina St *Web:* www.methodistchicago.org	Chicago	IL	60640	773-271-9040	989-1321

Phone Fax

Methodist Medical Ctr of Illinois
221 NE Glen Oak Ave .... Peoria IL 61636 309-672-5522
Web: unitypoint.org/peoria

Metro South Medical Ctr
12935 S Gregory St .... Blue Island IL 60406 708-597-2000 489-7773
Web: www.metrosouthmedicalcenter.com

Morris Hospital 150 W High St .... Morris IL 60450 815-942-2932 942-3154
TF: 877-743-3123 ■ *Web:* www.morrishospital.org

Mount Sinai Hospital Medical Ctr of Chicago
California Ave 15th St............ Chicago IL 60608 773-542-2000
TF: 877-448-7848 ■ *Web:* www.sinai.org

North Shore Skokie Hospital 9600 Gross Pt Rd .... Skokie IL 60076 847-677-9600 933-6012
Web: www.northshore.org/emergency-medicine/skokie-hospital

Northwest Community Hospital
800 W Central Rd............ Arlington Heights IL 60005 847-618-1000 618-5209
Web: www.nch.org

Norwegian-American Hospital
1044 N Francisco St............ Chicago IL 60622 773-292-8200 278-3531
TF: 877-624-9333 ■ *Web:* www.nahospital.org

OSF HealthCare 1100 E Norris Dr............ Ottawa IL 61350 815-433-3100 451-1354*
*Fax Area Code: 309 ■ *TF:* 800-635-1440 ■ *Web:* www.osfsaintelizabeth.org

OSF Saint Anthony Medical Ctr
5666 E State St............ Rockford IL 61108 815-226-2000 395-5449
TF: 800-343-3185 ■ *Web:* www.osfsaintanthony.org

OSF Saint Francis Medical Ctr
530 NE Glen Oak Ave .... Peoria IL 61637 309-655-2000 655-2303
TF: 888-627-5673 ■ *Web:* www.osfsaintfrancis.org

OSF Saint Joseph Medical Ctr
2200 E Washington St .... Bloomington IL 61701 309-662-3311
Web: www.osfstjoseph.org

OSF Saint Mary Medical Ctr
3333 N Seminary St .... Galesburg IL 61401 309-344-3161 451-8278
TF: 877-795-0416 ■ *Web:* www.osfstmary.org

Our Lady of Resurrection Medical Ctr
5645 W Addison St............ Chicago IL 60634 773-282-7000 794-7651
Web: www.reshealth.org

Palos Community Hospital
12251 S 80th Ave............ Palos Heights IL 60463 708-923-4000
Web: www.paloscommunityhospital.org

Passavant Area Hospital (PAH)
1600 W Walnut St............ Jacksonville IL 62650 217-245-9541
Web: www.passavanthospital.com

Pekin Hospital 600 S 13th St............ Pekin IL 61554 309-347-1151 353-0908
Web: www.pekinhospital.org

Proctor Hospital 5409 N Knoxville Ave .... Peoria IL 61614 309-691-1000 683-6190
Web: unitypoint.org/peoria/default.aspx

Provena Covenant Medical Ctr 1400 W Pk St............ Urbana IL 61801 217-337-2000
TF: 800-245-6697 ■ *Web:* www.provena.org

Provena Mercy Ctr 1325 N Highland Ave............ Aurora IL 60506 630-859-2222 859-9014
Web: provena.org

Provena Saint Joseph Hospital 77 N Airlite St............ Elgin IL 60123 847-695-3200 931-5511
Web: www.provena.org

Provena Saint Joseph Medical Ctr (PSJMC)
333 N Madison St............ Joliet IL 60435 815-725-7133 741-7579
Web: www.provena.org/stjoes

Provena Saint Mary's Hospital 500 W Ct St............ Kankakee IL 60901 815-937-2400
TF: 888-740-4111 ■ *Web:* www.provena.org

Provena United Samaritans Medical Ctr
812 N Logan Ave .... Danville IL 61832 217-443-5000
Web: www.provena.org

Resurrection Medical Ctr 7435 W Talcott Ave .... Chicago IL 60631 773-774-8000
Web: www.reshealth.org

Riverside Medical Ctr (RMC) 350 N Wall St............ Kankakee IL 60901 815-933-1671 935-7823
Web: www.riversidehealthcare.org

Rockford Memorial Hospital
2400 N Rockton Ave............ Rockford IL 61103 815-971-5000
Web: www.rockfordhealthsystem.org

Roseland Community Hospital 45 W 111th St............ Chicago IL 60628 773-995-3000 995-1052
Web: roselandhospital.org

Rush Oak Park Hospital (ROPH) 520 S Maple Ave .... Oak Park IL 60304 708-383-9300
Web: www.roph.org

Rush University Medical Ctr
1653 W Congress Pkwy .... Chicago IL 60612 312-942-5000 942-3212
Web: www.rush.edu

Rush-Copley Medical Ctr (RCMC) 2000 Ogden Ave .... Aurora IL 60504 630-978-6200 978-6888
TF: 866-426-7539 ■ *Web:* www.rushcopley.com

Saint Alexius Medical Ctr
1555 Barrigton Rd .... Hoffman Estates IL 60169 847-843-2000 490-2570
Web: www.alexianbrothershealth.org

Saint Anthony's Memorial Hospital
503 N Maple St............ Effingham IL 62401 217-342-2121 347-1563
Web: www.stanthonyshospital.org

Saint Francis Hospital of Evanston
355 Ridge Ave............ Evanston IL 60202 847-316-4000 316-4500
Web: www.reshealth.org

Saint John's Hospital 800 E Carpenter St............ Springfield IL 62702 217-544-6464
Web: www.st-johns.org

Saint Joseph Hospital & Health Care Ctr
2900 N Lk Shore Dr .... Chicago IL 60657 773-665-3000 665-3861
Web: www.reshealth.org

Saint Mary of Nazareth Hospital Ctr
2233 W Div St .... Chicago IL 60622 312-770-2000 770-3391
Web: www.reshealth.org

Sarah Bush Lincoln Health Ctr (SBLHC)
1000 Health Ctr Dr PO Box 372 .... Mattoon IL 61938 217-258-2525 258-4117
TF: 800-345-3191 ■ *Web:* www.sarahbush.org

St Bernard Hospital & Health Care Ctr
326 W 64th St............ Chicago IL 60621 773-962-3900 962-4219
Web: www.stbernardhospital.com

Swedish Covenant Hospital
5145 N California Ave............ Chicago IL 60625 773-878-8200 878-6152
Web: www.swedishcovenant.org

SwedishAmerican Hospital 1401 E State St .... Rockford IL 61104 815-968-4400 966-3999
TF: 800-322-4724 ■ *Web:* www.swedishamerican.org

Thorek Memorial Hospital 850 W Irving Pk Rd............ Chicago IL 60613 773-525-6780 975-6703
Web: thorek.org

Touchette Regional Hospital (TRH)
5900 Bond Ave............ Centreville IL 62207 618-332-3060 332-5256
Web: www.touchette.org

Trinity Medical Ctr West Campus (TMC)
2701 17th St............ Rock Island IL 61201 309-779-2800 779-2303
Web: www.unitypoint.org

University of Chicago Medical Ctr
5841 S Maryland Ave............ Chicago IL 60637 773-702-1000 702-4846
TF: 888-824-0200 ■ *Web:* www.uchospitals.edu

University of Illinois Medical Ctr
1740 W Taylor St .... Chicago IL 60612 312-996-3900 996-7049
TF: 866-600-2273 ■ *Web:* hospital.uillinois.edu

Vista Medical Center East
1324 N Sheridan Rd .... Waukegan IL 60085 847-360-3000
Web: www.vistahealth.com

Vista Medical Ctr 1324 N Sheridan Rd .... Waukegan IL 60085 847-360-3000 360-4109
Web: www.vistahealth.com

Vista West Ctr 2615 Washington St............ Waukegan IL 60085 847-249-3900 360-4109
Web: www.vistahealth.com/stmcvmh

West Suburban Hospital Medical Ctr
Three Erie Ct............ Oak Park IL 60302 708-383-6200
TF: 866-938-7256 ■ *Web:* www.westsuburbanmc.com/home.aspx

Westlake Hospital 1225 W Lake St............ Melrose Park IL 60160 708-681-3000 938-7975
Web: westlakehosp.com/home.aspx

Indiana

Phone Fax

Clark Memorial Hospital (CMH)
1220 Missouri Ave............ Jeffersonville IN 47130 812-282-6631 283-6330
Web: www.clarkmemorial.org

Columbus Regional Hospital 2400 E 17th St .... Columbus IN 47201 812-379-4441 376-5001
TF: 800-841-4938 ■ *Web:* www.crh.org

Community Hospital Anderson (CHA)
1515 N Madison Ave .... Anderson IN 46011 765-298-4242 298-5848
TF: 800-777-7775 ■ *Web:* www.communityanderson.com

Community Hospital East
1500 N Ritter Ave .... Indianapolis IN 46219 317-355-1411 355-1668
Web: ecommunity.com

Community Westview Hospital
3630 Guion Rd .... Indianapolis IN 46222 317-920-8439
Web: www.westviewhospital.org

De Kalb Memorial Hospital Inc
1316 E Seventh St .... Auburn IN 46706 260-925-4600
Web: dekalbhealth.com/

Elkhart General Hospital 600 E Blvd............ Elkhart IN 46514 574-294-2621 523-3495
Web: www.egh.org

Fayette Regional Health System (FRHS)
1941 Virginia Ave............ Connersville IN 47331 765-825-5131 827-7980
Web: www.fayetteregional.org

Floyd Memorial Hospital 1850 State St............ New Albany IN 47150 812-944-7701 949-5642
TF: 800-423-1513 ■ *Web:* floydmemorial.com

Franciscan St. Elizabeth Health
1501 Hartford St............ Lafayette IN 47904 765-423-6011
TF: 800-371-6011 ■ *Web:* franciscanste.org

Franciscan St. Margaret Health
5454 Hohman Ave .... Hammond IN 46320 219-932-2300 933-2585
Web: franciscanstmargaret.org

Hendricks Regional Health Danville
1000 E Main St............ Danville IN 46122 317-745-4451
Web: www.hendricks.org

Henry County Memorial Hospital (HCM)
1000 N 16th St .... New Castle IN 47362 765-521-0890 521-1555
Web: www.hcmhcares.org

Howard Regional Health System Main Campus (HRHS)
3500 S Lafountain St .... Kokomo IN 46902 765-453-0702
Web: ecommunity.com/howard

Indiana University Hospital
550 N University Blvd............ Indianapolis IN 46202 317-274-5000 274-1088
TF: 800-248-1199 ■ *Web:* www.iuhealth.org

IU Health Ball Memorial Hospital
2401 W University Ave............ Muncie IN 47303 765-747-3111 741-2848
Web: www.iuhealth.org

Johnson Memorial Hospital (JMH)
1125 W Jefferson St............ Franklin IN 46131 317-736-3300 736-2692
Web: www.johnsonmemorial.org

King's Daughters' Hospital
1373 E State Rd 62............ Madison IN 47250 812-801-0800 801-0680
Web: www.kdhmadison.org/

La Porte Hospital (LPH)
1007 Lincolnway PO Box 250............ La Porte IN 46350 219-326-1234 325-5403
TF: 800-235-6204 ■ *Web:* www.iuhealth.org/laporte

Lutheran Hospital of Indiana
7950 W Jefferson Blvd .... Fort Wayne IN 46804 260-435-7001 435-7632
TF: 800-444-2001 ■ *Web:* www.lutheranhospital.com

Major Hospital 150 W Washington St .... Shelbyville IN 46176 317-392-3211
Web: www.majorhospital.com

Margaret Mary Community Hospital Inc
321 Mitchell Ave PO Box 226............ Batesville IN 47006 812-934-6624 934-5373
Web: www.mmhealth.org/

Marion General Hospital (MGH) 441 N Wabash Ave............ Marion IN 46952 765-662-4000 651-7351
Web: www.mgh.net

Memorial Hospital & Health Care Ctr
800 W Ninth St............ Jasper IN 47546 812-996-2345
Web: www.mhhcc.org

Memorial Hospital of South Bend
615 N Michigan St............ South Bend IN 46601 574-647-1000 647-3670
TF: 800-850-7913 ■ *Web:* www.qualityoflife.org

	City	State	Zip	Phone	Fax
Parkview Hospital 2200 Randallia Dr. TF: 888-737-9311 ■ Web: www.parkview.com	Fort Wayne	IN	46805	260-373-4000	
Reid Hospital & Health Care Services 1100 Reid Pkwy Web: www.reidhosp.com	Richmond	IN	47374	765-983-3000	983-3260
Riverview Hospital 395 Westfield Rd TF: 800-523-6001 ■ Web: riverview.org	Noblesville	IN	46060	317-773-0760	776-7134
Saint Catherine Hospital 4321 Fir St Web: www.comhs.org	East Chicago	IN	46312	219-392-1700	392-7002
Saint Joseph Regional Medical Ctr Mishawaka 5215 Holy Cross Pkwy Web: www.sjmed.com	Mishawaka	IN	46545	574-335-5000	
Saint Mary Medical Ctr 1500 S Lk Pk Ave Web: www.comhs.org/stmary	Hobart	IN	46342	219-942-0551	947-6037
Saint Mary's Medical Ctr of Evansville 3700 Washington Ave Web: www.stmarys.org/smlocation	Evansville	IN	47750	812-485-4000	485-7080
Schneck Medical Ctr 411 W Tipton St TF: 800-234-9222 ■ Web: www.schneckmed.org	Seymour	IN	47274	812-522-2349	522-0792
St Vincent Dunn Hospital 1600 23rd St Web: www.stvincent.org	Bedford	IN	47421	812-275-3331	276-1211
Terre Haute Regional Hospital (THRH) 3901 S Seventh St *Fax Area Code: 877 ■ TF: 866-270-2311 ■ Web: www.regionalhospital.com	Terre Haute	IN	47802	812-232-0021	865-9738*
Urology of Indiana LLC 679 E County Line Rd Web: www.urologyin.com	Greenwood	IN	46143	317-885-1250	
Wishard Health Services 1001 W Tenth St Web: eskenazihealth.edu/	Indianapolis	IN	46202	317-639-6671	630-7678
Witham Memorial Hospital PO Box 1200 Web: witham.org	Lebanon	IN	46052	765-485-8000	
Women's Health Partnership PC 11595 N Meridian St Ste 110 Web: www.obgynindiana.com	Carmel	IN	46032	317-575-7300	575-7333

Iowa

	City	State	Zip	Phone	Fax
Allen Memorial Hospital 1825 Logan Ave TF: 888-343-4165 ■ Web: unitypoint.org/waterloo/default.aspx	Waterloo	IA	50703	319-235-3941	235-3906
Broadlawns Medical Ctr 1801 Hickman Rd TF: 866-904-5755 ■ Web: www.broadlawns.org	Des Moines	IA	50314	515-282-2200	282-8874
Buena Vista Regional Medical Ctr PO Box 309 TF: 877-401-8030 ■ Web: www.bvrmc.org	Storm Lake	IA	50588	712-732-4030	
Covenant Medical Ctr 3421 W Ninth St Web: www.wheatoniowa.org	Waterloo	IA	50702	319-272-8000	272-7313
Dallas County Hospital 610 10th St TF: 800-877-7541 ■ Web: www.dallascohospital.org	Perry	IA	50220	515-465-3547	465-7654
Finley Hospital 350 N Grandview Ave TF: 800-582-1891 ■ Web: www.unitypoint.org	Dubuque	IA	52001	563-582-1881	589-2562
Genesis Medical Ctr 1227 E Rusholme St Web: www.genesishealth.com	Davenport	IA	52803	563-421-1000	421-6500
Great River Health Systems 1221 S Gear Ave Web: www.greatrivermedical.org	West Burlington	IA	52655	319-768-1000	
Great River Medical Ctr 1221 S Gear Ave Web: www.greatrivermedical.org	West Burlington	IA	52655	319-768-1000	768-3266
Iowa Methodist Medical Ctr (IMMC) 1200 Pleasant St Web: unitypoint.org/desmoines/iowa-methodist-medical-center.aspx	Des Moines	IA	50309	515-241-6212	
Jennie Edmundson Hospital 933 E Pierce St Web: www.bestcare.org	Council Bluffs	IA	51503	712-396-6000	396-6288
Keokuk Area Hospital 1600 Morgan St Web: www.keokukhealthsystems.org	Keokuk	IA	52632	319-524-7150	524-5317
Madison County Healthcare System 300 Hutchings St Web: www.madisonhealth.com	Winterset	IA	50273	515-462-2373	462-5132
Marshalltown Medical & Surgical Ctr Three S Fourth Ave Web: marshmed.com/	Marshalltown	IA	50158	641-754-5151	754-5181
Mary Greeley Medical Ctr 1111 Duff Ave Web: www.mgmc.org	Ames	IA	50010	515-239-2011	239-2007
Mercy Iowa City 500 E Market St TF: 800-637-2942 ■ Web: www.mercyiowacity.org	Iowa City	IA	52245	319-339-0300	339-3788
Mercy Medical Ctr 1111 Sixth Ave TF: 800-637-2993 ■ Web: www.mercydesmoines.org	Des Moines	IA	50314	515-247-3121	247-4259
Mercy Medical Ctr North Iowa 1000 Fourth St SW TF: 800-433-3883 ■ Web: www.mercynorthiowa.com	Mason City	IA	50401	641-428-7000	
Orange City Area Health System 1000 Lincoln Cir SE TF: 800-808-6264 ■ Web: www.ochealthsystem.org	Orange City	IA	51041	712-737-4984	
Ottumwa Regional Health Ctr 1001 Pennsylvania Ave Web: www.ottumwaregionalhealth.com	Ottumwa	IA	52501	641-684-2300	684-2324
Saint Luke's Regional Medical Ctr 2720 Stone Pk Blvd TF: 800-352-4660 ■ Web: www.unitypoint.org	Sioux City	IA	51104	712-279-3500	279-7958
Trinity Regional Medical Ctr (TRMC) 802 Kenyon Rd Web: www.unitypoint.org	Fort Dodge	IA	50501	515-573-3101	573-8710
University of Iowa Hospitals & Clinics 200 Hawkins Dr Web: uihealthcare.org	Iowa City	IA	52242	319-356-1616	356-3862

Kansas

	City	State	Zip	Phone	Fax
Coffeyville Regional Medical Ctr 1400 W Fourth St TF: 800-540-2762 ■ Web: www.crmcinc.com	Coffeyville	KS	67337	620-251-1200	252-1651
Hays Medical Ctr (HMC) 2220 Canterbury Dr TF: 800-248-0073 ■ Web: haysmed.com	Hays	KS	67601	785-650-2759	623-2291
Lawrence Memorial Hospital (LMH) 325 Maine St TF: 800-749-4144 ■ Web: www.lmh.org	Lawrence	KS	66044	785-505-5000	
Menorah Medical Ctr 5721 W 119th St Web: www.menorahmedicalcenter.com	Overland Park	KS	66209	913-498-6000	345-3716
Mercy Health Ctr Fort Scott 401 Woodland Hills Blvd Web: mercy.net	Fort Scott	KS	66701	620-223-2200	223-5327
Newman Regional Health 1201 W 12th Ave Web: www.newmanrh.org	Emporia	KS	66801	620-343-6800	341-7801
Olathe Medical Ctr 20333 W 151st St Web: www.olathehealth.org	Olathe	KS	66061	913-791-4200	791-4313
Overland Park Regional Medical Ctr 10500 Quivira Rd Web: www.oprmc.com	Overland Park	KS	66215	913-541-5000	541-5035
Pratt Regional Medical Ctr Corp 200 Commodore St TF: 877-572-2787 ■ Web: www.prmc.org	Pratt	KS	67124	620-672-7451	672-2113
Promise Regional Medical Ctr-Hutchinson 1701 E 23rd Ave TF: 800-267-6891 ■ Web: www.promiseregional.com	Hutchinson	KS	67502	620-665-2000	
Providence Medical Ctr 8929 Parallel Pkwy TF: 800-281-7777 ■ Web: providence-health.org	Kansas City	KS	66112	913-596-4000	596-4801
Robert J Dole VA Medical Center 5500 E Kellogg St TF: 888-878-6881 ■ Web: www.wichita.va.gov/index.asp	Wichita	KS	67218	316-685-2221	651-3666
Saint Francis Health Ctr 1700 SW Seventh St TF: 855-578-3726 ■ Web: www.stfrancistopeka.org	Topeka	KS	66606	785-295-8000	295-5479
Saint John Hospital Inc of Kansas 3500 S Fourth St Web: www.providencekc.com	Leavenworth	KS	66048	913-680-6000	680-6013
Salina Regional Health Ctr 400 S Santa Fe Ave Web: www.srhc.com	Salina	KS	67401	785-452-7000	452-6963
Shawnee Mission Medical Ctr 9100 W 74th St Web: www.shawneemission.org	Shawnee Mission	KS	66204	913-676-2000	676-7792
St. Rose Ambulatory & Surgery Center 3515 Broadway St Web: www.stroseasc.org	Great Bend	KS	67530	620-792-2511	786-6298
Stormont-Vail Regional Health Ctr 1500 SW Tenth Ave TF: 800-432-2951 ■ Web: www.stormontvail.org	Topeka	KS	66604	785-354-6000	354-6926
University of Kansas Hospital 3901 Rainbow Blvd Web: www.kumed.com	Kansas City	KS	66160	913-588-1227	588-5785
Via Christi Regional Medical Ctr 929 N St Francis St Web: www.via-christi.org	Wichita	KS	67214	316-268-5000	291-7999
Western Plains Medical Complex 3001 Ave A Web: www.westernplainsmc.com	Dodge City	KS	67801	620-225-8400	225-8403

Kentucky

	City	State	Zip	Phone	Fax
ARH Regional Medical Ctr 100 Medical Ctr Dr Web: www.arh.org	Hazard	KY	41701	606-439-1331	439-6682
Baptist Health 1 Trillium Way TF: 800-395-4435 ■ Web: baptisthealthcorbin.com	Corbin	KY	40701	606-528-1212	528-3223
Baptist Health Louisville 4000 Kresge Way *Fax Area Code: 859 ■ TF: 800-489-3002 ■ Web: www.baptisteast.com	Louisville	KY	40207	502-897-8100	276-3765*
Baptist Health Paducah (WBH) 2501 Kentucky Ave *Fax Area Code: 859 ■ TF: 877-271-4176 ■ Web: westernbaptist.com	Paducah	KY	42003	270-575-2100	276-3765*
Central Baptist Hospital 1740 Nicholasville Rd Web: www.baptisthealthkentucky.com/lexington	Lexington	KY	40503	859-260-6100	
Clark Regional Medical Ctr Inc 175 Hospital Dr Web: www.clarkregional.org	Winchester	KY	40391	859-745-3500	
Ephraim McDowell Regional Medical Ctr 217 S Third St TF: 800-686-4121 ■ Web: www.emhealth.org	Danville	KY	40422	859-239-1000	239-6709
Frankfort Regional Medical Ctr 299 King's Daughters Dr TF: 888-696-4505 ■ Web: www.frankfortregional.com	Frankfort	KY	40601	502-875-5240	226-7936
Greenview Regional Hospital 1801 Ashley Cir Web: tristargreenviewregional.com	Bowling Green	KY	42104	270-793-1000	793-5205
Hardin Memorial Hospital 913 W Dixie Ave *Fax Area Code: 419 ■ Web: www.hmh.net	Elizabethtown	KY	42701	270-737-1212	673-1097*
Harlan ARH Hospital 81 Ballpark Rd TF: 800-274-9375 ■ Web: www.arh.org	Harlan	KY	40831	606-573-8100	573-8200
Highlands Regional Medical Ctr 5000 KY Rt 321 TF: 800-533-4762 ■ Web: www.hrmc.org	Prestonsburg	KY	41653	606-886-8511	886-1316
Jackson Purchase Medical Ctr 1099 Medical Ctr Cir TF: 800-994-6610 ■ Web: www.jacksonpurchase.com	Mayfield	KY	42066	270-251-4100	251-4507
Jennie Stuart Medical Ctr 320 W 18th St PO Box 2400 TF: 800-887-5762 ■ Web: www.jsmc.org	Hopkinsville	KY	42241	270-887-0100	
Kindred Hospital Louisville 1313 St Anthony Pl Web: www.kindredlouisville.com	Louisville	KY	40204	502-587-7001	587-0060

				Phone	*Fax*
Lake Cumberland Regional Hospital 305 Langdon St	Somerset	KY	42503	606-679-7441	678-9919
Web: lakecumberlandhospital.com					
Lourdes Hospital 1530 Lone Oak Rd	Paducah	KY	42003	270-444-2444	444-2980
Web: www.elourdes.com					
Meadowview Regional Medical Ctr (MRMC) 989 Medical Pk Dr	Maysville	KY	41056	606-759-5311	759-5616
Web: www.meadowviewregional.com					
Medical Ctr, The 250 Pk St	Bowling Green	KY	42101	270-780-2660	842-0765
Web: www.mcbg.org					
Middlesboro Appalachian Regional Hospital 3600 W Cumberland Ave	Middlesboro	KY	40965	606-242-1100	248-1018
Web: arh.org/locations/middlesboro.aspx					
Muhlenberg Community Hospital 440 Hopkinsville St	Greenville	KY	42345	270-338-8000	338-8278
Web: www.mchky.org					
Murray-Calloway County Hospital 803 Poplar St	Murray	KY	42071	270-762-1100	767-3600
Web: www.murrayhospital.org					
Norton Audubon Hospital One Audobon Plz Dr	Louisville	KY	40217	502-636-7111	
Web: www.nortonhealthcare.com					
Norton Hospital 200 E Chestnut St	Louisville	KY	40202	502-629-8000	629-8417
Web: www.nortonhealthcare.com					
Norton Suburban Hospital 4001 Dutchmans Ln	Louisville	KY	40207	502-893-1000	899-6131
Web: www.nortonhealthcare.com					
Our Lady of Bellefonte Hospital 1000 St Christopher Dr	Ashland	KY	41101	606-833-3333	
Web: www.olbh.com					
Owensboro Medical Health Systems (OMHS) 811 E Parish Ave PO Box 20007	Owensboro	KY	42303	270-688-2000	
TF: 877-888-6647 ■ *Web:* www.owensborohealth.org					
Pikeville Medical Ctr 911 Bypass Rd	Pikeville	KY	41501	606-218-4509	432-9479
Web: www.medicalleader.org					
Pineville Community Hospital 850 Riverview Ave	Pineville	KY	40977	606-337-3051	337-4284
Web: pinevillehospital.com					
Saint Claire Regional Medical Ctr 222 Medical Cir	Morehead	KY	40351	606-783-6500	783-6503
Web: www.st-claire.org					
Saint Joseph Hospital One St Joseph Dr	Lexington	KY	40504	859-313-1000	313-3000*
*Fax: Admitting ■ *Web:* kentuckyonehealth.org					
Saint Joseph Hospital East 150 N Eagle Creek Dr	Lexington	KY	40509	859-967-5000	967-5332
Web: kentuckyonehealth.org					
Saints Mary & Elizabeth Hospital 1850 Bluegrass Ave	Louisville	KY	40215	502-361-6000	361-6799
Web: www.jhsmh.org					
Taylor Regional Hospital 1700 Old Lebanon Rd	Campbellsville	KY	42718	270-465-3561	465-5386
Web: www.tchosp.org					
TJ Samson Community Hospital 1301 N Race St	Glasgow	KY	42141	270-651-4444	651-4848
TF: 800-651-5635 ■ *Web:* www.tjsamson.org					
UK Good Samaritan Hospital 310 S Limestone St	Lexington	KY	40508	859-226-7000	226-7154
Web: ukhealthcare.uky.edu					
University of Kentucky Chandler Medical Ctr 800 Rose St	Lexington	KY	40536	859-323-5000	323-2044
Web: www.mc.uky.edu					
University of Louisville Hospital 530 S Jackson St	Louisville	KY	40202	502-562-3000	
TF: 800-891-0947 ■ *Web:* www.kentuckyonehealth.org					
Whitesburg Appalachian Regional Hospital (ARH) 240 Hospital Rd	Whitesburg	KY	41858	606-633-3500	633-3652
Web: arh.org/locations/whitesburg.aspx					
Williamson ARH Hospital 260 Hospital Dr	South Williamson	KY	41503	606-237-1700	237-1701
TF General: 800-283-9375 ■ *Web:* arh.org/locations/williamson.aspx					

Louisiana

				Phone	*Fax*
American Legion Hospital 1305 Crowley Rayne Hwy	Crowley	LA	70526	337-783-3222	788-6413
Web: www.alh.org					
Baton Rouge General Medical Ctr (BRGMC) 3600 Florida Blvd	Baton Rouge	LA	70806	225-387-7000	381-6165*
*Fax: Admissions ■ *Web:* www.brgeneral.org					
CHRISTUS Bossier Medical Ctr 4241 Woodcock Dr Ste A-100	San Antonio,	TX	78228	210-785-5200	681-4215*
*Fax Area Code: 318 ■ *Web:* www.christushealth.org					
CHRISTUS Schumpert Highland 1453 E Bert Kouns	Shreveport	LA	71105	318-681-4500	
Web: christushealthsb.org					
Dauterive Hospital 600 N Lewis St	New Iberia	LA	70563	337-365-7311	374-4377
Web: www.dauterivehospital.com					
Earl K Long Medical Ctr 5825 Airline Hwy	Baton Rouge	LA	70805	225-358-1000	
Web: legis.state.la.us					
East Jefferson General Hospital (EJGH) 4200 Houma Blvd	Metairie	LA	70006	504-454-4000	456-8151
TF: 866-280-7737 ■ *Web:* www.ejgh.org					
Glenwood Regional Medical Ctr 503 McMillan Rd	West Monroe	LA	71291	318-329-4200	329-4710
Web: www.grmc.com					
Homer Memorial Hospital 620 E College St	Homer	LA	71040	318-927-2024	
Web: www.homerhospital.com					
Huey P Long Medical Ctr 352 Hospital Blvd PO Box 5352	Pineville	LA	71361	318-448-0811	473-6360
Web: lsuhscshreveport.edu					
Iberia Medical Ctr (IMC) 2315 E Main St	New Iberia	LA	70560	337-364-0441	374-7641
Web: www.iberiamedicalcenter.com					
Lady of The Sea General Hospital (LOSGH) 200 W 134th Pl	Cut Off	LA	70345	985-632-6401	632-8263
Web: www.losgh.org					
Lafayette General Medical Ctr 1214 Coolidge Blvd	Lafayette	LA	70505	337-289-7991	289-8671
Web: lafayettegeneral.com					
Lake Charles Memorial Health System (LCMH) 1701 Oak Pk Blvd	Lake Charles	LA	70601	337-494-3000	494-3299
Web: www.lcmh.com					
Lakeview Regional Medical Ctr 95 Judge Tanner Blvd	Covington	LA	70433	985-867-3800	
Web: www.lakeviewregional.com					
Lane Regional Medical Ctr 6300 Main St	Zachary	LA	70791	225-658-4000	658-4287
Web: www.lanermc.org					
Louisiana State University Health Sciences Ctr (LSUHSC) 1501 Kings Hwy	Shreveport	LA	71130	318-675-5000	
Web: www.lsuhscshreveport.edu/lsuhealthshreveport/lsuhealthshreveport.aspx					
Minden Medical Ctr One Medical Plz	Minden	LA	71055	318-377-2321	371-5606
Web: www.mindenmedicalcenter.com					
Natchitoches Parish Hospital 501 Keyser Ave	Natchitoches	LA	71457	318-214-4200	
Web: www.natchitocheshospital.org					
North Oaks Health System (NOHS) PO Box 2668	Hammond	LA	70404	985-345-2700	230-7655
Web: www.northoaks.org					
Northern Louisiana Medical Ctr 401 E Vaughn St	Ruston	LA	71270	318-254-2100	254-2728
Web: www.northernlouisianamedicalcenter.com					
NorthShore Regional Medical Ctr (NRMC) 100 Medical Ctr Dr	Slidell	LA	70461	985-649-7070	646-5552
Web: www.ochsner.org/locations/north_shore					
Ochsner Clinic Foundation Hospital 1514 Jefferson Hwy	New Orleans	LA	70121	504-842-3000	394-0840
TF: 800-343-0269 ■ *Web:* www.ochsner.org					
Ochsner Medical Ctr Baton Rouge 17000 Medical Ctr Dr	Baton Rouge	LA	70816	225-752-2470	755-4891*
*Fax: Admissions ■ *Web:* www.ochsner.org					
Ochsner Medical Ctr West Bank 2500 Belle Chasse Hwy	Gretna	LA	70056	504-391-5454	
TF: 800-231-5257 ■ *Web:* www.ochsner.org					
Our Lady of Lourdes Regional Medical Ctr 4801 Ambassador Caffery Pkwy	Lafayette	LA	70508	337-289-2000	
Web: fmolhs.org/lourdesrmc/pages/home.aspx					
Our Lady of the Lake Regional Medical Ctr 5000 Hennessy Blvd	Baton Rouge	LA	70808	225-765-6565	765-5290*
*Fax: Admissions ■ *Web:* fmolhs.org/ololrmc/pages/home.aspx					
Rapides Regional Medical Ctr 211 Fourth St	Alexandria	LA	71301	318-769-3000	449-7575
Web: www.rapidesregional.com					
River Oaks Hospital 1525 River Oaks Rd W	New Orleans	LA	70123	504-734-1740	733-3229
TF: 800-366-1740 ■ *Web:* www.riveroakshospital.com					
River Parishes Hospital 500 Rue De Sante	Laplace	LA	70068	985-652-7000	
TF: 800-231-5275 ■ *Web:* www.riverparisheshospital.com					
Saint Patrick Hospital of Lake Charles 524 Dr Michael DeBakey Dr	Lake Charles	LA	70601	337-436-2511	491-7157
Web: christusstpatrick.org					
Saint Tammany Parish Hospital 1202 S Tyler St	Covington	LA	70433	985-898-4000	898-4394
Web: www.stph.org					
Savoy Medical Ctr 801 Poinciana Ave	Mamou	LA	70554	337-468-0346	
Web: www.savoymedical.com					
Slidell Memorial Hospital (SMH) 1001 Gause Blvd	Slidell	LA	70458	985-643-2200	649-8626
Web: slidellmemorial.org					
St. Francis Medical Center 3421 Medical Pk Dr	Monroe	LA	71203	318-966-4000	966-7737
Web: fmolhs.org/stfran/pages/home.aspx					
Teche Regional Medical Ctr 1125 Marguerite St	Morgan City	LA	70380	985-384-2200	380-4546
Web: www.techeregional.com					
Terrebonne General Medical Ctr (TGMC) 8166 Main St	Houma	LA	70360	985-873-4141	873-5306
TF: 888-850-6270 ■ *Web:* www.tgmc.com					
Thibodaux Regional Medical Ctr (TRMC) 602 N Acadia Rd	Thibodaux	LA	70301	985-447-5500	446-5033
TF: 800-822-8442 ■ *Web:* thibodaux.com					
Touro Infirmary 1401 Foucher St	New Orleans	LA	70115	504-897-7011	897-8769
Web: www.touro.com					
Tulane Medical Ctr (TMC) 1415 Tulane Ave	New Orleans	LA	70112	504-588-5108	988-7973
TF: 800-588-5800 ■ *Web:* www.tulanehealthcare.com					
University Medical Ctr 2390 W Congress St	Lafayette	LA	70506	337-261-6000	261-6003
Web: lafayettegeneral.com					
West Calcasieu Cameron Hospital 701 E Cypress St	Sulphur	LA	70663	337-527-7034	527-4163*
*Fax: Administration ■ *Web:* www.wcch.com					
West Jefferson Medical Ctr 1101 Medical Ctr Blvd	Marrero	LA	70072	504-349-1134	349-6299
Web: www.wjmc.org					
Willis-Knighton Medical Ctr (WKMC) 2600 Greenwood Rd	Shreveport	LA	71103	318-212-4000	212-4195
Web: www.wkhs.com/home.aspx					

Maine

				Phone	*Fax*
Aroostook Medical Ctr, The (TAMC) 140 Academy St	Presque Isle	ME	04769	207-768-4000	768-4116
Web: www.tamc.org					
Central Maine Medical Ctr 300 Main St	Lewiston	ME	04240	207-795-0111	795-2303
Web: www.cmmc.org					
Eastern Maine Medical Ctr 489 State St	Bangor	ME	04401	207-973-7000	973-7348
Web: www.emmc.org					
Franklin Community Health Network 111 Franklin Health Commons	Farmington	ME	04938	207-778-6031	778-2548
TF: 800-398-6031 ■ *Web:* www.fchn.org					

Phone Fax

Maine General Medical Ctr (MGMC)
Augusta 361 Old Belgrade Rd .... Augusta ME 04330 207-626-1000 621-8801
Web: www.mainegeneral.org
Maine Medical Ctr (MMC) 22 Bramhall St. .... Portland ME 04102 207-662-0111
TF: 877-339-3107 ■ *Web:* www.mmc.org
Brighton Campus 335 Brighton Ave. .... Portland ME 04102 207-662-8000 662-8198
Web: www.mmc.org/mmc_body.cfm?id=2291
Mid Coast Hospital 123 Medical Ctr Dr. .... Brunswick ME 04011 207-729-0181 721-1230
TF: 800-994-6610 ■ *Web:* www.midcoasthealth.com
Miles Memorial Hospital 35 Miles St .... Damariscotta ME 04543 207-563-1234 563-4572
Web: www.mileshealthcare.org
Northern Maine Medical Ctr (NMMC)
194 E Main St. .... Fort Kent ME 04743 207-834-3155 834-2949
Web: www.nmmc.org
Penobscot Bay Medical Ctr
Four Glen Cove Dr # 101 .... Rockport ME 04856 207-596-8000 593-5287
Web: www.penbayhealthcare.org
Southern Maine Medical Ctr (SMMC)
One Medical Ctr Dr PO Box 626 .... Biddeford ME 04005 207-283-7000 283-7020
Web: smhc.org/
St. Joseph Healthcare 360 Broadway PO Box 403 .... Bangor ME 04402 207-262-1000 262-1240
Web: www.stjoeshealing.org

Maryland

Phone Fax

Anne Arundel Medical Ctr 2001 Medical Pkwy .... Annapolis MD 21401 443-481-1000 481-1313
Web: www.aahs.org
Baltimore Washington Medical Ctr
301 Hospital Dr .... Glen Burnie MD 21061 410-787-4000 595-1958
TF: 800-994-6610 ■ *Web:* www.mybwmc.org
Braddock Hospital 12500 Willowbrook Rd. .... Cumberland MD 21502 240-964-7000
Web: www.wmhs.com
Carroll Hospital Ctr 200 Memorial Ave. .... Westminster MD 21157 410-848-3000 871-7474
Web: carrollhospitalcenter.org
Doctors Community Hospital (DCH)
8118 Good Luck Rd .... Lanham MD 20706 301-552-8118 552-8521
Web: www.dchweb.org
Franklin Square Hospital Ctr
9000 Franklin Sq Dr .... Baltimore MD 21237 443-777-7000 777-7904
TF: 855-633-8880 ■ *Web:* www.medstarhealth.org
Frederick Memorial Hospital
400 W Seventh St. .... Frederick MD 21701 240-566-3300 566-3066*
**Fax:* Admitting ■ *Web:* www.fmh.org
Good Samaritan Hospital of Maryland
5601 Loch Raven Blvd .... Baltimore MD 21239 410-532-8000
Web: www.medstarhealth.org
Greater Baltimore Medical Ctr (GBMC)
6701 N Charles St .... Baltimore MD 21204 443-849-2000 849-8679
Web: www.gbmc.org
Harbor Hospital Ctr 3001 S Hanover St. .... Baltimore MD 21225 410-350-3200 354-4440
TF: 800-280-9006 ■ *Web:* www.medstarhealth.org
Howard County General Hospital
5755 Cedar Ln .... Columbia MD 21044 410-740-7890 740-7610
TF: 866-323-4615 ■ *Web:* www.hopkinsmedicine.org
Johns Hopkins Bayview Medical Ctr
4940 Eastern Ave .... Baltimore MD 21224 410-550-0100 550-7996
Web: www.hopkinsmedicine.org
Johns Hopkins Hospital 600 N Wolfe St. .... Baltimore MD 21287 410-955-5000
Web: www.hopkinsmedicine.org/the_johns_hopkins_hospital
Laurel Regional Hospital (LRH) 7300 Van Dusen Rd .... Laurel MD 20707 301-725-4300 497-7953
Web: dimensionshealth.org
Maryland General Hospital 827 Linden Ave .... Baltimore MD 21201 410-225-8000 462-5834
Web: ummidtown.org
Memorial Hospital at Easton (MHE)
219 S Washington St .... Easton MD 21601 410-822-1000 820-7831
Meritus Health 11116 Medical Campus Rd. .... Hagerstown MD 21742 301-790-8000
TF: 800-735-2258 ■ *Web:* www.meritushealth.com
Montgomery General Hospital
18101 Prince Philip Dr .... Olney MD 20832 301-774-8882
Web: www.medstarhealth.org
Northwest Hospital Ctr 5401 Old Ct Rd. .... Randallstown MD 21133 410-521-2200 521-7977
TF: 800-876-1175 ■ *Web:* www.lifebridgehealth.org
Peninsula Regional Medical Ctr
100 E Carroll St .... Salisbury MD 21801 410-546-6400 543-7102
TF: 800-543-7780 ■ *Web:* www.peninsula.org
Prince George's Hospital Ctr
3001 Hospital Dr .... Cheverly MD 20785 301-618-2000 618-3966
Web: princegeorgeshospital.org
Saint Agnes HealthCare 900 S Caton Ave .... Baltimore MD 21229 410-368-6000 368-2109
TF: 800-875-8750 ■ *Web:* www.stagnes.org
Shady Grove Adventist Hospital
9901 Medical Ctr Dr. .... Rockville MD 20850 301-279-6000
Web: www.shadygroveadventisthospital.com
Sinai Hospital of Baltimore
2401 W Belvedere Ave .... Baltimore MD 21215 410-601-9000 601-8356
TF: 800-444-8233 ■ *Web:* www.sinai-balt.com
Southern Maryland Hospital Ctr
7503 Surratts Rd. .... Clinton MD 20735 301-868-8000 868-5015*
Web: www.medstarhealth.org/southern-maryland/pages/default.aspx
Suburban Hospital 8600 Old Georgetown Rd .... Bethesda MD 20814 301-896-3100 493-5583
Web: hopkinsmedicine.org/suburban_hospital/
Total Health Care Inc 1501 Div St .... Baltimore MD 21217 410-383-8300 728-4412
Web: www.totalhealthcare.org
Union Memorial Hospital
201 E University Pkwy .... Baltimore MD 21218 410-554-2000 554-2652
Web: www.medstarhealth.org
University of Maryland Medical Ctr
22 S Greene St .... Baltimore MD 21201 410-328-8667
TF: 800-492-5538 ■ *Web:* www.umm.edu/center
University of Maryland Shore Regional Health
501 S Union Ave. .... Havre de Grace MD 21078 443-843-5000
Web: www.uchs.org

Phone Fax

Upper Chesapeake Medical Ctr
500 Upper Chesapeake Dr .... Bel Air MD 21014 443-643-1000
Web: uchs.org
Washington Adventist Hospital
7600 Carroll Ave. .... Takoma Park MD 20912 301-891-7600 891-5991
Web: www.adventisthealthcare.com

Massachusetts

Phone Fax

Anna Jaques Hospital (AJH) 25 Highland Ave .... Newburyport MA 01950 978-463-1000 463-1250
Web: www.ajh.org
Baystate Franklin Medical Ctr 164 High St. .... Greenfield MA 01301 413-773-0211
Web: www.baystatehealth.com
Baystate Medical Ctr 759 Chestnut St. .... Springfield MA 01199 413-794-0000
Web: www.baystatehealth.com/baystate
Berkshire Medical Ctr 725 N St. .... Pittsfield MA 01201 413-447-2000 447-2206
Web: www.berkshirehealthsystems.org
Beth Israel Deaconess Hospital-Milton
199 Reedsdale Rd. .... Milton MA 02186 617-696-4600 696-7380
Web: www.miltonhospital.org
Beth Israel Deaconess Medical Ctr (BIDMC)
330 Brookline Ave. .... Boston MA 02215 617-667-7000 754-2224
TF: 800-667-5356 ■ *Web:* www.bidmc.org
Boston Medical Ctr One Boston Medical Ctr Pl .... Boston MA 02118 617-638-8000 638-6905
Web: www.bmc.org
Brockton Hospital 680 Centre St .... Brockton MA 02302 508-941-7000 941-6201
Web: www.signature-healthcare.org
Cambridge Hospital 1493 Cambridge St .... Cambridge MA 02139 617-665-1000 665-1003
Web: www.challiance.org
Cape Cod Hospital 27 Pk St. .... Hyannis MA 02601 508-771-1800 862-7337
Web: www.capecodhealth.org/capecodhospital
Charlton Memorial Hospital
363 Highland Ave. .... Fall River MA 02720 508-679-3131 679-7692
Web: www.southcoast.org
Cooley Dickinson Hospital 30 Locust St. .... NorthHampton MA 01060 413-582-2000 582-2952
Web: www.cooley-dickinson.org
Emerson Hospital 133 Old Rd To 9 Acre Corner .... Concord MA 01742 978-369-1400 287-3655
Web: www.emersonhospital.org
Falmouth Hospital 100 Terr Heun Dr .... Falmouth MA 02540 508-548-5300
Web: www.capecodhealth.org
Faulkner Hospital 1153 Centre St. .... Jamaica Plain MA 02130 617-983-7000 524-8663
Web: www.brighamandwomensfaulkner.org
Good Samaritan Medical Ctr 235 N Pearl St. .... Brockton MA 02301 508-427-3000 427-3010
Web: steward.org
Harrington Memorial Hospital (HMH) 100 S St. .... Southbridge MA 01550 508-765-9771 765-3147
TF: 800-416-6072 ■ *Web:* www.harringtonhospital.org
HealthAlliance Leominster Hospital
60 Hospital Rd .... Leominster MA 01453 978-466-2000
Web: umassmemorialhealthcare.org/umass-memorial-medical-center/
Heywood Hospital 242 Green St .... Gardner MA 01440 978-632-3420 630-6529
Web: www.heywood.org
Holy Family Hospital 70 E St. .... Methuen MA 01844 978-687-0151 688-7689
Web: steward.org
Holyoke Medical Ctr 575 Beech St. .... Holyoke MA 01040 413-534-2500 534-2633
Web: www.holyokehealth.com
Hubbard Regional Hospital 340 Thompson Rd. .... Webster MA 01570 508-943-2600
Web: harringtonhospital.org
Jordan Hospital 275 Sandwich St .... Plymouth MA 02360 508-746-2000 830-1131
TF: 800-256-7326 ■ *Web:* bidplymouth.org/
Lahey Clinic Foundation Inc 41 Mall Rd. .... Burlington MA 01805 781-744-8000
TF: 800-524-3955 ■ *Web:* www.lahey.org
Lawrence General Hospital 1 General St .... Lawrence MA 01842 978-683-4000 946-8059
Web: www.lawrencegeneral.org
Lawrence Memorial Hospital of Medford
170 Governors Ave. .... Medford MA 02155 781-306-6000 306-6361
Web: www.hallmarkhealth.org
Lowell General Hospital (LGH) 295 Varnum Ave. .... Lowell MA 01854 978-937-6000 937-6869
Web: www.lowellgeneral.org
Massachusetts General Hospital 55 Fruit St .... Boston MA 02114 617-726-2000
Web: www.massgeneral.org
Melrose-Wakefield Hospital 585 Lebanon St. .... Melrose MA 02176 781-979-3000 979-3015
Web: www.hallmarkhealth.org
Merrimack Valley Hospital 140 Lincoln Ave .... Haverhill MA 01830 978-374-2000 521-8121
Web: merrimackvalley-hospital.org
MetroWest Medical Ctr 115 Lincoln St. .... Framingham MA 01702 508-383-1000 383-1166
TF: 800-357-6060 ■ *Web:* www.mwmc.com
Leonard Morse Campus 67 Union St. .... Natick MA 01760 508-650-7000 650-7777
Web: www.mwmc.com
Milford Regional Medical Ctr 14 Prospect St. .... Milford MA 01757 508-473-1190 473-2744
Web: www.milfordregional.org
Morton Hospital & Medical Ctr
88 Washington St .... Taunton MA 02780 508-828-7000 824-6941
Web: www.mortonhospital.org
Mount Auburn Hospital (MAH) 330 Mt Auburn St. .... Cambridge MA 02138 617-492-3500 491-0678
Web: www.mountauburnhospital.org
New England Baptist Hospital
125 Parker Hill Ave. .... Boston MA 02120 617-754-5000 734-7804
TF: 800-370-6324 ■ *Web:* www.nebh.org
Newton-Wellesley Hospital 2014 Washington St .... Newton MA 02462 617-243-6000 243-6954
Web: www.nwh.org
North Adams Regional Hospital (NARH)
71 Hospital Ave. .... North Adams MA 01247 413-664-5000 664-5028
Web: www.nbhealth.org
Quincy Medical Ctr 114 Whitwell St .... Quincy MA 02169 617-773-6100 376-1604
Web: steward.org
Saint Anne's Hospital 795 Middle St .... Fall River MA 02721 508-674-5600 235-5647
Web: steward.org
Saint Elizabeth's Medical Ctr
736 Cambridge St. .... Brighton MA 02135 617-789-3000 562-7568
Web: www.stemc.org/

Phone *Fax*

Saint Luke's Hospital of New Bedford
101 Page St .... New Bedford MA 02740 508-997-1515 979-8115
TF: 800-497-1727 ■ *Web:* www.southcoast.org/stlukes

Saint Vincent Hospital-Worcester Medical Ctr
123 Summer St.................................. Worcester MA 01608 508-363-5000
TF: 877-633-2368 ■ *Web:* www.stvincenthospital.com

South Shore Hospital 55 Fogg Rd............South Weymouth MA 02190 781-340-8000 337-3768
TF: 800-439-2370 ■ *Web:* www.southshorehospital.org

Southboro Medical Group Inc
24 Newton St ....Southborough MA 01772 508-481-5500 460-3221
Web: www.southboromedical.com

Sturdy Memorial Hospital 211 Pk St................Attleboro MA 02703 508-222-5200 236-8409
Web: www.sturdymemorial.org

Tufts Medical Ctr (TMC) 800 Washington St...........Boston MA 02111 617-636-5000 636-8199
TF: 866-220-3699 ■ *Web:* www.tuftsmedicalcenter.org/default

UMass Memorial Medical Ctr
Bone Marrow Transplant Program
55 Lake Ave N .... Worcester MA 01655 508-334-1000 334-7983
Web: umassmemorialhealthcare.org/umass-memorial-medical-center/
Memorial Campus 119 Belmont St .... Worcester MA 01605 508-334-1000
Web: umassmemorialhealthcare.org/umass-memorial-medical-center/
University Campus 55 Lake Ave N.............. Worcester MA 01655 508-334-1000
Web: umassmemorialhealthcare.org/umass-memorial-medical-center/

Upham's Corner Health Ctr 500 Columbia Rd........Dorchester MA 02125 617-287-8000 282-8625
Web: www.uphamscornerhealthctr.com

Whidden Memorial Hospital 103 Garland St ....Everett MA 02149 617-389-6270 389-3883
Web: www.challiance.org

Winchester Hospital 41 Highland Ave............. Winchester MA 01890 781-729-9000 756-2908
Web: www.winchesterhospital.org

Michigan

Phone *Fax*

Allegan General Hospital 555 Linn St................ Allegan MI 49010 269-673-8424 686-4239
Web: www.aghosp.org

Allegiance Health 205 NE Ave......................Jackson MI 49201 517-788-4800
TF: 800-872-6480 ■ *Web:* www.alleqiancehealth.org

Alpena Regional Medical Ctr
1501 W Chisholm St ....Alpena MI 49707 989-356-7000 356-7305
TF: 800-556-8842 ■ *Web:* www.alpenaregionalmedicalcenter.org

Bay Regional Medical Ctr (BRMC)
1900 Columbus Ave................................Bay City MI 48708 989-894-3000
TF: 800-656-3950 ■ *Web:* www.mclaren.org

Borgess Medical Ctr 1521 Gull Rd.................Kalamazoo MI 49048 269-226-7000 226-5966
Web: www.borgess.com

Botsford Hospital
28050 Grand River Ave...................... Farmington Hills MI 48336 248-471-8000 471-8896
Web: www.botsford.org

Bronson Methodist Hospital 601 John St...........Kalamazoo MI 49007 269-341-7654 341-8314
TF: 800-276-6766 ■ *Web:* www.bronsonhealth.com

Chelsea Community Hospital 775 S Main St ....Chelsea MI 48118 734-475-1311 475-4066
Web: stjoeschelsea.org/

Community Health Ctr of Branch County (CHCBC)
274 E Chicago St .... Coldwater MI 49036 517-279-5400 279-8830
TF: 800-994-6610 ■ *Web:* www.chcbc.com

Covenant Medical Ctr Cooper 700 Cooper Ave........Saginaw MI 48602 989-583-0000 583-6314*
*Fax: Admitting ■ *Web:* www.covenanthealthcare.com

Covenant Medical Ctr Harrison
1447 N Harrison St.................................Saginaw MI 48602 989-583-0000 583-4784
Web: www.covenanthealthcare.com

Crittenton Hospital
1101 W University Dr......................... Rochester Hills MI 48307 248-652-5000
Web: www.crittenton.com

Detroit Receiving Hospital & University Health Ctr
4201 St Antoine Blvd ....Detroit MI 48201 313-745-3100 745-3455
Web: www.drhuhc.org

Dickinson County Healthcare System
1721 S Stephenson Ave .... Iron Mountain MI 49801 906-774-1313 582-5599*
*Fax Area Code: 501 ■ *Web:* www.dchs.org

Doctors Hospital of Michigan 461 W Huron St .... Pontiac MI 48341 248-857-7200
Web: www.dhofm.com

Eaton Rapids Medical Ctr 1500 S Main St .... Eaton Rapids MI 48827 517-663-2671 663-4920
Web: www.eatonrapidsmedicalcenter.org

Emergency Physicians Medical Group Pc Inc
2000 Green Rd Ste 300........................... Ann Arbor MI 48105 734-995-3764 995-2913
Web: www.epmgpc.com

Garden City Hospital (GCH) 6245 Inkster Rd ....Garden City MI 48135 734-458-3300 421-3530
Web: www.gch.org

Harper University Hospital 3990 John R St............ Detroit MI 48201 313-745-8040 745-1520
Web: www.harperhutzel.org

Henry Ford Bi-County Hospital
13355 E Ten-Mile Rd ....Warren MI 48089 586-759-7300 759-7357
Web: hospital-data.com

Henry Ford Hospital 2799 W Grand Blvd .... Detroit MI 48202 313-916-2600
TF: 800-999-4340 ■ *Web:* www.henryford.com

Henry Ford Macomb Hospital
15855 19-Mile Rd .... Clinton Township MI 48038 586-263-2300 263-2614
Web: henryford.com/homepage_macomb.cfm?id=48346

Henry Ford Wyandotte Hospital
2333 Biddle Ave..................................Wyandotte MI 48192 734-246-6000 246-6904
Web: henryford.com/homepage_wyandotte.cfm?id=37472&otopid=33690

Holland Community Hospital 602 Michigan Ave........ Holland MI 49423 616-392-5141 394-3572
Web: www.hollandhospital.org

Hurley Medical Ctr One Hurley Plz ....Flint MI 48503 810-262-9000 762-6585
TF: 800-336-8999 ■ *Web:* www.hurleymc.com

Huron Valley Sinai Hospital (HVSH)
One William Carls Dr..............................Commerce MI 48382 248-937-3300 937-3378
Web: www.hvsh.org

Ingham Regional Medical Ctr
401 W Greenlawn Ave.............................Lansing MI 48910 517-975-6000 334-2939
Web: www.mclaren.org

Phone *Fax*

Lakeland Medical Center-Niles
31 N St Joseph Ave.................................... Niles MI 49120 269-683-5510 683-2337
TF: 800-968-0115 ■ *Web:* www.lakelandhealth.org

Lapeer Regional Hospital 1375 N Main St .... Lapeer MI 48446 810-667-5500 667-5582
TF: 888-327-0671 ■ *Web:* www.mclaren.org

Marquette General Hospital
580 W College Ave............................... Marquette MI 49855 906-228-9440 225-3084
Web: www.mgh.org

McLaren Regional Medical Ctr
401 S Ballenger Hwy ....Flint MI 48532 810-342-2000 342-2428
TF: 800-821-6517 ■ *Web:* www.mclaren.org

Memorial Healthcare Ctr 826 W King St............. Owosso MI 48867 989-723-5211 725-7902
TF: 800-206-8706 ■ *Web:* www.memorialhealthcare.org

Mercy General Health Partners
Muskegon Campus 1500 E Sherman Blvd........Muskegon MI 49444 231-672-2000
Web: www.mercyhealthmuskegon.com

Mercy Hospital Cadillac 400 Hobart St..............Cadillac MI 49601 231-876-7473
Web: www.munsonhealthcare.org

Mercy Memorial Hospital (MMH) 718 N Macomb St.... Monroe MI 48162 734-240-8400 240-4424
Web: www.mercymemorial.org

Metro Health Hospital 5900 Byron Ctr Ave ....Wyoming MI 49519 616-252-7200 252-0630
TF: 800-968-0051 ■ *Web:* www.metrohealth.net

MidMichigan Medical Ctr 4005 Orchard Dr...........Midland MI 48670 989-839-3000 839-1399
Web: www.midmichigan.org

Mount Clemens General Hospital
1000 Harrington Blvd........................Mount Clemens MI 48043 586-493-8000 493-8700
Web: www.mclaren.org

Munson Medical Ctr 1105 Sixth St.............. Traverse City MI 49684 231-935-5000
Web: www.munsonhealthcare.org

Oakwood Annapolis Hospital 33155 Annapolis Rd ...... Wayne MI 48184 734-467-4000 467-4017
TF: 800-543-9355 ■ *Web:* www.oakwood.org

Oakwood Heritage Hospital 10000 Telegraph Rd.........Taylor MI 48180 313-295-5000 295-5085
TF: 800-543-9355 ■ *Web:* www.oakwood.org

Oakwood Hospital & Medical Ctr
18101 Oakwood Blvd ....Dearborn MI 48124 313-593-7000 436-2038
TF: 800-543-9355 ■ *Web:* www.oakwood.org

Oakwood Southshore Medical Ctr 5450 Fort St .... Trenton MI 48183 734-671-3800 671-3891
TF: 800-543-9355 ■ *Web:* www.oakwood.org

POH Regional Medical Ctr 50 N Perry St............. Pontiac MI 48342 248-338-5000 338-5667
TF: 888-327-0671 ■ *Web:* www.mclaren.org

Port Huron Hospital (PHH)
1221 Pine Grove Ave ....Port Huron MI 48060 810-987-5000 502-1567*
*Fax Area Code: 877 ■ *TF:* 888-327-0671 ■ *Web:* www.porthuronhospital.org

Saint John Macomb-Oakland Hospital
Oakland Ctr 27351 Dequindre Rd ....Madison Heights MI 48071 248-967-7000
Web: www.stjohnprovidence.org/oakland

Saint Joseph Mercy Ann Arbor
5301 McAuley Dr .... Ypsilanti MI 48197 734-712-3456 712-3855
TF: 866-522-8268 ■ *Web:* www.stjoeshealth.org

Saint Joseph Mercy Hospital Port Huron
2601 Electric Ave ....Port Huron MI 48060 810-985-1500 985-1579
Web: www.mymercy.us/welcom-port-huron

Saint Joseph Mercy Oakland
44405 Woodward Ave................................ Pontiac MI 48341 248-858-3000 858-3155
TF: 800-396-1313 ■ *Web:* www.stjoesoakland.org

Saint Mary Mercy Hospital 36475 Five-Mile Rd........ Livonia MI 48154 734-655-4800
TF: 800-464-7492 ■ *Web:* www.stmarymercy.org

Saint Mary's Health Care
200 Jefferson St SE ....Grand Rapids MI 49503 616-685-5000
Web: www.mercyhealthsaintmarys.com

Scheurer Hospital Inc 170 N Caseville Rd.............Pigeon MI 48755 989-453-3223 856-2209
TF: 800-208-9060 ■ *Web:* www.scheurer.org

Sinai Grace Hospital 6071 W Outer Dr................ Detroit MI 48235 313-966-3300 966-3160
TF: 888-362-2500 ■ *Web:* www.sinaigrace.org

Sparrow Health System 1215 E Michigan Ave.......... Lansing MI 48912 517-364-1000 364-8002
TF: 800-772-7769 ■ *Web:* www.sparrow.org

Spectrum Health Blodgett Campus
100 Michigan St NE ....Grand Rapids MI 49503 616-774-7444 391-1883
TF: 866-989-7999 ■ *Web:* www.spectrumhealth.org

St John Detroit Riverview Ctr
7733 E Jefferson Ave ....Detroit MI 48214 866-501-3627
Web: www.stjohnprovidence.org/DetroitRiverView

St John Providence Health System
28000 Dequindre ....Warren MI 48092 866-501-3627
TF: 866-501-3627 ■ *Web:* www.stjohnprovidence.org

St Mary's of Michigan (STMH)
800 S Washington Ave ....Saginaw MI 48601 989-907-8115
Web: www.stmarysofmichigan.org

St. John Providence 28000 Dequindre.................Warren MI 48092 586-573-5000 573-5541
Web: www.stjohnprovidence.org

Three Rivers Health 701 S Health Pkwy .... Three Rivers MI 49093 269-278-1145 273-9703
Web: www.threerivershealth.org

Minnesota

Phone *Fax*

Abbott Northwestern Hospital
800 E 28th St .... Minneapolis MN 55407 612-863-4000 863-5667
Web: www.allinahealth.org

Affiliated Community Medical Centers (ACMC)
101 Willmar Ave SW.............................. Willmar MN 56201 320-231-5000
TF: 888-225-6580 ■ *Web:* www.acmc.com

Cambridge Medical Ctr (CMC) 701 S Dellwood St....Cambridge MN 55008 763-689-7700
TF: 800-252-4133 ■ *Web:* www.allinahealth.org

Douglas County Hospital (DCH) 111 17th Ave E...... Alexandria MN 56308 320-762-1511 762-6120
Web: www.dchospital.com

Essentia Health 502 E Second St .... Duluth MN 55805 218-786-8376 720-6406
Web: www.essentiahealth.org

Fairview Ridges Hospital - Burnsville
201 Nicollet Blvd .... Burnsville MN 55337 952-892-2000
Web: www.fairview.org

	City	State	Zip	Phone	Fax
Fairview Southdale Hospital 6401 France Ave S *Web:* www.fairview.org/hospitals/southdale/index.htm	Edina	MN	55435	952-924-5000	924-5382
Fairview University Medical Ctr Mesabi 750 E 34th St *TF:* 888-870-8626 ■ *Web:* www.range.fairview.org	Hibbing	MN	55746	218-262-4881	362-6619
Glacial Ridge Hospital Foundation Inc 10 Fourth Ave SE *TF:* 866-667-4747 ■ *Web:* www.glacialridge.org	Glenwood	MN	56334	320-634-4521	634-2269
Hennepin County Medical Ctr (HCMC) 701 Pk Ave *Web:* www.hcmc.org	Minneapolis	MN	55415	612-873-3000	904-4214
Lake Region Hospital 712 S Cascade St *TF:* 800-439-6424 ■ *Web:* www.lrhc.org	Fergus Falls	MN	56537	218-736-8000	
Mayo Clinic 200 First St SW *Web:* mayoclinic.org	Rochester	MN	55905	507-284-2511	284-0161
Mayo Clinic Health System Austin 1000 First Dr NW *TF:* 888-609-4065 ■ *Web:* mayoclinichealthsystem.org	Austin	MN	55912	507-433-7351	434-1992
Mayo Clinic Health System Southwest Minnesota 1025 Marsh St *TF:* 800-327-3721 ■ *Web:* mayoclinichealthsystem.org	Mankato	MN	56001	507-625-4031	
Mille Lacs Health System 200 Elm St N *TF:* 877-535-3154 ■ *Web:* www.mlhealth.org	Onamia	MN	56359	320-532-3154	
North Memorial Health Care 3300 Oakdale Ave N *Web:* www.northmemorial.com	Robbinsdale	MN	55422	763-520-5200	520-1454
Regions Hospital 640 Jackson St *Web:* www.regionshospital.com	Saint Paul	MN	55101	651-254-3456	254-9426
Rice Memorial Hospital 301 Becker Ave SW *Web:* www.ricehospital.com	Willmar	MN	56201	320-235-4543	
Ridgeview Medical Ctr (RMC) 500 S Maple St *TF:* 800-967-4620 ■ *Web:* www.ridgeviewmedical.org	Waconia	MN	55387	952-442-2191	442-6524
Rochester Methodist Hospital 201 W Ctr St *Web:* mayoclinic.org	Rochester	MN	55902	507-284-2511	284-1445
Saint Cloud Hospital 1406 Sixth Ave *TF:* 800-835-6652 ■ *Web:* www.centracare.com	Saint Cloud	MN	56303	320-251-2700	255-5711
Saint Luke's Hospital & Regional Trauma Ctr 915 E First St **Fax Area Code:* 816 ■ *TF:* 866-261-5915 ■ *Web:* www.saintlukeshealthsystem.org/services	Duluth	MN	55805	218-249-5555	932-6871*
Sanford Health 1300 Anne St NW *Web:* www.nchs.com	Bemidji	MN	56601	218-751-5430	333-5880
United Hospital 333 N Smith Ave *TF:* 800-869-1320 ■ *Web:* www.allinahealth.org	Saint Paul	MN	55102	651-241-8000	241-5189
Unity Hospital 550 Osborne Rd *Web:* www.allinahealth.org	Fridley	MN	55432	763-236-4111	236-4120
University of Minnesota Medical Ctr Fairview *Riverside Campus* 2450 Riverside Ave *TF:* 888-702-4073 ■ *Web:* www.uofmmedicalcenter.org	Minneapolis	MN	55454	612-273-3000	273-4098
University of Minnesota Medical Ctr Fairview - University Campus 500 Harvard St *TF:* 800-688-5252 ■ *Web:* www.uofmmedicalcenter.org	Minneapolis	MN	55455	612-273-3000	273-1919

Mississippi

	City	State	Zip	Phone	Fax
Baptist Memorial Hospital DeSoto 7601 Southcrest Pkwy *Web:* www.baptistonline.org	Southaven	MS	38671	662-772-4000	772-2111
Baptist Memorial Hospital Golden Triangle 2520 Fifth St N *TF:* 800-422-7847 ■ *Web:* www.baptistonline.org	Columbus	MS	39703	662-244-1000	244-1651
Baptist Memorial Hospital North Mississippi 2301 S Lamar Blvd *Web:* www.baptistonline.org	Oxford	MS	38655	662-232-8100	232-8391
Baptist Memorial Hospital Union County 200 Hwy 30 W *Web:* www.baptistonline.org	New Albany	MS	38652	662-538-7631	538-2591
Bolivar Medical Ctr 901 Hwy 8 E PO Box 1380 *Web:* www.bolivarmedical.com	Cleveland	MS	38732	662-846-2496	846-2380
Central Mississippi Medical Ctr 1850 Chadwick Dr *Web:* www.merithealthcentral.com	Jackson	MS	39204	601-376-1000	
Delta Regional Medical Ctr (DRMC) 1400 E Union St *Web:* www.deltaregional.com	Greenville	MS	38703	662-378-3783	
Forrest General Hospital 6051 US Hwy 49 *TF:* 800-503-5980 ■ *Web:* www.forrestgeneral.com	Hattiesburg	MS	39402	601-288-7000	288-4180
George County Hospital PO Box 607 *Web:* www.georgeregional.com	Lucedale	MS	39452	601-947-3161	
Greenwood Leflore Hospital 1401 River Rd *Web:* www.glh.org	Greenwood	MS	38930	662-459-7000	459-2719
Grenada Lake Medical Ctr (GLMC) 960 Avent Dr *Web:* www.glmc.net	Grenada	MS	38901	662-227-7000	227-7021
Jeff Anderson Regional Medical Ctr 2124 14th St *Web:* www.jarmc.org	Meridian	MS	39301	601-553-6000	553-6144
King's Daughters Medical Ctr 427 Hwy 51 N *Web:* www.kdmc.org	Brookhaven	MS	39601	601-833-6011	
Magnolia Regional Health Ctr 611 Alcorn Dr *Web:* www.mrhc.org	Corinth	MS	38834	662-293-1000	293-7667
Memorial Hospital at Gulfport 4500 13th St *Web:* www.gulfportmemorial.com	Gulfport	MS	39501	228-867-4000	867-4747
Merit Health Biloxi 150 Reynoir St *Web:* www.biloxiregional.net	Biloxi	MS	39530	228-432-1571	436-1205
Merit Health Gilmore Memorial (GMRMC) 1105 Earl Frye Blvd *Web:* www.gilmorehealth.com	Amory	MS	38821	662-256-7111	
Merit Health Rankin 350 Crossgates Blvd *Web:* www.crossgatesriveroaks.com	Brandon	MS	39042	601-825-2811	824-8519
Natchez Regional Medical Ctr 54 Sergeant S Prentiss Dr *Web:* www.natchezregional.com	Natchez	MS	39120	601-443-2100	445-0362
North Mississippi Medical Ctr 830 S Gloster St *Web:* www.nmhs.net/tupelo	Tupelo	MS	38801	662-377-3000	377-3564
Northwest Mississippi Regional Medical Ctr 1970 Hospital Dr *Web:* www.merithealthnorthwestms.com	Clarksdale	MS	38614	662-627-3211	
Oktibbeha County Hospital 400 Hospital Rd *Web:* www.och.org	Starkville	MS	39759	662-323-4320	
River Region Medical Ctr 2100 Hwy 61 N *Web:* www.riverregion.com	Vicksburg	MS	39183	601-883-5000	883-5196
River Region West Campus 2100 Highway 61 North/1111 N Frontage Road *TF:* 800-843-2131 ■ *Web:* www.riverregion.com	Vicksburg	MS	39183	601-883-5000	
Rush Foundation Hospital 1314 19th Ave *Web:* www.rushhealthsystems.org	Meridian	MS	39301	601-483-0011	703-4427
Saint Dominic-Jackson Memorial Hospital 969 Lakeland Dr *Web:* www.stdom.com	Jackson	MS	39216	601-200-2000	200-6800
Singing River Hospital 2809 Denny Ave *Web:* www.mysrhs.com	Pascagoula	MS	39581	228-809-5000	
South Central Regional Medical Ctr (SCRMC) 1220 Jefferson St *Web:* www.scrmc.com	Laurel	MS	39440	601-426-4000	
Southwest Mississippi Regional Medical Ctr 215 Marion Ave *Web:* www.smrmc.com	McComb	MS	39648	601-249-5500	249-1709
University of Mississippi Medical Ctr 2500 N State St *Web:* www.umc.edu	Jackson	MS	39216	601-984-1000	984-4125
Wesley Medical Ctr 5001 Hardy St *TF:* 800-622-8892 ■ *Web:* www.wesley.com	Hattiesburg	MS	39402	601-268-8000	268-5008

Missouri

	City	State	Zip	Phone	Fax
Barnes-Jewish Hospital One Barnes-Jewish Hospital Plz *Web:* www.barnesjewish.org	Saint Louis	MO	63110	314-362-5000	362-3725
Barnes-Jewish Saint Peters Hospital 4901 Forest Park Ave **Fax Area Code:* 636 ■ *Web:* www.bjc.org	St. Louis	MI	63108	314-747-9322	916-9414*
Boone Hospital Ctr 1600 E Broadway *Web:* www.boone.org	Columbia	MO	65201	573-815-8000	815-2638
Bothwell Regional Health Ctr 601 E 14th St *Web:* www.brhc.org	Sedalia	MO	65301	660-826-8833	
Capital Region Medical Ctr 1125 Madison St *Web:* www.crmc.org	Jefferson City	MO	65101	573-632-5000	632-5880
Centerpoint Medical Ctr 19600 E 39th St *Web:* www.centerpointmedical.com	Independence	MO	64057	816-698-7000	698-7003
Cox Hospital North 1423 N Jefferson Ave *Web:* www.coxhealth.com	Springfield	MO	65802	417-269-3000	269-8204
Cox Medical Center South 3801 S National Ave *Web:* www.coxhealth.com	Springfield	MO	65807	417-269-6000	269-4108
DesPeres Hospital 2345 Dougherty Ferry Rd *TF:* 888-457-5203 ■ *Web:* www.despereshospital.com	Saint Louis	MO	63122	314-966-9100	966-9274
Freeman Health System 1102 W 32nd St *Web:* www.freemanhealth.com	Joplin	MO	64804	417-347-1111	
Golden Valley Memorial Hospital 1600 N Second St *TF:* 888-225-6903 ■ *Web:* www.gvmh.org	Clinton	MO	64735	660-885-5511	885-8496
Hannibal Regional Hospital 6500 Hospital Dr *Web:* www.hrhonline.org	Hannibal	MO	63401	573-248-1300	248-5264
Kindred Hospital - Saint Louis 4930 Lindell Blvd *Web:* www.kindredstlouis.com	Saint Louis	MO	63108	314-361-8700	361-1210
Lake Regional Health System 54 Hospital Dr *Web:* www.lakeregional.com	Osage Beach	MO	65065	573-348-8000	348-8326
Liberty Hospital 2525 Glenn Hendren Dr *TF:* 800-344-3829 ■ *Web:* www.libertyhospital.org	Liberty	MO	64068	816-781-7200	781-7550
Mercy 615 S New Ballas Rd *Web:* www.mercy.net	Saint Louis	MO	63141	314-251-6000	
Mineral Area Regional Medical Ctr (WARMC) 1212 Weber Rd *Web:* www.mineralarearegional.com	Farmington	MO	63640	573-756-4581	
Missouri Baptist Hospital of Sullivan 751 Sappington Bridge Rd *TF:* 866-888-8918 ■ *Web:* www.missouribaptistsullivan.org	Sullivan	MO	63080	573-468-4186	860-2696
Missouri Baptist Medical Ctr 3015 N Ballas Rd *TF:* 800-392-0936 ■ *Web:* www.missouribaptist.org	Saint Louis	MO	63131	314-996-5000	996-5373
Missouri Delta Medical Ctr 1019 N Main St *Web:* www.missouridelta.com	Sikeston	MO	63801	573-471-1600	472-7606
North Kansas City Hospital 2800 Clay Edwards Dr *Web:* www.nkch.org	North Kansas City	MO	64116	816-691-2000	346-7020
Ozarks Medical Ctr 1100 N Kentucky Ave *Web:* www.ozarksmedicalcenter.com	West Plains	MO	65775	417-256-9111	257-6770
Parkland Health Ctr 1101 W Liberty St *Web:* www.parklandhealthcenter.org	Farmington	MO	63640	573-756-6451	760-8354
Poplar Bluff Regional Medical Ctr 2620 N Westwood Blvd *TF:* 800-327-0275 ■ *Web:* www.poplarbluffregional.com	Poplar Bluff	MO	63901	573-785-7721	
Poplar Bluff Regional Medical Ctr South Campus 621 WPine Blvd *TF:* 800-327-0275 ■ *Web:* www.poplarbluffregional.com	Poplar Bluff	MO	63901	573-686-4111	
Research Medical Ctr 2316 E Meyer Blvd *Web:* researchmedicalcenter.com	Kansas City	MO	64132	816-276-4000	276-4387

				Phone	Fax
Saint Alexius Hospital *Broadway Campus* 3933 S Broadway	Saint Louis	MO	63118	314-865-7000	865-7983
TF: 800-245-1431 ■ *Web:* www.stalexiushospital.com					
Saint Anthony's Medical Ctr 10010 Kennerly Rd	Saint Louis	MO	63128	314-525-1000	525-1228
Web: www.stanthonysmedcenter.com					
Saint Francis Medical Ctr 211 St Francis Dr	Cape Girardeau	MO	63703	573-331-3000	331-5009
Web: sfmc.net					
Saint Joseph Health Ctr 1000 Carondelet Dr	Kansas City	MO	64114	816-942-4400	943-3131
Web: www.carondelethealth.org					
Saint Louis University Hospital 3635 Vista Ave	Saint Louis	MO	63110	314-577-8000	577-8003
Web: www.sluhospital.com					
Saint Luke's Hospital 4401 Wornall Rd	Kansas City	MO	64111	816-932-2000	932-5990
Web: www.saintlukeshealthsystem.org					
Saint Mary's Health Ctr 6420 Clayton Rd	Richmond Heights	MO	63117	314-768-8000	768-8011
TF: 877-783-4193 ■ *Web:* www.ssmhealth.com					
Saint Mary's Medical Ctr 201 NW Rd Mize Rd	Blue Springs	MO	64014	816-228-5900	655-5408
Web: www.stmaryskc.com					
Skaggs Community Health Ctr 545 Branson Landing Blvd PO Box 650	Branson	MO	65615	417-335-7000	334-1505
TF: 800-994-6610 ■ *Web:* www.skaggs.net					
Southeast Missouri Hospital (SMH) 1701 Lacey St	Cape Girardeau	MO	63701	573-334-4822	651-5850
TF: 800-800-5123 ■ *Web:* www.sehealth.org					
SSM Health 620 E Monroe St	Mexico	MO	65265	573-582-5000	
TF: 844-776-9355 ■ *Web:* www.ssmhealthmidmo.com/locations/stmarysaudrain					
SSM Saint Joseph Health Ctr 300 First Capitol Dr	Saint Charles	MO	63301	636-949-7077	
Web: www.ssmhealth.com					
Truman Medical Ctr Hospital Hill 2301 Holmes St	Kansas City	MO	64108	816-404-1000	404-2828
Web: www.trumed.org					
Twin Rivers Regional Medical Ctr (TRRMC) 1301 First St	Kennett	MO	63857	573-888-4522	888-5525
Web: www.twinriversregional.com					
US Medical Ctr for Federal Prisoners 1900 W Sunshine St	Springfield	MO	65807	417-862-7041	837-1711
Web: www.bop.gov					

Montana

				Phone	Fax
Benefis Health Care *West Campus* 1101 26th St S	Great Falls	MT	59405	406-455-5000	455-3530
Web: www.benefis.org					
Benefis Healthcare *East Campus* 1101 26th St S	Great Falls	MT	59405	406-455-5000	455-4587
TF: 800-648-6632 ■ *Web:* www.benefis.org					
Billings Clinic 2800 Tenth Ave N	Billings	MT	59101	406-657-4000	
TF: 800-332-7156 ■ *Web:* www.billingsclinic.com					
Bozeman Deaconess Hospital 915 Highland Blvd	Bozeman	MT	59715	406-585-5000	585-1070
Web: www.bozemandeaconess.org					
Holy Rosary Healthcare 2600 Wilson St	Miles City	MT	59301	406-233-2600	233-4214
TF: 800-843-3820 ■ *Web:* www.holyrosaryhealthcare.org					
Kalispell Regional Medical Ctr 310 Sunnyview Ln	Kalispell	MT	59901	406-752-5111	756-2703
TF: 800-228-1574 ■ *Web:* www.kalispellregional.org					
Livingston Healtcare 504 S 13th St	Livingston	MT	59047	406-222-3541	222-5099
Web: www.livingstonhealthcare.org					
Saint James Healthcare 400 S Clark St	Butte	MT	59701	406-723-2500	723-2443
Web: www.stjameshealthcare.org					
Saint Patrick Hospital 500 W Broadway St	Missoula	MT	59802	406-543-7271	329-5693
Web: montana.providence.org/hospitals/st-patrick/					
St Luke Community Hospital (Inc) 107 Sixth Ave SW	Ronan	MT	59864	406-676-4441	
Web: www.stlukehealthnet.org					

Nebraska

				Phone	Fax
Bryan LGH Medical Ctr East 1600 S 48th St	Lincoln	NE	68506	402-481-7333	481-8306
TF: 800-742-7844 ■ *Web:* www.bryanhealth.com					
Bryan LGH Medical Ctr West 2300 S 16th St	Lincoln	NE	68502	402-481-1111	
Web: www.bryanhealth.com					
Creighton University Medical Ctr 601 N 30th St	Omaha	NE	68131	402-449-4000	449-5020
Web: www.creighton.edu					
Faith Regional Health Services 2700 W Norfolk Ave	Norfolk	NE	68701	402-371-4880	644-7468
Web: www.frhs.org					
Fremont Area Medical Ctr 450 E 23rd St	Fremont	NE	68025	402-721-1610	727-3656
Web: www.famc.org					
Great Plains Regional Medical Ctr (GPRMC) 601 W Leota St PO Box 1167	North Platte	NE	69101	308-696-8000	535-3410
TF: 800-662-0011 ■ *Web:* www.gprmc.com					
Immanuel Medical Ctr 6901 N 72nd St	Omaha	NE	68122	402-572-2121	572-3177
Web: chihealth.com/immanuel-medical-center					
Mary Lanning Memorial Hospital 715 N St Joseph Ave	Hastings	NE	68901	402-463-4521	461-5321
Web: www.marylanning.org					
Midlands Community Hospital 11111 S 84th St	Papillion	NE	68046	402-593-3000	593-3100
Web: chihealth.com/					
Nebraska Medical Ctr, The 4350 Dewey Ave	Omaha	NE	68105	402-552-2000	552-3267
Web: www.nebraskamed.com					
Nebraska Methodist Hospital 8303 Dodge St	Omaha	NE	68114	402-354-4000	354-8735
Web: www.bestcare.org					
Regional West Medical Ctr 4021 Ave B	Scottsbluff	NE	69361	308-635-3711	630-1815
Web: www.rwmc.net					
Saint Elizabeth Regional Medical Ctr 555 S 70th St	Lincoln	NE	68510	402-219-8000	219-8973
Web: www.saintelizabethonline.com					
University of Nebraska Medical Ctr 42nd and Emile	Omaha	NE	68198	402-559-4000	559-7866
TF: 800-642-1095 ■ *Web:* www.unmc.edu					

Nevada

				Phone	Fax
Carson Tahoe Hospital 1600 Medical Pkwy	Carson City	NV	89703	775-445-8000	887-4580
Web: www.carsontahoehospital.com					
Desert Springs Hospital Medical Ctr 2075 E Flamingo Rd	Las Vegas	NV	89119	702-733-8800	
Web: www.desertspringshospital.com					
MountainView Hospital 3100 N Tenaya Way	Las Vegas	NV	89128	702-255-5000	255-5074
Web: www.mountainview-hospital.com					
Northern Nevada Medical Ctr 2375 E Prater Way	Sparks	NV	89434	775-331-7000	356-4986
Web: www.nnmc.com					
Renown Regional Medical Ctr 1155 Mill St	Reno	NV	89502	775-982-4100	982-4111
Web: www.renown.org					
Saint Mary's Regional Medical Ctr 235 W Sixth St	Reno	NV	89503	775-770-3000	770-7474
Web: www.saintmarysreno.com					
Saint Rose Dominican Hospital *Rose de Lima Campus* 102 E Lk Mead Blvd	Henderson	NV	89015	702-564-2622	616-7549
Web: www.strosehospitals.org/medical_services/our_hospitals/185510					
Summerlin Hospital Medical Ctr 657 Town Ctr Dr	Las Vegas	NV	89144	702-233-7000	
Web: www.summerlinhospital.com					
Sunrise Hospital & Medical Ctr 3186 S Maryland Pkwy	Las Vegas	NV	89109	702-731-8000	731-8739
Web: www.sunrisehospital.com					
Valley Hospital Medical Ctr 620 Shadow Ln	Las Vegas	NV	89106	702-388-4000	388-4636
Web: www.valleyhospital.net					

New Hampshire

				Phone	Fax
Catholic Medical Ctr (CMC) 100 McGregor St	Manchester	NH	03102	603-668-3545	663-6989
TF: 800-437-9666 ■ *Web:* www.catholicmedicalcenter.org					
Cheshire Medical Ctr 590 Ct St	Keene	NH	03431	603-354-5400	354-5402
Web: www.cheshire-med.com					
Concord Hospital 250 Pleasant St	Concord	NH	03301	603-225-2711	224-6527
Web: www.concordhospital.org					
Dartmouth-Hitchcock Medical Ctr One Medical Ctr Dr	Lebanon	NH	03756	603-650-5000	650-8765
Web: www.dartmouth-hitchcock.org					
Elliot Hospital 1 Elliot Way Ste 100	Manchester	NH	03103	603-627-1669	624-2297
TF: 800-922-4999 ■ *Web:* www.elliothospital.org					
Exeter Hospital 5 Alumni Dr	Exeter	NH	03833	603-580-6668	778-6592
Web: www.exeterhospital.com					
Frisbie Memorial Hospital 11 Whitehall Road	Rochester	NH	03867	603-332-5211	335-8488
Web: www.frisbiehospital.com					
Lakes Region General Hospital 80 Highland St	Laconia	NH	03246	603-524-3211	527-2887
Web: www.lrgh.org					
Parkland Medical Ctr One Parkland Dr	Derry	NH	03038	603-432-1500	421-2111
Web: www.parklandmedicalcenter.com					
Portsmouth Regional Hospital 333 Borthwick Ave	Portsmouth	NH	03801	603-436-5110	431-3783
TF: 800-685-8282 ■ *Web:* www.portsmouthhospital.com					
Southern New Hampshire Medical Ctr Eight Prospect St PO Box 2014	Nashua	NH	03061	603-577-2000	577-5630
Web: snhhs.org					
Speare Memorial Hospital Assn 16 Hospital Rd	Plymouth	NH	03264	603-536-1120	
Web: www.spearehospital.com					
Wentworth-Douglass Hospital 789 Central Ave	Dover	NH	03820	603-742-5252	740-2242
TF: 877-201-7100 ■ *Web:* www.wdhospital.com					

New Jersey

				Phone	Fax
Atlantic Health System 475 South St	Morristown	NJ	07960	973-971-5000	290-7561
Web: www.atlantichealth.org					
Atlanticare Regional Medical Ctr 1925 Pacific Ave	Atlantic City	NJ	08401	609-344-4081	569-7020
Web: atlanticare.org					
Bayonne Medical Center 29th St & Ave E	Bayonne	NJ	07002	201-858-5000	858-5000
Web: bayonnemedicalcenter.org					
Bayshore Community Hospital 727 N Beers St	Holmdel	NJ	07733	732-739-5900	888-7334
Web: www.bayshorehospital.org					
Bergen Regional Medical Ctr 230 E Ridgewood Ave	Paramus	NJ	07652	201-967-4000	967-4277
Web: www.bergenregional.com					
Cape Regional Medical Ctr Inc (CRMC) Two Stone Harbor Blvd	Cape May Court House	NJ	08210	609-463-2000	465-9391
Web: www.caperegional.com					
Capital Health System at Fuld 750 Brunswick Ave	Trenton	NJ	08638	609-394-6000	394-6687
Web: www.capitalhealth.org					
Capital Health System at Mercer 446 Bellevue Ave	Trenton	NJ	08618	609-394-4000	
Web: www.capitalhealth.org					
CentraState Medical Ctr 901 W Main St	Freehold	NJ	07728	732-431-2000	462-5129
Web: www.centrastate.com					
Chilton Hospital 97 W Pkwy	Pompton Plains	NJ	07444	973-831-5000	831-5516
Web: www.chiltonhealth.org					

Phone | Fax

Clara Maass Medical Ctr
One Clara Maass Dr .... Belleville NJ 07109 973-450-2000 450-0181
Web: www.barnabashealth.org

Columbus Hospital 495 N 13th St .... Newark NJ 07107 973-587-7777 587-7829
Web: www.columbusltach.org/

Community Medical Ctr (CMC) 99 Hwy 37 W .... Toms River NJ 08755 732-557-8000 557-8935
TF: 888-724-7123 ■ *Web:* www.barnabashealth.org

Cooper University Hospital Three Cooper Plz .... Camden NJ 08103 856-342-2000 342-3299
TF: 800-826-6737 ■ *Web:* www.cooperhealth.org

East Orange General Hospital
300 Central Ave .... East Orange NJ 07018 973-672-8400
Web: www.evh.org

Englewood Hospital & Medical Ctr
350 Engle St .... Englewood NJ 07631 201-894-3000 894-1473
Web: www.englewoodhospital.com

Hackensack University Medical Ctr
30 Prospect Ave .... Hackensack NJ 07601 201-996-2000 489-7275
Web: hackensackumc.org

Hoboken University Medical Ctr
308 Willow Ave .... Hoboken NJ 07030 201-418-1000
Web: www.carepointhealth.org

Holy Name Hospital 718 Teaneck Rd .... Teaneck NJ 07666 201-833-3000 227-6048
Web: www.holyname.org

Hunterdon Medical Ctr 2100 Westcott Dr .... Flemington NJ 08822 908-788-6100 788-6111
Web: www.hunterdonhealthcare.org

Irvington General Hospital
95 Old Short Hills Rd .... West Orange NJ 07052 888-724-7123 322-6361*
**Fax Area Code:* 973 ■ *TF:* 888-724-7123 ■ *Web:* www.barnabashealth.org

Jersey City Medical Ctr 355 Grand St .... Jersey City NJ 07302 201-915-2000 915-2002
Web: www.libertyhealth.org

Jersey Shore University Medical Ctr
1945 Rt 33 .... Neptune NJ 07753 732-775-5500 751-5120
TF: 800-560-9990 ■ *Web:* www.jerseyshoreuniversitymedicalcenter.com

JFK Medical Ctr 65 James St .... Edison NJ 08818 732-321-7000 549-8532
Web: www.jfkmc.org

Kennedy Health System-Cherry Hill
2201 Chapel Ave W .... Cherry Hill NJ 08002 856-488-6500 488-6526
TF: 866-224-0264 ■ *Web:* www.kennedyhealth.org

Kimball Medical Ctr 600 River Ave .... Lakewood NJ 08701 732-363-1900 886-4406
Web: www.barnabashealth.org

Lifeline Medical Assoc LLC
99 Cherry Hill Rd Ste 220 .... Parsippany NJ 07054 973-316-0307
TF: 800-845-2785 ■ *Web:* www.lma-llc.com

Lourdes Medical Ctr of Burlington County
218 Sunset Rd .... Willingboro NJ 08046 609-835-2900
Web: www.lourdesnet.org

Memorial Hospital of Salem County
310 Woodstown Rd .... Salem NJ 08079 856-935-1000 935-3175
Web: www.mhschealth.com

Monmouth Medical Ctr 300 Second Ave .... Long Branch NJ 07740 732-222-5200 923-7544
TF: 888-724-7123 ■ *Web:* www.barnabashealth.org

Morristown Medical Ctr 100 Madison Ave .... Morristown NJ 07960 973-971-5000 290-7010
Web: www.atlantichealth.org

Muhlenberg Regional Medical Ctr
Park Ave & Randolph Rd .... Plainfield NJ 07060 908-668-2000
Web: jfkmc.org/jfk-muhlenberg-campus

Newark Beth Israel Medical Ctr 201 Lyons Ave .... Newark NJ 07112 973-926-7000 923-2886
Web: www.barnabashealth.org

Newton Memorial Hospital (NMH) 175 High St .... Newton NJ 07860 973-383-2121 383-8973
Web: atlantichealth.org/newton

Ocean Medical Ctr (OMC) 425 Jack Martin Blvd .... Brick NJ 08724 732-840-2200 840-3284
TF: 800-560-9990 ■ *Web:* www.oceanmedicalcenter.com/omc

Our Lady of Lourdes Medical Ctr
1600 Haddon Ave .... Camden NJ 08103 856-757-3500 757-3611
TF: 888-568-7337 ■ *Web:* www.lourdesnet.org

Overlook Medical Ctr 99 Beauvoir Ave .... Summit NJ 07902 908-522-2000 273-5134
Web: www.atlantichealth.org

Palisades Medical Ctr 7600 River Rd .... North Bergen NJ 07047 201-854-5000 854-5272*
**Fax:* Admitting ■ *Web:* www.palisadesmedical.org

Raritan Bay Medical Ctr
530 New Brunswick Ave .... Perth Amboy NJ 08861 732-442-3700 293-2297*
**Fax:* Hum Res ■ *Web:* www.rbmc.org

Riverview Medical Ctr One Riverview Plz .... Red Bank NJ 07701 732-741-2700 224-8408
Web: www.meridianhealth.com/rmc.cfm

Robert Wood Johnson University Hospital
1 Robert Wood Johnson Pl .... New Brunswick NJ 08901 732-828-3000 937-8837
TF: 888-637-9584 ■ *Web:* www.rwjuh.edu

Robert Wood Johnson University Hospital at Rahway (RWJUHR)
865 Stone St .... Rahway NJ 07065 732-381-4200 586-7900*
**Fax Area Code:* 609 ■ *Web:* www.rwjuhr.com

RWJ University Hospital at Hamilton
One Hamilton Health Pl .... Hamilton NJ 08690 609-586-7900 584-6429
Web: www.rwjhamilton.org

Saint Barnabas Medical Ctr
94 Old Short Hills Rd .... West Orange NJ 07052 973-322-5000 322-8790*
**Fax:* Admitting ■ *TF:* 888-724-7123 ■ *Web:* www.barnabashealth.org

Saint Clare's Hospital 25 Pocono Rd .... Denville NJ 07834 973-625-6000 625-6037
Web: www.saintclares.org

Saint Joseph's Regional Medical Ctr
703 Main St .... Paterson NJ 07503 973-754-2000 754-2208
Web: www.stjosephshealth.org

Saint Michael's Medical Ctr 111 Central Ave .... Newark NJ 07102 973-877-5000
Web: www.smmcnj.org

Saint Peter's University Hospital
254 Easton Ave .... New Brunswick NJ 08901 732-745-8600 247-8159*
**Fax:* Admitting ■ *Web:* www.saintpetershcs.com

SJH Elmer Hospital 501 W Front St .... Elmer NJ 08318 856-363-1000 358-3476
Web: www.inspirahealthnetwork.org

SJH Regional Medical Ctr (SJHRMC)
1505 W Sheman Ave .... Vineland NJ 08360 856-641-8000
Web: www.inspirahealthnetwork.org

Somerset Medical Ctr (SMC) 110 Rehill Ave .... Somerville NJ 08876 908-685-2200 685-2894
Web: rwjuh.edu

Phone | Fax

Southern Jersey Family Medical Centers Inc
860 S White Horse Pke .... Hammonton NJ 08037 609-567-0200
Web: www.sjfmc.org/

Southern Ocean Medical Ctr 1140 Rt 72 W .... Manahawkin NJ 08050 609-978-8900
TF: 888-864-4203 ■ *Web:* www.ultracare-dialysis.com

St Joseph's Wayne Hospital 224 Hamburg Tpke .... Wayne NJ 07470 973-942-6900 389-4044
Web: www.stjosephshealth.org

Trinitas Hospital 225 Williamson St .... Elizabeth NJ 07207 908-994-5000 994-5756
Web: www.trinitashospital.com

Underwood-Memorial Hospital 509 N Broad St .... Woodbury NJ 08096 856-845-0100 845-5322
Web: inspirahealthnetwork.org

Union Hospital 1000 Galloping Hill Rd .... Union NJ 07083 908-964-7333
Web: www.barnabashealth.org

University Medical Ctr at Princeton (UMCP)
253 Witherspoon St .... Princeton NJ 08540 609-497-4304 497-4306
TF: 877-932-8935 ■ *Web:* princetonhcs.org

University of Medicine & Dentistry of New Jersey
Graduate School of Biomedical Sciences (GSBS)
185 S Orange Ave MSB B640 .... Newark NJ 07107 973-972-4511
Web: rbhs.rutgers.edu
University Hospital, The 150 Bergen St C- 431 .... Newark NJ 07103 973-972-4300 972-6932
Web: www.uhnj.org

Valley Health System 223 N Van Dien Ave .... Ridgewood NJ 07450 201-447-8000
TF: 800-825-5391 ■ *Web:* www.valleyhealth.com

Virtua Voorhees 101 Carnie Blvd .... Voorhees NJ 08043 856-322-3000
Web: www.virtua.org

Virtua-Memorial Hospital Burlington County
175 Madison Ave .... Mount Holly NJ 08060 609-267-0700 702-9751
Web: www.virtua.org

Warren Hospital 185 Roseberry St .... Phillipsburg NJ 08865 908-859-6700
Web: www.warrenhospital.org

West Jersey Hospital Berlin 100 Townsend Ave .... Berlin NJ 08009 856-322-3000 322-3201
Web: www.virtua.org

New Mexico

Phone | Fax

Carlsbad Medical Ctr 2430 W Pierce St .... Carlsbad NM 88220 505-887-4100 887-4256
Web: www.carlsbadmedicalcenter.com

Eastern New Mexico Medical Ctr
405 W Country Club Rd .... Roswell NM 88201 575-622-8170
TF: 800-222-1222 ■ *Web:* www.enmmc.com

Gallup Indian Medical Ctr
516 E Nizhoni Blvd PO Box 1337 .... Gallup NM 87301 505-722-1000 722-1397

Gila Regional Medical Ctr 1313 E 32nd St .... Silver City NM 88061 575-538-4000 538-9714*
**Fax Area Code:* 505 ■ *Web:* www.grmc.org

Lea Regional Medical Ctr 5419 N Lovington Hwy .... Hobbs NM 88240 575-492-5000 492-5505
TF: 877-492-8001 ■ *Web:* www.learegionalmedical.com

Lovelace Medical Ctr 5400 Gibson Blvd SE .... Albuquerque NM 87108 505-262-7000 727-8000
TF: 888-281-6531 ■ *Web:* www.lovelace.com

MountainView Regional Medical Ctr
4311 E Lohman Ave .... Las Cruces NM 88001 575-556-7600 556-7619
Web: www.mountainviewregional.com

Nor-Lea General Hospital Inc
1600 N Main Ave .... Lovington NM 88260 575-396-6611
Web: norlea.org

Plains Regional Medical Ctr
2100 N ML King Blvd .... Clovis NM 88101 505-769-2141 769-7337
TF: 800-923-6980 ■ *Web:* www.phs.org

Presbyterian Espanola Hospital
1010 Spruce St .... Espanola NM 87532 505-753-7111
Web: www.phs.org/

Presbyterian Hospital
1100 Central Ave SE .... Albuquerque NM 87106 505-841-1234 462-7756
TF: 888-977-2333 ■ *Web:* www.phs.org

Presbyterian Kaseman Hospital
8300 Constitution Ave NE .... Albuquerque NM 87110 505-291-2000 291-2983
TF: 800-432-4600 ■ *Web:* www.phs.org

Rehoboth McKinley Christian Hospital
1900 Redrock Dr .... Gallup NM 87301 505-863-7000 863-5806
Web: www.rmch.org

Saint Vincent Regional Medical Ctr
455 St Michael's Dr .... Santa Fe NM 87505 505-983-3361 820-5210
Web: www.stvin.org

San Juan Regional Medical Ctr
801 W Maple St .... Farmington NM 87401 505-609-2000
Web: www.sanjuanregional.com

New York

Phone | Fax

Albany Medical Ctr 47 New Scotland Ave .... Albany NY 12208 518-262-3125 262-3398
Web: www.amc.edu

Albany Memorial Hospital 600 Northern Blvd .... Albany NY 12204 518-471-3221
Web: www.nehealth.com

Alice Hyde Medical Ctr 133 Pk St .... Malone NY 12953 518-483-3000 481-2320
Web: www.alicehyde.com

Arnot Ogden Medical Ctr 600 Roe Ave .... Elmira NY 14905 607-737-4100 737-4447
Web: www.arnothealth.org

Auburn Memorial Hospital 17 Lansing St .... Auburn NY 13021 315-255-7011 255-7382
Web: www.auburnhospital.org

Aurelia Osborn Fox Memorial Hospital
1 Norton Ave .... Oneonta NY 13820 607-432-2000 431-5006
Web: www.bassett.org

Bassett Healthcare Network 1 Atwell Rd .... Cooperstown NY 13326 607-547-3456 547-3921
TF: 800-227-7388 ■ *Web:* www.bassett.org

Bellevue Hospital Ctr 462 First Ave .... New York NY 10016 212-562-4141 562-4036
Web: nyc.gov

Beth Israel Medical Ctr First Ave & 16th St .... New York NY 10003 212-420-2000 844-1565
Web: www.bethisraelny.org

				Phone	Fax
Bon Secours Community Hospital					
160 E Main St	Port Jervis	NY	12771	845-858-7000	858-7415
Web: www.bonsecourscommunityhosp.org					
BronxCare Family Wellness Center					
1276 Fulton Ave	Bronx	NY	10456	718-590-1800	901-8247
TF: 877-451-9361 ■ *Web:* www.bronxcare.org					
Brookdale University Hospital & Medical Ctr					
One Brookdale Plz	Brooklyn	NY	11212	718-240-5000	240-5042
Web: www.brookdalehospital.org					
Brookhaven Memorial Hospital Medical Ctr					
101 Hospital Rd	Patchogue	NY	11772	631-654-7100	
Web: www.brookhavenhospital.org					
Brooklyn Hospital Ctr 121 DeKalb Ave	Brooklyn	NY	11201	718-250-8000	
Web: www.tbh.org					
Brooks Memorial Hospital 529 Central Ave	Dunkirk	NY	14048	716-366-1111	363-7288
Web: www.brookshospital.org					
Buffalo General Hospital 100 High St	Buffalo	NY	14203	716-859-5600	
TF: 800-506-6480 ■ *Web:* www.kaleidahealth.org					
Catskill Regional Medical Ctr					
68 Harris-Bushville Rd PO Box 800	Harris	NY	12742	845-794-3300	794-3240
TF: 888-846-5945 ■ *Web:* www.crmcny.org					
Cayuga Medical Ctr 101 Dates Dr	Ithaca	NY	14850	607-274-4011	274-4527
Web: www.cayugamed.org					
Claxton-Hepburn Medical Ctr 214 King St	Ogdensburg	NY	13669	315-393-3600	393-8506*
**Fax:* Hum Res ■ *Web:* www.claxtonhepburn.org					
Clifton Springs Hospital & Clinic					
2 Coulter Rd	Clifton Springs	NY	14432	315-462-9561	462-3492
TF: 888-786-4347 ■ *Web:* www.cliftonspringshospital.com					
Columbia Memorial Hospital 71 Prospect Ave	Hudson	NY	12534	518-828-7601	828-9980
TF: 866-539-1370 ■ *Web:* www.columbiamemorial.com					
Coney Island Hospital 2601 Ocean Pkwy	Brooklyn	NY	11235	718-616-3000	616-4512
Web: coneyislandhospital.com					
Corning Hospital 176 Denison Pkwy E	Corning	NY	14830	607-937-7200	937-7693
TF: 877-750-2042 ■ *Web:* www.guthrie.org					
Cortland Regional Medical Ctr (CRMC)					
134 Homer Ave PO Box 2010	Cortland	NY	13045	607-756-3500	756-3590
Web: www.cortlandregional.org					
Crouse Hospital 736 Irving Ave	Syracuse	NY	13210	315-470-7111	470-7014
Web: www.crouse.org					
CVPH Medical Ctr (CPVH) 75 Beekman St	Plattsburgh	NY	12901	518-561-2000	561-0881
Web: www.cvph.org					
De Graff Memorial Hospital					
445 Tremont St	North Tonawanda	NY	14120	716-694-4500	690-2300
Web: www.kaleidahealth.org					
Eastern Long Island Hospital Assn, The					
201 Manor Pl	Greenport	NY	11944	631-477-1000	
Web: www.elih.org					
Ellis Hospital 1101 Nott St	Schenectady	NY	12308	518-243-4000	
Web: www.ellismedicine.org/home/ellishospitalmain.aspx					
Elmhurst Hospital Ctr 79-01 Broadway	Elmhurst	NY	11373	718-334-4000	334-5161
Web: nyc.gov					
Erie County Medical Ctr 462 Grider St	Buffalo	NY	14215	716-898-3000	898-5178
Web: www.ecmc.edu					
Faxton Campus 1676 Sunset Ave	Utica	NY	13502	315-624-6000	
Web: www.faxtonstlukes.com					
Faxton Saint Luke's Healthcare					
Saint Luke's Campus 1656 Champlin Ave	New Hartford	NY	13413	315-624-6000	624-6269
Web: www.faxtonstlukes.com					
FF Thompson Hospital 350 Parrish St	Canandaigua	NY	14424	585-396-6000	396-6481
Web: www.thompsonhealth.com					
Flushing Hospital Medical Ctr					
4500 Parsons Blvd	Flushing	NY	11355	718-670-5000	670-3077
Web: www.flushinghospital.org					
Forest Hills Hospital (FHH) 102-01 66th Rd	Forest Hills	NY	11375	718-830-4000	830-4168
Web: northshorelij.com/hospitals/location/forest-hills					
Franklin Hospital 900 Franklin Ave	Valley Stream	NY	11580	516-256-6000	256-6503
Web: www.northshorelij.com/body.cfm?id=58					
Geneva General Hospital 196 N St	Geneva	NY	14456	315-787-4000	
Web: www.flhealth.org					
Glen Cove Hospital 101 St Andrews Ln	Glen Cove	NY	11542	516-674-7300	674-7588
Web: www.northshorelij.com/body.cfm?id=53					
Glens Falls Hospital 100 Pk St	Glens Falls	NY	12801	518-926-1000	926-1919
TF: 800-994-6610 ■ *Web:* www.glensfallshospital.org					
Harlem Hospital Ctr 506 Lenox Ave	New York	NY	10037	212-939-1000	939-1974
Web: nyc.gov					
Highland Hospital of Rochester 1000 S Ave	Rochester	NY	14620	585-473-2200	341-8350
Web: www.urmc.rochester.edu					
Hudson Valley Hospital Ctr					
1980 Crompond Rd	Cortlandt Manor	NY	10567	914-737-9000	
Web: www.hvhc.org					
Huntington Hospital 270 Pk Ave	Huntington	NY	11743	631-351-2000	351-2586
Web: www.northshorelij.com					
Interfaith Medical Ctr 1545 Atlantic Ave	Brooklyn	NY	11213	718-613-4000	613-4101
Web: www.interfaithmedical.com					
Ira Davenport Memorial Hospital Inc					
7571 State Rt 54	Bath	NY	14810	607-776-8500	
Web: www.arnothealth.org					
Jacobi Medical Ctr 1400 Pelham Pkwy S	Bronx	NY	10461	718-918-8141	918-4607
Web: www.nyc.gov/html/hhc/jacobi/home.html					
Jamaica Hospital Medical Ctr					
8900 Van Wyck Expy	Jamaica	NY	11418	718-206-6000	657-0545
Web: www.jamaicahospital.org					
John T Mather Memorial Hospital					
75 N Country Rd	Port Jefferson	NY	11777	631-473-1320	476-2792
Web: www.matherhospital.org					
Kenmore Mercy Hospital 2950 Elmwood Ave	Kenmore	NY	14217	716-706-2112	447-6090
Web: www.chsbuffalo.org/body.cfm?id=49					
Kings County Hospital Ctr 451 Clarkson Ave	Brooklyn	NY	11203	718-245-3131	613-8019
Web: www1.nyc.gov					
Kingsbrook Jewish Medical Ctr					
585 Schenectady Ave	Brooklyn	NY	11203	718-604-5000	604-5243
Web: www.kingsbrook.org					
Lawrence Hospital 55 Palmer Ave	Bronxville	NY	10708	914-787-1000	787-3113
Web: nyplawrence.org/					
Lenox Hill Hospital 100 E 77th St	New York	NY	10021	212-434-2000	
Web: www.lenoxhillhospital.org					
Lincoln Medical & Mental Health Ctr					
234 E 149th St	Bronx	NY	10451	718-579-5016	
Web: nyc.gov					
Little Falls Hospital 140 Burwell St	Little Falls	NY	13365	315-823-1000	
Web: www.bassett.org					
Long Beach Medical Ctr 455 E Bay Dr	Long Beach	NY	11561	516-897-1000	897-1214
Web: longbeachmedicalcenter.org					
Long Island College Hospital (LICH)					
339 Hicks St	Brooklyn	NY	11201	718-780-1000	270-4775
TF: 800-227-8922 ■ *Web:* www.downstate.edu/lich					
Long Island Jewish Medical Ctr					
270-05 76th Ave	New Hyde Park	NY	11040	718-470-7000	
Web: www.northshorelij.com					
Lutheran Medical Ctr (LHC) 150 55th St	Brooklyn	NY	11220	718-630-7000	630-8228
Web: lutheranhealthcare.org/main/home.aspx					
Maimonides Medical Ctr (MMC) 4802 Tenth Ave	Brooklyn	NY	11219	718-283-6000	635-8157
Web: www.maimonidesmed.org					
Mercy Hospital of Buffalo 565 Abbott Rd	Buffalo	NY	14220	716-826-7000	828-2700
Web: www.chsbuffalo.org					
MidHudson Regional Hospital 241 N Rd	Poughkeepsie	NY	12601	845-483-5000	485-3762
Web: www.sfhospital.org					
Millard Fillmore Gates Cir Hospital					
726 Exchange St	Buffalo	NY	14210	716-859-8000	
Web: www.kaleidahealth.org					
Montefiore Medical Ctr 111 E 210th St	Bronx	NY	10467	718-920-4321	920-8543
Web: www.montefiore.org					
Mount Saint Mary's Hospital					
5300 Military Rd	Lewiston	NY	14092	716-297-4800	298-2001
Web: www.msmh.org					
Mount Sinai Medical Ctr, The					
1 Gustave L Levy Pl	New York	NY	10029	212-241-6500	731-3418
TF: 800-637-4627 ■ *Web:* www.mountsinai.org					
Mount Sinai of Queens 25-10 30th Ave	Astoria	NY	11102	718-932-1000	278-1786
Web: www.mshq.org					
Mount Vernon Hospital 12 N Seventh Ave	Mount Vernon	NY	10550	914-664-8000	632-2927
Nassau University Medical Ctr					
2201 Hempstead Tpke	East Meadow	NY	11554	516-572-0123	572-6252
Web: www.ncmc.edu					
New York Community Hospital 2525 Kings Hwy	Brooklyn	NY	11229	718-692-5300	692-8454
Web: www.nych.com					
New York Downtown Hospital 170 William St	New York	NY	10038	212-312-5000	312-5977
Web: nyp.org					
New York Hospital Medical Ctr of Queens					
56-45 Main St	Flushing	NY	11355	718-670-2000	661-7704
Web: www.nyhq.org					
New York Methodist Hospital 506 Sixth St	Brooklyn	NY	11215	718-780-3000	965-4324
Web: www.nym.org					
New York Presbyterian Hospital					
525 E 68th St	New York	NY	10021	212-746-5454	746-4293
Web: www.nyp.org					
Newark-Wayne Community Hospital					
1250 Driving Pk Ave	Newark	NY	14513	315-332-2427	332-2371
Web: www.rochestergeneral.org					
Niagara Falls Memorial Medical Ctr					
621 Tenth St	Niagara Falls	NY	14302	716-278-4000	278-4054
Web: www.nfmmc.org					
North Central Bronx Hospital 3424 Kossuth Ave	Bronx	NY	10467	718-519-5000	639-2473*
**Fax Area Code:* 917 ■ *TF:* 877-207-2134 ■ *Web:* nyc.gov					
North Fork Radiology PC					
1333 Roanoke Ave Ste 202	Riverhead	NY	11901	631-727-2755	
Web: www.northforkrad.com					
North Shore University Hospital					
888 Old Country Rd	Plainview	NY	11803	516-719-3000	719-2719
Web: www.northshorelij.com					
Northern Westchester Hospital					
400 E Main St	Mount Kisco	NY	10549	914-666-1200	666-1055
Web: www.nwhc.net					
Nyack Hospital 160 N Midland Ave	Nyack	NY	10960	845-348-2000	348-2160
Web: www.nyackhospital.org					
NYU Langone Medical Ctr 550 First Ave	New York	NY	10016	212-263-7300	263-8460
Web: www.med.nyu.edu					
Olean General Hospital 515 Main St	Olean	NY	14760	716-373-2600	375-6393
Web: www.ogh.org					
Oneida Healthcare Ctr 321 Genesee St	Oneida	NY	13421	315-363-6000	361-2043
Web: www.oneidahealthcare.org					
Orange Regional Medical Ctr					
60 Prospect Ave	Middletown	NY	10940	845-343-2424	333-1560
TF: 888-321-6762 ■ *Web:* www.ormc.org					
Arden Hill Campus Four Harriman Dr	Goshen	NY	10924	845-294-5441	
Web: www.ormc.org					
Oswego Hospital 110 W Sixth St	Oswego	NY	13126	315-349-5511	349-5732
Web: oswegohealth.org					
Our Lady of Lourdes Memorial Hospital					
169 Riverside Dr	Binghamton	NY	13905	607-798-5111	798-5989
Web: www.lourdes.com					
Park Ridge Hospital 1555 Long Pond Rd	Rochester	NY	14626	585-723-7000	368-3888
Web: www.unityhealth.org/parkridge.asp					
Parkway Hospital 70-35 113th St	Forest Hills	NY	11375	718-990-4100	
Web: hospitals.nyhealth.gov					
Peconic Bay Medical Ctr 1300 Roanoke Ave	Riverhead	NY	11901	631-548-6000	548-6048
Web: www.pbmchealth.org					
Peninsula Hospital Ctr (PHC)					
51-15 Beach Ch Dr	Far Rockaway	NY	11691	718-734-2000	
Phelps Memorial Hospital Ctr (PMHC)					
701 N Broadway Rt 9	Sleepy Hollow	NY	10591	914-366-3000	366-1017
Web: www.phelpshospital.org					
Putnam Hospital Ctr 670 Stoneleigh Ave	Carmel	NY	10512	845-279-5711	279-2821
Web: www.health-quest.org					

				Phone	Fax
Queens Hospital Ctr 82-68 164th St.	Jamaica	NY	11432	718-883-3000	274-4988*
**Fax Area Code: 212* ■ *TF:* 888-692-6116 ■ *Web:* nyc.gov					
Richmond University Medical Ctr 355 Bard Ave	Staten Island	NY	10310	718-818-1234	
Web: rumcsi.org					
Rochester General Health System (RGHS) 1425 Portland Ave	Rochester	NY	14621	585-922-4000	
TF: 877-922-5465 ■ *Web:* www.rochestergeneral.org					
Rome Memorial Hospital 1500 N James St	Rome	NY	13440	315-338-7000	338-7695
Web: www.romehosp.org					
Saint Catherine of Siena Medical Ctr 50 Rt 25 A	Smithtown	NY	11787	631-862-3000	862-3105
Saint Elizabeth Medical Ctr 2209 Genesee St	Utica	NY	13501	315-798-8100	798-8344
Web: www.stemc.org					
Saint James Mercy Hospital 411 Canisteo St	Hornell	NY	14843	607-324-8000	324-8115
Web: www.stjamesmercy.org					
Saint John's Riverside Hospital *ParkCare Pavilion* Two Pk Ave	Yonkers	NY	10703	914-964-7300	964-7704
Web: www.riversidehealth.org					
Saint Joseph's Hospital Health Ctr 301 Prospect Ave	Syracuse	NY	13203	315-448-5111	448-6161
TF: 888-785-6371 ■ *Web:* www.sjhsyr.org					
Saint Luke's Cornwall Hospital *Cornwall Campus* 19 Laurel Ave	Cornwall	NY	12518	845-458-4512	
Saint Peter's Health Care Services 315 S Manning Blvd.	Albany	NY	12208	518-525-1550	
Web: www.sphcs.org					
Samaritan Hospital 2215 Burdett Ave.	Troy	NY	12180	518-271-3300	271-3203
Web: www.nehealth.com					
Samaritan Medical Ctr 830 Washington St	Watertown	NY	13601	315-785-4000	785-4343
TF: 877-888-6138 ■ *Web:* www.samaritanhealth.com					
Saratoga Hospital 211 Church St	Saratoga Springs	NY	12866	518-587-3222	580-4122
Web: www.saratogahospital.org					
Sisters of Charity Hospital of Buffalo 2157 Main St	Buffalo	NY	14214	716-862-1000	862-1899
Web: www.chsbuffalo.org/facilities/hospitals/soch					
Sisters of Charity Hospital, St. Joseph Campus 2605 Harlem Rd	Cheektowaga	NY	14225	716-891-2400	862-2006
Web: www.chsbuffalo.org					
South Nassau Communities Hospital 1 Healthy Way.	Oceanside	NY	11572	516-632-3000	377-5385
TF: 877-768-8462					
Southampton Hospital 240 Meeting House Ln	SouthHampton	NY	11968	631-726-8200	283-5730
Web: www.southamptonhospital.org					
Southside Hospital 301 E Main St	Bay Shore	NY	11706	631-968-3000	968-3315
Web: northshorelij.com/hospitals/location/southside-hospital					
Staten Island University Hospital 475 Seaview Ave.	Staten Island	NY	10305	718-226-9000	226-8255
Web: www.siuh.edu					
Stony Brook University Hospital (SBUH) 101 Nicolls Rd	Stony Brook	NY	11794	631-444-4000	444-6649
Web: www.stonybrookmedicine.edu					
Stem Cell Transplantation Ctr 601 Elmwood Ave	Rochester	NY	14642	585-275-1941	275-5590
Web: www.urmc.rochester.edu					
Strong Memorial Hospital *University of Rochester Medical Ctr* 601 Elmwood Ave	Rochester	NY	14642	585-275-2100	273-1118
TF: 800-999-6673 ■ *Web:* www.urmc.rochester.edu					
United Memorial Medical Ctr 127 N St	Batavia	NY	14020	585-343-6030	344-7434
Web: www.ummc.org					
University Hospital SUNY Upstate Medical University 750 E Adams St	Syracuse	NY	13210	315-464-5540	464-4841
TF: 877-464-5540 ■ *Web:* upstate.edu/hospital					
Upstate University Hospital at Community General 4900 Broad Rd	Syracuse	NY	13215	315-492-5011	492-5418
Web: upstate.edu					
Vassar Bros Medical Ctr 45 Reade Pl	Poughkeepsie	NY	12601	845-454-8500	
TF: 877-729-2444 ■ *Web:* www.health-quest.org					
Westchester Medical Ctr 100 Woods Rd	Valhalla	NY	10595	914-493-7000	
Web: www.westchestermedicalcenter.com					
White Plains Hospital Ctr 41 E Post Rd.	White Plains	NY	10601	914-681-0600	681-2902
Web: www.wphospital.org					
Winthrop University Hospital 259 First St	Mineola	NY	11501	516-663-0333	663-2946
Web: www.winthrop.org					
Woodhull Medical & Mental Health Ctr 760 Broadway	Brooklyn	NY	11206	718-963-8000	963-8999
Web: nyc.gov					

North Carolina

				Phone	Fax
Alamance Regional Medical Ctr 1240 Huffman Mill Rd	Burlington	NC	27215	336-538-7000	538-7425
Web: www.armc.com					
Albemarle Hospital 1144 N Rd St.	Elizabeth City	NC	27909	252-335-0531	384-4654
Web: www.albemarlehealth.org					
Annie Penn Hospital 618 S Main St	Reidsville	NC	27320	336-951-4000	951-4561
Web: www.conehealth.com					
Anson Community Hospital 500 Morven Rd	Wadesboro	NC	28170	704-695-3482	
Web: carolinashealthcare.org					
Betsy Johnson Regional Hospital 803 Tilghman Dr, Ste 100 PO Box 1706	Dunn	NC	28334	910-892-7161	
Web: myharnetthealth.org					
Caldwell Memorial Hospital 321 Mulberry St SW	Lenoir	NC	28645	828-757-5100	757-5247
Web: www.caldwellmemorial.org					
Cape Fear Hospital 5301 Wrightsville Ave	Wilmington	NC	28403	910-452-8100	452-8121
Web: www.nhrmc.org					
Cape Fear Valley Medical Ctr (CFVMC) 1638 Owen Dr PO Box 2000	Fayetteville	NC	28304	910-609-4000	609-6160
Web: www.capefearvalley.com					
CarolinaEast Health System 2000 Neuse Blvd.	New Bern	NC	28561	252-633-8111	633-8144
Web: www.carolinaeasthealth.com					
Carolinas Medical Center-NorthEast 920 Church St N.	Concord	NC	28025	704-403-1275	403-3000
TF: 800-575-1275 ■ *Web:* www.carolinashealthcare.org					
Carolinas Medical Center-University 8800 N Tryon St	Charlotte	NC	28262	704-863-6000	863-6236
TF: 800-821-1535 ■ *Web:* www.carolinashealthcare.org					
Carolinas Medical Ctr 1000 Blythe Blvd	Charlotte	NC	28203	704-355-2000	355-5577
Web: www.carolinashealthcare.org					
Carolinas Medical Ctr Mercy 2001 Vail Ave	Charlotte	NC	28207	800-821-1535	304-5695*
**Fax Area Code: 704* ■ *TF:* 800-821-1535 ■ *Web:* www.carolinashealthcare.org					
Carolinas Medical Ctr Union (CMCU) 600 Hospital Dr	Monroe	NC	28112	704-283-3100	
Web: www.carolinashealthcare.org					
Carteret General Hospital 3500 Arendell St PO Box 1619	Morehead City	NC	28557	252-808-6000	808-6573
Web: www.carteretgeneral.com					
Catawba Valley Medical Ctr 810 Fairgrove Church Rd SE	Hickory	NC	28602	828-326-3000	326-3371
Web: www.catawbavalleymedical.org					
Central Carolina Hospital 1135 Carthage St	Sanford	NC	27330	919-774-2100	774-2295
TF: 800-292-2262 ■ *Web:* www.centralcarolinahosp.com					
Columbus Regional Healthcare System 500 Jefferson St	Whiteville	NC	28472	910-642-8011	642-9305
Web: www.crhealthcare.org					
Davis Regional Medical Ctr 218 Old Mocksville Rd PO Box 1823	Statesville	NC	28625	704-873-0281	838-7287
Web: www.davisregional.com					
Duke Health Raleigh Hospital 3400 Wake Forest Rd	Raleigh	NC	27609	919-954-3000	954-3900
Web: www.dukeraleighhospital.org					
Duke University Hospital 2301 Erwin Rd	Durham	NC	27710	919-684-8111	
Web: dukemedicine.org/					
Durham Regional Hospital 3643 N Roxboro Rd	Durham	NC	27704	919-470-4000	477-1931
Web: www.dukeregional.org					
Forsyth Medical Ctr 3333 Silas Creek Pkwy	Winston-Salem	NC	27103	336-718-5000	718-9258
Web: novanthealth.org/forsythmedicalcenter.aspx					
Frye Regional Medical Ctr (FRMC) 420 N Ctr St	Hickory	NC	28601	828-315-5000	315-3901
Web: www.fryemedctr.com					
Grace Hospital 2201 S Sterling St	Morganton	NC	28655	828-580-5000	
Web: www.blueridgehealth.org/grace-hospital.html					
Halifax Regional Medical Ctr 250 Smith Church Rd	Roanoke Rapids	NC	27870	252-535-8011	535-8466
Web: halifaxregional.org					
Heritage Hospital 111 Hospital Dr	Tarboro	NC	27886	252-641-7700	641-7484
Web: www.vidanthealth.com					
High Point Regional Health System (HPRHS) 601 N Elm St PO Box HP-5	High Point	NC	27262	336-878-6000	
TF: 877-878-7644 ■ *Web:* www.highpointregional.com					
Hugh Chatham Memorial Hospital 180 Parkwood Dr PO Box 560	Elkin	NC	28621	336-527-7000	526-2783
Web: www.hughchatham.org					
Iredell Health Systemÿ 557 Brookdale Dr	Statesville	NC	28677	704-873-5661	872-7924
Web: www.iredellmemorial.org					
Johnston Memorial Hospital 509 N Bright Leaf Blvd	Smithfield	NC	27577	919-934-8171	989-7297
Web: www.johnstonhealth.org					
Kernodle Clinic Inc 1234 Huffman Mill Rd	Burlington	NC	27215	336-538-1234	
Web: kernodle.duhs.duke.edu/					
Lake Norman Regional Medical Ctr 171 Fairview Rd	Mooresville	NC	28117	704-660-4000	660-4005
Web: www.lnrmc.com					
Lenoir Memorial Hospital 100 Airport Rd	Kinston	NC	28501	252-522-7000	522-7007
Web: www.lenoirmemorial.org					
Margaret R Pardee Memorial Hospital 800 N Justice St	Hendersonville	NC	28791	828-696-1000	696-1128
Web: www.pardeehospital.org					
Maria Parham Medical Ctr 566 Ruin Creek Rd PO Box 59	Henderson	NC	27536	252-438-4143	436-1114
Web: www.mariaparham.com					
Mission Hospital-St Joseph Campus 428 Biltmore Ave	Asheville	NC	28801	828-213-1111	213-0763
Web: mission-health.org					
Moore Regional Hospital 155 Memorial Dr PO Box 3000.	Pinehurst	NC	28374	910-715-1000	428-1567
TF: 866-415-2778 ■ *Web:* www.firsthealth.org					
Morehead Memorial Hospital 117 E King's Hwy	Eden	NC	27288	336-623-9711	623-7660
Web: www.morehead.org					
Moses H Cone Memorial Hospital 1200 N Elm St	Greensboro	NC	27401	336-832-7000	832-8192
TF: 866-391-2734 ■ *Web:* www.conehealth.com					
Nash Health Care Systems (NHCS) 2460 Curtis Ellis Dr	Rocky Mount	NC	27804	252-443-8000	962-8067
Web: www.nhcs.org					
New Hanover Regional Medical Ctr 2131 S 17th St	Wilmington	NC	28401	910-343-7000	452-8799
TF: 877-228-8135 ■ *Web:* www.nhrmc.org					
Northern Hospital of Surry County 830 Rockford St	Mount Airy	NC	27030	336-719-7000	
Web: www.northernhospital.com					
Onslow Memorial Hospital 317 Western Blvd	Jacksonville	NC	28541	910-577-2345	577-2246
Web: www.onslow.org					
Pender Memorial Hospital 507 E Fremont St	Burgaw	NC	28425	910-259-5451	259-6182
TF: 888-468-5474 ■ *Web:* www.nhrmc.org					
Pitt County Memorial Hospital 2100 Stantonsburg Rd	Greenville	NC	27835	252-847-4100	847-5147
Web: www.vidanthealth.com					
Presbyterian Hospital Charlotte 200 Hawthorne Ln	Charlotte	NC	28204	704-384-4000	384-5600
Web: novanthealth.org/presbyterianmedicalcenter.aspx					

	City	State	Zip	Phone	Fax
Randolph Hospital 364 White Oak St PO Box 1048 *Web:* www.randolphhospital.org	Asheboro	NC	27204	336-625-5151	625-4393
Rex Healthcare 4420 Lk Boone Trl *Web:* www.rexhealth.com	Raleigh	NC	27607	919-784-3100	
Richmond Memorial Hospital 925 Long Dr *Web:* www.firsthealth.org	Rockingham	NC	28379	910-417-3000	
Roanoke-Chowan Hospital 500 S Academy St *Web:* www.vidanthealth.com	Ahoskie	NC	27910	252-209-3148	209-3146
Rowan Regional Medical Ctr (RRMC) 612 Mocksville Ave *TF:* 888-844-0080	Salisbury	NC	28144	704-210-5000	210-5562
Rutherford Regional Health System 288 S Ridgecrest Ave *Web:* www.rutherfordhosp.org	Rutherfordton	NC	28139	828-286-5000	
Sampson Regional Medical Ctr 607 Beaman St *Web:* www.sampsonrmc.org	Clinton	NC	28328	910-592-8511	590-2321
Scotland Memorial Hospital 500 Lauchwood Dr *Web:* www.scotlandhealth.org	Laurinburg	NC	28352	910-291-7000	291-7499
Southeastern Regional Medical Ctr 300 W 27th St *Web:* www.srmc.org	Lumberton	NC	28358	910-671-5000	671-5200
Stanly Memorial Hospital 301 Yadkin St *Web:* www.stanly.org	Albemarle	NC	28001	704-984-4000	983-3562
Thomasville Medical Ctr 207 Old Lexington Rd **Fax Area Code:* 919 ■ *TF:* 888-844-0080 ■ *Web:* novanthealth.org/thomasvillemedicalcenter.aspx	Thomasville	NC	27360	336-472-2000	496-0191*
Triangle Orthopedic Assoc PA 120 William Penn Plz *TF:* 800-359-3053 ■ *Web:* www.triangleortho.com	Durham	NC	27704	919-220-5255	220-0520
Valdese General Hospital (VGH) 720 Malcolm Blvd Ste 200 *TF:* 800-994-6610 ■ *Web:* www.blueridgehealth.org	Valdese	NC	28690	828-874-2251	397-3226
Wake Forest University Baptist Medical Ctr Medical Ctr Blvd *Web:* www.wakehealth.edu	Winston-Salem	NC	27157	336-716-2011	716-2067
WakeMed Raleigh Campus 3000 New Bern Ave *Web:* www.wakemed.org	Raleigh	NC	27610	919-350-7000	350-8868
Watauga Medical Ctr 336 Deerfield Rd *Web:* www.apprhs.org	Boone	NC	28607	828-262-4100	262-4103
Wesley Long Community Hospital 501 N Elam Ave *TF:* 866-391-2734 ■ *Web:* mosescone.com/body.cfm/?id=41	Greensboro	NC	27403	336-832-1000	832-7869
Wilkes Regional Medical Ctr 1370 W D St PO Box 609 *Web:* wilkesregional.com	North Wilkesboro	NC	28659	336-651-8100	651-8465
Wilson Medical Ctr 1705 SW Tarboro St *Web:* www.wilsonmedical.com	Wilson	NC	27893	252-399-8040	
Women's Hospital of Greensboro 801 Green Vly Rd *Web:* www.conehealth.com/womens-hospital	Greensboro	NC	27408	336-832-6500	

North Dakota

	City	State	Zip	Phone	Fax
Altru Hospital 1200 S Columbia Rd *TF:* 800-732-4277 ■ *Web:* www.altru.org	Grand Forks	ND	58201	701-780-5000	780-5238
CHI St. Joseph's Health 2500 Fairway St *TF General:* 800-446-6215 ■ *Web:* www.stjoeshospital.org	Dickinson	ND	58601	701-456-4000	
Medcenter One Hospital 300 N Seventh St *TF:* 800-932-8758 ■ *Web:* bismarck.sanfordhealth.org	Bismarck	ND	58501	701-323-6000	323-5221
St Alexius Medical Ctr 900 E Broadway Ave *TF:* 877-530-5550 ■ *Web:* www.st.alexius.org	Bismarck	ND	58501	701-530-7755	530-8984
Trinity Hospital Saint Joseph's One W Burdick Expy *TF:* 800-247-1316 ■ *Web:* www.trinityhealth.org	Minot	ND	58701	701-857-5000	857-5117
Trinity Medical Ctr One Burdick Expy W PO Box 5020 *Web:* www.trinityhealth.org	Minot	ND	58702	701-857-5000	857-5117

Ohio

	City	State	Zip	Phone	Fax
Adena Regional Medical Ctr 272 Hospital Rd *Web:* www.adena.org	Chillicothe	OH	45601	740-779-7500	779-7934
Affinity Medical Ctr 875 Eigth St NE *TF:* 800-999-6673 ■ *Web:* www.affinitymedicalcenter.com	Massillon	OH	44646	330-832-8761	837-6814
Akron General Medical Ctr 400 Wabash Ave **Fax:* Admitting ■ *TF:* 800-221-4601 ■ *Web:* www.akrongeneral.org	Akron	OH	44307	330-344-6000	344-1752*
Alliance Community Hospital (ACH) 200 E State St *Web:* www.achosp.org	Alliance	OH	44601	330-596-6000	596-7079
Ashtabula County Medical Ctr (ACMC) 2420 Lake Ave *Web:* www.acmchealth.org	Ashtabula	OH	44004	440-997-2262	997-6644
Atrium Medical Ctr One Medical Ctr Dr *TF:* 800-338-4057 ■ *Web:* www.atriummedcenter.org	Middletown	OH	45005	513-424-2111	
Aultman Hospital 2600 Sixth St SW *Web:* www.aultman.org	Canton	OH	44710	330-452-9911	438-6356
Bethesda Hospital 2951 Maple Ave *TF:* 800-322-4762 ■ *Web:* genesishcs.org	Zanesville	OH	43701	740-454-4000	454-4781
Bethesda North Hospital 10500 Montgomery Rd *Web:* www.trihealth.com	Cincinnati	OH	45242	513-569-5400	745-1441
Blanchard Valley Hospital 1900 S Main St *Web:* www.bvhealthsystem.org	Findlay	OH	45840	419-423-4500	423-5358
Bryan Hospital (CHWC) 433 W High St *Web:* www.chwchospital.com/default.asp	Bryan	OH	43506	419-636-1131	630-2155
Charles F Kettering Memorial Hospital 3535 Southern Blvd *Web:* www.ketteringhealth.org	Kettering	OH	45429	937-298-4331	395-8423
Christ Hospital 2139 Auburn Ave *TF:* 800-527-8919 ■ *Web:* thechristhospital.com	Cincinnati	OH	45219	513-585-2000	585-3200
Clermont Mercy Hospital 3000 Hospital Dr	Batavia	OH	45103	513-732-8200	732-8550
Cleveland Clinic 9500 Euclid Ave *TF:* 800-223-2273 ■ *Web:* my.clevelandclinic.org	Cleveland	OH	44195	216-444-2200	444-0271
Clinton Memorial Hospital (CMH) 610 W Main St PO Box 600 *TF:* 800-803-9648 ■ *Web:* www.cmhregional.com	Wilmington	OH	45177	937-382-6611	382-6633
Coshocton County Memorial Hospital Assn Inc 1460 Orange St *Web:* www.ccmh.com	Coshocton	OH	43812	740-622-6411	
Deaconess Hospital 311 Straight St **Fax Area Code:* 937 ■ *TF:* 800-398-5699 ■ *Web:* www.deaconess-healthcare.com	Cincinnati	OH	45219	513-559-2100	783-5820*
Doctors Hospital 5100 W Broad St *Web:* www.ohiohealth.com/doctors	Columbus	OH	43228	614-544-1000	
East Liverpool City Hospital (ELCH) 425 W Fifth St *Web:* www.elch.org	East Liverpool	OH	43920	330-385-7200	
Euclid Hospital 18901 Lk Shore Blvd *Web:* my.clevelandclinic.org	Euclid	OH	44119	216-531-9000	692-7488
Fairfield Medical Ctr (FMC) 401 N Ewing St *TF:* 800-548-2627 ■ *Web:* www.fmchealth.org	Lancaster	OH	43130	740-687-8000	
Fairview Hospital 18101 Lorain Ave *TF:* 800-801-2273 ■ *Web:* my.clevelandclinic.org	Cleveland	OH	44111	216-476-7000	476-4064
Firelands Regional Medical Ctr 1111 Hayes Ave *TF:* 800-342-1177 ■ *Web:* www.firelands.com	Sandusky	OH	44870	419-557-7400	557-6977
Fisher-Titus Medical Ctr (FTMC) 272 Benedict Ave *TF:* 800-589-3862 ■ *Web:* www.fisher-titus.org	Norwalk	OH	44857	419-668-8101	
Flower Hospital 5200 Harroun Rd *Web:* www.promedica.org	Sylvania	OH	43560	419-824-1444	882-2342
Fort Hamilton Hospital 630 Eaton Ave *Web:* www.ketteringhealth.org	Hamilton	OH	45013	513-867-2000	867-2119
Grandview Medical Ctr 405 W Grand Ave *Web:* www.ketteringhealth.org	Dayton	OH	45405	937-395-3963	395-8327
Grant Medical Ctr 111 S Grant Ave *Web:* www.ohiohealth.com	Columbus	OH	43215	614-566-9000	566-8043
Greene Memorial Hospital 1141 N Monroe Dr *Web:* ketteringhealth.org	Xenia	OH	45385	937-352-2000	352-3233
Hillcrest Hospital 6780 Mayfield Rd *Web:* my.clevelandclinic.org	Mayfield Heights	OH	44124	440-312-4500	
Holzer Health Systems 100 Jackson Pk *Web:* www.holzer.org	Gallipolis	OH	45631	740-446-5000	446-5522
Jewish Hospital 4777 E Galbraith Rd *Web:* e-mercy.com/jewish-hospital.aspx	Cincinnati	OH	45236	513-686-3000	686-3003
Kaiser Permanente Parma Medical Ctr 12301 Snow Rd *TF:* 800-524-7372 ■ *Web:* kaiserpermanente.org	Cleveland	OH	44130	216-362-2000	362-2093
Knox Community Hospital 1330 Coshocton Rd *Web:* www.knoxcommhosp.org	Mount Vernon	OH	43050	740-393-9000	393-3487
Lakewood Hospital 14519 Detroit Ave *TF:* 866-588-2264 ■ *Web:* my.clevelandclinic.org	Lakewood	OH	44107	216-521-4200	529-7161
Licking Memorial Hospital 1320 W Main St *Web:* www.lmhealth.org	Newark	OH	43055	740-348-4000	348-4106
Lima Memorial Hospital 1001 Bellefontaine Ave *TF:* 800-252-3337 ■ *Web:* www.limamemorial.org	Lima	OH	45804	419-228-3335	226-5013
Lutheran Hospital 1730 W 25th St *Web:* my.clevelandclinic.org	Cleveland	OH	44113	216-696-4300	363-2082
Marietta Memorial Hospital 401 Matthew St *TF:* 800-523-3977 ■ *Web:* mhsystem.org/	Marietta	OH	45750	740-374-1400	374-1787
Marymount Hospital 12300 McCracken Rd *TF:* 800-801-2273 ■ *Web:* my.clevelandclinic.org	Garfield Heights	OH	44125	216-581-0500	587-8882
Medcentral Health System Mansfield Hospital 335 Glessner Ave *Web:* www.medcentral.org	Mansfield	OH	44903	419-526-8000	521-7960
Memorial Hospital 715 S Taft Ave *TF:* 800-971-8203 ■ *Web:* www.memorialhcs.org	Fremont	OH	43420	419-332-7321	332-5875
Mercer County Joint Township Community Hospital 800 W Main St *TF:* 888-844-2341 ■ *Web:* www.mercer-health.com	Coldwater	OH	45828	419-678-2341	
Mercy Hospital Anderson 7500 State Rd *Web:* e-mercy.com	Cincinnati	OH	45255	513-624-4500	624-3299
Mercy Hospital Western Hills 3131 Queen City Ave *Web:* e-mercy.com	Cincinnati	OH	45238	513-389-5000	389-5201
Mercy Regional Medical Ctr 3700 Kolbe Rd *Web:* www.mercyonline.org	Lorain	OH	44053	440-960-4000	
Mercy St Anne Hospital 3404 W Sylvania Ave *Web:* www.mercyweb.org	Toledo	OH	43623	419-407-2663	407-3889
MetroHealth Medical Ctr 2500 MetroHealth Dr *TF:* 800-554-5251 ■ *Web:* www.metrohealth.org	Cleveland	OH	44109	216-778-7800	
Miami Valley Hospital One Wyoming St *TF All:* 800-544-0630 ■ *Web:* www.miamivalleyhospital.org	Dayton	OH	45409	937-208-8000	208-2225
Mount Carmel Saint Ann's Hospital 500 S Cleveland Ave *Web:* www.mountcarmelhealth.com	Westerville	OH	43081	614-898-4000	898-8668
Mount Carmel West Hospital 793 W State St *TF:* 800-346-1009 ■ *Web:* mountcarmelhealth.com	Columbus	OH	43222	614-234-5000	944-5070
Northside Medical Ctr (NMC) 500 Gypsy Ln *Web:* valleycareofohio.net/pages/home.aspx	Youngstown	OH	44501	330-884-1000	
Ohio State University Wexner Medical Center, The 410 W Tenth Ave *Web:* www.medicalcenter.osu.edu	Columbus	OH	43210	614-293-8652	
ProMedica 2142 N Cove Blvd **Fax:* Admitting ■ *Web:* www.promedica.org	Toledo	OH	43606	419-291-5437	291-6901*

Phone | Fax

Riverside Methodist Hospital
3535 Olentangy River Rd ... Columbus OH 43214 614-566-5000 566-6760
TF: 800-837-7555 ■ *Web:* www.ohiohealth.com/facilities/riverside

Robinson Memorial Hospital
6847 N Chestnut St ... Ravenna OH 44266 330-297-0811 297-2353
Web: www.robinsonmemorial.org

Saint Charles Mercy Hospital 2600 Navarre Ave ... Oregon OH 43616 419-696-7200 696-7328
TF: 888-987-6372 ■ *Web:* www.mercyweb.org/st_charles.aspx

Saint Rita's Medical Ctr (SRMC) 730 W Market St ... Lima OH 45801 419-227-3361 226-9750
TF: 800-232-7762 ■ *Web:* ehealthconnection.com/regions/st%5fritas/

Saint Vincent Charity Hospital (SVCH)
2351 E 22nd St ... Cleveland OH 44115 216-861-6200 363-2519
TF: 800-750-0750 ■ *Web:* www.stvincentcharity.com

Salem Community Hospital 1995 E State St ... Salem OH 44460 330-332-1551 332-7691
Web: www.salemhosp.com

Southeastern Ohio Regional Medical Ctr
1341 Clark St ... Cambridge OH 43725 740-439-8000 439-8175
Web: www.seormc.org

Southern Ohio Medical Ctr (SOMC)
1805 27th St ... Portsmouth OH 45662 740-356-5000 353-2981
Web: www.somc.org

Southwest General Health Ctr
18697 Bagley Rd ... Middleburg Heights OH 44130 440-816-8000 816-5348
Web: www.swgeneral.com

St Joseph Health Ctr 667 Eastland Ave SE ... Warren OH 44484 330-841-4000
Web: mercy.com

Summa Barberton Hospital 155 Fifth St NE ... Barberton OH 44203 330-615-3000
TF: 888-905-6071 ■ *Web:* summahealth.org

Trinity Medical Ctr West
4000 Johnson Rd ... Steubenville OH 43952 740-264-8000 283-7104
TF: 877-271-4176 ■ *Web:* www.trinityhealth.com

Trumbull Memorial Hospital (TMH)
1350 E Market St ... Warren OH 44482 330-841-9011
Web: valleycareofohio.net

UH Parma Medical Center (PCGH) 7007 Powers Blvd ... Parma OH 44129 440-743-3000 743-4386
TF: 855-292-4292 ■ *Web:* www.parmahospital.org

University Hospital Bedford Medical Ctr
44 Blaine Ave ... Bedford OH 44146 440-735-3900 735-3631
Web: www.uhhospitals.org

University Hospitals of Cleveland
11100 Euclid Ave ... Cleveland OH 44106 216-844-1000 844-7497
TF: 866-844-2273 ■ *Web:* www.uhhospitals.org

University of Toledo Medical Center, The
3000 Arlington Ave ... Toledo OH 43614 419-383-4000 383-3850
TF: 800-321-8383

Upper Valley Medical Ctr (UVMC)
3130 N County Rd 25-A ... Troy OH 45373 937-440-4000 440-7337
TF: 866-608-3463 ■ *Web:* www.uvmc.com

Wayne HealthCare 835 Sweitzer St ... Greenville OH 45331 937-548-1141
Web: www.waynehealthcare.org

Wilson Memorial Hospital 915 W Michigan St ... Sidney OH 45365 937-498-2311 497-8251
TF: 800-589-9641 ■ *Web:* www.wilsonhospital.com

Wood County Hospital 950 W Wooster St ... Bowling Green OH 43402 419-354-8900 354-8957
Web: www.woodcountyhospital.org

Oklahoma

Phone | Fax

Children's Hospital at OU Medical Ctr, The
1200 N Everett Dr ... Oklahoma City OK 73104 405-271-5656 271-1773
Web: www.oumedicine.com

Claremore Regional Hospital LLC
1202 N Muskogee Pl ... Claremore OK 74017 918-341-2556
Web: hillcrestclaremore.com

Comanche County Memorial Hospital
3401 NW Gore Blvd ... Lawton OK 73505 580-355-8620 585-5458
Web: www.ccmhonline.com

Duncan Regional Hospital 1407 Whisenant Dr ... Duncan OK 73533 580-252-5300 251-8829
Web: www.duncanregional.com

Grady Memorial Hospital 2220 Iowa Ave ... Chickasha OK 73018 405-224-2300 779-2413
TF: 800-299-9665 ■ *Web:* www.gradymem.org

Hillcrest Medical Ctr 1120 S Utica Ave ... Tulsa OK 74104 918-579-1000
Web: www.hillcrest.com

INTEGRIS Baptist Medical Ctr
3300 NW Expy ... Oklahoma City OK 73112 405-949-3011
Web: www.integrisok.com

INTEGRIS Baptist Regional Health Ctr
200 Second Ave SW ... Miami OK 74355 918-542-6611 540-7605
TF: 888-951-2277 ■ *Web:* www.integrisok.com

INTEGRIS Bass Baptist Health Ctr 600 S Monroe ... Enid OK 73701 580-233-2300
TF: 888-951-2277 ■
Web: integrisok.com/bass-baptist-health-center-enid-ok

INTEGRIS Southwest Medical Ctr
4401 S Western St ... Oklahoma City OK 73109 405-636-7000 540-7702*
**Fax Area Code:* 918 ■ *TF:* 888-949-3816 ■ *Web:* www.integrisok.com/southwest

Jackson County Memorial Hospital
1200 E Pecan St ... Altus OK 73521 580-379-5000
TF: 800-595-0455 ■ *Web:* www.jcmh.com

Jane Phillips Medical Ctr
3500 SE Frank Phillips Blvd ... Bartlesville OK 74006 918-333-7200 331-1529
Web: www.jpmc.org

McAlester Regional Health Ctr
One Clark Bass Blvd ... McAlester OK 74501 918-426-1800 421-8066
Web: www.mrhcok.com

Medical Ctr of Southeastern Oklahoma
1800 University Blvd ... Durant OK 74701 580-924-3080 924-0422
TF: 888-280-6276 ■ *Web:* www.mymcso.com

Mercy Health Ctr (MHC) 4300 W Memorial Rd ... Oklahoma City OK 73120 405-755-1515 936-5794
Web: www.mercy.net

Mercy Memorial Health Ctr (MMHC)
1011 14th Ave NW ... Ardmore OK 73401 580-223-5400 220-6580
TF: 888-637-2937 ■ *Web:* www.mercy.net

Phone | Fax

Midwest Regional Medical Ctr
2825 Parklawn Dr ... Midwest City OK 73110 405-610-4411 610-1380
TF: 877-456-9617 ■ *Web:* www.midwestregional.com

Muskogee Regional Medical Ctr
300 Rockefeller Dr ... Muskogee OK 74401 918-682-5501 684-2552
Web: www.eastarhealth.com

Norman Regional Hospital 901 N Porter St ... Norman OK 73071 405-307-1000 307-1076
Web: www.normanregional.com

OSU Medical Ctr 744 W Ninth St ... Tulsa OK 74127 918-599-1000 599-5892
Web: www.osumc.net

OU Medical Ctr Edmond One S Bryant St ... Edmond OK 73034 405-341-6100 359-5500
Web: www.oumedicine.com

Ponca City Medical Ctr 1900 N 14th St ... Ponca City OK 74601 580-765-3321 765-0341
TF: 800-222-1222 ■ *Web:* www.poncamedcenter.com

Saint Anthony Hospital 1000 N Lee St ... Oklahoma City OK 73101 405-272-7000 272-6592
TF: 800-227-6964 ■ *Web:* www.saintsok.com

SouthCrest Hospital 8801 S 101st E Ave ... Tulsa OK 74133 918-294-4000 294-4809
Web: hillcrestsouth.com

Southwestern Medical Ctr (SWMC) 5602 SW Lee Blvd ... Lawton OK 73505 580-531-4700 531-4702
TF: 877-707-1780 ■ *Web:* www.southwesternmedcenter.com

Stillwater Medical Ctr 1323 W Sixth St ... Stillwater OK 74074 405-372-1480
Web: www.stillwater-medical.org

Unity Health Ctr 1102 W MacArthur St ... Shawnee OK 74804 405-273-2270 878-8101
Web: stanthonyshawnee.com

Valley View Regional Hospital
430 N Monte Vista St ... Ada OK 74820 580-332-2323 421-1386
Web: www.mercy.net

Oregon

Phone | Fax

Adventist Medical Ctr 10123 SE Market St ... Portland OR 97216 503-257-2500 261-6638
Web: www.adventisthealth.org/nw/pages/default.aspx

Bay Area Hospital 1775 Thompson Rd ... Coos Bay OR 97420 541-269-8111
Web: www.bayareahospital.org

Good Samaritan Regional Medical Ctr
3600 NW Samaritan Dr ... Corvallis OR 97330 541-768-5111
TF: 888-872-0760 ■ *Web:* www.samhealth.org

Legacy Emanuel Hospital & Health Ctr
2801 N Gantenbein Ave ... Portland OR 97227 503-413-2200 413-2428
TF: 888-598-4232 ■ *Web:* www.legacyhealth.org

Legacy Good Samaritan Hospital
1015 NW 22nd Ave ... Portland OR 97210 503-335-3500 413-6919
TF: 800-733-9959 ■ *Web:* www.legacyhealth.org

Legacy Meridian Park Hospital
19300 SW 65th Ave ... Tualatin OR 97062 503-692-1212
Web: www.legacyhealth.org

McKenzie-Willamette Hospital 1460 G St ... Springfield OR 97477 541-726-4400
Web: www.mckweb.com

Oregon Health & Science University Hospital
3181 SW Sam Jackson Pk Rd ... Portland OR 97239 503-494-8311 494-3400
TF: 800-292-4466 ■ *Web:* www.ohsu.edu

Peace Health Medical Group 1162 Willamette St ... Eugene OR 97401 360-734-5400 253-1781
Web: peacehealth.org

Providence Medford Medical Ctr
1111 Crater Lk Ave ... Medford OR 97504 541-732-5000 732-5872
TF: 877-541-0588 ■ *Web:* www.oregon.providence.org

Providence Portland Medical Ctr
4805 NE Glisan St ... Portland OR 97213 503-215-1111 215-6858
TF: 800-833-8899 ■ *Web:* www.oregon.providence.org

Providence Saint Vincent Medical Ctr
9205 SW Barnes Rd Ste 20 ... Portland OR 97225 503-216-2401 216-4041
TF: 800-677-6752 ■ *Web:* www.oregon.providence.org

Sacred Heart Medical Ctr 1255 Hilyard St ... Eugene OR 97401 541-686-7300 686-3699
TF: 800-288-7444 ■ *Web:* www.peacehealth.org

Salem Hospital 665 Winter St SE ... Salem OR 97301 800-876-1718 561-4844*
**Fax Area Code:* 503 ■ *TF:* 800-876-1718 ■ *Web:* www.salemhealth.org

Samaritan Albany General Hospital
1046 Sixth Ave SW ... Albany OR 97321 541-812-4000 812-4610
Web: www.samhealth.org

Sky Lakes Medical Ctr 2865 Daggett Ave ... Klamath Falls OR 97601 541-882-6311 274-6725
Web: www.skylakes.org

Tuality Community Hospital
335 SE Eigth Ave ... Hillsboro OR 97123 503-681-1111 681-1608
Web: www.tuality.org

Willamette Falls Hospital 1500 Div St ... Oregon City OR 97045 503-656-1631 650-6807
Web: oregon.providence.org

Pennsylvania

Phone | Fax

Abington Memorial Hospital 1200 Old York Rd ... Abington PA 19001 215-481-2000 481-4014
Web: abingtonhealth.org/

Albert Einstein Medical Ctr
5501 Old York Rd ... Philadelphia PA 19141 800-346-7834 456-6242*
**Fax Area Code:* 215 ■ *TF:* 800-346-7834 ■ *Web:* www.einstein.edu

Allegheny General Hospital 320 E N Ave ... Pittsburgh PA 15212 412-359-3131 359-8786
Web: ahn.org

Allegheny Health Network
1301 Carlisle St ... Natrona Heights PA 15065 724-224-5100 226-7385
Web: ahn.org

Altoona Regional Health System Altoona Hospital
620 Howard Ave ... Altoona PA 16601 814-889-2011
TF: 877-855-8152 ■ *Web:* www.altoonaregional.org

Aria Health Bucks County Campus
380 N Oxford Vly Rd ... Langhorne PA 19047 215-949-5000 949-5105
Web: www.ariahealth.org

Aria Health System
Frankford Campus 4900 Frankford Ave ... Philadelphia PA 19124 215-831-2000 831-2331
Web: www.ariahealth.org

Phone | Fax

Armstrong County Memorial Hospital (ACMH)
One Nolte Dr. . . . Kittanning PA 16201 724-543-8500 543-8704
Web: www.acmh.org

Berwick Hospital Ctr, The 701 E 16th St. . . . Berwick PA 18603 570-759-5000 759-3473
Web: commonwealthhealth.net/

Bradford Regional Medical Ctr
116 Interstate Pk. . . . Bradford PA 16701 814-368-4143 368-5722
Web: www.brmc.com

Brandywine Hospital 201 Reeceville Rd. . . . Coatesville PA 19320 610-383-8000 383-8360
Web: www.brandywinehospital.com

Bryn Mawr Hospital 130 S Bryn Mawr Ave . . . Bryn Mawr PA 19010 610-526-3000 526-4488
Web: www.mainlinehealth.org/bmh

Butler Health System One Hospital Way. . . . Butler PA 16001 724-283-6666 284-4645
Web: butlerhealthsystem.org

Canonsburg General Hospital
100 Medical Blvd . . . Canonsburg PA 15317 724-745-6100 873-5876
Web: ahn.org

Carlisle Regional Medical Ctr
361 Alexander Spring Rd . . . Carlisle PA 17015 717-249-1212 249-0770
Web: carlislermc.com

Chambersburg Hospital 112 N Seventh St . . . Chambersburg PA 17201 717-267-3000 267-7704
Web: www.summithealth.org

Charles Cole Memorial Hospital
1001 E Second St . . . Coudersport PA 16915 814-274-9300 274-0884
Web: www.charlescolehospital.com

Chester County Hospital
701 E Marshall St . . . West Chester PA 19380 610-431-5000 430-2958*
**Fax:* Admitting ■ *Web:* www.cchosp.com

Chestnut Hill Hospital
8835 Germantown Ave . . . Philadelphia PA 19118 215-248-8200 242-2601
Web: www.chhealthsystem.com

Clarion Hospital (CH) One Hospital Dr . . . Clarion PA 16214 814-226-9500 226-1224
TF: 800-522-0505 ■ *Web:* www.clarionhospital.org

Clearfield Hospital
809 Tpke Ave PO Box 992 . . . Clearfield PA 16830 814-765-5341 768-2421
TF: 800-281-8000 ■ *Web:* phhealthcare.org/

Crozer-Chester Medical Ctr (CCMC)
One Medical Ctr Blvd . . . Upland PA 19013 610-447-2000 447-2234
Web: www.crozerkeystone.org

Delaware County Memorial Hospital
501 N Lansdowne Ave . . . Drexel Hill PA 19026 610-284-8100 284-8993
Web: www.crozerkeystone.org

Divine Providence Hospital
1100 Grampian Blvd. . . . Williamsport PA 17701 570-326-8000
Web: susquehannahealth.org

Doylestown Hospital 595 W State St . . . Doylestown PA 18901 215-345-2200 345-2532
Web: www.dh.org

DuBois Regional Medical Ctr 100 Hospital Ave . . . Du Bois PA 15801 814-371-2200 375-3562
Web: phhealthcare.org/

Easton Hospital 250 S 21st St. . . . Easton PA 18042 610-250-4000 250-4078
Web: www.easton-hospital.com

Einstein at Elkins Park
60 E Township Line Rd . . . Elkins Park PA 19027 215-663-6000 663-6002
Web: einstein.edu/locations/einstein-medical-center-elkins-park/

Ellwood City Hospital 724 Pershing St. . . . Ellwood City PA 16117 724-752-0081 752-0966
Web: www.echospital.org

Ephrata Community Hospital
169 Martin Ave PO Box 1002 . . . Ephrata PA 17522 717-733-0311 738-6675
Web: www.ephratahospital.org

Evangelical Community Hospital
1 Hospital Dr . . . Lewisburg PA 17837 570-522-2000 522-4136
Web: www.evanhospital.com

Forbes Regional Hospital
2570 Haymaker Rd . . . Monroeville PA 15146 412-858-2000 858-2088
Web: ahn.org

Frick Hospital 508 S Church St . . . Mount Pleasant PA 15666 724-547-1500 542-1815
TF: 877-771-1234 ■ *Web:* excelahealth.org

Geisinger Health System (CMC) 1800 Mulberry St . . . Scranton PA 18510 570-703-8000
Web: www.geisinger.org

Geisinger Medical Ctr 100 N Academy Ave. . . . Danville PA 17822 570-271-6211 271-6927
Web: www.geisinger.org

Geisinger South Wilkes-Barre (GSWB)
25 Church St . . . Wilkes-Barre PA 18765 570-808-3100
Web: www.geisinger.org

Geisinger Wyoming Valley Medical Ctr
1000 E Mountain Dr . . . Danville PA 17822 570-271-8600
Web: www.geisinger.org

Gettysburg Hospital
147 Gettys St PO Box 3786 . . . Gettysburg PA 17325 717-334-2121 334-1302
Web: wellspan.org/offices-locations/hospitals

Gnaden Huetten Memorial Hospital
211 N 12th St . . . Lehighton PA 18235 610-377-1300 377-7000
Web: www.ghmh.org

Grand View Hospital 700 Lawn Ave . . . Sellersville PA 18960 215-453-4000 453-9151
Web: www.gvh.org

Grove City Medical Ctr (GCMC)
631 N Broad St Ext . . . Grove City PA 16127 724-450-7000 450-7179
Web: www.gcmcpa.org

Hahnemann University Hospital
230 N Broad St . . . Philadelphia PA 19102 215-762-7000 762-3272*
**Fax:* Admitting ■ *Web:* www.hahnemannhospital.com

Hanover Hospital 300 Highland Ave . . . Hanover PA 17331 717-637-3711 633-2187
TF: 800-673-2426 ■ *Web:* www.hanoverhospital.org

Harrisburg Hospital 111 S Front St . . . Harrisburg PA 17101 717-782-3131 782-5536
TF: 888-782-5678 ■ *Web:* www.pinnaclehealth.org

Heart of Lancaster Regional Medical Ctr
1500 Highland Dr . . . Lititz PA 17543 717-625-5000 507-3618*
**Fax Area Code:* 727 ■ *TF:* 800-999-6673 ■ *Web:* www.heartoflancaster.com

Heritage Valley Health System
1000 Dutch Ridge Rd . . . Beaver PA 15009 724-728-7000 773-4675
Web: www.heritagevalley.org/

Holy Redeemer Hospital & Medical Ctr
1648 Huntingdon Pk. . . . Meadowbrook PA 19046 215-947-3000 938-2023
TF: 800-818-4747 ■ *Web:* www.holyredeemer.com

Holy Spirit Hospital 503 N 21st St. . . . Camp Hill PA 17011 717-763-2100 972-7676
Web: www.hsh.org

Hospital of the University of Pennsylvania
3400 Spruce St. . . . Philadelphia PA 19104 215-662-4000
Web: www.pennmedicine.org

Indiana Regional Medical Ctr 835 Hospital Rd . . . Indiana PA 15701 724-357-7000 357-7449
Web: www.indianarmc.org

JC Blair Memorial Hospital
1225 Warm Springs Ave. . . . Huntingdon PA 16652 814-643-2290 643-9718
Web: www.jcblair.org

Jeanes Hospital 7600 Central Ave. . . . Philadelphia PA 19111 215-728-2000 728-3365
Web: www.jeanes.com

Lancaster General Hospital 555 N Duke St . . . Lancaster PA 17604 717-544-5511 544-5966
Web: www.lancastergeneralhealth.org

Lancaster Regional Medical Ctr
250 College Ave . . . Lancaster PA 17603 717-291-8211 291-8090
TF: 800-999-6673 ■ *Web:* www.lancastermedicalcenters.com

Lankenau Medical Ctr 100 E Lancaster Ave. . . . Wynnewood PA 19096 484-476-2000
TF: 866-225-5654 ■ *Web:* www.mainlinehealth.org/lh

Latrobe Area Hospital 121 W Second Ave . . . Latrobe PA 15650 724-537-1000 539-8834
Web: www.lah.com

Lehigh Valley Health Network 700 E Broad St . . . Hazleton PA 18201 570-501-4000 501-6971
TF: 800-528-1234 ■ *Web:* lvhn.org/hazleton/

Lewistown Hospital 400 Highland Ave. . . . Lewistown PA 17044 717-248-5411 242-7132
TF: 800-248-0505 ■ *Web:* www.lewistownhospital.org

Lower Bucks Hospital 501 Bath Rd . . . Bristol PA 19007 215-785-9200 785-9825
Web: www.lowerbuckshosp.com

Marian Community Hospital (MCH)
100 Lincoln Ave . . . Carbondale PA 18407 570-281-1000 222-5201
Web: www.marianhospital.org

Meadville Medical Ctr (MMC) 751 Liberty St. . . . Meadville PA 16335 814-333-5000 333-9456
TF: 800-254-5164 ■ *Web:* www.mmchs.org

Mercy Hospital of Philadelphia
501 S 54th St . . . Philadelphia PA 19143 215-748-9000 748-9366
Web: www.mercyhealth.org

Mercy Suburban Hospital (MSH)
2701 De Kalb Pk. . . . Norristown PA 19401 610-278-2000 272-4642
Web: www.mercyhealth.org/suburban

Millcreek Community Hospital 5515 Peach St . . . Erie PA 16509 814-864-4031 868-8249
Web: www.millcreekcommunityhospital.com

Monongahela Valley Hospital
1163 Country Club Rd . . . Monongahela PA 15063 724-258-1000 258-1830
Web: www.monvalleyhospital.com

Montgomery Hospital 1301 Powell St. . . . Norristown PA 19401 610-270-2000
Web: www.montgomeryhospital.org

Moses Taylor Hospital 700 Quincy Ave . . . Scranton PA 18510 570-340-2100
Web: commonwealthhealth.net/

Mount Nittany Medical Ctr
1800 E Pk Ave. . . . State College PA 16803 814-231-7000 231-7200
TF: 866-686-6171 ■ *Web:* www.mountnittany.org

Nazareth Hospital 2601 Holme Ave . . . Philadelphia PA 19152 215-335-6000 335-7740
Web: www.mercyhealth.org/nazareth

Northeastern Hospital School of Nursing
2301 E Allegheny Ave. . . . Philadelphia PA 19134 215-926-3145
Web: www.nehson.templehealth.org

Ohio Valley General Hospital
25 Heckel Rd Kennedy Township . . . McKees Rocks PA 15136 412-777-6161 777-6363
Web: www.ohiovalleyhospital.org

Paoli Hospital (PH) 255 W Lancaster Ave . . . Paoli PA 19301 610-648-1000 647-0450
Web: mainlinehealth.org/paoli

Penn Presbyterian Medical Ctr (PPMC)
39th & Market Sts. . . . Philadelphia PA 19104 215-662-8000 662-9212
TF: 800-789-7366 ■
Web: pennmedicine.org/penn-presbyterian-medical-center/

Penn State Milton S Hershey Medical Ctr
500 University Dr . . . Hershey PA 17033 717-531-8521 531-4162
Web: www.pennstatehershey.org

Pennsylvania Hospital 800 Spruce St. . . . Philadelphia PA 19107 215-829-3000 829-6363
TF: 800-789-7366 ■ *Web:* www.pennmedicine.org

Phoenixville Hospital 140 Nutt Rd. . . . Phoenixville PA 19460 610-983-1000 983-1488
Web: www.phoenixvillehospital.com

Pinnacle Health Hospital at Community General
4300 Londonderry Rd. . . . Harrisburg PA 17109 717-652-3000 782-5911
TF: 888-782-5678 ■ *Web:* pinnaclehealth.org

Pocono Medical Ctr 206 E Brown St . . . East Stroudsburg PA 18301 570-421-4000 476-3469
Web: www.poconohealthsystem.org

Pottstown Memorial Medical Ctr (PMMC)
1600 E High St. . . . Pottstown PA 19464 610-327-7000 327-7432
Web: www.pottstownmemorial.com

Punxsutawney Area Hospital Inc (PAH)
81 Hillcrest Dr . . . Punxsutawney PA 15767 814-938-1800 938-1453
Web: www.pah.org

Reading Hospital & Medical Ctr PO Box 16052 . . . Reading PA 19612 610-988-8000 988-5192
Web: www.readinghealth.org

Regional Hospital of Scranton
746 Jefferson Ave. . . . Scranton PA 18510 570-348-7100 348-7639
Web: commonwealthhealth.net/

Riddle Memorial Hospital 1068 W Baltimore Pike. . . . Media PA 19063 484-227-9400 891-3592*
**Fax Area Code:* 610 ■ *TF:* 866-225-5654 ■ *Web:* www.mainlinehealth.org

Robert Packer Hospital One Guthrie Sq. . . . Sayre PA 18840 570-888-6666
TF: 888-448-8474 ■ *Web:* www.guthrie.org

Roxborough Memorial Hospital (RMH)
5800 Ridge Ave. . . . Philadelphia PA 19128 215-483-9900 487-4221
Web: www.roxboroughmemorial.com

Sacred Heart HealthCare System 421 Chew St . . . Allentown PA 18102 610-776-4500
TF: 800-994-6610 ■ *Web:* www.shh.org

Saint Vincent Health Ctr 232 W 25th St . . . Erie PA 16544 814-452-5000 455-1724
Web: ahn.org/locations/saint-vincent-hospital

Schuylkill Medical Center
420 S Jackson St . . . Pottsville PA 17901 570-621-5000 622-8221

	City	State	ZIP	Phone	Fax
Sewickley Valley Hospital 720 Blackburn Rd *Web:* www.heritagevalley.org	Sewickley	PA	15143	412-741-6600	749-7400
Sharon Regional Health System 740 E State St *Web:* www.sharonregional.com	Sharon	PA	16146	724-983-3911	983-3842
Soldiers + Sailors Memorial Hospital 32-36 Central Ave *TF:* 800-808-5287 ■ *Web:* www.laurelhs.org	Wellsboro	PA	16901	570-723-7764	724-2126
Somerset Hospital 225 S Ctr Ave *Web:* www.somersethospital.com	Somerset	PA	15501	814-443-5000	443-4937
Southwest Regional Medical Ctr 350 Bonar Ave *Web:* www.southwestregionalmedical.com	Waynesburg	PA	15370	724-627-3101	627-8653
St Joseph's Hospital 16th St at Girard Ave *Web:* www.nphs.com	Philadelphia	PA	19130	215-787-9000	787-2115
Sunbury Community Hospital (SCH) 350 N 11th St *Web:* www.sunburyhospital.com	Sunbury	PA	17801	570-286-3333	286-3500
Taylor Hospital 175 E Chester Pk *Web:* www.crozerkeystone.org	Ridley Park	PA	19078	610-595-6000	595-6198
Temple University Hospital 3401 N Broad St *Web:* www.tuh.templehealth.org	Philadelphia	PA	19140	215-707-2000	707-3679
Temple University Hospital Episcopal Campus 100 E Lehigh Ave *Web:* www.episcopal.templehealth.org	Philadelphia	PA	19125	215-707-1200	707-0953
Thomas Jefferson University Hospital 111 S 11th St *TF:* 800-533-3669 ■ *Web:* hospitals.jefferson.edu/	Philadelphia	PA	19107	215-955-6000	955-6464
Uniontown Hospital (UH) 500 W Berkeley St *Web:* www.uniontownhospital.com	Uniontown	PA	15401	724-430 5000	430-3342
Horizon 110 N Main St *TF:* 888-447-1122 ■ *Web:* www.upmc.com	Greenville	PA	16125	724-588-2100	
University of Pittsburgh Medical Ctr					
Northwest 100 Fairfield Dr *Web:* www.upmc.com	Seneca	PA	16346	814-676-7600	676-7150
Passavant 9100 Babcock Blvd *Web:* www.upmc.com	Pittsburgh	PA	15237	412-367-6700	
Shadyside 5230 Centre Ave *Web:* www.upmc.com	Pittsburgh	PA	15232	412-623-2121	
South Side 2000 Mary St *TF:* 800-533-8762 ■ *Web:* www.upmc.com	Pittsburgh	PA	15203	412-488-5550	
UPMC Hamot 201 State St *Web:* www.upmc.com	Erie	PA	16550	814-877-6000	877-6104
UPMC McKeesport 1500 Fifth Ave *Web:* www.upmc.com	McKeesport	PA	15132	412-664-2000	
UPMC Mercy Hospital 1400 Locust St *Web:* www.upmc.com	Pittsburgh	PA	15219	412-232-8111	232-7380
UPMC Presbyterian 200 Lothrop St *Web:* www.upmc.com	Pittsburgh	PA	15213	412-647-8762	647-3496
Warren General Hospital Two Crescent Pk W *Web:* www.wgh.org	Warren	PA	16365	814-723-3300	723-2248
Washington Hospital, The 155 Wilson Ave *Web:* www.washingtonhospital.org	Washington	PA	15301	724-225-7000	222-7316
Western Pennsylvania Hospital 4800 Friendship Ave *Web:* ahn.org	Pittsburgh	PA	15224	412-578-5000	578-4321
Wilkes-Barre General Hospital 575 N River St **Fax:* Admitting ■ *Web:* commonwealthhealth.net/	Wilkes-Barre	PA	18764	570-829-8111	552-3030*
Williamsport Hospital & Medical Ctr 777 Rural Ave *Web:* www.susquehannahealth.org	Williamsport	PA	17701	570-321-1000	
York Hospital 1001 S George St *Web:* www.wellspan.org	York	PA	17405	717-851-2345	851-2968

Rhode Island

	City	State	ZIP	Phone	Fax
Kent Hospital 455 Toll Gate Rd *Web:* www.kentri.org	Warwick	RI	02886	401-737-7000	736-1000
KOCH EYE Assoc 566 Toll Gate Rd *Web:* kocheye.com	Warwick	RI	02886	401-738-4800	738-8153
Landmark Medical Ctr 115 Cass Ave *Web:* www.landmarkmedical.org	Woonsocket	RI	02895	401-769-4100	766-5488
Memorial Hospital of Rhode Island (MHRI) 111 Brewster St *TF:* 800-647-4362 ■ *Web:* www.mhri.org	Pawtucket	RI	02860	401-729-2000	
Miriam Hospital, The 164 Summit Ave *Web:* www.miriamhospital.org	Providence	RI	02906	401-793-2500	793-7587
Newport Hospital (NH) 11 Friendship St *Web:* www.newporthospital.org	Newport	RI	02840	401-845-1646	
Our Lady of Fatima Hospital 200 High Service Ave *Web:* www.saintjosephri.com	North Providence	RI	02904	401-456-3000	752-8248
Rhode Island Hospital 593 Eddy St *Web:* www.rhodeislandhospital.org	Providence	RI	02903	401-444-4000	444-6572
Roger Williams Medical Ctr 825 Chalkstone Ave *Web:* rwmcmedicine.org	Providence	RI	02908	401-456-2000	456-2029
South County Hospital 100 Kenyon Ave *Web:* www.schospital.com	Wakefield	RI	02879	401-782-8000	783-6330
Westerly Hospital 25 Wells St *TF:* 800-933-5960 ■ *Web:* westerlyhospital.org	Westerly	RI	02891	401-596-6000	348-0350

South Carolina

	City	State	ZIP	Phone	Fax
Aiken Regional Medical Centers 302 University Pkwy *TF:* 800-245-3679 ■ *Web:* www.aikenregional.com	Aiken	SC	29801	803-641-5000	641-5000
AnMed Health 800 N Fant St *Web:* www.anmedhealth.org	Anderson	SC	29621	864-512-1000	512-1552
Beaufort Memorial Hospital 955 Ribaut Rd *TF:* 877-532-6472 ■ *Web:* www.bmhsc.org	Beaufort	SC	29902	843-522-5200	
Bon Secours Saint Francis Hospital 2095 Henry Tecklenburg Dr *Web:* rsfh.com/	Charleston	SC	29414	843-402-1000	402-1769
Carolina Pines Regional Medical Ctr 1304 W Bobo Newsome Hwy *Web:* www.cprmc.com	Hartsville	SC	29550	843-339-2100	339-4116
Carolinas Hospital System 805 Pamplico Hwy *Web:* www.carolinashospital.com	Florence	SC	29505	843-674-5000	674-2519
Colleton Medical Ctr (CMC) 501 Robertson Blvd *Web:* www.colletonmedical.com	Walterboro	SC	29488	843-782-2000	549-0246
Conway Medical Ctr 300 Singleton Ridge Rd *Web:* www.conwaymedicalcenter.com	Conway	SC	29526	843-347-7111	347-8056
East Cooper Medical Center 2000 Hospital Dr *Web:* www.eastcoopermedctr.com	Mount Pleasant	SC	29464	843-881-0100	881-4396
Georgetown Memorial Hospital PO Box 421718 *Web:* www.georgetownhospitalsystem.org	Georgetown	SC	29442	843-527-7000	520-7887
Grand Strand Regional Medical Ctr 809 82nd Pkwy *TF:* 800-342-2383 ■ *Web:* www.grandstrandmed.com	Myrtle Beach	SC	29572	843-692-1000	692-1109
Greenville Memorial Hospital 701 Grove Rd *Web:* www.ghs.org	Greenville	SC	29605	864-455-7000	455-8921
Hilton Head Regional Medical Ctr 25 Hospital Ctr Blvd *TF:* 888-689-8207 ■ *Web:* www.hiltonheadregional.com	Hilton Head Island	SC	29926	843-681-6122	689-3670
KershawHealth Medical Ctr 1315 Roberts St PO Box 7003 *Web:* www.kershawhealth.org	Camden	SC	29020	803-432-4311	713-6380
Lexington Medical Ctr 2720 Sunset Blvd *Web:* www.lexmed.com	West Columbia	SC	29169	803-791-2000	791-2660
Marion County Medical Ctr 2829 E Hwy 76 *Web:* www.carolinashospitalmarion.com	Mullins	SC	29574	843-431-2000	
Mary Black Memorial Hospital 1700 Skylyn Dr *Web:* www.maryblackhealthsystem.com	Spartanburg	SC	29307	864-573-3000	573-3240
McLeod Medical Ctr Dillon 301 E Jackson St *Web:* www.mcleodhealth.org	Dillon	SC	29536	843-774-4111	774-1563
McLeod Regional Medical Ctr 555 E Cheves St *Web:* www.mcleodhealth.org	Florence	SC	29506	843-777-2000	777-5465
Medical University of South Carolina Medical Ctr 171 Ashley Ave *TF:* 800-424-6872 ■ *Web:* www.musc.edu	Charleston	SC	29425	843-792-2300	792-3126
Oconee Medical Campus (OMC) 298 Memorial Dr *Web:* www.oconeemed.org	Seneca	SC	29672	864-882-3351	
Palmetto Health Baptist Columbia 1330 Taylor St *Web:* www.palmettohealth.org	Columbia	SC	29221	803-296-5010	296-5462
Palmetto Health Baptist Medical Ctr Easley 200 Fleetwood Dr *Web:* www.palmettohealth.org	Easley	SC	29640	864-442-7200	442-7521
Palmetto Health Richland Five Richland Medical Pk *Web:* palmettohealth.org/body.cfm?id=961	Columbia	SC	29203	803-434-7000	434-3571
Piedmont Medical Ctr 222 S Herlong Ave *TF:* 800-222-4218 ■ *Web:* www.piedmontmedicalcenter.com	Rock Hill	SC	29732	803-329-1234	329-0979
Providence Hospitals 2435 Forest Dr *TF:* 877-256-5381 ■ *Web:* www.providencehospitals.com	Columbia	SC	29204	803-256-5300	256-5935
Regional Medical Ctr, The 3000 St Matthews Rd *TF:* 800-476-3377 ■ *Web:* www.trmchealth.org	Orangeburg	SC	29118	803-395-2200	
Roper Hospital 316 Calhoun St *Web:* rsfh.com/	Charleston	SC	29401	843-724-2000	724-2995
Self Regional Hospital 1325 Spring St *Web:* www.selfregional.org	Greenwood	SC	29646	864-725-4111	725-4260
Spartanburg Regional Medical Ctr (SRMC) 101 E Wood St *TF:* 800-318-2596 ■ *Web:* spartanburgregional.com	Spartanburg	SC	29303	864-560-6000	560-3974
Springs Memorial Hospital 800 W Meeting St *Web:* www.springsmemorial.com	Lancaster	SC	29720	803-286-1214	
Trident Medical Ctr 9330 Medical Plz Dr *TF:* 866-492-9085 ■ *Web:* www.tridenthealthsystem.com	Charleston	SC	29406	843-797-7000	847-4086
Tuomey Regional Medical Ctr 129 N Washington St *Web:* www.tuomey.com	Sumter	SC	29150	803-774-9000	774-9489
Upstate Carolina Medical Ctr 1530 N Limestone St *Web:* novanthealth.org/gaffneymedicalcenter.aspx	Gaffney	SC	29340	864-487-4271	489-0585
Wallace Thomson Hospital 322 W S St *TF General:* 800-277-5633 ■ *Web:* www.wallacethomson.com	Union	SC	29379	864-301-2000	429-2524

South Dakota

	City	State	ZIP	Phone	Fax
Avera McKennan Hospital & University Health Ctr 1325 S Cliff Ave PO Box 5045 *Web:* www.avera.org/mckennan	Sioux Falls	SD	57117	605-322-8000	
Avera Queen of Peace Hospital 525 N Foster St *TF:* 888-531-1685 ■ *Web:* www.avera.org/queen-of-peace	Mitchell	SD	57301	605-995-2000	995-2441
Avera Sacred Heart Hospital 501 Summit *Web:* www.avera.org/sacred-heart	Yankton	SD	57078	605-668-8000	
Avera Saint Luke's Hospital 305 S State St *TF:* 800-658-3535 ■ *Web:* www.avera.org/st-lukes-hospital	Aberdeen	SD	57401	605-622-5000	622-5127
Huron Regional Medical Ctr (HRMC) 172 Fourth St SE *Web:* www.huronregional.org	Huron	SD	57350	605-353-6200	353-6300
Mobridge Regional Hospital Inc PO Box 580 *Web:* www.mobridgehospital.org	Mobridge	SD	57601	605-845-3692	

	City	State	Zip	Phone	Fax
Prairie Lakes Hospital & Care Ctr 401 Ninth Ave NW *TF:* 877-917-7547 ■ *Web:* www.prairielakes.com	Watertown	SD	57201	605-882-7000	882-7607
Rapid City Regional Health 353 Fairmont Blvd *Web:* www.regionalhealth.com	Rapid City	SD	57701	605-719-1000	719-8988
Sanford USD Medical Ctr 1305 W 18th St *Web:* www.sanfordhealth.org	Sioux Falls	SD	57117	605-333-1000	333-1531

Tennessee

	City	State	Zip	Phone	Fax
Baptist Memorial Hospital Memphis 6019 Walnut Grove Rd *Web:* www.baptistonline.org	Memphis	TN	38120	901-226-5000	226-5618
Baptist Memorial Hospital Union City 1201 Bishop St *Web:* www.baptistonline.org/facilities/unioncity	Union City	TN	38261	731-885-2410	884-8603
Blount Memorial Hospital 907 E Lamar Alexander Pkwy *Web:* www.blountmemorial.org	Maryville	TN	37804	865-983-7211	980-4868
Bristol Regional Medical Ctr One Medical Pk Blvd *Web:* www.wellmont.org/facilities/bristol/wbrmc/wbrmc.html	Bristol	TN	37620	423-844-1121	844-4204
Centennial Medical Ctr 2300 Patterson St *Web:* tristarcentennial.com	Nashville	TN	37203	615-342-1000	342-1045
Claiborne County Hospital & Nursing Home 1850 Old Knoxville Rd *Web:* www.claibornehospital.org	Tazewell	TN	37879	423-626-4211	
Cookeville Regional Medical Ctr (CRMC) One Medical Ctr Blvd *Web:* www.crmchealth.org	Cookeville	TN	38501	931-528-2541	526-8814
Cumberland Medical Ctr (CMC) 421 S Main St *Web:* www.cmchealthcare.org	Crossville	TN	38555	931-484-9511	707-8148
Delta Medical Ctr (DMC) 3000 Getwell Rd *Web:* www.deltamedcenter.com	Memphis	TN	38118	901-369-8100	369-4603
Dyersburg Regional Medical Ctr 400 E Tickle St *Web:* www.dyersburgregionalmc.com	Dyersburg	TN	38024	731-285-2410	
Erlanger Medical Ctr 975 E Third St *TF:* 877-849-8338 ■ *Web:* www.erlanger.org	Chattanooga	TN	37403	423-778-7000	778-8068
Fort Sanders Regional Medical Ctr 1901 W Clinch Ave *Web:* www.fsregional.com	Knoxville	TN	37916	865-541-1111	541-1262
Gateway Medical Ctr (GMC) 651 Dunlop Ln *Web:* www.todaysgateway.com/pages/home.aspx	Clarksville	TN	37040	931-502-1000	
Harton Regional Medical Ctr 1801 N Jackson St *TF General:* 800-999-6673 ■ *Web:* www.hartonmedicalcenter.com	Tullahoma	TN	37388	931-393-3000	393-7855
Henry County Medical Ctr 301 Tyson Ave *Web:* www.hcmc-tn.org	Paris	TN	38242	731-642-1220	642-9588
Holston Valley Hospital & Medical Ctr 130 W Ravine Rd *Web:* www.wellmont.org	Kingsport	TN	37660	423-224-4000	224-5037
Horizon Medical Ctr 111 Hwy 70 E *Web:* beta.ehc.com	Dickson	TN	37055	615-446-0446	
Indian Path Medical Ctr 2000 Brookside Dr *Web:* ipmc.msha.com	Kingsport	TN	37660	423-857-7000	
Jackson-Madison County General Hospital 620 Skyline Dr *Web:* wth.org/	Jackson	TN	38301	731-541-5000	541-3157
Johnson City Medical Ctr 400 N State of Franklin Rd *Web:* www.msha.com	Johnson City	TN	37604	423-431-6111	
Lakeway Regional Hospital (LRH) 726 McFarland St *Web:* www.lakewayregionalhospital.com	Morristown	TN	37814	423-522-6000	587-8548
Laughlin Memorial Hospital 1420 Tuscolum Blvd *TF:* 800-852-7157 ■ *Web:* www.laughlinmemorial.org	Greeneville	TN	37745	423-787-5000	787-5083
Livingston Regional Hospital 315 Oak St *Web:* mylivingstonhospital.com	Livingston	TN	38570	931-823-5611	
Maury Regional Hospital 1224 Trotwood Ave *Web:* www.mauryregional.com	Columbia	TN	38401	931-381-1111	
Memorial North Park Hospital 2051 Hamill Rd *Web:* www.memorial.org	Hixson	TN	37343	423-495-7100	495-7388
Methodist Hospital South (MHS) 1300 Wesley Dr *Web:* www.methodisthealth.org/methodist	Memphis	TN	38116	901-516-3700	516-3085
Methodist Medical Ctr of Oak Ridge 990 Oak Ridge Tpke *Web:* www.mmcoakridge.com	Oak Ridge	TN	37831	865-835-1000	835-4054
Methodist North Hospital 3960 New Covington Pk *Web:* www.methodisthealth.org	Memphis	TN	38128	901-516-5200	516-5323
Middle Tennessee Medical Ctr 1700 Medical Center Pkwy *TF General:* 800-400-5800 ■ *Web:* www.sths.com	Murfreesboro	TN	37129	615-396-4100	301-2329
Nashville General Hospital 1818 Albion St *TF:* 800-318-2596 ■ *Web:* nashville.gov/hospital-authority.aspx	Nashville	TN	37208	615-341-4000	341-4493
Northcrest Medical Ctr 100 Northcrest Dr *Web:* www.northcrest.com	Springfield	TN	37172	615-384-2411	384-1509
Parkridge East Hospital 941 Spring Creek Rd *TF:* 800-605-1527 ■ *Web:* www.parkridgeeasthospital.com	Chattanooga	TN	37412	423-894-7870	855-3648
Parkridge Medical Ctr 2333 McCallie Ave *Web:* www.parkridgemedicalcenter.com	Chattanooga	TN	37404	423-698-6061	493-1208
Parkwest Medical Ctr 9352 Pk W Blvd *Web:* www.treatedwell.com	Knoxville	TN	37923	865-373-1000	373-1012
Premier Medical Group Pc 1850 Business Pk Dr PO Box 3799 *Web:* www.premiermed.com	Clarksville	TN	37043	931-245-7000	
Regional Hospital of Jackson 367 Hospital Blvd **Fax Area Code:* 651 ■ *TF:* 800-454-9970 ■ *Web:* www.regionalhospitaljackson.com	Jackson	TN	38305	731-661-2000	254-9426*
Regional Medical Ctr at Memphis 877 Jefferson Ave *Web:* www.the-med.org	Memphis	TN	38103	901-545-7100	545-7037
Roane Medical Ctr 412 Devonia St *Web:* www.covenanthealth.com	Harriman	TN	37748	865-882-1323	
Saint Francis Hospital 5959 Pk Ave *Web:* www.saintfrancishosp.com/en-us/pages/default.aspx	Memphis	TN	38119	901-765-1000	765-1799
Saint Thomas Hospital 4220 HaRding Rd *TF:* 800-400-5800 ■ *Web:* www.sths.com	Nashville	TN	37205	615-222-2111	222-6502
Skyline Madison Campus 500 Hospital Dr *Web:* tristarskylinemadison.com	Madison	TN	37115	615-769-5000	
Skyline Medical Ctr 3441 Dickerson Pike *TF:* 800-242-5662 ■ *Web:* tristarskyline.com	Nashville	TN	37207	615-769-2000	769-7102
SkyRidge Medical Ctr 2305 Chambliss Ave *Web:* www.skyridgemedicalcenter.net	Cleveland	TN	37311	423-559-6000	559-6653
Summit Medical Ctr 5655 Frist Blvd *Web:* tristarsummit.com	Hermitage	TN	37076	615-316-3000	316-4912
Sumner Regional Medical Ctr 555 Hartsville Pike **Fax Area Code:* 312 ■ *TF:* 888-863-6198 ■ *Web:* ultracare-dialysis.com	Gallatin	TN	37066	615-328-8888	321-1505*
Takoma Regional Hospital 401 Takoma Ave *Web:* www.takoma.org	Greeneville	TN	37743	423-639-3151	636-2374
Tristar Southern Hills Medical Ctr 391 Wallace Rd *TF:* 800-242-5662 ■ *Web:* tristarsouthernhills.com	Nashville	TN	37211	615-781-4000	781-4113
Vanderbilt University Medical Ctr 1215 21st Ave S *TF:* 877-936-8422 ■ *Web:* www.mc.vanderbilt.edu	Nashville	TN	37232	615-322-5000	343-7317
Williamson Medical Ctr (WMC) 4321 Carothers Pkwy *Web:* www.williamsonmedicalcenter.org	Franklin	TN	37067	615-435-5000	435-5161

Texas

	City	State	Zip	Phone	Fax
Abilene Regional Medical Ctr 6250 S Hwy 83-84 *Web:* www.abileneregional.com	Abilene	TX	79606	325-428-1000	795-2113
Arlington Memorial Hospital 800 W Randol Mill Rd *Web:* www.texashealth.org	Arlington	TX	76012	817-960-6100	
Baylor All Saints Medical Ctr 1400 Eigth Ave *Web:* baylorhealth.com	Fort Worth	TX	76104	817-926-2544	927-6226
Baylor Medical Center (TMC) 4343 N Josey Ln	Carrollton	TX	75010	972-492-1010	394-4783
Baylor Medical Ctr at Garland 2300 Marie Curie Blvd *Web:* baylorhealth.com	Garland	TX	75042	972-487-5000	485-3051
Baylor Medical Ctr at Irving 1901 N MacArthur Blvd *Web:* www.baylorhealth.com/physicianslocations/irving	Irving	TX	75061	972-579-8100	579-5254
Baylor Regional Medical Ctr at Grapevine 1650 W College St *TF:* 800-422-9567 ■ *Web:* www.baylorhealth.com	Grapevine	TX	76051	817-481-1588	
Baylor University Medical Ctr at Dallas 3500 Gaston Ave *Web:* www.baylorhealth.com	Dallas	TX	75246	214-820-0111	820-2411
Bayshore Medical Ctr 4000 Spencer Hwy *TF:* 866-503-7546 ■ *Web:* www.bayshoremedical.com	Pasadena	TX	77504	713-359-2000	359-1004
Ben Taub General Hospital 1504 Taub Loop *Web:* www.harrishealth.org	Houston	TX	77030	713-873-2000	873-2305
Brackenridge Hospital 601 E 15th St *Web:* www.seton.net	Austin	TX	78701	512-324-7000	324-7051
Brazosport Regional Health System (BRHS) 100 Medical Dr *Web:* brazosportregional.org/	Lake Jackson	TX	77566	979-297-4411	285-1203
Brownwood Regional Medical Ctr 1501 Burnet Dr *Web:* www.brmc-cares.com	Brownwood	TX	76801	325-646-8541	646-5459
Central Texas Medical Ctr (CTMC) 1301 Wonder World Dr *TF:* 800-927-9004 ■ *Web:* www.ctmc.org	San Marcos	TX	78666	512-353-8979	753-3598
CHRISTUS Hospital - St Elizabeth 2830 Calder St *TF:* 866-683-3627 ■ *Web:* www.christushospital.org	Beaumont	TX	77702	409-892-7171	924-3959
CHRISTUS Saint Mary Hospital 3600 Gates Blvd Ste 3 *TF:* 866-683-3627 ■ *Web:* www.christushospital.org	Port Arthur	TX	77642	409-985-7431	989-1033
CHRISTUS Saint Michael Health System 2600 St Michael Dr *Web:* www.christusstmichael.org	Texarkana	TX	75503	903-614-1000	614-2212
CHRISTUS Santa Rosa Hospital 333 N Santa Rosa St *Web:* www.christussantarosa.org	San Antonio	TX	78207	210-704-2011	704-3632
CHRISTUS Spohn Hospital Corpus Christi Shoreline 600 Elizabeth St Third Fl *Web:* www.christushealth.org	Corpus Christi	TX	78404	361-881-3640	881-3149
CHRISTUS Spohn Hospital Corpus Christi-South 5950 Saratoga Blvd *Web:* www.christusspohn.org	Corpus Christi	TX	78414	361-985-5000	985-5173
CHRISTUS Spohn Hospital Kleberg 1311 General Cavazos Blvd *Web:* www.christusspohn.org	Kingsville	TX	78363	361-595-1661	595-5005
CHRISTUS Spohn Hospital Memorial 2606 Hospital Blvd *Web:* www.christusspohn.org	Corpus Christi	TX	78405	361-902-4000	902-4968
Citizens Medical Ctr 2701 Hospital Dr *Web:* citizensmedicalcenter.org	Victoria	TX	77901	361-573-9181	572-5070

Name / Address	City	State	Zip	Phone	Fax
Clear Lake Regional Medical Ctr 500 W Medical Ctr Blvd	Webster	TX	77598	281-332-2511	338-3352
Web: www.clearlakermc.com					
Cleveland Regional Medical Ctr 300 E Crockett St	Cleveland	TX	77327	281-593-1811	432-4370
Web: www.clevelandregionalmedicalcenter.com					
College Station Medical Ctr 1604 Rock Prairie Rd	College Station	TX	77845	979-764-5100	696-7373
Web: www.csmedcenter.com					
Conroe Regional Medical Ctr 504 Medical Ctr Blvd	Conroe	TX	77304	936-539-1111	539-5620
TF: 888-633-2687 ■ *Web:* www.conroeregional.com					
Corpus Christi Medical Ctr 13725 NW Blvd	Corpus Christi	TX	78410	361-767-4300	387-2798
Web: www.ccmedicalcenter.com					
Corpus Christi Medical Ctr Bay Area 7101 S Padre Island Dr	Corpus Christi	TX	78412	361-761-1200	761-3670
Web: www.ccmedicalcenter.com					
Cypress Fairbanks Medical Ctr 10655 Steepletop Dr	Houston	TX	77065	281-890-4285	890-5341
Web: www.cyfairhospital.com					
Dallas Medical Center 7 Medical Pkwy	Dallas	TX	75234	972-888-7000	888-7090
Web: www.dallasmedcenter.com					
Dallas Regional Medical Ctr (DRMC) 1011 N Galloway Ave	Mesquite	TX	75149	214-320-7000	289-9468*
**Fax Area Code:* 972 ■ *Web:* www.dallasregionalmedicalcenter.com					
Del Sol Medical Ctr 10301 Gateway W	El Paso	TX	79925	915-595-9000	
Web: www.laspalmasdelsolhealthcare.com/locations-facilities/del-sol-medical-center.aspx					
Denton Regional Medical Ctr 3535 S I-35 E	Denton	TX	76210	940-384-3535	384-4702
Web: www.dentonregional.com					
Detar Hospital Navarro 506 E San Antonio St	Victoria	TX	77901	361-575-7441	788-6114
Web: www.detar.com					
Detar Hospital North 101 Medical Dr	Victoria	TX	77904	361-573-6100	
Web: www.detar.com					
Doctors Hospital at White Rock Lake 9440 Poppy Dr	Dallas	TX	75218	214-324-6100	324-0612
TF: 866-893-8446 ■ *Web:* www.doctorshospitaldallas.com					
Doctors Hospital of Laredo 10700 McPherson Rd	Laredo	TX	78045	956-523-2000	523-0444
TF: 844-244-4874 ■ *Web:* www.doctorshosplaredo.com					
East Houston Regional Medical Ctr 13111 E Fwy	Houston	TX	77015	713-393-2000	393-2714
Web: www.easthoustonrmc.com					
East Texas Medical Ctr Athens 2000 S Palestine St	Athens	TX	75751	903-676-1000	676-3337
Web: www.etmc.org					
East Texas Medical Ctr Tyler 1000 S Beckham Ave	Tyler	TX	75701	903-597-0351	535-6334
Web: www.etmc.org					
Edinburg Regional Medical Ctr (ERMC) 1102 W Trenton Rd	Edinburg	TX	78539	956-388-6000	388-6020
TF: 800-465-5585 ■ *Web:* www.southtexashealthsystem.com					
Fort Duncan Regional Medical Ctr 3333 N Foster Maldonado Blvd	Eagle Pass	TX	78852	830-773-5321	872-2549*
**Fax:* Admissions ■ *Web:* www.fortduncanmedicalcenter.com					
Good Shepherd Medical Ctr 700 E Marshall Ave	Longview	TX	75601	903-315-2000	315-2479
Web: www.gsmc.org					
Harris Methodist Fort Worth 1301 Pennsylvania Ave	Fort Worth	TX	76104	817-882-2000	882-3169
Web: www.texashealth.org					
Harris Methodist-HEB 1600 Hospital Pkwy	Bedford	TX	76022	817-848-4000	
Web: www.texashealth.org					
Hendrick Health System 1900 Pine St	Abilene	TX	79601	325-670-2000	670-4417
Web: www.hendrickhealth.org					
Hillcrest Baptist Medical Ctr 3000 Herring Ave	Waco	TX	76708	254-202-2000	202-8978
Web: sw.org/location/waco-hillcrest-hospital					
Houston Northwest Medical Ctr 710 FM 1960 W	Houston	TX	77090	281-440-1000	440-2666
Web: www.hnmc.com					
Huguley Memorial Medical Ctr 11801 S Fwy	Burleson	TX	76028	817-293-9110	568-1298
Web: www.texashealthhuguley.org					
Hunt Regional Healthcare 4215 Joe Ramsey Blvd	Greenville	TX	75401	903-408-5000	408-1669
TF: 800-984-9223 ■ *Web:* www.hmhd.org					
Huntsville Memorial Hospital 110 Memorial Hospital Dr	Huntsville	TX	77340	936-291-3411	291-4373
Web: www.huntsvillememorial.com					
John Peter Smith Hospital 1500 S Main St	Fort Worth	TX	76104	817-921-3431	927-1604
Web: www.jpshealthnet.org					
Kingwood Medical Ctr 22999 US Hwy 59	Kingwood	TX	77339	281-348-8000	348-8010
Web: www.kingwoodmedical.com					
Knapp Medical Ctr (KMC) 1401 E Eigth St PO Box 1110	Weslaco	TX	78596	956-968-8567	968-0764
Web: www.knappmed.org					
Lake Pointe Medical Ctr (LPMC) 6800 Scenic Dr	Rowlett	TX	75088	972-412-2273	412-3276
TF: 866-525-5762 ■ *Web:* www.lakepointemedical.com					
Laredo Medical Ctr (LMC) 1700 E Saunders Ave	Laredo	TX	78041	956-796-5000	796-3175
Web: www.laredomedical.com					
Las Colinas Medical Ctr 6800 N MacArthur Blvd	Irving	TX	75039	972-969-2000	969-2080
Web: www.lascolinasmedical.com					
Las Palmas Medical Ctr 1801 N Oregon St	El Paso	TX	79902	915-521-1200	544-5203
Web: www.laspalmasdelsolhealthcare.com					
Live centre speciality 1111 Gallagher Dr	Sherman	TX	75090	903-870-7000	
Longview Regional Medical Ctr 2901 N Fourth St	Longview	TX	75605	903-758-1818	758-5167
Web: www.longviewregional.com					
Mainland Medical Ctr 6801 Emmett Lowry Expy	Texas City	TX	77591	409-938-5000	938-5001
Web: www.mainlandmedical.com					
McAllen Medical Ctr 301 W Expy 83	McAllen	TX	78503	956-632-4000	632-4010
Web: www.southtexashealthsystem.com					
Medical City Hospital 7777 Forest Ln	Dallas	TX	75230	972-566-7000	566-6560
Web: www.medicalcityhospital.com					
Medical Ctr Hospital (MCH) 500 W Fourth St	Odessa	TX	79761	432-640-6000	640-1118
Web: www.medicalcenterhealthsystem.com					
Medical Ctr of Arlington (MCA) 3301 Matlock Rd	Arlington	TX	76015	817-465-3241	472-4878
Web: www.medicalcenterarlington.com					
Medical Ctr of Lewisville 500 W Main St	Lewisville	TX	75057	972-420-1000	353-1789
Web: www.lewisvillemedical.com					
Medical Ctr of McKinney 4500 Medical Ctr Dr	McKinney	TX	75069	972-569-8000	
Web: www.medicalcenterofmckinney.com/home					
Medical Ctr of Plano, The 3901 W 15th St	Plano	TX	75075	972-596-6800	519-1409
Web: www.themedicalcenterofplano.com					
Medical Ctr of Southeast Texas, The 2555 Jimmy Johnson Blvd	Port Arthur	TX	77640	409-724-7389	
Web: www.medicalcentersetexas.com					
Memorial Hermann - Texas Medical Ctr 6411 Fannin St	Houston	TX	77030	713-704-4000	704-5872
Web: www.memorialhermann.org					
Memorial Hermann Katy Hospital 23900 Katy Fwy	Katy	TX	77494	281-644-7000	644-7280
Web: memorialhermann.org/locations/					
Memorial Hermann Memorial City Hospital 921 Gessner Rd	Houston	TX	77024	713-242-3000	359-3340*
**Fax Area Code:* 281 ■ *TF:* 800-526-2121 ■ *Web:* www.memorialhermann.org					
Memorial Hermann Southwest Hospital 7600 Beechnut St	Houston	TX	77074	713-456-5000	456-8363
Web: www.memorialhermann.org					
Methodist Charlton Medical Ctr 3500 W Wheatland Rd	Dallas	TX	75237	214-947-7777	947-7525
Web: methodisthealthsystem.org					
Methodist Dallas Medical Ctr 1441 N Beckley Ave	Dallas	TX	75203	214-947-8181	947-3403
Web: www.methodisthealthsystem.org					
Methodist Hospital 6565 Fannin St	Houston	TX	77030	713-790-3311	441-7465
Web: www.houstonmethodist.org					
Methodist Hospital System, The 6447 Main St	Houston	TX	77030	713-790-3333	790-2605
Web: www.houstonmethodist.org					
Methodist Richardson Medical Ctr 401 W Campbell Rd	Richardson	TX	75080	972-498-4000	498-4931
Web: methodisthealthsystem.org					
Metroplex Hospital 2201 S Clear Creek Rd	Killeen	TX	76549	254-526-7523	526-3483
TF: 800-926-7664 ■ *Web:* www.mplex.org					
Metropolitan Methodist Hospital 1310 McCullough Ave	San Antonio	TX	78212	210-757-2200	
Web: sahealth.com					
Midland Memorial Hospital 2200 W Illinois Ave	Midland	TX	79701	432-685-1111	685-4970
TF: 800-833-2916 ■ *Web:* www.midland-memorial.com					
Mission Regional Medical Ctr 900 S Bryan Rd	Mission	TX	78572	956-323-9000	323-1360
Web: www.missionhospital.com					
Mother Frances Hospital 800 E Dawson St	Tyler	TX	75701	903-593-8441	525-1201
Web: tmfhc.org/					
Nacogdoches Medical Ctr 4920 NE Stallings Dr	Nacogdoches	TX	75965	936-569-9481	568-3400
TF: 866-898-8446 ■ *Web:* www.nacmedicalcenter.com					
Nacogdoches Memorial Hospital 1204 N Mound St	Nacogdoches	TX	75961	936-564-4611	568-8588
Web: www.nacmem.org					
Navarro Regional Hospital (NRH) 3201 W Hwy 22	Corsicana	TX	75110	903-654-6800	654-6955
Web: www.navarrohospital.com					
Nix Medical Ctr 414 Navarro St	San Antonio	TX	78205	210-271-1800	271-2023
Web: www.nixhealth.com					
North Hills Hospital 4401 Booth Calloway Rd	North Richland Hills	TX	76180	817-255-1000	255-1991
Web: www.northhillshospital.com					
Northeast Baptist Hospital 8811 Village Dr	San Antonio	TX	78217	210-297-2000	297-0200
Web: www.baptisthealthsystem.com					
Northeast Medical Ctr Hospital 18951 Memorial N	Humble	TX	77338	281-540-7700	540-7846
Web: www.memorialhermann.org					
Northeast Methodist Hospital 12412 Judson Rd	San Antonio	TX	78233	210-757-7000	757-5072
Web: www.sahealth.com					
Northwest Texas Hospital 1501 S Coulter	Amarillo	TX	79106	806-354-1000	354-1122
TF: 800-887-1114 ■ *Web:* www.nwtexashealthcare.com					
OakBend Medical Ctr 1705 Jackson St	Richmond	TX	77469	281-341-3000	341-3056
Web: www.oakbendmedcenter.org					
Palestine Regional Medical Ctr 2900 S Loop 256	Palestine	TX	75801	903-731-1000	731-2236
TF: 800-222-1222 ■ *Web:* www.palestineregional.com					
Pampa Regional Medical Ctr One Medical Plz	Pampa	TX	79065	806-665-3721	665-2361
Web: www.prmctx.com					
Paris Regional Medical Ctr 820 Clarksville St	Paris	TX	75460	903-785-4521	737-3848
Web: www.parisregionalmedical.com					
Parkland Health & Hospital System 5201 Harry Hines Blvd	Dallas	TX	75235	214-590-8000	590-2713*
**Fax:* Admitting ■ *Web:* www.parklandhospital.com					
Peterson Regional Medical Ctr 551 Hill Country Dr	Kerrville	TX	78028	830-896-4200	258-7833
Web: www.petersonrmc.com					
Plaza Medical Ctr 900 Eigth Ave	Fort Worth	TX	76104	817-877-5292	347-1989
Web: www.plazamedicalcenter.com					
Presbyterian Hospital of Dallas 8200 Walnut Hill Ln	Dallas	TX	75231	214-345-6789	345-4603
Web: www.texashealth.org					
Providence Healthcare Network 6901 Medical Pkwy	Waco	TX	76712	254-751-4000	751-4769
Web: www.providence.net					
Providence Memorial Hospital (PMH) 2001 N Oregon St	El Paso	TX	79902	915-577-6011	577-6549
Web: www.sphn.com/en-us/aboutus/pages/providence%20memorial%20hospital.aspx					
Rio Grande Regional Hospital 101 E Ridge Rd	McAllen	TX	78503	956-632-6000	632-6621
Web: www.riohealth.com					
Saint David's Medical Ctr 919 E 32nd St	Austin	TX	78705	512-476-7111	544-8102
Web: www.stdavids.com					

				Phone	Fax
Saint Joseph Regional Health Ctr 2801 Franciscan Dr *Web:* www.st-joseph.org	Bryan	TX	77802	979-776-3777	774-4590
San Angelo Community Medical Ctr 3501 Knickerbocker Rd *Web:* www.sacmc.com	San Angelo	TX	76904	325-949-9511	947-6550
San Jacinto Methodist Hospital (SJMH) 4401 Garth Rd **Fax:* Admitting ■ *Web:* www.houstonmethodist.org	Baytown	TX	77521	281-420-8600	420-8672*
Scott & White Memorial Hospital 2401 S 31st St *TF:* 800-792-3710 ■ *Web:* www.sw.org	Temple	TX	76508	254-724-2111	724-2786
Seton Medical Ctr 1201 W 38th St *Web:* www.seton.net	Austin	TX	78705	512-324-1000	324-1924
Shannon Medical Ctr (SMC) 120 E Harris Ave *TF:* 888-657-5202 ■ *Web:* www.shannonhealth.com	San Angelo	TX	76903	325-653-6741	658-8295
Sierra Medical Ctr 1625 Medical Ctr Dr *TF:* 800-994-6610 ■ *Web:* www.sphn.com	El Paso	TX	79902	915-747-4000	577-7969
Southwest General Hospital (SGH) 7400 Barlite Blvd *TF:* 877-215-9355 ■ *Web:* www.swgeneralhospital.com	San Antonio	TX	78224	210-921-2000	921-3508
Southwestern University Hospital 5151 Harry Hines Blvd *Web:* www.utswmedicine.org	Dallas	TX	75390	214-645-5555	
St David's Round Rock Medical Ctr 2400 Round Rock Ave *Web:* www.stdavids.com	Round Rock	TX	78681	512-341-1000	238-1799
Texas Health Presbyterian Hospital Denton 3000 N I-35 *Web:* www.texashealth.org	Denton	TX	76201	940-898-7000	898-7071
Texas Health Presbyterian Hospital-WNJ Therapy Services 500 N Highland Ave *Web:* www.wnj.org	Sherman	TX	75092	903-870-4611	870-4409
Texas Healthcare PLLC 2821 Lackland Rd Ste 300 *TF:* 800-844-8850 ■ *Web:* www.txhealthcare.com	Fort Worth	TX	76116	817-378-3640	740-8516
Texoma Medical Ctr 5016 S US Hwy 75 *Web:* www.texomamedicalcenter.net	Denison	TX	75020	903-416-4000	416-4129
Titus Regional Medical Ctr 2001 N Jefferson Ave *Web:* www.titusregional.com	Mount Pleasant	TX	75455	903-577-6000	577-6027
Tomball Regional Hospital (TRMC) 605 Holderrieth St *Web:* www.tomballregionalmedicalcenter.com	Tomball	TX	77375	281-401-7500	
United Regional Health Care System *Eleventh Street Campus* 1600 11th St *Web:* www.unitedregional.org	Wichita Falls	TX	76301	940-764-7000	764-3041
United Regional Hospital *Eighth Street Campus* 1600 11th St 2nd Fl *Web:* www.unitedregional.org	Wichita Falls	TX	76301	940-764-7000	766-8711
University Medical Ctr of El Paso (UMCEP) 4815 Alameda Ave *Web:* www.umcelpaso.org	El Paso	TX	79905	915-544-1200	521-7612
University of Texas Health Ctr at Tyler (UTHCT) 11937 US Hwy 271 *Web:* www.uthealth.org	Tyler	TX	75708	903-877-7777	877-7759
University of Texas Medical Branch Hospitals 301 University Blvd *TF:* 800-201-0527 ■ *Web:* www.utmb.edu	Galveston	TX	77555	409-772-1011	772-5119
Valley Baptist Medical Ctr Brownsville 1040 W Jefferson St **Fax:* Hum Res ■ *Web:* www.valleybaptist.net/brownsville	Brownsville	TX	78520	956-698-5400	541-0712*
Valley Baptist Medical Ctr Harlingen 2101 Pease St *Web:* www.valleybaptist.net	Harlingen	TX	78550	956-389-1100	389-1632
Valley Regional Medical Ctr 100-A E Alton Gloor Blvd *TF:* 877-422-2030 ■ *Web:* www.valleyregionalmedicalcenter.com	Brownsville	TX	78526	956-350-7000	574-9730
Wadley Regional Medical Ctr 1000 Pine St *Web:* www.wadleyhealth.com	Texarkana	TX	75501	903-798-8000	798-8030
West Houston Medical Ctr 12141 Richmond Ave *Web:* westhoustonmedical.com	Houston	TX	77082	281-558-3444	596-5989
Woodland Heights Medical Ctr 505 S John Redditt Dr *TF:* 800-222-1222 ■ *Web:* www.woodlandheights.net	Lufkin	TX	75904	936-634-8311	637-8600
Zale Lipshy University Hospital 5151 Harry Hines Blvd *Web:* www.utsouthwestern.edu	Dallas	TX	75390	214-645-5555	

Utah

				Phone	Fax
Alta View Hospital 9660 South 1300 East *Web:* www.intermountainhealthcare.org/xp/public/altaview	Sandy	UT	84094	801-501-2600	501-4327
American Fork Hospital 170 North 1100 East *Web:* www.intermountainhealthcare.org	American Fork	UT	84003	801-763-3300	855-3548
Davis Hospital & Medical Ctr (DHMC) 1600 W Antelope Dr *TF:* 877-898-6080 ■ *Web:* www.davishospital.com	Layton	UT	84041	801-807-1000	807-7610
Intermountain Healthcare Logan Regional Hospital 500 E 1400 N *TF:* 800-442-4845 ■ *Web:* www.intermountainhealthcare.org	Logan	UT	84341	435-716-1000	716-5409
Jordan Valley Medical Center 3460 S Pioneer Pkwy *Web:* www.pioneervalleyhospital.com	West Valley City	UT	84120	801-964-3100	964-3279
Lakeview Hospital 630 E Medical Dr *Web:* www.lakeviewhospital.com	Bountiful	UT	84010	801-299-2200	299-2534
LDS Hospital 8th Ave & C St *TF:* 888-301-3880 ■ *Web:* intermountainhealthcare.org	Salt Lake City	UT	84143	801-408-1100	408-1665
McKay-Dee Hospital Ctr 4401 Harrison Blvd *Web:* www.intermountainhealthcare.org/hospitals/mckaydee/pages/home.aspx	Ogden	UT	84403	801-627-2800	
Mountain View Hospital 1000 East 100 North *Web:* www.mvhpayson.com	Payson	UT	84651	801-465-7000	465-7170
Ogden Regional Medical Ctr 5475 Adams Ave Pkwy *TF:* 877-870-3745 ■ *Web:* www.ogdenregional.com	Ogden	UT	84405	801-479-2111	479-2091
Saint Mark's Hospital 1200 East 3900 South *Web:* www.stmarkshospital.com	Salt Lake City	UT	84124	801-268-7111	270-3489
Salt Lake Regional Medical Ctr 1050 East South Temple *Web:* www.saltlakeregional.com	Salt Lake City	UT	84102	801-350-4111	350-4522
University of Utah Hospital & Clinics 50 N Medical Dr *Web:* healthcare.utah.edu	Salt Lake City	UT	84132	801-581-2121	585-5280
Utah Valley Regional Medical Ctr 1034 N 500 W *Web:* www.intermountainhealthcare.org/xp/public/uvrmc	Provo	UT	84604	801-373-7850	357-7780

Vermont

				Phone	Fax
Brattleboro Memorial Hospital Inc 17 Belmont Ave Ste 1 *TF:* 866-972-5266 ■ *Web:* www.bmhvt.org	Brattleboro	VT	05301	802-257-0341	257-8822
Central Vermont Medical Ctr (CVMC) 130 Fisher Rd *Web:* www.cvmc.org	Berlin	VT	05602	802-371-4100	371-4401
Copley Hospital Inc 528 Washington Hwy *Web:* www.copleyvt.org	Morrisville	VT	05661	802-888-8888	
Rutland Regional Medical Ctr 160 Allen St *Web:* www.rrmc.org	Rutland	VT	05701	802-775-7111	747-1620
Southwestern Vermont Medical Ctr 100 Hospital Dr *TF:* 800-543-1624 ■ *Web:* www.svhealthcare.org/hospital	Bennington	VT	05201	802-442-6361	447-5013
Springfield Hospital 25 Ridgewood Rd PO Box 2003 *Web:* www.springfieldhospital.org	Springfield	VT	05156	802-885-2151	885-7357
University of Vermont Medical Center, The (FAHC) 111 Colchester Ave *TF:* 800-358-1144 ■ *Web:* www.fletcherallen.org	Burlington	VT	05401	802-847-0000	656-2790

Virginia

				Phone	Fax
Alleghany Regional Hospital 1 ARH Ln *Web:* lewisgale.com/locations/lewisgale-hospital-alleghany/index.dot	Low Moor	VA	24457	540-862-6879	862-6589
Augusta Medical Ctr (AMC) 78 Medical Ctr Dr PO Box 1000 *TF:* 800-932-0262 ■ *Web:* www.augustahealth.com	Fishersville	VA	22939	540-932-4000	932-4809
Bon Secours DePaul Medical Ctr 150 Kingsley Ln *Web:* bshr.com/	Norfolk	VA	23505	757-889-5112	889-5837
Bon Secours Maryview Medical Ctr 3636 High St *Web:* bshr.com/facilities/maryview.html	Portsmouth	VA	23707	757-398-4444	
Bon Secours Memorial Regional Medical Ctr 8260 Atlee Rd *TF:* 888-455-3766 ■ *Web:* richmond.bonsecours.com	Mechanicsville	VA	23116	804-764-6000	764-6420
Bon Secours Saint Mary's Hospital 5801 Bremo Rd *TF:* 877-342-1500 ■ *Web:* richmond.bonsecours.com	Richmond	VA	23226	804-285-2011	559-0356
Buchanan General Hospital (BGH) 1535 Slate Creek Rd *Web:* www.bgh.org	Grundy	VA	24614	276-935-1000	935-1354
Carilion New River Valley Medical Ctr 2900 Lamb Cir *TF:* 800-432-7874 ■ *Web:* www.carilionclinic.org	Christiansburg	VA	24073	540-731-2000	731-2505
Carilion Roanoke Community Hospital (CRCH) 101 Elm Ave SE *Web:* carilionclinic.org	Roanoke	VA	24013	540-985-8000	
Carilion Roanoke Memorial Hospital 1906 Belleview Ave *Web:* www.carilionclinic.org	Roanoke	VA	24014	540-981-7000	981-7670
Chesapeake Regional Medical Ctr 736 Battlefield Blvd N *TF:* 800-582-8350 ■ *Web:* www.chesapeakeregional.com	Chesapeake	VA	23320	757-312-8121	312-6154
CJW Medical Ctr 7101 Jahnke Rd *TF:* 800-468-6620 ■ *Web:* hcavirginia.com	Richmond	VA	23225	804-320-3911	323-8049
Community Memorial Healthcenter 412 Bracey Ln *Web:* vcu-cmh.org/	South Hill	VA	23970	434-447-3151	774-2401
Danville Regional Medical Ctr 142 S Main St *TF:* 800-688-3762 ■ *Web:* danvilleregional.com	Danville	VA	24541	434-799-2100	
Fauquier Hospital 500 Hospital Dr *Web:* www.fauquierhealth.org	Warrenton	VA	20186	540-316-5000	
Halifax Regional Health System (HRHS) 2204 Wilborn Ave *Web:* www.hrhs.org	South Boston	VA	24592	434-517-3100	517-3626
Henrico Doctor's Hospital 1602 Skipwith Rd *Web:* hcavirginia.com	Richmond	VA	23229	804-289-4500	289-4801
Inova Alexandria Hospital 4320 Seminary Rd *Web:* www.inova.org	Alexandria	VA	22304	703-504-3000	504-3700
Inova Fair Oaks Hospital 3600 Joseph Siewick Dr *Web:* www.inova.org	Fairfax	VA	22033	703-391-3600	391-3273
Inova Fairfax Hospital 3300 Gallows Rd *Web:* www.inova.org	Falls Church	VA	22042	703-776-4001	776-6128
Inova Mount Vernon Hospital 2501 Parkers Ln *Web:* www.inova.org	Alexandria	VA	22306	703-664-7000	664-7235
John Randolph Medical Ctr 411 W Randolph Rd PO Box 971 *Web:* hcavirginia.com	Hopewell	VA	23860	804-541-1600	452-3699

Phone Fax

Lewis-Gale Medical Ctr 1900 Electric Rd Salem VA 24153 540-776-4000 953-5372
TF: 800-722-4673 ■ *Web:* lewisgale.com

Lynchburg General Hospital
1901 Tate Springs Rd Lynchburg VA 24501 434-947-3000
Web: web.lynchburgchamber.org

Martha Jefferson Hospital (MJH)
500 Martha Jefferson Dr Charlottesville VA 22902 434-982-7000
TF: 888-652-6663 ■ *Web:* www.marthajefferson.org

Mary Immaculate Hospital
Two Bernardine Dr Newport News VA 23602 757-886-6000 886-6751
Web: www.bshsi.com

Mary Washington Hospital
1001 Sam Perry Blvd Fredericksburg VA 22401 540-741-1100 310-0100
TF: 800-395-2455 ■ *Web:* www.marywashingtonhealthcare.com

Montgomery Regional Hospital
3700 S Main St Blacksburg VA 24060 540-951-1111 953-5372
Web: lewisgale.com

Norton Community Hospital (NCH) 100 15th St NW Norton VA 24273 276-679-9600
Web: www.msha.com

Prince William Hospital 8700 Sudly Rd Manassas VA 20110 703-369-8000 396-5297
Web: novanthealth.org/princewilliammedicalcenter.aspx

Reston Hospital Ctr 1850 Town Ctr Pkwy Reston VA 20190 703-689-9000
TF General: 888-327-8882 ■ *Web:* www.restonhospital.com

Retreat Hospital 2621 Grove Ave Richmond VA 23220 804-254-5100 254-5187
TF: 800-888-3627 ■ *Web:* hcavirginia.com

Riverside Regional Medical Ctr
500 J Clyde Morris Blvd Newport News VA 23601 757-594-2000 594-2084
Web: riversideonline.com

Rockingham Memorial Hospital (RMH)
2010 Health Campus Dr Harrisonburg VA 22801 540-689-1000
TF: 800-736-8272 ■ *Web:* www.rmhonline.com

Sentara Careplex Hospital 3000 Colliseum Dr Hampton VA 23666 757-736-1000 736-2659
TF: 800-736-8272 ■ *Web:* www.sentara.com

Sentara Leigh Hospital 830 Kempsville Rd Norfolk VA 23502 757-261-6000
Web: www.sentara.com/hospitals

Sentara Norfolk General Hospital
600 Gresham Dr Ste 8630 Norfolk VA 23507 757-388-6105 388-6106
Web: www.sentara.com/hospitals

Sentara Obici Hospital 2800 Godwin Blvd Suffolk VA 23434 757-934-4000 934-4284
TF: 800-736-8272 ■ *Web:* www.sentara.com

Sentara Virginia Beach General Hospital
1060 First Colonial Rd Virginia Beach VA 23454 757-395-8000
TF: 800-736-8272 ■ *Web:* www.sentara.com/hospitals

Sentara Williamsburg Regional Medical Ctr
100 Sentara Cir Williamsburg VA 23188 757-984-6000 984-8145
Web: www.sentara.com

Shore Memorial Hospital
9507 Hospital Ave PO Box 17 Nassawadox VA 23413 757-414-8000 414-8633
TF: 800-834-7035 ■ *Web:* shorehealthservices.org

Smyth County Community Hospital
565 Radio Hill Rd Marion VA 24354 276-782-1234
Web: www.msha.com

Southampton Memorial Hospital
100 Fairview Dr Franklin VA 23851 757-569-6100 569-6390
Web: www.smhfranklin.com

Southside Community Hospital (SCH) 800 Oak St Farmville VA 23901 434-392-8811 392-7654
Web: sch.centrahealth.com

Southside Regional Medical Ctr
200 Medical Park Blvd Petersburg VA 23805 804-765-5000
Web: www.srmconline.com

Tidewater Physicians Multispecialty Group PC
860 Omni Blvd Ste 304 Newport News VA 23606 757-232-8764 232-8865
Web: mytpmg.com

Twin County Regional Hospital 200 Hospital Dr Galax VA 24333 276-236-8181 236-1715
TF: 800-295-3342 ■ *Web:* www.tcrh.org

University of Virginia Health System
1215 Lee St Charlottesville VA 22908 434-924-0211 982-3759
TF: 800-251-3627 ■
Web: www.healthsystem.virginia.edu/toplevel/home/home.cfm

UVA Culpeper Hospital 501 Sunset Ln Culpeper VA 22701 540-829-4100
TF: 866-608-4749 ■ *Web:* www.culpeperhealth.org

Virginia Baptist Hospital
3300 Rivermont Ave Lynchburg VA 24503 434-947-4000
Web: www.centrahealth.com

Virginia Hospital Ctr
1701 N George Mason Dr Arlington VA 22205 703-558-5000 558-6583
Web: www.virginiahospitalcenter.com

Winchester Medical Ctr 1840 Amherst St Winchester VA 22601 540-536-8000 536-8606
Web: www.valleyhealthlink.com

Washington

Phone Fax

Auburn Regional Medical Ctr
202 N Div St Plaza 1 Auburn WA 98001 253-833-7711 697-7293
TF: 866-268-7223 ■ *Web:* www.multicare.org

Capital Medical Ctr 3900 Capital Mall Dr SW Olympia WA 98502 360-754-5858 956-2574
TF: 888-677-9757 ■ *Web:* www.capitalmedical.com

Deaconess Medical Ctr 800 W Fifth Ave Spokane WA 99204 509-458-5800 473-7286
Web: www.deaconessspokane.com

Evergreen Hospital Medical Ctr
12040 NE 128th St Kirkland WA 98034 425-899-1000 899-2624
Web: www.evergreenhealth.com

Grays Harbor Community Hospital
920 Anderson Dr Aberdeen WA 98520 360-532-5122 537-5039
Web: www.ghchwa.org

Harrison Memorial Hospital 2520 Cherry Ave Bremerton WA 98310 360-377-3911 792-6503
Web: www.harrisonhospital.org

Highline Medical Ctr 16251 Sylvester Rd SW Burien WA 98166 206-244-9970 246-5385
Web: highlinemedicalcenter.org

Kadlec Regional Medical Ctr 888 Swift Blvd Richland WA 99352 509-946-4611 942-2679
TF: 800-780-6067 ■ *Web:* www.kadlec.org

Kennewick General Hospital (KGH)
900 S Auburn St Kennewick WA 99336 509-586-6111 586-5892
Web: www.trioshealth.org

Legacy Salmon Creek Hospital
2211 NE 139th St Vancouver WA 98686 360-487-1000 487-3459
TF: 877-270-5566 ■ *Web:* www.legacyhealth.org

Lourdes Medical Ctr 520 N Fourth Ave Pasco WA 99301 509-547-7704 546-2291
Web: www.lourdeshealth.net

Northwest Hospital & Medical Ctr
1550 N 115th St Seattle WA 98133 206-364-0500 368-1949
TF: 877-694-4677 ■ *Web:* www.nwhospital.org

Olympic Medical Ctr 939 Caroline St Port Angeles WA 98362 360-417-7000 417-7333
TF: 888-362-6260 ■ *Web:* www.olympicmedical.org

Overlake Hospital Medical Ctr
1035 116th Ave NE Bellevue WA 98004 425-688-5000 688-5087
Web: www.overlakehospital.org

PeaceHealth 1615 Delaware St PO Box 3002 Longview WA 98632 360-414-2000
Web: www.peacehealth.org

PeaceHealth St Joseph Medical Ctr
2901 Squalicum Pkwy Bellingham WA 98225 360-734-5400 738-6393
TF: 800-541-7209 ■ *Web:* www.peacehealth.org

Peninsula Community Health Services
PO Box 960 Bremerton WA 98337 360-377-3776 373-2096
Web: www.pchsweb.org

Proliance Surgeons Inc 805 Madison Ste 901 Seattle WA 98104 206-264-8100
Web: www.proliancesurgeons.com

Providence Centralia Hospital
914 S Scheuber Rd Centralia WA 98531 360-736-2803 330-8614
TF Help Line: 877-736-2803 ■ *Web:* washington.providence.org

Providence Everett Medical Ctr
Colby Campus 1321 Colby Ave Everett WA 98201 425-261-2000 261-4030
Web: www2.providence.org

Providence Holy Family Hospital
5633 N Lidgerwood St Spokane WA 99208 509-482-0111 482-2456
Web: www2.providence.org

Providence Regional Medical Ctr Everett
916 Pacific Ave Everett WA 98201 425-261-2000 261-4051
Web: www2.providence.org

Providence Sacred Heart Medical Ctr
101 W Eigth Ave Spokane WA 99204 509-474-3170 474-4925
TF: 800-442-8534 ■ *Web:* washington.providence.org

Providence Saint Peter Hospital (PSPH)
413 Lilly Rd NE Olympia WA 98506 360-491-9480 493-4277
TF: 888-492-9480 ■ *Web:* www2.providence.org

Providence St Mary Medical Ctr
401 W Poplar St PO Box 1477 Walla Walla WA 99362 509-525-3320
TF: 877-215-7833 ■ *Web:* www2.providence.org

Qualis Health PO Box 33400 Seattle WA 98133 206-364-9700 368-2419
TF: 800-949-7536 ■ *Web:* www.qualishealth.org

Saint Joseph Medical Ctr (SJMC) 1717 S J St Tacoma WA 98405 888-825-3227 426-6260*
**Fax Area Code:* 253 ■ *Web:* chifranciscan.org/

Skagit Valley Hospital
1415 E Kincaid St Mount Vernon WA 98273 360-424-4111 428-2416
Web: www.skagitvalleyhospital.org

Southwest Washington Medical Ctr (SWMC)
400 NE Mother Joseph Pl PO Box 1600 Vancouver WA 98664 360-514-2000 514-2006
Web: peacehealth.org/southwest

Swedish Medical Ctr Cherry Hill Campus
500 17th Ave Seattle WA 98122 206-320-2000 320-2140
Web: www.swedish.org

Swedish Medical Ctr First Hill 747 Broadway Seattle WA 98122 206-386-6000 386-2277
Web: www.swedish.org

Swedish Medical Ctr/Edmonds 21601 76th Ave W Edmonds WA 98026 425-640-4000 640-4010
Web: www.swedish.org

Tacoma General Hospital 315 MLK Jr Way Tacoma WA 98405 253-403-1000 403-1180
TF: 800-552-1419 ■ *Web:* www.multicare.org

University of Washington Medical Ctr
1959 NE Pacific St Seattle WA 98195 206-685-8973 598-2343
Web: www.washington.edu

UW Medicine Eastside Hospital & Specialty
3100 Northup Way Bellevue WA 98004 425-646-7777
Web: eastside.uwmedicine.org

Valley Hospital & Medical Ctr (VHMC)
12606 E Mission Ave Spokane Valley WA 99216 509-924-6650 473-5903
Web: www.spokanevalleyhospital.com/pages/home.aspx

Valley Medical Ctr 400 S 43rd St Renton WA 98055 425-228-3450
TF: 855-923-4633 ■ *Web:* www.valleymed.org

Virginia Mason Medical Ctr 925 Seneca St Seattle WA 98101 206-624-1144 223-6976
Web: www.virginiamason.org

Yakima Regional Medical & Heart Ctr
110 S Ninth Ave Yakima WA 98902 509-575-5000 454-6193
Web: yakimaregional.com

Yakima Valley Memorial Hospital
2811 Tieton Dr Yakima WA 98902 509-575-8000 574-5800
Web: www.yakimamemorial.org

West Virginia

Phone Fax

Beckley Appalachian Regional Hospital
306 Stanaford Rd Beckley WV 25801 304-255-3000 255-3544
Web: www.arh.org

Bluefield Regional Medical Ctr (BRMC)
500 Cherry St Bluefield WV 24701 304-327-1100 792-5636*
**Fax Area Code:* 630 ■ *TF:* 800-994-6610 ■ *Web:* www.bluefieldregional.net/pages/home.aspx

Cabell Huntington Hospital
1340 Hal Greer Blvd Huntington WV 25701 304-526-2000 526-2008
Web: www.cabellhuntington.org

Camden-Clark Memorial Hospital (CCMH)
800 Garfield Ave Parkersburg WV 26101 304-424-2111 424-2782
TF: 800-541-3160 ■ *Web:* www.camdenclark.org

Charleston Area Medical Ctr 501 Morris St Charleston WV 25301 304-388-5432 388-3604
Web: www.camc.org

	City	State	ZIP	Phone	Fax
City Hospital 2500 Hospital Dr *TF:* 888-988-1362 ■ *Web:* www.wvuniversityhealthcare.com	Martinsburg	WV	25401	304-264-1000	260-1437
Davis Memorial Hospital 812 Gorman Ave *Web:* www.davishealthsystem.org	Elkins	WV	26241	304-636-3300	637-3184
Fairmont General Hospital (FGH) 1325 Locust Ave *Web:* www.fghi.com	Fairmont	WV	26554	304-367-7100	367-7246
Grafton City Hospital Inc 500 Market St *Web:* www.graftonhospital.com	Grafton	WV	26354	304-265-0400	
Greenbrier Valley Medical Ctr 202 Maplewood Ave *Web:* www.gvmc.com	Ronceverte	WV	24970	304-647-4411	647-6010
Logan Regional Medical Ctr 20 Hospital Dr *TF:* 888-982-9144 ■ *Web:* www.loganregionalmedicalcenter.com	Logan	WV	25601	304-831-1101	831-1871
Monongalia General Hospital 1200 JD Anderson Dr *TF:* 800-992-7600 ■ *Web:* mongeneral.com	Morgantown	WV	26505	304-598-1200	
Ohio Valley Medical Ctr 2000 Eoff St *Web:* ovmc-eorh.com	Wheeling	WV	26003	304-234-0123	234-8229
Pleasant Valley Hospital 2520 Valley Dr *Web:* www.pvalley.org	Point Pleasant	WV	25550	304-675-4340	
Princeton Community Hospital 122 12th St *Web:* www.pchonline.org	Princeton	WV	24740	304-487-7000	487-2161
Raleigh General Hospital 1710 Harper Rd *Web:* www.raleighgeneral.com	Beckley	WV	25801	304-256-4100	256-4009
Reynolds Memorial Hospital (RMH) 800 Wheeling Ave *Web:* www.reynoldsmemorial.com	Glen Dale	WV	26038	304-845-3211	843-3202
Stonewall Jackson Memorial Hospital (SJMH) 230 Hospital Plaza *TF:* 866-637-0471 ■ *Web:* www.stonewalljacksonhospital.com	Weston	WV	26452	304-269-8000	269-8090
Thomas Memorial Hospital 4605 MacCorkle Ave SW *Web:* www.thomaswv.org	South Charleston	WV	25309	304-766-3600	766-4359
United Hospital Ctr Three Hospital Plz *Web:* www.uhcwv.org	Clarksburg	WV	26301	304-624-2121	624-2909
Weirton Medical Ctr 601 Colliers Way *TF:* 800-994-6610 ■ *Web:* www.weirtonmedical.com	Weirton	WV	26062	304-797-6000	797-6176
West Virginia University Hospitals 1 Medical Ctr Dr *Web:* www.wvuhealthcare.com	Morgantown	WV	26506	304-598-4200	598-4073
Wetzel County Hospital Three E Benjamin Dr *Web:* www.wetzelcountyhospital.com	New Martinsville	WV	26155	304-455-8000	455-4259
Wheeling Hospital One Medical Pk *Web:* wheelinghospital.org	Wheeling	WV	26003	304-243-3000	

Wisconsin

	City	State	ZIP	Phone	Fax
Appleton Medical Ctr 1818 N Meade St *TF:* 800-236-4101 ■ *Web:* www.thedacare.org	Appleton	WI	54911	920-731-4101	738-6319
Aspirus Wausau Hospital 333 Pine Ridge Blvd *TF:* 800-283-2881 ■ *Web:* www.aspirus.org	Wausau	WI	54401	715-847-2121	847-0095
Aurora Lakeland Medical Ctr (ALMC) W3985 County Rd NN *Web:* www.aurorahealthcare.org	Elkhorn	WI	53121	262-741-2000	741-2759
Aurora Sinai Medical Ctr 945 N 12th St *TF:* 888-863-5502 ■ *Web:* www.aurorahealthcare.org	Milwaukee	WI	53201	414-219-2000	219-6735
Bay Area Medical Ctr (BAMC) 3100 Shore Dr *TF:* 888-788-2070 ■ *Web:* bamc.org	Marinette	WI	54143	715-735-4200	
Beaver Dam Community Hospital 707 S University Ave *Web:* www.bdch.com	Beaver Dam	WI	53916	920-887-7181	887-7973
Bellin Hospital 744 S Webster Ave *Web:* www.bellin.org	Green Bay	WI	54301	920-433-3500	431-5568
Beloit Health System 1969 W Hart Rd *TF:* 800-637-2641 ■ *Web:* www.beloithealthsystem.org	Beloit	WI	53511	608-363-5724	363-5702
Columbia Saint Mary's Hospital 2025 E Newport Ave *Web:* www.columbia-stmarys.org	Milwaukee	WI	53211	414-961-3300	
Columbia Saint Mary's Hospital Ozaukee 13111 N Port Washington Rd *Web:* www.columbia-stmarys.org	Mequon	WI	53097	262-243-7300	
Community Memorial Hospital (CMH) W 180 N 8085 Town Hall Rd *Web:* froedtert.com/	Menomonee Falls	WI	53051	262-251-1000	253-7169
Elmbrook Memorial Hospital 19333 W N Ave *Web:* www.mywheaton.org/locations/elmbrook_memorial	Brookfield	WI	53045	262-785-2000	
Fort Atkinson Memorial Hospital 611 Sherman Ave E *Web:* www.forthealthcare.com	Fort Atkinson	WI	53538	920-568-5000	568-5412
Franciscan Skemp Health Care 700 W Ave S *Web:* mayoclinichealthsystem.org/	La Crosse	WI	54601	608-785-0940	
Froedtert Hospital 9200 W Wisconsin Ave *Web:* www.froedtert.com	Milwaukee	WI	53226	414-805-4311	805-7790
Gundersen Lutheran Medical Ctr 1836 S Ave *TF:* 800-362-9567 ■ *Web:* www.gundersenhealth.org	La Crosse	WI	54601	608-782-7300	372-3253
Holy Family Memorial Medical Ctr 2300 Western Ave PO Box 1450 *TF:* 800-994-3662 ■ *Web:* www.hfmhealth.org	Manitowoc	WI	54220	920-320-2011	
Kenosha Medical Ctr 6308 Eigth Ave *TF:* 800-994-6610 ■ *Web:* www.uhsi.org	Kenosha	WI	53143	262-656-2011	656-2124
Lakeview Medical Ctr 1100 N Main St *Web:* www.lakeviewmedical.com	Rice Lake	WI	54868	715-234-1515	236-6342
Mayo Foundation for Medical Education & Research 1221 Whipple St PO Box 4105 *Web:* mayoclinichealthsystem.org	Eau Claire	WI	54702	715-838-3219	838-3268
Mercy Hospital & Trauma Ctr 1000 Mineral Pt Ave *TF:* 800-756-4147 ■ *Web:* www.mercyhealthsystem.com	Janesville	WI	53548	608-756-6000	756-6236
Meriter Hospital 202 S Pk St *Web:* www.meriter.com/mhs	Madison	WI	53715	608-417-6000	
Ministry Saint Joseph's Hospital (MSJH) 611 St Joseph Ave *Web:* www.ministryhealth.org/sjh/home.nws	Marshfield	WI	54449	715-387-1713	
Monroe Clinic Hospital 515 22nd Ave *TF:* 800-338-0568 ■ *Web:* www.monroeclinic.org	Monroe	WI	53566	608-324-2000	324-1114
Oconomowoc Memorial Hospital 791 Summit Ave *TF:* 800-242-0313 ■ *Web:* www.prohealthcare.org	Oconomowoc	WI	53066	262-569-9400	569-0336
Prairie Du Chien Memorial Hospital 705 E Taylor St *Web:* www.pdcmemorialhospital.org	Prairie Du Chien	WI	53821	608-357-2000	
Richland Hospital Inc, The 333 E Second St *TF:* 888-467-7485 ■ *Web:* www.richlandhospital.com	Richland Center	WI	53581	608-647-6321	647-6325
Sacred Heart Hospital 900 W Clairemont Ave *TF:* 888-445-4554 ■ *Web:* www.sacredhearteauclaire.org	Eau Claire	WI	54701	715-717-4121	
Saint Elizabeth Hospital 1506 S Oneida St *TF:* 800-223-7332 ■ *Web:* www.affinityhealth.org	Appleton	WI	54915	920-738-2000	
Saint Joseph's Hospital 2661 County Hwy I *TF:* 877-723-1811 ■ *Web:* www.stjoeschipfalls.com	Chippewa Falls	WI	54729	715-723-1811	726-3204
Saint Mary's Hospital 2251 N Shore Dr *TF Cust Svc:* 800-578-0840 ■ *Web:* www.ministryhealth.org	Rhinelander	WI	54501	715-361-2000	361-2011
Saint Mary's Hospital Medical Ctr 1726 Shawano Ave *TF:* 800-666-5606 ■ *Web:* www.stmgb.org	Green Bay	WI	54303	920-498-4200	436-1326
Saint Michael's Hospital 900 Illinois Ave *Web:* www.ministryhealth.org	Stevens Point	WI	54481	715-346-5000	346-5088
Saint Vincent Hospital 835 S Van Buren St *TF:* 800-236-3030 ■ *Web:* www.stvincenthospital.org	Green Bay	WI	54301	920-433-0111	431-3215
Southwest Health Ctr Inc 1400 Eastside Rd *Web:* www.southwesthealth.org	Platteville	WI	53818	608-348-2331	
St Agnes Hospital 430 E Div St *TF:* 800-922-3400 ■ *Web:* www.agnesian.com	Fond du Lac	WI	54935	920-929-2300	926-4866
Stoughton Hospital 900 Ridge St *TF:* 888-816-3831 ■ *Web:* www.stoughtonhospital.com	Stoughton	WI	53589	608-873-6611	873-2355
Theda Clark Medical Ctr 130 Second St *TF:* 800-236-3122 ■ *Web:* www.thedacare.org	Neenah	WI	54956	920-729-3100	729-3167
University of Wisconsin Hospital & Clinics 600 Highland Ave *TF:* 800-323-8942 ■ *Web:* www.uwhealth.org	Madison	WI	53792	608-263-6400	263-9830
Waukesha Memorial Hospital 725 American Ave *TF:* 800-326-2011 ■ *Web:* www.prohealthcare.org	Waukesha	WI	53188	262-928-1000	
West Allis Memorial Hospital 8901 W Lincoln Ave Second Fl *Web:* www.aurorahealthcare.org	West Allis	WI	53227	414-328-6000	328-8536
Wheaton Franciscan - Saint Joseph 5000 W Chambers St *Web:* www.mywheaton.org	Milwaukee	WI	53210	414-447-2000	
Wheaton Franciscan Healthcare *All Saints* 3801 Spring St *TF:* 877-304-6332 ■ *Web:* www.mywheaton.org	Racine	WI	53405	262-687-4011	687-5116
Wheaton Franciscan Healthcare - St. Francis 3237 S 16th St *Web:* www.mywheaton.org	Milwaukee	WI	53215	414-647-5000	647-5565

Wyoming

	City	State	ZIP	Phone	Fax
Campbell County Memorial Hospital 501 S Burma PO Box 3011 **Fax:* Hum Res ■ *Web:* www.ccmh.net	Gillette	WY	82717	307-688-1000	688-1516*
Cheyenne Regional Medical Ctr (CRMC) 214 E 23rd St *Web:* www.crmcwy.org	Cheyenne	WY	82001	307-634-2273	633-3569
Ivinson Memorial Hospital 255 N 30th St *TF:* 877-858-0990 ■ *Web:* www2.ivinsonhospital.org	Laramie	WY	82072	307-742-2141	742-2150
Memorial Hospital of Sweetwater County 1200 College Dr *TF General:* 866-571-0944 ■ *Web:* www.sweetwatermemorial.com	Rock Springs	WY	82901	307-362-3711	
Riverton Memorial Hospital LLC 2100 W Sunset Dr *TF:* 888-982-9144 ■ *Web:* sagewesthealthcare.com	Riverton	WY	82501	307-856-4161	856-9587
Sheridan Memorial Hospital 1401 W Fifth St *Web:* www.sheridanhospital.org	Sheridan	WY	82801	307-672-1000	672-1007
Wyoming Medical Ctr 1233 E Second St *TF:* 800-822-7201 ■ *Web:* wyomingmedicalcenter.org	Casper	WY	82601	307-577-7201	233-8230

377-4 Military Hospitals

	City	State	ZIP	Phone	Fax
Brooke Army Medical Ctr (BAMC) 3551 Roger Brooke Dr *TF:* 800-443-2262 ■ *Web:* www.bamc.amedd.army.mil	Fort Sam Houston	TX	78234	210-916-4141	
Charleston Naval Hospital 110 NNPTC Cir *Web:* www.med.navy.mil/sites/chas/pages/default.aspx	Goose Creek	SC	29445	843-794-6221	
Colonel Florence A Blanchfield Army Community Hospital 650 Joel Dr *Web:* www.campbell.amedd.army.mil/	Fort Campbell	KY	42223	270-798-8400	
Darnall Army Medical Ctr 36000 Darnall Loop *TF:* 800-305-6421 ■ *Web:* www.crdamc.amedd.army.mil	Fort Hood	TX	76544	254-288-8000	286-7372
David Grant US Air Force Medical Ctr 101 Bodin Cir *TF:* 800-264-3462 ■ *Web:* www.travis.af.mil/units/dgmc/	Travis AFB	CA	94535	707-423-3735	423-7416

Phone Fax

Dwight David Eisenhower Army Medical Ctr (DDAMC)
300 Hospital Rd . . . . . Fort Gordon GA 30905 706-787-5811 787-5342*
*Fax: Admitting ■ Web: www.ddeamc.amedd.army.mil

Evans Army Community Hospital
1650 Cochran Cir . . . . . Fort Carson CO 80913 719-526-7000
Web: www.evans.amedd.army.mil

Ireland Army Community Hospital
289 Ireland Ave . . . . . Fort Knox KY 40121 502-624-9333 624-9255
Web: www.iach.knox.amedd.army.mil

Irwin Army Community Hospital
600 Caisson Hill Rd . . . . . Fort Riley KS 66442 785-239-7000
Web: iach.amedd.army.mil

Keller Army Community Hospital
900 Washington Rd . . . . . West Point NY 10996 845-938-7992
TF: 800-552-2907 ■ Web: kach.amedd.army.mil

Lyster Army Health Clinic Andrews Ave . . . . . Fort Rucker AL 36362 334-255-7000
Web: www.rucker.amedd.army.mil

Madigan Army Medical Ctr 9040 Jackson Ave . . . . . Tacoma WA 98431 253-968-1110 968-1633*

Martin Army Community Hospital
7950 Martin Loop Bldg 9200 . . . . . Fort Benning GA 31905 706-544-2041
Web: martin.amedd.army.mil

National Naval Medical Ctr
8901 Wisconsin Ave . . . . . Bethesda MD 20889 301-295-4611

Naval Hospital 100 Brewster Blvd . . . . . Camp Lejeune NC 28547 910-450-4300 450-4012
Web: www.med.navy.mil/sites/nhcl/pages/default.aspx

Naval Hospital Bremerton One Boone Rd . . . . . Bremerton WA 98312 360-475-4000
TF: 800-422-1383 ■ Web: www.med.navy.mil

Naval Hospital Pensacola 6000 W Hwy 98 . . . . . Pensacola FL 32512 850-505-6601 505-6213
Web: www.med.navy.mil

Naval Medical Ctr Portsmouth
620 John Paul Jones Cir . . . . . Portsmouth VA 23708 757-953-5000

Naval Medical Ctr San Diego
34800 Bob Wilson Dr . . . . . San Diego CA 92134 619-532-6400
Web: www.med.navy.mil

Tripler Army Medical Ctr
1 Jarrett White Rd Tripler AMC . . . . . Honolulu HI 96859 808-433-6661 433-4899
TF: 877-880-2184 ■ Web: www.tamc.amedd.army.mil

US Air Force 375th Medical Group
310 W Losey St . . . . . Scott AFB IL 62225 866-683-2778
TF: 866-683-2778 ■ Web: www.scott.af.mil

US Air Force 96th Medical Group
307 Boatner Rd . . . . . Eglin AFB FL 32542 850-883-8600
Web: www.eglin.af.mil/units/eglinhospital.asp

US Air Force Medical Ctr Keesler 81st Medical Group
301 Fisher St . . . . . Keesler AFB MS 39534 228-376-8225 377-9748
Web: www.keesler.af.mil

William Beaumont Army Medical Ctr
5005 N Piedras St . . . . . El Paso TX 79920 915-742-2121
Web: www.wbamc.amedd.army.mil/

Winn Army Community Hospital
1061 Harmon Ave . . . . . Fort Stewart GA 31314 912-435-6837

Womack Army Medical Ctr
Bldg 4-2817 Reilly Rd . . . . . Fort Bragg NC 28310 910-907-6000 907-8473
Web: www.wamc.amedd.army.mil

377-5 Psychiatric Hospitals

Listings here include state psychiatric facilities as well as private psychiatric hospitals.

Phone Fax

Adventist Behavioral Health
14901 Broschart Rd . . . . . Rockville MD 20850 301-251-4500 315-3000
TF: 800-204-8600 ■ Web: www.adventistbehavioralhealth.com

Alaska Psychiatric Institute 3700 Piper St . . . . . Anchorage AK 99508 907-269-7100 269-7128
Web: dhss.alaska.gov

Alton Mental Health Ctr 4500 College Ave . . . . . Alton IL 62002 618-474-3200 474-3807
Web: 'www.agacistore.com/

Ancora Psychiatric Hospital
301 Spring Garden Rd . . . . . Hammonton NJ 08037 609-561-1700 561-2509
Web: nj.gov

Appalachian Behavioral Healthcare
100 Hospital Dr . . . . . Athens OH 45701 740-594-5000
Web: mha.ohio.gov

Arizona State Hospital 2500 E Van Buren St . . . . . Phoenix AZ 85008 602-244-1331 220-6355
TF: 877-588-5163 ■ Web: www.azdhs.gov/azsh

Arkansas State Hospital
4313 W Markham St . . . . . Little Rock AR 72205 501-686-9000 686-9483
Web: humanservices.arkansas.gov

Atascadero State Hospital
10333 S Camino Real . . . . . Atascadero CA 93422 805-468-2000 468-3386
TF: 844-210-6207 ■ Web: dsh.ca.gov

Aurora Las Encinas Hospital
2900 E Del Mar Blvd . . . . . Pasadena CA 91107 626-795-9901 792-2919
TF: 800-792-2345 ■ Web: www.lasencinashospital.com

Austin State Hospital 4110 Guadalupe St . . . . . Austin TX 78751 512-452-0381 419-2163
TF: 866-407-3773 ■ Web: dshs.state.tx.us

Banner Behavioral Health Hospital
7575 E Earll Dr . . . . . Scottsdale AZ 85251 480-941-7500
TF: 800-254-4357 ■ Web: www.bannerhealth.com

Bellevue Hospital Ctr 462 First Ave . . . . . New York NY 10016 212-562-4141 562-4036
Web: nyc.gov

Belmont Ctr for Comprehensive Treatment
4200 Monument Rd . . . . . Philadelphia PA 19131 215-877-2000 581-9141*
*Fax: Admissions ■ Web: www.einstein.edu

Big Spring State Hospital 1901 N Hwy 87 . . . . . Big Spring TX 79720 432-267-8216 268-7263
Web: dshs.state.tx.us

Brentwood A Behavioral Health Co
1006 Highland Ave . . . . . Shreveport LA 71101 318-678-7500 227-9296
TF: 877-678-7500 ■ Web: www.brentwoodbehavioral.com

Bridgewater State Hospital 20 Admin Rd . . . . . Bridgewater MA 02324 508-279-4500 279-4832
Web: mass.gov

Bronx Psychiatric Ctr 1500 Waters Pl . . . . . Bronx NY 10461 718-931-0600 862-4858
TF: 800-597-8481 ■ Web: omh.ny.gov

Phone Fax

Broughton Hospital 1000 S Sterling St . . . . . Morganton NC 28655 828-433-2111
Web: ncdhhs.gov

BryLin Hospitals 1263 Delaware Ave . . . . . Buffalo NY 14209 716-886-8200
TF: 800-727-9546 ■ Web: www.brylin.com

Buffalo Psychiatric Ctr 400 Forest Ave . . . . . Buffalo NY 14213 716-885-2261 885-4852
TF: 800-597-8481 ■ Web: www.omh.ny.gov

Butler Hospital 345 Blackstone Blvd . . . . . Providence RI 02906 401-455-6200 455-6309*
*Fax: Admitting ■ Web: www.butler.org

Capital District Psychiatric Ctr
75 New Scotland Ave . . . . . Albany NY 12208 518-447-9611 434-0041
Web: www.omh.ny.gov/omhweb/facilities/cdpc/

Caro Ctr 2000 Chambers Rd . . . . . Caro MI 48723 989-673-3191 673-6749
Web: michigan.gov

Carrier Clinic 252 County Rd 601 . . . . . Belle Mead NJ 08502 908-281-1000 281-1680
TF: 800-933-3579 ■ Web: carrierclinic.org

Catawba Hospital 5525 Catawba Hospital Dr . . . . . Catawba VA 24070 540-375-4200
TF: 800-451-5544 ■ Web: www.catawba.dbhds.virginia.gov

Cedar Springs Behavioral Health System
2135 Southgate Rd . . . . . Colorado Springs CO 80906 719-633-4114 578-0857
TF: 800-888-1088 ■ Web: cedarspringsbhs.com

Cedarcrest Hospital 525 Russell Rd . . . . . Newington CT 06111 860-666-4613

Central Louisiana State Hospital
242 W Shamrock St . . . . . Pineville LA 71360 318-484-6200 484-6501
TF: 866-666-8335 ■ Web: www.dhh.louisiana.gov

Central State Hospital
26317 W Washington St . . . . . Petersburg VA 23803 804-524-7000
Web: www.csh.dbhds.virginia.gov

Central Washington Hospital
1201 S Miller St . . . . . Wenatchee WA 98801 509-662-1511 665-6132
TF: 800-365-6428 ■ Web: www.cwhs.com

Cherry Hospital 201 Stevens Mill Rd . . . . . Goldsboro NC 27530 919-731-3200 731-3785
Web: www.ncdhhs.gov/dsohf/cherry

Chester Mental Health Ctr 1315 Lehman Dr . . . . . Chester IL 62233 618-826-4571
TF: 800-843-6154 ■ Web: www.dhs.state.il.us/

Chicago Lakeshore Hospital 4840 N Marine Dr . . . . . Chicago IL 60640 773-878-9700 907-4607
TF Cust Svc: 800-888-0560 ■ Web: www.chicagolakeshorehospital.com

Chicago-Read Mental Health Ctr
4200 N Oak Pk Ave . . . . . Chicago IL 60634 773-794-4000 794-4046
Web: www.dhs.state.il.us

Clarks Summit State Hospital
1451 Hillside Dr . . . . . Clarks Summit PA 18411 570-586-2011 587-7415
Web: dpw.state.pa.us

Clifton T Perkins Hospital Ctr
8450 Dorsey Run Rd . . . . . Jessup MD 20794 410-724-3000 724-3009
TF: 877-463-3464 ■ Web: dhmh.maryland.gov

Coastal Harbor Treatment Ctr
1150 Cornell Ave . . . . . Savannah GA 31406 912-354-3911 355-1336
Web: coastalharbor.com

College Hospital 10802 College Pl . . . . . Cerritos CA 90703 562-924-9581 809-0981
TF: 800-352-3301 ■ Web: www.collegehospitals.com

College Hospital Costa Mesa
301 Victoria St . . . . . Costa Mesa CA 92627 949-642-2734 574-3320
TF: 800-773-8001 ■ Web: www.collegehospitals.com

Colorado Mental Health Institute at Fort Logan (CMHIFL)
3520 W Oxford Ave . . . . . Denver CO 80236 303-866-7066 866-7101*
Web: www.colorado.gov/cs/satellite/cdhs-behavioralhealth/cbon/1251580627038

Colorado Mental Health Institute at Pueblo (CMHIP)
1600 W 24th St . . . . . Pueblo CO 81003 719-546-4000 546-4484
Web: www.colorado.gov

Connecticut Valley Hospital
1000 Silver St . . . . . Middletown CT 06457 860-262-5000 262-5989
Web: ct.gov

Creedmoor Psychiatric Ctr
79-25 Winchester Blvd . . . . . Queens Village NY 11427 718-464-7500 264-3636
TF: 800-597-8481 ■
Web: www.omh.ny.gov/omhweb/facilities/crpc/facility.htm

Danville State Hospital
200 State Hospital Dr . . . . . Danville PA 1782 570-271-4500
Web: dsh.thomas-industriesinc.com

Del Amo Hospital 23700 Camino Del Sol . . . . . Torrance CA 90505 310-530-1151
TF: 800-533-5266 ■ Web: www.delamohospital.com

Delaware Psychiatric Ctr
1901 N Dupont Hwy Main Bldg . . . . . New Castle DE 19720 302-255-9399 255-4428
TF: 800-652-2929 ■ Web: dhss.delaware.gov

Dominion Hospital 2960 Sleepy Hollow Rd . . . . . Falls Church VA 22044 703-536-2000 533-9650
Web: www.dominionhospital.com

Dorothea Dix Hospital 820 S Boylan Ave . . . . . Raleigh NC 27699 919-733-5540
Web: www.ncdhhs.gov/dsohf/services/dix

East Central Regional Hospital
Augusta 3405 Mike Padgett Hwy . . . . . Augusta GA 30906 706-792-7000

East Louisiana State Hospital 4502 Hwy 951 . . . . . Jackson LA 70748 225-634-0100
Web: new.dhh.louisiana.gov

Eastern Louisiana Mental Health System Greenwell Springs Campus
4502 Hwy 951 PO Box 549 . . . . . Greenwell Springs LA 70739 225-634-0100
Web: www.dhh.state.la.us

Eastern State Hospital (ESH)
4601 Ironbound Rd . . . . . Williamsburg VA 23188 757-253-5161 253-5065
TF: 800-994-6610 ■ Web: esh.dbhds.virginia.gov

Elgin Mental Health Ctr 750 S State St . . . . . Elgin IL 60123 847-742-1040

Elmira Psychiatric Ctr 100 Washington St . . . . . Elmira NY 14901 607-737-4711 737-9080
TF: 800-597-8481 ■ Web: omh.ny.gov

Essex County Hospital Ctr 204 Grove Ave . . . . . Cedar Grove NJ 07009 973-571-2800
Web: www.essex-countynj.org

Fair Oaks Hospital 5352 Linton Blvd . . . . . Delray Beach FL 33484 561-498-4440 495-3103
TF: 866-904-6871 ■ Web: www.delraymedicalctr.com

Fairfax Hospital 10200 NE 132nd St . . . . . Kirkland WA 98034 425-821-2000
TF: 800-435-7221 ■ Web: www.fairfaxhospital.com

Fairmount Behavioral Health System
561 Fairthorne Ave . . . . . Philadelphia PA 19128 215-487-4000 483-8187
TF: 800-235-0200 ■ Web: www.fairmountbhs.com

Fort Lauderdale Hospital
1601 E Las Olas Blvd . . . . . Fort Lauderdale FL 33301 954-463-4321 453-5497
TF: 800-585-7527 ■ Web: www.fortlauderdalehospital.org

				Phone	Fax
Four Winds Hospital 800 Cross River Rd *TF:* 800-528-6624 ■ *Web:* www.fourwindshospital.com	Katonah	NY	10536	914-763-8151	763-9597
Friends Hospital 4641 Roosevelt Blvd. *TF:* 800-889-0548 ■ *Web:* www.friendshospital.com	Philadelphia	PA	19124	215-831-4600	
Fulton State Hospital 600 E Fifth St *Web:* dmh.mo.gov	Fulton	MO	65251	573-592-4100	592-3000
GEO Care South Florida State Hospital 800 E Cypress Dr *Web:* geocarellc.com	Pembroke Pines	FL	33025	954-392-3000	
Georgia Regional Hospital at Atlanta 3073 Panthersville Rd. *Web:* dbhdd.georgia.gov	Atlanta	GA	30034	404-243-2100	
Georgia Regional Hospital at Savannah 1915 Eisenhower Dr *TF:* 800-436-7442	Savannah	GA	31406	912-356-2011	356-2691
Greater Binghamton Health Ctr 425 Robinson St. *Web:* www.omh.ny.gov/omhweb	Binghamton	NY	13904	607-724-1391	773-4387
Green Oaks Hospital 7808 Clodus Fields Dr. *TF:* 800-866-6554 ■ *Web:* www.greenoakspsych.com	Dallas	TX	75251	972-991-9504	789-1865
Greystone Park Psychiatric Hospital 59 Koch Ave *Web:* www.nj.gov/humanservices/dmhs/oshm/gpph	Morris Plains	NJ	07950	973-538-1800	
Griffin Memorial Hospital 900 E Main St. *TF General:* 800-955-3468 ■ *Web:* ok.gov	Norman	OK	73071	405-321-4880	
H Douglas Singer Mental Health & Development Ctr 4402 N Main St	Rockford	IL	61103	815-987-7096	
Hamilton Ctr Inc PO Box 4323 *TF:* 800-742-0787 ■ *Web:* www.hamiltoncenter.org	Terre Haute	IN	47804	812-231-8323	
Hampstead Hospital 218 E Rd *Web:* www.hampsteadhospital.com	Hampstead	NH	03841	603-329-5311	329-4746
Harris County Psychiatric Ctr 2800 S MacGregor Way *Web:* hcpc.uth.tmc.edu	Houston	TX	77021	713-741-5000	741-5939
Hartgrove Hospital 5730 W Roosevelt Rd. *TF:* 800-478-4783 ■ *Web:* hartgrovehospital.com	Chicago	IL	60644	773-722-3113	
Havenwyck Hospital 1525 University Dr *Fax: Admitting ■ *TF:* 800-401-2727 ■ *Web:* havenwyckhospital.com	Auburn Hills	MI	48326	248-373-9200	377-8160*
Hawaii State Hospital 45-710 Keaahala Rd	Kaneohe	HI	96744	808-247-2191	247-7335
Heartland Behavioral Healthcare 3000 S Erie St. *Web:* mha.ohio.gov	Massillon	OH	44646	330-833-3135	833-6564
Hill Crest Behavioral Health Services 6869 Fifth Ave S *TF:* 800-292-8553 ■ *Web:* www.hillcrestbhs.com	Birmingham	AL	35212	205-833-9000	
Holly Hill Hospital 3019 Falstaff Rd. *TF:* 800-447-1800 ■ *Web:* www.hollyhillhospital.com	Raleigh	NC	27610	919-250-7000	231-3231
Horsham Clinic 722 E Butler Pk *Fax: Admissions ■ *TF:* 800-237-4447 ■ *Web:* www.horshamclinic.com	Ambler	PA	19002	215-643-7800	654-1148*
Intracare Medical Ctr Hospital 7601 Fannin St *Web:* www.intracarehospital.com	Houston	TX	77054	713-790-0949	790-0456
Jewish Hospital & St Mary's HealthCare 2020 Newburg Rd. *TF:* 800-451-3637 ■ *Web:* www.jhsmh.org	Louisville	KY	40205	502-451-3330	479-4350
John J Madden Mental Health Ctr 1200 S First Ave *Web:* illinois.gov	Hines	IL	60141	708-338-7400	338-7057
John Umstead Hospital 1003 12th St.	Butner	NC	27509	919-575-7211	575-7013
Kalamazoo Psychiatric Hospital 1312 Oakland Dr. *Fax: Admitting ■ *Web:* michigan.gov	Kalamazoo	MI	49008	269-337-3000	337-3007*
Kerrville State Hospital 721 Thompson Dr *TF:* 888-963-7111 ■ *Web:* dshs.state.tx.us	Kerrville	TX	78028	830-896-2211	792-4926
Kingsboro Psychiatric Ctr 681 Clarkson Ave *Fax Area Code: 718 ■ *Fax: Admitting ■ *Web:* www.omh.ny.gov	Brooklyn	NY	11203	800-597-8481	221-7633*
Lakeside Behavioral Health System 2911 Brunswick Rd. *TF:* 800-232-5253 ■ *Web:* lakesidebhs.com	Memphis	TN	38133	901-377-4700	373-0912
Langley Porter Psychiatric Institute 401 Parnassus Ave *TF:* 800-723-7140 ■ *Web:* psych.ucsf.edu	San Francisco	CA	94143	415-476-7000	476-7320
Lincoln Medical & Mental Health Ctr 234 E 149th St *Web:* nyc.gov	Bronx	NY	10451	718-579-5016	
McLean Hospital 115 Mill St. *Web:* mcleanhospital.org/	Belmont	MA	02478	617-855-2000	855-3735
Meadows Psychiatric Ctr 132 The Meadows Dr *TF:* 800-641-7529 ■ *Web:* www.themeadows.net	Centre Hall	PA	16828	814-364-2161	
Meadowview Psychiatric Hospital 595 County Ave *Web:* hudsoncountynj.org	Secaucus	NJ	07094	201-369-5252	
Memorial Hermann Prevention & Recovery Ctr (MHPARC) 3043 Gessner *TF:* 800-464-7272 ■ *Web:* parc.memorialhermann.org	Houston	TX	77080	713-939-7272	939-7272
Mendota Mental Health Institute 301 Troy Dr *Web:* www.dhs.wisconsin.gov	Madison	WI	53704	608-301-1000	301-1358
Menninger Clinic 2801 Gessner Dr PO Box 809045 *TF:* 800-351-9058 ■ *Web:* www.menningerclinic.com	Houston	TX	77080	713-275-5000	275-5107
Mental Health Institute 2277 Iowa Ave *Web:* independenceia.com	Independence	IA	50644	319-334-2583	334-5252
Metropolitan State Hospital 11401 Bloomfield Ave. *Web:* dsh.ca.gov	Norwalk	CA	90650	562-863-7011	868-6920
Middle Tennessee Mental Health Institute 221 Stewarts Ferry Pike *TF:* 800-770-8277 ■ *Web:* tn.gov	Nashville	TN	37214	615-902-7400	741-8953
Milwaukee County Mental Health Complex 9455 Watertown Plank Rd. *Web:* www.county.milwaukee.gov	Milwaukee	WI	53226	414-257-6995	

				Phone	Fax
Mississippi State Hospital PO Box 157A *Web:* www.msh.state.ms.us	Whitfield	MS	39193	601-351-8000	351-8228
Moccasin Bend Mental Health Institute 100 Moccasin Bend Rd. *Web:* tn.gov	Chattanooga	TN	37405	423-265-2271	785-3333
Mohawk Valley Psychiatric Ctr 1400 Noyes St *TF:* 800-597-8481 ■ *Web:* omh.ny.gov	Utica	NY	13502	315-738-3800	738-4414
Napa State Hospital 2100 Napa-Vallejo Hwy *TF:* 866-762-0972 ■ *Web:* www.dsh.ca.gov	Napa	CA	94558	707-253-5000	253-5513
New Hampshire Hospital 36 Clinton St *Web:* www.dhhs.nh.gov	Concord	NH	03301	603-271-5200	271-5395
New Mexico Behavioral Health Institute 3695 Hot Springs Blvd *Fax: Admissions ■ *TF:* 800-446-5970 ■ *Web:* nmhealth.org/about/ofm/ltcf/nmbhi/	Las Vegas	NM	87701	505-454-2100	454-5172*
Norfolk Regional Ctr 1700 N Victory Rd. *Web:* dhhs.ne.gov	Norfolk	NE	68702	402-370-3400	
Norristown State Hospital 1001 Sterigere St	Norristown	PA	19401	610-313-1000	313-1013
North Dakota State Hospital 2605 Cir Dr *TF:* 888-862-7342 ■ *Web:* www.nd.gov	Jamestown	ND	58401	701-253-3650	253-3999
North Texas State Hospital 6515 Kemp Blvd	Wichita Falls	TX	76308	940-692-1220	
Northcoast Behavioral Healthcare System *South Campus* 1756 Sagamore Rd PO Box 305 *Web:* mha.ohio.gov	Northfield	OH	44067	330-467-7131	467-2420
Northwest Georgia Regional Hospital 705 N Div St *Web:* ngoc.com	Rome	GA	30165	706-295-6011	
Northwest Missouri Psychiatric Rehabilitation Ctr 3505 Frederick Ave *Fax Area Code: 573 ■ *Fax: Admitting ■ *TF:* 800-273-8255	Saint Joseph	MO	64506	816-387-2300	751-8224*
Oklahoma Forensic Ctr 24800 S 4420 Rd *Web:* ok.gov	Vinita	OK	74301	918-256-7841	
Oregon State Hospital 2600 Ctr St NE *Web:* oregon.gov	Salem	OR	97301	503-945-2800	945-2807
Patton State Hospital 3102 E Highland Ave. *Fax: Admitting ■ *Web:* dsh.ca.gov	Patton	CA	92369	909-425-7000	425-6370*
Peachford Behavioral Health System (PBHS) 2151 Peachford Rd *Web:* www.peachford.com	Atlanta	GA	30338	770-455-3200	
Pembroke Hospital 199 Oak St. *TF:* 800-222-2237 ■ *Web:* arbourhealth.com	Pembroke	MA	02359	781-829-7000	826-2061
Peninsula Hospital 2347 Jones Bend Rd *Fax: Admitting ■ *TF:* 800-526-8215 ■ *Web:* www.peninsulabehavioralhealth.org/hospital	Louisville	TN	37777	865-970-9800	970-6317*
Pilgrim Psychiatric Ctr 998 Crooked Hill Rd *TF:* 800-597-8481 ■ *Web:* www.omh.ny.gov	West Brentwood	NY	11717	631-761-3500	761-2600
Pine Rest Christian Mental Health Services 300 68th St SE PO Box 165 *Fax: Hum Res ■ *TF:* 800-678-5500 ■ *Web:* www.pinerest.org	Grand Rapids	MI	49501	616-455-5000	831-2608*
Poplar Springs Hospital 350 Poplar Dr PO Box 3060 *Fax: Admitting ■ *TF:* 866-546-2229 ■ *Web:* www.poplarsprings.com	Petersburg	VA	23805	804-733-6874	862-6322*
Psychiatric Institute of Washington 4228 Wisconsin Ave NW *TF:* 800-369-2273 ■ *Web:* www.psychinstitute.com	Washington	DC	20016	202-885-5600	885-5614
Research Psychiatric Ctr 2323 E 63rd St *Web:* researchpsychiatriccenter.com	Kansas City	MO	64130	816-444-8161	333-4495
Richard H Hutchings Psychiatric Ctr 620 Madison St	Syracuse	NY	13210	315-426-3600	
Richmond State Hospital (RSH) 498 NW 18th St *Web:* www.in.gov/fssa/dmha/6914.htm	Richmond	IN	47374	765-966-0511	939-0622
Ridge Behavioral Health System 3050 Rio Dosa Dr *TF:* 800-753-4673 ■ *Web:* www.ridgebhs.com	Lexington	KY	40509	859-269-2325	268-6451
River Park Hospital 1230 Sixth Ave *TF:* 800-621-2673 ■ *Web:* www.riverparkhospital.net	Huntington	WV	25701	304-526-9111	526-9140
Riverview Psychiatric Ctr 250 Arsenal St 11 State House Stn *TF:* 888-261-6684 ■ *Web:* maine.gov	Augusta	ME	04330	207-624-4600	287-2601
Rochester Psychiatric Ctr 1111 Elmwood Ave *Web:* rochesterhealth.com	Rochester	NY	14620	585-241-1200	241-1424
Rockland Psychiatric Ctr 140 Old Orangeburg Rd *Fax: Admitting ■ *Web:* omh.ny.gov	Orangeburg	NY	10962	845-359-1000	680-5580*
Rogers Memorial Hospital Inc 34700 Valley Rd *TF:* 800-767-4411 ■ *Web:* www.rogershospital.org	Oconomowoc	WI	53066	262-646-4411	646-3158
Rusk State Hospital 805 N Dickinson Dr *Web:* www.dshs.state.tx.us	Rusk	TX	75785	903-683-3421	683-7400
Saint Elizabeths Hospital 1100 Alabama Ave SE *Web:* www.stelizabethseast.com/	Washington	DC	20032	202-299-5000	
San Antonio State Hospital 6711 S Braunfels Ave *Web:* dshs.state.tx.us	San Antonio	TX	78223	210-532-8811	531-7780
San Diego County Psychiatric Hospital 3853 Rosecrans St *Web:* www.sdcounty.ca.gov	San Diego	CA	92110	619-692-8200	
Seton Shoal Creek Hospital 3501 Mills Ave *Web:* www.seton.net	Austin	TX	78731	512-324-2000	324-2003
Sharp-Mesa Vista Hospital 7850 Vista Hill Ave *Web:* www.sharp.com	San Diego	CA	92123	858-278-4110	
Sheppard Pratt at Ellicott City 4100 College Ave PO Box 836 *Web:* www.sheppardpratt.org	Ellicott City	MD	21041	443-364-5500	
Sheppard Pratt Health System (SPHS) 6501 N Charles St *Fax: Admissions ■ *TF:* 800-627-0330 ■ *Web:* www.sheppardpratt.org	Baltimore	MD	21285	410-938-3000	938-4532*
South Beach Psychiatric Ctr 777 Seaview Ave. *Web:* omh.ny.gov	Staten Island	NY	10305	718-667-2300	

	City	State	Zip	Phone	Fax
South Oaks Hospital 400 Sunrise Hwy *Web:* south-oaks.org	Amityville	NY	11701	631-264-4000	264-5259
Southeast Missouri Mental Health Ctr 1010 W Columbia St *Web:* dmh.mo.gov	Farmington	MO	63640	573-218-6792	218-6785
Southwest Behavioral Health Services Inc 3450 N Third St *Web:* www.sbhservices.org	Phoenix	AZ	85012	602-257-9339	265-8377
Southwestern Virginia Mental Health Institute 340 Bagley Cir **Fax:* Admitting ■ *Web:* www.swvmhi.dbhds.virginia.gov	Marion	VA	24354	276-783-1200	783-1216*
Spring Grove Hospital Ctr 55 Wade Ave *TF General:* 866-734-3337 ■ *Web:* www.springgrove.com	Catonsville	MD	21228	410-402-6000	402-7983
Spring Harbor Hospital 123 Andover Rd *TF:* 888-524-0080 ■ *Web:* www.springharbor.org	Westbrook	ME	04092	207-761-2200	761-2108
Springfield Hospital Ctr 6655 Sykesville Rd **Fax:* Hum Res ■ *TF:* 800-333-7564 ■ *Web:* dhmh.maryland.gov	Sykesville	MD	21784	410-970-7000	970-7024*
Summit Behavioral Healthcare 1101 Summit Rd *Web:* mha.ohio.gov	Cincinnati	OH	45237	513-948-3600	948-3080
Taunton State Hospital 60 Hodges Ave	Taunton	MA	02780	508-977-3000	
Thomas B Finan Ctr 10102 Country Club Rd SE PO Box 1722 *TF:* 888-854-0035 ■ *Web:* msa.maryland.gov	Cumberland	MD	21502	301-777-2405	777-2364
Timberlawn Mental Health System 4600 Samuell Blvd *TF:* 800-426-4944 ■ *Web:* www.timberlawn.com	Dallas	TX	75228	214-381-7181	388-6453
Torrance State Hospital 121 Longview Dr PO Box 111 **Fax:* Admitting ■ *TF:* 866-816-9212 ■ *Web:* www.dpw.state.pa.us/foradults/statehospitals/torrancestatehospital	Torrance	PA	15779	724-459-8000	459-1212*
Trenton Psychiatric Hospital PO Box 7500 *Web:* www.nj.gov	West Trenton	NJ	08628	609-633-1500	
UCLA Neuropsychiatric Institute & Hospital 760 Westwood Plz *Web:* www.semel.ucla.edu	Los Angeles	CA	90095	310-825-0511	
University Behavioral Ctr 2500 Discovery Dr *TF:* 800-999-0807 ■ *Web:* www.universitybehavioral.com	Orlando	FL	32826	407-281-7000	282-7012
Utah State Hospital 1300 E Ctr St *Web:* www.ush.utah.gov	Provo	UT	84606	801-344-4400	344-4225
Walter P Reuther Psychiatric Hospital 30901 Palmer Rd **Fax:* Mail Rm ■ *TF:* 877-765-8388 ■ *Web:* michigan.gov	Westland	MI	48186	734-367-8400	722-5562*
Warren State Hospital 33 Main Dr *Web:* dpw.state.pa.us	North Warren	PA	16365	814-723-5500	
Wernersville State Hospital PO Box 300 *Web:* www.dpw.state.pa.us	Wernersville	PA	19565	610-670-4173	
West Oaks Hospital 6500 Hornwood Dr *Web:* westoakshospital.com	Houston	TX	77074	713-995-0909	995-0221
Western Mental Health Institute 11100 Hwy 64 W **Fax Area Code:* 865 ■ *TF:* 800-770-8277 ■ *Web:* tn.gov	Bolivar	TN	38008	731-228-2000	457-0335*
Western State Hospital 1301 Richmond Ave *Web:* www.healthsystem.virginia.edu	Staunton	VA	24401	540-332-8000	332-8144
Westwood Lodge Hospital 45 Clapboardtree St *TF:* 800-222-2237 ■ *Web:* arbourhealth.com	Westwood	MA	02090	781-762-7764	762-0550
William R Sharpe Jr Hospital 936 Sharpe Hospital Rd *TF:* 866-384-5250	Weston	WV	26452	304-269-1210	436-6380
Winnebago Mental Health Institute (WMHI) 1300 S Dr PO Box 9 *Web:* dhs.wisconsin.gov/mh%5fwinnebago/	Winnebago	WI	54985	920-235-4910	237-2047
Wyoming State Hospital (WSH) 831 Hwy 150 S *Web:* www.health.wyo.gov/statehospital	Evanston	WY	82930	307-789-3464	789-7213

377-6 Rehabilitation Hospitals

	City	State	Zip	Phone	Fax
Allied Services Rehabilitation Hospital 475 Morgan Hwy *TF:* 888-734-2272 ■ *Web:* www.allied-services.org	Scranton	PA	18508	570-348-1300	341-4548
Bacharach Institute for Rehabilitation 61 W Jimmie Leads Rd *Web:* www.bacharach.org	Pomona	NJ	08240	609-652-7000	652-7487
Baptist Rehabilitation Germantown 2100 Exeter Rd *Web:* www.baptistonline.org	Germantown	TN	38138	901-757-1350	757-3496
Baton Rouge Rehab Hospital 8595 United Plaza Blvd	Baton Rouge	LA	70809	225-927-0567	231-3003
Baylor Institute for Rehabilitation 909 N Washington Ave *Web:* www.baylorhealth.com	Dallas	TX	75246	214-820-9300	818-8177
Bryn Mawr Rehab Hospital 414 Paoli Pike *TF:* 888-876-8764 ■ *Web:* www.mainlinehealth.org	Malvern	PA	19355	484-596-5400	
Burke Rehabilitation Hospital 785 Mamaroneck Ave *TF:* 888-992-8753 ■ *Web:* www.burke.org	White Plains	NY	10605	914-597-2500	
Cardinal Hill Healthcare System 2050 Versailles Rd **Fax:* Admitting ■ *TF:* 877-794-7328 ■ *Web:* www.cardinalhill.org	Lexington	KY	40504	859-254-5701	*
Charlotte Institute of Rehabilitation 1100 Blythe Blvd *TF:* 800-634-2256 ■ *Web:* www.carolinashealthcare.org	Charlotte	NC	28203	704-355-4300	355-4231
Craig Hospital 3425 S Clarkson St *TF:* 800-247-0257 ■ *Web:* www.craighospital.org	Englewood	CO	80113	303-789-8000	789-8219
Crotched Mountain Rehabilitation Ctr One Verney Dr *Web:* www.cmf.org	Greenfield	NH	03047	603-547-3311	547-3232
Drake Ctr 151 W Galbraith Rd *TF:* 800-948-0003 ■ *Web:* www.uchealth.com/danieldrakecenter	Cincinnati	OH	45216	513-418-2500	948-2501
Edwin Shaw Rehab 1621 Flickinger Rd *TF:* 800-221-4601 ■ *Web:* www.akrongeneral.org	Akron	OH	44312	330-784-1271	948-8332
Fairlawn Rehabilitation Hospital 189 May St *Web:* www.fairlawnrehab.org	Worcester	MA	01602	508-791-6351	753-2087
Frazier Rehabilitation Institute 220 Abraham Flexner Way *TF:* 800-333-2230 ■ *Web:* kentuckyonehealth.org	Louisville	KY	40202	502-582-7400	582-7477
Gaylord Hospital Gaylord Farms Rd PO Box 400 *TF:* 866-429-5673 ■ *Web:* www.gaylord.org	Wallingford	CT	06492	203-284-2800	294-8705
Good Shepherd Rehabilitation Hospital 850 S Fifth St **Fax:* Admitting ■ *Web:* www.goodshepherdrehab.org	Allentown	PA	18103	610-776-3585	776-3503*
Harmon Medical & Rehabilitation Hospital 2170 E Harmon Ave *Web:* fundltc.com	Las Vegas	NV	89119	702-794-0100	794-0041
HealthSouth Bakersfield Rehabilitation Hospital 5001 Commerce Dr *Web:* healthsouthbakersfield.com	Bakersfield	CA	93309	661-323-5500	633-5254
HealthSouth Braintree Rehabilitation Hospital 250 Pond St *Web:* www.gettingbacktolife.com	Braintree	MA	02184	781-348-2500	356-2748
HealthSouth Chattanooga Rehabilitation Hospital 3660 Grandview Pkwy Ste 200 *TF:* 800-765-4772 ■ *Web:* www.healthsouth.com	Birmingham	AL	35243	205-967-7116	
HealthSouth City View Rehabilitation Hospital 6701 Oakmont Blvd *Web:* healthsouthcityview.com	Fort Worth	TX	76132	817-370-4700	370-4986
HealthSouth Deaconess Rehabilitation Hospital 4100 Covert Ave *Web:* healthsouthdeaconess.com	Evansville	IN	47714	812-476-9983	476-4270
HealthSouth Harmarville Rehabilitation Hospital 320 Guys Run Rd *TF:* 800-765-4772 ■ *Web:* www.healthsouthharmarville.com	Pittsburgh	PA	15238	412-828-1300	
HealthSouth Hospital of Pittsburgh 320 Guys Run Rd *TF:* 800-765-4772 ■ *Web:* www.healthsouthharmarville.com	Pittsburgh	PA	15238	412-828-1300	
HealthSouth Houston Rehabilitation Institute 13031 Wortham Ctr Dr *Web:* www.healthsouth.com	Houston	TX	77065	832-280-2500	
HealthSouth Humble Rehabilitation Hospital 19002 McKay Dr *Web:* www.healthsouthhumble.com	Humble	TX	77338	281-319-9541	446-8022
HealthSouth Lakeshore Rehabilitation Hospital 3660 Grandview Pkwy Ste 200 *Web:* www.healthsouth.com	Birmingham	AL	35243	205-967-7116	
HealthSouth MountainView Regional Rehabilitation Hospital 1160 Van Voorhis Rd *TF:* 800-388-2451 ■ *Web:* www.healthsouthmountainview.com	Morgantown	WV	26505	304-598-1100	598-1103
HealthSouth Nittany Valley Rehabilitation Hospital 550 W College Ave *TF:* 800-842-6026 ■ *Web:* www.nittanyvalleyrehab.com	Pleasant Gap	PA	16823	814-359-3421	359-5898
HealthSouth Plano Rehabilitation Hospital 2800 W 15th St *TF:* 800-765-4772 ■ *Web:* www.healthsouthplano.com	Plano	TX	75075	972-612-9000	
HealthSouth Reading Rehabilitation Hospital 1623 Morgantown Rd *Web:* www.healthsouthreading.com	Reading	PA	19607	610-796-6000	796-6306
HealthSouth Rehabilitation Hospital of Albuquerque 7000 Jefferson St NE *Web:* www.healthsouthnewmexico.com	Albuquerque	NM	87109	505-344-9478	345-6722
HealthSouth Rehabilitation Hospital of Altoona 2005 Vly View Blvd *TF:* 800-873-4220 ■ *Web:* www.healthsouthaltoona.com	Altoona	PA	16602	814-944-3535	944-6160
HealthSouth Rehabilitation Hospital of Arlington 3200 Matlock Rd *Web:* www.healthsoutharlington.com	Arlington	TX	76015	817-468-4000	468-3055
HealthSouth Rehabilitation Hospital of Austin 1215 Red River *TF:* 800-765-4772 ■ *Web:* www.healthsouthaustin.com	Austin	TX	78701	512-474-5700	
HealthSouth Rehabilitation Hospital of Beaumont 3340 Plz 10 Blvd *Web:* www.healthsouthbeaumont.com	Beaumont	TX	77707	409-835-0835	835-1401
HealthSouth Rehabilitation Hospital of Columbia 2935 Colonial Dr *Web:* www.healthsouthcolumbia.com	Columbia	SC	29203	803-254-7777	401-1414
HealthSouth Rehabilitation Hospital of Erie 143 E Second St *TF:* 800-765-4772 ■ *Web:* healthsoutherie.com	Erie	PA	16507	814-878-1230	878-1470
HealthSouth Rehabilitation Hospital of Fayetteville 153 E Monte Painter *Web:* www.healthsouth.com	Fayetteville	AR	72703	479-444-2200	
HealthSouth Rehabilitation Hospital of Florence 900 E Cheves St *Web:* www.healthsouthflorence.com	Florence	SC	29506	843-679-9000	678-3767
HealthSouth Rehabilitation Hospital of Fort Smith 1401 S J St *Web:* www.healthsouthfortsmith.com	Fort Smith	AR	72901	479-785-3300	
HealthSouth Rehabilitation Hospital of Fort Worth 1212 W Lancaster *Web:* www.healthsouthfortworth.com	Fort Worth	TX	76102	817-870-2336	
HealthSouth Rehabilitation Hospital of Jonesboro 1201 Fleming Ave *Web:* www.healthsouthjonesboro.com	Jonesboro	AR	72401	870-932-0440	932-6792
HealthSouth Rehabilitation Hospital of Kingsport 113 Cassel Dr *TF:* 800-454-7422 ■ *Web:* www.healthsouthkingsport.com	Kingsport	TN	37660	423-246-7240	246-3441
HealthSouth Rehabilitation Hospital of Largo 901 N Clearwater-Largo Rd *Web:* healthsouthlargo.com	Largo	FL	33770	727-586-2999	588-3404
HealthSouth Rehabilitation Hospital of Memphis 4100 Austin Peay Hwy *Web:* www.healthsouthnorthmemphis.com	Memphis	TN	38128	901-213-5400	729-5171

Name / Address	City	State	Zip	Phone	Fax
HealthSouth Rehabilitation Hospital of Montgomery 4465 Narrow Ln Rd — *Web:* www.healthsouthmontgomery.com	Montgomery	AL	36116	334-284-7700	
HealthSouth Rehabilitation Hospital of New Jersey 14 Hospital Dr — *Web:* www.rehabnjtomsriver.com	Toms River	NJ	08755	732-244-3100	
HealthSouth Rehabilitation Hospital of North Alabama 107 Governors Dr — *Web:* healthsouth.com	Huntsville	AL	35801	800-467-3422	
HealthSouth Rehabilitation Hospital of Sarasota 6400 Edgelake Dr — *Web:* healthsouth.com	Sarasota	FL	34240	941-921-8600	
HealthSouth Rehabilitation Hospital of Tallahassee 1675 Riggins Rd — *Web:* www.healthsouthtallahassee.com	Tallahassee	FL	32308	850-656-4800	656-4892
HealthSouth Rehabilitation Hospital of Texarkana 515 W 12th St — *Web:* www.healthsouthtexarkana.com	Texarkana	TX	75501	903-735-5011	793-0899
HealthSouth Rehabilitation Hospital of Utah 8074 South 1300 East — *Web:* www.healthsouthutah.com	Sandy	UT	84094	801-565-6666	565-6576
HealthSouth Rehabilitation Institute of Tucson 2650 N Wyatt Dr — *Web:* www.rehabinstituteoftucson.com	Tucson	AZ	85712	520-325-1300	
HealthSouth Riosa 9119 Cinnamon Hill — *Web:* www.hsriosa.com	San Antonio	TX	78240	210-691-0737	
HealthSouth Sea Pines Rehabilitation Hospital 101 E Florida Ave — *Web:* www.healthsouthseapines.com	Melbourne	FL	32901	321-984-4662	984-4627
HealthSouth Sunrise Rehabilitation Hospital 4399 Nob Hill Rd — *Web:* healthsouthsunrise.com	Sunrise	FL	33351	954-749-0300	746-1562
HealthSouth Treasure Coast Rehabilitation Hospital 1600 37th St — *Web:* healthsouthtreasurecoast.com	Vero Beach	FL	32960	772-778-2100	562-9763
HealthSouth Tustin Rehabilitation Hospital 14851 Yorba St — *Web:* tustinrehab.com	Tustin	CA	92780	714-832-9200	734-4851
Hillside Rehabilitation Hospital (HRH) 8747 Squires Ln NE — *Web:* valleycareofohio.com/	Warren	OH	44484	330-841-3700	841-3647
Hospital for Special Care 2150 Corbin Ave — *Web:* www.hfsc.org	New Britain	CT	06053	860-223-2761	612-6304
Howard Regional Health System West Campus Specialty Hospital 829 N Dixon Rd — *Web:* ecommunity.com/howard	Kokomo	IN	46901	765-452-6700	452-7470
James H & Cecile C Quillen Rehabilitation Hospital 2511 Wesley St — *Web:* www.msha.com	Johnson City	TN	37601	423-431-6111	
JFK Johnson Rehabilitation Institute 65 James St — *Web:* www.jfkmc.org/clinical-services/	Edison	NJ	08818	732-321-7733	632-1671
John Heinz Institute of Rehabilitation Medicine 150 Mundy St Ste 3 — *Web:* allied-services.org	Wilkes-Barre	PA	18702	570-826-3800	826-3898
Kansas Rehabilitation Hospital 1504 SW Eigth Ave — *Web:* www.kansasrehabhospital.com	Topeka	KS	66606	785-235-6600	
Kentfield Rehabilitation Hospital 1125 Sir Francis Drake Blvd — *Web:* www.kentfieldrehab.com	Kentfield	CA	94904	415-456-9680	
Kernan Hospital 2200 Kernan Dr — *Web:* umrehabortho.org/	Baltimore	MD	21207	410-448-2500	448-6825
Laguna Honda Hospital & Rehabilitation Ctr 375 Laguna Honda Blvd — *Web:* www.lagunahonda.org	San Francisco	CA	94116	415-759-2300	759-2374
Madonna Rehabilitation Hospital 5401 S St — *TF:* 800-676-5448 ■ *Web:* www.madonna.org	Lincoln	NE	68506	402-489-7102	
Magee Rehabilitation Hospital 1513 Race St — *TF:* 800-966-2433 ■ *Web:* www.mageerehab.org	Philadelphia	PA	19102	215-587-3000	568-3736
Marianjoy Rehabilitation Hospital 26 W 171 Roosevelt Rd — *TF:* 800-462-2366 ■ *Web:* www.marianjoy.org	Wheaton	IL	60187	630-462-4000	
Mary Free Bed Rehabilitation Hospital 235 Wealthy St SE — *TF:* 800-528-8989 ■ *Web:* www.maryfreebed.com	Grand Rapids	MI	49503	616-242-0300	454-3939
Methodist Rehabilitation Ctr 1350 E Woodrow Wilson Dr — **Fax:* Admitting ■ *TF:* 800-223-6672 ■ *Web:* www.methodistonline.org/	Jackson	MS	39216	601-981-2611	364-3465*
Mid-America Rehabilitation Hospital 5701 W 110th St — *Web:* midamericarehabhospital.com	Overland Park	KS	66211	913-491-2400	338-3762
Missouri Rehabilitation Ctr 600 N Main St — *Web:* www.muhealth.org	Mount Vernon	MO	65712	417-466-3711	461-5775
National Rehabilitation Hospital 102 Irving St NW — *Web:* www.medstarhealth.org	Washington	DC	20010	202-877-1000	877-1602
New England Rehabilitation Hospital of Portland 335 Brighton Ave — *Web:* www.mainehealth.org/mmc_body.cfm?id=2169	Portland	ME	04102	207-775-4000	662-8446
New England Rehabilitation Hospital of Woburn Two Rehabilitation Way — *Web:* www.gettingbacktolife.com	Woburn	MA	01801	781-935-5050	935-3555
Northeast Rehabilitation Hospital 70 Butler St — *TF:* 800-439-2370 ■ *Web:* www.northeastrehab.com	Salem	NH	03079	603-893-2900	893-1628
Pinecrest Rehabilitation Hospital 5360 Linton Blvd — *Web:* www.delraymedicalctr.com	Delray Beach	FL	33484	561-495-0400	
Rancho Los Amigos National Rehabilitation Ctr 7601 E Imperial Hwy — **Fax:* Admitting ■ *TF:* 877-726-2461 ■ *Web:* dhs.lacounty.gov/wps/portal/dhs/rancho	Downey	CA	90242	562-401-7111	401-7022*
Rehabilitation Hospital of Indiana 4141 Shore Dr — *TF:* 866-510-2273 ■ *Web:* www.rhin.com	Indianapolis	IN	46254	317-329-2000	566-9111
Rehabilitation Hospital of New Mexico 4441 E Lohman Ave — *TF:* 888-659-3952 ■ *Web:* rhsnm.ernesthealth.com	Las Cruces	NM	88011	575-521-6400	521-6423
Rehabilitation Hospital of the Pacific 226 N Kuakini St — *TF:* 800-973-4226 ■ *Web:* www.rehabhospital.org	Honolulu	HI	96817	808-531-3511	544-3335
Rehabilitation Institute of Chicago 345 E Superior St — **Fax:* Admitting ■ *TF Admitting:* 800-354-7342 ■ *Web:* www.ric.org	Chicago	IL	60611	312-238-1000	238-5846*
Rehabilitation Institute of Michigan 261 Mack Blvd — *Web:* www.rimrehab.org	Detroit	MI	48201	313-745-1203	993-0808
Roosevelt Warm Springs Institute for Rehabilitation 6135 Roosevelt Hwy — **Fax:* Admissions ■ *Web:* www.rooseveltrehab.org	Warm Springs	GA	31830	706-655-5000	655-5258*
Sacred Heart Rehabilitation Institute 2323 N Lake Dr — *Web:* www.columbia-stmarys.org/	Milwaukee	WI	53211	414-298-6750	298-6770
Saint Lawrence Rehabilitation Ctr 2381 Lawrenceville Rd — *Web:* www.slrc.org	Lawrenceville	NJ	08648	609-896-9500	
Saint Luke's Rehabilitation Institute 711 S Cowley St — *Web:* www.st-lukes.org	Spokane	WA	99202	509-473-6000	473-6978
Saint Vincent Rehabilitation Hospital 2201 Wildwood Ave — *Web:* stvincentrehabhospital.com	Sherwood	AR	72120	501-834-1800	834-2227
San Joaquin Valley Rehabilitation Hospital 7173 N Sharon Ave — *Web:* www.sanjoaquinrehab.com	Fresno	CA	93720	559-436-3600	436-3688
Shadyside Nursing & Rehabilitation Ctr 5609 Fifth Ave — *TF:* 800-366-1232 ■ *Web:* manorcare.com	Pittsburgh	PA	15232	412-362-3500	362-1951
Shepherd Ctr 2020 Peachtree Rd NE — *Web:* www.shepherd.org	Atlanta	GA	30309	404-352-2020	350-7341
Sierra Providence Physical Rehabilitation Hospital 1740 Curie Dr — *TF:* 800-252-5400 ■ *Web:* www.sphn.com	El Paso	TX	79902	915-544-3399	
Siskin Hospital for Physical Rehabilitation 1 Siskin Plaza — **Fax Area Code:* 630 ■ *TF:* 800-994-6610 ■ *Web:* www.siskinrehab.org	Chattanooga	TN	37403	423-634-1200	792-5636*
Southern Indiana Rehabilitation Hospital 3104 Blackiston Blvd — *TF:* 800-737-7090 ■ *Web:* www.sirh.org	New Albany	IN	47150	812-941-8300	941-6276
Southern Kentucky Rehabilitation Hospital 1300 Campbell Ln — *Web:* www.skyrehab.com	Bowling Green	KY	42104	270-782-6900	782-7228
Spalding Rehabilitation Hospital 900 Potomac St — *TF:* 800-367-3309 ■ *Web:* www.spaldingrehab.com	Aurora	CO	80011	303-367-1166	360-8208
Spaulding Rehabilitation Hospital 125 Nashua St — *Web:* www.spauldingrehab.org	Boston	MA	02114	617-573-7000	573-7009
SSM Rehabilitation Hospital 6420 Clayton Rd — *TF:* 800-818-9494 ■ *Web:* www.ssm-select.com	Saint Louis	MO	63117	314-768-5300	768-5355
Sunnyview Rehabilitation Hospital 1270 Belmont Ave — *Web:* www.nehealth.com	Schenectady	NY	12308	518-382-4500	
TIRR Memorial Hermann Hospital 1333 Moursund St — *TF:* 800-447-3422 ■ *Web:* www.memorialhermann.org	Houston	TX	77030	713-799-5000	799-7095
Trinity Mother Frances Rehabilitation Hospital - Tyler 3131 Troup Hwy	Tyler	TX	75701	903-510-7000	510-7005
Trinity Neurological Rehabilitation Ctr 1400 Lindberg Dr — *Web:* trinityneurorehab.com	Slidell	LA	70458	985-641-4985	646-0793
Villa Maria Nursing Center 1050 NE 125th St — **Fax Area Code:* 954	North Miami	FL	33161	305-891-8850	485-4023*
Walton Rehabilitation Hospital 1355 Independence Dr — *Web:* www.wrh.org	Augusta	GA	30901	706-724-7746	724-5752
Warm Springs Rehabilitation Hospital of San Antonio 5101 Medical Dr — *Web:* www.warmsprings.org	San Antonio	TX	78229	210-595-2380	614-0649
Warm Springs Specialty Hospital 200 Memorial Dr — *Web:* www.warmsprings.org	Luling	TX	78648	830-875-8400	875-5029
Wesley Rehabilitation Hospital 8338 W 13th St N — *Web:* www.wesleyrehabhospital.com	Wichita	KS	67212	316-729-9999	729-8888

377-7 Specialty Hospitals

Name / Address	City	State	Zip	Phone	Fax
Barbara Ann Karmanos Cancer Institute 4100 John R St — *TF:* 800-527-6266 ■ *Web:* www.karmanos.org	Detroit	MI	48201	800-527-6266	
Bascom Palmer Eye Institute 900 NW 17th St — *TF:* 800-329-7000 ■ *Web:* www.bascompalmer.org/site	Miami	FL	33136	305-326-6000	326-6374
Bone & Joint Hospital 1111 N Dewey Ave — *Web:* www.boneandjoint.com	Oklahoma City	OK	73103	405-272-9671	
Brigham & Women's Hospital 75 Francis St — **Fax:* Admitting ■ *TF:* 800-722-5520 ■ *Web:* www.brighamandwomens.org	Boston	MA	02115	617-732-5500	264-5181*
Callahan Eye Foundation Hospital 1720 University Blvd — *Web:* uabmedicine.org	Birmingham	AL	35233	205-325-8100	

				Phone	Fax
Coler-Goldwater Specialty Hospital & Nursing Facility One Main St Franklin D Roosevelt Is *Web:* www.nyc.gov	New York	NY	10044	212-318-8000	318-4370
Cornerstone Hospital of Austin 4207 Burnet Rd *Web:* chghospitals.com	Austin	TX	78756	512-706-1900	
Dana-Farber Cancer Institute 44 Binney St **Fax:* PR ■ *TF:* 866-408-3324 ■ *Web:* www.dana-farber.org	Boston	MA	02115	617-632-3000	632-5520*
Deborah Heart & Lung Ctr 200 Trenton Rd *Web:* www.deborah.org	Browns Mills	NJ	08015	609-893-6611	893-1213
Delaware Hospital for the Chronically Ill 100 Sunnyside Rd *Web:* dhss.delaware.gov	Smyrna	DE	19977	302-233-1000	
Dermatology Assoc of Atlanta 5555 Pchtrdnwyd Ste 190 *TF:* 800-233-0706 ■ *Web:* www.dermatlanta.com	Atlanta	GA	30324	404-256-4457	255-3603
Doheny Eye Institute 1450 San Pablo St *TF:* 800-872-2273 ■ *Web:* www.doheny.org	Los Angeles	CA	90033	323-442-7100	442-7127
Eleanor Slater Hospital 14 Harrington Rd *TF:* 800-438-8477 ■ *Web:* www.bhddh.ri.gov	Cranston	RI	02920	401-462-2339	462-3204
Elmwood Healthcare Ctr & Specialty Hospital (SFHCC) 401 N Broadway *Web:* elmwoodcommunities.com	Green Springs	OH	44836	419-639-2626	639-6225
Fox Chase Cancer Ctr 333 Cottman Ave *TF:* 888-369-2427 ■ *Web:* www.fccc.edu	Philadelphia	PA	19111	215-728-6900	728-2682
Georgia Cancer Specialists Pc (GCS) 1872 Montreal Rd *TF:* 800-491-5991 ■ *Web:* www.gacancer.com	Tucker	GA	30084	770-496-9443	496-9490
H Lee Moffitt Cancer Ctr & Research Institute University of S Florida 12902 Magnolia Dr **Fax Area Code:* 813 ■ *TF:* 800-456-3434 ■ *Web:* www.moffitt.org	Tampa	FL	33612	888-663-3488	745-4064*
Hebrew Hospital Home Continuum of Care 61 Grasslands Rd *Web:* www.hebrewhospitalhome.org	Valhalla	NY	10595	914-681-8400	
Hospice of Washington County Inc 747 Northern Ave *Web:* www.hwc-md.org	Hagerstown	MD	21742	301-791-6360	791-6579
Hospital for Special Surgery 535 E 70th St *Web:* www.hss.edu	New York	NY	10021	212-606-1000	606-1930
Hughston Orthopedic Hospital 100 Frist Ct *TF:* 866-272-9452 ■ *Web:* columbusregional.com	Columbus	GA	31908	706-494-2100	494-2446
James Cancer Hospital & Solove Research Institute, The 300 W Tenth Ave Ste 519 *Web:* cancer.osu.edu/	Columbus	OH	43210	614-293-5066	293-3132
Kapiolani Medical Ctr for Women & Children (KMCWC) 1319 Punahou St *Web:* www.kapiolani.org/women-and-children/default.aspx	Honolulu	HI	96826	808-983-6000	983-6173
Kindred Hospital Atlanta 705 Juniper St *TF:* 800-255-0135 ■ *Web:* www.kindredatlanta.com	Atlanta	GA	30308	404-873-2871	873-4516
Kindred Hospital Dallas 9525 Greenville Ave *Web:* www.khdallas.com	Dallas	TX	75243	214-355-2600	355-2630
Kindred Hospital Fort Worth Southwest 7800 Oakmont Blvd *Web:* www.kindredhospitalfwsw.com	Fort Worth	TX	76132	817-346-0094	263-4071
Kindred Hospital Kansas City 8701 Troost Ave *TF:* 800-545-0749 ■ *Web:* www.kindredhospitalkc.com	Kansas City	MO	64131	816-995-2000	995-2171
Lake Taylor Transitional Hospital 1309 Kempsville Rd *Web:* www.laketaylor.org	Norfolk	VA	23502	757-461-5001	461-4282
Leahi Hospital 3675 Kilauea Ave *TF:* 800-845-6733 ■ *Web:* www.hhsc.org	Honolulu	HI	96816	808-733-8000	733-7914
Life Care Hospital of Pittsburgh 225 Penn Ave *Web:* lifecare-hospitals.com	Pittsburgh	PA	15221	412-247-2424	247-2333
Lombardi Comprehensive Cancer Ctr at Georgetown University 3800 Reservoir Rd NW *Web:* lombardi.georgetown.edu	Washington	DC	20007	202-444-2198	444-9429
Magee-Womens Hospital 300 Halket St *Web:* www.magee.edu	Pittsburgh	PA	15213	412-641-6361	641-4343
Mary Rutan Hospital 205 E Palmer Rd *Web:* www.maryrutan.org	Bellefontaine	OH	43311	937-592-5015	592-0207
Massachusetts Eye & Ear 243 Charles St **Fax:* Admitting ■ *Web:* www.masseyeandear.org	Boston	MA	02114	617-523-7900	573-4017*
Matheny Medical & Educational Ctr 65 Highland Ave *Web:* www.matheny.org	Peapack	NJ	07977	908-234-0011	719-2137
MD Anderson Cancer Ctr 1515 Holcombe Blvd **Fax:* Admitting ■ *TF:* 800-889-2094 ■ *Web:* www.mdanderson.org	Houston	TX	77030	713-792-2121	794-4915*
Memorial Sloan-Kettering Cancer Ctr 1275 York Ave *TF:* 800-525-2225 ■ *Web:* www.mskcc.org	New York	NY	10065	212-639-2000	
Miami Heart Institute 4701 N Meridian Ave *Web:* www.msmc.com	Miami Beach	FL	33140	305-672-1111	674-3006
Midwestern Regional Medical Ctr (MRMC) 2520 Elisha Ave *TF:* 800-615-3055 ■ *Web:* www.cancercenter.com	Zion	IL	60099	847-872-4561	872-6419
Monroe Community Hospital 435 E Henrietta Rd *Web:* www.monroehosp.org	Rochester	NY	14620	585-760-6500	760-6066
National Jewish Medical & Research Ctr 1400 Jackson St PO Box 17169 *TF:* 877-225-5654 ■ *Web:* www.nationaljewish.org	Denver	CO	80206	303-388-4461	
New York Eye & Ear Infirmary 310 E 14th St *TF:* 800-522-4582 ■ *Web:* www.nyee.edu	New York	NY	10003	212-979-4000	979-4512
Oak Forest Hospital of Cook County 15900 S Cicero Ave	Oak Forest	IL	60452	708-687-7200	
Odessa Regional Medical Ctr 520 E Sixth St *TF:* 877-898-6080 ■ *Web:* www.odessaregionalmedicalcenter.com	Odessa	TX	79761	432-582-8000	
Orthopaedic Hospital 2400 S Flower St *Web:* www.orthohospital.org	Los Angeles	CA	90007	213-742-1000	741-8338
Phillips Eye Institute 2215 Pk Ave S *Web:* www.allinahealth.org	Minneapolis	MN	55404	612-775-8800	
Piedmont Geriatric Hospital 5001 E Patrick Henry Hwy PO Box 427 *Web:* www.pgh.dbhds.virginia.gov	Burkeville	VA	23922	434-767-4401	
Presbyterian Orthopaedic Hospital 1901 Randolph Rd *Web:* novanthealth.org/presbyterianmedicalcenter.aspx	Charlotte	NC	28207	704-316-2000	316-1803
Princess Margaret Hospital 610 University Ave *Web:* www.uhn.ca	Toronto	ON	M5G2M9	416-946-2000	
Roswell Park Cancer Institute Elm and Carlton St *TF:* 877-275-7724 ■ *Web:* www.roswellpark.org	Buffalo	NY	14263	716-845-2300	845-8335
Runnells Specialized Hospital of Union County 40 Watchung Way *Web:* www.ucnj.org/government/runnells-specialized-hospital	Berkeley Heights	NJ	07922	908-771-5700	771-0376
Saint Vincent Women's Hospital 8111 Township Line Rd **Fax Area Code:* 765 ■ **Fax:* Admitting ■ *TF:* 800-582-8258 ■ *Web:* www.stvincent.org	Indianapolis	IN	46260	317-415-8111	236-8785*
Samuel Mahelona Memorial Hospital 4800 Kawaihau Rd *TF:* 800-845-6733 ■ *Web:* www.smmh.hhsc.org	Kapaa	HI	96746	808-822-4961	823-4100
Select Specialty Hospital Houston Heights 1917 Ashland St *Web:* selectspecialtyhospitals.com	Houston	TX	77008	713-861-6161	802-8653
Sidney Kimmel Comprehensive Cancer Ctr at Johns Hopkins 401 N Broadway The Harry & Jeanette Weinberg Bldg Ste 1100 *Web:* www.hopkinsmedicine.org	Baltimore	MD	21231	410-955-5222	955-6787
Siteman Cancer Ctr 4921 Parkview Pl *TF:* 800-600-3606 ■ *Web:* www.siteman.wustl.edu	Saint Louis	MO	63110	314-362-5196	
Specialty Hospital Jacksonville 4901 Richard St **Fax Area Code:* 615 ■ *Web:* www.specialtyhospitaljax.com	Jacksonville	FL	32207	904-737-3120	242-5826*
Stanford Cancer Ctr 875 Lake Blake Wilbur Dr *TF:* 800-422-6237 ■ *Web:* cancer.stanford.edu/	Stanford	CA	94305	650-498-6000	724-1433
Stony Point Surgical Ctr 8700 Stony Pt Pkwy *Web:* www.stonypointsc.com	Richmond	VA	23235	804-775-4500	643-3542
Straith Hospital for Special Surgery 23901 Lahser Rd *TF:* 800-994-6610 ■ *Web:* straith.org	Southfield	MI	48034	248-357-3360	357-0915
Tewksbury Hospital 365 E St **Fax:* Mail Rm ■ *Web:* mass.gov	Tewksbury	MA	01876	978-851-7321	851-5648*
Texas Ctr for Infectious Diseases 2303 SE Military Dr *TF:* 800-839-5864 ■ *Web:* www.dshs.state.tx.us/tcid/default.shtm	San Antonio	TX	78223	210-534-8857	531-4502
Texas Orthopedic Hospital 7401 Main St *TF:* 866-783-4549 ■ *Web:* www.texasorthopedic.com	Houston	TX	77030	713-799-8600	794-3580
UC Davis Cancer Ctr 4501 X St *TF:* 800-362-5566 ■ *Web:* www.ucdmc.ucdavis.edu/cancer	Sacramento	CA	95817	916-734-5800	703-5067
University of Michigan Trauma Burn Ctr 1500 E Medical Ctr Dr *Web:* www.traumaburn.org	Ann Arbor	MI	48109	734-936-9666	936-9657
Vanderbilt-Ingram Cancer Ctr 691 Preston Bldg *Web:* www.vicc.org	Nashville	TN	37232	615-936-1793	936-5879
Veterans Home & Hospital 287 W St **Fax:* Admitting ■ *Web:* ct.gov	Rocky Hill	CT	06067	860-529-2571	721-5979*
Villa Feliciana Chronic Disease Hospital 5002 Hwy 10 *Web:* dhh.louisiana.gov	Jackson	LA	70748	225-634-4000	634-4191
Wills Eye 840 Walnut St *Web:* www.willseye.org	Philadelphia	PA	19107	215-928-3000	928-0634
Woman's Hospital 100 Woman's Wy *Web:* www.womans.org	Baton Rouge	LA	70815	225-927-1300	924-8110
Woman's Hospital of Texas 7600 Fannin St *Web:* www.womanshospital.com	Houston	TX	77054	713-790-1234	790-0028
Women & Infants Hospital of Rhode Island 101 Dudley St *Web:* www.womenandinfants.org	Providence	RI	02905	401-274-1100	453-7666
Women's & Children's Hospital (WCH) 4600 Ambassador Caffery Pkwy *Web:* www.womens-childrens.com	Lafayette	LA	70508	337-521-9100	521-9102
Women's Christian Assn Hospital 207 Foote Ave *Web:* www.wcahospital.org	Jamestown	NY	14701	716-487-0141	

377-8 Veterans Hospitals

Listings for veterans hospitals are organized by states, and then by city names within those groupings.

				Phone	Fax
Birmingham VA Medical Ctr 700 S 19th St **Fax:* Admitting ■ *Web:* birmingham.va.gov	Birmingham	AL	35233	205-933-8101	933-4498*
Tuscaloosa VA Medical Ctr 3701 Loop Rd E *TF:* 888-269-3045 ■ *Web:* tuscaloosa.va.gov	Tuscaloosa	AL	35404	205-554-2000	
Northern Arizona VA Health Care System 500 Hwy 89 N *TF:* 800-949-1005 ■ *Web:* www.prescott.va.gov	Prescott	AZ	86313	928-445-4860	
Southern Arizona Veterans Healthcare System 3601 S Sixth Ave *TF:* 800-470-8262 ■ *Web:* tucson.va.gov	Tucson	AZ	85723	520-792-1450	
VA Central California Health Care System 2615 E Clinton Ave *Web:* fresno.va.gov	Fresno	CA	93703	559-225-6100	
Jerry L Pettis Memorial Veterans Affairs Medical Ctr 11201 Benton St **Fax:* Admitting ■ *TF:* 800-827-1000 ■ *Web:* www.lomalinda.va.gov	Loma Linda	CA	92357	909-825-7084	422-3140*
Veterans Affairs Long Beach Medical Ctr 5901 E Seventh St *TF:* 888-769-8387 ■ *Web:* www.longbeach.va.gov	Long Beach	CA	90822	562-826-8000	826-5906

Phone *Fax*

VA Greater Los Angeles Healthcare System
11301 Wilshire Blvd. . . . Los Angeles CA 90073 310-478-3711 268-3494
Web: www.losangeles.va.gov

San Francisco VA Medical Ctr
4150 Clement St. . . . San Francisco CA 94121 415-221-4810 750-2177
Web: www2.va.gov

Denver Veterans Affairs Medical Ctr
1055 Clermont St. . . . Denver CO 80220 303-399-8020 393-2861*
**Fax:* Mail Rm ■ *TF:* 888-336-8262 ■ *Web:* Www.denver.va.gov

Grand Junction VA Medical Ctr
2121 N Ave. . . . Grand Junction CO 81501 970-242-0731 244-1323
Web: grandjunction.va.gov

Malcom Randall VAMC NF/SGVHS
1601 SW Archer Rd . . . . Gainesville FL 32608 352-376-1611 374-6113*
**Fax:* Mail Rm ■ *TF:* 800-324-8387 ■ *Web:* www2.va.gov/directory/guide/facility.asp?id=54

Carl Vinson Veterans Affairs Medical Ctr
1826 Veterans Blvd. . . . Dublin GA 31021 478-272-1210 277-2717*
**Fax:* Mail Rm ■ *TF:* 800-595-5229 ■ *Web:* va.gov

Edward Hines Jr Veterans Affairs Hospital
5000 S Fifth Ave PO Box 5000 . . . . Hines IL 60141 708-202-8387 202-2506
Web: www.hines.va.gov

Richard L. Roudebush VA Medical Ctr
1481 W Tenth St. . . . Indianapolis IN 46202 317-988-4498
TF: 888-878-6889 ■ *Web:* www1.va.gov/directory/guide/facility.asp?id=62

Veterans Affairs Outpatient Clinic
1515 W Pleasant St Bldg 1. . . . Knoxville IA 50138 641-842-3101
TF: 800-816-8878 ■ *Web:* www.centraliowa.va.gov

Dwight D Eisenhower V A Medical Ctr
4101 South 4th St. . . . Leavenworth KS 66048 913-682-2000
TF: 800-952-8387 ■ *Web:* www.leavenworth.va.gov

Colmery-O'Neil Veterans Affairs Medical Ctr
2200 SW Gage Blvd . . . . Topeka KS 66622 785-350-3111 350-4336
TF: 800-574-8387 ■ *Web:* topeka.va.gov

Alexandria Veterans Affairs Medical Ctr
2495 Shreveport Hwy 71 N. . . . Pineville LA 71360 318-473-0010 483-5093*
**Fax:* Hum Res ■ *TF:* 800-375-8387 ■ *Web:* www.alexandria.va.gov

Overton Brooks Veterans Affairs Medical Ctr
510 E Stoner Ave . . . . Shreveport LA 71101 318-221-8411 990-5556
TF: 800-863-7441 ■ *Web:* www.shreveport.va.gov

Edith Nourse Rogers Memorial Veterans Hospital
200 Springs Rd. . . . Bedford MA 01730 415-839-6885 882-0495
Web: en.wikipedia.org

U.S. Department of Veterans Affairs
325 E 'H' St. . . . Iron Mountain MI 49801 906-774-3300
TF: 800-215-8262 ■ *Web:* www.ironmountain.va.gov

Paragon Health Pc 2318 Gull Rd Ste B. . . . Kalamazoo MI 49048 269-341-4554 381-3063
Web: www.paragonhealthpc.com

G.V. (Sonny) Montgomery VA Medical Ctr
1500 E Woodrow Wilson Dr . . . . Jackson MS 39216 601-362-4471 368-3811*
**Fax:* Hum Res ■ *Web:* jackson.va.gov

Harry S Truman Memorial Veterans Hospital
800 Hospital Dr . . . . Columbia MO 65201 573-814-6000 814-6600
TF: 877-222-8387 ■ *Web:* columbiamo.va.gov

John J Pershing Veterans Affairs Medical Ctr
1500 N Westwood Blvd. . . . Poplar Bluff MO 63901 573-686-4151 778-4559
TF: 888-557-8262 ■ *Web:* poplarbluff.va.gov

VA Medical Ctr 3687 Veterans Dr. . . . Fort Harrison MT 59636 406-442-6410 447-7904
Web: montana.va.gov

Sierra NV Healthcare Systems (VA Medical Ctr)
975 Kirman Ave . . . . Reno NV 89502 775-786-7200
TF: 888-838-6256 ■ *Web:* www.reno.va.gov

East Orange Campus of the VA New Jersey Health Care System (NJHCS)
385 Tremont Ave. . . . East Orange NJ 07018 844-872-4681 456-1414*
**Fax Area Code:* 202 ■ **Fax:* Hum Res ■ *Web:* www.usa.gov

Stratton Veterans Affairs Medical Ctr
113 Holland Ave . . . . Albany NY 12208 518-626-5000 626-6709*
**Fax:* Admitting ■ *TF:* 800-223-4810 ■ *Web:* www.albany.va.gov

Batavia VA Medical Ctr 222 Richmond Ave. . . . Batavia NY 14020 585-297-1000 297-1069
TF: 800-273-8255 ■ *Web:* buffalo.va.gov

Bath Veterans Affairs Medical Ctr
76 Veterans Ave . . . . Bath NY 14810 607-664-4000 664-4915*
**Fax:* Admissions ■ *TF:* 877-845-3247 ■ *Web:* www.bath.va.gov

James J Peters Veterans Affairs Medical Ctr
130 W Kingsbridge Rd . . . . Bronx NY 10468 718-584-9000 741-4571
Web: bronx.va.gov

VA Hudson Valley Health Care System
Montrose Campus
2094 Albany Post Rd PO Box 100 . . . . Montrose NY 10548 914-737-4400 788-4244
TF: 800-269-8749 ■ *Web:* www.hudsonvalley.va.gov

VA NY Harbor Healthcare System
423 E 23rd St . . . . New York NY 10010 212-686-7500 951-3375
Web: nyharbor.va.gov
Castle Point Campus 41 Castle Pt Rd . . . . Wappingers Falls NY 12590 845-831-2000 838-5193
TF: 877-222-8387 ■ *Web:* www.hudsonvalley.va.gov

WG Bill Hefner Veterans Affairs Medical Ctr
1601 Brenner Ave . . . . Salisbury NC 28144 704-638-9000 *
**Fax:* Admissions ■ *TF:* 800-469-8262 ■ *Web:* www.salisbury.va.gov

Louis Stokes Cleveland Veterans Affairs Medical Ctr
10701 E Blvd . . . . Cleveland OH 44106 216-791-3800
TF: 888-838-6446 ■ *Web:* cleveland.va.gov

Dayton Va Medical Ctr 4100 W Third St . . . . Dayton OH 45428 937-268-6511 262-2187
TF: 800-368-8262 ■ *Web:* dayton.va.gov

Altoona VA Medical Ctr
2907 Pleasant Vly Blvd. . . . Altoona PA 16602 877-626-2500 940-7898*
**Fax Area Code:* 814 ■ *TF:* 877-626-2500 ■ *Web:* www.altoona.va.gov

Erie VA Medical Ctr 135 E 38th St . . . . Erie PA 16504 814-868-8661
TF: 800-274-8387 ■ *Web:* www.erie.va.gov

Veterans Affairs Medical Ctr
1700 S Lincoln Ave. . . . Lebanon PA 17042 800-409-8771
TF: 800-409-8771 ■ *Web:* www.lebanon.va.gov

Ralph H Johnson Veterans Affairs Medical Ctr
109 Bee St . . . . Charleston SC 29401 843-577-5011
Web: charleston.va.gov

James H Quillen Veterans Affairs Medical Ctr
Corner of Lamont & Veterans Way
PO Box 4000 . . . . Mountain Home TN 37684 423-926-1171 979-3519
TF: 877-573-3529 ■ *Web:* www.mountainhome.va.gov

Alvin C York Medical Ctr
3400 Lebanon Pike. . . . Murfreesboro TN 37129 615-867-6000
TF: 800-228-4973 ■ *Web:* tennesseevalley.va.gov

Thomas E Creek Veterans Affairs Medical Ctr
6010 Amarillo Blvd W. . . . Amarillo TX 79106 806-355-9703
TF: 800-687-8262 ■ *Web:* www.amarillo.va.gov

South Texas Veterans Health Care System
7400 Merton Minter St . . . . San Antonio TX 78229 210-617-5300
Web: www.southtexas.va.gov

Central Texas Veterans Health Care System
1901 Veterans Memorial Dr . . . . Temple TX 76504 254-778-4811
TF: 800-423-2111 ■ *Web:* www2.va.gov

White River Junction Veterans Affairs Medical Ctr
215 N Main St . . . . White River Junction VT 05009 802-295-9363 296-5138
TF: 866-687-8387 ■ *Web:* www.whiteriver.va.gov

Salem Veterans Affairs Medical Ctr
1970 Roanoke Blvd. . . . Salem VA 24153 540-982-2463 983-1093*
**Fax:* Admitting ■ *Web:* va.gov

Veterans Affairs Puget Sound Medical Ctr
1660 S Columbian Way . . . . Seattle WA 98108 206-762-1010 764-2270*
**Fax:* Admitting ■ *TF:* 800-329-8387 ■ *Web:* www.pugetsound.va.gov

Louis A Johnson Veterans Affairs Medical Ctr
1 Medical Ctr Dr. . . . Clarksburg WV 26301 304-623-3461 626-7724
TF: 800-733-0512 ■ *Web:* clarksburg.va.gov

Huntington Veterans Affairs Medical Ctr
1540 Spring Valley Dr. . . . Huntington WV 25704 304-429-6741 429-0270
TF: 800-827-8244 ■ *Web:* huntington.va.gov

Tomah Veterans Affairs Medical Ctr
500 E Veterans St . . . . Tomah WI 54660 608-372-3971 372-1692*
**Fax:* Admissions ■ *TF:* 800-872-8662 ■ *Web:* tomah.va.gov

378 HOT TUBS, SPAS, WHIRLPOOL BATHS

Phone *Fax*

Alaglass Swimming Pools
165 Sweet Bay Rd. . . . Saint Matthews SC 29135 877-655-7179
TF: 877-655-7179 ■ *Web:* alaglas.com

Atlantic Spas & Billiards 8721 Glenwood Ave . . . . Raleigh NC 27617 919-783-7447 783-0146
TF: 800-849-8827 ■ *Web:* www.atlanticspasandbilliards.com

Bath-Tec Inc PO Box 1118. . . . Ennis TX 75120 972-646-5279 646-5688
TF: 800-526-3301 ■ *Web:* www.bathtec.com

Best Bath Systems 723 Garber St . . . . Caldwell ID 83605 208-342-6823 333-8657
TF: 866-333-8657 ■ *Web:* www.best-bath.com

Cal Spas Inc 1462 E Ninth St . . . . Pomona CA 91766 909-623-8781 629-0751
TF: 800-225-7727 ■ *Web:* www.calspas.com

Dimension One Spas 2611 Business Pk Dr . . . . Vista CA 92081 760-727-7727 734-4425
Web: www.d1spas.com

Galaxy Aquatics Inc
1075 W Sam Houston Pkwy N Ste 210. . . . Houston TX 77043 713-464-0303 464-0399
Web: www.galaxy-aquatics.com

Hydra Baths 1632 West 139th St . . . . Gardena CA 90249 714-556-9133 708-0632
Web: www.hydrabaths.com

Hydro Systems Inc 29132 Ave Paine. . . . Valencia CA 91355 661-775-0686 775-0668
TF: 800-747-9990 ■ *Web:* www.hydrosystem.com

Jason International Inc
8328 MacArthur Dr. . . . North Little Rock AR 72118 501-771-4477 771-2333
TF: 800-255-5766 ■ *Web:* www.jasoninternational.com

Kallista Inc 1227 N Eigth St Ste 2 . . . . Sheboygan WI 53081 920-457-4441 803-4867
TF Cust Svc: 888-452-5547 ■ *Web:* www.kallista.com

Koral Industries Inc 1504 S Kaufman St. . . . Ennis TX 75119 972-875-6555 875-9558
TF: 800-627-2441 ■ *Web:* www.koralco.com

Marquis Spas Corp 596 Hoffman Rd. . . . Independence OR 97351 503-838-0888 838-3849
TF: 800-275-0888 ■ *Web:* www.marquisspas.com

Master Spas Inc 6927 Lincoln Pkwy . . . . Fort Wayne IN 46804 260-436-9100 432-7935
TF: 800-860-7727 ■ *Web:* www.masterspas.com

Plastic Development Co Inc
75 Palmer Industrial Rd PO Box 4007 . . . . Williamsport PA 17701 800-451-1420 323-8485*
**Fax Area Code:* 570 ■ *TF:* 800-451-1420 ■ *Web:* www.pdcspas.com

Royal Baths Manufacturing Co
14635 Chrisman Rd . . . . Houston TX 77039 281-442-3400 442-1455
TF: 800-826-0074 ■ *Web:* www.royalbaths.com

Spa Manufacturers 6060 Ulmerton Rd . . . . Clearwater FL 33760 727-530-9493 539-8151
TF: 877-530-9493 ■ *Web:* www.spamanufacturers.com

Spurlin Industries Inc 625 Main St . . . . Palmetto GA 30268 770-463-1644 463-2932
TF: 800-749-4475 ■ *Web:* www.spurlinindustries.com

Thermo Spas Inc 155 E St. . . . Wallingford CT 06492 800-876-0158 265-7133*
**Fax Area Code:* 203 ■ *TF:* 800-876-0158 ■ *Web:* www.thermospas.com

Watertech Whirlpool Bath & Spa
2507 Plymouth Rd . . . . Johnson City TN 37601 423-926-1470 926-6438
TF: 800-289-8827 ■ *Web:* www.watertechtn.com

Watkins Mfg Corp 1280 Pk Ctr Dr. . . . Vista CA 92081 800-999-4688
TF: 800-999-4688 ■ *Web:* www.hotspring.com

379 HOTEL RESERVATIONS SERVICES

Phone *Fax*

AC Central Reservations Inc
201 Tilton Rd London Sq Mall Ste 17B . . . . Northfield NJ 08225 609-383-8880 383-8616
TF: 888-227-6667 ■ *Web:* www.acrooms.com

Accommodations Plus Inc 1200 Route 109. . . . Lindenhurst NY 11757 516-798-4444
Web: www.apihotels.com

Advance Reservations Inn Arizona PO Box 950 . . . . Tempe AZ 85280 480-990-0682 990-3390
TF: 800-456-0682 ■ *Web:* www.azres.com

Agile Ticketing Solutions 4124 Central Pk . . . . Hermitage TN 37076 615-360-6700
Web: tickettogo.com

				Phone	Fax
Alexandria & Arlington Bed & Breakfast Networks (AABBN) 4938 Hampden Ln Ste 164	Bethesda	MD	20814	703-549-3415	517-9179*
*Fax Area Code: 202 ■ TF: 888-549-3415 ■ Web: www.aabbn.com					
Alliance Reservations Network 21640 N 19th Ave Ste C102	Phoenix	AZ	85027	602-444-9993	207-4911*
*Fax Area Code: 515 ■ TF Cust Svc: 800-419-1545 ■ Web: www.reservetravel.com					
Anchorage Alaska Bed & Breakfast Assn (AABBA) PO Box 242623	Anchorage	AK	99524	907-272-5909	
TF: 888-584-5147 ■ Web: www.anchorage-bnb.com					
Annapolis Accommodations 41 Maryland Ave	Annapolis	MD	21401	410-263-3262	263-1703
Web: www.stayannapolis.com					
Arsenault Associates Inc Six Terri Ln Ste 700	Burlington	NJ	08016	609-747-8800	
Web: www.arsenault.com					
B & B Agency of Boston 47 Commercial Wharf Ste 3	Boston	MA	02110	800-248-9262	
TF: 800-248-9262 ■ Web: www.boston-bnbagency.com					
Barclay International Group 6800 Jericho Tpke	Syosset	NY	11791	516-364-0064	364-4468
TF: 800-845-6636 ■ Web: www.barclayweb.com					
Bed & Breakfast Assn of Downtown Toronto PO Box 190 Stn B	Toronto	ON	M5T2W1	416-410-3938	483-8822
Web: www.bnbinfo.com					
Bed & Breakfast Atlanta 790 N Ave Ste 202	Atlanta	GA	30306	404-875-0525	876-6544
TF: 800-967-3224 ■ Web: www.bedandbreakfastatlanta.com					
Bed & Breakfast Cape Cod PO Box 2250	Mashpee	MA	02649	508-255-3824	240-0599
TF: 800-556-3815 ■ Web: www.bookcapecod.com					
Bed & Breakfast of Hawaii PO Box 449	Kapaa	HI	96746	808-822-7771	822-2723
TF: 800-733-1632 ■ Web: www.bandb-hawaii.com					
Branson's Best Reservations 2875 Green Mtn Dr	Branson	MO	65616	417-339-2204	339-4051
TF: 800-335-2555 ■ Web: www.bransonbest.com					
Branson/Lakes Area Lodging Assn PO Box 430	Branson	MO	65615	417-332-1400	335-3643
TF: 877-781-1218 ■ Web: www.bransonarealodging.com					
Capitol Reservations 1730 Rhode Island Ave NW Ste 1210	Washington	DC	20036	202-452-1270	452-0537
Web: www.visitdc.com					
Central Reservation Service of New England Inc 300 Terminal C Logan International Airport	East Boston	MA	02128	617-569-3800	561-4840
Colonial Williamsburg Reservation Ctr PO Box 1776	Williamsburg	VA	23187	757-229-1000	565-8797
TF: 800-447-8679 ■ Web: www.history.org					
COMM Group Inc 2003 S Easton Rd Ste 100	Doylestown	PA	18901	215-348-8775	
Web: www.cheapcaribbean.com					
Daniel's Group of Companies Inc, The 10520 Seven Mile Rd	Caledonia	WI	53108	262-835-3553	
Web: www.meetings-incentives.com					
Greater Miami & The Beaches Hotel Assn (GMBHA) 1674 Meridian Ave Ste 420	Miami Beach	FL	33139	305-531-3553	531-8954
Web: gmbha.com					
Greater New Orleans Hotel & Lodging Assn 2020 St Charles Ave 5th Fl	New Orleans	LA	70130	504-525-2264	210-0356
TF: 866-366-1121 ■ Web: www.gnohla.com					
Hawaii's Best Bed & Breakfasts 571 Pauku St	Kailua	HI	96734	808-263-3100	262-5030
TF: 800-262-9912 ■ Web: www.bestbnb.com					
Holiday Inn Express & Suites 5001 Brougham Dr	Drayton Valley	AB	T7A0A1	780-515-9888	514-2734
TF: 877-444-3110 ■ Web: www.hiedraytonvalley.com					
Hot Rooms 875 N. Michigan Ave Ste 3100	Chicago	IL	60611	773-468-7666	649-0559*
*Fax Area Code: 312 ■ TF: 800-468-3500 ■ Web: www.hotrooms.com					
Jackson Hole Central Reservations (JHCR) 140 E Broadway Ste 24 PO Box 2618	Jackson	WY	83001	307-733-4005	733-1286
TF: 888-838-6606 ■ Web: www.jacksonholewy.com					
Key West Key 726 Passover Ln	Key West	FL	33040	800-881-7321	294-2974*
*Fax Area Code: 305 ■ TF: 800-881-7321 ■ Web: www.keywestkey.com					
Know Before You Go Reservations 8000 International Dr	Orlando	FL	32819	407-352-9813	
TF: 800-749-1993 ■ Web: www.knowbeforeugo.com					
Lasvegastickets.com 5030 Paradise Rd Ste B108	Las Vegas	NV	89119	702-597-1588	
Web: lasvegastickets.com					
Leading Hotels of the World 99 Pk Ave	New York	NY	10017	212-515-5600	515-5899
TF: 800-223-6800 ■ Web: www.lhw.com					
Luxe Worldwide Hotels 11461 W Sunset Blvd	Los Angeles	CA	90049	310-440-3090	440-0821
TF: 866-589-3411 ■ Web: www.luxehotels.com					
Martha's Vineyard & Nantucket Reservations 73 Lagoon Pond Rd	Vineyard Haven	MA	02568	508-693-7200	
Web: www.mvreservations.com					
Myrtle Beach Reservation Service 1200 N Oak St Ste 20	Myrtle Beach	SC	29577	843-626-9668	448-8143
Web: www.mbhospitality.org					
Nantucket Accommodations Two Windy Way	Nantucket	MA	02554	508-228-9559	901-4032
TF: 866-743-3330 ■ Web: nantucketaccommodations.com					
National Corporate Housing 365 Herndon Pkwy Ste 111	Herndon	VA	20170	866-229-4720	
TF: 866-229-4720 ■ Web: www.nationalcorporatehousing.com					
New Otani North America Reservation Ctr 120 S Los Angeles St	Los Angeles	CA	90012	213-629-1200	473-1416
TF Cust Svc: 800-421-8795 ■ Web: newotani.co.jp					
Ocean City Hotel-Motel-Restaurant Assn PO Box 340	Ocean City	MD	21843	410-289-6733	289-5645
TF: 800-626-2326 ■ Web: www.ocvisitor.com					
Private Lodging Service 1978 Coltman Rd	Cleveland	OH	44106	216-291-1209	
Web: privatelodgings.com					
Quikbook 381 Pk Ave S 3rd Fl	New York	NY	10016	212-686-7666	779-6120
TF: 800-789-9887 ■ Web: www.quikbook.com					
Resort 2 Me 975 Cass St	Monterey	CA	93940	831-642-6622	
TF: 800-757-5646 ■ Web: www.resort2me.com					
San Diego Concierge 4379 30th St Ste 4	San Diego	CA	92104	619-280-4121	280-4119
TF: 800-979-9091 ■ Web: www.sandiegoconcierge.com					
San Francisco Reservations 360 22nd St Ste 300	Oakland	CA	94612	510-628-4400	
Stay Aspen Snowmass 425 Rio Grande Pl	Aspen	CO	81611	970-925-9000	925-9008
TF: 888-649-5982 ■ Web: www.stayaspensnowmass.com					
Sundance Vacations Inc 264 Highland Park Blvd	Wilkes Barre	PA	18702	570-820-0900	
Web: www.sundancevacations.com					
Travel Planners Inc 381 Pk Ave S	New York	NY	10016	212-532-1660	779-6128
TF: 800-221-3531 ■ Web: www.tphousing.com					
Travelocity.com LP 3150 Sabre Dr	Southlake	TX	76092	888-872-8356	
TF: 888-872-8356 ■ Web: www.travelocity.com					
Vacation Co 42 New Orleans Rd Ste 102	Hilton Head Island	SC	29928	843-686-6100	686-3255
TF: 800-845-7018 ■ Web: www.vacationcompany.com					
Washington DC Accommodations 2201 Wisconsin Ave NW Ste C-120	Washington	DC	20007	202-293-8000	338-1365
TF: 800-503-3330 ■ Web: www.wdcahotels.com					
Winter Park Resort 85 Parsenn Rd	Winter Park	CO	80482	970-726-5514	726-1690
TF Resv: 800-903-7275 ■ Web: www.winterparkresort.com					
Worldhotels 152 W 57th St Sixth Fl	New York	NY	10019	212-956-0200	
Web: www.worldhotels.com					
WorldRes Ltd 15333 N Pima Rd Ste 245	Scottsdale	AZ	85260	480-946-5100	946-0450
Web: www.worldres.com					
Xanterra South Rim LLC 10 Albright St PO Box 699	Grand Canyon	AZ	86023	928-638-2631	638-9810
Web: www.grandcanyonlodges.com					

380 HOTELS - CONFERENCE CENTER

				Phone	Fax
ACE Conference Ctr 800 Ridge Pk	Lafayette Hill	PA	19444	610-825-8000	940-4343
TF: 800-523-3000 ■ Web: www.aceconferencecenter.com					
Airlie Conference Ctr 6809 Airlie Rd	Warrenton	VA	20187	540-347-1300	341-3207
TF: 800-288-9573 ■ Web: www.airlie.com					
Aspen Wye River Conference Ctr 600 Aspen Dr	Queenstown	MD	21658	410-827-7400	827-9295
Web: www.marriott.com					
Banff Centre, The 107 Tunnel Mtn Dr PO Box 1020	Banff	AB	T1L1H5	403-762-6100	762-6444
TF: 800-884-7574 ■ Web: www.banffcentre.ca					
Chaminade One Chaminade Ln	Santa Cruz	CA	95065	831-475-5600	476-4798
TF: 800-283-6569 ■ Web: www.chaminade.com					
Chateau Elan Resort & Conference Ctr 100 Rue Charlemagne	Braselton	GA	30517	678-425-0900	425-6000
TF: 800-233-9463 ■ Web: www.chateauelan.com					
Chattanoogan, The 1201 Broad St	Chattanooga	TN	37402	423-756-3400	756-3404
TF: 877-756-1684 ■ Web: www.chattanooganhotel.com					
Chauncey Conference Ctr 660 Rosedale Rd PO Box 6652	Princeton	NJ	08541	609-921-3600	683-4958
Web: www.acc-chaunceyconferencecenter.com					
Cheyenne Mountain Conference Resort 3225 Broadmoor Vly Rd	Colorado Springs	CO	80906	719-538-4000	576-4186
TF: 800-428-8886 ■ Web: www.cheyennemountain.com					
Clarion Hotel & Conference Ctr Antietam Creek 901 Dual Hwy	Hagerstown	MD	21740	301-733-5100	733-9192
TF: 888-528-6738 ■ Web: www.clarionhagerstown.com					
Conference Ctr at NorthPointe 100 Green Meadows Dr S	Lewis Center	OH	43035	614-880-4300	880-4167
TF: 866-233-9393 ■ Web: northpointecenter.com					
Cook Hotel & Conference Ctr 3848 W Lakeshore Dr	Baton Rouge	LA	70808	225-383-2665	383-4200
TF: 866-610-2665 ■ Web: www.thecookhotel.com					
Country Springs Hotel & Conference Ctr 2810 Golf Rd	Pewaukee	WI	53072	262-547-0201	547-0207
TF: 800-247-6640 ■ Web: www.countryspringshotel.com					
Crystal Mountain Resort 12500 Crystal Mtn Dr	Thompsonville	MI	49683	231-378-2000	378-2998
TF: 800-968-7686 ■ Web: www.crystalmountain.com					
Delta Sherbrooke Hotel & Conference Centre 2685 Rue King O	Sherbrooke	QC	J1L1C1	819-822-1989	822-8990
TF: 800-268-1133 ■ Web: www.deltahotels.com					
Dolce Atlanta-Peachtree 201 Aberdeen Pkwy	Peachtree City	GA	30269	770-487-2666	631-4096
TF: 800-983-6523 ■ Web: www.dolceatlantapeachtree.com					
Dolce Hayes Mansion 200 Edenvale Ave	San Jose	CA	95136	408-226-3200	362-2377
TF: 866-981-3300 ■ Web: www.hayesmansion.com					
Doral Arrowwood Conference Resort 975 Anderson Hill Rd	Rye Brook	NY	10573	844-214-5500	323-5500*
*Fax Area Code: 914 ■ TF: 844-211-0512 ■ Web: www.arrowwood.com					
Edith Macy Conference Ctr 550 Chappaqua Rd	Briarcliff Manor	NY	10510	914-945-8000	945-8009
Web: www.edithmacy.com					
Emory Conference Ctr Hotel 1615 Clifton Rd	Atlanta	GA	30329	404-712-6000	712-6025
TF: 800-933-6679 ■ Web: www.emoryconferencecenter.com					
Evergreen Marriott Conference Resort 4021 Lakeview Dr	Stone Mountain	GA	30083	770-879-9900	465-3264
TF: 800-228-9290 ■ Web: marriott.com/vanityredirect/atleg/					
Fogelman Executive Conference Ctr 330 Innovation Dr University of Memphis	Memphis	TN	38152	901-678-2021	678-5329
Web: www.wilsonhotels.com					
Founders Inn 5641 Indian River Rd	Virginia Beach	VA	23464	757-424-5511	366-0613
TF: 800-926-4466 ■ Web: www.foundersinn.com					
Four Points by Sheraton Norwood Hotel & Conference Ctr 1125 Boston-Providence Tpke (Rt 1)	Norwood	MA	02062	781-769-7900	551-3552
Web: www.fourpointsnorwood.com					
Georgetown University Hotel & Conference Ctr 3800 Reservoir Rd NW	Washington	DC	20057	202-687-3200	687-3297
TF: 800-228-9290 ■ Web: www.acc-guhotelandconferencecenter.com					
Glen Cove Mansion Hotel & Conference Ctr 200 Dosoris Ln	Glen Cove	NY	11542	516-671-6400	705-0147
TF: 877-782-9426 ■ Web: www.glencovemansion.com					

Phone Fax

Grandover Resort & Conference Ctr
1000 Club Rd .... Greensboro NC 27407 336-294-1800 856-9991
TF: 800-472-6301 ■ *Web:* www.grandover.com

H Hotel, The 111 W Main St .... Midland MI 48640 989-839-0500 837-6000
Web: www.thehhotel.com

Hamilton Park Hotel & Conference Ctr
175 Pk Ave .... Florham Park NJ 07932 973-377-2424 377-9560
TF: 800-321-6000 ■ *Web:* www.hamiltonparkhotel.com

Heritage Hotel 522 Heritage Rd .... Southbury CT 06488 203-264-8200 264-5035
TF: 800-932-3466 ■ *Web:* www.heritagesouthbury.com

Hickory Ridge Marriott Conference Hotel
10400 Fernwood Rd .... Bethesda IL 20817 301-380-3000 971-6956*
**Fax Area Code:* 630 ■ *TF:* 800-334-0344 ■ *Web:* www.marriott.com

Hidden Valley Resort & Conference Ctr
1 Craighead Dr PO Box 4420 .... Hidden Valley PA 15502 814-443-8000 443-8254
TF: 800-452-2223 ■ *Web:* www.hiddenvalleyresort.com

Hilton Scranton & Conference Ctr
100 Adams Ave .... Scranton PA 18503 570-343-3000 343-8415
TF: 800-445-8667 ■ *Web:* www.hilton.com

Hilton University of Florida Conference Ctr
1714 SW 34th St .... Gainesville FL 32607 352-371-3600 371-0306
TF: 800-774-1500 ■ *Web:* www1.hilton.com

Hotel at Auburn University & Dixon Conference Ctr, The
241 S College St .... Auburn AL 36830 334-821-8200 826-8746
TF: 800-228-2876 ■ *Web:* www.auhcc.com

Hotel Roanoke & Conference Ctr
110 Shenandoah Ave .... Roanoke VA 24016 540-985-5900 853-8264
TF: 800-222-8733 ■ *Web:* www.hotelroanoke.com

IBM Palisades Conference Ctr 334 Rt 9 W .... Palisades NY 10964 845-732-6000 732-6004
TF: 800-426-0889 ■ *Web:* www.dolcepalisades.com

Inn at Aspen 38750 Hwy 82 .... Aspen CO 81611 800-222-7736 925-9037*
**Fax Area Code:* 970 ■ *TF:* 800-222-7736 ■ *Web:* wyndhamvacationrentals.com

Inn at Virginia Tech & Skelton Conference Ctr
901 Prices Fork Rd MS 0104 .... Blacksburg VA 24061 540-231-8000 231-0146
TF: 877-200-3360 ■ *Web:* www.innatvirginiatech.com

InterContinental Hotel Cleveland
9801 Carnegie Ave .... Cleveland OH 44106 216-707-4100
TF: 877-707-8999 ■ *Web:* www.ihg.com

Ivey Spencer Leadership Centre
551 Windermere Rd .... London ON N5X2T1 519-679-4546 645-0733
TF: 888-678-6926 ■ *Web:* www.iveyspencerleadershipcentre.com

James L Allen Ctr 2169 Campus Dr .... Evanston IL 60208 847-467-7000 491-8002
TF: 877-755-2227 ■ *Web:* www.kellogg.northwestern.edu

Kingbridge Centre, The 12750 Jane St .... King City ON L7B1A3 905-833-3086 833-3075
TF: 800-827-7221 ■ *Web:* www.kingbridgecentre.com

Kingsgate Marriott Conference Ctr at the University of Cincinnati
151 Goodman St .... Cincinnati OH 45219 513-487-3800 487-3810
TF: 800-228-9290 ■ *Web:* www.marriott.com/hotels/travel/cvgkg

Kingsmill Resort & Spa
1010 Kingsmill Rd .... Williamsburg VA 23185 757-253-1703 253-8246
TF: 800-832-5665 ■ *Web:* www.kingsmill.com

Lakeview Golf Resort & Spa
One Lakeview Dr .... Morgantown WV 26508 304-594-1111
TF: 800-624-8300 ■ *Web:* www.lakeviewresort.com

Lakeway Inn & Resort 101 Lakeway Dr .... Austin TX 78734 512-261-6600 261-7311
Web: www.lakewayresortandspa.com

Lodge At Breckenridge, The
112 Overlook Dr .... Breckenridge CO 80424 970-453-9300
TF: 800-736-1607 ■ *Web:* thelodgeandspaatbreck.com

Marietta Conference Ctr & Resort
500 Powder Springs St .... Marietta GA 30064 770-427-2500 819-3224*
**Fax Area Code:* 678 ■ *TF:* 888-685-2500 ■ *Web:* www1.hilton.com

Marriott Montgomery Prattville at Capitol Hill
2500 Legends Cir .... Prattville AL 36066 334-290-1235 290-2222
TF Resv: 800-593-6429 ■ *Web:* www.marriott.com

Millennium Broadway Hotel New York
145 W 44th St .... New York NY 10036 212-768-4400 768-0847
TF: 800-622-5569 ■ *Web:* www.millenniumhotels.com

National Ctr for Employee Development (NCED)
2701 E Imhoff Rd .... Norman OK 73071 405-366-4420 366-4319
TF: 866-438-6233 ■ *Web:* www.nced.com

NAV Canada Training & Conference Ctr
1950 Montreal Rd .... Cornwall ON K6H6L2 613-936-5800 936-5010
TF: 877-832-6416 ■ *Web:* www.navcentre.ca

Northland Inn & Executive Conference Ctr, The
7025 Northland Dr .... Minneapolis MN 55428 763-536-8300 535-8221
TF: 800-441-6422 ■ *Web:* www.minneapolismarriottnw.com

Oak Brook Hills Marriott Resort
3500 Midwest Rd .... Oak Brook IL 60523 630-850-5555 850-5567
TF: 800-228-9290 ■ *Web:* marriott.com/hotels/propertypage/chimc

Oak Ridge Hotel & Conference Ctr
1 Oak Ridge Dr .... Chaska MN 55318 952-368-3100 368-1488
TF Sales: 800-737-9588 ■ *Web:* oakridgeminneapolis.com

Paul J Rizzo Conference Ctr
Rizzo Conference Ctr 150 DuBose House Ln ..... Chapel Hill NC 27517 919-913-2098 913-2099
Web: www.rizzoconferencecenter.com

Penn Stater Conference Ctr Hotel
215 Innovation Blvd .... State College PA 16803 814-863-5000 863-5002
TF: 800-233-7505 ■ *Web:* www.pshs.psu.edu

R David Thomas Executive Conference Ctr (RDTC)
One Science Dr PO Box 90344 .... Durham NC 27708 919-660-6400 660-3607
Web: www.fuqua.duke.edu

Renaissance Portsmouth Hotel & Waterfront Conference Ctr
425 Water St .... Portsmouth VA 23704 757-673-3000 673-3030
TF: 888-839-1775 ■ *Web:* renaissance-hotels.marriott.com

Resort at Squaw Creek
400 Squaw Creek Rd PO Box 3333 .... Olympic Valley CA 96146 530-583-6300 581-6632
TF: 800-327-3353 ■ *Web:* www.squawcreek.com

San Ramon Valley Conference Ctr
3301 Crow Canyon Rd .... San Ramon CA 94583 925-866-7500 866-7378
Web: www.sanramonvalleyconferencecenter.com

Saratoga Hilton 534 Broadway .... Saratoga Springs NY 12866 518-584-4000 584-7430
TF: 800-445-8667 ■ *Web:* www.hilton.com

Phone Fax

Scottsdale Resort & Conference Ctr
7700 E McCormick Pkwy .... Scottsdale AZ 85258 480-991-9000 596-7428
TF: 800-528-0293 ■ *Web:* www.thescottsdaleresort.com

Skamania Lodge
1131 SW Skamania Lodge Way PO Box 189 .... Stevenson WA 98648 509-427-7700 427-2547
TF: 800-221-7117 ■ *Web:* www.skamania.com

Snowbird Ski & Summer Resort
Hwy 210 PO Box 929000 .... Snowbird UT 84092 801-742-2222 947-8227
TF: 800-453-3000 ■ *Web:* www.snowbird.com

Stoweflake Mountain Resort & Spa
1746 Mountain Rd PO Box 369 .... Stowe VT 05672 802-253-7355 253-6858
TF: 800-253-2232 ■ *Web:* www.stoweflake.com

Talaris Conference Ctr 4000 NE 41st St .... Seattle WA 98105 206-268-7000 268-7001
Web: www.talarisconferencecenter.com

University of Maryland University College Marriott Conference Ctr Hotel
3501 University Blvd E .... Adelphi MD 20783 301-985-7300 985-7517
TF: 800-721-7033 ■ *Web:* www.marriott.com

University Place Conference Ctr & Hotel-Indianapolis
850 W Michigan St .... Indianapolis IN 46202 317-269-9000 278-8176
Web: eventservices.iupui.edu

University Plaza Hotel & Convention Ctr
333 John Q Hammons Pkwy .... Springfield MO 65806 417-864-7333 831-5893
Web: www.upspringfield.com

White Oaks Conference Resort & Spa
253 Taylor Rd SS4 .... Niagara-on-the-Lake ON L0S1J0 905-688-2550 688-2220
TF Resv: 800-263-5766 ■ *Web:* www.whiteoaksresort.com

Woodlands Resort & Conference Ctr, The
2301 N Millbend Dr .... The Woodlands TX 77380 281-367-1100 364-6275
TF Resv: 800-433-2624 ■ *Web:* www.woodlandsresort.com

Wyndham Peachtree Conference Ctr
2443 Hwy 54 W .... Peachtree City GA 30269 770-487-2000
TF: 800-996-3426 ■ *Web:* www.wyndham.com

381 HOTELS - FREQUENT STAY PROGRAMS

Phone Fax

45 Allen Plaza Development LLC
45 Ivan Allen Jr Blvd .... Atlanta GA 30308 404-582-5800
Web: www.watlantadowntown.com

Aava Whistler Hotel Ltd 4005 Whistler Way .... Whistler BC V0N1B4 604-932-2522
Web: www.aavawhistlerhotel.com

Afton Alps Inc 6600 Peller Ave S .... Hastings MN 55033 651-436-5245
Web: www.aftonalps.com

Alliance Hospitality Management LLC
1001 Wade Ave Ste 215 .... Raleigh NC 27605 919-791-1801
Web: www.alliancehospitality.com

Alta Mira Recovery Programs LLC
125 Bulkley Ave .... Sausalito CA 94965 415-332-1350
Web: www.altamirarecovery.com

Amara Resort LLC 100 Amara Ln .... Sedona AZ 86336 928-282-4828
Web: www.amararesort.com

Ambassador Hotel Inc 2040 Kuhio Ave .... Honolulu HI 96815 808-941-7777
Web: www.ambassadorwaikiki.com

Americas Best Value Inn
2393 Townsgate Rd Ste 100 .... Westlake Village OH 91361 805-557-7300
Web: www.americasbestvalueinn.com

AmericInn Inn-Pressive Club 250 Lake Dr E .... Chanhassen MN 55317 952-294-5000 294-5001
TF: 800-634-3444 ■ *Web:* www.americinn.com

Andaz 5th Avenue 485 Fifth Ave 41st St .... New York NY 10017 212-601-1234
Web: www.newyork.5thavenue.andaz.hyatt.com

Apple Farm Bakery 2015 Monterey St .... San Luis Obispo CA 93401 805-544-6100
Web: www.applefarm.com

Aqua Waikiki Pearl Hotel 415 Nahua St .... Waikiki Beach HI 96815 808-922-1616
Web: www.aquawaikikipearl.com

Ascent Hospitality LLC 715 College Dr .... Dalton GA 30720 706-529-6900
Web: www.ascent-hospitality.com

Auberge Resorts LLC
591 Redwood Hwy Ste 3150 .... Mill Valley CA 94941 415-380-3460
Web: www.aubergeresorts.com

Avalon Hotel, The 16 E 32nd St .... New York NY 10016 212-299-7000
Web: www.avalonhotelnyc.com

Bavarian Lion Company of California
2777 Fourth St .... Santa Rosa CA 95405 707-545-8530
Web: www.flamingoresort.com

Bay Landing Hotel 1550 Bayshore Hwy Fl 2 .... Burlingame CA 94010 650-259-9000 259-9099
Web: www.baylandinghotel.com

Baywood Hotels Inc 7871 Belle Point Dr .... Greenbelt MD 20770 301-345-8700
Web: www.baywoodhotels.com

BBL Hospitality LLC 302 Washington Ave Ext .... Albany NY 12203 518-640-6464
Web: www.bblhospitality.com

Beach Terrace Motor Inn 3400 Atlantic Ave .... Wildwood NJ 08260 609-522-8100
Web: www.beachterrace.com

Bear Creek Mountain Resort 101 Doe Mtn Ln .... Macungie PA 18062 610-641-7101
Web: www.bcmountainresort.com

Belleclaire Hotel Corp 250 W 77th St .... New York NY 10024 212-362-7700
Web: www.hotelbelleclaire.com

Best Western Edgewater 2400 London Rd .... Duluth MN 55812 218-728-3601
Web: www.zmchotels.com

Best Western InnTowner, The
2424 University Ave .... Madison WI 53726 608-233-8778
Web: inntowner.com

BEST WESTERN PLUS Heritage Inn
151 E McLeod Rd .... Bellingham WA 98226 360-647-1912
Web: www.bestwesternheritageinn.com

Beverly Hills Plaza Hotel
10300 Wilshire Blvd .... Los Angeles CA 90024 310-275-5575
Web: www.beverlyhillsplazahotel.com

Billings Ventures LP 1801 Majestic Ln .... Billings MT 59102 406-839-9300
Web: www.thebighornresort.com

Bjork Construction Company Inc
4420 Enterprise Pl .... Fremont CA 94538 510-656-4688
Web: www.bjorkconstruction.com

				Phone	Fax
Blue Harbor Resort & Conference Center 725 Blue Harbor Dr. *Web:* www.blueharborresort.com	Sheboygan	WI	53081	920-452-2900	
Bluewater Resort & Casino 11300 Resort Dr *Web:* www.bluewaterfun.com	Parker	AZ	85344	928-669-7000	
Boston Common Hotel & Conference Center 40 Trinity Pl *Web:* www.bostoncommonhotel.com	Boston	MA	02116	617-933-7700	
Breakers Hotel & Restaurant 1507 Ocean Ave *Web:* www.breakershotel.com	Spring Lake	NJ	07762	732-449-7700	
Breckenridge Grand Vacations LLC PO Box 6879 *Web:* www.breckenridgegrandvacations.com	Breckenridge	CO	80424	970-547-3630	
Brendan's Camarillo LLC 1755 E Daily Dr *Web:* brendans.com	Camarillo	CA	93010	805-383-7528	
Broadway Plaza Hotel 1155 Broadway *Web:* www.broadwayplazahotel.com	New York	NY	10001	212-679-7665	
Bromley Mountain Ski Resort 3984 Vt Rt 11 *Web:* www.bromley.com	Peru	VT	05152	802-824-5522	
Buena Vista Motor Inn 1599 Lombard St *Web:* www.buenavistamotorinn.com	San Francisco	CA	94123	415-923-9600	
Buffalo Lodging Associates LLC 570 Delaware Ave *Web:* www.buffalolodging.com	Buffalo	NY	14202	716-858-3163	
Burke Mountain Operating Co 223 Sherburne Lodge Rd *Web:* www.skiburke.com	East Burke	VT	05832	802-626-7300	
Caneel Bay Inc North Shore Rd *Web:* www.caneelbay.com	Cruz Bay	VI	00831	340-776-6111	
Capstone Hotel Ltd 320 Paul W Bryant Dr *Web:* www.hotelcapstone.com	Tuscaloosa	AL	35401	205-752-3200	
Carson Doubletree Hotel Civic Plaza, The Two Civic Plz *Web:* www.carsondoubletree.com	Carson	CA	90745	310-830-9200	
Celebrity Hotel Inc 629 Main St *Web:* www.celebritycasinos.com	Deadwood	SD	57732	605-578-1909	
Champion Hotels LLC 3048 N Grand Blvd *Web:* www.championhotels.com	Oklahoma City	OK	73107	405-606-7400	
Chena Hot Springs Resort LLC PO Box 58740 *Web:* www.chenahotsprings.com	Fairbanks	AK	99711	907-451-8104	
Chestnut Mountain Resort 8700 Chestnut Dr *TF:* 800-397-1320 ■ *Web:* www.chestnutmtn.com	Galena	IL	61036	800-397-1320	
Chicago South Loop Hotel 11 W 26th St *Web:* www.chicagosouthloophotel.com	Chicago	IL	60616	312-225-7000	
Chimney Rock Inn 800 Thompson Ave *Web:* www.chimneyrockinn.com	Bound Brook	NJ	08805	732-469-4600	
Choice Hotels Canada Inc 5090 Explorer Dr Ste 500 *Web:* www.choicehotels.ca	Mississauga	ON	L4W4T9	905-602-2222	
Christian Brothers Retreat 4401 Redwood Rd *Web:* www.christianbrosretreat.com	Napa	CA	94558	707-252-3810	
Christie Lodge PO Box 1196 *Web:* www.christielodge.com	Avon	CO	81620	970-845-4504	
Chukchansi Gold Resort & Casino 711 Lucky Ln *TF:* 866-794-6946 ■ *Web:* chukchansigold.com	Coarsegold	CA	93614	866-794-6946	
ClubHouse Rewards Program 2320 South Louise Ave *Web:* www.clubhouseinn.com	Sioux Falls	SD	57106	605-361-8700	361-5950
Coach Stop Inn, The 4755 Rt 6 *Web:* www.coachstopinn.com	Wellsboro	PA	16901	570-724-5361	
Comfort Inn & Suites 2201 Hotel Cir S *Web:* www.comfortinnhotelcircle.com	San Diego	CA	92108	619-881-6800	
Commonwealth Hotels LLC 100 E Rivercenter Blvd Ste 1050 *Web:* www.commonwealthhotels.com	Covington	KY	41011	859-261-5522	
Conrad Chicago 521 N Rush St *Web:* www.conradchicagohotel.com	Chicago	IL	60611	312-645-1500	
Copper Beech Inn, The 46 Main St *Web:* www.copperbeechinn.com	Ivoryton	CT	06442	860-767-0330	
Coral Hospitality LLC 9180 Galleria Ct Ste 600 *Web:* www.coralhospitality.com	Naples	FL	34109	239-449-1800	
Country Hearth Inn Inc 50 Glenlake Pkwy NE Ste 350 *Web:* www.countryhearth.com	Atlanta	GA	30328	770-393-2662	
Courtyard Anaheim at Disneyland, The 2045 S Harbor Blvd *Web:* www.courtyardanaheim.com	Anaheim	CA	92802	714-740-2645	
Cromwell Morgan 244 Fifth Ave Ste 2400 *Web:* www.cromwellmorgan.com	New York	NY	10001	212-726-2994	
Crowne Plaza Hotel Phoenix 2532 W Peoria Ave *Web:* www.cpphoenix.com	Phoenix	AZ	85029	602-943-2341	
Crowne Plaza Hotel St Louis-Clayton 7750 Carondelet Ave Clayton *Web:* www.cpclayton.com	Clayton	MO	63105	314-726-5400	719-7126
Crowne Plaza Hotels & Resorts 2701 Summer St *Web:* www.stamfordplazahotel.com	Stamford	CT	06905	203-359-1300	
Crowne Plaza Minneapolis Airport West 5401 Green Vly Dr *Web:* www.cpmsp.com	Minneapolis	MN	55437	952-831-8000	
Crowne Plaza Niagara Falls - Fallsview 5685 Falls Ave *Web:* www.niagarafallscrowneplazahotel.com	Niagara Falls	ON	L2E6W7	905-374-4447	
Crowne Plaza Ravinia 4355 Ashford Dunwoody Rd *Web:* www.cpravinia.com	Atlanta	GA	30346	770-395-7700	
CS&M Associates 500 Canal St *Web:* www.sheratonneworleans.com	New Orleans	LA	70130	504-525-2500	
Danfords Hotel & Marina 25 E Broadway *TF:* 800-332-6367 ■ *Web:* www.danfords.com	Port Jefferson	NY	11777	800-332-6367	
Days Inn Hinton-Jasper Hotel 358 Smith St *Web:* www.daysinnhinton.com	Hinton	AB	T7V2A1	780-817-1960	
Dearborn Partners LLC 200 W Madison St Ste 1950 *Web:* www.dearbornpartners.com	Chicago	IL	60606	312-795-1000	
Decatur Conference Center & Hotel 4191 W US Hwy 36 Wyckles Rd *Web:* www.hoteldecatur.com	Decatur	IL	62522	217-422-8800	
Discovery Inn Hotel 4701 Franklin Ave *Web:* www.discoveryinn.ca	Yellowknife	NT	X1A2N6	867-873-4151	
DKN Hotels LLC 42 Corporate Park Ste 200 *Web:* www.dknhotels.com	Irvine	CA	92626	714-427-4320	
Donovan House 1155 14th St NW *Web:* www.inndc.com	Washington	DC	20005	202-737-1200	
DoubleTree 2200 Fwy Blvd *Web:* www.minneapolisboulevardhotel.com	Minneapolis	MN	55430	763-566-8000	
DoubleTree by Hilton Baltimore - BWI Airport 890 Elkridge Landing Rd *Web:* www.doubletreebwiairporthotel.com	Linthicum	MD	21090	410-859-8400	
DoubleTree by Hilton Hotel Bethesda - Washington DC 8120 Wisconsin Ave *Web:* www.doubletreebethesda.com	Bethesda	MD	20814	301-652-2000	
Doubletree by Hilton Hotel Tucson-Reid Park 445 S Alvernon Way *Web:* www.dtreidpark.com	Tucson	AZ	85711	520-881-4200	
Dow Hotel Company LLC, The 16400 Southcenter Pkwy Ste 405 *Web:* www.dowhotelco.com	Seattle	WA	98188	206-575-3600	
Easton's Group of Hotels Inc 3100 Steeles Ave E Gateway Centre Ste 601 *Web:* www.eastonsgroup.com	Markham	ON	L3R8T3	905-940-9409	
Eastover Hotel & Resort LLC 430 East St *Web:* www.eastover.com	Lenox	MA	01240	413-637-0625	
Edgewater Beach Resort Management 11212 Front Beach Rd *Web:* www.edgewaterbeachresort.com	Panama City	FL	32407	850-235-4044	
Embassy Suites Hotel & Casino-San Juan Puerto Rico 8000 Tartak St Isla Verde Carolina *Web:* www.embassysuitessanjuan.com	San Juan	PR	00979	787-791-0505	
Embassy Suites Hotel Orlando - International Drive South 8978 International Dr *Web:* www.embassysuitesorlando.com	Orlando	FL	32819	407-352-1400	
Embassy Suites Memphis 1022 S Shady Grove Rd *Web:* www.indianaroof.com	Memphis	TN	38120	901-684-1777	
FairBridge Inns LLC 421 W Riverside Ave Ste 407 *TF:* 877-866-8090 ■ *Web:* www.fairbridgeinns.com	Spokane	WA	99201	877-866-8090	
Fairmont Hotel Management Lp 950 Mason St *Web:* www.tongaroom.com	San Francisco	CA	94108	415-982-6500	
Fairmont Olympic Hotel Seattle, The 411 University St *Web:* www.seattleskal.org	Seattle	WA	98101	206-621-1700	
Fairmont San Francisco Hotel, The 950 Mason St *TF:* 800-257-7544 ■ *Web:* fairmont.com	San Francisco	CA	94108	415-772-5000	
Fort William Henry Corp, The 48 Canada St *Web:* www.fortwilliamhenry.com	Lake George	NY	12845	518-668-3081	
Fountain Grove Inn, The 101 Fountaingrove Pkwy *Web:* www.fountaingroveinn.com	Santa Rosa	CA	95403	707-578-6101	
Gainey Suites Hotel 7300 E Gainey *Web:* www.gaineysuiteshotel.com	Scottsdale	AZ	85258	480-922-6969	
GF Management Inc 1628 John F Kennedy Blvd 8 Penn Ctr 23rd Fl *Web:* www.gfhotels.com	Philadelphia	PA	19103	215-972-2222	
Golden Inn Hotel 7849 Dune Dr *Web:* www.goldeninn.com	Avalon	NJ	08202	609-368-5155	
Grand Hyatt Denver 1750 Welton St *Web:* www.granddenver.hyatt.com	Denver	CO	80202	303-295-1234	
Grand Hyatt Tampa Bay 2900 Bayport Dr *Web:* www.grandtampabay.hyatt.com	Tampa	FL	33607	813-874-1234	
Grand Pacific Resorts Inc Grand Pacific Plz 5900 Pasteur Ct Ste 200 *Web:* www.grandpacificresorts.com	Carlsbad	CA	92008	760-431-8500	
Grand Seas Resort Partners 2424 N Atlantic Ave *Web:* www.grandseas.com	Daytona Beach	FL	32118	386-677-7880	
GrandLife Hotels Inc 310 W Broadway *Web:* www.grandlifehotels.com	New York	NY	10013	212-965-3000	
Great Wolf Lodge of Sandusky LLC 4600 Milan Rd US 250 *Web:* www.greatbearlodge.com	Sandusky	OH	44870	419-609-6000	
Green Turtle Bay Inc 239 Jetty Dr *Web:* www.greenturtlebay.com	Grand Rivers	KY	42045	270-362-8364	
Greenwich Hospitality Group LLC 500 Steamboat Rd *Web:* www.thedelamar.com	Greenwich	CT	06830	203-661-9800	
Greenwich Hotel, The 377 Greenwich St *Web:* www.thegreenwichhotel.com	New York	NY	10013	212-941-8900	
Gulf Bay Hotels Inc 3470 Club Ctr Blvd *Web:* www.gulfbay.com	Naples	FL	34114	239-732-9400	
Gunstock Recreation Area 719 Cherry Vly Rd *Web:* www.gunstock.com	Gilford	NH	03249	603-293-4341	
Hampton Inn Brookhaven 2000 N Ocean Ave *Web:* www.hamptoninnbrookhaven.com	Farmingville	NY	11738	631-732-7300	
Hampton Inn (Pittsburgh Pennsylvania) 3315 Hamlet St *Web:* www.pittsburghhamptoninn.com	Pittsburgh	PA	15213	412-681-1000	
Hampton Marina Hotel 700 Settlers Landing Rd *Web:* www.hamptonmarinahotel.com	Hampton	VA	23669	757-727-9700	

Phone | Fax

Harbor Hotel Provincetown
698 Commercial St Cape Cod .... Provincetown MA 02657 800-422-4224
Web: www.harborhotelptown.com

Harbour Towers Hotel & Suites 345 Quebec St .... Victoria BC V8V1W4 250-385-2405
Web: www.harbourtowers.com

Hawkeye Hotels Inc 1601 N Roosevelt Ave .... Burlington IA 52601 319-752-7400
Web: www.hawkeyehotels.com

HEI Hospitality LLC
101 Merritt 7 Corporate Park First Fl .... Norwalk CT 06851 203-849-8844
Web: www.heihotels.com

Hi-lo Motel Cafe & Rv Park 88 S Weed Blvd............ Weed CA 96094 530-938-2904
Web: www.sisdevco.com

Highgate Hotels Inc
545 E John Carpenter Fwy Ste 1400..................... Irving TX 75062 972-444-9700
Web: www.highgateholdings.com

HighPointe Hotel Corp
311 Gulf Breeze Pkwy........................... Gulf Breeze FL 32561 850-932-9314
Web: www.highpointe.com

Hilton Concord 1970 Diamond Boulevard .... Concord CA 94520 925-827-2000
Web: www.concordhilton.com

Hilton Garden Inn Baton Rouge Airport
3330 Harding Blvd .... Baton Rouge LA 70807 225-357-6177
Web: www.pinkshell.com

Hilton Hotel Waco 113 S University Parks Dr............. Waco TX 76701 254-754-8484
Web: www.hiltonwaco.com

Hilton Meadowlands Hotel & Conference Center
Two Meadowlands Plz........................ East Rutherford NJ 07073 201-896-0500
Web: www.hiltonmeadowlands.com

Hilton Miami Downtown 1601 Biscayne Blvd............ Miami FL 33132 305-374-0000
Web: www.hiltonmiamidowntown.com

Hilton Savannah Desoto 15 E Liberty St............. Savannah GA 31401 912-232-9000
Web: www.desotohilton.com

Hilton Suites Winnipeg Airport
1800 Wellington Ave............................. Winnipeg MB R3H1B2 204-783-1700
Web: www.fortisproperties.com

Hilton Woodcliff Lake 200 Tice Blvd .... Woodcliff Lake NJ 07677 201-391-3600
Web: www.hiltonwoodclifflake.com

Hinton Lakeview Inns & Suites 500 Smith St........... Hinton AB T7V2A1 780-865-2575
Web: www.lakeviewhotels.com

Holiday Inn Ann Arbor-Near the Univ of MI
3600 Plymouth Rd .... Ann Arbor MI 48105 734-769-9800
Web: www.hiannarbor.com

Holiday Inn Baltimore Inner Harbor Hotel
301 W Lombard St .... Baltimore MD 21201 410-685-3500
Web: www.innerharborhi.com

Holiday Inn By the Bay 88 Spring St .... Portland ME 04101 207-775-2311
Web: www.innbythebay.com

Holiday Inn Los Angeles International Airport
9901 La Cienega Blvd........................... Los Angeles CA 90045 310-649-5151
Web: www.hilax.com

Holiday Inn Select Hotel & Suites in Oakville
2525 Wyecroft Rd................................. Oakville ON L6L6P8 905-847-1000
Web: www.oakvillehotel.com

Holiday Inn Select in Windsor Canada
1855 Huron Church Rd............................. Windsor ON N9C2L6 519-966-1200
Web: www.his-windsor.com

HOOVER DAM LODGE Hwy 93 .... Boulder City NV 89005 702-293-5000
Web: www.haciendaonline.com

Horizon Hotel Resort & Spa Inc
1050 E Palm Canyon Dr........................ Palm Springs CA 92264 760-323-1858
Web: www.thehorizonhotel.com

Horseshoe Valley Resort Ltd
1101 Horseshoe Vly Rd - Comp 10 RR 1 .... Barrie ON L4M4Y8 705-835-2790
Web: www.horseshoeresort.com

Hospitality International INNcentive Card Program
1726 Montreal Cir .... Tucker GA 30084 800-247-4677 270-1077*
**Fax Area Code:* 770 ■ *TF:* 800-247-4677 ■ *Web:* bookroomsnow.com/discounts/

Hotel Blue 717 Central Ave Nw.................. Albuquerque NM 87102 505-924-2400
Web: www.thehotelblue.com

Hotel Carter 250 W 43rd St .... New York NY 10036 212-944-6000
Web: www.carterhotel.com

Hotel Equities Inc 41 Perimeter Ctr E Ste 510............ Atlanta GA 30346 678-578-4444
Web: www.hotelequities.com

Hotel ML, The 915 Rt 73.......................... Mt. Laurel NJ 08054 856-234-7300
Web: www.thehotelml.com

Hotel Modera 515 SW Clay St .... Portland OR 97201 503-484-1084
Web: hotelmodera.com

Hotel of Rivington 107 Rivington St .... New York NY 10002 212-475-2600
Web: www.hotelonrivington.com

Hotel Palomar Washington DC 2121 P St NW ...... Washington DC 20037 202-448-1800
Web: www.hotelpalomar-dc.com

Hotel Shangri La 1301 Ocean Ave .... Santa Monica CA 90401 310-394-2791
Web: www.shangrila-hotel.com

Hunt Valley Inn Baltimore 245 Shawan Rd .... Hunt Valley MD 21031 410-785-7000
Web: www.huntvalleyinn.com

Hyatt at Fisherman's Wharf
555 N Point St .... San Francisco CA 94133 415-563-1234
Web: fishermanswharf.hyatt.com

Hyatt Chicago Magnificent Mile
633 N Saint Clair St .... Chicago IL 60611 312-787-1234
Web: www.chicagomagnificentmile.hyatt.com

Hyatt Dulles 2300 Dulles Corner Blvd .... Herndon VA 20171 703-713-1234
Web: www.dulles.hyatt.com

Hyatt Gold Passport Program
9805 Q St PO Box 27089............................ Omaha NE 68127 800-233-1234 593-4030*
**Fax Area Code:* 402 ■ *TF:* 800-233-1234 ■ *Web:* www.goldpassport.com

Hyatt Key West Resort & Spa 601 Front St.......... Key West FL 33040 305-809-1234
Web: keywest.hyatt.com

Hyatt Place East End & Resort Marina
451 E Main St.................................. Riverhead NY 11901 631-208-0002
Web: www.hyattplaceeastend.com

Hyatt Place North Charleston Hotel
7331 Mazyck Rd........................... North Charleston SC 29406 843-735-7100
Web: northcharleston.place.hyatt.com

Hyatt Place San Jose Downtown
282 Almaden Blvd .... San Jose CA 95113 408-998-0400
Web: www.sanjose.place.hyatt.com

Hyatt Regency Albuquerque 330 Tijeras NW ...... Albuquerque NM 87102 505-842-1234
Web: www.albuquerque.hyatt.com

Hyatt Regency Bethesda
One Bethesda Metro Ctr 7400 Wisconsin Ave........... Bethesda MD 20814 301-657-1234
Web: bethesda.hyatt.com

Hyatt Regency Boston One Ave de Lafayette............ Boston MA 02111 617-912-1234
Web: www.regencyboston.hyatt.com

Hyatt Regency Century Plaza
2025 Ave of the Stars .... Los Angeles CA 90067 310-228-1234
Web: www.centuryplaza.hyatt.com

Hyatt Regency Columbus 350 N High St .... Columbus OH 43215 614-463-1234
Web: www.columbusregency.hyatt.com

Hyatt Regency Jacksonville Riverfront
225 E Coastline Dr.............................. Jacksonville FL 32202 904-588-1234
Web: www.jacksonville.hyatt.com

Hyatt Regency La Jolla at Aventine
3777 La Jolla Village Dr .... San Diego CA 92122 858-552-1234
Web: lajolla.hyatt.com

Hyatt Regency Lexington 401 W High St............ Lexington KY 40507 859-253-1234
Web: lexington.hyatt.com

Hyatt Regency Minneapolis
1300 Nicollet Mall .... Minneapolis MN 55403 612-370-1234
Web: minneapolis.hyatt.com

Hyatt Regency Montreal 1255 Jeanne-Mance......... Montreal QC H5B1E5 514-982-1234
Web: www.montreal.hyatt.com

Hyatt Regency North Dallas
701 E Campbell Rd............................. Richardson TX 75081 972-231-9600
Web: www.therichardsonhotel.com

Hyatt Regency Phoenix 122 N Second St .... Phoenix AZ 85004 602-252-1234
Web: www.phoenix.hyatt.com

Hyatt Regency Pittsburgh International Airport
1111 Airport Blvd PO Box 12420 .... Pittsburgh PA 15231 724-899-1234
Web: www.pittsburghairport.hyatt.com

Hyatt Regency Rochester 125 E Main St............ Rochester NY 14604 585-546-1234
Web: rochester.hyatt.com

Hyatt Regency San Francisco
Five Embarcadero Ctr .... San Francisco CA 94111 415-788-1234
Web: www.sanfranciscoregency.hyatt.com

Hyatt Regency Santa Clara
5101 Great America Pkwy........................ Santa Clara CA 95054 408-200-1234
Web: www.santaclara.hyatt.com

Hyatt Regency Savannah Two W Bay St............. Savannah GA 31401 912-238-1234
Web: www.savannah.hyatt.com

Hyatt Regency Suites Atlanta Northwest
2999 Windy Hill Rd .... Marietta GA 30067 770-956-1234
Web: atlantasuites.hyatt.com

Hyatt Regency Tulsa 100 E Second St .... Tulsa OK 74103 918-582-9000
Web: www.tulsa.hyatt.com

Hyatt Regency Valencia 24500 Town Ctr Dr .... Valencia CA 91355 661-799-1234
Web: valencia.hyatt.com

Hyatt Regency Washington DC on Capitol Hill
400 New Jersey Ave NW......................... Washington DC 20001 202-737-1234
Web: washingtonregency.hyatt.com

Indianapolis Marriott Downtown
350 W Maryland St............................ Indianapolis IN 46225 317-822-3500
Web: www.indymarriott.com

Inn at Ellis Square 201 W Bay St.................... Savannah GA 31401 877-542-7666
TF: 877-542-7666 ■ *Web:* www.innatellissquare.com

Inn at Jackson Hole, The
3345 W Village Dr PO Box 328.................. Teton Village WY 83025 307-733-2311
Web: www.innatjh.com

Inn at Mamas Fish House 799 Poho Pl .... Paia HI 96779 808-579-8488
Web: mamasfishhouse.com

Inn at USC Columbia South Caolina Hotel
1619 Pendleton St .... Columbia SC 29201 803-779-7779
Web: www.innatusc.com

InterContinental Mark Hopkins San Francisco
999 California St............................ San Francisco CA 94108 415-392-3434
Web: www.intercontinentalmarkhopkins.com

InterContinental Montreal
360 St-Antoine St W.............................. Montreal QC H2Y3X4 514-987-9900
Web: www.montreal.intercontinental.com

Intercontinental San Francisco
888 Howard St .... San Francisco CA 94103 888-811-4273
TF: 888-811-4273 ■ *Web:* www.intercontinentalsanfrancisco.com

InterContinental Stephen F Austin Hotel
701 Congress Ave.................................. Austin TX 78701 512-457-8800
Web: www.austin.intercontinental.com

JW Marriott Denver Cherry Creek Hotel
150 Clayton Ln................................... Denver CO 80206 303-316-2700
Web: www.jwmarriottdenver.com

Keating Hotel, The 432 F St...................... San Diego CA 92101 619-814-5700
Web: www.thekeating.com

King George Hotel 334 Mason St .... San Fran CA 94102 415-781-5050
Web: www.kinggeorge.com

Kontiki Beach Resort 2290 N Fulton Beach Rd .... Rockport TX 78382 361-729-2318 729-3212
Web: www.kontikibeach.com

KSL Resorts 50-905 Avenida Bermudas .... La Quinta CA 92253 760-564-8000
Web: www.kslresorts.com

Kyo-Ya Company Ltd 2255 Kalakaua Ave .... Honolulu HI 96815 808-931-8600
Web: kyoyahotelsandresorts.com

Lahaina Shores Beach Resort 475 Front St .... Lahaina HI 96761 866-934-9176
Web: www.classicresorts.com

Lancaster Group Inc, The
3411 Richmond Ave Ste 460 .... Houston TX 77046 713-224-6000
Web: www.lancaster.com

Name / Address	City	State	Zip	Phone	Fax
Landmark Hotel Group LLC 4453 Bonney Rd. Web: www.landmarkhotelgroup.com	Virginia Beach	VA	23462	757-213-4380	
Landsby, The 1576 Mission Dr Ofc. Web: www.thelandsby.com	Solvang	CA	93463	805-688-3121	
LBO Holding Inc Route 302. Web: www.attitash.com	Bartlett	NH	03812	603-374-2368	
LeisureLink Inc 90 S 400 W Ste 300. TF: 855-840-2249 ■ Web: www.leisurelink.com	Salt Lake City	UT	84101	855-840-2249	
Liberty Hotel, The 215 Charles St. Web: www.libertyhotel.com	Boston	MA	02114	617-224-4000	
Lodge at Big Sky LLC, The 75 Sitting Bull Rd. Web: www.lodgeatbigsky.com	Big Sky	MT	59716	406-995-7858	
Lodge at Tiburon, The 1651 Tiburon Blvd. Web: www.lodgeattiburon.com	Tiburon	CA	94920	415-435-3133	
London West Hollywood Hotel 1020 N San Vicente Blvd. TF: 866-282-4560 ■ Web: www.thelondonwesthollywood.com	West Hollywood	CA	90069	866-282-4560	
Lord Amherst Inc 5000 Main St. Web: www.lordamherst.com	Amherst	NY	14226	716-839-2200	
Los Gatos Hotel Corp 210 E Main St. Web: hotellosgatos.com	Los Gatos	CA	95030	408-335-1700	
LTD Hospitality Group LLC 1564 Crossways Blvd. Web: ltdhospitality.com	Chesapeake	VA	23320	757-420-0900	
M Gibson Hotels Group 409 Montbrook Ln. Web: www.mgibsonhotels.com	Knoxville	TN	37919	865-539-0588	
Maidstone Hotel, The 207 Main St. Web: www.themaidstone.com	East Hampton	NY	11937	631-324-5006	
Maine Course Hospitality Group Inc 15 Main St Ste 210. Web: www.mchg.com	Freeport	ME	04032	207-865-6105	
Mainsail Management Group Inc 5108 Eisenhower Blvd. Web: www.mainsailtampa.com	Tampa	FL	33634	813-243-2600	
Manchester Grand Hyatt San Diego One Market Pl. Web: www.manchestergrandhyattsandiego.com	San Diego	CA	92101	619-232-1234	
Manhattan at Times Square Hotel, The 790 Seventh Ave. Web: www.manhattanhoteltimessquare.com	New York	NY	10019	212-581-3300	
Marin Suites Hotel LLC 45 Tamal Vista Blvd. Web: www.marinsuites.com	Corte Madera	CA	94925	415-924-3608	
Mark Scott Construction 2835 Contra Costa Blvd. Web: www.msconstruction.com	Pleasant Hill	CA	94523	925-944-0502	
Marshall Hotels & Resorts Inc 1315 S Division St. Web: www.marshallhotels.com	Salisbury	MD	21804	410-749-8464	
Mayfair Hotel 1256 W Seventh St. Web: www.mayfairla.com	Los Angeles	CA	90017	213-484-9789	
McGuires Motor Inn 120 S Telegraph Rd. Web: www.mcguiresmotorinn.com	Waterford	MI	48328	248-682-5100	
Meadowmere Resort 74 Main St. Web: www.meadowmere.com	Ogunquit	ME	03907	207-646-9661	
Melrose Hotel Washington DC, The 2430 Pennsylvania Ave NW. Web: www.melrosehoteldc.com	Washington	DC	20037	202-955-6400	
Menominee Hotel PO Box 760. Web: www.menomineecasinoresort.com	Keshena	WI	54135	715-799-3600	
Microtel Inn & Suites 11274 S Fortuna Rd. Web: www.underhilltransfer.com	Yuma	AZ	85367	928-345-1777	
Midamerica Hotels Corp 105 S Mount Auburn Rd. Web: www.midamcorp.com	Cape Girardeau	MO	63703	573-334-0546	
Midas Hospitality LLC 11701 Borman Dr Ste 295. Web: www.midashospitality.com	St. Louis	MO	63146	314-692-0100	
Mont Saint-Sauveur International Inc 350 Saint-Denis Ave. Web: www.montsaintsauveur.com	Saint-sauveur	QC	J0R1R3	450-227-4671	
Mountaineer Inn 3343 Mountain Rd. Web: www.stowemountaineerinn.com	Stowe	VT	05672	802-253-7525	
Neil Locke & Associates 550 E Devon Ave Ste 130. Web: www.neillocke.com	Itasca	IL	60143	630-285-9085	
Noble Investment Group Ltd 2000 Monarch Tower 3424 Peachtree Rd NE. Web: www.nobleinvestment.com	Atlanta	GA	30326	404-419-1000	
Norfolk Marriott Waterside 235 E Main St. Web: www.norfolkmarriott.com	Norfolk	VA	23510	757-627-4200	
Norwich Partners LLC 10 Morgan Dr Ste 1. Web: www.norwichpartners.com	Lebanon	NH	03766	603-643-2206	
Nu Hotel 85 Smith St. Web: www.nuhotelbrooklyn.com	Brooklyn	NY	11201	718-852-8585	
Nylo Hotels LLC 260 Peachtree St NW Ste 2301. Web: www.nylohotels.com	Atlanta	GA	30303	404-221-0600	
Oak Plantation Resort & Suites Condominium Association Inc 4090 Enchanted Oaks Cir. TF: 888-411-4141 ■ Web: www.oakplantationresort.com	Kissimmee	FL	34741	888-411-4141	
Oceanfront Lodging Inc 305 N First St. Web: www.bestwesternjacksonvillebeach.com	Jacksonville Beach	FL	32250	904-249-4949	
Oceano Hotel & Spa Half Moon Bay Harbor 280 Capistrano Rd. Web: www.oceanohalfmoonbay.com	Half Moon Bay	CA	94019	650-726-5400	
Omni Hotels Select Guest Loyalty Program 11819 Miami St Third Fl. TF Cust Svc: 800-843-6664 ■ Web: omnihotels.com/loyalty	Omaha	NE	68164	800-843-6664	
OTO Development LLC 100 Dunbar St Ste 402. Web: www.otodevelopment.com	Spartanburg	SC	29306	864-596-8930	
Overland Park Convention Center Hotel 6100 College Blvd. Web: www.opconventioncenter.com	Overland Park	KS	66211	913-234-2100	
Pacific Plaza Hotels Inc 1000 Marina Village Pkwy Ste 100. Web: www.pacificplazahotels.com	Alameda	CA	94501	510-832-6868	
Paramount Hospitality Management LLC 12562 International Dr. Web: www.paramounthospitality.com	Orlando	FL	32821	321-329-4054	
Parke Hotel & Conference Center 1413 Leslie Dr. Web: www.parkehotel.com	Bloomington	IL	61704	309-662-4300	
Perry Group International One Market Plz Ste 3500. Web: www.perrygroup.com	San Francisco	CA	94105	415-434-0135	
Pharos Hospitality LLC 320 S Tryon St Ste 202. Web: www.pharoshospitality.com	Charlotte	NC	28202	704-333-1818	
Plaza Hotel, The 5th Ave at Central Park S. TF: 888-850-0909 ■ Web: www.theplazany.com	New York	NY	10019	212-759-3000	
Ponderosa Motor Inn 1206 Trans Canada Hwy. Web: www.ponderosamotorinn.bc.ca	Golden	BC	V0A1H0	250-344-2205	
Prince Preferred Guest Program 100 Holomoana St. *Fax Area Code: 808 ■ TF: 800-774-6234 ■ Web: www.princepreferred.com	Honolulu	HI	96815	800-774-6234	943-4158*
Pueblo Bonito Hotels & Resorts 4350 La Jolla Village Dr. Web: www.pueblobonito.com	San Diego	CA	92122	858-642-2050	
Purple Sage Motel 1501 E Coliseum Dr. TF: 800-388-8255 ■ Web: www.placestostay.com	Snyder	TX	79549	325-573-5491	573-9027
Pyramid Hotel Group LLC One Post Office Sq Ste 3100. Web: www.pyramidadvisors.com	Boston	MA	02109	617-412-2800	
Raintree Resorts Management Company LLC PO Box 350. Web: www.tetonclub.com	Teton Village	WY	83025	307-734-9777	
Ramada Inn Airport 2275 Marina Mile Blvd STATE Rd 84. Web: www.ramadainnairport.com	Fort Lauderdale	FL	33312	954-584-4000	
Ramada Plaza Beach Resort 1500 Miracle Strip Pkwy Se. Web: www.ramadafwb.com	Fort Walton Beach	FL	32548	850-243-9161	
Red Lion Hotel 621 21St St. Web: www.redlionlewiston.com	Lewiston	ID	83501	208-799-1000	
Redbury Hotel, The 1717 Vine St. Web: theredbury.com	Los Angeles	CA	90028	323-962-1717	
Resorts of the Canadian Rockies Inc 1505 17th Ave SW. Web: www.skircr.com	Calgary	AB	T2T0E2	403-254-7669	
Rim Hospitality 3990 Westerly Pl Ste 120. Web: www.rimcorp.net	Newport Beach	CA	92660	949-783-2500	
Rocky Gap Lodge Inc 16701 Lakeview Rd NE Flintstone. Web: www.rockygapresort.com	Cumberland	MD	21530	301-784-8400	
Roedel Companies LLC 1134 Gibbons Hwy. Web: www.roedelcompanies.com	Wilton	NH	03086	603-654-2040	
Rosemont Suites 181 W Town St. Web: www.whghotels.com	Norwich	CT	06360	860-889-2671	
Royal St Charles Hotel LLC 135 Saint Charles Ave. Web: www.royalsaintcharles.com	New Orleans	LA	70130	504-587-3700	
Sainte Claire Hotel, The 302 S Market St. Web: www.thesainteclaire.com	San Jose	CA	95113	408-295-2000	
San Antonio 2000 Ltd 123 Losoya. Web: sanantonioregency.hyatt.com	San Antonio	TX	78205	210-222-1234	
San Jose Airport Hotel LLC 1740 N First St. Web: www.sjcairporthotel.com	San Jose	CA	95112	408-793-3300	
Sand Pearl Resort LLC 500 Mandalay Ave. Web: www.sandpearl.com	Clearwater Beach	FL	33767	727-441-2425	
Sandals Life Style 4950 SW 72nd Ave. *Fax Area Code: 305 ■ TF: 888-726-3257 ■ Web: sandals.com/ssg/	Miami	FL	33155	876-952-5510	667-8996*
Santa Maria Hostel 7807 Long Point Rd Ste 375. Web: www.santamariahostel.org	Houston	TX	77055	281-657-0898	
Saskatoon Inn Hotel & Conference Centre 2002 Airport Dr. Web: www.saskatooninn.com	Saskatoon	SK	S7L6M4	306-242-1440	
Sea Breeze Ocean View Motel, The 323 State Hwy 3. Web: www.seabreeze.us	Bar Harbor	ME	04609	207-288-3565	
Seattle Marriott Waterfront Hotel 2100 Alaskan Way. Web: www.gowestmarriott.com	Seattle	WA	98121	206-443-5000	
Seldovia Native Association Inc 700 E Dimond Blvd. Web: www.dimondcenterhotel.com	Anchorage	AK	99515	907-868-8006	
Seven Crown Resorts Inc PO Box 16247. Web: www.sevencrown.com	Irvine	CA	92623	949-588-7400	
Shamin Hotels Inc 2000 Ware Bottom Spring Rd. Web: www.shaminhotels.com	Chester	VA	23836	804-777-9000	
Shane's Rib Shack 9404 W Westgate Blvd #C101. Web: www.shanesribshack.com	Glendale	AZ	85305	623-877-7427	
Sheraton Atlanta 165 Courtland St Ne. Web: www.sheratonatlantahotel.com	Atlanta	GA	30303	404-659-6500	
Sheraton Columbia Hotel 10207 Wincopin Cir. Web: www.sheratoncolumbia.com	Columbia	MD	21044	410-730-3900	
Sheraton Crescent Hotel 2620 W Dunlap Ave. Web: www.sheratoncrescent.com	Phoenix	AZ	85021	602-943-8200	
Sheraton Iowa City Hotel 210 S Dubuque St. Web: www.sheratoniowacity.com	Iowa City	IA	52240	319-337-4058	

Phone | Fax

Sheraton Music City Hotel (Nashville Tenn)
777 McGavock Pk — Nashville TN 37214 — 615-885-2200
Web: www.sheratonmusiccity.com

Sheraton Nashville Downtown Hotel
623 Union St — Nashville TN 37219 — 615-259-2000
Web: www.sheratonnashvilledowntown.com

Sheraton Oklahoma City Hotel
One N Broadway — Oklahoma City OK 73102 — 405-235-2780
Web: www.sheratonokc.com

Sheraton Premiere at Tysons Corner
8661 Leesburg Pk — Tysons VA 22182 — 703-448-1234
Web: www.sheratontysonscorner.com

Sheraton Universal Hotel
333 Universal Hollywood Dr — Universal City CA 91608 — 818-980-1212
Web: www.sheratonuniversal.com

Silver Lake Resort Owners Association Inc
7751 Black Lk Rd — Kissimmee FL 34747 — 407-397-2828
Web: www.takeme2orlando.com

Sky Lodge, The 201 Heber Ave Main St — Park City UT 84068 — 435-658-2500
Web: www.theskylodge.com

Spectra Co 2510 Supply St — Pomona CA 91767 — 909-599-0760
Web: www.spectracompany.com

Sree Hotels LLC
Palladium at Piper Glen 5113 Piper Sta Dr
Ste 300 — Charlotte NC 28277 — 704-364-6008
Web: www.sree.com

St Anthony Riverwalk Wyndham Hotel, The
300 E Travis St — San Antonio TX 78205 — 210-227-4392
Web: www.thestanthonyhotel.com

Starwood Hotels Preferred Guest Program
111 Westchester Ave — White Plains NY 10604 — 512-834-2426
TF: 888-625-4988 ■ *Web:* www.starwoodhotels.com

Sterling Hotel Dallas 1055 Regal Row — Dallas TX 75247 — 214-634-8550

Stevens Pass Mountain Resort LLC
Summit Stevens Pass US Hwy 2 — Skykomish WA 98288 — 206-812-4510
Web: www.stevenspass.com

Stillman Development International LLC
505 Park Ave 17th Fl — New York NY 10022 — 212-686-2400
Web: www.stillmandevelopment.com

Stonebridge McWhinney LLC
9100 E Panorama Dr Ste 300 — Englewood CO 80112 — 303-785-3100
Web: www.stonebridgecompanies.com

Summit Hospitality Group Ltd
3141 John Humphries Wynd Ste 200 — Raleigh NC 27612 — 919-787-5100
Web: www.summithospitality.com

Sunshine Village Corp
Calgary Snow Central 1037 11th Ave SW — Calgary AB T2R0G1 — 403-705-4000
Web: www.skibanff.com

Sunstream Hotels & Resorts
6231 Estero Blvd — Fort Myers Beach FL 33931 — 239-765-4111
Web: www.sunstream.com

Swissotel Management (USA) LLC
323 E Wacker Dr — Chicago IL 60601 — 312-565-0565
Web: www.swissotel.com

Sybaris Clubs International Inc
2430 E Rand Rd — Arlington Heights IL 60004 — 847-637-3000
Web: www.sybaris.com

T Bar m Inc 2549 W State Hwy 46 — New Braunfels TX 78132 — 830-625-7738
Web: www.tbarm.com

T2 Development LLC
620 Newport Ctr Dr 14th Fl — Newport Beach CA 92660 — 949-610-8200
Web: www.t2dev.com

Tahoe Biltmore Lodge & Casino PO Box 115 — Crystal Bay NV 89402 — 775-831-0660
Web: www.tahoebiltmore.com

Terranea Resort & Spa
6610 Palos Verdes Dr S — Rancho Palos Verdes CA 90275 — 310-265-2800
Web: www.terranea.com

Tramz Hotels LLC 776 Mountain Blvd Ste 200 — Watchung NJ 07069 — 908-753-7400
Web: www.tramzhotels.com

Trust Hospitality LLC
806 Douglas Rd 4th Fl — Coral Gables FL 33134 — 305-537-7040
Web: www.trusthospitality.com

TRYP Hotels Worldwide Inc
395 Rue De La Couronne — Quebec City QC G1K7X4 — 418-647-2611
Web: www.hotelpur.com

Turf Hotels Inc 792 Watervliet Shaker Rd — Latham NY 12110 — 518-786-0976
Web: www.turfhotels.com

Twin Pine Casino 22223 Hwy 29 — Middletown CA 95461 — 707-987-0197 — 987-0375
Web: twinpine.com

UCF Hotel Venture 6800 Lakewood Plz Dr — Orlando FL 32819 — 407-503-9000
Web: www.ucfalumni.com

Ultima Hospitality LLC
30 S Wacker Dr Ste 3600 — Chicago IL 60606 — 312-948-4500
Web: www.ultimahospitality.com

Union Station Hotel 1001 Broadway — Nashville TN 37203 — 615-726-1001
Web: www.unionstationhotelnashville.com

Vacationer RV Resort 1581 East Main St — El Cajon CA 92021 — 619-442-4865
Web: www.vacationerrv.com

Value Place LLC 8621 E 21st St N Ste 250 — Wichita KS 67206 — 316-631-1370
Web: www.valueplace.com

Vantage Hospitality Group Inc
3300 N University Dr — Coral Springs FL 33065 — 954-575-2668
Web: www.vantagehospitality.com

Virgin River Casino Corp 100 Pioneer Blvd — Mesquite NV 89027 — 702-346-7777
Web: www.virginriver.com

W New York- Union Square 201 Park Ave S — New York NY 10003 — 212-253-9119
Web: www.wnewyorkunionsquare.com

Wampanoag Tribe of Gay Head Aquinnah
20 Black Brook Rd — Aquinnah MA 02535 — 508-645-9265
Web: www.wampanoagtribe.net

Warner Center Marriott Woodland Hills
21850 Oxnard St — Woodland Hills CA 91367 — 818-887-4800
Web: www.warnercentermarriott.com

Washington Jefferson LLC 318 W 51st St — New York NY 10019 — 212-246-7550
Web: www.wjhotel.com

Waterfront Place Hotel Two Waterfront Pl — Morgantown WV 26501 — 304-296-1700
Web: www.waterfrontplacehotel.com

Wedmore Place LLC 5810 Wessex Hundred — Williamsburg VA 23185 — 866-933-6673
TF: 866-933-6673 ■ *Web:* www.wedmoreplace.com

Wellesley Inn & Suites 1377 Virginia Ave — Atlanta GA 30344 — 404-762-5111
Web: www.wellesleyinnatlanta.com

Western Camp Services Ltd 7668 - 69 St — Edmonton AB T6B2J7 — 780-468-1568 — 468-1948
Web: www.westerncampservices.com

Westin Atlanta Airport, The 4736 Best Rd — Atlanta GA 30337 — 404-762-7676
Web: www.westinatlantaairport.com

Westin Atlanta Perimeter North, The
Seven Concourse Pkwy — Atlanta GA 30328 — 770-395-3900
Web: www.westinatlantanorth.com

Westin Chicago River North, The
320 N Dearborn St — Chicago IL 60654 — 312-744-1900
Web: www.westinchicago.com

Westin Governor Morris Hotel, The
Two Whippany Rd — Morristown NJ 07960 — 973-539-7300
Web: www.westingovernormorris.com

Westin Long Beach, The 333 E Ocean Blvd — Long Beach CA 90802 — 562-436-3000
Web: westinlb.com

Westin Michigan Avenue Hotel
909 N Michigan Ave — Chicago IL 60611 — 312-943-7200
Web: www.thewestinmichiganavenue.com

Westin O'Hare, The 6100 N River Rd — Rosemont IL 60018 — 847-698-6000
Web: www.westinohare.com

Westin Reston Heights, The
11750 Sunrise Vly Dr — Reston VA 20191 — 703-391-9000
Web: www.westinreston.com

Westin San Diego Gaslamp Quarter, The
910 Broadway Cir — San Diego CA 92101 — 619-239-2200
Web: www.westingaslamp.com

Westin Westminster Hotel, The
10600 Westminster Blvd — Westminster CO 80020 — 303-410-5000
Web: www.westindenverboulder.com

Westminster Hotel LLC
550 W Mount Pleasant Ave — Livingston NJ 07039 — 973-533-0600
Web: www.westminsterhotel.net

Whiteface Lodge, The
Seven Whiteface Inn Ln — Lake Placid NY 12946 — 518-523-0500
Web: www.thewhitefacelodge.com

Wilderness Hotel & Resort Inc
511 E Adams St — Wisconsin Dells WI 53965 — 608-253-9729
Web: www.wildernessresort.com

Wyndham ByRequest Program PO Box 4090 — Aberdeen SD 57401 — 800-996-3426
TF: 800-996-3426 ■ *Web:* www.wyndham.com

YOTEL 570 Tenth Ave Times Sq — New York NY 10036 — 646-449-7700
Web: www.yotelnewyork.com

382 HOTELS & HOTEL COMPANIES

SEE ALSO Casino Companies p. 1904; Corporate Housing p. 2167; Hotel Reservations Services p. 2524; Hotels - Conference Center p. 2525; Hotels - Frequent Stay Programs p. 2526; Resorts & Resort Companies p. 3058

Phone | Fax

1859 Historic Hotels Ltd PO Box 59 — Galveston TX 77553 — 409-763-8536 — 763-5304
Web: www.1859historichotels.com

1886 Crescent Hotel & Spa
75 Prospect Ave — Eureka Springs AR 72632 — 479-253-9766 — 253-5296
TF: 877-342-9766 ■ *Web:* www.crescent-hotel.com

21c Museum Hotel 700 W Main St — Louisville KY 40202 — 502-217-6300 — 578-6601*
**Fax Area Code:* 513 ■ *Web:* www.21chotel.com

35th Street Hotel Corp 45 W 35th St — New York NY 10001 — 212-947-2500
Web: www.hotelmetronyc.com

500 West Hotel 500 W Broadway — San Diego CA 92101 — 619-234-5252 — 234-5272
Web: www.500westhotelsd.com

70 Park Avenue Hotel 70 Pk Ave at 38th St — New York NY 10016 — 212-973-2400 — 973-2401
TF: 877-707-2752 ■ *Web:* www.70parkave.com

A La Carte Event Pavilion Ltd
4050 Dana Shores Dr — Tampa FL 33634 — 813-831-5390
Web: www.alacarteevents.com

AAA Properties 330 W Fifth St — Chico CA 95928 — 530-895-3500
Web: aaapropertieschico.com

Academy Hotel Colorado Springs, The
8110 N Academy Blvd — Colorado Springs CO 80920 — 719-598-5770 — 598-5965
TF: 800-766-8524 ■ *Web:* www.theacademyhotel.com

Acadia Inn 98 Eden St — Bar Harbor ME 04609 — 207-288-3500 — 288-8428
TF: 800-638-3636 ■ *Web:* www.acadiainn.com

Acapulco Hotel & Resort
2505 S Atlantic Ave — Daytona Beach Shores FL 32118 — 386-761-2210
TF: 855-922-3224 ■ *Web:* acapulcohoteldaytona.com

Accent Inns Vancouver Airport
10551 St Edwards Dr — Richmond BC V6X3L8 — 604-273-3311 — 273-9522
TF: 800-663-0298 ■
Web: www.accentinns.com/vancouver-airport/hotel-directions

Accent Inns Vancouver-Burnaby
3777 Henning Dr — Burnaby BC V5C6N5 — 604-473-5000 — 473-5095
TF: 800-663-0298 ■ *Web:* www.accentinns.com/burnaby/hotel-amenities

Accor North America
4001 International Pkwy — Carrollton TX 75007 — 972-360-9000
Web: accor.com

Acqua Hotel 555 Redwood Hwy — Mill Valley CA 94941 — 415-380-0400 — 380-9696
TF: 888-662-9555 ■ *Web:* www.marinhotels.com

Acqualina 17875 Collins Ave — Sunny Isles Beach FL 33160 — 305-918-8000 — 918-8100
TF: 877-312-9742 ■ *Web:* www.acqualinaresort.com

Phone Fax

Adam's Mark Hotels & Resorts 120 Church St .... Buffalo NY 14202 716-845-5100
Web: www.adamsmark.com

Adams Oceanfront Resort Four Read St .... Dewey Beach DE 19971 302-227-3030
TF: 800-448-8080 ■ *Web:* www.adamsoceanfront.com

Admiral Fell Inn
888 S Broadway Historic Fell's Pt.................... Baltimore MD 21231 410-522-7377 522-0707
TF: 866-583-4162 ■ *Web:* www.harbormagic.com

Admiral on Baltimore 2 Baltimore Ave .... Rehoboth Beach DE 19971 302-227-1300
TF: 888-882-4188 ■ *Web:* www.admiralonbaltimore.com

Adolphus, The 1321 Commerce St .... Dallas TX 75202 214-742-8200 651-3588
TF: 800-221-9083 ■ *Web:* www.hoteladolphus.com

Adventureland Inn 305 34th Ave NW................. Altoona IA 50009 515-265-7321 265-3506
TF: 800-910-5382 ■ *Web:* www.adventurelandpark.com

Affina Dumont 150 E 34th St .... New York NY 10016 212-481-7600 889-8856
TF: 866-233-4642 ■ *Web:* www.affinia.com

Affinia 50 155 E 50th St .... New York NY 10022 212-751-5710 753-1468
TF: 866-246-2203 ■ *Web:* www.affinia.com

Affinia Chicago 155 E 50th St....................... New York NY 10022 212-751-5710 753-1468
TF: 866-246-2203 ■ *Web:* www.affinia.com

Affinia Gardens 215 E 64th St....................... New York NY 10065 212-355-1230 758-7858
TF: 866-233-4642 ■ *Web:* www.affinia.com

Affinia Manhattan 371 Seventh Ave .... New York NY 10001 212-563-1800 643-8028
TF: 866-246-2203 ■ *Web:* www.affinia.com

Airport Settle Inn 2620 S Packerland Dr............. Green Bay WI 54313 920-499-1900 499-1973
TF: 800-688-9052 ■ *Web:* www.settle-inn.com

Airtel Plaza Hotel 7277 Valjean Ave .... Van Nuys CA 91406 818-997-7676 785-8864
TF: 800-224-7835 ■ *Web:* www.airtelplaza.com

Ala Moana Hotel 410 Atkinson Dr .... Honolulu HI 96814 808-955-4811 944-6839
TF: 800-367-6025 ■
Web: www.outrigger.com/hotels-resorts/hawaiian-islands/oahu-waikiki/ala-moana-hotel

Alamo Inn 2203 E Commerce St .... San Antonio TX 78203 210-227-2203 222-2860
Web: alamoinnmotel.com

Albert at Bay Suite Hotel 435 Albert St................ Ottawa ON K1R7X4 613-238-8858 238-1433
TF: 800-267-6644 ■ *Web:* www.albertatbay.com

Alberta Place Suite Hotel 10049 103rd St .... Edmonton AB T5J2W7 780-423-1565 426-6260

Albion Hotel 1650 James Ave.................... Miami Beach FL 33139 305-913-1000 674-0507
TF General: 877-782-3557 ■ *Web:* www.rubellhotels.com

Alexis Hotel 1007 First Ave........................... Seattle WA 98104 206-624-4844 621-9009
TF: 866-356-8894 ■ *Web:* www.alexishotel.com

Algonquin Hotel 59 W 44th St...................... New York NY 10036 212-840-6800 944-1419
Web: www.thealgonquin.net

Alliance Hospitality Inc
600 Enterprise Dr .... Lewis Center OH 43035 614-846-6600
Web: www.alliancehospitalityinc.com

Alpenhof Lodge
3255 W Village Dr PO Box 288................... Teton Village WY 83025 307-733-3242
TF: 800-732-3244 ■ *Web:* alpenhoflodgereservations.com

Ambassador Hotel 3100 I-40 W .... Amarillo TX 79102 806-358-6161
Web: ambassador-amarillo-hotel.com

Ambrosia House Tropical Lodging
622 Fleming St.................................. Key West FL 33040 305-296-9838 296-2425
TF: 800-535-9838 ■ *Web:* www.ambrosiakeywest.com

America's Best Franchising Inc
50 Glenlake Pkwy Ste 350 .... Atlanta GA 30328 770-393-2662
Web: Website Not Working
America's Best Inns & Suites
50 Glen Lake Pkwy NE Ste 350 .... Atlanta GA 30328 770-393-2662 393-2480
TF: 800-237-8466 ■ *Web:* www.americasbestinn.com

American Liberty Hospitality Inc
10700 Richmond Ave Ste 120 .... Houston TX 77042 713-977-5556
Web: www.amliberty.com

AmericInn International LLC 250 Lake Dr E........ Chanhassen MN 55317 952-294-5000 294-5001
TF Resv: 800-396-5007 ■ *Web:* www.americinn.com

Ameristar Casino & Hotel
3200 N Ameristar Dr........................... Kansas City MO 64161 816-414-7000 *
**Fax:* Mktg ■ *TF:* 888-777-8700 ■ *Web:* www.ameristar.com

Ameristar Casino Hotel Council Bluffs
2200 River Rd................................ Council Bluffs IA 51501 712-328-8888
TF: 866-667-3386 ■ *Web:* www.ameristar.com

Ameritel Inn Boise Towne Square
7965 W Emerald St.................................. Boise ID 83704 208-378-7000 378-7040
TF: 800-600-6001 ■ *Web:* www.ameritelinns.com

Ameritel Inn Pocatello
1440 Pocatello Bench Rd .... Pocatello ID 83201 208-234-7500 234-0000
TF: 800-600-6001 ■ *Web:* www.ameritelinns.com

Amsterdam Hospitality
888 Seventh Ave 20th Fl......................... New York NY 10019 212-292-3600 292-7495

Amway Grand Plaza Hotel
187 Monroe Ave NW........................... Grand Rapids MI 49503 616-774-2000 776-6489
TF: 800-253-3590 ■ *Web:* www.amwaygrand.com

Anaheim Plaza Hotel & Suites
1700 S Harbor Blvd .... Anaheim CA 92802 714-772-5900 772-8386
TF: 800-631-4144 ■ *Web:* www.anaheimplazahotel.com

Anchor-In One S St................................ Hyannis MA 02601 508-775-0357 775-1313
Web: anchorin.com

Anchorage Uptown Suites 235 E 2nd Court .... Anchorage AK 99501 907-279-4232
Web: www.anchorageuptownsuites.com

Andaluz 125 Second St NW.................. Albuquerque NM 87102 505-242-9090
TF: 877-987-9090 ■ *Web:* www.hotelandaluz.com

Andaz San Diego 600 F St......................... San Diego CA 92101 619-849-1234 531-7955
TF: 877-489-4489 ■
Web: sandiego.andaz.hyatt.com/hyatt/hotels/index.jsp?null

Andrews Hotel 624 Post St .... San Francisco CA 94109 415-563-6877 928-6919
TF: 800-926-3739 ■ *Web:* www.andrewshotel.com

Angler's Inn 265 N Millward........................ Jackson WY 83001 307-733-3682 733-8662
TF: 800-867-4667 ■ *Web:* anglersinn.net

Antler Inn 43 W Pearl St PO Box 575 .... Jackson WY 83001 307-733-2535
TF: 800-483-8667 ■ *Web:* www.townsquareinns.com

Apple Tree Inn 9508 N Div St....................... Spokane WA 99218 509-466-3020 467-4377
TF: 800-323-5796 ■ *Web:* www.appletreeinnmotel.com

Applewood Manor Inn 62 Cumberland Cir.......... Asheville NC 28801 828-254-2244 254-0899
TF: 800-442-2197 ■ *Web:* www.applewoodmanor.com

Phone Fax

Aqua Bamboo 2425 Kuhio Ave .... Honolulu HI 96815 808-922-7777 943-8555
TF: 855-747-0754 ■ *Web:* www.aquaresorts.com

Aqua Hospitality Corp 445 Seaside Ave .... Honolulu HI 96815 808-923-2345 943-8555
TF: 855-747-0755 ■ *Web:* www.aquaresorts.com

Aqua Hotel & Lounge 1530 Collins Ave .... Miami Beach FL 33139 305-538-4361 673-8109
Web: www.aquamiami.com

Aqua Waikiki Wave 2299 Kuhio Ave................. Honolulu HI 96815 808-922-1262 943-8555
TF: 855-747-0754 ■ *Web:* www.aquaresorts.com

ARC the Hotel Ottawa 140 Slater St .... Ottawa ON K1P5H6 613-238-2888 235-8421
TF: 800-699-2516 ■ *Web:* www.arcthehotel.com

Arena Hotel 817 The Alameda.......................... San Jose CA 95126 408-294-6500 294-6585
TF: 800-954-6835 ■ *Web:* www.pacifichotels.com

Argonaut Hotel 495 Jefferson St................ San Francisco CA 94109 415-563-0800 563-2800
TF: 866-415-0704 ■ *Web:* www.argonauthotel.com

Arizona Charlie's Boulder Casino & Hotel
4575 Boulder Hwy .... Las Vegas NV 89121 702-951-5800
TF: 888-236-9066 ■ *Web:* www.arizonacharliesboulder.com

Arizona Charlie's Decatur Casino & Hotel
740 S Decatur Blvd.............................. Las Vegas NV 89107 702-258-5200 258-5192
TF: 888-236-8645 ■ *Web:* www.arizonacharliesdecatur.com

Arizona Inn 2200 E Elm St .... Tucson AZ 85719 520-325-1541 881-5830
TF: 800-933-1093 ■ *Web:* arizonainn.com

Asano of Hawaii Corp 3159 Koapaka St Ste D .... Honolulu HI 96819 808-836-3939

Ashland Springs Hotel 212 E Main St .... Ashland OR 97520 541-488-1700 488-0240
TF: 888-795-4545 ■ *Web:* www.ashlandspringshotel.com

Ashmore Inn & Suites 4019 S Loop 289 .... Lubbock TX 79423 806-785-0060 785-6001
TF: 800-785-0061 ■ *Web:* www.ashmoreinn.com

Ashton Hotel 610 Main St .... Fort Worth TX 76102 817-332-0100 332-0110
TF: 866-327-4866 ■ *Web:* www.theashtonhotel.com

Assiniboine Gordon Inn on the Park
1975 Portage Ave................................. Winnipeg MB R3J0J9 204-888-4806 897-9870
Web: gordonhotels.com

Associated Hotels LLC
29 S La Salle St Ste 705........................... Chicago IL 60603 312-782-6008 782-2356
Web: www.associatedhotelsllc.com

Asticou Inn 15 Peabody Dr.................. Northeast Harbor ME 04662 207-276-3344 276-3373
TF: 800-258-3373 ■ *Web:* www.asticou.com

Aston Hotels & Resorts
2155 Kalakaua Ave Ste 500 .... Honolulu HI 96815 808-931-1400 931-1414
TF: 800-775-4228 ■ *Web:* www.astonhotels.com

Astor Crowne Plaza 739 Canal St............... New Orleans LA 70130 504-962-0500 962-0503
TF: 877-408-9661 ■ *Web:* www.astorneworleans.com

Astor Hotel, The 924 E Juneau Ave .... Milwaukee WI 53202 414-271-4220 271-6370
TF: 800-558-0200 ■ *Web:* astormilwaukee.com

Atheneum Suite Hotel & Conference Ctr
1000 Brush Ave .... Detroit MI 48226 313-962-2323 962-2424
TF: 800-772-2323 ■ *Web:* www.atheneumsuites.com

Atlantic Eyrie Lodge Six Norman Rd .... Bar Harbor ME 04609 800-422-2883 288-8500*
**Fax Area Code:* 207 ■ *TF:* 800-422-2883 ■ *Web:* www.atlanticeyrielodge.com

Atlantic Palace Suites Hotel
1507 Boardwalk .... Atlantic City NJ 08401 609-344-1200 345-0733
Web: www.atlanticpalacesuites.com

Atlantic Sands Hotel 101 N Boardwalk......... Rehoboth Beach DE 19971 302-227-2511 227-9476
TF: 800-422-0600 ■ *Web:* www.atlanticsandshotel.com

Atlantic, The
601 N Ft Lauderdale Beach Blvd................ Fort Lauderdale FL 33304 954-567-8020 567-8040
Web: www.atlantichotelfl.com

Atrium Holding Co
6900 E Camelback Rd Ste 607 .... Scottsdale AZ 85251 480-222-6035

Atrium Hotel 18700 MacArthur Blvd...................... Irvine CA 92612 949-833-2770 757-1228
TF: 800-854-3012 ■ *Web:* www.atriumhotel.com

Auberge du Soleil 180 Rutherford Hill Rd........... Rutherford CA 94573 707-963-1211 963-8764
TF: 800-348-5406 ■ *Web:* www.aubergedusoleil.com

Auberge du Vieux-Port
97 Rue de la Commune E .... Montreal QC H2Y1J1 514-876-0081 876-8923
TF: 888-660-7678 ■ *Web:* www.aubergeduvieuxport.com

Auberge Saint-Antoine Eight rue Saint-Antoine......... Quebec QC G1K4C9 418-692-2211 692-1177
TF: 888-692-2211 ■ *Web:* www.saint-antoine.com

Aurora Inn 68 Mt Desert St Rt 3 .... Bar Harbor ME 04609 207-288-3771
Web: www.aurorainn.com

Austin Hotel & Spa 305 Malvern Ave .... Hot Springs AR 71901 501-623-6600 624-7160
TF: 877-623-6697 ■ *Web:* www.theaustinhotel.com

Avalon Beverly Hills
9400 W Olympic Blvd.......................... Beverly Hills CA 90212 310-277-5221 277-4928
TF: 800-670-6183 ■ *Web:* www.viceroyhotelgroup.com

Avalon Corporate Furnished Apartments
1553 Empire Blvd................................ Webster NY 14580 585-671-4421 671-9771
TF: 800-934-9763 ■ *Web:* www.rochesterfurnished.com

Avalon Hotel 16 W Tenth St .... Erie PA 16501 814-459-2220 459-2322
TF: 888-295-4949 ■ *Web:* www.avalonerie.com

Avalon Motel Corp 1529 Broadway.................. Saugus MA 01906 781-233-4200
Web: avalon-motel.com

Avendra LLC 702 King Farm Blvd Ste 600 .... Rockville MD 20850 301-825-0500 825-0497
Web: www.avendra.com

Avenue Inn & Spa 33 Wilmington Ave.......... Rehoboth Beach DE 19971 800-433-5870
TF: 800-433-5870 ■ *Web:* www.avenueinn.com

Avenue Plaza Resort 2111 St Charles Ave......... New Orleans LA 70130 504-566-1212 525-6899
TF: 800-614-8685 ■ *Web:* www.avenueplazaresort.com

Ayres Hotel Anaheim 2550 E Katella Ave .... Anaheim CA 92806 714-634-2106
TF: 800-595-5692 ■ *Web:* www.ayreshotels.com

Bahama House
2001 S Atlantic Ave.................... Daytona Beach Shores FL 32118 888-687-1894 248-0991*
**Fax Area Code:* 386 ■ *TF:* 888-687-1894 ■ *Web:* www.daytonabahamahouse.com

Balance Rock Inn 21 Albert Meadow .... Bar Harbor ME 04609 207-288-2610 288-5534
TF: 800-753-0494 ■ *Web:* www.balancerockinn.com

Balboa Park Inn 3402 Pk Blvd..................... San Diego CA 92103 619-298-0823 294-8070
TF: 800-938-8181 ■ *Web:* www.balboaparkinn.com

Bally's Casino Tunica
1450 Bally's Blvd .... Robinsonville MS 38664 866-422-5597
TF: 866-422-5597 ■ *Web:* www.ballystunica.com

Balmoral Inn 120 Balmoral Ave .... Biloxi MS 39531 228-388-6776 388-5450
TF: 800-393-9131 ■ *Web:* www.balmoralinn.com

Name / Address	City	State	ZIP	Phone	Fax
Bar Harbor Hotel-Bluenose Inn 90 Eden St. TF: 800-445-4077 ■ Web: barharborhotel.com	Bar Harbor	ME	04609	207-288-3348	288-2183
Barclay Hotel 1348 Robson St. Web: www.barclayhotel.com	Vancouver	BC	V5E1C5	604-688-8850	688-2534
Barnstead Inn 349 Bonnet St. TF: 800-331-1619 ■ Web: www.barnsteadinn.com	Manchester Center	VT	05255	802-362-1619	362-0688
Baronne Plaza Hotel 201 Baronne St TF: 888-756-0083 ■ Web: www.baronneplaza.com	New Orleans	LA	70112	504-522-0083	522-0053
Barrington Hotel & Suites 263 Shepherd of the Hills Expy. TF: 800-760-8866 ■ Web: www.barringtonhotel.com	Branson	MO	65616	417-334-8866	336-2585
Bavarian Inn 855 N Fifth St Web: www.bavarianinnsd.com	Custer	SD	57730	605-673-2802	673-4777
Bay Club Hotel & Marina 2131 Shelter Island Dr TF: 800-672-0800 ■ Web: www.bayclubhotel.com	San Diego	CA	92106	619-224-8888	225-1604
Bay Harbor Inn & Suites *Daddy O Miami* 9660 E Bay Harbor Dr. Web: www.daddyohotel.com/miami	Bay Harbor Island	FL	33154	305-868-4141	675-6488
Bay Park Hotel 1425 Munras Ave. TF Resv: 800-338-3564 ■ Web: www.bayparkhotel.com	Monterey	CA	93940	831-649-1020	373-4258
Bayfront Inn 138 Avenida Menendez TF: 800-558-3455 ■ Web: www.bayfrontinn.com	Saint Augustine	FL	32084	904-824-1681	829-8721
Baymont Inn 4025 McDonald Dr TF: 800-337-0550 ■ Web: www.baymontinns.com	Dubuque	IA	52003	563-582-3752	
Beach Haven Inn 4740 Mission Blvd. TF: 800-831-6323 ■ Web: www.beachhaveninn.com	San Diego	CA	92109	858-272-3812	272-3532
Beach Plaza - Ft Lauderdale 625 N Ft Lauderdale Beach Blvd. Web: 3palmshotels.com	Fort Lauderdale	FL	33304	954-566-7631	
Beacher's Lodge 6970 A1A S TF: 800-527-8849 ■ Web: www.beacherslodge.com	Saint Augustine	FL	32080	904-471-8849	471-3002
Beacon Hotel 720 Ocean Dr. TF: 877-674-8200 ■ Web: www.beaconsouthbeach.com	Miami Beach	FL	33139	305-674-8200	
Beacon Hotel & Corporate Quarters 1615 Rhode Island Ave NW TF: 800-823-1700 ■ Web: www.openhospitality.com	Washington	DC	20036	202-296-2100	
Beaver Creek Lodge 26 Avon Dale Ln. TF: 800-525-7280 ■ Web: www.beavercreeklodge.net	Beaver Creek	CO	81620	970-845-9800	845-8242
Beecher Hill LLC 9991 Beecher Hill Rd Web: beecherhill.com	Peshastin	WA	98847	509-548-0559	
Beechwood Hotel 363 Plantation St TF: 800-344-2589 ■ Web: www.beechwoodhotel.com	Worcester	MA	01605	508-754-5789	752-2060
Beekman Tower Hotel 606 W 42nd St 3rd Fl. Web: silversuitesresidences.com	New York	NY	10036	212-695-3400	
Bell Tower Hotel 300 S Thayer St. TF: 800-562-3559 ■ Web: www.belltowerhotel.com	Ann Arbor	MI	48104	734-769-3010	769-4339
Bell Tower Inn 1235 Second St SW TF: 800-448-7583 ■ Web: www.rochesterlodging.com	Rochester	MN	55902	507-289-2233	289-2233
Bellasera Hotel 221 Ninth St S TF: 855-990-0301 ■ Web: www.bellaseranaples.com	Naples	FL	34102	239-649-7333	649-6233
Bellevue Club Hotel 11200 SE Sixth St TF: 800-579-1110 ■ Web: www.bellevueclub.com	Bellevue	WA	98004	425-454-4424	688-3101
Bellmoor, The Six Christian St. TF: 800-425-2355 ■ Web: www.thebellmoor.com	Rehoboth Beach	DE	19971	302-227-5800	227-0323
Belvedere Hotel 319 W 48th St. TF: 800-492-8122 ■ Web: www.newyorkhotel.com	New York	NY	10036	212-245-7000	245-4455
Ben Lomond Suites LLC 2510 Washington Blvd TF: 877-627-1900 ■ Web: benlomondsuites.com	Ogden	UT	84401	801-627-1900	394-5342
Benchmark Hospitality International Four Waterway Sq Ste 300 Web: www.benchmarkresortsandhotels.com	The Woodlands	TX	77380	281-367-5757	367-1407
Bendel Executive Suites 213 Bendel Rd Web: www.bendelexec.com	Lafayette	LA	70503	337-261-0604	233-4296
Benjamin, The 125 E 50th St. TF: 866-233-4642 ■ Web: www.thebenjamin.com	New York	NY	10022	212-715-2500	715-2525
Bennett Enterprises Inc PO Box 670. Web: www.bennett-enterprises.com	Perrysburg	OH	43552	419-874-1933	874-0198
Benson, The 309 SW Broadway TF: 800-663-1144 ■ Web: www.coasthotels.com	Portland	OR	97205	503-228-2000	471-3920
Bentley Hotel New York 500 E 62nd St Web: www.hotelbentleynewyork.com	New York	NY	10065	212-644-6000	
Bergen County Community Action Program I 241 Moore St Web: www.bergencap.org	Hackensack	NJ	07601	201-968-0200	
Berkeley Hotel, The 1200 E Cary St. TF: 888-780-4422 ■ Web: www.berkeleyhotel.com	Richmond	VA	23219	804-780-1300	648-4728
Bernards Inn 27 Mine Brook Rd. TF: 888-766-0002 ■ Web: www.bernardsinn.com	Bernardsville	NJ	07924	908-766-0002	766-4604
Bernardus Lodge 415 Carmel Valley Rd TF: 800-223-2533 ■ Web: www.bernardus.com	Carmel Valley	CA	93924	831-658-3400	659-3529
Best Western Chincoteague Island 7105 Maddox Blvd TF: 800-553-6117 ■ Web: www.bestwestern.com	Chincoteague Island	VA	23336	757-336-6557	336-6558
Best Western International Inc 6201 N 24th Pkwy *Fax: Mktg ■ TF: 800-528-1234 ■ Web: www.bestwestern.com	Phoenix	AZ	85016	602-957-4200	957-5942*
Best Western Laguna Brisas Spa Hotel 1600 S Coast Hwy TF: 888-296-6834 ■ Web: www.lagunabrisas.com	Laguna Beach	CA	92651	949-497-7272	497-8306
Best Western Victorian Inn 487 Foam St TF: 800-232-4141 ■ Web: www.victorianinn.com	Monterey	CA	93940	831-373-8000	655-8174
Betsy Hotel 1440 Ocean Dr. TF: 866-792-3879 ■ Web: www.thebetsyhotel.com	Miami Beach	FL	33139	305-531-6100	531-9009
Beverly Heritage Hotel 1820 Barber Ln. Web: www.beverlyheritage.com	Milpitas	CA	95035	408-943-9080	432-8617
Beverly Hills Hotel 9641 Sunset Blvd TF: 800-283-8885 ■ Web: www.dorchestercollection.com	Beverly Hills	CA	90210	310-276-2251	887-2887
Beverly Hilton 9876 Wilshire Blvd. TF: 800-605-8896 ■ Web: www.beverlyhilton.com	Beverly Hills	CA	90210	310-274-7777	285-1313
Beverly Wilshire - A Four Seasons Hotel 9500 Wilshire Blvd TF: 800-545-4000 ■ Web: www.fourseasons.com/beverlywilshire	Beverly Hills	CA	90212	310-275-5200	274-2851
Bienville House Hotel 320 Decatur St TF: 800-535-7836 ■ Web: www.bienvillehouse.com	New Orleans	LA	70130	504-529-2345	525-6079
Bigelow Management Inc 4640 S Eastern Ave Web: budgetsuites.com	Las Vegas	NV	89119	702-456-1606	
Billings C'mon Inn Hotel 2020 Overland Ave. TF: 800-655-1170 ■ Web: www.cmoninn.com	Billings	MT	59102	406-655-1100	652-7672
Billings Hotel & Convention Ctr 1223 Mullowney Ln TF: 800-537-7286 ■ Web: www.billingshotel.net	Billings	MT	59101	406-248-7151	259-5338
Biltmore Greensboro Hotel 111 W Washington St. TF General: 800-332-0303 ■ Web: www.thebiltmoregreensboro.com	Greensboro	NC	27401	336-272-3474	275-2523
Biltmore Hotel & Suites 2151 Laurelwood Rd. TF: 800-255-9925 ■ Web: www.hotelbiltmore.com	Santa Clara	CA	95054	408-988-8411	988-0225
Biltmore Hotel Oklahoma 401 S Meridian Ave TF: 800-522-6620 ■ Web: www.biltmoreokc.com	Oklahoma City	OK	73108	405-947-7681	947-4253
Biltmore Suites 205 W Madison St. TF: 800-868-5064 ■ Web: www.biltmoresuites.com	Baltimore	MD	21201	410-728-6550	728-5829
Bismarck Expressway Suites 180 E Bismarck Expy TF: 888-774-5566 ■ Web: expresswayhotels.com	Bismarck	ND	58504	701-222-3311	222-3311
Black Swan Inn 746 E Ctr St Web: www.blackswaninn.com	Pocatello	ID	83201	208-233-3051	478-8516
Blackfoot Inn 5940 Blackfoot Trl SE TF: 800-661-1151 ■ Web: www.hotelblackfoot.com	Calgary	AB	T2H2B5	403-252-2253	252-3574
Blacktail Mountain Ski Area LLC 13990 Blacktail Mtn Rd Web: www.blacktailmountain.com	Lakeside	MT	59922	406-844-0999	
Blackwell, The 2110 Tuttle Pk Pl TF: 866-247-4003 ■ Web: www.theblackwell.com	Columbus	OH	43210	614-247-4000	247-4040
Blakely New York 136 W 55th St. TF: 800-735-0710 ■ Web: www.blakelynewyork.com	New York	NY	10019	212-245-1800	582-8332
Blantyre 16 Blantyre Rd PO Box 995. TF: 844-881-0104 ■ Web: blantyre.com	Lenox	MA	01240	413-637-3556	637-4282
Blue Horizon Hotel 1225 Robson St TF: 800-663-1333 ■ Web: www.bluehorizonhotel.com	Vancouver	BC	V6E1C3	604-688-1411	688-4461
Blue Moon Hotel 944 Collins Ave TF: 800-553-7739 ■ Web: www.bluemoonhotel.com	Miami Beach	FL	33139	305-673-2262	534-1546
Blue Parrot Inn 916 Elizabeth St. TF: 800-231-2473 ■ Web: www.blueparrotinn.com	Key West	FL	33040	305-296-0033	296-5697
Bluenose Inn & Suites 636 Bedford Hwy TF: 800-553-5339	Halifax	NS	B3M2L8	902-443-3171	
Boardwalk Plaza Hotel Two Olive Ave TF: 800-332-3224 ■ Web: www.boardwalkplaza.com	Rehoboth Beach	DE	19971	302-227-7169	227-0561
Bodega Bay Lodge 103 Coast Hwy 1. *Fax: Resv ■ TF Resv: 888-875-2250 ■ Web: www.bodegabaylodge.com	Bodega Bay	CA	94923	707-875-3525	875-2428*
Bohemian Hotel Celebration 700 Bloom St TF: 888-249-4007 ■ Web: www.celebrationhotel.com	Celebration	FL	34747	407-566-6000	566-1844
Bond Place Hotel 65 Dundas St E TF: 800-268-9390 ■ Web: bondplace.ca	Toronto	ON	M5B2G8	416-362-6061	360-6406
Boomtown Hotel Casino 300 Riverside Dr. Web: www.boomtownbossier.com	Bossier City	LA	71111	318-746-0711	226-9434
Boone Tavern Hotel of Berea College 100 S Main St. TF: 800-366-9358 ■ Web: www.boonetavernhotel.com	Berea	KY	40403	859-985-3700	985-3715
Borgata Hotel Casino & Spa 1 Borgata Way. TF: 877-786-9900 ■ Web: www.theborgata.com	Atlantic City	NJ	08401	609-317-1000	317-1039
Boston Harbor Hotel 70 Rowes Wharf. TF: 800-752-7077 ■ Web: www.bhh.com	Boston	MA	02110	617-439-7000	330-9450
Boston Marriott Copley Place 110 Huntington Ave Web: marriott.com	Boston	MA	02116	617-236-5800	
Boston Park Plaza Hotel & Towers 50 Pk Plz TF: 800-225-2008 ■ Web: www.bostonparkplaza.com	Boston	MA	02116	617-426-2000	426-5545
Boulder Mountain Lodge 91 Four Mile Canyon Rd. TF: 800-458-0882 ■ Web: www.bouldermountainlodge.com	Boulder	CO	80302	303-444-0882	541-0665
Boulder Station Hotel & Casino 4111 Boulder Hwy *Fax: Circulation Desk ■ TF: 800-683-7777 ■ Web: boulderstation.sclv.com	Las Vegas	NV	89121	702-432-7777	367-6138*
Bourbon Orleans - A Wyndham Historic Hotel 717 Orleans St TF: 866-513-9744 ■ Web: www.bourbonorleans.com	New Orleans	LA	70116	504-523-2222	571-4666
Bradley Boulder Inn 2040 16th St. Web: www.thebradleyboulder.com	Boulder	CO	80302	303-545-5200	440-6740
Bradley Inn 3063 Bristol Rd TF: 800-942-5560 ■ Web: www.bradleyinn.com	New Harbor	ME	04554	207-677-2105	677-3367
Brandywine Suites Hotel 1110 Baltimore Pk *Fax Area Code: 302 ■ Web: concordvillesuites.com	Glen Mills	PA	19342	610-358-1700	656-2459*
Brazilian Court, The 301 Australian Ave. TF: 800-552-0335 ■ Web: www.thebraziliancourt.com	Palm Beach	FL	33480	561-655-7740	655-0801
Breakers at Waikiki, The 250 Beach Walk TF: 800-426-0494 ■ Web: www.breakers-hawaii.com	Honolulu	HI	96815	808-923-3181	923-7174
Breakers Hotel & Suites 105 Second St TF: 800-441-8009 ■ Web: www.thebreakershotel.com	Rehoboth Beach	DE	19971	302-227-6688	227-2013
Breakwater Inn 1711 Glacier Ave TF: 888-586-6303 ■ Web: www.breakwaterinn.com	Juneau	AK	99801	907-586-6303	463-4820
Breckinridge Inn 2800 Breckinridge Ln Web: www.breckinridgeinn.com	Louisville	KY	40220	502-456-5050	451-1577
Brent House Hotel 1512 Jefferson Hwy. TF: 800-535-3986 ■ Web: www.brenthouse.com	New Orleans	LA	70121	504-842-4140	842-4160
Bridgewater Hotel 723 First Ave *Fax Area Code: 907 ■ TF: 800-528-4916 ■ Web: www.fountainheadhotels.com	Fairbanks	AK	99701	800-528-4916	452-6126*
Bristol Hotel 1055 First Ave TF: 800-662-4477 ■ Web: www.thebristolsandiego.com	San Diego	CA	92101	619-232-6141	232-0118

				Phone	Fax
Brookfield Suites Hotel & Convention Ctr 1200 S Moorland Rd *TF:* 800-444-6404 ■ *Web:* www.brookfieldsuiteshotel.com	Brookfield	WI	53005	262-782-2900	796-9159
Brookshire Suites 120 E Lombard St *TF:* 855-345-5033 ■ *Web:* www.brookshiresuites.com	Baltimore	MD	21202	410-625-1300	522-9602
Brookside Inn 1297 S Perry St *Web:* www.bsmc.com	Castle Rock	CO	80104	303-688-2500	
Brookstown Inn 200 Brookstown Ave *TF:* 800-845-4262 ■ *Web:* www.brookstowninn.com	Winston-Salem	NC	27101	336-725-1120	773-0147
Brookstreet Hotel 525 Legget Dr *TF:* 888-826-2220 ■ *Web:* www.brookstreethotel.com	Ottawa	ON	K2K2W2	613-271-1800	271-1850
Brown County Inn 51 State Rd 46 *TF:* 800-772-5249 ■ *Web:* www.browncountyinn.com	Nashville	IN	47448	812-988-2291	988-8312
Brown Hotel, The 335 W Broadway St *TF:* 888-387-0498 ■ *Web:* www.brownhotel.com	Louisville	KY	40202	502-583-1234	587-7006
Brown Palace Hotel 321 17th St *TF:* 800-321-2599 ■ *Web:* www.brownpalace.com	Denver	CO	80202	303-297-3111	312-5900
Brown's Wharf Inn 121 Atlantic Ave *TF:* 800-334-8110 ■ *Web:* www.brownswharfinn.com	Boothbay Harbor	ME	04538	207-633-5440	633-5440
Bryant Park Hotel 40 W 40th St *Web:* www.bryantparkhotel.com	New York	NY	10018	212-869-0100	869-4446
Buckingham Hotel 101 W 57th St *Web:* tripadvisor.com.au	New York	NY	10019	212-246-1500	262-0698
Buckrail Lodge 110 E Karns Ave PO Box 23 *Web:* www.buckraillodge.com	Jackson	WY	83001	307-733-2079	734-1663
Budget Host Inn 116 Kenyon Rd W *Web:* budgethost.com	Fort Dodge	IA	50501	515-955-8501	
Budget Host International 2307 Roosevelt Dr *TF:* 800-283-4678 ■ *Web:* www.budgethost.com	Arlington	TX	76016	817-861-6088	861-6089
Budget Suites of America 2770 N Hwy 360 *TF:* 866-877-2000 ■ *Web:* www.budgetsuites.com	Grand Prairie	TX	75050	972-647-2500	602-3549
Buena Vista Suites 8203 World Ctr Dr *TF Resv:* 800-537-7737 ■ *Web:* www.thecaribehotelsorlando.com	Orlando	FL	32821	407-239-8588	239-1401
Burnside Hotel 739 Windmill Rd *Web:* www.burnsidehotel.com	Dartmouth	NS	B3B1C1	902-468-7117	468-1770
Business Inn 180 MacLaren St *TF:* 800-363-1777 ■ *Web:* thebusinessinn.com	Ottawa	ON	K2P0L3	613-232-1121	232-8143
C'mon Inn Grand Forks 3051 32nd Ave S *TF:* 800-255-2323 ■ *Web:* www.cmoninn.com	Grand Forks	ND	58201	701-775-3320	780-8141
California Hotel & Casino 12 E Ogden Ave *TF:* 800-634-6505 ■ *Web:* www.thecal.com	Las Vegas	NV	89101	702-385-1222	388-2660
Cambridge Suites Hotel Halifax 1583 Brunswick St *TF:* 800-565-1263 ■ *Web:* www.cambridgesuiteshalifax.com	Halifax	NS	B3J3P5	902-420-0555	420-9379
Cambridge Suites Hotel Toronto 15 Richmond St E *TF:* 800-463-1990 ■ *Web:* www.cambridgesuitestoronto.com	Toronto	ON	M5C1N2	416-368-1990	601-3751
Camino Real El Paso 101 S El Paso St *Web:* www.caminoreal.com	El Paso	TX	79901	915-534-3050	534-3024
Camino Real Hotel LLC 2856 E Main St	Eagle Pass	TX	78852	830-757-8111	
Campus Inn & Suites 390 E Broadway *TF:* 800-888-6313 ■ *Web:* www.campus-inn.com	Eugene	OR	97401	541-343-3376	485-9392
Canad Inns - Club Regent Casino Hotel 1415 Regent Ave W *TF:* 888-332-2623 ■ *Web:* www.canadinns.com	Winnipeg	MB	R2C3B2	204-667-5560	667-5913
Canad Inns Fort Garry 1824 Pembina Hwy *TF:* 888-332-2623 ■ *Web:* www.canadinns.com	Winnipeg	MB	R3T2G2	204-261-7450	261-5433
Canad Inns Garden City 2100 McPhillips St *TF:* 888-332-2623 ■ *Web:* www.canadinns.com	Winnipeg	MB	R2V3T9	204-633-0024	697-3377
Canad Inns Polo Park 1405 St Matthews Ave *TF:* 888-332-2623 ■ *Web:* www.canadinns.com	Winnipeg	MB	R3G0K5	204-775-8791	783-4039
Canal Park Lodge 250 Canal Pk Dr *TF:* 800-777-8560 ■ *Web:* www.canalparklodge.com	Duluth	MN	55802	218-279-6000	279-4055
Canandaigua Inn on the Lake 770 S Main St *TF:* 800-228-2801 ■ *Web:* www.theinnonthelake.com	Canandaigua	NY	14424	585-394-7800	394-5003
Canary Hotel 31 W Carrillo *TF:* 866-999-5401 ■ *Web:* www.canarysantabarbara.com	Santa Barbara	CA	93101	805-884-0300	884-8153
Cannery Casino & Hotel, The *Cannery Casino Resorts LLC* 2121 E Craig Rd *TF:* 866-999-4899 ■ *Web:* www.cannerycasinos.com	North Las Vegas	NV	89030	702-507-5700	507-5750
Canoe Bay PO Box 28 *Web:* www.canoebay.com	Chetek	WI	54728	715-924-4594	924-2078
Cape Cod Irish Village 822 Rt 28 *Web:* www.capecod-irishvillage.com	S.Yarmouth	MA	02664	508-771-0100	
Capella Hotel Group 3384 Peachtree Rd Ste 375 *Web:* www.capellahotelgroup.com	Atlanta	GA	30326	404-842-7280	
Capital Hill Hotel & Suites 88 Albert St *TF:* 800-463-7705 ■ *Web:* www.capitalhill.com	Ottawa	ON	K1P5E9	613-235-1413	235-6047
Capital Hotel 111 W Markham St *TF:* 877-637-0037 ■ *Web:* www.capitalhotel.com/site	Little Rock	AR	72201	501-374-7474	370-7091
Capital Hotel Management LLC 548 Cabot St *Web:* www.chmhotel.com	Beverly	MA	01915	978-522-7000	
Capitol Hill Hotel 200 C St SE *Web:* capitolhillhotel-dc.com	Washington	DC	20003	202-543-6000	547-2608
Capitol Plaza Hotel & Conference Ctr 100 State St *TF:* 800-274-5252 ■ *Web:* www.capitolplaza.com	Montpelier	VT	05602	802-223-5252	229-5427
Capitol Plaza Hotel Jefferson City 415 W McCarty St *TF:* 800-338-8088 ■ *Web:* www.capitolplazajeffersoncity.com	Jefferson City	MO	65101	573-635-1234	635-4565
Capt Hirams Resort 1606 Indian River Dr *TF:* 888-447-2671 ■ *Web:* www.hirams.com	Sebastian	FL	32958	772-589-4345	
Captain Daniel Stone Inn 10 Water St *TF:* 877-573-2374 ■ *Web:* thedanielhotel.com/	Brunswick	ME	04011	207-373-1824	373-1857
Caretel Inns of America Inc 910 S Washington Ave	Royal Oak	MI	48067	248-543-7300	

				Phone	Fax
Caribbean Cove Hotel & Water Park 3850 Depauw Blvd *Web:* www.caribbeancovewaterpark.com	Indianapolis	IN	46268	317-872-9790	
Caribe Royale Orlando All-Suites Hotel & Convention Ctr 8101 World Ctr Dr *TF Resv:* 800-823-8300 ■ *Web:* www.thecaribehotelsorlando.com	Orlando	FL	32821	407-238-8000	238-8050
Carlson *Radisson Hotels & Resorts* 701 Carlson Pkwy *TF:* 800-333-3333 ■ *Web:* www.carlson.com	Minnetonka	MN	55305	763-212-5000	
Carlson Hotels Worldwide 701 Carlson Pkwy *Web:* www.carlsonhotels.com	Minneapolis	MN	55305	763-212-5000	
Country Inns & Suites by Carlson 11340 Blondo St Ste 100 *TF:* 800-600-7275 ■ *Web:* www.countryinns.com	Omaha	NE	68164	800-600-7275	
Carlton Arms 160 E 25th St *Web:* www.carltonarms.com	New York	NY	10010	212-679-0680	
Carlton on Madison Ave 88 Madison Ave *TF Resv:* 800-601-8500 ■ *Web:* www.carltonhotelny.com	New York	NY	10016	212-532-4100	696-9758
Carlyle Hotel, The 1731 New Hampshire Ave NW *TF:* 877-301-0019 ■ *Web:* www.carlylehoteldc.com	Washington	DC	20009	202-234-3200	
Carmel River Inn 26600 Oliver Rd *TF:* 800-882-8142 ■ *Web:* www.carmelriverinn.com	Carmel	CA	93923	831-624-1575	624-0290
Carnegie Hotel 1216 W State of Franklin Rd *TF:* 866-757-8277 ■ *Web:* www.carnegiehotel.com	Johnson City	TN	37604	423-979-6400	979-6424
Carolina Inn 211 Pittsboro St *TF:* 800-962-8519 ■ *Web:* www.carolinainn.com	Chapel Hill	NC	27516	919-933-2001	962-3400
Carousel Beachfront Hotel & Suites 11700 Coastal Hwy *TF:* 800-641-0011 ■ *Web:* www.carouselhotel.com	Ocean City	MD	21842	410-524-1000	524-7766
Carousel Inn & Suites 1530 S Harbor Blvd *TF:* 800-854-6767 ■ *Web:* www.carouselinnandsuites.com	Anaheim	CA	92802	714-758-0444	772-9960
Carroll Properties Partnership 12734 Kenwood Ln Ste 35 *Web:* carroll-properties.com	Fort Myers	FL	33907	239-278-5900	
Cartier Place Suite Hotel 180 Cooper St *TF:* 800-236-8399 ■ *Web:* www.suitedreams.com	Ottawa	ON	K2P2L5	613-236-5000	238-3842
Casa Blanca Motor Lodge Ltd 2728 Victoria Ave	Brandon	MB	R7B2V9	204-728-1500	
Casa Grande Suite Hotel 834 Ocean Dr *Web:* www.casagrandesuitehotel.com	Miami Beach	FL	33139	305-672-7003	673-3669
Casa Madrona Hotel 801 Bridgeway *TF General:* 800-288-0502 ■ *Web:* www.casamadrona.com	Sausalito	CA	94965	415-332-0502	331-3125
Casa Monica Hotel 95 Cordova St *TF Help Line:* 800-648-1888 ■ *Web:* www.casamonica.com	Saint Augustine	FL	32084	904-827-1888	819-6065
Casa Munras Hotel 700 Munras Ave *TF:* 800-222-2446 ■ *Web:* www.hotelcasamunras.com	Monterey	CA	93940	831-375-2411	375-1365
Casa Via Mar Inn & Tennis Club 377 W Ch Islands Blvd *TF:* 800-992-5522 ■ *Web:* www.casaviamar.com	Port Hueneme	CA	93041	805-984-6222	984-9490
Casablanca Hotel 147 W 43rd St *TF:* 888-922-7225 ■ *Web:* www.casablancahotel.com	New York	NY	10036	212-869-1212	391-7585
Cascades Inn 3226 Shepherd of the Hills Expy *TF:* 800-588-8424 ■ *Web:* www.cascadesinn.com	Branson	MO	65616	417-335-8424	334-1927
Casino Royale Hotel 3411 Las Vegas Blvd S *TF:* 800-854-7666 ■ *Web:* www.casinoroyalehotel.com	Las Vegas	NV	89109	702-737-3500	650-4743
Castle in the Sand Hotel 3701 Atlantic Ave *TF:* 800-552-7263 ■ *Web:* www.castleinthesand.com	Ocean City	MD	21842	410-289-6846	289-9446
Castle Inn & Suites 1734 S Harbor Blvd *TF:* 800-227-8530 ■ *Web:* www.castleinn.com	Anaheim	CA	92802	714-774-8111	956-4736
Castle on the Hudson 400 Benedict Ave *TF:* 800-616-4487 ■ *Web:* www.castleonthehudson.com	Tarrytown	NY	10591	914-631-1980	631-4612
Centennial Hotel 96 Pleasant St *TF:* 800-360-4839 ■ *Web:* www.thecentennialhotel.com	Concord	NH	03301	603-227-9000	225-5031
Center Court Historic Inn & Cottages 1075 Duval St C-19 *TF:* 800-797-8787 ■ *Web:* www.centercourtkw.com	Key West	FL	33040	305-296-9292	
Century Hotel South Beach 140 Ocean Dr *TF:* 877-659-8855 ■ *Web:* centurymiamibeach.com	Miami Beach	FL	33139	305-674-8855	
Century Plaza Hotel & Spa 1015 Burrard St *TF:* 800-663-1818 ■ *Web:* www.century-plaza.com	Vancouver	BC	V6Z1Y5	604-687-0575	682-5790
Century Suites Hotel 300 SR-446 *TF:* 800-766-5446 ■ *Web:* www.centurysuites.com	Bloomington	IN	47401	812-336-7777	336-0436
Chamberlain West Hollywood 1000 Westmount Dr *TF:* 800-201-9652 ■ *Web:* www.chamberlainwesthollywood.com	West Hollywood	CA	90069	310-657-7400	854-6744
Chambers Hotel 15 W 56th St *Web:* www.chambershotel.com	New York	NY	10019	212-974-5656	974-5657
Chancellor Hotel on Union Square 433 Powell St *TF:* 800-428-4748 ■ *Web:* www.chancellorhotel.com	San Francisco	CA	94102	415-362-2004	362-1403
Chandler Inn 26 Chandler St *TF:* 800-842-3450 ■ *Web:* www.chandlerinn.com	Boston	MA	02116	617-482-3450	542-3428
Charles Hotel Harvard Square One Bennett St *TF:* 800-882-1818 ■ *Web:* www.charleshotel.com	Cambridge	MA	02138	617-864-1200	864-5715
Charles Inn, The 20 Broad St *Web:* www.thecharlesinn.com	Bangor	ME	04401	207-992-2820	992-2826
Charleston Place 205 Meeting St *TF:* 800-611-5545 ■ *Web:* belmond.com/charleston-place/	Charleston	SC	29401	843-722-4900	722-0728
Charter at Beaver Creek 120 Offerson Rd PO Box 5310 *TF:* 800-525-6660 ■ *Web:* www.wyndhamvacationrentals.com	Avon	CO	81620	970-949-6660	949-6709
Charter One Hotels & Resorts Inc 2032 Hillview St *Web:* www.charteronehotels.com	Sarasota	FL	34239	941-364-9224	921-5246
Chartwell Hospitality LLC 2000 Meridian Blvd Ste 200 *Web:* www.chartwellhospitality.com	Franklin	TN	37067	615-550-1270	

Name / Address	City	State	Zip	Phone	Fax
Chase Hotel at Palm Springs 200 W Arenas Rd TF: 877-532-4273 ■ Web: www.chasehotelpalmsprings.com	Palm Springs	CA	92262	760-320-8866	323-1501
Chase Park Plaza 212 N KingsHwy Blvd TF Resv: 877-587-2427 ■ Web: www.chaseparkplaza.com	Saint Louis	MO	63108	314-633-3000	633-3077
Chateau du Sureau 48688 Victoria Ln PO Box 577 Web: www.chateausureau.com	Oakhurst	CA	93644	559-683-6860	683-0800
Chateau Dupre Hotel 131 Rue Decatur Web: www.bestneworleanshotels.com	New Orleans	LA	70130	504-569-0600	
Chateau Hotel & Conference Ctr, The 1601 Jumer Dr Web: www.chateauhotel.biz	Bloomington	IL	61704	309-662-2020	662-6522
Chateau Louis Hotel & Conference Centre 11727 Kingsway TF: 800-661-9843 ■ Web: www.chateaulouis.com	Edmonton	AB	T5G3A1	780-452-7770	454-3436
Chateau Marmont Hotel 8221 Sunset Blvd Web: www.chateaumarmont.com	Los Angeles	CA	90046	323-656-1010	655-5311
Chateau on the Lake 415 N State Hwy 265 TF: 888-333-5253 ■ Web: www.chateauonthelake.com	Branson	MO	65616	417-334-1161	339-5566
Chateau Vaudreuil Suites Hotel 21700 Rt Transcanada Hwy TF: 800-363-7896 ■ Web: chateauvaudreuil.ca	Vaudreuil-Dorion	QC	J7V8P3	450-455-0955	455-6617
Chateau Versailles 1659 Sherbrooke St W TF: 888-933-8111 ■ Web: www.chateauversaillesmontreal.com	Montreal	QC	H3H1E3	514-933-3611	
Chelsea Savoy Hotel 204 W 23rd St TF: 866-929-9353 ■ Web: www.chelseasavoynyc.com	New York	NY	10011	212-929-9353	741-6309
Cheshire, The 6300 Clayton Rd Web: www.cheshirestl.com	Saint Louis	MO	63117	314-647-7300	647-0442
Chesterfield Hotel 363 Cocoanut Row TF: 800-243-7871 ■ Web: www.chesterfieldpb.com	Palm Beach	FL	33480	561-659-5800	659-6707
Chestnut Hill Hotel 8229 Germantown Ave TF: 800-628-9744 ■ Web: www.chestnuthillhotel.com	Philadelphia	PA	19118	215-242-5905	242-8778
Chiltern Inn 11 Cromwell Harbor Rd TF: 800-709-0114 ■ Web: www.chilterninnbarharbor.com	Bar Harbor	ME	04609	207-288-3371	
Chimo Hotel 1199 Joseph Cyr St TF: 800-387-9779 ■ Web: www.chimohotel.com	Ottawa	ON	K1J7T4	613-744-1060	744-7076
Choice Hotels International, Inc. 997 New Loudon Rd TF: 800-424-6423 ■ Web: clarionhotel.com	Latham	NY	12110	518-785-0931	782-2578
Choice Hotelsÿ 3050 University Pkwy Web: www.clarionhotel.com	Winston-Salem	NC	27105	336-723-2911	714-4578
Chrysalis Inn & Spa 804 Tenth St TF: 888-808-0005 ■ Web: www.thechrysalisinn.com	Bellingham	WA	98225	360-756-1005	647-0342
Churchill Hotel 1914 Connecticut Ave NW TF: 800-424-2464 ■ Web: www.thechurchillhotel.com	Washington	DC	20009	202-797-2000	462-0944
Cincinnatian Hotel 601 Vine St TF: 800-942-9000 ■ Web: www.cincinnatianhotel.com	Cincinnati	OH	45202	513-381-3000	651-0256
Circa39 Hotel 3900 Collins Ave TF Resv: 877-824-7223 ■ Web: www.circa39.com	Miami Beach	FL	33140	305-538-4900	538-4998
Circus Circus Hotel & Casino Reno 500 N Sierra St TF: 800-648-5010 ■ Web: www.circusreno.com	Reno	NV	89503	775-329-0711	328-9652
Circus Circus Hotel Casino & Theme Park Las Vegas 2880 Las Vegas Blvd S TF Resv: 800-634-3450 ■ Web: www.circuscircus.com	Las Vegas	NV	89109	702-734-0410	
City Suites Hotel 933 W Belmont Ave Web: www.chicagocitysuites.com	Chicago	IL	60657	773-404-3400	404-3405
Civic Plaza Hotel 505 Pine St	Abilene	TX	79601	325-676-0222	676-0513
CJ Grand Hotel & Spa 67585 Hacienda Ave Web: cjmineralspa.com	Desert Hot Springs	CA	92240	760-329-4488	
Clarendon Hotel & Suites 401 W Clarendon Ave Web: goclarendon.com/	Phoenix	AZ	85013	602-252-7363	274-9009
Clayton on the Park 7343 Scottsdale Mall Web: www.theclaytononthepark.com	Scottsdale	AZ	85251	480-990-7300	
Cleftstone Manor 92 Eden St TF: 888-288-4951 ■ Web: www.cleftstone.com	Bar Harbor	ME	04609	207-288-8086	
Cliff House at Pikes Peak 306 Canyon Ave *Fax Area Code: 719 ■ TF: 888-212-7000 ■ Web: www.thecliffhouse.com	Manitou Springs	CO	80829	888-212-7000	685-3913*
Clift, The 495 Geary St Web: morganshotelgroup.com	San Francisco	CA	94102	415-775-4700	
Clinton Inn Hotel 145 Dean Dr TF: 800-275-4411 ■ Web: www.clinton-inn.com	Tenafly	NJ	07670	201-871-3200	871-3435
Clocktower Inn Hotel 181 E Santa Clara St TF: 800-727-1027 ■ Web: www.clocktowerinn.com	Ventura	CA	93001	805-652-0141	643-1432
ClubHouse Hotel & Suites Sioux Falls 2320 S Louise Ave TF: 866-534-8700 ■ Web: siouxfalls.clubhouseinn.com	Sioux Falls	SD	57106	605-361-8700	361-5950
Coachman Inn 32959 SR-Hwy 20 TF: 800-635-0043 ■ Web: www.thecoachmaninn.com	Oak Harbor	WA	98277	360-675-0727	675-1419
Coast Edmonton House Suite Hotel 1090 W Georgia S Ste 900 *Fax Area Code: 780 ■ TF: 800-716-6199 ■ Web: www.coasthotels.com	Vancouver	BC	V6E3V7	604-682-7982	420-4364*
Coast Hotels & Resorts Canada 1090 W Georgia St Web: www.coasthotels.com	Vancouver	BC	V6E3V7	604-682-7982	682-8942
Coast Hotels & Resorts USA 2003 Western Ave Ste 500 Web: www.coasthotels.com	Seattle	WA	98121	206-826-2700	826-2701
Coast Plaza Hotel 1316 33 St Ne Web: www.calgaryplaza.com	Calgary	AB	T2A6B6	403-248-8888	
Coastal Hotel Group 18525 36th Ave S Web: www.coastalhotels.com	Seattle	WA	98188	206-388-0400	388-0400
Coastal Inn Concorde 379 Windmill Rd TF: 800-565-1565 ■ Web: coastalinns.com/coastal-inn-halifax-dartmouth-ns.php	Dartmouth	NS	B3A1J6	902-465-7777	465-3956
Coastal Inns Inc 111 Warwick St Box 280 *Fax Area Code: 506 ■ TF: 800-665-7829 ■ Web: www.coastalinns.com	Digby	NS	B0V1A0	800-401-1155	857-1791*
Coastal Palms Hotel 120th St Coastal Hwy TF: 800-641-0011 ■ Web: www.coastalpalmshotel.com	Ocean City	MD	21842	800-641-0011	
Cocca's Inn & Suites Corner of Wolf Rd & Central Ave TF: 888-426-2227 ■ Web: www.coccas.com	Albany	NY	12205	518-459-2240	459-9758
Coffee Exchange 207 Wickenden St Web: www.coffeexchange.com	Providence	RI	02903	401-273-1198	
Cohasset Harbor Inn 124 Elm St TF: 800-252-5287 ■ Web: cohassetharborresort.com	Cohasset	MA	02025	781-383-6650	383-2872
Colby Hill Inn 33 The Oaks PO Box 779 TF: 800-531-0330 ■ Web: www.colbyhillinn.com	Henniker	NH	03242	603-428-3281	428-9218
Colcord Hotel 15 N Robinson Ave TF: 866-781-3800 ■ Web: www.colcordhotel.com	Oklahoma City	OK	73102	405-601-4300	208-4399
Colgate Inn 1 Payne St Web: www.colgateinn.com	Hamilton	NY	13346	315-824-2300	824-4500
College Houses Co-ops 1906 Pearl St Ofc 101 Web: collegehouses.org	Austin	TX	78705	512-476-5678	
Colonnade Hotel 120 Huntington Ave TF: 800-962-3030 ■ Web: www.colonnadehotel.com	Boston	MA	02116	617-424-7000	424-1717
Colony Hotel & Cabana Club 525 E Atlantic Ave Web: www.thecolonyhotel.com	Delray Beach	FL	33483	561-276-4123	276-0123
Colony South Hotel 7401 Surratts Rd TF: 800-537-1147 ■ Web: www.colonysouth.com	Clinton	MD	20735	301-856-4500	856-4500
Colorado Belle Hotel & Casino 2100 S Casino Dr TF Resv: 877-460-0777 ■ Web: www.coloradobelle.com	Laughlin	NV	89029	702-298-4000	
Columbia Gorge Hotel 4000 Westcliff Dr TF: 800-345-1921 ■ Web: www.columbiagorgehotel.com	Hood River	OR	97031	541-386-5566	386-9141
Columbia Hospitality 2223 Alaskan Way Ste 200 Web: www.columbiahospitality.com	Seattle	WA	98121	206-239-1800	239-1801
Columbia Sussex Corp 740 Centre View Blvd Web: www.columbiasussex.com	Crestview Hills	KY	41017	859-578-1100	578-1154
Columns, The 3811 St Charles Ave TF: 800-445-9308 ■ Web: www.thecolumns.com	New Orleans	LA	70115	504-899-9308	899-8170
Come Back in 508 E Wilson St Web: comebackintavern.com	Madison	WI	53703	608-258-8619	
Comfort Inn & Suites Milwaukee 916 E State St *Fax Area Code: 916 ■ TF: 800-424-6423 ■ Web: www.choicehotels.com	Milwaukee	WI	53202	414-276-8800	442-1100*
Commander Hotel 1401 Atlantic Ave TF: 888-289-6166 ■ Web: www.commanderhotel.com	Ocean City	MD	21842	410-289-6166	289-3998
Commonwealth Park Suites Hotel 901 Bank St TF: 888-343-7301 ■ Web: www.commonwealthparksuites.com	Richmond	VA	23219	804-343-7300	343-1025
Conch House Heritage Inn 625 Truman Ave TF: 800-207-5806 ■ Web: www.conchhouse.com	Key West	FL	33040	305-293-0020	293-8447
Conch House Marina Resort 57 Comares Ave TF: 800-940-6256 ■ Web: www.conch-house.com	Saint Augustine	FL	32080	904-829-8646	829-5414
Congress Plaza Hotel & Convention Ctr 520 S Michigan Ave TF: 800-635-1666 ■ Web: www.congressplazahotel.com	Chicago	IL	60605	312-427-3800	427-2919
Conrad Miami 1395 Brickell Ave TF: 800-002-6672 ■ Web: conradhotels3.hilton.com	Miami	FL	33131	305-503-6500	503-6599
Conrad Motel 100 Conrad Ct	Glenville	WV	26351	304-462-7316	
Contactpointe of Pittsburgh 2593 Wexford Bayne Rd Ste 200 Web: contactpointe.com	Sewickley	PA	15143	412-788-0680	
Continental Bayside Hotel 146 Biscayne Blvd Web: www.crshotels.com	Miami	FL	33132	305-358-4555	
Cooper Hotel & Conference Ctr 12230 Preston Rd TF: 800-444-5187 ■ Web: www.cooperaerobics.com	Dallas	TX	75230	972-386-0306	
Cooper Hotels 1661 Arrion Brainner Dr Ste 200 Web: www.cooperhotels.com	Memphis	TN	38120	901-322-1400	322-1403
Copley Square Hotel 47 Huntington Ave TF: 800-225-7062 ■ Web: www.copleysquarehotel.com	Boston	MA	02116	617-536-9000	267-3547
Cornhusker Hotel, The 333 S 13th St TF: 866-706-7706 ■ Web: www.marriott.com	Lincoln	NE	68508	402-474-7474	474-1847
Cosmopolitan Hotel Toronto Eight Colborne St TF: 800-958-3488 ■ Web: www.cosmotoronto.com	Toronto	ON	M5E1E1	416-350-2000	350-2460
Country Hearth 3450 S Clack St Web: www.countryhearthabilene.com	Abilene	TX	79606	325-695-7700	698-0546
Country Inn at the Mall 936 Stillwater Ave TF Resv: 800-244-3961 ■ Web: www.countryinnatthemall.net	Bangor	ME	04401	207-941-0200	
Country Inn Lake Resort 1332 Airport Rd TF: 800-822-7402 ■ Web: www.countryinnlakeresort.com	Hot Springs	AR	71913	501-767-3535	
Courtyard by Marriott Waikiki Beach 400 Royal Hawaiian Ave Web: marriott.com	Honolulu	HI	96815	808-954-4000	954-4047
Courtyard Fort Lauderdale Beach 440 Seabreeze Blvd TF: 888-236-2427 ■ Web: www.marriott.com/courtyard/travel.mi	Fort Lauderdale	FL	33316	954-524-8733	525-8145
Courtyard San Diego Oceanside 3501 Seagate Way Web: marriott.com	Oceanside	CA	92056	760-966-1000	
Cove Inn 900 Broad Ave S TF: 800-255-4365 ■ Web: www.coveinnnaples.com	Naples	FL	34102	239-262-7161	261-6905
Cowboy Village Resort 120 S Flat Creek Dr PO Box 38 TF: 800-962-4988 ■ Web: www.townsquareinns.com/cowboy-village	Jackson	WY	83001	307-733-3121	739-1955
Cozy Country Inn 103 Frederick Rd	Thurmont	MD	21788	301-271-4301	271-3107
Craftsman Inn 7300 E Genesee St Web: www.craftsmaninn.com	Fayetteville	NY	13066	315-637-8000	637-2440
Creekside Inn 3400 El Camino Real Web: www.greystonehotels.com	Palo Alto	CA	94306	650-493-2411	493-6787
Crescent Hotel 403 N Crescent Dr Web: www.crescentbh.com	Beverly Hills	CA	90210	310-247-0505	247-9053
Crescent Hotels & Resorts LLC 10306 Eaton Pl Ste 430	Fairfax	VA	22030	703-279-7820	
Crest Hotel & Suites 1670 James Ave TF: 800-531-3880 ■ Web: www.crestgrouphotels.com	Miami Beach	FL	33139	305-531-0321	531-8180

Phone | Fax

Cresthill Suites Hotel 1415 Washington Ave Albany NY 12206 518-454-0007
Web: www.cresthillsuites.com

Crestline Hotels & Resorts
3950 University Dr Ste 301 Fairfax VA 22030 571-529-6100 529-6095
Web: www.crestlinehotels.com

Crockett Hotel 320 Bonham St San Antonio TX 78205 210-225-6500 225-6251
TF: 800-292-1050 ■ *Web:* www.crockettthotel.com

Cross Creek Resort 3815 Pennsylvania 8 Titusville PA 16354 814-827-9611 827-2062
TF: 800-461-3173 ■ *Web:* www.crosscreekresort.com

Crown American Hotels Co Pasquerilla Plz Johnstown PA 15907 814-533-4600 535-9323
Web: www.crownamericanhotels.com

Crown Reef Resort 2913 S Ocean Blvd Myrtle Beach SC 29577 843-626-8077 916-0735
TF: 877-435-9125 ■ *Web:* www.crownreef.com

Crowne Plaza Campbell House
1375 S Broadway Rd Lexington KY 40504 859-255-4281 254-4368
Web: www.thecampbellhouse.com/

Crowne Plaza Chateau Lacombe
10111 Bellamy Hill Edmonton AB T5J1N7 780-428-6611
Web: www.chateaulacombe.com

Crowne Plaza Hollywood Beach Resort
4000 S Ocean Dr Hollywood FL 33019 954-454-4334
Web: cphollywoodbeach.com

Crowne Plaza St Paul Riverfront
11 E Kellogg Blvd St Paul MN 55101 651-292-1900
Web: ihg.com

Crowne Plaza Syracuse 701 E Genesee St Syracuse NY 13210 315-479-7000 472-2700
TF: 888-227-6963 ■ *Web:* cpsyracuse.com

Crowne Plaza Times Square Manhattan
1605 Broadway New York NY 10019 212-977-4000

Crystal Beach Suites & Health Club
6985 Collins Ave Miami Beach FL 33141 305-865-9555 866-3514
TF: 888-643-4630 ■ *Web:* www.crystalbeachsuites.com

Crystal Inn 185 S State St Ste 202 Salt Lake City UT 84111 801-320-7200 320-7201
TF General: 800-662-2525 ■ *Web:* www.crystalinns.com

Crystal Inn Salt Lake City Downtown
230 W 500 S Salt Lake City UT 84101 801-328-4466 320-7201
TF: 800-662-2525 ■ *Web:* crystalinns.com/

Curtis, The 1405 Curtis St Denver CO 80202 303-571-0300 825-4301
TF: 800-525-6651 ■ *Web:* www.thecurtis.com

Custom Hotel 8639 Lincoln Blvd Los Angeles CA 90045 310-645-0400 645-0700
TF: 877-287-8601 ■ *Web:* www.jdvhotels.com

Dahlmann Campus Inn 615 E Huron St Ann Arbor MI 48104 734-769-2200 769-6222
TF: 800-666-8693 ■ *Web:* campusinn.com

Daly Seven Inc 4829 Riverside Dr Danville VA 24541 434-822-2161
TF: 800-466-5337 ■ *Web:* dalyseven.com

Dan'l Webster Inn 149 Main St Sandwich MA 02563 508-888-3622 888-5156
TF: 800-444-3566 ■ *Web:* www.danlwebsterinn.com

Dauphine Orleans Hotel 415 Dauphine St New Orleans LA 70112 504-586-1800 586-1409
TF: 800-521-7111 ■ *Web:* www.dauphineorleans.com

Davenport Hotel, The 10 S Post St Spokane WA 99201 509-455-8888 624-4455
TF: 800-899-1482 ■ *Web:* www.davenporthotelcollection.com

David William Hotel Condo Assn
700 Biltmore Way Coral Gables FL 33134 305-445-7821
Web: davidwilliamcondo.com

Davidson & Jones Hotel Corp 1207 Front St Raleigh NC 27609 919-828-0880
Web: davidsonandjones.com

Days Inns Worldwide Inc
215 W 94th St Broadway New York NY 10025 212-866-6400 866-1357
TF: 800-834-2972 ■ *Web:* www.daysinn.com

Daytona Beach Resort & Conference Ctr
2700 N Atlantic Ave Daytona Beach FL 32118 386-672-3770 673-7262
TF: 800-654-6216 ■ *Web:* www.daytonabeachresort.com

Daytona Inn Beach Resort
219 S Atlantic Ave Daytona Beach FL 32118 386-252-3626 255-3680
TF General: 800-874-1822 ■ *Web:* daytonainnbeachresort.com

Dearborn Inn the - A Marriott Hotel
20301 Oakwood Blvd Dearborn MI 48124 313-271-2700 271-2700
TF: 800-228-9290 ■ *Web:* www.marriott.com

Deer Path Inn 255 E Illinois Rd Lake Forest IL 60045 847-234-2280 234-3352
TF: 800-788-9480 ■ *Web:* www.dpihotel.com

Deerfoot Inn & Casino 1000 11500 35th St SE Calgary AB T2Z3W4 403-236-7529 252-4767
TF: 877-236-5225 ■ *Web:* www.deerfootinn.com

Defender Resorts Inc 6301 N Kings Hwy Myrtle Beach SC 29572 843-449-1354
Web: defenderresorts.com

Del Monte Lodge Renaissance Rochester Hotel & Spa, The
41 N Main St Pittsford NY 14534 585-381-9900 381-9825
TF: 866-237-5979 ■ *Web:* marriott.com/hotels/propertypage/rocdl

DELAMAR Greenwich Harbor 500 Steamboat Rd Greenwich CT 06830 203-661-9800
TF: 866-335-2627 ■ *Web:* www.delamargreenwich.com

Delta King Riverboat Hotel 1000 Front St Sacramento CA 95814 916-444-5464
TF: 800-825-5464 ■ *Web:* www.deltaking.com

Deluxe Inn Odessa Hotel 1518 S Grant Ave Odessa TX 79761 432-333-1486
Web: deluxeinnodessa.com

DePalma Hotel Corp
700 Highlander Blvd Ste 400 Arlington TX 76015 817-557-1811 557-4333
Web: www.depalmahotels.com

Desert Inn Resort 900 N Atlantic Ave Daytona Beach FL 32118 386-258-6555 238-1635

Desert Riviera Hotel
610 E Palm Canyon Dr Palm Springs CA 92264 760-327-5314
Web: www.desertrivierahotel.com

Destination Hotels & Resorts Inc
10333 E Dry Creek Rd Ste 450 Englewood CO 80112 303-799-3830 799-6011
TF: 855-893-1011 ■ *Web:* www.destinationhotels.com

Diamond Head Inn 605 Diamond St San Diego CA 92109 858-273-1900 273-8532
TF: 888-478-7829 ■ *Web:* www.diamondheadinn.com

Dimension Development Co 769 Hwy 494 Natchitoches LA 71457 318-352-8238 352-8276
Web: www.dimdev.com

Dinah's Garden Hotel 4261 El Camino Real Palo Alto CA 94306 650-493-2844 856-4713
TF: 800-227-8220 ■ *Web:* www.dinahshotel.com

Disney's Paradise Pier Hotel
1717 S Disneyland Dr Anaheim CA 92802 714-999-0990
Web: www.disneyworld.disney.go.com

Disney's Saratoga Springs Resort & Spa
1960 Broadway St Lake Buena Vista FL 32830 407-827-1100 827-4444
Web: disneyworld.disney.go.com/resorts/saratoga-springs-resort-and-spa

Disneyland Hotel 1150 Magic Way Anaheim CA 92802 714-778-6600 956-6597
Web: disneyland.disney.go.com

Dockers Inn 3060 Green Mtn Dr Branson MO 65616 417-334-3600
Web: www.dockersinn.com

Dolce International 28 W Grand Ave Montvale NJ 07645 201-307-8700 307-8837
Web: www.dolce.com

Dolphin Beach Resort 4900 Gulf Blvd Saint Pete Beach FL 33706 727-360-7011 367-5909
Web: www.dolphinbeach.com

Dolphin Inn 1705 Atlantic Ave Virginia Beach VA 23451 757-491-1420 425-8390
TF: 800-365-3467 ■ *Web:* www.vbeach.com/hotels/dolphin.htm

Dominion Lodging Inc 658 Roanoke Rd Daleville VA 24083 540-992-4077
Web: www.dominionlodging.com

Don Hall's Guesthouse
1313 W Washington Ctr Rd Fort Wayne IN 46825 260-489-2524 489-7067
TF General: 800-348-1999 ■ *Web:* www.donhalls.com

Donatello, The 501 Post St San Francisco CA 94102 415-441-7100 441-7100
TF: 800-258-2366 ■ *Web:* www.clubdonatello.org

Dora Hotel Company LLC 10734 Sky Prairie St Fishers IN 46037 317-863-5700
Web: www.dorahotelco.com

Doubletree Claremont 555 W Foothill Blvd Claremont CA 91711 909-626-2411 624-0756
TF: 800-222-8733 ■ *Web:* www3.hilton.com

Doubletree Hotel 2800 Via Cabrillo Marina San Pedro CA 90731 310-514-3344 514-8945
Web: sanpedrodoubletree.com

Doubletree Hotel Downtown Wilmington Legal District
700 N King St Wilmington DE 19801 302-655-0400
TF: 800-222-8733 ■ *Web:* www3.hilton.com

Doubletree North Shore Hotel 9599 Skokie Blvd Skokie IL 60077 847-679-7000 679-0904
TF: 800-445-8667 ■ *Web:* www3.hilton.com

Downtown Erie Hotel 18 W 18th St Erie PA 16501 814-456-2961 456-7067
Web: www.downtownueriehotel.com

Drake Hotel, The 140 E Walton Pl Chicago IL 60611 312-787-2200 787-1431
TF: 800-553-7253 ■ *Web:* www.thedrakehotel.com

Dream 210 W 55th St New York NY 10019 212-247-2000
Web: www.dreamhotels.com

Driftwood Hospitality Management LLC
11770 Us Hwy One Ste 202 North Palm Beach FL 33408 561-207-2700
Web: www.driftwoodhospitality.com

Driftwood Hotel 435 Willoughby Ave Juneau AK 99801 907-586-2280 586-1034
TF: 800-544-2239 ■ *Web:* www.driftwoodalaska.com

Driftwood on the Oceanfront
Oceanfront at 16th Ave N Myrtle Beach SC 29578 843-448-1544 626-5001
TF: 855-741-7986 ■ *Web:* driftwoodattheboardwalk.com/

Driftwood Shores Resort 88416 First Ave Florence OR 97439 541-997-8263 997-3253
TF: 800-422-5091 ■ *Web:* www.driftwoodshores.com

Driskill Hotel 604 Brazos St Austin TX 78701 512-474-5911 474-2214
TF: 800-252-9367 ■ *Web:* www.driskillhotel.com

Drury Hotels Company LLC
721 Emerson Rd Ste 400 Saint Louis MO 63141 314-429-2255 429-5166
TF: 800-378-7946 ■ *Web:* www.druryhotels.com

Duane Street Hotel 130 Duane St New York NY 10013 212-964-4600 964-4800
Web: www.duanestreethotel.com

Dude Rancher Lodge 415 N 29th St Billings MT 59101 406-259-5561 259-0095
TF: 800-221-3302 ■ *Web:* www.duderancherlodge.com

Duke Towers- All Condominium Hotel
807 W Trinity Ave Durham NC 27701 919-687-4444 683-1215
TF: 866-385-3869 ■ *Web:* www.duketower.com

Duke's 8th Avenue Hotel 630 W Eigth Ave Anchorage AK 99501 907-274-6213 272-6308
TF: 800-478-4837 ■ *Web:* www.dukesalaskahotel.com

Dunes Manor Hotel 2800 Baltimore Ave Ocean City MD 21842 410-289-1100 289-4905
TF: 800-523-2888 ■ *Web:* www.dunesmanor.com

Dunhill Hotel 237 N Tryon St Charlotte NC 28202 704-332-4141 376-4117
TF: 800-354-4141 ■ *Web:* www.dunhillhotel.com

Dunn Hospitality Group LLC
300 SE Riverside Dr Ste 100 Evansville IN 47713 812-471-9300
Web: www.dunnhospitalitygroup.com

Dylan Hotel 52 E 41st St New York NY 10017 212-338-0500 227-1206*
*Fax Area Code: 646 ■ *TF:* 866-553-9526 ■ *Web:* www.dylanhotel.com

Dynasty Suites 1235 W Colton Ave Redlands CA 92374 909-793-6648 792-5219
TF General: 800-874-8958 ■ *Web:* www.dynastysuites.com

Eagle Mountain House
179 Carter Notch Rd PO Box 804 Jackson NH 03846 603-383-9111 383-0854
TF: 800-966-5779 ■ *Web:* www.eaglemt.com

East Canyon Hotel & Spa
288 E Camino Monte Vista Palm Springs CA 92262 760-320-1928 320-0599
TF: 877-324-6835 ■ *Web:* www.eastcanyonps.com

Eastland Park Hotel 157 High St Portland ME 04101 207-775-5411 775-0148
Web: www.westinportlandharborview.com

Eden House 1015 Fleming St Key West FL 33040 800-533-5397 294-1221*
*Fax Area Code: 305 ■ *TF:* 800-533-5397 ■ *Web:* www.edenhouse.com

Edgewater Beach Hotel 1901 Gulf Shore Blvd N Naples FL 34102 888-564-1308 403-2100*
*Fax Area Code: 239 ■ *TF:* 888-564-1308 ■ *Web:* www.edgewaternaples.com

Edgewater Hotel 2411 Alaskan Way Pier 67 Seattle WA 98121 206-728-7000 441-4119
TF: 800-624-0670 ■ *Web:* www.edgewaterhotel.com

Edgewater Resort 200 Edgewater Cir Hot Springs AR 71913 501-767-3311
TF: 800-234-3687 ■ *Web:* www.ewresort.com

Edgewater Resort & Waterpark 2400 London Rd Duluth MN 55812 218-728-3601 728-3727
TF: 800-777-7925 ■ *Web:* www.duluthwaterpark.com

Edmonds Harbor Inn & Suites 130 W Dayton Edmonds WA 98020 425-771-5021 672-2880
TF: 800-441-8033 ■ *Web:* www.bestwestern.com

Eisenhower Inn & Conference Ctr
2634 Emmitsburg Rd Gettysburg PA 17325 717-334-8121 334-6066
Web: www.eisenhower.com

EJ Del Monte Corp 909 Linden Ave Rochester NY 14625 585-586-3121
Web: delmontehotelgroup.com

El Cortez Hotel & Casino 600 E Fremont St Las Vegas NV 89101 702-385-5200 474-3633
TF: 800-634-6703 ■ *Web:* www.elcortezhotelcasino.com

El Rey Inn 1862 Cerillos Rd Santa Fe NM 87505 505-982-1931 989-9249
TF: 800-521-1349 ■ *Web:* www.elreyinnsantafe.com

Phone | Fax

El Tovar Hotel 1 Main Street .... Grand Canyon AZ 86023 928-638-2631
TF: 888-297-2757 ■ *Web:* www.grandcanyonlodges.com/el-tovar-409.html
Elan Hotel 8435 Beverly Blvd .... Los Angeles CA 90048 323-658-6663 658-6640
TF: 866-203-2212 ■ *Web:* www.greystonehotels.com
Elbow River Casino (ERC) 218 18th Ave SE .... Calgary AB T2G1L1 403-289-8880
Web: elbowrivercasino.com
Eldorado Hotel 309 W San Francisco St .... Santa Fe NM 87501 505-988-4455 995-4543
TF: 800-955-4455 ■ *Web:* www.eldoradohotel.com
Eldorado Hotel Casino 345 N Virginia St .... Reno NV 89501 775-786-5700 322-7124
TF Resv: 800-879-8879 ■ *Web:* www.eldoradoreno.com
Eldridge Hotel 701 Massachusetts St .... Lawrence KS 66044 785-749-5011 749-4512
TF: 800-527-0909 ■ *Web:* www.eldridgehotel.com
Eliot Hotel, The 370 Commonwealth Ave .... Boston MA 02215 617-267-1607 536-9114
TF: 800-443-5468 ■ *Web:* www.eliothotel.com
Elk Country Inn 480 W Pearl St PO Box 1255 .... Jackson WY 83001 307-733-2364 733-4465
Web: www.townsquareinns.com
Elvis Presley's Heartbreak Hotel
3677 Elvis Presley Blvd .... Memphis TN 38116 901-332-1000 332-2107
TF: 877-777-0606 ■ *Web:* www.elvis.com
Embarcadero Resort Hotel & Marina
1000 SE Bay Blvd .... Newport OR 97365 541-265-8521 265-7844
Web: embarcaderoresort.com/
Embassy Hotel 610 Polk St .... San Francisco CA 94102 415-673-1404 474-4188
Web: www.theembassyhotelsf.com
Embassy Hotel & Suites 25 Cartier St .... Ottawa ON K2P1J2 613-237-2111 563-1353
TF: 800-661-5495 ■ *Web:* www.embassyhotelottawa.com
Embassy Suites Chicago Downtown Lakefront
511 N Columbus Dr .... Chicago IL 60611 312-836-5900
Web: embassysuites3.hilton.com
Embassy Suites Columbus-Dublin
5100 Upper Metro Pl .... Dublin OH 43017 614-790-9000
Web: embassysuites3.hilton.com
Embassy West Hotel 1400 Carling Ave .... Ottawa ON K1Z7L8 613-729-4331 729-1600
TF: 800-267-8696 ■ *Web:* www.embassywesthotel.com
Emerald Queen Hotel & Casino 5700 Pacific Hwy E .... Fife WA 98424 253-922-2000
TF: 888-820-3555 ■ *Web:* emeraldqueen.com
Emerson Resort & Spa 5340 Rt 28 .... Mount Tremper NY 12457 845-688-7900 688-2829
TF: 877-688-2828 ■ *Web:* www.emersonresort.com
Emily Morgan Hotel 705 E Houston St .... San Antonio TX 78205 210-225-5100
TF: 800-824-6674 ■ *Web:* www.emilymorganhotel.com
Empire Landmark Hotel & Conference Centre
1400 Robson St .... Vancouver BC V6G1B9 604-687-0511
TF: 800-830-6144 ■ *Web:* www.empirelandmarkhotel.com
Empress Hotel 7766 Fay Ave .... La Jolla CA 92037 858-454-3001 454-6387
TF: 888-369-9900 ■ *Web:* www.empress-hotel.com
Enclave Suites of Orlando 6165 Carrier Dr .... Orlando FL 32819 407-351-1155 351-2001
TF: 800-457-0077 ■ *Web:* www.enclavesuites.com
Epoque Hotels 2500 NE 135th St Ste 502 .... North Miami FL 33181 305-538-9697
Web: www.epoquehotels.com
Ethan Allen Hotel 21 Lake Ave Ext .... Danbury CT 06811 203-744-1776 791-9673
TF: 800-742-1776 ■ *Web:* www.ethanallenhotel.com
Euro-American Finance Network Inc
1212 S Main St Ste B .... Wildwood FL 34785 352-504-1641
Web: www.eafninc.com
Euro-Suites Hotel
University Centre 501 Chestnut Ridge Rd .... Morgantown WV 26505 800-678-4837
TF: 800-678-4837 ■ *Web:* www.euro-suites.com
Evergreen Lodge 250 S Frontage Rd W .... Vail CO 81657 970-476-7810 476-4504
TF: 800-284-8245 ■ *Web:* www.evergreenvail.com
Excalibur Hotel & Casino
3850 Las Vegas Blvd S PO Box 96776 .... Las Vegas NV 89109 702-597-7777 597-7009
TF: 877-750-5464 ■ *Web:* www.excalibur.com
Executive Hotel Vintage Court
650 Bush St .... San Francisco CA 94108 415-392-4666 433-4065
TF: 888-388-3932 ■ *Web:* www.executivehotels.net
Executive Inn 978 Phillips Ln .... Louisville KY 40209 502-367-6161 367-6161
TF: 888-205-8144 ■ *Web:* hotelplanner.com
Executive Inn Group Corp
Executive Hotels & Resorts
1080 Howe St Eighth Fl .... Vancouver BC V6Z2T1 604-642-5250 642-5255
TF: 866-642-6888 ■ *Web:* www.executivehotels.net
Executive Pacific Plaza Hotel 400 Spring St .... Seattle WA 98104 206-623-3900 623-2059
TF: 888-388-3932 ■ *Web:* executivehotels.net/downtownseattlehotel/
Executive Suite Hotel 4360 SpenaRd Rd .... Anchorage AK 99517 907-243-6366 248-2161
TF: 800-770-6366 ■ *Web:* www.executivesuitehotel.com
Expressway Hotels 4303 17th Ave S .... Fargo ND 58103 701-239-4303 239-4303
TF: 877-239-4303 ■ *Web:* expresswaysuitesfargo.com
Extended Stay America
11525 N Community House Rd Ste 100 .... Charlotte NC 28277 980-345-1600 573-1695*
**Fax Area Code:* 864 ■ *TF:* 800-804-3724 ■ *Web:* www.extendedstayamerica.com
Crossland Economy Studios
11525 N Community House Rd Ste 100 .... Charlotte NC 28277 980-345-1600
TF: 800-804-3724 ■ *Web:* www.crosslandstudios.com
Extended StayAmerica
11525 N Community House Rd Ste 100 .... Charlotte NC 28277 980-345-1600
TF: 800-804-3724 ■ *Web:* www.extendedstayamerica.com
Extended Stay Hotels
StudioPLUS Deluxe Studios
530 Woods Lake Rd .... Greenville SC 29607 864-288-4300
TF: 800-804-3724 ■ *Web:* www.extendedstayamerica.com
Fairbanks Golden Nugget Hotel, The
900 Noble St .... Fairbanks AK 99701 907-452-5141 452-5458
Web: www.golden-nuggethotel.com
Fairbanks Princess Riverside Lodge
4477 Pikes Landing Rd .... Fairbanks AK 99709 907-455-4477 455-4476
TF: 800-426-0500 ■ *Web:* princesslodges.com
Fairmont Hotels & Resorts Inc
100 Wellington St W TD Ctr Ste 1600 .... Toronto ON M5K1B7 416-874-2600 874-2601
TF General: 800-441-3313 ■ *Web:* www.fairmont.com
Fairmount Hotel, The 401 S Alamo St .... San Antonio TX 78205 210-224-8800 475-0082
TF: 877-229-8808 ■ *Web:* www.thefairmounthotel-sanantonio.com
Falmouth Inn 824 Main St .... Falmouth MA 02540 508-540-2500 540-9256
TF: 800-255-4157 ■ *Web:* www.falmouthinn.com

Phone | Fax

Fargo C'mon Inn Hotel 4338 20th Ave SW .... Fargo ND 58103 701-277-9944 277-9117
TF: 800-334-1570 ■ *Web:* www.cmoninn.com
Fearrington House
2000 Fearrington Village Ctr .... Pittsboro NC 27312 919-542-2121 542-4202
Web: www.fearrington.com
Federal Square Inn & Extended Stay
8781 Madison Blvd .... Madison AL 35758 256-772-8470 772-0620
Fenwick Inn 13801 Coastal Hwy .... Ocean City MD 21842 410-250-1100 250-0087
TF: 800-492-1873 ■ *Web:* www.fenwickinn.com
Fiesta Henderson 777 W Lk Mead Pkwy .... Henderson NV 89015 702-558-7000
TF: 888-899-7770 ■ *Web:* www.fiestahenderson.sclv.com
Fifteen Beacon Hotel 15 Beacon St .... Boston MA 02108 617-670-1500 670-6925
TF: 877-982-3226 ■ *Web:* www.xvbeacon.com
Figueroa Hotel 939 S Figueroa St .... Los Angeles CA 90015 213-627-8971 689-0305
TF General: 800-421-9092 ■ *Web:* www.figueroahotel.com
Fiksdal Hotel & Suites 1215 Second St SW .... Rochester MN 55902 507-288-2671 285-9325*
**Fax:* Resv ■ *TF:* 800-366-3451 ■ *Web:* www.fiksdalhotel.com
Findlay Inn & Conference Ctr
200 E Main Cross St .... Findlay OH 45840 419-422-5682 422-5581
TF Cust Svc: 800-825-1455 ■ *Web:* www.findlayinn.com
Fireside Inn & Suites 25 Airport Rd .... West Lebanon NH 03784 603-298-5900 298-0340
TF: 877-258-5900 ■ *Web:* www.firesideinnwestlebanon.com
First Gold Hotel 270 Main St .... Deadwood SD 57732 605-578-9777 578-3979
TF: 800-274-1876 ■ *Web:* www.firstgold.com
First Interstate Inn 20 SE Wyoming Blvd .... Casper WY 82609 307-234-9125
Fisherman's Wharf Inn
22 Commercial St .... Boothbay Harbor ME 04538 207-633-5090 633-5092
TF: 800-628-6872 ■ *Web:* fishermanswharfinn.com
Fitger's Inn 600 E Superior St .... Duluth MN 55802 218-722-8826 722-8826
Web: www.fitgers.com
Fitzgerald Hotel 620 Post St .... San Francisco CA 94109 415-775-8100 775-1278
Web: www.fitzgeraldhotel.com
Fitzpatrick Manhattan Hotel
687 Lexington Ave .... New York NY 10022 212-355-0100 355-1371
TF: 800-367-7701 ■ *Web:* www.fitzpatrickhotels.com
Flagship All Suites Resort
60 N Maine Ave .... Atlantic City NJ 08401 609-343-7447 347-9597
TF: 800-647-7890 ■ *Web:* www.fantasearesorts.com
Foley House Inn 14 W Hull St Chippewa Sq .... Savannah GA 31401 912-232-6622 231-1218
TF: 800-647-3708 ■ *Web:* www.foleyinn.com
Foot of the Mountain Motel
200 W Arapahoe Ave .... Boulder CO 80302 303-442-5688 442-5719
TF: 866-773-5489 ■ *Web:* www.footofthemountainmotel.com
Foothills Inn 1625 N La Crosse St .... Rapid City SD 57701 605-348-5640 348-0073
TF: 877-428-5666 ■ *Web:* www.thefoothillsinn.com
Fort Garry, The 222 Broadway .... Winnipeg MB R3C0R3 204-942-8251 956-2351
TF: 800-665-8088 ■ *Web:* www.fortgarryhotel.com
Fort Marcy Hotel Suites 321 Kearney Ave .... Santa Fe NM 87501 505-988-2800 992-1804
TF: 888-667-2775 ■ *Web:* www.allseasonsresortlodging.com
Forum Motor Inn
800-814 Atlantic Ave PO Box 448 .... Ocean City NJ 08226 609-399-8700
Web: www.theforuminoc.homestead.com
Four Points by Sheraton Charlotte
315 E Woodlawn Rd .... Charlotte NC 28217 704-522-0852 522-1634
TF: 800-368-7764 ■ *Web:* www.starwoodhotels.com
Four Points by Sheraton French Quarter
541 Bourbon St .... New Orleans LA 70130 504-524-7611 524-8273
TF: 800-535-7891 ■ *Web:* www.fourpointsfrenchquarter.com
Four Queens Hotel & Casino 202 Fremont St .... Las Vegas NV 89101 702-385-4011 387-5158
TF: 800-634-6045 ■ *Web:* www.fourqueens.com
Four Sails Resort Hotel
3301 Atlantic Ave .... Virginia Beach VA 23451 757-491-8100 491-0573
TF: 800-227-4213 ■ *Web:* www.foursails.com
Four Seasons Hotels Inc 1165 Leslie St .... Toronto ON M3C2K8 416-449-1750 441-4374
TF: 800-332-3442 ■ *Web:* www.fourseasons.com
Francis Marion Hotel, The 387 King St .... Charleston SC 29403 843-722-0600 853-2186
TF: 877-756-2121 ■ *Web:* www.francismarionhotel.com
Franklin, The 164 E 87th St .... New York NY 10128 212-369-1000 369-8000
Web: www.franklinhotel.com
Fremont Hotel & Casino 200 Fremont St .... Las Vegas NV 89101 702-385-3232 385-6270
TF: 800-634-6460 ■ *Web:* www.fremontcasino.com
French Quarter Suites Hotel
1119 N Rampart St .... New Orleans LA 70116 504-524-7725 522-9716
TF: 800-457-2253 ■ *Web:* www.frenchquartersuites.com
Frost Valley Ymca 2000 Frost Vly Rd .... Claryville NY 12725 845-985-2291
Web: www.frostvalley.org
Future Inns 30 Fairfax Dr .... Halifax NS B3S1P1 902-443-4333
Web: www.futureinns.co.uk
G6 Hospitality LLC
Motel 6 4001 International Pkwy .... Carrollton TX 75007 972-360-9000 716-6416
TF: 800-466-8356 ■ *Web:* www.motel6.com
Galleria Park Hotel 191 Sutter St .... San Francisco CA 94104 415-781-3060
Web: www.jdvhotels.com
Galt House Hotel 140 N Fourth St .... Louisville KY 40202 502-589-5200
TF: 800-843-4258 ■ *Web:* www.galthouse.com
Galveston Computer Solutions LLC
523 24th St Ste 101 .... Galveston TX 77550 409-762-4326
Web: galvestoncs.com
Garden City Hotel 45 Seventh St .... Garden City NY 11530 516-747-3000 747-1414
TF: 877-549-0400 ■ *Web:* www.gardencityhotel.com
Garden Court Hotel 520 Cowper St .... Palo Alto CA 94301 650-322-9000 324-3609
TF: 800-824-9028 ■ *Web:* www.gardencourt.com
Garden Place Hotel 6461 Transit Rd .... Depew NY 14043 716-683-7990
TF: 877-456-4097 ■ *Web:* www.salvatores.net/garden_place/index.html
Gardens Hotel 526 Angela St .... Key West FL 33040 305-294-2661 292-1007
TF: 800-526-2664 ■ *Web:* www.gardenshotel.com
Gardner Hotel 311 E Franklin Ave .... El Paso TX 79901 915-532-3661 532-0302
Web: www.gardnerhotel.com
Garfield Suites Hotel Two Garfield Pl .... Cincinnati OH 45202 513-421-3355 421-3729
TF: 800-367-2155 ■ *Web:* www.garfieldsuitehotel.com
Garland, The 4222 Vineland Ave .... North Hollywood CA 91602 818-980-8000 766-0112
TF: 800-238-3759 ■ *Web:* www.beverlygarland.com

	City	State	Zip	Phone	Fax
Garrett's Desert Inn 311 Old Santa Fe Trl *TF:* 800-888-2145 ■ *Web:* www.garrettsdesertinn.com	Santa Fe	NM	87501	505-982-1851	989-1647
Gaslamp Plaza Suites 520 E St *TF:* 800-874-8770 ■ *Web:* www.gaslampplaza.com	San Diego	CA	92101	619-232-9500	238-9945
Gastonian, The 220 E Gaston St *TF:* 800-322-6603 ■ *Web:* www.gastonian.com	Savannah	GA	31401	912-232-2869	232-0710
Gateway Hospitality LLC 111 Stonemark Ln Ste 202 *Web:* gatewayhospitality.com	Columbia	SC	29210	803-798-7979	
Gateways Inn 51 Walker St *TF:* 888-492-9466 ■ *Web:* www.gatewaysinn.com	Lenox	MA	01240	413-637-2532	637-1432
Gaylord Opryland Hotel & Convention Ctr 2800 Opryland Dr *TF:* 888-236-2427 ■ *Web:* www.marriott.com	Nashville	TN	37214	615-889-1000	885-3054
General Morgan Inn 111 N Main St *TF:* 800-223-2679 ■ *Web:* generalmorganinn.com	Greeneville	TN	37743	423-787-1000	
Genesee Grande Hotel 1060 E Genesee St *TF:* 800-365-4663 ■ *Web:* www.geneseegrande.com	Syracuse	NY	13210	315-476-4212	471-4663
Geneva on the Lake 1001 Lochland Rd *TF:* 800-343-6382 ■ *Web:* www.genevaonthelake.com	Geneva	NY	14456	315-789-7190	682-6306
George Washington University Inn 824 New Hampshire Ave NW *TF:* 800-426-4455 ■ *Web:* www.gwuinn.com	Washington	DC	20037	202-337-6620	298-7499
Georgetown Inn 1310 Wisconsin Ave *TF:* 866-971-6618 ■ *Web:* www.georgetowninn.com	Washington	DC	20007	202-333-8900	333-8308
Georgian Court Hotel 773 Beatty St *TF:* 800-663-1155 ■ *Web:* www.georgiancourthotelvancouver.com	Vancouver	BC	V6B2M4	604-682-5555	682-8830
Georgian Hotel 1415 Ocean Ave *TF:* 800-538-8147 ■ *Web:* www.georgianhotel.com	Santa Monica	CA	90401	310-395-9945	451-3374
Georgian Resort 384 Canada St *TF:* 800-525-3436 ■ *Web:* www.georgianresort.com	Lake George	NY	12845	518-668-5401	668-5870
Georgian Terrace Hotel 659 Peachtree St NE *TF:* 800-651-2316 ■ *Web:* www.thegeorgianterrace.com	Atlanta	GA	30308	404-897-1991	724-9116
Gershwin Hotel 7 E 27th St *TF:* 855-468-3501 ■ *Web:* www.theevelyn.com	New York	NY	10016	212-545-8000	532-5008
Gideon Putnam Resort & Spa 24 Gideon Putnam Rd *TF:* 800-452-7275 ■ *Web:* www.gideonputnam.com	Saratoga Springs	NY	12866	518-584-3000	584-1354
Giusto Enterprises Inc 7525 Mission St *Web:* elcaminoinn.com	Daly City	CA	94014	650-992-7090	
Glacier Bay Country Inn 35 Tong Rd *TF:* 800-628-0912 ■ *Web:* www.glacierbayalaska.com	Gustavus	AK	99826	800-628-0912	
Glass House Inn 3202 W 26th St *TF:* 800-956-7222 ■ *Web:* www.glasshouseinn.com	Erie	PA	16506	814-833-7751	833-4222
Glen Grove Suites 2837 Yonge St *TF:* 800-565-3024 ■ *Web:* www.glengrove.com	Toronto	ON	M4N2J6	416-489-8441	440-3065
Glendorn 1000 Glendorn Dr *TF:* 800-843-8568 ■ *Web:* www.glendorn.com	Bradford	PA	16701	814-362-6511	368-9923
Glenerin Inn, The 1695 The Collegeway *TF:* 877-991-9971 ■ *Web:* www.glenerininn.com	Mississauga	ON	L5L3S7	905-828-6103	828-0891
Glenmore Inn 2720 Glenmore Trl SE *TF:* 800-661-3163 ■ *Web:* www.glenmoreinn.com	Calgary	AB	T2C2E6	403-279-8611	236-8035
Glidden House 1901 Ford Dr *TF:* 866-812-4537 ■ *Web:* www.gliddenhouse.com	Cleveland	OH	44106	216-231-8900	231-2130
Glorietta Bay Inn 1630 Glorietta Blvd *TF:* 800-283-9383 ■ *Web:* www.gloriettabayinn.com	Coronado	CA	92118	619-435-3101	435-6182
Gold Coast Hotel & Casino 4000 W Flamingo Rd *TF:* 800-331-5334 ■ *Web:* www.goldcoastcasino.com	Las Vegas	NV	89103	702-367-7111	367-8575
Goldbelt Hotel Juneau 51 Egan Dr *TF:* 888-478-6909 ■ *Web:* www.goldbelt.com/subsidiaries/gbhj.html	Juneau	AK	99801	907-586-6900	463-3567
Golden Eagle Resort 511 Mountain Rd PO Box 1090 *TF:* 800-626-1010 ■ *Web:* www.goldeneagleresort.com	Stowe	VT	05672	802-253-4811	253-2561
Golden Hotel, The 800 11th St *TF:* 800-233-7214 ■ *Web:* www.thegoldenhotel.com	Golden	CO	80401	303-279-0100	279-9353
Goldener Hirsch Inn 7570 Royal St E *TF Cust Svc:* 800-252-3373 ■ *Web:* www.goldenerhirschinn.com	Park City	UT	84060	435-649-7770	649-7901
Good Hospitality Services Inc 1051 Southpoint Dr Ste A *Web:* goodhsi.com	Valparaiso	IN	46385	219-462-6265	
Good Hotel *Good Hotel* 112 Seventh St *TF:* 800-444-5819 ■ *Web:* www.thegoodhotel.com	San Francisco	CA	94103	415-621-7001	626-3974
Good-Nite Inn Fremont 4135 Cushing Pkwy *TF:* 800-648-3466 ■ *Web:* www.goodnite.com	Fremont	CA	94538	510-656-9307	656-9110
Goodmanagement 603 Pilot House Dr Ste 225 *Web:* www.goodmanagement.com	Newport News	VA	23606	757-596-5215	
Gouverneur Hotel Montreal (Place-Dupuis) 1000 Sherbrooke St W Ste 2300 *TF:* 888-910-1111 ■ *Web:* www.gouverneur.com	Montreal	QC	H3A3R3	888-910-1111	
Gouverneur Hotels 1000 Sherbrooke St W Ste 2300 **Fax Area Code:* 819 ■ *Web:* www.gouverneur.com	Montreal	QC	H3A3R3	514-875-8822	762-8991*
Governor Calvert House 58 State Cir *TF:* 800-847-8882 ■ *Web:* www.historicinnsofannapolis.com	Annapolis	MD	21401	410-263-2641	268-3613
Governor Hotel 621 S Capitol Way *TF:* 800-716-6199 ■ *Web:* olympiagovernorhotel.com/	Olympia	WA	98501	360-352-7700	943-9349
Governor's Inn 210 Richards Blvd *TF:* 800-999-6689 ■ *Web:* www.governorsinnhotel.com	Sacramento	CA	95814	916-448-7224	448-7382
Governors Inn 209 S Adams St *Web:* thegovinn.org	Tallahassee	FL	32301	850-681-6855	222-3105
Grafton on Sunset 8462 W Sunset Blvd *TF:* 800-821-3660 ■ *Web:* www.graftononsunset.com	West Hollywood	CA	90069	323-654-4600	654-5918
Graham, The 1075 Thomas Jefferson St NW *TF:* 855-341-1292 ■ *Web:* thegrahamgeorgetown.com	Washington	DC	20007	202-337-0900	333-6526
Gramercy Park Hotel 2 Lexington Ave *TF:* 866-784-1300 ■ *Web:* www.gramercyparkhotel.com	New York	NY	10010	212-920-3300	673-5890
Grand America Hotel 555 S Main St *TF:* 800-621-4505 ■ *Web:* www.grandamerica.com	Salt Lake City	UT	84111	801-258-6000	258-6911
Grand Beach Inn (GBI) 198 E Grand Ave *Web:* grandbeachinnmaine.com	Old Orchard Beach	ME	04064	207-934-4621	934-3435
Grand Country Inn Grand Country Sq 1945 W Hwy 76 *TF:* 888-505-4096 ■ *Web:* www.grandcountry.com/lodging	Branson	MO	65616	417-335-3535	
Grand Del Mar 5300 Grand Del Mar Ct *TF:* 855-314-2030 ■ *Web:* www.thegranddelmar.com	San Diego	CA	92130	858-314-2000	314-2001
Grand Gateway Hotel 1721 N LaCrosse St *TF:* 866-742-1300 ■ *Web:* www.grandgatewayhotel.com	Rapid City	SD	57701	605-342-8853	342-0663
Grand Hotel & Suites Toronto 225 Jarvis St *TF:* 877-324-7263 ■ *Web:* www.grandhoteltoronto.com	Toronto	ON	M5B2C1	416-863-9000	863-1100
Grand Hotel Edmonton 10266 103rd St *Web:* www.thegrandedmonton.ca	Edmonton	AB	T5J0Y8	780-422-6365	
Grand Hotel Minneapolis, The 615 Second Ave S *TF:* 866-843-4726 ■ *Web:* www.grandhotelminneapolis.com	Minneapolis	MN	55402	612-288-8888	373-0407
Grand Hotel of Cape May Beach Ave *Web:* www.grandhotelcapemay.com	Cape May	NJ	08204	609-884-5611	
Grand Hotel, The 149 State Rt 64 *Web:* www.grandcanyongrandhotel.com	Tusayan	AZ	86023	928-638-3333	
Grand Hyatt Washington 1000 H St NW *Web:* grandwashington.hyatt.com	Washington	DC	20001	202-582-1234	
Grand Oaks Hotel 2315 Green Mountain Dr *TF:* 800-553-6423 ■ *Web:* www.grandoakshotel.net	Branson	MO	65616	800-553-6423	
Grand Summit Hotel 570 Springfield Ave *TF:* 800-346-0773 ■ *Web:* grandsummit.com	Summit	NJ	07901	908-273-3000	273-4228
Grande Colonial 910 Prospect St **Fax Area Code:* 858 ■ *TF:* 888-828-5498 ■ *Web:* www.thegrandecolonial.com	La Jolla	CA	92037	888-828-5498	454-5679*
Grandmark Lodging 3300 28th St SW	Grandville	MI	49418	616-534-7641	
Grant Plaza Hotel 465 Grant Ave *TF:* 800-472-6899 ■ *Web:* www.grantplaza.com	San Francisco	CA	94108	415-434-3883	434-3886
Granville Island Hotel 1253 Johnston St **Fax:* Admin ■ *TF Resv:* 800-663-1840 ■ *Web:* www.granvilleislandhotel.com	Vancouver	BC	V6H3R9	604-683-7373	683-3061*
Graycote Inn 40 Holland Ave *Web:* www.graycoteinn.com	Bar Harbor	ME	04609	207-288-3044	288-2719
Great Divide Lodge 550 Village Rd PO Box 8059 *TF:* 888-400-9590 ■ *Web:* www.breckresorts.com	Breckenridge	CO	80424	970-547-5550	
Green Harbor Resort 182 Baxter Ave *Web:* www.greenharborresort.com	West Yarmouth	MA	02673	508-771-1126	771-0701
Green Mountain Inn 18 Main St PO Box 60 *TF:* 800-253-7302 ■ *Web:* www.greenmountaininn.com	Stowe	VT	05672	802-253-7301	253-5096
Green Park Inn 9239 Valley Blvd *Web:* www.greenparkinn.com	Blowing Rock	NC	28605	828-414-9230	
Green Valley Ranch Resort Casino & Spa 2300 Paseo Verde Pkwy *TF Resv:* 866-782-9487 ■ *Web:* greenvalleyranch.sclv.com	Henderson	NV	89052	702-617-7777	
Grey Bonnet Inn 831 Rt 100 N *TF:* 800-342-2086 ■ *Web:* www.greybonnetinn.com	Killington	VT	05751	802-775-2537	775-3371
Greyfield Inn Four N Second St Ste 300 *TF:* 866-401-8581 ■ *Web:* www.greyfieldinn.com	Fernandina Beach	FL	32034	904-261-6408	321-0666
Grove Hotel, The 245 S Capitol Blvd *Web:* www.grovehotelboise.com	Boise	ID	83702	208-333-8000	333-8800
Grove Isle Hotel & Spa Four Grove Isle Dr *Web:* www.groveisle.com	Miami	FL	33133	305-858-8300	858-5908
Guest Inn 2533 N Piccoli Rd	Stockton	CA	95215	209-931-6675	931-8351
GuestHouse International LLC 100 Bluegrass Commons Blvd Ste 110 **Fax Area Code:* 770 ■ *TF:* 800-214-8378 ■ *Web:* www.guesthouseintl.com	Hendersonville	TN	37075	800-214-8378	951-0307*
Habana Inn 2200 NW 40th St *TF:* 800-988-2221 ■ *Web:* www.habanainn.com	Oklahoma City	OK	73112	405-525-0730	528-0496
Habitat Suites 500 E Highland Mall Blvd *TF:* 800-535-4663 ■ *Web:* www.habitatsuites.com	Austin	TX	78752	512-467-6000	467-6000
Hacienda Hotel 525 N Sepulveda Blvd	El Segundo	CA	90245	310-615-0015	615-0217
Hacienda The at Hotel Santa Fe 1501 Paseo del Peralta *TF:* 855-825-9876 ■ *Web:* www.hotelsantafe.com/the_hacienda	Santa Fe	NM	87501	505-955-7805	
Halekulani Hotel 2199 Kalia Rd *TF:* 800-367-2343 ■ *Web:* www.halekulani.com	Honolulu	HI	96815	808-923-2311	926-8004
Half Moon Bay Lodge & Conference Ctr 2400 S Cabrillo Hwy *TF:* 800-710-0778 ■ *Web:* pacificahotels.com/halfmoonbaylodge	Half Moon Bay	CA	94019	650-726-9000	726-7951
Halifax Marriott Harborfront Hotel 1919 Upper Water St *TF:* 800-450-4442 ■ *Web:* www.marriott.com/hotels/travel/yhzmc-halifax-marriott-harbourfront-hotel	Halifax	NS	B3J3J5	902-421-1700	422-5805
Halliburton House Inn 5184 Morris St *TF:* 888-512-3344 ■ *Web:* www.thehalliburton.com	Halifax	NS	B3J1B3	902-420-0658	423-2324
Hallmark Inns & Resorts 15455 Hallmark Dr Ste 200 **Fax Area Code:* 503 ■ *TF:* 888-448-4449 ■ *Web:* www.hallmarkinns.com	Lake Oswego	OR	97035	888-448-4449	436-0324*
Hampton Inn & Suites Atlanta Downtown Hotel 161 Spring St NW *Web:* hamptoninn.hilton.com	Atlanta	GA	30303	404-589-1111	
Hampton Inn Phoenix-Biltmore 2310 E Highland Ave *Web:* www.hotelhighlandatbiltmore.com	Phoenix	AZ	85016	602-956-5221	
Handlery Union Square Hotel 351 Geary St *TF:* 800-995-4874 ■ *Web:* www.handlery.com	San Francisco	CA	94102	415-781-7800	781-0216
Hanover Inn Two E Wheelock St *TF:* 800-443-7024 ■ *Web:* www.hanoverinn.com	Hanover	NH	03755	603-643-4300	643-4433
Harbor Court Hotel 550 Light St *TF:* 800-766-3782 ■ *Web:* www.sonesta.com	Baltimore	MD	21202	410-234-0550	659-5925
Harbor House 28 Pier 21 *Web:* www.harborhousepier21.com	Galveston	TX	77550	409-763-3321	765-6421
Harbor View Hotel 131 N Water St Martha's Vineyard PO Box 7 *TF:* 800-225-6005 ■ *Web:* www.harbor-view.com	Edgartown	MA	02539	508-627-7000	627-8417
Harborside Hotel & Marina 55 W St *TF:* 800-328-5033 ■ *Web:* www.theharborsidehotel.com	Bar Harbor	ME	04609	207-288-5033	288-3661
Harborside Inn One Christie's Landing *TF:* 800-427-9444 ■ *Web:* www.newportharborsideinn.com	Newport	RI	02840	401-846-6600	849-8510

				Phone	Fax
Harborside Inn of Boston 185 State St *Web:* www.harborsideinnboston.com	Boston	MA	02109	617-723-7500	670-6015
Hard Rock Hotel & Casino Biloxi 777 Beach Blvd *TF:* 877-877-6256 ■ *Web:* www.hardrockbiloxi.com	Biloxi	MS	39530	228-374-7625	276-7655
Hard Rock Hotel Chicago 230 N Michigan Ave *Web:* www.hardrockhotelchicago.com	Chicago	IL	60601	312-345-1000	
Hard Rock Hotel San Diego 207 Fifth Ave *TF:* 866-751-7625 ■ *Web:* www.hardrockhotelsd.com	San Diego	CA	92101	619-702-3000	702-3007
Harrah's Council Bluffs 1 Harrahs Blvd *TF:* 800-342-7724 ■ *Web:* www.harrahscouncilbluffs.com	Council Bluffs	IA	51501	712-329-6000	329-6491
Harrah's Joliet 151 N Joliet St *TF:* 800-522-4700 ■ *Web:* www.harrahsjoliet.com	Joliet	IL	60432	815-740-7800	740-2223
Harrah's Las Vegas 3475 Las Vegas Blvd S *TF:* 800-214-9110 ■ *Web:* www.harrahslasvegas.com	Las Vegas	NV	89109	800-214-9110	
Harrah's Reno 219 N Ctr St *TF:* 866-736-6427 ■ *Web:* www.harrahsreno.com	Reno	NV	89501	775-788-3044	
Harraseeket Inn 162 Main St *TF:* 800-342-6423 ■ *Web:* www.harraseeketinn.com	Freeport	ME	04032	207-865-9377	865-1684
Harrison Plaza Suite Hotel 409 S Cole Rd	Boise	ID	83709	208-376-3608	376-3608
Hartness House Inn 30 Orchard St *TF:* 800-732-4789 ■ *Web:* hartnesshouse.com	Springfield	VT	05156	802-885-2115	885-2207
Harvard Square Hotel 110 Mt Auburn St Harvard Sq *TF:* 800-458-5886 ■ *Web:* www.harvardsquarehotel.com	Cambridge	MA	02138	617-864-5200	864-2409
Harvest Inn 1 Main St *TF:* 800-950-8466 ■ *Web:* www.harvestinn.com	Saint Helena	CA	94574	707-963-9463	963-4402
Hassayampa Inn 122 E Gurley St **Fax Area Code:* 928 ■ *TF Cust Svc:* 800-322-1927 ■ *Web:* www.hassayampainn.com	Prescott	AZ	86301	800-322-1927	445-8590*
Hastings House Country House Hotel 160 Upper Ganges Rd *TF:* 800-661-9255 ■ *Web:* www.hastingshouse.com	Salt Spring Island	BC	V8K2S2	250-537-2362	537-5333
Hawaiian Inn 2301 S Atlantic Ave *TF:* 800-922-3023 ■ *Web:* www.hawaiianinn.com	Daytona Beach Shores	FL	32118	386-255-5411	253-1209
Hawthorne Hotel 18 Washington Sq W *TF:* 800-729-7829 ■ *Web:* www.hawthornehotel.com	Salem	MA	01970	978-744-4080	745-9842
Hawthorne Inn & Conference Ctr 420 High St *TF:* 877-777-3099 ■ *Web:* www.wakehealth.edu	Winston-Salem	NC	27101	336-777-3000	777-3282
Hay-Adams Hotel 800 16th St NE *Web:* www.hayadams.com	Washington	DC	20006	202-638-6600	638-2716
Haywood Park Hotel One Battery Pk Ave *Web:* www.haywoodpark.com	Asheville	NC	28801	828-252-2522	253-0481
Heartland Inns 87-2nd St *TF Resv:* 800-334-3277 ■ *Web:* www.heartlandinns.com	Coralville	IA	52241	319-351-8132	
Heathman Lodge 7801 NE Greenwood Dr *Web:* www.heathmanlodge.com	Vancouver	WA	98662	360-254-3100	254-6100
Helmsley Sandcastle Hotel 1540 Ben Franklin Dr *TF:* 800-225-2181 ■ *Web:* www.helmsleysandcastle.com	Sarasota	FL	34236	941-388-2181	388-2655
Henley Park Hotel 926 Massachusetts Ave NW *TF:* 800-222-8474 ■ *Web:* www.henleypark.com	Washington	DC	20001	202-638-5200	638-6740
Henlopen Hotel 511 N Boardwalk *TF:* 800-441-8450 ■ *Web:* www.henlopenhotel.com	Rehoboth Beach	DE	19971	302-227-2551	227-8147
Heritage Hotels & Resorts Inc 201 Third St NW Ste 1500 *Web:* www.heritagehotelsandresorts.com	Albuquerque	NM	87102	505-836-6700	
Heritage Inn 1350 Richmond Rd	Williamsburg	VA	23185	757-229-2455	
Heritage Inn, The 34521 Postal Ln *TF:* 800-669-9399 ■ *Web:* www.rehobothheritage.com	Lewes	DE	19958	800-669-9399	
Hermitage Hotel 231 Sixth Ave N *TF:* 888-888-9414 ■ *Web:* www.thehermitagehotel.com	Nashville	TN	37219	615-244-3121	254-6909
Hermosa Inn 5532 N Palo Cristi Rd *TF:* 800-241-1210 ■ *Web:* www.hermosainn.com	Paradise Valley	AZ	85253	602-955-8614	955-8299
Hershey Entertainment & Resorts Co 27 W Chocolate Ave **Fax Area Code:* 717 ■ *TF:* 800-437-7439 ■ *Web:* www.hersheypa.com	Hershey	PA	17033	800-437-7439	534-3324*
Hershey Lodge 325 University Dr *TF:* 800-437-7439 ■ *Web:* www.hersheylodge.com	Hershey	PA	17033	717-533-3311	533-9642
HI Development Corp 111 W Fortune St *Web:* www.hidevelopment.com	Tampa	FL	33602	813-229-6686	
Hilgard House Hotel & Suites 927 Hilgard Ave *TF:* 800-826-3934 ■ *Web:* www.hilgardhouse.com	Los Angeles	CA	90024	310-208-3945	208-1972
Hilltop Inn of Vermont 3472 Airport Rd *TF:* 877-609-0003 ■ *Web:* www.hilltopinnvt.net	Montpelier	VT	05602	802-229-5766	229-5766
Hilton Anaheim 777 W Convention Way *Web:* www.hiltonanaheimhotel.com	Anaheim	CA	92802	714-750-4321	
Hilton Atlanta Northeast 5993 Peachtree Industrial Blvd *Web:* hilton.com	Norcross	GA	30092	770-447-4747	
Hilton Garden Inn (Burlington Canada) 985 Syscon Rd *Web:* hiltongardeninn3.hilton.com	Burlington	ON	L7L5S3	905-631-7000	
Hilton Garden Inn Greenville 108 Carolina Point Pkwy *Web:* hiltongardeninn3.hilton.com	Greenville	SC	29605	864-284-0111	
Hilton Jackson 1001 E County Line Rd *Web:* www.hiltonjackson.com	Jackson	MS	39211	601-957-2800	
Hilton La Jolla Torrey Pines 10950 N Torrey Pines Rd *Web:* hilton.com	La Jolla	CA	92037	858-558-1500	
Hilton Long Beach Hotel & Executive Meeting Center 701 W Ocean Blvd *Web:* hiltonlb.com	Long Beach	CA	90831	562-983-3400	
Hilton Providence 21 Atwells Ave *Web:* hilton.com	Providence	RI	02903	401-831-3900	
Hilton St Louis Hotel at BaLLPark One S Broadway *Web:* www.hiltonstlouis.com	Saint Louis	MO	63102	314-421-1776	
Hilton Suites Atlanta Perimeter 6120 Peachtree Dunwoody Rd Ne *Web:* hilton.com	Atlanta	GA	30328	770-668-0808	
Hilton Worldwide 7930 Jones Branch Dr *TF:* 800-445-8667 ■ *Web:* www.hiltonworldwide.com	McLean	VA	22102	703-883-1000	
Historic Bullock Hotel 633 Main St **Fax Area Code:* 605 ■ *TF:* 800-336-1876 ■ *Web:* www.historicbullock.com	Deadwood	SD	57732	800-336-1876	578-1382*
Historic French Market Inn 509 Decatur St *TF:* 800-366-2743 ■ *Web:* www.frenchmarketinn.com	New Orleans	LA	70130	504-561-5621	581-3802
Historic Inns of Annapolis 58 State Cir *TF:* 800-847-8882 ■ *Web:* www.historicinnsofannapolis.com	Annapolis	MD	21401	410-263-2641	268-3613
HLC Hotels Inc 7080 Abercorn St PO Box 13069 *TF:* 800-344-4378 ■ *Web:* www.hlchotels.com	Savannah	GA	31416	912-352-4493	352-0314
Holiday Inn 301 Government St *TF:* 888-465-4329 ■ *Web:* www.ihg.com	Mobile	AL	36602	251-694-0100	694-0160
Holiday Inn Express DFW North 4550 W John Carpenter Fwy **Fax Area Code:* 972 ■ *TF:* 800-465-4329 ■ *Web:* www.ihg.com	Irving	TX	75063	800-465-4329	929-0774*
Holiday Inn Resort Daytona Beach Oceanfront 1615 S Atlantic Ave *TF:* 800-874-0975 ■ *Web:* www.hiresortdaytona.com	Daytona Beach	FL	32118	386-255-0921	
Hollow Inn 278 S Main St *Web:* www.hollowinn.com	Barre	VT	05641	802-479-9313	476-5242
Hollywood Roosevelt Hotel 7000 Hollywood Blvd *TF:* 800-950-7667 ■ *Web:* www.thompsonhotels.com	Los Angeles	CA	90028	323-466-7000	462-8056
Hollywood Standard Hotel 8300 Sunset Blvd *Web:* www.standardhotels.com	West Hollywood	CA	90069	323-650-9090	650-2820
Homestead Inn 420 Field Pt Rd *Web:* www.homesteadinn.com	Greenwich	CT	06830	203-869-7500	869-7502
Horton Grand Hotel 311 Island Ave *TF:* 800-542-1886 ■ *Web:* www.hortongrand.com	San Diego	CA	92101	619-544-1886	
Hospitality Inn 3709 NW 39th St	Oklahoma City	OK	73112	405-942-7730	
Master Hosts Inns & Resorts 1726 Montreal Cir **Fax Area Code:* 770 ■ *TF:* 800-247-4677 ■ *Web:* www.bookroomsnow.com	Tucker	GA	30084	800-247-4677	270-1077*
Passport Inn 1726 Montreal Cir **Fax Area Code:* 770 ■ *TF:* 800-251-1962 ■ *Web:* www.bookroomsnow.com	Tucker	GA	30084	800-251-1962	270-1077*
Red Carpet Inn 1726 Montreal Cir **Fax Area Code:* 770 ■ *TF:* 800-247-4677 ■ *Web:* www.bookroomsnow.com	Tucker	GA	30084	800-247-4677	270-1077*
Hospitality International Inc *Scottish Inns* 1726 Montreal Cir **Fax Area Code:* 770 ■ *TF:* 800-251-1962 ■ *Web:* www.bookroomsnow.com	Tucker	GA	30084	800-251-1962	270-1077*
Hospitality Suites Resort 409 N Scottsdale Rd *TF:* 800-445-5115 ■ *Web:* www.hospitalitysuites.com	Scottsdale	AZ	85257	480-949-5115	941-8014
Hostmark Hospitality Group 1300 E Woodfield Rd Ste 400 *Web:* www.hostmark.com	Schaumburg	IL	60173	847-517-9100	517-9797
Hotel & Suites Normandin 4700 Pierre-Bertrand Blvd *TF:* 800-463-6721 ■ *Web:* www.hotelnormandin.com	Quebec	QC	G2J1A4	418-622-1611	622-9277
Hotel 1000 1000 First Ave *TF:* 877-315-1088 ■ *Web:* www.hotel1000seattle.com	Seattle	WA	98104	206-957-1000	357-9457
Hotel 140 140 Clarendon St *TF:* 800-714-0140 ■ *Web:* www.hotel140.com	Boston	MA	02116	617-585-5600	585-5699
Hotel 43 981 Grove St *TF:* 800-243-4622 ■ *Web:* www.hotel43.com	Boise	ID	83702	208-342-4622	344-5751
Hotel 71 71 St Pierre St *TF:* 888-692-1171 ■ *Web:* www.hotel71.ca	Quebec City	QC	G1K4A4	418-692-1171	692-0669
Hotel Abri 127 Ellis St *TF:* 866-778-6169 ■ *Web:* www.hotelabrisf.com	San Francisco	CA	94102	415-392-8800	
Hotel Adagio 550 Geary St *TF:* 800-738-7477 ■ *Web:* www.jdvhotels.com	San Francisco	CA	94102	415-775-5000	775-9388
Hotel Alex Johnson 523 Sixth St *TF:* 800-888-2539 ■ *Web:* www.alexjohnson.com	Rapid City	SD	57701	605-342-1210	342-9326
Hotel Allegro Chicago 171 W Randolph St *TF:* 800-643-1500 ■ *Web:* www.allegrochicago.com	Chicago	IL	60601	312-236-0123	236-3440
Hotel Ambassadeur 3401 Blvd Ste-Anne *TF:* 800-363-4619 ■ *Web:* www.hotelambassadeur.ca	Qu,bec	QC	G1E3L4	418-666-2828	666-2775
Hotel Ambassador 1324 S Main St *TF General:* 888-408-8282 ■ *Web:* www.ambassadorhotelcollection.com	Tulsa	OK	74119	918-587-8200	587-8208
Hotel Andra 2000 Fourth Ave *TF:* 877-448-8600 ■ *Web:* www.hotelandra.com	Seattle	WA	98121	206-448-8600	441-7140
Hotel Andrew Jackson 919 Royal St *TF:* 844-561-5881 ■ *Web:* www.frenchquarterinns.com	New Orleans	LA	70116	504-561-5881	
Hotel Angeleno 170 N Church Ln *Web:* hotelangeleno.com	Los Angeles	CA	90049	310-476-6411	472-1157
Hotel Astor 956 Washington Ave *TF:* 800-270-4981 ■ *Web:* www.hotelastor.com	Miami Beach	FL	33139	305-531-8081	531-3193
Hotel at Old Town Wichita 830 E First St *TF:* 877-265-3869 ■ *Web:* www.hotelatoldtown.com	Wichita	KS	67202	316-267-4800	267-4840
Hotel Avante 860 E El Camino Real *TF:* 800-538-1600 ■ *Web:* jdvhotels.com/hotels/california/silicon-valley-hotels/hotel-avante	Mountain View	CA	94040	650-940-1000	968-7870
Hotel Beacon 2130 Broadway *TF:* 800-572-4969 ■ *Web:* www.beaconhotel.com	New York	NY	10023	212-787-1100	724-0839
Hotel Bedford 118 E 40th St *TF:* 800-221-6881 ■ *Web:* www.hotelbedfordny.com	New York	NY	10016	212-697-4800	697-1093
Hotel Bel-Air 701 Stone Canyon Rd *TF:* 800-648-4097 ■ *Web:* www.dorchestercollection.com	Los Angeles	CA	90077	310-472-1211	276-2251
Hotel Bethlehem 437 Main St *TF:* 800-607-2384 ■ *Web:* www.hotelbethlehem.com	Bethlehem	PA	18018	610-625-5000	625-2218
Hotel Bijou 111 Mason St *TF:* 877-568-2733 ■ *Web:* www.jdvhotels.com	San Francisco	CA	94102	415-771-1200	
Hotel Blake 500 S Dearborn St *Web:* www.hotelblake.com	Chicago	IL	60605	312-986-1234	939-2468
Hotel Boulderado 2115 13th St *TF:* 800-433-4344 ■ *Web:* www.boulderado.com	Boulder	CO	80302	303-442-4344	442-4378
Hotel Burnham One W Washington St *TF:* 866-690-1986 ■ *Web:* www.burnhamhotel.com	Chicago	IL	60602	312-782-1111	782-0899

				Phone	Fax
Hotel Captain Cook 939 W Fifth Ave	Anchorage	AK	99501	907-276-6000	343-2298
TF: 800-843-1950 ■ *Web:* www.captaincook.com					
Hotel Carlton 1075 Sutter St	San Francisco	CA	94109	415-673-0242	
Web: www.jdvhotels.com					
Hotel Casa del Mar 1910 Ocean Way	Santa Monica	CA	90405	310-581-5533	581-5503
TF: 800-898-6999 ■ *Web:* www.hotelcasadelmar.com					
Hotel Chateau Bellevue 16 Rue de la Porte	Quebec	QC	G1R4M9	418-692-2573	692-4876
TF: 877-849-1877 ■ *Web:* www.hotelchateaubellevue.com/en					
Hotel Chateau Laurier 1220 Pl George-V Ouest	Quebec	QC	G1R5B8	418-522-8108	524-8768
TF: 877-522-8108 ■ *Web:* hotelchateaulaurier.com					
Hotel Classique 2815 Laurier Blvd	Quebec	QC	G1V4H3	418-658-2793	658-6816
TF: 800-463-1885 ■ *Web:* www.hotelclassique.com					
Hotel Colorado 526 Pine St	Glenwood Springs	CO	81601	970-945-6511	945-7030
TF: 800-544-3998 ■ *Web:* www.hotelcolorado.com					
Hotel Commonwealth 500 Commonwealth Ave	Boston	MA	02215	617-933-5000	266-6888
TF: 866-784-4000 ■ *Web:* www.hotelcommonwealth.com					
Hotel Congress 311 E Congress St	Tucson	AZ	85701	520-622-8848	792-6366
TF: 800-722-8848 ■ *Web:* www.hotelcongress.com					
Hotel Contessa 306 W Market St	San Antonio	TX	78205	210-229-9222	229-9228
TF: 866-435-0900 ■ *Web:* www.thehotelcontessa.com					
Hotel Crescent Court 400 Crescent Ct	Dallas	TX	75201	214-871-3200	871-3272
Web: www.rosewoodhotels.com					
Hotel de Anza 233 W Santa Clara St	San Jose	CA	95113	408-286-1000	286-0500
TF: 800-843-3700 ■ *Web:* www.hoteldeanza.com					
Hotel De La Monnaie Owners Association Inc					
405 Esplanade Ave	New Orleans	LA	70116	504-947-0009	
Web: hoteldelamonnaie.com					
Hotel Deca 4507 Brooklyn Ave NE	Seattle	WA	98105	206-634-2000	
TF: 800-899-0251 ■ *Web:* www.hoteldeca.com					
Hotel Del Sol 3100 Webster St	San Francisco	CA	94123	415-921-5520	931-4137
TF: 877-433-5765 ■ *Web:* www.jdvhotels.com					
Hotel Deluxe 729 SW 15th Ave	Portland	OR	97205	503-219-2094	219-2095
TF: 866-895-2094 ■ *Web:* www.hoteldeluxeportland.com					
Hotel Derek 2525 W Loop S	Houston	TX	77027	713-961-3000	297-4392
TF: 866-292-4100 ■ *Web:* www.hotelderek.com					
Hotel Drisco 2901 Pacific Ave	San Francisco	CA	94115	415-346-2880	832-6228*
**Fax Area Code:* 510 ■ *TF:* 800-738-7477 ■ *Web:* jdvhotels.com/hotels/california					
Hotel du Pont 11th & Market Sts	Wilmington	DE	19801	302-594-3100	594-3108
TF: 800-441-9019 ■ *Web:* www.hoteldupont.com					
Hotel Durant 2600 Durant Ave	Berkeley	CA	94704	510-845-8981	832-6228
TF: 855-687-7262 ■ *Web:* www.jdvhotels.com					
Hotel Edison 228 W 47th St	New York	NY	10036	212-840-5000	596-6868
TF: 800-637-7070 ■ *Web:* www.edisonhotelnyc.com					
Hotel El Convento					
100 Cristo St Old San Juan	San Juan	PR	00901	787-723-9020	
Web: www.elconvento.com					
Hotel Elysee 60 E 54th St	New York	NY	10022	212-753-1066	980-9278
Web: www.elyseehotel.com					
Hotel Encanto de Las Cruces					
705 S Telshor Blvd	Las Cruces	NM	88011	575-522-4300	522-4300
Web: www.hotelencanto.com/					
Hotel Financial Strategies					
9107 Wilshire Blvd Ste 250	Beverly Hills	CA	90210	310-247-2101	
Web: www.hotelfinancial.com					
Hotel Fort Des Moines 1000 Walnut St	Des Moines	IA	50309	515-243-1161	243-4317
TF: 800-532-1466 ■ *Web:* hotelfortdesmoines.com					
Hotel Galvez - A Wyndham Historic Hotel					
2024 Seawall Blvd	Galveston	TX	77550	409-765-7721	765-5623
TF: 800-996-3426 ■ *Web:* www.wyndham.com					
Hotel Gault 449 Rue St-Helene St	Montreal	QC	H2Y2K9	514-904-1616	904-1717
Web: www.hotelgault.com					
Hotel George 15 E St NW	Washington	DC	20001	202-347-4200	347-4213
TF General: 800-546-7866 ■ *Web:* www.hotelgeorge.com					
Hotel Giraffe 365 Pk Ave S at 26th St	New York	NY	10016	212-685-7700	685-7771
Web: www.hotelgiraffe.com					
Hotel Grand Pacific 463 Belleville St	Victoria	BC	V8V1X3	250-386-0450	380-4475
TF: 800-663-7550 ■ *Web:* www.hotelgrandpacific.com					
Hotel Grand Victorian 2325 W Hwy 76	Branson	MO	65616	417-336-2935	
TF: 800-324-8751 ■ *Web:* www.hotelgrandvictorian.com					
Hotel Granduca 1080 Uptown Pk Blvd	Houston	TX	77056	713-418-1000	418-1001
TF: 888-472-6382 ■ *Web:* www.granducahouston.com					
Hotel Griffon 155 Steuart St	San Francisco	CA	94105	415-495-2100	495-3522
TF: 800-321-2201 ■ *Web:* www.hotelgriffon.com					
Hotel Group, The (THG) 110 James St Ste 102	Edmonds	WA	98020	425-771-1788	672-8280
Web: www.thehotelgroup.com					
Hotel Helix 1430 Rhode Island Ave NW	Washington	DC	20005	202-462-9001	521-2714
Web: www.hotelhelix.com					
Hotel Highland 1023 20th St S	Birmingham	AL	35205	205-933-9555	933-6918
Web: ascendcollection.com					
Hotel Huntington Beach 7667 Ctr Ave	Huntington Beach	CA	92647	714-891-0123	
Web: www.hotelhb.com					
Hotel Icon 220 Main St	Houston	TX	77002	713-224-4266	223-3223*
**Fax Area Code:* 832 ■ *Web:* www.hotelicon.com					
Hotel Indigo San Diego 509 Ninth Ave	San Diego	CA	92101	619-727-4000	
Web: www.hotelinsd.com					
Hotel Jerome 330 E Main St	Aspen	CO	81611	970-429-5028	920-2050
TF: 855-331-7213 ■ *Web:* hoteljerome.aubergeresorts.com					
Hotel Kabuki San Francisco					
1625 Post St	San Francisco	CA	94115	415-922-3200	614-5498
Web: jdvhotels.com/hotels/california/san-francisco-hotels/hotel-kabuki					
Hotel La Jolla 7955 La Jolla Shores Dr	La Jolla	CA	92037	858-459-0261	459-7649
TF: 800-941-1149 ■ *Web:* www.hotellajolla.com					
Hotel La Rose 308 Wilson St	Santa Rosa	CA	95401	707-579-3200	579-3247
TF: 800-527-6738 ■ *Web:* www.hotellarose.com					
Hotel Lawrence 302 S Houston St	Dallas	TX	75202	214-761-9090	761-0740
TF: 877-396-0334 ■ *Web:* www.hotellawrence.com					
Hotel Le Bleu 370 Fourth Ave	Brooklyn	NY	11215	718-625-1500	625-2600
TF: 866-427-6073 ■ *Web:* www.hotellebleu.com					
Hotel Le Cantlie Suites					
1110 Sherbrooke St W	Montreal	QC	H3A1G9	514-842-2000	844-7808
TF: 800-567-1110 ■ *Web:* www.hotelcantlie.com					
Hotel Le Capitole 972 St Jean St	Quebec	QC	G1R1R5	418-694-4040	694-9924
TF: 800-363-4040 ■ *Web:* www.lecapitole.com					
Hotel Le Clos Saint-Louis 69 St Louis St	Quebec	QC	G1R3Z2	418-694-1311	694-9411
TF: 800-461-1311 ■ *Web:* www.clossaintlouis.com					
Hotel Le Germain 2050 Mansfield St	Montreal	QC	H3A1Y9	514-849-2050	849-1437
TF: 877-333-2050 ■ *Web:* www.germainmontreal.com					
Hotel Le Germain Toronto 30 Mercer St	Toronto	ON	M5V1H3	416-345-9500	345-9501
TF: 866-345-9501 ■ *Web:* www.germaintoronto.com					
Hotel Le Marais 717 Conti St	New Orleans	LA	70130	504-525-2300	
TF: 800-935-8740 ■ *Web:* www.hotellemarais.com					
Hotel le Priori 15 du Sault-au-Matelot St	Quebec	QC	G1K3Y7	418-692-3992	692-0883
TF: 800-351-3992 ■ *Web:* www.hotellepriori.com					
Hotel Le Soleil 567 Hornby St	Vancouver	BC	V6C2E8	604-632-3000	632-3001
TF: 877-632-3030 ■ *Web:* www.hotellesoleil.com					
Hotel Le St-James 355 St Jacques St	Montreal	QC	H2Y1N9	514-841-3111	841-1232
TF: 866-841-3111 ■ *Web:* www.hotellestjames.com					
Hotel Lombardy 2019 Pennsylvania Ave NW	Washington	DC	20006	202-828-2600	
TF: 800-424-5486 ■ *Web:* www.hotellombardy.com					
Hotel Lord-Berri 1199 Berri St	Montreal	QC	H2L4C6	514-845-9236	849-9855
TF: 888-363-0363 ■ *Web:* www.lordberri.com					
Hotel Los Gatos 210 E Main St	Los Gatos	CA	95030	408-335-1700	335-1750
Web: www.jdvhotels.com					
Hotel Lucia 400 SW Broadway	Portland	OR	97205	503-225-1717	225-1919
TF: 877-225-1717 ■ *Web:* www.hotellucia.com					
Hotel Lumen 6101 Hillcrest Ave	Dallas	TX	75205	214-219-2400	219-2402
TF: 800-908-1140 ■ *Web:* www.hotellumen.com					
Hotel Lusso 808 West Sprague Avenue	Spokane	WA	99201	509-747-9750	747-9751
TF General: 800-899-1482 ■ *Web:* www.davenporthotelcollection.com					
Hotel Madera 1310 New Hampshire Ave NW	Washington	DC	20036	202-296-7600	293-2476
TF: 800-546-7866 ■ *Web:* www.hotelmadera.com					
Hotel Majestic 1500 Sutter St	San Francisco	CA	94109	415-441-1100	673-7331
Web: www.thehotelmajestic.com					
Hotel Manoir Victoria 44 Cote du Palais	Quebec	QC	G1R4H8	418-692-1030	692-3822
TF: 800-463-6283 ■ *Web:* www.manoir-victoria.com					
Hotel Maritime Plaza 1155 Guy St	Montreal	QC	H3H2K5	514-932-1411	932-0446
TF: 877-768-4326 ■ *Web:* www.tidanhotels.com					
Hotel Mark Twain 345 Taylor St	San Francisco	CA	94102	415-673-2332	673-0529
TF: 877-854-4106 ■ *Web:* www.hotelmarktwain.com					
Hotel Marlowe Cambridge					
25 Edwind H Land Blvd	Cambridge	MA	02141	617-868-8000	868-8001
TF: 800-825-7140 ■ *Web:* www.hotelmarlowe.com					
Hotel Max 620 Stewart St	Seattle	WA	98101	206-728-6299	443-5754
TF: 866-833-6299 ■ *Web:* www.hotelmaxseattle.com					
Hotel Mead 451 E Grand Ave	Wisconsin Rapids	WI	54494	715-423-1500	423-1510
TF: 800-843-6323 ■ *Web:* www.hotelmead.com					
Hotel Mela 120 W 44th St	New York	NY	10036	212-710-7000	704-9680
TF: 877-452-6352 ■ *Web:* www.hotelmela.com					
Hotel Metro 411 E Mason St	Milwaukee	WI	53202	414-272-1937	223-1158
TF: 877-638-7620 ■ *Web:* www.hotelmetro.com					
Hotel Monaco Chicago 225 N Wabash Ave	Chicago	IL	60601	312-960-8500	960-1883
TF: 800-397-7661 ■ *Web:* www.monaco-chicago.com					
Hotel Monaco Denver 1717 Champa St	Denver	CO	80202	303-296-1717	296-1818
TF: 800-990-1303 ■ *Web:* www.monaco-denver.com					
Hotel Monaco Portland					
506 SW Washington at Fifth Ave	Portland	OR	97204	503-222-0001	222-0004
TF: 866-861-9514 ■ *Web:* www.monaco-portland.com					
Hotel Monaco Salt Lake City					
15 West 200 South	Salt Lake City	UT	84101	801-595-0000	532-8500
TF Resv: 800-805-1801 ■ *Web:* www.monaco-saltlakecity.com					
Hotel Monaco San Francisco					
501 Geary St	San Francisco	CA	94102	415-292-0100	292-0111
TF: 866-622-5284 ■ *Web:* www.monaco-sf.com					
Hotel Monaco Seattle 1101 Fourth Ave	Seattle	WA	98101	206-621-1770	621-7779
TF: 800-715-6513 ■ *Web:* www.monaco-seattle.com					
Hotel Monte Vista 100 N San Francisco St	Flagstaff	AZ	86001	928-779-6971	779-2904
TF: 800-545-3068 ■ *Web:* www.hotelmontevista.com					
Hotel Monteleone 214 Royal St	New Orleans	LA	70130	504-523-3341	681-4413
TF: 800-535-9595 ■ *Web:* www.hotelmonteleone.com					
Hotel Murano 1320 Broadway Plz	Tacoma	WA	98402	253-238-8000	591-4105
TF: 888-862-3255 ■ *Web:* www.hotelmuranotacoma.com					
Hotel Nikko San Francisco 222 Mason St	San Francisco	CA	94102	415-394-1111	394-1106
TF: 866-636-4556 ■ *Web:* www.hotelnikkosf.com					
Hotel Northampton 36 King St	NorthHampton	MA	01060	413-584-3100	584-9455
TF: 800-547-3529 ■ *Web:* www.hotelnorthampton.com					
Hotel Ocean 1230 Ocean Dr	Miami Beach	FL	33139	305-672-2579	672-7665
Web: www.hotelocean.com					
Oceana Santa Monica 849 Ocean Ave	Santa Monica	CA	90403	310-393-0486	458-1182
Web: www.hoteloceanasantamonica.com					
Hotel Oceana					
Santa Barbara 202 W Cabrillo Blvd	Santa Barbara	CA	93101	805-965-4577	965-9937
TF: 800-965-9776 ■ *Web:* hotelmilosantabarbara.com					
Hotel Omni Mont-Royal 1050 Sherbrooke St W	Montreal	QC	H3A2R6	514-284-1110	845-3025
TF: 800-843-6664 ■ *Web:* www.omnihotels.com					
Hotel Orrington 1710 Orrington Ave	Evanston	IL	60201	847-866-8700	866-8724
TF: 888-677-4648 ■ *Web:* www.hotelorrington.com					
Hotel Pacific 300 Pacific St	Monterey	CA	93940	831-373-5700	373-6921
TF: 800-554-5542 ■ *Web:* www.hotelpacific.com					
Hotel Palomar San Francisco					
12 Fourth St	San Francisco	CA	94103	415-348-1111	348-0302
TF: 866-373-4941 ■ *Web:* www.hotelpalomar-sf.com					
Hotel Park City (HPC) 2001 Pk Ave	Park City	UT	84060	435-200-2000	940-5001
TF: 866-933-0347 ■ *Web:* www.hotelparkcity.com					
Hotel Phillips 106 W 12th St	Kansas City	MO	64105	816-221-7000	221-3477
TF: 800-433-1426 ■ *Web:* www.hotelphillips.com					
Hotel Plaza Athenee 37 E 64th St	New York	NY	10065	212-734-9100	772-0958
TF: 800-447-8800 ■ *Web:* www.plaza-athenee.com					
Hotel Plaza Quebec 3031 Laurier Blvd	Sainte-Foy	QC	G1V2M2	418-658-2727	658-6587
TF: 800-567-5276 ■ *Web:* www.hotelsjaro.com/plazaquebec/index-en.aspx					
Hotel Plaza Real 125 Washington Ave	Santa Fe	NM	87501	505-988-4900	983-9322
TF: 855-752-9273 ■ *Web:* hotelchimayo.com					
Hotel Preston 733 Briley Pkwy	Nashville	TN	37217	615-361-5900	
TF: 800-407-4324 ■ *Web:* www.hotelpreston.com					

				Phone	Fax
Hotel Provincial 1024 Rue Chartres *TF:* 800-535-7922 ■ *Web:* www.hotelprovincial.com	New Orleans	LA	70116	504-581-4995	581-1018
Hotel Rex 562 Sutter St *TF Resv:* 800-433-4434 ■ *Web:* jdvhotels.com/hotels/california/san-francisco-hotels/hotel-rex	San Francisco	CA	94102	415-433-4434	433-3695
Hotel Rodney 142 Second St *TF:* 800-824-8754 ■ *Web:* www.hotelrodneydelaware.com	Lewes	DE	19958	302-645-6466	645-7196
Hotel Roger Williams 131 Madison Ave *TF Resv:* 888-448-7788 ■ *Web:* www.therogernewyork.com	New York	NY	10016	212-448-7000	448-7007
Hotel Rouge 1315 16th St NW *TF:* 800-738-1202 ■ *Web:* www.rougehotel.com	Washington	DC	20036	202-232-8000	667-9827
Hotel Royal Plaza 1905 Hotel Plaza Blvd *TF:* 888-662-4683 ■ *Web:* bhotelsandresorts.com/b-walt-disney-world/	Lake Buena Vista	FL	32830	407-828-2828	
Hotel Ruby Foo's 7655 Decarie Blvd *TF:* 800-361-5419 ■ *Web:* www.hotelrubyfoos.com	Montreal	QC	H4P2H2	514-731-7701	731-7158
Hotel Saint Francis 210 Don Gaspar Ave *TF:* 800-529-5700 ■ *Web:* www.hotelstfrancis.com	Santa Fe	NM	87501	505-983-5700	989-7690
Hotel Saint Marie 827 Toulouse St *TF:* 800-366-2743 ■ *Web:* www.hotelstmarie.com	New Orleans	LA	70112	504-561-8951	571-2802
Hotel Saint Pierre 911 Burgundy St *TF Resv:* 800-225-4040 ■ *Web:* www.frenchquarterinns.com	New Orleans	LA	70116	504-524-4401	
Hotel Saint Regis Detroit 3071 W Grand Blvd *Web:* www.hotelstregisdetroit.com	Detroit	MI	48202	313-873-3000	481-8408
Hotel San Carlos 202 N Central Ave *TF:* 866-253-4121 ■ *Web:* hotelsancarlos.com	Phoenix	AZ	85004	602-253-4121	253-6668
Hotel Santa Barbara 533 State St *TF:* 888-259-7700 ■ *Web:* www.hotelsantabarbara.com	Santa Barbara	CA	93101	805-957-9300	962-2412
Hotel Santa Fe 1501 Paseo de Peralta *TF:* 855-825-9876 ■ *Web:* www.hotelsantafe.com	Santa Fe	NM	87501	505-982-1200	984-2211
Hotel Sax Chicago 333 N Dearborn St **Fax Area Code:* 416 ■ *TF:* 855-880-1240 ■ *Web:* www.thompsonhotels.com	Chicago	IL	60610	312-245-0333	640-7779*
Hotel Sepia 3135 Ch St-Louis *TF:* 888-301-6837 ■ *Web:* www.hotelsepia.ca	Sainte-Foy	QC	G1W1R9	418-653-4941	653-0774
Hotel Shelley 844 Collins Ave *TF:* 877-762-3477 ■ *Web:* www.hotelshelley.com	Miami Beach	FL	33139	305-531-3341	674-0811
Hotel Solamar 435 Sixth Ave *TF:* 877-230-0300 ■ *Web:* www.hotelsolamar.com	San Diego	CA	92101	619-819-9500	819-9539
Hotel St Germain 2516 Maple Ave *Web:* www.hotelstgermain.com	Dallas	TX	75201	214-871-2516	871-0740
Hotel st James Inc 109 W 45th St *Web:* hotel-st-james.hotelapp.me	New York	NY	10036	212-221-3600	
Hotel Strasburg, The 213 S Holliday St *TF:* 800-348-8327 ■ *Web:* www.hotelstrasburg.com	Strasburg	VA	22657	540-465-9191	465-4788
Hotel Teatro 1100 14th St *TF:* 888-727-1200 ■ *Web:* www.hotelteatro.com	Denver	CO	80202	303-228-1100	228-1101
Hotel The Queen Mary 1126 Queens Hwy *TF:* 877-342-0738 ■ *Web:* www.queenmary.com	Long Beach	CA	90802	562-435-3511	437-4531
Hotel Triton 342 Grant Ave *TF:* 800-800-1299 ■ *Web:* www.hoteltriton.com	San Francisco	CA	94108	415-394-0500	394-0555
Hotel Tybee 1401 Strand Ave *Web:* www.oceanplaza.com	Tybee Island	GA	31328	912-786-7777	
Hotel Universel 2300 Ch St-Foy *TF:* 800-463-4495 ■ *Web:* www.hoteluniversel.qc.ca	Qu,bec	QC	G1V1S5	418-653-5250	653-4486
Hotel Utica 102 Lafayette St *TF:* 877-906-1912 ■ *Web:* www.hotelutica.com	Utica	NY	13502	315-724-7829	733-7663
Hotel Valencia Santana Row 355 Santana Row *TF:* 866-842-0100 ■ *Web:* www.hotelvalencia-santanarow.com	San Jose	CA	95128	408-551-0010	551-0550
Hotel Valley Ho 6850 E Main St **Fax Area Code:* 480 ■ *TF:* 866-882-4484 ■ *Web:* www.hotelvalleyho.com	Scottsdale	AZ	85251	844-993-9601	421-7782*
Hotel Victoria 56 Yonge St *TF:* 800-363-8228 ■ *Web:* www.hotelvictoria-toronto.com	Toronto	ON	M5E1G5	416-363-1666	363-7327
Hotel Viking One Bellevue Ave *TF:* 800-556-7126 ■ *Web:* www.hotelviking.com	Newport	RI	02840	401-847-3300	
Hotel Vintage Park 1100 Fifth Ave *TF:* 800-853-3914 ■ *Web:* hotelvintage-seattle.com/	Seattle	WA	98101	206-624-8000	623-0568
Hotel Vitale 8 Mission St *TF:* 888-890-8688 ■ *Web:* www.hotelvitale.com	San Francisco	CA	94105	415-278-3700	278-3750
Hotel Wales 1295 Madison Ave *TF:* 866-925-3746 ■ *Web:* www.hotelwalesnyc.com	New York	NY	10128	212-876-6000	860-7000
Hotel Weatherford, The 23 N Leroux St *Web:* www.weatherfordhotel.com	Flagstaff	AZ	86001	928-779-1919	773-8951
Hotel Wolcott Four W 31st St *Web:* www.wolcott.com	New York	NY	10001	212-268-2900	563-0096
Hotel XIXe Siecle *Lhotel* 262 St Jacques St W *TF:* 877-553-0019 ■ *Web:* www.lhotelmontreal.com	Vieux Montreal	QC	H2Y1N1	514-985-0019	985-0059
Hotel ZaZa Dallas 2332 Leonard St *TF:* 800-597-8399 ■ *Web:* www.hotelzaza.com	Dallas	TX	75201	214-468-8399	468-8397
Hotel ZaZa Houston 5701 Main St *TF Resv:* 888-880-3244 ■ *Web:* www.hotelzaza.com/houston	Houston	TX	77005	713-526-1991	526-0359
Hotel, The 801 Collins Ave *Web:* www.thehotelofsouthbeach.com	Miami Beach	FL	33139	305-531-2222	531-3222
Hotels Unlimited Inc 399 Monmouth St	East Windsor	NJ	08520	609-632-0006	
HP Hotels Inc One Chase Corporate Dr Ste 210 *Web:* hp-hotels.com	Birmingham	AL	35244	205-879-7004	
Humphrey's Half Moon Inn & Suites 2303 Shelter Island Dr *TF:* 800-542-7400 ■ *Web:* www.halfmooninn.com	San Diego	CA	92106	619-224-3411	224-3478
Huntington Hotel & Nob Hill Spa 1075 California St *Web:* thescarlethotels.com/huntington-hotel-san-francisco	San Francisco	CA	94108	415-474-5400	474-6227
Hyannis Holiday Motel 131 Ocean St *TF:* 800-423-1551 ■ *Web:* hyannisholiday.com	Hyannis	MA	02601	508-775-1639	775-1672
Hyannis Travel Inn 18 N St *TF:* 800-352-7190 ■ *Web:* www.hyannistravelinn.com	Hyannis	MA	02601	508-775-8200	775-8201
Hyatt Carmel Highlands 120 Highlands Dr *TF:* 800-633-7313 ■ *Web:* www.highlandsinn.hyatt.com	Carmel	CA	93923	831-620-1234	626-1574
Hyatt Fair Lakes Hotel 12777 Fair Lakes Cir *Web:* fairpo.com	Fairfax	VA	22033	703-818-1234	
Grand Hyatt Hotels 71 S Wacker Dr **Fax:* Mktg ■ *TF Resv:* 800-233-1234 ■ *Web:* www.hyatt.com	Chicago	IL	60606	312-750-1234	780-5289*
Hyatt Place Hotels 71 S Wacker Dr *TF:* 888-492-8847 ■ *Web:* www.place.hyatt.com	Chicago	IL	60606	312-750-1234	
Hyatt Regency Hotels 71 S Wacker Dr **Fax:* Mktg ■ *TF Resv:* 800-233-1234 ■ *Web:* www.hyatt.com	Chicago	IL	60606	312-750-1234	780-5289*
Hyatt Summerfield Suites 71 S Wacker Dr *Web:* www.house.hyatt.com	Chicago	IL	60606	312-750-1234	
Hyatt Hotels Corp *Park Hyatt Hotels* 71 S Wacker Dr **Fax:* Mktg ■ *TF Resv:* 800-233-1234 ■ *Web:* www.hyatt.com	Chicago	IL	60606	312-750-1234	780-5289*
Hyatt Summerfield Suites Herndon 467 Herndon Pkwy *Web:* herndon.house.hyatt.com	Herndon	VA	20170	703-437-5000	
Hyatt Westlake Plaza in ThoUSAnd Oaks 880 S Wlake Blvd *Web:* www.westlake.hyatt.com	Westlake Village	CA	91361	805-557-1234	
Ilikai Hotel & Suites 1777 Ala Moana Blvd *TF:* 866-536-7973 ■ *Web:* www.ilikaihotel.com	Honolulu	HI	96815	808-949-3811	947-0892
Imperial of Waikiki 205 Lewers St *TF:* 800-347-2582 ■ *Web:* www.imperialofwaikiki.com	Honolulu	HI	96815	808-923-1827	921-7586
Imperial Swan Hotel 4141 S Florida Ave *Web:* www.imperialswanlakeland.com	Lakeland	FL	33813	863-647-3000	647-0467
Indian Creek Hotel 2727 Indian Creek Dr *Web:* www.thefreehand.com	Miami Beach	FL	33140	305-531-2727	531-5651
Indiana Memorial Union Board 900 E Seventh St Rm 270 *Web:* www.imu.indiana.edu	Bloomington	IN	47405	812-855-4682	
Indigo Inn One Maiden Ln *TF:* 800-845-7639 ■ *Web:* www.indigoinn.com	Charleston	SC	29401	843-577-5900	577-0378
Ingleside Inn 200 W Ramon Rd *TF:* 800-772-6655 ■ *Web:* www.inglesideinn.com	Palm Springs	CA	92264	760-325-0046	325-0710
Inhance Corp 609 Eighth St	Fort Madison	IA	52627	319-372-4920	
Inlet Tower Suites 1200 L St *TF:* 800-544-0786 ■ *Web:* www.inlettower.com	Anchorage	AK	99501	907-276-0110	258-4914
Inn & Spa at Loretto 211 Old Santa Fe Trl *TF:* 800-727-5531 ■ *Web:* www.innatloretto.com	Santa Fe	NM	87501	505-988-5531	984-7968
Inn Above Tide, The 30 El Portal *Web:* innabovetide.com	Sausalito	CA	94965	415-332-9535	
Inn at Camachee Harbor 201 Yacht Club Dr *TF:* 800-688-5379 ■ *Web:* www.camacheeinn.com	Saint Augustine	FL	32084	904-825-0003	825-0048
Inn at Gig Harbor 3211 56th St NW *TF:* 800-795-9980 ■ *Web:* www.innatgigharbor.com	Gig Harbor	WA	98335	253-858-1111	851-5402
Inn at Harbour Town Seven Lighthouse Ln *TF Resv:* 800-732-7463 ■ *Web:* www.seapines.com/accommodations/inn_at_harbour_town.cfm	Hilton Head Island	SC	29928	843-363-8100	363-8155
Inn at Henderson's Wharf 1000 Fell St *TF:* 888-995-9560 ■ *Web:* www.hendersonswharf.com	Baltimore	MD	21231	410-522-7777	522-7087
Inn at Lambertville Station 11 Bridge St *Web:* www.lambertvillestation.com	Lambertville	NJ	08530	609-397-4400	397-9744
Inn at Langley 400 First St PO Box 835 *TF:* 800-843-3779 ■ *Web:* www.innatlangley.com	Langley	WA	98260	360-221-3033	221-3033
Inn at Little Washington Middle & Main St PO Box 300 *Web:* www.theinnatlittlewashington.com	Washington	VA	22747	540-675-3800	675-3100
Inn at Longshore 260 Compo Rd S *Web:* www.innatlongshore.com	Westport	CT	06880	203-226-3316	226-5723
Inn at Mayo Clinic 4420 Mary Brigh Dr *TF:* 888-255-4458 ■ *Web:* www.mayoclinic.org	Jacksonville	FL	32224	904-992-9992	992-4463
Inn at Montchanin Village 528 Montchanin Rd *TF:* 800-269-2473 ■ *Web:* www.montchanin.com	Montchanin	DE	19710	302-888-2133	691-0198
Inn at Montpelier, The 147 Main St *Web:* www.innatmontpelier.com	Montpelier	VT	05602	802-223-2727	223-0722
Inn at Morro Bay 60 State Pk Rd *TF:* 800-321-9566 ■ *Web:* www.innatmorrobay.com	Morro Bay	CA	93442	805-772-5651	772-4779
Inn at Mystic 3 Williams Ave PO Box 526 *TF:* 800-237-2415 ■ *Web:* www.innatmystic.com	Mystic	CT	06355	860-536-9604	
Inn at National Hall 100 W Putnam Ave *Web:* www.innatnationalhall.com	Greenwich	CT	06830	203-221-1351	
Inn at Nichols Village 1101 Northern Blvd *Web:* www.nicholsvillage.com	Clarks Summit	PA	18411	570-587-1135	586-7140
Inn at Otter Crest 301 Otter Crest Loop *TF:* 800-452-2101 ■ *Web:* www.innatottercrest.com	Otter Rock	OR	97369	541-765-2111	765-2047
Inn at Oyster Point 425 Marina Blvd *Web:* www.innatoysterpoint.com	South San Francisco	CA	94080	650-737-7633	737-0795
Inn at Pelican Bay 800 Vanderbilt Beach Rd *TF:* 800-597-8770 ■ *Web:* www.innatpelicanbay.com	Naples	FL	34108	239-597-8777	597-8012
Inn at Perry Cabin 308 Watkins Ln *TF:* 800-722-2949 ■ *Web:* belmond.com/inn-at-perry-cabin-st-michaels/	Saint Michaels	MD	21663	410-745-2200	745-3348
Inn at Queen Anne 505 First Ave N *Web:* www.innatqueenanne.com	Seattle	WA	98109	206-282-7357	217-9719
Inn at Reading, The 1040 N Pk Rd *TF:* 800-383-9713 ■ *Web:* www.innatreading.com	Wyomissing	PA	19610	610-372-7811	372-4545
Inn at Saint John 939 Congress St *TF:* 800-636-9127 ■ *Web:* www.innatstjohn.com	Portland	ME	04102	207-773-6481	
Inn at Saint Mary's 53993 US Hwy 31-33 N *Web:* www.innatsaintmarys.com	South Bend	IN	46637	574-232-4000	289-0986
Inn at Sawmill Farm, The Seven Crosstown Rd PO Box 367 *Web:* www.theinnatsawmillfarm.com	West Dover	VT	05356	802-464-8131	
Inn at Spanish Head 4009 SW Hwy 101 *TF:* 800-452-8127 ■ *Web:* www.spanishhead.com	Lincoln City	OR	97367	541-996-2161	996-4089
Inn at Tallgrass, The 2280 N Tara Cir *Web:* www.theinnattallgrass.com	Wichita	KS	67226	316-684-3466	685-3466
Inn at the Market 86 Pine St *TF:* 800-446-4484 ■ *Web:* www.innatthemarket.com	Seattle	WA	98101	206-443-3600	448-0631

	City	State	Zip	Phone	Fax
Inn At The Quay 900 Quayside Dr.	New Westminster	BC	V3M6G1	604-520-1776	520-5645
TF: 800-663-2001 ■ *Web:* www.innatwestminsterquay.com					
Inn at Union Square 440 Post St	San Francisco	CA	94102	415-397-3510	989-0529
TF: 800-288-4346 ■ *Web:* www.greystonehotels.com					
Inn at, The Tides, The					
800 Coast Hwy 1 PO Box 640	Bodega Bay	CA	94923	707-875-2751	875-2669
TF: 800-541-7788 ■ *Web:* www.innatthetides.com					
Inn by the Lake 3300 Lk Tahoe Blvd.	South Lake Tahoe	CA	96150	530-542-0330	541-6250
TF: 800-877-1466 ■ *Web:* www.innbythelake.com					
Inn of Chicago Magnificent Mile					
162 E Ohio St	Chicago	IL	60611	312-787-3100	573-3159
TF Resv: 800-424-6423 ■ *Web:* www.innofchicago.com					
Inn of Long Beach 185 Atlantic Ave	Long Beach	CA	90802	562-435-3791	436-7510
TF: 800-230-7500 ■ *Web:* www.innoflongbeach.com					
Inn of the Anasazi 113 Washington Ave	Santa Fe	NM	87501	505-988-3030	988-3277
TF: 888-767-3966 ■ *Web:* www.rosewoodhotels.com					
Inn of the Governors 101 W Alameda St	Santa Fe	NM	87501	505-982-4333	989-9149
TF: 800-234-4534 ■ *Web:* www.innofthegovernors.com					
Inn of the Six Mountains					
2617 Killington Rd	Killington	VT	05751	802-422-4302	422-4321
TF: 800-228-4676 ■ *Web:* www.sixmountains.com					
Inn on Biltmore Estate 1 Antler Hill Rd.	Asheville	NC	28803	828-225-1333	225-6185
TF: 800-411-3812 ■ *Web:* www.biltmore.com					
Inn on Fifth 699 Fifth Ave S.	Naples	FL	34102	239-403-8777	403-8778
TF: 888-403-8778 ■ *Web:* innonfifth.com					
Inn on Gitche Gumee 8517 Congdon Blvd	Duluth	MN	55804	218-525-4979	
TF: 800-317-4979 ■ *Web:* www.innongitchegumee.com					
Inn on Lake Superior 350 Canal Pk Dr	Duluth	MN	55802	218-726-1111	727-3976
TF: 888-668-4352 ■ *Web:* www.theinnonlakesuperior.com					
Inn on the Alameda 303 E Alameda St	Santa Fe	NM	87501	505-984-2121	986-8325
TF: 888-984-2121 ■ *Web:* www.innonthealameda.com					
Inn on the Creek 295 N Millward Ave.	Jackson	WY	83001	307-739-1565	
Web: bedandbreakfast.com					
Inn on the Paseo 630 Paseo de Peralta	Santa Fe	NM	87501	505-984-8200	
TF: 855-984-8200 ■ *Web:* www.innonthepaseo.com					
Inns at Mill Falls 312 Daniel Webster Hwy	Meredith	NH	03253	800-622-6455	279-6797*
**Fax Area Code:* 603 ■ *TF:* 800-622-6455 ■ *Web:* www.millfalls.com					
Inns of America Suites 755 Raintree Dr	Carlsbad	CA	92011	760-438-6661	
Web: hotelringingbell.com					
InnSuites Hospitality Trust InnSuites Hotels & Suites					
475 N Granada Ave Ste 102	Tucson	AZ	85701	520-622-0923	678-0281*
**Fax Area Code:* 602 ■ *TF:* 800-842-4242 ■ *Web:* www.innsuites.com					
InnSuites Hotel Tempe/Phoenix Airport					
1651 W Baseline Rd	Tempe	AZ	85283	480-897-7900	491-1008
TF: 800-841-4242 ■ *Web:* www.innsuites.com/tempe					
InnSuites Hotel Tucson City Ctr					
475 N Granada Ave.	Tucson	AZ	85701	520-622-3000	623-8922
TF: 888-784-8324 ■ *Web:* www.innsuites.com/tucson_citycenter					
Crowne Plaza Hotels & Resorts					
3 Ravinia Dr Ste 2900	Atlanta	GA	30346	770-858-5035	
Web: ihg.com					
Holiday Inn Express 3 Ravinia Dr Ste 100	Atlanta	GA	30346	770-604-2000	604-5403
TF: 800-725-8232 ■ *Web:* www.ihgplc.com					
Holiday Inn Hotels & Resorts					
3 Ravinia Dr Ste 100	Atlanta	GA	30346	770-604-2000	604-5403
TF: 800-725-8232 ■ *Web:* www.ihgplc.com					
InterContinental Hotels Group					
Hotel Indigo 3 Ravinia Dr Ste 100	Atlanta	GA	30346	770-604-2000	604-5403
TF: 800-334-5194 ■ *Web:* www.ihgplc.com					
Staybridge Suites Three Ravinia Dr Ste 100	Atlanta	GA	30346	770-604-2000	604-5403
TF: 800-465-4329 ■ *Web:* www.ihgplc.com					
InterMountain Management LLC 2390 Tower Dr	Monroe	LA	71201	318-325-5561	
Web: www.intermtn.biz					
International Hotel 20 Second Ave SW	Rochester	MN	55902	800-940-6811	285-2767*
**Fax Area Code:* 507 ■ *TF:* 800-940-6811 ■ *Web:* www.towersatkahlergrand.com					
International Hotel of Calgary					
220 Fourth Ave SW.	Calgary	AB	T2P0H5	403-265-9600	
Web: internationalhotel.ca					
International House Hotel 221 Camp St.	New Orleans	LA	70130	504-553-9550	553-9560
TF: 800-633-5770 ■ *Web:* www.ihhotel.com					
Interstate Hotels & Resorts Inc					
4501 N Fairfax Dr	Arlington	VA	22203	703-387-3100	387-3101
Web: www.interstatehotels.com					
Iroquois New York 49 W 44th St	New York City	NY	10036	212-840-3080	719-0006
TF: 800-332-7220 ■ *Web:* www.iroquoisny.com					
Island Hotel, The 690 Newport Ctr Dr	Newport Beach	CA	92660	949-759-0808	759-0568
TF: 866-554-4620 ■ *Web:* www.islandhotel.com					
Jack London Inn 444 Embarcadero W	Oakland	CA	94607	510-444-2032	834-3074
TF: 800-549-8780 ■ *Web:* www.jacklondoninn.com					
Jackson Hole Lodge 420 W Broadway PO Box 1805	Jackson	WY	83001	307-733-2992	739-2144
TF: 800-604-9404 ■ *Web:* www.jacksonholelodge.com					
Jailhouse Inn 13 Marlborough St	Newport	RI	02840	401-847-4638	849-0605
Web: www.jailhouse.com					
James Chicago, The 55 E Ontario.	Chicago	IL	60611	312-337-1000	337-7217
TF: 888-526-3778 ■ *Web:* www.jameshotels.com					
James Gettys Hotel 27 Chambersburg St.	Gettysburg	PA	17325	717-337-1334	334-2103
TF: 888-900-5275 ■ *Web:* www.jamesgettyshotel.com					
Jameson Inns					
Jameson Inns 115 Ann Denard Dr	Washington	GA	30673	706-678-7925	
TF: 800-526-3766 ■ *Web:* www.jamesoninns.com					
Janus Hotels & Resorts Inc					
2300 Corporate Blvd NW Ste 232	Boca Raton	FL	33431	561-997-2325	997-5331
TF: 800-327-2110 ■ *Web:* www.janushotels.com					
Jared Coffin House 29 Broad St	Nantucket	MA	02554	508-228-2400	228-8549
TF Cust Svc: 800-248-2405 ■ *Web:* www.jaredcoffinhouse.com					
JC Resorts LLC 533 Coast Blvd S	La Jolla	CA	92037	858-605-2700	
Web: www.jcresorts.com					
Jefferson Hotel 101 W Franklin St	Richmond	VA	23220	804-788-8000	225-0334
TF: 800-424-8014 ■ *Web:* jeffersonhotel.com					
JHM Hotels Inc 60 Pointe Cir	Greenville	SC	29615	864-232-9944	248-1600*
**Fax:* PR ■ *Web:* www.jhmhotels.com					
John Q Hammons Hotel Management LLC					
300 S John Q Hammons Pkwy #900	Springfield	MO	65806	417-864-4300	873-3540
Web: www.jqhhotels.com					
Joie de Vivre Hospitality Inc					
530 Bush St Ste 501	San Francisco	CA	94108	415-835-0300	835-0317
Web: www.jdvhotels.com					
Jolly Hotel Madison Towers 22 E 38th St	New York	NY	10016	212-802-0600	447-0747
TF Resv: 888-726-0528 ■ *Web:* www.jollymadison.com					
Jolly Roger Inn 640 W Katella Ave	Anaheim	CA	92802	714-782-7500	772-2308
TF: 888-296-5986 ■ *Web:* www.jollyrogerhotel.com					
Jorgenson's Inn & Suites 1714 11th Ave	Helena	MT	59601	406-442-1770	449-0155
Web: www.jorgensonsinn.com					
Kahala Mandarin Oriental Hotel Hawaii Resort					
5000 Kahala Ave.	Honolulu	HI	96816	808-739-8888	739-8800
TF: 800-367-2525 ■ *Web:* www.kahalaresort.com					
Kawada Hotel 200 S Hill St	Los Angeles	CA	90012	213-621-4455	687-4455
TF: 800-752-9232 ■ *Web:* www.kawadahotel.com					
Kawailoa Development Company LP					
1571 Poipu Rd Ste 307 PO Box 369	Koloa	HI	96756	808-742-6300	742-7197
Web: www.kawailoa.com					
Kellogg Hotel & Conference Ctr					
219 S Harrison Rd					
Michigan State University Campus	East Lansing	MI	48824	517-432-4000	353-1872
TF: 800-875-5090 ■ *Web:* kelloggcenter.com					
Kelly Inns Ltd 3205 W Sencore Dr	Sioux Falls	SD	57107	605-965-1440	965-1450
Web: www.kellyinns.com					
Kensington Court Ann Arbor 610 Hilton Blvd.	Ann Arbor	MI	48108	734-761-7800	761-1040
TF Orders: 800-344-7829 ■ *Web:* www.kcourtaa.com					
Kensington Park Hotel 450 Post St.	San Francisco	CA	94102	415-202-8700	
TF: 800-553-1900 ■ *Web:* www.kensingtonparkhotel.com					
Kensington Riverside Inn 1126 Memorial Dr NW	Calgary	AB	T2N3E3	403-228-4442	228-9608
TF: 877-313-3733 ■ *Web:* www.kensingtonriversideinn.com					
Kent, The 1131 Collins Ave.	Miami Beach	FL	33139	305-604-5068	531-0720
TF: 866-826-5368 ■ *Web:* www.thekenthotel.com					
Keswick Hall 701 Club Dr	Keswick	VA	22947	434-979-3440	977-4171
TF: 888-778-2565 ■ *Web:* www.keswick.com					
Key Lime Inn 725 Truman Ave.	Key West	FL	33040	305-294-5229	294-9623
TF: 800-549-4430 ■ *Web:* www.historickeywestinns.com					
Keystone Lodge & Spa 22010 US Hwy 6	Keystone	CO	80435	970-496-3000	
Web: keystoneresort.com					
Killington Grand Resort Hotel & Conference Ctr					
4763 Killington Rd	Killington	VT	05751	802-422-5001	422-1399
TF: 800-621-6867 ■ *Web:* www.killington.com					
Kimball Terrace Inn					
10 Huntington Rd	Northeast Harbor	ME	04662	207-276-3383	276-4102
TF: 800-454-6225 ■ *Web:* www.kimballterraceinn.com					
Kimberly Hotel 145 E 50th St.	New York	NY	10022	212-755-0400	355-4318
TF: 800-683-0400 ■ *Web:* www.kimberlyhotel.com					
Kimpton Hotel & Restaurant Group					
422 SW Broadway	Portland	OR	97205	503-228-1212	228-3598
TF: 800-263-2305 ■ *Web:* www.vintageplaza.com					
Kimpton Hotel & Restaurant Group LLC					
222 Kearny St Ste 200	San Francisco	CA	94108	415-397-5572	296-8031
TF: 800-546-7866 ■ *Web:* www.kimptonhotels.com					
Kimpton Hotel & Restaurant Group, LLC					
10050 S DeAnza Blvd	Cupertino	CA	95014	408-253-8900	
TF: 800-499-1408 ■ *Web:* www.thecypresshotel.com					
King Kamehameha's Kona Beach Hotel					
75-5660 Palani Rd	Kailua-Kona	HI	96740	808-329-2911	329-4602
TF: 800-367-2111 ■ *Web:* www.konabeachhotel.com					
King Pacific Lodge 255 W First St.	North Vancouver	BC	V7M3G8	604-987-5452	
TF: 855-825-9378					
Kings Island Resort & Conference Ctr					
5691 Kings Island Dr	Mason	OH	45040	513-398-0115	
Kinseth Hotel Corp Two Quail Creek Cir	North Liberty	IA	52317	319-626-5600	
Web: www.kinseth.com					
Kinzie Hotel 20 W Kinzie St	Chicago	IL	60654	312-395-9000	395-9001
TF: 877-262-5341 ■ *Web:* kinziehotel.com					
Kitano New York 66 Pk Ave E 38th St	New York	NY	10016	212-885-7000	885-7100
TF: 800-548-2666 ■ *Web:* www.kitano.com					
Knickerbocker on, The Lake, The					
1028 E Juneau Ave.	Milwaukee	WI	53202	414-276-8500	276-3668
Web: www.knickerbockeronthelake.com					
Knob Hill Inn 960 N Main St PO Box 1327	Ketchum	ID	83340	208-726-8010	726-2712
TF: 800-526-8010 ■ *Web:* www.knobhillinn.com					
Koko Inn 5201 Ave Q	Lubbock	TX	79412	806-747-2591	747-2591
Kona Kai Resort 1551 Shelter Island Dr.	San Diego	CA	92106	619-221-8000	819-8101
TF: 800-566-2524 ■ *Web:* www.resortkonakai.com					
L' Appartement Hotel 455 Sherbrooke W	Montreal	QC	H3A1B7	514-284-3634	287-1431
TF: 800-363-3010 ■ *Web:* www.appartementhotel.com					
L'Enfant Plaza Hotel					
480 L'Enfant Plaza SW	Washington	DC	20024	202-484-1000	646-4456
Web: www.lenfantplazahotel.com					
L'Ermitage Beverly Hills Hotel					
9291 Burton Way	Beverly Hills	CA	90210	310-278-3344	278-8247
TF: 877-235-7582 ■ *Web:* www.viceroyhotelsandresorts.com					
L'Hotel du Vieux-Quebec 1190 St Jean St	Quebec	QC	G1R1S6	418-692-1850	692-5637
TF: 800-361-7787 ■ *Web:* www.hvq.com					
L'Hotel Quebec 3115 des Hotels Ave	Sainte-Foy	QC	G1W3Z6	418-658-5120	658-4504
TF: 800-567-5276 ■ *Web:* www.hotelsjaro.com					
La Colombe D'Or Inn 3410 Montrose Blvd.	Houston	TX	77006	713-469-4750	524-8923
Web: www.lacolombedor.com					
La Fonda 100 E San Francisco St.	Santa Fe	NM	87501	505-982-5511	988-2952
TF: 800-523-5002 ■ *Web:* www.lafondasantafe.com					
La Pensione Hotel 606 W Date St	San Diego	CA	92101	619-236-8000	236-8088
TF: 800-232-4683 ■ *Web:* www.lapensionehotel.com					
La Posada Hotel & Suites 1000 Zaragoza St	Laredo	TX	78040	956-722-1701	
TF Resv: 800-444-2099 ■ *Web:* www.laposada.com					
La Quinta Inn & Suites Secaucus Meadowlands					
350 Lighting Way	Secaucus	NJ	07094	201-863-8700	863-6209
TF General: 800-753-3757 ■ *Web:* www.7719.lq.com/lq/index.jsp					
La Valencia Hotel 1132 Prospect St.	La Jolla	CA	92037	858-454-0771	456-3921
Web: www.lavalencia.com					

				Phone	Fax
Lafayette Hotel 600 St Charles Ave. New Orleans	LA	70130		504-524-4441	523-7327

TF: 800-366-2743 ■ *Web:* www.lafayettehotelneworleans.com

Lafayette Hotel & Suites San Diego 2223 El Cajon Blvd. San Diego CA 92104 619-296-2101 296-0512
Web: www.lafayettehotelsd.com

Lafayette Park Hotel 3287 Mt Diablo Blvd. Lafayette CA 94549 925-283-3700 284-1621
TF: 877-283-8787 ■ *Web:* www.lafayetteparkhotel.com

Lake Louise Inn 210 Village Rd PO Box 209. Lake Louise AB T0L1E0 403-522-3791 522-2018
TF: 800-661-9237 ■ *Web:* www.lakelouiseinn.com

Lake Lure Inn & Spa, The 2771 Memorial Hwy. Lake Lure NC 28746 828-625-2526 625-9655
TF: 888-434-4970 ■ *Web:* www.lakelure.com

Lake Merritt, The 1800 Madison St. Oakland CA 94612 510-903-3600
Web: www.thelakemerritt.com

Lake Placid Lodge 144 Lodge Way. Lake Placid NY 12946 518-523-2700 523-1124
TF: 877-523-2700 ■ *Web:* www.lakeplacidlodge.com

Lakeside Inn 100 N Alexander St. Mount Dora FL 32757 352-383-4101 385-1615
TF: 800-556-5016 ■ *Web:* www.lakeside-inn.com

Lakeview on the Lake 8696 E Lake Rd. Erie PA 16511 814-899-6948
TF: 888-558-8439 ■ *Web:* www.lakevieweriе.com

Lakewoods Resort & Lodge 21540 County Hwy M. Cable WI 54821 715-794-2561
Web: lakewoodsresort.com

Lamothe House Hotel 621 Esplanade Ave. New Orleans LA 70116 800-535-7815 302-2019*
**Fax Area Code:* 504 ■ *TF:* 800-535-7815 ■ *Web:* www.frenchquarterguesthouses.com

Lamp Post Inn 2424 E Stadium Blvd. Ann Arbor MI 48104 734-971-8000 971-7483
Web: www.lamppostinn.com

Lamplighter Inn & Suites South 1772 S Glenstone Ave. Springfield MO 65804 417-882-1113 882-8869
Web: www.lamplighter-sgf.com

Lancaster Hotel 701 Texas St. Houston TX 77002 713-228-9500 223-4528
TF: 800-231-0336 ■ *Web:* www.thelancaster.com

Landmark Inn 230 N Front St. Marquette MI 49855 906-228-2580 228-5676
TF General: 888-752-6362 ■ *Web:* www.thelandmarkinn.com

Langdon Hall Country House Hotel & Spa One Langdon Dr. Cambridge ON N3H4R8 519-740-2100 740-8161
TF: 800-268-1898 ■ *Web:* www.langdonhall.ca

Langham Boston, The 250 Franklin St. Boston MA 02110 617-451-1900 423-2844
TF: 800-791-7781 ■ *Web:* www.langhamhotels.com

Lantern Lodge Motor Inn 411 N College St. Myerstown PA 17067 717-866-6536 866-8857
TF: 800-262-5564 ■ *Web:* www.thelanternlodge.com

LaPlaya Resort & Suites 2500 N Atlantic Ave. Daytona Beach Shores FL 32118 386-672-0990
Web: laplayadaytona.com

Larkspur Hotels & Restaurants Inc 550 W Hamilton Ave Ste 200. Campbell CA 95008 408-364-1514 945-5001*
**Fax Area Code:* 415 ■ *Web:* www.larkspurhotels.com

Las Vegas Club Hotel & Casino (LVC) 18 E Fremont St. Las Vegas NV 89101 702-385-1664
TF: 800-634-6532 ■ *Web:* www.lasvegasclubcasino.com

Las Vegas Sands Corp 3355 Las Vegas Blvd S. Las Vegas NV 89109 702-414-1000 414-4884
NYSE: LVS ■ *Web:* www.sands.com

LaSalle Hotel 120 S Main St. Bryan TX 77803 979-822-2000 779-4343
Web: www.lasalle-hotel.com

LaSalle Hotel Properties Three Bethesda Metro Ctr Ste 1200. Bethesda MD 20814 301-941-1500 941-1553
NYSE: LHO ■ *Web:* www.lasallehotels.com

Latham Hotel, The 135 S 17th St. Philadelphia PA 19103 215-563-7474 568-0110
TF: 877-528-4261 ■ *Web:* www.lathamhotelphiladelphia.com

Laurel Inn 444 Presidio Ave. San Francisco CA 94115 415-567-8467
TF: 800-738-7477 ■
Web: jdvhotels.com/hotels/california/san-francisco-hotels/laurel-inn

Laurel Lodge Enterprises Inc 1909 Harper Rd. Beckley WV 25801 304-255-0228
Web: lleinc.com

Le Chamois 4557 Blackcomb Way. Whistler BC V0N1B4 604-932-8700
TF: 866-944-7853 ■ *Web:* www.lechamoiswhistlerhotel.com

Le Meridian 20 Sidney St. Cambridge MA 02139 617-577-0200 494-8366
TF: 800-543-4300 ■ *Web:* starwoodhotels.com

Le Meridien Chambers Minneapolis 901 Hennepin Ave. Minneapolis MN 55403 612-767-6900 767-6801
TF General: 866-961-2861 ■ *Web:* www.lemeridienchambers.com

Le M,ridien Dallas, The Stoneleigh 2927 Maple Ave. Dallas TX 75201 214-871-7111
TF: 800-650-1458 ■ *Web:* lemeridiendallasstoneleigh.com

Le Merigot - A JW Marriott Beach Hotel & Spa 1740 Ocean Ave. Santa Monica CA 90401 310-395-9700 395-9200
TF: 888-539-7899 ■ *Web:* www.marriott.com

Le Montrose Suite Hotel 900 Hammond St. West Hollywood CA 90069 310-855-1115 657-9192
TF: 800-776-0666 ■ *Web:* www.lemontrose.com

Le Nouvel Montreal Hotel & Spa 1740 Rene-Levesque Blvd W. Montreal QC H3H1R3 514-931-8841 931-5581
TF: 800-363-6063 ■ *Web:* www.lenouvelhotel.com

Le Parc Suite Hotel 733 NW Knoll Dr. West Hollywood CA 90069 310-855-8888 659-7812
TF Resv: 800-578-4837 ■ *Web:* www.leparcsuites.com

Le Pavillon Hotel 833 Poydras St. New Orleans LA 70112 504-581-3111 620-4130
Web: www.lepavillon.com

Le Port-Royal Hotel & Suites 144 St Pierre St. Quebec QC G1K8N8 418-692-2777 692-2778
TF: 866-417-2777 ■ *Web:* www.leportroyal.com

Le Richelieu Hotel 1234 Chartres St. New Orleans LA 70116 504-529-2492 524-8179
TF: 800-535-9653 ■ *Web:* www.lerichelieuhotel.com

Le Saint Sulpice 414 Rue St Sulpice. Montreal QC H2Y2V5 514-288-1000 288-0077
TF General: 877-785-7423 ■ *Web:* www.lesaintsulpice.com

Leisure Hotels LLC
Leisure Hotel Corp
5000 W 95th St Ste 100. Prairie Village KS 66207 913-905-1460 905-1461
Web: www.leisurehotel.com

Leisure Sports Inc 7077 Koll Ctr Pkwy Ste 110. Pleasanton CA 94566 925-600-1966 643-7950*
**Fax Area Code:* 949 ■ *TF:* 888-239-0930 ■ *Web:* clubsports.com

Leland, The 400 Bagley St. Detroit MI 48226 313-962-2300 962-1045
Web: theleland.net

Lenox Hotel 61 Exeter St. Boston MA 02116 617-536-5300 267-1237
TF: 800-225-7676 ■ *Web:* www.lenoxhotel.com

Lenox Hotel & Suites 140 N St. Buffalo NY 14201 716-884-1700
Web: www.lenoxhotelandsuites.com

Leola Village Inn & Suites 38 Deborah Dr. Leola PA 17540 717-656-7002 656-7648
Web: www.theinnatleolavillage.com

Les Mars Hotel 27 N St. Healdsburg CA 95448 707-433-4211 433-4611
Web: www.hotellesmars.com

Les Suites Hotel Ottawa 130 Besserer St. Ottawa ON K1N9M9 613-232-2000 232-1242
TF: 866-682-0879 ■ *Web:* www.les-suites.com

Lexington Downtown Hotel & Conference Center 369 W Vine St. Lexington KY 40507 859-231-9000
Web: www.lexingtondowntownhotel.com

Lexington Hotel-George Washington Inn & Conference Ctr 500 Merrimac Trl. Williamsburg VA 23185 757-259-5500
Web: lexingtonhotelwilliamsburg.com

Library Hotel 299 Madison Ave. New York NY 10017 212-983-4500 499-9099
TF: 877-793-7323 ■ *Web:* www.libraryhotel.com

Lighthouse Club Hotel 201 60th St. Ocean City MD 21842 410-524-5400 524-3928
TF: 888-371-5400 ■ *Web:* fagers.com

Lighthouse Lodge & Suites 1150 Lighthouse Ave. Pacific Grove CA 93950 800-858-1249 655-4922*
**Fax Area Code:* 831 ■ *TF:* 800-858-1249 ■ *Web:* www.lighthouselodgecottages.com

Linden Row Inn 100 E Franklin St. Richmond VA 23219 804-783-7000 648-7504
TF: 800-348-7424 ■ *Web:* www.lindenrowinn.com

Listel Hotel, The 1300 Robson St. Vancouver BC V6E1C5 604-684-8461 684-7092
TF: 800-663-5491 ■ *Web:* www.thelistelhotel.com

Litchfield Plantation 24 Ave of the Oaks. Pawleys Island SC 29585 843-543-3146
Web: www.litchfieldplantation.net

Little America Hotel & Resort Cheyenne 2800 W Lincolnway. Cheyenne WY 82009 307-775-8400 775-8425
TF: 800-445-6945 ■ *Web:* www.cheyenne.littleamerica.com

Little America Hotel & Towers Salt Lake City 555 S Main St. Salt Lake City UT 84101 801-258-6568 596-5911
TF: 800-453-9450 ■ *Web:* www.littleamerica.com

Little America Hotel Flagstaff 2515 E Butler Ave. Flagstaff AZ 86004 928-779-7900 779-7983
TF: 800-352-4386 ■ *Web:* flagstaff.littleamerica.com

Little America Hotels & Resorts 500 S Main St. Salt Lake City UT 84101 801-596-5700
TF: 800-281-7899 ■ *Web:* www.littleamerica.com

Little Nell, The 675 E Durant Ave. Aspen CO 81611 970-920-4600 920-4670
TF: 888-843-6355 ■ *Web:* www.thelittlenell.com

Lodge & Spa at Cordillera 2205 Cordillera Way. Edwards CO 81632 970-926-2200 926-2486
TF: 800-877-3529 ■ *Web:* www.cordilleralodge.com

Lodge At Breckenridge, The 112 Overlook Dr. Breckenridge CO 80424 970-453-9300
TF: 800-736-1607 ■ *Web:* thelodgeandspaatbreck.com

Lodge at the Mountain Village 1415 Lowell Ave. Park City UT 84060 435-649-0800 649-1464
TF: 800-453-1360 ■ *Web:* visitparkcity.com

Lodge Hotel & Conference Ctr 900 Spruce Hills Dr. Bettendorf IA 52722 563-359-7141 359-7141
TF: 866-690-4006 ■ *Web:* www.lodgehotel.com

Lodge on the Desert 306 N Alvernon Way. Tucson AZ 85711 520-320-2000 327-5834
TF: 877-498-6776 ■ *Web:* www.lodgeonthedesert.com

LodgeWorks LP 8100 E 22nd St Bldg 500. Wichita KS 67226 316-681-5100 681-0905
Web: www.lodgeworks.com

Lodgian Inc 2002 Summit Blvd Ste 300. Atlanta GA 30319 404-364-9400 812-3102
NYSE: LGN ■ *TF:* 888-750-5834 ■ *Web:* www.lodgian.com

Lodging Hospitality Management Corp 111 W Port Plz Ste 500. St Louis MO 63146 314-434-9500
Web: www.lhmc.com

Lofts Hotel & Suites 55 E Nationwide Blvd. Columbus OH 43215 614-461-2663 461-2630
TF General: 877-902-9022 ■ *Web:* www.55lofts.com

Lombardy Hotel, The 111 E Fifth St. New York NY 10022 212-753-8600
Web: www.lombardyhotel.com

Lone Oak Lodge 2221 N Fremont St. Monterey CA 93940 831-372-4924 372-4985
TF General: 800-283-5663 ■ *Web:* www.loneoaklodge.com

Long House Alaskan Hotel 4335 Wisconsin St. Anchorage AK 99517 907-243-2133 243-6060
TF: 888-243-2133 ■ *Web:* www.longhousehotel.com

Long Island Hotels LLC 1757 Veteran'S Memorial Hwy Ste 22. Islandia NY 11749 631-234-9700
Web: www.longislandhotelsllc.com

Longhouse Hospitality 4770 S Atlanta Rd. Smyrna GA 30080 404-351-9700 350-6106
Web: www.longhousehospitality.com

Lonsdale Quay Hotel 123 Carrie Cates Ct. North Vancouver BC V7M3K7 604-986-6111 986-8782
TF: 800-836-6111 ■ *Web:* www.lonsdalequayhotel.com

Lookout Inn 6901 Lookout Rd. Boulder CO 80301 303-530-1513 530-4573
TF: 800-530-1513 ■ *Web:* www.lookoutinnguesthouse.com

Lord Elgin Hotel 100 Elgin St. Ottawa ON K1P5K8 613-235-3333 235-3223
TF: 800-267-4298 ■ *Web:* www.lordelginhotel.ca

Lord Nelson Hotel & Suites 1515 S Pk St. Halifax NS B3J2L2 902-423-6331 423-7148
TF: 800-565-2020 ■ *Web:* www.lordnelsonhotel.com

Lord Stanley Suites on the Park 1889 Alberni St. Vancouver BC V6G3G7 604-688-9299 688-9297
TF: 888-767-7829 ■ *Web:* www.lordstanley.com

Los Angeles Athletic Club 431 W Seventh St. Los Angeles CA 90014 213-625-2211 689-1194
TF: 800-421-8777 ■ *Web:* www.laac.com

Los Willows Inn & Spa 530 Stewart Canyon Rd. Fallbrook CA 92028 760-731-9400 728-3622
Web: www.loswillows.com

Lowell Inn 102 N Second St. Stillwater MN 55082 651-439-1100 439-0253
Web: www.lowellinn.com

LQ Management LLC
La Quinta Inn & Suites
909 Hidden Ridge Ste 600. Irving TX 75038 214-492-6600 492-6785*
**Fax:* Mktg ■ *TF:* 800-753-3757 ■ *Web:* www.lq.com

Luxe Hotel Rodeo Drive 360 N Rodeo Dr. Beverly Hills CA 90210 310-273-0300 859-8730
TF: 800-468-3541 ■ *Web:* www.luxehotels.com

Phone | Fax

Luxe Hotel Sunset Blvd 11461 Sunset Blvd — Los Angeles CA 90049 — 310-476-6571 — 471-6310
TF: 800-468-3541 ■ *Web:* www.luxehotels.com

Luxe Worldwide Hotels
11461 W Sunset Blvd — Los Angeles CA 90049 — 310-440-3090 — 440-0821
TF: 866-589-3411 ■ *Web:* www.luxehotels.com

Luxor Hotel & Casino 3900 Las Vegas Blvd S — Las Vegas NV 89119 — 702-262-4000 — 262-4404
TF Resv: 800-288-1000 ■ *Web:* www.luxor.com

LXR Luxury Resorts 501 E Camino Real Blvd — Boca Raton FL 33432 — 561-447-5300
Web: www.luxuryresorts.com

MacArthur Place 29 E MacArthur St — Sonoma CA 95476 — 707-938-2929 — 933-9833
TF: 800-722-1866 ■ *Web:* www.macarthurplace.com

Madison Concourse Hotel & Governors Club
1 W Dayton St — Madison WI 53703 — 608-257-6000 — 257-5280
TF: 800-356-8293 ■ *Web:* www.concoursehotel.com

Madison Hotel 79 Madison Ave — Memphis TN 38103 — 901-333-1200 — 333-1210
Web: www.madisonhotelmemphis.com

Madison Hotel, The One Convent Rd — Morristown NJ 07960 — 973-285-1800 — 540-8566
TF: 800-526-0729 ■ *Web:* www.themadisonhotel.com

Madison the - A Loews Hotel 667 Madison Ave — New York NY 10065 — 212-521-2000
TF: 800-235-6397 ■ *Web:* www.loewshotels.com

Magic Castle Hotel 7025 Franklin Ave — Los Angeles CA 90028 — 323-851-0800
Web: magiccastlehotel.com

Magnolia Hotel & Spa, The 623 Courtney St — Victoria BC V8W1B8 — 250-381-0999 — 381-0988
TF: 877-624-6654 ■ *Web:* www.magnoliahotel.com

Magnolia Hotel Dallas 1401 Commerce St — Dallas TX 75201 — 214-915-6500 — 253-0053
TF: 888-915-1110 ■ *Web:* www.magnoliahotels.com

Magnolia Hotel Denver 818 17th St — Denver CO 80202 — 303-607-9000 — 607-0101
TF: 888-915-1110 ■ *Web:* www.magnoliahotels.com

Magnolia Hotel Houston 1100 Texas Ave — Houston TX 77002 — 713-221-0011 — 221-0022
TF: 888-915-1110 ■ *Web:* www.magnoliahotels.com

Main Street Station Hotel & Casino
200 N Main St — Las Vegas NV 89101 — 702-387-1896 — 386-4421
TF: 800-713-8933 ■ *Web:* www.mainstreetcasino.com

Maison 140 Beverly Hills 140 Lasky Dr — Beverly Hills CA 90212 — 310-281-4000 — 281-4001
Web: maison140.com

Maison Dupuy Hotel 1001 Toulouse St — New Orleans LA 70112 — 504-586-8000 — 648-6180
TF: 800-535-9177 ■ *Web:* www.maisondupuy.com

Majestic Hotel 528 W Brompton — Chicago IL 60657 — 773-404-3499 — 404-3495
Web: www.majestic-chicago.com

Malaga Inn 359 Church St — Mobile AL 36602 — 251-438-4701 — 438-4701
TF: 800-235-1586 ■ *Web:* malagainn.com

Malibu Beach Inn 22878 Pacific Coast Hwy — Malibu CA 90265 — 310-456-6444 — 456-1499
Web: www.malibubeachinn.com

Mandarin Oriental Hotel Group (USA)
345 California St Ste 1250 — San Francisco CA 94104 — 415-772-8800 — 782-3778
TF: 800-526-6566 ■ *Web:* www.mandarinoriental.com

Mandarin Oriental Miami 500 Brickell Key Dr — Miami FL 33131 — 305-913-8288 — 913-8300
TF: 800-526-6566 ■ *Web:* www.mandarinoriental.com

Mandarin Oriental New York 80 Columbus Cir — New York NY 10023 — 212-805-8800 — 805-8888
TF: 866-801-8880 ■ *Web:* www.mandarinoriental.com

Mandarin Oriental San Francisco
222 Sansome St — San Francisco CA 94104 — 415-276-9888 — 433-0289
TF: 800-526-6566 ■ *Web:* www.mandarinoriental.com

Mandarin Oriental Washington DC
1330 Maryland Ave SW — Washington DC 20024 — 202-554-8588 — 554-8999
TF: 888-888-1778 ■ *Web:* www.mandarinoriental.com

Manor House Inn 106 W St — Bar Harbor ME 04609 — 207-288-3759 — 288-2974
TF: 800-437-0088 ■ *Web:* www.barharbormanorhouse.com

Mansfield, The 12 W 44th St — New York NY 10036 — 212-277-8700 — 764-4477
TF: 800-255-5167 ■ *Web:* www.mansfieldhotel.com

Mansion on Forsyth Park 700 Drayton St — Savannah GA 31401 — 912-238-5158 — 238-5146
TF: 888-213-3671 ■ *Web:* www.mansiononforsythpark.com

Mansion View Inn & Suites
529 S Fourth St — Springfield IL 62701 — 217-544-7411 — 544-6211
TF: 800-252-1083 ■ *Web:* www.mansionview.com

Maple Hill Farm Bed & Breakfast Inn
11 Inn Rd — Hallowell ME 04347 — 207-622-2708 — 622-0655
TF: 800-622-2708 ■ *Web:* www.maplebb.com

Marcus Corp 100 E Wisconsin Ave — Milwaukee WI 53202 — 414-905-1000
NYSE: MCS ■ *TF:* 800-461-9330 ■ *Web:* www.marcuscorp.com

Marcus Hotels & Resorts
100 E Wisconsin Ave Ste 1950 — Milwaukee WI 53202 — 414-905-1200 — 905-2250
TF: 800-294-2812 ■ *Web:* www.marcushotels.com

Marina Del Mar Resort & Marina
527 Caribbean Dr — Key Largo FL 33037 — 305-451-4107 — 451-1891
Web: www.marinadelmarkeylargo.com

Marina Inn at Grande Dunes
8121 Amalfi Pl — Myrtle Beach SC 29572 — 843-913-1333 — 913-1334
TF Resv: 877-913-1333 ■ *Web:* www.marinainnatgrandedunes.com

Marine Surf Waikiki Hotel 364 Seaside Ave — Honolulu HI 96815 — 808-779-3261
Web: www.waikikiview.com

Mariner's Point Resort of Cape Cod
425 Grand Ave — Falmouth MA 02540 — 508-457-0300
Web: www.marinerspointresort.com

Mark Spencer Hotel 409 SW 11th Ave — Portland OR 97205 — 503-224-3293 — 223-7848
TF: 800-548-3934 ■ *Web:* www.markspencer.com

Mark Twain Hotel 225 NE Adams St — Peoria IL 61602 — 309-676-3600 — 636-6118
TF: 866-325-6351 ■ *Web:* www.marktwainhotel.com

Market Pavilion Hotel 225 E Bay St — Charleston SC 29401 — 843-723-0500 — 723-4320
TF: 877-440-2250 ■ *Web:* www.marketpavilion.com

Maron Hotel & Suites
42 Lk Ave Ext Mill Plain Rd — Danbury CT 06811 — 203-791-2200 — 791-2201
Web: www.maronhotel.com

MarQueen Hotel 600 Queen Anne Ave N — Seattle WA 98109 — 206-282-7407 — 283-1499
Web: www.marqueen.com

Marquesa Hotel 600 Fleming St — Key West FL 33040 — 305-292-1919 — 294-2121
TF: 800-869-4631 ■ *Web:* www.marquesa.com

Marquette Hotel, The 710 Marquette Ave — Minneapolis MN 55402 — 612-333-4545 — 288-2188
TF: 800-328-4782 ■ *Web:* www.marquettehotel.com

Marriott Charleston Hotel
170 Lockwood Blvd — Charleston SC 29403 — 843-723-3000 — 723-0276
TF: 888-236-2427 ■ *Web:* www.marriott.com

Marriott Columbus 800 Front Ave — Columbus GA 31901 — 706-324-1800 — 576-4413
TF: 800-455-9261 ■ *Web:* www.marriott.com

Marriott International Inc
10400 Fernwood Road — Bethesda MD 20817 — 301-380-3000 — 665-6522*
NASDAQ: MAR ■ **Fax Area Code:* 336 ■ **Fax:* Mail Rm ■ *TF:* 800-450-4442 ■ *Web:* www.marriott.com
Ritz-Carlton Hotel Co LLC
4445 Willard Ave Ste 800 — Chevy Chase MD 20815 — 301-547-4700 — 547-4740
TF: 800-241-3333 ■ *Web:* www.ritzcarlton.com

Martha Washington Hotel & Spa, The
150 W Main St — Abingdon VA 24210 — 276-628-3161 — 628-8885
TF: 888-999-8078 ■ *Web:* www.marthawashingtoninn.com

Maryland Inn 16 Church Cir — Annapolis MD 21401 — 410-263-2641 — 268-3613
TF: 800-847-8882 ■ *Web:* www.historicinnsofannapolis.com

Matrix Hotel 10640-100 Ave — Edmonton AB T5J3N8 — 780-429-2861
TF: 866-465-8150 ■ *Web:* www.matrixedmonton.com

Maumee Bay Lodge & Conference Ctr
1750 Pk Rd Ste 2 — Oregon OH 43616 — 419-836-1466 — 836-2438
TF: 800-282-7275 ■ *Web:* www.maumeebaystateparklodge.com

Mayfair Hotel & Spa 3000 Florida Ave — Coconut Grove FL 33133 — 305-441-0000 — 447-9173
TF: 800-433-4555 ■ *Web:* www.mayfairhotelandspa.com

Mayflower Inn 118 Woodbury Rd Rt 47 — Washington CT 06793 — 860-868-9466 — 868-1497
TF: 800-585-7198 ■ *Web:* gracehotels.com/mayflower/

Mayflower Park Hotel 405 Olive Way — Seattle WA 98101 — 206-623-8700 — 382-6996
TF: 800-426-5100 ■ *Web:* www.mayflowerpark.com

McCamly Plaza Hotel 50 Capital Ave SW — Battle Creek MI 49017 — 269-963-7050
Web: www.mccamlyplaza.com

McKibbon Hotel Management Inc
5315 Avion Park Dr Ste 120 — Tampa FL 33607 — 813-241-2399
Web: www.mckibbonhotels.com

McKinley Grand Hotel 320 Market Ave S — Canton OH 44702 — 330-454-5000 — 454-5494
TF: 877-454-5008 ■ *Web:* www.mckinleygrandhotel.com

McLure Hotel, The 1200 Market St — Wheeling WI 26003 — 304-232-0300 — 233-1653

MCM Elegante Suites 4250 Ridgemont Dr — Abilene TX 79606 — 325-698-1234 — 698-2771
TF: 888-897-9644 ■ *Web:* www.mcmelegantesuites.com

Mediterranean Inn 425 Queen Anne Ave N — Seattle WA 98109 — 206-428-4700 — 428-4699
TF: 866-525-4700 ■ *Web:* www.mediterranean-inn.com

Meeting Street Inn 173 Meeting St — Charleston SC 29401 — 843-723-1882 — 577-0851
TF: 800-842-8022 ■ *Web:* www.meetingstreetinn.com

Mendocino Hotel & Garden Suites
45080 Main St — Mendocino CA 95460 — 707-937-0511 — 937-0513
Web: www.mendocinohotel.com

Menger Hotel 204 Alamo Plz — San Antonio TX 78205 — 210-223-4361 — 228-0022
TF: 800-345-9285 ■ *Web:* www.mengerhotel.com

Mercer Hotel 147 Mercer St — New York NY 10012 — 212-966-6060 — 965-3838
TF: 888-918-6060 ■ *Web:* www.mercerhotel.com

Meridian Plaza Resort 2310 N Ocean Blvd — Myrtle Beach SC 29577 — 843-626-4734 — 448-4569
TF: 800-323-3011 ■ *Web:* www.meridianplaza.com

Metropolitan Hotel Vancouver 645 Howe St — Vancouver BC V6C2Y9 — 604-687-1122 — 643-7267
TF: 800-667-2300 ■ *Web:* www.metropolitan.com/vanc

Metterra Hotel on Whyte 10454 82nd Ave — Edmonton AB T6E4Z7 — 780-465-8150 — 465-8174
TF: 866-465-8150 ■ *Web:* www.metterra.com

Meyer Crest Ltd 725 Folger Ave — Berkeley CA 94710 — 510-845-1077 — 845-1544
Web: www.meyercrest.com

Meyer Jabara Hotels
1601 Belvedere Rd Ste 407 S — West Palm Beach FL 33406 — 561-689-6602 — 689-4363
TF: 877-696-8671 ■ *Web:* www.meyerjabarahotels.com

Miami International Airport Hotel
NW 20th St & Le Jeune Rd — Miami FL 33122 — 305-871-4100 — 871-0800
TF: 800-327-1276 ■ *Web:* miahotel.miami-airport.com/

Michelangelo Hotel 152 W 51st St — New York NY 10019 — 212-765-1900 — 541-6604
TF: 800-237-0990 ■ *Web:* www.michelangelohotel.com

Midtown Hotel 220 Huntington Ave — Boston MA 02115 — 617-262-1000 — 262-8739
TF: 800-343-1177 ■ *Web:* www.midtownhotel.com

Mill Street Inn 75 Mill St — Newport RI 02840 — 401-849-9500 — 848-5131
TF: 800-392-1316 ■ *Web:* www.millstreetinn.com

Mill Valley Inn 165 Throckmorton Ave — Mill Valley CA 94941 — 415-389-6608 — 389-5051
Web: www.marinhotels.com

Mills House Hotel 115 Meeting St — Charleston SC 29401 — 843-577-2400 — 722-0623
TF: 800-874-9600 ■ *Web:* www.millshouse.com

Milner Hotel Boston 78 Charles St S — Boston MA 02116 — 617-426-6220 — 350-0360
TF: 877-645-6377 ■ *Web:* www.milner-hotels.com

Milner Hotels Inc 1538 Centre St — Detroit MI 48226 — 313-963-3950 — 962-0410
TF: 877-645-6377 ■ *Web:* www.milner-hotels.com

Minto Place Suite Hotel 185 Lyons St N — Ottawa ON K1R7X5 — 613-232-2200 — 232-6962
TF: 800-267-3377 ■ *Web:* www.minto.com

Mira Monte Inn & Suites 69 Mt Desert St — Bar Harbor ME 04609 — 800-553-5109 — 288-3115*
**Fax Area Code:* 207 ■ *TF:* 800-553-5109 ■ *Web:* www.miramonte.com

Mirabeau Park Hotel
1100 N Sullivan Rd — Spokane Valley WA 99037 — 509-924-9000 — 922-4965
TF: 866-584-4674 ■ *Web:* www.mirabeauparkhotel.com

Mirbeau Inn & Spa 851 W Genesee St — Skaneateles NY 13152 — 315-685-5006 — 685-5150
TF: 877-647-2328 ■ *Web:* www.mirbeau.com

Mission Inn 3649 Mission Inn Ave — Riverside CA 92501 — 951-784-0300 — 683-1342
TF: 800-843-7755 ■ *Web:* www.missioninn.com

Misty Harbor & Barefoot Beach Resort
118 Weirs Rd — Gilford NH 03249 — 603-293-4500
TF: 800-336-4789 ■ *Web:* www.mistyharbor.com

Miyako Hotel Los Angeles 328 E First St — Los Angeles CA 90012 — 213-617-2000 — 617-2700
TF: 800-228-6596 ■ *Web:* www.miyakoinn.com

MMI Hotel Group PO Box 320009 — Jackson MS 39232 — 601-936-3666 — 939-5685
Web: mmihospitality.com

MODA Hotel 900 Seymour St — Vancouver BC V6B3L9 — 604-683-4251 — 683-0611
TF: 877-683-5522 ■ *Web:* www.modahotel.ca

Moderne Hotel, The 243 W 55th St — New York NY 10019 — 212-397-6767 — 397-8787
Web: modernehotelnyc.com

Mojave A Desert Resort
73721 Shadow Mtn Dr — Palm Desert CA 92260 — 760-346-6121 — 674-9072
TF Resv: 800-391-1104 ■ *Web:* www.resortmojave.com

Molly Pitcher Inn 88 Riverside Ave — Red Bank NJ 07701 — 732-747-2500
Web: www.mollypitcher-oysterpoint.com

	City	State	Zip	Phone	Fax
Monarch Hotel & Conference Ctr					
12566 SE 93rd Ave	Clackamas	OR	97015	503-652-1515	652-7509
TF: 800-492-8700 ■ *Web:* www.monarchhotel.cc					
Mondrian Hotel 8440 Sunset Blvd	West Hollywood	CA	90069	323-650-8999	650-5215
TF: 800-525-8029 ■ *Web:* www.morganshotelgroup.com					
Monmouth Plantation 36 Melrose Ave	Natchez	MS	39120	601-442-5852	446-7762
TF: 800-828-4531 ■ *Web:* www.monmouthhistoricinn.com					
Monte Carlo Inn-Airport Suites					
7035 Edwards Blvd	Mississauga	ON	L5T2H8	905-564-8500	564-8400
TF: 800-363-6400 ■ *Web:* www.montecarloinns.com					
Monterey Bay Inn 242 Cannery Row	Monterey	CA	93940	831-373-6242	655-8174
TF: 800-424-6242 ■ *Web:* www.montereybayinn.com					
Monterey Hotel 406 Alvarado St	Monterey	CA	93940	831-375-3184	373-2899
TF: 800-727-0960 ■ *Web:* www.montereyhotel.com					
Monterey Inn Resort & Conference Centre					
2259 Prince of Wales Dr	Ottawa	ON	K2E6Z8	613-288-3500	226-5900
TF: 800-565-1311 ■ *Web:* www.monterey.ca					
Monterey Plaza Hotel & Spa 400 Cannery Row	Monterey	CA	93940	831-646-1700	646-0285
TF: 800-334-3999 ■ *Web:* www.woodsidehotels.com					
Moody Gardens Hotel Seven Hope Blvd	Galveston	TX	77554	409-741-8484	683-4937
TF: 888-388-8484 ■ *Web:* www.moodygardenshotel.com					
Morgans Hotel 237 Madison Ave	New York	NY	10016	212-686-0300	779-8352
TF: 800-606-6090 ■ *Web:* www.morganshotelgroup.com					
Morgans Hotel Group Co 475 Tenth Ave	New York	NY	10018	212-277-4100	532-0099*
NASDAQ: MHGC ■ **Fax Area Code:* 305 ■ *TF:* 800-606-6090 ■ *Web:* www.morganshotelgroup.com					
Morris Inn					
Notre Dame Ave University of Notre Dame	Notre Dame	IN	46556	574-631-2000	631-2340
Web: www.morrisinn.nd.edu					
Morrison-Clark Historic Inn & Restaurant					
1015 L St NW	Washington	DC	20001	202-898-1200	
TF: 800-332-7898 ■ *Web:* www.morrisonclark.com					
Mosaic Hotel 125 S Spalding Dr	Beverly Hills	CA	90212	310-278-0303	278-1728
TF: 800-463-4466 ■ *Web:* www.mosaichotel.com					
Mosser Hotel 54 Fourth St	San Francisco	CA	94103	415-986-4400	495-7653
TF: 800-227-3804 ■ *Web:* www.themosser.com					
Motel 6					
Red Roof Inn 4001 International Pkwy	Carrollton	TX	75007	972-360-9000	
TF: 800-466-8356 ■ *Web:* www.motel6.com					
Motel 6 Wichita 465 S Webb Rd	Wichita	KS	67207	316-684-6363	684-6363
TF: 800-466-8356 ■ *Web:* www.motel6.com					
Mount View Hotel & Spa 1457 Lincoln Ave	Calistoga	CA	94515	707-942-6877	942-6904
TF: 800-816-6877 ■ *Web:* www.mountviewhotel.com					
Mountain Haus 292 E Meadow Dr	Vail	CO	81657	970-476-2434	476-3007
TF: 800-237-0922 ■ *Web:* www.mountainhaus.com					
Mountain Lake Hotel 115 Hotel Cir	Pembroke	VA	24136	540-626-7121	626-7172
TF: 800-346-3334 ■ *Web:* www.mtnlakelodge.com					
Mountain Villas 9525 W Skyline Pkwy	Duluth	MN	55810	218-624-5784	624-1949
TF: 866-688-4552 ■ *Web:* www.mtvillas.com					
Movie Colony Hotel					
726 N Indian Canyon Dr	Palm Springs	CA	92262	760-320-6340	320-1640
TF: 888-953-5700 ■ *Web:* www.moviecolonyhotel.com					
Muse, The 130 W 46th St	New York	NY	10036	212-485-2400	485-2789
TF: 877-692-6873 ■ *Web:* www.themusehotel.com					
Mutiny Hotel 2951 S Bayshore Dr	Miami	FL	33133	305-441-2100	441-2822
TF: 888-868-8469 ■ *Web:* www.providentresorts.com					
Napa River Inn 500 Main St	Napa	CA	94559	707-251-8500	251-8504
TF: 877-251-8500 ■ *Web:* www.napariverinn.com					
Nassau Inn, The 10 Palmer Sq	Princeton	NJ	08542	609-921-7500	921-9385
TF: 800-862-7728 ■ *Web:* www.nassauinn.com					
Nathan Hale Inn & Conference Ctr					
855 Bolton Rd	Storrs	CT	06268	860-427-7888	427-7850
Web: www.nathanhaleinn.com					
National Hotel 1677 Collins Ave	Miami Beach	FL	33139	305-532-2311	534-1426
TF: 800-327-8370 ■ *Web:* www.nationalhotel.com					
Nativo Lodge Hotel					
6000 Pan American Fwy NE	Albuquerque	NM	87109	505-798-4300	798-4305
TF: 888-628-4861 ■ *Web:* www.hhandr.com					
New Castle Hotels & Resorts 2 Corporate Dr	Shelton	CT	06484	203-925-8370	
TF: 800-321-2211 ■ *Web:* www.newcastlehotels.com					
New Haven Hotel 229 George St	New Haven	CT	06510	203-498-3100	498-0911
TF: 800-644-6835 ■ *Web:* www.newhavenhotel.com					
New Haven Premier Suites Hotel					
Three Long Wharf Dr	New Haven	CT	06511	203-777-5337	777-2808
TF: 866-458-0232 ■ *Web:* www.newhavensuites.com					
New Otani Kaimana Beach Hotel					
2863 Kalakaua Ave	Honolulu	HI	96815	808-923-1555	922-9404
TF: 800-356-8264 ■ *Web:* www.kaimana.com					
New York Marriott East Side					
525 Lexington Ave	New York	NY	10017	212-755-4000	
Web: marriott.com					
New York Palace Hotel 455 Madison Ave	New York	NY	10022	212-888-7000	303-6000
TF: 800-697-2522 ■ *Web:* www.newyorkpalace.com					
New York's Hotel Pennsylvania					
401 Seventh Ave	New York	NY	10001	212-736-5000	502-8712
TF: 800-223-8585 ■ *Web:* www.hotelpenn.com/thehotel.html					
New Yorker Hotel 481 Eigth Ave	New York	NY	10001	212-971-0101	629-6536
Web: www.newyorkerhotel.com					
Newport Bay Club & Hotel					
337 Thames St PO Box 1440	Newport	RI	02840	401-849-8600	846-6857
Web: www.newportbayclub.com					
Newport Beach Hotel & Suites One Wave Ave	Middletown	RI	02842	401-846-0310	847-2621
TF: 800-655-1778 ■ *Web:* www.newportbeachhotelandsuites.com					
Newport Beachside Hotel & Resort					
16701 Collins Ave	Miami Beach	FL	33160	305-949-1300	956-2733
TF: 800-327-5476 ■ *Web:* www.newportbeachsideresort.com					
Newport Harbor Corp 366 Thames St	Newport	RI	02840	401-848-7010	
Web: www.newportharbor.com					
Newport Harbor Hotel & Marina					
49 America's Cup Ave	Newport	RI	02840	401-847-9000	849-6380
TF: 800-955-2558 ■ *Web:* www.newporthotel.com					
Nine Zero Hotel 90 Tremont St	Boston	MA	02108	617-772-5800	772-5810
TF: 866-906-9090 ■ *Web:* www.ninezero.com					
Nittany Lion Inn 200 W Pk Ave	State College	PA	16803	814-865-8500	865-8501
TF: 800-233-7505 ■ *Web:* www.pshs.psu.edu					
Noble House Hotels & Resorts 600 Sixth St S	Kirkland	WA	98033	425-827-8737	827-6707
Web: www.noblehousehotels.com					
North Forty Resort LLC					
3765 Mt Hwy 40 W	Columbia Falls	MT	59912	406-862-7740	
Web: northfortyresort.com					
Northland Properties Corp					
310 1755 W Broadway	Vancouver	BC	V6J4S5	604-730-6610	
Web: www.northland.ca					
Norwood Hotel 112 Marion St	Winnipeg	MB	R2H0T1	204-233-4475	231-1910
TF: 888-888-1878 ■ *Web:* www.norwood-hotel.com					
O Henry Hotel 624 Green Vly Rd	Greensboro	NC	27408	336-854-2000	854-2223
TF: 800-965-8259 ■ *Web:* www.ohenryhotel.com					
O Hotel 819 S Flower St	Los Angeles	CA	90017	213-623-9904	614-8010
Web: ohotelgroup.com					
O'Neill Hotels & Resorts Management Ltd					
401 W Georgia St Ste 1690	Vancouver	BC	V6B5A1	604-684-0444	684-0482
Web: www.oneillhotels.com					
Oberlin Inn Seven N Main St	Oberlin	OH	44074	440-775-1111	775-6356
TF: 800-376-4173 ■ *Web:* www.oberlininn.com					
Ocean Five Hotel 436 Ocean Dr	Miami Beach	FL	33139	305-532-7093	534-7353
TF Resv: 877-666-0505 ■ *Web:* www.oceanfive.com					
Ocean Forest Plaza 5523 N Ocean Blvd	Myrtle Beach	SC	29577	843-497-0044	692-5234
TF General: 800-845-6701 ■ *Web:* www.sandsresorts.com					
Ocean Key Resort 424 Atlantic Ave	Virginia Beach	VA	23451	757-425-2200	491-1186
TF: 800-955-9700 ■ *Web:* www.vsaresorts.com					
Ocean Park Hotels Inc					
710 Fiero Ln Ste 14	San Luis Obispo	CA	93401	805-544-0812	
Ocean Pointe Suites at Key Largo					
500 Burton Dr	Tavernier	FL	33070	305-853-3000	853-3007
TF: 800-882-9464 ■ *Web:* www.providentresorts.com/ocean-pointe-suites					
Ocean Reef Club 35 Ocean Reef Dr Ste 200	Key Largo	FL	33037	305-367-2611	
Web: www.oceanreef.com					
Ocean Resort Hotel Waikiki					
175 Paoakalani Ave	Honolulu	HI	96815	808-922-3861	922-3773
TF: 877-367-1912 ■ *Web:* www.castleresorts.com					
Ocean Sky Hotel & Resort					
4060 Galt Ocean Dr	Fort Lauderdale	FL	33308	954-565-6611	564-7730
TF: 800-678-9022 ■ *Web:* www.oceanskyresort.com					
Ocean Walk Resort 300 N Atlantic	Daytona Beach	FL	32118	386-323-4800	
TF: 888-743-2561 ■ *Web:* www.wyndhamoceanwalk.com					
Oceancliff Hotel & Resort 65 Ridge Rd	Newport	RI	02840	401-841-8868	849-3927
Web: www.newportexperience.com					
OHANA Waikiki Beachcomber Hotel					
2300 Kalakaua Ave	Honolulu	HI	96815	808-922-4646	622-4852*
**Fax Area Code:* 800 ■ *TF:* 866-956-4262 ■ *Web:* www.outrigger.com					
Old City House Inn 115 Cordova St	Saint Augustine	FL	32084	904-826-0113	
Web: www.oldcityhouse.com					
Old Mill Toronto 21 Old Mill Rd	Toronto	ON	M8X1G5	416-236-2641	236-2749
TF: 866-653-6455 ■ *Web:* oldmilltoronto.com					
Olde Mill Inn 5835 Dixie Hwy	Clarkston	MI	48346	248-623-0300	
Web: oldemillinnofclarkston.com					
Omaha Downtown Lodging Investors II LLC					
1005 Dodge St	Omaha	NE	68102	402-341-4400	
Omni Hotels 4001 Maple Ave	Dallas	TX	75219	402-952-6664	
TF: 800-843-6664 ■ *Web:* www.omnihotels.com					
Omni La Mansion del Rio 112 College St	San Antonio	TX	78205	210-518-1000	226-0389
TF: 800-292-7300 ■ *Web:* www.omnihotels.com					
One Washington Cir Hotel					
One Washington Cir NW	Washington	DC	20037	202-872-1680	887-4989
TF: 800-424-9671 ■ *Web:* www.thecirclehotel.com					
Onyx Hotel 155 Portland St	Boston	MA	02114	617-557-9955	557-0005
TF: 866-660-6699 ■ *Web:* www.onyxhotel.com					
Opus Hotel 322 Davie St	Vancouver	BC	V6B5Z6	866-642-6787	
TF: 866-642-6787 ■ *Web:* vancouver.opushotel.com					
Orchard Garden Hotel 466 Bush St	San Francisco	CA	94108	415-399-9807	393-9917
TF: 888-717-2881 ■ *Web:* www.theorchardgardenhotel.com					
Orchard Hotel 665 Bush St	San Francisco	CA	94108	415-362-8878	362-8088
TF: 888-717-2881 ■ *Web:* www.theorchardhotel.com					
Orchards Hotel, The 222 Adams Rd	Williamstown	MA	01267	413-458-9611	458-3273
TF: 800-225-1517 ■ *Web:* www.orchardshotel.com					
Orchards Inn of Sedona 254 Hwy N 89 A	Sedona	AZ	86336	855-474-7719	282-5710*
**Fax Area Code:* 928 ■ *TF:* 855-474-7719 ■ *Web:* www.orchardsinn.com					
Orient Express Hotels Inc					
1114 Ave of the Americas	New York	NY	10036	212-302-5055	302-5203
NYSE: OEH ■ *TF:* 800-237-1236 ■ *Web:* belmond.com/					
Orlando, The 8384 W Third St	Los Angeles	CA	90048	323-658-6600	653-3464
TF: 800-624-6835 ■ *Web:* www.theorlando.com					
Orleans Las Vegas Hotel & Casino					
4500 W Tropicana Ave	Las Vegas	NV	89103	702-365-7111	365-7500
TF: 800-675-3267 ■ *Web:* www.orleanscasino.com					
Outrigger Enterprises Group 2375 Kuhio Ave	Honolulu	HI	96815	808-921-6941	369-9403*
**Fax Area Code:* 303 ■ *TF:* 800-462-6262 ■ *Web:* www.outrigger.com					
OHANA Hotels & Resorts 2375 Kuhio Ave	Honolulu	HI	96815	866-254-1605	
TF: 866-254-1605 ■ *Web:* www.ohanahotelsoahu.com					
Outrigger Hotels & Resorts 2375 Kuhio Ave	Honolulu	HI	96815	808-921-6941	926-4368*
**Fax:* Sales ■ *TF:* 800-688-7444 ■ *Web:* www.outrigger.com					
Outrigger Waikiki on the Beach					
2335 Kalakaua Ave	Honolulu	HI	96815	808-923-0711	921-9749
TF: 800-688-7444 ■ *Web:* www.outrigger.com					
Overlook Lodge PO Box 351	Bear Mountain	NY	10911	845-786-2731	786-2543
Web: www.visitbearmountain.com					
Owyhee Plaza Hotel 1109 Main St	Boise	ID	83702	208-343-4611	
Web: www.owyheeplaza.com					
Oxford Hotel 1600 17th St	Denver	CO	80202	303-628-5400	628-5413
TF: 800-228-5838 ■ *Web:* www.theoxfordhotel.com					
Oxford Palace 745 S Oxford Ave	Los Angeles	CA	90005	213-389-8000	389-8500
TF: 800-532-7887 ■ *Web:* www.oxfordhotel.com					
Oxford Suites Boise 1426 S Entertainment Ave	Boise	ID	83709	208-322-8000	322-8002
TF General: 888-322-8001 ■ *Web:* www.oxfordsuitesboise.com					

Phone Fax

Oxford Suites Spokane Valley
15015 E Indiana Ave ... Spokane Valley WA 99216 509-847-1000 847-1001
TF: 866-668-7848 ■ *Web:* www.oxfordsuitesspokanevalley.com

Oxford Suites Spokane-Downtown
115 W N River Dr ... Spokane WA 99201 509-353-9000 353-9164
TF: 800-774-1877 ■ *Web:* www.oxfordsuitesspokane.com

Oyster Point Hotel, The 146 Bodman Pl ... Red Bank NJ 07701 732-530-8200 747-1875
TF: 800-345-3484 ■ *Web:* www.theoysterpointhotel.com

Pace's Lodging Corp 4265 45th St S Ste 200 ... Fargo ND 58104 701-281-9500 281-9501
Web: propertyresourcesgroup.com

Pacific Beach Hotel 2490 Kalakaua Ave ... Honolulu HI 96815 808-922-1233 922-0129
TF: 800-367-6060 ■ *Web:* www.pacificbeachhotel.com

Pacific Edge Hotel 647 S Coast Hwy ... Laguna Beach CA 92651 949-494-8566
Web: www.pacificedgehotel.com

Pacific Inn 600 Marina Dr ... Seal Beach CA 90740 562-493-7501 596-3448
TF: 866-466-0300 ■ *Web:* thepacificinn.com

Pacific Inn Resort & Conference Centre
1160 King George Hwy ... Surrey BC V4A4Z2 604-535-1432 531-6979
TF: 800-667-2248 ■ *Web:* www.pacificinn.com

Pacific Shores Inn 4802 Mission Blvd ... San Diego CA 92109 858-483-6300 483-9276
TF: 888-478-7829 ■ *Web:* www.pacificshoresinn.com

Pacific Terrace Hotel 610 Diamond St ... San Diego CA 92109 858-581-3500 274-2534
TF: 800-344-3370 ■ *Web:* www.pacificterrace.com

Painted Buffalo Inn
400 W Broadway PO Box 2547 ... Jackson WY 83001 307-733-4340 733-7953
TF: 800-288-3866 ■ *Web:* www.paintedbuffaloinn.com

Palace Hotel 2 New Montgomery St ... San Francisco CA 94105 415-512-1111 543-0671
TF: 866-716-8136 ■ *Web:* www.sfpalace.com

Palace Station Hotel & Casino
2411 W Sahara Ave ... Las Vegas NV 89102 702-367-2411
TF Resv: 800-634-3101 ■ *Web:* palacestation.sclv.com

Palmer House Hilton 17 E Monroe St ... Chicago IL 60603 312-726-7500 922-5240
TF: 800-445-8667 ■ *Web:* www.hiltonchicagohotel.com

Palmer Inn, The 3499 US 1 ... Princeton NJ 08540 609-452-2500
Web: www.palmerinnprinceton.com

Palo Verde Inn & Suites 5251 S Julian Dr ... Tucson AZ 85706 520-294-5250 889-1982
Web: www.paloverdeinn.com

Palos Verdes Inn
1700 S Pacific Coast Hwy ... Redondo Beach CA 90277 310-316-4211 316-4863
TF: 800-421-9241 ■ *Web:* www.palosverdesinn.com

Pan Pacific Hotel Vancouver
999 Canada Pl Ste 300 ... Vancouver BC V6C3B5 604-662-8111 685-8690
TF: 800-937-1515 ■ *Web:* www.panpacific.com

Pan Pacific Seattle 2125 Terry Ave ... Seattle WA 98121 206-264-8111 654-5049
Web: www.panpacific.com

Pantages Hotel 200 Victoria St ... Toronto ON M5B1V8 416-362-1777 214-5618
TF: 866-852-1777 ■ *Web:* www.pantageshotel.com

Par-A-Dice Hotel 21 Blackjack Blvd ... East Peoria IL 61611 309-699-7711 699-9317
TF: 800-727-2342 ■ *Web:* www.paradicecasino.com

Paragon Hotel Corp
5333 N Seventh St Ste A-100 ... Phoenix AZ 85014 602-248-0811 279-6765
Web: www.paragonhotels.com

Paramount Hotel 235 W 46th St ... New York NY 10036 212-764-5500 354-5237
TF Resv: 855-234-2074 ■ *Web:* www.nycparamount.com

Paramount Hotel Group 710 Rt 46 E Ste 206 ... Fairfield NJ 07004 973-882-0505 882-0043
Web: www.paramounthotelgroup.com

Parc 55 Hotel 55 Cyril Magnin St ... San Francisco CA 94102 415-392-8000 403-6602
Web: www.parc55hotel.com

Paris Las Vegas 3655 Las Vegas Blvd S ... Las Vegas NV 89109 800-522-4700 662-5339*
**Fax Area Code:* 216 ■ *TF:* 800-342-7724 ■ *Web:* www.totalrewards.com

Park Central Hotel 1010 Houston St ... Fort Worth TX 76102 817-336-2011 336-2011
Web: www.parkcentralhotel.com

Park Central New York 870 Seventh Ave ... New York NY 10019 212-247-8000 707-5557
Web: www.parkcentralny.com

Park Central, The 640 Ocean Dr ... Miami Beach FL 33139 305-538-1611 534-7520
Web: www.theparkcentral.com

Park Plaza Hotel Oakland 150 Hegenberger Rd ... Oakland CA 94621 510-635-5300 635-9661
Web: www.redlion.com

Park Shore Waikiki Hotel 2586 Kalakaua Ave ... Honolulu HI 96815 808-954-7426 923-0311
TF: 866-536-7975 ■ *Web:* www.parkshorewaikiki.com

Park South Hotel 124 E 28th St ... New York NY 10016 212-448-0888 448-0811
TF: 800-315-4642 ■ *Web:* www.parksouthhotel.com

Park Vista Resort Hotel
705 Cherokee OrchaRd Rd PO Box 30 ... Gatlinburg TN 37738 865-436-9211 430-7533
TF Sales: 800-227-5622 ■ *Web:* www.parkvista.com

Parkway Inn 125 N Jackson St PO Box 494 ... Jackson WY 83001 800-247-8390
TF: 800-247-8390 ■ *Web:* www.parkwayinn.com

Parkway Plaza Hotel 123 W E St ... Casper WY 82601 307-235-1777 266-4665
Web: www.parkwayplaza.net

Partridge Inn 2110 Walton Way ... Augusta GA 30904 706-737-8888 731-0826
TF: 800-476-6888 ■ *Web:* www.partridgeinn.com

Paso Robles Inn 1103 Spring St ... Paso Robles CA 93446 805-238-2660 238-4707
TF: 800-676-1713 ■ *Web:* www.pasoroblesinn.com

Peabody Hotel Group 5118 Park Ave Ste 245 ... Memphis TN 38117 901-762-5400 762-5464
Web: www.phg.net

Peabody Memphis 149 Union Ave ... Memphis TN 38103 901-529-4000 529-3600
TF: 800-732-2639 ■ *Web:* www.peabodymemphis.com

Peabody Orlando 5118 Park Ave Ste 245 ... Memphis TN 38117 901-762-5400 762-5464
Web: www.phg.net

Peachtree Hotel Group LLC
Two Premier Plaza 5607 Glenridge Dr Ste 430 ... Atlanta GA 30342 404-497-4111
Web: www.peachtreehotelgroup.com

Peacock Suites 1745 S Anaheim Blvd ... Anaheim CA 92805 714-535-8255 535-8914
TF: 800-522-6401 ■ *Web:* www.shellhospitality.com

Pearl Hotel, The 1410 Rosecrans St ... San Diego CA 92106 619-226-6100 226-6161
TF: 877-732-7573 ■ *Web:* www.thepearlsd.com

Peery Hotel 110 West 300 South ... Salt Lake City UT 84101 801-521-4300
TF: 800-331-0073 ■ *Web:* www.peeryhotel.com

Pegasus International Hotel 501 Southard St ... Key West FL 33040 305-294-9323 294-4741
TF: 800-397-8148 ■ *Web:* www.pegasuskeywest.com

Pelham Hotel 444 Common St ... New Orleans LA 70130 504-522-4444 539-9010
TF: 888-856-4486 ■ *Web:* www.thepelhamhotel.com

Phone Fax

Pelican Grand Beach Resort Condominium Associati
2000 N Ocean Blvd ... Fort Lauderdale FL 33305 954-568-9431
Web: pelicanbeach.com

Penguin Hotel 1418 Ocean Dr ... Miami Beach FL 33139 305-534-9334
TF: 800-499-7964 ■ *Web:* www.penguinhotel.com

Peninsula Beverly Hills
9882 S Santa Monica Blvd ... Beverly Hills CA 90212 310-551-2888 788-2319
TF: 800-462-7899 ■ *Web:* www.peninsula.com

Peninsula Chicago 108 E Superior St ... Chicago IL 60611 312-337-2888 751-2888
TF: 866-288-8889 ■ *Web:* www.peninsula.com

Peninsula New York 700 Fifth Ave ... New York NY 10019 212-956-2888 903-3949
TF: 800-262-9467 ■ *Web:* www.peninsula.com

Penn's View Hotel 14 N Front St ... Philadelphia PA 19106 215-922-7600 922-7642
TF: 800-331-7634 ■ *Web:* www.pennsviewhotel.com

Peppermill Hotel & Casino 2707 S Virginia St ... Reno NV 89502 775-826-2121 689-7041
TF: 800-648-6992 ■ *Web:* www.peppermillreno.com

Perfect North Slopes Inc
19074 Perfect Pl Ln ... Lawrenceburg IN 47025 812-537-3754
Web: perfectnorth.com

Petite Auberge 863 Bush St ... San Francisco CA 94108 415-928-6000 673-7214
Web: jdvhotels.com/hotels/california/

Pfister Hotel 424 E Wisconsin Ave ... Milwaukee WI 53202 414-273-8222 273-5025
TF: 800-558-8222 ■ *Web:* www.thepfisterhotel.com

Phillips Beach Plaza Hotel
1301 Atlantic Ave ... Ocean City MD 21842 410-289-9121 289-3041
TF: 800-492-5834 ■ *Web:* www.beachplazaoc.com

Phoenix Grand Hotel Salem 201 Liberty St SE ... Salem OR 97301 503-540-7800 540-7830
TF: 877-540-7800 ■ *Web:* www.grandhotelsalem.com

Phoenix Hotel 601 Eddy St ... San Francisco CA 94109 415-776-1380 885-3109
TF: 800-248-9466 ■
Web: jdvhotels.com/hotels/california/san-francisco-hotels/phoenix-hotel

Phoenix Park Hotel 520 N Capitol St ... Washington DC 20001 202-638-6900 393-3236
TF: 800-824-5419 ■ *Web:* www.phoenixparkhotel.com

Piccadilly Inn Airport 5115 E McKinley Ave ... Fresno CA 93727 559-375-7760
Web: www.piccadillyinn.com

Piccadilly Inn Express 2305 W Shaw Ave ... Fresno CA 93711 559-348-5520 456-4643
Web: www.piccadillyinn.com

Piccadilly Inn Hotels 2305 W Shaw Ave ... Fresno CA 93711 559-348-5520
TF: 888-286-2645 ■ *Web:* www.piccadillyinn.com

Piccadilly Inn Shaw 2305 W Shaw Ave ... Fresno CA 93711 559-348-5520
Web: www.piccadillyinn.com

Pier 5 Hotel 711 Eastern Ave ... Baltimore MD 21202 410-539-2000 783-1787
TF: 866-583-4162 ■ *Web:* www.harbormagic.com

Pierpont Inn 550 Sanjon Rd ... Ventura CA 93001 805-643-6144 643-9167
Web: www.pierpontinn.com

Pierre, The Two E 61st St ... New York NY 10065 212-838-8000 940-8109
Web: www.tajhotels.com

Pillar Hotels & Resorts LP
6031 Connection Dr Ste 500 ... Irving TX 75039 972-830-3100
Web: pillarhotels.com

Pillars Hotel at New River Sound
111 N Birch Rd ... Fort Lauderdale FL 33304 954-467-9639 763-2845
TF: 800-241-3333 ■ *Web:* www.pillarshotel.com

Pine Crest Inn 85 Pine Crest Ln ... Tryon NC 28782 828-859-9135 859-9136
TF: 800-633-3001 ■ *Web:* www.pinecrestinn.com

Pines Lodge 141 Scott Hill Rd ... Beaver Creek CO 81620 970-429-5043 845-7809
TF Resv: 800-859-8242 ■ *Web:* www.pineslodge.rockresorts.com

Pisgah Inn PO Box 749 ... Waynesville NC 28786 828-235-8228 648-9719
Web: www.pisgahinn.com

Pitcher Inn 275 Main St PO Box 347 ... Warren VT 05674 802-496-6350 496-6354
Web: www.pitcherinn.com

Place D'Armes Hotel 625 St Ann St ... New Orleans LA 70116 504-524-4531
TF: 800-366-2743 ■ *Web:* www.placedarmes.com

Place Louis Riel All-Suite Hotel
190 Smith St ... Winnipeg MB R3C1J8 204-947-6961 947-3029
TF: 800-665-0569 ■ *Web:* www.placelouisriel.com

Plains Hotel, The 1600 Central Ave ... Cheyenne WY 82001 307-638-3311 635-2022
TF: 866-275-2467 ■ *Web:* www.theplainshotel.com

Plantation Inn of New England
295 Burnett Rd ... Chicopee MA 01020 413-592-8200 592-9671

Planters Inn 112 N Market St ... Charleston SC 29401 843-722-2345 577-2125
TF: 800-845-7082 ■ *Web:* www.plantersinn.com

Platinum Hotel 211 E Flamingo Rd ... Las Vegas NV 89169 702-365-5000 636-2500
TF General: 877-211-9211 ■ *Web:* www.theplatinumhotel.com

Plaza Hotel & Casino One Main St PO Box 760 ... Las Vegas NV 89101 702-386-2110
TF: 800-634-6575 ■ *Web:* www.plazahotelcasino.com

Plaza Inn 900 Medical Arts NE ... Albuquerque NM 87102 505-243-5693 843-6229
Web: www.plazainnabq.com

Plaza on the River Resort Club Hotel 121 W St ... Reno NV 89501 775-786-2200
TF: 800-628-5974 ■ *Web:* www.plazaresortclub.com

Plaza Square Motor Lodge
2255 Central Blvd ... Brownsville TX 78520 956-546-5104 548-0243

Plaza Suite Hotel Resort 620 S Peters St ... New Orleans LA 70130 800-770-6721 524-2135*
**Fax Area Code:* 504 ■ *TF:* 800-770-6721 ■ *Web:* www.plazaresort.com

Plaza Suites Silicon Valley
3100 Lakeside Dr ... Santa Clara CA 95054 408-748-9800 748-1476
TF: 800-345-1554 ■ *Web:* www.theplazasuites.com

PLJ Restaurant 333 Fulton St ... San Francisco CA 94102 415-294-8925

Plump Jack's Squaw Valley Inn
1920 Squaw Vly Rd PO Box 2407 ... Olympic Valley CA 96146 530-583-1576 583-1734
TF: 800-323-7666 ■ *Web:* www.plumpjacksquawvalleyinn.com

Point Plaza Suites & Conference Hotel
950 J Clyde Morris Blvd ... Newport News VA 23601 757-599-4460 599-4336
TF: 800-841-1112 ■ *Web:* www.pointplazasuites.com

Pollard, The Two N Broadway PO Box 650 ... Red Lodge MT 59068 406-446-0001 446-0002
Web: www.thepollard.com

Pontchartrain Hotel 2031 St Charles Ave ... New Orleans LA 70130 504-524-0581
TF: 800-777-6193 ■ *Web:* www.pontchartrainhotel.com

Port Ludlow Assoc LLC 70 Breaker Ln ... Port Ludlow WA 98365 360-437-2101
Web: portludlowresort.com

Port-O-Call Hotel 1510 Boardwalk ... Ocean City NJ 08226 609-399-8812 399-0387
TF: 800-334-4546 ■ *Web:* www.portocallhotel.com

Phone Fax

Portland Harbor Hotel 468 Fore St. . . . . .Portland ME 04101 207-775-9090 775-9990
TF: 888-798-9090 ■ *Web:* www.portlandharborhotel.com

Portland Regency Hotel 20 Milk St. . . . . .Portland ME 04101 207-774-4200 775-2150
TF: 800-727-3436 ■ *Web:* www.theregency.com

Portofino Hotel & Yacht Club
260 Portofino Way . . . . .Redondo Beach CA 90277 310-379-8481 372-7329
TF: 800-468-4292 ■ *Web:* www.hotelportofino.com

Portofino Inn & Suites Anaheim
1831 S Harbor Blvd . . . . Anaheim CA 92802 714-782-7600 782-7619
TF Resv: 800-398-3963 ■ *Web:* www.portofinoinnanaheim.com

Portola Plaza Hotel 2 Portola Plaza . . . . Monterey CA 93940 831-649-4511 649-4511
TF: 888-222-5851 ■ *Web:* www.portolahotel.com

Post Hotel, The
200 Pipestone Rd PO Box 69 . . . . Lake Louise AB T0L1E0 403-522-3989 522-3966
TF: 800-661-1586 ■ *Web:* www.posthotel.com

Prairie Band Casino & Resort 12305 150th Rd . . . . Mayetta KS 66509 785-966-7777 966-7799
TF: 888-727-4946 ■ *Web:* www.pbpgaming.com

Prairie Hotel 700 Prairie Pk Ln PO Box 5210. . . . . Yelm WA 98597 360-458-8300 458-8301
Web: www.prairiehotel.com

Preferred Hotels & Resorts Worldwide Inc
311 S Wacker Dr Ste 1900. . . . . .Chicago IL 60606 312-913-0400 913-5124
TF: 800-650-1281 ■ *Web:* preferredhotels.com

Preferred Hotel Group
Sterling Hotels Corp 311 S Wacker Dr Ste 1900 . . . . Chicago IL 60606 312-913-0400 913-5124
Web: preferredhotelgroup.com
Summit Hotels & Resorts
311 S Wacker Dr Ste 1900. . . . . .Chicago IL 60606 312-913-0400 913-5124
TF: 800-650-1281 ■ *Web:* preferredhotelgroup.com

Premier Hotel Times Square, The
133 W 44th St. . . . . .New York NY 10036 212-789-7670
Web: millenniumhotels.com

Prescott Hotel 545 Post St . . . . San Francisco CA 94102 415-563-0303 563-6831
TF: 866-271-3632 ■ *Web:* www.prescotthotel.com

President Abraham Lincoln Hotel & Conference Ctr (PALHACC)
701 E Adams St . . . . .Springfield IL 62701 217-544-8800 544-9607
TF: 855-610-8733 ■ *Web:* doubletree3.hilton.com

Prestige Harbourfront Resort & Convention Centre
251 Harbourfront Dr Ne . . . . Salmon Arm BC V1E2W7 250-833-5800
Web: prestigehotelsandresorts.com

Priced Rite Suites 2327 University Ave. . . . . Green Bay WI 54302 920-469-2130
Web: www.pricedritesuites.com

Prince Conti Hotel 830 Conti St . . . . New Orleans LA 70112 504-529-4172 636-1046
TF: 800-366-2743 ■ *Web:* www.princecontihotel.com

Prince George Hotel, The 1725 Market St. . . . . .Halifax NS B3J3N9 902-425-1986 429-6048
TF: 800-565-1567 ■ *Web:* www.princegeorgehotel.com

Princess Bayside Beach Hotel & Golf Ctr
4801 Coastal Hwy. . . . . .Ocean City MD 21842 410-723-2900 723-0207
TF General: 888-622-9743 ■ *Web:* www.princessbayside.com

Princess Royale Oceanfront Hotel & Conference Ctr
9100 Coastal Hwy. . . . . .Ocean City MD 21842 410-524-7777 524-7787
TF: 800-476-9253 ■ *Web:* www.princessroyale.com

Priory, The 614 Pressley St. . . . . Pittsburgh PA 15212 412-231-3338 231-4838
Web: www.thepriory.com

Prism Hotels & Resorts
14800 Landmark Blvd Ste 800 . . . . Dallas TX 75254 214-987-9300
Web: www.prismhotels.com

Procaccianti Group, The 1140 Reservoir Ave. . . . . Cranston RI 02920 401-946-4600

Prospector Hotel 375 Whittier St . . . . Juneau AK 99801 907-586-3737 586-1204
TF: 800-331-2711 ■ *Web:* www.prospectorhotel.com

Providence Biltmore Hotel 11 Dorrance St. . . . . Providence RI 02903 800-294-7709
TF: 800-294-7709 ■ *Web:* www.providencebiltmore.com

Publick House Historic Resort
277 Main St Rt 131. . . . . .Sturbridge MA 01566 508-347-3313 347-1460
TF Cust Svc: 800-782-5425 ■ *Web:* www.publickhouse.com

Puffin Inn 4400 SpenaRd Rd. . . . . .Anchorage AK 99517 907-243-4044 248-6853
TF: 800-478-3346 ■ *Web:* puffininn.net

Q Hotel, The 560 Westport Rd. . . . . Kansas City MO 64111 816-931-0001
Web: achotelskansascity.com/new-ac-hotel

Quail Run Lodge 1130 Bob Harman Rd . . . . .Savannah GA 31408 912-964-1421 966-5646
Web: www.quailrunlodge.com

Quaintance-Weaver Inc 324 W Wendover Ave. . . . . . Greensboro NC 27408 336-370-0966 370-0965
Web: www.qwrh.com

Quality Hotel-airport 7228 Wminster Hwy . . . . Richmond BC V6X1A1 604-244-3051
Web: qualityhotelvancouverairport.com

Quality Inn Flamingo 1300 N Stone Ave. . . . . .Tucson AZ 85705 520-770-1910 770-0750
Web: www.flamingohoteltucson.com

Quality Inn Halifax Airport Hotel
60 Sky Blvd Halifax International Airport . . . . Goffs NS B2T1K3 902-873-3000 873-3001
TF: 800-667-3333 ■ *Web:* www.airporthotelhalifax.com

Quality Inn West Harvest
17803 Stony Plain Rd. . . . . Edmonton AB T5S1B4 780-484-8000 486-6060
TF: 800-661-2133 ■ *Web:* www.westharvest.ca

Quarterpath Inn & Suites 614 York St. . . . . .Williamsburg VA 23185 757-220-0960 591-7320
TF: 800-581-7245 ■ *Web:* www.quarterpathinnandsuites.com

Quebec Inn 7175 Blvd Hamel Ouest . . . . .Quebec City QC G2G1B6 418-872-9831 872-1336
TF: 800-567-5276 ■ *Web:* www.hotelsjaro.com/quebecinn/index-en.aspx

Queen & Crescent Hotel
535 Tchoupitoulas St . . . . New Orleans LA 70130 800-455-3417 587-9701*
**Fax Area Code:* 504 ■ *TF:* 800-455-3417 ■ *Web:* www.neworleansboutiquehotels.com

Queen Anne Hotel 1590 Sutter St . . . . San Francisco CA 94109 415-441-2828 775-5212
TF: 800-227-3970 ■ *Web:* www.queenanne.com

Queen Kapiolani Hotel 150 Kapahulu Ave . . . . .Honolulu HI 96815 808-922-1941 922-2694
TF: 866-970-4164 ■ *Web:* www.queenkapiolani.com

Quimby House Inn 109 Cottage St. . . . . .Bar Harbor ME 04609 207-288-5811
TF: 800-344-5811 ■ *Web:* www.quimbyhouse.com

Quincy Hotel 1823 L St NW . . . . .Washington DC 20036 202-223-4320 293-4977
TF: 800-424-2970 ■ *Web:* www.thequincy.com

Quorum Hotels & Resorts
5429 Lyndon B Johnson Fwy #625. . . . . Dallas TX 75240 972-458-7265 991-5647
Web: www.quorumhotels.com

Rabbit Hill Inn
48 Lower Waterford Rd PO Box 55 . . . . Lower Waterford VT 05848 802-748-5168 748-8342
TF: 800-626-3215 ■ *Web:* www.rabbithillinn.com

Radisson Butler Blvd 4700 Salisbury Rd . . . . .Jacksonville FL 32256 904-281-9700 281-1957
TF: 888-201-1718 ■ *Web:* www.radisson.com

Radisson Chicago-O'Hare Hotel
1450 E Touhy Ave. . . . . Des Plaines IL 60018 847-296-8866 296-8268
TF: 888-201-1718 ■ *Web:* www.radisson.com

Radisson Hotel & Suites Fort Mc Murray
435 Gregoire Dr . . . . .Fort Mcmurray AB T9H4K7 780-743-2400
Web: www.radissonfortmcmurray.com

Radisson Hotel Bloomington Mall of America
1700 American Blvd E . . . . Bloomington MN 55425 952-854-8700 854-8701
TF Resv: 800-967-9033 ■
Web: www.radisson.com/bloomington-hotel-mn-55425/mnblmmal

Radisson Hotel Gateway Seattle-Tacoma Airport
18118 International Blvd. . . . . Seattle WA 98188 206-244-6666 244-6679
Web: www.radisson.com

Radisson Milwaukee North Shore
7065 N Port Washington Rd . . . . .Milwaukee WI 53217 414-351-6960 351-5194
TF: 800-395-7046 ■ *Web:* www.radisson.com

Raffaello Hotel 201 E Delaware Pl. . . . . .Chicago IL 60611 312-943-5000 924-9158
Web: www.chicagoraffaello.com

Railroad Pass Hotel & Casino
2800 S Boulder Hwy. . . . . .Henderson NV 89002 702-294-5000 294-0092
TF: 800-654-0877 ■ *Web:* www.railroadpass.com

Ramada Middletown 425 E Main Rd . . . . Middletown RI 02842 401-846-3555 846-3666
TF: 800-854-9517 ■ *Web:* ramada.com

Ramada Plaza & Conference Ctr
4900 Sinclair Rd. . . . . Columbus OH 43229 614-846-0300 847-1022
TF: 800-272-6232 ■ *Web:* www.ramada.com

Ranch at Steamboat 1800 Ranch Rd . . . . Steamboat Springs CO 80487 970-879-3000 879-5409
TF: 888-686-8075 ■ *Web:* www.ranch-steamboat.com

Ranch Inn 45 E Pearl St. . . . . .Jackson WY 83001 307-733-6363 733-0623
TF: 800-348-5599 ■ *Web:* www.ranchinn.com

Rancho Alegre Lodge
3600 S Pk Loop Rd PO Box 998. . . . . .Jackson WY 83001 307-733-7988
Web: www.ranchoalegre.com

Raphael Kansas City 325 Ward Pkwy. . . . . Kansas City MO 64112 816-756-3800 802-2131
TF: 800-821-5343 ■ *Web:* www.raphaelkc.com

Red Jacket Beach Resort 39 Todd Rd . . . . .South Yarmouth MA 02664 508-398-6941 398-1830
TF: 800-227-3263 ■ *Web:* www.redjacketresorts.com

Red Lion Hotels Corp 201 W N River Dr Ste 100. . . . . Spokane WA 99201 800-733-5466 325-7324*
NYSE: RLH ■ **Fax Area Code:* 509 ■ *TF Resv:* 800-733-5466 ■ *Web:* www.redlion.com

Red Lion Inn 30 Main St PO Box 954 . . . . Stockbridge MA 01262 413-298-5545 298-5130
Web: www.redlioninn.com

Red Rock Resort Spa & Casino
11011 W Charleston Blvd. . . . . Las Vegas NV 89135 702-797-7777 797-7890
TF: 866-767-7773 ■ *Web:* redrock.sclv.com

Red Roof Inn 4271 Sidco Dr . . . . Nashville TN 37204 615-832-0093
Web: www.redroof.com

Red Roof Inn Monterey 2227 N Fremont St . . . . .Monterey CA 93940 831-372-7586
Web: www.redroofinnmonterey.com

Red Roof Inn Nashville Airport
510 Claridge Dr . . . . .Nashville TN 37214 615-872-0735
Web: redroof.com

Redstone Inn 82 Redstone Blvd . . . . Redstone CO 81623 970-963-2526
Web: www.redstoneinn.thegilmorecollection.com

Redstone Inn & Suites 504 Bluff St . . . . Dubuque IA 52001 563-582-1894
Web: www.theredstoneinn.com

Regency Fairbanks Hotel 95 Tenth Ave. . . . . .Fairbanks AK 99701 907-459-2700
TF: 800-478-1320 ■ *Web:* www.regencyfairbankshotel.com

Regency House Hotel 140 Rt 23 N. . . . . .Pompton Plains NJ 07444 973-696-0900 696-0201
Web: www.regencyhousehotel.com

Regency Suites Calgary 610 Fourth Ave SW. . . . . Calgary AB T2P0K1 403-231-1000
TF: 800-468-4044 ■ *Web:* www.regencycalgary.com

Regency Suites Hotel Midtown Atlanta
975 W Peachtree St . . . . Atlanta GA 30309 404-876-5003 817-7511
TF: 800-642-3629 ■ *Web:* www.regencysuites.com

Remington Hotel Corp
14185 Dallas Pkwy Ste 1150 . . . . Dallas TX 75254 972-980-2700 980-2705
Web: www.remingtonhospitalityservices.com

Remington Suite Hotel 220 Travis St. . . . . .Shreveport LA 71101 318-425-5000 425-5011
TF: 800-444-6750 ■ *Web:* www.remingtonsuite.com

Residence & Conference Centre - Toronto
1760 Finch Ave E . . . . Toronto ON M2J5G3 416-491-8811 491-0486
TF: 877-225-8664 ■ *Web:* www.stayrcc.com

Residences on Georgia
101-1288 W Georgia St . . . . .Vancouver BC V6E4R3 604-891-6101 891-6103
Web: www.respal.com

Rhett House Inn 1009 Craven St .Beaufort SC 29902 843-524-9030 524-1310
TF: 888-480-9530 ■ *Web:* www.rhetthouseinn.com

Richfield Hospitality Services
7600 E OrchaRd Rd Ste 230-S . . . . Greenwood Village CO 80111 303-220-2000
Web: www.richfield.com

Richmond, The 1757 Collins Ave . . . . Miami Beach FL 33139 305-538-2331 531-9021
TF: 855-627-3767 ■ *Web:* www.richmondhotel.com

Rittenhouse Hotel 210 W Rittenhouse Sq . . . . Philadelphia PA 19103 215-546-9000 732-3364
TF: 800-635-1042 ■ *Web:* www.rittenhousehotel.com

Ritz-Carlton Dallas 2121 McKinney Ave . . . . Dallas TX 75201 214-922-0200 922-4702
TF Resv: 800-960-7082 ■ *Web:* www.ritzcarlton.com

Riu Hotel Florida Beach 3101 Collins Ave. . . . . Miami FL 33140 305-673-5333 673-9335
TF: 888-666-8816 ■ *Web:* www.riu.com

River Inn 924 25th St NW . . . . .Washington DC 20037 202-337-7600 337-6520
Web: www.theriverinn.com

River Street Inn 124 E Bay St. . . . . .Savannah GA 31401 912-234-6400 234-1478
Web: www.riverstreetinn.com

River Terrace Inn 1600 Soscol Ave . . . . Napa CA 94559 707-320-6910
Web: riverterraceinn.com

River's Edge Hotel & Spa
0455 SW Hamilton Ct. . . . . .Portland OR 97239 503-802-5800
Web: www.riversedgehotel.com

River's Edge Resort Cottages 4200 Boat St . . . . .Fairbanks AK 99709 907-474-0286 474-3665
TF: 800-770-3343 ■ *Web:* www.riversedge.net

Riveredge Resort Hotel 17 Holland St. . . . . .Alexandria Bay NY 13607 315-482-9917 482-5010
TF: 800-365-6987 ■ *Web:* www.riveredge.com

Name / Address	City	State	Zip	Phone	Fax
Riverside Hotel 620 E Las Olas Blvd *TF:* 800-325-3280 ■ *Web:* www.riversidehotel.com	Fort Lauderdale	FL	33301	954-467-0671	462-2148
Riverside Inn 1 Fountain Ave *Web:* www.theriversideinn.com	Cambridge Springs	PA	16403	814-398-4645	398-8161
Riverstone Billings Inn 880 N 29th St *TF:* 800-231-7782 ■ *Web:* www.billingsinn.com	Billings	MT	59101	406-252-6800	252-6800
Riverview Plaza Hotel 64 S Water St *Web:* marriott.com	Mobile	AL	36602	251-438-4000	415-0123
Riviera Hotel 1431 Robson St *TF:* 888-699-5222 ■ *Web:* rivieravancouver.com/	Vancouver	BC	V6G1C3	604-685-1301	685-1335
Road King Inn Columbia Mall 3300 30th Ave S **Fax Area Code:* 701 ■ *TF:* 800-707-1391 ■ *Web:* www.roadkinginn.com/	Grand Forks	ND	58201	800-707-1391	746-8586*
Robert Treat Hotel 50 Pk Pl *TF:* 800-569-2300 ■ *Web:* www.rthotel.com	Newark	NJ	07102	973-622-1000	622-6410
Rock View Resort 1049 Parkview Dr *TF:* 800-375-9530 ■ *Web:* www.rockviewresort.com	Hollister	MO	65672	417-334-4678	334-1808
Rocklin Park Hotel 5450 China Garden Rd *TF:* 888-630-9400 ■ *Web:* www.rocklinpark.com	Rocklin	CA	95677	916-630-9400	630-9448
Rodeway Inn 1315 N 27th St	Billings	MT	59101	406-245-4128	
Roger Sherman Inn 195 Oenoke Ridge *Web:* www.rogershermaninn.com	New Canaan	CT	06840	203-966-4541	966-0503
Roger Smith Hotel 501 Lexington Ave *TF:* 800-445-0277 ■ *Web:* www.rogersmith.com	New York	NY	10017	212-755-1400	758-4061
Roosevelt Hotel 45 E 45th St *TF:* 888-833-3969 ■ *Web:* www.theroosevelthotel.com	New York	NY	10017	212-661-9600	885-6161
Rose Hotel 807 Main St *TF:* 800-843-9540 ■ *Web:* www.rosehotel.net	Pleasanton	CA	94566	925-846-8802	846-2272
Rosedale on Robson Suite Hotel 838 Hamilton St *TF:* 800-661-8870 ■ *Web:* www.rosedaleonrobson.com	Vancouver	BC	V6B6A2	604-689-8033	689-4426
Rosellen Suites at Stanley Park 2030 Barclay St *TF:* 888-317-6648 ■ *Web:* www.rosellensuites.com	Vancouver	BC	V6G1L5	604-689-4807	684-3327
Rosen Centre Hotel 9840 International Dr *TF:* 800-204-7234 ■ *Web:* www.rosencentre.com	Orlando	FL	32819	407-996-9840	996-0865
Rosen Hotels & Resorts Inc 9840 International Dr *TF:* 800-204-7234 ■ *Web:* www.rosenhotels.com	Orlando	FL	32819	407-996-9840	996-0865
Rosen Plaza Hotel 9700 International Dr *TF:* 800-366-9700 ■ *Web:* www.rosenplaza.com	Orlando	FL	32819	407-996-9700	354-5774
Rosen Shingle Creek 9939 Universal Blvd *TF:* 866-996-9939 ■ *Web:* www.rosenshinglecreek.com	Orlando	FL	32819	407-996-9939	996-9938
Rosewood Hotels & Resorts 500 Crescent Ct Ste 300 *TF:* 888-767-3966 ■ *Web:* www.rosewoodhotels.com	Dallas	TX	75201	214-880-4200	880-4201
Roslyn Claremont Hotel 1221 Old Northern Blvd *TF:* 800-626-9005 ■ *Web:* theroslynhotel.com	Roslyn	NY	11576	516-625-2700	625-2731
Rough Creek Lodge 5165 County Rd 2013 *TF:* 877-907-0754 ■ *Web:* www.roughcreek.com	Glen Rose	TX	76043	254-965-3700	918-2571
Royal Garden at Waikiki Hotel 440 Olohana St *TF:* 800-989-0971 ■ *Web:* www.extraholidays.com	Honolulu	HI	96815	808-943-0202	
Royal Holiday Beach Resort 1988 Beach Blvd *TF Resv:* 800-874-0402 ■ *Web:* www.holidaybeachresort.com	Biloxi	MS	39531	228-388-7553	
Royal Hotel South Beach 763 Pennsylvania Ave *Web:* www.royalsouthbeach.com	Miami Beach	FL	33139	305-673-9009	673-9244
Royal Park Hotel-brookshire & The Commons 600 E University Dr *Web:* royalparkhotel.net	Rochester	MI	48307	248-652-2600	
Royal Regency Hotel 165 Tuckahoe Rd **Fax Area Code:* 914 ■ *TF:* 800-215-3858 ■ *Web:* www.royalregencyhotelny.com	Yonkers	NY	10710	800-215-3858	375-7017*
Royal Sonesta Hotel Boston 40 Edwin H Land Blvd *TF:* 800-766-3782 ■ *Web:* www.sonesta.com/boston	Cambridge	MA	02142	617-806-4200	806-4232
Royal Sonesta Hotel New Orleans 300 Bourbon St *TF:* 800-766-3782 ■ *Web:* sonesta.com/royalneworleans/	New Orleans	LA	70130	504-586-0300	586-0335
Royal Suite Lodge 3811 Minnesota Dr	Anchorage	AK	99503	907-563-3114	563-4296
Royal Sun Inn 1700 S Palm Canyon Dr *TF:* 800-619-4786 ■ *Web:* www.royalsuninn.com	Palm Springs	CA	92264	760-327-1564	323-9092
Royalton Hotel 44 W 44th St *TF:* 800-606-6090 ■ *Web:* www.morganshotelgroup.com	New York	NY	10036	212-869-4400	869-8965
Ruffin Hotels Lp Dba Long Beach Marriott 4700 Airport Plz Dr	Long Beach	CA	90815	562-425-5210	
Rushmore View Inn 610 Hwy 16A	Keystone	SD	57751	605-666-4466	
Sage Hospitality Resources LLC 1575 Welton St Ste 300 *Web:* www.sagehospitality.com	Denver	CO	80202	303-595-7200	595-7219
Saint Anthony the - A Wyndham Historic Hotel 300 E Travis St *TF:* 800-996-3426 ■ *Web:* www.wyndham.com	San Antonio	TX	78205	210-227-4392	227-0915
Saint Gregory Luxury Hotel & Suites 2033 M St NW *TF:* 800-821-4367 ■ *Web:* www.capitalhotelswdc.com	Washington	DC	20036	202-530-3600	466-6770
Saint James Hotel 330 Magazine St *Web:* www.saintjameshotel.com	New Orleans	LA	70130	504-304-4000	304-4444
Saint Michaels Harbour Inn & Marina 101 N Harbor Rd *TF:* 800-955-9001 ■ *Web:* www.harbourinn.com	Saint Michaels	MD	21663	410-745-9001	745-9150
Saint Paul Hotel 350 Market St *TF:* 800-292-9292 ■ *Web:* www.saintpaulhotel.com	Saint Paul	MN	55102	651-292-9292	228-9506
Saint Regis Hotel 602 Dunsmuir St *TF:* 800-770-7929 ■ *Web:* www.stregishotel.com	Vancouver	BC	V6B1Y6	604-681-1135	683-1126
Saint Regis Hotel Winnipeg 285 Smith St *TF:* 800-663-7344 ■ *Web:* www.stregishotel.net	Winnipeg	MB	R3C1K9	204-942-0171	943-3077
Saint Tropez Hotel *Rumor* 455 E Harmon Ave *TF:* 877-997-8667 ■ *Web:* www.rumorvegas.com	Las Vegas	NV	89109	702-369-5400	369-8901
Salisbury Hotel 123 W 57th St *TF:* 888-692-5757 ■ *Web:* www.nycsalisbury.com	New York	NY	10019	212-246-1300	977-7752
Sam's Town Hotel & Casino Shreveport 315 Clyde Fant Pkwy **Fax Area Code:* 318 ■ *TF:* 877-770-7867 ■ *Web:* www.samstownshreveport.com	Shreveport	LA	71101	877-770-7867	424-5658*
Sam's Town Hotel & Gambling Hall 5111 Boulder Hwy *TF:* 800-897-8696 ■ *Web:* www.samstownlv.com	Las Vegas	NV	89122	702-456-7777	454-8107
San Carlos Hotel 150 E 50th St *TF:* 800-722-2012 ■ *Web:* www.sancarloshotel.com	New York	NY	10022	212-755-1800	688-9778
San Joaquin Hotel 1309 W Shaw Ave *TF General:* 800-775-1309 ■ *Web:* www.sjhotel.com	Fresno	CA	93711	559-225-1309	225-6021
San Mateo Marriott 1770 S Amphlett Blvd *Web:* www.sanmateomarriott.com	San Mateo	CA	94402	650-653-6000	
Sandman Hotels Inns & Suites 1755 W Broadway Ste 310 *Web:* www.sandmanhotels.ca	Vancouver	BC	V6J4S5	604-730-6600	730-4645
Sands Casino Resort Bethlehem 77 Sands Blvd *TF:* 877-726-3777 ■ *Web:* www.pasands.com	Bethlehem	PA	18015	877-726-3777	
Sands Central Inn 1525 Central Ave	Hot Springs	AR	71901	501-624-1258	624-2800
Sands Ocean Club Resort 9550 Shore Dr **Fax Area Code:* 843 ■ *TF General:* 888-999-8485 ■ *Web:* www.sandsresorts.com	Myrtle Beach	SC	29572	888-999-8485	449-1837*
Sands Regency Casino Hotel 345 N Arlington Ave **Fax:* Hum Res ■ *TF Resv:* 866-337-1555 ■ *Web:* www.sandsregency.com	Reno	NV	89501	775-348-2200	348-2278*
Sandwich Lodge & Resort 54 Rt 6A - Old King's Hwy PO Box 1038 *TF:* 800-282-5353 ■ *Web:* sandwichlodge.com	Sandwich	MA	02563	508-888-2275	888-8102
Sanibel Inn 937 E Gulf Dr *TF:* 866-565-5480 ■ *Web:* www.theinnsofsanibel.com	Sanibel	FL	33957	239-472-3181	472-5234
Santa Barbara Inn 901 E Cabrillo Blvd *TF:* 800-231-0431 ■ *Web:* www.santabarbarainn.com	Santa Barbara	CA	93103	805-966-2285	966-6584
Santa Maria Inn 801 S Broadway *TF:* 800-462-4276 ■ *Web:* www.santamariainn.com	Santa Maria	CA	93454	805-928-7777	928-5690
Saratoga Hilton 534 Broadway *TF:* 800-445-8667 ■ *Web:* www.hilton.com	Saratoga Springs	NY	12866	518-584-4000	584-7430
Satellite Hotel 411 Lakewood Cir *TF:* 800-423-8409 ■ *Web:* www.satellitehotel.net	Colorado Springs	CO	80910	719-596-6800	570-4499
Saunders Hotel Group Ltd 240 Newbury St *Web:* www.saundershotelgroup.net	Boston	MA	02116	617-861-9000	861-9010
Savoy Suites Georgetown 2505 Wisconsin Ave NW *TF:* 877-301-0002 ■ *Web:* www.savoysuites.com	Washington	DC	20007	202-337-9700	
Scotsman Inn West 5922 W Kellogg St *TF:* 800-950-7268 ■ *Web:* www.scotsmaninnwichita.com	Wichita	KS	67209	316-943-3800	943-3800
Sea Chambers Motel 67 Shore Rd *Web:* www.seachambers.com	Ogunquit	ME	03907	207-646-9311	646-0938
Sea Gull Motel on the Beach 2613 Atlantic Ave *Web:* www.seagullinn.net	Virginia Beach	VA	23451	757-425-5711	425-5710
Sea Ranch Lodge 60 Sea Walk Dr PO Box 44 *TF:* 800-732-7262 ■ *Web:* www.searanchlodge.com	The Sea Ranch	CA	95497	707-785-2371	785-2917
Sea View Hotel 9909 Collins Ave *TF:* 800-447-1010 ■ *Web:* www.seaview-hotel.com	Bal Harbour	FL	33154	305-866-4441	866-1898
Seacoast Suites Hotel 5101 Collins Ave *Web:* www.seacoastsuites.com	Miami Beach	FL	33140	305-865-5152	868-4090
Seafarer Motel 2079 Main St *Web:* www.chathamseafarer.com	Chatham	MA	02633	508-432-1739	432-8969
Seaport Hotel & World Trade Ctr One Seaport Ln *TF:* 877-732-7678 ■ *Web:* www.seaportboston.com	Boston	MA	02210	617-385-4000	385-4001
Seaport Marina Hotel 6400 E Pacific Coast Hwy *Web:* www.seaportmarinahotel.com	Long Beach	CA	90803	562-434-8451	598-6028
Seaside Inn 541 E Gulf Dr *TF:* 866-565-5092 ■ *Web:* www.theinnsofsanibel.com	Sanibel Island	FL	33957	239-472-1400	
Seattle Convention Ctr Pike Street 1011 Pike St *TF:* 800-225-5466 ■ *Web:* homewoodsuites3.hilton.com	Seattle	WA	98101	206-682-8282	682-5315
Sedona Rouge Hotel & Spa 2250 W SR- 89A *Web:* www.sedonarouge.com	Sedona	AZ	86336	928-203-4111	
Seelbach Hilton Louisville 500 S Fourth St *TF:* 800-333-3399 ■ *Web:* www.seelbachhilton.com	Louisville	KY	40202	502-585-3200	585-9239
Senate Luxury Suites 900 SW Tyler St *TF:* 800-488-3188 ■ *Web:* www.senatesuites.com	Topeka	KS	66612	785-233-5050	233-1614
Sentinel Hotel 614 SW 11th Ave *TF:* 888-246-5631 ■ *Web:* www.governorhotel.com	Portland	OR	97205	503-224-3400	241-2122
Serrano Hotel 405 Taylor St *TF:* 866-575-9941 ■ *Web:* www.serranohotel.com	San Francisco	CA	94102	415-885-2500	474-4879
Setai, The 2001 Collins Ave *TF:* 888-625-7500 ■ *Web:* www.thesetaihotel.com	Miami Beach	FL	33139	305-520-6000	
Seven Gables Inn 26 N Meramec Ave *Web:* sevengablesinn.com	Saint Louis	MO	63105	314-863-8400	863-8846
Shades of Green on Walt Disney World Resort 1950 W Magnolia Palm Dr *TF:* 888-593-2242 ■ *Web:* www.shadesofgreen.org	Lake Buena Vista	FL	32830	407-824-3400	824-3665
Shaner Hotel Group 1965 Waddle Rd **Fax:* Hum Res ■ *Web:* www.shanercorp.com	State College	PA	16803	814-234-4460	278-7295*
Shangri-La Hotel Toronto 188 University Ave *Web:* www.shangri-la.com	Toronto	ON	M5H0A3	647-788-8888	
Shelborne Wyndham Grand South Beach 1801 Collins Ave *Web:* www.shelbornewyndhamgrand.com	Miami Beach	FL	33139	305-531-1271	531-2206
Shelburne Murray Hill 303 Lexington Ave *TF:* 866-233-4642 ■ *Web:* www.affinia.com	New York	NY	10016	212-689-5200	779-7068
Shephard's Beach Resort 619 S Gulfview Blvd *TF:* 800-237-8477 ■ *Web:* www.shephards.com	Clearwater Beach	FL	33767	727-441-6875	442-7321
Sheraton Colonial Hotel & Golf Club Boston North 1 Audubon Rd *Web:* www.starwoodhotels.com	Wakefield	MA	01880	781-245-9300	245-9300

	City	State	Zip	Phone	Fax
Sheraton Delfina Santa Monica 530 W Pico Blvd	Santa Monica	CA	90405	310-399-9344	399-2504
TF: 888-627-8532 ■ *Web:* www.lemeridiendelfina.com					
Sheraton Gateway Hotel Los Angeles 6101 W Century Blvd	Los Angeles	CA	90045	310-642-1111	645-1414
TF: 888-627-7104 ■ *Web:* www.sheratonlax.com					
Sheraton Suites Calgary Eau Claire 255 Barclay Parade SW	Calgary	AB	T2P5C2	403-266-7200	
Web: sheratonsuites.com					
Sheridan Pond 8130 S Lakewood Pl	Tulsa	OK	74137	918-481-6598	
Web: www.sheridanpond.com					
Sherry-Netherland Hotel 781 Fifth Ave	New York	NY	10022	212-355-2800	319-4306
TF: 877-743-7710 ■ *Web:* t.sherrynetherland.com					
Shilo Inn Hotel Salt Lake City 206 SW Temple	Salt Lake City	UT	84101	800-222-2244	
TF: 800-222-2244 ■ *Web:* www.shiloinns.com					
Shilo Inn Suites Hotel Portland Airport 117707 NE Airport Way	Portland	OR	97220	503-252-7500	254-0794
TF: 800-222-2244 ■ *Web:* www.shiloinns.com					
Shilo Inn Suites Salem 3304 Market St	Salem	OR	97301	503-581-4001	399-9385
TF: 800-222-2244 ■ *Web:* www.shiloinns.com					
Shilo Inns Suites Hotels 11600 SW Shilo Ln	Portland	OR	97225	503-641-6565	644-0868*
**Fax:* Mktg ■ *TF:* 800-222-2244 ■ *Web:* www.shiloinns.com					
Shores Resort & Spa, The 2637 S Atlantic Ave	Daytona Beach Shores	FL	32118	386-767-7350	760-3651
Web: www.shoresresort.com					
Shutters on the Beach One Pico Blvd	Santa Monica	CA	90405	310-458-0030	458-4589
TF: 800-334-9000 ■ *Web:* www.shuttersonthebeach.com					
Siena Hotel 1505 E Franklin St	Chapel Hill	NC	27514	919-929-4000	968-8527
TF: 800-223-7379 ■ *Web:* www.sienahotel.com					
Sierra Land Group Inc 801 N Brand Blvd Ste 1010	Glendale	CA	91203	818-247-3681	
Sigma Sigma Sigma Foundation 225 N Muhlenberg St	Woodstock	VA	22664	540-459-4212	
Web: trisigma.org					
Silver Cloud Hotel Seattle Broadway 1100 Broadway	Seattle	WA	98122	206-325-1400	324-1995
TF: 800-590-1801 ■ *Web:* www.silvercloud.com					
Silver Cloud Inn Seattle-Lake Union 1150 Fairview Ave N	Seattle	WA	98109	206-447-9500	812-4900
TF General: 800-330-5812 ■ *Web:* www.silvercloud.com					
Silver Cloud Inn University District 5036 25th Ave NE	Seattle	WA	98105	206-526-5200	522-1450
TF: 800-205-6940 ■ *Web:* www.silvercloud.com					
Silver King Hotel 1485 Empire Ave	Park City	UT	84060	435-649-5500	649-6647
TF: 888-667-2775 ■ *Web:* www.allseasonsresortlodging.com					
Silver Smith Hotel & Suites 10 S Wabash Ave	Chicago	IL	60603	312-372-7696	372-7320
TF: 800-979-0084 ■ *Web:* www.silversmithchicagohotel.com					
SilverBirch Hotels & Resorts 1600 - 1030 W Georgia St	Vancouver	BC	V6E2Y3	604-646-2447	431-5802*
**Fax Area Code:* 780 ■ *TF:* 800-661-1232 ■ *Web:* www.silverbirchhotels.com					
Silverdale Beach Hotel 3073 NW Bucklin Hill Rd	Silverdale	WA	98383	360-698-1000	692-0932
TF: 800-544-9799 ■ *Web:* www.silverdalebeachhotel.com					
Simonton Court Historic Inn & Cottages 320 Simonton St	Key West	FL	33040	800-944-2687	293-8447*
**Fax Area Code:* 305 ■ *TF:* 800-944-2687 ■ *Web:* www.simontoncourt.com					
Sir Francis Drake Hotel 450 Powell St	San Francisco	CA	94102	415-392-7755	391-8719
TF: 800-795-7129 ■ *Web:* www.sirfrancisdrake.com					
Sise Inn, The 40 Ct St	Portsmouth	NH	03801	603-433-1200	
Web: thehotelportsmouth.com					
Ski Bromont 150 Champlain	Bromont	QC	J2L1A2	450-534-2200	
TF: 866-276-6668 ■ *Web:* www.skibromont.com					
Sky Hotel 709 E Durant Ave	Aspen	CO	81611	970-925-6760	925-6778
TF: 800-882-2582 ■ *Web:* www.theskyhotel.com					
Skyline Hotel 725 Tenth Ave	New York	NY	10019	212-586-3400	582-4604
Web: www.skylinehotelny.com					
Smoky Shadows Motel & Conference Ctr 4215 Pkwy	Pigeon Forge	TN	37863	865-453-7155	453-0308
Web: www.smokyshadows.com					
Snell House 21 Atlantic Ave	Bar Harbor	ME	04609	207-288-8004	
TF: 866-763-5524 ■ *Web:* www.snellhouse.com					
Snowbird Mountain Lodge 4633 Santeetlah Rd	Robbinsville	NC	28771	828-479-3433	479-3473
TF: 800-941-9290 ■ *Web:* www.snowbirdlodge.com					
Snowy Owl Inn 41 Village Rd	Waterville Valley	NH	03215	603-236-8383	236-4890
TF: 800-766-9969 ■ *Web:* www.snowyowlinn.com					
Sofia Hotel 150 W Broadway	San Diego	CA	92101	619-234-9200	544-9879
TF: 800-826-0009 ■ *Web:* www.thesofiahotel.com					
SoHo Grand Hotel 310 W Broadway	New York	NY	10013	212-965-3000	965-3200
TF: 800-965-3000 ■ *Web:* www.sohogrand.com					
SoHo Metropolitan Hotel 318 Wellington St W	Toronto	ON	M5V3T4	416-599-8800	599-8801
TF: 866-764-6638 ■ *Web:* www.metropolitan.com/soho					
Somerset Hills Hotel (SSH) 200 Liberty Corner Rd	Warren	NJ	07059	908-647-6700	647-8053
Web: www.thesomersethillshotel.com/					
Somerset Inn 2601 W Big Beaver Rd	Troy	MI	48084	248-643-7800	643-2296
TF: 800-228-8769 ■ *Web:* www.somersetinn.com					
Sonesta Hotel & Suites Coconut Grove 2889 McFarlane Rd	Miami	FL	33133	305-529-2828	529-2008
TF: 800-766-3782 ■ *Web:* sonesta.com/coconutgrove/					
Soniat House 1133 Chartres St	New Orleans	LA	70116	504-522-0570	522-7208
TF: 800-544-8808 ■ *Web:* www.soniathouse.com					
Sophie Station Suites 1717 University Ave	Fairbanks	AK	99709	800-528-4916	479-7951*
**Fax Area Code:* 907 ■ *TF:* 800-528-4916 ■ *Web:* www.fountainheadhotels.com					
South Beach Marina Inn & Vacation Rentals 232 S Sea Pines Dr	Hilton Head Island	SC	29928	843-671-6498	671-7495
TF: 800-367-3909 ■ *Web:* www.sbinn.com					
South Pier Inn on the Canal 701 Lake Ave S	Duluth	MN	55802	218-786-9007	786-9015
TF: 800-430-7437 ■ *Web:* www.southpierinn.com					
South Point Hotel & Casino 9777 Las Vegas Blvd S	Las Vegas	NV	89183	702-796-7111	797-8041
TF: 866-796-7111 ■ *Web:* www.southpointcasino.com					
Southampton Inn 91 Hill St	SoutHampton	NY	11968	631-283-6500	283-6559
TF: 800-832-6500 ■ *Web:* www.southamptoninn.com					
Southernmost On the Beach 508 S St	Key West	FL	33040	800-354-4455	294-2108*
**Fax Area Code:* 305 ■ *TF:* 800-354-4455 ■ *Web:* www.southernmostresorts.com					
Southfork Hotel 1600 N Central Expy	Plano	TX	75074	972-578-8555	423-7147
TF: 877-386-4383 ■ *Web:* www.southforkhotel.com					
Southway Inn 2431 Bank St	Ottawa	ON	K1V8R9	613-737-0811	737-3207
TF: 877-688-4929 ■ *Web:* www.southway.com					
Spindrift Inn 652 Cannery Row	Monterey	CA	93940	831-646-8900	655-8174
TF: 800-841-1879 ■ *Web:* www.spindriftinn.com					
Spring Creek Ranch 1800 Spirit Dance Rd	Jackson	WY	83001	307-733-8833	733-1964
TF: 800-443-6139 ■ *Web:* www.springcreekranch.com					
St James Hotel 406 Main St	Red Wing	MN	55066	651-388-2846	388-5226
TF: 800-252-1875 ■ *Web:* www.st-james-hotel.com					
St Julien Hotel & Spa 900 Walnut St	Boulder	CO	80302	720-406-9696	406-9668
TF: 877-303-0900 ■ *Web:* www.stjulien.com					
Stamford Suites 720 Bedford St	Stamford	CT	06901	203-359-7300	359-7304
TF: 866-394-4365 ■ *Web:* www.stamfordsuites.com					
Stanford Court - A Renaissance Hotel 905 California St	San Francisco	CA	94108	415-989-3500	
Web: www.marriott.com/default.mi					
Stanley Hotel 333 Wonderview Ave	Estes Park	CO	80517	970-586-3371	586-4964
TF: 800-976-1377 ■ *Web:* www.stanleyhotel.com					
Stanyan Park Hotel 750 Stanyan St	San Francisco	CA	94117	415-751-1000	668-5454
Web: www.stanyanpark.com					
Star Island Resort 5000 Ave of the Stars	Kissimmee	FL	34746	407-997-8000	997-5252
TF: 800-513-2820 ■ *Web:* www.star-island.com					
Starwood Hotels & Resorts Worldwide Inc					
Saint Regis Hotels & Resorts 1111 Westchester Ave	White Plains	NY	10604	914-640-8100	640-8310
TF: 888-625-4988 ■ *Web:* www.starwoodhotels.com					
Westin Hotels & Resorts 1111 Westchester Ave	White Plains	NY	10604	914-640-8100	640-8310
TF: 888-625-5144 ■ *Web:* www.starwoodhotels.com					
State Plaza Hotel 2117 E St NW	Washington	DC	20037	202-861-8200	659-8601
TF: 800-424-2859 ■ *Web:* www.stateplaza.com					
Staten Island Hotel 1415 Richmond Ave	Staten Island	NY	10314	718-698-5000	737-7294
TF: 800-230-4134 ■ *Web:* esplanadesi.com					
Sterling Hotel 1300 H St	Sacramento	CA	95814	916-448-1300	448-8066
Web: sterlinghotelsacramento.com					
Stockyards Hotel 109 E Exchange Ave	Fort Worth	TX	76164	817-625-6427	624-2571
TF: 800-423-8471 ■ *Web:* www.stockyardshotel.com					
Stone Castle Hotel & Conference Ctr, The 3050 Green Mtn Dr	Branson	MO	65616	417-335-4700	335-3906
TF: 800-677-6906 ■ *Web:* bransonstonecastle.com					
Stonebridge Inn 300 Carriage Way PO Box 5008	Snowmass Village	CO	81615	970-923-2420	923-5889
TF: 800-922-7242 ■ *Web:* www.stonebridgeinn.com					
Stonehedge Inn 160 Pawtucket Blvd	Tyngsboro	MA	01879	978-649-4400	649-9256
Web: www.stonehedgeinnandspa.com					
Stonewall Jackson Hotel & Conference Ctr 24 S Market St	Staunton	VA	24401	540-885-4848	885-4840
TF: 866-880-0024 ■ *Web:* www.stonewalljacksonhotel.com					
Stoney Creek Inn 101 Mariner's Way	East Peoria	IL	61611	309-694-1300	694-9303
TF: 800-659-2220 ■ *Web:* stoneycreekhotels.com/home.do					
Strater Hotel 699 Main Ave	Durango	CO	81301	970-247-4431	259-2208
TF: 800-247-4431 ■ *Web:* www.strater.com					
Stratford Hotel 242 Powell St	San Francisco	CA	94102	415-397-7080	397-7087
TF: 888-688-0038 ■ *Web:* www.hotelstratford.com					
Strathallan Hotel 550 E Ave	Rochester	NY	14607	585-461-5010	461-2503
Web: www.strathallan.com					
Strathcona Hotel 60 York St	Toronto	ON	M5J1S8	416-363-3321	363-4679
TF: 800-268-8304 ■ *Web:* www.thestrathconahotel.com					
Strathcona Hotel, The 919 Douglas St	Victoria	BC	V8W2C2	250-383-7137	383-6893
TF: 800-663-7476 ■ *Web:* www.strathconahotel.com					
Stratosphere Tower Hotel & Casino 2000 S Las Vegas Blvd	Las Vegas	NV	89104	702-380-7777	383-4755*
**Fax:* Sales ■ *TF:* 800-998-6937 ■ *Web:* www.stratospherehotel.com					
Sturbridge Host Hotel & Conference Ctr 366 Main St	Sturbridge	MA	01566	508-347-7393	347-3944
TF: 800-582-3232 ■ *Web:* www.sturbridgehosthotel.com					
Sugar Magnolia 804 Edgewood Ave NE	Atlanta	GA	30307	404-222-0226	681-1067
Web: www.sugarmagnoliabb.com					
Suites at Fisherman's Wharf 2655 Hyde St	San Francisco	CA	94109	415-771-0200	346-8058
TF: 800-227-3608 ■ *Web:* www.shellhospitality.com					
Suites Hotel in Canal Park, The 325 Lake Ave S	Duluth	MN	55802	218-727-4663	722-0572
TF: 877-766-2665 ■ *Web:* www.thesuitesduluth.com					
Summit Lodge & Spa 4359 Main St	Whistler	BC	V0N1B4	604-932-2778	932-2716
TF: 888-913-8811 ■ *Web:* summitlodge.com					
Sun Viking Lodge 2411 S Atlantic Ave	Daytona Beach Shores	FL	32118	386-252-6252	252-5463
TF: 800-874-4469 ■ *Web:* www.sunviking.com					
Sunburst Hospitality Corp 10770 Columbia Pk Ste 200	Silver Spring	MD	20901	301-592-3800	592-3830
Web: www.snbhotels.com					
Suncoast Hotel & Casino 9090 Alta Dr	Las Vegas	NV	89145	702-636-7111	636-7288
TF: 877-677-7111 ■ *Web:* www.suncoastcasino.com					
Sundial Boutique Hotel 4340 Sundial Crescent	Whistler	BC	V0N1B4	604-932-2321	935-0554
TF: 800-661-2321 ■ *Web:* www.sundialhotel.com					
Sunrise Suites Resort Key West 3685 Seaside Dr	Key West	FL	33040	305-296-6661	296-6665
Web: www.sunrisesuiteskeywest.com					
Sunset Inn Travel Apartments 1111 Burnaby St	Vancouver	BC	V6E1P4	604-688-2474	669-3340
TF: 800-786-1997 ■ *Web:* www.sunsetinn.com					
Sunset Marquis Hotel & Villas 1200 N Alta Loma Rd	West Hollywood	CA	90069	310-657-1333	652-5300
TF: 800-858-9758 ■ *Web:* www.sunsetmarquis.com					

Name / Address	City	State	Zip	Phone	Fax
Sunset Station Hotel & Casino 1301 W Sunset Rd *TF:* 888-786-7389 ■ *Web:* sunsetstation.sclv.com	Henderson	NV	89014	702-547-7777	
Sunset Tower Hotel 8358 Sunset Blvd *Web:* www.sunsettowerhotel.com	West Hollywood	CA	90069	323-654-7100	654-9287
Surf & Sand Resort 1555 S Coast Hwy *TF:* 888-869-7569 ■ *Web:* www.surfandsandresort.com	Laguna Beach	CA	92651	949-497-4477	494-2897
Surfsand Resort 148 W Gower Rd *TF:* 800-547-6100 ■ *Web:* www.surfsand.com	Cannon Beach	OR	97110	503-436-2274	436-9116
Surfside Inn 1211 Atlantic Ave *TF:* 800-437-2497 ■ *Web:* www.virginiabeachsurfside.com	Virginia Beach	VA	23451	757-428-1183	428-2243
Surrey Hotel 20 E 76th St *TF:* 866-233-4642 ■ *Web:* www.affinia.com	New York	NY	10021	212-288-3700	628-1549
Sutton Place Hotel Edmonton 10235 101st St *TF:* 866-378-8866 ■ *Web:* www.edmonton.suttonplace.com	Edmonton	AB	T5J3E9	780-428-7111	441-3098
Swag, The 2300 Swag Rd *TF:* 800-789-7672 ■ *Web:* www.theswag.com	Waynesville	NC	28785	828-926-0430	926-2036
Sweden House 4605 E State St	Rockford	IL	61108	815-398-4130	
Taj Boston 15 Arlington St *TF:* 877-482-5267 ■ *Web:* www.tajhotels.com	Boston	MA	02116	617-536-5700	536-1335
Taj Campton Place 340 Stockton St *TF:* 866-969-1825 ■ *Web:* www.tajhotels.com	San Francisco	CA	94108	415-781-5555	955-5536
Talbott Hotel 20 E Delaware Pl *TF:* 800-825-2688 ■ *Web:* www.talbotthotel.com	Chicago	IL	60611	312-944-4970	944-7241
Tarsadia Investments, 620 Newport Ctr Dr *Web:* tarsadiainvestments.com	Newport Beach	CA	92660	949-610-8000	
Tazewell Hotel & Suites 245 Granby St *Web:* www.thetazewell.com	Norfolk	VA	23510	757-623-6200	457-1516
Terminal City Club 837 W Hastings St *TF:* 888-253-8777 ■ *Web:* tcclub.com	Vancouver	BC	V6C1B6	604-681-4121	681-9634
Teton Mountain Lodge & Spa 3385 Cody Ln PO Box 564 *TF:* 800-631-6271 ■ *Web:* www.tetonlodge.com	Teton Village	WY	83025	307-201-6066	
Thayer Hotel 674 Thayer Rd *TF:* 800-247-5047 ■ *Web:* www.thethayerhotel.com	West Point	NY	10996	845-446-4731	446-0338
Tickle Pink Inn at Carmel Highlands 155 Highland Dr *TF:* 800-635-4774 ■ *Web:* www.ticklepinkinn.com	Carmel	CA	93923	831-624-1244	626-9516
Tidewater Inn & Conference Ctr 101 E Dover St *TF:* 800-237-8775 ■ *Web:* www.tidewaterinn.com	Easton	MD	21601	410-822-1300	820-8847
Timbers Hotel, The 4411 Peoria St	Denver	CO	80239	303-373-1444	373-1975
Time, The 224 W 49th St *TF:* 877-846-3692 ■ *Web:* www.thetimeny.com	New York	NY	10019	212-246-5252	245-2305
Times Hotel & Suites 6515 Wilfrid-Hamel Blvd *Web:* grandtimeshotel.com	L'Ancienne-Lorette	QC	G2E5W3	418-877-7788	877-3333
Tivoli Lodge 386 Hanson Ranch Rd *TF:* 800-451-4756 ■ *Web:* www.tivolilodge.com	Vail	CO	81657	970-476-5615	476-6601
Topaz Hotel 1733 N St NW *TF:* 800-546-7866 ■ *Web:* www.topazhotel.com	Washington	DC	20036	202-393-3000	785-9581
TOWER23 Hotel 723 Felspar St *Web:* tower23hotel.com	San Diego	CA	92109	858-270-2323	
Town & Country Inn 20 State RT 2 PO Box 220 *TF General:* 800-325-4386 ■ *Web:* www.townandcountryinn.com	Gorham	NH	03581	603-466-3315	466-3315
Town & Country Inn & Conference Ctr 2008 Savannah Hwy *TF:* 800-334-6660 ■ *Web:* www.thetownandcountryinn.com	Charleston	SC	29407	843-571-1000	
Town Inn Suites 620 Church St *TF:* 800-387-2755 ■ *Web:* www.towninn.com	Toronto	ON	M4Y2G2	416-964-3311	924-9466
TownHouse Inn 1411 Tenth Ave S *TF:* 800-442-4667 ■ *Web:* townhouseinngreatfalls.com	Great Falls	MT	59405	406-761-4600	761-7603
Townsend Hotel 100 Townsend St *TF:* 800-548-4172 ■ *Web:* www.townsendhotel.com	Birmingham	MI	48009	248-642-7900	645-9061
Townsend Manor Inn 714 Main St *Web:* www.townsendinn.com	Greenport	NY	11944	631-477-2000	477-2371
Tradewinds Carmel Mission St at Third Ave *Web:* www.tradewindscarmel.com	Carmel By The Sea	CA	93921	831-624-2776	624-0634
Trans World Corp (TWC) 545 Fifth Ave Ste 940 *OTC:* TWOC ■ *TF:* 877-407-9037 ■ *Web:* www.transwc.com	New York	NY	10017	212-983-3355	983-8129
Travelodge Virginia Beach 1909 Atlantic Ave *TF:* 800-578-7878 ■ *Web:* www.travelodge.com	Virginia Beach	VA	23451	757-425-0650	425-8898
Tremont Chicago 100 E Chestnut St *TF:* 888-627-8281 ■ *Web:* www.tremontchicago.com	Chicago	IL	60611	312-751-1900	751-8691
Tremont House - A Wyndham Historic Hotel, The 2300 Ship Mechanic Row *Web:* www.wyndham.com	Galveston	TX	77550	409-763-0300	763-1539
Trianon Old Naples 955 Seventh Ave S *TF:* 877-482-5228 ■ *Web:* www.trianon.com	Naples	FL	34102	239-435-9600	261-0025
Tribeca Grand Hotel Two Ave of the Americas *Web:* www.tribecagrand.com	New York	NY	10013	212-519-6600	519-6700
Tropical Winds Oceanfront Hotel 1398 N Atlantic Ave *TF:* 800-245-6099 ■ *Web:* tropicalwindshotel.com	Daytona Beach	FL	32118	386-258-1016	255-6462
Tropicana Inn & Suites 1540 S Harbor Blvd *TF:* 800-828-4898 ■ *Web:* tropicanainn-anaheim.com	Anaheim	CA	92802	714-635-4082	635-1535
Truman Hotel & Conference Ctr 1510 Jefferson St *TF:* 800-392-0202 ■ *Web:* www.trumanjeffersoncity.com	Jefferson City	MO	65109	573-635-7171	635-8006
Trump International Hotel & Tower 725 Fifth Ave **Fax Area Code:* 212 ■ *TF:* 888-448-7867 ■ *Web:* www.trumphotelcollection.com	New York	NY	10022	312-588-8000	299-1150*
Tugboat Inn 80 Commercial St PO Box 267 *TF:* 800-248-2628 ■ *Web:* www.tugboatinn.com	Boothbay Harbor	ME	04538	207-633-4434	633-5892
Tuscany Suites & Casino 255 E Flamingo Rd *TF Resv:* 877-887-2261 ■ *Web:* www.tuscanylv.com	Las Vegas	NV	89169	702-893-8933	947-5994
TWELVE Atlantic Station 361 17th St *Web:* www.twelvehotels.com	Atlanta	GA	30363	404-961-1212	961-1221
TWELVE Centennial Park 400 W Peachtree St *Web:* www.twelvehotels.com	Atlanta	GA	30308	404-418-1212	418-1221
Twin Farms 452 Royalton Tpke PO Box 115 *TF:* 800-894-6327 ■ *Web:* www.twinfarms.com	Barnard	VT	05031	802-234-9999	234-9990
UMass Hotel at the Campus Ctr 1 Campus Ctr Way *TF:* 877-822-2110 ■ *Web:* umasshotel.com	Amherst	MA	01003	413-549-6000	
Umstead Hotel & Spa 100 Woodland Pond *TF:* 866-877-4141 ■ *Web:* www.theumstead.com	Cary	NC	27513	919-447-4000	447-4100
Union Station A Wyndham Historic Hotel PO Box 4090 *TF:* 800-996-3426 ■ *Web:* www.wyndham.com	Aberdeen	SD	57401	800-996-3426	
University Inn Seattle 4140 Roosevelt Way NE *TF:* 800-733-3855 ■ *Web:* www.universityinnseattle.com	Seattle	WA	98105	206-632-5055	547-4937
University Place 310 SW Lincoln St *TF:* 866-845-4647 ■ *Web:* www.pdx.edu/cegs/university-place-hotel-conference-center	Portland	OR	97201	503-221-0140	226-6260
University Plaza Hotel & Conference Ctr 3110 Olentangy River Rd **Fax Area Code:* 417	Columbus	OH	43202	614-267-7461	831-5893*
University Plaza Hotel & Convention Ctr 333 John Q Hammons Pkwy *Web:* www.upspringfield.com	Springfield	MO	65806	417-864-7333	831-5893
US Grant, The 326 Broadway *TF:* 800-237-5029 ■ *Web:* www.usgrant.net	San Diego	CA	92101	619-232-3121	232-3626
US Suites 4970 Windplay Dr C1 *TF Cust Svc:* 800-877-8483 ■ *Web:* www.ussuites.com	El Dorado Hills	CA	95762	916-941-7970	
Vacation Resorts International Inc 23041 Avenida De La Carlota Ste 400 *Web:* www.vriresorts.com	Laguna Hills	CA	92653	949-587-2299	
Valley Park Hotel 2404 Stevens Creek Blvd *Web:* thevalleyparkhotel.com	San Jose	CA	95128	408-293-5000	293-5287
Valley River Inn 1000 Vly River Way *TF:* 800-543-8266 ■ *Web:* www.valleyriverinn.com	Eugene	OR	97401	541-743-1000	683-5121
Vancouver Extended-Stay Suites 1288 W Georgia St Ste 101 *Web:* www.vancouverextendedstay.com	Vancouver	BC	V6E4R3	604-891-6181	891-6151
Vanderbilt Grace 41 Mary St *TF:* 888-826-4255 ■ *Web:* www.gracehotels.com	Newport	RI	02840	401-846-6200	847-7689
Varscona Hotel 8208 106th St *TF:* 866-465-8150 ■ *Web:* www.varscona.com	Edmonton	AB	T6E6R9	780-434-6111	439-1195
Velvet Cloak Inn, The 1505 Hillsborough St *TF:* 888-828-0335 ■ *Web:* www.thevelvetcloak.com	Raleigh	NC	27605	919-828-0333	828-2656
Viceroy Palm Springs 415 S BelaRdo Rd **Fax Area Code:* 786 ■ *TF:* 866-781-9923 ■ *Web:* www.viceroyhotelsandresorts.com	Palm Springs	CA	92262	760-320-4117	329-5739*
Viceroy Santa Monica 1819 Ocean Ave *TF:* 888-622-4567 ■ *Web:* viceroyhotelsandresorts.com	Santa Monica	CA	90401	310-260-7500	260-7515
Victoria Inn Winnipeg 1808 Wellington Ave *TF:* 877-842-4667 ■ *Web:* www.vicinn.com	Winnipeg	MB	R3H0G3	204-786-4801	786-1329
Victoria Regent Hotel, The 1234 Wharf St *TF:* 800-663-7472 ■ *Web:* www.victoriaregent.com	Victoria	BC	V8W3H9	250-386-2211	386-2622
Victorian Condo-Hotel & Conference Ctr 6300 Seawall Blvd *TF:* 800-231-6363 ■ *Web:* www.victoriancondo.com	Galveston	TX	77551	409-740-3555	741-1676
Villa Florence 225 Powell St *TF:* 866-980-9684 ■ *Web:* www.larkspurhotels.com	San Francisco	CA	94102	415-397-7700	397-1006
Villa Royale Inn 1620 Indian Trl *TF:* 800-245-2314 ■ *Web:* www.villaroyale.com	Palm Springs	CA	92264	760-327-2314	322-3794
Village Latch Inn 101 Hill St PO Box 3000 *TF:* 800-545-2824 ■ *Web:* www.villagelatch.com	SouthHampton	NY	11968	631-283-2160	283-3236
Villagio Inn & Spa 6481 Washington St *TF:* 800-351-1133 ■ *Web:* www.villagio.com	Yountville	CA	94599	707-944-8877	944-8855
Villas de Santa Fe 400 Griffin St *Web:* www.diamondresorts.com	Santa Fe	NM	87501	505-988-3000	988-4700
Villas on the Bay 105 Marine St *Web:* thevillas.com	Saint Augustine	FL	32084	904-599-7301	
Vintage Inn Napa Valley 6541 Washington St **Fax Area Code:* 707 ■ *TF Cust Svc:* 800-351-1133 ■ *Web:* www.vintageinn.com	Yountville	CA	94599	800-351-1133	944-1617*
Vintners Inn 4350 Barnes Rd *TF:* 800-421-2584 ■ *Web:* www.vintnersinn.com	Santa Rosa	CA	95403	707-575-7350	575-1426
Virginian Lodge 750 W Broadway PO Box 1052 *TF:* 800-262-4999 ■ *Web:* www.virginianlodge.com	Jackson Hole	WY	83001	307-733-2792	733-9513
Virginian Suites 1500 Arlington Blvd *TF:* 866-371-1446 ■ *Web:* www.virginiansuites.com	Arlington	VA	22209	703-522-9600	525-4462
Viscount Gort Hotel 1670 Portage Ave *TF:* 800-665-1122 ■ *Web:* www.viscount-gort.com	Winnipeg	MB	R3J0C9	204-775-0451	772-2161
Viscount Suite Hotel 4855 E Broadway Blvd *TF Resv:* 800-527-9666 ■ *Web:* www.viscountsuite.com	Tucson	AZ	85711	520-745-6500	790-5114
Vista Host Inc 10370 Richmond Ave Ste 150 *TF:* 800-257-3000 ■ *Web:* vistahost.com	Houston	TX	77042	713-267-5800	267-5820
Voyageur Inn 200 Viking Dr *TF:* 800-444-4493 ■ *Web:* www.voyageurinn.net	Reedsburg	WI	53959	608-524-6431	524-0036
Voyageur Lakewalk Inn 333 E Superior St *TF:* 800-258-3911 ■ *Web:* www.voyageurlakewalkinn.com	Duluth	MN	55802	218-722-3911	722-3124
Waikiki Gateway Hotel 2070 Kalakaua Ave *TF:* 866-444-4352 ■ *Web:* www.waikikigateway.com	Honolulu	HI	96815	808-955-3741	
Waikiki Parc Hotel 2233 Helumoa Rd *TF:* 800-422-0450 ■ *Web:* www.waikikiparc.com	Honolulu	HI	96815	808-921-7272	923-1336
Waikiki Resort Hotel 2460 Koa Ave *TF:* 800-367-5116 ■ *Web:* www.waikikiresort.com	Honolulu	HI	96815	808-922-4911	922-9468
Waldorf Towers, The 100 E 50th St *TF:* 800-925-3673 ■ *Web:* www.waldorfnewyork.com	New York	NY	10022	212-355-3100	872-4799
Warwick Denver Hotel 1776 Grant St *TF:* 800-203-3232 ■ *Web:* warwickhotels.com/denver/	Denver	CO	80203	303-861-2000	832-0320
Warwick Melrose Hotel 3015 Oak Lawn Ave *TF:* 800-521-7172 ■ *Web:* warwickhotels.com/dallas/	Dallas	TX	75219	214-521-5151	521-2470
Warwick New York Hotel 65 W 54th St **Fax:* Sales ■ *TF:* 800-223-4099 ■ *Web:* warwickhotels.com/new-york/	New York	NY	10019	212-247-2700	247-2725*

				Phone	Fax
Warwick Regis Hotel San Francisco 490 Geary St	San Francisco	CA	94102	415-928-7900	441-8788
Web: warwickhotels.com/san-francisco/					
Warwick Seattle Hotel 401 Lenora St	Seattle	WA	98121	206-443-4300	448-1662
TF: 800-426-9280 ■ *Web:* warwickhotels.com/seattle/					
Washington Court Hotel 525 New Jersey Ave NW	Washington	DC	20001	202-628-2100	
TF: 800-321-3010 ■ *Web:* www.washingtoncourthotel.com					
Washington Duke Inn & Golf Club 3001 Cameron Blvd	Durham	NC	27705	919-490-0999	688-0105
TF: 800-443-3853 ■ *Web:* www.washingtondukeinn.com					
Washington Inn Hotel, The 495 Tenth St	Oakland	CA	94607	510-452-1776	452-4436
Web: www.thewashingtoninn.com					
Washington Plaza Hotel 10 Thomas Cir NW Massachusetts Ave at 14th St	Washington	DC	20005	202-842-1300	371-9602
TF: 800-424-1140 ■ *Web:* www.washingtonplazahotel.com					
Washington Square Hotel 103 Waverly Pl	New York	NY	10011	212-777-9515	979-8373
TF: 800-222-0418 ■ *Web:* www.washingtonsquarehotel.com					
Washington Suites 100 S Reynolds St	Alexandria	VA	22304	703-370-9600	370-0467
Waterfront Hotel 10 Washington St	Oakland	CA	94607	510-836-3800	832-5695
TF: 888-842-5333 ■ *Web:* www.jdvhotels.com					
Waters Edge Hotel 25 Main St	Tiburon	CA	94920	415-789-5999	789-5888
TF: 888-662-9555 ■ *Web:* www.marinhotels.com					
Wauwinet, The 120 Wauwinet Rd PO Box 2580	Nantucket	MA	02584	508-228-0145	228-6712
TF: 800-426-8718 ■ *Web:* www.wauwinet.com					
Weber's Inn 3050 Jackson Rd	Ann Arbor	MI	48103	734-769-2500	769-4743
TF Resv: 800-443-3050 ■ *Web:* www.webersinn.com					
Wedgewood Hotel 845 Hornby St	Vancouver	BC	V6Z1V1	604-689-7777	608-5348
TF: 800-663-0666 ■ *Web:* www.wedgewoodhotel.com					
Wedgewood Resort Hotel 212 Wedgewood Dr	Fairbanks	AK	99701	800-528-4916	451-8184*
**Fax Area Code:* 907 ■ *TF:* 800-528-4916 ■ *Web:* www.fountainheadhotels.com					
Wellington Hotel 871 Seventh Ave	New York	NY	10019	212-247-3900	581-1350
TF: 800-652-1212 ■ *Web:* www.wellingtonhotel.com					
Wellington Resort 551 Thames St	Newport	RI	02840	401-849-1770	847-6250
TF: 800-228-2968 ■ *Web:* www.wellingtonresort.com					
Wentworth Mansion 149 Wentworth St	Charleston	SC	29401	843-853-1886	720-5290
TF: 888-466-1886 ■ *Web:* www.wentworthmansion.com					
Western States Lodging 1018 W Atherton Dr	Taylorsville	UT	84123	801-269-0700	269-1512
Web: www.westernstateslodging.com					
Westford Regency Inn & Conference Ctr 219 Littleton Rd	Westford	MA	01886	978-692-8200	692-7403
TF: 800-543-7801 ■ *Web:* www.westfordregency.com					
Westgate Branson Woods 2201 Roark Vly Rd	Branson	MO	65616	417-334-2324	334-0834
TF: 877-253-8572 ■ *Web:* westgatedestinations.com/missouri/branson/westgate-branson-woods/					
Westgate Painted Mountain Country Club 6302 E McKellips Rd	Mesa	AZ	85215	480-654-3611	654-3613
TF: 888-433-3707 ■ *Web:* www.wgpaintedmountain.com					
Westin Houston Downtown, The 1520 Texas Ave	Houston	TX	77002	713-228-1520	228-1555
TF: 800-427-4697 ■ *Web:* www.westinhoustondowntown.com					
Westin San Francisco Market Street 50 Third St	San Francisco	CA	94103	415-974-6400	543-8268
TF: 888-627-8561 ■ *Web:* www.starwoodhotels.com					
Westmark Hotels Inc 300 Elliott Ave W	Seattle	WA	98119	800-544-0970	285-7152*
**Fax Area Code:* 206 ■ *TF:* 800-544-0970 ■ *Web:* www.westmarkhotels.com					
Westmont Hospitality Group Inc 5847 San Felipe St Ste 4650	Houston	TX	77057	713-782-9100	782-9600
Web: www.whg.com					
Westport Inn, The 1595 Post Rd E	Westport	CT	06880	203-557-8124	254-8439
Web: www.westportinn.com					
Wheatleigh 11 Hawthorne Rd	Lenox	MA	01240	413-637-0610	637-4507
Web: wheatleigh.com					
White Barn Inn 37 Beach Ave PO Box 560C	Kennebunk	ME	04043	207-967-2321	967-1100
Web: www.whitebarninn.com					
White Elephant Inn & Cottages 50 Easton St	Nantucket	MA	02554	508-228-2500	325-1195
TF: 800-475-2637 ■ *Web:* www.whiteelephanthotel.com					
White Inn, The 52 E Main St	Fredonia	NY	14063	716-672-2103	672-2107
Web: www.whiteinn.com					
White Lodging Services Inc 701 E 83rd Ave	Merrillville	IN	46410	219-472-2900	756-2902
Web: www.whitelodging.com					
White Swan Inn 845 Bush St	San Francisco	CA	94108	415-775-1755	
TF: 800-999-9570 ■ *Web:* www.whiteswaninnsf.com					
Whitehall Hotel 105 E Delaware Pl	Chicago	IL	60611	312-944-6300	944-8552
Web: www.thewhitehallhotel.com					
Whitelaw Hotel 808 Collins Ave	Miami Beach	FL	33139	305-398-7000	398-7010
Web: www.whitelawhotel.com					
Whitney the - A Wyndham Historic Hotel 610 Poydras St	New Orleans	LA	70130	504-581-4222	207-0101
TF: 800-996-3426 ■ *Web:* www.wyndham.com					
Wickaninnish Inn 500 Osprey Ln PO Box 250	Tofino	BC	V0R2Z0	250-725-3100	725-3110*
**Fax:* Resv ■ *TF:* 800-333-4604 ■ *Web:* www.wickinn.com					
Wild Palms Hotel 910 E Fremont Ave	Sunnyvale	CA	94087	408-738-0500	736-8302
TF: 800-738-7477 ■ *Web:* www.jdvhotels.com					
Williamsburg Lodge 310 S England St	Williamsburg	VA	23185	757-229-1000	220-7799
TF Cust Svc: 800-447-8679 ■ *Web:* www.history.org					
Willows Historic Palm Springs Inn 412 W Tahquitz Canyon Way	Palm Springs	CA	92262	760-320-0771	320-0780
TF: 800-966-9597 ■ *Web:* www.thewillowspalmsprings.com					
Willows Hotel 555 W Surf St	Chicago	IL	60657	773-528-8400	528-8483
TF: 877-207-2111 ■ *Web:* www.willowshotelchicago.com					
Willows Lodge 14580 NE 145th St	Woodinville	WA	98072	425-424-3900	424-2585
TF: 877-424-3930 ■ *Web:* www.willowslodge.com					
Wilson Hotel Management Company Inc 8700 Trl Lk Dr W Ste 300	Memphis	TN	38125	901-346-8800	346-5808
TF: 800-945-7661 ■ *Web:* www.wilsonhotels.com					
Windsor Arms Hotel 18 St Thomas St	Toronto	ON	M5S3E7	416-971-9666	921-9121
TF: 877-999-2767 ■ *Web:* www.windsorarmshotel.com					
Windsor Capital Group Inc 3000 Ocean Pk Blvd Ste 3010	Santa Monica	CA	90405	310-566-1100	566-1199
Web: www.wcghotels.com					
Windsor Court Hotel 300 Gravier St	New Orleans	LA	70130	504-523-6000	596-4513
TF: 888-596-0955 ■ *Web:* www.windsorcourthotel.com					
Windsor Hotel 125 W Lamar St	Americus	GA	31709	229-924-1555	924-1555
Web: www.windsor-americus.com					
Winegardner & Hammons Inc 4243 Hunt Rd	Cincinnati	OH	45242	513-891-1066	794-2590
Web: www.whihotels.com					
Wonder View Inn & Suites 50 Eden St PO Box 25	Bar Harbor	ME	04609	207-288-3358	288-2005
TF: 888-439-8439 ■ *Web:* www.wonderviewinn.com					
Woodloch Pines Inc 731 Welcome Lk Rd	Hawley	PA	18428	570-685-8000	685-8093
TF: 800-966-3562 ■ *Web:* www.woodloch.com					
Woodmark Hotel on Lake Washington 1200 Carillon Pt	Kirkland	WA	98033	425-822-3700	822-3699
TF: 800-822-3700 ■ *Web:* www.thewoodmark.com					
Wort Hotel 50 N Glenwood	Jackson	WY	83001	307-733-2190	733-2067
TF Cust Svc: 800-322-2727 ■ *Web:* www.worthotel.com					
Wyndham Grand Chicago Riverfront 71 E Wacker Dr	Chicago	IL	60601	312-346-7100	346-1721
Web: wyndhamgrandchicagoriverfront.com/					
AmeriHost Inn 8001 International Dr	Orlando	FL	32819	407-351-2420	
TF Resv: 877-999-3223 ■ *Web:* www.wyndham.com					
Baymont Inn & Suites PO Box 4090	Aberdeen	SD	57401	866-464-2321	
TF: 866-464-2321 ■ *Web:* www.baymontinns.com					
Ramada 949 Route 46	Parsippany	NJ	07054	877-212-2733	
TF Resv: 877-212-2733 ■ *Web:* www.ramada.com					
Wyndham Hotel Group *Travelodge* PO Box 4090	Aberdeen	SD	57041	312-427-8000	
TF Resv: 800-525-4055 ■ *Web:* www.travelodge.com					
Wyndham Vacation Resorts 6277 Sea Harbor Dr	Orlando	FL	32821	800-251-8736	
TF: 800-251-8736 ■ *Web:* www.clubwyndham.com					
Wyndham Lake Buena Vista 1850 Hotel Plaza Blvd	Lake Buena Vista	FL	32830	407-828-4444	
TF: 800-624-4109 ■ *Web:* www.wyndhamlakebuenavista.com					
Wyndham Midtown 45 205 E 45th St	New York	NY	10017	212-867-5100	867-7878
Web: www.thealexhotel.com					
Wyndham Worldwide Corp *Wyndham Hotel Group* 22 Sylvan Way	Parsippany	NJ	07054	973-753-6000	753-6000
NYSE: WYN ■ *Web:* www.wyndhamworldwide.com					
Wynfrey Hotel 1000 Riverchase Galleria	Birmingham	AL	35244	205-987-1600	988-4597
TF: 800-633-7313 ■ *Web:* wynfrey.regency.hyatt.com					
Wynn Las Vegas 3131 Las Vegas Blvd S	Las Vegas	NV	89109	702-770-7000	770-1571
TF: 877-321-9966 ■ *Web:* www.wynnlasvegas.com					
Yankee Inn 461 Pittsfield Lenox Rd	Lenox	MA	01240	413-499-3700	499-3634
Web: www.yankeeinn.com					
Yankee Peddler Inn 113 Touro St	Newport	RI	02840	401-846-1323	
Web: www.yankeepeddlerinn.com					
Yarmouth Resort 343 Main St Rt 28	West Yarmouth	MA	02673	508-775-5155	
Web: www.yarmouthresort.com					
Yarrow Hotel & Conference Ctr 1800 Pk Ave	Park City	UT	84060	435-649-7000	645-7007
TF: 800-445-8667 ■ *Web:* www.yarrowhotelparkcity.com					
Yogo Inn 211 E Main St	Lewistown	MT	59457	406-535-8721	535-8969
TF: 800-860-9646 ■ *Web:* www.yogoinn.com					
Yorktowne Hotel 48 E Market St	York	PA	17401	717-848-1111	845-4707
TF: 800-233-9324 ■ *Web:* www.yorktowne.com					

383 ICE - MANUFACTURED

				Phone	Fax
Arctic Glacier USA Inc 1654 Marthaler Ln	West Saint Paul	MN	55118	651-455-0410	455-7799
CV Ice Company Inc 83796 Date Ave	Indio	CA	92201	760-347-3529	347-3529
Web: www.cvice.com					
Dusing Bros Ice Manufacturing Co 3607 Dixie Hwy	Elsmere	KY	41018	859-727-2720	727-2780
Hanover Foods Corp 1550 York St PO Box 334	Hanover	PA	17331	717-632-6000	632-6681
OTC: HNFSA ■ *TF:* 800-888-4646 ■ *Web:* www.hanoverfoods.com					
House of Flavors Inc 110 N William St	Ludington	MI	49431	231-845-7369	845-7371
TF: 800-930-7740 ■ *Web:* www.houseofflavors.com					
Icemakers Inc 3711 Fifth Ct N	Birmingham	AL	35222	205-591-2791	591-2389
TF General: 800-467-2181 ■ *Web:* www.icemakers.net					
Pelesys Learning Systems Inc Ste 125 - 13500 Maycrest Way	Richmond	BC	V6V2N8	604-233-6268	
Web: www.pelesys.com					
Pelican Ice & Cold Storage Inc 711 Oxley St	Kenner	LA	70062	504-602-0013	
Web: pelicanice.com/					
Reddy Ice Holdings Inc 8750 N Central Expy Ste 1800	Dallas	TX	75231	214-526-6740	528-1532
OTC: RDDYQ ■ *TF:* 800-683-4423 ■ *Web:* www.reddyice.com					
Toyo Pumps North America Corp 2853 Douglas Rd	Burnaby	BC	V5C6H2	604-296-3900	
Web: www.toyopumps.com					

384 ICE CREAM & DAIRY STORES

				Phone	Fax
Amy's Ice Creams 3500 Guadalupe St	Austin	TX	78705	512-458-6895	458-4971
Web: www.amysicecreams.com					
Bahama Buck's Original Shaved Ice Co 5123 69th St	Lubbock	TX	79424	806-771-2189	771-2190
Web: www.bahamabucks.com					
Baskin-Robbins Inc 130 Royall St	Canton	MA	02021	781-737-3000	
TF: 800-859-5339 ■ *Web:* www.baskinrobbins.com					
Ben & Jerry's Homemade Inc 30 Community Dr	South Burlington	VT	05403	802-846-1500	846-1538
Web: www.benjerry.com					
Carvel Express 200 Glenridge Pt Pkwy Ste 200	Atlanta	GA	30342	800-322-4848	255-4978*
**Fax Area Code:* 404 ■ *TF:* 800-322-4848 ■ *Web:* www.carvel.com					
Cloverland Green Spring Dairy Inc 2701 Loch Raven Rd	Baltimore	MD	21218	410-235-4477	
TF Orders: 800-492-0094 ■ *Web:* www.cloverlanddairy.com					

Phone | Fax

Cold Stone Creamery Inc
9311 E Via De Ventura .... Scottsdale AZ 85258 480-362-4800 362-4812
TF Cust Svc: 866-452-4252 ■ *Web:* www.coldstonecreamery.com

Dairy Queen 7505 Metro Blvd .... Minneapolis MN 55439 952-830-0200 830-0227
TF: 800-883-4279 ■ *Web:* www.dairyqueen.com

Freshens Quality Brands 1750 The Exchange .... Atlanta GA 30339 678-627-5400 627-5454
Web: www.freshens.com

Kilwins Quality Confections Inc (KQC)
1050 Bay View Rd .... Petoskey MI 49770 888-454-5946
TF: 888-454-5946 ■ *Web:* www.kilwins.com

Newport Creamery Inc
35 Stockanosset Cross Rd PO Box 8819 .... Cranston RI 02920 401-946-4000 946-4392
Web: www.newportcreamery.com

Rita's Water Ice Franchise Co LLC
1401 Bridgetown Pike .... Feasterville PA 19053 215-322-8774
Web: www.ritasice.com

Royal Crest Dairy Inc 350 S Pearl St .... Denver CO 80209 303-777-2227 744-9173
TF: 888-226-6455 ■ *Web:* www.royalcrestdairy.com

Stewart's Shops PO Box 435 .... Saratoga Springs NY 12866 518-581-1201 581-1209
Web: stewartsshops.com

385 IMAGING EQUIPMENT & SYSTEMS - MEDICAL

SEE ALSO Medical Instruments & Apparatus - Mfr p. 2729

Phone | Fax

Agfa Corp 611 River Dr .... Elmwood Park NJ 07407 201-440-2500
TF: 888-274-8626 ■
Web: www.agfagraphics.com/gs/usa/en/internet/maings/

Alpine Solutions Inc
3222 Corte Malpaso Ste 204 .... Camarillo CA 93012 805-388-1699 388-2373
Web: www.alpinesolutionsinc.com

BrainLAB Inc
Three Westbrook Corp Ctr Ste 400 .... Westchester IL 60154 708-409-1343 409-1619
TF: 800-784-7700 ■ *Web:* www.brainlab.com

CIVCO Medical Instruments 102 First St .... Kalona IA 52247 319-656-4447 656-4451
TF: 800-445-6741 ■ *Web:* www.civcomedical.com

Dentsply International Inc
221 W Philadelphia St PO Box 872 .... York PA 17405 717-845-7511 849-4762
NASDAQ: XRAY ■ *TF:* 800-877-0020 ■ *Web:* www.dentsply.com

Digirad Corp 13950 Stowe Dr .... Poway CA 92064 858-726-1600 726-1700
NASDAQ: DRAD ■ *TF:* 800-947-6134 ■ *Web:* www.digirad.com

Dornier MedTech America Inc
1155 Roberts Blvd .... Kennesaw GA 30144 770-426-1315 426-6115
TF: 800-367-6437 ■ *Web:* www.dornier.com

Eastman Kodak Co 343 State St .... Rochester NY 14650 585-724-4000 724-0663
OTC: EKDKQ ■ *Web:* www.kodak.com

Fonar Corp 110 Marcus Dr .... Melville NY 11747 631-694-2929 390-7766
NASDAQ: FONR ■ *TF:* 877-694-2929 ■ *Web:* www.fonar.com

Given Imaging Ltd 3950 Shackleford Rd Ste 500 .... Duluth GA 30096 770-662-0870 662-0510
NASDAQ: GIVN ■ *Web:* www.givenimaging.com

Hitachi Medical Systems America Inc
1959 Summit Commerce Pk .... Twinsburg OH 44087 330-425-1313 425-1410
TF: 800-800-3106 ■ *Web:* www.hitachimed.com

Hologic Inc 35 Crosby Dr .... Bedford MA 01730 781-999-7300 280-0669
NASDAQ: HOLX ■ *TF:* 800-523-5001 ■ *Web:* www.hologic.com

Holorad 2929 S Main St .... Salt Lake City UT 84115 801-983-6075 802-8004
Web: www.holorad.com

iCAD Inc Four Townsend W Ste 17 .... Nashua NH 03063 603-882-5200 880-3843
NASDAQ: ICAD ■ *TF:* 866-280-2239 ■ *Web:* www.icadmed.com

ImageWorks 250 Clearbrook Rd .... Elmsford NY 10523 914-592-6100 592-6148
TF: 800-592-6666 ■ *Web:* www.imageworkscorporation.com

Imaging Diagnostic Systems Inc
6531 NW 18th Ct .... Plantation FL 33313 954-581-9800 979-2420
OTC: IMDS ■ *TF:* 800-992-9008 ■ *Web:* www.imds.com

IRIS International Inc 9172 Eton Ave .... Chatsworth CA 91311 818-709-1244 700-9661
NASDAQ: IRIS ■ *TF:* 877-920-4747 ■ *Web:* www.proiris.com

ITT Night Vision & Imaging
7635 Plantation Rd .... Roanoke VA 24019 540-563-0371 362-4979
TF: 800-448-8678 ■ *Web:* www.nightvision.com

Konica Minolta Medical Imaging
411 Newark Pompton Tpke .... Wayne NJ 07470 973-633-1500 523-7408
Web: konicaminolta.us

Merge Helathcare 350 N Orleans St First Fl .... Chicago IL 60654 312-565-6868 565-6870
TF: 877-446-3743 ■ *Web:* www.merge.com

Novadaq Technologies Inc
5090 Explorer Dr Ste 202 .... Mississauga ON L4W4T9 905-629-3822 247-0656
TSE: NDQ ■ *Web:* www.novadaq.com

One Call Medical Inc (OCM)
20 Waterview Blvd PO Box 614 .... Parsippany NJ 07054 973-257-1000 257-0044
TF: 800-872-2875 ■ *Web:* www.onecallcm.com

PerkinElmer Inc 940 Winter St .... Waltham MA 02451 203-925-4602 944-4904
NYSE: PKI ■ *Web:* www.perkinelmer.com

Philips Global PACS 5000 Marina Blvd Ste 100 .... Brisbane CA 94005 650-228-5555 228-5580
TF Cust Svc: 877-328-2808 ■ *Web:* www.healthcare.philips.com

Philips Medical Systems 3000 Minuteman Rd .... Andover MA 01810 978-659-3000
TF: 800-934-7372 ■ *Web:* www.healthcare.philips.com

Precision Optics Corp Inc 22 E Broadway .... Gardner MA 01440 978-630-1800 630-1487
OTC: PEYE ■ *TF:* 800-447-2812 ■ *Web:* www.poci.com

Quest Diagnostics 1311 Calle Batido .... San Clemente CA 92673 949-940-7200

S & S Technology 10625 Telge Rd .... Houston TX 77095 281-815-1300 815-1444
TF: 800-231-1747 ■ *Web:* www.ssxray.com

Shimadzu Medical Systems
20101 S Vermont Ave .... Torrance CA 90502 310-217-8855 217-0661
TF General: 800-477-1227 ■ *Web:* www.shimadzu.com

Siemens Medical Solutions Inc
51 Valley Stream Pkwy .... Malvern PA 19355 800-225-5336 219-3124*
**Fax Area Code:* 610 ■ *TF:* 800-888-7436 ■ *Web:* healthcare.siemens.com

Siemens Molecular Imaging Inc
810 Innovation Dr .... Knoxville TN 37932 865-218-2000 218-3000
Web: healthcare.siemens.com

SonoSite Inc 21919 30th Dr SE .... Bothell WA 98021 425-951-1200 951-1201
NASDAQ: SONO ■ *TF:* 888-482-9449 ■ *Web:* www.sonosite.com

Phone | Fax

Stereotaxis Inc 4320 Forest Pk Ave .... Saint Louis MO 63108 314-678-6100 678-6159
NASDAQ: STXS ■ *TF:* 866-646-2346 ■ *Web:* www.stereotaxis.com

Topcon Medical Systems Inc 111 Bauer Dr .... Oakland NJ 07436 201-599-5100 599-5250
TF: 800-223-1130 ■ *Web:* www.topconmedical.com

Toshiba America Inc
1251 Ave of the Americas Ste 4100 .... New York NY 10020 212-596-0600 593-3875
TF: 800-457-7777 ■ *Web:* www.toshiba.com

Toshiba America Medical Systems Inc
2441 Michelle Dr .... Tustin CA 92780 714-730-5000 730-4022
TF Cust Svc: 800-521-1968 ■ *Web:* www.medical.toshiba.com

Varian Medical Systems Inc 3100 Hansen Way .... Palo Alto CA 94304 650-493-4000
NYSE: VAR ■ *TF:* 800-544-4636 ■ *Web:* www.varian.com

Vision-Sciences Inc 40 Ramland Rd S .... Orangeburg NY 10962 845-365-0600 365-0620
NASDAQ: VSCI ■ *TF:* 800-874-9975 ■ *Web:* www.visionsciences.com

Wolf X-Ray Corp 100 W Industry Ct .... Deer Park NY 11729 631-242-9729 925-5003
TF Cust Svc: 800-356-9729 ■ *Web:* www.wolfxray.com

386 IMAGING SERVICES - DIAGNOSTIC

Phone | Fax

Alliance Imaging Inc
100 Bayview Cir Ste 400 .... Newport Beach CA 92660 949-242-5300 662-2730*
**Fax Area Code:* 888 ■ *TF:* 800-544-3215 ■ *Web:* www.alliancehealthcareservices-us.com

Center for Diagnostic Imaging
5775 Wayzata Blvd Ste 400 .... Saint Louis Park MN 55416 952-541-1840 847-1152
TF: 877-885-8797 ■ *Web:* mycdi.com

Excel Diagnostic Imaging Clinics
9701 Richmond Ave Ste 122 .... Houston TX 77042 713-781 6200
Web: exceldiagnostics.com

Insight Imaging
26250 Enterprise Ct Ste 100 .... Lake Forest CA 92630 949-282-6000 452-0161
TF: 800-344-9555 ■ *Web:* www.insighthealth.com

Johns Dental Laboratory Inc
423 S 13th St .... Terre Haute IN 47807 812-232-6026
Web: www.johnsdental.com

Medical Resources Inc 1455 Broad St .... Bloomfield NJ 07003 973-707-1100 707-1118
TF: 800-537-7272

Medquest Assoc Inc
3480 Preston Ridge Rd Ste 600 .... Alpharetta GA 30005 678-992-7200
Web: www.mqimaging.com

Memorial MRI & Diagnostic Center LP
1241 Campbell Rd .... Houston TX 77055 713-461-3399
Web: www.memorialdiagnostic.com

MNAP Medical Solutions Inc
9908 E Roosevelt Blvd .... Philadelphia PA 19115 215-464-3300
Web: mnap.com

Quality Electrodynamics LLC
700 Beta Dr .... Mayfield Village OH 44143 440-638-5106
Web: www.qualedyn.com

V-rad Systems Inc 4504 Maple St .... Bellaire TX 77401 713-667-6056
Web: v-radsystems.com

387 INCENTIVE PROGRAM MANAGEMENT SERVICES

SEE ALSO Conference & Events Coordinators p. 2069
Many of the companies listed here provide travel as a reward for employees or corporate customers in order to boost sales or employee performance. Most of these companies are members of the Society of Incentive & Travel Executives. Some of the companies listed offer merchandise or other types of incentives as well.

Phone | Fax

ADI Meetings & Events
4801 S Lakeshore Dr Ste 108 .... Tempe AZ 85282 480-350-9090 350-9393
Web: www.adimi.com

Beatty Group International
9800 Beaverton Hillsdale Ste 105 .... Beaverton OR 97005 503-644-3340 644-2219
TF: 800-285-6215 ■ *Web:* www.beattygroup.com

Don Jagoda Assoc Inc 100 Marcus Dr .... Melville NY 11747 631-454-1800 454-1834
Web: www.dja.com

Eaton Incentives Inc
271 Rt 46W Ste H 212-215 .... Fairfield NJ 07004 973-882-7700
Web: www.eatonincentives.com

Fennell Promotions Inc 951 Hornet Dr .... Hazelwood MO 63042 314-592-3300 495-9845*
**Fax Area Code:* 800 ■ *Web:* www.fennellpromotions.com

Fields Group Inc 12335 Bridgewater Rd .... Indianapolis IN 46256 317-578-4414 578-4411
TF: 800-600-2969 ■ *Web:* www.thefieldsgroupinc.com

Global Ministries Inc
2120 Main St Ste 130 .... Huntington Beach CA 92648 714-960-2300
Web: www.globalinc.net

Impact Incentives & Meetings Inc
23 Vreeland Rd Ste 204 .... Florham Park NJ 07932 973-952-9052 952-1024
Web: www.impactincentives.com

Incentive Travel & Meetings (ITM)
970 Clementstone Dr Ste 100 .... Atlanta GA 30342 404-252-2728 252-8328
Web: www.usaitm.com

ITAGroup 4600 Westown Pkwy .... West Des Moines IA 50266 800-257-1985
TF: 800-257-1985 ■ *Web:* www.itagroup.com

Marketing Innovators International Inc
9701 W Higgins Rd .... Rosemont IL 60018 800-543-7373 696-3194*
**Fax Area Code:* 847 ■ *TF:* 800-543-7373 ■ *Web:* www.marketinginnovators.com

Maxcel Co 6600 LBJ Fwy Ste 109 .... Dallas TX 75240 972-644-0880 680-2488
Web: www.maxcel.net

MotivAction 16355 36th Ave N Ste 100 .... Minneapolis MN 55446 763-412-3000
TF: 866-277-3420 ■ *Web:* www.motivaction.com

Motivation Through Incentives Inc
10400 W 103 St Ste 10 .... Overland Park KS 66214 800-826-3464
TF: 800-826-3464 ■ *Web:* www.mtievents.com

Performance Strategies Inc
6862 Hillsdale Ct .... Indianapolis IN 46250 317-842-0393 578-4711
Web: www.performancestrategies.com

	City	State	Zip	Phone	Fax
Premier Incentives 6 Admiral Ln	Salem	MA	01970	978-607-0135	607-0136
Web: www.premierincentives.com					
Pro Logic Consumer Marketing Services					
1625 S Congress Ave	Delray Beach	FL	33445	561-454-7600	265-2493
Web: www.prologicretail.com/consumer-marketing-services/					
PROVIDENT TRAVEL 11309 Montgomery Rd.	Cincinnati	OH	45249	513-247-1100	
TF: 800-354-8108 ■ *Web:* www.providenttravel.com					
Student Advantage LLC 280 Summer St	Boston	MA	02210	800-333-2920	912-2012*
**Fax Area Code:* 617 ■ *TF:* 800-333-2920 ■ *Web:* www.studentadvantage.com					
United Incentives Inc 131 N Third St.	Philadelphia	PA	19106	215-625-2700	625-2502
Web: www.unitedincentives.com					
Universal Odyssey Inc					
1601 Dove St Ste 260.	Newport Beach	CA	92660	949-263-1222	263-0983
Web: www.universalodyssey.com					
USMotivation					
7840 Roswell Rd Bldg 100 Third Fl	Atlanta	GA	30350	866-885-4702	290-4701*
**Fax Area Code:* 770 ■ *TF:* 866-885-4702 ■ *Web:* www.usmotivation.com					
Vertrue Inc 20 Glover Ave.	Norwalk	CT	06850	203-324-7635	674-7080
Viktor Incentives & Meetings					
4020 Copper View Ste 130.	Traverse City	MI	49684	231-947-0882	947-2532
TF: 800-748-0478 ■ *Web:* www.viktorwithak.com					

388 INDUSTRIAL EQUIPMENT & SUPPLIES (MISC) - WHOL

	City	State	Zip	Phone	Fax
AaronEquipment Company Inc					
735 E Green St PO Box 80	Bensenville	IL	60106	630-350-2200	350-9047
TF: 800-492-2766 ■ *Web:* www.aaronequipment.com					
Abatix Corp 2400 Skyline Dr Ste 400	Mesquite	TX	75149	214-381-0322	388-0443
TF: 800-426-3983 ■ *Web:* www.abatix.com					
Accurate Air Engineering Inc					
16207 Carmennita Rd.	Cerritos	CA	90703	562-484-6370	484-6371
TF: 800-438-5577 ■ *Web:* www.accurateair.com					
Adco Manufacturing Inc 2170 Academy Ave.	Sanger	CA	93657	559-875-5563	875-7665
Web: www.adcomfg.com					
AIM Supply Co 7337 Bryan Dairy Rd.	Largo	FL	33777	727-544-6211	544-6211
TF: 800-999-0125 ■ *Web:* www.aimsupply.com					
Aimco 10000 SE Pine St	Portland	OR	97216	800-852-1368	582-9015
TF: 800-852-1368 ■ *Web:* www.aimco-global.com					
Airgas Inc 259 N Radnor-Chester Rd Ste 100.	Radnor	PA	19087	610-687-5253	687-1052
NYSE: ARG ■ *TF:* 800-255-2165 ■ *Web:* www.airgas.com					
Airgas North Central					
1250 W Washington St.	West Chicago	IL	60185	630-231-9260	231-7768
Web: www.airgas.com					
AIV LP 7140 W Sam Houston Pkwy N Ste100.	Houston	TX	77040	713-462-4181	
Web: www.aivinc.com					
Alamo Iron Works Inc 943 AT&T Ctr Pkwy.	San Antonio	TX	78219	210-223-6161	704-8351
TF: 800-292-7817 ■ *Web:* www.aiwdirect.com					
Allied Automation Inc 5220 E 64th St	Indianapolis	IN	46220	317-253-5900	
Web: www.allied-automation.com					
Ames Supply Co 1936C University Ln	Lisle	IL	60532	630-964-2440	964-0497
AMI Bearings Inc 570 N Wheeling Rd	Mount Prospect	IL	60056	847-759-0620	
Web: www.amibearings.com					
Applied Industrial Technologies Inc					
One Applied Plz Eulid Ave.	Cleveland	OH	44115	216-426-4000	426-4845
NYSE: AIT ■ *Web:* www.applied.com					
Associated Packaging Inc 435 Calvert Dr	Gallatin	TN	37066	615-452-2131	452-7890
Web: www.associatedpackaging.com					
Atlantic Lift Truck Inc					
2945 Whittington Ave	Baltimore	MD	21230	410-644-7777	
TF: 800-638-4566 ■ *Web:* www.atlanticlift.com					
Austin Pump & Supply Co PO Box 17037	Austin	TX	78760	512-442-2348	442-2932
TF: 800-252-9692 ■ *Web:* www.austinpump.com					
Barnes Distribution 1301 E Ninth St Ste 700	Cleveland	OH	44114	216-416-7200	
TF: 800-726-9626 ■ *Web:* classc.mscdirect.com/					
Bearing Distributors Inc 8000 Hub Pkwy	Cleveland	OH	44125	216-642-9100	642-9573
TF: 888-435-7234 ■ *Web:* www.bdi-usa.com					
Bearing Headquarters Co 2550 S 25th Ave.	Broadview	IL	60155	708-681-4400	681-4462
Web: www.bearingheadquarters.com					
Bearings & Drives Inc					
607 Lower Poplar St PO Box 4325	Macon	GA	31208	478-746-7623	742-7836
Web: www.bdindustrial.com					
Bearings Ltd 2100 Pacific St	Hauppauge	NY	11788	631-273-8200	
Web: www.bearingslimited.com					
Berendsen Fluid Power 401 S Boston Ave Ste 1200.	Tulsa	OK	74103	918-592-3781	581-5080
TF: 800-360-2327 ■ *Web:* www.bfpna.com					
Bolttech Mannings 501 Mosside Blvd	North Versailles	PA	15137	724-872-4873	829-1834*
**Fax Area Code:* 412 ■ *TF:* 888-846-8827 ■ *Web:* www.bolttechmannings.com					
Brake Supply Company Inc					
5501 Foundation Blvd	Evansville	IN	47725	812-467-1000	429-9493
TF: 800-457-5788 ■ *Web:* www.brake.com					
Brauer Material Handling Systems Inc					
226 Molly Walton Dr.	Hendersonville	TN	37075	615-859-2930	859-2937
TF: 800-645-6083 ■ *Web:* www.braueronline.com					
Briggs Equipment 10540 N Stemmons Fwy Ste 1525	Dallas	TX	75220	214-630-0808	631-3560
TF: 800-606-1833 ■ *Web:* www.briggsequipment.com					
Briggs Industrial Equipment					
10550 N Stemmons Fwy.	Dallas	TX	75220	214-630-0808	631-3560
TF: 800-516-9206 ■ *Web:* www.briggsindustrial.com					
Brinker Brown Fastener & Supply Inc					
12290 Crystal Commerce Loop	Fort Myers	FL	33966	239-939-3535	
Web: www.brinkerbrown.com					
C & H Distributors LLC 770 S 70th St	Milwaukee	WI	53214	414-443-1700	336-1331*
**Fax Area Code:* 800 ■ *TF Sales:* 800-558-9966 ■ *Web:* www.chdist.com					
Canadian Bearings Ltd 1600 Drew Rd.	Mississauga	ON	L5S1S5	905-670-6700	670-0459
TF: 800-229-2327 ■ *Web:* www.canadianbearings.com					
Carolina Material Handling Services Inc					
PO Box 6	Columbia	SC	29202	803-695-0149	783-1659
TF: 800-922-6709 ■ *Web:* www.cmhservices.net					
Cascade Machinery & Electric Inc					
4600 E Marginal Way S PO Box 3575	Seattle	WA	98134	206-762-0500	767-5122
TF: 800-289-0500 ■ *Web:* www.cascade-machinery.com					
Cee Kay Supply Co 5835 Manchester Ave	Saint Louis	MO	63110	314-644-3500	644-4336
Web: www.ceekay.com					
Central Power Systems & Services					
9200 W Liberty Dr	Liberty	MO	64068	816-781-8070	781-2207*
**Fax:* Sales ■ *Web:* www.cpower.com					
Certified Slings & Supply Inc					
PO Box 180127	Casselberry	FL	32718	407-331-6677	260-9196
Web: www.certifiedslings.com					
Cisco-Eagle 2120 Valley View Ln.	Dallas	TX	75234	972-406-9330	406-9577
TF: 888-877-3861 ■ *Web:* www.cisco-eagle.com					
Clean Rooms West Inc 1392 Industrial Dr	Tustin	CA	92780	714-258-7700	
Web: www.cleanroomswest.com					
CMC Construction Services 9103 E Almeda Rd	Houston	TX	77054	713-799-1150	799-8431
TF: 877-297-9111 ■ *Web:* www.cmcconstructionservices.com					
Cohn & Gregory Inc 5450 Midway Rd.	Fort Worth	TX	76117	817-831-9998	
Web: www.cgsupply.com					
Conveyco Technologies Inc PO Box 1000	Bristol	CT	06011	860-589-8215	583-1384
TF: 800-229-8215 ■ *Web:* www.conveyco.com					
Crane Engineering Inc 707 Ford St PO Box 38	Kimberly	WI	54136	920-733-4425	733-0211
Web: www.craneengineering.net					
Cross Co 4400 Piedmont Pkwy	Greensboro	NC	27410	336-856-6000	856-6999
TF: 800-858-1737 ■ *Web:* www.crossco.com					
Cummins Southern Plains Inc PO Box 90027	Arlington	TX	76004	817-640-6801	640-6852
TF: 800-516-4354 ■ *Web:* www.cummins-sp.com					
Cvg International America Inc					
7200 NW 19th St Ste 110.	Miami	FL	33126	305-470-8100	470-8199
Danco Inc 486 Lakewood Rd.	Waterbury	CT	06704	203-753-5121	
Web: www.danco-inc.com					
Deacon Industrial Supply Co Inc					
165 Boro Line Rd	King of Prussia	PA	19406	610-265-5322	265-6470
TF: 800-726-9800 ■ *Web:* www.deaconind.com					
Detroit Pump & Mfg Co 450 Fair St Bldg D	Ferndale	MI	48220	248-544-4242	544-4141
TF: 800-686-1662 ■ *Web:* www.detroitpump.com					
DoALL Co 1480 S Wolf Rd	Wheeling	IL	60090	847-495-6800	484-2045
Web: www.doall.com					
Drago Supply Co 740 Houston Ave	Port Arthur	TX	77640	409-983-4911	985-6542*
**Fax:* Sales ■ *Web:* www.dragosupply.com					
Dueco N4 W22610 Bluemound Rd.	Waukesha	WI	53186	262-547-8500	547-8407
TF: 800-558-4004 ■ *Web:* www.dueco.com					
Duncan Industrial Solutions					
3450 S MacArthur Blvd	Oklahoma City	OK	73179	405-688-2300	
TF: 800-375-9470 ■ *Web:* www.duncanindustrial.com					
Duo-Fast Carolinas Inc					
1923 John Crossland Jr Dr.	Charlotte	NC	28208	704-377-5721	377-2368
Web: www.duofast.net					
DXP Enterprises Inc 7272 Pinemont Dr	Houston	TX	77040	713-996-4700	996-4701
NASDAQ: DXPE ■ *TF:* 800-830-3973 ■ *Web:* www.dxpe.com					
Eastern Lift Truck Company Inc					
549 E Linwood Ave.	Maple Shade	NJ	08052	856-779-8880	482-8804
TF: 866-980-7175 ■ *Web:* www.easternlifttruck.com					
Edgen Corp 18444 Highland Rd	Baton Rouge	LA	70809	225-756-9868	756-9868
TF: 866-334-3648 ■ *Web:* www.edgenmurray.com					
Ellison Machinery Co					
9912 S Pioneer Blvd.	Santa Fe Springs	CA	90670	562-949-8311	949-9091
Web: www.ellisontechnologies.com					
Endries International Inc					
714 W Ryan St PO Box 69	Brillion	WI	54110	920-756-5381	756-3772
TF: 800-852-5821 ■ *Web:* www.endries.com					
Engman-Taylor Company Inc (ETCO)					
W142 N9351 Fountain Blvd	Menomonee Falls	WI	53051	262-255-9300	255-6512
TF: 800-236-1975 ■ *Web:* www.engman-taylor.com					
Enpro Inc 121 S LombaRd Rd	Addison	IL	60101	630-629-3504	629-3512
TF: 800-323-2416 ■ *Web:* www.enproinc.com					
Erie Bearings Company Inc 1432 E 12th St.	Erie	PA	16503	814-453-6871	
Web: www.eriebearings.com					
Exterran 16666 Northchase Dr	Houston	TX	77060	281-836-7000	
TF Sales: 800-975-9090 ■ *Web:* www.exterran.com					
Fairmont Supply Co 1001 Consol Energy Dr	Canonsburg	PA	15317	724-514-3900	261-5310
Web: www.fairmontsupply.com					
FCx Performance 3000 E 14th Ave	Columbus	OH	43219	614-324-6050	253-2033
TF: 800-253-6223 ■ *Web:* www.fcxperformance.com					
Flexlink Systems Inc					
6580 Snowdrift Rd Ste 200.	Allentown	PA	18106	610-973-8200	973-8345
Web: www.flexlink.com					
Florida Detroit Diesel-Allison Inc					
5040 University Blvd W	Jacksonville	FL	32216	904-737-7330	733-5871
TF: 888-812-4440 ■ *Web:* www.fdda.com					
Forklifts of Minnesota Inc					
2201 W 94th St.	Bloomington	MN	55431	952-887-5400	881-3030
TF: 800-752-4300 ■ *Web:* www.forkliftsofmn.com					
FUJIFILM Graphic System USA Inc 45 Crosby Dr	Bedford	MA	01730	781-271-4400	
TF: 800-755-3854 ■ *Web:* www.fujifilmusa.com					
FW Webb Co 160 Middlesex Tpke.	Bedford	MA	01730	781-272-6600	275-3354
TF: 800-343-7555 ■ *Web:* www.fwwebb.com					
Gaffney-Kroese Supply Corp					
60 Kingsbridge Rd	Piscataway	NJ	08854	732-885-9000	885-9555
Web: gaffney-kroese.com					
Ganesh Machinery 20869 Plummer St	Chatsworth	CA	91311	818-349-9166	
Web: www.ganeshmachinery.com					
Garner 825 E Cooley Ave	San Bernardino	CA	92408	909-799-3030	
Web: www.garnerholt.com					
Gas Equipment Company Inc					
11616 Harry Hines Blvd	Dallas	TX	75229	972-241-2333	620-1403
Web: www.gasequipment.com					
General Tool & Supply Co Inc					
2705 NW Nicolai St	Portland	OR	97210	503-226-3411	
TF: 800-526-9328 ■ *Web:* www.motionindustries.com					
Geneva Scientific Inc 11 N Batavia Ave	Batavia	IL	60510	800-338-2697	879-8687*
**Fax Area Code:* 630 ■ *TF:* 800-338-2697 ■ *Web:* www.barcoproducts.com					

Company	City	State	ZIP	Phone	Fax
Genuine Parts Co 2999 Cir 75 Pkwy *NYSE:* GPC ■ *Web:* www.genpt.com	Atlanta	GA	30339	770-953-1700	
Gerotech Inc 29220 Commerce Dr. *Web:* www.gerotechinc.com	Flat Rock	MI	48134	734-379-7788	379-2244
Glatt Air Techniques Inc 20 Spear Rd *Web:* www.glattair.com	Ramsey	NJ	07446	201-825-8700	825-0389
Gosiger Inc 108 McDonough St *TF:* 877-288-1538 ■ *Web:* www.gosiger.com	Dayton	OH	45402	937-228-5174	228-5189
Greene Rubber Company Inc 20 Cross St. *Web:* www.greenerubber.com	Woburn	MA	01801	781-937-9909	
H G Makelim Co 219 Shaw Rd *TF:* 800-471-0590 ■ *Web:* www.hgmakelim.com	South San Francisco	CA	94080	650-873-4757	872-5438
Hagemeyer North America Inc 1460 Tobias Gadson Blvd *TF:* 877-462-7070 ■ *Web:* www.hagemeyerna.com	Charleston	SC	29407	843-745-2400	745-6942
Haggard & Stocking Assoc 5318 Victory Dr *TF:* 800-622-4824 ■ *Web:* www.haggard-stocking.com	Indianapolis	IN	46203	317-788-4661	788-1645
Hahn Systems Co Inc 6312 SE Ave *TF:* 800-201-4246 ■ *Web:* www.hahnsystems.com	Indianapolis	IN	46203	317-243-3796	244-9079
Harrington Industrial Plastics LLC 14480 Yorba Ave. *TF:* 800-213-4528 ■ *Web:* www.harringtonplastics.com	Chino	CA	91710	909-597-8641	597-9826
HD Supply Waterworks Ltd PO Box 1419 *TF:* 800-492-6909 ■ *Web:* www.hdswaterworks.com	Thomasville	GA	31799	800-950-7659	
Herc-U-Lift Inc 5655 Hwy 12 W PO Box 69 *TF:* 800-362-3500 ■ *Web:* www.herculift.com	Maple Plain	MN	55359	763-479-2501	479-2296
HJM Precision Inc Ninc New Tpke Rd *Web:* www.hjmprecision.com	Troy	NY	12182	518-235-7407	
Hope Group 70 Bearfoot Rd *Web:* www.thehopegroup.com	Northborough	MA	01532	508-393-7660	393-8203
Hughes Machinery Co 14400 College Blvd *Web:* www.hughesmachinery.com	Lenexa	KS	66215	913-492-0355	492-1420
Hull Lift Truck Inc 28747 Old US 33 W *TF:* 888-284-0364 ■ *Web:* www.hulllifttruck.com	Elkhart	IN	46516	574-293-8651	293-9769
Hydraulics International Inc 9201 Independence Ave *Web:* www.hiinet.com	Chatsworth	CA	91311	818-998-1231	718-2459
IBT Inc 9400 W 55th St *TF:* 800-332-2114 ■ *Web:* www.ibtinc.com	Merriam	KS	66203	913-677-3151	677-3752
IKO International Inc 91 Walsh Dr Fox Hill Industrial Park *Web:* www.ikont.com	Parsippany	NJ	07054	973-402-0254	
Illinois Auto Electric Co 700 Enterprise St *TF:* 800-683-8484 ■ *Web:* www.illinoisautoelectric.com	Aurora	IL	60504	630-862-3300	862-3137
Indeck Power Equipment Co 1111 Willis Ave. *TF:* 800-446-3325 ■ *Web:* www.indeck.com	Wheeling	IL	60090	847-541-8300	541-9984
Indoff Inc 11816 Lackland Rd *TF:* 800-486-7867 ■ *Web:* www.indoff.com	Saint Louis	MO	63146	314-997-1122	812-3932
Industrial Controls Distributors Inc (ICD) 1776 Bloomsbury Ave *TF Sales:* 800-281-4788 ■ *Web:* www.industrialcontrolsonline.com	Ocean	NJ	07712	732-918-9000	922-4417
Industrial Diesel Inc 8705 Harmon Rd. *TF:* 800-323-3659 ■ *Web:* www.industrialdiesel.net	Fort Worth	TX	76177	817-232-1071	232-0354
Industrial Supply Solutions Inc 520 Elizabeth St *TF:* 800-346-5341 ■ *Web:* www.issimro.com	Charleston	WV	25311	304-346-5341	346-5347
Innerstave LLC 21660 Eighth St E *Web:* www.innerstave.com	Sonoma	CA	95476	707-996-8781	
Integra Services Technologies Inc 3238 E Pasadena Fwy *Web:* www.integratechnologies.com	Pasadena	TX	77503	713-920-2400	
J. H. Bennett & Company Inc PO Box 8028 *TF General:* 800-837-5426 ■ *Web:* www.jhbennett.com	Novi	MI	48376	248-596-5100	596-0640
Jabo Supply Corp 5164 County Rd 64/66 *TF:* 800-334-5226 ■ *Web:* www.jabosupply.com	Huntington	WV	25705	304-736-8333	736-8551
Jefferds Corp 652 Winfield Rd PO Box 757 *TF:* 888-848-6216 ■ *Web:* www.jefferds.com	Saint Albans	WV	25177	304-755-8111	755-7544
Kaplan Industries Inc Route 73 & Morris Ave *Web:* www.kaplanindustries.com	Maple Shade	NJ	08052	856-779-8181	
Keen Compressed Gas Company Inc 4063 New Castle Ave *Web:* www.keengas.com	New Castle	DE	19720	302-594-4545	
Kemper Equipment Inc 5051 Horseshoe Pk. *Web:* www.kemperequipment.com	Honey Brook	PA	19344	610-273-2066	273-3537
Kennametal Inc 1600 Technology Way PO Box 231 *NYSE:* KMT ■ *TF Cust Svc:* 800-446-7738 ■ *Web:* www.kennametal.com	Latrobe	PA	15650	724-539-5000	539-8787
Kimball Midwest 4800 Robert Rd *TF:* 800-233-1294 ■ *Web:* www.kimballmidwest.com	Columbus	OH	43228	614-219-6100	219-6101
Knickerbocker Russell Company Inc 4759 Campbells Run *Web:* www.knickerbockerrussell.com	Pittsburgh	PA	15205	412-494-9233	787-7991
Lawson Products Inc 1666 E Touhy Ave. **Fax:* Sales ■ *Web:* www.lawsonproducts.com	Des Plaines	IL	60018	847-827-9666	827-1525*
Lewis Goetz & Company Inc 1571 Grandview Ave. *TF:* 800-257-6239 ■ *Web:* www.lewis-goetz.com	Paulsboro	NJ	08066	856-579-1421	579-1429
Lewis-Goetz & Co Inc 650 Washington Rd Ste 210 *TF:* 888-327-8882 ■ *Web:* www.lewis-goetz.com	Pittsburgh	PA	15228	412-341-7100	341-7192
Lipten Company LLC 28054 Ctr Oaks Ct *TF:* 800-860-0790 ■ *Web:* www.lipten.com	Wixom	MI	48393	248-374-8910	374-8906
Lister-Petter Americas Inc 815 E 56 Hwy *Web:* www.lister-petter.com	Olathe	KS	66061	913-764-3512	764-5493
Livingston & Haven 11529 Wilmar Blvd PO Box 7207 *Web:* www.livhaven.com	Charlotte	NC	28273	704-588-3670	504-2530
Logan Corp 555 Seventh Ave. *TF:* 888-853-4751 ■ *Web:* www.logancorp.com	Huntington	WV	25701	304-526-4700	526-4747
M & L Industries Inc 1210 St Charles St *TF General:* 800-969-0068 ■ *Web:* www.mlind.net	Houma	LA	70360	985-876-2280	872-9596
Mac-Gray Corp 404 Wyman St Ste 400 *NYSE:* TUC ■ *TF:* 888-622-4729 ■ *Web:* www.macgray.com	Waltham	MA	02451	781-487-7600	487-7601
Machine & Welding Supply Co 1660 Hwy 301 S PO Box 1708 *Web:* www.mwsc.com	Dunn	NC	28335	910-892-4016	892-3575
Machinery Sales Co 17253 Chestnut St *TF:* 800-588-8111 ■ *Web:* www.mchysales.com	City of Industry	CA	91748	626-581-9211	581-9277
Machinery Systems Inc 614 E State Pkwy. *TF:* 888-650-5424 ■ *Web:* www.machsys.com	Schaumburg	IL	60173	847-882-8085	882-2894
Mack Boring & Parts Co 2365 US Hwy 22 W *Web:* www.mackboring.com	Union	NJ	07083	908-964-0700	964-8475
Mahar Tool Supply Co Inc 112 Williams St *TF:* 800-456-2427 ■ *Web:* www.mahartool.com	Saginaw	MI	48605	989-799-5530	799-0830
Martin Supply Co 200 Appleton Ave *TF:* 800-828-8116 ■ *Web:* www.mscoinc.com	Sheffield	AL	35660	256-383-3131	389-9447
McCall Handling Co 8801 Wise Ave Ste 200 *TF:* 888-870-0685 ■ *Web:* www.mccallhandling.com	Dundalk	MD	21222	410-388-2600	388-2607
McGill Hose & Coupling Inc 41 Benton Dr PO Box 408 *Web:* www.mcgillhose.com	East Longmeadow	MA	01028	413-525-3977	
McKinley Equipment Corp 17611 Armstrong Ave. *TF:* 800-770-6094 ■ *Web:* www.mckinleyequipment.com	Irvine	CA	92614	949-261-9222	250-7301
Medart Inc 124 Manufacturers Dr. **Fax Area Code:* 888 ■ *TF Cust Svc:* 800-888-7181 ■ *Web:* www.medartinc.com	Arnold	MO	63010	636-282-2300	510-3100*
Midway Industrial Supply Inc 51 Wurz Ave *Web:* www.midwayindustries.net	Utica	NY	13502	315-797-6660	
Minnesota Supply Company Inc 6470 Flying Cloud Dr *TF:* 800-869-1028 ■ *Web:* www.mnsupply.com	Eden Prairie	MN	55344	952-828-7300	828-7301
Mitsubishi International Corp 655 Third Ave *Web:* www.mitsubishicorp.com	New York	NY	10017	212-605-2000	
Modern Group Ltd 2501 Durham Rd *TF:* 800-223-3827 ■ *Web:* www.moderngroup.com	Bristol	PA	19007	215-943-9100	943-4978
Motion Industries Inc 1605 Alton Rd *TF:* 800-526-9328 ■ *Web:* www.motionindustries.com	Birmingham	AL	35210	205-956-1122	951-1172
MSC Industrial Direct Co 75 Maxess Rd *NYSE:* MSM ■ **Fax Area Code:* 800 ■ *TF:* 800-645-7270 ■ *Web:* www.mscdirect.com	Melville	NY	11747	516-812-2000	255-5067*
Multiquip Inc 18910 Wilmington Ave *TF:* 800-421-1244 ■ *Web:* www.multiquip.com	Carson	CA	90746	310-537-3700	537-3927
Nachi Robotic Systems Inc 22285 Roethel Dr. *Web:* www.nachirobotics.com	Novi	MI	48375	248-305-6545	305-6542
NC Machinery Co 17025 W Valley Hwy *TF:* 800-562-4735 ■ *Web:* www.ncmachinery.com	Tukwila	WA	98188	425-251-9800	251-5886
Nebraska Machinery Co Inc 3501 S Jeffers St PO Box 809 *TF:* 800-494-9560 ■ *Web:* www.nmc-corp.com	North Platte	NE	69101	308-532-3100	532-3173
Nelson-Jameson Inc 2400 E Fifth St PO Box 647 *TF:* 800-826-8302 ■ *Web:* www.nelsonjameson.com	Marshfield	WI	54449	715-387-1151	387-8746
New England Industrial Truck Inc 195 Wildwood Ave *Web:* www.neit.com	Woburn	MA	01801	781-935-9105	938-3879
Newman's Inc 3003 Texas 225 *TF:* 800-231-3505 ■ *Web:* www.c-a-m.com	Pasadena	TX	77503	713-675-8631	675-1589
Nitta Corporation of America 7605 Nitta Dr *Web:* www.nitta.com	Suwanee	GA	30024	770-497-0212	
NSC International 7090 Central Ave **Fax Area Code:* 800 ■ *TF:* 800-643-1520 ■ *Web:* www.binding.com	Hot Springs	AR	71913	501-525-0133	960-2727*
Nu-Life Environmental Inc PO Box 1527 *TF:* 800-654-1752 ■ *Web:* www.nulifeenv.com	Easley	SC	29641	864-855-5155	295-2707
O Berk Co 3 Milltown Ct. *TF:* 800-631-7392 ■ *Web:* www.oberk.com	Union	NJ	07083	908-851-9500	851-9367
Pacific Power Group 600 S 56th Pl *TF:* 800-882-3860 ■ *Web:* www.pacificdda.com	Ridgefield	WA	98642	360-887-7400	887-5901
Piping & Equipment Inc 9100 Canniff St *TF:* 888-889-9683 ■ *Web:* www.pipingequipment.com	Houston	TX	77017	713-947-9393	
Poclain Hydraulics Inc PO Box 801 *Web:* www.poclain-hydraulics.com	Sturtevant	WI	53177	262-321-0676	554-4860
Premier Equipment Inc 990 Sunshine Ln *Web:* www.premierequipment.com	Altamonte Springs	FL	32714	407-786-2000	786-2001
ProAct Services Corp 1140 Conrad Industrial Dr *Web:* www.proact-usa.com	Ludington	MI	49431	231-843-2711	
Production Tool Supply 8655 E Eight Mile Rd. **Fax:* Sales ■ *TF:* 800-366-3600 ■ *Web:* www.pts-tools.com	Warren	MI	48089	586-755-7770	755-4921*
Provoast Automation Controls 12635 Danielson Court Ste 205 *Web:* www.proautocon.com	Poway	CA	92064	858-748-2237	
R & M Energy Systems 301 Premier Rd **Fax Area Code:* 281 ■ *TF Sales:* 888-262-8645 ■ *Web:* www.rmenergy.com	Borger	TX	79007	806-274-5293	820-0034*
R B M Co 2700 Texas Ave PO Box 12 *TF:* 800-521-5656 ■ *Web:* www.rbmcompany.com	Knoxville	TN	37921	865-524-8621	546-7326
Red Ball Oxygen Co Inc 609 N Market *TF:* 800-551-8150 ■ *Web:* www.redballoxygen.com	Shreveport	LA	71107	318-425-3211	425-6323
Rem Sales Inc 910 Gay Hill Rd *TF:* 877-689-1860 ■ *Web:* www.remsales.com	Windsor	CT	06095	860-687-3400	687-3401
Remstar International Inc 41 Eisenhower Dr **Fax Area Code:* 207 ■ *TF:* 800-639-5805 ■ *Web:* www.kardexremstar.com	Westbrook	ME	04092	800-639-5805	854-1610*
Renishaw Inc 5277 Trillium Blvd *Web:* www.renishaw.com	Hoffman Estates	IL	60192	847-286-9953	286-9974
Rex Supply Co 3715 Harrisburg Blvd *TF:* 800-369-0669 ■ *Web:* www.rex-supply.com	Houston	TX	77003	713-222-2251	225-5739
RHM Fluid Power Inc 375 Manufacturers Dr. *Web:* www.rhmfluidpower.com	Westland	MI	48186	734-326-5400	326-0339
Riekes Equipment Co PO Box 3392 *TF:* 800-856-0931 ■ *Web:* www.riekesequipment.com	Omaha	NE	68103	402-593-1181	593-9295
Road Builders Machinery & Supply Company Inc 1001 S Seventh St *Web:* www.roadbuildersmachinery.com	Kansas City	KS	66105	913-371-3822	371-3870

				Phone	Fax
Robert Dietrick Co Inc PO Box 605	Fishers	IN	46038	317-842-1991	842-2698
TF: 866-767-1888 ■ *Web:* www.rd-co.com					
Robert E Morris Co 910 Gay Hill Rd	Windsor	CT	06095	860-687-3300	687-3301
TF: 877-689-1860 ■ *Web:* www.robertemorris.com					
Royal Bearing Inc 17719 NE Sandy Blvd	Portland	OR	97230	503-231-0992	
Web: www.royalbearing.com					
RS Hughes Company Inc 10639 Glenoaks Blvd	Pacoima	CA	91331	818-686-9111	686-1973
TF: 877-774-8443 ■ *Web:* www.rshughes.com					
Ryan Herco Products Corp 3010 N San Fernando Blvd	Burbank	CA	91504	818-841-1141	973-2600
TF: 800-848-1141 ■ *Web:* www.ryanherco.com					
S&K /Air Power 317 Dewitt Ave E PO Box 1279	Mattoon	IL	61938	217-258-8500	258-8571
Web: www.skairpower.com					
S. J. Smith Company Inc 3707 W River Dr	Davenport	IA	52802	563-263-1829	324-1336
Web: www.sjsmith.com					
S.l.c. Meter Service Inc 10375 Dixie Hwy	Davisburg	MI	48350	248-625-0667	625-8650
TF: 800-433-4332 ■ *Web:* www.slcmeter.com					
Serenity Packaging Corp 1601 E Main St Ste 2E	Saint Charles	IL	60174	630-762-9870	
Web: www.serenitypkg.com					
Service Motor Co PO Box 170	Dale	WI	54931	920-779-4311	667-5330
Web: www.servicemotor.com					
Shively Bros Inc 2919 S Grand Travers St PO Box 1520	Flint	MI	48501	810-232-7401	232-3219
TF: 800-530-9352 ■ *Web:* www.shivelybros.com					
SKS Bottle & Packaging Inc 2600 Seventh Ave Bldg 60 W	Watervliet	NY	12189	518-880-6980	
Web: www.sks-bottle.com					
Smith Power Products Inc 3065 W California Ave	Salt Lake City	UT	84104	801-415-5000	415-5700
TF: 800-658-5352 ■ *Web:* www.smithpowerproducts.com					
So. Cal. Sandbags Inc 12620 Bosley Ln	Corona	CA	92883	951-277-3404	
Web: www.socalsandbags.com					
Sooner Pipe LLC 1331 Lamar St Ste 970 4 Houston Ctr	Houston	TX	77010	713-759-1200	759-0442
TF: 800-888-9161 ■ *Web:* www.soonerpipe.com					
Southern Pump & Tank Co 4800 N Graham St	Charlotte	NC	28269	704-596-4373	599-7700
TF Cust Svc: 800-477-2826 ■ *Web:* www.southernpump.com					
Stanley M Proctor Co 2016 Midway Dr	Twinsburg	OH	44087	330-425-7814	425-3222
Web: www.stanleyproctor.com					
Star CNC Machine Tool Corp 123 Powerhouse Rd	Roslyn Heights	NY	11577	516-484-0500	484-5820
Web: www.starcnc.com					
Strategic Distribution Inc 1414 Radcliffe St Ste 300	Bristol	PA	19007	215-633-1900	633-4426
TF: 800-322-2644 ■ *Web:* www.sdi.com					
Swift Industrial Power Inc 10917 McBride Ln	Knoxville	TN	37932	865-966-9758	
Web: www.swiftpower.com					
Teeco Products Inc 16881 Armstrong Ave	Irvine	CA	92606	949-261-6295	474-8663
TF: 800-854-3463 ■ *Web:* www.teecoproducts.com					
Tencarva Machinery Company Inc 12200 Wilfong Ct	Midlothian	VA	23112	804-639-4646	639-2400
Web: www.tencarva.com					
Texas Process Equipment Co 5215 Ted St	Houston	TX	77040	713-460-5555	460-4807
TF: 800-828-4114 ■ *Web:* www.texasprocess.com					
TF Hudgins Inc 4405 Directors Row	Houston	TX	77092	713-682-3651	
Web: www.tfhudgins.com					
Timco Rubber Products Inc 12300 Sprecher Ave	Cleveland	OH	44135	216-267-6242	
Web: www.timcorubber.com					
Tool Service Corp 2942 N 117th St	Milwaukee	WI	53226	414-476-7600	
Web: www.toolservice.com					
Total Equipment Co 400 Fifth Ave	Coraopolis	PA	15108	412-269-0999	269-0262
Web: www.totalequipment.com					
Total Filtration Services Inc 2725 Commerce Pkwy	Auburn Hills	MI	48326	248-377-4004	
Web: www.tfsi1.com					
Tox-Pressotechnik LLC 4250 Weaver Pkwy	Warrenville	IL	60555	630-393-0300	393-6800
Web: www.tox-us.com					
Travers Tool Company Inc 128-15 26th Ave	Flushing	NY	11354	718-886-7200	722-0703*
**Fax Area Code:* 800 ■ *TF Cust Svc:* 800-221-0270 ■ *Web:* www.travers.com					
Trio Pines U.S.A. Inc 16233 Heron Ave	La Mirada	CA	90638	714-523-5800	
Web: www.triopines.com					
Troy Belting & Supply Co 70 Cohoes Rd	Watervliet	NY	12189	518-272-4920	
Web: www.troyindustrialsolutions.com					
Turck Inc 3000 Campus Dr	Minneapolis	MN	55441	763-553-7300	553-0708
Web: www.turck.com					
Ulvac Technologies Inc 401 Griffin Brook Dr	Methuen	MA	01844	978-686-7550	689-6300
Web: www.ulvac.com					
Valtra Inc 7141 Paramount Blvd	Pico Rivera	CA	90660	562-949-8625	
TF: 800-989-5244 ■ *Web:* www.valtrainc.com					
Vellano Bros Inc Seven Hemlock St	Latham	NY	12110	518-785-5537	785-5578
TF: 800-342-9855 ■ *Web:* www.vellano.com					
Voto Manufacturers Sales Co 500 N Third St PO Box 1299	Steubenville	OH	43952	740-282-3621	282-5441
TF: 800-848-4010 ■ *Web:* www.votosales.com					
W.P. & R.S. Mars Co 4319 W First St	Duluth	MN	55807	218-628-0303	
Web: www.marssupply.com					
Waukesha-Pearce Industries Inc (WPI) 12320 S Main	Houston	TX	77235	713-723-1050	551-0454
Web: www.wpi.com					
WELSCO Inc 9006 Crystal Hill Rd	North Little Rock	AR	72113	501-771-1204	
Web: www.welsco.com					
Werres Corp 807 E S St	Frederick	MD	21701	301-620-4000	662-1028*
**Fax:* Sales ■ *TF:* 800-638-6563 ■ *Web:* www.werres.com					
Wilson Supply Co 1302 Conti St	Houston	TX	77002	713-237-3700	
TF: 800-874-5930					
Wind River Holdings LP 555 Croton Rd Croton Rd Corporate Ctr Ste 300	King Of Prussia	PA	19406	610-962-3770	
Web: www.windriverholdings.com					
Windsor Factory Supply Ltd 730 N Service Rd	Windsor	ON	N8X3J3	519-966-2202	966-2740
TF: 800-387-2659 ■ *Web:* www.wfsltd.com					
Yamazen Inc 735 E Remington Rd	Schaumburg	IL	60173	847-490-8130	490-3192
TF: 800-882-8558 ■ *Web:* www.yamazen.com					
Yanmar America Corp 101 International Pkwy	Adairsville	GA	30103	770-877-9894	877-9009
Web: www.yanmar.com					
Zatkoff Seals & Packings 23230 Industrial Pk Dr	Farmington Hills	MI	48335	248-478-2400	478-3392
Web: www.zatkoff.com					
Zuckerman Honickman 191 S Gulph Rd	King Of Prussia	PA	19406	610-962-0100	962-1080
Web: www.zh-inc.com					

389 INDUSTRIAL MACHINERY, EQUIPMENT, & SUPPLIES

SEE ALSO Conveyors & Conveying Equipment p. 2165; Food Products Machinery p. 2319; Furnaces & Ovens - Industrial Process p. 2343; Machine Shops p. 2680; Material Handling Equipment p. 2720; Packaging Machinery & Equipment p. 2849; Paper Industries Machinery p. 2855; Printing & Publishing Equipment & Systems p. 2975; Rolling Mill Machinery p. 3129; Textile Machinery p. 3230; Woodworking Machinery p. 3301

				Phone	Fax
3G Tech Inc 6910 Hayvenhurst Ave Unit 100	Van Nuys	CA	91406	818-510-4709	510-4716
Web: www.gggtech.com					
ABB Inc 501 Merritt 7	Norwalk	CT	06851	203-750-2200	435-7365
TF Prod Info: 800-626-4999 ■ *Web:* new.abb.com/us					
Accu Therm Inc PO Box 249	Monroe City	MO	63456	573-735-1060	735-1066
TF: 888-925-4332 ■ *Web:* www.accutherm.com					
Acme Electric N85 W12545 Westbrook Crossing	Menomonee Falls	WI	53051	910-738-1121	293-7022*
**Fax Area Code:* 262 ■ *TF:* 800-334-5214 ■ *Web:* acmetransformer.com					
Acorn Gencon Plastics Inc 15125 Proctor Ave	City of Industry	CA	91746	626-968-6681	855-4860
Web: www.whitehallmfg.com					
Adept Technology Inc 5960 Inglewood Dr	Pleasanton	CA	94588	925-245-3400	960-0452
NASDAQ: ADEP ■ *TF:* 800-292-3378 ■ *Web:* www.adept.com					
Advent Design Corp Canal St & Jefferson Ave	Bristol	PA	19007	215-781-0500	781-0508
Web: adventdesign.com					
Aeroglide Corp 100 Aeroglide Dr	Cary	NC	27511	919-851-2000	851-6029
TF: 800-722-7483 ■ *Web:* www.buhlergroup.com					
Airtech International Inc 5700 Skylab Rd	Huntington Beach	CA	92647	714-899-8100	899-8179
Web: www.airtechintl.com					
Alemite LLC 1057-521 Corporate Ctr Dr Ste 100	Fort Mill	SC	29715	803-802-0001	802-0246
TF: 800-267-8022 ■ *Web:* www.alemite.com					
Allen-Sherman-Hoff Co 457 Creamery Way	Exton	PA	19341	484-875-1600	875-2080
Web: www.diamondpower.com					
Allentown Equipment 1733 90th St	Sturtevant	WI	53177	800-553-3414	884-3070*
**Fax Area Code:* 262 ■ *TF:* 800-553-3414 ■ *Web:* www.putzmeisteramerica.com					
Allentown Inc 165 County Rd	Allentown	NJ	08501	609-259-7951	259-0449
Web: www.allentowninc.com					
American Baler Co 800 E Centre St	Bellevue	OH	44811	419-483-5790	483-3815
TF: 800-843-7512 ■ *Web:* www.americanbaler.com					
AO Smith Water Products Co 500 Tennessee Waltz Pkwy	Ashland City	TN	37015	800-527-1953	792-2163*
**Fax Area Code:* 615 ■ *TF:* 800-527-1953 ■ *Web:* www.hotwater.com					
Apache Stainless Equipment Corp 200 W Industrial Dr PO Box 538	Beaver Dam	WI	53916	920-356-9900	887-0206
TF: 800-444-0398 ■ *Web:* www.apachestainless.com					
Ats Systems Oregon Inc 2121 NE Jack London St	Corvallis	OR	97330	541-758-3329	758-9022
TF: 800-564-6253 ■ *Web:* www.atsautomation.com					
Auto Chlor System 450 Ferguson Dr	Mountain View	CA	94043	650-967-3085	
Web: autochlor.net					
Azon USA Inc 643 W Crosstown Pkwy	Kalamazoo	MI	49008	269-385-5942	373-9295
TF: 800-788-5942 ■ *Web:* www.azonintl.com					
Bauer-Pileco Inc 100 N FM 3083 E	Conroe	TX	77303	713-691-3000	691-0089
TF: 800-474-5326 ■ *Web:* www.bauerpileco.com					
Besser Co 801 Johnson St	Alpena	MI	49707	989-354-4111	354-3120
TF: 800-530-9980 ■ *Web:* www.besser.com					
Billco Manufacturing Inc 100 Halstead Blvd	Zelienople	PA	16063	724-452-7390	452-0217
Web: www.billco-mfg.com					
Blower Application Company Inc N 114 W 19125 Clinton Dr	Germantown	WI	53022	262-255-5580	255-3446
TF: 800-959-0880 ■ *Web:* www.bloapco.com					
Burke E Porter Machinery Co 730 Plymouth Ave NE	Grand Rapids	MI	49505	616-234-1200	459-1032
Web: www.bepco.com					
CHA Industries 4201 Business Ctr Dr	Fremont	CA	94538	510-683-8554	683-3848*
**Fax:* Sales ■ *Web:* www.chaindustries.com					
Charles Ross & Son Co 710 Old Willets Path	Hauppauge	NY	11788	631-234-0500	234-0691
TF: 800-243-7677 ■ *Web:* www.mixers.com					
Chemineer Inc 5870 Poe Ave	Dayton	OH	45414	937-454-3200	454-3379*
**Fax:* Sales ■ *TF:* 800-643-0641 ■ *Web:* www.chemineer.com					
Chemithon Corp 5430 W Marginal Way SW	Seattle	WA	98106	206-937-9954	932-3786
Web: www.chemithon.com					
Chief Automotive Systems Inc 1924 E Fourth St	Grand Island	NE	68802	308-384-9747	384-8966*
**Fax:* Mktg ■ *TF:* 800-445-9262 ■ *Web:* www.chiefautomotive.com					
Clean Diesel Technologies Inc 4567 Telephone Rd Ste 206	Ventura	CA	93003	805-639-9458	707-7746*
NASDAQ: CDTI ■ **Fax Area Code:* 905 ■ *TF:* 800-661-9963 ■ *Web:* www.cdti.com					
Clemco Industries Corp I Cable Car Dr	Washington	MO	63090	636-239-0300	726-7559*
**Fax Area Code:* 800 ■ *Web:* www.clemcoindustries.com					
CMA Dishmachines 12700 Knott St	Garden Grove	CA	92841	714-898-8781	891-9836
TF: 800-854-6417 ■ *Web:* www.cmadishmachines.com					
Corotec Corp 145 Hyde Rd	Farmington	CT	06032	860-678-0038	674-5229
TF: 800-423-0348 ■ *Web:* www.corotec.com					

Company	City	State	ZIP	Phone	Fax
CUNO Inc 400 Research Pkwy *TF:* 800-243-6894 ■ *Web:* solutions.3m.com	Meriden	CT	06450	203-237-5541	238-8701
Davis-Ulmer Sprinkler Company Inc One Commerce Dr *TF:* 877-691-3200 ■ *Web:* www.davisulmer.com	Amherst	NY	14228	716-691-3200	691-1230
Despatch Industries Inc 8860 207th St W *TF:* 800-726-0110 ■ *Web:* www.despatch.com	Lakeville	MN	55044	952-469-5424	469-4513
Diamond Power International Inc 2600 E Main St *TF:* 800-848-5086 ■ *Web:* www.diamondpower.com	Lancaster	OH	43130	740-687-6500	687-4229
Dings Co 4740 W Electric Ave *TF:* 800-494-1918 ■ *Web:* www.dingsbrakes.com	Milwaukee	WI	53219	414-672-7830	672-7830
Dom-Ex LLC 109 Grant St PO Box 877 *Web:* www.dom-ex.com	Hibbing	MN	55746	218-262-6116	263-8611
Dresser-Rand 10205 Westheimer Rd W 8 Twr Ste 1000 *NYSE: DRC* ■ *Web:* www.dresser-rand.com	Houston	TX	77042	713-354-6100	354-6110
Dynamic Manufacturing Inc 1930 N Mannheim Rd *Web:* www.dynamicmanufacturinginc.com	Melrose Park	IL	60160	708-343-8753	343-8768
Easom Automation Systems Inc 32471 Industrial Dr *Web:* www.easomeng.com	Madison Heights	MI	48071	248-307-0650	307-0701
Ecodyne Ltd 4475 Corporate Dr *TF:* 888-326-3963 ■ *Web:* www.ecodyne.com	Burlington	ON	L7L5T9	905-332-1404	332-6726
EFD Induction Inc 31511 Dequindre Rd *Web:* www.efd-induction.com	Madison Heights	MI	48071	248-658-0700	658-0701
Elliott Tape Inc 1882 Pond Run *Web:* www.egitape.com	Auburn Hills	MI	48326	248-475-2000	475-5893
Enerflex Systems Ltd 1331 Macleod Trail SE Ste 904 *TSE: EFX* ■ *TF:* 800-242-3178 ■ *Web:* www.enerflex.com	Calgary	AB	T2G0K3	403-387-6377	236-6816
Energy Sciences Inc 42 Industrial Way *Web:* www.ebeam.com	Wilmington	MA	01887	978-694-9000	694-9046
Engis Corp 105 W Hintz Rd *TF:* 800-993-6447 ■ *Web:* www.engis.com	Wheeling	IL	60090	847-808-9400	808-9430
Enterprise Co 616 S Santa Fe St *Web:* www.enterpriseco.com	Santa Ana	CA	92705	714-835-0541	543-2856
Entwistle Co, The Six Bigelow St *Web:* www.entwistleco.com	Hudson	MA	01749	508-481-4000	481-4004
Equipment Manufacturing Corp (EMC) 14930 Marquardt Ave *TF:* 888-833-9000 ■ *Web:* www.equipmentmanufacturing.com	Santa Fe Springs	CA	90670	562-623-9394	623-9342
FANUC America Corp 3900 W Hamlin Rd *TF:* 800-477-6268 ■ *Web:* www.fanucrobotics.com	Rochester Hills	MI	48309	248-377-7000	377-7832
Farrel Corp 25 Main St *TF:* 800-800-7290 ■ *Web:* www.farrel-pomini.com	Ansonia	CT	06401	203-736-5500	736-5580
Fluid Management Inc 1023 S Wheeling Rd *TF:* 800-462-2466 ■ *Web:* www.fluidman.com	Wheeling	IL	60090	847-537-0880	537-3221
Formaloy Corp 1080 W Jefferson St	Morton	IL	61550	309-266-5381	
Forward Technology Inc 260 Jenks Ave *TF Cust Svc:* 800-307-6040 ■ *Web:* www.forwardtech.com	Cokato	MN	55321	320-286-2578	286-2467
Foster Wheeler Energy International Inc Perryville Corporate Pk *Web:* www.fwc.com	Clinton	NJ	08809	908-730-4000	730-5315
French Oil Mill Machinery Co 1035 W Greene St *Web:* www.frenchoil.com	Piqua	OH	45356	937-773-3420	773-3424
Fusion Inc 4658 E 355th St *TF:* 800-626-9501 ■ *Web:* www.fusion-inc.com	Willoughby	OH	44094	440-946-3300	942-9083
Gamajet Cleaning Systems Inc 604 Jeffers Cir *TF Sales:* 877-426-2538 ■ *Web:* www.gamajet.com	Exton	PA	19341	610-408-9940	408-9945
GEA Niro Inc 9165 Rumsey Rd *Web:* www.niroinc.com	Columbia	MD	21045	410-997-8700	997-5021
General Equipment Co 620 Alexander Dr SW PO Box 334 *TF Cust Svc:* 800-533-0524 ■ *Web:* www.generalequip.com	Owatonna	MN	55060	507-451-5510	451-5511
Genmark Automation Inc 1201 Cadillac Ct *TF:* 866-467-6268 ■ *Web:* www.genmarkautomation.com	Milpitas	CA	95035	408-678-8500	942-7561
George Koch Sons LLC 10 S 11th Ave **Fax:* Sales ■ *TF:* 888-873-5624 ■ *Web:* www.kochllc.com	Evansville	IN	47712	812-465-9600	465-9814*
Gerber Scientific Inc 24 Industrial Pk Rd W *Web:* www.gerberscientific.com	Tolland	CT	06084	860-870-2890	
Glastender Inc 5400 N Michigan Rd *TF:* 800-748-0423 ■ *Web:* www.glastender.com	Saginaw	MI	48604	989-752-4275	752-4444
Globe Products Inc 5051 Kitridge Rd *Web:* www.globe-usa.com	Dayton	OH	45424	937-233-0233	233-5290
Glunt Industries Inc 319 N River Rd NW *Web:* www.glunt.com	Warren	OH	44483	330-399-7585	393-0387
Gougler Industries Inc 711 Lake St *TF:* 800-527-2282 ■ *Web:* www.frdusa.com	Kent	OH	44240	330-673-5826	677-1616
Graham Corp 20 Florence Ave *NYSE: GHM* ■ *TF Orders:* 800-828-8150 ■ *Web:* www.graham-mfg.com	Batavia	NY	14020	585-343-2216	343-1097
Gregory Poole Equipment Co 4807 Beryl Rd PO Box 469 *TF:* 800-451-7278 ■ *Web:* www.gregorypoole.com	Raleigh	NC	27606	919-828-0641	890-4621
Grenzebach Corp 10 Herring Rd *Web:* www.grenzebach.com	Newnan	GA	30265	770-253-4980	253-5189
Guzzler Manufacturing Inc 1621 S Illinois St **Fax:* Sales ■ *Web:* www.guzzler.com	Streator	IL	61364	815-672-3171	672-2779*
GWI Engineering Inc 1411 Michigan St NE *Web:* www.gwiengineering.com	Grand Rapids	MI	49503	616-459-8274	459-3390
Hamon Research-Cottrell Inc 58 E Main St *TF:* 800-722-7580 ■ *Web:* www.hamon-researchcottrell.com	Somerville	NJ	08876	908-685-4000	333-2152
Harrington Hoists Inc 401 W End Ave *TF:* 800-233-3010 ■ *Web:* www.harringtonhoists.com	Manheim	PA	17545	717-665-2000	665-2861
Helgesen Industries Inc 7261 Hwy 60 W *Web:* www.helgesen.com	Hartford	WI	53027	262-673-4444	709-4409
Hfw Industries Inc 196 Philadelphia St PO Box 8 *TF:* 800-937-9311 ■ *Web:* www.hfwindustries.com	Buffalo	NY	14207	716-875-3380	875-3385
Hirotec America Inc 4567 Glenmeade Ln *Web:* www.hirotecamerica.com	Auburn Hills	MI	48326	248-836-5100	836-5101
Hosokawa Micron Powder Systems 10 Chatham Rd *Web:* www.hosokawamicron.com	Summit	NJ	07901	908-273-6360	273-6344
Hosokawa Polymer Systems 63 Fuller Way *TF:* 800-233-6112 ■ *Web:* www.polysys.com	Berlin	CT	06037	860-828-0541	829-1313
Husky Injection Molding Systems Ltd 500 Queen St S *Web:* www.husky.co	Bolton	ON	L7E5S5	905-951-5000	951-5384
Hydro-Thermal Corp 400 Pilot Ct *TF:* 800-952-0121 ■ *Web:* www.hydro-thermal.com	Waukesha	WI	53188	262-548-8900	548-8908
Illinois Tool Works Inc (ITW) 3600 W Lake Ave *NYSE: ITW* ■ *Web:* www.itw.com	Glenview	IL	60026	847-724-7500	657-4261
Industrial Fabricators Inc 403 N Cemetery St *Web:* industrialfabinc.com	Thorp	WI	54771	715-669-5512	669-5514
ITW United Silicone 4471 Walden Ave *Web:* www.unitedsilicone.com	Lancaster	NY	14086	716-681-8222	681-8789
Jesco-Wipco Industries Inc 950 Anderson Rd PO Box 388 *TF:* 800-455-0019 ■ *Web:* www.jescoonline.com	Litchfield	MI	49252	517-542-2903	542-2501
JV Manufacturing Inc 1603 Burtner Rd PO Box 229 **Fax Area Code:* 479	Natrona Heights	PA	15065	724-224-1704	872-0037*
K & B Machine Works Inc 212 Redmond Rd PO Box 10265 *TF:* 800-256-1526 ■ *Web:* www.kb-machine.com	Houma	LA	70363	985-868-6730	851-7863
Kanematsu USA Inc 500 Fifth Ave 29th Fl *Web:* www.kanematsuusa.com	New York	NY	10110	212-704-9400	704-9483
Kawasaki Robotics Inc 28140 Lakeview Dr *Web:* www.kawasakirobotics.com	Wixom	MI	48393	248-446-4100	446-4200
Kobelco Stewart Bolling Inc (KSBI) 1600 Terex Rd *TF:* 800-464-0064 ■ *Web:* www.ksbiusa.com	Hudson	OH	44236	330-655-3111	655-2982
Koch Membrane Systems Inc 850 Main St *TF:* 888-677-5624 ■ *Web:* www.kochmembrane.com	Wilmington	MA	01887	978-694-7000	657-5208
Koch-Glitsch Inc 4111 E 37th St N *Web:* www.koch-glitsch.com	Wichita	KS	67220	316-828-5110	828-5263
Kois Bros Equipment Company Inc 5200 Colorado Blvd *TF:* 800-672-6010 ■ *Web:* www.koisbrothers.com	Commerce City	CO	80022	303-298-7370	298-8527
Komatsu America Industries LLC 1701 W Golf Rd Ste 300 *Web:* www.komatsupress.com	Rolling Meadows	IL	60008	847-437-3888	437-1811
Komline-Sanderson Engineering Corp 12 Holland Ave *TF:* 800-225-5457 ■ *Web:* www.komline.com	Peapack	NJ	07977	908-234-1000	234-9487
Lawton Industries Inc 4353 Pacific St *TF:* 800-692-2600 ■ *Web:* www.lawtonindustries.com	Rocklin	CA	95677	916-624-7895	624-7898
Lee Industries Inc 50 W Pine St *Web:* www.leeind.com	Philipsburg	PA	16866	814-342-0461	342-5660
Lesman Instrument Co 135 Bernice Dr *TF:* 800-953-7626 ■ *Web:* www.lesman.com	Bensenville	IL	60106	630-595-8400	595-2386
Leviathan Corp 20 Jay St *Web:* www.leviathancorp.com	Brooklyn	NY	11201	718-701-5718	701-5745
Lightnin 135 Mt Read Blvd *TF:* 877-247-3797 ■ *Web:* www.spx.com	Rochester	NY	14611	585-436-5550	436-5589
Ligon Industries LLC 1927 First Ave N Fifth Fl *Web:* www.ligonindustries.com	Birmingham	AL	35203	205-322-3302	322-3188
Lincoln Industrial Corp One Lincoln Way **Fax Area Code:* 800 ■ **Fax:* Cust Svc ■ *Web:* www.lincolnindustrial.com	Saint Louis	MO	63120	314-679-4200	424-5359*
Littleford Day Inc 7451 Empire Dr *TF:* 800-365-8555 ■ *Web:* www.littleford.com	Florence	KY	41042	859-525-7600	525-1446
Lmt USA Inc 1081 S Northpoint Blvd **Fax Area Code:* 630 ■ *Web:* www.lmtfette.com	Waukegan	IL	60085	800-225-0852	969-5492*
Marathon Equipment Co PO Box 1798 *TF:* 800-633-8974 ■ *Web:* www.marathonequipment.com	Vernon	AL	35592	205-695-9105	695-8813
Mark-Costello Co, The 1145 E Dominguez St *Web:* www.mark-costello.com	Carson	CA	90746	310-637-1851	762-2330
Maruka USA Inc 400 Commons Way *TF:* 800-631-0426 ■ *Web:* www.marukausa.com	Rockaway	NJ	07866	973-983-1000	983-8647
Materials Transportation Co (MTC) 1408 S Commerce PO Box 1358 *TF:* 800-433-3110 ■ *Web:* www.mtcworldwide.com	Temple	TX	76503	254-298-2900	771-0287
McCarty Equipment Co Ltd 1103 Industrial Blvd PO Box 1841 *Web:* www.mccartyequipment.com	Abilene	TX	79602	325-691-5558	691-5453
McNeil & NRM Inc 96 E Crosier St *TF:* 800-669-2525 ■ *Web:* www.mcneilnrm.com	Akron	OH	44311	330-253-2525	253-7022
MEGTEC Systems Inc 830 Prosper Rd *TF Cust Svc:* 800-558-5535 ■ *Web:* www.megtec.com	De Pere	WI	54115	920-336-5715	339-2784
Metem Corp 700 Parsippany Rd *Web:* www.metem.com	Parsippany	NJ	07054	973-887-6635	887-1755
MFRI Inc 7720 N Lehigh Ave *NASDAQ: MFRI* ■ *Web:* www.mfri.com	Niles	IL	60714	847-966-1000	966-8563
Michigan Fluid Power Inc 4556 Spartan Industrial Dr SW *TF:* 800-635-0289 ■ *Web:* www.mifp.com	Grandville	MI	49418	616-538-5700	538-0888
Michigan Wheel Corp 1501 Buchanan Ave SW *TF:* 800-369-4335 ■ *Web:* www.miwheel.com	Grand Rapids	MI	49507	616-452-6941	247-0227
Mico Inc 1911 Lee Blvd *TF:* 800-477-6426 ■ *Web:* www.mico.com	North Mankato	MN	56003	507-625-6426	625-3212
Micro-Poise Measurment Systems LLC 1624 Englewood Ave *TF:* 800-428-3812 ■ *Web:* www.micropoise.com	Akron	OH	44305	330-784-1251	798-0250
Milacron Inc 3010 Disney St *Web:* www.milacron.com	Cincinnati	OH	45209	513-487-5000	487-5086
Minuteman International Inc 111 S Rohlwing Rd *TF:* 800-323-9420 ■ *Web:* www.minutemanintl.com	Addison	IL	60101	630-627-6900	627-1130
Mississippi Welders Supply Co 5150 W Sixth St PO Box 1036 *TF:* 800-657-4422 ■ *Web:* store.mwsco.com	Winona	MN	55987	507-454-5231	454-8104

Company	City	State	Zip	Phone	Fax
Monroe Environmental Corp 810 W Front St *TF:* 800-992-7707 ■ *Web:* www.monroeenvironmental.com	Monroe	MI	48161	734-242-7654	242-5275
Moody-Price LLC 18320 Petroleum Dr **Fax Area Code:* 225 ■ *TF:* 800-272-9832 ■ *Web:* www.moodyprice.com	Baton Rouge	LA	70809	800-272-9832	763-6005*
Morrell Inc 333 Bald Mtn Rd *Web:* www.morrellinc.com	Auburn Hills	MI	48326	248-373-1600	373-0612
Mueller Graphic Supply Inc 11475 W Thdore Trcker Way *Web:* www.muellergraphics.com	Milwaukee	WI	53214	414-475-0990	475-0454
Mueller Steam Specialty 1491 NC Hwy 20 W *TF:* 800-334-6259 ■ *Web:* www.muellersteam.com	Saint Pauls	NC	28384	910-865-8241	865-8245
National Super Service Company Inc 3115 Frenchman Rd *TF Cust Svc:* 800-677-1663 ■ *Web:* www.nss.com	Toledo	OH	43607	419-531-2121	531-3761
Netzsch Inc 119 Pickering Way *Web:* www.netzschusa.com	Exton	PA	19341	610-363-8010	363-0971
Neumayer Equipment Company Inc 5060 Arsenal St *TF:* 800-843-4563 ■ *Web:* www.neumayerequipment.com	Saint Louis	MO	63139	314-772-4501	772-2311
Nexen Group Inc 560 Oak Grove Pkwy *TF:* 800-843-7445 ■ *Web:* www.nexengroup.com	Vadnais Heights	MN	55127	651-484-5900	286-1099
Nilfisk-Advance Inc 14600 21st Ave N *TF Cust Svc:* 800-989-2235 ■ *Web:* www.nilfisk.com/en	Plymouth	MN	55447	800-989-2235	989-6566
Nordson Corp 28601 Clemens Rd *NASDAQ: NDSN* ■ *TF:* 800-321-2881 ■ *Web:* www.nordson.com	Westlake	OH	44145	440-892-1580	892-9507
North Light Color Inc 5008 Hillsboro Ave N *Web:* www.northlightcolor.com	Minneapolis	MN	55428	763-531-8222	531-8224
Oil & Gas Equipment Corp Eight Rd 350 *TF:* 800-868-9624 ■ *Web:* www.ogequip.com	Flora Vista	NM	87415	505-333-2300	333-2301
Oscar Wilson Engines & Parts Inc 826 Lone Star Dr **Fax Area Code:* 800 ■ *TF:* 800-233-3723 ■ *Web:* www.oscar-wilson.com	O Fallon	MO	63366	636-978-1313	873-6720*
Ovivo Inc 2001 Mc Gill College Ste 2100 *TSE: OVI.A* ■ *Web:* www.glv.com	Montreal	QC	H3A1G1	514-284-2224	284-2225
Pall Corp 2200 Northern Blvd *NYSE: PLL* ■ *TF:* 800-645-6532 ■ *Web:* www.pall.com	East Hills	NY	11548	516-484-5400	801-9754
Parker Industries Inc 1650 Sycamore Ave *Web:* www.parkerind.com	Bohemia	NY	11716	631-567-1000	567-1355
Parkson Corp 1401 W Cypress Creek Rd **Fax Area Code:* 954 ■ *TF:* 888-727-5766 ■ *Web:* www.parkson.com	Fort Lauderdale	FL	33309	888-727-5766	974-6182*
Paul Mueller Co 1600 W Phelps St *OTC: MUEL* ■ *TF:* 800-683-5537 ■ *Web:* www.muel.com	Springfield	MO	65802	417-831-3000	831-3528
PDQ Manufacturing Inc 1698 Scheuring Rd *TF:* 800-227-3373 ■ *Web:* www.pdqinc.com	De Pere	WI	54115	920-983-8333	983-8330
Peach State Integrated Technologies Inc 3005 Business Pk Dr *TF:* 800-998-6517 ■ *Web:* www.peachstate.com	Norcross	GA	30071	678-327-2000	327-2030
Peerless Manufacturing Co 14651 N Dallas Pkwy Ste 500 *NASDAQ: PMFG* ■ *TF:* 877-879-7634 ■ *Web:* www.peerlessmfg.com	Dallas	TX	75254	214-357-6181	351-0194
Pengate Handling Systems Inc Three Interchange Pl *Web:* www.pengate.com	York	PA	17406	717-764-3050	764-5854
Permadur Industries Inc 186 Rt 206 S *TF:* 800-392-0146 ■ *Web:* www.permadur.com	Hillsborough	NJ	08844	908-359-9767	359-9773
Perry Videx LLC 25 Mount Laurel Rd *Web:* www.perryvidex.com	Hainesport	NJ	08036	609-267-1600	267-4499
Peterson Machine Tool Inc 1100 N Union St **Fax Area Code:* 620 ■ *TF:* 800-835-3528 ■ *Web:* petersonwashandblast.com	Council Grove	KS	66846	800-835-3528	767-6415*
Pfaudler Inc 1000 W Ave *Web:* www.pfaudler.com	Rochester	NY	14611	585-235-1000	235-6393
Phillips Machine Service Inc 367 George St *TF:* 800-733-1521 ■ *Web:* www.phillipsmachine.com	Beckley	WV	25801	304-255-0537	255-0565
Phoenix Process Equipment Co 2402 Watterson Trial *Web:* www.dewater.com	Louisville	KY	40299	502-499-6198	499-1079
Pioneer/Eclipse Corp One Eclipse Rd *TF Cust Svc:* 800-367-3550 ■ *Web:* pioneereclipse.com/	Sparta	NC	28675	336-372-8080	372-2895
Pipe & Tube Supply Inc 1407 N Cypress *TF:* 800-770-8823 ■ *Web:* www.pipeandtubesupply.com	North Little Rock	AR	72114	501-372-6556	372-7694
Powerboss Inc 175 Anderson St *Web:* powerboss.com	Aberdeen	NC	28315	910-944-2105	944-7409
PPC Industries - Electrostatic Precipitator 3000 E Marshall Ave *Web:* www.ppcesp.com	Longview	TX	75601	903-758-3395	758-6487
Premier Safety & Service Inc Two Industrial Pk Dr *TF:* 800-828-1080 ■ *Web:* www.premiersafety.com	Oakdale	PA	15071	724-693-8699	693-8698
PSB Industries Inc PO Box 1318 *Web:* www.psbindustries.com	Erie	PA	16512	814-453-3651	455-9082
PTI Technologies Inc 501 Del Norte Blvd *TF:* 800-331-2701 ■ *Web:* www.ptitechnologies.com	Oxnard	CA	93030	805-604-3700	604-3701
Pullman/Holt Corp 10702 N 46th St *TF:* 800-237-7582 ■ *Web:* www.pullman-holt.com	Tampa	FL	33617	813-971-2223	971-6090
R&R Products Inc 3334 E Milber St *TF:* 800-528-3446 ■ *Web:* www.rrproducts.com	Tucson	AZ	85714	520-889-3593	294-1045
R-V Industries Inc 584 Poplar Rd **Fax:* Sales ■ *Web:* www.rvii.com	Honey Brook	PA	19344	610-273-2457	273-3361*
Retech Systems LLC 100 Henry Stn Rd *Web:* www.retechsystemsllc.com	Ukiah	CA	95482	707-462-6522	
Roberts Sinto Corp 3001 W Main St *Web:* www.robertssinto.com	Lansing	MI	48917	517-371-2460	371-4930
Rockford Industrial Welding Supply Inc 4646 Linden Rd *TF:* 800-226-1904 ■ *Web:* www.riws.com	Rockford	IL	61109	815-226-1900	226-5617
Rotary Lift 2700 Lanier Dr *TF:* 800-445-5438 ■ *Web:* www.rotarylift.com	Madison	IN	47250	812-273-1622	273-3404
SAES Pure Gas Inc 4175 Santa Fe Rd *Web:* www.saespuregas.com	San Luis Obispo	CA	93401	805-541-9299	541-9399
Salem Tools Inc 1602 Midland Rd *TF:* 800-390-4348 ■ *Web:* www.salemtools.com	Salem	VA	24153	540-389-0233	375-3807
Salvagnini America Inc 27 Bicentennial Ct *Web:* www.salvagnini.com	Hamilton	OH	45015	513-874-8284	874-2229
Schutte & Koerting LLC 2510 Metropolitan *Web:* www.s-k.com	Feasterville Trevose	PA	19053	215-639-0900	639-1597
Scott Fetzer Co 28800 Clemens Rd *Web:* scottfetzer.com	Westlake	OH	44145	440-892-3000	892-3033
Senior Flexonics Inc Metal Bellows Div 1075 Providence Hwy *Web:* www.metalbellows.com	Sharon	MA	02067	781-784-1400	784-1405
Sentry Equipment & Erectors Inc 13150 E Lynchburg Salem Tpke *Web:* www.sentryequipment.com	Forest	VA	24551	434-525-0769	525-1701
Shop-Vac Corp 2323 Reach Rd *TF:* 800-356-0783 ■ *Web:* www.shopvac.com	Williamsport	PA	17701	570-326-0502	321-7089
SJF Material Handling Equipment 211 Baker Ave *TF:* 800-598-5532 ■ *Web:* www.sjf.com	Winsted	MN	55395	320-485-2824	485-2832
Sterling Production Control Units 2280 W Dorothy Ln *TF:* 800-968-7728 ■ *Web:* www.pcuinc.com	Dayton	OH	45439	937-299-5594	299-3843
STI Electronics Inc 261 Palmer Rd *TF:* 888-650-3006 ■ *Web:* www.solderingtech.com	Madison	AL	35758	256-461-9191	461-7524
Strasbaugh 825 Buckley Rd *OTC: STRB* ■ *Web:* www.strasbaugh.com	San Luis Obispo	CA	93401	805-541-6424	541-6425
Super Products LLC 17000 W Cleveland Ave *TF:* 800-837-9711 ■ *Web:* www.superproductsllc.com	New Berlin	WI	53151	262-784-7100	784-9561
Superior Crane Corp (SCC) 208 Wilmont Dr PO Box 1464 *Web:* www.superiorcrane.com	Waukesha	WI	53189	262-542-0099	542-7767
Swiss Precision Instruments Inc 11450 Markon Dr **Fax Area Code:* 800 ■ *TF:* 888-774-8200 ■ *Web:* www.swissprec.com	Garden Grove	CA	92841	714-799-1555	842-5164*
Synventive Molding Solutions Inc 10 Centennial Dr *TF:* 800-367-5662 ■ *Web:* www.synventive.com	Peabody	MA	01960	978-750-8065	646-3600
Tennant Co 701 N Lilac Dr *NYSE: TNC* ■ *TF Cust Svc:* 800-553-8033 ■ *Web:* www.tennantco.com	Minneapolis	MN	55422	763-540-1200	540-1437
Thermotron Industries Co 291 Kollen Pk Dr *Web:* www.thermotron.com	Holland	MI	49423	616-393-4580	392-5643
Thomas Engineering Inc 575 W Central Rd *TF:* 800-634-9910 ■ *Web:* www.thomaseng.com	Hoffman Estates	IL	60192	847-358-5800	358-5817
Thompson International Inc PO Box 656 *TF:* 800-626-7054 ■ *Web:* www.thompsoninternational.com	Henderson	KY	42420	270-826-3751	826-3881
Timesavers Inc 11123 89th Ave N *TF:* 800-537-3611 ■ *Web:* www.timesaversinc.com	Maple Grove	MN	55369	763-488-6600	488-6601
Tool Smith Company Inc 1300 Fourth Ave S PO Box 2384 *TF:* 800-317-8665 ■ *Web:* www.toolsmith.ws	Birmingham	AL	35233	205-323-2576	323-9060
Tulsa Rig Iron Inc 4457 W 151st PO Box 880 *Web:* www.tulsarigiron.com	Kiefer	OK	74041	918-321-3330	321-3099
Unified Brands 1055 Mendell Davis Dr *TF:* 888-994-7636 ■ *Web:* www.unifiedbrands.net	Jackson	MS	39272	888-994-7636	864-7636
Universal Machine & Engineering Corp 645 Old Reading Pk *Web:* www.umc-oscar.com	Stowe	PA	19464	610-323-1810	
USM Corp 32 Stevens St *TF:* 800-361-2056 ■ *Web:* www.usm-canada.com	Haverhill	MA	01830	978-374-0303	521-5519
Vactor Manufacturing Inc 1621 S Illinois St **Fax:* Sales ■ *Web:* www.vactor.com	Streator	IL	61364	815-672-3171	672-2779*
Vacudyne Inc 375 E Joe Orr Rd *TF:* 800-459-9591 ■ *Web:* www.vacudyne.com	Chicago Heights	IL	60411	708-757-5200	757-7180
Van Air Systems Inc 2950 Mechanic St *TF:* 800-840-9906 ■ *Web:* www.vanairsystems.com	Lake City	PA	16423	814-774-2631	774-3482
Van Dam Machine Corp 81-B Walsh Dr *Web:* www.vandammachine.com	Parsippany	NJ	07054	973-257-7050	257-7398
Vermeer Midsouth Inc 1200 Vermeer Cv *TF:* 800-264-4123 ■ *Web:* www.vermeermidsouth.com	Cordova	TN	38018	901-758-1928	758-1929
Videojet Technologies Inc 1500 Mittel Blvd **Fax:* Mktg ■ *TF Cust Svc:* 800-843-3610 ■ *Web:* www.videojet.com	Wood Dale	IL	60191	630-860-7300	616-3657*
Vulcan Engineering Co 1 Vulcan Dr Helena Industrial Pk *Web:* www.vulcangroup.com	Helena	AL	35080	205-663-0732	663-9103
W M Sprinkman Corp 4234 Courtney Rd PO Box 390 *TF:* 800-816-1610 ■ *Web:* www.sprinkman.com	Franksville	WI	53126	262-835-2390	835-4325
Welex Inc 1600 Union Meeting Rd *Web:* www.welex.com	Blue Bell	PA	19422	215-542-8000	542-9841
Western Hydro Corp 3449 Enterprise Ave *TF:* 800-972-5945 ■ *Web:* www.westernhydro.com	Hayward	CA	94545	510-783-9166	732-0250
WH Bagshaw Company Inc One Pine St Ext PO Box 766 *TF:* 800-343-7467 ■ *Web:* www.whbagshaw.com	Nashua	NH	03061	603-883-7758	882-2651
Williams Form Engineering Corp 8165 Graphic Dr *Web:* www.williamsform.com	Belmont	MI	49306	616-866-0815	866-1810
Windsor K„rcher Group 1351 W Stanford Ave *TF:* 800-444-7654 ■ *Web:* www.windsorind.com	Englewood	CO	80110	303-762-1800	865-2800
Wood Group Pratt & Whitney Industrial Turbine Services LLC 1460 Blue Hills Ave PO Box 45 *Web:* www.wgpw.com	Bloomfield	CT	06002	860-286-4600	769-7337
Wright Metal Products Inc 100 Ben Hamby Dr PO Box 6763 *Web:* www.wrightmetalproducts.com	Greenville	SC	29606	864-297-6610	281-0594
Yale Carolinas Inc (YCI) 9839 S Tryon St *TF:* 800-844-1454 ■ *Web:* www.yalecarolinas.com	Charlotte	NC	28273	704-588-6930	588-6047
Young Welding Supply Inc 101 E First St PO Box 700 *Web:* www.youngwelding.com	Sheffield	AL	35660	256-383-5429	383-1385

390 INFORMATION RETRIEVAL SERVICES (GENERAL)

SEE ALSO Investigative Services p. 2590

Company	City	State	ZIP	Phone	Fax
2KDirect Inc 3000 Broad St Ste 115 — *Web:* www.ipromote.com	San Luis Obispo	CA	93401	805-597-5000	
33Across Inc 229 W 28th St 12th Fl — *Web:* www.33across.com	New York	NY	10001	888-297-4094	
411 Local Search Corp Inc 1200 Eglinton Ave E Ste 300 N York — *Web:* www.411.ca	Toronto	ON	M3C1H9	416-849-1432	
Accesso LLC 1025 Greenwood Blvd Ste 500 — *Web:* www.accesso.com	Lake Mary	FL	32746	407-333-7311	
AccuData Holdings Inc 5220 Summerlin Commons Blvd Ste 200 — *Web:* www.accudata.com	Fort Myers	FL	33907	239-425-4400	
Acculynk Inc 3225 Cumberland Blvd SE Ste 550 — *Web:* www.acculynk.com	Atlanta	GA	30339	678-894-7010	
Acquire Media Corp Three Becker Farm Rd Ste 401 — *Web:* www.acquiremedia.com	Roseland	NJ	07068	973-422-0800	
Acquizition.biz Inc 1100 Rene-Levesque Blvd W 24th Fl — *Web:* www.acquizition.biz	Montreal	QC	H3B4X9	514-499-0334	
Adaptive Networks Inc 123 Highland Ave — *Web:* www.adaptivenetworks.com	Needham	MA	02494	781-444-4170	
ADCI of Delaware LLC 5550 Friendship Blvd Ste 340 — *Web:* www.adcit.com	Chevy Chase	MD	20815	301-951-4423	
AdMobilize LLC 1680 Michigan Ave Ste 736 — *TF:* 855-236-6245 ■ *Web:* www.admobilize.com	Miami	FL	33139	855-236-6245	
Adpay Inc 391 Inverness Pkwy Ste 300-B — *Web:* www.adpay.com	Englewood	CO	80112	303-268-1527	
Advantix Solutions Group 1202 Richardson Dr Ste 200 — *TF:* 866-238-2684 ■ *Web:* www.advantixsolutions.com	Richardson	TX	75080	866-238-2684	
Aeneas Communications LLC 300 N Cumberland St Ste 200 — *Web:* www.aeneas.com	Jackson	TN	38301	731-554-9200	
Aeris 2350 Mission College Blvd Ste 600 — *Web:* www.aeris.net	Santa Clara	CA	95054	408-557-1993	
Aerospike Inc 2525 E Charleston Rd Ste 201 — *Web:* www.aerospike.com	Mountain View	CA	94043	408-462-2376	
Affant Communication Inc Affant Communication 3146 Red Hill Ave Ste 100 — *Web:* www.affant.com	Costa Mesa	CA	92626	714-338-7100	
Affinity Circles Inc 701 N Shoreline Blvd First Fl — *Web:* www.affinitycircles.com	Mountain View	CA	94043	650-810-1500	
Affinity Labs Inc 799 Market St Ste 500 — *Web:* www.affinitylabs.com	San Francisco	CA	94103	415-365-1400	
Agentis Inc 222 W Hubbard St — *Web:* agentisenergy.com	Chicago	IL	60654	630-359-6210	
Airborne Mobile Inc 3575 Saint Laurent Blvd Ste 750	Montreal	QC	H2X2T7	514-289-9111	
Airespring Inc 6060 Sepulveda Blvd Ste 220 — *Web:* www.airespring.com	Van Nuys	CA	91411	818-786-8990	
airG 1133 Melville St Ste 710 — *Web:* www.airg.com	Vancouver	BC	V6E4E5	604-408-2228	
AirPair Inc 875 Howard St — *TF:* 800-487-0668 ■ *Web:* www.airpair.com	San Francisco	CA	94103	800-487-0668	
Airphrame Inc 25 Taylor St — *Web:* www.airphrame.com	San Francisco	CA	94102	415-857-5387	
Akimbo Systems Inc 411 Borel Ave Ste 100 — *Web:* www.akimbo.com	San Mateo	CA	94402	650-292-3330	
Albion Telephone Company Inc 225 W N St — *Web:* www.atcnet.net	Albion	ID	83311	208-673-5335	
All Property Management LLC 2505 Third Ave Ste 226 — *Web:* www.allpropertymanagement.com	Seattle	WA	98121	206-577-0029	
All Web Leads Inc 7300 FM 2222 Bldg 2 Ste 100 — *Web:* www.allwebleads.com	Austin	TX	78730	512-349-7900	349-7910
Allcharge Inc 15 W 39th St Rm 501 — *Web:* www.allcharge.com	New York	NY	10018	212-679-9445	
Allclasses Inc 109 Kingston St 5th Fl — *Web:* allclasses.com	Boston	MA	02111	772-589-5050	
Alli Alliance of Action Sports LLC 150 Harvester Dr Ste 140 — *Web:* www.allisports.com	Burr Ridge	IL	60527	304-284-0084	
ALOT Inc 143 Varick St — *Web:* www.alot.com	New York	NY	10013	212-231-2000	
Altocloud Inc 800 W El Camino Real — *Web:* www.altocloud.com	Mountain View	CA	94040	650-492-5218	
American Broadband Communications LLC 153 W Dave Dugas Rd — *Web:* www.americanbroadband.com	Sulphur	LA	70665	337-583-2111	
American Robotics Corp 880 Peru Ave Unit 2 — *Web:* www.swapbox.com	San Francisco	CA	94112	562-546-2659	
Amernet 315 Montgomery St — *Web:* www.amer.net	San Francisco	CA	94104	415-616-5100	
Amigos Library Services 14400 Midway Rd — *TF:* 800-843-8482 ■ *Web:* www.amigos.org	Dallas	TX	75244	972-851-8000	991-6061
Ancero LLC 1001 Briggs Rd Ste 220 — *Web:* www.ancero.com	Mount Laurel	NJ	08054	856-210-5800	
AnswerDash Inc 4000 Mason Rd New Ventures Facility Fluke Hall — *TF:* 800-311-5786 ■ *Web:* www.answerdash.com	Seattle	WA	98195	800-311-5786	
AOAExcel Inc 243 N Lindbergh Blvd Fl 1 — *Web:* www.excelod.com	St. Louis	MO	63141	314-983-4105	
Apkudo LLC 3500 Boston St Ste 333 — *Web:* www.apkudo.com	Baltimore	MD	21224	410-777-8612	
Apmetrix Inc 5414 Oberlin Dr Ste 200 — *TF:* 800-490-3184 ■ *Web:* www.apmetrix.com	San Diego	CA	92121	800-490-3184	
appAttach Inc 401 Parkplace Ctr Ste 305 — *Web:* www.appattach.com	Kirkland	WA	98033	425-202-5676	
Applanix Corp 85 Leek Cresent — *Web:* www.applanix.com	Richmond Hill	ON	L4B3B3	905-709-4600	
appMobi Inc 35-37 E Orange St — *Web:* www.flycast.fm	Lancaster	PA	17603	717-666-3151	
AppsHosting Inc 13772 Goldenwest St Ste 321 — *TF:* 877-625-6610 ■ *Web:* www.appshosting.com	Westminster	CA	92683	877-625-6610	
Apptopia Inc 71 Summer St Fourth Fl — *Web:* apptopia.com	Boston	MA	02110	617-758-8165	
Arcestra Inc 197 Spadina Ave Ste 200 — *Web:* www.arcestra.com	Toronto	ON	M5T2C8	416-596-9561	
Architelos Inc 43622 Merchant Mill Ter — *Web:* architelos.com	Leesburg	VA	20176	571-248-5830	
Ardmore Telephone Company Inc 30190 Ardmore Ave — *Web:* www.ardmore.net	Ardmore	AL	35739	256-423-2131	
Arkadin Inc Five Concourse Pkwy Ste 1600 — *TF:* 866-551-1432 ■ *Web:* www.arkadin.com	Atlanta	GA	30328	866-551-1432	
AroundWire.Com LLC 18107 Sherman Way Ste 206 — *TF:* 888-382-3793 ■ *Web:* www.aroundwire.com	Reseda	CA	91335	888-382-3793	
Artisan Communications Inc 12400 Hwy W Hwy 71 Ste 350-407 — *Web:* www.artisan.tv	Austin	TX	78738	512-600-4200	
Artsicle Inc 25 W 13th St — *Web:* www.artsicle.com	New York	NY	10011	646-470-4219	
Ash Creek Enterprises LLC 2226 Black Rock Tpke Ste 202 — *Web:* www.ashcreek.com	Fairfield	CT	06825	203-331-1685	
Association Resource Group 7926 Jones Branch Dr Ste 1150 — *Web:* www.myarg.com	Mc Lean	VA	22102	703-734-3500	
Astor & Sanders 9900 Belward Campus Dr Ste 275 — *Web:* www.astor-sanders.com	Rockville	MD	20850	301-838-3420	
Audability Inc 5915 Airport Rd Ste 700 — *Web:* www.audability.com	Mississauga	ON	L4V1T1	416-915-1301	
Audio Authority Corp 2048 Mercer Rd — *Web:* www.audioauthority.com	Lexington	KY	40511	859-233-4599	
Avangate Inc 555 Twin Dolphin Dr Ste 155 — *Web:* www.avangate.com	Redwood Shores	CA	94065	650-249-5280	
Avfinity LLC 11782 Jollyville Rd — *Web:* www.avfinity.com	Austin	TX	78759	512-535-3416	
Avvo Inc 705 Fifth Ave S Ste 600 — *Web:* www.avvo.com	Seattle	WA	98104	206-734-4111	
Axiom Education LLC Four Research Dr — *Web:* www.axiomeducation.com	Shelton	CT	06484	203-242-3070	
Axon Sports LLC 2100 Stewart Ave Ste 201 — *Web:* www.axonsports.com	Wausau	WI	54401	715-848-1024	
Azulstar Inc 1051 Jackson St Ste D — *Web:* www.azulstar.com	Grand Haven	MI	49417	616-842-2763	
Balance Financial Inc 1800 - 112th Ave NE Ste 260-E — *Web:* www.balancefinancial.com	Bellevue	WA	98004	425-458-4400	
BDNA Corp 339 N Bernardo Ave Ste 206 — *Web:* www.bdna.com	Mountain View	CA	94043	650-625-9530	
Beach.com Inc Five Penn Plz 23rd Fl — *Web:* www.beach.com	New York	NY	10001	212-835-1529	
Beaver Creek Cooperative Telephone Co 15223 Henrici Rd — *Web:* www.bctelco.com	Oregon City	OR	97045	503-632-3113	632-4159
Beepi 5050 El Camino Real Ste 116 — *TF:* 888-542-3374 ■ *Web:* www.beepi.com	Los Altos	CA	94022	888-542-3374	
Best Telecom Inc 262 E End Ave — *TF:* 888-365-2273 ■ *Web:* www.besttelecom.com	Beaver	PA	15009	888-365-2273	
BestTel 360 E. 1st St — *Web:* www.besttel.net	Tustin	CA	92780	714-612-7333	
BigDoor Media Inc 511 Boren Ave N Second Fl — *Web:* www.bigdoor.com	Seattle	WA	98109	425-296-0805	
BigTent Design Inc 350 Brannan St Third Fl — *Web:* www.bigtent.com	San Francisco	CA	94107	415-992-6550	
Binary Group Inc 1911 Ft Myer Dr Ste 300 — *Web:* www.binarygroup.com	Arlington	VA	22209	571-480-4444	480-4445
BitNami 650 Mission St Second Fl — *Web:* bitnami.com	San Francisco	CA	94105	415-318-3470	
Bliss Direct Media 641 15Th Ave Ne — *Web:* www.blissdirect.com	Saint Joseph	MN	56374	320-271-1600	
BlogHer Inc 805 Veterans Blvd Ste 305 — *Web:* www.blogher.com	Redwood City	CA	94063	650-363-2564	
Blogster.com LLC 20545 Ctr Ridge Rd Ste 135 — *Web:* www.blogster.com	Rocky River	OH	44116	440-333-7805	
BloomNet Inc One Old Country Rd Ste 500 — *TF:* 866-256-6663 ■ *Web:* www.mybloomnet.net	Carle Place	NY	11514	866-256-6663	
Blue Box Group Inc 119 Pine St Ste 200 — *TF:* 800-613-4305 ■ *Web:* www.bluebox.net	Seattle	WA	98101	800-613-4305	
Blue Jeans Network Inc 516 Clyde Ave — *Web:* www.bluejeans.com	Mountain View	CA	94043	408-550-2828	
Blue Ridge Internet Works 321 E Main St — *Web:* www.brnets.com	Charlottesville	VA	22902	434-817-0707	
BlueGenesisCom Corp 5915 Airport Rd Ste 1100 — *Web:* www.bluegenesis.com	Mississauga	ON	L4V1T1	905-673-3232	

			Phone	Fax
BoardBookit Inc One Altoona Pl . . . Pittsburgh *Web:* www.boardbookit.com	PA	15228	412-436-5180	
Bobber Interactive Corp 2505 Third Ave Ste 300A . . . Seattle *Web:* www.bobberinteractive.com	WA	98121	206-443-3863	
Bocada Inc 5555 Lakeview Dr. . . . Kirkland *TF:* 866-262-2321 ■ *Web:* www.bocada.com	WA	98033	425-818-4400	818-4455
BoeFly LLC 50 W 72nd St Ste C6 . . . New York *TF:* 800-277-3158 ■ *Web:* www.boefly.com	NY	10023	800-277-3158	
Boston Illiquid Securities Offering Network Inc 205 Portland St Ste 200 . . . Boston *Web:* www.bison.co	MA	02114	617-752-1921	
Brand Thunder LLC 6588 Dalmore Ln . . . Dublin *Web:* brandthunder.com	OH	43016	614-408-8202	
Branding Brand 2313 East Carson St Ste 100 . . . Pittsburgh *Web:* www.brandingbrand.com	PA	15203	888-979-5018	
Broadband Dynamics LLC 8757 E Via De Commercio . . . Scottsdale *TF:* 888-801-1034 ■ *Web:* www.broadbanddynamics.net	AZ	85258	888-801-1034	801-1038
BroadVoice Inc 20847 Sherman Way . . . Winnetka *Web:* www.broadvoice.com	CA	91306	978-418-7300	
BuildingSearch.com Inc 90 Railway Ave . . . Campbell *Web:* www.buildingsearch.com	CA	95008	408-426-8424	
BUMP Network Inc 1295 Prospect St Ste A . . . La Jolla *Web:* www.bump.com	CA	92037	858-459-4489	
BurrellesLuce 30 B Vreeland Rd PO Box 674 . . . Florham Park *TF:* 800-631-1160 ■ *Web:* www.burrellesluce.com	NJ	07932	973-992-6600	992-7675
Buyers Best Friend Inc 38 Lyon St . . . San Francisco *Web:* www.bbfdirect.com	CA	94117	415-375-0439	
Buzzwire Inc 1123 Auraria Pkwy . . . Denver **Fax Area Code:* 303	CO	80204	720-259-0100	557-0668*
C R T & Associates Inc 806 Hastings St Ste 8 . . . Traverse City *Web:* www.crt-a.com	MI	49686	231-946-1680	
C Spire 1018 Highland Colony Pkwy Ste 300 . . . Ridgeland *TF:* 855-277-4735 ■ *Web:* www.cspire.com	MS	39157	855-277-4735	
Cal Info 316 W Second St Ste 1102 . . . Los Angeles *Web:* www.calinfo.net	CA	90012	213-687-8710	687-8778
Calient Networks Inc 2665 N First St Ste 204 . . . San Jose *Web:* www.calient.net	CA	95134	408-232-6400	
California Regional Multiple Listing Service Inc 3201 W Temple Ave Ste 250 . . . Pomona *Web:* www.imrmls.com	CA	91768	909-859-2040	
CallDirek 2200 S Dixie Hwy Ste 401 . . . Miami *TF:* 866-673-4735 ■ *Web:* www.calldirek.com	FL	33133	866-673-4735	
Camperoo Inc 2900 Weslayan St Ste 545 . . . Houston *TF:* 888-538-8809 ■ *Web:* www.camperoo.com	TX	77027	888-538-8809	
Canadian Institute, The 1329 Bay St . . . Toronto *Web:* www.canadianinstitute.com	ON	M5R2C4	416-927-7936	
CaptainU LLC 5807 S Woodlawn Dr Ste 207 . . . Chicago *Web:* www.captainu.com	IL	60637	773-834-9097	
Care Zone Inc 1463 East Republican St Ste 198 . . . Seattle *Web:* carezone.com	WA	98112	888-407-7785	
CARIS-Universal Systems Ltd 115 Waggoners Ln . . . Fredericton *Web:* www.caris.com	NB	E3B2L4	506-458-8533	
Carriercom Lp 200 s Tenth st . . . McAllen *Web:* www.carriercom.net	TX	78501	956-682-3656	
CatholicMatch LLC 211 E Grandview Ave . . . Zelienople *TF:* 888-605-3977 ■ *Web:* www.catholicmatch.com	PA	16063	888-605-3977	
Catura Systems Inc 4677 Old Ironsides Dr Ste 180 . . . Santa Clara *Web:* www.caturasystems.com	CA	95054	408-986-8933	
CB Information Services Inc 104 W 27th St Fl 3 . . . New York *Web:* www.cbinsights.com	NY	10001	212-292-3148	
CBT Sports LLC 12 Cadillac Dr Ste 230 . . . Brentwood *Web:* 247sports.com	TN	37027	615-879-3786	
CCG Investor Relations Inc 10960 Wilshire Blvd Ste 2050 . . . Los Angeles *Web:* www.ccgir.com	CA	90024	310-231-8600	
CCI Communications Inc 155 North 400 West Ste 100 . . . Salt Lake *Web:* www.ccicom.com	UT	84103	801-994-4100	
CCT Telecommunications Inc 1106 E Turner Rd . . . Lodi *Web:* www.4cct.com	CA	95240	209-365-9500	
CDNetworks Inc 441 W Trimble Rd . . . San Jose *Web:* www.cdnetworks.com	CA	95131	408-228-3700	
Cellular Properties Inc 28 Towne Centre . . . Danville *Web:* www.cellular1.net	IL	61832	217-442-2355	
ChannelMeter Inc 1061 Market St Ste 504 . . . San Francisco *Web:* channelmeter.com	CA	94103	510-228-4395	
CharityUSA.com LLC 600 University St Ste 1000 One Union Square . . . Seattle *TF:* 888-811-5271 ■ *Web:* www.charityusa.com	WA	98101	206-268-5400	264-8448
Chartbeat Inc 826 Broadway 12th St Sixth Fl . . . New York *Web:* www.chartbeat.com	NY	10003	646-786-8472	
ChatID Inc 900 Broadway Ste 706 . . . New York *Web:* www.chatid.com	NY	10003	646-494-5678	
Chemical Abstracts Service (CAS) 2540 Olentangy River Rd . . . Columbus *TF:* 800-848-6538 ■ *Web:* cas.org	OH	43202	614-447-3600	447-3713
Chirpify Inc 317 SW Alder St Ste 1100 . . . Portland *Web:* www.chirpify.com	OR	97204	503-208-3068	
Choose Digital Inc 4040 Aurora St . . . Coral Gables *Web:* www.choosedigital.com	FL	33146	305-443-5981	
CHT Global Corp 2107 N First St Ste 580 . . . San Jose *Web:* www.chtglobal.com	CA	95131	408-988-1898	
CIMCO Communications Inc 1901 S Meyers Rd Seventh Fl . . . Oakbrook Terrace *Web:* www.cimco.net	IL	60181	630-691-8080	

			Phone	Fax
Circle 1 Network Inc 131 W Seeboth St . . . Milwaukee *Web:* www.circle1network.com	WI	53204	414-271-5437	
Citation Communications Inc 1855 Indian Rd Ste 207 . . . West Palm Beach *Web:* citation2way.com	FL	33409	561-688-0330	
Cityfone Telecommunications Inc 3991 Henning Dr Ste 101 . . . Burnaby *Web:* www.cityfone.net	BC	V5C6N5	604-298-5900	
ClearShot Communications LLC Five Great Vly Pkwy Ste 333 . . . Malvern *Web:* www.clearshotcom.com	PA	19355	610-648-3895	
clickworker.com Inc PO Box 601 . . . Penfield *Web:* www.clickworker.com	NY	14526	585-210-3912	
Clinical Media Ltd 887 Great Northern Way Ste 115 . . . Vancouver *Web:* www.clinicbook.com	BC	V7E4G1	604-639-1624	
CloudCheckr Inc 339 East Ave Ste 202-1 . . . Rochester *Web:* cloudcheckr.com	NY	14604	585-413-0869	
CloudSway LLC 711 Pacific Ave . . . Tacoma *TF:* 855-212-5683 ■ *Web:* www.cloudsway.com	WA	98402	855-212-5683	
Clustrix Inc 201 Mission St Ste 800 . . . San Francisco *Web:* www.clustrix.com	CA	94105	415-501-9560	
Collector Car Network Inc 1345 E Chandler Blvd Ste 101 . . . Phoenix *Web:* classiccars.com	AZ	85048	480-285-1600	
CollegeDegrees.com LLC 1001 McKinney St Ste 650 . . . Houston *Web:* www.collegedegrees.com	TX	77002	713-534-1948	
Commnet Wireless LLC 400 Northridge Rd Ste 325 . . . Atlanta *Web:* www.commnetwireless.com	GA	30350	678-338-5960	
CommSPEED LLC 33725 N Scottsdale Rd . . . Scottsdale *Web:* www.commspeed.net	AZ	85266	480-305-0584	
Communication Wiring Specialists Inc 8909 Complex Dr Ste F . . . San Diego *Web:* www.cwssandiego.com	CA	92123	858-278-4545	
Compass Healthcare Marketers 200 princeton S corporate ctr . . . Ewing *Web:* www.compasshc.com	NJ	08628	609-688-8440	
CompleteCampaigns.com Inc 3635 Ruffin Rd Third Fl . . . San Diego *TF:* 888-217-9600 ■ *Web:* www.completecampaigns.com	CA	92123	888-217-9600	
Computers & Tele-Comm Inc 1307 S Sterling Ave . . . Independence *Web:* www.ctcwi.com	MO	64052	816-252-4080	
ComTech21 One Barnes Park S . . . Wallingford *TF:* 877-312-5564 ■ *Web:* www.comtech21.com	CT	06492	877-312-5564	
Comwave Networks Inc 61 Wildcat Rd . . . Toronto *Web:* www.comwave.net	ON	M3J2P5	416-663-9700	
ConceptShare Inc 130 Slater St . . . Ottawa *Web:* www.conceptshare.com	ON	K1P6E2	613-903-4431	
Conjur Inc 55 Cambridge Pkwy Ste 103 . . . Cambridge *Web:* www.conjur.net	MA	02142	617-914-0016	
ConnXus Inc 5155 Financial Way . . . Mason *Web:* connxus.com	OH	45040	513-204-2873	
Contingent Network Services LLC 4400 Port Union Rd . . . West Chester *Web:* www.contingent.com	OH	45011	513-860-2573	
ConvergeOne LLC 175B Rennell Dr . . . Southport *TF:* 888-321-6227 ■ *Web:* www.converge-one.com	CT	06890	888-321-6227	
Cornerstone SMR Inc 4620 N State Rd 7 Ste 120 . . . Fort Lauderdale *Web:* www.cornerstonesmr.com	FL	33319	954-714-7030	
Cozi Group Inc 506 Second Ave Ste 800 . . . Seattle *Web:* www.cozi.com	WA	98104	206-957-8447	
creativeLIVE Inc 757 Thomas St . . . Seattle *Web:* www.creativelive.com	WA	98109	206-403-1395	
CrossFit Inc 1250 Connecticut Ave NW Ste 200 . . . Washington *Web:* www.crossfit.com	DC	20036	202-449-8533	
Crosslake Communications 35910 County Rd 66 PO Box 70 . . . Crosslake *Web:* www.crosslake.net	MN	56442	218-692-2777	
CU Conferences 8711 Watson Rd Ste 200 . . . St. Louis *TF:* 888-465-6010 ■ *Web:* www.cuconferences.com	MO	63119	888-465-6010	
Curatel LLC 1605 W Olympic Blvd Ste 800 . . . Los Angeles *TF:* 866-287-2366 ■ *Web:* www.curatel.com	CA	90015	866-287-2366	
Currensee Inc 54 Canal St Fourth Fl . . . Boston *Web:* www.currensee.com	MA	02114	978-964-1023	
Curriculum Technology LLC 3520 Seagate Way Ste 115 . . . Oceanside *Web:* www.curriculumtechnology.com	CA	92056	760-295-0863	
Custom Toll Free 914 164Th St SE #1670 . . . Mill Creek *TF:* 800-222-2222 ■ *Web:* www.customtollfree.com	WA	98012	800-222-2222	
Cybereason Inc One Broadway 15th Fl . . . Cambridge *Web:* www.cybereason.com	MA	02142	781-768-6065	
CyDesign Labs Inc 1810A Embarcadero Rd . . . Palo Alto *Web:* cydesign.com	CA	94303	650-855-9516	
CypherWorX Inc 3349 Monroe Ave . . . Rochester *TF:* 888-685-4440 ■ *Web:* nptrainingworks.com	NY	14618	888-685-4440	
DadLabs Inc 4612 Burleson Rd Ste L . . . Austin *Web:* www.dadlabs.com	TX	78744	512-215-4026	
Dailybreak Inc 100 N Washington St . . . Boston *Web:* www.dailybreak.com	MA	02114	617-451-1790	
DailyFeats Inc 22 Pearl St . . . Cambridge *Web:* www.dailyfeats.com	MA	02139	781-573-3287	
DashGo Inc 1620 Broadway Ste C . . . Santa Monica *Web:* www.dashgo.com	CA	90404	310-997-0675	
Data Center West Inc 739 Welch St . . . Medford *Web:* www.datacenterwest.com	OR	97501	541-326-4212	
Data Transmission Network Corp 9110 W Dodge Rd Ste 200 . . . Omaha *TF:* 800-485-4000 ■ *Web:* www.dtn.com	NE	68114	402-390-2328	390-7188

				Phone	*Fax*
DataCore Software Corp 6300 NW Fifth Way Corporate Park *Web:* www.datacore.com	Fort Lauderdale	FL	33309	954-377-6000	
Datadrill Communications Inc 6701 Fairmount Dr Se *Web:* www.datadrill.ca	Calgary	AB	T2H0X6	403-269-7500	
DataGravity Inc 100 Innovative Way Ste 3410 *Web:* www.datagravity.com	Nashua	NH	03062	603-943-8500	
Dataium LLC 2525 Perimeter Pl Dr Ste 105 *TF:* 877-896-3282 ■ *Web:* www.dataium.com	Nashville	TN	37214	877-896-3282	
Dataminr Inc 99 Madison Ave Third Fl *TF:* 888-764-4959 ■ *Web:* www.dataminr.com	New York	NY	10016	888-764-4959	
DataPop Inc 5762 W Jefferson Blvd *Web:* www.datapop.com	Los Angeles	CA	90016	323-302-4987	
DataTrail Inc 6223 2 St SE Ste 205 *Web:* www.datatrail.com	Calgary	AB	T2H1J5	403-253-3651	
Datonics LLC 84 Wooster St Ste 300 *Web:* datonics.com	New York	NY	10012	646-867-0647	
Datotel LLC 710 N Tucker Ste 400 *Web:* www.datotel.com	St. Louis	MO	63101	314-241-9101	
Deal Interactive LLC Three Park Ave 39th Fl *TF:* 888-415-4888 ■ *Web:* www.dealinteractive.com	New York	NY	10016	888-415-4888	
Dealertrack CentralDispatch Inc 26387 Network Pl *Web:* www.centraldispatch.com	Chicago	IL	60673	858-259-6084	
DealFlow Analytics Inc 131 Jericho Tpke PH3 *Web:* dealflow.com	Jericho	NY	11753	516-876-8006	
Dealmaker Media Inc Five Lucerne St Ste 2 *Web:* www.dealmakermedia.com	San Francisco	CA	94103	415-864-2885	
Dealtaker Inc 5360 Legacy Dr Ste 115 *Web:* www.dealtaker.com	Plano	TX	75024	214-234-9145	
DebtFolio Inc 384 Merrow Rd Ste G *TF:* 866-876-3654 ■ *Web:* www.geezeo.com	Tolland	CT	06084	866-876-3654	
Declara Inc 977 Commercial St *TF:* 877-216-0604 ■ *Web:* www.declara.com	Palo Alto	CA	94303	877-216-0604	
Delivery.com LLC 199 Water St Fl 23 *Web:* www.delivery.com	New York	NY	10038	212-294-7700	
Demeure Operating Company Ltd 187 King St S Unit 202 *Web:* demeure.com	Waterloo	ON	N2J1R1	519-886-8881	
Desmos Inc 1061 Market St *Web:* www.desmos.com	San Francisco	CA	94103	415-484-5342	
DFT Communications 40 Temple St *Web:* www.dftcommunications.com	Fredonia	NY	14063	716-673-3000	
Dialink Corp 1660 S Amphlett Blvd Ste 314 *Web:* www.dialink.com	San Mateo	CA	94402	650-691-9330	
Dialog 2250 Perimeter Pk Dr Ste 300 *TF:* 800-334-2564 ■ *Web:* proquest.com/	Morrisville	NC	27560	919-804-6400	804-6410
Dig Media Inc L200 560 Beatty St *Web:* www.digmediasolutions.com	Vancouver	BC	V6B2L3	604-688-8231	
Digital Datavoice Corp (DDV) 1210 Northland Dr Ste 160 *Web:* www.ddvc.com	Mendota Heights	MN	55120	651-994-2284	452-5470
Digital Reef Inc 85 Swanson Rd Ste 310 *Web:* www.digitalreefinc.com	Boxborough	MA	01719	978-893-1000	
Dimensional Insight Inc 60 Mall Rd Ste 210 *Web:* www.dimins.com	Burlington	MA	01803	781-229-9111	
Disqus Inc 301 Howard St Ste 300 *Web:* www.disqus.com	San Francisco	CA	94105	415-738-8848	
DMG Events Inc 3 Stamford Landing Ste 400 46 Southfield Avenue *Web:* www.dmgevents.com	Stamford	CT	06902	203-973-2940	
DocAuto Inc 3500 Pkwy Ln Ste 270 *Web:* www.docauto.com	Norcross	GA	30092	770-242-6747	
Doctor's Channel LLC, The 1133 Broadway Second Fl *Web:* www.thedoctorschannel.com	New York	NY	10010	646-257-5739	
doggyloot LLC 213 N Racine Ave *Web:* www.doggyloot.com	Chicago	IL	60607	312-566-8122	
Domain7 Solutions Inc 33820 S Fraser Way Unit 2A *Web:* www.domain7.com	Abbotsford	BC	V2S2C5	604-855-3772	
DotLoop LLC 700 W Pete Rose Way Ste 446 *Web:* www.dotloop.com	Cincinnati	OH	45203	513-257-0550	
DOTmed.com Inc 29 Broadway Ste 2500 *Web:* www.dotmed.com	New York	NY	10006	212-742-1200	
DoubleVerify Inc 575 Eigth Ave Seventh Fl *Web:* www.doubleverify.com	New York	NY	10018	212-631-2111	
DPL Group, The 53 Clark Rd *Web:* www.dpl.ca	Rothesay	NB	E2E2K9	506-847-2347	847-2348
DrivingSales LLC 8871 S Sandy Pkwy Ste 250 *TF:* 866-943-8371 ■ *Web:* www.drivingsales.com	Sandy	UT	84070	866-943-8371	
Dropcam Inc 301 Howard St 4th Fl *Web:* www.dropcam.com	San Francisco	CA	94105	855-469-6378	
Druva Software Inc 150 Mathilda Place, STE 450 *TF:* 888-248-4976 ■ *Web:* www.druva.com	Sunnyvale	CA	94086	888-248-4976	
DSG Tag Systems Inc 5455 152nd St Ste 214 *TF:* 877-589-8806 ■ *Web:* www.dsgtag.com	Surrey	BC	V3S5A5	877-589-8806	
Dubblee Media Inc 33 W 26th St Third Fl *Web:* lover.ly	New York	NY	10010	646-726-4395	
DVI Communications Inc 11 Park Pl Ste 906 *Web:* www.dvicomm.com	New York	NY	10007	212-267-2929	
EAGLE-Net Alliance 11800 Ridge Pkwy Ste 450 *Web:* www.co-eaglenet.net	Broomfield	CO	80021	720-210-9500	
Earth911 Inc 1375 N Scottsdale Rd Ste 140 *Web:* earth911.com	Scottsdale	AZ	85257	480-889-2650	
East Kentucky Network LLC 101 Technology Trl *Web:* www.appalachianwireless.com	Ivel	KY	41642	606-477-2355	

				Phone	*Fax*
Easy Analytic Software Inc 101 Haag Ave *Web:* www.easidemographics.com	Bellmawr	NJ	08031	856-931-5780	
EatStreet Inc 131 W Wilson St Ste 400 *TF:* 866-654-8777 ■ *Web:* eatstreet.com	Madison	WI	53715	866-654-8777	
EBSCO Information Services PO Box 1943 *TF:* 800-758-5995 ■ *Web:* www.ebsco.com	Birmingham	AL	35201	205-991-6600	991-1264
EC Suite LLC 2353 W University Dr *Web:* www.ecsuite.com	Tempe	AZ	85281	480-449-8817	
Ecliptic Enterprises Corp 398 W Washington Blvd Ste 100 *Web:* www.eclipticenterprises.com	Pasadena	CA	91103	626-798-2436	
Edison Carrier Solutions 4900 Rivergrade Rd Bldg 2B First Fl *Web:* www.edisoncarriersolutions.com	Irwindale	CA	91706	626-543-8156	
Education Online Services Corp 3303 W Commercial Blvd *Web:* www.educationonlineservices.com	Fort Lauderdale	FL	33309	954-606-5658	
Education.com Inc 2317 Broadway St Ste 200 *Web:* www.education.com	Redwood City	CA	94063	650-366-3380	
Edufii Inc 2078 Parker St Ste 200 *TF:* 800-439-8505 ■ *Web:* edufii.com	San Luis Obispo	CA	93401	800-439-8505	
Eduplanet21 LLC 401 East Winding Hill Rd Ste 200 *Web:* www.eduplanet21.com	Mechanicsburg	PA	17055	717-884-9900	
Efonica FZ-LLC 420 Lexington Ave Ste 518 *Web:* www.efonica.com	New York	NY	10170	212-214-0642	
Ekahau Inc 1851 Alexander Bell Dr Ste 300 *TF:* 866-435-2428 ■ *Web:* www.ekahau.com	Reston	VA	20191	866-435-2428	
Ellipse Communications Inc 14800 Quorum Dr Ste 420 *Web:* www.ellipseinc.com/	Dallas	TX	75254	214-237-0199	
ELM Resources 12950 Race Track Rd Ste 201 *TF:* 866-524-8198 ■ *Web:* www.elmresources.com	Tampa	FL	33626	866-524-8198	
Embark Corp 32 E 57th St 18th Fl *Web:* www.embark.com	New York	NY	10022	646-368-8394	
EMC Corporation of Canada 120 Adelaide St W 14th Fl Ste 1400 *Web:* www.canada.emc.com	Toronto	ON	M5H1T1	416-628-5973	
ENBALA Power Networks Ltd 360 Bay St Ste 401 **Fax Area Code:* 647 ■ *Web:* www.enbala.com	Toronto	ON	M5H2V6	416-623-2626	427-7041*
Endstream Communications LLC 401 E 34Th St *Web:* www.endstream.com	New York	NY	10016	212-786-7289	
Engineering.com Inc 5285 Solar Dr Ste 101 *Web:* www.engineering.com	Mississauga	ON	L4W5B8	905-273-9991	
Enprecis Inc 901 Fifth Ave Ste 820 *Web:* www.enprecis.com	Seattle	WA	98164	206-274-0122	
Environmental Data Resources Inc 440 Wheelers Farms Rd **Fax Area Code:* 800 ■ *TF:* 800-352-0050 ■ *Web:* www.edrnet.com	Milford	CT	06460	203-783-0300	231-6802*
Epicurious LLC Four Times Sq 17th Fl *Web:* www.epicurious.com	New York	NY	10036	212-381-7057	
eScreen Inc 7500 W 110th St Ste 500 *TF:* 800-881-0722 ■ *Web:* www.escreen.com	Overland Park	KS	66210	913-327-5915	327-8606
ESI Software Inc 1465 Kelly Johnson Blvd Ste 305 *Web:* www.esisoft.us	Colorado Springs	CO	80920	719-638-7033	
ESIS Inc 7920 Arjons Dr Ste H *Web:* www.esisinc.com	San Diego	CA	92126	858-625-0060	
eSnipe Inc 12819 SE 38th St *Web:* www.esnipe.com	Bellevue	WA	98006	425-260-5292	
ESP Solutions Group Inc 8627 N Mopac Ste 400 *Web:* www.espsolutionsgroup.com	Austin	TX	78759	512-879-5300	
EthoStream LLC 10200 Innovation Dr Ste 300 *Web:* www.ethostream.com	Milwaukee	WI	53226	414-223-0473	
Everlaw 2020 Milvia St Ste 220 *TF:* 844-383-7529 ■ *Web:* everlaw.com	Berkeley	CA	94704	844-383-7529	
EverTrue LLC 330 Congress St Second Fl *TF:* 855-387-8783 ■ *Web:* www.evertrue.com	Boston	MA	02210	855-387-8783	
Everwise Corp 1178 Broadway Fourth Fl *TF:* 888-734-0011 ■ *Web:* www.geteverwise.com	New York	NY	10001	888-734-0011	
EveryScape Inc 65 Chapel St *Web:* www.everyscape.com	Newton	MA	02458	781-250-4800	
Evidentio Inc 11501 Dublin Blvd Ste 200 *Web:* evident.io	Dublin	CA	94568	408-802-0724	
Evisors Inc 55 Broad St Ste 15F *Web:* www.evisors.com	New York	NY	10004	813-384-7677	
Evite LLC 8800 W Sunset Blvd *Web:* www.evite.com	West Hollywood	CA	90069	310-360-2427	
Exactearth Ltd 60 Struck Ct *Web:* www.exactearth.com	Cambridge	ON	N1R8L2	519-622-4445	
Exec Inc 277 Carolina St *Web:* iamexec.com	San Francisco	CA	94103	415-275-8094	
Experis Data Centers Inc 7272 Wisconsin Ave Ste 330 *Web:* www.experisdatacenters.com	Bethesda	MD	20814	240-223-0607	
Expoships LLLP 27598 Riverview Ctr Blvd *Web:* www.expoships.com	Bonita Springs	FL	34134	239-949-5411	
Eyejot Inc 315 5th Ave S Ste 800 *Web:* www.eyejot.com	Seattle	WA	98104	206-274-7374	
ezCater Inc 101 Arch St Ste 410 *TF:* 800-488-1803 ■ *Web:* www.ezcater.com	Boston	MA	02110	800-488-1803	
Ezzi Net 882 Third Ave Ninth Fl *Web:* www.ezzi.net	Brooklyn	NY	11232	646-375-3390	
FamilySearch 35 N W Temple St *TF:* 866-406-1830 ■ *Web:* www.familysearch.org	Salt Lake City	UT	84150	866-406-1830	
FamilyTime LLC 101 Merritt Blvd Ste 102 *Web:* www.familytime.com	Trumbull	CT	06611	203-610-8265	
Fanhattan Inc 489 S El Camino Real *Web:* www.vuze.com	San Mateo	CA	94402	408-236-7525	

				Phone	Fax
Fanlala Inc 2099 Mount Diablo Blvd Ste 204 — *Web:* imbee.com	Walnut Creek	CA	94596	925-954-1224	
Fidelity ActionsXchange Inc 200 Seaport Blvd — *Web:* www.actionsxchange.com	Boston	MA	02210	617-392-2900	
Figment LLC 118 E 64th St — *Web:* www.figment.com	New York	NY	10065	212-893-8790	
FirstFuel Software Inc 420 Bedford St Ste 200 — *Web:* www.firstfuel.com	Lexington	MA	02420	781-862-6500	
FirstGiving Inc 34 Farnsworth St Third Fl — *Web:* www.firstgiving.com	Boston	MA	02210	617-542-0010	
FishHound LLC 15720 Ventura Blvd Ste 220 — *TF:* 800-469-0224 ■ *Web:* www.fishhound.com	Encino	CA	91436	800-469-0224	
Fitocracy Inc 51 E 12th St Fourth Fl — *Web:* www.fitocracy.com	New York	NY	10003	646-450-3029	
FitOrbit Inc 11611 San Vicente Blvd Ste 515 — *Web:* www.fitorbit.com	Los Angeles	CA	90049	424-652-9650	
Flowroute LLC 1221 Second ave — *Web:* www.flowroute.com	Seattle	WA	98101	206-641-8000	
Fluidware 12 York St Second Fl — *TF:* 866-218-5127 ■ *Web:* www.fluidware.com	Ottawa	ON	K1N5S6	866-218-5127	
Flywheel Communications Inc 2501 Harrison St — *Web:* www.flywheel.com	San Francisco	CA	94110	415-401-7290	
FMS InfoServ Inc 6053 W Century Blvd Ninth Fl — *Web:* www.fmsinfoserv.com	Los Angeles	CA	90045	310-981-9510	
FocusVision Worldwide Inc 1266 E Main St — *Web:* www.focusvision.com	Stamford	CT	06902	203-961-1715	
FOI Services Inc 704 Quince OrchaRd Rd Ste 275 — *Web:* www.foiservices.com	Gaithersburg	MD	20878	301-975-9400	975-0702
FOIA Group Inc (FGI) 1250 Connecticut Ave NW Ste 200 — **Fax Area Code: 202* ■ *TF:* 888-461-7951 ■ *Web:* www.foia.com	Washington	DC	20036	888-461-7951	347-8419*
FoodLink Online LLC 475 Alberto Way Ste 100 — *Web:* www.foodlink.net	Los Gatos	CA	95032	408-395-7280	
Forex Newscom 55 Water St 50th Fl — *TF:* 888-503-6739 ■ *Web:* www.forexnews.com	New York	NY	10041	888-503-6739	
ForSaleByOwnercom Corp 435 N Michigan Ave Fl 5 — *Web:* www.forsalebyowner.com	Chicago	IL	60611	312-222-4653	
Fotolia LLC 41 E 11th St 11th Fl — *Web:* www.fotolia.com	New York	NY	10003	718-577-1321	
Fotomedia Technologies LLC 155 Fleet St — *Web:* www.fotomedialabs.com	Portsmouth	NH	03801	603-570-4843	
Franchise Information Services Inc 4300 Wilson Blvd Ste 480 — *TF:* 800-485-9570 ■ *Web:* www.frandata.com	Arlington	VA	22203	703-740-4700	
Frontier Networks Inc 530 Kipling Ave — *Web:* frontiernetworks.ca	Toronto	ON	M8Z5E3	416-847-5240	252-2301
FTJ FundChoice LLC 2300 Litton Ln Ste 102 — *TF:* 800-379-2513 ■ *Web:* www.ftjfundchoice.com	Hebron	KY	41048	800-379-2513	
G3 Telecom Inc 1039 McNicoll Ave — *Web:* www.g3telecom.com	Toronto	ON	M1W3W6	416-499-2121	
G4 Communications One Sundial Ave Ste 210 — *Web:* www.g4.net	Manchester	NH	03103	603-625-0555	
GDKN Corp 1779 N University Dr Ste 102 — *Web:* www.gdkn.com	Pembroke Pines	FL	33024	954-985-6650	
GDS Publishing Ltd 40 Wall St Trump Bldg Fl 5 — *Web:* www.gdsinternational.com	New York	NY	10005	212-796-2000	
GEENIUS Inc 4464 Long Lk Rd — *Web:* www.geenius.com	Melbourne	FL	32934	321-308-5330	
Genability 221 Main St Ste 400 — *Web:* www.genability.com	San Francisco	CA	94105	415-371-0136	
Genares Worldwide Reservation Services Ltd 5201 N O'Connor Blvd Ste 400 — *Web:* www.genares.com	Irving	TX	75039	817-722-2800	
Genius SIS Inc 1401 Sawgrass Corporate Pkwy Ste 136 — *Web:* www.geniussis.com	Sunrise	FL	33323	954-667-7747	
Genus Technologies LLC 6600 France Ave S Ste 425 — *Web:* www.genusllc.com	Minneapolis	MN	55435	952-844-2644	
GeoStrut 1374 W 200 S — *Web:* www.geostrut.net	Lindon	UT	84042	801-356-1311	
Geotab Inc 1081 S Service Rd W — *Web:* www.geotab.com	Oakville	ON	L6L6K3	416-434-4309	
Get It LLC 128 N Pitt St Ste 2 — *Web:* www.getit.me	Alexandria	VA	22314	703-880-6630	
Get Smart Content Inc 3000 E Cesar Chavez St — *Web:* www.getsmartcontent.com	Austin	TX	78702	512-583-1853	
Getabl Inc 11 Elkins St — *Web:* pingup.com	Boston	MA	02127	617-752-1691	
Giant Realm Inc 254 W 31St St Eighth Fl — *Web:* www.giantrealm.com	New York	NY	10001	212-488-1740	
GigMasters.com Inc 33 S Main St — *TF:* 866-342-9794 ■ *Web:* www.gigmasters.com	Norwalk	CT	06854	866-342-9794	
GitHub Inc 548 Fourth St — *Web:* github.com	San Francisco	CA	94107	415-448-6673	
Giveanything.com LLC 307 Fifth Ave Fourth Fl — *Web:* www.giveanything.com	New York	NY	10016	212-689-1200	
GIVINGTRAX 220 Second Ave S Ste 51 — *Web:* www.givingtrax.com	Seattle	WA	98104	206-486-0185	
GlobaFone Inc 1950 Lafayette Rd Ste 207 — *Web:* globafone.com	Portsmouth	NH	03801	603-433-7232	
Global Science & Technology Inc 7855 Walker Dr Ste 200 — *Web:* www.gst.com	Greenbelt	MD	20770	301-474-9696	
GoDaddy Inc 14455 N Hayden Rd — *Web:* www.godaddy.com	Scottsdale	AZ	85260	480-505-8800	
Gogo Inc 1250 N Arlington Heights Rd Ste 500 — *Web:* www.gogoair.com	Itasca	IL	60143	630-647-1400	
GoodGuide Inc 98 Battery St Ste 400 — *Web:* www.goodguide.com	San Francisco	CA	94111	415-732-7722	
Goomzee Corp 4852 Kendrick Pl Ste 1 — *Web:* www.goomzee.com	Missoula	MT	59808	406-542-9955	
Grab LLC 1100 Glendon Ave Ste 800 — *Web:* www.grab.com	Los Angeles	CA	90024	310-443-2758	
Graphight 2400 N Lincoln Ave Ste 212 — *Web:* rexter.com	Altadena	CA	91001	661-727-3446	
Green Job Interview 3050 Pullman Ave Ste D — *Web:* greenjobinterview.com	Costa Mesa	CA	92626	714-444-5500	
Grid4 Communications Inc 2107 Crooks Rd — *Web:* www.grid4.com	Troy	MI	48084	248-244-8100	
GridSpeak Corp 555 12th St Ste 2040 — *Web:* www.gridspeak.com	Oakland	CA	94607	510-463-8800	
Grockit 500 Third St Ste 260 — *Web:* www.grockit.com	San Francisco	CA	94107	415-512-1040	
GroupGifting.com Inc 445 Broad Hollow Rd Ste 25 — *Web:* www.egifter.com	Melville	NY	11747	516-882-1200	
HarborLink Network Ltd 3131 S Dixie Dr Ste 500 — *Web:* www.harborlink.net	Dayton	OH	45439	937-294-2954	
Harris CapRock Communications Inc 4400 S Sam Houston Pkwy E — *Web:* www.caprock.com	Houston	TX	77048	832-668-2300	
Havasu Newspapers Inc 2225 Acoma Blvd W — *Web:* www.havasunews.com	Lake Havasu City	AZ	86403	928-453-4237	
Healthcare Management Systems Inc (HMS) 3102 W End Ave Ste 400 — *TF:* 800-383-3317 ■ *Web:* www.hmstn.com	Nashville	TN	37203	615-383-7300	383-6093
HELIO LLC 10960 Wilshire Blvd Ste 700 — *Web:* www.helio.com	Los Angeles	CA	90024	310-445-7000	
Helixstorm Inc 29975 Technology Dr Ste 101 — *Web:* www.helixstorm.com	Murrieta	CA	92563	888-434-3549	
Helpjuice Inc 211 E Seventh St Ste 620 — *TF:* 888-230-3420 ■ *Web:* helpjuice.com	Austin	TX	78701	888-230-3420	
Hibernia Atlantic US LLC 35 Beechwood Rd Melrose Bldg Ste 3C — *Web:* www.hiberniaatlantic.com	Summit	NJ	07901	201-454-0777	
Hibernia Networks LLC 25 DeForest Ave Ste 108 — *Web:* www.hibernianetworks.com	Summit	NJ	07901	908-516-4200	
HipSwap Inc 2436 Second St — *Web:* www.hipswap.com	Santa Monica	CA	90405	310-396-5400	
HireAbility.com LLC 25 Nashua Rd Ste C6 — *Web:* www.hireability.com	Londonderry	NH	03053	603-432-6653	
Hireology Inc 640 N Lasalle St Ste 650 — *Web:* www.hireology.com	Chicago	IL	60654	312-253-7870	
Hollywood.com LLC 560 Broadway Ste 404 — *Web:* www.hollywood.com	New York	NY	10012	212-817-9105	
Homes.com Inc 150 Granby St — *TF:* 866-675-1058 ■ *Web:* www.homes.com	Norfolk	VA	23510	866-675-1058	
Host Department LLC 45277 Fremont Blvd Ste 11 — *TF:* 866-887-4678 ■ *Web:* www.hostdepartment.com	Fremont	CA	94538	866-887-4678	
Hubris Communications Inc 209 N Main — *Web:* www.hubris.net	Garden City	KS	67846	620-275-1900	
HyperCube LLC 3200 W Pleasant Run Rd Ste 300 — *Web:* www.hypercube-llc.com	Lancaster	TX	75146	469-727-1510	
I Am Athlete LLC PO Box 667 — *TF:* 877-462-7979 ■ *Web:* www.imathlete.com	Santa Monica	CA	90406	877-462-7979	
I-engineeringcom Inc Four Armstrong Rd Ste 2 — *Web:* www.i-engineering.com	Shelton	CT	06484	203-402-0800	
IBISWorld Inc 11755 Wilshire blvd 11th fl — *TF:* 800-330-3772 ■ *Web:* www.ibisworld.com	Los Angeles	CA	90025	800-330-3772	
iChange Networks Inc 801 N Harbor — *Web:* www.ichange.com	Fullerton	CA	92832	714-447-4098	
ICSA Labs 1000 Bent Creek Blvd Ste 200 — *Web:* www.icsalabs.com	Mechanicsburg	PA	17050	717-790-8100	
IdeaTek Communications LLC 102 N Main PO Box 258 — *Web:* www.idkcom.net	Buhler	KS	67522	620-543-5000	
Ifonoclast Inc 4620 Fortran Dr Ste 207 — *Web:* www.phonevite.com	San Jose	CA	95134	408-946-9700	
iForem Inc 350 Marine Pkwy Ste 200	Redwood Shores	CA	94065	650-352-4750	
iLearning Gateway Inc 2650 Vly View Ln Bldg 1 Ste 200 — *Web:* www.ilearninggateway.com	Dallas	TX	75234	972-488-2298	
Illuminate Education Inc 47 Discovery Ste 100 — *Web:* www.illuminateed.com	Irvine	CA	92618	949-242-0343	
ImageShack Corp 236 N. Santa Cruz Ave. Ste 100 — *Web:* www.imageshack.us	Los Gatos	CA	95030	408-354-5166	
IMshopping Inc 4699 Old Ironsides Dr Ste 450 — *Web:* www.imshopping.com	Santa Clara	CA	95054	408-228-4456	
IMVU Inc PO Box 390012 — *Web:* www.imvu.com	Mountain View	CA	94039	650-321-8334	
InComm Conferencing Inc 208 Harristown Rd Ste 101 — *TF:* 877-804-2062 ■ *Web:* www.incommconferencing.com	Glen Rock	NJ	07452	877-804-2062	
InDorse Technologies Inc 424 W 33rd St	New York	NY	10001	646-495-0966	
Information Systems Consulting 401 E East St — *Web:* www.isccorp.net	Casper	WY	82601	307-473-8933	
Information Tycoon LLC 3424 Peachtree Rd NE Ste 300 — *Web:* infotycoon.com	Atlanta	GA	30326	404-267-1506	
Infotrieve Inc 20 Westport Rd PO Box 7102 — *TF Cust Svc:* 800-422-4633 ■ *Web:* www.infotrieve.com	Wilton	CT	06897	203-423-2130	423-2155

				Phone	Fax
infoUSA Inc 5711 S 86th Cir	Omaha	NE	68127	800-835-5856	331-1505*
**Fax Area Code:* 402 ■ **Fax:* Sales ■ *TF:* 800-321-0869 ■ *Web:* www.infousa.com					
Infrastructure Networks Inc 1718 Fry Rd Ste 116	Houston	TX	77084	281-740-3226	
TF: 855-333-4638 ■ *Web:* www.infrastructurenetworks.com					
Innflux LLC 850 W Jackson Blvd Ste 250	Chicago	IL	60607	312-850-3399	
Web: www.innflux.com					
Innovative Telecom Solutions Inc Nine Vela Way	Edgewater	NJ	07020	800-510-3000	
TF: 800-510-3000 ■ *Web:* www.innovativetel.com					
Insur IQ LLC Two Corporate Dr Ste 636	Shelton	CT	06484	203-446-8070	
Web: www.insuriq.com					
Integrated Tower Systems 2703 Dawson Rd	Tulsa	OK	74110	918-749-8535	
Web: www.intelcotowers.com					
inTelesystems 17400 Dallas Pkwy	Dallas	TX	75287	972-852-8200	
Web: www.intelesystems.com					
Intelletrace Inc 448 Ignacio Blvd	Novato	CA	94945	800-618-5877	
TF: 800-618-5877 ■ *Web:* www.intelletrace.com					
Intelsat General Corp 6550 Rock Spring Dr Ste 450	Bethesda	MD	20817	301-571-1210	
Web: www.intelsatgeneral.com					
Interactive Data LLC 3057 Peachtree Industrial Blvd Ste 100	Duluth	GA	30097	678-584-5252	
Web: www.id-info.com					
Interactive Innovation Group Inc 413 W Channel Rd	Santa Monica	CA	90402	310-454-3023	
Web: www.panjo.com					
Interactive One Inc 850 Third Ave Third Fl	New York	NY	10022	212-431-4477	
Web: www.interactiveone.com					
International Automotive Technicians' Network Inc PO Box 1599	Brea	CA	92822	714-257-1335	
Web: www.iatn.net					
Internet Movie Database Inc 410 Terry Ave N	Seattle	WA	98109	206-266-4064	
Web: www.imdb.com					
Interschola 1004 Oreilly Ave	San Francisco	CA	94129	415-563-4100	
Web: www.interschola.com					
Iowa Communications Network Inc Grimes State Office Bldg 400 E 14th St	Des Moines	IA	50319	515-725-4692	
Web: icn.iowa.gov					
iPayStation LLC 213 School St Ste 101	Gardner	MA	01440	978-632-6798	
Web: www.ipaystation.com					
IrishCentral LLC 875 Sixth Ave	New York	NY	10001	212-871-0111	
Web: www.irishcentral.com					
ISLC Inc 14 Savannah Hwy	Beaufort	SC	29906	843-770-1000	
Web: www.islc.net					
iSnap 808 R St Ste 208	Sacramento	CA	95811	916-333-0330	
Web: www.isnap.com					
ITI TranscenData 5303 DuPont Cir	Milford	OH	45150	513-576-3900	
Web: www.transcendata.com					
ITworld.com Inc One Speen St	Framingham	MA	01701	508-879-0700	
Web: www.itworld.com					
Jibe Mobile Inc 990 N Rengstorff Ave	Mountain View	CO	94043	650-336-5423	
Web: www.jibemobile.com					
JMD Communications Inc 760 Calle Bolivar	Santurce	PR	00907	787-728-3030	
Web: www.jmdcom.com					
JNJ Mobile Inc 186 S St	Boston	MA	02111	617-542-1614	
Web: www.jnjmobile.com					
Jobaline Inc 620 Kirkland Way Ste 208	Kirkland	WA	98033	425-242-0866	
Web: www.jobaline.com					
Journal Media Group Inc 218 Adelaide St W Ste 400	Toronto	ON	M5H1W7	647-724-7059	
Web: www.jmg.com					
Junction Networks Inc 55 Broad St 20th Fl	New York	NY	10004	212-933-9190	
Web: www.junctionnetworks.com					
k-eCommerce 666 St-Martin W Blvd Ste 330	Laval	QC	H7M5G4	514-973-2510	372-5413*
**Fax Area Code:* 888 ■ *Web:* www.k-ecommerce.com					
Kagi Inc 1442-A Walnut St Ste 392	Berkeley	CA	94709	510-658-5244	
Web: www.kagi.com					
Kahuna Inc 555 Bryant St Ste 322	Palo Alto	CA	94301	844-465-2486	
Web: www.usekahuna.com					
Kaleo Software Inc 841 Apollo St Ste 330	El Segundo	CA	90245	888-937-8945	
TF: 888-937-8945 ■ *Web:* www.kaleosoftware.com					
Kalida Telephone Co 121 E Main St PO Box 267	Kalida	OH	45853	419-532-3218	
Web: www.kalidatel.com					
Kaneva Inc 5901-C Peachtree Dunwoody Rd	Atlanta	GA	30328	678-367-0555	
Web: www.kaneva.com					
Kanjoya Inc 456 Montgomery St Ste 500	San Francisco	CA	94104	650-745-1054	
Web: www.experienceproject.com					
Karma Gaming International Inc 1498 Lower Water St	Halifax	NS	B3J3R5	902-463-2280	
Web: www.karmagaming.com					
KBA2 Inc 400 Treat Ave Ste E	San Francisco	CA	94110	415-528-5500	
Web: www.crowdoptic.com					
Kiwibox Media Inc 330 W 38th St Ste 1602	New York	NY	10018	212-239-8210	
Web: www.kiwibox.com					
Knew Deal Inc 1528 Woodward Ave Fourth Fl	Detroit	MI	48226	313-373-7844	
Web: www.stik.com					
KoinzMedia 1851 McCarthy Blvd Ste 101	Milpitas	CA	95035	408-217-0304	
Web: www.rewardspay.com					
Koozoo Inc 880 Harrison St	San Francisco	CA	94107	415-778-6374	
KORE Telematics Inc 3700 Mansell Rd Ste 250	Alpharetta	GA	30022	203-478-5281	
Web: www.koretelematics.com					
Kuratur Inc 68 White St Ste 7-315	Red Bank	NJ	07701	732-676-3183	
Web: www.kuratur.com					
KX Systems Inc 530 Lytton St Second Fl	Palo Alto	CA	94301	650-798-5155	
Web: www.kx.com					
KYCK Inc 619 S Cedar St Ste M	Charlotte	NC	28202	704-951-5925	
Web: www.kyck.com					
Landel Telecom 6830 Via Del Oro Ste 260	San Jose	CA	95119	408-360-0480	
Web: www.landel.com					
LaughStub LLC 2038 Armacost Ave	Los Angeles	CA	90025	800-927-0939	
TF: 800-927-0939 ■ *Web:* www.laughstub.com					
LD Telecommunications Inc 121 Ponce de Leon Ste 200	Miami	FL	33134	305-358-8952	
Web: www.nexogy.com					
Lexicon International Corp 1400A Adams Rd	Bensalem	PA	19020	215-639-8220	
Web: lexicon-int.com					
LexisNexis Martindale-Hubbell 121 Chanlon Rd	New Providence	NJ	07974	800-526-4902	665-3593*
**Fax Area Code:* 908 ■ **Fax:* Sales ■ *TF:* 800-526-4902 ■ *Web:* www.martindale.com					
Liberty Communications Business Office 413 N Calhoun St	West Liberty	IA	52776	319-627-2145	
Web: www.libertycommunications.com					
LifeShare Technologies LLC 2177 Intelliplex Dr Ste 150	Shelbyville	IN	46176	317-825-0320	
Web: www.lifesharetech.com					
Lingo Inc 7901 Jones Branch Dr Ninth Fl	Mclean	VA	22102	888-546-4699	
TF: 888-546-4699 ■ *Web:* www.lingo.com					
LINQ Services 6679 Santa Barbara Rd Ste D	Elkridge	MD	21075	800-421-5467	
TF: 800-421-5467 ■ *Web:* www.linqservices.com					
Linq3 Technologies LLC 75 Rockefeller Plz 14th Fl	New York	NY	10019	646-837-7070	
Web: www.linq3.com					
LiveMocha Inc 1011 Western Ave, Ste 1000	Seattle	WA	98104	206-257-2500	
TF: 800-399-6212 ■ *Web:* www.livemocha.com					
LiveRelay Inc 10815 Rancho Bernardo Rd Ste 300	San Diego	CA	92127	858-348-1710	
Web: www.relaytv.com					
Localstake LLC 212 W Tenth St Ste A480	Indianapolis	IN	46202	317-602-4790	
Web: www.localstake.com					
LocalVox Media Inc Five Hanover Sq	New York	NY	10005	646-545-3400	
Web: localvox.com					
LocaModa Inc 160 Sidney St	Cambridge	MA	02139	617-864-9600	
Web: locamoda.com					
Loctronix Corp 18815 139th Ave NE Ste A-1	Woodinville	WA	98072	425-307-3480	
Web: www.loctronix.com					
Logical Net Corp 1462 Erie Blvd	Schenectady	NY	12305	518-292-4500	
Web: www.logical.net					
Lotsa Helping Hands Inc 34 Washington St Ste 310	Wellesley Hills	MA	02481	301-942-6430	
Web: www.lotsahelpinghands.com					
LOYAL3 Holdings Inc 150 California St Ste 400	San Francisco	CA	94111	415-981-0700	
Web: www.loyal3.com					
LTI DataComm Inc 23020 Eaglewood Dr Ste 600	Sterling	VA	20166	703-581-6868	
Web: www.ltidata.com					
M2M Datasmart Inc 2010 Jimmy Durante Blvd Ste 220	Del Mar	CA	92014	858-350-5855	
Web: www.m2mdatasmart.com					
Mainstream Data Inc 375 Chipeta Way Ste B	Salt Lake City	UT	84108	801-584-2800	
Web: www.mainstreamdata.com					
Manhattan Telecommunications Corp 55 Water St 31st Fl	New York	NY	10041	212-607-2000	
Web: www.mettel.net					
Marcus Evans Inc 455 N Cityfront Plz Dr The NBC Tower Ninth Fl	Chicago	IL	60611	312-540-3000	
Web: www.marcusevans.com					
Market Velocity Inc 1305 Mall of Georgia Blvd Ste 190	Buford	GA	30519	770-325-6300	
Web: www.marketvelocity.com					
MarketResearch.com 11200 Rockville Pk Ste 504	Rockville	MD	20852	240-747-3000	747-3004
Web: www.marketresearch.com					
Marshall Graphics Systems 1625 Galleria Blvd	Brentwood	TN	37027	615-399-8896	
Web: www.marshallgraphics.com					
MaxTradeIn.com LLC 9102 N Meridian St Ste 450	Indianapolis	IN	46260	317-218-3612	
Web: www.maxtradein.com					
MBO Partners Inc 13454 Sunrise Vly Dr Ste 300	Herndon	VA	20171	703-793-6000	
Web: www.mbopartners.com					
MBS Dev Inc 7887 E Belleview Ave Ste 600	Englewood	CO	80111	303-469-2346	
Web: www.mbsdev.com					
MCNC Inc 3021 E Cornwallis Rd PO Box 12889	Research Triangle Park	NC	27709	919-248-1900	
Web: www.mcnc.org					
MDSL 1410 Broadway Ste 2101	New York	NY	10018	212-201-6199	
Web: www.mdsl.com					
Media Convergence Group Inc 904 Elm St Ste 208	Columbia	MO	65201	573-442-4557	
Web: www.newsy.com					
Medialets Inc 80 Eighth Ave	New York	NY	10014	212-300-5670	
Web: www.medialets.com					
MedTrust Online LLC 14358 N Frank Lloyd Wright Blvd Ste 4	Scottsdale	AZ	85260	480-889-8955	
Web: www.medtrust-online.com					
Meer.net LLC 202 S Randolph Ave	Elkins	WV	26241	304-636-5722	
Web: www.meer.net					
MeetingOne Corp 501 S Cherry St One Cherry Ctr Ste 1000	Denver	CO	80246	303-623-2530	
Web: www.meetingone.com					
MemberPlanet Inc 23224 Crenshaw Blvd	Torrance	CA	94065	916-445-1254	
Web: www.memberplanet.com					
MENTISoftware Solutions LLC 311 E 72nd St Ste 9A	New York	NY	10021	212-861-2235	
Web: www.mentisoftware.com					
MerchantCircle Inc 201 Main St Ste 100	Los Altos	CA	94022	650-352-1335	
Web: www.merchantcircle.com					
Merrill DataSite 225 Varick St	New York	NY	10014	866-399-3770	
TF: 866-399-3770 ■ *Web:* www.datasite.com					

Company	City	State	ZIP	Phone	Fax
MERX Networks Inc 38 Antares Dr Ste 1000 *Web:* www.merx.com	Ottawa	ON	K2E7V2	613-727-4900	
Mesh Systems LLC 12400 N Meridian St Ste 175 *Web:* www.mesh-systems.com	Carmel	IN	46032	317-661-4800	
MessageBank LLC 250 W 57Th St Ste 1001 *TF:* 800-989-8001 ■ *Web:* www.messagebank.com	New York	NY	10107	212-333-9300	
MexGrocer.com LLC 4060 Morena Blvd Ste C *Web:* www.mexgrocer.com	San Diego	CA	92117	858-270-0577	
MindSnacks Inc 1479 Folsom St *Web:* www.mindsnacks.com	San Francisco	CA	94103	415-400-4626	
Mixamo Inc 2415 Third St Ste 239 *Web:* www.mixamo.com	San Francisco	CA	94107	415-255-7455	
Mobi PCS Inc 733 Bishop St Ste 1200 *Web:* www.mobipcs.com	Honolulu	HI	96813	808-723-1111	
Mobile Accord Inc 2150 W 29th Ave Second Fl *Web:* www.mobileaccord.com	Denver	CO	80211	303-531-5505	
MobileIQ Inc 4800 Baseline Rd Ste E104-247 *TF:* 866-261-8600 ■ *Web:* www.gomobileiq.com	Boulder	CO	80303	866-261-8600	
MOGL Loyalty Services Inc 9645 Scranton Rd Ste 110 *TF:* 888-664-5669 ■ *Web:* www.mogl.com	San Diego	CA	92121	888-664-5669	
MoJiva Inc 136 Baxter St *Web:* www.mojiva.com	New York	NY	10013	646-862-6201	
Mojo Motors Inc 150 W 30th St Ste 1200 *Web:* www.mojomotors.com	New York	NY	10001	917-398-4060	
Moseo Corp 2722 Elake Ave E *Web:* www.seniorhomes.com	Seattle	WA	98102	206-905-8774	
Motista Inc 1777 Borel Pl Ste 500 *TF:* 877-966-8478 ■ *Web:* www.motista.com	San Mateo	CA	94402	877-966-8478	
Mountain Telephone Co 405 Main St *Web:* www.mrtc.com	West Liberty	KY	41472	606-743-3121	
Mpathix Inc 87 Skyway Ave Ste 200 *Web:* www.mpathix.com	Toronto	ON	M9W6R3	416-849-4210	
MTN Government Services Inc 161 Ft Evans Rd NE Ste 220 *Web:* www.mtngs.com	Leesburg	VA	20176	703-443-6738	
MVS Group 1086 Goffle Rd *Web:* www.themvsgroup.com	Hawthorne	NJ	07506	201-447-1505	
MYCOM North America Inc 1080 Holcomb Bridge Rd Bldg 200 Ste 350 *Web:* www.mycom-usa.com	Roswell	GA	30076	770-776-0000	
MyCorporation Business Services Inc 23586 Calabasas Rd Ste 102 *Web:* www.mycorporation.com	Calabasas	CA	91302	818-224-7639	
myITForum.com 588 West 400 South *Web:* www.myitforum.com	Lindon	UT	84042	801-226-8500	
MyNewPlace.com 343 Sansome St Ste 700 *Web:* www.mynewplace.com	San Francisco	CA	94104	415-348-2009	
NADAguides.com 3186 K Airway Ave *Web:* www.nadaguides.com	Costa Mesa	CA	92626	714-556-8511	
National Technical Information Service (NTIS) 5285 Port Royal Rd *TF Orders:* 800-553-6847 ■ *Web:* www.ntis.gov	Springfield	VA	22161	703-605-6000	605-6900
NERAC Inc 1 Technology Dr *Web:* www.nerac.com	Tolland	CT	06084	860-872-7000	872-6026
NetStream Communications LLC 200 Sandy Springs Pl Ste 200 *Web:* www.netstreamcom.net	Atlanta	GA	30328	404-585-3535	
Netswitch 400 Oy Ste 226 *Web:* www.netswitch.net	South San Francisco	CA	94080	650-583-3066	
New Pros Data Inc 155 Hidden Ravines Dr *Web:* www.newpros.com	Powell	OH	43065	740-201-0410	
New Visions Powerline Communications Inc PO Box 11815 *Web:* www.nvplc.com	Syracuse	NY	13218	315-472-6300	
NewCloud Networks 160 Inverness Dr W *TF:* 855-255-5001 ■ *Web:* www.newcloudnetworks.com	Englewood	CO	80112	855-255-5001	
Newmark Advertising 15821 Ventura Blvd Ste 570 *Web:* www.newmarkad.com	Encino	CA	91436	818-461-0300	
Newsbank Inc 5801 Pelican Bay Blvd Ste 600 *TF:* 800-243-7694 ■ *Web:* www.newsbank.com	Naples	FL	34108	239-263-6004	263-3004
Next Net Media LLC 316 California Ave Ste 804 *TF:* 800-737-5820 ■ *Web:* nextnetmedia.com	Reno	NV	89509	800-737-5820	
Nextiva 8800 E Chaparral Rd Ste 300 *Web:* www.nextiva.com	Scottsdale	AZ	85250	602-753-4000	
nexVortex Inc 510 Spring St Ste 120 *Web:* www.nexvortex.com	Herndon	VA	20170	703-579-0200	
Nexxtworks Inc 30798 Us Hwy 19 N *TF:* 888-533-8353 ■ *Web:* www.nexxtworks.com	Palm Harbor	FL	34684	888-533-8353	
Niche Directories LLC 909 N Sepulveda Blvd 11th Fl *TF:* 877-242-9330 ■ *Web:* www.nichedirectories.com	El Segundo	CA	90026	877-242-9330	
NobelBiz Inc 5973 Avenida Encinas Ste 202 *Web:* www.nobelbiz.com	Carlsbad	CA	92008	760-405-0105	
North Africa Journal, The PO Box 1001 *Web:* www.north-africa.com	Concord	MA	01742	508-471-3899	
North Florida Broadband Authority 164 Nw Madison St *Web:* www.nfba.net	Lake City	FL	32055	386-438-5042	
Northeast Florida Telephone Company Inc 130 N Fourth St *Web:* www.nefcom.net	Macclenny	FL	32063	904-259-2261	
Northwest Communications Coop 111 Railroad Ave PO Box 38 *Web:* www.nccray.com	Ray	ND	58849	701-568-3331	
Nsight 450 Security Blvd *Web:* www.nsight.com	Green Bay	WI	54313	920-617-7000	
Oceus Networks Inc 1895 Preston White Dr Ste 300 *Web:* www.oceusnetworks.com	Reston	VA	20191	703-234-9200	
Ogmento Inc 134 Spring St *Web:* www.flybymedia.com	New York	NY	10012	212-226-2736	
Oklahoma Telephone & Telegraph Inc 26 N Otis Ave *TF:* 800-869-1989 ■ *Web:* www.oklatel.net	Dustin	OK	74839	800-869-1989	
OLogic 544 E Weddell Dr #7 *Web:* www.ologicinc.com	Sunnyvale	CA	94089	650-996-1490	
Omitron Inc 7051 Muirkirk Meadows Dr Ste A *Web:* www.omitron.com	Beltsville	MD	20705	301-474-1700	345-4594
On Campus Marketing LLC 10411 Motor City Dr Ste 650 *Web:* www.ocm.com	Bethesda	MD	20817	301-652-1580	
OneClass 415 Yonge St Unit 1205 *TF:* 855-392-6946 ■ *Web:* oneclass.com	Toronto	ON	M5B2E7	855-392-6946	
OneID Inc 580 Howard St Ste 303 *Web:* www.oneid.com	San Francisco	CA	94105	415-590-3712	
OneMorePallet.com 9891 Montgomery Rd Ste 122 *TF:* 855-438-1667 ■ *Web:* www.onemorepallet.com	Cincinnati	OH	45242	855-438-1667	
Oneplanetweb Inc 322 E Arrellaga St *Web:* www.1planetweb.com	Santa Barbara	CA	93101	805-963-1056	
Onvoy Inc 300 S Hwy 169 Ste 700 *Web:* www.onvoy.com	Minneapolis	MN	55426	952-230-4100	
Openbay Inc 222 Third St Ste 4000 *Web:* www.openbay.com	Cambridge	MA	02142	617-398-8888	
Openfilm LLC 1450 S Miami Ave *Web:* www.openfilm.com	Miami	FL	33130	305-396-2636	
OpenSesame Inc 2828 SW Corbett Ste135 *Web:* www.opensesame.com	Portland	OR	97201	503-808-1268	
Optimum Lead Generation LLC 12230 Forest Hill Blvd Ste 300 *Web:* www.optimumleadgeneration.com	Wellington	FL	33414	561-227-1507	
Orbitel Communications LLC 21116 N John Wayne Pkwy Ste B-9 *Web:* www.orbitelcom.com	Maricopa	AZ	85239	520-568-8890	
Oricom Internet Inc 400 Rue Nolin Bureau Ste 150 *Web:* orion.oricom.ca	Vanier	QC	G1M1E7	418-683-4557	
Otelco Inc. 505 Third Ave East *Web:* www3.otelco.net	Oneonta	AL	35121	205-625-3574	
OurParents Inc 8521 Leesburg Pk Ste 310 *TF:* 866-629-1634 ■ *Web:* www.ourparents.com	Vienna	VA	22182	866-629-1634	
Ovid Technologies Inc 333 Seventh Ave 20th Fl *TF:* 800-950-2035 ■ *Web:* www.ovid.com	New York	NY	10001	646-674-6300	674-6301
Oxford County Telephone & Telegraph Company Inc 491 Lisbon St *Web:* oxfordnetworks.com/	Lewiston	ME	04240	207-333-6900	
Oxygen Cloud Inc 1600 Seaport Blvd Ste 310 *Web:* www.oxygencloud.com	Redwood City	CA	94063	650-241-6210	
P Marshall & Associates LLC 1000 Holcomb Woods Pkwy Ste 210 *Web:* pmass.com	Roswell	GA	30076	678-280-2325	
P4RC Inc 10001 Venice Blvd Ste 421 *Web:* www.p4rc.com	Los Angeles	CA	90034	310-621-9555	
Pacific Centrex Services Inc 6855 Tujunga Ave *Web:* www.pcs1.net	North Hollywood	CA	91605	818-623-2300	
PackLate.com Inc 100 Four Falls Corporate Ctr Ste 104 *TF:* 877-472-2552 ■ *Web:* packlate.com	West Conshohocken	PA	19428	877-472-2552	
Pageplus Cellular 1615 Timberwolf Dr *Web:* www.pagepluscellular.com	Holland	OH	43528	419-382-8603	
Paniagua's Enterprises Development Company LLC 6400 Frankford Ave Ste 30 *Web:* www.paniaguas.net	Baltimore	MD	21206	410-485-9327	
Paramount Defenses Inc 620 Newport Ctr Dr Ste 1100 *Web:* www.paramountdefenses.com	Newport Beach	CA	92660	949-468-5770	
Patent Calls Inc 2802 Flintrock Trace Ste 202 *Web:* www.patentcalls.com	Austin	TX	78738	512-371-4120	287-5366
PayEase Inc 2332 Walsh Ave *Web:* www.w-phone.com	Santa Clara	CA	95051	408-567-9300	567-9370
Peerless Network Inc 222 S Riverside Plz Ste 2730 *Web:* www.peerlessnetwork.com	Chicago	IL	60606	312-506-0920	
PerspecSys Inc 86 Healey Rd *Web:* www.perspecsys.com	Bolton	ON	L7E5A7	905-857-0411	
Phone.com Inc 211 Warren St Ste 116 *Web:* www.phone.com	Newark	NJ	07103	973-577-6380	
Pineland Telephone Cooperative Inc 30 S Rountree St *Web:* www.pineland.net	Metter	GA	30439	912-685-2121	
Pinnacle Communications Corp 19821 Executive Park Cir *Web:* www.pinnaclecommunications.com	Germantown	MD	20874	301-601-0777	
Pixelgate 733 Lakefield Rd Ste A *Web:* www.pixelgate.net	Westlake Village	CA	91361	805-446-6251	
PK4 Media Inc 1600 E Franklin Ave Ste C *TF:* 888-320-6281 ■ *Web:* www.pk4media.com	El Segundo	CA	90245	888-320-6281	
PlaceFull Inc 122 S Jackson St Ste 310 *Web:* placefull.com	Seattle	WA	98104	206-624-0295	
Platfora Inc 1300 S El Camino Real Sixth Fl *Web:* www.platfora.com	San Mateo	CA	94402	650-918-1100	
Plum Analytics Inc 808 Firethorn Cir *Web:* www.plumanalytics.com	Dresher	PA	19025	206-331-7297	
Pong Marketing & Promotions Inc 201 Creditview Rd *Web:* www.pongmarketing.com	Woodbridge	ON	L4L9T1	905-264-3555	264-3556
Popp Telecom Inc 620 Mendelssohn Ave N *Web:* www.popp.com	Golden Valley	MN	55427	763-797-7900	
Postmasters Inc 701 Brazos St Ste 1616 *Web:* www.postmaster.io	Austin	TX	78701	512-693-4040	

Company / Address	City	State	Zip	Phone	Fax
PresiNET Systems Corp 645 Fort St Ste L109	Victoria	BC	V8W1G2	250-405-5380	405-5362
Web: www.presinet.com					
PrestoTech Solutions 4595 Broadmoor Ave Se Ste 236	Grand Rapids	MI	49512	616-891-4100	
Web: www.prestotech.net					
PriceWaiter LLC 426 Market St	Chattanooga	TN	37421	855-671-9889	
TF: 855-671-9889 ■ *Web:* www.pricewaiter.com					
Profisee Group Inc 2520 Northwinds Pkwy Two Northwinds Ctr	Alpharetta	GA	30009	678-202-8990	
Web: www.profisee.com					
Proformative Inc 99 Almaden Blvd Ste 975	San Jose	CA	95113	408-400-3993	
Web: www.proformative.com					
ProofSpace Inc 900 Clancy Ave NE	Grand Rapids	MI	49503	312-933-8823	
Web: www.proofspace.com					
Property Line International Inc 2525 Box Canyon Dr	Las Vegas	NV	89128	702-889-1063	
Web: www.propertyline.com					
PropertyMaps Inc 435 Aspen Dr	Austin	TX	78737	512-791-3527	
Web: www.propertymaps.com					
Proximic Inc 4400 Bohannon Dr	Menlo Park	CA	94025	650-549-7800	
Web: www.proximic.com					
Pulpo Media Inc 1767 Alcatraz Ave	Berkeley	CA	94703	510-594-2294	
Web: www.pulpomedia.com					
Pure Auto LLC 164 Market St Ste 250	Charleston	SC	29401	877-860-7873	
TF: 877-860-7873 ■ *Web:* www.purecars.com					
Purple Communications Inc 595 Menlo Dr	Rocklin	CA	95765	800-900-9478	
TF: 800-900-9478 ■ *Web:* www.purple.us					
Qualaroo Inc 1901 Newport Blvd Ste 175	Costa Mesa	CA	92627	650-485-3415	
Web: qualaroo.com					
Quality Communications & Alarm Co 1985 Swarthmore Ave Ste 4	Lakewood	NJ	08701	732-730-9000	
Web: www.qualitywireless.com					
QualVu Inc 12039 W Alameda Pkwy Ste Z-2	Lakewood	CO	80228	303-640-6222	
Web: www.qualvu.com					
Quantcast Corp 201 Third St Second Fl	San Francisco	CA	94103	415-738-4755	
Web: www.quantcast.com					
Quantopian Inc 77 Summer St	Boston	MA	02110	617-752-1454	
Web: www.quantopian.com					
Questia Media America Inc 1 N State St Ste 900	Chicago	IL	60602	800-889-0097	782-3901*
**Fax Area Code:* 312 ■ *TF:* 800-759-4726 ■ *Web:* www.questia.com					
Quip Inc 988 Market St Seventh Fl	San Francisco	CA	94102	650-804-5075	
Web: quip.com					
Quizzle LLC 1042 Woodward Ave	Detroit	MI	48226	313-373-3900	
Web: www.quizzle.com					
Rallyorg 580 Howard St Ste 402	San Francisco	CA	94105	888-648-2220	
TF: 888-648-2220 ■ *Web:* rally.org					
RateMyProfessors.com LLC 1515 Broadway	New York	NY	10036	212-654-7763	
Web: www.ratemyprofessors.com					
RC Telecom Inc 6250 W Tenth St Ste 1	Greeley	CO	80634	970-356-4572	
Web: rctelecom.com					
Reachable Inc 855 El Camino Real Ste 260	Palo Alto	CA	94301	650-324-1400	
Web: www.reachable.com					
ReadOz LLC 350 W Ontario St Ste 4W	Chicago	IL	60654	312-929-2500	
Web: www.readoz.com					
Ready Set Work LLC 1487 Dunwoody Dr	West Chester	PA	19380	215-689-4323	
Web: www.readysetwork.com					
Real Girls Media Network Inc 575 Market St Ninth Fl	San Francisco	CA	94105	415-295-8506	
Web: www.realgirlsmedia.com					
Real Time Translation Inc 1107 Hazeltine Blvd	Chaska	MN	55318	952-479-6180	
Web: www.rttmobile.com					
RealtyShares Inc 637 Natoma St Ste 5	San Francisco	CA	94103	415-450-6234	
Web: www.realtyshares.com					
Reaslo Inc 5214F Diamond Heights Blvd Ste 217	San Francisco	CA	94131	888-870-7889	
TF: 888-870-7889 ■ *Web:* www.reesio.com					
Rebellion Media Group Corp 150 Caroline St Ste 406	Waterloo	ON	N2L0A5	519-827-1999	
Web: www.rebellionmedia.com					
RecordSetter LLC 228 Park Ave S Ste 29280	New York	NY	10003	646-912-6611	
Web: recordsetter.com					
RecycleMatch LLC 3375 Westpark Dr Ste 321	Houston	TX	77005	713-581-0466	
Web: www.recyclematch.com					
Red Lambda Inc 2180 W State Rd 434 Ste 6200	Longwood	FL	32779	407-682-4940	445-5367*
**Fax Area Code:* 321 ■ *Web:* www.redlambda.com					
Redi-Data Inc Five Audrey Pl	Fairfield	NJ	07004	973-227-4380	
Web: www.redidata.com					
RefluxMD Inc 10804 Willow Ct Ste B	San Diego	CA	92127	760-668-9904	
Web: www.refluxmd.com					
RefWorks LLC 7200 Wisconsin Ave Ste 601	Bethesda	MD	20814	301-961-6700	
Web: www.refworks.com					
Regaalo Inc 75 Rochester Ave	Portsmouth	NH	03801	603-570-3200	
Web: www.regaalo.com					
RelayHealth Corp 1564 Northeast Expy Ste 600	Atlanta	GA	30329	404-728-2000	
Web: www.relayhealth.com					
Reliance Connects 61 W Mesquite Blvd	Mesquite	NV	89027	702-346-5211	
Web: www.relianceconnects.com					
Rentals Inc 3585 Engineering Dr	Norcross	GA	30092	888-501-7368	
TF: 888-501-7368 ■ *Web:* www.rentals.com					
rentbits.com Inc 1062 Delaware St Ste 5	Denver	CO	80204	303-640-3160	
Web: rentbits.com					
Reputation Rhino LLC 711 Third Ave 12th Fl	New York	NY	10017	888-975-3331	
TF: 888-975-3331 ■ *Web:* reputationrhino.com					
Research on Demand Inc 2629 State St	Santa Barbara	CA	93105	805-963-4095	
Web: www.researchondemand.com					
Research Wizard of Tulsa City-County Library 400 Civic Ctr	Tulsa	OK	74103	918-596-7991	596-2598
Web: www.researchwizard.org					
Resort Internet 2130 Resort Dr Ste 100	Steamboat Springs	CO	80487	970-870-1818	
Web: www.resortbroadband.com					
Resultly LLC 116 W Hubbard St Fourth Fl	Chicago	IL	60654	312-273-9400	
Web: www.result.ly					
Retailigence Corp 2400 Broadway Ste 220	Redwood City	CA	94063	650-716-4748	
Web: retailigence.com					
RetailMLS LLC 12 W 23rd St Fourth Fl	New York	NY	10010	212-729-1041	
Web: retailmls.com					
Revestor LLC 505 Montgomery St 11th Fl	San Francisco	CA	94111	415-689-4942	
Web: revestor.com					
ReviewPush 12885 N Hwy Ste 110A	Austin	TX	78750	512-814-8046	
Web: www.reviewpush.com					
Rhythm Organism LLC, The 400 N State St Ste 410	Chicago	IL	60654	312-321-0111	
Web: www.fanfueled.com					
RidgeviewTel LLC 1880 Industrial Cir Ste C	Longmont	CO	80501	303-309-4005	
RightAnswer.com Inc 2900 Rodd St	Midland	MI	48641	989-835-5000	
Web: www.rightanswer.com					
Rightside Group Ltd 5808 Lk Washington Blvd NE	Kirkland	WA	98033	425-298-2500	
Web: www.rightside.co					
Rise Broadband 400 Inverness Pkwy Ste 330	Englewood	CO	80112	303-705-6522	
Web: www.jabbroadband.com					
RISQ Inc 625 Rene-Levesque Blvd W Bureau 300	Montreal	QC	H3B1R2	514-845-7181	
Web: www.risq.qc.ca					
RivalHealth LLC 6601 Hillsborough St Ste 109	Raleigh	NC	27606	919-803-6709	
Web: www.rivalhealth.com					
Riviera Cellular & Telecommunicat PO Box 997	Riviera	TX	78379	361-296-3232	
Web: www.rivnet.com					
RobotsApps.com Inc 50 California St 15th Fl Ste 1500	San Francisco	CA	94111	415-439-5291	
Web: www.robotappstore.com					
Rockefeller Group Technology Solutions Inc 1221 Ave of the Americas	New York	NY	10020	212-282-2200	
Web: www.rgts.com					
Rockhouse Partners LLC 631 Second Ave S Ste 2R	Nashville	TN	37210	615-873-0924	
Web: www.rockhousepartners.com					
RoundPegg Inc 1433 Pearl St Ste 300	Boulder	CO	80302	720-663-7344	
Web: www.roundpegg.com					
SaaS Markets LLC 1720 S Amphlett Blvd Ste 210	San Mateo	CA	94402	650-458-0748	
Web: www.saasmarkets.com					
Salesconx Inc 701 Seventh Ave Ste 9E	New York	NY	10036	212-453-9880	
Web: www.salesconx.com					
Savant Technology Group Inc 2682 Bishop Dr Ste 210	San Ramon	CA	94583	925-461-4510	
Web: www.savant-us.com					
SaveUp Inc 480 Second St Ste 202	San Francisco	CA	94107	415-578-9949	
Web: www.saveup.com					
ScanAps 6133 Bristol Pkwy Ste 301	Culver City	CA	90230	310-670-1700	
Web: www.scanaps.com					
Schaller Telephone Co 111 w Second st	Schaller	IA	51053	712-275-4211	
Web: www.schallertel.net					
School Systems Group of Pearson 10911 White Rock Rd Ste 200	Rancho Cordova	CA	95670	916-288-1600	
Web: www.pearsonschoolsystems.com					
SchoolDocs LLC 5944 Luther Ln Ste 600	Dallas	TX	75225	866-311-2293	
TF: 866-311-2293 ■ *Web:* www.schooldocs.com					
Scoot & Doodle Inc 2625 Middlefield Rd Ste 223	Palo Alto	CA	94306	888-563-9224	
TF: 888-563-9224 ■ *Web:* scootdoodle.com					
Scott Enterprises Inc 2225 Downs Dr Sixth Fl Exce Stes	Erie	PA	16509	814-868-9500	866-0463
TF: 877-866-3445 ■ *Web:* www.scottenterprises.org					
Scripted Inc 135 Stillman St	San Francisco	CA	94107	415-795-4053	
Web: scripted.com					
SECOS Inc 18301 Von Karman Ave Ste 460	Irvine	CA	92612	949-794-0021	
Web: www.secos.com					
Sedo.com LLC 161 First St Fourth Fl	Cambridge	MA	02142	617-499-7200	
Web: www.sedo.com					
SeeClickFix Inc 746 Chapel St Ste 207	New Haven	CT	06510	203-752-0777	
Web: www.seeclickfix.com					
Seize The Deal LLC 1851 N Greenville Ave Ste 100	Richardson	TX	75081	866-210-0881	
TF: 866-210-0881 ■ *Web:* www.seizethedeal.com					
SelectPath Inc 10820 Central Ave SE	Albuquerque	NM	87123	505-275-4601	
Web: www.selectpath.com					
Sell My Timeshare Now LLC 383 Central Ave Ste 260	Dover	NH	03820	603-516-0200	
Web: www.sellmytimesharenow.com					
Senior-Living.com Inc 8521 Leesburg Pk Ste 310	Vienna	VA	22182	866-342-4297	
TF: 866-342-4297 ■ *Web:* www.seniorliving.net					
SERPs Inc 1410 NW Johnson St	Portland	OR	97209	503-683-3470	
Web: serps.com					
Setel 1165 s Sixth st	Macclenny	FL	32063	904-259-1300	
Web: www.mpittweather.com					
Shaadi Karoge Inc 108 W 13th St	Wilmington	DE	19801	510-402-4486	
Web: www.shaadikaroge.com					
Shapeways BV 419 Park Ave S	New York	NY	10016	718-974-8010	
Web: www.shapeways.com					
ShopVisible LLC 945 East Paces Ferry Rd Ste 1475	Atlanta	GA	30326	866-493-7037	745-0790*
**Fax Area Code:* 404 ■ *TF:* 866-493-7037 ■ *Web:* www.shopvisible.com					
Shoutlet Inc One Erdman Pl Ste 102	Madison	WI	53717	608-833-0088	
Web: www.swayonline.com					
SilverRail Technologies Inc 300 Trade Ctr Ste 5500	Woburn	MA	01801	617-934-6786	
Web: www.silverrailtech.com					
SimpleTuition Inc 268 Summer St Ste 502	Boston	MA	02210	617-630-6100	
Web: simpletuition.com					
Skinny Mom Inc 602 Main St Ste 410	Cincinnati	OH	45202	513-621-6364	
Web: skinnymom.com					

	City	State	Zip	Phone	Fax
SkyBlox LLC 244 Peters St Ste 7 *Web:* www.skyblox.com	Atlanta	GA	30313	866-632-9685	
Skype Inc 3210 Porter Dr *Web:* www.skype.com	Palo Alto	CA	94304	650-493-7900	
SkyWeaver Inc 1501 Broadway 25th Fl *Web:* www.skyweaver.com	New York	NY	10036	646-571-8596	
SlingShot Communications Inc 8723 E Via de Commercio Ste A-203 *Web:* www.slingshot.com	Scottsdale	AZ	85258	480-626-8625	
Smart Choice Communications LLC 16 W 45Th St *Web:* www.smartchoiceus.com	New York	NY	10036	212-660-7300	
SMART IT Services Inc 34715 Van Dyke Ave *Web:* www.smartservices.com	Sterling Heights	MI	48312	586-258-0650	
SmartAction Company LLC 390 N Sepulveda Blvd Ste 2150 *Web:* www.smartaction.com	El Segundo	CA	90245	310-776-9200	
SmartProcure LLC 700 W Hillsboro Blvd Ste 4-100 *Web:* smartprocure.us	Deerfield Beach	FL	33441	954-420-9900	
Smartsat Inc 8222 118th Ave Ste 600 *Web:* smartsat.com	Largo	FL	33773	727-535-6880	
Smarty Ants Inc 1400 Rollins Rd *TF:* 877-905-2687 ■ *Web:* www.smartyants.com	Burlingame	CA	94010	877-905-2687	
Smith Bagley Inc 1500 S White Mtn Rd Ste 103 *Web:* www.cellularoneonline.com	Show Low	AZ	85901	928-537-0690	
Snapfinger 3025 Windward Plz Ste 150 *Web:* www.snapfinger.com	Alpharetta	GA	30005	678-739-4650	
SnapGoods Inc 155 Water St *Web:* www.snapgoods.com	Brooklyn	NY	11201	347-651-0845	
Snooth Inc 162 Madison Ave Fl 4 *Web:* www.snooth.com	New York	NY	10016	646-723-4328	
Social Annex Inc 5301 Beethoven St Ste 260 *TF:* 866-802-8806 ■ *Web:* www.socialannex.com	Los Angeles	CA	90066	866-802-8806	
Social Strategy1 5000 Sawgrass Village Cir Ste 30 *Web:* www.socialstrategy1.com	Ponte Vedra Beach	FL	32082	877-771-3366	
SocialChorus 703 Market St Ste 470 *Web:* www.socialchorus.com	San Francisco	CA	94103	415-655-2700	
SocialFlow Inc 52 Vanderbilt Ave 12th Fl *Web:* www.socialflow.com	New York	NY	10017	212-883-9844	
Sogetel Inc 111, rue du 12-Novembre *Web:* www.sogetel.com	Nicolet	QC	J3T1S3	866-764-3835	
SOLOMO Technology Inc 222 W Washington Ave Ste 705 *Web:* solomotechnology.com	Madison	WI	53703	608-220-1900	
Sopheon Corp 3001 Metro Dr Ste 460 *TF:* 800-367-8358 ■ *Web:* www.sopheon.com	Bloomington	MN	55425	952-851-7500	851-7599
Sorvive Technologies Inc 2090 Buford Hwy Ste 1b *Web:* www.sorvive.com	Buford	GA	30518	770-614-3122	
Southwest Communications Inc 4100 N Mulberry Dr Ste 100 *Web:* www.scitel.net	Kansas City	MO	64116	816-298-4100	
SPACECONNECTION Inc, The 10530 Victory Blvd *Web:* www.thespaceconnection.com	North Hollywood	CA	91606	818-754-1100	
SpaceCurve Inc 710 Second Ave Ste 620 *Web:* www.spacecurve.com	Seattle	WA	98104	206-453-2225	
Spanfeller Media Group Inc 156 Fifth Ave Fourth Fl *Web:* www.spanfellergroup.com	New York	NY	10010	646-459-0604	
SpeakWorks Inc 815 West 1250 South Ste 119 *Web:* www.speakworks.com	Orem	UT	84058	801-717-3499	
Spectrum Networks Inc 2200 Sixth Ave Ste 905 *Web:* www.spectrumnet.us	Seattle	WA	98121	206-973-8300	
SpeedDate.com Inc PO Box 5545 *Web:* www.speeddate.com	Redwood City	CA	94063	650-692-9000	
SpinGo Solutions Inc 14193 S Minuteman Dr Ste 100 *TF:* 877-377-4646 ■ *Web:* www.spingo.com	Draper	UT	84020	877-377-4646	
Spira Data Corp 630 - Eigth Ave SW Ste 500 *Web:* www.spiradata.com	Calgary	AB	T2P1G6	403-263-6475	263-2513
Sport Ngin LLC 1400 Van Buren St NE Ste 200 *Web:* www.sportngin.com	Minneapolis	MN	55413	612-379-1030	
Spot411 Technologies Inc 10 Plz Sq Ste C *Web:* www.tvplus.com	Orange	CA	92866	714-771-2050	
SpotOn Inc 2350 Kerner Blvd Ste 380 *TF:* 877-814-4102 ■ *Web:* www.spoton.com	San Rafael	CA	94901	877-814-4102	
Spredfast Inc 200 W Cesar Chavez Ste 600 *Web:* www.spredfast.com	Austin	TX	78701	512-542-9900	
Spreedly Inc 116 W Main St *Web:* spreedly.com	Durham	NC	27701	919-432-5008	
Sqrrl Data Inc 275 Third St *Web:* sqrrl.com	Cambridge	MA	02142	617-902-0784	
SquaredOut Inc 2900 Bristol St Ste J203 *Web:* www.squaredout.com	Costa Mesa	CA	92626	714-668-0262	
Squire Tech Solutions LLC 6304 Fallwater Trl Ste 100 *Web:* www.squiretechsolutions.com	The Colony	TX	75056	214-306-6704	
Stage 2 Networks LLC 70 W 40th St Seventh Fl *Web:* www.stage2.net	New York	NY	10018	212-497-8000	
Star-Tech Inc PO Box 672932 *Web:* www.star-tech.net	Marietta	GA	30006	678-905-1171	
StarQuest Software Inc 1288 Ninth St *Web:* starquest.com	Berkeley	CA	94710	510-528-2900	
StataCorp LP 4905 Lakeway Dr *Web:* www.stata.com	College Station	TX	77845	979-696-4600	696-4601
Stibo Systems Inc 3550 George Busbee Pkwy NW Ste 350 *Web:* www.stibosystems.com	Kennesaw	GA	30144	770-425-3282	
Stickk.com LLC 39 E 30th St Ste 4 *TF:* 866-578-4255 ■ *Web:* www.stickk.com	New York	NY	10016	866-578-4255	
StudioNow Inc 4017 Hillsboro Pk *Web:* www.studionow.com	Nashville	TN	37215	615-577-9400	
StumbleUpon Inc 301 Brannan St *Web:* www.stumbleupon.com	San Francisco	CA	94107	415-979-0640	
StyleCaster Media Group LLC 49 W 27th St Studio A *Web:* www.stylecaster.com	New York	NY	10001	646-300-8350	
Summit Broadband Inc 4558 SW 35th St *Web:* www.summit-broadband.com	Orlando	FL	32811	407-996-8900	
Suncast Network Inc 2407 E Oakton St Ste B-10 *Web:* www.suncastv.com	Arlington Heights	IL	60005	847-364-4008	
Super Technologies Inc 6005 Keating Rd *Web:* www.supertec.com	Pensacola	FL	32504	850-433-8555	
SupportLocal LLC 1062 Delaware St Ste 4	Denver	CO	80204	720-432-8160	
SupremeBytes LLC PO Box 13746 *Web:* www.supremebytes.com	Columbus	OH	43213	614-636-4875	
Sureflix Digital Distribution Inc 229 Yonge St *Web:* www.corporate.sureflix.com	Toronto	ON	M5B1N9	416-907-7859	
Sutherland Global Services 1160 Pittsford-Victor Rd *Web:* www.sutherlandglobal.com	Pittsford	NY	14534	585-586-5757	784-2154
SystemMetrics Corp 900 Ft St Mall Ste 250 *Web:* www.platinumlimousinehawaii.com	Honolulu	HI	96813	808-791-7000	
Tandem Transit LLC 3611 14th Ave 3611 Ste 209 *Web:* tandemtransit.com	Brooklyn	NY	11218	718-689-1303	
Tapjoy Inc 111 Sutter St 13th Fl *Web:* www.tapjoy.com	San Francisco	CA	94104	415-766-6900	
TargetSpot Inc 149 Fifth Ave 10th Fl *Web:* www.targetspot.com	New York	NY	10010	212-631-0500	
Taurad LLC 6733 S Sepulveda Blvd Ste 135 *Web:* taurad.com	Los Angeles	CA	90045	310-281-3360	
Technorati Inc 360 Post St Ste 1100 *Web:* www.technorati.com	San Francisco	CA	94108	415-896-3000	
Telamon Corp 1000 E 116th St *Web:* www.telamon.com	Carmel	IN	46032	317-818-6888	
TelcoIQ 4300 Forbes Blvd Ste 110 *Web:* www.telcoiq.com	Lanham	MD	20706	202-595-1500	
Tele Atlas North America Inc 11 Lafayette St *Web:* www.tomtom.com	Lebanon	NH	03766	603-643-0330	653-0249
TeleGuam Holdings LLC 624 N Marine Corps Dr *Web:* www.gta.net	Tamuning	GU	96913	671-644-4482	
TelePacific Communications 1181 Grier Dr #F *Web:* www.telepacific.com	Las Vegas	NV	89119	702-851-6000	
Telephone Electronics Corp 236 E Capitol St *Web:* www.tec.com	Jackson	MS	39201	601-354-9070	
TeliaSonera International Carrier Inc 2201 Cooperative Way Ste 302 *Web:* www.teliasoneraic.com	Herndon	VA	20171	888-436-1133	
TelSpan Inc 101 W Washington St E Tower Ste 1200 *TF:* 800-800-1729 ■ *Web:* www.telspan.com	Indianapolis	IN	46204	800-800-1729	
TelTel Inc 2620 Augustine Dr Ste 100 *Web:* www.teltel.com	Santa Clara	CA	95054	408-970-3318	
Telx Group Inc, The One State St 24th Fl *Web:* www.telx.com	New York	NY	10004	212-480-3300	
Tendo Communications 340 Brannan St Ste 500 *Web:* www.tendocom.com	San Francisco	CA	94107	415-369-8200	
TennisHub Inc 95 Chestnut St	Providence	RI	02903	401-626-4280	
tenXer Inc 101 Townsend St Ste 209 *Web:* www.tenxer.com	San Francisco	CA	94107	415-500-2982	
Therapydia Inc 18 E Blithedale Ave Ste 21 *Web:* www.therapydia.com	Mill Valley	CA	94941	415-389-8677	
TheSquareFoot LLC 1776 Yorktown Dr Ste 610 *Web:* www.thesquarefoot.com	Houston	TX	77056	281-701-9697	
Thomson Financial 22 Thomson Pl *TF:* 888-216-1929 ■ *Web:* www.thomsonreuters.com	Boston	MA	02210	617-856-2000	
TIBCO Software Inc 707 State Rd Ste 212 *Web:* www.netrics.com	Princeton	NJ	08540	609-683-4002	
TicketBiscuit LLC 1550 Woods of Riverchase Dr Ste 330 *Web:* www.ticketbiscuit.com	Birmingham	AL	35244	205-757-8330	
Tie National Accounts 1723 Simms St Ste 206 *Web:* tienational.com	Aurora	IL	60504	630-301-7444	
TinyPass Inc 105 Hudson St *Web:* www.tinypass.com	New York	NY	10013	646-350-1999	
TodoCast Inc 31831 Camino Capistrano Ste 301 *TF:* 866-510-7889 ■ *Web:* todocast.tv	San Juan Capistrano	CA	92675	866-510-7889	
Tongal Inc 1918 Main St Second Fl *Web:* www.tongal.com	Santa Monica	CA	90405	310-579-9260	
Topix LLC 1001 Elwell Ct *Web:* www.topix.net	Palo Alto	CA	94303	650-461-8300	
TouchLogic Corp 30 Kinnear Ct Ste 602 *TF:* 877-707-0207 ■ *Web:* www.touchlogic.com	Richmond Hill	ON	L4B1K8	877-707-0207	
Touchstorm LLC 355 Lexington Ave 12th Fl *TF:* 877-794-6101 ■ *Web:* www.touchstorm.com	New York	NY	10017	877-794-6101	
Townes Tele-Communications Inc 120 E First St *Web:* www.walnuthilltel.com	Lewisville	AR	71845	870-921-4224	
Trada Inc 1023 Walnut St *TF:* 877-871-1835 ■ *Web:* www.trada.com	Boulder	CO	80302	877-871-1835	

Company / Address	City	State	Zip	Phone	Fax
Transcom Telecommunications Co 3744 Industry Ave. *Web:* www.transcomla.com	Lakewood	CA	90712	562-663-2000	
TransWorld Network Corp 255 Pine Ave N *Web:* www.twncorp.com	Oldsmar	FL	34677	813-891-4700	
Trapit Inc 2390 El Camino Real Ste 220 *Web:* www.trapit.com	Palo Alto	CA	94306	844-987-2748	
Travelport Ltd 300 Galleria Pkwy. *Web:* www.travelport.com	Atlanta	GA	30339	770-563-7400	
Tribe Networks Inc 208 Utah St. *Web:* www.tribe.net	San Francisco	CA	94103	415-861-2286	
Trillion Partners Inc 9208 Waterford Centre Blvd Ste 150 *Web:* www.trillion.net	Austin	TX	78758	512-334-4100	
Trisys Telecom Inc 215 Ridgedale Ave Ste 2 *Web:* www.trisys.com	Florham Park	NJ	07932	973-360-2300	
Trover Inc 307 Third Ave S Ste 520 *Web:* www.trover.com	Seattle	WA	98104	206-812-8700	
Truaxis Inc 959 Skyway Rd	San Carlos	CA	94070	650-654-7440	
True Fit Corp 800 W Cummings Park Ste 6400 *Web:* www.truefit.com	Woburn	MA	01801	617-848-3740	
TruMarx Data Partners Inc 30 S Wacker Dr Ste 2200 *Web:* www.trumarx.com	Chicago	IL	60606	312-707-9000	
TruSignal LLC 25 6th Ave N *TF:* 855-569-0426 ■ *Web:* www.tru-signal.com	St. Cloud	MN	56303	855-569-0426	
TTS LLC 2595 Dallas Pkwy Ste 300 *Web:* www.tts-us.com	Frisco	TX	75034	214-778-0800	778-0880
Tungle Corp 410 rue Saint-Nicolas Ste 260 *Web:* www.tungle.com	Montreal	QC	H2Y2P5	514-678-9181	
TurfNet Media Network 5276 Wynterhall Way *Web:* www.turfnet.com	Atlanta	GA	30338	770-395-9850	
Tutum Inc 2302 Environ Way *Web:* www.tutum.co	Chapel Hill	NC	27517	415-742-2442	
Twin Oaks Computing Inc 755 Maleta Ln Ste 203 *Web:* www.twinoakscomputing.com	Castle Rock	CO	80108	720-733-7906	
Tyze Personal Networks Ltd 210 W Broadway Sixth Fl *Web:* www.tyze.com	Vancouver	BC	V5Y3W2	604-628-9594	
Ultimate Information Systems 1815 W Missouri Ave Ste 211 *Web:* azgolfcommunities.com	Phoenix	AZ	85015	602-735-1010	
UrbanDaddy Inc 900 Broadway Ste 808 *Web:* www.urbandaddy.com	New York	NY	10003	212-929-7905	
US Farm Data Inc 10824 Old Mill Rd Ste 8 *Web:* www.usfarmdata.com	Omaha	NE	68154	402-334-1824	
US News University Connection LLC 9417 Princess Palm Ave *TF:* 866-442-6587 ■ *Web:* www.usnewsuniversitydirectory.com	Tampa	FL	33619	866-442-6587	
USA Communications Inc 920 E 56th St Ste B *TF:* 877-234-0102 ■ *Web:* www.usacommunications.tv	Kearney	NE	68847	877-234-0102	
uShip Inc 205 Brazos St. *TF:* 800-698-7447 ■ *Web:* www.uship.com	Austin	TX	78701	800-698-7447	
UsingMiles Inc 6400 S Fiddler's Green Cir Ste 975 *Web:* www.usingmiles.com	Greenwood Village	CO	80111	303-645-0531	
VALMARC Corp 109 Highland Ave *Web:* www.valmarc.com	Needham	MA	02494	339-225-4544	
Vanguard Systems Inc 2901 Dutton Mill Rd Ste 220 *Web:* www.vansystems.com	Aston	PA	19014	610-891-7703	
Vanilla Forums Inc 414 McGill St, Ste 800 *TF:* 866-845-0815 ■ *Web:* www.vanillaforums.com	Montreal	QC	H2Y1S1	866-845-0815	
Vectus Inc 18685 Main St 101 PMB 360 *TF:* 866-483-2887 ■ *Web:* www.vectus.com	Huntington Beach	CA	92648	866-483-2887	
Ventura County Employees' Retirement Association 1190 S Victoria Ave Ste 200 *Web:* portal.countyofventura.org	Ventura	CA	93003	805-339-4250	
Vermont Telephone Company Inc 354 River St *Web:* www.vermontel.com	Springfield	VT	05156	802-885-9000	
Vertical Web Media LLC 125 S Wacker Dr Ste 2900 *Web:* www.internetretailer.com	Chicago	IL	60606	312-362-9527	
Vessel Metrics LLC Three Church Cir Ste 325 *TF:* 888-214-1710 ■ *Web:* www.vesselvanguard.com	Annapolis	MD	21401	888-214-1710	
Vetstreet 780 Township Line Rd. *Web:* www.vetstreet.com	Yardley	PA	19067	215-493-0621	
Vianet Internet Solutions Inc 128 Larch St Ste 301 *Web:* www.vianet.ca	Sudbury	ON	P3E5J8	705-675-0400	
VideoGenie Inc 314 Lytton Ave Ste 100 *TF:* 877-392-2235 ■ *Web:* www.videogenie.com	Palo Alto	CA	94301	877-392-2235	
Vidmaker Inc 612 W Main St Ste 300 *Web:* www.vidmaker.com	Madison	WI	53703	608-620-6002	
Vinely One Kendall Sq Bldg 400 B4202 *TF:* 888-294-1128 ■ *Web:* www.vinely.com	Cambridge	MA	02139	888-294-1128	
Virgin Media Inc 65 Bleecker St Sixth Fl *Web:* www.virginmedia.com	New York	NY	10022	212-906-8440	
VirtualPBX.com Inc 111 N Market St Ste 1000 *Web:* www.virtualpbx.com	San Jose	CA	95113	408-414-7646	
VirtualWorks Group Inc 5301 N Federal Hwy Ste 230 *Web:* www.virtualworks.com	Boca Raton	FL	33487	561-327-4900	
Vista Broadband Networks Inc 3020 Santa Rosa Ave *Web:* www.vbbn.com	Santa Rosa	CA	95407	707-527-0545	
Viva Group Inc 11766 Wilshire Blvd Ste 300 *TF:* 866-432-7368 ■ *Web:* www.rent.com	Los Angeles	CA	90025	866-432-7368	
Voice123 30 E 23rd St *Web:* www.voice123.com	New York	NY	10010	212-461-1873	
VoIP Innovations Inc Eight Penn Ctr W Ste 101 *TF:* 877-478-6471 ■ *Web:* www.voipinnovations.com	Pittsburgh	PA	15276	877-478-6471	
Voxox Inc 9276 Scranton Rd Ste 300 *Web:* www.voxox.com	San Diego	CA	92121	619-900-9000	
VuFind Inc 1290 Oakmead Pkwy Ste 107 *Web:* www.vufind.com	Sunnyvale	CA	94508	408-739-2880	
Waveguide Inc 10 N Southwood Dr. *Web:* www.waveguidefiber.com	Nashua	NH	03063	603-598-0096	
WAVSYS LLC 101 Broadway Ste 406 *Web:* www.wavsys.com	Brooklyn	NY	11249	347-292-8797	
WealthForge Holdings Inc 6800 Paragon Pl Ste 237 *Web:* www.fundroom.com	Richmond	VA	23230	804-658-5280	
Weblo.com Inc 930-2075 University St. *Web:* www.weblo.com	Montreal	QC	H3A2L1	514-364-3636	
WEbook Inc 307 Fifth Ave Seventh Fl *Web:* www.webook.com	New York	NY	10016	646-453-8575	
WebReply.com Inc 1085 Worcester Rd *Web:* www.webreply.com	Natick	MA	01760	508-318-4600	
WellAware Holdings Inc 2330 N Loop 1604 W Ste 110 *Web:* www.wellaware.us	San Antonio	TX	78248	210-816-4600	
Wellsphere Inc 2300 Wilson Blvd Ste 600 *Web:* www.wellsphere.com	Arlington	VA	22201	703-302-1040	
WeSpire Inc 125 Kingston St Sixth Fl. *Web:* www.wespire.com	Boston	MA	02111	617-531-8970	
West Coast Green Institute 760 Market St Ste 1028 *Web:* westcoastgreen.com	San Francisco	CA	94102	415-955-1935	
West Group 610 Opperman Dr. *TF Cust Svc:* 800-328-4880 ■ *Web:* legalsolutions.thomsonreuters.com	Eagan	MN	55123	651-687-7000	687-7551
WhamTech Inc 12001 N Central Expy Ste 300 *Web:* www.whamtech.com	Dallas	TX	75243	972-991-5700	
WhoKnows Inc 800 W El Camino Real Ste 180 *TF:* 877-338-2763 ■ *Web:* corp.whoknows.com	Mountain View	CA	94040	877-338-2763	
Wholeshare Inc 2431 Mission St *TF:* 800-625-4605 ■ *Web:* www.wholeshare.com	San Francisco	CA	94110	800-625-4605	
WibiData Inc 375 Alabama St Ste 350 *Web:* www.wibidata.com	San Francisco	CA	94110	415-496-9424	
Wisetail 212 S Wallace Ave Ste B2 *Web:* www.wisetail.com	Bozeman	MT	59715	406-545-4662	
Wisper High Speed Internet 831 Main St S *Web:* www.wisperhighspeed.com	Sauk Centre	MN	56378	320-351-9477	
Wolfram Alpha LLC 100 Trade Ctr Dr *Web:* www.wolframalpha.com	Champaign	IL	61820	217-398-0700	
WyzAnt Inc 1714 N Damen Ave Ste 3N *Web:* www.wyzant.com	Chicago	IL	60647	312-646-6365	
X17 Inc PO Box 2362 *Web:* x17agency.com	Beverly Hills	CA	90213	310-230-3332	
Xacti Global LLC 999 W Yamato Rd Ste 100 *Web:* www.xactiglobal.com	Boca Raton	FL	33431	561-989-7400	
Xtel Communications Inc 401 Rt 73 n *Web:* www.xtel.net	Marlton	NJ	08053	856-596-4000	
XTRAC LLC 245 Summer St *TF:* 855-975-3569 ■ *Web:* www.xtracsolutions.com	Boston	MA	02210	855-975-3569	
Ya Sabe Inc 13755 Sunrise Vly Dr Ste 325 *Web:* www.yasabe.com	Herndon	VA	20171	703-793-3270	
Yesware Inc 75 Kneeland St Fl 15 *TF:* 855-937-9273 ■ *Web:* www.yesware.com	Boston	MA	02111	855-937-9273	
YouDocs Beauty Inc 648 Broadway *Web:* www.youbeauty.com	New York	NY	10012	646-449-9445	
YouVisit LLC 20533 Biscayne Blvd Ste 1322 *TF:* 866-585-7158 ■ *Web:* www.youvisit.com	Aventura	FL	33180	866-585-7158	
ZEFR Inc 1621 Abbot Kinney Blvd *Web:* zefr.com	Venice	CA	90291	310-392-3555	
Zenfolio Inc 3515-A Edison Way *Web:* www.zenfolio.com	Menlo Park	CA	94025	650-412-1888	
Zenovia Digital Exchange Corp 3141 Fairview Park Dr Ste 160 *TF:* 855-936-6842 ■ *Web:* www.zenoviaexchange.com	Falls Church	VA	22042	703-813-6400	
Zetta Inc 1362 Borregas Ave *Web:* www.zetta.net	Sunnyvale	CA	94089	650-590-0950	
Zignal Labs Inc 244 Jackson St Second Fl *Web:* www.zignallabs.com	San Francisco	CA	94111	415-683-7871	
Zindigo Inc 2401 PGA Blvd Ste 280-A *Web:* www.zindigo.com	Palm Beach Gardens	FL	33410	561-694-1314	
Zooppa.com Inc 911 Western Ave Ste 420 *Web:* zooppa.com	Seattle	WA	98104	206-866-0516	
Zootoo LLC 400 Plz Dr First Fl. *TF:* 877-580-7387 ■ *Web:* www.zootoo.com	Secaucus	NJ	07094	877-580-7387	
Ztar Mobile Inc 951 N Walnut Creek Dr Ste C *Web:* www.ztarmobile.com	Mansfield	TX	76063	214-231-0103	
ZUUS Media Inc Three Columbus Cir 15th Fl. *Web:* www.zuus.com	New York	NY	10019	646-664-1702	
Zypcom Inc 29400 Kohoutek Way Ste 170 *Web:* www.zypcom.com	Union City	CA	94587	510-324-2501	

391 INK

Company / Address	City	State	Zip	Phone	Fax
AJ Daw Printing Ink Co 608 E Compton Blvd E	Rancho Dmngz	CA	90221	323-723-3253	
Braden Sutphin Ink Co 3650 E 93rd St. *TF:* 800-289-6872 ■ *Web:* www.bsink.com	Cleveland	OH	44105	216-271-2300	271-0515

Company	City	State	ZIP	Phone	Fax
Central Ink Corp 1100 Harvester Rd	West Chicago	IL	60185	630-231-6500	231-6554
TF: 800-345-2541 ■ *Web:* www.cicink.com					
Color Resolutions International					
575 Quality Blvd	Fairfield	OH	45014	513-552-7200	552-7141
TF: 800-346-8570 ■ *Web:* new.colorresolutions.com					
Cudner & O'Connor Co 4035 W Kinzie St	Chicago	IL	60624	773-826-0200	826-0477
Web: www.candocinks.com					
Deco Chem Inc 3502 N Home St	Mishawaka	IN	46545	574-259-3787	
Web: www.decochem.com					
Gans Ink & Supply Company Inc					
1441 Boyd St	Los Angeles	CA	90033	323-264-2200	264-2916
TF: 800-421-6167 ■ *Web:* www.gansink.com					
Independent Ink Inc 13700 Gramercy Pl	Gardena	CA	90249	310-523-4657	329-0943
TF: 800-446-5538 ■ *Web:* www.independentink.com					
International Coatings Co 13929 166th St	Cerritos	CA	90703	562-926-1010	926-9486
TF: 800-423-4103 ■ *Web:* www.iccink.com					
Kerley Ink Engineers Inc 2700 S 12th Ave	Broadview	IL	60155	708-344-1295	865-5759
Web: www.kerleyink.com					
Keystone Printing Ink Co					
2700 Roberts Ave	Philadelphia	PA	19129	215-228-8100	
Web: www.keystoneink.com					
Matsui International Company Inc					
1501 W 178th St	Gardena	CA	90248	310-767-7812	767-7836
TF: 800-359-5679 ■ *Web:* www.matsui-color.com					
Nazdar 8501 Hedge Ln Terr	Shawnee	KS	66227	913-422-1888	422-2296
TF: 800-767-9942 ■ *Web:* www.nazdar.com					
Nor-Cote International Inc					
506 Lafayette Ave	Crawfordsville	IN	47933	765-362-9180	364-5408
TF: 800-488-9180 ■ *Web:* www.norcote.com					
Polytex 820 E 140th St	Bronx	NY	10454	718-402-3057	402-2984
Web: www.polytexink.com					
Ranger Industries Inc 15 Park Rd	Tinton Falls	NJ	07724	732-389-3535	
Web: www.rangerink.com					
Reaxis Inc 941 Robinson Hwy	Mcdonald	PA	15057	800-426-7273	
TF: 800-426-7273 ■ *Web:* www.reaxis.com					
Sensient Technologies Corp					
777 E Wisconsin Ave 11th Fl	Milwaukee	WI	53202	414-271-6755	347-3785
NYSE: SXT ■ *TF:* 800-558-9892 ■ *Web:* www.sensient-tech.com					
Sericol Inc 1101 W Cambridge Dr	Kansas City	KS	66103	913-342-4060	342-4752
TF: 800-737-4265 ■ *Web:* www.sericol.com					
Siegwerk USA Co 3535 SW 56th St	Des Moines	IA	50321	515-471-2100	471-2200
TF: 800-728-8200 ■ *Web:* www.siegwerk.com					
Spectrachem 10 Dell Glen Ave	Lodi	NJ	07644	973-253-3553	253-3663
Web: www.spectrachem.net					
Sun Chemical Corp 35 Waterview Blvd	Parsippany	NJ	07054	973-404-6000	404-6001
TF: 800-543-2323 ■ *Web:* www.sunchemical.com					
Superior Printing Ink Co Inc 100 N St	Teterboro	NJ	07608	201-478-5600	478-5650
Web: www.superiorink.com					
Tonertype of Florida LLC 5313 Johns Rd Ste 210	Tampa	FL	33634	813-915-1300	
Web: www.tonertype.com					
Toyo Ink America LLC 1225 N Michael Dr	Wood Dale	IL	60191	866-969-8696	628-1769*
**Fax Area Code:* 630 ■ *TF General:* 866-969-8696 ■ *Web:* www.toyoink.com					
U-mark Inc 102 Iowa Ave	Belleville	IL	62220	618-235-7500	
Web: www.umarkers.com					
US Ink Corp 651 Garden St	Carlstadt	NJ	07072	201-935-8666	933-3728*
**Fax:* Mktg ■ *TF:* 800-423-8838 ■ *Web:* www.usink.com					
Wikoff Color Corp 1886 Merritt Rd	Fort Mill	SC	29715	803-548-2210	548-5728
Web: www.wikoff.com					

392 INSULATION & ACOUSTICAL PRODUCTS

Company	City	State	ZIP	Phone	Fax
Anco Products Inc (API) 2500 S 17th St	Elkhart	IN	46517	574-293-5574	295-6235
TF: 800-837-2626 ■ *Web:* www.ancoproductsinc.com					
Applegate Insulation Manufacturing Inc					
1000 Highview Dr	Webberville	MI	48892	517-521-3545	521-3597
TF: 800-627-7536 ■ *Web:* www.applegateinsulation.com					
CertainTeed Corp 750 E Swedesford Rd	Valley Forge	PA	19482	610-341-7000	341-7777
TF Prod Info: 800-782-8777 ■ *Web:* www.certainteed.com					
Claremont Sales Corp 35 Winsome Dr PO Box 430	Durham	CT	06422	860-349-4499	349-7977
TF: 800-222-4448 ■ *Web:* claremontcorporation.com					
CTA Acoustics Inc 100 CTA Blvd PO Box 448	Corbin	KY	40702	606-528-8050	528-8074
Web: www.ctaacoustics.com					
Dryvit Systems Inc 1 Energy Way	West Warwick	RI	02893	401-822-4100	822-4510
TF: 800-556-7752 ■ *Web:* www.dryvit.com					
F Rodgers Corp 7901 National Dr	Livermore	CA	94550	925-960-2300	
Hi-Temp Insulation Inc 4700 Calle Alto	Camarillo	CA	93012	805-484-2774	484-7551
Web: www.hi-tempinsulation.com					
Industrial Acoustics Company Inc					
1160 Commerce Ave	Bronx	NY	10462	718-931-8000	863-1138
Web: www.iac-acoustics.com					
Industrial Insulation Group LLC (IIG)					
2100 Line St	Brunswick	GA	31520	800-334-7997	267-6096*
**Fax Area Code:* 912 ■ *TF:* 800-334-7997 ■ *Web:* www.iig-llc.com					
Isolatek International Inc 41 Furnace St	Stanhope	NJ	07874	973-347-1200	347-5131
TF: 800-631-9600 ■ *Web:* www.cafco.com					
ITW Insulation Systems					
1370 E 40th St Ste 1 Bldg 7	Houston	TX	77022	800-231-1024	691-7492*
**Fax Area Code:* 713 ■ *TF:* 800-231-1024 ■ *Web:* www.itwinsulation.com					
Johns Manville Corp 717 17th St PO Box 5108	Denver	CO	80217	303-978-2000	
TF Prod Info: 800-654-3103 ■ *Web:* www.jm.com					
Knauf Insulation One Knauf Dr	Shelbyville	IN	46176	317-398-4434	398-3675
TF: 800-825-4434 ■ *Web:* www.knaufinsulation.com					
MIT International 77 Massachusetts Ave	Cambridge	TX	02139	617-253-1000	283-1190*
**Fax Area Code:* 480 ■ *TF General:* 800-228-9290 ■ *Web:* web.mit.edu/					
Molded Acoustical Products of Easton Inc					
Three Danforth Dr	Easton	PA	18045	610-253-7135	253-1664
Web: www.map-easton.com					
Nu-Wool Company Inc 2472 Port Sheldon Rd	Jenison	MI	49428	616-669-0100	669-2370
TF: 800-748-0128 ■ *Web:* www.nuwool.com					
Owens Corning One Owens Corning Pkwy	Toledo	OH	43659	419-248-8000	325-1538
NYSE: OC ■ *Web:* www.owenscorning.com					
Pittsburgh Corning Corp					
800 Presque Isle Dr	Pittsburgh	PA	15239	724-327-6100	387-3806
Web: www.pittsburghcorning.com					
Premier Manufacturing Corp					
12117 Bennington Ave	Cleveland	OH	44135	216-941-9700	941-9719
Rock Wool Manufacturing Co					
1400 Seventh Ct PO Box 506	Leeds	AL	35094	205-699-6121	699-3132
TF Sales: 800-874-7625 ■ *Web:* www.deltainsulation.com					
Scott Industries Inc					
1573 Hwy 136 W PO Box 7	Henderson	KY	42419	270-831-2037	831-2039
TF: 800-951-9276 ■ *Web:* www.scott-mfg.com					
Sloss Industries Corp 3500 35th Ave N	Birmingham	AL	35207	205-808-7803	808-7715*
**Fax:* Sales ■ *Web:* www.walterenergy.com					
Soundcoat Co One Burt Dr	Deer Park	NY	11729	631-242-2200	242-2246
TF: 800-394-8913 ■ *Web:* www.soundcoat.com					
Thermafiber Inc 3711 W Mill St	Wabash	IN	46992	260-563-2111	563-7022
TF: 888-834-2371 ■ *Web:* www.thermafiber.com					
Thermwell Products Co 420 Rt 17 S	Mahwah	NJ	07430	201-684-4400	684-1214
TF: 800-526-5265 ■ *Web:* www.frostking.com					
TIGHITCO Inc 1375 Seaboard Industrial Blvd	Atlanta	GA	30318	404-355-1205	351-4458
Web: www.tighitco.com					
Transco Products Inc 1215 E 12th St Ste 2100	Streator	IL	61364	312-427-2818	427-4975
Web: www.transcoproducts.com					
Unifrax Corp 2351 Whirlpool St	Niagara Falls	NY	14305	716-278-3800	278-3904*
**Fax:* Cust Svc ■ *Web:* www.unifrax.com					
Ward Process Inc 311 Hopping Brook Rd	Holliston	MA	01746	508-429-1165	429-8543
Web: www.aapusa.com					

393 INSURANCE AGENTS, BROKERS, SERVICES

Company	City	State	ZIP	Phone	Fax
A Plus Benefits Inc 395 West 600 North	Lindon	UT	84042	801-443-1090	
TF: 800-748-5102 ■ *Web:* www.aplusbenefits.com					
Abacus Group LLC, The 2541 Lafayette Plz Dr	Albany	GA	31707	229-436-6032	
ACB Insurance Inc 7715 Loma Ct Ste E	Fishers	IN	46038	317-915-8601	
Web: acb-insurance.com					
Accredited Surety & Casualty Company Inc					
4798 New Broad St Ste 200	Orlando	FL	32814	407-629-2131	
Web: www.accredited-inc.com					
Accurate Insurance Inc 416 First St	Glenwood	IA	51534	712-527-9106	
Web: accurateinsinc.com					
Actuarial Systems Corp 15840 Monte St Ste 108	Sylmar	CA	91342	800-950-2082	
TF: 800-950-2082 ■ *Web:* www.asc-net.com					
Adorno-Denker Assoc Inc					
4502 Broadway	Long Island City	NY	11103	718-278-8660	
Advisornet Financial Inc					
701 Fourth Ave S Ste 1500	Minneapolis	MN	55415	612-347-8600	
Web: advisornet.com					
Affinion Group Inc 6 High Ridge Pk	Stamford	CT	06905	203-956-1000	956-8789
TF: 800-251-2148 ■ *Web:* www.affiniongroup.com					
Agency Software Inc 215 W Commerce Dr	Hayden Lake	ID	83835	208-762-7188	762-1265
TF: 800-342-7327 ■ *Web:* www.agencysoftware.com					
Albert J Marchionne Insurance Agency Inc					
11 Independence Ave	Quincy	MA	02169	617-471-5010	
Web: marchionneinsurance.com					
All Motorists Insurance Agency					
5230 Las Virgenes Rd Ste 100	Calabasas	CA	91302	818-880-9070	
Web: westerngeneral.com					
Allen Agency 34-36 Elm St PO Box 578	Camden	ME	04843	207-236-4311	
Alley Rehbaum & Capes Inc					
2433 Gulf To Bay Blvd	Clearwater	FL	33758	727-797-5193	
Web: www.arc-insurance.com					
Alliance Abstract LLC Two Mott St Ste 605	New York	NY	10013	212-962-2228	
Alliance Brokerage Corp 990 Wbury Rd	Westbury	NY	11590	516-333-7300	333-5698
Web: alliancebrokeragecorp.com					
Alliance of Transylvanian Saxons					
5393 Pearl Rd	Cleveland	OH	44129	440-842-8442	
Web: atsaxons.com					
Alliance Worldwide Investigative Group Inc					
Four Executive Park Dr	Clifton Park	NY	12065	518-514-2944	
TF: 800-579-2911 ■ *Web:* www.allianceinvestigative.com					
Allied Solutions LLC 1320 City Ctr Dr Ste 300	Carmel	IN	46032	317-706-7600	706-7606
Web: alliedsolutions.net					
Allstate Insurance Company					
2955 Pineda Plaza Way Ste 103	Viera	FL	32940	321-242-1002	
Web: agents.allstate.com					
Alpena Agency Inc 102 S Third Ave	Alpena	MI	49707	989-354-2175	
Web: alpenaagency.com					
AM Skier Agency Inc 209 Main Ave	Hawley	PA	18428	570-226-4571	
Web: amskier.com					
Amano Enzyme USA Company Ltd 1415 Madeline Ln	Elgin	IL	60124	847-649-0101	
Web: www.amano-enzyme.co.jp					
American Classic Agency					
201 Atp Tour Blvd	Ponte Vedra	FL	32082	904-285-4030	
Web: www.aclassic.com					
American Mutual Share Insurance Corp					
5656 Frantz Rd	Dublin	OH	43017	614-764-1900	
Web: www.excessshare.com					
Amfed Cos LLC 576 Highland Colony Pkwy	Ridgeland	MS	39157	601-853-4949	853-2727
TF: 800-264-8085 ■ *Web:* www.amfed.com					
Anchor Financial Group					
415 Fallowfield Rd Ste 300	Camp Hill	PA	17011	717-975-0509	
Web: www.anchorfinancialgroup.com					
ANCO Insurance 1111 Briarcrest Dr PO Box 3889	Bryan	TX	77802	979-776-2626	327-3219*
**Fax Area Code:* 936 ■ *TF:* 800-749-1733 ■ *Web:* www.anco.com					
Anderson Shumaker Co 824 S Central Ave	Chicago	IL	60644	773-287-0874	
Web: www.andersonshumaker.com					
Andover Co, The 95 Old River Rd	Andover	MA	01810	978-475-3300	
Web: andovercos.com					

Company / Address	City	State	ZIP	Phone	Fax
Andreini & Co 220 W 20th Ave *TF:* 800-969-2522 ■ *Web:* www.andreini.com	San Mateo	CA	94403	650-573-1111	378-4361
Andrew G Gordon Inc 306 Washington St *Web:* agordon.com	Norwell	MA	02061	781-659-2262	
Annette Willis Insurance Agency Inc 18401 NW 27th Ave *Web:* annettewillisinsurance.com	Miami	FL	33056	305-625-2403	
Aon Risk Services Inc 200 E Randolph St *TF:* 877-384-4276 ■ *Web:* www.aon.com	Chicago	IL	60601	312-381-1000	701-4580
Arch Capital Group (US) Inc One Liberty Plz 53rd Fl *Web:* www.archinsurance.com	New York	NY	10006	212-651-6500	
Argenia LLC 11524 Fairview Rd *Web:* argenia.com	Little Rock	AR	72212	501-227-9670	
Argus Research Inc. 887 W Marietta St Studio N-108 *Web:* www.argusbenefits.com	Atlanta	GA	30318	404-846-8883	
Arthur J Gallagher & Co 2 Pierce Pl *NYSE: AJG* ■ *TF:* 888-285-5106 ■ *Web:* www.ajg.com	Itasca	IL	60143	630-773-3800	285-4000
Arthur J. Glatfelter Agency Inc PO Box 2726 *TF:* 800-233-1957 ■ *Web:* www.glatfelters.com	York	PA	17405	717-741-0911	741-4160
Ash Brokerage Corp 7609 W Jefferson Blvd *Web:* www.ashbrokerage.com	Fort Wayne	IN	46804	260-478-0600	
Associated Administrators LLC 911 Ridgebrook Rd *Web:* www.associated-admin.com	Sparks	MD	21152	410-683-6500	
Associated Agencies Inc 1701 Golf Rd Tower 3 7th Fl *Web:* www.assocagencies.com	Rolling Meadows	IL	60008	847-427-8400	427-3559
Assurity Life Insurance Co 1526 K St *TF:* 800-869-0355 ■ *Web:* assurity.com	Lincoln	NE	68508	402-476-6500	
Atkinson & Assoc Insurance Inc 1537 Brantley Rd Bldg C *Web:* atkinsoninsurance.com	Fort Myers	FL	33907	239-437-5555	
Automated Benefit Services Inc 8220 Irving Rd *Web:* www.abs-tpa.com	Sterling Heights	MI	48312	586-693-4300	
Automobile Protection Corp 6010 Atlantic Blvd **Fax Area Code:* 678 ■ *TF Cust Svc:* 800-230-2434 ■ *Web:* www.easycare.com	Norcross	GA	30071	800-230-2434	225-1597*
B C Szerlip Insurance Agency Inc 34 Sycamore Ave *Web:* bcszerlip.com	Little Silver	NJ	07739	732-842-2020	
Badger Mutual Insurance Co 1635 W National Ave *TF:* 800-837-7833 ■ *Web:* www.badgermutual.com	Milwaukee	WI	53204	414-383-1234	
Barney J Belleci 26555 Carmel Rancho Blvd *Web:* belleci.net	Carmel	CA	93923	831-624-6466	
Bateman Gordon & Sands Inc 3050 N Federal Hwy *Web:* bgsagency.com	Lighthouse Point	FL	33064	954-941-0900	
BBR Benefits Solutions LLC 8150 Perry Hwy Ste 100 *Web:* bbrbenefits.com	Pittsburgh	PA	15237	412-847-3100	
Beazley Insurance Company Inc 30 Batterson Park Rd *Web:* www.beazley.com	Farmington	CT	06032	860-677-3700	
Beckerman & Co 430 Lake Ave *Web:* www.beckermanco.com	Colonia	NJ	07067	732-499-9200	
Bedford Underwriters Ltd 315 E Mill St *Web:* bedfordunderwriters.com	Plymouth	WI	53073	920-892-8795	
BeneCard Services Inc 3131 Princeton Pike Bldg 2B Ste 103 *Web:* www.benecard.com	Lawrenceville	NJ	08648	609-219-0400	
Benefit & Risk Management Services Inc 10860 Gold Ctr Dr Ste 300 *TF:* 888-326-2555 ■ *Web:* www.brmsonline.com	Rancho Cordova	CA	95670	916-858-2950	
Benefit Communications Inc 2126 21st Ave S *Web:* benefitcommunications.com	Nashville	TN	37212	615-292-3786	
Benefit Concepts Inc 1173 Brittmoore Rd *Web:* mybciteam.com	Houston	TX	77043	713-722-8779	728-7201
Benefit Resource Group LLC 5985 Home Gardens Dr Ste A *Web:* benresgroup.com	Reno	NV	89502	775-688-4400	
Benefits Div Inc 125 S Swoope Ave Ste 210 *Web:* benefits-division.com	Maitland	FL	32751	407-629-9085	
Beneplace Inc PO Box 203550 *Web:* bp.beneplace.com	Austin	TX	78720	512-346-3300	
BeneSys Inc 700 Tower Dr Ste 300 *Web:* www.benesysinc.com	Troy	MI	48098	248-813-9800	
Berkley Risk Administrators Company LLC 222 S Ninth St Ste 1300 *TF:* 800-449-7707 ■ *Web:* www.berkleyrisk.com	Minneapolis	MN	55402	612-766-3000	
Bernheimer-Lincoln Insurance Group 779 Farmington Ave *Web:* bernheimerinsurance.com	West Hartford	CT	06119	860-232-3810	
Bidlake Agency Inc 2905 Millennium Ste 3 *Web:* billingsinsurance.com	Billings	MT	59102	406-245-6224	
Bilbrey Insurance Services Inc 5701 Greendale Rd *Web:* icapiowa.com	Johnston	IA	50131	800-383-0116	
Bill Farris Insurance Agency Inc 390 Cypress Gardens Blvd *Web:* billfarris.com	Winter Haven	FL	33880	863-299-2153	
Bischoff Insurance Agency Inc 1300 Oakridge Dr Ste 100 *Web:* bradbischoff.com	Fort Collins	CO	80525	970-223-9400	
Black Sand Technologies Inc 3316 Bee Cave Rd Ste C *Web:* www.blacksand.com	Austin	TX	78746	512-329-9400	
Bliss Mcknight Inc 2801 E Empire *Web:* blissmcknight.com	Bloomington	IL	61704	309-663-1393	
Block Insurance Agency Inc 2333 Highland St *Web:* blockins.com	Allentown	PA	18104	610-433-4131	433-1531
Body-Borneman Insurance PO Box 584 *TF:* 800-326-5290 ■ *Web:* www.body-borneman.com	Boyertown	PA	19512	610-367-1100	367-1140
Boeck & Assoc Inc 930 Town Centre Dr *Web:* boeckinsurance.com	Medford	OR	97504	541-770-9400	
Bogart & Brownell 7529 Standish Pl Ste 320 *Web:* www.bogartandbrownell.com	Rockville	MD	20855	301-654-2277	907-0926
Bollinger Insurance 101 JFK Pkwy *TF:* 800-526-1379 ■ *Web:* www.bollingerinsurance.com	Short Hills	NJ	07078	973-467-0444	921-2876
Bolte Real Estate Inc & Bolte Insurance Inc 134 E Second St *Web:* bolterealty.com	Port Clinton	OH	43452	419-732-3111	
Bolton & Co 3475 E Foothill Blvd Ste 100 *Web:* www.boltonco.com	Pasadena	CA	91107	626-799-7000	441-3233
Boston Partners Financial Group LLC 138 River Rd Ste 310 *Web:* www.bostonpartnersfinancialgroup.com	Andover	MA	01810	978-689-9303	
Brad Peters Agency Inc 2028 N State St	Belvidere	IL	61008	815-544-2950	
Brady Chapman Holland & Assoc Inc 10055 W Gulf Bank *Web:* bch-insurance.com	Houston	TX	77040	713-688-1500	
Brown & Brown Agency of Insurance Professionals Inc 208 N Mill *Web:* www.bbinsurance.com	Pryor	OK	74361	918-825-3295	825-2727
Brown & Brown Inc 220 S Ridgewood Ave *NYSE: BRO* ■ *Web:* www.bbinsurance.com	Daytona Beach	FL	32114	386-252-9601	239-5729
Brown Smith Wallace LLC Six Cityplace Dr Ste 900 *Web:* bswllc.com	St Louis	MO	63141	314-983-1200	
Bruen Deldin Didio Assoc Three Starr Ridge Rd *Web:* bddinsurance.com	Brewster	NY	10509	845-279-5151	
Burnham & Flower Group Inc 315 S Kalamazoo Mall *Web:* bfgroup.com	Kalamazoo	MI	49007	269-381-1173	
Burnham Financial Services LLC 2038 Saranac Ave *Web:* burnhambenefitadvisors.com	Lake Placid	NY	12946	518-523-8100	
Buursma Agency 728 E Eighth St Ste 4 *Web:* buursmaagency.com	Holland	MI	49423	616-392-2105	
BWD Group LLC 45 Executive Dr BWD Plz *Web:* www.bwd.us	Plainview	NY	11803	516-327-2700	327-2800
Byrnes Agency Inc 394 Lake Rd *Web:* byrnesagency.com	Dayville	CT	06241	860-774-8549	
C & A Financial Group 2431 Atlantic Ave	Manasquan	NJ	08736	732-528-4800	
C p H & Associates 711 S Dearborn St Unit 205 *Web:* www.cphins.com	Chicago	IL	60605	312-987-9823	
CAA Saskatchewan 200 N Albert St *Web:* www.caasask.sk.ca	Regina	SK	S4R5E2	306-791-4314	
Cailor Fleming & Assoc Inc 4610 Market St *Web:* cailorfleming.com	Youngstown	OH	44512	330-782-8068	
Callbright Corp 6700 Hollister *TF:* 877-462-2552 ■ *Web:* www.callbright.com	Houston	TX	77040	877-462-2552	
CalSurance 681 S Parker St Ste 300 *TF:* 800-762-7800 ■ *Web:* www.calsurance.com	Orange	CA	92868	714-939-0800	939-1641
CAM Administrative Services Inc 25800 Northwestern Hwy Ste 700 *Web:* www.camads.com	Southfield	MI	48075	248-827-1050	
Cantella & Company Inc 101 Federal St 13th Fl *Web:* www.cantella.com	Boston	MA	02110	617-521-8630	
Capital Analysts Inc 218 Glenside Ave *TF:* 800-242-1421 ■ *Web:* www.capitalanalysts.com	Wyncote	PA	19095	800-242-1421	
Capital Strategies Group Inc 850 Shades Creek Pkwy Ste 300 *Web:* www.csginc.us	Birmingham	AL	35209	205-263-2400	
Carl E Mellen & Co 601 W Greenwood Ave *Web:* carlmellen.com	Waukegan	IL	60087	847-244-3500	
Carl Nelson Insurance Agency I 1519 N 11th Ave *Web:* carlnelsonins.com	Hanford	CA	93230	559-584-4495	
Carl Warren & Company Inc 770 S Placentia Ave *Web:* www.carlwarren.com	Placentia	CA	92870	714-572-5200	
Carol Drake 1913 N Green Vly Pkwy *Web:* caroldrake.com	Henderson	NV	89074	702-361-0300	
Casswood Insurance Agency Ltd Five Executive Pk Dr *TF:* 800-972-2242 ■ *Web:* www.casswood.com	Clifton Park	NY	12065	518-373-8700	373-8799
Castle Lake Insurance LLC 3385 S Holmes Ave *Web:* castlelakeinsurance.com	Idaho Falls	ID	83404	208-522-7778	
Caterpillar Financial Services Corp 2120 W End Ave *Web:* www.catfinancial.com	Nashville	TN	37203	615-341-1000	
Catholic United Financial 3499 Lexington Ave N *Web:* www.catholicunitedfinancial.org	St Paul	MN	55126	651-490-0170	
CBIZ Benefits & Insurance Services of Maryland Inc 44 Baltimore St **Fax:* Sales ■ *TF Cust Svc:* 800-615-8418 ■ *Web:* www.cbiz.com	Cumberland	MD	21502	301-777-1500	951-0425*
Century Coverage Corp 76 S Central Ave *Web:* centurycoverage.com	Valley Stream	NY	11580	516-791-1800	
Chamberlin Insurance Group Inc 485 Devon Park Dr Ste 111	Wayne	PA	19087	610-674-0999	
Charles L Crane Agency Co 100 N Broadway Ste 900 *Web:* www.craneagency.com	Saint Louis	MO	63102	314-241-8700	444-4970
Citizens Property Insurance Corp 6676 Corporate Ctr Pkwy *Web:* www.citizensfla.com	Jacksonville	FL	32216	904-296-6105	

Phone Fax

Claim Technologies Inc
100 Court Ave Ste 306 Des Moines IA 50309 515-244-7322
Web: www.claimtechnologies.com

Clark Insurance PO Box 3543 Portland ME 04104 207-774-6257
Web: clarkinsurance.com

Clifford & Rano Insurance Agency Inc
57 Cedar St Worcester MA 01609 508-752-8284
Web: cliffordrano.com

CLV Group Inc 485 Bank St Ste 200 Ottawa ON K2P1Z2 613-728-2000
Web: www.clvgroup.com

Cna National Warranty Corp
4150 N Drinkwater Blvd Ste 400 Scottsdale AZ 85251 480-941-1626
Web: cnanational.com

Cobb Strecker Dunphy & Zimmermann Inc
150 S Fifth St Ste 2800 Minneapolis MN 55402 612-349-2400
Web: www.csdz.com

Columbian Mutual Life Insurance Co
Vestal Pkwy E Binghamton NY 13902 607-724-2472
Web: www.cfglife.com

Combined Specialities International Inc
205 San Marin Dr Ste 5 Novato CA 94945 415-209-0012
Web: combinedspecialties.com

Combs Insurance Agency Inc 341 S Alaska St Palmer AK 99645 907-745-2144
Web: combsinsurance.com

Common Census Inc 90 Bridge St First Fl Westbrook ME 04092 207-854-5454
Web: www.commoncensus.com

Concepts Diversified 2509 Kesslersville Rd Easton PA 18040 610-250-9996

Concero Inc 10220 SW Greenburg Rd Portland OR 97223 971-222-1900
Web: concerogroup.com

Concklin Insurance Agency Inc
240 S Wmore Ave Lombard IL 60148 630-268-1600
Web: concklin.com

Connecture Inc 101 Marietta St Ste 1600 Atlanta GA 30303 404-879-4600
Web: www.connecture.com

Connexus Inc 10000 N Central Expy Dallas TX 75231 214-443-2600 443-2620
Web: www.idontwanttotravel.com

Continental American Insurance Company Inc
2801 Devine St Columbia SC 29205 803-256-6265

Core-Vens & Company Inc
2301 N Second St PO Box 1028 Clinton IA 52732 563-242-5423
Web: corevens.com

Cornerstone National Insurance Co
3100 Falling Leaf Ct Ste 200 POBox 6040 Columbia MO 65201 573-817-2481
Web: www.cornerstonenational.com

Corporate Synergies Group LLC
5000 Dearborn Cir Ste 100 Mount Laurel NJ 08054 856-813-1500
Web: corpsyn.com

Courtesy Insurance Agency
324 W Hefner Rd Oklahoma City OK 73114 405-755-4571
Web: ciaokc.com

Coverage Inc
4460-P Brookfield Corporate Dr Chantilly VA 20151 703-631-8000
Web: coverageinc.com

CPI-HR Inc 6830 Cochran Rd Solon OH 44139 440-542-7800
Web: www.cpihr.com

Cramer Johnson Wiggins & Assoc
1420 Edgewater Dr Ste 200 Orlando FL 32804 407-849-0044
Web: cjw-assoc.com

Cretcher Heartland LLC
4551 W 107th St Third Fl Overland Park KS 66207 913-341-8998
Web: cretcherheartland.com

Crosby Insurance Inc 8181 E Kaiser Blvd Anaheim CA 92808 714-221-5200
Web: crosbyinsurance.com

Cross Financial Corp 74 Gilman Rd PO Box 1388 Bangor ME 04401 207-947-7345 941-0849
TF: 800-999-7345 ■ *Web:* www.crossagency.com

Crown Polymers LLC 11111 Kiley Dr Huntley IL 60142 847-659-0300
Web: www.crownpolymers.com

CSP Information Group Inc
1100 Jorie Blvd Ste 260 Oak Brook IL 60523 630-574-5075
Web: www.cspnet.com

Cumbre Inc 3333 Concours Ste 5100 Ontario CA 91764 909-484-2456 484-2491
TF: 800-998-7986 ■ *Web:* www.cumbreinc.com

Cunningham Lindsey Group Ltd
3030 Rocky Point Dr Ste 530 Tampa FL 33607 813-830-7100
Web: www.cunninghamlindsey.com

Curtis Miller Insurance Agency Inc
1800 Blizzard Dr Parkersburg WV 26101 304-485-6431
Web: curtismillerins.com

CVP Systems Inc 2518 Wisconsin Ave Downers Grove IL 60515 630-852-1190
Web: www.cvpsystems.com

cynoSure Financial Inc
33490 Harper Ave Clinton Township MI 48035 586-771-3334
Web: www.cynosurefinancial.com

DailyAccess Corp
307 University Blvd N Bldg 3 Ste 1500 Mobile AL 36688 251-665-1800
TF: 877-859-5735 ■ *Web:* www.dailyaccess.com

Dale Barton Agency Inc
1100 East 6600 South Salt Lake City UT 84121 801-288-1600
Web: dalebarton.com

Daniel & Henry Co
1001 Highlands Plaza Dr W Ste 500 Saint Louis MO 63110 314-421-1525 444-1990
TF: 800-256-3462 ■ *Web:* www.danielandhenry.com

David Chapman Agency Inc 5700 W Mt Hope Rd Lansing MI 48917 517-321-4600
Web: davidchapmanagency.com

David T Andes 348 Pierce St Kingston PA 18704 570-288-6471
Web: daveandes.com

David Tate Insurance Agency Inc
2566 N Mcmullen Booth Rd Ste B Clearwater FL 33761 727-796-0408
Web: agents.allstate.com

Dawson Insurance Agency Inc 721 First Ave N Fargo ND 58107 701-237-3311
Web: dawsonins.com

Phone Fax

Dempsey Insurance Agency Inc
145 Railroad Ave Norwood MA 02062 781-762-0042
Web: demsure.com

Dennis M Doyle Jr 7807 Baymeadows Rd E Jacksonville FL 32256 904-737-3777
Web: dennydoyle.com

Derek Witham Insurance Agency 685 Salem St Malden MA 02148 781-322-2886

Dibrina Sure Benefits Consulting Inc
62 Frood Rd Sudbury ON P3C4Z3 705-688-9393
Web: dibrinasure.com

Dibuduo & Defendis 6873 N W Ave Ste 101 Fresno CA 93711 559-432-0222
Web: dibu.com

Distinguished Programs Group LLC, The
1180 Ave Of The Americas 16th Fl New York NY 10036 212-297-3100
TF: 888-355-4626 ■ *Web:* www.distinguished.com

Diversified Brokerage Services Inc
5501 Excelsior Blvd Minneapolis MN 55416 952-697-5001
Web: www.dbs-lifemark.com

Don Ferderer Insurance
1930 Brea Canyon Rd Diamond Bar CA 91765 909-396-1198
Web: insuranceplacecentral.com

DOT Integrated Financial Corp
155 Consumers Rd Ste 104 Toronto ON M2J0A3 416-920-8008
Web: www.dot-if.com

Duke Construction Inc 11307 Edgewater Dr Allendale MI 49401 616-895-4466
Web: www.dukeconstructioninc.net

Dyatech LLC 805 S Wheatley St Ste 600 Ridgeland MS 39157 601-914-1004
TF: 866-651-4222 ■ *Web:* www.dyatech.com

E M Schroeder Agency Inc 294 Town Ctr Dr Troy MI 48084 248-689-1020
Web: emschroeder.com

Eagan Insurance Agency Inc 2629 N Cswy Blvd Metairie LA 70002 504-836-9600 836-9621
TF: 888-882-9600 ■ *Web:* www.eaganins.com

Eaton & Berube Insurance Agency Inc
365 Nashua St Milford NH 03055 603-673-0500
Web: www.eatonberube.com

Elant Inc 46 Harriman Dr Goshen NY 10924 800-501-3936
TF: 800-501-3936 ■ *Web:* www.elant.org

Emery & Webb Inc 989 Main St Fishkill NY 12524 845-896-6727
Web: emerywebb.com

Employee benefits News
9221 Ravenna Rd Ste #D8 Twinsburg OH 44087 330-425-8399
Web: insurancebroadcasting.com

Employee Leasing Solutions Inc
1401 Manatee Ave W Ste 600 Bradenton FL 34205 941-746-6567

Employer Benefits Inc 31 Keystone Ave Reno NV 89503 775-786-6381
Web: ebi-nv.com

Employers Insurance Company of Nevada
9790 Gateway Dr Ste 100 Reno NV 89521 888-682-6671
TF: 888-682-6671 ■ *Web:* www.employers.com

Encon Group Inc 500-1400 Blair Pl Ottawa ON K1J9B8 613-786-2000
Web: www.encon.ca

Endurance Specialty Holdings Ltd
767 Third Ave 5th Fl New York NY 10017 212-209-6500 209-6501
NYSE: ENH ■ *TF:* 855-838-7792 ■ *Web:* www.endurance.bm

EOI Service Company Inc Flex
1820 E First St Ste 400 Santa Ana CA 92705 714-935-0503
Web: eoiservice.com

Esser Hayes Insurance Group Inc
1811 High Grove Naperville IL 60540 630-355-2077
Web: esserhayes.com

Evans Ewan & Brady Insurance Agency Inc
2404 Williams Dr Georgetown TX 78628 512-869-1511
Web: eebins.com

Everett Cash Mutual Insurance Co
10591 Lincoln Hwy Everett PA 15537 814-652-6111
Web: www.everettcash.com

F.B.P. Insurance Services LLC
130 Theory Ste 200 Irvine CA 92617 949-955-1430
Web: www.preceptgroup.com

FairMarket Life Settlements Corp
435 Ford Rd Ste 120 St Louis Park MN 55426 866-326-3757
TF: 866-326-3757 ■ *Web:* www.fairmarketlife.com

Faribo Insurance Agency Inc
1404 Seventh St NW Faribault MN 55021 507-334-3929
Web: insuranceagencymn.com

Farmers Fire Insurance Co 2875 Eastern Blvd York PA 17402 717-751-4435
TF: 800-537-0928 ■ *Web:* www.farmersfire.com

Farmers National Co, The
11516 Nicholas St Ste 100 Omaha NE 68154 402-496-3276
Web: www.farmers-national.com

Farris Evans Insurance Agency Inc
1568 Union Ave Memphis TN 38104 901-274-5424
TF: 800-395-8207 ■ *Web:* www.farrisevans.com

Faulkner Pontiac Buick Gmc Truck Inc
705 Autopark Blvd West Chester PA 19382 610-436-5600
Web: www.faulknerauto.com

FDI Group Inc 39500 High Pointe Blvd Ste 400 Novi MI 48375 248-348-8200
Web: www.hcaweb.net

Feingold & Feingold Insurance Agency Inc
22 Elm St Worcester MA 01608 508-831-9500
Web: feingoldco.com

Financial Designs Ltd 1775 Sherman St Ste 1800 Denver CO 80203 303-832-6100
Web: www.fdltd.com

First Delta Insurance Inc
400 Plz St PO Box 2398 West Helena AR 72390 870-572-1777
Web: firstdeltarealty.com

First Investors Financial Services Group Inc
380 Interstate N Pkwy Third Fl Atlanta GA 30339 713-977-2600
Web: www.fifsg.com

First Security Company Inc 212 Third Ave NW Hickory NC 28601 828-322-4171 322-5094
Web: www.1security.net

Flanary Group Inc, The
701 Decatur Ave North Golden Valley MN 55427 763-545-4564 545-4581
Web: theflanarygroup.com

Company / Address	City	State	ZIP	Phone	Fax
Flood & Peterson Insurance Inc 4687 W 18th St. *Web:* floodpeterson.com	Greeley	CO	80634	970-356-0123	
Forest Agency Inc 7310 W Madison St. *Web:* forestagency.com	Forest Park	IL	60130	708-383-9000	
Fortun Insurance Agency Inc 365 Palermo Ave. *TF:* 877-643-2055 ■ *Web:* www.fortuninsurance.com	Coral Gables	FL	33134	305-445-3535	
Fred C ChurchInc 41 Wellman St. *Web:* fredcchurch.com	Lowell	MA	01851	978-458-1865	
Fred Loya Insurance 1800 Lee Trevino Ste 201 **Fax Area Code:* 866 ■ *TF:* 800-554-0595 ■ *Web:* www.fredloya.com	El Paso	TX	79936	915-590-5692	685-6260*
Fringe Benefits Management Co 3101 Sessions Rd. *TF:* 800-872-0345 ■ *Web:* www.fbmc.com	Tallahassee	FL	32303	850-425-6200	425-6220
Frontier Adjusters of America Inc 4745 N Seventh St Ste 320 *TF:* 800-426-7228 ■ *Web:* www.frontieradjusters.com	Phoenix	AZ	85014	800-426-7228	553-4799
Gallagher Healthcare Insurance Services Inc 12621 Featherwood Dr Ste 300 *Web:* www.ajg.com	Houston	TX	77034	281-674-1420	
Garrison-Ross Agency Inc 602 W Flint PO Box 18 *Web:* www.garrisonross.com/	Davison	MI	48423	810-653-2101	
Gaylord Nelson Insurance Agency In 8516 S Pulaski Rd *Web:* gaylordnelson.net	Chicago	IL	60652	773-581-0844	
GCube Insurance Services Inc 3101 Wcoast Hwy Ste 100 *TF:* 877-903-4777 ■ *Web:* www.gcube-insurance.com	Newport Beach	CA	92663	949-515-9981	
Gebco Insurance Assoc 8600 LaSalle Rd Ste 338 *TF:* 800-464-3226 ■ *Web:* www.gogebco.com	Towson	MD	21286	410-668-3100	882-2872
Genatt Associates Inc 3333 New Hyde Park Rd Ste 400 *Web:* www.genatt.com	New Hyde Park	NY	11042	516-869-8666	
Gentle Dental 22 Alpine Ln *Web:* www.gentledental.com	Chelmsford	MA	01824	978-256-7581	
Gentry & Associates Claims Service Inc 1117-A Patricia Dr *Web:* www.gentryclaims.com	San Antonio	TX	78213	210-342-3036	
Gerald J Sullivan & Assoc Inc 800 W 6th St Ste 1800 *Web:* gjs.com	Los Angeles	CA	90017	213-626-1000	
Gerrity Baker Williams Inc Three Goldmine Rd. *Web:* gbwinsurance.com	Flanders	NJ	07836	973-426-1500	
Gibson Insurance Agency Inc 130 S Main St Ste 400 *Web:* gibsonins.com	South Bend	IN	46601	574-245-3500	
Glb Insurance Group of Nevada 4455 S Pecos Rd *Web:* glbins.com	Las Vegas	NV	89121	702-735-9333	
Glenn Miller Insurance Agency Inc 404 E N Ave *Web:* glennmilleragency.com	Northlake	IL	60164	708-562-3404	
Global Warranty Group LLC 500 Middle Country Rd	St. James	NY	11780	631-750-0300	
Gm Financial Consultants Corp 191 Presidental Blvd Ste W-1 *Web:* jackgrossman.metlife.com	Bala Cynwyd	PA	19004	610-664-4088	
Goetz Insurors Inc 227 Main St. *Web:* goetzinsurors.com	Fort Morgan	CO	80701	970-867-8246	
Graham Co, The One Penn Sq W 25th Fl. *TF:* 888-472-4262 ■ *Web:* www.grahamco.com	Philadelphia	PA	19102	215-567-6300	
Great American Custom Insurance Services Inc 725 S Figueroa St. *Web:* www.gamcustom.com	Los Angeles	CA	90017	213-430-4300	629-8223
Greene Wealth Management LLC 1301 Fifth Ave Ste 3410 *Web:* www.greenewealthmgmt.com	Seattle	WA	98101	206-623-2200	
Greene-Hazel & Assoc Inc 10739 Deerwood Park Blvd *Web:* greenehazel.com	Jacksonville	FL	32256	904-398-1234	
Greene-Niesen Insurance Agency Inc 6810 University Ave *Web:* greeneniesen.com	Middleton	WI	53562	608-831-3168	
Guy Ezzell Agency Inc 209 E High St	Lexington	KY	40507	859-264-1021	
Guy Hurley Blaser & Heuer LLC 1080 Kirts Blvd Ste 500 *Web:* www.ghbh.com	Troy	MI	48084	248-519-1400	
Haas & Wilkerson Inc 4300 Shawnee Mission Pkwy *TF:* 800-821-7703 ■ *Web:* www.hwins.com	Fairway	KS	66205	913-432-4400	432-6159
Hafetz & Assoc LLC 609 New Rd. *Web:* srhafetz.com	Linwood	NJ	08221	609-872-0001	
Hantz Group Inc 26200 America Dr Fifth Fl *Web:* hantzgroup.com	Southfield	MI	48034	248-304-2855	
Harmer Assoc 100 S Wacker Dr Ste 1950 *Web:* www.harmer.com	Chicago	IL	60606	312-407-7180	
Hauser Agency Inc 16 S Church St.	Mount Pleasant	PA	15666	724-547-3536	
Headliner Talent Marketing 39398 Moonlight Bay Trl *Web:* headlinertalent.com	Pelican Rapids	MN	56572	218-863-1367	
Health Network America Inc 745 Hope Rd. *Web:* www.healthnetworkamerica.com	Tinton Falls	NJ	07724	732-676-2630	
HealthSCOPE Benefits Inc 27 Corporate Hill Dr *TF:* 877-240-0135 ■ *Web:* www.healthscopebenefits.com	Little Rock	AR	72205	501-225-1551	
Healy Group Inc, The 53800 Generations Dr. *TF:* 800-667-4613 ■ *Web:* www.healygroup.com	South Bend	IN	46635	574-271-6000	
Heights Insurance Group Inc 2048 S Hacienda Blvd *Web:* www.kcal.net	Hacienda Heights	CA	91745	626-855-8288	
Hendricks & Assoc Inc 190 W Huffaker Ln Ste 403 *Web:* hendricks-inc.com	Reno	NV	89511	775-674-6000	
Herbert H. Landy Insurance Agency Inc 75 Second Ave Ste 410 **Fax Area Code:* 781 ■ *TF:* 800-336-5422 ■ *Web:* www.landy.com	Needham	MA	02494	800-336-5422	449-7908*
Herlong Bates Burnett Insurance Inc 28 Global Dr Ste 102 *Web:* hbbins.com	Greenville	SC	29607	864-527-0424	
Heuer Insurance Agency Inc 5050 Vista Blvd Ste 101 *Web:* heuerinsurance.com	Sparks	NV	89436	775-358-5554	
Hibbs Hallmark & Co 501 Shelley Dr **Fax Area Code:* 903 ■ *TF:* 800-765-6767 ■ *Web:* www.hibbshallmark.com	Tyler	TX	75701	800-765-6767	581-5988*
Hierl Insurance Inc 258 S Main St *Web:* hierl.com	Fond Du Lac	WI	54935	920-921-5921	
High & Assoc Inc Dba Financial Services Group 105 Old Hewitt Rd Ste 400 *Web:* highandassociates.net	Waco	TX	76712	254-776-7283	
Hill & Stone Insurance Agency Inc 900 N Shore Dr Ste 225	Lake Bluff	IL	60044	847-295-3030	
Hinkle Insurance Agency Inc 600 Olde Hickory Rd Ste 200 *Web:* hinkleinsurance.com	Lancaster	PA	17601	717-560-9733	
Holland Land Title & Abstract Company Inc 110 Pearl St *Web:* hollandtitle.com	Buffalo	NY	14202	716-853-6529	
Hollis D Segur Inc 156 Knotter Dr	Cheshire	CT	06410	203-699-4500	
Holliway Insurance Agcnoy Ino 5765 Olde Wadsworth Blvd.	Arvada	CO	80002	303-421-3046	
Holmes Murphy & Assoc Inc 3001 Westown Pkwy. *TF:* 800-247-7756 ■ *Web:* www.holmesmurphy.com	West Des Moines	IA	50266	515-223-6800	223-6944
Hometown Quotes LLC 133 Holiday Ct Ste 207 *Web:* www.hometownquotes.com	Franklin	TN	37067	615-599-5506	
Horton Group, The 10320 Orland Pkwy. *TF:* 800-383-8283 ■ *Web:* www.thehortongroup.com	Orland Park	IL	60467	708-845-3000	845-3001
Housing Authority Risk Retention Group Inc PO Box 189 *TF:* 800-873-0242 ■ *Web:* www.housingcenter.com	Cheshire	CT	06410	203-272-8220	271-2265
Hoyle Holt Allied Services Co 710 W Broadway	Ardmore	OK	73401	580-223-5434	
HUB International Insurance Services 1091 N Shoreline Blvd Ste 200 Ste 200 *Web:* hubinternational.com	Mountain View	CA	94043	650-237-3006	472-8000
Hub International Ltd 1065 Ave of the Americas *TF:* 800-456-5293 ■ *Web:* www.hubinternational.com	New York	NY	10018	212-338-2000	338-2100
Hudson Advisors LLC 2711 N Haskell Ave Ste 1800 *Web:* www.hudson-advisors.com	Dallas	TX	75204	214-754-8400	754-8440
Huggins Actuarial Services Inc 111 Veterans Sq Second Fl. *Web:* www.hugginsactuarial.com	Media	PA	19063	610-892-1824	
Hugh Rogers & Co 2100 Sawtelle Second Fl	Los Angeles	CA	90025	310-473-1171	
Human Arc Corp 1457 East 40th St *TF:* 800-828-6453 ■ *Web:* www.humanarc.com	Cleveland	OH	44103	216-431-5200	431-5201
Hunt Insurance Agency Inc 12000 S Harlem Ave. *TF:* 800-772-6484 ■ *Web:* thehuntgroup.com	Palos Heights	IL	60463	708-361-5300	361-5316
Huntley-Sheehy Inc 520 Olive St. *Web:* huntley-sheehy.com	Marysville	CA	95901	530-743-9264	
Hylant Group 811 Madison Ave *TF:* 800-249-5268 ■ *Web:* www.hylant.com	Toledo	OH	43624	419-255-1020	255-7557
Icim Services Inc 1401 H St Nw Fl 10 *Web:* www.icimutual.com	Washington	DC	20005	202-682-4150	
IIP Insurance Agency Inc 823 Clinton St. *Web:* mylocalagent.com	Ottawa	IL	61350	815-433-2680	
IMA Financial Group Inc 8200 E 32nd St N PO Box 2992 *Web:* www.imacorp.com	Wichita	KS	67226	316-267-9221	266-6254
IMPACT Financial Services LLC 381 Riverside Dr Ste 460 *Web:* www.impactfinancial.com	Franklin	TN	37064	615-771-9494	
Independant Insurance Services In 1736 W Locust St. *Web:* yourqcagent.com	Davenport	IA	52804	563-383-5555	
Independent Financial Agents Inc 14 Walnut Ave *Web:* www.ifaauto.com	Clark	NJ	07066	732-815-1202	
Insurance Services Office Inc (ISO) 545 Washington Blvd **Fax:* Hum Res ■ *TF:* 800-888-4476 ■ *Web:* www.iso.com	Jersey City	NJ	07310	201-469-2000	748-1472*
Insurance Unlimited of La Inc 3111 Ryan St *Web:* insunlimited.com	Lake Charles	LA	70601	337-477-6922	
InterContinental Insurance Brokers LLC 175 Federal St Ste 725 *Web:* www.iibweb.com	Boston	MA	02110	617-648-5100	
InterWest Insurance Services Inc 3636 American River Dr 2nd Fl. *TF:* 800-444-4134 ■ *Web:* www.iwins.com	Sacramento	CA	95864	916-679-2960	979-7992
Iwv Insurance 1310 N Norma St. *Web:* www.iwvins.com	Ridgecrest	CA	93555	760-446-3544	
Izett & Assoc LLC 912 Killian Hill Rd.	Lilburn	GA	30047	770-935-9575	
J Byrne Agency Inc 5200 New Jersey Ave *Web:* jbyrneagency.com	Wildwood	NJ	08260	609-522-3406	
J C Taylor Antique Automobile Agency Inc 320 S 69th St Ste 2. *Web:* www.jctaylor.com	Upper Darby	PA	19082	610-853-1300	
J Smith Lanier & Co 300 W Tenth St *TF:* 800-226-4522 ■ *Web:* www.jsmithlanier.com	West Point	GA	31833	706-645-2211	643-0606
Jack Ogren & Company Inc 6929 Hohman Ave. *Web:* ogreninsurance.com	Hammond	IN	46324	219-933-0076	

				Phone	Fax
Jake A Parrott Insurance Agency Inc 2508 N Herritage St	Kinston	NC	28501	252-523-1041	
Web: parrottins.com					
James A Normoyle Insurance Agency 669 Palmetto Ave Ste E	Chico	CA	95926	530-891-1122	
James Greene & Assoc Inc 275 W Kiehl Ave	Sherwood	AR	72120	501-834-4001	
Web: jamesgreeneins.com					
Jas. D. Collier & Co 606 S Mendenhall Rd Ste 200	Memphis	TN	38117	800-511-1548	529-2916*
**Fax Area Code:* 901 ■ *TF General:* 800-511-1548 ■ *Web:* www.collierinsurance.com					
Jeppesen Marine Inc 15242 NW Greenbrier Pkwy	Beaverton	OR	97006	503-579-1414	
Web: www.nobeltec.com					
Jim Marshall Insurance Inc 2084 Ninth St Ste D	Los Osos	CA	93402	805-528-4739	
Web: jimmarshallinsurance.com					
Jimcor Agency 60 Craig Rd	Montvale	NJ	07645	201-573-8200	
Web: jimcor.com					
Jmd Group LLC 720 Walnut St	Chattanooga	TN	37402	423-265-8111	
Web: jmdgroupllc.com					
John Callahan Agency Inc 294 New York Ave	Huntington	NY	11743	631-271-1615	
Web: statefarm.com					
John E Ernst 126 N 30th St Ste 103	Quincy	IL	62301	217-223-4127	
John F Sutherland & Assoc Ins Svcs Inc 6275 Lusk Blvd	San Diego	CA	92121	858-535-1139	
John L Wortham & Son LP 2727 Allen Pkwy	Houston	TX	77019	713-526-3366	526-5872
Web: www.worthaminsurance.com					
John Morgan Mclachlan Agency, The 75 E Main St	Somerville	NJ	08876	908-526-4600	
John Nuzzo 7428 W Belmont	Chicago	IL	60634	773-889-3900	
Web: johnnuzzo.com					
John Ratzlaff 515 Glen Creek Rd NW	Salem	OR	97304	503-399-1081	
Web: johnratzlaff.com					
Johns Eastern Co Inc PO Box 110259 Lakewood Branch	Sarasota	FL	34211	941-907-3100	402-7913*
**Fax Area Code:* 813 ■ *TF General:* 800-452-4682 ■ *Web:* www.johnseastern.com					
Joseph A Paine Inc 4301 S Pine St Ste 26	Tacoma	WA	98409	253-472-3055	
Web: paineinsurance.com					
Joseph Distel & Company Inc Five Two Mile Rd	Farmington	CT	06032	860-677-6505	
Web: distelgroup.com					
Joseph P O'Brien Agency Inc 454 New York Ave	Huntington	NY	11743	631-421-0505	
KAFL Inc 85 Allen St Ste 300	Rochester	NY	14608	585-271-6400	
Web: kafl.com					
Keenan & Assoc 2355 Crenshaw Blvd Ste 200 PO Box 4328	Torrance	CA	90501	310-212-3344	212-0300
TF: 800-654-8102 ■ *Web:* www.keenan.com					
Keenan Agency Inc, The 6805 Avery Muirfield Dr Ste 200	Dublin	OH	43016	614-764-7000	
Web: keenanins.com					
Kelleher Associates LLC 1255 Drummers Ln Four Glenhardie Corporate Ctr Ste 103	Wayne	PA	19087	610-293-1115	
Web: www.kelleherllc.com					
Kelsey National Corp 3030 S Bundy Dr	Los Angeles	CA	90066	310-390-1000	
Web: kelsey.com					
Kenney & Assoc 1754 Noirth Washington St	Naperville	IL	60563	630-505-4333	
Kentucky National Insurance Co 2709 Old Rosebud Rd	Lexington	KY	40509	859-367-5200	367-5293
Web: www.kynatins.com					
Keyes Coverage Inc 5900 Hiatus Rd	Tamarac	FL	33321	954-724-7000	
Web: keyescoverage.com					
Kraus-Anderson Insurance 420 Gateway Blvd	Burnsville	MN	55337	952-707-8200	890-0535
TF: 800-207-9261 ■ *Web:* www.kainsurance.com					
KRW Insurance Agency Inc 338 Memorial Dr	Crystal Lake	IL	60014	815-459-6300	
Web: krw-insurance.com					
Land Title Guarantee Co Inc 3033 E First Ave Ste 600 PO Box 5440	Denver	CO	80206	303-321-1880	322-7603
Web: www.ltgc.com					
Landry harris & Co 600 Jefferson St Ste 200 PO Box 2456	Lafayette	LA	70501	337-266-2150	266-2151
Web: www.landryharris.com					
Lanz & Mcardle Agency Inc 1022 17th Ave	Monroe	WI	53566	608-325-9126	
Laporte & Assoc Inc 5515 Se Milwaukie Ave	Portland	OR	97202	503-239-4116	
Web: laporte-insurance.com					
Larry Murphy Insurance Agency Inc 113 E Grand	Ponca City	OK	74601	580-767-1520	
Web: larrymurphyinsurance.com					
Lawley Service Insurance 361 Delaware Ave	Buffalo	NY	14202	716-849-8618	849-8291
TF Cust Svc: 800-860-5741 ■ *Web:* www.lawleyinsurance.com					
Le Mars Insurance Co PO Box 1608	Le Mars	IA	51031	800-545-6480	
TF: 800-545-6480 ■ *Web:* www.lemm.com					
Leap/Carpenter/Kemps Insurance Agency 3187 Collins Dr	Merced	CA	95348	209-384-0727	
Web: lckinsurance.com					
Leavell Insurance & Real Estate 117 E Broadway	Hobbs	NM	88241	575-393-2550	
Web: leavellinsurance.com					
leavitt group Enterprises 216 S 200 W PO Box 130	Cedar City	UT	84720	435-586-6553	586-1510
TF: 800-264-8085 ■ *Web:* www.leavitt.com					
Legacy Partners Inc 4000 E Third Ave Ste 600	Foster City	CA	94404	650-571-2200	
Web: www.legacypartners.com					
Leonard Insurance Services Agency Inc 4244 Mt Pleasant St NW	North Canton	OH	44720	330-266-1904	
Web: leonardinsurance.com					
Lewer Agency Inc 4534 Wornall Rd	Kansas City	MO	64111	800-821-7715	561-6840*
**Fax Area Code:* 816 ■ *TF:* 800-821-7715 ■ *Web:* www.lewer.com					
Lewis & Assoc Insurance Brokers Inc 700 W Center Ave	Visalia	CA	93291	559-733-7272	
Web: since1927.com					
Lincoln General Insurance Co 3501 Concord Rd	York	PA	17402	717-757-0000	
TF: 800-876-3350 ■ *Web:* www.lincolngeneral.com					
Linden Group Health Services Inc 2800 River Rd Ste 310	Des Plaines	IL	60018	847-294-0000	
Web: www.lindengrouphealth.com					
Linkfield & Cross Agency Inc 1600 E Beltline Ne Ste 211	Grand Rapids	MI	49525	616-447-2777	
Web: linkfieldcross.com					
Lipparelli & Assoc Inc 517 Idaho St	Elko	NV	89801	775-738-7131	
Web: progressive.com					
LISI Inc 1600 W Hillsdale Blvd	San Mateo	CA	94402	650-348-4131	
Web: lisibroker.com					
Lockton Cos 444 W 47th St Ste 900	Kansas City	MO	64112	816-960-9000	960-9099
Web: www.lockton.com					
Loesel Schaaf Insurance Agency Inc 3537 W 12th St	Erie	PA	16505	814-833-5433	
Web: lsinsure.com					
Lombardo Insurance Agency 25 Prescott St	West Hartford	CT	06110	860-236-6064	
Web: lombardo-ins.com					
Lone Star Abstract & Title Company Inc 600 N Loraine	Midland	TX	79701	432-683-1818	
Web: lonestarabstract.com					
Loomis Co 850 N Pk Rd	Wyomissing	PA	19610	610-374-4040	374-6578
TF: 800-782-0392 ■ *Web:* www.loomisco.com					
Lovitt & Touche Inc 7202 E Rosewood St Ste 200 PO Box 32702	Tucson	AZ	85710	520-722-3000	722-7245
TF: 800-426-2756 ■ *Web:* www.lovitt-touche.com					
Loyd Keith Friedlander Partners Ltd 18 Prospect St	Huntington	NY	11743	631-424-2600	
Mack & Associates Ltd 100 N La Salle St Ste 2110	Chicago	IL	60602	312-368-0677	
Web: www.mackltd.com					
Mackintire Insurance Agency Inc 11 W Main St	Westborough	MA	01581	508-366-6161	
Web: mackintire.com					
Maga Ltd 2610 Lk Cook Rd	Riverwoods	IL	60015	847-940-8866	
Web: magaltc.com					
Managed Care of America Inc 1910 Cochran Rd Ste 605	Pittsburgh	PA	15220	412-922-2803	
TF: 800-922-4966 ■ *Web:* www.mcoa.com					
Managed HealthCare Northwest Inc 422 East Burnside St Suite 215 P.O. Box 4629	Portland	OR	97208	503-413-5800	413-5801
TF: 800-648-6356 ■ *Web:* www.mhninc.com					
Mark R Veenstra 8501 75th St	Kenosha	WI	53142	262-694-4800	
Web: statefarm.com					
Marsh Saldana 1166 Ave of the Americas New York	New York	NY	10036	787-721-2600	721-1093
Web: latinamerica.marsh.com					
Marshall & Sterling Inc 110 Main St	Poughkeepsie	NY	12601	845-454-0800	454-0880
TF: 800-333-3766 ■ *Web:* marshallsterling.com					
Marwood Group LLC 733 Third Ave 11th Fl	New York	NY	10017	212-532-3651	
Web: www.marwoodgroup.com					
Masters & Assoc Insurance Inc 24 E Linden Ave PO Box 840	Miamisburg	OH	45343	937-866-3361	
Web: mastersins.com					
Matson & Cuprill LLC 7361 Kemper Rd Ste B	Cincinnati	OH	45249	513-563-7526	
Web: matsonandcuprill.com					
Mazzeo Agency Inc, The 178 Main St	Woodbridge	NJ	07095	732-636-5400	
McClone Agency Inc 150 Main St Ste 102 PO Box 389	Menasha	WI	54952	920-725-3232	
Web: www.mcclone.com					
Mcgohan Brabender Inc 3931 S Dixie Dr	Dayton	OH	45439	937-293-1600	
Web: mcgohanbrabender.com					
McGriff Seibels & Williams Inc 2211 Seventh Ave S PO Box 10265	Birmingham	AL	35233	205-252-9871	581-9293
TF: 800-476-2211 ■ *Web:* www.mcgriff.com					
McLaughlin Co, The 9210 Corporate Blvd Ste 250	Rockville	MD	20850	202-293-5566	857-8355
Web: www.mclaughlin-online.com					
Mcleod Insurance Inc 14425 N Seventh St Ste 100	Phoenix	AZ	85022	602-843-0005	
Web: mcleodinsinc.com					
Mcsweeney & Ricci Insurance Agency Inc 420 Washington St	Braintree	MA	02184	781-848-8600	
Web: mcsweeneyricci.com					
Medical Eye Services Inc 345 Baker St E	Costa Mesa	CA	92626	714-619-4660	
Web: www.mesvision.com					
Medical Risk Managers Inc 1170 Ellington Rd	South Windsor	CT	06074	860-732-3248	
Web: www.mrm-mgu.com					
MercyCare Insurance Company Inc 3430 Palmer Dr	Janesville	WI	53547	608-752-3431	
Web: www.mercycarehealthplans.com					
Mesirow Financial Insurance Services Div 353 N Clark St	Chicago	IL	60654	312-595-6200	
Web: www.mesirowfinancial.com					
MGM Industries Inc 287 Freehill Rd	Hendersonville	TN	37075	615-824-6572	
Web: www.mgmindustries.com					
MIC Services Insurance Inc 170 Kinnelon Rd - Ste 11	Kinnelon	NJ	07405	973-492-2828	
Web: micinsurance.com					
Michael Ashe Inc 1840 E Warm Springs Rd Ste 105	Las Vegas	NV	89119	702-641-1000	
Web: farmersagent.com					
Michael P Randolph 1001 E Wt Harris Blvd	Charlotte	NC	28213	704-549-1710	
Web: agents.allstate.com					
Michigan Insurance Co 1700 E Beltline Ne P.O. Box 152120, Suite 100	Grand Rapids	MI	49515	616-447-3600	
TF: 888-606-6426 ■ *Web:* www.michiganinsurance.com					

Company / Address	City	State	ZIP	Phone	Fax
MidCap Advisors LLC 1556 Third Ave Ste 410	New York	NY	10128	212-722-5683	
Web: www.midcapadvisors.com					
Miers Insurance Inc 2222 S 12th St	Allentown	PA	18103	610-797-7900	
Web: miersinsurance.com					
Mike Moss Agency Inc 803 S Dogwood	Siloam Springs	AR	72761	479-524-5111	
Web: mossins.com					
Miller Buettner & Parrott Inc 1515 S Meridian Rd	Rockford	IL	61102	815-986-0059	
Miller-Lewis Benefit Consultants 121 E Sixth Ave	Lancaster	OH	43130	740-654-4055	687-2236
TF: 800-734-3198 ■ *Web:* miller-lewis.com					
Minnesota Lawyers Mutual Insurance Co 333 S Seventh St Ste 2200	Minneapolis	MN	55402	800-422-1370	305-1510
TF: 800-422-1370 ■ *Web:* www.mlmins.com					
Mintz Girgan & Brightly Inc 18 W Passaic St	Rochelle Park	NJ	07662	201-507-5100	
Web: mgbinsurance.com					
Mj Insurance Inc 9225 Priority Way W Dr	Indianapolis	IN	46240	317-805-7500	
Web: mjinsurance.com					
MMG Insurance Co 44 Maysville St	Presque Isle	ME	04769	207-764-6611	
Web: www.mmgins.com					
MML Investors Services Inc 1295 State St	Springfield	MA	01111	413-737-8400	
Web: www.mmlinvestors.com					
Moloney Securities Company Inc 13537 Barrett Pkwy Dr Ste 300	Manchester	MO	63021	314-909-0600	
Web: www.moseco.com					
Morstan General Agency Inc 600 Community Dr PO Box 4500	Manhasset	NY	11030	516-488-4747	437-5050
Web: www.morstan.com					
Mother Lode Holding Co 189 Fulweiler Ave	Auburn	CA	95603	530-887-2410	
Web: placertitle.com					
MRops Inc 865 Easton Rd Ste 200	Warrington	PA	18976	267-895-9480	
Web: mrops.com					
MSI Benefits Group Inc 245 Townpark Dr Ste 100	Kennesaw	GA	30144	770-425-1231	425-4722
TF: 800-580-1629 ■ *Web:* www.msibenefitsgroup.com					
Multiplan inc 115 Fifth Ave	New York	NY	10003	212-780-2000	780-0420
TF: 800-922-4362 ■ *Web:* www.multiplan.com					
Murray & Zuckerman Inc 128 Erie Blvd	Schenectady	NY	12305	518-382-5483	
Web: mandzinc.com					
Nansemond Insurance Agency Inc 453 W Washington St	Suffolk	VA	23434	757-539-3421	
Web: nansemondins.com					
Naomi Taylor-Kenney Insurance Inc 4322 W El Prado Blvd	Tampa	FL	33629	813-902-8300	
Web: agents.allstate.com					
National Catastrophe Adjusters Inc 9725 Windermere Blvd	Fishers	IN	46037	317-915-8888	
Web: www.ncagroup.com					
National Electronic Attachment Inc 3577 Pkwy Ln Ste 250	Norcross	GA	30092	770-441-3203	
Web: www.nea-fast.com					
National Farm Life Insurance Co 6001 Bridge St	Fort Worth	TX	76112	817-451-9550	
TF: 800-772-7557 ■ *Web:* www.nflic.com					
NCCI Holdings Inc 901 Peninsula Corporate Cir	Boca Raton	FL	33487	561-893-1000	893-1191
TF Cust Svc: 800-622-4123 ■ *Web:* www.ncci.com					
Neal W Farinholt 9939 Hibert St	San Diego	CA	92131	858-578-6605	
Web: nealfarinholt.com					
Nease Lagana Eden & Culley Inc 2100 Riveredge Pkwy	Atlanta	GA	30328	770-956-1800	
Web: nlec.com					
NEBCO Inc 1815 Y St PO Box 80268	Lincoln	NE	68501	402-434-1212	
Web: www.nebraskaash.com					
Nevada Title Co 2500 N Buffalo Dr Ste 150	Las Vegas	NV	89128	702-251-5000	
Web: www.nevadatitle.com					
Newbury Corp 222 Ames St	Dedham	MA	02026	800-688-1825	
Web: www.ndgroup.com					
Newton One Advisors LLC 131 Continental Dr	Newark	DE	19713	302-731-1326	
Web: newtonone.com					
NIA Group Inc 490 E Monument Ave Ste 400	Saddle Brook	NJ	07663	201-845-6600	795-1158*
**Fax Area Code:* 866 ■ *TF:* 800-669-6330 ■ *Web:* www.mma-ne.com					
Norbert Cronin & Co 582 Market St Ste 1104	San Francisco	CA	94104	415-981-2222	
North Star Resource Group Inc 2701 University Ave SE N Star Professional Ctr	Minneapolis	MN	55414	612-617-6000	
Web: www.northstarfinancial.com					
Northwest Administrators Inc 2323 Eastlake Ave E	Seattle	WA	98102	206-329-4900	726-3209
TF: 877-304-6702 ■ *Web:* www.nwadmin.com					
Northwest Insurance Network Inc 330 S Wells St 16th Fl	Chicago	IL	60606	312-427-1777	
Web: www.northwestinsurance.com					
NSM Insurance Group Inc 555 N Ln Ste 6060	Conshohocken	PA	19428	610-941-9877	
Web: www.nsminc.com					
O'Connor Insurance Agency 12101 Olive Blvd	St Louis	MO	63141	314-434-0038	
Web: oconnor-ins.com					
Omni Life Assocates Inc 375 N Broadway Ste 203	Jericho	NY	11753	516-938-2465	
Web: omniquote.net					
Oriska Insurance Co 1310 Utica St	Oriskany	NY	13424	315-768-2726	
Web: oriskainsurance.com					
Oryx Insurance Brokerage Inc Two Ct St	Binghamton	NY	13901	607-724-0173	462-6799*
**Fax Area Code:* 888 ■ *Web:* www.oryxinsurance.com					
Oswald Cos 1100 Superior Ave Ste 1500	Cleveland	OH	44114	216-367-8787	839-2815
TF: 800-975-9468 ■ *Web:* www.oswaldcompanies.com					
Otis-Magie Insurance Agency Inc 332 W Superior St Ste 700	Duluth	MN	55802	218-722-7753	722-7756
TF: 800-241-2425 ■ *Web:* www.otismagie.com					
Otsego Mutual Fire Insurance Co 143 Arnold Rd PO Box 40	Burlington Flats	NY	13315	607-965-8211	
Web: otsegomutual.com					
Pacesetter Claims Service Inc 2871 N Hwy 167	Catoosa	Ok	74015	918-665-8887	
TF: 888-218-4880 ■ *Web:* www.pacesetterclaims.com					
Paradigm Equity Strategies LLC 1611 - A Akron Peninsula Rd	Akron	OH	44313	330-475-1690	
Web: paradigmequity.com					
Parker Smith & Feek Inc 2233 112th Ave NE	Bellevue	WA	98004	425-709-3600	709-7460
TF Cust Svc: 800-457-0220 ■ *Web:* www.psfinc.com					
Parkville Insurances Services Inc 15242 E Whittier Blvd PO Box 1275	Whittier	CA	90603	562-945-2702	945-4297
TF: 800-350-2702 ■ *Web:* parkvilleinsurance.com					
Paul Cribbs Insurance Agency Inc 3565 N Crossing Cir	Valdosta	GA	31602	229-247-7127	
Web: paulcribbs.net					
PCC Natural Markets Inc 4201 Roosevelt Way NE	Seattle	WA	98105	206-547-1222	
Web: www.pccnaturalmarkets.com					
Per-Se Technologies Inc 1145 Sanctuary Pkwy Ste 200	Alpharetta	GA	30004	770-237-4300	
Web: www.per-se.com					
Perry Insurance 522 Chickering Rd	North Andover	MA	01845	978-685-7690	
Web: perryins.com					
Piedmont Community Health Plan Inc 2512 Langhorne Rd	Lynchburg	VA	24501	434-947-4463	
Web: www.pchp.net					
Platinum Select LP 5001 Statesman Dr	Irving	TX	75201	866-953-0011	
TF: 866-953-0011 ■ *Web:* platinumselect.org					
Policemen's Annuity & Benefit Fund of Chicago 221 N LaSalle St Ste 1626	Chicago	IL	60601	312-744-3891	
Web: www.chipabf.org					
POMCO 2425 James St	Syracuse	NY	13206	315-432-9171	432-9171
TF: 800-934-2459 ■ *Web:* www.pomcogroup.com					
Preferred Professional Insurance Company Inc 11605 Miracle Hills Dr Ste 200	Omaha	NE	68154	402-392-1566	
Web: www.ppicins.com					
Premier Insurance Corp Inc 1326 Cape Coral Pkwy E	Cape Coral	FL	33904	239-542-7101	
Web: premierinsurancecorp.com					
Premins Company Inc, The 1407 Ave M	Brooklyn	NY	11230	718-375-8300	
Web: preminsco.com					
Pritchard & Jerden Inc 3565 Piedmont Rd Ste2000	Atlanta	GA	30305	404-238-9090	
Web: pritchardjerden.com					
Professional Risk Solutions LLC 37 Mountain Blvd Ste 3	Warren	NJ	07059	908-834-8401	
Web: www.prsbrokers.com					
Prospera Financial Services Inc 5429 LBJ Fwy Ste 400	Dallas	TX	75240	972-581-3000	
Web: www.prosperafinancial.com					
Protegrity Services Inc 260 Wekiva Springs Rd Ste 1040	Longwood	FL	32779	407-551-3962	788-0812
TF: 800-883-4000 ■ *Web:* protegrityproperties.com					
PS & Assoc Underwriting Agency Inc 1776 Legacy Cir Ste 104	Naperville	IL	60563	630-416-0004	416-2246
Web: www.psassociate.com/					
Purves & Assoc Insurance 500 Fourth St	Davis	CA	95616	530-756-5561	
Web: purvesinsurance.com					
Quincy & Company Inc 144 Gould St	Needham Heights	MA	02494	781-431-9600	
Web: quincyinsurance.net					
R Mcclure Electric 706 Portal St Ste D	Cotati	CA	94931	707-792-2101	
Web: rmcclure.com					
Rain & Hail LLC 9200 Northpark Dr Ste 250	Johnston	IA	50131	515-559-1200	
Web: www.rainhail.com					
Ralph C Mehler Agency Inc 62 E Shenango St	Sharpsville	PA	16150	724-962-5757	
Web: mehlerinsurance.com					
Rampart Brokerage Corp 1983 Marcus Ave Ste C130	New Hyde Park	NY	11042	516-538-7000	390-3555
TF: 800-772-6727 ■ *Web:* www.rampartinsurance.com					
Rand Insurance Inc 1100 E Putnam Ave	Riverside	CT	06878	203-637-1006	
Web: randinsurance.com					
RC Knox & Co One Goodwin Sq 24th Fl	Hartford	CT	06103	860-524-7600	240-1599
TF: 800-742-2765 ■ *Web:* www.peoples.com					
Real Estate Errors & Omissions Insurance Corp 1604 700 W Pender St	Vancouver	BC	V6C1G8	604-669-0019	
Web: www.reeoic.com					
Regional Care Inc 905 W 27th St	Scottsbluff	NE	69361	308-635-2260	
Web: www.regionalcare.com					
Reid Jones McRorie & Williams Inc PO Box 18527	Charlotte	NC	28218	704-537-0012	
TF: 800-785-2604 ■ *Web:* www.rjmw.com					
Reller Risk Management 6315 Fly Rd	East Syracuse	NY	13057	315-432-8210	
Web: rellerrisk.com					
Renaissance Group 981 Worcester St	Wellesley	MA	02482	800-514-2667	
TF: 800-514-2667 ■ *Web:* www.renaissanceins.com					
RF Ougheltree & Assoc LLC 1050 Wall St W	Lyndhurst	NJ	07071	201-964-9881	
Web: rfoins.com					
RH Nicholson & Company Inc 3998 Fair Ridge Dr Ste 200	Fairfax	VA	22033	703-261-6100	
Web: rhnicholson.com					
Rhythm Band Instruments LLC 1316 E Lancaster Ave	Fort Worth	TX	76102	817-335-2561	
Web: www.rhythmband.com					
Richard Hennessy Insurance Agency Inc 6335A SW Capitol Hwy	Portland	OR	97239	503-245-9345	
Web: statefarm.com					
Richmond & Associates 491 Maple St Ste 107	Danvers	MA	01923	978-777-8688	
Web: richmond.com					
Rigg Darlington Group Inc, The 14 E Welsh Pool Rd	Exton	PA	19341	484-876-2222	

Phone Fax

Robert J Hanafin Inc
204 Washington Ave PO Box 509 .... Endicott NY 13760 607-754-3500 754-9797

Robert M Degregorio Insurance Agency Inc
34 Woodside Ave .... Winthrop MA 02152 617-846-3313

Robert Moreno Insurance Services
1400 N Harbor Blvd .... Fullerton CA 92835 714-738-1383
Web: rmismga.com

Robert Runia 1270 East 8600 Souh Ste 8 .... Sandy UT 84094 801-566-5111
Web: robertrunia.com

Robertson Ryan & Assoc Inc
330 E Kilbourn Ave .... Milwaukee WI 53202 414-271-3575
Web: www.robertsonryan.com

Rosenthal Bros Inc 740 Waukegan Rd Ste 402 .... Deerfield IL 60015 847-940-4300
Web: www.rosenthalbros.com

Roy H Reeve Agency Inc 13400 Main Rd .... Mattituck NY 11952 631-298-4700
Web: royreeve.com

RpmOne Inc 4495 Military Trl Ste 207 .... Jupiter FL 33458 561-741-4447
Web: www.rpmone.com

RSI Insurance Brokers Inc
2801 Bristol St Ste 200 .... Costa Mesa CA 92626 714-546-6616
Web: rsiinsurancebrokers.com

Rutherfoord Thomas Inc One S Jefferson St .... Roanoke VA 24011 540-982-3511 342-9747
Web: www.rutherfoord.com

S L Nusbaum Insurance Agency Inc
500 W 21st St Ste 300 .... Norfolk VA 23517 757-622-4653
Web: nusbauminsurance.com

Sahouri Insurance & Associates Inc
8200 Grnsburg Dr Ste 1440 .... Mclean VA 22102 703-883-0500
Web: sahouri.com

Santo Insurance & Financial Services Inc
224 Main St .... Salem NH 03079 603-890-6439
Web: santoinsurance.com

SCF Securities Inc 155 E Shaw Ave Ste 102 .... Fresno CA 93710 559-456-6100
Web: www.scfsecurities.com

Scharer Insurance Inc 454 E Ctr St .... Marion OH 43302 740-387-4311
Web: scharerinsurance.com

Scott Danahy Naylon Company Inc (SDN)
300 Spindrift Dr .... Williamsville NY 14221 716-633-3400 633-4306
TF: 800-728-6362 ■ *Web:* www.sdnins.com

Scott N Schumaker 217 E Maple Rd .... Troy MI 48083 248-457-0800
Web: statefarm.com

Sean Wong - State Farm Insurance Agent
7035 Hwy 6 N .... Houston TX 77095 281-550-0555 550-0100
Web: statefarm.com

Security Escrow & Title Insurance Agency
337 South Main Ste 110 .... Cedar City UT 84720 435-867-0402
Web: securityescrowutah.com

Selectpath Benefits & Financial Inc
310-700 Richmond St .... London ON N6A5C7 519-675-1177 675-1331
Web: www.selectpath.ca

Selectquote Insurance Services
595 Market St 10th Fl .... San Francisco CA 94105 415-543-7338 436-7000*
**Fax Area Code:* 800 ■ *TF:* 800-670-3213 ■ *Web:* www.selectquote.com

Self Funding Administrators Corp
339 Busch'S Frontage Rd .... Annapolis MD 21409 410-757-4200

Senior Market Sales Inc (SMS)
8420 W Dodge Rd Fifth Fl .... Omaha NE 68114 402-397-3311 397-0455
TF: 800-786-5566 ■ *Web:* www.seniormarketsales.com

Seniority Benefit Group 6365 Riverside Dr .... Dublin OH 43017 614-799-1404
Web: www.ccibenefitsolutions.com

Sherzer & Assoc Insurance Inc
110 Stony Point Rd Ste 120 .... Santa Rosa CA 95401 707-573-1010
Web: www.sherzer.com

Sica Consultants Inc
883 Briarwoods Rd .... Franklin Lakes NJ 07417 201-805-1561
Web: www.sicaconsultants.com

SilverStone Group
11516 Miracle Hills Dr Ste 100 .... Omaha NE 68154 402-964-5400 964-5454
TF: 800-288-5501 ■ *Web:* www.silverstonegroup.com

Simkiss Cos Two Paoli Office Pk PO Box 1787 .... Paoli PA 19301 610-727-5300 727-5414
Web: www.simkiss.com

Sintz & Assoc Inc 57 S Park Blvd .... Greenwood IN 46143 317-889-3000

Smith Nadenbousch Insurance Inc
132 S Queen St .... Martinsburg WV 25401 304-263-3388
Web: smnains.com

Snellings Walters Insurance Agency
1117 Perimeter Ctr W W101 .... Atlanta GA 30338 770-396-9600
Web: www.snellingswalters.com

Southwest Business Corp
9311 San Pedro Ave Ste 600 .... San Antonio TX 78216 210-635-1231 525-1240
Web: www.swbc.com

SPAAN Tech Inc 311 S Wacker Dr Ste 2400 .... Chicago IL 60606 312-277-8800
Web: www.spaantech.com

SPARTA Insurance Holdings Inc
185 Asylum St Cityplace Ii .... Hartford CT 06103 860-275-6500
Web: www.spartainsurance.com

Stailey Insurance Corp 2084 S Milwaukee St .... Denver CO 80210 303-759-2796
Web: staileycorp.com

Stallings Crop Insurance Corp PO Box 6100 .... Lakeland FL 33807 863-647-2747
TF: 800-721-7099 ■ *Web:* www.stallingscrop.com

Standard Insurance Agency Corp 620 W Pipeline .... Hurst TX 76053 817-285-1800
Web: www.siatexas.com

Standard Life Financial Inc
1245 Sherbrooke St W .... Montreal QC H3G1G3 514-499-8855
Web: www.standardlife.ca

Standard Life Investments (USA) Ltd
One Beacon St 34th Fl .... Boston MA 02108 617-720-7900
Web: us.standardlifeinvestments.com

Stanley Mcdonald Agency of Illinois
2018 State Rd .... La Crosse WI 54601 608-788-6160
Web: armitageinconline.com

Phone Fax

Stanton Insurance Agency Inc
230 Second Ave Ste 105 .... Waltham MA 02451 781-893-3200
Web: stantonins.com

Star Casualty Insurance Company Inc
PO Box 451037 .... Miami FL 33134 877-782-7210 363-1954*
**Fax Area Code:* 786 ■ *TF:* 877-782-7210 ■ *Web:* www.starcasualty.com

Starkweather & Shepley Inc
60 Catamore Blvd .... East Providence RI 02914 401-435-3600 438-0150
TF: 800-854-4625 ■ *Web:* www.starkweathershepley.com

Starr Group, The 5005 W Loomis Rd Ste 300 .... Greenfield WI 53220 414-421-3800
Web: starrgroup.com

State Farm Mutual Automobile Insurance Company
800 Metairie Rd Ste P .... Metairie LA 70005 504-832-4127
Web: abflynt.net

State Mutual Insurance Co 210 E Second Ave .... Rome GA 30161 706-291-1054
Web: statemutualinsurance.com

Stephen Mahoney 380 W Portal Ave Ste D .... San Francisco CA 94127 415-681-7120
Web: agents.allstate.com

Sterling & Sterling Inc
135 Crossways Park Dr .... Woodbury NY 11797 516-487-0300

Stieg & Assoc Insurance Inc 3319 Gabel Rd .... Billings MT 59102 406-656-9666
Web: stieginsurance.com

Stoner-Johnson Insurance Agency
2330 Airport Hwy .... Toledo OH 43609 419-385-3101
Web: stonerjohnson.com

Strassman Insurance Services Inc
26351 Curtiss Wright Pkwy .... Richmond Heights OH 44143 216-289-1500
Web: strassman.net

Stratose Two Concourse Pkwy NE # 300 Ste 300 .... Atlanta GA 30328 404-459-7201 459-6645
Web: www.coalitionamerica.com

Succession Capital Alliance Insurance Services LLC
4695 MacArthur Ct 10th Fl .... Newport Beach CA 92660 949-794-1882
Web: www.successioncapital.com

Sullivan Curtis Monroe 1920 Main St .... Irvine CA 92614 949-250-7172 852-9762
TF: 800-427-3253 ■ *Web:* www.sullivancurtismonroe.com

Summit Financial Resources Inc
Four Campus Dr .... Parsippany NJ 07054 973-285-3600
Web: www.summitfinancial.com

Sundel & Milford Inc 11 Scovill St .... Waterbury CT 06720 203-753-0114
Web: sundelmilford.com

Surry Insurance Agency & Realty Company Inc
119 W Atkins St .... Dobson NC 27017 336-386-8228
Web: surryinsurance.com

Swan & Sons-Morss Company Inc 309 E Water St .... Elmira NY 14902 607-734-6283
Web: swanmorss.com

Synergy Investment Group Ltd
8320 University Exec Park Dr Ste 112 .... Charlotte NC 28262 704-333-7637
Web: synergyinvestments.com

Tabb Brockenbrough & Ragland LLC
4905 Dickens Rd .... Richmond VA 23230 804-355-7984
TF: 800-296-0531 ■ *Web:* www.tbrinsurance.com

Talladega Insurance Agency 109 Spring St N .... Talladega AL 35160 256-362-4153
Web: talladega-insurance.com

Tamrac Group Inc, The
10946 C Beaver Dam Rd .... Hunt Valley MD 21030 410-568-1200
Web: tamracinsurance.com

Teachers Protective Mutual Life Insurance Co
116-118 N Prince St .... Lancaster PA 17603 717-394-7156
TF: 800-555-3122 ■ *Web:* www.tpmins.com

Tetrault Insurance Agency Inc
4317 Acushnet Ave .... New Bedford MA 02745 508-995-8365
Web: tetraultinsurance.com

Texas Women Ventures 3625 N Hall St Ste 615 .... Dallas TX 75219 214-444-7890
Web: www.texaswomenventures.com

Thomas George Associates Ltd
10 Larkfield Rd .... East Northport NY 11731 631-261-8800
Web: www.tgaltd.com

Thomas Venturi 5616 Wmontrose Ave .... Chicago IL 60634 773-777-5151

Three Rivers Holdings Inc
Unison Plz 1001 Brinton Rd .... Pittsburgh PA 15221 412-858-4000
Web: www.unisonhealthplan.com

Thurston Group LLC
John Hancock Ctr 875 N Michigan Ave Ste 3640 .... Chicago IL 60611 312-255-0077
Web: www.thurstongroup.com

Title Security of Arizona Inc
6390 E Tanque Verde Rd .... Tucson AZ 85715 520-885-1600
Web: titlesecurity.com

Todd Organization Inc, The
24610 Detroit Rd Ste 210 .... Cleveland OH 44145 440-871-7700
Web: www.toddorg.com

Toler & Toler Insurance 1564 SR- 160 .... Gallipolis OH 45631 740-446-9445

Total Care Inc 819 S Salina St .... Syracuse NY 13202 315-634-5555
Web: www.totalcareny.com

Trans-Century Resources Inc
8716 N Mopac Expy Ste 100 .... Austin TX 78759 512-345-0280
Web: www.trans-century.com

Transguard Insurance Company of America Inc
215 S Human Blvd .... Naperville IL 60563 630-864-3500
Web: www.transguard.com

TRICOR Insurance & Financial Services Inc
230 W Cherry St .... Lancaster WI 53813 608-723-6441
Web: www.tricorinsurance.com

Trimble-Batjer Insurance Assoc
201 S Chadbourne St .... San Angelo TX 76903 325-653-6733
Web: trimble-batjer.com

U S Risk Insurance Group Inc
10210 N Central Expy .... Dallas TX 75231 214-265-7090 739-1421
TF: 800-926-9155 ■ *Web:* www.usrisk.com

Underwriters Safety & Claims Inc
1700 Eastpoint Pkwy .... Louisville KY 40223 502-244-1343
Web: www.uscky.com

Phone / Fax

Uni-Ter Underwriting Management Corp
500 Northridge Rd Ste 330 .... Atlanta GA 30350 678-781-2400
Web: www.usre.com

Union Central Life Insurance Co, The
1876 Waycross Rd PO Box 40888 .... Cincinnati OH 45240 513-595-2200
Web: www.unioncentral.com

United Funeral Directors Benefit Life Insurance Co
351 S Sherman Ste 102 .... Richardson TX 75081 469-330-2200
Web: unitedbenefitsinc.com

United States Warranty Corp
22 NE 22nd Ave .... Pompano Beach FL 33062 954-784-9400
Web: www.uswarranty.com

United Underwriters Inc PO Box 971000 .... Orem UT 84097 801-226-2662 229-2662
Web: www.uuinsurance.com

Usasia Insurance Services 319 Union Ave .... Pomona CA 91768 909-618-0288
Web: usasia-ins.com

USI Holdings Corp
555 Pleasantville Rd Ste 160 S .... Briarcliff Manor NY 10510 914-749-8500 749-8550
Web: www.usi.biz

Van Dyk Group Inc, The
12800 Long Beach Blvd .... Beach Haven NJ 08008 609-492-1511 492-7643
TF: 800-222-0131 ■ *Web:* www.vandykgroup.com

Van Gilder Insurance Corp 1515 Wine Coop .... Denver CO 80202 303-837-8500 831-5295
TF General: 800-872-8500 ■ *Web:* www.vgic.com

Van Zandt Emrich & Cary Inc
12401 Plantside Dr .... Louisville KY 40299 502-456-2001 454-5137
TF: 800-928-7355 ■ *Web:* www.vzecins.com

VanBeurden Insurance Services Inc
1600 Draper St PO Box 67 .... Kingsburg CA 93631 559-897-2975 897-4070
Web: www.vanbeurden.com

VIVA Health Inc 1222 14th Ave S .... Birmingham AL 35205 205-939-1718
TF: 800-633-1542 ■ *Web:* www.vivahealth.com

Wallace Welch Willingham
300 First Ave S Fifth Fl .... Saint Petersburg FL 33701 727-522-7777 521-2902
TF: 800-783-5085 ■ *Web:* www.marineins.com

Weaver Bros Insurance Assoc Inc
4550 Montgomery Ave Ste 300 North Tower .... Bethesda MD 20814 301-986-4400 986-4422
Web: www.weaverbros.com

Weber Insurance Corp 505 Corporate Dr W .... Langhorne PA 19047 215-860-0400
Web: weberinsurance.com

WellCare of Georgia Inc
211 Perimeter Ctr Pkwy Ste 800 .... Atlanta GA 30346 678-327-0939
Web: georgia.wellcare.com

Weller/Obrien Insurance Services
720 Kelly Ave .... Half Moon Bay CA 94019 650-726-6328
Web: wellerobrien.com

Wells Fargo Insurance Inc
600 S Hwy 169 .... Saint Louis Park MN 55426 612-667-5600 667-2681
Web: www.wellsfargo.com

West Boylston Insurance AgencyInc
12 W Boylston St .... West Boylston MA 01583 508-835-3877
Web: westboylstoninsurance.com

West Point Underwriters LLC
7785 66th St .... Pinellas Park FL 33781 727-507-7565
Web: westpointuw.com

Westcor Land Title Insurance Co
201 N New York Ave Ste 200 .... Winter Park FL 32789 407-629-5842
Web: www.wltic.com

Western Group Inc 511 W 10Th .... Pueblo CO 81003 719-543-3604
Web: wgiinsurance.com

Wharton Group 101 S Livingston Ave .... Livingston NJ 07039 973-992-5775 992-6660
TF: 800-521-2725 ■ *Web:* www.whartoninsurance.com

White Pigeon Mutual Insurance Assn
105 W Fourth St .... Wilton IA 52778 563-732-2072
Web: wpigeon.com

White Planning Group 602 Virginia St E .... Charleston WV 25301 304-346-3295
Web: whiteplanninggroup.com

William Gallagher Assoc Investment Services Group Inc (WGA)
470 Atlantic Ave .... Boston MA 02210 617-261-6700
Web: www.wgains.com

William Penn Assn 709 Brighton Rd .... Pittsburgh PA 15233 412-231-2979
TF: 800-848-7366 ■ *Web:* www.williampennassociation.org

Willis Group Holdings Ltd
200 Liberty St 1 World Financial Ctr .... New York NY 10281 212-915-8888 915-8511
NYSE: WSH ■ *TF:* 800-234-8596 ■ *Web:* www.willis.com

Wilshire Insurance Co 1206 W Ave J Ste 100 .... Lancaster CA 93534 661-940-7300
Web: www.wilshireinsurance.com

Wolverine Mutual Insurance Co
One Wolverine Way .... Dowagiac MI 49047 269-782-3451
TF: 800-733-3320 ■ *Web:* www.wolverinemutual.com

Word & Brown Insurance Administrators Inc
721 S Parker Ste 300 .... Orange CA 92868 714-835-6752
Web: www.wordandbrown.com

World Financial Group Inc
11315 Johns Creek Pkwy .... Johns Creek GA 30097 770-453-9300
Web: www.worldfinancialgroup.com

XL Capital Group 1540 Broadway .... New York NY 10036 212-915-6177
Web: www.xlgroup.com

394 INSURANCE COMPANIES

SEE ALSO Home Warranty Services p. 2478; Viatical Settlement Companies p. 3285

394-1 Animal Insurance

Phone / Fax

Ark Agency 310 Washburne Ave .... Paynesville MN 56362 320-243-7250 243-7224
TF: 800-328-8894 ■ *Web:* www.arkagency-naha.com

Canadian Livestock Insurance
480 University Ave Ste 412 .... Toronto ON M5G1V2 416-510-8191 510-8186
TF: 800-727-1502 ■ *Web:* www.cdnlivestock.ca

Equisport Agency Inc
2306 Eastways Rd PO Box 269 .... Bloomfield Hills MI 48304 248-644-1215 644-1404
TF: 800-432-1215 ■ *Web:* www.equisportagency.com

Henry Equestrian Insurance Brokers
28 Victoria St .... Aurora ON L4G1P9 905-727-1144 727-4986
TF: 800-565-4321 ■ *Web:* www.hep.ca

Merry Rama Insurance 4236 County Hwy 18 .... Delhi NY 13753 607-746-2226 746-2911
Web: www.cattlexchange.com/insurance.htm

Pet's Health Plan 3840 Greentree Ave SW .... Canton OH 44706 330-484-8080 484-8081
TF: 800-807-6724 ■ *Web:* www.petshealthplan.com

Veterinary Pet Insurance Inc PO Box 2344 .... Brea CA 92822 800-872-7387 989-0533*
**Fax Area Code:* 714 ■ *TF:* 800-872-7387 ■ *Web:* www.petinsurance.com

394-2 Life & Accident Insurance

Phone / Fax

Acacia Life Insurance Co 7315 Wisconsin Ave .... Bethesda MD 20814 301-280-1000 280-1161*
**Fax:* Cust Svc ■ *TF:* 800-444-1889 ■ *Web:* www.unificompanies.com

Acacia National Life 7315 Wisconsin Ave .... Bethesda MD 20814 800-368-2745 657-1982*
**Fax Area Code:* 301 ■ *TF:* 800-444-1889 ■ *Web:* www.unificompanies.com

Advance Insurance Company of Kansas
1133 SW Topeka Blvd .... Topeka KS 66629 785-273-9804 273-6121
TF: 800-530-5989 ■ *Web:* www.advanceinsurance.com

Aetna Inc 151 Farmington Ave .... Hartford CT 06156 860-273-0123 273-8909
NYSE: AET ■ *TF:* 800-872-3862 ■ *Web:* www.aetna.com

Alliant Insurance Services Inc
1301 Dove St .... Newport Beach CA 92660 949-756-0271 756-2713
Web: www.alliant.com

Allianz Life Insurance Company of North America
PO Box 1344 .... Minneapolis MN 55416 800-950-5872
TF: 800-950-5872 ■ *Web:* www.allianzlife.com

Allstate Life Insurance Co
3100 Sanders Rd Allstate W Plz .... Northbrook IL 60062 847-402-5000
TF Cust Svc: 800-366-1411 ■ *Web:* www.allstate.com

Amalgamated Life Insurance Co 730 Broadway .... New York NY 10003 212-539-5826
Web: www.amalgamatedlife.com

American Amicable Life Insurance Co PO Box 2549 .... Waco TX 76702 254-297-2777 297-2733
TF: 800-736-7311 ■ *Web:* americanamicable.com

American Equity Investment Life Insurance Co
6000 Westown Pkwy .... West Des Moines IA 50266 515-221-0002 221-9947
TF: 888-221-1234 ■ *Web:* www.american-equity.com

American Family Life Assurance Company of Columbus (AFLAC)
1932 Wynnton Rd .... Columbus GA 31999 706-323-3431 448-8922*
**Fax Area Code:* 800 ■ **Fax:* Cust Svc ■ *TF Cust Svc:* 800-992-3522 ■ *Web:* www.aflac.com

American Family Life Insurance Co
6000 American Pkwy .... Madison WI 53783 608-249-2111 243-4921
TF: 800-692-6326 ■ *Web:* www.amfam.com

American Family Mutual Insurance Co
6000 American Pkwy .... Madison WI 53783 608-249-2111 243-4917*
**Fax:* Hum Res ■ *TF Cust Svc:* 800-374-0008 ■ *Web:* www.amfam.com

American Fidelity Life Insurance Co
4060 Barrancas Ave .... Pensacola FL 32507 850-456-7401 453-5440
Web: www.americanfidelitylifeins.com

American Foreign Service Protective Assn
1716 N St NW .... Washington DC 20036 202-833-4910 833-4918
Web: www.afspa.org

American Income Life Insurance Co (AIL)
1200 Wooded Acres .... Waco TX 76710 254-761-6400 761-5724
TF: 800-433-3405 ■ *Web:* www.ailife.com

American National Insurance Co
One Moody Plz .... Galveston TX 77550 409-763-4661 763-4545
NASDAQ: ANAT ■ *Web:* anico.com

American Republic Insurance Co
601 Sixth Ave .... Des Moines IA 50309 800-247-2190 247-2435*
**Fax Area Code:* 515 ■ *TF Cust Svc:* 800-247-2190 ■ *Web:* americanrepublic.com

American Standard Insurance Company of Wisconsin
6000 American Pkwy .... Madison WI 53783 608-249-2111
TF: 800-692-6326 ■ *Web:* www.amfam.com

American Trust Administrators Inc
255 NW Blue Pkwy Ste 100 .... Lees Summit MO 64063 816-251-7700
Web: www.ataamerica.com

American United Life Insurance Co
One American Sq 510A PO Box 6010 .... Indianapolis IN 46282 317-285-1877 285-1855
TF: 800-537-6442 ■ *Web:* www.oneamerica.com

Americo Financial Life & Annuity Insurance Co
PO Box 410288 .... Kansas City MO 64141 800-231-0801
TF: 800-231-0801 ■ *Web:* www.americo.com

Ameritas Direct 5900 'O' St .... Lincoln NE 68510 800-555-4655 467-7935*
**Fax Area Code:* 402 ■ *TF:* 800-555-4655 ■ *Web:* www.ameritasdirect.com

Ameritas Life Insurance Corp 5900 'O' St .... Lincoln NE 68510 402-467-1122 467-7935*
**Fax:* Hum Res ■ *TF:* 800-745-1112 ■ *Web:* www.ameritas.com

Ameritas Variable Life Insurance Co
5900 'O' St .... Lincoln NE 68510 402-467-1122 467-7935*
**Fax:* Hum Res ■ *TF:* 800-634-8353 ■ *Web:* ameritas.com

Anthem Life Insurance Co
6740 N High St Ste 200 .... Worthington OH 43085 614-436-0688
TF: 800-551-7265 ■ *Web:* www.anthem.com

Arch Insurance Group Inc
One Liberty Plz 53rd Fl .... New York NY 10006 212-651-6500
TF: 866-993-9978 ■ *Web:* www.archinsurance.com

Assurant Employee Benefits
2323 Grand Blvd .... Kansas City MO 64108 816-474-2345 881-8996
TF: 800-733-7879 ■ *Web:* www.assurantemployeebenefits.com

Aurora National Life Assurance Co
PO Box 4490 .... Hartford CT 06147 800-265-2652 333-2311*
**Fax Area Code:* 803 ■ *TF:* 800-265-2652 ■ *Web:* www.auroralife.com

Auto-Owners Life Insurance Co
6101 Anacapri Blvd .... Lansing MI 48917 517-323-1200 323-8796
TF: 800-288-8740 ■ *Web:* www.auto-owners.com

Axa Distributors LLC
1290 Ave of the Americas .... New York NY 10104 212-314-3731 314-3583

Phone Fax

AXA Equitable Life Insurance Co
1290 Ave of the Americas New York NY 10104 212-554-1234
Web: us.axa.com

Baltimore Life Cos 10075 Red Run Blvd. Owings Mills MD 21117 410-581-6600 581-6601*
**Fax:* Claims ■ *TF:* 800-628-5433 ■ *Web:* www.baltlife.com

Bankers Fidelity Life Insurance Co
4370 Peachtree Rd Atlanta GA 30319 404-266-5500 266-5699*
NASDAQ: AAME ■ **Fax:* Sales ■ *TF:* 800-241-1439 ■ *Web:* www.bflic.com

Bankers Insurance LLC 4490 Cox Rd. Glen Allen VA 23060 804-497-3634 643-0938
Web: www.bankersinsurance.net

Bankers Life & Casualty Co
111 E Wacker Dr Ste 2100 Chicago IL 60601 312-396-6000
TF: 800-231-9150 ■ *Web:* www.bankers.com

Banner Life Insurance Co
1701 Research Blvd Rockville MD 20850 301-279-4800 294-6961
TF: 800-638-8428 ■ *Web:* www.lgamerica.com

Beneficial Financial Group 55 N 300 W Salt Lake City UT 84145 801-933-1100 531-3317*
**Fax:* Cust Svc ■ *TF:* 800-233-7979 ■ *Web:* www.beneficialfinancialgroup.com

Benevolent Life Insurance Company Inc
1624 Milam St Shreveport LA 71103 318-425-1522 221-1761

Best Life & Health Insurance Co
2505 McCabe Way Irvine CA 92614 949-253-4080 222-1004
Web: www.bestlife.com

Booker T Washington Insurance Co
1728 Third Ave N Birmingham AL 35203 205-328-5454

Boston Mutual Life Insurance Co 120 Royall St Canton MA 02021 781-463-6068 770-0490
TF: 800-669-2668 ■ *Web:* www.bostonmutual.com

Bristol West Insurance Group
5701 Stirling Rd PO Box 229080 Davie FL 33314 954-513-2500 316-5275
Web: www.bristolwest.com

Catalyst Health Solutions Inc
800 King Farm Blvd Ste 400 Rockville MD 20850 301-548-2900 268-3119*
NASDAQ: CHSI ■ **Fax Area Code:* 240 ■ *Web:* catamaranrx.com/

Catholic Order of Foresters
355 Shuman Blvd Naperville IL 60563 630-983-4900
Web: catholicforester.org

Central Security Life Insurance Co
2175 N Glenville Dr PO Box 833879 Richardson TX 75082 972-699-2770 699-2788
Web: www.cslic.com

Central States Health & Life Company of Omaha
1212 N 96th St Omaha NE 68114 402-397-1111
TF: 800-826-6587 ■ *Web:* www.cso.com

CIGNA 900 Cottage Grove Rd Hartford CT 06002 860-226-6000 351-3616*
**Fax Area Code:* 800 ■ *TF:* 800-997-1654 ■ *Web:* www.cigna.com

Citizens Insurance Company of America
400 E Anderson Ln Austin TX 78752 512-837-7100 836-9785
TF: 800-880-5044 ■ *Web:* www.citizensinc.com

Citizens Security Life Insurance Co
12910 Shelbyville Rd Ste 300 Louisville KY 40243 502-244-2420 254-4059
TF: 800-843-7752 ■ *Web:* www.citizenssecuritylife.com

Colonial Life & Accident Insurance Co
1200 Colonial Life Blvd Columbia SC 29210 803-213-7250 731-2618
TF: 800-325-4368 ■ *Web:* www.coloniallife.com

Colonial Penn Life Insurance Co
399 Market St Philadelphia PA 19181 215-928-8000
TF: 800-523-9100 ■ *Web:* www.colonialpenn.com

Columbus Life Insurance Co
400 E Fourth St PO Box 5737 Cincinnati OH 45201 800-677-9696 361-6939*
**Fax Area Code:* 513 ■ *TF:* 800-677-9595 ■ *Web:* www.columbuslife.com

Companion Life Insurance Co
7909 Parklane Rd Ste 200 Columbia SC 29223 803-735-1251 735-0736
TF: 800-753-0404 ■ *Web:* www.companionlife.com

Concord Group Insurance Cos Four Bouton St. Concord NH 03301 800-852-3380
TF: 800-852-3380 ■ *Web:* www.concordgroupinsurance.com

Conseco Annuity Assurance Co
11825 N Pennsylvania St Carmel IN 46032 866-595-2255 817-5704*
**Fax Area Code:* 317 ■ *TF:* 866-595-2255 ■ *Web:* www.conseco.com

Conseco Health Insurance Co
11825 N Pennsylvania St Carmel IN 46032 866-595-2255 817-2161*
**Fax Area Code:* 317 ■ *TF:* 866-595-2255 ■ *Web:* www.conseco.com

Conseco Life Insurance Co
11815 N Pennsylvania St Carmel IN 46032 317-817-3012 817-3773
Web: www.conseco.com

Conseco Senior Health Insurance Co
11825 N Pennsylvania St PO Box 1980 Carmel IN 46032 866-595-2255 817-6721*
**Fax Area Code:* 317 ■ *TF:* 866-595-2255 ■ *Web:* www.conseco.com

Continental Assurance Co 333 S Wabash Ave Chicago IL 60604 312-822-5000 260-4376
TF: 800-251-2148 ■ *Web:* www.cna.com

COUNTRY Insurance & Financial Services
1705 Towanda Ave Bloomington IL 61701 866-268-6879
TF: 888-211-2555 ■ *Web:* www.countryfinancial.com

Creative Mktg International Corp
11460 Tomahawk Creek Pkwy. Leawood KS 66211 913-814-0510
Web: www.creativeone.com/

Crump Insurance Services Inc
105 Eisenhower Pkwy Roseland NJ 07068 973-461-2100 461-2128
Web: crumplifeinsurance.com

Educators Mutual Insurance Assn Utah
852 East Arrowhead Ln Salt Lake City UT 84107 801-262-7476
Web: www.educatorsmutual.com

ELCO Mutual Life & Annuity
916 Sherwood Dr Lake Bluff IL 60044 847-295-6000
TF: 888-872-7954 ■ *Web:* www.elcomutual.com

Elite Mktg Group 800 Bering Dr. Houston TX 77057 713-507-1000
Web: www.elitemktg.net

Epic Life Insurance Co 1765 W Broadway Madison WI 53713 608-223-2100 223-2159
TF Sales: 800-236-8809 ■ *Web:* www.epiclife.com

Equitable Life & Casualty Insurance Co
Three Triad Ctr Salt Lake City UT 84180 877-358-4060 579-3790*
**Fax Area Code:* 801 ■ *TF Cust Svc:* 877-358-4060 ■ *Web:* www.equilife.com

Erie & Niagara Insurance Assn
8800 Sheridan Dr Williamsville NY 14221 716-632-5433
Web: www.enia.com

Erie Family Life Insurance Co
100 Erie Insurance Pl Erie PA 16530 814-870-2000 870-4040
TF: 800-458-0811 ■ *Web:* www.erieinsurance.com

Farm Bureau Life Insurance Co
5400 University Ave West Des Moines IA 50266 515-225-5400 226-6966*
**Fax:* Hum Res ■ *TF:* 800-247-4170 ■ *Web:* www.fbfs.com

Farm Family Life Insurance Co PO Box 656 Albany NY 12201 518-431-5000
TF: 800-948-3276 ■ *Web:* www.farmfamily.com

Farmers New World Life Insurance
3003 77th Ave SE Mercer Island WA 98040 206-232-8400 236-6642
Web: farmers.com

Federal Life Insurance Co Mutual
3750 W Deerfield Rd Ste A Riverwoods IL 60015 847-520-1900 520-1916
TF: 800-233-3750 ■ *Web:* www.federallife.com

Federated Life Insurance Co
121 E Pk Sq PO Box 328 Owatonna MN 55060 507-455-5200 455-7840
TF: 800-533-0472 ■ *Web:* federatedinsurance.com

Federated Mutual Insurance Co
121 E Pk Sq PO Box 328 Owatonna MN 55060 507-455-5200
TF: 800-533-0472 ■ *Web:* federatedinsurance.com

FEDUSA 7500 Ulmerton Rd Ste 35 Largo FL 33771 727-535-5671 610-1947*
**Fax Area Code:* 866 ■ *Web:* www.fedusa.com

First Investors Life Insurance Co
Raritan Plz 1 PO Box 7836 Edison NJ 08818 800-423-4026 510-4209*
**Fax Area Code:* 732 ■ *TF:* 800-423-4026 ■ *Web:* www.firstinvestors.com

First UNUM Life Insurance Co
2211 Congress St Portland ME 04122 207-575-2211 328-8977*
**Fax Area Code:* 212 ■ *TF:* 800-633-7491 ■ *Web:* www.unum.com

FirstCare 1901 W Loop 289 Ste #9 Lubbock TX 79407 806-784-4300
TF: 800-884-4901 ■ *Web:* www.firstcare.com

Forethought Financial Services Inc
Forethought Ctr Batesville IN 47006 713-212-4600 212-4656
TF: 877-454-4777 ■ *Web:* www.forethought.com

Gerber Life Insurance Co
1311 Mamaroneck Ave White Plains NY 10605 914-272-4000 272-4099
TF: 800-704-2180 ■ *Web:* www.gerberlife.com

Global Benefits Group Inc
26000 Towne Centre Dr Ste 100 Foothill Ranch CA 92610 949-470-2100
Web: www.gbg.com

Go Medico 1515 S 75th St Omaha NE 68124 402-391-6900
Web: gomedico.com

Grange Insurance 671 S High St Columbus OH 43206 800-422-0550 445-2337*
**Fax Area Code:* 614 ■ *TF:* 800-422-0550 ■ *Web:* grangeinsurance.com

Great-West Life & Annuity Insurance Co
8515 E OrchaRd Rd Greenwood Village CO 80111 303-737-3000
TF: 800-537-2033 ■ *Web:* www.greatwest.com

Great-West Life Assurance Co 100 Osborne St. Winnipeg MB R3C3A5 204-946-1190 946-4129*
**Fax:* Investor Rel ■ *TF:* 800-990-6654 ■ *Web:* www.greatwestlife.com

Greek Catholic Union of the USA
5400 Tuscarawas Rd Beaver PA 15009 724-495-3400
TF: 800-722-4428 ■ *Web:* www.gcuusa.com

Guarantee Trust Life Insurance Co
1275 Milwaukee Ave Glenview IL 60025 847-699-0600 699-2355
TF: 800-338-7452 ■ *Web:* www.gtlic.com

Guardian Life Insurance Company of America
Seven Hanover Sq New York NY 10004 212-598-8000 919-2762*
**Fax:* Hum Res ■ *TF:* 888-600-4667 ■ *Web:* www.guardianlife.com

GuideOne Mutual Insurance Co
1111 Ashworth Rd West Des Moines IA 50265 515-267-5000 267-5530*
**Fax:* Hum Res ■ *TF:* 877-448-4331 ■ *Web:* www.guideone.com

Hannover Life Reassurance Co of America
200 South Orange Avenue Suite 1900 Orlando FL 32801 407-649-8411
Web: www.hannoverre.com

Harleysville Life Insurance Co
355 Maple Ave Harleysville PA 19438 800-222-1981 256-7683*
**Fax Area Code:* 215 ■ *TF General:* 800-222-1981 ■ *Web:* www.harleysvillegroup.com

Harleysville Mutual Insurance Co
355 Maple Ave Harleysville PA 19438 215-256-5000
TF: 800-523-6344 ■ *Web:* www.harleysville.com

Hartford Life & Accident Insurance Co
One Hartford Plz Hartford CT 06155 860-547-5000
TF: 800-833-5575 ■ *Web:* www.thehartford.com

Harvey Watt & Co 475 N Central Ave Atlanta GA 30354 404-767-7501 761-8326
TF: 800-241-6103 ■ *Web:* www.harveywatt.com

HCC Life Insurance Co
225 Townpark Dr Ste 145 Kennesaw GA 30144 770-973-9851 973-9854
TF: 800-447-0460 ■ *Web:* www.hcc.com

Horace Mann Life Insurance Co
1 Horace Mann Plaza Springfield IL 62715 217-789-2500 788-5161
TF: 800-999-1030 ■ *Web:* www.horacemann.com

Hudson Health Plan Inc
303 S Broadway Ste 321 Tarrytown NY 10591 914-631-1611 631-1746
TF: 800-339-4557 ■ *Web:* www.hudsonhealthplan.org

Humana Inc 500 W Main St Louisville KY 40202 502-580-1000 580-3690
NYSE: HUM ■ *TF:* 800-486-2620 ■ *Web:* www.humana.com

Illinois Mutual Life Insurance Co
300 SW Adams St Peoria IL 61634 309-674-8255 674-8637
TF: 800-380-6688 ■ *Web:* www.illinoismutual.com

Indiana Farm Bureau Insurance Co
225 SE St PO Box 1250 Indianapolis IN 46206 317-692-7200 692-7009*
**Fax:* Sales ■ *TF:* 800-723-3276 ■ *Web:* www.infarmbureau.com

Industrial Alliance Insurance & Financial Services
1080 Grande Allee W
PO Box 1907 Stn Therminus Quebec City QC G1K7M3 418-684-5000 684-5050
TF: 800-463-6236 ■ *Web:* ia.ca/individuals

Insurance Marketing Agencies Inc
306 Main St Worcester MA 01608 508-753-7233 754-0487
TF: 800-891-1226 ■ *Web:* www.imaagency.com

Investors Heritage Life Insurance Co (IHLIC)
200 Capital Ave PO Box 717 Frankfort KY 40602 502-223-2361 875-7084
TF: 800-422-2011 ■ *Web:* www.investorsheritage.com

Jackson National Life Insurance Co
One Corporate Way Lansing MI 48951 517-381-5500
TF: 800-644-4565 ■ *Web:* www.jackson.com

Company	City	State	Zip	Phone	Fax
John Hancock Life Insurance Co One John Hancock Way Ste 1101	Boston	MA	02117	617-572-6000	
Web: www.johnhancock.com					
John Hancock New York 100 Summit Lake Dr 2nd Fl	Valhalla	NY	10595	877-391-3748	
TF: 800-732-5543 ■ *Web:* www.johnhancock.com					
Kilpatrick Life Insurance Co 1818 Marshall St	Shreveport	LA	71101	318-222-0555	
Web: www.klic.com					
Lafayette Life Insurance Co 400 Broadway	Cincinnati	OH	45202	800-443-8793	362-4900*
*Fax Area Code: 513 ■ *TF:* 800-443-8793 ■ *Web:* www.llic.com					
LDS Group, The PO Box 83480	Baton Rouge	LA	70884	225-769-9923	769-9112
Web: www.theldsgroup.com					
Liberty Life Insurance Co 2000 Wade Hampton Blvd	Greenville	SC	29615	864-609-1000	
TF: 855-428-4363 ■ *Web:* atheneannuity.com					
Life Insurance Co of Alabama 302 Broad St	Gadsden	AL	35901	256-543-2022	543-0019
TF: 800-226-2371 ■ *Web:* www.licoa.com					
Life Insurance Company of the Southwest 15455 Dallas Pkwy Ste 800	Addison	TX	75001	800-579-2878	638-9162*
*Fax Area Code: 214 ■ *TF:* 800-579-2878 ■ *Web:* www.nationallifegroup.com					
Lincoln Heritage Life Insurance Co PO Box 29045	Phoenix	AZ	85038	800-433-8181	840-0969*
*Fax Area Code: 602 ■ *TF:* 800-433-8181 ■ *Web:* www.lhlic.com					
Lincoln National Life Insurance Co 1300 S Clinton St	Fort Wayne	IN	46802	260-455-2000	455-4268*
*Fax: Hum Res ■ *TF:* 800-454-6265 ■ *Web:* www.lfg.com					
London Life Insurance Co 255 Dufferin Ave	London	ON	N6A4K1	519-432-5281	435-7679
TF: 800-990-6654 ■ *Web:* www.londonlife.com					
Loyal American Life Insurance Co *Great American Financial Resources Inc* PO Box 26580	Austin	TX	78755	800-545-4269	369-4172*
*Fax Area Code: 352 ■ *TF:* 800-315-5522 ■ *Web:* www.gafri.com					
Madison National Life Insurance Company Inc PO Box 5008	Madison	WI	53705	608-830-2000	830-2700
TF: 800-356-9601 ■ *Web:* www.madisonlife.com					
Manulife Mutual Funds 200 Bloor St E N Twr 3	Toronto	ON	M4W1E5	888-588-7999	
TF: 888-588-7999 ■ *Web:* www.manulife.ca					
May-mcconville Insurance Brokers Ltd 123 St George St Ste 100	London	ON	N6A3A1	519-673-0880	645-8764
TF: 877-629-6226 ■ *Web:* www.may-mcconville.com					
Medico Group 1515 S 75th St	Omaha	NE	68124	402-391-6900	391-6489
TF: 800-228-6080 ■ *Web:* gomedico.com					
MetLife Inc 200 Pk Ave	New York	NY	10166	212-578-2211	578-3320
NYSE: MET ■ *TF:* 800-638-5433 ■ *Web:* global.metlife.com					
MetLife Investors Insurance Co Five Pk Plz Ste 1900	Irvine	CA	92614	800-848-3854	
TF: 800-848-3854 ■ *Web:* www.metlifeinvestors.com					
Midland National Life Insurance Co One Sammons Plz	Sioux Falls	SD	57193	605-335-5700	335-3621
TF: 800-923-3223 ■ *Web:* midlandnational.com					
MML Bay State Life Insurance Co 100 Bright Meadow Blvd	Enfield	CT	06082	860-562-1000	
Web: www.massmutual.com					
Modern Woodmen of America 1701 First Ave	Rock Island	IL	61201	309-786-6481	793-5547
TF: 800-447-9811 ■ *Web:* www.modern-woodmen.org					
Motorists Life Insurance Co 471 E Broad St	Columbus	OH	43215	614-225-8211	225-8365
Web: www.motoristsmutual.com					
Mutual Insurance Company of Arizona PO Box 33180	Phoenix	AZ	85067	602-956-5276	468-1710
TF: 800-352-0402 ■ *Web:* www.mica-insurance.com					
Mutual of America Life Insurance Co 320 Pk Ave	New York	NY	10022	212-224-1600	224-2500*
*Fax: Mail Rm ■ *TF:* 800-468-3785 ■ *Web:* www.mutualofamerica.com					
Mutual of Omaha Insurance Co Mutual of Omaha Plaza	Omaha	NE	68175	402-342-7600	351-2775
TF: 800-775-6000 ■ *Web:* www.mutualofomaha.com					
Mutual Trust Life Insurance Co 1200 Jorie Blvd	Oak Brook	IL	60522	630-990-1000	990-7083
TF: 800-323-7320 ■ *Web:* www.mutualtrust.com					
National Guardian Life Insurance Co (NGL) 2 E Gilman St	Madison	WI	53703	608-257-5611	257-3940
TF: 800-548-2962 ■ *Web:* www.nglic.com/					
National Mutual Benefit 6522 Grand Teton Plaza	Madison	WI	53719	608-833-1936	833-8714
TF: 800-779-1936 ■ *Web:* www.nmblife.org					
National Western Life Insurance Co 850 E Anderson Ln	Austin	TX	78752	512-836-1010	719-0104*
NASDAQ: NWLI ■ *Fax: Hum Res ■ *TF:* 800-531-5442 ■ *Web:* www.nationalwesternlife.com					
Nationwide Life & Annuity Insurance Co One Nationwide Pl	Columbus	OH	43215	614-249-7111	249-2205*
*Fax: Hum Res ■ *TF:* 800-882-2822 ■ *Web:* www.nationwide.com					
Nationwide Mutual Insurance Company 5100 Rings Rd	Dublin	OH	43017	877-669-6877	854-2348*
*Fax Area Code: 614 ■ *TF:* 800-543-3747 ■ *Web:* nationwide.com					
New England Life Insurance Co 699 Boylston St	Boston	MA	02116	617-585-4574	
Web: metlife.com					
New York Life Insurance & Annuity Corp 51 Madison Ave	New York	NY	10010	212-576-7000	348-7660*
*Fax Area Code: 646 ■ *Fax: Hum Res ■ *TF:* 800-598-2019 ■ *Web:* nylinvestments.com					
New York Life Insurance Co 51 Madison Ave	New York	NY	10010	212-576-7000	576-8145
Web: www.newyorklife.com					
North Carolina Mutual Life Insurance Co 411 W Chapel Hill St	Durham	NC	27701	919-682-9201	682-1685
TF: 800-626-1899 ■ *Web:* www.ncmutuallife.com					
Ohio State Life Insurance Co PO Box 410288	Kansas City	MO	64141	800-752-1387	
TF: 800-752-1387 ■ *Web:* www.ohiostatelife.com					
Old American Insurance Co 3520 Broadway	Kansas City	MO	64111	816-753-7000	753-4902
TF: 800-733-6242 ■ *Web:* www.oaic.com					
OneAmerica Financial Partners Inc (PML) PO Box 368	Indianapolis	IN	46206	317-285-1877	285-6462
TF: 800-249-6269 ■ *Web:* www.oneamerica.com					
Oxford Life Insurance Co 2721 N Central Ave	Phoenix	AZ	85004	602-263-6666	277-5901
TF Cust Svc: 800-308-2318 ■ *Web:* www.oxfordlife.com					
Ozark National Life Insurance Inc 500 E Ninth St	Kansas City	MO	64106	816-842-6300	842-8373
Web: www.ozark-national.com					
Pacific Guardian Life Insurance Company Ltd 1440 Kapiolani Blvd Ste 1700	Honolulu	HI	96814	808-955-2236	942-1284
TF: 800-367-5354 ■ *Web:* www.pacificguardian.com					
Pacific Life Insurance Co 700 Newport Ctr Dr	Newport Beach	CA	92660	949-219-3011	219-3706*
*Fax: Hum Res ■ *TF:* 800-800-7646 ■ *Web:* www.pacificlife.com					
Pan-American Life Insurance Co 601 Poydras St	New Orleans	LA	70130	877-939-4550	
TF Life Ins: 877-939-4550 ■ *Web:* www.palig.com					
Partner Reinsurance Co of the US 1 Greenwich Plaza	Greenwich	CT	06830	203-485-4200	485-4300
TF: 800-831-9146 ■ *Web:* www.partnerre.com					
Pekin Life Insurance Co 2505 Ct St	Pekin	IL	61558	309-346-1161	346-8512
OTC: PKIN ■ *TF:* 800-322-0160 ■ *Web:* www.pekininsurance.com					
Penn Insurance & Annuity Co 600 Dresher Rd	Horsham	PA	19044	215-956-8000	956-7699
TF Cust Svc: 800-523-0650 ■ *Web:* www.pennmutual.com					
Penn Mutual Life Insurance Co 600 Dresher Rd	Horsham	PA	19044	215-956-8000	956-7699
TF Cust Svc: 800-523-0650 ■ *Web:* www.pennmutual.com					
Penn Treaty Network America Insurance Co 3440 Lehigh St	Allentown	PA	18103	800-362-0700	967-4616*
*Fax Area Code: 610 ■ *TF:* 800-362-0700 ■ *Web:* www.penntreaty.com					
Physicians Life Insurance Co 2600 Dodge St	Omaha	NE	68131	402-633-1000	
TF: 800-228-9100 ■ *Web:* physiciansmutual.com					
Physicians Mutual Insurance Co 2600 Dodge St	Omaha	NE	68131	402-633-1000	633-1604
TF: 800-228-9100 ■ *Web:* physiciansmutual.com					
Polish National Alliance of the US of North America 6100 N Cicero Ave	Chicago	IL	60646	773-286-0500	
Web: www.pna-znp.org					
Presidential Life Insurance Co 69 Lydecker St	Nyack	NY	10960	845-358-2300	353-0273
TF: 800-926-7599 ■ *Web:* www.presidentiallife.com					
Pro Assurance Corp 1250 23rd St NW Ste 250	Washington	DC	20037	202-969-1866	969-1881
TF: 800-613-3615 ■ *Web:* www.proassurance.com					
Property-Owners Insurance Co PO Box 30660	Lansing	MI	48909	517-323-1200	323-8796
TF: 800-288-8740 ■ *Web:* auto-owners.com					
Protective Life & Annuity Insurance Co 2801 Hwy 280 S	Birmingham	AL	35223	205-268-1000	
TF: 844-733-5433 ■ *Web:* www.protective.com					
Prudential Financial Inc 751 Broad St	Newark	NJ	07102	973-802-6000	367-6476
NYSE: PRU ■ *TF:* 800-843-7625 ■ *Web:* www.prudential.com					
RBC Liberty Insurance PO Box 789	Greenville	SC	29602	864-609-8111	
TF: 800-551-8354 ■ *Web:* www.rbcinsurance.com					
Reliable Life Insurance Co 100 King St W PO Box 557	Hamilton	ON	L8N3K9	905-523-5587	551-1704*
*Fax Area Code: 866 ■ *Fax: Claims ■ *TF:* 800-465-0661 ■ *Web:* www.reliablelifeinsurance.com					
Reliance Standard Life Insurance 2001 Market St Ste 1500	Philadelphia	PA	19103	267-256-3500	
TF: 800-351-7500 ■ *Web:* www.reliancestandard.com					
Reserve National Insurance Co 601 E Britton Rd	Oklahoma City	OK	73114	405-848-7931	
Web: www.reservenational.com					
Royal State National Insurance Company Ltd 819 S Beretania St	Honolulu	HI	96813	808-539-1600	
Web: www.royalstate.com					
Sabre Healthdirect Inc 590 Alden Rd	Markham	ON	L3R8N2	905-305-9900	
Web: sabrelife.com					
Savings Bank Life Insurance Company of Massachusetts, The (SBLI) One Linscott Rd	Woburn	MA	01801	781-938-3500	
Web: www.sbli.com					
Security Benefit Life Insurance Co One Security Benefit Pl	Topeka	KS	66636	785-438-3000	438-5177*
*Fax: Cust Svc ■ *TF:* 800-888-2461 ■ *Web:* www.securitybenefit.com					
Security Life Insurance Co of America 10901 Red Cir Dr	Minnetonka	MN	55343	952-544-2121	945-3419
TF: 800-328-4667 ■ *Web:* www.securitylife.com					
Security Mutual Life Insurance Co of New York 100 Court St PO Box 1625	Binghamton	NY	13901	607-723-3551	723-8665*
*Fax: Cust Svc ■ *TF:* 800-927-8846 ■ *Web:* www.smlny.com					
Security National Financial Corp (SNFC) 5300 South 360 West Ste 250 PO Box 57250	Salt Lake City	UT	84123	801-264-1060	265-9882
NASDAQ: SNFCA ■ *TF:* 800-574-7117 ■ *Web:* www.securitynational.com					
Selected Funeral & Life Insurance Co 119 Convention Blvd	Hot Springs National Park	AR	71902	501-624-2172	
Web: sflic.net					
Sentry Life Insurance Co 1800 N Pt Dr	Stevens Point	WI	54481	715-346-6000	346-7516
TF: 800-373-6879 ■ *Web:* www.sentry.com					
Sequoia Insurance Co 31 Upper Ragsdale Dr	Monterey	CA	93940	831-333-9880	632-5246*
*Fax Area Code: 866					
Settlers Life Insurance Co 1969 Lee Hwy Ste U1	Bristol	VA	24203	276-645-4300	645-4399
TF: 800-523-2650 ■ *Web:* settlerslife.com					
Shenandoah Life Insurance Co 2301 Brambleton Ave	Roanoke	VA	24015	540-985-4400	985-4444
TF: 800-848-5433 ■ *Web:* www.shenlife.com					
Slovene National Benefit Society 247 W Allegheny Rd	Imperial	PA	15126	724-695-1100	
Web: www.snpj.org					
Southern Farm Bureau Life Insurance Co PO Box 78	Jackson	MS	39205	601-981-7422	366-5808*
*Fax: Hum Res ■ *Web:* www.sfbli.com					
Southwestern Life Insurance Co 110 W Clinton St Ste 150	Hobbs	NM	88240	575-393-4577	333-7833*
*Fax Area Code: 803					
Standard Life Insurance Company of Indiana 10689 N Pennsylvania St	Indianapolis	IN	46280	317-574-6201	574-6278*
*Fax: Mktg ■ *TF:* 800-222-3216 ■ *Web:* www.standardagents.com					

Phone Fax

Standard Security Life Insurance Company of New York
485 Madison Ave 14th Fl . . . New York NY 10022 212-355-4141 644-5786
Web: www.sslicny.com

State Farm Insurance One State Farm Plz . . . Bloomington IL 61710 309-766-2311
TF: 800-447-4930 ■ *Web:* www.statefarm.com/insuranc/life/life.htm

State Farm Life & Accident Assurance Co
1 State Farm Plaza . . . Bloomington IL 61710 309-766-2311 766-3621*
*Fax: Mktg ■ *Web:* www.statefarm.com

State Life Insurance Co
One American Sq PO Box 368 . . . Indianapolis IN 46206 317-285-2300 285-2380
TF Cust Svc: 800-537-6442 ■ *Web:* www.oneamerica.com/home

Sun Life Assurance Company of Canada
One Sun Life Executive Pk
PO Box 9133 . . . Wellesley Hills MA 02481 781-237-6030
TF: 800-786-5433 ■ *Web:* www.sunlife.com/us

Symetra Life Insurance Co
777 108th Ave Ne Ste 1200 . . . Bellevue WA 98004 425-256-8000
Web: www.symetra.com

Texas Life Insurance Co
900 Washington PO Box 830 . . . Waco TX 76703 254-752-6521 754-7629*
*Fax: Sales ■ *Web:* www.texaslife.com

Thrivent Financial for Lutherans
4321 N BallaRd Rd . . . Appleton WI 54919 920-684-3225 340-5143*
*Fax Area Code: 612 ■ *TF:* 800-847-4836 ■ *Web:* www.thrivent.com

TIAA-CREF 730 Third Ave . . . New York NY 10017 212-490-9000 913-2803
TF: 866-842-2442 ■ *Web:* www.tiaa-cref.org

Transamerica Occidental Life Insurance Co
1150 S Olive St . . . Los Angeles CA 90015 213-742-2111 741-7939*
*Fax: Mail Rm ■ *TF Cust Svc:* 800-852-4678 ■ *Web:* transamerica.com

Trustmark Insurance Co 400 Field Dr . . . Lake Forest IL 60045 847-615-1500 615-3910
TF: 888-246-9949 ■ *Web:* www.trustmarkinsurance.com

United American Insurance Company Inc
PO Box 8080 . . . McKinney TX 75070 972-529-5085 569-3709
Web: www.unitedamerican.com

United Heritage Life Insurance Co
PO Box 7777 . . . Meridian ID 83680 208-493-6100 466-0825
TF: 800-657-6351 ■ *Web:* www.unitedheritage.com

United Insurance Holdings Corp
360 Central Ave Ste 900 . . . Saint Petersburg FL 33701 800-295-8016
NASDAQ: UIHC ■ *TF:* 800-861-4370 ■ *Web:* www.upcinsurance.com

United Investors Life Insurance Co
2801 Hwy 280 S . . . Birmingham AL 35223 205-268-1000 268-5547
TF: 800-866-9933 ■ *Web:* www.protective.com

United Life Insurance Co PO Box 73909 . . . Cedar Rapids IA 52407 319-399-5700 399-5499
TF: 800-332-7977 ■ *Web:* www.unitedfiregroup.com

United of Omaha Life Insurance Co
Mutual of Omaha Plaza . . . Omaha NE 68175 402-342-7600 351-2775
TF: 800-775-6000 ■ *Web:* www.mutualofomaha.com

United Security Life Insurance Company of Illinois (Inc)
6640 S Cicero Ave . . . Bedford Park IL 60638 800-875-4422 475-6121*
*Fax Area Code: 708 ■ *TF:* 800-875-4422 ■ *Web:* www.unitedsecuritylandh.com

United World Life Insurance Co
Mutual of Omaha Plz . . . Omaha NE 68175 402-342-7600 351-2775
TF: 800-775-6000 ■ *Web:* www.mutualofomaha.com

USAA Life Insurance Co (USAA)
9800 Fredericksburg Rd . . . San Antonio TX 78288 210-531-8722 531-8877*
*Fax Area Code: 800 ■ *Fax: Sales ■ *TF:* 800-531-8000 ■ *Web:* www.usaa.com

Utica National Insurance Group
180 Genesee St . . . New Hartford NY 13413 315-734-2000 734-2680
TF: 800-274-1914 ■ *Web:* www.uticanational.com

Variable Annuity Life Insurance Co (VALIC)
2929 Allen Pkwy . . . Houston TX 77019 800-448-2542
TF: 800-448-2542 ■ *Web:* www.valic.com

Washington National Insurance Co
11825 N Pennsylvania St . . . Carmel IN 46032 866-595-2255 757-6324*
*Fax Area Code: 800 ■ *TF:* 866-595-2255 ■ *Web:* www.conseco.com

Wawanesa Life Insurance Co
191 Broadway Ste 501 . . . Winnipeg MB R3C3P1 204-985-0684
Web: wawanesa.com/life/index.html

website not working 8485 Goodwood Blvd . . . Baton Rouge LA 70806 225-926-2888

Western & Southern Life Insurance Co
400 Broadway . . . Cincinnati OH 45202 800-926-1993 629-1212*
*Fax Area Code: 513 ■ *Fax: Hum Res ■ *TF:* 800-926-1993 ■ *Web:* www.westernsouthernlife.com

Western Fraternal Life Assn (WFLA)
1900 First Ave NE . . . Cedar Rapids IA 52402 319-363-2653
TF: 877-935-2467 ■ *Web:* www.wflains.org

Western United Life Assurance Co
929 W Sprague Ave PO Box 2290 . . . Spokane WA 99210 509-835-2500 835-3191
TF General: 800-247-2045 ■ *Web:* www.wula.com

Western-Southern Life Assurance Co
400 Broadway . . . Cincinnati OH 45202 866-832-7719 629-1212*
*Fax Area Code: 513 ■ *TF:* 866-832-7719 ■ *Web:* www.westernsouthernlife.com

William Penn Life Insurance Co of New York
100 Quentin Roosevelt Blvd . . . Garden City NY 11530 516-794-3700 229-3004*
*Fax: Hum Res ■ *TF:* 800-346-4773 ■ *Web:* www.lgamerica.com

Woman's Life Insurance Society
1338 Military St PO Box 5020 . . . Port Huron MI 48061 810-985-5191 985-6970
TF: 800-521-9292 ■ *Web:* www.womanslife.org

Woodmen of the World Life Insurance Society
1700 Farnam St . . . Omaha NE 68102 877-664-3332 271-7269*
*Fax Area Code: 402 ■ *TF:* 877-664-3332 ■ *Web:* www.woodmen.com

394-3 Medical & Hospitalization Insurance

Companies listed here provide managed care and/or traditional hospital and medical service plans to individuals and/or groups. Managed care companies typically offer plans as Health Maintenance Organizations (HMOs), Preferred Provider Organizations (PPOs), Exclusive Provider Organizations (EPOs), and/or Point of Service (POS) plans. Other types of hospital and medical service plans offered by companies listed here include indemnity plans and medical savings accounts.

Phone Fax

AARP Health Care Options PO Box 1017 . . . Montgomeryville PA 18936 800-523-5800 391-6259*
*Fax Area Code: 610 ■ *TF:* 800-523-5800 ■ *Web:* www.aarphealthcare.com

Phone Fax

Aetna Inc 151 Farmington Ave . . . Hartford CT 06156 860-273-0123 273-8909
NYSE: AET ■ *TF:* 800-872-3862 ■ *Web:* www.aetna.com

Aetna US Healthcare Inc 980 Jolly Rd . . . Blue Bell PA 19422 215-775-4800 775-6775*
*Fax: Hum Res ■ *TF:* 800-872-3862 ■ *Web:* www.aetna.com

AF & L Insurance Co
165 Veterans Way Ste 300 PO Box 5005 . . . Warminster PA 18974 215-918-0515
Web: www.aflltc.com

Alberta Blue Cross 10009 108th St NW . . . Edmonton AB T5J3C5 780-498-8100 425-4627
TF: 800-661-6995 ■ *Web:* www.ab.bluecross.ca

Altius Health Plans
10421 S Jordan Gateway Ste 400 . . . South Jordan UT 84095 801-355-1234 323-6100
TF: 800-365-1334 ■ *Web:* altiushealthplans.com

American Specialty Health Plans
10221 Wateridge Cir . . . San Diego CA 92121 800-848-3555 237-3810*
*Fax Area Code: 619 ■ *TF:* 800-848-3555 ■ *Web:* www.ashcompanies.com

Americhoice Corp 8045 Leesburg Pk Sixth Fl . . . Vienna VA 22182 703-506-3555
Web: www.americhoice.com

AMERIGROUP Corp 4425 Corporation Ln . . . Virginia Beach VA 23462 757-490-6900 518-3600
NYSE: AGP ■ *TF:* 800-600-4441 ■ *Web:* www.amerigroup.com

Ameritas Managed Dental Plan Inc 5900 'O' St . . . Lincoln NE 68510 402-467-1122 467-7338
TF: 800-404-8019 ■ *Web:* www.group.ameritas.com

Anthem Blue Cross & Blue Shield
2015 Staples Mill Rd . . . Richmond VA 23230 804-354-7000 354-3897
TF: 800-451-1527 ■ *Web:* www.anthem.com

Anthem Blue Cross & Blue Shield Maine
Two Gannett Dr . . . South Portland ME 04106 207-822-7000 822-7375
TF Cust Svc: 800-482-0966 ■ *Web:* www.anthem.com

Anthem Blue Cross & Blue Shield of Connecticut
370 Bassett Rd . . . North Haven CT 06473 800-922-4670 234-5347*
*Fax Area Code: 203 ■ *TF:* 800-922-1742 ■ *Web:* www.anthem.com

Anthem Blue Cross & Blue Shield of Nevada
9133 W Russell Rd . . . Las Vegas NV 89148 702-228-2583 763-3142*
*Fax Area Code: 800 ■ *TF:* 800-332-3842 ■ *Web:* www.anthem.com

Anthem Blue Cross Blue Shield Colorado
700 Broadway . . . Denver CO 80273 303-831-2131 764-7047
TF: 800-654-9338 ■ *Web:* www.anthem.com

Arkansas Blue Cross Blue Shield
PO Box 2181 . . . Little Rock AR 72203 501-378-2000 378-2969
TF: 800-238-8379 ■ *Web:* www.arkansasbluecross.com

AvMed 4300 NW 89th Blvd . . . Gainesville FL 32606 352-372-8400 337-8575*
*Fax: Hum Res ■ *TF:* 800-346-0231 ■ *Web:* www.avmed.org

Benecaid Health Benefit Solutions Inc
185 The W Mall Ste 1700 . . . Toronto ON M9C5L5 416-626-8786
Web: www.benecaid.com

Blue Care Network of Michigan
20500 Civic Ctr Dr . . . Southfield MI 48076 248-799-6400 799-6969*
*Fax: Cust Svc ■ *TF:* 800-662-6667 ■ *Web:* bcbsm.com/

Blue Cross & Blue Shield of Alabama
450 Riverchase Pkwy E . . . Birmingham AL 35244 205-988-2200 220-2902*
*Fax: Hum Res ■ *TF:* 800-292-8868 ■ *Web:* www.bcbsal.org

Blue Cross & Blue Shield of Kansas City
2301 Main St . . . Kansas City MO 64108 816-395-2222 395-2726*
*Fax: Hum Res ■ *TF:* 800-892-6048 ■ *Web:* www.bluekc.com

Blue Cross & Blue Shield of Michigan
600 Lafayette Blvd E . . . Detroit MI 48226 313-225-9000 225-5629*
*Fax: Hum Res ■ *Web:* www.bcbsm.com

Blue Cross & Blue Shield of Mississippi
PO Box 1043 . . . Jackson MS 39215 601-932-3704 939-7035
TF: 800-222-8046 ■ *Web:* www.bcbsms.com

Blue Cross & Blue Shield of Montana
560 N Pk Ave PO Box 4309 . . . Helena MT 59604 406-437-5000
TF: 800-447-7828 ■ *Web:* www.bcbsmt.com

Blue Cross & Blue Shield of Nebraska
1919 Aksarben Dr PO Box 3248 . . . Omaha NE 68180 402-982-7000
TF: 800-422-2763 ■ *Web:* www.nebraskablue.com

Blue Cross & Blue Shield of New Mexico
PO Box 27630 . . . Albuquerque NM 87125 505-291-3500
TF: 800-835-8699 ■ *Web:* www.bcbsnm.com

Blue Cross & Blue Shield of North Carolina
1965 Ivory Creek Blvd . . . Durham NC 27702 919-489-7431 765-3521*
*Fax: Hum Res ■ *TF Cust Svc:* 800 446 8053 ■ *Web:* www.bcbsnc.com

Blue Cross & Blue Shield of Oklahoma
1215 S Boulder Ave . . . Tulsa OK 74119 918-560-3500 560-3060
TF Cust Svc: 800-942-5837 ■ *Web:* www.bcbsok.com

Blue Cross & Blue Shield of Rhode Island
500 Exchange St . . . Providence RI 02903 401-459-1000 459-1996
TF: 800-637-3718 ■ *Web:* www.bcbsri.com

Blue Cross & Blue Shield of Texas Inc
1001 E Lookout Dr . . . Richardson TX 75082 972-766-6900 766-6060
TF: 800-521-2227 ■ *Web:* www.bcbstx.com

Blue Cross & Blue Shield of Vermont
445 Industrial Ln . . . Montpelier VT 05602 802-223-6131 223-4229*
*Fax: Hum Res ■ *TF Cust Svc:* 800-247-2583 ■ *Web:* www.bcbsvt.com

Blue Cross Blue Shield of Arizona
2444 W Las Palmaritas Dr . . . Phoenix AZ 85021 602-864-4400 864-4041*
*Fax: Cust Svc ■ *TF:* 800-232-2345 ■ *Web:* www.azblue.com

Blue Cross Blue Shield of Delaware
PO Box 1991 . . . Wilmington DE 19899 800-876-7639 421-2089*
*Fax Area Code: 302 ■ *Fax: Mktg ■ *TF:* 800-572-4400 ■ *Web:* www.highmarkbcbsde.com

Blue Cross Blue Shield of Georgia
3350 Peachtree Rd NE . . . Atlanta GA 30326 404-842-8000 842-8010
TF Cust Svc: 800-441-2273 ■ *Web:* www.bcbsga.com

Blue Cross Blue Shield of Illinois
300 E Randolph St . . . Chicago IL 60601 312-653-6000 938-8847*
*Fax: Hum Res ■ *Web:* www.bcbsil.com

Blue Cross Blue Shield of Kansas
1133 SW Topeka Blvd . . . Topeka KS 66629 785-291-7000 290-0711
TF: 800-432-0216 ■ *Web:* www.bcbsks.com

Blue Cross Blue Shield of Louisiana
5525 Reitz Ave . . . Baton Rouge LA 70898 225-295-3307 295-2054
TF: 800-599-2583 ■ *Web:* bcbsla.com

Phone Fax

Blue Cross Blue Shield of Massachusetts
401 Pk Dr Boston MA 02215 617-246-5000 636-9494*
Fax Area Code: 800 ■ **Fax:* PR ■ *TF:* 888-247-2583 ■ *Web:* www.bluecrossma.com
Blue Cross Blue Shield of North Dakota
4510 13th Ave S Fargo ND 58121 701-282-1100 277-2216*
**Fax:* Hum Res ■ *TF:* 800-342-4718 ■ *Web:* www.bcbsnd.com
Blue Cross Blue Shield of Wyoming
4000 House Ave Cheyenne WY 82001 307-634-1393 778-8582
TF: 800-851-9145 ■ *Web:* www.bcbswy.com
Blue Cross of California
Two Gannett Dr South Portland ME 04106 800-482-0966 438-6811*
**Fax Area Code:* 888 ■ *TF:* 800-999-3643 ■ *Web:* www.anthem.com
Blue Cross of Idaho 3000 E Pine Ave Meridian ID 83642 208-345-4550 331-7311
TF: 800-274-4018 ■ *Web:* www.bcidaho.com
Blue Cross of Northeastern Pennsylvania
19 N Main St Wilkes-Barre PA 18711 800-577-3742 200-6710*
**Fax Area Code:* 570 ■ *TF Cust Svc:* 800-577-3742 ■ *Web:* www.bcnepa.com
Blue Shield of California 50 Beale St San Francisco CA 94105 415-229-5000 229-6230*
**Fax:* Hum Res ■ *Web:* www.blueshieldca.com
BlueCross BlueShield of Western New York
257 W Genesee St Buffalo NY 14240 716-887-6900 887-7912
TF: 800-888-0757 ■ *Web:* bcbswny.com
Capital District Physicians' Health Plan
500 Patroon Creek Blvd Albany NY 12206 518-641-3000 641-3507
TF: 888-258-0477 ■ *Web:* www.cdphp.com
Capital Health Plan PO Box 15349 Tallahassee FL 32317 850-383-3333 383-3339
TF: 800-390-1434 ■ *Web:* www.capitalhealth.com
Capital Management Enterprises Inc
1111 W Dekalb Pk Wayne PA 19087 610-265-9600
Web: www.cms-advisors.com
CareFirst BlueCross BlueShield
10455 Mill Run Cir Owings Mills MD 21117 410-581-3000 998-6132
Web: www.carefirst.com
Carelink Health Plans
500 Virginia St E Ste 400 Charleston WV 25301 304-348-2900 348-2064
TF: 800-348-2922 ■ *Web:* coventryhealthcare.com
Cdspi 155 Lesmill Rd Toronto ON M3B2T8 416-296-9401
TF: 800-561-9401 ■ *Web:* cdspi.com
Centene Corp 7700 Forsyth Blvd Saint Louis MO 63105 314-725-4477 725-2065
NYSE: CNC ■ *TF General:* 800-293-0056 ■ *Web:* www.centene.com
Chiropractic Health Plan of California
PO Box 190 Clayton CA 94517 310-210-5400 844-3124*
**Fax Area Code:* 925 ■ *TF:* 800-995-2442 ■ *Web:* www.chpc.com
CIGNA Healthcare 900 Cottage Grove Rd Hartford CT 06152 860-226-6000
TF: 800-997-1654 ■ *Web:* www.cigna.com/health
CIGNA Healthcare of North Carolina Inc
701 Corporate Ctr Dr Raleigh NC 27607 919-854-7000 *
**Fax:* Hum Res ■ *TF:* 800-997-1654 ■ *Web:* www.cigna.com
Community Care 218 W Sixth St Tulsa OK 74119 918-594-5200 594-5209
TF: 800-278-7563 ■ *Web:* www.ccok.com
CompBenefits Corp 100 Mansell Ct E Ste 400 Roswell GA 30076 770-552-7101 998-6871*
**Fax:* Cust Svc ■ *TF:* 800-633-1262 ■ *Web:* www.compbenefits.com
Comprehensive Health Services Inc (CHSI)
10701 Parkridge Blvd Ste 200 Reston VA 20191 703-760-0700 760-0894
TF: 800-638-8083 ■ *Web:* chsimedical.com
ConnectiCare Inc 175 Scott Swamp Rd Farmington CT 06032 860-674-5700 674-5728
TF Cust Svc: 800-251-7722 ■ *Web:* www.connecticare.com
Coventry Health Care Inc
6705 Rockledge Dr Ste 900 Bethesda MD 20817 301-581-0600 581-0600*
NYSE: CVH ■ **Fax:* Hum Res ■ *TF:* 866-667-3062 ■ *Web:* www.coventryhealthcare.com
Coventry Health Care of Delaware Inc
750 Prides Crossing Ste 200 Newark DE 19713 800-833-7423
TF: 800-833-7423 ■ *Web:* coventryhealthcare.com
Coventry Health Care of Georgia Inc
1100 Cir 75 Pkwy Ste 1400 Atlanta GA 30339 678-202-2100
TF: 800-470-2004 ■ *Web:* chcgeorgia.coventryhealthcare.com
Coventry Health Care of Iowa Inc
4320 114th St Urbandale IA 50322 515-225-1234
TF: 800-470-6352 ■ *Web:* chciowa.coventryhealthcare.com
Coventry Health Care of Kansas Inc
8320 Ward Pkwy Kansas City MO 64114 800-969-3343
TF: 800-969-3343 ■ *Web:* chckansas.coventryhealthcare.com
Coventry Health Care of Louisiana Inc
1720 S Sykes Dr Bismarck ND 58504 800-341-6613
TF Sales: 800-341-6613 ■ *Web:* chclouisiana.coventryhealthcare.com
Coventry Health Care of Nebraska Inc
15950 W Dodge Rd Ste 100 Omaha NE 68164 402-498-9030
TF: 855-449-2889 ■ *Web:* chcnebraska.coventryhealthcare.com
Dakotacare 2600 W 49th St PO Box 7406 Sioux Falls SD 57117 605-334-4000 334-8717
TF: 800-325-5598 ■ *Web:* www.dakotacare.com
Davis Vision Inc 711 Troy-Schenectady Rd Latham NY 12110 800-999-5431 328-4761*
**Fax Area Code:* 888 ■ **Fax:* Claims ■ *TF:* 800-999-5431 ■ *Web:* www.davisvision.com
Dean Health Insurance Inc 1277 Deming Way Madison WI 53717 608-836-1400 827-4212
TF: 800-279-1301 ■ *Web:* www.deancare.com
Delta Dental Insurance Company of Alaska
PO Box 1809 Alpharetta GA 30023 800-521-2651
TF: 800-521-2651 ■ *Web:* www.deltadentalins.com
Delta Dental of Arizona PO Box 43026 Phoenix AZ 85080 800-352-6132 588-3636*
**Fax Area Code:* 602 ■ *TF:* 800-352-6132 ■ *Web:* www.deltadentalaz.com
Delta Dental of Arkansas
1513 Country Club Rd PO Box 15965 Sherwood AR 72120 501-835-3400 835-2733
TF: 800-462-5410 ■ *Web:* www.deltadentalar.com
Delta Dental of Colorado
4582 S Ulster St Ste 800 Denver CO 80237 303-741-9300 741-9338
TF: 800-233-0860 ■ *Web:* www.deltadentalco.com
Delta Dental of Georgia PO Box 1803 Alpharetta GA 30023 800-422-4234
TF: 800-422-4234 ■ *Web:* www.deltadentalins.com
Delta Dental of Idaho
555 E Parkcenter Blvd PO Box 2870 Boise ID 83706 208-489-3580 344-4649
TF: 800-356-7586 ■ *Web:* www.deltadentalid.com
Delta Dental of Indiana PO Box 30416 Lansing MI 48909 800-524-0149
TF: 800-524-0149 ■ *Web:* www.deltadentalin.com

Phone Fax

Delta Dental of Iowa
9000 Northpark Dr Ste 13 Johnston IA 50131 515-261-5500 261-5577
TF Cust Svc: 800-544-0718 ■ *Web:* www.deltadentalia.com
Delta Dental of Kansas
1619 N Waterfront Pkwy PO Box 789769 Wichita KS 67201 316-264-4511 462-3392
TF: 800-234-3375 ■ *Web:* www.deltadentalks.com
Delta Dental of Kentucky
10100 Linn Stn Rd PO Box 242810 Louisville KY 40223 800-955-2030 736-4823*
**Fax Area Code:* 502 ■ *TF Cust Svc:* 800-955-2030 ■ *Web:* www.deltadentalky.com
Delta Dental of Louisiana PO Box 1803 Alpharetta GA 30023 800-422-4234
TF: 800-422-4234 ■ *Web:* www.deltadentalins.com
Delta Dental of Maryland One Delta Dr Mechanicsburg PA 17055 717-766-8500 691-6653
TF: 800-932-0783 ■ *Web:* www.deltadentalins.com
Delta Dental of Massachusetts 465 Medford St Boston MA 02129 617-886-1000 886-1199
TF Cust Svc: 800-872-0500 ■ *Web:* www.deltadentalma.com
Delta Dental of Michigan PO Box 30416 Lansing MI 48909 800-524-0149
TF: 800-524-0149 ■ *Web:* www.deltadentalmi.com
Delta Dental of Minnesota PO Box 330 Minneapolis MN 55440 651-406-5900
TF: 800-553-9536 ■ *Web:* www.deltadentalmn.org
Delta Dental of Mississippi PO Box 1803 Alpharetta GA 30023 800-422-4234
TF: 800-422-4234 ■ *Web:* www.deltadentalins.com
Delta Dental of Missouri
12399 Gravois Rd Ste 2 Saint Louis MO 63127 314-656-3000 656-2900
TF: 800-392-1167 ■ *Web:* www.deltadentalmo.com
Delta Dental of Montana PO Box 1803 Alpharetta GA 30023 800-422-4234
TF: 800-422-4234 ■ *Web:* www.deltadentalins.com
Delta Dental of New Jersey
1639 State Rt 10 Parsippany NJ 07054 973-285-4000 285-4141
TF: 800-624-2633 ■ *Web:* deltadentalnj.com
Delta Dental of New Jersey Inc PO Box 222 Parsippany NJ 07054 800-452-9310 285-4141*
**Fax Area Code:* 973 ■ *TF:* 800-452-9310 ■ *Web:* deltadentalnj.com
Delta Dental of New Mexico
2500 Louisiana Blvd NE Ste 600 Albuquerque NM 87110 505-883-4777 883-7444
TF: 800-999-0963 ■ *Web:* www.deltadentalnm.com
Delta Dental of New York One Delta Dr Mechanicsburg PA 17055 717-766-8500
TF: 800-932-0783 ■ *Web:* www.deltadentalins.com
Delta Dental of Ohio PO Box 30416 Lansing MI 48909 800-524-0149
TF: 800-524-0149 ■ *Web:* www.deltadentaloh.com
Delta Dental of Oklahoma
16 NW 63rd St Ste 201 Oklahoma City OK 73116 405-607-2100 607-2190
TF: 800-522-0188 ■ *Web:* www.deltadentalok.org
Delta Dental of Pennsylvania
One Delta Dr Mechanicsburg PA 17055 800-932-0783
TF: 800-932-0783 ■ *Web:* www.deltadentalins.com
Delta Dental of Rhode Island
10 Charles St Providence RI 02904 401-752-6000 752-6060*
**Fax:* Cust Svc ■ *TF:* 800-598-6684 ■ *Web:* www.deltadentalri.com
Delta Dental of South Dakota
720 N Euclid Ave PO Box 1157 Pierre SD 57501 605-224-7345 224-0909
TF: 800-627-3961 ■ *Web:* www.deltadentalsd.com
Delta Dental of Tennessee 240 Venture Cir Nashville TN 37228 615-255-3175 244-8108
TF Cust Svc: 800-223-3104 ■ *Web:* www.deltadentaltn.com
Delta Dental of Texas PO Box 1803 Alpharetta GA 30023 800-422-4234
TF: 800-422-4234 ■ *Web:* www.deltadentalins.com
Delta Dental of Utah PO Box 1803 Alpharetta GA 30023 800-422-4234
TF: 800-422-4234 ■ *Web:* www.deltadentalins.com
Delta Dental of Virginia 4818 Starkey Rd Roanoke VA 24014 540-989-8000 725-3890
TF: 800-367-3531 ■ *Web:* www.deltadentalva.com
Delta Dental of West Virginia
One Delta Dr Mechanicsburg PA 17055 717-766-8500
TF: 800-932-0783 ■ *Web:* www.deltadentalins.com
Delta Dental of Wisconsin
2801 Hoover Rd PO Box 828 Stevens Point WI 54481 715-344-6087 344-9058
TF: 800-236-3713 ■ *Web:* www.deltadentalwi.com
Delta Dental of Wyoming
6234 Yellowstone Rd Ste 100 Cheyenne WY 82009 307-632-3313 632-7309
TF: 800-735-3379 ■ *Web:* www.deltadentalwy.org
Delta Dental Plan of North Carolina
343 E Six Forks Rd Ste 180 Raleigh NC 27609 919-832-6015 832-6549
TF: 800-662-8856
EmblemHealth Co 55 Water St New York NY 10041 646-447-5000
TF: 800-447-8255 ■ *Web:* www.emblemhealth.com
Excellus BlueCross BlueShield PO Box 22999 Rochester NY 14692 585-454-1700 238-4400
TF: 800-278-1247 ■ *Web:* www.excellusbcbs.com
Excellus BlueCross BlueShield of Central New York
333 Butternut Dr Syracuse NY 13214 315-671-6400 671-6752*
**Fax:* Cust Svc ■ *TF:* 800-633-6066 ■ *Web:* www.excellusbcbs.com
EyeMed Vision Care 4000 Luxottica Pl Mason OH 45040 513-765-4321 765-6050
TF: 800-521-3605 ■ *Web:* portal.eyemedvisioncare.com
Fallon Community Health Plan Inc
10 Chestnut St Ste 7 Worcester MA 01608 508-799-2100 797-9621
TF: 800-333-2535 ■ *Web:* www.fchp.org
First Choice Health Plan
600 University St Ste 1400 Seattle WA 98101 800-467-5281 667-8062*
**Fax Area Code:* 206 ■ **Fax:* Cust Svc ■ *TF:* 800-467-5281 ■ *Web:* www.fchn.com
First Priority Health 19 N Main St Wilkes-Barre PA 18711 800-822-8753 200-6730*
**Fax Area Code:* 570 ■ *TF:* 800-822-8753 ■ *Web:* www.bcnepa.com
Foster Thomas Inc 1788 Forest Dr Annapolis MD 21401 800-372-3626
Web: www.fosterthomas.com
Geisinger Health Plan 100 N Academy Ave Danville PA 17822 570-271-8760 271-7218
TF: 800-447-4000 ■ *Web:* www.thehealthplan.com
Golden Rule Insurance Co 7440 Woodlands Indianapolis IN 46278 800-444-8990 298-0875*
**Fax Area Code:* 317 ■ *TF Cust Svc:* 800-444-8990 ■ *Web:* www.goldenrule.com
Great American Supplemental Benefits
PO Box 26580 Austin TX 78755 866-459-4272
TF: 866-459-4272 ■ *Web:* www.cigna.com
Group Health Co-op 320 Westlake Ave N Ste 100 Seattle WA 98109 206-448-5600 448-2137
TF: 888-901-4636 ■ *Web:* www.ghc.org
Hanover Insurance Co 440 Lincoln St Worcester MA 01653 508-855-1000 855-6313
TF: 800-853-0456 ■ *Web:* www.hanover.com
Harvard Pilgrim Health Care Inc
93 Worcester St Wellesley MA 02481 617-509-1000 509-2515
TF: 888-888-4742 ■ *Web:* www.harvardpilgrim.org

Phone Fax

Hawaii Dental Service 700 Bishop St Ste 700 ... Honolulu HI 96813 808-521-1431 529-9368
TF: 800-232-2533 ■ *Web:* www.hawaiidentalservice.com

Hawaii Medical Service Assn
818 Keaeumoku St ... Honolulu HI 96822 808-948-6111 948-5567*
**Fax:* Cust Svc ■ *TF:* 800-776-4672 ■ *Web:* www.hmsa.com

Health Alliance Plan 2850 W Grand Blvd ... Detroit MI 48202 313-872-8100 664-5866*
**Fax:* Hum Res ■ *TF:* 800-422-4641 ■ *Web:* www.hap.org

Health Net Inc 21650 Oxnard St ... Woodland Hills CA 91367 818-676-6000
NYSE: HNT ■ *TF:* 800-848-4747 ■ *Web:* www.healthnet.com

Health Plan of Nevada Inc PO Box 15645 ... Las Vegas NV 89114 702-242-7716 242-7920
Web: www.healthplanofnevada.com

Health Tradition Health Plan 1808 E Main St ... Onalaska WI 54650 608-781-9692
TF: 800-545-8499 ■ *Web:* www.healthtradition.com

HealthAmerica Pennsylvania Inc
3721 Tecport Dr PO Box 67103 ... Harrisburg PA 17111 800-788-6445
TF: 800-788-6445 ■ *Web:* healthamerica.coventryhealthcare.com

HealthCare USA 10 S Broadway Ste 1200 ... Saint Louis MO 63102 314-241-5300 241-8010
TF: 800-213-7792 ■ *Web:* coventryhealthcare.com

HealthPartners Inc PO Box 1309 ... Minneapolis MN 55440 952-883-5000 967-5666*
**Fax:* Cust Svc ■ *TF:* 800-883-2177 ■ *Web:* www.healthpartners.com

Healthplex Inc 333 Earl Ovington Blvd ... Uniondale NY 11553 516-542-2200 794-3186
TF Cust Svc: 800-468-0608 ■ *Web:* www.healthplex.com

HealthPlus of Michigan 2050 S Linden Rd ... Flint MI 48532 810-230-2000
TF: 800-332-9161 ■ *Web:* www.healthplus.org

Heritage Summit HealthCare of Florida Inc
PO Box 2928 ... Lakeland FL 33806 863-665-6629 665-5177
TF: 800-282-7644 ■ *Web:* www.summitholdings.com

Highmark Inc 120 Fifth Ave Pl ... Pittsburgh PA 15222 412-544-7000 302-7182*
**Fax Area Code:* 717 ■ **Fax:* Hum Res ■ *TF:* 800-992-0246 ■ *Web:* www.highmark.com

Humana Inc 500 W Main St ... Louisville KY 40202 502-580-1000 580-3690
NYSE: HUM ■ *TF:* 800-486-2620 ■ *Web:* www.humana.com

Humana Military Healthcare Services
500 W Main St ... Louisville KY 40201 502-580-3200
TF General: 800-444-5445 ■ *Web:* www.humana-military.com

Independence Blue Cross 1901 Market St ... Philadelphia PA 19103 800-275-2583 241-0403*
**Fax Area Code:* 215 ■ **Fax:* Hum Res ■ *TF:* 800-275-2583 ■ *Web:* www.ibx.com

Independent Health 511 Farber Lakes Dr ... Buffalo NY 14221 716-631-3001 635-3838*
**Fax:* Hum Res ■ *TF:* 800-247-1466 ■ *Web:* www.independenthealth.com

IOA Re Inc 190 W Germantown Pk Ste 200 ... East Norriton PA 19401 610-940-9000
TF: 800-462-2300 ■ *Web:* www.ioare.com

Kaiser Foundation Health Plan & Hospitals Inc
1 Kaiser Plaza 27th Fl ... Oakland CA 94612 510-271-5800 271-6493
Web: healthy.kaiserpermanente.org

Kaiser Foundation Health Plan Inc
One Kaiser Plz 27th Fl ... Oakland CA 94612 510-271-5800 271-6493
TF: 800-464-4000 ■ *Web:* kaiserpermanente.org

Kaiser Permanente Colorado Denver/Boulder
2500 S Havanna ... Aurora CO 80014 303-338-3817
Web: www.kaiserpermanente.org

Kaiser Permanente Hawaii 711 Kapiolani Blvd ... Honolulu HI 96813 808-432-0000 432-5070
TF: 800-966-5955 ■ *Web:* kaiserpermanente.org

Kaiser Permanente Northwest
500 NE Multnomah St Ste 100 ... Portland OR 97232 503-813-2000
TF: 800-813-2000 ■ *Web:* healthy.kaiserpermanente.org

LA Care Health Plan
555 W Fifth St 29th Fl ... Los Angeles CA 90013 213-694-1250
TF: 888-839-9909 ■ *Web:* www.lacare.org

Lexington Veteran Affairs Medical Center
1101 Veterans Dr ... Lexington KY 40502 859-233-4511
TF: 877-222-8387 ■ *Web:* lexington.va.gov

Markel American Insurance Co
N14 W23800 Stone Ridge Dr ... Waukesha WI 53188 262-548-9880
Web: www.markelinsuresfun.com

MEDICA 401 Carlson Pkwy ... Minnetonka MN 55305 952-992-2900 992-3700*
**Fax:* Sales ■ *TF Cust Svc:* 800-952-3455 ■ *Web:* www.medica.com

Medical Benefits Mutual Life Insurance Co
1975 Tamarack Rd ... Newark OH 43058 740-522-8425
TF: 800-423-3151 ■ *Web:* www.medben.com

Medical Mutual of Ohio 2060 E Ninth St ... Cleveland OH 44115 216-687-7000 687-6585*
**Fax:* Hum Res ■ *TF:* 800-700-2583 ■ *Web:* www.medmutual.com

Memorial Health Partners
4700 Waters Ave Ste 13 ... Savannah GA 31404 912-350-8000 350-5976
TF: 800-537-0690 ■ *Web:* www.memorialhealth.com

MetLife Inc 200 Pk Ave ... New York NY 10166 212-578-2211 578-3320
NYSE: MET ■ *TF:* 800-638-5433 ■ *Web:* global.metlife.com

Molina Healthcare Inc
200 Oceangate Ste 100 ... Long Beach CA 90802 562-435-3666 437-7235
NYSE: MOH ■ *TF:* 888-562-5442 ■ *Web:* www.molinahealthcare.com

MVP Health Care 625 State St ... Schenectady NY 12305 518-370-4793 370-0830*
**Fax:* Hum Res ■ *TF:* 800-777-4793 ■ *Web:* www.mvphealthcare.com

Neighborhood Health Partnership Inc
7600 NW 19th St Ste 200 ... Miami FL 33126 877-972-8845
TF: 877-972-8845 ■ *Web:* www.neighborhood-health.com

ODS Cos 601 SW Second Ave ... Portland OR 97204 503-228-6554 521-7898*
**Fax Area Code:* 804 ■ *TF:* 888-221-0802 ■ *Web:* ods-security.com/about-ods/

Optima Health 4417 Corporation Ln ... Virginia Beach VA 23462 757-552-7174 552-8919
Web: www.optimahealth.com

Oxford Health Plans LLC 48 Monroe Tpke ... Trumbull CT 06611 203-459-9100 459-6464
TF: 800-444-6222 ■ *Web:* www.oxhp.com

Oxford Health Plans (NJ) Inc
111 Wood Ave S Ste 2 ... Iselin NJ 08830 732-623-1000
TF: 800-201-6920 ■ *Web:* www.oxhp.com

Pacificare of Texas 6200 NW Pkwy ... San Antonio TX 78249 210-474-5000
TF: 800-624-7272 ■ *Web:* uhcwest.com

Paramount Health Care 1901 Indian Wood Cir ... Maumee OH 43537 419-887-2525 887-2034*
**Fax:* Hum Res ■ *TF:* 800-462-3589 ■ *Web:* www.paramounthealthcare.com

Physicians Plus Insurance Corp
2650 Novation Pkwy Ste 200 ... Madison WI 53713 608-282-8900
TF: 800-545-5015 ■ *Web:* www.pplusic.com

Preferred CommunityChoice PPO 218 W Sixth St ... Tulsa OK 74119 918-594-5200 594-5210
TF: 800-884-4776 ■ *Web:* www.ccok.com

Preferred Health Systems Inc
8535 E 21st St N ... Wichita KS 67206 316-609-2345 609-2346
TF: 800-990-0345 ■ *Web:* chckansas.coventryhealthcare.com

Premera Blue Cross
7001 220th St SW ... Mountlake Terrace WA 98043 425-918-4000
TF Cust Svc: 800-722-1471 ■ *Web:* www.premera.com

Premera Blue Cross Blue Shield of Alaska
2550 Denali St Ste 1404 ... Anchorage AK 99503 907-258-5065
TF Cust Svc: 800-508-4722 ■ *Web:* premera.com

Prescription Corp of America
66 Ford Rd Ste 230 ... Denville NJ 07834 973-983-6300

Priority Health 1231 E Beltline NE ... Grand Rapids MI 49525 616-942-0954 942-0145
TF: 800-942-0954 ■ *Web:* www.priorityhealth.com

Regence Blue Cross Blue Shield of Oregon
PO Box 1071 ... Portland OR 97207 503-225-5351 226-8795*
**Fax:* Hum Res ■ *TF:* 888-734-3623 ■ *Web:* www.regence.com

Regence BlueCross BlueShield of Utah
2890 E Cottonwood Pkwy ... Salt Lake City UT 84121 801-333-2100 333-6516*
**Fax:* Hum Res ■ *TF Cust Svc:* 800-624-6519 ■ *Web:* www.regence.com

Rocky Mountain Health Plans
2775 Crossroads Blvd PO Box 10600 ... Grand Junction CO 81502 970-244-7760 244-7880
TF: 800-843-0719 ■ *Web:* www.rmhp.org

SafeGuard Health Enterprises Inc
95 Enterprise Ste 100 ... Aliso Viejo CA 92656 949-425-4300 425-4586
TF: 800-880-1800 ■ *Web:* www.metlife.com

Sagamore Health Network
11555 N Meridian St Ste 400 ... Carmel IN 46032 317-573-2886 580-8488
TF: 800-364-3469 ■ *Web:* www.sagamorehn.com

Scott & White Health Plan 2401 S 31st St ... Temple TX 76508 254-298-3000 298-3011
TF: 800-321-7947 ■ *Web:* www.sw.org

Sharp Health Plan
4305 University Ave Ste 200 ... San Diego CA 92105 619-228-2300
Web: www.sharphealthplan.com

Sierra Military Health Services Inc
111 Market Pl Ste 410 ... Baltimore MD 21202 410-547-9040

Spectera Inc
6220 Old Dobbin Ln Liberty 6, Ste 200 ... Columbia MD 21045 800-638-3120 265-6260*
**Fax Area Code:* 410 ■ *TF:* 800-638-3120 ■ *Web:* www.spectera.com

Trillium Community Health Plan Inc
1800 Millrace Dr ... Eugene OR 97403 541-431-1950
Web: trilliumchp.com

Tufts Associated Health Plans
705 Mt Auburn Street ... Watertown MA 02472 617-972-9400 972-9409
TF: 800-462-0224 ■ *Web:* www.tuftshealthplan.com

Union Pacific Railroad Employees' Health Systems
1040 North 2200 West ... Salt Lake City UT 84116 801-595-4300 595-4399
TF: 800-547-0421 ■ *Web:* www.uphealth.com

UnitedHealth Group Inc 9900 Bren Rd E ... Minnetonka MN 55343 952-936-1300
NYSE: UNH ■ *TF:* 800-328-5979 ■ *Web:* www.unitedhealthgroup.com

UnitedHealthcare 9900 Bren Rd E ... Minnetonka MN 55343 952-936-1300 771-1734*
**Fax Area Code:* 216 ■ **Fax:* Hum Res ■ *TF:* 800-362-0655 ■ *Web:* www.uhc.com

Unity Health Insurance 840 Carolina St ... Sauk City WI 53583 608-643-2491 643-2564
TF: 800-362-3308 ■ *Web:* www.unityhealth.com

Univera Healthcare 205 Pk Club Ln ... Buffalo NY 14221 716-847-1480 956-2397*
**Fax Area Code:* 800 ■ **Fax:* Hum Res ■ *TF:* 877-883-9577 ■ *Web:* www.univerahealthcare.com

Universal Care Inc 1600 E Hill St ... Signal Hill CA 90755 562-424-6200

Va Premier Health Plan Inc
625 Piney Forest Rd ... Danville VA 24540 434-799-4623
Web: vapremier.com

Voya Services Company 1 Orange Way ... Windsor CT 06095 860-580-4646
TF: 855-663-8692 ■ *Web:* www.voya.com

Washington Dental Service 9706 Fourth Ave NE ... Seattle WA 98115 206-522-1300 525-2330
TF: 800-367-4104 ■ *Web:* www.deltadentalwa.com

WellCare Group Inc 8735 Henderson Rd Rm 3 ... Tampa FL 33634 813-290-6200 675-2929
TF: 866-765-4385 ■ *Web:* www.wellcare.com

WellCare Health Plans Inc PO Box 31372 ... Tampa FL 33631 866-530-9491
TF: 866-530-9491 ■ *Web:* www.wellcare.com/healthplans/newyork/home.aspx

394-4 Property & Casualty Insurance

Phone Fax

Acceptance Insurance Cos Inc
300 W Broadway Ste 1600 ... Council Bluffs IA 51503 712-329-3600
Web: www.aicins.com

Access Management Group
1100 Northmeadow Pkwy Ste 114 ... Roswell GA 30076 770-777-6890 777-6916
Web: www.accessmgt.com

Accident Fund Co
232 S Capitol Ave PO Box 40790 ... Lansing MI 48901 517-342-4200 367-6712*
**Fax:* Mktg ■ *TF Mktg:* 888-276-0327 ■ *Web:* www.accidentfund.com

ACE USA 436 Walnut St PO Box 1000 ... Philadelphia PA 19106 215-640-1000 640-2489
Web: www.acegroup.com

Acuity Insurance 2800 S Taylor Dr ... Sheboygan WI 53081 920-458-9131 458-1618
Web: www.acuity.com

Addison Insurance Co
118 Second Ave SE PO Box 73909 ... Cedar Rapids IA 52401 319-399-5700 399-5499
TF: 800-332-7977 ■ *Web:* www.unitedfiregroup.com

Aegis Security Inc PO Box 3153 ... Harrisburg PA 17105 717-657-9671 657-0340
TF: 800-233-2160 ■ *Web:* www.aegisfirst.com

Agricultural Workers Mutual Auto Insurance Co
PO Box 88 ... Fort Worth TX 76101 817-831-9900 831-7565
TF: 800-772-7424 ■ *Web:* www.agworkers.com

ALLIED Group Inc 1100 Locust St ... Des Moines IA 50391 515-508-4211 280-4904
TF: 800-532-1436 ■ *Web:* www.alliedinsurance.com

Allied Insurance 1601 Exposition Blvd ... Sacramento CA 95815 916-924-4000
TF: 800-552-2437 ■ *Web:* www.alliedinsurance.com

American Agricultural Insurance Co
1501 E Woodfield Rd Ste 300 W ... Schaumburg IL 60173 847-969-2900 969-2752
Web: www.aaic.com

American Commerce Insurance Co
3590 Twin Creeks Dr ... Columbus OH 43204 614-308-3366 308-3365
TF: 800-848-2945 ■ *Web:* www.mapfreinsurance.com

Company / Address	City	State	Zip	Phone	Fax
American Family Mutual Insurance Co 6000 American Pkwy *Fax: Hum Res ■ TF Cust Svc: 800-374-0008 ■ Web: www.amfam.com	Madison	WI	53783	608-249-2111	243-4917*
American Modern Home Insurance Co PO Box 5323 TF: 800-543-2644 ■ Web: www.amig.com	Cincinnati	OH	45201	513-943-7200	943-7368
American National Property & Casualty Co 1949 E Sunshine St *Fax: Hum Res ■ TF: 800-333-2860 ■ Web: www.anpac.com	Springfield	MO	65899	417-887-0220	887-1801*
American Road Insurance Co, The 1 American Rd	Dearborn	MI	48126	313-845-5850	
American Southern Insurance Co 3715 Northside Pkwy NW Bldg 400 Ste 800 TF: 800-241-1172 ■ Web: www.amsou.com	Atlanta	GA	30327	404-266-9599	266-8327
AMERISAFE Inc 2301 Hwy 190 W NASDAQ: AMSF ■ TF: 800-256-9052 ■ Web: www.amerisafe.com	DeRidder	LA	70634	337-463-9052	463-7298
Amerisure Insurance Co 26777 Halsted Rd Ste 200 TF: 800-257-1900 ■ Web: www.amerisure.com	Farmington Hills	MI	48331	248-615-9000	615-8548
Amica Mutual Insurance Co 100 Amica Way *Fax Area Code: 401 ■ TF: 800-652-6422 ■ Web: www.amica.com	Lincoln	RI	02865	800-652-6422	334-4241*
Arbella Mutual Insurance Co 1100 Crown Colony Dr TF: 800-972-5348 ■ Web: www.arbella.com	Quincy	MA	02169	617-328-2800	328-2970
Arizona Farm Bureau Federation 325 S Higley Rd Web: www.azfb.org/	Higley	AZ	85296	480-635-3600	
Armed Forces Insurance Exchange (AFI) PO Box G TF: 800-255-0187 ■ Web: www.afi.org	Fort Leavenworth	KS	66027	800-255-6792	828-7731
Armour Risk Management Inc 1735 Market St Ste 3000 Web: www.armourholdings.com	Philadelphia	PA	19103	215-665-5000	
Arrowpoint Capital Whitehall Corporate Ctr Ste 3 3600 Arco Corporate Dr TF: 866-236-7750 ■ Web: www.arrowpointcap.com	Charlotte	NC	28273	704-522-2000	
Associated Industries Of Massachusetts Mutual Insurance Com PO Box 4070 TF: 866-270-3354 ■ Web: www.aimmutual.com	Burlington	MA	01803	781-221-1600	270-5599
AssuranceAmerica Corp 5500 I- N Pkwy Ste 600 TF: 800-450-7857 ■ Web: www.assuranceamerica.com	Atlanta	GA	30328	770-952-0200	952-0258
Auto-Owners Insurance Co 6101 Anacapri Blvd TF: 800-346-0346 ■ Web: www.auto-owners.com	Lansing	MI	48917	517-323-1200	323-8796
Avemco Insurance Co 411 Aviation Way TF: 800-874-9125 ■ Web: avemco.com	Frederick	MD	21701	301-694-5700	694-4376
Baldwin & Lyons Inc 111 Congressional Blvd Ste 500 NASDAQ: BWINB ■ TF: 800-644-5501 ■ Web: www.baldwinandlyons.com	Carmel	IN	46032	317-636-9800	632-9444
Berkshire Hathaway Group (BHG) 3024 Harney St *Fax Area Code: 212 ■ TF: 800-223-2064 ■ Web: berkshirehathaway.com	Omaha	NE	68131	402-536-3100	298-1915*
Berkshire Hathaway Homestates Cos (BHHC) PO Box 2048 TF: 888-495-8949 ■ Web: www.bhhc.com	Omaha	NE	68103	888-495-8949	
Bituminous Insurance Cos 320 18th St *Fax Area Code: 309 ■ TF: 800-475-4477 ■ Web: www.bitco.com	Rock Island	IL	61201	800-475-4477	786-3847*
Brotherhood Mutual Insurance Co (BMI) 6400 Brotherhood Way PO Box 2589 *Fax Area Code: 260 ■ TF Cust Svc: 800-333-3735 ■ Web: www.brotherhoodmutual.com	Fort Wayne	IN	46825	800-333-3735	482-7709*
Brown & Brown Insurance PO Box 1718 TF: 800-562-8171 ■ Web: www.bbtacoma.com	Tacoma	WA	98401	253-396-5500	396-4500
C Na Insurance 100 Centerview Dr	Nashville	TN	37214	615-871-1400	886-1883
California Casualty Insurance Group 1900 Alameda De Las Pulgas TF: 866-680-5143 ■ Web: www.calcas.com	San Mateo	CA	94403	650-574-4000	572-4608
Canada Life Assurance Co, The 330 University Ave TF: 888-252-1847 ■ Web: www.canadalife.com	Toronto	ON	M5G1R8	416-597-1456	597-6520
Canal Insurance Co 400 E Stone Ave PO Box 7 *Fax Area Code: 864 ■ TF: 800-452-6911 ■ Web: canalinsurance.com	Greenville	SC	29601	800-452-6911	232-5707*
Capitol Indemnity Corp 1600 Aspen Commons TF: 800-475-4450 ■ Web: www.capspecialty.com/	Middleton	WI	53562	608-829-4200	829-7408
Capitol Insurance Cos 1600 Aspen Commons PO Box 5900 TF: 800-475-4450 ■ Web: www.capspecialty.com/	Middleton	WI	53562	608-829-4200	829-7408
Carolina Casualty Insurance Co 4600 Touchton Rd E Bldg 100 Ste 400 TF: 800-874-8053 ■ Web: www.carolinacas.com	Jacksonville	FL	32246	904-363-0900	363-8098
Central Insurance Cos 800 S Washington St *Fax: Claims ■ TF: 800-736-7000 ■ Web: www.central-insurance.com	Van Wert	OH	45891	419-238-1010	238-7626*
Century-National Insurance Co 12200 Sylvan St PO Box 3999 TF Cust Svc: 800-894-8384 ■ Web: www.centurynational.com	North Hollywood	CA	91606	818-760-0880	
Chubb & Son 15 Mountain View Rd TF: 800-252-4670 ■ Web: www.chubb.com	Warren	NJ	07059	908-903-2000	903-2027
Chubb Group of Insurance Cos 15 Mtn View Rd Web: www.chubb.com	Warren	NJ	07059	908-903-2000	903-2027
Church Mutual Insurance Co 3000 Schuster Ln TF: 800-554-2642 ■ Web: www.churchmutual.com	Merrill	WI	54452	715-536-5577	539-4650
Cincinnati Indemnity Co 6200 S Gilmore Rd Web: cinfin.com	Fairfield	OH	45014	513-870-2000	
Cincinnati Insurance Co 6200 S Gilmore Rd Web: cinfin.com	Fairfield	OH	45014	513-870-2000	
Civil Service Employees Insurance Co 2121 N California Blvd Ste 555 *Fax Area Code: 925 ■ TF: 800-282-6848 ■ Web: www.cseinsurance.com	Walnut Creek	CA	94596	800-282-6848	817-6383*
Colorado Farm Bureau Mutual Insurance Co PO Box 5647 TF: 800-315-5998 ■ Web: www.cfbmic.com	Denver	CO	80217	303-749-7500	660-1694
Commerce Insurance Co 211 Main St TF: 800-221-1605 ■ Web: www.commerceinsurance.com	Webster	MA	01570	508-943-9000	949-4921
Community Assn Underwriters of America (CAU) Two Caufield Pl Web: www.cauinsure.com	Newtown	PA	18940	267-757-7100	757-7410
Concord Group Insurance Cos Four Bouton St TF: 800-852-3380 ■ Web: www.concordgroupinsurance.com	Concord	NH	03301	800-852-3380	
Continental Casualty Co 333 S Wabash Ave TF: 800-303-9744 ■ Web: www.cna.com	Chicago	IL	60685	312-822-5000	822-6419
Continental Western Group 11201 Douglas Ave *Fax: Hum Res ■ TF: 800-235-2942 ■ Web: www.cwgins.com	Urbandale	IA	50322	515-473-3000	473-3015*
Cornhusker Casualty Co PO Box 2048 TF: 888-495-8949 ■ Web: www.bhhc.com	Omaha	NE	68103	888-495-8949	
Country Mutual Insurance Co 1701 Towanda Ave TF Cust Svc: 888-211-2555 ■ Web: www.countryfinancial.com	Bloomington	IL	61701	309-821-3000	821-5160
Crum & Forster Insurance Inc 305 Madison Ave PO Box 1973 *Fax: Hum Res ■ TF: 800-690-5520 ■ Web: www.cfins.com	Morristown	NJ	07962	973-490-6600	490-6600*
Cumberland Insurance Group 633 Shiloh Pike *Fax Area Code: 856 ■ TF: 800-232-6992 ■ Web: www.cumberlandgroup.com	Bridgeton	NJ	08302	800-232-6992	451-7564*
Cumberland Mutual Fire Insurance Co 633 Shiloh Pk *Fax Area Code: 856 ■ TF: 800-232-6992 ■ Web: www.cumberlandgroup.com	Bridgeton	NJ	08302	800-232-6992	451-7564*
Dairyland Insurance Co 1800 N Pt Dr *Fax Area Code: 800 ■ *Fax: Sales ■ TF Sales: 866-445-5364 ■ Web: www.sentry.com	Stevens Point	WI	54481	715-346-6000	999-4642*
Donegal Mutual Insurance Co 1195 River Rd PO Box 302 TF: 800-877-0600 ■ Web: www.donegalgroup.com	Marietta	PA	17547	717-426-1931	426-7009
Dorinco Reinsurance Co 1320 Waldo Ave Web: www.dorinco.com	Midland	MI	48642	989-636-0047	638-9963
Economical Insurance Group, The 111 Westmount Rd S PO Box 2000 TF: 800-265-2180 ■ Web: www.economicalinsurance.com	Waterloo	ON	N2J4S4	519-570-8200	570-8389
Endurance Reinsurance Corp of America 750 Third Ave Fl 2 & 10 TF: 888-221-3894 ■ Web: endurance.bm	New York	NY	10017	212-471-2800	471-1748
Erie Indemnity Co Erie Insurance Group 100 Erie Insurance Pl NASDAQ: ERIE ■ *Fax: Mail Rm ■ TF: 800-458-0811 ■ Web: www.erieinsurance.com	Erie	PA	16530	814-870-2000	870-3126*
Erie Insurance Exchange 100 Erie Insurance Pl TF: 800-458-0811 ■ Web: www.erieinsurance.com	Erie	PA	16530	814-870-2000	870-3126
Erie Insurance Property & Casualty Co 100 Erie Insurance Pl TF: 800-458-0811 ■ Web: www.erieinsurance.com	Erie	PA	16530	814-870-2000	870-4408
Everest Reinsurance Co 477 Martinsville Rd TF: 800-269-6660 ■ Web: www.everestregroup.com	Liberty Corner	NJ	07938	908-604-3000	604-3322
Farm Family Casualty Insurance Co PO Box 656 TF: 800-843-3276 ■ Web: www.farmfamily.com	Albany	NY	12201	518-431-5000	
Farmers Alliance Mutual Insurance Co 1122 N Main PO Box 1401 TF: 800-362-1075 ■ Web: www.fami.com	McPherson	KS	67460	620-241-2200	241-5482
Farmers Insurance Exchange 4680 Wilshire Blvd *Fax Area Code: 877 ■ *Fax: Hum Res ■ TF: 855-808-6599 ■ Web: www.farmers.com	Los Angeles	CA	90010	323-932-3200	217-1389*
Farmers Mutual Hail Insurance Company of Iowa 6785 Westown Pkwy TF: 800-247-5248 ■ Web: www.fmh.com	West Des Moines	IA	50266	515-282-9104	282-1220
Farmers Mutual Insurance Company of Nebraska 1220 Lincoln Mall TF: 800-742-7433 ■ Web: www.fmne.com	Lincoln	NE	68508	402-434-8300	434-8385
FCCI Insurance Group 6300 University Pkwy PO Box 58004 TF: 800-226-3224 ■ Web: www.fcci-group.com	Sarasota	FL	34232	941-907-3224	
Federated Mutual Insurance Co 121 E Pk Sq PO Box 328 TF: 800-533-0472 ■ Web: federatedinsurance.com	Owatonna	MN	55060	507-455-5200	
FEDUSA 7500 Ulmerton Rd Ste 35 *Fax Area Code: 866 ■ Web: www.fedusa.com	Largo	FL	33771	727-535-5671	610-1947*
Fhm Insurance Co 4601 Touchton Rd E Bldg 300 Ste 3150 *Fax Area Code: 407 ■ TF: 800-393-0001 ■ Web: www.fhmic.com	Jacksonville	FL	32246	904-724-9890	926-9419*
Fireman's Fund Insurance Co 777 San Marin Dr *Fax Area Code: 888 ■ *Fax: Mail Rm ■ TF: 866-386-3932 ■ Web: www.firemansfund.com	Novato	CA	94998	800-558-1606	323-6450*
First Insurance Company of Hawaii Ltd 1100 Ward Ave PO Box 2866 TF: 800-272-5202 ■ Web: www.ficoh.com	Honolulu	HI	96803	808-527-7777	527-3200
Florida Family Insurance Services LLC 27599 Riverview Ctr Blvd Ste 100 PO Box 136001 TF: 888-850-4663 ■ Web: www.floridafamily.com	Bonita Springs	FL	34136	239-495-4700	948-7381
Florida Farm Bureau Casualty Insurance Co 5700 SW 34th St Web: floridafarmbureau.com	Gainesville	FL	32608	352-378-1321	374-1577
Florida Farm Bureau General Insurance Co 5700 SW 34th St Web: floridafarmbureau.com	Gainesville	FL	32608	352-378-1321	374-1577
Florida Farm Bureau Insurance Cos 5700 SW 34th St TF: 866-275-7322 ■ Web: floridafarmbureau.com	Gainesville	FL	32608	352-378-1321	374-1577
FM Global 270 Central Ave PO Box 7500 TF: 800-343-7722 ■ Web: www.fmglobal.com	Johnston	RI	02919	401-275-3000	275-3029
Foremost Insurance Co 5600 Beech Tree Ln TF: 800-532-4221 ■ Web: www.foremost.com	Caledonia	MI	49316	800-532-4221	
Frankenmuth Insurance 1 Mutual Ave TF: 800-234-4433 ■ Web: www.fmins.com	Frankenmuth	MI	48787	989-652-6121	652-3588
Franklin Mutual Insurance Co Five Broad St TF: 800-842-0551 ■ Web: www.fmiweb.com	Branchville	NJ	07826	973-948-3120	948-7190
GAINSCO County Mutual Insurance Co PO Box 199023 Web: gainsco.com	Dallas	TX	75219	972-629-4301	629-4335

				Phone	Fax
General Star National Insurance Co 695 E Main St Financial Ctr	Stamford	CT	06901	203-328-5000	328-6423
TF: 800-431-9994 ■ *Web:* www.generalstar.com					
Germania Farm Mutual Insurance Assn 507 Hwy 290 E	Brenham	TX	77833	979-836-5224	836-1977
TF: 800-392-2202 ■ *Web:* www.germania-ins.com					
Golden Eagle Insurance Corp 525 B St	San Diego	CA	92101	619-744-6000	
TF: 888-398-8924 ■ *Web:* libertymutualgroup.com/business					
Grain Dealers Mutual Insurance Co 6201 Corporate Dr	Indianapolis	IN	46278	317-388-4500	295-9434
TF: 800-428-7081 ■ *Web:* www.graindealers.com					
Grange Mutual Casualty Co 671 S High St	Columbus	OH	43206	800-422-0550	
Web: grangeinsurance.com					
Great American Insurance Co 580 Walnut St	Cincinnati	OH	45202	513-369-5000	
Web: www.greatamericaninsurancegroup.com					
Great Northern Insurance Co 15 Mtn View Rd	Warren	NJ	07059	908-903-2000	903-2027
TF Cust Svc: 800-252-4670 ■ *Web:* www.chubb.com					
Great West Casualty Co 1100 W 29th St PO Box 277	South Sioux City	NE	68776	402-494-2084	
TF: 800-228-8602 ■ *Web:* gwccnet.com					
Grinnell Mutual Reinsurance Co 4215 Hwy 146 PO Box 790	Grinnell	IA	50112	641-269-8000	236-2840
TF: 800-362-2041 ■ *Web:* grinnellmutual.com					
GuideOne Insurance Co 1111 Ashworth Rd	West Des Moines	IA	50265	515-267-5000	267-5730*
**Fax:* Hum Res ■ *TF:* 877-448-4331 ■ *Web:* www.guideone.com					
GuideOne Mutual Insurance Co 1111 Ashworth Rd	West Des Moines	IA	50265	515-267-5000	267-5530*
**Fax:* Hum Res ■ *TF:* 877-448-4331 ■ *Web:* www.guideone.com					
GuideOne Specialty Mutual Insurance Co 1111 Ashworth Rd	West Des Moines	IA	50265	515-267-5000	267-5730*
**Fax:* Hum Res ■ *TF:* 877-448-4331 ■ *Web:* www.guideone.com					
Hagerty Insurance Agency LLC 141 River's Edge Dr Ste 200 PO Box 1303	Traverse City	MI	49684	231-947-6868	941-8227
TF: 877-922-9701 ■ *Web:* www.hagerty.com					
Hanover Insurance Co 440 Lincoln St	Worcester	MA	01653	508-855-1000	855-6313
TF: 800-853-0456 ■ *Web:* www.hanover.com					
Harco National Insurance Co PO Box 68309	Schaumburg	IL	60168	800-448-4642	472-6015*
**Fax Area Code:* 847 ■ *TF:* 800-448-4642 ■ *Web:* iat-harco.com					
Harleysville Insurance Co of New Jersey 112 W Park Dr	Mount Laurel	NJ	08054	856-642-9779	642-9412*
**Fax:* Claims ■ *TF:* 800-322-5521 ■ *Web:* www.harleysvillegroup.com					
Harleysville Pennland Insurance Co 355 Maple Ave	Harleysville	PA	19438	215-256-5000	256-5602*
**Fax:* Hum Res ■ *TF:* 800-523-6344 ■ *Web:* www.harleysvillegroup.com					
Harleysville Preferred Insurance Co 355 Maple Ave	Harleysville	PA	19438	215-256-5000	256-5602*
**Fax:* Hum Res ■ *TF:* 800-523-6344 ■ *Web:* www.harleysvillegroup.com					
Harleysville Worcester Insurance Co 120 Front St Ste 400	Worcester	MA	01608	508-754-6666	752-7903*
**Fax:* Hum Res ■ *TF:* 800-225-7387 ■ *Web:* www.harleysvillegroup.com					
Hartford Casualty Insurance Co 1 Hartford Plaza	Hartford	CT	06155	860-547-5000	
Web: www.thehartford.com					
Hartford Fire Insurance Co One Hartford Plz	Hartford	CT	06115	860-547-5000	
Web: www.thehartford.com					
Hartford Steam Boiler Inspection & Insurance Co, The (HSB) One State St PO Box 5024	Hartford	CT	06102	800-472-1866	722-5106*
**Fax Area Code:* 860 ■ *TF:* 800-472-1866 ■ *Web:* www.hsb.com					
Hartford's Omni Auto Plan PO Box 105440	Atlanta	GA	30348	770-952-4500	983-3633*
**Fax Area Code:* 800 ■ *TF:* 800-243-5860 ■ *Web:* www.thehartford.com					
Hingham Mutual Fire Insurance Co 230 Beal St	Hingham	MA	02043	781-749-0841	749-4477
TF: 800-341-8200 ■ *Web:* www.hinghammutual.com					
Hortica Insurance One Horticultural Ln PO Box 428	Edwardsville	IL	62025	618-656-4240	656-7581
TF: 800-851-7740 ■ *Web:* www.hortica.com					
HSB Group Inc 1 State St	Hartford	CT	06103	860-722-1866	722-5106
TF: 800-472-1866					
ICW Group 11455 El Camino Real	San Diego	CA	92130	858-350-2400	350-2704
TF: 800-877-1111 ■ *Web:* www.icwgroup.com					
IMT Group, The PO Box 1336	Des Moines	IA	50266	800-274-3531	
TF: 800-274-3531 ■ *Web:* imtins.com					
Indiana Farmers Mutual Insurance Co 10 W 106th St	Indianapolis	IN	46290	317-846-4211	848-8629
TF: 800-666-6460 ■ *Web:* www.indianafarmers.com					
Injured Workers Insurance Fund 8722 Loch Raven Blvd	Towson	MD	21286	410-494-2000	494-2154
TF: 800-264-4943 ■ *Web:* www.ceiwc.com					
Insurance Company of the West 11455 El Camino Real	San Diego	CA	92130	858-350-2400	350-2616
TF: 800-877-1111 ■ *Web:* www.icwgroup.com					
Intact Insurance 700 University Ave Mn 3 Ste 1500	Toronto	ON	M5G0A1	416-341-1464	344-8030*
**Fax:* Claims ■ *TF:* 877-341-1464					
Jacobs Financial Group Inc 300 Summers St Ste 970	Charleston	WV	25301	304-343-8171	
Web: www.thejacobsfinancialgroup.com/					
James A Scott & Son Inc PO Box 10489	Lynchburg	VA	24506	434-832-2100	832-2190
TF: 800-365-0101 ■ *Web:* www.scottins.com					
Keen Battle Mead & Co (KBMCO) 7850 NW 146th St Ste 200 PO Box 171870	Hialeah	FL	33016	305-558-1101	822-4722
Web: www.kbmco.com					
Kentucky Farm Bureau Mutual Insurance Co 9201 Bunsen Pkwy	Louisville	KY	40220	502-495-5000	495-7703
Web: kyfb.com					
Kingstone Companies Inc 1154 Broadway	Hewlett	NY	11557	516-374-7600	295-7216
NASDAQ: KINS ■ *Web:* www.kingstonecompanies.com					
Kingsway Financial Services Inc 45 St Clair Ave W Ste 400	Toronto	ON	M4V1K9	416-848-1171	848-1171
NYSE: KFS ■ *Web:* www.kingsway-financial.com					
Koch Supply & Trading LP 4111 E 37th St N	Wichita	KS	67220	713-544-4123	828-5739*
**Fax Area Code:* 316 ■ *TF:* 800-245-2243 ■ *Web:* www.kochoil.com					

				Phone	Fax
Lexington Insurance Company Inc 99 High St Fl 23	Boston	MA	02110	617-330-1100	
Web: www.lexingtoninsurance.com					
Liberty Mutual Group 175 Berkeley St	Boston	MA	02116	617-357-9500	
Web: www.libertymutual.com					
Lititz Mutual Insurance Co Two N Broad St PO Box 900	Lititz	PA	17543	717-626-4751	626-0970
TF: 800-626-4751 ■ *Web:* www.lititzmutual.com					
Lumbermen's Underwriting Alliance (LUA) 1905 NW Corporate Blvd PO Box 3061	Boca Raton	FL	33431	561-994-1900	997-9489*
**Fax:* Hum Res ■ *TF:* 800-327-0630 ■ *Web:* www.lumbermensunderwriting.com					
Lykes Insurance Inc 400 N Tampa St	Tampa	FL	33602	813-223-3911	221-1857
TF: 800-243-0491 ■ *Web:* www.lykesinsurance.com					
Main Street America Group 55 W St	Keene	NH	03431	603-352-4000	358-1173
TF: 800-258-5310 ■ *Web:* www.msagroup.com					
Manuel Lujan Insurance Inc 4801 Indian School Rd NE	Albuquerque	NM	87110	505-266-7771	255-8140
TF: 888-652-7771 ■ *Web:* newmexico.hubinternational.com/					
MAPFRE USA Corp 211 Main St	Webster	MA	01570	800-922-8276	
TF: 800-922-8276 ■ *Web:* www.commerceinsurance.com					
Markel Specialty Commercial 4600 Cox Rd	Glen Allen	VA	23060	800-416-4364	527-7915*
**Fax Area Code:* 804 ■ *TF:* 800-416-4364 ■ *Web:* www.markelinsurance.com					
Mercer Insurance Group Inc 10 N Hwy 31 PO Box 278	Pennington	NJ	08534	609-737-0426	737-8719
TF: 800-223-0534 ■ *Web:* www.unitedfiregroup.com					
Merchants Insurance Group 250 Main St	Buffalo	NY	14202	716-849-3333	849-3246
TF: 800-462-1077 ■ *Web:* merchantsgroup.com					
Mercury Casualty Co 555 W Imperial Hwy	Brea	CA	92821	714-671-6600	857-7116*
**Fax Area Code:* 323 ■ **Fax:* Hum Res ■ *Web:* mercuryinsurance.com					
Mercury Insurance Co 555 W Imperial Hwy	Brea	CA	92821	714-671-6600	857-7116*
**Fax Area Code:* 323 ■ **Fax:* Hum Res					
Mercury Insurance Group 4484 Wilshire Blvd	Los Angeles	CA	90010	323-937-1060	857-7116
NYSE: MCY ■ *TF:* 800-956-3728 ■ *Web:* www.mercuryinsurance.com					
Michigan Millers Mutual Insurance Co 2425 E Grand River Ave PO Box 30060	Lansing	MI	48912	800-888-1914	
TF: 800-888-1914 ■ *Web:* www.mimillers.com					
Mid-Continent Group 1437 S Boulder Ave W PO Box 1409	Tulsa	OK	74119	918-587-7221	588-1293*
**Fax:* Hum Res ■ *TF:* 800-722-4994 ■ *Web:* www.mcg-ins.com					
Middlesex Mutual Assurance Co 213 Ct St PO Box 891	Middletown	CT	06457	800-622-3780	
TF: 800-622-3780 ■ *Web:* www.middleoak.com					
Midwest Employers Casualty Co 14755 N Outer 40 Dr Ste 300	Chesterfield	MO	63017	636-449-7000	449-7199
TF: 877-975-2667 ■ *Web:* www.mwecc.com					
Millers First Insurance Co 111 E Fourth St	Alton	IL	62002	618-463-3636	811-8305*
**Fax Area Code:* 888 ■ **Fax:* Cust Svc ■ *TF:* 800-558-0500 ■ *Web:* www.millersfirst.com					
Montgomery Mutual Insurance Co 13830 Ballantyne Corporate Pl Ste 300	Charlotte	NC	28277	704-759-7661	544-2971*
**Fax:* Hum Res ■ *TF:* 800-561-0178 ■ *Web:* www.montgomery-ins.com					
Motorists Mutual Insurance Co 471 E Broad St	Columbus	OH	43215	614-225-8211	225-1889*
**Fax Area Code:* 866 ■ *Web:* www.motoristsmutual.com					
Mutual of Enumclaw Insurance Co 1460 Wells St	Enumclaw	WA	98022	360-825-2591	825-6885
TF: 800-366-5551 ■ *Web:* www.mutualofenumclaw.com					
National Farmers Union Property & Casualty Co 5619 DTC Pkwy Ste 300	Greenwood Village	CO	80111	303-337-5500	338-2211
TF: 800-347-1961 ■ *Web:* www.farmersunioninsurance.com					
National Fire & Marine Insurance Co 3024 Harney St	Omaha	NE	68131	402-536-3000	916-3030
TF: 866-720-7861 ■ *Web:* www.nationalindemnity.com					
National Grange Mutual Insurance Co 55 W St	Keene	NH	03431	603-352-4000	358-1173
TF: 800-258-5310 ■ *Web:* msagroup.com					
National Indemnity Co 3024 Harney St	Omaha	NE	68131	402-536-3000	536-3030
Web: www.nationalindemnity.com					
National Interstate Corp 3250 I- Dr	Richfield	OH	44286	330-659-8900	659-8901
NASDAQ: NATL ■ *TF:* 800-929-1500 ■ *Web:* www.nationalinterstate.com					
Nationwide Mutual Fire Insurance Co 1 Nationwide Plaza	Columbus	OH	43215	614-249-7111	249-9071
TF: 877-669-6877 ■ *Web:* www.nationwide.com					
Nationwide Mutual Insurance Co 1 Nationwide Plaza	Columbus	OH	43215	614-249-7111	249-7705*
**Fax:* Cust Svc ■ *TF:* 877-669-6877 ■ *Web:* www.nationwide.com					
Nautilus Insurance Group LLC 7233 E Butherus Dr	Scottsdale	AZ	85260	480-951-0905	951-9730
TF: 800-842-8972 ■ *Web:* www.nautilusagents.com					
Navigator's Management Company Inc One Penn Plz	New York	NY	10119	212-244-2333	244-4077
Web: www.navg.com					
New Era Life Insurance Co PO Box 4884	Houston	TX	77210	800-552-7879	386-7286*
**Fax Area Code:* 281 ■ *TF:* 800-552-7879 ■ *Web:* www.neweralife.com					
New Jersey Manufacturers Insurance Co 301 Sullivan Way	West Trenton	NJ	08628	609-883-1300	882-3457
TF: 800-232-6600 ■ *Web:* www.njm.com					
New Mexico Mutual Casualty Co PO Box 27825	Albuquerque	NM	87125	505-345-7260	345-0816
TF: 800-788-8851 ■ *Web:* www.nmmcc.com					
New York Central Mutual Fire Insurance Co (NYCM) 1899 Central Plz E	Edmeston	NY	13335	800-234-6926	965-2712*
**Fax Area Code:* 607 ■ *TF:* 800-234-6926 ■ *Web:* www.nycm.com					
North American Specialty Insurance Co 650 Elm St Ste 600	Manchester	NH	03101	603-644-6600	644-6613
TF: 800-542-9200 ■ *Web:* swissre.com					
North Carolina Farm Bureau Mutual Insurance Co (NCFBMIC) PO Box 27427	Raleigh	NC	27611	919-782-1705	783-3593
Web: www.ncfbins.com					
Northern Security Insurance Co PO Box 188	Montpelier	VT	05601	802-223-2341	229-7646
TF: 800-451-5000 ■ *Web:* www.vermontmutual.com					
Northland Insurance Co 385 Washington St	Saint Paul	MN	55102	800-237-9334	310-4949*
**Fax Area Code:* 651 ■ *TF:* 800-237-9334 ■ *Web:* www.northlandins.com					

Phone Fax

Northwestern Pacific Indemnity Co
15 Mtn View Rd ... Warren NJ 07059 908-903-2000 903-2027
TF Claims: 800-252-4670 ■ *Web:* www.chubb.com

Odyssey Re Holdings Corp
300 First Stamford Pl ... Stamford CT 06902 203-977-8000 356-0196
TF: 866-745-4440 ■ *Web:* www.odysseyre.com

Ohio Casualty Insurance Co 9450 SewaRd Rd ... Fairfield OH 45014 513-603-2400 867-3840
TF: 800-843-6446 ■ *Web:* ohiocasualty-ins.com

Ohio Indemnity Co 250 E Broad St 7th Fl ... Columbus OH 43215 614-228-2800 228-5552
TF: 800-628-8581 ■ *Web:* www.ohioindemnity.com

Oklahoma Farm Bureau Mutual Insurance Co (OFB)
2501 N Stiles Ave ... Oklahoma City OK 73105 405-523-2300 523-2362
Web: www.okfarmbureau.org

Old Dominion Insurance Co
4601 Touchton Rd E Ste 330 Ste 3400 ... Jacksonville FL 32246 904-642-3000
TF: 800-226-0875 ■ *Web:* msagroup.com

Old Republic Insurance Co 133 Oakland Ave. ... Greensburg PA 15601 724-834-5000 834-4025
Web: orinsco.com

Old Republic International Corp
307 N Michigan Ave ... Chicago IL 60601 312-346-8100
Web: oldrepublic.com

OneBeacon Insurance Group
601 Carlson Pkwy Ste 600 ... Minnetonka MN 55305 781-332-7000 332-7904
TF: 877-434-3900 ■ *Web:* onebeacon.com

Oregon Mutual Insurance Co PO Box 808 ... McMinnville OR 97128 503-472-2141 565-3846
TF: 800-888-2141 ■ *Web:* www.ormutual.com

Pacific Specialty Insurance Co
3601 Haven Ave ... Menlo Park CA 94025 800-962-1172 780-4820*
**Fax Area Code:* 650 ■ *TF:* 800-962-1172 ■ *Web:* www.pacificspecialty.com

Peerless Insurance Co 62 Maple Ave ... Keene NH 03431 603-352-3221 422-7900
TF: 800-542-5385 ■ *Web:* www.peerless-ins.com

Pekin Insurance (FAIA) 2505 Ct St ... Pekin IL 61558 309-346-1161 346-1589
TF: 800-322-0160 ■ *Web:* pekininsurance.com

Penn Millers Insurance Co
72 N Franklin St PO Box P ... Wilkes-Barre PA 18773 800-233-8347 822-2165*
**Fax Area Code:* 570 ■ *TF:* 800-233-8347 ■ *Web:* www.aceagribusiness.com

Penn National Insurance Co
2 N Second St PO Box 2361 ... Harrisburg PA 17101 717-234-4941 255-6850
TF: 800-388-4764 ■ *Web:* www.pennnationalinsurance.com

Penn-America Insurance Co Three Bala Plz. ... Bala Cynwyd PA 19004 215-443-3600 660-8885*
**Fax Area Code:* 610 ■ *Web:* www.penn-america.com

Pennsylvania Manufacturers Assn Co
380 Sentry Pkwy ... Blue Bell PA 19422 800-222-2749
TF: 800-222-2749 ■ *Web:* pmacompanies.com

Pharmacists Mutual Insurance Co
808 Hwy 18 W PO Box 370 ... Algona IA 50511 800-247-5930 295-9306*
**Fax Area Code:* 515 ■ *TF General:* 800-247-5930 ■ *Web:* www.phmic.com/Default.aspx

Philadelphia Consolidated Holding Corp
231 Saint Asaph's Rd Ste 100 ... Bala Cynwyd PA 19004 610-617-7900 617-7940
TF: 888-647-8639 ■ *Web:* www.phly.com

Philadelphia Contributionship Insurance Co
212 S Fourth St ... Philadelphia PA 19106 215-627-1752 765-4611*
**Fax Area Code:* 267 ■ *TF Cust Svc:* 888-627-1752 ■ *Web:* www.contributionship.com

Pinnacol Assurance 7501 E Lowry Blvd ... Denver CO 80230 303-361-4000 361-5000
TF: 800-873-7242 ■ *Web:* www.pinnacol.com

Preferred Employers Group Inc
10800 Biscayne Blvd ... Miami FL 33161 305-899-0404

Preferred Employers Insurance Co
PO Box 85478 ... San Diego CA 92186 866-472-9602 688-3913*
**Fax Area Code:* 619 ■ *TF Cust Svc:* 888-472-9001 ■ *Web:* www.preferredworkcomp.com

Preferred Mutual Insurance Co
One Preferred Way ... New Berlin NY 13411 607-847-6161 847-8046*
**Fax:* Mail Rm ■ *TF:* 800-333-7642 ■ *Web:* www.preferredmutual.com

Princeton Excess & Surplus Lines Insurance Co
555 College Rd E ... Princeton NJ 08543 609-243-4200 243-4257
TF: 800-544-2378 ■ *Web:* ambest.com

Princeton Insurance Co
746 Alexander Rd PO Box 5322 ... Princeton NJ 08540 609-452-9404 734-8461
TF: 800-334-0588 ■ *Web:* www.princetoninsurance.com

Progressive Casualty Insurance Co
6300 Wilson Mills Rd Campus E ... Mayfield Village OH 44143 440-461-5000 446-4092
TF: 800-776-4737 ■ *Web:* progressive.com/

Providence Mutual Fire Insurance Co
340 E Ave ... Warwick RI 02886 401-827-1800 822-1872
TF: 877-763-1800 ■ *Web:* www.providencemutual.com

Prudential Financial Inc 751 Broad St ... Newark NJ 07102 973-802-6000 367-6476
NYSE: PRU ■ *TF:* 800-843-7625 ■ *Web:* www.prudential.com

QBE Holdings Inc Wall St Plz 88 Pine St ... New York NY 10005 212-422-1212 422-1313
TF: 800-456-1626 ■ *Web:* qbena.com

QBE Reinsurance Corp
88 Pine St Wall St Plz 16th Fl ... New York NY 10005 212-422-1212 422-1313
Web: qbena.com/

Quincy Mutual Fire Insurance Co
57 Washington St ... Quincy MA 02169 800-899-1116 899-7790
TF: 800-899-1116 ■ *Web:* www.quincymutual.com

Republic Western Insurance Co
2721 N Central Ave ... Phoenix AZ 85004 800-528-7134 745-6439*
**Fax Area Code:* 602 ■ *TF Claims:* 800-528-7134 ■ *Web:* www.repwest.com

RLI Insurance Co 9025 N Lindbergh Dr ... Peoria IL 61615 309-692-1000 692-1068
TF: 800-331-4929 ■ *Web:* www.rlicorp.com

Royal & SunAlliance Insurance Co of Canada (RSA)
18 York Street Suite 800 ... Toronto ON M5J2T8 416-366-7511 367-9869
TF: 800-268-8406 ■ *Web:* www.rsagroup.ca

RTW Inc
8500 Normandale Lk Blvd Ste 1400
PO Box 390327 ... Bloomington MN 55437 952-893-0403 893-3700
TF Sales: 800-789-2242 ■ *Web:* www.rtwi.com

Rural Mutual Insurance Company Inc
1241 John Q Hammons Dr PO Box 5555 ... Madison WI 53705 608-836-5525 828-5582
TF: 800-362-7881 ■ *Web:* www.ruralins.com

Safe Auto Insurance Co
Four Easton Oval PO Box 182109 ... Columbus OH 43219 614-231-0200
TF: 800-723-3288 ■ *Web:* www.safeauto.com

Phone Fax

Safeco Insurance Co of America
1001 Fourth Ave ... Seattle WA 98154 206-545-5000 *
**Fax:* Hum Res ■ *Web:* www.safeco.com

Safety Insurance Group Inc 20 Custom House St ... Boston MA 02110 617-951-0600
NASDAQ: SAFT ■ *Web:* safetyinsurance.com

Safeway Insurance Group 790 Pasquinelli Dr ... Westmont IL 60559 630-887-8300 887-9886*
**Fax:* Hum Res ■ *TF:* 800-273-0300 ■ *Web:* www.safewayinsurance.com

Sagamore Insurance Co
111 Congressional Blvd Ste 500 ... Carmel IN 46032 800-317-9402 348-3671
TF: 800-317-9402 ■ *Web:* www.sagamoreinsurance.com

Savers Property & Casualty Insurance Co
26255 American Dr ... Southfield MI 48034 248-204-8299 358-1614
TF: 800-482-2726 ■ *Web:* www.meadowbrookinsgrp.com/savers.html

Scottsdale Insurance Co
8877 N Gainey Ctr Dr ... Scottsdale AZ 85258 480-365-4000 483-6752
TF: 800-423-7675 ■ *Web:* www.scottsdaleins.com

Secura Insurance Cos PO Box 819 ... Appleton WI 54912 920-739-3161 739-6795
TF: 800-558-3405 ■ *Web:* www.secura.net

Selective Insurance Company of America
40 Wantage Ave ... Branchville NJ 07890 973-948-3000 948-0292*
**Fax:* Hum Res ■ *TF:* 800-777-9656 ■ *Web:* www.selective.com

Seneca Insurance Company Inc
160 Water St 16th Fl ... New York NY 10038 212-344-3000 344-4545
Web: www.senecainsurance.com

Sentry Insurance A Mutual Co
1800 N Pt Dr ... Stevens Point WI 54481 715-346-6000
Web: www.sentry.com

Sentry Insurance Co 2 Technology Park Dr ... Westford MA 01886 978-392-7119 999-4642*
**Fax Area Code:* 800 ■ *TF:* 800-373-6879 ■ *Web:* Www.sentry.com

Sompo Japan Insurance Co of America
777 Third Ave 28th Fl ... New York NY 10017 212-416-1200 416-1205
TF: 800-208-3614 ■ *Web:* www.sompous.com

Southern Farm Bureau Casualty Insurance Co
1800 E County Line Rd Ste 400 ... Ridgeland MS 39157 601-957-7777 957-4329
TF: 800-272-7977 ■ *Web:* www.sfbcic.com

SS Nesbitt & Co Inc 3500 Blue Lake Dr ... Birmingham AL 35243 205-262-2700 262-2701
TF: 800-422-3223 ■ *Web:* www.ssnesbitt.com

Star Insurance Co 26255 American Dr ... Southfield MI 48034 248-204-8299 358-1614
TF: 800-482-2726 ■ *Web:* www.meadowbrook.com/star.html

State Auto Insurance Cos 518 E Broad St ... Columbus OH 43215 614-464-5000
Web: www.state-auto-ins.com

State Auto National Insurance Co
518 E Broad St ... Columbus OH 43215 614-464-5000 464-5341*
**Fax:* Hum Res ■ *TF:* 800-444-9950 ■ *Web:* www.stateauto.com

State Auto Property & Casualty Insurance Co
518 E Broad St ... Columbus OH 43215 614-464-5000 719-0866*
**Fax:* Hum Res ■ *TF:* 800-444-9950 ■ *Web:* www.stateauto.com

State Automobile Mutual Insurance Co
518 E Broad St ... Columbus OH 43215 614-464-5000 464-5374*
**Fax:* Hum Res ■ *TF:* 800-444-9950 ■ *Web:* www.stateauto.com

State Compensation Insurance Fund
1275 Market St ... San Francisco CA 94103 415-565-1234 565-3127
TF: 866-721-3498 ■ *Web:* www.statefundca.com

State Farm Fire & Casualty Co
One State Farm Plz ... Bloomington IL 61710 309-766-2311
Web: statefarm.com

State Farm General Insurance Co
One State Farm Plz ... Bloomington IL 61710 309-766-2311
Web: www.statefarm.com

State Farm Indemnity Co
One State Farm Plz ... Bloomington IL 61710 309-766-2311 763-8777*
**Fax:* Mktg ■ *Web:* statefarm.com

State Farm Mutual Automobile Insurance Co
One State Farm Plz ... Bloomington IL 61710 309-766-2311
Web: www.statefarm.com

STOPS Inc 8855 Grissom Pkwy ... Titusville FL 32780 321-383-4111 632-2161*
**Fax Area Code:* 866 ■ *TF:* 866-632-2161 ■ *Web:* www.onecallcm.com

Stratford Insurance Co
400 Parson's Pond Dr ... Franklin Lakes NJ 07417 201-847-8600 847-1010
Web: www.westernworld.com

Swiss Re America Corp 175 King St ... Armonk NY 10504 914-828-8000 828-7000
Web: www.swissre.com

Texas Mutual Insurance Co 6210 E Hwy 290 ... Austin TX 78723 512-224-3800 224-3889
TF: 888-532-5246 ■ *Web:* www.texasmutual.com

Toa Reinsurance Company of America
177 Madison Ave PO Box 1930 ... Morristown NJ 07962 973-898-9480 898-9495
Web: www.toare.com

Tokio Marine Life 230 Pk Ave ... New York NY 10169 212-297-6600 297-6062
TF: 800-628-2796 ■ *Web:* www.tokiomarine.us

Topa Insurance Corp
1800 Ave of the Stars ... Los Angeles CA 90067 310-201-0451 843-9409
TF: 800-949-6505 ■ *Web:* www.topains.com

Tower Group Inc 120 Broadway 14th Fl ... New York NY 10271 212-655-2000 655-2199
NASDAQ: TWGP ■ *TF:* 877-883-6599 ■ *Web:* www.twrgrp.com

Transatlantic Reinsurance Co 80 Pine St ... New York NY 10005 212-365-2200 785-7230
Web: www.transre.com

Transcontinental Insurance Co
333 S Wabash Ave CNA Ctr ... Chicago IL 60604 312-822-5000 822-6419
TF: 800-437-8854 ■ *Web:* www.cna.com

Transportation Insurance Co 333 S Wabash Ave. ... Chicago IL 60604 312-822-5000 822-6419
TF: 800-437-8854 ■ *Web:* www.cna.com

ULLICO Casualty Co 1625 I St NW ... Washington DC 20006 800-431-5425 682-4911*
**Fax Area Code:* 202 ■ *TF:* 800-431-5425 ■ *Web:* www.ullico.com

Unico American Corp
23251 Mulholland Dr ... Woodland Hills CA 91364 818-591-9800
TF: 800-669-9800 ■ *Web:* www.crusaderinsurance.com

Union National Life Insurance
3636 S Sherwood Forest Blvd ... Baton Rouge LA 70816 225-291-0585

Union Standard Insurance Co
122 W Carpenter Fwy Ste 350 ... Irving TX 75039 972-719-2400 719-2401
TF: 800-444-0049 ■ *Web:* www.usic.com

				Phone	Fax
United Fire & Casualty Co 118 Second Ave SE *NASDAQ: UFCS* ■ *TF:* 800-332-7977 ■ *Web:* www.unitedfiregroup.com	Cedar Rapids	IA	52407	319-399-5700	399-5499
United Heartland Inc PO Box 3026 **Fax Area Code:* 262 ■ *TF:* 866-206-5851 ■ *Web:* www.unitedheartland.biz	Milwaukee	WI	53201	866-206-5851	787-7701*
United National Group Three Bala Plz E Ste 300 *TF:* 800-333-0352 ■ *Web:* www.unitednat.com	Bala Cynwyd	PA	19004	610-664-1500	660-8882
United National Insurance Co Three Bala Plz E Ste 300 *TF:* 800-333-0352 ■ *Web:* www.unitednat.com	Bala Cynwyd	PA	19004	610-664-1500	660-8882
Universal Insurance Holding Inc (UIH) 1110 W Commerical Blvd Ste 100 *NYSE: UVE* ■ **Fax Area Code:* 954 ■ *Web:* www.universalinsuranceholdings.com	Fort Lauderdale	FL	33309	800-509-5586	958-1201*
USA Workers' Injury Network 1250 S Capital of Texas Hwy Bldg 3 Ste 500 **Fax Area Code:* 512 ■ *TF Cust Svc:* 800-872-0020 ■ *Web:* www.usamco.com	Austin	TX	78746	800-872-0020	328-6785*
USAA Property & Casualty Insurance Group 9800 Fredericksburg Rd **Fax Area Code:* 800 ■ *TF:* 800-531-8722 ■ *Web:* www.usaa.com/inet/pages/newsroom_factsheets_pnc	San Antonio	TX	78288	210-531-8722	531-8877*
Utica First Insurance Co 5981 Airport Rd *TF:* 800-456-4556 ■ *Web:* www.uticafirst.com	Oriskany	NY	13424	315-736-8211	768-4408
Utica National Insurance Group 180 Genesee St *TF:* 800-274-1914 ■ *Web:* www.uticanational.com	New Hartford	NY	13413	315-734-2000	734-2680
Vermont Mutual Insurance Co 89 State St PO Box 188 *TF:* 800-451-5000 ■ *Web:* www.vermontmutual.com	Montpelier	VT	05601	802-223-2341	229-7670
Victoria Insurance 22901 Millcreek Blvd **Fax Area Code:* 440 ■ *TF:* 800-888-8424 ■ *Web:* www.victoriainsurance.com	Cleveland	OH	44122	216-896-6990	461-0958*
Vigilant Insurance Co 15 Mtn View Rd *TF Claims:* 800-252-4670 ■ *Web:* www.chubb.com	Warren	NJ	07059	908-903-2000	903-2027
Wawanesa Insurance 900-191 Broadway **Fax Area Code:* 204 ■ *Web:* www.wawanesa.com	Winnipeg	MB	R3C3P1	858-874-5300	942-7724*
West Bend Mutual Insurance Co 1900 S 18th Ave *TF:* 800-236-5010 ■ *Web:* www.thesilverlining.com	West Bend	WI	53095	262-334-5571	334-9109
Western National Mutual Insurance Co 5350 W 78th St **Fax:* Hum Res ■ *TF:* 800-862-6070 ■ *Web:* www.wnins.com	Edina	MN	55439	952-835-5350	921-3159*
Western Reserve Group, The 1685 Cleveland Rd **Fax:* Hum Res ■ *TF:* 800-362-0426 ■ *Web:* www.wrg-ins.com	Wooster	OH	44691	330-262-9060	262-3259*
Windham Injury Management Group Inc 500 N Comercial St Ste 301 **Fax Area Code:* 866 ■ *Web:* www.windhamgroup.com	Manchester	NH	03101	603-626-5789	404-0557*
Wisconsin Reinsurance Corp 2810 City View Dr *TF:* 800-939-9473 ■ *Web:* www.thewrcgroup.com	Madison	WI	53707	608-242-4500	242-4514
Zenith Insurance Co PO Box 9055 **Fax Area Code:* 877 ■ *TF:* 800-440-5020 ■ *Web:* www.thezenith.com	Van Nuys	CA	91409	818-713-1000	280-4701*
Zenithstar Insurance Co *Zenith Insurance Co* 1101 Capital of Texas Hwy S Bldg J PO Box 163510 *TF:* 800-841-3987 ■ *Web:* www.thezenith.com	Austin	TX	78746	512-306-1700	327-6497

394-5 Surety Insurance

				Phone	Fax
ACMAT Corp 233 Main St *OTC: ACMT* ■ *Web:* www.acmatcorp.com	New Britain	CT	06051	860-229-9000	
Acstar Insurance Co 233 Main St *Web:* www.acstarins.com	New Britain	CT	06051	860-224-2000	
AMBAC Assurance Corp 1 State St Plaza 15th Fl *TF:* 800-221-1854 ■ *Web:* www.ambac.com	New York	NY	10004	212-658-7470	208-3414
American Public Life Insurance Co 2305 Lakeland Dr PO Box 925 *TF:* 800-256-8606 ■ *Web:* ampublic.com	Jackson	MS	39205	601-936-6600	936-2157
Assurant Solutions 260 I- N Cir SE *Web:* www.assurantsolutions.com	Atlanta	GA	30339	770-763-1000	859-4403
Assured Guaranty Corp 31 W 52nd St *Web:* www.assuredguaranty.com	New York	NY	10019	212-974-0100	581-3268
Balboa Life & Casualty Insurance Co 3349 Michelson Dr Ste 200	Irvine	CA	92612	949-222-8000	222-8716
Bond Pro LLC 1501 E Second Ave *TF:* 888-789-4985 ■ *Web:* www.cumberlandtech.com	Tampa	FL	33605	888-789-4985	
Catholic Mutual Group 10843 Old Mill Rd *TF:* 800-228-6108 ■ *Web:* www.catholicmutual.org	Omaha	NE	68154	402-551-8765	551-2943
Central Insurance Cos 800 S Washington St **Fax:* Claims ■ *TF:* 800-736-7000 ■ *Web:* www.central-insurance.com	Van Wert	OH	45891	419-238-1010	238-7626*
Central States Indemnity Company of Omaha (CSI) 1212 N 96th St *Web:* www.csi-omaha.com	Omaha	NE	68114	402-997-8000	
Century Insurance Group 465 Cleveland Ave **Fax Area Code:* 800 ■ *TF:* 877-855-8462 ■ *Web:* www.meadowbrook.com	Westerville	OH	43082	614-895-2000	832-8793*
Chubb Specialty Insurance 82 Hopmeadow St *TF:* 800-252-4670 ■ *Web:* www.chubb.com	Simsbury	CT	06070	860-408-2000	408-2002
Cincinnati Casualty Co 6200 S Gilmore Rd	Fairfield	OH	45014	513-870-2000	870-2911
CNA Surety Corp 333 S Wabash Ave *NYSE: L* ■ *TF:* 877-672-6115 ■ *Web:* www.cnasurety.com	Chicago	IL	60604	312-822-5000	
Connecticut Medical Insurance Co (CMIC) 80 Glastonbury Blvd Third Fl	Glastonbury	CT	06033	860-633-7788	633-8237
Copic Insurance Co 7351 Lowry Blvd *TF:* 800-421-1834 ■ *Web:* www.callcopic.com/cic	Denver	CO	80230	720-858-6000	858-6001
Dentists Insurance Co 1201 K St 17th Fl **Fax Area Code:* 916 ■ *TF:* 800-733-0634 ■ *Web:* www.thedentists.com	Sacramento	CA	95814	800-733-0634	498-6162*
Doctors' Co, The 185 Greenwood Rd **Fax Area Code:* 707 ■ *TF:* 800-421-2368 ■ *Web:* www.thedoctors.com	Napa	CA	94558	800-421-2368	226-0165*
Euler Hermes ACI 800 Red Brook Blvd Fourth Fl *TF:* 877-883-3224 ■ *Web:* eulerhermes.us	Owings Mills	MD	21117	410-753-0753	554-0883
Everest Reinsurance Co 477 Martinsville Rd *TF:* 800-269-6660 ■ *Web:* www.everestregroup.com	Liberty Corner	NJ	07938	908-604-3000	604-3322
Federated Mutual Insurance Co 121 E Pk Sq PO Box 328 *TF:* 800-533-0472 ■ *Web:* federatedinsurance.com	Owatonna	MN	55060	507-455-5200	
Financial Guaranty Insurance Co 125 Pk Ave Sixth Fl *TF:* 800-352-0001 ■ *Web:* www.fgic.com	New York	NY	10017	212-312-3000	312-3231
Fireman's Fund Insurance Co 777 San Marin Dr **Fax Area Code:* 888 ■ **Fax:* Mail Rm ■ *TF:* 866-386-3932 ■ *Web:* www.firemansfund.com	Novato	CA	94998	800-558-1606	323-6450*
First Insurance Company of Hawaii Ltd 1100 Ward Ave PO Box 2866 *TF:* 800-272-5202 ■ *Web:* www.ficoh.com	Honolulu	HI	96803	808-527-7777	527-3200
Great American Insurance Co 580 Walnut St *Web:* www.greatamericaninsurancegroup.com	Cincinnati	OH	45202	513-369-5000	
Hartford Underwriters Insurance Co One Hartford Plz *Web:* www.thehartford.com	Hartford	CT	06115	860-547-5000	
Heritage Insurance Managers Inc 922 Isom Rd	San Antonio	TX	78216	210-829-7467	
Illinois State Medical Inter-Insurance Exchange (ISMIE) 20 N Michigan Ave Ste 700 *TF:* 800-782-4767 ■ *Web:* www.ismie.com	Chicago	IL	60602	312-782-2749	782-2023
Indemnity Company of California 17780 Fitch Ste 200 *TF:* 800-782-1546 ■ *Web:* www.inscodico.com	Irvine	CA	92614	949-263-3300	553-8149
Insco Dico Group 17780 Fitch Ste 200 *TF:* 800-782-1546 ■ *Web:* www.inscodico.com	Irvine	CA	92614	949-263-3300	
Insurance Company of the West 11455 El Camino Real *TF:* 800-877-1111 ■ *Web:* www.icwgroup.com	San Diego	CA	92130	858-350-2400	350-2616
International Fidelity Insurance Co (IFIC) One Newark Ctr 20th Fl *TF:* 800-333-4167 ■ *Web:* www.ific.com	Newark	NJ	07102	973-624-7200	643-7116
JP Everhart & Co 1840 N Greenville Ave Ste 178 **Fax Area Code:* 972 ■ *TF:* 888-622-8575 ■ *Web:* txnotaryapplication.com	Richardson	TX	75081	888-622-8575	808-9012*
Kansas Bankers Surety Co 1220 SW Executive Dr	Topeka	KS	66615	785-228-0000	228-0079
Kansas Medical Mutual Insurance Co (KaMMCO) 623 SW Tenth Ave Ste 200 *TF:* 800-232-2259 ■ *Web:* www.kammco.com	Topeka	KS	66612	785-232-2224	232-4704
Lexington Insurance Company Inc 99 High St Fl 23 *Web:* www.lexingtoninsurance.com	Boston	MA	02110	617-330-1100	
Life of the South Insurance Co 10151 Deerwood Pk Blvd Bldg 100 *TF:* 800-888-2738 ■ *Web:* www.life-south.com	Jacksonville	FL	32256	904-350-9660	354-4525
Louisiana Medical Mutual Insurance Co 1 Galleria Blvd Ste 700 **Fax Area Code:* 504 ■ *TF:* 800-452-2120 ■ *Web:* www.lammico.com	Metairie	LA	70001	800-452-2120	841-5300*
MBIA Insurance Corp 113 King St *TF:* 800-765-6242 ■ *Web:* www.mbia.com	Armonk	NY	10504	914-273-4545	765-3163
Media/Professional Insurance Inc 1201 Walnut Ste 1800 *TF:* 866-282-0565 ■ *Web:* www.axiscapital.com	Kansas City	MO	64106	816-471-6118	471-6119
Medical Assurance Inc 100 Brookwood Pl Ste 300 *TF Cust Svc:* 800-282-6242 ■ *Web:* www.proassurance.com	Birmingham	AL	35209	205-877-4400	802-4799
Medical Mutual Group 700 Spring Forest Rd *TF:* 800-662-7917 ■ *Web:* www.medicalmutualgroup.com	Raleigh	NC	27609	919-872-7117	878-7550
Medical Mutual Insurance Company of Maine One City Ctr Ste 9 *TF:* 800-942-2791 ■ *Web:* www.medicalmutual.com	Portland	ME	04101	207-775-2791	775-6576
Medical Mutual Liability Insurance Society of Maryland 225 International Cir PO Box 8016 *TF:* 800-492-0193 ■ *Web:* www.medicalmutualofmd.com	Hunt Valley	MD	21030	410-785-0050	785-2631
Medical Protective Co 5814 Reed Rd **Fax Area Code:* 800 ■ *TF:* 800-463-3776 ■ *Web:* www.medpro.com	Fort Wayne	IN	46835	260-485-9622	398-6726*
Mortgage Guaranty Insurance Corp 270 E Kilbourn Ave *TF:* 800-558-9900 ■ *Web:* www.mgic.com	Milwaukee	WI	53202	414-347-6480	347-6696
NCMIC Insurance Co 14001 University Ave **Fax Area Code:* 800 ■ *TF:* 800-769-2000 ■ *Web:* www.ncmic.com	Clive	IA	50325	515-313-4500	996-2642*
Norcal Mutual Insurance Company Inc 560 Davis St *TF:* 800-652-1051 ■ *Web:* www.norcalmutual.com	San Francisco	CA	94111	415-397-9700	835-9817
Old Republic Insured Automotive Services Inc 8282 S Memorial Dr **Fax Area Code:* 800 ■ *TF:* 800-331-3780 ■ *Web:* www.orias.com	Tulsa	OK	74133	918-307-1000	874-9559*
Old Republic Surety 445 S Moorlands Rd Ste 200 *TF:* 800-217-1792 ■ *Web:* www.orsurety.com	Brookfield	WI	53005	262-797-2640	797-8353
Pekin Life Insurance Co 2505 Ct St *OTC: PKIN* ■ *TF:* 800-322-0160 ■ *Web:* www.pekininsurance.com	Pekin	IL	61558	309-346-1161	346-8512
Penn National Insurance Co 2 N Second St PO Box 2361 *TF:* 800-388-4764 ■ *Web:* www.pennnationalinsurance.com	Harrisburg	PA	17101	717-234-4941	255-6850
Pennsylvania Medical Society Liability Insurance Co (PMSLIC) 1700 Bent Creek Blvd PO Box 2080 *TF:* 800-445-1212 ■ *Web:* www.pmslic.com	Mechanicsburg	PA	17050	717-791-1212	796-8080
PMI Mortgage Insurance Co 3003 Oak Rd *TF:* 800-288-1970 ■ *Web:* www.pmi-us.com	Walnut Creek	CA	94597	925-658-7878	658-6931
Podiatry Insurance Company of America 3000 Meridian Blvd Ste 400 *TF:* 800-251-5727 ■ *Web:* www.picagroup.com	Franklin	TN	37067	615-984-2005	370-9021
Pre-Paid Legal Services Inc one Pre-Paid Way **Fax:* Cust Svc ■ *TF:* 800-654-7757 ■ *Web:* www.legalshield.com	Ada	OK	74820	580-436-1234	436-7565*

				Phone	Fax
Princeton Insurance Co 746 Alexander Rd PO Box 5322	Princeton	NJ	08540	609-452-9404	734-8461
TF: 800-334-0588 ■ *Web:* www.princetoninsurance.com					
ProAssurance 20 Allen Ave Ste 430	Saint Louis	MO	63119	314-961-7700	918-0530
Web: www.proassurance.com					
ProMutual Group 101 Arch St 4th Fl	Boston	MA	02110	800-225-6168	330-1748*
**Fax Area Code:* 617 ■ *TF:* 800-225-6168 ■ *Web:* www.coverys.com					
Protective Insurance Co 111 Congressional Blvd Ste 500	Carmel	IN	46032	317-636-9800	632-9444
TF: 800-644-5501 ■ *Web:* www.protectiveinsurance.com					
Radian Asset Assurance Inc *Radian Group Inc, The* 335 Madison Ave 25th Fl	New York	NY	10017	212-983-3100	682-5377
TF: 877-723-4261 ■ *Web:* www.radian.biz					
Radian Group Inc 1601 Market St	Philadelphia	PA	19103	215-564-6600	
NYSE: RDN ■ *TF:* 800-523-1988 ■ *Web:* www.radian.biz					
Reciprocal of America 4200 Innslake Dr Ste 102	Glen Allen	VA	23060	804-747-8600	270-5281
TF: 800-284-8847 ■ *Web:* www.reciprocalgroup.com					
Republic Mortgage Insurance Co 101 N Cherry St Ste 101	Winston-Salem	NC	27101	800-999-7642	661-3275*
**Fax Area Code:* 336 ■ *TF:* 800-999-7642 ■ *Web:* www.rmic.com					
RLI Insurance Co 9025 N Lindbergh Dr	Peoria	IL	61615	309-692-1000	692-1068
TF: 800-331-4929 ■ *Web:* www.rlicorp.com					
Rose & Kiernan Inc 99 Troy Rd	East Greenbush	NY	12061	518-244-4245	244-4262
TF: 866-488-6582 ■ *Web:* www.rkinsurance.com					
Securities Investors Protection Corp 805 15th St NW Ste 800	Washington	DC	20005	202-371-8300	371-6728
Web: www.sipc.org					
State Volunteer Mutual Insurance Co 101 W Pk Dr Ste 300	Brentwood	TN	37027	615-377-1999	370-1343
TF: 800-342-2239 ■ *Web:* www.svmic.com					
Surety Group Inc 3715 Northside Pkwy NW Ste 1-315	Atlanta	GA	30327	404-352-8211	351-3237
TF: 800-486-8211 ■ *Web:* www.suretygroup.com					
Texas Hospital Insurance Exchange 8310 N Capital of Texas Hwy Ste 250	Austin	TX	78731	512-451-5775	451-3101
TF: 800-792-0060 ■ *Web:* www.thie.com					
Texas Lawyers Insurance Exchange (TLIE) 900 Congress Ave Ste 500	Austin	TX	78701	512-480-9074	482-8738
TF: 800-252-9332 ■ *Web:* www.tlie.org					
Transamerica 4333 Edgewood Rd NE	Cedar Rapids	IA	52499	319-355-8511	
TF: 800-852-4678 ■ *Web:* www.transamerica.com					
Transatlantic Reinsurance Co 80 Pine St	New York	NY	10005	212-365-2200	785-7230
Web: www.transre.com					
Triad Guaranty Insurance Corp 101 S Stratford Rd	Winston-Salem	NC	27104	336-723-1282	723-2824
TF Cust Svc: 888-691-8074 ■ *Web:* www.tgic.com					
ULLICO Casualty Co 1625 I St NW	Washington	DC	20006	800-431-5425	682-4911*
**Fax Area Code:* 202 ■ *TF:* 800-431-5425 ■ *Web:* www.ullico.com					
United Guaranty Corp (UGC) 230 N Elm St	Greensboro	NC	27401	800-334-8966	230-1946*
**Fax Area Code:* 336 ■ **Fax:* Hum Res ■ *TF:* 800-334-8966 ■ *Web:* www.ugcorp.com					
United National Group Three Bala Plz E Ste 300	Bala Cynwyd	PA	19004	610-664-1500	660-8882
TF: 800-333-0352 ■ *Web:* www.unitednat.com					
Utica National Insurance Group 180 Genesee St	New Hartford	NY	13413	315-734-2000	734-2680
TF: 800-274-1914 ■ *Web:* www.uticanational.com					
Victor O Schinnerer & Co Inc 2 Wisconsin Cir Ste 200	Chevy Chase	MD	20815	301-961-9800	951-5444
TF: 888-867-9327 ■ *Web:* www.schinnerer.com					
Vision Financial Corp PO Box 506	Keene	NH	03431	800-793-0223	357-0250*
**Fax Area Code:* 603 ■ *TF:* 800-793-0223 ■ *Web:* www.visfin.com					
Warranty Group Inc, The 175 W Jackson 11th Fl	Chicago	IL	60604	312-356-3000	
TF: 800-621-2130 ■ *Web:* www.thewarrantygroup.com					
Western World Insurance Co 400 Parson's Pond Dr	Franklin Lakes	NJ	07417	201-847-8600	847-1010
TF: 888-847-8600 ■ *Web:* www.westernworld.com					
Western World Insurance Group Inc 400 Parson's Pond Dr	Franklin Lakes	NJ	07417	201-847-8600	847-1010
Web: www.westernworld.com					
XL Specialty Insurance Co 70 Seaview Ave	Stamford	CT	06902	203-964-5200	526-2092*
**Fax Area Code:* 573 ■ *TF:* 877-263-7995 ■ *Web:* insurance.mo.gov					
Zurich North America 1400 American Ln	Schaumburg	IL	60196	847-605-6000	962-2567*
**Fax Area Code:* 877 ■ **Fax:* Claims ■ *TF:* 800-382-2150 ■ *Web:* www.zurichna.com					

394-6 Title Insurance

Most title insurance companies also provide other real estate services such as escrow, flood certification, appraisals, etc.

				Phone	Fax
Advantage Title Agency Inc 201 Old Country Rd Ste 200	Melville	NY	11747	631-424-6100	
Web: www.advantagegroupny.com					
Alamo Title Insurance 9600 N Mo Pac Expy Ste 125	Austin	TX	78759	512-459-7222	459-7460
Web: austintitle.com					
AmeriPoint Title Inc 10101 Reunion Pl Ste 250	San Antonio	TX	78216	210-340-2921	
Attorney's Title Insurance Fund Inc 6545 Corporate Ctr Blvd	Orlando	FL	32822	407-240-3863	240-0750
TF: 800-336-3863 ■ *Web:* thefund.com					
Chicago Title & Trust Co 171 N Clark St	Chicago	IL	60601	312-223-2000	223-2942*
**Fax:* Hum Res ■ *TF:* 800-621-1919 ■ *Web:* www.ctic.com					
Chicago Title Company of Oregon 10135 SE Sunnyside Rd Ste 130	Clackamas	OR	97015	503-794-5860	
Web: ctoregon.com					
Commonwealth Land Title Insurance Co 601 Riverside Ave	Jacksonville	FL	32204	888-866-3684	
TF: 888-866-3684 ■ *Web:* www.cltic.com					
Community Title & Escrow Ltd 2600 State St Bldg D	Alton	IL	62002	618-466-7755	466-7782
TF: 800-854-4049 ■ *Web:* communitytitle.net					
Dakota Homestead Title Insurance Co 315 S Phillips Ave	Sioux Falls	SD	57104	605-336-0388	996-3270
TF: 800-425-0388 ■ *Web:* www.tsptitle.com					
Entitle Direct Group Inc 281 Tresser Blvd Sixth Fl	Stamford	CT	06901	203-724-1150	
TF: 877-936-8485 ■ *Web:* www.entitledirect.com					
Fidelity National Title Group Inc 601 Riverside Ave	Jacksonville	FL	32204	904-854-8100	357-1007
TF: 888-866-3684 ■ *Web:* www.fntg.com					
Fidelity National Title Insurance Co 7025 N Scottsdale Rd	Scottsdale	AZ	85258	480-344-6400	
TF: 888-934-3354 ■ *Web:* www.fntic.com					
Fidelity National Title Insurance Company of Oregon 900 SW Fifth Ave Mezzanine Level	Portland	OR	97204	503-223-8338	796-6611
TF: 888-934-3354 ■ *Web:* www.fntic.com					
First American Corp One First American Way	Santa Ana	CA	92707	714-250-3000	
NYSE: FAF ■ *TF:* 800-854-3643 ■ *Web:* www.firstam.com					
GeoVera Holdings Inc 4820 Business Ctr Dr Ste 200	Fairfield	CA	94534	707-863-3700	
Web: www.geoveraholdingsinc.com					
Gracy Title Co 524 N Lamar Blvd Ste 200	Austin	TX	78703	512-472-8421	478-6038
Web: www.gracytitle.com					
Greater Illinois Title Co 120 N La Salle St Ste 900	Chicago	IL	60602	312-236-7300	236-0284
Web: www.gitc.com					
Hanover Insurance Co 440 Lincoln St	Worcester	MA	01653	508-855-1000	855-6313
TF: 800-853-0456 ■ *Web:* www.hanover.com					
Meridian Title Corp 202 S Michigan St	South Bend	IN	46601	574-232-5845	289-1514
TF: 800-777-1574 ■ *Web:* www.meridiantitle.com					
Mississippi Valley Title Insurance Co 315 Tom Bigbee St	Jackson	MS	39201	601-969-0222	969-2215
TF: 800-647-2124 ■ *Web:* www.mvt.com					
Monroe Title Insurance Corp 47 W Main St	Rochester	NY	14614	585-232-4950	232-4988
TF: 800-966-6763 ■ *Web:* www.monroetitle.com					
North American Title Co 1855 Gateway Blvd Ste 600	Concord	CA	94520	925-935-5599	933-4851
TF: 800-566-0370 ■ *Web:* classic.nat.com					
Northpoint Escrow & Title LLC 10800 NE Eighth St Ste 200	Bellevue	WA	98004	425-453-8880	
TF: 877-678-1678 ■ *Web:* www.onenorthpoint.com					
Old Republic National Title Insurance Co (ORTIG) 400 Second Ave S	Minneapolis	MN	55401	612-371-1111	371-1191
TF: 800-328-4441 ■ *Web:* www.oldrepublictitle.com					
Orange Coast Title Company Inc 640 N Tustin Ave Ste 106	Santa Ana	CA	92705	714-558-2836	
Web: www.octitle.com					
Placer Title Co 2394 Fair Oaks Blvd	Sacramento	CA	95825	916-973-1002	482-3049
Web: www.placertitle.com					
Rattikin Title Co 201 Main St Ste 800	Fort Worth	TX	76102	817-332-1171	882-9886
Web: rattikintitle.com					
Security Mutual Insurance Co 2417 N Triphammer Rd PO Box 4620	Ithaca	NY	14852	607-257-5000	
Web: www.securitymutual.com					
Southland Title LLC 6710 Stewart Rd Ste 300	Galveston	TX	77551	409-744-0727	744-3909
Web: www.southlandtitle.net					
Stewart Information Services Corp 1980 Post Oak Blvd Ste 800	Houston	TX	77056	713-625-8100	552-9523
NYSE: STC ■ *TF:* 800-729-1900 ■ *Web:* www.stewart.com					
Stewart REI Data Inc 1980 Post Oak Blvd Ste 800	Houston	TX	77056	212-922-0050	705-9377*
**Fax Area Code:* 630 ■ *TF:* 800-729-1900 ■ *Web:* www.stewart.com					
Stewart Title & Trust of Phoenix 244 W Osborn Rd	Phoenix	AZ	85013	602-462-8000	230-6209*
**Fax:* Cust Svc ■ *Web:* www.stewartaz.com					
Stewart Title Guaranty Co 1980 Post Oak Blvd Ste 800	Houston	TX	77056	713-625-8100	552-9523
TF: 800-729-1900 ■ *Web:* www.stewart.com					
Title Guaranty of Hawaii Inc 235 Queen St	Honolulu	HI	96813	808-533-6261	521-0210
TF: 800-222-3229 ■ *Web:* www.tghawaii.com					
Title Resource Group LLC 3001 Leadenhall Rd	Mount Laurel	NJ	08054	856-914-8500	
Web: www.trgc.com					
Title Resources Guaranty Co (TRGC) 8111 LBJ Fwy Ste 1200	Dallas	TX	75251	972-644-6500	485-3630*
**Fax Area Code:* 888 ■ *TF:* 800-526-8018 ■ *Web:* www.titleresources.com					
US Recordings Inc 2925 Country Dr	Little Canada	MN	55117	651-765-6400	
TF: 877-272-5250 ■ *Web:* www.usrecordings.com					
USHEALTH Group Inc 300 Burnett St Ste 200	Fort Worth	TX	76102	800-387-9027	
TF: 800-387-9027 ■ *Web:* www.ushealthgroup.com					

394-7 Travel Insurance

Most of the companies listed here are insurance agencies and brokerages that specialize in selling travel insurance policies, rather than the insurers who underwrite the policies.

				Phone	Fax
All Aboard Benefits 6162 E Mockingird Ln Ste 104	Dallas	TX	75214	214-821-6677	821-6676
TF: 800-462-2322 ■ *Web:* www.allaboardbenefits.com					
Continental Assurance Co 333 S Wabash Ave	Chicago	IL	60604	312-822-5000	260-4376
TF: 800-251-2148 ■ *Web:* www.cna.com					
Highway To Health Inc One Radnor Corporate Ctr Ste 100	Radnor	PA	19087	888-243-2358	254-8797*
**Fax Area Code:* 610 ■ *TF:* 888-243-2358 ■ *Web:* www.hthtravelinsurance.com					
Ingle International 460 Richmond St W Ste 100	Toronto	ON	M5V1Y1	416-730-8488	730-1878
TF: 800-360-3234 ■ *Web:* ingleinternational.com/					
Insurance Consultants International 19760 Knights Crossing Ste 1C	Monument	CO	80132	719-573-9080	
TF: 800-576-2674 ■ *Web:* www.globalhealthinsurance.com					

Phone Fax

International SOS Assistance Inc
3600 Horizon Blvd Ste 300 .... Trevose PA 19053 215-244-1500 942-8299
TF: 888-413-9071 ■ *Web:* www.internationalsos.com

Lloyd's America Inc 25 W 53rd St 14th Fl .... New York NY 10019 212-382-4060 382-4070
Web: www.lloyds.com

Pan-American Life Insurance Co
601 Poydras St .... New Orleans LA 70130 877-939-4550
TF Life Ins: 877-939-4550 ■ *Web:* www.palig.com

Travel Insured International
52-S Oakland Ave PO Box 280568 .... East Hartford CT 06128 800-243-3174 528-8005*
**Fax Area Code:* 860 ■ *TF:* 800-243-3174 ■ *Web:* www.travelinsured.com

Wallach & Company Inc 107 W Federal St .... Middleburg VA 20117 540-687-3166 687-3172
TF: 800-237-6615 ■ *Web:* www.wallach.com

395 INTERCOM EQUIPMENT & SYSTEMS

Phone Fax

Anacom General Corp 1240 S Claudina St .... Anaheim CA 92805 714-774-8484 774-7388*
**Fax:* Sales ■ *TF:* 800-955-9540 ■ *Web:* www.anacom-medtek.com

Clear-Com USA 850 Marina Village Pkwy .... Alameda CA 94501 510-337-6600
Web: www.clearcom.com

Clever Devices Ltd 300 Crossways Pk Dr .... Woodbury NY 11797 516-433-6100
TF: 800-872-6129 ■ *Web:* www.cleverdevices.com

Crest Healthcare Supply 195 Third St .... Dassel MN 55325 320-275-3382 275-2306
TF: 800-328-8908 ■ *Web:* www.cresthealthcare.com

David Clark Company Inc 360 Franklin St .... Worcester MA 01615 508-751-5800 753-5827*
**Fax:* Sales ■ *TF Cust Svc:* 800-298-6235 ■ *Web:* www.davidclark.com

Lee Dan Communications Inc 155 Adams Ave .... Hauppauge NY 11788 631-231-1414 231-1498
TF: 800-231-1414 ■ *Web:* www.leedan.com

396 INTERIOR DESIGN

Phone Fax

24 Asset Management Corp
2020 Camino del Rio N Ste 900 .... San Diego CA 92108 855-414-2424
TF: 855-414-2424 ■ *Web:* www.24asset.com

A Caring Exprnce Hm Healthcare
21 Douglas Ave .... Providence RI 02908 401-453-4545
Web: www.acaringexperience.com

A-1 Crane Services Ltd 1148 Sta Main .... Grande Prairie AB T8V4B5 780-532-8212
Web: ncsg.com

A.C. Schultes of Maryland Inc
8221 Cloverleaf Dr .... Millersville MD 21108 410-841-6710
Web: www.acschultes.com

ABBYY Language Services
Three Harrowgate Dr .... Cherry Hill NJ 08003 856-782-8106
Web: abbyy-ls.com

Academy Fire Protection Inc
48-81 Maspeth Ave .... Maspeth NY 11378 347-473-7200
Web: www.academyfire.com

Accent 7171 Mercy Rd Ste 200 .... Omaha NE 68106 402-397-9920
Web: www.onlineaccent.com

Accent Display Corp 1655 Elmwood Ave Ste 9 .... Cranston RI 02910 401-461-8787
Web: www.accentdisplay.com

Accent Office Interiors Inc
2108 Gilliam Ln # 3 .... Tallahassee FL 32308 850-386-5201
Web: www.accentoffice.com

Accord Creditor Services LLC PO Box 10005 .... Newnan GA 30271 800-373-0760
TF: 800-373-0760 ■ *Web:* www.accordcreditorservices.com

AdHub LLC, The 146 Alexander St .... Rochester NY 14607 585-442-2585
Web: www.adhub.com

Advance Central Services Inc
1313 N Market St 10th Fl .... Wilmington DE 19801 302-830-9732
Web: www.newspapersupport.com

Advance Relocation & Storage Inc
195 Sweet Hollow Rd .... Old Bethpage NY 11804 212-809-1988
Web: www.theadvancegrp.com

AGR Group Inc 1540 E Warner Ave .... Santa Ana CA 92705 714-245-7151
Web: www.agrgroupinc.com

Ak-Chin Indian Community
42507 W Peters & Nall Rd .... Maricopa AZ 85238 520-568-1000
Web: www.ak-chin.nsn.us

AKA Enterprise Solutions
875 Sixth Ave 20th Fl .... New York NY 10001 212-502-3900
Web: www.akaes.com

Alan Ferguson Associates 1212 N Main St .... High Point NC 27262 336-889-3866
Web: alanferguson.com

Alberta Workers' Compensation Board
9912-107 St PO Box 2415 .... Edmonton AB T5J2S5 780-498-3999
Web: www.wcb.ab.ca

Aldinger Company Inc 1440 Prudential Dr .... Dallas TX 75235 214-638-1808
Web: www.aldingercompany.com

Allen Commercial Industries Inc
11301 Mosier Vly Rd .... Euless TX 76040 817-267-4919
Web: www.allen-commercial.com

AllStar Deals Inc 150 Fifth Ave Fourth Fl .... New York NY 10010 240-876-5388
Web: www.giftconnect.co

AM Technical Solutions Inc
2213 RR 620 N Ste 105 .... Austin TX 78734 512-266-7259
Web: www.amts.com

Ambix Manufacturing Inc 71 Hobbs St Ste 104 .... Conway NH 03818 603-452-5247
Web: www.ambixllc.com

Ansol Inc 13766 Torrey Glenn Rd .... San Diego CA 92129 858-538-0128
Web: www.ansolinc.com

Apollo Retail Specialists LLC 1234 Tech Blvd .... Tampa FL 33619 813-712-2525
Web: www.apolloretail.com

Applied Merchandising Concepts LLC
15 Beechwood Ave .... New Rochelle NY 10801 914-738-5200
Web: www.appliedmerchandising.com

Phone Fax

ArabMedicare.com PO Box 12547 .... Research Triangle Park NC 27709 919-781-5838
Web: www.arabmedicare.com

Aram A. Kaz Co, The 383 Silas Deane Hwy .... Wethersfield CT 06109 860-529-6900
Web: www.aramkaz.com

Arch Communications Inc 1327 Hampton Ave .... St. Louis MO 63139 314-645-8000
Web: archcom.net

Ark TeleServices Two E Merrick Rd .... Valley Stream NY 11580 800-898-5367
TF: 800-898-5367 ■ *Web:* www.arktele.com

ArroHealth 49 Wireless Blvd Ste 140 .... Hauppauge NY 11788 631-780-5000
Web: www.medsaveusa.com

ARS National Services Inc 201 W Grand Ave .... Escondido CA 92025 760-735-2700
Web: www.arsnational.com

Arvato Digital Services LLC
29011 Commerce Ctr Dr .... Valencia CA 91355 800-223-1478
TF: 800-223-1478 ■ *Web:* www.arvatoservices.com

Ashland Partners & Company LLP
3549 Lear Way Ste 105 .... Medford OR 97504 541-857-8800
Web: www.ashlandpartners.com

Assured Packaging Inc 6080 Vipond Dr .... Mississauga ON L5T2V4 905-565-1410
Web: www.assuredpackaging.com

Asurion Canada Inc 1222 Main St Second Fl .... Moncton NB E1C1H6 506-386-9204
Web: www.knowmoncton.com

Atelka Inc 1000 St Antoine St W Ste 500 .... Montreal QC H3C3R7 514-448-4905
Web: www.atelka.com

ATIS Elevator Inspections LLC
1976 Innerbelt Business Center .... St. Louis MO 63114 314-441-3999
Web: www.americantesting.com

ATL Inc W140 N9504 Fountain Blvd .... Menomonee Falls WI 53051 262-255-6150
Web: www.atlco.com

Atlantic Skyline
4605 Brookfield Corporate Dr .... Chantilly VA 20151 703-802-6800
Web: www.atlanticexhibits.com

Azzur Group LLC
726 Fitzwatertown Rd Ste 6 .... Willow Grove PA 19090 215-322-8322
Web: azzurgroup.com

Baltimore Development Corp
36 S Charles St Ste 1600 .... Baltimore MD 21201 410-837-9305
Web: www.baltimoredevelopment.com

Bay Area Exhibits Inc 2900 Mead Ave .... Santa Clara CA 95051 408-566-8888
Web: www.baexhibits.com

Bellwyck Packaging Inc 21 Finchdene Sq .... Toronto ON M1X1A7 416-752-1210
Web: www.bellwyck.ca

BestPass Inc 828 Washington Ave .... Albany NY 12203 518-458-1579
Web: www.bestpass.com

Beveridge Seay Inc 2000 P St Nw Ste 700 .... Washington DC 20036 202-822-3800
Web: www.bevseay.com

Bill A. Duffy International Inc
700 Ygnacio Vly Rd Ste 330 .... Walnut Creek CA 94596 925-279-1040
Web: www.bdasports.com

BizUnite 670 N Commercial St .... Manchester NH 03101 603-628-2340
Web: www.bizunite.com

BlackBridge Geomatics Corp 3528 30th St N .... Lethbridge AB T1H6Z4 403-381-2800
Web: blackbridge.com

BlueLink Marketing LLC 306 W 37th St 11th Fl .... New York NY 10018 212-730-5785
Web: www.bluelinkmarketing.com

Boardroom Events LLC 5409 Overseas Hwy #295 .... Marathon FL 33050 786-361-0454
Web: www.boardroomevents.com

Broadcast Communications Media Inc
3101 Ocean Park Blvd Ste 309 .... Santa Monica CA 90405 310-452-6585
Web: www.bcmedia.tv

Broadcast Promotions Inc 1775 Bald Hill Rd .... Warwick RI 02886 401-826-3600
Web: www.ginsuguys.com

Building Service Inc (BSI)
W222 N630 Cheaney Rd .... Waukesha WI 53186 262-955-6400
TF: 866-353-3600 ■ *Web:* www.buildingservice.com

C m Buck & Associates Inc 6850 Guion Rd .... Indianapolis IN 46268 317-293-5704
Web: www.cmbuck.com

Canada Media Fund
50 Wellington St E Fourth Fl .... Toronto ON M5E1C8 416-214-4400
Web: www.cmf-fmc.ca

Carenet Healthcare Services
11845 Interstate 10 W Ste 400 .... San Antonio TX 78230 800-809-7000
TF: 800-809-7000 ■ *Web:* www.callcarenet.com

Carr & Assoc 22964 Professional Ln .... Lebanon MO 65536 586-465-0914
Web: www.carrassessment.com

Cascade Receivables Management LLC
101 Second St Ste 100 .... Petaluma CA 94952 888-417-1531
TF: 888-417-1531 ■ *Web:* www.cascadereceivables.com

Cathedral Village 600 E Cathedral Rd .... Philadelphia PA 19128 215-487-1300
Web: www.cathedralvillage.com

Cecconi Simone Inc 1335 Dundas St W .... Toronto ON M6J1Y3 416-588-5900
Web: www.cecconisimone.com

Center Stage Productions Inc
20-10 Maple Ave .... Fair Lawn NJ 07410 973-423-5000
Web: www.cspdisplay.com

Cgs Motorsports 3227 Producer Way Ste 134 .... Pomona CA 91768 909-444-5536
Web: www.cgsmotorsports.com

ChemRite CoPac 19725 W Edgewood Dr Bldg A101 .... Lannon WI 53046 262-255-3880
Web: www.chemritecopac.com

Chickasaw Telecommunications Services Inc
Five N McCormick .... Oklahoma City OK 73127 405-694-2000
Web: stillwater.brightok.net

Choice Translating Inc Tryon Plz .... Charlotte NC 28284 704-717-0043
Web: www.choicetranslating.com

Ci Radar LLC 4046 Wetherburn Way Ste 1 .... Norcross GA 30092 678-680-2103
Web: www.ciradar.com

City of Leawood, Kansas 4800 Town Ctr Dr .... Leawood KS 66211 913-339-6700
Web: www.leawood.org

Clean Uniform Co 1316 S Seventh St .... St. Louis MO 63104 314-421-1220
Web: www.cleanuniform.com

Cleanwise Inc 1100 E Woodfield Rd Ste 200 .... Schaumburg IL 60173 877-255-5230
TF: 877-255-5230 ■ *Web:* www.cleanwise.com

Phone | Fax

CLS Lexi-tech Ltd 10 Dawson Ave . . . Moncton NB E1A6C8 506-859-5200
Web: www.cls-lexitech.ca

CMS Mid-Atlantic Inc 295 Totowa Rd. . . . Totowa NJ 07512 800-267-1981
TF: 800-267-1981 ■ *Web:* www.cmsmidatlantic.com

CO-OP Financial Services Inc
9692 Haven Ave . . . Rancho Cucamonga CA 91730 800-782-9042
TF: 800-782-9042 ■ *Web:* www.co-opfs.org

Cole Martinez Curtis & Assoc
4040 Del Rey Ave # 7 . . . Marina del Rey CA 90292 310-827-7200 822-5803
Web: www.cmcadesign.com

CollabWorks 650 El Camino Real Ste O. . . . Redwood City CA 94063 650-368-2523
Web: www.collabworks.com

Commercial Furniture Interiors Inc
1154 Rt 22 W . . . Mountainside NJ 07092 908-518-1670 654-8436
Web: www.cfioffice.com

Compadre LLC 9330 United Dr Ste 110 . . . Austin TX 78758 512-334-1000
Web: compadre.com

Competition Bureau Canada 50 Victoria St . . . Gatineau QC K1A0C9 819-997-4282
Web: www.competitionbureau.gc.ca

Convince & Convert 4463 Forest Hill Dr . . . Bloomington IN 47401 602-616-1895
Web: www.convinceandconvert.com

Coregistics 240 Northpoint Pkwy. . . . Acworth GA 30102 678-453-5900
Web: www.coregistics.com

Cosmic Cart Inc 521 Lansdowne Rd . . . Charlotte NC 28270 704-651-8534
Web: cosmiccart.com

Cova Hotel 655 Ellis St . . . San Francisco CA 94109 415-771-3000
Web: www.covahotel.com

Credigy Solutions Inc
3715 Davinci Court Ste 200 . . . Norcross GA 30092 678-728-7310
Web: www.credigy.net

CUNA Strategic Services Inc
5710 Mineral Point Rd . . . Madison WI 53705 608-231-4340
Web: www.cunastrategicservices.com

Custom Exhibits Corp
1830 N Indianwood Ave . . . Broken Arrow OK 74012 918-250-2121
Web: www.customexhibits.com

D P Brown of Saginaw Inc 2845 Universal Dr . . . Saginaw MI 48603 989-799-9400
Web: www.dpbrowntech.com

Daroff Design Inc 2121 Market St Fl 1 . . . Philadelphia PA 19103 215-636-9900
Web: www.daroffdesign.com

Dawson Design Associates Inc
315 Second Ave S 300 . . . Seattle WA 98104 206-932-3102
Web: www.dawsondesignassociates.com

Dawson School 199 N School Ave. . . . Dawson TX 76639 254-578-1416
Web: www.dawsonisd.net

DCL Corp 48641 Milmont Dr . . . Fremont CA 94538 510-651-5100
Web: www.dclcorp.com

Decorating Den Systems Inc 8659 Commerce Dr . . . Easton MD 21601 410-822-9001
TF: 800-332-3367 ■ *Web:* www.decoratingden.com

Decorative Plant Service Inc
1150 Phelps St. . . . San Francisco CA 94124 415-826-8181
Web: www.decorative.com

Dekra America Inc 3901 Roswell Rd Ste 120 . . . Marietta GA 30062 770-971-3788
Web: www.dekra-na.com

Denison Yacht Sales Inc
401 SW First Ave Ste 102. . . . Fort Lauderdale FL 33301 954-763-3971
Web: www.denisonyachtsales.com

DeNuke Services Inc
702 S Illinois Ave Ste B-203. . . . Oak Ridge TN 37830 865-483-8620
Web: www.denuke.com

Design Phase Inc 1771 S Lakeside Dr. . . . Waukegan IL 60085 847-473-0077
Web: dphase.com

DGM Services Inc 1813 Greens Rd . . . Houston TX 77032 281-821-0500
Web: www.dgm-usa.com

DirectEmployers.com
9002 N Purdue Rd Quad III Ste 100 . . . Indianapolis IN 46268 317-874-9000
Web: www.directemployers.com

Display Producers Inc 1260 Zerega Ave. . . . Bronx NY 10462 718-904-1200
Web: www.displayproducersinc.com

EAST COAST GRAPHICS 125 Wireless Blvd. . . . Hauppauge NY 11788 631-231-9300
Web: www.ecoastgraphics.com

Eclipse Design Technologies Inc
33 W Higgins Rd Ste 650. . . . South Barrington IL 60010 847-844-8822
Web: eclipsedt.com

eCollect LLC 5000 Euclid Ave Ste 303 . . . Cleveland OH 44103 888-569-6001
TF: 888-569-6001 ■ *Web:* www.ecollectohio.com

Economy Linen & Towel Service Inc 80 Mead St . . . Dayton OH 45402 937-222-4625
Web: www.economylinen.com

Eg Tax Service 2475 Niagara Falls Blvd . . . Buffalo NY 14228 716-632-7886
Web: www.egtax.com

Elyse Connolly Inc 23 W 16th St. . . . New York NY 10011 212-255-0886
Web: www.elyseconnolly.com

EML LLC 318 Seaboard Ln Ste 106 . . . Franklin TN 37067 615-771-2560
Web: www.eml1.com

Engage3 Inc 109 Stevenson St Ste 200 . . . San Francisco CA 94105 415-240-4819
Web: www.engage3.com

Erik Johnson & Assoc 758 N Larrabee Unit 415. . . . Chicago IL 60654 312-644-2202 645-5883
Web: www.erikjohnsonassociates.com

EscrowTech International Inc
3290 W Mayflower Way . . . Lehi UT 84043 801-852-8202
Web: www.escrowtech.com

eSupply Systems LLC 7800 W IH-10 Ste 130. . . . San Antonio TX 78230 210-979-6670
Web: www.esupplysystems.com

Etheridge Printing Co 4434 Mcewen Rd . . . Dallas TX 75244 214-827-8151
TF: 800-834-2709 ■ *Web:* www.etheridge.com

Eureka Lighting 225 De Li ge ouest Ste 200 . . . Montreal QC H2P1H4 514-385-3515
Web: www.eurekalighting.com

Event Solutions International Inc
1757 Larchwood Dr . . . Troy MI 48083 248-307-9400
Web: www.eventman.com

Eventa Global Inc
1420 Celebration Blvd Ste 312. . . . Celebration FL 34747 407-476-9412
Web: www.eventaglobal.com

EWIE Company Inc 1099 Highland Dr Ste D . . . Ann Arbor MI 48108 734-971-6265
Web: www.ewie.com

Express Packaging of Ohio Inc
301 Enterprise Dr. . . . Newcomerstown OH 43832 740-498-4700
Web: www.expresspackaging.net

Farm First Dairy Cooperative
4001 Nakoosa Trl Ste 100. . . . Madison WI 53714 608-244-3373
Web: www.farmfirstdairycooperative.com

FCI Lender Services Inc
8180 E Kaiser Blvd. . . . Anaheim Hills CA 92808 714-282-2424
Web: www.trustfci.com

Fifth Sun Inc 495 Ryan Ave. . . . Chico CA 95973 530-343-8725
Web: www.5sun.com

FirstPoint Inc 225 Commerce Pl. . . . Greensboro NC 27401 336-378-6300
Web: www.firstpointresources.com

Focus Services Inc 4102 South 1900 West Ste 7. . . . Roy UT 84067 888-362-8711
TF: 888-362-8711 ■ *Web:* www.focusservices.com

Fortitude Business Solutions LLC PO Box 2095. . . . Daphne AL 36526 877-577-2644
TF: 877-577-2644 ■ *Web:* www.fortitudebusiness.com

Freedom Lights Our World (FLOW) Inc
1510 Falcon Ledge Dr . . . Austin TX 78746 512-327-8860
Web: www.flowidealism.org

Fusicology LLC
2658 Griffith Park Blvd #128 . . . Los Angeles CA 90039 323-988-2424
Web: fusicology.com

Fusion Packaging Solutions Inc
3333 Welborn St - Ste 400. . . . Dallas TX 75219 214-747-2004
Web: fusionpkg.com

G2 Secure Staff LLC
400 E Las Colians Blvd Ste 750. . . . Irving TX 75039 972-915-6979
Web: www.g2securestaff.com

Gardien Services USA Inc
5289 NE Elam Young Pkwy Ste 120. . . . Hillsboro OR 97124 503-430-8980
Web: www.gardien.com

Gary Raub Assoc 4345 Murphy Canyon Rd. . . . San Diego CA 92123 858-565-2775

GCS Service Inc 370 Wabasha St N. . . . St. Paul MN 55102 800-822-2303
TF: 800-822-2303 ■ *Web:* www.equipmentcare.com

Gehring LP 24800 Drake Rd . . . Farmington Hills MI 48335 248-478-8060
Web: www.gehringlp.com

Genesis Plastics Welding Inc
720 E Broadway . . . Fortville IN 46040 317-485-7887
Web: www.genesisplasticswelding.com

GGLO LLC 1301 First Ave Ste 301. . . . Seattle WA 98101 206-467-5828
Web: www.gglo.com

Global R&D Consulting Group
555 N Point Ctr E. . . . Alpharetta GA 30022 866-770-5577
TF: 866-770-5577 ■ *Web:* www.globalr-d.com

GLP Inc 360 W Superior St. . . . Chicago IL 60654 312-640-8300
Web: www.garyleepartners.com

Goldec Hamm's Manufacturing Ltd 6760 65 Ave . . . Red Deer AB T4P1A5 403-343-6607
Web: www.goldec.com

Good Leads 395 Main St. . . . Salem NH 03079 603-870-8150
Web: www.goodleads.com

Goodwin & Associates Hospitality Services LLC
91 A N State St . . . Concord NH 03301 603-223-0303
Web: www.goodwin-associates.com

Grant & Weber Inc 26610 Agoura Rd Ste 209. . . . Calabasas CA 91302 818-871-7700
Web: www.grantweber.com

GreenSeed Contract Packaging
1025 Paramount Pkwy . . . Batavia IL 60510 630-761-8544
Web: greenseedcp.com

Groople Inc 1732 Wazee St Ste 202 . . . Denver CO 80202 817-987-9004
Web: www.groople.com

Growing Leaders Inc
270 Scientific Dr NW Ste 10. . . . Norcross GA 30092 770-495-3332
Web: www.growingleaders.com

Gumas Advertising LLC 99 Shotwell St. . . . San Francisco CA 94103 415-621-7575
Web: www.gumas.com

Gyford Productions 891 Trademark Dr . . . Reno NV 89521 775-829-7272
Web: www.standoffsystems.com

H & O Centerless Grinding Inc
45 Bathurst Dr . . . Waterloo ON N2V1N2 519-884-0322
Web: www.cylindricalprecision.com

H Chambers Co 1800 Washington Blvd Ste 111. . . . Baltimore MD 21230 410-727-4535 727-6982
Web: www.chambersusa.com

Haas Environmental Inc
Seven Red Lion Rd PO Box 2082. . . . Vincentown NJ 08088 609-859-3100
Web: www.haasenvironmental.com

Hallcon Corp 5775 Yonge St Ste 1010. . . . Toronto ON M2M4J1 416-964-9191
Web: www.hallconcorp.com

Hand Era 2859 104th St. . . . Des Moines IA 50322 515-252-7522
Web: www.handera.com

HELIOS Group Utilities & Facilities Management Inc
101 Roland-Therrien Blvd Ste 110. . . . Longueuil QC J4H4B9 450-646-1903
Web: www.helios-group.com

Hignell Printing Ltd 488 Burnell St. . . . Winnipeg MB R3G2B4 204-784-1030
Web: www.hignell.mb.ca

Hileman Enterprises LLC
2217 E Ninth St Ste 200. . . . Cleveland OH 44115 216-923-1445
Web: www.hilemangroup.com

Homeowner Protection Office
1055 W Georgia St Ste 2270 Royal Centre. . . . Vancouver BC V6E3P3 604-646-7055
Web: www.hpo.bc.ca

hovelstay.com LLC 121 W Lexington Dr . . . Glendale CA 91203 818-480-5770
Web: hovelstay.com

hss LLC 5446 Dixie Hwy. . . . Saginaw MI 48601 989-777-2983
Web: www.valuepointsolutions.com

Hubbuch & Co 324 W Main St. . . . Louisville KY 40202 502-583-2713 582-7375
Web: www.hubbuch.com

Hypertec BCDR Inc
9300 Trans Canada Hwy. . . . Saint-laurent QC H4S1K5 514-789-9442
Web: www.hypertecbcdr.com

				Phone	Fax
ICON Creative Technologies Group 202 E Huron St Ste 100	Ann Arbor	MI	48104	734-239-3586	
Web: www.iconicweb.com					
Id Group LLC, The 2641 Irving Blvd	Dallas	TX	75207	214-638-6800	
Web: www.idgroupdallas.com					
Idem Translations Inc 550 California Ave Ste 310	Palo Alto	CA	94306	650-858-4336	
Web: www.idemtranslations.com					
Imagine Advertising & Publishing Inc 6141 Crooked Creek Rd	Norcross	GA	30092	770-734-0966	
Web: www.imagineadv.com					
iMirus 7715 E 111th St Ste 100	Tulsa	OK	74133	918-492-0660	
Web: www.imirus.com					
Infinite Scale Design Group LLC 16 E Exchange Pl	Salt Lake City	UT	84111	801-363-1881	
Web: www.infinitescale.com					
InfoSend Inc 4240 E La Palma Ave	Anaheim	CA	92807	714-993-2690	
Web: www.infosend.com					
Infusion Marketing Group LLC 18 Knights Bridge Rd	Sherwood	AR	72120	501-519-1969	
Web: www.profitgenerator.com					
Innovadex LLC 7930 Santa Fe Third Fl	Overland Park	KS	66204	913-307-9010	
Web: www.ulprospector.com					
Inovar Inc 1073 West 1700 North	Logan	UT	84321	435-792-4949	
Web: www.inovar-inc.com					
Interiors by Steven G Inc 2818 Centre Port Cir	Pompano Beach	FL	33064	954-735-8223	
Web: www.interiorsbysteveng.com					
Intland GmbH 968 Inverness Way	Sunnyvale	CA	94087	866-468-5210	
TF: 866-468-5210 ■ *Web:* www.intland.com					
Invisible Hand Networks Inc 670 Broadway Ste 302	New York	NY	10012	212-400-7416	
Web: www.invisiblehand.net					
ISPN Inc 14303 W 95th St	Lenexa	KS	66215	913-859-9500	
Web: www.ispn.net					
iTOK Inc 3400 North Ashton Blvd Ste 260	Lehi	UT	84043	866-515-4865	
TF: 866-515-4865 ■ *Web:* www.itok.net					
ITW Sexton Can Company Inc 3101 Sexton Rd	Decatur	AL	35603	256-355-5850	
Web: www.sextoncan.com					
J. Krug & Associates Inc 1350 W Northwest Hwy Ste 100	Mount Prospect	IL	60056	847-392-8585	
Web: www.jkrug.com					
Jameson Group 287 S Robertson Blvd Ste 474	Beverly Hills	CA	90211	310-289-5085	
Web: www.thejamesongroup.com					
Jamie Gibbs & Associates 120 W 73rd St	Indianapolis	IN	46260	917-862-5313	
Web: www.jamiegibbsassociates.com					
JBS Group Inc 260 S Los Robles Ave Ste 217	Pasadena	CA	91101	626-397-2886	
Web: www.jbshotels.com					
JDL Technologies Inc 5450 NW 33rd Ave Ft Lauderdale Commerce Ste 106	Fort Lauderdale	FL	33309	954-334-0650	
Web: www.jdltech.com					
Jomax LLC 14100 N 83rd Ave Ste 235	Peoria	AZ	85381	888-866-0721	
TF: 888-866-0721 ■ *Web:* jomaxrecovery.com					
K&T Switching Services Inc 3901 Colorado Ave	Sheffield Village	OH	44054	440-949-1910	
Web: www.ktswitching.com					
Kay Green Design Inc 859 Outer Rd	Orlando	FL	32814	407-246-7155	426-7873
TF: 800-226-5186 ■ *Web:* www.kaygreendesign.com					
Kinark Child 500 Hood Rd Ste 200	Markham	ON	L3R9Z3	905-474-9595	
Web: www.kinark.on.ca					
Kishimoto.gordon.dalaya PC 1300 Wilson Blvd Ste 250	Rosslyn	VA	22209	202-338-3800	
Web: www.kgdarchitecture.com					
Language Scientific Inc 10 Cabot Rd Ste 209	Medford	MA	02155	617-621-0940	
Web: www.ricintl.com					
LatPro Inc 3980 N Broadway Ste 103-147	Boulder	CO	80304	954-727-3844	
Web: www.latpro.com					
LBL Architects Inc 1106 W Randol Mill Rd Ste 300	Arlington	TX	76012	817-265-1510	
Web: www.lblarchitects.com					
Lehman Hardware & Appliances Inc 4779 Kidron Rd	Dalton	OH	44618	888-438-5346	
TF: 888-438-5346 ■ *Web:* www.lehmans.com					
LeTip International Inc 4838 E Baseline Rd Ste 123	Mesa	AZ	85206	480-264-4600	
Web: www.letip.com					
Lewellen & Best Displays Inc 101 Knell St	Montgomery	IL	60538	630-896-2500	
Web: lbexhibits.com					
Linxx Security Inc 272 Bedix Rd Ste 220	Virginia Beach	VA	23452	757-222-0300	
Web: www.linxxsecurity.com					
Logic PD Inc 6201 Bury Dr	Eden Prairie	MN	55346	952-941-8071	
Web: www.logicpd.com					
LUZ Inc 221 Main St Ste 1300	San Francisco	CA	94105	415-981-5890	
Web: www.luz.com					
M & W Transportation Company Inc 1110 Pumping Sta Rd	Nashville	TN	37210	615-726-3568	
Web: www.mwtrans.com					
Mactus Group 4034 148th Ave NE Ste K1C1	Redmond	WA	98052	425-883-3640	
Web: www.mactusgroup.com					
Maddalena Design Ltd 36801 Woodward Ave Ste 300	Birmingham	MI	48009	248-644-4919	
Web: www.maddalenadesign.com					
Mancini Duffy 275 Seventh Ave 19th Fl	New York	NY	10001	212-938-1260	
Web: www.manciniduffy.com					
Mandil Inc 846 Elati St	Denver	CO	80204	303-892-5805	
Web: www.mandilinc.com					
Mary Jurek Design Inc 2301 W 205th St Ste 114	Torrance	CA	90501	310-533-1196	
Web: maryjurekdesign.com					
Matric Group LLC 2099 Hill City Rd	Seneca	PA	16346	814-677-0716	
Web: www.matricgroup.com					
Matrix Companies, The 7162 Reading Rd Ste 250	Cincinnati	OH	45237	513-351-1222	
Web: www.matrixtpa.com					
MaxBounty Inc PO Box 17039	Ottawa	ON	K4A4W8	613-834-3955	
Web: www.maxbounty.com					
MDA Geospatial Services International 13800 Commerce Pkwy	Richmond	BC	V6V2J3	604-244-0400	
Web: gs.mdacorporation.com					
Med-RT 27758 Santa Margarita Pkwy	Mission Viejo	CA	92691	949-502-2800	
Web: www.med-rt.com					
Mennonite Economic Development Associates of Canada 155 Frobisher Dr Ste I-106	Waterloo	ON	N2V2E1	519-725-1633	
Web: www.meda.org					
Meta5 Inc 122 W Main St Ste 204	Babylon	NY	11702	631-587-6800	
Web: www.meta5.com					
Metcalfe Group Inc, The 30405 Solon Rd Ste 5	Solon	OH	44139	440-349-5995	
Web: www.metcalfegroup.com					
MGM Mirage Design Group Inc 3260 Industrial Rd	Las Vegas	NV	89109	702-650-7400	
TF: 800-929-1111 ■ *Web:* www.mgmresortsdiversity.com					
Microdynamics Group 1400 Shore Rd	Naperville	IL	60563	630-527-8400	
Web: www.microdg.com					
Midco Connections Inc 4901 E 26th St	Sioux Falls	SD	57110	605-330-4125	
Web: www.midcoconnections.com					
Milestone Technologies Inc 3101 Skyway Ct	Fremont	CA	94539	510-651-2454	
Web: www.milestn.com					
Miller/Zell Inc 4715 Frederick Dr SW	Atlanta	GA	30336	404-691-7400	699-2189
Web: www.millerzell.com					
Mo-Tires Ltd 2830 5 Ave N	Lethbridge	AB	T1H0P1	403-329-4533	
Web: www.mo-tires.com					
Monterey Financial Services Inc 4095 Avenida De La Plata	Oceanside	CA	92056	760-639-3500	
Web: www.montereyfinancial.com					
Motor City Computer 1610 E Highwood Dr	Pontiac	MI	48340	248-454-2000	
Web: www.motorcitycomputer.com					
Msa Planning & Design Consultants Inc 642 Harrison St Fl 3	San Francisco	CA	94107	415-541-0977	
Web: www.msasf.com					
MTI America POBox 667140	Pompano Beach	FL	33066	800-553-2155	
TF: 800-553-2155 ■ *Web:* www.mtiamerica.com					
myFreightWorld LLC 7133 W 95th St	Overland Park	KS	66211	877-549-9438	
TF: 877-549-9438 ■ *Web:* www.myfreightworld.com					
NEEBCO Limited Partnership 15 Chenell Dr	Concord	NH	03301	603-228-1133	
Web: www.neebco.com					
NEI Global Relocation Inc 8701 W Dodge Rd	Omaha	NE	68114	402-397-8486	
Web: www.neirelo.com					
Nemer Fieger 6250 Excelsior Blvd Ste 203	Minneapolis	MN	55416	952-278-3133	
Web: nemerfieger.com					
NetCenergy Corp 231 Elm St	Warwick	RI	02888	401-921-3100	
Web: www.netcenergy.com					
NetworkOmni Multilingual Communications Inc 4353 Park Ter Dr	Westlake Village	CA	91361	818-706-7890	
Web: www.networkomni.com					
Networld Media Group LLC 13100 Eastpoint Park Blvd Ste 100	Louisville	KY	40223	877-441-7545	
TF: 877-441-7545 ■ *Web:* www.networldalliance.com					
Nfusion Design Studio LLC 400 Fourth Ave S	Nashville	TN	37201	615-850-5530	
Web: www.nfusiondesignstudio.com					
Niermann Weeks Company Inc 760 Generals Hwy	Millersville	MD	21108	410-923-0123	923-0647
Web: www.niermannweeks.com					
O' Sullivan Menu Publishing Lp One FAIRFIELD CRES	West Caldwell	NJ	07006	973-227-5112	
Web: www.airlinemenus.com					
O'Currance Teleservices Inc 11747 South Lonepeak Pkwy Ste 100	Draper	UT	84020	801-736-0500	
Web: www.ocurrance.com					
Oak Brook Golf Club 1200 Oak Brook Rd	Oak Brook	IL	60523	630-990-4233	
Web: www.oak-brook.org					
Omnifics Inc 5845 Richmond Hwy Ste 300	Alexandria	VA	22303	703-548-4040	836-8159
Web: www.omnifics.com					
On-Ramp Medical Communications LLC 8770 Purdue Rd	Indianapolis	IN	46268	317-202-3300	
Web: www.frontlineindy.com					
OpEx Pros 1320 Main St Ste 300	Columbia	SC	29201	803-537-1021	
Web: opexpros.com					
Optoro Inc 5001-A Forbes Blvd	Lanham	MD	20706	301-760-7003	
Web: www.optoro.com					
Pacific Design Engineering (1996) Ltd 8505 Eastlake Dr	Burnaby	BC	V5A4T7	604-421-1311	
Web: www.pde.com					
Pacific Office Interiors 5304 Derry Ave Ste U	Agoura Hills	CA	91301	818-735-0333	
Web: www.poi.bz					
Paragon International Inc 2885 N Berkeley Lk Rd Ste 17	Duluth	GA	30096	678-481-6762	
Web: www.paragonint.net					
Paws Up Outfitters 40060 Paws Up Rd	Greenough	MT	59823	406-244-5200	
Web: www.pawsup.com					
Payroll Success 2701 Fondren Dr Ste 124	Dallas	TX	75206	214-265-1011	
Web: www.payrollsuccess.com					
PDS Development 15190 Marsh Ln	Addison	TX	75001	972-497-9000	
Web: www.pointinnovation.com					
PerformLine Inc 30 W Park Pl Third Fl	Morristown	NJ	07960	973-590-2305	
Web: performline.com					
Philpotts 40 S School St Ste 100	Honolulu	HI	96813	808-523-6771	521-9569
Web: www.philpotts.net					
Phoenix Engineering & Consulting Inc 107 Fairway Overlook	Woodstock	GA	30188	404-216-0140	
Web: www.phoenix-engineer.com					

Company	City	State	ZIP	Phone	Fax
Pioneer Magnetics 1745 Berkeley St *Web:* www.pioneermagnetics.com	Santa Monica	CA	90404	310-829-6751	
Placemaking Group 299 Third St Ste 101 *Web:* www.placemakinggroup.com	Oakland	CA	94607	510-835-7900	
Plant Affair, The 1931 Blake Ave *Web:* plantaffair.com	Los Angeles	CA	90039	323-661-4571	
Plantscape Inc 3101 Liberty Ave *Web:* www.plantscape.com	Pittsburgh	PA	15201	412-281-6352	
Polygon Network PO Box 4806 *TF:* 800-221-4435 ■ *Web:* www.polygon.net	Dillon	CO	80435	800-221-4435	
Potawatomi Business Development Corp 3215 W State St Ste 300 *Web:* www.potawatomibdc.com	Milwaukee	WI	53208	414-290-9490	
Potter-Randall Appraisal District 5701 Hollywood Rd (Loop 335) Po Box 7190 *Web:* www.prad.org	Amarillo	TX	79114	806-355-8426	
Premier BPO Inc 102 Country Ln Ste B *Web:* www.premierbpo.com	Clarksville	TN	37043	931-551-8888	
Press-A-Print International LLC 1463 Commerce Way *Web:* www.pressaprint.com	Idaho Falls	ID	83401	208-523-7620	
Primeritus Financial Services Inc 440 Metroplex Dr *TF:* 888-833-4238 ■ *Web:* www.primeritus.com	Nashville	TN	37211	888-833-4238	
Progrexion Marketing Inc 330 N Cutler Dr *Web:* www.progrexion.com	North Salt Lake	UT	84054	801-384-4100	
Propco Marketing Inc 7360 N Lincoln Ave Ste 100 *Web:* www.propco.com	Lincolnwood	IL	60712	773-463-9193	
Protectolite Inc 84 Railside Rd *Web:* www.protectolite.com	North York	ON	M3A1A3	416-444-4484	
Pump Audio Inc Five Pine St *Web:* www.pumpaudio.com	Tivoli	NY	12583	845-757-5555	
QualiTest Ltd 1139 Post Rd *TF:* 877-882-9540 ■ *Web:* www.qualitestgroup.com	Fairfield	CT	06824	877-882-9540	
R d Jones & Associates Inc 729 E Pratt St Ste 210 *Web:* www.rdjones.com	Baltimore	MD	21202	410-332-4700	
R.P.C. Contracting Inc 934 W Kitty Hawk Rd *Web:* www.rpccontracting.com	Kitty Hawk	NC	27949	252-261-3336	
Ravenswood Studio Inc 6900 N Central Pk Ave *Web:* www.ravenswoodstudio.com	Lincolnwood	IL	60712	847-679-2800	679-2805
Re Goodspeed & Sons Distr 11211 g ave *Web:* www.godspeednet.com	Hesperia	CA	92345	760-949-3356	
RealtyBid International Inc 3225 Rainbow Dr Ste 248 *TF:* 877-518-5600 ■ *Web:* www.realtybid.com	Rainbow City	AL	35906	877-518-5600	
Recruiting Toolbox PO Box 2573 *Web:* www.recruitingtoolbox.com	Redmond	WA	98073	425-557-2100	
RED Inc 298 E First St *Web:* www.redinc.com	Idaho Falls	ID	83401	208-528-0051	
Regatta Travel Solutions Inc 325 Winding River Ln Ste 201B *TF:* 800-605-5093 ■ *Web:* www.regattatravelsolutions.com	Charlottesville	VA	22911	800-605-5093	
Religence Inc 2090 Green St *Web:* www.religence.com	San Francisco	CA	94123	415-771-7473	
Remote Logistics International LLC 6430 Richmond Ave Ste 320 *Web:* www.remotelogisticsinternational.com	Houston	TX	77057	713-780-9933	
Renbor Sales Solutions Inc 256 Thornway Ave *Web:* www.sellbetter.ca	Thornhill	ON	L4J7X8	416-671-3555	
Rescraft Plastic Products Inc Nine Woodslee Ave *Web:* www.rescraft.com	Paris	ON	N3L3V1	519-442-4339	
Rev.com Inc 251 Kearny St Eighth Fl *TF:* 888-369-0701 ■ *Web:* www.foxtranslate.com	San Francisco	CA	94108	888-369-0701	
RevenueWire Inc Ste 102 3962 Borden St *Web:* www.revenuewire.com	Victoria	BC	V8P3H8	250-590-2273	
Rex Pak Ltd 85 Thornmount Dr *Web:* www.rexpak.com	Toronto	ON	M1B5V3	416-755-3324	
RightHand Technologies Inc 6545 N Olmsted Ave *Web:* www.righthandtech.com	Chicago	IL	60631	773-774-7600	
RJE Business Interiors Inc 623 Broadway St *Web:* www.rjecincy.com	Cincinnati	OH	45202	513-641-3700	
RMW Architecture & Interiors 160 Pine St Ste 509 *Web:* www.rmw.com	San Francisco	CA	94111	415-781-9800	
Rocketship Inc 110 South 300 West *Web:* www.rocketshipdesign.com	Provo	UT	84601	801-373-1922	
Rockford Mercantile Agency Inc 2502 S Alpine Rd *Web:* www.rmacollections.com	Rockford	IL	61108	815-229-3328	
Rodriguez Chavez Corp 10543 Fisher Rd *Web:* www.rchind.com	Houston	TX	77041	713-457-0570	
Rome Research Corp 421 Ridge St *Web:* www.pargovernment.com	Rome	NY	13440	315-339-0491	
Run Energy LP 4802 S Treadaway *Web:* www.runenergy.com	Abilene	TX	79602	325-795-1550	
Sacor Financial Inc 1911 Douglas Blvd 85-126 *TF:* 866-556-0231 ■ *Web:* www.sacor.net	Roseville	CA	95661	866-556-0231	
Sales Gauge 1186 Old Marlborough Rd *Web:* www.sales-gauge.com	Concord	MA	01742	781-910-0077	
ScentSational Technologies LLC 425 Old York Rd *Web:* www.scentsationaltechnologies.com	Jenkintown	PA	19046	215-886-7777	

Company	City	State	ZIP	Phone	Fax
Scribendi Inc 405 Riverview Dr Ste 304 *Web:* www.scribendi.com	Chatham	ON	N7M5J5	519-351-1626	
Sea Pearl Seafood Company Inc 14120 Shell Belt Rd *Web:* sea-pearl.com	Bayou La Batre	AL	36509	251-824-2129	
Securit Records Management 2794 S Sheridan Way *Web:* www.securit.com	Oakville	ON	L6J7T4	905-829-2794	
Service Companies Inc, The 14750 NW 77th Court Ste 100 *Web:* www.theservicecompanies.com	Miami Lakes	FL	33016	305-681-8800	
Setina Manufacturing Company Inc 2926 Yelm Hwy Se *TF:* 800-426-2627 ■ *Web:* www.setina.com	Olympia	WA	98501	800-426-2627	
ShareASale.com Inc 15 W Hubbard St Ste 500 *Web:* www.shareasale.com	Chicago	IL	60654	312-321-0487	
Sheila Greco Associates LLC 174 State Hwy 67 *Web:* www.sheilagreco.com	Amsterdam	NY	12010	518-843-4611	
Simard 1212 32nd ave *Web:* www.simard.ca	Lachine	QC	H8T3K7	905-670-2005	
Simplegrid Technology Inc 40 Baldwin Rd *Web:* www.simplegrid.com	Parsippany	NJ	07054	973-265-2838	
Sky Climber Wind Solutions LLC 1800 Pittsburgh Dr *Web:* www.skyclimberwindsolutions.com	Delaware	OH	43015	740-203-3900	
Skyline North 1604 Wayneport Rd *Web:* www.skylinenorth.com	Macedon	NY	14502	315-986-4600	
Slifer Designs 216 Main St Ste C-100 *Web:* www.sliferdesigns.com	Edwards	CO	81632	970-926-8200	
Sloan Accoustics Inc 38 Fairfield Pl PO Box CN 2845 *Web:* www.sloanandcompany.com	Caldwell	NJ	07006	973-227-3555	227-8731
Smart LLC Smart TuitionOne Woodbridge Ctr Ste 800 *TF:* 866-395-2986 ■ *Web:* www.smarttuition.com	Woodbridge	NJ	07095	866-395-2986	
Smart System Technology & Commercialization Center 5450 Campus Dr *Web:* www.stcmems.com	Canandaigua	NY	14424	585-919-3000	
sortimat Technology 2242 N Palmer Dr *Web:* www.sortimat.com	Schaumburg	IL	60173	630-484-3194	
Space Inc 3142 E Vantage Point Dr Ste 2 *Web:* workplayce.com	Midland	MI	48642	989-835-5151	
Speck Design Inc 3221 Porter Dr *Web:* www.speckdesign.com	Palo Alto	CA	94304	650-462-9080	
Spur Communications Inc 4200 Pennsylvania Ave Ste 250 *Web:* www.spurcommunications.com	Kansas City	MO	64111	816-471-7373	
Spyre Solutions Inc 91 Rylander Blvd Ste 7-250 *Web:* www.spyresolutions.com	Toronto	ON	M1B5M5	416-444-4924	
Staffelbach Design Associates Inc 2525 McKinnon Ste 800 *Web:* www.staffelbach.com	Dallas	TX	75201	214-747-2511	
Star Displays Inc 38w636 Us Hwy 20 *Web:* www.starincorporated.com	Elgin	IL	60124	847-695-2040	
Star Exhibits & Environments Inc 6920 93rd Ave N *Web:* www.starexhibits.com	Minneapolis	MN	55445	763-561-4655	
State Science & Technology Institute 5015 Pine Creek Dr *Web:* www.ssti.org	Westerville	OH	43081	614-901-1690	
StreamSend 78 York St *Web:* www.streamsend.com	Sacramento	CA	95814	916-326-5407	
StreetLinks LLC 7551 S Shelby St *Web:* www.streetlinks.com	Indianapolis	IN	46227	317-215-8800	
Strite Industries Ltd 298 Shepherd Ave *Web:* www.strite.com	Cambridge	ON	N3C1V1	519-658-9361	
Stroma Service Consulting Inc 19 Legault St *Web:* www.stroma.ca	North Bay	ON	P1A4K6	705-840-6000	
Stromberg Architectural Products Inc 4400 Oneal St *Web:* www.strombergarchitectural.com	Greenville	TX	75402	903-454-0904	
Studio Di Architectura 45 East 20 St *Web:* www.ma.com	New York	NY	10003	212-982-2020	
Summit Account Resolution 12201 Champlin Dr *Web:* www.summitcollects.com	Champlin	MN	55316	763-712-3700	
Sunset Farm Foods Inc 1201 Madison Hwy *Web:* www.sunsetfarmfoods.com	Valdosta	GA	31601	229-242-3389	
SweetLabs Inc 510 Market St Ste 301 *Web:* www.sweetlabs.com	San Diego	CA	92101	619-269-0150	
TCG Continuum LLC 4251 Leap Rd *Web:* www.thinktcg.com	Hilliard	OH	43026	614-876-8600	
TCS 168 Thatcher Rd *Web:* www.tcsusa.com	Greensboro	NC	27409	336-632-0860	
TECMA Group LLC, The 2000 Wyoming Ave *Web:* www.tecma.com	El Paso	TX	79903	915-534-4252	
Tektronix Component Solutions Inc 2905 SW Hocken Ave *Web:* component-solutions.tek.com	Beaverton	OR	97005	503-627-4521	
Telvista Inc 1605 LBJ Fwy Ste 200 *Web:* www.telvista.com	Dallas	TX	75234	972-919-7800	
Tetra Tech Architects & Engineers Cornell Business & Technology Park 10 Brown Rd *Web:* www.tetratechae.com	Ithaca	NY	14850	607-277-7100	
ThinkDirect Marketing Group Inc 8285 Bryan Dairy Rd Ste 150 *Web:* www.tdmg.com	Largo	FL	33773	727-369-2700	
Thomas Pheasant Inc 1029 33rd St NW *Web:* www.thomaspheasant.com	Washington	DC	20007	202-337-6596	

Company / Address	City	State	ZIP	Phone	Fax
Thomson Scientific Inc 3501 Market St. *Web:* scientific.thomson.com	Philadelphia	PA	19104	215-386-0100	
TJ Metzgers Inc 207 Arco Dr *Web:* www.metzgers.com	Toledo	OH	43607	419-861-8611	
Total Comfort of Wisconsin Inc W234 N2830 Paul Rd. *Web:* www.total-mechanical.com	Pewaukee	WI	53072	262-523-2500	
Trading Post of Kittery 301 US Route 1 *Web:* www.usaguns.com	Kittery	ME	03904	207-439-2700	
Training Industry Inc 401 Harrison Oaks Blvd Ste 300 *TF:* 866-298-4203 ■ *Web:* www.trainingindustry.com	Cary	NC	27513	866-298-4203	
Trak-1 Technology Co PO Box 52028 *Web:* www.trak-1.com	Tulsa	OK	74152	918-779-6500	
Transformit Inc 33 Sanford Dr. *Web:* transformitdesign.com	Gorham	ME	04038	207-856-9911	
TranslateMedia LLC 414 Broadway Fourth Fl *Web:* www.translatemedia.com	New York	NY	10013	212-796-5636	
Triad Creative Group 3130 Intertech Dr. *Web:* www.triadcreativegroup.com	Brookfield	WI	53045	262-781-3100	
tripBAM LLC 7318 Marquette *Web:* www.tripbam.com	Dallas	TX	75225	214-363-9630	
TS3 LLC 1870 General George Patton Dr *Web:* www.ts3technology.com	Franklin	TN	37067	615-523-5300	
Uhl Company Inc 9065 zachary ln n *Web:* www.uhlcompany.com	Maple grove	MN	55369	763-425-7226	
V. G. Reed & Sons Inc 1002 S 12th St. *Web:* www.vgreed.com	Louisville	KY	40210	502-560-0100	
Veenendaalcave Inc 1170 Peachtree St NE *Web:* www.vcave.com	Atlanta	GA	30309	404-881-1811	876-1289
Venuelabs 505 Fifth Ave S Ste 300 *TF:* 866-333-7328 ■ *Web:* venuelabs.com	Seattle	WA	98104	866-333-7328	
Verve 1127 Gregg St *Web:* www.verveinteriors.com	Columbia	SC	29201	803-799-0045	
Viking Client Services Inc 7500 Office Ridge Cir Ste 100 *Web:* www.vikingservice.com	Eden Prairie	MN	55344	952-944-7575	
Villa Lighting Supply Inc 2929 Chouteau Ave. **Fax Area Code:* 866 ■ *TF:* 800-325-0963 ■ *Web:* www.villalighting.com	Saint Louis	MO	63103	800-325-0963	531-8720*
Voith Industrial Services Inc 9395 Kenwood Rd Ste 200 *Web:* redirect.voith.com	Cincinnati	OH	45242	513-731-3590	
W. Caslon & Company Inc 1240 Jefferson Rd *Web:* www.caslon.net	Rochester	NY	14623	585-239-6063	
Walker Macy 111 SW Oak St *Web:* www.walkermacy.com	Portland	OR	97204	503-228-3122	
Walls 360 Inc 5054 Bond St *TF:* 888-244-9969 ■ *Web:* www.walls360.com	Las Vegas	NV	89118	888-244-9969	
Walton Signage Corp 3419 E Commerce *Web:* www.waltonsignage.com	San Antonio	TX	78220	210-886-0644	
Warranty Life Services Inc 4152 Meridian St Ste 105-29 *TF:* 888-927-7269 ■ *Web:* www.warrantylife.com	Bellingham	WA	98226	888-927-7269	
Wilson Office Interiors 1444 Oak Lawn Ave Ste 105 *Web:* www.wilsonoi.com	Dallas	TX	75207	972-488-4100	488-8815
Wirt Design Group 617 W Seventh St Ste 201 *Web:* www.wirtdesign.com	Los Angeles	CA	90017	213-239-0990	
Workspace Inc 309 Locust St *Web:* www.workspaceinc.net	Des Moines	IA	50309	515-288-7090	
WorldPantry.com Inc 1192 Illinois St. *Web:* www.worldpantry.com	San Francisco	CA	94107	415-401-0080	
Worldwide Court Reporters 3000 Weslayan St Ste 235 *Web:* www.worldwidecourtreporters.com	Houston	TX	77027	713-572-2000	
WS Live LLC 131 W 10th St. *Web:* www.wslive.com	Dubuque	IA	52001	563-582-9501	
Wyse Meter Solutions Inc RPO Newmarket Court PO Box 95530 *TF:* 866-681-9465 ■ *Web:* www.wysemeter.com	Newmarket	ON	L3Y8J8	866-681-9465	
xDefenders Inc 1100 Pittsford-Victor Rd. *Web:* www.xdefenders.com	Pittsford	NY	14534	585-385-2770	
Yale Club of New York City, The 50 Vanderbilt Ave *Web:* www.yaleclubnyc.org	New York	NY	10017	212-716-2100	
Yazaki Energy 701 E Plano Pkwy Ste 305 *Web:* www.yazakienergy.com	Plano	TX	75074	469-229-5443	
Yub Inc 321 Castro St Ste 1 *Web:* yub.com	Mountain View	CA	94041	650-265-7316	

397 INTERNET BACKBONE PROVIDERS

Companies that are, in effect, Internet service providers for Internet Service Providers (ISPs).

Company / Address	City	State	ZIP	Phone	Fax
BT Americas Inc 2160 E Grand Ave *TF:* 888-767-2988 ■ *Web:* www.globalservices.bt.com	El Segundo	CA	90245	408-330-2700	330-2701
Cogent Communications Group Inc 1015 31st St NW *NASDAQ: CCOI* ■ *TF:* 877-875-4432 ■ *Web:* www.cogentco.com	Washington	DC	20007	202-295-4200	338-8798
IDT Corp 520 Broad St *NYSE: IDT* ■ *Web:* www.idt.net	Newark	NJ	07102	973-438-1000	438-1453
iPass Inc 3800 Bridge Pkwy *NASDAQ: IPAS* ■ *TF:* 877-236-3807 ■ *Web:* www3.ipass.com	Redwood Shores	CA	94065	650-232-4100	232-4111
Level 3 Communications Inc 1025 Eldorado Blvd *NYSE: LVLT* ■ *TF:* 877-453-8353 ■ *Web:* www.level3.com	Broomfield	CO	80021	720-888-1000	
nFrame Inc 701 Congressional Blvd Ste 100 *TF:* 877-570-7827 ■ *Web:* expedient.com/nframe/index.html?url=www.expedient.com	Carmel	IN	46032	317-805-3759	
SAVVIS Inc One Savvis Pkwy *TF:* 800-728-8471 ■ *Web:* centurylinktechnology.com/	Town & Country	MO	63017	314-628-7000	
SunGard Availability Services 680 E Swedesford Rd **Fax Area Code:* 610 ■ *TF:* 800-468-7483 ■ *Web:* www.sungardas.com	Wayne	PA	19087	484-582-2000	687-4726*
Verio Inc 8005 S Chester St Ste 200 *TF Sales:* 800-438-8374 ■ *Web:* www.verio.com	Centennial	CO	80112	561-912-2555	
Verizon Business 1 Verizon Way *TF Cust Svc:* 877-297-7816 ■ *Web:* www.verizonenterprise.com	Basking Ridge	NJ	07920	908-559-2000	
XO Communications Inc 13865 Sunrise Vly Dr *TF:* 866-349-0134 ■ *Web:* www.xo.com	Herndon	VA	20171	703-547-2000	547-2881

398 INTERNET BROADCASTING

Company / Address	City	State	ZIP	Phone	Fax
Admeris Payment Systems Inc 326 Adelaide St W Ste 400 *Web:* www.admeris.com	Toronto	ON	M5V1R3	647-723-6346	
Audible Inc One Washington Pk *TF:* 888-283-5051 ■ *Web:* www.audible.com	Newark	NJ	07102	973-820-0400	
BankCard Services 3055 Wilshire Blvd Third Fl. *Web:* www.e-bankcard.com	Los Angeles	CA	90010	213-365-1122	
CareerBuilder Inc 200 N LaSalle St Ste 1100 *Web:* www.careerbuilder.com	Chicago	IL	60601	773-527-3600	
Caxy Consulting LLC 1812 W Hubbard St Ste 1 *Web:* www.caxy.com	Chicago	IL	60622	312-207-6200	
Compugen Inc 100 Via Renzo Dr *Web:* www.compugen.com	Richmond Hill	ON	L4S0B8	905-707-2000	
DigitalTown Inc 11974 Portland Ave. *Web:* www.digitaltown.com	Burnsville	MN	55337	952-890-2362	
Dynanet Corp 8182 Lark Brown Rd Ste 300 *Web:* www.dynanetcorp.com	Elkridge	MD	21075	443-661-1403	
Eventure Interactive Inc 3420 Bristol St Fl 6 *Web:* www.eventure.com	Costa Mesa	CA	92626	949-500-6960	
Gilbane Report, The 763 Massachusetts Ave *Web:* gilbane.com	Cambridge	MA	02139	617-497-9443	
iovation Inc 111 SW Fifth Ave Ste 3200 *Web:* www.iovation.com	Portland	OR	97204	503-224-6010	
Kelliher Samets Volk 212 Battery St. *Web:* www.ksvc.com	Burlington	VT	05401	802-862-8261	
LabRoots Inc 18340 Yorba Linda Blvd Ste 107 *Web:* labroots.com	Yorba Linda	CA	92886	714-269-2986	
Live365 Inc 950 Tower Ln Ste 400 *Web:* www.live365.com	Foster City	CA	94404	650-345-7400	345-7497
M3 USA Corp 1215 17th St NW Ste 100 *Web:* usa.m3.com	Washington	DC	20036	202-293-2288	
Mary Fisher Design LLC 1731 Emerson St. *Web:* www.maryfisherdesign.com	Jacksonville	FL	32207	904-398-3699	
MedAltus Inc 3567 County Rd 37 *Web:* www.medaltus.com	Bloomfield	NY	14469	585-582-1310	
MedCAREERS Group Inc 758 E Bethel School Rd *Web:* www.medcareersgroup.com	Coppell	TX	75019	972-393-5892	
Media Temple Inc 8520 National Blvd Bldg A *TF:* 877-578-4000 ■ *Web:* www.mediatemple.net	Culver City	CA	90232	877-578-4000	
MeetMe Inc 100 Union Sq Dr *Web:* www.meetmecorp.com	New Hope	PA	18938	215-862-1162	
NeuLion Inc 1600 Old Country Rd *Web:* www.neulion.com	Plainview	NY	11803	516-622-8300	
Ning Inc 735 Emerson St *Web:* www.ning.com	Palo Alto	CA	94301	270-514-7000	
Nstreams Technologies Inc 1914 Junction Ave *Web:* www.nstreams.com	San Jose	CA	95131	408-734-8889	734-8886
OMT Inc 1-1717 Dublin Ave. *TF:* 888-665-0501 ■ *Web:* www.omt.net	Winnipeg	MB	R3H0H2	204-786-3994	783-5805
ON24 Inc 201 Third St 3rd Fl *Web:* www.on24.com	San Francisco	CA	94103	415-369-8000	369-8388
Perfect World Entertainment Inc 1001 E Hillsdale Blvd Ste 800 *Web:* www.perfectworld.com	Foster City	CA	94404	650-590-7700	
Pictage Inc 1580 Francisco St Ste 101 *Web:* www.pictage.com	Torrance	CA	90501	310-525-1600	
Pulse Network Inc 10 Oceana Way *Web:* www.thepulsenetwork.com	Norwood	MA	02062	781-821-6600	
Real Capital Analytics Inc 110 Fifth Ave. *Web:* www.rcanalytics.com	New York	NY	10011	212-387-7103	
Richter10.2 Media Group LLC 600 Cleveland St Bank of America Tower Ste 920 *Web:* www.richter10point2.com	Clearwater	FL	33755	727-447-3600	
Santeon Group Inc Ste 150 11720 Plz America Dr *Web:* www.santeon.com	Reston	VA	20190	703-970-9200	
Synacor Inc 40 La Riviere Dr Ste 300 *Web:* www.synacor.com	Buffalo	NY	14202	716-853-1362	
Tine 4 Learning 6300 Ne First Ave Ste 203 *Web:* www.time4learning.com	Fort Lauderdale	FL	33334	954-771-0914	
Trulia Inc 535 Mission St Ste 700 *Web:* www.trulia.com	San Francisco	CA	94105	415-648-4358	
Virtual Piggy Inc 1221 Hermosa Ave Ste 210 *Web:* www.virtualpiggy.com	Hermosa Beach	CA	90254	310-853-1950	
Weather Decision Technologies Inc 201 David L Boren Blvd Ste 270 *Web:* wdtinc.com	Norman	OK	73072	405-579-7675	

399 INTERNET DOMAIN NAME REGISTRARS

	City	State	ZIP	Phone	Fax
@Com Technology LLC 1353 Pine St Ste E	Walnut Creek	CA	94596	480-624-2500	
Web: www.atcomtechnology.com					
AITDomains.com 421 Maiden Ln	Fayetteville	NC	28301	877-549-2881	321-1390*
**Fax Area Code:* 910 ■ *TF:* 877-549-2881 ■ *Web:* ait.com/domains/					
Best Registration Services Inc 1418 S Third St	Louisville	KY	40208	502-637-4528	
TF: 800-977-3475 ■ *Web:* www.bestregistrar.com					
Domain Registration Services PO Box 447	Palmyra	NJ	08065	888-339-9001	922-4961*
**Fax Area Code:* 215 ■ *TF:* 888-339-9001 ■ *Web:* www.dotearth.com					
Domain-It! 9891 Montgomery Rd	Cincinnati	OH	45242	513-351-4222	351-8222
TF General: 866-269-2355 ■ *Web:* www.domainit.com					
DomainPeople Inc 550 Burrard St Ste 200 Bentall Twr 5	Vancouver	BC	V6C2B5	604-639-1680	688-9013
TF: 877-734-3667 ■ *Web:* www.domainpeople.com					
DomainRegistry.com Inc 2301 E. Evesham Rd Ste 204	Voorhees	NJ	08043	856-335-5950	
Web: www.domainregistry.com					
Dotster 8100 NE Pkwy Dr Ste 300 PO Box 821066	Vancouver	WA	98682	360-449-5800	253-4234
TF: 800-401-5250 ■ *Web:* www.dotster.com					
Dotster Inc PO Box 821066	Vancouver	WA	98682	360-253-2210	
TF: 800-401-5250 ■ *Web:* www.dotster.com					
Dynadot LLC PO Box 345	San Mateo	CA	94401	650-585-1961	869-2893*
**Fax Area Code:* 415 ■ *TF Cust Svc:* 866-652-2039 ■ *Web:* www.dynadot.com					
easyDNS 219 Dufferin St Ste 304A	Toronto	ON	M6K3J1	416-535-8672	535-0237
TF: 888-677-4741 ■ *Web:* easydns.com					
EnCirca Inc 400 W Cummings Pk Ste 1725-307	Woburn	MA	01801	781-942-9975	823-8911
Web: www.encirca.com					
eNom Inc 5808 Lake Washington Blvd Ste 300	Kirkland	WA	98033	425-974-4689	974-4791*
**Fax:* Acctg ■ *Web:* www.enom.com					
Moniker Online Services LLC 20 SW 27th Ave Ste 201	Pompano Beach	FL	33069	800-688-6311	
Web: www.moniker.com					
Name.com LLC 2500 E Second Ave 2nd Fl	Denver	CO	80206	720-249-2374	399-3167*
**Fax Area Code:* 303 ■ *TF:* 800-365-0006 ■ *Web:* www.name.com					
Network Solutions LLC 13861 Sunrise Valley Dr Ste 300	Herndon	VA	20171	703-668-4600	668-5888
TF: 800-361-5712 ■ *Web:* www.networksolutions.com					
Register.com Inc 575 Eigth Ave Eighth Fl	New York	NY	10018	888-734-4783	
TF: 888-734-4783 ■ *Web:* www.register.com					
Tiger Technologies LLC PO Box 7596	Berkeley	CA	94707	510-527-3131	539-5032*
**Fax Area Code:* 866 ■ *Web:* www.tigertech.net					

400 INTERNET SEARCH ENGINES, PORTALS, DIRECTORIES

	City	State	ZIP	Phone	Fax
About Inc 1440 Broadway 19th Fl	New York	NY	10018	212-204-4000	
Web: www.about.com					
Adknowledge Inc 4600 Madison Ave 10th Fl	Kansas City	MO	64112	816-931-1771	
Web: www.adknowledge.com/					
America Online Inc (AOL) 22000 AOL Way	Dulles	VA	20166	703-265-1000	
Web: www.aol.com					
Ancestry 360 W 4800 N	Provo	UT	84604	801-705-7000	705-7001
TF: 800-262-3787 ■ *Web:* www.myfamily.com					
Ancestry.com 360 W 4800 N	Provo	UT	84604	801-705-7000	705-7001
TF Cust Svc: 800-262-3787 ■ *Web:* www.ancestry.com					
Ask.com 555 12th St Ste 500	Oakland	CA	94607	510-985-7400	985-7410
Web: www.ask.com					
BioSpace Inc 90 New Montgomery St Ste 414	San Francisco	CA	94105	877-277-7585	576-7585*
**Fax Area Code:* 415 ■ *TF:* 888-246-7722 ■ *Web:* www.biospace.com					
CEOExpress Co 1 Broadway 14th Fl	Cambridge	MA	02142	617-482-1200	225-4440
TF: 888-686-1181 ■ *Web:* www.ceoexpress.com					
Congress.Org 77 K St NE	Washington	DC	20002	715-232-1677	
Web: www.congress.org					
EarthCam Inc 84 Kennedy St	Hackensack	NJ	07601	201-488-1111	488-1119
Web: www.earthcam.com					
Encyclopedia.com 360 N Michigan Ave Ste 1900	Chicago	IL	60601	312-224-5000	224-5001
Web: www.encyclopedia.com					
FindLaw 610 Opperman Dr	Eagan	MN	55123	651-687-6393	392-6206*
**Fax Area Code:* 800 ■ *Web:* www.findlaw.com					
Fine Arts Museums of San Francisco 50 Hagiwara Tea Garden Dr	San Francisco	CA	94118	415-750-3600	
Web: deyoung.famsf.org					
Genealogy.com 360 West 4800 North	Provo	UT	84604	801-705-7000	705-7001
TF: 800-262-3787 ■ *Web:* www.genealogy.com					
Google Inc 1600 Amphitheatre Pkwy	Mountain View	CA	94043	650-253-0000	253-0001
NASDAQ: GOOG ■ *Web:* www.google.co.in					
GourmetSpot StartSport Mediaworks Inc 1840 Oak Ave	Evanston	IL	60201	847-866-1830	866-1880
Web: www.gourmetspot.com					
HighBeam Research Inc 65 E Wacker Pl Ste 400	Chicago	IL	60601	312-782-3900	782-3901
Web: www.highbeam.com					
HomeAdvisor 14023 Denver W Pkwy Ste 200	Golden	CO	80401	303-963-7200	980-3003
TF: 800-474-1596 ■ *Web:* www.homeadvisor.com					
Hotelrooms.com Inc 108-18 Queens Blvd	Forest Hills	NY	11375	718-730-6000	261-4598
TF: 800-486-7000 ■ *Web:* www.hotelrooms.com					
HowStuffWorks Inc 3350 Peachtree Rd NE Ste 1500	Atlanta	GA	30326	404-760-4729	
Web: www.howstuffworks.com					
InfoSpace Inc 601 108th Ave NE Ste 1200	Bellevue	WA	98004	425-201-6100	201-6150
Web: www.blucora.com					
Internet Archive 300 Funston Ave	San Francisco	CA	94118	415-561-6767	840-0391
Web: www.archive.org					
Internet Public Library University of Michigan School of Information 304 W Hall	Ann Arbor	MI	48109	734-763-2285	764-2475
TF: 800-545-2433 ■ *Web:* www.ipl.org					
Jayde.com iEntry Inc 2549 Richmond Rd Second Fl	Lexington	KY	40509	859-514-2720	219-9065
Web: www.jayde.com					
Law Engine 7660-H Fay Avenue Ste 342	La Jolla	CA	92037	858-456-1234	454-3375
TF: 800-894-2889 ■ *Web:* www.thelawengine.com					
Lycos Inc 52 2nd Ave	Waltham	MA	02451	781-370-2700	370-2886
Web: www.lycos.com					
MagPortal.com PO Box 463	Bryn Mawr	PA	19010	610-581-7702	
Web: www.magportal.com					
MindEdge Inc 465 Waverley Oaks Rd Ste 202	Waltham	MA	02452	781-250-1805	250-1810
TF: 877-592-8000 ■ *Web:* www.mindedge.com					
Nerd World Media Eight New England Executive Pk	Burlington	MA	01803	781-272-6599	
NewsHub 100 Lombard St Suite 203	Toronto	ON	M5C1M3	416-536-4827	536-0859
TF: 800-889-9487 ■ *Web:* nabet700.com					
Nursing Ctr 323 Norristown Rd Ste 200	Ambler	PA	19002	800-787-8985	
TF: 800-346-7844 ■ *Web:* www.nursingcenter.com					
RootsWeb.com 360 W 4800 N	Provo	UT	84604	801-705-7000	705-7001
TF: 800-262-3787 ■ *Web:* www.rootsweb.ancestry.com					
ShoppingSpot 1840 Oak Ave	Evanston	IL	60201	847-866-1830	866-1880
Web: www.shoppingspot.com					
Tucows Inc 96 Mowat Ave	Toronto	ON	M6K3M1	416-535-0123	531-5584
TSE: TC ■ *TF:* 800-371-6992 ■ *Web:* www.tucows.com					
USGS Education United States Geological Survey 12201 Sunrise Vly Dr MS 801	Reston	VA	20192	703-648-5953	648-4454
Web: education.usgs.gov					
Wired News Wired 520 Third St Ste 305	San Francisco	CA	94107	800-769-4733	276-8500*
**Fax Area Code:* 415 ■ *TF:* 800-769-4733 ■ *Web:* www.wired.com					
Yahoo! Inc 701 First Ave	Sunnyvale	CA	94089	408-349-3300	349-3301
NASDAQ: YHOO ■ *Web:* info.yahoo.com					
YELLOWPAGES.com LLC 208 S Akard Ste 1825	Dallas	TX	75202	866-329-7118	
TF: 866-329-7118 ■ *Web:* www.yellowpages.com					

401 INTERNET SERVICE PROVIDERS (ISPS)

	City	State	ZIP	Phone	Fax
ABT Internet Inc 175 E Shore Rd	Great Neck	NY	11023	516-829-5484	829-2955
TF: 800-367-3414 ■ *Web:* www.abt.net					
Access US 712 N Second St Ste 300	Saint Louis	MO	63102	314-655-7700	655-7701
TF: 800-638-6373 ■ *Web:* accessus.net					
America Online Inc (AOL) 22000 AOL Way	Dulles	VA	20166	703-265-1000	
Web: www.aol.com					
Aplus.net Internet Services 10350 Barnes Canyon Rd	San Diego	CA	92121	858-410-6929	
TF: 877-275-8763 ■ *Web:* www.aplus.net					
AT & T Inc 175 E Houston St PO Box 2933	San Antonio	TX	78299	210-821-4105	
NYSE: AT&T ■ *TF:* 800-351-7221 ■ *Web:* www.att.com					
Cable One Inc 210 E Earll Drive	Phoenix	AZ	85012	602-364-6000	364-6010
TF: 877-692-2253 ■ *Web:* www.cableone.net					
Cincinnati Bell Inc 221 E Fourth St	Cincinnati	OH	45202	513-397-9900	241-1264
NYSE: CBB ■ *TF:* 800-387-3638 ■ *Web:* www.cincinnatibell.com					
ClearSail Communications LLC 3950 Braxton	Houston	TX	77063	713-230-2800	
TF: 888-905-0888 ■ *Web:* www.clearsail.net					
Direct Internet Access 141 Desiard St PO Box 7263	Monroe	LA	71201	800-296-2249	835-2121*
**Fax Area Code:* 888 ■ *TF:* 800-296-2249 ■ *Web:* www.directinternet.net					
DSLextreme.com 21540 Plummer St Ste A	Chatsworth	CA	91311	866-243-8638	206-0326*
**Fax Area Code:* 818 ■ *TF:* 866-243-8638 ■ *Web:* www.dslextreme.com					
EarthLink Inc 1375 Peachtree St NE	Atlanta	GA	30309	404-815-0770	795-1034*
NASDAQ: ELNK ■ **Fax:* Sales ■ *TF:* 866-383-3080 ■ *Web:* www.earthlink.net					
Expedient Communications 810 Parish St	Pittsburgh	PA	15220	412-316-7800	
TF: 877-570-7827 ■ *Web:* www.expedient.com					
Frontline Communications PO Box 98	Orangeburg	NY	10962	888-376-6854	680-6541*
**Fax Area Code:* 845 ■ **Fax:* Sales ■ *TF:* 888-376-6854 ■ *Web:* www.frontline.net					
HughesNet 11717 Exploration Ln	Germantown	MD	20876	301-428-5500	428-1868
TF: 866-347-3292 ■ *Web:* www.hughesnet.com					
Internet America Inc 12853 Capricorn St	Stafford	TX	77477	800-232-4335	
TF: 800-232-4335 ■ *Web:* www.internetamerica.com					
iSelect Internet Inc 1420 W Kettleman Ln Ste E	Lodi	CA	95242	209-334-0496	837-1427*
**Fax Area Code:* 877 ■ *Web:* www.iselect.net					
J2 Interactive LLC Two 13th St	Charlestown	MA	02129	617-241-7266	241-8636
Web: www.j2interactive.com					
Net Access Corp Nine Wing Dr	Cedar Knolls	NJ	07927	973-590-5000	590-5080
TF: 800-638-6336 ■ *Web:* www.nac.net					
NetZero Inc 21301 Burbank Blvd	Woodland Hills	CA	91367	818-287-3000	287-3010
TF: 800-638-9376 ■ *Web:* www.netzero.net					
New Edge Networks 3000 Columbia House Blvd Ste 106	Vancouver	WA	98661	360-693-9009	
TF: 877-725-3343 ■ *Web:* www.newedgenetworks.com					
Nova Internet Services Inc PO Box 703696 Ste 230	Dallas	TX	75370	214-904-9600	357-1431
TF: 877-668-2663 ■ *Web:* www.novaone.net					
ProtoSource Network 2511 W Shaw Ave Ste 102	Fresno	CA	93711	866-490-8600	
TF: 866-490-8600 ■ *Web:* www.psnw.com					
Road Runner Group 60 Columbus Cir 60 Columbus Cir	New York	NY	10023	703-345-3422	697-4911*
**Fax Area Code:* 704 ■ *TF:* 866-689-3678 ■ *Web:* www.timewarnercable.com					
TOAST.net 4841 Monroe St Ste 307	Toledo	OH	43623	419-292-2200	474-1762
TF: 888-862-7863 ■ *Web:* www.toast.net					
Verio Inc 8005 S Chester St Ste 200	Centennial	CO	80112	561-912-2555	
TF Sales: 800-438-8374 ■ *Web:* www.verio.com					
Verizon Business 1 Verizon Way	Basking Ridge	NJ	07920	908-559-2000	
TF Cust Svc: 877-297-7816 ■ *Web:* www.verizonenterprise.com					
WorldGate Communications Inc 3800 Horizon Blvd Ste 103	Trevose	PA	19053	215-354-5100	
OTC: WGATQ					

402 INVENTORY SERVICES

Phone Fax

Douglas-Guardian Services Corp
14800 St Mary's Ln. Houston TX 77079 281-531-0500 531-1777
TF: 800-255-0552 ■ *Web:* www.douglasguardian.com

MSI Inventory Service Corp PO Box 320129 Flowood MS 39232 601-939-0130 939-0061
TF: 800-820-1460 ■ *Web:* www.msi-inv.com

MST Steel Corp 24417 Groesbeck Hwy Warren MI 48089 586-773-5460 773-5486
Web: www.mststeel.com

WIS International 9265 Sky Park Ct Ste 100 San Diego CA 92123 858-565-8111 677-1945*
**Fax Area Code:* 905 ■ *TF:* 800-268-6848 ■ *Web:* w3.wisintl.com

403 INVESTIGATIVE SERVICES

SEE ALSO Information Retrieval Services (General) p. 2557; Public Records Search Services p. 2980; Security & Protective Services p. 3161

Phone Fax

Accurate Biometrics Inc
4849 N Milwaukee Ave Ste 101 Chicago IL 60630 773-685-5699
Web: www.accuratebiometrics.com

Alliance Investigations LLC
240 S Montezuma St Ste 100 Prescott AZ 86303 928-717-1196
Web: az-pi.com

American Guard Services Inc
1299 E Artesia Blvd Carson CA 90746 310-645-6200
Web: www.americanguardservices.com

American Professional Services Inc
111 Harrison Ave Ste 500 Oklahoma City OK 73104 405-636-4222 632-7667
Web: www.americanpi.net

Amtex Security Inc 4814 Neptune St Corpus Christi TX 78405 361-882-1222
Web: www.amtexservices.com

ASK Services Inc 42180 Ford Rd Ste 101 Canton MI 48187 734-983-9040 983-9041
TF: 888-416-1313 ■ *Web:* www.ask-services.com

Aurico Reports Inc
116 W Eastman St Arlington Heights IL 60004 866-255-1852
TF: 866-255-1852 ■ *Web:* www.aurico.com

Bombet Cashio & Assoc
11220 N Harrells Ferry Rd Baton Rouge LA 70816 225-275-0796 272-3631
TF: 800-256-5333 ■ *Web:* www.bombet.com

Camping Investigations
24 W Mayflower Ave North Las Vegas NV 89030 702-258-1947
Web: www.campingcompanies.com

Capitol Detective Agency 2922 N 18th Pl Phoenix AZ 85016 602-265-3462
TF: 800-346-0347

Claims Verification Inc
6700 N Andrews Ave Ste 200 Ft. Lauderdale FL 33309 888-284-2000
TF: 888-284-2000 ■ *Web:* www.cvi.com

Culpepper Investigations Po Box 21594 El Sobrante CA 94820 510-243-9860
Web: mail2web.com

Donan Engineering Co Inc
11321 Plantside Dr Louisville KY 40299 800-482-5611 267-6973*
**Fax Area Code:* 502 ■ *TF:* 800-482-5611 ■ *Web:* www.donan.com

Douglas Baldwin & Assoc PO Box 1249 La Canada CA 91012 818-952-4433 790-4622
TF: 800-392-3950 ■ *Web:* www.baldwinpi.com

Gregg Investigations Inc
222 S Hamilton St Ste 17 Madison WI 53703 800-866-1976 755-5853*
**Fax Area Code:* 608 ■ *TF:* 800-866-1976 ■ *Web:* www.gregginvestigations.com

Hettrick Cyr & Assoc Inc 287 Main St East Hartford CT 06118 860-568-2999
Web: www.hettrickcyr.com

Hrodey & Assoc 114 W Calhoun St Woodstock IL 60098 815-337-4636 337-4638
Web: www.hrodey.com

Inquiries Inc 129 N W St Easton MD 21601 410-819-3711
Web: www.inquiriesinc.com

International Investigators Inc
3216 N Pennsylvania St Indianapolis IN 46205 317-925-1496 926-1177
TF: 800-403-8111 ■ *Web:* www.iiiweb.net

Internet Crimes Group Inc PO Box 3599 Princeton NJ 08543 609-806-5000 806-5001
Web: ithreat.com/

Investigative Services Inc 4381 S 153rd Cir Omaha NE 68137 402-894-5625 896-0621

Kessler International
45 Rockefeller Plz Ste 2000 New York NY 10111 212-286-9100 730-2433
TF: 800-932-2221 ■ *Web:* www.investigation.com

L&R Security Services Inc
3930 Old Gentilly Rd New Orleans LA 70126 504-943-3191
Web: www.lrsecurity.com

M2SYS LLC 1050 Crown Pointe Pkwy Ste 850 Atlanta GA 30338 770-393-0986
Web: www.m2sys.com

Michael Ramey & Assoc Inc PO Box 744 Danville CA 94526 800-321-0505 820-8082*
**Fax Area Code:* 925 ■ *TF:* 800-321-0505 ■ *Web:* www.rameypi.com

North Winds Investigations Inc
119 S Second St PO Box 1654 Rogers AR 72756 479-925-1612 878-5989
TF: 800-530-4514 ■ *Web:* www.napps.org

Owens & Assoc Investigations
8765 Aero Dr Ste 306 San Diego CA 92123 800-297-1343 297-1343*
**Fax Area Code:* 619 ■ *TF:* 800-297-1343 ■ *Web:* www.owenspi.com

PADIC Inc 1609 E Broadway Gainesville TX 76240 940-665-6130 665-7486
Web: www.padic.com

Palmer Investigative Services
624 W Gurley St Ste A Prescott AZ 86304 928-778-2951 445-7204
TF: 800-280-2951 ■ *Web:* www.palmerinvestigative.com

PI & Information Services LLC PO Box 157 Beaverton OR 97075 503-643-4274 643-5474
Web: www.pi-info.com

Pre-employ.com Inc 2301 Balls Ferry Rd Anderson CA 96007 530-378-7680
Web: www.pre-employ.com

Private Eyes Inc 190 N Wiget Ln Ste 220 Walnut Creek CA 94598 925-927-3333
Web: www.privateeyesinc.com

Research Assoc Inc 27999 Clemens Rd Cleveland OH 44145 440-892-9439 892-9439
TF: 800-255-9693 ■ *Web:* www.researchassociatesinc.com

Phone Fax

Rick Johnson & Assoc of Colorado
1649 Downing St Denver CO 80218 303-296-2200 296-3038
TF: 800-530-2300 ■ *Web:* www.denverpi.com

Seventrees Corp 2181 M-139 South Benton Harbor MI 49022 269-925-8111
Web: www.7trees.com

Shawver & Assoc 6262 Weber Rd Ste 112 Corpus Christi TX 78413 361-880-8968 880-8971
Web: www.stxpi.com

Southern Research Company Inc
2850 Centenary Blvd Shreveport LA 71104 318-227-9700 424-1801
TF: 888-772-6952 ■ *Web:* www.southernresearchinc.com

Starside Security & Investigation Inc
1930 S Brea Canyon Rd Ste 220 Diamond Bar CA 91765 909-396-9999
Web: www.starside.com

State Information Bureau 842 E Pk Ave Tallahassee FL 32301 850-561-3990 561-3995
Web: www.sibflorida.com

Stewart & Assoc Inc 50 W Douglas St Ste 1200 Freeport IL 61032 815-235-3807 235-1290
TF: 888-310-2840 ■ *Web:* www.bwstewart.com

Thillens Inc 4242 N Elston Ave Chicago IL 60618 773-539-4444
Web: www.thillens.com

Vericon Resources Inc
3550 Engineering Dr Ste 225 Norcross GA 30092 770-457-9922 457-5006
TF: 800-795-3784 ■ *Web:* www.vericon.com

VTS Investigations LLC PO Box 971 Elgin IL 60121 800-538-4464 888-8588*
**Fax Area Code:* 847 ■ *TF:* 800-538-4464 ■ *Web:* www.pichicago.com

Watkins Security Agency of D.c. Inc
5325 E Capitol St Se Washington DC 20019 202-581-2871
Web: thewatkinsgroup.com

Wood & Tait Inc 64-5249 Kauakea Rd Kamuela HI 96743 808-885-5090 630-0500*
**Fax Area Code:* 888 ■ *TF:* 800-774-8585 ■ *Web:* www.woodtait.com

404 INVESTMENT ADVICE & MANAGEMENT

SEE ALSO Commodity Contracts Brokers & Dealers p. 2010; Investment Guides - Online p. 2604; Mutual Funds p. 2807; Securities Brokers & Dealers p. 3151

Phone Fax

13D Research (USVI) LLC
6115 Estate Smith Bay PO Box 2 Ste 333 St Thomas VI 00802 340-775-3330
Web: www.13d.com

300 North Capital LLC 300 N Lake Ave Ste 210 Pasadena CA 91101 626-449-8500
Web: www.300northcapital.com

A N Culbertson & Company Inc
One Boars Head Pointe Ste 101 Charlottesville VA 22903 434-972-7766
Web: www.anculbertson.com

A&J Capital Investment Inc
1609 W Valley Blvd Ste 328 Alhambra CA 91803 626-289-8887
Web: www.ajcap.com

Aaron Bell International Inc
9101 E Kenyon Ave Ste 2300 Denver CO 80237 720-200-0470
Web: www.aaron-bell.com

Aberdeen Asset Management Inc
1735 Market St 32nd Fl Philadelphia PA 19103 215-405-5700
Web: www.aberdeen-asset.com

Abingdon Capital Management LLC
1650 Tysons Blvd Ste 1575 Mclean VA 22102 703-269-3400
Web: www.abingdoncapital.com

Absolute Investment Advisers LLC
18 Shipyard Dr Ste 3C Hingham MA 02043 781-740-1904
Web: www.absoluteadvisers.com

Acadian Asset Management Inc 260 Franklin St Boston MA 02110 617-850-3500 850-3501
TF: 800-946-0166 ■ *Web:* www.acadian-asset.com

Acquisitions Northwest Inc
210 SW Morrison Ste 600 Portland OR 97204 503-225-0479
Web: www.acquisitionsnw.com

Acumen Capital Finance Partners Ltd
404 Sixth Ave S W Ste 700 Calgary AB T2P0R9 403-571-0300
Web: www.acumencapital.com

Acupay System LLC 30 Broad St 46th Fl New York NY 10004 212-422-1222
Web: www.acupay.com

Addison Capital Partners
319 Clematis St Ste 211 West Palm Beach FL 33401 561-835-4041
Web: www.addisoncapitalpartners.com

Admedia Partners Three Park Ave 31st Fl New York NY 10016 212-759-1870
Web: www.admediapartners.com

Adroit Investment Management Ltd
12th Fl Canadian Western Bank Pl 10303 Jasper Ave
Edmonton AB T5J3N6 780-429-3500
Web: www.adroitinvestments.ca

Advanced Materials Partners Inc
45 Pine St New Canaan CT 06840 203-966-6415
Web: www.amplink.com

Advent Capital Management LLC
1065 Ave of the Americas 31st Fl New York NY 10018 212-482-1600 480-9655
TF: 888-523-8368 ■ *Web:* www.adventcap.com

Advisory Research Holdings Inc
180 N. Stetson Ave
Ste 5500 180 North Stetson Avenue Chicago IL 60601 312-565-1414
Web: www.advisoryresearch.com

Aegis Asset Management Inc
2331 W Lincoln Ave Anaheim CA 92801 714-635-9900
Web: www.catanzarite.com

AEL Financial LLC
600 N Buffalo Grove Rd Buffalo Grove IL 60089 847-465-2009
Web: aelfinancial.com

AEW Capital Management LP (AEW) 2 Seaport Ln Boston MA 02210 617-261-9000 261-9555
Web: www.aew.com

AGF Management Ltd 66 Wellington St W 31st Fl Toronto ON M5K1E9 905-214-8203 214-8243
TF: 800-268-8583 ■ *Web:* www.agf.com

Akanthos Capital Management LLC
21700 Oxnard St Ste 1520 Woodland Hills CA 91367 818-883-8270
Web: www.akanthoscapital.com

Phone | Fax

Aksia LLC 599 Lexington Ave 46th Fl .... New York NY 10022 212-710-5710
Web: www.aksia.com

Aldebaran Capital LLC
10293 N Meridian St Ste 100 .... Indianapolis IN 46290 317-818-7827
Web: www.aldebarancapital.com

Alderman & Company Capital LLC
20 Silver Brook Rd .... Ridgefield CT 06877 203-244-5680
Web: www.aldermancapital.com

Alembic Global Advisors 780 Third Ave 3rd Fl .... New York NY 10017 212-907-5350
Web: www.alembicglobal.com

Allegheny Investments Ltd
Stone Quarry Crossing 811 Camp Horne Rd
Ste 100 .... Pittsburgh PA 15237 412-367-3880
Web: www.alleghenyfinancial.com

Allegiance Financial Group Inc
2935 Country Dr Ste 102 .... Little Canada MN 55117 651-294-4550 294-4551
Web: www.afg2000.com

Allegis Residential Services Inc
7857 Convoy Ct Ste 211 .... San Diego CA 92111 858-430-5700
Web: www.allegisresidentialservices.com

AllianceBernstein Holding LP (AB)
1345 Ave of the Americas .... New York NY 10105 212-486-5800 969-2293*
NYSE: AB ■ **Fax:* Hum Res ■ *TF Cust Svc:* 800-221-5672 ■ *Web:* www.alliancebernstein.com

Allianz Global Investors of America LP
680 Newport Ctr Dr Ste 250 .... Newport Beach CA 92660 949-219-2200
Web: us.allianzgi.com

Allianz Real Estate of America
55 Green Farms Rd PO Box 5160 .... Westport CT 06881 203-221-8500 341-5722
Web: allianz-realestate.com

Alloy Silverstein Financial Services
900 Kings Hwy N Ste 101 .... Cherry Hill NJ 08034 856-667-6228
Web: www.alloysilverstein.com

Alpha Windward LLC
200 Lowder Brook Dr Ste 2400 .... Westwood MA 02090 781-326-8880
Web: www.alphawindward.com

Alphamark Advisors LLC
250 Grandview Dr Ste 175 .... Fort Mitchell KY 41017 859-957-1803
Web: www.alphamarkadvisors.com

Altair Advisers LLC 303 W Madison St Ste 600 .... Chicago IL 60606 312-429-3000
Web: www.altairadvisers.com

AltaVista Research LLC 243 Fifth Ave Ste 235 .... New York NY 10016 646-435-0569
Web: www.altavista-research.com

Alternative Strategy Advisers LLC
601 Carlson Pkwy Ste 1125 .... Minnetonka MN 55305 952-847-2450
Web: www.asallc.com

AM Private Investments Inc
45 Pine St E Wing .... New Canaan CT 06840 203-972-5095
Web: www.aminet.com

Ambassador Capital Management LLC
500 Griswold St Ste 2800 .... Detroit MI 48226 313-961-3111

Ambassador Financial Group Inc
1605 N Cedar Crest Blvd Ste 508 .... Allentown PA 18104 610-351-1633
Web: www.ambfg.com

American Capital Partners LLC 205 Oser Ave ...... Hauppauge NY 11788 631-851-0918
Web: www.americancapitalpartners.com

American Century Investments Inc
4500 Main St PO Box 419200 .... Kansas City MO 64111 816-531-5575 340-7962*
**Fax:* Cust Svc ■ *TF:* 800-345-2021 ■ *Web:* www.americancentury.com

American Portfolios Holdings Inc
4250 Veterans Memorial Hwy Ste 420E .... Holbrook NY 11741 631-439-4600
Web: www.americanportfolios.com

American Research & Management Co
145 Front St .... Marion MA 02738 508-748-1665
Web: www.arm-co.com

Ameriprise Financial Inc
834 Ameriprise Financial Ctr .... Minneapolis MN 55474 612-671-3131
NYSE: AMP ■ *TF:* 866-673-3673 ■ *Web:* www.ameriprise.com

Ameriprise Financial Services Inc
70100 Ameriprise Financial Ctr .... Minneapolis MN 55474 866-483-8434 671-8880*
**Fax Area Code:* 612 ■ *TF:* 866-483-8434 ■ *Web:* www.ameriprise.com

AMI Asset Management Corp
10866 Wilshire Blvd Ste 770 .... Los Angeles CA 90024 310-446-2740
Web: www.amiassetmanagement.com

Amivest Capital Management
703 Market St 18th Fl .... San Francisco CA 94103 800-541-7774 541-9760*
**Fax Area Code:* 415 ■ *TF:* 800-541-7774 ■ *Web:* www.wrapmanager.com

AmSouth Investment Services Inc (AIS)
250 Riverchase Pkwy E 4th Fl .... Birmingham AL 35244 866-512-3479 560-7923*
**Fax Area Code:* 205 ■ *TF:* 866-512-3479 ■ *Web:* www.regions.com

Amundi Smith Breeden 280 S Mangum St Ste 301 ...... Durham NC 27701 919-967-7221
Web: www.smithbreeden.com

Analytic Investors LLC
555 W Fifth St 50th Fl .... Los Angeles CA 90013 213-688-3015 688-8856
TF: 800-618-1872 ■ *Web:* www.aninvestor.com

Anchor Capital Advisors LLC
One Post Office Sq Ste 3850 .... Boston MA 02109 617-338-3800
Web: www.anchorcapital.com

Angeles Investment Advisors LLC
429 Santa Monica Blvd Ste 650 .... Santa Monica CA 90401 310-393-6300
Web: www.angelesadvisors.com

Apache Capital Management LLC
230 Park Ave Ste 664 .... New York NY 10169 212-972-0991
Web: www.apachecapital.com

Aperio Group LLC Three Harbor Dr Ste 315 .... Sausalito CA 94965 415-339-4300
Web: www.aperiogroup.com

Apex Capital LLC 25 Orinda Way Ste 300 .... Orinda CA 94563 925-253-1800
Web: www.apexcapitalfunds.com

Appleton Group Wealth Management LLC
100 W Lawrence St 3/F Apple .... Wisconsin WI 54911 920-993-7727
Web: www.appletongrouponline.com

Appleton Partners Inc
One Post Office Sq 6th Fl .... Boston MA 02109 617-338-0700
TF: 800-338-0745 ■ *Web:* www.appletonpartners.com

Aragon Ventures Inc 1455 Adams Dr Ste 1010 ...... Menlo Park CA 94025 650-566-8000
Web: www.aragonventures.com

Arbor Capital Management Inc
1400 W Benson Blvd Ste 575 .... Anchorage AK 99503 907-222-7581
Web: www.acminc.com

Arcade Partners LLC
62 La Salle Rd Ste 304 .... West Hartford CT 06107 860-236-6320
Web: www.arcadepartners.com

Arden Asset Management LLC
375 Park Ave 32nd Fl .... New York NY 10152 212-751-5252
Web: www.ardenasset.com

ARGI Investment Services LLC
1914 Stanley Gault Pkwy .... Louisville KY 40223 502-753-0609
Web: www.argifinancialgroup.com

Aristotle Capital Management LLC
11100 Santa Monica Blvd Ste 1700 .... Los Angeles CA 90025 310-478-4005 478-8496
TF: 877-478-4722 ■ *Web:* www.aristotlecap.com

Armstrong Shaw Associates Inc 45 Grove St ..... New Canaan CT 06840 203-972-9600
Web: www.armstrongshaw.com

Arnerich Massena & Associates Inc
2045 NE Martin Luther King Jr Blvd .... Portland OR 97212 503-239-0475
Web: www.am-a.com

Ashfield Capital Partners LLC
750 Battery St Ste 600 .... San Francisco CA 94111 415-391-4747
Web: www.ashfield.com

Assante Financial Management Ltd
4145 N Service Rd Ste 100 .... Burlington ON L7L6A3 905-335-2291
Web: assante.com

Asset Allocation & Management Co
30 W Monroe St Third Fl .... Chicago IL 60603 312-263-2900
Web: www.aamcompany.com

Asset Consulting Group LLC
231 S Bemiston Ave 14th Fl .... St Louis MO 63105 314-862-4848
Web: www.acgnet.com

Asset Strategy Consultants LLC
Six N Park Dr Ste 208 .... Hunt Valley MD 21030 410-528-8282
Web: www.assetstrategyconsultants.com

Assetbuilder Inc 1255 W 15th St Ste 1000 .... Plano TX 75075 972-535-4040
Web: assetbuilder.com

AssetMark Inc 1655 Grant St 10th Fl .... Concord CA 94520 800-664-5345
TF: 800-664-5345 ■ *Web:* www.assetmark.com

Assurex International 8200 E 32nd St N .... Wichita KS 67226 316-266-6222
Web: www.truenorth.net

Atalanta/Sosnoff Capital LLC
101 Pk Ave Sixth Fl .... New York NY 10178 212-867-5000 922-1820
Web: www.atalantasosnoff.com

Atlanta Capital Management Company LLC
1075 Peachtree St NW Ste 2100 .... Atlanta GA 30309 404-876-9411 872-1672
Web: www.atlcap.com

Atlantic Trust 100 E Pratt St 23rd Fl .... Baltimore MD 21202 410-539-4660 539-4661
TF: 866-644-4144 ■ *Web:* www.atlantictrust.com

Atlantic-Pacific Capital Inc
102 Greenwich Ave Second Fl .... Greenwich CT 06830 203-862-9182
Web: www.apcap.com

Attain Capital Management LLC
One E Wacher Dr 30th Fl .... Chicago IL 60601 312-604-0926
Web: attaincapital.com

Aurora Investment Management LLC
300 N LaSalle St 52nd Fl .... Chicago IL 60654 312-762-6700
Web: www.aurorallc.com

Austin Associates LLC 7205 W Central Ave .... Toledo OH 43617 419-841-8521
Web: www.austinassociates.com

Avalon Capital Management
495 Seaport Ct Ste 106 .... Redwood City CA 94063 650-306-1500
Web: www.avaloncapital.com

Avalon Trust Co 125 Lincoln Ave Ste 301 .... Santa Fe NM 87501 505-983-1111
Web: www.avalontrust.com

AXA Rosenberg Investment Management LLC
4 Orinda Way Bldg E .... Orinda CA 94563 925-254-6464 253-0141
Web: www.axa-rosenberg.com

Ayco Company LP One Wall St .... Albany NY 12205 518-464-2000 464-2122
Web: www.ayco.com

Aznar Financial Advisors 14 Raymond Rd .... Morris Plains NJ 07950 973-540-8850
Web: www.aznaradvisors.com

Backstrom McCarley Berry & Company LLC
115 Sansome St Mezzanine A .... San Francisco CA 94104 415-392-5505
Web: www.bmcbco.com

Badgley Phelps & Bell Inc
1420 Fifth Ave Ste 3200 .... Seattle WA 98101 206-623-6172
Web: badgley.com

Bahl & Gaynor Inc 212 E Third St Ste 200 .... Cincinnati OH 45202 513-287-6100 287-6110
TF: 800-341-1810 ■ *Web:* www.bahl-gaynor.com

Bailard Biehl & Kaiser Group
950 Tower Ln Ste 1900 .... Foster City CA 94404 650-571-5800 573-7128
Web: www.bailard.com

Baker-Meekins Company Inc, The
1404 Front Ave .... Lutherville Timonium MD 21093 410-823-2600
Web: www.bakermeekins.com

Banorte Securities International Ltd
140 E 45th St 32nd Fl .... New York NY 10017 212-484-5200
Web: www.banortesecurities.com

Barclay Financial Group
4851 Lyndon B Johnson Fwy Ste 510 .... Dallas TX 75244 972-774-9100
Web: www.barclayfg.com

Baring Asset Management Co Inc
470 Atlantic Ave Independence Wharf .... Boston MA 02210 617-946-5200 946-5400
Web: www.barings.com

Barnum Financial Group Six Corporate Dr .... Shelton CT 06484 203-513-6000
Web: www.barnumfinancialgroup.com

Barometer Capital Management Inc
One University Ave Ste 1910 PO Box 25 .... Toronto ON M5J2P1 416-601-6888
Web: www.barometercapital.ca

				Phone	Fax
Barrett & Co 42 Weybosset St Ste 2 ... Providence	RI	02903		401-351-1000	
Web: www.barrett.net					
Barrington Research Associates Inc 161 N Clark St Ste 2950 ... Chicago	IL	60601		312-634-6000	
Web: brai.com					
Barrow Hanley Mewhinney & Strauss LLC 2200 Ross Ave 31st Fl ... Dallas	TX	75201		214-665-1900	
Web: www.barrowhanley.com					
Barry Financial Group Inc 40 Se Fifth St Ste 600 ... Boca Raton	FL	33432		561-368-9120	
Web: www.talkmoney.com					
Bartlett & Co 600 Vine St Ste 2100 ... Cincinnati	OH	45202		513-621-4612	621-6462
TF: 800-800-4612 ■ *Web:* www.bartlett1898.com					
Batterymarch Financial Management Inc 200 Clarendon St ... Boston	MA	02116		617-266-8300	266-0633
Web: www.batterymarch.com					
Battle Road Research Ltd 465 Waverley Oaks Rd Ste 209 ... Waltham	MA	02452		781-894-0705	
Web: www.battleroad.com					
Beacon Hill Financial Corp 120 Water St ... Boston	MA	02109		617-973-6900	
Web: www.beaconhillfinancial.com					
Beacon Pointe Advisors LLC 500 Newport Ctr Dr Ste 125 ... Newport Beach	CA	92660		949-718-1600	
Web: www.bpadvisors.com					
Beacon Trust Co 163 Madison Ave Ste 600 ... Morristown	NJ	07960		973-377-8090	
Web: www.beacontrust.com					
Beck Mack & Oliver LLC 360 Madison Ave Ste 18 ... New York	NY	10017		212-661-2640	
Web: www.beckmack.com					
Becker Capital Management Inc 1211 S W Fifth Ave Ste 2185 ... Portland	OR	97204		503-223-1720	
TF: 800-551-3998 ■ *Web:* www.beckercap.com					
Bedell Frazier Investment Counselling LLC Two Walnut Creek Ctr 200 Pringle Ave Ste 555 ... Walnut Creek	CA	94596		925-932-0344	
Web: www.bedellinvest.com					
Bedrock Capital Management Inc 5050 El Camino Real Ste 204 ... Los Altos Hills	CA	94022		650-964-7024	
Web: www.bedrockcap.com					
Beecher Investors Inc 1266 E Main St Ste 700R ... Stamford	CT	06902		212-779-2200	
Web: www.beecherinvestors.com					
Bel Air Investment Advisors LLC 1999 Ave of the Stars Ste 2800 ... Los Angeles	CA	90067		310-229-1500	
Web: www.belair-llc.com					
Bell Investment Advisors 1111 Broadway Ste 1630 ... Oakland	CA	94607		510-433-1066	
Web: www.bellinvest.com					
Benchmark Plus Management LLC 820 A St Ste 700 ... Tacoma	WA	98402		253-573-0657	
Web: www.bpfunds.com					
Benham & Green Capital Management LLC 1299 Prospect St Ste 301 ... La Jolla	CA	92037		858-551-3130	
Berkshire Advisors Inc 2240 Ridgewood Rd ... Wyomissing	PA	19610		610-376-6970	
Web: www.berkshireadvisors.net					
Bernicke & Associates Ltd 4813 Keystone Crossing ... Eau Claire	WI	54701		715-832-1173	
Web: www.bernicke.com					
Bessemer Trust Co 630 Fifth Ave 6th Fl ... New York	NY	10111		212-708-9100	265-5826
TF: 800-255-7688 ■ *Web:* www.bessemertrust.com					
Beverly Hills Wealth Management LLC 9454 Wilshire Blvd ... Beverly Hills	CA	90212		310-859-1600	
Web: www.beverlyhillswealthmanagement.com					
BG Financial Services Group 160 Main St ... Gloucester	MA	01930		978-675-9941	
Web: www.nsfgma.com					
Birch Hill Investment Advisors LLC 24 Federal St 10th Fl ... Boston	MA	02110		617-502-8300	
Web: www.birchhilladvisors.com					
Bison Capital Asset Management LLC 233 Wilshire Blvd Ste 425 ... Santa Monica	CA	90401		310-260-6573	
Web: www.bisoncapital.com					
BlackRock Inc 40 E 52nd St 25th Fl ... New York	NY	10055		212-810-5300	
NYSE: BLK ■ *Web:* www.blackrock.com					
Blue Point Capital Partners 127 Public Sq Ste 5100 ... Cleveland	OH	44114		216-535-4700	
Web: www.bluepointcapital.com					
Blue Rock Advisors Inc 445 E Lk St Ste 120 ... Wayzata	MN	55391		952-229-8700	
Web: blue-rock.com					
Boenning & Scattergood Inc 200 Barr Harbor Dr Four Tower Bridge Ste 300 ... West Conshohocken	PA	19428		610-832-1212	
Web: www.boenninginc.com					
Bogdahn Group, The 4901 Vineland Rd Ste 600 ... Orlando	FL	32811		866-240-7932	
TF: 866-240-7932 ■ *Web:* www.bogdahngroup.com					
Bornhoft Group Corp, The 1775 Sherman St Ste 2500 ... Denver	CO	80203		303-572-1000	
Web: www.bornhoftgroup.com					
Boston Advisors Inc One Liberty Sq 10th Fl ... Boston	MA	02109		617-348-3100	348-0081
TF: 800-523-5903 ■ *Web:* www.bostonadvisors.com					
Boston Family Office LLC, The 88 Broad St Second Fl ... Boston	MA	02110		617-624-0800	
Web: www.bosfam.com					
Boston Financial Data Services 2000 Crown Colony Dr ... Quincy	MA	02169		617-483-5000	
TF: 888-772-2337 ■ *Web:* www.bostonfinancial.com					
Boston Portfolio Advisors Inc 800 Corporate Dr Ste 408 ... Fort Lauderdale	FL	33334		954-938-3000	
Web: www.bostonportfolio.com					
Bouchey Financial Group Ltd 1819 Fifth Ave ... Troy	NY	12180		518-720-3333	
Web: www.boucheyfinancial.com					
Bowling Portfolio Management LLC 4030 Smith Rd Ste 140 ... Cincinnati	OH	45209		513-871-7776	
Web: www.bowlingpm.com					
Boyar's Intrinsic Value Research LLC Six E 32nd St Seventh Fl ... New York	NY	10016		212-995-8300	
Web: boyarresearch.com					
Boys Arnold & Company Inc 1272 Hendersonville Rd ... Asheville	NC	28803		828-274-1542	
Web: manageyourinvestments.com					
Bragg Financial Advisors Inc 1031 S Caldwell St Ste 200 ... Charlotte	NC	28203		704-377-0261	
Web: www.braggfinancial.com					
Brandes Investment Partners LP 11988 El Camino Real Ste 500 ... San Diego	CA	92130		858-755-0239	755-0916
TF: 800-237-7119 ■ *Web:* www.brandes.com					
Brandywine Capital Associates 113 East Evans St ... West Chester	PA	19380		610-344-2910	
TF: 888-344-2920 ■ *Web:* brandywinecapitalassociates.com					
Brandywine Global Investment Management LLC 2929 Arch St Eighth Fl ... Philadelphia	PA	19104		215-609-3500	609-3501
TF: 800-348-2499 ■ *Web:* www.brandywineglobal.com					
Branson Fowlkes & Company Inc 3300 Chimney Rock Rd Ste 100-B ... Houston	TX	77056		713-780-0606	
Web: www.bransonfowlkes.com					
Brass Ring Capital Inc 301 Carlson Pkwy Ste 265 ... Minnetonka	MN	55305		952-473-2710	
Web: www.brassringcapital.com					
Breckinridge Capital Advisors Inc 200 High St Fl 2 ... Boston	MA	02110		617-443-0779	
Web: www.breckinridge.com					
Brenner Group Inc, The 19200 Stevens Creek Blvd Ste 200 ... Cupertino	CA	95014		408-873-3400	
Web: thebrennergroup.com					
Brentwood Capital Advisors LLC 5000 Meridian Blvd Ste 350 ... Franklin	TN	37067		615-224-3830	
Web: www.brentwoodcapital.com					
Bridgewater Assoc Inc One Glendinning Pl ... Westport	CT	06880		203-226-3030	291-7300
Web: www.bwater.com					
Briggs Capital LLC 858 Washington St Ste 100 ... Dedham	MA	02026		781-493-6581	
Web: www.briggscapital.com					
Brighton Jones LLC 506 Second Ave Ste 1800 ... Seattle	WA	98104		206-329-5546	
Web: www.brightonjones.com					
Brooke Private Equity Associates 84 State St Ste 320 ... Boston	MA	02109		617-227-3160	
Web: www.brookepea.com					
Brookmont Capital Management LLC 2000 McKinney Ave Ste 1230 ... Dallas	TX	75201		214-953-0190	
Web: www.brookmontcapital.com					
Brown &Tedstrom Inc 1700 Broadway Ste 500 ... Denver	CO	80290		303-863-7231	
Web: www.brown-tedstrom.com					
Brown Bros Harriman & Co 140 Broadway ... New York	NY	10005		212-483-1818	493-7287*
**Fax:* Hum Res ■ *Web:* www.bbh.com					
Brown Capital Management Inc 1201 N Calvert St ... Baltimore	MD	21202		410-837-3234	837-6525
TF: 800-809-3863 ■ *Web:* www.browncapital.com					
Brown Investment Advisory & Trust Co 901 S Bond St Ste 400 ... Baltimore	MD	21231		410-537-5400	
Web: www.brownadvisory.com					
Broyhill Asset Management LLC 800 Golfview Pk PO Box 500 ... Lenoir	NC	28645		828-758-6100	758-8919
Web: www.broyhillasset.com					
BTS Asset Management Inc 420 Bedford St Ste 340 ... Lexington	MA	02420		800-343-3040	
TF: 800-343-3040 ■ *Web:* www.btsmanagement.com					
Buckhead Capital Management LLC 3330 Cumberland Blvd Ste 650 ... Atlanta	GA	30339		404-720-8800	
Web: www.buckheadcapital.com					
Buckingham Family of Financial Services, The 8182 Maryland Ave Ste 900 ... St Louis	MO	63105		314-725-0455	
Web: www.investmentadvisornow.com					
Buckman Buckman & Reid Inc 174 Patterson Ave ... Shrewsbury	NJ	07702		732-530-0303	
Web: www.buckmanbuckman.com					
Burgeonvest Bick Securities Ltd 21 King St W Ste 1100 ... Hamilton	ON	L8P4W7		905-528-6505	
Web: www.burgeonvest.com					
Cadence Capital Management 265 Franklin St 4th Fl ... Boston	MA	02110		617-624-3500	624-3591
TF: 800-298-2194 ■ *Web:* www.cadencecapital.com					
Cafa Corporate Finance 4269 Sainte-Catherine W Office 200 ... Westmount	QC	H3Z1P7		514-989-5508	
Web: www.cafa.ca					
Calamos Asset Management Inc 2020 Calamos Ct ... Naperville	IL	60563		630-245-7200	245-6335
NASDAQ: CLMS ■ *TF:* 800-582-6959 ■ *Web:* www.calamos.com					
Caldwell Trust Co 201 Center Rd Ste Two ... Venice	FL	34285		941-493-3600	
Web: www.ctrust.com					
Calera Capital 580 California St Ste 2200 ... San Francisco	CA	94104		415-632-5200	
Web: www.caleracapital.com					
Caliber Advisors Inc 514 Via De La Valle Ste 210 ... Solana Beach	CA	92075		858-792-8990	
Web: www.caliberadvisors.com					
California Technology Ventures LLC 670 N Rosemead Blvd Ste 201 ... Pasadena	CA	91107		626-351-3700	
Web: www.ctventures.com					
Callan Assoc Inc 101 California St Ste 3500 ... San Francisco	CA	94111		415-974-5060	291-4014
TF: 800-227-3288 ■ *Web:* www.callan.com					
Calvert Investment Counsel LLC 4 N Park Dr Ste 201 ... Hunt Valley	MD	21030		410-435-3270	
Web: www.calvertinvcnsl.com					
Cambiar Investors Inc 2401 E Second Ave Ste 500 ... Denver	CO	80206		888-673-9950	302-9050*
**Fax Area Code:* 303 ■ *TF:* 888-673-9950 ■ *Web:* www.cambiar.com					

				Phone	Fax
Cambria Capital LLC 488 E Winchester St Ste 200 TF: 877-226-0477 ■ Web: www.cambriacapital.com	Salt Lake City	UT	84107	877-226-0477	
Cambridge Associates LLC 125 High St Web: www.cambridgeassociates.com	Boston	MA	02110	617-457-7500	
Cambridge Eating Disorder Center PC Three Bow St Ste 1 Web: www.eatingdisordercenter.org	Cambridge	MA	02138	617-547-2255	
Cambridge Financial Group Inc 4100 Horizons Dr Ste 200 Web: www.cfginc.net	Columbus	OH	43220	614-457-1530	
Camcor Capital Inc 525 Eigth Ave S W Ste 4080 Web: www.camcorpartners.com	Calgary	AB	T2P1G1	403-508-2950	
Cameron Thomson Group Ltd 390 Bay St Ste 1706 TF: 800-395-9943 ■ Web: www.cameronthomson.com	Toronto	ON	M5H2Y2	416-350-5009	
Canaccord Genuity, Research Division Pacific Centre 609 Granville St Ste 2200 PO Box 10337 Web: www.canaccordgenuity.com	Vancouver	BC	V7Y1H2	604-643-7300	
Cantor Fitzgerald Canada Corp 1100 Rene-Levesque Blvd W Ste 1310 Web: www.versantpartners.com	Montreal	QC	H3B4N4	514-845-8111	
CapFinancial Partners LLC 4208 Six Forks Rd Ste 1700 TF: 800-216-0645 ■ Web: www.captrustadvisors.com	Raleigh	NC	27609	919-870-6822	
Capital Advisors Group Inc Chatham Ctr 29 Crafts St Ste 270 Web: www.capitaladvisors.com	Newton	MA	02458	617-630-8100	
Capital Advisors Inc 2200 S Utica Pl Ste 150 Web: www.capitaladv.com	Tulsa	OK	74114	918-599-0045	
Capital Alpha Partners LLC 600 Pennsylvania Ave SE Ste 220 Web: www.capalphadc.com	Washington	DC	20003	202-548-0111	
Capital Concepts Group Inc 1030-4720 Kingsway	Burnaby	BC	V5H4N2	604-432-7743	
Capital Financial Group Inc 6600 Rockledge Dr Sixth Fl Web: www.cfginc.com	Bethesda	MD	20817	301-468-0100	
Capital Group Cos Inc 333 S Hope St TF: 800-421-8511 ■ Web: thecapitalgroup.com	Los Angeles	CA	90071	213-615-0514	486-9217
Capital Growth Management LP 1 International Pl TF: 800-345-4048 ■ Web: www.cgmfunds.com	Boston	MA	02110	617-737-3225	261-0572
Capital Innovations LLC 325 Forest Grove Dr Ste 100 Web: www.capinnovations.com	Pewaukee	WI	53072	262-746-3100	
Capital Institutional Services Inc 1601 Elm St Ste 3900 Web: www.capis.com	Dallas	TX	75201	214-720-0055	
Capital Link Inc 230 Park Ave Ste 1536 Web: www.capitallink.com	New York	NY	10169	212-661-7566	
Capital Management Corp, The 4101 Cox Rd Ste 110 Web: www.the-cmc.com	Glen Allen	VA	23060	804-270-4000	
Capital Premium Financing Inc 12235 South 800 East Web: www.capitalpremium.net	Draper	UT	84020	801-571-0775	
Capital Research & Management Co (CRMC) 333 S Hope St TF: 800-421-4225 ■ Web: thecapitalgroup.com	Los Angeles	CA	90071	213-486-9200	486-9217
CapitalSouth Growth Fund 4201 Congress St Ste 360 Web: www.capitalsouthpartners.com	Charlotte	NC	28209	704-376-5502	
Capmark Investments LP 116 Welsh Rd Web: capmark.com	Horsham	PA	19044	215-328-4622	
Cappello Capital Corp 100 Wilshire Blvd Ste 1200 Web: www.cappellocorp.com	Santa Monica	CA	90401	310-393-6632	
CapTrust Advisors LLC 102 W Whiting St Ste 400 Web: www.captrustadv.com	Tampa	FL	33602	813-218-5000	
Carderock Capital Management Inc Two Wisconsin Cir Ste 600 Web: www.carderockcapital.com	Chevy Chase	MD	20815	301-951-5288	
Cardinal Capital Management LLC Four Greenwich Office Park Web: www.cardcap.com	Greenwich	CT	06831	203-863-8990	
Carl Domino Inc 515 N Flagler Dr Ste 808 Web: www.carldomino.com	West Palm Beach	FL	33401	561-833-2882	
Carolinas Investment Consulting LLC 5605 Carnegie Blvd Ste 400 Web: www.carolinasinvest.com	Charlotte	NC	28209	704-643-2455	
Carty & Company Inc 6263 Poplar Ave Ste 800 Web: www.cartyco.com	Memphis	TN	38119	901-767-8940	
CarVal Investors LLC 9320 Excelsior Blvd Seventh Fl Web: www.carvalinvestors.com	Hopkins	MN	55343	952-984-3774	
Casey Research LLC PO Box 1427 TF: 888-512-2739 ■ Web: www.caseyresearch.com	Stowe	VT	05672	602-445-2736	
Casgrain & Company Ltd 1200 Mcgill College Ave 21st Fl TF: 800-361-8738 ■ Web: www.casgrain.ca	Montreal	QC	H3B4G7	514-871-8080	
Castle Creek Capital LLC 6051 El Tordo Web: www.castlecreek.com	Rancho Santa Fe	CA	92067	858-756-8300	
Cavallino LLC 599 Bridgeway Web: www.cavallinollc.com	Sausalito	CA	94965	415-285-9300	
Cavanal Hill Investment Management Inc One Williams Ctr 15th Fl Web: www.axiaim.com	Tulsa	OK	74172	918-588-8688	
Cedar Brook Financial Partners LLC 5885 Landerbrook Dr Ste 200 Web: cedarbrookfinancial.com	Cleveland	OH	44124	440-683-9200	
Cedar Financial Advisors Inc 3853 SW Hall Blvd Web: www.cedaradvisors.com	Beaverton	OR	97005	503-512-5890	
Centaur Capital Partners LP Southlake Town Sq 1460 Main St Ste 234 Web: www.centaurcapital.com	Southlake	TX	76092	817-488-9632	
Central Park Group LLC 805 Third Ave 18th Fl Web: www.centralparkgroup.com	New York	NY	10022	212-317-9200	
Century Wealth Management LLC 1770 Kirby Pkwy Ste 117 Web: www.centurywealth.com	Memphis	TN	38138	901-850-5532	
CFS Investment Advisory Services LLC 97 Lackawanna Ave Ste 101 Web: www.cfsias.com	Totowa	NJ	07512	973-826-8800	
Cherokee Investment Partners LLC 111 E Hargett St Ste 300 Web: www.cherokeefund.com	Raleigh	NC	27601	919-743-2500	
Chevy Chase Trust Co 7501 Wisconsin Ave W Tower Ste 1500W Web: www.chevychasetrust.com	Bethesda	MD	20814	240-497-5000	
Childs Company LLC 3438 Peachtree Raod Phipps Tower Ste 1400-B Web: www.childscompany.com	Atlanta	GA	30326	404-751-3049	
Churchill Corporate Services 56 Utter Ave TF: 800-941-7458 ■ Web: www.furnishedhousing.com	Hawthorne	NJ	07506	973-636-9400	636-0179
Cincinnati Asset Management Inc 4350 Glndl Milford Rd 1 Web: www.cambonds.com	Cincinnati	OH	45242	513-554-8500	
Cirrus Research LLC 303 S Broadway Ste 212 Tarrytown Web: www.cirrus-res.com	New York	NY	10591	914-289-1400	
Citco Fund Services San Francisco Inc 560 Mission St Fl 26 Web: www.citco.com	San Francisco	CA	94105	415-228-0390	
Clark Capital Management Group Inc (CCMG) 1650 Market St 1 Liberty Pl 53rd Fl TF: 800-766-2264 ■ Web: www.ccmg.com	Philadelphia	PA	19103	215-569-2224	569-3639
Clearspring Capital Group 11000 Richmond Ste 550 Web: www.clearspringcapitalgroup.com	Houston	TX	77042	713-339-1903	
Cleveland Research Co 1375 East Ninth St Ste 2700 Web: www.cleveland-research.com	Cleveland	OH	44114	216-649-7250	
CM Bidwell & Associates Ltd 20 Old Pali Pl Web: www.cmbidwellandassociates.com	Honolulu	HI	96817	808-595-1099	
Coastal Credit LLC 3852 Virginia Beach Boulvard Web: www.coastalcreditllc.com	Virginia Beach	VA	23452	757-340-6000	
Cohen & Steers Inc 280 Pk Ave 10th Fl NYSE: CNS ■ *Fax: Mktg ■ TF: 800-330-7348 ■ Web: www.cohenandsteers.com	New York	NY	10017	212-832-3232	832-3498*
Coho Partners Ltd 300 Berwyn Park 801 Cassatt Rd Ste 100 Web: www.cohopartners.com	Berwyn	PA	19312	484-318-7575	
Collins Barrow Ottawa LLP 400-301 Moodie Dr Web: www.collinsbarrowottawa.com	Ottawa	ON	K2H9C4	613-820-8010	
Collins Capital Management Inc 7077 Bonneval Rd Ste 340 Web: www.collinscmi.com	Jacksonville	FL	32216	904-493-7500	
Colony Capital Management 3050 Peachtree Rd NW Suite 200 TF: 877-365-5050 ■ Web: www.colonycapital.com	Atlanta	GA	30305	404-365-5050	523-7877
Columbia Management Investment Advisers LLC 1 Financial Ctr TF: 800-426-3750 ■ Web: www.columbiamanagement.com	Boston	MA	02111	800-426-3750	
Columbus Cir Investors Inc (CCI) 1 Stn Pl Metro Ctr 8th Fl Web: www.columbuscircle.com	Stamford	CT	06902	203-353-6000	353-5772
Commonfund Inc 15 Old Danbury Rd Web: www.commonfund.org	Wilton	CT	06897	203-563-5000	
Commonwealth Capital Advisors LLC 30 S Wacker Dr 22nd Fl Web: www.commonwealthcapital.com	Chicago	IL	60606	808-744-9713	
Commonwealth Financial Network 29 Sawyer Rd *Fax Area Code: 866 ■ TF: 800-237-0081 ■ Web: www.commonwealth.com	Waltham	MA	02453	781-736-0700	316-8357*
Compak Asset Management 1801 Dove St TF: 800-388-9700 ■ Web: www.compak.com	Newport Beach	CA	92660	800-388-9700	
Concorde Asset Management LLC 1120 E Long Lk Rd Ste 250 Web: www.concordefinancial.com	Troy	MI	48085	248-740-8500	
Conestoga Capital Advisors LLC 259 N Radnor Chester Rd Radnor Ct Ste 120 Web: www.conestogacapital.com	Radnor	PA	19087	484-654-1380	
Conexus Financial Partners LP 721 Rt 202/206 Web: www.conexuscapital.com	Bridgewater	NJ	08807	908-231-9101	
Conning Asset Management Co one Financial Plaza Web: www.conning.com	Hartford	CT	06103	860-299-2000	
Connors Investor Services Inc 1210 Broadcasting Rd Ste 200 Web: www.connorsinvestor.com	Wyomissing	PA	19610	610-376-7418	
Conrad Capital Management Inc 425 Broadhollow Rd Web: www.conradcapital.com	Melville	NY	11747	631-439-7878	
Cook Pine Capital LLC 73 Arch St Greenwich Second Fl Web: www.cookpinecapital.com	Greenwich	CT	06830	203-861-2930	
Cooke & Bieler LP 1700 Market St Ste 3222 Web: www.cooke-bieler.com	Philadelphia	PA	19103	215-567-1101	567-1681
Cookson Peirce & Company Inc 555 Grant St Ste 380 Web: www.cooksonpeirce.com	Pittsburgh	PA	15219	412-471-5320	

Phone Fax

Copeland Capital Management LLC
Eight Tower Bridge 161 Washington St
Ste 1650 .... Conshohocken PA 19428 484-530-4300
Web: www.copelandcapital.com

Corbyn Investment Management Inc
2330 W Joppa Rd Ste 108 .... Lutherville MD 21093 410-832-5500
Web: corbyn.com

Cornerstone Advisors Asset Management Inc
74 W Broad St Ste 340 .... Bethlehem PA 18018 610-694-0900
Web: www.cornerstone-companies.com

Cornerstone Advisors Inc 1802 Hamilton St .... Allentown PA 18104 610-437-1375
Web: www.cornerstoneadvisers.com

Corporate Development Associates Inc
5335 Far Hills Ave Ste 304 .... Dayton OH 45429 937-439-4227
Web: www.cda-inc.net

Coughlin & Company Inc 140 E 19th Ave Ste 700 .... Denver CO 80203 303-863-1900
Web: www.coughlinandcompany.com

Courier Capital Corp 1114 Delaware Ave .... Buffalo NY 14209 716-883-9595
Web: www.couriercapital.com

Covington Capital Management
601 S Figueroa St Ste 2000 .... Los Angeles CA 90017 213-629-7500
Web: www.covingtoncapitalmanagement.com

CPM Group 30 Broad St 37th Fl .... New York NY 10004 212-785-8320
Web: www.cpmgroup.com

CPS Investment Advisors 1509 S Florida Ave .... Lakeland FL 33803 863-688-1725
Web: www.cpalliance.com

Craig-Hallum Capital Group LLC
222 S Ninth St Ste 350 .... Minneapolis MN 55402 612-334-6300
Web: www.craig-hallum.com

Cramer Rosenthal Mcglynn LLC
520 Madison Ave 20th Fl .... New York NY 10022 212-838-3830
Web: www.crmllc.com

Crawford Investment Counsel Inc
600 Galleria Pkwy Ste 1650 .... Atlanta GA 30339 770-859-0045
Web: www.crawfordinvestment.com

Creative Financial Group (CFG)
16 Campus Blvd .... Newtown Square PA 19073 610-325-6100 325-6240
TF: 800-893-4824 ■ *Web:* creativefinancialgroup.com

Creative Financial Group Ltd
1000 Abernathy Rd Bldg 400 Ste 1500 .... Atlanta GA 30328 770-913-9704
Web: www.cfgltd.com

Creative Global Investments LLC Research Div
115 E 57th St 11th Fl .... New York NY 10022 212-939-7256
Web: cg-inv.com

Cremac LLC 78 Delevan St .... Brooklyn NY 11231 718-222-4500
Web: www.cremac.com

Crestwood Advisors LLC 50 Federal St Ste 810 .... Boston MA 02110 617-523-8880
Web: www.crestwoodadvisors.com

CrossHarbor Capital Partners LLC
One Boston Pl 23rd Fl .... Boston MA 02108 617-624-8300
Web: www.crossharborcapital.com

Crown Financial Ministries
601 Broad St SE .... Gainesville GA 30501 770-534-1000
TF: 800-722-1976 ■ *Web:* www.crown.org

CRT Capital Group LLC 262 Harbor Dr .... Stamford CT 06902 203-569-6400
Web: www.crtllc.com

CSM Capital Corp 625 Madison Ave Third Fl .... New York NY 10022 212-400-9550
Web: www.csmcapitalcorp.com

Cullinan Associates Inc
Woodlawn Ctr 295 N Hubbards Ln Second Fl .... Louisville KY 40207 502-893-0300
Web: www.cullinan.com

Cumberland Private Wealth Management Inc
99 Yorkville Ave Ste 300 .... Toronto ON M5R3K5 416-929-1090
Web: www.cumberlandprivate.com

Curran Investment Management
30 S Pearl St Omni Plz Ninth Fl .... Albany NY 12207 518-391-4246
Web: www.curranllc.com

Curtis Financial Group LLC
One Liberty Pl Ste 4400 1650 Market St .... Philadelphia PA 19103 215-972-2375
Web: www.curtisfinancial.com

Cutler Investment Counsel LLC
525 Bigham Knoll .... Jacksonville OR 97530 541-770-9000
Web: www.cutler.com

Cypress Capital Group Inc
251 Royal Palm Way Ste 500 .... Palm Beach FL 33480 561-659-5889
Web: www.cypresscapitalgroup.com

Cypress Wealth Advisors LLC
101 California St Ste 1025 .... San Francisco CA 94111 415-489-2100
Web: www.cypresswealth.com

Dahab Assoc Inc 423 S Country Rd .... Bay Shore NY 11706 631-665-6181
Web: www.dahab.com

DailyFX 32 Old Slip Financial Sq 10th Fl .... New York NY 10005 212-897-7660
Web: www.dailyfx.com

Dale Scott & Co
650 California St Eighth Fl .... San Francisco CA 94108 415-956-1030
Web: www.dalescott.com

Dalton Greiner Hartman Maher & Company LLC
565 Fifth Ave Ste 2101 .... New York NY 10017 212-557-2445 557-4898
Web: www.dghm.com

Dalton Investments LLC
1601 Cloverfield Blvd Ste 5050 N .... Santa Monica CA 90404 424-231-9100
Web: www.daltoninvestments.com

Darrell & King LLC
410 White Gables Ln .... Charlottesville VA 22903 434-977-7010
Web: www.darrellandking.com

Davidson & Garrard Inc 810 Main St .... Lynchburg VA 24505 434-847-6600
Web: dg-g.com

DDJ Capital Management LLC
130 Turner St Bldg 3 Ste 600 .... Waltham MA 02453 781-283-8500 283-8555
Web: www.ddjcap.com

Deans Knight Capital Management Ltd
999 W Hastings St Ste 1500 .... Vancouver BC V6C2W2 604-669-0212
Web: www.deansknight.com

Phone Fax

Deltec Asset Management LLC
623 Fifth Ave 28th Fl .... New York NY 10022 212-546-6200
Web: www.deltec-ny.com

Denning & Company LLC
One California St Ste 2800 .... San Francisco CA 94111 415-399-3939
Web: www.denningandcompany.com

Denver Investment Advisors LLC
1225 17th St 26th Fl .... Denver CO 80202 303-312-5000 312-4900
Web: www.denvest.com

Depository Trust Co 55 Water St 22nd Fl .... New York NY 10041 212-855-1000 855-8707
Web: www.dtcc.com

Design ProfessionalXL Group
2959 Salinas Hwy .... Monterey CA 93940 831-649-5522
TF: 800-227-4284 ■ *Web:* xlgroup.com

Desjardins Securities Inc
1170 Peel St Ste 300 .... Montreal QC H3B0A9 514-987-1749
Web: www2.vmdconseil.ca

Developing World Markets Finance LLP
750 Washington Blvd Ste 500 .... Stamford CT 06901 203-655-5453
Web: www.dwmarkets.com

DH Corp Ste 201 939 Eglinton Ave E .... Toronto ON M4G4H7 416-696-7700
Web: www.dhbrochure.com

Dimeo Schneider & Assoc LLC
500 W Madison St Ste 3855 .... Chicago IL 60661 312-853-1000 853-3352
Web: www.dimeoschneider.com

Dinosaur Securities LLC
470 Park Ave S Ninth Fl .... New York NY 10016 212-448-9944
Web: www.dinogroup.com

DISCERN Investment Analytics Inc
100 Pine St Ste 1850 .... San Francisco CA 94111 415-817-9012
Web: www.discern.com

Disciplined Growth Investors Inc
Fifth St Towers 150 S Fifth St Ste 2550 .... Minneapolis MN 55402 612-317-4100
Web: www.dginv.com

DL Carlson Investment Group Inc
101 N State St .... Concord NH 03301 603-224-5977
Web: www.carlsoninvest.com

Dodge & Cox 555 California St 40th Fl .... San Francisco CA 94104 415-981-1710 986-1369
TF: 800-254-8494 ■ *Web:* www.dodgeandcoxworldwide.com

Don Park LP 842 York Mills Rd .... North York ON M3B3A8 416-449-7275
Web: www.donpark.com

Donald Smith & Company Inc
152 W 57th St 22nd Fl .... New York NY 10019 212-284-0990
Web: www.donaldsmithandco.com

Donaldson Capital Management LLC
20 NW First St Fifth Fl .... Evansville IN 47708 812-421-3211
Web: www.dcmol.com

Dorsey Wright & Associates Inc
1011 Boulder Springs Dr Ste 150 .... Richmond VA 23225 804-320-8511
Web: www.dorseywright.com

Dover Financial Research LLC 208 Dover Rd .... Westwood MA 02090 781-461-0922
Web: www.doverfr.com

Dragonfly Capital Partners LLC
The Packard Bldg 1310 S Tryon St Ste 109 .... Charlotte NC 28203 704-342-3491
Web: www.dragonflycapital.com

Drake Capital Advisors LLC
One Fawcett Pl Ste 140 .... Greenwich CT 06830 203-861-7500
Web: www.drakeadvisors.com

Driehaus Capital Management Inc 25 E Erie St .... Chicago IL 60611 312-587-3800 587-3234
TF: 800-688-8819 ■ *Web:* www.driehaus.com

Duff & Phelps Investment Management Co
200 S Wacker Dr Ste 500 .... Chicago IL 60606 312-263-2610
Web: www.dpimc.com

DUNN Capital Management LLC
309 SE Osceola St Dunn Bldg Ste 350 .... Stuart FL 34994 772-286-4777
Web: www.dunncapital.com

Eagle Asset Management
880 Carillon Pkwy .... Saint Petersburg FL 33716 800-237-3101 573-8655*
**Fax Area Code:* 727 ■ **Fax:* Mktg ■ *TF:* 800-237-3101 ■ *Web:* www.eagleasset.com

Eagle Global Advisors LLC
5847 San Felipe Ste 930 .... Houston TX 77057 713-952-3550
Web: www.eagleglobal.com

Eagle Investment Systems LLC
65 LaSalle Rd Ste 305 .... West Hartford CT 06107 860-561-4602
Web: www.eagleinvsys.com

Earnest Partners LLC
1180 Peachtree St Ste 2300 .... Atlanta GA 30309 404-815-8772 815-8948
TF: 800-322-0068 ■ *Web:* www.earnestpartners.com

Eastbourne Capital Management LLC
1101 Fifth Ave Ste 370 .... San Rafael CA 94901 415-448-1200
Web: www.eastbournecapital.com

Edgar Lomax Co 6564 Loisdale Ct Ste 310 .... Springfield VA 22150 703-719-0026
TF: 866-205-0524 ■ *Web:* www.edgarlomax.com

Eidelman Virant Capital
8000 Maryland Ave Ste 380 .... Saint Louis MO 63105 314-727-9686
Web: www.eidelmanvirant.com

Elan Financial Services
225 W Sta Sq Dr Ste 620 .... Pittsburgh PA 15219 877-935-2637
TF: 877-935-2637 ■ *Web:* www.elanfinancialservices.com

Electronic Entertainment Design & Research Inc
2075 Corte Del Nogal Ste B .... Carlsbad CA 92011 760-579-7100
Web: www.eedar.com

Eliot Rose Asset Management LLC
1000 Chapel View Blvd Ste 240 .... Cranston RI 02920 401-588-5100
Web: www.eliotrose.com

Elliott Cove Capital Management
1000 Second Ave Ste 1440 .... Seattle WA 98104 206-267-2683
Web: www.elliottcove.com

emat Capital Management LLC
7474 N Figueroa St Ste A .... Los Angeles CA 90041 323-255-1333
Web: www.ematcapital.com

Phone | Fax

Emerald Asset Advisors LLC
2843 Executive Park Dr. . . . . Weston FL 33331 954-385-9624
Web: www.emerald-eas.com

Encima Global LLC 645 Madison Ave Fifth Fl . . . . . New York NY 10022 212-876-4400
Web: www.encimaglobal.com

Encompass Financial Advisors Inc
6107 SW Murray Blvd Ste 403 . . . . . Beaverton OR 97008 503-643-8075
Web: fiadvisor.com

Energy Security Analysis Inc
401 Edgewater Pl Ste 640 . . . . . Wakefield MA 01880 781-245-2036
Web: www.esai.com

EnviroCap LLC 2111 W Swann Ave 3rd Fl . . . . . Tampa FL 33606 813-341-3650
Web: www.envirocap.com

Envision Capital Management Inc
11755 Wilshire Blvd 1140 . . . . . Los Angeles CA 90025 310-445-3252
Web: www.envisioncap.com

Epoch Investment Partners Inc
640 Fifth Ave 18th Fl . . . . . New York NY 10019 212-303-7200 202-4948
NASDAQ: EPHC ■ *Web:* www.eipny.com

Essex Investment Management Company LLC
125 High St 29th Fl . . . . . Boston MA 02110 617-342-3200 342-3280
Web: www.essexinvest.com

Estrada Hinojosa & Company Inc
1717 Main St LB47 . . . . . Dallas TX 75201 214-658-1670 658-1671
TF: 800-676-5352 ■ *Web:* www.estradahinojosa.com

Europlay Capital Advisors LLC
15260 Ventura Blvd 20th Fl . . . . . Sherman Oaks CA 91403 818-444-4400
Web: www.europlaycapital.com

EVC Group Inc 201 Mission St Ste 1930 . . . . . San Francisco CA 94105 415-896-6820
Web: www.evcgroup.com

Evercore Partners Inc 55 E 52nd St . . . . . New York NY 10055 212-857-3100
Web: www.evercore.com

Evergreen Advisors LLC
9256 Bendix Rd Ste 300 . . . . . Columbia MD 21045 410-997-6000
Web: www.evergreenadvisorsllc.com

Evergreen Capital Management LLC
10500 N East 8th Ste 950 . . . . . Bellevue WA 98004 425-467-4600
Web: www.evergreencapital.net

Excipio Consulting LLC
1216 E Kenosha St . . . . . Broken Arrow OK 74012 918-357-5507
Web: www.excipio.net

Executive Monetary Management LLC
220 E 42nd St 32nd Fl . . . . . New York NY 10017 212-476-5555
Web: www.michaelbolton.com

Exvere Inc 1301 Fifth Ave Ste 3405 . . . . . Seattle WA 98101 206-728-1800
Web: www.exvere.com

Fairfield Research Corp
65 Locust Ave Ste 200 . . . . . New Canaan CT 06840 203-972-0404
Web: www.frcinvest.com

Falkenberg Capital Corp
600 S Cherry St Cherry Creek Plz I Ste 1108 . . . . . Denver CO 80246 303-320-4800
Web: www.falkenbergcapital.com

Falls River Group LLC 305 Fifth Ave S Ste 206 . . . . . Naples FL 34102 239-649-4222
Web: www.fallsrivergroup.com

Farber Financial Group 150 York St Ste 1600 . . . . . Toronto ON M5H3S5 416-497-0150
Web: www.farberfinancial.com

Favus Institutional Research LLC
PO Box 1003 . . . . . New York NY 10276 917-952-8158
Web: favusinstitutionalresearch.com

Fayez Sarofim & Co 909 Fannin St Ste 2907 . . . . . Houston TX 77010 713-654-4484 654-8184
Web: www.sarofim.com

FCA Corp 791 Town & Country Blvd Ste 250 . . . . . Houston TX 77024 713-781-2856 781-7195
Web: www.fcacorp.com

FCM Investments 2200 Ross Ave Ste 4600 W . . . . . Dallas TX 75201 214-665-6900 665-6940
Web: www.fcminvest.com

Federated Investors
1001 Liberty Ave Federated Investors Twr . . . . . Pittsburgh PA 15222 412-288-1900 288-6751*
NYSE: FII ■ **Fax:* Hum Res ■ *TF:* 800-245-0242 ■ *Web:* www.federatedinvestors.com

Feltl & Company Inc
2100 LaSalle Plz 800 LaSalle Ave . . . . . Minneapolis MN 55402 612-492-8800
Web: www.feltl.com

FHL Capital Corp
Two N Twentieth St Ste 860 . . . . . Birmingham AL 35203 205-328-3098
Web: www.fhlcapital.com

FIC Capital Inc 286 Madison Ave 11th Fl . . . . . New York NY 10017 212-679-2100
Web: www.ficcapital.com

Fidelity Investments Institutional Services Company Inc
82 Devonshire St . . . . . Boston MA 02109 617-563-9840
TF: 800-343-3548 ■ *Web:* www.fidelity.com

Fiduciary Capital Management Inc
PO Box 80 . . . . . Wallingford CT 06492 203-269-0440 269-6440
Web: www.fcmstablevalue.com

Fiduciary Management Assoc LLC
55 W Monroe St Ste 2550 . . . . . Chicago IL 60603 312-930-6850 641-2511
Web: www.fmausa.com

Fiduciary Management Inc of Milwaukee
100 E Wisconsin Ave Ste 2200 . . . . . Milwaukee WI 53202 414-226-4545 226-4522
TF: 800-264-7684 ■ *Web:* www.fiduciarymgt.com

Financial Dimensions Group
3900 Northwoods Dr . . . . . Saint Paul MN 55112 651-490-3458
Web: www.fdg-advisors.com

Financial Resource Group LLC
12900 Preston Rd Ste 1030 LB-104 . . . . . Dallas TX 75230 972-960-7790
Web: www.frgroup.net

Financial Technology Partners LP
601 California St 22nd Fl . . . . . San Francisco CA 94108 415-512-8700
Web: www.ftpartners.com

First Affirmative Financial Network LLC
5475 Mark Dabling Blvd Ste 108 . . . . . Colorado Springs CO 80918 719-636-1045
Web: www.firstaffirmative.com

First Fidelity Capital Markets Inc
10463 Stonebridge Blvd Ste 400 . . . . . Boca Raton FL 33498 561-558-0730
Web: www.ffidelity.com

First Pacific Advisors Inc
11400 W Olympic Blvd Ste 1200 . . . . . Los Angeles CA 90064 310-473-0225 996-5450
TF: 800-982-4372 ■ *Web:* www.fpafunds.com

Firsthand Capital Management Inc
150 Almaden Blvd Ste 1250 . . . . . San Jose CA 95113 408-886-7096
Web: www.firsthandcapital.com

Fischer Francis Trees & Watts Inc
200 Pk Ave 11th Fl . . . . . New York NY 10166 212-681-3000 681-3250
TF: 888-367-3389 ■ *Web:* www.fftw.com

Fisher Investments 13100 Skyline Blvd . . . . . Woodside CA 94062 800-550-1071 851-3514*
**Fax Area Code:* 650 ■ *TF:* 800-550-1071 ■ *Web:* www.fi.com

Flexial Corp 1483 Gould Dr . . . . . Cookeville TN 38506 931-432-1853
Web: www.flexial.com

Flexible Plan Investments Ltd
3883 Telegraph Rd Ste 100 . . . . . Bloomfield Hills MI 48302 248-642-6640
Web: www.flexibleplan.com

FMR Corp 82 Devonshire St . . . . . Boston MA 02109 800-343-3548
TF: 800-343-3548 ■ *Web:* www.fidelity.com

Fogel Capital Management Inc 453 Riverside Dr . . . . . Stuart FL 34994 772-223-9686
Web: fogelcapital.com

Foothills Asset Management Ltd
8767 E Via de Ventura Ste 175 . . . . . Scottsdale AZ 85258 480-777-9870
Web: www.faml.net

Ford Equity Research Inc
11722 Sorrento Vly Rd Ste I . . . . . San Diego CA 92121 858-755-1327
TF: 800-842-0207 ■ *Web:* www.fordequity.com

Forefront Analytics LLC
One Tower Bridge 100 Front St
Ste 1111 . . . . . West Conshohocken PA 19428 610-341-3900
Web: www.forefrontanalytics.com

Forest Investment Assoc
15 Piedmont Ctr Ste 1250 . . . . . Atlanta GA 30305 404-261-9575 261-9574
Web: www.forestinvest.com

Formula Growth Ltd
1010 Sherbrooke St W Ste 2300 . . . . . Montreal QC H3A2R7 514-288-5136
Web: www.formulagrowth.ca

Fort Point Capital Partners LLC
275 Sacramento St Eighth Fl . . . . . San Francisco CA 94111 415-625-0909
Web: www.fortpointcap.com

Fort Washington Investment Advisors Inc
303 Broadway Ste 1200 . . . . . Cincinnati OH 45202 513-361-7600
Web: www.fortwashington.com

Foster & Motley Inc
7755 Montgomery Rd Ste 100 . . . . . Cincinnati OH 45236 513-561-6640
Web: www.fosterandmotley.com

Franklin Park Associates LLC
Franklin Park 251 St Asaphs Rd Three Bala Plz
Ste 500 W . . . . . Bala Cynwyd PA 19004 610-822-0500
Web: www.franklinparkllc.com

Franklin Resources Inc
One Franklin Pkwy Bdge 970 First Fl . . . . . San Mateo CA 94403 650-312-2000 525-7141*
NYSE: BEN ■ **Fax:* Hum Res ■ *TF:* 800-632-2301 ■ *Web:* www.franklintempleton.com

Fredericks Michael & Co 430 Park Ave . . . . . New York NY 10022 212-732-1600
Web: www.fm-co.com

Front Street Capital 87 Front St E Ste 400 . . . . . Toronto ON M5E1B8 416-364-1990
Web: www.frontstreetcapital.com

Frontier Asset Management LLC
201 N Connor St Ste 250 . . . . . Sheridan WY 82801 307-673-5675
Web: www.frontierasset.com

Frontier Investment Management Co
8401 N Central Expy Ste 300 . . . . . Dallas TX 75225 972-934-2590
Web: www.frontierinvest.com

Fundquest 1 Winthrop Sq . . . . . Boston MA 02110 617-526-0766
Web: www.fundquestadvisor.com

Gannett Welsh & Kotler LLC
222 Berkeley St 15th Fl . . . . . Boston MA 02116 617-236-8900 236-1815
TF: 800-225-4236 ■ *Web:* www.gwkinvest.com

Garcia Hamilton & Associates LP
Five Houston Ctr 1401 McKinney Ste 1600 . . . . . Houston TX 77010 713-853-2322
Web: www.dhja.com

GARP Research & Securities Co
406 Main St Reisterstown . . . . . Baltimore MD 21136 410-764-1300
Web: www.garpresearch.com

Garrison Investment Group LP
1290 Ave of the Americas Ste 914 . . . . . New York NY 10104 212-372-9500
Web: www.garrisoninv.com

Gates Capital Management Inc
1177 Ave of the Americas between 45th and 46th Sts
46th Fl . . . . . New York NY 10036 212-626-1421
Web: www.gatescap.com

GDBA Investments LLLP 1440 Blake St Ste 310 . . . . . Denver CO 80202 720-932-9395
Web: www.gdbainvestments.com

Gemini Fund Services LLC 450 Wireless Blvd . . . . . Hauppauge NY 11788 631-470-2600 951-0573
Web: www.geminifund.com

Genus Capital Management Inc
900 W Hastings St Sixth Fl . . . . . Vancouver BC V6C1E5 604-683-4554
Web: www.genuscap.com

Georgian Partners 1300 Yonge St Ste 410 . . . . . Toronto ON M4T1X3 416-868-9696
Web: www.georgianpartners.com

Glenmede Trust Co
1650 Market St Ste 1200 . . . . . Philadelphia PA 19103 215-419-6000 419-6199
TF: 800-966-3200 ■ *Web:* www.glenmede.com

Global Cash Card Seven Corporate Park Ste 130 . . . . . Irvine CA 92606 949-751-0360
Web: www.globalcashcard.com

Global Credit Advisers LLC
101 Park Ave 26th Fl . . . . . New York NY 10178 212-949-1860
Web: www.globalcreditadvisers.com

Goelzer Investment Management Inc
111 Monument Cir Ste 500 . . . . . Indianapolis IN 46204 317-264-2600
Web: www.goelzerinc.com

Goldcrest Investments 5956 Sherry Ln Ste 930 . . . . . Dallas TX 75225 214-303-1112
Web: www.goldcrestinvestments.com

	City	State	Zip	Phone	Fax
Golden Capital Management LLC 10715 David Taylor Dr Ste 400 *Web:* www.gcm1.com	Charlotte	NC	28262	704-593-1144	
Goldman Sachs Asset Management (GSAM) 200 W St *TF:* 800-526-7384 ■ *Web:* www.goldmansachs.com	New York	NY	10282	212-902-1000	
Gollob Morgan Peddy & Company CPA 1001 Ese Loop 323 Ste 300 *Web:* www.gmpcpa.com	Tyler	TX	75701	903-534-0088	
Goode Investment Management Inc 23220 Shaker Blvd Ste 1700	Shaker Heights	OH	44122	216-771-9000	771-1949
Gould Asset Management LLC 341 W First St Ste 200 *Web:* www.gouldasset.com	Claremont	CA	91711	909-445-1291	
Gramercy Advisors LLC 20 Dayton Ave *Web:* www.gramercyadvisors.com	Greenwich	CT	06830	203-552-1900	
Granahan Investment Management Inc 404 Wyman St Ste 460 *Web:* www.granahan.com	Waltham	MA	02451	781-890-4412	
Granite Point Capital 222 Berkeley St *Web:* www.granitepoint.com	Boston	MA	02116	617-587-7500	
Grantham Mayo Van Otterloo & Company LLC (GMO) 40 Rowes Wharf *Web:* www.gmo.com	Boston	MA	02110	617-330-7500	261-0134
Grassi Investment Management LLC 1804 N Shoreline Blvd Ste 140 *Web:* www.grassiinvest.com	Mountain View	CA	94043	650-934-0770	
Gratry & Company LLC 20600 Chagrin Blvd 320 Tower E *Web:* www.gratry.com	Shaker Heights	OH	44122	216-283-8423	
Graybill Bartz & Thompson 568 S Spring Rd *Web:* www.graybillbartz.com	Elmhurst	IL	60126	630-941-9460	832-3491
Great Point Investors LLC Two Center Plz Ste 410 *Web:* www.gpinvestors.com	Boston	MA	02108	617-526-8800	
Greenhill & Company Inc 300 Pk Ave 23rd Fl *NYSE: GHL* ■ *Web:* www.greenhill.com	New York	NY	10022	212-389-1500	389-1700
Greycroft Partners LLC 292 Madison Ave 41st St *Web:* www.greycroftpartners.com	New York	NY	10017	212-756-3508	
Greystone Managed Investments Inc 300 Park Centre 1230 Blackfoot Dr *Web:* www.greystone.ca	Regina	SK	S4S7G4	306-779-6400	
H A M Media Group 305 Madison St Ste 3016 *Web:* www.hammedia.com	New York	NY	10017	212-297-2575	297-2576
Hagerty Peterson & Company LLC 421 N Northwest Hwy Ste 201 *Web:* www.hagertypeterson.com	Barrington	IL	60010	847-277-9900	
Hahn Capital Management LLC 601 Montgomery St Ste 840 *Web:* www.hahncap.com	San Francisco	CA	94111	415-394-6512	
Haidar Capital Management LLC Carnegie Hall Tower 152 W 57th St *Web:* www.haidarcapital.com	New York	NY	10019	212-752-5077	
Hall Capital Partners LLC One Maritime Plz Fifth Fl *Web:* www.hallcapital.com	San Francisco	CA	94111	415-288-0544	
Halpern Capital Inc 20900 NE 30th Ave Ste 200 *Web:* www.halperncapital.com	Aventura	FL	33180	786-528-1400	
Hamilton Advisors Inc 373 Stanwich Rd *Web:* www.hamiltonadvisors.com	Greenwich	CT	06830	203-629-1112	629-1469
Hamilton Capital Management 5025 Arlington Centre Blvd *Web:* www.hamiltoncapital.com	Columbus	OH	43220	614-273-1000	
Hanseatic Management Services Inc 5600 Wyoming N E Ste 220 *Web:* www.hanseaticgroup.com	Albuquerque	NM	87109	505-828-2824	
Harbour Investments Inc 575 D'Onofrio Dr Ste 300 *Web:* www.harbourinv.com	Madison	WI	53719	608-662-6100	
Harrington Investments Inc 1001 Second St Ste 325 *Web:* harringtoninvestments.com	Napa	CA	94559	707-252-6166	
Harris Assoc LP 111 South Wacker Dr Ste 4600 *TF:* 800-731-0700 ■ *Web:* www.harrisassoc.com	Chicago	IL	60606	312-646-3600	268-5295
Hartford Investment Management Co 55 Farmington Ave Fl 9 *Web:* www.himco.com	Hartford	CT	06105	860-297-6700	
Hawthorn PNC Family Wealth 1600 Market St *TF:* 888-947-3762 ■ *Web:* www.hawthorn.pnc.com	Philadelphia	PA	19103	888-947-3762	
Haywood Securities Inc Waterfront Centre 200 Burrard St Ste 700 *Web:* www.haywood.com	Vancouver	BC	V6C3L6	604-697-7100	
HD Vest Financial Services 6333 N State Hwy 161 Fourth Fl *TF:* 866-218-8206 ■ *Web:* hdvest.com	Irving	TX	75038	972-870-6000	870-6128
HealthEdge Investment Partners 5550 W Executive Dr Ste 230 *Web:* www.healthedgepartners.com	Tampa	FL	33609	813-490-7100	
Heaton Adams & Co 333 W Fourth St *Web:* www.heatonadams.com	Waterloo	IA	50701	319-232-1943	235-6664
Hedgeye Risk Management LLC 111 Whitney Ave *Web:* www2.hedgeye.com	New Haven	CT	06510	203-562-6500	
Height Analytics LLC 1775 Pennsylvania Ave NW Fifth Fl *Web:* www.heightllc.com	Washington	DC	20006	202-629-0000	
Henderson Global Investors One Financial Plz Fl 19 *TF:* 888-832-6774 ■ *Web:* www.henderson.com	Hartford	CT	06103	860-723-8600	
Hengehold Capital Management LLC 6116 Harrison Ave *Web:* www.hengeholdcapital.com	Cincinnati	OH	45247	513-598-5120	
Hennessee Group LLC 500 Fifth Ave 47th Fl *Web:* www.hennesseegroup.com	New York	NY	10110	212-857-4400	
Herndon Plant Oakley Ltd 800 N Shoreline Blvd Ste 2200 South *Web:* www.hpo.com	Corpus Christi	TX	78401	361-888-7611	888-9342
Hershey Trust Co 100 Mansion Rd E *Web:* www.hersheytrust.com	Hershey	PA	17033	717-520-1100	
HFI Wealth Management Inc 8530 Shepherdstown Pk PO Box E *Web:* www.hfiwealth.com	Shepherdstown	WV	25443	304-876-2619	
HFS Consultants 505 Fourteenth St Fifth Fl *Web:* www.hfsconsultants.com	Oakland	CA	94612	510-768-0066	
HGK Asset Management Inc 525 Washington Blvd Newport Tower Ste 2000 *Web:* www.hgk.com	Jersey City	NJ	07310	201-659-3700	
Hid Inc 119 Starwood Cir Lot 16	Jacksonville	NC	28540	910-455-6664	
Hillsdale Investment Management Inc 100 Wellington St W Ste 2100 TD Centre *Web:* www.hillsdaleinv.com	Toronto	ON	M5K1J3	416-913-3900	913-3901
Hillview Capital Advisors LLC 170 N Radnor-Chester Rd Ste 150 *Web:* www.hillviewcap.com	Radnor	PA	19087	484-708-4720	
HLB Cinnamon Jang Willoughby Metro Tower II Ste 900-4720 Kingsway *Web:* www.cjw.com	Burnaby	BC	V5H4N2	604-435-4317	
Holland Capital Management LP 303 W Madison St Ste 700 *TF:* 800-295-9779 ■ *Web:* www.hollandcap.com	Chicago	IL	60606	312-553-4830	553-4848
Horizon Wealth Management 8280 Ymca Plaza Dr Bldg 5 *Web:* www.horizonfg.com	Baton Rouge	LA	70810	225-612-3820	
Houston Trust Co 1001 Fannin St Ste 700 *Web:* www.houstontrust.com	Houston	TX	77002	713-651-9400	651-9402
Howland Capital Management Inc 75 Federal St Ste 1100 *Web:* www.howlandcapital.com	Boston	MA	02110	617-357-9110	357-5540
HPA Development Group Inc 7800 Cooper Rd Ste 204 *Web:* www.hpadg.com	Cincinnati	OH	45242	513-793-2400	
Hughes Capital Management Inc 916 Prince St Third Fl *Web:* hughescm.com	Alexandria	VA	22314	703-684-7222	684-7799
Hyperion Capital Management Inc 200 Vessey St 3 World Financial Ctr *TF:* 800-497-3746 ■ *Web:* brookfieldim.com	New York	NY	10281	212-549-8400	549-8300
ICC Capital Management Inc 390 N Orange Ave Ste 2700 *Web:* www.icccapital.com	Orlando	FL	32801	407-839-8440	
ICM Asset Management Inc 601 W Main Ave *TF:* 800-488-4075 ■ *Web:* www.icmasset.com	Spokane	WA	99201	509-455-3588	777-0999
ICON Advisers Inc 5299 DTC Blvd Ste 1200 *Web:* www.iconadvisers.com	Greenwood Village	CO	80111	303-790-1600	
IGM Financial Inc 447 Portage Ave 1 Canada Ctr *NYSE: IGM* ■ **Fax Area Code:* 204 ■ *TF:* 888-746-6344 ■ *Web:* www.investorsgroup.com	Winnipeg	MB	R3C3B6	888-746-6344	956-7688*
Imperial Capital LLC 2000 Ave of the Stars S Tower Ninth Fl *Web:* www.imperialcapital.com	Los Angeles	CA	90067	310-246-3700	
Incentives Advisors LLC 1001 W Southern Ave Ste 135 *Web:* www.incentiveadvisors.com	Mesa	AZ	85210	480-302-6370	
Income Research & Management 100 Federal St 30th Fl *Web:* www.incomeresearch.com	Boston	MA	02110	617-330-9333	
Indaba Capital Management LP One Letterman Dr Bldg D Ste DM700 The Presidio of San Francisco *Web:* www.indabacapital.com	San Francisco	CA	94129	415-680-1180	
Independent Capital Management 4141 Inland Empire Blvd Ste 301 *Web:* www.icmfinancial.com	Ontario	CA	91764	909-948-1608	
Infinity Capital Partners LLC 1355 Peachtree St N E Ste 750 *Web:* www.infinityfunds.com	Atlanta	GA	30309	678-904-6301	
Innovest Portfolio Solutions LLC 4643 S Ulster St Ste 1040 *Web:* www.innovestinc.com	Denver	CO	80237	303-694-1900	
Institutional Shareholder Services Inc 2099 Gaither Rd Ste 501 *Web:* www.issgovernance.com	Rockville	MD	20850	301-556-0500	
Integra Capital Ltd 2020 Winston Park Dr Ste 200 *Web:* www.integra.com	Oakville	ON	L6H6X7	905-829-1131	
Integral Group LLC, The 191 Peachtree St NE Ste 4100 *Web:* www.integral-online.com	Atlanta	GA	30303	404-224-1860	224-1899
Integrated Wealth Counsel LLC 100 Clock Tower Pl Ste 210 *Web:* www.integratedwealth.com	Carmel	CA	93923	831-624-3317	
Intelligent Capital Inc Market at Third St The Hearst Bldg Ste 810 *Web:* www.intelligentcapital.com	San Francisco	CA	94103	415-974-1000	
Interlaken Capital Inc 475 Steamboat Rd Second Fl *Web:* www.interlakencapital.com	Greenwich	CT	06830	203-629-8750	
International Risk Management Institute Inc 12222 Merit Dr Ste 1450 *Web:* www.cvrdallas.com	Dallas	TX	75251	972-960-7693	

Company / Address	City	State	ZIP	Phone	Fax
InvestAmerica Investment Advisors Inc 101 Second St SE Ste 800 — Web: www.investamericaventure.com	Cedar Rapids	IA	52401	319-363-8249	363-9683
Investcorp International Inc 280 Park Ave Fl 37 — Web: www.investcorp.com	New York	NY	10017	212-599-4700	
Investment Counselors of Maryland LLC 803 Cathedral St — Web: www.icomd.com	Baltimore	MD	21201	410-539-3838	625-9016
Investment Performance Services LLC 7402 Hodgson Memorial Dr Ste 100 — Web: www.ips-net.com	Savannah	GA	31406	912-352-2862	
Investment Scorecard Inc 601 Grassmere Park Dr Ste 1 — Web: informais.com/	Nashville	TN	37211	615-665-1234	
Investor Growth Capital Inc 630 Fifth Ave Ste 1965 — Web: www.investorab.com	New York	NY	10111	212-515-9000	515-9009
IOS Partners 311 Mendoza Ave — Web: www.iospartners.com	Coral Gables	FL	33134	305-648-2877	
Ironbound Capital Management LP 902 Carnegie Ctr Ste 300 — Web: www.ironboundcapital.com	Princeton	NJ	08540	609-951-5000	
ISC Group Inc 3500 Oak Lawn Ave Ste 400 — Web: www.iscgroup.com	Dallas	TX	75219	214-520-1115	
Ivory Investment Management LP 11755 Wilshire Blvd Ste 1350 — Web: www.ivorycapital.com	Los Angeles	CA	90025	310-899-7300	
Jacob Securities Inc 199 Bay St Commerce Court W PO Box 322 Ste 2901 — Web: www.jacobsecurities.com	Toronto	ON	M5L1G1	416-866-8300	
Jacobus Wealth Management Inc 2323 N Mayfair Rd — Web: www.jwmfamilyoffices.com	Milwaukee	WI	53226	414-475-6565	
Jacuzzi Brands Inc 13925 City Ctr Dr Ste 200 — Web: www.jacuzzi.com	Chino Hills	CA	91709	909-247-2920	
James Investment Research Inc 1349 Fairgrounds Rd — Web: www.jamesfunds.com	Xenia	OH	45385	937-426-7640	
Janus Capital Management LLC 151 Detroit St — Web: www.janus.com	Denver	CO	80206	303-333-3863	
Jatheon Technologies Inc British Colonial Bldg 8 Wellington St E Mezzanine Level — TF: 888-528-4366 ■ Web: www.jatheon.com	Toronto	ON	M5E1C5	416-840-0418	849-9971
Jeffrey Matthews Financial Group LLC, The 30B Vreeland Rd Ste 210 — TF: 888-467-3636 ■ Web: www.jeffreymatthews.com	Florham Park	NJ	07932	973-805-6222	
Jetstream Capital LLC 12 Cadillac Dr Ste 280 — Web: www.jetstreamcapital.com	Brentwood	TN	37027	615-425-3400	425-3401
JFS Wealth Advisors LLC 1479 N Hermitage Rd — Web: www.jfswa.com	Hermitage	PA	16148	724-962-3200	
JMG Financial Group Ltd 2301 W 22nd St Ste 300 — Web: jmgfinancial.com	Oak Brook	IL	60523	630-571-5252	
JNBA Financial Advisors Inc 8500 Normandale Lk Blvd Ste 450 — Web: jnba.com	Minneapolis	MN	55437	952-844-0995	
JNK Securities Corp 902 Broadway 20th Fl — Web: www.jnksecurities.com	New York	NY	10010	212-885-6300	
John Hsu Capital Group Inc 747 Third Ave 26th Fl — Web: www.johnhsucapital.com	New York	NY	10017	212-223-7515	
John W Bristol & Company Inc 48 Wall St 18th Fl — Web: www.jwbristol.com	New York	NY	10005	212-389-5880	
Johnson Investment Counsel Inc 3777 W Fork Rd — Web: www.johnsoninv.com	Cincinnati	OH	45247	513-661-3100	
Johnston Asset Management Corp One Landmark Sq 20th Fl — Web: www.johnstonasset.com	Stamford	CT	06901	203-324-4722	
Jones & Roth PC 432 W 11th Ave PO Box 10086 — Web: www.jrcpa.com	Eugene	OR	97401	541-687-2320	485-0960
JPMorgan Fleming Asset Management PO Box 8528 — *Fax Area Code: 816 ■ TF: 800-480-4111 ■ Web: www.jpmorganfunds.com	Boston	MA	02266	800-480-4111	471-3053*
JPMorgan Worldwide Securities Services 270 Park Ave — Web: www.jpmorgan.com	New York	NY	10017	212-270-6000	
Jra Financial Advisors 7373 Kirkwood Ct Ste 300 — Web: www.jrafinancial.com	Maple Grove	MN	55369	763-315-8000	
Kalmar Investments Inc Barley Mill House 3701 Kennett Pk — Web: www.kalmarinvestments.com	Wilmington	DE	19807	302-658-7575	
Karr Barth Assoc Inc 40 Monument Rd — Web: karr-barthassociates.com	Bala Cynwyd	PA	19004	610-660-4459	
KARVY Global Services (US) 11 Broadway Ste 1568 — Web: www.karvyglobal.com	New York	NY	10004	212-267-4381	
Kaspick & Co 203 Redwood Shores Pkwy Ste 300 — Web: www.kaspick.com	Redwood Shores	CA	94065	650-585-4100	
Kayne Anderson Capital Advisors LP 1800 Ave of the Stars Third Fl — TF: 800-638-1496 ■ Web: www.kaynecapital.com	Los Angeles	CA	90067	800-638-1496	
KCD Financial Inc 3313 S Packerland Dr Ste E — Web: www.kcdfinancial.com	De Pere	WI	54115	920-347-3400	
KCM Investment Advisors LLC 750 Lindaro St Ste 250 — Web: www.kcmadvisors.com	San Rafael	CA	94901	415-461-7788	
KDI Capital Partners LLC 4101 Lk Boone Trl Ste 218 — Web: www.kdicapitalpartners.com	Raleigh	NC	27607	919-573-4124	
Keane Capital Management Inc 3440 Toringdon Way Ste 308 — Web: www.keanecapital.com	Charlotte	NC	28277	704-364-3250	
Keats, Connelly & Associates LLC 3336 N 32nd St Ste 100 — Web: www.keatsconnelly.com	Phoenix	AZ	85018	602-955-5007	
Kensico Capital Management Corp 55 RailRoad Ave Second Fl — Web: www.kensicocapital.com	Greenwich	CT	06830	203-862-5800	
Kerlin Capital Group LLC 555 S Flower St Ste 2750 — Web: www.kerlincapital.com	Los Angeles	CA	90071	213-627-3300	
Keystone Capital Corp 3511 Camino Del Rio S Ste 406 — Web: www.keystonecapcorp.com	San Diego	CA	92108	619-283-3107	
Keystone Capital Inc 155 N Wacker Dr Ste 4150 — Web: www.keystonecapital.com	Chicago	IL	60606	312-219-7900	
Killen Group Inc 1189 Lancaster Ave — TF: 877-454-5536 ■ Web: www.thekillengroup.com	Berwyn	PA	19312	610-296-7222	296-3168
Kirr Marbach & Co Investment Management 621 Washington St — Web: www.kirrmar.com	Columbus	IN	47201	812-376-9444	
Knightsbridge Asset Management LLC 660 Newport Ctr Dr Ste 460 — Web: www.knightsb.com	Newport Beach	CA	92660	949-644-4444	
Koler Wealth Management 6400 Pearl Rd — Web: www.kolerfinancialgroup.com	Parma	OH	44130	440-884-7042	
Koonce Securities Inc 6550 Rock Spring Dr Ste 600 — Web: www.koonce.net	Bethesda	MD	20817	301-897-9700	
Kootenay Savings Financial 300 - 1199 Cedar Ave — Web: www.kscu.com	Trail	BC	V1R4B8	250-368-2686	
Kornitzer Capital Management Inc 5420 W 61st Pl — Web: www.kornitzercapitalmanagement.com	Shawnee Mission	KS	66205	913-677-7778	
Koshinski Asset Management Inc 226 W Eldorado St — Web: www.investment-planners.com	Decatur	IL	62522	217-425-6340	
Kubera Partners LLC 1475 Franklin Ave Garden City — Web: www.kuberapartners.com	New York	NY	11530	212-202-7657	
Kuhns Brothers 558 Lime Rock Rd — Web: www.kuhnsbrothers.com	Lakeville	CT	06039	860-435-7000	
L. Roy Papp & Associates LLP 2201 E Camelback Rd Ste 227B — Web: www.roypapp.com	Phoenix	AZ	85016	602-956-0980	
Laidlaw Group LLC Two Depot Plz Ste 202C — Web: www.laidlawgrp.com	Bedford Hills	NY	10507	914-767-0650	
Laird Norton Tyee 801 Second Ave Ste 1600 — TF: 800-426-5105 ■ Web: lairdnortonwm.com	Seattle	WA	98104	206-464-5100	464-5267
Lakeside Capital Management LLC 50 S Sixth St Ste 1460 — Web: www.gmbmezz.com	Minneapolis	MN	55402	612-243-4400	
Lampo Group Inc, The 1749 Mallory Ln — Web: www.daveramsey.com	Brentwood	TN	37027	615-371-8881	
Lancaster Pollard Investment Advisory Group 65 E State St Ste 1600 — Web: www.lancasterpollard.com	Columbus	OH	43215	614-224-8800	
Landaas & Co 411 E Wisconsin Ave 20th Fl — Web: www.landaas.com	Milwaukee	WI	53202	414-223-1099	
Lara Shull & May LLC 7600 Leesburg Pk Ste 120 E — Web: www.larashullmay.com	Falls Church	VA	22043	703-827-2300	
Lau Associates LLC 20 Montchanin Rd Ste 110 — Web: www.lauassociates.net	Greenville	DE	19807	302-792-5955	
Laurentian Bank Securities Inc 1981 McGill College Ave Ste 100 — Web: www.vmbl.ca	Montreal	QC	H3A3K3	514-350-2800	
Lawson Kroeker Investment Management Inc 450 Regency Pkwy Ste 410 — Web: www.lawsonkroeker.com	Omaha	NE	68114	402-392-2606	
Lazenby & Associates Inc 1050 Indigo Dr Ste 130 — Web: www.lazenbyassociates.com	Las Vegas	NV	89145	702-304-9270	
LCG Assoc Inc 400 Galleria Pkwy SE — Web: www.lcgassociates.com	Atlanta	GA	30339	770-644-0100	644-0105
Leavitt Capital Management Inc 3000 Dundee Rd Ste 101 — Web: www.leavittcapital.com	Northbrook	IL	60062	847-205-1300	
Leconte Wealth Management LLC 703 William Blount Dr — Web: lecontewealth.com	Maryville	TN	37801	865-379-8200	
Leerink Swann & Co 1 Federal St 37th Fl — *Fax Area Code: 617 ■ TF: 800-808-7525 ■ Web: www.leerink.com	Boston	MA	02110	800-808-7525	918-4900*
Legend Financial Advisors Inc 5700 Corporate Dr Ste 350 — Web: www.legend-financial.com	Pittsburgh	PA	15237	412-635-9210	
Lenox Advisors Inc 530 Fifth Ave — Web: www.lenoxadvisors.com	New York	NY	10036	212-536-8700	
Lenox Wealth Management Inc 8044 Montgomery Rd Ste 480 — Web: www.lenoxwealth.com	Cincinnati	OH	45236	513-618-7080	
Lexington Wealth Management 12 Waltham St — Web: www.lexingtonwealth.com	Lexington	MA	02421	781-860-7745	

Phone Fax

Libbie Agran Financial Services & Seminars
2120 Colorado Ave Ste 100 .... Santa Monica CA 90404 310-586-1828
Web: www.lafs.net
Liberty Lane Service Company LLC Liberty Ln .... Hampton NH 03842 603-929-2600
Web: www.latonaassociates.com
LifeTech Capital 4431 Woodfield Blvd .... Boca Raton FL 33432 561-988-9129
Web: www.lifetechcapital.com
Lighthouse Investment Partners LLC
3801 PGA Blvd Ste 500 .... Palm Beach Gardens FL 33410 561-741-0820
Web: www.lighthousepartners.com
Lineage Capital LLC 399 Boylston St Ste 450 .... Boston MA 02116 617-778-0660
Web: www.lineagecap.com
Linscomb & Williams Inc
1400 Post Oak Blvd Ste 1000 .... Houston TX 77056 713-840-1000
Web: www.linscomb-williams.com
Litman Gregory Asset Management LLC
100 Larkspur Landing Cir Ste 204 .... Larkspur CA 94939 415-461-8999
Web: www.lginvestment.com
Litman Gregory Research Inc
Four Orinda Way Ste 200-D .... Orinda CA 94563 925-254-8999
Web: litmangregory.com
LivePlanet Inc 2644 30th St .... Santa Monica CA 90405 310-664-2400
Web: www.liveplanet.com
Llenroc Capital LLC
781 Lincoln Ave Ste 340 .... San Rafael CA 94901 415-785-3670
Web: www.llenroccap.com
LM Capital Group LLC 750 B St Ste 3010 .... San Diego CA 92101 619-814-1401
Web: www.lmcapital.com
Loeb Enterprises LLC 712 Fifth Ave 14th Fl .... New York NY 10019 646-442-5807
Web: www.loebenterprises.com
Logan Capital Management Inc
Six Coulter Ave Ste 2000 .... Ardmore PA 19003 800-215-1100
TF: 800-215-1100 ■ *Web:* www.logancapital.com
Logan Circle Partners LP
1717 Arch St Ste 1500 .... Philadelphia PA 19103 267-330-0000
Web: www.logancirclepartners.com
Lone Star Funds 2711 N Haskell Ave Ste 1700 .... Dallas TX 75204 214-754-8300 754-8301
Web: www.lonestarfunds.com
Longview Wealth Management LLC
15268 Boulder Pointe Rd .... Eden Prairie MN 55347 952-906-1289
Web: www.longviewwealth.com
Loomis Sayles & Company Inc LP
PO Box 219594 .... Kansas City MO 64121 800-633-3330 423-3065*
**Fax Area Code:* 617 ■ *TF:* 800-343-2029 ■ *Web:* www.loomissayles.com
Lord & Benoit LLC 1 W Boylston St .... Worcester MA 01605 508-853-6404
Lord Abbett & Co 90 Hudson St .... Jersey City NJ 07302 201-827-2000
TF: 888-522-2388 ■ *Web:* www.lordabbett.com
Mackenzie Financial Corp 180 Queen St W .... Toronto ON M5V3K1 416-922-5322 922-5660
TF: 888-653-7070 ■ *Web:* www.mackenzieinvestments.com
Mackie Research Capital Corp
199 Bay St Commerce Court W Ste 4500 .... Toronto ON M5L1G2 416-860-7600
Web: www.mackieresearch.com
Mackinac Partners LLC
180 High Oak Ste 100 .... Bloomfield Hills MI 48304 248-258-6900
Web: www.mackinacpartners.com
Madison Investment Advisors Inc
550 Science Dr .... Madison WI 53711 608-274-0300 274-7905
TF: 800-767-0300 ■ *Web:* www.madisonadv.com
Magee Thomson Investment Partners LLC
12531 High Bluff Dr Ste 120 .... San Diego CA 92130 858-350-5050
Web: www.mageethomson.com
Magnitude Capital LLC
601 Lexington Ave 56th Fl .... New York NY 10022 212-915-3900
Web: www.magnitudecapital.com
Main Street Advisors LLC 205 E Main St .... Westminster MD 21157 410-840-9200
Web: www.mainstadvisors.com
Mallory Capital Group LLC
19 Old King'S Hwy S Ste 14 .... Darien CT 06820 203-655-1571
Web: www.mallorycapital.com
Manarin Investment Counsel Ltd 505 N 210th St .... Omaha NE 68022 402-330-1166
Web: www.manarin.com
Manchester Financial Inc
2815 Townsgate Rd Ste 100 .... Westlake Village CA 91361 800-492-1107
TF: 800-492-1107 ■ *Web:* www.mfinvest.com
Mann Armistead & Epperson Ltd
119 Shockoe Slip .... Richmond VA 23219 804-644-1200
Web: www.maeltd.com
Manning & Napier Advisors Inc
290 Woodcliff Dr .... Fairport NY 14450 585-325-6880 325-1984
Web: www.manning-napier.com
Maplewood Investment Advisors Inc
8750 N Central Expy Ste 715 .... Dallas TX 75231 214-739-5677
Web: www.maplewoodinvestments.com
Marco Consulting Group Inc
550 W Washington Blvd Ste 900 .... Chicago IL 60661 312-575-9000
Web: www.marcoconsulting.com
Mark Asset Management Corp
667 Madison Ave Ninth Fl .... New York NY 10065 212-372-2500
Web: markasset.com
Market Street Partners LLC
477 Pacific Ave .... San Francisco CA 94133 415-445-3240
Web: www.marketstreetpartners.com
Marketocracy Inc 1208 W Magnolia Ste 236 .... Fort Worth TX 76104 877-462-4180 777-6181*
**Fax Area Code:* 888 ■ *TF:* 877-462-4180 ■ *Web:* www.marketocracy.com
Marque Millennium Capital Management LLC
850 Third Ave 13th Fl .... New York NY 10022 212-759-6801
Web: www.marqmil.com
Marquette Asset Management
60 S Sixth St Ste 3900 .... Minneapolis MN 55402 612-661-3770
TF: 866-661-3770 ■ *Web:* www.marquetteam.com
Marshall & Sullivan Inc
1109 First Ave Ste 200 .... Seattle WA 98101 206-621-9014
Web: www.msinvest.com

Phone Fax

Martin Capital Management LLP
300 NIBCO Pkwy Ste 301 .... Elkhart IN 46516 574-293-2077
Web: www.mcmadvisors.com
Marvin & Palmer Assoc Inc
1201 N Market St Ste 2300 .... Wilmington DE 19801 302-573-3570 573-6772
Web: www.marvinandpalmer.com
Maryanov Madsen Gordon & Campbell CPA
801 E Tahquitz Canyon Way Ste 200
PO Box 1826 .... Palm Springs CA 92263 760-320-6642 327-6854
Web: www.mmgccpa.com
MatlinPatterson Global Advisers LLC
520 Madison Ave 35 FL .... New York NY 10022 212-651-9500
Web: www.matlinpatterson.com
Matrix Capital Advisors LLC
200 S Wacker Dr Ste 680 .... Chicago IL 60606 312-612-6100
Web: matrixcapital.com
Matterhorn Capital Management LLC
3512 Paesanos Pkwy Ste 301 .... San Antonio TX 78231 210-694-4329
Web: www.matterhorncap.com
Maxim Group LLC 405 Lexington Ave .... New York NY 10174 212-895-3500
Web: www.maximgrp.com
Mazama Capital Management Inc
One S W Columbia St Ste 1500 .... Portland OR 97258 503-221-8725
Web: www.mazamacap.com
McAdams Wright Ragen Inc
925 Fourth Ave Ste 3900 .... Seattle WA 98104 206-664-8850 470-3512
TF: 888-212-8843 ■ *Web:* www.mwrinc.com
McCullough & Associates LLC
101 California St Ste 3260 .... San Francisco CA 94111 415-956-8700
Web: www.macinv.com
McCutchen Group LLC 925 Fourth Ave Ste 2288 .... Seattle WA 98104 206-816-6850
Web: www.mccutchengroup.com
McDonnell Investment Management LLC
1515 W 22nd St 11th Fl .... Oak Brook IL 60523 630-684-8600
Web: www.mcdmgmt.com
McGlinn Capital Management
850 N Wyomissing Blvd .... Wyomissing PA 19610 610-374-5125
Web: www.mcglinncap.com
McKinley Capital Management LLC
3301 C St Ste 500 .... Anchorage AK 99503 907-563-4488
Web: www.mckinleycapital.com
McMorgan & Co LLC 1 Front St Ste 500 .... San Francisco CA 94111 415-788-9300 616-9386
Web: www.nylinvestments.com
MCS Financial Advisors 360 E Tenth Ave Ste 200 .... Eugene OR 97401 541-345-7023
Web: www.mcsfa.com
MD Sass Investor Services Inc
1185 Ave of the Americas 18th Fl .... New York NY 10036 212-730-2000 764-0381
Web: www.mdsass.com
Megastar Financial Corp 1080 Cherokee St .... Denver CO 80204 303-321-8800
Web: www.libertyhomefinancial.com
Mellon Capital Management Corp
50 Fremont St Ste 3900 .... San Francisco CA 94105 415-546-6056 777-5699
Web: www.mcm.com
Mercadien Group
3625 Quakerbridge Rd Ste D .... Hamilton Township NJ 08619 609-689-9700 838-3331
Web: www.mercadien.com
Mercer Global Advisors Inc
1801 E Cabrillo Blvd .... Santa Barbara CA 93108 800-898-4642
Web: www.merceradvisors.com
Mercury Investment Management LLC
88 Union Ctr Ste 1150 .... Memphis TN 38103 901-521-4200
Web: www.mercuryprop.com
Merit Financial 150 River Rd Ste E1 .... Montville NJ 07045 973-331-5600
Web: www.meritfinancialcorp.com
Meritage Portfolio Management Inc
7500 College Blvd Ste 1212 .... Overland Park KS 66210 913-345-7000
Web: www.meritageportfolio.com
Merritt Capital Management Inc
30 Western Ave Ste 101 .... Gloucester MA 01930 978-282-0035
Web: www.merrittcapitalmanagement.com
Metropolitan West Asset Management LLC
865 S Figueroa St .... Los Angeles CA 90017 213-244-0000
Web: www.mwamllc.com
MFS Investment Management 500 Boylston St .... Boston MA 02116 617-954-5000 954-6621
TF: 877-960-6077 ■ *Web:* www.mfs.com
MFX Solutions Inc 1050 17th St NW Ste 550 .... Washington DC 20036 202-527-9947
Web: www.mfxsolutions.com
MidMark Capital 177 Madison Ave .... Morristown NJ 07960 973-971-9960 971-9963
Web: www.midmarkcapital.com
Milestone Investments Inc
315 Manitoba Ave Ste 310 .... Wayzata MN 55391 952-476-8516
Web: www.milestoneusa.com
Millbrook Capital Management Inc
1370 Ave of the Americas 25th Fl .... New York NY 10019 212-586-4333
Web: www.millcap.com
Miller-Green Financial Group
1330 Lk Robbins Dr Ste 360 .... The Woodlands TX 77380 281-364-9100
Web: www.miller-green.com
Mission Markets Inc 394 Broadway Sixth Fl .... New York NY 10013 646-837-6877
Web: www.missionmarkets.com
Mission Wealth Management LLC
1123 Chapala St 3rd Fl .... Santa Barbara CA 93101 805-882-2360
Web: www.missionwealthmanagement.com
Mitchell & Titus LLP
One Battery Pk Plz 27th Fl .... New York NY 10004 212-709-4500 709-4680
Web: www.mitchelltitus.com
MJ Whitman LLC 622 Third Ave 32nd Fl .... New York NY 10017 212-888-2290
Web: www.mjwhitman.com
MMA Financial LLC 621 E Pratt St Ste 300 .... Baltimore MD 21202 443-263-2900
Web: www.mmarealtycapital.com
MoffettNathanson LLC
1180 Ave Of The Americas Eighth Fl .... New York NY 10036 212-519-0020
Web: www.moffettnathanson.com

	City	State	ZIP	Phone	Fax
Monarch Capital Management Inc 127 W Berry St Ste 402	Fort Wayne	IN	46802	260-422-2765	
Web: www.monarchcapitalmgmt.com					
Monitor Clipper Partners LLC 116 Huntington Ave Ninth Fl	Boston	MA	02116	617-638-1100	
Web: www.monitorclipper.com					
Moody Aldrich Partners LLC 18 Sewall St.	Marblehead	MA	01945	781-639-2750	639-2751
Web: www.moodyaldrich.com					
Moody's Corp 250 Greenwich St 7 World Trade Ctr.	New York	NY	10007	212-553-0300	
NYSE: MCO ■ *Web:* www.moodys.com					
Mooreland Partners LLC 537 Steamboat Rd Ste 200	Greenwich	CT	06830	203-629-4400	
Web: www.moorelandpartners.com					
Morgan Dempsey Capital Management LLC 309 N Water St	Milwaukee	WI	53202	414-319-1080	
Web: www.morgandempsey.com					
Morley Financial Services Inc 1300 SW Fifth Ave Ste 3300	Portland	OR	97201	503-484-9300	
Web: www.morley.com					
Morningstar Inc 22 W Washington St.	Chicago	IL	60606	312-696-6000	696-6009
NASDAQ: MORN ■ *TF Orders:* 800-735-0700 ■ *Web:* www.corporate.morningstar.com					
Morrow & Co LLC 470 W Ave.	Stamford	CT	06902	203-658-9400	
TF: 800-662-5200 ■ *Web:* morrowco.com					
Morton Capital Management 23945 Calabasas Rd Ste 203	Calabasas	CA	91302	818-222-4727	
Web: www.mortoncapital.com					
MPS LORIA Financial Planners LLC 7500 S County Line Rd Ste 100	Burr Ridge	IL	60527	630-887-4404	
Web: www.mpsloria.com					
MRB Partners Inc 2001 Rue University Ste 810	Montreal	QC	H3A2A6	514-558-1515	
Web: www.mrbpartners.com					
Mt Eden Investment Advisors LLC 425 California St Ste 1500	San Francisco	CA	94104	415-288-3000	
Web: www.mtedeninvest.com					
Munder Capital Management 480 Pierce St Ste 300	Birmingham	MI	48009	248-647-9200	
Web: www.munder.com					
Murray Devine & Company Inc 1650 Arch St Ste 2700	Philadelphia	PA	19103	215-977-8700	
Web: www.murraydevine.com					
National Financial Partners Corp (NFP) 340 Madison Ave 20th Fl	New York	NY	10173	212-301-4000	301-4001
NYSE: NFP ■ *Web:* www.nfp.com					
Navellier Securities Corp 1 E Liberty St Ste 504	Reno	NV	89501	775-785-2300	
TF: 800-887-8671 ■ *Web:* www.navellier.com					
NCM Capital Management Group Inc 2634 Durham Chapel Hill Blvd Ste 206	Durham	NC	27707	919-688-0620	683-1352*
**Fax:* Mktg ■ *Web:* www.ncmcapital.com					
Neiman Funds Management LLC 6631 Main St	Williamsville	NY	14221	877-385-2720	
Web: www.neimanfunds.com					
Nelson Roberts Investment Advisors LLC 1950 University Ave Ste 202	East Palo Alto	CA	94303	650-322-4000	
Web: www.nelsonroberts.com					
NEPC LLC One Main St Eighth Fl	Cambridge	MA	02142	617-374-1300	
Web: www.nepc.com					
Neuberger Berman LLC 605 Third Ave.	New York	NY	10158	800-223-6448	476-9862*
**Fax Area Code:* 212 ■ *TF:* 800-223-6448 ■ *Web:* www.nb.com					
New Constructs LLC 210 Jamestown Park Ste 201	Brentwood	TN	37027	615-377-0443	
Web: www.newconstructs.com					
New Mexico State Investment Council 41 Plz la Prensa	Santa Fe	NM	87507	505-476-9500	
Web: www.sic.state.nm.us					
New York Global Group Inc The Trump Bldg 40 Wall St 38th Fl	New York	NY	10005	212-566-0499	
Web: www.nyggroup.com					
Newport Asia LLC 601 California St Ste 1168	San Francisco	CA	94108	415-677-8620	
Web: www.newportasiallc.com					
Newport Private Capital LLC 610 Newport Ctr Dr Ste 600	Newport Beach	CA	92660	949-644-7300	
Web: www.privatecapital.com					
Newsouth Capital Management Inc 999 S Shady Grove Rd Ste 501	Memphis	TN	38120	901-761-5561	
Web: www.newsouthcapital.com					
NGP Energy Capital Management 5221 N O'Connor Blvd Ste 1100	Irving	TX	75039	972-432-1440	
Web: www.ngpenergycapital.com					
Nogales Investors Management LLC 9229 W Sunset Blvd Ste 900	Los Angeles	CA	90069	310-276-7439	
Web: www.nogalesinvestors.com					
NorthCoast Asset Management LLC Six Glenville St	Greenwich	CT	06831	203-532-7000	
Web: www.northcoastam.com					
Northern Trust Company of Connecticut 300 Atlantic St Ste 400	Stamford	CT	06901	312-630-0779	356-9341*
**Fax Area Code:* 203 ■ *TF:* 866-876-9944 ■ *Web:* www.ntrs.com					
Northland Securities Inc 45 S Seventh St Ste 2000	Minneapolis	MN	55402	612-851-5900	
Web: www.northlandsecurities.com					
Northwestern Mutual Investment Services LLC 611 E Wisconsin Ave Ste 300	Milwaukee	WI	53202	866-664-7737	
TF: 866-664-7737 ■ *Web:* www.northwesternmutual.com					
Northwood Family Office LP 3650 Victoria Park Ave Ste 200	Toronto	ON	M2H3P7	416-502-1245	
Web: www.northwoodfamilyoffice.com					
Nottingham Management Company Inc, The 116 S Franklin St	Rocky Mount	NC	27804	252-972-9922	
Web: www.equityfund.com					
Obermeyer Wood Investment Counsel, LLLP 501 Rio Grande Pl Ste 107	Aspen	CO	81611	970-925-8747	
Web: www.obermeyerasset.com					
Oberon Asset Management LLC 51 Wooster St Fourth Fl	New York	NY	10013	917-237-0147	
Web: www.oberonasset.com					
Odlum Brown Ltd 250 Howe St Ste 1100	Vancouver	BC	V6C3S9	604-669-1600	844-5342
TF: 866-636-8222 ■ *Web:* www.odlumbrown.com					
Off Wall Street Consulting Group Inc 22 Hilliard St Ste 3	Cambridge	MA	02138	617-868-7880	
Web: www.riverviewpartners.com					
Offit Capital Advisors LLC 485 Lexington Ave 24th Fl	New York	NY	10017	212-588-3278	
Web: www.offitcapital.com					
Ohio Municipal Advisory Council 9321 Ravenna Rd Ste K	Twinsburg	OH	44087	330-963-7444	
Web: www.ohiomac.com					
Old Hill Partners 1120 Boston Post Rd Second Fl	Darien	CT	06820	203-656-3004	
Web: www.oldhill.com					
Oppenheimer & Company Inc 300 Madison Ave	New York	NY	10017	212-885-4646	
Web: www.opco.com					
Opus Capital Management LLC 221 E. 4th St Ste 2700	Cincinnati	OH	45202	513-621-6787	
Web: www.opusinc.com					
Osborne Partners Capital Management LLC 580 California St Ste 1900	San Francisco	CA	94104	415-362-5637	
Web: www.osbornepartners.com					
Otter Creek Management Inc 222 Lakeview Ave Ste 1100	West Palm Beach	FL	33401	561-832-4110	
Web: ottercreekmgt.com					
Oxford Financial Group Ltd 11711 N Meridian St Ste 600	Carmel	IN	46032	317-843-5678	
Web: www.ofgltd.com					
Pacer Financial Inc 16 Industrial Blvd	Paoli	PA	19301	610-644-8100	
Web: www.pacerfinancial.com					
Pacific Global Advisors LLC 535 Madison Ave Fl 14	New York	NY	10022	212-405-6300	
Web: pacificglobaladvisors.com					
Pacific Income Advisers Inc 1299 Ocean Ave Second Fl Ste 210	Santa Monica	CA	90401	310-393-1424	
Web: www.pacificincome.com					
Pacific Investment Management Company LLC 840 Newport Ctr Dr.	Newport Beach	CA	92660	949-720-6000	720-1376
TF: 800-387-4626 ■ *Web:* www.pimco.com					
Pacific Vista Capital LLC 2211 Encinitas Blvd	Encinitas	CA	92024	760-479-0601	
Web: www.pacvista.com					
Palisades Hudson Financial Group LLC Two Overhill Rd Ste 100	Scarsdale	NY	10583	914-723-5000	
Web: www.palisadeshudson.com					
Pan American Finance LLC 601 Brickell Key Dr Ste 604	Miami	FL	33131	305-577-9799	
Web: www.panamfinance.com					
Paradigm Capital Inc 95 Wellington St W Ste 2101	Toronto	ON	M5J2N7	416-361-9892	
Web: www.paradigmcapinc.com					
Paradigm Financial Advisors LLC 12231 Manchester Rd.	Des Peres	MO	63131	314-966-3400	
Web: www.pfaclient.com					
Parady Financial Group Inc 340 Heald Way Ste 226	The Villages	FL	32163	352-751-3016	
Web: www.paradyfinancial.com					
Park West Asset Management LLC 900 Larkspur Landing Cir Ste 165	Larkspur	CA	94939	415-524-2948	
Web: www.parkwestllc.com					
Parsons Capital Management Inc 10 Weybosset St Ste 1000	Providence	RI	02903	401-521-2440	
Web: www.parsonscapital.com					
Partners Capital Investment Group LLC 50 Rowes Wharf Fourth Fl	Boston	MA	02110	617-292-2570	
Web: www.partners-cap.com					
Payden & Rygel 333 S Grand Ave	Los Angeles	CA	90071	213-625-1900	628-8488
TF: 800-572-9336 ■ *Web:* www.payden.com					
Peak Financial Management Inc 281 Winter St Ste 160	Waltham	MA	02451	781-487-9500	
Web: www.peak-financial.com					
Peninsula Asset Management Inc 1111 Third Ave W Ste 340	Bradenton	FL	34205	800-269-6417	748-2654*
**Fax Area Code:* 941 ■ *TF:* 800-269-6417 ■ *Web:* www.peninsulaasset.com					
Penobscot Investment Management Company Inc 50 Congress St Ste 410	Boston	MA	02109	617-227-3111	
Web: www.pimboston.com					
Pensionmark Retirement Group 24 E Cota St	Santa Barbara	CA	93101	805-456-6260	
Web: www.pensionmark.com					
Pentalpha Capital Group LLC 1 Greenwich Office Park N Bldg	Greenwich	CT	06831	203-660-6100	629-8907
Web: www.pentalphaglobal.com					
Peregrine Capital Partners LLC 732 Pittsford-Victor Rd.	Pittsford	NY	14534	585-218-5220	
Web: www.peregrinecapitalpartners.com					
Perkins Capital Management Inc 730 E Lake St	Wayzata	MN	55391	952-473-8367	
Web: www.perkinscap.com					
Permal Group, The 900 Third Ave 28th Fl	New York	NY	10022	212-418-6500	
Web: www.permal.com					
Perryman Financial Advisory Inc 12221 Merit Dr Ste 1660	Dallas	TX	75251	972-770-4800	
Web: www.billperryman.com					
Personal Capital Corp 726 Main St	Redwood City	CA	94063	855-855-8005	
TF: 855-855-8005 ■ *Web:* www.personalcapital.com					

Phone Fax

Peter A Sokoloff & Co
550 N Brand Blvd Ste 1650 . . . Glendale CA 91203 818-547-4500
Web: www.sokoloffco.com

Petra Financial Advisors Inc
Two N Cascade Ave Ste 720 . . . Colorado Springs CO 80903 719-636-9000
Web: www.petrafinancial.com

Piedmont Investment Advisors LLC
300 W Morgan St Ste 1200 . . . Durham NC 27701 919-688-8600
Web: www.piedmontinvestment.com

Pillar Financial Advisors LLC
3046 Breckenridge Ln Ste 104 . . . Louisville KY 40220 502-384-3890
Web: www.pillar.net

Pin Oak Investment Advisors Inc
510 Bering Dr Ste 100 . . . Houston TX 77057 713-871-8300
Web: www.pinoakinc.com

Pittenger & Anderson Inc
5533 S 27th St Ste 201 . . . Lincoln NE 68512 402-328-8800
Web: www.pittand.com

Placemark Investments Inc 16633 Dallas Pkwy . . . Addison TX 75001 972-404-8100 404-4505
Web: www.placemark.com

PlanMember Financial Corp
6187 Carpinteria Ave . . . Carpinteria CA 93013 805-684-1199
Web: online.planmember.com

Platinum Advisors LLC 1215 K St Ste 1150 . . . Sacramento CA 95814 916-443-8891
Web: www.platinumadvisors.com

Portfolio 21 Investments Inc
721 N W Ninth Ave Ste 250 . . . Portland OR 97209 503-224-7828
Web: www.portfolio21.com

Portfolio Strategy Group Inc, The
81 Main St . . . White Plains NY 10601 914-328-6660
Web: www.portfoliostrategygroup.com

Portland Global Advisors LLC
217 Commercial St Ste 400 . . . Portland ME 04101 207-773-2773
Web: portlandglobal.com

Ppm America Inc 225 W Wacker Dr Ste 1200 . . . Chicago IL 60606 312-634-2500 634-0050
Web: www.ppmamerica.com

Prairie Capital Management LLC
4900 Main St Ste 700 . . . Kansas City MO 64112 816-531-1101
Web: www.prairiecapital.com

Primary Global Research LLC
1975 W El Camino Real Ste 300 . . . Mountain View CA 94040 888-893-1688
TF: 888-893-1688 ■ *Web:* www.pg-research.com

Prime Buchholz & Assoc Inc
273 Corporate Dr Ste 250 . . . Portsmouth NH 03801 603-433-1143 433-8661
Web: www.primebuchholz.com

PRIMECAP Management Co 225 S Lk Ave Ste 400 . . . Pasadena CA 91101 626-304-9222
Web: www.primecapmanagement.com

Primerica Financial Services
3120 Breckinridge Blvd . . . Duluth GA 30099 770-381-1000
TF: 800-257-4725 ■ *Web:* www.primerica.com

Private Advisors LLC
Riverfront Plz W 901 E Byrd St Ste 1400 . . . Richmond VA 23219 804-289-6000
Web: www.privateadvisors.com

Producers Financial
5350 Tomah Dr Ste 2300 . . . Colorado Springs CO 80918 719-535-0739
Web: www.pfnco.com

Progress Investment Management Co
33 New Montgomery St Ste 1900 . . . San Francisco CA 94105 415-512-3480 512-3475
Web: www.progressinvestment.com

Provident Advisors LLC 2800 Niagara Ln N . . . Plymouth MN 55447 952-345-5200
Web: www.providentadvisors.com

Prudential Financial Inc 751 Broad St . . . Newark NJ 07102 973-802-6000 367-6476
NYSE: PRU ■ *TF:* 800-843-7625 ■ *Web:* www.prudential.com

Pugh Capital Management Inc
520 Pk St Ste 2900 . . . Seattle WA 98101 206-322-4985 322-3025
Web: www.pughcapital.com

Puplava Securities Inc
10809 Thornmint Rd Second Fl . . . San Diego CA 92127 858-487-3939
Web: www.puplava.com

Pure Financial Advisors Inc
3131 Camino del Rio N Ste 1550 . . . San Diego CA 92108 619-814-4100
Web: www.purefinancial.com

Putnam Investments 30 Dan Rd PO Box 8383 . . . Canton MA 02021 617-292-1000
TF: 888-478-8626 ■ *Web:* www.putnam.com

PVG Asset Management Corp
24918 Genesee Trl Rd . . . Golden CO 80401 303-526-0548 526-1391
TF: 800-777-0818 ■ *Web:* www.pvgassetmanagement.com

Pzena Investment Management Inc
120 W 45th St 20th Fl . . . New York NY 10036 212-355-1600 308-0010
NYSE: PZN ■ *Web:* www.pzena.com

QCI Asset Management 40A Grove St . . . Pittsford NY 14534 585-218-2060 218-2013
TF: 800-836-3960 ■ *Web:* www.e-qci.com

Quabbin Capital Inc 160 Federal St . . . Boston MA 02110 617-330-9041
Web: www.quabbincapital.com

Quadravest Capital Management Inc
77 King St W Royal Trust Tower Ste 4500 . . . Toronto ON M5K1K7 416-304-4440
Web: www.quadravest.com

Quaker Funds Inc 309 Technology Dr . . . Malvern PA 19355 610-455-2200
Web: www.quakerfunds.com

Quantlab Financial LLC
4200 Montrose Blvd Ste 200 . . . Houston TX 77006 713-333-5440
Web: www.quantlab.com

Quantum Capital Management LLC
105 E Mill Rd . . . Northfield NJ 08225 609-677-4949
Web: www.quantumadv.com

Quazar Capital Corp
3535 Plymouth Blvd Ste 210 . . . Minneapolis MN 55447 763-550-9000
Web: quazarcapital.com

Quest Capital Management Inc
8117 Preston Rd Ste 700 . . . Dallas TX 75225 214-691-6090
Web: www.questadvisor.com

Phone Fax

Quest Investment Management Inc
One S W Columbia St Ste 1100 . . . Portland OR 97258 503-221-0158
Web: www.questinvestment.com

Quest Partners LLC 126 E 56th St 19th Fl . . . New York NY 10022 212-838-7222
Web: www.questpartnersllc.com

R N Croft Financial Group Inc
218 Steeles Ave E . . . Thornhill ON L3T1A6 905-695-7777
Web: www.croftgroup.com

R. M. Davis Inc 24 City Center . . . Portland ME 04101 207-774-0022
Web: www.rmdavis.com

R.H. Bluestein & Co 260 E Brown St Ste 100 . . . Birmingham MI 48009 248-646-4000
Web: www.rhbco.com

Radnor Financial Advisors Inc
485 Devon Park Dr Ste 119 . . . Wayne PA 19087 610-975-0280
Web: www.radnorfinancial.com

Raffles Capital Group Inc
One Burning Tree Rd . . . Greenwich CT 06830 203-629-5604
Web: www.rafflescapital.com

Rampart Investment Management Company LLC
One International Pl 14th Fl . . . Boston MA 02110 617-342-6900
Web: www.rimco.com

Raskob Kambourian Financial Advisors Ltd
4100 N First Ave . . . Tucson AZ 85719 520-690-1999
Web: www.rkfin.com

Raymond James Ltd
2200-925 W Georgia St Cathedral Pl . . . Vancouver BC V6C3L2 604-659-8000
Web: www.raymondjames.ca

RB Milestone Group LLC
420 Lexington Ave Ste 1626 . . . New York NY 10170 212-661-0075
Web: www.rbmilestone.com

RBC Global Asset Management
155 Federal St 16th Fl . . . Boston MA 02110 617-722-4700 722-4714

RCGT Inc 7950 Asheville Hwy . . . Spartanburg SC 29303 864-503-0879

Real Estate Management Services Group LLC
1100 Fifth Ave S Ste 305 . . . Naples FL 34102 239-262-3017
Web: www.remsgroup.com

Redhills Ventures LLC 908 Trophy Hills Dr . . . Las Vegas NV 89134 702-233-2160
Web: www.redhillsventures.com

Regiment Capital Advisors LLC
222 Berkeley St 12th Fl . . . Boston MA 02116 617-488-1600
Web: www.regimentcapital.com

Renaissance Macro Research LLC
116 E 16th St 12th Fl . . . New York NY 10003 212-537-8811
Web: www.renmac.com

Retirement Investment Advisors Inc
3001 United Founders Blvd Ste A . . . Oklahoma City OK 73112 405-842-3443
Web: www.wealthtrac.com

Retirement Plan Advisors LLC
105 W Adams St Ste 2125 . . . Chicago IL 60603 312-701-1100
Web: www.retirementplanadvisors.com

Retirement System Group Inc
108 Corporate Park Dr . . . White Plains NY 10604 212-503-0100
Web: www.rsgroup.com

RG Associates Inc 201 N Charles St Ste 806 . . . Baltimore MD 21201 410-783-0672
Web: www.accountingobserver.com

RGM Advisors LLC 221 W 6th St Ste 1600 . . . Austin TX 78701 512-807-5000 226-7599
Web: www.rgmadvisors.com

Rhodes Computer Services Inc
610 Ronald Reagan Dr . . . Evans GA 30809 706-868-1298
Web: www.rhodesmurphy.com

Rhumbline Advisers Corp
265 Franklin St 21st Fl . . . Boston MA 02110 617-345-0434 345-0675
Web: www.rhumblineadvisers.com

Rice Hall James & Assoc LLC
600 W Broadway Ste 1000 . . . San Diego CA 92101 619-239-9005
Web: www.ricehalljames.com

Richardson Partners Financial Ltd
1100 One Lombard Pl . . . Winnipeg MB R3B0X3 204-957-7735
Web: www.rpfl.com

Richland Investments LLC
4100 Newport Pl Dr Ste 800 . . . Newport Beach CA 92660 949-261-7010
Web: www.richlandcommunities.com

Richmond Capital Management Inc
10800 Midlothain Tpke Ste 217 . . . Richmond VA 23235 804-379-8280
Web: www.richmondcap.com

Ridgestone Corp
10880 Wilshire Blvd Ste 910 . . . Los Angeles CA 90024 310-209-5300
Web: www.ridgestonecorp.com

Riverfront Investment Group LLC
1214 E Cary St . . . Richmond VA 23219 804-549-4800
Web: www.riverfrontig.com

RNC Genter Capital Management
11601 Wilshire Blvd 25th Fl . . . Los Angeles CA 90025 310-477-6543 479-6406
TF: 800-877-7624 ■ *Web:* www.rncgenter.com

Roffman Miller Assoc Inc
1835 Market St Ste 500 . . . Philadelphia PA 19103 215-981-1030 981-0146
TF: 800-995-1030 ■ *Web:* www.roffmanmiller.com

Rogge Capital Management LP
401 Congress Ave Ste 2750 . . . Austin TX 78701 512-322-0909
Web: www.roggecapital.com

Ronald Blue & Company LLC
300 Colonial Ctr Pkwy Ste 300 . . . Roswell GA 30076 770-280-6000 280-6001
TF: 800-841-0362 ■ *Web:* www.ronblue.com

Roncelli Inc 6471 Metro Pkwy . . . Sterling Heights MI 48312 586-264-2060
Web: www.roncelli-inc.com

Rosenblatt Securities Inc
20 Broad St 26th Fl . . . New York NY 10005 212-607-3100
Web: rblt.com

Rosenblum-silverman-sutton Sf Inc
1388 Sutter St Ste 725 . . . San Francisco CA 94109 415-771-4500 771-0542
Web: www.rssic.com

	City	State	Zip	Phone	Fax
Rosenthal Retirement Planning LP 1412 Main St 6th Fl *Web:* www.rrp.com	Dallas	TX	75202	214-752-1000	
Rothschild North America Inc 1251 Ave of the Americas 51st Fl *TF:* 844-726-3863 ■ *Web:* www.rothschild.com	New York	NY	10020	212-403-3500	403-3501
Roundtable Investment Partners LLC 280 Park Ave E 23rd Fl *Web:* www.roundtableip.com	New York	NY	10017	212-488-4700	
Royal Capital Management LLC 623 Fifth Ave 24th Fl *Web:* www.royalcap.com	New York	NY	10022	212-920-3400	
Royce & Assoc LLC 745 Fifth Ave 24th Fl *TF:* 800-221-4268 ■ *Web:* www.roycefunds.com	New York	NY	10151	800-221-4268	
RREEF 101 California St 26th Fl **Fax Area Code:* 714 ■ *TF All:* 800-222-5885 ■ *Web:* realestate.deutscheawm.com/	San Francisco	CA	94111	415-781-3300	247-6022*
RS Investment Management Company LLC One Bush St Ste 900 *Web:* www.rsinvestments.com	San Francisco	CA	94104	415-591-2700	
RSF Social Finance 1002A O'Reilly Ave *Web:* www.rsfsocialfinance.org	San Francisco	CA	94129	415-561-3900	
Ruane Cunniff & Goldfarb Inc 9 W 57th St Ste 5000 *TF:* 800-686-6884 ■ *Web:* sequoiafund.com	New York	NY	10019	212-832-5280	832-5298
Russell Investment Group 909 A St *TF:* 800-787-7354 ■ *Web:* www.russell.com	Tacoma	WA	98402	800-787-7354	
Russell Investments 1301 Second Ave 18th Fl *TF:* 800-426-7969 ■ *Web:* www.russell.com	Seattle	WA	98101	206-505-7877	
RW Pressprich & Company Inc Research Div 452 Fifth Ave 12th Fl *Web:* www.pressprich.com	New York	NY	10018	212-832-6200	
RWI Ventures 545 Middlefield Rd Ste 220 *Web:* www.rwigroup.com	Menlo Park	CA	94025	650-543-3300	
Sage Advisory Services Ltd Co 5900 SW Pkwy Bldg 1 Ste 100 *Web:* www.sageadvisory.com	Austin	TX	78735	512-327-5530	
Sage Group LLC, The 11111 Santa Monica Blvd Ste 2200 *Web:* www.sagellc.com	Los Angeles	CA	90025	310-478-7899	
Sage Rutty & Company Inc 100 Corporate Woods Ste 300 *Web:* www.sagerutty.com	Rochester	NY	14623	585-232-3760	
Sagient Research Systems Inc 3655 Nobel Dr Ste 540 *Web:* www.sagientresearch.com	San Diego	CA	92122	858-623-1600	
Samco Capital Markets 11111 Katy Fwy Ste 820 *Web:* www.samcocapital.com	Houston	TX	77079	713-467-7344	
Sampers Financial Inc 79 Midland Ave *Web:* www.sampersfinancial.com	Montclair	NJ	07042	973-744-1014	
Sapers & Wallack Inc 275 Washington St Ste 205 *Web:* www.sapers-wallack.com	Newton	MA	02458	617-225-2600	
Sasco Capital Inc 10 Sasco Hill Rd *Web:* www.sascocap.com	Fairfield	CT	06430	203-254-6800	
Saturna Capital Corp 1300 N State St *Web:* www.saturna.com	Bellingham	WA	98225	360-734-9900	
Savant Investment Group LLC 461 Second St Ste 151 *Web:* www.savantig.com	San Francisco	CA	94107	415-926-7200	
Saybrook Capital LLC 11400 W Olympic Blvd *Web:* www.saybrook.net	Los Angeles	CA	90064	310-899-9200	899-9101
SBV Venture Partners 454 Ruthven Ave *Web:* www.sbvpartners.com	Palo Alto	CA	94301	650-522-0085	
Scharf Investments LLC 5619 Scotts Vly Dr Ste 140 *Web:* www.scharfinvestments.com	Scotts Valley	CA	95066	831-429-6513	
Schechter Wealth Strategies 251 Pierce St *Web:* www.schechterwealth.com	Birmingham	MI	48009	248-731-9500	
Schneider Capital Management Corp 460 E Swedesford Rd Ste 2000 *Web:* schneidercap.com	Wayne	PA	19087	610-687-8080	
Schreiner Capital Management Inc 111 Summit Dr Ste 100 *Web:* www.scminvest.com	Exton	PA	19341	610-524-7310	
Schultz Collins Lawson Chambers Inc 455 Market St Ste 1250 *TF:* 877-291-2205 ■ *Web:* www.schultzcollins.com	San Francisco	CA	94105	415-291-3000	
Schultze Asset Management LLC 3000 Westchester Ave Ste 204 *Web:* www.samco.net	Purchase	NY	10577	914-701-5260	
SDL Capital LP 480 San Antonio Rd Ste 200 *Web:* www.sdlventures.com	Mountain View	CA	94040	650-559-9355	
Seamans Capital Management LLC 500 Boylston St Ste 420 *Web:* www.seamanscapital.com	Boston	MA	02116	781-890-5225	
Seaport Group LLC Research Division, The 360 Madison Ave 22nd Fl *Web:* www.theseaportgroup.com	New York	NY	10017	212-616-7700	
Segal Advisors Inc 116 Huntington Ave Ste 8 *Web:* www.segaladvisors.com	Boston	MA	02116	617-424-7300	
Segal Rogerscasey One Parklands Dr *Web:* www.segalrc.com	Darien	CT	06820	203-621-3620	
Segall Bryant & Hamill 10 S Wacker Dr Ste 3500 *Web:* www.sbhic.com	Chicago	IL	60606	312-474-1222	
Select Portfolio Management Inc 120 Vantis *Web:* www.selectportfolio.com	Aliso Viejo	CA	92656	949-975-7900	
Sentinel Wealth Management Inc 11710 Plaza America Dr Ste 130 *Web:* www.sentinelwealth.com	Reston	VA	20190	703-787-5770	
Sharenet Inc 5600 Explorer Dr *Web:* www.sharenetinc.com	Mississauga	ON	L4W4Y2	905-206-0884	206-9783
Sheaff Brock Investment Advisors LLC 10401 N Meridian St Ste 100 *Web:* www.sheaffbrock.com	Indianapolis	IN	46290	317-705-5700	
Sherman Capital Markets LLC 200 Meeting St Ste 206	Charleston	SC	29401	843-266-1717	
Shields & Company Inc 890 Winter St Ste 160 *Web:* www.shieldsco.com	Waltham	MA	02451	781-890-7033	
Shine Investment Advisory Services Inc 9892 Rosemont Ave Ste 100 *Web:* www.shineinvestments.com	Lone Tree	CO	80124	303-740-8600	
Sidus Investment Management LLC 767 Third Ave 15th Fl *Web:* www.sidusfunds.com	New York	NY	10017	212-751-6644	
Sigma Analysis & Management Ltd 101 College St Ste 345 *Web:* www.sigmanalysis.com	Toronto	ON	M5G1L7	416-260-6291	
Signalert Corp 150 Great Neck Rd Ste 301 *TF:* 800-829-6229 ■ *Web:* www.systemsandforecasts.com	Great Neck	NY	11021	516-829-6444	829-9366
Signator Investors Inc 197 Clarendon St C-8 *TF:* 800-543-6611 ■ *Web:* www.signatorinvestors.com	Boston	MA	02116	800-543-6611	
Signature Estate & Investment Advisors LLC 2121 Ave Of The Stars Ste 1600 *Web:* www.seia.com	Los Angeles	CA	90067	310-712-2323	
Signia Capital Management LLC 108 N Washington St Ste 305 *Web:* www.signiacapital.com	Spokane	WA	99201	509-789-8970	
Silver Lake Technology Management LLC 2775 Sand Hill Rd Ste 100 *Web:* www.silverlake.com	Menlo Park	CA	94025	650-233-8120	233-8125
Silvercrest Asset Management Group LLC 1330 Ave of the Americas 38th Fl *Web:* www.silvercrestgroup.com	New York	NY	10019	212-649-0600	
Simmons & Company International 700 Louisiana Ste 1900 *Web:* www.simmonsco-intl.com	Houston	TX	77002	713-236-9999	
Sit Investment Assoc Inc 80 S Eigth St 3300 IDS Ctr *Web:* www.sitinvest.com	Minneapolis	MN	55402	612-332-3223	332-1911
SKBA Capital Management 44 Montgomery St Ste 3500 *Web:* www.skba.com	San Francisco	CA	94104	415-989-7852	989-2114
SKIRITAI Capital LLC One Ferry Bldg Ste 255 *Web:* www.skiritai.com	San Francisco	CA	94111	415-677-5460	
Smith Graham & Co 600 Travis St Ste 6900 *TF:* 800-739-4470 ■ *Web:* smithgraham.com	Houston	TX	77002	713-227-1100	223-0844
Sonata Capital Group Inc 2001 Sixth Ave Ste 3410 *Web:* www.sonatacap.com	Seattle	WA	98121	206-256-4400	
Sound Shore Management Inc Eight Sound Shore Dr Ste 180 *Web:* www.soundshore.com	Greenwich	CT	06830	203-629-1980	
South Texas Money Management Ltd 700 N Saint Mary's Ste 100 *Web:* stmmltd.com	San Antonio	TX	78205	210-824-8916	
Southeastern Asset Management Inc 6410 Poplar Ave Ste 900 *Web:* www.southeasternasset.com	Memphis	TN	38119	901-761-2474	
SouthernSun Asset Management LLC 6070 Poplar Ave Ste 300 *Web:* www.southernsunam.com	Memphis	TN	38119	901-333-6980	
Sovereign Society, The 98 S E Sixth Ave Ste 2 *TF:* 888-358-8125 ■ *Web:* www.sovereignsociety.com	Delray Beach	FL	33483	888-358-8125	
Speece Thorson Capital Group Inc 225 S Sixth St Ste 2575 *Web:* www.stcapital.com	Minneapolis	MN	55402	612-338-4649	
Spero-Smith Investment Advisers Inc 3601 Green Rd Ste 102 *Web:* www.sperosmith.com	Cleveland	OH	44122	216-464-6266	
Sperry, Mitchell & Company Inc 595 Madison Ave Thirtieth Fl *Web:* sperrymitchell.com	New York	NY	10022	212-832-6628	
Spire Investment Partners LLC 7918 Jones Branch Dr Ste 750 *Web:* www.spireip.com	Mclean	VA	22102	703-748-5800	
Springsted Inc 380 Jackson St Ste 300 *Web:* www.springsted.com	Saint Paul	MN	55101	651-223-3000	
Springvale Terrace 8505 Springvale Rd *Web:* www.springvaleterrace.com	Silver Spring	MD	20910	301-587-0190	
St Charles Capital LLC 1400 Sixteenth St Ste 300	Denver	CO	80202	303-339-9099	
Standard Pacific Capital LLC 101 California St 36th Fl *Web:* standardpacific.com	San Francisco	CA	94111	415-352-7100	
Standish Mellon One Boston Pl *Web:* www.standish.com	Boston	MA	02108	617-248-6000	248-6050
Stanford Investment Group Inc 2570 W El Camino Real Ste 520 *Web:* www.stanfordinvestment.com	Mountain View	CA	94040	650-941-1717	
Stansberry & Assoc Investment Research LLC 1217 Saint Paul St *Web:* www.stansberryresearch.com	Baltimore	MD	21202	888-261-2693	
Stanwich Advisors LLC One Dock St Ste 602 *Web:* www.stanwichadvisors.com	Stamford	CT	06902	203-406-1099	
StarMine Corp 49 Stevenson St *Web:* starmine.com	San Francisco	CA	94105	415-777-1147	
State Universities Retirement System of Illinois 1901 Fox Dr *Web:* www.surs.com	Champaign	IL	61820	217-378-8800	

Company / Address	City	State	ZIP	Phone	Fax
Stellar Capital Management LLC 2200 E Camelback Rd Ste 130 *Web:* www.stellarmgt.com	Phoenix	AZ	85016	602-778-0307	
Sterling Investment Partners 285 Riverside Ave Ste 300 *Web:* www.sterlinglp.com	Westport	CT	06880	203-226-8711	
Sterling Mutuals Inc 880 Ouellette Ave Ninth Fl *Web:* www.sterlingmutuals.com	Windsor	ON	N9A1C7	519-256-1002	
Stevens Capital Management LP 201 King Of Prussia Rd Ste 400 *Web:* www.scm-lp.com	Wayne	PA	19087	610-971-5000	
Stoever Glass & Company Inc 30 Wall St *TF:* 800-223-3881 ■ *Web:* stoeverglass.com	New York	NY	10005	800-223-3881	
StoneCreek Capital Inc 18500 Von Karman Ave Ste 590 *Web:* www.stonecreekcapital.com	Irvine	CA	92612	949-752-4580	
StoneRidge Investment Partners LLC 301 Lindenwood Dr Ste 310 *Web:* www.stoneridgeinvestments.com	Malvern	PA	19355	610-647-5253	
Stoneworth Financial LLC 6575 W Loop S Ste 468 *Web:* www.stoneworthfinancial.com	Houston	TX	77401	713-429-1838	
Strategic Financial Alliance Inc, The 2200 Century Pkwy Ste 500 *Web:* www.jointhesfa.com	Atlanta	GA	30345	678-954-4000	
Stratford Advisory Group Inc 500 W Madison St Ste 2740 *Web:* www.stratfordadvisorygroup.com	Chicago	IL	60661	312-798-3200	
StreetAuthority LLC 4601 Spicewood Springs Rd Bldg 3 Ste 100 *Web:* www.streetauthority.com	Austin	TX	78759	512-501-4001	
StreetInsider.com Inc 280 W Maple Ste 232 *Web:* www.streetinsider.com	Birmingham	MI	48009	248-593-6536	
Stretegic Mktg Ventures Inc 8262 Lees Ridge Rd *Web:* www.smvbpo.com	Warrenton	VA	20186	540-349-8888	
Summit Strategies Inc 8182 Maryland Ave Sixth Fl *Web:* www.summitstrategies.com	St. Louis	MO	63105	314-727-7211	
SunTrust Banks Inc 25 Pk Pl NE *NYSE: STI* ■ *Web:* suntrust.com	Atlanta	GA	30303	404-588-7610	575-2837
Swarthmore Group 1650 Arch St Ste 2100 *Web:* www.swarthmoregroup.com	Philadelphia	PA	19103	215-557-9300	557-9305
Systematic Financial Management LP 300 Frank W Burr Blvd Seventh Fl Glenpoint Ctr E 7th Fl *TF:* 800-258-0497 ■ *Web:* www.sfmlp.com	Teaneck	NJ	07666	201-928-1982	928-1401
T Rowe Price Assoc Inc 100 E Pratt St **Fax:* Cust Svc ■ *TF:* 800-638-7890 ■ *Web:* corporate.troweprice.com	Baltimore	MD	21202	410-345-2000	345-6244*
Tactical Allocation Group LLC 139 S Old Woodward Ave *Web:* www.tagllc.net	Birmingham	MI	48009	248-283-2520	
TAG Associates LLC 75 Rockefeller Plz *Web:* www.tagassoc.com	New York	NY	10019	212-275-1500	275-1510
Takenaka Partners LLC 801 S Figueroa St Ste 620 *Web:* www.takenakapartners.com	Los Angeles	CA	90017	213-891-0060	
Tamarac Inc 701 Fifth Ave 14th Fl *TF:* 866-525-8811 ■ *Web:* www.tamaracinc.com	Seattle	WA	98104	866-525-8811	
TAMRO Capital Partners LLC 1701 Duke St Ste 250 *Web:* www.tamrocapital.com	Alexandria	VA	22314	703-740-1000	
Taurus Asset Management LLC 590 Madison Ave 35th Fl *Web:* www.taurusassetmanagement.com	New York	NY	10022	212-457-9922	
TCI Wealth Advisors Inc 4011 E Sunrise Dr *Web:* www.tciwealth.com	Tucson	AZ	85718	520-733-1477	
TE Financial Consultants Ltd 26 Wellington St E Ste 710 *Web:* www.tewealth.com	Toronto	ON	M5E1S2	416-366-1451	
TeamCo Advisers LLC One Bush St Ste 550 *Web:* www.teamcoadvisers.com	San Francisco	CA	94104	415-445-9800	
Technomart RGA Inc 401 Washington Ave Ste 1101 *Web:* www.technomartrga.com	Baltimore	MD	21204	410-828-6555	
Telemus Capital Partners LLC Two Towne Sq Ste 800 *Web:* www.telemuscapital.com	Southfield	MI	48076	248-827-1800	
Telsey Advisory Group LLC 535 Fifth Ave 12th Fl *Web:* www.telseygroup.com	New York	NY	10017	212-973-9700	
Terry McDaniel & Co 2630 Exposition Blvd Ste 300 *Web:* www.tmcdanco.com	Austin	TX	78703	512-495-9500	
Third Coast Capital Advisors LLC One N Franklin St Ste 3200 *Web:* www.thirdcoastca.com	Chicago	IL	60606	312-332-6484	
Third River Capital Management LLC 221 N Lasalle St 32nd Fl Ste 3200 *Web:* www.thirdrivercap.com	Chicago	IL	60601	312-628-6700	
Thompson Research Group LLC 2525 W End Ave Ste 1440 *Web:* www.thompsonresearchgroup.com	Nashville	TN	37203	615-891-6200	
Thompson Siegel & Walmsley Inc 6806 Paragon Pl Ste 300 *TF:* 800-697-1056 ■ *Web:* www.tswinvest.com	Richmond	VA	23230	804-353-4500	353-0925
Thoroughbred Financial Services LLC 5110 Maryland Way Ste 300 *Web:* www.thoroughbredfinancial.com	Brentwood	TN	37027	615-371-0001	
TICC Capital Corp Eight Sound Shore Dr Ste 255 *Web:* www.ticc.com	Greenwich	CT	06830	203-983-5275	
TIF Fund Management LLC Four Woodbine Ave *Web:* www.tiffund.com	Greenwood Lake	NY	10925	845-477-0200	
Tirschwell & Loewy Inc 400 Park Ave *Web:* www.tirschwellandloewy.com	New York	NY	10022	212-888-7940	
Titlemax of South Carolina Inc 15 Bull St Ste 200 *Web:* www.gmlblaw.com	Savannah	GA	31401	901-236-0578	
TM Capital Corp 641 Lexington Ave 30th Fl *Web:* www.tmcapital.com	New York	NY	10022	212-809-1360	
Tom Johnson Investment Management Inc 201 Robert S Kerr Ave *Web:* tjim.com	Oklahoma City	OK	73102	405-236-2111	
Torch Energy Advisors Inc (TEAI) 1331 Lamar Ave Ste 1450 *Web:* www.teai.com	Houston	TX	77010	713-650-1246	655-1866
Toyon Associates Inc 1800 Sutter St Ste 600 *Web:* www.toyonassociates.com	Concord	CA	94520	925-685-9312	
Tradition Capital Management LLC 129 Summit Ave *Web:* www.traditioncm.com	Summit	NJ	07901	908-598-0909	
Transamerica Corporation 440 Mamaroneck Ave *Web:* www.divinvest.com	Harrison	NY	10528	914-627-3000	697-3743
Transmarket Group LLC 550 W Jackson Blvd Ste 1300 *Web:* www.transmarketgroup.com	Chicago	IL	60661	312-284-5500	284-5650
Treflie Capital Management 35 Ezekills Holw *Web:* www.treflie.com	Sag Harbor	NY	11963	631-725-2500	
Trellis Capital Corp 333 Wilson Ave Ste 600 *Web:* www.trelliscapital.com	Toronto	ON	M3H1T2	416-398-2299	
Trent Capital Management Inc 3150 N Elm St Ste 204 *Web:* www.trentcapital.com	Greensboro	NC	27408	336-282-9302	
Triangle Securities LLC 1301 Annapolis Dr *Web:* www.trianglesecurities.com	Raleigh	NC	27608	919-838-3221	
Trimaran Fund Management LLC 1325 Ave of the Americas *Web:* www.trimarancapital.com	New York	NY	10019	212-616-3700	616-3701
TrimTabs Investment Research Three Harbor Dr *Web:* www.trimtabs.com	Sausalito	CA	94965	415-324-5873	
TripleTree 7601 France Ave S Ste 150 *Web:* www.triple-tree.com	Minneapolis	MN	55435	952-253-5300	
Trustmont Financial Group Inc 200 Brush Run Rd Ste A *Web:* www.trustmontgroup.com	Greensburg	PA	15601	724-468-5665	
Tsg Equity Partners LLC 636 Great Rd *Web:* www.tsgequity.com	Stow	MA	01775	978-461-9900	461-9909
Turner Investment Partners Inc 1205 Westlakes Dr Ste 100 *Web:* www.turnerinvestments.com	Berwyn	PA	19312	484-329-2300	
TYGH Capital Management Inc 1211 S W Fifth Ave Ste 2100 *Web:* www.tyghcap.com	Portland	OR	97204	503-972-0150	
Ullman John & Associates Inc 51 E Market St *Web:* www.jgua.com	Corning	NY	14830	607-936-3785	
Unique Investment Corp 7028 Kearny Dr *Web:* www.uniquepartners.com	Huntington Beach	CA	92648	714-848-5900	
United Capital Financial Advisers LLC 500 Newport Ctr Dr Ste 500 *Web:* www.unitedcp.com	Newport Beach	CA	92660	949-999-8500	
Unity Financial Strategists Inc 100 Wall St 22nd Fl *Web:* www.unityfinancialadvisors.com	New York	NY	10005	212-785-4200	
US Capital Advisors LLC 1330 Post Oak Blvd Ste 900 *Web:* www.uscallc.com	Houston	TX	77056	713-366-0500	
US Global Investors Inc 7900 Callaghan Rd *NASDAQ: GROW* ■ *TF:* 800-873-8637 ■ *Web:* www.usfunds.com	San Antonio	TX	78229	210-308-1234	308-1223
US Renewables Group LLC 2425 Olympic Blvd Ste 4050 W *Web:* www.usregroup.com	Santa Monica	CA	90404	310-586-3900	
USAA Investment Management 9800 Fredericksburg Rd PO Box 659453 **Fax Area Code:* 210 ■ *TF:* 800-531-8722 ■ *Web:* www.usaa.com	San Antonio	TX	78288	800-531-8722	498-3999*
Valley Financial Solutions Inc 2847 Penn Forest Blvd Ste 100 *Web:* www.valleyfinancialsolutions.com	Roanoke	VA	24018	540-777-4302	
Value Line Asset Management 220 E 42nd St *TF:* 800-634-3583 ■ *Web:* www.valueline.com	New York	NY	10017	212-907-1500	818-9781
Value Line Inc 220 E 42nd St *NASDAQ: VALU* ■ *TF Cust Svc:* 800-634-3583 ■ *Web:* www.valueline.com	New York	NY	10017	212-907-1500	818-9747
Van Strum & Towne Inc 505 Sansome St Ste 1001 *Web:* www.vanstrum.com	San Francisco	CA	94111	415-981-3455	
Vanguard Group 455 Devon Pk Dr *TF:* 800-662-7447 ■ *Web:* investor.vanguard.com	Wayne	PA	19087	610-669-1000	669-6551
VCI Emergency Vehicle 43 jefferson ave *Web:* vciambulances.com	Berlin	NJ	08009	856-768-2162	
VectorVest Inc 20472 Chartwell Ctr Dr Ste D *Web:* www.vectorvest.com	Cornelius	NC	28031	704-895-4095	
Verisight Inc 35 Iron Point Cir Ste 300 *Web:* verisightgroup.com/	Folsom	CA	95630	916-932-1800	
Veritable LP 6022 W Chester Pk *Web:* www.finestimage.com	Newtown Square	PA	19073	610-640-9551	
Vertical Research Partners LLC One Landmark Sq Ste 400 *Web:* verticalresearchpartners.com	Stamford	CT	06901	203-276-5680	

Phone | Fax

Virtus Investment Partners Inc
100 Pearl St Ninth Fl .... Hartford CT 06103 860-263-4707
Web: www.virtus.com

Vontobel Asset Management Inc
1540 Broad Way Ave 38th Fl. .... New York NY 10036 212-415-7000 415-7087
TF General: 800-445-8872 ■ *Web:* www.vusa.com

VSR Financial Services Inc
8620 W 110th St Ste 200 .... Overland Park KS 66210 913-498-2900
Web: www.vsrfinancial.com

VTL Associates LLC
One Commerce Sq 2005 Market St Ste 2020 .... Philadelphia PA 19103 215-854-8181
Web: www.vtlassociates.com

WAB Capital LLC
1559 Michael Ln Pacific Palisades .... Los Angeles CA 90272 310-230-8664
Web: www.growthequities.com

Waddell & Reed Financial Inc
6300 Lamar Ave .... Overland Park KS 66201 913-236-2000 532-2749*
NYSE: WDR ■ **Fax Area Code:* 800 ■ *TF:* 888-923-3355 ■ *Web:* www.waddell.com

Wade Financial Advisory Inc
2105 S Bascom Ave Ste 110 .... Campbell CA 95008 408-369-7399
Web: www.wadefa.com

Warwick Investment Management Inc
4444 Carter Creek Pkwy Ste 109 .... Bryan TX 77802 979-260-9777
Web: www.warwickpartners.net

Washington Capital Management Inc
1301 Fifth Ave Ste 3100 .... Seattle WA 98101 206-382-0825 382-0950
Web: www.wcmadvisors.com

Wasmer Schroeder & Company Inc
600 Fifth Ave S Ste 210 .... Naples FL 34102 239-263-6877 263-8146
Web: www.wasmerschroeder.com

Waters Parkerson & Company LLC
228 St Charles Ave Ste 512 .... New Orleans LA 70130 504-581-2022
Web: www.wpcoinc.com

WCM Investment Management 281 Brooks St .... Laguna Beach CA 92651 949-380-0200
Web: www.wcminvest.com

WE Donoghue & Company Inc 629 Washington St .... Norwood MA 02062 800-642-4276
TF: 800-642-4276 ■ *Web:* www.donoghue.com

WE Family Offices LLC 701 Brickell Ave Ste 2100 .... Miami FL 33131 305-825-2225
Web: www.wefamilyoffices.com

Wealth Conservancy Inc, The
1525 Spruce St Ste 300 .... Boulder CO 80302 303-444-1919
Web: www.thewealthconservancy.com

Wealthfront Inc 541 Cowper St .... Palo Alto CA 94301 650-249-4250 223-1679*
**Fax Area Code:* 202 ■ *Web:* www.wealthfront.com

Webb Financial Group
7900 Xerxes Ave S Ste 1920 .... Minneapolis MN 55431 952-837-3200
Web: www.webbfinancial.com

Wedge Capital Management LLP
301 S College St Ste 2920 .... Charlotte NC 28202 704-334-6475 334-3542
Web: www.wedgecapital.com

Weil Co, The 12555 High Bluff Dr Ste 180 .... San Diego CA 92130 858-704-1444
Web: www.cweil.com

Weiss Research Inc 15430 Endeavour Dr .... Jupiter FL 33478 800-291-8545
TF: 800-291-8545 ■ *Web:* www.weissinc.com

Welch Capital Partners LLC 90 Park Ave .... New York NY 10016 212-754-6077
Web: www.welchcapital.com

Wellington Management Company LLP
280 Congress St .... Boston MA 02210 617-951-5000 951-5250
Web: www.wellington.com

Wentworth Hauser & Violich (WHV)
301 Battery St .... San Francisco CA 94111 415-981-6911 288-6153
TF: 800-204-2650 ■ *Web:* www.whv.com

Westfield Capital Management Company LP
One Financial Ctr 24th Fl .... Boston MA 02111 617-428-7100
Web: www.westfieldcapital.com

Weston Capital Management Inc
12424 Wilshire Blvd Ste 1115 .... Los Angeles CA 90025 310-826-0811
Web: www.westoncap.com

Wilbanks, Smith & Thomas Asset Management LLC
150 W Main St Ste 1700 .... Norfolk VA 23510 757-623-3676
Web: www.wstam.com

Wilkinson O'Grady & Company Inc
499 Park Ave Seventh Fl .... New York NY 10022 212-644-5252
Web: www.wilkinsonogrady.com

Williams, Jones & Associates LLC
717 Fifth Ave Ste 1700 .... New York NY 10022 212-935-8750
Web: www.williamsjones.com

Willis Investment Counsel Inc
710 Green St .... Gainesville GA 30501 770-718-0706
Web: www.wicinvest.com

Wilshire Assoc Inc
1299 Ocean Ave Ste 700 .... Santa Monica CA 90401 310-451-3051 458-0520
Web: www.wilshire.com

Windlake Capital Advisors LLC
980 N Michigan Ave Ste 1400 .... Chicago IL 60611 312-357-0900
Web: www.windlakeadvisors.com

Woodmont Investment Counsel LLC
401 Commerce St Ste 5400 .... Nashville TN 37219 615-297-6144
Web: www.woodmontcounsel.com

Woodridge Capital
800 Woodlands Pkwy Ste 201 .... Ridgeland MS 39157 601-957-6006
Web: www.woodridge-capital.com

Woodstock Corp 27 School St Ste 200 .... Boston MA 02108 617-227-0600
Web: www.woodstockcorp.com

Woodway Financial Advisors
10000 Memorial Dr Ste 650 .... Houston TX 77024 713-683-7070 683-0702
Web: www.woodwayfinancial.com

Workplace Answers LLC
3701 Executive Ctr Dr Ste 201 .... Austin TX 78731 866-861-4410
TF: 866-861-4410 ■ *Web:* www.workplaceanswers.com

Phone | Fax

WP Stewart & Company Ltd
527 Madison Ave 20th Fl .... New York NY 10022 212-750-8585 980-8039
OTC: WPSL ■ *TF:* 888-695-4092 ■
Web: www.alliancebernstein.com/microsites/abi/pub/wps/wpsab.htm

WRA Inc 2169 Francisco Blvd E Ste G .... San Rafael CA 94901 415-454-8868
Web: www.eahhousing.org

Wright Investors' Service
440 Wheelers Farms Rd .... Milford CT 06461 203-783-4400 783-4401
TF: 800-232-0013 ■ *Web:* www.wisi.com

XRoads Solutions Group
1821 E Dyer Rd Ste 225 .... Santa Ana CA 92705 949-567-1600
Web: www.xroadsllc.com

Yacktman Asset Management Co
6300 Bridgepoint Pkwy Bldg 1 Ste 320 .... Austin TX 78730 512-767-6700
TF: 800-835-3879 ■ *Web:* www.yacktman.com

YHB Investment Advisors Inc
29 S Main St Ste 306 .... West Hartford CT 06107 860-561-7050
Web: www.yhbia.com

Your Source Private Equity
707 E Northern Ave .... Phoenix AZ 85020 602-343-1700
Web: www.ysfi.com

Zebra Capital Management LLC
612 Wheelers Farm Rd .... Milford CT 06461 203-878-3223
Web: www.zebracapm.com

Zuk Financial Group 22936 El Toro Rd .... Lake Forest CA 92630 949-472-4550
Web: www.zukfinancial.com

405 INVESTMENT COMPANIES - SMALL BUSINESS

The companies listed here conform to the Small Business Administration's standards for investing.

Phone | Fax

Argentum Group, The 60 Madison Ave Ste 701 .... New York NY 10010 212-949-6262 949-8294
Web: www.argentumgroup.com

Atalanta Investment Company Inc
PO Box 7718 .... Incline Village NV 89452 775-833-1836 833-1890

Bankoh Investment Services Inc
130 Merchant St Ste 850 .... Honolulu HI 96813 808-537-8500 538-4891
Web: www.boh.com

Brynwood Partners LP
Eight Sound Shore Dr Ste 265 .... Greenwich CT 06830 203-622-1790 622-0559
Web: www.brynwoodpartners.com

Center for Innovation
University of N Dakota PO Box 8372 .... Grand Forks ND 58202 701-777-3132 777-2339
Web: www.innovators.net

Cypress Group LLC 437 Madison Ave 33rd Fl .... New York NY 10022 212-705-0150 705-0199
Web: www.cypressgp.com

El Dorado Ventures 850 Oak Grove Ave .... Menlo Park CA 94025 650-854-1200 854-1202
Web: www.eldorado.com

Elliott Management 40 W 57th St .... New York NY 10019 212-974-6000
Web: www.elliottmgmt.com

Eos Partners LP 320 Pk Ave Ninth Fl .... New York NY 10022 212-832-5800 832-5815
Web: www.eospartners.com

Federal Farm Credit Banks Funding Corp
10 Exchange Pl Ste 1401 .... Jersey City NJ 07302 201-200-8131 200-8109
Web: www.farmcreditfunding.com

Galliard Capital Management Inc
800 La Salle Ave Ste 1100 .... Minneapolis MN 55402 612-667-3220 667-3223
TF: 800-717-1617 ■ *Web:* www.galliard.com

GamePlan Financial Marketing LLC
300 ParkBrooke Pl Ste 200 .... Woodstock GA 30189 678-238-0601 718-1954
TF Cust Svc: 800-886-4757 ■ *Web:* www.gameplanfinancial.com

Gemini Investors LLC 20 William St Ste 250 .... Wellesley MA 02481 781-237-7001 237-7233
Web: www.gemini-investors.com

Hornor Townsend & Kent Inc (HTK)
600 Dresher Rd Ste C1C .... Horsham PA 19044 800-289-9999 956-7750*
**Fax Area Code:* 215 ■ *TF:* 800-289-9999 ■ *Web:* www.htk.com

Impact Seven Inc 147 Lk Almena Dr .... Almena WI 54805 715-357-3334 357-6233
TF: 800-685-9353 ■ *Web:* www.impactseven.org

Inverness Management LLC
21 Locust Ave Ste 1D .... New Canaan CT 06840 203-966-4177
Web: www.invernessmanagement.com

Kansas Venture Capital Inc (KVCI)
10601 Mission Rd Ste 250 .... Leawood KS 66206 913-262-7117 262-3509
Web: www.kvci.com

Kentucky Highlands Investment Corp
362 Old Whitley Rd .... London KY 40744 606-864-5175 864-5194
Web: www.khic.org

Marwit Capital LLC
100 Bayview Cir Ste 550 .... Newport Beach CA 92660 949-861-3636 861-3637
Web: www.marwit.com

Mason Wells 411 E Wisconsin Ave Ste 1280 .... Milwaukee WI 53202 414-727-6400 727-6410
Web: www.masonwells.com

MVP Capital Partners
259 N Radnor-Chester Rd Ste 130 .... Radnor PA 19087 610-254-2999 254-2996
Web: www.meridian-venture.com

Novus Ventures LP
20111 Stevens Creek Blvd Ste 130 .... Cupertino CA 95014 408-252-3900
Web: www.novusventures.com

Physical Optics Corp 20600 Gramercy Pl .... Torrance CA 90501 310-320-3088 320-4667
Web: www.poc.com

RFE Investment Partners 36 Grove St .... New Canaan CT 06840 203-966-2800 966-3109
Web: www.rfeip.com

River Cities Capital Funds
221 E Fourth St Ste 2400 .... Cincinnati OH 45202 513-621-9700 579-8939

Seacoast Capital Partners 55 Ferncroft Rd .... Danvers MA 01923 978-750-1300 750-1301
Web: www.seacoastcapital.com

Sorrento Assoc Inc
12250 El Camino Real Ste 100 .... San Diego CA 92130 858-792-2700 792-5070
Web: www.sorrentoventures.com

				Phone	Fax
Stonehenge Capital Company LLC 236 Third St. *Web:* www.stonehengecapital.com	Baton Rouge	LA	70801	225-408-3000	408-3090
TPG Capital LP 301 Commerce St Ste 3300 *Web:* www.tpg.com	Fort Worth	TX	76102	817-871-4000	871-4001
UMB Capital Corp 1010 Grand Blvd. *TF:* 800-821-2171 ■ *Web:* www.umb.com	Kansas City	MO	64106	816-860-7000	860-7143
Vestor Partners LP 607 Cerrillos Rd *Web:* www.vestor.com	Santa Fe	NM	87501	505-988-9100	988-1958
Virginia Capital Partners LLC 1801 Libbie Ave Ste 201 *Web:* www.vacapital.com	Richmond	VA	23226	804-648-4802	648-4809
Waterside Capital Corp 2505 Cheyne Walk *OTC: WSCC*	Virginia Beach	VA	23454	757-626-1111	

406 INVESTMENT COMPANIES - SPECIALIZED SMALL BUSINESS

Companies listed here conform to the Small Business Administration's requirements for investment in minority companies.

				Phone	Fax
Accord Financial Corp Ste 1803 77 Bloor St W *Web:* www.accordfinancial.com	Toronto	ON	M5S1M2	416-961-0007	
Al Copeland Investments Inc 1001 Harimaw Ct S. *TF:* 800-401-0401 ■ *Web:* www.alcopeland.com	Metairie	LA	70001	504-830-1000	401-0401
ALCO Inc 6925 - 104 St. *Web:* www.alcoinc.ca	Edmonton	AB	T6H2L5	780-435-3502	
American Small Bus Investment 4141 N Henderson Rd Ste 8	Arlington	VA	22203	703-527-5200	527-3700
Appaloosa Management LP 51 John F Kennedy Pkwy *Web:* www.dealbreaker.com	Short Hills	NJ	07078	973-701-7000	
Arlington Capital Partners 5425 Wisconsin Ave Ste 200 *Web:* www.arlingtoncap.com	Chevy Chase	MD	20815	202-337-7500	337-7525
Associated Southwest Investors Inc 6501 Americas Pkwy NE	Albuquerque	NM	87110	505-247-4050	247-1899
Bastion Capital Corp 1901 Ave of the Stars	Los Angeles	CA	90067	310-788-5700	277-7582
Brentwood Assoc 11150 Santa Monica Blvd Ste 1200 *Web:* www.brentwood.com	Los Angeles	CA	90025	310-477-6611	477-1011
Brown Gibbons Lang & Co LLC 1375 E 9th St Suite 2500 *Web:* www.bglco.com	Cleveland	OH	44114	216-241-2800	241-7417
Burney Co 121 Rowell Ct. *Web:* www.burney.com	Falls Church	VA	22046	703-241-5611	531-0418
Capricorn Management LLC 30 E Elm St *Web:* www.capricornholdings.com	Greenwich	CT	06830	203-861-6600	861-6671
Castle Harlan Inc 150 E 58th St *Web:* www.castleharlan.com	New York	NY	10155	212-644-8600	207-8042
Chatham Financial Corp 235 Whitehorse Ln *Web:* www.chathamfinancial.com	Kennett Square	PA	19348	610-925-3120	
Chicago Oakbrook Financial Group 903 Commerce Dr Ste 300 *Web:* www.cofgroup.com	Oak Brook	IL	60523	630-954-5572	
Clayton Dubilier & Rice Inc 375 Pk Ave 18th Fl *Web:* www.cdr-inc.com	New York	NY	10152	212-407-5200	407-5252
Community Mortgage Corp 142 Timber Creek Dr. *Web:* www.communitymtg.com	Cordova	TN	38018	901-759-4400	
Core Realty Holdings LLC 1600 Dove St Ste 450 *Web:* www.corerealtyholdings.com	Newport Beach	CA	92660	949-863-1031	
Cypress Sharpridge Investments Inc (CYS) 890 Winter St *NYSE: CYS* ■ *Web:* www.cysinv.com	Waltham	MA	02451	617-639-0440	
Goldner Hawn Johnson & Morrison Inc (GHJ&M) 90 S Seventh St 3700 Wells Fargo Ctr *Web:* www.ghjm.com	Minneapolis	MN	55402	612-338-5912	338-2860
Ibero American Investors Corp 817 E Main *Web:* www.iberoinvestors.com	Rochester	NY	14605	585-256-8900	
La Financiere Agricole Du Quebec 1400 Blvd de la Rive-Sud *Web:* www.fadq.qc.ca	Saint-romuald	QC	J2X3C7	418-838-5602	
Linx Partners LLC 100 Galleria Pkwy Ste 1150 *Web:* www.linxpartners.com	Atlanta	GA	30339	770-818-0335	
Littlejohn & Company LLC Eight Sound Shore Dr Ste 303 *Web:* www.littlejohnllc.com	Greenwich	CT	06830	203-552-3500	552-3550
Madison Capital Partners Corp 500 W Madison St Ste 3890 *Web:* www.madisoncapitalpartners.net	Chicago	IL	60661	312-277-0156	277-0163
MBN Corp 812 Memorial Dr NW *Web:* www.middlefield.com	Calgary	AB	T2N3C8	403-269-2100	
MCG Global LLC 300 Long Beach Blvd Ste 13 *Web:* www.mcgglobal.com	Stratford	CT	06615	203-386-0615	386-0771
Medallion Capital 3000 W County Rd 42 Ste 301 *Web:* www.medallionfinancial.com	Burnsville	MN	55337	952-831-2025	831-2945
Mennonite Savings & Credit Union (Ontario) Ltd 1265 Strasburg Rd *Web:* www.mscu.com	Kitchener	ON	N2R1S6	519-746-1010	
Milestone Growth Fund 527 Marquette Ave Ste 1915 *Web:* www.milestonegrowth.com	Minneapolis	MN	55402	612-338-0090	
MMG Ventures LP 826 E Baltimore St *TF:* 800-248-1960 ■ *Web:* www.mmgcapitalgroup.com	Baltimore	MD	21202	410-333-2548	333-2552
NCA Partners Inc 1200 Westlake Ave N Ste 600 *Web:* www.nwcap.com	Seattle	WA	98109	206-689-5615	689-5614
Nitze-Stagen & Company Inc 2401 Utah Ave S Ste 305 *Web:* www.nitze-stagen.com	Seattle	WA	98134	206-467-0420	467-0423
Opportunity Capital Corp 2201 Walnut Ave Ste 210 *Web:* www.opportunitycapitalpartners.com	Fremont	CA	94538	510-795-7000	
Polestar Capital Inc 180 N Michigan Ave Ste 1905 *Web:* www.polestarvc.com	Chicago	IL	60601	312-984-9090	984-9877
Princeton Financial Systems LLC 600 College Rd E *Web:* www.pfs.com	Princeton	NJ	08540	609-987-2400	987-9320
Pro Mujer Inc 253 W 35th St 11th Fl South *Web:* www.promujer.org	New York	NY	10001	646-626-7000	
Rainmaker Group Ventures LLC, The 4550 N Point Pkwy Ste 400 *Web:* www.letitrain.com	Alpharetta	GA	30022	678-578-5700	
Rayonier Inc 225 Water St Ste 1400 *Web:* www.rayonier.com	Jacksonville	FL	32202	904-357-9100	
RD Legal Funding LLC 45 Legion Dr *Web:* www.legalfunding.com	Cresskill	NJ	07626	201-568-9007	
Security Credit Services LLC 2653 W Oxford Loop Ste 108 *Web:* www.securitycreditservicesllc.com	Oxford	MS	38655	662-281-7220	
Smith Affiliated Capital (SAC) 800 Third Ave 12th Fl *TF:* 888-387-3298 ■ *Web:* www.smithcapital.com	New York	NY	10022	212-644-9440	644-1979
Stockbridge Capital Partners LLC Four Embarcadero Ctr Ste 3300 *Web:* www.sbfund.com	San Francisco	CA	94111	415-658-3300	
United FCS ACA 2616 US Hwy 45 *Web:* www.unitedfcs.com	Antigo	WI	54409	715-623-7644	

407 INVESTMENT GUIDES - ONLINE

SEE ALSO Buyer's Guides - Online p. 1896

				Phone	Fax
Briefing.com Inc 401 N Michigan Ste 2910 *TF General:* 800-752-3013 ■ *Web:* www.briefing.com	Chicago	IL	60611	312-670-4463	670-5761
EDGAR Online Inc 11200 Rockville Pk Ste 310 *NASDAQ: EDGR* ■ *TF:* 800-732-0330 ■ *Web:* edgar-online.com	Rockville	MD	20852	301-287-0300	287-0390
eSignal 3955 Pt Eden Way *TF:* 800-815-8256 ■ *Web:* www.esignal.com	Hayward	CA	94545	510-266-6000	266-6100
FactSet Research Systems Inc 601 Merritt 7 Third Fl *NYSE: FDS* ■ *TF:* 877-322-8738 ■ *Web:* www.factset.com	Norwalk	CT	06851	203-810-1000	810-1000
Harris myCFO Inc 2200 Geng Rd Ste 100 *TF:* 866-966-1130 ■ *Web:* ctcmycfo.com/	Palo Alto	CA	94303	650-210-5000	210-5010
Hoover's Inc 5800 Airport Blvd. *TF:* 800-486-8666 ■ *Web:* www.hoovers.com	Austin	TX	78752	512-374-4500	374-4501
InvestorPlace.com 2420A Gehman Ln 2420A Gehman Ln *TF:* 800-219-8592 ■ *Web:* www.investorplace.com	Lancaster	PA	17602	800-219-8592	
Motley Fool Inc 2000 Duke St Fourth Fl *Web:* www.fool.com	Alexandria	VA	22314	703-838-3665	254-1999
Stockwatch 700 W Georgia St PO Box 10371 *TF:* 800-268-6397 ■ *Web:* www.stockwatch.com	Vancouver	BC	V7Y1J6	604-687-1500	687-0541
TheStreet.com Inc 14 Wall St 15th Fl *NASDAQ: TST* ■ *TF:* 800-562-9571 ■ *Web:* www.thestreet.com	New York	NY	10005	212-321-5000	321-5016
Yahoo! Finance 701 First Ave *Web:* finance.yahoo.com	Sunnyvale	CA	94089	408-349-3300	349-3301

408 INVESTMENT (MISC)

SEE ALSO Commodity Contracts Brokers & Dealers p. 2010; Franchises p. 2330; Investment Guides - Online p. 2604; Mortgage Lenders & Loan Brokers p. 2766; Mutual Funds p. 2807; Investment Newsletters p. 2816; Real Estate Investment Trusts (REITs) p. 3039; Royalty Trusts p. 3129; Securities Brokers & Dealers p. 3151; Banks - Commercial & Savings p. 1848; Venture Capital Firms p. 3277

				Phone	Fax
ABRY Partners LLC 111 Huntington Ave 29th Fl *TF:* 800-777-3674 ■ *Web:* www.abry.com	Boston	MA	02199	617-859-2959	859-8797
Acacia Research Corp 500 Newport Ctr Dr Ste 700 *NASDAQ: ACTG* ■ *Web:* www.acaciaresearch.com	Newport Beach	CA	92660	949-480-8300	480-8301
Adams Express Co Seven St Paul St Ste 1140 *NYSE: ADX* ■ *TF:* 800-638-2479 ■ *Web:* www.adamsexpress.com	Baltimore	MD	21202	410-752-5900	659-0080
AEA Investors Inc 666 Fifth Ave 36th Fl *Web:* www.aeainvestors.com	New York	NY	10103	212-644-5900	888-1459
Anschutz Corp 555 17th St Ste 2400 *Web:* anschutz-exploration.com	Denver	CO	80202	303-298-1000	298-8881
Bancroft Fund Ltd 65 Madison Ave Ste 550 *NYSE: BCV* ■ *Web:* www.bancroftfund.com	Morristown	NJ	07960	973-631-1177	631-1313
Barry S. Nussbaum Company Inc 13151 Emily Rd Ste 250 *Web:* www.bncrealestate.com	Dallas	TX	75240	972-437-9900	437-9377
Central Securities Corp 630 Fifth Ave Ste 820 *NYSE: CET* ■ *TF:* 866-593-2507 ■ *Web:* www.centralsecurities.com	New York	NY	10111	212-698-2020	
Cerberus Capital Management LP 875 Third Ave *Web:* www.cerberuscapital.com	New York	NY	10022	212-891-2100	
Columbia Ventures Corp (CVC) 12503 SE Mill Plain Blvd Ste 120 *Web:* www.colventures.com	Vancouver	WA	98684	360-816-1840	816-1841
Counsel Corp 1211 Ave of the Americas Ste 2902 *NYSE: CXS* ■ *TF:* 866-296-3743 ■ *Web:* www.snl.com	New York	NY	10036	212-696-0100	696-9809

Phone Fax

DPEC Capital Inc 135 Fifth Ave New York NY 10010 301-590-6500
TF: 844-574-3577 ■ *Web:* finra.org

Dundee Wealth Management Inc
One Adelaide St E Toronto ON M5C2V9 416-350-3250 350-5105
Web: dundeecorp.com

Enerplus Resources Fund
333 Seventh Ave SW Ste 3000 Calgary AB T2P2Z1 403-298-2200 298-2211
TF: 800-319-6462 ■ *Web:* www.enerplus.com

Enstar USA Inc 7035 Halcyon Pk Dr Montgomery AL 36117 334-834-5483
NASDAQ: ESGR ■ *Web:* www.enstargroup.com

Eureka Growth Capital
1717 Arch St 3420 Bell Atlantic Twr Philadelphia PA 19103 267-238-4200 238-4201
Web: www.eurekagrowth.com

Fairmont Capital Inc 3350 E Birch St Ste 206 Brea CA 92821 714-524-4770 524-4775
Web: www.fairmontcapital.com

Fairview Capital Partners Inc
75 Isham Rd Ste 200 West Hartford CT 06107 860-674-8066 678-5108
Web: www.fairviewcapital.com

Fidelity Investments Charitable Gift Fund
PO Box 770001 Cincinnati OH 45277 800-262-6039 665-4274*
**Fax Area Code: 877* ■ *TF:* 800-262-6039 ■ *Web:* www.fidelitycharitable.org

Forstmann Little & Co 767 Fifth Ave New York NY 10153 212-355-5656 759-9059

Fremont Group Inc 199 Fremont St San Francisco CA 94105 415-284-8500 284-8191
Web: www.fremontgroup.com

Golden Gate Capital
One Embarcadero Ctr Fl 39 San Francisco CA 94111 415-983-2700 983-2701
Web: goldengatecap.com

Gores Technology Group
10877 Wilshire Blvd Ste 1805 Los Angeles CA 90024 310-209-3010 209-3310
Web: www.gores.com

Gould Investors LP
60 Cutter Mill Rd Ste 303 Great Neck NY 11021 516-466-3100 466-3132
Web: gouldlp.com

Haverford Trust Co
Three Radnor Corp Ctr Ste 450 Radnor PA 19087 610-995-8700 995-8796
TF: 888-995-1979 ■ *Web:* www.haverfordtrust.com

Hellman & Friedman LLC
1 Maritime Plaza 12th Fl San Francisco CA 94111 415-788-5111 788-0176
Web: www.hf.com

Highland Capital Management LP
300 Crescent Ct Ste 700 Dallas TX 75201 972-628-4100 628-4147
Web: www.hcmlp.com

Hold Bros On-Line Investment Services Inc
525 Washington Blvd Ste 2450 Jersey City NJ 07310 201-499-9700
Web: www.holdbrothers.com

HomeVestors of America Inc
6500 Greenville Ave Ste 400 Dallas TX 75206 972-761-0046 761-9022
TF: 800-442-8937 ■ *Web:* www.homevestors.com

ICV Capital Partners LLC
299 Park Ave 34th Fl New York NY 10171 212-455-9600 455-9603
Web: naicvc.com

JII Partners Inc 450 Lexington Ave 31st Fl New York NY 10017 212-286-8600 286-8626
Web: www.jllpartners.com

Kunath Karren Rinne & Atkin LLC
1000 Second Ave Ste 4000 Seattle WA 98104 206-621-7400 343-3085
Web: www.kkra.com

Lion Chemical Capital LLC
535 Madison Ave 4th Fl New York NY 10022 212-355-5500 355-6283
Web: www.lionchemicalcapital.com

Liquidnet Holdings Inc
498 Seventh Ave 12th Fl New York NY 10018 646-674-2000 674-2003
Web: www.liquidnet.com

Main Street Capital Corp 1300 Post Oak Blvd Houston TX 77056 713-350-6000 350-6042
NYSE: MAIN ■ *TF:* 800-966-1559 ■ *Web:* www.mainstcapital.com

McCown De Leeuw & Co (MDC)
950 Tower Ln Ste 800 Foster City CA 94404 650-854-6000 854-0853
Web: www.mdcpartners.com

Moors & Cabot Inc 111 Devonshire St Boston MA 02109 617-426-0500 426-9608
TF: 800-426-0501 ■ *Web:* www.moorscabot.com

Novitas Capital 435 Devon Pk Dr Ste 801 Wayne PA 19087 610-293-4075 254-4240
Web: www.novitascapital.com

Pembina Pipeline Corp 700 Ninth Ave SW Calgary AB T2P3V4 403-231-7500 237-0254
TSE: PPL ■ *TF:* 888-428-3222 ■ *Web:* www.pembina.com

Petroleum & Resources Corp
Seven St Paul St Ste 1140 Baltimore MD 21202 410-752-5900 659-0080
NYSE: PEO ■ *TF:* 800-638-2479 ■ *Web:* www.peteres.com

Platinum Equity Holdings
Platinum Equity LLC 360 N Crescent Dr Beverly Hills CA 90210 310-712-1850
Web: www.platinumequity.com

Provender Capital Group 1841 Broadway New York NY 10023 212-271-8888 271-8875

Rand Capital Corp 2200 Rand Bldg Buffalo NY 14203 716-853-0802 854-8480
NASDAQ: RAND ■ *Web:* www.randcapital.com

Safeguard International Fund LP
435 Devon Pk Dr Bldg 200 Wayne PA 19087 610-293-0838 293-0854

SCP Private Equity Partners
1200 Liberty Ridge Dr Ste 300 Wayne PA 19087 610-995-2900 975-9546
Web: www.scppartners.com

Sequoia Equities Inc
1777 Botelho Dr Ste 300 Walnut Creek CA 94596 925-945-0900 256-3780
Web: www.experiencesequoia.com

Smith Whiley & Co 242 Trumbull St Eighth Fl Hartford CT 06103 860-548-2513 548-2518
Web: www.smithwhiley.com

Spell Capital Partners LLC
222 S Ninth St Ste 2880 Minneapolis MN 55402 612-371-9650 371-9651
Web: www.spellcapital.com

Superior Plus Income Fund
840-7 Ave SW Ste 1400 Calgary AB T2P3G2 403-218-2970 218-2973
TF: 866-490-7587 ■ *Web:* www.superiorplus.ca

Technology Ventures Corp
1155 University Blvd SE Albuquerque NM 87106 505-246-2882 246-2891
Web: www.techventures.org

Thomas H Lee Partners 100 Federal St 35th Fl Boston MA 02110 617-227-1050 227-3514
TF: 877-456-3427 ■ *Web:* www.thl.com

Thomas Properties Group Inc
515 S Flower St Sixth Fl Los Angeles CA 90071 213-613-1900 633-4760
NYSE: TPGI

Tracinda Corp 150 Rodeo Dr Ste 250 Beverly Hills CA 90212 310-271-0638 271-3416

Welsh Carson Anderson & Stowe
320 Pk Ave Ste 2500 New York NY 10022 212-893-9500
Web: www.welshcarson.com

409 JANITORIAL & CLEANING SUPPLIES - WHOL

Phone Fax

Accutemp Products Inc 8415 N Clinton Park Fort Wayne IN 46825 260-493-0415
Web: accutemp.net

Advanced Vacuum Company Inc
1215 Business Pkwy N Westminster MD 21157 410-876-8200
Web: www.advaco.com

Alliance Fire Protection Co 2114 E Cedar St Tempe AZ 85281 480-966-9178
Web: www.afpc.com

AmSan 3031 N Andrews Ave Exd Pompano Beach FL 33064 954-972-1700
TF: 866-412-6726 ■ *Web:* amsan.com

Badger Land Car Wash Equipment & Supplies LLC
300A E Oak St Oak Creek WI 53154 414-764-4250
Web: www.badgerlandcarwashequipment.com

Brady Industries Inc 7055 Lindell Rd Las Vegas NV 89118 702-876-3990 876-1580
TF: 800-293-4698 ■ *Web:* www.bradyindustries.com

C&T Design & Equipment Company Inc
2750 Tobey Dr Indianapolis IN 46219 317-898-9602
Web: www.c-tdesign.com

Castle Sprinkler & Alalarm
5117 College Ave College Park MD 20740 301-927-7300
Web: www.csafire.com

Culinary Depot Inc Two Melnick Dr Monsey NY 10952 888-845-8200
TF: 888-845-8200 ■ *Web:* www.culinarydepotinc.com

EXSL/Ultra Labs Inc 30921 Wiegman Rd Hayward CA 94544 510-324-4567 324-8881
Web: exsl.net

Finley Fire Equipment Company Inc
5255 N State Rt 60 NW Mcconnelsville OH 43756 740-962-4328
Web: www.finleyfire.com

Fitch Co 2201 Russell St Baltimore MD 21230 410-539-1953 727-2244
TF: 800-933-4824 ■ *Web:* www.fitchco.com

I Janvey & Sons Inc 218 Front St Hempstead NY 11550 516-489-9300 486-3927
Web: www.janvey.com

Industrial Soap Co 722 S Vandeventer Ave Saint Louis MO 63110 314-241-6363 533-5556
Web: www.industrialsoap.com

J. Ennis Fabrics Ltd 12122 - 68 St Edmonton AB T5B1R1 800-663-6647
TF: 800-663-6647 ■ *Web:* www.jennisfabrics.com

Kellermeyer Co 475 W Woodland Cir Bowling Green OH 43402 419-255-3022 255-2752
TF: 800-445-7415 ■ *Web:* www.kellermeyer.com

Kenway Distributors Inc
6320 Strawberry Ln Louisville KY 40214 502-367-2201 368-5519
Web: www.kenway.net

Mobile Fixture & Equipment Company Inc
1155 Montlimar Dr Mobile AL 36609 251-342-0455
Web: www.mobilefixture.com

Mortech Manufacturing Inc 411 N Aerojet Ave Azusa CA 91702 626-334-1471
Web: mortechmfg.com

Rose Products & Services Inc 545 Stimmel Rd Columbus OH 43223 614-443-7647 443-2771
TF: 800-264-1568 ■ *Web:* hillyard.com

Sani-Clean Distributors 57 Industrial Way Portland ME 04103 207-797-8240

Shadow Beverages & Snacks LLC
4650 E Cotton Ctr Blvd Ste 240 Phoenix AZ 85040 480-371-1100
Web: www.shadowbev.com

Standard Companies Inc, The
2601 S Archer Ave Chicago IL 60608 312-225-2777
Web: www.thestandardcompanies.com

Taylor Freezers of California
221 Harris Ct South San Francisco CA 94080 877-978-4800
TF: 877-978-4800 ■ *Web:* www.taylorfreezers.com

410 JEWELERS' FINDINGS & MATERIALS

Phone Fax

10G LLC 100 Morey Dr Woodridge IL 60517 630-754-2400
Web: www.10g.com

A & D Technology Inc 4622 Runway Blvd Ann Arbor MI 48108 734-973-1111
Web: www.aanddtech.com

Absolute Analysis Inc
2393 Teller Rd Ste 109 Newbury Park CA 91320 805-376-6048
Web: www.absoluteanalysis.com

Advanced Mechanical Technology Inc
176 Waltham St Watertown MA 02472 617-926-6700
Web: www.amti.biz

Affinity Biosensors LLC
75D Robin Hill Rd Santa Barbara CA 93117 805-960-5100
Web: www.affinitybio.com

Ag Leader Technology Inc 2202 S River Side Dr Ames IA 50010 515-232-5363
Web: agleader.com

Amber Precision Instruments Inc
746 San Aleso Ave Sunnyvale CA 94085 408-752-0199
Web: www.amberpi.com

AmbiCom Holdings Inc 500 Alder Dr Milpitas CA 95035 408-321-0822
Web: www.ambicom.com

American Automatrix Inc One Technology Ln Export PA 15632 724-733-2000
Web: www.aamatrix.com

Ampex Casting Corp 23 W 47th St Fourth Fl New York NY 10036 212-719-1318 719-3493

ANDalyze Inc 2109 S Oak St Ste 102 Champaign IL 61820 217-328-0045
Web: www.andalyze.com

Andrews Industrial Controls 108 Rosslyn Rd Carnegie PA 15106 412-279-5335
Web: www.andrewsic.com

Phone Fax

Ashcroft Inc 250 E Main St .... Stratford CT 06614 203-378-8281
Web: www.ashcroftinc.com

Aspect Automation LLC 1185 Willow Lk Blvd .... Saint Paul MN 55110 651-643-3700
Web: www.aspectautomation.com

AutoSeis Inc 2101 Midway Rd Ste 310 .... Carrollton TX 75006 972-332-3388
Web: www.autoseis.net

Avalon Vision Solutions LLC
422 Thornton Rd Ste 104 .... Lithia Springs GA 30122 770-944-8445
Web: www.avalonvision.com

B&W Tek Inc 19 Shea Way Ste 301 .... Newark DE 19713 302-368-7824
Web: www.bwtek.com

Best Priced Products Inc
Three Westchester Plz .... Elmsford NY 10523 914-345-3800
Web: www.bpp2.com

Bizerba USA Inc 31 Gordon Rd .... Piscataway NJ 08854 732-565-6000
Web: www.bizerbausa.com

Boon Edam Inc 402 McKinney Pkwy .... Lillington NC 27546 910-814-3800
Web: www.boonedam.us

Boulder Innovation Group Inc
4824 Sterling Dr .... Boulder CO 80301 303-447-0248
Web: www.imageguided.com

BrightSign LLC 16795 Lark Ave Ste 200 .... Los Gatos CA 95032 408-852-9263
Web: www.brightsign.biz

Brooks Instrument LLC 407 W Vine St .... Hatfield PA 19440 215-362-3500
Web: www.brooksinstrument.com

Capstone Metering LLC 1600 Capital Ave Ste 200 .... Plano TX 75074 214-469-1065
Web: www.intellih2o.com

CDEX Inc 4555 S Palo Verde Ste 123 .... Tucson AZ 85714 520-745-5172
Web: www.cdex-inc.com

Chauvin Arnoux Inc 15 Faraday Dr .... Dover NH 03820 603-749-6434
Web: www.aemc.com

Coastal Environmental Systems Inc
820 First Ave S .... Seattle WA 98134 206-682-6048
Web: www.coastalenvironmental.com

Comark Instruments Inc
Bldg 50-209 PO Box 500 .... Beaverton OR 97077 503-643-5204
Web: www.comarkusa.com

Control Module Inc 89 Phoenix Ave .... Enfield CT 06082 860-745-2433
Web: www.controlmod.com

COSA Xentaur Corp 84G Horseblock Rd .... Yaphank NY 11980 631-345-3434
Web: www.cosaxentaur.com

Craftstones PO Box 847 .... Ramona CA 92065 760-789-1620 789-3432
Web: www.craftstones.com

Cranesmart Systems Inc 4908 97 St NW .... Edmonton AB T6E5S1 780-437-2986 438-9491
Web: cranesmart.com

CW Brabender Instruments Inc
50 E Wesley St .... South Hackensack NJ 07606 201-343-8425
Web: www.cwbrabender.com

Cyber-Rain Inc 6345 Balboa Blvd Ste 230 .... Encino CA 91316 877-888-1452
TF: 877-888-1452 ■ *Web:* www.cyber-rain.com

Data Physics Corp 1741 Technology Dr Ste 260 .... San Jose CA 95110 408-437-0100
Web: www.dataphysics.com

David H Fell & Company Inc
6009 Bandini Blvd .... Commerce CA 90040 323-722-9992 722-6567
TF: 800-822-1996 ■ *Web:* www.dhfco.com

Delta Controls Inc 17850 - 56th Ave .... Surrey BC V3S1C7 604-574-9444 574-7793
Web: www.deltacontrols.com

Delta M Corp 1003 Larsen Dr .... Oak Ridge TN 37830 800-922-0083
TF: 800-922-0083 ■ *Web:* www.deltamcorp.com

DEVAR Inc 706 Bostwick Ave .... Bridgeport CT 06605 203-368-6751
Web: www.devarinc.com

dpiX LLC 1635 Aeroplaza Dr .... Colorado Springs CO 80916 719-457-7700
Web: www.dpix.com

DTN.IQ Inc 9110 W Dodge Rd Ste 200 .... Omaha NE 68114 402-390-2328
Web: www.interquote.com

EHT International Inc
1340 Gay Lussac Ste 10 .... Boucherville QC J4B7G4 450-906-0705
Web: www.ehtinternational.com

Embraer Aircraft Maintenance Services Inc
10 Airways Blvd .... Nashville TN 37217 615-367-2100
Web: www.embraerexecutivejets.com

Emme E2MS LLC PO Box 2251 .... Bristol CT 06011 800-396-0523
TF: 800-396-0523 ■ *Web:* www.getemme.com

Environmental Systems Products Inc
Seven Kripes Rd .... East Granby CT 06026 860-392-2100
Web: www.esp-global.com

ET Water Systems LLC
384 Bel Marin Keys Blvd Ste 145 .... Novato CA 94949 415-945-9383
Web: www.etwater.com

Eyedro Green Solutions Inc
151 Charles St W Ste 100 .... Kitchener ON N2G1H6 226-499-0944
Web: eyedro.com

FBS Inc 3340 W College Ave .... State College PA 16801 814-234-3437
Web: www.fbsworldwide.com

FCT Assembly Inc 1309 N 17th Ave .... Greeley CO 80631 970-346-8002
Web: www.fctassembly.com

Findings Inc 160 Water St .... Keene NH 03431 603-352-3717
TF: 800-225-2706 ■ *Web:* leachgarner.com

Fireye Inc Three Manchester Rd .... Derry NH 03038 603-432-4100
Web: www.fireye.com

Flexstar Technology Inc 1965 Concourse Dr .... San Jose CA 95131 408-643-7000
Web: www.flexstar.com

FoodChek Systems Inc 1414 8 St. S.W. Ste 450 .... Calgary AB T2R1J6 403-269-9424
Web: www.foodcheksystems.com

Fossil Power Systems Inc
10 Mosher Dr Burnside Industrial Park .... Dartmouth AB B3B1N5 902-468-2743
Web: www.fossil.ca

Fugro-Roadware Inc 2505 Meadowvale Blvd .... Mississauga ON L5N5S2 905-567-2870
Web: www.roadware.com

GeoDigital International Inc
175 Longwood Rd S McMaster Innovation Park
Ste 400A .... Hamilton ON L8P0A1 250-388-0500 388-0501
Web: www.geodigital.net

George Kelk Corp 48 Lesmill Rd .... Toronto ON M3B2T5 416-445-5850
Web: www.kelk.com

Gordon-Darby Inc 2410 Ampere Dr .... Louisville KY 40299 502-266-5797
Web: www.gordon-darby.com

Governor Control Systems Inc
3101 SW Third Ave .... Fort Lauderdale FL 33315 954-462-7404
Web: www.govconsys.com

GroundMetrics Inc 4217 Ponderosa Ave Ste A .... San Diego CA 92123 619-786-8023
Web: www.groundmetrics.com

Guardian Interlock Systems of Northeast Georgia Inc
228 Church St .... Marietta GA 30060 770-499-0499
Web: www.guardianinterlock.com

Heat-Timer Corp 20 New Dutch Ln .... Fairfield NJ 07004 973-575-4004
Web: www.heat-timer.com

Helitune Inc 190 Gordon St .... Elk Grove Village IL 60007 847-228-0985
Web: www.helitune.com

Hortau Inc
1112, Blvd de la Rive-Sud Bureau 200 .... Saint-romuald QC G6W5M6 418-839-2852 839-2851
Web: www.hortau.com

Humboldt Manufacturing Co 875 Tollgate Rd .... Elgin IL 60123 708-456-6300
Web: www.humboldtmfg.com

HydroPoint Data Systems Inc
1720 Corporate Cir .... Petaluma CA 94954 707-769-9696
Web: www.hydropoint.com

Image Sensing Systems Inc
500 Spruce Tree Centre 1600 University Ave .... St. Paul MN 55104 651-603-7700
Web: www.imagesensing.com

Interocean Systems 3738 Ruffin Rd .... San Diego CA 92123 858-565-8400
Web: www.interoceansystems.com

Intoximeters Inc 2081 Craig Rd .... Saint Louis MO 63146 314-429-4000
Web: www.intox.com

IRD LLC 4740 Allmond Ave .... Louisville KY 40209 502-366-0916
Web: www.irdbalancing.com

James A Murphy & Son Inc
1879 County St PO Box 3006 .... South Attleboro MA 02703 508-761-5060 761-4580
Web: patch.com/attleboro

JASCO Inc 28600 Mary's Ct .... Easton MD 21601 410-822-1220
Web: www.jascoinc.com

Kahan Jewelry Corp 1156 Ave .... New York NY 10036 212-719-1055

Karbra Co 151 W 46th St 10th Fl .... New York NY 10036 212-736-9300 736-9303
Web: karbra.com

Kejr Inc 1835 Wall St .... Salina KS 67401 785-825-1842
Web: geoprobe.com

Kent Scientific Corp 1116 Litchfield St .... Torrington CT 06790 860-626-1172
Web: www.kentscientific.com

Kinemotive Corp 222 Central Ave .... Farmingdale NY 11735 631-249-6440
Web: www.kinemotive.com

Kratos Analytical Inc
100 Red Schoolhouse Rd Bldg A .... Spring Valley NY 10977 845-426-6700
Web: www.kratos.com

Krohn Industries Inc PO Box 98 .... Carlstadt NJ 07072 201-933-9696 933-9684
TF: 800-526-6299 ■ *Web:* www.krohnindustries.com

Kuster Co 2900 E 29th St .... Long Beach CA 90806 562-595-0661
Web: www.kusterco.com

Labsphere Inc 231 Shaker St .... North Sutton NH 03260 603-927-4266
Web: www.labsphere.com

Laser Atlanta LLC 6090 E Northbelt Pkwy .... Norcross GA 30071 770-446-3866
Web: www.laseratlanta.com

Lazare Kaplan International Inc
19 W 44th St 16th Fl .... New York NY 10036 212-764-7201 972-8561
OTC: LKII ■ *Web:* www.lazarediamonds.com

Lee's Morvillo Group 160 Niantic Ave .... Providence RI 02907 401-353-1740 353-0740
TF: 800-821-1700 ■ *Web:* www.leesmfg.com

Lifeloc Technologies Inc
12441 W 49th Ave Unit 4 .... Wheat Ridge CO 80033 303-431-9500
Web: www.lifeloc.com

Lighting Sciences Inc 7826 E Evans Rd .... Scottsdale AZ 85260 480-991-9260
Web: www.lightingsciences.com

LMG Holdings Inc 4290 Glendale Milford Rd .... Blue Ash OH 45242 513-651-9560
Web: www.lifesafer.com

Loadstar Sensors Inc
48501 Warm Springs Blvd Ste 109 .... Fremont CA 94539 510-274-1872
Web: www.loadstarsensors.com

LPA Designs 21 Gregory Dr Ste 140 .... South Burlington VT 05403 802-658-0038
Web: www.lpadesign.com

Magic Novelty Inc 308 Dyckman St .... New York NY 10034 212-304-2777 567-2809
Web: www.magicnovelty.com

Measurement Technology Group Inc
1310 Emerald Rd .... Greenwood SC 29646 864-223-1212
Web: www.redsealmeasurement.com

Meriam Process Technologies Inc
10920 Madison Ave .... Cleveland OH 44102 216-281-1100
Web: www.meriam.com

Met One Instruments Inc
1600 Washington Blvd .... Grants Pass OR 97526 541-471-7111
Web: www.metone.com

Micron Optics Inc 1852 Century Pl NE .... Atlanta GA 30345 404-325-0005
Web: www.micronoptics.com

MicroSense LLC 205 Industrial Ave E .... Lowell MA 01852 978-843-7673
Web: www.microsense.net

Modern Machine & Tool Company Inc
11844 Jefferson Ave .... Newport News VA 23606 757-873-1212
Web: www.mmtool.com

MRU Instruments Inc 6699 Portwest Dr Ste 130 .... Houston TX 77024 713-426-3260
Web: www.mru-instruments.com

MSP Corp 5910 Rice Creek Pkwy Ste 300 .... Shoreview MN 55126 651-287-8100
Web: www.mspcorp.com

MTI Instruments Inc 325 Washington Ave Ext .... Albany NY 12205 518-218-2550
Web: www.mtiinstruments.com

Nanovea Six Morgan .... Irvine CA 92618 949-461-9292
Web: nanovea.com

NCI Technologies Inc 636 Cure-Boivin Blvd .... Boisbriand QC J7G2A7 450-434-7222
Web: www.ncitech.ca

Company	City	State	Zip	Phone	Fax
New Frontier Electronics Inc 6131 Kellers Church Rd *Web:* www.surgex.com	Pipersville	PA	18947	215-766-1240	
Newage Testing Instruments Inc 820 Pennsylvania Blvd *Web:* www.hardnesstesters.com	Feasterville	PA	19053	215-355-6900	
Nidec Avtron Automation Corp 7555 E Pleasant Vly Rd Bldg 100 *Web:* www.nidec-avtron.com	Independence	OH	44131	216-642-1230	
Northern Digital Inc 103 Randall Dr *Web:* www.ndigital.com	Waterloo	ON	N2V1C5	519-884-5142	
Nutfield Technology Inc One Wall St Ste 113 *Web:* www.nutfieldtech.com	Hudson	NH	03051	603-893-6200	
OmniMetrix LLC 5225 Belle Wood Ct *Web:* www.omnimetrix.net	Buford	GA	30518	770-209-0012	
OndaVia Inc 26102 Eden Landing Rd Ste 1 *Web:* www.ondavia.com	Hayward	CA	94545	510-887-3180	
Optel Vision Inc 2680, boul. du Parc Technologique *Web:* www.optelvision.com	Quebec City	QC	G1P4S6	418-688-0334	688-9397
OptoAtmospherics Inc 1777 Highland Dr Ste B *Web:* www.optoatmospherics.com	Ann Arbor	MI	48108	734-975-8777	
Paroscientific Inc 4500 148th Ave Ne *Web:* www.paroscientific.com	Redmond	WA	98052	425-883-8700	
Paul H Gesswein & Co 255 Hancock Ave *TF:* 800-544-2043 ■ *Web:* www.gesswein.com	Bridgeport	CT	06605	203-366-5400	366-3953
Piezotech LLC 8431 Georgetown Rd Ste 300 *Web:* www.piezotechnologies.com	Indianapolis	IN	46268	317-876-4670	
Pillar Innovations LLC 164 Corporate Dr PO Box 550 *Web:* www.pillarinnovations.com	Grantsville	MD	21536	301-245-4007	
Polimaster Inc 2300 Clarendon Blvd Ste 708 *Web:* www.polimaster.us	Arlington	VA	22201	703-525-5075	
PowerOneData Inc 1201 S Alma School Rd Mesa Financial Ctr Ste 229 *Web:* www.p1di.com	Mesa	AZ	85210	480-668-0700	
Precision Specialties Co 1201 East Pecan St **Fax Area Code:* 903 ■ *TF:* 800-527-3295 ■ *Web:* www.presco.com	Sherman	TX	75090	800-527-3295	893-2328*
Precision Time Systems Inc 349 McKay Rd *Web:* www.precisiontime.com	Bolivia	NC	28422	910-253-9850	
ProvibTech Inc 11011 Brooklet Dr Ste 300 *Web:* www.provibtech.com	Houston	TX	77099	713-830-7601	
QualMark Corp 10390 E 48th Ave *Web:* www.qualmark.com	Denver	CO	80238	303-254-8800	
Rad-comm Systems Corp 7522 Bath Rd *Web:* www.radcommsystems.com	Mississauga	ON	L4T1L2	905-678-6503	
Radiant Zemax LLC 22908 NE Alder Crest Dr Ste 100 *Web:* www.radimg.com	Redmond	WA	98053	425-844-0152	
Rainwise Inc 25 Federal St *TF:* 800-762-5723 ■ *Web:* www.rainwise.com	Bar Harbor	ME	04609	207-288-5169	
Rees Scientific Corp 1007 Whitehead Rd Ext *Web:* www.reesscientific.com	Trenton	NJ	08638	609-530-1055	
ReVera Inc 3090 Oakmead Village Dr *Web:* www.revera.com	Santa Clara	CA	95051	408-510-7400	
Romanoff International Supply Corp Nine Deforest St *TF Cust Svc:* 800-221-7448 ■ *Web:* www.romanoff.com	Amityville	NY	11701	631-842-2400	842-0028
Romet Ltd 1080 Matheson Blvd East *Web:* www.rometlimited.com	Mississauga	ON	L4W2V2	905-624-1591	624-5668
S Himmelstein & Co 2490 Pembroke Ave *Web:* www.himmelstein.com	Hoffman Estates	IL	60169	847-843-3300	
Santa Barbara Control Systems 5375 Overpass Rd *Web:* www.sbcontrol.com	Santa Barbara	CA	93111	805-683-8833	
Satlantic Inc Richmond Terminal Pier 9 3481 N Marginal Rd *Web:* www.satlantic.com	Halifax	NS	B3K5X8	902-492-4780	
Saunders & Associates LLC 2520 E Rose Garden Ln *Web:* www.saunders-assoc.com	Phoenix	AZ	85050	602-971-9977	
Schenck AccuRate Inc 746 E Milwaukee St PO Box 208 *Web:* www.accuratefeeders.com	Whitewater	WI	53190	262-473-2441	
SECO Manufacturing Company Inc 4155 Oasis Rd *Web:* www.surveying.com	Redding	CA	96003	530-225-8155	
Senet Inc 94 River Rd Ste 101 *Web:* www.enertrac.com	Hudson	NH	03051	603-880-8484	
Sentient Energy Inc 880 Mitten Rd *Web:* www.sentient-energy.com	Burlingame	CA	94010	650-523-6680	
SepSensor Inc 257 Simarano Dr Annex II	Marlborough	MA	01752	508-229-2291	
SIE Computing Solutions Inc 10 Mupac Dr *Web:* sie-cs.com	Brockton	MA	02301	508-588-6110	
Signalisation Ver-Mac Inc 1781 Bresse *Web:* www.ver-mac.com	Quebec	QC	G2G2V2	418-654-1303	654-0517
SIX Safety Systems Inc 34 Griffin Industrial Point Ste 1 *Web:* www.sixsafetysystems.com	Cochrane	AB	T4C0A3	403-932-7955	
Solmetric Corp 117 Morris St Ste 100 *Web:* www.solmetric.com	Sebastopol	CA	95472	707-823-4600	
Sotax Corp 2400 Computer Dr *Web:* www.sotax.com	Westborough	MA	01581	508-417-1112	
Source Production & Equipment Company Inc 113 Teal St *Web:* www.spec150.com	Saint Rose	LA	70087	504-464-9471	
Space Optics Research Labs LLC Seven Stuart Rd *Web:* www.sorl.com	Chelmsford	MA	01824	978-250-8640	
Spectral Applied Research Inc 9078 Leslie St Unit 11 *Web:* www.spectral.ca	Richmond Hill	ON	L4B3L8	905-326-5040	
Sri Instruments Inc 6440 Sunset Corporate Dr *Web:* www.srigc.com	Las Vegas	NV	89120	702-361-2210	
Strainsert Inc 12 Union Hill Rd *Web:* www.strainsert.com	West Conshohocken	PA	19428	610-825-3310	
Stuller Settings Inc PO Box 87777 *TF:* 800-877-7777 ■ *Web:* www.stuller.com	Lafayette	LA	70598	800-877-7777	444-4741
Sumitomo (SHI) Cryogenics of America Inc 1833 Vultee Sreet *Web:* www.shicryogenics.com	Allentown	PA	18103	610-791-6700	
Super Systems Inc 7205 Edington Dr *Web:* www.supersystems.com	Cincinnati	OH	45249	513-772-0060	
SymCom Inc 222 Disk Dr *Web:* www.symcom.com	Rapid City	SD	57701	605-348-5580	
TAC Americas Inc 1650 W Crosby Rd *Web:* www.tac-global.com	Carrollton	TX	75006	972-323-1111	
Tavis Corp 3636 State Hwy 49 S *Web:* www.taviscorp.com	Mariposa	CA	95338	209-966-2027	
Techmor Inc 19911-D N Cove Rd *Web:* www.techmor.com	Cornelius	NC	28031	336-442-3686	
Test Evolution Corp 102 S St *Web:* www.testevolution.com	Hopkinton	MA	01748	781-644-2111	
Testek Inc 28320 Lakeview Dr *Web:* www.testek.com	Wixom	MI	48393	248-573-4980	
Tornado Spectral Systems 555 Richmond St W Ste 705 PO Box 218 *Web:* tornado-spectral.com	Toronto	ON	M5V3B1	416-361-3444	
Unholtz-Dickie Corp Six Brookside Dr *Web:* www.udco.com	Wallingford	CT	06492	203-265-3929	
Veris Industries Inc 16640 SW 72nd Ave *Web:* www.veris.com	Portland	OR	97224	503-598-4564	
Viconics Technologies Inc 9245 Langelier Blvd *Web:* www.viconics.com	St. Leonard	QC	H1P3K9	514-321-5660	
Victor Settings Inc 25 Brook Ave *TF:* 800-322-9008 ■ *Web:* www.victorsettings.com	Maywood	NJ	07607	201-845-4433	712-0818
William Goldberg Diamond Corp 589 Fifth Ave *Web:* www.williamgoldberg.com	New York	NY	10017	212-980-4343	980-6120
Wireless Seismic Inc 13100 Southwest Fwy Ste 150 *Web:* www.wirelessseismic.com	Sugar Land	TX	77478	832-532-5080	
Xensor Corp 4000 Bridge St *Web:* www.xensor.com	Drexel Hill	PA	19026	610-284-2508	
Zepp Labs Inc 20 S Santa Cruz Ave Ste 102 *Web:* www.zepp.com	Los Gatos	CA	95030	408-884-8077	

411 JEWELRY - COSTUME

Company	City	State	Zip	Phone	Fax
1928 Jewelry Co 3000 W Empire Ave *TF:* 800-227-1928 ■ *Web:* www.1928.com	Burbank	CA	91504	818-841-1928	526-4558
A & Z Hayward Co 655 Waterman Ave *TF:* 800-556-7462 ■ *Web:* www.azhayward.com	East Providence	RI	02914	401-438-0550	438-6970
American Ring Company Inc 19 Grosvenor Ave	East Providence	RI	02914	401-438-9060	438-3806
Arden Jewelry Manufacturing Co 10 Industrial Ln *Web:* www.ardenjewelry.com	Johnston	RI	02919	401-274-9800	
C & J Jewelry Company Inc 100 Dupont Dr *Web:* www.candjjewelry.com	Providence	RI	02907	401-944-2200	944-7915
Donald Bruce & Co 3600 N Talman Ave	Chicago	IL	60618	773-477-8100	
FGX International Inc 500 George Washington Hwy *TF:* 800-480-4846 ■ *Web:* fgxi.com	Smithfield	RI	02917	401-231-3800	
Gem-Craft Inc 1420 Elmwood Ave	Cranston	RI	02910	401-854-1200	
Jewelry Fashions Inc 385 Fifth Ave *Web:* www.robertrose.com/	New York	NY	10016	212-947-7700	
Kirk's Folly 236 Chapman St *Web:* www.kirksfolly.com	Providence	RI	02905	401-941-4300	467-2360
Shira Accessories Ltd 28 W 36th St	New York	NY	10018	212-594-4455	
Speidel Corp 1425 Cranston St **Fax Area Code:* 800 ■ *Web:* www.speidel.com	Cranston	RI	02920	401-519-2000	928-2423*
Swank Inc 656 Joseph Warner Blvd *Web:* swankinc.com	Taunton	MA	02780	508-822-2527	977-4428

412 JEWELRY - PRECIOUS METAL

Company	City	State	Zip	Phone	Fax
American Achievement Corp 7211 Cir S Rd *TF:* 800-531-5055 ■ *Web:* www.artcarved.com	Austin	TX	78745	512-444-0571	443-5213
Armbrust International Ltd 735 Allens Ave *Web:* www.armbrustintl.com	Providence	RI	02905	401-781-3300	781-2590
Balfour 7211 Cir S Rd *TF:* 800-225-3687 ■ *Web:* www.balfour.com	Austin	TX	78745	800-225-3687	
Byard F Brogan Inc PO Box 0369 *TF:* 800-232-7642 ■ *Web:* www.bfbrogan.com	Glenside	PA	19038	215-885-3550	885-1366
Danecraft Inc One Baker St *Web:* www.danecraft.com	Providence	RI	02905	401-941-7700	
David Yurman Designs Inc 24 Vestry St *Web:* www.davidyurman.com	New York	NY	10013	212-896-1550	
Diablo Mfg Company Inc 900 Golden Gate Terr PO Box 1108 *TF Cust Svc:* 800-551-2233 ■ *Web:* www.diablosilver.com	Grass Valley	CA	95945	530-272-2241	272-2243
Esposito Jewelry Inc 225 DuPont Dr	Providence	RI	02907	401-943-1900	
Gem East Corp 2124 Second Ave *Web:* www.gemeast.com	Seattle	WA	98121	206-441-1700	
Gemveto Jewelry Company Inc 18 E 48th St Ste 502 *Web:* www.gemveto.com	New York	NY	10017	212-755-2522	755-2027
George H Fuller & Son Co 151 Exchange St	Pawtucket	RI	02904	401-722-6530	

Company	City	State	ZIP	Phone	Fax
Hammerman Bros Inc 50 W 57th St 12th Fl *TF:* 800-223-6436 ■ *Web:* www.hammermanbrothers.com	New York	NY	10019	212-956-2800	956-2769
Harry Klitzner Co, The 530 Wellington Ave Ste 11 *TF:* 800-621-0161 ■ *Web:* www.klitzner.com	Cranston	RI	02910	800-621-0161	622-9802
Harry Winston Inc 718 Fifth Ave *TF:* 800-988-4110 ■ *Web:* www.harrywinston.com	New York	NY	10019	212-399-1000	489-6715
Ira Green Inc 177 Georgia Ave *TF General:* 800-663-7487 ■ *Web:* www.iragreen.com	Providence	RI	02905	401-467-4770	467-5557
Jacmel Jewelry Inc 3030 47th Ave *TF:* 800-945-4300 ■ *Web:* www.jacmel.com	Long Island City	NY	11101	800-945-4300	
James Avery Craftsman Inc 145 Avery Rd N *TF:* 800-283-1770 ■ *Web:* www.jamesavery.com	Kerrville	TX	78029	830-895-1122	895-6601
Jostens Inc 3601 Minnesota Ave Ste 400 **Fax:* Hum Res ■ *TF:* 800-235-4774 ■ *Web:* www.jostens.com	Minneapolis	MN	55435	952-830-3300	830-3293*
Kinsley & Sons Inc 24 S Church St Ste A *TF General:* 800-468-4428 ■ *Web:* www.gothic-jewelry.com	Union	MO	63084	800-468-4428	
Maui Divers of Hawaii 1520 Liona St *TF:* 800-462-4454 ■ *Web:* www.mauidivers.com	Honolulu	HI	96814	808-946-7979	946-0406
Mtm Recognition Corp 3201 SE 29th St *TF:* 877-686-7464 ■ *Web:* www.mtmrecognition.com	Oklahoma City	OK	73115	405-670-4545	670-0619
Novell Design Studio 129 Chestnut St **Fax Area Code:* 908 ■ *TF:* 888-668-3551 ■ *Web:* www.novelldesignstudio.com	Roselle	NJ	07203	888-668-3551	245-5090*
OC Tanner Co 1930 S State St **Fax Area Code:* 801 ■ *TF:* 800-453-7490 ■ *Web:* www.octanner.com	Salt Lake City	UT	84115	800-453-7490	493-3013*
Oro-Cal Mfg Company Inc 1720 Bird St *TF:* 800-367-6225 ■ *Web:* www.orocal.com	Oroville	CA	95965	530-533-5065	533-5067
Ostbye & Anderson Inc 10055 51st Ave N **Fax Area Code:* 877 ■ *TF:* 866-553-1515 ■ *Web:* www.ostbye.com	Minneapolis	MN	55442	763-553-1515	553-1515*
Paris 1624 Knowlton St *Web:* www.paristiaras.com	Cincinnati	OH	45223	513-542-8329	542-8329
Relios Inc 6815 Academy Pkwy W NE *TF:* 800-827-6543 ■ *Web:* www.carolynpollack.com	Albuquerque	NM	87109	505-345-5304	
Robert S Fisher & Company Inc 280 Sheffield St *TF:* 800-526-8052 ■ *Web:* www.rsfisher.com	Mountainside	NJ	07092	908-928-0002	928-0092
Stamper Black Hills Gold Jewelry 7201 S Hwy 16 *TF Cust Svc:* 800-843-8753 ■ *Web:* www.stamperbhg.com	Rapid City	SD	57702	605-342-0751	343-9783
Stanley Creations Inc 1414 Willow Ave *TF:* 800-220-1414 ■ *Web:* www.stanleycreations.com	Melrose Park	PA	19027	215-635-6200	635-2708
Sunshine Minting Inc 7600 Mineral Dr Ste 700 *TF:* 800-274-5837 ■ *Web:* www.sunshinemint.com	Coeur d'Alene	ID	83815	208-772-9592	772-9739
Tache USA Inc 550 Fifth Ave *Web:* www.tacheusa.com	New York	NY	10036	212-371-1234	852-4961
Terryberry Co 2033 Oak Industrial Dr NE *TF:* 800-253-0882 ■ *Web:* www.terryberry.com	Grand Rapids	MI	49505	616-458-1391	458-5292
Tiffany & Co 727 Fifth Ave *NYSE: TIF* ■ *TF Orders:* 800-526-0649 ■ *Web:* www.tiffany.com	New York	NY	10022	212-755-8000	
Trebor Enterprises Ltd 927 W Stephenson St	Freeport	IL	61032	815-235-1700	
Tru-Kay Manufacturing Co Two Carol Dr	Lincoln	RI	02865	401-333-2105	
Uncas Manufacturing Co 150 Niantic Ave *Web:* uncas.com	Providence	RI	02907	401-944-4700	943-2951
Wheeler Mfg Co Inc 107 Main Ave PO Box 629 *TF:* 800-843-1937 ■ *Web:* www.wheelerjewelry.com	Lemmon	SD	57638	605-374-3848	374-3655
Wright & Lato 2100 Felver Ct *TF:* 800-724-1855 ■ *Web:* www.wrightandlato.com	Rahway	NJ	07065	973-674-8700	674-6964

413 JEWELRY STORES

Company	City	State	ZIP	Phone	Fax
Aires Jewelers Co Three Harrison Ave *Web:* airesjewelers.com	Morris Plains	NJ	07950	973-292-0950	
Alvin Goldfarb Jeweler of Seattle Inc 305 Bellevue Way Ne *Web:* alvingoldfarbjeweler.com	Bellevue	WA	98004	425-454-9393	
Argo & Lehne Jewelers Inc 3100 Tremont Rd *Web:* argolehne.com	Columbus	OH	43221	614-457-6261	457-6716
Arthur Groom & Company Inc 262 E Ridgewood Ave *Web:* www.arthurgroom.com	Ridgewood	NJ	07450	201-670-0300	
Aucoin-Hart 1525 Metairie Rd *Web:* aucoinhart.com	Metairie	LA	70005	504-834-9999	
B C Clark Inc 12042 N May Ave *Web:* www.bcclark.com	Oklahoma City	OK	73120	405-755-4040	
Ben Amun Company Inc 246 W 38th St Fl 12a *Web:* www.ben-amun.com	New York	NY	10018	212-944-6480	944-9625
Ben Bridge Jeweler Inc PO Box 1908 *TF Cust Svc:* 888-917-9171 ■ *Web:* www.benbridge.com	Seattle	WA	98111	206-239-6811	448-7456
Ben Moss Jewellers 300-201 Portage Ave **Fax Area Code:* 204 ■ *TF:* 888-236-6677 ■ *Web:* www.benmoss.com	Winnipeg	MB	R3B3K6	888-236-6677	988-0148*
Bergstrom Jewelers Inc 1695 W End Blvd *Web:* bergstromjewelers.com	St Louis Park	MN	55416	952-767-0606	
Betteridge Jewelers Inc 117 Greenwich Ave *Web:* www.betteridge.com	Greenwich	CT	06830	203-869-0124	
Blue Nile Inc 705 Fifth Ave S Ste 900 *NASDAQ: NILE* ■ *TF:* 800-242-2728 ■ *Web:* www.bluenile.com	Seattle	WA	98104	206-336-6700	336-7950
Bluedial.com 3622 N Rancho Dr *Web:* www.bluedial.com	Las Vegas	NV	89130	702-645-5260	
Borsheim's Inc 120 Regency Pkwy *TF:* 800-642-4438 ■ *Web:* www.borsheims.com	Omaha	NE	68114	402-391-0400	391-6694
Brian Gavin Diamonds 7322 Southwest Frwy Ste 1810 - Arena One *Web:* www.briangavindiamonds.com	Houston	TX	77074	713-574-6666	
Charm Jewelry Ltd 140 Portland St *Web:* charmdiamondcentres.com	Dartmouth	NS	B2Y1J1	902-463-7177	
Coleman E Adler & Sons Inc 722 Canal St Third Fl *TF:* 800-925-7912 ■ *Web:* www.adlersjewelry.com	New Orleans	LA	70130	504-523-5292	568-0610
Color Merchants Six E 45th St Rm 1704 *Web:* www.colormerchants.com	New York	NY	10017	212-682-4788	
Cooper & Company Inc 10179 Commerce Park Dr *Web:* www.dakotawatchsales.com	Cincinnati	OH	45246	513-671-6067	
Corbo Jewelers Inc 58 Pk Ave *Web:* www.corbojewelers.com	Rutherford	NJ	07070	201-438-4454	438-3108
De Von's Jewelers Inc 1689 Arden Way *Web:* www.devonsjewelers.com	Sacramento	CA	95815	916-929-3991	
DGSE Cos Inc 11311 Reeder Rd *NYSE: DGSE* ■ *TF:* 800-527-5307 ■ *Web:* www.dgse.com	Dallas	TX	75229	972-484-3662	241-0646
Diamond Cellar Inc 6280 Sawmill Rd *Web:* www.diamondcellar.com	Dublin	OH	43017	614-336-4545	
Don Roberto Jewelers Inc 1020 Calle Recordo Ste 100 *Web:* www.donrobertojewelers.com	San Clemente	CA	92673	949-361-6700	
Dunkin's Diamonds Inc 897 Hebron Rd *Web:* www.dunkinsdiamonds.com	Heath	OH	43056	877-343-4883	
Ed Levin Inc 52 W Main St *Web:* www.edlevinjewelry.com	Cambridge	NY	12816	518-677-8595	
Elegant Illusions Inc 542 Lighthouse Ave Ste 5 *Web:* www.elegant-illusions.com	Pacific Grove	CA	93950	831-649-1814	649-1001
Ernest Bock Jewelers 226 W Portal Ave	San Francisco	CA	94127	415-681-5362	
Fantasy Diamond Corp 1550 W Carrol Ave *TF:* 800-621-4445 ■ *Web:* endlessdiamond.com/	Chicago	IL	60607	312-583-3200	583-3434
Fashion Time 2700 Potomac Mills Cir *Web:* www.shopfashiontime.com	Woodbridge	VA	22192	703-490-1556	
Finks Jewelry Inc 3545 Electric Rd *TF:* 800-699-7464 ■ *Web:* www.finks.com	Roanoke	VA	24018	540-342-2991	344-5385
Firestone & Parson Inc 30 Newbury St	Boston	MA	02116	617-266-1858	
Freeman Jewelers Inc 76 Merchants Row *TF:* 800-451-4167 ■ *Web:* rutlanddowntown.com	Rutland	VT	05701	802-773-2792	773-1685
Garfield Refining Co 810 East Cayuga St *Web:* www.garfieldrefining.com	Philadelphia	PA	19124	800-523-0968	
Girardin Jewelers Inc 3321 N Valdosta Rd *Web:* girardinjewelers.com	Valdosta	GA	31602	229-242-8546	
Gleim The Jeweler Inc 322 University Ave *Web:* www.gleimjewelers.com	Palo Alto	CA	94301	650-323-1331	
GN Diamond LLC 800 Chestnut St *Web:* www.gndiamond.com	Philadelphia	PA	19107	215-238-5778	
Green Lake Jewelry Works 550 Ne Northgate Way *Web:* www.seattlejewelry.com	Seattle	WA	98125	206-527-1108	
Gregg Ruth & Co 22809 Pacific Coast Hwy *Web:* greggruth.com	Malibu	CA	90265	310-456-1888	
H Stern Jewelers Inc 645 Fifth Ave *TF:* 800-747-8376 ■ *Web:* www.hstern.net	New York	NY	10022	212-688-0300	888-5137
H. E. Murdock Co Inc 88 Main St *Web:* www.daysjewelers.com	Waterville	ME	04901	207-873-7036	859-9729
Haltoms Jewelers 317 Main St *Web:* www.haltoms.com	Fort Worth	TX	76102	817-336-4051	336-0064
Handpicked Inc 150 Harbison Blvd Ste C *Web:* www.handpicked.net	Columbia	SC	29212	803-749-6024	
Harris Originals of NY Inc 800 Prime Pl *Web:* www.harrisjewelry.com	Hauppauge	NY	11788	631-348-0303	
Harry Ritchie's Jewelers Inc 956 Willamette St *TF Cust Svc:* 800-935-2850 ■ *Web:* www.harryritchies.com	Eugene	OR	97401	541-686-1787	485-8841
Harry Winston Inc 718 Fifth Ave *TF:* 800-988-4110 ■ *Web:* www.harrywinston.com	New York	NY	10019	212-399-1000	489-6715
Helzberg Diamonds 1825 Swift Ave **Fax:* Sales ■ *TF:* 800-669-7780 ■ *Web:* www.helzberg.com	North Kansas City	MO	64116	816-842-7780	627-1301*
Henry B Ball Co 5254 Dressler Rd NW *Web:* henrybball.com	Canton	OH	44718	330-499-3000	
Husar's House of Fine Diamonds 131 N Main St *Web:* www.husars.com	West Bend	WI	53095	262-334-3453	
Hyde Park Jewelers Inc 3000 E First Ave Ste 243 *Web:* www.hydeparkjewelers.com	Denver	CO	80206	303-333-4446	
Jay Roberts Jewelers 515 Rt 73 S *Web:* www.jayrobertsjewelers.com	Marlton	NJ	08053	856-596-8600	
Jewel-Osco 150 Pierce Rd *Web:* www.jewelosco.com	Itasca	IL	60143	630-948-6000	
Jewelers Inc, The 2400 Western Ave *Web:* www.thejewelers.com	Las Vegas	NV	89102	702-382-1234	
Jewelry Concepts Inc 41 Western Industrial Dr	Cranston	RI	02921	401-228-8586	
JewelryWeb.com Inc 98 Cuttermill Rd Ste 464 **Fax Area Code:* 800 ■ *TF:* 800-955-9245 ■ *Web:* www.jewelryweb.com	Great Neck	NY	11021	516-482-3982	955-2520*
Jewels by Park Lane 100 Commerce Dr *Web:* www.hallenspecialties.com	Schaumburg	IL	60173	847-884-9999	
Kay Jewelers 375 Ghent Rd *TF:* 800-681-8796 ■ *Web:* www.kay.com	Akron	OH	44333	330-668-5000	668-5187
King's Jewelry & Loan 800 S Vermont Ave *Web:* www.kingspawn.com	Los Angeles	CA	90005	213-383-5555	
Lauren Spencer Inc 40 Clairedan Dr *Web:* www.lauren-spencer.com	Powell	OH	43065	614-888-7773	
Lee Michaels Fine Jewelers Inc 11314 Cloverland Ave *Web:* lmfj.com	Baton Rouge	LA	70809	225-291-9094	
Lee Michaels Jewelers Inc 7560 Corporate Blvd *Web:* www.lmfj.com	Baton Rouge	LA	70809	225-926-4644	
Lester Lampert Corporate 57 E Oak St *Web:* www.lesterlampert.com	Chicago	IL	60611	312-944-6888	
Lori Bonn Jewelery 114 Linden St *Web:* www.loribonn.com	Oakland	CA	94607	877-507-4206	
Lux Bond & Green Inc 46 Lasalle Rd **Fax Area Code:* 860 ■ *TF:* 800-524-7336 ■ *Web:* www.lbgreen.com	West Hartford	CT	06107	800-524-7336	521-8693*

Company / Address	City	State	ZIP	Phone	Fax
Magnon Jewelers Inc 606 S Dale Mabry Hwy *Web:* magnon-jewelers.com	Tampa	FL	33609	813-872-9374	
Mann's Jewelers Inc 2945 Monroe Ave *Web:* www.mannsjewelers.com	Rochester	NY	14618	585-271-4000	
Mccarys Jewelers Inc 1409 E 70th St Ste 118 *Web:* mccarys.com	Shreveport	LA	71105	318-798-3050	
Mead Jewelers Inc 1309 13th St *Web:* meadjewelers.com	Woodward	OK	73801	580-256-6373	
Mervis Diamond Corp 1900 Mervis Way Tyson's Corner *Web:* www.mervisdiamond.com	Vienna	VA	22182	703-448-9000	
Michaels Creative Jewelry 4843 E Ray Rd *Web:* www.michaelscreative.com	Phoenix	AZ	85044	480-598-0306	
Morgan & Co 1131 Glendon Ave *Web:* www.morganjewellers.com	Los Angeles	CA	90024	310-208-3377	208-6920
Northville Clock & Watch Shop 132 W Dunlap St *Web:* www.clockone.com	Northville	MI	48167	248-349-4938	
Osterman Jewelers 375 Ghent Rd *Web:* ostermanjewelers.com	Akron	OH	44333	330-668-5000	668-5184
Painful Pleasures Inc 7410 Coca Cola Dr Ste 214 *Web:* www.painfulpleasures.com	Hanover	MD	21076	410-712-0145	
Peoples Jewellers 1100 Pembroke St E *Web:* www.peoplesjewellers.com	Pembroke	ON	K8A6Y7	613-735-1536	
Perrywinkles Fine Jewelry 227 Main St *Web:* www.perrywinkles.com	Burlington	VT	05401	802-865-2624	
Randy'S Jewelry Inc 309 S Main St *Web:* randys-jewelry.com	O Fallon	MO	63366	636-978-1953	
Reeds Jewelers Inc PO Box 2229 *TF Orders:* 877-406-3266 ■ *Web:* www.reeds.com	Wilmington	NC	28402	910-350-3100	350-3353
Reis Nichols Jewelers 789 Us Hwy 31 N Ste A *Web:* www.reisnichols.com	Greenwood	IN	46142	317-883-4467	
Republic Metals Corp 12900 NW 38th Ave *Web:* republicmetalscorp.com	Miami	FL	33054	305-685-8505	
Ringmaster Jewelers Inc 1990 Healy Dr. *Web:* ringmasterjewelers.com	Winston-Salem	NC	27103	336-722-2218	
Rogers Jewelry Co PO Box 3151 *TF:* 800-877-4221 ■ *Web:* www.thinkrogers.com	Modesto	CA	95353	800-877-4221	
Ross Simons Jewelers Inc Nine Ross Simons Dr **Fax Area Code:* 401 ■ *TF:* 800-835-0919 ■ *Web:* www.ross-simons.com	Cranston	RI	02920	800-835-0919	463-8599*
Samuels Jewelers 9607 Research Blvd Ste 100 Bldg F *TF:* 877-202-2870 ■ *Web:* www.samuelsjewelers.com	Austin	TX	78759	512-369-1400	
Satya Jewelry Inc 330 Bleecker St *Web:* www.satyajewelry.com	New York	NY	10014	212-243-7313	
Sea of Diamonds.com 606 S Olive St Ste 1026 *Web:* www.steindiamonds.com	Los Angeles	CA	90014	213-226-0150	
Shane Co 9790 E Arapahoe Rd *TF:* 866-467-4263 ■ *Web:* www.shaneco.com	Greenwood Village	CO	80112	866-467-4263	
Shreve Crump & Low Inc 440 Boylston St *Web:* www.shrevecrumpandlow.com	Boston	MA	02116	617-267-9100	
Silverberg Jewelry Co 6730 22nd Ave N Ste E *Web:* www.silverbergjewelry.com	St Petersburg	FL	33710	727-381-1286	
Simon G Jewelry Inc 528 State St *Web:* www.simongjewelry.com	Glendale	CA	91203	818-500-9697	
Smart Creations Inc 1799 St Johns Ave	Highland Park	IL	60035	847-433-3451	
Smith Jewelers C W 603 Wisconsin Ave *Web:* www.cwsmithjewelers.com	North Fond Du Lac	WI	54937	920-922-6259	
Sol Jewelry Designs Inc 550 S Hill St Ste 1020 *Web:* soljewelry.com	Los Angeles	CA	90013	213-622-7772	
Spark Creations Inc 10 W 46th St *Web:* www.sparkcreations.com	New York	NY	10036	212-575-8385	
Sultan Co 500 Ala Moana Blvd Ste 7-210 *Web:* obits.staradvertiser.com	Honolulu	HI	96819	808-833-7772	837-1358
Tapper's Fine Jewelry Inc Orchard Mall 6337 Orchard Lk Rd *Web:* www.tappers.com	West Bloomfield	MI	48322	248-932-7700	
TAWA Supermarket Inc 6281 Regio Ave *Web:* www.99ranch.com	Buena Park	CA	90620	714-521-8899	
Tiffany & Co 727 Fifth Ave *NYSE:* TIF ■ *TF Orders:* 800-526-0649 ■ *Web:* www.tiffany.com	New York	NY	10022	212-755-8000	
Tiny Jewel Box Inc 1147 Connecticut Ave Nw *Web:* www.tinyjewelbox.com	Washington	DC	20036	202-393-2747	
Trabert & Hoeffer 111 E Oak St *TF:* 800-539-3573 ■ *Web:* www.trabertandhoeffer.com	Chicago	IL	60611	312-787-1654	787-1446
Universal Jewelers Manufacturing Inc 4718 Admiralty Way *Web:* www.universaljewelersmfg.com	Marina Del Rey	CA	90292	310-301-9797	
Van Cleef & Arpels Inc 744 Fifth Ave *TF:* 877-826-2533 ■ *Web:* www.vancleefarpels.com	New York	NY	10019	212-896-9284	
Ware Jewelers 7268 Eastchase Pkwy *Web:* www.warejewelers.com	Montgomery	AL	36117	334-386-9273	
Wedding Day Diamonds 7901 Penn Ave S *Web:* www.weddingdaydiamonds.com	Bloomington	MN	55431	952-253-0235	
Wedding Ring Shop 1181 Kapiolani Blvd *Web:* www.weddingringshop.com	Honolulu	HI	96814	808-945-7766	
Wempe Jewelers 700 Fifth Ave *Web:* www.wempe.com	New York	NY	10019	212-397-9000	
William Crow Jewelry Inc 910 16th St Ste 320 *Web:* williamcrow.com	Denver	CO	80202	303-592-1695	
Wixon Jewelers Inc 9955 Lyndale Ave S *Web:* wixonjewelers.com	Minneapolis	MN	55420	952-881-8862	
Worthington Jewelers 692 High St *Web:* www.worthingtonjewelers.com	Worthington	OH	43085	614-430-8800	
Ybarras Jewelers Inc 678 N Wilson Way Space 28 *Web:* ybarrasjewelers.com	Stockton	CA	95205	209-547-0320	
Zale Corp *Zales Jewelers Div* 901 W Walnut Hill Ln *TF Cust Svc:* 800-311-5393 ■ *Web:* www.zales.com	Irving	TX	75038	972-580-4000	580-5907
Zale Corp Bailey Banks & Biddle Div 901 W Walnut Hill Ln *TF Cust Svc:* 800-468-9716 ■ *Web:* signetjewelers.com	Irving	TX	75038	866-249-2593	

414 JEWELRY, WATCHES, GEMS - WHOL

Company / Address	City	State	ZIP	Phone	Fax
AH Lisanti Capital Growth LLC 608 Fifth Ave Ste 301 *Web:* www.ahlisanti.com	New York	NY	10020	212-792-6990	
Alexa's Angels Inc 621 Innovation Cir *Web:* www.alexas-angels.com	Windsor	CO	80550	970-686-7247	
Alishaev Bros Inc 20 W 47th St Ste 203 *TF:* 877-859-6020 ■ *Web:* alishaevbros.com	New York	NY	10036	877-859-6020	
American Time & Signal Co 140 Third St *Web:* www.atsclock.com	Dassel	MN	55325	320-275-2101	
Anatometal 411 Ingalls St *Web:* www.anatometal.com	Santa Cruz	CA	95060	831-454-9880	
Anne Koplik Designs Inc 173 Main St Ste 1 *Web:* annekoplik.com	Brewster	NY	10509	845-279-8244	
Antwerp Diamond Distributors Six E 45th St Ste 302	New York	NY	10017	212-319-3300	207-8168
Ball Watch USA 1131 Fourth St N *Web:* www.ballwatchusa.com	Saint Petersburg	FL	33701	727-896-4278	
Barse & Company Inc 7800 John Carpenter Fwy *Web:* barse.com	Dallas	TX	75247	214-631-0925	
Bead Bazaar USA Inc 687 Lofstrand Ln Ste H *Web:* beadkit.com	Rockville	MD	20850	301-610-6022	
Bennett Brothers Inc 30 E Adams St *Web:* www.bennettbrothers.com	Chicago	IL	60603	312-263-4800	
Broco Products Inc 18624 Syracuse Ave *Web:* brocoproducts.com	Cleveland	OH	44110	216-531-0880	
Charles & Colvard Ltd 170 Southport Dr *NASDAQ:* CTHR ■ **Fax Area Code:* 919 ■ *TF:* 877-202-5467 ■ *Web:* www.moissanite.com	Morrisville	NC	27560	877-202-5467	468-0486*
Charles Wolf Couture 579 Fifth Ave Ste 1518	New York	NY	10017	212-371-6130	
Circa Inc 415 Madison Ave 19th Fl *TF:* 877-876-5493 ■ *Web:* circajewels.com	New York	NY	10017	212-486-6013	
Clyde Duneier Inc 415 Madison Ave Fl 6 *Web:* www.clydeduneier.com	New York	NY	10017	212-398-1122	
Combine International Inc 354 Indusco Ct *Web:* combine.com	Troy	MI	48083	248-585-9900	
Continental Coin Corp 5627 Sepulveda Blvd *TF:* 800-552-6467 ■ *Web:* continentalcoin.com	Van Nuys	CA	91411	818-781-4232	782-6779
Danforth Pewterers Ltd 52 Seymour St *Web:* www.danforthpewter.com	Middlebury	VT	05753	802-388-8666	
Dominion Diamond Corp PO Box 4569 Sta A *Web:* www.ddcorp.ca/	Toronto	ON	M5W4T9	416-362-2237	362-2230
EH Ashley & Company Inc One White Squadron Rd *Web:* ehashley.com	Riverside	RI	02915	401-431-0950	
Empire Diamond Corp 350 Fifth Ave Ste 4000 *TF:* 800-728-3425 ■ *Web:* www.dialadiamond.com	New York	NY	10118	212-564-4777	564-4960
Ettika LLC 714 S Hill St Ste 405 *Web:* ettika.com	Los Angeles	CA	90014	213-817-5510	
FAF Inc 26 Lark Industrial Pkwy *Web:* www.faf.com	Greenville	RI	02828	401-949-3000	
Frederick Goldman Inc 154 W 14th St *Web:* www.fgoldman.com	New York	NY	10011	212-924-6767	
Fremada Gold Inc Two W 45th St Ste 1605 *Web:* www.fremadaspecials.com	New York	NY	10036	212-921-8829	
Gemex Systems Inc 6040 W Executive Dr Ste A *TF:* 866-694-3639 ■ *Web:* www.gemex.com	Mequon	WI	53092	262-242-1111	
Genal Strap Inc 31-00 47th Ave *Web:* voguestrap.com	Long Island City	NY	11101	718-706-8700	
Genesis Diamonds Cool Springs LLC 3742 Hillsboro Pk *Web:* genesisdiamonds.net	Nashville	TN	37215	615-269-6996	
Gennaro Inc 1725 Pontiac Ave *Web:* www.gennaroinc.com	Cranston	RI	02920	401-632-4100	
Gerson Co 1450 S Lone Elm Rd *TF:* 800-444-8172 ■ *Web:* www.gersoncompany.com	Olathe	KS	66061	913-262-7400	535-7592
Gottlieb Bros Inc 55 E Washington	Chicago	IL	60602	312-609-2222	
HS Strygler & Company Inc 37 W 20th St Ste 1210	New York	NY	10011	212-727-7840	727-3700
Identification Plates Inc 1555 High Point Dr. *Web:* www.idplates.com	Mesquite	TX	75149	972-216-1616	216-1555
Jeff Cooper Inc 288 Wbury Ave *Web:* www.jeffcooperdesigns.com	Carle Place	NY	11514	516-333-8200	
Jewel-Craft Inc 4122 Olympic Blvd *TF:* 800-525-5482 ■ *Web:* www.jewel-craft.com	Erlanger	KY	41018	859-282-2400	
Joseph Blank Inc 62 W 47th St Ste 808 *TF:* 800-223-7666 ■ *Web:* www.josephblank.com	New York	NY	10036	212-575-9050	302-8521
Just Bead It 9514 Third Ave *Web:* www.justbeadit.net	Stone Harbor	NJ	08247	609-368-0400	
Kabana Inc 616 Indian School Rd NW *Web:* www.kabana.net	Albuquerque	NM	87102	505-843-9330	
Kendra Scott Design Inc 1400 S Congress Ave Ste A-170 *TF:* 866-677-7023 ■ *Web:* www.kendrascott.com	Austin	TX	78704	512-499-8400	499-8414
KMA Sunbelt Trading Corp 3696 Ulmerton Rd. *Web:* www.shopidc.com	Clearwater	FL	33762	727-572-7258	
La Vie Parisienne Corp 1837 Lincoln Blvd *Web:* lavieparisienne.com	Santa Monica	CA	90404	310-392-8428	

Phone | Fax

Lashbrook Designs 131 E 13065 S Draper UT 84020 888-252-7388
Web: lashbrookdesigns.com

Leo Wolleman Inc 45 W 45th St 10th Fl New York NY 10036 212-840-1881 869-4216
TF: 800-223-5667 ■ *Web:* www.leowolleman.com

Lyles-De Grazier Co
2050 N Stemmons Fwy Ste 7943 Dallas TX 75207 214-747-3558 741-3513
Web: www.lylesjewelry.com

MA Reich & Co Inc 481 Franklin St Buffalo NY 14202 716-856-4085
TF: 800-746-7062 ■ *Web:* www.mareich.com

Merchants Overseas Inc 41 Bassett St Providence RI 02903 401-331-5603

Metal Marketplace International (MMI)
718 Sansom St Philadelphia PA 19106 215-592-8777 592-8195
TF: 800-523-9191 ■ *Web:* www.metalmarketplace.com

Mikimoto (America) Company Ltd
680 Fifth Ave Fourth Fl New York NY 10019 212-457-4500
TF: 800-223-4008 ■ *Web:* www.mikimotoamerica.com

Morgan Advanced Materials 7331 William Ave Allentown PA 18106 610-366-7100
Web: www.diamonex.com

MR Diamonds Inc Five S Wabash Ave Ste 1709A Chicago IL 60603 312-346-3333

Paramount Sales Company Inc
10140 Gallows Pt Dr Knoxville TN 37931 865-470-9977 470-9801

PM Recovery Inc 106 Calvert St Harrison NY 10528 914-835-1900
Web: www.pmrecovery.com

Prime Time International Inc
135 W 36th St Fifth Fl New York NY 10018 212-695-5322
Web: www.waitex.com

Prime Time Manufacturing Inc
185 Jefferson Blvd Warwick RI 02888 401-738-1227
Web: www.primetimemfg.com

Pugster Inc 2835 Sierra Grande St Pasadena CA 91107 626-356-1881
Web: pugster.com

Rego Mfg Company Inc 1870 E Mansfield St Bucyrus OH 44820 419-562-0466
Web: www.regoonline.com

Seno Jewelry LLC 259 W 30th St 10th Fl New York NY 10001 888-468-0888
Web: www.ippolita.com

SKL Company Inc 545 Island Rd Ramsey NJ 07446 201-825-6633 825-8009

Tacori Enterprises 1736 Gardena Ave Glendale CA 91204 818-863-1536
Web: tacori.com

Tara Pearls 10 W 46th Ste 600 New York NY 10036 212-575-8191
Web: www.tarasons.com

Thunderbird Supply Co 1907 W Historic Rt 66 Gallup NM 87301 505-722-4323 722-6736
Web: www.thunderbirdsupply.com

TSI Accessory Group Inc 8350 Lehigh Ave Morton Grove IL 60053 847-965-1700
Web: www.tsiag.com

United Legwear Company LLC 48 W 38th St New York NY 10018 212-391-4143
Web: www.unitedlegwear.com

Variety Gem Company Inc 11 W 46th St Fl 3 New York NY 10036 212-921-1820
Web: www.varietygem.com

World Minerals Inc 130 Castilian Dr Goleta CA 93117 805-562-0200 562-0298
TF: 800-893-4445 ■ *Web:* www.worldminerals.com

415 JUVENILE DETENTION FACILITIES

SEE ALSO Correctional & Detention Management (Privatized) p. 2167; Correctional Facilities - Federal p. 2167; Correctional Facilities - State p. 2168
Listings are organized alphabetically by states.

Phone | Fax

LABELS - FABRIC

SEE Narrow Fabric Mills p. 3232

Bethel Youth Facility
301 W Northern Lights Blvd PO Box 1989 Bethel AK 99559 907-543-5200 543-2710
Web: dhss.alaska.gov

Fairbanks Youth Facility 1502 Wilbur St Fairbanks AK 99701 907-451-2150
TF: 800-478-2686

Johnson Youth Ctr 3252 Hospital Dr Juneau AK 99801 907-586-9433 463-4933
TF: 800-780-9972 ■ *Web:* dhss.alaska.gov

McLaughlin Youth Ctr 2600 Providence Dr Anchorage AK 99508 907-261-4399 261-4308
TF: 800-478-2221 ■ *Web:* dhss.alaska.gov

Nome Youth Facility 804 E Fourth St Nome AK 99762 907-443-5434 443-7295
Web: dhss.alaska.gov

Arkansas Juvenile Access & Treatment Ctr
425 W Capitol Ste 1620 Little Rock AR 72201 501-324-8900 324-8904
TF: 877-727-3468 ■ *Web:* www.arkansas.gov

Jack Jones Jefferson County Juvenile Detention Ctr
101 E Barraque St Pine Bluff AR 71611 870-541-5351 541-8504
Web: www.jeffcoso.org

Northwest Arkansas Regional Juvenile Program
36 Johnny Cake Pt Rd Mansfield AR 72944 479-928-0166 928-2060
Web: saysyouth.org

El Paso de Robles Youth Correctional Facility
4545 Airport Rd PO Box 7008 Paso Robles CA 93447 805-238-4040 227-2569
Web: www.cdcr.ca.gov

OH Close Youth Correctional Facility
7650 S Newcastle Rd PO Box 213001 Stockton CA 95213 209-944-6391
Web: cdcr.ca.gov

Ventura Youth Correctional Facility
3100 Wright Rd Camarillo CA 93010 805-485-7951 485-2801
TF: 866-232-5627 ■ *Web:* www.cdcr.ca.gov

Adams Youth Services Ctr 1933 E Bridge St Brighton CO 80601 303-659-4450 637-0471
Web: colorado.gov

Gilliam Youth Services Ctr 2844 Downing St Denver CO 80205 303-296-0941

Grand Mesa Youth Sevices Ctr
360 28th Rd Grand Junction CO 81501 970-242-1521 242-8127
Web: www.colorado.gov

Lookout Mountain Youth Services Ctr
2901 Ford St Golden CO 80401 303-273-2600 273-2622
Web: colorado.gov

Phone | Fax

Marvin W Foote Youth Services Ctr
13500 E Fremont Pl Englewood CO 80112 303-534-3468 768-7516
Web: www.colorado.gov

Mount View Youth Services Ctr
7862 W Mansfield Pkwy Denver CO 80235 303-987-4502
Web: www.colorado.gov

Platte Valley Youth Services Ctr 2200 'O' St Greeley CO 80631 970-304-6275 304-6228

Pueblo Youth Services Ctr 1406 W 17th St Pueblo CO 81003 719-546-4902
Web: www.colorado.gov

Spring Creek Youth Services Ctr
3190 E Las Vegas St Colorado Springs CO 80906 719-390-2710
Web: www.colorado.gov

Zebulon Pike Youth Services Ctr
1427 W Rio Grande Colorado Springs CO 80906 719-329-6924
Web: www.colorado.gov/

Connecticut Juvenile Training School
1225 Silver St Middletown CT 06457 860-638-2400

John R Manson Youth Institute 42 Jarvis St Cheshire CT 06410 203-806-2500 699-1845

Ferris School 959 Centre Rd Wilmington DE 19805 302-993-3800 993-3820
TF: 800-292-9582 ■ *Web:* kids.delaware.gov

New Castle County Detention Ctr
963 Centre Rd Wilmington DE 19805 302-633-3100 995-8393
TF: 800-969-4357 ■ *Web:* kids.delaware.gov

Stevenson House Detention Ctr
750 N Dupont Hwy Milford DE 19963 302-424-8100 422-1535

Bay Regional Juvenile Detention Ctr
450 E 11th St Panama City FL 32401 850-872-4706 873-7099
Web: www.djj.state.fl.us/programsfacilities/detentioncenters

Brevard Regional Juvenile Detention Ctr
5225 DeWitt Ave Cocoa FL 32927 321-690-3400 504-0907

Duval Regional Juvenile Detention Ctr
1241 E Eigth St Jacksonville FL 32206 904-798-4820

Hillsborough Regional Juvenile Detention Ctr West
3948 ML King Jr Blvd Tampa FL 33614 813-871-7650 871-4764
Web: www.djj.state.fl.us/programsfacilities/detentioncenters

Leon Regional Juvenile Detention Ctr
2303 Ronellis Dr Tallahassee FL 32310 850-488-7672 922-2842
Web: www.djj.state.fl.us/programsfacilities/detentioncenters

Manatee Regional Juvenile Detention Ctr
1803 Fifth St W Bradenton FL 34205 941-741-3023 741-3061
Web: manateeclerk.com

Marion Regional Juvenile Detention Ctr
3040 NW Tenth St Ocala FL 34475 352-732-1450 732-1457
Web: djj.state.fl.us

Orange Regional Juvenile Detention Ctr
2800 S Bumby Ave Orlando FL 32806 407-897-2800 897-2856
Web: www.djj.state.fl.us/programsfacilities/detentioncenters

Polk Regional Juvenile Detention Ctr
2155 Bob Phillips Rd Bartow FL 33830 863-534-7090

Saint Lucie Regional Juvenile Detention Ctr
1301 Bell Ave Fort Pierce FL 34982 772-468-3940 468-4005

Juvenile Corrections Center-Nampa
1650 11th Ave N Nampa ID 83687 208-465-8443 465-8484

Juvenile Corrections Center-Saint Anthony
2220 E 600 N PO Box 40 Saint Anthony ID 83445 208-624-3462 624-0973

Illinois Youth Ctr Harrisburg
1201 W Poplar St Harrisburg IL 62946 618-252-8681 795-6869*
**Fax Area Code: 815* ■ *Web:* idjj.state.il.us

Illinois Youth Ctr Saint Charles
3825 Campton Hills Rd Saint Charles IL 60175 630-584-0506 584-1014
Web: www.illinois.gov/idjj/pages/st_charles_iyc.aspx

Camp Summit Boot Camp 2407 N 500 W La Porte IN 46350 219-874-9898 326-9218
Web: in.gov

Logansport Juvenile Correctional Facility
1118 S St Rd 25 Logansport IN 46947 574-753-7571 732-0729
TF: 800-800-5556 ■ *Web:* www.in.gov/idoc

Plainfield Re-Entry Educational Facility
501 W Main St Plainfield IN 46168 317-839-7751 838-7548
Web: in.gov/idoc/

Iowa Juvenile Home 701 S Church St Toledo IA 52342 641-484-2560 484-2816

State Training School 3211 Edgington Ave Eldora IA 50627 641-858-5402 858-2416
TF: 800-362-2178 ■ *Web:* dhs.iowa.gov

Larned Juvenile Correctional Facility
1301 Kansas Hwy 264 Larned KS 67550 620-285-0300 285-0301

Topeka Juvenile Correctional Complex
1430 NW 25th St Topeka KS 66618 785-354-9800

Mountainview Youth Development Ctr
1182 Dover Rd Charleston ME 04422 207-285-0880 285-0836
Web: maine.gov

Pine Hills Youth Correctional Facility
Four N Haynes Ave Miles City MT 59301 406-232-1377 232-7432
Web: www.cor.mt.gov

Riverside Youth Correctional Facility
Two Riverside Rd PO Box 88 Boulder MT 59632 406-225-4500 225-4511
Web: mt.gov

Mountainview Youth Correctional Facility
31 Petticoat Ln Annandale NJ 08801 908-638-6191 638-4423

Youth Diagnostic Development Ctrl
4000 Edith NE Albuquerque NM 87107 505-841-2400 841-2428

Crossroads Juvenile Ctr 17 Bristol St Brooklyn NY 11212 718-495-8160 495-8254

Horizon Juvenile Ctr 560 Brook Ave Bronx NY 10455 718-292-0065 401-8109
Web: www1.nyc.gov/

Foothills Correctional Institution
5150 Western Ave Morganton NC 28655 828-438-5585 438-5598
Web: ncdps.gov

Morrison Correctional Institution
1573 McDonald Church Rd PO Box 169 Hoffman NC 28347 910-281-3161 281-3609
Web: www.ncdps.gov

Western Youth Institution 5155 Western Ave Morganton NC 28655 828-438-6037 438-6076
Web: doc.state.nc.us

Cuyahoga Hills Juvenile Correctional Facility
4321 Green Rd Highland Hills OH 44128 216-464-8200 464-3540
TF: 800-872-3132 ■ *Web:* dys.ohio.gov

				Phone	Fax
Indian River Juvenile Correctional Facility 2775 Indian River Rd SW *Web:* www.dys.ohio.gov	Massillon	OH	44648	330-837-4211	837-4740
Ohio Dept of Youth Services 51 N High St *Web:* www.dys.ohio.gov	Columbus	OH	43215	614-466-4314	
Ohio River Juvenile Correctional Facility 4696 Gallia Pk *Web:* dys.ohio.gov	Franklin Furnace	OH	45629	740-354-7000	
Scioto Juvenile Correctional Facility 5993 Home Rd *Web:* dys.ohio.gov	Delaware	OH	43015	740-881-3250	881-5944
Central Oklahoma Detention Juvenile Ctr 700 S Ninth St *Web:* www.ok.gov	Tecumseh	OK	74873	405-598-2135	598-8713
Southwest Oklahoma Juvenile Ctr 300 S Broadway	Manitou	OK	73555	580-397-3511	397-3491
Camp Florence 4859 S Jetty Rd *Web:* oregon.gov	Florence	OR	97439	541-997-2076	
Camp Tillamook 6820 Barracks Cir *Web:* www.oregon.gov/	Tillamook	OR	97141	503-842-4243	842-1476
Eastern Oregon Youth Correctional Facility 1800 W Monroe St *Web:* oregon.gov	Burns	OR	97720	541-573-3133	573-3665
Hillcrest Youth Correctional Facility 2450 Strong Rd SE *Web:* oregon.gov	Salem	OR	97302	503-986-0400	986-0406
MacLaren Youth Correctional Facility 2630 N Pacific Hwy *Web:* oregon.gov	Woodburn	OR	97071	503-981-9531	982-4439
Oregon Youth Authority Riverbend (OYA) 58231 Oregon Hwy 244 *Web:* www.oregon.gov/oya/pages/facilities/riverbend.aspx	La Grande	OR	97850	541-663-8801	663-9181
Rogue Valley Youth Correctional Facility 2001 NE 'F' St *Web:* oregon.gov	Grants Pass	OR	97526	541-471-2862	471-2861
Tillamook Youth Correctional Facility 6700 Officer Row *Web:* oregon.gov	Tillamook	OR	97141	503-842-2565	842-4918
Cresson Secure Treatment Unit 251 Corrections Rd *Web:* jri.org	Cresson	PA	16630	814-886-6903	886-6296
Loysville Youth Development Ctr 10 Opportunity Dr	Loysville	PA	17047	717-789-3841	789-5538
New Castle Youth Development Ctr 1745 Frew Mill Rd	New Castle	PA	16101	724-656-7300	
South Mountain Secure Treatment Unit 10056 S Mtn Rd	South Mountain	PA	17261	717-749-7904	749-7905
STAR Academy 12279 Brady Dr *Web:* www.doc.sd.gov	Custer	SD	57730	605-673-2521	673-5489
Mountain View Youth Development Ctr 809 Peal Ln	Dandridge	TN	37725	865-397-0174	397-0738
Woodland Hills Youth Development Ctr 3965 Stewarts Ln *TF:* 855-418-1622 ■ *Web:* www.tennessee.gov	Nashville	TN	37218	615-532-2000	532-8402
Evins Regional Juvenile Ctr 3801 E Monte Cristo Rd	Edinburg	TX	78542	956-289-5500	
Gainesville State School 1379 FM 678 *Web:* tjjd.texas.gov	Gainesville	TX	76240	940-665-0701	665-0469
Giddings State School 2261 James Turman Rd PO Box 600 *Web:* tjjd.texas.gov	Giddings	TX	78942	979-542-4500	542-0177
Woodside Juvenile Rehabilitation Ctr 26 Woodside Dr	Colchester	VT	05446	802-655-4990	
Beaumont Juvenile Correctional Ctr 3500 Beaumont Rd *Web:* djj.virginia.gov	Beaumont	VA	23014	804-556-3316	
Bon Air Juvenile Correctional Ctr 1900 Chatsworth Ave *Web:* djj.virginia.gov	Bon Air	VA	23235	804-323-2550	323-2440
Hanover Juvenile Correctional Ctr 7093 Broadneck Rd *Web:* djj.virginia.gov	Hanover	VA	23069	804-537-5316	537-5907
Oak Ridge Juvenile Correctional Ctr 1801 Old Bon Air Rd *Web:* www.djj.virginia.gov	Richmond	VA	23235	804-323-2335	323-2310
Davis Juvenile Correctional Ctr Blackwater Falls Rd *Web:* www.wvdjs.state.wv.us	Davis	WV	26260	304-259-5241	259-4851
Lincoln Hills School W4380 Copper Lk Rd *Web:* doc.wi.gov	Irma	WI	54442	715-536-8386	536-8236
Prairie du Chien Correctional Institution 500 E Parrish St *Web:* doc.wi.gov	Prairie du Chien	WI	53821	608-326-7828	326-5960

416 LABELS - OTHER THAN FABRIC

				Phone	Fax
Accurate Dial & Nameplate Inc 329 Mira Loma Ave **Fax Area Code:* 818 ■ *TF:* 800-400-4455 ■ *Web:* www.accuratedial.com	Glendale	CA	91204	323-245-9181	243-6793*
Acro Labels Inc 2530 Wyandotte Rd *TF:* 800-355-2235 ■ *Web:* www.acrolabels.com	Willow Grove	PA	19090	215-657-5366	657-3325
Alcop Adhesive Label Co 826 Perkins Ln *Web:* alcoplabels.com	Beverly	NJ	08010	609-871-4400	871-3017
AME Label Corp 25155 W Ave Stanford *TF:* 866-278-9268 ■ *Web:* www.amelabel.com	Valencia	CA	91355	661-257-2200	257-7981
American Law Label Inc 1674 S Research Loop Ste 436 *Web:* www.americanlawlabel.com	Tucson	AZ	85710	520-546-6200	546-6203
Arch Crown Tags Inc 460 Hillside Ave *TF:* 800-526-8353 ■ *Web:* www.archcrown.com	Hillside	NJ	07205	973-731-6300	731-2228
Avery Dennison Corp 17700 Foltz Industrial Pkwy	Strongsville	OH	44149	440-878-7000	
Best Label Co 2900 Faber St *TF:* 800-637-5333 ■ *Web:* www.bestlabel.com	Union City	CA	94587	510-489-5400	489-2914
Blue Ribbon Tag & Label Corp 4035 N 29th Ave *TF:* 800-433-4974 ■ *Web:* www.blueribbonlabel.com	Hollywood	FL	33020	954-922-9292	922-9977
Brady Corp 6555 W Good Hope Rd *NYSE:* BRC ■ **Fax Area Code:* 800 ■ **Fax:* Cust Svc ■ *TF Cust Svc:* 800-541-1686 ■ *Web:* www.bradycorp.com	Milwaukee	WI	53223	414-358-6600	292-2289*
Brady Identification Solutions 6555 W Good Hope Rd **Fax Area Code:* 800 ■ **Fax:* Cust Svc ■ *TF Cust Svc:* 800-537-8791 ■ *Web:* www.bradyid.com	Milwaukee	WI	53223	414-358-6600	292-2289*
CCL Label Inc 161 Worcester Rd Ste 502 **Fax Area Code:* 416 ■ *TF:* 877-240-9772 ■ *Web:* www.cclind.com	Framingham	MA	01701	508-872-4511	756-8555*
Cellotape Inc 47623 Fremont Blvd *TF:* 800-231-0608 ■ *Web:* www.cellotape.com	Fremont	CA	94538	510-651-5551	651-8091
Chase Corp 26 Summer St *NYSE:* CCF ■ **Fax Area Code:* 508 ■ *Web:* www.chasecorp.com	Bridgewater	MA	02324	781-332-0700	697-6419*
Clamp Swing Pricing Company Inc 8386 Capwell Dr *TF:* 800-227-7615 ■ *Web:* clampswing.com	Oakland	CA	94621	510-567-1600	
Data Label Inc 1000 Spruce St *TF:* 800-457-0676 ■ *Web:* www.data-label.com	Terre Haute	IN	47807	812-232-0408	238-1847
DeskTop Labels 7277 Boone Ave N **Fax Area Code:* 763 ■ *TF:* 800-241-9730 ■ *Web:* www.desktoplabels.com	Minneapolis	MN	55428	800-241-9730	531-5764*
Discount Labels Inc 4115 Profit Ct *TF:* 800-995-9500 ■ *Web:* www.discountlabels.com	New Albany	IN	47150	800-995-9500	995-9600
East West Label Co 1000 E Hector St *TF:* 800-441-7333 ■ *Web:* www.ewlabel.com	Conshohocken	PA	19428	610-825-0410	
Ennis Inc PO Box D *TF:* 800-527-1008 ■ *Web:* www.ennistagandlabel.com	Wolfe City	TX	75496	800-527-1008	453-2674
General Data Co Inc 4354 Ferguson Dr **Fax:* Sales ■ *TF:* 800-733-5252 ■ *Web:* www.general-data.com	Cincinnati	OH	45245	513-752-7978	752-6947*
Gilbreth Packaging Systems 3001 State Rd **Fax Area Code:* 215 ■ *TF:* 800-630-2413 ■ *Web:* www.gilbrethusa.com	Croydon	PA	19021	800-630-2413	785-4077*
Grand Rapids Label Co 2351 Oak Industrial Dr NE *TF:* 800-552-5215 ■ *Web:* www.grlabel.com	Grand Rapids	MI	49505	616-459-8134	459-4543
Green Bay Packaging Inc 1700 Webster Ct *TF:* 800-236-8400 ■ *Web:* www.gbp.com	Green Bay	WI	54302	920-433-5111	
Harris Industries Inc 5181 Argosy Ave *TF:* 800-222-6866 ■ *Web:* www.harrisind.com	Huntington Beach	CA	92649	714-898-8048	898-7108
Impact Label Corp 3434 S Burdick St *TF:* 800-820-0362 ■ *Web:* www.impactlabel.com	Kalamazoo	MI	49001	269-381-4280	381-1055
International Label & Printing Company Inc 2550 United Ln **Fax Area Code:* 630 ■ *TF:* 800-244-1442 ■ *Web:* www.internationallabel.com	Elk Grove Village	IL	60007	800-244-1442	595-1747*
Label Graphics Company Inc 1225 Carnegie St Ste 104B *Web:* labelgraphicscompany.com	Rolling Meadows	IL	60008	847-454-1005	454-1008
Labelmaster Co 5724 N Pulaski Rd *TF:* 800-621-5808 ■ *Web:* www.labelmaster.com	Chicago	IL	60646	773-478-0900	478-6054
Labeltape Inc 5100 Beltway Dr SE *TF:* 800-928-4537 ■ *Web:* www.labeltape-inc.com	Caledonia	MI	49316	616-698-1830	698-7831
Lancer Label 301 S 74th St **Fax Area Code:* 402 ■ *TF Cust Svc:* 800-228-7074 ■ *Web:* www.lancerlabel.com	Omaha	NE	68114	800-228-7074	390-9459*
LGInternational 6700 SW Bradbury Ct *TF:* 800-345-0534 ■ *Web:* www.lgintl.com	Portland	OR	97224	503-620-0520	620-3296
McCourt Label Co 20 Egbert Ln *TF:* 800-458-2390 ■ *Web:* www.mccourtlabel.com	Lewis Run	PA	16738	814-362-3851	362-4156
Morgan Fabrics Corp 4265 Exchange Ave *Web:* www.morganfabrics.com	Los Angeles	CA	90058	323-583-9981	923-2352
MPI Label Systems Inc 450 Courtney Rd *TF:* 800-423-0442 ■ *Web:* www.mpilabels.com	Sebring	OH	44672	330-938-2134	938-9878
Multi-Color Corp 4053 Clough Woods Dr *NASDAQ:* LABL ■ *Web:* www.multicolorcorp.com	Batavia	OH	45103	513-381-1480	381-2240
National Label Company Inc 2025 Joshua Rd *Web:* www.nationallabel.com	Lafayette Hill	PA	19444	610-825-3250	834-8854
National Printing Converters Inc 18 S Murphy Ave *TF:* 800-877-6724 ■ *Web:* www.npclabels.com	Brazil	IN	47834	812-448-2555	
Northeast Data Services 1316 College Ave *TF Cust Svc:* 800-699-5636 ■ *Web:* the-leader.com	Elmira	NY	14901	607-733-5541	
Pamco Label 2200 S Wolf Rd *Web:* www.pamcolabel.com	Des Plaines	IL	60018	847-803-2200	803-2209
Phifer Inc 4400 Kauloosa Ave PO Box 1700 *TF:* 800-633-5955 ■ *Web:* www.phifer.com	Tuscaloosa	AL	35401	205-345-2120	759-4450
Print-O-Tape Inc 755 Tower Rd *TF:* 800-346-6311 ■ *Web:* www.printotape.com	Mundelein	IL	60060	847-362-1476	949-7449
Printed Systems 1265 Gillingham Rd **Fax Area Code:* 888 ■ **Fax:* Sales ■ *TF Sales:* 800-352-2332 ■ *Web:* www.psdtag.com	Neenah	WI	54956	800-352-2332	321-8247*
Quikstik Labels 220 Broadway *TF:* 800-225-3496 ■ *Web:* www.qsxlabels.com	Everett	MA	02149	617-389-7570	381-9280
Reidler Decal Corp 264 Industrial Pk Rd PO Box 8 **Fax Area Code:* 570 ■ *TF:* 800-628-7770 ■ *Web:* www.reidlerdecal.com	Saint Clair	PA	17970	800-628-7770	429-1528*
Shamrock Scientific Specialty Systems Inc 34 Davis Dr **Fax Area Code:* 800 ■ *TF:* 800-323-0249 ■ *Web:* www.shamrocklabels.com	Bellwood	IL	60104	708-547-9005	248-1907*
Smyth Cos Inc 1085 Snelling Ave N *TF:* 800-473-3464 ■ *Web:* www.smythco.com	Saint Paul	MN	55108	651-646-4544	646-8949
Sohn Manufacturing Inc 544 Sohn Dr *Web:* www.sohnmanufacturing.com	Elkhart Lake	WI	53020	920-876-3361	876-2952
Spear Inc 5510 Courseview Dr *TF:* 800-627-7327 ■ *Web:* www.spearinc.com	Mason	OH	45040	513-459-1100	459-1362
Spectrum Label Corp 30803 San Clemente St *Web:* www.spectrumlabel.com	Hayward	CA	94544	510-477-0707	477-0787
Spinnaker Coating Inc 518 E Water St *TF:* 800-543-9452 ■ *Web:* spinnakercoating.com	Troy	OH	45373	937-332-6500	332-6518

Phone *Fax*

Strutz International Inc
440 Mars-Valencia Rd PO Box 509 .... Mars PA 16046 724-625-1501 625-3570
Web: www.strutz.com

Tag-It Pacific Inc
21900 Burbank Blvd Ste 270 .... Woodland Hills CA 91367 818-444-4100 444-4105
TF: 877-870-5176 ■ *Web:* www.talonzippers.com

Tape & Label Converters Inc
8231 Allport Ave.......................... Santa Fe Springs CA 90670 562-945-3486 696-8198
TF: 888-285-2462 ■ *Web:* www.stickybiz.com

Tapecon Inc 10 Latta Rd......................... Rochester NY 14612 585-621-8400
TF: 800-333-2407 ■ *Web:* www.tapecon.com

TAPEMARK Co 1685 Marthaler Ln.............. West Saint Paul MN 55118 651-455-1611 450-8403
TF: 800-535-1998 ■ *Web:* www.tapemark.com

Valmark Industries Inc 7900 National Dr............ Livermore CA 94550 925-960-9900 960-0900
TF: 800-770-7074 ■ *Web:* www.valmark.com

Weber Marking Systems Inc
711 W Algonquin Rd .... Arlington Heights IL 60005 847-364-8500 364-8575
TF Sales: 800-843-4242

West Coast Tag & Label Co PO Box 4099........... West Hills CA 91308 213-748-0244 710-7645*
**Fax Area Code:* 818

Whitlam Label Company Inc
24800 Sherwood Ave .... Center Line MI 48015 586-757-5100 757-1243
TF: 800-755-2235 ■ *Web:* www.whitlam.com

Wise Tag & Label Company Inc
1077 Thomas Busch Memorial Hwy................ Pennsauken NJ 08110 856-663-2400 663-8610
Web: www.wisetaglabel.com

Wright Global Graphics 5115 Prospect St.........Thomasville NC 27360 336-472-4200 476-8554
TF: 800-678-9019 ■ *Web:* www.wrightglobalgraphics.com

WS Packaging Group Inc 2571 S. Hemlock Rd .... Green Bay WI 54229 800-818-5481 866-6485*
**Fax Area Code:* 920 ■ *TF:* 800-236-3424 ■ *Web:* www.wspackaging.com

417 LABOR UNIONS

Phone *Fax*

Actors' Equity Assn 1560 Broadway................ New York NY 10036 212-869-8530 719-9815
Web: www.actorsequity.org

AFT Healthcare 555 New Jersey Ave NW........... Washington DC 20001 202-879-4491 393-5672
TF: 800-238-1133 ■ *Web:* www.aft.org

Air Line Pilots Assn 535 Herndon Pkwy .... Herndon VA 20170 703-689-2270 232-0438*
**Fax Area Code:* 202 ■ *TF:* 877-331-1223 ■ *Web:* www.alpa.org

Allied Pilots Association
14600 Trinity Blvd O'Connell Bldg Ste 500........... Fort Worth TX 76155 817-302-2272
Web: www.alliedpilots.org

Amalgamated Transit Union (ATU)
5025 Wisconsin Ave NW Third Fl................. Washington DC 20016 202-537-1645 244-7824
TF: 888-240-1196 ■ *Web:* www.atu.org

American Federation of Government Employees
80 F St NW.................................... Washington DC 20001 202-737-8700 639-6441
TF: 888-844-2343 ■ *Web:* www.afge.org

American Federation of Labor & Congress of Industrial Organizations (AFL-CIO)
815 16th St NW .... Washington DC 20006 202-637-5000 637-5058
TF: 877-850-4959 ■ *Web:* www.aflcio.org

American Federation of Musicians of the US & Canada (AFM)
1501 Broadway Ste 600 .... New York NY 10036 212-869-1330 764-6134
TF: 800-762-3444 ■ *Web:* www.afm.org

American Federation of State County & Municipal Employees
1625 L St NW.................................. Washington DC 20036 202-429-1000 429-1293
Web: www.afscme.org

American Federation of Teachers (AFT)
555 New Jersey Ave NW.......................... Washington DC 20001 202-879-4400 879-4556*
**Fax:* PR ■ *TF:* 800-238-1133 ■ *Web:* www.aft.org

American Federation of Television & Radio Artists (AFTRA)
260 Madison Ave Seventh Fl .... New York NY 10016 212-532-0800 532-2242
Web: www.sagaftra.org

American Postal Workers Union
1300 L St NW.................................. Washington DC 20005 202-842-4200 842-8500
Web: www.apwu.org

American Train Dispatchers Assn
4239 W 150th St................................ Cleveland OH 44135 216-251-7984

Apartment Association
333 W Broadway Ste 101 .... Long Beach CA 90802 562-426-8341
Web: www.apt-assoc.com

Association of Civilian Technicians (ACT)
12620 Lk Ridge Dr .... Woodbridge VA 22192 703-494-4845 494-0961
Web: www.actnat.com

Association of Flight Attendants
501 Third St NW................................ Washington DC 20001 202-434-1300 434-1319
Web: afacwa.org

Association of Professional Flight Attendants
1004 W Euless Blvd .... Euless TX 76040 817-540-0108 540-2077
TF: 800-395-2732 ■ *Web:* www.apfa.org

Association of Western Pulp & Paper Workers
1430 SW Clay St .... Portland OR 97208 503-228-7486 228-1346
Web: www.awppw.org

B.C. Government & Service Employees' Union
4911 Canada Way................................ Burnaby BC V5G3W3 604-291-9611
Web: www.bcgeu.ca

Bakery Confectionery Tobacco Workers & Grain Millers International Union
10401 Connecticut Ave.......................... Kensington MD 20895 301-933-8600 946-8452
Web: www.bctgm.org

Brotherhood of Locomotive Engineers & Trainmen (BLET)
1370 Ontario St Mezzanine Level .... Cleveland OH 44113 216-241-2630 241-6516
TF: 877-772-5772 ■ *Web:* www.ble-t.org

Brotherhood of Maintenance of Way Employees (BMWED)
41475 Gardenbrook Rd................................ Novi MI 48375 248-662-2660 662-2659
Web: www.bmwed.org

Brotherhood of Railroad Signalmen
917 Shenandoah Shores Rd .... Front Royal VA 22630 540-622-6522 622-6532
Web: www.brs.org

Canada Labour Congress 2841 Riverside Dr........... Ottawa ON K1V8X7 613-521-3400 521-4655
Web: www.clc-ctc.ca

Phone *Fax*

Chicago Teachers Union
222 Merchandise Mart Plz Ste 400.................... Chicago IL 60654 312-329-9100 329-6200
Web: www.ctunet.com

Communications Workers of America (CWA)
501 Third St NW.................................. Washington DC 20001 202-434-1100 434-1377*
**Fax Area Code:* 208 ■ **Fax:* Hum Res ■ *Web:* www.cwa-union.org

Directors Guild of America
7920 W Sunset Blvd............................ Los Angeles CA 90046 310-289-2000 289-2029
TF: 800-421-4173 ■ *Web:* www.dga.org

Federal Education Assn
1201 16th St NW Ste 117........................ Washington DC 20036 202-822-7850 822-7816
Web: www.feaonline.org

Glass Molders Pottery Plastics & Allied Workers International Union
608 E Baltimore Pike .... Media PA 19063 610-565-5051 565-0983
TF: 855-670-4787 ■ *Web:* www.gmpiu.org

Graphic Artists Guild Inc
32 Broadway Ste 1114 .... New York NY 10004 212-791-3400 791-0333
Web: www.graphicartistsguild.org

Graphic Communications International Union
1900 L St NW Ste 800 .... Washington DC 20036 202-462-1400
Web: www.teamster.org

Inlandboatmen's Union of the Pacific (IBU)
1711 W Nickerson St Ste D .... Seattle WA 98119 206-284-6001 284-5043
TF: 800-562-6000 ■ *Web:* www.ibu.org

International Alliance of Theatrical Stage Employees Moving Picture Technicians (IATSE)
1430 Broadway 20th Fl............................ New York NY 10018 212-730-1770 921-7699
TF: 800-456-3863 ■ *Web:* iatse.net/

International Assn of Bridge Structural Ornamental & Reinforcing Iron Workers
1750 New York Ave NW Ste 400.................... Washington DC 20006 202-383-4800 638-4856
TF: 800-368-0105 ■ *Web:* www.ironworkers.org

International Assn of Fire Fighters (IAFF)
1750 New York Ave NW Third Fl.................. Washington DC 20006 202-737-8484 737-8418
Web: www.iaff.org

International Assn of Heat & Frost Insulators & Asbestos Workers
9602 ML King Jr Hwy.............................. Lanham MD 20706 301-731-9101 731-5058
Web: www.insulators.org

International Assn of Machinists & Aerospace Workers
9000 Machinists Pl.......................... Upper Marlboro MD 20772 301-967-4500 967-4588
Web: www.goiam.org

International Brotherhood of Boilermakers Iron Shipbuilders Blacksmiths Forgers & Helpers
753 State Ave Ste 570.......................... Kansas City KS 66101 913-371-2640 281-8101
Web: www.boilermakers.org

International Brotherhood of Electrical Workers
900 Seventh St NW.............................. Washington DC 20001 202-833-7000
Web: www.ibew.org

International Brotherhood of Police Officers (IBPO)
159 Burgin Pkwy .... Quincy MA 02169 617-376-0220 376-0285*
**Fax:* Legal Dept ■ *Web:* www.ibpo.org

International Brotherhood of Teamsters
25 Louisiana Ave NW............................ Washington DC 20001 202-624-6800 624-6918*
**Fax:* PR ■ *Web:* www.teamster.org

International Chemical Workers Union Council
1799 Akron Peninsula Rd.............................. Akron OH 44313 330-926-1444 926-0816
Web: icwuc.net/

International Federation of Professional & Technical Engineers
8630 Fenton St Ste 400 .... Silver Spring MD 20910 301-565-9016 565-0018
Web: www.ifpte.org

International Longshore & Warehouse Union
1188 Franklin St 4th Fl........................ San Francisco CA 94109 415-775-0533 775-1302
TF: 866-266-0013 ■ *Web:* www.ilwu.org

International Organization of Masters Mates & Pilots
700 Maritime Blvd .... Linthicum Heights MD 21090 410-850-8700 850-0973
TF: 877-667-5522 ■ *Web:* www.bridgedeck.org

International Union of Bricklayers & Allied Craftworkers (BAC)
1776 eye St NW .... Washington DC 20006 202-783-3788 393-0219
TF: 888-880-8222 ■ *Web:* www.bacweb.org

International Union of Elevator Constructors (IUEC)
7154 Columbia Gateway Dr .... Columbia MD 21046 410-953-6150 953-6169
Web: www.iuec.org

International Union of Operating Engineers
1125 17th St NW .... Washington DC 20036 202-429-9100 778-2616
Web: www.iuoe.org

International Union of Painters & Allied Trades (IUPAT)
7234 Pkwy Dr..................................... Hanover MD 21076 410-564-5900
TF: 800-554-2479 ■ *Web:* www.ibpat.org

International Union of Police Assn
1549 Ringling Blvd Ste 600 .... Sarasota FL 34236 941-487-2560 487-2570
TF: 800-247-4872 ■ *Web:* iupa.org

International Union Security Police & Fire Professionals of America (SPFPA)
25510 Kelly Rd................................... Roseville MI 48066 586-772-7250 772-9644
TF: 800-228-7492 ■ *Web:* www.spfpa.org

International Union United Automobile Aerospace & Agricultural Implement Workers of America
8000 E Jefferson Ave .... Detroit MI 48214 313-926-5000 823-6016
Web: www.uaw.org

Laborers' International Union of North America
905 16th St NW .... Washington DC 20006 202-737-8320 737-2754
Web: www.liuna.org

Llorens Pharmaceuticals International Division
6830 NW 77th Ct .... Miami FL 33166 305-716-0595
Web: www.llorenspharm.com

Marine Engineers' Beneficial Assn (MEBA)
444 N Capitol St NW Ste 800.................... Washington DC 20001 202-638-5355 638-5369
Web: mebaunion.org

Missouri Afl-cio 227 Jefferson St .... Jefferson City MO 65101 573-634-2115
Web: moaflcio.org

Mont Pelerin Capital LLC
660 Newport Ctr Dr Ste 1220................. Newport Beach CA 92660 949-706-6707
Web: www.montpelerincapital.com

Mspta 1715 Abbey Rd Ste B .... East Lansing MI 48823 517-336-7782
Web: mspta.net

NA of Broadcast Employees & Technicians (NABET-CWA)
501 Third St NW................................ Washington DC 20001 202-434-1100 434-1426
Web: www.nabetcwa.org

Name / Address	City	State	ZIP	Phone	Fax
NA of Letter Carriers 100 Indiana Ave NW Web: www.nalc.org	Washington	DC	20001	202-393-4695	737-1540
National Air Traffic Controllers Assn (NATCA) 1325 Massachusetts Ave NW TF: 800-266-0895 ■ Web: www.natca.org	Washington	DC	20005	202-628-5451	628-5767
National Alliance of Postal & Federal Employees 1628 11th St NW Web: www.napfe.com	Washington	DC	20001	202-939-6325	939-6389
National Basketball Players Assn (NBPA) 310 Malcolm X Blvd Web: www.nbpa.com	New York	NY	10027	212-655-0880	655-0881
National Conference of Firemen & Oilers 1023 15th St NW 10th Fl Web: www.ncfo.org	Washington	DC	20005	202-962-0981	872-1222
National Federation of Federal Employees 805-15th St NW Ste 500 Web: www.nffe.org	Washington	DC	20036	202-216-4420	862-4432
National League of Postmasters of the US 5904 Richmond Hwy Ste 500 Web: www.postmasters.org	Alexandria	VA	22303	703-329-4550	329-0466
National Organization of Industrial Trade Unions 148-06 Hillside Ave Web: www.noitu.org	Jamaica	NY	11435	718-291-3434	
National Rural Letter Carriers' Assn 1630 Duke St Fourth Fl Web: www.nrlca.org	Alexandria	VA	22314	703-684-5545	548-8735
National Treasury Employees Union 1750 H St NW 10th Fl Web: www.nteu.org	Washington	DC	20006	202-572-5500	572-5643
National Writers Union (NWU) 256 W 38th St Ste 703 Web: www.nwu.org	New York	NY	10018	212-254-0279	254-0673
News Media Guild 424 W 33rd St Ste 260 Web: www.newsmediaguild.org	New York	NY	10001	212-869-9290	840-0687
Newspaper Guild-Communications Workers of America, The 501 Third St NW Sixth Fl Web: www.newsguild.org	Washington	DC	20001	202-434-7177	434-1472
Northern California Laborers Apprenticeship Program 1001 Westside Dr Web: www.norcalaborers.org	San Ramon	CA	94583	925-828-2513	
Ocsea-afscme Local 390 Worthington Rd Ste A Web: www.ocsea.org	Westerville	OH	43082	614-865-4700	
Ohio Federation of Teachers 1251 E Broad St Frnt Web: oh.aft.org	Columbus	OH	43205	614-258-3240	
Ontario Nurses Association 85 Grenville St Ste 400 Web: www.ona.org	Toronto	ON	M5S3A2	416-964-8833	
Pipeline Industry Benefit Fund 4845 S 83rd E Ave Web: www.pibf.org	Tulsa	OK	74145	918-280-4800	
Plumbers Local Union No 68 502 Link Rd Web: www.plu68.com	Houston	TX	77009	713-869-3592	
Plumbing Industry Board Trade Education Committee 3711 47th Ave Web: www.ualocal1.org	Long Island City	NY	11101	718-752-9630	
Power Worker's Union, The 244 Eglinton Ave E Web: www.pwu.ca	Toronto	ON	M4P1K2	416-481-4491	
Professional Security Officers Union 3411 E 12th St Ste 200 Web: www.seiu-usww.org	Oakland	CA	94601	510-437-8100	261-2039
Road Sprinkler Fitters Local Union 669 7050 Oakland Mills Rd Web: www.sprinklerfitters669.org	Columbia	MD	21046	410-381-4300	
RWDSU 30 E 29th St Web: rwdsu.info	New York	NY	10016	212-684-5300	779-2809
Screen Actors Guild (SAG) 5757 Wilshire Blvd TF: 800-724-0767 ■ Web: www.sagaftra.org	Los Angeles	CA	90036	323-954-1600	549-6775
Seafarers International Union 5201 Auth Way TF: 800-252-4674 ■ Web: www.seafarers.org	Camp Springs	MD	20746	301-899-0675	899-7355
Service Employees International Union 1800 Massachusetts Ave NW TF: 800-424-8592 ■ Web: www.seiu.org	Washington	DC	20036	202-730-7000	429-5660
Sheet Metal Workers International Assn (SMWIA) 1750 New York Ave NW Sixth Fl TF: 800-251-7045 ■ Web: www.smwia.org	Washington	DC	20006	202-783-5880	662-0894
Shopper Local 2222 Sedwick Rd # 102 TF: 877-251-4592 ■ Web: www.shopperlocal.com	Durham	NC	27713	877-251-4592	
Transportation Communications International Union 3 Research Pl TF: 877-772-5772 ■ Web: www.goiam.org	Rockville	MD	20850	301-948-4910	948-1369
UA Local 486 7830 Philadelphia Rd Web: www.ualocal486.com	Baltimore	MD	21237	410-866-4380	
Uflac Local 112 Dental In 1571 Beverly Blvd Web: www.uflac.org	Los Angeles	CA	90026	213-895-4006	
Unifor 301 Laurier Ave W Web: www.cep.ca	Ottawa	ON	K1P6M6	613-230-5200	
Union Des Producteurs Agricole L 555 Boul Roland-therrien Web: www.amsq.qc.ca	Longueuil	QC	J4H3Y9	450-679-0540	
Union of American Physicians & Dentists 180 Grand Ave Ste 1380 TF: 800-622-0909 ■ Web: www.uapd.com	Oakland	CA	94612	510-839-0193	763-8756
Union Roofers Health & Welfare 9901 Paramount Blvd Ste 211 Web: www.unionroofers.com	Downey	CA	90240	562-927-1434	
UNITE HERE 275 Seventh Ave Web: www.unitehere.org	New York	NY	10001	212-265-7000	
United Assn Three Park Pl Web: www.ua.org	Annapolis	MD	21401	410-269-2000	
United Brotherhood of Carpenters & Joiners of America 101 Constitution Ave NW TF: 800-530-5090 ■ Web: www.carpenters.org	Washington	DC	20001	202-546-6206	543-5724
United Electrical Radio & Machine Workers of America One Gateway Ctr Ste 1400 Web: www.ueunion.org	Pittsburgh	PA	15222	412-471-8919	471-8999
United Farm Workers of America 29700 Woodford Techachpi Rd PO Box 62 Web: www.ufw.org	Keene	CA	93531	661-823-6151	823-6174
United Food & Commercial Workers International Union (UFCW) 1775 K St NW TF: 800-551-4010 ■ Web: www.ufcw.org	Washington	DC	20006	202-223-3111	466-1562
United Food & Commercial Workers Union Local 555 7095 SW Sandburg St Web: www.ufcw555.com	Tigard	OR	97281	503-684-2822	
United Scenic Artists 29 W 38th St 15th Fl TF: 800-456-3863 ■ Web: www.usa829.org	New York	NY	10018	212-581-0300	977-2011
United Steel Workers (USW) 3340 Perimeter Hill Dr Web: www.usw.org	Nashville	TN	37211	615-834-8590	834-7741
United Steelworkers of America Five Gateway Ctr Rm 701 Web: www.usw.org	Pittsburgh	PA	15222	412-562-2575	562-2445
United Transportation Union 14600 Detroit Ave TF: 800-558-8842 ■ Web: www.utu.org	Cleveland	OH	44107	216-228-9400	228-5755
Utility Workers Union of America (UWUA) 888 16th St NW Ste 550 Web: www.uwua.net	Washington	DC	20006	202-974-8200	974-8201
Willamette Education Service District Employees Association Inc 2611 Pringle Rd Se Web: www.ddouglas.k12.or.us	Salem	OR	97302	503-588-5330	
Writers Guild of America East (WGAE) 250 Hudson St Web: www.wgaeast.org	New York	NY	10013	212-767-7800	582-1909
Writers Guild of America West (WGAw) 7000 W Third St TF: 800-421-4182 ■ Web: www.wga.org	Los Angeles	CA	90048	323-951-4000	782-4800

418 LABORATORIES - DENTAL

SEE ALSO Laboratories - Medical p. 2616

Name / Address	City	State	ZIP	Phone	Fax
1 Biotechnology PO Box 758 TF: 800-951-4246 ■ Web: www.1biotechnology.com	Oneco	FL	34264	941-355-8451	351-0026
A & M Dental Laboratories Inc 425 S Santa Fe St Web: www.aandmdental.com	Santa Ana	CA	92705	714-547-8051	
Able Imaging LLC 2051 Springdale Rd Web: www.ableimaging.com	Cherry Hill	NJ	08003	856-424-2929	
Access Bio Inc 65 Clyde Rd Ste A Web: www.accessbio.net	Somerset	NJ	08873	732-873-4040	
Accu Reference Medical Lab 1901 E Linden Ave Unit 4 Web: www.accureference.com	Linden	NJ	07036	908-474-1004	
Accurate Diagnostic Labs Inc 3000 Hadley Rd Web: www.adlabs.net	South Plainfield	NJ	07080	732-839-3300	
ACM Medical Laboratory Inc 160 Elmgrove Park Web: www.acmlab.com	Rochester	NY	14624	585-247-3500	
Aculabs Inc Two Kennedy Blvd Web: www.aculabs.com	East Brunswick	NJ	08816	732-777-2588	
Advanced Medical Analysis LLC 1941 Walker Ave Web: www.amalab.net	Monrovia	CA	91016	626-305-5709	
Advanced Radiology PA 7253 Ambassador Rd Web: www.advancedradiology.com	Baltimore	MD	21244	443-436-1100	
Affiliated Medical Services Laboratory Inc 2916 E Central Ave Web: www.amsreferencelab.com	Wichita	KS	67214	316-265-4533	
Afr Labs LLC 23891 Via Fabricante Ste 607 Web: afrlabs.com	Mission Viejo	CA	92691	949-462-9822	
Alcopro Inc 2547 Sutherland Ave Web: www.alcopro.com	Knoxville	TN	37919	865-525-4900	
Alfred Mann Foundation, The 25134 Rye Canyon Loop Web: www.aemf.org	Valencia	CA	91355	661-702-6700	
American Esoteric Laboratories Inc 1701 Century Ctr Cove Web: www.ael.com	Memphis	TN	38134	901-405-8200	
American Health Associates 671 Ohio Pk Ste K TF: 800-522-7556 ■ Web: www.thml.com	Cincinnati	IN	45245	800-522-7556	
Ami Imaging Systems Inc 7815 Telegraph Rd Web: www.ami-imaging.com	Bloomington	MN	55438	952-828-0080	
Any Lab Test Now 235 Bloomfield Dr Ste 110 Web: www.anylabtestnow.com	Lititz	PA	17543	717-823-6787	
Applied Diagnostics Inc 1140 Business Center Dr Ste 370 Web: www.applieddiagnostics.com	Houston	TX	77043	713-271-4133	271-6885
Ascend Clinical LLC 1400 Industrial Way Web: www.ascendclinical.com	Redwood City	CA	94063	650-780-5500	
Associated Clinical Laboratories 1526 Peach St Web: www.associatedclinicallabs.com	Erie	PA	16501	814-461-2420	
Aurora Diagnostics LLC 11025 RCA Ctr Dr Ste 300 Web: www.auroradx.com	Palm Beach Gardens	FL	33410	561-626-5512	

				Phone	Fax
Bio Analytical Research Corporation (USA) Inc Five Delaware Dr. *Web:* www.barclab.com	Lake Success	NY	11042	516-719-1052	
BlueLine Services LLC 448 East 6400 South Ste 425 *Web:* www.blueline-services.com	Salt Lake City	UT	84107	801-575-8378	
Boos Dental Laboratory 1000 Boone Ave N Ste 660 *TF:* 800-333-2667 ■ *Web:* www.dentalservices.net	Golden Valley	MN	55427	763-544-1446	546-1392
Boston Endoscopy Center LLC 175 Worcester St (Rte 9) *Web:* www.gmed.com	Wellesley Hills	MA	02481	617-754-0800	
Boyce & Bynum Pathology Laboratories PC 200 Portland St. *Web:* www.bpllab.com	Columbia	MO	65201	573-886-4600	
BRLI No 2 Acquisition Corp 207 Perry Pkwy. *Web:* www.genedx.com	Gaithersburg	MD	20877	301-519-2100	
C D D 11603 Crosswinds Way Ste 100 *Web:* www.cddmedical.com	San Antonio	TX	78233	210-590-3033	
C Dental X Ray 1050 Northgate Dr Ste 110. *Web:* www.cdental.com	San Rafael	CA	94903	415-472-1323	
Calgary Laboratory Services 3535 Research Rd NW *Web:* www.calgarylabservices.com	Calgary	AB	T2L2K8	403-770-3500	
Calloway Laboratories Inc 12 Gill St Ste 4000 *Web:* www.callowaylabs.com	Woburn	MA	01801	781-224-9899	
Candelis Inc 18821 Bardeen Ave *Web:* www.candelis.com	Irvine	CA	92612	949-852-1000	
Carolina Medical Lab 1815 Back Creek Dr Ste 100. *Web:* www.cmedlab.com	Charlotte	NC	28213	704-598-8818	
CBLPath Inc 2100 SE 17th St. *Web:* www.cblpath.com	Ocala	FL	34471	352-732-9990	
Celdara Medical LLC 16 Cavendish Court DRTC *Web:* www.celdaramedical.com	Lebanon	NH	03766	617-320-8521	
Central Coast Pathology Consultants Inc 3701 S Higuera St Ste 200 *Web:* www.ccpathology.com	San Luis Obispo	CA	93401	805-541-6033	
Chromosomal Labs Bode Technology 1825 W Crest Ln. *Web:* www.chromosomal-labs.com	Phoenix	AZ	85027	623-434-0292	
Cleveland HeartLab Inc 6701 Carnegie Ave Ste 500 *TF:* 866-358-9828 ■ *Web:* www.clevelandheartlab.com	Cleveland	OH	44103	866-358-9828	
Clinical Information Network Inc 8283 N Hayden Rd Hayden Corporate Ctr Ste 100. *Web:* www.clinicalinfonet.com	Scottsdale	AZ	85258	480-422-1811	
Clinical Laboratories of Hawaii LLP 91-2135 Ft Weaver Rd Ste 300. *Web:* www.clinicallabs.com	Ewa Beach	HI	96706	808-677-7999	
Clinical Laboratory Partners LLC 129 Patricia M. Genova Dr *Web:* www.clinicallaboratorypartners.com	Newington	CT	06111	860-545-2299	
Clinical Pathology Laboratories Inc 9200 Wall St. *Web:* www.cpllabs.com	Austin	TX	78754	512-339-1275	
Clinical Science Laboratory Inc 51 Francis Ave *Web:* clinicalsciencelab.com	Mansfield	MA	02048	508-339-6106	
Coast2Coast Diagnostics Inc 600 N Tustin Ave Ste 110 *TF:* 800-730-9263 ■ *Web:* www.c2cdiagnostics.net	Santa Ana	CA	92705	800-730-9263	
Consultants in Laboratory Medicine 3170 W Central Ave Ste A. *Web:* www.clm-pml.com	Toledo	OH	43606	419-534-6600	
ConVerge Diagnostic Services LLC 200 Corporate Pl Ste 7 *Web:* www.converge.com	Peabody	MA	01960	978-538-8000	
Cytolab Pathology Services 6825 216th St Sw. *TF:* 800-845-6167	Lynnwood	WA	98036	425-712-8020	
Delta Pathology Group LLP 2915 Missouri Ave *Web:* www.deltapathology.com	Shreveport	LA	71109	318-621-8820	
Dental Technologies Inc (DTI) 5601 Arnold Rd *TF:* 800-229-0936 ■ *Web:* www.dtidental.com	Dublin	CA	94568	925-829-3611	828-0153
Detroit Bio-med Laboratories 23955 Fwy Park Dr *Web:* www.detroitbio.com	Farmington Hills	MI	48335	248-471-4111	
Diagnostic Imaging Inc 4 Neshaminy Interplex Ste 209 *Web:* diiradiology.com/	Trevose	PA	19053	215-244-3070	
Diagnostic Laboratory of Oklahoma LLC 225 N East 97th St *Web:* www.dlolab.com	Oklahoma City	OK	73114	405-608-6100	
Diagnostic Laboratory Services Inc 99-859 Iwaiwa St *Web:* www.dlslab.com	Aiea	HI	96701	808-589-5100	
Diagnostic Pathology Medical Group Inc 3301 C St Ste 200e. *Web:* www.cafebleu.com	Sacramento	CA	95816	916-446-0424	
Diagnostic Radiology Associates of Edison 3830 & 3840 Park Ave	Edison	NJ	08820	732-494-9061	
DIATHERIX Laboratories Inc 601 Genome Way Ste 4208 *Web:* www.diatherix.com	Huntsville	AL	35806	256-327-0699	
Distinctive Dental Studio Ltd. Inc 1504 Wall St. *Web:* www.ddsltdlab.com	Naperville	IL	60563	630-369-4600	
DNA Labs International Inc 240 Sw Natura Ave *Web:* www.dnalabsinternational.com	Deerfield Beach	FL	33441	954-426-5163	
Duckworth Pathology Group Inc 1211 Union Ave Ste 300. *Web:* www.duckworthpathology.com	Memphis	TN	38104	901-725-7551	
Dynacare Laboratories Inc 9200 W Wisconsin Ave. *Web:* www.dynacaremilwaukee.com	Milwaukee	WI	53226	414-805-7600	
DynaLifeDX Diagnostic Laboratory Services 10150 - 102 St Ste 200 *Web:* www.dynalifedx.com	Edmonton	AB	T5J5E2	780-451-3702	
East Side Clinical Laboratory Inc 10 Risho Ave. *Web:* www.esclab.com	East Providence	RI	02914	401-455-8400	
Elisa Act Biotechnologies 109 Carpenter Dr. *TF:* 800-553-5472 ■ *Web:* www.elisaact.com	Sterling	VA	20165	800-553-5472	
Ella Health Inc One Lemoyne Sq Plz Ste 102 (On Camp Hill Bypass Rd) *Web:* www.ellahealth.com	Lemoyne	PA	17043	717-695-9464	
Ellis Bandt Birkin Kollins & Wong Prof Corp 2020 Palomino Ln Ste 100. *Web:* www.desertradiology.com	Las Vegas	NV	89106	702-759-8600	
ExamWorks Inc 3280 Peachtree Rd Ste 2625 *TF:* 877-628-4703 ■ *Web:* www.examworks.com	Atlanta	GA	30305	877-628-4703	
Express Diagnostics Int'l Inc 1550 Industrial Dr. *Web:* www.drugcheck.com	Blue Earth	MN	56013	507-526-3951	
First - Call Medical Inc 574 Boston Rd Unit 11 *Web:* www.fcminc.com	Billerica	MA	01821	978-670-5399	
First Dental Health 5771 Copley Dr Ste 101. *TF:* 800-334-7244 ■ *Web:* www.firstdentalhealth.com	San Diego	CA	92111	800-334-7244	
Foundation Laboratory 1716 W Holt Ave *Web:* www.foundationlaboratory.com	Pomona	CA	91768	909-623-9301	
Franciscan St Elizabeth Health - Lafayette Central 1501 Hartford St. *Web:* ste.org	Lafayette	IN	47904	765-423-6011	
Futurewise 2990 Richmond Ave Ste 444 *Web:* www.houstontraining.com	Houston	TX	77098	713-874-1990	
Gamma Dynacare Medical Laboratories Inc 115 Midair Ct *Web:* www.gamma-dynacare.com	Brampton	ON	L6T5M3	905-790-3000	
Gene By Gene LTD 1445 N Loop West 820. *Web:* www.genebygene.com	Houston	TX	77008	832-381-5410	
Genetic Assays Inc 4711 Trousdale Dr Ste 209 *Web:* www.geneticassays.com	Nashville	TN	37220	615-781-0709	
Genetics & IVF Institute Inc 3015 Williams Dr *Web:* www.givf.com	Fairfax	VA	22031	703-698-7355	
Genetics Associates Inc 1916 Patterson St Ste 400 *Web:* www.geneticsassociates.com	Nashville	TN	37203	615-327-4532	
Gw Technologies 1245 S Garfield Ave *Web:* www.goodwillnmi.org	Traverse City	MI	49686	231-941-2250	
Health Diagnostic Laboratory Inc 737 N Fifth St Ste 103 *Web:* www.hdlabinc.com	Richmond	VA	23219	804-343-2718	
HEALTHeLINK The Commons at Walden 2568 Walden Ave Ste 107. *Web:* www.wnyhealthelink.com	Buffalo	NY	14225	716-206-0993	
HEALTHEON Inc 201 St Charles Ave Ste 2500 *Web:* www.healtheoninc.com	New Orleans	LA	70170	504-599-5982	
Highlands Pathology Consultants Pc 10368 Wallace Alley St Ste 18 *Web:* www.asspalace.com	Kingsport	TN	37663	423-323-5290	
Histopath Billing 3853 S Alameda St *Web:* www.histopath.com	Corpus Christi	TX	78411	361-992-4040	992-3847
Imaging Healthcare Specialists Medical Group Inc 6256 Greenwich Dr Ste 150 *TF:* 866-558-4320 ■ *Web:* www.imaginghealthcare.com	San Diego	CA	92122	866-558-4320	
Implantech Dental Laboratory 72415 Parkview Dr *Web:* www.implantechlab.com	Palm Desert	CA	92260	760-341-7388	
Incyte Diagnostics 13103 E Mansfield Ave. *Web:* www.incytepathology.com	Spokane Valley	WA	99216	509-892-2700	
Industrial Health Council 3513 Seventh Ave S *Web:* www.i-h-c.org	Birmingham	AL	35222	205-326-4109	
Infuse Medical 3369 W Mayflower Ave Ste 100 *Web:* www.infusemed.com	Lehi	UT	84043	801-331-8610	
Integrated Regional Laboratories Inc 5361 NW 33rd Ave *TF:* 800-522-0232 ■ *Web:* www.irlfl.com	Ft. Lauderdale	FL	33309	800-522-0232	
Interactive Medical Connections Inc 700 Gemini St Ste 110 *Web:* www.edrugfree.com	Houston	TX	77058	281-486-4434	
International Medical Laboratory Inc 6419 Parkland Dr *Web:* www.internationalmedicallab.com	Sarasota	FL	34243	941-756-0000	
Interscope Pathology Medical Group Inc 21114 Vanowen St *Web:* www.interscopepath.com	Canoga Park	CA	91303	818-992-7848	
Kaylor Dental Laboratory Inc 619 N Florence St. *Web:* www.kaylordental.com	Wichita	KS	67212	316-943-3226	
Kimball Genetics Inc 8490 Upland Dr Ste 100. *TF:* 800-444-9111 ■ *Web:* www.kimballgenetics.com	Englewood	CO	80112	800-444-9111	
KMH Cardiology & Diagnostic Centres 2075 Hadwen Rd *Web:* www.kmhlabs.com	Mississauga	ON	L5K2L3	905-855-1860	

Name / Address	City	State	Zip	Phone	Fax
Knight Dental Group 3659 Tampa Rd *Web:* www.knightdentalgroup.com	Oldsmar	FL	34677	813-854-3333	
Landmark Imaging Medical Group Inc 11620 Wilshire Blvd Ste 100 *Web:* www.landmarkimaging.com	Los Angeles	CA	90025	310-914-7336	
Lawson Health Research Institute Inc 268 Grosvenor St *Web:* www.lawsonresearch.com	London	ON	N6A4V2	519-646-6005	
Lenox Hill Radiology & Medical Imaging Associates PC 61 E 77th St *Web:* www.lenoxhillradiology.com	New York	NY	10075	212-772-3111	
LifeScan Laboratory Inc 5255 W Golf *TF:* 800-270-0037 ■ *Web:* lifescanlab.com	Skokie	IL	60077	800-270-0037	
Litholink Corp 2250 W Campbell Park Dr *Web:* www.litholink.com	Chicago	IL	60612	312-243-0600	
Lous Clinical Laboratory Inc 706 Adams Ave *Web:* www.drug-screen.com	Odessa	TX	79761	432-332-9421	
Main Street Radiology 13625 37th Ave Fl 2 *Web:* www.mainstreetradiology.com	Flushing	NY	11354	718-428-1500	
Mayo Collaborative Services Inc 3050 Superior Dr NW *Web:* www.mayomedicallaboratories.com	Rochester	MN	55901	507-266-5700	
Med Fusion LLC 2501 S State Hwy 121 Business Ste 1100 *Web:* www.medfusionservices.com	Lewisville	TX	75067	972-966-7000	
Medical Instrument Development Laboratories Inc 557 McCormick St *Web:* www.midlabs.com	San Leandro	CA	94577	510-357-3952	
MEDomics LLC 426 N San Gabriel Ave *Web:* www.medomics.com	Azusa	CA	91702	626-804-3645	
Metallurgical Technologies Inc pa 160 Bevan Dr *Web:* www.met-tech.com	Mooresville	NC	28115	704-663-5108	
Mo Bio Laboratories Inc 2746 Loker Ave W Ste A *Web:* www.mobio.com	Carlsbad	CA	92010	760-929-9911	
Modern Dental Laboratory USA LLC 13228 SE 30th St Ste C-6 *TF:* 877-711-8778 ■ *Web:* www.moderndentalusa.com	Bellevue	WA	98005	877-711-8778	
Molecular Diagnostics Laboratories Inc 632 Russell St *Web:* www.mdl-labs.com	Covington	KY	41011	513-437-3000	
Molecular Imaging Services Inc 10 Whitaker Ct *TF:* 866-937-8855 ■ *Web:* www.mismedical.com	Bear	DE	19701	866-937-8855	
Moleculera Labs LLC 800 Research Pkwy Ste 384 *Web:* www.moleculera.com	Oklahoma City	OK	73104	405-239-5250	
MRI Group 2100 Harrisburg Pk *Web:* www.mrigroup.com	Lancaster	PA	17601	717-291-1016	
National Center for Drug Free Sport, The 2537 Madison Ave *Web:* www.drugfreesport.com	Kansas City	MO	64108	816-474-8655	
Navix Diagnostix Inc 100 Myles Standish Blvd *Web:* www.navixdiagnostix.com	Taunton	MA	02780	508-977-2807	
Nicholas Laboratories LLC 21 Argonaut Ste A *Web:* www.nicholaspiramal.com	Aliso Viejo	CA	92656	949-448-4360	
Northern Illinois Clinical Laboratory Ltd 306 Era Dr *Web:* www.nicl.com	Northbrook	IL	60062	847-509-9779	
O'Brien Dental Lab Inc 4311 SW Research Way *Web:* www.obriendentallab.com	Corvallis	OR	97333	541-754-1238	
OB-GYN Physicians Inc 621 S New Ballas Rd Ste 75B *Web:* www.obgynphysician.com	St. Louis	MO	63141	314-872-7400	
Occupational Care Consultants 3028 Navarre Ave *Web:* www.therapyworks.net	Oregon	OH	43616	419-697-6850	
Old Town Endoscopy Center LLC 5500 Greenville Ave Ste 1100 *Web:* www.dhat.com	Dallas	TX	75206	214-646-3470	
Omega Laboratories Inc 400 N Cleveland Ave *Web:* www.omegalabs.net	Mogadore	OH	44260	330-628-5748	
OncoMDx Inc 2458 Embarcadero Way *Web:* www.oncomdx.com	Palo Alto	CA	94303	650-532-9500	
One Source Toxicology Laboratory Inc 1213 Genoa Red Bluff Rd *Web:* www.onesourcetox.com	Pasadena	TX	77504	713-920-2559	
OralDNA Labs Inc 7400 Flying Cloud Dr Ste 150 *Web:* www.oraldna.com	Eden Prairie	MN	55344	952-400-7772	
Outpatient Imaging Affiliates LLC 4322 Harding Pk Ste 422 *Web:* www.oiarad.com	Nashville	TN	37205	615-846-7733	
Palo Alto Medical Foundation for Health Care Research & Education, The 795 El Camino Real *Web:* www.pamf.org	Palo Alto	CA	94301	650-853-2974	
Pathology & Cytology Laboratories Inc 290 Big Run Rd *Web:* www.pandclab.com	Lexington	KY	40503	859-278-9513	
Pathology Inc 19951 Mariner Ave Ste 150 *Web:* www.pathologyinc.com	Torrance	CA	90503	310-769-0561	
Pathology Laboratories Inc 1946 N 13th St Ste 301 *Web:* www.pathlabs.org	Toledo	OH	43604	419-255-4600	
PeaceHealth Laboratories 123 International Way *Web:* www.peacehealthlabs.org	Springfield	OR	97477	541-341-8010	
PersonalizeDx 17500 Red Hill Ave Ste 210 *TF:* 877-429-6643 ■ *Web:* www.cynogen.com	Irvine	CA	92614	877-429-6643	
Pharmacogenetics Diagnostic Laboratory LLC 201 E Jefferson St Ste 309 *Web:* www.pgxlab.com	Louisville	KY	40202	502-569-1584	
Pharmagra Labs Inc 158 Mclean Rd *Web:* www.pharmagra.com	Brevard	NC	28712	828-884-8656	
Phase 2 Medical Manufacturing Inc 88 Airport Dr Ste 100 *Web:* www.phase2medical.com	Rochester	NH	03867	603-332-8900	
Phenopath Laboratories PLLC 551 N 34th St Ste 100 *Web:* www.phenopath.com	Seattle	WA	98103	206-374-9000	
Physicians Laboratory Services Inc 4840 "F" St *Web:* www.physlab.com	Omaha	NE	68117	402-731-4145	
Physicians Reference Laboratory LLC 7800 W 110th St *Web:* www.prlnet.com	Overland Park	KS	66210	913-338-4070	
Pittman Dental Laboratory 2355 Centennial Cir *Web:* www.pittmandental.com	Gainesville	GA	30504	770-534-4457	
PLUS Diagnostics Inc 825 Rahway Ave *Web:* www.plusdx.com	Union	NJ	07083	732-901-7575	
Posca Bros Dental Laboratory Inc 641 W Willow St *TF:* 800-537-6722 ■ *Web:* www.poscabrothers.com	Long Beach	CA	90806	562-427-1811	595-5821
Precipio Diagnostics LLC Four Science Park Third Fl *Web:* precipiodx.com	New Haven	CT	06511	203-787-7888	
Premier Diagnostic Health Services Inc 3185 Willingdon Green Ste 301 *Web:* www.premierdiagnostics.ca	Burnaby	BC	V5G4P3	604-678-9115	
Primex Clinical Laboratories Inc 16742 Stagg St Ste 120 *Web:* www.primexlab.com	Van Nuys	CA	91406	818-779-0496	
Quality Bioresources Inc 1015 N Austin St *Web:* www.qualbio.com	Seguin	TX	78155	830-372-4797	
RadNet Inc 1516 Cotner Ave *Web:* www.radnet.com	Los Angeles	CA	90025	310-445-2800	445-2980
RedPath Integrated Pathology Inc 2515 Liberty Ave *Web:* www.redpathip.com	Pittsburgh	PA	15222	412-224-6100	
Regional Medical Laboratories Inc 175 College St *Web:* www.glplasticandhandsurgery.com	Battle Creek	MI	49037	269-969-6161	
Reliance Pathology Partners LLC 5755 Hoover Blvd *Web:* www.pims-inc.com	Tampa	FL	33634	813-884-2849	
Reproductive Genetics Institute Inc 2825 N Halsted *Web:* www.east-westmedical.net	Chicago	IL	60657	773-472-4900	
Roe Dental Laboratory Inc 9565 Midwest Ave *TF:* 800-228-6663 ■ *Web:* www.roedentallab.com	Garfield Heights	OH	44125	216-663-2233	663-2237
Rolling Oaks Radiology Inc 415 Rolling Oaks Dr *Web:* www.rollingoaksradiology.com	Thousand Oaks	CA	91361	805-778-1513	
Roman Research Inc 800 Franklin St *TF:* 800-225-8652 ■ *Web:* www.romanresearch.com	Hanson	MA	02341	800-225-8652	
Rose Radiology Boot Ranch 4133 Woodlands Pkwy *Web:* www.roseradiology.com	Palm Harbor	FL	34685	727-781-3888	
Sand Lake Imaging 9350 Turkey Lk Rd *Web:* www.sandlakeimaging.com	Orlando	FL	32819	407-363-2772	
Shiel Medical Laboratory Inc Brooklyn Navy Yard Bldg 292 63 Flushing Ave *Web:* www.shiel.com	Brooklyn	NY	11205	718-552-1000	
Siloam Biosciences LLC 413 Northland Blvd *Web:* www.siloambio.com	Cincinnati	OH	45240	513-429-2976	
Simonmed Imaging 9201 E Mtn View Rd Ste 137 *Web:* www.simonmed.com	Scottsdale	AZ	85258	480-614-8555	
Slater Technology Fund Three Davol Sq Ste A340 *Web:* www.slaterfund.com	Providence	RI	02903	401-831-6633	
Sonic Healthcare USA Inc 9737 Great Hills Trl Ste 100 *Web:* www.sonichealthcareusa.com	Austin	TX	78759	512-439-1600	
South Bay Expressway LP 1129 La Media Rd *Web:* www.southbayexpressway.com	San Diego	CA	92154	619-661-7070	
South Jersey Radiology Associates PA 100 Carnie Blvd *Web:* www.sjra.com	Voorhees	NJ	08043	856-751-5522	
SPSmedical Supply Corp 6789 W Henrietta Rd *Web:* www.spsmedical.com	Rush	NY	14543	585-359-0130	
STERLING Reference Laboratories 2617 East L St Ste A *Web:* www.sterlingreflabs.com	Tacoma	WA	98421	253-552-1551	
Stockton Endoscopy Center 415 E Harding Way Ste E *Web:* www.stocktonurology.com	Stockton	CA	95204	209-942-1179	
Studio 2 Digital Dental Design Inc 2405 32nd St SE *Web:* www.studio2dental.com	Kentwood	MI	49512	616-957-2140	
Suncoast Pathology Inc 446 Tamiami Trl S *Web:* www.defevercruisers.com	Venice	FL	34285	941-483-3319	
Touchstone Medical Imaging LLC 5214 Maryland Way Ste 200 *Web:* www.touchstoneimaging.com	Brentwood	TN	37027	615-661-9200	
TriCore Reference Laboratories 1001 Woodward Pl NE *Web:* www.tricore.org	Albuquerque	NM	87102	505-938-8888	

Phone | Fax

Truxtun Radiology Medical Group LP
1817 Truxtun Ave ... Bakersfield CA 93301 661-325-6800
Web: www.truxtunrad.com

Utah Imaging Associates Inc
380 N 200 W Ste 209 ... Bountiful UT 84010 801-924-0029
Web: www.utahimaging.com

VantagePoint Laboratory Partners LLC
4980 Carroll Canyon Rd ... San Diego CA 92121 858-638-8120
Web: www.vpointlabs.com

VDIC Inc 16900 SE 82nd Dr ... Clackamas OR 97015 503-722-8077
Web: www.vdic.com

Vista Imaging Services Inc
3941 Park Dr Ste 20-463 ... El Dorado Hills CA 95762 415-272-3925
Web: www.vistaimagingservices.com

Warde Medical Laboratory 300 W Textile Rd ... Ann Arbor MI 48108 734-214-0300
Web: www.wardelab.com

Weidmann Diagnostic Solutions Inc
4011 Power Inn Rd Ste G ... Sacramento CA 95826 916-455-2284
Web: www.weidmann-diagnostics.com

Weland Clinical Laboratories PC
1911 First Ave SE ... Cedar Rapids IA 52402 319-366-1503
Web: www.welandlaboratories.com

West End Diagnostic Imaging
2425 Bloor St W Ste 103 ... Toronto ON M6S4W4 416-763-4331
Web: www.wedi.ca

Yosemite Pathology Group Inc
2625 Coffee Rd Ste S ... Modesto CA 95355 209-577-1200
Web: www.ypmg.com

419 LABORATORIES - DRUG-TESTING

SEE ALSO Laboratories - Medical p. 2616

Phone | Fax

Bio-Reference Laboratories Inc
481 Edward H Ross Dr ... Elmwood Park NJ 07407 201-421-2001 791-1941
NASDAQ: BRLI ■ *TF:* 800-229-5227 ■ *Web:* www.bioreference.com

Drug Detection Laboratories Inc
9700 Business Pk Dr Ste 407 ... Sacramento CA 95827 916-366-3113 366-3917
Web: www.drugdetection.net

ElSohly Laboratories Inc
Five Industrial Pk Dr ... Oxford MS 38655 662-236-2609 234-0253
Web: www.elsohly.com

Industrial Laboratories Company Inc, The
4046 Youngfield St ... Wheat Ridge CO 80033 303-287-9691 287-0964
Web: www.industriallabs.net

LabOne Inc 10101 Renner Blvd ... Lenexa KS 66219 913-888-1770 888-1778*
**Fax:* Sales ■ *TF:* 800-646-7788 ■ *Web:* www.labone.com

MEDTOX Scientific Inc 402 W County Rd D ... Saint Paul MN 55112 651-636-7466 636-5351
NASDAQ: MTOX ■ *TF:* 800-832-3244 ■ *Web:* www.medtox.com

US Drug Testing Laboratories Inc
1700 S Mt Prospect Rd ... Des Plaines IL 60018 847-375-0770 375-0775
TF: 800-235-2367 ■ *Web:* www.usdtl.com

420 LABORATORIES - GENETIC TESTING

SEE ALSO Laboratories - Medical p. 2616

Phone | Fax

American Red Cross Pacific NorthWest Blood Service
3131 N Vancouver Ave ... Portland OR 97227 503-284-1234
Web: www.redcrossblood.org

Blood Systems Laboratories 2424 W Erie Dr ... Tempe AZ 85282 602-343-7000 343-7025
TF: 800-288-2199 ■ *Web:* www.bloodsystemslaboratories.org

BRT Laboratories Inc 400 W Franklin St ... Baltimore MD 21201 410-225-9595 383-0938
TF: 800-765-5170 ■ *Web:* www.brtlabs.com

Cellmark Forensics 13988 Diplomat Dr Ste 100 ... Dallas TX 75234 214-271-8400 271-8322
TF: 800-752-2774 ■ *Web:* www.orchidcellmark.com

Center for Genetic Testing at Saint Francis
6465 S Yale Ave ... Tulsa OK 74136 918-502-1720
TF: 877-789-6001 ■ *Web:* www.saintfrancis.com

Clinical Testing & Research Inc
20 Wilsey Sq ... Ridgewood NJ 07450 888-837-5267 652-2775*
**Fax Area Code:* 201 ■ *TF:* 888-837-5267 ■ *Web:* www.clinicaltesting.com

Commonwealth Biotechnologies Inc
601 Biotech Dr ... Richmond VA 23235 804-648-3820 648-2641
TF: 800-735-9224 ■ *Web:* cbi-biotech.com

DNA Diagnostics Ctr 1 DDC Way ... Fairfield OH 45014 513-881-7800 881-7803
TF: 800-362-2368 ■ *Web:* www.dnacenter.com

DNA Paternity Lab of Utah
2749 E Parleys Way Ste 100 ... Salt Lake City UT 84109 801-466-3872 582-8460
TF: 800-362-5559 ■ *Web:* www.affiliatedgenetics.com

Eurofins Scientific Inc
2200 Rittenhouse St Ste 150 ... Des Moines IA 50321 515-265-1461 266-5453
Web: www.eurofinsus.com

Genetic Profiles Corp
10675 Treena St Ste 103 ... San Diego CA 92131 800-551-7763 348-0048*
**Fax Area Code:* 858 ■ *TF:* 800-551-7763 ■ *Web:* www.geneticprofiles.com

Genetica DNA Laboratories Inc
8740 Montgomery Rd ... Cincinnati OH 45236 513-985-9777 985-9983
TF: 800-433-6848 ■ *Web:* www.genetica.com

GenQuest DNA Analysis Laboratory
133 Coney Island Dr ... Sparks NV 89431 775-358-0652
TF: 877-362-5227 ■ *Web:* www.genquestdnalab.com

Genzyme Genetics 3400 Computer Dr ... Westborough MA 01581 508-898-9001 331-5799*
**Fax Area Code:* 267 ■ *TF:* 800-255-7357 ■ *Web:* www.labcorp.com

Identity Genetics Inc 47927 213th St ... Aurora SD 57002 800-861-1054 697-5306*
**Fax Area Code:* 605 ■ *TF:* 800-861-1054 ■ *Web:* www.identitygenetics.com

Laboratory Corp of America Holdings
358 S Main St ... Burlington NC 27215 336-584-5171
NYSE: LH ■ *TF:* 800-334-5161 ■ *Web:* www.labcorp.com

LABS Inc 6933 S Revere Pkwy ... Centennial CO 80112 720-528-4750 528-4786
TF: 866-393-2244 ■ *Web:* www.labs-inc.org

Phone | Fax

Maxxam Analytics Inc 335 LaiRd Rd Unit 2 ... Guelph ON N1G4P7 905-288-2150 288-2169
TF: 877-706-7678 ■ *Web:* www.thednalab.com

Medical Genetics Consultants
819 DeSoto St ... Ocean Springs MS 39564 800-362-4363 872-1893*
**Fax Area Code:* 228 ■ *TF:* 800-362-4363 ■ *Web:* www.legalgenetics.com

Memorial Blood Centers (MBC) 737 Pelham Blvd ... Saint Paul MN 55114 651-332-7000 332-7001
TF Cust Svc: 888-448-3253 ■ *Web:* www.mbc.org

Molecular Pathology Laboratory Network Inc
250 E Broadway ... Maryville TN 37804 865-380-9746 380-9191
TF: 800-932-2943 ■ *Web:* www.mplnet.com

NMS Labs 3701 Welsh Rd ... Willow Grove PA 19090 215-657-4900 657-2972
TF: 800-522-6671 ■ *Web:* www.nmslabs.com

Paternity Testing Corp (PTC) 300 Portland St ... Columbia MO 65201 573-442-9948 442-9870
TF: 888-837-8323 ■ *Web:* www.ptclabs.com

Rhode Island Blood Ctr 405 Promenade St ... Providence RI 02908 401-453-8360 453-8557
TF: 800-283-8385 ■ *Web:* www.ribc.org

RJ Lee Group Inc 350 Hochberg Rd ... Monroeville PA 15146 724-325-1776 733-1799
Web: rjlg.com

South Texas Blood & Tissue Ctr
6211 IH-10 W ... San Antonio TX 78201 210-731-5555 731-5501
TF: 800-292-5534 ■ *Web:* southtexasblood.org

State University of New York Upstate Medical University Tissue Typing Laboratory
750 E Adams St ... Syracuse NY 13210 315-464-4775 464-9557
Web: www.upstate.edu

University of North Texas Health Science Ctr
3500 Camp Bowie Blvd ... Fort Worth TX 76107 817-735-2000 735-5016
TF: 800-687-7580 ■ *Web:* web.unthsc.edu

421 LABORATORIES - MEDICAL

SEE ALSO Laboratories - Dental p. 2613; Laboratories - Drug-Testing p. 2616; Laboratories - Genetic Testing p. 2616; Organ & Tissue Banks p. 2848; Blood Centers p. 1873

Phone | Fax

A b C Testing Inc 95 First St ... Bridgewater MA 02324 508-697-6068
Web: www.abcndt.com

Abc American Bio-clinical
616 N Garfield Ave Ste 101 ... Monterey Park CA 91754 626-288-0208
Web: www.abclab.com

Accugenix Inc 223 Lake Dr ... Newark DE 19702 302-292-8888
TF: 800-886-9654 ■ *Web:* criver.com/products-services

AdvanDx Inc 400 Tradecenter Ste 6990 ... Woburn MA 01801 781-376-0009
Web: www.advandx.com

Analyte Health Inc 328 S Jefferson St Ste 770 ... Chicago IL 60661 312-477-3000
Web: www.analytehealth.com

ANI Pharmaceuticals Inc 210 Main St W ... Baudette MN 56623 218-634-1809
Web: www.anipharmaceuticals.com

Applied Laboratories Inc
3240 N Indianapolis Rd PO Box 2127 ... Columbus IN 47202 812-372-2607 372-2631
Web: www.appliedlabs.com

Ariosa Diagnostics Inc 5945 Optical Ct ... San Jose CA 95138 855-927-4672
TF: 855-927-4672 ■ *Web:* www.ariosadx.com

Arkansas Anatomic Pathology Services pa
411 E Matthews Ave ... Jonesboro AR 72401 870-930-3518
Web: www.dapsonline.com

Atherotech Inc 201 London Pkwy ... Birmingham AL 35211 800-719-9807
TF: 800-719-9807 ■ *Web:* www.atherotech.com

Aurum Ceramic Dental Laboratories Ltd
115 17 Ave SW ... Calgary AB T2S0A1 403-228-5120
TF: 800-665-8815 ■ *Web:* www.aurumgroup.com

Bio-Reference Laboratories Inc
481 Edward H Ross Dr ... Elmwood Park NJ 07407 201-421-2001 791-1941
NASDAQ: BRLI ■ *TF:* 800-229-5227 ■ *Web:* www.bioreference.com

BioMarker Strategies LLC
855 N Wolfe St Ste 603 ... Baltimore MD 21205 410-522-1008
Web: www.biomarkerstrategies.com

Biometrix Inc 2419 Ocean Ave ... San Francisco CA 94127 415-333-0522
Web: biometrixinc.com

BioZone Laboratories Inc 580 Garcia Ave ... Pittsburg CA 94565 925-473-1000
Web: www.biozonelabs.com

Biron Groupe Sante Inc 4105-F Blvd Matte ... Brossard QC J4Y2P4 514-866-6146
Web: www.biron.ca

Boval Company LP 505 W Industrial Blvd ... Cleburne TX 76031 817-645-1706
Web: www.bovalco.com

Calvert Labs 1225 Crescent Green Ste 115 ... Cary NC 27518 919-459-8653
TF: 800-300-8114 ■ *Web:* www.calvertlabs.com

Canadian Medical Laboratories Ltd
6560 Kennedy Rd ... Mississauga ON L5T2X4 800-263-0801 565-6704*
**Fax Area Code:* 905 ■ *TF:* 800-263-0801 ■ *Web:* profilecanada.com

Cell Signaling Technology Inc Three Trask Ln ... Danvers MA 01923 978-867-2300 867-2400
TF: 877-678-8324 ■ *Web:* www.cellsignal.com

Centrex Clinical Laboratories Inc
28 Campion Rd ... New Hartford NY 13413 315-797-0791
TF: 800-753-8653 ■ *Web:* www.centrexlabs.com

Charlotte Radiological P.A 1701 East Blvd ... Charlotte NC 28203 704-334-7800
Web: www.charlotteradiology.com

CIS Biotech Inc 2675 N Decatur Rd Ste 212 ... Atlanta GA 30033 404-499-0303
Web: www.cisbiotech.com

ClearPath Diagnostics
600 E Genesee St Ste 305 ... Syracuse NY 13202 315-234-3300
Web: www.clearpathdiagnostics.com

Cmi 6704 Guada Coma Dr ... Schertz TX 78154 210-967-6169 967-9233
Web: www.cmi-satx.com

Cml Healthcare Inc
Unit 1 60 Courtneypark Dr W ... Mississauga ON L5W0B3 905-565-0043
Web: www.cmlhealthcare.com

Crown Valley Imaging LLC
27401 Los Altos Ste 150 ... Mission Viejo CA 92691 949-367-1010
Web: www.crownvalleyimaging.com

Phone Fax

David Chen Md Diagnostic Medical Group Inc
1129 S San Gabriel Blvd. . . . . San Gabriel CA 91776 626-287-6746
Web: www.dmg.net

DIANON Systems Inc One Forest Pkwy . . . . Shelton CT 06484 203-926-7100
TF: 800-328-2666 ■ *Web:* www.dianon.com

DNA Reference Lab Inc
7271 Wurzbach Rd Ste 125 . . . . San Antonio TX 78240 210-692-3800
Web: www.dnareferencelab.com

Doctors Pathology Services
1253 College Park Dr . . . . Dover DE 19904 302-677-0000
Web: dpspa.com

Donlevy Laboratories Inc
11165 Delaware Pkwy. . . . . Crown Point IN 46307 219-226-0001
Web: www.donlevylab.com

Doshi Diagnostic Imaging Services PC
560 S Broadway . . . . Hicksville NY 11801 516-933-2800
Web: www.doshidiagnostic.com

Equipoise Dental Laboratory Inc
85 Portland Ave . . . . Bergenfield NJ 07621 201-385-4750 385-3280
TF: 800-999-4950 ■ *Web:* www.equipoisedental.com

ESA Biosciences Inc 22 Alpha Rd. . . . . Chelmsford MA 01824 978-250-7000

Focus Diagnostics Inc 11331 Vly View St . . . . . . Cypress CA 90630 562-240-6500
Web: m.focusdx.com

Genetrack Biolabs Inc 401-1508 Broadway W . . . . Vancouver BC V6J1W8 604-325-7282
Web: www.genetrack.com

Genova Diagnostics 63 Zillicoa St . . . . Asheville NC 28801 828-253-0621 252-9303*
**Fax:* Cust Svc ■ *TF:* 800-522-4762 ■ *Web:* www.gdx.net

Global Neuro-Diagnostics LP
2670 Firewheel Dr Ste B. . . . . Flower Mound TX 75028 866-848-2522
TF: 866-848-2522 ■ *Web:* www.globalneuro.net

Global Safety & Security Inc
4713 Trenton St . . . . Metairie LA 70006 504-454-6933
Web: www.globalsafety.net

Great Plains Laboratory Inc
11813 W 77th St. . . . . Overland Park KS 66214 913-341-8949
Web: www.greatplainslaboratory.com

Green Dental Laboratories Inc
1099 Wilburn Rd . . . . Heber Springs AR 72543 501-362-3132
Web: greendentallab.com

Harmony Dental Lab 564 Marietta Hwy. . . . . Dallas GA 30157 770-443-4667
Web: www.harmonydental.com

Health Network Laboratory 2024 Lehigh St . . . . . Allentown PA 18103 610-402-8170 402-5592
TF: 877-402-4221 ■ *Web:* www.healthnetworklabs.com

Hydrogen Future Corp
2525 Robinhood St Ste 1100 . . . . Houston TX 77005 514-420-0333
Web: www.a5labs.com

Identigene LLC 2495 South West Temple . . . . . Salt Lake City UT 77005 801-462-1401
Web: www.dnatesting.com

Igenex 795 San Antonio Rd . . . . Palo Alto CA 94303 650-424-1191
Web: www.igenex.com

Immco Diagnostics Inc 60 Pineview Dr . . . . Buffalo NY 14228 716-691-0091
Web: www.immcodiagnostics.com

Keller Laboratories Inc
160 Larkin Williams Industrial Ct . . . . Fenton MO 63026 636-600-4200
TF: 800-325-3056 ■ *Web:* www.kellerlab.com

LabOne Inc 10101 Renner Blvd. . . . . Lenexa KS 66219 913-888-1770 888-1778*
**Fax:* Sales ■ *TF:* 800-646-7788 ■ *Web:* www.labone.com

Laboratory Corp of America Holdings
358 S Main St. . . . . Burlington NC 27215 336-584-5171
NYSE: LH ■ *TF:* 800-334-5161 ■ *Web:* www.labcorp.com

Lakeland Surgical & Diagnostic Center LLP
1315 N Florida Ave. . . . . Lakeland FL 33805 863-683-2268
Web: www.lsdc.net

LifeLabs Inc 3680 Gilmore Way . . . . Burnaby BC V5G4V8 604-431-5005
Web: www.mdsdx.com

Machaon Diagnostics Inc 3023 Summit St. . . . . . Oakland CA 94609 510-839-5600
Web: www.machaondiagnostics.com

Mcmahon Publishing Group 545 W 45th St . . . . . New York NY 10036 212-957-5300
Web: www.mcmahonmed.com

Medical Diagnostic Laboratories LLC
2439 Kuser Rd . . . . Hamilton NJ 08690 609-570-1000
TF: 877-269-0090 ■ *Web:* www.mdlab.com

Metametrix Inc 3425 Corporate Way . . . . Duluth GA 30096 770-446-5483
Web: www.metametrix.com

Midwest Clinical Laboratories
3267 S 16th St Ste 100. . . . . Milwaukee WI 53215 414-647-5505 256-5566

Mri Central 3301 S Shepherd Dr. . . . . Houston TX 77098 713-874-0111
Web: www.mricentral.com

National Genetics Institute
2440 S Blvd Ste 235. . . . . Los Angeles CA 90064 310-996-0036
TF: 800-352-7788 ■ *Web:* www.ngi.com

Nebraska Lablinc LLC 5440 S St Ste 100. . . . . . . Lincoln NE 68506 402-484-5462
Web: www.lablinc.com

NeoGenomics Inc
12701 Commonwealth Dr Ste 9 . . . . Fort Myers FL 33913 941-923-1949
Web: www.neogenomics.com

NeuroScience Inc 373 280th St . . . . Osceola WI 54020 715-294-2144
Web: www.neurorelief.com

NMS Labs 3701 Welsh Rd . . . . Willow Grove PA 19090 215-657-4900 657-2972
TF: 800-522-6671 ■ *Web:* www.nmslabs.com

Norgen Biotek Corp 3430 Schmon Pkwy . . . . Thorold ON L2V4Y6 905-227-8848 227-1061
Web: www.norgenbiotek.com

North Coast Clinical Laboratory Inc
2215 Cleveland Rd . . . . Sandusky OH 44870 419-626-6012
TF: 800-325-5737 ■ *Web:* www.northcoastlab.com

Northern Diagnostic Laboratories Inc
301A US Route 1 . . . . Scarborough ME 04074 207-396-7830
Web: www.nordx.org

Oklahoma Breast Care Center LLC
13509 N Meridian. . . . . Oklahoma City OK 73120 405-755-2273
Web: www.okbreastcare.com

Phone Fax

Opmedic Group Inc
1361 Beaumont Ave Ste 301. . . . . Mount-royal QC H3P2W3 514-345-8535
Web: www.groupeopmedic.com

OURLab Inc 1450 Elm Hill Pk . . . . Nashville TN 37210 615-874-0410
Web: www.ourlab.net

Parkway Clinical Laboratories Inc
3494 Progress Dr . . . . Bensalem PA 19020 215-245-5112
TF: 800-327-2764 ■ *Web:* www.parkwayclinical.com

Path Logic Inc
950 Riverside Pkwy Ste 90. . . . . West Sacramento CA 95605 855-291-4528
TF: 855-291-4528 ■ *Web:* www.pathlogic.com

Pathology Ctr, The 8303 Dodge St. . . . . Omaha NE 68114 402-354-4540
Web: thepathologycenter.org

Pekin Mri 1300 Park Ave. . . . . Pekin IL 61554 309-347-2143
Web: www.kingsmedicalgroup.com

Penta Laboratories 9740 Cozycroft Ave . . . . Chatsworth CA 91311 818-993-0153
Web: www.pentalaboratories.com

PerkinElmer Genetics Inc 90 Emerson Ln . . . . . . Bridgeville PA 15017 412-220-2300
Web: www.perkinelmergenetics.com

Persante Health Care Inc
130 Gaither Dr Ste 124. . . . . Mt. Laurel NJ 08054 856-234-0770
Web: www.persante.com

Personal Genome Diagnostics Inc
2809 Boston St Ste 503 . . . . Baltimore MD 21224 443-602-8833
Web: personalgenome.com

Physician's Automated Laboratory Inc (PALLAB)
9830 Brimhall Rd . . . . Bakersfield CA 93312 661-829-2260 829-1317
TF: 800-675-2271 ■ *Web:* www.pallab.org

Ponca Tribe 2602 J St. . . . . Omaha NE 68107 402-734-5275
Web: www.poncatribe-ne.org

Princeton Radiology Associates P.A. Inc
3674 Route 27 . . . . Kendall Park NJ 08824 732-821-5563
Web: www.prapa.com

ProPath Laboratory Inc 1355 River Bend Dr . . . . . Dallas TX 75247 214-638-2000
Web: www.propathlab.com

ProScan Imaging LLC 5400 Kennedy Ave. . . . . . . Cincinnati OH 45213 513-618-1063
Web: www.proscan.com

Quest Diagnostics at Nichols Institute
33608 Ortega Hwy . . . . San Juan Capistrano CA 92675 949-728-4000 728-4985*
**Fax:* Hum Res ■ *TF:* 800-642-4657 ■ *Web:* www.questdiagnostics.com

Quest Diagnostics Inc Three Giralda Farms . . . . . Madison NJ 07940 201-393-5000 462-4169*
NYSE: DGX ■ **Fax:* Cust Svc ■ *TF:* 800-222-0446 ■ *Web:* www.questdiagnostics.com

Scientific Molding Corp Ltd 330 SMC Dr. . . . . . . Somerset WI 54025 715-247-3500 247-3611
Web: www.smcltd.com

South Bend Medical Foundation
530 N Lafayette Blvd . . . . South Bend IN 46601 574-234-4176 234-1561
TF: 800-544-0925 ■ *Web:* www.sbmflab.org

Specialty Laboratories Inc 27027 Tourney Rd . . . . Valencia CA 91355 661-799-6543 799-6634
TF Sales: 800-421-7110 ■ *Web:* www.specialtylabs.com

Strand Analytical Laboratories LLC
5770 Decatur Blvd Ste A. . . . . Indianapolis IN 46241 317-455-2100
Web: www.strandlabs.com

Sunrise Medical Laboratories Inc
250 Miller Pl. . . . . Hicksville NY 11801 631-435-1515
TF Cust Svc: 800-782-0282 ■ *Web:* www.sunriselab.com

TeraRecon Inc 4000 E Third Ave Ste 200 . . . . . . Foster City CA 94404 650-372-1100
Web: www.terarecon.com

US Laboratory & Radiology Inc
Two Jonathan Dr. . . . . Brockton MA 02301 508-583-2000
Web: www.uslabrad.com

US LABS Inc 2601 Campus Dr. . . . . Irvine CA 92612 800-710-1800
TF: 888-875-2270 ■ *Web:* www.uslabs.net

VCA Antech Inc 12401 W Olympic Blvd. . . . . Los Angeles CA 90064 310-571-6500 571-6700
NASDAQ: WOOF ■ *TF:* 800-966-1822 ■ *Web:* www.vcaantech.com

Visalia Medical Lab 833 Sequoia Ave . . . . Lindsay CA 93247 559-562-1222
Web: www.vmchealth.com

Vista Biologicals Corp 2120-C Las Palmas Dr. . . . . Carlsbad CA 92009 760-438-5058
Web: www.vistabiologicals.com

422 LABORATORY ANALYTICAL INSTRUMENTS

SEE ALSO Glassware - Laboratory & Scientific p. 2358; Laboratory Apparatus & Furniture p. 2619

Phone Fax

1st Detect Corp 401 Congress Ave Ste 1650. . . . . Austin TX 78701 512-485-9530
Web: www.spacehab.com

4pi Analysis Inc 3500 Westgate Dr Ste 403 . . . . . Durham NC 27707 919-489-1757
Web: www.4pi.com

Abaxis Inc 3240 Whipple Rd. . . . . Union City CA 94587 510-675-6500 441-6150
NASDAQ: ABAX ■ *TF:* 800-822-2947 ■ *Web:* www.abaxis.com

Actinix Inc 1800 Green Hills Rd Ste 105 . . . . . Scotts Valley CA 95066 831-440-9388
Web: www.actinix.com

Advanced Technical Support Inc
231 Crosswicks Rd. . . . . Bordentown NJ 08505 609-298-2522
Web: www.atsrheosystems.com

Alden Research Laboratory Inc
30 Shrewsbury St . . . . Holden MA 01520 508-829-6000 829-5939
Web: www.aldenlab.com

Altamira Instruments Inc
149 Delta Dr Ste 200 . . . . Pittsburgh PA 15238 412-963-6385
Web: www.altamirainstruments.com

American Biologics 1180 Walnut Ave . . . . Chula Vista CA 91911 619-429-8200 429-8004
TF: 800-227-4473 ■ *Web:* www.americanbiologics.com

Analytical Sensors & Instruments Ltd
12800 Pk One Dr . . . . Sugar Land TX 77478 281-565-8818 565-8811
Web: www.asi-sensors.com

Analytical Spectral Devices Inc
2555 55th St Ste 100 . . . . Boulder CO 80301 303-444-6522
Web: www.asdi.com

Andor Technology Plc (USA)
425 Sullivan Ave Ste No3. . . . . South Windsor CT 06074 860-290-9211
Web: www.andor.com

	City	State	Zip	Phone	Fax
Ankom Technology 2052 Oneil Rd *Web:* www.ankom.com	Macedon	NY	14502	315-986-8090	
Applied Instrument Technologies Inc 2121 Aviation Dr. *Web:* www.aitanalyzers.com	Upland	CA	91786	909-204-3700	
Asylum Research Corp 6310 Hollister Ave *Web:* www.asylumresearch.com	Santa Barbara	CA	93117	805-696-6466	
BBI Source Scientific Inc 7390 Lincoln Way	Garden Grove	CA	92841	714-898-9001	
BD Biosciences 2350 Qume Dr *TF:* 800-223-8226 ■ *Web:* www.bdbiosciences.com	San Jose	CA	95131	408-432-9475	954-2347
Bio/Data Corp PO Box 347 *TF:* 800-257-3282 ■ *Web:* www.biodatacorp.com	Horsham	PA	19044	215-441-4000	443-8820
Bioanalytical Systems Inc 2701 Kent Ave. *NASDAQ: BASI* ■ *TF:* 800-845-4246 ■ *Web:* www.basinc.com	West Lafayette	IN	47906	765-463-4527	497-1102
BiOptix Inc 1775 38th St Ste A *Web:* www.bioptix.com	Boulder	CO	80301	303-545-5550	
BioTek Instruments Inc 100 Tigan St PO Box 998 *TF:* 888-451-5171 ■ *Web:* www.biotek.com	Winooski	VT	05404	802-655-4740	655-7941
Biovision Technologies 64 E Uwchlan Ave # 273 *Web:* www.biovis.com	Exton	PA	19341	610-524-9740	
Blanke Industries Inc 1099 Brown St Ste 103 *Web:* www.blankeindustries.com	Wauconda	IL	60084	847-487-2780	
Block Engineering Inc 377 Simarano Dr *Web:* www.blockeng.com	Marlborough	MA	01752	508-251-3100	
Brinkmann Instruments Inc 1819 Underwood Blvd *Web:* www.lauda-brinkmann.com	Delran	NJ	08075	856-764-7300	
Bruker Daltonics Inc 40 Manning Rd *Web:* www.bruker.com	Billerica	MA	01821	978-663-3660	667-5993
Buehler Ltd 41 Waukegan Rd *TF Sales:* 800-283-4537 ■ *Web:* buehler.com	Lake Bluff	IL	60044	847-295-6500	295-7979
California Analytical Instruments Inc 1312 W Grove Ave *TF:* 800-959-0949 ■ *Web:* www.gasanalyzers.com	Orange	CA	92865	714-974-5560	282-6280
Caliper Life Sciences Inc 68 Elm St *TF:* 800-762-4000 ■ *Web:* www.perkinelmer.com	Hopkinton	MA	01748	508-435-9500	435-3439
CAO Group Inc 4628 Skyhawk Dr *TF:* 877-877-9778 ■ *Web:* www.caogroup.com	West Jordan	UT	84084	801-256-9282	256-9287
CardioGenics Holdings Inc 6295 Northam Dr Unit 8 *Web:* www.cardiogenics.com	Mississauga	ON	L4V1W8	905-673-8501	
Cargille-Sacher Laboratories Inc 55 Commerce Rd *Web:* www.cargille.com	Cedar Grove	NJ	07009	973-239-6633	239-6096
CDS Analytical Inc 465 Limestone Rd PO Box 277 *TF:* 800-541-6593 ■ *Web:* www.cdsanalytical.com	Oxford	PA	19363	610-932-3636	932-4158
CEM Corp 3100 Smith Farm Rd *TF:* 800-726-3331 ■ *Web:* www.cem.com	Matthews	NC	28104	704-821-7015	821-7894
Cepheid 904 E Caribbean Dr *NASDAQ: CPHD* ■ *TF:* 888-838-3222 ■ *Web:* www.cepheid.com	Sunnyvale	CA	94089	408-541-4191	541-4192
Cetac Technologies Inc 14306 Industrial Rd *TF:* 800-369-2822 ■ *Web:* www.cetac.com	Omaha	NE	68144	402-733-2829	733-5292
CH Technologies (USA) Inc 263 Center Ave Ste 1 *Web:* www.envmed.com	Westwood	NJ	07675	201-666-2335	
Chemetrics Inc 4295 Catlett Rd *Web:* www.chemetrics.com	Calverton	VA	20138	540-788-9026	788-4856
Chrom Tech Inc 5995 149th St W Ste 102 *Web:* www.chromtech.com	Apple Valley	MN	55124	952-431-6000	
CMI Inc 316 E Ninth St *TF:* 866-835-0690 ■ *Web:* www.alcoholtest.com	Owensboro	KY	42303	270-685-6545	685-6678
CompuMed Inc 5777 W Century Blvd Ste 360 *TF:* 800-421-3395 ■ *Web:* compumed.ning.com	Los Angeles	CA	90045	310-258-5000	645-5880
Corning Inc Life Sciences Div 836 N St Bldg 300 Ste 3401 *TF:* 800-492-1110 ■ *Web:* www.corning.com/lifesciences	Tewksbury	MA	01876	978-442-2200	635-2476
CPI International Inc 5580 Skylane Blvd *Web:* www.cpiinternational.com	Santa Rosa	CA	95403	707-525-5788	
CRAIC Technologies Inc 948 N Amelia Ave *Web:* www.microspectra.com	San Dimas	CA	91773	310-573-8180	
Custom Sensors & Technology 531 Axminister Dr *Web:* www.customsensors.com	Fenton	MO	63026	636-305-0666	
Datacolor 5 Princess Rd *TF General:* 800-340-1007 ■ *Web:* www.datacolor.com	Lawrenceville	NJ	08648	609-924-2189	895-7414
Daxor Corp 350 Fifth Ave Ste 7120 *NYSE: DXR* ■ *Web:* www.daxor.com	New York	NY	10118	212-244-0555	244-0806
DeltaNu LLC 5452 Old Hwy 130 *Web:* www.deltanu.com	Laramie	WY	82070	307-745-9148	
Diba Industries Inc Four Precision Rd *Web:* www.dibaind.com	Danbury	CT	06810	203-744-0773	
Direct Dimensions Inc 10310 S Dolfield Rd Ste B *Web:* www.dirdim.com	Owings Mills	MD	21117	410-998-0880	
Eberbach Corp 505 S Maple Rd *Web:* www.eberbachlabtools.com	Ann Arbor	MI	48103	734-665-8877	
Eckert & Ziegler Isotope Products Inc 24937 Ave Tibbitts *Web:* www.isotopeproducts.com	Valencia	CA	91355	661-309-1010	
EDAX Inc 91 McKee Dr *Web:* www.edax.com	Mahwah	NJ	07430	201-529-4880	529-3156
Entech Instruments Inc 2207 Agate Ct *Web:* www.entechinst.com	Simi Valley	CA	93065	805-527-5939	
Environics Inc 69 Industrial Park Rd E *Web:* www.environics.com	Tolland	CT	06084	860-872-1111	
Environmental Express Ltd 2345A Charleston Regional Pkwy *Web:* www.envexp.com	Charleston	SC	29492	843-881-6560	
Eppendorf North America Inc One Cantiague Rd *Web:* www.eppendorfna.com	Westbury	NY	11590	516-334-7500	
Exergen Corp 400 Pleasant St *Web:* www.exergen.com	Watertown	MA	02472	617-923-9900	923-9911
FEI Co 5350 NE Dawson Creek Dr *NASDAQ: FEIC* ■ **Fax:* Sales ■ *TF Cust Svc:* 866-693-3426 ■ *Web:* www.fei.com	Hillsboro	OR	97124	503-640-7500	726-2570*
Fisher Scientific Company Inc 112 Colonnade Rd *Web:* www.fishersci.ca	Ottawa	ON	K2E7L6	613-228-6571	226-7658
Fluid Imaging Technologies Inc 65 Forest Falls Dr *Web:* www.fluidimaging.com	Yarmouth	ME	04096	207-846-6100	
FORNEY LLC 310 Seven Fields Blvd One Adams Pl *Web:* www.forneymaterialstesting.com	Seven Fields	PA	16046	724-346-7400	
Gambro BCT 10811 W Collins Ave *TF:* 877-339-4228 ■ *Web:* www.terumobct.com	Lakewood	CO	80215	303-231-4357	231-4357
Gamma Vacuum LLC 2915 133rd St W *Web:* www.gammavacuum.com	Shakopee	MN	55379	952-445-4841	
Gatan Inc 5794 W Las Positas Blvd *Web:* www.gatan.com	Pleasanton	CA	94588	925-463-0200	463-0204
GrayWolf Sensing Solutions LLC Six Research Dr *TF:* 800-218-7997 ■ *Web:* www.wolfsense.com	Shelton	CT	06484	203-402-0477	
Hach Co PO Box 389 *TF:* 800-227-4224 ■ *Web:* www.hach.com	Loveland	CO	80539	970-669-3050	669-2932
Hamilton Co 4970 Energy Way *TF:* 800-648-5950 ■ *Web:* www.hamiltonrobotics.com	Reno	NV	89502	775-858-3000	
Harvard Bioscience Inc 84 October Hill Rd *NASDAQ: HBIO* ■ *TF:* 800-272-2775 ■ *Web:* www.harvardbioscience.com	Holliston	MA	01746	508-893-8999	429-5732
Helena Laboratories Inc 1530 Lindbergh Dr *TF:* 800-231-5663 ■ *Web:* www.helena.com	Beaumont	TX	77704	409-842-3714	842-3094
Hitachi High Technologies America Inc 10 N Martingale Rd Ste 500 *Web:* www.hitachi-hta.com	Schaumburg	IL	60173	847-273-4141	273-4407
Horiba Instruments Inc 17671 Armstrong Ave *TF:* 800-446-7422 ■ *Web:* www.horiba.com	Irvine	CA	92614	949-250-4811	250-0924
hygiena LLC 941 Avenida Acaso *TF:* 877-494-4364 ■ *Web:* www.hygiena.net	Camarillo	CA	93012	805-388-8007	
Illumina Inc 9885 Towne Centre Dr *NASDAQ: ILMN* ■ *TF:* 800-809-4566 ■ *Web:* www.illumina.com	San Diego	CA	92121	858-202-4500	202-4545
Inanovate Inc Two Davis Dr Ste 13169 *Web:* www.inanovate.com	Research Triangle Park	NC	27709	919-354-1028	
Infolab Inc 17400 Hwy 61 N	Clarksdale	MS	38614	662-627-2283	627-1913
Instrumentation Laboratory Inc 180 Hartwell Rd *TF Sales:* 800-955-9525 ■ *Web:* www.instrumentationlaboratory.com	Bedford	MA	01730	781-861-0710	861-1908
IonField Systems LLC 1 Executive Dr Ste 8 *Web:* ionfieldsystems.com	Moorestown	NJ	08057	856-437-0330	823-1426
IonSense Inc 999 Broadway Ste 404 *Web:* www.ionsense.com	Saugus	MA	01906	781-484-1043	
IRIS International Inc 9172 Eton Ave *NASDAQ: IRIS* ■ *TF:* 877-920-4747 ■ *Web:* www.proiris.com	Chatsworth	CA	91311	818-709-1244	700-9661
ISCO Inc 4700 Superior St PO Box 82531 **Fax:* Cust Svc ■ *TF:* 800-228-4250 ■ *Web:* www.isco.com	Lincoln	NE	68501	402-464-0231	465-3022*
JEOL USA Inc 11 Dearborn Rd *Web:* www.jeol.com	Peabody	MA	01960	978-535-5900	536-2205
k-Space Associates Inc 2182 Bishop Cir E *Web:* www.k-space.com	Dexter	MI	48130	734-426-7977	
Kimble Chase Life Science & Research Products LLC 1022 Spruce St *Web:* www.kimble-chase.com	Vineland	NJ	08362	856-692-8500	
Kurt J Lesker Co 1925 Rt 51 *Web:* www.lesker.com	Jefferson Hills	PA	15025	412-387-9200	
Labcon North America Inc 3700 Lkeville Hwy *TF:* 800-227-1466 ■ *Web:* www.labcon.com	Petaluma	CA	94954	707-766-2100	766-2199
LaMotte Co 802 Washington Ave *TF:* 800-344-3100 ■ *Web:* www.lamotte.com	Chestertown	MD	21620	410-778-3100	778-6394
Leco Corp 3000 Lakeview Ave **Fax:* Sales ■ *TF:* 800-292-6141 ■ *Web:* www.leco.com	Saint Joseph	MI	49085	269-985-5496	982-8977*
Levitt-Safety Ltd 2872 Bristol Cir *Web:* www.levitt-safety.com	Oakville	ON	L6H5T5	905-829-3299	829-2919
Li Cor Inc PO Box 4425 *TF:* 800-447-3576 ■ *Web:* www.licor.com	Lincoln	NE	68504	402-467-3576	467-2819
Luminex Corp 12212 Technology Blvd *NASDAQ: LMNX* ■ *TF:* 888-219-8020 ■ *Web:* www.luminexcorp.com	Austin	TX	78727	512-219-8020	219-5195
M. Braun Inc 14 Marin Way *Web:* www.mbraun.com	Stratham	NH	03885	603-773-9333	773-0008
Malvern Instruments Inc 117 Flanders Rd *Web:* www.malvern.com	Westborough	MA	01581	508-768-6400	
Mandel Scientific Company Inc Two Admiral Pl *TF:* 888-883-3636 ■ *Web:* www.mandel.ca	Guelph	ON	N1G4N4	519-763-9292	763-2005
MassTech Inc 6992 Columbia Gateway Dr *Web:* www.apmaldi.com	Columbia	MD	21046	443-539-1758	
Matrix Technologies Corp 22 Friars Dr *Web:* www.matrixtechcorp.com	Hudson	NH	03051	603-595-0505	
Med-plus Medical Supplies 17 Vanderbilt Ave *Web:* www.medexsupply.com	Brooklyn	NY	11205	718-222-4416	
Mettler-Toledo International Inc 1900 Polaris Pkwy *Web:* www.mt.com	Columbus	OH	43240	614-438-4511	
Micromeritics Instrument Corp 1 Micromeritics Dr *TF:* 800-229-5052 ■ *Web:* www.micromeritics.com	Norcross	GA	30093	770-662-3620	662-3696
Microsonic Systems Inc 76 Bonaventura Dr *Web:* www.microsonics.com	San Jose	CA	95134	408-844-4980	
Microtrac Inc 148 Keystone Dr *Web:* www.microtrac.com	Montgomeryville	PA	18936	215-619-9920	
Modal Shop Inc, The 1776 Mentor Ave *TF:* 800-860-4867 ■ *Web:* www.modalshop.com	Cincinnati	OH	45212	513-351-9919	
Molecular Devices Inc (MDI) 1311 Orleans Dr Ste 408 *TF:* 800-635-5577 ■ *Web:* www.moleculardevices.com	Sunnyvale	CA	94089	408-747-1700	747-3601

				Phone	Fax
Monogram Biosciences Inc 345 Oyster Pt Blvd	South San Francisco	CA	94080	650-635-1100	635-1111
TF: 800-777-0177 ■ Web: www.monogrambio.com					
MPD Inc 316 E Ninth St	Owensboro	KY	42303	270-685-6200	685-6494
TF: 866-225-5673 ■ Web: www.mpdinc.com					
NanoDrop Technologies LLC 3411 Silverside Rd Bancroft Bldg	Wilmington	DE	19810	302-479-7707	
Web: www.nanodrop.com					
New Objective Inc Two Constitution Way	Woburn	MA	01801	781-933-9560	
Web: www.newobjective.com					
Nor-Cal Controls Inc 1952 Concourse Dr	San Jose	CA	95131	408-435-0400	
Web: www.norcal4air.com					
Noran Instruments Inc 5225 Verona Rd	Madison	WI	53711	608-276-6100	273-5045
Web: www.thermofisher.com/en/home.html					
Nova Biomedical Corp 200 Prospect St	Waltham	MA	02454	781-894-0800	894-5915
TF Sales: 800-458-5813 ■ Web: www.novabiomedical.com					
NOVA R & D Inc 1525 Third St Ste C	Riverside	CA	92507	951-781-7332	
Web: www.novarad.com					
NucSafe Inc 601 Oak Ridge Tpke	Oak Ridge	TN	37830	865-220-5050	
Web: www.nucsafe.com					
OI Corp 151 Graham Rd PO Box 9010	College Station	TX	77842	979-690-1711	690-0440
TF: 800-653-1711 ■ Web: www.oico.com					
Olis Inc 130 Conway Dr Ste A B & C	Bogart	GA	30622	706-353-6547	353-1972
TF: 800-852-3504 ■ Web: www.olisweb.com					
Pall Life Sciences 600 S Wagner Rd	Ann Arbor	MI	48103	734-665-0651	913-6495
TF: 800-521-1520 ■ Web: www.pall.com					
PANalytical Inc 117 Flanders Rd	Westborough	MA	01581	508-647-1100	
Web: www.panalytical.com					
Particle Measuring Systems Inc 5475 Airport Blvd	Boulder	CO	80301	303-443-7100	449-6870
TF Cust Svc: 800-238-1801 ■ Web: www.pmeasuring.com					
PerkinElmer Inc 940 Winter St	Waltham	MA	02451	203-925-4602	944-4904
NYSE: PKI ■ Web: www.perkinelmer.com					
Petroleum Analyzer Company LP 8824 Fallbrook Dr	Houston	TX	77064	281-940-1803	
Web: www.paclp.com					
Phenomenex Inc 411 Madrid Ave	Torrance	CA	90501	310-212-0555	328-7768
Web: www.phenomenex.com					
Photo Research Inc 9731 Topanga Canyon Pl	Chatsworth	CA	91311	818-341-5151	725-9770
TF: 877-424-6423 ■ Web: www.photoresearch.com					
Physical Electronics Inc 18725 Lake Dr E	Chanhassen	MN	55317	952-828-6100	828-6451
TF: 800-328-7515 ■ Web: www.phi.com					
Picarro Inc 480 Oakmead Pkwy	Sunnyvale	CA	94085	408-962-3900	
Web: www.picarro.com					
Qualigen Inc 2042 Corte Del Nogal	Carlsbad	CA	92011	760-918-9165	
Web: www.qualigeninc.com					
Quantum Design Inc 6325 Lusk Blvd	San Diego	CA	92121	858-481-4400	
Web: www.qdusa.com					
QUEST Integrated Inc 19823 58th Pl S	Kent	WA	98032	253-872-9500	
Web: www.qi2.com					
Real-Time Laboratories LLC 990 S Rogers Cir Ste 5	Boca Raton	FL	33487	561-988-8826	
Web: www.real-timelabs.com					
Response Biomedical Corp 1781 75th Ave W	Vancouver	BC	V6P6P2	604-456-6010	456-6066
TSE: RBM ■ TF: 888-591-5577 ■ Web: www.responsebio.com					
Sakura Finetek USA Inc 1750 W 214th St	Torrance	CA	90501	310-972-7800	972-7888
TF: 800-725-8723 ■ Web: www.sakura-americas.com					
Schroer Manufacturing Co 511 Osage Ave	Kansas City	KS	66105	913-281-1500	
TF: 800-444-1579 ■ Web: www.shor-line.com					
Scientific Industries Inc 70 Orville Dr	Bohemia	NY	11716	631-567-4700	
TF: 888-850-6208 ■ Web: www.scientificindustries.com					
SEER Technology Inc 2681 Parleys Way Ste 201	Salt Lake City	UT	84109	801-746-7888	
TF: 877-505-7337 ■ Web: www.seertechnology.com					
Senova Systems Inc 1230 Bordeaux Dr	Sunnyvale	CA	94089	415-324-8505	
Web: www.senovasystems.com					
Sentry Equipment Corp 966 Blue Ribbon Cir N	Oconomowoc	WI	53066	262-567-7256	567-4523
Web: www.sentry-equip.com					
Sheldon Laboratory Systems Inc 102 Kirk St PO Box 836	Crystal Springs	MS	39059	601-892-2731	
Web: www.sheldonlabs.com					
Shimadzu Scientific Instruments Inc 7102 Riverwood Dr	Columbia	MD	21046	410-381-1227	381-1222
TF: 800-477-1227 ■ Web: www.ssi.shimadzu.com					
Siskiyou Corp 110 Sw Booth St	Grants Pass	OR	97526	541-479-8697	
Web: www.siskiyou.com					
Smart Imaging Technologies Inc 1770 Saint James Pl Ste 414	Houston	TX	77056	713-589-3500	
Web: www.smartimtech.com					
Soilmoisture Equipment Corp 801 S Kellogg Ave	Goleta	CA	93117	805-964-3525	
TF: 888-964-0040 ■ Web: www.soilmoisture.com					
SonoPlot Inc 3030 Laura Ln Ste 120	Middleton	WI	53562	608-824-9311	
Web: www.sonoplot.com					
Soquelec Ltd 5757 Cavendish Blvd Ste 540	Montreal	QC	H4W2W8	514-482-6427	482-1929
Web: www.soquelec.com					
Sparton Corp 425 N Martingale Rd Ste 2050	Schaumburg	IL	60173	847-762-5800	
Web: sparton.com					
Spectech 106 Union Vly Rd	Oak Ridge	TN	37830	865-482-9948	
Web: www.spectrumtechniques.com					
Spectra Analysis Inc 257 Simarano Dr	Marlborough	MA	01752	508-281-6232	
Web: www.spectra-analysis.com					
Spectra Services Inc 6359 Dean Pkwy	Ontario	NY	14519	585-265-4320	
Web: www.spectraservices.com					
Spectro Inc One Executive Dr Ste 101	Chelmsford	MA	01824	978-486-0123	
Web: spectrosci.com/					
Spectrum Laboratories Inc 18617 Broadwick St	Rancho Dominguez	CA	90220	310-885-4600	885-4666
TF: 800-634-3300 ■ Web: www.spectrumlabs.com					
Spectrum Systems Inc 3410 W Nine-Mile Rd	Pensacola	FL	32526	850-944-3392	944-1011
TF: 800-432-6119 ■ Web: spectrumsystems.com					
STARR Life Sciences Corp 333 Alegheney Ave Ste 300	Oakmont	PA	15139	866-978-2779	
TF: 866-978-2779 ■ Web: www.starrlifesciences.com					
Stellarnet Inc 14390 Carlson Cir	Tampa	FL	33626	813-855-8687	
Web: www.stellarnet-inc.com					
Supelco Inc 595 N Harrison Rd	Bellefonte	PA	16823	814-359-3441	325-5052*
*Fax Area Code: 800 ■ TF: 800-247-6628 ■ Web: www.sigmaaldrich.com					
Supercritical Fluid Technologies Inc One Innovation Way	Newark	DE	19711	302-738-3420	
Web: www.supercriticalfluids.com					
TA Instruments Inc 159 Lukens Dr	New Castle	DE	19720	302-427-4000	
Web: www.tainstruments.com					
Techne Inc Three Terri Ln Ste 10	Burlington	NJ	08016	609-589-2560	
Web: www.techneusa.com					
Tekran Instruments Corp 230 Tech Ctr Dr	Knoxville	TN	37912	865-688-0688	
TF: 888-383-5726 ■ Web: www.tekran.com					
Teledyne Instruments Inc 16830 Chestnut St	City Of Industry	CA	91748	626-934-1500	
Web: www.teledyne-ai.com					
Teledyne Leeman Labs Inc Six Wentworth Dr	Hudson	NH	03051	603-886-8400	
Web: www.teledyneleemanlabs.com					
Teledyne Tekmar Company Inc 4736 Socialville Foster Rd	Mason	OH	45040	513-229-7000	
Web: www.teledynetekmar.com					
Temptronic Corp 41 Hampden Rd	Mansfield	MA	02048	781-688-2300	688-2301*
*Fax: Sales ■ TF Tech Support: 800-558-5080 ■ Web: www.temptronic.com					
Thermo Fisher Scientific Inc 81 Wyman St PO Box 9046	Waltham	MA	02454	781-622-1000	622-1207
NYSE: TMO ■ TF: 800-678-5599 ■ Web: www.thermofisher.com					
Thinky USA 23151 Verdugo Dr	Laguna Hills	CA	92653	949-768-9001	
Web: www.janustechsales.com					
Thoren Caging Systems Inc 815 W Seventh St	Hazleton	PA	18201	570-455-5041	
Web: www.thoren.com					
Toptica Photonics Inc 1286 Blossom Dr Ste 1	Victor	NY	14564	585-657-6663	
TF: 877-277-9897 ■ Web: www.toptica.com					
Transgenomic Inc 12325 Emmet St	Omaha	NE	68164	402-452-5400	452-5401
OTC: TBIO ■ TF: 888-233-9283 ■ Web: www.transgenomic.com					
Upchurch Scientific Inc 619 Oak St	Oak Harbor	WA	98277	866-339-4653	
TF: 866-339-4653 ■ Web: www.idex-hs.com					
Vernier Software & Technology LLC 13979 SW Millikan Way	Beaverton	OR	97005	503-277-2299	
Web: www.vernier.com					
WaferGen Bio-systems Inc 7400 Paseo Padre Pkwy	Fremont	CA	94555	510-651-4450	
Web: www.wafergen.com					
Waters Corp 34 Maple St	Milford	MA	01757	508-478-2000	872-1990
NYSE: WAT ■ TF: 800-252-4752 ■ Web: www.waters.com					
Westco Scientific Instruments Inc 117 Old State Rd Ste 1	Brookfield	CT	06804	203-740-2999	
Web: westcoscientific.com					
Wilks Enterprise Inc 25 Van Zant St Ste 8F	East Norwalk	CT	06855	203-855-9136	
Web: www.wilksir.com					
X-ray Instrumentation Associates 8450 Central Ave	Newark	CA	94560	510-494-9020	
Web: www.xia.com					
XiGo Nanotools Inc 116 Research Dr Ste 39	Bethlehem	PA	18015	610-849-5090	
Web: www.xigonanotools.com					
ZAPS Technologies Inc 4314 SW Research Way	Corvallis	OR	97333	541-207-1122	
Web: www.zapstechnologies.com					
ZTR Control Systems Inc 8050 County Rd 101 East	Minneapolis	MN	55379	855-724-5987	
Web: www.ztr.com					

423 LABORATORY APPARATUS & FURNITURE

SEE ALSO Glassware - Laboratory & Scientific p. 2358; Laboratory Analytical Instruments p. 2617; Scales & Balances p. 3134

				Phone	Fax
Baker Company Inc 161 Gatehouse Rd PO Box E	Sanford	ME	04073	207-324-8773	324-3869
TF: 800-992-2537 ■ Web: www.bakerco.com					
Bel-Art Products Inc Six Industrial Rd	Pequannock	NJ	07440	973-694-0500	694-7199
TF: 800-423-5278 ■ Web: www.belart.com					
Boekel Scientific 855 Pennsylvania Blvd	Feasterville	PA	19053	215-396-8200	396-8264
TF: 800-336-6929 ■ Web: www.boekelsci.com					
Caliper Life Sciences Inc 68 Elm St	Hopkinton	MA	01748	508-435-9500	435-3439
TF: 800-762-4000 ■ Web: www.perkinelmer.com					
Cole-Parmer Instrument Co 625 E Bunker Ct	Vernon Hills	IL	60061	847-549-7600	247-2929
TF: 800-323-4340 ■ Web: www.coleparmer.com					
Comet Technologies Inc 3400 Gilchrist Rd	Akron	OH	44260	330-798-4800	784-9854
Web: www.yxlon.com					
Corning Inc Life Sciences Div 836 N St Bldg 300 Ste 3401	Tewksbury	MA	01876	978-442-2200	635-2476
TF: 800-492-1110 ■ Web: www.corning.com/lifesciences					
Durcon Co 8464 Ronda Dr	Canton	MI	48187	734-455-4520	
Web: www.durcon.com					
Edstrom Industries Inc 819 Bakke Ave	Waterford	WI	53185	262-534-5181	534-5184
TF: 800-558-5913 ■ Web: www.edstrom.com					
Ets-Lindgren LP 1301 Arrow Pt Dr	Cedar Park	TX	78613	512-531-6400	531-6500
Web: www.ets-lindgren.com					
Ika-Works Inc 2635 Northchase Pkwy SE	Wilmington	NC	28405	910-452-7059	452-7693
TF: 800-733-3037 ■ Web: www.ika.com					
Infolab Inc 17400 Hwy 61 N	Clarksdale	MS	38614	662-627-2283	627-1913
Kalamazoo Technical Furniture 6450 Vly Industrial Dr	Kalamazoo	MI	49009	800-832-5227	
TF: 800-832-5227 ■ Web: www.teclab.com					
Kewaunee Scientific Corp 2700 W Front St PO Box 1842	Statesville	NC	28687	704-873-7202	873-5160*
NASDAQ: KEQU ■ *Fax: Sales ■ TF: 800-824-6626 ■ Web: www.kewaunee.com					

				Phone	Fax
Knf Neuberger Inc 2 Black Forest Rd. *TF:* 800-323-4340 ■ *Web:* www.knf.com	Trenton	NJ	08691	609-890-8600	890-2838
Koch Modular Process Systems LLC 45 Eisenhower Dr *Web:* www.modularprocess.com	Paramus	NJ	07652	201-368-2929	368-8989
Lab Fabricators Co 1802 E 47th St *Web:* www.labfabricators.com	Cleveland	OH	44103	216-431-5444	431-5447
Labconco Corp 8811 Prospect Ave *TF Cust Svc:* 800-821-5525 ■ *Web:* www.labconco.com	Kansas City	MO	64132	816-333-8811	363-0130
Nalge Nunc International 75 Panorama Creek Dr *TF:* 800-625-4327 ■ *Web:* www.thermoscientific.com	Rochester	NY	14625	585-586-8800	586-3294
New Brunswick Scientific Company Inc 44 Talmadge Rd PO Box 4005 *TF Cust Svc:* 800-631-5417 ■ *Web:* www.nbsc.com	Edison	NJ	08818	732-287-1200	287-4222
Omnicell Inc 1201 Charleston Rd. *NASDAQ: OMCL* ■ *TF:* 800-850-6664 ■ *Web:* www.omnicell.com	Mountain View	CA	94043	650-251-6100	251-6266
Pacific Combustion Engineering Co 2107 Border Ave *TF:* 800-342-4442 ■ *Web:* www.pacificcombustion.com	Torrance	CA	90501	310-212-6300	212-5333
Parr Instrument Co 211 53rd St *TF:* 800-872-7720 ■ *Web:* www.parrinst.com	Moline	IL	61265	309-762-7716	762-9453
Parter Medical Products Inc 17015 Kingsview Ave *TF:* 800-666-8282 ■ *Web:* www.partermedical.com	Carson	CA	90746	310-327-4417	327-8601
Percival Scientific Inc 505 Research Dr *TF:* 800-695-2743 ■ *Web:* www.percival-scientific.com	Perry	IA	50220	515-465-9363	465-9464
Preston Industries Inc 6600 W Touhy Ave *TF:* 800-229-7569 ■ *Web:* www.polyscience.com	Niles	IL	60714	847-647-0611	647-1155
Samco Scientific Corp 81 WYMAN ST PO Box 9046 **Fax Area Code:* 818 ■ *TF:* 800-522-3359 ■ *Web:* www.thermoscientific.com	Waltham	MA	02451	781-622-1000	838-2488*
SKC Inc 863 Vly View Rd *Web:* www.skcinc.com	Eighty Four	PA	15330	724-941-9701	941-1369
Thermo Fisher Scientific Inc 81 Wyman St PO Box 9046 *NYSE: TMO* ■ *TF:* 800-678-5599 ■ *Web:* www.thermofisher.com	Waltham	MA	02454	781-622-1000	622-1207
ThermoGenesis Corp 2711 Citrus Rd *NASDAQ: KOOL* ■ *TF:* 800-783-8357 ■ *Web:* cescatherapeutics.com/	Rancho Cordova	CA	95742	916-858-5100	858-5199
Thomas Scientific 1654 High Hill Rd PO Box 99 *TF:* 800-345-2100 ■ *Web:* www.thomassci.com	Swedesboro	NJ	08085	856-467-2000	467-3087
Valley City Mfg Co Ltd, The 64 Hatt St *TF:* 800-306-3319 ■ *Web:* www.valleycity.com	Dundas	ON	L9H2G3	905-628-2253	628-0753

424 LADDERS

				Phone	Fax
ALACO Ladder Co 5167 G St *TF:* 888-310-7040 ■ *Web:* www.alacoladder.com	Chino	CA	91710	909-591-7561	591-7565
Ballymore Co 501 Gunnard Carlson Dr *TF:* 800-762-8327 ■ *Web:* www.ballymore.com	Coatesville	PA	19365	610-593-5062	593-8615
Cotterman Co 130 Seltzer Rd *TF:* 800-552-3337 ■ *Web:* www.cotterman.com	Croswell	MI	48422	810-679-4400	679-4510
Duo-Safety Ladder Corp 513 W Ninth Ave *Web:* www.duosafety.com	Oshkosh	WI	54902	920-231-2740	231-2460
Lynn Ladder & Scaffolding Company Inc 20 Boston St *TF:* 800-225-2510 ■ *Web:* www.lynnladder.com	Lynn	MA	01904	781-598-6010	593-2915
Putnam Rolling Ladder Inc 32 Howard St *Web:* www.putnamrollingladder.com	New York	NY	10013	212-226-5147	941-1836
Werner Co 93 Werner Rd *TF:* 888-523-3371 ■ *Web:* us.wernerco.com	Greenville	PA	16125	888-523-3371	456-8459
Wing Enterprises Inc 1198 N Spring Creek *TF:* 866-872-5901 ■ *Web:* littlegiantladders.com	Springville	UT	84663	801-489-3684	489-3685

425 LANDSCAPE DESIGN & RELATED SERVICES

				Phone	Fax
Annco Services Inc 8892 152nd Pl S *Web:* www.anncoservices.com	Delray Beach	FL	33446	561-638-2540	638-3993
Artistic Maintenance Inc 23676 Birtcher Dr *TF General:* 800-698-9834 ■ *Web:* www.artisticmaintenance.com	Lake Forest	CA	92630	949-581-9817	581-0436
Brickman Group Ltd 375 S Flowers Mill Rd *Web:* brickman.com/	Langhorne	PA	19047	215-757-9400	891-1259
Cagwin & Dorward Inc 1565 S Novato Blvd Ste B *TF:* 800-891-7710 ■ *Web:* www.cagwin.com	Novato	CA	94947	415-892-7710	897-7864
Chapel Valley Landscape Co 3275 Jennings Chapel Rd PO Box 159 *Web:* www.chapelvalley.com	Woodbine	MD	21797	301-924-5400	854-6390
Creative Environments 8920 S Hardy Dr *TF:* 855-777-9305 ■ *Web:* www.creativeenvironments.com	Tempe	AZ	85284	480-458-4100	777-9296
D Schumacher Landscaping Inc 635 Manley St *Web:* www.dschumacher.com	West Bridgewater	MA	02379	508-427-7707	427-7714
Davids Clarence & Co 22901 S Ridgeland Ave *Web:* www.clarencedavids.com	Matteson	IL	60443	708-720-4100	720-4200
Environmental Earthscapes Inc 5075 S Swan Rd *TF:* 800-571-1575 ■ *Web:* www.groundskeeper.com	Tucson	AZ	85706	520-571-1575	750-7480
Golden Bear International Inc 11780 US Hwy 1 *Web:* www.nicklaus.com	North Palm Beach	FL	33408	561-626-3900	227-0302
Hindsdale Nurseries Inc 7200 S Madison Rd *Web:* www.hinsdalenurseries.com	Willowbrook	IL	60527	630-323-1411	323-0918
Horizon Distributors Inc 261 N Roosevelt Ave *Web:* www.horizononline.com	Chandler	AZ	85226	480-337-6750	337-6701
Jensen Corp 1983 Concourse Dr *Web:* www.jensencorp.com	San Jose	CA	95131	408-446-1118	446-4881
Landscape Concepts Management 31745 Alleghany Rd *TF:* 866-655-3800 ■ *Web:* www.landscapeconcepts.com	Grayslake	IL	60030	847-223-3800	223-0169
Landscape Development Inc 28447 Witherspoon Pkwy *Web:* www.landscapedevelopment.com	Valencia	CA	91355	661-295-1970	295-1969
Lied's Landscape Design & Construction N63 W22039 Hwy 74 *Web:* www.lieds.com/design	Sussex	WI	53089	262-246-6901	246-3569
Lipinski Landscape & Irrigation Contractors Inc 100 Sharp Rd **Fax Area Code:* 856 ■ *TF:* 800-644-6035 ■ *Web:* www.meritservicesolutions.com	Marlton	NJ	08053	800-644-6035	983-0500*
LMI Landscapes Inc 1437 Halsey Way *Web:* www.lmilandscapes.com	Carrollton	TX	75007	972-446-0020	446-0028
Mariani Enterprises Inc 300 Rockland Rd *Web:* www.marianilandscape.com	Lake Bluff	IL	60044	847-234-2172	234-2754
Mariposa Horticultural Enterprises Inc 15529 Arrow Hwy *Web:* mariposa-ca.com	Irwindale	CA	91706	626-960-0196	960-8477
Mission Landscape Services Inc 536 E Dyer Rd **Fax Area Code:* 714 ■ *TF:* 800-545-9963 ■ *Web:* www.missionlandscape.com	Santa Ana	CA	92707	800-545-9963	668-0119*
Park West Cos Inc 22421 Gilberto Ste A *Web:* www.parkwestlandscape.com	Rancho Santa Margarita	CA	92688	949-546-8300	546-8301
Peoria Landscaping Company Inc 2700 W Cedar Hills Dr *Web:* www.greenview.com	Dunlap	IL	61525	309-243-7761	243-9235
Schrickel Rollins & Assoc Inc 1161 Corporate Dr W Ste 200 *Web:* www.sradesign.com	Arlington	TX	76006	817-649-3216	649-7645
Spectrum Care Landscape 27181 Burbank *Web:* www.spectrumcarelandscape.com	Foothill Ranch	CA	92610	949-454-6900	454-6910
Summit Landscape Services Inc 12452 Cutten Rd *Web:* www.summitls.com	Houston	TX	77066	281-583-7900	583-7994
SWA Group 2200 Bridgeway Blvd *Web:* www.swagroup.com	Sausalito	CA	94965	415-332-5100	332-0719
Teufel Nursery Inc 3431 NW John Olsen Pl *TF:* 800-483-8335 ■ *Web:* www.teufellandscape.com	Hillsboro	OR	97124	503-646-1111	646-1112
Turf Management Systems LLC PO Box 26389 *Web:* www.turfmanagementsystems.com	Birmingham	AL	35260	205-979-8604	979-6063
Underwood Bros 3747 E Southern Ave *Web:* www.aaalandscape.com	Phoenix	AZ	85040	602-437-2690	437-2970
US Lawns 4700 Millenia Blvd Ste 240 **Fax Area Code:* 407 ■ *TF:* 800-875-2967 ■ *Web:* www.uslawns.com	Orlando	FL	32839	800-875-2967	246-1623*
ValleyCrest Cos 24151 Ventura Blvd. *Web:* www.valleycrest.com	Calabasas	CA	91302	818-223-8500	223-8142

426 LANGUAGE SCHOOLS

SEE ALSO Translation Services p. 3249

				Phone	Fax
Access International Business Institute 609 E Liberty St *Web:* www.accessesl.org	Ann Arbor	MI	48104	734-994-1456	994-7341
Agape English Language Institute (AELI) 610 Pickens St PO Box 12504 *TF:* 877-476-2354 ■ *Web:* www.aeliusa.com	Columbia	SC	29201	803-799-3452	252-5500
American Academy of English 530 Golden Gate Ave *Web:* www.aae.edu	San Francisco	CA	94102	415-567-0189	567-1475
American Language Communication Ctr 229 W 36th St *TF:* 800-364-5474 ■ *Web:* www.learnenglish.com	New York	NY	10018	212-736-2373	947-6403
AmeriSpan Unlimited 1334 Walnut St 6 Fl *TF:* 800-879-6640 ■ *Web:* www.amerispan.com	Philadelphia	PA	19107	215-751-1100	751-1986
Berlitz Languages Inc 400 Alexander Pk *Web:* www.berlitz.com	Princeton	NJ	08540	609-524-2514	514-9689
Boston Academy of English 38 Chauncy St Eighth Fl **Fax Area Code:* 617 ■ *TF:* 800-704-9313 ■ *Web:* www.bostonacademyofenglish.com	Boston	MA	02111	800-704-9313	695-9349*
Boston Academy of English inc 38 Chauncy St 8th Fl **Fax Area Code:* 617 ■ *TF:* 800-704-9313 ■ *Web:* bostonacademyofenglish.com	Boston	MA	02111	800-704-9313	695-9349*
Brandon College 944 Market St 2nd Fl *Web:* www.brandoncollege.com	San Francisco	CA	94102	415-391-5711	391-3918
Colorado School of English 331 14th St Ste 3 *Web:* www.englishamerica.com	Denver	CO	80202	720-932-8900	932-0315
Converse International School of Languages 636 Broadway Ste 210 *Web:* www.cisl.edu	San Diego	CA	92101	619-239-3363	239-3778
Cultural Ctr for Language Studies 3191 Coral Way Ste 114 *TF:* 800-704-8181 ■ *Web:* www.cclscorp.com	Miami	FL	33145	305-529-2257	443-8538
Diplomatic Language Services LLC 1901 N Ft Myer Dr Sixth Fl *TF:* 800-642-7974 ■ *Web:* dlsdc.com	Arlington	VA	22209	703-243-4855	243-7003
EC Boston 729 Boylston St *Web:* www.ecenglish.com	Boston	MA	02116	617-247-3033	247-2959
ELS Language Centers 7 Roszel Rd *TF:* 800-468-8978 ■ *Web:* www.els.edu	Princeton	NJ	08540	609-759-5500	750-3599
Embassy CES 328 Seventh Ave 6th Fl *Web:* embassyenglish.com/	New York	NY	10001	212-629-7300	497-0045
English Connection Inc 77 Railroad Pl *Web:* esldirectory.com	Saratoga Springs	NY	12866	518-581-1478	
English Language Ctr Inc (ELC) 11 Beacon St Fl 2 *Web:* www.elc.edu	Boston	MA	02108	617-536-9788	536-5789
ESL Instruction & Consulting Inc 42 Broad St NW *TF:* 877-579-2366 ■ *Web:* www.eslinstruction.com	Atlanta	GA	30303	404-577-2366	577-2360

				Phone	Fax
Global Village English Centres 888 Cambie St *Web:* www.gvenglish.com	Vancouver	BC	V6B2P6	604-684-1118	684-1117
Human International Academy 123 Camino de la Reina W-200 *Web:* www.hiausa.com	San Diego	CA	92108	619-501-8091	501-9027
ILSC Education Group Inc, The 555 Richards St *Web:* www.ilsc.ca	Vancouver	BC	V6B2Z5	604-689-9095	
inlingua International 551 Fifth Ave Ste 1625 *Web:* www.inlinguametrony.com	New York	NY	10017	212-682-8585	599-0977
Intercultural Communications College 810 Richards St Ste 200 *TF:* 800-545-2078 ■ *Web:* www.icchawaii.edu	Honolulu	HI	96813	808-946-2445	946-2231
International Ctr for Language Studies Inc 1133 15th St NW Ste 600 *TF:* 800-626-2427 ■ *Web:* www.icls.com	Washington	DC	20005	202-639-8800	783-6587
International English Institute 640 Spence Ln Ste 121 *Web:* www.iei.edu	Nashville	TN	37217	615-327-1715	399-9799
International House Vancouver 1215 W Broadway Ste 2001 *Web:* www.ihvancouver.com	Vancouver	BC	V6H1G7	604-739-9836	739-9839
International Language Institute 1337 Connecticut Ave NW 4th Fl *Web:* www.transemantics.com	Washington	DC	20036	202-362-2505	686-5603
Internexus 220 South 200 East Ste 200 *Web:* www.internexus.to	Salt Lake City	UT	84111	801-487-2499	487-2198
Intrax International Institute 600 California St 10th Fl *Web:* www.intrax.edu	San Francisco	CA	94108	415-434-1221	434-5404
Lado International College 401 Ninth St NW Ste C100 *Web:* www.lado.com	Washington	DC	20004	202-223-0023	337-1118
Language Academy 200 S Andrews Ave Ste 100 *Web:* www.languageacademy.com	Fort Lauderdale	FL	33301	954-462-8373	462-3738
Language Co 189 W 15th St *Web:* www.thelanguagecompany.com	Edmond	OK	73013	405-715-9996	715-1116
Language Door LLC 11870 Santa Monica Blvd Ste 202 *Web:* www.languagedoor.com	Los Angeles	CA	90025	310-826-4140	
Language Exchange International 500 NE Spanish River Blvd Ste 19 *TF:* 800-223-5836 ■ *Web:* www.languageexchange.com	Boca Raton	FL	33431	561-368-3913	368-9380
Language Pacifica 585 Glenwood Ave *Web:* www.languagepacifica.com	Menlo Park	CA	94025	650-321-1840	321-2510
Language Plus Inc 4110 Rio Bravo Ste 202 *Web:* www.languageplus.com	El Paso	TX	79902	915-544-8600	544-8640
Language Studies Canada 124 Eglinton Ave W Ste 400 *Web:* www.ecenglish.com	Toronto	ON	M4R2G8	416-488-2200	488-2225
Language Studies International 1706 Fifth Ave Third Fl *Web:* www.lsi.edu	San Diego	CA	92101	619-234-2881	234-2883
Lingua School Inc 225 E Las Olas Blvd Sixth Fl *TF:* 888-654-6482 ■ *Web:* www.linguaschool.com	Fort Lauderdale	FL	33301	954-577-9955	577-9977
Michigan Language Ctr 309 S State St *Web:* www.englishclasses.com	Ann Arbor	MI	48107	734-663-9415	663-9623
New England School of English 36 John F Kennedy St *Web:* www.nese.com	Cambridge	MA	02138	617-864-7170	864-7282
Nomen Global Language Centers 384 W Ctr St *Web:* www.nomenglobal.com	Provo	UT	84601	801-377-3223	377-3993
Pacific Language Institute 755 Burrard St Ste 300 *Web:* kaplaninternational.ca/	Vancouver	BC	V6Z1X6	604-688-8330	688-0638
POLY Languages Institute Inc (POLY) 5757 Wilshire Blvd Ste 510 *TF:* 877-738-5787 ■ *Web:* www.polylanguages.com	Los Angeles	CA	90036	323-933-9399	686-5384
Rennert Bilingual 216 E 45th St *Web:* www.rennert.com	New York	NY	10017	212-867-8700	867-7666
Rosemead College of English 8705 E Valley Blvd *Web:* www.rosemeadcollege.edu	Rosemead	CA	91770	626-285-9668	285-1351
Tamwood International College 300-909 Burrard St *Web:* www.tamwood.com	Vancouver	BC	V6Z2N2	604-899-4480	899-4481
University Language Institute 2448 E 81st St Ste 1400 *Web:* www.uli.net	Tulsa	OK	74137	918-493-8088	493-8084
Wisconsin English as a Second Language Institute 19 N Pinckney St *Web:* www.wesli.com	Madison	WI	53703	608-257-4300	257-4346
Zoni Language Centers 22 W 34th St *Web:* www.zoni.com	New York	NY	10001	212-736-9000	947-8030

427 LASER EQUIPMENT & SYSTEMS - MEDICAL

SEE ALSO Medical Instruments & Apparatus - Mfr p. 2729

				Phone	Fax
BioLase Technology Inc Four Cromwell *TF:* 800-699-9462 ■ *Web:* www.biolase.com	Irvine	CA	92618	888-424-6527	
Candela Corp 530 Boston Post Rd *NASDAQ: CLZR* ■ *TF:* 800-733-8550 ■ *Web:* syneron-candela.com	Wayland	MA	01778	508-358-7400	358-5602
Convergent Laser Technologies 1660 S Loop Rd *TF:* 800-848-8200 ■ *Web:* www.convergentlaser.com	Alameda	CA	94502	510-832-2130	832-1600
Cynosure Inc Five Carlisle Rd *NASDAQ: CYNO* ■ *TF:* 800-886-2966 ■ *Web:* www.cynosure.com	Westford	MA	01886	978-256-4200	256-6556
Iridex Corp 1212 Terra Bella Ave *NASDAQ: IRIX* ■ *TF Cust Svc:* 800-388-4747 ■ *Web:* www.iridex.com	Mountain View	CA	94043	650-940-4700	940-4710
Laserscope 3070 Orchard Dr **Fax:* Sales ■ *TF:* 800-878-3399 ■ *Web:* fundinguniverse.com	San Jose	CA	95134	408-943-0636	943-1051*
LaserSight Technologies Inc 931 S Semoran Blvd	Winter Park	FL	32792	407-678-9900	
Lumenis Ltd 2033 Gateway Pl Ste 200 *TF:* 877-586-3647 ■ *Web:* www.lumenis.com	San Jose	CA	95110	408-764-3000	764-3999
Palomar Medical Technologies Inc 15 Network Dr *NASDAQ: PMTI* ■ *Web:* www.palmed.com	Burlington	MA	01803	781-993-2300	993-2330
PhotoMedex Inc 147 Keystone Dr *NASDAQ: PHMD* ■ *TF:* 800-366-4758 ■ *Web:* www.photomedex.com	Montgomeryville	PA	18936	215-619-3600	619-3208
PLC Medical Systems Inc 459 Fortune Blvd *Web:* www.renalguard.com	Milford	MA	01757	508-541-8800	541-7980
Spectranetics Corp 9965 Federal Dr *NASDAQ: SPNC* ■ *TF:* 800-231-0978 ■ *Web:* www.spectranetics.com	Colorado Springs	CO	80921	719-447-2000	447-2022
Trimedyne Inc 15091 Bake Pkwy *OTC: TMED* ■ *TF:* 800-733-5273 ■ *Web:* www.trimedyne.com	Irvine	CA	92618	949-559-5300	855-8206

428 LASERS - INDUSTRIAL

				Phone	Fax
AGL Corp 2202 N Redmond Rd PO Box 189 *TF:* 800-643-9696 ■ *Web:* agl-lasers.com	Jacksonville	AR	72076	501-982-4433	982-0880
Baublys Control Laser Corp 7101 Tpc Dr Ste 100 *Web:* www.controllaser.com	Orlando	FL	32822	407-926-3500	926-3590
Coherent Inc 5100 Patrick Henry Dr *NASDAQ: COHR* ■ *TF Sales:* 800-527-3786 ■ *Web:* www.coherent.com	Santa Clara	CA	95054	408-764-4000	764-4000
Continuum 3150 Central Expy *TF:* 888-532-1064 ■ *Web:* www.continuumlasers.com	Santa Clara	CA	95051	408-727-3240	727-3550
Cymer Inc 17075 Thornmint Ct *NASDAQ: CYMI* ■ *Web:* www.cymer.com	San Diego	CA	92127	858-385-7300	385-7100
Electro Scientific Industries Inc 13900 NW Science Pk Dr *NASDAQ: ESIO* ■ **Fax:* Claims ■ *TF Cust Svc:* 800-331-4708 ■ *Web:* esi.com	Portland	OR	97229	503-641-4141	671-5544*
Ionatron Inc 3590 E Columbia St *OTC: AERG* ■ *Web:* www.appliedenergetics.com	Tucson	AZ	85714	520-628-7415	622-3835
IPG Photonics Corp 50 Old Webster Rd *NASDAQ: IPGP* ■ *TF:* 877-980-1550 ■ *Web:* www.ipgphotonics.com	Oxford	MA	01540	508-373-1100	373-1103
Isomet Corp 5263 Port Royal Rd *OTC: IOMT* ■ *Web:* www.isomet.com	Springfield	VA	22151	703-321-8301	321-8546
Jodon Engineering 62 Enterprise Dr *Web:* www.jodon.com	Ann Arbor	MI	48103	734-761-4044	
Kigre Inc 100 Marshland Rd *Web:* www.kigre.com	Hilton Head Island	SC	29926	843-681-5800	681-4559
Laser Excel N6323 Berlin Rd PO Box 279 *TF:* 800-285-6544 ■ *Web:* www.laserexcel.com	Green Lake	WI	54941	920-294-6544	294-6588
Leica Geosystems Inc 3498 Kraft Ave SE *TF Sales:* 800-367-9453 ■ *Web:* www.leica-geosystems.com	Grand Rapids	MI	49512	616-977-4189	942-4627
PRIMA North America Inc 711 E Main St *Web:* www.prima-na.com	Chicopee	MA	01020	413-598-5200	
PTR-Precision Technologies Inc 120 Post Rd *Web:* www.ptreb.com	Enfield	CT	06082	860-741-2281	745-7932
Rofin-Sinar Inc 40984 Concept Dr *NASDAQ: RSTI* ■ *Web:* www.rofin.com	Plymouth	MI	48170	734-455-5400	455-5587
STI Optronics Inc 2755 Northup Way *Web:* www.stioptronics.com	Bellevue	WA	98004	425-827-0460	828-3517
Synrad Inc 4600 Campus Pl *TF:* 800-796-7231 ■ *Web:* www.synrad.com	Mukilteo	WA	98275	425-349-3500	349-3667
TRUMPF Group 111 Hyde Rd **Fax:* Mktg ■ *Web:* www.trumpf.com	Farmington	CT	06032	860-255-6000	255-6424*

429 LAUNDRY & DRYCLEANING SERVICES

SEE ALSO Linen & Uniform Supply p. 2669

				Phone	Fax
ACW Management Corp 2019 Eastchester Dr PO Box 6535 *Web:* www.acleanerworld.com	High Point	NC	27265	336-841-4188	841-4117
Admiral Inc 10 Taylor Ave *TF:* 800-864-4429 ■ *Web:* www.admiralcleaners.com	Annapolis	MD	21401	410-267-8381	263-4225
Al Phillips the Cleaner 3250 W Ali Baba Ln Ste C-F *Web:* www.alphillipslv.com	Las Vegas	NV	89118	702-798-7333	798-1731
Anton'S Cleaners Inc 500 Clark Rd *Web:* antons.com	Tewksbury	MA	01876	978-851-3721	
Apparel Finishing America 250 Belmont Ave *Web:* www.apparelgroup.org	Haledon	NJ	07508	973-942-6800	
AW Zengeler Cleaners 550 Dundee Rd *Web:* www.zengelercleaners.com	Northbrook	IL	60062	847-272-6550	272-5465
Best Cleaners Inc 265 Osborne Rd *Web:* www.bestcleanersny.com	Loudonville	NY	12211	518-459-7440	
Broadway Laundry Cleaners 548 N Broadway St *Web:* www.linenservice.com	Greenville	MS	38701	662-332-5988	
Camelot Cleaners Co 8590 Frederick St *Web:* camelotcleanersomaha.com	Omaha	NE	68124	402-393-5257	
Champion Cleaners 2548 Rocky Ridge Rd *Web:* www.championcleaners.com	Vestavia	AL	35243	205-824-7737	
Coinmach Service Corp 303 Sunnyside Blvd Ste 70 *TF:* 877-264-6622 ■ *Web:* www.coinmachservicecorp.com	Plainview	NY	11803	516-349-8555	349-9125
Concord Custom Cleaners 1183 Brock Mcvey Dr Ste A *Web:* www.concordcustomcleaners.com	Lexington	KY	40509	859-422-4800	
Consumer Textile Corp 123 N 4Th	Clinton	OK	73601	580-323-3111	

				Phone	Fax
Crown Management Services Inc 1501 N Guillemard St. *TF:* 800-844-5280 ■ *Web:* crownlaundry.com	Pensacola	FL	32501	850-438-7578	438-9395
Dependable Clrs & Shirt Ldry 101 Adams St. *Web:* www.dependablecleaners.com	Denver	CO	80206	303-322-8822	
Division Laundry & Cleaners Inc 6649 Old Hwy 90 W. *Web:* divisionlaundry.com	San Antonio	TX	78227	210-674-5110	673-8510
Dove Cleaners Inc 1560 Yonge St. *Web:* www.dovecleaners.com	Toronto	ON	M4T2S9	416-413-7900	
Dry Cleaning Depot Inc 730 W Broward Blvd. *Web:* www.drycleaningdepot.com	Fort Lauderdale	FL	33312	954-522-3660	
Dryclean USA Inc 290 NE 68th St. *Web:* www.drycleanusa.com	Miami	FL	33138	305-754-9966	754-8010
Imperial Laundry Services LLC 1236 13th St. *Web:* www.imperiallaundrysystems.com	Racine	WI	53403	262-632-7997	
Lois Inc Dba Brown'S Cleaners 1223 Montana Ave	Santa Monica	CA	90403	310-451-8531	
Marberry Cleaners & Launderers 220 John St. *Web:* www.marberrycleaners.com	North Aurora	IL	60542	630-897-0579	
Martinizing Dry Cleaning 8944 Columbia Rd Ste J. **Fax Area Code:* 513 ■ *TF:* 800-827-0207 ■ *Web:* www.martinizing.com	Loveland	OH	45140	800-827-0207	731-0818*
Model Cleaners Uniforms & Apparel LLC 100 Third St. *Web:* www.modeluniforms.com	Charleroi	PA	15022	724-489-9553	
New System Laundry LLC 432 NE 10th Ave. *Web:* www.newsystemlaundry.com	Portland	OR	97232	503-232-8181	
North Texas Health Care Laundry Cooperation Assn 1080 Post Paddock. *Web:* nthcl.org	Grand Prairie	TX	75050	469-916-1150	
Nu-Yale Cleaners 6300 Hwy 62. *TF:* 888-644-7400 ■ *Web:* www.nuyale.com	Jeffersonville	IN	47130	812-285-7400	285-7421
PAC Industries Inc 5341 Jaycee Ave. *Web:* pacindustries.com	Harrisburg	PA	17112	717-657-0407	
Pressed4Time Inc Eight Clock Tower Pl Ste 110. **Fax Area Code:* 978 ■ *TF:* 800-423-8711 ■ *Web:* www.pressed4time.com	Maynard	MA	01754	800-423-8711	823-8301*
Prestige Cleaners Inc 7536 Taggart Ln. *Web:* prestigecleanersinc.net	Knoxville	TN	37938	865-938-7701	
Pride Cleaners Inc 300 E 51st St. *Web:* www.pridecleaners.com	Kansas City	MO	64112	816-753-8481	
Robison & Smith Inc 335 N Main St. *Web:* www.robison-smith.com	Gloversville	NY	12078	518-620-3720	
Rockwood Dry Cleaners 171 Granville St. *Web:* rockwoodcleaners.com	Gahanna	OH	43230	614-471-3700	
Sloan's Dry Cleaning Inc 3001 N Main St	Los Angeles	CA	90031	323-225-1303	223-5358
Spic & Span Inc 4301 N Richards St. *Web:* www.spicandspan.com	Milwaukee	WI	53212	414-964-5050	964-5042
Spot Lite Cleaners 120 Bradley Rd. *Web:* www.spotlite.com	Madison	CT	06443	203-245-9536	
Spotless Cleaners Inc 410 Fifth St	Dunmore	PA	18512	570-346-7577	
Star Gold Cleaners Inc 200 Wilson St. *Web:* www.goldstarcleaners.com	Brewer	ME	04412	207-989-5170	
Sun Country Cleaners Inc 2240 34th Way N. *Web:* www.suncountrycleaners.com	Largo	FL	33771	727-535-9930	
Superior Health Linens LLC 5005 S Packard Ave. *Web:* www.superiorhealthlinens.com	Cudahy	WI	53110	414-769-0670	
Swan Super Cleaners Inc 1535 Bethel Rd. *Web:* www.swancleaners.com	Columbus	OH	43220	614-442-5000	442-5007
Swiss Cleaners 35 Windsor Ave. *Web:* www.swisscleaners.com	Vernon	CT	06066	860-872-0166	
Up-To-Date Laundry Inc 1221 Desoto Rd. *Web:* www.carrolltonbank.com	Baltimore	MD	21223	410-646-0475	
Zips Dry Cleaners 7500 Greenway Center Dr Ste 400. *Web:* www.321zips.com	Greenbelt	MD	20770	301-306-1100	

LAUNDRY EQUIPMENT - HOUSEHOLD

SEE Appliances - Major - Mfr p. 1744; Appliances - Whol p. 1745

430 LAUNDRY EQUIPMENT & SUPPLIES - COMMERCIAL & INDUSTRIAL

				Phone	Fax
Alliance Laundry Systems LLC PO Box 990. *Web:* www.alliancelaundry.com	Ripon	WI	54971	920-748-3121	748-4564
American Dryer Corp 88 Currant Rd. *Web:* adclaundry.com/	Fall River	MA	02720	508-678-9000	678-9447
Chicago Dryer Co 2200 N Pulaski Rd. *Web:* www.chidry.com	Chicago	IL	60639	773-235-4430	235-4439
Coinmach Service Corp 303 Sunnyside Blvd Ste 70. *TF:* 877-264-6622 ■ *Web:* www.coinmachservicecorp.com	Plainview	NY	11803	516-349-8555	349-9125
Colmac Industries Inc PO Box 72. *TF:* 800-926-5622 ■ *Web:* www.colmacind.com	Colville	WA	99114	509-684-4505	684-4500
Dexter Co 2211 W Grimes Ave. *Web:* www.dexter.com	Fairfield	IA	52556	641-472-5131	472-5131
Edro Corp 37 Commerce St. *TF Sales:* 800-628-6434 ■ *Web:* www.edrodynawash.com	East Berlin	CT	06023	860-828-0311	828-5984
Ellis Corp 1400 W Bryn Mawr Ave. *TF:* 800-611-6806 ■ *Web:* www.elliscorp.com	Itasca	IL	60143	630-250-9222	250-9241
Forenta LP 2300 W Andrew Johnson Hwy Ste A. *Web:* www.forentausa.com	Morristown	TN	37814	423-586-5370	586-3470
GA Braun Inc 461 E Brighton Ave. *TF:* 800-432-7286 ■ *Web:* www.gabraun.com	Syracuse	NY	13212	315-475-3123	475-4130
Kemco Systems Inc 11500 47th St N. *TF:* 800-633-7055 ■ *Web:* www.kemcosystems.com	Clearwater	FL	33762	727-573-2323	573-2346
Minnesota Chemical Co 2285 Hampden Ave. *TF:* 800-328-5689 ■ *Web:* www.minnesotachemical.com	Saint Paul	MN	55114	651-646-7521	649-1101
Pellerin Milnor Corp 700 Jackson St. *Web:* www.milnor.com	Kenner	LA	70062	504-467-9591	469-1849
Rema Dri-Vac Corp 45 Ruby St. *Web:* www.remadrivac.com	Norwalk	CT	06850	203-847-2464	847-3609
Thermal Engineering of Arizona Inc 2250 W Wetmore Rd. *TF:* 866-832-7278 ■ *Web:* www.teatucson.com	Tucson	AZ	85705	520-888-4000	888-4457

431 LAW FIRMS

SEE ALSO Arbitration Services - Legal p. 1747; Litigation Support Services p. 2671; Legal Professionals Associations p. 1801; Bar Associations - State p. 1859

				Phone	Fax
A Ble Advocates for Basic Legal Equality Inc 525 Jefferson Ave. *Web:* www.lawolaw.org	Toledo	OH	43604	419-255-0814	
Aafedt, Forde, Gray, Monson & Hager PA 150 S Fifth St Ste 2600. *Web:* www.aafedt.com	Minneapolis	MN	55402	612-339-8965	
Abbey, Weitzenberg, Warren & Emery PC 100 Stony Point Rd Ste 200. *Web:* www.abbeylaw.com	Santa Rosa	CA	95401	707-542-5050	
Abelson Herron Halpern LLP 333 S Grand Ave Ste 1550. *Web:* www.abelsonherron.com	Los Angeles	CA	90071	213-402-1900	
Abraham Watkins Nichols Sorrels Agosto & Friend 800 Commerce St. *Web:* abrahamwatkins.com	Houston	TX	77002	713-222-7211	
Abrahamson Uiterwyk & Barnes 2639 Mccormick Dr. *Web:* www.theinjurylawyers.com	Clearwater	FL	33759	727-797-5297	
Acadiana Legal Service Corp 1020 Surrey St. *Web:* www.la-law.org	Lafayette	LA	70501	337-237-4320	
AccessAlpha Worldwide LLC 630 Davis St Ste 201. *Web:* www.accessalpha.com	Evanston	IL	60201	847-475-6000	
Adam Moore Law Firm, The 217 N Second St. *Web:* www.adammoorelaw.com	Yakima	WA	98901	509-575-0372	
Adams Jhonson & Duncan 3128 Colby Ave. *Web:* adamslawyers.com	Everett	WA	98201	425-339-8556	
Adelberg, Rudow, Dorf & Hendler LLC Seven Saint Paul St Ste 600. *Web:* www.adelbergrudow.com	Baltimore	MD	21202	410-539-5195	
Adelsberger Donna & Associates Six Royal Ave. *Web:* dlalawyers.com	Glenside	PA	19038	215-576-8690	
Advocacy Center for Persons With Disabilities 2728 Centerview Dr Ste 102. *Web:* www.disabilityrightsflorida.org	Tallahassee	FL	32301	850-488-9071	
Ahmad, Zavitsanos, Anaipakos, Alavi & Mensing PC One Houston Ctr 1221 McKinney St Ste 3460. *Web:* www.azalaw.com	Houston	TX	77010	713-655-1101	
Ahmuty, Demers & McManus 200 IU Willets Rd. *Web:* www.admlaw.com	Albertson	NY	11507	516-294-5433	
Akerman Senterfitt One SE Third Ave 25th Fl. *Web:* www.akerman.com	Miami	FL	33131	305-374-5600	374-5095
Akin Gump Strauss Hauer & Feld LLP 1333 New Hampshire Ave NW. *Web:* www.akingump.com	Washington	DC	20036	202-887-4000	887-4288
Alan b Harris Attorney at Law 409 N Texas Ave. *Web:* alanbharris.com	Odessa	TX	79761	432-580-3118	
Albert & Mackenzie A Professional Law Corp 28348 Roadside Dr Ste 105. *Web:* www.albmac.com	Agoura Hills	CA	91301	818-575-9876	
Alex m Greenberg, Dds PC 18 E 48th St Rm 1702. *Web:* www.dralexgreenberg.com	New York	NY	10017	212-319-9700	
Alleman Hall Mccoy Russell & Tuttle LLP 806 S W Broadway Ste 600. *Web:* www.ahmrt.com	Portland	OR	97205	503-459-4141	
Allen Dell PA 202 S Rome Ave Ste 100. *Web:* www.allendell.com	Tampa	FL	33606	813-223-5351	
Allen, Summers, Simpson, Lillie & Gresham PLLC 80 Monroe Ave Ste 650. *Web:* www.allensummers.com	Memphis	TN	38103	901-763-4200	
Alpern Myers Stuart LLC 14 N Sierra Madre St Ste A. *Web:* www.coloradolawyers.net	Colorado Springs	CO	80903	719-471-7955	
Alston & Bird LLP 1201 W Peachtree St. *Web:* www.alston.com	Atlanta	GA	30309	404-881-7000	881-7777
Altschul & Altschul Inc 18 E 12th St Frnt 1. *Web:* www.altschul.biz	New York	NY	10003	212-924-1505	
Alvarez, Sambol, Winthrop & Madson PA 100 S Orange Ave. *Web:* www.awtspa.com	Orlando	FL	32801	407-210-2796	
Alverson, Taylor, Mortensen & Sanders 7401 W Charleston Blvd. *Web:* www.alversontaylor.com	Las Vegas	NV	89117	702-384-7000	
Amal Law Group LLC 7804 W College Dr. *Web:* amallaw.com	Palos Heights	IL	60463	708-361-3600	
Amato Legal Search Inc 2321 Old Maple Ct. *Web:* amatolegalsearch.com	Ellicott City	MD	21042	410-750-7550	
American LegalNet Inc 16501 Ventura Blvd Ste 615. *Web:* alncorp.com	Encino	CA	91436	818-817-9225	
Anderson H Thomas 6160 Saint Andrews Rd. *Web:* hthomasanderson.com	Columbia	SC	29212	803-798-9586	
Anderson, Julian & Hull LLP C W Moore Plz 250 S Fifth St Ste 700. *Web:* www.ajhlaw.com	Boise	ID	83707	208-344-5800	

Firm	Address	City	State	ZIP	Phone	Fax	Web
Anderson, O'Brien, Bertz, Skrenes & Golla	1257 Main St	Stevens Point	WI	54481	715-344-0890		*Web:* www.andlaw.com
Anderson, Zeigler, Disharoon, Gallagher & Gray A Professional Corp	50 Old Courthouse Sq Fifth Fl	Santa Rosa	CA	95404	707-545-4910		*Web:* www.azdgg.com
Andreou & Casson Ltd	661 W Lk St Ste 2n	Chicago	IL	60661	312-935-2001		*Web:* www.andreou-casson.com
Andrew Moore & Associates	1132 Old York Rd	Abington	PA	19001	215-885-3500		*Web:* www.andrew-moore.com
Andrews Kurth LLP	600 Travis St Chase Towers Ste 4200	Houston	TX	77002	713-220-4200	220-4285	*Web:* www.andrewskurth.com
Anglin Flewelling Rasmussen Campbell & Trytten LLP	199 S Los Robles Ste 600	Pasadena	CA	91101	626-535-1900		*Web:* www.afrct.com
Anthony Ostlund Baer & Louwagie PA	3600 Wells Fargo Bldg 90 S Seventh St	Minneapolis	MN	55402	612-349-6969		*Web:* anthonyostlund.com
Arguedas Cassman & Headley	803 Hearst Ave	Berkeley	CA	94710	510-845-3000		*Web:* www.achlaw.com
Armbrecht Jackson LLP	63 S Royal St Riverview Plz 13th Fl	Mobile	AL	36602	251-405-1300		*Web:* www.ajlaw.com
Armentor Glenn Law Corp	300 Stewart St	Lafayette	LA	70501	337-233-1471		*Web:* www.glennarmentor.com
Armstrong Donohue & Ceppos	204 Monroe St Ste 101	Rockville	MD	20850	301-251-0440		*Web:* www.adclawfirm.com
Arnold & Itkin LLP	6009 Memorial Dr	Houston	TX	77007	713-222-3800		*Web:* www.arnolditkin.com
Arnold & Porter LLP	555 12th St NW	Washington	DC	20004	202-942-5000	942-5999	*TF:* 877-470-8792 ■ *Web:* www.arnoldporter.com
Arns Law Firm, The	515 Folsom St Fl 3	San Francisco	CA	94105	415-495-7800		*Web:* www.arnslaw.com
Arthur, Chapman, Kettering, Smetak & Pikala PA	500 Young Quinlan Bldg 81 S Ninth St	Minneapolis	MN	55402	612-339-3500		*Web:* www.arthurchapman.com
Ashbaugh Beal LLP	4400 Columbia Ctr 701 Fifth Ave	Seattle	WA	98104	206-386-5900		*Web:* www.lawasresults.com
Asian Pacific American Legal Center of Southern California	1145 Wilshire Blvd Fl 2	Los Angeles	CA	90017	213-977-7500		*Web:* advancingjustice-la.org
Asiatico & Associates Pllc	2201 N Central Expy Ste 225	Richardson	TX	75080	214-570-0700		*Web:* baalegal.com
Ater Wynne LLP	1331 NW Lovejoy St Lovejoy Bldg Ste 900	Portland	OR	97209	503-226-1191		*Web:* aterwynne.com
Atkinson Andelson Loya Ruud & Romo A Professional Law Corp	17871 Pk Plz Dr	Cerritos	CA	90703	562-653-3200		*Web:* www.aalrr.com
Atkinson Conway & Gagnon Inc	420 L St Ste 500	Anchorage	AK	99501	907-276-1700		*Web:* www.acglaw.com
Atlas Legal Research Lp	3402 Mcfarlin Blvd Ste 201	Dallas	TX	75205	214-526-8811		*Web:* www.atlaslegal.com
Attorney Aid Divorce & Bankruptcy Center Inc	3605 Long Beach Blvd Ste 300	Long Beach	CA	90807	562-988-0885		*Web:* www.attorneyaid.com
Attorney General	120 W Water St	Dover	DE	19904	302-739-4211		*Web:* www.state.de.us
Ausley McMullen	123 S Calhoun St	Tallahassee	FL	32302	850-224-9115		*Web:* ausley.com
Austin Davis & Mitchell Attorneys at Law	109 Cherry St	Dunlap	TN	37327	423-949-4159		*Web:* austindavismitchell.com
Babcock Law Firm	10101 Siegen Ln Ste 3C	Baton Rouge	LA	70810	225-344-0911		*Web:* www.babcockpartners.com
Backus Meyer & Branch LLP	116 Lowell St	Manchester	NH	03104	603-668-7272		*Web:* www.backusmeyer.com
Bailey & Galyen	1901 W Airport Fwy	Bedford	TX	76021	817-288-1101		*Web:* www.galyen.com
Bailey & Glasser LLP	209 Capitol St	Charleston	WV	25301	304-345-6555		*Web:* www.baileyglasser.com
Bailey Cavalieri LLC	One Columbus 10 W Broad St Ste 2100	Columbus	OH	43215	614-221-3155		*Web:* www.baileycavalieri.com
Baker & McKenzie LLP	130 E Randolph St Ste 3900	Chicago	IL	60601	312-861-8800	861-2899	*Web:* www.bakermckenzie.com
Baker Botts LLP	910 Louisiana St 1 Shell Plz	Houston	TX	77002	713-229-1234	229-1522	*Web:* www.bakerbotts.com
Baker Donelson Bearman Caldwell & Berkowitz PC	165 Madison Ave First Tennessee Bldg Ste 2000	Memphis	TN	38103	901-526-2000	577-2303	*Web:* www.bakerdonelson.com
Baker Hostetler LLP	1900 E Ninth St National City Ctr Ste 3200	Cleveland	OH	44114	216-621-0200	696-0740	*Web:* www.bakerlaw.com
Baker Manock & Jensen	5260 N Palm Ste 421	Fresno	CA	93704	559-432-5400		*Web:* www.bakermanock.com
Baker, Keener & Nahra LLP	633 W Fifth St Ste 5500	Los Angeles	CA	90071	213-241-0900		*Web:* www.bknlawyers.com
Balch & Bingham LLP	1710 Sixth Ave N	Birmingham	AL	35203	205-251-8100		*Web:* www.balch.com
Baldwin C. Mark Atty.	112 Old Bridge St	Jacksonville	NC	28540	910-455-4065		*Web:* www.bmklaw.net
Baldwin Haspel Burke & Mayer LLC	Energy Ctr 1100 Poydras St Ste 3600	New Orleans	LA	70163	504-569-2900		*Web:* www.bhbmlaw.com
Ball Janik	One Main Pl 101 Sw Main St Ste 1100	Portland	OR	97204	503-228-2525		*Web:* www.bjllp.com
Ball Kirk & Holm Pc	3324 Kimball Ave	Waterloo	IA	50702	319-234-2638		*Web:* www.ballkirkholm.com
Ballard Spahr Andrews & Ingersoll LLP	1735 Market St 51st Fl	Philadelphia	PA	19103	215-665-8500	864-8999	*Web:* www.ballardspahr.com
Ballon Stoll Bader & Nadler PC	729 Seventh Ave 17th Fl	New York	NY	10019	212-575-7900		*Web:* www.ballonstoll.com
Banner & Witcoff Ltd	Ten S Wacker Dr Ste 3000	Chicago	IL	60606	312-463-5000		*Web:* bannerwitcoff.com
Barg Coffin Lewis & Trapp LLP	350 California St 22nd Fl	San Francisco	CA	94104	415-228-5400		*Web:* www.bcltlaw.com
Baritz & Colman LLP	1075 Broken Sound Pkwy NW Ste 102	Boca Raton	FL	33487	561-864-5100		*Web:* www.baritzcolman.com
Barkan & Barkan Company LPA	81 S Fourth St Ste 300	Columbus	OH	43215	614-461-1551		*Web:* barkanlaw.com
Barker Martin PS	719 Second Ave Ste 1200	Seattle	WA	98104	360-756-9806		*Web:* www.barkermartin.com
Barley, Snyder, Senft & Cohen LLC	126 E King St	Lancaster	PA	17602	717-299-5201		*Web:* www.barley.com
Barlow Garsek & Simon LLP	920 Foch St	Fort Worth	TX	76107	817-731-4500		*Web:* www.bgsfirm.com
Barlow, Josephs & Holmes Ltd	101 Dyer St Fl 5	Providence	RI	02903	401-273-4446		*Web:* barjos.com
Barna, Guzy & Steffen Ltd	400 Northtown Financial Plz 200 Coon Rapids Blvd	Coon Rapids	MN	55433	763-780-8500		*Web:* www.bgslaw.com
Barnes & Thornburg	11 S Meridian St	Indianapolis	IN	46204	317-236-1313	231-7433	*TF:* 800-236-1352 ■ *Web:* www.btlaw.com
Barnwell Whaley Patterson & Helms LLC	288 Meeting St	Charleston	SC	29401	843-577-7700		*Web:* www.barnwell-whaley.com
Barran Liebman LLP	601 SW Second Ave Ste 2300	Portland	OR	97204	503-228-0500		*Web:* www.barran.com
Barrett & McNagny LLP	215 E Berry St	Fort Wayne	IN	46802	260-423-9551		*Web:* www.barrettlaw.com
Barris, Sott, Denn & Driker PLLC	211 W Ft St 15th Fl	Detroit	MI	48226	313-965-9725		*Web:* www.bsdd.com
Barron & Newburger PC	1212 Guadalupe St Ste 104	Austin	TX	78701	512-476-9103		*Web:* www.bnpclaw.com
Barton, Klugman & Oetting LLP	350 S Grand Ave Ste 2200	Los Angeles	CA	90071	213-621-4000		*Web:* bkolaw.com
Baxter, Baker, Sidle, Conn & Jones PA	120 E Baltimore St Ste 2100	Baltimore	MD	21202	410-385-8122		*Web:* www.bbsclaw.com
Bay Area Legal Aid	1735 Telegraph Ave	Oakland	CA	94612	510-663-4755		*Web:* www.baylegal.org
Bayard Firm, The	222 Delaware Ave Ste 900	Wilmington	DE	19899	302-655-5000		*Web:* www.bayardfirm.com
Bazelon Less & Feldman PC	One S Broad St Ste 1500	Philadelphia	PA	19107	215-568-1155		*Web:* www.bazless.com
BCF LLP	25th Fl 1100 Rene-Levesque Blvd W	Montreal	QC	H3B5C9	514-397-8500		*Web:* www.bcf.ca
Bean, Kinney & Korman A Professional Corp	2300 Wilson Blvd The Navy League Bldg Seventh Fl	Arlington	VA	22201	703-525-4000		*Web:* www.beankinney.com
Beasley Allen Crow Methvin	218 Commerce St	Montgomery	AL	36104	334-269-2343		*Web:* www.beasleyallen.com
Becherer Kannett & Schweitzer	The Water Tower 1255 Powell St	Emeryville	CA	94608	510-658-3600		*Web:* bkscal.com
Becket & Lee LLP	16 General Warren Blvd	Malvern	PA	19355	610-644-7800		*Web:* www.becket-lee.com
Begley, Carlin & Mandio LLP	680 Middletown Blvd	Langhorne	PA	19047	215-750-0110		*Web:* www.begleycarlin.com
Beliveau, Fradette, Doyle & Gallant PA	91 Bay St	Manchester	NH	03104	603-623-1234		*Web:* www.beliveau-fradette.com
Bell, Nunnally & Martin	1400 One McKinney Plz	Dallas	TX	75204	214-740-1400		*Web:* www.bellnunnally.com
Bennett Jones LLP	855 Second St S W 4500 Bankers Hall E	Calgary	AB	T2P4K7	403-298-3100		*Web:* www.bennettjones.ca
Bennington Johnson Biermann & Craigmile LLC	3500 Republic Plz 370 17th St Ste 3500	Denver	CO	80202	303-629-5200		*Web:* benningtonjohnson.com
Berding & Weil LLP	2175 N California Blvd Ste 500	Walnut Creek	CA	94596	925-838-2090		*Web:* www.berding-weil.com
Berg Hill Greenleaf & Ruscitti LLP	1712 Pearl St	Boulder	CO	80302	303-402-1600		*Web:* www.bhgrlaw.com

Firm	City	State	ZIP	Phone	Fax
Berger & Montague PC 1622 Locust St *Web:* www.bergermontague.com	Philadelphia	PA	19103	215-875-3000	
Berkowitz Oliver Williams Shaw & Eisenbrandt LLP Crown Ctr 2600 Grand Blvd Ste 1200 *Web:* www.bowse-law.com	Kansas City	MO	64108	816-561-7007	
Berman Myles L Law Offices 4665 Macarthur Ct Ste 240 *Web:* www.topgundui.com	Newport Beach	CA	92660	949-640-1860	
Berndt & Associates PC 30500 Van Dyke Ave Ste 702 *Web:* www.berndtlegal.com	Warren	MI	48093	586-558-9000	
Berry & Berry Law Offices 2930 Lakeshore Ave *Web:* berryandberry.com	Oakland	CA	94610	510-250-0200	
Best & Flanagan LLP 225 S Sixth St Ste 4000 *Web:* www.bestlaw.com	Minneapolis	MN	55402	612-339-7121	339-5897
Best, Vanderlaan & Harrington 25 E Washington St Ste 800 *Web:* www.bestfirm.com	Chicago	IL	60602	312-819-1100	
Beveridge & Diamond PC 1350 I St NW Ste 700 *Web:* www.bdlaw.com	Washington	DC	20005	202-789-6000	
Bilicki Law Firm Pc, The 1285 N Main St *Web:* www.patexia.com	Jamestown	NY	14701	716-664-5600	
Bishop, White, Marshall & Weibel PS 720 Olive Way Ste 1201 *Web:* www.bwmlegal.com	Seattle	WA	98101	206-622-5306	
Black Mann & Graham LLP 2905 Corporate Cir *Web:* www.blackmannandgraham.com	Flower Mound	TX	75028	972-353-4174	
Black Srebnick Kornspan & Stumpf PA 201 S Biscayne Blvd Ste 1300 *Web:* www.royblack.com	Miami	FL	33131	305-371-6421	
Blackwell Burke PA 431 S Seventh St 2500 *Web:* www.blackwellburke.com	Minneapolis	MN	55415	612-343-3200	
Blakinger Byler & Thomas PC 28 Penn Sq *Web:* www.bbt-law.com	Lancaster	PA	17603	717-299-1100	
Blalock Walters PA 802 11th St W *Web:* blalockwalters.com	Bradenton	FL	34205	941-748-0100	
Blaney McMurtry LLP Maritime Life Tower 2 Queen St E Ste 1500 *Web:* www.blaney.com	Toronto	ON	M5C3G5	416-593-1221	
Blank Rome LLP One Logan Sq 130 N 18th St *Web:* www.blankrome.com	Philadelphia	PA	19103	215-569-5500	569-5555
Blasingame, Burch, Garrard & Ashley PC 440 College Ave *Web:* www.bbgbalaw.com	Athens	GA	30603	706-354-4000	
Blecher & Collins 515 S Figueroa St Ste 1750 *Web:* www.blechercollins.com	Los Angeles	CA	90071	213-622-4222	
Blitt & Gaines Pc 661 Glenn Ave *Web:* www.blittandgaines.com	Wheeling	IL	60090	847-403-4900	
Blue Williams LLP 3421 N Causeway Blvd Ste 900 *Web:* bluewilliams.com	Metairie	LA	70002	504-831-4091	
Bodman PLC 1901 Saint Antoine St Sixth Fl at Ford Field *Web:* www.bodmanllp.com	Detroit	MI	48226	313-259-7777	
Boehl Stopher & Graves LLP 400 W Market St Ste 2300 *Web:* www.bsg-law.com	Louisville	KY	40202	502-589-5980	
Boies Schiller & Flexner LLP 5301 Wisconsin Ave NW *TF:* 877-224-0464 ■ *Web:* bsfllp.com	Washington	DC	20015	202-237-2727	237-6131
Bone McAllester Norton PLLC 511 Union St Nashville City Ctr Ste 1600 *Web:* www.bonelaw.com	Nashville	TN	37219	615-238-6300	
Boren, Oliver & Coffey LLP 59 N Jefferson St *Web:* www.boclawyers.com	Martinsville	IN	46151	765-342-0147	
Bose McKinney & Evans LLP 111 Monument Cir Ste 2700 *Web:* www.boselaw.com	Indianapolis	IN	46204	317-684-5000	684-5173
Boss Law Firm APLC, The 9710 Scranton Rd Ste 300 *Web:* bosslawfirm.com	San Diego	CA	92121	619-234-1776	
Boyle Fredrickson SC 840 N Plankinton Ave *Web:* www.boylefred.com	Milwaukee	WI	53203	414-225-9755	
Bracewell & Giuliani LLP 711 Louisiana St Ste 2300 *Web:* www.bracewellgiuliani.com	Houston	TX	77002	713-223-2300	221-1212
Bradford & Barthel LLP 2518 River Plz Dr *Web:* www.bradfordbarthel.com	Sacramento	CA	95833	916-569-0790	569-0799
Bradley & Riley PC PO Box 2804 *Web:* bradleyriley.com	Cedar Rapids	IA	52406	319-363-0101	
Bradley Arant Boult Cummings LLP 1819 Fifth Ave N *Web:* www.babc.com	Birmingham	AL	35203	205-521-8000	
Brady Connolly & Masuda Pc 705 E Lincoln St Ste 313 *Web:* bcm-law.com	Normal	IL	61761	309-862-4914	
Brann & Isaacson 184 Main St *Web:* www.brannlaw.com	Lewiston	ME	04243	207-786-3566	
Bremer Whyte Brown & O'Meara LLP 20320 SW Birch St Second Fl *Web:* www.bremerwhyte.com	Newport Beach	CA	92660	949-221-1000	
Brennan Manna & Diamond LLC 75 E Market St *Web:* www.bmdllc.com	Akron	OH	44308	330-253-5060	
Brewer & Pritchard Three Riverway Ste 1800 *Web:* www.bplaw.com	Houston	TX	77024	713-209-2950	
Brian Patrick Conry Pc 534 Sw Third Ave Ste 711 *Web:* www.brianpatrickconry.com	Portland	OR	97204	503-274-4430	
Brick Gentry Law Firm 6701 Westown Pkwy Ste 100 *Web:* www.brickgentrylaw.com	West Des Moines	IA	50266	515-274-1450	
Bricker & Eckler LLP 100 S Third St *Web:* www.bricker.com	Columbus	OH	43215	614-227-2300	
Brock & Scott PLLC 1315 Westbrook Plz Dr *Web:* www.brockandscott.com	Winston-salem	NC	27103	336-760-5526	
Brooklyn Legal Services Corp 105 Court St Fl 3 *Web:* www.sbls.org	Brooklyn	NY	11201	718-237-5500	
Brooks, Pierce, McLendon, Humphrey & Leonard LLP 230 N Elm St Ste 2000 *Web:* www.brookspierce.com	Greensboro	NC	27401	336-373-8850	
Brown & Charbonneau LLP 420 Exchange Ste 270 *Web:* bc-llp.com	Irvine	CA	92602	714-505-3000	
Brown & Connery LLP 360 Haddon Ave *Web:* brownconnery.com	Westmont	NJ	08108	856-854-8900	
Brown & Michaels 400 M T Bank Bldg Ste 400 *Web:* www.bpmlegal.com	Ithaca	NY	14850	607-256-2000	
Brown, Garganese, Weiss & D'Agresta PA 111 N Orange Ave Ste 2000 *Web:* www.orlandolaw.net	Orlando	FL	32802	407-425-9566	
Brownlee Fryett 530 8 Ave Sw *Web:* www.brownleelaw.com	Calgary	AB	T2P3S8	403-232-8408	
Broyles Kight & Ricafort PC 8250 Haverstick Rd Ste 100 *Web:* www.bkrlaw.com	Indianapolis	IN	46240	317-571-3600	
Brumund, Jacobs, Hammel & Davidson LLC 58 E Clinton St Ste 200 *Web:* www.brumund-jacobs.com	Joliet	IL	60432	815-723-0628	
Bucci Bailey & Javins Lc 213 Hale St *Web:* buccibaileyjavins.com	Charleston	WV	25301	304-345-0346	
Buchalter Nemer Pc 1000 Wilshire Blvd *Web:* www.buchalter.com	Los Angeles	CA	90017	213-891-0700	896-0400
Buchanan Ingersoll & Rooney PC 301 Grant St 1 Oxford Ctr 20th Fl *TF:* 800-444-6738 ■ *Web:* www.bipc.com	Pittsburgh	PA	15219	412-562-8800	562-1041
Budd Larner P C 150 John F Kennedy Pkwy *Web:* www.buddlarner.com	Short Hills	NJ	07078	973-379-4800	379-7734
Bull, Housser & Tupper LLP 900 Howe St Ste 900 *Web:* www.bht.com	Vancouver	BC	V6Z2M4	604-687-6575	
Bullivant Houser Bailey PC 888 SW Fifth Ave Ste 300 *Web:* www.bullivant.com	Portland	OR	97204	503-228-6351	
Burch & Cracchiolo PA 702 E Osborn Rd Ste 200 *Web:* www.bcattorneys.com	Phoenix	AZ	85014	602-274-7611	
Burch Porter & Johnson Pllc 130 N Ct Ave *Web:* www.bpjlaw.com	Memphis	TN	38103	901-524-5000	524-5024
Burg Simpson Eldredge Hersh Jardine PC 40 Inverness Dr E *Web:* www.burgsimpson.com	Englewood	CO	80112	303-792-5595	
Burns Burns Walsh & Walsh pa 704 Topeka Ave *Web:* bbwwlaw.com	Lyndon	KS	66451	785-828-4418	
Bush Ross PA 1801 N Highland Ave *Web:* www.bushross.com	Tampa	FL	33602	813-224-9255	
Butch Quinn Rosemurgy Jardis Burkhart Lewandowski & Miller Pc 816 Ludington St *Web:* www.bqrlaw.com	Escanaba	MI	49829	906-786-4422	
Bybel Rutledge LLP 1017 Mumma Rd *Web:* www.bybelrutledge.com	Lemoyne	PA	17043	717-731-1700	
Cabaniss, Johnston, Gardner, Dumas & O'Neal LLP Park Pl Tower 2001 Park Pl N Ste 700 *Web:* www.cabaniss.com	Birmingham	AL	35203	205-716-5200	
Cable Huston Benedic 1001 Sw Fifth Ave Ste 2000 *Web:* www.cablehuston.com	Portland	OR	97204	503-224-3092	
Caesar, Rivise, Bernstein, Cohen & Pokotilow Ltd 12th Fl 1635 Market St *Web:* www.crbcp.com	Philadelphia	PA	19103	215-567-2010	
Cain Lamarre Casgrain Wells Senc 630 boul Rene-Levesque Ouest Ste 2780 *Web:* www.clcw.ca	Montreal	QC	H3B1S6	514-393-4580	
Cairncross & Hempelmann PS 524 Second Ave Ste 500 *Web:* www.cairncross.com	Seattle	WA	98104	206-587-0700	
Cameron, Hodges, Coleman, LaPointe & Wright PA 111 N Magnolia Ave Ste 1350 *Web:* www.cameronhodges.com	Orlando	FL	32801	407-841-5030	
Campbell, Guin, Williams, Guy & Gidiere LLC Capitol Park Ctr 2711 University Blvd *Web:* www.tannerguin.com	Tuscaloosa	AL	35401	205-633-0200	
Cannon & Dunphy Sc 595 N Barker Rd *Web:* www.cannon-dunphy.com	Brookfield	WI	53045	262-780-7154	
Cantor Colburn LLP 22nd Fl 20 Church St *Web:* www.cantorcolburn.com	Hartford	CT	06103	860-286-2929	
Capell & Howard PC 150 S Perry St *Web:* capellhoward.com	Montgomery	AL	36104	334-241-8000	
Carlile Patchen & Murphy LLP 366 E Broad St *Web:* www.cpmlaw.com	Columbus	OH	43215	614-228-6135	221-0216
Carlsmith Ball LLP 1001 Bishop St Ste 2200 *Web:* www.carlsmith.com	Honolulu	HI	96813	808-523-2500	523-0842
Carlson, Caspers, Vandenburgh & Lindquist 225 S Sixth St Ste 4200 *Web:* carlsoncaspers.com	Minneapolis	MN	55402	612-436-9600	
Carlson, Gaskey & Olds A Professional Corp 400 W Maple Rd Ste 350 *Web:* www.cgolaw.com	Birmingham	MI	48009	248-988-8360	

Firm	City	State	Zip	Phone	Fax
Carlton Fields PA 4221 W Boy Scout Blvd Corporate Ctr Three Ste 1000 *Web:* www.carltonfields.com	Tampa	FL	33607	813-223-7000	
Carluccio, Leone, Dimon, Doyle & Sacks LLC Nine Robbins St *Web:* cldds.com	Toms River	NJ	08753	732-797-1600	
Carman Callahan & Ingham LLP Carman Bldg 280 Main St *Web:* www.carmancallahan.com	Farmingdale	NY	11735	516-249-3450	
Carmody Torrance Sandak & Hennessey LLP 50 Leavenworth St *Web:* carmodylaw.com	Waterbury	CT	06721	203-573-1200	
Carpenter Lipps & Leland LLP 280 N High St Ste 1300 *Web:* carpenterlipps.com	Columbus	OH	43215	614-365-4100	
Carr & Ferrell LLP 120 Constitution Dr *Web:* www.carrferrell.com	Menlo Park	CA	94025	650-812-3400	
Carr McClellan Ingersall Thompson 216 Park Rd *Web:* www.carr-mcclellan.com	Burlingame	CA	94010	650-342-9600	
Carroll Burdick & Mc Donough 44 Montgomery St Ste 400 *Web:* www.cbmlaw.com	San Francisco	CA	94104	415-989-5900	989-0932
Carter Ledyard & Milburn LLP Two Wall St Fl 13 *Web:* www.clm.com	New York	NY	10005	212-732-3200	732-3232
Carter Mario Injury Lawyers 176 Wethersfield Ave *Web:* cartermario.com	Hartford	CT	06114	860-525-2222	
Casey Gerry Schenk Francavilla Blatt & Penfield LLP 110 Laurel St *Web:* www.caseygerry.com	San Diego	CA	92101	619-238-1811	
Casner & Edwards LLP 303 Congress St *Web:* www.casneredwards.com	Boston	MA	02210	617-426-5900	
Cassels Brock & Blackwell LLP 2100 Scotia Plz 40 King St W *Web:* www.casselsbrock.com	Toronto	ON	M5H3C2	416-869-5300	
Cassin & Cassin LLP 711 Third Ave 20th Fl *Web:* www.cassinllp.com	New York	NY	10017	212-972-6161	
Cavanagh Law Firm, The 1850 N Central Ave *TF:* 888-824-3476 ■ *Web:* www.cavanaghlaw.com	Phoenix	AZ	85004	602-322-4000	322-4100
Cellino & Barnes PC 2500 Main Pl Tower 350 Main St *Web:* www.cellinoandbarnes.com	Buffalo	NY	14202	716-854-2020	
Center-battered Womens Services Po Box 1406 *Web:* www.sanctuaryforfamilies.org	New York	NY	10268	212-349-6009	
Cga Law Firm 106 Harrisburg St *Web:* www.cgalaw.com	East Berlin	PA	17316	717-259-9592	
Chaffetz Lindsey LLP 505 Fifth Ave Fourth Fl *Web:* www.chaffetzlindsey.com	New York	NY	10017	212-257-6960	
Chalker Flores LLP 14951 N Dallas Pkwy Ste 400 *Web:* www.chalkerflores.com	Dallas	TX	75254	817-820-0244	
Chang & Boos 1305 11th St Ste 301 *Web:* www.americanlaw.com	Bellingham	WA	98225	360-671-5945	
Chapman & Intrieri LLP 2236 Mariner Sq Dr Ste 300 *Web:* chapmanandintrieri.com	Alameda	CA	94501	510-864-3600	
Charles d Hankey Law Office PC 434 E New York St *Web:* www.hankeylawoffice.com	Indianapolis	IN	46202	317-634-8565	
Chasan Leyner & Lamparello A Professional Corp 300 Harmon Meadow Blvd *Web:* www.chasanlaw.com	Secaucus	NJ	07094	201-348-6000	
Cheng Cohen LLC 311 N Aberdeen Ste 400 *Web:* www.chengcohen.com	Chicago	IL	60607	312-243-1701	
Chilivis, Cochran, Larkins & Bever LLP 3127 Maple Dr NE *Web:* www.cclblawyers.com	Atlanta	GA	30305	404-233-4171	
Christensen O'Connor Johnson & Kindness PLLC 1201 Third Ave Ste 3600 *Web:* www.cojk.com	Seattle	WA	98101	206-682-8100	
Christie, Parker & Hale LLP 655 N Central Ave Ste 2300 *Web:* www.cph.com	Glendale	CA	91203	626-795-9900	
Clark, Gagliardi & Miller PC 99 Court St *TF:* 800-734-5694 ■ *Web:* www.cgmlaw.com	White Plains	NY	10601	800-734-5694	
Clarke Silverglate PA 799 Brickell Plz Ste 900 *Web:* www.cspalaw.com	Miami	FL	33131	305-377-0700	
Clifford Chance LLP 31 W 52nd St *Web:* www.cliffordchance.com	New York	NY	10019	212-878-8000	878-8375
Cloppert, Latanick, Sauter & Washburn LLP 225 E Broad St Fl 4 *Web:* www.cloppertlaw.com	Columbus	OH	43215	614-461-4455	
Cobb & Cole 150 Magnolia Ave *Web:* www.cobbcole.com	Daytona Beach	FL	32114	386-255-8171	
Cocciardi & Associates Inc Four Kacey Ct *Web:* www.cai.biz	Mechanicsburg	PA	17055	717-766-4500	
Cochran Firm LLC 111 E Main St *TF:* 800-843-3476 ■ *Web:* www.cochranfirm.com	Dothan	AL	36301	334-793-1555	793-8280
Codilis & Associates PC 15W030 N Frontage Rd *Web:* www.codilis.com	Burr Ridge	IL	60527	630-794-5300	
Cohen & Gresser LLP 800 Third Ave *Web:* www.cohengresser.com	New York	NY	10022	212-957-7600	
Cohen & Grigsby Pc 625 Liberty Ave *TF:* 800-235-8619 ■ *Web:* www.cohenlaw.com	Pittsburgh	PA	15222	412-297-4900	209-0672
Cohen Highley LLP 255 Queens Ave *Web:* www.cohenhighley.com	London	ON	N6A5R8	519-672-9330	
Cohen Seglias Pallas Greenhall & Furman PC 30 S 17th St 19th Fl United Plz *Web:* cohenseglias.com	Philadelphia	PA	19103	215-564-1700	
Cohen, Hurkin, Ehrenfeld, Pomerantz & Tenenbaum 25 Chapel St Ste 705 *Web:* www.cohenhurkin.com	Brooklyn	NY	11201	718-596-9000	
Cokinos Bosien & Young PC 2919 Allen Pkwy Ste 1500 *Web:* www.cbylaw.com	Houston	TX	77019	713-535-5500	
Cole Scott & Kissane pa 617 Whitehead St *Web:* www.csklegal.com	Key West	FL	33040	305-294-4440	
Collins & Lacy PC 1330 Lady St Sixth Fl *Web:* www.collinsandlacy.com	Columbia	SC	29201	803-256-2660	
Colten Cummins Watson & Vincent PC 3959 Pender Dr Ste 200 *Web:* www.coltenlaw.com	Fairfax	VA	22030	703-277-9700	
Colucci & Umans Inc 218 E 50th St *Web:* www.colucci-umans.com	New York	NY	10022	212-935-5700	
Coman & Anderson PC 2525 Cabot Dr Ste 300 *Web:* www.comananderson.com	Lisle	IL	60532	630-428-2660	
Connell Foley LLP 85 Livingston Ave *Web:* www.connellfoley.com	Roseland	NJ	07068	973-535-0500	
Connelly Baker Wotring LLP 700 JPMorgan Chase Tower 600 Travis St *Web:* www.connellybaker.com	Houston	TX	77002	713-980-1700	
Conrad & Scherer LLP 633 S Federal Hwy *Web:* www.conradscherer.com	Fort Lauderdale	FL	33301	954-462-5500	
Conrad, Trosch & Kemmy PA 5821 Fairview Rd Ste 405 Parkview Bldg *Web:* www.ctklawyers.com	Charlotte	NC	28209	704-553-8221	
Conroy, Simberg, Ganon, Krevans, Abel, Lurvey, Morrow & Schefer PA 3440 Hollywood Blvd Second Fl *Web:* www.conroysimberg.com	Hollywood	FL	33021	954-961-1400	
Constangy, Brooks & Smith LLC 230 Peachtree St N W Ste 2400 *Web:* constangy.com	Atlanta	GA	30303	404-525-8622	
Consumer Attorneys of California 770 L St Ste 1200 *Web:* www.caoc.org	Sacramento	CA	95814	916-442-6902	
Conway, Olejniczak & Jerry SC 231 S Adams St *Web:* www.lcojlaw.com	Green Bay	WI	54301	920-437-0476	
Cooch & Taylor 1000 W St The Brandywine Bldg 10th Fl *Web:* www.coochtaylor.com	Wilmington	DE	19801	302-984-3800	
Cooley Godward Kronish LLP 3000 El Camino Real *TF:* 888-654-2411 ■ *Web:* www.cooley.com	Palo Alto	CA	94306	650-843-5000	849-7400
Coon Brent & Associates Law Firm Pc 215 Orleans St *Web:* bcoonlaw.com	Beaumont	TX	77701	409-835-2666	
Cooper Legal Services Dwayne e Cooper Atty at Law 8411 Tuskin Way *Web:* cooperlegalservices.com	Indianapolis	IN	46278	317-873-3600	
Copple, Rockey, Mckeever & Schlecht PC LLO 2425 Taylor Ave *Web:* www.greatadvocates.com	Norfolk	NE	68701	402-371-4300	
Cors & Bassett 537 E Pete Rose Way Ste 400 *Web:* www.corsbassett.com	Cincinnati	OH	45202	513-852-8200	
Cory Watson Crowder & DeGaris 2131 Magnolia Ave *Web:* www.cwcd.com	Birmingham	AL	35205	205-328-2200	
Costello, Porter, Hill, Heisterkamp, Bushnell & Carpenter LLP Security Bldg 704 St Joseph St *Web:* www.costelloporter.com	Rapid City	SD	57709	605-343-2410	
Couch White LLP 540 Broadway *Web:* www.couchwhite.com	Albany	NY	12201	518-426-4600	
Covington & Burling LLP 1201 Pennsylvania Ave NW *Web:* www.cov.com	Washington	DC	20004	202-662-6000	662-6291
Covington Patrick Hagins Stern & Lewis pa Law Firm 211 Pettigru St *Web:* covpatlaw.com	Greenville	SC	29601	864-242-9000	
Cowles & Thompson A Professional Corp 901 Main St Ste 3900 *Web:* www.cowlesthompson.com	Dallas	TX	75202	214-672-2000	672-2020
Cox Smith Matthews Inc 112 E Pecan St Ste 1800 *Web:* www.coxsmith.com	San Antonio	TX	78205	210-554-5500	
Cozen O'Connor 1900 Market St *TF:* 800-523-2900 ■ *Web:* www.cozen.com	Philadelphia	PA	19103	215-665-2000	665-2013
Craige Brawley Liipfert & Walker LLP 110 Oakwood Dr Ste 300 *Web:* www.craigebrawley.com	Winston Salem	NC	27103	336-725-0583	
Cranfill Sumner & Hartzog LLP PO Box 27808 *Web:* www.cshlaw.com	Raleigh	NC	27611	919-828-5100	828-2277
Cravath Swaine & Moore LLP 825 Eigth Ave Worldwide Plz *Web:* www.cravath.com	New York	NY	10019	212-474-1000	474-3700
Critchfield, Critchfield & Johnston Ltd 225 N Market St *Web:* www.ccj.com	Wooster	OH	44691	330-264-4444	
Crivello Carlson Sc 710 N Plankinton Ave Ste 500 *Web:* www.milwlaw.com	Milwaukee	WI	53203	414-271-7722	
Crowley Fleck PLLP 490 N 31st St Fifth Fl *Web:* www.crowleyfleck.com	Billings	MT	59101	406-252-3441	
Cruser & Mitchell LLP 275 Scientific Dr *Web:* cmlawfirm.com	Norcross	GA	30092	404-881-2622	
Cullen, Weston, Pines & Bach LLP 122 W Washington Ave Ste 900 *Web:* www.cwpb.com	Madison	WI	53703	608-807-0752	

	Phone	Fax

Cummings & Lockwood LLC
8000 Health Ctr Blvd Unit 300 Bonita Springs FL 34135 239-947-8811
Web: www.cl-law.com

Curtin & Heefner 250 N Pennsylvania Morrisville PA 19067 215-736-2521
Web: www.curtinheefner.com

Dale L Buchanan & Associates PC
6576 E Brainerd Rd Chattanooga TN 37421 423-894-2552
Web: dalebuchanan.com

Daley & Heft LLP 462 Stevens Ave Ste 201 Solana Beach CA 92075 858-755-5666
Web: daley-heft.com

Daniel & Stark Law Offices 620 Owen Ln Waco TX 76710 254-776-6200
Web: www.danielstarklaw.com

Daniels & Porco LLP 517 Route 22 Pawling NY 12564 845-855-5900
Web: www.danielsporco.com

Dann, Dorfman, Herrell & Skillman PC
1601 Market St Ste 2400 Philadelphia PA 19103 215-563-4100
Web: www.ddhs.com

Dascenzo Intellectual Property Law PC
1000 S W Broadway Ste 1555 Portland OR 97205 503-224-7529
Web: www.dascenzoiplaw.com

Davenport, Evans, Hurwitz & Smith LLP
206 W 14th St Sioux Falls SD 57101 605-336-2880
Web: dehs.com

David L Martin Attorney 701 Pike St Ste 1800 Seattle WA 98101 206-624-7990
Web: www.leesmart.com

Davidson, Davidson & Kappel LLC
485 Seventh Ave Fl 14 New York NY 10018 212-736-1940
Web: www.ddkpatent.com

Davies Pearson PC 920 Fawcett Ave Tacoma WA 98401 253-620-1500
Web: www.dpearson.com

Davis & Gilbert 1740 Broadway New York NY 10019 212-468-4800
Web: www.dglaw.com

Davis & Wilkerson Pc
1801 S Mo Pac Expy Ste 300 Austin TX 78746 512-482-0614
Web: www.dwlaw.com

Davis Graham & Stubbs LLP 1550 17th St Ste 500 Denver CO 80202 303-892-9400 893-1379
Web: www.dgslaw.com

Davis Law Firm 5710 IH-10 W San Antonio TX 78201 210-734-3599
Web: www.jeffdavislawfirm.com

Davis Polk & Wardwell 450 Lexington Ave New York NY 10017 212-450-4000 701-5800
Web: www.davispolk.com

Davis Wright Tremaine LLP
1201 Third Ave #2200 Seattle WA 98101 206-622-3150 757-7700
Web: www.dwt.com

Dawda, Mann, Mulcahy & Sadler PLC
39533 Woodward Ave Ste 200 Bloomfield Hills MI 48304 248-642-3700
Web: www.dmms.com

Day Pitney LLP 242 Trumbull St Hartford CT 06103 860-275-0100 275-0343
TF: 800-882-8684 ■ *Web:* www.daypitney.com

De Cotiis Fitzpatrick Cole & Wisler LLP
500 Frank W Burr Blvd Teaneck NJ 07666 201-928-1100
Web: www.decotiislaw.com

Dean, Ringers, Morgan & Lawton PA
1200 Capital Plz I 201 E Pine St Ste 1200 Orlando FL 32801 407-422-4310
Web: www.drml-law.com

Debevoise & Plimpton LLP 919 Third Ave New York NY 10022 212-909-6000 909-6836
Web: www.debevoise.com

Dechert LLP 2929 Arch St Cira Ctr Philadelphia PA 19104 215-994-4000 994-2222
TF: 800-328-4880 ■ *Web:* www.dechert.com

Degan, Blanchard & Nash A Professional Law Corp
Texaco Ctr 400 Poydras St Ste 2600 New Orleans LA 70130 504-529-3333
Web: www.degan.com

Deily Mooney & Glastetter LLP
Eight Thurlow Ter Albany NY 12203 518-436-0344
Web: www.deilylawfirm.com

Delahousaye Angela Law Offices
1655 N Main St Ste 230 Walnut Creek CA 94596 925-944-3300
Web: www.delahousayelaw.com

Delaney, Wiles, Hayes, Gerety, Ellis & Young Inc
1007 W Third Ave Ste 400 Anchorage AK 99501 907-279-3581
Web: www.delaneywiles.com

Dennis, Corry, Porter & Smith LLP
14 Piedmont Ctr 3535 Piedmont Rd NE Ste 900 Atlanta GA 30305 404-365-0102
Web: www.dcplaw.com

Denton & Keuler Attonrnies Ofc
555 Jefferson St Ste 301 Paducah KY 42001 270-443-8253
Web: www.dklaw.com

Deutsch Williams Brooks DeRensis & Holland PC
One Design Ctr Pl Ste 600 Boston MA 02210 617-951-2300
Web: www.dwboston.com

Deutsch, Kerrigan & Stiles LLP
755 Magazine St New Orleans LA 70130 504-581-5141
Web: www.dkslaw.com

DeWitt Ross & Stevens SC
Two E Mifflin St Ste 600 Madison WI 53703 608-255-8891
Web: www.dewittross.com

Dickstein Shapiro LLP 1825 Eye St NW Washington DC 20006 202-420-2200 420-2201
TF: 800-733-2767 ■ *Web:* www.dicksteinshapiro.com

Diederiks & Whitelaw Plc
13663 Office Pl Ste 201 Woodbridge VA 22192 703-583-8300
Web: www.dwpatentlaw.com

DiFrancesco, Bateman, Coley, Yospin, Kunzman, Davis & Lehrer PC
15 Mountain Blvd Warren NJ 07059 908-757-7800
Web: www.newjerseylaw.net

Dinkes & Schwitzer 112 Madison Ave Fl 10 New York NY 10016 212-683-3800
Web: dandsatlaw.com

DLA Piper 203 N LaSalle St Ste 1900 Chicago IL 60601 312-368-4000 236-7516
Web: www.dlapiper.com

Dld Lawyers 150 Alhambra Cir Ph Coral Gables FL 33134 305-443-4850
Web: www.dldlawyers.com

Docken & Co 900-800 6 Ave Sw Calgary AB T2P3G3 403-269-3612
Web: docken.com

Dolden Wallace & Folick 888 Dunsmuir St Vancouver BC V6C3K4 604-689-3222
Web: www.dolden.com

Domengeaux Wright Roy & Edwards LLC
556 Jefferson St Ste 500 Lafayette LA 70501 337-233-3033
Web: www.wrightroy.com

Donald Harris Law Firm
158 E Market St Ste 302 Sandusky OH 44870 419-621-9388
Web: www.donaldharrislawfirm.com

Donati Law Firm LLP 1545 Union Ave Memphis TN 38104 901-278-1004
Web: www.donatilaw.com

Donohoe & Stapleton LLC 2781 Zelda Rd Montgomery AL 36106 334-269-3355
Web: donohoeandstapleton.com

Donohue Brown Mathewson & Smyth LLC
140 S Dearborn St Ste 800 Chicago IL 60603 312-422-0900
Web: www.dbmslaw.com

Dorsey & Whitney LLP
50 S Sixth St Ste 1500 Minneapolis MN 55402 612-340-2600 340-2868
TF: 800-759-4929 ■ *Web:* www.dorsey.com

Downey Brand LLP 621 Capitol Mall 18th Fl Sacramento CA 95814 916-444-1000
Web: www.downeybrand.com

Dozier, Miller, Pollard & Murphy LLP
Cameron Brown Bldg 301 S McDowell St
Ste 700 Charlotte NC 28204 704-372-6373
Web: www.dmpm.com

Drake, Loeb, Heller, Kennedy, Gogerty, Gaba, Rodd PLLC
555 Hudson Vly Ave Ste 100 New Windsor NY 12553 845-561-0550
Web: www.drakeloeb.com

Dreher Langer & Tomkies LLP
41 S High St Ste 2250 Columbus OH 43215 614-628-8000
Web: www.dltlaw.com

Drinker Biddle & Reath LLP
1 Logan Sq Ste 2000 Philadelphia PA 19103 215-988-2700 988-2757
Web: www.drinkerbiddle.com

Drummond Woodsum LLP 84 Marginal Way Ste 600 Portland ME 04101 207-772-1941
Web: www.dwmlaw.com

Duane Morris LLP 30 S 17th St United Plz Philadelphia PA 19103 215-979-1000 979-1020
Web: www.duanemorris.com

DuBois, Sheehan, Hamilton, Levin & Weissman LLC
511 Cooper St Camden NJ 08102 856-365-7665
Web: www.duboislaw.com

Dudley & Smith PA 101 Fifth St E Ste 2602 Saint Paul MN 55101 651-291-1717
Web: www.dudleyandsmith.com

Dunn Carney Allen Higgins & Tongue LLP
851 SW Sixth Ave Ste 1500 Portland OH 97204 503-224-6440
Web: www.dunncarney.com

Dunn Lambert LLC 80 W State Rt 4 Ste 170 Paramus NJ 07652 201-291-0700
Web: www.njbizlawyer.com

Dunnington Bartholow & Miller LLP
666 Third Ave New York NY 10017 212-682-8811
Web: www.dunnington.com

Durham Jones & Pinegar
111 East Broadway Ste 900 Salt Lake City UT 84111 801-415-3000
Web: www.durhamjones.com

Eagleton, Eagleton & Harrison Inc
320 S Boston Ave Ste 1700 Tulsa OK 74103 918-584-0462
Web: www.eehlaw.com

Eastham, Watson, Dale & Forney LLP
The Niels Esperson Bldg 808 Travis Ste 1300 Houston TX 77002 713-225-0905
Web: www.easthamlaw.com

Eastman & Smith Ltd One Seagate 24th Fl Toledo OH 43699 419-241-6000
Web: www.eastmansmith.com

Eckell, Sparks, Levy, Auerbach, Monte, Sloane, Matthews & Auslander PC
344 W Front St Media PA 19063 610-565-3700
Web: www.eckellsparks.com

Edward A. Williamson Law Firm Pllc, The
509 S Church Ave Philadelphia MS 39350 601-656-5634
Web: www.eawlaw.com

Edwards Angell Palmer & Dodge LLP
111 Huntington Ave Boston MA 02199 617-239-0100 227-4420
Web: www.edwardswildman.com

Edwards, Kenny & Bray
1900 - 1040 W Georgia St Vancouver BC V6E4H3 604-689-1811
Web: www.ekb.com

Einhorn, Harris, Ascher, Barbarito & Frost PC
165 E Main St Denville NJ 07834 973-627-7300
Web: www.einhornharris.com

Elarbee , Thompson , Sapp & Wilson LLP
800 International Tower 229 Peachtree St NE Atlanta GA 30303 404-659-6700
Web: www.elarbeethompson.com

Elderkin, Martin, Kelly & Messina PC
150 E Eighth St Fl 2 Erie PA 16501 814-456-4000
Web: www.elderkinlaw.com

Elliott, Ostrander & Preston PC
Union Bank Tower 707 SW Washington St
Ste 1500 Portland OR 97205 503-224-7112
Web: www.eoplaw.com

Ellis Ged & Bodden pa 7171 N Federal Hwy Boca Raton FL 33487 561-995-1966
Web: www.ellisandged.com

Ellis Law Group LLP
740 University Ave Ste 100 Sacramento CA 95825 916-283-8820
Web: www.womenlawyers-sacramento.org

Ellis, Li & McKinstry PLLC
Market Pl Tower 2025 First Ave Ph A Seattle WA 98121 206-682-0565
Web: www.elmlaw.com

Ellison, Schneider & Harris LLP 2015 H St Sacramento CA 95814 916-447-2166
Web: www.eslawfirm.com

Emerson Thomson & Bennett LLC
1914 Akron Peninsula Rd Akron OH 44313 330-434-9999
Web: www.etblaw.com

Empire Justice Center One W Main St Ste 200 Rochester NY 14614 585-454-4060
Web: www.empirejustice.org

Engelman Berger PC 3636 N Central Ave Ste 700 Phoenix AZ 85012 602-271-9090
Web: www.engelmanberger.com

Firm / Address	City	State	ZIP	Phone	Fax
English, Lucas, Priest & Owsley LLP 1101 College St *Web:* www.elpolaw.com	Bowling Green	KY	42102	270-781-6500	
Epstein Becker & Green PC 250 Pk Ave *Web:* www.ebglaw.com	New York	NY	10177	212-351-4500	661-0989
Epstein Cole LLP 393 University Ave *Web:* www.epsteincole.com	Toronto	ON	M5G1E6	416-862-9888	
Ervin Cohen & Jessup 9401 Wilshire Blvd Ninth Fl *Web:* www.ecjlaw.com	Beverly Hills	CA	90212	310-273-6333	
Escamilla, Poneck & Cruz LLP 850 Riverwalk Pl 700 N St Mary's St *Web:* www.escamillaponeck.com	San Antonio	TX	78205	210-225-0001	
Evan K Thalenberg Law Offices 216 E Lexington St *Web:* ektlaw.com	Baltimore	MD	21202	410-625-9100	
Evans Latham & Campisi One Post St Ste 600 *Web:* www.elc-law.com	San Francisco	CA	94104	415-421-0288	
Ezra Sutton Law Offices 900 Us Hwy 9 N Ste 201 *Web:* ezrasutton.com	Woodbridge	NJ	07095	732-634-3520	
Faegre & Benson LLP 90 S Seventh St 2200 Wells Fargo Bldg *TF:* 800-328-4393 ■ *Web:* www.faegrebd.com	Minneapolis	MN	55402	612-766-7000	766-1600
Fafinski Mark & Johnson PA Flagship Corporate Ctr 775 Prairie Ctr Dr Ste 400 *Web:* www.fmjlaw.com	Edon Prairie	MN	55344	952-995-9500	
Fann & Petruccelli PA 5100 N Federal Hwy Ste 300 B *Web:* fplawyers.com	Fort Lauderdale	FL	33308	954-771-4118	
Farah Afaf Vicky 201 E Liberty St Ste 7 *Web:* vickyfarah.com	Ann Arbor	MI	48104	734-663-9813	
Farr, Farr, Emerich, Hackett & Carr PA Earl D Farr Bldg 99 Nesbit St *Web:* www.farr.com	Punta Gorda	FL	33950	941-639-1158	
Farrell Fritz EAB Plz 14th Fl *Web:* www.farrellfritz.com	Uniondale	NY	11556	516-227-0700	
Farris, Riley & Pitt LLP 2025 Third Ave N Ste 400 *Web:* www.frplegal.com	Birmingham	AL	35203	205-324-1212	
Faruki Ireland & Cox PLL 500 Courthouse Plz SW 10 N Ludlow St *Web:* www.ficlaw.com	Dayton	OH	45402	937-227-3700	
Feldesman Tucker Leifer Fidell LLP 1129 20th St NW Fourth Fl *Web:* www.feldesmantucker.com	Washington	DC	20036	202-466-8960	
Feldman Gale & Weber PA Two S Biscayne Blvd One Biscayne Tower 30th Fl *Web:* www.feldmangale.com	Miami	FL	33131	305-358-5001	
Feldman, Kramer & Monaco PC 330 Vanderbilt Motor Pkwy *Web:* www.fkmlaw.com	Hauppauge	NY	11788	631-231-1450	
Fennemore Craig PC 3003 N Central Ave Ste 2600 *Web:* www.fclaw.com	Phoenix	AZ	85012	602-916-5000	
Ferguson, Case, Orr, Paterson, & Cunningham LLP 1050 S Kimball Rd *Web:* www.fcopc.com	Ventura	CA	93004	805-659-6800	
Ferrara Fiorenza Larrison Barrett & Reitz PC 5010 Campuswood Dr *Web:* www.ferrarafirm.com	East Syracuse	NY	13057	315-437-7600	
Fiddler Gonzalez & Rodriguez PSC 254 Munoz Rivera Ave Sixth Fl *Web:* www.fgrlaw.com	Hato Rey	PR	00918	787-753-3113	
Fieger Fieger Kenney & Giroux PC 19390 W 10-Mile Rd *Web:* www.fiegerlaw.com	Southfield	MI	48075	248-355-5555	355-5148
Field Law 10235 101 St Nw Ste 2000 *Web:* www.fieldlaw.com	Edmonton	AB	T5J3G1	780-423-3003	
Finkelstein & Partners LLP 1279 Route 300 *Web:* www.lawampm.com	Newburgh	NY	12551	845-562-0203	
Finley, Alt, Smith, Scharnberg, Craig, Hilmes & Gaffney PC 1900 Hub Tower 699 Walnut St *Web:* www.finleylaw.com	Des Moines	IA	50309	515-288-0145	
Fire-Safe Protection Services 1815 Sherwood Forest St *Web:* www.fire-safe.net	Houston	TX	77043	713-722-7800	
Fish & Richardson PC 225 Franklin St 31st Fl *TF:* 800-818-5070 ■ *Web:* www.fr.com	Boston	MA	02110	617-542-5070	542-8906
Fitelson Lasky Aslan & Couture Atty 551 Fifth Ave Rm 605 *Web:* agnesdemilledances.com	New York	NY	10176	212-586-4700	
Fitzpatrick Cella Harper & Scinto 1290 Ave of the Americas *Web:* www.fitzpatrickcella.com	New York	NY	10104	212-218-2100	218-2200
Flaster Greenberg 1810 Chapel Ave W *Web:* www.flastergreenberg.com	Cherry Hill	NJ	08002	856-661-1900	
Fletcher, Heald & Hildreth PLC 1300 N 17th St 11th Fl *Web:* www.fhhlaw.com	Arlington	VA	22209	703-812-0400	
Flicker, Kerin, Kruger & Bissada A Limited Liability Partnership 120 B Santa Margarita Ave *Web:* www.fkkblaw.com	Menlo Park	CA	94025	650-289-1400	
Flook & Graham Pc 11 E Kansas St Ste 100 *Web:* flookandgraham.com	Liberty	MO	64068	816-792-0500	
Foley & Lardner LLP 777 E Wisconsin Ave *TF:* 855-225-5341 ■ *Web:* www.foley.com	Milwaukee	WI	53202	414-271-2400	297-4900
Ford & Harrison LLP 271 17th St NW Ste 1900 *Web:* www.fordharrisonlaw.com	Atlanta	GA	30363	404-888-3800	
Ford Nassen & Baldwin PC 8080 N Central Expy Ste 1600 LB 65 *Web:* www.fordnassen.com	Dallas	TX	75206	214-523-5100	
Fortney Scott LLC 1750 K St Nw Ste 325 *Web:* fortneyscott.com	Washington	DC	20006	202-689-1200	
Foster Pepper Pllc 1111 Third Ave Ste 3400 *TF:* 800-995-5902 ■ *Web:* www.foster.com	Seattle	WA	98101	206-447-4400	447-9700
Foster Swift Collins & Smith 313 S Washington Sq *Web:* www.fosterswift.com	Lansing	MI	48933	517-371-8100	
Foulston & Siefkin LLP 1551 N Waterfront Pkwy Ste 100 *Web:* www.foulston.com	Wichita	KS	67206	316-267-6371	
Fox Galvin LLC One Memorial Dr Eighth Fl *Web:* www.foxgalvin.com	St. Louis	MO	63102	314-588-7000	
Fox Rothschild LLP 2000 Market St 10th Fl *Web:* www.foxrothschild.com	Philadelphia	PA	19103	215-299-2000	299-2150
Fraim & Fiorella PC 150 Boush St Ste 601 *Web:* fraimandfiorella.com	Norfolk	VA	23510	757-227-5900	
Framme Law Firm PC 2812 Emerywood Pkwy Ste 220 *Web:* www.frammelaw.com	Richmond	VA	23294	804-649-1334	
Franczek Sullivan Pc 300 S Wacker Dr Ste 3400 *Web:* www.franczek.com	Chicago	IL	60606	312-786-6119	
Frankfurt Kurnit Klein & Selz Pc 488 Madison Ave 10th Fl *Web:* www.fkks.com	New York	NY	10022	212-980-0120	593-9175
Franklin & Prokopik A Professional Corp The B & O Bldg 2 N Charles St Ste 600 *Web:* www.fandpnet.com	Baltimore	MD	21201	410-752-8700	
Fraser Stryker PC LLO 500 Energy Plz 409 S 17th St *Web:* www.fraserstryker.com	Omaha	NE	68102	402-341-6000	
Fraser Trebilcock Davis & Dunlap PC 124 W Allegan St Ste 1000 *Web:* www.fraserlawfirm.com	Lansing	MI	48933	517-482-5800	
Frederic Dorwart Lawyers Old City Hall 124 E Fourth St *Web:* www.fdlaw.com	Tulsa	OK	74103	918-583-9922	
Fredrickson, Mazeika & Grant LLP 5720 Oberlin Dr *Web:* fmglegal.com	San Diego	CA	92121	858-642-2002	
Freeborn & Peters 311 S Wacker Dr Ste 3000 *Web:* www.freeborn.com	Chicago	IL	60606	312-360-6000	360-6520
Freeland Cooper & Foreman LLP 150 Spear St Ste 1800 *Web:* www.freelandlaw.com	San Francisco	CA	94105	415-541-0200	
Freeman Freeman & Smiley LLP 1888 Century Pk E Ste 1900 *Web:* www.ffslaw.com	Los Angeles	CA	90067	310-255-6100	391-4042
Freund, Freeze & Arnold, A Legal Professional Association One S Main St Fifth Third Ctr Ste 1800 *Web:* ffalaw.com	Dayton	OH	45402	937-222-2424	
Friday, Eldredge & Clark LLP 400 W Capitol Ave Ste 2000 *Web:* www.fridayfirm.com	Little Rock	AR	72201	501-376-2011	
Fried Frank Harris Shriver & Jacobson LLP (FFHSJ) One New York Plz *Web:* www.friedfrank.com	New York	NY	10004	212-859-8000	859-4000
Friedemann Goldberg LLP 420 Aviation Blvd Ste 201 *Web:* www.frigolaw.com	Santa Rosa	CA	95403	707-543-4900	
Friedman & Feiger LLP 5301 Spring Vly Rd Ste 200 *Web:* www.fflawoffice.com	Dallas	TX	75254	972-788-1400	
Friedman Michael G. Atty. 77 N Bridge St *Web:* www.maurosavolaw.com	Somerville	NJ	08876	908-526-0707	
Frost Brown Todd LLC 201 E Fifth St 2200 PNC Ctr *TF:* 866-559-6446 ■ *Web:* www.frostbrowntodd.com	Cincinnati	OH	45202	513-651-6800	651-6981
Fulbright & Jaworski LLP 1301 McKinney St Ste 5100 *TF:* 866-385-2744 ■ *Web:* www.nortonrosefulbright.com	Houston	TX	77010	713-651-5151	651-5246
Fullerton & Knowles PC 12644 Chapel Rd Ste 206 *Web:* www.fullertonlaw.com	Clifton	VA	20124	703-818-2600	
Fultz Maddox Hovious & Dickens PLC 2700 National City Tower 101 S Fifth St *Web:* www.tmhd.com	Louisville	KY	40202	502-588-2000	
Gagen, McCoy, McMahon, Koss, Markowitz & Raines A Professional Corp 279 Front St *Web:* www.gagenmccoy.com	Danville	CA	94526	925-837-0585	
Gallagher, Gams, Pryor, Tallan & Littrell LLP 471 E Broad St Ste 1900 *Web:* www.ggptl.com	Columbus	OH	43215	614-228-5151	
Gallon Takacs Boissoneault & Schaffer Company LPA Jack Gallon Bldg 3516 Granite Cir *Web:* www.gallonlaw.com	Toledo	OH	43617	419-843-2001	
Galloon e s & Associates 40 W Fourth St Ste 2200 *Web:* esgallon.com	Dayton	OH	45402	937-586-3100	
Galloway, Lucchese, Everson & Picchi A Professional Corp 1676 N California Blvd Ste 500 *Web:* www.glattys.com	Walnut Creek	CA	94596	925-930-9090	
Garan Lucow Miller PC 1000 Woodbridge St *Web:* www.garanlucow.com	Detroit	MI	48207	313-446-1530	
Garden City Group LLC 105 Maxess Rd *TF:* 888-404-8013 ■ *Web:* www.gcginc.com	Melville	NY	11747	631-470-5000	470-5100
Gardner James Nakken Hugo & Nolan 429 First St *Web:* yololaw.com	Woodland	CA	95695	530-662-7367	

Phone Fax

Garfunkel Wild & Travis PC
111 Great Neck Rd Ste 503........Great Neck NY 11021 516-393-2200
Web: www.garfunkelwild.com

Garganigo, Goldsmith & Weiss
14 Penn Plz Ste 1020........New York NY 10122 212-643-6400
Web: www.ggw.com

Garrett & Tully A Professional Corp
225 S Lk Ave Ste 1400........Pasadena CA 91101 626-577-9500
Web: www.garrett-tully.com

Garvin & Hickey LLC 181 E Livingston Ave........Columbus OH 43215 614-225-9000
Web: garvin-hickey.com

Gary d Mccallister & Associates LLC
120 N La Salle St Ste 2800........Chicago IL 60602 312-345-0611
Web: www.gdmlawfirm.com

Gary K Walch 4768 Park Granada Fl 2........Calabasas CA 91302 818-222-3400
Web: www.walchlaw.com

Gates, O'Doherty, Gonter & Guy LLP
15373 Innovation Dr Ste 170........San Diego CA 92128 949-769-2481
Web: gogglaw.com

Gauntlett & Associates Attorneys at Law
18400 Von Karman Ave Ste 300........Irvine CA 92612 949-553-1010
Web: www.gauntlettlaw.com

Gawthrop Greenwood PC
17 E Gay St Ste 100........West Chester PA 19381 610-696-8225
Web: www.gawthrop.com

GCA Law Partners LLP 1891 Landings Dr........Mountain View CA 94043 650-428-3900
Web: www.gcalaw.com

General Code Publishers Corp 72 Hinchey Rd........Rochester NY 14624 585-328-1810
Web: www.generalcode.com

Gentry Locke Rakes & Moore LLP
SunTrust Plz 10 Franklin Rd S E........Roanoke VA 24022 540-983-9300
Web: www.gentrylocke.com

George Warshaw & Associates PC
77 Newbury St Fl 4........Boston MA 02116 617-262-7800
Web: warshawlaw.com

Geragos & Geragos PC 644 S Figueroa St........Los Angeles CA 90017 213-625-3900 625-1600
Web: www.geragos.com

Gerard Singer Levick & Busch Pc
16200 Addison Rd Ste 140........Addison TX 75001 972-380-5533
Web: www.singerlevick.com

Germer Gertz LLP 550 Fannin Ste 400........Beaumont TX 77701 409-654-6700
Web: www.germer.com

Gerrish McCreary Smith PC
700 Colonial Rd Ste 200........Memphis TN 38117 901-767-0900
Web: www.gerrish.com

Geygan & Geygan Ltd
8050 Hosbrook Rd Ste 107........Cincinnati OH 45236 513-793-6555
Web: geygan.net

Gibbons PC One Gateway Ctr........Newark NJ 07102 973-596-4500 596-0545
Web: www.gibbonslaw.com

Gibson Dunn & Crutcher LLP
333 S Grand Ave Ste 4600........Los Angeles CA 90071 213-229-7000 229-7520
TF: 888-203-1112 ■ *Web:* www.gibsondunn.com

Gilbert Kelly Crowley & Jennett LLP
1055 W Seventh St Ste 2000........Los Angeles CA 90017 213-615-7000
Web: www.gilbertkelly.com

Gilberti Stinziano Heintz & Smith PC
555 E Genesee St........Syracuse NY 13202 315-442-0100
Web: www.gilbertilaw.com

Gilbride, Tusa, Last & Spillane
31 Brookside Dr PO Box 658........Greenwich CT 06836 203-622-9360
Web: www.gtlslaw.com

Giles & Lambert PC 106 E Market St........Martinsville VA 24112 276-632-7000
Web: www.gileslambert.com

Gill Elrod Ragon Owen & Sherman pa
425 W Capitol Ave Ste 3801........Little Rock AR 72201 501-376-3800
Web: gill-law.com

Ginsburg & Misk Attys
21548 Jamaica Ave........Queens Village NY 11428 718-468-0500
Web: www.gmlawyers.net

Giordano, Halleran & Ciesla PC
125 Half Mile Rd........Middletown NJ 07748 732-741-3900
Web: www.ghclaw.com

Gipson Hoffman & Pancione
1901 Ave of The Stars 11th Fl........Los Angeles CA 90067 310-556-4660 356-8945
Web: www.ghplaw.com

Gislason & Hunter LLP 2700 S Broadway........New Ulm MN 56073 507-354-3111
Web: www.gislason.com

Glancy Prongay & Murray LLP
1801 Ave Of The Stars........Los Angeles CA 90067 310-201-9150
Web: www.glancylaw.com

Glaser Weil Fink Jacobs Howard Avchen & Shapiro LLP
10250 Constellation Blvd 19th Fl........Los Angeles CA 90067 310-553-3000 556-2920
Web: glaserweil.com

Gleason Law Offices PC 163 Merrimack St........Haverhill MA 01830 978-521-4044
Web: www.gleasonlawoffices.com

Glinsmann & Glinsmann, Chartered
12 Russell Ave........Gaithersburg MD 20877 301-987-0030
Web: mygreencardlawyer.com

Global Learning Resources Inc
46330 Sentinel Dr........Fremont CA 94539 510-659-0179
Web: www.glresources.com

Glynn & Finley LLP
100 Pringle Ave Ste 500........Walnut Creek CA 94596 925-210-2800
Web: www.glynnfinley.com

Godfrey & Kahn SC 780 N Water St Ste 1500........Milwaukee WI 53202 414-273-3500
Web: www.gklaw.com

Goehring, Rutter & Boehm
437 Grant St Ste 1424........Pittsburgh PA 15219 412-281-0587
Web: www.grblaw.com

Goldberg & Connolly
G&C Bldg 66 N Village Ave........Rockville Centre NY 11570 516-764-2800
Web: www.goldbergconnolly.com

Goldberg Weisman Cairo
One E Wacker Dr 38th & 39th Fl........Chicago IL 60601 312-464-1200
Web: www.injury-law-atty.com

Goldberg, Persky & White PC
1030 Fifth Ave........Pittsburgh PA 15219 412-471-3980
Web: www.gpwlaw.com

Goldfarb & Lipman LLP 1300 Clay St 11th Fl........Oakland CA 94612 510-836-6336
Web: www.goldfarblipman.com

Goldman Antonetti & Cordova
250 Munoz Rivera Ave Ste 1400........San Juan PR 00918 787-759-8000
Web: www.gaclaw.com

Goldwater Dube 3500 Boul De Maisonneuve O........Westmount QC H3Z3C1 514-861-4367
Web: www.goldwaterdube.com

Gonzales Hoblit Ferguson LLP
802 N Carancahua St Ste 2000........Corpus Christi TX 78401 361-888-9392
Web: www.ghf-lawfirm.com

Goode Casseb Jones Riklin Choate & Watson A Professional Corp
2122 N Main Ave........San Antonio TX 78212 210-733-6030
Web: www.goodelaw.com

Goodell Devries Leech & Dann LLP
One S St 20th Fl........Baltimore MD 21202 410-783-4000 783-4040
TF: 888-229-4354 ■ *Web:* www.gdldlaw.com

Goodman Allen & Filetti PLLC
4501 Highwoods Pkwy Ste 210........Glen Allen VA 23060 804-346-0600
Web: www.goodmanallen.com

Goodsill Anderson Quinn & Stifel
1099 Alakea St Ste 1800........Honolulu HI 96813 808-547-5600
Web: www.goodsill.com

Goodwin Procter LLP 53 State St........Boston MA 02109 617-570-1000 523-1231
Web: www.goodwinprocter.com

Gordon Feinblatt Rothman Hoffberger & Hollander LLC
233 E Redwood St........Baltimore MD 21202 410-576-4156 576-4246
Web: www.gfrlaw.com

Gordon Thomas Honeywell LLP
1201 Pacific Ave Ste 2100........Tacoma WA 98402 253-620-6500 620-6565
Web: www.gth-law.com

Gordon, Fournaris & Mammarella PA
1925 Lovering Ave........Wilmington DE 19806 302-652-2900
Web: gfmlaw.com

Goulston & Storrs 400 Atlantic Ave........Boston MA 02110 617-482-1776
Web: www.goulstonstorrs.com

Goyette & Associates Inc
11344 Coloma Rd Ste 145........Gold River CA 95670 916-851-1900
Web: goyetteassociates.com

Graham Curtin & Sheridan PA
Four Headquarters Plz........Morristown NJ 07962 973-292-1700
Web: www.grahamcurtin.com

Graham Lundberg & Peschei
2153 Bethel Rd Se........Port Orchard WA 98366 360-876-5005
Web: www.glpattorneys.com

Grant, Herrmann, Schwartz & Klinger
675 Third Ave........New York NY 10017 212-682-1800
Web: www.ghsklaw.com

Grant, Konvalinka & Harrison PC
Republic Ctr 633 Chestnut St Ninth Fl
Ste 900........Chattanooga TN 37450 423-756-8400
Web: www.gkhpc.com

Gravel & Shea 76 St Paul St PO Box 369........Burlington VT 05402 802-658-0220
Web: www.gravelshea.com

Gravely & Pearson LLP
425 Soledad St Ste 600........San Antonio TX 78205 210-472-1111
Web: www.gplawfirm.com

Gray Plant Mooty Inc
500 IDS Ctr 80 S Eighth St........Minneapolis MN 55402 612-632-3000
Web: www.gpmlaw.com

Gray, Layton, Kersh, Solomon, Sigmon, Furr & Smith PA
516 S New Hope Rd........Gastonia NC 28053 704-865-4400
Web: www.gastonlegal.com

Greenan, Peffer, Sallander & Lally LLP
6111 Bollinger Canyon Rd Ste 500........San Ramon CA 94583 925-866-1000
Web: www.gpsllp.com

Greenbaum, Rowe, Smith, Ravin, Davis & Himmel LLP
Metro Corporate Campus 99 Wood Ave South........Woodbridge NJ 07095 732-549-5600
Web: www.greenbaumlaw.com

Greenberg Glusker Fields Claman & Machtinger LLP
1900 Ave of the Stars 21st Fl........Los Angeles CA 90067 310-553-3610 553-0687
Web: www.greenbergglusker.com

Greer Herz & Adams LLP
2525 S Shore Blvd Ste 203........League City TX 77573 281-480-5278
Web: www.greerherz.com

Grey Law of Ventura County Inc
290 Maple Ct Ste 128........Ventura CA 93003 805-658-2266
Web: www.greylaw.us

Griffel, Dorshow & Johnson, Chartered
1809 Plymouth Rd Ste 333........Hopkins MN 55305 612-529-3333
Web: www.612law3333.com

Grossman, Tucker, Perreault & Pfleger PLLC
55 S Commercial St........Manchester NH 03101 603-668-6560
Web: gtpp.com

Group Wellesley 933 Wellesley Rd........Pittsburgh PA 15206 412-363-3481
Web: www.groupwellesley.com

Grower, Ketcham, Rutherford, Bronson, Eide & Telan PA
901 N Lk Destiny Rd Ste 450........Maitland FL 32751 407-423-9545
Web: www.growerketcham.com

Guida, Slavich & Flores PC
750 N Saint Paul St Ste 200........Dallas TX 75201 214-692-0009
Web: www.guidaslavichflores.com

Gullett, Sanford, Robinson & Martin PLLC
150 Third Ave S Ste 1700........Nashville TN 37201 615-244-4994
Web: www.gsrm.net

Gunster Yoakley & Stewart Pa
777 S Flagler Dr Ste 500 E........West Palm Beach FL 33401 561-655-1980 655-5677
TF: 800-749-1980 ■ *Web:* www.gunster.com

Firm	Address	City	State	Zip	Phone	Fax	Web
Gurstel Chargo LLP	6681 Country Club Dr	Golden Valley	MN	55427	763-267-6700		www.gurstel.com
Gutman, Mintz, Baker & Sonnenfeldt	813 Jericho Tpke	New Hyde Park	NY	11040	516-775-7007		www.gmbspc.com
Hagen Wilka & Archer LLP	600 S Main Ave Ste 102	Sioux Falls	SD	57104	605-334-0005		hagen-wilka-archer-p-c-.nhft.org
Hagens Berman Sobol Shapiro LLP	1918 Eighth Ave Ste 3300	Seattle	WA	98101	206-623-7292		www.hbsslaw.com
Haight Brown & Bonesteel LLP	555 S Flower St	Los Angeles	CA	90071	213-542-8000	542-8100	www.hbblaw.com
Hailey, McNamara, Hall, Larmann & Papale LLP	One Galleria Blvd Ste 1400	Metairie	LA	70001	504-836-6500		www.hmhlp.com
Hale Lane Peek Dennison & Howard	5441 Kietzke Ln Second Fl	Reno	NV	89511	775-327-3000		www.halelane.com
Hall & Evans	1125 17th St Ste 600	Denver	CO	80202	303-628-3300	293-3232	www.hallevans.com
Hall Render Killian Heath & Lyman Pc	1 American Sq Ste 2000 Ste 2000	Indianapolis	IN	46282	317-633-4884	633-4878	www.hallrender.com
Hall, Estill, Hardwick, Gable, Golden & Nelson PC	320 S Boston Ave Ste 400	Tulsa	OK	74103	918-594-0400		www.hallestill.com
Hangley Aronchick Segal & Pudlin PC	One Logan Sq 18th and Cherry Sts.	Philadelphia	PA	19103	215-568-6200		www.hangley.com
Hansen, Jacobson, Teller, Hoberman, Newman, Warren, Richman, Rush & Kaller LLP	450 N Roxbury Dr Eighth Fl	Beverly Hills	CA	90210	310-271-8777		www.hjth.com
Hanson Lulic & Krall LLC	700 Northstar E 608 Second Ave S	Minneapolis	MN	55402	612-333-2530		hlk.com
Harbour, Smith, Harris & Merritt	404 N Green St	Longview	TX	75601	903-757-4001		www.harbourlaw.com
Hardin, Kundla, McKeon & Poletto PA - A Professional Corp	673 Morris Ave	Springfield	NJ	07081	973-912-5222		www.hkmpp.com
Hargreaves & Taylor	750 B St Ste 2300	San Diego	CA	92101	619-238-5501		www.htfamlaw.com
Harman, Claytor, Corrigan & Wellman A Professional Corp	PO Box 70280	Richmond	VA	23255	804-747-5200		www.hccw.com
Harmon Curran Spielberg & Eisenberg	1726 M St Nw Ste 600	Washington	DC	20036	202-328-3500		www.harmoncurran.com
Harper Grey LLP	3200 Vancouver Centre 650 W Georgia St	Vancouver	BC	V6B4P7	604-687-0411		www.harpergrey.com
Harrang Long Gary Rudnick PC	360 E 10th Ave Ste 300	Eugene	OR	97401	541-485-0220		www.harrang.com
Harris Law Firm	30 Hempstead Ave Ste H11	Rockville Centre	NY	11570	516-569-2600		www.harrisfamilylaw.com
Harris Wyatt & Amala Attorneys at Law	5778 Commercial St Se	Salem	OR	97306	503-378-7744		www.salemattorneys.com
Harrison & Held LLP	333 W Wacker Dr Ste 1700	Chicago	IL	60606	312-753-6185		www.harrisonheld.com
Harrison, Eichenberg & Murphy LLP	155 E Wilbur Rd Ste 200	Thousand Oaks	CA	91360	805-495-7379		www.hem-law.com
Harter Secrest & Emery LLP (HSE)	1600 Bausch & Lomb Pl.	Rochester	NY	14604	585-232-6500	232-2152	www.hselaw.com
Hartley, Rowe & Fowler PC	6622 Broad St	Douglasville	GA	30134	770-920-2000		www.hrflegal.com
Hartline Dacus Barger Dreyer LLP	6688 N Central Expy Ste 1000	Dallas	TX	75206	214-369-2100		www.hdbdlaw.com
Hartman Underhill & Brubaker LLP	221 E Chestnut St	Lancaster	PA	17602	717-299-7254		hublaw.com
Hartman, Simons, Spielman & Wood LLP	6400 Powers Ferry Rd NW Ste 400	Atlanta	GA	30339	770-955-3555		www.hartmansimons.com
Hartnett Law Firm, The	2920 N Pearl St	Dallas	TX	75201	214-742-4655		www.hartnettlawfirm.com
Harwell Howard Hyne Gabbert & Manner PC	315 Deaderick St Ste 1800	Nashville	TN	37238	615-256-0500		www.h3gm.com
Harwood Lloyd LLC	130 Main St	Hackensack	NJ	07601	201-487-1080		www.harwoodlloyd.com
Haverstock & Owens LLP	162 N Wolfe Rd	Sunnyvale	CA	94086	408-530-9700		hollp.com
Hawkins Parnell Thackston & Young LLP	4000 SunTrust Plz 303 Peachtree St NE	Atlanta	GA	30308	404-614-7400		www.hptylaw.com
Hawley Troxell Ennis & Hawley LLP	877 Main St Ste 1000	Boise	ID	83702	208-344-6000		hteh.com
Haworth, Bradshaw, Stallknecht & Barber Inc	4420 Auburn Blvd.	Sacramento	CA	95841	916-484-4354		www.haworthlaw.com
Haynes & Boone LLP	2323 Victory Ave #700	Dallas	TX	75219	214-651-5000	651-5940	www.haynesboone.com
Haynsworth Sinkler Boyd PA	134 Meeting St Third Fl.	Charleston	SC	29402	843-722-3366		www.hsblawfirm.com
Heard & Smith LLP	3737 Broadway Ste 310	San Antonio	TX	78209	210-820-3737		www.heardandsmith.com
Heavner, Scott, Beyers & Mihlar LLC	111 E Main St Ste 200	Decatur	IL	62523	217-422-1719		hsbattys.com
Heidell, Pittoni, Murphy & Bach LLP	99 Park Ave.	New York	NY	10016	212-286-8585		www.hpmb.com
Henderson, Caverly, Pum & Charney LLP	12750 High Bluff Dr Ste 300	San Diego	CA	92130	858-755-3000		www.hcesq.com
Henson & Efron PA	220 S Sixth St Ste 1800	Minneapolis	MN	55402	612-339-2500		www.hensonefron.com
Herman Herman Katz & Cotlar LLP	820 Okeefe Ave	New Orleans	LA	70113	504-581-4892		hhklawfirm.com
Herold & Sager, Attorneys at Law	550 Second St Ste 200	Encinitas	CA	92024	760-487-1047		www.heroldsagerlaw.com
Herrick Feinstein LLP	Two Park Ave.	New York	NY	10016	212-592-1400		www.herrick.com
Hershner Hunter LLP	180 E 11th Ave	Eugene	OR	97401	541-686-8511		www.hershnerhunter.com
Hertz Schram & Saretsky Pc	1760 S Telegraph Rd Ste 300	Bloomfield Hills	MI	48302	248-335-5000		www.hsspc.com
Heslin, Rothenberg, Farley, & Mesiti PC	Five Columbia Cir.	Albany	NY	12203	518-452-5600		www.hrfmlaw.com
Heyl Royster Voelker & Allen Pc	124 SW Adams St Ste 600	Peoria	IL	61602	309-676-0400		www.hrva.com
Hicken, Scott, Howard & Anderson PA	2150 Third Ave Ste 300	Anoka	MN	55303	763-421-4110		www.hshalaw.com
Hiday & Ricke pa	4230 S Macdill Ave Ste 214	Tampa	FL	33611	813-805-0300		www.hidayricke.com
Hill Ward Henderson	101 E Kennedy Blvd Ste 3700	Tampa	FL	33602	813-221-3900		www.hwhlaw.com
Hill, Farrer & Burrill LLP	300 S Grand Ave One California Plz 37th Fl	Los Angeles	CA	90071	213-620-0460		www.hfbllp.com
Hillis, Clark, Martin & Peterson PS	1221 Second Ave Ste 500	Seattle	WA	98101	206-623-1745		www.hcmp.com
Hillman, Brown & Darrow PA	221 Duke Of Gloucester St	Annapolis	MD	21401	410-269-5555		www.hbdlaw.com
Hinckley Allen & Snyder LLP	28 State St	Boston	MA	02109	617-345-9000	345-9020	www.hinckleyallen.com
Hinkle Elkouri Law Firm LLC	2000 Epic Ctr 301 N Main St	Wichita	KS	67202	316-267-2000		hinklaw.com
Hinman, Howard & Kattell LLP	700 Security Mutual 80 Exchange St	Binghamton	NY	13901	607-723-5341		www.hhk.com
Hinshaw & Culbertson LLP	222 N LaSalle St Ste 300	Chicago	IL	60601	312-704-3000	704-3001	www.hinshawlaw.com
Hiscock & Barclay LLP	300 S State St	Syracuse	NY	13202	315-425-2700		hblaw.com
Hoagland, Longo, Moran, Dunst & Doukas	40 Paterson St	New Brunswick	NJ	08903	732-545-4717		www.hoaglandlongo.com
Hochman, Salkin, Rettig, Toscher & Perez PC	9150 Wilshire Blvd Ste 300	Beverly Hills	CA	90212	310-281-3200		taxlitigator.com
Hodes Keating & Pilon	134 N La Salle St Ste 1300	Chicago	IL	60602	312-553-1440		www.hkp-customs.com
Hodgson Russ LLP	140 Pearl St The Guaranty Bldg Ste 100	Buffalo	NY	14202	716-856-4000		www.hodgsonruss.com
Hoffman Alvary & Company LLC	Seven Wells Ave Ste 33	Newton Center	MA	02459	617-758-0500		hoffmanalvary.com
Hoffmann & Baron LLP	6900 Jericho Tpke	Syosset	NY	11791	516-822-3550		www.hbiplaw.com
Hogan Marren Ltd	321 N Clark St Ste 1301	Chicago	IL	60654	312-946-1800		www.hmltd.com
Holihan Law	1101 N Lk Destiny Rd Ste 275	Maitland	FL	32751	407-660-8575		www.holihanpc.com
Hopkins & Carley A Law Corp	PO Box 1469	San Jose	CA	95109	408-286-9800	998-4790	*TF:* 800-829-3676 ■ www.hopkinscarley.com
Horowitt, Darryl J. - Coleman & Horowitt LLP	499 W Shaw Ave Ste 116	Fresno	CA	93704	559-248-4820		www.ch-law.com
Horton, Oberrecht, Kirkpatrick & Martha, Attorneys At Law A Professional Corp	NBC Bldg 225 Broadway Ste 2200	San Diego	CA	92101	619-232-1183		www.hortonfirm.com
Horvitz & Levy LLP	15760 Ventura Blvd Ste 1800	Encino	CA	91436	818-995-0800		horvitzlevy.com
Houser & Allison APC	9970 Research Dr	Irvine	CA	92618	949-679-1111		www.houser-law.com
Howard & Howard Attorneys Pc	39400 Woodward Ave Ste 101	Bloomfield Hills	MI	48304	248-645-1483	645-1568	www.h2law.com
Howard N. Sobel Law Offices	507 Kresson Rd	Voorhees	NJ	08043	856-424-6400		sobellaw.com

	City	State	Zip	Phone	Fax
Howard, Kohn, Sprague & FitzGerald LLP 237 Buckingham St *Web:* www.hksflaw.com	Hartford	CT	06126	860-525-3101	
Howrey LLP 1299 Pennsylvania Ave NW	Washington	DC	20004	202-783-0800	
Hudson Cook LLP 7250 Pkwy Dr Fifth Fl *Web:* www.hudco.com	Hanover	MD	21076	410-684-3200	
Hudson, Mallaney, Shindler & Anderson PC 5015 Grand Ridge Dr Ste 100 *Web:* www.hudsonlaw.net	West Des Moines	IA	50265	515-223-4567	
Huff Poole & Mahoney Pc 4705 Columbus St Ste 100 *Web:* poolemahoney.com	Virginia Beach	VA	23462	757-499-1841	
Hughes Hubbard & Reed LLP One Battery Pk Plz *Web:* www.hugheshubbard.com	New York	NY	10004	212-837-6000	422-4726
Hunt Leibert Jacobson PC 50 Weston St *Web:* www.huntleibert.com	Hartford	CT	06120	860-808-0606	
Hunter, Smith & Davis LLP 1212 N Eastman Rd *Web:* www.hsdlaw.com	Kingsport	TN	37664	423-378-8800	
Hunton & Williams LLP 951 E Byrd St Riverfront Plaza E Tower *TF:* 800-669-6820 ■ *Web:* www.hunton.com	Richmond	VA	23219	804-788-8200	788-8218
Hurley Rogner Miller Cox 1560 Orange Ave # 500 *Web:* www.hrmcw.com	Winter Park	FL	32789	407-571-7400	422-1371
Hurley, Toevs, Styles, Hamblin & Panter PA 4155 Montgomery Blvd Ne *Web:* hurleyfirm.com	Albuquerque	NM	87109	505-888-1188	
Husch Blackwell LLP 4801 Main St Ste 1000 *Web:* www.husch.com	Kansas City	MO	64108	816-983-8000	
Hyland Levin LLP 6000 Sagemore Dr Ste 6301 *Web:* www.hylandlevin.com	Marlton	NJ	08053	856-355-2900	
Hyman Phelps & Mcnamara Pc 700 13th St NW Ste 1200 *Web:* www.hpm.com	Washington	DC	20005	202-737-5600	737-9329
Illinois Legal Aid Online 17 N State St Ste 1590 *Web:* illinoislegalaid.org	Chicago	IL	60602	312-977-9047	
Inner City Law Center 1309 E Seventh St *Web:* www.innercitylaw.org	Los Angeles	CA	90021	213-891-2880	
Innocence Project of Florida Inc 1100 E Park Ave *Web:* www.floridainnocence.org	Tallahassee	FL	32301	850-561-6767	
Iowa Legal Aid 1111 Ninth St Ste 230 *Web:* www.iowalegalaid.org	Des Moines	IA	50314	515-243-2151	
Iphorgan Ltd 1130 W Lk Cook Rd Ste 240 *Web:* iphorgan.com	Buffalo Grove	IL	60089	847-808-5500	
Ipwatch Corp 401 E Tuscaloosa St *Web:* www.ipwatch.com	Florence	AL	35630	256-718-0078	
Irell & Manella LLP 1800 Ave of the Stars Ste 900 *Web:* irell.com	Los Angeles	CA	90067	310-277-1010	203-7199
Iseman Cunningham Riester & Hyde LLP Nine Thurlow Ter *Web:* www.icrh.com	Albany	NY	12203	518-462-3000	
Ivey, Barnum & O'mara LLC 170 Mason St *Web:* www.ibolaw.com	Greenwich	CT	06830	203-661-6000	
Jacko Law Group PC 5920 Friars Rd Ste 208 *Web:* www.jackolg.com	San Diego	CA	92108	619-298-2880	
Jackson & Hertogs 170 Columbus Ave Fl 4 *Web:* jackson-hertogs.com	San Francisco	CA	94133	415-986-4559	
Jackson DeMarco Tidus & Peckenpaugh Law Corp 2030 Main St 12th Fl *Web:* www.jdtplaw.com	Irvine	CA	92614	949-752-8585	
Jackson Kelly PLLC 1600 Laidley Tower 500 Lee St *Web:* www.jacksonkelly.com	Charleston	WV	25322	304-340-1172	
JacksonWhite PC 40 N Center St Ste 200 *Web:* whitebuffaloclub.com	Mesa	AZ	85201	480-464-1111	
Jacob Medinger & Finnegan LLP (JMF) 1270 Ave of the Americas *Web:* jmfnylaw.com	New York	NY	10020	212-524-5000	332-7777
Jacobson Holman PLLC 400 Seventh St NW *Web:* www.jhip.com	Washington	DC	20004	202-638-6666	
Jacobson, Hansen, Najarian & Mcquillan 1690 W Shaw Ave Ste 201 *Web:* jhnmlaw.com	Fresno	CA	93711	559-448-0400	
Jaffe Raitt Heuer & Weiss PC 27777 Franklin Rd Ste 2500 *Web:* www.jaffelaw.com	Southfield	MI	48034	248-351-3000	
James Hoyer Newcomer & Smiljanich pa 3301 Thomasville Rd *Web:* www.jameshoyer.com	Tallahassee	FL	32308	850-325-2680	
James, McElroy & Diehl PA 600 S College St *Web:* www.jmdlaw.com	Charlotte	NC	28202	704-372-9870	
Jameson & Dunagan PC 3890 W Northwest Hwy Ste 550 *Web:* jamesondunagan.com	Dallas	TX	75220	214-369-6422	
Jan Dils Attorneys at Law Lc 107 Lb And T Way *Web:* www.jandils.com	Logan	WV	25601	304-831-0000	
Jardine, Logan & O'Brien PLLP 8519 Eagle Point Blvd Ste 100 *Web:* www.jlolaw.com	Lake Elmo	MN	55042	651-290-6500	
Jaspan Schlesinger Hoffman LLP 300 Garden City Plz *Web:* www.jaspanllp.com	Garden City	NY	11530	516-746-8000	
Javitch Block & Rathbone LLP 602 Main St Ste 500 *Web:* www.jbandr.com	Cincinnati	OH	45202	513-744-9600	
Jeansonne & Remondet LLC 200 W Congress St Ste 1100 *Web:* www.jeanrem.com	Lafayette	LA	70501	337-237-4370	
Jeffers, Danielson, Sonn & AylwardPS 2600 Chester Kimm Rd *Web:* www.jdsalaw.com	Wenatchee	WA	98801	509-662-3685	
Jenkins Fenstermaker PLLC 325 Eighth St *Web:* www.jenkinsfenstermaker.com	Huntington	WV	25701	304-523-2100	
Jenkins, Wilson, Taylor & Hunt PA 3100 Tower Blvd Ste 1200 *Web:* www.jenkinswilson.com	Durham	NC	27707	919-493-8000	
Jenner & Block LLP 353 N Clark St *Web:* www.jenner.com	Chicago	IL	60654	312-222-9350	527-0484
Jensen Baird Gardner & Henry 10 Free St *Web:* www.jbgh.com	Portland	ME	04112	207-775-7271	
John C. Heath, Attorney at Law PLLC 360 N Cutler Dr *TF:* 800-756-9681 ■ *Web:* www.lexingtonlaw.com	Salt Lake City	UT	84054	800-756-9681	
Johnson & Bell Ltd 33 W Monroe St Ste 2700 *Web:* johnsonandbell.com	Chicago	IL	60603	312-372-0770	372-9818
Johnston, Allison & Hord PA 1065 E Morehead St *Web:* www.jahlaw.com	Charlotte	NC	28204	704-332-1181	
Jones Day 51 Louisiana Ave NW *Web:* www.jonesday.com	Washington	DC	20001	202-879-3939	626-1700
Jones, Allen & Fuquay LLP 8828 Greenville Ave *Web:* www.jonesallen.com	Dallas	TX	75243	214-343-7400	
Jordan Price Wall Gray Jones & Carlton PLLC 1951 Clark Ave *Web:* www.jordanprice.com	Raleigh	NC	27605	919-828-2501	
Joseph, Greenwald & Laake PA 6404 Ivy Ln Ste 400 *Web:* www.jgllaw.com	Rockville	MD	20770	301-220-2200	
Judicare Wisconsin Inc Attys 300 N Third St Ste 210 *Web:* www.judicare.org	Wausau	WI	54403	715-842-1681	
Kagan Binder PLLC 221 Main St N Ste 200 *Web:* www.kaganbinder.com	Stillwater	MN	55082	651-351-2900	
Kahn Soares & Conway LLP 1415 L St Ste 400 *Web:* www.ksclawyers.com	Sacramento	CA	95814	916-448-3826	
Karbal, Cohen, Economou, Silk & Dunne LLC 150 S Wacker Dr Ste 1700 *Web:* www.karballaw.com	Chicago	IL	60606	312-431-3700	
Karl Truman Law Office LLC 420 Wall St *Web:* www.trumanlaw.com	Jeffersonville	IN	47130	812-282-8500	
Katten Muchin Rosenman LLP 525 W Monroe St Ste 1300 *TF:* 800-449-8114 ■ *Web:* www.kattenlaw.com	Chicago	IL	60661	312-902-5200	902-1061
Katz & Korin PC The Emelie Bldg 334 N Senate Ave *Web:* www.katzkorin.com	Indianapolis	IN	46204	317-464-1100	
Katz Goldstein & Warren Pc 2345 Waukegan Rd Ste 150 *Web:* kgwlaw.com	Bannockburn	IL	60015	847-317-9500	
Katz Law Office Ltd 2408 W Cermak Rd *Web:* katzlawchicago.com	Chicago	IL	60608	773-847-8982	
Kaufman Borgeest & Ryan LLP 23975 Park Sorrento Ste 370 *Web:* kbrlaw.com	Calabasas	CA	91302	818-880-0993	
Kay Casto & Chaney PLLC 1500 Chase Tower 707 Virginia St E *Web:* www.kaycasto.com	Charleston	WV	25301	304-345-8900	
Kaye Scholer LLP 425 Pk Ave *Web:* www.kayescholer.com	New York	NY	10022	212-836-8000	836-8689
Keating Muething & Klekamp Pll One E Fourth St Ste 1400 *Web:* www.kmklaw.com	Cincinnati	OH	45202	513-579-6400	579-6457
Keeney, Waite & Stevens 402 W Broadway Ste 1820 *Web:* www.keenlaw.com	San Diego	CA	92101	619-238-1661	
Keesal Young & Logan 400 Oceangate PO Box 1730 *Web:* www.kyl.com	Long Beach	CA	90801	562-436-2000	436-7416
Kegler, Brown, Hill & Ritter Company LPA 65 E State St Capitol Sq Ste 1800 *Web:* www.keglerbrown.com	Columbus	OH	43215	614-462-5400	
Keker & Van Nest LLP 633 Battery St *Web:* www.kvn.com	San Francisco	CA	94111	415-391-5400	
Kell, Alterman & Runstein LLP The Pacific Bldg 520 SW Yamhill St Ste 600 *Web:* www.kelrun.com	Portland	OR	97204	503-222-3531	
Keller & Heckman LLP 1001 G St NW Ste 500w *TF:* 888-364-1200 ■ *Web:* www.khlaw.com	Washington	DC	20001	202-434-4100	434-4646
Kelley & Ferraro LLP 2200 Key Tower 127 Pub Sq *Web:* www.kelley-ferraro.com	Cleveland	OH	44114	216-202-3450	
Kelley Drye & Warren LLP 101 Pk Ave *Web:* www.kelleydrye.com	New York	NY	10178	212-808-7800	808-7897
Kellogg, Huber, Hansen, Todd, Evans & Figel PLLC Sumner Sq 1615 M St NW Ste 400 *Web:* www.khhte.com	Washington	DC	20036	202-326-7900	
Kelly Mike Law Group LLC 500 Taylor St Ste 400 *Web:* www.mklawgroup.com	Columbia	SC	29201	803-726-0123	
Kemp & Smith LLP 221 N Kansas PO Box 1700 *Web:* www.kempsmith.com	El Paso	TX	79901	915-533-4424	546-5360
Ken Nunn Law Office 104 S Franklin Rd *Web:* kennunn.com	Bloomington	IN	47404	812-332-9451	
Killian Jensen & Davis Pc Martin Cheryl 202 N Seventh St *Web:* www.killianlaw.com	Grand Junction	CO	81501	970-241-0707	

Name / Address	City	State	Zip	Phone	Fax
Kilmer, Voorhees & Laurick PC 732 NW 19th Ave Web: www.kilmerlaw.com	Portland	OR	97209	503-224-0055	
Kilpatrick Townsend & Stockton LLP 1100 Peachtree St. Web: www.kilpatricktownsend.com	Atlanta	GA	30309	404-815-6500	815-6555
Kimball, Tirey & St. John LLP 7676 Hazard Ctr Dr Ste 900 Web: www.kts-law.com	San Diego	CA	92108	619-234-1690	
King & Partners Plc 170 College Ave Ste 230 Web: www.king-partners.com	Holland	MI	49423	616-355-0400	
King & Schickli PLLC 247 N Broadway Web: www.iplaw1.net	Lexington	KY	40507	859-252-0889	
King & Spalding 1180 Peachtree St NE Web: www.kslaw.com	Atlanta	GA	30309	404-572-4600	572-5100
King, Krebs & Jurgens PLLC Capital One Bldg 201 St Charles Ave 45th Fl Web: www.kingkrebs.com	New Orleans	LA	70170	504-582-3800	
Kinney & Lange PA 312 S Third St. Web: www.kinney.com	Minneapolis	MN	55415	612-339-1863	
Kirby Noonan Lance & Hoge LLP 350 Tenth Ave Ste 1300 Web: www.knlh.com	San Diego	CA	92101	619-231-8666	
Kirk Rankin Law Office 11501 Georgia Ave Ste 210 Web: kirkrankin.com	Silver Spring	MD	20902	301-933-4648	
Kirkland & Ellis LLP 200 E Randolph Dr. TF: 800-647-7600 ■ Web: www.kirkland.com	Chicago	IL	60601	312-861-2000	861-2200
Kirkpatrick & Lockhart Preston Gates Ellis LLP 210 Sixth Ave TF: 800-452-8260 ■ Web: www.klgates.com	Pittsburgh	PA	15222	412-355-6500	355-6501
Kissinger & Fellman PC 3773 Cherry Creek N Dr Web: www.kandf.com	Denver	CO	80209	303-320-6100	
Kitch Drutchas Wagner Valitutti & Sherbrook Pc One Woodward Ave Ste 2400 Web: www.kitch.com	Detroit	MI	48226	313-965-7900	
Kivell, Rayment & Francis PC 7666 E 61st St Ste 550 Web: www.kivell.com	Tulsa	OK	74133	918-254-0626	
Klafter & Mason LLC Manalapan Corporate Plz 195 Rt 9 South Web: www.kmrslaw.com	Manalapan	NJ	07726	732-358-2028	
Kleinfeld, Kaplan & Becker LLP 1140 19th St NW Ste 900 Web: www.kkblaw.com	Washington	DC	20036	202-223-5120	
Klenda Austerman LLC 1600 Epic Ctr 301 N Main St Web: klendalaw.com	Wichita	KS	67202	316-267-0331	
Kline & Specter A Professional Corp 1525 Locust St 19th Fl Web: www.klinespecter.com	Philadelphia	PA	19102	215-772-1000	
Klinedinst Law 801 K St Fl 28 Web: www.klinedinstlaw.com	Sacramento	CA	95814	916-444-7573	
Knox McLaughlin Gornall & Sennett PC 120 W Tenth St Web: kmgslaw.com	Erie	PA	16501	814-459-2800	
Kobayashi, Sugita & Goda LLP, Attorneys at Law 999 Bishop St Ste 2600 Web: www.ksglaw.com	Honolulu	HI	96813	808-535-5700	
Koenig Jacobsen LLP 16300 Bake Pkwy Web: kjattorneys.com	Irvine	CA	92618	949-756-0700	
Kohner Mann & Kailas SC Washington Bldg 4650 N Port Washington Rd Web: www.kmksc.com	Milwaukee	WI	53212	414-962-5110	
Kominiarek Bressler Harvick & Gudmundson LLC 33 N Dearborn St Ste 700 Web: www.kbhglaw.com	Chicago	IL	60602	312-322-1111	782-1432
Kope & Associates LLC 4660 Trindle Rd Ste 201 Web: www.kopelaw.com	Camp Hill	PA	17011	717-761-7573	
Korshak Kracoff Kong & Sugano LLP 1640 S Sepulveda Blvd Ste 520 Web: kkks.com	Los Angeles	CA	90025	310-996-2340	
Koskoff, Koskoff & Bieder PC 350 Fairfield Ave Web: www.koskoff.com	Bridgeport	CT	06604	203-583-8634	
Kotin, Crabtree & Strong LLP One Bowdoin Sq Web: www.kcslegal.com	Boston	MA	02114	617-227-7031	
Kramer, Dillof, Livingston & Moore 217 Broadway Fl 10 Web: kdlm.com	New York	NY	10007	212-267-4177	
Kream & Kream 536 Broad St Ste 5 Web: www.kreamandkream.com	East Weymouth	MA	02189	781-331-9333	
Kreis, Enderle, Hudgins & Borsos PC 8225 Moorsbridge Rd. Web: www.kreisenderle.com	Kalamazoo	MI	49003	269-324-3000	
Kremblas Foster Phillips & Pollick 7632 Slate Ridge Blvd Web: ohiopatent.com	Reynoldsburg	OH	43068	614-575-2100	
Krieg DeVault Alexander & Capehart One Indiana Sq Ste 2800 Web: www.kriegdevault.com	Indianapolis	IN	46204	317-636-4341	636-1507
Kring & Chung LLP 38 Corporate Park Web: www.kringandchung.com	Irvine	CA	92606	949-467-9164	
Kronick Moskovitz Tiedemann & Girard (KMTG) 400 Capitol Mall Fl 27 Web: www.kmtg.com	Sacramento	CA	95814	916-321-4500	321-4555
Krugliak, Wilkins, Griffiths & Dougherty Co 4775 Munson St NW Web: www.kwgd.com	Canton	OH	44735	330-497-0700	
Kutak Rock LLP 1650 Farnam St Web: www.kutakrock.com	Omaha	NE	68102	402-346-6000	346-1148
Kuzmich Law Firm Pc 335 W Main St Web: www.kuzmichlaw.com	Lewisville	TX	75057	972-434-1555	
L. Patrick Mulligan & Associates LPA Co 28 N Wilkinson St. Web: www.patrickmulligan.com	Dayton	OH	45402	937-228-9790	
Lackey Hershman LLP 3102 Oak Lawn Ave Ste 777 Web: www.lhlaw.net	Dallas	TX	75219	214-560-2201	
Lacy Katzen LLP 130 E Main St Second Fl. Web: www.lacykatzen.com	Rochester	NY	14604	585-454-5650	
Ladas & Parry LLP 1040 Ave of the Americas Web: www.ladas.com	New York	NY	10018	212-708-1800	246-8959
Lakin Spears LLP Embarcadero Pl 2400 Geng Rd Ste 110 Web: www.lakinspears.com	Palo Alto	CA	94303	650-328-7000	
Lamb & Barnosky LLP 534 Broadhollow Rd Ste 210 PO Box 9034 Web: www.lambbarnosky.com	Melville	NY	11747	631-694-2300	
Lamb McErlane PC 24 E Market St PO Box 565 Web: www.lambmcerlane.com	West Chester	PA	19381	610-430-8000	
Lamson, Dugan & Murray LLP Lamson Dugan & Murray Bldg 10306 Regency Pkwy Dr Web: www.ldmlaw.com	Omaha	NE	68114	402-397-7300	
Landrum & Shouse LLP 220 W Main St Ste 1900. Web: watsoninsurance.com	Louisville	KY	40202	502-589-7616	
Lane & Waterman LLP 220 N Main St Ste 600 Web: www.l-wlaw.com	Davenport	IA	52801	563-324-3246	324-1616
Lanier Ford Shaver & Payne PC 2101 W Clinton Ave Ste 102 Web: www.lanierford.com	Huntsville	AL	35805	256-535-1100	
Lanier Law Group PA 600 S Duke St Web: lanierlawgroup.com	Durham	NC	27701	919-682-2111	
LaRiviere, Grubman PC 19 Upper Ragsdale Dr Ste 200 Web: www.lgpatlaw.com	Monterey	CA	93942	831-649-8800	
Larson Berg & Perkins Pllc 105 N Third St Web: www.lplaw.com	Yakima	WA	98901	509-457-1515	
Larson King LLP 30 E Seventh St Ste 2800 TF: 877-373-5501 ■ Web: www.larsonking.com	Saint Paul	MN	55101	651-312-6500	312-6618
Lashly & Baer PC 714 Locust St Web: www.lashlybaer.com	St. Louis	MO	63101	314-621-2939	
Lassiter-taylor Law Firm, The 6215 Claret Dr Web: www.lassiterlawyers.com	Jacksonville	FL	32210	904-779-5585	
Latham & Watkins LLP 885 Third Ave Web: www.lw.com	New York	NY	10022	212-906-1200	751-4864
Latimer, Biaggi, Rachid, & Godreau LLP Firstbank Bldg 1519 Ponce de Leon Ave Ste 1205 Web: www.lbrglaw.com	San Juan	PR	00902	787-724-0230	
Lavin O'Neil Ricci Cedrone & Disipio 190 N Independence Mall W. Web: www.lavin-law.com	Philadelphia	PA	19106	215-627-0303	627-2551
Law Society of Manitoba 219 Kennedy St Web: www.lawsociety.mb.ca	Winnipeg	MB	R3C1S8	204-942-5571	
Law Weathers & Richardson Pc 333 Bridge St NW Ste 800 Web: www.lawweathers.com	Grand Rapids	MI	49504	616-459-1171	732-1740
Lawson & Weitzen LLP 88 Black Falcon Ave Web: www.lawson-weitzen.com	Boston	MA	02210	617-439-4990	
Lawson Lundell LLP 925 W Georgia St Cathedral Pl Ste 1600 Web: www.lawsonlundell.com	Vancouver	BC	V6C3L2	604-685-3456	
Lawton & Cates SC Ten E Doty St Ste 400 Web: www.lawtoncates.com	Madison	WI	53703	608-282-6200	
Lawyer Referral Service 123 Remsen St Web: www.brooklynbar.org	Brooklyn	NY	11201	718-624-0843	
Leason Ellis LLP One Barker Ave Fifth Fl Web: www.leasonellis.com	White Plains	NY	10601	914-821-9070	
Lee & Hayes PLLC 601 W Riverside Ave Ste 1400 Web: www.leehayes.com	Spokane	WA	99201	509-324-9256	
Leete Kosto & Wizner LLC 999 Asylum Ave Ste 202 Web: lkwvisa.com	Hartford	CT	06105	860-249-8100	
Legal Aid 126 W Adams St Fl 7 Web: www.jaxlegalaid.org	Jacksonville	FL	32202	904-356-8371	
Legal Aid Bureau Inc 500 E Lexington St Web: www.mdlab.org	Baltimore	MD	21202	410-951-7777	
Legal Aid Foundation of Los Angeles 1102 Crenshaw Blvd. Web: www.lafla.org	Los Angeles	CA	90019	323-801-7991	
Legal Aid Society of Palm Beach County Inc 423 Fern St Ste 200 Web: www.legalaidpbc.org	West Palm Beach	FL	33401	561-655-8944	
Legal Aid Society of San Mateo County, The 521 E Fifth Ave Web: www.legalaidsmc.org	San Mateo	CA	94402	650-558-0915	
Lehr Middlebrooks & Vreeland PC 2021 Third Ave N. Web: www.lehrmiddlebrooks.com	Birmingham	AL	35203	205-326-3002	
Lerman Senter PLLC 2000 K St NW Ste 600 Web: www.lermansenter.com	Washington	DC	20006	202-429-8970	
Lerner David Littenberg Krumholz & Mentlik 600 South Ave W Web: ldlkm.com	Westfield	NJ	07090	908-654-5000	
Lerner, Sampson & Rothfuss A Legal Professional Association 120 E Fourth St Ste 800 Web: www.lsrlaw.com	Cincinnati	OH	45202	513-241-3100	
Lesperance & Martineau 1440 Rue Sainte-catherine O Web: www.l-m.ca	Montreal	QC	H3G1R8	514-861-4831	

				Phone	Fax
Levasseur Dier & Associates Pc 3233 Coolidge Hwy *Web:* www.mortgage-foreclosures.com	Berkley	MI	48072	248-586-1200	
Levine Blaszak Block & Boothby LLP 2001 L St NW Ste 900 *Web:* www.lb3law.com	Washington	DC	20036	202-857-2550	
Lewis & Kappes 1700 One American Sq Box 82053 *Web:* www.lewis-kappes.com	Indianapolis	IN	46282	317-639-1210	
Lewis & Munday PC 2490 First National Bldg 660 Woodward Ave *Web:* www.lewismunday.com	Detroit	MI	48226	313-961-2550	
Lewis Brisbois Bisgaard & Smith LLP 221 N Figueroa St Ste 1200 *Web:* lewisbrisbois.com	Los Angeles	CA	90012	213-250-1800	250-7900
Lewis Wagner 501 Indiana Ave #200 *Web:* www.lewiswagner.com	Indianapolis	IN	46202	317-237-0500	
Liddle & Robinson LLP 800 Third Ave Fl 8 *Web:* www.liddlerobinson.com	New York	NY	10022	212-687-8500	
Lightfoot, Franklin & White LLC The Clark Bldg 400 20th St N *Web:* www.lfwlaw.com	Birmingham	AL	35203	205-581-0700	
Lind, Jensen, Sullivan & Peterson A Professional Association 1300 AT&T Tower 901 Marquette Ave South *Web:* www.lindjensen.com	Minneapolis	MN	55402	612-333-3637	
Lindquist & Vennum PLLP 4200 IDS Ctr 80 S Eighth St *Web:* www.lindquist.com	Minneapolis	MN	55402	612-371-3211	
Linowes & Blocher LLP 7200 Wisconsin Ave Ste 800 *Web:* linowes-law.com	Bethesda	MD	20814	301-654-0504	654-2801
Lippes Mathias Wexler Friedman LLP 665 Main St Ste 300 *Web:* www.lippes.com	Buffalo	NY	14203	716-853-5100	
Lipson, Neilson, Cole, Seltzer & Garin PC 3910 Telegraph Rd Ste 200 *Web:* www.lipsonneilson.com	Bloomfield Hills	MI	48302	248-593-5000	
Lipton Law Center Pc 18930 W 10 Mile Rd Ste 3000 *Web:* liptonlawcenter.com	Southfield	MI	48075	248-557-1688	
Liskow & Lewis 701 Poydras St Ste 5000 *Web:* www.liskow.com	New Orleans	LA	70139	504-581-7979	
Little Pedersen Fankhauser LLP 901 Main St Ste 4110 *Web:* www.lpf-law.com	Dallas	TX	75202	214-573-2300	
Littler Mendelson PC 650 California St 20th Fl *TF:* 888-548-8537 ■ *Web:* www.littler.com	San Francisco	CA	94108	415-433-1940	399-8490
Lloyd & McDaniel PLC 11405 Park Rd Ste 200 *Web:* www.lloydmc.com	Louisville	KY	40223	502-585-1880	
Lloyd Gray Whitehead & Monroe PC 2501 20th Pl S Ste 300 *Web:* www.lgwmlaw.com	Birmingham	AL	35223	205-967-8822	
Locke Lord Bissell & Liddell LLP (LLBL) 2200 Ross Ave Ste 2200 *Web:* www.lockelord.com	Dallas	TX	75201	214-740-8000	740-8000
Loewinsohn Flegle Deary LLP Lakeside Sq 12377 Merit Dr Ste 900 *Web:* lfdlaw.com	Dallas	TX	75251	214-572-1700	
Lone Star Legal Aid 1415 Fannin St Ste 300 *Web:* www.gclf.org	Houston	TX	77002	713-652-0077	
Longsworth Law Offices LLC 7030 Pointe Inverness Way Ste 330 *Web:* longsworthlaw.com	Fort Wayne	IN	46804	260-436-1555	
Lopez Mchugh LLP 1123 Admiral Peary Way *Web:* lopezmchugh.com	Philadelphia	PA	19112	215-952-6910	
Lorber Greenfield & Polito LLP 13985 Stowe Dr *Web:* lorberlaw.com	Poway	CA	92064	858-513-1020	
Lorge & Lorge Law Firm 1630 Fordem Ave Apt 112 *Web:* www.lawfirm.net	Madison	WI	53704	608-244-0608	
Lowenstein Sandler PC 65 Livingston Ave St 2 *Web:* www.lowenstein.com	Roseland	NJ	07068	973-597-2500	
Lozano Smith 7404 N Spalding Ave *Web:* www.lozanosmith.com	Fresno	CA	93720	559-431-5600	
Lukins & Annis PS 1600 WA Trust Financial Ctr 717 W Sprague Ave Ste 1600 *Web:* www.lukins.com	Spokane	WA	99201	509-455-9555	
Lynch, Traub, Keefe & Errante A Professional Corp 52 Trumbull St *Web:* www.ltke.com	New Haven	CT	06506	203-787-0275	
Lynn Todd m 12350 Jefferson Ave Ste 300 *Web:* www.pwhd.com	Newport News	VA	23602	757-223-4573	
Lyons & Lyons Attorneys at Law 8310 Princeton Glendale Rd *Web:* www.lyonsandlyonslaw.com	West Chester	OH	45069	513-942-5555	
Macdonald Devin PC 3800 Renaissance Tower 1201 Elm St *Web:* macdonalddevin.com	Dallas	TX	75270	214-744-3300	
MacElree Harvey Ltd 17 W Miner St *Web:* www.macelree.com	West Chester	PA	19381	610-436-0100	
Macera & Jarzyna LLP 1200-427 Laurier Ave W *Web:* www.macerajarzyna.com	Ottawa	ON	K1R7Y2	613-238-8173	
Mackall, Crounse & Moore PLC 1400 AT&T Tower 901 Marquette Ave *Web:* www.mcmlaw.com	Minneapolis	MN	55402	612-305-1400	
Magavern Magavern & Grimm LLP 1100 Rand Bldg *Web:* www.magavern.com	Buffalo	NY	14203	716-856-3500	
Mahaffey & Gore PC 300 NE First St *Web:* www.mahaffeygore.com	Oklahoma City	OK	73104	405-236-0478	
Maher, Guiley & Maher PA 631 W Morse Blvd Ste 200 *Web:* maherlawfirm.com	Winter Park	FL	32789	407-839-0866	
Mallilo & Grossman 16309 Northern Blvd *Web:* www.malliloandgrossman.com	Flushing	NY	11358	718-461-6633	
Manatt, Phelps & Phillips 11355 W Olympic Blvd *Web:* www.manatt.com	Los Angeles	CA	90064	310-312-4000	
Mandel, Katz & Brosnan LLP The Law Bldg 210 Rt 303 *Web:* www.mkbllp.com	Valley Cottage	NY	10989	845-639-7800	
Manley Deas & Kochalski LLC PO Box 165028 *Web:* mdk-llc.com	Columbus	OH	43216	614-220-5611	
Manning Fulton & Skinner PA 3605 Glenwood Ave *Web:* www.manningfulton.com	Raleigh	NC	27612	919-787-8880	
Marcari, Russotto, Spencer & Balaban PC 6801 Pleasant Pines Dr Ste 101 *Web:* www.donmarcari.com	Raleigh	NC	27613	919-787-9944	
Marcus & Pollack LLP 708 Third Ave Fl 11 *Web:* marcuspollack.com	New York	NY	10017	212-490-2900	
Marger Johnson & McCollom PC 210 S W Morrison St Ste 400 *Web:* techlaw.com	Portland	OR	97204	503-222-3613	
Margolis Edelstein 170 S Independence Mall W The Curtis Ctr Ste 400E *Web:* www.margolisedelstein.com	Philadelphia	PA	19106	215-922-1100	
Mariani & Reck LLC 83 Broad St *Web:* www.marianireck.com	New London	CT	06320	860-443-5023	
Mariscal Weeks Mcintyre & Friedlander Pa 2901 N Central Ave *Web:* www.dickinson-wright.com	Phoenix	AZ	85012	602-285-5000	285-5100
Marnen Mioduszewski Bordonaro Wagner & Sinnott LLC 516 W 10th St *Web:* mmbwslaw.com	Erie	PA	16502	814-874-3460	
Marrone, Robinson, Frederick & Foster 111 N First St Ste 300 *Web:* www.mrfflaw.net	Burbank	CA	91502	818-841-1144	
Marsh Fischmann & Breyfogle LLP 8055 E Tufts Ave Ste 450 *Web:* www.mfblaw.com	Denver	CO	80237	303-770-0051	
Marshall Dennehey Warner Coleman & Goggin 1845 Walnut St 16th Fl *Web:* www.marshalldennehey.com	Philadelphia	PA	19103	215-575-2600	575-0856
Marshall V Miller & Company Pc 4929 Main St *Web:* www.millerco.com	Kansas City	MO	64112	816-561-4999	
Marten Law 1191 Second Ave Ste 2200 *Web:* www.martenlaw.com	Seattle	WA	98101	206-292-2600	
Martin, Disiere, Jefferson & Wisdom LLP 808 Travis St # 1800 Houston Tx *Web:* www.mdjwlaw.com	Houston	TX	77002	512-610-4400	
Martin, Harding & Mazzotti LLP 1222 Troy-Schenectady Rd *Web:* www.1800law1010.com	Niskayuna	NY	12309	518-862-1200	
Martin, Leigh, Laws & Fritzlen Professional Corp 1044 Main St Ste 900 *Web:* www.mllfpc.com	Kansas City	MO	64105	816-221-1430	
Martin, Shudt, Wallace, DiLorenzo & Johnson 258 Hoosick St Ste 201 *Web:* www.martinshudt.com	Troy	NY	12180	518-272-6565	
Maslon Edelman Borman & Brand LLP 3300 Wells Fargo Ctr 90 S Seventh St *Web:* www.maslon.com	Minneapolis	MN	55402	612-672-8200	
Mason, Griffin & Pierson PC 101 Poor Farm Rd *Web:* www.mgplaw.com	Princeton	NJ	08540	609-921-6543	
Matheny Sears Linkert & Jaime LLP 3638 American River Dr *Web:* www.mathenysears.com	Sacramento	CA	95853	916-978-3434	
Mattioni LLP 1316 Kings Hwy *Web:* www.mattioni.com	Swedesboro	NJ	08085	856-241-9779	
Mawicke & Goisman SC 1509 N Prospect Ave *Web:* www.dmgr.com	Milwaukee	WI	53202	414-224-0600	
Maxwell Noll Inc 600 S Lk Ave Ste 502 *Web:* www.maxnoll.com	Pasadena	CA	91106	626-796-7133	
May, Adam, Gerdes & Thompson LLP 503 S Pierre St *Web:* www.magt.com	Pierre	SD	57501	605-224-8803	
Mazursky Constantine LLC 999 Peachtree St Ste 1500 *Web:* www.mazconlaw.com	Atlanta	GA	30309	404-888-8820	
McAfee & Taft A Professional Corp Two Leadership Sq 211 N Robinson Ste 1000 *Web:* www.mcafeetaft.com	Oklahoma City	OK	73102	405-235-9621	
McAndrews Held & Malloy 500 W Madison St 34th Fl *Web:* www.mcandrews-ip.com	Chicago	IL	60661	312-775-8000	775-8100
Mccallum, Hoaglund, Cook & Irby LLP 905 Montgomery Hwy Ste 201 *Web:* www.mhcilaw.com	Vestavia	AL	35216	205-824-7767	
McConnaughhay Duffy Coonrad Pope & Weaver Pa Drawer 229 *Web:* www.mcconnaughhay.com	Tallahassee	FL	32302	850-222-8121	
Mccranie, Sistrunk, Anzelmo, Hardy, Maxwell & Mcdaniel PC 3445 N Causeway Blvd Ste 800 *Web:* www.mcsalaw.com	Metairie	LA	70002	504-831-0946	
McDermott Will & Emery 227 W Monroe St Ste 4700 *Web:* www.mwe.com	Chicago	IL	60606	312-372-2000	984-7700
Mcdivitt Law Firm 19 E Cimarron St *Web:* mcdivittlaw.com	Colorado Springs	CO	80903	303-426-4878	

				Phone	Fax
McDougall Gauley 701 Broadway Ave Web: www.mcdougallgauley.com	Saskatoon	SK	S7K3L7	306-653-1212	
Mcdowell Rice Smith & Buchanan Pc 605 W 47th St Ste 350 Web: www.mcdowellrice.com	Kansas City	MO	64112	816-753-5400	753-9996
McElroy Deutsch & Mulvaney LLP PO Box 2075 Web: www.mdmc-law.com	Morristown	NJ	07962	973-993-8100	425-0161
Mcgarry Bair Pc 32 Market Ave Sw Ste 500 Web: www.mcgarrybair.com	Grand Rapids	MI	49503	616-742-3500	
Mcginnis Lochridge & Kilgore LLP 600 Congress Ave. Web: www.mcginnislaw.com	Austin	TX	78701	512-495-6000	495-6093
Mcgowan Hood & Felder LLC 1517 Hampton St. Web: louthianlaw.com	Columbia	SC	29201	803-779-0100	
McGuireWoods LLP 901 E Cary St 1 James Ctr TF: 877-712-8778 ■ Web: www.mcguirewoods.com	Richmond	VA	23219	804-775-1000	775-1061
McHale & Slavin PA 2855 PGA Blvd. Web: mspatents.com	Palm Beach Gardens	FL	33410	561-625-6575	
McKee, Voorhees & Sease PLC 801 Grand Ste 3200 Web: www.ipmvs.com	Des Moines	IA	50309	515-288-3667	
McKenna Long & Aldridge LLP 303 Peachtree St Ste 5300 TF: 866-643-2933 ■ Web: mckennalong.com	Atlanta	GA	30308	404-527-4000	527-4198
McKenna Storer 33 N LaSalle St 14th Fl. Web: mckenna-law.com	Chicago	IL	60602	312-558-3900	
Mckenzie Lake Lawyers LLP 300 Dundas St Web: www.mckenzielake.com	London	ON	N6B1T6	519-672-5666	
McLennan Ross LLP 600 W Chambers 12220 Stony Plain Rd. Web: www.mross.com	Edmonton	AB	T5N3Y4	780-482-9200	
McManis Faulkner Fairmont Plz 50 W San Fernando St 10th Fl Web: www.mcmanislaw.com	San Jose	CA	95113	408-279-8700	
Mcmillan & Terry pa 6101 Carnegie Blvd Ste 310 Web: mplawcarolinas.com	Charlotte	NC	28209	704-552-9997	
McNees Wallace & Nurick LLC 125 N Washington Ave Web: www.mwn.com	Scranton	PA	18503	570-209-7220	
McTeague Higbee Case Cohen Whitney & Toker PA Four Union Park Web: www.me-law.com	Topsham	ME	04086	207-725-5581	
Meisner & Associates Pc 30200 Telegraph Rd Ste 467 Web: meisner-law.com	Bingham Farms	MI	48025	248-644-4433	
Meissner Tierney Fisher & Nichols S.C 111 E Kilbourn Ave 19th Fl. Web: www.mtfn.com	Milwaukee	WI	53202	414-273-1300	
Meltzer Lippe Goldstein & Schissel LLP 190 Willis Ave. Web: www.mlg.com	Mineola	NY	11501	516-747-0300	
Mendes & Mount LLP 750 Seventh Ave Web: www.mendes.com	New York	NY	10019	212-261-8000	
Merchant & Gould 3200 IDS Ctr 80 S Eighth St Web: www.merchantgould.com	Minneapolis	MN	55402	612-332-5300	
Merrigan Brandt Ostenso & Cambre pa 25 Ninth Ave N Web: merriganlaw.com	Hopkins	MN	55343	952-933-2390	
Mesch, Clark & Rothschild PC 259 N Meyer Ave Web: www.mcrazlaw.com	Tucson	AZ	85701	520-624-8886	
Messa & Associates PC 123 S 22nd St. Web: messalaw.com	Philadelphia	PA	19103	215-568-3500	
Messerli & Kramer PA 1400 Fifth St Towers 100 S Fifth St Web: www.messerlikramer.com	Minneapolis	MN	55402	612-672-3600	672-3777
Meyer Unkovic & Scott LLP 535 Smithfield St Ste 1300. Web: www.muslaw.com	Pittsburgh	PA	15222	412-456-2800	456-2864
Midkiff, Muncie & Ross PC 300 Arboretum Pl Ste 420 Web: www.midkifflaw.com	Richmond	VA	23236	804-560-9600	
MidPenn Legal Services 213 A N Front St Web: www.midpenn.org	Harrisburg	PA	17101	717-234-0492	
Milbank Tweed Hadley & McCloy LLP 1 Chase Manhattan Plaza TF: 800-229-0543 ■ Web: www.milbank.com	New York	NY	10005	212-530-5000	530-5219
Miller & Chevalier Chartered 655 15th St NW Ste 900 TF: 866-628-4282 ■ Web: www.millerchevalier.com	Washington	DC	20005	202-626-5800	626-5801
Miller & Luring Company LPa 314 W Main St Web: www.millerluring.com	Troy	OH	45373	937-339-2627	
Miller & Martin PLLC 832 Georgia Ave Volunteer Bldg Ste 1000 Web: www.millermartin.com	Chattanooga	TN	37402	423-756-6600	
Miller Canfield Paddock & Stone PLC 150 W Jefferson Ave Ste 2500 Web: www.millercanfield.com	Detroit	MI	48226	313-963-6420	496-7500
Miller Johnson Snell & Cummiskey PLC 250 Monroe Ave NW Ste 800 PO Box 306 TF: 866-667-6572 ■ Web: www.millerjohnson.com	Grand Rapids	MI	49503	616-831-1700	831-1701
Miller Law Firm Pc, The 950 W University Dr Ste 300 Web: www.millerlawpc.com	Rochester	MI	48307	248-841-2200	
Miller Nash Graham & Dunn LLP 2801 Alaskan Way Ste 300 Web: www.grahamdunn.com	Seattle	WA	98121	206-624-8300	340-9599
Miller Nash LLP 3400 US Bancorp Tower Web: www.millernash.com	Portland	OR	97204	503-224-5858	
Miller Russell H. Law Offices 20 Park Rd Ste E Web: www.millerpoliticallaw.com	Burlingame	CA	94010	650-401-8735	
Miller Stratvert PA 500 Marquette Ave NW Ste 1100 Web: www.mstlaw.com	Albuquerque	NM	87125	505-842-1950	
Miner, Barnhill & Galland PC 14 W Erie St. Web: www.lawmbg.com	Chicago	IL	60654	312-751-1170	
Minerva & D'agostino PC 107 S Central Ave. Web: mindaglaw.com	Valley Stream	NY	11580	516-872-7400	
Mintz Levin Cohn Ferris Glovsky & Popeo PC One Financial Ctr Web: www.mintz.com	Boston	MA	02111	617-542-6000	542-2241
Mitchell Williams Selig Gates & Woodyard Pllc 425 W Capitol Ave Ste 1800. Web: mitchellwilliamslaw.com	Little Rock	AR	72201	501-688-8800	688-8807
Modrall Sperling Roehl Harris & Sisk P.a PO Box 2168 Web: www.modrall.com	Albuquerque	NM	87103	505-848-1800	
Moffatt Thomas Barrett Rock & Fields 101 S Capitol Blvd Fl 10 10th Fl. Web: www.moffatt.com	Boise	ID	83702	208-345-2000	
Montgomery Little & Soran PC 5445 Dtc Pkwy Ste 800. Web: www.montgomerylittle.com	Greenwood Village	CO	80111	303-773-8100	220-0412
Montlick & Associates PC 17 Executive Park Dr Ste 300 Web: www.montlick.com	Atlanta	GA	30329	404-235-5000	
Moore Ingram Johnson & Steele LLP Emerson Overlook 326 Roswell Rd. Web: www.mijs.com	Marietta	GA	30060	770-429-1499	
Morgan & Weisbrod 6800 S Loope. Web: www.morganweisbrod.com	Houston	TX	77087	713-838-0003	
Morgan Lewis & Bockius LLP 1701 Market St. TF: 866-963-7137 ■ Web: www.morganlewis.com	Philadelphia	PA	19103	215-963-5000	963-5001
Morgan Melhuish Abrutyn 651 W Mount Pleasant Ave Ste 200 Web: www.morganlawfirm.com	Livingston	NJ	07039	973-994-2500	
Morris Duffy Alonso & Faley Two Rector St 22nd Fl. Web: www.mdafny.com	New York	NY	10006	212-766-1888	
Morris Polich & Purdy 1055 W Seventh St Ste 2400 Web: www.mpplaw.com	Los Angeles	CA	90017	213-891-9100	488-1178
Morrison & Foerster LLP 425 Market St Web: www.mofo.com	San Francisco	CA	94105	415-268-7000	268-7522
Morrison Mahoney LLP 250 Summer St Fl 1 Web: www.morrisonmahoney.com	Boston	MA	02210	617-439-7500	439-7590
Morrison Scott Alan Law Offices of pa 141 W Patrick St Ste 300 Web: www.samlawoffice.com	Frederick	MD	21701	301-694-6262	
Morse, Barnes-Brown & Pendleton PC CityPoint 230 Third Ave Fourth Fl Web: www.mbbp.com	Waltham	MA	02451	781-622-5930	
Mulherin, Rehfeldt & Varchetto PC 211 S Wheaton Ave Ste 200 Web: www.mrvlaw.com	Wheaton	IL	60187	630-653-9300	
Mullen & Filippi LLP 1601 Response Rd Ste 300. Web: www.mulfil.com	Sacramento	CA	95815	916-442-4503	
Muller Muller Richmond Harms Myers & Sgroi Atty 33233 Woodward Ave. Web: www.mullerfirm.com	Birmingham	MI	48009	248-645-2440	
Mullin Hoard & Brown LLP Amarillo National Plz Two Ste 800 500 S Taylor Lobby Box Ste 213 Web: www.mullinhoard.com	Amarillo	TX	79101	806-372-5050	
Munck Wilson Mandala LLP 600 Banner Pl Tower 12770 Coit Rd. Web: www.munckwilson.com	Dallas	TX	75251	972-628-3600	
Munsch Hardt Kopf Harr Pc 500 N Akard St TF: 800-321-6742 ■ Web: www.munsch.com	Dallas	TX	75201	214-855-7500	855-7584
Murphy & Grantland PA 4406-B Forest Dr. Web: www.murphyandgrantland.com	Columbia	SC	29260	803-782-4100	
Murphy & McGonigle 4870 Sadler Rd Ste 301 Web: www.mmlawus.com	Glen Allen	VA	23060	804-762-5320	
Murphy Sullivan Kronk 275 College St Web: www.mskvt.com	Burlington	VT	05401	802-861-7000	
Murphy, Hesse, Toomey & Lehane LLP Crown Colony Plz 300 Crown Colony Dr Ste 410. Web: www.mhtl.com	Quincy	MA	02169	617-479-5000	
Murray, Plumb & Murray 75 Pearl St. Web: www.mpmlaw.com	Portland	ME	04101	207-773-5651	
Musick Peeler & Garrett LLP One Wilshire Blvd Ste 2000 Web: www.musickpeeler.com	Los Angeles	CA	90017	213-629-7600	
Myers, Oliver & Price PC 1401 Central Ave Nw Ste A. Web: moplaw.com	Albuquerque	NM	87104	505-247-9080	
Myers, Widders, Gibson, Jones & Feingold LLP 5425 Everglades St. Web: www.mwgjs.com	Ventura	CA	93003	805-644-7188	
Nagle & Associates pa 7780 Brier Creek Pkwy Ste 210 Web: www.naglefirm.com	Raleigh	NC	27617	919-433-0035	
Nahon, Saharovich & Trotz PLC 488 S Menhenhall Rd. Web: www.nstlaw.com	Memphis	TN	38117	901-683-7000	
Nason, Yeager, Gerson, White & Lioce PA Sabadell United Bank Tower 1645 Palm Beach Lakes Blvd Ste 1200 Web: nasonyeager.com	West Palm Beach	FL	33401	561-686-3307	

Phone Fax

Nauman Smith Shissler & Hall LLP
200 N Third St Fl 18 .... Harrisburg PA 17101 717-236-3010
Web: nssh.com

Neal & Harwell PLC
One Nashville Pl Ste 2000 150 Fourth Ave N .... Nashville TN 37219 615-244-1713
Web: www.nealharwell.com

Nelson & Kennard
2180 Harvard St Ste 160 PO Box 13807.... Sacramento CA 95853 866-920-2295
TF: 866-920-2295 ■ *Web:* nelson-kennard.com

Nelson Mullins Riley & Scarborough LLP
1320 Main St 17th Fl .... Columbia SC 29201 803-799-2000 256-7500
TF: 800-237-2000 ■ *Web:* www.nelsonmullins.com

Neuberger Quinn Gielen Rubin Gibber PA
One South St 27th Fl .... Baltimore MD 21202 410-332-8550
Web: www.nqgrg.com

Nevada Disability Advocacy & Law Center Inc
6039 Eldora Ave Ste C .... Las Vegas NV 89146 702-257-8150
Web: ndalc.org

New Haven Legal Assistance Association Inc
426 State St .... New Haven CT 06510 203-946-4811
Web: nhlegal.org

New York Prosecutors Training Institute
107 Columbia St.... Albany NY 12210 518-432-1100
Web: www.nypti.org

Newmeyer & Dillion LLP
895 Dove St Fifth Fl .... Newport Beach CA 92660 949-854-7000
Web: www.ndlf.com

Niedner, Bodeux, Carmichael, Huff, Lenox & Pashos LLP
131 Jefferson St.... Saint Charles MO 63301 636-949-9300
Web: www.niednerlaw.com

Nielsen, Merksamer, Parrinello, Gross & Leoni LLP
2350 Kerner Blvd Ste 250.... San Rafael CA 94901 415-389-6800
Web: www.nmgovlaw.com

Niles Barton & Wilmer
111 S Calvert St Ste 1400.... Baltimore MD 21202 410-783-6300 783-6363
Web: www.nilesbarton.com

Nirenstein, Horowitz & Associates PC
43 Woodland St Ste 520.... Hartford CT 06105 860-548-1000
Web: www.preserveyourestate.net

Niro Scavone Haller & Niro Ltd
181 W Madison St Ste 4600.... Chicago IL 60602 312-236-0733
Web: www.niroscavone.com

Nisen & Elliott LLC 200 W Adams St Ste 2500 .... Chicago IL 60606 312-346-7800
Web: www.nisen.com

Nolan & Heller LLP 39 N Pearl St Third Fl .... Albany NY 12207 518-449-3300
Web: www.nolanandheller.com

Norman, Wood, Kendrick & Turner
1130 22nd St S Ridge Park Pl Ste 3000.... Birmingham AL 35205 205-328-6643
Web: nwkt.com

Norris, McLaughlin & Marcus PA
721 Route 202-206.... Bridgewater NJ 08807 908-722-0700
Web: nmmlaw.com

North Berman & Beebe
1111 14th St Nw Ste 920 .... Washington DC 20005 202-371-1100
Web: northberman.com

Notaro & Michalos PC 100 Dutch Hill Rd.... Orangeburg NY 10962 845-359-7700
Web: www.notaromichalos.com

Nowell Amoroso Klein Bierman PA
155 Polifly Rd Third Fl.... Hackensack NJ 07601 201-343-5001
Web: nakblaw.com

Nuzzo & Roberts LLC One Town Ctr.... Cheshire CT 06410 203-250-2000
Web: www.nuzzo-roberts.com

Nysarc Inc 393 Delaware Ave .... Delmar NY 12054 518-439-8311 439-1893
TF: 800-735-8924 ■ *Web:* www.nysarc.org

O'Brien, Tanski & Young LLP
CityPlace II 185 Asylum St.... Hartford CT 06103 860-525-2700
Web: www.otylaw.com

O'connell, Tivin, Miller & Burns LLC
135 S La Salle St Ste 2300.... Chicago IL 60603 312-256-8800
Web: www.mwoodco.com

O'donnell Lee Mccowan & Phillips LLC
112 Silver St.... Waterville ME 04901 207-872-0112
Web: www.odonnellandlee.com

O'hagan Smith & Amundsen
308 W State St Ste 320.... Rockford IL 61101 815-987-0441
Web: salawus.com

O'Melveny & Myers LLP
400 S Hope St 10th Fl .... Los Angeles CA 90071 213-430-6000 430-6407
Web: www.omm.com

O'Reilly Rancilio PC
Sterling Town Ctr 12900 Hall Rd
Ste 350.... Sterling Heights MI 48313 586-726-1000
Web: www.orlaw.com

O'riordan Bethel Law Firm LLP, The
1314 19th St Nw.... Washington DC 20036 202-822-1720
Web: oriordan-law.com

Ogden, Gibson, Broocks, Longoria & Hall LLP
1900 Pennzoil Pl 711 Louisiana St.... Houston TX 77002 713-844-3000
Web: www.ogwbl.com

Ogne Alberts & Stuart Pc 1869 E Maple Rd.... Troy MI 48083 248-362-3707
Web: oaspc.com

Ohio Legal Assistance Foundation
10 W Broad St Ste 950.... Columbus OH 43215 614-715-8560
Web: www.olaf.org

Oliff & Berridge PLC
277 S Washington St Ste 500.... Alexandria VA 22314 703-836-6400
Web: www.oliff.com

Oliver, Price & Rhodes
1212 S Abington Rd.... Clarks Summit PA 18411 570-585-1200
Web: oprlaw.com

ONeill & Borges
American International Plz 250 Munoz Rivera Ave
Ste 800.... San Juan PR 00918 787-764-8181
Web: www.oneillborges.com

Orgain Bell & Tucker LLP 470 Orleans St .... Beaumont TX 77704 409-838-6412
Web: www.obt.com

Orlans Associates PC 1650 W Big Beaver Rd.... Troy MI 48084 248-502-1400
Web: www.orlans.com

Orrick Herrington & Sutcliffe LLP
666 Fifth Ave.... New York NY 10103 212-506-5000 506-5151
TF: 866-342-5259 ■ *Web:* www.orrick.com

Otten Johnson Robinson Neff & Ragonetti PC
950 17th St Ste 1600 .... Denver CO 80202 303-825-8400 825-6525
Web: www.ojrnr.com

Pachulski Stang Ziehl Young & Jones Professional Corp
10100 Santa Monica Blvd.... Los Angeles CA 90067 310-277-6910
Web: pszjlaw.com

Paine, Hamblen, Coffin, Brooke & Miller LLP
717 W Sprague Ave Washington Trust Financial Ctr
Ste 1200.... Spokane WA 99201 509-455-6000
Web: www.painehamblen.com

Paladin Law Group LLP 1176 Blvd Way .... Walnut Creek CA 94595 925-947-5700
Web: www.paladinlaw.com

Pallett Valo LLP
90 Burnhamthorpe Rd W Ste 1600.... Mississauga ON L5B3C3 905-273-3300
Web: www.pallettvalo.com

Parker McCay PA
9000 Midlantic Dr Ste 300.... Mount Laurel NJ 08054 856-596-8900
Web: www.parkermccay.com

Parker Poe Adams & Bernstein LLP
Three Wachovia Ctr 401 S Tryon St Ste 3000.... Charlotte NC 28202 704-372-9000
Web: www.parkerpoe.com

Parker Stanbury LLP
444 S Flower St Ste 1900.... Los Angeles CA 90071 619-528-1259
Web: www.parkstan.com

Parker, Kern, Nard & Wenzel
1111 E Herndon Ave Ste 202 .... Fresno CA 93720 559-449-2558
Web: pknwlaw.com

Parlee McLaws LLP
3400 Petro-Canada Centre 150-6th Ave SW.... Calgary AB T2P3Y7 403-294-7000
Web: www.parlee.com

Parr Brown Gee & Loveless
185 South State St Ste 800.... Slc UT 84111 801-532-7840
Web: www.parrbrown.com

Parr Richey Obremsky & Morton
201 N Illinois St Ste 300.... Indianapolis IN 46204 317-269-2500
Web: www.parrlaw.com

Parrett, Porto, Parese & Colwell PC
One Hamden Ctr 2319 Whitney Ave Ste 1-D.... Hamden CT 06518 203-281-2700
Web: www.byxbee.com

Partridge Snow & Hahn LLP 180 S Main St .... Providence RI 02903 401-861-8200
Web: www.psh.com

Passman & Jones
2500 Renaissance Tower 1201 Elm St .... Dallas TX 75270 214-742-2121
Web: www.passmanjones.com

Paul Hastings Janofsky & Walker LLP
515 S Flower St 25th Fl .... Los Angeles CA 90071 213-683-6000 627-0705
Web: www.paulhastings.com

Paul Weiss Rifkind Wharton & Garrison LLP
1285 Ave of the Americas.... New York NY 10019 212-373-3000 757-3990
Web: www.paulweiss.com

PDQ Legal Services 15876 N 76th St Ste 110.... Scottsdale AZ 85260 480-556-6660
Web: pdqlegal.com

Peabody & Arnold LLP 600 Atlantic Ave.... Boston MA 02210 617-951-2100 951-2125
Web: www.peabodyarnold.com

Pearce & Durick 314 E Thayer Ave .... Bismarck ND 58502 701-223-2890
Web: www.pearce-durick.com

Pearne & Gordon LLP
1801 E Ninth St Ste 1200.... Cleveland OH 44114 216-579-1700
Web: www.pearne.com

Peirson Patterson LLP
2310 W Interstate 20 Ste 100 .... Arlington TX 76017 817-461-5500
Web: www.peirsonpatterson.com

Pellettieri Rabstein & Altman
100 Nassau Pk Blvd .... Princeton NJ 08540 609-520-0900 452-8796
TF: 800-432-5297 ■ *Web:* www.pralaw.com

PennStuart 208 E Main St.... Abingdon VA 24210 276-628-5151
Web: www.pennstuart.com

Pepper Hamilton LLP
3000 Two Logan Sq 18th & Arch St .... Philadelphia PA 19103 215-981-4000 981-4750
Web: www.pepperlaw.com

Perantinides & Nolan Company LPa
80 S Summit St Ste 300.... Akron OH 44308 330-253-5454
Web: eyemg.com

Perkins Coie LLP 1201 Third Ave Ste 4800.... Seattle WA 98101 206-359-8000 359-9000
TF: 888-720-8382 ■ *Web:* www.perkinscoie.com

Perkins Thompson & Hinckley
One Canal Plz Ste 900 .... Portland ME 04101 207-774-2635
Web: perkinsthompson.com

Peter J. Jaensch Immigration 2198 Main St.... Sarasota FL 34237 941-366-9841
Web: visaamerica.com

Peters & Freedman LLP
191 Calle Magdalena Ste 220.... Encinitas CA 92024 760-436-3441
Web: www.hoalaw.com

Peters Murdaugh Parker Ellzr
123 S Walter St.... Walterboro SC 29488 843-549-9544
Web: www.pmped.com

Phelan Hallinan & Schmieg LLP
400 Fellowship Rd Ste 100.... Mount Laurel NJ 08054 856-813-5500
Web: fedphe.com

Phelps Dunbar LLP
Canal Pl 365 Canal St Ste 2000 .... New Orleans LA 70130 504-566-1311
Web: www.phelpsdunbar.com

Philips & Cohen LLP
2000 Massachusetts Ave Nw Ste 100.... Washington DC 20036 202-833-4567
Web: www.phillipsandcohen.com

Firm / Address	City	State	ZIP	Phone	Fax
Phillips & Webster Pllc Attys 13303 Ne 175th St	Woodinville	WA	98072	425-482-1111	
Web: phillipswebster.com					
Phillips Law Group LLC 1618 Thompson Ave	Atlanta	GA	30344	404-761-6800	
Web: www.phillipslawatlanta.com					
Phillips Murrah PC 101 N Robinson Ave Corporate Tower Thirteenth Fl	Oklahoma City	OK	73102	405-235-4100	
Web: www.phillipsmurrah.com					
Pickrel Schaeffer & Ebeling 40 N Main St - Kettering Tower	Dayton	OH	45423	937-223-1130	
Web: www.pselaw.com					
Pierce & Associates One N Dearborn St Ste 1300	Chicago	IL	60602	312-346-9088	
Web: www.atty-pierce.com					
Pierce & Shearer LLP 730 Polhemus Rd Ste 101	San Mateo	CA	94402	650-573-9300	
Web: www.pierceshearer.com					
Pietragallo Gordon Alfano Bosick & Raspanti LLP One Oxford Centre Fl 38	Pittsburgh	PA	15219	412-263-2000	
Web: www.pietragallo.com					
Pietrantoni Mendez & Alvarez LLP Popular Ctr Bldg 208 Ponce de Leon Ave 19th Fl	San Juan	PR	00918	787-274-1212	
Web: www.pmalaw.com					
Pillsbury Winthrop Shaw Pittman LLP 50 Fremont St	San Francisco	CA	94105	415-983-1000	983-1200
TF: 800-477-0770 ■ *Web:* www.pillsburylaw.com					
Plews Shadley Racher & Braun LLP 1346 N Delaware St	Indianapolis	IN	46202	317-637-0700	
Web: www.psrb.com					
Polsinelli Shalton Flanigan Suelthaus PC 700 W 47th St Ste 1000	Kansas City	MO	64112	816-753-1000	753-1536
TF: 888-572-7025 ■ *Web:* www.polsinelli.com					
Porteous, Hainkel & Johnson LLP 704 Carondelet St	New Orleans	LA	70130	504-581-3838	
Web: www.phjlaw.com					
Portnoff Law Associates Ltd 1000 Sandy Hill Rd Ste 1	Norristown	PA	19401	484-690-9300	
Web: portnoffonline.com					
Porzio Bromberg & Newman PC 100 Southgate Pkwy	Morristown	NJ	07962	973-538-4006	
Web: www.pbnlaw.com					
Post & Schell PC Four Penn Ctr 1600 John F Kennedy Blvd	Philadelphia	PA	19103	215-587-1000	
Web: postschell.com					
Potestivo & Associates PC 811 S Blvd Ste 100	Rochester Hills	MI	48307	248-853-4400	
Web: www.potestivolaw.com					
Potter Anderson & Corroon Hercules Plz 1313 N Market St	Wilmington	DE	19801	302-984-6000	
Web: www.potteranderson.com					
Powell, Trachtman, Logan, Carrle & Lombardo PC 475 Allendale Rd Ste 200	King Of Prussia	PA	19406	610-354-9700	
Web: www.powelltrachtman.com					
Powers Pyles Sutter & Verville PC 1501 M St NW Seventh Fl	Washington	DC	20005	202-466-6550	
Web: www.ppsv.com					
Powers Vincent m & Associates 411 S 13th St Ste 300	Lincoln	NE	68508	402-474-8000	
Web: vincepowerslaw.com					
Poyner & Spruill LLP 301 Fayetteville St Ste 1900	Raleigh	NC	27601	919-783-6400	
Web: www.poynerspruill.com					
Pray, Walker, Jackman, Williamson, & Marlar 900 Oneok Plz 100 W Fifth St	Tulsa	OK	74103	918-581-5500	
Web: www.praywalker.com					
Preis & Roy PLC Versailles Centre 102 Versailles Blvd Ste 400	Lafayette	LA	70501	337-237-6062	
Web: www.pkrlaw.com					
Pressler & Pressler LLP Seven Entin Rd	Parsippany	NJ	07054	973-753-5100	
Web: www.pressler-pressler.com					
Preti, Flaherty, Beliveau, Pachios & Haley LLC 45 Memorial Cir	Augusta	ME	04330	207-623-5300	
Web: www.preti.com					
Price Postel & Parma LLP 200 E Carrillo St Fl 4	Santa Barbara	CA	93101	805-962-0011	
Web: www.melfassett.com					
Price, Heneveld, Cooper, De Witt & Litton 695 Kenmoor Ave SE	Grand Rapids	MI	49546	616-949-9610	
Web: www.priceheneveld.com					
Prickett, Jones & Elliott PA 1310 King St Box 1328	Wilmington	DE	19899	302-888-6500	
Web: prickett.com					
Pro Bono Partnership 237 Mamaroneck Ave Ste 300	White Plains	NY	10605	914-328-0674	
Web: www.probonopartner.org					
Procopio Cory Hargreaves & Savitch LLP 525 B St Ste 2200	San Diego	CA	92101	619-238-1900	235-0398
Web: www.procopio.com					
Proskauer Rose LLP 1585 Broadway	New York	NY	10036	212-969-3000	969-2900
TF: 866-444-3272 ■ *Web:* www.proskauer.com					
Provost-Umphrey Law Firm LLP 490 Park St	Beaumont	TX	77704	409-835-6000	
Web: www.provostumphrey.com					
Quarles & Brady LLP 411 E Wisconsin Ave Ste 2040	Milwaukee	WI	53202	414-277-5000	271-3552
TF: 800-654-2200 ■ *Web:* www.quarles.com					
Quest Discovery Services Inc 981 Ridder Park Dr	San Jose	CA	95131	408-441-7000	
Web: www.questds.com					
Quine IP Law Group 2033 Clement Ave Ste 200	Alameda	CA	94501	510-337-7871	
Web: www.quinelaw.com					
Quinn, Johnston, Henderson, Pretorius & Cerulo Chartered 227 N E Jefferson St	Peoria	IL	61602	309-674-1133	
Web: www.qjhp.com					
Rachlin & Wolfson LLP 390 Bay St Ste 1500	Toronto	ON	M5H2Y2	416-367-0202	
Web: www.rachlinlaw.com					
Rad Law Firm 2001 Beach St Ste 600	Fort Worth	TX	76103	817-543-1990	
Web: www.radlawfirm.com					
Radey Thomas Yon & Clark 301 S Bronough St Ste 200	Tallahassee	FL	32301	850-425-6654	
Web: www.radeylaw.com					
Ragan & Ragan p C 3100 State Rt 138 Ste 3	Wall Township	NJ	07719	732-280-4100	
Web: www.raganlaw.com					
Rainwater, Holt & Sexton PA 6315 Ranch Dr	Little Rock	AR	72223	800-434-4800	
TF: 800-434-4800 ■ *Web:* www.callrainwater.com					
Rajkowski Hansmeier Ltd Daniel Bldg 11 Seventh Ave N	Saint Cloud	MN	56302	320-251-1055	
Web: www.rajhan.com					
Rankin, Hill, Porter & Clark LLP 23755 Lorain Rd Ste 200	North Olmsted	OH	44070	216-566-9700	
Web: www.rankinhill.com					
Rash, Chapman, Schreiber, Leaverton & Morrison LLP 2112 Rio Grande St	Austin	TX	78705	512-477-7543	
Web: www.rcsp.com					
Rathbun, Cservenyak & Kozol LLC 3260 Executive Dr Ste A	Joliet	IL	60431	815-730-1977	
Web: www.rcklawfirm.com					
Rawle & Henderson 1339 Chestnut St One S Penn Sq The Widener Bldg 16th Fl	Philadelphia	PA	19107	215-575-4200	
Web: www.rawle.com					
Recordtrak Inc 651 Allendale Rd PO Box 61591	King Of Prussia	PA	19406	610-992-5000	354-8946
Redmon, Peyton & Braswell LLP 510 King St Ste 301	Alexandria	VA	22314	703-684-2000	
Web: www.rpb-law.com					
Reed Smith 435 Sixth Ave	Pittsburgh	PA	15219	412-288-3131	288-3063
Web: www.reedsmith.com					
Rees Broome PC 1900 Gallows Rd	Tysons Corner	VA	22182	703-790-1911	
Web: www.reesbroome.com					
Reicker, Pfau, Pyle & McRoy LLP 1421 State St Ste B	Santa Barbara	CA	93101	805-966-2440	
Web: www.reickerpfau.com					
Reilly Like & Tenety 179 Little E Neck Rd	West Babylon	NY	11704	631-669-3000	
Web: rlt-law.com					
Relin, Goldstein & Crane LLP 28 E Main St Ste 1800	Rochester	NY	14614	585-325-6202	
Web: www.rgcattys.net					
Reminger & Reminger Company LPa 101 W Prospect Ave	Cleveland	OH	44115	216-687-1311	687-1841
TF: 800-486-1311 ■ *Web:* www.reminger.com					
Renaud Cook Drury Mesaros PA One N Central Ste 900	Phoenix	AZ	85004	602-307-9900	
Web: www.rcdmlaw.com					
Rendigs, Fry, Kiely & Dennis LLP 600 Vine St Ste 2650	Cincinnati	OH	45202	513-381-9200	
Web: www.rendigs.com					
Reuben & Junius LLP One Bush St Ste 600	San Francisco	CA	94104	415-567-9000	
Web: www.reubenlaw.com					
Reynolds, Mirth, Richards & Farmer LLP Manulife Pl 10180-101 St Ste 3200	Edmonton	AB	T5J0W2	780-425-9510	
Web: www.rmrf.com					
Rhoades McKee PC 161 Ottawa Ave NW Ste 600	Grand Rapids	MI	49503	616-235-3500	459-5102
Web: www.rhoadesmckee.com					
Richard a Kennedy Law Office 3773 Tibbetts St Ste D	Riverside	CA	92506	951-715-5000	
Web: www.richardakennedy.com					
Richards Layton & Finger PO Box 551	Wilmington	DE	19899	302-651-7700	651-7701
Web: www.rlf.com					
Rieders, Travis, Humphrey, Harris, Waters, Waffenschmidt & Dohrmann 161 W Third St	Williamsport	PA	17701	570-323-8711	
Web: www.riederstravis.com					
Riemer & Braunstein LLP Three Ctr Plz Sixth Fl	Boston	MA	02108	617-523-9000	
Web: www.riemerlaw.com					
Riggs Abney Neal Orbison & Lewis Inc 502 W Sixth St Frisco Bldg	Tulsa	OK	74119	918-587-3161	
Web: www.riggsabney.com					
Riker, Danzig, Scherer, Hyland & Perretti LLP Headquarters Plz One Speedwell Ave	Morristown	NJ	07962	973-538-0800	
Web: www.riker.com					
Riley Bennett & Egloff LLP 141 E Washington St Fourth Fl	Indianapolis	IN	46204	317-636-8000	
Web: www.rbelaw.com					
Rinke Noonan US Bank Plz 1015 W St Germain St Ste 300	Saint Cloud	MN	56302	320-251-6700	
Web: www.rnoon.com					
Ritchie, Dillard, Davies & Johnson PC 606 W Main St Ste 300	Knoxville	TN	37902	865-637-0661	
Web: www.rddjlaw.com					
Rivkin Radler LLP 926 RXR Plz	Uniondale	NY	11556	516-357-3000	
Web: www.rivkinradler.com					
Robbins Arroyo LLP 600 B St Ste 1900	San Diego	CA	92101	619-525-3990	
Web: www.robbinsarroyo.com					
Roberts & Holland LLP 825 Eighth Ave Ste 37	New York	NY	10019	212-903-8700	
Web: www.robertsandholland.com					
Robie & Matthai A Professional Corp Biltmore Tower 500 S Grand Ave Ste 1500	Los Angeles	CA	90071	213-706-8000	
Web: www.romalaw.com					

Firm	City	State	Zip	Phone	Fax
Robinson & Geraldo Prof Corp 4407 N Front St *Web:* www.rglaw.net	Harrisburg	PA	17110	717-232-8525	
Robinson & Mcelwee Pllc 700 Virginia St E Ste 400 *Web:* ramlaw.com	Charleston	WV	25301	304-344-5800	
Robinson & Wood Inc 227 N First St *Web:* www.robinsonwood.com	San Jose	CA	95113	408-298-7120	
Robinson Bradshaw & Hinson Pa 101 N Tryon St Ste 1900 *Web:* www.rbh.com	Charlotte	NC	28246	704-377-2536	378-4000
Rodey Dickason Sloan Akin & Robb P A 201 Third St NW Ste 2200 *TF:* 800-226-2935 ■ *Web:* www.rodey.com	Albuquerque	NM	87102	505-765-5900	768-7395
Rogers & Lapan PA 355 Windy Ridge Rd *Web:* rogerslapan.com	Chapel Hill	NC	27517	919-545-9259	
Roig, Kasperovich, Tutan & Woods PA 1255 S Military Trl Ste 100 *Web:* www.roiglawyers.com	Deerfield Beach	FL	33442	954-834-0330	
Ropes & Gray LLP One International Pl *Web:* www.ropesgray.com	Boston	MA	02110	617-951-7000	951-7050
Rose Law Firm A Professional Assn 120 E Fourth St *Web:* www.roselawfirm.com	Little Rock	AR	72201	501-375-9131	375-1309
Rosemarie Arnold Law Offices 1386 Palisade Ave *Web:* www.rosemariearnold.com	Fort Lee	NJ	07024	201-461-1111	
Rosen Law Firm LLC 18 Broad St Ste 201 *Web:* www.rosen-lawfirm.com	Charleston	SC	29401	843-377-1700	
Rosenn, Jenkins & Greenwald LLP 15 S Franklin St *Web:* www.rjglaw.com	Wilkes Barre	PA	18711	570-301-6118	
Ross & Matthews PC 3650 Lovell Ave *Web:* www.rossandmatthews.com	Fort Worth	TX	76107	817-255-2000	
Ross, Banks, May, Cron & Cavin PC Two Riverway Ste 700 *Web:* www.rossbanks.com	Houston	TX	77056	713-626-1200	
Ross, Brittain & Schonberg Company LPA Corporate Plz II 6480 Rockside Woods Blvd S Ste 350 *Web:* www.rbslaw.com	Cleveland	OH	44131	216-447-1551	
Rossi Kimms & Mcdowell LLC 20609 Gordon Park Sq Ste 150 *Web:* rkmllp.com	Ashburn	VA	20147	703-726-6020	
Rothberg Logan & Warsco LLP 505 E Washington Blvd *Web:* www.rlwlawfirm.com	Fort Wayne	IN	46802	260-422-9454	
Rothman Gordon P.C Grant Bldg Third Fl *Web:* www.rothmangordon.com	Pittsburgh	PA	15219	412-338-1100	
Rourke & Blumenthal LLP 495 S High St Ste 450 *Web:* www.randbllp.com	Columbus	OH	43215	614-220-9200	
Rowley Chapman & Barney Ltd 63 E Main St Ste 501 *Web:* www.azlegal.com	Mesa	AZ	85201	480-833-1113	
Royse Law Firm PC 1717 Embarcadero Rd *Web:* www.rroyselaw.com	Palo Alto	CA	94303	650-813-9700	
Rubin & Levin PC 500 Marott Ctr 342 Massachusetts Ave *Web:* www.rubin-levin.com	Indianapolis	IN	46204	317-634-0300	
Rush Moore LLP 737 BISHOP St Ste 2400 *Web:* www.rmhawaii.com	Honolulu	HI	96813	808-521-0400	521-0497
Ruskin Moscou Faltischek PC East Tower 15th Fl 1425 RXR Plz *Web:* www.rmfpc.com	Uniondale	NY	11556	516-663-6600	
Rusty Hardin & Associates LLP Five Houston Ctr 1401 McKinney Ste 2250 *Web:* rustyhardin.com	Houston	TX	77010	713-652-9000	
Ryan Smith & Carbine Ltd Mead Bldg 98 Merchants Row *Web:* www.rsclaw.com	Rutland	VT	05702	802-786-1000	
Ryley Carlock & Applewhite Pa One N Central Ave Ste 1200 *Web:* www.rcalaw.com	Phoenix	AZ	85004	602-258-7701	257-9582
Rywant Alvarez Jones Russo & Guyton pa 407 Courthouse Sq *Web:* rywantalvarez.com	Inverness	FL	34450	352-341-4441	
Saalfeld Griggs PC Park Pl 250 Church St SE Ste 300 *Web:* www.sglaw.com	Salem	OR	97308	503-399-1070	
Sachs Waldman Pc 1000 Farmer St *Web:* www.sachswaldman.com	Detroit	MI	48226	313-965-3464	
Sackett & Associates 1055 Lincoln Ave *Web:* www.sackettlaw.com	San Jose	CA	95125	408-295-7755	
Sacks Tierney PA 4250 N Drinkwater Blvd Fourth Fl *Web:* www.sackstierney.com	Scottsdale	AZ	85251	480-425-2600	
Salvi & Schostok Pc 218 N Martin Luther King Jr Ave *Web:* www.salvilaw.com	Waukegan	IL	60085	847-249-1227	
Samuels, Miller, Schroeder, Jackson & Sly LLP 225 N Water St Ste 301 *Web:* www.smsjslaw.com	Decatur	IL	62523	217-429-4325	
Saul Ewing LLP Centre Sq W 1500 Market St 38th Fl *Web:* www.saul.com	Philadelphia	PA	19102	215-972-7777	
Saxe Doernberger & Vita PC 1952 Whitney Ave *Web:* www.sdvlaw.com	Hamden	CT	06517	203-287-2100	
Schaefer The Law Firm of John f 380 N Old Woodward Ave Ste 320 *Web:* lfjfs.com	Birmingham	MI	48009	248-642-6655	
Scheef & Stone LLP 500 N Akard St Ste 2700 *Web:* www.solidcounsel.com	Dallas	TX	75201	214-706-4200	

Firm	City	State	Zip	Phone	Fax
Schiff Hardin LLP 233 S Wacker Dr 6600 Sears Tower *Web:* www.schiffhardin.com	Chicago	IL	60606	312-258-5500	258-5600
Schiller & Knapp LLP 950 New Loudon Rd Ste 310 *Web:* www.schillerknapp.com	Latham	NY	12110	518-786-9069	
Schindler Cohen & Hochman LLP 100 Wall St 15th Fl *Web:* www.schlaw.com	New York	NY	10005	212-277-6300	
Schlachman, Belsky & Weiner PA 300 E Lombard St Ste 1100 *Web:* www.sbwlaw.com	Baltimore	MD	21202	410-685-2022	
Schlichter, Bogard & Denton 100 S Fourth St Ste 900 *Web:* uselaws.com	St. Louis	MO	63102	314-621-6115	
Schneiderman & Sherman 23938 Research Dr Ste 300 *Web:* sspclegal.com	Farmington Hills	MI	48335	248-539-7400	
Schroeder Group, The 20800 Swenson Dr Ste 475 *Web:* www.tsglaw.com	Waukesha	WI	53186	262-798-8220	
Schulte Roth & Zabel LLP 919 Third Ave *Web:* www.srz.com	New York	NY	10022	212-756-2000	593-5955
Schwartz Hannum PC 11 Chestnut St *Web:* shpclaw.com	Andover	MA	01810	978-623-0900	
Schwartz Semerdjian Ballard & Cauley LLP 101 W Broadway Ste 810 *Web:* www.sshbclaw.com	San Diego	CA	92101	619-236-8821	
Scolaro, Shulman, Cohen, Fetter & Burstein PC Franklin Sq 507 Plum St Ste 300 *Web:* www.scolaro.com	Syracuse	NY	13204	315-471-8111	
Scopelitis , Garvin , Light , Hanson & Feary PLC 600 Republic Centre 633 Chestnut St *Web:* www.scopelitis.com	Chattanooga	TN	37450	423-266-2769	
Searcy Denney Scarola Barnhart Po Box 3626 *Web:* www.searcylaw.com	West Palm Beach	FL	33402	561-686-6300	
Sebaly Shillito & Dyer 1900 Kettering Tower 40 N Main St *Web:* ssdlaw.com	Dayton	OH	45423	937-222-2500	
Secrest Wardle Lynch Hampton Po Box 3040 *Web:* www.secrestwardle.com	Farmington Hills	MI	48333	248-851-9500	
Seder & Chandler 339 Main St Burnside Bldg *Web:* www.sederlaw.com	Worcester	MA	01608	508-757-7721	
Sedgwick Detert Moran & Arnold LLP One Market Plz Steuart Twr Eighth Fl *TF:* 800-826-3262 ■ *Web:* www.sdma.com	San Francisco	CA	94105	415-781-7900	781-2635
Seed Mackall & Cole LLP 1332 Anacapa St Ste 200 *Web:* seedmackall.com	Santa Barbara	CA	93101	805-963-0669	
Segel, Goldman, Mazzotta & Siegel PC Nine Washington Sq Washington Ave Ext *Web:* www.msvlawfirm.com	Albany	NY	12205	518-452-0941	
Selman Breitman LLP 11766 Wilshire Blvd *Web:* selmanbreitman.com	Los Angeles	CA	90025	310-445-0800	473-2525
Seltzer Caplan Mcmahon Vitek 2100 Symphony Towers 750 B St *Web:* www.scmv.com	San Diego	CA	92101	619-685-3003	
Serratelli Schiffman Brown & Calhoon 2080 Linglestown Rd Ste 201 *Web:* www.skellydrc.com	Harrisburg	PA	17110	717-540-9170	
Settle & Pou PC 3333 Lee Pkwy Ste 800 *Web:* www.settlepou.com	Dallas	TX	75219	214-520-3300	
Seward & Kissel 1 Battery Pk Plaza Ste 19 *Web:* www.sewkis.com	New York	NY	10004	212-574-1200	480-8421
Seyfarth Shaw LLP 131 S Dearborn St Ste 2400 *Web:* www.seyfarth.com	Chicago	IL	60603	312-460-5000	460-7000
Sharp & Cobos PC 4705 Spicewood Springs Rd Ste 100 *Web:* sharpcobos.com	Austin	TX	78759	512-473-2265	
Shartsis Friese & Ginsburg LLP One Maritime Plz 18th Fl *Web:* www.sflaw.com	San Francisco	CA	94111	415-421-6500	421-2922
Shean Law Offices 1114 N College Ave *Web:* www.sheanlaw.com	Bloomington	IN	47404	812-332-3643	
Shearman & Sterling LLP 599 Lexington Ave *Web:* www.shearman.com	New York	NY	10022	212-848-4000	848-7179
Shepherd, Finkelman, Miller & Shah LLP 65 Main St *Web:* www.sfmslaw.com	Chester	CT	06412	860-526-1100	
Sheppard Mullin Richter & Hampton LLP 333 S Hope St 48th Fl *Web:* www.sheppardmullin.com	Los Angeles	CA	90071	213-620-1780	620-1398
Shermeta, Adams & Von Allmen PC 901 Tower Dr Ste 400 *Web:* www.shermeta.com	Troy	MI	48098	248-519-1700	
Shernoff Bidart Darras & Echeverria LLP 600 S Indian Hill Blvd *Web:* www.sbd-law.com	Claremont	CA	91711	909-621-4935	
Sherrard Kuzz LLP 155 University Ave *Web:* www.sherrardkuzz.com	Toronto	ON	M5H3B7	416-603-0700	
Shook & Stone Attorneys at Law 710 S Fourth St *Web:* www.shookandstone.com	Las Vegas	NV	89101	702-385-2220	
Shook Hardy & Bacon LLP 2555 Grand Blvd *TF:* 800-821-7962 ■ *Web:* www.shb.com	Kansas City	MO	64108	816-474-6550	421-5547
Siben & Siben LLP 90 E Mn St *Web:* www.sibensiben.com	Bay Shore	NY	11706	631-665-3400	
Sidley Austin LLP 1 S Dearborn St *TF:* 800-306-5230 ■ *Web:* www.sidley.com	Chicago	IL	60603	312-853-7000	853-7036
Sieben Polk PA 1640 S Frontage Rd Ste 200 *Web:* www.siebenpolklaw.com	Hastings	MN	55033	651-437-3148	

Firm	City	State	ZIP	Phone	Fax
Siemer, Austin, Resch, Fuhr & Totten 307 N Third St *Web:* siemeraustin.com	Effingham	IL	62401	217-342-9291	
Sigman Janssen Stack Sewall & Pitz 303 S Memorial Dr *Web:* www.sigmanlegal.com	Appleton	WI	54911	920-731-5201	
Sills Cummis & Gross PC One Riverfront Plz The Legal Center *Web:* www.sillscummis.com	Newark	NJ	07102	973-643-7000	
Silver & Archibald LLP 997 S Milledge Ave *Web:* silverandarchibald.com	Athens	GA	30605	706-548-8122	
Silver Golub & Teitell LLP 184 Atlantic St *Web:* www.sgtlaw.com	Stamford	CT	06904	203-325-4491	
Simmons Perrine Moyer Bergman PLC 115 Third St SE Ste 1200 *Web:* www.simmonsperrine.com	Cedar Rapids	IA	52401	319-366-7641	
Simon & Geherin PLLC 1310 S Main St Ste 11 *Web:* www.simongeherin.com	Ann Arbor	MI	48104	734-997-0870	
Simpson Thacher & Bartlett LLP 425 Lexington Ave *Web:* www.stblaw.com	New York	NY	10017	212-455-2000	455-2502
Sindel, Sindel & Noble PC 8008 Carondelet Ave Ste 301 *Web:* www.sindellaw.com	Saint Louis	MO	63105	314-721-6040	
Sirote & Permutt Pc 2311 Highland Ave S PO Box 55727 *Web:* www.sirote.com	Birmingham	AL	35205	205-930-5100	930-5101
Siskinds LLP 680 Waterloo St PO Box 2520 *Web:* www.siskinds.com	London	ON	N6A3V8	519-672-2121	
Skadden Arps Slate Meagher & Flom LLP Four Times Sq *Web:* www.skadden.com	New York	NY	10036	212-735-3000	735-2000
Skoler, Abbott & Presser PC One Monarch Pl Ste 2000 *Web:* skoler-abbott.com	Springfield	MA	01144	413-737-4753	
Slack & Davis LLP 2705 Bee Caves Rd Ste 220 *Web:* www.slackdavis.com	Austin	TX	78746	512-795-8686	
Slater, Tenaglia, Fritz & Hunt PA Corp 301 Third St *Web:* www.stfhlaw.com	Ocean City	NJ	08226	609-399-9960	
Slevin & Hart PC 1625 Massachusetts Ave NW Ste 450 *Web:* www.slevinhart.com	Washington	DC	20036	202-797-8700	
Slover & Loftus LLP 1224 17th St NW *Web:* www.sloverandloftus.com	Washington	DC	20036	202-347-7170	
Slutzky Wolfe & Bailey LLP 2255 Cumberland Pkwy Se Ste 1300 *Web:* swbatl.com	Atlanta	GA	30339	770-438-8000	
Smith Bovill Pc 200 Saint Andrews Rd *Web:* www.smithbovill.com	Saginaw	MI	48638	989-792-9641	
Smith Hartvigsen PLLC The Walker Ctr 175 South Main St Ste 300 *Web:* www.smithhartvigsen.com	Salt Lake City	UT	84111	801-413-1600	
Smith Hulsey & Busey 225 Water St Ste 1800 *Web:* www.smithhulsey.com	Jacksonville	FL	32202	904-359-7700	359-7708
Smith Katzenstein & Furlow LLP The Corporate Plz 800 Delaware Ave *Web:* www.skfdelaware.com	Wilmington	DE	19899	302-652-8400	
Smith Keller Miner & O'shea 69 Delaware Ave Rm 1212 *Web:* www.smithminerlaw.com	Buffalo	NY	14202	716-855-3611	
Smith Mazure Director Wilkins Young & Yagerman PC 111 John St 20th Fl *Web:* www.smithmazure.com	New York	NY	10038	212-964-7400	
Smith Peterson Law Office 35 Main Pl Ste 300 *Web:* www.smithpeterson.com	Council Bluffs	IA	51503	712-328-1833	
Smith, Anderson, Blount, Dorsett, Mitchell & Jernigan LLP 2500 First Union Capitol Center *Web:* www.smithlaw.com	Raleigh	NC	27602	919-821-1220	
Smith, Sovik, Kendrick & Sugnet PC 250 S Clinton St Ste 600 *Web:* www.smithsovik.com	Syracuse	NY	13202	315-474-2911	
Snell & Wilmer LLP One Arizona Ctr 400 E Van Buren St Ste 1900 *TF:* 800-322-0430 ■ *Web:* www.swlaw.com	Phoenix	AZ	85004	602-382-6000	382-6070
Snow Christensen & Martineau 10 Exchange Pl *Web:* www.scmlaw.com	Salt Lake City	UT	84111	801-521-9000	
Solem, Mack & Steinhoff PC 3333 S Bannock St Ste 900 *Web:* solemlaw.com	Englewood	CO	80110	303-761-4900	
Somach Simmons & Dunn 500 Capitol Mall Ste 1000 *Web:* www.somachlaw.com	Sacramento	CA	95814	916-446-7979	
Sorling, Northrup, Hanna, Cullen & et al 607 E Adams St Illinois Bldg Ste 800 *Web:* www.sorlinglaw.com	Springfield	IL	62705	217-544-1144	
Southern Environmental Law Center 201 W Main St Ste 14 *Web:* www.southernenvironment.org	Charlottesville	VA	22902	434-977-4090	
Sowell Gray Stepp & Laffitte LLC 1310 Gadsden St *Web:* www.sowell.com	Columbia	SC	29211	803-929-1400	
Spangler, Jennings & Dougherty PC 8396 Mississippi St *Web:* www.sjdlaw.com	Merrillville	IN	46410	219-769-2323	
Spector Gadon & Rosen PC Seven Penn Ctr Seventh Fl 1635 Market St *Web:* www.lawsgr.com	Philadelphia	PA	19103	215-241-8888	
Spence Law Firm LLC 15 S Jackson St *TF:* 800-967-2117 ■ *Web:* www.spencelawyers.com	Jackson	WY	83001	307-733-7290	733-5248
Spencer Fane Britt & Browne LLP 1000 Walnut St Ste 1400 *Web:* www.spencerfane.com	Kansas City	MO	64106	816-474-8100	474-3216
Spilman Thomas & Battle PLLC Spilman Cntr 300 Knwh Blv Spilman Ctr Spilman Center *Web:* www.spilmanlaw.com	Charleston	WV	25301	304-340-3838	
Squire Patton Boggs 127 Public Sq 4900 Key Tower *TF:* 800-743-2773 ■ *Web:* www.squirepattonboggs.com	Cleveland	OH	44114	216-479-8500	479-8780
St. Onge Steward Johnston & Reens LLC 986 Bedford St *Web:* mobile.ssjr.com	Stamford	CT	06905	203-324-6155	
Stanley, Lande & Hunter A Professional Corp 301 Iowa Ave Ste 400 *Web:* www.slhlaw.com	Muscatine	IA	52761	563-264-5000	
Stark & Knoll Company LPA 3475 Ridgewood Rd *Web:* www.stark-knoll.com	Akron	OH	44333	330-376-3300	
Stark & Stark 993 Lenox Dr Bldg 2 *TF:* 800-535-3425 ■ *Web:* www.stark-stark.com	Lawrenceville	NJ	08648	609-896-9060	896-0629
Starr & Associates PC 4245 N Central Expy Ste 350 *Web:* www.starrattorneys.com	Dallas	TX	75205	214-219-8440	
Stearns Weaver Miller Weissler Alhadeff & Sitterson P.A. 150 W Flagler St Ste 2200 *TF:* 866-293-7866 ■ *Web:* stearnsweaver.com/	Miami	FL	33130	305-789-3200	789-3395
Steele Law Firm p C The 949 County Rt 53 *Web:* www.thesteelelawfirm.com	Oswego	NY	13126	315-216-4721	
Stein Monast LLP 70 rue Dalhousie Bureau 300 *Web:* www.steinmonast.ca	Quebec	QC	G1K4B2	418-529-6531	
Stein Sperling Bennett De Jong Driscoll & Greenfeig PC 25 W Middle Ln *Web:* www.steinsperling.com	Rockville	MD	20850	301-340-2020	
Steptoe & Johnson LLP 1330 Connecticut Ave NW *Web:* www.steptoe.com	Washington	DC	20036	202-429-3000	429-3902
Steptoe & Johnson PLLC 400 White Oaks Blvd *Web:* www.steptoe-johnson.com	Bridgeport	WV	26330	304-933-8000	
Steven Brian Davis Law Offices 12396 World Trade Dr Ste 115 *Web:* www.prestonestateplanning.com	San Diego	CA	92128	858-451-1004	
Stevens & Lee PC 111 N Sixth St *Web:* www.stevenslee.com	Reading	PA	19603	610-478-2000	
Stewart Sokol & Gray LLC 2300 Sw First Ave Ste 200 *Web:* lawssg.com	Portland	OR	97201	503-221-0699	
Stichter, Riedel, Blain & Prosser PA 110 E Madison St Ste 200 *Web:* www.srbp.com	Tampa	FL	33602	813-229-0144	
Stidham & Associates PSC 401 Lewis Hargett Cir Ste 250 *Web:* www.stidhamlaw.com	Lexington	KY	40503	859-219-2255	
Stikeman Elliott LLP 1155 Rene-levesque Blvd W 40th Fl *Web:* www.stikeman.com	Montreal	QC	H3B3V2	514-397-3000	
Stoel Rives LLP 900 S W Fifth Ave Ste 2600 *Web:* www.stoel.com	Portland	OR	97204	503-224-3380	
Stokes Lazarus & Carmichael 80 Peachtree Park Dr Ne *Web:* slclaw.com	Atlanta	GA	30309	404-352-1465	
Stoll Stoll Berne Lokting & Shlachter PC 209 SW Oak St Ste 500 *Web:* www.ssbls.com	Portland	OR	97204	503-227-1600	
Stone Pigman Walther Wittmann LLC 546 Carondelet St *Web:* www.stonepigman.com	New Orleans	LA	70130	504-581-3200	
Storch Amini & Munves PC Two Grand Central Tower 140 E 45th St 25th Fl *Web:* samlegal.com	New York	NY	10017	212-490-4100	
Strauss & Troy 150 E Fourth St *Web:* www.strausstroy.com	Cincinnati	OH	45202	513-621-2120	241-8259
Strip Hoppers Leithart Mcgrath 575 S Third St *Web:* www.columbuslawyer.org	Columbus	OH	43215	614-228-6345	
Stroock & Stroock & Lavan LLP 180 Maiden Ln *Web:* www.stroock.com	New York	NY	10038	212-806-5400	
Stroud, Willink & Howard LLC 25 W Main St Ste 300 PO Box 2236 *Web:* www.stroudlaw.com	Madison	WI	53701	608-257-2281	
Stueve Siegel Hanson LLP 460 Nichols Rd Ste 200 *Web:* stuevesiegel.com	Kansas City	MO	64112	816-714-7100	
Sturgill, Turner, Barker & Moloney PLLC 333 W Vine St Ste 1400 *Web:* www.sturgillturner.com	Lexington	KY	40507	859-255-8581	
Sughrue Mion PLLC 2100 Pennsylvania Ave NW Ste 800 *Web:* www.sughrue.com	Washington	DC	20037	202-293-7060	
Suiter Swantz Pc Llo 14301 Fnb Pkwy Ste 220 *Web:* www.suiter.com	Omaha	NE	68154	402-496-0300	
Sullivan & Cromwell LLP 125 Broad St *Web:* www.sullcrom.com	New York	NY	10004	212-558-4000	558-3588
Sullivan Hincks & Conway 120 W 22nd St Ste 100 *Web:* www.shlawfirm.com	Oak Brook	IL	60523	630-573-5021	
Sulloway & Hollis Nine Capitol St & 29 School St *Web:* www.sulloway.com	Concord	NH	03301	603-224-2341	

Phone | Fax

Summit Law Group PLLC
315 Fifth Ave S Ste 1000 .... Seattle WA 98104 206-676-7000
Web: www.summitlaw.com

Sundahl Powers Kapp & Martin LLC
1725 Carey Ave. .... Cheyenne WY 82001 307-632-6421
Web: www.spkm.org

Sutherland Asbill & Brennan LLP
999 Peachtree St NE .... Atlanta GA 30309 404-853-8000 853-8806
TF: 855-857-9769 ■ *Web:* www.sutherland.com

Sutin Thayer & Browne
6565 Americas Pkwy N E Two Park Sq
Ste 1000 .... Albuquerque NM 87110 505-883-2500
Web: sutinfirm.com

Swanson & Bratschun LLC 8210 SouthPark Ter .... Littleton CO 80120 303-268-0066
Web: www.sbiplaw.com

Sweeney Law Firm 8109 Lima Rd .... Fort Wayne IN 46818 260-420-3137
Web: sweeneylawfirm.com

Sweet, Stevens, Katz & Williams LLP
331 E Butler Ave .... New Britain PA 18901 215-345-9111
Web: sweetstevens.com

Szabo, Zelnick & Erickson PC
12610 Lk Ridge Dr .... Woodbridge VA 22192 703-494-7171
Web: zelnickerickson.com

Tabet DiVito & Rothstein LLC
The Rookery Bldg 209 S LaSalle St Seventh Fl .... Chicago IL 60604 312-762-9450
Web: www.tdrlawfirm.com

Taggart Morton LLC
2100 Energy Ctr 1100 Poydras St .... New Orleans LA 70163 504-599-8500
Web: www.taggartmortonlaw.com

Taylor Financial Corp
100 Winners Cir N Ste 100 .... Brentwood TN 37027 615-373-4111
Web: taylorcos.com

Taylor Law Offices Pc 122 E Washington Ave .... Effingham IL 62401 800-879-2250
TF: 800-879-2250 ■ *Web:* taylorlaw.net

Taylor Wellons Politz & Duhe Aplc
7924 Wrenwood Blvd Ste C .... Baton Rouge LA 70809 225-387-9888
Web: www.twpdlaw.com

Taylor, Porter, Brooks & Phillips
451 Florida St Eighth Fl .... Baton Rouge LA 70801 225-387-3221
Web: www.taylorporter.com

Teplitsky, Colson LLP 70 Bond St Ste 200 .... Toronto ON M5B1X3 416-365-9320
Web: www.teplitskycolson.com

Terra Law LLP 177 Park Ave Third Fl .... San Jose CA 95113 408-299-1200
Web: www.terra-law.com

Texas Legal Services Center Inc
815 Brazos St Ste 1100 .... Austin TX 78701 512-477-6000
Web: www.tlsc.org

Thompson & Bowie LLP Three Canal Plz .... Portland ME 04112 207-774-2500
Web: thompsonbowie.com

Thompson & Knight LLP
1700 Pacific Ave Ste 3300 .... Dallas TX 75201 214-969-1700 969-1751
Web: www.tklaw.com

Thompson & McMullan 100 Shockoe Slip .... Richmond VA 23219 804-649-7545
Web: www.t-mlaw.com

Thompson Coe Cousins & irons
700 N Pearl St 25th Fl .... Dallas TX 75201 214-871-8200 871-8209
Web: www.thompsoncoe.com

Thompson Hine LLP
127 Public Sq 3900 Key Ctr .... Cleveland OH 44114 216-566-5500 566-5800
TF: 877-257-3382 ■ *Web:* www.thompsonhine.com

Thompson, O'Brien, Kemp & Nasuti PC
40 Technology Pkwy S Ste 300 .... Norcross GA 30092 770-925-0111
Web: www.tokn.com

Thornton, Davis & Fein PA
Brickell Bayview Ctr 80 SW Eighth St Ste 2900 .... Miami FL 33130 305-446-2646
Web: www.tdflaw.com

Thorp Reed & Armstrong LLP
301 Grant St 14th Fl .... Pittsburgh PA 15219 412-394-7711 394-2555
TF: 800-949-3120 ■ *Web:* clarkhill.com

Thorpe, North & Western LLP
8180 South 700 East Ste 200 .... Sandy UT 84070 801-566-6633
Web: www.tnw.com

Thorsnes Bartolotta McGuire
2550 Fifth Ave 11th Fl .... San Diego CA 92103 619-236-9363
Web: tbmlawyers.com

Timoney Knox LLP 400 Maryland Dr .... Fort Washington PA 19034 215-646-6000
Web: www.timoneyknox.com

Timothy M. Cary & Associates
3300 Cameron Park Dr Ste 2000 .... Cameron Park CA 95682 530-672-7601
Web: carylaw.com

Tompkins Mc Guire Wachenfeld & Barry
100 Mulberry St .... Newark NJ 07102 973-622-3000 623-7780
Web: www.tompkinsmcguire.com

Tousley Brain Stephens PLLC
1700 Seventh Ave Ste 2200 .... Seattle WA 98101 206-682-5600
Web: www.tousley.com

Townsend James r 150 Dufferin Ave .... London ON N6A5N6 519-672-5272
Web: www.ftgalaw.com

Triplett Woolf & Garretson LLC
2959 N Rock Rd -Ste 300 .... Wichita KS 67226 316-630-8100
Web: www.twgfirm.com

Tripp Scott 110 SE Sixth St 15th Fl .... Fort Lauderdale FL 33301 954-525-7500
Web: www.trippscott.com

Trojan Law Offices
9250 Wilshire Blvd Ste 325 .... Beverly Hills CA 90212 310-777-8399
Web: www.trojanlawoffices.com

Troutman Sanders LLP
600 Peachtree St NE Ste 5200 .... Atlanta GA 30308 404-885-3000 885-3900
Web: www.troutmansanders.com

Tucker Arensberg Inc 1500 1 PPG Pl .... Pittsburgh PA 15222 412-594-5521 594-5619
Web: www.tuckerlaw.com

Tucker Ellis & West LLP 925 Euclid Ave .... Cleveland OH 44115 216-592-5000 592-5009
Web: tuckerellis.com

Phone | Fax

Tully Rinckey PLLC 441 New Karner Rd .... Albany NY 12205 518-218-7100
Web: www.tullylegal.com

Turner & Burney Pc Attorneys 105 W Public Sq .... Laurens SC 29360 864-984-6565
Web: www.tandblaw.net

Turner, Padget, Graham & Laney PA
1901 Main St 17th Fl .... Columbia SC 29202 803-254-2200
Web: www.turnerpadget.com

Turocy & Watson LLP
Key Tower 127 Public Sq 57th Fl .... Cleveland OH 44114 216-696-8730
Web: www.thepatentattorneys.com

Twomey, Latham, Shea, Kelley, Dubin & Quartararo LLP
33 W Second St PO Box 9398 .... Riverhead NY 11901 631-727-2180
Web: www.suffolklaw.com

Udall Shumway PLC 1138 N Alma School Rd Ste 101 .... Mesa AZ 85201 480-461-5300
Web: www.udallshumway.com

Ulmer & Berne 1660 W Second St Ste 1100 .... Cleveland OH 44113 216-583-7000
Web: www.ulmer.com

Underwood Attorneys & Counselors at Law
1111 W Loop 289 .... Lubbock TX 79416 806-793-1711
Web: www.uwlaw.com

Unruh, Turner, Burke & Frees PC
17 W Gay St .... West Chester PA 19381 610-692-1371
Web: www.utbf.com

Updike Kelly & Spellacy Pc PO Box 231277 .... Hartford CT 06123 860-548-2600
Web: www.uks.com

Urban League of Philadelphia Administrative Offices
121 S Broad St Fl 9 .... Philadelphia PA 19107 215-985-3220
Web: golombhonik.com

Valensi Rose PLC
1888 Century Park E Ste 1100 .... Los Angeles CA 90067 310-277-8011
Web: www.vrmlaw.com

Van Der Hout Brigagliano & Nightingale LLP
180 Sutter St Fl 5 .... San Francisco CA 94104 650-688-6020
Web: www.vblaw.com

Van Winkle Buck Wall Starnes & Davis PA
11 N Market St .... Asheville NC 28801 828-258-2991
Web: www.vwlawfirm.com

Vann & Sheridan LLP
1720 Hillsborough St Ste 200 .... Raleigh NC 27605 919-510-8585
Web: vannattorneys.com

Venable LLP 575 Seventh St NW .... Washington DC 20004 202-344-4000 344-8300
Web: www.venable.com

Ver Ploeg & Lumpkin PA
Miami Twr 100 SE Second St 30th Fl .... Miami FL 33131 305-577-3996
Web: www.vpl-law.com

Vernis & Bowling of Miami PA 1680 NE 135th St .... Miami FL 33181 305-895-3035
Web: www.florida-law.com

Verrill Dana LLP PO Box 586 .... Portland ME 04112 207-774-4000 774-7499
Web: www.verrilldana.com

Victim Rights Law Center Inc
115 Broad St Fl 3 .... Boston MA 02110 617-399-6720
Web: www.victimrights.org

Vinson & Elkins LLP
1001 Fannin St 1st City Tower Ste 2500 .... Houston TX 77002 713-758-2222 758-2346
TF: 877-610-2009 ■ *Web:* www.velaw.com

Visa Law Group 1806 11th St Nw .... Washington DC 20001 202-265-7530
Web: www.visalawgroup.com

Vogel Law Firm 218 NP Ave .... Fargo ND 58107 701-237-6983
Web: www.vogellaw.com

Vorys Sater Seymour & Pease LLP (VSSP)
52 E Gay St PO Box 1008 .... Columbus OH 43216 614-464-6400 464-6350
Web: www.vorys.com

Vrdolyak Law Group LLC 741 N Dearborn St .... Chicago IL 60654 312-482-8200
Web: www.vrdolyak.com

Wagner Falconer & Judd Ltd
80 S Eighth St Ste 1700 .... Minneapolis MN 55402 612-339-1421
Web: www.wfjlawfirm.com

Wagner Johnston & Rosenthal
5855 Sandy Springs Cir Ste 300 .... Atlanta GA 30328 404-261-0500
Web: www.wjrlaw.com

Wagstaff & Cartmell LLP
4740 Grand Ave Ste 300 .... Kansas City MO 64112 816-701-1100
Web: www.wagstaffcartmell.com

Wai & Connor LLP
2566 Overland Ave Ste 570 .... Los Angeles CA 90064 310-838-6800
Web: www.waiconnor.com

Walker & Jocke Company LPA 231 S Broadway .... Medina OH 44256 330-721-0000
Web: www.walkerandjocke.com

Walker, Morgan & Kinard 135 E Main St .... Lexington SC 29072 803-359-6194
Web: walkermorgan.com

Wallace Saunders Austin Brown Enochs
200 W Douglas Ave Ste 400 .... Wichita KS 67202 316-269-2100
Web: wallacesaunders.com

Waller Lansden Dortch & Davis
Nashville City Ctr 511 Union St Ste 2100 .... Nashville TN 37219 615-850-8487
Web: www.wallerlaw.com

Walter J Haverfield LLP
1300 Terminal Tower .... Cleveland OH 44113 216-781-1212
Web: www.walterhav.com

Walton Lantaff Schroeder & Carson LLP
9350 S Dixie Hwy 10th Fl .... Miami FL 33156 305-671-1300
Web: www.atlanticcivil.com

Ward & Smith 1001 College Ct .... New Bern NC 28563 252-672-5400
Web: www.wardandsmith.com

Ward, Murray, Pace & Johnson PC
202 E Fifth St .... Sterling IL 61081 815-625-8200
Web: www.wmpj.com

Waters & Kraus LLP 3219 McKinney Ave .... Dallas TX 75204 214-357-6244
Web: www.waterskraus.com

Watt, Beckworth, Thompson Henneman & Sullivan LLP
1800 Pennzoil Pl 711 Louisiana St .... Houston TX 77002 713-650-8100
Web: www.wattbeckworth.com

Name / Address	City	State	Zip	Phone	Fax
Weber Gallagher Simpson Stapleton Fires & Newby LLP					
2000 Market St Ste 1300	Philadelphia	PA	19103	215-972-7900	
Web: www.wglaw.com					
Weil Gotshal & Manges LLP 767 Fifth Ave	New York	NY	10153	212-310-8000	310-8007
Web: www.weil.com					
Weiner Lesniak LLP 629 Parsippany Rd	Parsippany	NJ	07054	973-403-1100	
Web: www.weinerlesniak.com					
Weir & Partners LLP					
The Widener Bldg 1339 Chestnut St Ste 500	Philadelphia	PA	19107	215-665-8181	
Web: www.weirpartners.com					
WeirFoulds LLP					
4100 - 66 Wellington St W Toronto-Dominion Centre PO Box 35	Toronto	ON	M5K1B7	416-365-1110	
Web: www.weirfoulds.com					
Welborn Sullivan Meck & Tooley					
821 17th St Ste 500	Denver	CO	80202	303-830-2500	
Web: www.wsmtlaw.com					
Welch Gold & Siegel Pc					
428 Forbes Ave Ste 1240	Pittsburgh	PA	15219	412-391-1014	
Web: www.wgspc.com					
Wendel, Rosen, Black & Dean LLP					
1111 Broadway 24th Fl	Oakland	CA	94607	510-834-6600	
Web: www.wendel.com					
Westchase Law Group pa 12027 Whitmarsh Ln	Tampa	FL	33626	813-490-5211	
Web: www.westchaselaw.com					
Westman Champlin & Kelly					
900 Second Ave S	Minneapolis	MN	55402	612-334-3222	
Web: www.wck.com					
Weston Hurd LLP					
The Tower at Erieview 1301 E Ninth St Ste 1900	Cleveland	OH	44114	216-241-6602	
Web: www.westonhurd.com					
Wharton Levin Ehrmantraut & Klein Profit Sharing Plan					
104 W St	Annapolis	MD	21404	410-263-5900	
Web: www.wlekn.com					
Wheeler, Van Sickle & Anderson SC					
25 W Main St Ste 801	Madison	WI	53703	608-255-7277	
Web: wheelerlaw.com					
Whiteford, Taylor & Preston LLP					
Seven Saint Paul St	Baltimore	MD	21202	410-347-8700	
Web: www.wtplaw.com					
Whitfield & Eddy PLC					
317 Sixth Ave Ste 1200	Des Moines	IA	50309	515-288-6041	246-1474
Web: www.whitfieldlaw.com					
Wiggins, Childs, Quinn & Pantazis LLC					
The Kress Bldg 301 19th St N	Birmingham	AL	35203	205-314-0500	
Web: www.wcqp.com					
Wiley Rein LLP 1776 K St N W	Washington	DC	20006	202-719-7000	
Web: www.wileyrein.com					
Wilhelm Law Service					
100 W Lawrence St Ste 309	Appleton	WI	54911	920-831-0100	
Web: www.wilhelmlaw.com					
Wilkinson Barker Knauer LLP					
2300 N St NW Ste 700	Washington	DC	20037	202-783-4141	
Web: www.wbklaw.com					
Willcox, Buyck & Williams PA 248 W Evans St	Florence	SC	29501	843-662-3258	
Web: www.willcoxlaw.com					
William W Price PA 320 Fern St	West Palm Beach	FL	33401	561-659-3212	
Web: www.wpricepa.com					
Williams & Anderson PLC					
111 Ctr St 22nd Fl	Little Rock	AR	72201	501-372-0800	372-6453
Web: williamsanderson.com					
Williams & Connolly LLP 725 12th St NW	Washington	DC	20005	202-434-5000	434-5029
Web: www.wc.com					
Williams & Petro Company LLC					
338 S High St Second Fl	Columbus	OH	43215	614-224-0531	
Web: williamsandpetro.com					
Williams Mullen					
1021 E Cary St James Ctr Two	Richmond	VA	23219	804-643-1991	
Web: www.williamsmullen.com					
Williams Parker Harrison Dietz & Getzen Professional Association					
200 S Orange Ave	Sarasota	FL	34236	941-366-4800	
Web: www.williamsparker.com					
Williams, Kastner & Gibbs PLLC					
Two Union Sq 601 Union St Ste 4100	Seattle	WA	98101	206-628-6600	
Web: www.williamskastner.com					
Williams, Turner & Holmes PC					
200 N Sixth St Ste 103	Grand Junction	CO	81501	970-242-6262	
Web: www.wth-law.com					
Willkie Farr & Gallagher LLP					
787 Seventh Ave Second Fl	New York	NY	10019	212-728-8000	728-8111
Web: www.willkie.com					
Wilmer Cutler Pickering Hale & Dorr LLP					
1875 Pennsylvania Ave	Washington	DC	20006	202-663-6000	663-6363
Web: www.wilmerhale.com					
Wilson Elser Moskowitz Edelman & Dicker LLP					
150 E 42nd St	New York	NY	10017	212-490-3000	490-3038
Web: www.wilsonelser.com					
Wilson Sonsini Goodrich & Rosati					
650 Page Mill Rd	Palo Alto	CA	94304	650-493-9300	493-6811
Web: www.wsgr.com					
Wilson, Sheehy, Knowles, Robertson & Cornelius PC					
909 ESE Loop 323 Ste 400	Tyler	TX	75701	903-509-5000	
Web: www.wilsonlawfirm.com					
Windels Marx Ln Mittendorf LLP					
156 W 56th St	New York	NY	10019	212-237-1000	262-1215
Web: www.windelsmarx.com					
Winderweedle, Haines, Ward & Woodman PA					
329 Park Ave N Second Fl 32789 Post Office Box 880	Winter Park	FL	32790	407-423-4246	
Web: www.whww.com					
Winet, Patrick & Weaver 1215 W Vista Way	Vista	CA	92083	760-758-4261	
Web: www.wpwlaw.com					
Winstead PC					
1201 Elm St 5400 Renaissance Tower	Dallas	TX	75270	214-745-5400	
Web: www.winstead.com					
Winthrop & Weinstine PA					
225 S Sixth St Ste 3500	Minneapolis	MN	55402	612-604-6400	
Web: www.winthrop.com					
Wisler Pearlstine LLP					
460 Norristown Rd Ste 110	Blue Bell	PA	19422	610-825-8400	
Web: www.wislerpearlstine.com					
Wojtalewicz Law Firm Ltd 139 N Miles St	Appleton	MN	56208	320-289-2363	
Web: wojtalewiczlawfirm.com					
Wolfe Jones Boswell & Wolfe Hancock & Daniel LLC					
905 Bob Wallace Ave Sw	Huntsville	AL	35801	256-534-2205	
Web: www.wjb-law.com					
Wolff & Samson PC					
One Boland Dr The Offices at Crystal Lake	West Orange	NJ	07052	973-325-1500	
Web: www.wolffsamson.com					
Wolff, Hill, McFarlin & Herron PA					
1851 W Colonial Dr	Orlando	FL	32804	407-648-0058	
Web: www.whmh.com					
Wolk Law Firm, The 1712 Locust St	Philadelphia	PA	19103	215-545-4220	
Web: airlaw.com					
Womble Carlyle Sandridge & Rice PLLC					
One W Fourth St	Winston-Salem	NC	27101	336-721-3600	721-3660
Web: www.wcsr.com					
Wong Fleming PC 821 Alexander Rd Ste 200	Princeton	NJ	08540	609-951-9520	
Web: wongfleming.com					
Woodcock Washburn LLP 2929 Arch St Fl 12	Philadelphia	PA	19104	215-568-3100	568-3439
Web: bakerlaw.com/_wwmerge.html					
Woods Fuller Shultz & Smith					
300 S Phillips Ave Ste 300	Sioux Falls	SD	57117	605-336-3890	
Web: www.woodsfuller.com					
Woods Rogers PLC 10 S Jefferson St Ste 1400	Roanoke	VA	24011	540-983-7600	
Web: www.woodsrogers.com					
Workman Nydegger PC					
60 East South Temple Ste 1000	Salt Lake City	UT	84111	801-533-9800	
Web: www.wnlaw.com					
Wright Ginsberg Brusilow PC					
14755 Preston Rd Ste 600	Dallas	TX	75254	972-788-1600	
Web: www.wgblawfirm.com					
Wright Lindsey & Jennings LLP					
200 W Capitol Ave Ste 2300	Little Rock	AR	72201	501-371-0808	376-9442
Web: www.wlj.com					
Wulfsberg, Reese, Colvig & Firstman PC					
Kaiser Ctr 300 Lakeside Dr 24th Fl	Oakland	CA	94612	510-835-9100	
Web: www.wulfslaw.com					
Wyatt Early Harris Wheeler LLP					
PO Drawer 2086	High Point	NC	27261	336-884-4444	
Web: www.wehwlaw.com					
Wyatt Tarrant & Combs					
PNC Plz 500 W Jefferson St	Louisville	KY	40202	502-589-5235	
Web: www.wyattfirm.com					
Yavenditti Kate Esq Cfls 1901 First Ave	San Diego	CA	92101	619-531-9300	
Web: www.thedeanlawgroup.com					
Young Clement Rivers LLP 28 Broad St	Charleston	SC	29401	843-577-4000	
Web: www.ycrt.com					
Youth Advocate Programs Inc					
2007 N Third St	Harrisburg	PA	17102	717-232-7580	
Web: www.yapinc.org					
Yturri Rose LLP 89 SW Third Ave	Ontario	OR	97914	541-889-5368	
Web: www.yturrirose.com					
Yukevich | Cavanaugh					
355 S Grand Ave 15th Fl	Los Angeles	CA	90071	213-362-7777	
Web: www.yukelaw.com					
Zager Fuchs PC 268 Broad St	Red Bank	NJ	07701	732-747-3700	
Web: zagerfuchs.com					
Zimmerman Reed PLLP					
1100 IDS Ctr 80 S Eighth St	Minneapolis	MN	55402	612-341-0400	
Web: www.zimmreed.com					
Zucker Goldberg & Ackerman					
200 Sheffield St Ste 301	Mountainside	NJ	07092	908-233-8500	
Web: www.zuckergoldberg.com					
Zumpano, Patricios & Winker PA					
312 Minorca Ave	Coral Gables	FL	33134	305-444-5565	
Web: www.zpwlaw.com					

432 LAWN & GARDEN EQUIPMENT

SEE ALSO Farm Machinery & Equipment - Mfr p. 2282

Name / Address	City	State	Zip	Phone	Fax
American Biophysics Corp					
140 Frenchtown Rd	North Kingstown	RI	02852	800-953-5737	
TF: 877-699-8727 ■ *Web:* www.mosquitomagnet.com					
American Lawn Mower Co 2100 N Grandville Ave	Muncie	IN	47303	765-288-6624	
Web: www.americanlawnmower.com					
Ames True Temper Inc 465 Railroad Ave	Camp Hill	PA	17011	800-393-1846	
TF: 800-393-1846 ■ *Web:* www.ames.com					
Ariens Co 655 W Ryan St	Brillion	WI	54110	920-756-2141	756-2407
Web: www.ariens.com					
Armatron International Inc 15 Highland Ave	Malden	MA	02148	781-321-2300	321-2309
TF: 800-343-3280 ■ *Web:* www.slowtron.com					
Artcraft Company Inc, The					
200 John L Dietsch Blvd	North Attleboro	MA	02763	508-695-4042	
TF: 800-659-4042 ■ *Web:* www.artcraft.com					
Automatic Irrigation Supply Co 4877 SR- 261	Newburgh	IN	47630	812-858-1809	
Web: www.automaticirrigation.com					
Binkley & Hurst LP 133 Rothsville Stn Rd	Lititz	PA	17543	717-626-4705	
TF: 800-414-4705 ■ *Web:* www.binkleyhurst.com					
Blount Inc Oregon Cutting Systems Div					
4909 SE International Way	Portland	OR	97222	503-653-8881	653-4201
TF: 800-223-5168 ■ *Web:* www.oregonproducts.com					

Company	City	State	Zip	Phone	Fax
Blount Outdoor Products Group 4909 SE International Way *Web:* blount.com	Portland	OR	97222	503-653-8881	653-4402
Bondioli & Pavesi Inc 10252 Sycamore Dr *Web:* bondioli-pavesi.com	Ashland	VA	23005	804-550-2224	
Bosmere Inc 323 Corban Ave SW *Web:* bosmereusa.com	Concord	NC	28025	704-784-1608	
Brinly-Hardy Co 3230 Industrial Pkwy *TF:* 800-626-5329 ■ *Web:* www.brinly.com	Jeffersonville	IN	47130	812-218-7200	218-6085
Brown Dairy Equipment 6500 W Gerwoude Dr **Fax Area Code:* 989 ■ *Web:* browndairyequip.com	Mc Bain	MI	49657	231-825-4144	269-1953*
California Flexrake Corp 9620 Gidley St *TF:* 800-266-4200 ■ *Web:* www.flexrake.com	Temple City	CA	91780	626-443-4026	443-6887
Carswell Distributing Co 3750 N Liberty St *TF:* 800-929-1948 ■ *Web:* www.carswelldist.com	Winston Salem	NC	27105	336-767-7700	
CMD Products 1410 Flightline Dr Ste D *TF:* 800-210-9949 ■ *Web:* www.cmdproducts.com	Lincoln	CA	95648	916-434-0228	434-0214
Coast Pump Water Technologies Inc 610 Groveland Ave *Web:* www.coastpumpwatertechnology.com	Venice	FL	34285	941-484-3738	
Commerce Corp 7603 Energy Pkwy *TF:* 800-883-0234 ■ *Web:* bfgsupply.com/	Baltimore	MD	21226	410-255-3500	
Corona Clipper Inc 22440 Tomasco Canyon Rd *TF:* 800-234-2547 ■ *Web:* www.coronatoolsusa.com	Corona	CA	92883	951-737-6515	737-6515
Dultmeier Sales LLC 13808 Industrial Rd *TF:* 888-677-5054 ■ *Web:* www.dultmeier.com	Omaha	NE	68137	402-333-1444	
EarthWay Products Inc 1009 Maple St *TF:* 800-294-0671 ■ *Web:* www.earthway.com	Bristol	IN	46507	574-848-7491	848-4249
Echo Inc 400 Oakwood Rd *TF:* 800-673-1558 ■ *Web:* www.echo-usa.com	Lake Zurich	IL	60047	847-540-8400	540-9741
Emco Wheaton USA Inc 9111 Jackrabbit Rd *Web:* www.emcowheaton.com	Houston	TX	77095	281-856-1300	856-1325
Encore Manufacturing Company Inc 2415 Ashland Ave *Web:* www.encoreequipment.com	Beatrice	NE	68310	800-267-4255	
Future Harvest Development Ltd 725 Evans Crt *Web:* futureharvest.com	Kelowna	BC	V1X6G4	250-491-0255	
Gilmour Mfg Group 492 Drum Ave Somerset *TF Cust Svc:* 800-458-0107 ■ *Web:* www.gilmour.com	Somerset	PA	15501	814-443-4802	
Grasshopper Co, The 105 Old US Hwy 81 PO Box 637 *Web:* www.grasshoppermower.com	Moundridge	KS	67107	620-345-8621	345-2301
Grassland Equipment & Irrigation Corp 892-898 Troy Schenectady Rd *TF:* 800-564-5587 ■ *Web:* www.grasslandcorp.com	Latham	NY	12110	518-785-5841	785-5740
Green Depot Inc One Ivy Hill Rd *Web:* greendepot.com	Brooklyn	NY	11211	718-782-2991	
Greenscapes Home & Garden Products Inc 200 Union Grove Rd SE *Web:* www.greenscapesinc.net	Calhoun	GA	30701	706-629-6652	
Handy Tv Inc 224 Oxmoor Cir *Web:* www.handytv.com	Birmingham	AL	35209	205-290-0300	
Harnack Co 6016 Nordic Dr **Fax Area Code:* 800 ■ *TF Cust Svc:* 800-772-2022 ■ *Web:* www.harnack.net	Cedar Falls	IA	50613	319-277-0660	772-2027*
Holt Equipment Co LLC PO Box 436317 *Web:* www.holtgascompression.com	Louisville	KY	40223	502-797-5075	
Howard Price Turf Equipment Inc 18155 Edison Ave *Web:* www.howardpriceturf.com	Chesterfield	MO	63005	636-532-7000	532-0201
Hutson 2804 Pembroke Rd *Web:* www.hutsoninc.com/h2/	Hopkinsville	KY	42240	270-886-3994	
Imperial Sprinkler Supply Inc 1485 N Manassero St *Web:* www.imperialsprinklersupply.com	Anaheim	CA	92807	714-792-2925	
Jacobsen 11108 Quality Dr *TF:* 866-522-6273 ■ *Web:* www.jacobsen.com	Charlotte	NC	28273	704-504-6600	504-6661
Kanequip Inc 1451 S Second Ave *Web:* kanequip.com	Dodge City	KS	67801	620-225-0016	
Kenney Corp 8420 Zionsville Rd *Web:* www.kmcturf.com	Indianapolis	IN	46268	317-872-4793	879-2331
Kusel Equipment Co 820 W St *Web:* www.kuselequipment.com	Watertown	WI	53094	920-261-4112	
Landmark Equipment Company Inc 1309 Haltom Rd *Web:* www.landmarkeq.com	Fort Worth	TX	76117	972-579-9999	
Lang Diesel Inc 1366 Toulon Ave *Web:* langdieselinc.com	Hays	KS	67601	785-735-2651	
Lawn & Golf Supply Co Inc 647 Nutt Rd PO Box 447 *TF:* 800-362-5650 ■ *Web:* www.lawn-golf.com	Phoenixville	PA	19460	610-933-5801	933-8890
Lawn Equipment Parts Co 1475 River Rd *TF:* 800-365-3726 ■ *Web:* www.lepcoonline.com	Marietta	PA	17547	717-426-5200	
Lawn-Boy Inc 8111 S Lyndale Ave *Web:* www.lawn-boy.com	Bloomington	MN	55420	952-888-8801	887-8258
LL Johnson Distributing Co 4700 Holly St *Web:* www.lljohnson.com	Denver	CO	80216	303-320-1270	
Lodi Irrigation 1301 E Armstrong Rd *TF:* 800-634-7272 ■ *Web:* www.lodiirrigation.com	Lodi	CA	95242	800-634-7272	
MacKissic Inc PO Box 111 *TF:* 800-348-1117 ■ *Web:* www.mackissic.com	Parker Ford	PA	19457	610-495-7181	495-5951
Master Mark Plastics 210 Ampe Dr *TF Cust Svc:* 800-535-4838 ■ *Web:* www.mastermark.com	Paynesville	MN	56362	320-845-2111	845-7093
McLane Manufacturing Inc 7110 E Rosecrans Ave *Web:* mclanemower.com	Paramount	CA	90723	562-633-8158	602-0651
Melnor Inc 109 Tyson Dr **Fax Area Code:* 888 ■ *TF:* 877-283-0697 ■ *Web:* www.melnor.com	Winchester	VA	22603	540-722-5600	411-2500*
Mid West Products Inc PO Box 301 *Web:* www.lambertmfg.com	Phillipsburg	OH	45354	847-214-6261	756-3831
Midwest Bio-systems Inc 28933 35 E St *Web:* www.midwestbiosystems.com	Tampico	IL	61283	815-438-7200	
MTD Products Inc 5965 Grafton Rd *TF:* 800-800-7310 ■ *Web:* www.mtdproducts.com	Valley City	OH	44280	330-225-2600	273-4617
Ohio Steel Industries Inc 2575 Ferris Rd *Web:* www.ohiosteel.com	Columbus	OH	43224	614-471-4800	
Oliver M Dean Inc 125 Brooks St *TF:* 800-648-3326 ■ *Web:* www.omdean.com	Worcester	MA	01606	508-856-9100	
Poly-clip System Corp 1000 Tower Rd *Web:* www.polyclip-usa.com	Mundelein	IL	60060	847-949-2800	
Precision Products Inc 316 Limit St *TF Cust Svc:* 800-225-5891 ■ *Web:* www.precisionprodinc.com	Lincoln	IL	62656	217-735-1590	735-2435
Rio Delmar Enterprises 8338 Elliott Rd *Web:* www.stihldealer.net	Easton	MD	21601	410-822-8866	
Rugg Mfg Company Inc 105 Newton St *TF:* 800-633-8772 ■ *Web:* www.rugg.com	Greenfield	MA	01302	413-773-5471	774-4354
Schiller Grounds Care Inc 1028 St Rd *Web:* www.littlewonder.com	Southampton	PA	18966	215-357-5110	
Simplicity Manufacturing Inc PO Box 702 *TF:* 800-837-6836 ■ *Web:* www.simplicitymfg.com	Milwaukee	WI	53201	800-837-6836	
Smithco Inc 34 W Ave *TF:* 877-833-7648 ■ *Web:* www.smithco.com	Wayne	PA	19087	610-688-4009	688-6069
Stens Corp 2424 Cathy Ln *TF:* 800-457-7444 ■ *Web:* www.stens.com	Jasper	IN	47546	812-482-2526	482-1275
Stihl Inc 536 Viking Dr **Fax Area Code:* 303 ■ *TF Cust Svc:* 800-467-8445 ■ *Web:* www.stihlusa.com	Virginia Beach	VA	23452	757-486-9100	340-0377*
Storr Tractor Co 3191 Rt 22 *TF:* 800-526-3802 ■ *Web:* www.storrtractor.com	Branchburg	NJ	08876	908-722-9830	722-9847
Swisher Mower & Machine Company Inc 1602 Corporate Dr *TF:* 800-222-8183 ■ *Web:* www.swisherinc.com	Warrensburg	MO	64093	660-747-8183	747-8650
Toro Co 8111 Lyndale Ave *NYSE:* TTC ■ **Fax Area Code:* 952 ■ *TF:* 888-384-9939 ■ *Web:* www.toro.com	Bloomington	MN	55420	888-384-9939	887-8258*
Toro Company Commercial Products Div 8111 Lyndale Ave *TF Cust Svc:* 800-348-2424 ■ *Web:* www.toro.com	Bloomington	MN	55420	952-888-8801	887-8258
Tuff Torq Corp 5943 Commerce Blvd *TF:* 866-572-3441 ■ *Web:* www.tufftorq.com	Morristown	TN	37814	423-585-2000	585-2003
Weathermatic 3301 W Kingsley Rd *TF:* 888-484-3776 ■ *Web:* www.weathermatic.com	Garland	TX	75041	972-278-6131	271-5710
Wesspur Tree Equipment 2121 Iron St *TF:* 800-268-2141 ■ *Web:* www.wesspur.com	Bellingham	WA	98225	360-734-5242	

433 LEATHER GOODS - PERSONAL

SEE ALSO Clothing & Accessories - Mfr p. 1952; Footwear p. 2321; Handbags, Totes, Backpacks p. 2444; Leather Goods (Misc) p. 2640; Luggage, Bags, Cases p. 2680

Company	City	State	Zip	Phone	Fax
AD Sutton & Sons Inc 20 W 33rd St Second Fl *Web:* www.adsutton.com	New York	NY	10001	212-695-7070	947-6253
Bottega Veneta Inc 699 Fifth Ave *Web:* www.bottegaveneta.com	New York	NY	10022	212-371-5511	371-4361
Buxton Co 245 Cadwell Dr PO Box 1650 *TF:* 800-426-3638 ■ *Web:* www.buxton.co	Springfield	MA	01104	413-734-5900	785-1367
Carroll Cos Inc 1640 Old Hwy 421 S *TF:* 800-884-2521 ■ *Web:* www.clgco.com	Boone	NC	28607	828-264-2521	264-2633
Coach Inc 516 W 34th St *NYSE:* COH ■ *TF:* 800-444-3611 ■ *Web:* world.coach.com	New York	NY	10001	212-594-1850	594-1682
Dooney & Bourke Inc 1 Regent St **Fax Area Code:* 800 ■ *TF Cust Svc:* 800-347-5000 ■ *Web:* www.dooney.com	East Norwalk	CT	06855	203-853-7515	326-1496*
Jaclyn Inc 197 W Spring Vly Ave *OTC:* JCLY ■ *Web:* www.jaclyninc.com	Maywood	NJ	07607	201-909-6000	
Sharif Designs Ltd 34-12 36th Ave	Long Island City	NY	11106	718-472-1100	937-2561
Westport Corp 331 Changdridge Rd *Web:* www.mundiwestport.com	Pine Brook	NJ	07058	973-575-0110	575-8197

434 LEATHER GOODS (MISC)

Company	City	State	Zip	Phone	Fax
Action Co 1425 N Tennessee St *TF Sales:* 800-937-3700 ■ *Web:* www.actioncompany.com	McKinney	TX	75069	972-542-8700	562-7300
Auburn Leather Co 125 N Caldwell St *TF:* 800-635-0617 ■ *Web:* www.auburnleather.com	Auburn	KY	42206	270-542-4116	542-7107
Capitol Saddlery 8121 N Research Blvd *Web:* capsaddlery.com	Austin	TX	78758	512-478-9309	
Carroll Cos Inc 1640 Old Hwy 421 S *TF:* 800-884-2521 ■ *Web:* www.clgco.com	Boone	NC	28607	828-264-2521	264-2633
Garlin-Neumann Leathers Company Inc 66-D River Rd *Web:* leatherusa.com	Hudson	NH	03051	603-595-6319	881-9431
Gould & Goodrich Leather Inc 709 E McNeil St *TF:* 800-277-0732 ■ *Web:* www.gouldusa.com	Lillington	NC	27546	910-893-2071	893-4742
Hunter Company Inc 3300 W 71st Ave *TF:* 800-676-4868 ■ *Web:* www.huntercompany.com	Westminster	CO	80030	303-427-4626	
Tex Shoemaker & Son Inc 131 S Eucla Ave *Web:* www.texshoemaker.com	San Dimas	CA	91773	909-592-2071	592-2378

435 LEATHER TANNING & FINISHING

Company	City	State	Zip	Phone	Fax
Agora Leather Products 2101 28th St N *Web:* agoraleather.com	St Petersburg	FL	33713	727-321-0707	
Bernardo Fashions LLC 463 Seventh Ave Seventh Fl *Web:* www.bernardofashions.com	New York	NY	10018	212-594-3900	
Carville National Leather Corp 10 Knox Ave PO Box 40	Johnstown	NY	12095	518-762-1634	762-8973

				Phone	Fax
Creative Extrusion & Technologies Inc 230 Elliot St *Web:* creativeet.com	Brockton	MA	02302	508-587-2290	
Cromwell Leather Company Inc 147 Palmer Ave *Web:* www.cromwellgroup.com	Mamaroneck	NY	10543	914-381-0100	381-0046
Eagle Ottawa Leather Company LLC 2930 W Auburn Rd *Web:* www.eagleottawa.com	Rochester Hills	MI	48309	248-853-3122	853-6135
GST AutoLeather Inc 20 Oak Hollow Dr Ste 300 *Web:* www.gstautoleather.com	Southfield	MI	48033	248-436-2300	436-2390
Hermann Oak Leather Co 4050 N First St *TF:* 800-325-7950 ■ *Web:* www.hermannoakleather.com	Saint Louis	MO	63147	314-421-1173	421-6152
Horween Leather Co 2015 N Elston Ave *Web:* www.horween.com	Chicago	IL	60614	773-772-2026	772-9235
Leather Bros Inc 1314 Nabholz Ave *Web:* www.leatherbrothers.com	Conway	AR	72034	501-329-9471	
Leatherock International Inc 5285 Lovelock St *Web:* www.leatherock.com	San Diego	CA	92110	619-299-7625	299-7629
North American Tanning Corp 248 W 35th St Ste 505 *Web:* www.natanning.com	New York	NY	10001	212-643-1702	967-0068
Robus Leather Corp 4010 W 86th St Ste C *Web:* www.robus.com	Indianapolis	IN	46268	317-704-7000	702-7001
Seidel Tanning Corp 1306 E Meinecke Ave *Web:* www.seideltanning.com	Milwaukee	WI	53212	414-562-4030	562-4445
Showa Best Glove Inc 579 Edison St *Web:* showabestglove.com	Menlo	GA	30731	706-862-2302	
Simco Leather Corp 99 Pleasant Ave	Johnstown	NY	12095	518-762-7100	736-1514
Stahl USA 13 Corwin St *Web:* www.stahl.com	Peabody	MA	01960	978-531-0371	532-9062
Wood & Hyde Leather Company Inc PO Box 786 *Web:* www.woodandhyde.com	Gloversville	NY	12078	518-725-7105	725-5158

436 LEGISLATION HOTLINES

				Phone	Fax
Alabama Bill Status-House State House 11 S Union St *Web:* www.legislature.state.al.us	Montgomery	AL	36130	334-242-7600	242-2489
Alabama State Legislature State House 11 S Union St *TF:* 800-499-3051 ■ *Web:* www.legislature.state.al.us/senate/senate.html	Montgomery	AL	36130	334-242-7600	
Alaska Bill Status State Capitol MS 3100 *Web:* www.legis.state.ak.us/basis	Juneau	AK	99811	907-465-4930	465-2864
Arkansas Bill Status-Senate State Capitol Rm 320 *Web:* www.arkleg.state.ar.us	Little Rock	AR	72201	501-682-5951	
California Bill Status-Assembly State Capitol Rm 3196 *Web:* www.leginfo.ca.gov/bilinfo.html	Sacramento	CA	95814	916-445-2323	
District of Columbia Bill Status 1350 Pennsylvania Ave NW *Web:* dccouncil.us	Washington	DC	20004	202-724-8080	347-3070
Florida Bill Status 111 W Madison St Rm 704 *TF:* 800-342-1827 ■ *Web:* www.leg.state.fl.us	Tallahassee	FL	32399	850-488-4371	
Georgia Bill Status-House 309 State Capitol *Web:* www.house.ga.gov	Atlanta	GA	30334	404-656-5015	
Hawaii Bill Status 415 S Beretania St Rm 401 *Web:* www.capitol.hawaii.gov	Honolulu	HI	96813	808-587-0478	587-0793
Idaho Bill Status PO Box 83720 *Web:* www.legislature.idaho.gov	Boise	ID	83720	208-334-2475	334-2125
Illinois Bill Status 705 Stratton Bldg *Web:* www.ilga.gov/legislation	Springfield	IL	62706	217-782-3944	524-6059
Indiana Bill Status State House 200 W Washington St Ste 220 *Web:* www.in.gov/apps/lsa/session/billwatch	Indianapolis	IN	46204	317-233-5293	
Kansas Bill Status 300 SW Tenth Ave State Capitol Bldg Rm 343N *Web:* www.kslegislature.org	Topeka	KS	66612	785-296-2391	296-1153
Kentucky Bill Status 702 Capitol Ave Rm 424F *Web:* kentuckyhouserepublicans.org	Frankfort	KY	40601	502-564-8100	
Maryland Dept of Legislative Services 90 State Cir *TF:* 800-492-7122 ■ *Web:* www.mlis.state.md.us	Annapolis	MD	21401	410-946-5400	946-5405
Massachusetts Bill Status 1 Ashburton Pl Rm 1611 *TF:* 800-392-6090 ■ *Web:* malegislature.gov	Boston	MA	02108	617-727-7030	742-4528
Minnesota Bill Status-Senate 100 Rev Dr Martin Luther King Junior Blvd *Web:* www.house.leg.state.mn.us	Saint Paul	MN	55155	651-296-2146	
Mississippi Bill Status PO Box 2611 *Web:* billstatus.ls.state.ms.us	Jackson	MS	39215	601-359-2420	
Montana Legislative Services 1301 E Sixth Ave PO Box 201706 *Web:* leg.mt.gov	Helena	MT	59620	406-444-3064	444-3036
Nevada Bill Status 401 S Carson St *TF:* 800-978-2878 ■ *Web:* www.leg.state.nv.us	Carson City	NV	89701	775-684-3360	684-3330
New Hampshire Bill Status 107 N Main St *Web:* www.gencourt.state.nh.us	Concord	NH	03301	603-271-3435	
New Jersey Bill Status State House Annex PO Box 068 *TF:* 800-792-8630 ■ *Web:* www.njleg.state.nj.us	Trenton	NJ	08625	609-292-4840	777-2440
New Mexico Legislative Council Services 625 Don Gaspar Ave *Web:* www.nmlegis.gov	Santa Fe	NM	87501	505-986-4600	
New York Bill Status 202 Legislative Office Bldg *TF:* 800-342-9860 ■ *Web:* www.assembly.state.ny.us	Albany	NY	12248	518-455-4218	
North Carolina Bill Status 16 W Jones St *Web:* www.ncleg.net	Raleigh	NC	27601	919-733-4111	
North Dakota Legislative Council Services State Capitol Bldg 600 E Blvd Ave *TF:* 800-366-6888 ■ *Web:* www.legis.nd.gov	Bismarck	ND	58505	701-328-2916	328-3615
Ohio Legislative Information Office 77 S High St *Web:* www.lis.state.oh.us/	Columbus	OH	43215	614-728-0711	
Oklahoma Legislation Service Bureau 2300 N Lincoln Blvd *Web:* www.oklegislature.gov	State Capitol Bldg	OK	73105	405-521-4081	521-5507
Oregon Publication & Distribution Services 900 Ct St NE Rm 49 *Web:* Www.oregonlegislature.gov	Salem	OR	97310	503-986-1360	373-1527
Pennsylvania Bill Status 462 Main Capitol Bldg *Web:* www.legis.state.pa.us	Harrisburg	PA	17120	717-787-5920	
Rhode Island Bill Status 82 Smith St Rm 217 *Web:* www.rilin.state.ri.us	Providence	RI	02903	401-222-3580	
South Carolina Bill Status PO Box 142 *Web:* www.scstatehouse.gov	Columbia	SC	29201	803-212-6200	
South Dakota Bill Status 500 E Capitol *Web:* legis.sd.gov	Pierre	SD	57501	605-773-3251	
Tennessee Bill Status 320 Sixth Ave N 1st Fl *Web:* www.tn.gov/directory	Nashville	TN	37243	615-741-1000	
Utah State Legislature 350 North State St Ste 320 PO Box 145115 *Web:* le.utah.gov/documents/bills.htm	Salt Lake City	UT	84114	801-538-1035	538-1728
Vermont Bill Status 115 State St State House *Web:* www.leg.state.vt.us	Montpelier	VT	05633	802-828-2231	828-2424
Washington Bill Status PO Box 40600 *TF:* 800-562-6000 ■ *Web:* www.leg.wa.gov	Olympia	WA	98504	360-786-7573	
West Virginia Bill Status State Capitol Complex Rm MB27 Bldg 1 *TF:* 877-565-3447 ■ *Web:* www.legis.state.wv.us	Charleston	WV	25305	304-347-4836	347-4901
Wisconsin Bill Status 1 E Main St *TF:* 800-362-9472 ■ *Web:* legis.wisconsin.gov	Madison	WI	53708	608-266-9960	
Wyoming Legislative Service Office 3001 E Pershing Blvd *TF:* 800-342-9570 ■ *Web:* legisweb.state.wy.us	Cheyenne	WY	82002	307-777-7881	777-5466

437 LIBRARIES

SEE ALSO Library Systems - Regional - Canadian p. 2667

				Phone	Fax
Budgetext Corp 1936 N Shiloh Dr *TF:* 800-621-4272 ■ *Web:* www.fes.follett.com	Fayetteville	AR	72704	479-684-3300	

437-1 Medical Libraries

				Phone	Fax
Alfred Taubman Medical Library University of Michigan 1135 E Catherine St *Web:* www.lib.umich.edu	Ann Arbor	MI	48109	734-764-1210	763-1473
Allen Memorial Medical Library Case Western Reserve University 11000 Euclid Ave *Web:* www.case.edu/chsl/allen.htm	Cleveland	OH	44106	216-368-3643	368-6396
Allyn & Betty Taylor Library University of Western Ontario Natural Sciences Ctr *Web:* www.lib.uwo.ca/taylor	London	ON	N6A5B7	519-661-3168	661-3435
Augustus C Long Health Sciences Library Columbia University Medical Ctr 701 W 168th St *Web:* library.cumc.columbia.edu	New York	NY	10032	212-305-3605	
Boston University School of Medicine Alumni Medical Library 80 E Concord St R-806 *Web:* www.bumc.bu.edu/busm/about/library	Boston	MA	02118	617-638-1950	
Brown University Sciences Library 201 Thayer St PO Box 'I' *Web:* www.brown.edu	Providence	RI	02912	401-863-3333	863-2753
Chandler Medical Ctr Library 500 S Limestone St *Web:* libraries.uky.edu	Lexington	KY	40506	859-323-5300	323-1040
Cleveland Health Sciences Library (CHSL) *Case Western Reserve University Robbins Bldg* 2109 Adelbert Rd *Web:* www.case.edu/chsl/library/index.html	Cleveland	OH	44106	216-368-4540	368-3008
Coy C Carpenter Library *Wake Forest University School of Medicine* Medical Ctr Blvd *Web:* www.wakehealth.edu/library	Winston-Salem	NC	27157	336-716-2011	716-2186
Creighton University Health Sciences Library 2500 California Plz *Web:* www.creighton.edu	Omaha	NE	68178	402-280-5108	280-5134
D Samuel Gottesman Library 1300 Morris Pk Ave # 132 *Web:* library.einstein.yu.edu	Bronx	NY	10461	718-430-3108	430-8795
Dahlgren Memorial Library Georgetown University Medical Ctr 3900 Reservoir Rd NW PO Box 571420 *Web:* dml.georgetown.edu	Washington	DC	20057	202-687-1448	687-1862

				Phone	Fax

Dana Biomedical Library Dartmouth College........... Hanover NH 03755 603-650-1658 650-1354
Web: www.dartmouth.edu

Del E Webb Memorial Library
Loma Linda University 11072 Anderson St........... Loma Linda CA 92350 909-558-4550 558-4188
Web: www.llu.edu/llu/library

Duke University Medical Ctr Library
103 Seeley Mudd Bldg DUMC 3702.................. Durham NC 27710 919-660-1150 681-7599
Web: www.mclibrary.duke.edu

Dykes Library
University of Kansas Medical Ctr
2100 W 39th Ave MS 1050....................... Kansas City KS 66106 913-588-7166 588-7304
Web: library.kumc.edu

Francis A Countway Library of Medicine, The
10 Shattuck St .... Boston MA 02115 617-432-2136 432-4739
Web: www.countway.harvard.edu

Frederick L Ehrman Medical Library
New York University Medical Ctr School of Medicine
Medical Science Bldg Elevator B.................. New York NY 10016 212-263-5395 263-6534
Web: hsl.med.nyu.edu

George F Smith Library of the Health Sciences
Univ of Medicine & Dentistry of New Jersey
30 12th Ave.................................... Newark NJ 07101 973-972-4580 972-7474
Web: rbhs.rutgers.edu

George T Harrell Health Sciences Library
Pennsylvania State University College of Medicine
500 University Dr Milton S Hershey Medical .... Hershey PA 17033 717-531-8626 531-8635
Web: med.psu.edu

Gerstein Science Information Centre
University of Toronto
Nine King's College Cir
Sigmund Samuel Library Bldg..................... Toronto ON M5S1A5 416-978-2280
Web: gerstein.library.utoronto.ca

Hardin Library for the Health Sciences
University of Iowa 100 Hardin Library................. Iowa City IA 52242 319-335-9871 353-3752
Web: www.lib.uiowa.edu/hardin

Harvey Cushing/John Hay Whitney Medical Library
333 Cedar St PO Box 208014..................... New Haven CT 06520 203-785-5352 785-5636
Web: medicine.yale.edu

Himmelfarb Health Sciences Library
George Washington University Medical Ctr
2300 Eye St NW................................ Washington DC 20037 202-994-2850 994-4343
Web: www.gwumc.edu/library

Houston Academy of Medicine - Texas Medical Ctr Library
1133 John Freeman Blvd.......................... Houston TX 77030 713-795-4200 790-7052
Web: www.library.tmc.edu

John A Prior Health Sciences Library
Ohio State University 376 W Tenth Ave .... Columbus OH 43210 614-292-4861 292-1920
Web: www.hsl.osu.edu

Kornhauser Health Sciences Library
University of Louisville 500 S Preston St......... Louisville KY 40292 502-852-5771 852-1631
Web: www.louisville.edu

Lamar Soutter Library 55 N Lake Ave.............. Worcester MA 01655 508-856-6099 856-5899
Web: library.umassmed.edu

Lane Medical Library
Stanford University Medical Ctr
300 Pasteur Dr Rm L-109.......................... Stanford CA 94305 650-723-6831 725-7471
Web: www.lane.stanford.edu

Leon S McGoogan Library of Medicine
University of Nebraska Medical Ctr
986705 Nebraska Medical Ctr .... Omaha NE 68198 402-559-6221 559-5498
TF: 866-800-5209 ■ *Web:* www.unmc.edu/library

Library of Rush University
Rush University Medical Ctr
600 S Paulina St Ste 571......................... Chicago IL 60612 312-942-5950 942-3143
Web: rushu.libguides.com

Louis Calder Memorial Library
University of Miami School of Medicine R-950
PO Box 016950 .... Miami FL 33101 305-243-6648 325-9670
Web: www.calder.med.miami.edu

Mayo Foundation Mayo Medical Ctr Libraries
200 First St SW .... Rochester MN 55905 480-301-8000 301-9310
Web: mayoclinic.com

McGill University Life Sciences Library & Osler Library of the History of Medicine
3655 Sir William Osler........................... Montreal QC H3G1Y6 514-398-4475 398-3890
Web: www.mcgill.ca

McMaster University Health Sciences Library
1200 Main St W................................. Hamilton ON L8N3Z5 905-525-9140 528-3733
Web: hsl.mcmaster.ca

Medical University of South Carolina Library
171 Ashley Ave Ste 300 PO Box 250403 .... Charleston SC 29425 843-792-2372 792-4900
Web: www.library.musc.edu

Meharry Medical College Library
1005 DB Todd Blvd................................ Nashville TN 37208 615-327-6318 327-6448
Web: www.mmc.edu

Moody Medical Library 914 Market st.............. Galveston TX 77555 409-772-2371 202-2689*
**Fax Area Code:* 832 ■ *TF:* 866-235-5223
Library 9000 Rockville Pike Bldg 10 .... Bethesda MD 20892 301-496-4000 402-2984
Web: www.nih.gov/
National Library of Medicine
8600 Rockville Pike Bldg 38 .... Bethesda MD 20894 301-594-5983 402-1384
TF: 888-346-3656 ■ *Web:* www.nlm.nih.gov

New York Academy of Medicine Library
1216 Fifth Ave.................................. New York NY 10029 212-822-7315 423-0266
Web: www.nyam.org/library

Norris Medical Library
University of Southern California
2003 Zonal Ave.................................. Los Angeles CA 90089 323-442-1111 221-1235
Web: www.usc.edu/hsc/nml

Oregon Health & Science University
Bone Marrow Transplant Program (OHSU)
3181 SW Sam Jackson Pk Rd .... Portland OR 97239 503-494-1617 494-7086
TF: 800-799-7233 ■ *Web:* www.ohsu.edu
Library 3181 SW Sam Jackson Pk Rd .... Portland OR 97239 503-494-3460 494-3322
Web: www.ohsu.edu/xd/education/library

Raymon H Mulford Library
Medical College of Ohio Toledo
3000 Arlington Ave .... Toledo OH 43614 419-383-4225
Web: www.utoledo.edu/library/mulford/index.html

Robert B Greenblatt MD Library
Medical College of Georgia
1439 Lny Walker Blvd .... Augusta GA 30912 706-721-3441
Web: www.gru.edu

Robert M Bird Health Sciences Library
OUHSC 1000 Stanton L Young Blvd
PO Box 26901 .... Oklahoma City OK 73126 405-271-2285 271-3297
Web: library.ouhsc.edu

Rosalind Franklin University of Medicine & Science Learning Resource Ctr
3333 Green Bay Rd.......................... North Chicago IL 60064 847-578-3000
Web: www.rosalindfranklin.edu

Rowland Medical Library
University of Mississippi 2500 N State St.............. Jackson MS 39216 601-984-1231 984-1251
Web: www.umc.edu
Camden 406 Penn St......................... Camden NJ 08102 856-225-6104 225-6498*
**Fax:* Admissions ■ *Web:* www.camden.rutgers.edu
Library of Science & Medicine
165 Bevier Rd .... Piscataway NJ 08854 732-445-3854 445-5703
Web: www.libraries.rutgers.edu

Ruth Lilly Medical Library
975 W Walnut St IB 100......................... Indianapolis IN 46202 317-274-7182 278-2349
TF: 877-952-1988 ■ *Web:* www.library.medicine.iu.edu

Saint Louis University 221 N Grand Blvd........... Saint Louis MO 63103 314-977-7288 977-7136*
**Fax:* Admissions ■ *TF:* 800-758-3678 ■ *Web:* www.slu.edu

Schaffer Library of the Health Sciences
Albany Medical College 47 New Scotland Ave .... Albany NY 12208 518-262-5586 262-5820
Web: www.amc.edu/academic/schaffer

Scott Memorial Library
1020 Walnut St Ste 310 .... Philadelphia PA 19107 215-503-8848 923-3203

Southern Illinois University School of Medicine Medical Library (SIU)
801 N Rutledge St PO Box 19625.................. Springfield IL 62794 217-545-2122 545-0988
Web: www.siumed.edu/lib

State University of New York at Buffalo
Health Sciences Library (HSL)
3435 Main St Abbott Hall Rm 102.................. Buffalo NY 14214 716-829-3900 829-2211
TF: 866-432-5849 ■ *Web:* library.buffalo.edu/hsl

State University of New York Upstate Medical University Health Sciences Library
766 Irving Ave .... Syracuse NY 13210 315-464-7087 464-7199
Web: library.upstate.edu

Stony Brook University Health Sciences Library
8034 Suny HSC Level 3 Rm 136 .... Stony Brook NY 11794 631-444-2512 444-6649
Web: library.stonybrook.edu/healthsciences

SUNY Downstate Medical Ctr
Medical Research Library of Brooklyn, The
450 Clarkson Ave PO Box 14..................... Brooklyn NY 11203 718-270-1000 270-7471
Web: www.downstate.edu
Medical Sciences Library MS 4462......... College Station TX 77843 979-845-7428
Web: msl.library.tamu.edu

Texas Tech University Health Sciences Ctr
Preston Smith Library of the Health Sciences
3601 Fourth St MS 7781........................ Lubbock TX 79430 806-743-2200 743-2218
Web: www.ttuhsc.edu/libraries/guides/lubbockguide.aspx#welcome

Tompkins-McCaw Library 509 N 12th St........... Richmond VA 23298 804-828-0636 828-6089
Web: www.library.vcu.edu

Tufts University Hirsh Health Sciences Library
145 Harrison Ave .... Boston MA 02111 617-636-6705 636-4039
Web: www.library.tufts.edu/hsl

Uniformed Services University of the Health Sciences Learning Resource Ctr
4301 Jones Bridge Rd .... Bethesda MD 20814 301-295-3350

Universite de Montreal Bibliotheque de la Sante
2900 Blvd Edouard-Montpetit Rm L623............... Montreal QC H3T1J4 514-343-6111 343-2350
Web: www.bib.umontreal.ca/sa

Universite Laval
Bibliotheque Scientifique
Pavillon Alexandre-Vachon 1045 Ave .... Quebec QC G1V0A6 418-656-3967 656-7699
Web: www.bibl.ulaval.ca

University of Arizona Arizona Health Sciences Library
1501 N Campbell Ave PO Box 245079................. Tucson AZ 85724 520-626-6125 626-2922
Web: www.ahsl.arizona.edu

University of Arkansas for Medical Sciences
Bone Marrow Transplantation Ctr
4301 W Markham Ave Slot 816................. Little Rock AR 72205 501-686-8250 526-2273
Web: www.uams.edu
Medical Library
4301 W Markham St Slot 586 .... Little Rock AR 72205 501-686-6734 686-6745

University of California Irvine
Library PO Box 19557 .... Irvine CA 92623 949-824-6836 824-3644
TF: 800-848-4722 ■ *Web:* www.lib.uci.edu

University of California San Diego (UCSD)
Biomedical Library 9500 Gilman Dr............... La Jolla CA 92093 858-534-3253 534-6609
Web: www.libraries.ucsd.edu

University of California San Diego Medical Ctr Library
200 W Arbor Dr .... San Diego CA 92103 619-543-6222
Web: health.ucsd.edu

University of California San Francisco
Kalmanovitz Library 530 Parnassus Ave ...... San Francisco CA 94143 415-476-8293 476-4653
Web: www.library.ucsf.edu
Library & Center for Knowledge Management
530 Parnassus Ave PO Box 0840............. San Francisco CA 94143 415-476-8293 476-4653
Web: www.library.ucsf.edu

University of Cincinnati
51 Goodman Dr PO Box 670550 .... Cincinnati OH 45267 513-558-4553 558-2910
Web: www.health.uc.edu

University of Florida Health Science Ctr Libraries
1600 SW Archer Rd PO Box 100206 .... Gainesville FL 32610 352-273-8408 392-2565
Web: www.library.health.ufl.edu

University of Illinois Chicago
Daley Library 801 S Morgan St Rm 1-280......... Chicago IL 60607 312-996-2716 413-0424
TF: 866-904-5843 ■ *Web:* www.uic.edu/depts/lib

				Phone	Fax
Library of the Health Sciences 1750 W Polk St MC 763 *Web:* www.uic.edu/depts/lib/lhsc	Chicago	IL	60612	312-996-8974	996-1899
University of Maryland Baltimore *Health Sciences & Human Services Library (HSHSL)* 601 W Lombard St *Web:* www.hshsl.umaryland.edu	Baltimore	MD	21201	410-706-7995	706-8403
Bio-Medical Library 505 Essex St SE 325 Diehl Hall *Web:* www.hsl.lib.umn.edu/biomed	Minneapolis	MN	55455	612-626-4045	
University of Nebraska Medical Ctr McGoogan Library of Medicine 986705 Nebraska Medical Ctr *Web:* www.unmc.edu/library	Omaha	NE	68198	402-559-4006	559-5498
Davis Library CB 3900 *Web:* library.unc.edu	Chapel Hill	NC	27514	919-962-1356	843-8936
University of North Carolina Chapel Hill *Health Sciences Library* CB 7585 *Web:* hsl.lib.unc.edu	Chapel Hill	NC	27599	919-962-0800	966-5592
University of Ottawa Health Sciences Library 65 University *Web:* www.biblio.uottawa.ca	Ottawa	ON	K1N6N5	613-562-5407	
University of Pennsylvania *Biomedical Library* 3610 Hamilton Walk Johnson Pavilion *Web:* www.library.upenn.edu/biomed	Philadelphia	PA	19104	215-898-5815	573-4143
University of Saskatchewan *Health Sciences Library* 107 Wiggins Rd Ste B-205 *Web:* library.usask.ca/hsl	Saskatoon	SK	S7N5E5	306-966-5991	966-5918
University of Tennessee Health Science Ctr *Health Sciences Library & Biocommunications Ctr* 877 Madison Ave *TF:* 877-747-0004 ■ *Web:* www.uthsc.edu	Memphis	TN	38103	901-448-5634	
University of Texas Health Science Ctr San Antonio *Libraries* 7703 Floyd Curl Dr MSC 7940 *Web:* www.library.uthscsa.edu	San Antonio	TX	78229	210-567-2400	567-2490
University of Texas Southwestern Medical Ctr at Dallas Library, The 5323 Harry Hines Blvd *TF:* 866-645-6455 ■ *Web:* utsouthwestern.edu/	Dallas	TX	75390	214-648-2001	648-2826
University of Washington Health Sciences Libraries & Information Ctr 1959 NE Pacific St PO Box 357155 *Web:* hsl.uw.edu	Seattle	WA	98195	206-543-3390	543-8066
Ebling Library 750 Highland Ave *Web:* www.ebling.library.wisc.edu	Madison	WI	53705	608-262-2020	262-4732
Weill Cornell Medical Library Weill Medical College of Cornell University 1300 York Ave *Web:* weill.cornell.edu	New York	NY	10065	212-746-6050	746-6494
West Virginia University PO Box 6009 *TF:* 800-344-9881 ■ *Web:* www.wvu.edu	Morgantown	WV	26506	304-293-2121	293-3080
William E Laupus Health Sciences Library 500 Health Science Dr 600 Moye Blvd Health Sciences Bldg *Web:* www.ecu.edu/cs-dhs/laupuslibrary	Greenville	NC	27834	252-744-2230	744-1376
William H Welch Medical Library Johns Hopkins University 1900 E Monument St *Web:* welch.jhmi.edu	Baltimore	MD	21205	410-955-3410	
WK Kellogg Health Sciences Library 5850 College St Sir Charles Tupper Medical Bldg *Web:* libraries.dal.ca	Halifax	NS	B3H1X5	902-494-2458	494-3798
Woodruff Health Sciences Ctr Library *Emory University* 1462 Clifton Rd NE *Web:* health.library.emory.edu	Atlanta	GA	30322	404-727-8727	727-9821
Woodward Biomedical Library 2198 Health Sciences Mall *Web:* woodward.library.ubc.ca	Vancouver	BC	V6T1Z3	604-822-2883	822-5596

437-2 Presidential Libraries

				Phone	Fax
Abraham Lincoln Presidential Library & Museum 112 N Sixth St *TF:* 800-610-2094 ■ *Web:* www.alplm.org	Springfield	IL	62701	217-557-6250	
Dwight D Eisenhower Presidential Library & Museum 200 SE Fourth St *TF:* 877-746-4453 ■ *Web:* www.eisenhower.utexas.edu	Abilene	KS	67410	785-263-6700	263-6715
Franklin D Roosevelt Presidential Library & Museum 4079 Albany Post Rd *TF:* 800-337-8474 ■ *Web:* www.fdrlibrary.marist.edu	Hyde Park	NY	12538	845-486-7770	486-1147
George Bush Library & Museum 1000 George Bush Dr W *Fax Area Code: 214	College Station	TX	77845	979-691-4000	346-1699*
Gerald R Ford Library 1000 Beal Ave *Web:* www.fordlibrarymuseum.gov	Ann Arbor	MI	48109	734-205-0555	205-0571
Harry S Truman Presidential Library & Museum 500 W Hwy 24 *TF:* 800-833-1225 ■ *Web:* www.trumanlibrary.org	Independence	MO	64050	816-268-8200	268-8295
Herbert Hoover Presidential Library & Museum 210 Parkside Dr *Web:* www.hoover.archives.gov	West Branch	IA	52358	319-643-5301	643-6045
Jimmy Carter Library & Museum 441 Freedom Pkwy *Web:* www.jimmycarterlibrary.gov	Atlanta	GA	30307	404-865-7100	865-7102
John F Kennedy Presidential Library & Museum Columbia Pt *TF:* 866-535-1960 ■ *Web:* www.jfklibrary.org	Boston	MA	02125	617-514-1600	514-1652
LBJ Library & Museum 2313 Red River St *TF:* 800-874-6451 ■ *Web:* www.lbjlib.utexas.edu	Austin	TX	78705	512-721-0216	721-0170
Richard Nixon Foundation, The 18001 Yorba Linda Blvd *Web:* www.nixonfoundation.org	Yorba Linda	CA	92886	714-993-5075	528-0544
Ronald Reagan Presidential Library & Museum 40 Presidential Dr *TF:* 800-410-8354 ■ *Web:* www.reagan.utexas.edu	Simi Valley	CA	93065	805-577-4000	577-4074
Rutherford B Hayes Presidential Ctr Spiegel Grove *TF:* 800-998-7737 ■ *Web:* www.rbhayes.org	Fremont	OH	43420	419-332-2081	332-4952
William J Clinton Presidential Ctr 1200 President Clinton Ave *Web:* www.clintonfoundation.org	Little Rock	AR	72201	501-370-8000	375-0512
Woodrow Wilson Presidential Library 20 N Coalter St PO Box 24 *TF:* 888-496-6376 ■ *Web:* www.woodrowwilson.org	Staunton	VA	24401	540-885-0897	886-9874

437-3 Public Libraries

Listings for public libraries are alphabetized by city name within each state grouping.

Alabama

				Phone	Fax
Aliceville Public Library (APL) 416 Third Ave NE *Web:* pickenslibrary.com	Aliceville	AL	35442	205-373-6691	373-3731
Auburn Public Library 749 E Thach Ave *Web:* www.auburnalabama.org	Auburn	AL	36830	334-501-3190	
Bay Minette Public Library 205 W Second St *Web:* cityofbayminette.org	Bay Minette	AL	36507	251-580-1648	937-0339
Bessemer Public Library 400 19th St *Web:* www.bessemerlibrary.org	Bessemer	AL	35020	205-428-7882	428-7882
Birmingham Public Library 2100 Pk Pl *Web:* www.bham.lib.al.us	Birmingham	AL	35203	205-226-3600	226-3731
Choctaw County Public Library 124 N Academy Ave	Butler	AL	36904	205-459-2542	
Harrison Regional Library 50 Lester St *Web:* www.shelbycounty-al.org	Columbiana	AL	35051	205-669-3910	669-3940
Cullman County Public Library System 200 Clark St NE *TF:* 800-752-7389 ■ *Web:* www.ccpls.com	Cullman	AL	35055	256-734-1068	734-6902
Horseshoe Bend Regional Library 207 NW St *TF:* 855-336-0333 ■ *Web:* www.horseshoebendlibrary.org	Dadeville	AL	36853	256-825-9232	
Florence-Lauderdale Public Library (FLPL) 350 N Wood Ave *Web:* www.flpl.org	Florence	AL	35630	256-764-6564	
Gadsden Public Library 254 College St *Web:* www.gadsdenlibrary.org	Gadsden	AL	35901	256-549-4699	
Guntersville Public Library 1240 O'Brig Ave *Web:* www.guntersvillelibrary.org	Guntersville	AL	35976	256-571-7595	571-7596
Cheaha Regional Library 935 Coleman St *Web:* www.cheaharegionallibrary.org	Heflin	AL	36264	256-463-7125	463-7125
Hoover Public Library (HPL) 200 Municipal Dr *Web:* www.hooverlibrary.org	Hoover	AL	35216	205-444-7800	444-7878
Hueytown Public Library 1372 Hueytown Rd *Web:* www.hueytown.com	Hueytown	AL	35023	205-491-1443	491-6319
Huntsville-Madison County Public Library 915 Monroe St *Web:* hmcpl.org	Huntsville	AL	35801	256-532-5940	532-5997
Carl Elliott Regional Library 98 E 18th St	Jasper	AL	35501	205-221-2568	221-2584
Mobile Public Library 701 Government St *TF:* 877-322-8228 ■ *Web:* www.mplonline.org	Mobile	AL	36602	251-208-7073	208-7137
Montgomery City-County Public Library 245 High St *Web:* www.mccpl.lib.al.us	Montgomery	AL	36104	334-240-4999	240-4980
Tuscaloosa Public Library 1801 Jack Warner Pkwy *Web:* www.tuscaloosa-library.org	Tuscaloosa	AL	35401	205-345-5820	758-1735
Bradshaw-Chambers County Public Library 3419 20th Ave *Web:* www.chamberscountylibrary.org	Valley	AL	36854	334-768-2161	768-7272

Alaska

				Phone	Fax
ZJ Loussac Public Library 3600 Denali St *Web:* www.muni.org	Anchorage	AK	99503	907-343-2975	343-2930
Big Lake Public Library 3140 S Big Lk Rd *Web:* matsulibraries.org	Big Lake	AK	99652	907-892-6475	
Fairbanks North Star Borough Public Library 1215 Cowles St *Fax: Admin ■ *Web:* library.fnsb.lib.ak.us	Fairbanks	AK	99701	907-459-1022	459-1024*
Homer Public Library 500 Hazel Ave *Web:* www.cityofhomer-ak.gov/library	Homer	AK	99603	907-235-3180	235-3136
Juneau Public Libraries 292 Marine Way *TF:* 800-478-4176 ■ *Web:* www.juneau.org	Juneau	AK	99801	907-586-5324	586-3419

Arizona

				Phone	Fax
Apache Junction Public Library 1177 N Idaho Rd *Web:* www.ajpl.org	Apache Junction	AZ	85119	480-983-6012	983-4540
Cochise County Library District 100 Quality Hill Rd *Web:* cochise.az.gov	Bisbee	AZ	85603	520-432-8930	432-7339
Chandler Public Library 22 S Delaware St *Web:* www.chandlerlibrary.org	Chandler	AZ	85225	480-782-2800	782-2823
Cottonwood Public Library 100 S Sixth St *Web:* ctwpl.info	Cottonwood	AZ	86326	928-634-7559	634-0253
Flagstaff City-Coconino County Public Library System 300 W Aspen Ave *Web:* www.flagstaffpubliclibrary.org	Flagstaff	AZ	86001	928-213-2330	774-9573

	City	State	Zip	Phone	Fax
Pinal County Library District (PCLD) 92 W Butte Ave *Web:* www.pinalcountyaz.gov/departments/library	Florence	AZ	85132	520-866-6457	866-6533
Southeast Regional Library 775 N Greenfield Rd *Web:* mcldaz.org	Gilbert	AZ	85234	602-652-3000	
Glendale Public Library 5959 W Brown St *Web:* www.glendaleaz.com	Glendale	AZ	85302	623-930-3530	842-4209
Mohave Educational Services Cooperative Inc 625 E Beale St *Web:* www.mesc.org	Kingman	AZ	86401	928-753-6945	
Mesa Public Library 64 E First St *Web:* www.mesalibrary.org	Mesa	AZ	85201	480-644-2207	644-3490
Nogales City/Santa Cruz County Public Library 518 N Grand Ave *Web:* nogalesaz.gov	Nogales	AZ	85621	520-287-3343	287-4823
Page Public Library 479 Lk Powell Blvd *Web:* www.pagepubliclibrary.org	Page	AZ	86040	928-645-4270	645-5804
Maricopa County Library District 2700 N Central Ave Ste 700 *Web:* www.mcldaz.org	Phoenix	AZ	85004	602-652-3000	
Phoenix Public Library 1221 N Central Ave *Web:* www.phoenixpubliclibrary.org	Phoenix	AZ	85004	602-261-8847	261-8836
Safford City - Graham County Library 808 Seventh Ave *Web:* www.cityofsafford.us	Safford	AZ	85546	928-432-4165	348-3209
Pima County Public Library 101 N Stone Ave *TF:* 877-705-5437 ■ *Web:* www.library.pima.gov	Tucson	AZ	85701	520-594-5600	594-5621

Arkansas

	City	State	Zip	Phone	Fax
Saline County Public Library 1800 Smithers *Web:* www.saline.lib.ar.us	Benton	AR	72015	501-778-4766	
Arkansas River Valley Regional Library 501 N Front St *Web:* www.arvrls.com	Dardanelle	AR	72834	479-229-4418	229-2595
Barton Library 200 E Fifth St	El Dorado	AR	71730	870-875-1330	
Washington County Library System 1080 W Clydesdale Dr *Web:* www.co.washington.ar.us	Fayetteville	AR	72701	479-442-6253	442-6812
Fort Smith Public Library 3201 Rogers Ave *TF:* 866-660-0885 ■ *Web:* fortsmithlibrary.org	Fort Smith	AR	72903	479-783-0229	783-5129
Crowley Ridge Regional Library 315 W Oak St *Web:* www.libraryinjonesboro.org	Jonesboro	AR	72401	870-935-5133	935-7987
William F. Laman Public Library System 2801 Orange St *Web:* www.lamanlibrary.org	North Little Rock	AR	72114	501-758-1720	758-3539
Pope County Library System 116 E Third St *Web:* popelibrary.org	Russellville	AR	72801	479-968-4368	968-3222
White County Public Library 113 E Pleasure St *Web:* whitecountylibraries.org/locations/searcy	Searcy	AR	72143	501-268-2449	268-5682

California

	City	State	Zip	Phone	Fax
Alameda Free Library 1550 Oak St *Web:* alamedaca.gov	Alameda	CA	94501	510-747-7777	337-1471
Alhambra Civic Ctr Library 101 S First St *Web:* www.alhambralibrary.org	Alhambra	CA	91801	626-570-5008	457-1104
Anaheim Public Library 500 W Broadway *Web:* library.anaheim.net	Anaheim	CA	92805	714-765-1880	765-1730
Placer County Library 350 Nevada St *TF:* 800-488-4308 ■ *Web:* www.placer.ca.gov	Auburn	CA	95603	530-886-4500	886-4555
Azusa City Library 729 N Dalton Ave *Web:* www.ci.azusa.ca.us	Azusa	CA	91702	626-812-5232	334-4868
Beale Memorial Library 701 Truxtun Ave *Web:* www.kerncountylibrary.org	Bakersfield	CA	93301	661-868-0701	868-0799
Beaumont Library District 125 E Eigth St	Beaumont	CA	92223	951-845-1357	845-6217
Benicia Public Library 150 E 'L' St *Web:* www.ci.benicia.ca.us	Benicia	CA	94510	707-746-4343	747-8122
Berkeley Public Library 2090 Kittredge St *Web:* www.berkeleypubliclibrary.org	Berkeley	CA	94704	510-981-6100	981-6111
Beverly Hills Public Library 444 N Rexford Dr *Web:* www.beverlyhills.org	Beverly Hills	CA	90210	310-288-2220	278-3387
Burbank Central Library 110 N Glenoaks Blvd *Web:* www.burbank.lib.ca.us	Burbank	CA	91502	818-238-5600	238-5553
City of Carlsbad Library 1250 Carlsbad Village Dr *TF:* 866-230-2273 ■ *Web:* carlsbadca.gov	Carlsbad	CA	92008	760-434-2870	929-0256
Cerritos Civic Ctr 18025 Bloomfield Ave *TF:* 866-402-7433 ■ *Web:* www.cerritos.us	Cerritos	CA	90703	562-916-1350	916-1375
Chula Vista Public Library 365 F St *Web:* www.chulavistalibrary.com	Chula Vista	CA	91910	619-691-5069	427-4246
Colton Public Library 656 N Ninth St *Web:* ci.colton.ca.us	Colton	CA	92324	909-370-5083	422-0873
Corona Public Library 650 S Main St *Web:* www.coronapubliclibrary.org	Corona	CA	92882	951-736-2381	736-2499
Coronado Public Library 640 Orange Ave *Web:* www.coronado.ca.us	Coronado	CA	92118	619-522-7390	
Covina Public Library 234 N Second Ave *Web:* covinaca.gov	Covina	CA	91723	626-384-5300	384-5315
Daly City Public Library 40 Wembley Dr *TF:* 888-227-7669 ■ *Web:* www.dalycity.org	Daly City	CA	94015	650-991-8025	991-8225
Dixon Public Library 230 N First St *Web:* www.dixonlibrary.com	Dixon	CA	95620	707-678-5447	678-3515
Downey City Library (DCL) 11121 Brookshire Ave *TF:* 877-846-3452 ■ *Web:* www.downeyca.org	Downey	CA	90241	562-904-7360	923-3763
Los Angeles County Public Library 7400 E Imperial Hwy *TF:* 888-794-9466 ■ *Web:* www.colapublib.org	Downey	CA	90242	562-940-8462	803-3032
El Centro Public Library 539 State St *TF:* 877-482-5656 ■ *Web:* www.cityofelcentro.org/library	El Centro	CA	92243	760-337-4565	352-1384
Imperial County Free Library 1125 W Main St *Web:* www.imperialcounty.net	El Centro	CA	92243	760-482-4986	482-4792
Escondido Public Library 239 S Kalmia St *Web:* www.library.escondido.org	Escondido	CA	92025	760-839-4601	741-4255
Humboldt County Library 1313 Third St *Web:* www.co.humboldt.ca.us/library	Eureka	CA	95501	707-269-1900	269-1999
Alameda County Library 2450 Stevenson Blvd *Web:* aclibrary.org	Fremont	CA	94538	510-745-1500	793-2987
Fremont Main Library 2400 Stevenson Blvd *TF:* 800-434-0222 ■ *Web:* www.aclibrary.org	Fremont	CA	94538	510-745-1400	797-6557
Fresno County Public Library 2420 Mariposa St *Web:* www.fresnolibrary.org	Fresno	CA	93721	559-600-7323	488-1971
Fullerton Public Library 353 W Commonwealth Ave *Web:* www.ci.fullerton.ca.us	Fullerton	CA	92832	714-738-6333	447-3280
Garden Grove Regional Library 11200 Stanford Ave *Web:* www.ocsd.org/ocgov/ocpubliclibraries/librarylocator/gardengroveregional	Garden Grove	CA	92840	714-530-0711	
Glendora Public Library & Cultural Ctr 140 S Glendora Ave *TF:* 866-275-3772 ■ *Web:* www.ci.glendora.ca.us	Glendora	CA	91741	626-852-4891	852-4899
Kings County Library 401 N Douty St *Web:* www.kingscountylibrary.org	Hanford	CA	93230	559-582-0261	583-6163
Hayward Public Library 835 C St *Web:* www.library.ci.hayward.ca.us	Hayward	CA	94541	510-293-8685	
Hemet Public Library 300 E Latham Ave *Web:* hemetpubliclibrary.org	Hemet	CA	92543	951-765-2440	765-2446
San Benito County Free Library 470 Fifth St *Web:* www.sanbenitofl.org	Hollister	CA	95023	831-636-4107	636-4099
Huntington Beach Public Library (HBPL) 7111 Talbert Ave *TF:* 800-565-0148 ■ *Web:* www.huntingtonbeachca.gov/government/departments/library	Huntington Beach	CA	92648	714-842-4481	375-5180
Inglewood Public Library 101 W Manchester Blvd *Web:* www.cityofinglewood.org/depts/library	Inglewood	CA	90301	310-412-5380	
Amador County Library 530 Sutter St *Web:* www.co.amador.ca.us	Jackson	CA	95642	209-223-6400	223-6303
Lake County Library 1425 N High St *Web:* library.co.lake.ca.us	Lakeport	CA	95453	707-263-8817	
Livermore Public Library 1188 S Livermore Ave *Web:* www.cityoflivermore.net	Livermore	CA	94550	925-373-5500	
Lodi Public Library 201 W Locust St *Web:* www.lodi.gov	Lodi	CA	95240	209-333-5566	367-5944
Lompoc Public Library 501 E N Ave *Web:* www.cityoflompoc.com	Lompoc	CA	93436	805-736-3477	
Long Beach Public Library 101 Pacific Ave *Web:* www.lbpl.org	Long Beach	CA	90822	562-570-7500	570-7408
Braille Institute of America Library Services (BILS) 741 N Vermont Ave *TF:* 800-808-2555 ■ *Web:* www.brailleinstitute.org	Los Angeles	CA	90029	323-660-3880	663-0867
Los Angeles Public Library 630 W Fifth St *Web:* www.lapl.org	Los Angeles	CA	90071	213-228-7000	228-7369
Los Gatos Public Library (LGPL) 110 E Main St *Web:* www.losgatosca.gov	Los Gatos	CA	95030	408-354-8600	354-0578
Santa Clara County Library 14600 Winchester Blvd *TF:* 800-286-1991 ■ *Web:* www.sccl.org	Los Gatos	CA	95032	408-293-2326	364-0161
Madera County Library 121 N 'G' St *Web:* www.madera-county.com	Madera	CA	93637	559-675-7871	675-7998
Yuba County Library 303 Second St *Web:* www.co.yuba.ca.us	Marysville	CA	95901	530-749-7380	741-3098
Menlo Park Public Library 800 Alma St *Web:* www.menloparklibrary.org	Menlo Park	CA	94025	650-330-2501	327-7030
Merced County Library 2100 O St *TF:* 866-249-0773 ■ *Web:* www.co.merced.ca.us	Merced	CA	95340	209-385-7643	726-7912
Mill Valley Public Library 375 Throckmorton Ave *Web:* www.millvalleylibrary.org	Mill Valley	CA	94941	415-389-4292	388-8929
Monrovia Public Library 321 S Myrtle Ave *TF:* 888-620-1749 ■ *Web:* www.cityofmonrovia.org	Monrovia	CA	91016	626-256-8274	256-8255
Monterey Public Library 625 Pacific St *TF:* 800-338-0505 ■ *Web:* www.monterey.org	Monterey	CA	93940	831-646-3932	646-5618
Mountain View Public Library 585 Franklin St *Web:* mountainview.gov	Mountain View	CA	94041	650-903-6335	962-0438
Napa City-County Library 580 Coombs St *TF:* 877-848-7030 ■ *Web:* countyofnapa.org	Napa	CA	94559	707-253-4241	253-4615
National City Public Library 1401 National City Blvd *Web:* www.ci.national-city.ca.us	National City	CA	91950	619-470-5800	470-5880
Nevada County Library 980 Helling Way *Web:* mynevadacounty.com/nc/library	Nevada City	CA	95959	530-265-7050	265-9863
Oakland Public Library 125 14th St *Web:* www.oaklandlibrary.org	Oakland	CA	94612	510-238-3144	238-2232
Oceanside Public Library 330 N Coast Hwy *Web:* www.ci.oceanside.ca.us	Oceanside	CA	92054	760-435-5600	
Ontario City Library 215 E C St *Web:* www.ci.ontario.ca.us/library	Ontario	CA	91764	909-395-2004	
Butte County Library 1820 Mitchell Ave *Web:* www.buttecounty.net/bclibrary	Oroville	CA	95966	530-538-7641	538-7235
Oxnard Public Library (OPL) 251 S 'A' St *Web:* www.oxnardlibrary.net	Oxnard	CA	93030	805-385-7532	385-7526

Library	City	State	ZIP	Phone	Fax
City of Palm Springs 300 S Sunrise Way *TF:* 800-611-1911 ■ *Web:* palmspringslibrary.org	Palm Springs	CA	92262	760-322-7323	
Palmdale City Library 700 E Palmdale Blvd *Web:* cityofpalmdale.org	Palmdale	CA	93550	661-267-5222	
Palo Alto City Library 1213 Newell Rd *Web:* cityofpaloalto.org/gov/depts/lib/default.asp	Palo Alto	CA	94303	650-329-2436	327-2033
Pasadena Public Library 285 E Walnut St *Web:* www.cityofpasadena.net	Pasadena	CA	91101	626-744-4052	585-8396
El Dorado County Library 345 Fair Ln *Web:* www.eldoradolibrary.org	Placerville	CA	95667	530-621-5540	622-3911
Contra Costa County Library 75 Santa Barbara Rd *TF:* 800-984-4636 ■ *Web:* www.ccclib.org	Pleasant Hill	CA	94523	925-646-6423	646-6461
Pomona Public Library 625 S Garey Ave *Web:* www.youseemore.com	Pomona	CA	91766	909-620-2043	620-3713
Porterville Public Library 41 W Thurman Ave *Web:* portervillelibrary.org	Porterville	CA	93257	559-784-0177	781-4396
Rancho Cucamonga Public Library 7368 Archibald Ave *TF:* 800-655-4555 ■ *Web:* www.rcpl.lib.ca.us	Rancho Cucamonga	CA	91730	909-477-2720	477-2721
Tehama County Library 645 Madison St *Web:* tehamacountylibrary.org	Red Bluff	CA	96080	530-527-0604	527-1562
Shasta Public Library 1100 Parkview Ave *Web:* www.shastalibraries.org	Redding	CA	96001	530-245-7250	
AK Smiley Public Library 125 W Vine St *Web:* www.akspl.org	Redlands	CA	92373	909-798-7565	798-7566
Redondo Beach Public Library 303 N Pacific Coast Hwy *Web:* redondo.org	Redondo Beach	CA	90277	310-318-0675	318-3809
Redwood City Public Library 1044 Middlefield Rd *Web:* www.redwoodcity.org/library	Redwood City	CA	94063	650-780-7018	
Riverside City Public Library 3581 Mission Inn Ave *TF:* 888-225-7377 ■ *Web:* www.riversideca.gov/library	Riverside	CA	92501	951-826-5201	826-5407
Palos Verdes Library District 701 Silver Spur Rd *Web:* www.pvld.org	Rolling Hills Estates	CA	90274	310-377-9584	
Sacramento Public Library 828 'I' St *Web:* www.saclibrary.org	Sacramento	CA	95814	916-264-2770	264-2755
John Steinbeck Library 350 Lincoln Ave *Web:* www.salinaspubliclibrary.org	Salinas	CA	93901	831-758-7311	758-7336
Calaveras County Library 891 Mtn Ranch Rd *Web:* calaverasgov.us	San Andreas	CA	95249	209-754-6510	754-6512
San Bruno Public Library 701 Angus Ave W *Web:* www.sanbruno.ca.gov	San Bruno	CA	94066	650-616-7078	876-0848
San Diego County Library System 5560 Overland Ave Ste 110 *Web:* www.sdcl.org	San Diego	CA	92123	858-694-2415	495-5981
San Diego Public Library 820 E St *TF:* 866-470-1308 ■ *Web:* www.sandiego.gov/public-library	San Diego	CA	92101	619-236-5800	236-5878
San Francisco Public Library 100 Larkin St *Web:* www.sfpl.org	San Francisco	CA	94102	415-557-4400	557-4239
San Jose Public Library 150 E San Fernando St *Web:* www.sjpl.org	San Jose	CA	95113	408-808-2000	
City of San Leandro Public Library, The 835 E 14th St *Web:* www.sanleandro.org	San Leandro	CA	94577	510-577-3351	278-3095
San Luis Obispo City-County Library 995 Palm St *Web:* www.slolibrary.org	San Luis Obispo	CA	93401	805-781-5991	781-1166
San Mateo County Library 25 Tower Rd *Web:* www.smcl.org	San Mateo	CA	94402	650-312-5258	312-5382
Marin County Free Library 3501 Civic Ctr Dr Ste 414 *Web:* marinlibrary.org	San Rafael	CA	94903	415-499-3220	499-3726
San Rafael Public Library 1400 Fifth Ave *Web:* www.cityofsanrafael.org	San Rafael	CA	94901	415-485-3323	485-3112
Orange County Public Library 1501 E St Andrew Pl *Web:* ocpl.org	Santa Ana	CA	92705	714-566-3000	566-3042
Santa Ana Public Library 26 Civic Ctr Dr *Web:* www.ci.santa-ana.ca.us/library	Santa Ana	CA	92701	714-647-5250	
Santa Barbara Public Library 40 E Anapamu St *Web:* santabarbaraca.gov	Santa Barbara	CA	93101	805-962-7653	564-5660
Santa Clara City Library 2635 Homestead Rd *Web:* library.santaclaraca.gov	Santa Clara	CA	95051	408-615-2900	
Garfield Park Library 705 Woodrow Ave *Web:* www.santacruzpl.org	Santa Cruz	CA	95060	831-427-7713	
Santa Maria Public Library 420 S Broadway *Web:* www.cityofsantamaria.org	Santa Maria	CA	93454	805-925-0994	928-7432
Santa Monica Public Library 1343 Sixth St *Web:* www.smpl.org	Santa Monica	CA	90401	310-458-8608	394-8951
Sonoma County Library Third & E Sts *Web:* sonomalibrary.org/	Santa Rosa	CA	95404	707-545-0831	575-0437
South San Francisco Public Library 840 W Orange Ave *Web:* www.ssf.net	South San Francisco	CA	94080	650-829-3860	829-3866
Stockton-San Joaquin County Public Library (SSJCPL) 605 N El Dorado St *TF:* 866-805-7323 ■ *Web:* www.ssjcpl.org	Stockton	CA	95202	209-937-8416	937-8683
Sunnyvale Public Library (SPL) 665 W Olive Ave *Web:* www.sunnyvale.ca.gov/Departments/SunnyvalePublicLibrary.aspx	Sunnyvale	CA	94086	408-730-7300	730-7715
Thousand Oaks Library 1401 E Janss Rd *Web:* www.tol.lib.ca.us	Thousand Oaks	CA	91362	805-449-2660	373-6858
Belvedere-Tiburon Public Library 1501 Tiburon Blvd *Web:* www.bel-tib-lib.org	Tiburon	CA	94920	415-789-2665	789-2650
Torrance Public Library 3301 Torrance Blvd *Web:* www.torranceca.gov	Torrance	CA	90503	310-618-5959	618-5952
Tulare Public Library 475 N M St *Web:* www.tularepubliclibrary.org	Tulare	CA	93274	559-685-4500	
Mendocino County Library 105 N Main St *Web:* www.co.mendocino.ca.us	Ukiah	CA	95482	707-463-4491	463-5472
Upland Public Library 450 N Euclid Ave *Web:* www.uplandpl.lib.ca.us	Upland	CA	91786	909-931-4200	931-4209
EP Foster Library 651 E Main St *Web:* www.vencolibrary.org	Ventura	CA	93001	805-648-2716	648-3696
Ventura County Libraries 646 County Sq Dr Ste 150 *Web:* www.vencolibrary.org	Ventura	CA	93003	805-477-7331	477-7340
Tulare County Library System 200 W Oak Ave *Web:* www.tularecountylibrary.org	Visalia	CA	93291	559-713-2700	737-4586
Watsonville Public Library 275 Main St Ste 100 *Web:* cityofwatsonville.org	Watsonville	CA	95076	831-768-3400	763-4015
Woodland Public Library 250 First St *TF:* 800-321-2752 ■ *Web:* www.cityofwoodland.org/library	Woodland	CA	95695	530-661-5980	666-5408
Yolo County Library 226 Buckeye St *Web:* yolocounty.org	Woodland	CA	95695	530-666-8005	666-8006
Yorba Linda Public Library 18181 Imperial Hwy *Web:* ylpl.lib.ca.us/	Yorba Linda	CA	92886	714-777-2873	777-0640
Siskiyou County Library 719 Fourth St *Web:* www.snowcrest.net/siskiyoulibrary	Yreka	CA	96097	530-841-4175	842-7001
Sutter County Library 750 Forbes Ave *TF:* 800-533-2873 ■ *Web:* co.sutter.ca.us	Yuba City	CA	95991	530-822-7137	671-6539

Colorado

Library	City	State	ZIP	Phone	Fax
Basalt Regional Library 14 Midland Ave *Web:* basaltrld.org	Basalt	CO	81621	970-927-4311	927-1351
Boulder Public Library 1000 Canyon Blvd *Web:* www.boulderlibrary.org	Boulder	CO	80302	303-441-3100	442-1808
Mamie Doud Eisenhower Public Library Three Community Pk Rd *Web:* www.ci.broomfield.co.us	Broomfield	CO	80020	720-887-2300	887-1384
Douglas County Libraries 100 S Wilcox *Web:* douglascountylibraries.org	Castle Rock	CO	80104	303-791-7323	
Pikes Peak Library District PO Box 1579 *Web:* www.ppld.org	Colorado Springs	CO	80901	719-531-6333	528-2810
Denver Public Library 10 W 14th Ave Pkwy *Web:* www.denverlibrary.org	Denver	CO	80204	720-865-1111	
Poudre River Public Library 201 Peterson St *Web:* www.poudrelibraries.org	Fort Collins	CO	80524	970-221-6740	221-6398
American Alpine Club 710 Tenth St Ste 15 *Web:* americanalpineclub.org	Golden	CO	80401	303-384-0112	
Farr Regional Library 1939 61st Ave *TF:* 888-861-7323 ■ *Web:* www.mylibrary.us	Greeley	CO	80634	970-506-8550	506-8551
Bemis Public Library 6014 S Datura St *Web:* www.littletongov.org	Littleton	CO	80120	303-795-3961	795-3996
Longmont Public Library 409 Fourth Ave *Web:* longmontcolorado.gov	Longmont	CO	80501	303-651-8470	
Bud Werner Memorial Library 1289 Lincoln Ave *Web:* www.steamboatlibrary.org	Steamboat Springs	CO	80487	970-879-0240	
Rangeview Library District 5877 E 120th Ave *TF:* 800-222-3937 ■ *Web:* www.anythinklibraries.org	Thornton	CO	80602	303-288-2001	451-0190
Westminster Public Library 7392 Irving St *Web:* www.ci.westminster.co.us	Westminster	CO	80030	303-430-2400	

Connecticut

Library	City	State	ZIP	Phone	Fax
Avon Free Public Library 281 Country Club Rd *Web:* www.avonctlibrary.info	Avon	CT	06001	860-673-9712	675-6364
Bridgeport Public Library 925 Broad St *Web:* www.bportlibrary.org	Bridgeport	CT	06604	203-576-7403	576-8255
Cheshire Public Library 104 Main St *Web:* cheshirelibrary.com	Cheshire	CT	06410	203-272-2245	272-7714
Danbury Public Library 170 Main St *Web:* www.danburylibrary.org	Danbury	CT	06810	203-797-4505	796-1677
Town of East Hampton Senior Center 105 Main St *Web:* www.easthamptonct.org	East Hampton	CT	06424	860-267-4426	
East Hartford Public Library 840 Main St *Web:* www.ehtfdlib.info	East Hartford	CT	06108	860-289-6429	291-9166
Enfield Public Library 104 Middle Rd *Web:* www.enfield-ct.gov	Enfield	CT	06082	860-763-7510	763-7514
Fairfield Public Library 1080 Old Post Rd *Web:* www.fairfieldpubliclibrary.org	Fairfield	CT	06824	203-256-3155	256-3162
Welles-Turner Memorial Library 2407 Main St *TF:* 800-411-9671 ■ *Web:* www.wtmlib.com	Glastonbury	CT	06033	860-652-7719	652-7721
Groton Public Library 52 Newtown Rd Rt 117 *Web:* grotonpl.org	Groton	CT	06340	860-441-6750	448-0363
Hamden Library 2901 Dixwell Ave *Web:* www.hamdenlibrary.org	Hamden	CT	06518	203-287-2686	287-2685
Hartford Public Library 500 Main St *Web:* www.hplct.org	Hartford	CT	06103	860-695-6300	722-6900

Phone *Fax*

Mary Cheney Library 586 Main St .... Manchester CT 06040 860-643-2471 643-9453
Web: library.townofmanchester.org
Meriden Public Library 105 Miller St .... Meriden CT 06450 203-238-2344 238-3647
TF: 800-567-0902 ■ *Web:* meridenlibrary.org
Milford Public Library 57 New Haven Ave .... Milford CT 06460 203-783-3304
New Canaan Library 151 Main St .... New Canaan CT 06840 203-594-5000 594-5026
TF: 800-545-2433 ■ *Web:* www.newcanaanlibrary.org
New Fairfield Free Public Library
2 Brush Hill Rd PO Box F .... New Fairfield CT 06812 203-312-5679 312-5685
TF: 877-227-7487 ■ *Web:* www.newfairfieldlibrary.org
Haskins Laboratories Library
300 George St Ste 900 .... New Haven CT 06511 203-865-6163
Web: www.haskins.yale.edu
New Haven Free Public Library 133 Elm St .... New Haven CT 06510 203-946-8130 946-8140
Web: www.cityofnewhaven.com/library
Lucy Robbins Welles Library 95 Cedar St........... Newington CT 06111 860-665-8700 667-1255
TF: 800-842-1423 ■ *Web:* www.newingtonct.gov
Norwalk Public Library 1 Belden Ave................ Norwalk CT 06850 203-899-2780 866-7982
Web: www.norwalklib.org
Plumb Memorial Library 65 Wooster St.............. Shelton CT 06484 203-924-1580 924-8422
Web: www.sheltonlibrarysystem.org
Simsbury Public Library 725 Hopmeadow St .... Simsbury CT 06070 860-658-7663 658-6732
Web: www.simsburylibrary.info
Southington Public Library 255 Main St .... Southington CT 06489 860-628-0947 628-0488
Web: www.southingtonlibrary.org
Ferguson Library One Public Library Plz............. Stamford CT 06904 203-964-1000 357-9098
Web: www.fergusonlibrary.org
Willoughby Wallace Memorial Library (WWML)
146 Thimble Islands Rd .... Stony Creek CT 06405 203-488-8702 315-3347
Web: www.wwml.org
Trumbull Library 33 Quality St..................... Trumbull CT 06611 203-452-5197 452-5125
Web: www.trumbullct-library.org
Silas Bronson Library (SBL) 267 Grand St........... Waterbury CT 06702 203-574-8222 574-8055
Web: www.bronsonlibrary.org
West Hartford Public Library
20 S Main St............................... West Hartford CT 06107 860-561-6950 561-6990
Web: www.westhartfordlibrary.org
Windsor Public Library 323 Broad St................ Windsor CT 06095 860-285-1910 285-1889
Web: www.windsorlibrary.com

Delaware

Phone *Fax*

Kent County Library 2319 S Dupont Hwy .... Dover DE 19901 302-698-6440 698-6441
Web: www.co.kent.de.us/departments/communitysvcs/library
Hockessin Library 1023 Valley Rd .... Hockessin DE 19707 302-239-5160 239-1519
TF: 888-352-7722 ■ *Web:* www.nccde.org
New Castle Public Library 424 Delaware St......... New Castle DE 19720 302-328-1995 378-5594
TF: 877-225-7351
New Castle County Library 750 Library Ave .... Newark DE 19711 302-731-7550 731-4019
TF: 877-225-7351 ■ *Web:* nccde.org
Rehoboth Beach Public Library
226 Rehoboth Ave.......................... Rehoboth Beach DE 19971 302-227-8044 227-0597
Web: www.rehobothlibrary.org
Kirkwood Library 6000 Kirkwood Hwy .... Wilmington DE 19808 302-995-7663 995-7687
TF: 888-352-7722 ■ *Web:* www.nccde.org
Wilmington Public Library 10 E Tenth St .... Wilmington DE 19801 302-571-7400 654-9132
Web: wilmington.lib.de.us

District of Columbia

Phone *Fax*

Martin Luther King Jr Memorial Library (MLK)
901 G St NW................................ Washington DC 20001 202-727-0321
Web: www.dclibrary.org
Medicare Payment Advisory Comm
601 New Jersey Ave Nw .... Washington DC 20001 202-220-3700
Web: www.medpac.gov

Florida

Phone *Fax*

DeSoto County Library 125 N Hillsboro Ave........... Arcadia FL 34266 863-993-4851 491-4095
Web: www.myhlc.org
Citrus County Library System
425 W Roosevelt Blvd.......................... Beverly Hills FL 34465 352-746-9077 746-9493
Web: www.cclib.org
Boca Raton Public Library
400 NW Second Ave........................... Boca Raton FL 33432 561-393-7852 393-7823
Web: www.bocalibrary.org
Boynton Beach City Library
208 S Seacrest Blvd .... Boynton Beach FL 33435 561-742-6390
Web: www.boyntonlibrary.org
Manatee County Public Library System
PO Box 1000 .... Bradenton FL 34206 941-748-4501 749-7191
Web: www.mymanatee.org
Hernando County Public Library System
238 Howell Ave................................ Brooksville FL 34601 352-754-4043 754-4044
Web: www.hcpl.lib.fl.us
Seminole County Public Library
215 N Oxford Rd............................... Casselberry FL 32707 407-665-0000
Web: www.seminolecountyfl.gov/lls/library
Clearwater Public Library
100 N Osceola Ave............................. Clearwater FL 33755 727-562-4970 562-4977
TF: 800-342-8060 ■ *Web:* www.myclearwater.com/cpl
Clewiston Public Library System
120 W Osceola Ave............................. Clewiston FL 33440 863-983-1493 983-9194
Web: www.hendrylibraries.org
Central Brevard Library 308 Forest Ave................ Cocoa FL 32922 321-633-1792 633-1806
Web: www.brevardcounty.us

Phone *Fax*

Volusia County Public Library
105 E Magnolia Ave .... Daytona Beach FL 32114 386-257-6036 257-6026
Web: www.volusialibrary.org
Walton-De Funiak Library 3 Cir Dr.......... DeFuniak Springs FL 32435 850-892-3624 892-4438
TF: 800-342-0141 ■ *Web:* co.walton.fl.us
Delray Beach Library 100 W Atlantic Ave.......... Delray Beach FL 33444 561-266-0194 266-9757
Web: www.delraylibrary.org
Broward County Library
100 S Andrews Ave.......................... Fort Lauderdale FL 33301 954-357-7444
Web: www.browardlibrary.org
Lee County Library 2050 Central Ave............... Fort Myers FL 33901 239-479-4636
Web: leelibrary.net
Saint Lucie County Library System
2300 Virginia Ave............................... Fort Pierce FL 34950 772-462-1100 462-2750
Web: www.st-lucie.lib.fl.us
Alachua County Library District
401 E University Ave............................ Gainesville FL 32601 352-334-3900 334-3918
TF: 866-341-2730 ■ *Web:* www.aclib.us
Pasco County Library System 8012 Library Rd......... Hudson FL 34667 727-861-3020 861-3025
Web: www.pascolibraries.org
Monroe County Public Library System
700 Fleming St.................................. Key West FL 33040 305-292-3595 295-3626
TF: 877-772-8346 ■ *Web:* keyslibraries.org
Columbia County Public Library
308 NW Columbia Ave PO Box 1529 .... Lake City FL 32055 386-758-2101 758-2135
Web: www.columbiacountyfla.com/default.asp
Lake Worth Public Library 15 N 'M' St............. Lake Worth FL 33460 561-533-7354 586-1651
Web: www.lakeworth.org
Lakeland Public Library 100 Lk Morton Dr........... Lakeland FL 33801 863-834-4270
Web: www.lakelandgov.net/library/home.aspx
Leesburg Public Library 100 E Main St............. Leesburg FL 34748 352-728-9790 728-9794
Web: www.leesburgflorida.gov
Collier County Public Library (CCPL)
2385 Orange Blossom Dr .... Naples FL 34109 239-593-0177
Web: www.colliergov.net
North Miami Public Library
835 NE 132nd St .... North Miami FL 33161 305-891-5535 892-0843
Web: northmiamifl.gov
North Miami Beach Public Library
1601 NE 164th St...................... North Miami Beach FL 33162 305-948-2970 787-6007
Web: nmblib.com
Orange County Library System
101 E Central Blvd .... Orlando FL 32801 407-835-7323 835-7650
Web: www.ocls.lib.fl.us
Flagler County Public Library (FCPL)
2500 Palm Coast Pkwy NW .... Palm Coast FL 32137 386-446-6763 446-6773
TF: 877-863-5244 ■ *Web:* www.flaglercounty.org
Bay County Public Library 898 W 11th St......... Panama City FL 32401 850-522-2100
Web: www.nwrls.lib.fl.us
Northwest Regional Library System
898 W 11th St................................ Panama City FL 32401 850-522-2100 522-2138
Web: www.nwrls.com
West Florida Regional Library
200 W Gregory St............................... Pensacola FL 32501 850-436-5060 436-5039
TF: 800-435-7352 ■ *Web:* www.cityofpensacola.com
Helen B Hoffman Plantation Library
501 N Fig Tree Ln............................... Plantation FL 33317 954-797-2140 797-2767
TF: 800-774-5866 ■ *Web:* plantation.org
Gadsden County Public Library
732 Pat Thomas Pkwy .... Quincy FL 32351 850-627-7106
Web: www.gcpls.org
Riviera Beach Public Library
600 W Blue Heron Blvd .... Riviera Beach FL 33404 561-845-4195 881-7308
Web: rivierabch.com
St Johns County Public Library
1960 N Ponce de Leon Blvd .... Saint Augustine FL 32084 904-827-6940 827-6945
Web: www.sjcpls.org
Saint Petersburg Public Library
3745 Ninth Ave N......................... Saint Petersburg FL 33713 727-893-7724 892-5432
Web: www.splibraries.org
Seminole County Public Library - North Branch
150 N Palmetto Ave .... Sanford FL 32771 407-665-1620 330-3120
Web: www.seminolecountyfl.gov/lls/library
Selby Public Library 1331 First St .... Sarasota FL 34236 941-365-5228 316-1188
Web: www.selbylibraryfriends.org/
Heartland Library Co-op 319 W Ctr Ave .... Sebring FL 33870 863-402-6716
Web: www.myhlc.org
Martin County Public Library
2401 SE Monterey Rd................................ Stuart FL 34996 772-288-5702 219-4959
Web: www.martin.fl.us
College Center for Library Automation
1753 W Paul Dirac Dr.......................... Tallahassee FL 32310 850-922-6044
Web: www.cclaflorida.org
Leon County Public Library System
200 W Pk Ave .... Tallahassee FL 32301 850-487-2665
Web: cms.leoncountyfl.gov/library
Tampa-Hillsborough County Public Library
900 N Ashley Dr.................................... Tampa FL 33602 813-273-3652 272-5640
Web: www.hcplc.org
Indian River County Library (IRCL)
1600 21st St.................................... Vero Beach FL 32960 772-770-5060 770-5066
Web: www.irclibrary.org
Palm Beach County Public Library System
3650 Summit Blvd .... West Palm Beach FL 33406 561-233-2600 233-2622
Web: www.pbclibrary.org
West Palm Beach Public Library
411 Clematis St .... West Palm Beach FL 33401 561-868-7700 822-1892
TF: 866-472-7275 ■ *Web:* www.wpbpl.com

Georgia

				Phone	Fax
Dougherty County Public Library 300 N Pine Ave *Web:* www.docolib.org	Albany	GA	31701	229-420-3200	
Athens/Clarke County Library 2025 Baxter St *Web:* athenslibrary.org	Athens	GA	30606	706-613-3650	613-3660
Atlanta-Fulton Public Library One Margaret Mitchell Sq *Web:* www.afpls.org/locations/locations2	Atlanta	GA	30303	404-730-1700	730-1990
Augusta-Richmond County Library 823 Telfair St *Web:* ecgrl.public.lib.ga.us	Augusta	GA	30901	706-821-2600	724-6762
Brunswick-Glynn County Regional Library 208 Gloucester St *TF:* 800-222-6748	Brunswick	GA	31520	912-267-1212	261-3849
West Georgia Regional Library 710 Rome St *Web:* www.wgrl.net	Carrollton	GA	30117	770-836-6711	836-4787
Bartow County Public Library 429 W Main St *Web:* www.bartowlibraryonline.org	Cartersville	GA	30120	770-382-4203	386-3056
Columbus Public Library 3000 Macon Rd *Web:* www.cvlga.org/branches/columbus	Columbus	GA	31906	706-243-2669	
Northwest Georgia Regional Library 310 Cappes St *Web:* www.ngrl.org	Dalton	GA	30720	706-876-1360	272-2977
DeKalb County Public Library 215 Sycamore St *TF:* 800-677-1116 ■ *Web:* dekalblibrary.org	Decatur	GA	30030	404-370-3070	370-8469
Flint River Regional Library 800 Memorial Dr *Web:* frrls.net	Griffin	GA	30223	770-412-4770	412-4771
Clayton County Library System 865 Battle Creek Rd *Web:* claytonpl.org	Jonesboro	GA	30236	770-473-3850	473-3858
LaFayette-Walker County Library 305 S Duke St *TF:* 877-842-9733 ■ *Web:* www.chrl.org	La Fayette	GA	30728	706-638-2992	638-4028
Gwinnett County Public Library 1001 Lawrenceville Hwy *Web:* www.gwinnettpl.org	Lawrenceville	GA	30046	770-822-4522	822-5379
Middle Georgia Regional Library System 1180 Washington Ave *Web:* maconbibb.us	Macon	GA	31201	478-744-0800	621-5823
Cobb County Public Library System 266 Roswell St *Web:* www.cobbcat.org	Marietta	GA	30060	770-528-2320	528-2349
Henry County Public Library System 1001 Florence McGarity Blvd *TF:* 877-527-3712 ■ *Web:* www.henry.public.lib.ga.us	McDonough	GA	30252	770-954-2806	954-2808
Sara Hightower Regional Library 205 Riverside Pkwy NE *Web:* www.romelibrary.org	Rome	GA	30161	706-236-4600	236-4631
Live Oak Public Libraries 2002 Bull St *Web:* www.liveoakpl.org	Savannah	GA	31401	912-652-3600	652-3638
South Georgia Regional Library 300 Woodrow Wilson Dr *Web:* www.sgrl.org	Valdosta	GA	31602	229-333-0086	333-7669

Idaho

				Phone	Fax
Boise Public Library 715 S Capitol Blvd *Web:* www.boisepubliclibrary.org	Boise	ID	83702	208-384-4076	384-4025
Coeur d'Alene Public Library 702 E Front *Web:* www.cdalibrary.org	Coeur d'Alene	ID	83814	208-769-2315	769-2381
Idaho Falls Public Library 457 W Broadway *Web:* www.ifpl.org	Idaho Falls	ID	83402	208-612-8460	612-8467
Lewiston City Library 428 Thain Rd *Web:* www.cityoflewiston.org	Lewiston	ID	83501	208-743-6519	798-4446
Nampa Public Library (NPL) 101 11th Ave S *Web:* www.nampalibrary.org	Nampa	ID	83651	208-468-5800	465-2277
East Bonner County Library District 1407 W Cedar St *Web:* ebonnerlibrary.org	Sandpoint	ID	83864	208-263-6930	
Twin Falls Public Library 201 Fourth Ave E *Web:* www.twinfallspubliclibrary.org	Twin Falls	ID	83301	208-733-2964	733-2965

Illinois

				Phone	Fax
Addison Public Library 4 Friendship Plaza *Web:* www.addisonlibrary.org	Addison	IL	60101	630-543-3617	543-7275
Algonquin Area Public Library District 2600 Harnish *Web:* www.aapld.org	Algonquin	IL	60102	847-658-4343	
Arlington Heights Memorial Library 500 N Dunton Ave *Web:* www.ahml.info	Arlington Heights	IL	60004	847-392-0100	506-2650
Aurora Public Library One E Benton St *Web:* www.aurora.lib.il.us	Aurora	IL	60505	630-264-4100	896-3209
Batavia Public Library District 10 S Batavia Ave *Web:* www.batavia.lib.il.us	Batavia	IL	60510	630-879-1393	
Bensenville Community Public Library 200 S Church Rd *Web:* www.bensenville.lib.il.us	Bensenville	IL	60106	630-766-4642	766-0788
Berwyn Public Library (BPL) 2701 S Harlem Ave *Web:* www.berwynlibrary.org	Berwyn	IL	60402	708-795-8000	795-8101
Bloomington Public Library 205 E Olive St *Web:* blpl.ent.sirsi.net	Bloomington	IL	61701	309-828-6091	
Fountaindale Public Library 300 W Briarcliff Rd *Web:* www.fountaindale.org	Bolingbrook	IL	60440	630-759-2102	759-9519
Calumet City Public Library 660 Manistee Ave *Web:* calumetcitypl.org	Calumet City	IL	60409	708-862-6220	862-0872
Carbondale Public Library 405 W Main St *Web:* www.carbondale.lib.il.us	Carbondale	IL	62901	618-457-0354	457-0353
Carol Stream Public Library 616 Hiawatha Dr *TF:* 800-829-1040 ■ *Web:* www.cslibrary.org	Carol Stream	IL	60188	630-653-0755	653-6809
Chicago Public Library 400 S State St *Web:* www.chipublib.org	Chicago	IL	60605	312-747-4999	747-4968
Gerber/Hart Library & Archives 6500 N Clark St *Web:* www.gerberhart.org	Chicago	IL	60626	773-381-8030	381-8030
Cicero Public Library 5225 W Cermak Rd *Web:* cicerolibrary.org	Cicero	IL	60804	708-652-8084	652-8095
Crystal Lake Public Library 126 W Paddock St *Web:* www.crystallakelibrary.org	Crystal Lake	IL	60014	815-459-1687	459-5845
Decatur Public Library 130 N Franklin St *Web:* decaturlibrary.org	Decatur	IL	62523	217-424-2900	233-4071
DeKalb Public Library 309 Oak St *TF:* 888-268-2824 ■ *Web:* www.dkpl.org	DeKalb	IL	60115	815-756-9568	756-7837
Des Plaines Public Library 1501 Ellinwood Ave *TF:* 800-829-1040 ■ *Web:* www.dppl.org	Des Plaines	IL	60016	847-827-5551	827-7974
Downers Grove Public Library 1050 Curtiss St *Web:* www.downersgrovelibrary.org	Downers Grove	IL	60515	630-960-1200	960-9374
Elk Grove Village Public Library 1001 Wellington Ave *TF:* 800-252-8980 ■ *Web:* www.egvpl.org	Elk Grove Village	IL	60007	847-439-0447	439-0475
Elmhurst Public Library 125 S Prospect Ave *Web:* www.elmhurstpubliclibrary.org	Elmhurst	IL	60126	630-279-8696	279-0636
Evanston Public Library 1703 Orrington Ave *TF:* 888-253-7003 ■ *Web:* epl.org	Evanston	IL	60201	847-448-8600	866-0313
Freeport Public Library 100 E Douglas St *Web:* www.freeportpubliclibrary.org	Freeport	IL	61032	815-233-3000	297-8236
Galesburg Public Library 40 E Simmons St *Web:* www.galesburglibrary.org	Galesburg	IL	61401	309-343-6118	343-4877
DuPage Library System 127 S First St *Web:* www.dupagels.lib.il.us	Geneva	IL	60134	630-232-8457	232-0699
Glenview Public Library 1930 Glenview Rd *Web:* www.glenviewpl.org	Glenview	IL	60025	847-729-7500	729-7558
Grande Prairie Public Library 3479 W 183rd St *TF:* 800-321-9511 ■ *Web:* www.grandeprairie.org	Hazel Crest	IL	60429	708-798-5563	798-5874
Highland Park Public Library 494 Laurel Ave *Web:* www.hplibrary.org	Highland Park	IL	60035	847-432-0216	432-9139
Joliet Public Library 150 N Ottawa St *Web:* jolietlibrary.org	Joliet	IL	60432	815-740-2660	740-6161
Kankakee Public Library 201 E Ct St *Web:* www.lions-online.org	Kankakee	IL	60901	815-939-4564	939-9057
Lake Villa Illinois Public Library District 1001 E Grand Ave *Web:* www.lvdl.org	Lake Villa	IL	60046	847-356-7711	
Ela Area Public Library District 275 Mohawk Trl *Web:* www.eapl.org	Lake Zurich	IL	60047	847-438-3433	438-9290
Lewis O Flom Lansing Public Library 2750 Indiana Ave *Web:* www.lansingpl.org	Lansing	IL	60438	708-474-2447	474-9466
Lexington Public Library District 207 S Cedar St *Web:* lexington.lib.il.us	Lexington	IL	61753	309-365-7801	
Cook Memorial Public Library District 413-n Milwaukee Ave *Web:* www.cooklib.org	Libertyville	IL	60048	847-362-2330	
Lisle Library District 777 Front St *Web:* www.lislelibrary.org	Lisle	IL	60532	630-971-1675	
Helen M Plum Memorial Library 110 W Maple St *Web:* helenplum.org	Lombard	IL	60148	630-627-0316	627-0336
Maywood Public Library 121 S Fifth Ave *Web:* www.maywood.org	Maywood	IL	60153	708-343-1847	343-2115
McHenry Public Library District 809 N Front St *Web:* mchenrylibrary.org	Mchenry	IL	60050	815-385-0036	
Morton Grove Public Library 6140 Lincoln Ave *Web:* www.mgpl.org	Morton Grove	IL	60053	847-965-4220	965-7903
Mount Prospect Public Library 10 S Emerson St *Web:* www.mppl.org	Mount Prospect	IL	60056	847-253-5675	253-5677
Naperville Public Libraries 200 W Jefferson Ave *Web:* www.naperville-lib.org	Naperville	IL	60540	630-961-4100	637-4870
Normal Public Library 206 W College *Web:* www.normalpl.org	Normal	IL	61761	309-452-1757	452-5312
North Chicago Public Library 2100 Argonne Dr *Web:* ncplibrary.org	North Chicago	IL	60064	847-689-0125	689-9117
Northbrook Public Library 1201 Cedar Ln *Web:* northbrook.info	Northbrook	IL	60062	847-272-6224	498-0440
Oak Lawn Public Library 9427 Raymond Ave *Web:* www.lib.oak-lawn.il.us	Oak Lawn	IL	60453	708-422-4990	422-5061
Oak Park Public Library 834 Lake St *Web:* www.oppl.org	Oak Park	IL	60301	708-383-8200	383-6384

Library	City	State	ZIP	Phone	Fax
Orland Park Public Library 14921 Ravinia Ave; *Web:* www.orlandparklibrary.org	Orland Park	IL	60462	708-428-5100	349-8196
Park Forest Public Library 400 Lakewood Blvd; *Web:* www.pfpl.org	Park Forest	IL	60466	708-748-3731	748-8829
Park Ridge Public Library 20 S Prospect Ave.; *Web:* www.parkridgelibrary.org	Park Ridge	IL	60068	847-825-3123	825-0001
Pekin Public Library 301 S Fourth St; *Web:* www.pekinpubliclibrary.org	Pekin	IL	61554	309-347-7111	347-6587
Peoria Public Library 107 NE Monroe St; *Web:* www.peoriapubliclibrary.org	Peoria	IL	61602	309-497-2135	674-0116
Quincy Public Library 526 Jersey St.; *Web:* www.quincylibrary.org	Quincy	IL	62301	217-223-1309	222-3052
Rock Island Public Library 401 19th St.; *Web:* www.rockislandlibrary.org	Rock Island	IL	61201	309-732-7323	732-7342
Rockford Public Library 215 N Wyman St.; *Web:* www.rockfordpubliclibrary.org	Rockford	IL	61101	815-965-6731	965-6735
Schaumburg Township District Library (STDL) 130 S Roselle Rd; *Web:* www.schaumburglibrary.org	Schaumburg	IL	60193	847-985-4000	923-3335
Shorewood-Troy Public Library District 650 Deerwood Dr; *Web:* www.shorewood.lib.il.us	Shorewood	IL	60404	815-725-1715	725-1722
Skokie Public Library 5215 Oakton St; *Web:* www.skokielibrary.info	Skokie	IL	60077	847-673-7774	673-7797
Lincoln Library 326 S Seventh St.; *Web:* www.lincolnlibrary.info	Springfield	IL	62701	217-753-4900	
Tinley Park Public Library 7851 Timber Dr.; *Web:* www.tplibrary.org	Tinley Park	IL	60477	708-532-0160	532-2981
Urbana Free Library 210 W Green St; *Web:* www.urbanafreelibrary.org	Urbana	IL	61801	217-367-4057	367-4061
Waukegan Public Library 128 N County St.; *Web:* www.waukeganpl.org	Waukegan	IL	60085	847-623-2041	623-2092
Wheaton Public Library 225 N Cross St; *Web:* www.wheaton.lib.il.us	Wheaton	IL	60187	630-668-1374	668-8950
Winnetka-Northfield Public Library District 768 Oak St; *Web:* winnetkalibrary.org	Winnetka	IL	60093	847-446-7220	
Woodridge Public Library 3 Plaza Dr; *TF:* 800-279-0400 ■ *Web:* www.woodridgelibrary.org	Woodridge	IL	60517	630-964-7899	964-0175

Indiana

Library	City	State	ZIP	Phone	Fax
Anderson Public Library 111 E 12th St; *Web:* www.and.lib.in.us	Anderson	IN	46016	765-641-2456	641-2197
Eckhart Public Library 603 S Jackson St.; *Web:* www.epl.lib.in.us	Auburn	IN	46706	260-925-2414	
Batesville Memorial Public Library (BMPL) 131 N Walnut St; *Web:* www.ebatesville.com/library	Batesville	IN	47006	812-934-4706	934-6288
Bedford Public Library 1323 K St; *Web:* www.bedlib.org	Bedford	IN	47421	812-275-4471	277-1145
Monroe County Public Library 303 E Kirkwood Ave; *Web:* www.monroe.lib.in.us	Bloomington	IN	47408	812-349-3050	349-3051
Wells County Public Library 200 W Washington St.; *TF:* 800-824-6111 ■ *Web:* www.wellscolibrary.org	Bluffton	IN	46714	260-824-1612	824-3129
Carmel Clay Public Library 55 Fourth Ave SE; *TF:* 800-908-4490 ■ *Web:* www.carmel.lib.in.us	Carmel	IN	46032	317-844-3361	571-4285
Charlestown Clark County Public Library 51 Clark Rd.; *Web:* www.clarkco.lib.in.us	Charlestown	IN	47111	812-256-3337	256-3890
Bartholomew County Public Library 536 Fifth St.; *Web:* mybcpl.org/	Columbus	IN	47201	812-379-1255	379-1275
Harrison County Public Library District 105 N Capital Ave.; *Web:* www.hcpl.lib.in.us	Corydon	IN	47112	812-738-4110	
Lincoln Heritage Public Library 105 N Wallace St; *Web:* www.lincolnheritage.lib.in.us	Dale	IN	47523	812-937-7170	
East Chicago Public Library (ECPL) 2401 E Columbus Dr; *Web:* www.ecpl.org	East Chicago	IN	46312	219-397-2453	397-6715
Evansville Vanderburgh Public Library 200 SE ML King Jr Blvd; *Web:* www.evpl.org	Evansville	IN	47713	812-428-8200	428-8397
Allen County Public Library 900 Library Plaza; *TF:* 800-448-6160 ■ *Web:* www.acpl.lib.in.us	Fort Wayne	IN	46802	260-421-1200	421-1386
Frankfort Community Public Library (FCPL) 208 W Clinton St; *Web:* fcpl.accs.net	Frankfort	IN	46041	765-654-8746	654-8747
Johnson County Public Library 401 S State St.; *Web:* pageafterpage.org/	Franklin	IN	46131	317-738-2833	738-9635
Gary Public Library 220 W Fifth Ave; *Web:* www.garypubliclibrary.org	Gary	IN	46402	219-886-2484	886-6829
Putnam County Public Library 103 E Poplar St PO Box 116; *Web:* www.putnam.lib.in.us	Greencastle	IN	46135	765-653-2755	653-2756
Hammond Public Library 564 State St.; *Web:* www.hammond.lib.in.us	Hammond	IN	46320	219-931-5100	931-3474
Federal Home Loan Bank of Indianapolis 8250 Woodfield Crossing Blvd; *Web:* www.fhlbi.com	Indianapolis	IN	46240	317-465-0200	
Indianapolis-Marion County Public Library (IMCPL) PO Box 211; *Web:* www.imcpl.org	Indianapolis	IN	46206	317-275-4100	
Jasper Public Library 1116 Main St.; *Web:* jdcpl.lib.in.us	Jasper	IN	47546	812-482-2712	482-7123
Kokomo-Howard County Public Library 220 N Union St.; *TF:* 800-257-4762 ■ *Web:* www.kokomo.lib.in.us	Kokomo	IN	46901	765-457-3242	457-3683
La Porte County Public Library 904 Indiana Ave; *Web:* www.laportelibrary.org	La Porte	IN	46350	219-362-6156	362-6158
Tippecanoe County Public Library 627 S St.; *TF:* 800-542-7818 ■ *Web:* www.tcpl.lib.in.us	Lafayette	IN	47901	765-429-0100	429-0150
LaGrange County Public Library 203 W Spring St; *Web:* www.lagrange.lib.in.us	LaGrange	IN	46761	260-463-2841	
Logansport-Cass County Public Library 616 E Broadway; *Web:* www.logan.lib.in.us	Logansport	IN	46947	574-753-6383	722-5889
Madison-Jefferson County Public Library 420 W Main St; *Web:* www.madison-jeffco.lib.in.us	Madison	IN	47250	812-265-2744	265-2217
Lake County Public Library 1919 W 81st Ave.; *Web:* lcplin.org	Merrillville	IN	46410	219-769-3541	769-0690
Mooresville Public Library 220 W Harrison St; *Web:* www.mooresvillelib.org	Mooresville	IN	46158	317-831-7323	831-7383
New Albany-Floyd County Public Library 180 W Spring St; *Web:* newalbany.boundless.ly/	New Albany	IN	47150	812-944-8464	949-3734
New Castle-Henry County Public Library (NCHC) 376 S 15th St; *Web:* nchcpl.org	New Castle	IN	47362	765-529-0362	521-3581
Jasper County Public Library 208 W Susan St; *Web:* www.jasperco.lib.in.us	Rensselaer	IN	47978	219-866-5881	
Morrisson-Reeves Public Library 80 N Sixth St; *Web:* mrlinfo.org	Richmond	IN	47374	765-966-8291	962-1318
Jackson County Public Library (JCPL) 303 W Second St; *TF:* 877-275-7673 ■ *Web:* www.myjclibrary.org	Seymour	IN	47274	812-522-3412	522-5456
Shelbyville-Shelby County Public Library 57 W Broadway; *TF:* 866-466-l438	Shelbyville	IN	46176	317-398-7121	421-2758
Saint Joseph County Public Library 304 S Main St; *Web:* www.sjcpl.lib.in.us	South Bend	IN	46601	574-282-4630	
Vigo County Public Library One Library Sq; *Web:* www.vigo.lib.in.us	Terre Haute	IN	47807	812-232-1113	232-3208
Valparaiso Public Library 103 Jefferson St; *Web:* pcpls.org/	Valparaiso	IN	46383	219-462-0524	477-4867
Knox County Public Library 502 N Seventh St; *Web:* www.kcpl.lib.in.us	Vincennes	IN	47591	812-886-4380	886-0342
West Lafayette Public Library 208 W Columbia St; *Web:* www.wlaf.lib.in.us	West Lafayette	IN	47906	765-743-2261	743-0540

Iowa

Library	City	State	ZIP	Phone	Fax
Ames Public Library 515 Douglas Ave; *Web:* www.amespubliclibrary.org	Ames	IA	50010	515-239-5630	232-4571
Kirkendall Public Library 1210 NW Prairie Ridge Dr; *Web:* www.ankenyiowa.gov	Ankeny	IA	50023	515-965-6460	289-9122
Bettendorf Public Library 2950 Learning Campus Dr; *Web:* www.bettendorflibrary.com	Bettendorf	IA	52722	563-344-4175	344-4185
Burlington Public Library 210 Ct St; *Web:* www.burlington.lib.ia.us	Burlington	IA	52601	319-753-1647	229-0406
Cedar Falls Public Library 524 Main St; *Web:* www.cedarfallspubliclibrary.org	Cedar Falls	IA	50613	319-273-8643	273-8648
Cedar Rapids Public Library 2600 Edgewood Rd SW Ste 330; *Web:* www.crlibrary.org	Cedar Rapids	IA	52404	319-398-5123	398-0476
Clinton Public Library 306 Eigth Ave S; *Web:* clinton.lib.ia.us	Clinton	IA	52732	563-242-8441	242-8162
Council Bluffs Public Library 400 Willow Ave.; *Web:* www.councilbluffslibrary.org	Council Bluffs	IA	51503	712-323-7553	323-1269
Davenport Public Library 321 Main St; *Web:* www.davenportlibrary.com	Davenport	IA	52801	563-326-7832	326-7809
Des Moines Public Library 1000 Grand Ave; *Web:* dmpl.org/	Des Moines	IA	50309	515-283-4152	237-1654
Carnegie-Stout Public Library 360 W 11th St.; *Web:* www.dubuque.lib.ia.us	Dubuque	IA	52001	563-589-4225	589-4217
Fort Dodge Public Library 424 Central Ave; *Web:* www.fortdodgeiowa.org	Fort Dodge	IA	50501	515-573-8167	573-5422
Iowa City Public Library 123 S Linn St; *TF:* 866-862-6877 ■ *Web:* www.icpl.org	Iowa City	IA	52240	319-356-5200	356-5494
Marion Public Library 1095 Sixth Ave; *Web:* www.marionpubliclibrary.org	Marion	IA	52302	319-377-3412	377-0113
Marshalltown Public Library 105 W Boone St; *Web:* www.marshalltownlibrary.org	Marshalltown	IA	50158	641-754-5738	754-5708
Mason City Public Library 225 Second St SE; *Web:* www.mcpl.org	Mason City	IA	50401	641-421-3668	423-2615

Library	City	State	ZIP	Phone	Fax
Musser Public Library 304 Iowa Ave *Web:* www.musserpubliclibrary.org	Muscatine	IA	52761	563-263-3065	264-1033
Newton Public Library (NPL) 100 N Third Ave W PO Box 746 *Web:* newton.lib.ia.us	Newton	IA	50208	641-792-4108	791-0729
Ottumwa Public Library 102 W Fourth St *Web:* ottumwapubliclibrary.org	Ottumwa	IA	52501	641-682-7563	682-4970
Sioux City Public Library 529 Pierce St *Web:* www.siouxcitylibrary.org	Sioux City	IA	51101	712-255-2933	279-6432
Urbandale Public Library 3520 86th St *Web:* www.urbandalelibrary.org	Urbandale	IA	50322	515-278-3945	278-3918
West Des Moines Public Library 4000 Mills Civic Pkwy *Web:* www.wdmlibrary.org	West Des Moines	IA	50265	515-222-3400	222-3401

Kansas

Library	City	State	ZIP	Phone	Fax
Belleville Public Library 1327 19th St *Web:* www.bellevillepl.blogspot.in	Belleville	KS	66935	785-527-5305	527-5305
Finney County Public Library Garden City 605 E Walnut St *Web:* finneylibrary.org	Garden City	KS	67846	620-272-3680	272-3682
Hutchinson Public Library 901 N Main St *Web:* www.hutchpl.org	Hutchinson	KS	67501	620-663-5441	663-9506
Dorothy Bramlage Public Library Junction City 230 W Seventh St *Web:* www.jclib.org	Junction City	KS	66441	785-238-4311	238-7873
Kansas City Kansas Public Library 625 Minnesota Ave *Web:* links.kckpl.org/	Kansas City	KS	66101	913-551-3280	279-2032
Lawrence Public Library 707 Vermont St *TF:* 888-657-7323 ■ *Web:* www.lawrence.lib.ks.us	Lawrence	KS	66044	785-843-3833	843-3368
Leavenworth Public Library 417 Spruce St *Web:* leavenworthpubliclibrary.org	Leavenworth	KS	66048	913-682-5666	682-1248
Manhattan Public Library 629 Poyntz Ave *TF:* 800-432-2796 ■ *Web:* mhklibrary.org/	Manhattan	KS	66502	785-776-4741	776-1545
Salina Public Library 301 W Elm St *Web:* www.salinapubliclibrary.org	Salina	KS	67401	785-825-4624	823-0706
Johnson County Library PO Box 2933 *TF:* 800-386-8501 ■ *Web:* www.jocolibrary.org	Shawnee Mission	KS	66201	913-826-4600	826-4453
Topeka & Shawnee County Public Library 1515 SW Tenth Ave *Web:* www.tscpl.org	Topeka	KS	66604	785-580-4400	580-4496
Wichita Public Library 223 S Main St *Web:* www.wichita.lib.ks.us	Wichita	KS	67202	316-261-8500	262-4540

Kentucky

Library	City	State	ZIP	Phone	Fax
Boyd County Public Library 1740 Central Ave *Web:* www.thebookplace.org	Ashland	KY	41101	606-329-0518	329-0578
Kenton County Public Library 502 Scott Blvd *Web:* www.kenton.lib.ky.us	Covington	KY	41011	859-962-4060	962-4096
Boyle County Public Library 307 W Broadway *Web:* boylepublib.org	Danville	KY	40422	859-236-8466	236-7692
Hardin County Public Library 100 Jim Owen Dr *Web:* www.hcpl.info	Elizabethtown	KY	42701	270-769-6337	769-0437
Paul Sawyier Public Library 319 Wapping St *TF:* 800-829-3676 ■ *Web:* www.pspl.org	Frankfort	KY	40601	502-352-2665	227-2250
Anderson County Public Library 114 N Main St *Web:* www.andersonpubliclibrary.org	Lawrenceburg	KY	40342	502-839-6420	
Lexington Public Library 140 E Main St *Web:* www.lexpublib.org	Lexington	KY	40507	859-231-5504	231-5598
Louisville Free Public Library 301 York St *Web:* www.lfpl.org	Louisville	KY	40203	502-574-1611	574-1666
Daviess County Public Library 2020 Frederica St *Web:* www.dcplibrary.org	Owensboro	KY	42301	270-684-0211	684-0218
McCracken County Public Library 555 Washington St *Web:* www.mclib.net	Paducah	KY	42003	270-442-2510	
Pulaski County Public Library 304 S Main St *Web:* www.pulaskipubliclibrary.org	Somerset	KY	42501	606-679-8401	679-1779

Louisiana

Library	City	State	ZIP	Phone	Fax
Rapides Parish Library 411 Washington St *Web:* www.rpl.org	Alexandria	LA	71301	318-445-2411	445-6478
East Baton Rouge Parish Library (EBRPL) 7711 Goodwood Blvd *Web:* www.ebrpl.com	Baton Rouge	LA	70806	225-231-3750	231-3759
Bossier Parish Library (BPL) 2206 Beckett St *Web:* www.bossierlibrary.org	Bossier City	LA	71111	318-746-1693	746-7768
Saint Bernard Parish Library 2600 Palmisano Blvd *Web:* www.stbernard.lib.la.us	Chalmette	LA	70043	504-279-0448	
Saint Tammany Parish Library 310 W 21st Ave *Web:* www.sttammany.lib.la.us/	Covington	LA	70433	985-893-6280	871-1271
Acadia Parish Library 1125 N Parkerson Ave *Web:* www.acadia.lib.la.us	Crowley	LA	70526	337-788-1880	788-3759
Beauregard Parish Library 205 S Washington Ave *TF:* 800-524-6239 ■ *Web:* www.library.beau.org	DeRidder	LA	70634	337-463-6217	462-5434
St Mary Parish Library 206 Iberia St *Web:* stmary.lib.la.us	Franklin	LA	70538	337-828-1624	828-2329
Washington Parish Library System 825 Free St *Web:* www.washington.lib.la.us	Franklinton	LA	70438	985-839-7806	839-7808
Terrebonne Parish Library System 151 Library Dr *Web:* www.terrebonne.lib.la.us	Houma	LA	70360	985-876-5861	917-0582
Jefferson Davis Parish Library 118 W Plaquemine St *Web:* www.jefferson-davis.lib.la.us	Jennings	LA	70546	337-824-1210	824-5444
Lafayette Parish Public Library 301 W Congress St *Web:* lafayettepubliclibrary.org	Lafayette	LA	70501	337-261-5775	261-5782
Calcasieu Parish Public Library System 301 W Claude St *Web:* www.calcasieulibrary.org	Lake Charles	LA	70605	337-721-7116	475-8806
Vernon Parish Library 1401 Nolan Trace *TF:* 800-737-2231 ■ *Web:* www.youseemore.com	Leesville	LA	71446	337-239-2027	238-0666
Livingston Parish Library 20390 Iowa St PO Box 397 *Web:* mylpl.info	Livingston	LA	70754	225-686-2436	686-3888
DeSoto Parish Library 109 Crosby St *Web:* desotoparishlibrary.com	Mansfield	LA	71052	318-872-6100	872-6120
Avoyelles Parish Library 104 N Washington St *Web:* www.avoyelles.lib.la.us	Marksville	LA	71351	318-253-7559	253-6361
Jefferson Parish Library 4747 W Napoleon Ave *Web:* www.jefferson.lib.la.us	Metairie	LA	70001	504-838-1100	838-1110
Webster Parish Library 521 E & W Sts *Web:* www.webster.lib.la.us	Minden	LA	71055	318-371-3080	371-3081
Ouachita Parish Public Library 1800 Stubbs Ave *Web:* www.oplib.org	Monroe	LA	71201	318-327-1490	327-1373
Natchitoches Parish Library 450 Second St *Web:* www.youseemore.com	Natchitoches	LA	71457	318-357-3280	357-7073
Iberia Parish Library 445 E Main St *Web:* www.iberia.lib.la.us	New Iberia	LA	70560	337-364-7024	373-0086
Opelousas-Eunice Public Libraries 212 E Grolee St *Web:* opelousaseunicepubliclibrary.org	Opelousas	LA	70570	337-948-3693	948-5200
Iberville Parish Library 24605 J Gerald Berret Blvd *Web:* www.iberville.lib.la.us	Plaquemine	LA	70765	225-687-2520	687-9719
Lincoln Parish Library 910 N Trenton St *Web:* www.mylpl.org	Ruston	LA	71270	318-251-5030	251-5045
Saint Martin Parish Library 201 Porter St *Web:* stmartinparishlibrary.org/site.php	Saint Martinville	LA	70582	337-394-2207	394-2248
Shreve Memorial Library 424 Texas St *TF:* 866-783-5462 ■ *Web:* www.shreve-lib.org	Shreveport	LA	71101	318-226-5897	226-4780
Evangeline Parish Library 242 W Main St *Web:* www.evangeline.lib.la.us	Ville Platte	LA	70586	337-363-1369	363-2353

Maine

Library	City	State	ZIP	Phone	Fax
Lithgow Public Library 45 Winthrop St *Web:* www.lithgow.lib.me.us	Augusta	ME	04330	207-626-2415	626-2419
Bangor Public Library 145 Harlow St *TF:* 800-442-4293 ■ *Web:* www.bpl.lib.me.us	Bangor	ME	04401	207-947-8336	947-8336
Camden Public Library (CPL) 55 Main St *Web:* www.librarycamden.org	Camden	ME	04843	207-236-3440	236-6673
Lewiston Public Library 200 Lisbon St *Web:* www.lplonline.org	Lewiston	ME	04240	207-513-3004	784-3011
Portland Public Library 5 Monument Sq *Web:* www.portlandlibrary.com	Portland	ME	04101	207-871-1700	871-1703

Maryland

Library	City	State	ZIP	Phone	Fax
Anne Arundel County Public Library Five Harry S Truman Pkwy *Web:* aacpl.net	Annapolis	MD	21401	410-222-7371	222-7188
Enoch Pratt Free Library 400 Cathedral St *Web:* www.prattlibrary.org	Baltimore	MD	21201	410-396-5283	396-8134
Harford County Public Library 1221-A Brass Mill Rd *TF:* 800-944-7403 ■ *Web:* www.hcplonline.org	Belcamp	MD	21017	410-575-6761	273-5606
Dorchester County Public Library 303 Gay St *Web:* www.dorchesterlibrary.org	Cambridge	MD	21613	410-228-7331	228-6313
Queen Anne's County Library 121 S Commerce St *Web:* www.quan.lib.md.us	Centreville	MD	21617	410-758-0980	758-0614
Howard County Central Library 10375 Little Patuxent Pkwy *TF:* 800-848-1555 ■ *Web:* www.hclibrary.org	Columbia	MD	21044	410-313-7800	313-7864
Allegany County Public Library System 31 Washington St *Web:* www.alleganycountylibrary.info	Cumberland	MD	21502	301-777-1200	777-7299
Caroline County Public Library 100 Market St *TF:* 800-832-3277 ■ *Web:* www.carolib.org	Denton	MD	21629	410-479-1343	479-1443
Talbot County Free Library 100 W Dover St *Web:* www.tcfl.org/library	Easton	MD	21601	410-822-1626	820-8217
Cecil County Public Library (CCPL) 301 Newark Ave *Web:* www.cecil.ebranch.info	Elkton	MD	21921	410-996-1055	996-5604

				Phone	Fax
Frederick County Public Libraries (FCPL) 110 E Patrick St *Web:* www.fcpl.org	Frederick	MD	21701	301-600-1613	631-3789
Prince George's County Memorial Library 6532 Adelphi Rd *Web:* pgcmls.info	Hyattsville	MD	20782	301-699-3500	699-0122
St Mary's County Maryland Libraries 23250 Hollywood Rd *TF:* 800-783-3625 ■ *Web:* www.stmalib.org	Leonardtown	MD	20650	301-475-2846	884-4415
Ruth Enlow Library Six N Second St *Web:* www.relib.net	Oakland	MD	21550	301-334-3996	334-4152
Calvert County Public Library 850 Costley Way *Web:* www.calvert.lib.md.us	Prince Frederick	MD	20678	410-535-0291	535-3022
Wicomico County Free Library 122 S Div St *Web:* www.wicomicolibrary.org	Salisbury	MD	21801	410-749-3612	548-2968
Worcester County Library 307 N Washington St *Web:* www.worc.lib.md.us	Snow Hill	MD	21863	410-632-2600	632-1159
Baltimore County Public Library 320 York Rd *TF:* 800-705-3493 ■ *Web:* www.bcpl.info	Towson	MD	21204	410-887-6100	887-6103
Washington Research Library Consortium Inc, The 901 Commerce Dr *Web:* www.wrlc.org	Upper Marlboro	MD	20774	301-390-2000	
Carroll County Public Library 1100 Green Vly Rd New *Web:* www.library.carr.org	Windsor	MD	21776	410-386-4500	386-4509

Massachusetts

				Phone	Fax
Agawam Public Library 750 Cooper St *Web:* www.agawamlibrary.org	Agawam	MA	01001	413-789-1550	789-1552
Jones Library Inc 43 Amity St *TF:* 800-439-2370 ■ *Web:* www.joneslibrary.org	Amherst	MA	01002	413-256-4090	256-4096
Memorial Hall Library Two N Main St *Web:* www.mhl.org	Andover	MA	01810	978-623-8400	623-8407
Robbins Library 700 Massachusetts Ave *Web:* robbinslibrary.org	Arlington	MA	02476	781-316-3200	
Attleboro Public Library 74 N Main St *Web:* www.sailsinc.org	Attleboro	MA	02703	508-222-0157	226-3326
Sturgis Library 3090 Main St *Web:* www.sturgislibrary.org	Barnstable	MA	02630	508-362-6636	362-5467
Beverly Public Library 32 Essex St *Web:* www.noblenet.org	Beverly	MA	01915	978-921-6062	922-8329
Billerica Public Library 15 Concord Rd *Web:* www.billericalibrary.org	Billerica	MA	01821	978-671-0948	667-4242
Boston Public Library 700 Boylston St Copley Sq *Web:* www.bpl.org	Boston	MA	02116	617-536-5400	236-4306
New England Historic Genealogical Society 101 Newbury St *Web:* www.historicbostons.com	Boston	MA	02116	617-536-5740	
Thayer Public Library 798 Washington St *Web:* www.thayerpubliclibrary.org	Braintree	MA	02184	781-848-0405	356-5447
Brockton Public Library 304 Main St *Web:* www.brocktonpubliclibrary.org	Brockton	MA	02301	508-580-7890	580-7898
Brookline Public Library 361 Washington St *Web:* www.brooklinelibrary.com	Brookline	MA	02445	617-730-2370	730-2160
Cambridge Public Library 449 Broadway *Web:* www.cambridgema.gov/cpl	Cambridge	MA	02138	617-349-4040	
Centerville Public Library 585 Main St *Web:* www.centervillelibrary.org	Centerville	MA	02632	508-790-6220	790-6218
Chelmsford Public Library 25 Boston Rd *Web:* www.chelmsfordlibrary.org	Chelmsford	MA	01824	978-256-5521	256-8511
Chicopee Public Library 449 Front St *Web:* www.chicopeepubliclibrary.org	Chicopee	MA	01013	413-594-1800	594-1819
Dartmouth Public Libraries 732 Dartmouth St *Web:* www.dplma.org	Dartmouth	MA	02748	508-999-0726	992-9914
Moses Greeley Parker Memorial Library 28 Arlington St *Web:* www.dracutlibrary.org	Dracut	MA	01826	978-454-5474	454-9120
Parlin Memorial Library 410 Broadway *Web:* www.noblenet.org/everett	Everett	MA	02149	617-394-2300	389-1230
Millicent Library 45 Ctr St *Web:* www.millicentlibrary.org	Fairhaven	MA	02719	508-992-5342	993-7288
Fall River Public Library 104 N Main St *TF:* 800-331-3764 ■ *Web:* www.sailsinc.org	Fall River	MA	02720	508-324-2700	324-2707
Falmouth Public Library 300 Main St *Web:* www.falmouthpubliclibrary.org	Falmouth	MA	02540	508-457-2555	457-2559
Fitchburg Public Library 610 Main St *Web:* fitchburgpubliclibrary.org	Fitchburg	MA	01420	978-345-9635	345-9631
Sawyer Free Library Two Dale Ave *Web:* www.sawyerfreelibrary.org	Gloucester	MA	01930	978-281-9763	281-9770
Holmes Public Library 470 Plymouth St *Web:* holmespubliclibrary.org	Halifax	MA	02338	781-293-2271	294-8518
Haverhill Public Library 99 Main St *Web:* www.haverhillpl.org	Haverhill	MA	01830	978-373-1586	373-8466
Holyoke Public Library 335 Maple St *Web:* www.holyokelibrary.org	Holyoke	MA	01040	413-322-5640	532-4230
Hyannis Public Library (HPL) 401 Main St *Web:* www.hyannislibrary.org	Hyannis	MA	02601	508-775-2280	790-0087
Leominster Public Library 30 W St *Web:* www.leominsterlibrary.org	Leominster	MA	01453	978-534-7522	
Cary Memorial Library 1874 Massachusetts Ave *Web:* www.carylibrary.org	Lexington	MA	02420	781-862-6288	862-7355
Pollard Memorial Library 401 Merrimack St *Web:* www.pollardml.org	Lowell	MA	01852	978-970-4120	
Lynn Public Library Five N Common St *Web:* www.noblenet.org/lynn	Lynn	MA	01902	781-595-0567	592-5050
Malden Public Library 36 Salem St *Web:* www.maldenpubliclibrary.org	Malden	MA	02148	781-324-0218	324-4467
Marlborough Public Library 35 W Main St *Web:* www.marlborough-ma.gov	Marlborough	MA	01752	508-624-6900	485-1494
Ventress Memorial Library 15 Library Plz *Web:* www.ventresslibrary.org	Marshfield	MA	02050	781-834-5535	837-8362
Marstons Mills Public Library 2160 Main St *Web:* www.mmpl.org	Marstons Mills	MA	02648	508-428-5175	420-5194
Medford Public Library 111 High St *TF:* 800-392-6089 ■ *Web:* www.medfordlibrary.org	Medford	MA	02155	781-395-7950	391-2261
Melrose Public Library 69 W Emerson St *Web:* www.melrosepubliclibrary.org	Melrose	MA	02176	781-665-2313	662-4229
Milford Town Library 80 Spruce St *Web:* www.milfordtownlibrary.org	Milford	MA	01757	508-473-2145	473-8651
Milton Public Library 476 Canton Ave *Web:* www.miltonlibrary.org	Milton	MA	02186	617-698-5757	698-0441
Morse Institute Library 14 E Central St *Web:* www.morseinstitute.org	Natick	MA	01760	508-647-6520	647-6527
Needham Public Library 1139 Highland Ave *Web:* www.town.needham.ma.us	Needham	MA	02494	781-455-7559	455-7591
New Bedford Free Public Library (NBFPL) 613 Pleasant St *TF:* 877-336-2627 ■ *Web:* www.newbedford-ma.gov/library	New Bedford	MA	02740	508-991-6275	991-6368
Newton Free Library 330 Homer St *Web:* newtonfreelibrary.net	Newton Center	MA	02459	617-796-1360	965-8457
Norfolk Public Library, The 139 Main St *Web:* library.virtualnorfolk.org	Norfolk	MA	02056	508-528-3380	528-6417
Richards Memorial Library 118 N Washington St *Web:* rmlonline.org	North Attleboro	MA	02760	508-699-0122	699-0122
Forbes Library 20 W St *Web:* www.forbeslibrary.org	NorthHampton	MA	01060	413-587-1012	587-1015
Northborough Free Library 34 Main St *Web:* northboroughlibrary.org	Northborough	MA	01532	508-393-5025	393-5027
Morrill Memorial Library 33 Walpole St PO Box 220 *Web:* www.norwoodlibrary.org	Norwood	MA	02062	781-769-0200	
Osterville Free Library 43 Wianno Ave *Web:* www.ostervillefreelibrary.org	Osterville	MA	02655	508-428-5757	428-5557
Peabody Institute Library 82 Main St *Web:* www.peabodylibrary.org	Peabody	MA	01960	978-531-0100	532-1797
Berkshire Athenaeum One Wendell Ave *Web:* www.berkshire.net	Pittsfield	MA	01201	413-499-9480	499-9489
Plymouth Public Library 132 S St *Web:* plymouthpubliclibrary.org	Plymouth	MA	02360	508-830-4250	830-4258
Provincetown Public Library 356 Commercial St *Web:* provincetownlibrary.org	Provincetown	MA	02657	508-487-7094	
Thomas Crane Public Library 40 Washington St *Web:* www.thomascranelibrary.org	Quincy	MA	02169	617-376-1301	
Turner Free Library Two N Main St *Web:* turnerfreelibrary.org	Randolph	MA	02368	781-961-0932	961-0933
Revere Public Library 179 Beach St *Web:* reverepubliclibrary.org	Revere	MA	02151	781-286-8380	286-8382
Saugus Free Public Library 295 Central St *Web:* www.noblenet.org	Saugus	MA	01906	781-231-4168	231-4169
Sharon Public Library 11 N Main St *Web:* www.townofsharon.net	Sharon	MA	02067	781-784-1578	784-4728
Somerville Public Library (SPL) 79 Highland Ave *Web:* www.somervillepubliclibrary.org	Somerville	MA	02143	617-623-5000	628-4052
Bacon Free Library 58 Eliot St *Web:* baconfreelibrary.net	South Natick	MA	01760	508-653-6730	
Springfield City Library 220 State St *Web:* www.springfieldlibrary.org	Springfield	MA	01103	413-263-6828	263-6817
Stoughton Public Library 84 Pk St *Web:* stoughtonlibrary.org	Stoughton	MA	02072	781-344-2711	344-7340
Taunton Public Library 12 Pleasant St *Web:* www.tauntonlibrary.org	Taunton	MA	02780	508-821-1411	821-1414
Tewksbury Public Library 300 Chandler St *Web:* www.tewksburypl.org	Tewksbury	MA	01876	978-640-4490	
Lucius Beebe Memorial Library 345 Main St *Web:* www.wakefieldlibrary.org	Wakefield	MA	01880	781-246-6334	246-6385
Walpole Public Library 143 School St *Web:* www.walpolelibrary.org/walpolenew	Walpole	MA	02081	508-660-7340	
Waltham Public Library 735 Main St *Web:* www.waltham.lib.ma.us	Waltham	MA	02451	781-314-3425	647-5873
Watertown Free Public Library 123 Main St *TF:* 800-829-3676 ■ *Web:* www.watertownlib.org	Watertown	MA	02472	617-972-6431	926-4375
Wayland Free Public Library Five Concord Rd *Web:* www.wayland.ma.us	Wayland	MA	01778	508-358-2311	358-5249
Wellesley Free Library 530 Washington St *Web:* www.ci.wellesley.ma.us	Wellesley	MA	02482	781-235-1610	237-4875
Whelden Memorial Library 2401 Meetinghouse Way PO Box 147 *Web:* wheldenlibrary.org/	West Barnstable	MA	02668	508-362-2262	362-1344
Westfield Athenaeum Six Elm St *Web:* www.westath.org	Westfield	MA	01085	413-568-7833	568-0988
Tufts Library 46 Broad St *TF:* 888-283-3757 ■ *Web:* weymouth.ma.us	Weymouth	MA	02188	781-337-1402	682-6123
Milne Public Library 1095 Main St *Web:* www.milnelibrary.org	Williamstown	MA	01267	413-458-5369	458-3085
Woburn Public Library 45 Pleasant St *TF:* 800-392-6089 ■ *Web:* www.woburnpubliclibrary.org	Woburn	MA	01801	781-933-0148	938-7860
Woods Hole Public Library 581 Woods Hole Rd PO Box 185 *Web:* woodsholepubliclibrary.org	Woods Hole	MA	02543	508-548-8961	540-1969

Michigan

Library	City	State	ZIP	Phone	Fax
Lenawee County Library 4459 W US 223 *Web:* www.lenawee.lib.mi.us	Adrian	MI	49221	517-263-1011	
Alpena County George N Fletcher Public Library 211 N First Ave *TF:* 877-737-4106 ■ *Web:* alpenalibrary.org	Alpena	MI	49707	989-356-6188	356-2765
Ann Arbor District Library (AADL) 343 S Fifth Ave *Web:* www.aadl.org	Ann Arbor	MI	48104	734-327-4200	327-8309
Bay County Library System 500 Ctr Ave *Web:* www.baycountylibrary.org	Bay City	MI	48708	989-894-2837	894-2021
Baldwin Public Library 300 W Merrill St *Web:* www.baldwinlib.org	Birmingham	MI	48009	248-647-1700	644-7297
Bloomfield Township Public Library 1099 Lone Pine Rd *TF:* 800-318-2596 ■ *Web:* www.btpl.org	Bloomfield Hills	MI	48302	248-642-5800	642-4175
Cadillac-Wexford County Public Library 411 S Lake St *Web:* www.cadillaclibrary.org	Cadillac	MI	49601	231-775-6541	775-1749
Canton Public Library 1200 S Canton Ctr Rd *TF:* 888-988-6300 ■ *Web:* www.cantonpl.org	Canton	MI	48188	734-397-0999	397-1130
Chelsea District Library 221 S Main St *Web:* chelsea.lib.mi.us	Chelsea	MI	48118	734-475-8732	
Kent District Library 814 W River Ctr Dr NE *TF:* 877-243-2466 ■ *Web:* www.kdl.org	Comstock Park	MI	49321	616-784-2007	647-3908
Henry Ford Centennial Library 16301 Michigan Ave *Web:* dearbornlibrary.org	Dearborn	MI	48126	313-943-2330	943-3063
Detroit Public Library 5201 Woodward Ave *Web:* www.detroitpubliclibrary.org	Detroit	MI	48202	313-481-1300	832-0877
East Lansing Public Library 950 Abbott Rd *TF:* 866-861-2010 ■ *Web:* www.elpl.org	East Lansing	MI	48823	517-351-2420	351-9536
Eastpointe Memorial Library 15875 Oak St *Web:* cityofeastpointe.net	Eastpointe	MI	48021	586-445-5096	775-0150
Escanaba Public Library 400 Ludington St *TF:* 800-992-9012 ■ *Web:* www.uproc.lib.mi.us	Escanaba	MI	49829	906-786-4463	786-0942
Ferndale Public Library 222 E Nine-Mile Rd *Web:* www.ferndale.lib.mi.us	Ferndale	MI	48220	248-546-2504	545-5840
Flint Public Library 1026 E Kearsley St *Web:* fpl.info	Flint	MI	48502	810-232-7111	
Genesee District Library G-4195 W Pasadena Ave *TF:* 866-732-1120 ■ *Web:* www.thegdl.org	Flint	MI	48504	810-732-0110	732-3146
Garden City Public Library 31735 Maplewood St *Web:* www.garden-city.lib.mi.us	Garden City	MI	48135	734-793-1830	793-1831
Loutit District Library 407 Columbus St *Web:* www.loutitlibrary.org	Grand Haven	MI	49417	616-842-5560	847-0570
Grand Rapids Public Library 111 Library St NE *Web:* grpl.org	Grand Rapids	MI	49503	616-988-5400	988-5429
Dickinson County Library 401 Iron Mtn St *Web:* www.dcl-lib.org	Iron Mountain	MI	49801	906-774-1218	774-4079
Jackson District Library 244 W Michigan Ave *Web:* www.myjdl.com	Jackson	MI	49201	517-788-4087	782-8635
Georgetown Township Library 1525 Baldwin St *Web:* www.georgetown-mi.gov	Jenison	MI	49428	616-457-9620	457-3666
Kalamazoo Public Library 315 S Rose St *Web:* www.kpl.gov	Kalamazoo	MI	49007	269-342-9837	553-7921
Orion Township Public Library 825 Joslyn Rd *TF:* 877-924-7467 ■ *Web:* www.orionlibrary.org	Lake Orion	MI	48362	248-693-3000	693-3009
Capital Area District Library 401 S Capitol Ave *Web:* www.cadl.org	Lansing	MI	48933	517-367-6300	374-1068
Lapeer District Library 201 Village W Dr S *TF:* 866-746-7252 ■ *Web:* www.library.lapeer.org	Lapeer	MI	48446	810-664-9521	664-8527
Livonia Public Library 32777 Five Mile Rd *Web:* www.livonia.lib.mi.us	Livonia	MI	48154	734-466-2491	458-6011
Madison Heights Public Library 240 W 13 Mile Rd *Web:* www.madison-heights.org/departments/library	Madison Heights	MI	48071	248-588-7763	588-2470
Peter White Public Library 217 N Front St *TF:* 800-992-9012 ■ *Web:* www.uproc.lib.mi.us	Marquette	MI	49855	906-228-9510	226-1783
Grace A Dow Memorial Library 1710 W St Andrews Rd *TF:* 888-400-5530 ■ *Web:* cityofmidlandmi.gov/1208/welcome-to-our-new-website	Midland	MI	48640	989-837-3430	837-3468
Monroe County Library System 3700 S Custer Rd *TF:* 800-462-2050 ■ *Web:* www.monroe.lib.mi.us	Monroe	MI	48161	734-241-5277	241-4722
Veterans Memorial Library 301 S University Ave **Fax Area Code:* 541 ■ *TF:* 888-520-8103	Mount Pleasant	MI	48858	989-773-3242	247-4411*
Muskegon Area District Library 4845 Airline Rd *TF:* 877-569-4801 ■ *Web:* www.madl.org	Muskegon	MI	49444	231-737-6248	737-6307
Novi Public Library 45255 W 10 Mile Rd *Web:* www.novilibrary.org	Novi	MI	48375	248-349-0720	349-6520
Owosso Public Library 502 W Main St *Web:* sdl.lib.mi.us	Owosso	MI	48867	989-725-5134	723-5444
Pontiac Public Library 60 E Pike St *Web:* www.pontiac.lib.mi.us	Pontiac	MI	48342	248-758-3942	758-3990
Saint Clair County Library System 210 McMorran Blvd *TF:* 877-987-7323 ■ *Web:* www.sccl.lib.mi.us	Port Huron	MI	48060	810-987-7323	987-7874
Portage District Library 300 Library Ln *Web:* www.portagelibrary.info	Portage	MI	49002	269-329-4544	324-9222
Rochester Hills Public Library 500 Olde Towne Rd *Web:* www.rhpl.org	Rochester	MI	48307	248-656-2900	650-7131
Roseville Public Library 29777 Gratiot Ave *Web:* www.libcoop.net	Roseville	MI	48066	586-445-5407	445-5499
Royal Oak Public Library 222 E Eleven Mile Rd *Web:* ropl.org	Royal Oak	MI	48067	248-246-3700	545-6220
Public Libraries of Saginaw 505 Janes St *Web:* www.saginawlibrary.org	Saginaw	MI	48607	989-755-0904	755-9829
Shelby Township Library 51680 Van Dyke Hwy *Web:* www.shelbytwplib.org	Shelby Township	MI	48316	586-739-7414	726-0535
Southfield Public Library 26300 Evergreen Rd *Web:* www.sfldlib.org	Southfield	MI	48076	248-796-4200	796-4245
Sterling Heights Public Library 40255 Dodge Pk Rd *Web:* www.shpl.net	Sterling Heights	MI	48313	586-446-2665	276-4067
Troy Public Library 510 W Big Beaver Rd *TF:* 855-203-5274 ■ *Web:* www.libcoop.net	Troy	MI	48084	248-524-3538	524-0112
Warren Public Library 5460 Arden *Web:* www.warrenlibrary.net	Warren	MI	48092	586-751-5377	264-2811
Waterford Township Public Library 5168 Civic Ctr Dr *TF:* 800-318-2596 ■ *Web:* www.waterford.lib.mi.us	Waterford	MI	48329	248-674-4831	674-1910
West Bloomfield Township Public Library 4600 Walnut Lake Rd *Web:* www.wblib.org	West Bloomfield	MI	48323	248-682-2120	232-2333

Minnesota

Library	City	State	ZIP	Phone	Fax
Albert Lea Public Library 211 E Clark St *Web:* alplonline.org	Albert Lea	MN	56007	507-377-4350	
Anoka County Library 711 County Rd 10 *Web:* www.anoka.lib.mn.us	Blaine	MN	55434	763-717-3267	717-3259
Carver County Library 4 City Hall Plaza *Web:* www.carverlib.org	Chaska	MN	55318	952-448-9395	448-9392
Hill Museum & Manuscript Library PO Box 7300 *Web:* www.hmml.org	Collegeville	MN	56321	320-363-3514	
Duluth Public Library 520 W Superior St *Web:* www.duluth.lib.mn.us	Duluth	MN	55802	218-730-4200	723-3822
Buckham Memorial Library 11 Div St E *Web:* www.ci.faribault.mn.us	Faribault	MN	55021	507-334-2089	
Library Foundation of Hennepin County, The 300 Nicollet Mall *Web:* www.supporthclib.org	Minneapolis	MN	55401	952-847-8105	
Hennepin County Library (HCL) 12601 Ridgedale Dr **Fax Area Code:* 952 ■ *Web:* www.hclib.org	Minnetonka	MN	55305	612-543-5669	847-8600*
Lake Agassiz Regional Library (LARL) 118 Fifth St S PO Box 900 *TF:* 800-247-0449 ■ *Web:* www.larl.org	Moorhead	MN	56560	218-233-3757	233-7556
Owatonna Public Library 105 N Elm St *TF:* 800-657-3864 ■ *Web:* ci.owatonna.mn.us	Owatonna	MN	55060	507-444-2460	444-2465
Rochester Public Library 101 Second St SE *Web:* www.rochesterpubliclibrary.org	Rochester	MN	55904	507-285-8000	
Great River Regional Library 1300 W St Germain St *Web:* www.griver.org	Saint Cloud	MN	56301	320-650-2500	650-2501
Saint Paul Public Library 90 W Fourth St *TF:* 888-335-9632 ■ *Web:* www.sppl.org	Saint Paul	MN	55102	651-266-7000	266-7060
Scott County Library System 13090 Alabama Ave S *TF:* 877-772-8346 ■ *Web:* www.scott.lib.mn.us	Savage	MN	55378	952-707-1770	707-1775
Ramsey County Public Library 4570 N Victoria St *TF:* 888-335-9632 ■ *Web:* www.rclreads.org	Shoreview	MN	55126	651-486-2200	486-2220
Pioneerland Library System 410 SW Fifth St *Web:* www.pioneerland.lib.mn.us	Willmar	MN	56201	320-235-6106	214-0187
Winona Public Library 151 W Fifth St PO Box 1247 *Web:* www.selco.lib.mn.us	Winona	MN	55987	507-452-4582	452-5842
Washington County Library 8595 Central Pk Pl *TF:* 800-657-3750 ■ *Web:* www.co.washington.mn.us	Woodbury	MN	55125	651-275-8500	275-8509

Mississippi

Library	City	State	ZIP	Phone	Fax
Hancock County Library 312 Hwy 90 *Web:* hancocklibraries.info/	Bay Saint Louis	MS	39520	228-467-5282	467-5503
Bolivar County Library 104 S Leflore Ave *TF:* 888-268-8076 ■ *Web:* www.bolivar.lib.ms.us	Cleveland	MS	38732	662-843-2774	843-4701
Columbus-Lowndes County Library 314 N Seventh St *Web:* www.lowndes.lib.ms.us	Columbus	MS	39701	662-329-5300	329-5156
Greenwood-Leflore Public Library 405 W Washington St *Web:* glpls.com	Greenwood	MS	38930	662-453-3634	453-0683
Library of Hattiesburg Petal & Forrest County 329 Hardy St *Web:* hattlibrary.com	Hattiesburg	MS	39401	601-582-4461	
First Regional Library 370 W Commerce St *TF:* 800-446-0892 ■ *Web:* firstregional.org	Hernando	MS	38632	662-429-4439	429-8853
Marshall County Library 109 E Gholson Ave *Web:* www.marshall.lib.ms.us	Holly Springs	MS	38635	662-252-3823	252-3066
Eudora Welty Library, The 300 N State St *TF:* 800-968-5803 ■ *Web:* www.jhlibrary.com	Jackson	MS	39201	601-968-5811	968-5817

Library	City	State	ZIP	Phone	Fax
Laurel-Jones County Library 530 Commerce St *Web:* www.laurel.lib.ms.us	Laurel	MS	39440	601-428-4313	428-4314
Meridian-Lauderdale County Public Library 2517 Seventh St *TF:* 800-318-2596 ■ *Web:* www.meridian.lib.ms.us	Meridian	MS	39301	601-693-6771	486-2260
Jackson-George Regional Library System 3214 S Pascagoula St *Web:* www.jgrls.org	Pascagoula	MS	39567	228-769-3060	769-3113
Pearl River County Library System 900 Goodyear Blvd *Web:* www.pearlriver.lib.ms.us	Picayune	MS	39466	601-798-5081	798-5082
Starkville Public Library 326 University Dr *Web:* www.starkville.lib.ms.us	Starkville	MS	39759	662-323-2766	323-9140
Warren County-Vicksburg Public Library 700 Veto St *TF:* 800-721-7222 ■ *Web:* www.warren.lib.ms.us	Vicksburg	MS	39180	601-636-6411	634-4809

Missouri

Library	City	State	ZIP	Phone	Fax
Bowling Green Public Library 201 W Locust St *Web:* www.bgmopl.org	Bowling Green	MO	63334	573-324-5030	324-6367
Camden County Library District 89 Rodeo Rd PO Box 1320 *Web:* www.ccld.us	Camdenton	MO	65020	573-346-5954	346-1263
Cape Girardeau Public Library 711 N Clark St *Web:* www.capelibrary.org	Cape Girardeau	MO	63701	573-334-5279	334-8334
Daniel Boone Regional Library 100 W Broadway *TF:* 800-324-4806 ■ *Web:* www.dbrl.org	Columbia	MO	65203	573-443-3161	443-3281
Cass County Public Library 400 E Mechanic St *Web:* www.casscolibrary.org	Harrisonville	MO	64701	816-380-4600	884-2301
Mid-Continent Public Library 15616 E 24 Hwy *TF:* 800-318-2596 ■ *Web:* www.mymcpl.org	Independence	MO	64050	816-836-5200	521-7253
Missouri River Regional Library 214 Adams St *TF:* 800-949-7323 ■ *Web:* www.mrrl.org	Jefferson City	MO	65101	573-634-2464	634-7028
Joplin Public Library 300 S Main St *Web:* www.joplinpubliclibrary.org	Joplin	MO	64801	417-623-7953	624-5217
ALFA International 2400 Pershing Rd Ste 500 *Web:* www.alfainternational.com	Kansas City	MO	64108	816-471-2121	
Kansas City Public Library, The (KCPL) 14 W Tenth St *Web:* www.kclibrary.org	Kansas City	MO	64105	816-701-3400	701-3401
Linda Hall Library 5109 Cherry St *TF:* 800-662-1545 ■ *Web:* www.lindahall.org	Kansas City	MO	64110	816-363-4600	926-8790
Kirkwood Public Library 140 E Jefferson Ave *Web:* www.kirkwoodpubliclibrary.org	Kirkwood	MO	63122	314-821-5770	822-3755
Christian County Library 1005 N Fourth Ave *Web:* www.christiancounty.lib.mo.us	Ozark	MO	65721	417-581-2432	581-8855
Saint Louis County Library (SLCL) 1640 S Lindbergh Blvd *Web:* www.slcl.org	Saint Louis	MO	63131	314-994-3300	997-7602
Saint Louis Public Library (SLPL) 1301 Olive St *Web:* www.slpl.org	Saint Louis	MO	63103	314-241-2288	539-0393
St Louis Public Library 4234 N Grand Blvd *Web:* www.slpl.lib.mo.us	Saint Louis	MO	63107	314-534-0313	
Saint Charles City County Library District 77 Boone Hill Dr	Saint Peters	MO	63376	636-441-2300	
Rolling Hills Consolidated Library 1904 N Belt Hwy *Web:* rhcl.org	St Joseph	MO	64506	816-236-2106	
University City Public Library 6701 Delmar Blvd *Web:* www.ucpl.lib.mo.us	University City	MO	63130	314-727-3150	727-6005

Montana

Library	City	State	ZIP	Phone	Fax
Parmly Billings Library 510 N Broadway *Web:* www.ci.billings.mt.us	Billings	MT	59101	406-657-8258	657-8293
Bozeman Public Library 626 E Main St *Web:* www.bozemanlibrary.org	Bozeman	MT	59715	406-582-2400	582-2424
Butte-Silver Bow Public Library 226 W Broadway *Web:* www.buttepubliclibrary.info	Butte	MT	59701	406-723-3361	
Great Falls Public Library 301 Second Ave N *Web:* www.greatfallslibrary.org	Great Falls	MT	59401	406-453-0349	453-0181
Lewis & Clark Library 120 S Last Chance Gulch *TF:* 800-733-2767 ■ *Web:* www.lewisandclarklibrary.org	Helena	MT	59601	406-447-1690	447-1687
Missoula Public Library 301 E Main St *Web:* www.missoula.lib.mt.us	Missoula	MT	59802	406-721-2665	728-5900

Nebraska

Library	City	State	ZIP	Phone	Fax
Bellevue Public Library 1003 Lincoln Rd *Web:* bellevuelibrary.org	Bellevue	NE	68005	402-293-3157	293-3163
Edith Abbott Memorial Library 211 N Washington St *Web:* www.grand-island.com	Grand Island	NE	68801	308-385-5333	385-5339
Hastings Public Library 517 W Fourth St *TF:* 800-318-2596 ■ *Web:* www.hastings.lib.ne.us	Hastings	NE	68901	402-461-2346	461-2359
Kearney Public Library & Information Ctr 2020 First Ave *Web:* www.cityofkearney.org	Kearney	NE	68847	308-233-3282	233-3291
Lincoln City Libraries 136 S 14th St *Web:* www.lincolnlibraries.org	Lincoln	NE	68508	402-441-8500	441-8586
North Platte Public Library 120 W Fourth St *Web:* ci.north-platte.ne.us	North Platte	NE	69101	308-535-8036	535-8296
Omaha Public Library 215 S 15th St *Web:* www.omaha.lib.ne.us	Omaha	NE	68102	402-444-4800	444-4504

Nevada

Library	City	State	ZIP	Phone	Fax
Carson City Library 900 N Roop St *Web:* carsoncitylibrary.org	Carson City	NV	89701	775-887-2244	887-2273
Douglas County Library 1625 Library Ln *Web:* douglas.lib.nv.us	Minden	NV	89423	775-782-9841	782-5754
Washoe County Library (WCL) 301 S Ctr St *Web:* www.washoecounty.us/library	Reno	NV	89501	775-327-8300	327-8341

New Hampshire

Library	City	State	ZIP	Phone	Fax
Amherst Town Library 14 Main St *Web:* www.amherstlibrary.org	Amherst	NH	03031	603-673-2288	672-6063
Concord Public Library 45 Green St *Web:* www.concordnh.gov	Concord	NH	03301	603-225-8670	230-3693
Derry Public Library 64 E Broadway *Web:* www.derry.lib.nh.us	Derry	NH	03038	603-432-6140	432-6128
Dover Public Library 73 Locust St *Web:* www.dover.lib.nh.us	Dover	NH	03820	603-516-6050	516-6053
Howe Library 13 S St *Web:* www.thehowe.org	Hanover	NH	03755	603-643-4120	643-0725
Hollis Social Library Two Monument Sq *Web:* hollislibrary.org	Hollis	NH	03049	603-465-7721	465-3507
Manchester City Library 405 Pine St *Web:* www.manchesternh.gov	Manchester	NH	03104	603-624-6550	624-6559
Nashua Public Library Two Ct St *Web:* www.nashualibrary.org	Nashua	NH	03060	603-589-4600	594-3457
Wing Group LLC 20 Trafalgar Sq Ste 455 *Web:* www.wing-group.com	Nashua	NH	03063	603-589-4076	
Kelley Library 234 Main St *Web:* www.kelleylibrary.org	Salem	NH	03079	603-898-7064	898-8583

New Jersey

Library	City	State	ZIP	Phone	Fax
Atlantic City Free Public Library 1 N Tennessee Ave *TF:* 800-621-3362 ■ *Web:* acfpl.org	Atlantic City	NJ	08401	609-345-2269	345-5570
Bayonne Free Public Library 697 Ave C *Web:* www.bayonnenj.org	Bayonne	NJ	07002	201-858-6970	437-6928
Dillon Clarence Public Library 2336 Lamington Rd *Web:* www.clarencedillonpl.org	Bedminster	NJ	07921	908-234-2325	
Warren County Library 199 Hardwick St *Web:* warrenlib.com	Belvidere	NJ	07823	908-475-6322	
Bloomfield Public Library 90 Broad St *Web:* bplnj.org	Bloomfield	NJ	07003	973-566-6200	566-6217
Cumberland County Library 800 E Commerce St *Web:* www.clueslibs.org	Bridgeton	NJ	08302	856-453-2210	451-1940
Somerset County Library 1 Vogt Dr *TF:* 888-313-3532 ■ *Web:* www.somerset.lib.nj.us	Bridgewater	NJ	08807	908-526-4016	526-5221
Cape May County Library (CMCL) 30 Mechanic St *Web:* www.cmclibrary.org	Cape May Court House	NJ	08210	609-463-6350	465-3895
Clark Public Library 303 Westfield Ave *Web:* www.youseemore.com	Clark	NJ	07066	732-388-5999	388-7866
Clifton Public Library 292 Piaget Ave *Web:* www.cliftonpl.org	Clifton	NJ	07011	973-772-5500	772-2926
East Brunswick Public Library 2 Jean Walling Civic Ctr *TF:* 800-829-1040 ■ *Web:* www.ebpl.org	East Brunswick	NJ	08816	732-390-6950	390-6869
East Orange Public Library 21 S Arlington Ave *Web:* www.eopl.org	East Orange	NJ	07018	973-266-5600	674-1991
Edison Township Free Public Library 340 Plainfield Ave *Web:* www.edisonpubliclibrary.net	Edison	NJ	08817	732-287-2298	819-9134
Elizabeth Public Library 11 S Broad St *Web:* www.elizpl.org	Elizabeth	NJ	07202	908-354-6060	354-5845
Englewood Public Library 31 Engle St *Web:* www.englewoodlibrary.org	Englewood	NJ	07631	201-568-2215	568-6895
Maurice M Pine Free Public Library 10-01 Fair Lawn Ave *Web:* www.bccls.org/fairlawn	Fair Lawn	NJ	07410	201-796-3400	
Hunterdon County Library 314 State Hwy 12 Bldg Ste 3 *Web:* www.hclibrary.us	Flemington	NJ	08822	908-788-1444	806-4862
Fort Lee Free Public Library 320 Main St *Web:* www.bccls.org	Fort Lee	NJ	07024	201-592-3614	585-0375
Garfield Free Public Library 500 Midland Ave *Web:* www.bccls.org	Garfield	NJ	07026	973-478-3800	478-7162
Johnson Public Library 274 Main St *Web:* www.bccls.org	Hackensack	NJ	07601	201-343-4169	343-1395
Hoboken Public Library (HPL) 500 Pk Ave *Web:* hobokenfol.org	Hoboken	NJ	07030	201-420-2346	

Library	City	State	ZIP	Phone	Fax
Irvington Public Library Five Civic Sq. *Web:* www.irvingtonpubliclibrary.org	Irvington	NJ	07111	973-372-6400	372-6860
Jersey City Free Public Library 472 Jersey Ave *Web:* jclibrary.org	Jersey City	NJ	07302	201-547-4501	547-4584
Kearny Public Library 318 Kearny Ave *Web:* www.kearnylibrary.org	Kearny	NJ	07032	201-998-2666	998-1141
Mercer County Library System (MCL) 2751 Brunswick Pk *Web:* www.mcl.org	Lawrenceville	NJ	08648	609-882-9246	
Linden Public Library 31 E Henry St. *Web:* www2.youseemore.com/lindenfreepl/default.asp	Linden	NJ	07036	908-298-3830	486-2636
Livingston Public Library 10 Robert H Harp Dr *Web:* livingston.bccls.org	Livingston	NJ	07039	973-992-4600	994-2346
Long Branch Free Public Library 328 Broadway *Web:* www.lmxac.org/longbranch	Long Branch	NJ	07740	732-222-3900	222-3799
Monmouth County Library (MCL) 125 Symmes Rd *Web:* www.monmouthcountylib.org	Manalapan	NJ	07726	732-431-7220	409-2556
Atlantic County Library-Mays Landing 40 Farragut Ave. *Web:* www.atlanticlibrary.org	Mays Landing	NJ	08330	609-646-8699	625-8143
Middletown Township Library 55 New Monmouth Rd *Web:* www.mtpl.org	Middletown	NJ	07748	732-671-3700	671-5839
South Brunswick Public Library 110 Kingston Ln *Web:* www.lmxac.org	Monmouth Junction	NJ	08852	732-329-4000	842-4191
Mount Arlington Public Library 333 Howard Blvd *Web:* mountarlingtonlibrary.org	Mount Arlington	NJ	07856	973-398-1516	
Burlington County Library Five Pioneer Blvd *Web:* www.bcls.lib.nj.us	Mount Holly	NJ	08060	609-267-9660	267-4091
Mount Laurel Library 100 Walt Whitman Ave *TF:* 888-576-5529 ■ *Web:* www.mtlaurel.lib.nj.us	Mount Laurel	NJ	08054	856-234-7319	234-6916
Gloucester County Library System 389 Wolfert Stn Rd *Web:* www.gcls.org	Mullica Hill	NJ	08062	856-223-6000	223-6039
Neptune Public Library 25 Neptune Blvd *Web:* www.neptunepubliclibrary.org	Neptune	NJ	07753	732-775-8241	774-1132
New Brunswick Free Public Library 60 Livingston Ave *Web:* www.lmxac.org	New Brunswick	NJ	08901	732-745-5108	846-0226
Newark Public Library Five Washington St *Web:* www.npl.org	Newark	NJ	07101	973-733-7784	733-5919
Sussex County Library 125 Morris Tpke. *TF:* 800-318-2596 ■ *Web:* www.sussexcountylibrary.org	Newton	NJ	07860	973-948-3660	948-2071
North Bergen Free Public Library 8411 Bergenline Ave. *Web:* nbpl.org	North Bergen	NJ	07047	201-869-4715	868-0968
North Brunswick Public Library 880 Hermann Rd. *Web:* northbrunswicklibrary.org	North Brunswick	NJ	08902	732-246-3545	246-1341
Nutley Free Public Library 93 Booth Dr *Web:* www.bccls.org	Nutley	NJ	07110	973-667-0405	667-4673
Ocean City Public Library 1735 Simpson Ave Ste 4 *Web:* oceancitylibrary.org	Ocean City	NJ	08226	609-399-2434	398-8944
Old Bridge Public Library One Old Bridge Plz *TF:* 800-829-1040 ■ *Web:* www.oldbridgelibrary.org	Old Bridge	NJ	08857	732-721-5600	607-4816
Orange Public Library 348 Main St *Web:* www.orangepl.org	Orange	NJ	07050	973-673-0153	673-1847
Sayreville Free Public Library 1050 Washington Rd *Web:* www.lmxac.org	Parlin	NJ	08859	732-727-0212	553-0776
Parsippany-Troy Hills Public Library 449 Halsey Rd *Web:* www.parsippanylibrary.org	Parsippany	NJ	07054	973-887-5150	887-5150
Paterson Free Public Library 250 Broadway *Web:* www.patersonpl.org	Paterson	NJ	07501	973-321-1223	321-1205
Pennsauken Free Public Library 5605 N Crescent Blvd. *Web:* www.pennsaukenlibrary.org	Pennsauken	NJ	08110	856-665-5959	486-0142
Perth Amboy Public Library 196 Jefferson St *Web:* ci.perthamboy.nj.us	Perth Amboy	NJ	08861	732-826-2600	324-8079
John F Kennedy Library 500 Hoes Ln. *Web:* piscatawaylibrary.org	Piscataway	NJ	08854	732-463-1633	463-9022
Plainfield Public Library 800 Pk Ave. *Web:* www.plainfieldlibrary.info	Plainfield	NJ	07060	908-757-1111	754-0063
Rahway Public Library Two City Hall Plz *Web:* www.rahwaylibrary.org	Rahway	NJ	07065	732-340-1551	340-0393
Margaret E Heggan Public Library 606 Delsea Dr. *Web:* www.hegganlibrary.org	Sewell	NJ	08080	856-589-3334	582-2042
Franklin Township Public Library 485 DeMott Ln *Web:* www.franklintwp.org	Somerset	NJ	08873	732-873-8700	873-0746
Teaneck Public Library 840 Teaneck Rd *TF:* 800-245-1377 ■ *Web:* www.teaneck.org	Teaneck	NJ	07666	201-837-4171	837-0410
Ocean County Library 101 Washington St *Web:* theoceancountylibrary.org	Toms River	NJ	08753	732-349-6200	473-1356
Trenton Public Library 120 Academy St. *Web:* www.trentonlib.org	Trenton	NJ	08608	609-392-7188	695-8631
Union Township Public Library 1980 Morris Ave *Web:* www.uplnj.org	Union	NJ	07083	908-851-5450	851-4671
Union City Public Library 324 43rd St. *Web:* uclibrary.org	Union City	NJ	07087	201-866-7500	866-0962
Vineland Public Library 1058 E Landis Ave. *Web:* www.vineland.lib.nj.us	Vineland	NJ	08360	856-794-4244	
Camden County Library 203 Laurel Rd *TF:* 877-222-3737 ■ *Web:* www.camdencountylibrary.org	Voorhees	NJ	08043	856-772-1636	772-6105
Wayne Public Library 461 Valley Rd. *Web:* www.waynepubliclibrary.org	Wayne	NJ	07470	973-694-4272	692-0637
West Milford Township Library 1490 Union Vly Rd *Web:* www.wmtl.org	West Milford	NJ	07480	973-728-2820	728-2106
West New York Public Library 425 60th St. *Web:* wnypl.org	West New York	NJ	07093	201-295-5135	662-1473
West Orange Public Library 46 Mt Pleasant Ave. *TF:* 800-345-7587 ■ *Web:* www.wopl.lib.nj.us	West Orange	NJ	07052	973-736-0198	733-7240
Westfield Memorial Library 550 E Broad St *Web:* www.wmlnj.org	Westfield	NJ	07090	908-789-4090	789-0921
Morris County Library (MCL) 30 E Hanover Ave *Web:* www.gti.net/mocolib1	Whippany	NJ	07981	973-285-6930	
Monroe Township Free Public Library 713 Marsha Ave *Web:* www.monroetpl.org	Williamstown	NJ	08094	856-629-1212	875-0191
Willingboro Public Library 220 Willingboro Pkwy *TF:* 866-321-9571 ■ *Web:* www.willingboro.org	Willingboro	NJ	08046	609-877-6668	835-1699
Woodbridge Public Library George Frederick Plz. *Web:* www.woodbridge.lib.nj.us	Woodbridge	NJ	07095	732-634-4450	

New Mexico

Library	City	State	ZIP	Phone	Fax
Rio Grande Valley Library System 501 Copper Ave NW *Web:* abclibrary.org	Albuquerque	NM	87102	505-768-5170	768-5191
Marshall Memorial Library 110 S Diamond Ave.	Deming	NM	88030	575-546-9202	
Farmington Public Library 2101 Farmington Ave *Web:* infoway.org	Farmington	NM	87401	505-599-1270	599-1257
Hobbs Public Library 509 N Shipp St **Fax Area Code:* 505 ■ *Web:* www.hobbspubliclibrary.org	Hobbs	NM	88240	575-397-9328	397-1508*
Thomas Branigan Memorial Library 200 E Picacho Ave *Web:* www.las-cruces.org	Las Cruces	NM	88001	575-528-4000	528-4030
Santa Fe Public Library 145 Washington Ave *Web:* www.santafelibrary.org	Santa Fe	NM	87501	505-955-6780	955-6676

New York

Library	City	State	ZIP	Phone	Fax
Albany Public Library (APL) 161 Washington Ave. *TF:* 800-733-2767 ■ *Web:* www.albanypubliclibrary.org	Albany	NY	12210	518-427-4300	449-3386
Amherst Public Library 350 John James Audubon Pkwy. *Web:* buffalolib.org	Amherst	NY	14228	716-689-4922	689-6116
Baldwinsville Public Library 33 E Genesee St *Web:* www.bville.lib.ny.us	Baldwinsville	NY	13027	315-635-5631	635-6760
Suffolk Co-op Library System 627 N Sunrise Service Rd PO Box 9000 *Web:* portal.suffolklibrarysystem.org/	Bellport	NY	11713	631-286-1600	286-1647
Brentwood Public Library (BPL) 34 Second Ave *Web:* brentwoodnylibrary.org	Brentwood	NY	11717	631-273-7883	273-7896
Bronx Library Ctr 310 E Kings Bridge Rd. **Fax Area Code:* 646 ■ *TF:* 800-342-3688	Bronx	NY	10458	718-579-4244	312-4781*
Brooklyn Public Library (BPL) 496 Franklin Ave. *Web:* bklynlibrary.org/	Brooklyn	NY	11238	718-623-0012	230-2097
Buffalo & Erie County Public Library One Lafayette Sq. *Web:* www.buffalolib.org	Buffalo	NY	14203	716-858-8900	858-6211
Middle Country Public Library 101 Eastwood Blvd *Web:* middlecountrypubliclibrary.org	Centereach	NY	11720	631-585-9393	
Reinstein Public Library 2580 Harlem Rd. *Web:* buffalolib.org	Cheektowaga	NY	14225	716-892-8089	
Half Hollow Hills Community Library 55 Vanderbilt Pkwy. *Web:* hhhlibrary.org	Dix Hills	NY	11746	631-421-4530	
East Meadow Public Library Front St & E Meadow Ave. *Web:* eastmeadow.info	East Meadow	NY	11554	516-794-2570	
East Rochester Public Library 111 W Elm St *Web:* www.libraryweb.org	East Rochester	NY	14445	585-586-8302	
Steele Memorial Library 101 E Church St. *Web:* www.steele.lib.ny.us	Elmira	NY	14901	607-733-9173	733-9176
Fayetteville Free Library Inc 300 Orchard St *Web:* fflib.org	Fayetteville	NY	13066	315-637-6374	
Franklin Square Public Library, The 19 Lincoln Rd. *Web:* franklinsquarepl.org	Franklin Square	NY	11010	516-488-3444	
Crandall Public Library 251 Glen St *Web:* www.crandalllibrary.org	Glens Falls	NY	12801	518-792-6508	
Greece Public Library Two Vince Tofany Blvd *Web:* greecepubliclibrary.org	Greece	NY	14612	585-225-8951	
Hamburg Public Library 102 Buffalo St *Web:* buffalolib.org	Hamburg	NY	14075	716-649-4415	649-4160
Hempstead Public Library 115 Nichols Ct *Web:* www.nassaulibrary.org	Hempstead	NY	11550	516-481-6990	481-6719
Islip Public Library 71 Monell Ave *Web:* www.islipliibrary.org	Islip	NY	11751	631-581-5933	

Phone | Fax

Cornell University School of Hotel Administration
Cornell University School of Hotel Aministration .... Ithaca NY 14853 607-255-8702
Web: www.hotelschool.cornell.edu

Finger Lakes Library System 119 E Green St .... Ithaca NY 14850 607-273-4074 273-3618
TF: 800-909-3557 ■ *Web:* www.flls.org

Tompkins County Public Library 101 E Green St .... Ithaca NY 14850 607-272-4557 272-8111
TF: 800-772-7267 ■ *Web:* www.tcpl.org

Queens Borough Public Library
89-11 Merrick Blvd. .... Jamaica NY 11432 718-990-0700 658-2919*
**Fax:* Hum Res ■ *Web:* www.queenslibrary.org

Chautauqua-Cattaraugus Library System
106 W Fifth St. .... Jamestown NY 14701 716-484-7135 483-6880
Web: www.cclslib.org

Town of Tonawanda Public Library Kenmore Branch
160 Delaware Rd. .... Kenmore NY 14217 716-873-2842 873-8416
Web: www.buffalolib.org

William K Sanford Town Library
629 Albany Shaker Rd .... Loudonville NY 12211 518-458-9274 438-0988
Web: www.colonie.org

Ramapo Catskill Library System
619 Rt 17-M .... Middletown NY 10940 845-343-1131
TF: 800-327-7343 ■ *Web:* www.rcls.org

Hendrick Hudson Free Library
185 Kings Ferry Rd. .... Montrose NY 10548 914-739-5654
Web: www.westchesterlibraries.org

Mount Vernon Public Library
28 S First Ave .... Mount Vernon NY 10550 914-668-1840 668-1018
Web: mountvernonpubliclibrary.org

Medical Lette, The 1000 Main St. .... New Rochelle NY 10801 914-235-0500
Web: www.medletter.com

Film Movement LLC 109 W 27th St Rm 9b .... New York NY 10001 212-941-7744
Web: www.filmmovement.com

Jump Film Editing 625 Broadway 8th Fl .... New York NY 10012 212-228-7474
Web: www.nycjump.com

New York Public Library 5th Ave & 42nd St. .... New York NY 10018 917-275-6975
Web: www.nypl.org

Saturn Production Inc 305 E 86th St .... New York NY 10028 212-348-7300
Web: www.iperceptions.com

Niagara Falls Public Library
1425 Main St .... Niagara Falls NY 14305 716-286-4894 286-4885
Web: www.niagarafallspubliclib.org

Patchogue-Medford Library
54-60 E Main St Ste 60 .... Patchogue NY 11772 631-654-4700
Web: www.pmlib.org

Clinton-Essex-Franklin Library System
33 Oak St .... Plattsburgh NY 12901 518-563-5190 563-0421
Web: www.cefls.org

Mount Pleasant Public Library NY
350 Bedford Rd. .... Pleasantville NY 10570 914-769-0548
Web: www.mountpleasantlibrary.org

Northern New York Library Network
6721 Us Hwy 11 .... Potsdam NY 13676 315-265-1119
Web: nnyln.org

Mid-Hudson Library System 103 Market St ...... Poughkeepsie NY 12601 845-471-6060 454-5940
Web: www.midhudson.org

Brighton Memorial Library 2300 Elmwood Ave ...... Rochester NY 14618 585-784-5300 784-5333
Web: www.brightonlibrary.org

Central Library of Rochester & Monroe County
115 S Ave .... Rochester NY 14604 585-428-7300 428-8353
Web: www.rochester.lib.ny.us/central

Chili Public Library 3333 Chili Ave .... Rochester NY 14624 585-889-2200 889-5819
Web: www.libraryweb.org/chili

Gates Public Library 1605 Buffalo Rd. .... Rochester NY 14624 585-247-6446 426-5733
Web: www.gateslibrary.org

Henrietta Public Library 455 Calkins Rd. .... Rochester NY 14623 585-359-7092 334-6369
Web: www.hpl.org

Irondequoit Public Library 45 Cooper Rd. .... Rochester NY 14617 585-336-6062 336-6066
Web: www.libraryweb.org/irondequoit

Southern Adirondack Library System
22 Whitney Pl .... Saratoga Springs NY 12866 518-584-7300
Web: www.sals.edu

Mohawk Valley Library System
858 Duanesburg Rd .... Schenectady NY 12306 518-355-2010
Web: www.mvls.info

Schenectady County Public Library System
99 Clinton St .... Schenectady NY 12305 518-388-4500 386-2241
Web: www.scpl.org

Mastics-moriches-shirley Community Library
407 William Floyd Pkwy. .... Shirley NY 11967 631-399-1511
Web: www.communitylibrary.org

John C Hart Memorial Library
1130 E Main St. .... Shrub Oak NY 10588 914-245-5262 245-5936
Web: yorktownlibrary.org

Saint George Library Ctr 5 Central Ave .... Staten Island NY 10301 718-442-8560 312-4781*
**Fax Area Code:* 646 ■ *TF:* 800-342-3688

Onondaga County Public Library
447 S Salina St. .... Syracuse NY 13202 315-435-1900
Web: www.onlib.org

Nassau Library System 900 Jerusalem Ave .... Uniondale NY 11553 516-292-8920 481-4777
TF: 800-662-1220 ■ *Web:* www.nassaulibrary.org

Mid-York Library System 1600 Lincoln Ave .... Utica NY 13502 315-735-8328 735-0943
Web: myls.ent.sirsi.net

Henry Waldinger Memorial Library
60 Verona Pl .... Valley Stream NY 11582 516-825-6422 825-6551
Web: www.nassaulibrary.org

Four County Library System 304 Clubhouse Rd .... Vestal NY 13850 607-723-8236 723-1722
Web: www.4cls.org

Vestal Public Library 320 Vestal Pkwy E .... Vestal NY 13850 607-754-4244 754-7936
Web: www.4cls.org

Flower Memorial Library 229 Washington St .... Watertown NY 13601 315-785-7705 788-2584

North Country Library System 22072 CR 190. .... Watertown NY 13601 315-782-5540 782-6883
Web: ncls.northcountrylibraries.org

Webster Public Library
980 Ridge Rd ; Webster Plz. .... Webster NY 14580 585-872-7075 872-7073
Web: www.websterlibrary.org

West Islip Public Library 3 Higbie Ln .... West Islip NY 11795 631-661-7080 661-7137
TF: 866-833-1122 ■ *Web:* www.wipublib.org

West Seneca Public Library 1300 Union Rd .... West Seneca NY 14224 716-674-2928
Web: buffalolib.org

White Plains Public Library
100 Martine Ave .... White Plains NY 10601 914-422-1400 422-1462
TF: 877-772-8346 ■ *Web:* whiteplainslibrary.org

Yonkers Public Library One Larkin Ctr. .... Yonkers NY 10701 914-337-1500 376-3676
Web: www.ypl.org

North Carolina

Phone | Fax

Randolph Public Library 201 Worth St .... Asheboro NC 27203 336-318-6800 318-6823
Web: www.randolphlibrary.org

Asheville-Buncombe Library System
67 Haywood St .... Asheville NC 28801 828-250-4746 255-5213
Web: www.buncombecounty.org/governing/depts/library

Transylvania County Library (TCL)
212 S Gaston St .... Brevard NC 28712 828-884-3151
Web: library.transylvaniacounty.org

Fontana Regional Library 33 Fryemont Rd .... Bryson City NC 28713 828-488-2382
Web: www.fontanalib.org

Pender County Public Library
103 S Cowan St PO Box 879 .... Burgaw NC 28425 910-259-1234
Web: youseemore.com

May Memorial Library 342 S Spring St .... Burlington NC 27215 336-229-3588 229-3592
Web: www.alamancelibraries.org

Chapel Hill Public Library
100 Library Dr .... Chapel Hill NC 27514 919-968-2780 968-2838
Web: chapelhillpubliclibrary.org

Charlotte Mecklenburg Library
310 N Tryon St .... Charlotte NC 28202 704-416-0100
Web: cmlibrary.org/

J C Holliday Library 217 Graham St. .... Clinton NC 28328 910-592-4153
Web: www.iis.net/

Durham County Library 300 N Roxboro St. .... Durham NC 27701 919-560-0100 560-0106
Web: www.durhamcountylibrary.org

Rockingham County Public Library 527 Boone Rd. .... Eden NC 27288 336-627-1106 623-1258
Web: www.rcpl.org

Cumberland County Public Library
300 Maiden Ln .... Fayetteville NC 28301 910-483-1580 486-5372
TF: 866-488-7386 ■ *Web:* www.cumberland.lib.nc.us

Gaston County Public Library
1555 E Garrison Blvd .... Gastonia NC 28054 704-868-2164 853-0609
TF: 888-241-3115 ■ *Web:* gastonlibrary.org

Greensboro Public Library 219 N Church St .... Greensboro NC 27401 336-373-2471 333-6781
Web: www.greensboro-nc.gov

Halifax County Library System PO Box 97 .... Halifax NC 27839 252-583-3631 583-8661
Web: www.halifaxnc.libguides.com

H. Leslie Perry Memorial Library
205 Breckenridge St .... Henderson NC 27536 252-438-3316 438-3744
Web: www.perrylibrary.org

Henderson County Public Library
301 N Washington St .... Hendersonville NC 28739 828-697-4725 692-8449
TF: 866-866-2362 ■ *Web:* www.henderson.lib.nc.us

High Point Public Library (HPPL)
901 N Main St .... High Point NC 27262 336-883-3660 883-3636
TF: 877-772-8346 ■ *Web:* www.highpointpubliclibrary.com

Onslow County Public Library
58 Doris Ave E .... Jacksonville NC 28540 910-455-7350 455-1661
TF: 800-351-1697 ■ *Web:* www.onslowcountync.gov/Library

Duplin County Library 107 Bowdens Rd .... Kenansville NC 28349 910-296-2117 296-2172
Web: library.duplincounty.org

Caldwell County Public Library
120 Hospital Ave. .... Lenoir NC 28645 828-757-1270 757-1413
Web: www.ccpl.us

Harnett County Public Library PO Box 1149 .... Lillington NC 27546 910-893-3446 893-3001
Web: www.harnett.org/library

Franklin County Library 906 N Main St. .... Louisburg NC 27549 919-496-2111 496-1339
Web: fcnclibrary.wordpress.com

McDowell County Public Library 90 W Ct St. .... Marion NC 28752 828-652-3858 652-2098
Web: www.main.nc.us

McDowell County Schools 334 S Main St. .... Marion NC 28752 828-652-4535
Web: www.mcdowell.k12.nc.us

Davie County Public Library 371 N Main St .... Mocksville NC 27028 336-753-6030 751-1370
Web: www.daviecountync.gov

Union County Public Library 316 E Windsor St. .... Monroe NC 28112 704-283-8184 282-0657
Web: www.union.lib.nc.us

Burke County Public Library 204 S King St .... Morganton NC 28655 828-437-5638 433-1914
Web: www.bcpls.org

New Bern-Craven County Public Library
400 Johnson St .... New Bern NC 28560 252-638-7800 638-7817
Web: newbern.cpclib.org

Catawba County Library 115 W C St. .... Newton NC 28658 828-465-8664 465-8293
Web: www.catawbacountync.gov/library

Richard H Thornton Public Library 210 Main St .... Oxford NC 27565 919-693-1121 693-2244
Web: www.granville.lib.nc.us

Wake County Public Library System
4020 Carya Dr .... Raleigh NC 27610 919-250-1200 250-1209
Web: www.wakegov.com

Sandhill Regional Library System
412 E Franklin St .... Rockingham NC 28379 910-997-3388
Web: www.ncmail.net

Rowan Public Library PO Box 4039 .... Salisbury NC 28145 704-216-8243 638-3002
Web: www.rowancountync.gov

Brunswick County Library 109 W Moore St .... Southport NC 28461 910-457-6237 457-6977
Web: library.brunsco.net

Library	City	State	ZIP	Phone	Fax
Iredell County Library PO Box 1810 *Web:* www.iredell.lib.nc.us	Statesville	NC	28687	704-878-3090	878-5449
Edgecombe County Memorial Library 909 N Main St *Web:* www.edgecombelibrary.org	Tarboro	NC	27886	252-823-1141	823-7699
Alexander County Library 77 First Ave SW *Web:* www.alexanderlibrary.org	Taylorsville	NC	28681	828-632-4058	632-1094
Montgomery Community College Foundation Inc 1011 Page St *Web:* www.montgomery.edu	Troy	NC	27371	910-576-6222	
Haywood County Public Library 678 S Haywood St *Web:* haywoodlibrary.libguides.com	Waynesville	NC	28786	828-452-5169	452-6746
New Hanover County Public Library 201 Chestnut St *Web:* www.nhcgov.com/library/pages/default.aspx	Wilmington	NC	28401	910-798-6301	798-6312
Wilson County Public Library 249 W Nash St *TF:* 877-321-2652 ■ *Web:* www.wilson-co.com	Wilson	NC	27893	252-237-5355	243-4311
Forsyth County Public Library 660 W Fifth St *TF:* 866-345-1884 ■ *Web:* www.forsyth.cc	Winston-Salem	NC	27101	336-703-2665	727-2549
Gunn Memorial Public Library 161 Main St E *Web:* caswellcountync.gov	Yanceyville	NC	27379	336-694-6241	694-9846

North Dakota

Library	City	State	ZIP	Phone	Fax
Bismarck Veterans Memorial Public Library 515 N Fifth St *Web:* www.bismarck.org	Bismarck	ND	58501	701-355-1480	221-3729
City of Fargo 200 Third St N *Web:* cityoffargo.com/cityinfo/departments/library/	Fargo	ND	58102	701-241-1310	
Carnegie Regional Library 49 W Seventh St *TF:* 800-568-5964	Grafton	ND	58237	701-352-2754	352-2757
Minot Public Library 516 Second Ave SW *Web:* www.minotlibrary.org	Minot	ND	58701	701-852-1045	852-2595

Ohio

Library	City	State	ZIP	Phone	Fax
Akron-Summit County Public Library 60 S High St *Web:* www.ascpl.lib.oh.us	Akron	OH	44326	330-643-9000	
Rodman Public Library 215 E Broadway St *Web:* www.rodmanlibrary.com	Alliance	OH	44601	330-821-2665	821-5053
Ashtabula County District Library 335 W 44th St *Web:* www.ashtabula.lib.oh.us	Ashtabula	OH	44004	440-997-9341	992-7714
Clermont County Public Library System 326 Broadway St *Web:* clermontlibrary.org	Batavia	OH	45103	513-732-2736	732-3177
Logan County District Library 220 N Main St *Web:* www.logancountylibraries.org	Bellefontaine	OH	43311	937-599-4189	599-5503
Bexley Public Library 2411 E Main St *Web:* www.bexlib.org	Bexley	OH	43209	614-231-9709	231-0794
Wood County District Public Library 251 N Main St *Web:* www.wcdpl.lib.oh.us	Bowling Green	OH	43402	419-352-5104	354-0405
Guernsey County District Public Library 800 Steubenville Ave *Web:* www.gcdpl.lib.oh.us	Cambridge	OH	43725	740-432-5946	432-7142
Stark County District Library 715 Market Ave N *Web:* www.starklibrary.org	Canton	OH	44702	330-452-0665	452-0403
Carroll County District Library 70 Second St NE *TF:* 800-827-1000 ■ *Web:* carrolllibrary.org	Carrollton	OH	44615	330-627-2613	627-2523
Geauga County Public Library 12701 Ravenwood Dr *Web:* www.geauga.lib.oh.us	Chardon	OH	44024	440-286-6811	286-7419
Chillicothe & Ross County Public Library 140 S Paint St *Web:* crcpl.org	Chillicothe	OH	45601	740-702-4145	702-4156
Public Library of Cincinnati & Hamilton County 800 Vine St *Web:* www.cincinnatilibrary.org	Cincinnati	OH	45202	513-369-6900	369-3123
Pickaway County District Public Library 1160 N Ct St *TF:* 888-268-3756 ■ *Web:* www.pickawaylib.org	Circleville	OH	43113	740-477-1644	474-2855
Cleveland Public Library 325 Superior Ave *Web:* www.cpl.org	Cleveland	OH	44114	216-623-2800	623-7015
Shaker Heights Public Library 16500 Van Aken Blvd *Web:* www.shakerlibrary.org	Cleveland	OH	44120	216-991-2030	
Cleveland Heights-University Heights Public Library 2345 Lee Rd *Web:* www.heightslibrary.org	Cleveland Heights	OH	44118	216-932-3600	932-0932
Columbus Metropolitan Library 96 S Grant Ave *Web:* www.columbuslibrary.org	Columbus	OH	43215	614-645-2275	645-2050
Dayton Metro Library 215 E Third St *Web:* www.daytonmetrolibrary.org	Dayton	OH	45402	937-463-2665	
Defiance Public Library 320 Ft St *Web:* www.defiancelibrary.org	Defiance	OH	43512	419-782-1456	782-6235
Delaware County District Library 84 E Winter St *TF:* 866-862-7286 ■ *Web:* www.delawarelibrary.org	Delaware	OH	43015	740-362-3861	369-0196
Brooke-Gould Memorial Library 450 S Barron St *Web:* www.pcdl.lib.oh.us/locations/eaton.html	Eaton	OH	45320	937-456-4331	456-4774
Euclid Public Library 631 E 222nd St *Web:* www.euclidlibrary.org	Euclid	OH	44123	216-261-5300	
Findlay Hancock County District Public Library 206 Broadway *Web:* www.findlaylibrary.org	Findlay	OH	45840	419-422-1712	422-0638
Birchard Public Library of Sandusky County 423 Croghan St *Web:* www.birchard.lib.oh.us	Fremont	OH	43420	419-334-7101	334-4788
Dr Samuel L Bossard Memorial Library Seven Spruce St *Web:* www.bossard.lib.oh.us	Gallipolis	OH	45631	740-446-7323	446-1701
Portage County District Library 10482 S St *TF:* 800-500-5179 ■ *Web:* www.portagecounty.lib.oh.us	Garrettsville	OH	44231	330-527-4378	527-4370
Lane Public Library 300 N Third St *Web:* www.lanepl.org	Hamilton	OH	45011	513-894-7156	894-2718
Highland County District Library 10 Willettsville Pk *Web:* highlandco.org	Hillsboro	OH	45133	937-393-3114	393-2985
Hudson Library & Historical Society 96 Library St *Web:* www.hudsonlibrary.org	Hudson	OH	44236	330-653-6658	
Briggs Lawrence County Public Library 321 S Fourth St *Web:* www.briggslibrary.com	Ironton	OH	45638	740-532-1124	
Lakewood Public Library 15425 Detroit Ave *Web:* lakewoodpubliclibrary.org/	Lakewood	OH	44107	216-226-8275	521-4327
Fairfield County District Library 219 N Broad St *Web:* www.fcdlibrary.org	Lancaster	OH	43130	740-653-2745	653-4199
Lebanon Public Library 101 S Broadway *Web:* www.lebanonlibrary.org	Lebanon	OH	45036	513-932-2665	
Lima Public Library 650 W Market St *Web:* www.limalibrary.com	Lima	OH	45801	419-228-5113	
Logan-Hocking County District Library 230 E Main St *Web:* www.hocking.lib.oh.us	Logan	OH	43138	740-385-2348	385-9093
Lorain Public Library System 351 W Sixth St *TF:* 800-322-7323 ■ *Web:* lorainpubliclibrary.org/	Lorain	OH	44052	440-244-1192	244-4888
Mansfield-Richland County Public Library 43 W Third St *TF:* 877-795-2111 ■ *Web:* www.mrcpl.org	Mansfield	OH	44902	419-521-3100	525-4750
Washington County Public Library 615 Fifth St *Web:* wcplib.info	Marietta	OH	45750	740-373-1057	373-2860
Medina County District Library 210 S Broadway *Web:* www.mcdl.info	Medina	OH	44256	330-725-0588	725-2053
Middletown Public Library 125 S Broad St *Web:* www.midpointelibrary.org	Middletown	OH	45044	513-424-1251	424-6585
Holmes County District Public Library (HCDPL) 3102 Glen Dr *Web:* www.holmeslibrary.org	Millersburg	OH	44654	330-674-5972	674-1938
Mount Vernon & Knox County Public Library 201 N Mulberry St	Mount Vernon	OH	43050	740-392-2665	397-3866
Perry County District Library 117 S Jackson St *Web:* www.pcdl.org	New Lexington	OH	43764	740-342-4194	342-4204
Tuscarawas County Public Library 121 Fair Ave NW *Web:* www.tusclibrary.org	New Philadelphia	OH	44663	330-364-4474	364-8217
Putnam County District Library 136 Putnam Pkwy PO Box 230 *Web:* www.mypcdl.org	Ottawa	OH	45875	419-523-3747	523-6477
Morely Library 184 Phelps St *Web:* www.morleylibrary.org	Painesville	OH	44077	440-352-3383	352-9079
Cuyahoga County Public Library 2111 Snow Rd *TF:* 800-749-5560 ■ *Web:* www.cuyahogalibrary.org	Parma	OH	44134	216-398-1800	749-9479
Paulding County Carnegie Library 205 S Main St *Web:* www.pauldingcountylibrary.org	Paulding	OH	45879	419-399-2032	399-2114
Ida Rupp Public Library 310 Madison St *Web:* www.idarupp.lib.oh.us	Port Clinton	OH	43452	419-732-3212	
Portsmouth Public Library 1220 Gallia St *Web:* www.portsmouth.lib.oh.us	Portsmouth	OH	45662	740-354-5688	353-3483
Clark County Public Library 201 S Fountain Ave *Web:* www.ccpl.lib.oh.us	Springfield	OH	45501	937-328-6903	328-6908
Public Library of Steubenville & Jefferson County 407 S Fourth St *Web:* www.steubenville.lib.oh.us	Steubenville	OH	43952	740-282-9782	282-2919
Tiffin-Seneca Public Library 77 Jefferson St *Web:* tiffinsenecalibrary.org/	Tiffin	OH	44883	419-447-3751	447-3045
Toledo-Lucas County Public Library 325 N Michigan St *Web:* www.toledolibrary.org	Toledo	OH	43604	419-259-5200	255-1334
Troy-Miami County Public Library 419 W Main St *Web:* www.troypubliclibrary.org	Troy	OH	45373	937-339-0502	335-4880
Upper Arlington Public Library 2800 Tremont Rd *Web:* www.ualibrary.org	Upper Arlington	OH	43221	614-486-9621	486-4530
Brumback Library 215 W Main St *Web:* www.brumbacklib.com	Van Wert	OH	45891	419-238-2168	238-3180
Wadsworth Public Library 132 Broad St *Web:* www.wadsworthlibrary.com	Wadsworth	OH	44281	330-334-5761	
Warren-Trumbull County Public Library 444 Mahoning Ave NW *Web:* www.wtcpl.lib.oh.us	Warren	OH	44483	330-399-8807	395-3988
Carnegie Public Library 127 S N St *Web:* www.cplwcho.org	Washington Courthouse	OH	43160	740-335-2540	335-2928
Garnet A Wilson Public Library of Pike County 207 N Market St *Web:* www.pike.lib.oh.us	Waverly	OH	45690	740-947-4921	947-2918

Library	City	State	ZIP	Phone	Fax
Westerville Public Library 126 S State St *TF:* 800-816-0662 ■ *Web:* westervillelibrary.org/	Westerville	OH	43081	614-882-7277	882-4160
Greene County Public Library 76 E Market St PO Box 520 *Web:* greenelibrary.info	Xenia	OH	45385	937-352-4000	372-4673
Public Library of Youngstown & Mahoning County 305 Wick Ave *Web:* libraryvisit.org	Youngstown	OH	44503	330-744-8636	744-2258
Reuben Mc Millan Free Library Association Inc, The 305 Wick Ave *Web:* www.libraryvisit.org	Youngstown	OH	44503	330-744-8636	
Muskingum County Library System 220 N Fifth St *Web:* www.muskingumlibrary.org	Zanesville	OH	43701	740-453-0391	455-6357

Oklahoma

Library	City	State	ZIP	Phone	Fax
J W Martin Library 709 Oklahoma Blvd *Web:* www.nwosu.edu	Alva	OK	73717	580-327-8574	
Bartlesville Public Library 600 S Johnstone Ave *Web:* www.bartlesville.lib.ok.us	Bartlesville	OK	74003	918-337-5353	337-5338
Edmond Public Library 10 S Blvd *Web:* www.metrolibrary.org	Edmond	OK	73034	405-341-9282	
Lawton Public Library 110 SW Fourth St *TF:* 855-895-8064 ■ *Web:* www.cityof.lawton.ok.us	Lawton	OK	73501	580-581-3450	248-0243
Southeastern Library System of Oklahoma (SEPLSO) 401 N Second St *TF:* 800-215-6494 ■ *Web:* oklibrary.net	McAlester	OK	74501	918-426-0456	423-5731
Eastern Oklahoma District Library System 814 W Okmulgee St *Web:* www.eodls.lib.ok.us	Muskogee	OK	74401	918-683-2846	683-0436
Pioneer Library System 300 Norman Center Court *Web:* pioneerlibrarysystem.org	Norman	OK	73072	405-801-4500	701-2608
Ponca City Library 515 E Grand Ave *TF:* 800-522-8165 ■ *Web:* poncacitylibrary.com	Ponca City	OK	74601	580-767-0345	767-0374
Stillwater Public Library 1107 S Duck St *Web:* library.stillwater.org	Stillwater	OK	74074	405-372-3633	624-0552
Tulsa City-County Library (TCCL) 400 Civic Ctr *Web:* www.tulsalibrary.org	Tulsa	OK	74103	918-549-7323	596-7990
Tulsa Zoological Park Library 5701 E 36th St N *Web:* www.tulsazoo.org	Tulsa	OK	74115	918-669-6600	

Ontario

Library	City	State	ZIP	Phone	Fax
Waterloo Public Library 35 Albert St *Web:* www.wpl.ca	Waterloo	ON	N2L5E2	519-886-1310	886-7936

Oregon

Library	City	State	ZIP	Phone	Fax
Beaverton City Library 12375 SW Fifth St *Web:* www.beavertonlibrary.org	Beaverton	OR	97005	503-644-2197	
Deschutes Public Library 507 NW Wall St *TF:* 855-268-3767 ■ *Web:* www.deschuteslibrary.org	Bend	OR	97701	541-312-1020	389-2982
Coos Bay Public Library 525 W Anderson Ave *Web:* bay.cooslibraries.org	Coos Bay	OR	97420	541-269-1101	269-7567
Corvallis-Benton County Library 645 NW Monroe Ave *Web:* www.library.ci.corvallis.or.us	Corvallis	OR	97330	541-766-6793	766-6915
Eugene Public Library 100 W Tenth Ave *Web:* www.eugene-or.gov	Eugene	OR	97401	541-682-5450	682-5898
Josephine County Library System 200 NW 'C' St PO Box 1684 *Web:* www.josephinelibrary.org	Grants Pass	OR	97526	541-476-0571	660-6531
Hillsboro Public Library 2850 NE Brookwood Pkwy *TF:* 855-870-0049 ■ *Web:* www.ci.hillsboro.or.us	Hillsboro	OR	97124	503-615-6500	615-6501
Klamath County Library 126 S Third St *Web:* klamathlibrary.plinkit.org	Klamath Falls	OR	97601	541-882-8894	882-6166
Lake Oswego Public Library 706 Fourth St *Web:* www.ci.oswego.or.us	Lake Oswego	OR	97034	503-636-7628	635-4171
McMinnville Public Library 225 NW Adams St *Web:* www.maclibrary.org	McMinnville	OR	97128	503-435-5555	435-5560
Jackson County Library System 205 S Central Ave *Web:* www.jcls.org	Medford	OR	97501	541-774-8679	774-6748
Ledding Library 10660 SE 21st Ave *Web:* www.milwaukieoregon.gov	Milwaukie	OR	97222	503-786-7580	659-9497
Clackamas County Library 16201 SE McLoughlin Blvd *Web:* www.clackamas.us/lib/hours.html	Oak Grove	OR	97267	503-655-8543	
Oregon City Public Library 606 John Adams *Web:* orcity.org	Oregon City	OR	97045	503-657-8269	657-3702
Multnomah County Library 801 SW Tenth Ave *Web:* www.multcolib.org	Portland	OR	97205	503-988-5123	988-5226
Douglas County Library System 1409 NE Diamond Lk Blvd *Web:* www.dclibrary.us	Roseburg	OR	97470	541-440-4311	440-4315
Salem Public Library 585 Liberty St SE *Web:* www.cityofsalem.net/departments/library	Salem	OR	97301	503-588-6071	588-6055
Springfield Public Library 225 N Fifth St *Web:* ci.springfield.or.us	Springfield	OR	97477	541-726-3766	726-3747
Tigard Public Library 13500 SW Hall Blvd *Web:* tigard-or.gov	Tigard	OR	97223	503-684-6537	598-7515

Pennsylvania

Library	City	State	ZIP	Phone	Fax
Allentown Public Library 1210 Hamilton St *Web:* www.allentownpl.org	Allentown	PA	18102	610-820-2400	820-0640
Altoona Area Public Library 1600 Fifth Ave *Web:* www.altoonalibrary.org	Altoona	PA	16602	814-946-0417	946-3230
LTK Engineering Services Inc 100 W Butler Ave *Web:* www.ltk.com	Ambler	PA	19002	215-542-0700	
Bethlehem Area Public Library 11 W Church St *TF:* 800-732-0999 ■ *Web:* www.bapl.org	Bethlehem	PA	18018	610-867-3761	867-2767
Bucks County Free Library 150 S Pine St *Web:* www.buckslib.org	Doylestown	PA	18901	215-348-9081	348-4760
Erie County Library System 160 E Front St *Web:* www.erielibrary.org	Erie	PA	16507	814-451-6900	451-6969
Raymond M Blasco MD Memorial Library 160 E Front St *Web:* www.erielibrary.org	Erie	PA	16507	814-451-6900	
Chester County Library 450 Exton Sq Pkwy *Web:* www.ccls.org	Exton	PA	19341	610-280-2600	280-2694
Adams County Public Library 140 Baltimore St *Web:* www.adamslibrary.org	Gettysburg	PA	17325	717-334-5716	334-7992
Dauphin County Library System 101 Walnut St *Web:* www.dcls.org	Harrisburg	PA	17101	717-234-4961	234-7479
Cambria County Library System 248 Main St *Web:* www.cclsys.org	Johnstown	PA	15901	814-536-5131	536-6905
Lancaster Public Library 125 N Duke St *Web:* www.lancaster.lib.pa.us	Lancaster	PA	17602	717-394-2651	394-3083
Library System of Lebanon County 125 N Seventh St *Web:* www.lebanoncountylibraries.org	Lebanon	PA	17046	717-273-7624	273-2719
Montgomery County-Norristown Public Library 1001 Powell St *Web:* mnl.mclinc.org	Norristown	PA	19401	610-278-5100	277-0344
Oil Creek District Library Ctr Two Central Ave *Web:* www.oilcreekdistrictlibrary.org	Oil City	PA	16301	814-678-3054	676-0359
Osceola Mills Public Library 600 Lingle St	Osceola Mills	PA	16666	814-339-7229	
Free Library of Philadelphia 1901 Vine St *TF:* 800-732-0999 ■ *Web:* www.freelibrary.org	Philadelphia	PA	19103	215-686-5322	563-3628
University of Pennsylvania Lippincott Library at Wharton 3420 Walnut St Van Pelt-Dietrich Library Ctr Second Fl *Web:* www.library.upenn.edu	Philadelphia	PA	19104	215-898-6248	
Carnegie Library of Pittsburgh 4400 Forbes Ave *Web:* carnegielibrary.org	Pittsburgh	PA	15213	412-622-3114	622-6278
Northland Public Library 300 Cumberland Rd *Web:* www.northlandlibrary.org	Pittsburgh	PA	15237	412-366-8100	
Upper st Clair Township Lbrry 1820 Mclaughlin Run Rd *Web:* www.twpusc.org	Pittsburgh	PA	15241	412-835-5540	
Pottsville Free Public Library 215 W Market St *Web:* www.pottsvillelibrary.org	Pottsville	PA	17901	570-622-8880	622-2157
Reading Public Library 100 S Fifth St *Web:* www.reading.lib.pa.us	Reading	PA	19602	610-655-6355	655-6609
Albright Memorial Library 500 Vine St *Web:* www.lclshome.org	Scranton	PA	18509	570-348-3000	348-3020
Scranton Public Library 500 Vine St *Web:* www.albright.org	Scranton	PA	18509	570-348-3000	
Osterhout Free Library 71 S Franklin St *Web:* www.osterhout.lib.pa.us	Wilkes-Barre	PA	18701	570-823-0156	
James V Brown Library of Williamsport & Lycoming County 19 E Fourth St *Web:* www.jvbrown.edu	Williamsport	PA	17701	570-326-0536	326-1671
Martin Memorial Library 159 E Market St *Web:* www.yorklibraries.org	York	PA	17401	717-846-5300	848-2330

Rhode Island

Library	City	State	ZIP	Phone	Fax
Coventry Public Library 1672 Flat River Rd *Web:* www.coventrylibrary.org	Coventry	RI	02816	401-822-9100	822-9133
Cranston Public Library 140 Sockanosset Cross Rd *Web:* www.cranstonlibrary.org	Cranston	RI	02920	401-943-9080	946-5079
Cumberland Public Library 1464 Diamond Hill Rd *Web:* www.cumberlandlibrary.org	Cumberland	RI	02864	401-333-2552	334-0578
East Providence Public Library 41 Grove Ave *Web:* www.eastprovidencelibrary.org	East Providence	RI	02914	401-434-2453	
Marion J Mohr Memorial Library One Memorial Ave *Web:* mohrlibrary.net	Johnston	RI	02919	401-231-4980	231-4984
Newport Public Library 300 Spring St *Web:* www.newportlibraryri.org	Newport	RI	02840	401-847-8720	842-0841
Pawtucket Public Library 13 Summer St *Web:* www.pawtucketlibrary.org	Pawtucket	RI	02860	401-725-3714	
Providence Public Library 150 Empire St *Web:* www.provlib.org	Providence	RI	02903	401-455-8000	455-8080
Warwick Public Library (WPL) 600 Sandy Ln *Web:* warwicklibrary.org	Warwick	RI	02886	401-739-5440	732-2055

Library	City	State	ZIP	Phone	Fax
West Warwick Public Library System 1043 Main St *Web:* www.wwlibrary.org	West Warwick	RI	02893	401-828-3750	828-8493
Westerly Public Library 44 Broad St *Web:* www.westerlylibrary.org	Westerly	RI	02891	401-596-2877	596-5600
Woonsocket Harris Public Library 303 Clinton St *TF:* 800-359-3090 ■ *Web:* www.woonsocketlibrary.org	Woonsocket	RI	02895	401-769-9044	767-4140

South Carolina

Library	City	State	ZIP	Phone	Fax
Aiken-Bamberg-Barnwell-Edgefield Regional Library System 314 Chesterfield St *Web:* www.abbe-lib.org	Aiken	SC	29801	803-642-7575	642-7597
Anderson County Library 300 S McDuffie St *Web:* www.andersonlibrary.org	Anderson	SC	29621	864-260-4500	260-4510
Marlboro County Library 203 Fayetteville Ave *Web:* www.edelmanpubliclibrary.org	Bennettsville	SC	29512	843-479-5630	479-5645
Charleston County Public Library 68 Calhoun St *Web:* www.ccpl.org	Charleston	SC	29401	843-805-6930	727-3741
Chesterfield County Library 119 Main St *Web:* chesterfield.lib.sc.us	Chesterfield	SC	29709	843-623-7489	623-3295
Richland County Public Library (RCPL) 1431 Assembly St *Web:* www.richlandlibrary.com	Columbia	SC	29201	803-799-9084	
State Library 1430 Senate St *Web:* www.statelibrary.sc.gov	Columbia	SC	29201	803-734-4611	
Darlington County Library 204 N Main St *Web:* www.darlington-lib.org	Darlington	SC	29532	843-398-4940	398-4942
Dillon County Library 600 E Main St *Web:* dillon.lib.sc.us	Dillon	SC	29536	843-774-0330	774-0733
Pickens County Library 304 Biltmore Rd *Web:* pickens.lib.sc.us	Easley	SC	29640	864-850-7077	850-7088
Florence County Library 509 S Dargan St *Web:* www.florencelibrary.org	Florence	SC	29506	843-662-8424	661-7544
Cherokee County Public Library 300 E Rutledge Ave	Gaffney	SC	29340	864-487-2711	487-2752
Greenville County Library 25 Heritage Green Pl *TF:* 866-275-7273 ■ *Web:* www.greenvillelibrary.org	Greenville	SC	29601	864-242-5000	235-8375
Hilton Head Library 11 Beach City Rd *TF:* 800-860-1444 ■ *Web:* beaufortcountylibrary.org	Hilton Head Island	SC	29926	843-255-6500	342-9220
Williamsburg County Library 215 N Jackson St *Web:* www.mywcl.org	Kingstree	SC	29556	843-355-9486	355-9991
Lancaster County Library 313 S White St *Web:* www.lanclib.org	Lancaster	SC	29720	803-285-1502	285-6004
Laurens County Library 1017 W Main St *Web:* lcpl.org	Laurens	SC	29360	864-681-7323	681-0598
Harvin Clarendon County Library 215 N Brooks St *Web:* www.clarendoncountylibrary.com	Manning	SC	29102	803-435-8633	435-8101
Marion County Library (MCL) 101 E Ct St *Web:* www.marioncountylibrary.org	Marion	SC	29571	843-423-8300	423-8302
Berkeley County Library 1003 Hwy 52	Moncks Corner	SC	29461	843-719-4223	719-4732
Chapin Memorial Library 400 14th Ave N *Web:* www.cityofmyrtlebeach.com	Myrtle Beach	SC	29577	843-918-1275	918-1288
Orangeburg County Library (OCL) 510 Louis St *Web:* www.orangeburgcounty.org	Orangeburg	SC	29115	803-531-4636	533-5860
York County Library 138 E Black St *Web:* www.yclibrary.org	Rock Hill	SC	29730	803-981-5858	328-9290
Dorchester County Library 506 N Parler Ave *Web:* www.dcl.lib.sc.us	Saint George	SC	29477	843-563-9189	563-7823
Spartanburg County Public Library 151 S Church St *Web:* www.infodepot.org	Spartanburg	SC	29306	864-596-3507	596-3518
Sumter County Library 111 N Harvin St *Web:* www.sumtercountylibrary.org	Sumter	SC	29150	803-773-7273	773-4875
Union County Carnegie Library 300 E S St *Web:* www.unionlibrary.org	Union	SC	29379	864-427-7140	427-5155
Oconee County Library 501 W S Broad St *Web:* oconeelibrary.org	Walhalla	SC	29691	864-638-4133	
Colleton County Memorial Library 600 Hampton St *Web:* www.colletonlibrary.org	Walterboro	SC	29488	843-549-5621	549-5122

South Dakota

Library	City	State	ZIP	Phone	Fax
Brookings Public Library 515 Third St *Web:* www.brookingslibrary.org	Brookings	SD	57006	605-692-9407	692-9386
RE Rawlins Municipal Library 1000 E Church St	Pierre	SD	57501	605-773-7421	773-7423
Rapid City Public Library (RCPL) 610 Quincy St *Web:* www.rcgov.org/library	Rapid City	SD	57701	605-394-4171	394-4064

Tennessee

Library	City	State	ZIP	Phone	Fax
Cheatham County Public Library 188 County Services Dr Ste 200 **Fax Area Code:* 305	Ashland City	TN	37015	615-792-4828	393-8193*
EG Fisher Public Library 1289 Ingleside Ave *TF:* 800-552-6843 ■ *Web:* fisherlibrary.org	Athens	TN	37303	423-745-7782	745-1763
Sullivan County Public Library 1655 Blountville Blvd PO Box 510 *Web:* sullivancountylibrarytn.org	Blountville	TN	37617	423-279-2714	279-2836
Chattanooga-Hamilton County Bicentennial Library 1001 Broad St *Web:* www.lib.chattanooga.gov	Chattanooga	TN	37402	423-757-5310	757-4994
Clarksville Montgomery County Public Library 350 Pageant Ln *TF:* 877-239-6635 ■ *Web:* www.mcgtn.org/library	Clarksville	TN	37040	931-648-8826	648-8831
Cleveland Bradley County Public Library 795 N Church St NE *Web:* www.clevelandlibrary.org	Cleveland	TN	37311	423-472-2163	339-9791
Blue Grass Regional Library 104 E Sixth St **Fax Area Code:* 865 ■ *TF:* 888-345-5575	Columbia	TN	38401	931-388-9282	981-4587*
Putnam County Library 50 E Broad St *Web:* www.pclibrary.org	Cookeville	TN	38501	931-526-2416	372-8517
Art Cir Public Library Three E St *Web:* www.artcirclelibrary.info	Crossville	TN	38555	931-484-6790	484-2350
Dickson County Public Library 206 Henslee Dr *Web:* www.youseemore.com	Dickson	TN	37055	615-446-8293	446-9130
McIver's Grant Public Library 204 N Mill Ave *Web:* www.dyersburgdyercolibrary.com	Dyersburg	TN	38024	731-285-5032	
Elizabethton-Carter County Public Library 201 N Sycamore St *Web:* eccpl.info	Elizabethton	TN	37643	423-547-6360	
Williamson County Public Library 1314 Columbia Ave *Web:* www.lib.williamson-tn.org	Franklin	TN	37064	615-794-3105	595-1245
Martin Curtis-Hendersonville Public Library 140 Saundersville Rd	Hendersonville	TN	37075	615-824-0656	
Jacksboro Public Library 585 Main St Ste 201 *Web:* www.jacksboropubliclibrary.org	Jacksboro	TN	37757	423-562-3675	562-9587
Jackson-Madison County Library 433 E Lafayette St *Web:* www.jmcl.tn.org	Jackson	TN	38301	731-425-8600	425-8609
Johnson City Public Library 100 W Millard St *Web:* www.jcpl.net	Johnson City	TN	37604	423-434-4450	434-4469
Washington County-Jonesborough Library 200 E Sabine Dr *Web:* wclibrarytn.org	Jonesborough	TN	37659	423-753-1800	753-1802
Kingsport Public Library 400 Broad St *Web:* www.kingsportlibrary.org	Kingsport	TN	37660	423-224-2559	224-2558
Lawrence County Public Library 519 E Gaines St *Web:* lawrencecountytn.gov	Lawrenceburg	TN	38464	931-762-4627	766-1597
Lebanon-Wilson County Public Library 108 S Hatton Ave *Web:* www2.youseemore.com/lebanon-wilson/default.asp	Lebanon	TN	37087	615-444-0632	444-0535
Lenoir City Public Library 100 W Broadway St Ste 103	Lenoir City	TN	37771	865-986-3210	
Reelfoot Regional Library Ctr 542 N Lindell St *Web:* tennessee.gov	Martin	TN	38237	731-587-2347	
Blount County Public Library 508 N Cusick St *Web:* www.blountlibrary.org	Maryville	TN	37804	865-982-0981	977-1142
Morristown-Hamblen Public Library 417 W Main St *Web:* morristownhamblenlibrary.org	Morristown	TN	37814	423-586-6410	587-6226
Highland Rim Regional Library Ctr 2118 E Main St *Web:* tennessee.gov	Murfreesboro	TN	37130	615-893-3380	895-6727
Linebaugh Public Library 105 W Vine St *Web:* www.linebaugh.org	Murfreesboro	TN	37130	615-893-4131	848-5038
Nashville Public Library 615 Church St *Web:* www.library.nashville.org	Nashville	TN	37219	615-862-5800	880-2119
Stokely Memorial Library 383 E Broadway	Newport	TN	37821	423-623-3832	623-3832
Oak Ridge Public Library 1401 Oak Ridge Tpke *Web:* www.orpl.org	Oak Ridge	TN	37830	865-425-3455	425-3429
WG Rhea Library 400 W Washington St *Web:* rheapubliclibrary.org	Paris	TN	38242	731-642-1702	
Giles County Public Library 122 S Second St *Web:* www.gilescountylibrary.org	Pulaski	TN	38478	931-363-2720	424-7032
Hawkins County Library System 407 E Main St *Web:* www.hawkinslibraries.org	Rogersville	TN	37857	423-272-8710	272-9261
Sevier County Public Library 408 High St *Web:* www.sevierlibrary.org	Sevierville	TN	37862	865-453-3532	365-1667
Argie Cooper Public Library 100 S Main St *Web:* www.acolibrary.com	Shelbyville	TN	37160	931-684-7323	685-4848
Fayette County Library 216 W Market St *TF:* 866-465-3591 ■ *Web:* www.fayettetn.us	Somerville	TN	38068	901-465-5248	465-5271
Gorham MacBane Public Library 405 White St *Web:* www1.youseemore.com	Springfield	TN	37172	615-384-5123	
County Library 1304 Old Knoxville Rd	Tazewell	TN	37879	423-626-5414	626-9481
Obion County Public Library 1221 E Reelfoot Ave *Web:* www.oclibrary.org	Union City	TN	38261	731-885-7000	885-9638

Texas

Library	City	State	ZIP	Phone	Fax
Abilene Public Library 202 Cedar St *Web:* www.abilenetx.com	Abilene	TX	79601	325-677-2474	676-6024
Alice Public Library 401 E Third St	Alice	TX	78332	361-664-9506	668-3248

Library	City	State	ZIP	Phone	Fax
Amarillo Public Library 413 SE Fourth Ave *Web:* www.amarillolibrary.org	Amarillo	TX	79101	806-378-3054	378-9327
Brazoria County Library System 451 N Velasco Ste 250 *Web:* bcls.lib.tx.us/	Angleton	TX	77515	979-864-1505	864-1298
Arlington Public Library 101 E Abram St *TF:* 888-227-7669 ■ *Web:* www.arlingtonlibrary.org	Arlington	TX	76010	817-459-6900	459-6902
Henderson County CW Murchison Memorial Library 121 S Prairieville *Web:* www.koha.org	Athens	TX	75751	903-677-7295	
Austin Public Library 800 Guadalupe St *Web:* library.austintexas.gov	Austin	TX	78701	512-974-7400	499-7403
Sterling Municipal Library Mary Elizabeth Wilbanks Ave *Web:* www.baytownlibrary.org	Baytown	TX	77520	281-427-7331	420-5347
Beaumont Public Library System 801 Pearl St *Web:* beaumontlibrary.org	Beaumont	TX	77701	409-838-6606	838-6838
Howard County Library 500 S Main St **Fax Area Code:* 410	Big Spring	TX	79720	432-264-2260	750-8588*
Nancy Carol Roberts Memorial Library 100 Martin Luther King Junior Pkwy *Web:* cityofbrenham.org	Brenham	TX	77833	979-337-7201	
Brownsville Public Library 4320 Southmost Rd *Web:* www.bpl.us	Brownsville	TX	78521	956-548-1055	548-0684
Brownwood Public Library 600 Carnegie Blvd *Web:* www.brownwoodpubliclibrary.com	Brownwood	TX	76801	325-646-0155	646-6503
Bryan Public Library 201 E 26th St *Web:* www.bcslibrary.org	Bryan	TX	77803	979-209-5600	209-5610
Van Zandt County Library 317 First Monday Ln *Web:* vanzandtlibrary.org	Canton	TX	75103	903-567-4276	567-6981
Carrollton Public Library 4220 N Josey Ln *TF:* 888-727-2978 ■ *Web:* www.cityofcarrollton.com/library	Carrollton	TX	75010	972-466-4800	466-4722
Montgomery County Library 104 I-45 N *Web:* www.countylibrary.org	Conroe	TX	77301	936-442-7712	788-8398
Corpus Christi Public Libraries 805 Comanche St *Web:* www.cclibraries.com	Corpus Christi	TX	78401	361-826-7000	880-7046
Corsicana Public Library 100 N 12th St *Web:* www.cityofcorsicana.com	Corsicana	TX	75110	903-654-4810	
J Erik Jonsson Central Library 1515 Young St *Web:* www.dallaslibrary2.org/central	Dallas	TX	75201	214-670-1400	
Deer Park Public Library 3009 Ctr St *Web:* deerparktx.gov	Deer Park	TX	77536	281-478-7208	478-7212
Val Verde County Library 300 Spring St *Web:* valverdecounty.org	Del Rio	TX	78840	830-774-7595	774-7607
Denison Public Library 300 W Gandy St *Web:* www.barr.org	Denison	TX	75020	903-465-1797	465-1130
Emily Fowler Central Library 502 Oakland St	Denton	TX	76201	940-349-8752	349-8101
DeSoto Public Library 211 E Pleasant Run Rd Ste C *TF:* 800-886-9008 ■ *Web:* www.ci.desoto.tx.us	DeSoto	TX	75115	972-230-9656	230-5797
Diboll Texas Independent School District 215 N Temple Dr *Web:* www.dibollisd.com	Diboll	TX	75941	936-829-4718	
Duncanville Public Library 201 James Collins Blvd *TF:* 866-332-4558 ■ *Web:* duncanville.com	Duncanville	TX	75116	972-780-5050	780-6426
Eagle Pass Public Library 243 Bliss St *Web:* eaglepasstx.us	Eagle Pass	TX	78852	830-773-2516	
Edinburg Public Library 1906 S Closner *Web:* www.edinburg.lib.tx.us	Edinburg	TX	78539	956-383-6246	318-3446
Euless Public Library 201 N Ector Dr *Web:* eulesstx.gov	Euless	TX	76039	817-685-1480	267-1979
City of Farmers Branch 13000 William Dodson Pkwy *Web:* www.dallascremations-funerals.com	Farmers Branch	TX	75234	972-247-3131	
Fort Worth Public Library 500 W Third St *Web:* fortworthtexas.gov	Fort Worth	TX	76102	817-871-7323	871-7734
Friendswood Public Library 416 S Friendswood Dr *TF:* 800-696-3493 ■ *Web:* www.friendswood.lib.tx.us	Friendswood	TX	77546	281-482-7135	482-2685
Rosenberg Library 2310 Sealy Ave *Web:* www.rosenberg-library.org	Galveston	TX	77550	409-763-8854	763-0275
Nicholson Memorial Library System 200 N 5th St *Web:* www.nmls.lib.tx.us	Garland	TX	75040	972-205-2000	205-2523
Upshur County Library 702 W Tyler St *Web:* countyofupshur.com	Gilmer	TX	75644	903-843-5001	843-3995
Hood County Public Library 222 N Travis St *TF:* 800-452-9292 ■ *Web:* www.co.hood.tx.us	Granbury	TX	76048	817-573-3569	573-3969
Grapevine Public Library 1201 Municipal Way *Web:* grapevinetexas.gov	Grapevine	TX	76051	817-410-3400	410-3080
Greenville Library One Lou Finney Ln *Web:* www.ci.greenville.tx.us	Greenville	TX	75401	903-457-2992	457-2961
Haltom City Public Library 4809 Haltom Rd *Web:* www.haltomcitytx.com	Haltom City	TX	76117	817-222-7786	834-1446
Harlingen Public Library 410 76th Dr	Harlingen	TX	78550	956-216-5888	
Rusk County Library (RCL) 106 E Main St *Web:* www.rclib.org	Henderson	TX	75652	903-657-8557	657-7637
Harris County Public Library System 8080 El Rio St *Web:* www.hcpl.net	Houston	TX	77054	713-749-9000	749-9090
Houston Public Library 500 McKinney St *TF:* 800-318-2596 ■ *Web:* www.houstonlibrary.org	Houston	TX	77002	832-393-1313	393-1324
Hurst Public Library 901 Precinct Line Rd *TF:* 800-344-8377 ■ *Web:* hursttx.gov	Hurst	TX	76053	817-788-7300	590-9515
Irving Public Library 801 W Irving Blvd *Web:* irvingwiki.cityofirving.org	Irving	TX	75060	972-721-2606	721-2463
Butt-Holdsworth Memorial Library 505 Water St *Web:* www.kerrville.org	Kerrville	TX	78028	830-257-8422	792-5552
Robert J Kleberg Public Library 220 N Fourth St *Web:* kleberglibrary.com	Kingsville	TX	78363	361-592-6381	
Laredo Public Library 1120 E Calton Rd *Web:* www.laredolibrary.org	Laredo	TX	78041	956-795-2400	795-2403
Helen Hall Library (HHL) 100 W Walker St *Web:* www.leaguecity.com	League City	TX	77573	281-554-1111	
Lewisville Public Library 1197 W Main St *Web:* www.cityoflewisville.com	Lewisville	TX	75067	972-219-3570	219-5094
Lubbock Public Library 1306 Ninth St *Web:* www.mylubbock.us/departmental-websites/departments/library/library-home	Lubbock	TX	79401	806-775-2835	775-2827
Marshall Public Library 300 S Alamo St *Web:* marshalltexas.net	Marshall	TX	75670	903-935-4465	935-4463
McAllen Memorial Library 601 N Main St *Web:* www.mcallenlibrary.net	McAllen	TX	78501	956-688-3300	
Mesquite Public Library 300 W Grubb Dr *TF:* 866-797-8268 ■ *Web:* www.cityofmesquite.com	Mesquite	TX	75149	972-216-6220	216-6740
Midland County Public Library 301 W Missouri Ave *Web:* www.co.midland.tx.us	Midland	TX	79701	432-688-4320	688-4939
Speer Memorial Library 801 E 12th St *Web:* www.mission.lib.tx.us	Mission	TX	78572	956-580-8750	580-8756
Nacogdoches Public Library 1112 N St *TF:* 800-252-5400 ■ *Web:* ci.nacogdoches.tx.us	Nacogdoches	TX	75961	936-559-2970	569-8282
New Braunfels Public Library 700 E Common St *TF:* 800-434-8013 ■ *Web:* www.nbtexas.org	New Braunfels	TX	78130	830-221-4300	608-2151
North Richland Hills Public Library 9015 Grand Ave *Web:* www.library.nrhtx.com	North Richland Hills	TX	76180	817-427-6800	427-6808
Ector County Library 321 W Fifth St *Web:* www.ector.lib.tx.us	Odessa	TX	79761	432-332-0633	337-6502
Palestine Public Library 2000 S Loop 256 #42 *Web:* www.youseemore.com	Palestine	TX	75801	903-729-4121	729-4062
Lee Davis Library 8060 Spencer Hwy *Web:* www.sjcd.edu	Pasadena	TX	77505	281-476-1850	478-2734
Pharr Memorial Library 121 E Cherokee St *Web:* pharr-tx.gov	Pharr	TX	78577	956-787-3966	787-3345
Unger Memorial Library 825 N Austin St *Web:* whc.net/	Plainview	TX	79072	806-296-1148	291-1245
Plano Public Library System 5024 Custer Rd *Web:* planolibrary.org	Plano	TX	75023	972-769-4200	769-4210
Port Arthur Public Library 4615 Ninth Ave *Web:* www.pap.lib.tx.us	Port Arthur	TX	77642	409-985-8838	985-5969
Richardson Public Library 900 Civic Ctr Dr *TF:* 800-735-2989 ■ *Web:* www.cor.net	Richardson	TX	75080	972-744-4350	744-5806
George Memorial Library 1001 Golfview Dr *Web:* www.fortbend.lib.tx.us	Richmond	TX	77469	281-342-4455	341-2689
Round Rock Public Library 216 E Main St *Web:* www.roundrocktexas.gov	Round Rock	TX	78664	512-218-7001	218-7061
Tom Green County Library System 33 W Beauregard Ave *Web:* tgclibrary.com	San Angelo	TX	76903	325-655-7321	
Daughters of the Republic of Texas Library PO Box 1401 *Web:* www.drtl.org	San Antonio	TX	78295	210-225-1071	212-8514
Marcive Inc 12100 Crownpoint Dr Ste 160 *Web:* www.marcive.com	San Antonio	TX	78233	210-646-6161	
San Antonio Public Library 600 Soledad St *Web:* www.sanantonio.gov/library	San Antonio	TX	78205	210-207-2500	271-9497
San Benito Public Library 101 W Rose St *TF:* 800-444-1187 ■ *Web:* www.cityofsanbenito.com	San Benito	TX	78586	956-361-3860	361-3867
San Marcos Public Library 625 E Hopkins St *Web:* www.ci.san-marcos.tx.us	San Marcos	TX	78666	512-393-8200	754-8131
Sherman Public Library 421 N Travis St *Web:* www.barr.org	Sherman	TX	75090	903-892-7240	892-7101
Taylor Public Library 400 Porter St *Web:* www.ci.taylor.tx.us	Taylor	TX	76574	512-352-3434	352-8080
Temple Public Library 100 W Adams Ave *Web:* youseemore.com	Temple	TX	76501	254-298-5555	
Terrell Public Library 301 N Rockwell Ave *Web:* cityofterrell.org	Terrell	TX	75160	972-551-6663	551-6662
Texarkana Public Library 600 W Third St *Web:* www.txar-publib.org	Texarkana	TX	75501	903-794-2149	794-2139
Moore Memorial Public Library 1701 Ninth Ave N *Web:* www.texascity-library.org	Texas City	TX	77590	409-643-5979	948-1106
Colony Public Library, The 6800 Main St *Web:* thecolonytx.gov	The Colony	TX	75056	972-625-1900	624-2245
Tyler Public Library 201 S College Ave *Web:* library.cityoftyler.org/	Tyler	TX	75702	903-593-7323	531-1329
Waco-McLennan County Library 1717 Austin Ave *TF:* 800-433-7300 ■ *Web:* www.waco-texas.com	Waco	TX	76701	254-750-5941	750-5940
Watauga Public Library 7109 Whitley Rd *Web:* www.cowtx.org	Watauga	TX	76148	817-514-5855	581-3910
Weatherford Public Library 1014 Charles St *TF:* 800-489-0190 ■ *Web:* ci.weatherford.tx.us	Weatherford	TX	76086	817-598-4150	598-4161
Weslaco Public Library 525 S Kansas Ave *Web:* www.weslaco.lib.tx.us	Weslaco	TX	78596	956-968-4533	969-4069
Wharton County Library 1920 N Fulton St *TF:* 800-244-5492 ■ *Web:* www.whartonco.lib.tx.us	Wharton	TX	77488	979-532-8080	532-2792
Wichita Falls Public Library 600 11th St *Web:* www.wfpl.net	Wichita Falls	TX	76301	940-767-0868	720-6672

Utah

				Phone	Fax
Davis County Library 61 S Main St PO Box 618 *Web:* www.co.davis.ut.us	Farmington	UT	84025	801-451-2322	451-3281
Logan Library 255 N Main St *Web:* library.loganutah.org	Logan	UT	84321	435-716-9123	716-9145
Murray Public Library 166 East 5300 South *Web:* www.murray.lib.ut.us	Murray	UT	84107	801-264-2580	264-2586
Weber County Library 2464 Jefferson Ave *TF:* 866-678-5342 ■ *Web:* www.weberpl.lib.ut.us	Ogden	UT	84401	801-337-2632	337-2615
Orem Public Library 58 N State St *Web:* lib.orem.org	Orem	UT	84057	801-229-7050	229-7130
Provo City Library 550 N University Ave *TF:* 800-914-8931 ■ *Web:* provolibrary.com	Provo	UT	84601	801-852-6650	852-6688
Salt Lake City Public Library 210 East 400 South *Web:* www.slcpl.lib.ut.us	Salt Lake City	UT	84111	801-524-8200	322-8196
Salt Lake County Library System 2197 E Ft Union Blvd *Web:* www.slcolibrary.org	Salt Lake City	UT	84121	801-943-4636	942-6323

Vermont

				Phone	Fax
Fletcher Free Public Library 235 College St *Web:* www.fletcherfree.org	Burlington	VT	05401	802-863-3403	865-7227
Kellogg-Hubbard Library 135 Main St *Web:* www.kellogghubbard.org	Montpelier	VT	05602	802-223-3338	223-3338

Virginia

				Phone	Fax
Amherst County Virgina 382 S Main St PO Box 370 *Web:* www.countyofamherst.com	Amherst	VA	24521	434-946-9400	946-9348
Arlington County Central Library 1015 N Quincy St *Web:* www.arlingtonva.us	Arlington	VA	22201	703-228-5990	228-7720
Bristol Public Library 701 Goode St *Web:* www.bristol-library.org	Bristol	VA	24201	276-645-8780	669-5593
Jefferson-Madison Regional Library 201 E Market St *TF:* 866-979-1555 ■ *Web:* www.jmrl.org	Charlottesville	VA	22902	434-979-7151	971-7035
Pittsylvania County Public Library 24 Military Dr *Web:* www.pcplib.org	Chatham	VA	24531	434-432-3271	432-1405
Chesapeake Public Library 298 Cedar Rd *Web:* www.chesapeake.lib.va.us	Chesapeake	VA	23322	757-410-7100	410-7122
Montgomery-Floyd Regional Library 125 Sheltman St *Web:* www.mfrl.org	Christiansburg	VA	24073	540-382-6965	382-6964
Culpeper County Library 271 Southgate Shopping Ctr *Web:* www2.youseemore.com/culpeper/	Culpeper	VA	22701	540-825-8691	825-7486
Danville Public Library 511 Patton St *Web:* readdanvilleva.org	Danville	VA	24541	434-799-5195	
Shenandoah County Library 514 Stoney Creek Blvd *TF:* 800-829-5137 ■ *Web:* www.shenandoah.co.lib.va.us	Edinburg	VA	22824	540-984-8200	984-8207
Fairfax County Public Library 12000 Government Ctr Pkwy Ste 324 *Web:* www.fairfaxcounty.gov/library	Fairfax	VA	22035	703-324-3100	222-3193
Augusta County Library 1759 Jefferson Hwy *Web:* www.augustacountylibrary.org	Fishersville	VA	22939	540-949-6354	
Samuels Public Library 330 E Criser Rd *Web:* www.samuelslibrary.net	Front Royal	VA	22630	540-635-3153	635-5653
Gloucester County Library 6920 Main St *Web:* gloucesterva.info	Gloucester	VA	23061	804-693-2998	693-1477
Buchanan County Public Library 1185 Poe Town St *Web:* www.bcplnet.org	Grundy	VA	24614	276-935-5721	
Hampton Public Library 4207 Victoria Blvd *Web:* www.hampton.gov	Hampton	VA	23669	757-727-1154	727-1152
Massanutten Regional Library 174 S Main St **Fax Area Code:* 888 ■ *Web:* www.mrlib.org	Harrisonburg	VA	22801	540-434-4475	334-5211*
Henrico County Public Library 1001 N Laburnum Ave *Web:* www.henricolibrary.org	Henrico	VA	23223	804-290-9300	222-5566
Appomattox Regional Library 209 E Cawson St *Web:* www.arls.org	Hopewell	VA	23860	804-458-6329	
Russell County Public Library 248 W Main St PO Box 247 *Web:* www.russell.lib.va.us	Lebanon	VA	24266	276-889-8044	889-8045
Loudoun County Public Library Administration 380 Old Waterford Rd *Web:* www.library.loudoun.gov	Leesburg	VA	20175	703-777-0368	771-5620
Lynchburg Public Library 2315 Memorial Ave *Web:* www.lynchburgva.gov/publiclibrary	Lynchburg	VA	24501	434-455-6300	845-1479
Newport News Public Library System 700 Town Ctr Dr Ste 300 *Web:* www.nngov.com	Newport News	VA	23606	757-926-1350	926-1365
Norfolk Public Library 235 E Plume St *Web:* www.npl.lib.va.us	Norfolk	VA	23510	757-664-7323	664-7320
Petersburg Public Library 137 S Sycamore St *Web:* www.ppls.org	Petersburg	VA	23803	804-733-2387	733-7972
Pulaski County Library 60 W Third St *Web:* www.pclibs.org	Pulaski	VA	24301	540-980-7770	980-7775
Richmond Public Library 101 E Franklin St *Web:* www.richmondpubliclibrary.org	Richmond	VA	23219	804-646-7223	646-7685
Roanoke County Public Library 3131 Electric Rd *Web:* www.roanokecountyva.gov	Roanoke	VA	24018	540-772-7507	989-3129
Tazewell County Public Library 310 E Main St PO Box 929 *Web:* www.tcplweb.org	Tazewell	VA	24651	276-988-2541	988-5980
Bridgeborn LLC 596 Lynnhaven Pkwy Ste 100 *Web:* www.bridgeborn.com	Virginia Beach	VA	23452	757-437-5000	
Virginia Beach Public Library 4100 Virginia Beach Blvd *Web:* vbgov.com/government/departments/libraries	Virginia Beach	VA	23452	757-385-0150	
Williamsburg Regional Library 7770 Croaker Rd *Web:* www.wrl.org	Williamsburg	VA	23188	757-259-4071	259-4077
Lonesome Pine Regional Library 124 Library Rd *Web:* lprlibrary.org	Wise	VA	24293	276-328-8325	328-1739
York County Public Library 8500 George Washington Memorial Hwy *Web:* yorkcounty.gov	Yorktown	VA	23692	757-890-3377	890-2956

Washington

				Phone	Fax
Anacortes Public Library 1220 Tenth St	Anacortes	WA	98221	360-293-1910	293-1929
Bellingham Public Library 210 Central Ave *Web:* www.bellinghampubliclibrary.org	Bellingham	WA	98225	360-778-7323	676-7795
Kitsap Regional Library 1301 Sylvan Way *TF:* 877-883-9900 ■ *Web:* www.krl.org	Bremerton	WA	98310	360-405-9100	405-9156
Everett Public Library 2702 Hoyt Ave *Web:* www.epls.org	Everett	WA	98201	425-257-8010	257-8016
King County Library System 960 Newport Way NW *Web:* www.kcls.org	Issaquah	WA	98027	425-369-3224	369-3214
Mid-Columbia Libraries 405 S Dayton St *Web:* www.mcl-lib.org	Kennewick	WA	99336	509-586-3156	
Longview Public Library 1600 Louisiana St *Web:* www.longviewlibrary.org	Longview	WA	98632	360-442-5300	442-5954
Puyallup Public Library 324 S Meridian *TF:* 866-862-4232 ■ *Web:* www.cityofpuyallup.org	Puyallup	WA	98371	253-841-5454	841-5483
Richland Public Library 955 Northgate Dr *Web:* www.richland.lib.wa.us	Richland	WA	99352	509-942-7454	942-7447
Seattle Public Library 1000 Fourth Ave *Web:* www.spl.org	Seattle	WA	98104	206-386-4636	386-4119
Spokane Public Library 906 W Main Ave *Web:* www.spokanelibrary.org	Spokane	WA	99201	509-444-5300	444-5365
Pierce County Library System 3005 112th St E *TF:* 800-346-0995 ■ *Web:* www.piercecountylibrary.org	Tacoma	WA	98446	253-536-6500	537-4600
Tacoma Public Library 1102 Tacoma Ave S *Web:* www.tpl.lib.wa.us	Tacoma	WA	98402	253-591-5666	591-5470
Timberland Regional Library 415 Tumwater Blvd SW *TF:* 877-284-6237 ■ *Web:* trl.org	Tumwater	WA	98501	360-943-5001	586-6838
Fort Vancouver Regional Library 1007 E Mill Plain Blvd *Web:* fvrl.ent.sirsi.net	Vancouver	WA	98663	360-906-5000	
Walla Walla Public Library 238 E Alder St *Web:* wallawallapubliclibrary.org	Walla Walla	WA	99362	509-527-4550	527-3748
North Central Regional Library 16 N Columbia St *Web:* www.ncrl.org	Wenatchee	WA	98801	509-663-1117	662-8060
Yakima Valley Regional Library 102 N Third St *Web:* www.yvrl.org	Yakima	WA	98901	509-452-8541	575-2093

West Virginia

				Phone	Fax
Raleigh County Public Library 221 N Kanawha St	Beckley	WV	25801	304-255-0511	255-9161
Craft Memorial Library 600 Commerce St *Web:* craftmemorial.lib.wv.us	Bluefield	WV	24701	304-325-3943	325-3702
Cabell County Public Library 455 Ninth St Plz *Web:* www.cabell.lib.wv.us	Huntington	WV	25701	304-528-5700	528-5701
Ceredo-Kenova Public Library 1200 Oak St *Web:* www.wcpl.lib.wv.us	Kenova	WV	25530	304-453-2462	453-2462
Martinsburg-Berkeley County Public Library 101 W King St *Web:* www.youseemore.com	Martinsburg	WV	25401	304-267-8933	267-9720
Morgantown Public Library 373 Spruce St *Web:* morgantown.lib.wv.us	Morgantown	WV	26505	304-291-7425	291-7437
Fayette County Public Library 531 Summit St *TF:* 855-275-5737 ■ *Web:* fayette.lib.wv.us	Oak Hill	WV	25901	304-465-0121	465-5306
Parkersburg & Wood County Public Library 3100 Emerson Ave *TF:* 800-642-8674 ■ *Web:* parkersburg.lib.wv.us	Parkersburg	WV	26104	304-420-4587	420-4589
Mason County Public Library 508 Viand St *Web:* masoncounty.lib.wv.us	Point Pleasant	WV	25550	304-675-0894	675-0895
Mary H Weirton Public Library 3442 Main St *Web:* www.weirton.lib.wv.us	Weirton	WV	26062	304-797-8510	797-8526
McDowell Public Library 90 Howard St *Web:* mcdowell.lib.wv.us	Welch	WV	24801	304-436-3070	436-8079
Ohio County Public Library 52 16th St *Web:* ohiocountylibrary.org	Wheeling	WV	26003	304-232-0244	232-6848

Wisconsin

Library	City	State	ZIP	Phone	Fax
Northern Waters Library Service 3200 E Lakeshore Dr *TF:* 800-228-5684 ■ *Web:* www.nwls.lib.wi.us	Ashland	WI	54806	715-682-2365	685-2704
Beloit Public Library 605 Eclipse Blvd *Web:* www.als.lib.wi.us	Beloit	WI	53511	608-364-2905	364-2907
Brookfield Public Library 1900 N Calhoun Rd *TF:* 866-868-3947 ■ *Web:* www.ci.brookfield.wi.us/index.aspx?NID=38	Brookfield	WI	53005	262-782-4140	796-6670
Chippewa Falls Public Library 105 W Central St *Web:* www.chippewafallslibrary.org	Chippewa Falls	WI	54729	715-723-1146	720-6922
Indianhead Federated Library System 1538 Truax Blvd *TF:* 800-321-5427 ■ *Web:* iflsweb.org/	Eau Claire	WI	54703	715-839-5082	839-5151
LE Phillips Memorial Public Library 400 Eau Claire St *Web:* www.ecpubliclibrary.info	Eau Claire	WI	54701	715-839-5004	839-3822
Southwest Wisconsin Library System 1775 Fourth St *TF:* 866-866-3393 ■ *Web:* www.swls.org	Fennimore	WI	53809	608-822-3393	
Fond du Lac Public Library 32 Sheboygan St *Web:* fdlpl.org	Fond du Lac	WI	54935	920-929-7080	929-7082
Germantown Community Library N112 W16957 Mequon Rd *Web:* germantownlibrarywi.org	Germantown	WI	53022	262-253-7760	253-7763
USS Liberty Memorial Public 1620 11th Ave.	Grafton	WI	53024	262-375-5315	375-5317
Brown County Library 515 Pine St *Web:* www.co.brown.wi.us	Green Bay	WI	54301	920-448-4400	448-4388
Greenfield Public Library 5310 W Layton Ave. *Web:* www.greenfieldlibrary.org	Greenfield	WI	53220	414-321-9595	321-8595
La Crosse County Library 103 State St *Web:* www.lacrossecountylibrary.org	Holmen	WI	54636	608-526-9600	
Mid Wisconsin Federated Library System 112 Clinton St *Web:* www.mwfls.org	Horicon	WI	53032	920-485-0833	
Arrowhead Library System 210 Dodge St. *TF:* 855-352-9003 ■ *Web:* www.als.lib.wi.us	Janesville	WI	53548	608-758-6690	758-6689
Hedberg Public Library (HPL) 316 S Main St *Web:* www.hedbergpubliclibrary.org	Janesville	WI	53545	608-758-6600	758-6583
Kenosha Public Library 7979 38th Ave *Web:* www.mykpl.info	Kenosha	WI	53142	262-564-6100	564-6370
La Crosse Public Library 800 Main St *Web:* www.lacrosselibrary.org	La Crosse	WI	54601	608-789-7100	789-7106
Madison Public Library 201 W Mifflin St. *Web:* www.madisonpubliclibrary.org	Madison	WI	53703	608-266-6300	266-4338
S Central Library Syst 4610 S Biltmore Ln *Web:* www.scls.info	Madison	WI	53718	608-246-7970	
Manitowoc-Calumet Library System 707 Quay St *Web:* www.manitowoclibrary.org	Manitowoc	WI	54220	920-686-3010	683-4873
Stephenson Public Library 1700 Hall Ave	Marinette	WI	54143	715-732-7570	732-7575
Marshfield Public Library 211 E Second St *Web:* www.marshfieldlibrary.org	Marshfield	WI	54449	715-387-8494	
Menasha Public Library 440 First St. *Web:* www.menashalibrary.org	Menasha	WI	54952	920-967-5166	967-5159
Menomonee Falls Public Library W156 N8436 Pilgrim Rd. *Web:* www.mf.lib.wi.us	Menomonee Falls	WI	53051	262-532-8900	532-8939
Menomonie Public Library 600 Wolske Bay Rd *Web:* www.menomonielibrary.org	Menomonie	WI	54751	715-232-2164	232-2324
Middleton Public Library 7425 Hubbard Ave *Web:* www.midlibrary.org	Middleton	WI	53562	608-831-5564	836-5724
Milwaukee Public Library 814 W Wisconsin Ave. *TF:* 866-947-7363 ■ *Web:* www.mpl.org	Milwaukee	WI	53233	414-286-3000	286-2798
Neenah Public Library 240 E Wisconsin Ave PO Box 569 *Web:* www.neenahlibrary.org	Neenah	WI	54956	920-886-6315	
New Berlin Public Library 15105 Library Ln *Web:* www.newberlinlibrary.org	New Berlin	WI	53151	262-785-4980	
Oshkosh Public Library 106 Washington Ave *Web:* www.oshkoshpubliclibrary.org	Oshkosh	WI	54901	920-236-5200	236-5227
Winnefox Library System 106 Washington Ave. *Web:* www.winnefox.org	Oshkosh	WI	54901	920-236-5220	236-5228
Oxford Public Library 129 S Franklin Ave. *Web:* www.oxfordlibrary.org	Oxford	WI	53952	608-586-4458	586-4559
Racine Public Library 75 Seventh St *TF:* 888-529-0061 ■ *Web:* www.racinelib.lib.wi.us	Racine	WI	53403	262-636-9241	636-9260
River Falls Public Library 115 E Elm St. *Web:* www.rfcity.org	River Falls	WI	54022	715-425-0908	
Mead Public Library 710 N Eigth St *Web:* www.meadpubliclibrary.org	Sheboygan	WI	53081	920-459-3400	459-0204
Portage County Public Library 1001 Main St *Web:* www.uwsp.edu	Stevens Point	WI	54481	715-346-1544	346-1239
Door County Library (DCL) 107 S Fourth Ave *Web:* www.doorcountylibrary.org	Sturgeon Bay	WI	54235	920-743-6578	743-6697
Superior Public Library 1530 Tower Ave *TF:* 866-894-4899 ■ *Web:* www.ci.superior.wi.us	Superior	WI	54880	715-394-8860	394-8870
Lakeshores Library System (LLS) 725 Cornerstone Crossing Ste C *Web:* www.lakeshores.lib.wi.us	Waterford	WI	53185	262-514-4500	514-4544
Watertown Public Library 100 S Water St *TF:* 800-829-3676 ■ *Web:* www.watertownpubliclibrary.org	Watertown	WI	53094	920-262-4090	261-8943
Waukesha Public Library 321 Wisconsin Ave. *Web:* www.waukesha.lib.wi.us	Waukesha	WI	53186	262-524-3680	650-2502
Marathon County Public Library (MCPL) 300 N First St *Web:* www.mcpl.us	Wausau	WI	54403	715-261-7200	261-7204
Wauwatosa Public Library 7635 W N Ave *Web:* www.wauwatosalibrary.org	Wauwatosa	WI	53213	414-471-8484	
West Allis Public Library 7421 W National Ave *TF:* 800-877-8339 ■ *Web:* www.westalliswi.gov	West Allis	WI	53214	414-302-8500	302-8545
West Bend Community Memorial Library 630 Poplar St *Web:* www.west-bendlibrary.org	West Bend	WI	53095	262-335-5151	335-5150
McMillan Memorial Library 490 E Grand Ave *Web:* www.mcmillanlibrary.org	Wisconsin Rapids	WI	54494	715-423-1040	423-2665

Wyoming

Library	City	State	ZIP	Phone	Fax
Natrona County Public Library 307 E Second St *Web:* natronacountylibrary.org	Casper	WY	82601	307-237-4935	266-3734
Laramie County Public Library 2200 Pioneer Ave *Web:* www.lclsonline.org	Cheyenne	WY	82001	307-634-3561	634-2082
Campbell County Public Library 2101 S 4-J Rd *TF:* 888-250-1879 ■ *Web:* ccgov.net/384/library	Gillette	WY	82718	307-682-3223	686-4009
Sweetwater County Library System 300 N First E St *Web:* www.sweetwaterlibraries.com	Green River	WY	82935	307-875-3615	872-3203
Teton County Public Library 125 Virginian Ln *TF:* 800-878-2167 ■ *Web:* www.tclib.org	Jackson	WY	83001	307-733-2164	733-4568
Fremont County Library System 451 N Second St *Web:* fclsonline.org	Lander	WY	82520	307-332-5194	332-3909
Albany County Public Library 310 S Eigth St *Web:* www.albanycountylibrary.org	Laramie	WY	82070	307-721-2580	721-2584

437-4 Special Collections Libraries

Library	City	State	ZIP	Phone	Fax
Academy of Motion Picture Arts & Sciences Herrick Library 333 S La Cienega Blvd *Web:* www.oscars.org	Beverly Hills	CA	90211	310-247-3020	657-5193
African American Museum & Library in Oakland 659 14th St *Web:* oaklandlibrary.org/locations/african-american-museum-library-oakland	Oakland	CA	94612	510-637-0200	637-0204
AIDS Library 1233 Locust St 2nd Fl *TF:* 877-613-4533 ■ *Web:* www.aidslibrary.org	Philadelphia	PA	19107	215-985-4851	985-4492
American Craft Council Library 72 Spring St *Web:* www.craftcouncil.org	New York	NY	10012	212-274-0630	274-0650
American Film Institute Mayer Library 2021 N Western Ave *Web:* www.afi.com	Los Angeles	CA	90027	323-856-7600	
American Kennel Club Library 260 Madison Ave 4th Fl *Web:* www.akc.org	New York	NY	10016	212-696-8200	696-8281
American Library Assn Library 50 E Huron St *TF:* 800-545-2433 ■ *Web:* americanlibrariesmagazine.org	Chicago	IL	60611	312-944-6780	280-3255
American Museum of Natural History *Library* Central Pk W at 79th St *Web:* www.amnh.org	New York	NY	10024	212-769-5400	769-5009
American Philatelic Research Library (APRL) 100 Match Factory Pl *Web:* www.stamps.org/TheLibrary/lib_AbouttheAPRL.htm	Bellefonte	PA	16823	814-933-3803	933-6128
Association for Research & Enlightenment Library 215 67th St. *TF:* 800-333-4499 ■ *Web:* edgarcayce.org	Virginia Beach	VA	23451	757-428-3588	
Athenaeum of Philadelphia 219 S Sixth St. *Web:* www.philaathenaeum.org	Philadelphia	PA	19106	215-925-2688	925-3755
Bentley Historical Library 1150 Beal Ave *TF:* 866-233-6661 ■ *Web:* www.bentley.umich.edu	Ann Arbor	MI	48109	734-764-3482	936-1333
Boston Athenaeum 10 1/2 Beacon St *Web:* www.bostonathenaeum.org	Boston	MA	02108	617-227-0270	227-5266
Brookings Institution Library 1775 Massachusetts Ave NW *Web:* www.brookings.edu	Washington	DC	20036	202-797-6000	797-2970
Center for Migration Studies of New York Inc *Library & Archives* 307 E 60th St 4th Fl. **Fax Area Code:* 646 ■ *Web:* cmsny.org/archives	New York	NY	10022	212-337-3080	998-4625*
Ernie Pyle Library 900 Girard Blvd SE *Web:* abclibrary.org	Albuquerque	NM	87106	505-256-2065	
Folger Shakespeare Library 201 E Capitol St SE *Web:* www.folger.edu	Washington	DC	20003	202-544-4600	544-4623
Frank Lloyd Wright Preservation Trust *Special Collections* 931 Chicago Ave **Fax Area Code:* 708 ■ *Web:* flwright.org	Oak Park	IL	60302	312-994-4000	848-1248*
George Eastman House *Menschel Library* 900 E Ave *Web:* eastmanhouse.org/visit/research.php	Rochester	NY	14607	585-271-3361	271-3970
Gettysburg National Military Park Library & Research Ctr 97 Taneytown Rd. *Web:* nps.gov/nps/404.htm	Gettysburg	PA	17325	717-334-1124	334-1997
Juilliard School, The *Wallace Library* 60 Lincoln Ctr Plz. *Web:* juilliard.edu	New York	NY	10023	212-799-5000	787-9722
Karpeles Manuscript Library 453 Porter Ave *Web:* www.rain.org/~karpeles	Buffalo	NY	14201	716-885-4139	
Library Company of Philadelphia 1314 Locust St *Web:* www.librarycompany.org	Philadelphia	PA	19107	215-546-3181	546-5167

Phone | Fax

Lincoln Memorial Shrine 125 W Vine St Redlands CA 92373 909-798-7632 798-7566
Web: www.lincolnshrine.org

National Baseball Hall of Fame & Museum Library
25 Main St Cooperstown NY 13326 607-547-0330 547-4094
Web: www.baseballhall.org

Portsmouth Athenaeum Nine Market Sq Portsmouth NH 03801 603-431-2538 433-8933
Web: www.portsmouthathenaeum.org

Providence Athenaeum 251 Benefit St Providence RI 02903 401-421-6970 421-2860
Web: www.providenceathenaeum.org

Redwood Library & Athenaeum 50 Bellevue Ave Newport RI 02840 401-847-0292 841-5680
Web: www.redwoodlibrary.org

Rosenbach Museum & Library
2008-2010 Delancey St Philadelphia PA 19103 215-732-1600 545-7529
Web: www.rosenbach.org

Salem Athenaeum, The 337 Essex St Salem MA 01970 978-744-2540 744-7536
Web: www.salemathenaeum.net

Schomburg Ctr for Research in Black Culture
515 Malcolm X Blvd New York NY 10037 212-491-2200
Web: nypl.org

Smithsonian Institution Cullman Library
1000 Constitution Ave NW
Natural History Bldg Washington DC 20560 202-633-2240 633-0219
Web: library.si.edu

Smithsonian Institution Dibner Library of the History of Science & Technology
Smithsonian Institution NMAH 1041 MRC 672
PO Box 37012 Washington DC 20013 202-633-3872 633-9102
Web: library.si.edu

US Holocaust Memorial Museum Library
100 Raoul Wallenburg Pl SW Washington DC 20024 202-488-0400 488-2613
Web: ushmm.org/research/research-in-collections/search-the-collections

Vietnam Archive, The
Texas Tech University PO Box 1041 Lubbock TX 79409 806-742-9010 742-0496
Web: www.vietnam.ttu.edu

Yale University Beinecke Rare Book & Manuscript Library
121 Wall St New Haven CT 06511 203-432-2977 432-4047
Web: web.library.yale.edu

437-5 State Libraries

Phone | Fax

Alabama Public Library Service
6030 Monticello Dr Montgomery AL 36130 334-213-3900 213-3993
Web: webmini.apls.state.al.us

Alaska State Library PO Box 110571 Juneau AK 99811 907-465-2920 465-2665
Web: library.alaska.gov

Arizona State Library
1700 W Washington St Rm 200 Phoenix AZ 85007 602-542-4035 542-4972
Web: www.azlibrary.gov

Arkansas State Library
900 W Capitol Ste 100 Little Rock AR 72201 501-682-2053 682-1529
TF: 866-801-3435 ■ *Web:* www.library.arkansas.gov

California State Library 900 N St Sacramento CA 95814 916-654-0261 654-0241
TF: 800-952-5666 ■ *Web:* www.library.ca.gov

Colorado State Library 201 E Colfax Ave Rm 309 Denver CO 80203 303-866-6900 866-6940
Web: www.cde.state.co.us

Connecticut State Library 231 Capitol Ave Hartford CT 06106 860-757-6510 757-6503
TF: 866-886-4478 ■ *Web:* www.ctstatelibrary.org

Delaware Div of Libraries 497 S Red Haven Ln Dover DE 19901 302-739-4748 739-6787
TF: 800-829-4059 ■ *Web:* www.lib.de.us

Hawaii State Public Library System (HSPLS)
44 Merchant St Honolulu HI 96813 808-586-3704 586-3715
Web: hawaii.sdp.sirsi.net

Idaho Commission for Libraries (ICFL)
325 W State St Boise ID 83702 208-334-2150 334-4016
TF: 800-458-3271 ■ *Web:* www.libraries.idaho.gov

Illinois State Library 300 S Second St Springfield IL 62701 217-782-2994 785-4326
Web: www.cyberdriveillinois.com/departments/library/home.html

Indiana State Library (ISL)
140 N Senate Ave Indianapolis IN 46204 317-232-3694 232-3728
Web: www.in.gov/library

Iowa State Library 112 E Grand Ave Des Moines IA 50319 515-281-4105 281-6191
Web: www.statelibraryofiowa.org

Kentucky Dept for Libraries & Archives
300 Coffee Tree Rd Frankfort KY 40602 502-564-8300 564-5773
TF: 800-372-2968 ■ *Web:* www.kdla.ky.gov

Library of Michigan, The
702 W Kalamazoo St PO Box 30007 Lansing MI 48909 517-373-1580 373-4480
Web: www.michigan.gov/mde/0,1607,7-140-54504---,00.html

Library of Virginia 800 E Broad St Richmond VA 23219 804-692-3500 692-3594
Web: www.lva.virginia.gov

Louisiana State Library 701 N Fourth St Baton Rouge LA 70821 225-342-4915 219-4725
Web: www.state.lib.la.us

Maine State Library 64 State House Stn Augusta ME 04333 207-287-5600 287-5615
Web: www.maine.gov

Massachusetts Board of Library Commissioners
98 N Washington St Boston MA 02114 617-725-1860 725-0140
TF: 800-952-7403 ■ *Web:* mblc.state.ma.us

Missouri State Library
600 W Main St PO Box 387 Jefferson City MO 65102 573-751-3615 526-1142
Web: www.sos.mo.gov/library

Montana State Library (MSL)
1515 E Sixth Ave PO Box 201800 Helena MT 59620 406-444-3115 444-0266
Web: home.montanastatelibrary.org

Nebraska Library Commission 1200 N St Ste 120 Lincoln NE 68508 402-471-2045 471-2083
TF: 800-307-2665 ■ *Web:* nlc.nebraska.gov

Nevada State Library & Archives (NSLA)
100 N Stewart St Carson City NV 89701 775-684-3360 684-3311
TF: 800-922-2880 ■ *Web:* www.nsla.nevadaculture.org

New Hampshire State Library 20 Pk St Concord NH 03301 603-271-2144 271-2205
Web: www.nh.gov

New York State Library Empire State Plaza Albany NY 12230 518-474-5355 474-5786
Web: www.nysl.nysed.gov

North Dakota State Library (NDSL)
604 E Blvd Ave Dept 250 Bismarck ND 58505 701-328-4622 328-2040
TF: 800-472-2104 ■ *Web:* www.library.nd.gov

Oklahoma Dept of Libraries
200 NE 18th St Oklahoma City OK 73105 405-521-2502 525-7804
TF: 800-522-8116 ■ *Web:* www.odl.state.ok.us

Oregon State Library
250 Winter NE State Library Bldg Salem OR 97301 503-378-4243 588-7119
Web: www.oregon.gov/osl

South Carolina State Library 1430 Senate St Columbia SC 29201 803-734-8666 734-8676
Web: www.state.sc.us

South Dakota State Library 800 Governors Dr Pierre SD 57501 605-773-3131 773-4950
TF: 800-423-6665 ■ *Web:* www.library.sd.gov

State Library of Ohio
274 E First Ave Ste 100 Columbus OH 43201 614-644-7061 466-3584
TF: 800-686-1532 ■ *Web:* library.ohio.gov

Tennessee State Library & Archives
403 Seventh Ave N Nashville TN 37243 615-741-2764 741-6471
TF: 877-850-4959 ■ *Web:* www.state.tn.us/tsla

Texas State Library & Archives Commission
PO Box 12927 Austin TX 78711 512-463-5455
Web: www.tsl.texas.gov/

Utah State Library 250 N 1950 W Ste A Salt Lake City UT 84116 801-715-6777 715-6767
TF: 800-662-9150 ■ *Web:* heritage.utah.gov

Vermont Dept of Libraries 109 State St Montpelier VT 05609 802-828-3261 828-2199
TF: 888-350-0950 ■ *Web:* libraries.vermont.gov

Washington State Library PO Box 40220 Olympia WA 98504 360-902-4151 586-7575
Web: www.sos.wa.gov

West Virginia Library Commission
1900 Kanawha Blvd E Charleston WV 25305 304-558-2041 558-2044
TF: 800-642-9021 ■ *Web:* www.librarycommission.lib.wv.us

Wisconsin Department of Public Instruction
125 S Webster St PO Box 7841 Madison WI 53707 608-266-3390 267-1052
TF: 800-441-4563 ■ *Web:* www.dpi.state.wi.us

Wyoming State Library 2800 Central Ave Cheyenne WY 82001 307-777-6333 777-6289
Web: www-wsl.state.wy.us

437-6 University Libraries

Listings for university libraries are arranged by states.

Phone | Fax

Alabama Agricultural & Mechanical University J F Drake Memorial Learning Resources Ctr
PO Box 489 Normal AL 35762 256-372-5000 372-5768
Web: www.aamu.edu

Auburn University
Draughon Library 231 Mell St Auburn University AL 36849 334-844-4500 844-4424*
**Fax:* Admin ■ *Web:* www.lib.auburn.edu

Tuskegee University Ford Motor Co Library/Learning Resource Ctr
Hollis Burke Frissell Library Bldg Tuskegee AL 36088 334-727-8894 727-9282
TF: 800-622-6531 ■ *Web:* www.tuskegee.edu

University of Alabama PO Box 870132 Tuscaloosa AL 35487 205-348-6010 348-9046*
**Fax:* Admissions ■ *TF Admissions:* 800-933-2262 ■ *Web:* www.ua.edu
Gorgas Library Information Ctr First Fl Tuscaloosa AL 35487 205-348-6047 348-0760
TF: 888-764-5603 ■ *Web:* www.lib.ua.edu/libraries/gorgas

UAA/APU Consortium Library
3211 Providence Dr Anchorage AK 99508 907-786-1848
Web: www.consortiumlibrary.org
Rasmuson Library PO Box 756800 Fairbanks AK 99775 907-474-7481 474-6841
Web: library.uaf.edu

Arizona State University
1151 S Forest Ave PO Box 870312 Tempe AZ 85281 480-965-9011 727-6453
Web: www.asu.edu
Hayden Library 300 E Orange Mall Tempe AZ 85281 480-965-3417 965-9169
Web: www.asu.edu

University of Arizona Library
1510 E University Blvd Tucson AZ 85721 520-621-6442 621-9733*
**Fax:* Admin ■ *Web:* www.library.arizona.edu

University of Arkansas
232 Silas Hunt Hall Fayetteville AR 72701 479-575-5346 575-7515*
**Fax:* Admissions ■ *TF Admissions:* 800-377-8632 ■ *Web:* www.uark.edu

University of Central Arkansas Torreyson Library
201 Donaghey Ave Conway AR 72035 501-450-5000 450-5208
Web: www.uca.edu/library

California Institute of Technology Library
1200 E California Blvd MC I-32 Pasadena CA 91125 626-395-3405 792-7540
Web: www.library.caltech.edu

California Lutheran University Pearson Library
60 W Olsen Rd Thousand Oaks CA 91360 805-493-3250 493-3842
TF: 877-258-3678 ■ *Web:* www.callutheran.edu

California Polytechnic State University Kennedy Library
One Grand Ave Bldg 35 San Luis Obispo CA 93407 805-756-2305 756-2346
Web: www.lib.calpoly.edu

California State University Chico
Meriam Library 400 W First St Chico CA 95929 530-898-6502 898-4443
Web: www.csuchico.edu/library

California State University Dominguez Hills
Library 1000 E Victoria St Carson CA 90747 310-243-3696 516-4219
Web: library.csudh.edu

California State University Long Beach
University Library 1250 Bellflower Blvd Long Beach CA 90840 562-985-4047 985-1703
Web: www.csulb.edu/library

California State University Los Angeles
Kennedy Memorial Library
5151 State University Dr Los Angeles CA 90032 323-343-3988 343-6401
Web: www.calstatela.edu/library

California State University Northridge
Oviatt Library 18111 Nordhoff St Northridge CA 91330 818-677-2285 677-2676
Web: library.csun.edu

California State University Sacramento
Library 2000 State University Dr E Sacramento CA 95819 916-278-5679 278-4160
Web: www.library.csus.edu

Phone *Fax*

California State University San Bernardino
Pfau Library 5500 University Pkwy San Bernardino CA 92407 909-537-3447 537-7079
Web: www.lib.csusb.edu
California State University San Marcos
Library 333 S Twin Oaks Vly Rd San Marcos CA 92096 760-750-4340
Web: www.csusm.edu/
California State University Stanislaus
Library One University Cir Turlock CA 95382 209-667-3234 667-3164
Web: ivy.csustan.edu
Humboldt State University Library
One Harpst St Arcata CA 95521 707-826-3431 826-3440
Web: library.humboldt.edu
John F Kennedy University Library (JFKU)
100 Ellinwood Way Pleasant Hill CA 94523 925-969-3300 969-3101
Web: library.jfku.edu
Occidental College Clapp Library
1600 Campus Rd Los Angeles CA 90041 323-259-2640 341-4991
Web: www.oxy.edu
Pepperdine University Payson Library
24255 Pacific Coast Hwy Malibu CA 90263 310-506-4252 506-4117
Web: www.library.pepperdine.edu
San Francisco State University Leonard Library
1630 Holloway Ave San Francisco CA 94132 415-338-1854 338-1504
Web: www.library.sfsu.edu
Sonoma State University University Library
1801 E Cotati Ave Rohnert Park CA 94928 707-664-2397 664-2090
Web: library.sonoma.edu
Stanford University Green Library
557 Escondido Mall Stanford CA 94305 650-723-2300 725-6874
TF: 800-521-0600 ■ *Web:* library.stanford.edu
University of California Davis
Shields Library 100 NW Quad Davis CA 95616 530-752-6561 752-7815
TF: 877-772-5772 ■ *Web:* www.lib.ucdavis.edu
University of California Irvine
Library PO Box 19557 Irvine CA 92623 949-824-6836 824-3644
TF: 800-848-4722 ■ *Web:* www.lib.uci.edu
University of California Los Angeles
Library System
Charles E Young Research Library
PO Box 951575 Los Angeles CA 90095 310-825-4732
Web: www.library.ucla.edu
University of California Riverside
Libraries PO Box 5900 Riverside CA 92517 951-827-3220 827-3281
Web: libraries.universityofcalifornia.edu
University of California San Diego (UCSD)
Biomedical Library 9500 Gilman Dr La Jolla CA 92093 858-534-3253 534-6609
Web: www.libraries.ucsd.edu
Libraries 9500 Gilman Dr Ste 0175 La Jolla CA 92093 858-534-3336
Web: libraries.ucsd.edu
University of California San Francisco
Kalmanovitz Library 530 Parnassus Ave San Francisco CA 94143 415-476-8293 476-4653
Web: www.library.ucsf.edu
University of California Santa Cruz
McHenry Library 1156 High St Santa Cruz CA 95064 831-459-2076 459-8206
Web: www.library.ucsc.edu
University of San Francisco Gleeson Library
2130 Fulton St San Francisco CA 94117 415-422-5555 422-2233
TF: 800-225-5873 ■ *Web:* www.usfca.edu/library
Doheny Memorial Library
3550 Trousdale Pkwy University Pk Campus Los Angeles CA 90089 213-740-4039 740-3488
TF: 800-775-7330 ■ *Web:* www.usc.edu/libraries/locations/doheny
Colorado State University 200 W Lake St Fort Collins CO 80523 970-491-1101 491-7799*
*Fax: Admissions ■ *Web:* www.colostate.edu
Morgan Library
501 University Ave 1019 Campus Delivery Fort Collins CO 80523 970-491-1833 491-1195
Web: www.lib.colostate.edu
University of Colorado at Colorado Springs
Kraemer Family Library
1420 Austin Bluffs Pkwy PO Box 7150 Colorado Springs CO 80918 719-255-3295 528-5227
TF: 800-990-8227 ■ *Web:* www.uccs.edu/~library
University of Denver Westminster Law Library
2255 E Evans Ave Denver CO 80208 303-871-6190 871-6999
Web: www.law.du.edu/library
University of Northern Colorado Michener Library
501 20th St Greeley CO 80639 970-351-2601 351-2963
Web: www.unco.edu
Central Connecticut State University Burritt Library
1615 Stanley St New Britain CT 06050 860-832-2055 832-2118
Web: www.library.ccsu.edu
Connecticut College Shain Library
270 Mohegan Ave New London CT 06320 860-447-1911
Web: www.conncoll.edu/is/charles-e-shain-library.htm
Eastern Connecticut State University Smith Library
83 Windham St Willimantic CT 06226 860-465-4506 465-5522
TF: 800-578-1449 ■ *Web:* www.easternct.edu
Southern Connecticut State University Buley Library
501 Crescent St New Haven CT 06515 203-392-5750 392-5775
Web: library.southernct.edu
Trinity College Raether Library
300 Summit St Hartford CT 06106 860-297-2000 297-2251
Web: www.trincoll.edu/depts/library
University of Connecticut
Babbidge Library 369 Fairfield Rd Unit 2005 Storrs CT 06269 860-486-2219 486-0584*
*Fax: Admin ■ *TF:* 888-603-9635 ■ *Web:* www.lib.uconn.edu
Wesleyan University Olin Library
252 Church St Middletown CT 06459 860-685-2660 685-2661
TF: 800-421-1561 ■ *Web:* www.wesleyan.edu
Yale University Sterling Memorial Library
120 High St New Haven CT 06511 203-432-1775 432-1294
Web: web.library.yale.edu
University of Delaware Library
181 S College Ave Newark DE 19717 302-831-2965 831-1046
Web: library.udel.edu

Phone *Fax*

American University Bender Library
4400 Massachusetts Ave NW Washington DC 20016 202-885-3200 885-3226
Web: american.edu
Gallaudet University Library
800 Florida Ave NE Washington DC 20002 202-651-5217 651-5213
TF: 800-995-0550 ■ *Web:* www.gallaudet.edu/library.html
Gelman Library 2130 H St NW Washington DC 20052 202-994-6558
Web: library.gwu.edu/
Georgetown University Lauinger Library
37th 'O' St NW PO Box 57174 Washington DC 20057 202-687-7452 687-1215
Web: www.library.georgetown.edu
Barry University
Barry Memorial Library
11300 NE Second Ave Miami Shores FL 33161 305-899-3000 899-4792
TF: 800-756-6000 ■ *Web:* www.barry.edu/libraryservices
Florida A & M University
Coleman Memorial Library
1500 S Martin Luther King Blvd Tallahassee FL 32307 850-599-3370 561-2293
TF: 800-540-6754 ■ *Web:* www.famu.edu/library
Florida Atlantic University (FAU)
777 Glades Rd Boca Raton FL 33431 561-297-3000 297-2758*
*Fax: Admissions ■ *TF Admissions:* 800-299-4328 ■ *Web:* www.fau.edu
Florida State University Strozier Library
Rm 314 Tallahassee FL 32306 850-644-5211 644-5016*
*Fax: Admin ■ *Web:* www.lib.fsu.edu
Stetson University DuPont-Ball Library
421 N Woodland Blvd DeLand FL 32723 386-822-7183 740-3626
TF: 800-688-0101 ■ *Web:* secure.stetson.edu
University of Florida Libraries
PO Box 117001 Gainesville FL 32611 352-392-0342 392-7251
TF: 877-351-2377 ■ *Web:* www.uflib.ufl.edu
University of Miami Richter Library
PO Box 248214 Coral Gables FL 33124 305-284-3551 284-4027*
*Fax: Admin ■ *TF:* 800-708-6754 ■ *Web:* www.library.miami.edu
University of South Florida
Libraries 4202 E Fowler Ave LIB 122 Tampa FL 33620 813-974-2729 974-5153
Web: www.lib.usf.edu
University of South Florida Polytechnic
Lakeland 3433 Winter Lake Rd Lakeland FL 33803 863-667-7017 667-7096*
*Fax: Admissions ■ *TF:* 800-873-5636 ■ *Web:* poly.usf.edu
Emory University Woodruff Library
540 Asbury Cir Atlanta GA 30322 404-727-6861 727-0805
Web: emory.edu/home/academics/libraries/index.html
Georgia Institute of Technology Library
225 N Ave NW Atlanta GA 30332 404-894-4500 894-0399
TF: 888-225-7804 ■ *Web:* www.library.gatech.edu
Mercer University 1400 Coleman Ave Macon GA 31207 478-301-2650 301-2828*
*Fax: Admissions ■ *TF:* 800-637-2378 ■ *Web:* www.mercer.edu
Tarver Library 1300 Edgewood Ave Macon GA 31207 478-301-2960 301-2111
Web: libraries.mercer.edu
University of Georgia Library
320 S Jackson St Athens GA 30602 706-542-0621 542-4144*
*Fax: Admin ■ *TF:* 877-314-5560 ■ *Web:* www.libs.uga.edu
Valdosta State University Odum Library
1500 N Patterson St Valdosta GA 31698 229-333-5869 219-1362
Web: www.valdosta.edu
Meader Library 1060 Bishop St Honolulu HI 96813 808-544-0210 521-7998
TF: 866-225-5478 ■ *Web:* www.hpu.edu
University of Hawaii at Hilo
Edwin H. Mookini Library 200 W Kawili St Hilo HI 96720 808-974-7344 974-4106
Web: hilo.hawaii.edu
Hamilton Library 2500 Campus Rd Honolulu HI 96822 808-956-6911 956-7109
Web: www.manoa.hawaii.edu/
Boise State University Albertsons Library
1910 University Dr Boise ID 83725 208-426-1204
Web: library.boisestate.edu
Idaho State University Oboler Library
850 S Ninth Ave Bldg 50 CB 8089 Pocatello ID 83209 208-282-2958 282-5847
Web: www.isu.edu/library
Library PO Box 442350 Moscow ID 83844 208-885-6534 885-6817
Web: www.lib.uidaho.edu
Bradley University Cullom-Davis Library
1501 W Bradley Ave Peoria IL 61625 309-677-2850 677-2558
TF: 800-858-6843 ■ *Web:* www.bradley.edu
DePaul University Library
1 E Jackson Blvd 10th Fl Chicago IL 60605 312-362-8433 362-6186
Web: www.lib.depaul.edu
Illinois Institute of Technology
Galvin Library 35 W 33rd St Chicago IL 60616 312-567-3616 567-5318
Web: www.gl.iit.edu
Illinois State University Milner Library
201 N School St Normal IL 61790 309-438-3451 438-3676*
*Fax: Admin ■ *Web:* www.illinoisstate.edu
Cudahy Library 1032 W Sheridan Rd Chicago IL 60660 773-508-2632
Web: libraries.luc.edu/cudahy
Northeastern Illinois University Williams Library
5500 N St Louis Ave Chicago IL 60625 773-442-4470 442-4531
TF: 800-393-0865 ■ *Web:* www.neiu.edu
Northern Illinois University University Libraries
1425 W Lincoln Hwy DeKalb IL 60115 815-753-1000 753-9803
Web: www.niu.edu
Northwestern University Library
1970 Campus Dr Evanston IL 60208 847-491-7658 491-8306
Web: www.library.northwestern.edu
Southern Illinois University Carbondale Morris Library
605 Agriculture Dr MC 6632 Carbondale IL 62901 618-453-2522 453-3440
Web: www.lib.siu.edu
Southern Illinois University Edwardsville
Lovejoy Library
30 Hairpin Dr PO Box 1063 Edwardsville IL 62026 618-650-4636 650-2717
TF: 888-328-5168 ■ *Web:* www.siue.edu/lovejoylibrary
University of Chicago Library 1100 E 57th St Chicago IL 60637 773-702-8740 702-6623
Web: www.lib.uchicago.edu

	City	State	ZIP	Phone	Fax
University of Illinois Chicago					
Daley Library 801 S Morgan St Rm 1-280	Chicago	IL	60607	312-996-2716	413-0424
TF: 866-904-5843 ■ *Web:* www.uic.edu/depts/lib					
University of Illinois Springfield					
Brookens Library One University Plz	Springfield	IL	62703	217-206-6605	
Web: library.uis.edu					
University of Illinois Urbana-Champaign					
Library 1408 W Gregory Dr MC-522	Urbana	IL	61801	217-333-2290	333-2214
Web: www.library.illinois.edu					
Western Illinois University					
Malpass Library One University Cir	Macomb	IL	61455	309-298-2762	298-2791
Web: www.wiu.edu/library					
Butler University Irwin Library					
4600 Sunset Ave.	Indianapolis	IN	46208	317-940-9227	940-9711
TF: 888-940-8100 ■ *Web:* www.butler.edu/library					
Cunningham Memorial Library					
510 N 6 1/2 St	Terre Haute	IN	47809	812-237-2580	
TF: 800-851-4279 ■ *Web:* odin.indstate.edu					
DePauw University West Library					
11 E Larabee St.	Greencastle	IN	46135	765-658-4420	658-4445
TF: 800-447-2495 ■ *Web:* depauw.edu/libraries/					
Indiana University Bloomington					
Libraries 1320 E Tenth St.	Bloomington	IN	47405	812-855-8028	855-2576
Web: www.libraries.iub.edu					
Indiana University South Bend					
Schurz Library					
1700 Mishawaka Ave PO Box 7111	South Bend	IN	46634	574-520-4440	
Web: www.iusb.edu					
Indiana University-Purdue University Fort Wayne					
Helmke Library 2101 E Coliseum Blvd.	Fort Wayne	IN	46805	260-481-5404	481-6509
Web: usdirectoryfinder.com					
Indiana University-Purdue University Indianapolis					
Library 755 W Michigan St	Indianapolis	IN	46202	317-274-0462	278-2300
TF: 888-422-0499 ■ *Web:* www.ulib.iupui.edu					
Purdue University					
Schleman Hall 475 Stadium Mall Dr.	West Lafayette	IN	47907	765-494-1776	494-0544*
**Fax:* Admissions ■ *Web:* www.purdue.edu					
Libraries ADMN 504 W State St.	West Lafayette	IN	47907	765-494-2900	494-0156*
**Fax:* Admin ■ *Web:* www.lib.purdue.edu					
University of Notre Dame Hesburgh Library					
221 Hesburgh Library	Notre Dame	IN	46556	574-631-5252	631-6772
Web: www.library.nd.edu					
Drake University Cowles Library					
2507 University Ave	Des Moines	IA	50311	515-271-2111	271-3933
Web: www.library.drake.edu					
Grinnell College Burling Library					
6th Ave High St.	Grinnell	IA	50112	641-269-3371	269-4283
TF: 800-247-0113 ■ *Web:* www.grinnell.edu					
Iowa State University Parks Library					
Osborn Dr & Morrill Rd	Ames	IA	50011	515-294-3642	294-5525
Web: www.lib.iastate.edu					
University of Iowa Libraries					
100 Main Library	Iowa City	IA	52242	319-335-5299	335-5900*
**Fax:* Library ■ *Web:* www.lib.uiowa.edu					
Kansas State University Hale Library					
137 Hale Library 1100 Mid-Campus Dr	Manhattan	KS	66506	785-532-3014	532-7415
Web: www.lib.k-state.edu					
Pittsburg State University Axe Library					
1701 S Broadway	Pittsburg	KS	66762	620-235-4882	235-4090
Web: axe.pittstate.edu					
Wichita State University Ablah Library (WSU)					
1845 Fairmount St PO Box 68	Wichita	KS	67260	316-978-3481	978-3048
Web: libraries.wichita.edu					
Kentucky State University Blazer Library					
400 E Main St.	Frankfort	KY	40601	502-597-6852	597-5068
Web: www.kysu.edu					
University of Kentucky Young Library					
500 S Limestone St	Lexington	KY	40506	859-257-0500	257-0505
Web: www.uky.edu					
University of Louisville Ekstrom Library					
2301 S Third St	Louisville	KY	40292	502-852-6747	852-7394
Web: www.louisville.edu					
Grambling State University Lewis Memorial Library (GSU)					
403 Main St PO Box 4256	Grambling	LA	71245	318-274-3354	274-3268
Web: www.gram.edu/research/library					
Louisiana Tech University Prescott Memorial Library					
PO Box 10408	Ruston	LA	71272	318-257-3555	257-2447
TF: 877-557-2575 ■ *Web:* www.latech.edu/library					
Monroe Library 6363 St Charles Ave.	New Orleans	LA	70118	504-864-7111	864-7247
Web: library.loyno.edu					
Nicholls State University Ellender Memorial Library					
906 E First St	Thibodaux	LA	70301	985-448-4646	448-4925
Web: www.nicholls.edu/library					
Northwestern State University Watson Memorial Library					
913 University Pkwy	Natchitoches	LA	71497	318-357-4477	357-4470
TF: 888-540-9657 ■ *Web:* library.nsula.edu					
Southeastern Louisiana University Sims Memorial Library					
SLU 10896	Hammond	LA	70402	985-549-3860	549-3995
Web: www.southeastern.edu					
Tulane University Howard-Tilton Memorial Library					
7001 Freret St.	New Orleans	LA	70118	504-865-5131	865-6773
Web: www.library.tulane.edu					
University of New Orleans Long Library					
2000 Lakeshore Dr	New Orleans	LA	70148	504-280-6556	280-7277
Web: www.library.uno.edu					
Xavier University of Louisiana Library					
One Drexel Dr	New Orleans	LA	70125	504-486-7411	520-7917
Web: www.xula.edu/library					
Bates College Ladd Library 48 Campus Ave.	Lewiston	ME	04240	207-786-6226	786-6055
Web: www.bates.edu					
Bowdoin College Hawthorne-Longfellow Library					
3000 College Stn	Brunswick	ME	04011	207-725-3280	725-3083
Web: library.bowdoin.edu					
Colby College Miller Library					
5100 Mayflower Hill	Waterville	ME	04901	207-859-5147	859-5105
Web: libguides.colby.edu					
Fogler Library 5729 Fogler Library	Orono	ME	04469	207-581-1666	581-1653*
**Fax:* Admin ■ *Web:* www.library.umaine.edu					
Frostburg State University Ort Library					
One Stadium Dr	Frostburg	MD	21532	301-687-4395	687-7069
Web: frostburg.edu/lewis-ort-library/					
Johns Hopkins University Sheridan Libraries					
3400 N Charles St	Baltimore	MD	21218	410-516-8335	516-5080
Web: www.library.jhu.edu					
Salisbury University Blackwell Library					
1101 Camden Ave.	Salisbury	MD	21801	410-543-6130	543-6203
Web: www.salisbury.edu/library					
Towson University Cook Library 8000 York Rd	Towson	MD	21252	410-704-2461	704-3292
Web: cooklibrary.towson.edu					
McKeldin Library McKeldin Library	College Park	MD	20742	301-405-9075	
Web: www.lib.umd.edu					
University of Maryland Baltimore county					
Kuhn Library 1000 Hilltop Cir	Baltimore	MD	21250	410-455-2232	
Web: www.umbc.edu/aok					
Amherst College Frost Library PO Box 5000	Amherst	MA	01002	413-542-2373	542-2662
Web: www.amherst.edu/library					
Boston College Libraries					
140 Commonwealth Ave.	Chestnut Hill	MA	02467	617-552-4472	552-0599
Web: www.bc.edu/libraries					
Boston University Mugar Memorial Library					
771 Commonwealth Ave.	Boston	MA	02215	617-353-3710	353-2084
Web: www.bu.edu/library					
Brandeis University Library 415 S St	Waltham	MA	02454	781-736-7777	736-4719
Web: lts.brandeis.edu					
Bridgewater State College Maxwell Library					
10 Shaw Rd	Bridgewater	MA	02325	508-531-1392	
Web: www.bridgew.edu/library					
College of the Holy Cross Dinand Library					
1 College St	Worcester	MA	01610	508-793-2642	793-2372
TF: 877-433-1843 ■ *Web:* www.holycross.edu					
Harvard University Widener Library					
Hardvar Yard Rm 110	Cambridge	MA	02138	617-495-3650	496-8740
Web: harvard.edu					
Massachusetts Institute of Technology Libraries					
77 Massachusetts Ave	Cambridge	MA	02139	617-253-5282	253-8894
Web: libraries.mit.edu					
Mount Holyoke College Williston Memorial Library					
50 College St	South Hadley	MA	01075	413-538-2000	538-2370
TF: 800-642-4483 ■ *Web:* www.mtholyoke.edu/lits/library					
Northeastern University Snell Library					
360 Huntington Ave	Boston	MA	02115	617-373-2350	373-5409
Web: www.lib.neu.edu					
Simmons College Beatley Library					
300 The Fenway	Boston	MA	02115	617-521-2780	521-3093
TF: 800-831-4284 ■ *Web:* www.simmons.edu					
Suffolk University Sawyer Library					
Eight Ashburton Pl	Boston	MA	02108	617-573-8000	573-8756
Web: www.suffolk.edu/sawlib					
Tufts University Tisch Library					
35 Professors Row	Medford	MA	02155	617-627-3345	627-3002
Web: tischlibrary.tufts.edu					
University of Massachusetts Amherst					
Du Bois Library 154 Hicks Way	Amherst	MA	01003	413-545-0284	545-6873
Web: www.library.umass.edu					
University of Massachusetts Boston					
Healey Library 100 Morrissey Blvd	Boston	MA	02125	617-287-5900	287-5955
Web: www.umb.edu					
University of Massachusetts Dartmouth					
Library 285 Old Westport Rd	North Dartmouth	MA	02747	508-999-8675	999-9142
Web: www.lib.umassd.edu					
University of Massachusetts Lowell					
Lydon Library 84 University Ave	Lowell	MA	01854	978-934-3205	934-3014
Web: www.library.uml.edu					
Andrews University James White Library					
4190 Admin Dr.	Berrien Springs	MI	49104	269-471-3264	471-6166
TF: 800-253-2874 ■ *Web:* www.andrews.edu/library					
Calvin College Hekman Library					
3201 Burton St SE	Grand Rapids	MI	49546	616-526-6000	526-6470
TF: 800-688-0122 ■ *Web:* www.calvin.edu					
Eastern Michigan University Halle Library					
955 W Cir Dr	Ypsilanti	MI	48197	734-487-0020	487-8861
TF: 888-888-3465 ■ *Web:* emich.edu/library/index.php					
Ferris State University					
FLITE Library 1010 Campus Dr	Big Rapids	MI	49307	231-591-3602	591-3724
TF: 800-433-7747 ■ *Web:* www.ferris.edu/library					
Grand Valley State University Zumberge Library					
One Campus Dr	Allendale	MI	49401	616-331-3252	
TF: 800-879-0581 ■ *Web:* www.gvsu.edu/library					
Hope College Van Wylen Library 53 Graves Pl.	Holland	MI	49423	616-395-7790	395-7965
TF: 800-968-7850 ■ *Web:* www.hope.edu					
Lake Superior State University Shouldice Library					
650 W Easterday Ave	Sault Sainte Marie	MI	49783	906-632-6841	635-2111
Web: www.lssu.edu/library					
Michigan State University Library					
100 Library	East Lansing	MI	48824	517-353-8700	432-1191
TF: 800-500-1554 ■ *Web:* www.lib.msu.edu					
Michigan Technological University J R Van Pelt Library					
1400 Townsend Dr	Houghton	MI	49931	906-487-2507	487-2357
TF: 877-688-2586 ■ *Web:* www.mtu.edu/library					
Saginaw Valley State University Zahnow Library					
7400 Bay Rd	University Center	MI	48710	989-964-4240	964-4383
TF: 800-968-9500 ■ *Web:* www.svsu.edu/library					
University of Michigan 515 E Jefferson St.	Ann Arbor	MI	48109	734-764-1817	
Web: www.umich.edu					
Libraries 920 S University Ave.	Ann Arbor	MI	48109	734-764-9356	763-5080
Web: www.lib.umich.edu					

Library	City	State	ZIP	Phone	Fax
University of Michigan Dearborn					
Mardigian Library 4901 Evergreen Rd	Dearborn	MI	48128	313-593-5445	593-5561
TF: 877-619-6650 ■ *Web:* umdearborn.edu/					
Wayne State University Libraries					
5150 Anthony Wayne Dr Ste 1210	Detroit	MI	48202	313-577-4023	577-5265
Web: www.lib.wayne.edu					
Western Michigan University Waldo Library					
1903 W Michigan Ave MS 5353	Kalamazoo	MI	49008	269-387-5202	387-5077
TF: 866-533-3438 ■ *Web:* www.wmich.edu					
Bemidji State University Clark Library					
1500 Birchmont Dr NE	Bemidji	MN	56601	218-755-3345	
Web: www.bemidjistate.edu/library					
Bethel University Library 3900 Bethel Dr	Saint Paul	MN	55112	651-638-6400	
Web: www.bethel.edu					
Hamline University Bush Memorial Library					
1536 Hewitt Ave	Saint Paul	MN	55104	651-523-2375	523-2199
TF: 800-753-9753 ■ *Web:* www.hamline.edu					
Minnesota State University Mankato					
Memorial Library PO Box 8419	Mankato	MN	56002	507-389-5952	389-5155
TF: 800-722-0544 ■ *Web:* www.lib.mnsu.edu					
Saint John's University Alcuin Library					
2835 Abbey Plaza PO Box 2500	Collegeville	MN	56321	320-363-2122	363-2126
TF: 800-544-1489 ■ *Web:* csbsju.edu/libraries					
University of Minnesota Crookston					
UMC Library 2900 University Ave	Crookston	MN	56716	218-281-8399	281-8080
TF: 800-862-6466 ■ *Web:* www1.crk.umn.edu					
University of Minnesota Duluth					
UMD Library 416 Library Dr	Duluth	MN	55812	218-726-8102	726-8019
TF: 866-999-6995 ■ *Web:* www.d.umn.edu/lib					
University of Minnesota Morris					
Briggs Library 600 E Fourth St	Morris	MN	56267	320-589-6176	589-6168
Web: www.morris.umn.edu					
Bio-Medical Library					
505 Essex St SE 325 Diehl Hall	Minneapolis	MN	55455	612-626-4045	
Web: www.hsl.lib.umn.edu/biomed					
University of Minnesota Twin Cities					
Wilson Library 309 19th Ave S	Minneapolis	MN	55455	612-624-3321	626-9353
Web: www.lib.umn.edu/wilson					
University of Saint Thomas O'Shaughnessy-Frey Library					
2115 Summit Ave	Saint Paul	MN	55105	651-962-5494	962-5406
TF: 800-328-6819 ■ *Web:* www.stthomas.edu/libraries					
Winona State University Krueger Library					
PO Box 5838	Winona	MN	55987	507-457-5140	457-5594
Web: www.winona.edu/library					
University of Mississippi PO Box 1848	University	MS	38677	662-915-7211	915-5869*
**Fax:* Admissions ■ *Web:* www.olemiss.edu					
Williams Library 1 Library Loop	University	MS	38677	662-915-7091	915-5734
TF: 800-891-4596 ■ *Web:* www.olemiss.edu					
University of Missouri Kansas City					
Nichols Library 800 E 51st St	Kansas City	MO	64110	816-235-1534	333-5584
TF: 800-775-8652 ■ *Web:* www.umkc.edu					
Washington University in Saint Louis Olin Library					
1 Brookings Dr PO Box 1061	Saint Louis	MO	63130	314-935-5400	935-4045
TF: 800-779-3272 ■ *Web:* library.wustl.edu					
Billings 1500 University Dr	Billings	MT	59101	406-657-2011	657-2302*
**Fax:* Admissions ■ *Web:* www.msubillings.edu					
Library Renne Library PO Box 173320	Bozeman	MT	59717	406-994-3171	994-2851
Web: www.lib.montana.edu					
University of Montana Missoula					
Mansfield Library 32 Campus Dr	Missoula	MT	59812	406-243-2053	243-4067
TF: 800-240-4939 ■ *Web:* www.lib.umt.edu					
Peru State College Library 600 Hoyt St PO Box 10	Peru	NE	68421	402-872-2218	872-2311
Web: www.peru.edu					
University of Nebraska Lincoln					
Love Memorial Library					
318 Love Library PO Box 884100	Lincoln	NE	68588	402-472-2848	472-5131
Web: www.libraries.unl.edu					
University of Nevada Las Vegas					
Lied Library 4505 S Maryland Pkwy	Las Vegas	NV	89154	702-895-3011	
Web: www.unlv.edu					
Dartmouth College Baker-Berry Library					
6025 Baker-Berry Library	Hanover	NH	03755	603-646-2704	
Web: www.dartmouth.edu/~library/bakerberry					
Keene State College Mason Library 229 Main St	Keene	NH	03435	603-358-2711	
TF: 800-572-1909 ■ *Web:* www.keene.edu					
Plymouth State University Lamson Library					
17 High St	Plymouth	NH	03264	603-535-2258	535-2445
Web: library.plymouth.edu					
University of New Hampshire					
Three Garrison Ave Grant House	Durham	NH	03824	603-862-1234	862-0077*
**Fax:* Admissions ■ *Web:* www.unh.edu					
Dimond Library 18 Library Way	Durham	NH	03824	603-862-1540	862-0247*
**Fax:* Admin ■ *Web:* www.library.unh.edu					
Princeton University Library					
One Washington Rd	Princeton	NJ	08544	609-258-4820	258-0441*
**Fax:* Library ■ *Web:* library.princeton.edu					
Camden 406 Penn St	Camden	NJ	08102	856-225-6104	225-6498*
**Fax:* Admissions ■ *Web:* www.camden.rutgers.edu					
Libraries 169 College Ave	New Brunswick	NJ	08901	732-932-7505	932-1101
Web: www.libraries.rutgers.edu					
William Paterson University Cheng Library					
300 Pompton Rd	Wayne	NJ	07470	973-720-2541	720-2585
Web: www.wpunj.edu/library					
New Mexico Institute of Mining & Technology Skeen Library					
801 Leroy Pl	Socorro	NM	87801	575-835-5614	835-6666*
**Fax Area Code:* 505 ■ *Web:* www.nmt.edu					
New Mexico State University (NMSU)					
MSC-3A PO Box 30001	Las Cruces	NM	88003	575-646-3121	646-6330*
**Fax:* Admissions ■ *TF Admissions:* 800-662-6678 ■ *Web:* www.nmsu.edu					
Baruch College The William & Anita Newman Library					
151 E 25th St	New York	NY	10010	646-312-1600	
Web: www.baruch.cuny.edu					
Brooklyn College Library 2900 Bedford Ave	Brooklyn	NY	11210	718-951-5335	951-4540
Web: library.brooklyn.cuny.edu					
Buffalo State College EH Butler Library					
1300 Elmwood Ave	Buffalo	NY	14222	716-878-6314	878-3134
Web: www.buffalostate.edu/library					
City College of New York Cohen Library					
160 Convent Ave	New York	NY	10031	212-650-7155	650-7604
Web: www.ccny.cuny.edu/library					
Colgate University Case Library 13 Oak Dr	Hamilton	NY	13346	315-228-7300	228-7934
TF: 888-827-4434 ■ *Web:* www.colgate.edu					
Columbia University Butler Library					
535 W 114th St	New York	NY	10027	212-854-2271	854-9099
Web: library.columbia.edu					
Cornell University Olin Library					
Olin & Uris Libraries	Ithaca	NY	14853	607-255-4144	255-6788
Web: olinuris.library.cornell.edu					
Hamilton College Burke Library					
198 College Hill Rd	Clinton	NY	13323	315-859-4475	859-4578
Web: www.hamilton.edu/library					
Hofstra University Axinn Library					
123 Hofstra University	Hempstead	NY	11549	516-463-5940	463-6387
Web: www.hofstra.edu					
Hunter College Library 695 Pk Ave	New York	NY	10065	212-772-4179	772-4142
Web: hunter.cuny.edu					
Ithaca College Library 953 Danby Rd	Ithaca	NY	14850	607-274-3206	
Web: www.ithacalibrary.com					
Jewish Theological Seminary Library					
3080 Broadway	New York	NY	10027	212-678-8075	678-8891
Web: jtsa.edu/x166.xml					
Lehman College Library 250 Bedford Pk Blvd W	Bronx	NY	10468	718-960-8577	960-8952
Web: www.lehman.edu/provost/library					
New York University Bobst Library					
70 Washington Sq S	New York	NY	10012	212-998-2500	995-4829
Web: www.library.nyu.edu					
Niagara University Library					
5795 Lewison Rd	Niagara University	NY	14109	716-286-8000	286-8009
Web: library.niagara.edu					
Pace University					
Birnbaum Library One Pace Plz	New York	NY	10038	212-346-1332	346-1516
Web: www.pace.edu/library					
Rensselaer Polytechnic Institute Folsom Library					
110 Eigth St	Troy	NY	12180	518-276-6000	276-8559
Web: library.rpi.edu					
Rockefeller University					
Library 1230 York Ave PO Box 263	New York	NY	10065	212-327-8904	
Web: rockefeller.edu					
State University of New York College at Geneseo					
Milne Library One College Cir	Geneseo	NY	14454	585-245-5594	245-5769
Web: www.geneseo.edu					
Syracuse University Bird Library					
222 Waverly Ave	Syracuse	NY	13244	315-443-2093	443-9510*
**Fax:* Admin ■ *TF:* 866-722-7858 ■ *Web:* library.syr.edu					
University at Albany University Libraries					
1400 Washington Ave	Albany	NY	12222	518-442-3600	442-3567
TF: 800-342-4146 ■ *Web:* library.albany.edu					
University at Buffalo					
University Libraries 433 Capen Hall	Buffalo	NY	14260	716-645-2965	645-3844
Web: library.buffalo.edu					
University of Rochester River Campus Libraries					
755 Library Rd PO Box 270055	Rochester	NY	14627	585-275-5804	273-5309
Web: www.library.rochester.edu					
Vassar College Library					
124 Raymond Ave PO Box 20	Poughkeepsie	NY	12604	845-437-5760	437-5864
Web: library.vassar.edu					
Wells College Long Library 170 Main St	Aurora	NY	13026	315-364-3266	
TF: 800-952-9355 ■ *Web:* www.wells.edu					
Appalachian State University					
Belk Library 218 College St PO Box 32026	Boone	NC	28608	828-262-2300	262-3001*
**Fax:* Administration ■ *TF:* 877-423-0086 ■ *Web:* www.library.appstate.edu					
Duke University Perkins Library PO Box 90193	Durham	NC	27708	919-660-5800	660-5923
Web: www.library.duke.edu					
East Carolina University Joyner Library					
E Fifth St	Greenville	NC	27858	252-328-6518	328-4834
Web: www.ecu.edu/cs-lib					
North Carolina State University Libraries					
CB 7111	Raleigh	NC	27695	919-515-2843	515-3628*
**Fax:* Admin ■ *TF:* 877-601-0590 ■ *Web:* www.lib.ncsu.edu					
Davis Library CB 3900	Chapel Hill	NC	27514	919-962-1356	843-8936
Web: library.unc.edu					
Wake Forest University Reynolds Library					
PO Box 7777	Winston-Salem	NC	27109	336-758-4931	758-5605
Web: www.zsr.wfu.edu					
University of North Dakota Chester Fritz Library					
3051 University Ave Stop 9000	Grand Forks	ND	58202	701-777-2189	777-3319
Web: www.library.und.edu					
Ashland University Library 509 College Ave	Ashland	OH	44805	419-289-5400	289-5422
TF: 866-434-5222 ■ *Web:* www.ashland.edu					
Bowling Green State University Jerome Library (BGSU)					
1001 E Wooster St	Bowling Green	OH	43403	419-372-2051	372-0475
TF: 866-246-6732 ■ *Web:* bgsu.edu/library.html					
Case Western Reserve University kelvin Smith Library					
11055 Euclid Ave	Cleveland	OH	44106	216-368-3506	368-3669
Web: library.case.edu					
Cedarville University Centennial Library					
251 N Main St	Cedarville	OH	45314	937-766-7700	766-2337
TF: 800-233-2784 ■ *Web:* www.cedarville.edu/academics/library					
Cleveland State University University Library					
2121 Euclid Ave Rhodes Tower	Cleveland	OH	44115	216-687-5300	687-5098
Web: www.ulib.csuohio.edu					
Denison University Doane Library					
400 W Loop PO Box L	Granville	OH	43023	740-587-6235	587-6285
TF: 800-336-4766 ■ *Web:* www.denison.edu/library					

	City	State	ZIP	Phone	Fax
Kent State University					
Libraries 1125 Risman Dr	Kent	OH	44242	330-672-3456	672-4811*
**Fax:* Admin ■ *Web:* www.library.kent.edu					
Oberlin College Library 148 W College St	Oberlin	OH	44074	440-775-8285	775-8739
Web: home.oberlin.edu					
Ohio Northern University Heterick Memorial Library					
525 S Main St	Ada	OH	45810	419-772-2181	772-1927
TF: 866-943-5787 ■ *Web:* onu.edu/academics/heterick_memorial_library					
Ohio State University 154 W 12th Ave	Columbus	OH	43210	614-292-3980	292-4818*
**Fax:* Admissions ■ *TF:* 800-426-5046 ■ *Web:* www.osu.edu					
Libraries 1858 Neil Ave Mall	Columbus	OH	43210	614-292-6175	292-7859
TF: 800-555-1212 ■ *Web:* www.library.osu.edu					
Alden Library Park Pl	Athens	OH	45701	740-593-2699	593-0138*
**Fax:* Admin ■ *Web:* www.library.ohiou.edu					
Shawnee State University Clark Memorial Library					
940 Second St	Portsmouth	OH	45662	740-351-4778	
Web: shawnee.edu					
University of Cincinnati Langsam Library					
PO Box 210033	Cincinnati	OH	45221	513-556-1515	556-0325*
**Fax:* Admin ■ *TF:* 866-397-3382 ■ *Web:* www.libraries.uc.edu					
University of Library 302 Buchtel Common	Akron	OH	44325	330-972-5355	972-5106
Web: www.uakron.edu/libraries					
University of Toledo Carlson Library					
2801 W Bancroft St MS 509	Toledo	OH	43606	419-530-2324	530-2726
TF: 800-586-5336 ■ *Web:* www.utoledo.edu/library					
Wittenberg University Thomas Library					
807 Woodlawn Ave PO Box 7207	Springfield	OH	45504	937-327-7511	327-6139
TF: 800-677-7558 ■ *Web:* www6.wittenberg.edu/lib					
Wright State University Dunbar Library					
3640 Colonel Glenn Hwy	Dayton	OH	45435	937-775-4125	775-2356
Web: www.libraries.wright.edu					
Xavier University Library					
3800 Victory Pkwy	Cincinnati	OH	45207	513-745-3881	745-1932
TF: 877-382-2293 ■ *Web:* www.xavier.edu/library					
Youngstown State University Maag Library					
One University Plz	Youngstown	OH	44555	330-941-3675	941-3734
Web: www.maag.ysu.edu					
East Central University Linscheid Library					
1100 E 14th St	Ada	OK	74820	580-332-8000	436-3242
TF: 800-772-1213 ■ *Web:* www.ecok.edu					
Broken Arrow 3100 E New Orleans	Broken Arrow	OK	74014	918-449-6000	449-6190*
**Fax:* Admissions ■ *Web:* www.nsuba.edu					
Vaughan Library 711 N Grand Ave	Tahlequah	OK	74464	918-456-5511	
Web: library.nsuok.edu					
Oklahoma State University					
219 Student Union Bldg	Stillwater	OK	74078	405-744-5000	744-7092
TF: 800-852-1255 ■ *Web:* www.okstate.edu					
Oral Roberts University Library					
7777 S Lewis Ave	Tulsa	OK	74171	918-495-6723	495-6893
TF: 800-678-8876 ■ *Web:* oru.edu/library					
University of Oklahoma Bizzell Memorial Library					
401 W Brooks St	Norman	OK	73019	405-325-4142	325-7550*
**Fax:* Admin ■ *Web:* www.libraries.ou.edu					
University of Tulsa McFarlin Library					
2933 E Sixth St	Tulsa	OK	74104	918-631-2873	631-3791
Web: www.lib.utulsa.edu					
Eastern Oregon University Pierce Library					
One University Blvd	La Grande	OR	97850	541-962-3579	962-3335
Web: library.eou.edu					
Lewis & Clark College Watzek Library					
0615 Palatine Hill Rd	Portland	OR	97219	503-768-7270	768-7282
Web: library.lclark.edu					
Oregon State University Valley Library					
121 Vly Library	Corvallis	OR	97331	541-737-3411	737-3453*
**Fax:* Admin ■ *Web:* osulibrary.oregonstate.edu					
Pacific University Library					
2043 College Way	Forest Grove	OR	97116	503-352-1400	352-1416
TF: 800-677-6712 ■ *Web:* pacificu.edu/libraries					
Portland State University Millar Library					
1875 SW Pk Ave	Portland	OR	97201	503-725-5874	
Web: library.pdx.edu					
Reed College Library 3203 SE Woodstock Blvd	Portland	OR	97202	503-777-7702	777-7786
Web: library.reed.edu					
Southern Oregon University Hannon Library					
1250 Siskiyou Blvd	Ashland	OR	97520	541-552-6441	552-6429
Web: hanlib.sou.edu					
University of Oregon Knight Library					
1299 University of Oregon	Eugene	OR	97403	541-346-3053	346-3485*
**Fax:* Library ■ *Web:* library.uoregon.edu					
Western Oregon University Hamersly Library					
345 N Monmouth Ave	Monmouth	OR	97361	503-838-8418	838-8645
Web: www.wou.edu/provost/library					
Willamette University Hatfield Library					
900 State St	Salem	OR	97301	503-370-6312	370-6141
Web: library.willamette.edu					
Bloomsburg University Harvey A. Andruss Library					
400 E Second St	Bloomsburg	PA	17815	570-389-4000	389-3895
Web: bloomu.edu					
Bucknell University Bertrand Library					
69 Coleman Hall Rd	Lewisburg	PA	17837	570-577-1557	577-3313
Web: www.bucknell.edu/isr					
California University of Pennsylvania Louis L Manderino Library					
250 University Ave	California	PA	15419	724-938-4091	938-5901
Web: www.library.calu.edu					
Dickinson College Waidner-Spahr Library					
PO Box 1773	Carlisle	PA	17013	717-245-1397	245-1439
Web: dickinson.edu/homepage/604/library_information_services					
Drexel University Hagerty Library					
33rd St & Market St	Philadelphia	PA	19104	215-895-2767	895-2070
TF: 888-278-8825 ■ *Web:* www.library.drexel.edu					
Duquesne University Gumberg Library					
600 Forbes Ave	Pittsburgh	PA	15282	412-396-6130	396-1658
TF: 800-283-3853 ■ *Web:* www.duq.edu/library					
East Stroudsburg University Kemp Library					
200 Prospect St	East Stroudsburg	PA	18301	570-422-3465	422-3151
TF: 877-422-1378 ■ *Web:* www.esu.edu/library					
Edinboro University of Pennsylvania Baron-Forness Library (EUB)					
200 Tartan Rd	Edinboro	PA	16444	814-732-2273	732-2883
TF: 888-845-2890 ■ *Web:* edinboro.edu/home/page_not_found.dot					
Franklin & Marshall College Shadek-Fackenthal Library					
450 College Ave	Lancaster	PA	17604	717-291-4223	291-4160
TF: 866-366-7655 ■ *Web:* www.fandm.edu					
Haverford College Magill Library					
370 Lancaster Ave	Haverford	PA	19041	610-896-1163	896-1102
Web: library.haverford.edu					
Indiana University of Pennsylvania Stapleton Library					
431 S 11th St	Indiana	PA	15705	724-357-2340	357-4891
TF: 888-342-2383 ■ *Web:* www.iup.edu/library					
Kutztown University Rohrbach Library					
15200 Kutztown Rd Bldg 5	Kutztown	PA	19530	610-683-4480	683-4483
Web: www.kutztown.edu/library					
La Salle University Connelly Library					
1900 W Olney Ave	Philadelphia	PA	19141	215-951-1287	
Web: www.lasalle.edu/library					
Lafayette College Skillman Library					
710 Sullivan Rd	Easton	PA	18042	610-330-5151	252-0370
Web: library.lafayette.edu					
Pennsylvania State University					
201 Shields Bldg Ofc of Admissions	University Park	PA	16802	814-865-4700	863-7590
Web: www.psu.edu					
Libraries 510 Paterno Library	University Park	PA	16802	814-865-6368	865-3665
Web: www.libraries.psu.edu					
Swarthmore College McCabe Library					
500 College Ave	Swarthmore	PA	19081	610-328-8477	
Web: www.swarthmore.edu					
Temple University Paley Library					
1210 W Berks St MS 017-00	Philadelphia	PA	19122	215-204-8231	204-5201
Web: www.library.temple.edu					
University of Pennsylvania Van Pelt Library					
3420 Walnut St	Philadelphia	PA	19104	215-898-7091	898-0559
TF: 877-784-8379 ■ *Web:* www.library.upenn.edu/vanpelt					
Hillman Library 3960 Forbes Ave	Pittsburgh	PA	15260	412-648-7710	648-7887
TF: 888-465-4329 ■ *Web:* www.library.pitt.edu					
Villanova University Falvey Memorial Library					
800 Lancaster Ave	Villanova	PA	19085	610-519-4270	519-5018
Web: www.library.villanova.edu					
West Chester University Green Library					
700 S High St	West Chester	PA	19383	610-436-1000	738-0555
TF: 800-886-9654 ■ *Web:* www.wcupa.edu/library.fhg					
Brown University Rockefeller Library					
10 Prospect St	Providence	RI	02912	401-863-2162	863-1272
TF: 877-668-4493 ■ *Web:* www.brown.edu					
Bryant University Krupp Library					
1150 Douglas Pk	Smithfield	RI	02917	401-232-6125	232-6126
Web: bryant.edu					
Salve Regina University McKillop Library					
100 Ochre Pt Ave	Newport	RI	02840	401-341-2291	341-2951
Web: library.salve.edu					
University of Rhode Island (URI)					
45 Upper College Rd	Kingston	RI	02881	401-874-1000	874-5523
Web: ww2.uri.edu					
Libraries 15 Lippitt Rd	Kingston	RI	02881	401-874-2666	874-4608
Web: ww2.uri.edu					
Clemson University Library					
413 Cooper Library PO Box 343001	Clemson	SC	29634	864-656-5186	
Web: www.clemson.edu					
Francis Marion University Rogers Library					
PO Box 100547	Florence	SC	29502	800-368-7551	661-1309*
**Fax Area Code:* 843 ■ *TF:* 800-368-7551 ■ *Web:* www.fmarion.edu/rogerslibrary/directory					
University of South Carolina					
1600 Hampton St	Columbia	SC	29208	803-777-7000	777-0101*
**Fax:* Admissions ■ *TF:* 800-868-5872 ■ *Web:* www.sc.edu					
Cooper Library 1322 Greene St	Columbia	SC	29208	803-777-2805	777-9503*
**Fax:* Admin ■ *Web:* library.sc.edu					
South Dakota State University Briggs Library					
N Campus Dr PO Box 2115	Brookings	SD	57007	605-688-5106	688-6133
TF: 800-786-2038 ■ *Web:* www.sdstate.edu					
University of South Dakota Weeks Library					
414 E Clark St	Vermillion	SD	57069	605-677-5371	677-5488
Web: www.usd.edu					
Middle Tennessee State University Walker Library					
1301 E Main St	Murfreesboro	TN	37132	615-898-2300	904-8505
Web: library.mtsu.edu					
Rhodes College Barret Library 2000 N Pkwy	Memphis	TN	38112	901-843-3900	843-3404
Web: www.rhodes.edu					
University of Memphis McWherter Library					
126 Ned R McWherter Library	Memphis	TN	38152	901-678-2201	678-8218
TF: 866-670-6147 ■ *Web:* www.memphis.edu					
University of Tennessee Chattanooga					
Lupton Library					
University of Tennessee at Chattanooga					
700 Vine St	Chattanooga	TN	37403	423-425-4501	425-4775
Web: utc.edu/library					
University of Tennessee Knoxville					
Hodges Library 1015 Volunteer Blvd	Knoxville	TN	37996	865-974-4351	974-0555
TF: 800-426-9119 ■ *Web:* www.lib.utk.edu					
Vanderbilt University Heard Library					
419 21st Ave S	Nashville	TN	37240	615-322-7100	343-8279
Web: www.library.vanderbilt.edu					
Abilene Christian University Brown Library (ACU)					
760 Library Ct	Abilene	TX	79699	325-674-2000	674-2202
TF: 800-460-6228 ■ *Web:* www.acu.edu/academics/library					
Angelo State University Henderson Library					
2025 S Johnson St	San Angelo	TX	76909	325-942-2051	942-2198
TF: 800-946-8627 ■ *Web:* www.angelo.edu					

	City	State	Zip	Phone	Fax
Baylor University Moody Memorial Library & Jones Library PO Box 97148 *Web:* www.baylor.edu/lib	Waco	TX	76798	254-710-2112	752-5332
Lamar University Gray Library 211 Redbird Ln PO Box 10021 *Web:* vmlibweb.lamar.edu	Beaumont	TX	77710	409-880-8118	880-2318
McMurry University Jay-Rollins Library 1601 War Hawk Way *Web:* www.mcm.edu/newsite/web/library	Abilene	TX	79605	325-793-4692	
Rice University Fondren Library 6100 Main St MS 44 *Web:* library.rice.edu	Houston	TX	77005	713-348-4022	348-5258
Sixth Floor Museum 411 Elm St Ste 120 Dealey Plz *TF:* 888-485-4854 ■ *Web:* www.jfk.org	Dallas	TX	75202	214-747-6660	747-6662
Southern Methodist University Central University Libraries 6425 Boaz Ln PO Box 750135 *Web:* www.smu.edu/libraries	Dallas	TX	75205	214-768-2000	768-3815
Stephen F Austin State University Steen Library (SFASU) 1936 N St *Web:* www.sfasu.edu	Nacogdoches	TX	75962	936-468-3401	
Texas A & M University *Evans Library* 5000 Tamu *Web:* library.tamu.edu	College Station	TX	77843	979-845-5741	845-6238
Texas Christian University Mary Couts Burnett Library 2800 S University Dr *TF:* 866-321-7428 ■ *Web:* www.tcu.edu	Fort Worth	TX	76129	817-257-7000	257-7282
Texas State University San Marcos *Alkek Library* 601 University Dr *Web:* www.library.txstate.edu	San Marcos	TX	78666	512-245-2133	245-3002
Texas Tech University Libraries 18th & Boston Ave PO Box 40002 *TF:* 888-270-3369 ■ *Web:* library.ttu.edu	Lubbock	TX	79409	806-742-2265	742-0737
University of Houston 4800 Calhoun Rd *Web:* www.uh.edu	Houston	TX	77004	713-743-1000	743-9665
University of North Texas Libraries 1155 Union Cir PO Box 305190 **Fax:* Circulation Desk ■ *TF:* 877-872-0264 ■ *Web:* www.library.unt.edu	Denton	TX	76203	940-565-2413	565-4949*
Allied Health Sciences School 5323 Harry Hines Blvd **Fax Area Code:* 512	Dallas	TX	75390	214-648-3111	475-7641*
Libraries PO Box P *Web:* www.lib.utexas.edu	Austin	TX	78713	512-495-4250	495-4347
Brigham Young University 770 E University Pkwy	Provo	UT	84602	801-422-4636	
Lee Library 2060 HBLL **Fax:* Admin ■ *Web:* www.lib.byu.edu	Provo	UT	84602	801-422-2905	422-0466*
University of Utah Marriott Library Marriott Library 295 S 1500 E **Fax:* Admin ■ *TF:* 800-458-0145 ■ *Web:* www.lib.utah.edu	Salt Lake City	UT	84112	801-581-8558	585-3464*
Utah State University Merrill-Cazier Library 3000 Old Main Hill **Fax:* Admin ■ *Web:* www.library.usu.edu	Logan	UT	84322	435-797-2631	797-2880*
Weber State University *Stewart Library* 2901 University Cir *TF:* 877-306-3140 ■ *Web:* www.library.weber.edu	Ogden	UT	84408	801-626-6403	626-7045
Middlebury College Library 110 Storrs Ave *TF:* 800-829-1040 ■ *Web:* www.middlebury.edu	Middlebury	VT	05753	802-443-5494	443-5698
University of Vermont Bailey/Howe Library 538 Main St *Web:* library.uvm.edu	Burlington	VT	05405	802-656-2023	656-4038
Christopher Newport University Smith Library One University Pl *Web:* cnu.edu	Newport News	VA	23606	757-594-7133	594-7776
College of William & Mary Swem Library PO Box 8794 *TF:* 800-462-3683 ■ *Web:* www.swem.wm.edu	Williamsburg	VA	23187	757-221-3072	221-2635
Emory & Henry College Kelly Library 30450 Armbrister Dr *Web:* www.ehc.edu	Emory	VA	24327	276-944-6208	944-4592
Fenwick Library 4400 University Dr *Web:* library.gmu.edu	Fairfax	VA	22030	703-993-2240	
James Madison University Library 880 Madison Dr MSC 1704 *Web:* www.lib.jmu.edu	Harrisonburg	VA	22807	540-568-6150	
Radford University McConnell Library PO Box 6881 *Web:* library.radford.edu	Radford	VA	24142	540-831-5471	831-6138
Regent University *Library* 1000 Regent University Dr *TF:* 888-249-1822 ■ *Web:* www.regent.edu/general/library	Virginia Beach	VA	23464	757-352-4916	226-4167
Sweet Briar College Cochran Library 134 Chapel Rd *Web:* sbc.libguides.com/content.php?pid=168514	Sweet Briar	VA	24595	434-381-6138	381-6173
Boatwright Memorial Library 28 Westhampton Way *Web:* library.richmond.edu	Richmond	VA	23173	804-289-8454	287-1840
Virginia Commonwealth University Cabell Library 901 Pk Ave PO Box 842033 *TF:* 844-352-7399 ■ *Web:* library.vcu.edu/about/libraries/cabell	Richmond	VA	23284	804-828-1105	828-0151
Virginia Polytechnic Institute & State University Libraries PO Box 90001 **Fax:* Admin ■ *Web:* www.lib.vt.edu	Blacksburg	VA	24062	540-231-6170	231-7808*
Central Washington University Brooks Library 400 E University Way *Web:* www.lib.cwu.edu	Ellensburg	WA	98926	509-963-3682	963-3684
Evergreen State College Evans Library 2700 Evergreen Pkwy NW *Web:* library.evergreen.edu	Olympia	WA	98505	360-867-6250	
Gonzaga University Foley Library 502 E Boone Ave *TF:* 800-498-5941 ■ *Web:* gonzaga.edu/campus%2dresources/	Spokane	WA	99258	509-323-5931	323-5904
Pacific Lutheran University Mortvedt Library 12180 Pk Ave S *Web:* www.plu.edu/~libr	Tacoma	WA	98447	253-535-7500	535-7315
Seattle University Lemieux Library 901 12th Ave *TF:* 800-426-7123 ■ *Web:* www.seattleu.edu/lemlib	Seattle	WA	98122	206-296-6210	296-2572
University of Washington Libraries PO Box 352900 *Web:* www.lib.washington.edu	Seattle	WA	98195	206-543-0242	
Washington State University PO Box 641040 *TF:* 888-468-6978 ■ *Web:* www.wsu.edu	Pullman	WA	99164	509-335-3564	335-4902
West Virginia University PO Box 6009 *TF:* 800-344-9881 ■ *Web:* www.wvu.edu	Morgantown	WV	26506	304-293-2121	293-3080
Libraries PO Box 6069 *Web:* www.libraries.wvu.edu	Morgantown	WV	26506	304-293-2440	293-6638
Lawrence University Mudd Library 711 E Boldt Way *TF:* 888-300-4473 ■ *Web:* www.lawrence.edu/library	Appleton	WI	54911	920-832-6750	832-6967
Marquette University Raynor Memorial Library 1355 W Wisconsin Ave *TF:* 800-876-1715 ■ *Web:* www.marquette.edu/library	Milwaukee	WI	53233	414-288-7556	288-5324
University of Wisconsin Eau Claire *McIntyre Library* 105 Garfield Ave *TF:* 877-267-1384 ■ *Web:* www.uwec.edu	Eau Claire	WI	54702	715-836-3715	836-2949
University of Wisconsin Green Bay *Cofrin Library* 2420 Nicolet Dr *Web:* www.uwgb.edu/library	Green Bay	WI	54311	920-465-2333	465-2388
University of Wisconsin La Crosse *Murphy Library* 1631 Pine St *Web:* www.uwlax.edu/murphylibrary	La Crosse	WI	54601	608-785-8000	785-8639
Ebling Library 750 Highland Ave *Web:* www.ebling.library.wisc.edu	Madison	WI	53705	608-262-2020	262-4732
University of Wisconsin Madison *Libraries* 728 State St *Web:* www.library.wisc.edu	Madison	WI	53706	608-262-3193	265-2754
University of Wisconsin Milwaukee (UWM) *Golda Meir Library* 2311 E Hartford Ave PO Box 604 *Web:* www4.uwm.edu	Milwaukee	WI	53211	414-229-4785	
University of Wisconsin Oshkosh *Polk Library* 800 Algoma Blvd *Web:* www.uwosh.edu/library	Oshkosh	WI	54901	920-424-3334	424-7338
University of Wisconsin Parkside *Library* 900 Wood Rd *Web:* www.uwp.edu	Kenosha	WI	53141	262-595-2360	595-2545
University of Wisconsin Stevens Point *University Library* 900 Reserve St *Web:* www.uwsp.edu	Stevens Point	WI	54481	715-346-2540	346-2367
University of Wisconsin Stout *Library* 315 Tenth Ave E *TF:* 866-716-6685 ■ *Web:* www.uwstout.edu/lib	Menomonie	WI	54751	715-232-1215	
University of Wisconsin Superior *Jim Dan Hill Library* PO Box 2000 *TF:* 877-232-1727 ■ *Web:* www.uwsuper.edu/library	Superior	WI	54880	715-394-8343	
University of Wisconsin Whitewater *Andersen Library* 800 W Main St *Web:* library.uww.edu	Whitewater	WI	53190	262-472-5511	
University of Wyoming Libraries PO Box 3334 **Fax:* Admin ■ *TF:* 800-442-6757 ■ *Web:* www-lib.uwyo.edu	Laramie	WY	82071	307-766-3190	766-2510*

438 LIBRARY ASSOCIATIONS - STATE & PROVINCE

	City	State	Zip	Phone	Fax
Adriance Memorial Library 93 Market St *Web:* www.poklib.org	Poughkeepsie	NY	12601	845-485-3445	
Arizona Library Assn (AzLA) 1030 E Baseline Rd Ste 105-1025 *Web:* www.azla.org	Tempe	AZ	85283	480-609-3999	609-3939
Barrie Public Library 60 Worsley St *Web:* library.barrie.ca	Barrie	ON	L4M1L6	705-728-1010	
Cariboo Regional District A-180 Third Ave N *Web:* cariboord.bc.ca	Williams Lake	BC	V2G2A4	250-392-3351	
Castle Branch Inc 1845 Sir Tyler Dr *Web:* www.castlebranch.com	Wilmington	NC	28405	910-815-3880	
Crystal Springs City Water Department 306 W Railroad Ave S *Web:* www.crystalspringsmiss.com	Crystal Springs	MS	39059	601-892-4111	
Deerfield Public Library Inc 920 Waukegan Rd *Web:* deerfieldlibrary.org	Deerfield	IL	60015	847-945-3311	
El Paso Public Library 501 N Oregon St *Web:* elpasolibrary.org	El Paso	TX	79901	915-543-5413	
Glen Ellyn Public Library 400 Duane St *Web:* www.gepl.org	Glen Ellyn	IL	60137	630-790-0034	
Illinois Library Assn (ILA) 33 W Grand Ave Ste 301 *Web:* www.ila.org	Chicago	IL	60610	312-644-1896	644-1899
Indiana Library Federation (ILF) 941 E 86th St Ste 260 *Web:* www.ilfonline.org	Indianapolis	IN	46240	317-257-2040	257-1389
Lake Bluff Public Library 123 E Scranton Ave *Web:* lakeblufflibrary.org	Lake Bluff	IL	60044	847-234-1507	
Lethbridge Public Library 810 5 Ave S *Web:* www.lethlib.ca	Lethbridge	AB	T1J4C4	403-380-7310	
Maryland Library Assn (MLA) 1401 Hollins St *Web:* www.mdlib.org	Baltimore	MD	21223	410-947-5090	947-5089
Messaging Solutions LLC 8203 Shoregrove Dr Ste 200 *Web:* www.messagingsolutions.com	Humble	TX	77346	281-852-1301	

Phone | Fax

Midlothian Public Library
14701 Kenton Ave. .... Midlothian IL 60445 708-535-2027
Web: www.midlothianlibrary.org

Minnesota Library Assn (MLA)
1821 University Ave W Ste S256 .... Saint Paul MN 55104 651-999-5343 917-1835
TF: 877-867-0982 ■ *Web:* www.mnlibraryassociation.org

Mishawaka-Penn-Harris Public Library Indiana
209 Lincoln Way E .... Mishawaka IN 46544 574-259-5277
Web: mphpl.org

Montclair Public Library
50 S Fullerton Ave .... Montclair NJ 07042 973-744-0500
Web: www.montclairlibrary.org

Nanuet Public Library 149 Church St. .... Nanuet NY 10954 845-623-4281
Web: www.nanuetlibrary.org

Nelson Public Library 201 Cathedral Mnr .... Bardstown KY 40004 502-348-3714
Web: www.nelsoncopublib.org

New Jersey Library Assn (NJLA) PO Box 1534 .... Trenton NJ 08607 609-394-8032 394-8164
Web: www.njla.org

New York Library Assn (NYLA)
6021 State Farm Rd .... Guilderland NY 12084 518-432-6952 427-1697
Web: www.nyla.org

North Carolina Library Assn (NCLA)
1811 Capital Blvd. .... Raleigh NC 27604 919-839-6252 839-6253
Web: www.nclaonline.org

Orangeburg Public Library 20 Greenbush Rd .... Orangeburg NY 10962 845-359-2244
Web: www.orangeburg-library.org

Orcas Island Library District 500 Rose St. .... East Sound WA 98245 360-376-4985
Web: orcaslibrary.org

Parkland Community Library
4422 Walbert Ave .... Allentown PA 18104 610-398-1361
Web: www.parklandlibrary.org

Pennsylvania Library Assn (PaLA)
220 Cumberland Pkwy Ste 10. .... Mechanicsburg PA 17055 717-766-7663 766-5440
Web: www.palibraries.org

Perry County Public Library
289 Black Gold Blvd .... Hazard KY 41701 606-436-4747
Web: www.perrycountylibrary.org

Powell River Public Library
4411 Michigan Ave. .... Powell River BC V8A2S3 604-485-4796
Web: www.powellriverlibrary.ca

Red Deer Public Library 4818 49 St. .... Red Deer AB T4N1T9 403-346-4576
Web: www.rdpl.org

Rockwall County Library
1215 E Yellowjacket Ln. .... Rockwall TX 75087 972-882-0340
Web: www.rockwallcountytexas.com

Rocky River Public Library
1600 Hampton Rd. .... Rocky River OH 44116 440-333-7610
Web: www.rrpl.org

Rolling Meadows Library
3110 Martin Ln. .... Rolling Meadows IL 60008 847-259-6050
Web: www.rmlib.org

Solano County Library 1150 Kentucky St .... Fairfield CA 94533 707-421-6500
Web: www.solanocounty.com

South Carolina Library Assn (SCLA) PO Box 1763. .... Columbia SC 29202 803-252-1087 252-0589
Web: www.scla.org

South Holland Public Library
16250 Wausau .... South Holland IL 60473 708-331-5262
Web: www.southhollandlibrary.org

St Albert Public Library Five St Anne St. .... St Albert AB T8N3Z9 780-459-1530
Web: www.sapl.ca

State Education Resource Center
25 Industrial Park Rd .... Middletown CT 06457 860-632-1485
Web: ctserc.org

Tennessee Library Assn (TLA) PO Box 241074 .... Memphis TN 38124 901-485-6952
Web: www.tnla.org

Texas Library Association
3355 Bee Cave Rd Ste 401 .... West Lake Hills TX 78746 512-328-1518
Web: www.txla.org

Vernon Area Public Library District
300 Olde Half Day Rd .... Lincolnshire IL 60069 847-634-3650
Web: vapld.info

Westport Public Library 20 Jesup Rd .... Westport CT 06880 203-227-8411
Web: westportlibrary.org

Wisconsin Library Assn (WLA)
4610 S Biltmore Ln Ste 100 .... Madison WI 53718 608-245-3640 245-3646
Web: wla.memberclicks.net

439 LIBRARY SYSTEMS - REGIONAL - CANADIAN

Phone | Fax

Cape Breton Regional Library 50 Falmouth St .... Sydney NS B1P6X9 902-562-3279 564-0765
Web: cbrl.ca

Centre Regional de Services Aux Bibliotheques Publiques de L'Estrie Inc
4155 Rue Brodeur. .... Sherbrooke QC J1L1K4 819-565-9744 565-9157
Web: www.reseaubibliioduquebec.qc.ca

Centre Regional de Services Aux Bibliotheques Publiques de L'Outaouais Inc
2295 Rue St Louis .... Gatineau QC J8T5L8 819-561-6008 561-6767
Web: crsbpo.qc.ca

Centre Regional de Services Aux Bibliotheques Publiques de la Monteregie Inc
275 Rue Conrad-Pelletier .... La Prairie QC J5R4V1 450-444-5433 659-3364
Web: www.reseaubiblioduquebec.qc.ca

Centre Regional de Services Aux Bibliotheques Publiques des Laurentides Inc
29 Rue Brissette .... Sainte-Agathe-des-Monts QC J8C3L1 819-326-6440 326-0885
Web: www.reseaubiblioduquebec.qc.ca

Evergreen Regional Library 55 1st Ave. .... Gimli MB R0C1B0 204-642-7912 642-8319
Web: erlibrary.ca

Lakeland Regional Library 318 Williams Ave .... Killarney MB R0K1G0 204-523-4949 523-7460
Web: www.lakelandregionallibrary.ca

North Ontario Library Service 334 Regent St .... Sudbury ON P3C4E2 705-675-6467 675-2285
Web: olsn.ca

Palliser Regional Library 366 Coteau St W. .... Moose Jaw SK S6H5C9 306-693-3669 692-5657
Web: www.palliserlibrary.ca

Phone | Fax

Provincial Information & Library Resources Board
Eastern Div 48 St Georges Ave. .... Stephenville NL A2N1L1 709-737-3508 737-3571
Web: www.nlpl.ca
West Newfoundl and-Labrador Div
Five Union St. .... Corner Brook NL A2H5M7 709-634-7333 634-7313
Web: www.nlpl.ca

Saint John Regional Library One Market Sq .... Saint John NB E2L4Z6 506-643-7220 643-7225
Web: saintjohnlibrary.com

Southwestern Manitoba Regional Library
149 Main St PO Box 670 .... Melita MB R0M1L0 204-522-3923 522-3923
Web: www.wix.com

Wapiti Regional Library 145 12th St E. .... Prince Albert SK S6V1B7 306-764-0712 922-1516
Web: wapitilibrary.ca

Western Manitoba Regional Library
710 Rosser Ave Unit 1 .... Brandon MB R7A0K9 204-727-6648 727-4447
Web: www.wmrl.ca

440 LIGHT BULBS & TUBES

Phone | Fax

Advanced Lighting Technologies Inc
32000 Aurora Rd .... Solon OH 44139 440-519-0500 519-0501
TF: 888-440-2358 ■ *Web:* www.adlt.com

AETEK UV Systems 1229 Lakeview Ct .... Romeoville IL 60446 630-226-4200 226-4215
TF: 800-333-2304 ■ *Web:* www.americanultraviolet.com

Amglo Kemlight Laboratories Inc
215 Gateway Rd .... Bensenville IL 60106 630-350-9470 350-9474
Web: www.amglo.com

Bayco Products Inc 640 Sanden Blvd. .... Wylie TX 75098 469-326-9400 326-9401
TF: 800-233-2155 ■ *Web:* www.baycoproducts.com

Carley Lamps Inc 1502 W 228th St. .... Torrance CA 90501 310-325-8474 534-2912
Web: www.carleylamps.com

Empire Wire & Supply 2119 Austin Ave .... Rochester Hills MI 48309 800-826-1265 853-6667*
**Fax Area Code:* 248 ■ *TF:* 800-826-1265 ■ *Web:* www.empirewc.com

Eye Lighting International NA
9150 Hendricks Rd. .... Mentor OH 44060 440-350-7000 350-7001
TF Cust Svc: 888-665-2677 ■ *Web:* www.eyelighting.com

Hanovia Corp Six Evans St. .... Fairfield NJ 07004 973-651-5510 651-5550
Web: www.hanovia-uv.com

Interlectric Corp 1401 Lexington Ave. .... Warren PA 16365 814-723-6061 723-1074
TF: 800-722-2184 ■ *Web:* www.interlectric.com

LCD Lighting Inc 37 Robinson Blvd .... Orange CT 06477 203-795-1520 795-2874
TF: 800-826-9465 ■ *Web:* www.light-sources.com

Ledtronics Inc 23105 Kashiwa Ct .... Torrance CA 90505 310-534-1505 534-1424
TF: 800-579-4875 ■ *Web:* www.led.net

Light Sources Inc 37 Robinson Blvd .... Orange CT 06477 203-799-7877 795-5267
TF: 800-826-9465 ■ *Web:* www.light-sources.com

Litetronics International Inc 4101 W 123rd St .... Alsip IL 60803 708-389-8000 371-0627
TF: 800-860-3392 ■ *Web:* www.litetronics.com

Magnet Sales & Mfg Company Inc
11248 Playa Ct. .... Culver City CA 90230 310-391-7213
TF: 800-421-6692 ■ *Web:* www.magnetsales.com

OSRAM Sylvania Glass Technologies
131 Portsmouth Ave. .... Exeter NH 03833 603-772-4331 778-4554
TF: 800-258-8290 ■ *Web:* www.sylvania.com

OSRAM Sylvania Inc 100 Endicott St .... Danvers MA 01923 978-777-1900 750-2152
Web: www.sylvania.com

PerkinElmer Inc 940 Winter St. .... Waltham MA 02451 203-925-4602 944-4904
NYSE: PKI ■ *Web:* www.perkinelmer.com

Philips Lighting Co 200 Franklin Sq Dr. .... Somerset NJ 08873 800-555-0050
TF: 800-555-0050 ■ *Web:* www.usa.lighting.philips.com

Rogers Corp Durel Div 2225 W Chandler Blvd .... Chandler AZ 85224 480-917-6000 917-6049
Web: www.rogerscorp.com

Sun Ergoline Inc 1 Walter Kratz Dr. .... Jonesboro AR 72401 888-771-0996 935-3618*
**Fax Area Code:* 870 ■ *TF:* 888-771-0996 ■ *Web:* sunergoline.com/

Technical Consumer Products Inc 325 Campus Dr .... Aurora OH 44202 800-324-1496 995-6188*
**Fax Area Code:* 330 ■ *TF:* 800-324-1496 ■ *Web:* www.tcpi.com

Trojan Inc 198 Trojan St PO Box 850 .... Mount Sterling KY 40353 859-498-0526 498-0528
TF: 800-264-0526 ■ *Web:* www.trojaninc.com

Ushio America Inc 5440 Cerritos Ave .... Cypress CA 90630 714-236-8600 776-3641*
**Fax Area Code:* 800 ■ **Fax:* Mktg ■ *TF:* 800-326-1960 ■ *Web:* www.ushio.com

UVP Inc 2066 W 11th St. .... Upland CA 91786 909-946-3197 946-3597
TF Cust Svc: 800-452-6788 ■ *Web:* www.uvp.com

Venmar Ventilation Inc 550 Lemire Blvd. .... Drummondville QC J2C7W9 819-477-6226 475-2660
Web: www.venmar.ca

Venture Lighting International Inc
32000 Aurora Rd .... Solon OH 44139 440-248-3510 349-7771
TF: 800-451-2606 ■ *Web:* www.venturelighting.com

441 LIGHTING EQUIPMENT - VEHICULAR

Phone | Fax

Able 2 Products Company Inc PO Box 543. .... Cassville MO 65625 417-847-4791 847-2222
TF: 800-641-4098 ■ *Web:* www.able2products.com

Astronics Corp 130 Commerce Way .... East Aurora NY 14052 716-805-1599 655-0309
NASDAQ: ATRO ■ *Web:* www.astronics.com

ATC Lighting & Plastics Inc 101 Parker Dr .... Andover OH 44003 440-293-4064 293-4591
Web: www.atc-lighting-plastics.com

Aurora Cord & Cable Co 325 S Union St .... Aurora IL 60505 630-851-1616 851-1626
Web: www.auroracord.com

Avtec Inc Six Industrial Pk .... Cahokia IL 62206 618-337-7800 337-7976
TF: 800-552-8832 ■ *Web:* www.avteclighting.com

Bruce Industries Inc 101 Evans Ave. .... Dayton NV 89403 775-246-0101
Web: www.bruceind.com

Federal Signal Corp Emergency Products Div
2645 Federal Signal Dr. .... University Park IL 60466 708-534-3400 534-9050
Web: www.fedsig.com

JW Speaker Corp
N 120 W 19434 Freistadt Rd PO Box 1011. .... Germantown WI 53022 262-251-6660 251-2918
TF: 800-558-7288 ■ *Web:* www.jwspeaker.com

Phone Fax

KC Hilites Inc PO Box 155 Williams AZ 86046 928-635-2607 635-2486
Web: kchilites.com

Luminator 900 Klein Rd Plano TX 75074 972-424-6511 423-1540
TF: 800-388-8205 ■ *Web:* luminatortechnologygroup.com/mass-transit

North American Lighting Inc 2275 S Main St Paris IL 61944 217-465-6600 465-6610
Web: www.nal.com

Nova Electronics Inc 36 Doctor Foote Rd Colchester CT 06415 860-537-3471 537-0656
Web: www.strobe.com

Peterson Manufacturing Co 4200 E 135th St Grandview MO 64030 816-765-2000 761-6693
TF: 800-821-3490 ■ *Web:* www.pmlights.com

Soderberg Mfg Company Inc 20821 Currier Rd Walnut CA 91789 909-595-1291
Web: www.soderberg.aero

Teledyne Lighting & Display Products
12964 Panama St Los Angeles CA 90066 310-823-5491 574-2070
Web: www.teledynelighting.com

Trans-Lite Inc 120 Wampus Ln Milford CT 06460 203-878-8567 877-2630
Web: www.teknowareinc.com

Truck-Lite Company Inc 310 E Elmwood Ave Falconer NY 14733 716-665-6214 665-6403
TF Cust Svc: 800-562-5012 ■ *Web:* www.truck-lite.com

Unity Manufacturing Co 1260 N Clybourn Ave Chicago IL 60610 312-943-5200 943-5681
Web: www.unityusa.com

Vehicle Safety Mfg LLC 408 Central Ave Newark NJ 07107 973-643-3000 643-2167
TF General: 800-832-7233 ■ *Web:* www.vehiclesafetymfg.com

Whelen Engineering Company Inc
51 Winthrop Rd & Rt 145 Chester CT 06412 860-526-9504 526-4078
Web: www.whelen.com

442 LIGHTING FIXTURES & EQUIPMENT

Phone Fax

ALP Lighting Components Inc
6333 Gross Point Rd Niles IL 60714 773-774-9550 774-9331
Web: alplighting.com

Altman Lighting Inc 57 Alexander St Yonkers NY 10701 914-476-7987 966-1980
TF: 800-425-8626 ■ *Web:* www.altmanltg.com

American Fluorescent Corp
2345 Ernie Krueger Cir Waukegan IL 60087 847-249-5970 249-2618
TF: 800-873-2326 ■ *Web:* www.afxinc.com

American Louver Co 7700 N Austin Ave Skokie IL 60077 847-470-3300 966-8074
TF: 800-772-0355 ■ *Web:* www.americanlouver.com

AmerillumBrands 3728 Maritime Way Oceanside CA 92056 760-727-7675
Web: www.amerillum.com

Antique Street Lamps Inc 2011-B W Rundberg Ln Austin TX 78758 512-977-8444 977-9622
Web: antiquestreetlamps.acuitybrands.com

Ashley Lighting Inc 405 Industrial Dr Trumann AR 72472 870-483-6181 483-7140
Web: ashleylighting.com

Automatic Power Inc
10810 W Little York Rd Ste 130 Houston TX 77041 713-228-5208 228-3717
Web: www.automaticpower.com

Big Beam Emergency Systems Inc
290 E Prairie St PO Box 518 Crystal Lake IL 60039 815-459-6100 459-6126
Web: www.bigbeam.com

Boyd Corp 6325 San Pedro Ave San Antonio TX 78216 210-344-9222 349-2693
Web: www.boydlightingsa.com

Boyd Lighting Co 944 Folsom St San Francisco CA 94107 415-778-4300 778-4319
Web: www.boydlighting.com

Brinkmann Corp 4215 McEwen Rd Dallas TX 75244 972-770-8500 770-8545
TF: 800-527-0717 ■ *Web:* www.brinkmann.net

California Lighting Sales Inc (CLS)
4900 Rivergrade Rd Ste D110 Irwindale CA 91706 626-775-6000 775-6001
Web: www.californialightingsales.com

Carlisle & Finch Co 4562 W Mitchell Ave Cincinnati OH 45232 513-681-6080 681-6226
Web: www.carlislefinch.com

Chapman Mfg Company Inc PO Box 359 Avon MA 02322 508-588-3200 587-7592
Web: www.chapmanco.com

Commercial Lighting Industries
81161 Indio Blvd Indio CA 92201 760-343-2704 262-3940
TF: 800-755-0155 ■ *Web:* www.commercial-lighting.net

Con-Tech Lighting 2783 Shermer Rd Northbrook IL 60062 847-559-5500 559-5505
TF: 800-728-0312 ■ *Web:* www.con-techlighting.com

Cooper Industries 600 Travis St Ste 5400 Houston TX 77002 713-209-8400 209-8995
NYSE: ETN ■ *TF:* 866-853-4293 ■ *Web:* www.cooperindustries.com

Cooper Lighting Inc 1121 Hwy 74 S Peachtree City GA 30269 770-486-4800 486-4801
Web: www.cooperindustries.com

Corbett Lighting Inc
14508 Nelson Ave City of Industry CA 91744 626-336-4511 336-5121
TF: 800-533-8769 ■ *Web:* www.corbettlighting.com

Coronet Lighting PO Box 2065 Gardena CA 90248 310-327-6700 532-8092
TF: 800-421-2748 ■ *Web:* www.coronetlighting.com

CW Cole & Company Inc
2560 Rosemead Blvd South El Monte CA 91733 626-443-2473 443-9253
Web: www.colelighting.com

Dazor Manufacturing Corp
2079 Congressional Saint Louis MO 63146 314-652-2400 652-2069
TF: 800-345-9103 ■ *Web:* www.dazor.com

Deaver Industries Inc 3120 Morgan Rd Bessemer AL 35022 205-426-4309 426-4364
Web: www.deaverind.com

Dual-Lite Inc 701 Millennium Blvd Greenville SC 29607 864-678-1000 678-1415
Web: www.dual-lite.com

Duray Lighting Inc 2050 W Balmoral Ave Chicago IL 60625 773-271-2800 271-4410
Web: www.durayinc.com

Edison Price Lighting Inc (EPL)
41-50 22nd St Long Island City NY 11101 718-685-0700 786-8530
Web: www.epl.com

Electrix Inc 45 Spring St New Haven CT 06519 203-776-5577 624-7545
Web: www.electrix.com

ELK Lighting 12 Willow Ln Nesquehoning PA 18240 800-613-3261 613-3264*
**Fax Area Code:* 866 ■ *TF:* 800-613-3261 ■ *Web:* www.nulcolighting.com

Elk Lighting Inc 12 Willow Lane Nesquehoning PA 18240 866-283-1953 388-6052*
**Fax Area Code:* 800 ■ *TF:* 866-283-1953 ■ *Web:* www.elkhospitality.com

Energy Focus Inc 32000 Aurora Rd Solon OH 44139 440-715-1300 715-1314
OTC: EFOI ■ *TF:* 800-327-7877 ■ *Web:* www.energyfocusinc.com

EZ Electric Inc 1250 Birchwood Dr Sunnyvale CA 94089 408-734-4282 734-0798
Web: www.ez-electric.com

Finelite Inc 30500 Whipple Rd Union City CA 94587 510-441-1100 441-1510
Web: www.finelite.com

Fulton Industries Inc
135 E Linfoot St PO Box 377 Wauseon OH 43567 419-335-3015 335-3215
TF: 800-537-5012 ■ *Web:* www.fultonindoh.com

Gardco Lighting 1611 Clovis Barker Rd San Marcos TX 78666 512-753-1000
TF: 800-227-0758 ■ *Web:* www.sitelighting.com

GE Lighting Systems Inc
3010 Spartanburg Hwy East Flat Rock NC 28726 828-693-2000 693-2112
TF: 888-694-3533 ■ *Web:* gelighting.com/lightingweb/na/

Good Earth Lighting Inc 5260 Capitol Dr Wheeling IL 60090 847-808-1133 808-0838
Web: www.goodearthlighting.com

HE Williams Inc 831 W Fairview Ave Carthage MO 64836 417-358-4065 358-6015
TF: 866-358-4065 ■ *Web:* www.hewilliams.com

High End Systems Inc 2105 Gracy Farms Ln Austin TX 78758 512-836-2242 837-5290
TF: 800-890-8989 ■ *Web:* www.highend.com

High Q Lighting Inc 11439 E Lakewood Blvd Holland MI 49424 616-396-3591
Web: www.hql.net

Hinkley Lighting 12600 Berea Rd Cleveland OH 44111 216-671-3300 671-4537
TF: 800-446-5539 ■ *Web:* www.hinkleylighting.com

Holophane 214 Oakwood Ave PO Box 3004 Newark OH 43058 740-345-9631 349-4426
TF: 866-465-6742 ■ *Web:* www.holophane.com

Hubbell Lighting Inc 701 Millennium Blvd Greenville SC 29607 864-678-1000 678-1065
TF: 800-465-7051 ■ *Web:* www.hubbelllighting.com

Hydrel 12881 Bradley Ave Sylmar CA 91342 866-533-9901 362-6548*
**Fax Area Code:* 818 ■ *TF:* 866-533-9901 ■ *Web:* hydrel.acuitybrands.com

Justice Design Group (JDG)
500 S Grand Ave Ste 110 Los Angeles CA 90071 213-437-0102 437-0860
TF: 800-533-4799 ■ *Web:* www.jdg.com

Kenall Mfg 1020 Lakeside Dr Gurnee IL 60031 847-360-8200 360-1781
TF: 800-453-6255 ■ *Web:* www.kenall.com

Kichler Lighting
7711 E Pleasant Vly Rd PO Box 318010 Cleveland OH 44131 866-558-5706 659-8808*
**Fax Area Code:* 888 ■ **Fax:* Cust Svc ■ *TF:* 866-558-5706 ■ *Web:* www.kichler.com

Kim Lighting Inc
16555 E Gale Ave PO Box 60080 City of Industry CA 91745 626-968-5666 968-5716
Web: www.kimlighting.com

Kirlin Co 3401 E Jefferson Ave Detroit MI 48207 313-259-6400 259-3121
Web: www.kirlinlighting.com

Koehler-Bright Star Inc
380 Stewart Rd Hanover Township PA 18706 570-825-1900 825-7108
TF Cust Svc: 800-788-1696 ■ *Web:* www.flashlight.com

Kurt Versen Co 10 Charles St Westwood NJ 07675 201-664-8200 664-4801
Web: www.kurtversen.com

Kurtzon Lighting Inc 1420 S Talman Ave Chicago IL 60608 773-277-2121 277-9164
TF: 800-837-8937 ■ *Web:* www.kurtzon.com

Lamplight Farms Inc
W140 N4900 Lilly Rd Menomonee Falls WI 53051 262-781-9590 781-6774
TF Cust Svc: 888-473-1088 ■ *Web:* www.tikibrand.com

LC Doane Co 110 Pond Meadow Rd PO Box 700 Ivoryton CT 06442 860-767-8295 767-1397
TF: 800-447-5006 ■ *Web:* www.lcdoane.com

Ledalite Architectural Products
19750-92A Ave Langley BC V1M3B2 604-888-6811 888-2003
TF: 800-665-5332 ■ *Web:* www.ledalite.com

Legion Lighting Company Inc
221 Glenmore Ave Brooklyn NY 11207 718-498-1770 498-0128
TF: 800-453-4466 ■ *Web:* www.legionlighting.com

Lighting Alliance Inc, The
2700 Esters Blvd Ste 100 PO Box 613079 Dallas TX 75261 972-456-9800
Web: www.thelightingalliance.com

Lighting Quotient, The 114 Boston Post Rd West Haven CT 06516 203-931-4455 931-4464
TF: 800-222-0193

Lights of America 611 Reyes Dr Walnut CA 91789 909-594-7883 594-6758
TF Cust Svc: 800-321-8100 ■ *Web:* www.lightsofamerica.com

Lite Energy 780 Salaberry Laval QC H7S1H3 450-668-9620 668-9625
Web: www.liteenergy.com

Litecontrol 100 Hawks Ave Hanson MA 02341 781-294-0100 293-2849
Web: www.litecontrol.com

Lithonia Lighting One Lithonia Way Conyers GA 30012 770-922-9000 483-2635
TF: 800-858-7763 ■ *Web:* www.lithonia.com

LSI Industries Inc 10000 Alliance Rd Cincinnati OH 45242 513-793-3200 984-1335
NASDAQ: LYTS ■ *Web:* www.lsi-industries.com

Lumec Inc 640 Blvd Cur-Boivin Boisbriand QC J7G2A7 450-430-7040 430-1453
Web: www.lumec.com

Luxo Corp Five Westchester Plz Elmsford NY 10523 914-345-0067 345-0068*
**Fax:* Sales ■ *TF:* 800-222-5896 ■ *Web:* www.luxous.com

Mag Instrument Inc 2001 S Hillman Ave Ontario CA 91761 909-947-1006 947-3116
TF: 800-289-6241 ■ *Web:* www.maglite.com

Manning Lighting 1810 N Ave PO Box 1063 Sheboygan WI 53083 920-458-2184 458-2491
Web: www.manningltg.com

Mario Industries of Virginia Inc
2490 Patterson Ave SW PO Box 3190 Roanoke VA 24016 540-342-1111 345-4813
Web: www.marioindustries.com

Mark Architectural Lighting Three Kilmer Rd Edison NJ 08817 732-985-2600 985-8441
Web: www.marklighting.com

Mercury Lighting Products Company Inc
20 Audrey Pl Fairfield NJ 07004 973-244-9444 244-9522
TF: 800-637-2584 ■ *Web:* www.mercltg.com

Minka Group 1151 W Bradford Ct Corona CA 92882 951-735-9220 735-9758
TF: 800-221-7977 ■ *Web:* www.minkagroup.net

Mole-Richardson Company Inc
937 N Sycamore Ave Hollywood CA 90038 323-851-0111 851-5593
Web: www.mole.com

Mule Lighting Inc 46 Baker St Providence RI 02905 401-941-4446 941-2929
TF: 800-556-7690 ■ *Web:* www.mulelighting.com

Multi-Electric Manufacturing Inc
4223 W Lake St Chicago IL 60624 773-722-1900 722-5694
Web: www.multielectric.com

Phone Fax

Musco Sports Lighting LLC
100 First Ave W PO Box 808 .... Oskaloosa IA 52577 641-673-0411 673-4852
TF: 800-825-6020 ■ *Web:* www.musco.com

National Lighting Company Inc
522 Cortlandt St .... Belleville NJ 07109 973-751-1600 751-4931
Web: www.natltg.com

Nightscaping 1705 E Colton Ave .... Redlands CA 92374 909-794-2121
TF: 800-544-4840 ■ *Web:* www.nightscaping.com

North Star Lighting Inc 2150 Parkes Dr .... Broadview IL 60155 708-681-4330 681-4006
TF: 800-229-4330 ■ *Web:* www.northstarlightingsite.com

Norwell Manufacturing Inc 82 Stevens St .... East Taunton MA 02718 508-823-1751 823-9431
TF: 800-822-2831 ■ *Web:* www.norwellinc.com

Omniglow LLC 865 Memorial Ave .... West Springfield MA 01089 413-241-6010 543-5470

OSRAM Sylvania Inc 100 Endicott St .... Danvers MA 01923 978-777-1900 750-2152
Web: www.sylvania.com

Pacific Coast Lighting 20238 Plummer St .... Chatsworth CA 91311 818-886-9751 886-5751
TF: 800-709-9004 ■ *Web:* www.pacificcoastlighting.com

Paraflex Industries 2006 Inc 222 New Rd .... Parsippany NJ 07054 973-340-6040 340-6043
Web: www.paraflex.com

Paramount Industries Inc 304 N Howard St .... Croswell MI 48422 810-679-2551 679-4045
TF: 800-521-5405 ■ *Web:* www.paramount-lighting.com

Paul C Buff Inc 2725 Bransford Ave .... Nashville TN 37204 615-383-3982 383-0676
TF: 800-443-5542 ■ *Web:* www.paulcbuff.com

Peerless Lighting Corp 2246 Fifth St .... Berkeley CA 94710 510-845-2760 845-2776
Web: www.peerlesslighting.com

Philips Canlyte, Inc 3015 Louis Amos .... Lachine QC H8T1C4 514-636-0670 636-0460
TF All: 800-668-2770 ■ *Web:* www.canlyte.com

Philips Day-Brite 776 S Green St .... Tupclo MS 38804 800-234-1890 841-5501*
**Fax Area Code:* 662 ■ **Fax:* Hum Res ■ *TF:* 800-234-1890 ■ *Web:* daybrite.com/day%2dbrite/

Philips Holding USA Inc
1251 Ave of the Americas .... New York NY 10020 212-536-0500 536-0506
TF: 800-453-6860 ■ *Web:* usa.philips.com/

Prescolite Inc 701 Millennium Blvd .... Greenville SC 29607 864-678-1000 678-1415
TF: 888-777-4832 ■ *Web:* www.prescolite.com

Prudential Ltd 1737 E 22nd St .... Los Angeles CA 90058 213-746-0360 741-8590
Web: www.prulite.com

Quoizel Inc 6 Corporate Pkwy .... Goose Creek SC 29445 843-553-6700 553-1002
Web: www.quoizel.com

RAB Lighting 170 Ludlow Ave .... Northvale NJ 07647 201-784-8600 722-1232*
**Fax Area Code:* 888 ■ *TF:* 888-722-1000 ■ *Web:* www.rabweb.com

Rejuvenation Inc 2550 NW Nicolai St .... Portland OR 97210 503-231-1900 526-7329*
**Fax Area Code:* 800 ■ *TF:* 888-401-1900 ■ *Web:* www.rejuvenation.com

Renova Lighting Systems Inc
20 Middlesex Rd .... Mansfield MA 02048 401-682-1850 682-1860
TF: 800-635-6682 ■ *Web:* www.renova.com

Schonbek Worldwide Lighting Inc
61 Industrial Blvd .... Plattsburgh NY 12901 518-563-7500 563-4228
TF: 800-836-1892 ■ *Web:* www.schonbek.com

Sea Gull Lighting Products LLC A Generations Brands Co
301 W Washington St .... Riverside NJ 08075 856-764-0500
TF: 800-347-5483 ■ *Web:* www.seagulllighting.com

Sentry Electric 185 Buffalo Ave .... Freeport NY 11520 516-379-4660 378-0624
Web: www.sentrylighting.com

Sesco Lighting Inc
1133 W Morse Blvd Ste 100 .... Winter Park FL 32789 407-629-6100 629-6168
Web: www.sescolighting.com

SIMKAR Corp 700 Ramona Ave .... Philadelphia PA 19120 215-831-7700 831-7703*
**Fax:* Cust Svc ■ *TF:* 800-523-3602 ■ *Web:* www.simkar.com

Spectrolab Inc 12500 Gladstone Ave .... Sylmar CA 91342 818-365-4611 361-5102
TF: 800-936-4888 ■ *Web:* www.spectrolab.com

Spring City Electrical Manufacturing Co
PO Box 19 .... Spring City PA 19475 610-948-4000 948-5577
Web: www.springcity.com

Stonco Lighting 2345 Vauxhall Rd .... Union NJ 07083 908-964-7000
TF: 800-334-2212 ■ *Web:* www.stoncolighting.com

Strand Lighting 10911 Petal St .... Dallas TX 75238 214-647-7880 647-8031
TF: 800-733-0564 ■ *Web:* www.strandlighting.com

Streamlight Inc 30 Eagleville Rd .... Eagleville PA 19403 610-631-0600 631-0712
TF: 800-523-7488 ■ *Web:* www.streamlight.com

Super Sky Products Inc 10301 N Enterprise Dr .... Mequon WI 53092 262-242-2000 242-7409
TF: 800-558-0467 ■ *Web:* www.supersky.com

Swivelier Company Inc 600 Bradley Hill Rd .... Blauvelt NY 10913 845-353-1455 353-1512
Web: www.swivelier.com

Tech Lighting LLC 7400 Linda Ave .... Skokie IL 60077 847-410-4400 410-4500
TF: 800-522-5315 ■ *Web:* www.techlighting.com

Tri-Lite Inc 1642 N Besly Ct .... Chicago IL 60642 773-384-7765 384-5115
TF: 800-322-5250 ■ *Web:* www.triliteinc.com

Troy-CSL Lighting Inc
14508 Nelson Ave .... City of Industry CA 91744 626-336-4511 330-4266
TF: 800-533-8769 ■ *Web:* www.troy-lighting.com

Western Reflections 261 Commerce Way .... Gallatin TN 37066 615-451-9700 452-0283
TF Cust Svc: 800-507-8302 ■ *Web:* www.western-reflections.com

Wildwood Lamps & Accents
516 Paul St PO Box 672 .... Rocky Mount NC 27803 252-446-3266 977-6669
Web: www.wildwoodlamps.com

Wilshire Manufacturing Co
645 Myles Standish Blvd .... Taunton MA 02780 508-824-1970
Web: wilshiremfg.com

443 LIME

Phone Fax

Austin White Lime Company Ltd 4900 Howard Ln .... Austin TX 78728 512-255-3646
Web: www.austinwhitelime.com

Carmeuse North America
11 Stanwix St 11th Fl .... Pittsburgh PA 15222 412-995-5500 995-5570
TF: 866-243-0965 ■ *Web:* www.carmeusena.com

Cheney Lime & Cement
478 Graystone Rd PO Box 160 .... Allgood AL 35013 205-625-3031 625-3032
TF: 800-752-8282 ■ *Web:* www.cheneylime.com

Phone Fax

Graymont Inc 10991 Shellbridge Way Ste 200 .... Richmond BC V6X3C6 604-276-9331 276-9337
Web: www.graymont.com

Martin Limestone Inc PO Box 550 .... Blue Ball PA 17506 717-354-1300 766-0202*
**Fax Area Code:* 814 ■ *Web:* www.martinlimestone.com

Martin Marietta Materials Inc
2710 Wycliff Rd .... Raleigh NC 27607 919-781-4550
NYSE: MLM ■ *Web:* www.martinmarietta.com

Mercer Lime & Stone Co
50 Abele Rd Ste 1006 .... Bridgeville PA 15017 412-220-0316 220-0347
Web: www.mercerlime.com

Schildberg Construction Co PO Box 358 .... Greenfield IA 50849 641-743-2131
Web: schildberg.com

Texas Lime Co 15865 Farm Rd 1434 PO Box 851 .... Cleburne TX 76033 817-641-4433 556-0905
TF: 800-772-8000 ■ *Web:* uslm.com

US Lime & Minerals Inc 5429 LBJ Fwy Ste 230 .... Dallas TX 75240 972-991-8400 385-1340
NASDAQ: USLM ■ *Web:* www.uslm.com

Western Lime Corp 206 N Sixth Ave PO Box 57 .... West Bend WI 53095 262-334-2874
TF: 800-433-0036 ■ *Web:* www.westernlime.com

444 LIMOUSINE SERVICES

Phone Fax

Advantage Limousine Services Inc
8310 Castleford St Ste 200 .... Houston TX 77040 713-983-9991 983-9959
TF: 888-983-9991 ■ *Web:* www.advantagelimos.com

Alliance Limousine Inc
14553 Delano St Unit 210 .... Van Nuys CA 91411 800-954-5466 786-8810*
**Fax Area Code:* 818 ■ *TF:* 800-954-5466 ■ *Web:* www.alliancelimo.net

American Coach Limousine
1100 Jorie Blvd Ste 314 .... Oak Brook IL 60523 630-629-0001 629-0002
TF: 888-709-5466 ■ *Web:* www.americancoachlimousine.com

American Limousines Inc
4401 E Fairmount Ave .... Baltimore MD 21224 410-522-0400
Web: www.amerlimo.com

Arizona Limousines Inc
8900 N Central Ave Ste 101 .... Phoenix AZ 85020 602-267-7097 870-3388
TF: 800-678-0033 ■ *Web:* www.arizonalimos.com

Atlantic Services Group Inc 2131 K St NW .... Washington DC 20037 202-466-5050
Web: atlanticservicesgroup.com

Bayview Limousine Service 15701 Nelson Pl S .... Seattle WA 98188 206-824-6200 277-5895*
**Fax Area Code:* 425 ■ *TF:* 800-606-7880 ■ *Web:* www.bayviewlimo.com

Carey Executive Limousine 245 University Ave .... Atlanta GA 30315 404-223-2000 933-9937*
**Fax Area Code:* 770 ■ *TF:* 800-241-3943 ■ *Web:* www.careyatlanta.com

Carey International Inc
4530 Wisconsin Ave NW 5th Fl .... Washington DC 20016 202-895-1200 895-1251
TF: 800-336-4646 ■ *Web:* www.carey.com

Classic Transportation Group 1600 Locust Ave .... Bohemia NY 11716 631-567-5100 244-9006
TF: 800-291-8090 ■ *Web:* www.classictrans.com

Elite Limousine Service Inc
1059 12th Ave Ste E .... Honolulu HI 96816 808-735-2431 735-5159
TF: 800-776-2098 ■ *Web:* www.elitelimohawaii.com

Gateway Limousines 1550 Gilbreth Rd .... Burlingame CA 94010 650-697-5548 697-7739
TF: 800-486-7077 ■ *Web:* gatewayglobalsf.com

Gold Coast Limousines Po Box 6345 .... Santa Barbara CA 93160 805-966-5466
Web: www.goldcoastlimos.com

International Chauffeured Service Worldwide
53 E 34th St Fourth Fl .... New York NY 10016 212-213-0302 266-5254*
**Fax Area Code:* 877 ■ *TF:* 800-266-5254 ■ *Web:* www.bookalimo.com

Mears Transportation Group 324 W Gore St .... Orlando FL 32806 407-422-4561 422-6923
TF: 800-759-5219 ■ *Web:* www.mearstransportation.com

Park Cities Limousine 7129 Harry Hines Blvd .... Dallas TX 75235 214-824-0011 827-0136
TF: 888-559-0708 ■ *Web:* www.limodfw.com

Pontarelli Limousine Service
2225 W Hubbard St .... Chicago IL 60612 312-226-5466 226-1300
TF: 800-322-5466 ■ *Web:* www.pontarelliischicago.com

R & R Limousine 4403 Kiln Ct .... Louisville KY 40218 502-458-1862 458-3608
TF: 800-582-5576 ■ *Web:* www.rrlimo.com

Regency Limousine International
83-03 24th Ave .... East Elmhurst NY 11370 718-507-4000 507-8283
TF: 866-302-2201 ■ *Web:* www.regencylimo.com

Ritz Transportation 4676 Wynn Rd .... Las Vegas NV 89103 702-889-4242
Web: www.awgambassador.com

Royal Coachman Worldwide 88 Ford Rd Ste 26 .... Denville NJ 07834 973-400-3200 675-4365
TF: 800-472-7433 ■ *Web:* www.royalcoachman.com

Starlite Limousines LLC PO Box 13542 .... Scottsdale AZ 85267 480-422-3619 671-0522*
**Fax Area Code:* 617 ■ *TF:* 800-875-4104 ■ *Web:* www.starlitelimos.com

SuperShuttle International Inc
14500 N Northsight Blvd Ste 329 .... Scottsdale AZ 85260 480-609-3000 607-9317
Web: www.supershuttle.com

Teddy's Transportation System Inc
18 Rowan St .... Norwalk CT 06855 203-866-2231
Web: teddyslimo.com

US Coachways Inc
100 St Mary's Ave Ste 2B .... Staten Island NY 10305 718-477-4242
TF: 800-359-5991 ■ *Web:* www.uscoachways.com

Wild Goose Storage LLC
2780 W Liberty Rd Ste 2500 .... Gridley CA 95948 530-846-7350
Web: www.niskapartners.com

XYZ Two Way Radio Inc 275 20th St .... Brooklyn NY 11215 718-499-2007
Web: xyzcar.com

445 LINEN & UNIFORM SUPPLY

Phone Fax

Ace ImageWear 4120 Truman Rd .... Kansas City MO 64127 816-231-5737 231-3550
TF: 800-366-0564 ■ *Web:* www.aceimagewear.com

Ace-Tex Enterprises 7601 Central St .... Detroit MI 48210 313-834-4000 834-0260
TF: 800-444-3800 ■ *Web:* www.ace-tex.com

Admiral Linen Service Inc 2030 Kipling St .... Houston TX 77098 713-529-2608
Web: www.admiralservices.com

Company	City	State	ZIP	Phone	Fax
AmeriPride Services Inc 10801 Wayzata Blvd *TF Cust Svc:* 800-750-4628 ■ *Web:* www.ameripride.com	Minnetonka	MN	55305	952-738-4200	738-4252
Apparelmaster 123 Harrison Ave *TF:* 877-543-1678 ■ *Web:* companycasuals.com	Harrison	OH	45030	513-202-1600	202-1660
Arrow Uniform Rental Inc 6400 Monroe Blvd *TF:* 888-332-7769 ■ *Web:* www.arrowuniform.com	Taylor	MI	48180	313-299-5000	299-5093
Bates Troy Health Care Linen Supply 151 Laurel Ave *Web:* www.batestroy.com	Binghamton	NY	13905	607-723-5333	
Berkshire Blanket Inc 44 E Main St *Web:* www.berkshireblanket.com	Ware	MA	01082	413-967-5964	
Capitol Uniform & Linen Service 195 Commerce Way *Web:* www.capitollinen.com/	Dover	DE	19904	302-674-1511	
Cintas Corp PO Box 625737 *NASDAQ: CTAS* ■ *TF:* 800-786-4367 ■ *Web:* www.cintas.com	Cincinnati	OH	45262	513-459-1200	
Continental Linen Services 4200 Manchester Rd **Fax Area Code:* 269 ■ *TF:* 800-878-4357 ■ *Web:* www.clsimage.com	Kalamazoo	MI	49001	800-878-4357	343-2515*
Coyne Textile Services Inc 140 Cortland Ave *TF:* 800-672-6963 ■ *Web:* www.coynetextileservices.com	Syracuse	NY	13202	315-475-1626	
David Hughes Custom Linen 14332 Wadkins Ave *Web:* customlinenservice.com	Gardena	CA	90249	310-324-2465	
Domestic Linen Supply & Laundry Co Inc 30555 NW Hwy *TF:* 800-344-3555 ■ *Web:* www.domesticuniform.com	Farmington Hills	MI	48334	248-737-2000	
Faultless Linen 330 W 19th Ter *Web:* www.faultlesslinen.com	Kansas City	MO	64108	816-421-2373	
FDR Services Corp of New Jersey Inc 179 Lafayette St Ste 204 *Web:* www.fdrservicescorp.com	Paterson	NJ	07501	973-977-9300	
Frette North America Inc 850 Third Ave 10th Fl *Web:* www.cifg.com	New York	NY	10022	212-299-0400	
G & K Services Inc 5995 Opus Pkwy Ste 500 *TF:* 800-452-2737 ■ *Web:* www.gkservices.com	Minnetonka	MN	55343	952-912-5500	912-5999
Healthcare Services Group Inc (HCSG) 3220 Tillman Dr Ste 300 *TF:* 800-486-3289 ■ *Web:* www.hcsgcorp.com	Bensalem	PA	19020	215-639-4274	
Hospital Laundry Services Inc (HLS) 45 W Hintz Rd *Web:* www.hlschicago.com	Wheeling	IL	60090	847-941-7000	537-9198
Industrial Towel & Uniform Inc 2700 S 160th St *TF:* 800-767-2487 ■ *Web:* www.ituabsorbtech.com	New Berlin	WI	53151	262-782-1950	782-1802
Iron City Uniform Rental 6640 Frankstown Ave *TF:* 800-532-2010 ■ *Web:* www.ironcityuniform.com	Pittsburgh	PA	15206	412-661-2001	661-9356
Knights Apparel Inc 5475 N Blackstone Rd *Web:* futurespark.com/	Spartanburg	SC	29303	864-587-9690	
Kobe Sportswear Inc 791 Tapscott Rd *Web:* kobesportswear.com	Scarborough	ON	M1X1A2	416-754-7024	291-0146
Linens of the Week 713 Lamont St NW *Web:* www.linensoftheweek.com	Washington	DC	20010	202-291-9200	291-6485
Majestic Athletic Ltd 2320 Newlins Mill Rd *Web:* www.majesticathletic.com	Easton	PA	18045	610-746-6800	
Medical Linen Service Inc 290 S Maple Ave *Web:* www.completelinen.com	South San Francisco	CA	94080	650-873-1221	
Mickey's Linen & Towel Supply 4601 W Addison St *Web:* mickeyslinen.com	Chicago	IL	60641	773-545-7211	545-9111
Model Coverall Service Inc 100 28th St SE *TF:* 800-968-6491 ■ *Web:* www.modelcoverall.com	Grand Rapids	MI	49548	616-241-6491	241-0677
Morgan Linen Service Inc 145 Broadway Menands *Web:* www.morganlinenservice.com	Albany	NY	12204	518-465-3337	
Morgan Services Inc 323 N Michigan Ave *TF:* 888-966-7426 ■ *Web:* www.morganservices.com	Chicago	IL	60601	312-346-3181	346-0144
Overall Laundry Services Inc 7200 HaRdeson Rd	Everett	WA	98203	425-347-0123	
Prudential Overall Supply PO Box 11210 *TF:* 800-767-5536 ■ *Web:* www.prudentialuniforms.com	Santa Ana	CA	92711	949-250-4855	261-1947
Roscoe Co 3535 W Harrison St *TF Cust Svc:* 888-476-7263 ■ *Web:* www.eroscoe.com	Chicago	IL	60624	773-722-5000	722-0827
Service Linen Supply Inc 903 S Fourth St *Web:* www.servicelinen.com	Renton	WA	98057	425-255-8686	
Sitex Corp 1300 Commonwealth Dr *TF:* 800-278-3537 ■ *Web:* www.sitex-corp.com	Henderson	KY	42420	270-827-3537	
Summit Golf Brands Inc 8 W 40th St 2nd Fl *Web:* www.summitgolfbrands.com	New York	NY	10018	212-302-7255	
Superior Linen Service 1012 S Ctr St *Web:* suplinen.com	Tacoma	WA	98409	253-383-2636	383-1061
Tennier Industries Inc 978 Rt 45 - Northside Plz	Pomona	NY	10970	845-362-0800	
Textile Care Services Inc 225 Wood Lk Dr SE **Fax Area Code:* 507 ■ *TF:* 800-422-0945 ■ *Web:* www.textilecs.com	Rochester	MN	55904	800-422-0945	252-7550*
Unitech Services Group 295 Parker St *TF:* 800-344-3824 ■ *Web:* www.unitechus.com	Springfield	MA	01151	413-543-6911	543-6989
US Linen & Uniform Inc 1106 Harding St *Web:* www.uslinen.com	Richland	WA	99352	509-946-6125	
Valiant Products Corp 2727 Fifth Ave W *TF Cust Svc:* 800-347-2727 ■ *Web:* www.valiantproducts.com	Denver	CO	80204	303-892-1234	892-5535
WH Christian & Sons Inc 22 - 28 Franklin St *Web:* www.whchristian.com	Brooklyn	NY	11222	718-389-7000	389-9644

446 LIQUOR STORES

Company	City	State	ZIP	Phone	Fax
21st Amendment Inc 1158 W 86th St *Web:* www.21stamendment.com	Indianapolis	IN	46260	317-846-1678	846-5687
ABC Fine Wines & Spirits 8989 S Orange Ave *TF:* 800-854-7283 ■ *Web:* abcfws.com	Orlando	FL	32824	407-851-0000	857-5500
Acker Merrall & Condit Company Inc 160 W 72nd St *Web:* www.ackerwines.com	New York	NY	10023	212-787-1700	
All Star Wine & Spirits 579 Troy Schenectady Rd Ste 209 *Web:* www.allstarwine.com	Latham	NY	12110	518-220-9463	
B P Lesky Distributing Company Inc 120 Western Maryland Pkwy	Hagerstown	MD	21740	301-733-0787	
B-21 Liquors Inc 43380 US Hwy 19 N *Web:* b-21.com	Tarpon Springs	FL	34689	727-937-5049	
Berbiglia Inc 1114 W 103 St *Web:* www.berbiglia.com	Kansas City	MO	64114	816-942-0070	942-1777
Bevmax Wines & Liquors 835 E Main St *Web:* www.bevmax.com	Stamford	CT	06902	203-357-9151	359-9967
BevMo! 1470 Enea Cir Ste 1600 *Web:* www.bevmo.com	Concord	CA	94520	925-609-6000	
Big Red Liquors Inc 1110 N College Ave PO Box 2209 *Web:* www.bigredliquors.com	Bloomington	IN	47404	812-332-0653	
Bouchaine Vineyards Inc 1075 Buchli Sta Rd *Web:* www.bouchaine.com	Napa	CA	94559	707-252-9065	
Bowser's Lucky Dog Casino 3140 Dredge Dr *Web:* orofinogroup.com	Helena	MT	59602	406-442-1555	
Cap n Cork 1031 Broadway *Web:* www.capncork.com	Fort Wayne	IN	46802	260-423-1496	
Cheers Liquor Mart 1105 N Circle Dr *Web:* www.cheersliquormart.com	Colorado Springs	CO	80909	719-574-2244	
Chicago Wine Co 835 N Central Ave *Web:* www.tcwc.com	Wood Dale	IL	60191	630-594-2972	
Clark Distributing Co 1300 Us Hwy 51 Byp S *Web:* www.clarkdistributingco.com	Dyersburg	TN	38024	731-285-1500	
Colonial Spirits, The 87 Great Rd *Web:* colonialspirits.com	Acton	MA	01720	978-263-7775	
Consumer'S Beverages Company Inc 2230 S Park Ave *Web:* consumersbeverages.com	Buffalo	NY	14220	716-826-9200	
Creekside Cellars 28036 Hwy 74 *Web:* www.creeksidecellars.net	Evergreen	CO	80439	303-674-5460	
Curtis Liquor Stores Inc 790 Chief Justice Cushing Hwy *Web:* www.curtisliquors.com	Cohasset	MA	02025	781-383-9800	
Druley Enterprises Inc 3305 N Anthony Blvd # 41 *Web:* www.belmontbev.com	Fort Wayne	IN	46805	260-424-4604	
Dufry Houston Inc 10300 Nw 19th St Ste 114 *Web:* www.dufry.com	Doral	FL	33172	305-591-1763	
Eagle Brands Inc 3201 NW 72nd Ave *Web:* www.eaglebrands.com	Miami	FL	33122	305-599-2337	
Eureka Casino Hotel 275 Mesa Blvd *Web:* www.eurekamesquite.com	Mesquite	NV	89027	702-346-4600	
Ferry Plaza Wine Merchant Administration Offices 101 The Embarcadero *Web:* www.fpwm.com	San Francisco	CA	94105	415-288-0470	
FINE WINE BROKERS 4621 N Lincoln Ave *Web:* www.fwbchicago.com	Chicago	IL	60625	773-989-8166	989-8166
Flanigan's Enterprises Inc 5059 NE 18th Ave *NYSE: BDL* ■ *Web:* www.flanigans.net	Fort Lauderdale	FL	33334	954-377-1961	377-1980
Foppiano Wine Co 12707 Old Redwood Hwy *Web:* www.foppiano.com	Healdsburg	CA	95448	707-433-7272	
Fox Run Vineyards 670 State Rt 14 *Web:* www.foxrunvineyards.com	Penn Yan	NY	14527	315-536-4616	
Frank Family Vineyards LLC 1091 Larkmead Ln *Web:* www.frankfamilyvineyards.com	Calistoga	CA	94515	707-942-0859	
Frey Vineyards Winery 14000 Tomki Rd *Web:* freywine.com	Redwood Valley	CA	95470	707-485-5177	
Gary's Wine & Marketplace 121 Main St *Web:* www.garyswine.com	Madison	NJ	07940	973-822-0200	
Gold Standard Enterprises Inc 5100 W Dempster St *TF:* 888-942-9463 ■ *Web:* www.binnys.com	Skokie	IL	60077	847-674-4200	568-9905
Goody-Goody Liquors Inc 10301 Harry Hines Blvd *Web:* www.goodygoody.com	Dallas	TX	75220	214-459-9962	350-4258
Grape Wine Company of San Antonio Inc, The 1747 Citadel Plz Ste 112	San Antonio	TX	78209	210-828-2222	
Hart Davis Hart Wine Co 363 W Erie St Ste 500W *Web:* www.hdhwine.com	Chicago	IL	60654	312-482-9996	
Hartwell Vineyards 5795 Silverado Trl *Web:* www.hartwellvineyards.com	Napa	CA	94558	707-255-4269	
K & L Wine Merchants 638 Fourth St *Web:* www.klwines.com	San Francisco	CA	94107	415-896-1734	
Kappy s Liquors 325 Bennett Hwy *Web:* www.kappys.com	Malden	MA	02148	781-321-1000	
Kings Liquor Inc 2810 W Berry St *Web:* www.kingsliquor.com	Fort Worth	TX	76109	817-923-3737	
L&N Enterprises Inc 5720 Daltry Ln	Colorado Springs	CO	80906	719-576-7925	
Left Bank Wine Co 4910 Triangle St *Web:* www.leftbankwine.com	Mc Farland	WI	53558	608-838-8400	
Liquor Barn Inc 4301 Towne Ctr Dr *Web:* www.liquorbarn.com	Louisville	KY	40241	502-426-4222	

	City	State	ZIP	Phone	Fax
Liquor Mart Inc 1750 15th St. *Web:* www.liquormart.com	Boulder	CO	80302	303-449-3374	
Localwineeventscom 2042 General Alexander Dr *Web:* www.localwineevents.com	Malvern	PA	19355	610-647-4888	
Lombard Liquor Inc 420 W 22nd St *Web:* lombardliquors.com	Lombard	IL	60148	630-376-6040	
Luna Vineyards Inc 2921 Silverado Trl *Web:* www.lunavineyards.com	Napa	CA	94558	707-255-5862	
McDonald Oil Company Inc 1700 Lukken Indus Dr W *Web:* www.mcdonaldoil.com	Lagrange	GA	30240	706-884-6191	
Midwest Aero Support Inc 1303 Turret Dr. *Web:* www.midwestaerosupport.com	Machesney Park	IL	61115	815-398-9202	
Mozingo Liquors Inc 120 S Sixth St	Hartsville	SC	29550	843-332-6554	332-6921
Old World Gourmet Deli & Wine Shop 117 Us Rt 1 *Web:* www.oldworldgourmet.com	Freeport	ME	04032	207-865-4477	
Owens Liquors Inc 8000 N Kings Hwy. *Web:* owensliquors.com	Myrtle Beach	SC	29572	843-449-6833	
P J Liquor Whse 4898 Broadway *Web:* www.pjwine.com	New York	NY	10034	212-567-5500	
Patz & Hall Wine Co 851 Napa Vly Corporate Way Ste A. *Web:* www.patzhall.com	Napa	CA	94558	707-265-7700	
Pearlstine Distributors Inc (PDI) 1600 Christon Rgonal Pkwy *TF:* 800-922-1048 ■ *Web:* sc.soeagle.net	Charleston	SC	29492	843-388-6800	388-6799
Pinkie's Inc 1426 E Eigth St *Web:* www.pinkiestexas.com	Odessa	TX	79761	432-580-0439	580-0918
Rocky Mountain Wine Co 133 Big Horn Dr *Web:* www.rockymountainwine.com	Kalispell	MT	59901	406-752-9463	
Saratoga Liquor Company Inc 3215 James Day Ave. *Web:* www.saratogaliquor.com	Superior	WI	54880	715-394-4487	
Shafer Vineyards 6154 Silverado Trl *Web:* www.shafervineyards.com	Napa	CA	94558	707-944-2877	
Sherry-Lehmann Wine & Spirits 505 Pk Ave. *Web:* www.sherry-lehmann.com	New York	NY	10022	212-838-7500	838-9285
Shop 'N Save Liquors 20 Independence Ave *Web:* shopnsaveliquors.com	Quincy	MA	02169	617-773-2060	786-9797
Sigel's Beverages LP 2960 Anode Ln. *Web:* www.sigels.com	Dallas	TX	75220	214-350-1271	357-3490
Spec's Wines Spirits & Finer Foods 2410 Smith St. *TF:* 888-526-8787 ■ *Web:* www.specsonline.com	Houston	TX	77006	713-526-8787	526-6129
State Liquor Store 15015 Main St Ste 117 *Web:* www.liq.wa.gov	Bellevue	WA	98007	617-419-3900	
Touring & Tasting 125 S Quarantina St. *TF:* 800-850-4370 ■ *Web:* www.touringandtasting.com	Santa Barbara	CA	93103	805-965-2813	965-2873
Twin Liquors Lp 5639 Airport Blvd *Web:* twinliquors.com	Austin	TX	78751	512-222-0700	
United Package Liquors Inc 6350 Rucker Rd Ste 105 *Web:* www.unitedpackageliquors.com	Indianapolis	IN	46220	317-205-9266	
Vintage Wines 2277 Westbrooke Dr *Web:* www.vintwine.com	Columbus	OH	43228	614-876-2580	
Wally's Wine & Spirits 2107 Westwood Blvd *Web:* www.wallywine.com	Los Angeles	CA	90025	310-475-0606	
Westchester Wine Warehouse 53 Tarrytown Rd Ste 1. *Web:* www.westchesterwine.com	White Plains	NY	10607	914-824-1400	
Wiederkehr Wine Cellars Inc 3324 Swiss Family Dr. *Web:* www.wiederkehrwines.com	Altus	AR	72821	479-468-3551	
Willow Park Wines & Spirits Ltd 10801 Bonaventure Dr SE. *Web:* www.willowpark.net	Calgary	AB	T2J6Z8	403-296-1640	
Wine Cask Inc, The 407 Washington St *Web:* thewineandcheesecask.com	Somerville	MA	02143	617-623-8656	
Wine Club, The 1431 S Village Way. *TF:* 800-966-5432 ■ *Web:* www.thewineclub.com	Santa Ana	CA	92705	714-835-6485	835-5062
Wine of The Month Club Inc 907 S Magnolia Ave *Web:* wineofthemonthclub.com	Monrovia	CA	91016	626-303-1690	
Wine.com Inc 114 Sansome St 3rd Fl *TF:* 800-592-5870 ■ *Web:* www.wine.com	San Francisco	CA	94104	415-291-9500	248-4400
WineShop At Home 525 Airpark Rd. *Web:* www.wineshopathome.com	Napa	CA	94558	707-253-0200	
Zachys Wine & Liquor Inc 16 E Pkwy *TF:* 800-723-0241 ■ *Web:* www.zachys.com	Scarsdale	NY	10583	914-723-0241	723-1033

447 LITERARY AGENTS

	City	State	ZIP	Phone	Fax
Aaron M Priest Literary Agency 708 Third Ave 23rd Fl. *Web:* aaronpriest.com	New York	NY	10017	212-818-0344	573-9417
Browne & Miller Literary Assoc LLC 410 S Michigan Ave Ste 460 *Web:* www.browneandmiller.com	Chicago	IL	60605	312-922-3063	922-1905
David Black Agency 335 Adams St Ste 2707 *Web:* www.davidblackagency.com	Brooklyn	NY	11201	718-852-5500	852-5539
Dominick Abel Literary Agency Inc 146 W 82nd St Ste 1A *Web:* dalainc.com	New York	NY	10024	212-877-0710	595-3133
Don Congdon Assoc Inc 110 William St Ste 2202. *Web:* www.doncongdon.com	New York	NY	10038	212-727-2688	727-2688
Donadio & Olsen Inc 121 W 27th St Ste 704 *Web:* donadio.com	New York	NY	10001	212-691-8077	633-2837
Dystel & Goderich Literary Management One Union Sq W Ste 904 *Web:* www.dystel.com	New York	NY	10003	212-627-9100	627-9313
Frances Collin Literary Agent PO Box 33 *Web:* www.francescollin.com	Wayne	PA	19087	610-254-0555	254-5029
George Borchardt Inc 136 E 57th St. *Web:* gbagency.com	New York	NY	10022	212-753-5785	838-6518
Harold Ober Assoc Inc 425 Madison Ave 10th Fl *Web:* www.haroldober.com	New York	NY	10017	212-759-8600	759-9428
Harvey Klinger Inc 300 W 55th St. *Web:* www.harveyklinger.com	New York	NY	10019	212-581-7068	315-3823
InkWell Management 521 Fifth Ave Ste 2600 *Web:* www.inkwellmanagement.com	New York	NY	10175	212-922-3500	922-0535
Jane Rotrosen Agency 318 E 51st St *Web:* janerotrosen.com	New York	NY	10022	212-593-4330	935-6985
Jean V Naggar Literary Agency Inc 216 E 75th St Ste 1E. *Web:* www.jvnla.com	New York	NY	10021	212-794-1082	794-3605
Larsen Pomada Literary Agents 1029 Jones St. *Web:* www.larsenpomada.com	San Francisco	CA	94109	415-673-0939	
Lowenstein-Yost Assoc Inc 121 W 27th St Ste 501 *Web:* www.lowensteinassociates.com	New York	NY	10001	212-206-1630	727-0280
Manus & Assoc Literary Agency Inc 425 Sherman Ave Ste 200 *Web:* www.manuslit.com	Palo Alto	CA	94306	650-470-5151	470-5159
Richard Curtis Assoc Inc 171 E 74th St Second Fl. *Web:* www.curtisagency.com	New York	NY	10021	212-772-7363	772-7393
Sanford J Greenburger Assoc Inc 55 Fifth Ave 15th Fl *Web:* www.greenburger.com	New York	NY	10003	212-206-5600	463-8718
Trident Media Group LLC 41 Madison Ave 36th Fl *Web:* www.tridentmediagroup.com	New York	NY	10010	212-333-1511	262-4849
Wallace Literary Agencies Inc 301 E 79th St Ste 14-J	New York	NY	10075	212-570-9090	
William Morris Agency 1325 Ave of the Americas *Web:* www.wma.com	New York	NY	10019	212-586-5100	246-3583
Writers House 21 W 26th St. *Web:* www.writershouse.com	New York	NY	10010	212-685-2400	685-1781

448 LITIGATION SUPPORT SERVICES

	City	State	ZIP	Phone	Fax
Al Betz & Assoc Inc 125 Airport Dr Ste 30 *TF:* 877-402-3376 ■ *Web:* www.albetzreporting.com	Westminster	MD	21157	410-875-3376	875-2857
Alderson Reporting Co 1155 Connecticut Ave NW Ste 200. *TF:* 800-367-3376 ■ *Web:* www.aldersonreporting.com	Washington	DC	20036	202-289-2260	289-2221
Allied Court Reporters Inc 115 Phenix Ave. *TF:* 888-443-3767 ■ *Web:* www.alliedcourtreporters.com	Cranston	RI	02920	401-946-5500	946-9228
Atkinson-Baker Inc (ABI) 500 N Brand Blvd 3rd Fl. *TF:* 800-288-3376 ■ *Web:* www.depo.com	Glendale	CA	91203	818-551-7300	
Compex Legal Services Inc 325 S Maple Ave. *TF Cust Svc:* 800-426-6739 ■ *Web:* www.cpxlegal.com	Torrance	CA	90503	800-426-6739	479-3365
Courtroom Sciences Inc 4950 N O'Connor Rd Corporate Plaza 1 1st Fl *TF:* 800-514-5879 ■ *Web:* www.courtroomsciences.com	Irving	TX	75062	972-717-1773	717-3985
DecisionQuest 21535 Hawthorne Blvd Ste 310. *TF:* 877-833-2474 ■ *Web:* www.decisionquest.com	Torrance	CA	90503	310-618-9600	618-1122
Depobook Reporting Services 1600 G St Ste 101 *TF:* 800-830-8885 ■ *Web:* www.depobook.com	Modesto	CA	95354	209-544-6466	544-6566
DepoNet 2700 Centennial Tower 101 Marietta St 101 Marietta St. **Fax Area Code: 723* ■ *TF:* 800-337-6638 ■ *Web:* www.esquiresolutions.com	Atlanta	GA	30303	404-495-0777	288-2473*
DOAR Litigation Consulting 170 Earle Ave *TF:* 800-875-8705 ■ *Web:* www.doar.com	Lynbrook	NY	11563	516-823-4000	823-4400
FTI Consulting 909 Commerce Rd Ste 1400. *NYSE: FCN* ■ *TF:* 800-334-5701 ■ *Web:* www.fticonsulting.com	Annapolis	MD	21401	410-224-8770	224-9740
Hahn & Bowersock Corp 151 Kalmus Dr Ste L1. **Fax Area Code: 714* ■ *TF:* 800-660-3187 ■ *Web:* www.hahnbowersock.com	Costa Mesa	CA	92626	800-660-3187	662-1398*
Hutchings Court Reporters LLC 6055 E Washington Blvd Eighth Fl *TF Cust Svc:* 800-697-3210 ■ *Web:* www.hutchings.com	Los Angeles	CA	90040	323-888-6300	888-6333
Jane Rose Reporting 80 Fifth Ave. *TF:* 800-825-3341 ■ *Web:* www.janerose.net/janeroseflash.swf	New York	NY	10011	212-727-7773	
Jury Research Institute 2617 Danville Blvd PO Box 100 *TF:* 800-233-5879 ■ *Web:* www.juryresearchinstitute.com	Alamo	CA	94507	925-932-5663	932-8409
Professional Shorthand Reporters Inc (PSR) 601 Poydras St Ste 1615 *TF:* 800-536-5255 ■ *Web:* www.psrdepo.com	New Orleans	LA	70130	504-529-5255	529-5257
Ralph Rosenberg Court Reporters Inc 1001 Bishop St Ste 2460 *TF:* 888-524-5888 ■ *Web:* www.hawaiicourtreporters.com	Honolulu	HI	96813	888-524-5888	
Starr Litigation Services Inc 1201 Grand Ave	West Des Moines	IA	50265	515-224-1616	
Trial Behavior Consulting Inc 505 Sansome St Ste 1701 *Web:* www.trialbehavior.com	San Francisco	CA	94111	415-781-5879	362-8775
US Legal Support Inc 363 N Sam Houston Pkwy E Ste 900 *TF:* 800-567-8757 ■ *Web:* www.uslegalsupport.com	Houston	TX	77060	713-653-7100	653-7171

				Phone	Fax
Veritext LLC 290 W Mt Pleasant Ave Ste 3200	Livingston	NJ	07039	800-567-8658	410-1313*

**Fax Area Code:* 973 ■ *TF:* 800-567-8658 ■ *Web:* www.veritext.com

449 LIVESTOCK - WHOL

SEE ALSO Cattle Ranches, Farms, Feedlots (Beef Cattle) p. 1721; Hog Farms p. 1723

Name / Address	City	State	Zip	Phone	Fax
101 Livestock Market Inc 4400 Hwy 101 *Web:* www.101livestock.com	Aromas	CA	95004	831-726-3303	
Adams Cattle LLC 327 S First Ave *Web:* www.adamslandandcattle.com	Broken Bow	NE	68822	308-872-6494	
Alabama Livestock Auction Inc Hwy 80 E *Web:* www.allivestock.com	Uniontown	AL	36786	334-628-2371	628-6268
All West Select Sires 450 N Hill Blvd *TF:* 800-426-2697 ■ *Web:* www.allwestselectsires.com	Burlington	WA	98233	800-426-2697	
Bales Continental Commission Co 39763 US Hwy 14 PO Box 1337 *Web:* www.balesccc.com	Huron	SD	57350	605-352-8682	352-9374
Billings Livestock Commission Co 2443 N Frontage Rd *Web:* www.billingslivestock.com	Billings	MT	59101	406-245-4151	
Blackfoot Livestock Auction 93 Rich Ln PO Box 830 *Web:* www.blackfootlivestockauction.com	Blackfoot	ID	83221	208-785-0500	785-0503
Blue Grass Stockyard 375 Lisle Industrial Ave PO Box 1023 *TF:* 800-621-3972 ■ *Web:* www.bgstockyards.com	Lexington	KY	40588	859-255-7701	255-5495
Cattle Empire LLC 1174 Empire Cir *Web:* www.cattle-empire.net	Satanta	KS	67870	620-649-2235	
Circle X Land & Cattle Company Ltd 3131 Briarcrest Dr Ste 220 *Web:* www.bre.com	Bryan	TX	77802	979-776-5760	776-4818
D & S Cattle Co 2167 SR 66 PO Box 172	Zolfo Springs	FL	33890	863-735-1112	735-1282
Delta Sales Yard Inc 700 W Fifth St *Web:* www.deltasalesyard.com	Delta	CO	81416	970-874-4612	874-3087
Empire Livestock Marketing LLC 5001 Brittonfield Pkwy *TF:* 800-462-8802 ■ *Web:* www.empirelivestock.com	East Syracuse	NY	13057	315-433-9129	433-0068
Equity Co-op Livestock Sales Assn 401 Commerce Ave *TF:* 800-362-3989 ■ *Web:* www.equitycoop.com	Baraboo	WI	53913	608-356-8311	356-0117
Farmers Livestock Auction Inc 1581 E Emma Ave	Springdale	AR	72764	479-751-5727	751-5896
Finger Lakes Livestock Exchange Inc 3865 Rts 5 & 20 Geneva Tpke *Web:* www.fingerlakeslivestockex.com	Canandaigua	NY	14424	585-394-1515	394-9151
Four States Livestock Sales 501 E First St *Web:* fourstateslivestocksales.com	Hagerstown	MD	21740	301-733-8120	733-7318
High Plains Livestock Exchange LLC 28601 US Hwy 34 *TF:* 866-842-5115 ■ *Web:* www.hplivestock.com	Brush	CO	80723	970-842-5115	842-5088
Houston Livestock Show & Rodeo Inc NRG Ctr Three NRG Park *Web:* www.rodeohouston.com	Houston	TX	77054	832-667-1000	
Jamestown Livestock Auction 3443 82nd Ave SE *Web:* www.jamestownlivestock.com	Jamestown	ND	58401	701-252-2111	252-1520
Keeneland Association Inc 4201 Versailles Rd *Web:* www.keeneland.com	Lexington	KY	40510	859-254-3412	
Kidron Auction Inc 4885 Kidron Rd *TF:* 800-589-9749 ■ *Web:* kidronauction.com	Kidron	OH	44636	330-857-2641	698-3088
Lewiston Sales Inc 21241 Dutchmans Crossing Rd *TF:* 800-732-6334 ■ *Web:* www.lewistonsales.com	Lewiston	MN	55952	507-523-2112	523-2400
Lexington Livestock Market Inc 300 Plum Creek Pkwy *Web:* www.lexlivestock.com	Lexington	NE	68850	308-324-4663	
Lexington Trots Breeders Association 1200 Red Mile Rd *Web:* www.theredmile.com	Lexington	KY	40504	859-255-0752	
Lynch Livestock Co 331 Third St NW *Web:* www.lynchlivestock.com	Waucoma	IA	52171	563-776-3311	
Midwest Land & Cattle Company Inc 503 N Mur-Len Rd	Olathe	KS	66062	913-782-6677	
Midwest Livestock Systems Inc 3600 N Sixth St *Web:* www.midwestlivestock.com	Beatrice	NE	68310	402-223-5281	
Miller Livestock Markets Inc 100 Sale Barn Rd *Web:* millerlivestockinc.com	Dequincy	LA	70633	337-786-2995	786-3270
National Commission Assn 2501 Exchange Ave Ste 102 *Web:* www.nationallivestock.com	Oklahoma City	OK	73108	405-232-3128	
O & S Cattle Co 100 StockyaRds Rd	South Saint Paul	MN	55075	651-455-5459	455-8394
Overland Stockyard Inc 10565 Ninth Ave *Web:* www.overlandstockyards.com	Hanford	CA	93230	559-582-0404	
Pipestone Livestock Auction Market 1500 Seventh St SE *Web:* www.pipestonelivestock.com	Pipestone	MN	56164	507-825-3306	825-3308
Prairie Livestock LLC 2139 Barton Ferry Rd PO Box 636 *TF:* 800-647-6350 ■ *Web:* www.prairielivestock.net	West Point	MS	39773	662-494-5651	
Producers Livestock Auction Co 1131 N Bell St *Web:* www.producersandcargile.com	San Angelo	TX	76903	325-653-3371	653-3370
Producers Livestock Marketing Assn 4809 S 114th St *TF:* 800-257-4046 ■ *Web:* producerslivestock.net	Omaha	NE	68137	402-597-9189	597-9505
Roswell Livestock Auction Sales Inc 900 N Garden PO Box 2041 **Fax Area Code:* 505 ■ *Web:* www.roswelllivestockauction.com	Roswell	NM	88202	575-622-5580	623-5680*
San Antonio Livestock Exposition Inc PO Box 200230 *Web:* www.sarodeo.com	San Antonio	TX	78220	210-225-0575	
Sheridan Livestock Auction Company Inc Sale Barn Rd *Web:* sheridanlivestock.com	Rushville	NE	69360	308-327-2406	327-2383
Stockmen's Livestock Market Inc 1200 E Hwy 50 PO Box 528 *TF:* 800-532-0952 ■ *Web:* stockmenslivestock.com	Yankton	SD	57078	605-665-9641	665-9644
Topeka Livestock Auction 601 E Lake St *Web:* topekalivestock.com	Topeka	IN	46571	260-593-2522	593-2258
Turner County Stockyard 1315 US Hwy 41 S *Web:* turnercountystockyard.com	Ashburn	GA	31714	229-567-3371	567-3785
United Producers Inc 8351 N High St Ste 250 *TF:* 800-456-3276 ■ *Web:* www.uproducers.com	Columbus	OH	43235	800-456-3276	
Wayland Hopkins Livestock 3634 Tenth St	Wayland	MI	49348	269-792-2296	792-8055
Winner Livestock Auction Co 31690 Livestock Barn Rd *TF:* 800-201-0451 ■ *Web:* www.winnerlivestock.com	Winner	SD	57580	605-842-0451	842-3562
Winter Livestock Inc P.O. Box 909 PO Box 909 *Web:* www.winterlivestock.com	Enid	OK	73702	580-237-4600	237-4604

450 LIVESTOCK & POULTRY FEEDS - PREPARED

Name / Address	City	State	Zip	Phone	Fax
AC Nutrition 158 N Main St *TF:* 800-588-3333 ■ *Web:* www.acnutrition.com	Winters	TX	79567	325-754-4546	754-4546
ADM Alliance Nutrition Inc 1000 N 30th St *TF:* 800-292-3333 ■ *Web:* www.admani.com	Quincy	IL	62301	217-222-7100	
AG Partners Inc 512 S Eigth St PO Box 467 *TF:* 800-772-2990 ■ *Web:* agpartners.net	Lake City	MN	55041	651-345-3328	345-2212
Ag Processing Inc 12700 W Dodge Rd PO Box 2047 *TF:* 800-247-1345 ■ *Web:* www.agp.com	Omaha	NE	68103	402-496-7809	498-2215
Agri-King Inc 18246 Waller Rd *TF:* 800-435-9560 ■ *Web:* www.agriking.com	Fulton	IL	61252	815-589-2525	589-4565
Ahrberg Milling Co 200 S Depot St PO Box 968 *TF:* 800-324-0267 ■ *Web:* www.ahrbergmilling.com	Cushing	OK	74023	918-225-0267	225-0275
AL Gilbert Co 304 N Yosemite Ave *Web:* farmerswarehouse.com	Oakdale	CA	95361	209-847-1721	
Alabama Farmers Co-op Inc PO Box 2227 *TF:* 888-255-2667 ■ *Web:* www.alafarm.com	Decatur	AL	35601	256-353-6843	350-1770
Albion Laboratories Inc 101 N Main St *TF:* 800-453-2406 ■ *Web:* www.albionminerals.com	Clearfield	UT	84015	801-773-4631	773-4633
American Proteins Inc 4705 Leland Dr *Web:* www.americanproteins.com	Cumming	GA	30041	770-886-2250	886-2296
Bagdad Roller Mills Inc 5740 Elmburg Rd PO Box 7 *TF:* 800-928-3333 ■ *Web:* www.bagdadrollermillsfeed.com	Bagdad	KY	40003	502-747-8968	747-8960
Belstra Milling Company Inc 424 15th St PO Box 460 **Fax Area Code:* 219 ■ *TF:* 800-276-2789 ■ *Web:* www.belstramilling.com	Demotte	IN	46310	800-276-2789	987-5227*
BioZyme Inc 6010 Stockyards Expy *TF:* 800-821-3070 ■ *Web:* www.biozymeinc.com	Saint Joseph	MO	64504	816-238-3326	238-7549
Blue Seal Feeds Inc 2905 US Hwy 61 N *TF Cust Svc:* 866-647-1212 ■ *Web:* www.blueseal.com	Muscatine	IA	52761	866-647-1212	
Buckeye Nutrition 330 E Schultz Ave PO Box 505 **Fax Area Code:* 330 ■ *TF:* 800-417-6460 ■ *Web:* www.buckeyenutrition.com	Dalton	OH	44618	800-417-6460	828-2309*
Cargill Inc North America 15407 McGinty Rd *Web:* cargill.com	Wayzata	MN	55391	952-742-7575	
Central AG Services 209 N Bridge St PO Box 98	Clarissa	MN	56440	218-756-2112	756-2451
Circle S Ranch Inc 1604 Cir S Ranch Rd	Monroe	NC	28112	704-764-7414	764-7646
Cumberland Valley Co-op Assn 908 Mt Rock Rd *TF:* 800-488-2197 ■ *Web:* agmap.psu.edu	Shippensburg	PA	17257	717-532-2197	
Cutler-Dickerson Company Inc 507 College Ave *Web:* cutlerdickerson.com	Adrian	MI	49221	517-265-5191	263-4213
D & D Commodities Ltd PO Box 359 **Fax Area Code:* 218 ■ *TF:* 800-543-3308 ■ *Web:* www.ddcommodities.com	Stephen	MN	56757	800-543-3308	478-3533*
Dairymen's Feed & Supply Co 323 E Washington St	Petaluma	CA	94952	707-763-1585	763-5239
Darling International Inc 251 O'Connor Ridge Blvd Ste 300 *NYSE: DAR* ■ *TF:* 855-327-7761 ■ *Web:* www.darlingii.com	Irving	TX	75038	972-717-0300	717-1588
DeKalb Feeds Inc 105 Dixon Ave *Web:* dekalbfeeds.com	Rock Falls	IL	61071	815-625-4546	
Diamond V Mills Inc PO Box 74570 *TF:* 800-373-7234 ■ *Web:* www.diamondv.com	Cedar Rapids	IA	52407	319-366-0745	366-6333
Eagle Roller Mill Co 1101 Airport Rd *TF:* 800-223-9108 ■ *Web:* www.eaglerollermill.com	Shelby	NC	28150	704-487-5061	482-1263
Effingham Equity Inc 201 W Roadway Ave *TF:* 800-223-1337 ■ *Web:* www.effinghamequity.com	Effingham	IL	62401	217-342-4101	347-7601
Elenbaas Co 411 W Front St *TF:* 800-808-6954 ■ *Web:* www.elenbaasco.com	Sumas	WA	98295	360-988-5811	988-0411
Farmers Co-op Elevator Co 177 W Main St PO Box 108 *Web:* www.farmerscoopelevator.com	Cottonwood	MN	56229	507-423-5412	423-5551
Farmers Union Co-op 1913 Co Rd B32	Ossian	IA	52161	563-532-9381	
Feed Products Inc 1000 W 47th Ave	Denver	CO	80211	303-455-3646	477-6206
First Co-op Assn (FCA) 960 Riverview Dr PO Box 60 *TF:* 877-753-5400 ■ *Web:* www.firstcoop.com	Cherokee	IA	51012	712-225-5400	225-5493
FL Emmert Co Inc 2007 Dunlap St *TF:* 800-441-3343 ■ *Web:* www.emmert.com	Cincinnati	OH	45214	513-721-5808	721-6087
Flint River Mills Inc 1100 Dothan Rd PO Box 280 **Fax:* Cust Svc ■ *TF Cust Svc:* 800-841-8502 ■ *Web:* frmfeeds.com	Bainbridge	GA	39817	229-246-2232	243-7376*

				Phone	Fax
FM Brown's Sons Inc 205 Woodrow Ave PO Box 2116	Sinking Spring	PA	19608	610-678-4567	678-7023
TF: 800-334-8816 ■ *Web:* www.fmbrown.com					
Form-A-Feed Inc (FAF) 740 Bowman St	Stewart	MN	55385	320-562-2413	
TF: 800-422-3649 ■ *Web:* www.formafeed.com					
Franklin Feed & Supply Co 1977 Philadelphia Ave	Chambersburg	PA	17201	717-264-6148	264-7865
Web: franklinhardwareandpetcenter.com					
Friona Industries LP 500 S Taylor St Ste 601 PO Box 15568	Amarillo	TX	79101	806-374-1811	374-1324
TF: 800-658-6014 ■ *Web:* www.frionaind.com					
Furst-McNess Co 120 E Clark St	Freeport	IL	61032	815-235-6151	232-9724
TF: 800-435-5100 ■ *Web:* www.mcness.com					
Goldsboro Milling Co 938 Millers Chapel Rd	Goldsboro	NC	27534	919-778-3130	
Web: cals.ncsu.edu					
Harvest Land Co-op 711 Front St PO Box 278	Morgan	MN	56266	507-249-3196	
TF: 800-245-5819 ■ *Web:* www.harvestland.com					
Hog Slat 200 N Meridian Line Rd	Camden	IN	46917	574-967-3776	
TF: 800-949-4647 ■ *Web:* www.hogslat.com/					
Hubbard Feeds Inc 424 N Riverfront Dr PO Box 8500	Mankato	MN	56001	507-388-9400	388-9453
TF: 800-869-7219 ■ *Web:* www.hubbardfeeds.com					
Hunt & Behrens Inc 30 Lakeville St	Petaluma	CA	94952	707-762-4594	762-9164
Web: hbfeeds.com					
International Ingredient Corp 150 Larkin Williams Industrial Ct PO Box 26377	Fenton	MO	63026	636-343-4111	349-4845
Web: www.iicag.com					
JBS United Inc 4310 State Rd 38 W	Sheridan	IN	46069	317-758-4495	
TF: 800-382-9909 ■ *Web:* www.jbsunited.com					
JD Heiskell & Co 116 W Cedar St	Tulare	CA	93274	559-685-6100	686-8697
TF: 800-366-1886 ■ *Web:* www.heiskell.com					
John A Van Den Bosch Co 4511 Holland Ave	Holland	MI	49424	800-968-6477	
TF: 800-968-6477 ■ *Web:* www.vbosch.com					
Kay Dee Feed Company Inc 1919 Grand Ave	Sioux City	IA	51106	712-277-2011	279-1946
TF Cust Svc: 800-831-4815 ■ *Web:* kaydeefeed.com					
Keith Smith Company Inc 130 K-Tech Ln PO Box 3800	Hot Springs	AR	71914	501-760-0100	760-9199
Web: www.keith-smith.com					
Kemin Industries Inc 2100 Maury St	Des Moines	IA	50317	515-559-5100	559-5232
TF: 800-777-8307 ■ *Web:* www.kemin.com					
Lakeland Animal Nutrition 2801 S Combee Rd	Lakeland	FL	33803	863-665-5722	686-9427
Land O'Lakes Inc Western Feed Div 4001 Lexington Ave N	Arden Hills	MN	55126	800-328-9680	
TF: 800-328-9680 ■ *Web:* www.landolakesinc.com					
Lucta USA Inc Pine Meadow Corporate Ctr 950 Technology Way Ste 110	Libertyville	IL	60048	847-996-3400	996-3401
TF: 800-323-5341 ■ *Web:* www.lucta.com					
Manna Pro Corp 707 Spirit 40 Pk Dr Ste 150	Chesterfield	MO	63005	800-690-9908	
TF: 800-690-9908 ■ *Web:* www.mannapro.com					
Mark Hershey Farms Inc 479 Horseshoe Pk	Lebanon	PA	17042	717-867-4624	867-4313
TF: 888-801-3301 ■ *Web:* www.markhersheyfarms.com					
Merrick's Inc 2415 Parview Rd PO Box 620307	Middleton	WI	53562	608-831-3440	836-8943
TF: 800-637-7425 ■ *Web:* www.merricks.com					
MFA Inc 201 Ray Young Dr	Columbia	MO	65201	573-874-5111	876-5505
Web: www.mfaincorporated.com					
Milk Specialties Co 260 S Washington St	Carpentersville	IL	60110	952-942-7310	426-4121*
**Fax Area Code:* 847 ■ *TF:* 800-323-4274 ■ *Web:* www.milkspecialties.com					
Moroni Feed Co 15 East 1900 South Feed Mill Rd	Moroni	UT	84646	435-436-8225	436-8101
Web: www.moroni.openfos.com					
Mountaire Corp PO Box 1320	Millsboro	DE	19966	302-934-1100	
TF: 877-887-1490 ■ *Web:* www.mountaire.com					
Mountaire Farms of North Carolina 203 Morris Farm Rd	Candor	NC	27229	910-974-3232	974-3165
Web: mountaire.com					
Moyer & Son Inc 113 E Reliance Rd	Souderton	PA	18964	215-799-2000	721-2814
TF: 866-669-3747 ■ *Web:* www.emoyer.com					
NRV Inc N8155 American St	Ixonia	WI	53036	920-261-7000	261-1685
TF: 800-558-0002 ■ *Web:* www.calfmax1.com					
Oberbeck Grain Co 700 Walnut St	Highland	IL	62249	618-654-2387	654-5862
TF: 800-632-2012 ■ *Web:* www.oberbeckgrainco.com					
OMCO Inc 214 E Mill St	Odon	IN	47562	812-636-7362	636-4777
TF: 800-525-0272 ■ *Web:* marketplaceindiana.com					
Pennfield Corp 2260 Erin Ct PO Box 4366	Lancaster	PA	17601	717-299-2561	295-8766
Pied Piper Mills Inc 423 E Lake Dr	Hamlin	TX	79520	325-576-3684	576-3460
Web: www.piedpiperpetfood.net					
Preble Feed & Grain Inc 6035 N 400 W	Preble	IN	46782	260-547-4452	
Web: kentfeeds.com					
Prince Agri Products Inc 229 Radio Rd	Quincy	IL	62306	217-222-8854	222-5098
Web: www.princeagri.com					
Prince Minerals 21 W 46th St 14th Fl	New York	NY	10036	646-747-4222	
Web: www.princeminerals.com					
Producers Co-op Assoc 300 E Buffalo St PO Box 323	Girard	KS	66743	620-724-8241	724-8243
Web: www.girardcoop.com					
Provimi North America Inc 10 Collective Way	Brookville	OH	45309	937-770-2400	
TF: 888-522-2420 ■ *Web:* www.provimi-na.com					
Quali Tech Inc 318 Lake Hazeltine Dr	Chaska	MN	55318	952-448-5151	448-3603
TF: 800-328-5870 ■ *Web:* www.qualitechco.com					
Ragland Mills Inc 14079 Hammer Rd	Neosho	MO	64850	417-451-2510	451-7499
Web: www.raglandmills.com					
Ralco Nutrition Inc 1600 Hahn Rd	Marshall	MN	56258	800-533-5306	532-5740*
**Fax Area Code:* 507 ■ *TF:* 800-533-5306 ■ *Web:* www.ralconutrition.com					
Rangen Inc 115 13th Ave S	Buhl	ID	83316	208-543-6421	543-6090
TF Cust Svc: 800-657-6446 ■ *Web:* www.rangen.com					
Seminole Feed 335 NE Watula Ave PO Box 940	Ocala	FL	34470	352-732-4143	732-5968
TF: 800-683-1881 ■ *Web:* www.seminolefeed.com					
Star Milling Co 24067 Water St	Perris	CA	92570	951-657-3143	657-3114
TF: 800-733-6455 ■ *Web:* www.starmilling.com					
Triple Crown Nutrition Inc 319 Barry Ave S Ste 303	Wayzata	MN	55391	800-451-9916	473-6571*
**Fax Area Code:* 952 ■ *TF:* 800-451-9916 ■ *Web:* www.triplecrownfeed.com					
Trouw Nutrition 115 Executive Dr	Highland	IL	62249	618-654-2070	654-7012
TF: 800-365-1357 ■ *Web:* trouwnutritionusa.com					
Ursa Farmers Co-op Inc 202 W Maple Ave PO Box 8	Ursa	IL	62376	217-964-2111	964-2260
Web: www.ursacoop.com					
Valley Proteins Inc 151 Valpro Dr	Winchester	VA	22603	540-877-2590	877-3215
Web: www.valleyproteins.com					
Vita Plus Corp 2514 Fish Hatchery Rd	Madison	WI	53713	608-256-1988	283-7990
TF: 800-362-8334 ■ *Web:* www.vitaplus.com					
Zeigler Bros Inc 400 GaRdner Stn Rd PO Box 95	Gardners	PA	17324	717-677-6181	677-6826
TF: 800-841-6800 ■ *Web:* www.zeiglerfeed.com					

451 LOGGING

				Phone	Fax
B & S Logging Inc 4411 NW Elliott Ln	Prineville	OR	97754	541-447-3175	447-7141
Besse Forest Products Group Inc 933 N Eigth St	Gladstone	MI	49837	906-428-3113	
Web: www.bessegroup.com					
Canal Wood LLC 2430 Main St	Conway	SC	29526	843-488-9663	
TF: 866-587-1460 ■ *Web:* www.canalwood.com					
Cousineau Inc Three Valley Rd	North Anson	ME	04958	207-635-4445	
Web: www.cousineaus.com					
Crane Mills Inc 22938 S Ave	Corning	CA	96021	530-824-5427	824-3157
Croman Corp 801 Ave C	White City	OR	97503	541-826-4455	826-7430
Web: www.croman.net					
Freres Lumber Company Inc PO Box 276	Lyons	OR	97358	503-859-2121	859-2112
Web: www.frereslumber.com					
Green Crow Corp 727 E Eigth St PO Box 2469	Port Angeles	WA	98362	360-452-3325	
Web: www.greencrow.com					
Greif Inc 425 Winter Rd	Delaware	OH	43015	740-549-6000	657-6592
NYSE: GEF ■ *TF:* 877-781-9797 ■ *Web:* www.greif.com					
Hopkes Logging Company Inc 2235 Hadley Rd N	Tillamook	OR	97141	503-842-2491	842-9858
Huffman & Wright Logging Inc 801 SE Third St PO Box 910	Canyonville	OR	97417	541-839-4251	
Midwest Walnut Co 1914 Postevin St	Council Bluffs	IA	51503	712-325-9191	325-0156
TF: 800-592-5688 ■ *Web:* www.midwestwalnut.com					
Morbark Inc 8507 S Winn Rd	Winn	MI	48896	989-866-2381	
Web: www.morbark.com					
Plum Creek Timber Company Inc 601 Union St Ste 3100	Seattle	WA	98101	206-467-3600	467-3795
NYSE: PCL ■ *TF:* 800-858-5347 ■ *Web:* www.plumcreek.com					
Roseburg Forest Products Co PO Box 1088	Roseburg	OR	97470	541-679-3311	
TF: 800-245-1115 ■ *Web:* www.roseburg.com					
Sealaska Corp One Sealaska Plz Ste 400	Juneau	AK	99801	907-586-1512	586-2304
Web: www.sealaska.com					
Sierra Pacific Industries 19794 Riverside Ave	Anderson	CA	96007	530-378-8000	378-8109
Web: spi-ind.com					
Swanson Group Inc 2695 Glendale Vly Rd PO Box 250	Glendale	OR	97442	541-832-1121	
Web: www.swansongroupinc.com					
Western Forest Products Inc (WFP) 510 - 700 W Georgia St PO Box 10032	Vancouver	BC	V7Y1A1	604-648-4500	681-9584
TSE: WEF ■ *Web:* www.westernforest.com					
Yeomans Wood & Timber Inc 714 Empire Expy	Swainsboro	GA	30401	478-237-9940	
Web: yeomanswood.com					

452 LOGISTICS SERVICES (TRANSPORTATION & WAREHOUSING)

SEE ALSO Freight Forwarders p. 2333; Marine Services p. 2715; Rail Transport Services p. 3029; Trucking Companies p. 3260; Commercial Warehousing p. 3292

				Phone	Fax
A Duie Pyle Inc 650 Westtown Rd	West Chester	PA	19382	610-696-5800	
TF: 800-523-5020					
Access Business Group 7575 Fulton St E	Ada	MI	49355	616-787-6000	
TF Cust Svc: 800-253-6500 ■ *Web:* www.accessbusinessgroup.com					
Accomack County School District 23296 Courthouse Ave PO Box 330	Accomac	VA	23301	757-787-5754	787-2951
Web: www.accomack.k12.va.us					
Acme Wire Products Co Seven Broadway Ave	Mystic	CT	06355	860-572-0511	
Web: www.acmewire.com					
ADS Tactical Inc Lynnwood Plz 621 Lynnhaven Pkwy Ste 400	Virginia Beach	VA	23452	757-481-7758	
TF: 800-948-9433 ■ *Web:* www.adsinc.com					
Advantage Learning Solutions Inc 160-9521 Franklin Ave	Fort Mcmurray	AB	T9H3Z7	780-743-5001	
Web: www.advantagels.ca					
American Cargo Express Inc PO Box 483	Elizabeth	NJ	07207	908-351-3400	289-2490
Web: www.americancargoexpress.com					
AN Deringer Inc 64 N Main St	Saint Albans	VT	05478	802-524-8110	524-5970
TF: 800-448-8108 ■ *Web:* www.anderinger.com					
APL Logistics Inc 16220 N Scottsdale Rd Ste 300	Scottsdale	AZ	85254	866-896-2005	586-4861*
**Fax Area Code:* 602 ■ *TF:* 866-896-2005 ■ *Web:* www.apllogistics.com					
Associated Global Systems Inc 3333 New Hyde Pk Rd	New Hyde Park	NY	11042	516-627-8910	627-8851
TF Cust Svc: 800-645-8300 ■ *Web:* www.agsystems.com					
Atlantic Bulk Carrier Corp PO Box 112	Providence Forge	VA	23140	804-966-5459	966-5081
TF: 800-966-0030 ■ *Web:* www.atlanticbulk.com					
B-H Transfer Co 750 Sparta Rd PO Box 151	Sandersville	GA	31082	478-552-5119	552-0384
TF: 888-786-3664 ■ *Web:* www.b-htransfer.com					

	City	State	Zip	Phone	Fax
Bantam Group Inc 50 Bay Colony Dr.	Westwood	MA	02090	781-329-2020	
Web: www.bantamgroup.com					
BDP International Inc 510 Walnut St	Philadelphia	PA	19106	215-629-8900	629-8940
Web: www.bdpinternational.com					
Bender Group 345 Parr Cir.	Reno	NV	89512	775-788-8800	788-8811
TF: 800-621-9402 ■ *Web:* www.bendergroup.com					
Bestway Systems Inc 5755 Granger Rd Ste 400	Independence	OH	44131	216-398-6090	398-0674
Web: www.bestwaysystems.com					
Bridger LLC 15510 Wright Brothers Dr	Addison	TX	75001	214-722-6960	
Web: www.bridgergroup.com					
Bulldog Hiway Express 3390 Buffalo Ave.	Charleston	SC	29418	843-744-1651	529-3345
TF: 800-331-9515 ■ *Web:* www.bulldoghiway.com					
Cardinal Logistics Management Corp 5333 Davidson Hwy	Concord	NC	28027	704-786-6125	788-6618
Web: www.cardlog.com					
Cargo Solution Express Inc 14589 Valley Blvd	Fontana	CA	92335	909-350-1644	350-4349
Web: www.cargosolutionexpress.com					
Caterpillar Logistics Services Inc 500 N Morton Ave.	Morton	IL	61550	309-266-3591	
Web: www.caterpillar.com					
Cdo Technologies Inc 5200 Sprngfeld St Ste 320.	Dayton	OH	45431	937-258-0022	258-1614
TF: 866-307-6616 ■ *Web:* www.cdotech.com					
Central Transportation Systems Inc 4105 Rio Bravo Ste 100	El Paso	TX	79902	800-283-3106	
TF: 800-283-3106 ■ *Web:* www.centralsystems.com					
CH Robinson Worldwide Inc 14701 Charlson Rd.	Eden Prairie	MN	55347	952-683-3950	
NASDAQ: CHRW ■ *TF Cust Svc:* 855-229-6128 ■ *Web:* www.chrobinson.com					
Clarion Associates Inc 601 S La Salle St Ste 600	Chicago	IL	60605	312-630-9400	
Web: clarionassociates.com					
Classical Academy 975 Stout Rd	Colorado Springs	CO	80921	719-484-0091	
Web: www.tcatitans.org					
Clean Air Technology Inc 41105 Capital Dr.	Canton	MI	48187	734-459-6320	459-9437
TF: 800-459-6320 ■ *Web:* www.cleanairtechnology.com					
Clipper Exxpress Inc 9014 Heritage Pkwy Ste 300.	Woodridge	IL	60517	630-739-0700	739-1817
TF: 800-678-2547 ■ *Web:* www.clippergroup.com					
Coleman American Cos Inc PO Box 960.	Midland City	AL	36350	334-983-6500	983-5532
TF: 877-693-7060 ■ *Web:* www.colemanallied.com					
Conley Transport Ii Inc 2104 Eastline Rd.	Searcy	AR	72143	501-268-4672	268-6810
TF: 800-338-8700 ■ *Web:* www.conleytransport.com					
Cord Moving & Storage 4101 Rider Trl N.	Saint Louis	MO	63045	314-720-2147	291-6127
Web: www.cordmoving.com					
Coyote Logistics LLC 191 E Deerpath Rd	Lake Forest	IL	60045	847-295-2424	295-2828
TF: 877-626-9683 ■ *Web:* www.coyotelogistics.com					
Crane Worldwide Logistics LLC 1500 Rankin Rd	Houston	TX	77073	281-443-2777	443-3777
TF: 888-870-2726 ■ *Web:* www.craneww.com					
Customer Insight Group Inc 6711 Secrest Cir	Arvada	CO	80007	303-422-9758	
Web: www.customerinsightgroup.com					
Daniel F Young Inc 1235 Westlakes Dr Ste 255	Berwyn	PA	19312	610-725-4000	725-0570
TF: 866-407-0083 ■ *Web:* www.dfyoung.com					
Daniel Group Ltd, The 400 Clarice Ave Ste 200	Charlotte	NC	28204	704-367-4242	
Web: thedanielgroup.com					
Danny Herman Trucking Inc PO Box 55	Mountain City	TN	37683	423-727-9061	727-5675
TF: 800-251-7500 ■ *Web:* www.dannyherman.com					
Dennis K Burke Inc 284 Eastern Ave PO Box 6069	Chelsea	MA	02150	617-884-7800	884-7638
TF: 800-289-2875 ■ *Web:* www.burkeoil.com					
Dependable Highway Express Inc 2440 S 48th Ave	Phoenix	AZ	85043	602-278-4401	278-4473
TF: 800-472-2037 ■ *Web:* www.godependable.com					
Distribution & Marking Services Inc (DMSI) 10708 Granite St Ste J	Charlotte	NC	28273	704-749-7300	749-7301
Web: www.dmsi.net					
Dohrn Transfer Co 625 Third Ave.	Rock Island	IL	61201	309-794-0723	794-1693
TF: 888-364-7621 ■ *Web:* www.dohrn.com					
DSC Logistics 1750 S Wolf Rd	Des Plaines	IL	60018	800-372-1960	390-7276*
**Fax Area Code:* 847 ■ *TF:* 800-372-1960 ■ *Web:* www.dsclogistics.com					
DTI Assoc Inc 2920 S Glebe Rd	Arlington	VA	22206	703-299-1600	706-0474
Web: www.dtiassociates.com					
Eagle Support Services Corp 2705 Artie St Bldg 400 Ste 30	Huntsville	AL	35805	256-534-2274	534-0606
Web: www.eaglesupport.com					
Elston-Richards Inc 5738 Eagle Dr SE Ste B	Grand Rapids	MI	49512	616-698-2698	698-8090
Web: www.elstonrichards.com					
EMBASSY Products & Logistics PO Box 8066	Falls Church	VA	22041	703-845-0800	820-9385
Web: www.embassy-usa.com					
EnteGreat Inc 1500 Urban Ctr Dr Ste 415	Vestavia Hills	AL	35242	205-968-3050	
Web: www.entegreat.com					
Ervin Equipment Inc 608 N Ohio St	Toledo	IL	62468	217-849-3125	
Web: www.ervinusa.com					
Ethier Associates 736 6 Ave Sw	Calgary	AB	T2P3T7	403-234-8960	
Web: www.ethier.ca					
Exel 570 Polaris Pkwy.	Westerville	OH	43082	614-865-8500	865-8875
TF: 800-272-1052 ■ *Web:* www.exel.com					
Expeditors International of Washington Inc 1015 Third Ave 12th Fl	Seattle	WA	98104	206-674-3400	682-9777
NASDAQ: EXPD ■ *TF:* 800-284-7474 ■ *Web:* www.expeditors.com					
Extron Logistics LLC 496 S Abbott Ave.	Milpitas	CA	95035	510-353-0177	
Web: www.extroninc.com					
FedEx Supply Chain Services Inc 5455 Darrow Rd	Hudson	OH	44236	901-369-3600	
TF: 800-463-3339 ■ *Web:* www.fedex.com					
FedEx Trade Networks Inc 6075 Poplar Ave Ste 300 Third Fl.	Memphis	TN	38119	901-684-4800	684-4843
NYSE: FDX ■ *Web:* www.ftn.fedex.com					
Fremont Contract Carriers Inc (FCC) 865 S Bud Blvd.	Fremont	NE	68025	800-228-9842	727-8712*
**Fax Area Code:* 402 ■ *TF:* 800-228-9842 ■ *Web:* www.fcc-inc.com					
Frontier Logistic Services 1700 N Alameda St	Compton	CA	90222	310-604-8208	604-8135
Web: www.frontier-logistics.com					
Gellman Research Associates Inc 115 W Ave Ste 201	Jenkintown	PA	19046	215-884-7500	
Web: gra-inc.com					
Global Logistics 1085 Rockaway Ave Vly stream Sixth Fl	New York	NY	11581	516-825-2922	825-1143
Web: www.globallog.com					
Griffin Transport Services 5360 Capital Ct	Reno	NV	89502	775-331-8010	
Web: legacyscs.com					
Groton-Dunstable Regional School District PO Box 729	Groton	MA	01450	978-448-5505	448-9402
Web: www.gdrsd.org					
Gypsum Express Ltd 8280 Sixty Rd PO Box 268	Baldwinsville	NY	13027	315-638-2201	638-2453
TF: 800-621-7901 ■ *Web:* www.gypsumexpress.com					
H E Whitlock Inc 4808 Dillon Dr	Pueblo	CO	81008	866-933-0709	544-1832*
**Fax Area Code:* 719 ■ *TF:* 866-933-0709 ■ *Web:* www.hewhitlock.com					
Hanson Logistics 2900 S State St Ste 4 E	Saint Joseph	MI	49085	269-982-1390	982-1506
TF: 888-772-1197 ■ *Web:* www.hansonlogisticsgroup.com					
Higher Ed Growth LLC 5400 S Lakeshore Dr Ste 101	Tempe	AZ	85283	866-433-8532	
TF: 866-433-8532 ■ *Web:* www.higheredgrowth.com					
Highway Transport Logistics Inc (HTL) 6420 Baum Dr	Knoxville	TN	37919	865-584-8631	
Web: www.hytt.com					
Horizon Air Freight Inc 152-15 Rockaway Blvd	Jamaica	NY	11434	718-528-3800	949-0655
TF: 800-221-6028 ■ *Web:* www.haf.com					
Hoyt, Shepston & Sciaroni Inc 161a Starlite St # B	South San Francisco	CA	94080	650-952-6930	
Web: www.hoyt-shepston.com					
Hub Group Inc 3050 Highland Pkwy Ste 100	Downers Grove	IL	60515	630-271-3600	964-6475
NASDAQ: HUBG ■ *TF:* 800-377-5833 ■ *Web:* www.hubgroup.com					
InterChez Logistics Systems Inc 600 Alpha Pkwy.	Stow	OH	44224	330-923-5080	
Web: www.interchez.com					
J A Moss Construction PO Box 180460	Richland	MS	39218	601-939-4141	939-4142
Web: www.jamossconstruction.com					
James Group International 4335 W Ft St	Detroit	MI	48209	313-841-0070	841-5074
Web: www.jamesgroupintl.com					
Jarrett Logistics Systems Inc 1347 N Main St	Orrville	OH	44667	330-682-0099	
Web: www.jarrettlogistics.com					
JB Hunt Transport Services Inc 615 JB Hunt Corporate Dr	Lowell	AR	72745	479-820-0000	820-8249*
NASDAQ: JBHT ■ **Fax:* Hum Res ■ *TF:* 800-643-3622 ■ *Web:* www.jbhunt.com					
Jon Peddie Research Inc Four Saint Gabrielle Ct	Tiburon	CA	94920	415-435-9368	
Web: www.jonpeddie.com					
Kenco Group Inc 2001 Riverside Dr.	Chattanooga	TN	37406	800-758-3289	643-3500*
**Fax Area Code:* 423 ■ *TF:* 800-758-3289 ■ *Web:* www.kencogroup.com					
Kintetsu World Express USA Inc One Jericho Plz Ste 100	Jericho	NY	11753	516-933-7100	933-7731
TF: 800-275-4045 ■ *Web:* www.kweusa.com					
Kom International 300 St-Sacrement Ste 307	Montreal	QC	H2Y1X4	514-849-4000	849-8888
Web: www.komintl.com					
Kuehne & Nagel Inc 10 Exchange Pl.	Jersey City	NJ	07302	201-413-5500	413-5777
TF: 866-914-0444 ■ *Web:* www.kn-portal.com					
L&B Transport LLC 708 US190 PO Box 74870	Port Allen	LA	70767	225-387-0894	387-0126
TF: 800-545-9401 ■ *Web:* www.landbtransport.com					
L-3 Vertex Aerospace Llc 555 Industrial Dr S	Madison	MS	39110	601-607-6288	
Web: www.l-3vertex.com					
Landstar Logistics Inc 13410 Sutton Pk Dr S.	Jacksonville	FL	32224	904-398-9400	872-8574*
**Fax Area Code:* 800 ■ *TF:* 800-872-9400 ■ *Web:* www.landstar.com					
Leicht Transfer & Storage Co 1401 State St PO Box 2447	Green Bay	WI	54304	920-432-8632	432-4130
Web: www.rgllogistics.com					
LeSaint Logistics 868 W Crossroads Pkwy.	Romeoville	IL	60446	630-243-5950	
TF: 877-566-9375 ■ *Web:* www.lesaint.com					
LJG Partners Inc 680 W Beech St.	San Diego	CA	92101	619-232-3000	
Web: www.ljg.com					
Loggins Logistics Inc 5706 Commerce Sq.	Jonesboro	AR	72401	870-932-9231	802-2190
Web: www.logginslogistics.com					
Logical Solution Services Inc 200 Union Ave	Lakehurst	NJ	08733	732-657-7777	
Web: www.solutionservices.us					
Lucas County Educational Service Ctr 2275 Collingwood Blvd	Toledo	OH	43620	419-245-4150	245-4186
Web: www.esclakeeriewest.org					
Lynden International Logistics Co 10 Corrine Ct	Vaughan	ON	L4K4T7	905-879-0114	
Web: www.lilco.lynden.com					
M & J Transportation 3536 Nicholson Ave	Kansas City	MO	64120	816-231-6733	231-7645
TF: 866-298-3858 ■ *Web:* www.mjtransportationkc.com					
Majestic Transportation 283 Lockhaven Ste 100	Houston	TX	77073	281-869-8031	
Web: www.majestictransportation.com					
Matson Logistics Inc 555 12th St	Oakland	CA	94607	510-628-4000	
TF: 800-492-8766 ■ *Web:* www.matson.com					
Maximus Federal Services Inc 3750 Monroe Ave Ste 702	Pittsford	NY	14534	585-348-3300	
Web: www.medicareappeal.com					
McElroy Truck Lines Inc 111 80 Spur PO Box 104	Cuba	AL	36907	205-392-5579	392-7992
TF: 800-992-7863 ■ *Web:* www.mcelroytrucklines.com					
McLaughlin Consulting Group Inc 945 Hamilton Ave	Menlo Park	CA	94025	650-366-5999	
Web: www.mcgweb.com					
Menlo Worldwide Inc *Con-Way Inc* 2855 Campus Dr Ste 300	San Mateo	CA	94403	650-378-5200	357-9160
TF: 800-426-6929 ■ *Web:* www.con-way.com					

Company	City	State	ZIP	Phone	Fax
Mercator Transport Group Corp Ste 220 8200 Boul Decarie *Web:* www.corpgmt.com	Montreal	QC	H4T1M4	514-874-1616	
Meridian IQ 11501 Outlook St Ste 500 **Fax Area Code:* 913 ■ *TF:* 877-246-4909 ■ *Web:* www2.miq.com	Overland Park	KS	66211	877-246-4909	696-7501*
Meteor Express Inc PO Box 248 *Web:* www.meteorx.com	Scottsboro	AL	35768	256-218-3000	259-3990
Metropolitan Trucking Inc (MRTK) 299 Market St Ste 300 **Fax Area Code:* 201 ■ *TF:* 800-967-3278 ■ *Web:* www.mtrk.com	Saddle Brook	NJ	07663	800-967-3278	843-6179*
MHD Enterprises 9715 Burnet Rd #125 *Web:* www.mhdenterprises.com	Austin	TX	78758	512-992-2565	
Midwest Specialized Transportation Inc PO Box 6418 **Fax Area Code:* 507 ■ *TF:* 800-927-8007 ■ *Web:* www.midspec.com	Rochester	MN	55903	800-927-8007	288-6859*
Millard Refrigerated Services Inc 4715 S 132nd St *Web:* www.millardref.com	Omaha	NE	68137	402-896-6600	896-6700
Miller Bros Express LC 560 West 400 North *TF:* 800-366-6239 ■ *Web:* www.mbexlc.com	Hyrum	UT	84319	435-245-6025	245-4853
Mitsui & Co (USA) Inc 200 Pk Ave *TF:* 877-248-4237 ■ *Web:* www.mitsui.com/us	New York	NY	10166	212-878-4000	878-4800
Modern Transportation Service Inc 2605 Nicholson Rd Ste 110 *Web:* www.moderntrans.com	Sewickley	PA	15143	412-489-4800	200-5050
Mount Vernon City School Dist 80 2710 N St *Web:* www.mtv80.org	Mount Vernon	IL	62864	618-244-8080	244-8082
Muscle Shoals City School District 3200 Wilson Dam Rd *Web:* www.mscs.k12.al.us	Muscle Shoals	AL	35661	256-389-2600	389-2662
MySupplyChainGroup LLC 1500 First Ave N Ste A111 *Web:* www.mysupplychaingroup.com	Birmingham	AL	35203	205-706-4300	
National Distributors Inc 1517 Avco Blvd *TF:* 800-334-9677	Sellersburg	IN	47172	812-246-6306	246-6821
National Freight Inc (NFI) 1515 Burnt Mill Rd *TF General:* 877-634-3777 ■ *Web:* www.natlfreight.com	Cherry Hill	NJ	08003	877-634-3777	
Navigator Development Group Inc 116 S Main St Ste 214 *Web:* www.ndgi.com	Enterprise	AL	36330	334-347-7612	
Navis Logistics Network 6551 S Revere Pkwy Ste 250 **Fax Area Code:* 303 ■ *TF:* 800-344-3528 ■ *Web:* www.gonavis.com	Centennial	CO	80111	800-344-3528	741-6653*
Neuger Communications Group Inc 25 Bridge Sq *Web:* www.neuger.com	Northfield	MN	55057	507-664-0700	
NNR Global Logistics USA Inc 450 E Devon Ave Ste 260 *Web:* www.staffingnetwork.com	Itasca	IL	60143	630-773-1490	
Oakley Transport Inc 101 ABC Rd PO Box 4170 *TF:* 800-969-8265 ■ *Web:* oakleytransport.com	Lake Wales	FL	33859	863-638-1435	638-1927
ODW Logistics Inc 1580 Williams Rd *TF:* 800-743-7062 ■ *Web:* www.odwlogistics.com	Columbus	OH	43207	614-497-1660	497-1426
Odyssey Logistics & Technology Corp 39 Old Ridgebury Rd - N1 *Web:* www.odysseylogistics.com	Danbury	CT	06810	203-448-3900	
Omnitrans Inc 4300 Jean-Talon W *Web:* www.omnitrans.com	Montreal	QC	H4P1W3	514-288-6664	
Open Roads Consulting Inc 103 Watson Rd *Web:* www.openroadsconsulting.com	Chesapeake	VA	23320	757-546-3401	
Panalpina 1776 On-the-Green 67 E Pk Pl *TF:* 866-202-0377 ■ *Web:* www.panalpina.com	Morristown	NJ	07960	973-683-9000	254-5712
Park-Ohio Holdings Corp (PKOH) 6065 Parkland Blvd *NASDAQ: PKOH* ■ *Web:* www.pkoh.com	Cleveland	OH	44124	440-947-2000	947-2099
Pegasus Logistics Group Inc 615 Freeport Pkwy Ste 100 *TF:* 800-997-7226 ■ *Web:* www.pegasuslogistics.com	Coppell	TX	75019	469-671-0300	671-0317
Pierce Distribution Services Co PO Box 15600 **Fax Area Code:* 815 ■ *TF:* 800-466-7397 ■ *Web:* www.piercedistribution.com	Loves Park	IL	61132	800-466-7397	636-5660*
Ponvia Technology Inc 49-T Sherwood Ter *TF:* 877-217-0875 ■ *Web:* www.ponvia.com	Lake Bluff	IL	60045	877-217-0875	
R.C. Dolner LLC 307 5th Ave 9th Fl *Web:* www.rcdolner.com	New York	NY	10016	212-531-8600	633-1108
Radiant Logistics Inc Third Fl 405 114Th Ave Se *Web:* www.radiantdelivers.com	Bellevue	WA	98004	425-943-4599	
Red Rock Distributing Co One NW 50th St *TF:* 800-323-7109 ■ *Web:* www.redrockdist.com	Oklahoma City	OK	73118	405-677-3373	557-7795
Red Star Oil 802 Purser Dr *TF:* 800-774-6033 ■ *Web:* www.redstaroil.com	Raleigh	NC	27603	919-772-1944	779-8871
Reliant Transportation Inc 4411 S 86th St Ste 101 PO Box 67009 *Web:* www.reliant-transportation.com	Lincoln	NE	68526	402-464-7771	464-8124
Renodis Inc 476 Robert St N *Web:* www.renodis.com	Saint Paul	MN	55101	651-556-1200	
Ridgewood High School 7500 W Montrose Ave *Web:* www.ridgenet.org	Norridge	IL	60706	708-456-4242	456-0342
RIM Logistics Ltd 200 N Gary Ave Ste B *TF:* 888-275-0937 ■ *Web:* www.rimlogistics.com	Roselle	IL	60172	630-595-0610	595-0614
Rinchem Company Inc 6133 Edith Blvd NE *TF:* 888-375-2436 ■ *Web:* www.rinchem.com	Albuquerque	NM	87107	505-345-3655	
ROACO Logistics Services 500 Country Club Dr	Bensenville	IL	60106	630-595-8631	
Rural Health Resource Center 600 W Superior St Apt 404 *Web:* ruralcenter.org	Duluth	MN	55802	218-727-9390	
Ryder System Inc 11690 NW 105th St *NYSE: R* ■ *TF:* 800-297-9337 ■ *Web:* www.ryder.com	Miami	FL	33178	305-500-3726	500-4599
S & H Express Inc 400 Mulberry St PO Box 20219 *TF:* 800-637-9782 ■ *Web:* www.sandhexpress.com	York	PA	17403	717-848-5015	852-8722
Saddle Creek Corp 3010 Saddle Creek Rd *Web:* www.sclogistics.com	Lakeland	FL	33801	863-665-0966	666-8295
Schirm USA Inc 2801 Oak Grove Rd *Web:* www.schirm.com	Ennis	TX	75119	972-878-4400	875-9859
Schneider National Inc 3101 S Packerland Dr PO Box 2545 *TF:* 800-558-6767 ■ *Web:* www.schneider.com	Green Bay	WI	54306	920-592-2000	592-3063
School District of Hartford 675 E Rossman St *Web:* www.hartfordjt1.k12.wi.us	Hartford	WI	53027	262-673-3155	673-3548
Scully Oil Company & Svc Station 150 E Flint St PO Box 398 *Web:* www.scullyoil.com	Lyndon Station	WI	53944	608-666-2662	666-2239
Sds Consulting Corp 3115 12 St Ne Ste 310 *Web:* www.sdsconsulting.ca	Calgary	AB	T2E7J2	403-221-8077	
Seko Worldwide Inc 1100 Arlington Heights Rd Ste 600 **Fax Area Code:* 518 ■ *TF:* 800-323-1235 ■ *Web:* www.sekologistics.com	Itasca	IL	60143	630-919-4800	785-4594*
Shaker Group Inc, The 862 Albany Shaker Rd *TF:* 800-267-0314 ■ *Web:* www.theshakergroup.com	Latham	NY	12110	518-786-9286	782-7226
Sierra West Express Inc 850 Bergin Way	Sparks	NV	89431	775-355-9595	
Slay Industries Inc 1441 Hampton Ave *TF:* 800-852-7529 ■ *Web:* www.slay.com	Saint Louis	MO	63139	314-647-7529	647-5240
Southeast Delco School District 1560 Delmar Dr *Web:* www.sedelco.org	Folcroft	PA	19032	610-522-4300	
Speegle Construction Inc 210 Government Ave *Web:* www.speegleconstruction.com	Niceville	FL	32578	850-729-2484	
Star Line Trucking Corp 18480 W Lincoln Ave *Web:* www.starlinetrucking.com	New Berlin	WI	53146	262-786-8280	786-0071
Store Opening Solutions (SOS) 800 Middle Tennessee Blvd **Fax Area Code:* 615 ■ *TF:* 877-388-9262 ■ *Web:* www.store-solutions.com	Murfreesboro	TN	37129	877-388-9262	867-4740*
Sunteck Transport Group 6413 Congress Ave Ste 260 *PINK: AUTO* ■ *TF:* 800-759-7910 ■ *Web:* suntecking.net/	Boca Raton	FL	33487	561-988-9456	
Support Kansas City Inc 5960 Dearborn St Ste 200 *Web:* www.supportkc.org	Mission	KS	66202	913-831-4752	
Survival Systems Training Ltd 40 Mount Hope Ave *Web:* www.sstl.com	Dartmouth	NS	B2Y4K9	902-465-3888	
Taylor Protocols Inc 16040 Christensen Rd Ste 315 *Web:* www.taylorprotocols.com	Tukwila	WA	98188	206-283-8144	
Tbb Global Logistics Inc 802 Far Hills Dr *TF:* 800-937-8224 ■ *Web:* www.tbbgl.com	New Freedom	PA	17349	717-227-5000	227-5500
Technical Transportation Inc 1701 W Northwest Hwy Ste 100 **Fax Area Code:* 817 ■ *TF:* 800-852-8726 ■ *Web:* www.techtrans.com	Grapevine	TX	76051	800-852-8726	488-0306*
Thoroughbred Direct Intermodal Services 5165 Campus Dr Ste 400 *TF:* 877-250-2902 ■ *Web:* www.ns-direct.com	Plymouth Meeting	PA	19462	610-567-3360	567-3370
Titan Global Distribution 1100 Corporate Sq Dr *Web:* titan-global.com	Saint Louis	MO	63132	314-817-0051	
TRANSFLO Terminal Services Inc 500 Water St Ste J975 *TF:* 866-872-6735 ■ *Web:* transflo.net	Jacksonville	FL	32202	866-872-6735	
TransMontaigne Inc 1670 Broadway Ste 3100 Ste 3100 *Web:* www.transmontaigne.com	Denver	CO	80202	303-626-8200	626-8228
Transplace 3010 Gaylord Pkwy Ste 200 **Fax Area Code:* 972 ■ *TF:* 866-413-9266 ■ *Web:* www.transplace.com	Frisco	TX	75034	866-413-9266	731-4501*
Transportation Insight LLC 328 First Ave NW *Web:* www.t-insight.com	Hickory	NC	28601	828-485-5000	
Transportation Solutions Inc 1900 Brannan Rd *Web:* www.tsilogistics.com	McDonough	GA	30253	770-474-1555	954-0055
Trimar Construction Inc 1720 W Cass St *Web:* 0350766.netsolhost.com	Tampa	FL	33606	813-258-5524	258-4743
TSS Inc 110 E Old Settlers Blvd *Web:* www.totalsitesolutions.com	Round Rock	TX	78664	512-310-1000	
United Nations International School 24-50 Fdr Dr *Web:* www.unis.org	New York	NY	10010	212-684-7400	
Unitrans International Corp 709 S Hindry Ave *Web:* www.unitrans-us.com	Inglewood	CA	90301	310-410-7676	410-1719
University City School Dst 8136 Groby Rd *Web:* www.ucityschools.org	Saint Louis	MO	63130	314-290-4000	
Uplogix Inc 7600B N Capital of Texas Hwy Ste 220 *Web:* www.uplogix.com	Austin	TX	78731	512-857-7000	
UPS Supply Chain Solutions 12380 Morris Rd *TF:* 800-742-5727 ■ *Web:* www.ups-scs.com	Alpharetta	GA	30005	913-693-6151	
UTi Worldwide Inc 100 Oceangate Ste 1500 *NASDAQ: UTIW* ■ *Web:* www.go2uti.com	Long Beach	CA	90802	562-552-9400	
VectorCSP LLC 405 E Main St *Web:* www.vectorcsp.com	Elizabeth City	NC	27909	252-338-2264	
Vimich Traffic Logistics 12201 Tecumseh Rd E **Fax Area Code:* 519 ■ *TF:* 800-284-1045 ■ *Web:* www.vimich.com	Tecumseh	ON	N8N1M3	800-284-1045	735-4309*

				Phone	Fax
Virginkar & Associates Inc 3350 E Birch St Ste 101 *Web:* www.va-inc.com	Brea	CA	92821	714-993-1000	
W M Schlosser Company Inc 2400 51st Pl *Web:* www.wmschlosser.com	Hyattsville	MD	20781	301-773-1300	773-9263
Weber Logistics 13530 Rosecrans Ave *TF:* 855-469-3237 ■ *Web:* www.weberlogistics.com	Santa Fe Springs	CA	90670	855-469-3237	
Whitehall Management Consultants Inc 9815 N 95th St *Web:* www.whitehallmgt.com	Scottsdale	AZ	85258	480-860-5700	
Wiefling Consulting LLC 2332 Harding Ave *Web:* www.wiefling.com	Redwood City	CA	94062	650-867-0847	
Wiley Sanders Truck Lines Inc PO Box 707 *TF:* 800-633-8740 ■ *Web:* www.wsanders.com	Troy	AL	36081	334-566-5184	566-3257
Wilheit Packaging LLC 1527 May Dr *TF:* 800-727-4421 ■ *Web:* www.wilheit.com	Gainesville	GA	30507	770-532-4421	532-8956
Willson International Ltd 2345 Argentia Rd Ste 201 *Web:* www.willsonintl.com	Mississauga	ON	L5N8K4	905-363-1133	
Wise Consulting Associates Inc 54 Scott Adam Rd Ste 206 *Web:* www.wiseconsulting.com	Hunt Valley	MD	21030	410-628-0100	
XPO Logistics Inc 6805 Perimeter Dr *TF:* 800-837-7584 ■ *Web:* www.pacer.com	Dublin	OH	43016	614-923-1400	

453 LONG-TERM CARE FACILITIES

SEE ALSO Long-Term Care Facilities Operators p. 2679; Retirement Communities p. 3124; Veterans Nursing Homes - State p. 3282

Free-standing facilities accredited by the Joint Commission on Accreditation of Healthcare Organizations. Listings in this category are organized alphabetically by states.

				Phone	Fax
Canterbury Health Facility 1720 Knowles Rd	Phenix City	AL	36869	334-291-0486	
Mercy Medical 101 Villa Dr PO Box 1090 *Web:* mercymedical.com	Daphne	AL	36526	251-621-4200	621-4463
Northside Health Care 700 Hutchins Ave *Web:* northsidehealthcare.com	Gadsden	AL	35901	256-543-7101	543-2367
Catalina Care Ctr 2611 N Warren Ave *Web:* nursingfacilitytucson.com	Tucson	AZ	85719	520-795-9574	321-4983
Coronado Care Ctr 11411 N 19th Ave *Web:* www.coronadocare.com	Phoenix	AZ	85029	602-256-7500	943-7697
Osborn Health & Rehabilitation 3333 N Civic Ctr Plz *Web:* osbornhealth.com	Scottsdale	AZ	85251	480-994-1333	990-3895
Casa Colina Ctr for Rehabilitation 255 E Bonita Ave *TF:* 800-926-5462 ■ *Web:* www.casacolina.org	Pomona	CA	91769	909-596-7733	596-7845
Clear View Sanitarium & Convalescent Ctr 15823 S Western Ave *Web:* clearviewcare.com	Gardena	CA	90247	310-538-2323	538-3509
English Oaks Nursing & Rehabilitation Ctr 2633 W Rumble Rd *Web:* lifegen.net	Modesto	CA	95350	209-577-1001	577-0366
Ensign Group Inc, The 27101 Puerta Real Ste 450 *NASDAQ: ENSG* ■ *Web:* www.ensigngroup.net	Mission Viejo	CA	92691	949-487-9500	
Evergreen Rehabilitation & Care Ctr 2030 Evergreen Ave *Web:* www.evergreencare.com	Modesto	CA	95350	209-577-1055	550-3615
Extended Care Hospital Westminster 206 Hospital Cir **Fax Area Code:* 909 ■ *TF:* 800-236-9747	Westminster	CA	92683	714-891-2769	580-6196*
French Park Care Ctr 600 E Washington Ave *Web:* frenchparkcarecenter.com	Santa Ana	CA	92701	714-973-1656	836-4349
Front Porch Communities & Services 303 N Glenoaks Blvd *TF:* 800-233-3709 ■ *Web:* www.frontporch.net	Burbank	CA	91502	800-233-3709	
Gladstone Care & Rehabilitation Ctr 435 E Gladstone St *Web:* www.gladstonecare.com	Glendora	CA	91740	626-963-5955	963-8683
Grand Terrace Healthcare Ctr 12000 Mt Vernon Ave *Web:* grandterracecare.com	Grand Terrace	CA	92313	909-825-5221	783-4811
Hanford Nursing & Rehabilitation Hospital 1007 W Lacey Blvd *Web:* missioncg.com	Hanford	CA	93230	559-582-2871	582-5853
Heritage Rehabilitation Ctr 21414 S Vermont Ave *Web:* heritagerehabcenter.com	Torrance	CA	90502	310-320-8714	320-1809
Huntington Valley Health Care Ctr 8382 Newman Ave *Web:* hvhcc.com	Huntington Beach	CA	92647	714-842-5551	848-5359
Kisco Senior Living LLC 5790 Fleet St Ste 300 *Web:* kiscoseniorliving.com	Carlsbad	CA	92008	760-804-5900	804-5909
La Jolla Nursing & Rehabilitation Ctr 2552 Torrey Pines Rd *TF:* 800-861-0086 ■ *Web:* covenantcare.com/locations/la-jolla-nursing-and-rehabilitation-center	La Jolla	CA	92037	858-453-5810	452-4301
La Mariposa Nursing & Rehab 1244 Travis Blvd	Fairfield	CA	94533	707-422-7750	422-7452
New Orange Hills 5017 E Chapman Ave *Web:* www.neworangehills.com	Orange	CA	92869	714-997-7090	997-4631
Pacific Coast Manor 1935 Wharf Rd *Web:* covenantcare.com	Capitola	CA	95010	831-476-0770	476-0737
Pacifica Nursing & Rehabilitation Ctr 385 Esplanade Ave *Web:* pacificarehab.com	Pacifica	CA	94044	650-993-5576	359-9388
Park Anaheim HealthCare Ctr 3435 W Ball Rd	Anaheim	CA	92804	714-827-5880	827-5880
Park Regency Care Ctr 1770 W La Habra Blvd **Fax Area Code:* 562 ■ *Web:* www.parkregencycare.com	La Habra	CA	90631	714-773-0750	697-8478*
Seton Medical Ctr Coastside 600 Marine Blvd *Web:* www.dochs.org	Moss Beach	CA	94038	650-563-7100	728-5314
Subacute Saratoga Children's Hospital 13425 Sousa Ln *Web:* www.subacutesaratoga.com	Saratoga	CA	95070	408-378-8875	378-7419
Tulare Nursing & Rehabilitation 680 E Merritt Ave *Web:* missioncaregroup.com	Tulare	CA	93274	559-686-8581	686-5393
Tunnell Ctr for Rehabilitation & Healthcare 1359 Pine St *Web:* www.tunnellrehab.com	San Francisco	CA	94109	415-673-8405	563-2174
Villa Maria Healthcare Ctr 425 E Barcellus Ave *Web:* villamariacarecenter.com	Santa Maria	CA	93454	805-922-3558	922-5548
Village Square Nursing & Rehabilitation Ctr 1586 W San Marcos Blvd *Web:* www.villagesquarerehab.com	San Marcos	CA	92078	760-471-2986	471-5176
Windsor Rehabilitation Care Ctr 3806 Clayton Rd *Web:* www.windsorcares.com	Concord	CA	94521	925-689-2266	689-0509
Apple Rehab 46 Maple St *TF General:* 800-353-5368 ■ *Web:* www.apple-rehab.com	Kent	CT	06757	860-927-5368	927-1594
Avon Health Ctr Inc 652 W Avon Rd *Web:* avonhealthcenter.com	Avon	CT	06001	860-673-2521	675-1101
Branford Hills Health Care Ctr 189 Alps Rd *Web:* www.bhhcc.com	Branford	CT	06405	203-481-6221	483-1893
Elim Park Baptist Home Inc 140 Cook Hill Rd *TF:* 800-994-1776 ■ *Web:* www.elimpark.org	Cheshire	CT	06410	203-272-7550	271-7794
Golden Hill Health Care Ctr 2028 Bridgeport Ave **Fax Area Code:* 908 ■ *Web:* healthbridgemanagement.com	Milford	CT	06460	203-877-0371	378-7868*
HealthBridge Management 57 Old Road to Nine Acre Corner **Fax Area Code:* 908 ■ **Fax:* Admitting ■ *Web:* healthbridgemanagement.com	Concord	MA	01742	203-792-8102	378-7868*
Hebrew Health Care Inc One Abrahms Blvd *Web:* www.hebrewhealthcare.org	West Hartford	CT	06117	860-523-3800	523-3949
Jewish Senior Services of Fairfield County Inc 175 Jefferson St *Web:* jhe.org	Fairfield	CT	06825	203-365-6400	374-8082
Manchester Manor Health Care Ctr 385 W Ctr St *Web:* www.manchestermanorct.com	Manchester	CT	06040	860-646-0129	645-0313
Masonic Healthcare Ctr 22 Masonic Ave *Web:* masonicare.org	Wallingford	CT	06492	203-679-5900	679-6459
Miller Memorial Community 360 Broad St *Web:* www.millercommunity.org	Meriden	CT	06450	203-237-8815	
Montowese Health & Rehabilitation Ctr Inc 163 Quinnipiac Ave *Web:* www.montowesehealth.com	North Haven	CT	06473	203-624-3303	787-9243
Noble Horizons 17 Cobble Rd *Web:* www.noblehorizons.org	Salisbury	CT	06068	860-435-9851	435-0636
Pendleton Health & Rehabilitation Ctr 44 Maritime Dr *Web:* savaseniorcare.com	Mystic	CT	06355	860-572-1700	572-7830
River Glen Health Care Ctr 162 S Britain Rd *Web:* www.healthbridgemanagement.com	Southbury	CT	06488	203-264-9600	264-9603
Sharon Health Care Ctr 27 Hospital Hill Rd *Web:* athenahealthcare.com	Sharon	CT	06069	860-364-1002	364-0237
Summit at Plantsville 261 Summit St *Web:* athenahealthcare.com	Plantsville	CT	06479	860-628-0364	628-9166
Valerie Manor Inc 1360 Torringford St *Web:* athenahealthcare.com	Torrington	CT	06790	860-489-1008	496-9252
Village Green of Waterbury 128 Cedar Ave *Web:* www.reverawaterbury.com	Waterbury	CT	06705	203-757-9271	757-2988
Watrous Nursing Ctr 9 Neck Rd *TF:* 800-353-5368 ■ *Web:* apple-rehab.com	Madison	CT	06443	203-245-9483	245-4668
Waveny Care Ctr Three Farm Rd *Web:* www.waveny.org	New Canaan	CT	06840	203-594-5200	594-5327
West Hartford Health & Rehabilitation Ctr 130 Loomis Dr *Web:* www.westhartfordhealth.com	West Hartford	CT	06107	860-521-8700	521-7452
Westport Health Care Ctr 7300 Forest Avenue	Richmond	VA	23226	804-288-3152	285-9348
Wethersfield Health Care Ctr 341 Jordan Ln *Web:* healthbridgemanagement.com	Wethersfield	CT	06109	860-563-0101	257-6107
Armed Forces Retirement Home - Washington 3700 N Capitol St NW **Fax Area Code:* 202 ■ *TF Admissions:* 800-422-9988 ■ *Web:* www.afrh.gov/afrh	Washington	DC	20011	800-422-9988	541-7519*
Area Agency On Aging 9549 Koger Blvd Gadsden Bldg Ste 100 *TF:* 800-963-5337 ■ *Web:* www.agingcarefl.org	St Petersburg	FL	33702	727-570-9696	234-4401
Bay Pointe Nursing Pavilion 4201 31st St S *Web:* baypointenursingpavilion.com	Saint Petersburg	FL	33712	727-867-1104	867-9837
Boca Raton Rehabilitation Ctr 755 Meadows Rd *Web:* bocaratonhealthandrehab.com	Boca Raton	FL	33486	561-391-5200	391-0685
Consulate Health Care at Lake Parker 2020 W Lk Parker Dr *Web:* www.consulatemgt.com	Lakeland	FL	33805	863-682-7580	683-9564
Consulate Health Care of Brandon 701 Victoria St *Web:* consulatehealthcare.com	Brandon	FL	33510	813-681-4220	689-5685
Consulate Health Care of Tallahassee 800 Concourse Pkwy S Ste 200 *Web:* www.consulatehealthcare.com	Maitland	FL	32751	407-571-1550	571-1599
Heartland Health Care & Rehabilitation Ctr 5401 Sawyer Rd	Sarasota	FL	34233	941-925-3427	925-8469

Facility	City	State	Zip	Phone	Fax
Heartland Health Care Ctr Boynton Beach 3600 Old Boynton Rd *Web:* heartlandnursing.com	Boynton Beach	FL	33436	561-736-9992	364-9527
Heartland Health Care Ctr-South Jacksonville 3648 University Blvd S *Web:* www.heartland-manorcare.com	Jacksonville	FL	32216	904-733-7440	448-9425
Leesburg Health & Rehabiltation LLC 715 E Dixie Ave	Leesburg	FL	34748	352-728-3020	323-5061
Manatee Springs Care & Rehab 5627 Ninth St E *Web:* manateespringsrehab.com	Bradenton	FL	34203	941-753-8941	753-7576
ManorCare Health Services - Carrollwood 3030 W Bearss Ave *Web:* www.hcr-manorcare.com	Tampa	FL	33618	813-968-8777	961-5189
River Garden Hebrew Home for the Aged 11401 Old St Augustine Rd *TF:* 800-468-3571 ■ *Web:* rivergarden.org	Jacksonville	FL	32258	904-260-1818	260-9733
Southern Pines Nursing Ctr 6140 Congress St *Web:* southernpineshealthcare.com	New Port Richey	FL	34653	727-842-8402	841-8060
Magnolia Manor Inc 2001 S Lee St *Web:* www.magnoliamanor.com	Americus	GA	31709	229-924-9352	
Uhs Pruitt Corp 1626 Jeurgens Ct *Web:* pruitthealth.com/	Norcross	GA	30093	770-279-6200	925-4619
Kula Hospital 100 Keokea Pl *TF:* 800-845-6733 ■ *Web:* www.hhsc.org	Kula	HI	96790	808-878-1221	878-1791
Apostolic Christian Restmor Inc 1500 Parkside Ave *Web:* www.acrestmor.org	Morton	IL	61550	309-284-1400	266-7877
Barton W Stone Christian Home 873 Grove St *Web:* heritageofcare.com	Jacksonville	IL	62650	217-479-3400	243-8553
Brentwood North Nursing & Rehabilitation Ctr 3705 Deerfield Rd *Web:* brentwoodnorthrehab.com	Riverwoods	IL	60015	847-947-9000	
Brentwood Subacute Rehabilitation Ctr 5400 W 87th St *Web:* savaseniorcare.com	Burbank	IL	60459	708-423-1200	423-8405
Community Nursing & Rehabilitation Ctr 1136 N Mill St *Web:* www.cnrcllc.com	Naperville	IL	60563	630-355-3300	355-1417
Evenglow Lodge Inc 215 E Washington St *Web:* www.evenglowlodge.org	Pontiac	IL	61764	815-844-6131	842-3558
Heritage Enterprises Inc 115 W Jefferson St *Web:* www.heritageofcare.com	Bloomington	IL	61702	309-828-4361	
John C Proctor Endowment 2724 W Reservoir Blvd *Web:* proctorplace.org	Peoria	IL	61615	309-685-6580	566-4292
Lieberman Ctr for Health & Rehabilitation 9700 Gross Pt Rd *Web:* cje.net	Skokie	IL	60076	847-674-7210	674-6366
ManorCare Health Services - Arlington Heights 715 W Central Rd *Web:* manorcare.com	Arlington Heights	IL	60005	847-392-2020	392-0174
ManorCare Health Services - Homewood 940 Maple Ave *Web:* www.heartland-manorcare.com	Homewood	IL	60430	708-799-0244	799-1505
ManorCare Health Services - Oak Lawn East 9401 S Kostner Ave *Web:* www.heartland-manorcare.com	Oak Lawn	IL	60453	708-423-7882	423-7947
Norridge Health Care & Rehabilitation Centre 7001 W Cullom Ave	Norridge	IL	60706	708-457-0700	457-8852
North Adams Home Inc 2259 E 1100th St *Web:* www.northadamshome.org	Mendon	IL	62351	217-936-2137	936-2818
Oakton Pavilion Healthcare Facility Inc 1660 Oakton Pl	Des Plaines	IL	60018	847-299-5588	493-6525
OSF Saint Clare Home 5533 N Galena Rd *Web:* www.osfhealthcare.org	Peoria Heights	IL	61616	309-682-5428	682-8478
Plymouth Place Inc 315 N LaGrange Rd *Web:* www.plymouthplace.org	La Grange Park	IL	60526	708-354-0340	482-6843
Regency Nursing Centre 6631 N Milwaukee Ave *Web:* www.regencyrehabcenter.com	Niles	IL	60714	847-647-7444	647-6403
Sherman West Court 1950 Larkin Ave *Web:* shermanwestcourt.com	Elgin	IL	60123	847-742-7070	742-7248
Sherwin Manor Nursing Ctr 7350 N Sheridan Rd *Web:* www.sherwinmanor.com	Chicago	IL	60626	773-274-1000	274-2353
Heritage Ctr 1201 W Buena Vista Rd *TF:* 800-704-0700 ■ *Web:* www.holidayhealthcare.com	Evansville	IN	47710	812-429-0700	429-1849
Miller's Merry Manor 1500 Grant St *Web:* www.millersmerrymanor.com	Huntington	IN	46750	260-356-5713	356-8671
Northwest Manor Health Care Ctr 6440 W 34th St *Web:* northwesthealthcare.net	Indianapolis	IN	46224	317-293-4930	291-1543
Pyramid Point Post-Acute Rehabilitation Ctr 8530 Township Line Rd *TF:* 800-861-0086 ■ *Web:* covenantcare.com/locations	Indianapolis	IN	46260	317-876-9955	876-6016
St.Vincent Health 2001 W 86th St *TF:* 866-338-2345 ■ *Web:* www.stvincent.org	Indianapolis	IN	46260	317-338-2345	338-6491
Waters of Covington 1600 E Liberty St *Web:* www.watersofcovington.com	Covington	IN	47932	765-793-4818	
Abcm Corp 1320 Fourth St NE PO Box 436 *Web:* www.abcmcorp.com	Hampton	IA	50441	641-456-5636	456-2320
Edgewood Convalescent Home Inc 513 S Bell St	Edgewood	IA	52042	563-928-6461	928-6462
Monticello Nursing & Rehabilitation Ctr 500 Pinehaven Dr *Web:* monticellocampus.com	Monticello	IA	52310	319-465-5415	465-3205
New Hampton Nursing & Rehabilitation Ctr 703 S Fourth Ave *Web:* nhnrc.com	New Hampton	IA	50659	641-394-4153	394-5483
New London Nursing & Rehabilitation Ctr 100 Care Cir PO Box 136 *Web:* careinitiatives.org	New London	IA	52645	319-367-5753	367-2003
Wheatland Manor Inc 316 E Lincolnway St *Web:* wheatmanor.com	Wheatland	IA	52777	563-374-1295	
Fountain Circle Care & Rehabilitation Center 200 Glenway Rd *Web:* www.fountaincirclecare.com	Winchester	KY	40391	859-744-1800	
Signature Health Care LLC 12201 Bluegrass Pkwy *Web:* ltcrevolution.com	Louisville	KY	40299	502-568-7800	
Fox Chase Rehabilitation & Nursing Ctr 2015 E W Hwy *Web:* reverafoxchase.com	Silver Spring	MD	20910	301-587-2400	587-2404
FutureCare Canton Harbor 1300 S Ellwood Ave *Web:* futurecare.com	Baltimore	MD	21224	410-342-6644	327-3949
Keswick Multi-Care Ctr 700 W 40th St *Web:* www.keswick-multicare.org	Baltimore	MD	21211	410-235-8860	662-4324
Levindale Hebrew Geriatric Ctr & Hospital 2434 W Belvedere Ave *Web:* www.lifebridgehealth.org/levindale	Baltimore	MD	21215	410-601-2400	601-2890
ManorCare Health Services - Rossville 6600 Ridge Rd *Web:* manorcare.com	Baltimore	MD	21237	410-574-4950	391-4386
ManorCare Health Services - Ruxton 7001 N Charles St *Web:* manorcare.com	Towson	MD	21204	410-821-9600	337-8313
Woodside Ctr 9101 Second Ave *Web:* genesishcc.com	Silver Spring	MD	20910	301-588-5544	588-5547
Brookline Health Care Ctr 99 Pk St *Web:* healthbridgemanagement.com	Brookline	MA	02446	617-731-1050	731-6516
Cedar Hill Health Care Ctr 49 Thomas Patten Dr *Web:* www.healthbridgemanagement.com/cedar-hill	Randolph	MA	02368	781-961-1160	963-8610
Central Boston Elder Services Inc 2315 Washington St *TF:* 800-922-2275 ■ *Web:* www.centralboston.org	Boston	MA	02119	617-277-7416	277-2005
Colonial Nursing & Rehabilitation Inc 125 Broad St *Web:* welchhrg.com	Weymouth	MA	02188	781-337-3121	337-9831
Eastpointe Rehabilitation & Skilled Care Ctr 255 Central Ave *Web:* www.eastpointerehab.com	Chelsea	MA	02150	617-884-5700	884-7005
Essex Park Rehabilitation Ctr 265 Essex St *Web:* healthbridgemanagement.com	Beverly	MA	01915	978-927-3260	922-8347
Fairview Commons Nursing & Rehabilitation Ctr 151 Christian Hill Rd *Web:* www.fairviewcommons.org	Great Barrington	MA	01230	413-528-4560	528-5767
Holyoke Rehabilitation Ctr 260 Easthampton Rd *Fax Area Code: 908 ■ *TF:* 800-811-3535 ■ *Web:* www.healthbridgemanagement.com/holyoke	Holyoke	MA	01040	413-538-9733	378-1187*
Jewish Nursing Home of Western Massachusetts Inc 770 Converse St *Fax: Admitting ■ *Web:* jewishgeriatric.org	Longmeadow	MA	01106	413-567-6211	567-2477*
JML Care Ctr 184 Terr Heun Dr *Web:* capecodhealth.org	Falmouth	MA	02540	508-457-4621	457-1218
Kindred Transitional Care and Rehabilitation 160 Main St *Web:* kindredharrington.com	Walpole	MA	02081	508-660-3080	660-1634
Lowell Health Care Ctr 19 Varnum St *TF:* 800-811-3535 ■ *Web:* www.healthbridgemanagement.com/lowell	Lowell	MA	01850	978-454-5644	452-0201
Marlborough Hills Healthcare Ctr 121 Northboro Rd E	Marlborough	MA	01752	508-485-4040	481-5585
Meadow Green Nursing & Rehabilitation Ctr 45 Woburn St *Web:* www.meadowgreen.org	Waltham	MA	02454	781-899-8600	899-3124
Newton Health Care Ctr 2101 Washington St *Web:* www.healthbridgemanagement.com	Newton	MA	02462	617-969-4660	928-0737
North Adams Common Nursing Home 175 Franklin St *TF:* 800-445-4560 ■ *Web:* www.northadamscommons.org	North Adams	MA	01247	413-664-4041	664-8447
Peabody Glen Health Care Ctr 199 Andover St *Web:* www.healthbridgemanagement.com	Peabody	MA	01960	978-531-0772	531-7809
Port Health Care 113 Low St *Web:* whittierhealth.com	Newburyport	MA	01950	978-462-7373	462-6510
Sacred Heart Home 359 Summer St *Web:* www.dhfo.org	New Bedford	MA	02740	508-996-6751	996-5189
Sherrill House Inc (SH) 135 S Huntington Ave *Web:* www.sherrillhouse.org	Jamaica Plain	MA	02130	617-731-2400	731-8671
Vinfen Corp 950 Cambridge St *Web:* www.vinfen.org	Cambridge	MA	02141	617-441-1800	441-1858
Williamstown Commons Nursing & Rehabilitation Ctr 25 Adams Rd *TF:* 800-445-4560 ■ *Web:* www.williamstowncommons.org	Williamstown	MA	01267	413-458-2111	458-3156
Wilmington Health Care Ctr 750 Woburn St *Web:* healthbridgemanagement.com	Wilmington	MA	01887	978-988-0888	658-6470
Worcester Skilled Care Ctr 59 Acton St *Web:* www.wingatehealthcare.com	Worcester	MA	01604	508-791-3147	753-6267
Bay County Medical Care Facility 564 W Hampton Rd *Web:* www.baycountymcf.com	Essexville	MI	48732	989-892-3591	892-6991
Clarkston Specialty Healthcare Ctr 4800 Clintonville Rd *Web:* savaseniorcare.com	Clarkston	MI	48346	248-674-0903	674-3431
Crestmont Health Care Ctr 111 Trealout Dr *Web:* savaseniorcare.com	Fenton	MI	48430	810-629-4105	629-7538
Farmington HealthCare Ctr 34225 Grand River Ave	Farmington	MI	48335	248-477-7373	477-2888
Grand Blanc Rehabilitation & Nursing Ctr 11941 Belsay Rd *Web:* healthbridgemanagement.com	Grand Blanc	MI	48439	810-694-1970	694-4081

Facility	City	State	Zip	Phone	Fax
Heartland Health Care Ctr Bloomfield Hills 2975 N Adams Rd *Fax Area Code: 614 ■ *TF:* 800-622-6757 ■ *Web:* www.hcr-manorcare.com	Bloomfield Hills	MI	48304	248-645-2900	895-1094*
Heartland Health Care Ctr University 28550 Five Mile Rd *Web:* heartland-manorcare.com	Livonia	MI	48154	734-427-8270	427-2135
Hope Network 3075 Orchard Vista Dr SE *TF:* 800-695-7273 ■ *Web:* www.hopenetwork.org	Grand Rapids	MI	49546	616-301-8000	301-8010
Howell Care Ctr 3003 W Grand River Ave	Howell	MI	48843	517-546-4210	546-9495
Isabella Medical Care Facility 1222 N Dr *Web:* mcf.isabellacounty.org	Mount Pleasant	MI	48858	989-772-2957	772-3669
Martha T Berry Memorial Medical Care Facility 43533 Elizabeth Rd *Web:* www.macombcountymi.gov	Mount Clemens	MI	48043	586-469-5265	466-7418
Sanctuary at Bellbrook 873 W Avon Rd *Web:* www.trinityseniorsanctuary.org/communities/sanctuary-bellbrook	Rochester Hills	MI	48307	248-656-6300	656-8160
Tendercare Clare 600 SE Fourth St *Web:* tendercareclare.com	Clare	MI	48617	989-386-7723	
Sunset Hills Health & Rehabilitation Ctr 10954 Kennerly Rd *Web:* sunsethillshrc.com	Saint Louis	MO	63128	314-843-4242	843-4031
Village North Health Ctr 11160 Village N Dr *Web:* www.bjc.org	Saint Louis	MO	63136	314-355-8010	653-4880
Good Shepherd Rehabilitation & Nursing Ctr 20 Plantation Dr *Web:* nh-cc.org	Jaffrey	NH	03452	603-532-8762	593-0006
Kindred Transitional Care & Rehabilitation - Greenbriar 55 Harris Rd *Web:* www.greenbriarterrace.com	Nashua	NH	03062	603-888-1573	888-5089
Pleasant Valley Nursing Ctr Eight Peabody Rd	Derry	NH	03038	603-434-1566	434-2299
Camden County Health Services Ctr 425 Woodbury Turnersville Rd *Web:* www.cchsc.com	Blackwood	NJ	08012	856-374-6600	
CareOne At Valley 300 Old Hook Rd *Web:* www.care-one.com	Westwood	NJ	07675	201-664-8888	242-4010
Daughters of Miriam Ctr/Gallen Institute 155 Hazel St *Web:* www.daughtersofmiriamcenter.org	Clifton	NJ	07011	973-772-3700	
Linwood Care Ctr 201 New Rd & Central Ave *Web:* www.reveralinwood.com	Linwood	NJ	08221	609-927-6131	927-6131
ManorCare Health Services - Mountainside 1180 Rt 22 W *TF:* 800-366-1232 ■ *Web:* www.hcr-manorcare.com	Mountainside	NJ	07092	908-654-0020	
Somerset Valley Rehab Ctr 1621 Rt 22 W *Web:* care-one.com	Bound Brook	NJ	08805	732-469-2000	469-8917
Voorhees Pediatric Facility 1304 Laurel Oak Rd *TF:* 888-873-5437 ■ *Web:* www.forkidcare.com	Voorhees	NJ	08043	856-346-3300	346-3462
Willow Creek Rehabilitation & Care Ctr 1165 Easton Ave *Web:* reverawillowcreek.com	Somerset	NJ	08873	732-246-4100	246-3926
At Rosewood 284 Troy Rd *Web:* wwwrosewoodrehabilitation.com	Rensselaer	NY	12144	518-286-1621	286-1691
Clove Lakes Health Care & Rehabilitation Ctr 25 Fanning St *Web:* www.clovelakes.com	Staten Island	NY	10314	718-289-7900	761-8701
Comprehensive Care Management Corp (CCM) 1250 Waters Pl Tower 1 Ste 602 *TF:* 877-226-8500 ■ *Web:* www.centerlighthealthcare.org	Bronx	NY	10461	877-226-8500	
Diamond Hill Nursing & Rehabilitation 100 New Tpke Rd *TF:* 800-697-5374 ■ *Web:* news10.com	Troy	NY	12182	518-235-1410	426-4792
Dumont Ctr for Rehabilitation & Nursing Care 676 Pelham Rd *Web:* www.dumontcenter.com	New Rochelle	NY	10805	914-632-9600	632-9247
Golden Gate Rehabilitation & Health Care Ctr 191 Bradley Ave *Web:* goldengaterehab.com	Staten Island	NY	10314	718-698-8800	698-5536
Grace Plaza of Great Neck Inc 15 St Paul's Pl *Web:* www.graceplaza.com	Great Neck	NY	11021	516-466-3001	466-7624
Haven Manor Health Care Ctr 1441 Gateway Blvd *Web:* nursinghomes.nyhealth.gov	Far Rockaway	NY	11691	718-471-1500	471-9606
Jewish Home Lifecare 120 W 106th St *TF:* 800-544-0304 ■ *Web:* www.jewishhome.org	New York	NY	10025	212-870-5000	870-4715
Lutheran Social Services 715 Falconer St *Web:* www.lutheran-jamestown.org	Jamestown	NY	14701	716-665-4905	665-8055
Margaret Tietz Ctr for Nursing Care 164-11 Chapin Pkwy *Web:* www.margarettietz.org	Jamaica	NY	11432	718-298-7800	262-8839
Mosholu Parkway Nursing & Rehabilitation Ctr 3356 Perry Ave	Bronx	NY	10467	718-655-3568	
Palm Gardens Ctr for Nursing & Rehabilitation 615 Ave C *Web:* www.palmgardenscenter.com	Brooklyn	NY	11218	718-633-3300	853-8680
Promenade Rehabilitation & Health Care Ctr 140 Beach 114th St	Rockaway Park	NY	11694	718-945-4600	634-8237
Providence Rest 3304 Waterbury Ave *Web:* www.providencerest.org	Bronx	NY	10465	718-931-3000	863-0185
Robinson Terrace 28652 New York 23 *Web:* www.robinsonterrace.com	Stamford	NY	12167	607-652-7521	652-3362
Saint Mary's Hospital for Children Inc 29-01 216th St *Web:* www.stmaryskids.org	Bayside	NY	11360	718-281-8800	281-8523
Victory Lake Nursing Ctr 419 N Quaker Ln *Web:* victorylakenursing.com	Hyde Park	NY	12538	845-229-9177	229-9819
Wesley Gardens 3 Upton Pk *Web:* wesleygardens.com	Rochester	NY	14607	585-241-2100	241-2180
Kindred Hospital Greensboro 2401 Southside Blvd *TF:* 877-836-2671 ■ *Web:* www.khgreensboro.com	Greensboro	NC	27406	336-271-2800	271-2734
Long Leaf Medical Treatment Ctr 4761 Ward Blvd	Wilson	NC	27893	252-399-2112	399-2138
Valley Nursing Ctr 581 NC Hwy 16 S *Web:* valleyrehab.com	Taylorsville	NC	28681	828-632-8146	635-0300
Arbors at Delaware 2270 Warrensburg Rd *Web:* extendicareus.com	Delaware	OH	43015	740-369-9614	
Arbors at Marietta 400 Seventh St *Web:* extendicareus.com	Marietta	OH	45750	740-373-3597	373-3915
Arbors East Subacute Nursing & Rehabilitation Ctr 5500 E Broad St *Web:* arborseastskillednursing.com	Columbus	OH	43213	614-575-9003	575-9101
Area Agency On Aging 10b Inc 1550 Corporate Woods Pkwy *TF:* 800-421-7277 ■ *Web:* www.services4aging.org	Uniontown	OH	44685	330-896-9172	896-6644
Cedarwood Plaza 12504 Cedar Rd *Web:* lhshealth.com	Cleveland Heights	OH	44106	216-371-3600	371-4661
Columbus Rehabilitation & Subacute Institute 44 S Souder Ave *Web:* columbusrehabskillednursing.com	Columbus	OH	43222	614-228-5900	228-3989
Communi Care At Waterford 955 Garden Lk Pkwy *Web:* www.communicarehealth.com	Toledo	OH	43614	419-382-2200	
Deaconess Long Term Care Inc (DLTC) 440 Lafayette Ave PO Box 198027 *Web:* www.deaconess-healthcare.com	Cincinnati	OH	45220	513-487-3600	
Heartland of Beavercreek 1974 N Fairfield Rd *Web:* heartlandnursing.com	Dayton	OH	45432	937-429-1106	429-0902
Heartland of Centerburg 212 Fairview Ave *Web:* hcr-manorcare.com	Centerburg	OH	43011	740-625-5774	625-7426
Heartland of Marysville 755 S Plum St *Web:* heartlandnursing.com	Marysville	OH	43040	937-644-8836	644-1811
Hennis Care Centre 1720 Cross St *TF:* 800-241-1044 ■ *Web:* www.henniscarecentre.com	Dover	OH	44622	330-364-8849	364-2128
ManorCare Health Services - North Olmsted 23225 Lorain Rd *Web:* www.hcr-manorcare.com	North Olmsted	OH	44070	440-779-6900	779-8091
St Augustine Health Ministries 7801 Detroit Ave *Web:* staugministries.org	Cleveland	OH	44102	216-634-7400	643-7483
Villa Angela Nursing Rehabilitation Ctr 5700 Karl Rd *Web:* villa-angela.net	Columbus	OH	43229	614-846-5420	854-7830
Walton Manor Health Care Ctr 19859 Alexander Rd *Web:* www.saberhealth.com	Walton Hills	OH	44146	440-652-5212	
Oklahoma Veterans Ctr Norman 1776 E Robinson St *TF:* 800-782-5218 ■ *Web:* www.ok.gov/	Norman	OK	73071	405-360-5600	
Golden Living Ctr 350 Old Gilkeson Rd *Web:* goldenlivingcenters.com	Pittsburgh	PA	15228	412-564-3988	257-8226
Golden LivingCenter - Western Reserve 1521 W 54th St *Web:* local.goldenlivingcenters.com	Erie	PA	16509	814-864-0671	
Greenery Speciality Care 2200 Hill Church-Houston Rd *Web:* greenerysccc.com	Canonsburg	PA	15317	724-745-8000	746-8780
Kindred Hospital Philadelphia 6129 Palmetto St *TF:* 800-654-5988 ■ *Web:* www.kindredphila.com	Philadelphia	PA	19111	215-722-8555	725-8998
Kindred Hospital Pittsburgh 7777 Steubenville Pk *TF:* 800-654-5988 ■ *Web:* www.kindredhospitalpittsburgh.com	Oakdale	PA	15071	412-494-5500	494-5511
Laurel Ctr 125 Holly Rd *Web:* genesishcc.com	Hamburg	PA	19526	610-562-2284	562-0775
Liberty Nursing & Rehabilitation Ctr 535 N 17th St *Web:* heartland-manorcare.com	Allentown	PA	18104	610-432-4351	435-4470
Presbyterian SeniorCare-Southminster Place 835 S Main St *Web:* www.srcare.org	Washington	PA	15301	724-222-4300	250-4998
Presbyterian SeniorCare-Westminster Place 1215 Hulton Rd *TF:* 877-772-6500 ■ *Web:* www.srcare.org	Oakmont	PA	15139	412-828-5600	826-6059
Redstone Highlands Health Care Ctr 6 Garden Ctr Dr *TF:* 800-732-0999 ■ *Web:* www.redstonehighlands.org	Greensburg	PA	15601	724-832-8400	836-3710
Rest Haven-York 1050 S George St *TF:* 800-368-1019 ■ *Web:* www.resthavenyork.com	York	PA	17403	717-843-9866	846-5894
South Mountain Restoration Ctr 10058 S Mountain Rd *Web:* dpw.state.pa.us	South Mountain	PA	17261	717-749-3121	
Woodhaven Care Ctr 2400 McGinley Rd *Web:* mywoodhavencarecenter.com	Monroeville	PA	15146	412-856-4770	856-6856
Oak Hill Nursing & Rehabilitation Ctr 544 Pleasant St *Fax: Admitting ■ *Web:* kindredhealthcare.com/	Pawtucket	RI	02904	401-725-8888	*
Saint Elizabeth Home One Saint Elizabeth Way *Web:* www.stelizabethcommunity.org	East Greenwich	RI	02818	401-471-6060	471-6072
Heartland Health Care Ctr Charleston 1800 Eagle Landing Blvd *Web:* heartlandnursing.com	Hanahan	SC	29406	843-553-0656	553-9773
Allen Morgan Health Ctr 177 N Highland Ave *Web:* trezevantmanor.org	Memphis	TN	38111	901-325-4003	325-4011
Diversicare Healthcare Services Inc 537 Spring St *Web:* manorhouseofdover.com	Dover	TN	37058	931-232-6902	
Diversicare Healthcare Services Inc. 100 Elmhurst Dr *Web:* briarcliffhealthcare.com	Oak Ridge	TN	37830	865-481-3367	

				Phone	Fax
Fairfield Nursing & Rehabilitation 420 Moody St. *Web:* fairfieldnursingandrehab.com	Fairfield	TX	75840	903-389-1236	
Hearthstone of Round Rock 401 Oakwood Blvd *Web:* www.seniorcarecentersltc.com	Round Rock	TX	78681	512-388-7494	388-2166
Heartland Health Care Ctr Bedford 2001 Forest Ridge Dr *Web:* heartlandnursing.com	Bedford	TX	76021	817-571-6804	267-4176
Heartland of San Antonio One Heartland Dr *Web:* heartlandnursing.com	San Antonio	TX	78247	210-653-1219	653-8977
Kindred Hospital Fort Worth 815 Eigth Ave *Web:* kindredfortworth.com	Fort Worth	TX	76104	817-332-4812	332-8843
Plum Creek Specialty Hospital 5601 Plum Creek Dr	Amarillo	TX	79121	806-351-1000	351-8117
Treemont Nursing & Rehabilitation Ctr 5550 Harvest Hill Rd. **Fax Area Code:* 615 ■ *Web:* www.treemonthealthcare.com	Dallas	TX	75230	972-661-1862	261-0050*
South Davis Community Hospital 401 S 400 E. *Web:* www.sdch.com	Bountiful	UT	84010	801-295-2361	295-1398
Sunshine Terrace Foundation Inc 248 West 300 North *Web:* www.sunshineterrace.com	Logan	UT	84321	435-752-0411	752-1318
Berkshire Health & Rehabilitation Ctr 705 Clearview Dr *Web:* www.berkshirehealthrehab.com	Vinton	VA	24179	540-982-6691	985-4899
James River Convalescent Ctr 540 Aberthaw Ave. *Web:* vahs.com	Newport News	VA	23601	757-595-2273	595-2271
Laurels of University Park, The 2420 Pemberton Rd *Web:* www.laurelsofuniversitypark.com	Richmond	VA	23233	804-747-9200	747-1574
Lucy Corr Village 6800 Lucy Corr Blvd *Web:* www.lucycorrvillage.com	Chesterfield	VA	23832	804-748-1511	706-5572
Lynchburg Health & Rehabilitation Ctr 5615 Seminole Ave. *Web:* lynchburghealthrehab.com	Lynchburg	VA	24502	434-239-2657	239-4062
ManorCare Health Services - Arlington 550 S Carlin Springs Rd *Web:* www.hcr-manorcare.com	Arlington	VA	22204	703-379-7200	578-5524
ManorCare Health Services - Fair Oaks 12475 Lee Jackson Memorial Hwy *Web:* manorcare.com	Fairfax	VA	22033	703-352-7172	352-1455
Riverside Regional Convalescent Ctr 1000 Old Denbigh Blvd *Web:* riversideonline.com	Newport News	VA	23602	757-875-2000	875-2036
Ballard Care & RehabilitationCenter 820 NW 95th St *Web:* genesishcc.com	Seattle	WA	98117	206-782-0100	781-1448
Kitsap Mental Health Services 5455 Almira Dr NE *Web:* www.kitsapmentalhealth.org	Bremerton	WA	98311	360-405-4010	
Seattle Medical & Rehabilitation Ctr 555 16th Ave. *Web:* seattlemedicalpostacute.com	Seattle	WA	98122	206-324-8200	324-0780
Glenwood Park Retirement Village 1924 Glenwood Pk Rd **Fax:* Admitting ■ *Web:* www.gwpinc.org	Princeton	WV	24739	304-425-8128	487-1338*
Brewster Village 3300 W Brewster St *Web:* www.outagamie.org	Appleton	WI	54914	920-832-5400	832-4922
Clement Manor 3939 S 92nd St *Web:* www.clementmanor.com	Greenfield	WI	53228	414-321-1800	546-7357
Franciscan Villa 3601 S Chicago Ave. *Web:* www.franciscanvilla.org	South Milwaukee	WI	53172	414-764-4100	764-0706
Middleton Village Nursing & Rehabilitation Ctr 6201 Elmwood Ave.	Middleton	WI	53562	608-831-8300	831-4253

454 LONG-TERM CARE FACILITIES OPERATORS

				Phone	Fax
Active Day/Senior Care Inc 400 Redland Ct Ste 114 *TF:* 866-724-9599 ■ *Web:* www.seniorcarectrs.com	Owings Mills	MD	21117	866-724-9599	
Aegis Assisted Living 17602 NE Union Hill Rd *TF:* 888-252-3447 ■ *Web:* www.aegisliving.com	Redmond	WA	98052	425-861-9993	861-7278
American Religious Town Hall Meeting Inc PO Box 180118 *TF:* 800-783-9828 ■ *Web:* www.americanreligious.org	Dallas	TX	75218	214-328-9828	328-3042
Americare Systems Inc 214 N Scott St *Web:* www.americareusa.net	Sikeston	MO	63801	573-471-1113	
Atria Senior Living Group 300 E Market St Ste 100 *Web:* www.atriaseniorliving.com	Louisville	KY	40202	502-779-4700	
Autumn Corp 451 N Winstead Ave *Web:* www.autumncorp.com	Rocky Mount	NC	27804	252-443-6265	443-2703
CabelTel International Corp 1603 Lyndon B Johnson Fwy **Fax Area Code:* 469 ■ *TF:* 888-407-8400 ■ *Web:* www.newconceptenergy.com	Dallas	TX	75234	972-407-8400	522-4240*
Cardinal Ritter Senior Services 7601 Watson Rd *Web:* www.ccstl.org	Saint Louis	MO	63119	314-961-8000	961-1934
Comprehensive Systems Inc 1700 Clark St. *Web:* comprehensivesystems.org	Charles City	IA	50616	641-228-4842	228-4675
ElderWood Senior Care Seven Limestone Dr *TF:* 888-826-9663 ■ *Web:* www.elderwood.com	Williamsville	NY	14221	716-633-3900	633-1153
Emeritus Corp 3131 Elliott Ave Ste 500 *NYSE: ESC* ■ *TF:* 855-444-7658 ■ *Web:* www.emeritus.com	Seattle	WA	98121	206-298-2909	
Extendicare Inc 3000 Steeles Ave E *NYSE: EXE* ■ *Web:* www.extendicare.com	Markham	ON	L3R9W2	905-470-4000	470-5588
Five Star Quality Care Inc 400 Centre St *NYSE: FVE* ■ *TF:* 866-230-1286 ■ *Web:* www.fivestarseniorliving.com	Newton	MA	02458	617-796-8387	796-8385
Genesis HealthCare Corp 101 E State St *TF:* 800-944-7776 ■ *Web:* www.genesishcc.com	Kennett Square	PA	19348	610-444-6350	925-4000
HCF Inc 1100 Shawnee Rd *Web:* www.hcfinc.com	Lima	OH	45805	419-999-2010	999-6284
HCR Manor Care 333 N Summit St PO Box 10086 **Fax:* Hum Res ■ *Web:* www.hcr-manorcare.com	Toledo	OH	43699	419-252-5500	252-6404*
Kindred Healthcare Inc 680 S Fourth Ave *NYSE: KND* ■ *TF:* 800-545-0749 ■ *Web:* www.kindredhealthcare.com	Louisville	KY	40202	502-596-7300	596-4052
Life Care Centers of America Inc 3570 Keith St NW PO Box 3480 *Web:* www.lcca.com	Cleveland	TN	37320	423-472-9585	476-5974
National HealthCare Corp 100 E Vine St PO Box 1398 *NYSE: NHC* ■ *Web:* www.nhccare.com	Murfreesboro	TN	37133	615-890-2020	890-0123
Odyssey HealthCare Inc 717 N Harwood St. *TF:* 888-922-9711 ■ *Web:* gentiva.com	Dallas	TX	75201	214-922-9711	
Royal Management Corp 665 W N Ave *Web:* www.lexingtonhealth.com	Lombard	IL	60148	630-458-4700	748-3701
Sun Healthcare Group Inc 18831 Von Karman Ste 400 *NASDAQ: SUNH* ■ *TF:* 800-729-6600	Irvine	CA	92612	949-255-7100	
Sunrise Senior Living Inc 7902 Westpark Dr Ste T-900. *NYSE: SRZ* ■ *TF:* 800-929-4124 ■ *Web:* www.sunriseseniorliving.com	McLean	VA	22102	703-273-7500	744-1601

455 LOTTERIES, GAMES, SWEEPSTAKES

SEE ALSO Games & Gaming p. 2353

				Phone	Fax
7 Cedars Casino 170756 Hwy 101 *Web:* www.7cedarsresort.com	Sequim	WA	98382	360-683-7777	
Alta Ski Lifts Co Alta Ski Area Hwy 210 Little Cottonwood Canyon *Web:* www.alta.com	Alta	UT	84092	801-359-1078	
Arizona Lottery 4740 E University Dr. *Web:* arizonalottery.com	Phoenix	AZ	85034	480-921-4400	
AVI Casino Enterprise Inc 10000 Aha Macav Pkwy *Web:* www.avicasino.com	Laughlin	NV	89029	702-535-5555	
Bartons Club 93 93 Jackpot *Web:* www.bartonsclub93.com	Jackpot	NV	89825	775-755-2341	
Bay Mills Resort & Casinos 11386 W Lakeshore Dr *Web:* www.4baymills.com	Brimley	MI	49715	906-248-3715	
Bishop Paiute Gaming Corp 2742 N Sierra Hwy *Web:* www.bishoppaiutetribe.com	Bishop	CA	93514	760-873-4150	
Boot Hill Casino & Resort 4000 W Comanche St. *Web:* boothillcasino.com	Dodge City	KS	67801	620-682-7777	
British Columbia Lottery Corp (BCLC) 74 W Seymour St *Web:* www.bclc.com	Kamloops	BC	V2C1E2	250-828-5500	828-5631
Casino San Pablo of Lytton Rancheria 13255 San Pablo Ave *Web:* www.sanpablolytton.com	San Pablo	CA	94806	510-215-7888	
Catfish Bend Casinos II LLC 3001 Winegard Dr *Web:* www.thepzazz.com	Burlington	IA	52601	319-753-2946	
Chinook Winds Casino Resort 1777 NW 44th St *Web:* www.chinookwindscasino.com	Lincoln City	OR	97367	541-996-5825	
Choctaw Casino Resorts 3735 Choctaw Rd *Web:* www.choctawcasinos.com	Durant	OK	74701	580-920-0160	
Chumash Casino Resort 3400 E Hwy 246 *Web:* chumashcasino.com	Santa Ynez	CA	93460	805-686-0855	
Cliff Castle Casino 555 W Middle Verde Rd *Web:* www.cliffcastlecasinohotel.com	Camp Verde	AZ	86322	928-567-7999	
Colorado Lottery 212 W Third St Ste 210 *TF:* 800-999-2959 ■ *Web:* www.coloradolottery.com	Pueblo	CO	81003	719-546-2400	546-5208
Cypress Bayou Casino 832 Martin Luther King Rd *TF:* 800-284-4386 ■ *Web:* www.cypressbayou.com	Charenton	LA	70523	800-284-4386	
Delaware State Lottery 1575 McKee Rd Ste 102 *Web:* www.delottery.com	Dover	DE	19904	302-739-5291	739-7586
District of Columbia Lottery & Charitable Games Control Board 2101 ML King Jr Ave SE *Web:* www.dclottery.com	Washington	DC	20020	202-645-8000	
Florida Lottery Dept 250 Marriott Dr **Fax:* Hum Res ■ *Web:* www.flalottery.com	Tallahassee	FL	32301	850-487-7777	*
Fortune Bay Resort & Casino 1430 Bois Forte Rd *Web:* fortunebay.com	Tower	MN	55790	218-753-6400	
Gamesville Inc 100 Fifth Ave. *Web:* www.gamesville.com	Waltham	MA	02451	781-370-2700	
Georgia Lottery Corp 250 Williams St NW Ste 3000 *Web:* www.galottery.com	Atlanta	GA	30303	404-215-5000	215-8871
Grand Lake Casino 24701 S 655 Rd *Web:* grandlakecasino.com	Grove	OK	74344	918-786-8528	
High Winds Casino 61475 E 100 Rd *Web:* highwindscasino.com	Miami	OK	74354	918-541-9463	
Idaho Lottery 1199 Shoreline Ln Ste 100 *TF:* 800-432-5688 ■ *Web:* www.idaholottery.com	Boise	ID	83702	208-334-2600	334-2610
Illinois Lottery 101 W Jefferson St. **Fax Area Code:* 866 ■ *TF:* 800-252-1775 ■ *Web:* www.illinoislottery.com	Springfield	IL	62702	217-524-6435	877-0436*
Indiana Lottery 201 S Capitol Ave Ste 1100 *TF:* 800-955-6886 ■ *Web:* www.in.gov	Indianapolis	IN	46225	317-264-4800	
Iowa Lottery 2323 Grand Ave **Fax:* Hum Res ■ *Web:* www.ialottery.com/	Des Moines	IA	50312	5-3-23--4633	*

	City	State	ZIP	Phone	Fax
Kansas Lottery 128 N Kansas Ave *TF:* 800-544-9467 ■ *Web:* kslottery.com	Topeka	KS	66603	785-296-5700	
Kentucky Lottery Corp 1011 W Main St *TF:* 800-937-8946 ■ *Web:* www.kylottery.com	Louisville	KY	40202	502-560-1500	560-1532
Lco Casino Lodge & Convention Center 13767 W County Rd B *Web:* lcocasino.com	Hayward	WI	54843	715-634-5643	
Louisiana Lottery Corp 555 Laurel St *Web:* louisianalottery.com	Baton Rouge	LA	70801	225-297-2000	297-2005
Lucky Chances Casino 1700 Hillside Blvd *Web:* www.grubgirl.com	Colma	CA	94014	650-758-2237	
Maryland State Lottery 1800 Washington Blvd Ste 330 *Web:* www.mdlottery.com	Baltimore	MD	21230	410-230-8790	230-8728
Massachusetts State Lottery Commission 60 Columbian St *Web:* www.masslottery.com	Braintree	MA	02184	781-849-5555	849-5546
Michigan State Lottery 101 E Hillsdale St PO Box 30023 *Web:* www.michigan.gov/lottery	Lansing	MI	48909	517-335-5600	335-5644
Minnesota State Lottery 2645 Long Lake Rd *Web:* www.mnlottery.com	Saint Paul	MN	55113	651-635-8273	
Missouri Lottery 1823 Southridge Dr PO Box 1603 *Web:* www.molottery.com	Jefferson City	MO	65109	573-751-4050	751-5188
Montana Lottery 2525 N Montana Ave *TF:* 800-425-1435 ■ *Web:* www.montanalottery.com	Helena	MT	59601	406-444-5825	444-5830
Multi-State Lottery Association 4400 NW Urbandale Dr *Web:* www.musl.com	Urbandale	IA	50322	515-453-1400	
Nassau Regional Off Track Betting Corp 220 Fulton Ave *Web:* www.nassauotb.com	Hempstead	NY	11550	516-572-2800	
Nebraska Lottery 1800 "O" St PO Box 98901 *TF:* 800-587-5200 ■ *Web:* www.nelottery.com	Lincoln	NE	68509	402-471-6100	471-6108
New Hampshire Lottery Commission 14 Integra Dr *TF:* 800-852-3324 ■ *Web:* www.nhlottery.com	Concord	NH	03301	603-271-3391	271-1160
New Jersey Lottery PO Box 041 *Web:* www.state.nj.us	Trenton	NJ	08625	609-599-5800	599-5935
New Mexico Lottery *Lottery* 4511 Osuna Rd NE PO Box 93190 *Web:* www.nmlottery.com	Albuquerque	NM	87199	505-342-7600	342-7511
Ocean's Eleven Casino 121 Brooks St *Web:* www.oceans11.com	Oceanside	CA	92054	760-439-6988	
Ohio Lottery Commission 615 W Superior Ave *TF:* 800-686-4208 ■ *Web:* www.ohiolottery.com	Cleveland	OH	44113	216-787-3200	787-3313
Ohiya Casino 53142 Hwy 12 *Web:* ohiyacasino.com	Niobrara	NE	68760	402-857-3860	
Oregon Lottery 500 Airport Rd SE *Web:* oregonlottery.org	Salem	OR	97301	503-540-1000	540-1001
Pahrump Nugget Hotel & Gambling Hall 681 S Hwy 160 *Web:* pahrumpnugget.com	Pahrump	NV	89048	775-751-6500	
Patriot Gaming & Electronics Inc 217 N Lindberg St *Web:* patriotgaming.com	Griffith	IN	46319	219-922-6400	
Prairie's Edge Casino Resort 5616 Prairies Edge Ln *Web:* www.prairiesedgecasino.com	Granite Falls	MN	56241	320-564-2121	
Rail City Casino 2121 Victorian Ave *Web:* www.railcity.com	Sparks	NV	89431	775-359-9440	
Red Hawk Casino One Red Hawk Pkwy *Web:* www.redhawkcasino.com	Placerville	CA	95667	530-677-7000	
Rhode Island Lottery 1425 Pontiac Ave *Web:* www.rilot.com	Cranston	RI	02920	401-463-6500	
River Rock Entertainment Authority 3250 Hwy 128 E *Web:* www.riverrockcasino.com	Geyserville	CA	95441	707-857-2777	
Riverwalk Casino Hotel 1046 Warrenton Rd *Web:* www.riverwalkvicksburg.com	Vicksburg	MS	39180	601-634-0100	
San Felipe's Casino Hollywood 25 Hagon Rd *Web:* sanfelipecasino.com	Algodones	NM	87001	505-867-6700	
Santa Ana Star Casino 54 Jemez Dam Rd *Web:* www.santaanastar.com	Bernalillo	NM	87004	505-867-0000	
Shooting Star Casino Hotel & Event Center 777 Se Casino Rd *Web:* www.starcasino.com	Mahnomen	MN	56557	218-935-2711	
Soboba Casino 23333 Soboba Rd *Web:* soboba.net	San Jacinto	CA	92583	951-654-2883	
South Carolina Education Lottery 1333 Main St 4th Fl *Web:* www.sceducationlottery.com	Columbia	SC	29201	803-737-2002	737-2005
Spirit Lake Casino & Resort 7889 Hwy 57 *Web:* www.spiritlakecasino.com	Saint Michael	ND	58370	701-766-4747	
Stockman's Casino 1560 W Williams Ave *Web:* www.stockmanscasino.com	Fallon	NV	89406	775-423-2117	
Sun Ray Park & Casino LLC 39 Rd 5568 *Web:* sunraygaming.com	Farmington	NM	87401	505-566-1200	
Tennessee Lottery 200 Athens Way Ste 200 **Fax:* Hum Res ■ *Web:* www.tnlottery.com/	Nashville	TN	37228	615-324-6500	*
Vermont Lottery Commission 1311 US Rt 302 Ste 100 *Web:* wherezit.com	Barre	VT	05641	802-479-5686	479-4294
Virginia Lottery 900 E Main St *Web:* www.valottery.com	Richmond	VA	23219	804-692-7777	692-7775
Washington State Lottery PO Box 43000 *TF:* 800-732-5101 ■ *Web:* www.walottery.com	Olympia	WA	98504	360-664-4720	664-2630
West Virginia Lottery 900 Pennsylvania Ave *Web:* www.wvlottery.com/	Charleston	WV	25302	304-558-0500	
Western Canada Lottery Corp 125 Garry St 10th Fl *Web:* www.wclc.com	Winnipeg	MB	R3C4J1	204-942-8217	946-1442
Wisconsin Lottery PO Box 8941 *Web:* www.wilottery.com	Madison	WI	53708	608-261-4916	264-6644
Wyandotte Nation Casino 100 Jackpot Pl *Web:* wyandottecasinos.com	Wyandotte	OK	74370	918-678-4946	
Zdi Gaming Inc 2124 196th St Sw *Web:* www.zdigaming.com	Lynnwood	WA	98036	425-775-7991	

456 LUGGAGE, BAGS, CASES

SEE ALSO Handbags, Totes, Backpacks p. 2444; Leather Goods - Personal p. 2640

	City	State	ZIP	Phone	Fax
Anvil Cases 15730 Salt Lake Ave *TF:* 800-359-2684 ■ *Web:* www.anvilcase.com	City of Industry	CA	91745	626-968-4100	968-1703
Award Winner Group 202 W Third St *Web:* www.awardwinnergroup.com	Mount Vernon	NY	10550	914-664-7134	668-2858
Bergman Luggage Co 401 NE Northgate Way Ste 914 *Web:* www.bergmanluggage.com	Seattle	WA	98125	206-365-5775	
Brewer-Cantelmo Company Inc 55 W 39th St Ste 205 *TF:* 800-246-1233 ■ *Web:* www.brewer-cantelmo.com	New York	NY	10018	212-244-4600	244-1640
Calzone Case Co 225 Black Rock Ave *TF Cust Svc:* 800-243-5152 ■ *Web:* www.calzonecase.com	Bridgeport	CT	06605	203-367-5766	336-4406
CH Ellis Co Inc 2432 SE Ave *TF Sales:* 800-466-3351 ■ *Web:* www.chellis.com	Indianapolis	IN	46201	317-636-3351	635-5140
Coach Inc 516 W 34th St *NYSE: COH* ■ *TF:* 800-444-3611 ■ *Web:* world.coach.com	New York	NY	10001	212-594-1850	594-1682
Delsey Luggage 6735 Business Pkwy Ste A *TF:* 800-558-3344 ■ *Web:* www.delsey.com	Elkridge	MD	21075	410-796-5655	796-4192
Forward Industries Inc 477 S Rosemary Ave Suite 219 *Web:* www.forwardindustries.com	West Palm Beach	FL	33401	561-465-0030	
Johnston Manufacturing Co 19406 E Parlier Ave	Reedley	CA	93654	559-638-2737	
LC Industries 401 N Western Ave *Web:* lewisnclark.com	Chicago	IL	60612	312-455-0500	
Leather Specialty Co 1088 Business Ln	Naples	FL	34110	239-333-1000	
Mercury Luggage Manufacturing Co 4843 Victor St *TF:* 800-874-1885 ■ *Web:* www.mercuryluggage.com	Jacksonville	FL	32207	904-334-8801	733-9671
Platt Luggage Inc 4051 W 51st St *TF:* 800-222-1555 ■ *Web:* www.plattcases.com/default.asp	Chicago	IL	60632	773-838-2000	838-2010
RJ Singer International Inc 4801 W Jefferson Blvd *Web:* www.rjsinger.com	Los Angeles	CA	90016	323-735-1717	735-3753
Royal Case Company Inc 419 E Lamar St *Web:* www.royalcase.com	Sherman	TX	75090	903-868-0288	893-7984
SKB Corp 434 W Levers Pl *TF Sales:* 800-410-2024 ■ *Web:* www.skbcases.com	Orange	CA	92867	714-637-1252	637-0491
Targus Inc 1211 N Miller St *TF:* 877-482-7487 ■ *Web:* www.targus.com	Anaheim	CA	92806	714-765-5555	765-5599
Travelpro USA 700 Banyan Trl *TF:* 800-741-7471 ■ *Web:* www.travelpro.com	Boca Raton	FL	33431	561-998-2824	998-8487
Zero Manufacturing Inc 500 West 200 North *TF:* 800-959-5050 ■ *Web:* www.zerocases.com	North Salt Lake	UT	84054	801-298-5900	292-9450

457 MACHINE SHOPS

SEE ALSO Precision Machined Products p. 2957

	City	State	ZIP	Phone	Fax
A-1 Jays Machinery 2228 Oakland Rd *Web:* www.a1jays.com	San Jose	CA	95131	408-577-0282	
Ability Engineering Technology inc 16140 S Vincennes Ave *Web:* www.abilityengineering.com	South Holland	IL	60473	708-331-0025	
Accudynamics LLC 240 Kenneth Welch Dr *Web:* www.accudynamics.com	Lakeville	MA	02347	508-946-4545	
Accura Technics LLC 310 Marlboro St *Web:* www.accuratechnics.com	Keene	NH	03431	603-355-2727	
Accuturn Corp 6510 Box Springs Blvd Ste A *Web:* www.accuturninc.com	Riverside	CA	92507	951-656-6621	
Ace Precision Machining Corp 977 Blue Ribbon Cir N *Web:* www.aceprecision.com	Oconomowoc	WI	53066	262-252-4003	
Acme Cryogenics Inc 2801 Mitchell Ave *TF:* 800-422-2790 ■ *Web:* www.acmecryo.com	Allentown	PA	18103	610-966-4488	
Acme Industries Inc 1325 Pratt Blvd *Web:* www.acmeind.com	Elk Grove Village	IL	60007	847-296-3346	296-8622
Acro Industries Inc 554 Colfax St *Web:* www.acroind.com	Rochester	NY	14606	585-254-3661	254-0415
Acutec Precision Machining Inc 16891 State Hwy 198 *Web:* www.acutecprecision.com	Saegertown	PA	16433	814-763-3214	763-3817
Addison Precision Manufacturing 500 Avis St *Web:* www.addisonprec.com	Rochester	NY	14615	585-254-1386	
Advance Mfg Company Inc Eight Tpke Industrial Rd PO Box 726 *Web:* www.advancemfg.com	Westfield	MA	01085	413-568-2411	568-6011
Advanced Integration Technologies (AIT) 481 N Dean Ave **Fax Area Code:* 972	Chandler	AZ	85226	480-940-0036	423-8469*

Company / Address	City	State	Zip	Phone	Fax
Advanced Machine & Tool Corp 3706 Transportation Dr *Web:* www.amt-corp.com	Fort Wayne	IN	46818	260-489-3572	
Aero Business Group. ÿ151 S Whittier *Web:* theaerogroup.com	Wichita	KS	67207	316-689-4272	
Aero Fab 1600 W 41st St *Web:* www.netzermetalcraftinc.com	Baltimore	MD	21211	410-467-9762	
Aerospace Techniques Inc 1100 Country Club Rd *Web:* www.aerospacetechniques.com	Middletown	CT	06457	860-347-1200	
AFC Tool Company Inc 4900 Webster St *Web:* www.afctool.com	Dayton	OH	45414	937-275-8700	
Airfasco Industries Inc 2655 Harrison Ave Sw *Web:* www.airfasco.com	Canton	OH	44706	330-430-6190	
Aitkin Iron Works Inc 301 Bunker Hill Dr *Web:* www.aiw.com	Aitkin	MN	56431	218-927-2400	
AJL Manufacturing Corp 100 Holleder Pkwy *Web:* www.ajlmfg.com	Rochester	NY	14615	585-254-1128	458-6400
AJR Industries Inc 117 Gordon St *Web:* www.ajrindustries.com	Elk Grove Village	IL	60007	847-439-0380	439-0230
All Tech Engineering 1030 58th St Sw *Web:* www.alltech-eng.com	Wyoming	MI	49509	616-406-0681	
Allied Engineering & Production Corp 2421 Blanding Ave *Web:* www.alliedeng.com	Alameda	CA	94501	510-522-1500	522-2868
Alpha Lehigh Tool & Machine Co 41 Industrial Rd *Web:* www.alphalehigh.com	Alpha	NJ	08865	908-454-6481	
American Grinding & Machine Co 2000 N Mango Ave *TF:* 877-988-4343 ■ *Web:* www.americangrinding.com	Chicago	IL	60639	773-889-4343	889-3781
American Metal Technologies LLC 8213 Durand Ave *Web:* www.amermetals.com	Sturtevant	WI	53177	262-633-1756	
American Precision Prototyping Inc 19503 E Sixth St *Web:* www.approto.com	Tulsa	OK	74108	918-266-1004	
AMG Inc 301 Jefferson Ridge Pkwy Lynchpin Industrial Ctr *Web:* www.amg-inc.net	Lynchburg	VA	24501	434-385-7525	
Amity Machine of Alburtis 3750 Chestnut Rd *Web:* www.amityindustries.com	Alburtis	PA	18011	610-966-3115	
Anderson Machining Service Inc 211 Collins Rd *Web:* www.amscnc.com	Jefferson	WI	53549	920-674-6003	
Anderson Tool & Engineering Co Inc 1735 W 53 St *Web:* www.iupui.edu/	Anderson	IN	46013	765-643-6691	
Andrew Tool & Machining Inc 15300 28th Ave N Ste A *Web:* www.andrewtool.com	Minneapolis	MN	55447	763-559-0402	
Apparent Technologies Inc 11202 Georgian Dr Unit A *Web:* www.apparenttech.com	Austin	TX	78753	512-873-0023	
Archer Screw Products Inc 11341 Melrose Ave *Web:* www.archerscrew.com	Franklin Park	IL	60131	847-451-1150	
Armec Corp 8113 Beaver Ridge Rd *Web:* armec.us	Knoxville	TN	37931	865-483-9969	
Arwood Machine Corp 95 Parker St *Web:* www.arwoodmachine.com	Newburyport	MA	01950	978-463-3777	
Autotool 8150 Business Way *Web:* www.autotoolinc.com	Plain City	OH	43064	614-733-0222	
B & B Precision Manufacturing Inc 310 W Main St *Web:* www.bbprecision.com	Avon	NY	14414	585-226-6226	
B M C Bil Mac Corp 2995 44th St Sw *Web:* www.bmcbil-mac.com	Grandville	MI	49418	616-538-1930	
B&B Manufacturing Company Inc 27940 Beale Ct *Web:* www.bbmfg.com	Valencia	CA	91355	661-257-2161	
B-tec Solutions Inc 913 Cedar Ave *Web:* www.btecsolutions.com	Croydon	PA	19021	215-785-2400	
Barth Industries Company LP 12650 Brookpark Rd *Web:* www.barth-landis.com	Cleveland	OH	44130	216-267-1950	
Barton Air Fabrications Inc 394 Sherman Ave N *Web:* www.bartonairfab.com	Hamilton	ON	L8L6N7	905-524-2234	526-6580
Bayless Engineering Inc 26100 Ave Hall *Web:* www.baylessengineering.com	Valencia	CA	91355	661-257-3373	
Bayne Machine Works Inc 910 Fork Shoals Rd *Web:* www.baynethinline.com	Greenville	SC	29605	864-288-3877	
Biax-fiberfilm Corp N1001 Tower View Dr *Web:* www.biax-fiberfilm.com	Greenville	WI	54942	920-757-9000	
Bley LLC 700 Chase Ave *Web:* acmeind.com	Elk Grove Village	IL	60007	847-290-0117	
Blue Ridge Tool & Machine Company Inc 115 Hollow Oaks Ln *Web:* www.blueridgetool.com	Easley	SC	29642	864-859-4758	
Bob Inc 8740 49th Ave N *Web:* www.bobinc.com	North Minneapolis	MN	55428	763-533-2261	533-1735
Boston Centerless Inc 11 Presidential Way *Web:* www.bostoncenterless.com	Woburn	MA	01801	781-994-5000	
Bradhart Products Inc 7747 Lochlin Dr *Web:* www.bradhart.com	Brighton	MI	48116	248-437-8700	
Brandywine Machine Company Inc 300 Creek Rd *Web:* www.bramcostainless.com	Downingtown	PA	19335	800-523-7128	
BTL Machine Inc 1168 Sherborn St *Web:* www.btlmachine.com	Corona	CA	92879	951-808-9929	
Burger & Brown Engineering Inc 4500 E 142nd St *Web:* www.smartflow-usa.com	Grandview	MO	64030	816-878-6675	
Bystronic Inc 200 Airport Rd *Web:* www.bystronic.com	Elgin	IL	60123	847-214-0300	
C & F Tool & Die Co 7206 Eckhert Rd *Web:* www.c-ftool.com	San Antonio	TX	78238	210-522-9310	
Cadence Aerospace 2600 94th St SW Bomarc Industrial Park Ste 150 *Web:* www.giddens.com	Everett	WA	98204	425-353-0405	
Cambridge Valley Machining Inc 28 Perry Ln *Web:* www.cvmusa.com	Cambridge	NY	12816	518-677-5617	
Cardo Systems Inc 100 High Tower Blvd *Web:* www.cardowireless.com	Pittsburgh	PA	15205	412-788-4533	
CARMANAH Design & Manufacturing Inc 15050 - 54A Ave Unit 8 *Web:* www.carmanahdesign.com	Surrey	BC	V3S5X7	604-299-3431	
Century Precision Machine Inc 1130 W Grove Ave *Web:* www.centuryindustriesinc.com	Orange	CA	92865	714-637-3691	
Chalmers & Kubeck Inc 150 Commerce Dr *TF:* 800-242-5637 ■ *Web:* www.candk.com	Aston	PA	19014	610-494-4300	485-1484
Chamberlain Group Inc, The 845 N Larch Ave *Web:* www.chamberlain.com	Elmhurst	IL	60126	630-279-3600	
Chant Engineering 59 Industrial Dr *Web:* www.chantengineering.com	New Britain	PA	18901	215-230-4260	
Chapel Steel Co 590 N Bethlehem Pk PO Box 1000 *TF:* 800-570-7674 ■ *Web:* www.chapelsteel.com	Lower Gwynedd	PA	19002	215-793-0899	793-0919
Cleveland Tool & Machine 5240 Smith Rd Ste 3 *Web:* www.clevtool.com	Brook Park	OH	44142	216-267-6010	
Cling's Manufacturing 6628 S Dateland Dr *Web:* www.clingsmfg.com	Tempe	AZ	85283	480-968-1778	
Cloeren Inc 401 16th St *Web:* www.cloeren.com	Orange	TX	77630	409-886-5820	
CNC Industries Ltd 9331 39 Ave *Web:* www.cncindustries.com	Edmonton	AB	T6E5T3	780-469-2346	
Columbus Jack Corp 2222 S Third St *Web:* www.columbusjack.com	Columbus	OH	43207	614-443-7492	
Commercial Jet Inc 4600 NW 36 St Miami International Airport Bldg 896 *Web:* www.commercialjet.com	Miami	FL	33166	305-341-5150	
Competitive Engineering Inc 3371 E Hemisphere Loop *Web:* www.ceiglobal.com	Tucson	AZ	85706	520-746-0270	
Complete Prototype Services Inc 44783 Morley Dr *Web:* www.completeprototype.com	Clinton Township	MI	48036	586-469-9155	
Component Engineers Inc 108 N Plains Industrial Rd *Web:* www.componenteng.com	Wallingford	CT	06492	203-269-0557	269-1357
Consolidated Bottle Corp 77 Union St *Web:* www.consbottle.com	Toronto	ON	M6N3N2	416-656-7777	
Control Alt Design Ltd 1760 Britannia Dr Ste 8 *Web:* www.controlalt.com	Elgin	IL	60124	847-695-4050	
Covert Manufacturing Inc 328 S East St *Web:* www.covertmfg.com	Galion	OH	44833	419-468-1761	
Craft Machine Works Inc 2102 48th St *Web:* www.craftmachine.com	Hampton	VA	23661	757-380-8615	380-9120
Cremach Tech Inc 369 Meyers Cir *Web:* www.cmtus.com	Corona	CA	92879	951-735-3194	
Custom Air Products & Services Inc 35 Southbelt Industrial Dr *Web:* www.customairproducts.com	Houston	TX	77047	713-460-9009	
Custom Brackets 32 Alpha Park *Web:* www.custombrackets.com	Cleveland	OH	44143	440-446-0819	
D&E Machining LTD 150 Industrial Dr *Web:* www.demachining.com	Corry	PA	16407	814-664-3531	
D&G Machine Products Inc 50 Eisenhower Dr *Web:* www.dgmachine.com	Westbrook	ME	04092	207-854-1500	
Daman Industrial Services Inc 754 Kittanning Hollow Rd PO Box 486 *Web:* www.damanindustrial.com	East Brady	PA	16028	724-526-5714	526-5277
De Dietrich Process Systems Inc 244 Sheffield St *Web:* www.ddpsinc.com	Mountainside	NJ	07092	908-317-2585	
Dechert Dynamics Corp 713 W Main St *Web:* www.decherts.com	Palmyra	PA	17078	717-838-1326	838-1525
Digital Machining Systems LLC 929 Ridge Rd *Web:* www.digitalmachining.com	Duson	LA	70529	337-984-6013	
Downey Grinding Co 12323 Bellflower Blvd *Web:* www.downeygrinding.com	Downey	CA	90242	562-803-5556	803-3237
DP Products Inc 2015 Stone Ave *Web:* www.dpprod.com	San Jose	CA	95125	408-299-0190	
DYE Precision Inc 10637 Scripps Summit Ct *Web:* dyeprecisioncnc.com	San Diego	CA	92131	858-536-5183	
Dynomax Inc 1535 Abbott Dr *Web:* www.dynomaxinc.com	Wheeling	IL	60090	847-680-8833	
Ebco Industries Ltd 7851 Alderbridge Way *Web:* www.ebco.com	Richmond	BC	V6X2A4	604-278-5578	
Ebtec Corp 120 Shoemaker Ln *Web:* www.ebteccorp.com	Agawam	MA	01001	413-786-0393	789-2851
Echo Industrial Inc 1615 Ritner Hwy *Web:* www.echoindustrial.com	Carlisle	PA	17013	717-249-6319	
Edward Segal Inc 360 Reynolds Bridge Rd *Web:* www.edwardsegalinc.com	Thomaston	CT	06787	860-283-5821	
Egge Machine Company Inc 11707 Slauson Ave *Web:* www.egge.com	Santa Fe Springs	CA	90670	562-945-3419	

Company	City	State	ZIP	Phone	Fax
Electro-Tech Machining 2000 W Gaylord St	Long Beach	CA	90813	562-436-9281	436-9281
Web: www.etmgraphite.com					
Elizabeth Companies, The 601 Linden St	Mckeesport	PA	15132	412-751-3000	635-7850*
*Fax Area Code: 502 ■ *Web:* www.eliz.com/					
Empire Bakery Equipment 171 Greenwich St	Hempstead	NY	11550	516-538-1210	
Web: empirebake.com					
Energetiq Technology Inc Seven Constitution Way	Woburn	MA	01801	781-939-0763	
Web: www.energetiq.com					
Enser Corp 1902 Taylor's Ln	Cinnaminson	NJ	08077	856-829-5522	
Web: www.enser.com					
Erdman Automation Corp 1603 14th St S	Princeton	MN	55371	763-389-9475	
Web: www.eacy.com					
Express Manufacturing Inc 3519 W Warner Ave	Santa Ana	CA	92704	714-979-2228	556-0575
Web: www.eminc.com					
F Ziegler Enterprises Ltd 528 Harrison Ct	North Fond Du Lac	WI	54937	920-921-4084	
Web: www.fziegler.com					
Farmington Engineering Inc Seven Orchard Park Rd	Madison	CT	06443	203-245-1100	
Web: www.farmingtoneng.com					
Faxon Machining Inc 11101 Adwood Dr	Cincinnati	OH	45240	513-851-4644	
Web: www.faxon-machining.com					
Femco Machine Co 754 S Main St Ext	Punxsutawney	PA	15767	814-938-9763	938-8332
TF: 800-458-3445 ■ *Web:* www.femcomachine.com					
Fixtureworks LLC 33792 Doreka	Fraser	MI	48026	586-294-1188	
Web: www.fixtureworks.net					
FM Industries Inc 221 Warren Ave	Fremont	CA	94539	510-668-1900	668-1920
Web: www.fmindustries.com					
Forged Components Inc 14527 Smith Rd	Humble	TX	77396	281-441-4088	441-8899
Web: forgedcomponents.com					
Framingham Welding & Engineering Corp 120 Leland St PO Box 112	Framingham	MA	01702	508-875-3563	626-4234
Web: www.framinghamwelding.com					
Fraser Manufacturing Corp 7235 Boyington St	Lexington	MI	48450	810-359-5338	359-8731
Furmanite America 101 Old Underwood Rd Unit E	La Porte	TX	77571	281-842-5100	842-5111
TF: 800-444-5572 ■ *Web:* www.furmanite.com					
Gatterdam Industrial Services 114 N 30th St	Louisville	KY	40212	502-776-3937	
Web: www.gatterdam.com					
GBF Enterpnrises Inc 2709 Halladay St	Santa Ana	CA	92705	714-979-7131	
Web: www.gbfenterprises.com					
GCH International Inc 330 Boxley Ave	Louisville	KY	40209	502-636-1374	
Web: www.gchintl.com					
Gill Manufacturing Ltd Nine Kenview Blvd	Brampton	ON	L6T5G5	905-792-0999	
Web: www.gillmanufacturing.com					
GKI Inc 6204 Factory Rd	Crystal Lake	IL	60014	815-459-2330	
Web: www.gkitool.com					
Golden State Engineering Inc 15338 Garfield Ave	Paramount	CA	90723	562-634-3125	
Web: www.goldenstateeng.com					
Grand Valley Mfg Co (GVM) 701 E Spring St Bldg 52	Titusville	PA	16354	814-827-2707	827-4349
Web: www.grandvalleymfg.com					
Granite State Manufacturing Co 124 Joliette St	Manchester	NH	03102	800-464-7646	668-1906*
*Fax Area Code: 603 ■ *TF:* 800-464-7646 ■ *Web:* gogsmgo.com					
Greno Industries Inc 2820 Amsterdam Rd	Scotia	NY	12302	518-393-4195	
Web: www.greno.com					
Groupe Meloche Inc 491 Boul. Des Rables	Salaberry-de-valleyfield	QC	J6T6G3	450-371-4646	371-4957
Web: www.melocheinc.com					
H & S Swansons' Tool Co 9000 68th St N	Pinellas Park	FL	33782	727-541-3575	
Web: www.hsswansons.com					
H.M. Dunn Co 3301 House Anderson Rd	Euless	TX	76040	817-283-3722	283-8402
Web: www.hmdunn.com					
Haas Automation Inc 2800 Sturgis Rd	Oxnard	CA	93030	805-278-1800	278-2255
TF: 800-331-6746 ■ *Web:* int.haascnc.com					
Hamill Manufacturing Co 500 Pleasant Vly Rd	Trafford	PA	15085	724-744-2131	
Web: www.hamillmfg.com					
Hayward Quartz Technology Inc 1700 Corporate Way	Fremont	CA	94539	510-657-9605	
Web: www.haywardquartz.com					
Hfw Industries Inc 196 Philadelphia St PO Box 8	Buffalo	NY	14207	716-875-3380	875-3385
TF: 800-937-9311 ■ *Web:* www.hfwindustries.com					
Highway Machine Company Inc (HMC) 3010 S Old US Hwy 41	Princeton	IN	47670	812-385-3639	385-8186
TF: 866-990-9462 ■ *Web:* www.hmcgears.com					
Hitachi High Technologies America Inc 10 N Martingale Rd Ste 500	Schaumburg	IL	60173	847-273-4141	273-4407
Web: www.hitachi-hta.com					
HMS Products Co 1200 E Big Beaver Rd	Troy	MI	48083	248-689-8120	
Web: www.hmsproducts.com					
HNH Mach Inc 110 Towerline Pl	London	ON	N6E2T1	519-680-3880	
Web: www.hnhmachine.com					
Howard Engineering Company Inc 687 Wooster St PO Box 1315	Naugatuck	CT	06770	203-729-5213	729-3843
Web: www.howardengineering.com					
Hti Cybernetics 6701 Center Dr	Sterling Heights	MI	48312	586-826-8346	
Web: www.htitool.com					
Hughes Supply Company of Thomasville Inc 175 Kanoy Rd PO Box 1003	Thomasville	NC	27360	336-475-8146	472-0404
TF: 800-747-8141 ■ *Web:* www.hughessupplyco.com					
Illinois Machine & Tool Works 1961 Edgewater Dr	North Pekin	IL	61554	309-382-3045	382-2644
Web: www.illmachtool.com					
IMT Precision Inc 31902 Hayman St	Hayward	CA	94544	510-324-8926	
Web: www.imtp.com					
Indiana Technology & Mfg Cos 6100 Michigan Rd	Plymouth	IN	46563	574-936-2112	
Web: www.itamco.com					
Industrial Tool Inc 9210 52nd Ave N	New Hope	MN	55428	763-533-7244	
TF Sales: 800-776-4455 ■ *Web:* www.industrial-tool.com					
IntriPlex Technologies Inc 751 S Kellogg Ave	Santa Barbara	CA	93117	805-683-3414	
Web: www.intri-plex.com					
Invena Corp 416 E Fifth St	Eureka	KS	67045	620-583-8630	
Web: www.invena.com					
Island Timberlands LP 65 Front St Fourth Fl	Nanaimo	BC	V9R5H9	250-755-3500	
Web: www.islandtimberlands.com					
J C Steele & Sons Inc 710 S Mulberry St	Statesville	NC	28677	704-872-3681	
TF: 800-278-3353 ■ *Web:* www.jcsteele.com					
Jamco Aerospace Inc 121 E Industry Ct	Deer Park	NY	11729	631-586-7900	
Web: www.jamco-aerospace.com					
Janicki Industries Inc 1476 Moore St	Sedro-woolley	WA	98284	360-856-5143	
Web: www.janicki.com					
JBL Enterprises International Inc 3219 Roymar Rd	Oceanside	CA	92058	760-754-2727	
Web: www.jblspearguns.com					
Jewell Tool Technology 3129 State St	Bettendorf	IA	52722	563-355-5010	
Web: www.jewellgroup.com					
JF Fredericks Tool Company Inc 25 Spring Ln	Farmington	CT	06032	860-677-2646	674-8679
Web: www.jffaero.com					
Johnson Technology Corp 2034 Latimer Dr	Muskegon	MI	49442	231-777-2685	773-1397
JWD Machine Inc 7215 45th St Court E	Fife	WA	98424	253-922-3806	
Web: www.jwdmachine.net					
K & M Machine-Fabricating Inc 20745 Michigan 60	Cassopolis	MI	49031	269-445-2495	445-3002
Web: www.k-mm.com					
Kamet Manufacturing Solutions 171 Commercial St	Sunnyvale	CA	94086	408-522-8000	
Web: www.kamet.com					
Kay Manufacturing Co 602 State St	Calumet City	IL	60409	708-862-6800	862-8122
Web: www.kaymfg.com					
Kenona Industries Inc 3044 Wilson Dr NW	Grand Rapids	MI	49534	616-735-6228	
Web: www.kenona.com					
Kessington Machine Products Inc 27217 County Rd 6 W	Elkhart	IN	46514	574-266-4500	
Web: www.kessington.com					
Kewaunee Fabrications LLC 520 N Main St	Kewaunee	WI	54216	920-388-2000	388-0263
Web: www.kewauneefabrications.com					
Keystone Honing Co 1000 Industrial Dr	Titusville	PA	16354	814-827-9641	
Komar Industries Inc 4425 Marketing Pl	Groveport	OH	43125	614-836-2366	
Web: www.komarindustries.com					
Kurt Manufacturing Co 5280 Main St NE	Minneapolis	MN	55421	763-572-1500	571-8466*
*Fax: Sales ■ *TF:* 800-458-7855 ■ *Web:* www.kurt.com					
Laser Excel N6323 Berlin Rd PO Box 279	Green Lake	WI	54941	920-294-6544	294-6588
TF: 800-285-6544 ■ *Web:* www.laserexcel.com					
Laser Technologies Inc 1120 N Frontenac Rd	Naperville	IL	60563	630-761-1200	
Web: lasertechnologiesinc.com					
LaVezzi Precision Inc 999 Regency Dr	Glendale Heights	IL	60139	630-582-1230	582-1238
TF: 800-323-1772 ■ *Web:* www.lavezzi.com					
Lb Steel LLC 15700 Lathrop Ave	Harvey	IL	60426	708-331-2600	331-8500
Web: www.lbsteel.com					
Leiss Tool & Die Co 801 N Pleasant Ave	Somerset	PA	15501	814-444-1444	445-3456
Web: www.leiss.com					
Lemco Tool Corp 1850 Metzger Ave	Cogan Station	PA	17728	570-494-0620	494-0860
TF: 800-233-8713 ■ *Web:* www.lemco-tool.com					
LHM Technologies Inc 446 Rowtree Dairy Rd	Woodbridge	ON	L4L8H2	905-856-2466	856-2474
Web: www.lhmtech.com					
Liburdi Engineering Ltd 400 Hwy 6 N	Dundas	ON	L9H7K4	905-689-0734	689-0739
Web: www.liburdi.com					
Lindquist Machine Corp 610 Baeten Rd	Green Bay	WI	54304	920-713-4100	499-8482
Web: www.lmc-corp.com					
Lith-O-Roll Corp 9521 Telstar Ave	El Monte	CA	91731	626-579-0340	548-4676*
*Fax Area Code: 800 ■ *TF:* 800-423-4176 ■ *Web:* www.lithoroll.com					
Litton Engineering Laboratories 200 Litton Dr Ste 200	Grass Valley	CA	95945	530-273-6176	
Web: www.littonengr.com					
LKM Industries Inc 44 Sixth Rd	Woburn	MA	01801	781-935-9210	
Web: www.lkm.com					
Logan Machine Co 1405 Home Ave	Akron	OH	44310	330-633-6163	633-6362
Web: www.loganmachine.com					
Mac Machine Company Inc 7209 Rutherford Rd	Baltimore	MD	21244	410-944-6171	
Web: www.macmachine.com					
Magna Machine & Tool Company Inc 3722 N Messick Rd	New Castle	IN	47362	765-766-5388	766-5300
Web: www.magnamachine.com					
Major Tool & Machine Inc 1458 E 19th St	Indianapolis	IN	46218	317-636-6433	634-9420
Web: www.majortool.com					
Manor Tool & Manufacturing Co 9200 Ivanhoe St	Schiller Park	IL	60176	847-678-2020	678-6937
Web: www.manortool.com					
Manufacturing & Design Technology Inc 1033a Cavalier Blvd	Chesapeake	VA	23323	757-485-8924	
Web: www.m-d-t.com					
Marberry Machine Co 6210 Cunningham Rd	Houston	TX	77041	713-466-9666	
Web: www.marberrymachine.com					
Marine Exhaust Systems of Alabama Inc 757 Nichols Ave	Fairhope	AL	36532	251-928-1234	928-1234
Web: www.mesamarine.com					
Marmen Inc 845 Berlinguet St	Trois-rivieres	QC	G8T8N9	819-379-0453	
Web: www.marmeninc.com					
Marshall Screw Products Co 3820 Chandler Dr Ne	Minneapolis	MN	55421	800-321-6727	
TF: 800-321-6727 ■ *Web:* www.marshallmfg.com					
Martinez & Turek Inc 300 S Cedar Ave	Rialto	CA	92376	909-820-6800	
Web: www.martinezandturek.com					

Company	City	State	Zip	Phone	Fax
Marton Precision Manufacturing LLC 1365 S Acacia Ave *Web:* www.martoninc.com	Fullerton	CA	92831	714-808-6523	
Master Automatic Inc 40485 Schoolcraft Rd *Web:* www.masterautomatic.com	Plymouth	MI	48170	734-414-0500	
McElroy Manufacturing Inc 833 N Fulton Ave *Web:* www.mcelroy.com	Tulsa	OK	74115	918-836-8611	
McGill Maintenance Partnership Ltd 6402 E Hwy 332 *Web:* www.mcgillmaintenance.com	Freeport	TX	77542	979-233-5438	
Mellott Manufacturing Co 13156 Long Ln *Web:* www.mellottmfg.com	Mercersburg	PA	17236	717-369-3125	
Merit Gage Inc 3954 Meadowbrook Rd *Web:* www.meritgage.com	Minneapolis	MN	55426	952-935-0113	935-2641
Metal Craft Machine & Engineering Inc 13760 Business Ctr Dr *Web:* www.metal-craft.com	Elk River	MN	55330	763-441-1855	
Metalex Manufacturing Inc 5750 Cornell Rd *Web:* www.metalexmfg.com	Cincinnati	OH	45242	513-489-0507	489-1020
Meyer Tool Inc 3055 Colerain Ave *Web:* www.meyertool.com	Cincinnati	OH	45225	513-853-4400	853-4439
Michigan Production Machining Inc 16700 23 Mile Rd *Web:* www.michpro.com	Macomb	MI	48044	586-228-9700	228-7347
Micro Instrument Corp (MIC) 1199 Emerson St PO Box 60619 *TF:* 800-200-3150 ■ *Web:* www.microinst.com	Rochester	NY	14606	585-458-3150	254-0922
Micro Machine Company LLC 2429 N Burdick *Web:* www.micromachineco.com	Kalamazoo	MI	49007	269-388-2440	
Micro-Tronics Inc 2905 S Potter Dr *Web:* www.micro-tronics.com	Tempe	AZ	85282	602-437-8995	431-9480
Mid-America Machining Inc 11530 Brooklyn Rd *Web:* www.mid-americamachining.com	Brooklyn	MI	49230	517-592-8988	
Milltech Manufacturing Co 537 Easy St *Web:* www.milltechmfg.com	Garland	TX	75042	972-276-1786	
Mitee-bite Products Inc PO Box 430 *Web:* www.miteebite.com	Center Ossipee	NH	03814	603-539-4538	
Mittler Corp 10 Cooperative Way *Web:* www.mittlerbros.com	Wright City	MO	63390	636-745-7757	
Morrison Container Handling Solutions 335 W 194th St *Web:* www.morrison-chs.com	Glenwood	IL	60425	708-756-6660	
Moss Precision Inc 3200 Arden Rd *Web:* www.mossprecision.com	Hayward	CA	94545	510-785-2235	
Mulgrew Aircraft Components Inc 1810 S Shamrock Ave *Web:* www.mulgrewaircraft.com	Monrovia	CA	91016	626-256-1375	
MVS Saegertown 1 Crawford St *Web:* www.macleanfoggcs.com	Saegertown	PA	16433	814-763-2655	763-2069
Myrmo & Sons Inc 3600 Franklin Blvd *TF:* 800-683-7040 ■ *Web:* www.myrmo.com	Eugene	OR	97403	541-747-4565	747-6832
Nassau Tool Works Inc 34 Lamar St	West Babylon	NY	11704	631-643-5000	643-5062
Nationwide Precision Products Corp 200 Tech Park Dr *Web:* www.nationwideprecision.com	Rochester	NY	14623	585-272-7100	
NC Dynamics Inc (NCDI) 3401 E 69th St *Web:* www.ncdi.aero	Long Beach	CA	90805	562-634-7392	634-6220
Neosho Trompler Inc 580 S Industrial Dr Stop 1 *Web:* www.neoshotrompler.com	Hartland	WI	53029	262-367-5600	
New Dimensions Precision Machining Inc 6614 S Union Rd *Web:* www.newdims.com	Union	IL	60180	815-923-8300	
New Era Ohio LLC 520 W Mulberry St *Web:* www.neweraohio.com	Bryan	OH	43506	419-633-1616	
Norotos Inc 201 E Alton Ave *Web:* www.norotos.com	Santa Ana	CA	92707	714-662-3113	662-7950
Norsco Inc 1816 Ackley Cir *Web:* www.norscoinc.com	Oakdale	CA	95361	209-845-2327	
Northstar Machine & Tool Company Inc 4212 Enterprise Cir *Web:* www.northstaraerospace.com	Duluth	MN	55811	218-720-2920	
Novacro Machining Inc 380 Dewitt Rd *Web:* www.novacromachininginc.com	Stoney Creek	ON	L8E2T2	905-664-2721	
Numerical Precision Inc 2200 Foster Ave *Web:* www.numericalprecision.com	Wheeling	IL	60090	847-394-3610	394-3962
O & F Machine Products Company Inc 3020 W 20th St PO Box 1363 *Web:* www.ofmachine.com	Joplin	MO	64802	417-623-7476	623-4736
Ohio Fabricators Co 111 N 14th St *Web:* www.ohfab.com	Coshocton	OH	43812	740-622-5922	622-3307
OMW Corp 21 Pamaron Way Ste G *Web:* www.omwcorp.com	Novato	CA	94949	415-382-1669	
Onamac Industries Inc 11504 Airport Rd Bldg G *Web:* www.onamac.com	Everett	WA	98204	425-743-6676	742-2718
OP Schuman & Sons Inc 2001 County Line Rd *Web:* www.opschuman.com	Warrington	PA	18976	215-343-1530	343-1633
Owens Design Inc 47427 Fremont Blvd *Web:* www.owensdesign.com	Fremont	CA	94538	510-659-1800	
Owens Industries Inc 7815 S Sixth St *Web:* www.owensind.com	Oak Creek	WI	53154	414-764-1212	764-6030
P & J Machining Inc 2601 Inter Ave *Web:* www.pnjmachining.com	Puyallup	WA	98372	253-841-0500	
Palcam Technologies Ltd 1300 Ringwell Dr *Web:* www.palcam.com	Newmarket	ON	L3Y9C7	905-853-1675	853-1584
Paradigm Precision Holdings 404 W Guadalupe Rd	Tempe	AZ	85283	480-839-0501	
Parsons Company Inc 1386 SR- 117 *Web:* www.parsonscompany.com	Roanoke	IL	61561	309-467-9100	
PDC Machines Inc 1875 Stout Dr *Web:* www.pdcmachines.com	Warminster	PA	18974	215-443-9442	
Peeco 7050 W Ridge Rd *Web:* www.autodev.com	Fairview	PA	16415	814-474-5561	

Company	City	State	Zip	Phone	Fax
Peko Precision Products Inc 1400 Emerson St *Web:* www.pekoprecision.com	Rochester	NY	14606	585-647-3010	647-1366
PEMCO-Naval Engineering Works Inc 3614 Frederic St *Web:* www.pemco-inc.com	Pascagoula	MS	39567	228-769-7081	769-6520
Perfekta Inc 480 E 21st St N *Web:* www.perfekta-inc.com	Wichita	KS	67214	316-263-2056	263-0106
Peterson Tool Company Inc 739 Fesslers Ln PO Box 100830 *Web:* www.petersontool.com	Nashville	TN	37224	615-242-7341	242-7362
PFI Precision Inc 2011 N Dayton Lakeview Rd *Web:* www.pfiprecision.com	New Carlisle	OH	45344	937-845-3563	
Pioneer Products Inc 1917 S Memorial Dr PO Box 1348 *Web:* www.pioneerproducts.com	Racine	WI	53403	262-633-6304	633-0465
Poly Cycle Inc 5501 Campbells Run Rd *TF:* 800-394-4333 ■ *Web:* www.polycycle.com	Pittsburgh	PA	15205	412-747-1101	747-0749
Prattville Machine & Tool Company Inc 240 Jubilee Dr Second Fl *Web:* www.prattvillemachine.com	Peabody	MA	01960	978-538-5229	
Precision Gears Inc N 13 W 24705 Bluemound Rd *Web:* www.precisiongears.com	Pewaukee	WI	53072	262-542-4261	542-1592
Precision Machine & Manufacturing Inc 1290 S Bertelsen Rd *Web:* www.premach.com	Eugene	OR	97402	541-484-9841	
Precision Roll Grinders Inc 6356 Chapmans Rd *Web:* www.precisionrollgrinders.com	Allentown	PA	18106	610-395-6966	481-9130
Precision Screw Thread Corp S 82 W 19275 Apollo Dr *Web:* www.precisionscrewthread.com	Muskego	WI	53150	262-679-9000	679-9004
Pro-line Water Screen Services Inc PO Box 2565 *Web:* www.intakescreens.com	Pearland	TX	77588	281-992-6730	
Process Equipment Co 6555 S SR-202 *Web:* www.peco-us.com	Tipp City	OH	45371	937-667-4451	667-9322
Process Fab Inc 15644 Clanton Cir *Web:* www.processfab.com	Santa Fe Springs	CA	90670	562-921-1979	921-3145
Prototype & Plastic Mold Co 35 Industrial Pk Pl *Web:* www.proppm.com	Middletown	CT	06457	860-632-2800	632-2249
Prototype Machine Co 818 Prototype Rd PO Box 249	Flatonia	TX	78941	361-865-3230	
Pyramid Precision Machine Inc 6721 Cobra Way *Web:* www.pyramidprecision.com	San Diego	CA	92121	858-642-0713	
Quality Engineering & Tool Company Inc 380 S Wheatfield St *Web:* qes1.com	York	PA	17403	717-854-3875	843-0297
Quality Mfg Company Inc (QMI) PO Box 616 *TF:* 866-460-6459 ■ *Web:* www.qmiky.com	Winchester	KY	40392	859-744-0420	744-0696
R & d Machine & Engineering Inc 130 Scarlet Blvd *Web:* www.rdmachine.com	Oldsmar	FL	34677	813-891-9109	
R A Zweig Inc 2500 Ravine Way *Web:* www.zweig-cnc.com	Glenview	IL	60025	847-832-9001	
Ram Precision Industries Inc 11125 Yankee Rd Ste A *Web:* www.ramprecision.com	Dayton	OH	45458	937-885-7700	
Revzero Inc 2431 Galpin Ct Ste 150 *Web:* www.revzeroinc.com	Chanhassen	MN	55317	952-380-9966	
Ridge Engineering Inc 3987 Hampstead Mexico Rd *Web:* www.ridgeeng.com	Hampstead	MD	21074	410-239-7716	239-8710
Rite Track Inc 8655 Rite Track Way *Web:* www.ritetrack.com	West Chester	OH	45069	513-881-7820	
RM Kerner Co 2208 E 33rd St *Web:* www.rmkco.com	Erie	PA	16510	814-898-2000	
RMS-Ross Corp 44325 Yale Rd W *Web:* www.rmsross.com	Chilliwack	BC	V2R4H2	604-792-5911	792-7148
Robinson Metal Inc 1740 Eisenhower Dr *Web:* www.robinsonmetal.com	De Pere	WI	54115	920-494-7411	
RS Hughes Company Inc Saunders Div 975 N Todd Ave *TF Sales:* 888-932-8836 ■ *Web:* www.saunderscorp.com	Azusa	CA	91702	626-691-1111	691-0116
Santinelli International Inc 325 Oser Ave *TF:* 800-644-3343 ■ *Web:* www.santinelli.com	Hauppauge	NY	11788	631-435-3343	
Schaffer Grinding Co 848 S Maple Ave *Web:* www.schaffergrinding.com	Montebello	CA	90640	323-724-4476	724-2635
Scheirer Machine Company Inc 3200 Industrial Blvd *TF:* 800-448-4590 ■ *Web:* www.scheirer.com	Bethel Park	PA	15102	412-833-6500	833-8110
Schmiede Corp 1865 Riley Creek Rd PO Box 1630 *TF:* 800-535-1851 ■ *Web:* www.schmiedecorp.com	Tullahoma	TN	37388	931-455-4801	455-1703
Schwartz Industries Inc 6909 E 11-Mile Rd *Web:* sharedvision.net/	Warren	MI	48092	586-759-1777	759-0808
Scicon Technologies Corp 27525 Newhall Ranch Rd *Web:* www.scicontech.com	Valencia	CA	91355	661-295-8630	295-6611
Service Guide Inc 3605 Warren Meadville Rd *Web:* usa.siemens.com/rolling-mill-maintenance	Cortland	OH	44410	330-637-6060	637-6229
Sintel Inc 18437 171st Ave *Web:* www.sintelinc.com	Spring Lake	MI	49456	616-842-6960	
SMF Inc 1550 Industrial Pk PO Box 157 *Web:* www.smf-inc.com	Minonk	IL	61760	309-432-2586	432-2390
Solid Concepts Inc 28309 Ave Crocker *TF:* 888-311-1017 ■ *Web:* www.solidconcepts.com	Valencia	CA	91355	661-295-4400	257-9311
Sonfarrel Inc 3000-3010 E La Jolla St *Web:* www.sonfarrel.com	Anaheim	CA	92806	714-630-7280	632-7239

Company / Address	City	State	ZIP	Phone	Fax
South Side Machine Works Inc 3761 Eiler St. Web: www.southsidemachine.net	Saint Louis	MO	63116	314-481-7171	481-9271
Southern Prestige Industries Inc 113 Hatfield Rd. Web: www.southernprestige.com	Statesville	NC	28625	704-872-9524	
Specialty Bar Products Co 200 Martha St PO Box 127 Web: www.specialty-bar.com	Blairsville	PA	15717	724-459-7500	459-0944
St George Steel Fabrication Inc 1301 East 700 North Web: www.stgeorgesteel.com	Saint George	UT	84770	435-673-4856	628-4139
Standard Locknut Inc 1045 E 169th St TF: 800-783-6887 ■ Web: www.stdlocknut.com	Westfield	IN	46074	317-867-0100	867-4231
Stellar Technology Inc 237 Commerce Dr Web: www.stellartech.com	Amherst	NY	14228	716-250-1900	
Sterling Engineering Corp 236 Newhartford Rd Web: www.sterlingeng.com	Barkhamsted	CT	06063	860-379-3366	379-3278
Steward Machine Company Inc 3911 13th Ave N. Web: www.stewardmachine.com	Birmingham	AL	35234	205-841-6461	849-8029
Stewart Assembly & Machining 7234 Blue Ash Rd. Web: www.pmcworldwide.net	Cincinnati	OH	45236	513-891-9000	
Stillwater Technologies Inc 1040 S Dorset Web: www.stlwtr.com	Troy	OH	45373	937-440-2500	
Straton Industries Inc 180 Surf Ave. Web: www.straton.com	Stratford	CT	06615	203-375-4488	
Supreme Gear Company Inc 17430 Malyn Blvd Web: www.dorrisco.com	Fraser	MI	48026	586-294-7625	
Sussek Machine Corp 805 Pierce St Web: www.sussek.com	Waterloo	WI	53594	920-478-2126	478-3452
T & K Machine Inc 2220 W Park St Web: www.tkparis.com	Paris	TX	75460	903-785-5574	
T & S Machine Shop Inc 1396 Hwy 471 Web: www.tandsmachine.com	Brandon	MS	39042	601-825-8627	
T R C Hydraulics Inc Seven Mosher Dr Web: www.trchydraulics.com	Dartmouth	NS	B3B1E5	902-468-4605	
Tacoma Screw Products Inc 2001 Center St. Web: www.tacomascrew.com	Tacoma	WA	98409	253-572-3444	
Tecmotiv (USA) Inc 1500 James Ave. Web: www.tecmotiv.com	Niagara Falls	NY	14305	716-282-1211	
Tell Tool Inc 35 Tpke Industrial Rd Web: www.telltool.com	Westfield	MA	01085	413-568-1671	562-7237
Tibor Machine Products Inc 7400 W 100th Pl. Web: www.tibormachine.com	Bridgeview	IL	60455	708-499-3700	499-6803
Tier One LLC 31 Pecks Ln TF: 877-251-2228 ■ Web: www.tieronemachining.com	Newtown	CT	06470	203-426-3030	
Total Components Solutions Corp 2080 Tenth St Web: www.tcsiowa.com	Rock Valley	IA	51247	712-476-5315	
Tree City Tool 1954 N Montgomery Rd. Web: www.treecitytool.com	Greensburg	IN	47240	812-663-4196	
Tri-State Machine Inc 3301 Mccolloch St. Web: www.tri-statemachine.com	Wheeling	WV	26003	304-234-0170	
True Position Technologies Inc 24900 Ave Standford Web: www.truepositiontech.com	Valencia	CA	91355	661-294-0030	294-1240
True-Tech Corp 4050 Technology Pl Web: www.true-tech.com	Fremont	CA	94538	510-353-1000	353-9000
TSS Technologies Inc 8800 Global Way Web: tsstech.com/	West Chester	OH	45069	513-772-7000	772-2938
Tulsa Centerless Bar Processing 1605 N 168th E Ave Web: tulsacenterless.com	Tulsa	OK	74116	918-438-0000	
TurboCare Chicopee 2140 Westover Rd. Web: www.turbocare.com	Chicopee	MA	01022	413-593-0500	593-3424
Twin City EDM 7940 Rancher Rd NE. TF: 800-397-0338 ■ Web: www.twincityedm.com	Fridley	MN	55432	763-783-7808	783-7842
Ultra Tech Machinery Inc 297 Ascot Pkwy Web: www.utmachinery.com	Cuyahoga Falls	OH	44223	330-929-5544	
UMC Inc 500 Chelsea Rd Web: www.ultramc.com	Monticello	MN	55362	763-271-5200	271-5249
Unisource Manufacturing Inc 8040 NE 33rd Dr TF: 800-234-2566 ■ Web: www.unisource-mfg.com	Portland	OR	97211	503-281-4673	281-5845
Urban Manufacturing Inc 1288 Hickory St Web: www.urban-mfg.com	Pewaukee	WI	53072	262-691-2455	691-8938
Usitech Nov Inc 1295 1e Rue Parc Industriel Web: www.usitechnov.com	Sainte-marie De Beauce	QC	G6E3T3	418-387-3133	
V W Broaching Service Inc 3250 W Lake St Web: vwbroaching.com	Chicago	IL	60624	773-533-9000	
Vaga Industries Inc 2505 Loma Ave. Web: www.vaga.com	South El Monte	CA	91733	626-442-7436	442-4330
Vermont Aerospace Manufacturing Inc 966 Industrial Pwy PO Box 1148 Web: www.vtaerospace.com	Lyndonville	VT	05851	802-748-8705	748-8437
Vescio Threading Co 14002 Anson Ave TF: 800-361-4218 ■ Web: www.vesciothreading.com	Santa Fe Springs	CA	90670	562-802-1868	802-2073
Vickers Engineering Inc 3604 Glendora Rd PO Box 346 Web: www.vickerseng.com	New Troy	MI	49119	269-426-8545	426-8494
Wahlco Inc 2722 S Fairview St TF: 800-423-5432 ■ Web: www.wahlco.com	Santa Ana	CA	92704	714-979-7300	979-0603
Warren Fabricating & Machining 3240 Mahoning Ave NW. TF: 800-827-0596 ■ Web: www.warfab.com	Warren	OH	44483	330-847-0596	
Washington Tool & Machine Co One S Baird Ave PO Box 873 Web: www.washtool.com	Washington	PA	15301	724-225-7470	225-7484
Waterbury Swiss Automatics Inc 43 Mattatuck Heights Rd. Web: www.waterburyswiss.com	Waterbury	CT	06705	203-573-8584	
Wayne Metals LLC 400 E Logan St Web: waynemetals.com	Markle	IN	46770	260-758-3121	758-2521
Wayne Trail Technologies Inc 203 E Park St Web: www.waynetrail.com	Fort Loramie	OH	45845	937-295-2120	
Weaver Industries Inc 425 S Fourth St PO Box 326 Web: www.weaverind.com	Denver	PA	17517	717-336-7507	336-4182
Webber Metal Products Inc 120 Industrial Park Rd Web: www.webbermetals.com	Cascade	IA	52033	563-852-7122	
Weldmac Manufacturing Co 1451 N Johnson Ave TF: 800-252-1533 ■ Web: www.weldmac.com	El Cajon	CA	92020	619-440-2300	440-8723
West Coast Industrial Systems 1995 W Airway Rd Web: www.westcoastindustrial.com	Lebanon	OR	97355	541-451-6677	
West Engineering Company Inc 10106 Louistown Rd. Web: www.west-engineering.net	Ashland	VA	23005	804-798-3966	798-8590
Whelan Machine & Tool 134 Rochester Dr Web: www.whelanmachine.com	Louisville	KY	40214	502-364-6370	
Wilco Machine & Fab Inc 1326 S Broadway PO Box 48 Web: www.wilcofab.com	Marlow	OK	73055	580-658-6993	658-6767
Will-Burt Co 169 S Main St Web: willburt.com	Orrville	OH	44667	330-682-7015	684-1190
Williams Machine & Tool Company Inc 1009 Schermerhorn Rd. Web: www.wilmaco.com	Galena	KS	66739	620-783-5184	
Wind Turbine Industries Corp 16801 Industrial Cir SE Web: www.windturbine.net	Prior Lake	MN	55372	952-447-6064	
Windham Manufacturing Company Inc 8520 Forney Rd Web: www.windhammfg.com	Dallas	TX	75227	214-388-0511	
Windings Inc PO Box 566 TF: 800-795-8533 ■ Web: www.windings.com	New Ulm	MN	56073	507-359-2034	354-5383
Wise Plastics Technologies Inc 3810 Stern Ave Web: www.wise-hamlin.com	Saint Charles	IL	60174	847-697-2840	697-0103
World Class Manufacturing Group Inc, The 1101 S Pine St Web: www.worldcls.com	Weyauwega	WI	54983	920-867-2527	
Wright Plastic Products LLC 201 E Condensery Rd. Web: wppllc.com	Sheridan	MI	48884	989-291-3211	291-5321
WSI Industries Inc 213 Chelsea Rd NASDAQ: WSCI ■ Web: www.wsiindustries.com	Monticello	MN	55362	763-295-9202	295-9212
Xtek Inc 11451 Reading Rd TF: 888-332-9835 ■ Web: www.xtek.com	Cincinnati	OH	45241	513-733-7800	733-7939
Yates Industries Inc 23050 E Industrial Dr Web: www.yatesind.com	St. Clair Shores	MI	48080	586-778-7680	
Zach Halopoff Inc 15422 Assembly Ln Web: www.haloindustries.com	Huntington Beach	CA	92649	714-373-3333	

458 MACHINE TOOLS - METAL CUTTING TYPES

SEE ALSO Machine Tools - Metal Forming Types p. 2685; Metalworking Devices & Accessories p. 2756

Company / Address	City	State	ZIP	Phone	Fax
Abbco Inc 2401 American Ln TF: 866-986-6546 ■ Web: www.abbcoinc.net	Elkgrove Vlg	IL	60007	630-595-7115	595-6431
Accurate Boring Co 17420 Malyn Blvd Web: www.accurateboring.com	Fraser	MI	48026	586-294-7555	294-2530
Acme Manufacturing Co 4240 N Atlantic Blvd. Web: www.acmemfg.com	Auburn Hills	MI	48326	248-393-7300	393-4060
Airtronics Gage & Machine Co 516 Slade Ave. Web: www.airtronicsgauge.com	Elgin	IL	60120	847-695-0911	695-8745
Allied Tool Products 9334 N 107th St TF: 800-558-5147 ■ Web: www.atptools.com	Milwaukee	WI	53224	414-355-8280	355-8297
American GFM Corp 1200 Cavalier Blvd. Web: www.agfm.com	Chesapeake	VA	23323	757-487-2442	487-5274
Automation Assoc Inc 416 Campus Dr Web: www.autoinc.com	Arlington Heights	IL	60004	847-255-4500	255-9648
Babin Machine Works Inc 2510 N Ninth St.	Beaumont	TX	77703	409-892-1231	892-1236
Bardons & Oliver Inc 5800 Harper Rd Web: www.bardonsoliver.com	Solon	OH	44139	440-498-5800	498-2001
Barnes International Inc 814 Chestnut St PO Box 1203 TF: 800-435-4877 ■ Web: www.barnesintl.com	Rockford	IL	61105	815-964-8661	964-5074
Bourn & Koch Inc 2500 Kishwaukee St. Web: www.bourn-koch.com	Rockford	IL	61104	815-965-4013	965-0019
Bryant Grinder 65 Pearl St. Web: www.bryantgrinder.com	Springfield	VT	05156	802-885-5161	885-9444
Burr Oak Tool Inc 405 W S St Web: www.burroak.com	Sturgis	MI	49091	269-651-9393	651-4324
Carlson Tool & Machine Co 2300 Gary Ln Web: www.carlson-tool.com	Geneva	IL	60134	630-232-2460	232-2016
Chas G Allen Company Inc 25 Williamsville Rd. Web: www.chasgallen.com	Barre	MA	01005	978-355-2911	355-2917
Continental Machines Inc 5505 W 123rd St Web: continentalhydraulics.com	Savage	MN	55378	952-895-6400	
Crafts Technology 91 Joey Dr. TF: 800-323-6802 ■ Web: www.craftstech.net	Elk Grove Village	IL	60007	847-758-3100	758-0162
Darex 210 E Hersey St PO Box 730 TF: 800-418-1439 ■ Web: www.darex.com	Ashland	OR	97520	541-488-2224	488-2229

Company	City	State	ZIP	Phone	Fax
Davenport Machine Inc 167 Ames St *TF:* 800-344-5748 ■ *Web:* www.davenportmachine.com	Rochester	NY	14611	585-235-4545	235-7997
Dayton Machine Tool Co 1314 Webster St *Web:* www.dmtnet.com	Dayton	OH	45404	937-222-6444	222-6444
DoALL Co 1480 S Wolf Rd *Web:* www.doall.com	Wheeling	IL	60090	847-495-6800	484-2045
Eagle Tool Co 101 Woodward Ave *Web:* eaglebroach.com	Iron Mountain	MI	49801	906-774-0284	774-0342
EH Wachs Co 600 Knightsbridge Pkwy **Fax:* Sales ■ *TF:* 800-323-8185 ■ *Web:* www.ehwachs.com	Lincolnshire	IL	60069	847-537-8800	520-1147*
Entrust Mfg Technologies Inc N 58 W 14630 Shawn Cir *Web:* www.entrustmt.com	Menomonee Falls	WI	53051	262-252-3802	252-4075
Everite Machine Products Co 6995 Airport Hwy Ln *Web:* www.everite.net	Pennsauken	NJ	08110	856-330-6700	
Extrude Hone Corp 235 Industry Blvd *TF:* 800-367-1109 ■ *Web:* www.kennametal.com	Irwin	PA	15642	724-863-5900	863-8759
Flow International Corp 23500 64th Ave S *NASDAQ: FLOW* ■ *TF:* 800-446-3569 ■ *Web:* www.flowwaterjet.com	Kent	WA	98032	253-850-3500	813-9377
GF Machining Solutions 560 Bond St *TF:* 800-282-1336 ■ *Web:* www.gfac.com	Lincolnshire	IL	60069	847-913-5300	913-5340
Gleason Corp 1000 University Ave *TF:* 800-727-6333 ■ *Web:* www.gleason.com	Rochester	NY	14607	585-473-1000	461-4348
Grob Inc 1731 Tenth Ave *TF:* 800-225-6481 ■ *Web:* www.grobinc.com	Grafton	WI	53024	262-377-1400	377-2106
Hammond Roto-Finish 1600 Douglas Ave *Web:* www.hammondmach.com	Kalamazoo	MI	49007	269-345-7151	345-1710
Hanchett Manufacturing Inc 906 N State St *TF:* 800-454-7463 ■ *Web:* www.hanchett.com	Big Rapids	MI	49307	231-796-7678	796-4851
Hardinge Inc 1 Hardinge Dr *NASDAQ: HDNG* ■ *TF:* 800-843-8801 ■ *Web:* www.hardinge.com	Elmira	NY	14902	607-734-2281	
Harrington Tool Co 105 N Rath Ave *Web:* harringtontool.net	Ludington	MI	49431	231-843-3445	845-7477
Hause Machines 809 S Pleasant St *TF:* 800-932-8665 ■ *Web:* www.hausemachines.com	Montpelier	OH	43543	419-485-3158	485-3146
Hausermann Abrading Process Co 300 Laura Dr *Web:* www.hausermann.net	Addison	IL	60101	630-543-6688	543-6689
Hetran Inc 70 Pinedale Industrial Rd *Web:* www.hetraninc.com	Orwigsburg	PA	17961	570-366-1411	366-1829
Huffman Corp 1050 Huffman Way *TF:* 888-483-3626 ■ *Web:* huffman-llc.com	Clover	SC	29710	803-222-4561	222-7599
Hurco Cos Inc One Technology Way *NASDAQ: HURC* ■ *TF Sales:* 800-634-2416 ■ *Web:* www.hurco.com	Indianapolis	IN	46268	317-293-5309	298-2621
Hydromat Inc 11600 Adie Rd **Fax:* Sales ■ *TF:* 800-552-3288 ■ *Web:* www.hydromat.com	Saint Louis	MO	63043	314-432-4644	432-7552*
Hypertherm Inc 21 Great Hollow Rd PO Box 5010 *TF:* 800-643-0030 ■ *Web:* www.hypertherm.com	Hanover	NH	03755	603-643-3441	643-5352
Hypneumat Inc 5900 W Franklin Dr *Web:* www.hypneumat.com	Franklin	WI	53132	414-423-7400	423-7414
Industrial Steel & Machine Sales Inc 2712 Lackland Dr *Web:* www.is-ms.net	Waterloo	IA	50702	319-296-1816	296-3630
John J Adams Die Corp 10 Nebraska St	Worcester	MA	01604	508-757-3894	753-8016
Kaufman Mfg Co 547 S 29th St PO Box 1056 *TF:* 800-420-6641 ■ *Web:* www.kaufmanmfg.com	Manitowoc	WI	54221	920-684-6641	686-4103
Kennametal Inc 1600 Technology Way PO Box 231 *NYSE: KMT* ■ *TF Cust Svc:* 800-446-7738 ■ *Web:* www.kennametal.com	Latrobe	PA	15650	724-539-5000	539-8787
Kitamura Machinery of USA Inc 78 Century Dr *Web:* www.kitamura-machinery.com	Wheeling	IL	60090	847-520-7755	520-7763
Klingelhofer Corp 165 Mill Ln *TF:* 800-879-5546 ■ *Web:* www.klingelhofer.com	Mountainside	NJ	07092	908-232-7200	232-1841
Koike Aronson Inc 635 W Main St PO Box 307 *TF:* 800-252-5232 ■ *Web:* www.koike.com	Arcade	NY	14009	585-492-2400	457-3517
Kyocera Tycom Corp 3565 Cadillac *TF:* 800-823-7284 ■ *Web:* www.kyoceratycom.com	Costa Mesa	CA	92626	714-428-3600	428-3605
Lucas Precision LP 13020 St Clair Ave *Web:* www.lucasprecision.com	Cleveland	OH	44108	216-451-5588	451-5174
Makino 7680 Innovation Way *TF:* 888-625-4661 ■ *Web:* www.makino.com	Mason	OH	45040	513-573-7200	573-7360
McLean Inc 3409 E Miraloma Ave *TF Cust Svc:* 800-451-2424 ■ *Web:* mcleaninc.com	Anaheim	CA	92806	714-996-5451	996-5453
Metal Cutting Corp 89 Commerce Rd *Web:* www.metalcutting.com	Cedar Grove	NJ	07009	973-239-1100	239-6651
Metl-Saw Systems Inc 2950 Bay Vista Ct *Web:* www.metlsaw.com	Benicia	CA	94510	707-746-6200	746-5085
Monarch Lathes 615 N Oaks Ave PO Box 4609 *Web:* www.monarchlathe.com	Sidney	OH	45365	937-492-4111	492-7958
Morgood Tools Inc 940 Millstead Way *Web:* www.morgood.com	Rochester	NY	14624	585-436-8828	436-2426
NNT Corp 1320 Norwood Ave *TF:* 800-556-9999 ■ *Web:* www.nntcorp.com	Itasca	IL	60143	630-875-9600	875-8899
Normac Inc 10 Loop Rd PO Box 69 *Web:* www.normac.com	Arden	NC	28704	828-209-9000	209-9001
North American Products Corp 1180 Wernsing Rd **Fax Area Code:* 800 ■ *TF Cust Svc:* 800-457-7468 ■ *Web:* www.napgladu.com	Jasper	IN	47546	812-482-2000	457-7458*
Ohio Broach & Machine Co 35264 Topps Industrial Pkwy **Fax:* Sales ■ *Web:* www.ohiobroach.com	Willoughby	OH	44094	440-946-1040	946-0725*
Okuma America Corp 11900 W Hall Dr *Web:* www.okuma.com	Charlotte	NC	28278	704-588-7000	588-6503
Oliver of Adrian Inc 1111 E Beecher St PO Box 189 *TF:* 877-668-0885 ■ *Web:* www.oliverinstrument.com	Adrian	MI	49221	517-263-2132	265-8698
P & R Industries Inc 1524 Clinton Ave N *Web:* pandrindustries.com	Rochester	NY	14621	585-266-6725	266-0075
Parker Majestic Inc 300 N Pike Rd *TF:* 866-572-7537 ■ *Web:* www.pennunited.com	Sarver	PA	16055	724-352-1551	353-1196
Peddinghaus Corp 300 N Washington Ave *TF:* 800-786-2448 ■ *Web:* www.peddinghaus.com	Bradley	IL	60915	815-937-3800	937-4003
Pilz Automation Safety LP 7150 Commerce Blvd *Web:* www.pilz.com	Canton	MI	48187	734-354-0272	354-3355
Pioneer Broach Co 6434 Telegraph Rd *TF:* 800-621-1945 ■ *Web:* www.pioneerbroach.com	Los Angeles	CA	90040	323-728-1263	722-1699
PMC Industries Inc 29100 Lakeland Blvd *Web:* www.pmc-colinet.com/default.asp?id=50	Wickliffe	OH	44092	440-943-3300	944-1974
Reno Machine Company Inc 170 Pane Rd *Web:* www.reno-machine.com	Newington	CT	06111	860-666-5641	667-4496
RF Cook Manufacturing Co 4585 Allen Rd *Web:* www.rfcook.com	Stow	OH	44224	330-923-9797	923-8641
Rothenberger USA 4455 Boeing Dr **Fax Area Code:* 800 ■ *TF:* 800-545-7698 ■ *Web:* www.rothenberger-usa.com	Rockford	IL	61109	815-397-7617	451-2632*
Rottler Mfg 8029 S 200th St *TF:* 800-452-0534 ■ *Web:* www.rottlermfg.com	Kent	WA	98032	253-872-7050	395-0230
Royal Master Grinders Inc 143 Bauer Dr *Web:* www.royalmaster.com	Oakland	NJ	07436	201-337-8500	337-2324
RP Machine Enterprises Inc 820 Cochran St *Web:* www.rpmachine.com	Statesville	NC	28677	704-872-8888	872-5777
S & M Machine Service Inc 109 E Highland Dr *TF:* 800-323-1579 ■ *Web:* www.snmmachine.com	Oconto Falls	WI	54154	920-846-8130	846-4803
Saginaw Machine Systems (SMS) 800 N Hamilton St *Web:* www.saginawmachine.com	Saginaw	MI	48602	989-753-8465	753-1751
Sandvik Coromant Co 1702 Nevins Rd *TF Cust Svc:* 800-726-3845 ■ *Web:* www.sandvik.com	Fair Lawn	NJ	07410	201-794-5000	794-5165
Savage Saws 100 Indel Ave PO Box 156 *Web:* www.savagesaws.com	Rancocas	NJ	08073	609-267-8501	267-1366
Seneca Falls Technology Group 314 Fall St *Web:* www.sftg.com	Seneca Falls	NY	13148	315-568-5804	568-5800
Servo Products Co 34940 Lakeland Blvd *TF:* 800-521-7359 ■ *Web:* www.servoproductsco.com	Eastlake	OH	44095	440-942-9999	942-9100
Setco Sales Co 5880 Hillside Ave *TF:* 800-543-0470 ■ *Web:* www.setco.com	Cincinnati	OH	45233	513-941-5110	941-6913
SGS Tool Co 55 S Main St **Fax:* Hum Res ■ *Web:* www.sgstool.com	Munroe Falls	OH	44262	330-688-6667	686-2128*
Simmons Machine Tool Corp 1700 N Broadway *Web:* smtgroup.com	Albany	NY	12204	518-462-5431	462-0371
SNK America Inc 1150 Feehanville Dr *TF:* 888-765-6224 ■ *Web:* www.snkamerica.com	Mount Prospect	IL	60056	847-364-0801	364-4363
Southwestern Industries Inc 2615 Homestead Pl *TF:* 800-421-6875 ■ *Web:* www.southwesternindustries.com	Rancho Dominguez	CA	90220	310-608-4422	764-2668
Stephen Bader Co Inc 10 Charles St PO Box 297 *Web:* www.stephenbader.com	Valley Falls	NY	12185	518-753-4456	753-4962
Sunnen Products Co 7910 Manchester Ave **Fax:* Cust Svc ■ *TF:* 800-325-3670 ■ *Web:* www.sunnen.com	Saint Louis	MO	63143	314-781-2100	781-2268*
Technidrill Systems Inc 429 Portage Blvd *TF:* 800-914-5863 ■ *Web:* www.technidrillsystems.com	Kent	OH	44240	330-678-9980	678-9981
Thermal Dynamics Corp 82 Benning St *TF:* 800-752-7621 ■ *Web:* victortechnologies.com	West Lebanon	NH	03784	603-298-5711	298-0558
Thurston Mfg Company Inc 14 Thurber Blvd *Web:* www.thurstonmfg.com	Smithfield	RI	02917	401-232-9100	232-9101
Tiffin Foundry & Machine Inc 423 W Adams St PO Box 37 *Web:* www.tiffinfoundry.com	Tiffin	OH	44883	419-447-3991	447-7969
Tool-Flo Mfg Inc 7803 Hansen Rd *TF:* 800-345-2815 ■ *Web:* www.toolflo.com	Houston	TX	77061	713-941-1080	941-8099
Tornos Technologies US Corp 840 Parkview Blvd *Web:* www.tornos.com	Lombard	IL	60148	630-812-2040	812-2039
Toyoda Machinery USA Inc 316 W University Dr *TF:* 800-257-2985 ■ *Web:* www.toyodausa.com	Arlington Heights	IL	60004	847-253-0340	577-4680
TRU TECH Systems Inc 24550 N River Rd PO Box 46965 *TF:* 877-878-8324 ■ *Web:* www.trutechsystems.com	Mount Clemens	MI	48046	586-469-2700	469-1344
US Tool Grinding Inc 701 S Desloge Dr *TF:* 800-775-8665 ■ *Web:* www.ustg.net	Desloge	MO	63601	573-431-3856	431-6655
Vernon Tool Company Ltd 503 Jones Rd *TF:* 800-452-1542 ■ *Web:* www.vernontool.com	Oceanside	CA	92054	760-433-5860	757-2233
WF Meyers Co 1008 13th St PO Box 426 *TF:* 800-457-4055 ■ *Web:* www.wfmeyers.com	Bedford	IN	47421	812-275-4485	275-4488
WF Wells Inc 16645 Heimbach Rd *Web:* www.wfwells.com	Three Rivers	MI	49093	269-279-5123	279-6337
Whitney Tool Company Inc 906 R St PO Box 545 *TF:* 800-536-1971 ■ *Web:* www.whitneytool.com	Bedford	IN	47421	812-275-4491	275-6458
Wisconsin Machine Tool Corp 3225 Gateway Rd Ste 100 *TF:* 800-243-3078 ■ *Web:* www.machine-tool.com	Brookfield	WI	53045	262-317-3048	317-3079

459 MACHINE TOOLS - METAL FORMING TYPES

SEE ALSO Machine Tools - Metal Cutting Types p. 2684; Metalworking Devices & Accessories p. 2756; Rolling Mill Machinery p. 3129; Tool & Die Shops p. 3238

Company	City	State	ZIP	Phone	Fax
Advanced Hydraulics Inc 13568 Vintage Pl *TF:* 888-581-8079 ■ *Web:* www.advancedhydraulicsinc.com	Chino	CA	91710	909-590-7644	590-7049
Amada America Inc 7025 Firestone Blvd *TF:* 800-626-6612 ■ *Web:* www.amada.com	Buena Park	CA	90621	714-739-2111	739-4099
American Actuator Corp (AAC) PO Box 113096 *Web:* www.americanactuator.com	Stamford	CT	06911	203-324-6334	324-4471
Anderson Cook Inc 17650 15-Mile Rd *Web:* www.andersoncook.com	Fraser	MI	48026	586-293-0800	293-0833
Atlas Technologies Inc 3100 Cotter Ave *Web:* www.atlastechnologies.com	Fenton	MI	48430	810-629-6663	629-8145
Badge A Minit Ltd 345 N Lewis Ave *TF:* 800-223-4103 ■ *Web:* www.badgeaminit.com	Oglesby	IL	61348	815-883-8822	883-9696
Beatty Machine & Mfg Company Inc 940 150th St *Web:* www.beattymachine.com	Hammond	IN	46327	219-931-3000	937-1662

				Phone	Fax
Bedco Inc 4600 Bree Rd *Web:* www.bedcoinc.com	East China	MI	48054	810-329-2292	329-4017
Bliss Clearing Niagara (BCN) 1004 E State St *TF:* 800-642-5477 ■ *Web:* www.bcntechserv.com	Hastings	MI	49058	269-948-3300	948-3313
Bradbury Company Inc 1200 E Cole *TF:* 800-397-6394 ■ *Web:* bradburygroup.com	Moundridge	KS	67107	620-345-6394	345-6381
Bruderer Inc 1200 Hendricks Cswy *Web:* www.bruderer.com	Ridgefield	NJ	07657	201-941-2121	886-2010
CA Lawton Company Inc 1950 Enterprise Way *Web:* www.calawton.com	De Pere	WI	54115	920-337-2470	337-2477
Cincinnati Inc 7420 Kilby Rd *Web:* www.e-ci.com	Harrison	OH	45030	513-367-7100	367-7552
Cyril Bath Co 1610 Airport Rd *TF:* 800-801-1418 ■ *Web:* www.cyrilbath.com	Monroe	NC	28110	704-289-8531	289-3932
DR Sperry & Co 623 Rathbone Ave *TF:* 888-997-9297 ■ *Web:* www.drsperry.com	Aurora	IL	60506	630-892-4361	892-1664
Edwards Manufacturing Co 1107 Sykes St PO Box 166 *TF:* 800-373-8206 ■ *Web:* www.edwardsironworkers.com	Albert Lea	MN	56007	507-373-8206	373-9433
Eitel Presses Inc 97 Pinedale Industrial Rd *Web:* www.eitelpresses.com	Orwigsburg	PA	17961	570-366-0585	366-2536
Emery Corp PO Box 1104 *Web:* www.emerycorp.com	Morganton	NC	28680	828-433-1536	433-6809
Erie Press Systems 1253 W 12th St PO Box 4061 *TF:* 800-222-3608 ■ *Web:* www.eriepress.com	Erie	PA	16512	814-455-3941	456-4819
FH Peterson Machine Corp 143 S St *Web:* www.fhpetersonmachine.com	Stoughton	MA	02072	781-341-4930	341-6022
GEMCOR Corp 100 Gemcor Dr *Web:* www.gemcor.com	West Seneca	NY	14224	716-674-9300	674-3171
General Broach Company Spline Rolling Div 307 Salisbury St *Web:* www.generalbroach.com	Morenci	MI	49256	517-458-7555	458-6821
Grant Assembly Technologies 90 Silliman Ave *TF:* 800-227-2150 ■ *Web:* www.grantriveters.com	Bridgeport	CT	06605	203-366-4557	366-0370
Greenerd Press & Machine Company Inc 41 Crown St *TF:* 800-877-9110 ■ *Web:* www.greenerd.com	Nashua	NH	03060	603-889-4101	889-7601
Heim LP 6360 W 73rd St *Web:* www.theheimgroup.com	Chicago	IL	60638	708-496-7450	496-7428
Hudson Machinery Worldwide 32 Stevens St	Haverhill	MA	01830	978-373-7295	
Kinefac Corp 156 Goddard Memorial Dr *Web:* www.kinefac.com	Worcester	MA	01603	508-754-6891	756-5342
Lockformer Co 5480 Sixth St SW **Fax Area Code:* 319 ■ *Web:* mestekmachinery.com/	Cedar Rapids	IA	52404	630-964-8000	364-3436*
Manor Industries Inc 24400 Maplehurst *TF:* 800-921-1007 ■ *Web:* www.precisionboring.com	Clinton Township	MI	48036	586-463-4604	463-3905
Mate Precision Tooling Inc 1295 Lund Blvd *TF:* 800-328-4492 ■ *Web:* www.matept.com	Anoka	MN	55303	763-421-0230	421-0285
Mega Manufacturing Inc PO Box 457 *Web:* www.megafab.com	Hutchinson	KS	67504	620-663-1127	664-9658
Minster Machine Co 240 W Fifth St PO Box 120 *Web:* www.minster.com	Minster	OH	45865	419-628-2331	628-3517
Murata Machinery USA Inc 2120 Queen City Dr **Fax Area Code:* 704 ■ *TF:* 800-428-8469 ■ *Web:* www.muratec-usa.com	Charlotte	NC	28208	800-428-8469	392-6541*
National Machinery LLC 161 Greenfield St *Web:* www.nationalmachinery.com	Tiffin	OH	44883	419-447-5211	443-2379
NFM Welding Engineers 577 Oberlin Rd SW *Web:* www.nfm.net	Massillon	OH	44647	330-837-3868	837-2230
Oak Products Inc 504 Wade St *Web:* www.oakpresses.com	Sturgis	MI	49091	269-651-8513	651-8513
Pacific Press Technologies 714 Walnut St *TF:* 800-851-3586 ■ *Web:* www.pacific-press.com	Mount Carmel	IL	62863	618-262-8666	262-7000
Pacific Roller Die Co 1321 W Winton Ave *Web:* www.prdcompany.com	Hayward	CA	94545	510-782-7242	887-5639
Presses Inc 6360 W 73rd St *TF:* 800-927-9393 ■ *Web:* www.theheimgroup.com	Chicago	IL	60638	708-496-7400	496-7428
QPI Multipress Inc 2222 S Third St *Web:* www.multipress.com	Columbus	OH	43207	614-228-0185	228-2358
Reed 28 Sword St *TF:* 800-343-6068 ■ *Web:* ptgtools.com/	Auburn	MA	01501	508-753-6530	753-0127
Reno Machine Company Inc 170 Pane Rd *Web:* www.reno-machine.com	Newington	CT	06111	860-666-5641	667-4496
Rimrock Corp 1700 Jetway Blvd *Web:* www.rimrockcorp.com	Columbus	OH	43219	614-471-5926	471-7388
Roper Whitney of Rockford Inc 2833 Huffman Blvd **Fax:* Sales ■ *Web:* www.roperwhitney.com	Rockford	IL	61103	815-962-3011	962-2227*
Schleuniger Inc 87 Colin Dr *TF Tech Supp:* 877-902-1470 ■ *Web:* www.schleuniger.com	Manchester	NH	03103	603-668-8117	668-8119
Strippit Inc/LVD 12975 Clarence Ctr Rd *TF:* 800-828-1527 ■ *Web:* www.lvdgroup.com	Akron	NY	14001	716-542-4511	542-5957
Tetrahedron Assoc Inc PO Box 710157 *TF:* 800-958-3872 ■ *Web:* www.tetrahedronassociates.com	San Diego	CA	92171	619-661-0552	661-0559
Tools for Bending Inc 194 W Dakota Ave *TF Cust Svc:* 800-873-3305 ■ *Web:* www.toolsforbending.com	Denver	CO	80223	303-777-7170	777-4749
Vamco International 555 Epsilon Dr *Web:* www.vamcointernational.com	Pittsburgh	PA	15238	412-963-7100	963-7160
WA Whitney Co 650 Race St PO Box 1206 *Web:* www.megafab.com	Rockford	IL	61105	815-964-6771	964-3175
Wabash MPI 1569 Morris St PO Box 298 *Web:* www.wabashmpi.com	Wabash	IN	46992	260-563-1184	563-1396
Williams White & Co 600 River Dr **Fax Area Code:* 309 ■ *TF:* 877-797-7650 ■ *Web:* www.williamswhite.com	Moline	IL	61265	877-797-7650	797-7677*
Wysong Inc 4820 US 29 N *TF:* 800-299-7664 ■ *Web:* www.wysongpartsandservice.com	Greensboro	NC	27405	336-621-3960	621-8360

460 MAGAZINES & JOURNALS

SEE ALSO Periodicals Publishers p. 2991

460-1 Agriculture & Farming Magazines

				Phone	Fax
Alfa Corp 2108 E S Blvd *Web:* www.alfainsurance.com	Montgomery	AL	36116	334-288-0375	288-0905
American Agriculturist 5227-B Baltimore Pike *TF:* 800-441-1410 ■ *Web:* farmprogress.com	Littlestown	PA	17340	717-359-0150	359-0250
Beef Magazine 7900 International Dr Ste 300 *TF Cust Svc:* 800-722-5334 ■ *Web:* beefmagazine.com	Minneapolis	MN	55425	952-851-9329	851-4601
Dairy Herd Management 10901 W 84th Terr *TF:* 800-255-5113 ■ *Web:* www.dairyherd.com	Lenexa	KS	66214	913-438-8700	438-0695
Farm Bureau Press 10720 Kanis Rd *Web:* www.arfb.com	Little Rock	AR	72211	501-228-1300	
Farm Industry News 7900 International Dr Ste 300 *TF Cust Svc:* 800-722-5334 ■ *Web:* www.farmindustrynews.com	Minneapolis	MN	55425	952-851-9329	851-4601
Farm Journal 261 E Broadway PO Box 1167	Monticello	MN	55362	763-271-3363	271-3360
Farm Show Magazine 20088 Kenwood Trial **Fax Area Code:* 952 ■ *TF:* 800-834-9665 ■ *Web:* www.farmshow.com	Lakeville	MN	55044	800-834-9665	469-5575*
Floridagriculture Magazine PO Box 147030 *Web:* www.floridagriculture.org	Gainesville	FL	32614	352-378-1321	374-1530
Georgia Farm Bureau News 1620 Bass Rd *TF:* 800-342-1192 ■ *Web:* www.gfb.org	Macon	GA	31210	478-474-8411	474-8750
Hoard's Dairyman Magazine 28 Milwaukee Ave W PO Box 801 *TF:* 800-245-8222 ■ *Web:* www.hoards.com	Fort Atkinson	WI	53538	920-563-5551	563-7298
Iowa Farm Bureau Spokesman Magazine 5400 University Ave *TF:* 866-598-3693 ■ *Web:* iowafarmbureau.com	West Des Moines	IA	50266	515-225-5413	225-5419
Kansas Living Magazine 2627 KFB Plz *TF:* 800-406-3053 ■ *Web:* www.kfb.org	Manhattan	KS	66503	785-587-6000	587-6914
Neighbors Magazine 1324 Chippenham Dr **Fax Area Code:* 334 ■ *Web:* www.neighborsmag.com/contactus	Baton Rouge	LA	70808	225-767-8549	284-3957*
Pork Report 1776 NW 114th St PO Box 9114 *TF:* 800-456-7675 ■ *Web:* www.pork.org	Des Moines	IA	50325	515-223-2600	223-2646
Soybean Digest 7900 International Dr Ste 300 *TF Cust Svc:* 800-722-5334 ■ *Web:* www.cornandsoybeandigest.com	Minneapolis	MN	55425	952-851-4667	851-4601
Tennessee Farm Bureau News 147 Bear Creek Pike *TF:* 877-876-2222 ■ *Web:* www.tnfarmbureau.org	Columbia	TN	38401	931-388-7872	388-5818
Texas Agriculture Magazine 7420 Fish Pond Rd PO Box 2689 *TF:* 800-772-6535 ■ *Web:* www.texasfarmbureau.org	Waco	TX	76710	254-772-3030	772-1766
Texas Farm Bureau 7420 Fish Pond Rd PO Box 2689 *TF:* 800-488-7872 ■ *Web:* www.texasfarmbureau.org	Waco	TX	76710	254-772-3030	772-1766
Top Producer Magazine 1818 Market St 31st Fl *TF:* 800-320-7992 ■ *Web:* www.agweb.com	Philadelphia	PA	19103	800-320-7992	

460-2 Art & Architecture Magazines

				Phone	Fax
AmericanStyle Magazine 3000 Chestnut Ave Ste 304 *Web:* www.americanstyle.com	Baltimore	MD	21211	410-889-3093	243-7089
Architectural Digest Four Times Sq 18th Fl *TF:* 800-365-8032 ■ *Web:* www.architecturaldigest.com	New York	NY	10036	800-365-8032	
Architectural Record Magazine 2 Penn Plaza 9th Fl *TF:* 800-393-6343 ■ *Web:* archrecord.construction.com	New York	NY	10121	212-904-2594	904-4256
Art Calendar 1500 Pk Ctr Dr *Web:* www.professionalartistmag.com	Orlando	FL	32835	407-563-7000	563-7099
Art in America Magazine 575 Broadway **Fax:* Cust Svc ■ *TF Cust Svc:* 800-925-8059 ■ *Web:* www.artinamericamagazine.com	New York	NY	10012	212-941-2800	941-2870*
Artforum International Magazine 350 Seventh Ave 19th Fl *TF:* 800-966-2783 ■ *Web:* www.artforum.com	New York	NY	10001	212-475-4000	529-1257
Artist's Magazine, The 4700 E Galbraith Rd *TF:* 800-422-2550 ■ *Web:* www.artistsnetwork.com	Cincinnati	OH	45236	513-531-2222	891-7153
ARTnews Magazine 48 W 38th St Ninth Fl *TF:* 800-284-4625 ■ *Web:* artnews.com	New York	NY	10018	212-398-1690	819-0394
Bomb Magazine 80 Hanson Pl Ste 703 *Web:* www.bombsite.com	Brooklyn	NY	11217	718-636-9100	636-9200
Design Journal 23371 Mulholland Dr STE 253 *Web:* www.designjournalmag.com	Woodland Hills	CA	91364	310-394-4394	394-0966
Design/Build Business Magazine 3030 Salt Creek Ln Ste 200 *TF:* 800-547-7377 ■ *Web:* www.forresidentialpros.com	Arlington Heights	IL	60005	847-454-2714	454-2759
HOW Design Magazine 4700 E Galbraith Rd *TF Cust Svc:* 800-333-1115 ■ *Web:* www.howdesign.com	Cincinnati	OH	45236	513-531-2690	891-7153
Inland Architect Magazine 3500 W Peterson Ave Ste 103 *Web:* www.inlandarchitectmag.com	Chicago	IL	60659	773-866-9900	866-9881
Landscape Architecture Magazine 636 'I' St NW *Web:* www.asla.org/nonmembers/lam.cfm	Washington	DC	20001	202-898-2444	898-1185
Metropolis Magazine 61 W 23rd St Fourth Fl *TF:* 800-344-3046 ■ *Web:* www.metropolismag.com	New York	NY	10010	212-627-9977	627-9988
Modernism Magazine 199 George St *Web:* ragoarts.com	Lambertville	NJ	08530	609-397-4104	397-4409

Phone Fax

Pastel Journal 4700 E Galbraith Rd . . . . Cincinnati OH 45236 513-531-2222 891-7153
TF: 800-422-2550 ■ *Web:* www.artistsnetwork.com

Southwest Art Magazine
10901 W 120th Ave Ste 350 . . . . Broomfield CO 80021 303-442-0427 449-0279
TF: 877-212-1938 ■ *Web:* www.southwestart.com

Studio Photography & Design Magazine
1233 Janesville Ave . . . . Fort Atkinson WI 53538 631-963-6200 547-7377*
**Fax Area Code:* 800 ■ *Web:* www.imaginginfo.com

Sunshine Artist Magazine
4075 LB McLeod Rd Ste E . . . . Orlando FL 32811 407-648-7479 648-7454
TF: 800-597-2573 ■ *Web:* www.sunshineartist.com

460-3 Automotive Magazines

Phone Fax

American Iron Magazine 1010 Summer St . . . . Stamford CT 06905 203-425-8777
TF Cust Svc: 877-693-3572 ■ *Web:* www.aimag.com

Automobile Magazine 120 E Liberty St . . . . Ann Arbor MI 48104 310-531-9900 994-1153*
**Fax Area Code:* 734 ■ *Web:* www.automobilemag.com

AutoWeek Magazine 1155 Gratiot Ave . . . . Detroit MI 48207 313-446-6000 446-0347
TF Circ: 888-288-6954 ■ *Web:* www.autoweek.com

Backroads Magazine 160 Co Rd 521 . . . . Newton NJ 07860 973-948-4176 948-0823
Web: www.backroadsusa.com

Car Craft Magazine 6420 Wilshire Blvd . . . . Los Angeles CA 90048 323-782-2000 782-2263
TF: 800-230-3030 ■ *Web:* www.carcraft.com

Cycle World Magazine 1499 Monrovia Ave . . . . Newport Beach CA 92663 949-720-5300 631-0651
TF: 800-456-3084 ■ *Web:* www.cycleworld.com

Easyriders Magazine 28210 Dorothy Dr . . . . Agoura Hills CA 91301 818-889-8740
Web: www.paisanopub.com

Friction Zone Magazine
60166 Hop Patch Spring Rd . . . . Mountain Center CA 92561 951-659-9500 659-8182
Web: www.friction-zone.com

Grassroots Motorsports Magazine
915 Ridgewood Ave . . . . Holly Hill FL 32117 386-239-0523 239-0573
TF: 800-520-8292 ■ *Web:* www.grassrootsmotorsports.com

Hemmings Motor News 222 Main St . . . . Bennington VT 05201 802-442-3101 447-9631
TF: 800-227-4373 ■ *Web:* www.hemmings.com

Hot Rod Magazine 6420 Wilshire Blvd . . . . Los Angeles CA 90048 323-782-2000 782-2223
TF Orders: 800-800-4681 ■ *Web:* www.hotrod.com

Hot Rod Network 774 S Placentia Ave . . . . Placentia CA 92870 800-926-8207
TF: 800-926-8207 ■ *Web:* www.popularhotrodding.com

Lowrider Magazine 2400 E Katella Ave 11th Fl . . . . Anaheim CA 92806 714-939-2400 978-6390
Web: www.lowridermagazine.com

Motor Trend Magazine
6420 Wilshire Blvd Seventh Fl . . . . Los Angeles CA 90048 323-782-2000 782-2355
TF: 800-800-6848 ■ *Web:* www.motortrend.com

Motorcycle Consumer News Magazine
Three Burroughs . . . . Irvine CA 92618 949-855-8822 855-0654
TF: 888-333-0354 ■ *Web:* www.mcnews.com/mcnews

National Speed Sport News Magazine
142 F S Cardigan Way . . . . Mooresville NC 28117 704-489-5231
TF: 866-455-2531 ■ *Web:* www.nationalspeedsportnews.com

Off-Road Magazine 2400 E Katella Ave Ste 1100 . . . . Anaheim CA 92806 714-848-8880 978-6390
TF: 877-462-6752 ■ *Web:* www.fourwheeler.com

Road & Track Magazine
1499 Monrovia Ave . . . . Newport Beach CA 92663 949-720-5300 280-3971*
**Fax Area Code:* 646 ■ *TF:* 800-835-6422 ■ *Web:* www.roadandtrack.com

Sports Car Magazine
16842 Von Karman Ave Ste 125 . . . . Irvine CA 92606 949-417-6700 417-6116
TF: 800-722-7140 ■ *Web:* sportscarmag-digital.com

Stock Car Racing Magazine PO Box 420235 . . . . Palm Coast FL 32142 800-333-2633
TF: 800-333-2633 ■ *Web:* www.stockcarracing.com

Street & Smith's Sports Group Inc
120 W Morehead St Ste 320 . . . . Charlotte NC 28202 704-973-1300

460-4 Boating Magazines

Phone Fax

48 Degrees North 6327 Seaview Ave NW . . . . Seattle WA 98107 206-789-7350 789-6392
Web: www.48north.com

Blue Water Sailing Magazine
747 Aquidneck Ave Ste 201 Ste 201 . . . . Middletown RI 02842 401-847-7612 845-8580
TF: 888-800-7245 ■ *Web:* www.bwsailing.com

Boating Life Magazine
460 N Orlando Ave Ste 200 . . . . Winter Park FL 32789 407-571-4682 628-7061
Web: www.boatingmag.com

Boating Magazine 1633 Broadway . . . . New York NY 10019 212-767-4818 767-4831
Web: www.boatingmag.com

Cruising World Magazine
55 Hammerlund Way Ste A . . . . Middletown RI 02842 401-845-5100 845-5180
Web: www.cruisingworld.com

Duncan Mcintosh 17782 Cowan St Ste C . . . . Irvine CA 92614 949-660-6150 660-6172
Web: duncanmcintoshco.com

Good Old Boat Magazine 1501 Eigth Ave NW . . . . Jamestown ND 58401 701-952-9433 952-9434
Web: www.goodoldboat.com

PassageMaker Magazine
105 Eastern Ave Ste 203 . . . . Annapolis MD 21403 410-990-9086 990-9095
Web: www.passagemaker.com

Power & Motoryacht Magazine
260 Madison Ave Fourth Fl . . . . New York NY 10016 860-767-3200
TF: 800-284-8036 ■ *Web:* www.powerandmotoryacht.com

SAIL Magazine 98 N Washington St Ste 107 . . . . Boston MA 02114 617-720-8600 723-0911
TF: 877-388-7761 ■ *Web:* www.sailmagazine.com

Sailing World Magazine 55 Hammarlund Way . . . . Middletown RI 02842 401-845-5100 845-5180
TF Cust Svc: 866-436-2460 ■ *Web:* www.sailingworld.com

Sea Magazine 17782 Cowan St Ste C . . . . Irvine CA 92614 949-660-6150 660-6172
TF: 800-873-7327 ■ *Web:* www.seamagazine.com

Yachting Magazine 55 Hammarlund Way . . . . Middletown RI 02842 800-999-0869 845-5180*
**Fax Area Code:* 401 ■ *TF:* 800-999-0869 ■ *Web:* www.yachtingmagazine.com

Phone Fax

460-5 Business & Finance Magazines

Phone Fax

Advisor Today 2901 Telestar Ct . . . . Falls Church VA 22042 800-247-4074 770-8212*
**Fax Area Code:* 703 ■ *TF:* 800-247-4074 ■ *Web:* www.advisortoday.com

Alaska Business Monthly
501 W Northern Lights Blvd Ste 100 . . . . Anchorage AK 99503 907-276-4373 279-2900
TF: 800-770-4373 ■ *Web:* www.akbizmag.com

American Banker Magazine
one State St Plaza 27th Fl . . . . New York NY 10004 212-803-8200 843-9600
TF: 800-221-1809 ■ *Web:* www.americanbanker.com

American Journalism Review
University of Maryland
1117 Journalism Bldg
1117 Journalism Bldg Rm 2116 . . . . College Park MD 20742 301-405-8803 405-8323
TF: 800-827-0771 ■ *Web:* www.ajr.org

Appraisal Journal 200 W Madison Ste 1500 . . . . Chicago IL 60606 888-756-4624 335-4400*
**Fax Area Code:* 312 ■ *TF:* 888-756-4624 ■ *Web:* www.appraisalinstitute.org

Area Development Magazine
400 Post Ave Ste 304 . . . . Westbury NY 11590 516-338-0900 338-0100
TF: 800-735-2732 ■ *Web:* www.areadevelopment.com

Arkansas Business LP 122 E Second St . . . . Little Rock AR 72201 501-372-1443 375-7933
TF: 888-322-6397 ■ *Web:* www.arkansasbusiness.com

Association Management Magazine
1575 'I' St NW . . . . Washington DC 20005 202-371-0940 371-8825
Web: www.asaecenter.org

Atlanta Business Chronicle
3423 Piedmont Rd Ste 400 . . . . Atlanta GA 30305 404-249-1000 249-1048
Web: www.bizjournals.com

Austin Business Journal
111 Congress Ave Ste 750 . . . . Austin TX 78701 512-494-2500 494-2525*
**Fax:* Edit ■ *Web:* www.bizjournals.com

Baltimore Business Journal
111 Market Pl Ste 720 . . . . Baltimore MD 21202 410-576-1161 752-3112
Web: www.bizjournals.com

Banking Strategies Magazine
115 S LaSalle St Ste 3300 . . . . Chicago IL 60603 312-553-4600 683-2415
TF: 888-224-0037 ■ *Web:* www.bai.org/bankingstrategies/about.asp

Baton Rouge Business Report
445 N Blvd Ste 210 . . . . Baton Rouge LA 70802 225-928-1700 926-1329
Web: www.businessreport.com

Best's Review Ambest Rd . . . . Oldwick NJ 08858 908-439-2200 439-3363
Web: www.ambest.com/review

Birmingham Business Journal
2140 11th Ave S Ste 205 . . . . Birmingham AL 35205 205-322-0000 322-0040
Web: www.bizjournals.com

BizWest 3180 Sterling Cir Ste 201 . . . . Boulder CO 80301 303-440-4950 440-8954
Web: www.bcbr.com

Black Enterprise Magazine 130 Fifth Ave . . . . New York NY 10011 212-242-8000 886-9610
TF Cust Svc: 800-727-7777 ■ *Web:* www.blackenterprise.com

Boston Business Journal 160 Federal St 12th Fl . . . . Boston MA 02110 617-330-1000 330-1016
Web: www.bizjournals.com

Brandweek Magazine 770 Broadway Seventh Fl . . . . New York NY 10003 646-654-5000 654-5375
Web: www.adweek.com

British Standards Institution, The
12110 Sunset Hills Rd Ste 200 . . . . Reston VA 20190 703-437-9000 437-9001
TF: 800-862-4977 ■ *Web:* www.bsigroup.com

Business Facilities Magazine
44 Apple St Ste 3 . . . . Tinton Falls NJ 07724 732-842-7433 758-6634
TF: 800-524-0337 ■ *Web:* www.businessfacilities.com

Business First 465 Main St . . . . Buffalo NY 14203 716-854-5822 854-3394
Web: www.bizjournals.com

Business Insurance Magazine 711 Third Ave . . . . New York NY 10017 212-210-0100 280-3174*
**Fax Area Code:* 312 ■ *TF:* 877-812-1587 ■ *Web:* www.businessinsurance.com

Business Journal of Milwaukee
825 N Jefferson St Ste 200 . . . . Milwaukee WI 53202 414-278-7788 278-7028
Web: www.bizjournals.com/milwaukee

Business Journal of Phoenix
101 N First Ave Ste 2300 . . . . Phoenix AZ 85003 602-230-8400 230-0955
Web: www.bizjournals.com

Business Journal of Portland
851 SW Sixth Ave Ste 500 . . . . Portland OR 97204 503-274-8733 219-3450
Web: www.bizjournals.com

Business Journal of San Jose
96 N Third St Ste 100 . . . . San Jose CA 95112 408-295-3800 295-5028
Web: www.bizjournals.com

Business Journal of Tampa Bay
4890 W Kennedy Blvd Ste 850 . . . . Tampa FL 33609 813-873-8225 876-1827
Web: www.bizjournals.com/tampabay

Business Journal, The 25 E Boardman St . . . . Youngstown OH 44501 330-744-5023 744-5838
TF: 800-837-6397 ■ *Web:* businessjournaldaily.com

California Real Estate Magazine
525 S Virgil Ave . . . . Los Angeles CA 90020 213-739-8200 480-7724
TF: 888-811-5281 ■ *Web:* www.car.org

Central New York Business Journal, The
269 W Jefferson St . . . . Syracuse NY 13202 315-579-3919 641-3601
TF: 800-836-3539 ■ *Web:* www.cnybj.com

CFO Magazine 253 Summer St . . . . Boston MA 02210 617-345-9700 951-4090
TF: 800-772-1119 ■ *Web:* www2.cfo.com

Charlotte Business Journal
1100 S Tryon St Ste 100 . . . . Charlotte NC 28203 704-973-1100 973-1101*
**Fax:* Edit ■ *Web:* www.bizjournals.com

Chief Executive Magazine
One Sound Shore Dr Ste 100 . . . . Greenwich CT 06830 203-930-2700 930-2701
Web: www.chiefexecutive.net

Cincinnati Business Courier
101 W Seventh St . . . . Cincinnati OH 45202 513-621-6665 621-2462
Web: www.bizjournals.com

CIO Magazine
492 Old Connecticut Path PO Box 9208 . . . . Framingham MA 01701 508-872-0080 879-7784
Web: www.cio.com

Entry	Phone	Fax
Columbus Business First 303 W Nationwide Blvd, Columbus OH 43215 *TF:* 800-486-3289 ■ *Web:* www.bizjournals.com	614-461-4040	365-2980
Communications News PO Box 866, Osprey FL 34229 *TF:* 800-827-9715 ■ *Web:* www.comnews.com	941-539-7579	966-2590
Contract Design Magazine 770 Broadway, New York NY 10004 **Fax Area Code:* 646 ■ *TF:* 800-697-8859 ■ *Web:* www.contractdesign.com	800-697-8859	654-7205*
Crain's Chicago Business Magazine 150 N Michigan Ave 16th Fl, Chicago IL 60601 *TF:* 877-812-1590 ■ *Web:* www.chicagobusiness.com	312-649-5200	280-3150
Crain's Cleveland Business Magazine 700 W St Clair Ave Ste 310, Cleveland OH 44113 *TF:* 888-909-9111 ■ *Web:* www.crainscleveland.com	216-522-1383	694-4264
Crain's Detroit Business Magazine 1155 Gratiot Ave, Detroit MI 48207 *TF:* 888-909-9111 ■ *Web:* www.crainsdetroit.com	313-446-6000	446-1687
Crain's New York Business Magazine 685 Third Ave 3rd Fl, New York NY 10017 **Fax:* Edit ■ *TF:* 888-909-9111 ■ *Web:* www.crainsnewyork.com	212-210-0100	210-0799*
Denver Business Journal 1700 Broadway Ste 515, Denver CO 80290 *Web:* www.bizjournals.com/denver	303-837-3500	837-3535
Des Moines Business Record 100 Fourth St, Des Moines IA 50309 *Web:* www.businessrecord.com	515-288-3336	288-0309
Drug Topics Magazine 24950 Country Club Blvd Ste 200, North Olmsted OH 44070 *TF Cust Svc:* 877-922-2022 ■ *Web:* drugtopics.modernmedicine.com	440-891-2792	891-2735
E-Commerce Times (ECT) 16133 Ventura Blvd Ste 700, Encino CA 91436 *TF:* 877-328-5500 ■ *Web:* www.ectnews.com	818-461-9700	461-9710
Editor & Publisher Magazine 17782 Cowan Ste C, Irvine CA 92614 *TF:* 855-896-7433 ■ *Web:* www.editorandpublisher.com	949-660-6150	660-6172
Employee Benefit News 1325 G St NW Ste 900, Washington DC 20005 *TF:* 800-221-1809 ■ *Web:* ebn.benefitnews.com	202-504-1122	772-1448
Enterprise Magazine 825 North 300 West Ste C309, Salt Lake City UT 84103 *Web:* www.slenterprise.com	801-533-0556	533-0684
Entrepreneur Magazine 2445 McCabe Way Ste 400, Irvine CA 92614 *TF:* 800-274-6229 ■ *Web:* www.entrepreneur.com	949-261-2325	261-7729
Expansion Management Magazine 1300 E Ninth St, Cleveland OH 44114 *TF:* 866-505-7173 ■ *Web:* www.industryweek.com	216-696-7000	
Fast Company Magazine Seven World Trade Ctr, New York NY 10007 *TF:* 800-542-6029 ■ *Web:* www.fastcompany.com	212-389-5300	389-5496
Finance & Commerce 730 Second Ave S US Trust Bldg Ste 100, Minneapolis MN 55402 *TF:* 800-451-9998 ■ *Web:* www.finance-commerce.com	612-333-4244	333-3243
Fleet Owner Magazine 11 Riverbend Dr S PO Box 4211, Stamford CT 06907 *TF:* 800-776-1246 ■ *Web:* www.fleetowner.com	203-358-4205	358-5819
Forbes Magazine 60 Fifth Ave, New York NY 10011 *TF:* 800-295-0893 ■ *Web:* www.forbes.com	212-366-8900	
Fortune Small Business Magazine (FSB) 1271 Ave of the Americas Fourth Fl, New York NY 10020 *Web:* www.money.cnn.com/magazines/fsb	212-522-1212	
Franchising World Magazine 1501 K St NW Ste 350, Washington DC 20005 *TF:* 800-543-1038 ■ *Web:* www.franchise.org	202-628-8000	628-0812
Futures Magazine 222 S Riverside Plz Ste 620, Chicago IL 60606 *Web:* www.futuresmag.com	312-846-4600	846-4638
Global Finance Magazine E 20th St, New York NY 10003 *Web:* www.gfmag.com	212-447-7900	
Grand Rapids Business Journal (GRBJ) 549 Ottawa Ave NW Ste 201, Grand Rapids MI 49503 *Web:* grbj.com/	616-459-4545	459-4800
Greenville Business Magazine 303 Haywood Rd, Greenville SC 29607 *Web:* www.greenvillebusinessmag.com	864-271-1105	271-1165
Harvard Business Review 60 Harvard Way, Boston MA 02163 **Fax:* Cust Svc ■ *TF:* 800-274-3214 ■ *Web:* www.hbr.org	617-783-7500	783-7555*
Health Facilities Management Magazine 155 N Wacker Dr Ste 400, Chicago IL 60606 *TF:* 800-621-6902 ■ *Web:* www.hfmmagazine.com	312-893-6800	422-4500
Hospitals & Health Networks Magazine 155 N Wacker Ste 400, Chicago IL 60606 *TF:* 800-621-6902 ■ *Web:* www.hhnmag.com	312-893-6800	422-4500
Houston Business Journal 1233 W Loop S Ste 1300, Houston TX 77027 **Fax:* Edit ■ *Web:* www.bizjournals.com	713-688-8811	963-0482*
HRMagazine 1800 Duke St, Alexandria VA 22314 *TF:* 800-283-7476 ■ *Web:* www.shrm.org/hrmagazine	703-548-3440	836-0367
Human Resource Executive Magazine 747 Dresher Rd Ste 500, Horsham PA 19044 *TF:* 888-365-2763 ■ *Web:* www.hreonline.com	215-784-0910	784-0275
In Business Magazine 200 River Pl Ste 250, Madison WI 53716 *Web:* www.ibmadison.com	608-204-9655	204-9656
Inc Magazine 7 World Trade Ctr, New York NY 10007 *TF:* 800-234-0999 ■ *Web:* www.inc.com	212-389-5377	389-5379
Independent Agent Magazine 127 S Peyton St, Alexandria VA 22314 **Fax Area Code:* 866 ■ *Web:* www.iamagazine.com	800-221-7917	665-2756*
Indianapolis Business Journal 41 E Washington St Ste 200, Indianapolis IN 46204 **Fax:* Edit ■ *TF:* 800-428-7081 ■ *Web:* www.ibj.com	317-634-6200	263-5406*
Internal Auditor Magazine 247 Maitland Ave, Altamonte Springs FL 32701 *Web:* na.theiia.org	407-937-1100	937-1101
Journal of Accountancy 220 Leigh Farm Rd, Durham NC 27707 **Fax Area Code:* 919 ■ *TF:* 888-777-7077 ■ *Web:* www.journalofaccountancy.com	888-777-7077	419-5241*
Journal of Business 429 E Third Ave, Spokane WA 99202 *Web:* www.spokanejournal.com	509-456-5257	456-0624
Journal of Financial Planning Assn 7535 E Hampden Ave Ste 600, Denver CO 80231 *TF:* 800-322-4237 ■ *Web:* www.fpanet.org/journal	303-759-4900	759-0749
Journal of Housing & Community Development 630 'I' St NW, Washington DC 20001 *TF:* 877-866-2476 ■ *Web:* www.nahro.org	202-289-3500	289-8181
Journal of Property Management 430 N Michigan Ave, Chicago IL 60611 *TF:* 800-837-0706 ■ *Web:* irem.org/home/pagenotfound	800-837-0706	338-4736
Kansas City Business Journal 1100 Main St Ste 210, Kansas City MO 64105 *Web:* www.bizjournals.com	816-421-5900	472-4010
Law Enforcement Technology Magazine 1233 Janesville Ave, Fort Atkinson WI 53538 **Fax Area Code:* 920 ■ *TF:* 800-547-7377 ■ *Web:* www.officer.com	800-547-7377	563-1704*
Leadership Journal 465 Gundersen Dr, Carol Stream IL 60188 *TF:* 800-777-3136 ■ *Web:* christianitytoday.com/le/	630-260-6200	
Lodging Magazine 385 Oxford Vly Rd Ste 420, Yardley PA 19067 *TF:* 800-394-5157 ■ *Web:* www.lodgingmagazine.com	215-321-9662	321-5124
Los Angeles Business Journal 5700 Wilshire Blvd Ste 170, Los Angeles CA 90036 *Web:* www.labusinessjournal.com	323-549-5225	549-5255
Marketing News 311 S Wacker Dr Ste 5800, Chicago IL 60606 *TF:* 800-262-1150 ■ *Web:* www.ama.org	312-542-9000	922-3763
Meetings & Conventions Magazine 100 Lighting Way, Secaucus NJ 07094 *TF:* 877-705-8889 ■ *Web:* www.meetings-conventions.com	201-902-2000	902-1916
Memphis Business Journal 80 Monroe Ave Ste 600, Memphis TN 38103 *Web:* www.bizjournals.com	901-523-1000	526-5240
Mergers & Acquisitions Magazine One State St Plz, New York NY 10004 *TF Cust Svc:* 888-807-8667 ■ *Web:* www.themiddlemarket.com	212-803-6051	
Midlands Business Journal 1324 S 119th St, Omaha NE 68144 *Web:* www.mbj.com	402-330-1760	758-9315
Minneapolis-Saint Paul Business Journal 333 S Seventh St Ste 350, Minneapolis MN 55402 *Web:* www.bizjournals.com/twincities	612-288-2100	288-2121
Mississippi Business Journal 200 N Congress St, Jackson MS 39201 *TF:* 800-283-4625 ■ *Web:* www.msbusiness.com	601-364-1000	364-1007
Nashville Business Journal 1800 Church St Ste 300, Nashville TN 37203 *Web:* www.bizjournals.com	615-248-2222	248-6246
National Assn of Credit Management 8840 Columbia 100 Pkwy, Columbia MD 21045 *TF:* 800-955-8815 ■ *Web:* www.nacm.org	410-740-5560	740-5574
National Notary Magazine 9350 DeSoto Ave, Chatsworth CA 91311 *TF Cust Svc:* 800-876-6827 ■ *Web:* www.nationalnotary.org	818-739-4000	700-1942
National Real Estate Investor Magazine 6151 Powers Ferry Rd NW Ste 200, Atlanta GA 30339 *TF:* 877-829-2782 ■ *Web:* www.nreionline.com	770-955-2500	618-0348
New Accountant Magazine 3525 W Peterson Ave Ste 403, Chicago IL 60659 *Web:* www.newaccountantusa.com	773-866-9900	866-9881
New Jersey Business Magazine 310 Passaic Ave, Fairfield NJ 07004 *Web:* www.njbmagazine.com	973-882-5004	882-4648
New Orleans City Business 111 Veterans Memorial Blvd Ste 1440, Metairie LA 70005 *Web:* www.neworleanscitybusiness.com	504-834-9292	832-3550
Orange County Business Journal (OCBJ) 18500 Von Karman Ave Ste 150, Irvine CA 92612 *Web:* www.ocbj.com	949-833-8373	833-8751
Orlando Business Journal (OBJ) 255 S Orange Ave Ste 700, Orlando FL 32801 *Web:* www.bizjournals.com	407-649-8470	420-1625
Palm Beach Daily Business Review 324 Datura St Ste 140, West Palm Beach FL 33401 *TF:* 800-777-7300 ■ *Web:* www.dailybusinessreview.com	561-820-2060	820-2077
PCBE Inc PO Box 1575, Tacoma WA 98401 *TF:* 800-540-8322 ■ *Web:* www.businessexaminer.com	253-404-0891	404-0892
Pensions & Investments Magazine 711 Third Ave, New York NY 10017 **Fax Area Code:* 800 ■ *TF Cust Svc:* 888-446-1422 ■ *Web:* www.pionline.com	212-210-0100	545-3123*
Pharmaceutical Representative Magazine 641 Lexington Ave Eighth Fl, New York NY 10022 *Web:* www.pharmexec.com	212-951-6600	951-6604
Philadelphia Business Journal 400 Market St Ste 1200, Philadelphia PA 19106 *Web:* www.bizjournals.com/philadelphia	215-238-1450	238-9489
Pittsburgh Business Times 424 S 27th St Ste 211, Pittsburgh PA 15203 *Web:* www.bizjournals.com/pittsburgh	412-481-6397	481-9956
Print Magazine 10151 Carver Rd Ste 200, Blue Ash OH 45242 **Fax Area Code:* 212 ■ *TF:* 877-860-9145 ■ *Web:* www.printmag.com	513-531-2690	447-5231*
Providence Business News 220 W Exchange St Ste 210, Providence RI 02903 **Fax:* Hum Res ■ *Web:* www.pbn.com	401-273-2201	274-6580*
Purchasing Magazine 225 Wyman St, Waltham MA 02451 *TF:* 888-393-5000 ■ *Web:* www.buyerzone.com	888-393-5000	
Realtor Magazine 430 N Michigan Ave Ninth Fl, Chicago IL 60611 *TF:* 800-874-6500 ■ *Web:* www.realtor.org/rmodaily.nsf	312-329-8458	329-5978
Registered Representative Magazine 1166 Ave of the Americas 10th Fl, New York NY 10036 *Web:* www.penton.com	212-204-4200	
Rochester Business Journal 45 E Ave Ste 500, Rochester NY 14604 *Web:* www.rbj.net	585-546-8303	546-3398
Rough Notes Company Inc, The 11690 Technology Dr, Carmel IN 46032 *TF:* 800-428-4384 ■ *Web:* www.roughnotes.com	317-582-1600	816-1000
Sacramento Business Journal 1400 X St, Sacramento CA 95818 *Web:* www.bizjournals.com/sacramento	916-447-7661	444-7779
Sales & Marketing Management Magazine 27020 Noble Rd, Excelsior MN 55331 **Fax Area Code:* 952 ■ *Web:* www.salesandmarketing.com	510-772-7829	401-7899*

Phone Fax

San Antonio Business Journal
8200 IH 10 W Ste 820 .... San Antonio TX 78230 210-341-3202 341-3031
Web: www.bizjournals.com/sanantonio

San Diego Business Journal
4909 Murphy Canyon Rd Ste 200 .... San Diego CA 92123 858-277-6359 277-6398
TF: 888-425-7325 ■ *Web:* www.sdbj.com

Self-Employed America Magazine
PO Box 241 .... Annapolis Junction MD 20701 800-649-6273
TF: 800-649-6273 ■ *Web:* www.nase.org

Selling Power Magazine
1140 International Pkwy .... Fredericksburg VA 22406 540-752-7000 752-7001
TF: 800-752-7355 ■ *Web:* www.sellingpower.com

Signal Magazine 4400 Fair Lakes Ct .... Fairfax VA 22033 703-631-6100 631-6188
TF: 800-336-4583 ■ *Web:* www.afcea.org/signal

Sloan Management Review
77 Massachusetts Ave E60-100 .... Cambridge MA 02139 617-253-7170 258-9739
TF: 800-876-5764 ■ *Web:* www.sloanreview.mit.edu

Small Business Opportunities Magazine
1115 Broadway Eighth Fl .... New York NY 10010 212-807-7100 924-8416
Web: www.sbomag.com

South Florida Business Journal
6400 N Andrews Ave Ste 200 .... Fort Lauderdale FL 33309 954-949-7600 949-7591
Web: www.bizjournals.com

Springfield Business Journal
313 Pk Central W .... Springfield MO 65806 417-831-3238 831-5478
Web: www.sbj.net

Staffdigest Magazine PO Box 384 Ste H3 .... Alief TX 77411 281-498-2913 447-3168*
**Fax Area Code:* 866 ■ *TF General:* 800-444-0674 ■ *Web:* www.staffdigest.com

Strategic Finance Magazine
10 Paragon Dr Ste 1 .... Montvale NJ 07645 201-573-9000 474-1603
TF: 800-638-4427 ■ *Web:* imanet.org

Successful Meetings Magazine
100 Lighting Way .... Secaucus NJ 07094 201-902-2000
Web: www.successfulmeetings.com

Toledo Business Journal
5301 Southwyck Blvd Ste 104 .... Toledo OH 43614 419-865-0972 865-2429
Web: www.toledobiz.com

Training & Development Magazine
1640 King St. .... Alexandria VA 22313 703-683-8100 683-8103
TF: 800-628-2783 ■ *Web:* astd.org/publications/magazines/td

Training Magazine 27020 Noble Rd .... Excelsior MN 55331 847-559-7596
Web: www.trainingmag.com

Tri Cities Business Journal
1114 Sunset Dr Ste 2 .... Johnson City TN 37604 423-854-0140 929-3430
Web: www.bjournal.com

Triangle Business Journal
3600 Glenwood Ave Ste 100 .... Raleigh NC 27612 919-878-0010 954-4898
Web: www.bizjournals.com

Utah Business Magazine
90 S 400 W Ste 650 .... Salt Lake City UT 84101 801-568-0114
TF: 866-294-1660 ■ *Web:* www.utahbusiness.com

Vancouver Business Journal
1251 Officers Row .... Vancouver WA 98661 360-695-2442 695-3056
Web: www.vbjusa.com

Virginia Business Magazine
333 E Franklin St .... Richmond VA 23219 804-649-6999 649-6311
Web: www.virginiabusiness.com

Washington Business Journal
1555 Wilson Blvd Ste 400 .... Arlington VA 22209 703-258-0800 258-0802
Web: www.bizjournals.com

Wichita Business Journal
121 N Mead St Ste 100 .... Wichita KS 67202 316-267-6406 267-8570
Web: www.bizjournals.com

Your Church Magazine 465 Gundersen Dr .... Carol Stream IL 60188 630-260-6200 260-0114
TF: 877-247-4787 ■ *Web:* www.christianitytoday.com

460-6 Children's & Youth Magazines

Phone Fax

AppleSeeds Magazine 30 Grove St Ste C .... Peterborough NH 03458 800-821-0115 924-7380*
**Fax Area Code:* 603 ■ *TF:* 800-821-0115 ■ *Web:* www.cobblestonepub.com/magazine/app

Babybug Magazine 30 Grove St Ste C .... Peterborough NH 03458 800-821-0115 924-7380*
**Fax Area Code:* 603 ■ *TF:* 800-821-0115 ■ *Web:* www.cobblestonepub.com/magazine/bbb

Click Magazine 30 Grove St Ste C .... Peterborough NH 03458 800-821-0115 924-7380*
**Fax Area Code:* 603 ■ *TF:* 800-821-0115 ■ *Web:* www.cobblestonepub.com/magazine/clk

Cobblestone Magazine 30 Grove St Ste C .... Peterborough NH 03458 603-924-7209 924-7380
TF: 800-821-0115 ■ *Web:* www.cobblestonepub.com/magazine/cob

Creative Kids Magazine PO Box 8813 .... Waco TX 76714 254-756-3337 756-3339
TF: 800-998-2208 ■ *Web:* www.prufrock.com

Cricket Media Inc 30 Grove St Ste C .... Peterborough NH 03458 800-821-0115 924-7380*
**Fax Area Code:* 603 ■ *TF:* 800-821-0115 ■ *Web:* shop.cricketmedia.com

DECA Dimensions Magazine 1908 Assn Dr .... Reston VA 20191 703-860-5000 860-4013
Web: www.deca.org

Girls' Life Acqusition Co 4529 Hartford Rd .... Baltimore MD 21214 410-426-9600 254-0991
TF: 888-999-3222 ■ *Web:* www.girlslife.com

National Geographic Kids Magazine
1145 17th St NW .... Washington DC 20036 202-857-7000 775-6141
TF: 800-647-5463 ■ *Web:* www.kids.nationalgeographic.com/kids

New Moon Magazine PO Box 161287 .... Duluth MN 55816 218-878-9673
TF: 800-381-4743 ■ *Web:* www.newmoon.com

Odyssey Magazine 30 Grove St Ste C .... Peterborough NH 03458 603-924-7209 924-7380
TF: 800-821-0115 ■ *Web:* www.odysseymagazine.com

Owl Magazine 10 Lower Spadina Ave Ste 400 .... Toronto ON M5V2Z2 416-340-2700 340-9769
TF: 800-551-6957 ■ *Web:* www.owlkids.com

Teen People Magazine 1271 Sixth Ave Ste 3540 .... New York NY 10020 212-522-6699 522-0601*
**Fax:* Edit ■ *Web:* www.people.com

Turtle Magazine 1100 Waterway Blvd .... Indianapolis IN 46202 317-634-1100 684-8094
TF: 800-558-2376 ■ *Web:* uskidsmags.com

Wild Animal Baby Magazine
11100 Wildlife Ctr Dr .... Reston VA 20190 800-822-9919
TF: 800-822-9919 ■ *Web:* www.nwf.org/wildanimalbaby

Phone Fax

Your Big Backyard Magazine
11100 Wildlife Ctr Dr .... Reston VA 20190 800-822-9919 442-7332*
**Fax Area Code:* 703 ■ *TF:* 800-822-9919 ■ *Web:* www.nwf.org/yourbigbackyard

460-7 Computer & Internet Magazines

Phone Fax

2600 Magazine PO Box 752 .... Middle Island NY 11953 631-751-2600 474-2677
Web: www.2600.com

Computer Magazine
10662 Los Vaqueros Cir .... Los Alamitos CA 90720 714-821-8380 821-4010
TF Orders: 800-272-6657 ■ *Web:* www.computer.org

Computers in Libraries Magazine
143 Old Marlton Pk .... Medford NJ 08055 609-654-6266 654-4309
TF: 800-300-9868 ■ *Web:* www.infotoday.com/cilmag

Computerworld Magazine One Speen St .... Framingham MA 01701 508-879-0700
TF: 800-343-6474 ■ *Web:* www.computerworld.com

eContent Magazine 143 Old Marlton Pike Ste 3 .... Medford NJ 08055 609-654-6266 654-4309
TF: 800-300-9868 ■ *Web:* www.econtentmag.com

Federal Computer Week Magazine
3141 Fairview Pk Dr Ste 777 .... Falls Church VA 22042 703-876-5100 876-5100
TF: 877-534-2208 ■ *Web:* www.fcw.com

IEEE Computer Graphics & Applications Magazine
10662 Los Vaqueros Cir PO Box 3014 .... Los Alamitos CA 90720 714-821-8380 821-4641
TF: 800-272-6657 ■ *Web:* computer.org/portal/web/computingnow/cga

IEEE Micro Magazine
10662 Los Vaqueros Cir PO Box 3014 .... Los Alamitos CA 90720 714-821-8380 821-4641
TF: 800-272-6657 ■ *Web:* computer.org/portal/web/computingnow/micro

Information Today Magazine
143 Old Marlton Pk .... Medford NJ 08055 609-654-6266 654-4309
TF: 800-300-9868 ■ *Web:* www.infotoday.com

InformationWeek Magazine 600 Community Dr ..... Manhasset NY 11030 516-562-5000 562-5036
TF: 800-441-8826 ■ *Web:* www.informationweek.com

InfoWorld Magazine
501 Second St Ste 120 .... San Francisco CA 94107 415-243-4344 978-3120
TF: 800-227-8365 ■ *Web:* www.infoworld.com

Law Technology News 120 Broadway 5th Fl .... New York NY 10271 212-457-7905 822-5300*
**Fax Area Code:* 646 ■ *TF Cust Svc:* 800-888-8300 ■ *Web:* legaltechshow.com

Macworld Magazine 501 Second St Ste 600 ...... San Francisco CA 94107 415-243-0505 442-1891
TF Cust Svc: 800-288-6848 ■ *Web:* www.macworld.com

Maximum PC Magazine
4000 Shoreline Ct Ste 400 .... South San Francisco CA 94080 650-872-1642 872-2207
Web: www.maximumpc.com

MultiMedia Schools Magazine
143 Old Marlton Pk .... Medford NJ 08055 609-654-6266 654-4309
TF: 800-300-9868 ■ *Web:* www.infotoday.com/mmschools

Network Computing Magazine
600 Community Dr .... Manhasset NY 11030 516-562-5000
Web: www.networkcomputing.com

Network World Magazine
492 Old Connecticut Path Ste 200
PO Box 9208 .... Framingham MA 01701 800-622-1108 490-6417*
**Fax Area Code:* 508 ■ *TF:* 800-622-1108 ■ *Web:* www.networkworld.com

Oracle Magazine
500 Oracle Pkwy MS OPL3 .... Redwood Shores CA 94065 650-506-7000 633-2424*
**Fax:* Cust Svc ■ *TF:* 800-392-2999 ■ *Web:* www.oracle.com/oramag/index.html

PC Magazine 28 E 28th St .... New York NY 10016 212-503-3500
TF: 800-289-0429 ■ *Web:* www.pcmag.com

PC World Magazine 501 Second St Ste 600 .... San Francisco CA 94107 415-243-0505 442-1891
Web: www.pcworld.com

Searcher: The Magazine for Database Professionals
143 Old Marlton Pk .... Medford NJ 08055 609-654-6266 654-4309
TF: 800-300-9868 ■ *Web:* www.infotoday.com/searcher

460-8 Education Magazines & Journals

Phone Fax

Academe Magazine 1133 19th St NW Ste 200 ...... Washington DC 20036 202-737-5900 737-5526
TF: 800-424-2973 ■ *Web:* www.aaup.org

AEA Advocate Magazine 345 E Palm Ln .... Phoenix AZ 85004 602-264-1774 240-6887
TF: 800-352-5411 ■ *Web:* www.arizonaea.org

Alabama School Journal 422 Dexter Ave .... Montgomery AL 36104 334-834-9790 262-8377
TF: 800-392-5839 ■ *Web:* www.myaea.org

American Educator Magazine
555 New Jersey Ave NW .... Washington DC 20001 202-879-4400
TF: 800-238-1133 ■ *Web:* www.aft.org

American Libraries Magazine 50 E Huron St .... Chicago IL 60611 800-545-2433 440-0901*
**Fax Area Code:* 312 ■ *TF:* 800-545-2433 ■ *Web:* www.americanlibrariesmagazine.org

American Teacher Magazine
555 New Jersey Ave NW .... Washington DC 20001 202-879-4400
TF: 800-238-1133 ■ *Web:* www.aft.org/publications/american_teacher

Arkansas Educator Magazine
1500 W Fourth St .... Little Rock AR 72201 501-375-4611 375-4620
TF: 800-632-0624 ■ *Web:* aeaonline.org

California Educator Magazine
1705 Murchison Dr .... Burlingame CA 94010 650-697-1400 552-5002
Web: www.cta.org

Chronicle of Higher Education, The
1255 23rd St NW Ste 700 .... Washington DC 20037 202-466-1000 452-1033
TF: 800-728-2803 ■ *Web:* www.chronicle.com

Colorado School Journal 1500 Grant St .... Denver CO 80203 800-332-5939
TF: 800-336-7678 ■ *Web:* denverpost.com

Education Ctr Inc 3515 W Market St Ste 200 .... Greensboro NC 27403 336-854-0309 547-1587
TF: 800-714-7991 ■ *Web:* www.theeducationcenter.com

Education Week Magazine 6935 Arlington Rd .... Bethesda MD 20814 301-280-3100 280-3250
TF: 800-346-1834 ■ *Web:* www.edweek.org

Educational Leadership Magazine
1703 N Beauregard St .... Alexandria VA 22311 703-578-9600 575-5400
TF: 800-933-2723 ■ *Web:* www.ascd.org

	City	State	Zip	Phone	Fax
Harvard Educational Review Eight Story St First Fl *TF:* 877-930-4473 ■ *Web:* www.gse.harvard.edu	Cambridge	MA	02138	617-495-3432	496-3584
ISTA Advocate Magazine 150 W Market St Ste 900 *TF:* 800-382-4037 ■ *Web:* ista-in.org	Indianapolis	IN	46204	317-263-3400	655-3700
Journal of Physical Education Recreation & Dance (JOPERD) 1900 Assn Dr *Web:* shapeamerica.org	Reston	VA	20191	703-476-3400	476-9527
KEA News 401 Capital Ave *TF:* 800-231-4532 ■ *Web:* www.kea.org	Frankfort	KY	40601	502-875-2889	227-8062
Library Journal 160 Varick St 11th Fl *TF:* 800-588-1030 ■ *Web:* lj.libraryjournal.com	New York	NY	10013	646-380-0700	380-0756
Louisiana Association of Educators 8322 One Kalais Ave *TF:* 800-256-4523 ■ *Web:* www.lae.org	Baton Rouge	LA	70809	225-343-9243	343-9272
MAA FOCUS 1529 18th St NW *TF:* 800-741-9415 ■ *Web:* maa.org/publications/periodicals/maa-focus	Washington	DC	20036	202-387-5200	265-2384
Mailbox Bookbag Magazine 3515 W Market St Ste 200 *TF:* 800-714-7991 ■ *Web:* www.theeducationcenter.com	Greensboro	NC	27403	336-854-0309	547-1587
Mailbox Teacher Magazine 3515 W Market St Ste 200 *Web:* www.theeducationcenter.com	Greensboro	NC	27403	336-854-0309	547-1590
Maine Educator Magazine 35 Community Dr *TF:* 800-332-8529 ■ *Web:* centralmaine.com/	Augusta	ME	04330	207-622-5866	
MEA Voice Magazine 1216 Kendale Blvd PO Box 2573 *TF:* 800-292-1934 ■ *Web:* www.mea.org	East Lansing	MI	48826	517-332-6551	337-5414
Minnesota Educator Magazine 41 Sherburne Ave *TF:* 800-652-9073 ■ *Web:* educationminnesota.org	Saint Paul	MN	55103	651-227-9541	292-4802
Missouri State Teachers Assn 407 S Sixth St *TF General:* 800-392-0532 ■ *Web:* msta.org	Columbia	MO	65201	573-442-3127	443-5079
MTA Today Magazine 20 Ashburton Pl *TF:* 800-392-6175 ■ *Web:* www.massteacher.org	Boston	MA	02108	617-878-8000	742-7046
NCAE News Bulletin PO Box 27347 *TF:* 800-662-7924 ■ *Web:* www.ncae.org	Raleigh	NC	27611	919-832-3000	829-1626
NCTM News Bulletin 1906 Assn Dr *TF:* 800-235-7566 ■ *Web:* www.nctm.org/news	Reston	VA	20191	703-620-9840	476-2970
New Hampshire Educator Magazine 9 S Spring St *TF:* 866-556-3264 ■ *Web:* www.neanh.org	Concord	NH	03301	603-224-7751	224-2648
New York Teacher Magazine 800 Troy-Schenectady Rd *TF:* 800-342-9810 ■ *Web:* www.nysut.org	Latham	NY	12110	518-213-6000	213-6415
NJEA Review 180 W State St *Web:* www.njea.org	Trenton	NJ	08607	609-599-4561	392-6321
NSEA Voice Magazine 605 S 14th St Ste 200 *TF:* 800-742-0047 ■ *Web:* www.nsea.org	Lincoln	NE	68508	402-475-7611	475-2630
Ohio Education Assn (OEA) 225 E Broad St PO Box 2550 *TF:* 800-282-1500 ■ *Web:* www.ohea.org	Columbus	OH	43216	614-228-4526	228-8771
Oklahoma Education Association 323 E Madison PO Box 18485 *TF:* 800-522-8091 ■ *Web:* www.okea.org/about-oea/contact-the-staff	Oklahoma City	OK	73154	405-528-7785	524-0350
Oregon Education Magazine (OEA) 6900 SW Atlanta St Bldg 1 *TF:* 800-858-5505 ■ *Web:* www.oregoned.org	Portland	OR	97223	503-684-3300	684-8063
Scholastic Coach & Athletic Director Magazine 557 Broadway *TF General:* 800-724-6527 ■ *Web:* www.scholastic.com/coach	New York	NY	10012	212-343-6100	343-6930
Teacher Magazine 6935 Arlington Rd Ste 100 *TF:* 800-346-1834 ■ *Web:* www.edweek.org/tm	Bethesda	MD	20814	301-280-3100	280-3150
Teaching Tolerance Magazine 400 Washington Ave *Web:* www.tolerance.org	Montgomery	AL	36104	334-956-8200	
TSTA Advocate Magazine 316 W 12th St *TF:* 877-275-8782 ■ *Web:* www.tsta.org	Austin	TX	78701	512-476-5355	486-7049
Vermont NEA Today Magazine 10 Wheelock St *TF:* 800-649-6375 ■ *Web:* www.vtnea.org	Montpelier	VT	05602	802-223-6375	223-1253
Virginia Journal of Education 116 S Third St *TF:* 800-552-9554 ■ *Web:* www.veanea.org	Richmond	VA	23219	804-648-5801	775-8379
West Virginia School Journal 1558 Quarrier St *TF:* 800-642-8261 ■ *Web:* www.wvea.org	Charleston	WV	25311	304-346-5315	346-4325
Young Children Magazine 1313 L St NW Ste 500 PO Box 97156 *TF:* 800-424-2460 ■ *Web:* www.naeyc.org	Washington	DC	20005	202-232-8777	328-1846

460-9 Entertainment & Music Magazines

	City	State	Zip	Phone	Fax
American Cinematographer Magazine 1782 N Orange Dr *TF:* 800-448-0145 ■ *Web:* www.theasc.com	Los Angeles	CA	90028	323-969-4333	876-4973
Back Stage Magazine 770 Broadway *Web:* www.backstage.com	New York	NY	10003	212-493-4420	
Bass Player Magazine 28 E 28th St 12th Fl *TF Cust Svc:* 866-246-3595 ■ *Web:* www.bassplayer.com	New York	NY	10016	212-378-0400	378-0470
Broadcast Engineering Magazine 9800 Metcalf Ave *Web:* tvtechnology.com/	Overland Park	KS	66212	913-967-1737	967-1905
Cadence Magazine Cadence Bldg *Web:* www.cadencebuilding.com	Redwood	NY	13679	315-287-2852	287-2860
Canadian Musician Magazine 4056 Dorchester Rd *Fax Area Code: 888 ■ *TF:* 877-746-4692 ■ *Web:* www.canadianmusician.com	Niagara Falls	ON	L2E6M9	905-374-8878	665-1307*
Country Weekly Magazine 118 16th Ave S Ste 230 *Web:* www.countryweekly.com	Nashville	TN	37203	615-259-1111	255-1110
Dance Magazine 333 Seventh Ave 11th Fl *Fax Area Code: 646 ■ *TF:* 800-331-1750 ■ *Web:* www.dancemagazine.com	New York	NY	10001	212-979-4800	674-0102*
Down Beat Magazine 102 N Haven Rd PO Box 906 *Fax Area Code: 630 ■ *TF:* 800-554-7470 ■ *Web:* www.downbeat.com	Elmhurst	IL	60126	651-251-9682	941-3210*
Dramatics Magazine 2343 Auburn Ave *Web:* www.schooltheatre.org	Cincinnati	OH	45219	513-421-3900	421-7077
Emmy Magazine 5220 Lankershim Blvd *Web:* emmys.com/	North Hollywood	CA	91601	818-754-2800	
Entertainment Weekly Magazine 1675 Broadway 29th Fl *TF:* 800-828-6882 ■ *Web:* www.ew.com	New York	NY	10019	212-522-5600	467-1778
Film Comment Magazine 165 W 65th St *TF:* 888-313-6085 ■ *Web:* www.filmlinc.com	New York	NY	10023	212-875-5610	875-5636
Grammy Magazine 3030 Olympic Blvd *TF:* 800-423-2017 ■ *Web:* www.grammy.com	Santa Monica	CA	90404	310-392-3777	392-9262
Guitar Player Magazine 28 E 28th St 12th Fl *Fax Area Code: 917 ■ *TF Cust Svc:* 800-289-9839 ■ *Web:* www.guitarplayer.com	New York	NY	10016	212-378-0400	281-4704*
Hollywood Reporter 5055 Wilshire Blvd Ste 600 *Fax: Edit ■ *TF:* 866-525-2150 ■ *Web:* www.hollywoodreporter.com	Los Angeles	CA	90036	323-525-2000	525-2377*
Hollywood Scriptwriter Magazine PO Box 3761 *Fax Area Code: 562 ■ *Web:* www.hollywoodscriptwriter.com	Cerritos	CA	90703	310-283-1630	926-2060*
International Musician 120 Walton St *Web:* www.internationalmusician.org	Syracuse	NY	13202	315-422-4488	422-3837
Jazziz Magazine 2650 N Military Trail Ste 140 *TF:* 888-852-9987 ■ *Web:* www.jazziz.com	Boca Raton	FL	33431	561-893-6868	893-6867
JazzTimes Magazine 85 Quincy Ave Ste 2 *TF:* 800-437-5828 ■ *Web:* www.jazztimes.com	Quincy	MA	02169	617-706-9110	536-0102
Keyboard Magazine 28 E 28th St 12th Fl *Fax Area Code: 555 ■ *TF Cust Svc:* 800-483-2433 ■ *Web:* www.keyboardmag.com	New York	NY	10016	212-378-0400	555-4564*
Live Design 249 W 17th St *TF Sales:* 866-505-7173 ■ *Web:* www.livedesignonline.com	New York	NY	10011	212-204-4272	204-4291
Metal Edge Magazine 333 Seventh Ave Ste 1100	New York	NY	10001	212-780-3500	
Multichannel News 28 E 28th St 12th Fl *TF Cust Svc:* 888-343-5563 ■ *Web:* www.multichannel.com	New York	NY	10016	917-281-4700	281-4704
Opera News Magazine 70 Lincoln Ctr Plaza 6th Fl *Web:* operanews.com	New York	NY	10023	212-769-7080	769-8500
Playbill Magazine 525 Seventh Ave Ste 1801 *TF:* 800-533-4330 ■ *Web:* www.playbill.com	New York	NY	10018	212-557-5757	682-2932
Pollstar 4697 W Jacquelyn Ave *Fax: Edit ■ *TF:* 800-344-7383 ■ *Web:* www.pollstar.com	Fresno	CA	93722	559-271-7900	271-7979*
Rolling Stone Magazine 1290 Ave of the Americas 2nd Fl *Fax Area Code: 212 ■ *TF:* 800-283-1549 ■ *Web:* www.rollingstone.com	New York	NY	10104	800-283-1549	767-8203*
TV Guide Magazine LLC 11 West 42nd St 16th Fl *TF:* 800-866-1400 ■ *Web:* www.tvguide.com	New York	NY	10036	212-852-7500	852-7323
Video Age International Magazine 216 E 75th St Ste PW *Web:* www.videoageinternational.com	New York	NY	10021	212-288-3933	734-9033
Videomaker Magazine 1350 E Ninth St PO Box 4591 *TF:* 800-284-3226 ■ *Web:* www.videomaker.com	Chico	CA	95927	530-891-8410	891-8443

460-10 Fraternal & Special Interest Magazines

	City	State	Zip	Phone	Fax
AARP the Magazine 601 E St NW *TF:* 888-687-2277 ■ *Web:* www.aarp.org	Washington	DC	20049	202-434-3525	434-6883
AAUW Outlook Magazine 1111 16th St NW *TF:* 800-326-2289 ■ *Web:* www.aauw.org	Washington	DC	20036	202-785-7700	872-1425
Adoptive Families Magazine 108 West 39th St Ste 805 *TF:* 800-372-3300 ■ *Web:* www.adoptivefamilies.com	New York	NY	10018	646-366-0830	366-0842
American Legion Auxiliary National News 8945 N Meridian St Second Fl *Web:* www.alaforveterans.org/	Indianapolis	IN	46260	317-569-4500	569-4502
American Legion Magazine 700 N Pennsylvania St *Web:* www.legion.org	Indianapolis	IN	46204	317-630-1200	630-1280
American Scholar Magazine 1606 New Hampshire Ave NW *Web:* www.pbk.org	Washington	DC	20009	202-265-3808	986-1601
American Spirit 1776 D St NW *Web:* dar.org/national-society/american-spirit-magazine	Washington	DC	20006	202-628-1776	628-0820
Columbia Magazine 1 Columbus Plaza *TF:* 800-380-9995 ■ *Web:* www.kofc.org	New Haven	CT	06510	203-752-4000	752-4000
Commentary Magazine 561 7th Ave 16th Fl *TF:* 800-829-6270 ■ *Web:* www.commentarymagazine.com	New York	NY	10018	212-891-1400	891-6700
Disabled American Veterans Magazine 3725 Alexandria Pike PO Box 14301 *TF:* 877-426-2838 ■ *Web:* www.dav.org	Cold Spring	KY	41076	859-441-7300	441-1416
Eagle Magazine 1623 Gateway Cir S *TF:* 800-236-5450 ■ *Web:* www.foe.com	Grove City	OH	43123	614-883-2200	883-2201
Elks Magazine 425 W Diversey Pkwy *TF:* 800-273-8255 ■ *Web:* www.elks.org/elksmag	Chicago	IL	60614	773-755-4700	755-4745
Gettysburg Review 300 N Washington St *Web:* www.gettysburgreview.com	Gettysburg	PA	17325	717-337-6300	337-6775
Kiwanis Magazine 3636 Woodview Trace *TF:* 800-549-2647 ■ *Web:* kiwanis.org/kiwanis/stories/kiwanis-magazine#.ub9reedjm1i	Indianapolis	IN	46268	317-875-8755	879-0204
Ladies Auxiliary VFW Magazine 406 W 34th St *TF:* 800-843-1950 ■ *Web:* www.ladiesauxvfw.org	Kansas City	MO	64111	816-561-8655	931-4753
Lion Magazine 300 W 22nd St *TF Circ:* 800-710-7822 ■ *Web:* www.lionsclubs.org	Oak Brook	IL	60523	630-571-5466	571-8890
Moose Magazine 155 S International Dr *Web:* www.mooseintl.org/public/moose_magazine.aspx	Mooseheart	IL	60539	630-859-2000	
Phi Delta Kappan Magazine 408 N Union St *TF:* 800-766-1156 ■ *Web:* www.pdkintl.org	Bloomington	IN	47407	812-339-1156	339-0018

				Phone	Fax
Poets & Writers Magazine 90 Broad St Ste 2100 *Web:* www.pw.org	New York	NY	10004	212-226-3586	226-3963
Police Times Magazine 6350 Horizon Dr. *Web:* www.aphf.org	Titusville	FL	32780	321-264-0911	264-0033
Royal Neighbor Magazine 230 16th St *TF:* 800-627-4762 ■ *Web:* www.royalneighbors.org	Rock Island	IL	61201	309-788-4561	
Scouting Magazine 1325 W Walnut Hill Ln PO Box 152079 *Web:* www.scoutingmagazine.org	Irving	TX	75015	972-580-2000	580-2079
Tikkun Magazine 2342 Shattuck Ave Ste 1200 *Web:* www.tikkun.org	Berkeley	CA	94704	510-644-1200	644-1255
United Commercial Travellers 1801 Watermark Dr Ste 100 *TF:* 800-848-0123 ■ *Web:* www.uct.org	Columbus	OH	43215	614-228-3276	487-9675
WOODMEN Magazine 1700 Farnam St *TF:* 800-225-3108 ■ *Web:* woodmen.org	Omaha	NE	68102	402-342-1890	271-7269

460-11 General Interest Magazines

				Phone	Fax
Alfred Hitchcock Mystery Magazine 44 Wall St Ste 904 *TF:* 800-220-7443 ■ *Web:* www.themysteryplace.com	New York	NY	10005	212-686-7188	686-7414
American Baby Magazine 375 Lexington Ave *Web:* www.parents.com	New York	NY	10017	212-499-2000	
Asimov's Science Fiction Magazine 267 Broadway Fourth Fl *Web:* www.asimovs.com	New York	NY	10007	212-686-7188	686-7414
Atlantic Monthly Magazine 600 New Hampshire Ave NW *TF Cust Svc:* 800-234-2411 ■ *Web:* www.theatlantic.com	Washington	DC	20037	202-266-6000	266-6332
Avenue Magazine 79 Madison Ave 16th Fl *Web:* www.avenuemagazine.com	New York	NY	10016	212-268-8600	
Better Investing Magazine PO Box 220 *TF:* 877-275-6242 ■ *Web:* www.betterinvesting.org	Royal Oak	MI	48068	248-583-6242	583-4880
Black Enterprise Magazine 130 Fifth Ave *TF Cust Svc:* 800-727-7777 ■ *Web:* www.blackenterprise.com	New York	NY	10011	212-242-8000	886-9610
Booklist Magazine 50 E Huron St *TF:* 800-545-2433 ■ *Web:* www.ala.org	Chicago	IL	60611	800-545-2433	
Bridal Guide Magazine 330 Seventh Ave 10th Fl *TF:* 800-472-7744 ■ *Web:* www.bridalguide.com	New York	NY	10001	212-838-7733	308-7165
Canadian Living Magazine 25 Sheppard Ave W Ste 100 *TF:* 800-387-6332 ■ *Web:* www.canadianliving.com	Toronto	ON	M2N6S7	416-733-7600	733-3398
Christianity Today 465 Gundersen Dr *TF Cust Svc:* 800-222-1840 ■ *Web:* christianitytoday.com/iyf/	Carol Stream	IL	60188	630-260-6200	260-0114
College Outlook & Career Opportunities Magazine 20 E Gregory Blvd. *TF:* 800-274-8867 ■ *Web:* www.mymajors.com	Kansas City	MO	64114	816-361-0616	361-6164
Consumer Reports Magazine 101 Truman Ave *TF Orders:* 800-333-0663 ■ *Web:* www.consumerreports.org	Yonkers	NY	10703	914-378-2000	
Cook's Illustrated Magazine PO Box 470739 *TF Circ:* 800-526-8442 ■ *Web:* www.cooksillustrated.com	Brookline	MA	02447	617-232-1000	
Cosmopolitan Magazine 300 W 57th St *TF:* 800-888-2676 ■ *Web:* www.cosmopolitan.com	New York	NY	10019	212-649-2000	
Country Living Magazine 300 W 57th St **Fax Area Code:* 646 ■ *TF:* 800-888-0128 ■ *Web:* www.countryliving.com	New York	NY	10019	212-649-3204	280-3971*
Country Magazine 1610 North 2nd St Ste 102 *TF:* 888-861-1265 ■ *Web:* www.country-magazine.com	Milwaukee	WI	53212	414-423-0100	
Coup de Pouce Magazine 1100 boul Rene-Levesque O 24e Etage *TF:* 800-528-3836 ■ *Web:* www.coupdepouce.com	Montreal	QC	H3B4X9	514-392-9000	
Cuisine Magazine 2200 Grand Ave **Fax Area Code:* 515 ■ *TF:* 800-311-3995 ■ *Web:* www.cuisineathome.com	Des Moines	IA	50312	800-311-3995	283-2003*
Delicious Living Magazine 1401 Pearl St Ste 200 *TF:* 866-458-4935 ■ *Web:* deliciousliving.com	Boulder	CO	80302	303-939-8440	998-9020
Details Magazine 4 Times Sq 8th Fl *Web:* www.details.com	New York	NY	10036	212-286-8059	
Ebony Magazine 820 S Michigan Ave *Web:* www.ebony.com	Chicago	IL	60605	312-322-9200	
Elle Magazine 1633 Broadway 44th Fl *TF:* 800-876-8775 ■ *Web:* www.elle.com	New York	NY	10019	212-903-5000	
Ellery Queen Mystery Magazine (EQMM) 267 Broadway 4th Fl *Web:* www.themysteryplace.com/eqmm	New York	NY	10007	212-888-8171	686-7414
Entrepreneur Magazine 2445 McCabe Way Ste 400 *TF:* 800-274-6229 ■ *Web:* www.entrepreneur.com	Irvine	CA	92614	949-261-2325	261-7729
Esquire Magazine 300 W 57th St 21st Fl *TF:* 800-888-5400 ■ *Web:* www.esquire.com	New York	NY	10019	212-649-4020	649-2000
Essence Magazine 135 W 50th St Fourth Fl *TF:* 800-274-9398 ■ *Web:* www.essence.com	New York	NY	10020	800-274-9398	274-9398
Family Cir Magazine 375 Lexington Ave 9th Fl **Fax Area Code:* 212 ■ *TF:* 800-627-4444 ■ *Web:* www.familycircle.com	New York	NY	10017	800-627-4444	499-1987*
Food & Wine Magazine 1120 Ave of the Americas *TF:* 800-333-6569 ■ *Web:* www.foodandwine.com	New York	NY	10036	813-979-6625	
For the Bride Magazine 222 W 37th St *Web:* www.demetriosbride.com	New York	NY	10018	212-967-0751	
Franchise Handbook 5555 N Port Washington Rd Ste 305 **Fax Area Code:* 418 ■ *TF:* 800-272-0246 ■ *Web:* franchisehandbook.com	Milwaukee	WI	53217	414-882-2878	882-2877*
Futurist Magazine 7910 Woodmont Ave Ste 450 *TF:* 800-989-8274 ■ *Web:* www.wfs.org	Bethesda	MD	20814	301-656-8274	951-0394
Harper's Bazaar Magazine 300 W 57th St *TF General:* 800-285-4274 ■ *Web:* www.harpersbazaar.com	New York	NY	10019	212-903-5000	
Harper's Magazine 666 Broadway 11th Fl *TF:* 800-444-4653 ■ *Web:* www.harpers.org	New York	NY	10012	212-420-5720	228-5889
In Touch Weekly Magazine 270 Sylvan Ave *Web:* www.intouchweekly.com	Englewood Cliffs	NJ	07632	201-569-6699	569-2510
Interview Magazine 575 Broadway Fifth Fl *TF:* 800-925-9574 ■ *Web:* www.interviewmagazine.com	New York	NY	10012	212-941-2900	941-2885
Latina Media Ventures LLC 625 Madison Ave 3rd Fl *TF:* 888-489-7753 ■ *Web:* www.latina.com	New York	NY	10022	212-642-0200	575-3088
Lucky Inc 4 Times Sq *TF:* 888-959-5203 ■ *Web:* www.luckyshops.com	New York	NY	10036	800-405-8085	
Marie Claire Magazine 300 W 57th St 34th Fl **Fax Area Code:* 646 ■ *TF:* 800-925-0485 ■ *Web:* www.marieclaire.com	New York	NY	10019	800-925-0485	280-1089*
Martha Stewart Living Magazine 11 W 42nd St 25th Fl **Fax Area Code:* 212 ■ *TF:* 800-999-6518 ■ *Web:* www.marthastewart.com	New York	NY	10036	800-999-6518	827-8149*
Men's Journal LLC 1290 Ave of the Americas 2nd Fl **Fax Area Code:* 212 ■ *TF:* 800-677-6367 ■ *Web:* www.mensjournal.com	New York	NY	10104	800-677-6367	484-3435*
Ms Magazine 1600 Wilson Blvd Ste 801 *TF:* 866-672-6363 ■ *Web:* www.msmagazine.com	Arlington	VA	22209	703-522-4201	522-2219
National Geographic Adventure Magazine 1145 17th St NW *TF:* 800-647-5463 ■ *Web:* www.nationalgeographic.com/adventure	Washington	DC	20036	202-857-7000	775-6141
National Geographic Magazine 1145 17th St NW *TF:* 800-647-5463 ■ *Web:* nationalgeographic.com	Washington	DC	20036	202-857-7000	775-6141
New York Review of Books 435 Hudson St Third Fl *TF:* 800-354-0050 ■ *Web:* www.nybooks.com	New York	NY	10014	212-757-8070	333-5374
Nylon Magazine 110 Greene St Ste 607 *Web:* www.nylon.com	New York	NY	10012	212-226-6454	226-7738
O the Oprah Magazine 5700 Wilshire Blvd Ste 120 *Web:* www.oprah.com/omagazine	Los Angeles	CA	90036	323-602-5500	
People Magazine Rockefeller Ctr Time & Life Bldg. *TF:* 800-541-9000 ■ *Web:* www.people.com/people	New York	NY	10020	212-522-3347	522-0331
Psychology Today Magazine 115 E 23 St 9th Fl **Fax:* Edit ■ *TF:* 800-931-2237 ■ *Web:* www.psychologytoday.com	New York	NY	10010	212-260-7210	260-7445*
Reminisce Magazine 750 Third Ave Third Fl *TF:* 888-859-7838 ■ *Web:* www.reminisce.com	New York	WI	10017	414-423-0100	423-8463
Saturday Evening Post, The 1100 Waterway Blvd *TF:* 800-829-5576 ■ *Web:* www.saturdayeveningpost.com	Indianapolis	IN	46202	317-634-1100	637-0126
Saveur Magazine 15 E 32nd St 12th Fl *Web:* www.saveur.com	New York	NY	10016	212-219-7400	
Self Magazine 4 Times Sq *TF:* 800-274-6111 ■ *Web:* www.self.com	New York	NY	10036	212-286-2860	630-5883
Simple & Delicious 5400 S 60th St *TF:* 800-344-6913 ■ *Web:* www.tasteofhome.com	Greendale	WI	53129	414-423-0100	
Smithsonian Magazine 600 Maryland Ave Ste 6001 *TF:* 800-766-2149 ■ *Web:* www.smithsonianmag.com	Washington	DC	20024	202-633-6090	
Sun Magazine 8815 Conroy Windermere Rd Ste 130 *TF:* 888-218-9968 ■ *Web:* www.floridasunmagazine.com	Orlando	FL	32835	407-477-2815	293-1179
Taste of Home Magazine 5400 S 60th St *TF:* 800-344-6913 ■ *Web:* www.tasteofhome.com	Greendale	WI	53129	414-423-0100	423-8463
This Old House Magazine 135 W 50th St 10th Fl *Web:* www.thisoldhouse.com/toh/magazines	New York	NY	10020	212-522-9465	522-9435
Traditional Home Magazine 1716 Locust St **Fax:* Edit ■ *TF Circ:* 800-374-8791 ■ *Web:* www.traditionalhome.com	Des Moines	IA	50309	515-284-3762	284-2083*
Utne Reader Magazine 12 N 12th St Ste 400 *TF Cust Svc:* 800-736-8863 ■ *Web:* www.utne.com	Minneapolis	MN	55403	612-338-5040	338-6043
Vanity Fair Magazine Four Times Sq **Fax Area Code:* 212 ■ **Fax:* Edit ■ *TF:* 800-365-0635 ■ *Web:* www.vanityfair.com	New York	NY	10036	800-365-0635	286-6707*
Western Living Magazine 2608 Granville St Ste 560 *TF:* 800-363-3272 ■ *Web:* www.westernlivingmagazine.com	Vancouver	BC	V6H3V3	604-877-7732	877-4848
Wilson Quarterly Magazine 1300 Pennsylvania Ave NW 1 Woodrow Wilson Plaza *TF Orders:* 888-947-9018 ■ *Web:* www.wilsoncenter.org	Washington	DC	20004	202-691-4000	691-4247
Women's Wear Daily Magazine 750 Third Ave Fifth Fl *TF:* 800-289-0273 ■ *Web:* www.wwd.com	New York	NY	10017	212-630-4600	630-4580
Working Mother Magazine Two Park Ave 10th Fl *Web:* www.workingmother.com	New York	NY	10016	212-779-5000	351-6487

460-12 Government & Military Magazines

				Phone	Fax
Air Force Magazine 1501 Lee Hwy *TF:* 800-727-3337 ■ *Web:* www.afa.org/magazine/aboutmag.asp	Arlington	VA	22209	703-247-5800	247-5853
Air Force Times Magazine 6883 Commercial Dr *TF:* 800-368-5718 ■ *Web:* www.airforcetimes.com	Springfield	VA	22159	703-750-7400	750-8601
Airman Magazine 203 Norton St	San Antonio	TX	78226	210-925-7757	925-7219
ARMY Magazine 2425 Wilson Blvd *TF:* 800-336-4570 ■ *Web:* www.ausa.org	Arlington	VA	22201	703-841-4300	525-9039
FRA Today 125 NW St *TF:* 800-372-1924 ■ *Web:* www.fra.org	Alexandria	VA	22314	703-683-1400	549-6610
Governing Magazine 1100 Connecticut Ave NW Ste 1300 *TF:* 800-940-6039 ■ *Web:* www.governing.com	Washington	DC	20036	202-862-8802	862-0032
Military & Aerospace Electronics Magazine 98 Spit Brook Rd *TF:* 866-423-4837 ■ *Web:* www.militaryaerospace.com	Nashua	NH	03062	847-763-9540	763-9607
Military Engineer Magazine 607 Prince St *TF Cust Svc:* 800-336-3097 ■ *Web:* www.same.org	Alexandria	VA	22314	703-549-3800	684-0231

				Phone	Fax
Military Officer Magazine 201 N Washington St	Alexandria	VA	22314	703-549-2311	838-8179
TF: 800-234-6622 ■ *Web:* www.moaa.org/Magazine					
Navy Times Magazine 6883 Commercial Dr	Springfield	VA	22159	703-750-7400	750-8767
TF Cust Svc: 800-368-5718 ■ *Web:* www.navytimes.com					
Public Employee Magazine 1625 L St NW	Washington	DC	20036	202-429-1130	429-1120
TF: 800-792-0045 ■ *Web:* www.afscme.org					
Soldier of Fortune Magazine 2135 11th St	Boulder	CO	80302	303-449-3750	
TF: 800-377-2789 ■ *Web:* www.sofmag.com					

460-13 Health & Fitness Magazines

				Phone	Fax
American Fitness Magazine 15250 Ventura Blvd Ste 200	Sherman Oaks	CA	91403	818-905-0040	990-1139
TF: 800-446-2322 ■ *Web:* www.afaa.com					
Cooking Light Magazine 2100 Lakeshore Dr	Birmingham	AL	35209	205-445-6000	445-6600
TF: 800-366-4712 ■ *Web:* www.cookinglight.com					
Diabetes Forecast Magazine 1701 N Beauregard St	Alexandria	VA	22311	703-549-1500	549-6995
TF: 800-676-4065 ■ *Web:* www.diabetes.org					
Fitness Rx for Men Magazine 21 Bennetts Rd	Setauket	NY	11733	631-751-9696	751-9699
TF: 800-653-1151 ■ *Web:* www.fitnessrxformen.com					
Fitness Rx for Women Magazine 21 Bennetts Rd Ste101	Setauket	NY	11733	631-751-9696	
Web: www.fitnessrxwomen.com					
Flex Magazine 21100 Erwin St	Woodland Hills	CA	91367	412-235-0203	776-2610*
**Fax Area Code:* 888 ■ *TF:* 877-527-8342 ■ *Web:* www.flexonline.com					
Heart & Soul Magazine 15480 Annapolis Rd Ste 202-225	Bowie	MD	20715	800-834-8813	
TF: 800-834-8813 ■ *Web:* www.heartandsoul.com					
Ironman Magazine 1701 Ives Ave	Oxnard	CA	93033	805-385-3500	385-3515
TF: 800-447-0008 ■ *Web:* www.ironmanmagazine.com					
MediMedia ManagedÿMarkets 780 Township Line Rd	Yardley	PA	19067	267-685-2300	
Web: www.medimedia.com					
Men's Fitness Magazine one Pk Ave 3rd Fl	New York	NY	10016	212-223-8811	
Web: www.mensfitness.com					
Men's Health Magazine 400 S Tenth St	Emmaus	PA	18098	610-967-5171	967-7725
TF: 800-666-2303 ■ *Web:* www.menshealth.com					
Ms Fitness Magazine PO Box 2490	White City	OR	97503	541-830-0400	830-0410
Web: www.msfitness.com					
Muscle & Fitness Hers Magazine 21100 Erwin St	Woodland Hills	CA	91367	800-340-8954	226-0148*
**Fax Area Code:* 818 ■ *Web:* www.muscleandfitness.com/muscle-fitness-hers					
Muscle & Fitness Magazine 21100 Erwin St	Woodland Hills	CA	91367	818-884-6800	595-0463
TF Orders: 866-688-7679 ■ *Web:* www.muscleandfitness.com					
Prevention Magazine 400 S Tenth St	Emmaus	PA	18098	212-697-2040	
TF: 800-813-8070 ■ *Web:* www.prevention.com					
Runner's World Magazine 400 S Tenth St	Emmaus	PA	18098	610-967-5171	
TF Cust Svc: 800-666-2828 ■ *Web:* www.runnersworld.com					
Shape Magazine Four New York Pl	New York	NY	10004	212-545-4800	679-2091
Web: www.shape.com					
Vegetarian Times 300 N Continental Blvd Ste 650	El Segundo	CA	90245	310-356-4100	356-4110
TF: 800-573-1900 ■ *Web:* www.vegetariantimes.com					
Yoga Journal Magazine 475 Sansome St Ste 850	San Francisco	CA	94111	415-591-0555	591-0733
Web: www.yogajournal.com					

460-14 Hobby & Personal Interests Magazines

				Phone	Fax
American History Illustrated Magazine 19300 Promenade Dr	Leesburg	VA	20176	310-922-2159	
TF: 800-435-0715 ■ *Web:* www.historynet.com/ah					
American Photo Magazine 1633 Broadway 43rd Fl	New York	NY	10019	212-767-6000	767-5602
TF: 800-274-4514 ■ *Web:* www.popphoto.com					
Antique Trader 700 E State St	Iola	WI	54990	715-445-2214	445-4087
TF: 800-258-0929 ■ *Web:* www.antiquetrader.com					
AOPA Pilot Magazine 421 Aviation Way	Frederick	MD	21701	301-695-2000	695-2375
TF: 800-872-2672 ■ *Web:* www.aopa.org					
Aquarium Fish Magazine Three Burroughs	Irvine	CA	92618	949-855-8822	855-3045
Web: www.fishchannel.com					
Arabian Horse World Magazine 1316 Tamson Dr Ste 101	Cambria	CA	93428	805-771-2300	927-6522
TF: 800-955-9423 ■ *Web:* arabianhorseworld.com					
Backpacker Magazine 2520 55th St Ste 210	Boulder	CO	80301	610-967-8296	413-1602*
**Fax Area Code:* 303 ■ *Web:* www.backpacker.com					
Bead & Button Magazine 21027 Crossroads Cir	Waukesha	WI	53186	262-796-8776	796-1615*
**Fax:* Cust Svc ■ *TF Cust Svc:* 800-533-6644 ■ *Web:* bnb.jewelrymakingmagazines.com					
BeadStyle Magazine 21027 Crossroads Cir	Waukesha	WI	53186	262-796-8776	796-1615*
**Fax:* Cust Svc ■ *TF Cust Svc:* 800-533-6644 ■ *Web:* bds.jewelrymakingmagazines.com					
Better Homes & Gardens WOOD Magazine 1716 Locust St	Des Moines	IA	50309	800-374-9663	551-7114*
**Fax Area Code:* 212 ■ **Fax:* Edit ■ *TF:* 800-374-9663 ■ *Web:* www.woodmagazine.com					
Bicycling Magazine 400 S Tenth St	Emmaus	PA	18098	800-666-2806	
TF: 800-666-2806 ■ *Web:* www.bicycling.com					
Bird Talk Magazine Three Burroughs	Irvine	CA	92618	949-855-8822	855-3045
TF Resv: 800-695-6088 ■ *Web:* www.birdchannel.com					
Birds & Blooms Magazine 5400 S 60th St	Greendale	WI	53129	414-423-0100	*
**Fax:* Edit ■ *TF:* 888-860-8040 ■ *Web:* www.birdsandblooms.com					
BirdWatching Magazine 25 Braintree Hill Office Pk Ste 404	Braintree	MA	02184	877-252-8141	
TF: 877-252-8141 ■ *Web:* www.birdwatchingdaily.com					
Blood-Horse Magazine PO Box 911088	Lexington	KY	40591	859-278-2361	276-4450
TF: 800-866-2361 ■ *Web:* www.bloodhorse.com					
British Heritage Magazine 19300 Promenade Dr	Leesburg	VA	20176	800-358-6327	
TF: 800-358-6327 ■ *Web:* www.historynet.com/bh					
Cat Fancy Magazine Three Burroughs	Irvine	CA	92618	949-855-8822	855-3045
TF Cust Svc: 800-546-7730 ■ *Web:* www.catchannel.com					
Ceramics Monthly 600 N Cleveland Ave Ste 210	Westerville	OH	43082	614-794-5867	891-8960
TF: 800-342-3594 ■ *Web:* www.ceramicartsdaily.org					
Chess Life Magazine PO Box 3967	Crossville	TN	38557	931-787-1234	787-1200
TF Sales: 800-903-8723 ■ *Web:* www.uschess.org					
Classic Trains Magazine 21027 Crossroads Cir PO Box 1612	Waukesha	WI	53186	262-796-8776	796-1615
TF: 800-533-6644 ■ *Web:* ctr.trains.com					
Coin World Magazine 911 S Vandemark Rd	Sidney	OH	45365	937-498-0800	498-0812
TF: 866-519-7298 ■ *Web:* www.coinworld.com					
COINage Magazine PO Box 6925	Ventura	CA	93006	805-644-3824	
Web: coinagemag.com					
Country Sampler Magazine 707 Kautz Rd	Saint Charles	IL	60174	630-377-8000	377-8194
Web: www.countrysampler.com					
Country Woman Magazine 5400 S 60th St	Greendale	WI	53129	414-423-0100	423-8463*
**Fax:* Edit ■ *TF:* 800-828-4548 ■ *Web:* www.countrywomanmagazine.com					
Crafts 'n Things Magazine PO Box 926	Sidney	OH	45365	866-222-3621	498-0876*
**Fax Area Code:* 937 ■ *TF:* 866-222-3621 ■ *Web:* craftideas.com/					
Creating Keepsakes Magazine 14850 Pony Express Rd	Bluffdale	UT	84065	801-816-8300	816-8301
TF: 888-247-5282 ■ *Web:* www.creatingkeepsakes.com					
Crochet World Magazine 306 E Parr Rd	Berne	IN	46711	260-589-8741	589-8093
Web: www.crochet-world.com					
Daily Racing Form 100 Broadway Seventh Fl	New York	NY	10005	212-366-7600	366-7738
TF Cust Svc: 800-306-3676 ■ *Web:* www.drf.com					
Digital Photographer Magazine 12121 Wilshire Blvd 12th Fl	Los Angeles	CA	90025	310-820-1500	826-5008
TF: 800-537-4619 ■ *Web:* www.dpmag.com					
Dog Fancy Magazine Three Burroughs	Irvine	CA	92618	949-855-8822	855-3045
TF Cust Svc: 800-546-7730 ■ *Web:* www.dogchannel.com					
Equus Magazine 656 Quince OrchaRd Rd Ste 600	Gaithersburg	MD	20878	301-977-3900	990-9015
TF Cust Svc: 800-829-5910 ■ *Web:* equusmagazine.com/home					
Family Handyman Magazine 2915 Commers Dr Ste 700	Eagan	MN	55121	800-285-4961	994-2250*
**Fax Area Code:* 651 ■ *TF:* 800-285-4961 ■ *Web:* www.familyhandyman.com					
Family Tree Magazine 4700 E Galbraith Rd	Cincinnati	OH	45236	513-531-2690	422-9686*
**Fax Area Code:* 219 ■ *Web:* www.familytreemagazine.com					
Fine Woodworking Magazine 63 S Main St PO Box 5506	Newtown	CT	06470	203-426-8171	270-6753
TF: 800-283-7252 ■ *Web:* www.finewoodworking.com					
Flying Magazine 460 N. Orlando Ave. Suite 200	Winter Park	FL	32789	407-628-4802	628-7061
TF Cust Svc: 800-678-0797 ■ *Web:* www.flyingmag.com					
Horse Illustrated Magazine 3 Burroughs	Irvine	CA	92618	949-855-8822	580-5668*
**Fax Area Code:* 518 ■ *TF:* 888-588-4677 ■ *Web:* www.horsechannel.com					
McCall Patterns Magazine 120 Broadway	New York	NY	10271	800-782-0323	
Web: www.mccall.com					
McCall's Quilting Magazine 741 Corporate Cir Ste A	Golden	CO	80401	303-215-5600	
TF: 800-944-0736 ■ *Web:* www.mccallsquilting.com					
Model Airplane News 20 Westport Rd	Wilton	CT	06897	203-431-9000	259-6379*
**Fax Area Code:* 717 ■ *TF:* 800-827-0323 ■ *Web:* www.modelairplanenews.com					
Mountain Bike Magazine 400 S Tenth St	Emmaus	PA	18098	800-666-2806	
TF: 800-666-2806 ■ *Web:* www.mountainbike.com					
Nuts & Volts Magazine 430 Princeland Ct	Corona	CA	92879	951-371-8497	371-3052
TF Orders: 800-783-4624 ■ *Web:* www.nutsvolts.com					
Outdoor Photographer Magazine 12121 Wilshire Blvd 12th Fl	Los Angeles	CA	90025	310-820-1500	826-5008
TF Cust Svc: 800-283-4410 ■ *Web:* www.outdoorphotographer.com					
Outside Magazine 400 Market St	Santa Fe	NM	87501	505-989-7100	
TF General: 888-909-2382 ■ *Web:* www.outsideonline.com					
Paper Crafts Magazine 14850 Pony Express Rd	Bluffdale	UT	84065	801-816-8300	816-8301
TF: 800-727-2387 ■ *Web:* www.papercraftsmag.com					
PC Gamer Magazine 4000 Shoreline Ct Ste 400	South San Francisco	CA	94080	650-238-2505	872-2207
TF: 877-404-1337 ■ *Web:* www.pcgamer.com					
Plane & Pilot Magazine 12121 Wilshire Blvd 12th Fl	Los Angeles	CA	90025	310-820-1500	826-5008
TF: 800-283-4330 ■ *Web:* www.planeandpilotmag.com					
Popular Mechanics Magazine 300 W 57th St	New York	NY	10019	212-649-2904	280-1081*
**Fax Area Code:* 646 ■ *Web:* www.popularmechanics.com					
Popular Woodworking Magazine 4700 E Galbraith Rd	Cincinnati	OH	45236	513-531-2690	891-7196
TF Cust Svc: 877-860-9140 ■ *Web:* www.popularwoodworking.com					
Practical Horseman Magazine 656 Quince OrchaRd Rd Ste 600	Gaithersburg	MD	20878	301-977-3900	990-9015
Web: practicalhorsemanmag.com					
QST Magazine 225 Main St	Newington	CT	06111	860-594-0200	594-0259
Web: arrl.org/members-only/page/16609					
Quilter's Newsletter Magazine 741 Corporate Cir Ste A	Golden	CO	80401	303-215-5600	215-5601
TF: 800-477-6089 ■ *Web:* www.quiltersnewsletter.com					
Quiltmaker Magazine 741 Corporate Cir Ste A	Golden	CO	80401	800-881-6634	277-0370*
**Fax Area Code:* 303 ■ *TF:* 800-388-7023 ■ *Web:* www.quiltmaker.com					
Radio Control Boat Modeler 88 Danbury Rd	Wilton	CT	06897	203-431-9000	
TF: 888-235-2021 ■ *Web:* www.airagestore.com					
Rock & Gem Magazine 290 Maple Ct Ste 232	Ventura	CA	93003	805-644-3824	644-3875
TF: 866-377-4666 ■ *Web:* www.rockngem.com					
Rug Hooking Magazine 5067 Ritter Rd	Mechanicsburg	PA	17055	717-796-0411	750-6326*
**Fax Area Code:* 610 ■ *TF:* 866-375-8626 ■ *Web:* www.rughookingmagazine.com					
Scale Auto Magazine 21027 Crossroads Cir	Waukesha	WI	53186	262-796-8776	796-1615*
**Fax:* Cust Svc ■ *TF Cust Svc:* 800-533-6644 ■ *Web:* www.scaleautomag.com					
Shutterbug Magazine 1419 Chaffee Dr Ste 1	Titusville	FL	32780	386-447-6318	225-3149*
**Fax Area Code:* 321 ■ *TF:* 800-829-3340 ■ *Web:* www.shutterbug.com					
Smoke Magazine 26 Broadway	New York	NY	10004	212-391-2060	827-0945
TF: 800-766-2633 ■ *Web:* www.smokemag.com					

	City	State	Zip	Phone	Fax
Threads Magazine 63 S Main St PO Box 5506	Newtown	CT	06470	203-426-8171	270-6753
TF General: 800-283-7252 ■ *Web:* www.threadsmagazine.com					
Western Horseman Magazine 2112 Montgomery St	Fort Worth	TX	76107	817-737-6397	737-9266
Web: www.westernhorseman.com					
Wine Spectator Magazine 387 Pk Ave S Eighth Fl	New York	NY	10016	212-684-4224	481-1540
TF Orders: 800-752-7799 ■ *Web:* www.winespectator.com					
Woodshop News 10 Bokum Rd	Essex	CT	06426	860-767-8227	767-0645
TF: 800-444-7686 ■ *Web:* www.woodshopnews.com					
Woodsmith Magazine 2200 Grand Ave	Des Moines	IA	50312	800-333-5075	282-6741*
**Fax Area Code:* 515 ■ *TF Cust Svc:* 800-333-5075 ■ *Web:* www.woodsmith.com					

460-15 Law Magazines & Journals

	City	State	Zip	Phone	Fax
@Law Magazine 8159 E 41st St	Tulsa	OK	74145	918-582-5188	582-5907
Web: www.nals.org					
Advocate Magazine PO Box 895	Boise	ID	83701	208-334-4500	
Web: www.isb.idaho.gov					
Alabama Lawyer Magazine 415 Dexter Ave	Montgomery	AL	36104	334-269-1515	261-6310
TF: 800-354-6154 ■ *Web:* www.alabar.org					
Arizona Attorney Magazine 4201 N 24th St Ste 200	Phoenix	AZ	85016	602-252-4804	271-4930
TF: 866-482-9227 ■ *Web:* www.myazbar.org/AZAttorney					
Arkansas Lawyer Magazine 2224 Cottondale Ln	Little Rock	AR	72202	501-375-4606	375-4901
TF: 800-609-5668 ■ *Web:* arkbar.com					
Bench & Bar of Minnesota Magazine 600 Nicollet Mall Ste 380	Minneapolis	MN	55402	612-333-1183	333-4927
TF: 800-366-4812 ■ *Web:* mnbenchbar.com					
California Bar Journal 180 Howard St	San Francisco	CA	94105	415-538-2000	
Web: www.calbar.ca.gov					
California Lawyer Magazine 44 Montgomery St Ste 250	San Francisco	CA	94104	415-296-2400	296-2400
Web: www.dailyjournal.com					
Colorado Lawyer Magazine 1900 Grant St Ninth Fl	Denver	CO	80203	303-860-1115	830-3990
TF: 800-332-6736 ■ *Web:* www.cobar.org/tcl/index.cfm					
Connecticut Lawyer Magazine 30 Bank St PO Box 350	New Britain	CT	06050	860-223-4400	223-4488
Web: www.ctbar.org					
Florida Bar Journal 651 E Jefferson St	Tallahassee	FL	32399	850-561-5600	681-3859
TF: 800-342-8060 ■ *Web:* www.floridabar.org					
Georgia Bar Journal 104 Marietta St NW Ste 100	Atlanta	GA	30303	404-527-8700	527-8717
TF: 866-773-2782 ■ *Web:* gabar.org					
Harvard Law Review 1511 Massachusetts Ave Gannett House	Cambridge	MA	02138	617-495-4650	495-2748
Web: www.harvardlawreview.org					
Hawaii Bar Journal 1100 Alakea St Ste 1000	Honolulu	HI	96813	808-537-1868	521-7936
TF: 888-586-1056 ■ *Web:* hsba.org					
InsideCounsel 469 Seventh Ave 10th Fl	New York	NY	10018	312-654-3500	654-3525
Web: www.insidecounsel.com					
Journal of the Kansas Bar Assn 1200 SW Harrison St	Topeka	KS	66612	785-234-5696	234-3813
TF: 800-928-3111 ■ *Web:* www.ksbar.org					
Legal Management: Journal of the Assn of Legal Administrators (ALA) 75 Tri State International Ste 222	Lincolnshire	IL	60069	847-267-1252	267-1329
TF: 800-801-3830 ■ *Web:* www.alanet.org					
Los Angeles Lawyer Magazine 261 S Figueroa St Ste 300	Los Angeles	CA	90012	213-896-6503	613-1972
Web: www.lacba.org/showpage.cfm?pageid=40					
Maine Bar Journal 124 State St PO Box 788	Augusta	ME	04332	207-622-7523	623-0083
TF: 800-475-7523 ■ *Web:* www.mainebar.org					
Maryland Bar Journal 520 W Fayette St	Baltimore	MD	21201	410-685-7878	685-1016
TF: 800-492-1964 ■ *Web:* www.msba.org/departments					
Michigan Bar Journal 306 Townsend St	Lansing	MI	48933	517-346-6300	482-6248
TF: 888-726-3678 ■ *Web:* www.michbar.org/journal					
Mississippi Lawyer Magazine 643 N State St	Jackson	MS	39202	601-948-4471	355-8635
Web: www.msbar.org					
Montana Lawyer Magazine 7 W Sixth Ave Ste 2B	Helena	MT	59601	406-442-7660	442-7763
TF: 888-385-9119 ■ *Web:* www.montanabar.org					
National Jurist Magazine 7670 Opportunity Rd Ste 105	San Diego	CA	92111	858-300-3201	
TF: 800-296-9656 ■ *Web:* www.nationaljurist.com					
New Hampshire Bar News 2 Pillsbury St Ste 300	Concord	NH	03301	603-224-6942	224-2910
TF: 800-868-1212 ■ *Web:* www.nhbar.org					
New York Law Journal 120 Broadway Fifth Fl	New York	NY	10271	877-256-2472	822-5146*
**Fax Area Code:* 646 ■ *TF:* 877-256-2472 ■ *Web:* www.newyorklawjournal.com					
New York State Bar News One Elk St	Albany	NY	12207	518-463-3200	463-4276
Web: www.nysba.org					
Oregon State Bar Bulletin, The 16037 SW Upper Boones Ferry Rd PO Box 231935	Tigard	OR	97281	503-620-0222	684-1366
TF: 800-452-8260 ■ *Web:* www.osbar.org/publications/bulletin/bulletin.html					
Pennsylvania Bar News 100 S St	Harrisburg	PA	17101	717-238-6715	238-7182
TF: 800-932-0311 ■ *Web:* www.pabar.org/public/membership/barnews.asp					
Rhode Island Bar Journal 115 Cedar St	Providence	RI	02903	401-421-5740	421-2703
TF: 800-335-5701 ■ *Web:* www.ribar.com/About%20the%20Bar%20Association/BarJournal.aspx					
Texas Bar Journal 1414 Colorado St Ste 902	Austin	TX	78701	512-463-1463	427-4107
TF: 800-204-2222 ■ *Web:* www.texasbar.com					
Washington Lawyer Magazine 1101 K St NW Ste 200	Washington	DC	20005	202-737-4700	626-3471
TF: 877-333-2227 ■ *Web:* www.dcbar.org					
Washington State Bar News 1325 Fourth Ave Ste 600	Seattle	WA	98101	800-945-9722	727-8320*
**Fax Area Code:* 206 ■ *TF:* 800-945-9722 ■ *Web:* www.wsba.org					
Yale Law Journal PO Box 208215	New Haven	CT	06520	203-432-1666	432-7482
Web: www.yale.edu/yalelj					

460-16 Medical Magazines & Journals

	City	State	Zip	Phone	Fax
Access Magazine 444 N Michigan Ave Ste 3400	Chicago	IL	60611	312-440-8900	467-1806
TF: 800-243-2342 ■ *Web:* adha.org/publications					
Alaska Medicine Magazine 4107 Laurel St	Anchorage	AK	99508	907-562-0304	561-2063
Web: commerce.alaska.gov					
American Dental Assn News 211 E Chicago Ave	Chicago	IL	60611	312-440-2500	
American Journal of Psychiatry 1000 Wilson Blvd Ste 1825	Arlington	VA	22209	703-907-7300	907-1085
TF: 800-368-5777 ■ *Web:* www.ajp.psychiatryonline.org					
American Medical News 515 N State St	Chicago	IL	60654	312-464-4429	464-4445
Web: www.amednews.com					
American Nurse Magazine 8515 Georgia Ave Ste 400	Silver Spring	MD	20910	301-628-5000	628-5001
TF: 800-274-4262 ■ *Web:* www.nursingworld.org					
American Psychologist Magazine 750 First St NE	Washington	DC	20002	202-336-5500	336-6091
TF: 800-374-2721 ■ *Web:* apa.org/journals/amp.aspx					
Annals of Internal Medicine Magazine 190 N Independence Mall W	Philadelphia	PA	19106	215-351-2400	351-2644
TF: 800-523-1546 ■ *Web:* www.annals.org					
Connecticut Medicine Magazine 160 St Ronan St	New Haven	CT	06511	203-865-0587	865-4997
TF: 800-842-8440 ■ *Web:* www.csms.org					
Dental Economics Magazine 1421 S Sheridan Rd	Tulsa	OK	74112	800-331-4463	835-3161*
**Fax Area Code:* 918 ■ *TF:* 800-331-4463 ■ *Web:* www.dentaleconomics.com					
Diabetes Advisor Magazine 1701 N Beauregard St	Alexandria	VA	22311	800-806-7801	
TF: 800-342-2383 ■ *Web:* www.diabetesforecast.org					
Family Practice Management 11400 Tomahawk Creek Pkwy	Leawood	KS	66211	913-906-6000	906-6075
TF: 800-274-2237 ■ *Web:* aafp.org/journals/fpm.html					
Hospital Physician Magazine 125 Strafford Ave Ste 220	Wayne	PA	19087	610-975-4541	975-4564
Web: turner-white.com					
Infection Control Today Magazine 3300 N Central Ave Ste 300	Phoenix	AZ	85012	480-990-1101	990-0819
Web: www.infectioncontroltoday.com					
Internal Medicine News 5635 Fishers Ln Ste 6000	Rockville	MD	20852	240-221-2400	221-4400
TF: 877-524-9336 ■ *Web:* www.internalmedicinenews.com					
Iowa Medicine Magazine 1001 Grand Ave	West Des Moines	IA	50265	515-223-1401	223-0590
TF: 800-747-3070 ■ *Web:* www.iowamedical.org					
Journal of Kentucky Medical Assn 4965 US Hwy 42 KMA Bldg Ste 2000	Louisville	KY	40222	502-426-6200	426-6877
Web: www.kyma.org					
Journal of Practical Nursing (JPN) 1940 Duke St Ste 200	Alexandria	VA	22314	703-933-1003	940-4089
TF: 800-655-4845 ■ *Web:* www.napnes.org					
Journal of the American Dietetic Assn 1600 John F Kennedy Blvd	Philadelphia	PA	19103	212-633-3970	633-3820
Web: www.andjrnl.org					
Journal of the American Medical Assn (JAMA) PO Box 10946	Chicago	IL	60654	312-670-7827	
TF: 800-262-2350 ■ *Web:* jama.jamanetwork.com					
Journal of the American Pharmacists Assn 2215 Constitution Ave NW	Washington	DC	20037	202-628-4410	783-2351
TF: 800-237-2742 ■ *Web:* www.pharmacist.com					
Journal of the Louisiana State Medical Society 6767 Perkins Rd Ste 100	Baton Rouge	LA	70808	225-763-8500	768-5601
TF: 800-375-9508 ■ *Web:* www.lsms.org					
Journal of the Medical Assn of Georgia 1849 The Exchange Ste 200	Atlanta	GA	30339	678-303-9290	303-3732
TF: 800-282-0224 ■ *Web:* www.mag.org					
Journal of the Mississippi State Medical Assn PO Box 2548	Ridgeland	MS	39158	601-853-6733	853-6746
Web: www.msmaonline.com					
Mayo Clinic Proceedings Magazine 200 First St SW Siebens Bldg 7-70	Rochester	MN	55905	507-284-2094	284-0252
TF Cust Svc: 800-654-2452 ■ *Web:* www.mayoclinicproceedings.org					
Medicine & Health/Rhode Island Magazine 235 Promenade St Ste 500 PO Box 91055	Providence	RI	02908	401-331-3207	751-8050
Web: www.rimed.org					
Minnesota Medicine Magazine 1300 Godward St NE Ste 2500	Minneapolis	MN	55413	612-378-1875	378-3875
TF: 800-342-5662 ■ *Web:* www.minnesotamedicine.com					
Missouri Medicine Magazine PO Box 1028	Jefferson City	MO	65102	573-636-5151	636-8552
TF: 800-869-6762 ■ *Web:* www.msma.org					
Monitor on Psychology 750 First Ave NE	Washington	DC	20002	202-336-5500	336-6103
Web: www.apa.org/monitor					
NASW News 750 First St NE Ste 700	Washington	DC	20002	202-408-8600	336-8312
TF: 800-227-3590 ■ *Web:* www.naswpress.org					
NCMS Bulletin 222 N Person St	Raleigh	NC	27601	919-833-3836	833-2023
New England Journal of Medicine 10 Shattuck St	Boston	MA	02115	617-734-9800	739-9864
TF: 800-843-6356 ■ *Web:* www.nejm.org					
Nursing Spectrum Greater New York/New Jersey Metro Magazine 1721 Moon Lk Blvd Ste 540	Hoffman Estates	IL	60169	800-770-0866	
TF: 800-770-0866 ■ *Web:* www.nurse.com					
Ohio Medicine Magazine 3401 Mill Run Dr	Hilliard	OH	43026	614-527-6762	527-6763
TF: 800-766-6762 ■ *Web:* osma.org					
Pharmacy Today Magazine 2215 Constitution Ave NW	Washington	DC	20037	202-628-4410	783-2351
TF: 800-237-2742 ■ *Web:* www.pharmacist.com					
Postgraduate Medicine Magazine 1235 Westlakes Dr Ste 320	Berwyn	PA	19312	215-625-8900	
Web: postgradmed.org					

Phone | Fax

Psychotherapy Networker
5135 MacArthur Blvd NW .... Washington DC 20016 202-537-8950 537-6869
TF: 888-883-3782 ■ *Web:* www.psychotherapynetworker.org

Social Work Magazine
750 First St NE Ste 700 .... Washington DC 20002 202-408-8600 336-8312
TF: 800-227-3590 ■ *Web:* www.naswpress.org

South Dakota State Medical Assn (SDSMA)
2600 W 49th St Ste 200 PO Box 7406 .... Sioux Falls SD 57117 605-336-1965 274-3274
Web: sdsma.org

Southern Medical Journal 35 Lakeshore Dr .... Birmingham AL 35209 205-945-1840 945-1548
TF: 800-423-4992 ■
Web: journals.lww.com/smajournalonline/pages/default.aspx

Texas Medicine Magazine 401 W 15th St .... Austin TX 78701 512-370-1300 370-1693
TF: 800-880-1300 ■ *Web:* www.texmed.org/ata/nrm/tme/texmed_mag.asp

US Pharmacist Magazine
100 Ave of the Americas Ninth Fl .... New York NY 10013 800-825-4696 219-7835*
**Fax Area Code:* 212 ■ *TF:* 800-825-4696 ■ *Web:* www.uspharmacist.com

Virginia Medical News
2924 Emerywood Pkwy Ste 300 .... Richmond VA 23294 800-746-6768 355-6189*
**Fax Area Code:* 804 ■ *TF:* 800-746-6768 ■ *Web:* www.msv.org

West Virginia Medical Journal PO Box 4106 .... Charleston WV 25364 304-925-0342 925-0345
TF: 800-257-4747 ■ *Web:* www.wvsma.com

460-17 Political & Current Events Magazines

Phone | Fax

American Prospect
1710 Rhode Island Ave NW 12th Fl .... Washington DC 20036 202-776-0730 776-0740
Web: www.prospect.org

American Spectator Magazine
1611 N Kent St Ste 901 .... Arlington VA 22209 703-807-2011 807-2013
TF: 800-524-3469 ■ *Web:* www.spectator.org

Association on American Indian Affairs (AAIA)
966 Hungerford Dr Ste 12-B .... Rockville MD 20850 240-314-7155 314-7159
Web: www.indian-affairs.org

Commonweal Magazine 475 Riverside Dr Ste 405 .... New York NY 10115 212-662-4200 662-4183
Web: www.commonwealmagazine.org

Foreign Affairs 58 E 68th St .... New York NY 10065 212-434-9527 434-9859*
**Fax:* Edit ■ *TF Cust Svc:* 800-829-5539 ■ *Web:* foreignaffairs.com

Freeman, The 30 S Broadway .... Irvington-on-Hudson NY 10533 914-591-7230 591-8910
TF Sales: 800-960-4333 ■ *Web:* www.fee.org

Maclean's Magazine One Mt Pleasant Rd 11th Fl .... Toronto ON M4Y2Y5 416-764-1300 764-1332
TF: 800-268-9119 ■ *Web:* macleans.ca/

Mother Jones Magazine
222 Sutter St Ste 600 .... San Francisco CA 94108 415-321-1700 321-1701
TF: 800-438-6656 ■ *Web:* www.motherjones.com

Nation Magazine 33 Irving Pl Eighth Fl .... New York NY 10003 212-209-5400 982-9000
TF Cust Svc: 800-333-8536 ■ *Web:* www.thenation.com

National Journal 600 New Hampshire Ave NW .... Washington DC 20037 202-739-8400 833-8069
TF: 800-613-6701 ■ *Web:* www.nationaljournal.com

National Review 215 Lexington Ave 11th Fl .... New York NY 10016 212-679-7330 679-6174
Web: www.nationalreview.com

New Republic, The 1331 H St NW Ste 700 .... Washington DC 20005 202-508-4444 628-9383
TF: 800-827-1289 ■ *Web:* www.newrepublic.com

Newsweek Magazine Seven Hanover Sq .... New York NY 10004 800-631-1040
TF Cust Svc: 800-631-1040 ■ *Web:* www.newsweek.com

Reason Magazine
3415 S Sepulveda Blvd Ste 400 .... Los Angeles CA 90034 310-391-2245 391-4395
TF Cust Svc: 888-732-7668 ■ *Web:* www.reason.com

Slate Magazine 1350 Connecticut Ave NW .... Washington DC 20036 212-445-5330 261-1310*
**Fax Area Code:* 202 ■ *Web:* www.slate.com

US News & World Report
1050 Thomas Jefferson St NW .... Washington DC 20007 212-716-6800
TF: 800-836-6397 ■ *Web:* www.usnews.com

460-18 Religious & Spiritual Magazines

Phone | Fax

B'Nai B'Rith Magazine
2020 K St NW Seventh Fl .... Washington DC 20006 202-857-6600
TF: 888-388-4224 ■ *Web:* www.bnaibrith.org

Biblical Archaeology Review
4710 41st St NW .... Washington DC 20016 202-364-3300 364-2636
TF: 800-221-4644 ■ *Web:* www.biblicalarchaeology.org

Body & Soul 42 Pleasant St .... Watertown MA 02472 617-449-5506 647-0116*
**Fax Area Code:* 603 ■ *TF:* 800-755-1178 ■ *Web:* www.marthastewart.com

Catholic Digest PO Box 6015 .... New London CT 06320 860-437-3012
TF: 800-678-2836 ■ *Web:* www.catholicdigest.com

Charisma Magazine 600 Rinehart Rd .... Lake Mary FL 32746 407-333-0600 333-7100
TF: 800-749-6500 ■ *Web:* www.charismamag.com

Christianity Today Magazine
465 Gundersen Dr .... Carol Stream IL 60188 630-260-6200 260-0114
TF: 800-999-1704 ■ *Web:* www.christianitytoday.com

Episcopal Life Magazine
815 Second Ave Episcopal Church Ctr .... New York NY 10017 212-716-6000 716-6000
TF: 800-334-7626 ■ *Web:* www.episcopalchurch.org

Kashrus Magazine PO Box 204 .... Brooklyn NY 11204 718-336-8544 336-8550
Web: www.kashrusmagazine.com

Lutheran Magazine 8765 W Higgins Rd .... Chicago IL 60631 800-638-3522 380-2409*
**Fax Area Code:* 773 ■ *TF:* 800-638-3522 ■ *Web:* www.thelutheran.org

Ministries Today Magazine 600 Rinehart Rd .... Lake Mary FL 32746 407-333-0600 333-7100
Web: www.ministriestoday.com

Moment Magazine
4115 Wisconsin Ave NW Ste 10 .... Washington DC 20016 202-363-6422 362-2514
TF: 800-777-1005 ■ *Web:* www.momentmag.com

Presbyterians Today Magazine
100 Witherspoon St .... Louisville KY 40202 800-872-3283 569-8632*
**Fax Area Code:* 502 ■ *TF:* 800-728-7228 ■ *Web:* www.presbyterianmission.org

Reform Judaism Magazine 633 Third Ave .... New York NY 10017 212-650-4240 212-4249
Web: reformjudaismmag.org

Spiritled Woman - Charisma Magazine
600 Rinehart Rd .... Lake Mary FL 32746 407-333-0600 333-7100
TF: 866-776-6473 ■ *Web:* www.charismamag.com/index.php/spiritled-woman

Today's Christian Woman Magazine
465 Gundersen Dr .... Carol Stream IL 60188 630-260-6200 260-0114
TF Orders: 877-247-4787 ■ *Web:* www.christianitytoday.com/women

US Catholic Magazine 205 W Monroe .... Chicago IL 60606 312-236-7782 236-8207
TF Cust Svc: 800-328-6515 ■ *Web:* uscatholic.org

460-19 Science & Nature Magazines

Phone | Fax

American Laboratory
395 Oyster Pt Blvd Ste 321 .... South San Francisco CA 94080 650-243-5600
Web: www.americanlaboratory.com

American Scientist Magazine
3106 E NC Hwy 54 PO Box 13975 .... Research Triangle Park NC 27709 919-549-4691 549-0090
TF: 800-243-6534 ■ *Web:* www.americanscientist.org

Archaeology Magazine 36-36 33rd St .... Long Island City NY 11106 718-472-3050 472-3051
TF: 877-275-9782 ■ *Web:* www.archaeology.org

Audubon Magazine 225 Varick St Seventh Fl .... New York NY 10014 212-979-3000 477-9069
TF Cust Svc: 800-274-4201 ■ *Web:* mag.audubon.org

Aviation Week & Space Technology Magazine
1200 G St NW Ste 922 .... Washington DC 20005 800-525-5003 383-2346*
**Fax Area Code:* 202 ■ **Fax:* Edit ■ *TF:* 800-525-5003 ■ *Web:* www.aviationweek.com

BioScience 1444 'I' St NW Ste 200 .... Washington DC 20005 202-628-1500 628-1509
TF: 800-992-2427 ■ *Web:* www.aibs.org/bioscience

BioTechniques 52 Vanderbilt Ave 7th Fl .... New York NY 10017 212-520-2777 661-5052
TF: 800-606-6246 ■ *Web:* biotechniques.com

Defenders Magazine 1130 17th St NW .... Washington DC 20036 202-682-9400 682-1331
TF: 800-385-9712 ■ *Web:* defenders.org/newsletter

E/The Environmental Magazine
28 Knight St PO Box 5098 .... Norwalk CT 06851 203-854-5559 866-0602
TF: 800-321-6742 ■ *Web:* www.emagazine.com

Earth Island Journal
300 Broadway Ste 28 .... San Francisco CA 94133 415-788-3666 788-7324
Web: www.earthisland.org/eijournal

Friends of the Earth Magazine
1100 15th St NW .... Washington DC 20005 202-783-7400 783-0444
TF: 877-843-8687 ■ *Web:* www.foe.org

Garden Compass 1660 Union St .... San Diego CA 92101 619-239-2202
Web: gardencompass.com

National Parks Magazine
777 Sixth St NW Ste 700 .... Washington DC 20001 202-223-6722 454-3333
TF General: 800-628-7275 ■ *Web:* npca.org/news/magazine/

National Wildlife Magazine
11100 Wildlife Ctr Dr .... Reston VA 20190 703-438-6000 438-6040
TF Cust Svc: 800-822-9919 ■ *Web:* www.nwf.org/nationalwildlife

Natural History Magazine 105 W Hwy 54 Ste 265 .... Durham NC 27713 646-356-6500 933-1867*
**Fax Area Code:* 919 ■ *Web:* www.naturalhistorymag.com

Nature
National Press Bldg 529 14th St NW
Ste 968 .... Washington DC 20045 202-737-2355 628-1609
TF: 800-524-0384 ■ *Web:* www.nature.com

Orion Magazine 187 Main St .... Great Barrington MA 01230 413-528-4422 528-0676
TF: 888-909-6568 ■ *Web:* www.orionmagazine.org

Physics Today Magazine
One Physics Ellipse .... College Park MD 20740 301-209-3040 209-0842
TF: 800-344-6902 ■ *Web:* contact.physicstoday.org

R & D Magazine 100 Enterprise Dr Ste 600 .... Rockaway NJ 07866 973-920-7000 663-9177*
**Fax Area Code:* 978 ■ *TF:* 866-885-9794 ■ *Web:* www.rdmag.com

Science Magazine 1200 New York Ave NW .... Washington DC 20005 202-326-6500 842-1065
TF: 800-731-4939 ■ *Web:* www.sciencemag.org

Science News 1719 N St NW .... Washington DC 20036 202-785-2255 659-0365
TF Cust Svc: 800-552-4412 ■ *Web:* www.sciencenews.org

Scientist, The 400 Market St Ste 1250 .... Philadelphia PA 19106 215-351-1660 351-1146
Web: www.the-scientist.com

Sierra Magazine 85 Second St 2nd Fl .... San Francisco CA 94105 415-977-5500 977-5794
TF: 866-338-1015 ■ *Web:* www.sierraclub.org/sierra

Sky & Telescope Magazine 90 Sherman St .... Cambridge MA 02140 617-864-7360 864-6117
TF: 800-253-0245 ■ *Web:* www.skyandtelescope.com

Smithsonian Air & Space Magazine
PO Box 37012 .... Washington DC 20013 202-633-6070 633-6085
TF Cust Svc: 800-766-2149 ■ *Web:* www.airspacemag.com

Tech Briefs Media Group
261 Fifth Ave Ste 1901 .... New York NY 10016 212-490-3999
TF: 888-456-3398 ■ *Web:* www.techbriefs.com

Technology Review Magazine
One Main St Seventh Fl .... Cambridge MA 02142 617-475-8000 475-8042
Web: www.technologyreview.com

460-20 Sports Magazines

Phone | Fax

American Rifleman Magazine
11250 Waples Mill Rd .... Fairfax VA 22030 800-672-3888 267-3971*
**Fax Area Code:* 703 ■ *Web:* americanrifleman.org

Baseball America Magazine
4319 S Alston Ave Ste 103 .... Durham NC 27713 919-682-9635 682-2880
Web: baseballamerica.com/

Bassmaster Magazine
3500 Blue Lake Dr Suite 330 .... Birmingham FL 35243 877-227-7872
TF: 877-227-7872 ■
Web: www.bassmaster.com/topics/Bassmaster%20Magazine

Beckett Football Card Monthly 4635 McEwen Rd .... Dallas TX 75244 972-991-6657 991-8930
Web: www.beckett.com

Bowhunting World Magazine
6121 Baker Rd Ste 101 .... Minnetonka MN 55345 952-405-2280
TF: 800-766-0039 ■ *Web:* www.grandviewoutdoors.com

Phone | Fax

Climbing Magazine 2291 Arapahoe Ave ... Boulder CO 80302 800-829-5895
TF: 800-829-5895 ■ *Web:* www.climbing.com

Competitor Magazine 9477 Waples St Ste 150 ... San Diego CA 92121 800-311-1255 768-6801*
**Fax Area Code:* 858 ■ *TF:* 800-311-1255 ■ *Web:* running.competitor.com

Ducks Unlimited Magazine One Waterfowl Way ... Memphis TN 38120 901-758-3825 758-3850
TF: 800-453-8257 ■ *Web:* www.ducks.org

Florida Sportsman Magazine 2700 S Kanner Hwy ... Stuart FL 34994 772-219-7400 219-6900
Web: www.flsportsman.com

Gaebler Ventures 12301 Whitewater Dr ... Minnetonka MN 55343 952-936-9333 936-9755
Web: www.gaebler.com

Golf Digest 20 Westport Rd Ste 320 ... Wilton CT 06897 203-761-5100 761-5129
Web: www.golfdigest.com

Golf Tips Magazine
12121 Wilshire Blvd Ste 1200 ... Los Angeles CA 90025 310-820-1500 826-5008
TF: 877-505-9447 ■ *Web:* www.golftipsmag.com

Hockey News Magazine 25 Sheppard Ave Ste 100 ... Toronto ON M2N6S7 888-361-9768
TF: 888-361-9768 ■ *Web:* www.thehockeynews.com

In-Fisherman Magazine 7819 Highland Scenic Rd ... Baxter MN 56425 218-829-1648 829-3091
Web: www.in-fisherman.com

Journal of the Philosophy of Sport
1607 N Market St ... Champaign IL 61820 217-351-5076 351-1549
TF: 800-747-4457 ■ *Web:* www.humankinetics.com

Links Magazine 10 Executive Pk Rd ... Hilton Head Island SC 29928 843-842-6200 842-6233
Web: www.linksmagazine.com

Salt Water Sportsman Magazine
460 N Orlando Ave Ste 200 ... Winter Park FL 32789 407-628-4802 628-7061
TF: 800-759-2127 ■ *Web:* www.saltwatersportsman.com

Ski Magazine 5720 Flatiron Pkwy ... Boulder CO 80301 303-253-6300
TF: 888-444-8151 ■ *Web:* www.skinet.com

Snow Goer Magazine
3300 Fernbrook Ln N Ste 200 ... Plymouth MN 55447 800-710-5249 383-4499*
**Fax Area Code:* 763 ■ *TF:* 800-710-5249 ■ *Web:* www.snowgoer.com

Sport Fishing Magazine
460 N Orlando Ave Ste 200 ... Orlando FL 32789 305-253-0555 628-7061*
**Fax Area Code:* 407 ■ *Web:* www.sportfishingmag.com

Sports Afield Magazine
15621 Chemical Ln ... Huntington Beach CA 92649 714-373-4910 894-4949
TF: 800-451-4788 ■ *Web:* www.sportsafield.com

Sports Business Daily
120 W Morehead St Ste 310 ... Charlotte NC 28202 704-973-1410 973-1401
TF: 800-829-9839 ■ *Web:* www.sportsbusinessdaily.com

Sports Spectrum Magazine
105 Corporate Blvd Ste 2 ... Indian Trail NC 28079 704-821-2971 875-2669*
**Fax Area Code:* 866 ■ *TF:* 866-821-2971 ■ *Web:* www.sportsspectrum.com

Tennis Magazine 814 S Westgate Ste 100 ... Los Angeles NY 90049 310-893-5300
Web: www.tennis.com

TransWorld Surf Magazine
2052 Corte del Nogal Ste 100 ... Carlsbad CA 92011 760-722-7777 722-0653
Web: surf.transworld.net

Travel + Leisure Magazine
1120 Ave of the Americas 10th Fl ... New York NY 10036 212-382-5600 373-3681*
**Fax Area Code:* 718 ■ *TF:* 800-452-9292 ■ *Web:* www.travelandleisure.com

460-21 Trade & Industry Magazines

Phone | Fax

AAPG Explorer Magazine 1444 S Boulder Ave ... Tulsa OK 74119 918-584-2555 560-2636
TF: 800-364-2274 ■ *Web:* www.aapg.org

Aerospace America Magazine
1801 Alexander Bell Dr Ste 500 ... Reston VA 20191 703-264-7500 264-7551
TF: 800-639-2422 ■ *Web:* www.aiaa.org

Air Conditioning Heating & Refrigeration News
2401 W Big Beaver Rd Ste 700 ... Troy MI 48084 248-362-3700 362-0317
TF: 800-837-8337 ■ *Web:* www.achrnews.com

Air Transport World Magazine
8380 Colesville Rd Ste 500 ... Silver Spring MD 20910 301-755-0200 514-3909*
**Fax Area Code:* 913 ■ *Web:* www.atwonline.com

American Salon Magazine 757 Third Ave 5th Fl ... New York NY 10017 212-895-8200 376-9073*
**Fax Area Code:* 805 ■ *TF:* 866-871-0656 ■ *Web:* www.americansalon.com

American Society of Civil Engineers (ASCE)
1801 Alexander Bell Dr ... Reston VA 20191 703-295-6300 295-6211
TF: 800-548-2723 ■ *Web:* www.asce.org

Automotive Executive Magazine
8400 Westpark Dr ... McLean VA 22102 703-821-7150 821-7234
TF: 800-672-3888 ■ *Web:* insidenova.com

Automotive News Magazine 1155 Gratiot Ave ... Detroit MI 48207 313-446-0450 446-0383
TF: 877-812-1584 ■ *Web:* www.autonews.com

Bartender Magazine PO Box 158 ... Liberty Corner NJ 07938 908-766-6006 766-6607*
**Fax:* Edit ■ *TF Sales:* 800-463-7465 ■ *Web:* www.bartender.com

Builder Magazine 1 Thomas Cir NW Ste 600 ... Washington DC 20005 202-452-0800 785-1974
TF: 800-325-6180 ■ *Web:* www.builderonline.com

Building Design & Construction Magazine
3030 W Salt Creek Ln Ste 201 ... Arlington Heights IL 60005 847-391-1000 390-0408
TF: 888-811-3288 ■ *Web:* www.bdcnetwork.com

Chemical Processing Magazine
555 W Pierce Rd Ste 301 ... Itasca IL 60143 630-467-1300 467-1109
TF: 800-343-4048 ■ *Web:* www.chemicalprocessing.com

Chemical Week Magazine
140 East 45th Street
2 Grand Central Tower,40th Fl ... New York NY 10017 212-884-9528 884-9514
TF Cust Svc: 866-501-7540 ■ *Web:* www.chemweek.com

Civil Engineering Magazine
1801 Alexander Bell Dr ... Reston VA 20191 703-295-6300 295-6300*
**Fax:* Edit ■ *TF:* 800-548-2723 ■ *Web:* asce.org

Contract Employment Weekly
11711 N Creek Pkwy S # 112 ... Bothell WA 98011 425-806-5200
Web: www.ceweekly.com

Control Engineering Magazine
2000 Clearwater Dr ... Oak Brook IL 60523 630-288-8000 288-8580
Web: www.controleng.com

Controller Magazine 120 W Harvest Dr ... Lincoln NE 68521 402-479-2143 479-2135
TF: 800-247-4890 ■ *Web:* www.controller.com

Phone | Fax

DaySpa Magazine 7628 Densmore Ave ... Van Nuys CA 91406 818-782-7328 782-7450
TF: 800-442-5667 ■ *Web:* www.dayspamagazine.com

Design News 225 Wyman St ... Waltham MA 02451 763-746-2792
TF: 800-869-6882 ■ *Web:* www.designnews.com

Designfax Magazine 2506 Tamiami Trail North ... Nokomis FL 34275 941-966-9521 966-2590
TF: 877-245-6247 ■ *Web:* www.designfax.net

EC & M Magazine 9800 Metcalf Ave ... Overland Park KS 66212 913-967-1782 514-6782
Web: www.ecmweb.com

EDN Magazine 303 Second St ... San Francisco CA 94107 415-947-6000
TF Orders: 800-446-6551 ■ *Web:* www.edn.com

EE Times Magazine 600 Community Dr ... Manhasset NY 11030 408-930-7372 651-1651*
**Fax Area Code:* 856 ■ *TF:* 800-645-6278 ■ *Web:* www.eetimes.com

Electronic Component News
100 Enterprise Dr Ste 600 ... Rockaway NJ 07866 973-920-7000 607-5488
TF: 877-650-5160 ■ *Web:* www.ecnmag.com

Engineering News-Record (ENR)
Two Penn Plz Ninth Fl ... New York NY 10121 212-904-3507 904-2820
TF: 877-876-8208 ■ *Web:* enr.construction.com

EPRI Journal 3420 Hillview Ave ... Palo Alto CA 94304 650-855-2121 855-2121
TF: 800-313-3774 ■ *Web:* www.epri.com/journal

Equipment Today Magazine
1233 Janesville Ave ... Fort Atkinson WI 53538 920-563-1677

Fine Homebuilding Magazine
63 S Main St PO Box 5506 ... Newtown CT 06470 203-426-8171 270-6753
TF: 800-283-7252 ■ *Web:* www.finehomebuilding.com

Food Management Magazine 1300 E Ninth St ... Cleveland OH 44114 216-696-7000 514-6738*
**Fax Area Code:* 913 ■ *Web:* www.penton.com

Food Processing Magazine
555 W Pierce Rd Ste 301 ... Itasca IL 60143 630-467-1300 467-1179
TF: 800-755-5505 ■ *Web:* www.foodprocessing.com

Furniture/Today Magazine
7025 Albert Pick Rd Ste 200 ... Greensboro NC 27409 336-605-0121 605-1143
Web: www.furnituretoday.com

Giftware News 20 W Kinzie St 12th Fl ... Chicago IL 60654 312-849-2220 849-2174
TF: 800-229-1967 ■ *Web:* www.talcott.com

Glass Magazine 8200 Greensboro Dr Ste 302 ... McLean VA 22102 703-442-4890
Web: www.glassmagazine.com

Home Media Retailing
201 E Sandpointe Ave Ste 500 ... Santa Ana CA 92707 714-759-4661 248-4107*
**Fax Area Code:* 540 ■ **Fax:* Sales ■ *TF:* 800-371-6897 ■ *Web:* www.homemediamagazine.com

Industrial Equipment News Five Penn Plz ... New York NY 10001 212-695-0500 290-7362
Web: www.thomaspublishing.com

Inside Self Storage Magazine
3300 N Central Ave Ste 300 ... Phoenix AZ 85012 480-990-1101 990-0819
Web: www.insideselfstorage.com

Institute of Scrap Recycling Industries Magazine
1615 L St NW Ste 6000 ... Washington DC 20036 202-662-8500 626-0900
TF: 800-767-7236 ■ *Web:* www.isri.org

Journal of Petroleum Technology
222 Palisades Creek Dr ... Richardson TX 75080 972-952-9393 952-9435
TF: 800-456-6863 ■ *Web:* www.spe.org

Journal of Protective Coatings & Linings
2100 Wharton St Ste 310 ... Pittsburgh PA 15203 412-431-8300 431-5428
TF: 800-837-8303 ■ *Web:* www.paintsquare.com

Land Line Magazine One NW Oodia Dr ... Grain Valley MO 64029 816-229-5791 443-2227
TF: 800-444-5791 ■ *Web:* www.landlinemag.com

Looking Fit Magazine
3300 N Central Ave Ste 300 ... Phoenix AZ 85012 480-990-1101 567-6852*
**Fax Area Code:* 602 ■ *Web:* www.lookingfit.com

Machine Design Magazine 330 N. Wabash Ave ... Chicago IL 60611 312-840-8462 621-8469*
**Fax Area Code:* 216 ■ *Web:* machinedesign.com/?p=1

Modern Car Care Magazine
3300 N Central Ave Ste 300 ... Phoenix AZ 85012 480-990-1101 990-0819
Web: www.moderncarcare.com

Modern Machine Shop Magazine
6915 Valley Ave ... Cincinnati OH 45244 513-527-8800 527-8801
TF: 800-950-8020 ■ *Web:* www.mmsonline.com

Nailpro Magazine 7628 Densmore Ave ... Van Nuys CA 91406 818-782-7328 782-7450
TF: 800-442-5667 ■ *Web:* www.nailpro.com

Nails Magazine 3520 Challenger St ... Torrance CA 90503 310-533-2400 533-2507
TF: 888-624-5744 ■ *Web:* www.nailsmag.com

National Clothesline Magazine
801 Easton Rd Ste 2 ... Willow Grove PA 19090 215-830-8467 830-8490
Web: www.natclo.com

National Fisherman Magazine 121 Free St ... Portland ME 04101 207-842-5600 842-5603
TF: 800-959-5073 ■ *Web:* www.nationalfisherman.com

National Fitness Trade Journal
PO Box 2490 ... White City OR 97503 541-830-0400 830-0410
TF: 877-867-7835 ■
Web: www.msfitness.com/nationalfitness/tradejournal/nftj.html

Natural Products Insider Magazine
3300 N Central Ave Ste 3000 ... Phoenix AZ 85012 480-990-1101 990-0819
Web: www.naturalproductsinsider.com

New Equipment Digest 1300 E Ninth St ... Cleveland OH 44114 216-696-7000
Web: www.pentonmsc.com

NewBay Media LLC 28 E 28th St 12th Fl ... New York NY 10016 212-378-0400 378-0470
Web: www.newbaymedia.com

Oil & Gas Journal PO Box 2002 ... Tulsa OK 74101 918-831-9423 831-9482
TF: 800-633-1656 ■ *Web:* www.ogj.com

PHONE+ Magazine 3300 N Central Ave Ste 300 ... Phoenix AZ 85012 480-990-1101 990-0819
Web: www.channelpartnersonline.com

Plant Engineering Magazine
2000 Clearwater Dr ... Oak Brook IL 60523 630-288-8780 288-8781
Web: www.plantengineering.com

Plant Services Magazine
555 W Pierce Rd Ste 301 ... Itasca IL 60143 630-467-1300 467-1120
TF: 800-872-9141 ■ *Web:* www.plantservices.com

Plastics Technology Magazine
6915 Valley Ave ... Cincinnati OH 45244 513-527-8800 527-8801
Web: www.ptonline.com

Pro Lights & Staging News Magazine
6000 S Eastern Ste 14-J ... Las Vegas NV 89119 702-932-5585 932-5584
TF General: 888-667-7438 ■ *Web:* www.plsn.com

Phone | Fax

Proceedings of the IEEE Magazine
445 Hoes Ln ... Piscataway NJ 08855 732-562-5478 562-5456
TF: 800-678-4333 ■ *Web:* www.ieee.org

Product Design & Development Magazine
199 E Badger Rd Ste 201 ... Madison WI 53713 973-920-7000
Web: www.pddnet.com

Professional Surveyor Magazine
20 W Third St ... Frederick MD 21701 301-682-6101 682-6105
Web: xyht.com

Qualified Remodeler Magazine
1233 Janesville Ave ... Fort Atkinson WI 53538 920-563-6388 563-1707
TF: 800-547-7377 ■ *Web:* www.forresidentialpros.com

Quality Progress Magazine
600 N Plankinton Ave PO Box 3005 ... Milwaukee WI 53201 414-272-8575 272-1734
TF Cust Svc: 800-248-1946 ■ *Web:* www.asq.org/pub/qualityprogress

Retail Traffic 249 W 17th St ... New York NY 10011 212-204-4200 514-9050*
**Fax Area Code:* 914 ■ *Web:* nreionline.com

Street & Smith's SportsBusiness Journal
120 W Morehead St Ste 310 ... Charlotte NC 28202 704-973-1410 973-1401
Web: www.sportsbusinessdaily.com

Travel Weekly Crossroads Magazine
100 Lighting Way ... Secaucus NJ 07094 201-902-2000 902-1916
Web: www.travelweekly.com

Trucker's Connection
3651 Peachtree Pkwy Ste 103 ... Suwanee GA 30024 770-416-0927 253-7086*
**Fax Area Code:* 470

United Mine Workers of America
18354 Quantico Gateway Dr Ste 200 ... Triangle VA 22172 703-291-2400
Web: www.umwa.org

Urban Call Magazine
4265 Brownsboro Rd Ste 225 ... Winston-Salem NC 27106 336-759-7477 759-7212
Web: www.theurbancall.com

Women's Wear Daily Magazine
750 Third Ave Fifth Fl ... New York NY 10017 212-630-4600 630-4580
TF: 800-289-0273 ■ *Web:* www.wwd.com

Writer's Digest 4700 E Galbraith Rd ... Cincinnati OH 45236 513-531-2690
TF Cust Svc: 800-283-0963 ■ *Web:* www.writersdigest.com

460-22 Travel & Regional Interest Magazines

Phone | Fax

Alaska Airlines Magazine
2701 First Ave Ste 250 ... Seattle WA 98121 206-441-5871 448-6939
Web: www.alaskaairlinesmagazine.com

Alaska Magazine
301 Arctic Slope Ave Ste 300 ... Anchorage AK 99518 386-246-0444 275-2117*
**Fax Area Code:* 907 ■ *TF:* 800-288-5892 ■ *Web:* www.alaskamagazine.com

Arizona Highways Magazine 2039 W Lewis Ave ... Phoenix AZ 85009 800-543-5432 254-4505*
**Fax Area Code:* 602 ■ *TF:* 800-543-5432 ■ *Web:* www.arizonahighways.com

Atlanta Magazine 260 Peachtree St Ste 300 ... Atlanta GA 30303 404-527-5500 527-5575
Web: www.atlantamagazine.com

Baltimore Magazine
1000 Lancaster St Ste 400 ... Baltimore MD 21202 410-752-4200 625-0280
TF Cust Svc: 800-935-0838 ■ *Web:* www.baltimoremagazine.net

Buffalo Spree Magazine
100 Corporate Pkwy Ste 220 ... Buffalo NY 14226 716-783-9119 783-9983
TF: 855-697-7733 ■ *Web:* www.buffalospree.com

Cape Cod Life Magazine
13 Steeple St Ste 204 PO Box 1439 ... Mashpee MA 02649 508-419-7381 477-1225
TF: 800-698-1717 ■ *Web:* www.capecodlife.com

Caribbean Travel & Life Magazine
460 N Orlando Ave Ste 200 ... Winter Park FL 32789 407-628-4802 628-7061
TF Sales: 800-289-9399 ■ *Web:* www.bonniercorp.com

Carnegie Magazine 4400 Forbes Ave ... Pittsburgh PA 15213 412-622-3131 622-6258
Web: www.carnegiemuseums.org/cmag

Chesapeake Bay Magazine
1819 Bay Ridge Ave Ste 180 ... Annapolis MD 21403 410-263-2662 267-6924
TF: 800-283-2883 ■ *Web:* www.chesapeakeboating.net

Chicago Life Magazine PO Box 11311 ... Chicago IL 60611 773-549-1523
Web: www.chicagolife.net

Chicago Magazine 435 N Michigan Ave Ste 1100 ... Chicago IL 60611 312-222-8999 222-0699*
**Fax:* Edit ■ *TF:* 800-999-0879 ■ *Web:* www.chicagomag.com

Cincinnati Magazine 441 Vine St Ste 200 ... Cincinnati OH 45202 513-421-4300 562-2746
Web: www.cincinnatimagazine.com

Cleveland Magazine 1422 Euclid Ave Ste 730 ... Cleveland OH 44115 216-771-2833 781-6318
TF: 800-210-7293 ■ *Web:* www.clevelandmagazine.com

Columbus Monthly Magazine 34 South Third St ... Columbus OH 43215 614-888-4567 461-8746
Web: www.columbusmonthly.com

Conde Nast Traveler Magazine Four Times Sq ... New York NY 10036 212-286-2860 286-2190
Web: www.cntraveler.com

Connecticut Magazine 35 Nutmeg Dr ... Trumbull CT 06611 203-380-6600 380-6610
TF: 800-645-4328 ■ *Web:* www.connecticutmag.com

Cruise Travel Magazine 990 Grove St Ste 400 ... Evanston IL 60201 847-491-6440 491-0459
Web: cruisetravelmag.com

Departures Magazine
1120 Ave of the Americas ... New York NY 10036 212-642-1999 827-6413
TF: 800-333-7483 ■ *Web:* www.departures.com

Down East 680 Commercial St ... Rockport ME 04856 207-594-9544 594-5144
TF: 800-766-1670 ■ *Web:* downeast.com

Family Motor Coaching Magazine
8291 Clough Pk ... Cincinnati OH 45244 513-474-3622 474-2332
TF: 800-543-3622 ■ *Web:* www.fmca.com

Guest Informant Magazine 725 Broad St ... Augusta GA 30901 706-724-0851
TF: 800-622-6358 ■ *Web:* morris.com

Hamptons Magazine 67 Hampton Rd Ste 201 ... SouthHampton NY 11968 631-283-7125 283-7854
TF: 866-891-3144 ■ *Web:* www.hamptons-magazine.com

Hana Hou Magazine (Hawaiian Airlines)
1144 Tenth Ave Ste 401 ... Honolulu HI 96816 808-733-3333 733-3340
TF: 888-733-3336 ■ *Web:* www.hanahou.com

Home & Away Magazine 10703 J St Ste 100 ... Omaha NE 68127 402-592-5000 331-5194
TF: 800-710-2267 ■ *Web:* www.homeandawaymagazine.com

Honolulu Magazine 1000 Bishop St Ste 405 ... Honolulu HI 96813 808-534-7546
TF: 800-788-4230 ■ *Web:* www.honolulumagazine.com

Houston LifeStyle Magazine
10707 Corporate Dr Ste 170 ... Stafford TX 77477 281-240-2445 240-5079
TF: 866-505-4456 ■ *Web:* www.houstonlifestyles.com

Hudson Valley Magazine 2678 S Rd 2nd Fl ... Poughkeepsie NY 12601 845-463-0542 463-1544
TF General: 855-658-1850 ■ *Web:* www.hvmag.com

Indianapolis Monthly Magazine
40 Monument Cir Ste 100 ... Indianapolis IN 46204 317-237-9288 684-2080
TF Circ: 888-403-9005 ■ *Web:* www.indianapolismonthly.com

Inland Empire Magazine
3769 Tibbetts St Ste A ... Riverside CA 92506 951-682-3026 682-0246
TF General: 800-424-4232 ■ *Web:* www.inlandempiremagazine.com

InsideFlyer Magazine
1930 Frequent Flyer Pt ... Colorado Springs CO 80915 719-597-8889 597-6855
TF: 800-767-8896 ■ *Web:* www.insideflyer.com

Islands Magazine
460 N Orlando Ave Ste 200 ... Winter Park FL 32789 515-237-3697 524-8292*
**Fax Area Code:* 800 ■ *TF:* 800-250-1523 ■ *Web:* www.islands.com

Jacksonville Magazine 1261 King St ... Jacksonville FL 32204 904-389-3622 389-3628
TF: 800-962-0214 ■ *Web:* www.jacksonvillemag.com

Key Magazine PO Box 111266 ... Memphis TN 38111 901-458-3912 458-5723
TF: 866-446-3674 ■ *Web:* www.keymemphis.com

Key: This Week in Chicago Magazine
226 E Ontario St Ste 300 ... Chicago IL 60611 312-943-0838 664-6113
TF: 877-866-0966 ■ *Web:* www.keymagazinechicago.com

Los Angeles Confidential Magazine
8530 Wilshire Blvd Ste 500 ... Beverly Hills CA 90211 310-289-7300 289-0444
TF: 866-891-3144 ■ *Web:* www.la-confidential-magazine.com

Los Angeles Magazine
5900 Wilshire Blvd 10th Fl ... Los Angeles CA 90036 323-801-0100 801-0105*
**Fax:* Edit ■ *TF Cust Svc:* 800-876-5222 ■ *Web:* www.lamag.com

Louisville Magazine
137 W Muhammad Ali Blvd Ste 102 ... Louisville KY 40202 502-625-0100 625-0109
TF: 866-832-0011 ■ *Web:* www.louisville.com

Memphis Magazine 460 Tennessee St Ste 200 ... Memphis TN 38103 901-521-9000 521-0129
TF: 800-288-9999 ■ *Web:* www.memphismagazine.com

Michigan Out-of-Doors Magazine (MOOD)
2101 Wood St PO Box 30235 ... Lansing MI 48912 517-371-1041 371-1505
TF: 800-777-6720 ■ *Web:* www.mucc.org

Midwest Living Magazine 1716 Locust St ... Des Moines IA 50309 515-284-3808 284-3836
TF: 800-678-8093 ■ *Web:* www.midwestliving.com

Milwaukee Magazine 126 N Jefferson St ... Milwaukee WI 53202 414-273-1101 287-4373
TF: 800-662-4818 ■ *Web:* www.milwaukeemag.com

Minneapolis-Saint Paul Magazine
220 S Sixth St Ste 500 ... Minneapolis MN 55402 612-339-7571 339-5806
TF: 800-999-5589 ■ *Web:* www.mspmag.com

Mississippi Magazine
Five Lakeland Cir PO Box 16445 ... Jackson MS 39216 601-982-8418 982-8447
Web: www.mississippimagazine.com

MotorHome Magazine 2750 Park View Ct Ste 240 ... Oxnard CA 93036 805-667-4100 667-4484
TF Cust Svc: 800-678-1201 ■ *Web:* www.motorhome.com

National Geographic Traveler Magazine
1145 17th St NW ... Washington DC 20036 202-857-7000
TF: 800-647-5463 ■ *Web:* nationalgeographic.com

Nevada Magazine 401 N Carson St ... Carson City NV 89701 775-687-5416 687-6159
TF: 855-729-7117 ■ *Web:* www.nevadamagazine.com

New Jersey Monthly Magazine
55 Pk Pl PO Box 920 ... Morristown NJ 07963 973-539-8230 538-2953
TF: 888-419-0419 ■ *Web:* www.njmonthly.com

New Mexico Magazine PO Box 12002 ... Santa Fe NM 87504 800-898-6639 827-6496*
**Fax Area Code:* 505 ■ *TF:* 800-898-6639 ■ *Web:* www.nmmagazine.com

New Orleans Magazine
110 Veterans Blvd Ste 123 ... Metairie LA 70005 504-828-1380 828-1385
TF Edit: 877-221-3512 ■ *Web:* www.myneworleans.com/new-orleans-magazine

New York Magazine 75 Varick St ... New York NY 10013 212-508-0700
TF: 800-678-0900 ■ *Web:* www.nymag.com

Nob Hill Gazette 5 Third St Ste 222 ... San Francisco CA 94103 415-227-0190 974-5103
TF: 866-617-4578 ■ *Web:* www.nobhillgazette.com

Ohio Magazine 1422 Euclid Ave Ste 730 ... Cleveland OH 44115 216-771-2833 781-6318
TF: 800-210-7293 ■ *Web:* www.ohiomagazine.com

Orange Coast Magazine
3701 Birch St Ste 100 ... Newport Beach CA 92660 949-862-1133 862-0133
TF: 800-397-8179 ■ *Web:* www.orangecoast.com

Oregon Coast Magazine 4969 Hwy 101 Ste 2 ... Florence OR 97439 541-997-8401 997-1124
TF: 800-348-8401 ■ *Web:* www.oregoncoastmagazine.com

Orlando Magazine 801 N Magnolia Ave Ste 201 ... Orlando FL 32803 407-423-0618 237-6258
TF: 866-356-3075 ■ *Web:* www.orlandomagazine.com

Palm Beach Illustrated Magazine
1000 N Dixie Hwy Ste C ... West Palm Beach FL 33401 561-659-6160 659-1736
TF: 800-308-7346 ■ *Web:* www.palmbeachillustrated.com

Palm Springs Life Magazine
303 N Indian Canyon ... Palm Springs CA 92262 760-325-2333 325-7008
Web: www.palmspringslife.com

Philadelphia Magazine
1818 Market St 36th Fl ... Philadelphia PA 19103 215-564-7700 656-3500
Web: www.phillymag.com

Phoenix Magazine
15169 N Scottsdale Ste C10 ... Scottsdale AZ 85254 480-664-3960 664-3962
TF: 866-481-6970 ■ *Web:* www.phoenixmag.com

Saint Louis Bride Magazine
1006 Olive St Ste 202 ... Saint Louis MO 63101 314-588-8313
Web: bridestl.com

San Francisco Magazine 243 Vallejo St ... San Francisco CA 94111 415-398-2800 398-6777
TF: 866-736-2499 ■ *Web:* www.modernluxury.com

Savannah Magazine PO Box 1088 ... Savannah GA 31402 912-652-0423 525-0611
Web: www.savannahmagazine.com

Southern Accents Magazine
2100 Lakeshore Dr ... Birmingham AL 35209 205-445-6000 624-2910*
**Fax Area Code:* 678 ■ *TF:* 877-262-5866 ■ *Web:* www.southernliving.com

Southern Living Magazine
2100 Lakeshore Dr ... Birmingham AL 35209 205-445-6000 445-6700
TF: 800-366-4712 ■ *Web:* www.southernliving.com

Company	Address	City	State	Zip	Phone	Fax
Today's Chicago Woman Magazine	150 E Huron St Ste 1001	Chicago	IL	60611	312-951-7600	
Web: www.tcwmag.com						
Toronto Life Magazine	111 Queen St E Ste 320	Toronto	ON	M5C1S2	416-364-3333	861-1169
Web: www.torontolife.com						
Travel Agent Magazine	757 Third Ave 5th Fl	New York	NY	10017	212-895-8200	895-8210
TF: 855-424-6247 ■ *Web:* www.travelagentcentral.com						
TravelAge West Magazine	11400 W Olympic Blvd Ste 325	Los Angeles	CA	90064	310-954-2510	954-2525
Web: www.travelagewest.com						
Travelhost Magazine	10701 N Stemmons Fwy	Dallas	TX	75220	972-556-0541	432-8729
TF: 800-527-1782 ■ *Web:* www.travelhost.com						
Tucson Lifestyle Magazine	7000 E Tanque Verde Rd Ste 11	Tucson	AZ	85715	520-721-2929	721-8665
Web: www.tucsonlifestyle.com						
Vermont Life	One National Life Dr Sixth Fl	Montpelier	VT	05620	802-828-3241	828-3366
TF: 800-284-3243 ■ *Web:* www.vtlife.com						
Washingtonian Magazine	1828 L St NW Ste 200	Washington	DC	20036	202-296-3600	785-1822*
**Fax:* Edit ■ *Web:* www.washingtonian.com						
Western Outdoors Magazine	185 Avenida La Pata	San Clemente	CA	92673	949-366-0030	366-0804
TF: 800-290-2929 ■ *Web:* www.wonews.com						
Westways Magazine	3333 Fairview Rd	Costa Mesa	CA	92626	714-885-2376	
Where Chicago Magazine	1165 N Clark St Ste 302	Chicago	IL	60610	312-642-1896	642-5467
Web: www.wheretraveler.com						
Where Los Angeles Magazine	3679 Motor Ave Ste 300	Los Angeles	CA	90034	310-280-2880	280-2890
Web: www.wherela.com						
Where San Francisco Magazine	555 Montgomery St Ste 803	San Francisco	CA	94111	415-901-6260	901-6261
Web: www.wheretraveler.com						
Where Washington Magazine	1720 Eye St NW Ste 600	Washington	DC	20006	202-463-4550	463-4553
Web: www.wheretraveler.com						
Yankee Magazine	1121 Main St PO Box 520	Dublin	NH	03444	603-563-8111	563-8252
TF: 800-288-4284 ■ *Web:* www.yankeemagazine.com						

461 MAGNETS - PERMANENT

Company	Address	City	State	Zip	Phone	Fax
Bangor Electronics Co	100 Industrial Pk Dr	Bangor	MI	49013	269-427-7944	
Web: www.bangorelectronics.com						
Dexter Magnetic Technologies Inc	1050 Morse Ave	Elk Grove Village	IL	60007	847-956-1140	956-8205
Web: www.dextermag.com						
Electron Energy Corp	924 Links Ave	Landisville	PA	17538	717-898-2294	898-0660
TF: 800-824-2735 ■ *Web:* www.electronenergy.com						
Eneflux Armtek Magnetics Inc	700 Hicksville Rd Ste 110	Bethpage	NY	11714	516-576-3434	
Web: www.eamagnetics.com						
Flexmag Industries Inc	107 Industry Rd	Marietta	OH	45750	740-374-8024	374-5068
TF: 800-543-4426 ■ *Web:* www.arnoldmagnetics.com						
Magnaworks Technology Inc	36 Carlough Rd	Bohemia	NY	11716	631-218-3431	218-3432
Web: www.magnaworkstechnology.com						
Magnet Technology Inc	1599 Kingsview Dr	Lebanon	OH	45036	513-932-4416	932-4502
Web: www.magtech.cc						
Magnetic Component Engineering Inc	2830 Lomita Blvd	Torrance	CA	90505	800-989-5656	784-3192*
**Fax Area Code:* 310 ■ *TF:* 800-989-5656 ■ *Web:* www.mceproducts.com						
Magnum Magnetics Corp	801 Masonic Pk Rd	Marietta	OH	45750	740-373-7770	373-2880
TF: 800-258-0991 ■ *Web:* www.magnummagnetics.com						
Mohr Corp	PO Box 1600	Brighton	MI	48114	810-225-9494	225-4634
TF: 800-223-6647 ■ *Web:* www.mohrcorp.com						
National Magnetics Group Inc	1210 Win Dr	Bethlehem	PA	18017	610-867-7600	867-0200
Web: www.magneticsgroup.com						
Permanent Magnet Company Inc	4437 Bragdon St	Lawrence	IN	46226	317-547-1336	549-9259
Shin-etsu Magnetics Inc	2372 Qume Dr Ste B	San Jose	CA	95131	408-383-9240	383-9245
Web: www.shinetsumagnetics.com						
Thomas & Skinner Inc	1120 E 23rd St	Indianapolis	IN	46205	317-923-2501	923-5919
Web: www.thomas-skinner.com						

462 MAIL ORDER HOUSES

SEE ALSO Checks - Personal & Business p. 1943; Computer Stores p. 2051; Art Supply Stores p. 1752; Seed Companies p. 3165; Book, Music, Video Clubs p. 1877

Company	Address	City	State	Zip	Phone	Fax
1Mart Corp	570 El Camino Real Ste 150	Redwood City	CA	94063	650-363-7700	
Web: americangene.com						
2 Checkoutcom Inc	1785 O'Brien Rd	Columbus	OH	43228	614-921-2450	
Web: www.2checkout.com						
Advanced Image Direct	1415 S Acacia Ave	Fullerton	CA	92831	714-502-3900	502-3901
TF: 800-540-3848 ■ *Web:* www.advancedimagedirect.com						
Aeromedixcom LLC	Po Box 14730	Jackson	WY	83002	307-732-2642	
Web: www.aeromedix.com						
Allied Marketing Group Inc	1555 Regal Row	Dallas	TX	75247	214-915-7000	915-7458
Web: www.alliedmarketinggroup.com						
America's Hobby Ctr Inc	8300 Tonnelle Ave	North Bergen	NJ	07047	201-662-0777	
Backcountry.com	2607 South 3200 West Ste A	West Valley City	UT	84119	800-409-4502	746-7581*
**Fax Area Code:* 801 ■ *TF Orders:* 800-409-4502 ■ *Web:* www.backcountry.com						
Blueport Commerce Inc	580 Harrison Ave	Boston	MA	02118	617-275-7200	
Web: www.furniture.com						
Brokers Worldwide	701C Ashland Ave	Folcroft	PA	19032	610-461-3661	
TF: 800-624-5287 ■ *Web:* asendiausa.com						
Chadwick's of Boston	500 Bic Dr Bldg 4	Milford	CT	06461	877-330-3393	
TF: 877-330-3393 ■ *Web:* www.chadwicks.com						
Childcraft Education Corp	1156 Four Star Dr	Mount Joy	PA	17552	800-631-5652	532-4453*
**Fax Area Code:* 888						
Cinmar LLC	5566 W Chester Rd	West Chester	OH	45069	888-263-9850	603-1492*
**Fax Area Code:* 513 ■ *TF:* 888-263-9850 ■ *Web:* www.frontgate.com						
Colony Brands Inc	1112 Seventh Ave	Monroe	WI	53566	608-328-8400	328-8457
Web: www.theswisscolony.net						
Country Home Products Inc	75 Meigs Road	Vergennes	VT	05491	802-877-1200	877-1212
TF: 800-376-9637 ■ *Web:* www.chp.com						
Crutchfield Corp	One Crutchfield Pk	Charlottesville	VA	22911	434-817-1000	817-1010
TF Sales: 800-955-3000 ■ *Web:* www.crutchfield.com						
Current USA Inc	1005 E Woodmen Rd	Colorado Springs	CO	80920	800-848-2848	993-3232
TF Cust Svc: 800-848-2848 ■ *Web:* www.currentcatalog.com						
Daniel Smith Artist Materials	PO Box 84268	Seattle	WA	98124	206-223-9599	224-3567
TF: 800-426-6740 ■ *Web:* www.danielsmith.com						
Design Toscano Inc	1400 Morse Ave	Elk Grove Village	IL	60007	847-952-0100	
TF: 800-525-5141 ■ *Web:* www.designtoscano.com						
Digi-Key Corp	701 Brooks Ave S	Thief River Falls	MN	56701	218-681-6674	681-3380
TF: 800-344-4539 ■ *Web:* www.digikey.com						
E-filliate Inc	11321 White Rock Rd	Rancho Cordova	CA	95742	916-858-1000	
Web: www.efilliate.com						
ET Wright & Company Inc	1251 First Ave	Chippewa Falls	WI	54729	715-720-4288	
Everglades Direct	720 International Pkwy	Sunrise	FL	33325	954-846-8899	846-0777
Web: www.evergladesdirect.com						
EVINE Live Inc	6740 Shady Oak Rd	Eden Prairie	MN	55344	800-676-5523	*
**Fax:* Hum Res ■ *TF:* 800-676-5523 ■ *Web:* www.evine.com						
FarSounder Inc	43 Jefferson Blvd	Warwick	RI	02888	401-784-6700	
Web: www.farsounder.com						
Fingerhut	6509 Flying Cloud Dr	Eden Prairie	MN	55344	800-208-2500	
TF: 800-208-2500 ■ *Web:* www.fingerhut.com						
Forestry Suppliers Inc	205 W Rankin St	Jackson	MS	39201	601-354-3565	292-0165
TF Cust Svc: 800-752-8460 ■ *Web:* www.forestry-suppliers.com						
Gaiam Inc	833 W S Boulder Rd Ste C	Louisville	CO	80027	303-222-3600	222-3750
NASDAQ: GAIA ■ *TF:* 877-989-6321 ■ *Web:* www.gaiam.com						
Gardens Alive Inc	5100 Schenley Pl	Lawrenceburg	IN	47025	513-354-1482	354-1484
TF: 800-222-1222 ■ *Web:* www.gardensalive.com						
Hammacher Schlemmer & Co	9307 N Milwaukee Ave	Niles	IL	60714	800-321-1484	581-8616*
**Fax Area Code:* 847 ■ *TF:* 800-321-1484 ■ *Web:* www.hammacher.com						
Hanna Andersson Corp	1010 NW Flanders St	Portland	OR	97209	800-222-0544	222-0544*
**Fax Area Code:* 503 ■ *TF Cust Svc:* 800-222-0544 ■ *Web:* www.hannaandersson.com						
Hanover Direct Inc	1500 Harbor Blvd	Weehawken	NJ	07086	201-863-7300	272-3465
Web: www.hanoverdirect.com						
Harry & David Holdings Inc	2500 S Pacific Hwy	Medford	OR	97501	877-322-1200	233-2300
TF Cust Svc: 877-322-1200 ■ *Web:* www.harryanddavid.com						
Hello Direct Inc	77 NE Blvd	Nashua	NH	03062	800-435-5634	456-2566*
**Fax:* Sales ■ *TF:* 800-435-5634 ■ *Web:* www.hellodirect.com						
Houston Numismatic Exchange Inc	2486 Times Blvd	Houston	TX	77005	713-528-2135	528-7618
TF: 800-231-3650 ■ *Web:* www.hnex.com						
J Crew Group Inc	770 Broadway	New York	NY	10003	212-209-2500	209-2666
TF: 800-562-0258 ■ *Web:* www.jcrew.com						
Jackson & Perkins	Two Floral Ave	Hodges	SC	29653	800-292-4769	
TF Cust Svc: 800-292-4769 ■ *Web:* www.jacksonandperkins.com						
JC Whitney	761 Progress Pkwy	La Salle	IL	61301	866-529-5530	431-6095*
**Fax Area Code:* 312 ■ *TF:* 866-529-5530 ■ *Web:* www.jcwhitney.com						
JDR Microdevices Inc	229 Polaris Ave Ste 17	Mountain View	CA	94043	650-625-1400	538-5005*
**Fax Area Code:* 800 ■ *TF:* 800-538-5000 ■ *Web:* www.jdr.com						
Lands' End Inc	One Lands' End Ln	Dodgeville	WI	53595	800-963-4816	935-4260*
**Fax Area Code:* 608 ■ *TF Orders:* 800-963-4816 ■ *Web:* www.landsend.com						
Levenger	420 S Congress Ave	Delray Beach	FL	33445	561-276-2436	243-3629
TF Cust Svc: 800-544-0880 ■ *Web:* www.levenger.com						
Living Naturally LLC	6230 University Pkwy Ste 301	Sarasota	FL	34240	941-480-1910	
Web: www.livingnaturally.com						
LL Bean Inc	15 Casco St	Freeport	ME	04033	207-552-3080	552-3080
TF: 800-341-4341 ■ *Web:* www.llbean.com						
Mary Maxim Inc	2001 Holland Ave PO Box 5019	Port Huron	MI	48061	810-987-2000	987-5056
TF: 800-962-9504 ■ *Web:* www.marymaxim.com						
Maynards Industries Ltd	1837 Main St	Vancouver	BC	V5T3B8	604-876-6787	
Web: www.maynards.com						
MBI Inc	47 Richards Ave	Norwalk	CT	06857	203-853-2000	
Web: www.mbi-inc.com						
Miles Kimball Co	250 City Ctr Bldg	Oshkosh	WI	54906	920-231-3800	231-6942
TF Cust Svc: 855-202-7394 ■ *Web:* www.mileskimball.com						
Movies Unlimited Inc	3015 Darnell Rd	Philadelphia	PA	19154	215-637-4444	637-2350
TF: 800-668-4344 ■ *Web:* www.moviesunlimited.com						
Mystic Stamp Co	9700 Mill St	Camden	NY	13316	315-245-2690	385-4919*
**Fax Area Code:* 800 ■ *TF:* 866-660-7147 ■ *Web:* www.mysticstamp.com						
NASCO International Inc	901 Janesville Ave	Fort Atkinson	WI	53538	920-563-2446	563-8296
TF Orders: 800-558-9595 ■ *Web:* www.enasco.com						
National 4-H Council	7100 Connecticut Ave	Chevy Chase	MD	20815	301-961-2800	
Web: www.4-h.org						
National Wholesale Company Inc	400 National Blvd	Lexington	NC	27292	800-480-4673	249-9326*
**Fax Area Code:* 336 ■ *TF:* 800-480-4673 ■ *Web:* www.shopnational.com						
Newport News Inc	711 Third Ave Fourth Fl	New York	NY	10017	212-986-2585	
Web: www.spiegel.com						
NHT Global Inc	2050 Diplomat Dr	Dallas	TX	75234	972-241-6525	
Web: www.nhtglobal.com						
Norm Thompson Outfitters Inc	3188 NW Aloclek Dr	Hillsboro	OR	97124	503-614-4600	821-1282*
**Fax Area Code:* 800 ■ *TF:* 800-547-1160 ■ *Web:* normthompson.blair.com						
Northeast Data Services	1316 College Ave	Elmira	NY	14901	607-733-5541	
TF Cust Svc: 800-699-5636 ■ *Web:* the-leader.com						
Now Courier Inc	PO Box 6066	Indianapolis	IN	46206	800-543-6066	638-5750*
**Fax Area Code:* 317 ■ *TF:* 800-543-6066 ■ *Web:* www.nowcourier.com						

	Phone	Fax
NRC Sports Inc 603 Pleasant St . . . Paxton MA 01612 *Fax Area Code: 508 ■ TF: 800-243-5033 ■ Web: www.nrcsports.com	800-243-5033	852-8206*
One World Direct 10 First Ave E . . . Mobridge SD 57601 Web: www.owd.com	605-845-7172	
Oriental Trading Company Inc 5455 S 90th St . . . Omaha NE 68127 TF: 800-875-8480 ■ Web: www.orientaltrading.com	402-596-1200	596-2322
Patagonia Inc 259 W Santa Clara St PO Box 150 . . . Ventura CA 93001 TF Cust Svc: 800-638-6464 ■ Web: www.patagonia.com	805-643-8616	648-8020
Penzeys Spices Inc 12001 W Capitol Dr . . . Wauwatosa WI 53222 Web: www.penzeys.com	414-760-7307	
Phoenix Vintners LLC Four S Main St Ste 2 . . . Ipswich MA 01938 TF: 877-340-9869 ■ Web: www.travelingvineyard.com	877-340-9869	
Roaman's 2300 SE Ave . . . Indianapolis IN 46283 *Fax Area Code: 317 ■ TF: 800-677-0229 ■ Web: www.roamans.com	800-677-0229	266-3393*
RSVP Direct Inc 1019 Noel Ave . . . Wheeling IL 60090 Web: www.rsvpdirect.net	847-215-9054	
S & S Worldwide Inc 75 Mill St . . . Colchester CT 06415 TF Orders: 800-243-9232 ■ Web: www.ssww.com	860-537-3451	537-2563
Seta Corp 6400 E Rogers Cir . . . Boca Raton FL 33499 Web: www.setacorporation.com	561-994-2660	
SkyMall Inc 1520 E Pima St . . . Phoenix AZ 85034 *Fax Area Code: 602 ■ TF: 800-759-6255 ■ Web: www.skymall.com	800-759-6255	254-6075*
Southern Fulfillment Services LLC 1650 90th Ave . . . Vero Beach FL 32966 Web: www.southernfulfillment.com	772-226-3500	
Specialty Catalog Corp 400 Manley St . . . West Bridgewater MA 02379 TF: 800-364-9060 ■ Web: www.scdirect.com	508-638-7000	894-0181
StubHub Inc 199 Fremont St Fl 4 . . . San Francisco CA 94105 TF: 866-788-2482 ■ Web: www.stubhub.com	415-222-8400	
Sunnyland Farms Inc PO Box 8200 . . . Albany GA 31706 *Fax Area Code: 229 ■ TF: 800-999-2488 ■ Web: www.sunnylandfarms.com	800-999-2488	888-4979*
Super Duper Inc PO Box 24997 . . . Greenville SC 29616 Web: www.superduperinc.com	864-288-3536	288-3380
Taymark Inc 4875 White Bear Pkwy . . . White Bear Lake MN 55110 Web: www.handyart.com	651-426-1667	
Tech4Learning Inc 10981 San Diego Mission Rd Ste 120 . . . San Diego CA 92108 TF: 877-834-5453 ■ Web: www.tech4learning.com	619-563-5348	
Tog Shop Inc 30 Tozer Rd . . . Beverly MA 01915 *Fax Area Code: 800 ■ TF: 800-767-6666 ■ Web: togshop.com	978-922-2040	755-7557*
TravelSmith Outfitters 773 San Marin Dr Ste 2300 . . . Novato CA 94945 TF: 800-770-3387 ■ Web: www.travelsmith.com	800-770-3387	950-1656
Unicover Corp One Unicover Ctr . . . Cheyenne WY 82008 TF Cust Svc: 800-443-4225 ■ Web: www.unicover.com	307-771-3000	771-3134
Unistar-Sparco Computers Inc 7089 Ryburn Dr . . . Millington TN 38053 TF: 800-840-8400 ■ Web: www.sparco.com	901-872-2272	872-8482
Van Dyke Supply Co 39771 Sd Hwy 34 . . . Woonsocket SD 57385 TF: 800-279-7985 ■ Web: www.vandykestaxidermy.com	704-279-7985	
Victorian Trading Co 15600 W 99th St . . . Lenexa KS 66219 *Fax Area Code: 800 ■ TF Cust Svc: 800-700-2035 ■ Web: www.victoriantradingco.com	913-438-3995	724-7697*
Wild Wings LLC 2101 S Hwy 61 . . . Lake City MN 55041 TF: 800-445-4833 ■ Web: www.wildwings.com	651-345-5355	
Williams-Sonoma Inc 3250 Van Ness Ave . . . San Francisco CA 94109 NYSE: WSM ■ TF: 800-838-2589 ■ Web: www.williams-sonomainc.com	415-421-7900	616-8359
Wintersilks Inc PO Box 196 4th Fl . . . Jessup PA 18434 TF: 800-648-7455 ■ Web: wintersilks.blair.com	800-718-3687	
Women's International Pharmacy Inc PO Box 6468 . . . Madison WI 53716 TF: 800-279-5708 ■ Web: www.womensinternational.com	608-221-7800	221-7819
Woodcraft Supply LLC 1177 Rosemar Rd PO Box 1686 . . . Parkersburg WV 26105 *Fax Area Code: 304 ■ TF: 800-535-4482 ■ Web: www.woodcraft.com	800-535-4482	428-8271*
Your Electronic Warehouse 2828 Broadway St . . . Quincy IL 62301 Web: 4electronicwarehouse.com	217-224-8500	
Zappos.com 400 E Stewart Ave Ste 104 . . . Las Vegas KY 89101 TF: 800-927-7671 ■ Web: www.zappos.com	800-927-7671	

463 MALLS - SHOPPING

	Phone	Fax
57th Street Antique Row 875 57th St . . . Sacramento CA 95819 Web: 57thstreetantiquerow.com	916-451-3110	
Adams Avenue Business Assn 4649 Hawley Blvd . . . San Diego CA 92116 Web: www.adamsavenuebusiness.com	619-282-7329	282-8751
Ala Moana Shopping Ctr 1450 Ala Moana Blvd . . . Honolulu HI 96814 Web: www.alamoanacenter.com	808-955-9517	955-2193
Allen Premium Outlets 820 W Stacy Rd . . . Allen TX 75013 Web: www.premiumoutlets.com	972-678-7000	678-7011
Almeda Mall 555 Almeda Mall . . . Houston TX 77075 Web: www.almedamall.com	713-944-1010	944-5948
Altamonte Mall 451 E Altamonte Dr Ste 2165 . . . Altamonte Springs FL 32701 Web: www.altamontemall.com	407-830-4422	215-5125
American Antique Mall 3130 E Grant Rd . . . Tucson AZ 85716 Web: www.americanantiquemall.com	520-326-3070	
Anaheim Indoor Marketplace 1440 S Anaheim Blvd . . . Anaheim CA 92805 Web: www.anaheimindoormarketplace.com	714-999-0888	999-0885
Annapolis Harbour Shopping Center 2512A Solomon'S Island Rd . . . Annapolis MD 21401 *Fax Area Code: 301 ■ Web: www.annapolisharbourcenter.com	410-266-5857	970-2508*
Antique Mall 1251 S Virginia St . . . Reno NV 89502 TF: 888-316-6255 ■ Web: www.antiquemalls.com	775-324-4141	
Antique Village 10203 Chamberlayne Rd . . . Mechanicsville VA 23116 Web: www.antiquevillageva.com	804-746-8914	
Antique World 11111 Main St . . . Clarence NY 14031 TF: 800-321-2211 ■ Web: www.antiqueworldmarket.com	716-759-8483	759-0437
Antiques Mall of Madison 4748 Cottage Grove Rd . . . Madison WI 53716 Web: www.antiquesmadison.com	608-222-2049	
Arizona Mills 5000 Arizona Mills Cir . . . Tempe AZ 85282 TF: 877-746-6642 ■ Web: simon.com/mall/arizona-mills	480-491-7300	491-7400
Arrowhead Towne Ctr 7700 W Arrowhead Towne Ctr . . . Glendale AZ 85308 Web: www.arrowheadtownecenter.com	623-979-7777	979-4447
Aspen Grove Lifestyle Ctr 7301 S Santa Fe Dr . . . Littleton CO 80120 Web: www.shopaspengrove.com	303-794-0640	798-0238
Augusta Mall 3450 Wrightsboro Rd . . . Augusta GA 30909 Web: www.augustamall.com	706-733-1001	733-7980
Aventura Mall 19501 Biscayne Blvd . . . Aventura FL 33180 Web: aventuramall.com	305-935-1110	935-9360
Avenues Mall 10300 Southside Blvd . . . Jacksonville FL 32256 Web: www.simon.com	904-363-3054	363-3058
Barton Creek Square Mall 2901 S Capital of Texas Hwy . . . Austin TX 78746 Web: www.simon.com	512-327-7040	328-0923
Battlefield Mall 2825 S Glenstone Ave . . . Springfield MO 65804 Web: www.simon.com	417-883-7777	883-2641
Bayshore Town Center 5800 N Bayshore Dr Ste A256 . . . Glendale WI 53217 TF: 800-235-4636 ■ Web: www.bayshoretowncenter.com	414-963-8780	332-5304
Bearden Antique Mall 310 Mohican St . . . Knoxville TN 37919	865-584-1521	
Bel Air Mall 3299 Bel Air Mall . . . Mobile AL 36606 Web: www.shopatbelairmall.com	251-478-1893	476-5722
Bellevue Square 575 Bellevue Sq . . . Bellevue WA 98004 Web: www.bellevuesquare.com	425-646-3660	455-3631
Belmont Shore 200 Nieto Ave Ste 200-B . . . Long Beach CA 90803 Web: www.belmontshore.org	562-434-3066	
Boulder Arts & Crafts 1421 Pearl St Mall . . . Boulder CO 80302 TF: 866-656-2667 ■ Web: www.boulderartsandcrafts.com	303-443-3683	443-7998
Boulevard Mall 730 Alberta Dr . . . Amherst NY 14226 Web: www.boulevard-mall.com	716-834-8600	836-6127
Boynton Beach Mall 801 N Congress Ave . . . Boynton Beach FL 33426 TF: 877-746-6642 ■ Web: www.simon.com	561-736-7902	736-7907
Brea Mall 1065 Brea Mall . . . Brea CA 92821 Web: www.simon.com	714-990-2732	990-5048
Bronx Council on the Arts 1738 Hone Ave . . . Bronx NY 10461 TF: 866-564-5226 ■ Web: bronxarts.org	718-931-9500	409-6445
Buena Park Downtown 8308 On The Mall . . . Buena Park CA 90620 Web: www.buenaparkdowntown.com	714-503-5000	761-0748
Burbank Town Ctr 201 E Magnolia Blvd . . . Burbank CA 91502 Web: www.burbanktowncenter.com	818-566-8556	566-7936
Burlington Mall 75 Middlesex Tpke . . . Burlington MA 01803 TF: 877-746-6642 ■ Web: www.simon.com/mall/?id=146	781-272-8667	229-0420
Burnsville Ctr 1178 Burnsville Ctr . . . Burnsville MN 55306 Web: www.burnsvillecenter.com	952-435-8182	
Camarillo Premium Outlets 740 E Ventura Blvd . . . Camarillo CA 93010 Web: www.premiumoutlets.com	805-445-8520	445-8522
CambridgeSide Galleria 100 Cambridgeside Pl . . . Cambridge MA 02141 Web: www.cambridgesidegalleria.com	617-621-8666	621-6078
Carlsbad Premium Outlets 5620 Paseo del Norte . . . Carlsbad CA 92008 Web: www.premiumoutlets.com	760-804-9000	
Carolina Place Mall 11025 Carolina Pl Pkwy . . . Pineville NC 28134 Web: www.carolinaplace.com	704-543-9300	543-6355
Carousel Mall 295 Carousel Mall . . . San Bernardino CA 92401 Web: carouselmall.net	909-884-0106	885-6893
Cary Towne Ctr 1105 Walnut St . . . Cary NC 27511 Web: www.shopcarytownecentermall.com	919-467-0145	
Casino Factory Shoppes LLC 13118 Hwy 61 N Ste 110B . . . Robinsonville MS 38664 Web: www.casinofactoryshoppes.com	662-363-1940	363-1941
Castleton Square Mall 6020 E 82nd St . . . Indianapolis IN 46250 Web: www.simon.com	317-849-9993	849-4689
Centralia Square 201 S Pearl . . . Centralia WA 98531 Web: www.myantiquemall.com/centraliasquare.html	360-736-6406	
Centre at Salisbury 2300 N Salisbury Blvd . . . Salisbury MD 21801 Web: www.centreatsalisbury.com	410-548-1600	
Century III Mall 3075 Clairton Rd . . . West Mifflin PA 15123 Web: www.simon.com	412-653-1222	655-0202
Chapel Hills Mall 1710 Briargate Blvd . . . Colorado Springs CO 80920 Web: www.chapelhillsmall.com	719-594-0111	594-6439
Charlestowne Mall 3800 E Main St . . . Saint Charles IL 60174 Web: www.charlestownemall.com	630-513-1120	513-1459
Cherry Creek Shopping Ctr 3000 E First Ave . . . Denver CO 80206 Web: www.shopcherrycreek.com	303-388-3900	388-8203
Chicago Premium Outlets 1650 Premium Outlets Blvd . . . Aurora IL 60502 Web: www.premiumoutlets.com	630-585-2200	236-0036
Christiana Mall 132 Christiana Mal . . . Newark DE 19702 Web: www.christianamall.com	302-731-9815	731-9950
Christown Spectrum Mall 1703 W Bethany Home Rd . . . Phoenix AZ 85015 Web: www.christownspectrum.com	602-249-0670	246-8690
Cielo Vista Mall 8401 Gateway Blvd W . . . El Paso TX 79925 Web: www.simon.com	915-779-7071	772-4926
Citadel Mall 2070 Sam Rittenberg Blvd Ste 200 . . . Charleston SC 29407 Web: www.citadelmall.net	843-766-8321	763-8534
Citadel Mall, The 750 Citadel Dr E Ste 3114 . . . Colorado Springs CO 80909 Web: www.shopthecitadel.com	719-591-2900	597-4839
City Centre 1420 Fifth Ave Ste 212 . . . Seattle WA 98101	206-624-6851	623-4625
City Market Antique Mall 707 Gervais St . . . Columbia SC 29201	803-799-7722	

Name / Address	City	State	ZIP	Phone	Fax
Clackamas Town Ctr 12000 SE 82nd Ave *Web:* www.clackamastowncenter.com	Happy Valley	OR	97086	503-653-6913	
Clifton Square 3700 E Douglas *Web:* www.cliftonsquare.com	Wichita	KS	67208	316-686-2177	686-2266
Collin Creek Mall 811 N Central Expy *Web:* www.collincreekmall.com	Plano	TX	75075	972-543-0369	881-1642
Colonie Ctr Wolf Rd & Central Ave Northway Exit 2E *Web:* www.shopatcoloniecenter.com	Albany	NY	12205	518-459-9020	438-4835
Columbia Gorge Premium Outlets 450 NW 257th Way Ste 400 *Web:* www.premiumoutlets.com	Troutdale	OR	97060	503-669-8060	666-3062
Columbia Place 7201 Two Notch Rd *Web:* www.shopcolumbiaplace.com/shop/columbia.nsf/index	Columbia	SC	29223	803-788-4678	736-9168
Columbiana Centre Mall 100 Columbiana Cir *Web:* www.columbianacentre.com	Columbia	SC	29212	803-732-6255	732-3360
Commons, The 1928 S Commons *Web:* www.tcafw.com	Federal Way	WA	98003	253-839-6150	946-1413
Complexe Les Ailes 677 Sainte-Catherine St W *Web:* www.complexelesailes.com	Montreal	QC	H3A3T2	514-288-3759	288-3779
Concord Mall 4737 Concord Pk *Web:* www.concordmall.com	Wilmington	DE	19803	302-478-9271	479-8314
Concord Mills 8111 Concord Mills Blvd *TF:* 877-789-2327 ■ *Web:* simon.com/default.aspx	Concord	NC	28027	704-979-3000	
CoolSprings Galleria 1800 Galleria Blvd Ste 2075 *Web:* www.coolspringsgalleria.com	Franklin	TN	37067	615-771-2050	771-2127
Copley Place 100 Huntington Ave Ste 100 *TF:* 877-746-6642 ■ *Web:* simon.com	Boston	MA	02116	617-262-6600	369-5002
Coral Ridge Mall 1451 Coral Ridge Ave *Web:* www.coralridgemall.com	Coralville	IA	52241	319-625-5522	625-5501
Coronado Ctr 6600 Menaul Blvd NE Ste 1 *Web:* www.coronadocenter.com	Albuquerque	NM	87110	505-881-2700	
Cotton City Antique Mall 2012 Airport Blvd *Web:* antiquemalls.com	Mobile	AL	36606	251-479-9747	
Crabtree Valley Mall 4325 Glenwood Ave *Web:* www.crabtree-valley-mall.com	Raleigh	NC	27612	919-787-2506	787-7108
Crocker Galleria 50 Post St *Web:* www.thecrockergalleria.com	San Francisco	CA	94104	415-393-1505	
Cross County Shopping Ctr 8000 Mall Walk *Web:* www.crosscountycenter.com	Yonkers	NY	10704	914-968-9570	423-7760
Crossgates Mall One Crossgates Mall Rd *Web:* shopcrossgates.com	Albany	NY	12203	518-869-9565	
Crossroads Mall 7000 Crossroads Blvd *Web:* www.plazamayorok.com	Oklahoma City	OK	73149	405-631-4422	
Cumberland Mall 1000 Cumberland Mall *Web:* www.cumberlandmall.com	Atlanta	GA	30339	770-435-2206	435-0432
Dallas Galleria 13350 N Dallas Pkwy *Web:* www.galleriadallas.com	Dallas	TX	75240	972-702-7100	702-7130
Dayton Mall 2700 Miamisburg Centerville Rd *Web:* www.daytonmall.com	Dayton	OH	45459	937-433-9833	433-5289
Dedham Mall 300 Providence Hwy *Web:* www.dedham-mall.com	Dedham	MA	02026	781-329-1210	329-0513
Deerbrook Mall 20131 Hwy 59 N *Web:* www.shopdeerbrookmall.com	Humble	TX	77338	281-446-5300	446-1921
Del Amo Fashion Ctr 3525 Carson St *TF:* 877-746-6642 ■ *Web:* www.simon.com	Torrance	CA	90503	310-542-8525	793-9235
Derby City Antique Mall 3819 Bardstown Rd *Web:* www.derbycityantiquemall.com	Louisville	KY	40218	502-459-5151	459-3438
Desert Sky Mall 7611 W Thomas Rd *Web:* www.desertskymall.com	Phoenix	AZ	85033	623-245-1404	245-1411
Design Ctr of the Americas (DCOTA) 1855 Griffin Rd *TF:* 877-992-9204 ■ *Web:* www.dcota.com	Dania Beach	FL	33004	954-920-7997	
Dixie Outlet Mall 1250 S Service Rd *Web:* www.dixieoutletmall.com	Mississauga	ON	L5E1V4	905-278-3494	278-4283
Dolphin Mall 11401 NW 12 St *Web:* www.shopdolphinmall.com	Miami	FL	33172	305-365-7446	436-9000
Domain, The 11410 Century Oaks Terr *Web:* www.simon.com	Austin	TX	78758	512-795-4230	833-5173
Downtown Tempe Community 310 S Mill Ave Ste A-201 *Web:* www.millavenue.com	Tempe	AZ	85281	480-355-6060	968-7882
Dutch Square Center 421 Bush River Rd *Web:* www.dutchsquare.com	Columbia	SC	29210	803-772-3864	750-0036
East Towne Mall 89 E Towne Mall *Web:* www.shopeasttowne-mall.com	Madison	WI	53704	608-244-1387	244-8306
Eastern Shore Centre 30500 State Hwy 181 *Web:* easternshorecentre.com	Spanish Fort	AL	36527	251-625-0060	625-0039
Eastfield Mall 1655 Boston Rd *Web:* www.eastfieldmall.com	Springfield	MA	01129	413-543-8000	543-4221
Eastgate Mall 4601 Eastgate Blvd *Web:* www.shopeastgate-mall.com	Cincinnati	OH	45245	513-752-2294	752-2499
Eastland Center 18000 Vernier Rd *Web:* www.shopeastland.com	Harper Woods	MI	48225	313-371-1501	371-3511
Eastland Mall 800 N Green River Rd *Web:* www.simon.com	Evansville	IN	47715	812-477-7171	474-1691
Eastmont Town Ctr 7200 Bancroft Ave Ste 268	Oakland	CA	94605	510-638-7323	
Eastridge Mall 2200 Eastridge Loop Ste 2062 *Web:* www.eastridgecenter.com	San Jose	CA	95122	408-238-3600	274-9684
Eastview Mall 7979 Pittsford-Victor Rd *Web:* www.eastviewmall.com	Victor	NY	14564	585-223-4420	
Eastwood Mall 5555 Youngstown-Warren Rd *Web:* eastwoodmall.com	Niles	OH	44446	330-652-6980	544-5929
Eastwood Towne Ctr 3003 Preyde Blvd *Web:* www.shopeastwoodtownecenter.com	Lansing	MI	48912	517-316-9209	316-9214
Edens & Avant 2855 W Market St Ste 207	Fairlawn	OH	44333	330-836-9174	836-5139
Edmonton City Centre 10025-102A Ave *Web:* www.edmontoncitycentre.com	Edmonton	AB	T5J2Z2	780-426-8444	
El Con Mall 3601 E Broadway Blvd Ste 5B *Web:* www.elconcenter.com	Tucson	AZ	85716	520-795-9958	
Ellenton Premium Outlets 5461 Factory Shops Blvd *TF:* 888-267-2121 ■ *Web:* www.premiumoutlets.com	Ellenton	FL	34222	941-723-1150	723-9437
Emerald Square Mall 999 S Washington St *Web:* www.simon.com/mall/?id=335	North Attleboro	MA	02760	508-699-7979	
Empire Mall, The 5000 Empire Mall *Web:* simon.com/default.aspx	Sioux Falls	SD	57106	605-361-0586	362-0283
Enfield Square 90 Elm St *Web:* shopenfieldmall.com	Enfield	CT	06082	860-745-7000	745-3007
Essex Shoppes & Cinema 21 Essex Way Ste 107 *Web:* www.essexoutlets.com	Essex	VT	05451	802-878-4200	879-5080
Factory at Franklin 230 Franklin Rd PO Box 864 *Web:* www.factoryatfranklin.com	Franklin	TN	37064	615-791-1777	591-2511
Factory Stores at North Bend *North Bend Premium Outlets* 461 S Fork Ave SW Ste E-1 *Web:* www.premiumoutlets.com	North Bend	WA	98045	425-888-4505	888-4514
Fair Oaks Mall 11750 Lee Jackson Hwy *Web:* www.shopfairoaksmall.com	Fairfax	VA	22033	703-359-8300	
Fairfield Commons 4869 Nine Mile Rd	Richmond	VA	23223	804-222-4167	226-2510
Fairlane Town Ctr 18900 Michigan Ave *TF:* 800-992-9500 ■ *Web:* www.shopfairlane.com	Dearborn	MI	48126	800-992-9500	
Fallbrook Ctr 6633 Fallbrook Ave *TF:* 866-718-1649 ■ *Web:* www.ggp.com	West Hills	CA	91307	818-885-9700	885-0029
Fantastic Indoor Swap Meet 1717 S Decatur Blvd *Web:* www.fantasticindoorswapmeet.com	Las Vegas	NV	89102	702-877-0087	877-3102
Farm, The 5321 S Sheridan Ste 27 *Web:* www.farmshoppingcenter.com	Tulsa	OK	74145	918-622-3860	622-4675
Fashion Island Shopping Ctr 401 Newport Ctr Dr *Web:* www.shopfashionisland.com	Newport Beach	CA	92660	949-721-2000	720-3350
Fashion Place 6191 S State St *Web:* www.fashionplace.com	Murray	UT	84107	801-262-9447	261-0660
Fashion Show Mall 3200 Las Vegas Blvd S Ste 600 *Web:* www.thefashionshow.com	Las Vegas	NV	89109	702-369-8382	369-1613
Fashion Valley Mall 7007 Friars Rd *Web:* www.simon.com	San Diego	CA	92108	619-688-9113	294-8291
Fayette Mall 3401 Nicholasville Rd Ste 303 *Web:* www.shopfayette-mall.com	Lexington	KY	40503	859-272-3493	273-6376
Festival Flea Market Mall 2900 W Sample Rd *TF:* 800-353-2627 ■ *Web:* www.festival.com	Pompano Beach	FL	33073	954-979-4555	968-3980
Fiesta Mall 1445 W Southern Ave Ste 2104 *Web:* www.shopfiesta.com	Mesa	AZ	85202	480-833-4121	
Fig Garden Village 5082 N Palm Ave Ste A *Web:* www.shopfiggardenvillage.com	Fresno	CA	93704	559-226-4084	226-7960
First Colony Mall 16535 SW Fwy Ste 1 *Web:* www.firstcolonymall.com	Sugar Land	TX	77479	281-265-6123	265-6124
Fleaworld 4311 Orlando Ave *Web:* www.fleaworld.com	Sanford	FL	32773	407-330-1792	
Florida Mall 8001 S Orange Blossom Trl *Web:* www.simon.com	Orlando	FL	32809	407-851-6255	855-1827
Foothill Village 1400 S Foothill Dr *Web:* www.foothillvillage.com	Salt Lake City	UT	84108	801-487-6670	487-6671
Foothills Mall 7475 N La Cholla Blvd Ste 133 *Web:* www.shopfoothillsmall.com	Tucson	AZ	85741	520-742-7191	797-0936
Four Seasons Town Centre 410 Four Seasons Town Centre *Web:* www.shopfourseasons.com	Greensboro	NC	27427	336-292-0171	
Fox River Mall 4301 W Wisconsin Ave *Web:* www.foxrivermall.com	Appleton	WI	54913	920-739-4100	739-8210
Foyer, The 3655 Perkins Rd	Baton Rouge	LA	70808	225-343-3655	343-3652
Franklin Mills 1455 Franklin Mills Cir *TF General:* 877-746-6642 ■ *Web:* simon.com/mall/franklin-mills	Philadelphia	PA	19154	215-632-1500	632-7888
Fulton's Folly Antique Mall 920 E Olive Ave	Fresno	CA	93728	559-268-3856	
Galleria at Fort Lauderdale 2414 E Sunrise Blvd *Web:* www.galleriamall-fl.com	Fort Lauderdale	FL	33304	954-564-1015	566-9976
Galleria at Pittsburgh Mills 590 Pittsburgh Mills Cir *Web:* www.pittsburghmills.com	Tarentum	PA	15084	724-904-9010	904-9020
Galleria at Sunset 1300 W Sunset Rd Ste 1400 *Web:* www.galleriaatsunset.com	Henderson	NV	89014	702-434-2409	434-0259
Galleria at Tyler 1299 Galleria at Tyler St *Web:* www.galleriatyler.com	Riverside	CA	92503	951-351-3112	351-3139
Galleria at White Plains 100 Main St *Web:* simon.com/default.aspx	White Plains	NY	10601	914-682-0111	682-1609
Galleria, The 5085 Westheimer Rd Ste 4850 *Web:* www.simon.com	Houston	TX	77056	713-966-3500	966-3596
Galleries of Syracuse, The 441 S Salina St	Syracuse	NY	13202	315-475-5351	475-4263
Gallery at Market East, The 9th & Market Sts **Fax Area Code: 773* ■ *Web:* galleryatmarketeast.com	Philadelphia	PA	19107	215-625-4962	728-6999*
Garden City Center 100 Midway Rd Ste 14 *Web:* www.gardencitycenter.com	Cranston	RI	02920	401-942-2800	942-8240
Garden State Plaza One Garden State Plz *Web:* www.westfield.com	Paramus	NJ	07652	201-843-2121	
Gardens Mall, The 3101 PGA Blvd *Web:* www.thegardensmall.com	Palm Beach Gardens	FL	33410	561-622-2115	694-9380
Gardner Village 1100 West 7800 South *TF:* 800-662-4335 ■ *Web:* www.gardnervillage.com	West Jordan	UT	84088	801-566-8903	
Gateway Mall 3000 Gateway St *Web:* www.gatewaymall.com	Springfield	OR	97477	541-747-6294	747-5897

Name / Address	City	State	ZIP	Phone	Fax
Genesee Valley Ctr 3341 S Linden Rd *TF:* 866-236-1128 ■ *Web:* www.geneseemall.com	Flint	MI	48507	810-732-4000	732-4343
Glenbrook Square 4201 Coldwater Rd *Web:* www.glenbrooksquare.com	Fort Wayne	IN	46805	260-483-2121	483-7756
Glendale Galleria 100 W Broadway *Web:* www.glendalegalleria.com	Glendale	CA	91210	818-240-9481	
Golf Mill Shopping Ctr 239 Golf Mill Ctr. *TF:* 866-853-9491 ■ *Web:* www.golfmill.com	Niles	IL	60714	847-699-1070	699-1593
Governor's Square 1500 Apalachee Pkwy *Web:* www.governorssquare.com	Tallahassee	FL	32301	850-877-8106	942-0136
Grand Avenue 649 Grand Ave *Web:* www.grandave.com	Saint Paul	MN	55105	651-699-0029	699-7775
Grapevine Mills 3000 Grapevine Mills Pkwy *Web:* www.grapevinemills.com	Grapevine	TX	76051	972-724-4900	724-4920
Great Lakes Mall 7850 Mentor Ave *TF:* 877-746-6642 ■ *Web:* www.simon.com	Mentor	OH	44060	440-255-6900	255-0509
Great Mall 447 Great Mall Dr *Web:* www.simon.com	Milpitas	CA	95035	408-945-4022	945-4027
Green Acres Mall 2034 Green Acres Mall *Web:* www.greenacresmallonline.com	Valley Stream	NY	11581	516-561-7360	561-3870
Green Hills Antique Mall 4108 Hillsboro Pk *TF:* 888-316-6255 ■ *Web:* www.antiquemalls.com/stores/11101.aspx	Nashville	TN	37215	615-383-9851	383-4886
Greenbriar Mall 2841 Greenbriar Pkwy SW *Web:* www.shopgreenbriar.com	Atlanta	GA	30331	404-344-6611	344-6631
Greenspoint Mall 12300 IH-45 N Fwy *Web:* www.greenspointmall.com	Houston	TX	77060	281-875-6255	
Greenway Station 1650 Deming Way *Web:* www.greenwayshopping.com	Middleton	WI	53562	608-824-9111	824-9144
Greenwood Park Mall 1251 US Hwy 31 N *TF:* 877-746-6642 ■ *Web:* simon.com/mall?id=165	Greenwood	IN	46142	317-881-6758	887-8606
Grossmont Center 5500 Grossmont Ctr Dr *Web:* www.grossmontcenter.com	La Mesa	CA	91942	619-465-2900	465-9207
Grove, The 189 The Grove Dr *TF:* 888-315-8883 ■ *Web:* www.thegrovela.com	Los Angeles	CA	90036	323-900-8080	900-8001
Gurnee Mills 6170 W Grand Ave *Web:* www.simon.com	Gurnee	IL	60031	847-263-7500	
Gwinnett Place Mall 2100 Pleasant Hill Rd *Web:* www.simon.com	Duluth	GA	30096	770-813-6840	476-9355
Hamilton Mall 4403 Black Horse Pk *Web:* www.shophamilton.com	Mays Landing	NJ	08330	609-646-6392	645-7837
Hamilton Place 2100 Hamilton Pl Blvd *Web:* www.hamiltonplace.com	Chattanooga	TN	37421	423-855-0001	892-0765
Hanes Mall 3320 Silas Creek Pkwy Ste 264 *Web:* www.shophanesmall.com	Winston-Salem	NC	27103	336-765-8323	765-3738
Hanover Mall 1775 Washington St *Web:* www.hanovermall.com	Hanover	MA	02339	781-826-4392	826-1575
Hawthorne Boulevard Cutters 1744 Se Hawthorne Blvd	Portland	OR	97214	503-239-0382	
Haywood Mall 700 Haywood Rd *Web:* www.simon.com	Greenville	SC	29607	864-288-0511	297-6018
Hickory Hollow Mall 5262 Hickory Hollow Pkwy	Antioch	TN	37013	615-731-3500	
Hickory Ridge Mall 6075 Winchester Rd *Web:* www.hickoryridge.com	Memphis	TN	38115	901-795-8844	
Highland Mall 6001 Airport Blvd Ste 1199 *Web:* www.highlandmall.com	Austin	TX	78752	512-454-9656	452-1463
Hillsdale Shopping Ctr 60 31st Ave *Web:* www.hillsdale.com	San Mateo	CA	94403	650-345-8222	573-5457
Hilltop Mall 2200 Hilltop Mall Rd *Web:* www.shophilltop.com	Richmond	CA	94806	510-223-6900	223-1453
Historic Old Town Fort Collins 19 Old Town Sq Ste 230 *TF:* 866-203-5939 ■ *Web:* www.downtownfortcollins.com	Fort Collins	CO	80524	970-484-6500	484-2069
Historic Valley Junction 217 Fifth St *Web:* www.valleyjunction.com	West Des Moines	IA	50265	515-222-3642	274-8407
Holyoke Mall at Ingleside 50 Holyoke St *Web:* holyokemall.com	Holyoke	MA	01040	413-536-1441	536-5740
Hulen Mall 4800 S Hulen St *Web:* www.hulenmall.com	Fort Worth	TX	76132	817-294-1200	370-0932
Independence Ctr 2035 Independence Ctr Dr *TF:* 877-746-6642 ■ *Web:* www.simon.com	Independence	MO	64057	816-795-8600	795-7836
Independence Mall 3500 Oleander Dr *Web:* www.shopindependencemall.com	Wilmington	NC	28403	910-392-1776	
Indianapolis Downtown Antique Mall 1044 Virginia Ave	Indianapolis	IN	46203	317-635-5336	
Ingram Park Mall 6301 NW Loop 410 *TF:* 877-746-6642 ■ *Web:* www.simon.com	San Antonio	TX	78238	210-684-9570	681-4614
Irving Mall 3880 Irving Mall *TF:* 877-746-6642 ■ *Web:* www.simon.com	Irving	TX	75062	972-255-0571	570-7310
Janet's Antiques 2545 Central Ave *Web:* thepricefairy.com	Saint Petersburg	FL	33713	727-823-5700	
Jantzen Beach SuperCenter 1405 Jantzen Beach Centre	Portland	OR	97217	503-286-9103	
Jefferson Mall 4801 Outerloop Rd *Web:* www.shopjefferson-mall.com	Louisville	KY	40219	502-968-4101	969-0882
Jefferson Valley Mall 650 Lee Blvd *Web:* www.simon.com	Yorktown Heights	NY	10598	914-245-4200	245-3479
Katy Mills 5000 Katy Mills Cir *Web:* www.simon.com	Katy	TX	77494	281-644-5015	644-5001
Kenwood Towne Centre 7875 Montgomery Rd *Web:* www.kenwoodtownecentre.com	Cincinnati	OH	45236	513-745-9100	745-9974
Kierland Commons 15205 N Kierland Blvd Ste 150 *Web:* www.kierlandcommons.com	Scottsdale	AZ	85254	480-348-1577	348-1497
King of Prussia Mall 160 N Gulph Rd *TF:* 877-746-6642 ■ *Web:* simon.com/mall/king-of-prussia-mall	King of Prussia	PA	19406	610-265-5727	265-1640
La Gran Plaza 4200 S Fwy Ste 2500 *Web:* www.lagranplazamall.com	Fort Worth	TX	76115	817-922-8888	927-1833
Lafayette Antique Market 3108 Johnston St *Web:* lafayetteantiquemarket.com	Lafayette	LA	70503	337-981-9884	981-9828
Lake Buena Vista Factory Stores 15657 S Apopka Vineland Rd Sr 535 *Web:* www.lbvfs.com	Orlando	FL	32821	407-238-9301	238-9716
Lakeline Mall 11200 Lakeline Mall Dr *Web:* www.simon.com	Cedar Park	TX	78613	512-257-7467	257-0522
Lakeside Mall 14000 Lakeside Cir *Web:* www.shop-lakesidemall.com	Sterling Heights	MI	48313	586-247-1590	247-0762
Lakeside Shopping Center 3301 Veterans Memorial Blvd Ste 209 *Web:* www.lakesideshopping.com	Metairie	LA	70002	504-835-8000	831-1170
Lakewood Ctr Mall 500 Lakewood Ctr *Web:* www.shoplakewoodcenter.com	Lakewood	CA	90712	562-633-0437	633-1452
Landmark Mall 5801 Duke St *Web:* www.landmarkmall.com	Alexandria	VA	22304	703-354-8405	
Lansing City Market 325 City Market Dr *Web:* www.lansingcitymarket.com	Lansing	MI	48912	517-483-7460	483-7462
Las Vegas Premium Outlets 875 S Grand Central Pkwy *Web:* www.premiumoutlets.com	Las Vegas	NV	89106	702-474-7500	676-1184
Lehigh Valley Mall 250 Lehigh Vly Mall *Web:* www.lehighvalleymall.com	Whitehall	PA	18052	610-264-5511	264-5957
Lenox Square Mall 3393 Peachtree Rd NE *Web:* www.simon.com	Atlanta	GA	30326	404-233-6767	233-7868
Lexington Market 400 W Lexington St *Web:* www.lexingtonmarket.com	Baltimore	MD	21201	410-685-6169	547-1864
Liberty Tree Mall 100 Independence Way *TF:* 877-746-6642 ■ *Web:* www.simon.com	Danvers	MA	01923	978-777-0794	777-9857
Lincoln Center Shops 374 Lincoln Centre *Web:* www.lincolncentershops.com	Stockton	CA	95207	209-477-4868	477-8936
Lincoln Mall 208 Lincoln Mall Dr *Web:* www.lincoln-mall.com	Matteson	IL	60443	708-747-5600	747-5629
Lincoln Square Shopping Center 436 Lincoln Sq *Web:* www.lincolnsquarearlington.com	Arlington	TX	76011	817-461-7953	274-5574
Los Cerritos Ctr 239 Los Cerritos Ctr *Web:* www.shoploscerritos.com	Cerritos	CA	90703	562-860-0341	860-5289
Lower East Side Business Improvement District 54 Orchard St *TF:* 866-224-0206 ■ *Web:* lowereastside.org/	New York	NY	10002	212-226-9010	226-8161
Lynnhaven Mall 701 Lynnhaven Pkwy Ste 1068 *Web:* www.lynnhavenmall.com	Virginia Beach	VA	23452	757-340-9340	463-8150
MacArthur Center 300 Monticello Ave *Web:* www.shopmacarthur.com	Norfolk	VA	23510	757-627-6000	627-6624
Macomb Mall 32233 Gratiot Ave *Web:* www.shopmacombmall.com	Roseville	MI	48066	586-293-7800	293-2713
Macon Mall 3661 Eisenhower Pkwy *Web:* maconmall.com	Macon	GA	31206	478-477-8840	474-5238
Maine Mall 364 Maine Mall Rd *Web:* www.mainemall.com	South Portland	ME	04106	207-774-0303	774-6813
Mall at Cortana 9401 Cortana Pl *Web:* www.cortanamall.com	Baton Rouge	LA	70815	225-927-6747	928-7920
Mall at Fairfield Commons 2727 Fairfield Commons *Web:* www.mallatfairfieldcommons.com	Beavercreek	OH	45431	937-427-4300	427-3668
Mall at Greece Ridge, The 271 Greece Ridge Ctr Dr *Web:* www.themallatgreeceridge.com	Rochester	NY	14626	585-225-0430	227-2525
Mall at Millenia 4200 Conroy Rd *Web:* www.mallatmillenia.com	Orlando	FL	32839	407-363-3555	363-6877
Mall at Robinson 100 Robinson Centre Dr *Web:* www.shoprobinsonmall.com	Pittsburgh	PA	15205	412-788-0816	788-1156
Mall at Short Hills 1200 Morris Tpke *Web:* www.shopshorthills.com	Short Hills	NJ	07078	973-376-7350	376-2976
Mall at Steamtown, The 300 Lackawanna Ave *Web:* www.themallatsteamtown.com	Scranton	PA	18503	570-343-3400	941-8623
Mall at Wellington Green 10300 W Forest Hill Blvd *Web:* www.shopwellingtongreen.com	Wellington	FL	33414	561-227-6900	227-6920
Mall del Norte 5300 San Dario Ste 206C *Web:* www.malldelnorte.com	Laredo	TX	78041	956-724-8191	728-1537
Mall of America 60 E Broadway *Web:* www.mallofamerica.com	Bloomington	MN	55425	952-883-8810	
Mall of Louisiana 6401 Bluebonnet Blvd *Web:* www.mallofl ouisiana.com	Baton Rouge	LA	70836	225-761-7228	761-7225
Mall Saint Matthews 5000 Shelbyville Rd *Web:* www.mallstmatthews.com	Louisville	KY	40207	502-893-0311	897-5849
Mall Saint Vincent 1133 St Vincent Ave Ste 200 *Web:* www.mallstvincent.com	Shreveport	LA	71104	318-227-9880	424-0454
Manchester Center 1901 E Shields Ave Ste 203 *Web:* www.manchester-center.com	Fresno	CA	93726	559-227-1901	227-1602
Market, The 2628 S Glenstone Ave	Springfield	MO	65804	417-889-1145	882-0261
Marketplace Mall 1 Miracle Mile Dr *Web:* www.themarketplacemall.com	Rochester	NY	14623	585-424-6220	427-2745
Marshall Square Mall 720 University Ave	Syracuse	NY	13210	315-422-3234	475-2004
Mayfair Mall 2500 N Mayfair Rd *Web:* www.mayfairmall.com	Milwaukee	WI	53226	414-771-1300	771-1034
Mazza Gallerie 5300 Wisconsin Ave NW *Web:* www.mazzagallerie.com	Washington	DC	20015	202-966-6114	362-0471
McCain Mall 3929 Mccain Blvd *Web:* www.simon.com/mall	North Little Rock	AR	72116	501-758-6317	758-0131
Memorial City Mall 303 Memorial City *Web:* www.memorialcitymall.com	Houston	TX	77024	713-464-8640	464-7845
Meridian Mall 1982 W Grand River Ave *Web:* www.meridianmall.com	Okemos	MI	48864	517-349-2031	349-7737
Merle Hay Mall 3800 Merle Hay Rd *Web:* www.merlehaymall.com	Des Moines	IA	50310	515-276-8551	276-9227
Mesilla Valley Mall 700 S Telshor Blvd *Web:* www.mesillavalleymall.com	Las Cruces	NM	88011	575-522-1001	522-0956
Metrocenter Mall 3645 Hwy 80 W *Web:* www.shopmetrocentermall.com	Jackson	MS	39209	601-969-7633	969-6820

	City	State	ZIP	Phone	Fax
Meyerland Plaza 420 Meyerland Plaza *TF:* 888-675-2275 ■ *Web:* tx.houston.charmingcharlie.com/	Houston	TX	77096	713-349-0245	600-1017
Mic Mac Mall 21 MicMac Blvd *Web:* www.micmacmall.com	Dartmouth	NS	B3A4N3	902-463-5891	469-5268
Mid Rivers Mall 1600 Mid Rivers Mall *Web:* www.shopmidriversmall.com	Saint Peters	MO	63376	636-970-2610	970-2950
Midway Mall 3343 Midway Mall *Web:* www.midwaymallshopping.com	Elyria	OH	44035	440-324-5749	324-7276
Mill Creek Mall 654 Millcreek Mall *TF:* 800-615-3535 ■ *Web:* www.millcreekmall.net	Erie	PA	16565	814-868-9000	864-1193
Mills at Jersey Gardens, The 651 Kapkowski Rd *TF:* 877-789-2327 ■ *Web:* www.jerseygardens.com	Elizabeth	NJ	07201	908-354-5900	
Monroeville Mall 200 Mall Blvd *Web:* www.monroevillemall.com	Monroeville	PA	15146	412-243-8511	372-0205
Montclair Plaza 5060 Montclair Plz Ln *Web:* www.montclairplaza.com	Montclair	CA	91763	909-626-2442	
Montgomery Street Antique Mall 2601 Montgomery St *Web:* www.montgomerystreetantiques.com	Fort Worth	TX	76107	817-735-9685	735-9379
Moreno Valley Mall 22500 Town Cir Ste 1206 *Web:* www.morenovalleymall.com	Moreno Valley	CA	92553	951-653-1177	653-1171
Natick Mall 1245 Worcester St *Web:* www.natickmall.com	Natick	MA	01760	508-655-4800	650-9945
NCDA&CS Raleigh Farmers Market 1201 Agriculture St *Web:* www.ncagr.gov/markets/facilities/markets/raleigh	Raleigh	NC	27603	919-733-7417	733-9932
Newgate Mall 36th St & Wall Ave *Web:* www.newgatemall.com	Ogden	UT	84405	801-621-1161	392-2159
Newpark Mall 2086 Newpark Mall *Web:* www.newparkmall.com	Newark	CA	94560	510-794-5523	796-7968
North East Mall 1101 Melbourne St Ste 1000 *TF:* 877-746-6642 ■ *Web:* www.simon.com	Hurst	TX	76053	817-284-3427	595-4471
North Idaho Outlets 4300 W Riverbend Ave	Post Falls	ID	83854	208-773-4556	773-4556
North Market 59 Spruce St *Web:* www.northmarket.com	Columbus	OH	43215	614-463-9664	
North Star Mall 7400 San Pedro Ave Ste 2000 *Web:* www.northstarmall.com	San Antonio	TX	78216	210-342-2325	342-7023
North Town Mall 4750 N Div St *Web:* www.northtownmall.com	Spokane	WA	99207	509-482-0209	483-0360
Northbrook Court 2171 Northbrook Ct *Web:* www.northbrookcourt.com	Northbrook	IL	60062	847-498-8161	498-5194
Northgate Mall 9501 Colerain Ave *Web:* www.mynorthgatemall.com	Cincinnati	OH	45251	513-385-5600	385-5603
NorthPark Ctr 8687 N Central Expy *Web:* www.northparkcenter.com	Dallas	TX	75225	214-363-7441	363-0195
Northpoint Mall 1000 N Pt Cir *Web:* www.northpointmall.com	Alpharetta	GA	30022	770-740-9273	442-8396
Northridge Fashion Ctr 9301 Tampa Ave *Web:* www.northridgefashioncenter.com	Northridge	CA	91324	818-885-9700	885-0029
Northridge Mall 796 Northridge Mall *Web:* www.shop-northridge-mall.com	Salinas	CA	93906	831-449-7226	449-6756
Northshore Mall 210 Andover St *Web:* www.simon.com	Peabody	MA	01960	978-531-3440	532-9115
Northwoods Mall 2150 Northwoods Blvd Unit 60 *Web:* shopnorthwoodsmall.com	North Charleston	SC	29406	843-797-3062	797-8363
Oak Hollow Mall 921 Eastchester Dr *Web:* www.oakhollowmall.com	High Point	NC	27262	336-886-6255	886-6257
Oak Park Mall 11149 W 95th St *Web:* www.thenewoakparkmall.com	Overland Park	KS	66214	913-888-4400	599-5839
Oak View Mall 3001 S 144th St *Web:* www.oakviewmall.com	Omaha	NE	68144	402-330-3332	330-3255
Oakbrook Shopping Ctr 100 Oakbrook Ctr *Web:* www.oakbrookcenter.com	Oak Brook	IL	60523	630-573-0700	573-0710
Oaks, The 350 W Hillcrest Dr *Web:* www.shoptheoaksmall.com	Thousand Oaks	CA	91360	805-495-2032	
Oakwood Ctr 197 Westbank Expy *Web:* www.oakwoodcenter.com	Gretna	LA	70053	504-361-1550	
Oglethorpe Mall 7804 Abercorn Ext *Web:* www.oglethorpemall.com	Savannah	GA	31406	912-354-7038	
Ohio Valley Mall 67800 Mall Rd *Web:* www.ohiovalleymall.net	Saint Clairsville	OH	43950	740-695-4526	695-4451
Old Mill Antique Mall 310 State St *Web:* oldmillantiquemall.com	West Columbia	SC	29169	803-796-4229	
Old Orchard Ctr 4905 Old Orchard Ctr *Web:* www.westfield.com	Skokie	IL	60077	847-673-6800	
Ontario Mills One Mills Cir Ste 1 *Web:* www.simon.com	Ontario	CA	91764	909-484-8300	
Orland Square 288 Orland Sq *TF:* 877-746-6642 ■ *Web:* www.simon.com/mall/?id=189	Orland Park	IL	60462	708-349-1646	349-8419
Orlando Fashion Square 3201 E Colonial Dr	Orlando	FL	32803	407-896-1132	894-8381
Orlando Premium Outlets 8200 Vineland Ave *Web:* www.premiumoutlets.com	Orlando	FL	32821	407-238-7787	238-7649
Outlets at Anthem 4250 W Anthem Way *TF:* 888-482-5834 ■ *Web:* www.outletsanthem.com	Phoenix	AZ	85086	623-465-9500	465-9516
Outlets at Loveland 5661 McWhinney Blvd *Web:* www.outletsatloveland.com	Loveland	CO	80538	970-663-1916	663-2421
Over-the-Rhine Chamber of Commerce 111 E 13th St *Web:* www.otrchamber.com	Cincinnati	OH	45202	513-241-2690	241-6770
Owings Mills Mall 10300 Mill Run Cir *Web:* www.owingsmillsmall.com	Owings Mills	MD	21117	410-363-7000	363-7999
Oxford Valley Mall 225 W Washington St **Fax Area Code:* 215 ■ *Web:* www.oxfordvalleymall.com	Indianapolis	IN	46204	317-636-1600	750-0469*
Ozark Antique 200 S 20th St *Web:* ozarkantiquemall.com	Ozark	MO	65721	417-581-5233	
Pacific Place 600 Pine St *Web:* www.pacificplaceseattle.com	Seattle	WA	98101	206-405-2655	587-3955
Palmer Square 40 Nassau St *Web:* www.palmersquare.com	Princeton	NJ	08542	609-921-2333	921-3797
Paradise Valley Mall 4568 E Cactus Rd *Web:* www.theparadisevalleymall.com	Phoenix	AZ	85032	602-996-8840	
Park City Ctr 142 Pk City Ctr *Web:* www.parkcitycenter.com	Lancaster	PA	17601	717-393-3851	392-8577
Park Meadows Retail Resort 8401 Pk Meadows Ctr Dr *Web:* www.parkmeadows.com	Littleton	CO	80124	303-792-2533	792-3360
Park Meadows Town Ctr 8401 Pk Meadows Ctr Dr *Web:* www.parkmeadows.com	Lone Tree	CO	80124	303-792-2533	792-3360
Park Place 5870 E Broadway Blvd *Web:* www.parkplacemall.com	Tucson	AZ	85711	520-747-7575	
Park Plaza Mall 6000 W Markham St *Web:* www.parkplazamall.com	Little Rock	AR	72205	501-664-4956	666-2115
Parks at Arlington 3811 S Cooper St Ste 2206 *Web:* www.theparksatarlington.com	Arlington	TX	76015	817-467-0200	468-5356
Parkway Place Mall 2801 Memorial Pkwy SW *Web:* www.parkwayplacemall.com	Huntsville	AL	35801	256-533-0700	533-5637
Parmatown Mall 7899 W Ridgewood Dr *Web:* www.facebook.com	Parma	OH	44129	440-885-5506	884-9330
Patrick Henry Mall 12300 Jefferson Ave *Web:* www.shoppatrickhenrymall.com	Newport News	VA	23602	757-249-4305	249-2730
Pearlridge Ctr 98-1005 Moana Lua Rd Ste 231 *Web:* www.pearlridgeonline.com	Aiea	HI	96701	808-488-0981	488-9456
Pembroke Lakes Mall 11401 Pines Blvd Ste 546 *Web:* www.pembrokelakesmall.com	Pembroke Pines	FL	33026	954-436-3520	436-7992
Peninsula Town Ctr 4410 E Claiborne Sq Ste 212 *Web:* www.peninsulatowncenter.com	Hampton	VA	23666	757-838-1505	827-9166
Penn Square Mall 1901 NW Expy *Web:* www.simon.com	Oklahoma City	OK	73118	405-842-4424	842-4676
Perimeter Mall 4400 Ashford-Dunwoody Rd Ste 1360 *Web:* www.perimetermall.com	Atlanta	GA	30346	770-394-4270	396-4732
Place de la Cite 2600 Laurier Blvd *Web:* www.placedelacite.com	Quebec	QC	G1V4T3	418-657-6920	657-6924
Plaza, The 9500 S Western Ave	Evergreen Park	IL	60805	708-422-5454	422-9780
Polaris Fashion Place 1500 Polaris Pkwy *Web:* www.polarisfashionplace.com	Columbus	OH	43240	614-846-1500	846-4617
Potomac Mills 2700 Potomac Mills Cir Ste 307 *TF:* 877-746-6642 ■ *Web:* www.simon.com	Woodbridge	VA	22192	703-496-9301	643-1054
Prime Outlets San Marcos 3939 S IH-35 **Fax Area Code:* 973 ■ *TF:* 866-888-5530 ■ *Web:* www.premiumoutlets.com	San Marcos	TX	78666	512-396-2200	228-8513*
Princeton Forrestal Village 206 Rockingham Row *Web:* pfvillage.com/	Princeton	NJ	08540	609-799-7400	799-0245
Provo Towne Centre 1200 Towne Centre Blvd *Web:* www.provotownecentre.com	Provo	UT	84601	801-852-2400	852-2405
Puente Hills Mall 1600 Azusa Ave *Web:* www.puentehills-mall.com	City of Industry	CA	91748	626-912-8777	913-2719
Quail Springs Mall 2501 W Memorial Rd *Web:* www.quailspringsmall.com	Oklahoma City	OK	73134	405-755-6530	751-8344
Quaker Bridge Mall 150 Quaker Bridge Mall *Web:* simon.com/mall/quaker-bridge-mall	Lawrenceville	NJ	08648	609-799-8177	275-6523
Regency Mall 5538 Durand Ave *Web:* www.shopregency-mall.com	Racine	WI	53406	262-554-7903	
Regency Square Mall 9501 Arlington Expy Ste 100 *Web:* www.regencysquaremall.com	Jacksonville	FL	32225	904-725-3830	724-7109
Reynolda Village 2201 Reynolda Rd *Web:* www.reynoldavillage.com	Winston-Salem	NC	27106	336-758-5584	
Richland Mall 3400 Forest Dr *Web:* www.richlandmallsc.com	Columbia	SC	29204	803-782-7575	
Ridgedale Ctr 12401 Wayzata Blvd *Web:* www.ridgedalecenter.com	Minnetonka	MN	55305	952-541-4864	540-0154
Ridgmar Mall 1888 Green Oaks Rd *Web:* www.ridgmar.com	Fort Worth	TX	76116	817-731-0856	763-5146
River City Antique Mall & Collector's Market 6363 Hearne Ave	Shreveport	LA	71108	318-621-1009	
River Oaks Ctr 96 River Oaks Ctr Dr *TF:* 877-746-6642 ■ *Web:* simon.com/mall?id=190	Calumet City	IL	60409	708-868-0600	868-1402
Riverchase Galleria 3000 Riverchase Galleria Ste 400 *Web:* www.riverchasegalleria.com	Birmingham	AL	35244	205-985-3020	
Rivergate Mall 1000 Rivergate Pkwy Ste 1 *Web:* www.rivergate-mall.com	Goodlettsville	TN	37072	615-859-3458	851-9656
RiverTown Crossings 3700 Rivertown Pkwy *Web:* www.rivertowncrossings.com	Grandville	MI	49418	616-257-5000	257-0507
Riverwalk Marketplace 500 Port Of New Orleans Pl *Web:* riverwalkneworleans.com	New Orleans	LA	70130	504-522-1555	586-8532
Rockaway Townsquare Mall 301 Mt Hope Ave *Web:* www.simon.com	Rockaway	NJ	07866	973-361-4070	361-1561
Rolling Oaks Mall 6909 N Loop 1604 E *TF:* 877-746-6642 ■ *Web:* www.simon.com	San Antonio	TX	78247	210-651-5513	651-6326
Roosevelt Field Mall 630 Old Country Rd *TF:* 877-746-6642 ■ *Web:* www.simon.com	Garden City	NY	11530	516-742-8001	742-8004
Ross Park Mall 1000 Ross Pk Mall Dr *Web:* www.simon.com	Pittsburgh	PA	15237	412-369-4400	369-4408
Saint Clair Square 134 St Clair Sq *Web:* www.stclairsquare.com	Fairview Heights	IL	62208	618-632-7567	632-4452
Saint Louis Mills 5555 St Louis Mills Blvd **Fax Area Code:* 314 ■ *Web:* www.simon.com	Hazelwood	MO	63042	317-636-1600	227-5901*
Salem Center 401 Center St NE *Web:* www.salemcenter.com	Salem	OR	97301	503-399-9676	364-1284

Name / Address	City	State	Zip	Phone	Fax
San Jacinto Mall 1496 San Jacinto Mall *Web:* www.sanjacintomall.com	Baytown	TX	77521	281-421-4533	421-7377
Sangamon Antique Mall 3050 E Sangamon Ave	Springfield	IL	62702	217-522-7740	
Savannah Mall 14045 Abercorn St *Web:* www.savannahmall.com	Savannah	GA	31419	912-927-7467	927-0434
Sawgrass Mills 12801 W Sunrise Blvd *Web:* www.simon.com	Sunrise	FL	33323	954-846-2300	846-2312
Seattle Premium Outlets 10600 Quil Ceda Blvd Ste 750 *Web:* www.premiumoutlets.com	Tulalip	WA	98271	360-654-3000	
Security Square Mall 6901 Security Blvd *Web:* www.securitysquare.com	Baltimore	MD	21244	410-265-6000	281-1473
Seminole Towne Ctr 200 Towne Ctr Cir *TF:* 877-746-6642 ■ *Web:* www.simon.com	Sanford	FL	32771	407-323-2262	323-2464
Sharpstown Mall 201 Sharpstown Ctr Ste 201 *Web:* www.plazamericas.com	Houston	TX	77036	713-777-1111	
Sherwood Mall 5308 Pacific Ave *Web:* www.sherwoodmall.com	Stockton	CA	95207	209-952-6277	952-6282
Shop at North Bridge, The 520 N Michigan Ave *Web:* www.theshopsatnorthbridge.com	Chicago	IL	60611	312-327-2300	222-1757
ShoppingTown Mall 3649 Erie Blvd E *Web:* www.shoppingtownmall.com	Dewitt	NY	13214	315-446-9159	446-1955
Shops at Briargate 1885 Briargate Pkwy *Web:* thepromenadeshopsatbriargate.com	Colorado Springs	CO	80920	719-265-6264	268-0738
Shops at Hilltop North East & West Laskin Rd *Web:* www.hilltopshops.com	Virginia Beach	VA	23451	757-428-2224	
Shops at Houston Center 1200 Mckinney Ste 545 *Web:* www.shopsathc.com	Houston	TX	77010	713-759-1442	759-1337
Shops at La Cantera 15900 La Cantera Pkwy Ste 6698 *Web:* www.theshopsatlacantera.com	San Antonio	TX	78256	210-582-6255	582-6699
Shops at Liberty Place 1625 Chestnut St *Web:* www.shopsatliberty.com	Philadelphia	PA	19103	215-851-9055	851-9154
Shops at Riverwoods 4801 N University Ave *Web:* www.shopsatriverwoods.com	Provo	UT	84604	801-802-8430	802-8431
Shops at Tanforan, The 1150 El Camino Real *Web:* www.theshopsattanforan.com	San Bruno	CA	94066	650-873-2000	873-4210
Shops at Willow Bend 6121 W Pk Blvd Ste 1000 *Web:* www.shopwillowbend.com	Plano	TX	75093	972-202-7115	202-7118
Shops at Woodlake 725 Woodlake Rd *TF:* 855-444-2838 ■ *Web:* www.americanclubresort.com	Kohler	WI	53044	920-459-1713	
Sierra Vista Mall 1050 Shaw Ave *Web:* www.sierravistamall.com	Clovis	CA	93612	559-299-5070	
Solomon Pond Mall 601 Donald Lynch Blvd *TF:* 877-746-6642 ■ *Web:* simon.com/mall?id=339	Marlborough	MA	01752	508-303-6255	303-0206
South Bay Galleria 1815 Hawthorne Blvd Ste 201 *Web:* www.southbaygalleria.com	Redondo Beach	CA	90278	310-371-7546	697-0793
South Coast Plaza 3333 Bristol St **Fax Area Code: 714* ■ *TF:* 800-782-8888 ■ *Web:* www.southcoastplaza.com	Costa Mesa	CA	92626	800-782-8888	540-7334*
South County Ctr 18 S County Centerway *Web:* www.shopsouthcountycenter.com	Saint Louis	MO	63129	314-892-8954	892-0006
South Mall 3300 Lehigh St *Web:* www.shopsouthmall.com	Allentown	PA	18103	610-791-0606	797-4065
South Park Mall 2310 SW Military Dr *Web:* www.visitsouthpark.com	San Antonio	TX	78224	210-921-0534	921-0628
South Plains Mall 6002 Slide Rd *Web:* www.southplainsmall.com	Lubbock	TX	79414	806-792-4653	799-2331
South Shore Plaza 250 Granite St *TF:* 877-746-6642 ■ *Web:* www.simon.com	Braintree	MA	02184	781-843-8200	843-4708
Southcenter Mall 2800 Southcenter Mall *Web:* www.westfield.com	Seattle	WA	98188	206-246-7400	244-8607
Southdale Ctr 10 Southdale Ctr *TF:* 877-746-6642 ■ *Web:* simon.com/mall?id=1249	Edina	MN	55435	952-925-7874	925-7856
Southern Park Mall 7401 Market St *TF:* 877-746-6642 ■ *Web:* www.simon.com	Youngstown	OH	44512	330-758-4511	726-2719
Southlake Mall 1000 Southlake Mall *Web:* www.southlakemall.com	Morrow	GA	30260	770-961-1050	961-1113
Southland Mall 20505 S Dixie Hwy *Web:* www.mysouthlandmall.com	Miami	FL	33189	305-235-8880	235-7956
SouthPark Mall 4400 Sharon Rd *TF:* 888-726-5930 ■ *Web:* www.simon.com	Charlotte	NC	28211	704-364-4411	364-4913
SouthPointe Pavilions 2910 Pine Lake Rd Ste Q *TF:* 800-733-2767 ■ *Web:* www.southpointeshopping.com	Lincoln	NE	68516	402-421-2114	421-2191
Southport Antique Mall 2028 E Southport Rd *Web:* www.southportantiquemall.net	Indianapolis	IN	46227	317-786-8246	786-9926
Southridge Mall 1111 E Army Post Rd *Web:* www.shopsouthridgemall.com	Des Moines	IA	50315	515-287-3881	287-0983
Southwest Ctr Mall 3662 W Camp Wisdom Rd *Web:* swcmall.com	Dallas	TX	75237	972-296-1491	861-5798
Southwest Plaza Mall 8501 W Bowles Ave Ste 2A-483 *Web:* www.southwestplaza.com	Littleton	CO	80123	303-973-5300	972-9516
Spokane Valley Mall 14700 E Indiana Ave *TF:* 800-326-3264 ■ *Web:* www.spokanevalleymall.com	Spokane	WA	99216	509-926-3700	926-4411
Spring Hill Mall 1072 Spring Hill Mall *Web:* www.springhillmall.com	West Dundee	IL	60118	847-428-2200	428-2219
Square One Mall 1201 Broadway *TF:* 877-746-6642 ■ *Web:* simon.com/mall?id=340	Saugus	MA	01906	781-233-8787	231-9787
Stanford Shopping Ctr 660 Stanford Shopping Ctr *Web:* www.simon.com	Palo Alto	CA	94304	650-617-8200	
Staten Island Mall 2655 Richmond Ave *Web:* www.statenisland-mall.com	Staten Island	NY	10314	718-761-6800	494-6766
Stonebriar Centre 2601 Preston Rd *Web:* www.shopstonebriar.com	Frisco	TX	75034	972-668-6255	668-4902
Stoneridge Shopping Ctr 1 Stoneridge Mall *TF:* 877-746-6642 ■ *Web:* simon.com/mall/stoneridge-shopping-center	Pleasanton	CA	94588	925-463-2778	463-1467
Stonestown Galleria 3251 20th Ave *TF:* 800-326-3264 ■ *Web:* www.stonestowngalleria.com	San Francisco	CA	94132	415-564-8848	
Stratford Square Mall 152 Stratford Sq *Web:* stratfordmall.com	Bloomingdale	IL	60108	630-539-1000	351-9769
Summit Sierra 13925 S Virginia St Ste 212 *Web:* www.thesummitonline.com	Reno	NV	89511	775-853-7800	
Sunrise Mall 6041 Sunrise Mall *Web:* www.sunrisemallonline.com	Citrus Heights	CA	95610	916-961-7150	
Sunvalley Mall One Sunvalley Mall *Web:* www.shopsunvalley.com	Concord	CA	94520	925-825-0400	825-1392
SuperMall of the Great Northwest 1101 SuperMall Way *Web:* www.outletcollectionseattle.com	Auburn	WA	98001	253-833-9500	833-9006
Tacoma Mall 4502 S Steele St Ste 1177 *TF:* 877-746-6642 ■ *Web:* www.simon.com/mall/?id=238	Tacoma	WA	98409	253-475-4565	472-3413
Tanger Outlet Ctr San Marcos 4015 S IH-35 Ste 319 *TF:* 800-408-8424 ■ *Web:* www.tangeroutlet.com	San Marcos	TX	78666	512-396-7446	396-7449
Timeless Treasures Antique Mall 433 E Us Hwy 69	Kansas City	MO	64119	816-455-9400	
Town Ctr at Boca Raton 6000 Glades Rd Ste 100 *Web:* www.simon.com	Boca Raton	FL	33431	561-368-6000	338-0891
Town Ctr at Cobb 400 Ernest Barrett Pkwy NW Ste 100 *Web:* www.simon.com	Kennesaw	GA	30144	770-424-9486	424-7917
Town East Mall 2063 Town E Mall *Web:* www.towneastmall.com	Mesquite	TX	75150	972-270-4431	686-8974
Tracy Outlets 1005 E Pescadero Ave *Web:* www.mytracyoutlets.com	Tracy	CA	95304	209-833-1895	
Tri-County Mall 11700 Princeton Pike *TF:* 866-905-4675 ■ *Web:* tricountymall.com	Cincinnati	OH	45246	513-671-0120	671-2931
Tucson Mall 4500 N Oracle Rd *Web:* www.tucsonmall.com	Tucson	AZ	85705	520-293-7330	293-6824
Tulsa Promenade 4107 S Yale Ave *Web:* www.tulsapromenade.com	Tulsa	OK	74135	918-627-9282	663-9385
Tyrone Square Mall 6901 Tyrone Sq *Web:* www.simon.com/mall/?id=135	Saint Petersburg	FL	33710	727-345-0126	345-5699
Tysons Corner Ctr 1961 Chain Bridge Rd *TF:* 877-247-5223 ■ *Web:* tysonscornercenter.com	McLean	VA	22102	703-847-7300	847-3089
Tysons Galleria 2001 International Dr *Web:* www.tysonsgalleria.com	Mclean	VA	22102	703-827-7730	
University Mall 2200 E Fowler Ave *Web:* www.universitymalltampa.com	Tampa	FL	33612	813-971-3465	971-0923
University Park Mall 6501 N Grape Rd *TF:* 877-746-6642 ■ *Web:* www.simon.com	Mishawaka	IN	46545	574-277-2223	272-5924
University Village 2623 NE University Village St *Web:* www.uvillage.com	Seattle	WA	98105	206-523-0622	525-3859
Valley Fair Mall 3601 South 2700 West *Web:* www.shopvalleyfairmall.com	West Valley City	UT	84119	801-969-6211	969-6233
Valley Plaza Mall 2701 Ming Ave *Web:* www.valleyplazamall.com	Bakersfield	CA	93304	661-832-2436	
Valley River Center 293 Valley River Ctr *Web:* www.valleyrivercenter.com	Eugene	OR	97401	541-683-5513	343-2478
Valley View Ctr Mall 13331 Preston Rd *Web:* www.shopvalleyviewcenter.com	Dallas	TX	75240	972-661-2939	239-1344
Valley View Mall 4802 Vly View Blvd *Web:* www.valleyviewmall.com	Roanoke	VA	24012	540-563-4440	366-8742
Vaughan Mills One Bass Pro Mills Dr *Web:* www.vaughanmills.com	Vaughan	ON	L4K5W4	905-879-2110	879-1888
Viejas Outlet Ctr 5005 Willows *Web:* viejas.com	Alpine	CA	91901	619-659-2070	659-2077
Viewmont Mall 100 Viewmont Mall *Web:* www.shopviewmontmall.com	Scranton	PA	18508	570-346-9165	
Village on Venetian Bay 4200 Gulf Shore Blvd N *Web:* www.venetianvillage.com	Naples	FL	34103	239-261-6100	262-6315
Vinings Jubilee 4300 Paces Ferry Rd Se Ste 245 *Web:* www.viningsjubilee.com	Atlanta	GA	30339	770-438-8080	438-8181
Vintage Faire Mall 3401 Dale Rd Ste 483 *Web:* www.shopvintagefairemall.com	Modesto	CA	95356	209-527-3401	527-3428
Virginia Ctr Commons 10101 Brook Rd Ste 765 *Web:* www.simon.com	Glen Allen	VA	23059	804-266-9000	266-9148
Vista Ridge Mall 2401 S Stemmons Fwy *Web:* www.vistaridgemall.com	Lewisville	TX	75067	972-315-3641	315-3725
Voorhees Town Ctr 2120 Voorhees Town Ctr *Web:* www.voorheestowncenter.com	Voorhees	NJ	08043	856-772-1950	772-2831
Walden Galleria One Walden Galleria *Web:* waldengalleria.com	Buffalo	NY	14225	716-681-7600	681-1773
Warwick Mall 400 Bald Hill Rd Ste 100 *Web:* www.warwickmall.com	Warwick	RI	02886	401-739-7500	732-6052
Washington Square Mall 10202 E Washington St *Web:* www.simon.com	Indianapolis	IN	46229	317-899-4568	897-9428
Washington Square Shopping Ctr 9585 SW Washington Sq Rd *Web:* www.shopwashingtonsquare.com	Portland	OR	97223	503-639-8860	620-6602
West County Ctr 80 W County Ctr *Web:* www.shopwestcountycenter.com	Des Peres	MO	63131	314-288-2020	288-2030
West Oaks Mall 2600 Hwy 6 S *Web:* www.shopwestoaksmall.com	Houston	TX	77082	281-531-1332	531-1579
West Point Market 1711 W Market St *TF:* 800-838-2156 ■ *Web:* www.westpointmarket.com	Akron	OH	44313	330-864-2151	869-8666
West Ridge Mall 1801 SW Wanamaker Rd *Web:* www.simon.com	Topeka	KS	66604	785-272-5119	272-1483
West Shore Plaza 250 W Shore Blvd *Web:* www.westshoreplaza.com	Tampa	FL	33609	813-286-0790	286-1250

	City	State	Zip	Phone	Fax
West Town Mall 7600 Kingston Pk *Web:* www.simon.com	Knoxville	TN	37919	865-693-0292	531-0503
West Towne Mall 66 W Towne Mall *Web:* www.shopwesttowne-mall.com	Madison	WI	53719	608-833-6330	833-5878
Westchester, The 125 Westchester Ave Ste 925 *TF:* 877-746-6642 ■ *Web:* www.simon.com	White Plains	NY	10601	914-421-1333	421-1475
Westfarms Mall 1500 New Britian Ave *Web:* www.shopwestfarms.com	West Hartford	CT	06110	860-561-3420	521-8682
Westfield Broward Mall 8000 W Broward Blvd *Web:* www.westfield.com	Plantation	FL	33388	954-473-8100	472-4302
Westfield Century City 10250 Santa Monica Blvd *Web:* www.westfield.com/centurycity	West Los Angeles	CA	90067	310-553-5300	553-3812
Westfield Citrus Park 8021 Citrus Pk Dr *Web:* www.westfield.com	Tampa	FL	33625	813-926-4644	926-4601
Westfield Countryside 27001 US 19 N Ste 1039 *Web:* www.westfield.com/countryside	Clearwater	FL	33761	727-796-1079	791-8470
Westfield Downtown Plaza 547 L St *Web:* www.westfield.com/downtownplaza	Sacramento	CA	95814	916-442-4000	442-3117
Westfield Fashion Square 14006 Riverside Dr *Web:* www.westfield.com	Sherman Oaks	CA	91423	818-783-0550	783-5955
Westfield Fox Hills 6000 Sepulveda Blvd *Web:* www.westfield.com/foxhills	Culver City	CA	90230	310-390-5073	391-9576
Westfield Hawthorn R 122 Hawthorn Ctr *Web:* www.westfield.com	Vernon Hills	IL	60061	847-362-2600	362-2689
Westfield MainPlace 2800 N Main St *Web:* westfield.com/mainplace	Santa Ana	CA	92705	714-547-7800	547-2643
Westfield Mission Valley 1640 Camino del Rio N Ste 351 *Web:* www.westfield.com	San Diego	CA	92108	619-296-6375	692-0555
Westfield Montgomery 7101 Democracy Blvd *Web:* www.westfield.com/montgomery	Bethesda	MD	20817	301-469-6000	469-7612
Westfield San Francisco Centre 865 Market St PO Box A *Web:* www.westfield.com	San Francisco	CA	94103	415-495-5656	512-6770
Westfield Santa Anita 400 S Baldwin Ave Ste 231 *Web:* www.westfield.com/santaanita	Arcadia	CA	91007	626-445-6255	446-9320
Westfield Sarasota Square 8201 S Tamiami Tr *Web:* www.westfield.com	Sarasota	FL	34238	941-922-9609	921-2632
Westfield Shoppingtown Annapolis 2002 Annapolis Mall *Web:* www.westfield.com	Annapolis	MD	21401	410-266-5432	266-3572
Westfield Shoppingtown UTC 4545 La Jolla Village Dr *Web:* www.westfield.com	San Diego	CA	92122	858-546-8858	552-9065
Westfield Southgate 3501 S Tamiami Trl *Web:* www.westfield.com	Sarasota	FL	34239	941-955-0900	954-3087
Westfield Topanga 6600 Topanga Canyon Blvd *Web:* www.westfield.com	Canoga Park	CA	91303	818-594-8740	999-0878
Westfield Trumbull Town Shopping Mall 5065 Main St *Web:* www.westfield.com	Trumbull	CT	06611	203-372-4500	372-0197
Westfield Valley Fair 2855 Stevens Creek Blvd Ste 2178 *Web:* www.westfield.com	Santa Clara	CA	95050	408-248-4451	248-8614
Westfield Vancouver 8700 NE Vancouver Mall Dr *Web:* www.westfield.com/vancouver	Vancouver	WA	98662	360-892-6255	892-0124
WestGate Mall 205 W Blackstock Rd *Web:* www.westgate-mall.com	Spartanburg	SC	29301	864-574-0264	
Westlake Ctr 400 Pine St *Web:* www.westlakecenter.com	Seattle	WA	98101	206-467-1600	467-1603
Westland Shopping Ctr 35000 W Warren Rd *Web:* www.westlandcenter.com	Westland	MI	48185	734-425-5001	425-9205
Westminster Mall 1025 Westminster Mall *Web:* www.simon.com	Westminster	CA	92683	714-898-2558	892-8824
Westmoreland Mall 5256 Rt 30 E *TF:* 800-333-7310 ■ *Web:* www.westmorelandmall.com	Greensburg	PA	15601	724-836-5025	
Wet Seal 1401 W Esplanade Ave Ste 100	Kenner	LA	70065	504-468-1889	465-2166
White Marsh Mall 8200 Perry Hall Blvd *Web:* www.whitemarshmall.com	Baltimore	MD	21236	410-931-7100	931-7120
Willowbrook Mall 2000 Willowbrook Mall *Web:* www.shopwillowbrookmall.com	Houston	TX	77070	281-890-8000	890-3019
Wolfchase Galleria 2760 N Germantown Pkwy *Web:* www.simon.com	Memphis	TN	38133	901-381-2769	388-5542
Woodbridge Center Mall 250 Woodbridge Ctr Dr *Web:* www.woodbridgecenter.com	Woodbridge	NJ	07095	732-636-4600	
Woodburn Co Stores 1001 N Arney Rd **Fax Area Code:* 973 ■ *TF:* 866-888-5530 ■ *Web:* www.premiumoutlets.com	Woodburn	OR	97071	503-981-1900	228-8513*
Woodfield Mall 5 Woodfield Mall *Web:* www.shopwoodfield.com	Schaumburg	IL	60173	847-330-1537	330-0204
Woodland Hills Mall 7021 S Memorial Dr Ste 225B *Web:* www.simon.com	Tulsa	OK	74133	918-250-1449	250-9084
Woodland Mall 3195 28th St SE *Web:* www.shopwoodlandmall.com	Grand Rapids	MI	49512	616-949-0012	949-7348
Yorktown Shopping Ctr 203 Yorktown Ctr *Web:* www.yorktowncenter.com	Lombard	IL	60148	630-629-7330	629-7334

464 MALTING PRODUCTS

SEE ALSO Breweries p. 1887

	City	State	Zip	Phone	Fax
Briess Malting Co 625 S Irish Rd *Web:* www.briess.com	Chilton	WI	53014	920-849-7711	849-4277
Great Western Malting Co 1701 NW Harborside Dr *Web:* www.greatwesternmalting.com	Vancouver	WA	98660	360-693-3661	
LE Cooke Co 26333 Rd 140 *Web:* lecooke.com	Visalia	CA	93292	559-732-9146	732-3702
Premier Malt Products Inc 25760 Groesbeck Hwy Ste 103 *TF Cust Svc:* 800-521-1057 ■ *Web:* www.premiermalt.com	Warren	MI	48089	586-443-3355	443-4580
Schoenmann Produce Company Inc 6950 Neuhaus St *Web:* www.schoenmannproduce.com	Houston	TX	77061	713-923-2728	923-5897
United Canadian Malt Ltd 843 Pk St S *Web:* www.unitedcanadianmalt.ca	Peterborough	ON	K9J3V1	705-876-9110	876-9118

465 MANAGED CARE - BEHAVIORAL HEALTH

	City	State	Zip	Phone	Fax
Allen Group 50 Washington St Fifth Fl *Web:* www.theallengroup.com	Norwalk	CT	06854	203-855-5777	855-5779
American Behavioral Benefits Managers 2204 Lakeshore Dr Ste 135 *TF:* 800-925-5327 ■ *Web:* www.americanbehavioral.com	Birmingham	AL	35209	205-871-7814	868-9600
Anthem Inc 120 Monument Cir *TF:* 800-999-7222 ■ *Web:* www.wellpoint.com	Indianapolis	IN	46204	317-488-6000	
APC Hegeman 8-12 Dietz St Ste 201 *Web:* www.eap-counseling.com	Oneonta	NY	13820	607-432-9039	432-7029
APS Healthcare Inc 44 S Broadway Ste 1200 *TF:* 800-305-3720 ■ *Web:* www.apshealthcare.com	White Plains	NY	10601	800-305-3720	
Associated Behavioral Health Care Inc 4700 42nd Ave SW Ste 480 *TF:* 800-858-6702 ■ *Web:* www.abhc.com	Seattle	WA	98116	206-935-1282	937-1380
Baxter Assistance Services Inc 2800 E Broadway Ste C-416 *TF:* 866-443-0005 ■ *Web:* www.bas-employeeassistance.com	Pearland	TX	77581	866-443-0005	910-1600
Bensinger DuPont & Assoc (BDA) 134 N LaSalle St Ste 2200 *TF:* 800-227-8620 ■ *Web:* www.bensingerdupont.com	Chicago	IL	60602	312-726-8620	726-1061
CIGNA Behavioral Health Inc 11095 Viking Dr Ste 350 *TF:* 800-753-0540 ■ *Web:* www.cignabehavioral.com	Eden Prairie	MN	55344	703-907-7730	
Comprehensive EAP 5 Militia Dr **Fax Area Code:* 781 ■ *TF:* 800-344-1011 ■ *Web:* www.compeap.com	Lexington	MA	02421	800-344-1011	860-9839*
ComPsych Corp 455 N City Front Plaza Dr NBC Tower 13th Fl *TF:* 800-851-1714 ■ *Web:* www.compsych.com	Chicago	IL	60611	312-595-4000	595-4219
COPE Inc 1120 G St NW Ste 550 *TF:* 800-247-3054 ■ *Web:* www.cope-inc.com	Washington	DC	20005	202-628-5100	628-5111
CorpCare Assoc Inc 7000 Peachtree Dunwoody Rd Bldg 4 Ste 300 **Fax Area Code:* 770 ■ *TF:* 800-728-9444 ■ *Web:* www.corpcareeap.com	Atlanta	GA	30328	800-728-9444	396-9522*
Corporate Care Works 8649 Baypine Rd Ste 101 *TF:* 800-327-9757 ■ *Web:* ccw.healthadvocate.com	Jacksonville	FL	32256	904-296-9436	296-1511
EAP Consultants Inc 3901 Roswell Rd Ste 340 *TF:* 800-869-0276 ■ *Web:* www.eapconsultants.com	Marietta	GA	30062	770-951-9970	953-3174
EAP Systems 500 W Cummings Pk *TF:* 800-535-4841 ■ *Web:* www.theeap.com	Woburn	MA	01801	781-935-8850	
FEI Behavioral Health 11700 W Lk Pk Dr *TF:* 800-782-1948 ■ *Web:* www.feinet.com	Milwaukee	WI	53224	414-359-1055	359-1973
Frontier Health 1167 Spratlin Pk Dr PO Box 9054 *Web:* www.frontierhealth.org	Gray	TN	37615	423-467-3600	467-3710
Gilsbar Inc PO Box 998 *TF:* 800-445-7227 ■ *Web:* www.gilsbar.com	Covington	LA	70434	985-892-3520	898-1500
Holman Group 9451 Corbin Ave *TF:* 800-321-2843 ■ *Web:* www.holmangroup.com	Northridge	CA	91324	818-704-1444	704-9339
Human Management Services Inc 835 Springdale Dr *TF:* 800-343-2186 ■ *Web:* hms.healthadvocate.com	Exton	PA	19341	610-363-6175	644-1134
Hurst Place 209 Limeridge Rd E **Fax Area Code:* 905 ■ *TF:* 888-521-8300 ■ *Web:* www.mohawkssi.com	Hamilton	ON	L9A2S6	289-426-5302	521-8166*
Interface EAP Inc (IEAP) 10370 Richmond Ave Ste 1100 PO Box 421879 *TF:* 800-324-4327 ■ *Web:* www.ieap.com	Houston	TX	77042	713-781-3364	784-0425
Magellan Health Services Inc 55 Nod Rd *NASDAQ: MGLN* ■ *TF:* 800-424-4399 ■ *Web:* www.magellanhealth.com	Avon	CT	06001	860-507-1900	507-1990
Managed Health Network Inc 1600 Los Gamos Dr Ste 300 *TF:* 800-327-2133 ■ *Web:* www.mhn.com	San Rafael	CA	94903	800-327-2133	
MENTOR Network, The 313 Congress St 5th Fl *TF:* 800-388-5150 ■ *Web:* www.thementornetwork.com	Boston	MA	02210	617-790-4800	790-4848
MHNet Behavioral Health 9606 N MoPac Exwy Ste 600 **Fax Area Code:* 512 ■ *TF:* 888-646-6889 ■ *Web:* www.mhnet.com	Austin	TX	78759	888-646-6889	347-1810*
Midwest EAP Solutions Inc 1015 W St Germain St Ste 440 *TF:* 800-383-1908 ■ *Web:* www.midwesteap.com	Saint Cloud	MN	56301	320-253-1909	240-1501
National Employee Assistance Services Inc N 17 W 24100 Riverwood Dr Ste 300 *TF:* 800-634-6433 ■ *Web:* www.empathia.com	Waukesha	WI	53188	262-574-2500	798-3928
New Directions Behavioral Health LLC PO Box 6729 *TF:* 800-528-5763 ■ *Web:* www.ndbh.com	Leawood	KS	66206	913-982-8200	982-8401
Perspectives Ltd 20 N Clark St Ste 2650 *TF:* 800-866-7556 ■ *Web:* www.perspectivesltd.com	Chicago	IL	60602	312-558-5318	558-1570
Preferred Mental Health Management Inc 401 E Douglas Ave Ste 300 *Web:* www.pmhm.com	Wichita	KS	67202	316-262-0444	
Providence Service Corp 64 E Broadway *NASDAQ: PRSC* ■ *TF:* 800-747-6950 ■ *Web:* www.provcorp.com	Tucson	AZ	85701	520-748-7108	747-9787

Phone | Fax

Stuecker & Assoc Inc
1930 Bishop Ln Watterson Towers Ste 1001............Louisville KY 40218 502-452-9227
TF: 800-799-9327 ■ *Web:* www.stueckerandassoc.com

United Behavioral Health Inc
425 Market St 27th Fl..........................San Francisco CA 94105 415-547-5000 547-5800
TF: 800-888-2998 ■ *Web:* optum.com

ValueOptions Inc 12369 Sunrise Vly Dr Ste C...........Reston VA 20191 703-390-6800
TF: 877-334-0077 ■ *Web:* www.valueoptions.com

466 MANAGEMENT SERVICES

SEE ALSO Educational Institution Operators & Managers p. 2210; Facilities Management Services p. 2281; Hotels & Hotel Companies p. 2530; Incentive Program Management Services p. 2551; Investment Advice & Management p. 2590; Association Management Companies p. 1754; Pharmacy Benefits Management Services p. 2925

Phone | Fax

2 Places At 1 Time Inc
270 Peachtree St 20th Fl...........................Atlanta GA 30303 877-275-2237 800-7888*
**Fax Area Code: 404* ■ *TF:* 877-275-2237 ■ *Web:* www.2placesat1time.com

2030 Inc 607 Cerrillos Rd..........................Santa Fe NM 87505 505-988-5309
Web: www.architecture2030.org

360 Technologies Inc 15401 Debba Dr.................Austin TX 78734 512-266-7360
Web: www.360tech.com

3H Group Inc 505 Riverfront Parkway ....Chattanooga TN 37402 423-499-0497
Web: www.3hgrouphotels.com

A Plus Arts Academy 270 S Napoleon Ave ....Columbus OH 43213 614-338-0767
Web: aplusarts.com

Absolute Technologies Inc
4890 E La Palma Ave.................................Anaheim CA 92807 714-692-6570
Web: www.absolutetechnologies.com

Acc Technical Services Inc
106 Dwight Park Cir..............................Syracuse NY 13209 315-484-4500
Web: www.acctek.com

Accent Computer Solutions Inc
8438 Red Oak St........................Rancho Cucamonga CA 91730 909-204-4801
Web: www.acsinet.com

Accompass 1052 Yonge St..........................Toronto ON M4W2L1 416-969-8588
Web: www.accompass.com

Accu-Read Inc PO Box 18277......................Spokane WA 99228 509-670-5894
Web: accureadinc.com

ACE NET Consulting 5800 E Skelly Dr..................Tulsa OK 74135 918-496-4223
Web: www.acenetconsulting.com

Ace Products Management G
12801 W Silver Spring Rd ....Butler WI 53007 262-754-1289
Web: www.brandedproducts.com

Acentech Inc 33 Moulton St ....Cambridge MA 02138 617-499-8000
Web: www.acentech.com

ACES 4140 W 99th St...............................Carmel IN 46032 317-344-7000
Web: www.acespower.com

Acoustic Sounds Inc 1500 S Ninth St ....Salina KS 67401 785-825-8609
Web: store.acousticsounds.com

Act Too Consulting Inc
917 W Inyokern Rd Ste C........................Ridgecrest CA 93555 760-301-5566
Web: www.acttooconsulting.com

Action Pact Inc 7709 W Lisbon Ave ....Milwaukee WI 53222 414-258-3649
Web: www.actionpact.com

Actuarial Management Resources Inc
4964 University Pkwy......................Winston Salem NC 27106 336-759-0008
Web: www.actmanre.com

Adams-Gabbert & Associates LLC
7300 W 110th St Ste 700......................Overland Park KS 66210 913-735-4390
Web: www.adamsgabbert.com

Adelaide Environmental Health Associates
1511 Route 22 ....Brewster NY 10509 845-278-7710
Web: adelaidellc.com

ADI Technologies Inc
1487 Chain Bridge Rd Ste 204........................Mclean VA 22101 703-734-9626
Web: www.aditechnologies.com

Advanced Generation Telecom Group Inc
752 Walker Rd Ste H...............................Great Falls VA 22066 703-757-6757
Web: www.adgentelecom.com

Advantech Manufacturing Inc
2450 S Commerce Dr...........................New Berlin WI 53151 262-786-1600
Web: www.advantechmfg.com

Advisory Council Inc, The One Stiles Rd Ste 105........Salem NH 03079 781-791-9582
Web: www.tacadvisory.com

Aeromedevac Inc 681 Kenney St...................El Cajon CA 92020 619-284-7910
Web: www.aeromedevac.com

AG Communications LLC 909 Church Hill Rd...........Fairfield CT 06825 203-373-0599
Web: www.agcomm.com

AgreeYa Solutions Inc 605 Coolidge Dr...............Folsom CA 95630 916-294-0075
Web: www.agreeya.com

AIB International Inc
1213 Bakers Way PO Box 3999 ....Manhattan KS 66505 785-537-4750
Web: www.aibonline.org

AirTrav Inc 10 Delisle Ave 14th Fl Ste 1402 ....Toronto ON M4V3C6 289-346-0071
Web: www.airtrav.ca

Alan B Lancz & Assoc Inc 2400 N Reynolds Rd.........Toledo OH 43615 419-536-5200 536-5401
Web: www.ablonline.com

Alcazar Networks Inc
6366 Hamilton Blvd Ste B.........................Allentown PA 18106 484-664-2800
Web: www.alcazarnetworks.com

Alderney Advisors LLC
One Towne Sq Ste 1870..........................Southfield MI 48076 248-504-0690
Web: www.alderneyadvisors.com

Aldo Ventures Inc 7370 Viewpoint Rd..................Aptos CA 95003 831-662-2536
Web: www.aldo.com

Alliance Health Networks
Nine Exchange Pl Second Fl....................Salt Lake City UT 84111 801-355-6002
Web: www.alliancehealth.com

Phone | Fax

Alliance of Professionals & Consultants Inc
8200 Brownleigh Dr...............................Raleigh NC 27617 919-510-9696 510-9668
Web: www.apc-services.com

Alliant Consulting Inc 555 Cajon St Ste A............Redlands CA 92373 909-792-8812
Web: www.alliantconsulting.net

AllMed Healthcare Management Inc
621 SW Alder St Ste 740..........................Portland OR 97205 503-274-9916
Web: allmedmd.com

AllTranstek LLC 1101 W 31st St Ste 200.........Downers Grove IL 60515 630-325-9977
Web: www.alltranstek.com

Altus Consulting Corp
38699 Old Wheatland Rd ....Waterford VA 20197 703-929-4000
Web: www.altuscc.com

Amarillo Economic Development Corp
801 S Fillmore Ste 205.............................Amarillo TX 79101 806-379-6411
Web: www.amarilloedc.com

Amc Management Group Inc 34 Abby Rd.........Farmingdale NJ 07727 732-938-5457
Web: www.amcinc.biz

American Dental Partners Inc
401 Edgewater Pl Ste 430.........................Wakefield MA 01880 781-213-6500 224-4216
NASDAQ: ADPI ■ *TF:* 800-838-6563 ■ *Web:* www.amdpi.com

AMFM Inc 240 Capitol St Ste 500..................Charleston WV 25301 304-344-1623
TF: 800-348-1623 ■ *Web:* www.amfmwv.com

AMI Environmental 8802 S 135Th St Ste 100...........Omaha NE 68138 402-397-5001
Web: www.amienvironmental.com

AMTEK Information Service Inc 4001 Sherwood.......Houston TX 77092 713-956-0100
Web: www.amtekusa.com

AMTIS Inc 12124 High Tech Ave Ste 150 ....Orlando FL 32817 407-513-9490
Web: www.amtisinc.com

AMZ Financial Insurance Services LLC
4944 Windplay Dr Ste 115....................El Dorado Hills CA 95762 916-939-3765
Web: www.amzwebcenter.com

Andra Partners LLC
2550 Meridian Blvd Ste 200.........................Franklin TN 37067 615-567-8090
Web: www.andrapartners.com

Angie Herbers Inc 1228 Westloop Pl Ste 327.........Manhattan KS 66502 785-320-2349
Web: www.angieherbers.com

Ann Arbor Distribution 1942 Mcgregor Rd............Ypsilanti MI 48198 734-484-0100
Web: annarbordist.com

Annex Wealth Management LLC
12700 W Bluemound Rd Ste 200...................Elm Grove WI 53122 262-786-6363
Web: www.advisorsannex.com

Apto Solutions Inc 1910 MacArthur Blvd ....Atlanta GA 30318 404-605-0992
Web: www.aptosolutions.com

Archway Marketing Services Inc
19850 S Diamond Lake Rd............................Rogers MN 55374 763-428-3300 488-6801
TF: 866-779-9855 ■ *Web:* www.archway.com

Arcweb Technologies LLC
234 Market St Fifth Fl.........................Philadelphia PA 19106 800-846-7980
TF: 800-846-7980 ■ *Web:* arcweb.co

ARD Inc 159 Bank St Ste 300......................Burlington VT 05401 802-658-3890
Web: careers.tetratechintdev.com

Area Circulation Inc 5656 Shell Rd ....Virginia Beach VA 23455 757-499-8330
Web: www.areacirculation.net

Ares Management LLC
2000 Ave of the Stars 12th Fl.....................Los Angeles CA 90067 310-201-4100 201-4170
Web: www.aresmgmt.com

ARK Solutions Inc
14161-B Robert Paris Ct Westfield Corp Pk............Chantilly VA 20151 703-657-0670
Web: www.arksolutionsinc.com

ARS Technologies Inc 98 N Ward St............New Brunswick NJ 08901 732-296-6620
Web: www.arstechnologies.com

Arthur Agency Inc 104 E Jackson St..............Carbondale IL 62901 618-351-1599
Web: www.arthuragency.com

Ascend Analytics LLC 1877 Broadway Ste 706 ....Boulder CO 80302 303-415-1400
Web: www.ascendanalytics.com

Ascendiant Capital Group LLC
18881 Von Karman Ave 16th Fl ....Irvine CA 92612 949-259-4900
Web: www.ascendiant.com

Ascent LLC 2350 Ball Dr............................St. Louis MO 63146 314-989-1011
Web: www.ascent-corp.com

ASR International Corp
580 Old Willets Path.............................Hauppauge NY 11788 631-231-1086
Web: www.asrintl.com

Assurance Investment Management LLC
1920 Georgetown Rd ....Hudson OH 44236 330-650-1750
Web: www.assureim.com

Astro Studios Inc 348 Sixth St.................San Francisco CA 94103 415-487-6787
Web: www.astrostudios.com

ATCO Properties & Management Inc
555 Fifth Ave 16th Fl ....New York NY 10017 212-687-5154 682-7599
Web: www.atco555.com

Ath Power Consulting Corp 100 Burtt Rd.............Andover MA 01810 978-474-6464
Web: www.athpower.com

Atrilogy Solutions Group Inc
One Jenner Ste 240 ....Irvine CA 92618 949-777-4700 777-4777
Web: www.atrilogy.com

Audit Group Inc, The
16141 Swingley Ridge Rd Ste 310................Chesterfield MO 63017 636-536-6333
Web: theauditgroup.com

Augustine Inc 17 S 19th St ....Camp Hill PA 17011 717-221-0825
Web: www.method3.com

Aurora Systems Consulting Inc
2510 W 237th St Ste 202..........................Torrance CA 90505 310-530-8260
Web: www.auroraent.com

Aurora Worldwide Development Corp
215 Martin Luther King Jr Blvd Ste 32...............Madison WI 53701 608-268-3470
Web: www.aurorawdc.com

Auto Profit Masters 250 E Dry Creek Rd..............Littleton CO 80122 303-795-5838
Web: autoprofitmasters.com

Avascent Group, The 1615 L St NW 12th Fl.........Washington DC 20036 202-452-6990
Web: www.avascent.com

Company	City	State	ZIP	Phone	Fax
Avatar Management Services Inc 8157 Bavaria Dr E *Web:* www.avatarms.com	Macedonia	OH	44056	330-963-3900	
Avrick Direct Inc 1021 Tremonto Rd *Web:* www.avrickdirect.com	Santa Barbara	CA	93103	805-963-8888	
AWC Inc 6655 Exchequer Dr *Web:* www.awc-inc.com	Baton Rouge	LA	70809	225-752-1100	751-9029
aWhere Inc 4891 Independence St Ste 275 *Web:* www.awhere.com	Wheat Ridge	CO	80033	303-279-9293	
Axia Strategies Inc 8688 Eagle Creek Cir *Web:* www.axiastrategies.com	Savage	MN	55378	952-945-3535	
B.I.T. Group, The 219 E Blithedale Ave Ste 4 *Web:* www.thebitgroup.com	Mill Valley	CA	94941	415-388-3282	
B3 Solutions LLC 1225 W Beaver St Ste 108 *Web:* b3solutions.com	Jacksonville	FL	32204	904-695-4241	
Baker Krizner Financial Planning 2230 N Limestone St *Web:* www.bakerkrizner.com	Springfield	OH	45503	937-390-8750	
Bamboo Worldwide Inc 2141 W N Ave *Web:* bambooexperience.com	Chicago	IL	60647	773-227-4848	
Bankruptcy Management Solutions Inc Eight Corporate Park Ste 230 *TF:* 800-634-7734 ■ *Web:* www.bms7.com	Irvine	CA	92606	800-634-7734	
Banyan Water Inc 11002-B Metric Blvd *TF:* 800-276-1507 ■ *Web:* www.banyanwater.com	Austin	TX	78758	800-276-1507	
Barada Associates Inc 130 E Second St *Web:* baradainc.com	Rushville	IN	46173	765-932-5917	
Barnsider Management Corp 15 Newbury St Apt A *Web:* www.barnsiderrestaurants.com	Danvers	MA	01923	978-777-3885	
Bartell & Bartell Ltd 432 Rolling Rdg Dr *Web:* bartellbartell.com	State College	PA	16801	814-861-6606	
Bates White LLC 1300 Eye St N W Ste 600 *Web:* www.bateswhite.com	Washington	DC	20005	202-408-6110	
BC Johnson Associates LLC 3702 Old Chocolate Bayou Rd *Web:* www.bcjohnson.com	Manvel	TX	77578	281-489-4894	
Bcn Transportation Services 3650 W Liberty Rd *Web:* www.bcnservices.com	Ann Arbor	MI	48103	734-994-4100	
BCT Partners LLC 105 Lock St *Web:* www.bctpartners.com	Newark	NJ	07103	973-622-0900	
Beaird Group, The 236 S Washington St Ste 208 *Web:* www.beairdgroup.com	Naperville	IL	60540	630-637-0430	
Bedford Management Co 50 Route 46 *Web:* bedfordmanagement.com	Parsippany	NJ	07054	973-227-1366	
Beghou Consulting 1880 Oak Ave *Web:* www.beghouconsulting.com	Evanston	IL	60201	847-864-5320	
Benefact Consulting Group 6285 Northam Dr Ste 112 *TF:* 855-829-2225 ■ *Web:* www.benefact.ca	Mississauga	ON	L4V1X5	855-829-2225	
Benefit Advantage Inc 3431 Commodity Ln *Web:* www.benefitadvantage.com	Green Bay	WI	54304	920-339-0351	
Benetrends Inc 1180 Welsh Rd *Web:* www.benetrends.com	North Wales	PA	19454	267-498-0059	
Bernstein Crisis Management Inc 180 S Mountain Trl *Web:* www.bernsteincrisismanagement.com	Sierra Madre	CA	91024	626-825-3838	
Bexar Fax & Mail Ctr 2186 Jackson Keller Rd Ste 330 *Web:* www.bexarcountymanagement.com	San Antonio	TX	78213	210-228-0083	
Beyond Quota LLC 537 King Muir Rd *Web:* www.beyondquota.com	Lake Forest	IL	60045	847-234-9475	
Beyond the Arc Inc 2600 Tenth St Ste 616 *TF:* 877-676-3743 ■ *Web:* www.beyondthearc.com	Berkeley	CA	94710	877-676-3743	
Bill Dunbar & Associates LLC 2601 Fortune Cir E Ste 301a *Web:* www.billdunbar.com	Indianapolis	IN	46241	317-247-8014	
Billions Corp, The 3522 W Armitage Ave *Web:* billions.com	Chicago	IL	60647	312-997-9999	
Birner Dental Management Services Inc 1777 S Harrison St Ste 1400 *TF:* 877-898-1083 ■ *Web:* www.perfectteeth.com	Denver	CO	80210	303-691-0680	691-0889
Bithgroup Technologies Inc 113 W Monument St *Web:* www.bithgroup.com	Baltimore	MD	21201	410-962-1188	
Bitzone 4102 Barrett Ave *Web:* bitzone-torrent.org	Richmond	CA	94805	510-234-4046	
Bizport Ltd Nine N Third St *Web:* www.bizport.biz	Richmond	VA	23219	804-780-1060	
Blackhawk Management Corp 1335 Regents Pk Dr *Web:* www.blackhawkmgmt.com	Houston	TX	77058	281-286-5751	286-5752
Blenheim Pharmacal Inc 119 Creamery Rd *Web:* bpipack.com	North Blenheim	NY	12131	518-827-3121	
BlessingWhite Inc 23 Orchard Rd *Web:* blessingwhite.com	Skillman	NJ	08558	908-904-1000	
Bluewater Energy Inc 3459 Acworth Due W Rd Ste 206 *Web:* bluewaterenergysolutions.com	Acworth	GA	30101	678-594-2058	
Bonefish Capital LLC Rosewood Court 2101 Cedar Springs Rd Ste 1050 *Web:* www.bonefishcapital.com	Dallas	TX	75201	214-347-0780	
Bonfire Communications Inc 577 Second St Ste 200 *Web:* www.bonfirecommunications.com	San Francisco	CA	94107	415-597-9930	
Boston Benefit Partners LLC 177 Milk St Ste 310 *Web:* www.bosben.com	Boston	MA	02109	617-570-9100	
Boston Strategies International Inc 445 Washington St *Web:* www.bostonstrategies.com	Wellesley	MA	02482	781-250-8150	
Bowen Group 10 Ctr St Ste 103 *Web:* www.bowenconsulting.com	Stafford	VA	22556	540-658-0490	
Brandon Technology Consulting Inc 3012 Business Park Cir Ste 700 *Web:* www.brandontci.com	Goodlettsville	TN	37072	615-757-1200	
Brillio 100 Town Sq Pl Ste 308 *TF:* 800-317-0575 ■ *Web:* www.brillio.com	Jersey City	NJ	07310	800-317-0575	
Broadgate Inc 830 Kirts Blvd Ste 400 *Web:* www.broadgateinc.com	Troy	MI	48084	248-918-0110	
Brookwood Program Management LLC 1819 Peachtree Rd NE Ste 501 *Web:* www.brookwoodpm.com	Atlanta	GA	30309	404-350-9988	
Browning Phyllis Co 14855 Blanco Rd Ste 403 *Web:* www.phyllisbrowning.com	San Antonio	TX	78216	210-408-2500	
BSC America Inc 803 Bel Air Rd *TF:* 800-764-7400 ■ *Web:* www.bscamerica.com	Bel Air	MD	21014	800-764-7400	
Bulk Solutions Inc 4040 Waring Rd *Web:* bulksol.com	Lakeland	FL	33811	863-248-1136	
Business Valuation Center LLC 560 Herndon Pkwy Ste 130 *Web:* businessvaluationcenter.com	Herndon	VA	20170	703-787-0012	
Buy Gitomer 310 Arlington Ave *Web:* www.gitomer.com	Charlotte	NC	28203	704-333-1112	
Buying Alliance 16 Mtn Ash Trl *Web:* www.diningalliance.com	Webster	NY	14580	585-671-0650	
C d Barnes Associates Inc 3437 Eastern Ave Se *Web:* cdbarnes.com	Grand Rapids	MI	49508	616-241-4491	
C2 Group LLC 325 Seventh St NW Ste 400 Liberty Pl *Web:* www.thec2group.com	Washington	DC	20004	202-567-2900	
C3 Consulting 2975 Sidco Dr *Web:* www.c3-consult.com	Nashville	TN	37204	615-371-8612	
C5 Insight Inc 8701 Mallard Creek Rd Ste 230 *Web:* www.c5insight.com	Charlotte	NC	28262	704-895-2500	
Caled 550 Bercut Dr Ste G *Web:* www.caled.org	Sacramento	CA	95811	916-448-8252	
Cannon Cochran Management Services Inc Two E Main St Towne Centre Bldg Ste 208 *Web:* www.ccmsi.com	Danville	IL	61832	217-446-1089	
Cape Henry Associates Inc 1206 Laskin Rd Ste 100 *Web:* www.cape-henry.com	Virginia Beach	VA	23451	757-502-7424	
Capgemini US LLC 623 Fifth Ave # 33 *Web:* www.capgemini.com	New York	NY	10022	212-314-8000	
Capital Realty Advisors Inc 600 Sandtree Dr Ste 109 *Web:* www.capitalrealtyadvisors.com	Palm Beach Gardens	FL	33403	561-624-5888	
Capital Review Group 1430 E Missouri Ave Ste B-165 *Web:* www.capitalreviewgroup.com	Phoenix	AZ	85014	602-741-7776	
Capitol Creag LLC 1300 Penn Ave Nw *Web:* www.capitolcreag.com	Washington	DC	20004	202-355-1028	
CapSouth Partners 2216 W Main St *Web:* www.capsouthpartners.com	Dothan	AL	36301	334-673-8600	
CapWealth Advisors LLC 3000 Meridian Blvd Ste 250 *Web:* capwealthadvisors.com	Franklin	TN	37067	615-778-0740	
Cardon & Assoc Inc 2749 E Covenanter Dr *Web:* cardon.us	Bloomington	IN	47401	812-332-2265	
Careers Inc 208 Ave Ponce De Leon Ste 1100 *Web:* www.careersincpr.com	San Juan	PR	00918	787-764-2298	
Carnahan Group Inc 5005 W Laurel St Ste 204 *Web:* www.carnahangroup.com	Tampa	FL	33607	813-289-2588	
Carolina Advanced Digital Inc 133 Triangle Trade Dr *Web:* www.cadinc.com	Cary	NC	27513	919-663-2211	
Carpedia International Ltd 75 Navy St *TF:* 877-445-8288 ■ *Web:* www.carpedia.com	Oakville	ON	L6J2Z1	877-445-8288	
Cascadia Managing Brands 1109 First Ave Ste 400 *Web:* www.cascadiaconsulting.com	Seattle	WA	98101	206-343-9759	
Caswood Group Inc, The 811 Ayrault Rd Ste 2 *Web:* www.caswood.com	Fairport	NY	14450	585-425-0332	
Catalyst House Inc 32545 Golden Lantern St *Web:* www.catalysthouse.net	Dana Point	CA	92629	949-443-0096	
Catapult Technology Ltd 7500 Old Georgetown Rd 11th Fl **Fax Area Code:* 301 ■ *Web:* www.catapulttechnology.com	Bethesda	MD	20814	240-482-2100	986-8688*
Catchpole Corp, The 10 High St Ste 502 *Web:* www.catchpole.com	Boston	MA	02110	781-431-2666	
Cavanaugh Tocci Associates Inc 327 Boston Post Rd *Web:* cavtocci.com	Sudbury	MA	01776	978-443-7871	
CBR-Technology Corp 15581 Sunburst Ln *Web:* www.cbrtechnology.com	Huntington Beach	CA	92647	714-901-5740	
Ccg Automation Inc 3868 congress pkwy *Web:* www.ccgautomation.com	Richfield	OH	44286	330-659-5082	
CE Resource Inc 1482 Stone Point Dr Ste 100 *TF:* 800-707-5644 ■ *Web:* www.paragoncet.com	Roseville	CA	95661	800-707-5644	
CEBOS Ltd 5936 Ford Court Ste 203 *Web:* www.cebos.com	Brighton	MI	48116	810-534-2222	
Celenia Software NA Inc 1509 Johnson Ferry Rd Ste 150 *Web:* www.celenia.com	Marietta	GA	30062	404-614-1751	

Company	City	State	Zip	Phone	Fax
Cengea Solutions Inc Ste 1160 St Mary Ave *Web:* www.cengea.com	Winnipeg	MB	R3C3Z5	204-957-7566	
Center of Workforce Innovations Inc, The 2804 Boilermaker Ct Ste E *Web:* www.innovativeworkforce.com	Valparaiso	IN	46383	219-462-2940	
Central IQ Inc 14527 Cotswolds Dr *Web:* www.centraliq.com	Tampa	FL	33626	813-920-4001	
Centrilogy Consulting 3201 Walker Pl *Web:* centrilogy.com	Grapevine	TX	76051	817-416-9722	
Centuria Corp 11955 Democracy Dr Ste 1620 *Web:* www.centuria.com	Reston	VA	20190	703-435-4600	
CES USA Inc 235 Remington Blvd Ste H *Web:* www.cesltd.com	Bolingbrook	IL	60440	630-296-8939	
CFOs 2Go Inc 500 Ygnacio Vly Rd Ste 410 *Web:* www.2gocompanies.com	Walnut Creek	CA	94596	925-299-4450	
Chagrin Consulting Services 24800 Chagrin Blvd Ste 207 *Web:* www.chagrinconsulting.com	Beachwood	OH	44122	216-514-3301	
Chally Group Worldwide Inc 3123 Research Blvd *Web:* chally.com	Dayton	OH	45420	937-259-1200	
Chartis Group LLC 220 W Kinzie St Fifth Fl *TF:* 877-667-4700 ■ *Web:* www.chartisgroup.com	Chicago	IL	60654	877-667-4700	
Charton Management Inc 373 Timberline Pkwy *Web:* www.charton-mgmt.com	Vienna	WV	26105	304-865-2222	
ChemQuest Group Inc, The 8150 Corporate Dr Ste 250 *Web:* www.chemquest.com	Cincinnati	OH	45242	513-469-7555	
Chervon North America Inc 120 Ionia Ave SW Ste 102 *Web:* www.chervonpowertools.com	Grand Rapids	MI	49503	616-454-8410	
Chiro. Advance Services Inc W5240 Oak Hill Rd *Web:* chiroadvance.com	Trego	WI	54888	715-635-5211	
Chugach Management Services Inc 3800 Centerpoint Dr Ste 601 *Web:* www.chugach.com	Anchorage	AK	99503	907-563-8866	
CIC Energy Consulting 30 S Wacker Dr Ste 1700 *Web:* www.cicenergyconsulting.com	Chicago	IL	60606	312-466-0500	
Cimro of Nebraska 1230 O St Ste 120 *Web:* www.cimronebraska.org	Lincoln	NE	68508	402-476-1399	
Ciproms Inc 3600 Woodview Trce *Web:* www.ciproms.com	Indianapolis	IN	46268	317-870-0480	
Citent Inc 600 Anton Blvd *Web:* www.citent.com	Costa Mesa	CA	92626	714-436-6100	
Clara Abbott Foundation, The 1505 S White Oak Dr *Web:* www.clara.abbott.com	Waukegan	IL	60085	847-937-1090	
Clarity Partners LLC 227 W Monroe St Ste 3950 *Web:* www.claritypartners.com	Chicago	IL	60606	312-920-0550	
Clark Mc Dowall 404 E 11th St *Web:* www.clarkmcdowall.com	New York	NY	10009	212-473-3737	
Clayton L Scroggins Associates Inc 200 Northland Blvd *Web:* www.scroggins.com	Cincinnati	OH	45246	513-771-7070	
closerlook Inc 212 W Superior St Ste 300 *Web:* www.closerlook.com	Chicago	IL	60654	312-640-3700	
Clover Global Group 2431 W Irving Park Rd *Web:* www.cloverglobal.com	Chicago	IL	60618	773-267-6767	
Coalition of Health Services Inc 301 S Polk St Ste 740 *Web:* cohs.net	Amarillo	TX	79101	806-337-1700	
Coast Dental Services Inc 4010 W Boy Scout Blvd Ste 1100 *TF:* 800-327-6453 ■ *Web:* www.coastdental.com	Tampa	FL	33607	813-288-1999	289-4500
Cochran, Cochran & Yale LLC 955 E Henrietta Rd *Web:* www.ccy.com	Rochester	NY	14623	585-424-6060	
Coker Consulting 2400 Lakeview Pkwy Ste 400 *TF:* 800-345-5829 ■ *Web:* www.cokergroup.com	Alpharetta	GA	30009	800-345-5829	
Combustion Components Assoc Inc 884 MN St *Web:* www.cca-inc.net	Monroe	CT	06468	203-268-3139	261-7697
Commodity Sourcing Group (CSG) 19730 Ralston St	Detroit	MI	48203	313-366-0660	
Commongood Careers Inc 99 Chauncy St Ste 910 *Web:* www.cgcareers.org	Boston	MA	02111	617-542-1404	
Communibiz Inc Po Box 30062 *Web:* communibiz.com	Billings	MT	59107	406-259-1252	
Communico Ltd 19 Ludlow Rd *Web:* www.communicoltd.com	Westport	CT	06880	203-226-7117	
Community Eldercare Services LLC 2844 Traceland Dr	Tupelo	MS	38801	662-680-3148	844-6558
Compmanagement Inc PO Box 884 *TF:* 800-825-6755 ■ *Web:* www.compmgt.com	Dublin	OH	43017	614-376-5300	766-6888
Computer Sciences Corp Healthcare Group 1160 Swedesford Rd Ste 200 *Web:* www.csc.com	Berwyn	PA	19312	610-251-0660	647-4912
Comworks Multi Media 2192 Yorkshire Rd *Web:* www.comworksonline.com	Birmingham	MI	48009	248-649-5454	
Concentra Inc 5080 Spectrum Dr Ste 1200 W **Fax Area Code:* 972 ■ *TF:* 866-944-6046 ■ *Web:* www.concentra.com	Addison	TX	75001	866-944-6046	725-6439*
Conception To Reality Inc 6020 W 91 Ave *Web:* ctr-inc.com	Westminster	CO	80031	303-225-0230	
Concord Promotions Inc 2000 Bloomingdale Rd *Web:* www.concordpromotions.com	Glendale Heights	IL	60139	630-893-6453	
Conducive Consulting Inc 3445 Executive Ctr Dr Ste 216 *Web:* www.conduciveconsulting.com	Austin	TX	78731	512-551-0660	
Conklin & de Decker 62B Cranberry Hwy *Web:* www.conklindd.com	Orleans	MA	02653	508-255-5975	
Conquest Technologies Inc 9250 Rumsey Rd Ste B *Web:* www.conquesttechnologies.com	Columbia	MD	21045	410-740-4448	
CONSOR Inc 7342 Girard Ave Ste 8 *Web:* www.consor.com	La Jolla	CA	92037	858-454-9091	
Contact International Inc 3201 Old Glnvw Rd 50 *Web:* www.contactamt.com	Wilmette	IL	60091	847-324-4411	
Continuous Learning Group Inc, The 500 Cherrington Pkwy Ste 350 *Web:* www.clg.com	Pittsburgh	PA	15108	412-269-7240	
Corizon 105 Westpark Dr Ste 200 *TF:* 800-729-0069 ■ *Web:* www.corizonhealth.com	Brentwood	TN	37027	800-729-0069	
Cornell Technical Services LLC 9700 Patuxent Woods Dr Ste 140 *Web:* www.cts-llc.com	Columbia	MD	21046	301-560-2544	
Corporate Healthcare Strategies LLC 280 Granite Run Dr Ste 250 *Web:* www.stoudtadvisors.com	Lancaster	PA	17601	717-581-8382	
Corporate University Xchange 4900 Ritter Rd Ste 103 *Web:* www.corpu.com	Mechanicsburg	PA	17055	717-395-9267	
Cortex Consultants Inc 1218 Langley St *Web:* www.cortex.ca	Victoria	BC	V8W1W2	250-360-1492	
Corum Group Ltd 19805 N Creek Pkwy Ste 300 *Web:* www.corumgroup.com	Bothell	WA	98011	425-455-8281	
CorVel Corp 2010 Main St Ste 600 *NASDAQ: CRVL* ■ *TF:* 888-726-7835 ■ *Web:* www.corvel.com	Irvine	CA	92614	949-851-1473	851-1469
Corvirtus LLC 1011 N Weber St *TF:* 800-322-5329 ■ *Web:* www.corvirtus.com	Colorado Springs	CO	80903	800-322-5329	
Coyle Hospitality Group 244 Madison Ave Ste 369 *Web:* www.coylehospitality.com	New York	NY	10016	212-629-2083	
Craford Benefits Consultants 990 Fifth Ave *Web:* www.craford.com	San Rafael	CA	94901	415-456-9790	
CRAssoc Inc 8580 Cinderbed Rd Ste 2400 **Fax Area Code:* 830 ■ *TF:* 877-272-8960 ■ *Web:* www.crassoc.com	Newington	VA	22122	703-550-8145	249-3596*
CRC Sogema Inc 1111 Saint-Charles St W Saint-Charles Complex W Tower Ste 700 *Web:* crcsogema.com	Longueuil	QC	J4K5G4	450-651-2800	
Creative Support Solutions 5508 W Hwy 290 Ste 203 *Web:* csssolutions.com	Austin	TX	78735	512-330-0701	
Critigen LLC 7604 Technology Way Ste 300 *Web:* www.critigen.com	Denver	CO	80237	303-706-0990	706-1861
CRMPlus Consulting Inc 11531 Meridian Point Dr *Web:* www.crmplusconsulting.com	Tampa	FL	33626	813-343-2173	
Croner Company Inc, The 1028 Sir Francis Drake Blvd *Web:* www.croner.biz	Kentfield	CA	94904	415-485-5530	
Cross World Network 10 Van Winkle Rd *Web:* www.crossworldnetwork.com	Hudson	NY	12534	518-851-6688	
Crossmedia Inc 22 W 23rd St *Web:* www.xmedia.com	New York	NY	10010	212-206-0888	
Crown Asset Management LLC 3355 Breckinridge Blvd Ste 132 *Web:* www.crownasset.com	Duluth	GA	30096	770-817-6700	
Crowned Grace Inc 2582 Maguire Rd Ste 316 *Web:* www.crownedgrace.com	Ocoee	FL	34761	321-251-5236	
CSG Government Solutions Inc 180 N Stetson Ave Ste 3200 *Web:* www.csgdelivers.com	Chicago	IL	60601	312-444-2760	
Currie Management Consultants Inc 292 Lincoln St *Web:* www.curriemanagement.com	Worcester	MA	01605	508-752-9229	
D&S Communications Inc 1355 N Mclean Blvd *Web:* www.dscomm.com	Elgin	IL	60123	847-468-8082	
D. Pagan Communications Inc 175 Pinelawn Rd Ste 215 *Web:* www.dpagan.com	Melville	NY	11747	631-659-2309	
D. R. Payne & Associates Inc 119 N Robinson Ave Ste 400 *Web:* drpayne.com	Oklahoma City	OK	73102	405-272-0511	
Dane Holdings Inc 6997 W Firebird Dr *Web:* www.daneholdings.com	Glendale	AZ	85308	623-825-3173	
DatamanUSA LLC 6890 S Tucson Way Ste 100 *Web:* www.datamanusa.com	Centennial	CO	80112	720-248-3121	
Datum Corp 6009 Business Blvd *Web:* www.datumcorporation.com	Sarasota	FL	34240	941-256-8700	
Davidoff Communications 10 S La Salle St Ste 1450 *Web:* www.davidoffcommunications.com	Chicago	IL	60603	312-543-1932	
Davis & Company Inc 11 Harristown Rd Ste 3 *Web:* www.davisandco.com	Glen Rock	NJ	07452	201-445-5100	
Davis Demographics & Planning Inc 11850 Pierce St Ste 200 *Web:* www.davisdemographics.com	Riverside	CA	92505	951-270-5211	
Dci Consulting Group Inc 1920 I St Nw *Web:* dciconsult.com	Washington	DC	20006	202-828-6900	
DD&F Consulting Group 521 S Rock St *Web:* ddfconsulting.com	Little Rock	AR	72202	501-374-2600	
De Maximis Inc 450 Montbrook Ln *Web:* www.demaximis.com	Knoxville	TN	37919	865-691-5052	691-6485
DealNet Capital Corp 325 Milner Ave Ste 300 *TF:* 855-912-3444 ■ *Web:* www.dealnetcapital.com	Toronto	ON	M1B5N1	855-912-3444	
Decimal Technologies Inc 841 Jean-Paul-Vincent Blvd Ste 202 *Web:* www.decimal.ca	Longueuil	QC	J4G1R3	450-640-1222	
Deep East Texas Council of Governments 274 e lamar st *Web:* www.detcog.org	Jasper	TX	75951	409-384-5704	
Delta Training Partners Inc 4020 Oleander Dr *Web:* deltatraining.com	Wilmington	NC	28403	910-790-1985	

Company / Address	City	State	ZIP	Phone	Fax
Denmar Services Inc 605 SW B Ave Ste 2 *Web:* www.denmarservices.com	Lawton	OK	73501	580-355-8900	
Dental Care Alliance LLC 6240 Lk Osprey Dr *Web:* dentalcarealliance.net	Sarasota	FL	34240	941-955-3150	914-9684
Desai Systems Inc 199 Oakwood Ave *Web:* www.desai.com	West Hartford	CT	06119	860-233-0011	
Design Dimension Inc 901 N W St *Web:* www.designdimension.com	Raleigh	NC	27603	919-828-1485	
Designs on Talent LLC 1579 Monroe Dr F155 *TF:* 888-360-3360 ■ *Web:* www.designsontalent.com	Atlanta	GA	30324	888-360-3360	
Development Alternatives Inc (DAI) 7600 Wisconsin Ave Ste 200 *Web:* www.dai.com	Bethesda	MD	20814	301-771-7600	771-7777
DevFacto Technologies Inc 2250 Scotia Place Tower 1 10060 Jasper Ave *Web:* www.devfacto.com	Edmonton	AB	T5J3R8	587-520-9118	
Dickson Consulting 351 Old Babcock Trl *Web:* www.dicksonconsulting.biz	Gibsonia	PA	15044	724-272-1527	
Digital Street Inc 8000 centre park dr *Web:* www.digitalstreets.tv	Austin	TX	78754	512-870-8413	
Dirks, Van Essen & Murray 119 E Marcy St Ste 100 *Web:* www.dirksvanessen.com	Santa Fe	NM	87501	505-820-2700	
Discover Reinsurance Company Inc Five Batterson Pk	Farmington	CT	06032	860-674-2660	674-2671
Doctors Administrative Solutions LLC 3414 W Bay to Bay Blvd Ste 100 *Web:* www.dr-solutions.com	Tampa	FL	33629	813-774-9800	
Dodge County Board of Education PO Box 1029 *Web:* www.dodge.k12.ga.us	Eastman	GA	31023	478-374-3783	374-6697
Domain Systems Inc 117 West 200 South *Web:* www.domainsi.com	Farmington	UT	84025	801-447-3778	
Doran Consulting LLC 3101 Magic Hollow Blvd *Web:* doranconsulting.com	Virginia Beach	VA	23453	757-368-2208	
Doyletech Corp 28 Thorncliff Pl Ste 201 *Web:* www.doyletechcorp.com	Nepean	ON	K2H6L2	613-226-8900	
Dresser & Associates Inc 243 US Route 1 *Web:* www.dresserassociates.com	Scarborough	ME	04074	207-885-0809	
DTE Energy Services 414 S Main St Ste 600 *Web:* www.dtees.com	Ann Arbor	MI	48104	734-302-4800	
Ducker Worldwide LLC 1250 Maplelawn Dr *Web:* www.ducker.com	Troy	MI	48084	248-644-0086	
Dunthorpe Marketing Group Inc 8825 Se 11th Ave *Web:* www.dunthorpemarketing.com	Portland	OR	97202	503-236-4242	
Dyna Lync Corp 200 Consumer Rd Ste 604 *Web:* www.dynalync.ca	Toronto	ON	M2J4R4	416-398-2000	
Dynamic Links International LLC 8286 Daleview Rd *Web:* dynamiclinksint.com	Cincinnati	OH	45247	513-385-2600	
Eagle Construction Services Inc 1624 Jacksonville Rd *Web:* www.eagle1construction.com	Burlington	NJ	08016	609-239-8000	
Eagle's Flight, Creative Training Excellence Inc 489 Clair Rd W *Web:* www.eaglesflight.com	Guelph	ON	N1L0H7	519-767-1747	
Eberline Services Inc 7021 Pan American Fwy NE *Web:* www.eberlineservices.com	Albuquerque	NM	87109	505-262-2694	
EBUSINESS STRATEGIS LLC 18318 Fern Trl Ctr *Web:* askebiz.com	Houston	TX	77084	281-647-6183	
Economic Systems Inc 3141 Frview Pk Dr *Web:* www.econsys.com	Falls Church	VA	22042	703-642-5225	
Edelman Berland Inc 1875 Eye St NW Ste 900 *Web:* www.edelmanberland.com	Washington	DC	20006	202-326-1772	
Edgemark Partners 4510 cox rd *Web:* www.edgemarkpartners.com	Glen Allen	VA	23060	804-967-2000	
EDJ Associates Inc 2100 Reston Pkwy Ste 350 *Web:* edjassociates.com	Reston	VA	20191	703-738-9150	
Ellis-harper Advertising Inc 710 Stage Rd *Web:* www.ellisharper.com	Auburn	AL	36830	334-887-6536	
EMI Services Inc 301 A St *Web:* www.emiservices.com	Idaho Falls	ID	83402	208-522-1117	
Empowered Networks Inc 1315 Pickering Pkwy Ste 200 *Web:* empowered.ca	Pickering	ON	L1V7G5	905-837-6585	
Enaxis Consulting 24 E Greenway Plz *Web:* www.enaxisconsulting.com	Houston	TX	77046	713-881-9494	
Encore Cbt Co 5900 n high st *Web:* www.encorecbt.com	Columbus	OH	43085	614-888-4179	
Enderle Group Inc 389 Photinia Ln *Web:* www.enderlegroup.com	San Jose	CA	95127	408-272-8560	
Energy Ace Inc 160 Clairemont Ave Ste 600 *Web:* www.energyace.com	Decatur	GA	30030	404-378-7800	
Energy Authority Inc, The 301 W Bay St Ste 2600 *Web:* www.teainc.org	Jacksonville	FL	32202	904-356-3900	
Energy Management Solutions Inc 7935 Stone Creek Dr Ste 140 *Web:* www.emsenergy.com	Chanhassen	MN	55317	952-767-7450	
Energy Project, The One Larkin Plaza Fourth Fl *Web:* theenergyproject.com	Yonkers	NY	10701	914-207-8800	
EnergyWorks Inc 71 Old Mill Bottom Rd N Ste 101 *Web:* www.energyworks.com	Annapolis	MD	21409	410-349-2001	
Enernoc Inc 101 Federal St Ste 1100 *NASDAQ: ENOC* ■ *Web:* www.enernoc.com	Boston	MA	02110	617-224-9900	224-9910
Engineering Management Concepts Inc 5051 Verdugo Way Ste 200 *Web:* www.emc-inc.com	Camarillo	CA	93012	805-484-9082	484-4607
Enigma Marketing Trvl Solutions 8463 castlewood dr *Web:* www.enigma-marketing.com	Indianapolis	IN	46250	317-585-0100	
Entelechy Enterprises Inc 19 Springfield Cir *Web:* www.unlockit.com	Merrimack	NH	03054	603-424-1237	
Enterey Inc 9900 Irvine Ctr Dr Ste 100 *TF:* 800-691-2349 ■ *Web:* www.enterey.com	Irvine	CA	92618	800-691-2349	
Envisa Inc 281 Pleasant St *Web:* www.envisa.com	Framingham	MA	01701	508-405-1220	
Ephor Group LLC 24 E Greenway Plz Ste 440 *TF:* 800-379-9330 ■ *Web:* www.ephorgroup.com	Houston	TX	77046	800-379-9330	
Epi Marketing Group 30262 Crown Vly Pkwy Ste B458 *Web:* www.epi-marketing.com	Laguna Niguel	CA	92677	949-542-7743	
Epler Co 450 B St Ste 750 *Web:* eplercompany.com	San Diego	CA	92101	619-239-0831	
EPS Corp 150 Paularino Ave Ste A120 *TF:* 866-377-7834 ■ *Web:* www.epsway.com	Costa Mesa	CA	92626	866-377-7834	
Equitrust Financial Group Ltd 570 Lk Cook Rd Ste 101 *Web:* www.equitrustfinancial.com	Deerfield	IL	60015	847-317-0200	
ERA Herman Group Real Estate 4057 Battleground Ave *Web:* www.hermangroup.com	Greensboro	NC	27410	336-282-9370	
Eventech 1833 alford ave *Web:* www.eventech.com	Los Altos	CA	94024	650-961-7845	
Evidence Based Research Inc 1595 Spring Hill Rd *Web:* www.ebrinc.com	Vienna	VA	22182	703-893-6800	
Evision Systems I Inc 2852 Antoine Dr *Web:* www.evisionsys.com	Houston	TX	77092	713-807-9555	
Execustaff HR 1625 W Campbell Ave *Web:* www.execustaffhr.com	Campbell	CA	95008	408-364-2800	
Executive Business Media Inc 825 Old Country Rd *Web:* www.ebmpubs.com	Westbury	NY	11590	516-334-3030	334-3059
Executive Sounding Board Associates Inc Two Penn Ctr Plz 1500 John F Kennedy Blvd Ste 1730 *Web:* www.esba.com	Philadelphia	PA	19102	215-568-5788	
Expense Reduction Analysts Inc 16479 N Dallas Pkwy Bent Tree Twr II Ste 240 *Web:* www.expensereduction.com	Addison	TX	75001	469-310-2970	
Expotel Hospitality Services LLC 401 Veterans Memorial Blvd Ste 102 *Web:* www.expotelhospitality.com	Metairie	LA	70005	504-212-1492	
Fabrizio, McLaughlin & Associates 915 King St *Web:* www.fabriziolee.com	Alexandria	VA	22314	703-684-4510	
Falk Marques Group LLC 114 Waltham St Ste 22 *Web:* www.falkmarquesgroup.com	Lexington	MA	02421	781-652-0900	
Family Business Institute Inc, The 4700 Homewood Court Ste 340 *Web:* www.familybusinessinstitute.com	Raleigh	NC	27609	919-783-1880	
Family Circle Tennis Center 161 Seven Farms Dr *Web:* www.familycirclecup.com	Daniel Island	SC	29492	843-856-7900	
Fandel Retail Group 650 Fifth St Ste 405 *Web:* www.fandelretail.com	San Francisco	CA	94107	415-538-8355	
Farr Associates Inc 4194 Mendenhall Oaks Pkwy Ste 101 *Web:* www.farrleadership.com	High Point	NC	27265	336-812-8050	
Fast-Impact Consulting Inc 5190 Neil Rd Ste 430 *Web:* www.fast-impact.com	Reno	NV	89502	775-284-3704	
FCC Services 7951 E Maplewood Ave Ste 225 *TF:* 888-275-3227 ■ *Web:* www.fccservices.com	Greenwood Village	CO	80111	888-275-3227	
Fiedor Van Epps & Associates 964 Fifth Ave *Web:* fiedorvanepps.com	San Diego	CA	92101	619-544-1422	
Fieldman Rolapp & Assoc 19900 Macarthur Blvd *Web:* www.fieldman.com	Irvine	CA	92612	949-660-7300	474-8773
File Keepers LLC 6277 E Slauson Ave *TF:* 800-332-3463 ■ *Web:* www.filekeepers.com	Los Angeles	CA	90040	323-728-3133	728-0867
Fino Consulting LLC 20 W 37th St 12th Fl *Web:* www.finoconsulting.com	New York	NY	10018	212-532-0020	
Firm Consulting Group 2107 W Cass St Ste B *TF:* 877-636-9525 ■ *Web:* www.firmconsultinggrp.com	Tampa	FL	33606	877-636-9525	
First Carolina Management Inc 300 N Winstead Ave *Web:* www.1stcarolina.net	Rocky Mount	NC	27804	252-937-8111	
First Health Group Corp *Coventry* 3200 Highland Ave *TF:* 800-247-2898 ■ *Web:* www.firsthealth.com	Downers Grove	IL	60515	630-737-7900	
First Infrastructure LLC 15 Wendover Rd *Web:* www.1stinfrastructure.com	Montclair	NJ	07042	973-783-0088	
Fiserv Credit Processing Services Ste 100 901 International Pkwy *Web:* www.progressdata.com	Lake Mary	FL	32746	407-829-4200	
Fishkind & Associates Inc 12051 Corporate Blvd *Web:* www.fishkind.com	Orlando	FL	32817	407-382-3256	
Fitch & Associates LLC 303 Marshall Rd Ste 6 *Web:* www.fitchassoc.com	Platte City	MO	64079	816-431-2600	
FleetWeather Group, The 2566 Route 52 *Web:* fleetweathergroup.com	Hopewell Junction	NY	12533	845-226-8300	
Fletcher Csi LLC 237 Commerce St *Web:* www.fletchercsi.com	Williston	VT	05495	802-660-9636	

Phone Fax

Flippen Group, The 1199 Haywood Dr ... College Station TX 77845 979-693-7549
Web: www.flippengroup.com

Focus Center of Pittsburgh
2101 Greentree Rd # A106 ... Pittsburgh PA 15220 412-279-5900
Web: www.fcpresearch.com

Focus Healthcare Management Inc
720 Cool Springs Blvd ... Franklin TN 37067 615-778-4000 778-0801

Focus Management Group USA Inc 5001 W Lemon St ... Tampa FL 33609 813-281-0062
Web: www.focusmg.com

Fonkoze USA Inc
1700 Kalorama Rd NW Ste 102 ... Washington DC 20009 202-628-9033
Web: www.fonkoze.org

Food Concepts Inc 2551 Parmenter St ... Middleton WI 53562 608-831-5006
Web: foodconcepts.com

Force Management LLC 10815 Sikes Pl Ste 200 ... Charlotte NC 28277 704-246-2400
Web: www.forcemanagement.com

Forte Information Resources LLC
1140 Delaware St ... Denver CO 80204 303-321-3888
Web: www.forteinformation.com

Fortune Practice Management
2650 Camino Del Rio N ... San Diego CA 92108 619-564-7402

Foster Lake & Pond Management Inc
183 Donmoor Ct ... Garner NC 27529 919-772-8548
Web: www.fosterlake.com

Franchise Brands LLC 325 Bic Dr ... Milford CT 06461 800-797-2308
TF: 800-797-2308 ■ *Web:* www.franchisebrandsllc.com

Franchise Co, The (TFC)
5399 Eglinton Ave W Ste 110 ... Etobicoke ON M9C5K9 416-620-3960 620-3961
TF: 800-294-5591 ■ *Web:* www.thefranchisecompany.com

Francorp Inc 20200 Governors Dr ... Olympia Fields IL 60461 708-481-2900
Web: www.francorp.com

Fulcrum Financial Inquiry LLP
888 S Figueroa St Ste 2000 ... Los Angeles CA 90017 213-787-4100
Web: www.fulcruminquiry.com

Fuld & Company Inc 131 Oliver St Third Fl ... Boston MA 02110 617-492-5900
Web: www.fuld.com

Furtwengler & Associates Inc
2412 Oakmont Ct ... High Ridge MO 63049 314-707-3771
Web: www.furtwengler.com

Fusion Advisor Network
Fusion Financial 555 Taxter Rd Ste 190 ... Elmsford NY 10523 914-909-1518
Web: www.fusionfinancialgroup.com

Future Financial Planners Inc 847 Broadway ... Bayonne NJ 07002 201-823-1030
Web: ffpinc.com

G.S. Proctor & Associates Inc
14408 Old Mill Rd Ste 201 ... Upper Marlboro MD 20772 301-952-8885
Web: www.gsproctor.com

Ganim Group Inc, The 2429 N Ave ... Bridgeport CT 06604 203-335-0851
Web: www.ganimgroup.com

Gap International Inc 700 Old Marple Rd ... Springfield PA 19064 610-328-0308
Web: www.gapinternational.com

Gartland & Mellina Group Corp
1385 Broadway Ste 912 ... New York NY 10018 212-418-4780
Web: www.gartlandandmellina.com

GCR Inc 2021 Lakeshore Dr Ste 500 ... New Orleans LA 70122 504-304-2500
Web: www.gcrincorporated.com

Geehan Group 40 N Main St Ste 1570 ... Dayton OH 45423 937-226-1622
Web: www.geehangroup.com

Genscape Inc 445 E Main St Ste 200 ... Louisville KY 40202 502-583-3435 583-3464
Web: www.genscape.com

Geo-Cleanse International Inc
400 State Rt 34 Ste B ... Matawan NJ 07747 908-206-1250
Web: www.geocleanse.com

Geo-instruments Inc
24 Celestial Dr Ste B ... Narragansett RI 02882 800-477-2506
TF: 800-477-2506 ■ *Web:* www.geo-instruments.com

Georesults Inc 309 Pirkle Ferry Rd ... Cumming GA 30040 770-205-8111
Web: www.georesults.com

George Darling Consulting Group Inc
Towle Office Bldg 260 Merrimac St ... Newburyport MA 01950 978-463-0400
Web: www.darlingconsulting.com

GIC Group Inc, The 1434 Duke St ... Alexandria VA 22314 703-684-1366
Web: www.gicgroup.com

Gifford Fong Associates Inc
3658 Mount Diablo Blvd Ste 200 ... Lafayette CA 94549 925-299-7800
Web: www.gfong.com

Global Center for Economic Enabling Environments
273 24th Ave ... San Francisco CA 94121 206-877-2460
Web: www.gceee.com

Global New Beginnings Inc
4042 W 82nd Ct ... Merrillville IN 46410 219-738-3600
Web: www.gnbiusa.com

Global Sage Group LLC Po Box 1431 ... Salem NH 03079 603-425-9136
Web: globalsagegroup.com

Global Voyages Group LLC
320 120th Ave NE Ste 100 ... Bellevue WA 98005 425-637-8558
Web: www.globalvoyagesgroup.com

Gnarus Advisors LLC
4350 N Fairfax Dr Ste 830 ... Arlington VA 22203 571-384-2444
Web: www.gnarusllc.com

Gobbell Hays Partners Inc 10500 E 54th Ave J ... Denver CO 80239 303-574-0082
Web: www.ghp1.com

Gordon Energy Solutions LLC
11286 Hadley St ... Overland Park KS 66210 913-451-9539
Web: www.gordonenergysolutions.com

Gottlieb Martin & Associates Inc
4932 Sunbeam Rd ... Jacksonville FL 32257 904-346-3088
Web: www.gottlieb.com

Gravitant
Synergy Plz - N 11940 Jollyville Rd Ste 325-N ... Austin TX 78759 512-535-7399
Web: gravitant.com

Green Peak Partners PO Box 6064 ... Denver CO 80206 303-841-7098
Web: www.greenpeakpartners.com

Greencastle Associates Consulting LLC
627 Swedesford Rd ... Malvern PA 19355 610-640-9958
Web: www.greencastleconsulting.com

Greenline Emeritus Consulting
29 S Lasalle St Ste 333 ... Chicago IL 60603 312-436-1883
Web: www.greenlineemeritus.com

GreenTree Financial Group Inc
7951 SW Sixth St Ste 216 ... Plantation FL 33324 954-424-2345
Web: www.gtfinancial.com

Greentree Group Inc, The
1360 Technology Court Ste 100 ... Dayton OH 45430 937-490-5500
Web: www.greentreegroup.com

Griffin Communitcations Group
3101 Nasa Pkwy Ste L ... Seabrook TX 77586 281-335-0200
Web: griffincg.com

Group Management Services Inc
3296 Columbia Rd Ste 101 ... Richfield OH 44286 330-659-0100 659-0150
TF: 888-823-2084 ■ *Web:* www.groupmgmt.com

Groupe BBA Inc
375 Sir-Wilfrid-Laurier Blvd ... Mont-saint-hilaire QC J3H6C3 450-464-2111
Web: www.bba.ca

Grove Consultants International, The
1000 Oreilly Ave ... San Francisco CA 94129 415-561-2500
Web: www.grove.com

Growth Design Corp
225 E St Paul Ave Ste 201 ... Milwaukee WI 53202 414-224-0586
Web: www.growthdesign.com

GSVlabs Inc 425 Broadway St ... Redwood CA 94063 650-421-2000
Web: gsvlabs.com

Guidant Group Inc
3414 Peachtree Rd NE Ste 375 ... Atlanta GA 30326 404-920-6100
Web: www.guidantgroup.com

Gulf South Research Corp 8081 G S R I Rd ... Baton Rouge LA 70820 225-757-8088
Web: www.gsrcorp.com

H & W Management Co
1021 Majestic Dr Ste 380 ... Lexington KY 40513 859-263-0106
Web: www.hwhotels.com

H S C Foundation Inc 1808 I St Nw ... Washington DC 20006 202-454-1220
Web: www.hscfoundation.org

Hale Group Ltd, The Eight Cherry St ... Danvers MA 01923 978-777-9077
Web: www.halegroup.com

Harkcon 1390 Chain Bridge Rd 570 ... Mclean VA 22101 800-499-6456
TF: 800-499-6456 ■ *Web:* www.harkcon.com

Harkess-Ord LLC 25 W 45th St Ste 306 ... New York NY 10036 212-704-9989
Web: harkess.com

Harlan Consulting Services Inc
2515 Briarpark Dr ... Houston TX 77042 713-464-2484
Web: www.harlanconsulting.com

Hawthorne Corp
3955 Faber Pl Dr Ste 301 ... North Charleston SC 29405 843-553-2203
Web: www.hawthornecorp.com

Hayes Group International Inc, The
4400 Silas Creek Pkwy Ste 301 ... Winston-salem NC 27104 336-765-6764
Web: www.thehayesgroupintl.com

Hdl Companies 1340 Vly Vista Dr Ste 200 ... Diamond Bar CA 91765 909-861-4335
Web: www.hdlcompanies.com

Health Decisions Inc
2510 Meridian Pkwy Ste 300 ... Durham NC 27713 919-967-1111
Web: www.healthdec.com

HealthAxis Inc 7301 N State Hwy 161 Ste 300 ... Irving TX 75039 972-443-5000 556-0572
TF: 888-974-2947 ■ *Web:* www.healthaxis.com

Healthlinx Transitional Leadership Inc
1404 Goodale Blvd Ste 400 ... Columbus OH 43212 614-444-5400
Web: www.healthlinx.com

Helix Design Inc 175 Lincoln St Unit 201 ... Manchester NH 03103 603-644-1408
Web: www.helixdesign.net

Hempstead & Company Inc 807 Haddon Ave ... Haddonfield NJ 08033 856-795-6026
Web: www.hempsteadco.com

Hg Solutions 3701 S Lawrence St ... Tacoma WA 98409 253-588-2626
Web: www.hughesgroup.biz

Hidi Rae Consulting Engineers Inc
One Yonge St Ste 2100 ... Toronto ON M5E1E5 416-364-2100
Web: www.hidi.com

Higher Dimension Research Inc 570 Hale Ave ... Oakdale MN 55128 651-730-6203
Web: www.superfabric.com

Hill Physicians Medical Group Inc
2409 Camino Ramon PO Box 5080 ... San Ramon CA 94583 925-820-8300 820-8252
TF: 800-445-5747 ■ *Web:* www.hillphysicians.com

Hogan Assessment Systems Inc 2622 E 21st St ... Tulsa OK 74114 918-749-0632
Web: www.hoganassessments.com

Holdsworth Financial Group
40 Eagle Vly ct ... Broadview Heights OH 44147 440-746-8100
Web: www.holdsworthfinancial.com

Hospicomm Inc 41 N Third St ... Philadelphia PA 19106 215-925-5158
Web: www.hospicomm.com

Hospitality Ventures Management LLC
5 Concourse Pkwy Ste 2828 ... Atlanta GA 30328 404-467-9299 467-1962
Web: www.hvmg.com

Hotchkis & Wiley Capital Management LLC
725 S Figueroa St Fl 39 ... Los Angeles CA 90017 213-430-1000 430-1001
Web: www.hwcm.com

Howard Simon & Associates Inc
304 Saunders Rd ... Riverwoods IL 60015 847-945-0340
Web: hsimon.com

Howick Associates 111 N Fairchild St ... Madison WI 53703 608-233-3377
Web: www.howickassociates.com

HPM Corp 4304 W 24th Ave Ste 100 ... Kennewick WA 99338 509-737-8939
Web: www.hpmcorporation.com

Hpn Worldwide Inc 119 W Vallette St ... Elmhurst IL 60126 630-941-9030
Web: www.hpn.com

Hru Inc. Technical Resources 3451 Dunckel Rd ... Lansing MI 48911 517-272-5888
Web: www.hru-tech.com

				Phone	Fax
HRValue LLC 1010 E 20th St. Web: www.4hrv.com	Tulsa	OK	74120	614-266-5926	
Hudson Mann Inc 1092 Johnnie Dodds Blvd Web: www.hudsonmann.com	Mount Pleasant	SC	29464	843-884-5557	
Hurley Communications Inc 1113 Washington St. Web: hurleycommunications.com	Norwood	MA	02062	781-762-3313	
Huron Consulting Services LLC 550 W Van Buren St Web: www.huronconsultinggroup.com	Chicago	IL	60607	312-583-8700	
Hurwitz & Associates 13A Highland Cir. Web: hurwitz.com	Needham	MA	02494	617-597-1724	
HVS Executive Search 372 Willis Ave. Web: www.hvs.com	Mineola	NY	11501	516-248-8828	
Hygieneering Inc 7575 Plz Ct. Web: hygieneering.com	Willowbrook	IL	60527	630-654-2550	
Hypotenuse Enterprises Inc 1545 East Ave Web: www.hypot.com	Rochester	NY	14610	585-473-7799	
ICG Consulting Inc 8570 E Shea Blvd Ste 110 Web: www.icgconsulting.com	Scottsdale	AZ	85260	480-607-4040	
ICM Inc 310 N First St Web: www.icminc.com	Colwich	KS	67030	316-796-0900	
Icon International Inc Four Stamford Plz 15th Fl 107 Elm St. Web: www.icon-intl.com	Stamford	CT	06902	203-328-2300	328-2333
IDOM Inc 55 Madison Ave Ste 400 Web: www.idomusa.com	Morristown	NJ	07960	973-285-3328	
Iec Group 3449 e copper point dr Web: www.iecgroup.com	Meridian	ID	83642	208-947-9522	
ieLinks Inc 2701 E Thomas Rd Ste B Web: ielinks.net	Phoenix	AZ	85016	602-852-0101	
Ignite Venture Partners LLC 34522 N Scottsdale Rd Ste D7239 Web: www.ignite-vp.com	Scottsdale	AZ	85266	480-575-9717	
IHL Consulting Group 1064 Cedarview Ln. Web: www.ihlservices.com	Franklin	TN	37067	615-591-2955	
IM Group, The 1903 Post Rd Ste 201 Web: www.the-imgroup.com	Fairfield	CT	06824	203-256-9494	
Image Resource Group Inc 9010 Farrow Rd Web: www.imageresourcegroup.com	Columbia	SC	29203	803-790-2121	
Imagine Business Development 485 Ritchie Hwy Ste 201. Web: www.imaginellc.com	Severna Park	MD	21146	410-544-7878	
IMC Consulting 10529 Old Ct Rd Web: www.consultimc.com	Woodstock	MD	21163	410-505-4666	
IMEX Research 1474 Camino Robles. Web: www.imexresearch.com	San Jose	CA	95120	408-268-0800	
Impact Resources Inc 5910 Lone Oak Dr. Web: www.ir-tech.com	Bethesda	MD	20814	301-581-9676	
IMS Worldwide Inc 309 Henrietta Web: imsw.com	Webster	TX	77598	281-554-9099	
Incentive Group Inc, The 399 Knollwood Rd Web: www.incentivegroup.com	White Plains	NY	10603	914-948-0904	
Indigena Solutions LP Ste 301 - 800 Carleton Ct. Web: www.indigenasolutions.com	Delta	BC	V3M6Y6	604-549-5800	
InEdge 9900 Cavendish Blvd Ste 200 Web: www.inedge.com	Montreal	QC	H4M2V2	514-333-6600	
INFOCUS Marketing Inc 4245 Sigler Rd. TF: 800-708-5478 ■ Web: www.infocusmarketing.com	Warrenton	VA	20187	800-708-5478	
Ingenix Inc 12125 Technology Dr. TF: 888-445-8745 ■ Web: www.optuminsight.com	Eden Prairie	MN	55344	952-833-7100	833-7090
Initio Inc 2850 W Horizon Ridge Pkwy Ste 200 Web: initioinc.com	Henderson	NV	89052	201-621-0400	
Injury & Health Management Solutions Inc 441 Watertower Cir Ste 100 Web: www.ihmspt.com	Colchester	VT	05446	802-655-7575	
Innerspec Technologies Inc 4004 Murray Pl Web: www.innerspec.com	Lynchburg	VA	24501	434-948-1301	
Innosight LLC 92 Hayden Ave. Web: innosight.com	Lexington	MA	02421	781-652-7200	
Innovatia Inc One Germain St Web: www.innovatia.net	Saint John	NB	E2L4V1	506-640-4000	
Ino.Com Inc 4800 Atwell Rd Discovery Village Web: www.ino.com	Shady Side	MD	20764	410-867-2100	
Inprov Ltd 2150 E Continental Blvd. Web: www.inprov.biz	Southlake	TX	76092	817-748-0300	
Insperity Inc 19001 Crescent Springs Dr. Web: www.administaff.com	Kingwood	TX	77339	713-358-8986	
Inspire Excellence 657 n W ave Web: www.inspireexcellence.com	Elmhurst	IL	60126	630-279-7500	
Intech Enterprises Inc 3825 Grant St. Web: www.intechenterprises.com	Washougal	WA	98671	360-835-8785	
Integral Hospitality Solutions LLC 3522 Vann Rd Ste 102 Web: www.integralhospitality.com	Birmingham	AL	35235	205-655-2097	
Integrity Group, The 20333 Sh 249 Ste 500. Web: www.go-integrity.com	Houston	TX	77070	281-955-0707	
Intellithink LLC 630 Minnesota Ave Ste 200 Web: www.intelli-think.com	Kansas City	KS	66101	913-766-0303	
InterDent Inc 9800 S La Cienega Blvd Ste 800 Web: www.interdent.com	Inglewood	CA	90301	310-765-2400	765-2456
Internovo Inc 468 Shakespeare Dr. Web: www.internovo.com	Collegeville	PA	19426	610-409-9120	
Investco Financial Corp 1302 Puyallup St Web: www.investco.com	Sumner	WA	98390	253-863-6200	

				Phone	Fax
ipCapital Group Inc 426 Industrial Ave Ste 150 Web: www.ipcapitalgroup.com	Williston	VT	05495	802-859-7800	
IPD Analytics LLC 1170 Kane Concourse Ste 300 Web: www.ipdanalytics.com	Bay Harbor Islands	FL	33154	305-662-8515	
IQ Systems Inc 4655 Longley Ln Ste 106 Web: www.iqisit.com	Reno	NV	89502	775-352-2301	
Irc Building Sciences Group 7565 Danbro Cres Web: www.ircgroup.com	Mississauga	ON	L5N6P9	905-607-7244	
ISPA Inc 1100 Cir 75 Pkwy Ste 900 Web: www.ispainc.com	Atlanta	GA	30339	770-690-2900	
ISS Technologies 22 Business Park Cir Web: www.isstechnologies.com	Arden	NC	28704	828-684-4248	
Ivy Planning Group 15204 Omega Dr. Web: www.ivygroupllc.com	Rockville	MD	20850	301-963-1669	
Iwpc 610 Louis Dr Web: www.iwpc.org	Warminster	PA	18974	215-293-9000	
J. Calnan & Assoc Inc 1250 Hancock St Ste 302n Web: www.jcalnan.com	Quincy	MA	02169	617-801-0200	801-0201
J. Joseph Consulting 21732 Hardy Oak Blvd Web: www.jjosephconsulting.com	San Antonio	TX	78258	210-587-2770	
J. P. Farley Corp 29055 Clemens Rd Web: www.jpfarley.com	Westlake	OH	44145	440-250-4300	
J.F. Smith Group Inc 735 E Glenn Ave. Web: www.jfsg.com	Auburn	AL	36831	334-502-5374	
J.R. Henry Consulting Inc PO BOX 9724 Web: www.psmarketing.org	Pittsburgh	PA	15229	412-931-2833	
Jamsan Hotel Management Inc 440 Bedford St. Web: www.jamsanhotels.com	Lexington	MA	02420	781-863-8500	
Jarlette Health Services 689 Yonge St Web: www.jarlette.com	Midland	ON	L4R2E1	705-526-4238	
Jax Kneppers Associates Inc 2125 Ygnacio Vly Rd Web: www.jaxkneppers.com	Walnut Creek	CA	94598	925-933-3914	
Jay Electric Company Inc 5300 E Lake Blvd Web: www.jayelectric.com	Birmingham	AL	35217	205-595-9910	
Jdk Management Co Inc 1388 SR- 487 Web: www.jdkmgt.com	Bloomsburg	PA	17815	570-784-0111	784-4785
Jenaly Technology Group I One greenleaf woods dr Web: www.jenaly.com	Portsmouth	NH	03801	603-431-7864	
Jeskell Systems LLC 6201 chevy chase dr Web: www.jeskell.com	Laurel	MD	20707	301-230-1533	
JHPIEGO Corp 1615 Thames St Web: www.jhpiego.org	Baltimore	MD	21231	410-537-1800	
JHT Inc 2710 Discovery Dr Ste 100 Web: www.jht.com	Orlando	FL	32826	407-381-7797	381-0017
Jim Whitten Roof Consultants LLC Po Box 200925 Web: www.jimwhitten.com	Austin	TX	78720	512-250-0999	
Jiten Hotel Management Inc 495 Westgate Dr Web: www.jitenhotels.com	Brockton	MA	02301	508-427-1667	
JKM Consulting Inc PO Box 3250 Web: www.m2connections.com	Oxford	AL	36203	256-405-0613	
Job Performance Systems Inc 1240 N Pitt St Ste 200 Web: www.jps-usa.com	Alexandria	VA	22314	703-683-5805	
JobsOhio 41 S High St Ste 1500 Web: jobs-ohio.com	Columbus	OH	43215	614-224-6446	
John Levy Consulting 505 Mesa Rd Ste 1 Web: johnlevyconsulting.com	Point Reyes Station	CA	94956	415-663-1818	
Jolt Consulting Group 112 Spring St Ste 301 TF: 877-249-6262 ■ Web: www.joltconsultinggroup.com	Saratoga Springs	NY	12866	877-249-6262	
Jones Consulting Group LLC, The 3648 Carmel Dr Web: www.jconsultants.net	Troy	MI	48083	248-677-2236	
Jurinnov Ltd The Idea Ctr 1375 Euclid Ave Ste 400 Web: www.jurinnov.com	Cleveland	OH	44115	216-664-1100	
K2 Project Control Systems 4330 E W Hwy Ste 320 Web: www.k2consulting.com	Bethesda	MD	20814	301-656-2228	
Kaplan Devries Inc 1903 Ashwood Ct. Web: www.kaplandevries.com	Greensboro	NC	27455	336-288-8200	
Kawaller & Company LLC 162 State St Web: kawaller.com	Brooklyn	NY	11201	718-694-6270	
Keating Technologies Inc 25 Royal Crest Court Ste 120 Web: www.keating.com	Markham	ON	L3R9X4	905-479-0230	
Kehrer Saltzman & Associates LLC 9218 Skipaway Dr. Web: kehrerbielan.com	Waxhaw	NC	28173	704-243-4512	
Keiro Services 325 S Boyle Ave TF: 855-872-6060 ■ Web: www.keiro.org	Los Angeles	CA	90033	323-980-7555	
Kek Associates Inc 100 Josons Dr Web: kekdesign.com	Rochester	NY	14623	585-424-3380	
Kesselrun 8215 Roswell Rd Ste 925 Web: www.kesselrunconsulting.com	Atlanta	GA	30350	770-640-9100	
Kewin Consulting 62 Twenty Seventh St Web: www.kewin.ca	Toronto	ON	M8W2X4	416-802-2526	
KickStart Alliance PO Box 705 Web: www.kickstartall.com	Los Altos	CA	94023	650-464-7663	
Kirby Bates Associates Inc One Bala Ave Ste 234 Web: www.kirbybates.com	Bala Cynwyd	PA	19004	610-667-1800	
KKO & Associates LLC Five Vine St Web: kko.com	Andover	MA	01810	978-475-4079	

	City	State	Zip	Phone	Fax
Klemmer & Associates Leaders 1340 commerce st *Web:* www.klemmer.com	Petaluma	CA	94954	707-559-7722	
KLG Advisors 104 Fifth Ave 20th Fl *Web:* www.klgadvisors.com	New York	NY	10011	212-514-4600	
Km2 Solutions LLC 3481 Lakeside Dr Ste 2602 *Web:* www.km2solutions.com	Atlanta	GA	30326	404-848-8886	
Koski Research Inc Seven joost ave *Web:* www.koskiresearch.com	San Francisco	CA	94131	415-334-3400	
Kotter International Five Bennett St *Web:* www.kotterinternational.com	Cambridge	MA	02138	617-600-6787	
Kremer & Associates Inc 6400 Brooktree Ct Ste 240 *Web:* www.kremerassociates.com	Wexford	PA	15090	724-934-0808	
Kw Engineering 287 17th St Ste 300 *Web:* www.kw-engineering.com	Oakland	CA	94612	510-834-6420	
Lane Bridgers Schill 230 Marter Ave *Web:* lanebridgers.com	Moorestown	NJ	08057	856-638-1855	
Lassus Wherley & Associates Pc One Academy St *Web:* www.lassuswherley.com	New Providence	NJ	07974	908-464-0102	
Latitude Consulting Group Inc 100 E Michigan Ave Ste 200 *TF:* 888-577-2797 ■ *Web:* www.latitudecg.com	Saline	MI	48176	888-577-2797	
Lawrence Service Co 1405 Xenium Ln N Ste 250 *Web:* www.lmsvc.com	Plymouth	MN	55441	763-383-5700	
Learning Network, Inc, The 401 Glenneyre St Ste C *Web:* www.learning.net	Laguna Beach	CA	92651	949-497-1318	
Learning Unlimited 5810 E Skelly Dr Ste 500 *Web:* learningunlimited.com	Tulsa	OK	74135	918-622-3292	
Legal Club of America Corp 7771 W Oakland Park Blvd Ste 217 *Web:* www.legalclub.com	Sunrise	FL	33351	954-377-0222	
Leland Management Inc 8009 S Orange Ave *Web:* www.lelandmanagement.com	Orlando	FL	32809	407-447-9955	
Levin Group Inc 10 New Plant Ct *Web:* www.levingroup.com	Owings Mills	MD	21117	410-654-1234	
LexaMed Ltd 705 Front St *Web:* www.lexamed.net	Toledo	OH	43605	419-693-5307	
Lifewings Partners LLC 9198 Crestwyn Hills Dr *TF:* 800-290-9314 ■ *Web:* www.saferpatients.com	Memphis	TN	38125	800-290-9314	
Linchris Hotel Corp 269 Hanover St Ste 2 *Web:* www.linchris.com	Hanover	MA	02339	781-826-8824	826-2411
Lionshare Leadership Group Inc 7065 Moores Ln Ste 200 *Web:* lionshare.org	Brentwood	TN	37027	615-377-4688	
LogicData 3650 S Yosemite St Ste 202 *Web:* www.logicdata.com	Denver	CO	80237	303-694-4400	
Logistics Capital & Strategy LLC 1110 N Glebe Rd Ste 250 *Web:* www.mergeglobal.com	Arlington	VA	22201	703-276-9100	
Loren D Stark Company Inc 10750 Rockley Rd *Web:* www.ldsco.com	Houston	TX	77099	281-498-5777	
Lost Recovery Network Lrni 406 dixon st *Web:* www.lrni.com	Vidalia	GA	30474	912-537-3901	
Louddoor 1001 harden st *Web:* www.louddoor.com	Columbia	SC	29205	803-765-2995	
Loyalty Methods Inc 80 Yesler Way Ste 310 *Web:* www.loyaltymethods.com	Seattle	WA	98104	206-257-2111	
LS Gallegos & Associates Inc 9137 E Mineral Cir Ste 220 *Web:* www.lsgallegos.com	Centennial	CO	80112	303-790-8474	
LT&T (DW Consulting) 1556 Halford Ave #230 *Web:* www.lighthouse-tours.com	Santa Clara	CA	95051	408-260-5802	
Lunarpages. Inc 1360 N Hancock St *Web:* www.lunarpages.com	Anaheim	CA	92807	714-521-8150	
LWBJ Financial LLC 4200 University Ave Ste 410 *Web:* www.lwbj.com	West Des Moines	IA	50266	515-222-5680	
Lynchval Systems Worldwide Inc 4170 Lafayette Ctr Dr Ste 500 *Web:* www.lynchval.com	Chantilly	VA	20151	703-709-1000	
Lytica Inc 308 Legget Dr Ste 200 *Web:* www.lytica.com	Kanata	ON	K2K1Y6	613-271-1414	
M L s Data Mgt Solutions 200 N Mesquite St Ste 200 *Web:* www.mlsc.com	Arlington	TX	76011	817-804-6900	
M2 Logistics Inc 2413 Hazelwood Ln *Web:* www.m2logistics.com	Green Bay	WI	54304	920-569-8800	
Macadamian Technologies Inc 165 Rue Wellington *Web:* www.macadamian.com	Gatineau	QC	J8X2J3	819-772-0300	
MacMunnis Inc 1840 Oak Ave Ste 300 *Web:* www.macmunnis.com	Evanston	IL	60201	847-316-1100	
Macro Management Service 800 Navarro St *Web:* www.macromgt.com	San Antonio	TX	78205	210-226-1047	
Magee Resource Group LLC 920 Pierremont Rd *Web:* www.mageeresource.com	Shreveport	LA	71106	318-865-8411	
Magellan Medicaid Administration Inc 4300 Cox Rd *TF:* 800-884-2822 ■ *Web:* www1.magellanmedicaid.com	Glen Allen	VA	23060	804-965-7400	
Management & Engineering Technologies International Inc (METI) 8600 Boeing Dr *Web:* www.meticorp.com	El Paso	TX	79925	915-772-4975	772-2253
Manasco Marketing Partners 9600 Escarpment Blvd Ste 745-87 *Web:* www.manascomarketing.com	Austin	TX	78749	512-301-4881	
Manorhouse Management Inc 706 Old Stream Rd *Web:* www.manorhouseretirement.com	Manakin Sabot	VA	23103	804-784-7255	
Marakon Associates Inc 1155 Ave of the Americas 18th Fl *Web:* www.marakon.com	New York	NY	10036	212-520-7120	
Marble A D & Company Inc 375 E Elm St *Web:* www.admarble.com	Conshohocken	PA	19428	484-533-2500	
Mariner Partners Inc 12 Smythe St *Web:* www.marinerpartners.com	Saint John	NB	E2L5G5	506-642-9000	
Markon Inc 400 S Maple Ave Ste 230 *Web:* www.markonsolutions.com	Falls Church	VA	22046	703-884-0030	
Marlin Alliance 600 Marlin Ln *Web:* themarlinalliance.com	Carlsbad	CA	92011	760-431-8610	
Material & Contract Services LLC 5820 Stoneridge Mall Rd *Web:* www.macservices.us	Pleasanton	CA	94588	925-460-0397	
Matter Communications Inc 50 Water St Mill No 3 The Tannery *Web:* www.matternow.com	Newburyport	MA	01950	978-499-9250	
Mattersight Corp 200 S Wacker Ste 820 **Fax Area Code:* 312 ■ *TF:* 877-235-6925 ■ *Web:* www.mattersight.com	Chicago	IL	60606	877-235-6925	454-3501*
MavenWire LLC 630 Freedom Business Ctr Third Fl *TF:* 866-343-4870 ■ *Web:* www.mavenwire.com	King Of Prussia	PA	19406	866-343-4870	
McCormick Group Inc, The 1440 Central Park Blvd Ste 207 *Web:* www.mccormickgroup.com	Fredericksburg	VA	22401	540-786-9777	
McGraw Wentworth Inc 3331 W Big Beaver Rd Ste 200 *Web:* www.mcgrawwentworth.com	Troy	MI	48084	248-822-8000	
Mcintosh & Associates LLC 1955 Lakeway Dr Ste 270b *Web:* mcintoshassociates.com	Lewisville	TX	75057	214-488-2321	
McLagan Partners Inc 1600 Summer St Ste 601 *Web:* www.mclagan.com	Stamford	CT	06905	203-359-2878	
McLarty Associates 900 17th St NW Ste 800 *Web:* www.maglobal.com	Washington	DC	20006	202-419-1420	
Mcmanis Associates Inc 7518 Diplomat Dr Ste 201 *Web:* mcmanis-monsalve.com	Manassas	VA	20109	703-331-3890	
MDA Leadership Consulting Inc 150 S Fifth St *Web:* www.mdaleadership.com	Minneapolis	MN	55402	612-332-8182	
Medco Enterprises Inc 3530 Wayne Ave *Web:* www.medcoent.com	Bronx	NY	10467	718-655-1700	
Medcor Inc 4805 W Prime Pkwy *TF:* 877-696-6775 ■ *Web:* www.medcor.com	McHenry	IL	60050	815-363-9500	363-9696
Medefis Inc 10826 Old Mill Rd Suitte 101 *Web:* www.medefis.com	Omaha	NE	68154	402-393-6333	
Medexcel USA Inc 484 Temple Hill Rd *Web:* www.medexcelusa.com	New Windsor	NY	12553	845-565-3700	
Medical Strategic Planning Inc Five Shelbern Dr *Web:* www.medsp.com	Lincroft	NJ	07738	732-219-5090	
Meeting Incentive Experts 61 W 15th St Apt 301 *Web:* www.meetingincentiveexperts.com	Chicago	IL	60605	312-842-3600	
Meeting Systems Inc 600 N Curtis Rd Ste 170 *Web:* www.meetingsystems.com	Boise	ID	83706	208-288-0290	
MELE Associates Inc 11 Taft Court Ste 101 *Web:* www.meleassociates.com	Rockville	MD	20850	240-453-6990	
Mercatus Energy Advisors LLC 708 Main St Ste 880 *Web:* www.mercatusenergy.com	Houston	TX	77002	713-970-1003	
Met-L-Flo Inc 720 Heartland Dr Ste S *Web:* www.met-l-flo.com	Sugar Grove	IL	60554	630-409-9860	
Metasystems Inc 13700 State Rd Ste 1 *Web:* www.metasystems.com	North Royalton	OH	44133	440-526-1454	
Metis Strategy LLC 4607 NORWOOD Dr *Web:* www.metisstrategy.com	CHEVY CHASE	MD	20815	301-893-4610	
Metropolitan Health Networks Inc 777 Yamato Rd Ste 510 *NYSE: MDF* ■ *TF:* 800-221-5487 ■ *Web:* www.metcare.com	Boca Raton	FL	33431	561-805-8500	
Metrus Group Inc 953 Route 202 *Web:* www.metrus.com	Somerville	NJ	08876	908-231-1900	
MHM Services Inc 1593 Spring Hill Rd Ste 600 *TF:* 800-416-3649 ■ *Web:* www.mhm-services.com	Vienna	VA	22182	703-749-4600	749-4604
Michael Raiser Associates Inc Seven Doig Rd Ste 4 *Web:* teammra.com	Wayne	NJ	07470	973-305-0011	
Microbiology & Quality Associates Inc 2341 Stanwell Dr *Web:* microqa.com	Concord	CA	94520	925-270-3800	
Mid Ohio Regional Planning Commission 111 Liberty St Ste 100 *Web:* morpc.org	Columbus	OH	43215	614-228-2663	
Mid Peninsula Endoscopy Center 50 S San Mateo Dr Ste 400 *Web:* www.midpeninsulaendoscopy.com	San Mateo	CA	94401	650-373-1970	
MIDIOR Consulting Inc 22 Putnam Ave *Web:* www.midior.com	Cambridge	MA	02139	617-864-8813	
Midland Community Healthcare Services 600 N Marienfeld St *Web:* www.midlandchs.com	Midland	TX	79701	432-570-0238	
Midpoint National 1263 Southwest Blvd *Web:* www.midpt.com	Kansas City	KS	66103	913-362-7400	
Midwest Consulting Group 222 Las Colinas Blvd W *Web:* www.mcginfo.com	Irving	TX	75039	972-910-9200	
Midwest Hospitality Group Inc (MHG) 1220 Brookville Way *Web:* www.mhghotelsllc.com	Indianapolis	IN	46239	317-356-4000	356-4004

Company / Address	City	State	ZIP	Phone	Fax
Mikan Associates Consulting 101 SCHELTER Rd Ste A204 *Web:* www.mikanassociates.com	LINCOLNSHIRE	IL	60069	847-613-6010	
Mission1st Group Inc 1161 Broad St Ste 114 *Web:* www.mission1st.com	Shrewsbury	NJ	07702	732-542-5700	
Mitchell Selling Dynamics 1360 Puritan Ave *Web:* www.mitchellsell.com	Birmingham	MI	48009	248-644-8092	
MKP communications Inc Five E 16th St Third Fl *Web:* www.mkpteam.com	New York	NY	10003	212-983-5700	
ML Levin & Associates 4927 W 88TH ST *Web:* www.mllevin.com	Prairie Village	KS	66207	913-226-8840	
Modis Inc 10201 Centurion Pkwy N Ste 400 *TF:* 800-372-2788 ■ *Web:* www.modis.com	Jacksonville	FL	32256	904-360-2300	360-2110
Modular Process Control LLC 15455 Conway Rd *Web:* www.mpcenergyllc.com	Chesterfield	MO	63017	636-536-1000	
Montana Manufacturing Extension Center 2310 University Way Bldg 2 *Web:* www.mtmanufacturingcenter.com	Bozeman	MT	59715	406-994-3812	
Montreal International 380 Saint-Antoine St W Ste 8000 *Web:* www.montrealinternational.com	Montreal	QC	H2Y3X7	514-987-8191	
Monument Consulting LLC 3957 Westerre Pkwy Ste 330 *Web:* www.monumentconsulting.com	Richmond	VA	23233	804-622-9992	
Moreland Associates Corp 2532 Santa Clara Ave Ste 413 *Web:* www.morelandassoc.com	Alameda	CA	94501	510-748-8146	
Mortgage Banking Solutions Frost Bank Tower 401 Congress Ave Ste 1540 *Web:* www.mortgagebankingsolutions.com	Austin	TX	78701	512-977-9900	
Mosaic Financial Partners Inc 140 Geary St Sixth Fl *Web:* mosaicfp.com	San Francisco	CA	94108	415-788-1952	
Moseley Corp, The 31 Hayward St *Web:* www.moseleycorp.com	Franklin	MA	02038	508-520-4004	
Mosser Companies 308 Jessie St *Web:* www.mosserco.com	San Francisco	CA	94103	415-284-9000	
Mpa Media 5406 Bolsa Ave *Web:* www.mpamedia.com	Huntington Beach	CA	92649	714-230-3150	
MSS Services Inc 14200 Schaeffer Rd *Web:* mssserv.com	Germantown	MD	20874	301-528-5531	
Mutual Fund Store LLC, The 7301 College Blvd Ste 220 *Web:* www.mutualfundstore.com	Overland Park	KS	66210	913-319-8100	
MVS Inc 3630A Georgia Ave NW *Web:* www.mvsconsulting.com	Washington	DC	20010	202-722-7981	
MyLLC.com Inc 5716 Corsa Ave Ste 110 *TF:* 888-886-9552 ■ *Web:* www.myllc.com	Westlake Village	CA	91362	888-886-9552	
Napa Networks Inc 245 Stafford Rd West Ste 202 *Web:* www.talentmap.com	Ottawa	ON	K2H9E8	613-248-3417	
National Health Management Inc 4415 Fifth Ave Ste B *Web:* www.independencecourt.com	Pittsburgh	PA	15213	412-578-7800	681-8254
National Quality Assurance - U.S.A. Inc Four Post Office Sq *Web:* www.nqa-usa.com	Acton	MA	01720	978-635-9256	
Navigator Planning Group LLC 3091 Voyager Dr *Web:* www.navigatorpg.com	Green Bay	WI	54311	920-406-8500	
Navin, Haffty & Associates LLC 200 Cordwainer Dr Ste 100 *Web:* www.navinhaffty.com	Norwell	MA	02061	781-871-6770	
Navtech Seminars & Gps Supply 5501 Backlick Rd Ste 230 *Web:* www.navtechgps.com	Springfield	VA	22151	703-256-8900	
Neilson Associates Inc 42 Blue Stone Dr *Web:* www.neilsonassociates.com	Chadds Ford	PA	19317	610-793-0883	
Nellis Management Corp 2940 104th St *Web:* www.nellismanagement.com	Urbandale	IA	50322	515-252-1742	
Nelson, Tietz & Hoye Inc 81 S Ninth St Ste 330 *Web:* www.nth-inc.com	Minneapolis	MN	55402	612-344-1500	
NeoTech Incubator 6751 Columbia Gateway Dr Ste 500 *Web:* www.hceda.org	Columbia	MD	21046	410-313-6550	
Neset Consulting Service Inc 6844 Hwy 40 *Web:* www.nesetconsulting.com	Tioga	ND	58852	701-664-1492	
Net (net) Inc Baker Lofts Bldg 217 E 24th St - Ste 010 *Web:* www.netnetweb.com	Holland	MI	49423	616-546-3100	
Net Theory Inc Seven Dey St #300 *Web:* www.nettheory.com	New York	NY	10007	212-868-5950	
Netcracker Technology Corp 95 Sawyer Rd University Ofc Pk III *TF:* 800-477-5785 ■ *Web:* www.netcracker.com	Waltham	MA	02453	781-419-3300	419-3301
Netropole 5630 NE Martin Luther King Jr *Web:* www.portlandmanagedservices.com	Portland	OR	97211	503-241-3499	
Network Medical Management Inc 1668 S Garfield Ave Ste 2nd *Web:* www.networkmedmgmt.com	Alhambra	CA	91801	626-282-0288	
New Age Protection Inc 6320 Augusta Dr Ste 1200 *Web:* www.new-age-inc.com	Springfield	VA	22150	703-912-3057	
New Ventures West 3502 Geary Blvd Fl 2 *TF:* 800-332-4618 ■ *Web:* newventureswest.com	San Francisco	CA	94118	800-332-4618	
Nexgen Product Design & Development 3117 Almond Dr *Web:* www.nexgenpd.com	Flower Mound	TX	75028	972-333-3870	
NFC Global LLC 240 Gibraltar Rd Ste 150 *Web:* www.nfcglobal.com	Horsham	PA	19044	215-657-0800	
Noninvasive Medical Technologies Inc 6412 S Arville St *Web:* www.nmtinc.org	Las Vegas	NV	89118	702-614-3360	
North Channel Capital LLC 5550 S 59th St Ste 26 *Web:* www.wfafinet.com	Lincoln	NE	68516	402-421-6500	
Northbridge Group, The 30 Monument Sq Ste 105 *Web:* norbridgeinc.com	Concord	MA	01742	781-266-2600	
Northeast Utilities Service Company Inc 56 Prospect St *TF:* 800-286-5000 ■ *Web:* www.nu.com	Hartford	CT	06103	800-286-5000	
Northeast Veterans Business Resource Center Po Box 52113 *Web:* www.nevbrc.org	Boston	MA	02205	617-938-3933	
NorthStar Management Partners LLC Four Pleasant St South *Web:* www.northstarmp.com	Natick	MA	01760	508-651-0093	
Novatek Communications Inc 500 Helendale Rd Ste 280 *Web:* www.novatekcom.com	Rochester	NY	14609	585-482-4070	
Nulayer Inc 72 Fraser Ave Ste 201 *Web:* www.nulayer.com	Toronto	ON	M6K3J7	416-840-4384	
O'Connor Group Inc, The 10 Stearns Rd *Web:* www.theoconnorgroup.com	Bedford	MA	01730	781-275-2423	
Oak Grove Technologies LLC 4140 Parklake Ave Ste 330 *Web:* www.oakgrovetech.com	Raleigh	NC	27612	919-845-1038	
OB Sports Golf Management LLC 7025 E Greenway Pkwy Ste 550 *Web:* www.obsports.com	Scottsdale	AZ	85254	480-948-1300	
Oconomowoc Residential Programs Inc 1746 Executive Dr *Web:* www.orp.com	Oconomowoc	WI	53066	262-569-5515	
Ohm Systems Inc 10250 Chester Rd *Web:* www.ohmworld.com	Cincinnati	OH	45215	513-771-0008	771-0101
Olive Grove Consulting 540 Ralston Ave #2c *Web:* theolivegrove.com	Belmont	CA	94002	650-591-4155	
Ologie LLC 447 E Main St *Web:* ologie.com	Columbus	OH	43215	614-221-1107	
Olympique Expert Building Care 26232 Enterprise Ct *Web:* www.olympique.net	Lake Forest	CA	92630	949-455-0796	
Omega Waste Management Inc 957 Colusa St *Web:* www.omegawaste.com	Corning	CA	96021	530-824-1890	
Omegasys It Consulting 420 w fullerton pkwy *Web:* omegasysit.com	Chicago	IL	60614	773-857-2751	
OMNI Management Group LLC 5955 De Soto Ave Ste 100 *Web:* www.omnimgt.com	Woodland Hills	CA	91367	818-906-8300	
On Site Marketing 1901 Strasburg Rd *Web:* www.onsitemarketing.com	Coatesville	PA	19320	610-486-6900	
Onprocess Technology Inc 200 Homer Ave *Web:* www.onprocess.com	Ashland	MA	01721	508-520-2711	
Onset Marketing LLC 143 Cady Center *Web:* www.onsetmarketing.com	Northville	MI	48167	248-596-9788	
Open Options Corp 1203-20 Erb St W *Web:* www.openoptions.com	Waterloo	ON	N2L1T2	519-884-5898	
Operari Group LLC, The 6800 Park Ten Blvd Ste 170-W *Web:* www.operarigroup.com	San Antonio	TX	78213	210-298-1291	
OPTIMUS | SBR 30 Adelaide St E Ste 600 *Web:* optimussbr.com	Toronto	ON	M5C3G8	416-649-6000	
Opvantek Inc 28 S State St *Web:* www.opvantek.com	Newtown	PA	18940	215-968-7790	
Oriel Stat A Matrix One Quality Pl Edison *Web:* www.orielstat.com	Edison	NJ	08830	732-548-0600	
Orion Registrar Inc 7850 vance dr *Web:* www.orion4value.com	Arvada	CO	80003	303-456-6010	
Orr & Boss Inc 33900 Harper Ave Ste 103 *Web:* www.orrandboss.com	Clinton Township	MI	48035	586-416-9090	
OST Inc 2001 M St NW Ste 3000 *Web:* www.ostglobal.com	Washington	DC	20036	202-466-8099	
P.E.T. Terra Systems Inc 110 Evans Mill Dr *Web:* www.petsystems.com	Dallas	GA	30157	770-445-2233	
P3I Inc 77 Main St *Web:* www.p3i-inc.com	Hopkinton	MA	01748	508-435-7882	
Pak Technologies Inc 7025 W Marcia Rd *Web:* www.paktech.com	Milwaukee	WI	53223	414-371-3100	
Palladian Partners Inc 8484 Georgia Ave Ste 200 *Web:* www.palladianpartners.com	Silver Spring	MD	20910	301-650-8660	
Paradigm Construction Services Inc 9150 Chesapeake Dr Ste 190 *Web:* www.paradigm-cs.net	San Diego	CA	92123	858-300-8299	
Paradigm Transportation Solutions Ltd 43 Forest Rd *Web:* www.ptsl.com	Cambridge	ON	N1S3B4	519-896-3163	
Paradigms Consulting Group 18936 Congress Junction *Web:* paradigmsgroup.com	Saratoga	CA	95070	408-996-9880	
Paragon Audit & Consulting Inc 50 S Steele St Ste 325 *Web:* www.paragonaudit.com	Denver	CO	80209	720-245-6500	
Park Dietz & Associates Inc 2906 Lafayette Rd *Web:* www.parkdietzassociates.com	Newport Beach	CA	92663	949-723-2211	
Parker Ag Services LLC 53036 N Hwy 71 *Web:* www.parkerag.com	Limon	CO	80828	719-775-9870	
Partners Benefit Group Inc Five Crystal Pond Rd *TF:* 877-993-5600 ■ *Web:* www.partnersbenefitgroup.com	Southborough	MA	01772	877-993-5600	

Company	City	State	Zip	Phone	Fax
Pascal Enterprises Inc 2621 State St. *Web:* www.pascalent.com	Dallas	TX	75204	214-871-0300	
Patricia Lynch Associates Inc 677 Broadway Ste 1105 *Web:* www.plynchassociates.com	Albany	NY	12207	518-432-9220	
Patricia Seybold Group 210 Commercial St. *TF:* 855-310-0101 ■ *Web:* www.customers.com	Boston	MA	02109	617-742-5200	742-1028
Patricio Enterprises Inc 125 Wdstream Blvd. *Web:* www.patricioenterprises.com	Stafford	VA	22556	703-474-4100	
PCI Strategic Management LLC 6811 Benjamin Franklin Dr Ste 200 *Web:* www.pci-sm.com	Columbia	MD	21046	410-312-0885	
PDM Group LLC 27908 Orchard Lk Rd Ste B *Web:* www.thepdmgroup.com	Farmington Hills	MI	48334	248-626-5500	
Peak Organization Inc, The 25 W 31st St Fl 12 *Web:* www.peakorg.com	New York	NY	10001	212-947-6600	
Pediatrix Medical Group Inc 1301 Concord Terr *TF:* 800-243-3839 ■ *Web:* www.pediatrix.com	Sunrise	FL	33323	954-384-0175	838-9961
Pembroke Consulting 1515 Market St Ste 960 PO Box 58757 *Web:* www.pembrokeconsulting.com	Philadelphia	PA	19102	215-523-5700	
Pemco Ltd 1632 S King St Ste 100 *Web:* www.pemco-limited.com	Honolulu	HI	96826	808-949-0414	
Peoplesafe Inc 49 Jersey St *Web:* peoplesafe.com	Dedham	MA	02026	781-329-7588	
Persyst Consulting LLC 12345 Lk City Way NE Ste 396 *Web:* www.persystconsulting.com	Seattle	WA	98125	206-396-5825	
Petrie Raymond, Professional Chartered Accountants LLP 255 Cremazie Blvd E Ste 1000 *Web:* www.petrieraymond.qc.ca	Montreal	QC	H2M1M2	514-342-4740	
PFSweb Inc 505 Millennium Dr Ste 500 *NASDAQ: PFSW* ■ *TF:* 888-330-5504 ■ *Web:* www.pfsweb.com	Allen	TX	75013	972-881-2900	
PHM Hospitality Inc 3300 Oak Lawn Ave Ste 408 *Web:* phmhospitality.com	Dallas	TX	75219	214-521-0002	
Phoenix Group of Virginia Inc 630C Woodlake Dr *Web:* www.phoenix-group.com	Chesapeake	VA	23320	757-228-1730	
Pilbara Group 900 Commonwealth Pl Ste 214 *Web:* www.pilbaragroup.com	Virginia Beach	VA	23464	757-361-0341	
Pinnacle Hotels USA Inc 8369 Vickers St Ste 101 *Web:* www.pinnaclehotelsusa.com	San Diego	CA	92111	858-974-8201	
Pinpoint Technologies 17802 Irvine Blvd Ste 215 *Web:* www.pinpoint-tech.com	Tustin	CA	92780	714-505-7600	
Pinyon Environmental Engineering Resources 9100 W Jewell Ave Ste 200 *Web:* www.pinyon-env.com	Denver	CO	80232	303-980-5200	
Pitney Bowes Management Services 90 Pk Ave. *TF:* 800-322-8000 ■ *Web:* pitneybowes.com/us	New York	NY	10016	212-808-3800	
PK Network Communications Inc 11 E 47th St *Web:* www.pknetwork.com	New York	NY	10017	212-888-4700	
Plainfield Asset Management LLC 60 Arch St Second Fl *Web:* www.pfam.com	Greenwich	CT	06830	203-302-1700	
Planetfone Inc 120 S Euclid Ave. *Web:* planetfone.com	Pasadena	CA	91101	626-792-9978	
Planetmagpie 2762 Bayview Dr *Web:* www.planetmagpie.com	Fremont	CA	94538	408-341-8770	
Plasencia Group Inc, The 4107 N Himes Ave *Web:* www.tpghotels.com	Tampa	FL	33607	813-932-1234	
Playback Now Inc 3139 Campus Dr Ste 700 *Web:* www.playbacknow.com	Norcross	GA	30071	770-447-0616	
Plexus Ventures LLC 1701 Waterford Way *Web:* plexusventures.com	Maple Glen	PA	19002	215-542-2727	
Pmalliance Inc 2075 Spencers Way Ste 201 *Web:* www.pm-alliance.com	Stone Mountain	GA	30087	770-938-4947	
pmpm Consulting Group Inc 1900 Point W Way Ste 111 *Web:* www.pmpm.com	Sacramento	CA	95815	916-565-6130	
PointCross Inc 1291 E Hillsdale Blvd Ste 304 *Web:* pointcross.com	Foster City	CA	94404	650-350-1900	
Pool Management Group Inc 1210 Warsaw Rd Ste 900 *Web:* www.poolmanagementgroup.com	Roswell	GA	30076	770-993-4665	
Porter Khouw Consulting Inc PO Box 4028 *Web:* www.porterkhouwconsulting.com	Crofton	MD	21114	410-451-3617	
Porter Medical Ctr Inc 115 Porter Dr. *TF:* 800-994-6610 ■ *Web:* www.portermedical.org	Middlebury	VT	05753	802-388-4701	
Portico Healthnet 2610 University Ave W *Web:* www.porticohealthnet.org	Saint Paul	MN	55114	651-603-5100	
Power Management Concepts LLC 510 Grumman Rd W Ste 211 *Web:* www.powermanage.com	Bethpage	NY	11714	516-465-0188	
Power Wellness 2055 W Army Trl Rd Ste 124 *Web:* www.powerwellness.com	Addison	IL	60101	630-570-2600	
Praendex Inc 16 Laurel Ave *Web:* www.piworldwide.com	Wellesley Hills	MA	02481	781-235-8872	
Prairie Quest Inc 4211 Hobson Ct Ste A *Web:* www.prairiequest.com	Fort Wayne	IN	46815	260-420-7374	
PreferredOne Administrative Services Inc 6105 Golden Hills Dr *Web:* www.preferredone.com	Golden Valley	MN	55416	763-847-4000	
Premier Prizm Solutions LLC 10 E Stow Rd Ste 100 *Web:* www.premierprizm.com	Marlton	NJ	08053	856-596-5600	
PRI Group LLC 600 Thomas Dr *Web:* www.theprigroup.com	Bensenville	IL	60106	708-492-1777	
Pride Hospitality LLC 2129 S Germantown Rd Ste 1 *Web:* www.pridehospitality.com	Germantown	TN	38138	901-751-2212	
Primatech Inc 50 Northwoods Blvd. *Web:* www.primatech.com	Columbus	OH	43235	614-841-9800	
PrimeGenesis LLC 200 W Hill Rd *Web:* www.primegenesis.com	Stamford	CT	06902	203-323-8501	
Principal Maritime Management LLC 3530 Post Rd Ste 201 *Web:* princimar.com	Southport	CT	06890	203-292-9580	
Prism Companies Inc 2200 Western Court Ste 150 *Web:* www.prismretailservices.com	Lisle	IL	60532	630-324-3400	
Pritchard Management Associates Inc 517 Wilson Pl Ste 1000 *Web:* www.projectconnections.com	Frederick	MD	21702	301-662-7877	
Private Client Resources LLC Wilton Corporate Ctr - Riverview 187 Danbury Rd Ste 202 *Web:* www.pcrinsight.com	Wilton	CT	06897	203-762-9006	
Private Club Associates 2750 Holcomb Bridge Rd Ste 220 *Web:* www.privateclubassociates.com	Alpharetta	GA	30022	678-585-9120	
Progesys Inc 4020 Blvd le Corbusier Ste 201 *Web:* www.progesys.ca	Laval	QC	H7L5R2	450-667-7646	
ProMetrics Inc 480 American Ave. *Web:* www.prometrics.com	King Of Prussia	PA	19406	610-265-6344	
Prosci Inc 1367 S Garfield Ave *Web:* www.prosci.com	Loveland	CO	80537	970-203-9332	
Prospect Medical Holdings Inc 10780 Santa Monica Blvd Ste 400 *TF:* 800-708-3230 ■ *Web:* www.prospectmedical.com	Los Angeles	CA	90025	310-943-4500	
Protocol Driven Healthcare Inc 40 Morristown Rd Ste 2D *Web:* www.pdhi.com	Bernardsville	NJ	07924	515-277-1376	
Protocol Link Inc 175 E Hawthorn Pkwy Ste 210 *Web:* www.protocollink.com	Vernon Hills	IL	60061	847-549-0390	
ProtonMedia Inc 1690 Sumneytown Pike Ste 370 *Web:* www.protonmedia.com	Lansdale	PA	19446	215-631-1401	
Provell Inc 855 Village Center Drive Suite 116 **Fax:* Hum Res ■ *TF:* 800-624-2946 ■ *Web:* www.provell.com	North Oaks	MN	55127	952-258-2000	258-2100*
Pullan Consulting 4400 Paseo Santa Rosa *Web:* www.pullanconsulting.com	Newbury Park	CA	91320	805-558-0361	
PurEnergy LLC 4488 Onondaga Blvd *Web:* www.purenergyllc.com	Syracuse	NY	13219	315-448-2266	
PVA Consulting Group Inc 20865 Ch de la Cote Nord Ste 200 *Web:* www.pva.ca	Boisbriand	QC	J7E4H5	450-970-1970	
QED Group LLC, The 1250 Eye St NW Ste 1100 *Web:* www.qedgroupllc.com	Washington	DC	20005	202-521-1900	
Quality Administration 14466 N Us Hwy 169 *Web:* quality-admin.com	Smithville	MO	64089	816-532-2090	
Quality Fuel Networks Inc 15227 herriman blvd *Web:* www.qualityfuel.com	Noblesville	IN	46060	317-774-1076	
Quality Media Resources Inc 10929 Se 23rd St *Web:* qmr.com	Bellevue	WA	98004	425-455-0558	
QuantiTech Inc 7027 Old Madison Pike NW Ste 106 *Web:* www.quantitech.com	Huntsville	AL	35806	256-650-6263	
Quantum Automation Inc 4400 E La Palma Ave *Web:* www.quantumautomation.com	Anaheim	CA	92807	714-854-0800	
R Ms Risk Management Services 8227 Northwest Blvd Ste 230 *Web:* rms-safety.com	Indianapolis	IN	46278	317-872-8227	
Radar Media Group Inc 12 Blossom Hill Rd Ste 101a *Web:* www.radarmedia.com	Winchester	MA	01890	781-721-1910	
Ralm Inc 4620 Mercason Rd *Web:* www.ralminc.net	Fayetteville	NC	28311	910-486-4491	
Ralph Andersen & Assoc 5800 Stanford Ranch Rd. *Web:* www.ralphandersen.com	Rocklin	CA	95765	916-630-4900	
Ran One Inc 2100 Embarcadero Ste 100 *Web:* global.ranone.com	Oakland	CA	94606	510-535-9730	
Raving Consulting Co 475 Hill St # G *Web:* www.ravingconsulting.com	Reno	NV	89501	775-329-7864	
RBN Energy LLC 2323 S Shepherd Dr Ste 1010 *TF:* 888-400-9838 ■ *Web:* www.rbnenergy.com	Houston	TX	77019	888-400-9838	
RCS Services Inc 5506 Mitchelldale St *Web:* www.rcsservicesinc.com	Houston	TX	77092	713-461-4119	
ReachForce Inc 9020-I Capital of Texas Hwy N Ste 270 *Web:* www.reachforce.com	Austin	TX	78759	512-327-9000	
Real Story Group, The 3470 Olney-Laytonsville Rd Ste 131 *Web:* www.realstorygroup.com	Olney	MD	20832	617-340-6464	
Realstreet Staffing 2500 Wallington Way Ste 208 *Web:* www.realstreetstaffing.com	Marriottsville	MD	21104	410-480-8002	
RealTime Group Inc, The 3035 W 15th St *Web:* therealtimegroup.com	Plano	TX	75075	972-985-9100	
Record Center Innovations Inc 3919 W Washington St *Web:* recordcenterinnovations.com	Phoenix	AZ	85009	602-258-4000	
Rector-Dunan & Assoc 314 E Highland Mall Blvd.	Austin	TX	78752	512-454-5262	
Red Spot Interactive 1001 jupiter park dr. *TF:* 800-401-7931 ■ *Web:* www.redspotinteractive.com	Jupiter	FL	33458	800-401-7931	

	City	State	Zip	Phone	Fax
RedHouse Associates LLC 802 Lovett Blvd *Web:* www.redhouseassociates.com	Houston	TX	77006	713-338-2151	
Registrar Corp 144 Research Dr *Web:* www.registrarcorp.com	Hampton	VA	23666	757-224-0177	
Reingold Inc 1415 Elliot Pl Nw *Web:* www.reingold.com	Washington	DC	20007	202-333-0400	
Reinsel Kuntz Lesher 1330 Broadcasting Rd *Web:* www.rklcpa.com	Wyomissing	PA	19610	610-376-1595	
Remodelers Advantage Inc 14440 Cherry Ln Ct Ste 201 *Web:* www.remodelersadvantage.com	Laurel	MD	20707	301-490-5620	
Restaurant Partners Inc 1030 N Orange Ave Ste 200 *Web:* www.restaurantpartnersinc.com	Orlando	FL	32801	407-839-5070	839-3388
Retirement Advantage Inc, The 47 Park Pl Ste 850 *TF:* 888-872-2364 ■ *Web:* www.tra401k.com	Appleton	WI	54914	888-872-2364	
Revel Consulting 4020 Lk Washington Blvd NE Ste 210 *Web:* www.revelconsulting.com	Kirkland	WA	98033	206-407-3173	
Revenue Factors 325 Howard Ave No 945 *Web:* www.revenuefactors.com	Burlingame	CA	94010	650-685-8096	
RGFCC Corp 8507 Oxon Hill Rd Ste 301 *TF:* 888-389-1230 ■ *Web:* www.rgfcc.com	Fort Washington	MD	20744	888-389-1230	
Rgm & Associates 3230 Monument Way *Web:* www.rgmassociates.com	Concord	CA	94518	925-671-7717	
RHA Health Services Inc 17 Church St *TF:* 866-742-2428 ■ *Web:* www.rhahealthservices.org	Asheville	NC	28801	828-232-6844	665-1921
Rhodes-Joseph & Tobiason Advisors LLC 1177 High Ridge Rd *Web:* www.rjtadvisors.com	Stamford	CT	06905	203-883-8144	
Richards Energy Group 781 S Chiques Rd *Web:* www.richardsenergy.com	Manheim	PA	17545	717-898-6330	
Rideau Inc 473 Deslauriers *TF:* 800-363-6464 ■ *Web:* www.rideau.com	Montreal	QC	H4N1W2	800-363-6464	
River West Meeting Associates Inc 3616 N Lincoln Ave *Web:* www.riverwestmeetings.com	Chicago	IL	60613	773-755-3000	
Rizzetta & Company Inc 3434 Colwell Ave Ste 200 *Web:* www.rizzetta.com	Tampa	FL	33614	813-933-5571	
Rmc Project Management Inc 10953 Bren Rd E *Web:* www.rmcproject.com	Minnetonka	MN	55343	952-846-4484	
Robert Ferrilli LLC 414 W State St *Web:* ferrilli.com	Media	PA	19063	610-565-3710	
Robertson GeoConsultants Inc 580 Hornby St Ste 640 *Web:* www.robertsongeoconsultants.com	Vancouver	BC	V6C3B6	604-684-8072	
Rocket-Hire LLC 4537 N Robertson St *Web:* www.rocket-hire.com	New Orleans	LA	70117	504-236-7259	
Roco Rescue 7077 Exchequer Dr *Web:* www.rocorescue.com	Baton Rouge	LA	70809	225-755-7626	
ROI4Sales Inc 3355 Quaas Dr *Web:* www.roi4sales.com	West Bend	WI	53095	262-338-1851	
Roland Berger Strategy Consultants LLC 37000 Woodward Ave Ste 200 *Web:* www.rolandberger.us	Bloomfield Hills	MI	48304	248-729-5000	
Rs Marketing Services LLC 35 Ft Boone Ct *Web:* www.rsmsinsights.com	Clayton	NC	27527	919-585-4556	
RSD Solutions Inc 177 Lincolnshire Dr *Web:* www.rsdsolutions.com	Fall River	NS	B2T1P8	902-441-4102	
Rtm Consulting LLC 3221 Ivy Hills Blvd *Web:* www.rtmconsulting.net	Cincinnati	OH	45244	513-236-5585	
Rucker & Associates Inc 7009 N Ridge Dr Ste 300 *Web:* www.ruckerassociates.com	Raleigh	NC	27615	919-873-1268	
Ruggie Wealth Management 2100 Lk Eustis Dr *Web:* www.ruggiewealth.com	Tavares	FL	32778	352-343-2700	
Russell Phillips & Associates LLC 500 Cross Keys Office Park *Web:* www.phillipsllc.com	Fairport	NY	14450	585-223-1130	
RxResults LLC 320 Executive Court Ste 301 *Web:* rxresults.com	Little Rock	AR	72205	501-367-8402	
S4 NetQuest 580 N Fourth St Ste 600 *Web:* www.s4netquest.com	Columbus	OH	43215	614-220-5700	
Sales Effectiveness Inc 570 W Crssvlle Rd *Web:* www.saleseffectiveness.com	Roswell	GA	30075	770-552-6612	
Salt Lake Cable & Harness Inc 421 West 900 North *Web:* www.saltlakecable.com	North Salt Lake	UT	84054	801-292-4999	
Sand Cherry Associates Inc Eight Sand Cherry *Web:* www.sandcherryassociates.com	Denver	CO	80127	303-933-9494	
Satov Consultants Inc 250 The Esplanade Ste 200 *Web:* www.satovconsultants.com	Toronto	ON	M5A1J2	416-777-9000	
Scarritt Group Inc 7620 N Hartman Ln Ste 100 *Web:* www.scarrittgroup.com	Tucson	AZ	85743	520-529-0000	
Scheibel Halaska 735 N Water St Ste 200 *Web:* www.trefoilgroup.com	Milwaukee	WI	53202	414-272-6898	
Schreiber Law Firm PLLC, The 53 Stiles Rd Ste A102 *Web:* www.schreiblaw.com	Salem	NH	03079	603-870-5333	
Schroeder Measurement Technologies Inc 2494 Byshore Blvd Ste 201 *Web:* www.smttest.com	Dunedin	FL	34698	727-738-8727	
Schwartz Heslin Group Inc (SHG) Eight Airport Park Blvd *Web:* www.shggroup.com	Latham	NY	12110	518-786-7733	
Scott Sheldon LLC 3985 Medina Rd Ste 220 *Web:* www.scott-sheldon.com	Medina	OH	44256	330-952-1671	
SEA Ltd 7349 Worthington-Galena Rd *TF:* 800-782-6851 ■ *Web:* www.sealimited.com	Columbus	OH	43085	800-782-6851	
SearchDex 2602 McKinney Ave Ste 100 *Web:* www.searchdex.com	Dallas	TX	75204	214-999-0889	
Seccuris Inc 100-321 McDermot Ave *Web:* www.seccuris.com	Winnipeg	MB	R3A0A3	204-255-4136	
Select Medical Corp 4714 Gettysburg Rd *TF:* 888-735-6332 ■ *Web:* www.selectmedical.com	Mechanicsburg	PA	17055	717-972-1100	
Sendero Business Services LP 750 N Paul St Ste 700 *Web:* www.senderocorp.com	Dallas	TX	75201	972-388-5760	
Sentry Hospitality Ltd 136 E 57th St Ste 1003 *Web:* www.sentryhospitality.com	New York	NY	10022	212-753-5347	688-2772
Service Intelligence Inc 1061 Red Venture Dr Ste 175 *TF:* 800-263-2980 ■ *Web:* www.serviceintelligence.com	Fort Mill	SC	29707	800-263-2980	
SET Consulting Inc 5821 Windermere Ln *Web:* www.setconsulting.com	Fairfield	OH	45014	240-296-0800	
Seton Hotel 144 E 40th St *Web:* www.setonhotelny.com	New York	NY	10016	212-889-5301	
Sgv International LLC 8588 Kaity Fwy Ste 200 *Web:* www.sgvinternational.com	Houston	TX	77024	713-647-7555	
Shade Inc 5049 Russell Cir *Web:* www.shadeinc.com	Lincoln	NE	68507	402-466-3393	
Sheridan Healthcare Inc 1613 NW 136th Ave Ste 200 **Fax Area Code:* 954 ■ *TF:* 800-437-2672 ■ *Web:* www.sheridanhealthcare.com	Sunrise	FL	33323	800-437-2672	851-1775*
Shipley Associates Inc 532 North 900 West *Web:* www.shipleywins.com	Kaysville	UT	84037	801-544-9787	
SIB Development & Consulting Inc 796 Meeting St *Web:* www.sibdevelopment.com	Charleston	SC	29403	843-576-3606	
Sierra Infosys Inc 6001 Savoy Dr Ste 210 *Web:* www.sierratec.com	Houston	TX	77036	713-747-9693	
Sigma Breakthrough Technologies Inc 123 N Edward Gary Second Fl *Web:* www.sbtionline.com	San Marcos	TX	78666	512-353-7489	
Signum Group LLC 1900 The Exchange SE Bldg 200 *Web:* www.signumgroup.com	Atlanta	GA	30339	770-514-8111	
Silliman Associates Inc Thomas 425 N Lee St *Web:* www.tsilliman.com	Alexandria	VA	22314	703-548-4100	
Simione Healthcare Consultants LLC 4130 Whitney Ave *Web:* www.simioneconsultants.com	Hamden	CT	06518	203-287-9288	
Smart Inc Howard Triangle Bldg 833 Howard Ave *Web:* www.smartinc1.com	New Orleans	LA	70113	504-566-0900	
Smart Work Network Inc 135 S Main St Ste 402 *Web:* www.smartworknetwork.com	Greenville	SC	29601	864-233-3007	
Smith Research Inc 710 Estate Dr *Web:* www.smithresearch.com	Deerfield	IL	60015	847-948-0440	
Solomon Hardwick & Associates LLC 1160 Folly Rd *Web:* www.solomonhardwick.com	Charleston	SC	29412	843-406-6680	
Solutions 21 152 Wabash St *Web:* solutions21.com	Pittsburgh	PA	15220	412-921-2171	
Solutions AE Inc 236 Auburn Ave *TF:* 888-562-4441 ■ *Web:* www.solutionsae.org	Atlanta	GA	30303	888-562-4441	
Spaulding Group Inc, The 33 Clyde Rd Ste 103 *Web:* spauldinggrp.com	Somerset	NJ	08873	732-873-5700	
SpawGlass Construction Corp 13800 W Rd *TF:* 800-771-0422 ■ *Web:* www.spawglass.com	Houston	TX	77041	281-970-5300	970-5305
Spectrum Healthcare Resources Inc 12647 Olive Blvd Ste 600 **Fax Area Code:* 314 ■ **Fax:* Hum Res ■ *TF:* 800-325-3982 ■ *Web:* www.spectrumhealth.com	Saint Louis	MO	63141	800-325-3982	744-4181*
Speed Consulting LLC 2871 Howard Rd *Web:* www.speedconsulting.com	Waxahachie	TX	75165	972-938-0490	
Speer & Associates Inc 1165 Sanctuary Pkwy Ste 150 *Web:* www.speerandassociates.com	Alpharetta	GA	30009	770-396-2528	
Spencer Shenk Capers & Assoc 1515 W 190th St *Web:* www.ssca.com	Gardena	CA	90248	310-515-7555	
Sports Technologies Inc 10 Front St *Web:* www.sportstechinc.com	Collinsville	CT	06019	860-693-9561	
SSA Consultants Inc 9331 Bluebonnet Blvd *Web:* www.consultssa.com	Baton Rouge	LA	70810	225-769-2676	
SST Planners 1501 Wilson Blvd Ste 507 *Web:* www.sstplanners.com	Arlington	VA	22209	703-875-8787	
St. Michael's Inc 3310 Noble Pond Way *Web:* www.stmichaelsinc.com	Woodbridge	VA	22193	703-463-9463	
St. Onge Co 1400 Williams Rd *Web:* www.stonge.com	York	PA	17402	717-840-8181	
Sta 4100 Fairfax Dr Ste 910 *Web:* stassociates.com	Arlington	VA	22203	703-522-5123	
Staff Leasing Inc 149 Northern Concourse Ste 3 *Web:* www.staffleasing-peo.com	Syracuse	NY	13212	315-641-3600	
Staffing.org Inc 10 Burchard Ln *Web:* www.staffing.org	Rowayton	CT	06853	203-227-0186	
Standard Nine Inc 153 Kearny St Fourth Fl *Web:* www.inkling.com	San Francisco	CA	94108	415-975-4420	
Staples Construction Company Inc 1501 Eastman Ave *TF:* 800-881-4650 ■ *Web:* www.staplesconstruction.com	Ventura	CA	93003	805-658-8786	658-8785
Stern Group Inc, The 3314 Ross Pl NW *Web:* www.sterngroup.biz	Washington	DC	20008	202-966-7894	
Stieglitz Snyder Architecture 425 Franklin St *Web:* www.stieglitzsnyder.com	Buffalo	NY	14202	716-828-9166	

	City	State	ZIP	Phone	Fax
Stock & Option Solutions Inc 6399 San Ignacio Ave Ste 100 *Web:* www.sos-team.com	San Jose	CA	95119	408-979-8700	
Stop Hunger Now 2501 Clark Ave *Web:* www.stophungernow.org	Raleigh	NC	27607	919-839-0689	
Strayer Consulting Group Inc 16151 Wood Acres Rd *Web:* www.strayerconsulting.com	Los Gatos	CA	95030	408-399-1500	
Streebo Inc 10998 S Wilcrest Dr Ste 162 *Web:* www.streebo.com	Houston	TX	77099	832-426-2700	
Strong-Bridge Consulting LLC 545 Andover Park West Ste 215 *Web:* www.strong-bridge.com	Seattle	WA	98188	206-905-4631	
Sudler Property Management 875 N Michigan Ave Ste 3980 *Web:* www.sudlerathome.com	Chicago	IL	60611	312-751-0900	
Summit Energy Services Inc 10350 Ormsby Pk Pl Ste 400 *TF:* 866-907-8664 ■ *Web:* www.summitenergy.com	Louisville	KY	40223	502-429-3800	753-2248
Surge Resources 920 Candia Rd *Web:* www.surgeindustries.com	Manchester	NH	03109	603-623-0007	
Swiss Consulting Group 101 W 23 St Ste 2422 *Web:* www.swissconsultinggroup.com	New York	NY	10011	212-288-4858	
Synaptic Decisions LP 10700 N Fwy Ste 130 *Web:* www.synapticdecisions.com	Houston	TX	77037	832-300-9800	
Synaptis Inc 150 Cornerstone Dr Ste 201 *Web:* www.synaptis.com	Cary	NC	27519	919-844-5840	
Synthesis Professional Services Inc 12339 Carroll Ave. *Web:* www.synthesisps.com	Rockville	MD	20852	301-770-8970	
Szarka Financial Management 29691 Lorain Rd. *Web:* www.szarkafinancial.com	North Olmsted	OH	44070	440-779-1430	
Table Group Inc 3640 MT Diablo Blvd 202 *Web:* www.tablegroup.com	Lafayette	CA	94549	925-299-9700	
Tagos Group LLC, The Eight E Greenway Plz Ste 1340 *Web:* www.tagosgroup.com	Houston	TX	77046	713-850-7031	
Talent Curve 14 Bridle Path *TF:* 866-494-0248 ■ *Web:* www.talentcurve.com	Pittsboro	NC	27312	866-494-0248	
Taos Mountain 121 Daggett Dr. *Web:* www.taos.com	San Jose	CA	95134	408-588-1200	
Targeted Learning 706 Technology Ave *Web:* www.targetedlearning.com	Orem	UT	84097	801-235-9414	
Task Management Inc 99 Danbury Rd *Web:* www.taskmanagement.com	Ridgefield	CT	06877	203-438-9777	
TBN Consulting LLC 3301 Brunswick Ave N. *Web:* www.tonynelson.com	Minneapolis	MN	55422	763-971-8057	
Team Quality Services Inc 4483 County Rd 19 Ste B *Web:* teamqualityservices.com	Auburn	IN	46706	260-572-0060	
Technosphere 155 N Washington Ave. *Web:* www.technosphere.com	Bergenfield	NJ	07621	201-384-7400	
Tecolote Research Inc 420 S Fairview Ave Ste 201 *Web:* www.tecolote.com	Goleta	CA	93117	805-571-6366	571-6377
Telcom Corp 1499 W Palmetto Park Rd Ste 214 *Web:* www.telcomcorp.com	Boca Raton	FL	33486	561-394-5448	
Telecom Resources International Inc 7119 E Shea Blvd Ste 109-486 *Web:* tri-1.com	Scottsdale	AZ	85254	480-391-3800	
TeleSoft Systems 335 Wesley St Ste 203 *Web:* www.telesoftsystems.ca	Nanaimo	BC	V9R2R7	250-760-0142	
Tenox Appraisal Systems Inc 2140 Winston Park Dr Unit #31 *Web:* www.weshop4u.com	Oakville	ON	L6H5V5	905-829-9548	
TGC 3200 Travis St *Web:* www.thegoodmancorp.com	Houston	TX	77006	512-236-8002	
ThinkHR Corp 4457 Willow Rd Ste 120 *Web:* www.thinkhr.com	Pleasanton	CA	94588	925-225-1100	
Three Rivers Planning & Development District Inc 75 S Main St PO Box 690. *Web:* www.trpdd.com	Pontotoc	MS	38863	662-489-2415	489-6815
TigerSwan Inc 3452 Apex Peakway *Web:* www.tigerswan.com	Apex	NC	27502	919-439-7110	
Toeroek Associates Inc 300 Union Blvd Ste 520 *Web:* www.toeroek.com	Lakewood	CO	80228	303-420-7735	
Toshiba Global Commerce Solutions Inc 3039 Cornwallis Rd *Web:* www.toshibacommerce.com	Research Triangle Park	NC	27709	919-523-7241	
Total Contentz LLC 845 E Easy St Ste 102. *Web:* www.totalcontentz.com	Simi Valley	CA	93065	805-522-5900	
Total Logistics Solutions Inc PO Box 11146 *Web:* www.logisticsociety.com	Burbank	CA	91510	818-353-2962	
TraceSecurity Inc 6300 Corporate Blvd Ste 200 *Web:* www.tracesecurity.com	Baton Rouge	LA	70809	225-612-2121	
Traffic Group Inc, The 9900 Franklin Sq Dr *Web:* www.trafficgroup.com	Baltimore	MD	21236	410-931-6600	
Tragon Corp 365 Convention Way. *Web:* tragon.com	Redwood City	CA	94063	650-365-1833	
Trainertainment LLC 6829 Greenleaf Dr. *Web:* trainertainment.net	North Richland Hills	TX	76182	817-886-4840	
Tran Cert Marketing Inc 2295 Berry Ln Ste 880 *Web:* www.trancertmarketing.com	Point Roberts	WA	98281	360-945-2190	
Transverse LLC 620 Congress Ave Ste 200 *Web:* www.gotransverse.com	Austin	TX	78701	512-279-3119	
Treacy & Co 1220 South St. *Web:* www.treacyandco.com	Needham	MA	02492	781-559-3381	
Trellist Inc 117 N Market St *Web:* www.trellist.com	Wilmington	DE	19801	302-778-1300	
Trinity River Authority of Texas 5300 s collins st *Web:* www.trinityra.org	Arlington	TX	76018	817-467-4343	
TriReme Medical Inc 7060 Koll Ctr Pkwy Ste 300 *Web:* qtvascular.com	Pleasanton	CA	94566	925-931-1300	
Trissential Inc 1905 E Wayzata Blvd Ste 333 *Web:* www.trissential.com	Minneapolis	MN	55391	952-595-7970	
Trp Enterprises Inc 3978 Old Greensboro Rd *Web:* www.trpnet.com	Winston Salem	NC	27101	336-777-1947	
True Market Solutions Inc 82 Levant St. *Web:* truemarketsolutions.com	San Francisco	CA	94114	415-484-9044	
TTG Consultants 4727 Wilshire Blvd *Web:* www.ttgconsultants.com	Los Angeles	CA	90010	323-936-6600	
Turover-Straus Group Inc 4145 S Mccann Ct B. *Web:* tsgnpd.com	Springfield	MO	65804	417-889-0770	
Turpin Sales & Marketing Inc 330 Cold Spring Ave. *TF:* 877-377-7573 ■ *Web:* www.turpinsales.com	West Springfield	MA	01089	877-377-7573	
UCI Medical Affiliates Inc 1818 Henderson St. **Fax:* Executive Fax ■ *Web:* www.doctorscare.com	Columbia	SC	29201	803-782-4278	782-3445*
Ulterior Motives International Inc 1081 Ohio Dr Ste 2. *Web:* www.umi-inc.com	Plano	TX	75093	214-826-0011	
Unemed Corp 986099 Nebraska Medical Center *Web:* www.unemed.com	Omaha	NE	68198	402-559-2468	
Unemployment Services Corp 333 N Ave *Web:* www.uscorp.com	Wakefield	MA	01880	781-246-0262	
Unify Square Inc 411 108th Ave NE. *Web:* www.unifysquare.com	Bellevue	WA	98004	425-865-0700	
Unisource NTC 1560 Holly Court Ste 200 *TF:* 800-736-8470 ■ *Web:* www.unisourcentc.com	Thousand Oaks	CA	91360	800-736-8470	
United Sourcing Alliance 2105 Water Ridge Pkwy Ste 470. *Web:* usa-llc.com	Charlotte	NC	28217	704-697-9695	
United Temps Inc 1550 S Indiana Ave Ste 300 *Web:* unitedhq.com	Chicago	IL	60605	312-922-8558	
US-Reports Inc 5802 Wright Dr. *Web:* www.us-reports.com	Loveland	CO	80538	970-593-9888	
Valley Small Business Development 7035 N Fruit Ave. *Web:* www.vsbdc.com	Fresno	CA	93711	559-438-9680	
Vanir Construction Management Inc 4540 Duckhorn Dr Ste 300. *TF:* 888-912-1201 ■ *Web:* www.vanir.com	Sacramento	CA	95834	916-575-8887	575-8887
Vaya Ste 250 2111 Plum St *Web:* www.vayapath.com	Aurora	IL	60506	630-906-3046	
vCustomer Corp 4040 Lk Washington Blvd NE *Web:* www.vcustomer.com	Kirkland	WA	98033	206-802-0200	
Vectrus Inc 655 Space Ctr Dr. *Web:* www.vectrus.com	Colorado Springs	CO	80915	719-591-3600	
Veetech PC 113 Centrewest Ct. *Web:* www.veetechpc.com	Cary	NC	27513	919-388-0037	
Vega Energy Partners Ltd 3701 Kirby Ste 1290. *Web:* www.vegaenergy.com	Houston	TX	77098	713-527-0557	
Vendors Exchange International Inc 8700 Brookpark Rd. *Web:* www.veii.com	Cleveland	OH	44129	216-785-2611	
Venn Products Group 80 Skyline Dr *Web:* www.mciproducts.com	Plainview	NY	11803	516-822-1561	
Veracity Credit Consultants LLC 110 16th St Ste 1000 *Web:* www.veracitycredit.com	Denver	CO	80202	303-893-1801	
Verax Communications 499 Adams St. *Web:* www.veraxcom.com	Milton	MA	02186	617-698-0088	
Veri-Tax LLC 30 Executive Park Ste 200 *Web:* www.veri-tax.com	Irvine	CA	92614	949-783-2100	
Verifi Inc 8391 Beverly Blvd Ste 310. *Web:* www.verifi.com	Los Angeles	CA	90048	323-655-5789	
Verisk Analytics 545 Washington Blvd *NASDAQ: VRSK* ■ *Web:* www.verisk.com	Jersey City	NJ	07310	201-469-3000	748-1472
Vermont Energy Investment Corp 128 Lakeside Ave Ste 401. *Web:* www.veic.org	Burlington	VT	05401	802-658-6060	
Vertigraph Inc 12959 Jupiter Rd Ste 252 *Web:* www.vertigraph.com	Dallas	TX	75238	214-340-9436	
VetStrategy 780 Hwy 6 N. *TF:* 866-901-6471 ■ *Web:* www.vetstrategy.com	Waterdown	ON	L0R2H1	866-901-6471	
Vetter Health Services Inc 20220 Harney St. *TF:* 800-388-4264 ■ *Web:* www.vetterhealthservices.com	Elkhorn	NE	68022	402-895-3932	895-8165
VHA Inc 220 Las Colinas Blvd E PO Box 140909. *TF:* 800-842-5146 ■ *Web:* www.vha.com	Irving	TX	75039	972-830-7845	830-0012
Village Adelphoi 112 Porter Ave *Web:* www.adelphoiusa.org	Connellsville	PA	15425	724-626-7818	
VisionQuest National Ltd 600 N Swan Rd. *Web:* www.vq.com	Tucson	AZ	85732	520-881-3950	881-3269
ViTEX Inc 630 Williamson Rd *Web:* www.vitex.com	Mooresville	NC	28117	704-663-2544	
Vizant Technologies LLC Brandywine Two Bldg 5 Christy Dr Ste 202 *Web:* vizant.com	Chadds Ford	PA	19317	610-358-1003	
VizQuest Ventures LLC PO Box 920741 *Web:* www.vizquest.com	Needham	MA	02492	781-207-0311	
Volt VIEWtech Inc 4761 E Hunter Ave *TF:* 888-396-9927 ■ *Web:* www.volt.com	Anaheim	CA	92807	714-695-3377	

Phone | Fax

Von Lehman & CO
250 Grandview Dr Ste 300 .... Fort Mitchell KY 41017 859-331-3300
Web: www.vlcpa.com
Vortex Advisory Group 220 Pond St .... Hopkinton MA 01748 508-435-0220
Web: www.vortexadvisory.com
VStock Transfer LLC 18 Lafayette Pl .... Woodmere NY 11598 212-828-8436
Web: www.vstocktransfer.com
W H Meanor & Associates
216 N Mcdowell St Ste 200 .... Charlotte NC 28204 704-372-7640
Web: www.whmeanor.com
Warren Distribution Inc 727 S 13th St .... Omaha NE 68102 402-341-9397 977-5754
Web: www.wd-wpp.com
Warren Management Group Inc, The
1720 Jet Stream Dr Ste 200 .... Colorado Springs CO 80921 719-534-0266
Web: warrenmgmt.com
Warren Whitney Sherwood & Company Inc
7231 Forest Ave .... Richmond VA 23226 804-282-9566
Web: www.wwsmanagement.com
Wasmer Group, The 2001 Jackson St .... Alexandria LA 71301 318-443-6551
Web: www.wasmer.com
Waypoint Consulting 1450 E Boot Rd .... West Chester PA 19380 484-472-8611
Web: www.waypointco.com
Weber Marketing Group Inc
225 Terry Ave North Ste 400 .... Seattle WA 98109 206-340-6111
Web: www.webermarketing.com
Wellford Energy Group LLC 555 11th St NW .... Washington DC 20004 202-783-9193
Web: www.wellfordenergy.com
West Pacific Consulting Group
8988 Fraserton Crt .... Burnaby BC V5J5H8 604-294-1200
Web: www.wpcg.ca
Westin Engineering Inc
3100 Zinfandel Dr Ste 300 .... Rancho Cordova CA 95670 916-852-2121 852-2311
Westney Consulting Group Inc
2200 W Loop S Ste 500 .... Houston TX 77027 713-861-0800
Web: www.westney.com
Wheaton Partners LLC
1901 N Roselle Rd Ste 640 .... Schaumburg IL 60195 847-381-5465
Web: www.codemap.com
Wicklander Zulawski & Associates Inc
4932 Main St .... Downers Grove IL 60515 630-852-6800
Web: www.w-z.com
WideNet Consulting Group
11400 SE Sixth St Ste 130 .... Bellevue WA 98004 425-643-0366
Web: www.widenet-consulting.com
William Avery & Associates Inc
Three 1/2 N Santa Cruz Ave Ste A .... Los Gatos CA 95030 408-399-4424
Web: www.averyassoc.net
Willow Group Inc, The
8201 Norman Ctr Dr Ste 450 .... Bloomington MN 55437 952-897-3550
Web: willowg.com
Wilson Legal Solutions Inc
3817 W chester Pk .... Newtown Square PA 19073 484-422-0010
Web: www.wilsonlegalsol.com
Windward Environmental LLC
200 W Mercer St Ste 401 .... Seattle WA 98119 206-378-1364
Web: www.windwardenv.com
Winfree Marketing & Sales Institute
1905 Arnold Palmer Blvd .... Louisville KY 40245 502-253-0700
Web: www.winfree.org
Winning Edge Group LLC 2576 Euclid Crescent E .... Upland CA 91784 909-949-9083
Web: www.group50.com
Winning Proposals Inc 374 Maple Ave E Ste 305 .... Vienna VA 22180 703-242-6490
Web: www.win-pros.com
Winsby Inc 1854 Sherman Ave .... Evanston IL 60201 847-316-9800
Web: www.winsbyinc.com
Wise Agent, The 13014 N Saguaro Blvd .... Fountain Hills AZ 85268 480-836-0345
Web: www.thewiseagent.com
Words & Numbers Inc 2050 Rockrose Ave .... Baltimore MD 21211 410-467-7835
Web: www.wordsandnumbers.com
Worldview Solutions Inc 101 S 15th St .... Richmond VA 23219 804-915-7628
Web: www.worldviewsolutions.com
Wwc Enterprises Inc 19145 S Us Hwy 377 .... Dublin TX 76446 254-445-0100
Web: www.wwcenterprises.com
X Dot Inc 4500 Westgrove Dr Ste 395 .... Addison TX 75001 972-248-7243
Web: www.x-dot.com
Xand Corp 11 Skyline Dr .... Hawthorne NY 10532 914-592-8282 592-3482
TF: 800-522-2823 ■ *Web:* www.xand.com
Xtreme Consulting Group Inc
3500 Carillon Point .... Kirkland WA 98033 425-861-9460
Web: www.xtremeconsulting.com
Young Startup Ventures Inc
258 Crafton Ave .... Staten Island NY 10314 718-477-2208
Web: www.youngstartup.com
Youthbuild International 58 Day St Ste 300 .... Somerville MA 02144 617-623-9900
Web: www.youthbuild.org
Zerochaos LLC 420 S Orange Ave Ste 600 .... Orlando FL 32801 407-770-6161 888-9376*
**Fax Area Code:* 877 ■ *Web:* www.zerochaos.com
Zeus Development Corp 2424 Wilcrest Ste 100 .... Houston TX 77042 713-952-9500
Web: www.zeusintel.com
Zielinski Financial Advisors LLC
2403 High Hammock Rd .... Seabrook Island SC 29455 843-974-4964
Web: www.zfinancialadvisors.com
Zimmet Healthcare Consulting LLC
4006 Us Hwy 9 .... Morganville NJ 07751 732-970-0733
Web: zhealthcare.com
Zitter Group, The
290 W Mount Pleasant Ave Ste 2210 .... Livingston NJ 07039 973-376-1300
Web: www.zitter.com
Zoyto Inc 433 Northpark Central Dr .... Houston TX 77073 713-300-3000
Web: www.zoyto.com

467 MANNEQUINS & DISPLAY FORMS

Phone | Fax

Barnhart Display Inc 1170 Charming St .... Maitland FL 32751 407-637-2060 637-2053
Web: www.barnhartdisplay.com
Goldsmith New York at Studio 350
601 W 26th St Ste 350 .... New York NY 10001 212-366-9040
Web: www.goldsmith-inc.com
Ronis Bros 39 Harriet Pl .... Lynbrook NY 11563 516-887-5266 887-5288
TF: 888-555-1234 ■ *Web:* www.ronis.com
Siegel & Stockman USA 126 W 25th St .... New York NY 10001 212-633-0138 366-0575
TF: 888-515-8949 ■ *Web:* www.siegel-stockman.com
Silvestri Studio Inc 8125 Beach St .... Los Angeles CA 90001 323-277-4420 585-0861
TF: 800-647-8874 ■ *Web:* www.silvestricalifornia.com

468 MARINE SERVICES

SEE ALSO Freight Transport - Deep Sea (Domestic Ports) p. 2336; Freight Transport - Deep Sea (Foreign Ports) p. 2336; Freight Transport - Inland Waterways p. 2336; Logistics Services (Transportation & Warehousing) p. 2673

Phone | Fax

AEP River Operations
16150 Main Cir Dr Ste 400 .... Chesterfield MO 63017 636-530-2100 860-3215*
**Fax Area Code:* 281 ■ *TF:* 800-621-3362 ■ *Web:* www.aepriverops.com
American Port Service Inc 2901 Childs St .... Baltimore MD 21226 410-350-0400 354-8812
Web: www.amports.com
Andrie Inc 561 E Western Ave .... Muskegon MI 49442 231-728-2226 726-6747
TF: 800-722-2421 ■ *Web:* www.andrie.com
Bay Houston Towing Co 2243 Milford St .... Houston TX 77253 713-529-3755 529-2591
TF: 800-324-3755 ■ *Web:* www.bayhouston.com
Bisso Towboat Company Inc 8237 Oak St .... New Orleans LA 70178 504-861-1411 861-9298
Web: www.bissotowing.com
Bunkers International Corp
110 Timberlachen Cir Ste 1012 .... Lake Mary FL 32746 407-328-7757 328-0045
Web: www.bunkersinternational.com
Cargo Express Inc 1790 Yardley Stn Dr .... Yardley PA 19067 215-493-2662
Ceres Terminals Inc
Two Tower Ctr Blvd .... East Brunswick NJ 08816 201-974-3800 974-3850
Web: www.ceresglobal.com
Cooper/T Smith Stevedoring Co 118 N Royal St .... Mobile AL 36602 251-431-6100
Web: www.coopertsmith.com
Crowley Maritime Corp
9487 Regency Square Blvd Ste 2130 .... Jacksonville FL 32225 904-727-2200 727-2501
TF: 800-276-9539 ■ *Web:* www.crowley.com
Dix Industries Inc 5500 RL Ostos Rd .... Brownsville TX 78521 956-831-4228 831-2559
Web: www.dixshipping.com
Donjon Marine Company Inc 100 Central Ave .... Hillside NJ 07205 908-964-8812 964-7426
Web: www.donjon.com
Eagle Marine Industries Inc One Riverview Ave .... Sauget IL 62201 618-875-1153 875-1505
Edison Chouest Offshore 16201 E Main St .... Galliano LA 70354 985-601-4444 601-4237
TF: 866-925-5161 ■ *Web:* www.chouest.com
Eller-ITO Stevedoring Company LLC
1007 N America Way .... Miami FL 33132 305-379-3700 371-9969
Web: www.ellerito.com
Foss Maritime Co 660 W Ewing St .... Seattle WA 98119 800-562-2711 281-4702*
**Fax Area Code:* 206 ■ *TF:* 800-426-2885 ■ *Web:* www.foss.com
G & H Towing Company Inc PO Drawer 2270 .... Galveston TX 77553 409-744-6311 740-2575
Web: www.gandhtowing.com
General Steamship Agencies Inc
575 Redwood Hwy Ste 200 .... Mill Valley CA 94941 415-389-5200 389-9020
TF: 855-859-3123 ■ *Web:* www.gensteam.com
Great Lakes Towing Co 4500 Div Ave .... Cleveland OH 44102 216-621-4854 621-7616
TF: 800-321-3663 ■ *Web:* www.thegreatlakesgroup.com
Hawaii Stevedores Inc
1601 Sand Island Pkwy PO Box 2160 .... Honolulu HI 96819 808-527-3400
Web: www.hawaiistevedores.com
Hawaiian Tug & Barge
1331 N Nimitz Hwy PO Box 3288 .... Honolulu HI 96817 808-543-9311 543-9477
TF: 800-572-2743 ■ *Web:* www.htbyb.com
Higman Marine Services
1980 Post Oak Blvd Ste 1101 .... Houston TX 77056 713-552-1101 552-0732
Web: higman.com
Hopkins-Carter Company Inc 3300 NW 21st St .... Miami FL 33142 305-635-7377 633-1310
TF: 800-595-9656 ■ *Web:* www.hopkins-carter.com
Hornbeck Offshore Services Inc
103 Northpark Blvd Ste 300 .... Covington LA 70433 985-727-2000 727-2006
NYSE: HOS ■ *TF:* 800-642-9816 ■ *Web:* www.hornbeckoffshore.com
Houston Pilots 8150 S Loop E Ste 118 .... Houston TX 77017 713-645-9620
Web: www.houston-pilots.com
International Transportation Service Inc
1281 Pier J Way .... Long Beach CA 90802 562-435-7781 590-6761
Web: www.itslb.com
J. F. Brennan Co Inc 820 Bainbridge .... La Crosse WI 54603 608-784-7173 785-2090
Web: www.jfbrennan.com
James Marine Inc (JMI)
4500 Clarks River Rd P.O. Box 2305 .... Paducah KY 42002 270-898-7392 448-0015
Web: www.jamesmarine.com
Kinder Morgan Bulk Terminals Inc
7116 Hwy 22 .... Sorrento LA 70778 225-675-5387 675-5923
TF: 800-232-1627 ■ *Web:* www.kindermorgan.com
LeBeouf Brothers Towing LLC 124 Dry Dock Rd .... Bourg LA 70343 985-594-6691 594-5253
Web: www.lebeouftowing.com
Marquette Transportation Company LLC
5525 Mounes St PO Box 23521 .... New Orleans LA 70123 504-733-5845
TF: 800-735-5845 ■ *Web:* www.marquettetrans.com
McAllister Towing & Transportation Co Inc
17 Battery Pl Ste 1200 .... New York NY 10004 212-269-3200 509-1147
TF: 888-774-0400 ■ *Web:* www.mcallistertowing.com

				Phone	Fax
McCabe Hamilton & Renny Company Ltd (MHR) 1130 N Nimitz Hwy Rm A265 *Web:* www.mhrhawaii.com	Honolulu	HI	96817	808-524-3255	545-3101
Murphy Marine Services Inc 11 Gist Rd First Fl *Web:* murphymarine.com	Port of Wilmington	DE	19801	302-571-4700	571-4702
New Haven Terminal Inc 100 Waterfront St	New Haven	CT	06512	203-468-0805	469-6374
New York State Canal Corp 200 Southern Blvd PO Box 189 *TF:* 800-422-6254 ■ *Web:* www.canals.ny.gov	Albany	NY	12201	518-436-2700	
Nicholson Terminal & Dock Co 360 E Great Lakes *Web:* www.nicholson-terminal.com	Ecorse	MI	48229	313-842-4300	843-1091
North Star Terminal & Stevedore Company LLC 790 Ocean Dock Rd *Web:* www.northstarak.com	Anchorage	AK	99501	907-272-7537	272-8927
Odyssey Marine Exploration Inc 5215 W Laurel St *NASDAQ: OMEX* ■ *TF:* 800-458-4646 ■ *Web:* www.shipwreck.net	Tampa	FL	33607	813-876-1776	876-1777
Otto Candies LLC 17271 US 90 *Web:* www.ottocandies.com	Des Allemands	LA	70030	504-469-7700	469-7740
Parker Towing Company Inc PO Box 20908 *Web:* www.parkertowing.com	Tuscaloosa	AL	35402	205-349-1677	758-0061
Pelicans Perch Marina & Boatyard 40 Audusson Ave Bayou Chico *Web:* www.pelicansperchmarina.com	Pensacola	FL	32507	850-453-3471	457-1662
Port of Miami Terminal Operating Company LC 1007 N America Way Ste 400 *Web:* www.pomtoc.com	Miami	FL	33132	305-416-7600	374-6724
Ports America Inc 525 Washington Blvd Ste 1660 **Fax Area Code:* 201 ■ *Web:* www.portsamerica.com	Jersey City	NJ	07310	732-635-3899	216-9366*
RMS Titanic Inc 3340 Peachtree Rd NE *Web:* premierexhibitions.com/exhibitions/3/3/titanic-artifact-exhibition	Atlanta	GA	30326	404-842-2600	842-2626
Rukert Terminals Corp 2021 S Clinton St *Web:* www.rukert.com	Baltimore	MD	21224	410-276-1013	
Sause Bros 3710 NW Front Ave *TF:* 800-488-4167 ■ *Web:* www.sause.com	Portland	OR	97210	503-222-1811	222-2010
Sea Tow Services International Inc 1560 Youngs Ave PO Box 1178 *TF:* 800-473-2869 ■ *Web:* www.seatow.com	Southold	NY	11971	631-765-3660	
SSA Marine 1131 SW Klickitat Way *TF:* 800-422-3505 ■ *Web:* www.ssamarine.com	Seattle	WA	98134	206-623-0304	623-0179
Tidewater Inc 601 Poydras St Ste 1900 *NYSE: TDW* ■ *TF:* 800-678-8433 ■ *Web:* www.tdw.com	New Orleans	LA	70130	504-568-1010	566-4580
Virginia International Terminals Inc 7737 Hampton Blvd Ste D224 *TF General:* 800-541-2431 ■ *Web:* www.vit.org	Norfolk	VA	23505	757-440-7000	440-7221
Western Towboat Company Inc 617 NW 40th St *Web:* www.westerntowboat.com	Seattle	WA	98107	206-789-9000	789-9755

469 MARKET RESEARCH FIRMS

SEE ALSO

				Phone	Fax
1stWEST Financial Corp 32186 Castle Court Ste 220 *TF:* 866-670-3443 ■ *Web:* www.1stwest.com	Evergreen	CO	80439	866-670-3443	
Abbott Nicholson PC 300 River Pl Ste 3000 *Web:* www.abbottnicholson.com	Detroit	MI	48207	313-566-2500	
Aberdeen Group Inc 451 D St Seventh Fl Ste 710 *Web:* www.aberdeen.com	Boston	MA	02210	617-854-5200	
AbsolutData Technologies Inc 1851 Harbor Bay Pkwy Ste 125 *Web:* www.absolutdata.com	Alameda	CA	94502	510-748-9922	
Abt Assoc Inc 55 Wheeler St *Web:* www.abtassociates.com	Cambridge	MA	02138	617-492-7100	492-5219
Advanced Scientific Concepts Inc 135 E Ortega St *Web:* www.advancedscientificconcepts.com	Santa Barbara	CA	93101	805-966-3331	
Allan R Nelson Engineering (1997) Inc 17510-102 Ave 2nd Fl *Web:* www.arneng.ab.ca	Edmonton	AB	T5S1K2	780-483-3436	489-9557
Alliance Energy Services LLC 318 Armour Rd *Web:* www.alliancec3.com	Kansas City	MO	64116	816-421-5192	
Ameresco Canada Inc 90 Sheppard Ave E 7th Fl *TF:* 877-358-3853 ■ *Web:* www.ameresco.ca	North York	ON	M2N6X3	416-512-7700	218-2288
AML Partners LLC Four Grand Cove Way *TF:* 866-790-5095 ■ *Web:* www.amlpartners.com	Edgewater	NJ	07020	201-484-8835	
Amphenol Optimize Manufacturing Co 180 N Freeport Dr Bldg W-10 *TF:* 800-288-4746 ■ *Web:* www.amphenol-optimize.com	Nogales	AZ	85621	520-397-7015	397-7014
AMTEK Engineering Services Ltd 1676 Bank St Ste 200 *Web:* www.amtekcdn.com	Ottawa	ON	K1V7Y6	613-749-3990	
Anderson Analytics LLC 154 Cold Spring Rd Ste 80 *Web:* www.andersonanalytics.com	Stamford	CT	06905	203-912-7175	
Andrew Seybold Inc 315 Meigs Rd Ste A-267 *Web:* www.andrewseybold.com	Santa Barbara	CA	93109	805-898-2460	
Answers Research Inc 380 Stevens Ave Ste 214 *Web:* www.answersresearch.com	Solana Beach	CA	92075	858-792-4660	
Arbitron Inc 9705 Patuxent Woods Dr *NYSE: ARB* ■ **Fax:* Hum Res ■ *TF:* 800-543-7300 ■ *Web:* www.arbitron.com	Columbia	MD	21046	410-312-8000	312-8607*
Artafact LLC 43165 Sabercat *Web:* www.artafact.com	Fremont	CA	94539	510-651-9178	
Attitude Measurement Corp Five Sentry Pkwy W Ste 100 *Web:* www.amcglobal.com	Blue Bell	PA	19422	610-238-9200	
Bensussen Deutsch & Assoc Inc (BDA) 15525 Woodinville-Redmond Rd NE *TF:* 800-451-4764 ■ *Web:* www.bdainc.com	Woodinville	WA	98072	425-492-6111	492-7222
Beroe Inc 2054 Kildaire Farm Rd *Web:* www.beroe-inc.com	Cary	NC	27518	919-363-9058	
Biomod Concepts Inc 1821B Lavoisier *Web:* www.biomod.com	Sainte-julie	QC	J3E1Y6	514-905-5848	
Bishop & Associates Inc 1209 Fox Glen Dr *Web:* www.bishopinc.com	St. Charles	IL	60174	630-443-2702	
Brand Institute Inc 200 SE First St 12th Fl *Web:* www.brandinst.com	Miami	FL	33131	305-374-2500	
Bridge Metrics LLC 830 S Greenville Ave *TF:* 877-801-7158 ■ *Web:* www.bridgemetrics.com	Allen	TX	75002	877-801-7158	
Burke Inc 500 W Seventh St *Web:* www.burke.com	Cincinnati	OH	45203	513-241-5663	684-7500
Butler Pappas Weihmuller Katz Craig LLP 80 SW Eighth St Ste 3300 *Web:* www.butlerpappas.com	Miami	FL	33130	305-416-9998	
C & R Research Services Inc 500 N Michigan Ave Ste 1200 *TF:* 800-543-9393 ■ *Web:* crresearch.com	Chicago	IL	60611	312-828-9200	527-3113
CúSuite Communications 401 N Cattlemen Rd *Web:* www.clarkeadvertising.com	Sarasota	FL	34232	941-365-2710	
CA Walker Research Solutions Inc 100 W Broadway Ste 1170 *Web:* www.cawalker.com	Glendale	CA	91210	626-584-8180	584-8199
Cadence Research & Consulting 360 Via Las Brisas Ste 210 *Web:* www.cadenceresearch.com	Thousand Oaks	CA	91320	805-499-8603	
Carnegie Observatories 813 Santa Barbara St *Web:* obs.carnegiescience.edu	Pasadena	CA	91101	626-577-1122	
CattleLog 10305 102nd Terrace *TF:* 866-239-2665 ■ *Web:* www.cattlelog.com	Sebastian	FL	32958	866-239-2665	
CBR International Corp 2905 Wilderness Pl Ste 202 *Web:* www.cbrintl.com	Boulder	CO	80301	720-746-1190	
Celula Inc 11011 Torreyana Rd Ste 200 *Web:* www.celula-inc.com	San Diego	CA	92121	858-875-8800	
Centralized Supply Chain Services LLC 8140 Ward Pkwy *Web:* www.cscscoop.com	Kansas City	MO	64114	913-438-5552	
Chadwick Martin Bailey Inc 179 S St Third Fl *Web:* www.cmbinfo.com	Boston	MA	02111	617-350-8922	
CKR Global 17 Fawcett Rd Ste 225 *Web:* ckrglobal.com	Coquitlam	BC	V3K6V2	604-517-4545	
Clear Seas Research 2401 W Big Beaver Rd *Web:* clearseas.mobi	Troy	MI	48084	248-786-1683	
Clinical Research Advantage Inc 2141 E Broadway Rd *Web:* crastudies.com	Tempe	AZ	85282	480-820-5656	
Coleman Research Inc 909 Aviation Pkwy Ste 400 *Web:* www.colemaninsights.com	Morrisville	NC	27560	919-571-0000	
comScore Inc 11950 Democracy Dr # 600 *TF:* 866-276-6972 ■ *Web:* www.comscore.com	Reston	VA	20190	703-438-2000	438-2051
Corra Group 13011 W Washington Blvd *Web:* www.corragroup.com	Los Angeles	CA	90066	310-822-7788	
Crompco Corp 1815 Gallagher Rd *Web:* www.crompco.com	Plymouth Meeting	PA	19462	610-278-7203	
Crystal McKenzie Inc 30 E 20th St Fifth Fl *Web:* www.cminyc.com	New York	NY	10003	212-598-4567	
Davidson-Peterson Associates Inc 201 Lafayette Center *Web:* digitalresearch.com	Kennebunk	ME	04043	207-985-1790	
Decision Analyst Inc 604 Ave H E *Web:* www.decisionanalyst.com	Arlington	TX	76011	817-640-6166	640-6567
Demand Metric 562 Wellington St *Web:* www.demandmetric.com	London	ON	N6A3R5	519-495-9619	
Dieringer Research Group Inc, The 200 Bishops Way *Web:* www.thedrg.com	Brookfield	WI	53005	262-432-5200	
Digital Traffic Systems Inc 6020 Academy Rd NE Ste 202 *Web:* www.dtsits.com	Albuquerque	NM	87109	505-881-4470	
Directions Research Inc 401 E Ct St Ste 200 *Web:* www.directionsrsch.com	Cincinnati	OH	45202	513-651-2990	651-2998
Dodd Creative Group Holding Company Inc 3720 Canton St Ste 100 *Web:* doddcreative.com	Dallas	TX	75226	214-821-6990	
Dolcera Corp 3555 S El Camino Real Ste 305 *Web:* www.dolcera.com	San Mateo	CA	94403	650-425-6772	
Dunnhumby USA LLC 444 W Third St *Web:* www.dunnhumby.com	Cincinnati	OH	45202	513-632-1020	
Durie Tangri LLP 217 Leidesdorff St *Web:* www.durietangri.com	San Francisco	CA	94111	415-362-6666	
DYG Inc 36A Padanaram Rd *Web:* dyg.com	Danbury	CT	06811	203-744-9008	
Elder Research Inc 300 W Main Ste 301 *Web:* www.datamininglab.com	Charlottesville	VA	22903	434-973-7673	
Empire Advisory Group Inc 38 Chimney View Ln *Web:* www.empire4u.net	Springfield	IL	62707	217-528-0047	
EmployeeScreenIQ Inc 24500 Chagrin Blvd *Web:* www.employeescreen.com	Cleveland	OH	44122	216-514-2800	
Enclude Ltd 1220 19th St NW Ste 200 *Web:* www.encludesolutions.com	Washington	DC	20036	202-822-9100	
ENLASO Corp 9543 W Emerald St Ste 105 *Web:* www.enlaso.com	Boise	ID	83704	208-672-8500	
Envirosell Inc 907 Broadway	New York	NY	10010	212-673-9100	

Company / Address	City	State	Zip	Phone	Fax
eXelate Seven W 22nd St Ninth Fl *TF:* 877-896-3282 ■ *Web:* exelate.com	New York	NY	10010	646-380-4400	
Fashion Snoops Inc 39W 38th St *Web:* www.fashionsnoops.com	New York	NY	10018	212-768-8804	
Firefly 401 Merritt 7 3rd Fl. *Web:* www.fireflymb.com	Norwalk	CT	06851	203-221-0411	221-0791
Fox Lawson & Assoc LLC 1335 County Rd D Cir E *Web:* www.foxlawson.com	St Paul	MN	55109	651-635-0976	
Freedonia Group Inc, The 767 Beta Dr *Web:* freedoniagroup.com	Cleveland	OH	44143	440-684-9600	
FreeMind Group LLC 423 Brookline Ave *Web:* www.freemindconsultants.com	Boston	MA	02215	617-648-0340	
Futures Co, The 11 Madison Ave 12th flr *Web:* thefuturescompany.com	New York	NY	10010	212-896-8112	
Galloway Field Service Inc Dba Galloway Research Service 4751 Hamilton-Wolfe *Web:* gallowayresearch.com	San Antonio	TX	78229	210-734-4346	
Gallup Inc 1001 Gallup Dr *Web:* gallup.com	Omaha	NE	68102	402-951-2003	
Gallup Organization 901 F St NW *TF:* 877-242-5587 ■ *Web:* www.gallup.com	Washington	DC	20004	202-715-3030	715-3045
Gartner Inc 56 Top Gallant Rd *NYSE: IT* ■ *TF:* 800-863-8863 ■ *Web:* www.gartner.com	Stamford	CT	06902	203-964-0096	316-6300
GCG Marketing 2421 W Seventh St Ste 400 *Web:* www.gcgmarketing.com	Fort Worth	TX	76107	817-332-4600	
Geffen Mesher & Co 888 SW Fifth Ave Ste 800 *Web:* www.gmco.com	Portland	OR	97204	503-221-0141	
Genuine Interactive Inc 500 Harrison Ave 4 Fl *Web:* www.genuineinteractive.com	Boston	MA	02118	617-451-9700	
GFK Custom Research Inc 8401 Golden Vly Rd *Web:* gfk.com/us/pages/default.aspx	Minneapolis	MN	55427	763-542-0800	542-0864
Global Market Insite Inc 1100 112th Ave Ne Ste 200 *Web:* www.gmi-mr.com	Bellevue	WA	98004	206-315-9300	
Graham & Assoc 3000 Riverchase Galleria Ste 310 *Web:* www.grahammktres.com	Birmingham	AL	35244	205-443-5399	443-5389
Gravity Tank Inc 114 W Illinois St Fl 3 *Web:* www.gravitytank.com	Chicago	IL	60654	312-988-3000	
GRFI Ltd 400 E Randolph St Ste 700 *TF:* 888-856-5161 ■ *Web:* grfiltd.com	Chicago	IL	60601	888-856-5161	
Guidepoint Global LLC 730 Third Ave 11th Fl *Web:* guidepointglobal.com	New York	NY	10017	212-375-2980	
Gulf of Maine Research Institute, The 350 Commercial St *TF:* 866-447-2111 ■ *Web:* www.gmri.org	Portland	ME	04101	207-772-2321	
Harris Interactive Inc 60 Corporate Woods *NASDAQ: HPOL* ■ *TF:* 800-866-7655 ■ *Web:* www.harrisinteractive.com	Rochester	NY	14623	585-272-8400	272-7258
Harrison Edwards Inc 51 Babitt Rd *Web:* harrison-edwardspr.com	Bedford Hills	NY	10507	914-242-0010	
Harry Jernigan CPA Attorney PC 5101 Cleveland St Ste 200 *Web:* www.hjlaw.com	Virginia Beach	VA	23462	757-490-2200	
Hasd&ic 5575 Ruffin Rd Ste 225 *Web:* www.hasdic.org	San Diego	CA	92123	858-614-0200	
HCD Research Inc 260 US Hwy 202/31 Ste 1000 *Web:* www.hcdi.net	Flemington	NJ	08822	908-788-9393	
Heliae Development LLC 614 E Germann Rd *Web:* www.heliae.com	Gilbert	AZ	85297	480-424-2875	
Hotspex Inc 40 Eglinton Ave E Ste 801 *Web:* www.hotspex.biz	Toronto	ON	M4P3A2	416-487-5439	
HRA - Healthcare Research & Analytics LLC 400 Lanidex Plz *Web:* www.hraresearch.com	Parsippany	NJ	07054	973-240-1200	
HTG Peer Groups 653 Oak Rd *Web:* www.htgpeergroups.com	Harlan	IA	51537	712-744-3619	
i2E Inc 840 Research Pkwy Research Park Ste 250 *Web:* www.i2e.org	Oklahoma City	OK	73104	405-235-2305	
IBM Almaden Research Center 650 Harry Rd *Web:* www.almaden.ibm.com	San Jose	CA	95120	408-927-1080	
iCrossing Inc 300 W 57th St *Web:* www.icrossing.com	New York	NY	10019	212-649-3900	
iData Research Inc 850-777 W Broadway *Web:* www.idataresearch.net	Vancouver	BC	V5Z4J7	604-266-6933	
IMS Health Inc 901 Main Ave Ste 612 *Web:* www.imshealth.com	Norwalk	CT	06851	203-845-5200	845-5299
InBios International Inc 562 First Ave S Ste 600 *Web:* www.inbios.com	Seattle	WA	98104	206-344-5821	
Infinite Wellness Solutions 3300 Reynolda Rd *Web:* www.infinitewellnesssolutions.com	Winston Salem	NC	27106	336-725-8624	
Information Resources Inc 150 N Clinton St *TF:* 866-262-5973 ■ *Web:* www.iriworldwide.com	Chicago	IL	60661	312-726-1221	
Innovairre Communications LLC 825 Hylton Rd *Web:* www.innovairre.com	Pennsauken	NJ	08110	856-663-2500	
Instantly Inc 16501 Ventura Blvd *Web:* usamp.com	Encino	CA	91436	818-524-1218	
Institute for Corporate Productivity Inc 411 First Ave S Ste 403 *TF:* 866-375-4427 ■ *Web:* www.i4cp.com	Seattle	WA	98104	206-624-6565	
Institute for Trend Research 166 King St *Web:* www.itreconomics.com	Boscawen	NH	03303	603-796-2500	
International Communications Research 53 W Baltimore Pike *Web:* www.icrsurvey.com	Media	PA	19063	484-840-4300	840-4599

Company / Address	City	State	Zip	Phone	Fax
International Data Corp (IDC) Five Speen St *TF:* 800-343-4952 ■ *Web:* www.idcresearch.com	Framingham	MA	01701	508-872-8200	935-4015
Investment Metrics LLC Three Parklands Dr *Web:* www.invmetrics.com	Darien	CT	06820	203-662-8400	
Invoke Solutions Inc 375 Totten Pond Rd *TF:* 866-687-4367 ■ *Web:* www.invoke.com	Waltham	MA	02451	781-810-2700	810-2750
IPOfferings LLC 799 Dover St *Web:* www.ipofferings.com	Boca Raton	FL	33487	561-948-0672	
Ipsos Reid Corp 160 Bloor St E Ste 300 *Web:* www.ipsos.ca	Toronto	ON	M4W1B9	416-324-2900	
Ipsos-ASI Inc 301 Merritt 7 Corporate Pk *Web:* www.ipsos.com	Norwalk	CT	06851	203-840-3400	840-3450
Irving Burton Associates Inc 3150 Fairview Park Dr Ste 301 *Web:* www.ibacorp.us	Falls Church	VA	22042	703-575-8359	
J. Reckner Associates Inc 587 Bethlehem Pike Ste 800 *Web:* www.reckner.com	Montgomeryville	PA	18936	215-822-6220	
Jantzi-Sustainalytics Inc 215 Spadina Ave Ste 300 *Web:* www.sustainalytics.com	Toronto	ON	M5T2C7	416-861-0403	
JD Power & Assoc 2625 Townsgate Rd Ste 100 *TF:* 800-274-5372 ■ *Web:* www.jdpower.com	Westlake Village	CA	91361	805-418-8000	418-8900
Jim Jordan & Assoc LP 12941 N Fwy Ste 226 *Web:* www.jordan-associates.com	Houston	TX	77060	281-877-7009	
Kantar Group 501 Kings Hwy E Fourth Fl	Fairfield	CT	06825	203-330-5200	330-5201
Kaplan Mrd Inc 31 Chesley Rd *Web:* kaplanmrd.com	White Plains	NY	10605	914-686-1450	
Kazan, McClain, Abrams, Fernandez, Lyons & Farrise PLC Jack London Market 55 Harrison St Ste 400 *TF:* 877-995-6372 ■ *Web:* www.kazanlaw.com	Oakland	CA	94607	877-995-6372	
KL Communications Inc 50 English Plz Ste 6B *Web:* klcommunications.com	Red Bank	NJ	07701	732-224-9991	
Knowledge Works Inc 5750 Old Orchard Rd Ste 250 *TF:* 866-825-3400 ■ *Web:* www.paynetonline.com	Skokie	IL	60077	847-853-6117	
KNV Chartered Accountants LLP 200 - 15300 Croydon Dr *Web:* www.knv.com	Surrey	BC	V3S0Z5	604-536-7614	
LaneTerralever 425 S Mill Ave *Web:* terralever.com	Tempe	AZ	85281	480-839-1080	
Leger, The Research Intelligence Group 507 Pl d'Armes Ste 700 *Web:* leger360.com	Montreal	QC	H2Y2W8	514-982-2464	
Liberty Advisor Group LLC The Mercantile Exchange 30 S Wacker Dr 22nd Fl *Web:* www.libertyadvisorgroup.com	Chicago	IL	60606	312-869-9707	
Lieberman Research 98 Cutter Mill Rd *Web:* www.liebermanresearch.com	Great Neck	NY	11021	516-829-8880	829-8880
Lopez Research LLC 2269 Chestnut St Ste 202 *Web:* www.lopezresearch.com	San Francisco	CA	94123	415-894-5781	
Luth Research Inc 1365 Fourth Ave *Web:* www.luthresearch.com	San Diego	CA	92101	619-234-5884	
M/A/R/C Research 1660 Westridge Cir *TF:* 800-884-6272 ■ *Web:* www.marcresearch.com	Irving	TX	75038	972-983-0400	983-0444
m2M Strategies LLC 33 Buford Village Way Ste 329 *Web:* m2mstrategies.com	Buford	GA	30518	678-835-9080	
Maguire Associates Inc 555 Virginia Rd 5 Concord Farms Ste 201 *Web:* www.maguireassoc.com	Concord	MA	01742	978-371-1775	
Maher Duessel DL Clark Bldg 503 Martindale St Ste 600 *Web:* www.md-cpas.com	Pittsburgh	PA	15212	412-471-5500	
Maier Markey & Justic LLP 222 Bloomingdale Rd Ste 400 *Web:* mgroupusa.com	White Plains	NY	10605	914-644-9200	644-9300
Maillie LLP 1521 Concord Pike Ste 301 *Web:* www.maillie.com	Wilmington	DE	19803	302-358-2371	
Maritz Canada Inc 6900 Maritz Dr *Web:* aworldmoreloyal.com/	Mississauga	ON	L5W1L8	905-696-9400	
Maritz Inc 1375 N Hwy Dr **Fax:* Hum Res ■ *Web:* www.maritz.com	Fenton	MO	63099	636-827-4000	827-4336*
Maritz Research Inc 1355 N Hwy Dr *TF:* 877-462-7489 ■ *Web:* www.maritzresearch.com	Fenton	MO	63099	636-827-4000	
Market Decisions LLC 75 Washington Ave Ste 206 *TF:* 800-293-1538 ■ *Web:* www.marketdecisions.com	Portland	ME	04101	207-767-6440	767-8158
Market Strategies Inc 17430 College Pkwy *Web:* www.marketstrategies.com	Livonia	MI	48152	734-542-7600	542-7620
Market Track LLC 233 S Wacker Dr Ste 1801 *Web:* www.markettrack.com	Chicago	IL	60606	312-529-5102	
Marketing & Planning Systems 850 Winter St *Web:* www.mapsnet.com	Waltham	MA	02451	781-642-6277	642-9508
Marketing Analysts Inc (MAI) 7300 Carmel Executive Pk Ste 330 *Web:* www.mairesearch.com	Charlotte	NC	28226	704-405-2150	
Marketing Workshop Inc 3725 Da Vinci Ct *Web:* www.mwshop.com	Norcross	GA	30092	770-449-6767	449-6739
MarketVision Research Inc 10300 Alliance Rd Ste 200 *TF:* 800-232-4250 ■ *Web:* www.mv-research.com	Cincinnati	OH	45242	513-791-3100	794-3500
Mashwork Inc 11 W 25th St Seventh Fl *Web:* mashwork.com	New York	NY	10010	646-201-9124	
Micro-Tech Consultants Inc 1686 Jessica Pl *Web:* www.micro-techco.com	Santa Rosa	CA	95403	707-575-4820	
Millward Brown Group 33 Bloor St E Ste 701 *Web:* www.millwardbrown.com	Toronto	ON	M4W3H1	203-330-2581	

Company	City	State	ZIP	Phone	Fax
Millward Brown IntelliQuest 11 Madison Ave 12th Fl *Web:* www.millwardbrown.com	New York	NY	10010	212-548-7200	548-7201
MinoTech Engineering Inc JRD Technology Ctr 242 Sturbridge Rd *Web:* www.minotecheng.com	Charlton	MA	01507	978-474-8034	
Modellers LLC, The 6995 Union Park Ctr Ste 300 *Web:* www.themodellers.com	Salt Lake City	UT	84047	801-290-3800	
Monterey Technologies Inc 24600 Silver Cloud Court Ste 103 *Web:* www.montereytechnologies.com	Monterey	CA	93940	831-648-0190	
MORPACE International Inc 31700 Middlebelt Rd Ste 200 *TF General:* 800-881-1723 ■ *Web:* www.morpace.com	Farmington Hills	MI	48334	248-737-5300	737-5326
MP2 Energy Texas LLC 21 Waterway Ave Ste 500 *Web:* www.mp2energy.com	The Woodlands	TX	77380	832-510-1030	
Mustel Research Group Ltd 1505 W Second Ave Ste 402 *Web:* www.mustelgroup.com	Vancouver	BC	V6H3Y4	604-733-4213	
National Research Corp 1245 Q St *NASDAQ: NRCI* ■ *TF:* 800-388-4264 ■ *Web:* www.nationalresearch.com	Lincoln	NE	68508	402-475-2525	475-9061
Neal Analytics LLC 3240 Eastlake Ave E Ste 104 *Web:* www.nealanalytics.com	Seattle	WA	98102	206-286-9200	
Netpop Research LLC 322 Cortland Ave *Web:* netpop.com	San Francisco	CA	94110	415-647-1007	
New Home Trends Inc 4314 148th St SE *Web:* www.newhometrends.com	Bothell	WA	98012	425-742-8040	
News Generation Inc 7508 Wisconsin Ave Ste 300 *Web:* newsgeneration.com	Bethesda	MD	20814	301-664-6448	
Nichols Research Inc 333 W El Camino Real *Web:* nicholsresearch.com	Sunnyvale	CA	94087	408-773-8200	
NineSigma Inc 23611 Chagrin Blvd Ste 320 *Web:* ninesigma.com	Cleveland	OH	44122	216-295-4800	
Norman Hecht Research Inc 33 Queens St Third Fl *Web:* www.normanhechtresearch.com	Syosset	NY	11791	516-496-8866	
NPD Group Inc 900 W Shore Rd *TF:* 866-444-1411 ■ *Web:* www.npd.com	Port Washington	NY	11050	516-625-0700	625-2444
OnCard Marketing Inc 276 Fifth Ave Ste 608 *TF:* 866-996-8729 ■ *Web:* www.revtrax.com	New York	NY	10001	866-996-8729	
OneMedPlace 219 E 83rd St 4 Fl *Web:* www.onemedplace.com	New York	NY	10028	212-734-1008	
Open Minds 163 York St *Web:* www.openminds.com	Gettysburg	PA	17325	717-334-1329	
Opinion Research Corp (ORC) 902 Carnegie Ctr Ste 220 **Fax Area Code:* 609 ■ *TF:* 800-444-4672 ■ *Web:* www.orcinternational.com	Princeton	NJ	08540	800-444-4672	419-1892*
Opinionology Inc 701 East Timpanogos Pkwy Bldg M *Web:* www.westernwats.com	Orem	UT	84097	801-373-7735	
Pert Group Inc, The 270 Farmington Ave Ste 200 *Web:* thepertgroup.com	Farmington	CT	06032	860-242-2005	
Point Group, The 5949 Sherry Ln Ste 1800 *Web:* www.thepointgroup.com	Dallas	TX	75225	214-378-7970	378-7967
PQ Media LLC Two Stamford Landing Ste 100 *Web:* www.pqmedia.com	Stamford	CT	06902	203-921-0368	
Pragati Synergetic Research Inc 801 Moffett Blvd NASA Research Park NASA Ames Research Ctr MS 19-46Q Ste 1010 *Web:* www.pragati-inc.com	Moffett Field	CA	94035	650-625-0274	
PredictWallStreet LLC 1840 41st Ave Ste 102-171 *Web:* www.predictwallstreet.com	Capitola	CA	95010	831-464-0308	
PreTesting Group 38 Franklin St *Web:* www.pretesting.com	Tenafly	NJ	07670	201-569-4800	
PriMetrica Inc 5927 Priestly Dr Ste 111 *Web:* www.primetrica.com	Carlsbad	CA	92008	760-651-0030	
Princeton Survey Research Assoc 600 Alexander Rd *Web:* psrai.com	Princeton	NJ	08540	609-924-9204	
Prinzo Group, The 11260 Deerfield Pkwy Ste 100 *Web:* www.prinzogroup.com	Alpharetta	GA	30004	678-496-4615	
Pro-Tech Energy Solutions LLC 3322 Rt 22 W Bldg No 15 Ste 1502 *Web:* www.pro-techenergy.com	Branchburg	NJ	08876	908-526-3322	
Propane Resources LLC 6950 Squibb Rd Ste 306 *Web:* www.propaneresources.com	Mission	KS	66201	913-262-8345	
Public Partnerships LLC 40 Broad St Fourth Fl *Web:* www.publicpartnerships.com	Boston	MA	02109	617-426-2026	
RateHub.ca 103 Balliol St *TF:* 800-679-9622 ■ *Web:* www.ratehub.ca	Toronto	ON	M4S1C8	800-679-9622	
RDA Group 450 Enterprise Ct *TF:* 800-669-7324 ■ *Web:* www.rdagroup.com	Bloomfield Hills	MI	48302	248-332-5000	332-4168
RealityCheck Inc 2033 N Geyer Rd *Web:* www.realitycheckinc.com	Saint Louis	MO	63131	314-909-9095	
Reis Inc 530 Fifth Ave Fifth Fl *NASDAQ: REIS* ■ *TF:* 800-366-7347 ■ *Web:* www.reis.com	New York	NY	10036	212-921-1122	921-2533
REPUCOM America LLC 422 Summer St *Web:* www.repucom.net	Stamford	CT	06901	203-975-9000	
Reputation Institute Inc 55 Broad St *Web:* reputationinstitute.com	New York	NY	10004	212-495-3855	
Research Director Inc 914 Bay Ridge Rd Ste 215 *Web:* www.researchdirectorinc.com	Annapolis	MD	21403	410-295-6619	268-1915
Research Solutions Inc 5435 Balboa Blvd Ste 202 *Web:* www.reprintsdesk.com	Encino	CA	91316	310-477-0354	
Rincon Research Corp 101 N Wilmot Rd Ste 101 *Web:* rincon.com	Tucson	AZ	85711	520-519-4600	519-4747
Robert d Niehaus Inc 140 E Carrillo St *Web:* www.rdniehaus.com	Santa Barbara	CA	93101	805-962-0611	
Robert Hale & Assoc 5405 Morehouse Dr Ste 327 *Web:* www.roberthaleassociates.com	San Diego	CA	92121	858-404-0200	
Rockwood Service Corp 43 Arch St *Web:* www.rockwoodservice.com	Greenwich	CT	06830	203-869-6734	
Roland|Criss 2011 E Lamar Blvd Ste 150 *Web:* rolandcriss.com	Arlington	TX	76006	817-861-7963	
RRC Associates Inc 4940 Pearl E Cir Ste 103 *Web:* rrcassoc.com	Boulder	CO	80301	303-449-6558	
Ruf Strategic Solutions 1533 E Spruce St *Web:* www.ruf.com	Olathe	KS	66061	913-782-8544	
S2 Statistical Solutions Inc 11176 Main St *Web:* www.s2stats.com	Cincinnati	OH	45241	513-247-0561	
Salient Corp 203 Colonial Dr *Web:* www.salient.com	Horseheads	NY	14845	607-739-4511	
Sapphire Technologies Inc 6660 Taylor Dr Ste 105 *Web:* www.sapphiretech.org	Red Deer	AB	T4P1Y3	403-341-6284	
Savitz Research Solutions 13747 Montfort Dr Ste 211 *Web:* www.savitzresearch.com	Dallas	TX	75240	972-386-4050	661-3198
Scanner Applications Inc 400 Milford Pkwy *Web:* www.scanapps.com	Milford	OH	45150	513-248-5588	
Schulman Ronca & Bucuvalas Inc 275 Seventh Ave Ste 2700 *Web:* www.srbi.com	New York	NY	10001	212-779-7700	779-7785
SCRI International Inc 2023 N Atlantic Ave Ste 310 *Web:* www.scri.com	Cocoa Beach	FL	32931	321-868-8273	
Secret Ingredient Marketing 217 Knight Dr *Web:* www.secretingredientmarketing.com	San Rafael	CA	94901	415-963-4000	
Segmedica Inc 305 S First St Ste 120 *Web:* segmedica.com	Lewiston	NY	14092	716-754-8744	
Select Sales & Mktg Inc 549 Mercury Ln	Brea	CA	92821	714-990-3755	
Seneca Consulting Group Inc 68 S Service Rd Ste 100 *Web:* www.senecaconsulting.com	Melville	NY	11747	631-577-4092	
Shapard Research LLC 820 Ne 63rd St Uppr E *Web:* www.shapard.com	Oklahoma City	OK	73105	405-607-4664	
Sheiness, Glover & Grossman LLP 4544 Post Oak Pl Dr Ste 270 *Web:* www.sgglawyers.com	Houston	TX	77027	713-374-7000	
Smith Travel Research Inc 735 E Main St *Web:* www.str.com	Hendersonville	TN	37075	615-824-8664	
SPI Lasers 4000 Burton Dr *Web:* www.spioptics.com	Santa Clara	CA	95054	408-454-1170	
Standards Council of Canada 270 Albert St Ste 200 *TF:* 800-844-6790 ■ *Web:* www.scc.ca	Ottawa	ON	K1P6N7	613-238-3222	
Strategic Analysis Inc 4075 Wilson Blvd Ste 200 *Web:* www.sainc.com	Arlington	VA	22203	703-527-5410	527-5445
Strategy Institute 401 Richmond St W Ste 401 *TF:* 866-298-9343 ■ *Web:* www.strategyinstitute.com	Toronto	ON	M5V3A8	416-944-9200	
Stratus Consulting Inc 1881 Ninth St Ste 201 *Web:* www.stratusconsulting.com	Boulder	CO	80302	303-381-8000	
Strong & Hanni 102 South 200 East Ste 800 *Web:* www.strongandhanni.com	Salt Lake City	UT	84111	801-532-7080	
SuperData Research Inc 116 W 23rd St Fifth Fl *Web:* www.superdataresearch.com	New York	NY	10011	646-375-2273	
Survey Service Inc 1911 Sheridan Dr *Web:* www.surveyservice.com	Buffalo	NY	14223	716-876-6450	
Synovate Inc 222 S Riverside Plz	Chicago	IL	60606	312-526-4000	526-4099
Topspin Group Inc 415 Executive Dr *Web:* topspingroup.com	Princeton	NJ	08540	609-252-9515	
TRC Holdings Inc 1300 Virginia Dr Ste 200 *Web:* www.trchome.com	Fort Washington	PA	19034	215-641-2200	
TrendSource Inc 4891 Pacific Hwy Ste 200 *Web:* www.trendsource.com	San Diego	CA	92110	619-718-7467	
Uniform Industrial Corp 47436 Fremont Blvd *Web:* uicworld.com	Fremont	CA	94538	510-438-6799	
Unity Marketing Inc 206 E Church St *Web:* www.unitymarketingonline.com	Stevens	PA	17578	717-336-1600	
Urban Icons Marketing Inc 46 NW 36th St Loft 4 *Web:* www.urbaniconsmarketing.com	Miami	FL	33127	305-438-0107	
Verance Corp 4435 Eastgate Mall Ste 350 *Web:* verance.com	San Diego	CA	92121	858-202-2800	
VGMarket LLC 3860 Sheridan St Ste B *Web:* www.vgmarket.com	Hollywood	FL	33021	650-483-8384	
W5 Inc 3211 Shannon Rd *Web:* w5insight.com	Durham	NC	27707	919-932-1117	
Walker Information Inc 301 Pennsylvania Pkwy *TF:* 800-334-3939 ■ *Web:* www.walkerinfo.com	Indianapolis	IN	46280	317-843-3939	843-8584
Wendover Corp 130 S State Rd *Web:* www.wendovercorp.com	Upper Darby	PA	19082	610-449-2056	
West Technology Research Solutions LLC 2247A Old Middlefield Way *Web:* www.wtrs.net	Mountain View	CA	94043	650-940-1196	
Westat Inc 1600 Research Blvd *TF:* 800-669-6820 ■ *Web:* www.westat.com	Rockville	MD	20850	301-251-1500	294-2040

Phone | Fax

Wiese Research Associates Inc
9375 Burt St Ste 100 ... Omaha NE 68114 402-391-7734
Web: www.wraresearch.com

Wilkins Research Services LLC
1730 Gunbarrel Rd ... Chattanooga TN 37421 423-894-9478
Web: www.wilkinsresearch.net

WTI Inc 3737 E Broadway Rd ... Phoenix AZ 85040 602-437-8979
Web: www.wticompanies.com

Xpera Inc 153 N Hwy 101 Ste 103 ... Solana Beach CA 92075 858-436-7770
Web: www.xperagroup.com

XtremeEDA Corp 201-1339 Wellington St W ... Ottawa ON K1Y3B8 613-728-5912
TF: 800-586-0280 ■ *Web:* www.xtreme-eda.com

Zagada Markets Inc
Caribbean Commercial Bldg 145 Giralda Ave
... Coral Gables FL 33133 305-529-9028
Web: www.zagada.com

Zolato Inc 2801 First Ave Ste 306 ... Seattle WA 98121 866-557-6716
TF: 866-557-6716 ■ *Web:* www.discuss.io

470 MARKING DEVICES

Phone | Fax

American Marking Systems Inc
1015 Paulison Ave PO Box 1677 ... Clifton NJ 07011 973-478-5600 478-0039
TF: 800-782-6766 ■ *Web:* www.ams-stamps.com

Automark Marking Systems
13475 Lakefront Dr ... Earth City MO 63045 314-739-0430 739-1483
TF: 888-777-2303 ■ *Web:* www.automark.com

Cable Markers Company Inc 13805-C Alton Pkwy ... Irvine CA 92618 800-746-7655 699-1642*
**Fax Area Code:* 949 ■ *TF:* 800-746-7655 ■ *Web:* www.cablemarkers.com

Carco Inc 10333 Shoemaker PO Box 13859 ... Detroit MI 48213 313-925-9000 925-9602
Web: www.carcousa.com

CH Hanson Co 2000 N Aurora Rd ... Naperville IL 60563 630-848-2000 848-2515
TF: 800-827-3398 ■ *Web:* www.chhanson.com

Cosco Industries Inc
7220 W Wilson Ave ... Harwood Heights IL 60706 708-867-5800 323-0275*
**Fax Area Code:* 800 ■ *TF:* 800-296-8970 ■ *Web:* www.coscoindustries.com

DM Stamps & Specialties Inc
1101 N Riverfront Dr PO Box 1029 ... Mankato MN 56001 507-387-4444 387-4447
Web: dmstampsdiv.com

Excelsior Marking Products 888 W Waterloo Rd ... Akron OH 44314 330-745-2300 745-2333
TF: 800-433-3615 ■ *Web:* www.excelsiormarking.com

Hampton Technologies LLC 19 Scouting Blvd ... Medford NY 11763 631-924-1335
Web: www.hamptontech.net

Hitt Marking Devices Inc
3231 W MacArthur Blvd ... Santa Ana CA 92704 714-979-1405 979-1407
TF: 800-969-6699 ■ *Web:* www.hittmarking.com

Huntington Park Rubber Stamp
2761 E Slauson Ave PO Box 519 ... Huntington Park CA 90255 323-582-6461 582-8046
TF: 800-882-0029 ■ *Web:* www.hprubberstamp.com

Industrial Marking Products 1415 Grovenburg Rd ... Holt MI 48842 517-699-2160 699-1505
Web: www.industrialmarking.com

Infosight Corp PO Box 5000 ... Chillicothe OH 45601 740-642-3600 642-5001
TF: 800-401-0716 ■ *Web:* www.infosight.com

Jackson Marking Products Co
9105 N Rainbow Ln ... Mount Vernon IL 62864 618-242-1334 242-7732
TF: 800-782-6722 ■ *Web:* www.rubber-stamp.com

JP Nissen Co 2544 Fairhill Ave PO Box 339 ... Glenside PA 19038 215-886-2025 886-0707
Web: www.nissenmarkers.com

Krengel Enterprises 121 Fulton St ... New York NY 10038 212-239-6677 239-0041

La-Co/Markal Co 1201 Pratt Blvd ... Elk Grove Village IL 60007 847-956-7600 448-5436*
**Fax Area Code:* 800 ■ *TF:* 800-621-4025 ■ *Web:* www.laco.com

Matthews International Corp Marking Products Div
6515 Penn Ave ... Pittsburgh PA 15206 412-665-2500 665-2550
TF: 800-775-7775 ■ *Web:* www.matthewsmarking.com

Menke Marking Devices
13253 Alondra Blvd PO Box 2986 ... Santa Fe Springs CA 90670 562-921-1380 921-1184
TF: 800-231-6023 ■ *Web:* www.menkemarking.com

New Method Steel Stamps Inc 31313 Kendall Ave ... Fraser MI 48026 586-293-0200 296-1900
TF: 800-582-0199 ■ *Web:* www.newmethod.org

Norwood Marking Systems
2538 Wisconsin Ave ... Downers Grove IL 60515 630-968-0646 968-7672
TF: 800-626-3464 ■ *Web:* itwnorwood.com

Saint Paul Stamp Works Inc 87 Empire Dr ... Saint Paul MN 55103 651-222-2100 228-1314
Web: www.stpaulstamp.com

Schwaab Inc 11415 W Burleigh St ... Milwaukee WI 53222 414-771-4150 935-9866*
**Fax Area Code:* 800 ■ *TF:* 800-935-9877 ■ *Web:* www.schwaab.com

Schwerdtle Stamp Co 166 Elm St ... Bridgeport CT 06604 203-330-2750 330-2760
TF: 800-535-0004 ■ *Web:* www.schwerdtle.com

Signet Marking Devices 3121 Red Hill Ave ... Costa Mesa CA 92626 714-549-0341 549-0972
TF: 800-421-5150 ■ *Web:* www.signetmarking.com

Stamp-Rite Inc 154 S Larch St ... Lansing MI 48912 517-487-5071 487-6211
TF: 800-328-1988 ■ *Web:* www.stamprite.com

Tacoma Rubber Stamp & Sign 919 Market St ... Tacoma WA 98402 253-383-5433 383-0649
TF: 800-544-7281 ■ *Web:* www.tacomarubberstamp.com

Volk Corp 23936 Industrial Pk Dr ... Farmington Hills MI 48335 248-477-6700 478-6884
TF Cust Svc: 800-521-6799 ■ *Web:* www.volkcorp.com

Wendell's Inc
6601 Bunker Lk Blvd NW PO Box 458 ... Ramsey MN 55303 763-576-8200 576-0995
TF: 800-936-3355 ■ *Web:* www.wendellsinc.com

471 MASS TRANSPORTATION (LOCAL & SUBURBAN)

SEE ALSO Bus Services - Intercity & Rural p. 1891

Phone | Fax

Alameda-Contra Costa Transit District
1600 Franklin St 10th Fl ... Oakland CA 94612 510-891-4777 891-4705*
**Fax:* Cust Svc ■ *TF:* 877-878-8883 ■ *Web:* www.actransit.org

Alaska Marine Highway System
6858 Glacier Hwy PO Box 112505 ... Juneau AK 99801 907-465-3941 465-2476
TF: 800-642-0066 ■ *Web:* www.dot.state.ak.us/amhs

Altamont Commuter Express (ACE) 949 E Ch St ... Stockton CA 95202 800-411-7245 944-6273*
**Fax Area Code:* 209 ■ *TF:* 800-411-7245 ■ *Web:* www.acerail.com

Ann Arbor Transportation Authority
2700 S Industrial Hwy ... Ann Arbor MI 48104 734-973-6500 973-6338
Web: www.theride.org

Bay Area Rapid Transit District
300 Lakeside Dr ... Oakland CA 94612 510-464-6000 464-7175*
**Fax:* Mktg ■ *Web:* www.bart.gov

BC Transit 520 Gorge Rd E ... Victoria BC V8W2P3 250-385-2551 995-5639
Web: www.bctransit.com

Bi-State Development Agency
707 N First St ... Saint Louis MO 63102 314-982-1400 923-3019*
**Fax:* Cust Svc ■ *Web:* www.metrostlouis.org

Bonneville Transloaders Inc (BTI)
642 S Federal Blvd ... Riverton WY 82501 307-856-7480 856-4623
Web: www.bonntran.com

Caledonia Haulers LLC
420 W Lincoln St PO Box 31 ... Caledonia MN 55921 507-725-9000 725-9015
TF: 800-325-4728 ■ *Web:* www.caledoniahaulers.com

Cape Cod Regional Transit Authority (CCRTA)
215 Iyannough Rd PO Box 1988 ... Hyannis MA 02601 508-775-8504 775-8513
TF: 800-352-7155 ■ *Web:* www.capecodtransit.org

Capital District Transportation Authority (CDTA)
110 Watervliet Ave ... Albany NY 12206 518-482-8822 437-8318
Web: www.cdta.org

Catalina Express Berth 95 ... San Pedro CA 90731 310-519-7971 548-8425
TF: 800-481-3470 ■ *Web:* www.catalinaexpress.com

Central Florida Regional Transportation Authority (Inc)
455 N Garland Ave ... Orlando FL 32801 407-841-2279
Web: www.golynx.com

Central New York Regional Transportation Authority
200 Cortland Ave ... Syracuse NY 13205 315-442-3400 442-3337
Web: www.centro.org

Central Ohio Transit Authority (COTA)
33 N High St ... Columbus OH 43215 614-228-1776 275-5933
Web: www.cota.com

Central Puget Sound Regional Transit Authority
401 S Jackson St ... Seattle WA 98104 206-398-5000 689-3360*
**Fax:* Hum Res ■ *TF:* 800-201-4900 ■ *Web:* www.soundtransit.org

Champaign-Urbana Mass Transit District
1101 E University Ave ... Urbana IL 61802 217-384-8188 384-8215
Web: www.cumtd.com

Charleston Area Regional Transportation Authority (CARTA)
36 John St ... Charleston SC 29403 843-724-7304
Web: www.ridecarta.com

Chicago Transit Authority (CTA) 567 W Lake St ... Chicago IL 60661 312-664-7200 681-2725*
**Fax:* Cust Svc ■ *Web:* www.transitchicago.com

Cliff Viessman Inc 215 First Ave PO Box 175 ... Gary SD 57237 605-272-5241 272-5546
TF: 800-328-2408 ■ *Web:* www.viessmantrucking.com

Connecticut Transit 100 Leibert Rd ... Hartford CT 06141 860-522-8101 247-1810
Web: www.cttransit.com

Dallas Area Rapid Transit Authority (DART)
1401 Pacific Ave PO Box 660163 ... Dallas TX 75202 214-749-3278 749-3661
Web: www.dart.org

Delaware Transit Corp
119 Lower Beach St Ste 100 ... Wilmington DE 19805 302-576-6000 577-6066
TF: 800-652-3278 ■ *Web:* www.dartfirststate.com

Erie Metropolitan Transit Authority (EMTA)
127 E 14th St ... Erie PA 16503 814-452-3515
Web: www.ride-the-e.com

Escambia County Area Transit (ECAT)
1515 W Fairfield Dr ... Pensacola FL 32501 850-595-3228 595-3222
Web: www.goecat.com

Fort Wayne Public Transportation Corp
801 Leesburg Rd ... Fort Wayne IN 46808 260-432-4546 436-7729
Web: www.fwcitilink.com

Fresno Area Express 2223 G St ... Fresno CA 93706 559-621-7433 488-1065
Web: www.fresno.gov

GO Transit 20 Bay St Ste 600 ... Toronto ON M5J2W3 416-869-3200 869-3525
Web: www.gotransit.com

Gold Coast Transit (GCT) 301 E Third St ... Oxnard CA 93030 805-487-4222 487-0925
Web: www.goldcoasttransit.org

Golden Empire Transit District
1830 Golden State Ave ... Bakersfield CA 93301 661-324-9874 869-6394
Web: www.getbus.org

Greater Cleveland Regional Transit Authority (RTA)
1240 W Sixth St ... Cleveland OH 44113 216-566-5285 781-4483
Web: www.riderta.com

Greater Peoria Mass Transit District
2105 NE Jefferson St ... Peoria IL 61603 309-676-4040 676-8373
Web: www.ridecitylink.org

Greater Portland Transit District
114 Valley St ... Portland ME 04102 207-774-0351 774-6241
Web: gpmetrobus.net

Greater Vancouver Transportation Authority
4720 Kingsway Ste 1600 ... Burnaby BC V5H4N2 604-453-4500 453-4626
Web: www.translink.ca

GRTC Transit System 301 E Belt Blvd ... Richmond VA 23224 804-358-3871 342-1933
Web: www.ridegrtc.com

Honolulu Dept of Transportation Services
650 S King St Third Fl ... Honolulu HI 96813 808-768-8303 768-4954
Web: www1.honolulu.gov

Horizon Freight System Inc
6600 Bessemer Ave ... Cleveland OH 44127 216-341-7410 429-3523
TF: 800-480-6829 ■ *Web:* www.horizonfreightsystem.com

Idaho Milk Transport Inc PO Box 1185 ... Burley ID 83318 208-878-5000 878-5001
Web: www.idahomilktransport.com

Inter-Urban Transit Partnership
300 Ellsworth St SW ... Grand Rapids MI 49503 616-776-1100 456-1941
Web: www.ridetherapid.org

Intermodal Cartage Co Inc 5707 E Holmes Rd ... Memphis TN 38141 901-363-0050 432-6174
Web: www.imcg.com

Company / Address	City	State	ZIP	Phone	Fax
Karl's Transport Inc PO Box 333	Antigo	WI	54409	715-623-2033	623-2791
TF: 800-922-8707 ■ *Web:* www.karlstransport.com					
King County Dept of Transportation 201 S Jackson St	Seattle	WA	98104	206-684-1481	684-1224
Web: www.kingcounty.gov					
Los Angeles County Metropolitan Transportation Authority One Gateway Plz	Los Angeles	CA	90012	213-922-6000	
TF: 800-621-7828 ■ *Web:* www.metro.net					
Maryland Transit Administration (MTA) 6 St Paul St	Baltimore	MD	21202	410-539-5000	333-3279
Web: www.mta.maryland.gov					
Massachusetts Bay Transportation Authority (MBTA) 10 Pk Plaza Ste 3910	Boston	MA	02116	617-222-5000	222-3340*
**Fax:* Mktg ■ *Web:* www.mbta.com					
Memphis Area Transit Authority (MATA) 1370 Levee Rd	Memphis	TN	38108	901-722-7100	722-7123
Web: www.matatransit.com					
Metro Transit 200 Ilsley Ave	Dartmouth	NS	B3B1V1	902-490-4000	490-6688
Web: www.halifax.ca/metrotransit					
Metropolitan Atlanta Rapid Transit Authority (MARTA) 2424 Piedmont Rd NE	Atlanta	GA	30324	404-848-5000	
Web: www.itsmarta.com					
Metropolitan Transit Authority of Harris County 1900 Maine	Houston	TX	77002	713-739-4000	739-4096
Web: ridemetro.org/news/emergencyalerts/default.aspx					
Miami-Dade Transit (MDTA) 701 NW First Ct	Miami	FL	33136	305-468-5402	469-5580*
**Fax Area Code:* 786 ■ *Web:* miamidade.gov					
Milwaukee County Transit System 1942 N 17th St	Milwaukee	WI	53205	414-343-1700	343-1787*
**Fax:* Hum Res ■ *Web:* www.ridemcts.com					
Mission Petroleum Carriers Inc 8450 Mosley	Houston	TX	77075	713-943-8250	944-6080
TF: 800-737-9911 ■ *Web:* www.mipe.com					
Monterey-Salinas Transit (MST) One Ryan Ranch Rd	Monterey	CA	93940	831-899-2555	
Web: www.mst.org					
MV Transportation Inc 5910 N Central Expy Ste 1145	Dallas	TX	75206	972-391-4600	863-8944*
**Fax Area Code:* 707 ■ *Web:* www.mvtransit.com					
New Jersey Transit Corp One Penn Plz E	Newark	NJ	07105	973-491-7000	491-8247*
**Fax:* Cust Svc ■ *TF Cust Svc:* 800-772-3606 ■ *Web:* www.njtransit.com					
Niagara Frontier Transit Metro System Inc 181 Ellicott St Ste 1	Buffalo	NY	14203	716-855-7300	856-2524
TF: 877-294-9434					
Norfolk Southern Corp 3 Commercial Pl	Norfolk	VA	23510	855-667-3655	629-2361*
NYSE: NSC ■ **Fax Area Code:* 757 ■ **Fax:* Mktg ■ *TF Cust Svc:* 800-635-5768 ■ *Web:* www.nscorp.com					
North County Transit District (NCTD) 810 Mission Rd	Oceanside	CA	92054	760-966-6500	967-2001
Web: www.gonctd.com					
Northeast Illinois Regional Commuter Railroad Corp 547 W Jackson Blvd	Chicago	IL	60661	312-322-6777	322-6747*
**Fax:* Mktg ■ *Web:* www.metrarail.com					
Northern Indiana Commuter Transportation District 33 E US Hwy 12	Chesterton	IN	46304	219-926-5744	929-4438
TF: 800-323-5281 ■ *Web:* www.nictd.com					
Norwalk Transit District (NTD) 275 Wilson Ave	Norwalk	CT	06854	203-852-0000	853-6761
Web: www.norwalktransit.com					
Oahu Transit Services 811 Middle St	Honolulu	HI	96819	808-848-4500	848-4419
Web: www.thebus.org					
Office Movers Inc 6500 Kane Way	Elkridge	MD	21075	410-799-7704	799-3208
TF: 800-331-4025 ■ *Web:* www.officemovers.com					
Orange County Transportation Authority 550 S Main St PO Box 14184	Orange	CA	92863	714-560-6282	560-5899
Web: www.octa.net					
Pace Suburban Bus 550 W Algonquin Rd	Arlington Heights	IL	60005	847-364-8130	364-7236*
**Fax:* Cust Svc ■ *Web:* www.pacebus.com					
Packard Transport Inc 24021 S Municipal Dr PO Box 380	Channahon	IL	60410	815-467-9260	467-6939
TF: 800-467-9260 ■ *Web:* www.packardtransport.com					
Pierce Transit 3701 96th St SW PO Box 99070	Lakewood	WA	98499	253-581-8000	581-8075
TF: 800-562-8109 ■ *Web:* www.piercetransit.org					
Port Authority of Allegheny County 345 Sixth Ave Third Fl	Pittsburgh	PA	15222	412-566-5500	566-5406*
**Fax:* Cust Svc ■ *Web:* www.portauthority.org					
Regional Transit Authority (RTA) 2817 Canal St	New Orleans	LA	70118	504-827-8300	
Web: www.norta.com					
Regional Transit Service Inc 1372 E Main St	Rochester	NY	14609	585-654-0200	352-4596*
**Fax Area Code:* 951 ■ *Web:* www.myrts.com					
Regional Transit System (RTS) Station 5 PO Box 490	Gainesville	FL	32627	352-334-2600	334-2607
Web: www.go-rts.com					
Regional Transportation Authority 175 W Jackson Blvd Ste 1550	Chicago	IL	60604	312-913-3200	913-3206
Web: www.rtachicago.com					
Regional Transportation Commission of Southern Nevada (RTC) 600 S Grand Central Pkwy Ste 350	Las Vegas	NV	89106	702-676-1500	676-1518
TF: 800-228-3911 ■ *Web:* www.rtcsouthernnevada.com					
Regional Transportation District (RTD) 1600 Blake St	Denver	CO	80202	303-628-9000	299-2015
TF: 800-366-7433 ■ *Web:* www.rtd-denver.com					
Reliable Carriers Inc 41555 Koppernick Rd	Canton	MI	48187	734-453-6677	453-8609
TF: 800-521-6393 ■ *Web:* www.reliablecarriers.com					
Reliable Transportation Specialists Inc 139 Venturi Dr	Chesterton	IN	46304	219-926-8850	926-5174
Web: www.reliabletrans.com					
Rhode Island Public Transit Authority 265 Melrose St	Providence	RI	02907	401-781-9400	784-9595
Web: www.ripta.com					
Riverside Transit Agency (RTA) 1825 Third St PO Box 59968	Riverside	CA	92517	951-565-5000	684-1007
TF: 800-800-7821 ■ *Web:* www.riversidetransit.com					
Sacramento Regional Transit District 1400 29th St	Sacramento	CA	95816	916-321-2800	444-2156
Web: www.sacrt.com					
San Diego Transit Corp 100 16th St	San Diego	CA	92101	619-238-0100	696-5241
San Mateo County Transit District 1250 San Carlos Ave PO Box 3006	San Carlos	CA	94070	650-508-6200	508-6443
TF: 800-660-4287 ■ *Web:* www.smctd.com					
Santa Barbara Metropolitan Transit District 550 Olive St	Santa Barbara	CA	93101	805-963-3364	962-4794
Web: www.sbmtd.gov					
Santa Clara Valley Transportation Authority (VTA) 3331 N First St	San Jose	CA	95134	408-321-5555	
TF: 800-894-9908 ■ *Web:* www.vta.org					
Sonoma County Transit 355 W Robles Ave	Santa Rosa	CA	95407	707-585-7516	585-7713
TF: 800-345-7433 ■ *Web:* www.sctransit.com					
Southeastern Pennsylvania Transportation Authority (SEPTA) 1234 Market St	Philadelphia	PA	19107	215-580-7800	
Web: www.septa.org					
Southern California Regional Rail Authority 700 S Flower St Ste 2600	Los Angeles	CA	90017	213-452-0200	452-0429
TF: 800-371-5465 ■ *Web:* www.metrolinktrains.com					
Steamship Authority PO Box 284	Woods Hole	MA	02543	508-548-5011	548-8410
Web: www.steamshipauthority.com					
Suburban Mobility Authority for Regional Transportation (SMART) 535 Griswold St Ste 600 Buhl Bldg	Detroit	MI	48226	313-223-2100	
TF: 866-962-5515 ■ *Web:* www.smartbus.org					
TLD Distribution Company LLC 505 S Seventh Ave	City of Industry	CA	91746	310-324-5111	516-3960
Toronto Transit Commission (TTC) 1900 Yonge St	Toronto	ON	M4S1Z2	416-393-4000	338-0128*
**Fax:* PR ■ *Web:* www.ttc.ca					
Transcare Corp 1 Metrotech Ctr	Brooklyn	NY	11201	718-763-8888	209-1381
Web: www.transcare.com					
Transit Authority of River City (TARC) 1000 W Broadway	Louisville	KY	40203	502-585-1234	213-3243*
Tri-County Commuter Rail Authority 800 NW 33rd St Ste 100	Pompano Beach	FL	33064	954-942-7245	788-7878
Web: www.tri-rail.com					
Tri-County Metropolitan Transportation District of Oregon 4012 SE 17th Ave	Portland	OR	97202	503-962-5806	962-6469*
**Fax:* Mktg ■ *Web:* www.trimet.org					
Triangle Transit Authority PO Box 13787	Research Triangle Park	NC	27709	919-549-9999	485-7441
Web: www.triangletransit.org					
Utah Transit Authority 3600 S 700 W PO Box 30810	Salt Lake City	UT	84130	801-262-5626	
TF: 888-743-3882 ■ *Web:* www.rideuta.com					
VIA Metropolitan Transit 800 W Myrtle St	San Antonio	TX	78212	210-362-2000	362-2563*
**Fax:* Cust Svc ■ *TF:* 866-362-4200 ■ *Web:* www.viainfo.net					
Virginia Railway Express (VRE) 1500 King St Ste 202	Alexandria	VA	22314	703-684-1001	684-1313
TF: 800-743-3873 ■ *Web:* www.vre.org					
VPSI Inc 1220 Rankin Dr	Troy	MI	48083	248-597-3500	597-3501
TF: 800-826-7433 ■ *Web:* www.vride.com					
Washington Metropolitan Area Transit Authority 600 Fifth St NW	Washington	DC	20001	202-637-7000	962-6103
Web: www.wmata.com					
Westchester County Dept of Transportation 100 E First St	Mount Vernon	NY	10550	914-813-7777	813-7735
Web: www.co.westchester.ny.us/transportation					
Worcester Regional Transit Authority 287 Grove St	Worcester	MA	01605	508-791-9782	752-3153*
**Fax:* Cust Svc ■ *Web:* therta.com					
York County Transportation Authority 1230 Roosevelt Ave	York	PA	17404	717-846-5562	848-4853
TF: 800-632-9063 ■ *Web:* www.rabbittransit.org					

472 MATCHES & MATCHBOOKS

Company / Address	City	State	ZIP	Phone	Fax
DD Bean & Sons Co 207 Peterborough St	Jaffrey	NH	03452	603-532-8311	532-6001*
**Fax:* Sales ■ *TF:* 800-366-2824 ■ *Web:* www.ddbean.com					
Maryland Match Corp 605 Alluvion St	Baltimore	MD	21230	410-752-8164	752-3441
TF: 800-423-0013 ■ *Web:* www.marylandmatch.com					
Universal Creative Concepts Corp 10143 Royalton Rd Unit E	North Royalton	OH	44133	440-230-1366	230-1919
TF: 800-876-8626 ■ *Web:* www.uccpromo.com					

473 MATERIAL HANDLING EQUIPMENT

SEE ALSO Conveyors & Conveying Equipment p. 2165

Company / Address	City	State	ZIP	Phone	Fax
4Front Engineered Solutions Inc 1612 Hutton Dr Ste 140	Carrollton	TX	75006	972-466-0707	323-2661
TF: 877-778-3625 ■ *Web:* www.4frontes.com					
Abell-Howe Crane Inc 10321 Werch Dr Ste 100	Woodridge	IL	60517	800-366-0068	972-0897*
**Fax Area Code:* 630 ■ *TF:* 800-366-0068 ■ *Web:* www.abellhowe.com					
Advance Lifts Inc 701 Kirk Rd	Saint Charles	IL	60174	630-584-9881	584-9405
TF: 800-843-3625 ■ *Web:* www.advancelifts.com					
Air Technical Industries 7501 Clover Ave	Mentor	OH	44060	440-951-5191	953-9237
TF: 800-321-9680 ■ *Web:* www.airtechnical.com					
American Crane & Equipment Corp 531 Old Swede Rd	Douglassville	PA	19518	610-385-6061	385-3191*
**Fax:* Sales ■ *TF:* 877-877-6778 ■ *Web:* www.americancrane.com					
American Lifts 532 E Baili Ct	Greensburg	IN	47240	812-663-4085	
American Power Pull Corp 550 W Linfoot St PO Box 109	Wauseon	OH	43567	419-335-7050	335-7070
TF: 800-808-5922 ■ *Web:* www.americanpowerpull.com					
ATAP Inc PO Box 98	Eastaboga	AL	36260	256-362-2221	362-2221
TF: 800-362-2827 ■ *Web:* www.atap.com					

Company	City	State	ZIP	Phone	Fax
Autoquip Corp 1058 W Industrial Rd *TF:* 888-811-9876 ■ *Web:* www.autoquip.com	Guthrie	OK	73044	405-282-5200	282-8105
Bayhead Products Corp 173 Crosby Rd *TF:* 800-229-4323 ■ *Web:* www.bayheadproducts.com	Dover	NH	03820	603-742-3000	743-4701
Berns Co 1250 W 17th St *TF:* 800-421-3773 ■ *Web:* www.thebernsco.com	Long Beach	CA	90813	562-437-0471	436-1074
BGK Finishing Systems 4131 Pheasant Ridge Dr NE *TF:* 800-663-5498 ■ *Web:* www.bgk.com	Minneapolis	MN	55449	763-784-0466	784-1362
Breeze-Eastern Corp 700 Liberty Ave *Web:* www.breeze-eastern.com	Union	NJ	07083	973-602-1001	
Busse/SJI Corp 124 N Columbus St **Fax Area Code:* 920 ■ *TF:* 800-882-4995 ■ *Web:* www.arrowheadsystems.com	Randolph	WI	53956	800-882-4995	326-3134*
Cannon Equipment Co 15100 Business Pkwy *Web:* www.cannonequipment.com	Rosemount	MN	55068	651-322-6300	322-1583
Cascade Corp 2201 NE 201st Ave *NYSE: CASC* ■ *TF:* 800-227-2233 ■ *Web:* www.cascorp.com	Fairview	OR	97024	503-669-6300	669-6716
Clark Material Handling Co 700 Enterprise Dr *TF:* 866-252-5275 ■ *Web:* www.clarkmhc.com	Lexington	KY	40510	859-422-6400	
Clyde Machines Inc 1150 State Hwy 55 N PO Box 194 *Web:* www.clydemachines.com	Glenwood	MN	56334	320-634-4503	634-4506
Columbus McKinnon Corp 140 John James Audubon Pkwy *NASDAQ: CMCO* ■ *TF:* 800-888-0985 ■ *Web:* www.cmworks.com	Amherst	NY	14228	716-689-5400	639-4250
Cozzini Inc 4300 W Bryn Mawr Ave *Web:* www.cozzini.com	Chicago	IL	60646	773-478-9700	478-8689
Crane Tech Solutions LLC 2030 Ponderosa St *Web:* www.cranetechsolutions.com	Portsmouth	VA	23701	757-405-0311	405-0313
Craneveyor Corp 1524 Potrero Ave **Fax Area Code:* 626 ■ *TF:* 888-501-0050 ■ *Web:* www.craneveyor.com	South El Monte	CA	91733	888-501-0050	442-7308*
Crosby Group, The 2801 Dawson Rd *TF:* 800-772-1500 ■ *Web:* www.thecrosbygroup.com	Tulsa	OK	74110	918-834-4611	832-0940
Crown Equipment Corp 44 S Washington St *Web:* www.crown.com	New Bremen	OH	45869	419-629-2311	629-2900
Crysteel Mfg Inc 52182 Ember Rd *TF Orders:* 800-533-0494 ■ *Web:* www.crysteel.com	Lake Crystal	MN	56055	507-726-2728	726-2559
Dematic 507 Plymouth Ave NE **Fax Area Code:* 616 ■ *TF Cust Svc:* 877-725-7500 ■ *Web:* www.dematic.com	Grand Rapids	MI	49505	877-725-7500	913-7701*
Detroit Hoist Co 6650 Sterling Dr N *TF:* 800-521-9126 ■ *Web:* www.detroithoist.com	Sterling Heights	MI	48312	586-268-2600	268-0044
Downs Crane & Hoist Company Inc 8827 Juniper St *TF:* 800-748-5994 ■ *Web:* www.downscrane.com	Los Angeles	CA	90002	323-589-6061	589-6066
Drake-Scruggs Equipment Inc 2000 S Dirksen Pkwy *TF:* 877-799-0398 ■ *Web:* www.drake-scruggs.com	Springfield	IL	62703	217-753-3871	753-2760
Dynacon Inc 831 Industrial Blvd *Web:* www.dynacon.com	Bryan	TX	77803	979-823-2690	823-0947
Escalera Inc 708 S Industrial Dr PO Box 1359 *TF:* 800-622-1359 ■ *Web:* www.escalera.com	Yuba City	CA	95993	530-673-6318	673-6376
Excalibur Equipment LLC *Gregory Industrial Trucks* 285 Eldridge Rd *Web:* www.exequipment.com	Fairfield	NJ	07004	973-808-8399	808-8398
Excellon Automation Inc 20001 S Rancho Way *TF:* 800-392-3556 ■ *Web:* www.excellon.com	Rancho Dominguez	CA	90220	310-668-7700	668-7800
FL Smidth Inc 2040 Ave C *TF:* 800-523-9482 ■ *Web:* www.flsmidth.com	Bethlehem	PA	18017	610-264-6011	264-6170
Genie Industries Inc 18340 NE 76th St *TF:* 800-536-1800 ■ *Web:* www.genielift.com	Redmond	WA	98052	425-881-1800	883-3475
Gunnebo-Johnson Corp 1240 N Harvard Ave **Fax:* Cust Svc ■ *TF Sales:* 800-331-5460 ■ *Web:* www.gunnebojohnson.com	Tulsa	OK	74115	918-832-8933	834-0984*
Harlan Materials Handling Corp 27 Stanley Rd *TF:* 800-255-4262 ■ *Web:* www.harlan-corp.com	Kansas City	KS	66115	913-342-5650	321-5802
Harper Trucks Inc PO Box 12330 *TF:* 800-835-4099 ■ *Web:* www.harpertrucks.com	Wichita	KS	67277	316-942-1381	942-8508
Heyl & Patterson Inc 2000 Cliff Mine Rd PO Box 36 *Web:* www.heylpatterson.com	Pittsburgh	PA	15230	412-788-9810	788-9822
Hilman Inc 12 Timber Ln *TF Cust Svc:* 888-276-5548 ■ *Web:* www.hilmanrollers.com	Marlboro	NJ	07746	732-462-6277	462-6355
Indusco Group 1200 W Hamburg St *TF:* 800-727-0665 ■ *Web:* www.induscowirerope.com	Baltimore	MD	21230	410-727-0665	727-2538
Industrial Vehicles International Inc (IVI) 6737 E 12th St *Web:* www.indvehicles.com	Tulsa	OK	74112	918-836-6516	838-9529
Iowa Mold Tooling Co Inc (IMT) 500 W US Hwy 18 *TF:* 800-247-5958 ■ *Web:* www.imt.com	Garner	IA	50438	641-923-3711	923-6063
James Walker Co 7109 Milford Industrial Rd *Web:* jameswalker.com	Baltimore	MD	21215	410-486-3950	
Kelly Systems Inc 422 N Western Ave *TF:* 800-258-8237 ■ *Web:* www.kellytubesystems.com	Chicago	IL	60612	312-733-3224	733-6971
Key Handling Systems Inc 137 W Commercial Ave *Web:* www.keyhandling.com	Moonachie	NJ	07074	201-933-9333	933-4777
Konecranes America 7300 Chippewa Blvd *TF:* 800-231-0241 ■ *Web:* www.konecranesusa.com	Houston	TX	77086	281-445-2225	445-9355
Kornylak Corp 400 Heaton St *TF:* 800-837-5676 ■ *Web:* www.kornylak.com	Hamilton	OH	45011	513-863-1277	863-7644
KWD Manufacturing Co 2230 W Southcross Blvd	San Antonio	TX	78211	210-924-5999	924-6799
Landoll Corp 1900 N St **Fax Area Code:* 888 ■ **Fax:* Sales ■ *TF Cust Svc:* 800-446-5175 ■ *Web:* www.landoll.com	Marysville	KS	66508	785-562-5381	321-3865*
Leebaw Mfg Company Inc PO Box 553 *TF:* 800-841-8083 ■ *Web:* www.leebaw.com	Canfield	OH	44406	800-841-8083	
Lift-All Company Inc 1909 McFarland Dr **Fax:* Cust Svc ■ *TF:* 800-909-1964 ■ *Web:* www.lift-all.com	Landisville	PA	17538	717-898-6615	898-1215*
Liftone 440 E Westinghouse Blvd *Web:* www.liftone.net	Charlotte	NC	28273	855-543-8663	
Linde Hydraulics Corp 5089 W Western Reserve Rd PO Box 82 *Web:* www.linde-hydraulics.us	Canfield	OH	44406	330-533-6801	533-6893
Lovegreen Industrial Services Inc 2280 Sibley Ct *TF:* 800-262-8284 ■ *Web:* www.lovegreen.com	Eagan	MN	55122	651-890-1166	890-8370
MacCabe Electric Conductors Inc 426 Stump Rd PO Box 590 *Web:* www.maccabeelectric.com	Montgomeryville	PA	18936	215-368-9420	368-9220
Magline Inc 1205 W Cedar St **Fax Area Code:* 989 ■ *TF:* 800-624-5463 ■ *Web:* www.magliner.com	Standish	MI	48658	800-624-5463	879-5399*
Manitex Inc 3000 S Austin Ave *TF:* 877-314-3390 ■ *Web:* www.manitex.com	Georgetown	TX	78626	512-942-3000	869-7550
Manitou North America 6401 Imperial Dr *Web:* www.constructionequipment.com	Waco	TX	76712	254-799-0232	799-4433
Matot Inc 2501 Van Buren St *TF:* 800-369-1070 ■ *Web:* www.matot.com	Bellwood	IL	60104	708-547-1888	547-1608
Maxon Industries Inc 11921 Slauson Ave **Fax Area Code:* 888 ■ *TF:* 800-227-4116 ■ *Web:* www.maxonlift.com	Santa Fe Springs	CA	90670	562-464-0099	771-7713*
Mazzella Lifting Technologies 21000 Aerospace Pkwy *TF:* 800-362-4601 ■ *Web:* www.mazzellalifting.com	Cleveland	OH	44142	440-239-7000	239-7010
McGuire W194 N11481 McCormick Dr PO Box 309 **Fax Area Code:* 262 ■ *TF:* 800-624-8473 ■ *Web:* www.wbmcguire.com	Germantown	WI	53022	518-828-7652	255-9399*
Mertz Mfg LLC 1701 N Waverly St *TF:* 800-654-6433 ■ *Web:* www.mertzok.com	Ponca City	OK	74601	580-762-5646	767-8411
Mitsubishi Caterpillar Forklift America Inc 2121 W Sam Houston Pkwy N *Web:* www.mcfa.com	Houston	TX	77043	713-365-1000	365-1441
Morris Material Handling Inc 315 W Forest Hill Ave *TF:* 800-933-3001 ■ *Web:* www.morriscranes.com	Oak Creek	WI	53154	414-764-6200	570-2779
NACCO Materials Handling Group Inc 650 NE Holladay Liberty Centre Ste 1600 *Web:* www.hyster-yale.com	Portland	OR	97232	503-721-6000	721-6001
Nissan Forklift Corp North America (NFC) 240 N Prospect St *Web:* www.nissanforklift.com	Marengo	IL	60152	815-568-0061	568-0179
NMC-Wollard Inc 2021 Truax Blvd *TF:* 800-656-6867 ■ *Web:* www.nmc-wollard.com	Eau Claire	WI	54703	715-835-3151	835-6625
North American Industries Inc 80 Holton St *TF:* 800-847-8470 ■ *Web:* www.naicranes.com	Woburn	MA	01801	781-897-4100	729-3343
Nutting 450 Pheasant Ridge Dr **Fax Area Code:* 866 ■ *TF:* 800-533-0337 ■ *Web:* www.acconutting.com	Watertown	SD	57201	605-882-3000	688-8464*
Ohio Magnetics Inc 5400 Dunham Rd *TF:* 800-486-6446 ■ *Web:* www.ohiomagnetics.com	Maple Heights	OH	44137	216-662-8484	662-2911
P & H Mining Equipment 4400 W National Ave *Web:* www.phmining.com	Milwaukee	WI	53214	414-671-4400	671-7604
Paceco Corp 25503 Whitesell St *Web:* www.pacecocorp.com	Hayward	CA	94545	510-264-9288	264-9280
Paragon Technologies Inc 600 Kuebler Rd *OTC: PGNT* ■ *Web:* pgntgroup.com	Easton	PA	18040	610-252-3205	252-3102
Pettibone Michigan 1100 Superior Ave *TF:* 800-467-3884 ■ *Web:* www.gopettibone.com/	Baraga	MI	49908	906-353-4800	353-6325
Positech Corp 191 N Rush Lk Rd *TF:* 800-831-6026 ■ *Web:* www.positech-solutions.com	Laurens	IA	50554	712-841-4548	841-4765
Powell Systems Inc 162 Churchill-HubbaRd Rd *Web:* www.powellsystems.com	Youngstown	OH	44505	330-759-9220	759-9434
Process Equipment Inc 2770 Welborn St PO Box 1607 *TF:* 888-663-2028 ■ *Web:* www.processbarron.com	Pelham	AL	35124	205-663-5330	663-6037
Production Equipment Co 401 Liberty St **Fax Area Code:* 800 ■ *TF:* 800-758-5697 ■ *Web:* www.peco1938.com	Meriden	CT	06450	203-235-5795	563-4150*
Proserv Anchor Crane Group 455 Aldine Bender PO Box 670965 *TF:* 800-835-2223 ■ *Web:* www.proservanchor.com	Houston	TX	77060	281-405-9048	448-7508
PTR Baler & Compactor Co 2207 E Ontario St *TF:* 800-523-3654 ■ *Web:* www.ptrco.com	Philadelphia	PA	19134	215-533-5100	537-8536
Pucel Enterprises Inc 1440 E 36th St *TF:* 800-336-4986 ■ *Web:* www.pucelenterprises.com	Cleveland	OH	44114	216-881-4604	881-6731
Raymond Corp 22 S Canal St *TF General:* 800-235-7200 ■ *Web:* www.raymondcorp.com	Greene	NY	13778	607-656-2311	656-9005
RKI Inc 2301 Central Pkwy *TF:* 800-346-8988 ■ *Web:* www.rki-us.com	Houston	TX	77092	713-688-4414	688-8982
Royal Tractor Co Inc 109 Overland Pk Pl *TF:* 888-782-7278 ■ *Web:* www.royaltractor.com	New Century	KS	66031	913-782-2598	782-4588
Scott Industrial Systems Inc 4433 Interpoint Blvd PO Box 1387 **Fax Area Code:* 800 ■ *TF:* 800-416-6023 ■ *Web:* www.scottindustrialsystems.com	Dayton	OH	45401	937-233-8146	416-6023*
Shepard Niles 220 N Genesee St *TF:* 800-481-2260 ■ *Web:* www.shepard-niles.com	Montour Falls	NY	14865	607-535-7111	535-7323
Sherman & Reilly Inc 400 W 33rd St *TF Sales:* 800-251-7780 ■ *Web:* www.sherman-reilly.com	Chattanooga	TN	37401	423-756-5300	756-2948
Snorkel 2009 Roseport Rd *Web:* www.snorkellifts.com	Elwood	KS	66024	785-989-3000	989-3070
Solazyme Inc 225 Gateway Blvd *NASDAQ: SZYM* ■ *TF:* 877-917-9075 ■ *Web:* www.solazyme.com	South San Francisco	CA	94080	650-780-4777	989-6700
Southeast Industrial Equipment Inc 12200 Steele Creek Rd PO Box 39110 *TF:* 800-752-6368 ■ *Web:* www.sielift.com	Charlotte	NC	28273	704-399-9700	393-1714
Southworth Products Corp PO Box 1380 *TF:* 800-743-1000 ■ *Web:* www.southworthproducts.com	Portland	ME	04104	207-878-0700	797-4734
Steel King Industries Inc 2700 Chamber St *TF:* 800-826-0203 ■ *Web:* www.steelking.com	Stevens Point	WI	54481	715-341-3120	341-8792

				Phone	Fax
Stock Fairfield Corp 16490 Chillicothe Rd *Web:* www.fairfieldengineering.com	Chagrin Falls	OH	44023	440-543-6000	543-5944
Streator Dependable Manufacturing Co 1705 N Shabbona St *TF:* 800-795-0551 ■ *Web:* www.streatordependable.com	Streator	IL	61364	815-672-0551	672-7631
Taylor-Dunn Manufacturing Co 2114 W Ball Rd *TF:* 800-688-8680 ■ *Web:* www.taylor-dunn.com	Anaheim	CA	92804	714-956-4040	956-3130
TC/American Monorail Inc 12070 43rd St NE *Web:* www.tcamerican.com	Saint Michael	MN	55376	763-497-7000	497-7001
Terex Corp 200 Nyala Farm Rd *NYSE: TEX* ■ *Web:* www.terex.com	Westport	CT	06880	203-222-7170	222-7976
Terex Corp Crane Div 202 Raleigh St *TF:* 877-794-5284 ■ *Web:* www.terex.com	Wilmington	NC	28412	910-395-8500	
Terex-Telelect Inc 500 Oakwood Rd PO Box 1150 *TF:* 800-982-8975 ■ *Web:* www.terex.com	Watertown	SD	57201	605-882-4000	882-1842
Thern Inc 5712 Industrial Pk Rd PO Box 347 *TF:* 800-843-7648 ■ *Web:* thern.com	Winona	MN	55987	507-454-2996	454-5282
Triple/S Dynamics Inc 1031 S Haskell Ave PO Box 151027 *TF:* 800-527-2116 ■ *Web:* www.sssdynamics.com	Dallas	TX	75315	214-828-8600	828-8688
United Central Industrial Supply Company LLC 1241 Volunteer Pkwy Ste 1000 *Web:* www.unitedcentral.net	Bristol	TN	37620	423-573-7300	573-7392
Valley Craft 2001 S Hwy 61 *TF:* 800-328-1480 ■ *Web:* www.valleycraft.com	Lake City	MN	55041	651-345-3386	345-3606
Vibra Screw Inc 755 Union Blvd *Web:* www.vibrascrew.com	Totowa	NJ	07512	973-256-7410	256-7567
WA Charnstrom Co 5391 12th Ave E *TF Cust Svc:* 800-328-2962 ■ *Web:* www.charnstrom.com	Shakopee	MN	55379	800-328-2962	916-3215
Waldon Mfg LLC 201 W Oklahoma Ave *TF:* 866-283-2759 ■ *Web:* www.waldonequipment.com	Fiarview	OK	73737	580-227-3711	
Wayne Engineering Corp 701 Performance Dr *Web:* www.wayneusa.com	Cedar Falls	IA	50613	319-266-1721	266-8207
Wesco Industrial Products Inc PO Box 47 **Fax Area Code:* 800 ■ *Web:* www.wescomfg.com	Lansdale	PA	19446	215-699-7031	346-5511*
Western Hoist Inc 1839 Cleveland Ave *TF:* 888-994-6478 ■ *Web:* www.westernlift.org	National City	CA	91950	619-474-3361	474-8261
Whiting Corp 26000 Whiting Way **Fax Area Code:* 708 ■ *TF:* 800-861-5744 ■ *Web:* www.whitingcorp.com	Monee	IL	60449	800-861-5744	587-2001*
Wiggins Lift Company Inc 2571 Cortez St *TF:* 800-350-7821 ■ *Web:* www.wigginslift.com	Oxnard	CA	93031	805-485-7821	485-5230
WinHolt Equipment Group 141 Eileen Way *TF:* 800-444-3595 ■ *Web:* www.winholt.com	Syosset	NY	11791	516-222-0335	921-0538
Zenar Corp 7301 S Sixth St PO Box 107 *Web:* www.zenarcrane.com	Oak Creek	WI	53154	414-764-1800	764-1267

474 MATTRESSES & ADJUSTABLE BEDS

SEE ALSO Household Furniture p. 2345

				Phone	Fax
Bechik Products Inc 1020 Discovery Rd Ste 150 *TF:* 800-328-6569 ■ *Web:* www.bechik.com	Eagan	MN	55121	651-698-0364	698-1009
Bergad Inc 747 Eljer Way *TF:* 888-476-8664 ■ *Web:* www.bergad.com	Ford City	PA	16226	724-763-2883	
Bowles Mattress Co Inc 1220 Watt St *TF:* 800-223-7509 ■ *Web:* www.bowlesmattress.com	Jeffersonville	IN	47130	812-288-8614	288-8650
Classic Sleep Products Inc 8214 Wellmoor Ct **Fax Area Code:* 301 ■ *TF:* 877-707-7533 ■ *Web:* www.classicmattress.com	Jessup	MD	20794	410-904-0006	498-6149*
Comfortex Inc 1680 Wilkie Dr PO Box 850 *TF:* 800-445-4007 ■ *Web:* www.comfortexinc.com	Winona	MN	55987	507-454-6579	454-6581
Corsicana Bedding Inc PO Box 1050 *TF:* 800-323-4349 ■ *Web:* www.corsicanabedding.com	Corsicana	TX	75151	903-872-2591	872-9138
Cotton Belt Inc 401 E Sater St *TF:* 800-849-4192 ■ *Web:* www.edgecombe.com	Pinetops	NC	27864	252-827-4192	827-5683
Diamond Mattress Company Inc 3112 Las Hermanas St E *Web:* www.diamondmattress.com	Compton	CA	90221	310-638-0363	638-2005
Dreamline Mfg Inc 1514 S Second St PO Box 1250 *TF:* 800-888-3585 ■ *Web:* www.dreamlinebedding.com	Cabot	AR	72023	501-843-3585	843-2990
Englander Northeast 12 Esquire Rd **Fax Area Code:* 978 ■ *TF:* 800-370-8700 ■ *Web:* www.englander.com	North Billerica	MA	01862	800-370-8700	667-4914*
FXI, Inc 1241 Old Temescal Rd *Web:* www.anatomicglobal.com	Corona	CA	92881	951-371-8101	
HomeStyle Industries 1323 11th Ave N *Web:* www.home-style.com	Nampa	ID	83687	208-466-8481	
Imperial Bedding Co 720 11th St PO Box 5347 *TF:* 800-529-3321 ■ *Web:* www.imperialbedding.com	Huntington	WV	25703	304-529-3321	525-5317
Jackson Mattress Company Inc 3154 Camden Rd *TF:* 800-763-7378 ■ *Web:* restonic.com	Fayetteville	NC	28306	910-425-0131	425-1602
Jamison Bedding Inc PO Box 681948 *TF Cust Svc:* 800-255-1883 ■ *Web:* www.jamisonbedding.com	Franklin	TN	37068	615-794-1883	
King Koil Licensing Company Inc 7501 S Quincy St Ste 130 *TF:* 800-525-8331 ■ *Web:* www.kingkoil.com	Willowbrook	IL	60527	800-525-8331	
Kingsdown Inc 126 W Holt St **Fax:* Cust Svc ■ *TF Cust Svc:* 800-354-5464 ■ *Web:* www.kingsdown.com	Mebane	NC	27302	919-563-3531	563-6730*
Kolcraft Enterprises Inc 10832 NC Hwy 211 E *TF Cust Svc:* 800-453-7673 ■ *Web:* www.kolcraft.com	Aberdeen	NC	28315	910-944-9345	
Leggett & Platt Inc Number 1 Leggett Rd PO Box 757 *NYSE: LEG* ■ *TF:* 800-888-4569 ■ *Web:* www.leggett.com	Carthage	MO	64836	417-358-8131	358-6996
Meridian Mattress Factory Inc 200 Rubush Rd PO Box 5127 *TF:* 800-844-3875 ■ *Web:* mermat.com	Meridian	MS	39301	601-693-3875	693-5462
Northwest Bedding 6102 S Hayford Rd *TF:* 800-456-7686 ■ *Web:* www.nwbedding.com	Spokane	WA	99224	509-244-3000	244-9905
Omaha Bedding Co 4011 S 60th St *TF:* 800-279-9018 ■ *Web:* www.omahabeddingco.com	Omaha	NE	68117	402-733-8600	733-0586
Original Mattress Factory Inc, The 4930 State Rd *Web:* originalmattress.com/	Cleveland	OH	44134	216-661-8388	
Palliser Furniture Upholstery Ltd 70 Lexington Park *Web:* www.palliser.com	Winnipeg	MB	R2G4H2	204-988-5600	988-5604
Paramount Industrial Cos Inc 1112 Kingwood Ave *Web:* www.paramountsleep.com	Norfolk	VA	23502	757-855-3321	855-2029
Park Place Corp 6801 Augusta Rd *Web:* www.parkplacecorp.com	Greenville	SC	29605	864-422-8118	
Restonic Mattress 201 James E Casey Dr *TF:* 800-898-6075 ■ *Web:* www.restonic.com	Buffalo	NY	14206	716-895-1414	895-1416
Restonic Mattress Corp 737 Main St *TF:* 800-898-6075 ■ *Web:* www.restonic.com	Buffalo	NY	14203	800-898-6075	
Riverside Mattress Co 225 Dunn Rd *TF:* 888-288-5195 ■ *Web:* www.riversidemattressinc.com	Fayetteville	NC	28312	910-483-0461	484-2334
Serta Mattress/AW Inc 8415 ARdmore Rd *TF:* 888-557-3782 ■ *Web:* www.serta.com	Landover	MD	20785	301-322-1000	
Simmons Co 1 Concourse Pkwy Ste 800 *Web:* www.simmons.com	Atlanta	GA	30328	770-512-7700	392-2560
Sleep Design 5808 Berry Brook Dr *Web:* sleep-designs.com	Houston	TX	77017	713-227-0121	227-8159
Sleep Innovations Inc 187 Rt 36 Ste 101	West Long Branch	NJ	07764	732-263-0800	
Sleep Train Inc 2205 Plz Dr **Fax Area Code:* 866 ■ *TF:* 800-919-2337 ■ *Web:* www.sleeptrain.com	Rocklin	CA	95765	800-919-2337	293-5719*
Southerland Inc 1973 Southerland Dr *TF Cust Svc:* 800-443-1183 ■ *Web:* www.southerlandsleep.com	Nashville	TN	37207	615-226-9650	650-2653
Stress-O-Pedic Mattress Company Inc 2060 S Wineville Ave *Web:* www.stressopedic.com	Ontario	CA	91761	909-605-2010	
Symbol Mattress Co 1814 High Pt Ave *Web:* www.symbolmattress.com	Richmond	VA	23230	804-353-8965	
Tempur Production USA Inc 203 Tempur Pedic Dr Ste 102 *Web:* tempurpedic.com	Duffield	VA	24244	276-431-7150	
Tempur-Pedic International Inc 1713 Jaggie Fox Way *NYSE: TPX* ■ **Fax Area Code:* 859 ■ *TF:* 800-821-6621 ■ *Web:* www.tempurpedic.com	Lexington	KY	40511	800-821-6621	259-9843*
Therapedic International 1375 Jersey Ave *TF:* 800-233-7467 ■ *Web:* www.therapedic.com	North Brunswick	NJ	08902	800-233-7467	
VyMaC Corp W3130 State Rd 59 E	Whitewater	WI	53190	920-568-3130	
White Dove Ltd 3201 Harvard Ave *Web:* www.whitedoveusa.com	Cleveland	OH	44105	216-341-0200	341-3399
Winston-Salem Industries for the Blind 7730 N Pt Dr *Web:* www.wsifb.com	Winston-Salem	NC	27106	336-759-0551	759-0990

475 MEASURING, TESTING, CONTROLLING INSTRUMENTS

SEE ALSO Electrical Signals Measuring & Testing Instruments p. 2229

				Phone	Fax
ABB Inc 501 Merritt 7 *TF Prod Info:* 800-626-4999 ■ *Web:* new.abb.com/us	Norwalk	CT	06851	203-750-2200	435-7365
Adcole Corp 669 Forest St *Web:* www.adcole.com	Marlborough	MA	01752	508-485-9100	481-6142
AGR International Inc 615 Whitestown Rd *Web:* www.agrintl.com	Butler	PA	16001	724-482-2163	482-2767
All Weather Inc 1165 National Dr *TF:* 800-824-5873 ■ *Web:* www.allweatherinc.com	Sacramento	CA	95834	916-928-1000	928-1165
AMETEK Aerospace & Defense 50 Fordham Rd **Fax:* Cust Svc ■ *Web:* ametekaerodefense.com	Wilmington	MA	01887	978-988-4771	988-4944*
AMETEK Inc Test & Calibration Instruments Div 8600 Somerset Dr *TF:* 800-733-5427 ■ *Web:* www.ametek.com	Largo	FL	33773	727-538-6132	538-6121
AMETEK US Gauge 820 Pennsylvania Blvd *TF:* 888-631-5454 ■ *Web:* www.ametekusg.com	Feasterville	PA	19053	215-355-6900	354-1802
Beta LaserMike Inc 8001 Technology Blvd *TF:* 800-886-9935 ■ *Web:* www.betalasermike.com	Dayton	OH	45424	937-233-9935	233-7284
Bruel & Kjaer Instruments Inc 2815 Colonnades Ct Ste A *TF:* 800-332-2040 ■ *Web:* www.bkhome.com	Norcross	GA	30071	770-209-6907	448-3246
Cambridge Technology Inc 25 Hartwell Ave *TF:* 800-342-3757 ■ *Web:* www.camtech.com	Lexington	MA	02421	781-541-1600	541-1601
Canberra Industries Inc 800 Research Pkwy *TF Sales:* 800-243-3955 ■ *Web:* www.canberra.com	Meriden	CT	06450	203-238-2351	235-1347
Century Equipment Inc 5959 Angola Rd PO Box 352889 *Web:* www.centuryequip.com	Toledo	OH	43615	419-865-7400	865-8215
Clayton Industries 17477 Hurley St *TF:* 800-423-4585 ■ *Web:* www.claytonindustries.com	City of Industry	CA	91744	626-435-1200	435-0180
Copley Controls Corp 20 Dan Rd *Web:* www.copleycontrols.com	Canton	MA	02021	781-828-8090	828-6547
Crane Nuclear Inc 2825 Cobb International Blvd *TF:* 800-795-8013 ■ *Web:* www.cranenuclear.com	Kennesaw	GA	30152	770-424-6343	429-4750
Cubic Transportation Systems Inc 5650 Kearny Mesa Rd *TF:* 800-937-5449 ■ *Web:* www.cubic.com	San Diego	CA	92111	858-268-3100	292-9987
Danaher Corp 2200 Pennsylvania Ave NW Ste 800 *NYSE: DHR* ■ *TF:* 800-833-9200 ■ *Web:* www.danaher.com	Washington	DC	20037	202-828-0850	828-0860
Davis Instrument Corp 3465 Diablo Ave *TF:* 800-678-3669 ■ *Web:* www.davisnet.com	Hayward	CA	94545	510-732-9229	670-0589

Phone | Fax

Delta Cooling Towers Inc PO Box 315 .... Rockaway NJ 07866 973-586-2201 586-2243
TF: 800-289-3358 ■ *Web:* www.deltacooling.com

Dresser Inc 15455 Dallas Pkwy Ste 1100 .... Addison TX 75001 972-361-9800 361-9903
Web: www.ge-energy.com

Dynisco LLC 38 Forge Pkwy .... Franklin MA 02038 508-541-9400 541-6206
TF General: 800-396-4726 ■ *Web:* www.dynisco.com

Emerson Process Management CSI
835 Innovation Dr .... Knoxville TN 37932 865-675-2110 218-1764
TF: 800-675-4726 ■ *Web:* www2.emersonprocess.com

Endevco Corp
30700 Rancho Viejo Rd .... San Juan Capistrano CA 92675 949-493-8181 661-7231
TF: 800-982-6732 ■ *Web:* www.endevco.com

Enidine Inc 7 Centre Dr .... Orchard Park NY 14127 716-662-1900 662-1909
TF: 800-852-8508 ■ *Web:* www.enidine.com

Fairfield Industries Inc
1111 Gillingham Ln .... Sugar Land TX 77478 281-275-7500 275-7500
TF: 800-231-9809 ■ *Web:* www.fairfieldnodal.com

Fiber Instruments Sales Inc 161 Clear Rd .... Oriskany NY 13424 315-736-2206 736-2285
TF Sales: 800-500-0347 ■ *Web:* www.fiberinstrumentsales.com

Fisher Research Laboratory Inc
1465H Henry Brennan Ste H .... El Paso TX 79936 915-225-0333 225-0336
Web: www.fisherlab.com

Flowline Inc 10500 Humbolt St .... Los Alamitos CA 90720 562-598-3015 431-8507
Web: www.flowline.com

Garrett Metal Detectors 1881 W State St .... Garland TX 75042 972-494-6151 494-1881
TF: 800-234-6151 ■ *Web:* www.garrett.com

General Monitors Inc 26776 Simpatica Cir .... Lake Forest CA 92630 949-581-4464 581-1151
TF: 866-686-0741 ■ *Web:* www.generalmonitors.com

Geokon Inc 48 Spencer St .... Lebanon NH 03766 603-448-1562 448-3216
Web: www.geokon.com

Geometrics Inc 2190 Fortune Dr .... San Jose CA 95131 408-954-0522 954-0902
Web: www.geometrics.com

George Risk Industries Inc 802 S Elm St .... Kimball NE 69145 308-235-4645 235-2609
OTC: RSKIA ■ *TF Sales:* 800-523-1227 ■ *Web:* www.grisk.com

GFI Genfare 751 Pratt Blvd .... Elk Grove Village IL 60007 847-593-8855 593-1824
TF: 877-247-3797 ■ *Web:* www.spx.com

Gleason M & M Precision Systems Corp
300 Progress Rd .... Dayton OH 45449 937-859-8273 859-4452
TF: 800-727-6333 ■ *Web:* www.gleason.com

Goodrich Corp
2730 W Tyvola Rd 4 Coliseum Ctr .... Charlotte NC 28217 704-423-7000 423-7002
NYSE: GR ■ *TF:* 800-735-7899 ■ *Web:* utcaerospacesystems.com

Herman H Sticht Company Inc
45 Main St Ste 701 .... Brooklyn NY 11201 718-852-7602 852-7915
TF: 800-221-3203 ■ *Web:* www.stichtco.com

Hexagon Metrology Inc 250 Circuit Dr .... North Kingstown RI 02852 401-886-2000 886-2727
TF: 855-443-9638 ■ *Web:* www.sheffieldmeasurement.com

Howell Instruments Inc 8945 S Fwy .... Fort Worth TX 76140 817-336-7411 336-7874
Web: www.howellinst.com

Industrial Dynamics Company Ltd
3100 Fujita St .... Torrance CA 90505 310-325-5633
TF: 888-434-5832 ■ *Web:* www.filtec.com

Instron Corp 825 University Ave .... Norwood MA 02062 781-828-2500 575-5750
Web: www.instron.us

Instron Corp Wilson Instruments Div
825 University Ave .... Norwood MA 02062 781-828-2500 575-5751
TF: 800-695-4273 ■ *Web:* www.instron.us

Intra Corp 885 Manufacturers Dr .... Westland MI 48186 734-326-7030 326-1410
Web: www.intra-corp.net

Isra Surface Vision Inc
4470 Peachtree Lakes Dr .... Duluth GA 30096 770-449-7776 449-0399
Web: www.lasorsystronics.com

Kavlico Corp 14401 Princeton Ave .... Moorpark CA 93021 805-523-2000 523-7125
Web: www.kavlico.com

Kinemetrics Inc 222 Vista Ave .... Pasadena CA 91107 626-795-2220 795-0868
Web: www.kinemetrics.com

Kistler Instrument Corp 75 John Glenn Dr .... Amherst NY 14228 716-691-5100 691-5226
TF: 888-547-8537 ■ *Web:* www.kistler.com

Konica Minolta Sensing Americas Inc
101 Williams Dr .... Ramsey NJ 07446 201-825-4000 785-2480*
**Fax:* Sales ■ *TF:* 888-473-2656 ■ *Web:* www.konicaminolta.com

L-3 Avionics Systems 5353 52nd St SE .... Grand Rapids MI 49512 616-949-6600 285-4457*
**Fax:* Hum Res ■ *TF:* 800-253-9525 ■ *Web:* www.l-3avionics.com/

Leica Geosystems Inc 3498 Kraft Ave SE .... Grand Rapids MI 49512 616-977-4189 942-4627
TF Sales: 800-367-9453 ■ *Web:* www.leica-geosystems.com

Link Engineering Company Inc
43855 Plymouth Oaks Blvd .... Plymouth MI 48170 734-453-0800 453-0802
Web: www.linkeng.com

Lockheed Martin Sippican Seven Barnabas Rd .... Marion MA 02738 508-748-1160 748-3626
Web: www.sippican.com

Logis Tech Inc 9450 Innovation Dr Ste 1 .... Manassas VA 20110 703-393-0122
Web: www.logis-tech.com

Ludlum Measurements Inc 501 Oak St .... Sweetwater TX 79556 325-235-5494 235-4672
TF: 800-622-0828 ■ *Web:* www.ludlums.com

Magnetic Analysis Corp 103 Fairview Park Dr .... Elmsford NY 10523 914-699-9450 703-3790
TF: 800-463-8622 ■ *Web:* www.mac-ndt.com

Marposs Corp 3300 Cross Creek Pkwy .... Auburn Hills MI 48326 248-370-0404 370-0991
TF: 888-627-7677 ■ *Web:* www.marposs.com

Mason Industries Inc 350 Rabro Dr .... Hauppauge NY 11788 631-348-0282 348-0279
Web: www.mason-industries.com

Metrix Instrument Co 8824 Fallbrook Dr .... Houston TX 77064 713-461-2131 559-9417
TF: 800-638-7494 ■ *Web:* www.metrixvibration.com

Metrosonics 1060 Corporate Ctr Dr .... Oconomowoc WI 53066 262-567-9157 567-4047
TF: 800-245-0779 ■ *Web:* 3m.com/

Metrotech Corp 3251 Olcott St .... Santa Clara CA 95054 408-734-1400 734-1415
TF: 800-446-3392 ■ *Web:* www.vivax-metrotech.com

Morcom International Inc
3656 Centerview Dr Unit 1 .... Chantilly VA 20151 703-263-9305 263-9308
Web: www.morcom.com

MTS Systems Corp 14000 Technology Dr .... Eden Prairie MN 55344 952-937-4000 937-4515
NASDAQ: MTSC ■ *TF Cust Svc:* 800-328-2255 ■ *Web:* www.mts.com

Mustang Dynamometer 2300 Pinnacle Pkwy .... Twinsburg OH 44087 330-963-5400 425-3310
TF: 888-468-7826 ■ *Web:* www.mustangdyne.com

Phone | Fax

Nanometrics Inc 1550 Buckeye Dr .... Milpitas CA 95035 408-545-6000 232-5910
NASDAQ: NANO ■ *Web:* www.nanometrics.com

Nextest Systems Corp 875 Embedded Way .... San Jose CA 95138 408-960-2400 960-7660
Web: www.teradyne.com

Novatron Corp 401 Loop 59 .... Atlanta TX 75551 903-799-6560 799-6580

Ohmart/VEGA Corp 4241 Allendorf Dr .... Cincinnati OH 45209 513-272-0131 272-0133
TF: 800-367-5383 ■ *Web:* www.vega-americas.com

Oxford Instruments Measurement Systems
300 Bake Ave Ste 150 .... Concord MA 01742 800-447-4717 369-8287*
**Fax Area Code:* 978 ■ *TF:* 800-447-4717 ■ *Web:* www.oxford-instruments.com

Perceptron Inc 47827 Halyard Dr .... Plymouth MI 48170 734-414-6100 414-4700
NASDAQ: PRCP ■ *Web:* www.perceptron.com

Preco Electronics Inc 10335 W Emerald St .... Boise ID 83704 208-323-1000 323-1034
TF: 866-977-7326 ■ *Web:* www.preco.com

Princeton Gamma-Tech Instruments Inc
303-C College Rd E .... Princeton NJ 08540 609-924-7310 924-1729

Promess Inc PO Box 748 .... Brighton MI 48116 810-229-9334 229-8125
Web: www.promessinc.com

Radiation Monitoring Devices Inc (RMDINC)
44 Hunt St Ste 2 .... Watertown MA 02472 617-668-6800 926-9980
Web: www.rmdinc.com

Rochester Gauges Inc of Texas
11616 Harry Hines Blvd .... Dallas TX 75229 972-241-2161 620-1403
TF: 800-821-1829 ■ *Web:* www.rochestergauges.com

Rudolph Technologies Inc
One Rudolph Rd PO Box 1000 .... Flanders NJ 07836 973-691-1300 691-4863
NASDAQ: RTEC ■ *TF:* 877-467-8365 ■ *Web:* www.rudolphtech.com

Schmitt Industries Inc 2765 NW Nicolai St .... Portland OR 97210 503-227-7908 223-1258
NASDAQ: SMIT ■ *Web:* www.schmitt-ind.com

Schneeberger Inc 11 Deangelo Dr .... Bedford MA 01730 781-271-0140 275-4749
Web: www.schneeberger.com

Sensor Systems LLC 2800 Anvil St N .... Saint Petersburg FL 33710 727-347-2181 347-7520
Web: www.sensorsllc.com

Sercel Inc 17200 Pk Row .... Houston TX 77084 281-492-6688 579-6555
Web: www.sercel.com

Setra Systems Inc 159 Swanson Rd .... Boxborough MA 01719 978-263-1400 264-0292
TF: 800-257-3872 ■ *Web:* www.setra.com

Sierra Monitor Corp 1991 Tarob Ct .... Milpitas CA 95035 408-262-6611 262-9042
OTC: SRMC ■ *TF:* 888-509-1970 ■ *Web:* www.sierramonitor.com

Smiths Detection 2202 Lakeside Blvd .... Edgewood MD 21040 410-510-9100 510-9490
Web: www.smithsdetection.com

Sorrento Electronics Inc
4949 Greencraig Ln .... San Diego CA 92123 858-522-8300 522-8300
TF: 800-252-1180 ■ *Web:* ga.com

SuperFlow Technologies Group
4747 Centennial Blvd .... Colorado Springs CO 80919 719-471-1746 471-1490
TF: 800-471-7701 ■ *Web:* www.superflow.com

Taber Industries 455 Bryant St .... North Tonawanda NY 14120 716-694-4000 694-1450
Web: www.taberindustries.com

Taylor Hobson Inc 1725 Western Dr .... West Chicago IL 60185 630-621-3099 231-1739
Web: www.taylor-hobson.com

Tel-Instrument Electronics Corp
1 Branca Rd .... East Rutherford NJ 07073 201-933-1600 933-7340
NYSE: TIK ■ *Web:* www.telinstrument.com

Testing Machines Inc 40 McCullough Dr .... New Castle DE 19720 302-613-5600 613-5619
TF General: 800-678-3221 ■ *Web:* www.testingmachines.com

Thermo Fisher Scientific Inc
81 Wyman St PO Box 9046 .... Waltham MA 02454 781-622-1000 622-1207
NYSE: TMO ■ *TF:* 800-678-5599 ■ *Web:* www.thermofisher.com

Tinius Olsen Testing Machine Company Inc
1065 Easton Rd PO Box 1009 .... Horsham PA 19044 215-675-7100 441-0899
Web: www.tiniusolsen.com

Topcon Positioning Systems Inc
7400 National Dr .... Livermore CA 94551 925-245-8300 245-8599
Web: www.topconpositioning.com

Ues Inc 4401 Dayton Xenia Rd .... Dayton OH 45432 937-426-6900 429-5413
Web: www.ues.com

Unilux Inc 59 N Fifth St .... Saddle Brook NJ 07663 201-712-1266 712-1366
TF: 800-522-0801 ■ *Web:* www.unilux.com

Uster Technologies Inc
456 Troy Cir PO Box 51270 .... Knoxville TN 37919 865-588-9716 588-1414
Web: www.uster.com

Vaisala Inc 10-D Gill St .... Woburn MA 01801 781-933-4500 933-8029
TF: 888-824-7252 ■ *Web:* www.vaisala.com

Verity Instruments Inc 2901 Eisenhower St .... Carrollton TX 75007 972-446-9990 446-9586
Web: www.verityinst.com

White's Electronics Inc
1011 Pleasant Valley Rd .... Sweet Home OR 97386 800-547-6911 367-6629*
**Fax Area Code:* 541 ■ *TF Sales:* 800-999-9147 ■ *Web:* www.whitesdetectors.com

476 MEAT PACKING PLANTS

SEE ALSO Poultry Processing p. 2955

Phone | Fax

Abbott's Meat Inc 3623 Blackington Ave .... Flint MI 48532 810-232-7128
Web: www.abbottsmeat.com

Abbyland Foods Inc
502 E Linden St PO Box 69 .... Abbotsford WI 54405 715-223-6386 223-6388
TF: 800-732-5483 ■ *Web:* www.abbyland.com

Academy Packing Company Inc 2881 Wyoming St .... Dearborn MI 48120 313-841-4900 841-9760
Web: academypackingcompany.com

Allen Bros Inc 3737 S Halsted St .... Chicago IL 60609 773-890-5100 890-9146
TF: 800-548-7777 ■ *Web:* www.allenbrothers.com

Alpine Meats 9850 Lowr Sacramento Rd .... Stockton CA 95210 209-477-2691 477-1994
TF: 800-399-6328 ■ *Web:* www.alpinemeats.com

American Foods Group Inc 544 Acme St .... Green Bay WI 54302 920-437-6330 436-6510
TF: 800-345-0293 ■ *Web:* www.americanfoodsgroup.com

Atlantic Veal & Lamb Inc 275 Morgan Ave .... Brooklyn NY 11211 718-599-6400 302-3237
Web: atlanticveal.com

Company	City	State	Zip	Phone	Fax
ATRAHAN Transformation Inc 860 Chemin Des Acadiens; *Web:* www.atrahan.com	Yamachiche	QC	G0X3L0	819-296-3791	
Birchwood Foods 6009 Goshen Springs Rd; *Web:* www.bwfoods.com	Norcross	GA	30071	770-448-9101	447-0459
Burnett & Son Meat Co Inc 1420 S Myrtle Ave; *Web:* www.burnettandson.com	Monrovia	CA	91016	626-357-2165	357-7115
Cargill Meat Solutions 151 N Main PO Box 2519; **Fax:* Hum Res ■ *Web:* cargill.com	Wichita	KS	67201	316-291-2500	291-2589*
Carolina Packers Inc 2999 S Bright Leaf Blvd PO Box 1109; *TF:* 800-682-7675 ■ *Web:* www.carolinapackers.com	Smithfield	NC	27577	919-934-2181	989-6794
Central Beef Industry LLC 571 W Kings Hwy PO Box 399	Center Hill	FL	33514	352-793-3671	793-2227
Central Nebraska Packing Inc 2800 E Eigth St; *TF Cust Svc:* 800-445-2881 ■ *Web:* www.nebraskabrand.com	North Platte	NE	69103	308-532-1250	532-2744
Cherry Meat Packers Inc 4750 S California Ave	Chicago	IL	60632	773-927-1200	
Chip Steak & Provision Co 232 Dewey St	Mankato	MN	56001	507-388-6277	388-6279
Chisesi Bros Meat Packing Co 5221 Jefferson Hwy; *TF:* 800-966-3550 ■ *Web:* www.chisesibros.com	New Orleans	LA	70123	504-822-3550	822-3916
Clougherty Packing Co 3049 E Vernon Ave; **Fax Area Code:* 323 ■ *TF Sales:* 800-846-7635 ■ *Web:* www.farmerjohn.com	Los Angeles	CA	90058	800-846-7635	584-1699*
Comer Packing 1000 Poplar St PO Box 33; *TF:* 800-748-8916	Aberdeen	MS	39730	662-369-9325	369-9375
ConAgra Foods Retail Products Co Deli Foods Group 215 W Field Rd; *TF:* 877-266-2472 ■ *Web:* www.conagrafoods.com	Naperville	IL	60563	630-857-1000	
Cougle Commission Co 345 N Aberdeen St; *Web:* couglecommission.com	Chicago	IL	60607	312-666-7861	
Cudahy Patrick Inc One Sweet Apple-Wood Ln; *TF:* 800-486-6900 ■ *Web:* www.patrickcudahy.com	Cudahy	WI	53110	414-744-2000	744-2000
Curtis Packing Co 2416 Randolph Ave PO Box 1470; *TF:* 800-852-7890 ■ *Web:* www.curtispackingcompany.com	Greensboro	NC	27406	336-275-7684	275-1901
Dallas City Packing Inc 3049 Morrell St	Dallas	TX	75203	214-948-3901	942-2039
Demakes Enterprises Inc 37 Waterhill St; *Web:* oldneighborhoodfoods.com	Lynn	MA	01905	781-592-0016	595-7523
DL Lee & Sons Inc 927 Hwy 32 E; *Web:* www.dllee.com	Alma	GA	31510	912-632-4406	632-8298
Eddy Packing Company Inc 404 Airport Dr; *TF:* 800-292-2361 ■ *Web:* www.eddypacking.com	Yoakum	TX	77995	361-293-2361	293-2254
Esskay Inc 8422 Bellona Ln Ste 200; *Web:* www.esskaymeat.com	Towson	MD	21204	410-823-2100	823-2100
Fair Oaks Farms Inc 7600 95th St; *Web:* www.fairoaksfarms.com	Pleasant Prairie	WI	53158	262-947-0320	947-0348
Farm Boy Meats 2761 N Kentucky Ave; *TF:* 800-852-3976 ■ *Web:* www.farmboyfoodservice.com	Evansville	IN	47711	812-425-5231	425-5231
Food Consulting Co, The 13724 Recuerdo Dr; *Web:* www.foodlabels.com	Del Mar	CA	92014	858-793-4658	
Fresh Mark Inc 1888 Southway St SE; *Web:* www.freshmark.com	Massillon	OH	44646	330-832-7491	830-3174
Golden State Foods 18301 Von Karman Ave Ste 1100; *Web:* www.goldenstatefoods.com	Irvine	CA	92612	949-252-2000	252-2080
Greater Omaha Packing Company Inc 3001 L St; *TF:* 800-747-5400 ■ *Web:* www.greateromaha.com	Omaha	NE	68107	402-731-1700	731-8020
Hansel 'n Gretel Brand Inc 79-36 Cooper Ave; *Web:* www.healthydeli.com	Glendale	NY	11385	718-326-0041	326-2069
Harris Ranch Beef Co 16277 S McCall Ave PO Box 220; **Fax Area Code:* 559 ■ *TF:* 800-742-1955 ■ *Web:* www.harrisranchbeef.com	Selma	CA	93662	800-742-1955	896-3095*
Hatfield Quality Meats Inc 2700 Clemens Rd; *TF:* 800-743-1191 ■ *Web:* www.hatfieldqualitymeats.com	Hatfield	PA	19440	215-368-2500	
Isaly's Inc PO Box F; *Web:* www.isalys.com	Evans City	PA	16033	724-538-9044	538-3262
J Freirich Foods Inc 815 W Kerr St PO Box 1529; *TF:* 800-554-4788 ■ *Web:* freirich.com	Salisbury	NC	28144	704-636-2621	
JBS Five Rivers Cattle Feeding LLC 1770 Promontory Cir; *Web:* www.fiveriverscattle.com	Greeley	CO	80634	970-506-8363	
JF O'Neill Packing Company Inc 3120 G St	Omaha	NE	68107	402-733-1200	733-1724
JH Routh Packing Company Inc 4413 W Bogart Rd; *TF:* 800-446-6759 ■ *Web:* routhpacking.com	Sandusky	OH	44870	419-626-2251	625-4782
John Morrell & Co 805 E Kemper Rd; **Fax Area Code:* 408 ■ **Fax:* Cust Svc ■ *TF:* 800-722-1127 ■ *Web:* www.johnmorrell.com	Cincinnati	OH	45246	513-346-3540	220-9679*
L & H Packing Co PO Box 831368; *TF:* 800-999-3241 ■ *Web:* lhpacking.net	San Antonio	TX	78283	210-532-3241	532-5033
L Frankel Packing Company Inc 230 N Peoria St	Chicago	IL	60607	312-421-3200	421-6049
Land O'Frost Inc 16850 Chicago Ave; *TF:* 800-323-3308 ■ *Web:* www.landofrost.com	Lansing	IL	60438	708-474-7100	
Long Prairie Packing Co 10 Riverside Dr; **Fax Area Code:* 651 ■ *TF:* 800-996-6440	Long Prairie	MN	56347	320-732-2171	552-2107*
Morans Ground Beef Co 3425 E Vernon Ave; *Web:* www.moransgroundbeef.com	Vernon	CA	90058	323-585-0068	
Morrilton Packing Company Inc 51 Blue Diamond Dr; *TF:* 800-264-2475 ■ *Web:* petitjeanmeats.com	Morrilton	AR	72110	501-354-2474	354-2283
National Beef Packing Co LLC 12200 Ambassador Dr Ste 500 PO Box 20046; *TF:* 800-449-2333 ■ *Web:* www.nationalbeef.com	Kansas City	MO	64163	800-449-2333	
Ohio Packing Co 1306 Harmon Ave; *Web:* www.ohiopacking.com	Columbus	OH	43223	614-239-1600	237-0885
Olymel LP 2200 Pratte Ave Pratte; *TF:* 800-361-7990 ■ *Web:* www.olymel.com	Saint-Hyacinthe	QC	J2S4B6	450-771-0400	645-2869
OSI Industries LLC 1225 Corporate Blvd; *Web:* www.osigroup.com	Aurora	IL	60505	630-851-6600	692-2340
Pearl Meat Packing Company Inc 27 York Ave; *TF:* 800-462-3022 ■ *Web:* www.pearlmeat.com	Randolph	MA	02368	781-228-5100	228-5123
Plumrose USA Inc 1901 Butterfield Rd Ste 305; *TF:* 800-526-4909 ■ *Web:* www.plumroseusa.com	Downers Grove	IL	60515	732-624-4040	257-6644
Premium Standard Farms Inc Hwy 65 N PO Box 194	Princeton	MO	64673	660-748-4647	748-7341
Quality Meats & Seafoods 700 Ctr St; *TF:* 800-342-4250 ■ *Web:* www.qualitymeats.com	West Fargo	ND	58078	701-282-0202	
Quality Porks International Inc 10404 F Plz; *Web:* www.qpii.com	Omaha	NE	68127	402-339-1911	339-8383
Quincy Street Inc 13350 Quincy St; *TF:* 800-784-6290 ■ *Web:* www.quincystreetinc.com	Holland	MI	49424	616-399-3330	399-0952
Rochelle Foods Inc 1001 S Main St PO Box 45	Rochelle	IL	61068	815-562-4141	562-4149
Rose Packing Company Inc 65 S Barrington Rd; **Fax:* Cust Svc ■ *TF:* 800-323-7363 ■ *Web:* www.rosepacking.com	South Barrington	IL	60010	847-381-5700	381-9436*
Sam Hausman Meat Packer Inc 4261 Beacon; *TF:* 800-364-5521 ■ *Web:* www.hausmanfoods.com/	Corpus Christi	TX	78403	361-883-5521	883-1003
Sam Kane Beef Processors Inc 9001 Leopard St; *TF:* 800-242-4142 ■ *Web:* www.samkanebeef.com	Corpus Christi	TX	78409	361-241-5000	242-2999
Schenk Packing Co Inc 8204 288th St NW; *Web:* www.schenkpacking.com	Stanwood	WA	98292	360-629-6290	629-4451
Sioux-Preme Packing Co 4241 US 75th Ave; *TF General:* 800-735-7675 ■ *Web:* www.siouxpreme.com	Sioux Center	IA	51250	800-735-7675	
Smithfield Foods Inc 200 Commerce St; *NYSE:* SFD ■ *TF:* 800-276-6158 ■ *Web:* www.smithfieldfoods.com	Smithfield	VA	23430	757-365-3000	365-3017
Square-H Brands Inc 2731 S Soto St; *Web:* www.squarehbrands.com	Los Angeles	CA	90058	323-267-4600	261-7350
Superior Farms 1480 Drew Ave Ste 100; *TF:* 800-228-5262 ■ *Web:* www.superiorfarms.com	Davis	CA	95618	530-297-7299	757-1184
Thompson Packers Inc 550 Carnation St; *TF:* 800-989-6328 ■ *Web:* www.thompack.com	Slidell	LA	70460	985-641-6640	645-2112
Travis Meats Inc 7210 Clinton Hwy PO Box 670; *TF:* 800-247-7606 ■ *Web:* www.travismeats.com	Powell	TN	37849	865-938-9051	938-9211
Tyson Fresh Meats Inc 800 Stevens Port Dr; *TF:* 800-416-2269 ■ *Web:* www.tyson.com	Dakota Dunes	SD	57049	605-235-2061	
Washington Beef LLC 201 Elmwood Rd; *Web:* www.wabeef.org	Toppenish	WA	98948	509-865-2121	
Wolverine Packing Company Inc 2535 Rivard St; *Web:* www.wolverinepacking.com	Detroit	MI	48207	313-259-7500	568-1909

477 MEDICAL ASSOCIATIONS - STATE

SEE ALSO Health & Medical Professionals Associations p. 1796

Association	City	State	Zip	Phone	Fax
Alabama Medical Assn 19 S Jackson St; **Fax Area Code:* 334 ■ *TF:* 800-239-6272 ■ *Web:* www.masalink.org	Montgomery	AL	36104	800-239-6272	269-5200*
Alaska State Medical Assn 4107 Laurel St; *TF:* 800-951-8712 ■ *Web:* www.asmadocs.org	Anchorage	AK	99508	907-562-0304	561-2063
Arizona Medical Assn, The (ArMA) 810 W Bethany Home Rd; *TF:* 800-482-3480 ■ *Web:* www.azmed.org	Phoenix	AZ	85013	602-246-8901	242-6283
California Medical Assn 1201 J St Ste 200; *Web:* www.cmanet.org	Sacramento	CA	95814	916-444-5532	
Colorado Medical Society 7351 Lowry Blvd; *TF:* 800-654-5653 ■ *Web:* www.cms.org	Denver	CO	80230	720-859-1001	859-7509
Connecticut State Medical Society 160 St Ronan St; *TF:* 800-406-1527 ■ *Web:* www.csms.org	New Haven	CT	06511	203-865-0587	865-4997
Delmarva Foundation For Medical Care Inc (DFMC) 28464 Marlboro Ave; *TF:* 800-999-3362 ■ *Web:* delmarvafoundation.org	Easton	MD	21601	410-822-0697	822-7971
Hawaii Medical Assn 1360 S Beretania St Ste 200; *TF:* 888-536-2792 ■ *Web:* www.hmaonline.net	Honolulu	HI	96814	808-536-7702	528-2376
Idaho Medical Assn 305 W Jefferson St; *Web:* www.idmed.org	Boise	ID	83702	208-344-7888	344-7903
Illinois State Medical Society 20 N Michigan Ave Ste 700; *TF:* 800-782-4767 ■ *Web:* www.isms.org	Chicago	IL	60602	312-782-1654	782-2023
Indiana State Medical Assn 322 Canal Walk; *TF:* 800-257-4762 ■ *Web:* www.ismanet.org	Indianapolis	IN	46202	317-261-2060	261-2076
Iowa Medical Society 1001 Grand Ave; *TF:* 800-747-3070 ■ *Web:* www.iowamedical.org	West Des Moines	IA	50265	515-223-1401	223-0590
Journal Mississippi State Medical Assn 408 W PkwyPl; *Web:* msmaonline.com	Ridgeland	MS	39157	601-853-6733	
Kansas Medical Society 623 SW Tenth Ave; *TF:* 800-332-0156 ■ *Web:* kmsonline.org	Topeka	KS	66612	785-235-2383	235-5114
Kentucky Medical Assn 4965 US Hwy 42 KMA Bldg Ste 2000; *Web:* www.kyma.org	Louisville	KY	40222	502-426-6200	426-6877
Louisiana State Medical Society 6767 Perkins Rd Ste 100; *TF:* 800-375-9508 ■ *Web:* www.lsms.org	Baton Rouge	LA	70808	225-763-8500	763-6122
Maine Medical Assn 30 Assn Dr; *TF:* 800-772-0815 ■ *Web:* www.mainemed.com	Manchester	ME	04351	207-622-3374	622-3332
Maryland State Medical Society 1211 Cathedral St; *TF:* 800-492-1056 ■ *Web:* www.medchi.org	Baltimore	MD	21201	410-539-0872	547-0915
Massachusetts Medical Society (MMS) 860 Winter St; *TF:* 800-322-2303 ■ *Web:* www.massmed.org	Waltham	MA	02451	781-893-4610	893-8009
Medical Assn of Georgia (MAG) 1849 The Exchange Ste 200; *TF:* 800-282-0224 ■ *Web:* www.mag.org	Atlanta	GA	30339	678-303-9290	303-3732

				Phone	Fax
Michigan State Medical Society 120 W Saginaw St *Web:* www.msms.org	East Lansing	MI	48823	517-337-1351	337-2490
Minnesota Medical Assn 1300 Godward St NE Ste 2500 *TF:* 800-342-5662 ■ *Web:* www.mnmed.org	Minneapolis	MN	55413	612-378-1875	378-3875
Missouri State Medical Assn 113 Madison St *TF:* 800-869-6762 ■ *Web:* www.msma.org	Jefferson City	MO	65101	573-636-5151	636-8552
Montana Medical Assn 2021 11th Ave Ste 1 *TF:* 877-443-4000 ■ *Web:* www.mmaoffice.org	Helena	MT	59601	406-443-4000	443-4042
Nebraska Medical Assn 233 S 13th St Ste 1200 *Web:* www.nebmed.org	Lincoln	NE	68508	402-474-4472	474-2198
Nevada State Medical Assn (NSMA) 3660 Baker Ln Ste 101 *Web:* www.nsmadocs.org	Reno	NV	89509	775-825-6788	825-3202
New Hampshire Medical Society Seven N State St *TF:* 800-564-1909 ■ *Web:* www.nhms.org	Concord	NH	03301	603-224-1909	226-2432
New Jersey Medical Society 2 Princess Rd *TF:* 800-706-7893 ■ *Web:* www.msnj.org	Lawrenceville	NJ	08648	609-896-1766	
New Mexico Medical Society (NMMS) 316 Osuna Rd NE Ste 501 *TF:* 800-748-1596 ■ *Web:* www.nmms.org	Albuquerque	NM	87107	505-828-0237	828-0336
New York State Medical Society 865 Merrick Ave PO Box 5404 *TF:* 800-523-4405 ■ *Web:* www.mssny.org	Westbury	NY	11590	516-488-6100	488-1267
North Carolina Medical Society 222 N Person St *TF:* 800-722-1350 ■ *Web:* www.ncmedsoc.org	Raleigh	NC	27601	919-833-3836	833-2023
North Dakota Medical Assn (NDMA) 1622 I- Ave. *Web:* www.ndmed.org	Bismarck	ND	58503	701-223-9475	223-9476
Ohio State Medical Assn 3401 Mill Run Dr *TF:* 800-766-6762 ■ *Web:* www.osma.org	Hilliard	OH	43026	614-527-6762	527-6763
Oregon Medical Assn (OMA) 11740 SW 68th Pkwy Ste 100 *TF:* 877-605-3229 ■ *Web:* www.theoma.org	Portland	OR	97223	503-619-8000	619-0609
Pennsylvania Medical Society 777 E Pk Dr *Web:* www.pamedsoc.org	Harrisburg	PA	17111	717-558-7750	558-7840
Rhode Island Medical Society 235 Promenade St Ste 500 *TF:* 800-343-7776 ■ *Web:* www.rimed.org	Providence	RI	02908	401-331-3207	751-8050
South Carolina Medical Assn 132 W Pk Blvd *TF:* 800-327-1021 ■ *Web:* www.scmedical.org	Columbia	SC	29210	803-798-6207	772-6783
Texas Medical Assn 401 W 15th St *TF:* 800-880-1300 ■ *Web:* www.texmed.org	Austin	TX	78701	512-370-1300	370-1693
Vermont Medical Society 134 Main St *TF:* 800-640-8767 ■ *Web:* www.vtmd.org	Montpelier	VT	05601	802-223-7898	223-1201
Virginia Medical Society 4205 Dover Rd *TF:* 800-746-6768 ■ *Web:* www.msv.org	Richmond	VA	23221	804-353-2721	355-6189
Washington State Medical Assn 2033 Sixth Ave Ste 1100 *TF:* 800-552-0612 ■ *Web:* www.wsma.org	Seattle	WA	98121	206-441-9762	441-5863
West Virginia State Medical Assn 4307 MacCorkle Ave SE PO Box 4106 *TF:* 800-257-4747 ■ *Web:* www.wvsma.com	Charleston	WV	25364	304-925-0342	925-0345
Wisconsin State Medical Society 330 E Lakeside St **Fax Area Code: 608 ■ *TF:* 866-442-3800 ■ *Web:* www.wisconsinmedicalsociety.org	Madison	WI	53701	866-442-3800	442-3802*
Wyoming Medical Society 122 E 17th St *TF:* 888-879-3599 ■ *Web:* www.wyomed.org	Cheyenne	WY	82001	307-635-2424	632-1973

478 MEDICAL & DENTAL EQUIPMENT & SUPPLIES - WHOL

				Phone	Fax
180 Medical Inc 5324 W Reno Ste A *Web:* www.180medical.com	Oklahoma City	OK	73127	405-702-7700	
480 Biomedical Inc 480 Arsenal St *Web:* www.480biomedical.com	Watertown	MA	02472	617-393-4600	
A Plus International Inc 5138 Eucalyptus Ave *TF:* 800-762-1123 ■ *Web:* www.aplusgroup.net	Chino	CA	91710	909-591-5168	591-0359
A to Z Logos 3947 Catamarca Dr *Web:* www.a2zlogos.com	San Diego	CA	92124	858-715-4775	
ABC Home Medical Supply Inc 15 E Uwchlan Ave Ste 430 *TF:* 866-897-8588 ■ *Web:* www.abc-med.com	Exton	PA	19341	866-897-8588	
Ace Medical Inc 94-910 Moloalo St *TF:* 866-678-3601 ■ *Web:* www.acemedicalinc.com	Waipahu	HI	96797	808-678-3600	678-3604
Advacare Systems 2939 N Pulaski Rd *Web:* www.advacaresystems.com	Chicago	IL	60641	773-725-8858	
Advanced Diagnostics Inc 2440 Cinnabar Loop *Web:* www.adialaska.com	Anchorage	AK	99507	907-344-3456	
Advanced Imaging Research Inc 4700 Lakeside Ave Ste 400 *Web:* www.advimg.com	Cleveland	OH	44114	216-426-1461	
Advanced Medical Equipment Inc 2655 S Dixie Dr *Web:* www.advancedmedequipment.com	Kettering	OH	45409	937-534-1080	
Adventure Medical Kits LLC 7700 Edgewater Dr Ste 526 *Web:* www.adventuremedicalkits.com	Oakland	CA	94624	510-261-7414	
Aeroflow Inc 3165 Sweeten Creek Rd *TF:* 888-345-1780 ■ *Web:* www.aeroflowinc.com	Asheville	NC	28803	888-345-1780	
Aethon Inc 100 Business Ctr Dr *Web:* www.aethon.com	Pittsburgh	PA	15205	412-322-2975	
Aktina Medical Physics Corp 360 N Route 9W *Web:* www.aktina.com	Congers	NY	10920	845-268-0101	
Allegro Industries 7221 Orangewood Ave *Web:* www.allegrosafety.com	Garden Grove	CA	92841	714-899-9855	
Allied 100 LLC 1800 US Hwy 51 N *Web:* www.aedsuperstore.com	Woodruff	WI	54568	715-358-2329	
Alma Lasers Inc 485 Half Day Rd Ste 100 *Web:* www.almalasers.com	Buffalo Grove	IL	60089	224-377-2000	
Alpha Imaging Inc 4455 Glenbrook Rd *TF:* 800-331-7327 ■ *Web:* www.alpha-imaging.com	Willoughby	OH	44094	440-953-3800	953-1455
Alpha Source Inc 6619 W Calumet Rd *Web:* www.alphasource.com	Milwaukee	WI	53223	414-760-2222	
Amber Diagnostics Inc 2180 Premier Row *Web:* www.amberusa.com	Orlando	FL	32809	407-438-7847	
Amendia Inc 1755 W Oak Pkwy *Web:* www.amendia.com	Marietta	GA	30062	678-445-3784	
American Medical Alarms Inc 4414 SE 16th Pl Ste 4 *Web:* www.americanmedicalalarms.com	Cape Coral	FL	33904	239-540-4655	
American Medical ID 949 Wakefield Ste 100 *TF:* 800-363-5985 ■ *Web:* www.americanmedical-id.com	Houston	TX	77018	800-363-5985	
American Medical Supplies Inc 751 Park of Commerce Dr Ste 126 *Web:* www.americandiabetic.com	Boca Raton	FL	33487	561-362-7105	
Ampronix Inc 15 Whatney *TF:* 800-400-7972 ■ *Web:* www.ampronix.com	Irvine	CA	92618	949-273-8000	
Amvex Corp 25B E Pearce St *Web:* www.amvex.com	Richmond Hill	ON	L4B2M9	905-764-7736	
Andersen Products Inc 3202 Caroline Dr *Web:* www.anpro.com	Haw River	NC	27258	336-376-3000	
Andrew Technologies LLC 1421 Edinger Ave Ste D *TF:* 888-959-7674 ■ *Web:* hydrasolvc.com	Tustin	CA	92780	888-959-7674	
Anesthesia Service Inc 1821 N Classen Blvd Ste 100 *Web:* www.anesthesiaservice.com	Oklahoma City	OK	73106	405-525-3588	
Ansar Group Inc, The 240 S Eigth St *TF:* 888-883-7804 ■ *Web:* www.ans-hrv.com	Philadelphia	PA	19107	215-922-6088	922-6463
Ansell Sandel Medical Solutions LLC 19736 Dearborn St *Web:* www.sandelmedical.com	Chatsworth	CA	91311	818-534-2500	
Applied Medical Technology Inc 8000 Katherine Blvd *Web:* www.amtinnovation.com	Brecksville	OH	44141	440-717-4000	
Aqueduct Medical Inc 665 Third St Ste 20 *TF:* 877-365-4325 ■ *Web:* www.aqueductmedical.com	San Francisco	CA	94107	877-365-4325	
AR Medicom Inc 1200 55th Ave *Web:* www.medicom.com	Lachine	QC	H8T3J8	514-636-6262	
Aria Medical 1330 W Blanco Rd *Web:* www.ariamedical.com	San Antonio	TX	78232	210-281-9602	
Arteriocyte Medical Systems Inc 7100 Euclid Ave Research & Development Ctr *Web:* www.arteriocyte.com	Cleveland	OH	44103	216-456-9640	
Attentus Medical Sales Inc 5750 N Sam Houston Pkwy E Ste 406 *Web:* www.attentusmedical.com	Houston	TX	77032	281-776-5188	
Augmenix Inc 204 Second Ave *Web:* www.augmenix.com	Waltham	MA	02451	781-895-3235	
Avalign Technologies Inc 272 E Deerpath Rd Ste 208 *Web:* www.avaligntech.com	Lake Forest	IL	60045	847-739-3239	
aycan Medical Systems LLC 693 East Ave *Web:* www.aycanus.com	Rochester	NY	14607	585-473-1350	
Banyan International Corp PO Box 1779 *Web:* www.statkit.com	Abilene	TX	79604	325-677-1372	
Bard Electrophysiology Inc 55 Technology Dr	Lowell	MA	01851	978-441-6202	
Benco Dental Co 295 CenterPoint Blvd *Web:* www.benco.com	Pittston	PA	18640	800-462-3626	
BidMed LLC 321 N Clark St Ste 2550 *Web:* bidmed.com	Chicago	IL	60654	773-840-8140	
BioImagene Inc 919 Hermosa Ct *Web:* www.bioimagene.com	Sunnyvale	CA	94085	408-207-4200	
Bisco Dental Products (Canada) Inc 2571 Smith St *Web:* www.biscocanada.com	Richmond	BC	V6X2J1	604-276-8662	
BIT MedTech operation 15870 Bernardo Ctr Dr *Web:* www.calmedtech.com	San Diego	CA	92127	858-613-1200	
Blickman Inc 500 US Hwy 46 E *Web:* www.blickman.com	Clifton	NJ	07011	973-330-0557	
Block Scientific Inc 1620 Ocean Ave Unit 3 *Web:* www.blockscientific.com	Bohemia	NY	11716	631-589-1118	
Blue Belt Technologies Inc 2905 Northwest Blvd Ste 40 *Web:* www.bluebelttech.com	Plymouth	MN	55441	763-452-4950	
Blue Ridge X-Ray Company Inc 120 Vista Blvd *TF:* 800-727-7290 ■ *Web:* www.blueridgex-ray.com	Arden	NC	28704	800-727-7290	
Breathe Technologies Inc 175 Technology Dr Ste 100 *Web:* www.breathetechnologies.com	Irvine	CA	92618	949-988-7700	
BRIT Systems Inc 1909 Hi Line Dr *Web:* www.brit.com	Dallas	TX	75207	214-630-0636	
Broadley-James Corp 19 Thomas *Web:* www.broadleyjames.com	Irvine	CA	92618	949-829-5555	
Browns Medical Imaging 9880 Pflumm Rd *Web:* www.brownsmedicalimaging.com	Lenexa	KS	66215	913-888-6710	
Buffalo Hospital Supply Company Inc 4039 Genesee St *Web:* www.buffalohospital.com	Buffalo	NY	14225	716-626-9400	626-4307
Burkhart Dental Supply Co 2502 S 78th St *TF Cust Svc:* 800-562-8176 ■ *Web:* www.burkhartdental.com	Tacoma	WA	98409	253-474-7761	472-4773
Burlington Medical Supplies Inc Three Elmhurst St *Web:* www.burmed.com	Newport News	VA	23603	757-888-8994	

Name / Address	City	State	Zip	Phone	Fax
Butler Animal Health Supply LLC 400 Metro Pl N	Dublin	OH	43017	614-761-9095	659-1653
TF PR: 888-691-2724 ■ *Web:* www.accessbutler.com					
Byram Healthcare Centers Inc 120 Bloomingdale Rd	White Plains	NY	10605	914-286-2000	
TF: 800-354-4054 ■ *Web:* www.byramhealthcare.com					
Cameron Health Inc 905 Calle Amanecer Ste 300	San Clemente	CA	92673	949-498-5630	
Web: www.cameronhealth.com					
CAN-med Healthcare 200 Bluewater Rd	Bedford	NS	B4B1G9	902-455-4649	
Web: www.canmedhealthcare.com					
Canadian Hospital Specialties ULC 2810 Coventry Rd	Oakville	ON	L6H6R1	905-825-9300	
Web: www.chsltd.com					
Capital X-Ray Inc 2189 Notasulga Rd	Tallassee	AL	36078	334-283-8410	
Web: www.capitalxray.com					
Cardiac Dimensions Inc 5540 Lk Washington Blvd NE	Kirkland	WA	98033	425-605-5900	
Web: www.cardiacdimensions.com					
CardioMed Supplies Inc 199 Saint David St	Lindsay	ON	K9V5K7	705-328-2518	328-9747
Web: www.cardiomed.com					
Care Medical Systems 1840 S Central St	Visalia	CA	93277	559-741-9005	
Web: www.caremedical.com					
CAREstream Medical Ltd 20133 102 Ave Units 1	Langley	BC	V1M4B4	604-552-5486	310-2187*
**Fax Area Code:* 888 ■ *Web:* www.carestreammedical.com					
Carl Zeiss Canada Ltd 45 Valleybrook D	Toronto	ON	M3B2S6	416-449-4660	449-3524
Web: www.zeiss.ca					
Carolina Apothecary Inc 726 S Scales St	Reidsville	NC	27320	336-342-0071	
Web: www.carolinaapothecary.com					
Cascade Orthopedic Supply Inc 2638 Aztec Dr	Chico	CA	95928	530-879-1500	
Web: www.cascade-usa.com					
Cassling Diagnostic Imaging Inc 13808 F St	Omaha	NE	68137	402-334-5000	
Web: www.cassling.com					
Castlewood Surgical Inc 91 Main St Ste 302	Concord	MA	01742	978-610-6321	
Web: www.castlewoodsurgical.com					
Cbaia 1125 Jefferson Davis Hwy Ste 380	Fredericksburg	VA	22401	540-604-9731	
Web: www.cbaia.com					
CCS Medical Inc 1505 LBJ Fwy Ste 600	Farmers Branch	TX	75234	800-260-8193	
TF: 800-726-9811 ■ *Web:* www.ccsmed.com					
CellAegis Devices Inc 139 Mulock Ave First Fl	Toronto	ON	M6N1G9	647-722-9601	
Web: www.cellaegisdevices.com					
Centennial Optical Ltd 158 Norfinch Dr	Toronto	ON	M3N1X6	416-739-8539	
Web: www.centennialoptical.com					
CenTrak Inc Five Caufield Pl Ste 102	Newtown	PA	18940	215-860-2928	
Web: www.centrak.com					
Central Medical Equipment Rentals Inc 2850 Douglas Rd Third Fl	Coral Gables	FL	33134	305-441-0156	
Web: www.empmed.com					
CERAGEM International Inc 3699 Wilshire Blvd Ste 900	Los Angeles	CA	90010	213-480-7070	
Web: www.ceragem.com					
Charter Medical Ltd 3948-A Westpoint Blvd	Winston-Salem	NC	27103	336-768-6447	
Web: www.chartermedical.com					
CHME Inc 289 Foster City Blvd Ste A	Foster	CA	94404	650-357-8550	
Web: www.chme.org					
Citagenix Inc 1111 Autoroute Chomedy	Laval	QC	H7W5J8	450-688-8699	688-1977
Web: www.citagenix.com					
Clarion Medical Technologies Inc 125 Fleming Dr	Cambridge	ON	N1T2B8	519-620-3900	
Web: www.clarionmedical.com					
Colson Associates Inc One N Franklin St Site 2420	Chicago	IL	60606	312-980-1100	
Web: www.colsongroup.com					
Columbia Medical Manufacturing LLC 11724 Willake St	Santa Fe Springs	CA	90670	562-282-0244	
Web: www.columbiamedical.com					
Comedical Inc 7100 Roosevelt Way NE	Seattle	WA	98115	206-524-7424	
Web: www.comedical.com					
Companion Health Services Inc 284 N St	Boston	MA	02113	617-227-0830	
Web: www.companionhealthservices.com					
Connect America LLC 2193 W Chester Pk	Broomall	PA	19008	800-654-6100	
TF: 800-654-6100 ■ *Web:* connectamerica.com					
Core Medical Imaging Inc 6161 Ne 175th St Ste 201	Kenmore	WA	98028	425-485-4330	
Web: www.coremedicalimaging.com					
Cortech Solutions Inc 1409 Audubon Blvd Ste B1	Wilmington	NC	28403	910-362-1143	
Web: www.cortechsolutions.com					
Crest Services 735 Plz Blvd Ste 210	Coppell	TX	75019	214-488-9301	488-9299
Web: crestservices.org					
Current Solutions LLC 3814 Woodbury Dr	Austin	TX	78704	512-600-7080	
Web: www.currentsolutionsnow.com					
Cygnus Manufacturing Company LLC Victory Rd Business Park 491 Chantler Dr	Saxonburg	PA	16056	724-352-8000	
Web: www.cmc-usa.com					
D&B Industrial Group 21649 Cedar Creek Ave	Georgetown	DE	19947	302-855-0585	
Web: www.dbindustrialgroup.com					
Dalton Medical Corp 1435 Bradley Ln Ste 100	Carrollton	TX	75007	972-418-5129	
Web: www.daltonmedical.com					
Decision Diagnostics Corp 2660 Townsgate Rd Ste 300	Westlake Village	CA	91361	805-446-1973	
Web: www.instacare.net					
Dectro International Inc 1000 Blvd du Parc-Technologique	Quebec	QC	G1P4S3	418-650-0303	
Web: www.dectro.com					
Dedicated Distribution Inc 640 Miami Ave	Kansas City	KS	66105	913-371-2200	
TF: 800-325-8367 ■ *Web:* www.dedicateddistribution.com					
Delta Medical Systems Inc W239 N2890 Pewaukee Rd Unit E	Pewaukee	WI	53072	262-523-2300	
Web: www.deltamedicalsystems.com					
Dentsply Canada Ltd 161 Vinyl Ct	Woodbridge	ON	L4L4A3	905-851-6060	
Web: www.dentsply.ca					
Derma Sciences Inc 214 Carnegie Ctr Ste 100	Princeton	NJ	08540	609-514-4744	514-8554
TF: 800-825-4325 ■ *Web:* www.dermasciences.com					
DogLeggs LLC 2104 Thomas View Rd	Reston	VA	20191	703-715-0300	
Web: www.dogleggs.com					
Dr Fresh Inc 6645 Caballero Blvd	Buena Park	CA	90620	714-690-1573	
Web: www.drfreshdental.com					
DRE Inc 1800 Williamson Ct	Louisville	KY	40223	502-244-4444	
Web: www.dremed.com					
Dukal Corp Two Fleetwood Ct	Ronkonkoma	NY	11779	631-656-3800	
Web: www.dukal.com					
Dura Medical Equipment Inc 7835 NW 148 St	Miami Lakes	FL	33016	305-821-1202	
Web: www.bayshoreduramedical.com					
Dynamic Medical Systems Inc 2811 E Ana St	Rancho Dominguez	CA	90221	310-928-0251	
Web: www.godynamic.com					
Eagle Laboratories Inc 10201-A Trademark St	Rancho Cucamonga	CA	91730	909-481-0011	
Web: www.eaglelabs.com					
Electra-med Corp 5332 Hill 23 Dr	Flint	MI	48507	810-232-4856	
Web: www.electramed.com					
Electromek Diagnostic Systems Inc 412 W US Hwy 40	Troy	IL	62294	618-667-6761	
Web: www.electromek.com					
elliquence LLC 2455 Grand Ave	Baldwin	NY	11510	516-277-9000	
Web: www.elliquence.com					
Endomedix Inc 211 Warren St	Newark	NJ	07103	848-248-1883	
Web: www.endomedix.com					
Endoscopic Technologies Inc 2603 Camino Ramon Ste 100	San Ramon	CA	94583	925-866-7111	
Web: www.estech.com					
EndoShape Inc 2450 Central Ave Ste I	Boulder	CO	80301	303-951-6898	
Web: www.endoshape.com					
Endotec Inc 20 Valley St	South Orange	NJ	07079	973-762-6100	
Web: www.endotec.com					
Engineered Medical Systems Inc 2055 Executive Dr	Indianapolis	IN	46241	317-246-5500	
Web: www.engmedsys.com					
Enthermics Inc W164 N9221 Water St	Menomonee Falls	WI	53051	262-251-8356	
Web: www.enthermics.com					
Erchonia Corp 2021 Commerce Dr	Mckinney	TX	75069	214-544-2227	
Web: www.erchonia.com					
Evaheart Medical USA Inc 880 William Pitt Way Ste B1-330	Pittsburgh	PA	15238	412-828-7090	
Web: www.evaheart-usa.com					
Evans-Sherratt Co 13050 Northend Ave	Oak Park	MI	48237	248-584-5500	584-5510
TF: 800-248-3826 ■ *Web:* www.evans-sherratt.com					
eVent Medical Inc 971 Calle Amanecer Ste 101	San Clemente	CA	92673	949-492-8368	
Web: www.event-medical.com					
Evis Medical Equipment Inc 751 Maple Ave	Hartford	CT	06114	860-296-3565	
Web: www.evismedical.com					
Expeditor Systems Inc 4090 Nine McFarland Dr	Alpharetta	GA	30004	800-226-8158	
Web: www.expeditor.com					
Feta Med Inc 530 S Henderson Rd Ste D	King Of Prussia	PA	19406	610-205-0010	
Web: www.fetamed.com					
First Coast Hearing Clinic Inc 1835 Us Hwy 1 S Ste 127	Saint Augustine	FL	32084	904-824-6007	
Web: www.firstcoasthearing.com					
Flanagan Instruments Inc 633 Village Ln N	Mandeville	LA	70471	985-626-3786	
Web: www.flanagan.com					
FMI Inc 2382 United Ln	Elk Grove Village	IL	60007	847-350-1535	
Web: www.fmimed.com					
Freedom Designs Inc 2241 N Madera Rd	Simi Valley	CA	93065	805-582-0077	
Web: www.freedomdesigns.com					
GE Walker Inc 3502-C Queen Palm Dr	Tampa	FL	33619	813-623-2481	
Web: www.gewalker.com					
Global Medical Imaging LLC 222 Rampart St	Charlotte	NC	28203	800-958-9986	
TF: 800-958-9986 ■ *Web:* www.gmi3.com					
Global Medical LLC 8332 Bristol Ct Ste 108	Jessup	MD	20794	800-528-1001	
TF: 800-528-1001 ■ *Web:* www.globalmedical1.com					
Global Resources International Inc 4142 Industry Way	Flowery Branch	GA	30542	678-866-0550	
Web: www.gri-usa.com					
Goetze Dental 3939 NE 33 Terrace	Kansas City	MO	64117	816-413-1200	
Web: www.goetzedental.com					
Griffin Home Health Care Inc 4231 Monroe Rd	Charlotte	NC	28205	704-347-1993	
Web: www.griffinhomehealthcare.com					
Griswold Machine & Engineering Inc 8530 M 60	Union City	MI	49094	517-741-4300	
TF: 800-248-2054 ■ *Web:* www.gme-shields.com					
Grogans Health Care Supply Inc 1016 S Broadway St	Lexington	KY	40504	859-254-6661	254-6666
TF: 800-365-1020 ■ *Web:* www.grogans.com					
Halyard Health Inc 5405 Windward Pkwy	Alpharetta	GA	30004	678-425-9273	
Web: www.halyardhealth.com					
Hanson Medical Systems Inc 1954 Howell Branch Rd Ste 203	Winter Park	FL	32792	407-671-3883	
Web: www.hansonmedicalsystems.com					
Hardy Diagnostics Inc 1430 W Mccoy Ln	Santa Maria	CA	93455	805-346-2766	
Web: www.hardydiagnostics.com					
Hasco Medical Inc 15928 Midway Rd	Addison	TX	75001	214-302-0930	
Web: hascomed.com					
Healthcom 1600 W Jackson St	Sullivan	IL	61951	217-728-8331	
Web: www.healthcominc.com					
Hegele Logistic LLC 1460 Brummel Ave	Elk Grove	IL	60007	847-690-0430	
Web: www.hegelelogistic.com					

				Phone	Fax
Helm Surgical Systems LLC 5895 E Evans Ave Ste 100 *Web:* www.helmsurgical.com	Denver	CO	80222	720-524-1900	
HemaSource Inc 4158 Nike Dr Ste B *Web:* www.hemasource.com	West Jordan	UT	84088	801-280-5151	
Henry Schein Inc 135 Duryea Rd *NASDAQ: HSIC* ■ *TF:* 800-582-2702 ■ *Web:* www.henryschein.com	Melville	NY	11747	631-843-5500	843-5652
Hi-Tech Healthcare Inc 1805 Shackleford Ct Ste 100 *Web:* www.hitechcares.com	Norcross	GA	30093	770-449-6785	
Holt Dental Supply Inc N30 W22383 Green Rd Ste A *Web:* holtdentalsupply.com	Waukesha	WI	53186	262-896-9380	
Home Care Specialists Inc 113 Neck Rd PO Box 8237 *Web:* www.hcshme.com	Haverhill	MA	01835	978-373-7771	
Hospi Tel Manufacturing Corp 545 N Arlington Ave Ste 7 *Web:* www.hospitel.com	East Orange	NJ	07017	973-678-7100	
Hospira Healthcare Corp 1111 Dr Frederik-Philips Blvd Ste 600 *Web:* www.hospira.ca	Saint-laurent	QC	H4M2X6	514-905-2600	
HRM USA Inc 1039 Pulinski Rd *Web:* www.heartratemonitorsusa.com	Warminster	PA	18974	215-259-2700	
HyperBranch Medical Technology Inc 800-12 Capitola Dr *Web:* www.hyperbranch.com	Durham	NC	27713	919-433-3325	
IC Medical Inc 2340 W Shangri La Rd *Web:* www.icmedical.com	Phoenix	AZ	85029	623-780-0700	
Indigo ORB Inc 2454 Alton Pkwy *Web:* www.indigo-orb.com	Irvine	CA	92606	949-784-0303	
Innovative Optics Inc 6812 Hemlock Ln *Web:* www.innovativeoptics.com	Maple Grove	MN	55369	763-425-7789	
Instratek Inc 15200 Middlebrook Dr Ste G *Web:* www.instratek.com	Houston	TX	77058	281-890-8020	
Instrumed International Inc 626 Cooper Ct *Web:* www.instrumedinc.biz	Schaumburg	IL	60173	847-908-0292	
Intact Medical Corp 550 Cochituate Rd Ste 25 East Wing Fl 4 *Web:* www.intactmedical.com	Framingham	MA	01701	508-655-7820	
Integra LifeSciences Corp 15115 Park Row Ste 100 *Web:* www.metasurg.com	Houston	TX	77084	281-398-5656	
International Manufacturing Group Inc 879 F St Ste 120 *TF:* 800-775-6412 ■ *Web:* www.relyaid.com	West Sacramento	CA	95605	800-775-6412	
Interplex Medical LLC 25 Whitney Dr *Web:* www.interplexmedical.com	Milford	OH	45150	513-248-5120	
Intrinsic Therapeutics Inc 30 Commerce Way *Web:* www.intrinsic-therapeutics.com	Woburn	MA	01801	781-932-0222	
Invuity Inc 444 De Haro St *Web:* www.invuity.com	San Francisco	CA	94107	415-655-2100	
Iowa Veterinary Supply Co (IVESCO) 124 Country Club Rd *TF:* 800-457-0118 ■ *Web:* www.ivescollc.com	Iowa Falls	IA	50126	641-648-2529	648-5994
Jordan Reses Supply Company LLC 24 Frank Lloyd Wright Dr Ste A3300 *Web:* www.jrsupplyco.com	Ann Arbor	MI	48106	734-213-5528	
Jorgensen Laboratories Inc 1450 Van Buren Ave *TF:* 800-525-5614 ■ *Web:* www.jorvet.com	Loveland	CO	80538	970-669-2500	663-5042
Kapstone Medical LLC 100 E S Main St *Web:* www.kapstonemedical.com	Waxhaw	NC	28173	704-843-7852	
Karl Storz Endoscopy-america Inc 600 Corporate Pt Fl 5 *TF:* 800-321-1304 ■ *Web:* www.karlstorz.com	Culver City	CA	90230	310-338-8100	
KCI Medical Canada Inc 75 Courtneypark Dr W Unit No 2 *Web:* www.kci-medical.ca	Mississauga	ON	L5W0E3	905-565-7187	
KD Scientific Inc 84 October Hill Rd *Web:* www.kdscientific.com	Holliston	MA	01746	508-429-6809	
Keir Surgical Ltd 408 E Kent Ave S Ste 126 *Web:* www.keirsurgical.com	Vancouver	BC	V5X2X7	604-261-9596	
Kentec Medical Inc 17871 Fitch *TF:* 800-825-5996 ■ *Web:* www.kentecmedical.com	Irvine	CA	92614	949-863-0810	833-9730
Keystone Industries 480 S Democrat Rd *TF:* 800-333-3131 ■ *Web:* www.keystoneindustries.com	Gibbstown	NJ	08027	856-663-4700	224-9444
Laerdal Medical Corp 167 Myers Corners Rd PO Box 1840 *Web:* www.laerdal.com	Wappingers Falls	NY	12590	845-297-7770	
LaserBand LLC 120 S Central Ave Ste 450 *Web:* www.laserband.com	St. Louis	MO	63105	314-726-1060	
Leeches USA Ltd 300 Shames Dr *TF:* 800-645-3569 ■ *Web:* www.leechesusa.com	Westbury	NY	11590	516-333-2570	997-4948
LENSAR Inc 2800 Discovery Dr *TF:* 888-536-7271 ■ *Web:* www.lensar.com	Orlando	FL	32826	888-536-7271	
Les Wilkins & Assoc Inc 6850 35th Ave NE *Web:* www.leswilkins.com	Seattle	WA	98115	206-522-0908	522-5292
Life Systems Inc 515 Trade Ctr Blvd *Web:* www.lifesystemsinc.com	Chesterfield	MO	63005	636-787-2100	
Life-Assist Inc 11277 Sunrise Park Dr *TF:* 800-824-6016 ■ *Web:* www.life-assist.com	Rancho Cordova	CA	95742	800-824-6016	
Logi-D Holding Inc 5550 des Rossignols Blvd *Web:* www.logi-d.net	Laval	QC	H7L5W6	450-628-8800	
Mabis Healthcare Inc 1931 Norman Dr *TF:* 800-526-4753 ■ *Web:* www.mabisdmi.com	Waukegan	IL	60085	800-526-4753	479-7968
Mada Medical Products Inc 625 Washington Ave *TF:* 800-526-6370 ■ *Web:* www.madamedical.com	Carlstadt	NJ	07072	201-460-0454	460-3509
Magnaserv Enterprises Inc 2862 SE Monroe St *Web:* www.magnaserv.com	Stuart	FL	34997	772-219-2229	
Maquet-Dynamed Inc 235 Shields Ct *Web:* www.maquet-dynamed.com	Markham	ON	L3R8V2	905-752-3300	

				Phone	Fax
Marketlab Inc 6850 Southbelt Dr **Fax Area Code:* 616 ■ *TF:* 866-237-3722 ■ *Web:* marketlab.com	Caledonia	MI	49316	866-237-3722	656-2475*
MAST Biosurgery Inc 6749 Top Gun St Ste 108 *Web:* www.mastbio.com	San Diego	CA	92121	858-550-8050	
Mati Therapeutics Inc 4317 Dunning Ln *Web:* www.matitherapeutics.com	Austin	TX	78746	512-329-6360	
MC Healthcare Products Inc 4658 Ontario St **Fax Area Code:* 905 ■ *TF:* 800-268-8671 ■ *Web:* www.mchealthcare.com	Beamsville	ON	L0R1B4	800-268-8671	563-8680*
MCI Optonix LLC 253 E Washington Ave *Web:* www.mcio.com	Washington	NJ	07882	908-835-0004	
McKesson Medical Group Extended Care 8121 Tenth Ave N **Fax Area Code:* 763 ■ *TF:* 800-328-8111 ■ *Web:* www.mbbnet.umn.edu/company_folder/mckhboc-mgec.html	Golden Valley	MN	55427	800-328-8111	595-6677*
McKesson Medical-Surgical 8741 Landmark Rd **Fax Area Code:* 804 ■ *TF:* 800-446-3008 ■ *Web:* www.mckesson.com	Richmond	VA	23228	415-983-8300	264-7679*
MD International Inc 11300 NW 41st St *Web:* www.mdint.com	Miami	FL	33178	305-669-9003	
Med 4 Home Inc 10800 N Congress Ave *Web:* www.med4home.com	Kansas City	MO	64153	816-801-7400	
MED-EL Corp 2511 Old Cornwallis Rd Ste 100 *Web:* www.medel.com	Durham	NC	27713	919-572-2222	
Med-Fit Systems Inc 3553 Rosa Way *Web:* www.medfitsystems.com	Fallbrook	CA	92028	760-723-9618	
MedaCheck LLC 602 Main St Fourth Fl Ste 401 *Web:* www.medacheck.com	Cincinnati	OH	45202	513-488-1111	
MedAvail Technologies Inc 6665 Millcreek Dr Unit No1 *Web:* www.medavail.com	Mississauga	ON	L5N5M4	905-812-0023	
Medcare Products Inc 151 E Cliff Rd *Web:* medcarelifts.com	Burnsville	MN	55337	952-894-7076	
Medi-Globe Corp 110 W Orion St Ste 136 *Web:* www.mediglobe.com	Tempe	AZ	85283	480-897-2772	
Medical Treatment Systems Inc 6300 Westgate Rd Ste A	Raleigh	NC	27617	919-782-9050	
MedicaMetrix Inc One Old Sudbury Rd *Web:* www.medicametrix.com	Wayland	MA	01778	617-694-1713	
MediCapture Inc 580 W Germantown Pk Ste 103 *Web:* www.medicapture.com	Plymouth Meeting	PA	19462	610-238-0700	
Medigroup Services Corp 1360 S Fifth St Ste 334 *Web:* www.medigroup.com	St. Charles	MO	63301	636-947-7555	
Medison Econet Corp 7260 NW 58th St *Web:* www.medisoneconet.com	Miami	FL	33166	305-599-7161	
MedSignals Corp 217 Alamo Plz *Web:* www.medsignals.com	San Antonio	TX	78205	210-222-2067	
MedSupply 5850 E Shields Ave Ste 105 *Web:* www.gomedsupply.net	Fresno	CA	93727	559-292-1540	
MEI Development Corp 11772 W Sample Rd *Web:* www.meidevelopment.com	Coral Springs	FL	33065	954-341-3302	
Mergenet Solutions Inc 6601 Lyons Rd Ste B1-B4 *Web:* www.mergenetsolutions.com	Coconut Creek	FL	33073	561-208-3770	
Mesa Laboratories Inc 12100 W Sixth Ave *NASDAQ: MLAB* ■ *TF Sales:* 800-992-6372 ■ *Web:* www.mesalabs.com	Lakewood	CO	80228	303-987-8000	987-8989
Micro Bio-Medics Inc 14 Pelham Pkwy	Pelham	NY	10803	914-738-9200	
Midway Dental Supply Inc 701 N Michigan St *Web:* www.midwaydental.com	Lakeville	IN	46536	574-784-2533	
MinXray Inc 3611 Commercial Ave *Web:* www.minxray.com	Northbrook	IL	60062	847-564-0323	
Mio 2930 Arbutus St *Web:* www.mioglobal.com	Vancouver	BC	V6J3Y9	604-224-9184	
Mizuho OSI Inc 30031 Ahern Ave *Web:* www.mizuhosi.com	Union City	CA	94587	510-429-1500	
Mmar Medical Group Inc 9619 Yupondale Dr *Web:* www.mmarmedical.com	Houston	TX	77080	713-465-2003	465-2818
Mobile Medical International Corp 2176 Portland St PO Box 672 *Web:* www.mobile-medical.com	St. Johnsbury	VT	05819	802-748-2322	
Mobility Freedom Inc 20354 US Hwy 27 *Web:* www.mobilityfreedom.com	Clermont	FL	34715	352-429-3972	
Monarch Medical Imaging Equipment Inc 101 Ellis St *Web:* www.monarchmedical.com	Staten Island	NY	10307	718-317-0124	
Monebo Technologies Inc 1800 Barton Creek Blvd *Web:* www.monebo.com	Austin	TX	78735	512-732-0235	732-0285
Monteris Medical Inc 16305 36th Ave N Ste 200 *Web:* www.monteris.com	Plymouth	MN	55446	763-253-4710	
Moore Medical Corp 389 John Downey Dr **Fax Area Code:* 800 ■ *TF Sales:* 800-234-1464 ■ *Web:* www.mooremedical.com	New Britain	CT	06050	860-826-3600	944-6667*
Nashville Dental Inc 1229 Northgate Business Pkwy *Web:* www.nashvilledental.com	Madison	TN	37115	615-868-3911	
National HME Inc 7451 Airport Fwy *Web:* www.nationalhme.com	Richland Hills	TX	76118	817-332-4433	
Nationwide Medical Equipment Inc 1510 Stuart Rd Ste 109 *Web:* www.nme.cc	Cleveland	TN	37312	423-478-7433	
NCD Corp 33801 Curtis Blvd Ste 100 *Web:* www.ncdcorp.com	Eastlake	OH	44095	440-953-4488	
ndd Medical Technologies Inc Two Dundee Park *Web:* www.nddmed.com	Andover	MA	01810	978-470-0923	
NEI Treatment Systems LLC 3530 Wilshire Blvd Ste 1130 *Web:* www.nei-marine.com	Los Angeles	CA	90010	213-383-5855	
NeoForce Group Inc 35 Commerce Dr *Web:* www.neoforcegroup.com	Ivyland	PA	18974	215-672-6800	

Company	City	State	ZIP	Phone	Fax
NeoMed Inc 100 Londonderry Ct Ste 112 *Web:* www.neomedinc.com	Woodstock	GA	30188	770-516-2225	
NeoTract Inc 4473 Willow Rd Ste 100 *Web:* www.neotract.com	Pleasanton	CA	94588	925-401-0700	
Neoventa Medical Inc 226 Lowell St Ste 1a2 *Web:* www.neoventa.com	Wilmington	MA	01887	978-657-7750	
Nesch LLC 9800 Connecticut Dr *Web:* www.neschllc.com	Crown Point	IN	46307	219-644-3505	
Neta Scientific Inc 4206 Sylon Blvd *Web:* www.netascientific.com	Hainesport	NJ	08036	609-265-8210	
Neuro Kinetics Inc 128 Gamma Dr *Web:* www.neuro-kinetics.com	Pittsburgh	PA	15238	412-963-6649	
Neuro-Tec Inc 975 Cobb Pl Blvd Ste 301 *TF:* 800-554-3407 ■ *Web:* www.neurotec.net	Kennesaw	GA	30144	800-554-3407	
NeuroPace Inc 455 N Bernardo Ave *Web:* www.neuropace.com	Mountain View	CA	94043	650-237-2700	
New Star Lasers Inc 9085 Foothills Blvd. *Web:* www.newstarlasers.com	Roseville	CA	95747	916-677-1900	
Next Health LLC 112 Rowayton Ave *Web:* www.nexthealthinc.com	Rowayton	CT	06853	203-939-1153	
Nidek Inc 47651 Westinghouse Dr *Web:* usa.nidek.com	Fremont	CA	94539	510-226-5700	
Nihon Kohden America Inc 90 Icon *TF:* 800-325-0283 ■ *Web:* www.nkusa.com	Foothill Ranch	CA	92610	949-580-1555	580-1550
Nipro Medical Corp 3150 NW 107th Ave. *Web:* www.nipro.com	Miami	FL	33172	305-599-7174	
Noraxon U.S.A. Inc 15770 N Greenway-Hayden Loop Ste 100 *Web:* www.noraxon.com	Scottsdale	AZ	85260	480-443-3413	
North American Medical Corp 1649 Sands Pl SE Ste A *Web:* www.namcorporation.com	Marietta	GA	30067	770-541-0012	
North American Rescue LLC 35 Tedwall Ct *Web:* www.narescue.com	Greer	SC	29650	864-675-9800	
Northern X-ray Co 2118 Fourth Ave S *Web:* www.nxcimaging.com	Minneapolis	MN	55404	612-870-1561	
Nova Ortho-Med Inc 1470 Beachey Pl. *Web:* www.novamedicalproducts.com	Carson	CA	90746	310-352-3600	
Oakworks Inc 923 E Wellspring Rd *TF:* 800-558-8850 ■ *Web:* www.oakworks.com	New Freedom	PA	17349	717-235-6807	235-6798
Odyssey Medical Inc 2975 Brother Blvd. *Web:* www.odysseymed.com	Bartlett	TN	38133	901-383-7777	
OEC Medical Systems Inc 384 Wright Brothers Dr. *Web:* www.gehealthcare.com	Salt Lake City	UT	84116	801-328-9300	
Omar Medical Supplies Inc Holiday Plz Dr Ste 130 *Web:* www.omarinc.com	Matteson	IL	60443	708-679-0347	
Omega Medical Health Systems Inc 1200 E High St Ste 106 *TF:* 866-716-6342 ■ *Web:* www.omegamedicalsystems.com	Pottstown	PA	19464	866-716-6342	
Omron Healthcare Inc 1925 W Field Ct *Fax: Cust Svc ■ *TF:* 877-216-1333 ■ *Web:* www.omronhealthcare.com	Lake Forest	IL	60045	847-680-6200	680-6269*
Ondal USA 5140 Commerce Rd *Web:* ondal.com	Richmond	VA	23234	804-279-0320	
Online Engineering Inc 400 N Cedar St *Web:* www.online-engineering.com	Manistique	MI	49854	906-341-0090	
Onyx Medical Corp 1800 N Shelby Oaks Dr *Web:* www.onyxmedical.net	Memphis	TN	38134	901-323-6699	
OptiNose US Inc 1010 Stony Hill Rd Ste 375 *Web:* www.optinose.com	Yardley	PA	19067	267-364-3500	
Oral BioTech 812 Water Ave NE *Web:* www.carifree.com	Albany	OR	97321	541-928-4445	
Oral-B Laboratories 600 Clipper Dr Ste 200 *TF:* 800-566-7252 ■ *Web:* www.oralb.com	Belmont	CA	94002	800-566-7252	
Organ Recovery Systems Inc 2570 E Devon Ave. *Web:* www.organ-recovery.com	Des Plaines	IL	60018	847-824-2600	
Ortho Kinematics Inc 7004 Bee Cave Rd Bldg III Ste 315 *Web:* www.orthokinematics.com	Austin	TX	78746	512-334-5490	
Otologics LLC 5445 Airport Blvd *Web:* www.otologics.com	Boulder	CO	80301	303-448-9933	
Otto Bock Healthcare North America Inc Two Carlson Pkwy N Ste 100 *TF:* 800-328-4058 ■ *Web:* www.ottobockus.com	Minneapolis	MN	55447	763-553-9464	
Owens & Minor Inc 9120 Lockwood Blvd *NYSE: OMI* ■ *Web:* www.owens-minor.com	Mechanicsville	VA	23116	804-723-7000	723-7100
Paragon Medical Inc Eight Matchett Industrial Park Dr *Web:* www.paragonmedical.com	Pierceton	IN	46562	574-594-2140	
Parmenter Realty Partners 701 Brickell Ave Ste 2020 *Web:* www.parmco.com	Miami	FL	33131	305-379-7500	
PatientSafe Solutions Inc 5375 Mira Sorrento Pl Ste 500 *Web:* www.patientsafesolutions.com	San Diego	CA	92121	858-746-3100	
Patterson Cos Inc 1031 Mendota Heights Rd *NASDAQ: PDCO* ■ *TF:* 800-328-5536 ■ *Web:* www.pattersondental.com	Saint Paul	MN	55120	651-686-1600	686-9331
Patterson Dental Canada Inc 1205 Henri Bourassa Blvd *Web:* www.pattersondental.ca	West Montreal	QC	H3M3E6	514-745-4040	745-0596
Pearson Dental Supplies Inc 13161 Telfair Ave *Fax Area Code: 800 ■ *TF:* 800-535-4535 ■ *Web:* www.pearsondental.com	Sylmar	CA	91342	818-362-2600	835-3100*
PenRad Technologies Inc 114 Commerce Cir. *Web:* www.penrad.com	Buffalo	MN	55313	763-475-3388	
PerceptiMed Inc 365 San Antonio Rd *Web:* perceptimed.com	Mountain View	CA	94040	650-941-7000	
Permobil Inc 6961 Eastgate Blvd *Fax Area Code: 800 ■ *Web:* www.permobil.com	Lebanon	TN	37090	615-443-2839	231-3256*
PerSys Medical Co 5310 Elm St *Web:* www.ps-med.com	Houston	TX	77081	888-737-7978	
Pharmed Corp 24340 Sperry Dr. *Web:* www.pharmedcorp.com	Westlake	OH	44145	440-835-0660	
Philips Healthcare 22100 Bothell Everett Hwy *Web:* www.dunlee.com	Bothell	WA	98021	425-487-7000	
Physcient Inc 112 S Duke St Ste 4A *Web:* www.physcient.com	Durham	NC	27701	919-686-0300	
PickPoint Corp 4234 Hacienda Dr Ste 101 *Web:* www.pickpoint.com	Pleasanton	CA	94588	925-924-1700	
Pivot Medical Inc 247 Humboldt Courtyard *Web:* www.pivotmedical.com	Sunnyvale	CA	94089	408-774-1452	
PMT Corp 1500 Park Rd. *Web:* www.pmtcorp.com	Chanhassen	MN	55317	952-470-0866	
Portal Instruments Inc 148 Sidney St *Web:* www.portalinstruments.com	Cambridge	MA	02139	617-500-4348	
Precision BioLogic Inc 140 Eileen Stubbs Ave *Web:* www.precisionbiologic.com	Dartmouth	NS	B3B0A9	902-468-6422	
Precision X-Ray Inc 15 Commerce Dr *Web:* www.pxinc.com	North Branford	CT	06471	203-484-2011	
Prestige Medical Corporation International 8600 Wilbur Ave. *Web:* www.prestigemedical.com	Northridge	CA	91324	818-993-3030	
Prima Tooh USA 279 Faison McGowan Rd Ste 2 *TF:* 888-833-7099 ■ *Web:* neogen.com/primatech	Kenansville	NC	28349	910-296-6116	296-0306
PRN Medical Services LLC 2311 W Utopia Rd. *Web:* www.symbiusmedical.com	Phoenix	AZ	85027	623-780-8686	
Proa Medical Inc 2512 Artesia Blvd Ste 305-C *Web:* proamedical.com	Redondo Beach	CA	90278	310-592-3046	
Professional Hospital Supply Inc 41980 Winchester Rd *Web:* www.phsyes.com	Temecula	CA	92590	951-296-2600	
ProLabs Inc 137 Herricks Rd *Web:* www.prolabs.md	Garden City Park	NY	11040	516-877-9000	
ProMed Molded Products Inc 15600 Medina Rd *Web:* www.promedmolding.com	Plymouth	MN	55447	763-331-3800	
Promex Technologies LLC 3049 Hudson St. *Web:* www.promextech.com	Franklin	IN	46131	317-736-0128	
PSS World Medical Inc 4345 Southpoint Blvd. *NASDAQ: PSSI* ■ *Web:* www.pssworldmedical.com	Jacksonville	FL	32216	904-332-3000	
Pulsar Vascular Inc 4030 Moorpark Ave Ste 110 *Web:* www.pulsarvascular.com	San Jose	CA	95117	408-260-9264	
Pulse Biomedical Inc 1305 Catfish Ln *Web:* www.qrscard.com	Norristown	PA	19403	610-666-5510	
Radiancy Inc 40 Ramland Rd S Ste 200 *Web:* www.radiancy.com	Orangeburg	NY	10962	845-398-1647	
Rainier Surgical Inc 1144 29th St NW *Web:* www.rainiersurgical.com	Auburn	WA	98001	253-486-0500	
RedRick Technologies Inc 21624 Adelaide Rd *Web:* www.redricktechnologies.com	Mount Brydges	ON	N0L1W0	519-264-2400	
Reliable Medical Supply Inc 9401 Winnetka Ave N *Web:* www.reliamed.com	Brooklyn Park	MN	55445	763-255-3800	
Reshape Medical 100 Calle Iglesia *Web:* www.reshapemedical.com	San Clemente	CA	92672	949-429-6680	
Rgh Enterprises Inc 1810 Summit Commerce Pk *TF:* 800-307-5930 ■ *Web:* www.edgepark.com	Twinsburg	OH	44087	330-963-6998	963-6839
Rigaku Americas Corp 9009 New Trails Dr *Web:* www.rigaku.com	The Woodlands	TX	77381	281-362-2300	364-3628
Roberts Home Medical Inc 20465 Seneca Meadows Pkwy *Web:* www.robertshomemedical.com	Germantown	MD	20876	301-353-0300	
Roka Bioscience Inc 20 Independence Blvd Fourth Fl *Web:* www.rokabio.com	Warren	NJ	07059	908-605-4700	
Saebo Inc 2725 Water Ridge Pkwy Ste 320 Six LakePointe Plaza *Fax Area Code: 855 ■ *TF:* 888-284-5433 ■ *Web:* www.saebo.com	Charlotte	NC	28217	888-284-5433	414-0037*
SameDay Security Inc 133 S Church St *Web:* www.lifesupportmedical.com	Las Cruces	NM	88001	866-572-3274	
Savoy Technical Services Inc 4301 Hwy 27 South *Web:* savoyndt.com	Sulphur	LA	70665	337-558-6071	
SCHAERER MEDICAL USA Inc 675 Wilmer Ave *Web:* www.schaerermayfieldusa.com	Cincinnati	OH	45226	513-561-2241	
SciCan Ltd 1440 Don Mills Rd *Web:* www.scican.com	Toronto	ON	M3B3P9	416-445-1600	
Scisense Inc 3397 White Oak Rd Unit 3 *Web:* scisense.com	London	ON	N6E3A1	519-680-7677	
Sebacia Inc 2905 Premiere Pkwy Ste 150 *Web:* www.sebacia.com	Duluth	GA	30097	888-935-4411	
Secure Health Inc 1729 Red Oak Run *Web:* www.4securehealth.com	Fort Wayne	IN	46804	260-436-1436	
Securisyn Medical LLC 9150 Commerce Ctr Cir Ste 135 *Web:* www.securisyn.com	Highlands Ranch	CO	80129	303-952-4530	
SeQual Technologies Inc 11436 Sorrento Vly Rd *Web:* www.sequal.com	San Diego	CA	92121	858-202-3100	
Shared Imaging LLC 801 Phoenix Lk Ave *Web:* www.sharedimaging.com	Streamwood	IL	60107	630-483-3980	
Shared Service Systems Inc 1725 S 20th St. *Web:* www.sharedomaha.com	Omaha	NE	68108	402-536-5300	
Shifamed LLC 745 Camden Ave Ste A *Web:* www.shifamed.com	Campbell	CA	95008	408-637-2150	

Phone | Fax

Signus Medical LLC 18888 Lake Dr E .... Chanhassen MN 55317 952-294-8700
Web: www.signusmedical.com

Simbionix USA Corp
7100 Euclid Ave Baker Electric Bldg
Ste 180 .... Cleveland OH 44103 216-229-2040
Web: www.simbionix.com

Sinclair Dental Company Ltd
900 Harbourside Dr .... North Vancouver BC V7P3T8 604-986-1544
Web: www.sinclairdental.com

SinuSys Corp 4030 Fabian Way .... Palo Alto CA 94303 650-213-9988
Web: sinusys.com

SLMP LLC 407 Interchange St .... Mckinney TX 75071 972-436-1010
Web: www.statlab.com

SmartScrubs LLC 3400 E Mcdowell Rd .... Phoenix AZ 85008 800-800-5788
TF: 800-800-5788 ■ *Web:* www.smartscrubs.com

Somagen Diagnostics Inc 9220 25th Ave .... Edmonton AB T6N1E1 780-702-9500 438-6595
TF: 800-661-9993 ■ *Web:* www.somagen.com

Specialty Surgical Products Inc
1131 Us Hwy 93 N .... Victor MT 59875 406-961-0102
Web: www.ssp-inc.com

SST Group Inc 309 Laurelwood Rd Ste 20 .... Santa Clara CA 95054 408-350-3450
Web: www.sstgroup-inc.com

Strukmyer LLC 1801 Big Town Blvd Ste 100 .... Mesquite TX 75149 214-275-9595
Web: www.strukmyer.com

Sun Surgical Supply Co 302 NW Sixth St .... Gainesville FL 32601 352-377-2696
Web: www.sunsurgical.com

SureTek Medical 25 Maple Creek Cir Ste B .... Greenville SC 29607 864-299-9743
Web: www.suretekmedical.com

Surgical Principals Inc 1625 S Tacoma Way .... Tacoma WA 98409 888-801-9251
TF: 888-801-9251 ■ *Web:* www.surgicalprincipals.com

Synapse Biomedical Inc 300 Artino St .... Oberlin OH 44074 440-774-2488
Web: synapsebiomedical.com

Syneron Beauty Inc 11-380 Jamieson Pkwy .... Cambridge ON N3C4N4 519-651-1177
Web: www.tanda.com

Synovis Micro Companies Alliance Inc
439 Industrial Ln .... Birmingham AL 35211 205-941-0111
Web: www.synovismicro.com

Synthes Spine Inc 325 Paramount Dr .... Raynham MA 02767 508-880-8100
Web: www.depuysynthes.com

Sysmex America Inc One Nelson C White Pkwy .... Mundelein IL 60060 847-996-4500 996-4397
TF: 800-379-7639 ■ *Web:* www.sysmex.com

Systagenix Wound Management (US) Inc
400 Crown Colony Ste 302 .... Quincy MA 02169 617-774-5500
Web: www.systagenix.com

Talyst Inc 11100 NE Eigth St .... Bellevue WA 98004 425-289-5400 289-5663
Web: www.talyst.com

TCGRx N1671 Powers Lk Rd .... Powers Lake WI 53159 262-279-5307
Web: www.tcgrx.com

Tech West Vacuum Inc 2625 N Argyle Ave .... Fresno CA 93727 559-291-1650
Web: www.tech-west.com

Technical Instrument San Francisco
1826 Rollins Rd .... Burlingame CA 94010 650-651-3000
Web: www.techinst.com

Tegra Medical LLC Nine Forge Park .... Franklin MA 02038 508-541-4200
Web: www.tegramedical.com

Tendyne Holdings Inc 2825 Fairview Ave N .... Roseville MN 55113 651-289-5500
Web: www.tendyne.com

Tetra Medical Supply Corp 6364 W Gross Pt Rd .... Niles IL 60714 847-647-0590 647-9034
TF Cust Svc: 800-621-4041 ■ *Web:* www.tetramed.com

Therapy Support Inc 2803 N Oak Grove Ave .... Springfield MO 65803 417-890-7165
Web: www.therapysupport.com

Thermedx LLC 31200 Solon Rd Unit #1 .... Solon OH 44139 440-542-0883
Web: www.thermedx.com

Ti Ba Enterprises Inc 25 Hytec Cir .... Rochester NY 14606 585-247-1212
Web: www.ti-ba.com

Tiba Medical Inc 2701 NW Vaughn St Ste 470 .... Portland OR 97210 503-222-1500
Web: www.tibamedical.com

Tosoh Bioscience Inc
6000 Shoreline Court Ste 101 .... South San Francisco CA 94080 650-615-4970
Web: www.diagnostics.us.tosohbioscience.com

TPC Advance Technology Inc
18525 Gale Ave .... City Of Industry CA 91748 626-810-4337
Web: www.tpcdental.com

Trans Med USA Inc 31 Progress Ave .... Tyngsboro MA 01879 978-649-1970
TF: 800-442-1142 ■ *Web:* www.transmed-usa.com

Tri State Distribution Inc 600 Vista Dr .... Sparta TN 38583 800-392-9824
TF: 800-392-9824 ■ *Web:* www.provial.com

Tri-State Surgical Supply & Equipment Ltd
409 Hoyt St .... Brooklyn NY 11231 718-624-1000
Web: tristatesurgical.com

Triangle X-ray Co 4900 Thornton Rd Ste 117 .... Raleigh NC 27616 919-876-6156
Web: trianglexray.com

Tridien Medical Inc 4200 NW 120th Ave .... Coral Springs FL 33065 954-340-0500
Web: www.tridien.com

Trudell Medical Group Ltd 758 Third St .... London ON N5V5J7 519-685-8800
Web: www.tmml.com

Turn-key Medical Inc 365 Sw Fifth Ave .... Meridian ID 83642 208-888-1760
Web: turn-keymedical.com

Ultra Solutions Acquisition LLC
1137 E Philadelphia St .... Ontario CA 91761 909-628-1778
Web: www.ultrasolutions.com

US Med-Equip Inc 9777 W Gulf Bank Ste 20 .... Houston TX 77040 713-983-8860
Web: www.usmedequip.com

USDiagnostics Inc 2007 Bob Wallace Ave .... Huntsville AL 35805 256-534-4881
Web: www.usdiagnostics.com

Valeritas Inc 750 Rt 202 S Ste 600 .... Bridgewater NJ 08807 908-927-9920 927-9927
TF: 855-384-8848 ■ *Web:* www.valeritas.com

Vascular Dynamics Inc
2134 Old Middlefield Way Ste J .... Mountain View CA 94043 650-963-9370
Web: www.vasculardynamics.com

Vascular Pathways Inc 1847 Trade Ctr Way .... Naples FL 34109 239-254-0391
Web: www.vascularpathways.com

Phone | Fax

VasoHealthcare
Revolution Mill Studios 1150 Revolution Mill Dr Studio 1
.... Greensboro NC 27405 336-398-8276
Web: www.vasohealthcare.com

Venta Medical LLC 33170 Central Ave .... Union City CA 94587 510-429-9300
Web: ventamedical.com

Ventec Life Systems Inc
9800 29th Ave W Ste E101 .... Everett WA 98204 425-355-8038
Web: www.venteclife.com

VIOlight Inc One Executive Blvd Fourth Fl .... Yonkers NY 10701 914-207-1820
Web: www.violight.com

Virtual Imaging Inc
720 S Powerline Rd Ste E .... Deerfield Beach FL 33442 954-428-6191
Web: www.virtualimaging-fl.com

Vista Therapeutics Inc 3900 Paseo del Sol .... Sante Fe NM 87507 505-474-3143
Web: www.vistatherapeutics.org

Vital Diagnostics Inc 27 Wellington Rd .... Lincoln RI 02865 401-642-8400
Web: www.vitaldiagnosticsinc.com

VWR International
100 Matsonford Rd Bldg 1 Ste 200 .... Radnorpa PA 19087 610-431-1700 431-9174
TF: 800-932-5000 ■ *Web:* us.vwr.com

W Joe Shaw LTD 4200 Underwood Rd .... La Porte TX 77571 281-476-5392
Web: www.gosafe.com

Water-Jel Technologies LLC 50 Broad St .... Carlstadt NJ 07072 201-806-3040
Web: www.waterjel.com

Western Drug 3604 San Fernando Rd .... Glendale CA 91204 818-956-6691
Web: www.westerndrug.com

Westprime Healthcare 5751 Chino Ave .... Chino CA 91710 714-529-2027
Web: www.westprimehealthcare.com

William V MacGill & Co 1000 N LombaRd Rd .... Lombard IL 60148 630-889-0500 727-3433*
**Fax Area Code:* 800 ■ *TF:* 800-323-2841 ■ *Web:* www.macgill.com

Xenex Disinfection Services LLC
121 Interpark Ste 104 .... San Antonio TX 78216 210-538-9300
Web: www.xenex.com

XLV Diagnostics Inc 290 Munro St Ste 2311 .... Thunder Bay ON P7A7T1 807-766-3479
Web: xlvdiagnostics.com

Z-Medica Corp Four Fairfield Blvd .... Wallingford CT 06492 203-294-0000
Web: www.z-medica.com

Zee Medical Inc 22 Corporate Pk .... Irvine CA 92606 800-435-7763 252-9649*
**Fax Area Code:* 949 ■ *TF:* 800-435-7763 ■ *Web:* www.zeemedical.com

Zipline Medical Inc 747 Camden Ave Ste A .... Campbell CA 95008 408-412-7228
Web: www.ziplinemedical.com

Zosano Pharma Inc 34790 Ardentech Ct .... Fremont CA 94555 510-745-1200
Web: www.macroflux.com

MEDICAL FACILITIES

SEE Substance Abuse Treatment Centers p. 3199; Hospitals p. 2489; Imaging Services - Diagnostic p. 2551; Developmental Centers p. 2198; Health Care Providers - Ancillary p. 2448; Hospices p. 2479

479 MEDICAL INSTRUMENTS & APPARATUS - MFR

SEE ALSO Imaging Equipment & Systems - Medical p. 2551; Medical Supplies - Mfr p. 2733

Phone | Fax

AccessClosure Inc 645 Clyde Ave .... Mountain View CA 94043 408-610-6500
Web: www.accessclosure.com

Accurate Surgical & Scientific Instruments Corp
300 Shames Dr .... Westbury NY 11590 516-333-2570 997-4948
TF: 800-645-3569 ■ *Web:* www.accuratesurgical.com

Accuray Inc 1310 Chesapeake Terr .... Sunnyvale CA 94089 408-716-4600 716-4601
NASDAQ: ARAY ■ *TF:* 888-522-3740 ■ *Web:* www.accuray.com

AccuTech LLC 2641 La Mirada Dr .... Vista CA 92081 760-599-6555
Web: www.accutech-llc.com

ACIST Medical Systems Inc
7905 Fuller Rd .... Eden Prairie MN 55344 952-941-3507
Web: www.acist.com

Acme United Corp 60 Round Hill Rd .... Fairfield CT 06824 203-254-6060 254-6019
NYSE: ACU ■ *TF:* 800-835-2263 ■ *Web:* www.acmeunited.com

Ad-tech Medical Instrument Inc
1901 William St .... Racine WI 53404 262-634-1555
TF: 800-776-1555 ■ *Web:* www.adtechmedical.com

AESCULAP Inc 3773 Corporate Pkwy .... Center Valley PA 18034 800-282-9000 791-6886*
**Fax Area Code:* 610 ■ *TF:* 800-282-9000 ■ *Web:* www.aesculapusa.com

AirClean Systems Inc 3248 Lk Woodard Dr .... Raleigh NC 27604 919-255-3220
Web: www.aircleansystems.com

Alfa Scientific Designs Inc 13200 Gregg St .... Poway CA 92064 858-513-3888
Web: www.alfascientific.com

Alfa Wassermann Inc Four Henderson Dr .... West Caldwell NJ 07006 973-882-8630
Web: www.alfawassermannus.com

Allied Healthcare Products Inc
1720 Sublette Ave .... Saint Louis MO 63110 314-771-2400 477-7701*
NASDAQ: AHPI ■ **Fax Area Code:* 800 ■ **Fax:* Cust Svc ■ *TF:* 800-444-3954 ■ *Web:* www.alliedhpi.com

Altimate Medical Inc 262 W First St .... Morton MN 56270 507-697-6393
TF: 800-342-8968 ■ *Web:* www.easystand.com

Alto Development Corp
5206 Asbury Rd PO Box 758 .... Farmingdale NJ 07727 732-938-2266
Web: aemedical.com

Amaranth Medical Inc
1145 Terra Bella Ave Ste A .... Mountain View CA 94043 650-965-3830
Web: amaranthmedical.com

				Phone	Fax
Anchor Products Company Inc 52 Official Rd. *Web:* www.anchorsurgical.com	Addison	IL	60101	630-543-9124	
Andover Healthcare Inc 9 Fanaras Dr *TF:* 800-432-6686 ■ *Web:* www.andovercoated.com	Salisbury	MA	01952	978-465-0044	462-0003
Antares Pharma Inc 3905 Annapolis Ln N Ste 105 *AMEX: AIS* ■ *Web:* www.antarespharma.com	Minneapolis	MN	55447	763-475-7700	476-1009
Aperio Technologies Inc 1360 Park Ctr Dr Ste 106 *TF:* 866-478-4111 ■ *Web:* www.aperio.com	Vista	CA	92081	866-478-4111	
Apex Medical Technologies Inc 10064 Mesa Ridge Court Ste 202 *Web:* www.apexmedtech.com	San Diego	CA	92121	858-535-0012	
Aradigm Corp 3929 Pt Eden Way *OTC: ARDM* ■ *Web:* www.aradigm.com	Hayward	CA	94545	510-265-9000	265-0277
Armm Inc 17744 Sampson Ln *Web:* www.armminc.com	Huntington Beach	CA	92647	714-848-8190	
Artisan Laboratories Inc 2532 Se Hawthorne Blvd *Web:* www.artisandental.com	Portland	OR	97214	503-238-6006	
Aspect Imaging 60 St Clair Ave East Ste 703 *Web:* www.aspectimaging.com	Toronto	ON	M4T1N5	647-260-1991	
Aspen Medical Products 6481 Oak Cyn *TF:* 800-295-2776 ■ *Web:* www.aspenmp.com	Irvine	CA	92618	949-681-0200	681-0222
Asuragen Inc 2150 Woodward St Ste 100 *Web:* www.asuragen.com	Austin	TX	78744	512-681-5200	681-5201
Atrion Corp One Allentown Pkwy *NASDAQ: ATRI* ■ *Web:* www.atrioncorp.com	Allen	TX	75002	972-390-9800	396-7581
Atrium Medical Corp 5 Wentworth Dr. *TF:* 800-528-7486 ■ *Web:* www.atriummed.com	Hudson	NH	03051	603-880-1433	880-6718
Avantec Vascular Corp 605 W California Ave *Web:* www.avantecvascular.com	Sunnyvale	CA	94086	408-329-5400	
B Braun Medical Inc 824 12th Ave *TF:* 800-523-9676 ■ *Web:* www.bbraunusa.com	Bethlehem	PA	18018	610-691-5400	997-5510
Bard Access Systems Inc 605 North 5600 West *TF:* 800-443-5505 ■ *Web:* www.bardaccess.com	Salt Lake City	UT	84116	801-522-5000	
Bard Inc Peripheral Vascular 1625 W Third St. *TF:* 800-321-4254 ■ *Web:* www.bardpv.com	Tempe	AZ	85281	480-894-9515	966-7062
Baxter Healthcare Corp 1 Baxter Pkwy **Fax Area Code:* 224 ■ *Web:* www.baxter.com	Deerfield	IL	60015	847-948-2000	948-1813*
Baxter International Inc One Baxter Pkwy *NYSE: BAX* ■ *Web:* www.baxter.com	Deerfield	IL	60015	847-948-2000	948-3948
BD Medical 9450 S State St. *TF:* 888-237-2762 ■ *Web:* www.bd.com	Sandy	UT	84070	801-565-2300	565-2740
Becton Dickinson & Co One Becton Dr *NYSE: BDX* ■ **Fax:* Cust Svc ■ *TF Cust Svc:* 888-237-2762 ■ *Web:* www.bd.com	Franklin Lakes	NJ	07417	201-847-6800	847-4882*
Becton Dickinson Pharmaceutical Systems 1 Becton Dr MC407 **Fax Area Code:* 800 ■ *TF:* 800-638-8663 ■ *Web:* www.bd.com/pharmaceuticals	Franklin Lakes	NJ	07417	201-847-6800	847-2220*
Beekley Corp One Prestige Ln *Web:* www.beekley.com	Bristol	CT	06010	860-583-4700	
Benlan Inc 2760 Brighton Rd Winston Business Park *Web:* www.benlan.com	Oakville	ON	L6H5T4	905-829-5004	
Berkley Medical Resources Inc 700 Mtn View Dr. *Web:* www.business.com	Smithfield	PA	15478	724-564-5002	
Best Theratronics Ltd 413 March Rd *Web:* www.theratronics.ca	Ottawa	ON	K2K0E4	613-591-2100	
Best Vascular 4350 International Blvd Ste E *TF:* 800-668-6783 ■ *Web:* www.bestvascular.com	Norcross	GA	30093	770-717-0904	717-1283
Bio Compression Systems Inc 120 W Commercial Ave *Web:* www.biocompression.com	Moonachie	NJ	07074	201-939-0716	
BioCardia Inc 125 Shoreway Rd Ste B. *TF:* 800-624-1179 ■ *Web:* www.biocardia.com	San Carlos	CA	94070	650-226-0120	
Biocoat Inc 211 Witmer Rd. *Web:* www.biocoat.com	Horsham	PA	19044	215-734-0888	
BioCure Inc 2975 Gateway Dr Ste 100 *Web:* www.biocure.com	Norcross	GA	30071	678-966-3400	
Biodex Medical Systems Inc 20 Ramsay Rd. *TF:* 800-224-6339 ■ *Web:* www.biodex.com	Shirley	NY	11967	631-924-9000	924-8355
Bioflex Low Intensity Laser System 411 Horner Ave. *Web:* www.bioflexlaser.com	Etobicoke	ON	M8W4W3	416-251-1055	
Bioject Medical Technologies Inc 20245 SW 95 Ave. *OTC: BJCT* ■ *TF:* 800-683-7221 ■ *Web:* www.bioject.com	Tualatin	OR	97062	503-692-8001	692-6698
BioMerieux Inc 595 Anglum Rd **Fax Area Code:* 800 ■ *TF:* 800-634-7656 ■ *Web:* www.biomerieux.com	Hazelwood	MO	63042	314-731-8500	325-1598*
Biomet Microfixation Inc 1520 Tradeport Dr. *TF:* 800-874-7711 ■ *Web:* www.biomet.com	Jacksonville	FL	32218	904-741-4400	741-4500
Bioseal 167 W Orangethorpe Ave *Web:* www.biosealnet.com	Placentia	CA	92870	714-528-4695	
Biosense Webster Inc 3333 S Diamond Canyon Rd *TF:* 800-729-9010 ■ *Web:* www.biosensewebster.com	Diamond Bar	CA	91765	909-839-8500	468-2905
Biosign Technologies Inc 14-3715 Laird Rd. *Web:* www.biosign.com	Mississauga	ON	L5L0A3	416-218-9800	
Blackburn's Physicians Pharmacy Inc 301 Corbet St. *TF:* 800-472-2440 ■ *Web:* www.blackburnsmed.com	Tarentum	PA	15084	724-224-9100	224-9124
Blood Bank Computer Systems Inc 1002 15th St SW Ste 120 *Web:* www.bbcsinc.com	Auburn	WA	98001	253-333-0046	
Boston Scientific Corp One Boston Scientific Pl. *NYSE: BSX* ■ **Fax Area Code:* 888 ■ **Fax:* Cust Svc ■ *TF:* 888-272-1001 ■ *Web:* www.bostonscientific.com	Natick	MA	01760	508-650-8000	272-9444*
Braemar Inc 1285 Corporate Ctr Dr *TF:* 800-328-2719 ■ *Web:* www.braemarinc.com	Eagan	MN	55121	651-286-8620	286-8630
Braff Group, The 1665 Washington Rd Ste 3 *Web:* www.thebraffgroup.com	Pittsburgh	PA	15228	412-833-5733	
Braintree Laboratories Inc 60 Columbian St W *AMEX: AIS* ■ *Web:* www.braintreelabs.com	Braintree	MA	02185	781-843-2202	
Branan Medical Corp 140 Technology Ste 400 *Web:* www.brananmedical.com	Irvine	CA	92618	949-598-7166	
Brava LLC 14221 SW 142nd St Ste 725 *TF:* 800-422-5350 ■ *Web:* www.bravallc.com	Miami	FL	33186	305-856-4242	423-3254
Bunnell Inc 436 Lawndale Dr *Web:* www.bunl.com	Salt Lake City	UT	84115	801-467-0800	
Cadwell Laboratories Inc 909 N Kellogg St *TF:* 800-245-3001 ■ *Web:* www.cadwell.com	Kennewick	WA	99336	509-735-6481	783-6503
Cambridge Heart Inc 46 Jonspin Rd *TF:* 888-226-9283 ■ *Web:* www.cambridgeheart.com	Wilmington	MA	01887	978-654-7600	752-1330
Cantel Medical Corp 150 Clove Rd Ninth Fl *NYSE: CMN* ■ *Web:* www.cantelmedical.com	Little Falls	NJ	07424	973-890-7220	890-7270
CardiacAssist Inc 240 Alpha Dr. *TF:* 800-373-1607 ■ *Web:* www.cardiacassist.com	Pittsburgh	PA	15238	412-963-7770	
Cardica Inc 900 Saginaw Dr. *NASDAQ: CRDC* ■ *TF:* 888-544-7194 ■ *Web:* www.cardica.com	Redwood City	CA	94063	650-364-9975	364-3134
Cardinal Health Automation & Information Services 7000 Cardinal Pl. *Web:* cardinal.com/us/en/aboutus/ourbusinesses	Dublin	OH	43017	614-757-5000	
Cardiovascular Systems Inc 651 Campus Dr *TF:* 877-274-0360 ■ *Web:* www.csi360.com	St Paul	MN	55112	651-259-1600	
CareFusion Corp 3750 Torrey View Ct. *NYSE: CFN* ■ *TF:* 888-876-4287 ■ *Web:* www.carefusion.com	San Diego	CA	92130	858-617-2000	617-2900
CAS Medical Systems Inc 44 E Industrial Rd. *NASDAQ: CASM* ■ *TF:* 800-227-4414 ■ *Web:* www.casmed.com	Branford	CT	06405	203-488-6056	488-9438
Celsion Corp 10220-L Old Columbia Rd *NASDAQ: CLSN* ■ *TF:* 888-504-7965 ■ *Web:* www.celsion.com	Columbia	MD	21046	410-290-5390	290-5394
Certified Safety Manufacturing Inc 1400 Chestnut Ave *Web:* www.certifiedsafetymfg.com	Kansas City	MO	64127	816-483-9090	
Chad Therapeutics Inc 2975 Horseshoe Dr S Ste 600 *OTC: CHADQ* ■ *TF:* 800-423-8870 ■ *Web:* www.chadtherapeutics.com	Naples	FL	34104	239-687-1285	687-1280
Chemlink Laboratories Inc 1590 Roberts Rd Ste 111 *Web:* chemlinklabs.com	Kennesaw	GA	30144	770-499-8008	
Clementia Pharmaceuticals Inc 1375 TransCanada Hwy Ste 200 *Web:* clementiapharma.com	Montreal	QC	H9P2W8	514-940-3600	
CMP Industries LLC 413 N Pearl St. *Web:* cmpindustries.com	Albany	NY	12297	518-434-3147	
Command Medical Products Inc 15 Signal Ave *Web:* www.commandmedical.com	Ormond Beach	FL	32174	386-672-8116	
Compass Animal Health Inc 12872 141 St Nw *Web:* www.compass-ah.com	Edmonton	AB	T5L4S3	780-451-6517	
Composite Manufacturing Inc 970 Calle Amanecer Ste B *Web:* www.carbonfiber.com	San Clemente	CA	92673	949-361-7580	
Computerized Screening Inc 9550 Gateway Dr *Web:* www.computerizedscreening.com	Reno	NV	89521	775-359-1191	
Conmed Corp 525 French Rd *NASDAQ: CNMD* ■ **Fax Area Code:* 800 ■ **Fax:* Cust Svc ■ *TF:* 800-448-6506 ■ *Web:* www.conmed.com	Utica	NY	13502	315-797-8375	438-3051*
ConMed Endoscopic Technologie 525 French Rd. *TF:* 800-225-1332 ■ *Web:* www.conmed.com	Utica	NY	13502	315-797-8375	797-0321
CONMED Linvatec 11311 Concept Blvd **Fax:* Cust Svc ■ *TF Cust Svc:* 800-448-6506 ■ *Web:* www.conmed.com	Largo	FL	33773	727-392-6464	399-5256*
Cook Inc PO Box 4195 *TF:* 800-457-4500 ■ *Web:* www.cookmedical.com	Bloomington	IN	47402	812-339-2235	339-2235
Cook Medical Inc 1186 Montgomery Ln. *TF General:* 800-245-4715 ■ *Web:* www.cookmedical.com	Vandergrift	PA	15690	724-845-8621	845-2848
Cook Urological Inc 1100 W Morgan St PO Box 227 *TF:* 800-457-4500 ■ *Web:* www.cookmedical.com	Spencer	IN	47460	812-829-4891	829-1801
Cooper Cos Inc 6140 Stoneridge Mall Rd Ste 590 *NYSE: COO* ■ *TF:* 888-822-2660 ■ *Web:* www.coopercos.com	Pleasanton	CA	94588	925-460-3600	460-3649
CooperSurgical Inc 95 Corporate Dr **Fax Area Code:* 800 ■ **Fax:* Cust Svc ■ *TF:* 800-645-3760 ■ *Web:* www.coopersurgical.com	Trumbull	CT	06611	203-929-6321	262-0105*
Cordis Corp 14201 NW 60th Ave. **Fax Area Code:* 786 ■ *TF:* 800-327-7714 ■ *Web:* www.cordis.com	Miami Lakes	FL	33014	800-447-7585	313-2080*
Corpak Medsystems Inc 1001 Asbury Dr *TF:* 800-323-6305 ■ *Web:* www.corpakmedsystems.com	Buffalo Grove	IL	60089	847-403-3400	541-9526
CP Medical Inc 803 NE 25th Ave *Web:* www.cpmedical.com	Portland	OR	97232	503-232-1555	
CR Bard Inc 730 Central Ave *NYSE: BCR* ■ *Web:* www.crbard.com	Murray Hill	NJ	07974	908-277-8000	277-8412
CR Bard Inc Medical Div 8195 Industrial Blvd **Fax Area Code:* 800 ■ **Fax:* Cust Svc ■ *TF:* 800-526-4455 ■ *Web:* www.bardmedical.com	Covington	GA	30014	770-784-6100	852-1339*
CR Bard Inc Urological Div 8195 Industrial Blvd *TF:* 800-526-4455 ■ *Web:* www.bardmedical.com	Covington	GA	30014	770-784-6100	
Creative Laboratory Products Inc 6420 Guion Rd *Web:* www.clplipids.com	Indianapolis	IN	46268	317-293-2991	
CRH Medical Corp 999 Canada Pl Ste 522 *Web:* www.crhsystem.com	Vancouver	BC	V6C3E1	604-633-1440	
Criticare Systems Inc N7W22025 Johnson Dr *TF:* 800-458-4615 ■ *Web:* www.csiusa.com	Waukesha	WI	53186	262-798-8282	798-8290
Cutera Inc 3240 Bayshore Blvd. *NASDAQ: CUTR* ■ *TF:* 888-428-8372 ■ *Web:* www.cutera.com	Brisbane	CA	94005	415-657-5500	330-2444

Phone Fax

Cutting Edge Products LLC
350 Turk Hill Park . . . Fairport NY 14450 585-421-8080
Web: www.cuttingedgevet.com

Dale Medical Products Inc PO Box 1556 . . . Plainville MA 02762 800-343-3980 695-6587*
**Fax Area Code:* 508 ■ *TF:* 800-343-3980 ■ *Web:* www.dalemed.com

Davol Inc 100 Crossings Blvd . . . Warwick RI 02886 800-556-6756
TF Cust Svc: 800-556-6756 ■ *Web:* www.davol.com

Defibtech LLC 741 Boston Post Rd Ste 201 . . . Guilford CT 06437 203-453-4507
Web: www.defibtech.com

Delcath Systems Inc 810 Seventh Ave 35th Fl . . . New York NY 10019 212-489-2100
Web: www.delcath.com

Diopsys Inc 16 Chapin Rd Ste 911 . . . Pine Brook NJ 07058 973-244-0622
Web: www.diopsys.com

Disposable Instrument Co
14248 Santa Fe Trl Dr . . . Shawnee Mission KS 66215 913-492-6492
Web: www.disposableinstrument.com

Encision Inc 6797 Winchester Cir . . . Boulder CO 80301 303-444-2600 444-2693
OTC: ECIA ■ *TF:* 800-998-0986 ■ *Web:* www.encision.com

Endologix Inc 11 Studebaker . . . Irvine CA 92618 949-457-9546 843-1500*
NASDAQ: ELGX ■ **Fax Area Code:* 877 ■ *TF:* 800-983-2284 ■ *Web:* www.endologix.com

Epimed International Inc
141 Sal Landrio Dr . . . Johnstown NY 12095 518-725-0209
Web: www.epimedpain.com

Escalon Medical Corp 435 Devon Pk Dr Bldg 100 . . . Wayne PA 19087 610-688-6830 688-3641
NASDAQ: ESMC ■ *Web:* www.escalonmed.com

Eternity Healthcare Inc Ste 1 8755 Ash St . . . Vancouver BC V6P6T3 855-324-1110
TF: 855-324-1110 ■ *Web:* eternityhealthcare.com

Ethicon Endo-Surgery Inc 4545 Creek Rd . . . Cincinnati OH 45242 513-337-7000
Web: www.ethicon.com

ev3 Inc 3033 Campus Dr . . . Plymouth MN 55441 763-398-7000 398-7200
TF: 800-716-6700 ■ *Web:* www.ev3.net

First Quality Products Inc 121 N Rd . . . Mcelhattan PA 17748 570-769-6900
Web: www.firstquality.com

G & G Instrument Corp 466 Saw Mill River Rd . . . Ardsley NY 10502 914-693-6000 693-6738
TF: 800-882-2288 ■ *Web:* www.datacut.com

Gauthier Biomedical Inc 1235 Dakota Dr Ste G . . . Grafton WI 53024 262-546-0010
Web: www.gauthierbiomedical.com

Gaymar Industries Inc 10 Centre Dr . . . Orchard Park NY 14127 716-662-2551
TF: 800-828-7341 ■ *Web:* stryker.com/

GEM Edwards Inc
5640 Hudson Industrial Pkwy PO Box 429 . . . Hudson OH 44236 800-733-7976
TF: 800-733-7976 ■ *Web:* www.gemcomedical.com

Gemoscan Canada Inc
5000 Dufferin St Unit D1 . . . North York ON M3H5T5 416-650-1200
Web: www.hemocode.com

Gettig Technologies Inc
One Streamside Pl E . . . Spring Mills PA 16875 814-422-8892 422-8011
Web: springmillsmfg.com/

GF Health Products Inc 2935 NE Pkwy . . . Atlanta GA 30360 770-447-1609 726-0601*
**Fax Area Code:* 800 ■ *TF:* 800-347-5678 ■ *Web:* www.grahamfield.com

Great Basin Scientific Inc
2441 South 3850 West Ste 200A . . . West Valley City UT 84120 801-990-1055
Web: www.gbscience.com

GT Urological LLC 960 E Hennepin Ave . . . Minneapolis MN 55414 612-379-3578
Web: www.gturological.com

Gyrus ACMI 6655 Wedgwood Rd Ste 160 . . . Maple Grove MN 55311 763-416-3000
Web: medical.olympusamerica.com

Haemonetics Corp 400 Wood Rd . . . Braintree MA 02184 781-848-7100 860-1512*
NYSE: HAE ■ **Fax Area Code:* 800 ■ *TF:* 800-225-5242 ■ *Web:* www.haemonetics.com

Harmac Medical Products Inc 2201 Bailey Ave . . . Buffalo NY 14211 716-897-4500 897-0016
Web: www.harmac.com

Hartwell Medical Corp
6354 Corte Del Abeto Ste F . . . Carlsbad CA 92011 760-438-5500
Web: www.hartwellmedical.com

HeartSine Technologies Inc
121 Friends Ln Ste 400 . . . Newtown PA 18940 215-860-8100
Web: heartsine.com

Henry Troemner LLC 201 Wolf Dr . . . Thorofare NJ 08086 856-686-1600
TF: 800-352-7705 ■ *Web:* www.troemner.com

Hill-Rom Services Inc 1069 SR 46 E . . . Batesville IN 47006 812-934-7777 934-8189
TF: 800-267-2337 ■ *Web:* www.hill-rom.com

Hoggan Health Industries Inc
8020 South 1300 West . . . West Jordan UT 84088 801-572-6500 572-6514
TF: 800-678-7888 ■ *Web:* hogganhealth.net

Hospira Inc 275 N Field Dr . . . Lake Forest IL 60045 224-212-2000
NYSE: HSP ■ *TF:* 877-946-7747 ■ *Web:* www.hospira.com

Hospital Marketing Services Company Inc
162 Great Hill Rd . . . Naugatuck CT 06770 203-723-1466
Web: www.hmsmedical.com

Hypertension Diagnostics Inc
2915 Waters Rd Ste 108 . . . Eagan MN 55121 651-687-9999 687-0485
TF: 888-785-7392 ■ *Web:* www.hypertensiondiagnostics.com

Imaging Dynamics Company Ltd
Ste 1157 40 Ave NE . . . Calgary AB T2E6M9 403-251-9939
Web: www.imagingdynamics.com

Imalux Corp 11000 Cedar Ave Ste 250 . . . Cleveland OH 44106 216-502-0755

Immunalysis Corp 829 Towne Ctr Dr . . . Pomona CA 91767 909-482-0840
Web: immunalysis.com

ImmunoScience Inc 6670 Owens Dr . . . Pleasonton CA 94588 925-828-1000
Web: www.immunoscience.com

Implant Sciences Corp 500 Research Dr . . . Wilmington MA 01887 978-752-1700 752-1711
OTC: IMSC ■ *TF:* 877-732-7333 ■ *Web:* www.implantsciences.com

IND Diagnostic Inc 1629 Fosters Way . . . Delta BC V3M6S7 604-522-1619
Web: www.ind.ca

InfraReDx Inc 34 Third Ave . . . Burlington MA 01803 781-221-0053
Web: www.infraredx.com

Ingen Technologies Inc
3410 La Sierra Ave Ste F507 . . . Riverside CA 92503 951-688-7840
Web: www.ingen-tech.com

Inogen Inc 326 Bollay Dr . . . Goleta CA 93117 805-562-0500
Web: www.inogen.com

Phone Fax

Inovise Medical Inc
8770 SW Nimbus Ave Ste D . . . Beaverton OR 97008 503-431-3800
TF: 877-466-8473 ■ *Web:* www.inovise.com

Inrad Inc 4375 Donker Court SE . . . Kentwood MI 49512 616-301-7800
Web: www.inrad-inc.com

InSitu Technologies Inc 539 Phalen Blvd . . . St Paul MN 55130 651-389-1017
Web: www.insitu-tech.com

Insulet Corp Nine Oak Park Dr . . . Bedford MA 01730 781-457-5000
TF: 800-591-3455 ■ *Web:* investor.insulet.com

Integra LifeSciences Holdings Corp
311 Enterprise Dr . . . Plainsboro NJ 08536 609-275-0500 799-3297
NASDAQ: IART ■ *TF:* 800-654-2873 ■ *Web:* www.integra-ls.com

Interrad Medical Inc 181 Cheshire Ln Ste 100 . . . Plymouth MN 55441 763-225-6699
Web: www.interradmedical.com

Intersect ENT Inc 1555 Adams Dr . . . Menlo Park CA 94025 650-641-2100
Web: www.intersectent.com

Interventional Spine Inc
13700 Alton Pkwy Ste 160 . . . Irvine CA 92618 949-472-0006
Web: www.i-spineinc.com

Intuitive Surgical Inc
1266 Kifer Rd Bldg 101 . . . Sunnyvale CA 94086 408-523-2100 523-1390
NASDAQ: ISRG ■ *TF:* 888-868-4647 ■ *Web:* www.intuitivesurgical.com

Joerns Healthcare 5001 Joerns Dr . . . Stevens Point WI 54481 715-341-3600 457-8827*
**Fax Area Code:* 800 ■ *TF:* 800-826-0270

Johnson Matthey Medical Products
1401 King Rd . . . West Chester PA 19380 610-648-8000 648-8111
TF: 800-442-1405 ■ *Web:* www.jmmedical.com

JPI Healthcare Solutions Inc 52 Newton Plz . . . Plainview NY 11803 516-513-1330
Web: www.jpihealthcare.com

Katecho Inc 4020 Gannett Ave . . . Des Moines IA 50321 515-244-1212 244-4912
Web: www.katecho.com

Kensey Nash Corp 735 Pennsylvania Dr . . . Exton PA 19341 484-713-2100 713-2900
NASDAQ: KNSY ■ *TF General:* 800-322-2885 ■ *Web:* dsm.com/markets/medical/en_us/home.html

Kimberly-Clark/Ballard Medical Products
1400 Holcomb Bridge Rd . . . Roswell GA 30076 800-524-3577
TF: 800-524-3577 ■ *Web:* www.kchealthcare.com

Kinamed Inc 820 Flynn Rd . . . Camarillo CA 93012 805-384-2748
Web: www.kinamed.com

Kirwan Surgical Products Inc
180 Enterprise Dr . . . Marshfield MA 02050 781-834-9500
Web: www.ksp.com

Knit Rite Inc 120 Osage Ave . . . Kansas City KS 66105 913-281-4600 281-5455
TF: 800-821-3094 ■ *Web:* www.knitrite.com

Laborie Medical Technologies Inc
6415 Northwest Dr Unit 11 . . . Mississauga ON L4V1X1 905-612-1170
Web: www.laborie.com

Lake Region Mfg Company Inc
340 Lk Hazeltine Dr . . . Chaska MN 55318 952-361-2522 448-3441
Web: www.lakeregionmedical.com

Landice Inc 111 Canfield Ave . . . Randolph NJ 07869 973-927-9010
TF: 800-526-3423 ■ *Web:* www.landice.com

Laserage Technology Corp 3021 N Delany Rd . . . Waukegan IL 60087 847-249-5900 336-1103
Web: www.laserage.com

LeMaitre Vascular Inc 63 Second AVE . . . Burlington MA 01803 781-221-2266
Web: www.lemaitre.com

Life Measurement Inc 1850 Bates Ave . . . Concord CA 94520 925-676-6002
Web: www.bodpod.com

Life-tech Inc PO Box 1849 . . . Stafford TX 77497 281-491-6600 491-6646
TF: 800-231-9841 ■ *Web:* www.life-tech.com

Links Medical Products Inc 9247 Research Dr . . . Irvine CA 92618 949-753-0001
Web: www.linksmed.com

Mangar Industries Inc 97 Britain Dr . . . New Britain PA 18901 215-230-0300
Web: www.mangar.com

MAQUET Cardiac Assist 15 Law Dr . . . Fairfield NJ 07004 973-244-6100
TF: 800-777-4222 ■ *Web:* ca.maquet.com

Maxtec Inc 6526 S Cottonwood St . . . Salt Lake City UT 84107 801-266-5300
Web: www.maxtecinc.com

Med-I-Pant Inc 9100 Ray Lawson Blvd . . . Montreal QC H1J1K8 514-356-1224
Web: www.mipinc.info

Medarray Inc 3915 research park dr . . . Ann Arbor MI 48108 734-769-1066
Web: www.permselect.com

Medi-Nuclear Corp Inc
4610 Littlejohn St . . . Baldwin Park CA 91706 626-960-9822
Web: www.medinuclear.com

Medica Corp Five Oak Park Dr . . . Bedford MA 01730 781-275-4892
Web: www.medicacorp.com

Medical Components Inc 1499 Delp Dr . . . Harleysville PA 19438 215-256-4201
Web: www.medcompnet.com

Medical International Technology Inc
1872 Beaulac Ville Saint-Laurent . . . Montreal QC H4R2E7 514-339-9355
Web: www.mitcanada.ca

Medical Tactile Inc
5757 Century Blvd Ste 600 . . . Los Angeles CA 90045 310-641-8228
Web: www.medicaltactile.com

Medin Corp 90 Dayton Ave Bldg 16C . . . Passaic NJ 07055 973-779-2400
Web: www.medin.com

Medivance Inc 321 S Taylor Ave Ste 200 . . . Louisville CO 80027 303-926-1917
Web: www.medivance.com

MEDNOVUS Inc 664 Hymettus Ave . . . Leucadia CA 92024 760-390-1410
Web: www.mednovus.com

Medone Surgical Inc 670 Tallevast Rd . . . Sarasota FL 34243 941-359-3129
Web: www.medone.com

Medovations Inc 102 E Keefe Ave . . . Milwaukee WI 53212 414-265-7620 265-7628
TF: 800-558-6408 ■ *Web:* www.medovations.com

MedRx Inc 1200 Starkey Rd Ste 105 . . . Largo FL 33771 727-584-9600
Web: www.medrx-usa.com

Medtronic Inc 710 Medtronic Pkwy NE . . . Minneapolis MN 55432 763-514-4000 514-4879
NYSE: MDT ■ *TF Cust Svc:* 800-328-2518 ■ *Web:* www.medtronic.com

Medtronic Neurosurgery 125 Cremona Dr . . . Goleta CA 93117 800-633-8766 968-5038*
**Fax Area Code:* 805 ■ *TF Cust Svc:* 800-468-9710 ■ *Web:* medtronic.com

Medtronic Perfusion Systems
7611 Northland Dr . . . Brooklyn Park MN 55428 763-391-9000 391-9100
TF: 800-328-3320 ■ *Web:* www.medtronic.com

Phone | Fax

MedVenture Technology Corp
2301 Centennial Blvd ... Jeffersonville IN 47130 812-280-2400
Web: medventure.com

Megadyne Medical Products Inc
11506 S State St ... Draper UT 84020 801-576-9669 576-9698
TF: 800-747-6110 ■ *Web:* www.megadyne.com

Mercury Medical 11300 49th St N ... Clearwater FL 33762 727-573-0088 571-3922
TF: 800-237-6418 ■ *Web:* www.mercurymed.com

Meridian Medical Technologies Inc
6350 Stevens Forest Rd Ste 301 ... Columbia MD 21046 443-259-7800 259-7801
TF: 800-638-8093 ■ *Web:* www.meridianmeds.com

Merit Medical Systems Inc
1600 W Merit Pkwy ... South Jordan UT 84095 801-253-1600 253-1652
NASDAQ: MMSI ■ *TF:* 800-356-3748 ■ *Web:* www.merit.com

Michigan Instruments Inc
4717 Talon Ct SE ... Grand Rapids MI 49512 616-554-9696
Web: www.michiganinstruments.com

Micro-Tube Fabricators Inc 250 Lackland Dr ... Middlesex NJ 08846 732-469-7420 469-4314
Web: hhmtf.com

MicroAire Surgical Instruments Inc
3590 Grand Forks Blvd ... Charlottesville VA 22911 800-722-0822 975-4144*
**Fax Area Code:* 434 ■ *TF:* 800-722-0822 ■ *Web:* www.microaire.com

Microflex Corp 2301 Robb Dr ... Reno NV 89523 775-746-6600
Web: www.microflex.com

Microlife USA Inc
1617 Gulf to Bay Blvd Second Fl Ste B ... Clearwater FL 33755 727-451-0484
Web: www.microlifeusa.com

Microline Surgical Inc
800 Cummings Ctr Ste 157-X ... Beverly MA 01915 978-922-9810
Web: www.microlinesurgical.com

MicroLumen Inc One Microlumen Way ... Oldsmar FL 34677 813-886-1200
Web: www.microlumen.com

Micropace EP Inc 3205 W Warner Ave ... Santa Ana CA 92704 714-258-7025
Web: www.micropaceep.com

Midi Inc 125 Sandy Dr ... Newark DE 19713 302-824-4736
Web: www.midi-inc.com

Midmark Corp 60 Vista Dr ... Versailles OH 45380 937-526-3662
Web: www.midmark.com

MiMedx Group Inc 1775 W Oak Commons Ct Ne ... Marietta GA 30062 888-543-1917
TF: 888-543-1917 ■ *Web:* www.mimedx.com

Mindray DS USA Inc 800 MacArthur Blvd ... Mahwah NJ 07430 201-995-8000
Web: www.mindray.com

Mindways Software Inc
3001 S Lamar Blvd Ste 302 ... Austin TX 78704 512-912-0871
Web: www.qct.com

Minntech Corp 14605 28th Ave N ... Minneapolis MN 55447 763-553-3300 553-3387
TF: 800-328-3345 ■ *Web:* www.medivators.com

Moberg Research Inc 224 S Maple St ... Ambler PA 19002 215-283-0860
Web: www.moberg.com

Morgan Scientific Inc 151 Essex St ... Haverhill MA 01832 978-521-4440
Web: www.morgansci.com

Mott Corp 84 Spring Ln ... Farmington CT 06032 860-747-6333
TF: 800-289-6688 ■ *Web:* www.mottcorp.com

MPM Medical Inc 2301 Crown Ct ... Irving TX 75038 972-893-4090 893-4092
TF: 800-232-5512 ■ *Web:* www.mpmmedicalinc.com

Mui Scientific 145 Traders Blvd E ... Mississauga ON L4Z3L3 905-890-5525
Web: muiscientific.com

Myelotec Inc 4000 Northfield Way Ste 900 ... Roswell GA 30076 770-664-4656
Web: www.myelotec.com

Mytrex Inc 10321 South Beckstead Ln ... South Jordan UT 84095 801-571-4121
Web: www.rescuealert.com

Nasiff Associates 841 County Rt 37 ... Central Square NY 13036 315-676-2346
Web: nasiff.com

NDH Medical Inc
11001 Roosevelt Blvd N Ste 150 ... St. Petersburg FL 33716 727-570-2293
Web: www.ndhmedical.com

NeoMetrics Inc 2605 Fernbrook Ln N Ste J ... Plymouth MN 55447 763-559-4440
Web: www.neometricsinc.com

Neovasc Inc 13700 Mayfield Pl Ste 2135 ... Richmond BC V6V2E4 604-270-4344
Web: www.neovasc.com

Nephros Inc 41 Grand Ave ... River Edge NJ 07661 201-343-5202 343-5207
OTC: NEPH ■ *TF:* 800-732-0330 ■ *Web:* www.nephros.com

Neuroptics Inc 2082 Michelson Dr Ste 450 ... Irvine CA 92612 949-250-9792
Web: www.neuroptics.com

New World Medical Inc
10763 Edison Ct ... Rancho Cucamonga CA 91730 909-466-4304
Web: www.ahmedvalve.com

NormaTec Industries LP 44 Glen Ave ... Newton Center MA 02459 617-928-3400
Web: www.normatec.net

NovaBone Products LLC
1551 Atlantic Blvd Ste 105 ... Jacksonville FL 32207 904-807-0140
Web: www.novabone.com

NovaVision Inc 6401 Congress Ave Ste 140 ... Boca Raton FL 33487 561-558-2000
Web: www.novavision.com

Novosci 2021 Airport Rd ... Conroe TX 77301 281-363-4950 363-7080
TF: 800-854-0567 ■ *Web:* www.novosci.us

Nspire Health Inc 1830 Lefthand Cir ... Longmont CO 80501 303-666-5555 666-5588
TF: 800-574-7374 ■ *Web:* www.nspirehealth.com

Nubenco Medical One Kalisa Way Ste 207 ... Paramus NJ 07652 201-967-9000
Web: nubenco.com

Nutech Medical Inc 2641 Rocky Ridge Ln ... Birmingham AL 35216 205-290-2158
Web: www.nutechmedical.com

NuVasive Inc 7475 Lusk Blvd ... San Diego CA 92121 858-909-1800 909-2000
NASDAQ: NUVA ■ *TF:* 800-475-9131 ■ *Web:* www.nuvasive.com

NuVue Therapeutics Inc 11135 Sedgefield Rd ... Fairfax VA 22030 703-591-1691
Web: www.nuvuetherapeutics.com

NxStage Medical Inc 439 S Union St Fifth Fl ... Lawrence MA 01843 978-687-4700 687-4809
NASDAQ: NXTM ■ *TF:* 866-697-8243 ■ *Web:* www.nxstage.com

Occk Inc 1710 W Schilling Rd ... Salina KS 67401 785-827-9383
Web: www.occk.com

Oceanic Medical Products Inc
8005 Shannon Industrial Park Ln ... Atchison KS 66002 913-874-2000
Web: www.oceanicmedical.com

Phone | Fax

Oraya Therapeutics Inc 8000 Jarvis Ave Ste 200 ... Newark CA 94560 510-456-3700
Web: orayainc.com

Organ Transport Systems Inc
6170 Research Rd Ste 103 ... Frisco TX 75034 972-987-1312
Web: www.organtransportsystems.com

Ortho Technology Inc 17401 Commerce Park Blvd ... Tampa FL 33647 813-991-5896
TF: 800-999-3161 ■ *Web:* www.orthotechnology.com

Ortho-Clinical Diagnostics Inc
1001 US Rt 202 N PO Box 350 ... Raritan NJ 08869 800-828-6316 453-3660*
**Fax Area Code:* 585 ■ **Fax:* Cust Svc ■ *TF:* 800-828-6316 ■ *Web:* www.orthoclinical.com

ORTHOCON Inc One Bridge St Ste 121 ... Irvington NY 10533 914-357-2600
Web: www.orthocon.com

OSO BioPharmaceuticals Mfg LLC
4401 Alexander Blvd Ne ... Albuquerque NM 87107 505-923-2112
Web: www.osobio.com

Osseon LLC 2330 Circadian Way ... Santa Rosa CA 95407 707-636-5940
Web: www.osseon.com

Osteomed Corp 3885 Arapaho Rd ... Addison TX 75001 972-677-4600 677-4601
TF Cust Svc: 800-456-7779 ■ *Web:* www.osteomedcorp.com

Pace Tech Inc 2040 Calumet St ... Clearwater FL 33765 727-442-8118
Web: www.pacetech-med.com

Pacific Bioscience Laboratories Inc
16275 NE 67th Ct Suite 112 ... Redmond WA 98052 425-283-5700
TF: 888-525-2747 ■ *Web:* www.clarisonic.com

Paramit Corp 18735 Madrone Pkwy ... Morgan Hill CA 95037 408-782-5600 782-9991
Web: www.paramit.com

Parker Laboratories Inc 286 Eldridge Rd ... Fairfield NJ 07004 973-276-9500
Web: www.parkerlabs.com

Path-Tec LLC 1333-A Belfast Ave ... Columbus GA 31904 706-569-6368
Web: www.path-tec.com

Pepin Manufacturing Inc 1875 Hwy 61 South ... Lake City MN 55041 651-345-5655
Web: www.pepinmfg.com

Pepose Vision Institute PC
1815 Clarkson Rd ... Chesterfield MO 63017 636-728-0111
Web: www.peposevision.com

Peregrine Surgical Ltd 51 Britain Dr ... New Britain PA 18901 215-348-0456
Web: www.peregrinesurgical.com

PerkinElmer Inc 940 Winter St ... Waltham MA 02451 203-925-4602 944-4904
NYSE: PKI ■ *Web:* www.perkinelmer.com

Perry Baromedical Corp
3750 Prospect Ave ... Riviera Beach FL 33404 561-840-0395
Web: www.perrybaromedical.com

Pilling Surgical 2917 Weck Dr ... Research Triangle Park NC 27709 919-544-8000 361-3914
TF Cust Svc: 866-246-6990 ■
Web: www.teleflex.com/en/emea/brands/pilling/index.html

PneumRx Inc 530 Logue Ave ... Mountain View CA 94043 650-625-8910
Web: www.pneumrx.com

Point Medical Corp 891 E Summit St ... Crown Point IN 46307 219-663-1775
Web: pointmedical.com

Polyzen Inc 1041 Classic Rd ... Apex NC 27539 919-319-9599
Web: www.polyzen.com

Precision Edge Surgical Products Co
415 W 12th Ave ... Sault Sainte Marie MI 49783 906-632-4800 632-5619
Web: www.precisionedge.com

Prism Medical Ltd Unit 2 485 Millway Ave ... Concord ON L4K3V4 416-260-2145
Web: www.prismmedicalltd.com

Prizm Medical Inc 3400 Corporate Way Ste I ... Duluth GA 30096 770-622-0933
Web: www.prizm-medical.com

Prodigy Diabetes Care LLC
2701-A Hutchison McDonald Rd PO Box 481928 ... Charlotte NC 28269 800-366-5901
TF: 800-366-5901 ■ *Web:* www.prodigymeter.com

Promedica Inc 114 Douglas Rd E ... Oldsmar FL 34677 813-854-1905
Web: www.promedica-usa.com

Pronk Technologies Inc
8933 Lankershim Blvd ... Sun Valley CA 91352 818-768-5600
Web: www.pronktech.com

Propper Mfg Company Inc
36-04 Skillman Ave ... Long Island City NY 11101 718-392-6650 482-8909
TF Cust Svc: 800-832-4300 ■ *Web:* www.proppermfg.com

Prosurg Inc 2195 Trade Zone Blvd ... San Jose CA 95131 408-945-4044
Web: prosurg.com

Proteus Applied Technologies Inc
377 Oyster Point Blvd ... South San Francisco CA 94080 650-588-7774
Web: www.proteus-applied.com

Pryor Products 1819 Peacock Blvd ... Oceanside CA 92056 760-724-8244
Web: www.pryorproducts.com

Pulse Needlefree Systems Inc 8210 Marshall Dr ... Lenexa KS 66214 913-599-1590
Web: www.pulse-nfs.com

Qosina Corp 150-Q Executive Dr ... Edgewood NY 11717 631-242-3000
Web: www.qosina.com

Quality Tech Services Inc
10525 Hampshire Ave South ... Bloomington MN 55438 952-942-8321
Web: www.qtspackage.com

Radiology Support Devices Inc
1904 E Dominguez St ... Long Beach CA 90810 310-518-0527
Web: www.rsdphantoms.com

Ranfac Corp PO Box 635 ... Avon MA 02322 508-588-4400 584-8588
Web: www.ranfac.com

Reed-Lane Inc 359 Newark-Pompton Tpke ... Wayne NJ 07470 973-709-1090
Web: reedlane.com

ResMed Inc 9001 Spectrum Ctr Blvd ... San Diego CA 92123 858-836-5000 836-5501
NYSE: RMD ■ *TF:* 800-424-0737 ■ *Web:* www.resmed.com

Rex Medical LP 1100 E Hector St Ste 245 ... Conshohocken PA 19428 610-940-0665
Web: www.rexmedical.com

Rochester Medical Corp
1 Rochester Medical Dr ... Stewartville MN 55976 507-533-9600 533-4232
NASDAQ: ROCM ■ *TF:* 800-243-3315 ■ *Web:* www.rocm.com

ROHO Group, The 100 N Florida Ave ... Belleville IL 62221 618-277-9173 277-9561
Web: www.rohoinc.com

Safety Syringes Inc 2875 Loker Ave E ... Carlsbad CA 92010 760-918-9908 918-0565
Web: www.safetysyringes.com

Saint Jude Medical St Jude Medical Inc ... St Paul MN 55117 651-756-2000 756-3301
NYSE: STJ ■ *TF:* 800-328-9634 ■ *Web:* www.sjm.com

				Phone	Fax
Salter Labs 100 Sycamore Rd TF: 800-421-0024 ■ Web: www.salterlabs.com	Arvin	CA	93203	661-854-3166	854-3850
Sandstrom Trade & Technology Inc 610 Niagara St Web: www.sandstrom.on.ca	Welland	ON	L3B5Y5	905-732-1307	
SANUWAVE Health Inc 11475 Great Oaks Way Ste 150 Web: www.sanuwave.com	Alpharetta	GA	30022	678-581-6843	
Seabrook International LLC 15 Woodworkers Way Web: www.seabrookinternational.com	Seabrook	NH	03874	603-474-1919	474-1833
Sechrist Industries Inc 4225 E La Palma Ave TF: 800-732-4747 ■ Web: www.sechristusa.com	Anaheim	CA	92807	714-579-8400	579-0814
Sekisui Diagnostics LLC Four Hartwell Pl Web: www.sekisuidiagnostics.com	Lexington	MA	02421	781-652-7800	
Shofu Dental Corp 1225 Stone Dr Web: www.shofu.com	San Marcos	CA	92078	760-736-3277	
Siemens Medical Solutions Inc 51 Valley Stream Pkwy *Fax Area Code: 610 ■ TF: 800-888-7436 ■ Web: healthcare.siemens.com	Malvern	PA	19355	800-225-5336	219-3124*
Skyline Medical Inc 2915 Commers Dr Ste 900 Web: www.skylinemedical.com	Eagan	MN	55121	651-389-4800	
Smith & Nephew Inc Endoscopy Div 150 Minuteman Rd TF: 800-343-5717 ■ Web: www.smith-nephew.com	Andover	MA	01810	978-749-1000	749-1599
Smiths Medical MD Inc 1265 Grey Fox Rd TF: 800-258-5361 ■ Web: www.smiths-medical.com	Saint Paul	MN	55112	651-633-2556	628-7459
Sorin Group USA Inc 14401 W 65th Way TF: 800-289-5759 ■ Web: www.sorin.com	Arvada	CO	80004	303-424-0129	467-6584
Specialty Silicone Fabricators 3077 Rollie Gates Dr TF: 800-394-4284 ■ Web: www.ssfab.com	Paso Robles	CA	93446	805-239-4284	239-0523
Spinesmith Partners 5300 N Lamar Blvd Ste 107 Web: spinesmithusa.com	Austin	TX	78751	512-302-0086	
Starplex Scientific Inc 50 A Steinway Blvd Web: www.starplexscientific.com	Etobicoke	ON	M9W6Y3	416-674-7474	
STERIS Corp 5960 Heisley Rd NYSE: STE ■ *Fax: Cust Svc ■ TF: 800-548-4873 ■ Web: www.steris.com	Mentor	OH	44060	440-354-2600	639-4450*
Stryker Corp 2825 Airview Blvd NYSE: SYK ■ TF: 800-616-1406 ■ Web: www.stryker.com	Kalamazoo	MI	49002	269-385-2600	385-1062
Suburban Surgical Company Inc 275 Twelfth St Web: www.suburbansurgical.com	Wheeling	IL	60090	847-537-9320	
Synemed Inc 4562 E Second St Ste A Web: www.synemed.com	Benicia	CA	94510	707-745-8386	
Synergetics USA Inc 3845 Corporate Ctr Dr NASDAQ: SURG ■ TF: 800-600-0565 ■ Web: www.synergeticsusa.com	O'Fallon	MO	63368	636-939-5100	939-6885
Techno-Aide Inc 7117 Centennial Blvd TF: 800-251-2629 ■ Web: www.techno-aide.com	Nashville	TN	37209	615-350-7030	350-7879
TERATECH Corp 77-79 Terr Hall Ave TF: 866-837-2766 ■ Web: www.terason.com	Burlington	MA	01803	781-270-4143	
Terumo Cardiovascular Systems Corp 6200 Jackson Rd *Fax Area Code: 800 ■ *Fax: Cust Svc ■ TF: 800-262-3304 ■ Web: www.terumo-us.com	Ann Arbor	MI	48103	734-663-4145	292-6551*
Terumo Medical Corp 2101 Cottontail Ln TF: 800-283-7866 ■ Web: www.terumomedical.com	Somerset	NJ	08873	732-302-4900	302-3083
TFX Medical Inc 50 Plantation Dr TF: 800-548-6600 ■ Web: www.teleflexmedicaloem.com	Jaffrey	NH	03452	603-532-7706	532-6108
TheraTest Laboratories Inc 1111 N Main St Web: theratest.com	Lombard	IL	60148	630-627-6069	
Thermasolutions Inc 1889 Buerkle Rd Web: www.thermasolutions.com	Saint Paul	MN	55110	651-209-3900	
TherOx Inc 17500 Cartwright Rd Ste 100 Web: www.therox.com	Irvine	CA	92614	949-757-1999	
Topcon Medical Systems Inc 111 Bauer Dr TF: 800-223-1130 ■ Web: www.topconmedical.com	Oakland	NJ	07436	201-599-5100	599-5250
Trans1 Inc 301 Government Ctr Dr TF: 866-256-1206 ■ Web: baxanosurgical.com	Wilmington	NC	28403	910-332-1700	332-1701
Transenterix Inc 635 Davis Dr Ste 300 Web: www.transenterix.com	Morrisville	NC	27560	919-765-8400	
TransMedics Inc 200 Minuteman Rd Ste 302 Web: www.transmedics.com	Andover	MA	01810	978-552-0900	
Ultraviolet Devices Inc 26145 Technology Dr Web: www.uvdi.com	Valencia	CA	91355	661-295-8140	
Unilife Corp 250 Cross Farm Ln Web: www.unilife.com	York	PA	17406	717-384-3400	
United States Endoscopy Group Inc 5976 Heisley Rd TF: 800-769-8226 ■ Web: www.usendoscopy.com	Mentor	OH	44060	440-639-4494	639-4494
Urologix Inc 14405 21st Ave N TF: 800-475-1403 ■ Web: www.urologix.com	Minneapolis	MN	55447	763-475-1400	475-1443
Uroplasty Inc 5420 Feltl Rd NASDAQ: UPI ■ Web: www.uroplasty.com	Minnetonka	MN	55343	952-426-6140	426-6199
Utah Medical Products Inc 7043 S 300 W NASDAQ: UTMD ■ TF: 866-754-9789 ■ Web: www.utahmed.com	Midvale	UT	84047	801-566-1200	566-2062
Vasamed Inc 7615 Golden Triangle Dr Ste A *Fax Area Code: 952 ■ TF: 800-695-2737 ■ Web: www.vasamed.com	Eden Prairie	MN	55344	800-695-2737	944-6022*
Vascular Solutions Inc 6464 Sycamore Ct NASDAQ: VASC ■ *Fax Area Code: 877 ■ TF: 877-979-4300 ■ Web: www.vasc.com	Minneapolis	MN	55369	763-656-4300	656-4251*
Ventana Medical Systems Inc 1910 Innovation Pk Dr TF: 800-227-2155 ■ Web: www.ventana.com	Tucson	AZ	85755	520-887-2155	
VirtualScopics Inc 350 Linden Oaks NASDAQ: VSCP ■ Web: www.virtualscopics.com	Rochester	NY	14625	585-249-6231	218-7350
Visicon Technologies Inc 871 Latour Ct Web: www.visicontech.com	Napa	CA	94558	707-259-1300	
Vital Signs Inc 20 Campus Rd TF: 800-932-0760 ■ Web: www3.gehealthcare.com	Totowa	NJ	07512	973-790-1330	790-3307
Vivosonic Inc 120-5525 Eglinton Ave W Web: www.vivosonic.com	Toronto	ON	M9C5K5	416-231-9997	
W A Baum Company Inc 620 Oak St TF: 888-281-6061 ■ Web: www.wabaum.com	Copiague	NY	11726	631-226-3940	
WalkMed Infusion LLC 96 Inverness Dr E Ste J TF: 800-578-0555 ■ Web: www.walkmed.net	Englewood	CO	80112	303-420-9569	420-4545
Wells Johnson Co 8000 S Kolb Rd Web: www.wellsgrp.com	Tucson	AZ	85756	520-298-6069	
Wexler Surgical Supplies 11333 Chimney Rock Rd Web: www.wexlersurgical.com	Houston	TX	77035	713-723-6900	
Zonare Medical Systems Inc 420 N Bernardo Ave Web: www.zonare.com	Mountain View	CA	94043	650-230-2800	

480 MEDICAL SUPPLIES - MFR

SEE ALSO Personal Protective Equipment & Clothing p. 2914

				Phone	Fax
A-M Systems Inc 131 Business Park Loop Web: a-msystems.com	Sequim	WA	98382	360-683-8300	
Adhesives Research Inc 400 Seaks Run Rd PO Box 100 TF: 800-445-6240 ■ Web: www.adhesivesresearch.com	Glen Rock	PA	17327	717-235-7979	235-8320
Adroit Medical Systems Inc 1146 CaRding Machine Rd TF: 800-267-6077 ■ Web: www.adroitmedical.com	Loudon	TN	37774	800-267-6077	267-6077
Advanced Orthopro Inc 1820 N Illinois St Web: www.advancedorthopro.com	Indianapolis	IN	46202	317-924-4444	
Advanced Sterilization Products (ASP) 33 Technology Dr *Fax Area Code: 949 ■ *Fax: Sales ■ TF: 888-783-7723 ■ Web: www.aspjj.com	Irvine	CA	92618	888-783-7723	450-6800*
AESCULAP Inc 3773 Corporate Pkwy *Fax Area Code: 610 ■ TF: 800-282-9000 ■ Web: www.aesculapusa.com	Center Valley	PA	18034	800-282-9000	791-6886*
Agrilectric Power Inc 3063 Hwy 397 Web: www.agrilectric.com	Lake Charles	LA	70615	337-430-0006	
Allergan 2525 Dupont Dr PO Box 19534 TF: 800-347-4500 ■ Web: www.allergan.com	Irvine	CA	92612	714-246-4500	246-6987
Allied Healthcare Products Inc 1720 Sublette Ave NASDAQ: AHPI ■ *Fax Area Code: 800 ■ *Fax: Cust Svc ■ TF: 800-444-3954 ■ Web: www.alliedhpi.com	Saint Louis	MO	63110	314-771-2400	477-7701*
Alta Manufacturing Inc 47650 Westinghouse Dr Web: www.altamfg.com	Fremont	CA	94539	510-668-1870	
American Medical Systems Holdings Inc 10700 Bren Rd W TF: 800-328-3881 ■ Web: www.americanmedicalsystems.com	Minnetonka	MN	55343	952-930-6000	930-6373
AMG Medical Inc 8505 Dalton Web: www.amgmedical.com	Montreal	QC	H4T1V5	514-737-5251	
Animas Corp 200 Lawrence Dr TF: 877-937-7867 ■ Web: www.animas.com	West Chester	PA	19380	610-644-8990	644-8717
Armstrong Medical Industries Inc 575 Knightsbridge Pkwy TF Cust Svc: 800-323-4220 ■ Web: www.armstrongmedical.com	Lincolnshire	IL	60069	847-913-0101	913-0138
Arthrex Inc 1370 Creekside Blvd TF: 800-934-4404 ■ Web: www.arthrex.com	Naples	FL	34108	239-643-5553	598-5534
ASO LLC 300 Sarasota Ctr Blvd Web: www.asocorp.com	Sarasota	FL	34240	941-379-0300	378-9040
Aspen Surgical 6945 Southbelt Dr SE TF: 888-364-7004 ■ Web: www.aspensurgical.com	Caledonia	MI	49316	616-698-7100	698-0525
Baxter International Inc One Baxter Pkwy NYSE: BAX ■ Web: www.baxter.com	Deerfield	IL	60015	847-948-2000	948-3948
Baylis Medical Company Inc 5959 Trans-Canada Hwy TF: 800-850-9801 ■ Web: www.baylismedical.com	Montreal	QC	H4T1A1	514-488-9801	
Becton Dickinson & Co One Becton Dr NYSE: BDX ■ *Fax: Cust Svc ■ TF Cust Svc: 888-237-2762 ■ Web: www.bd.com	Franklin Lakes	NJ	07417	201-847-6800	847-4882*
Becton Dickinson Consumer Healthcare One Becton Dr TF: 888-237-2762 ■ Web: www.bd.com/consumer	Franklin Lakes	NJ	07417	201-847-6800	
Beltone Electronics Corp 2601 Patriot Blvd *Fax Area Code: 952 ■ TF: 800-235-8663 ■ Web: www.beltone.com	Glenview	IL	60026	847-832-3300	769-8417*
BioHorizons Inc 2300 Riverchase Ctr TF: 888-246-8338 ■ Web: www.biohorizons.com	Birmingham	AL	35244	205-967-7880	870-0304
Biomet Inc 56 E Bell Dr PO Box 587 TF: 800-348-9500 ■ Web: www.biomet.com	Warsaw	IN	46582	574-267-6639	267-8137
Bioventus LLC 4721 Emperor Blvd Ste 100 Web: www.bioventusglobal.com	Durham	NC	27703	919-474-6700	
Bristol-Myers Squibb Co 345 Pk Ave NYSE: BMY ■ Web: www.bms.com	New York	NY	10154	212-546-4000	546-4020
BSN Medical Inc 5825 Carnegie Blvd TF: 800-552-1157 ■ Web: www.bsnmedical.com	Charlotte	NC	28209	704-554-9933	331-8785
Capstone Therapeutics Corp 1275 W Washington St Ste 101 OTC: CAPS ■ TF: 800-937-5520 ■ Web: www.capstonethx.com	Tempe	AZ	85281	602-286-5520	
Cardiopulmonary Corp 200 Cascade Blvd Web: www.cardiopulmonarycorp.com	Milford	CT	06460	203-877-1999	
CarTika Medical Inc 6550 Wedgwood Rd N Ste 300 Web: www.cartikamedical.com	Maple Grove	MN	55311	763-545-5188	
Centurion Medical Products 100 Centurion Way TF: 800-248-4058 ■ Web: www.centurionmp.com	Williamston	MI	48895	517-546-5400	546-9388
Chattanooga Group 4717 Adams Rd TF: 800-592-7329 ■ Web: www.djoglobal.com	Hixson	TN	37343	423-870-2281	875-5497
ClearCount Medical Solutions Inc 101 Bellevue Rd Web: www.clearcount.com	Pittsburgh	PA	15229	412-931-7233	
Codman & Shurtleff Inc 325 Paramount Dr *Fax Area Code: 508 ■ TF: 800-225-0460 ■ Web: www.depuy.com/about-depuy/depuy-divisions/about-codman	Raynham	MA	02767	800-382-4682	880-8122*

Phone | Fax

Community Surgical Supply Inc
1390 Rt 37 W . . . Toms River NJ 08755 732-349-2990 244-7588
TF: 800-349-2990 ■ *Web:* www.communitysurgical.com

Connecticut Hypodermics Inc 519 Main St. . . . Yalesville CT 06492 203-265-4881 284-1520
Web: www.connhypo.com

Consensus Orthopedics Inc
1115 Windfield Way Ste 100 . . . El Dorado Hills CA 95762 916-355-7100
Web: www.consensusortho.com

Conventus Orthopaedics Inc
10200 73rd Ave N Ste 122 . . . Maple Grove MN 55369 763-515-5000
Web: www.conventusortho.com

CR Bard Inc 730 Central Ave . . . Murray Hill NJ 07974 908-277-8000 277-8412
NYSE: BCR ■ *Web:* www.crbard.com

Cramer Products Inc 153 W Warren St. . . . Gardner KS 66030 913-856-7511
TF: 800-345-2231 ■ *Web:* www.cramersportsmed.com

Cyberonics Inc
100 Cyberonics Blvd The Cyberonics Bldg. . . . Houston TX 77058 281-228-7262 218-9332
NASDAQ: CYBX ■ *TF:* 800-332-1375 ■ *Web:* www.cyberonics.com

DeRoyal Industries Inc 200 DeBusk Ln . . . Powell TN 37849 865-938-7828 362-1230*
**Fax:* Hum Res ■ *TF:* 800-251-9864 ■ *Web:* www.deroyal.com

DJ Orthopedics Inc 1430 Decision St . . . Vista CA 92081 760-727-1280 936-6569*
**Fax Area Code:* 800 ■ *TF:* 800-321-9549 ■ *Web:* www.djoglobal.com

DNA Genotek Inc Two Beaverbrook Rd. . . . Kanata ON K2K1L1 613-723-5757
Web: www.dnagenotek.com

Dynarex Corporation 10 Glenshaw St. . . . Orangeburg NY 10962 845-365-8200 365-8201
TF: 888-335-7500 ■ *Web:* www.dynarex.com

Ehob Inc 250 N Belmont Ave . . . Indianapolis IN 46222 317-972-4600 972-4601
TF: 800-899-5553 ■ *Web:* www.ehob.com

Environmental Tectonics Corp
125 James Way. . . . SouthHampton PA 18966 215-355-9100 357-4000
OTC: ETCC ■ *Web:* www.etcusa.com

Ergodyne Corp 1021 Bandana Blvd E Ste 220 . . . Saint Paul MN 55108 651-642-9889 642-1882
TF: 800-225-8238 ■ *Web:* www.ergodyne.com

Exactech Inc 2320 NW 66th Ct . . . Gainesville FL 32653 352-377-1140 378-2617
NASDAQ: EXAC ■ *TF:* 800-392-2832 ■ *Web:* www.exac.com

Female Health Co 515 N State St Ste 2225. . . . Chicago IL 60654 312-595-9123
TF: 800-860-2442 ■ *Web:* www.femalehealth.com

Ferno-Washington Inc 70 Weil Way. . . . Wilmington OH 45177 937-382-1451 382-1191
TF: 800-733-3766 ■ *Web:* www.ferno.com

Fillauer Inc PO Box 5189. . . . Chattanooga TN 37406 423-624-0946 629-7936
TF: 800-251-6398 ■ *Web:* www.fillauer.com

Flexible Lifeline Systems Inc
14325 W Hardy Rd . . . Houston TX 77060 832-448-2900
Web: www.fall-arrest.com

Freeman Manufacturing Co 900 W Chicago Rd. . . . Sturgis MI 49091 269-651-2371 651-8248
TF: 800-253-2091 ■ *Web:* www.freemanmfg.com

Getinge USA Inc 1777 E Henrietta Rd . . . Rochester NY 14623 585-475-1400
Web: www.getingeusa.com

GF Health Products Inc 2935 NE Pkwy. . . . Atlanta GA 30360 770-447-1609 726-0601*
**Fax Area Code:* 800 ■ *TF:* 800-347-5678 ■ *Web:* www.grahamfield.com

Guided Therapeutics Inc
5835 Peachtree Corners E Ste D. . . . Norcross GA 30092 770-242-8723 242-8639
OTC: GTHP ■ *Web:* www.guidedinc.com

Gyrus Medical Inc ENT Div
136 Turnpike Rd . . . Southborough MA 01772 508-804-2600
Web: www.gyrus-ent.com

Halyard Health 1400 Holcomb Bridge Rd . . . Roswell GA 30076 770-587-8000
Web: www.kchealthcare.com

Hanger Orthopedic Group Inc
10910 Domain Dr Ste 300 . . . Austin TX 78758 512-777-3800
TF: 877-442-6437 ■ *Web:* www.hanger.com

Hanger Prosthetics & Orthopedics Inc
10910 Domain Dr Ste 300 . . . Austin TX 78758 877-442-6437
TF: 877-442-6437 ■ *Web:* www.hanger.com

Hans Rudolph Inc 8325 Cole Pkwy . . . Shawnee KS 66227 913-422-7788
Web: www.rudolphkc.com

Helix Medical LLC 1110 Mark Ave. . . . Carpinteria CA 93013 805-684-3304 684-1934
TF: 800-266-4421 ■ *Web:* www.helixmedical.com

Helvoet Pharma Inc 9012 Pennsauken Hwy . . . Pennsauken NJ 08110 856-663-2202 663-2636
TF: 800-874-3586 ■ *Web:* www.datwyler.com

Hermell Products Inc Nine Britton Dr. . . . Bloomfield CT 06002 860-242-6550
Web: www.hermell.com

Hightech American Industrial Laboratories Inc (HAI)
320 Massachusetts Ave . . . Lexington MA 02420 781-862-9884 860-7722
Web: www.hailabs.com

Hollister Inc 2000 Hollister Dr . . . Libertyville IL 60048 847-680-1000 680-2123*
**Fax:* Hum Res ■ *TF:* 800-323-4060 ■ *Web:* www.hollister.com

Hosmer-Dorrance Corp 561 Div St . . . Campbell CA 95008 408-379-5151 379-5263
Web: www.hosmer.com

Hospira Inc 275 N Field Dr. . . . Lake Forest IL 60045 224-212-2000
NYSE: HSP ■ *TF:* 877-946-7747 ■ *Web:* www.hospira.com

Hoveround Corp
2151 Whitfield Industrial Way. . . . Sarasota FL 34243 941-739-6200 388-6912*
**Fax Area Code:* 800 ■ *TF:* 800-542-7236 ■ *Web:* www.hoveround.com

Howard Leight Industries
7828 Waterville Rd. . . . San Diego CA 92154 800-430-5490 232-3110*
**Fax Area Code:* 401 ■ *TF:* 800-430-5490 ■ *Web:* www.howardleight.com

Hy-Tape International Inc PO Box 540 . . . Patterson NY 12563 800-248-0101 878-4104*
**Fax Area Code:* 845 ■ *TF:* 800-248-0101 ■ *Web:* www.hytape.com

ICU Medical Inc 951 Calle Amanecer. . . . San Clemente CA 92673 949-366-2183 366-8368
NASDAQ: ICUI ■ *TF:* 800-824-7890 ■ *Web:* www.icumed.com

Ideal Tape Co 1400 Middlesex St. . . . Lowell MA 01851 800-284-3325 458-0302*
**Fax Area Code:* 978 ■ *TF:* 800-284-3325 ■ *Web:* www.idealtape.com

Independence Technology LLC 45 Technology Dr. . . . Warren NJ 07059 908-412-2200 412-2205

International Technidyne Corp Eight Olsen Ave . . . Edison NJ 08820 732-548-5700 548-2419
TF: 800-631-5945 ■ *Web:* www.itcmed.com

Invacare Corp One Invacare Way . . . Elyria OH 44036 440-329-6000 619-7996*
NYSE: IVC ■ **Fax Area Code:* 877 ■ *TF:* 800-333-6900 ■ *Web:* www.invacare.com

Iowa Veterinary Supply Co (IVESCO)
124 Country Club Rd . . . Iowa Falls IA 50126 641-648-2529 648-5994
TF: 800-457-0118 ■ *Web:* www.ivescollc.com

Phone | Fax

Johnson & Johnson Consumer Products Co
199 Grandview Rd . . . Skillman NJ 08558 908-874-1000
TF: 866-565-2229 ■ *Web:* www.johnsonsbaby.com

Johnson & Johnson Inc 7101 Notre-Dame E. . . . Montreal QC H1N2G4 514-251-5100 251-6233
TF: 800-361-8990 ■ *Web:* www.jnjcanada.com

K-Tube Technologies 13400 Kirkham Way. . . . Poway CA 92064 858-513-9229 513-9459
TF: 800-394-0058 ■ *Web:* www.k-tube.com

Kimberly-Clark/Ballard Medical Products
1400 Holcomb Bridge Rd . . . Roswell GA 30076 800-524-3577
TF: 800-524-3577 ■ *Web:* www.kchealthcare.com

Kinetic Concepts Inc (KCI) PO Box 659508 . . . San Antonio TX 78265 800-275-4524 311-9291*
**Fax:* Hum Res ■ *TF Cust Svc:* 800-275-4524 ■ *Web:* www.kci1.com

Kloehn Inc 10000 Banburry Cross Dr. . . . Las Vegas NV 89144 702-243-7727 243-6036
TF: 800-358-4342 ■ *Web:* www.norgren.com

Langer Inc 2905 Veterans' Memorial Hwy. . . . Ronkonkoma NY 11779 800-645-5520
TF: 800-645-5520 ■ *Web:* www.langerbiomechanics.com

LPS Industries Inc 10 Caesar Pl . . . Moonachie NJ 07074 201-438-3515 643-0180*
**Fax Area Code:* 732 ■ *TF Sales:* 800-275-6577 ■ *Web:* www.lpsind.com

M & C Specialties Co 90 James Way . . . SouthHampton PA 18966 215-322-1600 322-1620
TF Cust Svc: 800-441-6996 ■ *Web:* www.mcspecialties.com

Maetta Sciences Inc
75 De Mortagne Blvd Ste 109. . . . Boucherville QC J4B6Y4 450-641-7534
Web: www.maetta.ca

MAKO Surgical Corp 2555 Davie Rd . . . Fort Lauderdale FL 33317 954-927-2044
Web: www.makosurgical.com

Martech Medical Products Inc
1500 Delp Dr . . . Harleysville PA 19438 215-256-8833 256-8837
Web: www.martechmedical.com

Medaire Inc 1250 W Washington St Ste 442 . . . Tempe AZ 85281 480-333-3700 333-3592
Web: www.medaire.com

Medical Action Industries Inc (MAI)
500 Expy Dr S. . . . Brentwood NY 11717 631-231-4600
NASDAQ: MDCI ■ *TF:* 800-645-7042 ■ *Web:* www.medical-action.com

Medical Depot Inc 99 Seaview Blvd . . . Port Washington NY 11050 516-998-4600
Web: www.drivemedical.com

Medizone International Inc
4000 Bridgeway Ste 401. . . . Sausalito CA 94965 415-331-0303
Web: www.medizoneint.com

MEDport LLC 23 Acorn St. . . . Providence RI 02903 401-273-0444
Web: www.medport-llc.com

Medtronic Inc 710 Medtronic Pkwy NE. . . . Minneapolis MN 55432 763-514-4000 514-4879
NYSE: MDT ■ *TF Cust Svc:* 800-328-2518 ■ *Web:* www.medtronic.com

Medtronic Inc Heart Valve Div
710 Medtronic Pwy. . . . Minneapolis MN 55432 763-514-4000
TF: 800-633-8766 ■ *Web:* www.medtronic.com

Medtronic MiniMed Inc 18000 Devonshire St . . . Northridge CA 91325 800-646-4633
TF: 800-646-4633 ■ *Web:* www.medtronicdiabetes.com

Medtronic Powered Surgical Solutions
4620 N Beach St. . . . Fort Worth TX 76137 817-788-6400 788-6401*
**Fax:* Orders ■ *TF:* 800-643-2773 ■
Web: www.medtronic.com/for-healthcare-professionals/business-unit-landing-page

Medtronic Surgical Technologies
6743 Southpoint Dr N. . . . Jacksonville FL 32216 904-296-9600
TF: 800-874-5797 ■ *Web:* www.medtronic.com

Mentor Corp 201 Mentor Dr. . . . Santa Barbara CA 93111 805-879-6000
NASDAQ: MENT ■ *TF:* 800-525-0245 ■ *Web:* www.mentorwwllc.com

Merits Health Products Inc 730 NE 19th Pl . . . Cape Coral FL 33909 239-772-0579
Web: www.meritshealth.com

Mettler Electronics Corp 1333 S Claudina St. . . . Anaheim CA 92805 714-533-2221
TF: 800-854-9305 ■ *Web:* www.mettlerelectronics.com

Microtek Medical Holdings Inc
13000 Deerfield Pkwy Ste 300 . . . Alpharetta GA 30004 678-896-4400 327-5921*
**Fax Area Code:* 662 ■ *TF:* 800-777-7977 ■ *Web:* www.microtekmed.com

Microtek Medical Inc 512 N Lehmberg Rd . . . Columbus MS 39702 662-327-1863 327-5921
TF: 800-824-3027 ■ *Web:* www.microtekmed.com

MicroVention Inc 1311 Valencia Ave . . . Tustin CA 92780 714-247-8000
TF: 800-990-8368 ■ *Web:* www.microvention.com

Micrus Endovascular 821 Fox Ln. . . . San Jose CA 95131 408-433-1400 433-1401

Milestone Scientific Inc 220 S Orange Ave . . . Livingston NJ 07039 973-535-2717 535-2829
OTC: MLSS ■ *TF:* 800-862-1125 ■ *Web:* www.milestonescientific.com

Miracle-Ear Inc
5000 Cheshire Pkwy N Ste 1 . . . Minneapolis MN 55446 800-464-8002 268-4365*
**Fax Area Code:* 763 ■ *TF:* 800-464-8002 ■ *Web:* www.miracle-ear.com

Monaghan Medical Corp
Five Latour Ave Ste 1600 . . . Plattsburgh NY 12901 518-561-7330
Web: www.monaghanmed.com

Moximed Inc 26460 Corporate Ave Ste 100. . . . Hayward CA 94545 510-887-3300
Web: www.moximed.com

MP Biomedicals LLC
Three Hutton Ctr Dr Ste 100. . . . Santa Ana CA 92707 949-833-2500
TF: 800-633-1352 ■ *Web:* www.mpbio.com

National Fabrication Ctr 9561 Satellite Blvd. . . . Orlando FL 32837 407-852-6170
Web: hanger.com

Nearly Me Technolgies Po Box 21475 . . . Waco TX 76702 254-662-1752
Web: www.tgtransforms.com

NELCO Inc Three Gill St Unit D . . . Woburn MA 01801 781-933-1940 933-4763
TF: 800-635-2613 ■ *Web:* www.nelcoworldwide.com

Net Safety Monitoring Inc
2721 Hopewell Pl NE . . . Calgary AB T1Y7J7 403-219-0688
Web: www.net-safety.com

Nice-Pak Products Inc Two Nice-Pak Pk. . . . Orangeburg NY 10962 845-365-1700 365-1717
TF: 800-999-6423 ■ *Web:* www.nicepak.com

Nonin Medical Inc 13700 First Ave N Ste A . . . Plymouth MN 55441 763-553-9968 577-5500
Web: www.nonin.com

NorMed 4310 S 131 Pl . . . Seattle WA 98168 800-288-8200 242-3315*
**Fax Area Code:* 206 ■ *TF:* 800-288-8200 ■ *Web:* www.normed.com

Nu-Hope Laboratories Inc 12640 Branford St. . . . Pacoima CA 91331 818-899-7711
Web: www.nu-hope.com

NuOrtho Surgical Inc 151 Martine St . . . Fall River MA 02723 617-848-8999
Web: www.nuorthosurgical.com

Company	City	State	Zip	Phone	Fax
Ortho Development Corp 12187 S Business Pk Dr *TF:* 800-429-8339 ■ *Web:* www.odev.com	Draper	UT	84020	801-553-9991	553-9993
Orthofix Inc 1720 Bray Central Dr *TF:* 800-527-0404 ■ *Web:* www.orthofix.com	McKinney	TX	75069	469-742-2500	742-2556
OrthoPediatrics Corp 2850 Frontier Dr *Web:* www.orthopediatrics.com	Warsaw	IN	46582	574-268-6379	
OrthoSensor Inc 1855 Griffin Rd Ste A-310 *Web:* www.orthosensor.com	Dania Beach	FL	33004	954-577-7770	
Osborn Medical Corp 100 W Main St *Web:* www.osbornmedical.com	Utica	MN	55979	507-932-5028	
Osteomed Corp 3885 Arapaho Rd *TF Cust Svc:* 800-456-7779 ■ *Web:* www.osteomedcorp.com	Addison	TX	75001	972-677-4600	677-4601
Pacific Medical Inc 1700 N Chrisman Rd *TF:* 800-726-9180 ■ *Web:* www.pacmedical.com	Tracy	CA	95304	800-726-9180	861-5950
Passy-Muir Inc 4521 Campus Dr Pmb 273 *Web:* www.passy-muir.com	Irvine	CA	92612	949-833-8255	
Perma-Type Company Inc 83 NW Dr *Web:* www.perma-type.com	Plainville	CT	06062	860-747-9999	747-1986
Phonic Ear Inc 2080 Lakeville Hwy *TF:* 800-227-0735 ■ *Web:* www.phonicear.com	Petaluma	CA	94954	707-769-1110	781-9415
Phygen LLC 2301 Dupont Ave Ste 510 *TF:* 800-939-7008 ■ *Web:* www.phygenspine.com	Irvine	CA	92612	800-939-7008	
Pioneer Surgical Technology Inc 375 River Park Cir *Web:* www.pioneersurgical.com	Marquette	MI	49855	906-226-9909	
Posey Co 5635 Peck Rd **Fax Area Code:* 800 ■ *TF:* 800-447-6739 ■ *Web:* www.posey.com	Arcadia	CA	91006	626-443-3143	767-3933*
Precision Dynamics Corp 13880 Del Sur St *TF:* 800-847-0670 ■ *Web:* www.pdcorp.com	San Fernando	CA	91340	818-897-1111	899-4045
Precision Technology Inc 50 Maple St *Web:* www.ptiplastics.com	Norwood	NJ	07648	201-767-1600	
Pride Mobility Products Corp 182 Susquehanna Ave **Fax Area Code:* 570 ■ *TF:* 800-800-8586 ■ *Web:* www.pridemobility.com	Exeter	PA	18643	800-800-8586	655-2990*
Pro Orthopedic Devices Inc 2884 E Ganley Rd *Web:* www.proorthopedic.com	Tucson	AZ	85706	520-294-4401	
Prosthetic Design Inc 700 Harco Dr *Web:* prostheticdesign.com	Clayton	OH	45315	937-836-1464	
Rapid Fire Marketing Inc Ste 1234 311 W Third St *Web:* www.rapid-fire-marketing.com	Carson City	NV	89703	404-261-1196	
Redi-Medic Ind 1320 Alberta Ave	Saskatoon	SK	S7K1R5	306-955-8821	
Rehab Plus Therapeutic Products 6104 45th St	Lubbock	TX	79407	806-791-2288	
Retractable Technologies Inc 511 Lobo Ln *NYSE: RVP* ■ *TF:* 888-806-2626 ■ *Web:* www.vanishpoint.com	Little Elm	TX	75068	972-294-1010	292-3600
REVA Medical Inc 5751 Copley Dr *Web:* www.revamedical.com	San Diego	CA	92111	858-966-3000	
Rockford Medical & Safety Co 2420 Harrison Ave *Web:* www.firensafety.com	Rockford	IL	61108	815-394-0100	
Rusch Inc 2917 Weck Dr PO Box 12600 *TF:* 866-246-6990 ■ *Web:* teleflex.com/en/usa/notfound.html	Research Triangle Park	NC	27709	919-544-8000	361-3914
Sas Safety Corp 3031 Gardenia Ave **Fax Area Code:* 800 ■ *TF:* 800-262-0200 ■ *Web:* www.sassafety.com	Long Beach	CA	90807	562-427-2775	244-1938*
Siemens Hearing Instruments Inc 10 Constitution Ave PO Box 1397 **Fax Area Code:* 732 ■ *TF:* 800-766-4500 ■ *Web:* healthcare.siemens.com	Piscataway	NJ	08855	800-766-4500	562-6696*
Smith & Nephew Inc 970 Lk Carillon Dr 310 *TF Cust Svc:* 800-876-1261 ■ *Web:* smith-nephew.com	Saint Petersburg	FL	33716	727-392-1261	392-6914
Smith & Nephew Inc Orthopaedic Div 1450 Brooks Rd **Fax Area Code:* 800 ■ *TF:* 800-821-5700 ■ *Web:* www.smith-nephew.com	Memphis	TN	38116	901-396-2121	621-6924*
Smiths Medical ASD Inc 160 Weymouth St *TF:* 800-258-5361 ■ *Web:* www.smiths-medical.com	Rockland	MA	02370	781-878-8011	878-8201
Smiths Medical MD Inc 1265 Grey Fox Rd *TF:* 800-258-5361 ■ *Web:* www.smiths-medical.com	Saint Paul	MN	55112	651-633-2556	628-7459
Smiths Medical Respiratory Support Products 5200 Upper Metro Pl Ste 200 **Fax Area Code:* 614 ■ *TF:* 800-258-5361 ■ *Web:* www.smiths-medical.com	Dublin	OH	43017	214-618-0218	734-0254*
Sonic Innovations Inc 2501 Cottontail Ln Ste 300 **Fax Area Code:* 801 ■ *TF:* 888-678-4327 ■ *Web:* www.sonicinnovations.com	Somerset	NJ	08873	888-423-7834	365-3000*
Sophono Inc 5744 Central Ave Ste 100 *Web:* sophono.com	Boulder	CO	80301	720-407-5160	
Southmedic Inc 50 Alliance Blvd *Web:* southmedic.com	Barrie	ON	L4M5K3	705-726-9383	
Span-America Medical Systems Inc 70 Commerce Ctr *NASDAQ: SPAN* ■ *TF:* 800-888-6752 ■ *Web:* www.spanamerica.com	Greenville	SC	29615	864-288-8877	288-8692
Spenco Medical Corp PO Box 2501 *TF:* 800-877-3626 ■ *Web:* www.spenco.com	Waco	TX	76702	254-772-6000	772-3093
Standard Textile Company Inc One Knollcrest Dr *TF:* 800-999-0400 ■ *Web:* www.standardtextile.com	Cincinnati	OH	45237	513-761-9255	761-0467
Starkey Laboratories Inc 6700 Washington Ave S *TF:* 800-328-8602 ■ *Web:* www.starkey.com	Eden Prairie	MN	55344	952-941-6401	828-6972
STERIS Corp 5960 Heisley Rd *NYSE: STE* ■ **Fax:* Cust Svc ■ *TF:* 800-548-4873 ■ *Web:* www.steris.com	Mentor	OH	44060	440-354-2600	639-4450*
Stryker Endoscopy 5900 Optical Ct *Web:* strykerendo.com	San Jose	CA	95138	408-754-2000	
Sunrise Medical Inc 2842 Business Pk Ave *TF:* 800-333-4000 ■ *Web:* www.sunrisemedical.com	Fresno	CA	93727	800-333-4000	
Surgical Appliance Industries Inc 3960 Rosslyn Dr *TF:* 800-888-0867 ■ *Web:* www.surgicalappliance.com	Cincinnati	OH	45209	800-888-0867	309-9055
Symmetry Medical Inc 3724 N State Rd 15 *NYSE: SMA* ■ *Web:* www.symmetrymedical.com	Warsaw	IN	46582	574-267-8700	
SynCardia Systems Inc 1992 E Silverlake Rd *Web:* www.syncardia.com	Tucson	AZ	85713	520-545-1234	
Synovis Life Technologies Inc 2575 University Ave *NASDAQ: SYNO* ■ *TF:* 800-255-4018 ■ *Web:* www.synovislife.com	Saint Paul	MN	55114	651-796-7300	642-9018
Synthes USA 1302 Wrights Ln E **Fax:* Hum Res ■ *Web:* synthes.com	West Chester	PA	19380	610-719-5000	719-5140*
Tamarack Habilitation Technologies Inc 1670 94th Ln NE *Web:* www.tamarackhti.com	Blaine	MN	55449	763-795-0057	
TIDI Products LLC 570 Enterprise Dr *TF:* 800-521-1314 ■ *Web:* www.tidiproducts.com	Neenah	WI	54956	800-521-1314	837-7770
Treen Gloves & Safety Products Ltd 704 Alexander St *Web:* www.treensafety.com	Vancouver	BC	V6A1E3	604-253-4588	
Trulife 26296 Twelve Trees Ln NW *Web:* apexsystemsinc.com	Poulsbo	WA	98370	360-697-5656	697-5876
TSO3 Inc 2505 Dalton Ave *TF:* 866-715-0003 ■ *Web:* www.tso3.com	Quebec	QC	G1P3S5	418-651-0003	653-5726
Utah Medical Products Inc 7043 S 300 W *NASDAQ: UTMD* ■ *TF:* 866-754-9789 ■ *Web:* www.utahmed.com	Midvale	UT	84047	801-566-1200	566-2062
Venture Tape Corp 30 Commerce Rd *TF:* 800-343-1076 ■ *Web:* venturetape.com	Rockland	MA	02370	781-331-5900	871-0065
Vital Signs Inc 20 Campus Rd *TF:* 800-932-0760 ■ *Web:* www3.gehealthcare.com	Totowa	NJ	07512	973-790-1330	790-3307
Volcano Corp 3661 Vly Centre Dr Ste 200 **Fax Area Code:* 916 ■ *TF:* 800-228-4728 ■ *Web:* www.volcanocorp.com	San Diego	CA	92130	800-228-4728	638-8812*
West Pharmaceutical Services Inc 101 Gordon Dr *NYSE: WST* ■ *TF:* 800-345-9800 ■ *Web:* www.westpharma.com	Lionville	PA	19341	610-594-2900	594-3000
Widex Canada Ltd 5041 Mainway *Web:* www.widex.ca	Burlington	ON	L7L5H9	905-315-8303	
Wright & Filippis Inc 2845 Crooks Rd *Web:* www.firsttoserve.com	Rochester Hills	MI	48309	248-829-8200	853-1830
Wright Medical Group Inc 5677 Airline Rd *NASDAQ: WMGI* ■ *TF:* 800-238-7188 ■ *Web:* www.wmt.com	Arlington	TN	38002	901-867-9971	867-9534
Wright Medical Technology Inc 5677 Airline Rd **Fax:* Cust Svc ■ *TF:* 800-238-7188 ■ *Web:* www.wmt.com	Arlington	TN	38002	901-867-9971	867-9534*
Zimmer Inc 1800 W Ctr St PO Box 708 *TF:* 800-613-6131 ■ *Web:* www.zimmer.com	Warsaw	IN	46580	574-267-6131	372-4988

481 MEDICAL TRANSCRIPTION SERVICES

Companies listed here have a national or regional clientele base.

Company	City	State	Zip	Phone	Fax
Acusis LLC Four Smithfield St *Web:* www.acusis.com	Pittsburgh	PA	15222	412-209-1300	209-1299
ASL Distribution Services Ltd 2160 Buckingham Rd *Web:* www.asldistribution.com	Oakville	ON	L6H6M7	905-829-5141	
Carrier Services of Tennessee Inc 2532 N Mount Juliet Rd *Web:* www.carrierservtn.com	Mount Juliet	TN	37122	615-758-9757	
Comtrans 20651 Prism Pl *Web:* www.gocomtrans.com	Lake Forest	CA	92630	949-455-9890	
DCT Chambers Trucking Ltd 600 Waddington Dr *Web:* dctchambers.com	Vernon	BC	V1T8T6	250-549-2157	
Earth Auto Shippers LLC 2245 Keller Way Ste 300 *Web:* www.earthautoshippers.com	Carrollton	TX	75006	214-483-9028	
Energetic Services Inc Mile 54 Alaska Hwy *Web:* www.energeticservices.com	Fort St John	BC	V1J4J1	250-785-4761	
FreightPros 3307 Northland Dr Ste 360 *TF:* 888-297-6968 ■ *Web:* www.freightpros.com	Austin	TX	78731	888-297-6968	
Hybrid Transit Systems Inc 818 Dows Rd SE *Web:* www.hybridtrans.com	Cedar Rapids	IA	52403	319-261-0749	
Logistic Professionals Inc 1920 Pennsylvania Ave *Web:* www.logisticpros.com	Mcdonough	GA	30253	770-692-0431	
MediGrafix Inc 9 Fairway Ln Ste C **Fax Area Code:* 888 ■ *Web:* www.medi-grafix.com	Blythewood	SC	29016	803-261-6387	744-1301*
Moran Towing Corp 50 Locust Ave *Web:* www.morantug.com	New Canaan	CT	06840	203-442-2800	
Multivans Inc 13289 Coleraine Dr *Web:* www.multivans.com	Bolton	ON	L7E3B6	905-857-3171	
Rapid Transcript Inc 4311 Wilshire Blvd *Web:* www.rapidtranscript.com	Los Angeles	CA	90010	323-964-0400	
Southern Motor Carriers Rate Conference Inc 500 Westpark Dr *Web:* www.smc3.com	Peachtree City	GA	30269	770-486-5800	
Thomas Transcription Services Inc PO Box 26613 *TF:* 888-878-2889 ■ *Web:* www.thomastx.com	Jacksonville	FL	32226	904-751-5058	751-5240
Transport Jacques Auger Inc 860 Archimede St *Web:* www.tja.ca	Levis	QC	G6V7M5	418-835-9266	
Warren Gibson Ltd 206 Church St South PO Box 100 *Web:* www.warrengibson.com	Alliston	ON	L9R1T9	705-435-4342	
Webmedx Inc 564 Alpha Dr *Web:* corpweb.webmedx.com	Pittsburgh	PA	15238	412-968-9244	

482 MEDICINAL CHEMICALS & BOTANICAL PRODUCTS

SEE ALSO Diagnostic Products p. 2198; Pharmaceutical Companies p. 2921; Pharmaceutical Companies - Generic Drugs p. 2924; Vitamins & Nutritional Supplements p. 3286; Biotechnology Companies p. 1869

Companies listed here manufacture medicinal chemicals and botanical products in bulk for sale to pharmaceutical, vitamin, and nutritional product companies.

Company	City	State	Zip	Phone	Fax
Acic Fine Chemicals Inc 81 St Claire Blvd	Brantford	ON	N3S7X6	519-751-3668	751-1378
TF: 800-265-6727 ■ *Web:* www.acic.com					
AM Todd Co 1717 Douglas Ave	Kalamazoo	MI	49007	269-343-2603	343-3399
Web: www.wildflavors.com					
American Laboratories Inc (ALI) 4410 S 102nd St	Omaha	NE	68127	402-339-2494	339-0801
Web: www.americanlaboratories.com					
Anika Therapeutics Inc 32 Wiggins Ave	Bedford	MA	01730	781-457-9000	305-9720
NASDAQ: ANIK ■ *Web:* www.anikatherapeutics.com					
Apotex Pharmachem Inc 34 Spalding Dr	Brantford	ON	N3T6B8	519-756-8942	753-3051
Web: www.apotexpharmachem.com					
AQ Pharmaceuticals Inc 11555 Monarch St	Garden Grove	CA	92841	714-903-1000	
Web: www.aqpharmaceuticals.com					
Array BioPharma Inc 3200 Walnut St	Boulder	CO	80301	303-381-6600	449-5376
NASDAQ: ARRY ■ *TF:* 877-633-2436 ■ *Web:* www.arraybiopharma.com					
Avanti Polar Lipids Inc					
700 Industrial Pk Dr	Alabaster	AL	35007	205-663-2494	663-0756
TF: 800-227-0651 ■ *Web:* www.avantilipids.com					
Bachem Bioscience Inc 3132 Kashiwa St	Torrance	CA	90505	310-539-4171	239-0800*
**Fax Area Code:* 610 ■ *TF:* 800-634-3183 ■ *Web:* www.bachem.com					
Balchem Corp 52 Sunrise Pk Rd PO Box 600	New Hampton	NY	10958	845-326-5613	326-5742
NASDAQ: BCPC ■ *TF:* 877-407-8289 ■ *Web:* www.balchem.com					
Bedford Laboratories Inc 300 Northfield Rd	Bedford	OH	44146	440-232-3320	232-2772
TF: 800-562-4797 ■ *Web:* www.bedfordlabs.com					
Ben Venue Laboratories Inc 300 Northfield Rd	Bedford	OH	44146	440-232-3320	439-6398
TF General: 800-989-3320 ■ *Web:* www.benvenue.com					
Betachem Inc 58 Ware Rd	Upper Saddle River	NJ	07458	201-327-4100	327-9366
BI Nutraceuticals 2550 El Presidio St	Long Beach	CA	90810	310-669-2100	637-3644
Web: www.botanicals.com					
Bio-Botanica Inc 75 Commerce Dr	Hauppauge	NY	11788	631-231-5522	231-7332
TF: 800-645-5720 ■ *Web:* www.bio-botanica.com					
Cambrex Charles City Inc 1205 11th St	Charles City	IA	50616	641-257-1000	228-4152
Web: www.cambrex.com					
Cambrex Corp					
1 Meadowlands Plaza 15th Fl	East Rutherford	NJ	07073	201-804-3000	804-9852
NYSE: CBM ■ *TF:* 866-286-9133 ■ *Web:* www.cambrex.com					
Cell Marque Corp 6600 Sierra College Blvd	Rocklin	CA	95677	916-746-8900	
Web: www.cellmarque.com					
Charm Sciences Inc 659 Andover St	Lawrence	MA	01843	978-687-9200	687-9216
TF: 800-343-2170 ■ *Web:* www.charm.com					
ChemWerth Inc 1764 Litchfield Tpke	Woodbridge	CT	06525	203-387-7794	397-8132
Web: www.chemwerth.com					
Contract Pharmacal Corp 135 Adams Ave	Hauppauge	NY	11788	631-231-4610	231-4610
Web: www.cpc.com					
Creagen Biosciences Inc 23 Rainin Rd	Woburn	MA	01801	781-938-1122	
Web: www.creagenbio.com					
Cyanotech Corp					
73-4460 Queen Kaahumanu Hwy Ste 102	Kailua-Kona	HI	96740	808-326-1353	329-4533
NASDAQ: CYAN ■ *TF Sales:* 800-453-1187 ■ *Web:* www.cyanotech.com					
Designing Health Inc 28410 Witherspoon Pkwy	Valencia	CA	91355	661-257-1705	
Web: www.missinglinkproducts.com					
Diosynth RTP Inc 101 J Morris Commons Ln	Morrisville	NC	27560	919-337-4477	
Web: www.fujifilmdiosynth.com					
Down to Earth 2525 S King St	Honolulu	HI	96826	808-947-7678	
Web: www.downtoearth.org					
Elge Inc 1000 Cole Ave	Rosenberg	TX	77471	281-342-8228	232-0476
Web: www.elgeinc.com					
Flavine North America Inc 10 Reuten Dr	Closter	NJ	07624	201-768-4190	768-2854
Web: www.flavine.com					
Flora Mfg & Distributing Ltd					
7400 Fraser Park Dr	Burnaby	BC	V5J5B9	604-436-6000	
TF: 888-436-6697 ■ *Web:* www.florahealth.com					
Gemini Pharmaceuticals Inc 87 Modular Ave	Commack	NY	11725	631-543-3334	543-3335
Web: www.geminipharm.com					
George Uhe Company Inc 219 River Dr	Garfield	NJ	07026	201-843-4000	843-7517
TF: 800-850-4075 ■ *Web:* www.uhe.com					
Greer Laboratories Inc					
639 Nuway Cir NE PO Box 800	Lenoir	NC	28645	828-754-5327	754-5320
TF Cust Svc: 800-378-3906 ■ *Web:* www.greerlabs.com					
GYMA Laboratories of America Inc					
135 Cantiague Rock Rd	Westbury	NY	11590	516-933-0900	933-1075
Web: www.gyma.com					
Heel Inc 10421 Research Rd SE	Albuquerque	NM	87123	505-293-3843	
Web: www.heel.com					
ICC Industries Inc 460 Pk Ave	New York	NY	10022	212-521-1700	521-1970
TF: 800-422-1720 ■ *Web:* www.iccchem.com					
InCon Processing LLC 970 Douglas Rd	Batavia	IL	60510	630-761-1180	
Web: www.incontech.com					
Interchem Corp 120 Rt 17 N	Paramus	NJ	07652	201-261-7333	261-7339
TF: 800-261-7332 ■ *Web:* www.interchem.com					
Johnson Matthey Inc Pharmaceutical Materials Div					
2003 Nolte Dr	Paulsboro	NJ	08066	856-384-7001	384-7186
TF: 800-444-8544 ■ *Web:* www.jmpharma.com					
Johnson Matthey Pharma Services 25 Patton Rd	Devens	MA	01434	978-784-5000	784-5500
TF: 800-444-8544 ■ *Web:* www.jmpharmaservices.com					
Lannett Company Inc (LCI)					
13200 Townsend Rd	Philadelphia	PA	19154	215-333-9000	333-9004
NYSE: LCI ■ *TF:* 800-325-9994 ■ *Web:* www.lannett.com					
Libby Laboratories Inc 1700 Sixth St	Berkeley	CA	94710	510-527-5400	527-8687
Web: www.libbylabs.com					
LycoRed Corp 377 Crane St	Orange	NJ	07051	973-882-0322	882-0323
TF: 877-592-6733 ■ *Web:* www.lycored.com					
Natural Standard One Davis Sq	Somerville	MA	02144	617-591-3300	
Web: naturalmedicines.therapeuticresearch.com/					
Naturex Inc 375 Huyler St	South Hackensack	NJ	07606	201-440-5000	342-8000
Web: www.naturex.com					
NHK Laboratories Inc					
12230 E Florience Ave	Santa Fe Springs	CA	90670	562-944-5400	944-0266
TF: 866-645-5227 ■ *Web:* www.nhklabs.com					
NovaDigm Therapeutics Inc					
4201 James Ray Dr Reac 1 Bldg Ste 2200	Grand Forks	ND	58202	701-757-5161	335-7121
Web: www.novadigm.net					
Nutra Pharma Corp					
12502 W Atlantic Blvd	Coral Springs	FL	33071	954-509-0911	
TF: 877-895-5647 ■ *Web:* www.nutrapharma.com					
Nutraceutix Inc 9609 153rd Ave NE	Redmond	WA	98052	425-883-9518	869-1020
TF: 800-548-3222 ■ *Web:* www.nutraceutix.com					
NutriScience Innovations LLC					
2450 Reservoir Ave	Trumbull	CT	06611	203-372-8877	372-9977
Web: www.nutriscienceusa.com					
Nutrition 21 Inc Three Manhattanville Rd	Purchase	NY	10577	914-701-4500	696-0860
Web: www.nutrition21.com					
One Lambda Inc 21001 Kittridge St	Canoga Park	CA	91303	818-702-0042	702-6904
TF: 800-822-8824 ■ *Web:* www.onelambda.com					
Paddock Laboratories Inc					
3940 Quebec Ave N	Minneapolis	MN	55427	763-546-4676	
Web: www.paddocklabs.com					
Patheon Inc 2100 Syntex Ct	Mississauga	ON	L5N7K9	905-821-4001	812-6709
TF: 866-529-2922 ■ *Web:* www.patheon.com					
PendoPharm Inc 6111 Royalmount	Montreal	QC	H4P2T4	514-340-5045	733-9684
TF Cust Svc: 866-926-7653 ■ *Web:* www.pendopharm.com					
Pharma Tech Industries Inc 1310 Stylemaster Dr	Union	MO	63084	636-583-8664	583-5373
Web: www.pharma-tech.net					
Premier Micronutrient Corp					
1801 W End Ave Ste 910	Nashville	TN	37203	615-234-4020	
Web: www.premiermicronutrient.com					
Rainbow Light Nutritional Sys Inc					
100 Ave Tea	Santa Cruz	CA	95060	800-635-1233	429-0189*
**Fax Area Code:* 831 ■ *TF:* 800-635-1233 ■ *Web:* www.rainbowlight.com					
Sabinsa Corp 20 Lake Dr	East Windsor	NJ	08520	732-777-1111	777-1443
Web: www.sabinsa.com					
Salvona Technologies LLC 65 Stults Rd Bldg 1	Dayton	NJ	08810	609-655-0173	
Web: www.salvona.com					
Scientific Protein Laboratories Inc					
700 E Main St PO Box 158	Waunakee	WI	53597	608-849-5944	849-4053
TF: 800-334-4775 ■ *Web:* www.spl-pharma.com					
Siegfried USA LLC 33 Industrial Pk Rd	Pennsville	NJ	08070	856-678-3601	678-8201
TF Cust Svc: 877-763-8630 ■ *Web:* www.siegfried.ch					
Sigma-Aldrich Corp 3050 Spruce St	Saint Louis	MO	63103	314-771-5765	325-5052*
NASDAQ: SIAL ■ **Fax Area Code:* 800 ■ *TF:* 800-325-3010 ■ *Web:* www.sigmaaldrich.com					
Spectrum Laboratory Products Inc					
14422 S San Pedro St PO Box 290	Gardena	CA	90248	310-516-8000	516-7512*
**Fax:* Cust Svc ■ *TF General:* 800-772-8786 ■ *Web:* www.spectrumchemical.com					
SPI Pharma Rockwood Office Park Fl 2	Wilmington	DE	19809	302-576-8567	789-9755*
**Fax Area Code:* 800 ■ *TF:* 800-789-9755 ■ *Web:* www.spipharma.com					
SST Corp 635 Brighton Rd	Clifton	NJ	07012	973-473-4300	473-4326
TF: 800-222-0921 ■ *Web:* www.sst-corp.com					
Starwest Botanicals Inc					
11253 Trade Ctr Dr	Rancho Cordova	CA	95742	916-638-8100	638-8293
TF General: 800-800-4372 ■ *Web:* www.starwestherb.com					
Terry Laboratories Inc 7005 Technology Dr	Melbourne	FL	32904	321-259-1630	242-0625
TF: 800-367-2563 ■ *Web:* www.terrylabs.com					
Tri-K Industries Inc					
Two Stewart Ct PO Box 10	Denville	NJ	07834	973-298-8850	750-9785*
**Fax Area Code:* 201 ■ *TF:* 800-526-0372 ■ *Web:* www.tri-k.com					
TSI Health Sciences Inc					
305 S Fourth St E Ste 101	Missoula	MT	59801	406-549-9123	549-6139
TF: 877-549-9123 ■ *Web:* www.tsiinc.com					
Uluru Inc 4452 Beltway Dr	Addison	TX	75001	214-905-5145	905-5130
Web: www.uluruinc.com					
United-Guardian Inc (UGI)					
230 Marcus Blvd PO Box 18050	Hauppauge	NY	11788	631-273-0900	273-0858
NASDAQ: UG ■ *TF:* 800-645-5566 ■ *Web:* www.u-g.com					
Vinchem Inc 301 Main St	Chatham	NJ	07928	973-635-4841	635-1459
Web: www.vinchem.com					
Wilcox Emporium Warehouse 161 Howard St	Boone	NC	28607	828-262-1221	
Web: wilcoxemporium.com					

483 METAL - STRUCTURAL (FABRICATED)

Company	City	State	Zip	Phone	Fax
A J Sackett & Sons Co, The					
1701 S Highland Ave	Baltimore	MD	21224	410-276-4466	
Web: www.ajsackett.com					
Able Steel Fabricators Inc 4150 E Quartz Cir	Mesa	AZ	85215	480-830-2253	
Web: www.ablesteel.com					
Acme Architectural Products Inc					
251 Lombardy St	Brooklyn	NY	11222	718-384-7800	
Web: www.acmesteel.com					
Aerospace America Inc					
900 Harry Truman Pkwy PO Box 189	Bay City	MI	48706	989-684-2121	684-4486
TF: 800-237-6414 ■ *Web:* www.aerospaceamerica.com					
Afco Manufacturing Corp					
428 Cogshall St PO Box 230	Holly	MI	48442	248-634-4415	634-6301
Web: www.afcomfg.com					
Afco Steel Inc 1423 E Sixth St	Little Rock	AR	72202	501-340-6200	340-6260
Web: www.afcosteel.com					
Aircon Corp 2873 Chelsea Ave	Memphis	TN	38108	901-452-0230	
Web: www.aircon-corporation.com					
AJ Manufacturing Inc 1217 Oak St	Bloomer	WI	54724	715-568-2204	
Web: www.ajdoor.com					
All Metals Service & Warehousing Inc					
100 All Metals Dr	Cartersville	GA	30120	770-427-7379	
Web: www.allmetals.com					

				Phone	Fax
Allcan Distributors Inc 12612 - 124 St *Web:* www.allcan.com	Edmonton	AB	T5L0N7	780-451-2357	
Allied Steel Fabricators Inc 4604 148th Ave Ne *Web:* www.alliedsteelfab.com	Redmond	WA	98052	425-861-9558	
Alloy Engineering Co, The 844 Thacker St *Web:* www.alloyengineering.com	Berea	OH	44017	440-243-6800	
AmChel Communications Inc 2800 Capital St *Web:* www.amchel.com	Wylie	TX	75098	972-442-1030	
American Aerogel Corp 460 Buffalo Rd Ste 200A *Web:* www.americanaerogel.com	Rochester	NY	14611	585-328-2140	
American BOA Inc 1420 Redi Rd *Web:* www.americanboa.com	Cumming	GA	30040	770-889-9400	
American Commercial Inc 200 Bob Morrison Blvd *Web:* www.dsiunderground.com	Bristol	VA	24201	276-466-2743	
Amerimax Bldg Products Inc 5208 Tennyson Pkwy *Fax Area Code: 800 ■ *TF:* 800-448-4033 ■ *Web:* www.amerimaxbp.com	Plano	TX	75024	469-366-3200	448-8391*
Amerimax Home Products Inc 450 Richardson Dr *TF:* 800-347-2586 ■ *Web:* www.amerimax.com	Lancaster	PA	17603	717-299-3711	299-3014
Anasteel & Supply Company LLC 2272 Mabros Industrial Pkwy *Web:* www.anasteel.com	Ellenwood	GA	30294	404-675-9501	
Anchor Fabrication Ltd 1200 Lawson Rd *TF:* 800-635-0386 ■ *Web:* anchorfabrication.com	Fort Worth	TX	76131	817-498-2521	
Apex Industries Inc 100 Millennium Blvd *TF:* 800-268-3331 ■ *Web:* www.apexindustries.com	Moncton	NB	E1E2G8	506-857-1620	
APi Group Inc Fabrication & Mfg Group 1100 Old Hwy 8 NW *Fax Area Code: 651 ■ *TF:* 800-223-4922 ■ *Web:* apigroupinc.com/industries/	New Brighton	MN	55112	800-223-4922	636-0312*
Arcadia Mfg Group Inc 80 Cohoes Ave *Web:* www.arcadiamfg.com	Green Island	NY	12183	518-434-6213	
Artimex Iron Company Inc 315 Cypress Ln *Web:* www.artimexiron.com	El Cajon	CA	92020	619-444-3155	
ASTECH Engineered Products Inc 3030 Red Hill Ave	Santa Ana	CA	92705	949-250-1000	
Azimuth Three Communications 127 Delta Park Blvd *Web:* www.az3.com	Brampton	ON	L6T5M8	905-793-7793	793-0780
Baker Metal Products Inc 11140 Zodiac Ln *Web:* bakermetal.com	Dallas	TX	75229	972-241-3553	
Baker Tankhead Inc 10405 N fwy *Web:* www.bakertankhead.com	Fort Worth	TX	76177	817-232-8030	
Barker Steel Co Inc 55 Sumner St *Fax Area Code: 905 ■ *TF:* 866-977-3227 ■ *Web:* www.barker.com	Milford	MA	01757	508-473-8484	573-5263*
Baron Metal Industries Inc 101 Ashbridge Cir *Web:* www.baronmetal.com	Woodbridge	ON	L4L3R5	416-749-2111	
Benson Steel Ltd 72 Commercial Rd *Web:* www.bensonsteel.com	Bolton	ON	L7E1K4	905-857-0684	
Berlin Steel Construction Co 76 Depot Rd PO Box 428 *Web:* www.berlinsteel.com	Kensington	CT	06037	860-828-3531	828-5253
Bohn & Dawson Inc 3500 Tree Ct Industrial Blvd *Web:* www.bohnanddawson.com	Saint Louis	MO	63122	636-225-5011	825-6111
Boman Kemp Basement Window Systems 2393 South 1900 West *Web:* www.boman-kemp.com	Ogden	UT	84401	801-731-0615	
Braden Mfg LLC 5199 N Mingo Rd *Fax Area Code: 918 ■ *TF:* 800-272-3360 ■ *Web:* www.braden.com	Tulsa	OK	74117	800-272-3360	272-7414*
Brandywine Valley Fabricators Inc Brandywine Vly Fab *Web:* www.brandywinevalleyfab.com	Coatesville	PA	19320	610-384-7440	
Brilex Industries Inc PO Box 749 *Web:* www.brilex.com	Youngstown	OH	44501	330-744-1114	744-1125
Brookfield Fabricating Corp 111 Stanbury Industrial Dr *Web:* www.brookfieldfabricating.com	Brookfield	MO	64628	660-258-2214	
Busch Industries Inc 900 E Paris Ave Se Ste 304 *Web:* www.buschindustries.com	Grand Rapids	MI	49546	616-957-3737	
C&G Systems Corp 320 E Main St *Web:* www.cgsystems.com	Lake Zurich	IL	60047	847-816-9700	
Capital Tower & Communications Inc 13330 Amberly Rd *Web:* www.capitaltower.com	Waverly	NE	68462	402-786-3333	
Cauttrell Enterprises Inc 7618 N Broadway *Web:* www.cauttrellenterprises.com	St. Louis	MO	63147	314-385-4270	
Center Rock Inc 118 Schrock Dr *Web:* www.centerrock.com	Berlin	PA	15530	814-267-7100	
Central Aluminum Co 2045 Broehm Rd *Web:* www.centralaluminum.com	Columbus	OH	43207	614-491-5700	
Central Minnesota Fabricating Inc 2725 W Gorton Ave *TF:* 800-839-8857 ■ *Web:* www.cmf-inc.com	Willmar	MN	56201	320-235-4181	
Central Steel Fabricators Inc 1843 S 54th Ave *Web:* www.centralsteelfab.com	Cicero	IL	60804	708-652-2037	
Central Texas Iron Works Inc 1000 Winchell St PO Box 2555 *Web:* www.ctiw.com	Waco	TX	76712	254-776-8000	772-5811
CENTRIA 1005 Beaver Grade Rd *Fax: Hum Res ■ *TF:* 800-759-7474 ■ *Web:* www.centria.com	Moon Township	PA	15108	412-299-8000	299-8051*
Certified Stainless Service Inc 2704 Railroad Ave *Web:* www.west-mark.com	Ceres	CA	95307	209-537-4747	
Cessco Fabrication & Engineering Ltd 7310-99 St *Web:* www.cessco.ca	Edmonton	AB	T6E3R8	780-433-9531	432-7899
Chase Industries Inc 10021 Commerce Park Dr *TF:* 800-543-4455 ■ *Web:* www.chasedoors.com	Cincinnati	OH	45246	513-860-5565	
Cherubini Metal Works Ltd 570 Wilkinson Ave	Dartmouth	NS	B3B0J4	902-468-5630	
CHI Overhead Doors Inc 1485 Sunrise Dr *Web:* www.chiohd.com	Arthur	IL	61911	217-543-2135	
Cives Steel Co 210 Cives Ln *Web:* www.cives.com	Winchester	VA	22603	540-667-3480	662-2680
Clark Steel Fabricators Inc 12610 Vigilante Rd *Web:* www.clarksteelfab.com	Lakeside	CA	92040	619-390-1502	
Clermont Steel Fabricators LLC 2565 Old SR 32 *Web:* www.clermontsteel.com	Batavia	OH	45103	513-732-6033	732-5344
CMC Alamo Steel Co 2784 Old Dallas Rd *TF:* 800-500-0333 ■ *Web:* www.cmc.com	Waco	TX	76705	254-799-2471	799-6227
CMC Capitol City Steel 14501 S IH 35 *TF:* 888-682-7337 ■ *Web:* www.cmc.com	Buda	TX	78610	512-282-8820	295-2500
CMC Rebar Carolinas 2528 N Chester St *Web:* www.cmc.com	Gastonia	NC	28052	704-865-8571	865-2713
CMC Rebar Georgia 251 Hosea Rd *TF:* 888-682-7337 ■ *Web:* www.cmc.com	Lawrenceville	GA	30045	770-963-6251	339-6623
Coastal Steel Inc 870 Cidco Rd *Web:* www.coastalsteel.com	Cocoa	FL	32923	321-632-8228	
Collins Industries Ltd 3740-73 Ave *Web:* www.collins-industries-ltd.com	Edmonton	AB	T6B2Z2	780-440-1414	
Com-Tech Service Group Inc 17827 Commerce Dr *Web:* www.comtechservices.net	Westfield	IN	46074	317-867-4486	
Commercial Resins Company Inc 8100 E 96th Ave *Web:* commercialresins.com	Henderson	CO	80640	303-288-3914	
Compo Steel Products Inc 3637 N Holton St *Web:* www.composteel.com	Milwaukee	WI	53212	414-962-6800	
Contract Fabricators Inc 105 Rolfing Rd *Web:* www.contractfab.com	Holly Springs	MS	38635	662-252-6330	
Contractors Material Co 10320 S Medallion Dr *Web:* www.cmcmmi.com	Cincinnati	OH	45241	513-733-3000	
Cooper STEEL Inc 503 N Hillcrest Dr *Web:* www.coopersteel.com	Shelbyville	TN	37160	931-684-7962	
Cowelco a California Corp 1634 W 14th St *Web:* www.cowelco.com	Long Beach	CA	90813	562-432-5766	
Craig Manufacturing Ltd 96 Mclean Ave *Web:* www.craig-mfg.com	Hartland	NB	E7P2K5	506-375-4493	
Crane Hill Machine & Fabrication Inc 2476 E Us Hwy 50 *Web:* www.cranehillmachine.com	Seymour	IN	47274	812-358-3534	358-2351
Creative Door Services Ltd 14904 - 135 Ave *Web:* creativedoor.com	Edmonton	AB	T5V1R9	780-483-1789	
Cubic Designs Inc 5487 S Westridge Dr *Web:* www.cubicdesigns.com	New Berlin	WI	53151	262-789-1966	
Danny Byrd Inc 1416 Sandersville Sharon Rd *Web:* www.dannybyrdinc.com	Laurel	MS	39443	601-649-2524	
Dave Steel Company Inc 40 Meadow Rd *Web:* www.davesteel.com	Asheville	NC	28803	828-252-2771	
Day Wireless Systems Inc 4700 SE International Way *Web:* www.daywireless.com	Milwaukie	OR	97222	503-659-1240	
Dis-Tran Steel Fabrication LLC 529 Cenla Dr *Web:* www.distran.com	Pineville	LA	71360	318-640-6892	
Discount RampsCom LLC 760 S Indiana Ave *TF:* 888-651-3431 ■ *Web:* www.discountramps.com	West Bend	WI	53095	262-338-3431	
Don Young Co 8181 Ambassador Row *TF:* 800-367-0390 ■ *Web:* www.dycwindows.com	Dallas	TX	75247	214-630-0934	630-0406
Dover Tank & Plate Co, The 5725 Crown Rd Nw *Web:* www.dovertank.com	Dover	OH	44622	330-343-4443	
Dropbox Inc 1805 N Second St *TF:* 888-388-7768 ■ *Web:* www.dropboxinc.com	Ironton	OH	45638	888-388-7768	
Dura-Bond Industries Inc 2658 Puckety Dr *Web:* www.dura-bond.com	Export	PA	15632	724-327-0280	
Eberl Iron Works Inc 128 Sycamore St *Web:* www.eberliron.com	Buffalo	NY	14204	716-854-7633	
Ejcon Corp 5502 Shawland Rd *Web:* www.ejcon.com	Jacksonville	FL	32254	904-786-0622	
Energy Steel & Supply Co 3123 John Conley Dr *Web:* www.energysteel.com	Lapeer	MI	48446	810-538-4990	
Ennis Steel Industries Inc 204 Metro Park Blvd *Web:* www.ennissteel.com	Ennis	TX	75119	972-878-0400	878-9563
Etobicoke Ironworks Ltd 141 Rivalda Rd *Web:* www.eiw.ca	Weston	ON	M9M2M6	416-742-7111	
Euramax International Inc 5445 Triangle Pkwy Ste 350 *Web:* www.euramax.com	Norcross	GA	30092	770-449-7066	
Excel Bridge Manufacturing Co 12001 Shoemaker Ave *Web:* www.excelbridge.com	Santa Fe Springs	CA	90670	562-944-0701	
Exergy LLC 320 Endo Blvd *Web:* www.exergyllc.com	Garden City	NY	11530	516-832-9300	
F & r Installers Corp 63 Flushing Ave Ste 270	Brooklyn	NY	11205	718-855-1600	
Fabco Steel Fabrication Inc 14688 San Bernardino Ave *Web:* www.fabcosteel.com	Fontana	CA	92335	909-350-1535	
Fabral Inc 3449 Hempland Rd *TF:* 800-477-2741 ■ *Web:* www.fabral.com	Lancaster	PA	17601	717-397-2741	397-1040
Fabrication Products Inc 4201 Ne Minnehaha St *Web:* www.fabproducts.com	Vancouver	WA	98661	360-696-1324	

Company / Address	City	State	Zip	Phone	Fax
Florig R & J Industrial Company Inc 910 Brook Rd	Conshohocken	PA	19428	610-825-6655	825-7424
Web: www.rjflorig.com					
Franke Kindred Canada Ltd 1000 Kindred Rd	Midland	ON	L4R4K9	705-526-5427	227-3035*
**Fax Area Code:* 866 ■ *Web:* www.frankekindred.com					
FWT LLC 5750 E Interstate 20	Fort Worth	TX	76119	817-255-3060	
Web: fwtllc.com					
Garaga Inc 8500 25th Ave	St Georges	QC	G6A1K5	418-227-2828	227-6282
TF: 800-464-2724 ■ *Web:* www.garaga.com					
Gayle Mfg Company Inc 1455 E Kentucky Ave	Woodland	CA	95776	530-662-0284	
Web: gaylemfg.com					
GEA PHE Systems North America Inc 100 Gea Dr	York	PA	17402	717-268-6200	
TF: 800-774-0474 ■ *Web:* www.gea-phe.com					
Gerlinger Foundry & Machine Works Inc 1527 Sacramento St	Redding	CA	96099	530-243-1053	
Web: www.gerlinger.com					
Glenco Steel Corp 8657 Live Oak Ave	Fontana	CA	92335	909-854-9000	854-9008
GLM Industries LP 1508 - Eighth St	Nisku	AB	T9E7S6	780-955-2233	
TF: 800-661-9828 ■ *Web:* www.glmindustries.com					
Global Fabrication Inc 235 Beaver Dr	Dubois	PA	15801	814-372-1500	
Web: www.globalfabricationinc.com					
Grain Belt Supply Company Inc PO Box 615	Salina	KS	67402	785-827-4491	827-4494
TF: 800-447-0522 ■ *Web:* www.grainbeltsupply.com					
Heartland Engineered Products LLC 355 Industrial Dr	Harrison	OH	45030	513-367-0080	
Web: www.heartlandengineeredproducts.com					
Hemco Industries Inc 2408 Karbach St	Houston	TX	77092	713-681-2426	
Web: www.hemcoind.com					
Herber Aircraft Service Inc 1401 E Franklin Ave	El Segundo	CA	90245	310-322-9575	
Web: www.herberaircraft.com					
Herrick Corp 3003 E Hammer Ln	Stockton	CA	95212	209-956-4751	
Web: www.herricksteel.com					
Hirschfeld Industries LP 112 W 29th St PO Box 3768	San Angelo	TX	76903	325-486-4201	486-4380
Web: www.carolinasteel.com					
Hirschfeld Steel Company Inc 112 W 29th St	San Angelo	TX	76903	325-486-4201	486-4380
Web: www.hirschfeld.com					
Hogan Manufacturing Inc (HMI) PO Box 398	Escalon	CA	95320	209-838-7323	838-7329
Web: www.hoganmfg.com					
Hoosier Tank & Manufacturing Inc 1710 N Sheridan St	South Bend	IN	46628	574-232-8368	
Web: hoosiertank.com					
Hurco Technologies Inc 409 Enterprise St	Harrisburg	SD	57032	605-743-2466	
Web: www.gethurco.com					
Hyspan Precision Products Inc 1685 Brandywine Ave	Chula Vista	CA	91911	619-421-1355	421-1702
Web: www.hyspan.com					
Imprex Inc 3260 S 108th St	Milwaukee	WI	53227	414-321-9300	
Web: imprexusa.com					
InterLock Industries Inc 545 S Third St Ste 310	Louisville	KY	40202	502-569-2007	569-2016
Web: www.interlockindustries.com					
International Production Specialists Inc 35006 Washington Ave	Honey Creek	WI	53138	262-534-3130	
Web: www.ipstanks.com					
IP Systems Inc 2685 Industrial Ln	Broomfield	CO	80020	303-438-1570	
Web: www.ipsysinc.com					
Irwin Car and Equipment 9953 Broadway St	Irwin	PA	15642	724-864-8900	
Web: www.irwincar.com					
J V Northwest Inc 390 S Redwood St	Canby	OR	97013	503-263-2858	
Web: www.jvnw.com					
J. C. Macelroy Company Inc PO Box 850	Piscataway	NJ	08855	732-572-7100	572-7112
TF: 800-622-3576 ■ *Web:* www.macelroy.com					
Jebco Industries Inc 111 Ellis Dr	Barrie	ON	L4N8Z3	705-797-8888	797-8887
Web: jebcoindustries.com					
Jesse Engineering Co 1840 Marine View Dr	Tacoma	WA	98422	253-922-7433	922-1998
Web: www.jesseengineering.com					
JH Industries Inc 1981 E Aurora Rd	Twinsburg	OH	44087	330-963-4105	963-4111
TF: 800-321-4968 ■ *Web:* www.copperloy.com					
Johnson Bros Metal Forming Co 5744 McDermott Dr	Berkeley	IL	60163	708-449-7050	449-0042
Web: www.johnsonrollforming.com					
Kennedy Tank & Mfg Company Inc 833 E Sumner Ave	Indianapolis	IN	46227	317-787-1311	
Web: www,kennedytank.com					
Kern Steel Fabrication Inc 627 Williams St	Bakersfield	CA	93305	661-327-9588	
Web: kernsteel.com					
Lane Conveyors & Drives Inc 15 Industrial Plz	Brewer	ME	04412	207-989-4560	
Web: www.lanesupplyco.com					
Lapeer Industries Inc 400 Mccormick Dr	Lapeer	MI	48446	810-664-1816	
Web: www.lapeerind.com					
LeJeune Steel Co 118 W 60th St	Minneapolis	MN	55419	612-861-3321	861-2724
Web: www.lejeunesteel.com					
Lexicon Inc 8900 Fourche Dam Pk	Little Rock	AR	72206	501-490-4200	
Web: www.lexicon-inc.com					
Liberty Industries LC 2855 Hwy 261	Newburgh	IN	47630	812-853-0595	
Web: www.towerinnovations.net					
Lichtenwald-Johnston Iron Works Corp 7840 Lehigh St PO Box 1328	Morton Grove	IL	60053	847-966-1100	966-1159
Web: lichtenwald-johnston.com					
Linetec 725 S 75th Ave	Wausau	WI	54401	715-843-4100	
TF: 888-717-1472 ■ *Web:* www.linetec.com					
Lone Wolf Mfg LLC 19321 Stuebner Airline Rd	Spring	TX	77379	281-370-3087	
Web: lonewolfmfg.net					
M & J Materials Inc 7561 Gadsden Hwy PO Box 428	Trussville	AL	35173	205-655-7451	655-4100
M-13 Construction Management LLC 775 W Spring Creek Pl	Springville	UT	84663	801-489-3215	
Web: www.m-13.com					
M-5 Steel Manufacturing Inc 1450 Mirasol St	Los Angeles	CA	90023	323-263-9383	
Web: www.m5steel.com					
Magnolia Steel Company Inc PO Box 5007	Meridian	MS	39302	601-693-4301	693-3101
Web: www.magnoliasteel.com					
Maguire Iron Inc 1610 N Minnesota Ave	Sioux Falls	SD	57104	605-334-9749	
Web: www.maguireiron.com					
Manko Window Systems Inc 800 Hayes Dr	Manhattan	KS	66502	785-776-9643	
TF: 800-642-1488 ■ *Web:* www.mankowindows.com					
Mark Steel Corp 1230 West 200 South PO Box 16006	Salt Lake City	UT	84104	801-521-0670	303-2040
Web: www.marksteel.net					
Mascott Equipment Company Inc 435 NE Hancock St	Portland	OR	97212	503-282-2587	
Web: www.mascottec.com					
Mason Corp 123 W Oxmoor Rd	Birmingham	AL	35209	205-942-4100	
Web: www.masoncorp.com					
McElroy Metal Inc 1500 Hamilton Rd	Bossier City	LA	71111	318-747-8097	747-8657
TF: 800-562-3576 ■ *Web:* www.mcelroymetal.com					
Merchant & Evans Inc 308 Connecticut Dr	Burlington	NJ	08016	609-387-3033	
Web: www.ziprib.com					
Merrill Iron & Steel Inc 900 Alderson St	Schofield	WI	54476	715-355-8924	
Web: www.merrilliron.com					
Met-Con Inc 465 Canaveral Groves Blvd	Cocoa	FL	32926	321-632-4880	639-0158
Web: www.metconinc.com					
Midwest Metal Products Co 2100 W Mt Pleasant Rd	Muncie	IN	47302	888-741-1044	741-3167*
**Fax Area Code:* 765 ■ *TF:* 888-741-1044 ■ *Web:* www.midwestmetal.com					
Midwest Steeplejacks Inc 4623 Timberline Dr S	Fargo	ND	58104	701-241-7040	
Web: www.midweststeeplejacks.com					
Miller Metal Fabricators Inc 345 National Ave	Staunton	VA	24401	540-886-5575	
Misa Metal Fabricating Inc 7101 International Dr	Louisville	KY	40258	502-933-5555	
Web: www.misametalfab.com					
Mobility Center Inc 6693 Dixie Hwy	Bridgeport	MI	48722	989-777-0910	
Web: www.myamigo.com					
Monarch LLC 7050 N 76th St	Milwaukee	WI	53223	414-353-8820	
Web: www.monarchcorp.com					
Mound Technologies Inc 25 Mound Pk Dr	Springboro	OH	45066	937-748-2937	748-9763
Web: moundtechnologies.com					
Nabco Entrances Inc S82W18717 Gemini Dr	Muskego	WI	53150	262-679-0045	
TF: 888-679-3319 ■ *Web:* www.nabcoentrances.com					
Nello Capital Inc 211 W Washington St Ste 2000	South Bend	IN	46601	574-288-3632	
Web: www.nelloinc.com					
New Way Air Bearings Inc 50 McDonald Blvd	Aston	PA	19014	610-494-6700	
Web: www.newwayairbearings.com					
Norlen Inc 900 Grossman Dr	Schofield	WI	54476	715-359-0506	359-9935*
**Fax Area Code:* 713 ■ *Web:* www.norlen.com					
North Star Propellers Inc 2317 Newton Ave	San Diego	CA	92113	619-239-8309	
Web: www.northstarpropellers.com					
North State Steel Inc 1010 W Gum Rd	Greenville	NC	27834	252-830-8884	
Web: www.northstatesteel.com					
Northeast Towers 199 Brickyard Rd	Farmington	CT	06032	860-677-1999	
Web: www.northeasttowers.com					
Northern Pride Communications Inc 20 Ctr Park Rd	Topsham	ME	04086	207-798-5540	
Web: www.northernpridecommunications.com					
Nucor Corp 1915 Rexford Rd	Charlotte	NC	28211	704-366-7000	362-4208
NYSE: NUE ■ *TF:* 800-294-1322 ■ *Web:* www.nucor.com					
Nucor Corp Vulcraft Div 1501 W Darlington St	Florence	SC	29501	843-662-0381	662-3132
Web: www.vulcraft.com					
Ocean Steel & Construction Ltd 400 Chesley Dr	Saint John	NB	E2K5L6	506-632-2600	
Web: www.oceansteel.com					
Olson & Company Steel Inc 1941 Davis St	San Leandro	CA	94577	510-567-2200	
Web: www.olsonsteel.com					
Optimus Corp 5727 S Lewis Ave Ste 600	Tulsa	OK	74105	918-491-9191	
Web: www.optimus-tulsa.com					
Ornamental Metal Works Inc 2100 N Woodford St	Decatur	IL	62526	217-428-3446	
Owen Industries Inc 501 Ave H	Carter Lake	IA	51510	712-347-5500	347-6166
TF: 800-831-9252 ■ *Web:* www.owenind.com					
Owen Steel Co 727 Mauney Dr	Columbia	SC	29201	803-251-7680	251-7613
Web: www.owensteel.com					
Ozark Steel Fabricators Inc One Ozark Steel Dr	Farmington	MO	63640	573-756-5741	
Web: ozarksteel.com					
Pacificomm Systems LLC 73-5563 Olowalu St Ste B6	Kailua Kona	HI	96740	808-329-6440	
Paramount Components Ltd 2130 Paramount Cres	Abbotsford	BC	V2T6A5	604-852-2564	
Web: www.paramount.bc.ca					
Parkway Metal Products Inc 130 Rawls Rd	Des Plaines	IL	60018	847-789-4000	
Web: www.parkwaymetal.com					
Paxton & Vierling Steel Co 501 Ave H	Carter Lake	IA	51510	800-831-9252	347-5507*
**Fax Area Code:* 712 ■ *TF:* 800-831-9252 ■ *Web:* pvsteelfab.com					
Phoenix Fabricators & Erectors Inc 182 S Country Rd 900 E	Avon	IN	46123	317-271-7002	
Web: www.phoenixtank.com					
Pipe Welders Inc 2965 W State Rd 84	Fort Lauderdale	FL	33312	954-587-8400	
TF: 800-787-8401 ■ *Web:* www.pipewelders.com					
Precision Masking Inc 721 Lavoy Rd	Erie	MI	48133	734-848-4200	
Web: www.precisionmasking.com					
Price Steel Ltd 13500 156 St	Edmonton	AB	T5V1L3	780-447-9999	
Web: www.pricesteel.com					
Processed Metals Innovators LLC 600 21st Ave	Bloomer	WI	54724	715-568-1700	
Web: www.pmillc.com					
Qualico Steel Co Inc PO Box 149	Webb	AL	36376	334-793-1290	794-0996
TF: 866-234-5382 ■ *Web:* www.qualicosteel.com					

				Phone	Fax
Quality Machine & Welding Company Inc PO Box 27345 *Web:* www.qmwkx.com	Knoxville	TN	37927	865-524-2162	524-1830
R F R Metal Fabrication Inc 3204 Knotts Grove Rd *Web:* www.rfr-metalfab.com	Oxford	NC	27565	919-693-1354	
Ralston Metal Products Ltd 50 Watson Rd S **Fax Area Code:* 519 ■ *TF:* 800-265-7611 ■ *Web:* www.ralstonmetal.com	Guelph	ON	N1L1E2	800-265-7611	836-9763*
Ram Welding Company Inc 93 Rado Dr *Web:* www.ramwelding.com	Naugatuck	CT	06770	203-729-2289	
Ramgen Power Systems LLC 11808 Northup Way Ste W-190 *Web:* www.ramgen.com	Bellevue	WA	98005	425-828-4919	
Ranor Inc One Bella Dr *TF:* 800-225-9552 ■ *Web:* www.ranor.com	Westminster	MA	01473	978-874-0591	874-2748
Rast Iron Works 12895 Interstate 10 East *Web:* www.rastironworks.com	San Antonio	TX	78154	210-659-6704	659-6791
Rodney Hunt Co 46 Mill St *TF:* 800-448-8860 ■ *Web:* www.rodneyhunt.com	Orange	MA	01364	978-544-2511	544-7204
Roscoe Steel 1501 S 30th St W *Web:* www.truenorthsteel.com	Billings	MT	59102	406-656-2253	
Roth Fabricating Inc 9600 Skyline Dr *Web:* www.rothfabricatinginc.com	Morenci	MI	49256	517-458-7541	
RSDC of Michigan LLC 1775 Holloway Dr *Web:* www.rsdcmi.com	Holt	MI	48842	877-881-7732	
Safe Harbor Access Systems LLC 211 N Koppers Rd *Web:* www.safe-harbor.com	Florence	SC	29506	843-679-6888	
Schuff Steel Inc 1920 Ledo Rd *TF:* 800-248-5367 ■ *Web:* www.schuff.com	Albany	GA	31707	229-883 4506	
Security Metal Products Corp 5700 Hannum Ave Ste 250 *Web:* www.secmet.com	Culver City	CA	90230	310-641-6690	
Senior Flexonics Inc 300 E Devon Ave *Web:* www.senior-flexonics.com	Bartlett	IL	60103	630-837-1811	
Senior Flexonics Pathway Division 2400 Longhorn Industrial Dr *Web:* www.pathwayb.com	New Braunfels	TX	78130	830-629-8080	
SFI-Gray Steel Ltd 3511 W 12th St *Web:* www.sfigray.com	Houston	TX	77008	713-864-6450	
Shape Corp 1900 Hayes St *Web:* www.shapecorp.com	Grand Haven	MI	49417	616-846-8700	846-3464
Shepard Steel Company Inc 110 Meadow St *Web:* www.shepardsteel.com	Hartford	CT	06114	860-525-4446	
Shure-line Construction Inc PO Box 249 *Web:* www.shure-line.com	Kenton	DE	19955	302-653-4610	
Sims Cab Depot 200 Moulinette Rd *Web:* www.cabdepot.com	Long Sault	ON	K0C1P0	613-534-2289	
SiteMaster Inc 6914 S Yorktown Ave Ste 210 *Web:* www.sitemaster.com	Tulsa	OK	74136	918-663-2232	
Smardt Chiller Group Inc 1800 Trans Canada Hwy *Web:* www.smardt.com	Dorval	QC	H9P1H7	514-426-8989	
SnowBear Ltd 155 Dawson Rd *Web:* www.snowbear.com	Guelph	ON	N1H1C1	519-767-1115	
Southeast Fabricators Inc 7301 University Blvd E *Web:* www.sefab.com	Cottondale	AL	35453	205-556-3227	
Southern Steel Fabricators Inc 208 Wagon Wheel Rd *Web:* www.southernsteelfab.com	Monroe	LA	71202	318-345-2800	
Southland Steel Fabricators Inc 251 Greensburg St *Web:* www.southlandsteel.com	Greensburg	LA	70441	225-222-4141	
Specialty Manufacturing LLC 5601 San Francisco Rd NE *Web:* www.wirelesscomponents.com	Albuquerque	NM	87109	505-823-1832	
Speedway Steel Fabrication Inc 501 N Truman Blvd *Web:* www.speedwaysteel.net	Crystal City	MO	63019	636-931-6500	
Stainless LLC 1140 Welsh Rd Ste 250 *Web:* www.talltowers.com	North Wales	PA	19454	215-631-1400	
Standard Iron Inc 2516 Vance Ave *Web:* www.standardiron.com	Chattanooga	TN	37404	423-756-0940	756-0944
Starr Manufacturing Inc 4175 Warren-Sharon Rd *Web:* www.starrmfg.com	Vienna	OH	44473	330-394-9891	
Steel Fabricators LLC 721 NE 44th St **Fax:* Sales ■ *Web:* www.sfab.com	Fort Lauderdale	FL	33334	954-772-0440	938-7527*
Steel Fabricators of Monroe LLC 2101 Booth St Ste 4830 *Web:* www.steelfab.com	Monroe	LA	71201	318-387-9426	
Steele Solutions Inc 9909 S 57th St *Web:* www.steelesolutions.com	Franklin	WI	53132	414-367-5099	
SteelFab Inc 8623 Old Dowd Rd *Web:* www.steelfab-inc.com	Charlotte	NC	28214	704-394-5376	
Steffes Corp 3050 Hwy 22 N *Web:* www.steffes.com	Dickinson	ND	58601	701-483-5400	
Structural Steel of Carolina LLC 1725 Vargrave St *Web:* www.steelofcarolina.com	Winston Salem	NC	27107	336-725-0521	
Structural Steel Services 6210 St Louis St S Industrial Pk	Meridian	MS	39307	601-483-5381	
Stupp Bros Inc 3800 Weber Rd *TF:* 800-899-1856 ■ *Web:* www.stupp.com	Saint Louis	MO	63125	314-638-5000	638-2660
T. Bruce Sales Inc Nine Carbaugh St *TF:* 800-944-0738 ■ *Web:* www.tbrucesales.com	West Middlesex	PA	16159	724-528-9961	528-2050
TFT Inc 2976 N Florence Ave *Web:* tulsafintube.com	Tulsa	OK	74110	918-834-2366	
Thornton Steel Company Inc 2700 W Pafford St *Web:* www.thorntonsteel.com	Fort Worth	TX	76110	817-926-3324	
Tie Down Engineering Inc 255 Villanova Dr SW *TF:* 800-241-1806 ■ *Web:* www.danforthanchors.com	Atlanta	GA	30336	404-344-0000	
Tower Systems Inc 17226 447th Ave PO Box 1474 *Web:* www.towersystems.com	Watertown	SD	57201	605-886-0930	
Trans-tec Machine Ltd 6320 Ridgemont St *Web:* www.transtecmachine.com	Houston	TX	77087	713-643-9114	
Trinity Steel Fabricators Inc 13430 Northwest Fwy Ste 225 *Web:* www.trinitysteel.com	Trinity	TX	77040	713-460-5556	
Trinity Structural Towers Inc 2525 N Stemmons Fwy *Web:* www.trinitytowers.com	Dallas	TX	75207	214-631-4420	589-8640
Trulite Glass & Aluminum Solutions LLC 800 Fairway Dr Ste 200 *Web:* www.trulite.com	Deerfield Beach	FL	33441	954-724-1775	
Union Metal Corp 1432 Maple Ave NE *Web:* www.unionmetal.com	Canton	OH	44705	330-456-7653	456-0196
United Window & Door Manufacturing Inc 24-36 Fadem Rd *TF:* 800-848-4550 ■ *Web:* www.unitedwindowmfg.com	Springfield	NJ	07081	973-912-0600	
US Tower Corp 1099 W Ropes Ave *Web:* www.ustower.com	Woodlake	CA	93286	559-564-6000	
USP Structural Connectors Inc 703 Rogers Dr *Web:* www.uspconnectors.com	Montgomery	MN	56069	507-364-7333	
Val-Fab Inc 218 Jackson St *TF:* 888-482-5322 ■ *Web:* www.valfab.com	Neenah	WI	54956	920-722-1009	
Vibrant Power Inc 310 Courtneypark Dr E *Web:* www.vibrantpower.com	Mississauga	ON	L5T2S5	905-564-8644	
Vitols Tool & Machine Corp 10082 Sandmeyer Ln *Web:* www.vitolsgroup.com	Philadelphia	PA	19116	215-464-8240	
W & K Steel LLC 98 Antisbury Pl *Web:* www.wksteelfacts.com	Rankin	PA	15104	412-271-1620	271-3988
W & W Steel Co 1730 W Reno Ave *Web:* www.wwsteel.com	Oklahoma City	OK	73106	405-235-3621	236-4842
Wabi Iron & Steel Corp 330 Broadwood Ave *Web:* www.wabicorp.com	New Liskeard	ON	P0J1P0	705-647-4383	
Wagner Plate Works LLC 4142 W 49th St *Web:* www.wagnerplateworks.com	Tulsa	OK	74107	918-447-4488	
Wahlcometroflex Inc 29 Lexington St *TF:* 800-272-6652 ■ *Web:* sfpathway.com	Lewiston	ME	04240	207-784-2338	
Waiward Steel Fabricators Ltd 10030 - 34 St *Web:* www.waiward.com	Edmonton	AB	T6B2Y5	780-469-1258	
Walters Metal Fabrication 3660 State Rt 111 *Web:* www.waltersmetalfab.com	Granite City	IL	62040	618-931-5551	
WaUSAu Window & Wall Systems 7800 International Dr *TF:* 877-678-2983 ■ *Web:* www.wausauwindow.com	Wausau	WI	54401	715-845-2161	
Wear - Concepts Inc 106 NW Business Park Ln *Web:* www.wearcon.com	Riverside	MO	64150	816-587-1923	
Wojan Window & Door Corp 217 Stover Rd *TF:* 800-632-9827 ■ *Web:* www.wojan.com	Charlevoix	MI	49720	231-547-2931	
WSF Industries Inc Seven Hackett Dr *TF:* 800-874-8265 ■ *Web:* www.wsf-inc.com	Tonawanda	NY	14150	716-692-4930	
Zieman Manufacturing Co 168 S Spruce *Web:* www.zieman.com	Rialto	CA	92376	909-873-0061	
Zimmerman Metals Inc 201 E 58th Ave *Web:* www.zimmerman-metals.com	Denver	CO	80216	303-294-0180	

484 METAL COATING, PLATING, ENGRAVING

				Phone	Fax
A & L Metal Processing 1920 George St	Sandusky	OH	44870	419-627-0022	
A-Brite Plating Company Inc 3000 W 121st St *Web:* www.abriteplating.com	Cleveland	OH	44111	216-252-2995	
All Metals Processing of Orange County Inc 8401 Standustrial St *Web:* www.allmetalsprocessing.com	Stanton	CA	90680	714-828-8238	828-4552
Allegan Metal Finishing Co 1274 Lincoln Rd *Web:* www.amfco.biz	Allegan	MI	49010	269-673-6604	
Almond Products Inc 17150 148th Ave *Web:* www.almondproducts.com	Spring Lake	MI	49456	616-844-1813	
Alumicor Ltd 290 Humberline Dr *TF:* 877-258-6426 ■ *Web:* www.alumicor.com	Toronto	ON	M9W5S2	416-745-4222	
Aluminum Coil Anodizing Corp 501 E Lake St *Web:* www.acacorp.com	Streamwood	IL	60107	630-837-4000	837-0814
American Nickeloid Co 2900 Main St *TF:* 800-645-5643 ■ *Web:* www.nickeloid.com	Peru	IL	61354	815-223-0373	223-5344
Anomatic Corp 1650 Tamarack Rd *Web:* www.anomatic.com	Newark	OH	43055	740-522-2203	
Apex Anodizing Nev Inc 280 Coney Island Dr Ste B *Web:* apexanodizing.com	Sparks	NV	89431	775-355-8121	
Applied Thin-Film Products Inc 3439 Edison Way *Web:* www.thinfilm.com	Fremont	CA	94538	510-661-4287	
APS Materials Inc 4011 Riverside Dr *Web:* www.apsmaterials.com	Dayton	OH	45405	937-278-6547	
Archer Wire International Corp 7300 S Narragansett Ave *Web:* www.archerwire.com	Bedford Park	IL	60638	708-563-1700	563-1740
Arlington Plating Co 600 S Vermont St *Web:* www.arlingtonplating.com	Palatine	IL	60078	847-359-1490	
AST Products Inc Nine Linnell Cir *TF:* 877-667-4500 ■ *Web:* www.astp.com	Billerica	MA	01821	978-667-4500	

Phone *Fax*

ATI Precision Finishing 499 Delaware Ave .... Rochester PA 15074 724-775-1664 775-1668
Web: www.atimetals.com

Bayou Perma-Pipe Canada Ltd 5233 39th St .... Camrose AB T4V4R5 780-672-2345
Web: www.bayoupermapipe.com

Bel Air Finishing Supply Corp
101 Circuit Dr .... North Kingstown RI 02852 401-667-7902
Web: www.belairfinishing.com

Bennett Metal Products Inc
700 Rackaway St .... Mount Vernon IL 62864 618-244-1911
Web: bennettmetal.com

BF Inkjet Media Inc 116 Bethea Rd #322 .... Fayetteville GA 30214 770-719-2051
Web: www.bfinkjet.com

BL Downey Company LLC 2125 Gardner Rd .... Broadview IL 60155 708-345-8000
TF: 800-323-1206 ■ *Web:* www.bldowney.com

Bon Chef Inc 205 SR- 94 .... Lafayette NJ 07848 973-383-8848
Web: www.bonchef.com

Bowman Plating Company Inc 2631 126th St .... Compton CA 90222 310-639-4343
Web: www.bowmanplating.com

Bredero Shaw A ShawCor Co
3838 N Sam Houston Pkwy E Ste 300 .... Houston TX 77032 281-886-2350 886-2353
Web: www.brederoshaw.com

Central Metal Finishing Inc
80 Flagship Dr .... North Andover MA 01845 978-685-4811
Web: www.cenmet.com

Certified Enameling Inc 3342 Emery St .... Los Angeles CA 90023 323-264-4403 264-9599
Web: www.certifiedenameling.com

Certified Metal Finishing Inc
1420 SW 28th Ave .... Pompano Beach FL 33069 954-979-0707
Web: certifiedmetalfinishing.com

Charlotte Anodizing Products Inc
591 E Packard Hwy .... Charlotte MI 48813 517-543-1911
TF: 800-818-6945 ■ *Web:* www.charlotte-anodizing.com

Chem Processing Inc 3910 Linden Oaks Dr .... Rockford IL 61109 815-874-8118
TF: 800-262-2119 ■ *Web:* www.chemprocessing.com

Chemart Co 15 New England Way .... Lincoln RI 02865 401-333-9200 333-1634
TF: 800-521-5001 ■ *Web:* www.chemart.com

Chemline Inc 5151 Natural Bridge Rd .... Saint Louis MO 63115 314-664-2230
Web: www.chemline.net

Chemresearch Company Inc 1101 W Hilton Ave .... Phoenix AZ 85007 602-253-4175
Web: chemresearchco.com

Chicago Metallic Corp 4849 S Austin Ave .... Chicago IL 60638 708-563-4600 222-3744*
**Fax Area Code:* 800 ■ *TF:* 800-323-7164 ■ *Web:* www.chicago-metallic.com

Coast Coatings LLC 227 Calle Pintoresco .... San Clemente CA 92672 949-492-9037
Web: www.coastpowdercoating.com

Coast Plating Inc 128 W 154th St .... Gardena CA 90248 323-770-0240
Web: www.coastplating.com

Coastline Metal Finishing Corp
7061 Patterson Dr .... Garden Grove CA 92841 714-895-9099
Web: www.coastlinemetalfinishing.com

Cole a Die & Engraving 5515 Chantry Dr .... Columbus OH 43232 614-863-6866
Web: www.aecole.com

Conforma Clad Inc 501 Park E Blvd .... New Albany IN 47150 812-948-2118
Web: www.conformaclad.com

Continental Studwelding Ltd 35 Devon Rd .... Brampton ON L6T5B6 905-792-3650 792-3711
TF: 800-848-9442 ■ *Web:* www.constud.ca

Cork Industries Inc 500 Kaiser Dr .... Folcroft PA 19032 610-522-9550
Web: www.corkind.com

Corrosion Monitoring Services Inc
902 Equity Dr .... Saint Charles IL 60174 630-762-9300
Web: www.cmsinc.us

Craddock Finishing Corp
1400 W Illinois St .... Evansville IN 47710 812-425-2691
Web: www.craddockfinishing.com

Crest Coating Inc 1361 S Allec St .... Anaheim CA 92805 714-635-7090 758-8752
Web: www.crestcoating.com

Crown Tumbling Corp
32571 Stephenson Hwy .... Madison Heights MI 48071 248-588-4990

Crystal Finishing Systems Inc
2610 Ross Ave .... Schofield WI 54476 715-355-5351
Web: www.crystalfinishing.com

CuraFlo British Columbia Ltd
7436 Fraser Park Dr .... Burnaby BC V5J5B9 604-298-7278
Web: curaflo.com

Curtis Metal Finishing Co
6645 Sims Dr .... Sterling Heights MI 48313 586-939-2850
Web: www.curtismetal.com

CVD Diamond Corp 2061 Piper Ln .... London ON N5V3S5 519-457-9903
Web: www.cvddiamond.com

Deposition Sciences Inc 3300 Coffey Ln .... Santa Rosa CA 95403 707-573-6700 573-6748
TF: 866-433-7724 ■ *Web:* www.depsci.com

Dura Coat Products Inc 5361 Via Ricardo .... Riverside CA 92509 951-341-6500
Web: www.duracoatproducts.com

East Side Plating Inc 8400 SE 26th Pl .... Portland OR 97202 503-654-3774
TF: 800-394-8554 ■ *Web:* www.eastsideplating.com

Electric Coating Technologies (ECT)
4407 Railroad Ave .... East Chicago IN 46312 219-378-1930 378-1933
Web: www.ectllc.com

Electro-spec Inc 1800 Commerce Pkwy .... Franklin IN 46131 317-738-9199
Web: www.electro-spec.com

Endura Coatings LLC
42250 Yearego Dr .... Sterling Heights MI 48314 586-739-0101
Web: www.enduracoatings.com

Erler Industries Inc
418 Stockwell St PO Box 219 .... North Vernon IN 47265 812-346-4421 346-1892
Web: www.erler.com

Everlube Products 100 Cooper Cir .... Peachtree City GA 30269 770-261-4800
Web: everlubeproducts.com

Flame Control Coatings LLC
4120 Hyde Park Blvd .... Niagara Falls NY 14305 716-282-1399
Web: www.flamecontrol.com

Form Grind Corp
30062 Aventura .... Rancho Santa Margarita CA 92688 949-858-7000
Web: www.kellysearch.com

Phone *Fax*

FW Gartner Thermal Spraying Ltd
25 Southbelt Industrial Dr .... Houston TX 77047 713-225-0010
TF: 888-439-4872 ■ *Web:* www.fwgts.com

Galvan Industries Inc 7320 Millbrook Rd .... Harrisburg NC 28075 704-455-5102 455-5215
TF General: 888-256-6929 ■ *Web:* www.galvan-ize.com

General Extrusions Inc 4040 Lk Pk Rd .... Youngstown OH 44512 330-783-0270 788-1250
Web: www.genext.com

General Metal Finishing Company Inc (GMF)
42 Frank Mossberg Dr .... Attleboro MA 02703 508-226-5606
Web: www.pepgenmetal.com

GH International Inc 2540 Rena Rd .... Mississauga ON L4T3C9 905-677-5522
Web: www.ghinternational.ca

Giering Metal Finishing Inc 2655 State St .... Hamden CT 06517 203-248-5583
Web: www.gieringmetalfinishing.com

GM Nameplate Inc 2040 15th Ave W .... Seattle WA 98119 206-284-2200 284-3705
TF: 800-366-7668 ■ *Web:* www.gmnameplate.com

Hadronics Inc 4570 Steel Pl .... Cincinnati OH 45209 513-321-9350
TF: 800-829-0826 ■ *Web:* www.hadronics.com

Heyco Metals Inc 1069 Stinson Dr .... Reading PA 19605 610-926-4131
Web: www.heyco-metals.com

Hydratech Engineered Products LLC
10448 Chester Rd .... Cincinnati OH 45215 513-827-9169
Web: hydratechllc.com

Hytek Finishes Co 8127 S 216th St .... Kent WA 98032 253-872-7160
Web: www.hytekfinishes.com

IBC Coating Technologies 902 Hendricks Dr .... Lebanon IN 46052 765-482-9802
Web: www.ibccoatings.com

Ingot Metal Company Ltd 111 Fenmar Dr .... Weston ON M9L1M3 416-749-1372
TF: 800-567-7774 ■ *Web:* www.ingot.ca

Integrated Surface Technologies Inc
1455 Adams St Ste 1125 .... Menlo Park CA 94025 650-324-1824
Web: www.insurftech.com

Interplex Engineered Products 231 Ferris Ave .... Rumford RI 02916 401-434-6543 399-7655*
**Fax Area Code:* 508 ■ *Web:* www.interplex.com

IonBond LLC 200 Roundhill Dr .... Rockaway NJ 07866 973-586-4700 586-4729
Web: www.ionbond.com

IVC Industrial Coatings Inc
2831 E Industrial Pk .... Brazil IN 47834 812-442-5080
Web: www.teamivc.com

J & M Plating Inc 4500 Kishwaukee St .... Rockford IL 61109 815-964-4975
Web: www.jmplating.com

John C Dolph Co 320 New Rd .... Monmouth Junction NJ 08852 732-329-2333
Web: www.dolphs.com

KC Jones Plating Co 2845 E Ten Mile Rd .... Warren MI 48091 586-755-4900
Web: www.kcjplating.com

KNS Cos Inc 475 Randy Rd .... Carol Stream IL 60188 630-665-9010 665-1819
Web: www.knscompanies.com

Korns Galvanizing Co 75 Bridge St .... Johnstown PA 15902 814-535-3293
Web: kornsgalvanizing.com

Kuntz Electroplating Inc 851 Wilson Ave .... Kitchener ON N2C1J1 519-893-7680 893-5431
Web: www.kuntz.com

LB Foster Co 415 Holiday Dr .... Pittsburgh PA 15220 800-255-4500 928-7891*
NASDAQ: FSTR ■ **Fax Area Code:* 412 ■ **Fax:* Sales ■ *TF:* 800-255-4500 ■ *Web:* www.lbfoster.com

Liberty Coating Company LLC
21 S Steel Rd .... Morrisville PA 19067 215-736-1111
Web: www.libertycoating.com

Liquidmetal Coatings LLC
900 Rockmead Dr Ste 240 .... Kingwood TX 77339 281-359-1283

Lorin Industries 1960 S Roberts St .... Muskegon MI 49443 231-722-1631 728-3139
TF: 800-654-1159 ■ *Web:* www.lorin.com

Magna-Tech Manufacturing Corp 3416 S Hoyt Ave .... Muncie IN 47302 765-284-5050
Web: www.magnatechmfg.com

Magnetic Metals Corp 1900 Hayes Ave .... Camden NJ 08105 856-964-7842 963-8569
TF: 800-257-8174 ■ *Web:* www.magmet.com

Markland Industries Inc
1111 E McFadden Ave .... Santa Ana CA 92705 714-245-2850 245-2853
Web: www.marklandindustries.com

Master Finish Co
2020 Nelson SE PO Box 7505 .... Grand Rapids MI 49510 877-590-5819 245-0039*
**Fax Area Code:* 616 ■ *TF:* 877-590-5819 ■ *Web:* www.masterfinishco.com

Material Sciences Corp (MSC)
2200 E Pratt Blvd .... Elk Grove Village IL 60007 847-439-2210 439-0737
NASDAQ: MASC ■ *Web:* www.matsci.com

Max Levy Autograph Inc
2710 Commerce Way .... Philadelphia PA 19154 215-842-3675
Web: www.maxlevy.com

MesoCoat Inc 24112 Rockwell Dr .... Euclid OH 44117 216-453-0866
Web: www.mesocoat.com

Metal Arts Finishing Inc 1001 S Lake St .... Aurora IL 60506 630-892-6744

Metal Cladding Inc 230 S Niagara St .... Lockport NY 14094 800-432-5513 439-4010*
**Fax Area Code:* 716 ■ *TF:* 800-432-5513 ■ *Web:* www.metalcladding.com

Metal Coatings Corp 3700 Dunvale Rd .... Houston TX 77063 713-977-0123 977-0824
Web: www.metcoat.com

Metal Koting - Continuous Colour Coat Ltd
1430 Martin Grove Rd .... Rexdale ON M9W4Y1 416-743-7980 743-5980
TF: 855-656-8464 ■ *Web:* www.metalkoting.com

MetaLPlate Galvanizing LP 1120 39th St N .... Birmingham AL 35234 205-595-4703
Web: www.metalplate.com

MetoKote Corp 1340 Neubrecht Rd .... Lima OH 45801 419-996-7800 996-7801
Web: www.metokote.com

Meziere Enterprises Inc 220 S Hale Ave .... Escondido CA 92029 760-746-3273
TF: 800-208-1755 ■ *Web:* www.meziere.com

Microcast Technologies Corp (MTC)
1611 W Elizabeth Ave .... Linden NJ 07036 908-523-9503 523-0910
Web: www.mtcnj.com

Midwest Products Finishing Company Inc
6194 Section Rd .... Ottawa Lake MI 49267 734-856-5200 856-7267
Web: www.midwestecoat.com

National Coatings Inc
3520 Rennie School Rd .... Traverse City MI 49685 231-943-2557 943-4262
TF: 888-947-2557 ■ *Web:* www.nationalcoatings.biz

Nd Industries Inc 1000 N Crooks Rd .... Clawson MI 48017 248-288-0000 288-0022
TF: 800-471-5000 ■ *Web:* www.ndindustries.com

Phone Fax

NOF Metal Coatings NA 275 Industrial Pkwy .... Chardon OH 44024 440-285-2231 285-5009
Web: www.metal-coatings.com
Nor-Ell Inc 851 Hubbard Ave....................... Saint Paul MN 55104 651-487-1441 488-1626
Web: www.nor-ell.com
Northern Engraving Corp
803 S Black River St PO Box 377 .... Sparta WI 54656 608-269-6911 366-3725
Web: www.norcorp.com
O E C Graphics Inc
555 W Waukau Ave PO Box 2443.................... Oshkosh WI 54902 920-235-7770 235-2252
TF: 800-388-7770 ■ *Web:* www.oecgraphics.com
Passaic Engraving Company Inc 41 Brook Ave .... Passaic NJ 07055 973-777-0621 777-7791
Web: www.passaicengraving.com
Pioneer Metal Finishing LLC 486 Globe Ave .... Green Bay WI 54304 877-721-1100 884-1790*
**Fax Area Code:* 920 ■ *TF:* 877-721-1100 ■ *Web:* www.pioneermetal.com
Plasma Ruggedized Solutions Inc
2284 Ringwood Ave Ste A .... San Jose CA 95131 408-954-8405
TF: 800-994-7527 ■ *Web:* www.plasmarugged.com
Plasma Technology Inc 1754 Crenshaw Blvd ....Torrance CA 90501 310-320-3373 533-1677
Web: www.ptise.com
Precision Coating Company Inc 63 Sprague St.........Boston MA 02136 781-329-1420 329-3618
Web: www.precisioncoating.com
Precision Graphics Inc 21 County Line Rd ....Somerville NJ 08876 908-707-8880 707-8884
Web: www.precisiongraphics.us
Precoat Metals
8440 Woodfield Crossing Bldg 2 Ste 500...........Indianapolis IN 46240 317-462-7761
Web: www.precoat.com
Premier Die Casting Co 1177 Rahway Ave............. Avenel NJ 07001 732-634-3000 634-0590
TF: 800-394-3006 ■ *Web:* www.diecasting.com
Providence Metallizing Company Inc
51 Fairlawn Ave .... Pawtucket RI 02860 401-722-5300 724-3410
Web: www.providencemetallizing.com
Quick Tanks Inc PO Box 338 .... Kendallville IN 46755 260-347-3850 347-3853
Web: www.quicktanks.com
Rimex Metals (USA) Inc 2850 Woodbridge Ave ....Edison NJ 08837 732-549-3800 549-6435
Web: www.rimexmetals.com
Roehlen Engraving 5901 Lewis Rd ....Sandston VA 23150 804-222-2821 226-3462
Web: www.standexengraving.com
Roesch Inc 100 N 24th St......................... Belleville IL 62222 800-423-6243 233-1186*
**Fax Area Code:* 618 ■ *TF:* 800-423-6243 ■ *Web:* www.roeschinc.com
Sapa Inc 7933 NE 21st Ave ....Portland OR 97211 503-802-3000 802-3060
TF: 800-547-0790 ■ *Web:* www.sapagroup.com
Savon Plating & Powder Coating Inc
15523 Illinois Ave.............................Paramount CA 90723 562-634-6189
Web: sav-onplating.com
Sequa Corp Precoat Metals Div
1310 Papin St Third Fl.......................... Saint Louis MO 63103 314-436-7010 436-7050
Web: www.precoatmetals.com
Southwest Metal Finishing Inc
2445 S Calhoun Rd ....New Berlin WI 53151 262-784-1919 641-7086
Web: www.swmetalfinishing.com
Standex International Corp Engraving Group
5901 Lewis Rd ....Sandston VA 23150 804-222-2821 226-3462
Web: www.standexengraving.com
Sumco Inc 1351 S Girls School Rd.................Indianapolis IN 46231 317-241-7600 248-2352
Web: sumco.com
Summit Corp of America 1430 Waterbury Rd .... Thomaston CT 06787 860-283-4391 283-4010
Web: www.scact.com
Techno-Coat Inc 861 E 40th St...................... Holland MI 49423 616-396-6446 396-8211
Web: www.technocoat.com
Towne Technologies Inc
6-10 Bell Ave PO Box 460 ....Somerville NJ 08876 908-722-9500 722-8394
TF: 800-837-2515 ■ *Web:* www.townetech.com
Ulterion International Inc
1136 Zion Church Rd.............................Braselton GA 30517 706-654-2222
Web: www.ulterion.com
Ultra-tech Enterprises Inc
4701 Taylor Rd .... Punta Gorda FL 33950 941-575-2000
TF: 800-293-2001 ■ *Web:* www.ute-inc.com
Unicote Corp 33165 Groesbeck Hwy .... Fraser MI 48026 586-296-0700 296-3155
Web: www.unicotecorporation.com
United Galvanizing Inc 6123 Cunningham Rd ....Houston TX 77041 713-466-4161 466-7811
Web: unitedgalvinc.com
US Chrome Corp 175 Garfield Ave .... Stratford CT 06615 800-637-9019 386-0067*
**Fax Area Code:* 203 ■ *TF:* 800-637-9019 ■ *Web:* www.uschrome.com
Valley City Plating Co
3353 Eastern Ave SE...........................Grand Rapids MI 49508 616-245-1223
Web: www.brassplater.com
VAM Drilling USA Inc 6300 Navigation Blvd ....Houston TX 77011 713-844-3700
Web: www.vallourec.com
Voigt & Schweitzer Inc 1000 Buckeye Park Rd ....Columbus OH 43207 614-449-8281
Web: www.hotdipgalvanizing.com
W & m Manufacturing Inc 1000 N Morton St...........Portland IN 47371 260-726-9800
Web: www.wmmanufacturing.com
Watson Grinding & Mfg Co 4525 Gessner Dr ....Houston TX 77041 713-466-3053 466-8992
Web: www.watsongrinding.com
Westfield Electroplating Company Inc
68 N Elm St ....Westfield MA 01085 413-568-3716
Web: www.westfieldplating.com
Whitford Corp PO Box 80......................... Elverson PA 19520 610-296-3200 286-3510
Web: www.whitfordww.com
Whyco Finishing Technologies LLC
670 Waterbury Rd.............................. Thomaston CT 06787 860-283-5826
Web: www.whyco.com
Willington Cos 11 Middle River Dr .... Stafford Springs CT 06076 860-684-4281
TF: 877-892-2966 ■ *Web:* www.wnpinc.com
Wismarq Corp 930 Armour Rd................. Oconomowoc WI 53066 262-567-1112
Web: www.wismarq.com
Womble Company Inc 12821 Industrial Rd.............Houston TX 77015 713-635-8300 635-5209
Web: www.wombleco.com
Wright Coating Company Inc
1603 N Pitcher St...............................Kalamazoo MI 49007 269-344-8195
Web: www.wrightcoating.com

Phone Fax

Xccent Inc 5240 257th St..........................Wyoming MN 55092 651-462-9200
Web: www.xccentplay.com

485 METAL FABRICATING - CUSTOM

Phone Fax

Afco Industries Inc 3400 Roy St................... Alexandria LA 71302 800-551-6576
TF: 800-551-6576 ■ *Web:* www.afco-ind.com
Aldine Metal Products Corp
566 Danbury Rd Ste 1...........................New Milford CT 06776 860-350-2552 350-1061
Web: www.aldinemetal.com
Alpha Sintered Metals Inc 95 Mason Run Rd..........Ridgway PA 15853 814-773-3191 776-1009
Web: www.alphasintered.com
American Aluminum Co 230 Sheffield St......... Mountainside NJ 07092 908-233-3500 233-3241
Web: www.amalco.com
Angell & Giroux Inc 2727 Alcazar St...............Los Angeles CA 90033 323-269-8596 269-0454
Web: www.angellandgiroux.com
Applied Engineering Inc 2008 E Hwy 50.............. Yankton SD 57078 605-665-4425 665-1479
Web: www.appliedeng.com
Arlington Metals Corp
11355 Franklin Ave............................Franklin Park IL 60131 847-451-9100 451-9676
Web: www.arlingtonmetals.com
Ascension Industries 1254 Erie Ave ....North Tonawanda NY 14120 716-693-9381 693-9882
Web: www.asmfab.com
Associated Steel Workers Ltd
91-156 Kalaeloa Blvd .... Kapolei HI 96707 808-682-5588 682-7392
Autoswage Products Inc 726 River Rd .... Shelton CT 06484 203-929-1401 929-6187
Web: www.autoswage.com
Brakewell Steel Fabricator Inc 55 Leone Ln.......... Chester NY 10918 845-469-9131 469-7618
TF: 888-914-9131 ■ *Web:* www.brakewell.com
Cerro Fabricated Products Inc
300 Triangle Dr..............................Weyers Cave VA 24486 540-234-9252 234-8416
Web: www.cerrofabricated.com
Chandler Industries Inc 1654 N Ninth St........... Montevideo MN 56265 320-269-8893 269-5827
Web: www.chandlerindustries.com
Chicago Metal Fabricators Inc
3724 S Rockwell St................................Chicago IL 60632 773-523-5755 523-8680
Web: www.chicagometal.com
CMW Inc 70 S Gray St...........................Indianapolis IN 46201 317-634-8884 638-2706
Web: www.cmwinc.com
Compax Inc 1210 N Blue Gum St.................... Anaheim CA 92806 714-630-3670 632-1344
Web: www.compaxinc.com
Cross Bros Inc 5255 Sheila St ....Los Angeles CA 90040 323-266-2000 266-2106
TF: 866-939-1057 ■ *Web:* www.crossbrothersinc.com
CSM Metal Fabricating & Engineering Inc
1800 S San Pedro St ....Los Angeles CA 90015 213-748-7321 749-5106
TF: 800-272-4806 ■ *Web:* www.csmworks.com
D & S Manufacturing Inc
301 E Main St............................. Black River Falls WI 54615 715-284-5376 284-4084
Web: www.dsmfg.com
Daniel Tanney Company Inc 3268 Clive Ave..........Bensalem PA 19020 215-639-3131 638-3333
Web: dctanney.com
Delaco Steel Corp 8111 Tireman Ave .... Dearborn MI 48126 313-491-1200 491-6210
Web: www.delacosteel.com
Demsey Manufacturing Co 78 New Wood Rd........ Watertown CT 06795 860-274-6209 274-6209
TF: 800-533-6739 ■ *Web:* www.demseymfg.com
Fabricated Components Inc PO Box 431......... Stroudsburg PA 18360 570-421-4110 421-2553
TF: 800-233-8163 ■ *Web:* www.fabricatedcomponents.com
Harford Systems Inc
2225 Pulaski Hwy PO Box 700...................... Aberdeen MD 21001 410-272-3400
Web: harfordsystems.com
Harris Manufacturing Inc 4775 E Vine Ave............. Fresno CA 93725 559-268-7422 268-2846
Web: www.harrismfg.com
International Extrusions Inc
5800 Venoy Rd................................Garden City MI 48135 734-427-8700 427-9319
TF: 800-242-8876 ■ *Web:* www.extrusion.net
Johnson Matthey Noble Metals
1397 King Rd ....West Chester PA 19380 610-648-8067 648-8105
Web: www.noble.matthey.com
Lafayette Quality Products 111 Farabee Dr .... Lafayette IN 47905 765-447-3106
Web: lqp-mfg.com
Liquidmetal Technologies Inc (LQMT)
30452 Esperanza .... Rancho Santa Margarita CA 92688 949-635-2100 635-2188
OTC: LQMT ■ *TF:* 888-203-1112 ■ *Web:* www.liquidmetal.com
LTC Roll & Engineering Co
23500 John Gorsuch Dr.................... Clinton Township MI 48036 586-465-1023 465-0554
Web: www.ltcroll.com
Lucasey Manufacturing Corp
2744 E 11th St PO Box 14023 ....Oakland CA 94601 510-534-1435 534-6828
TF: 800-582-2739 ■ *Web:* www.lucasey.com
Manufacturers Industrial Group LLC
659 Natchez Trace Dr .... Lexington TN 38351 731-967-0001 968-3320
Web: www.migllc.com
MarathonNorco Aerospace Inc 8301 Imperial Dr........Waco TX 76712 254-776-0650 776-6558
Web: www.mnaerospace.com
Master Metal Products Co 495 Emory St .... San Jose CA 95110 408-275-1210 275-0523
Web: www.mastermetalproducts.com
Metal Fabricating Corp 10408 Berea Rd .... Cleveland OH 44102 216-631-2480 631-2453
Web: www.metalfabricatingcorp.com
MP Metal Products Inc W1250 Elmwood Ave .... Ixonia WI 53036 920-261-9650 261-9652
TF: 800-824-6744 ■ *Web:* www.mpmetals.com
National Sintered Alloys Inc
Heritage Pk Rt 145 PO Box 332 .... Clinton CT 06413 860-669-8653 669-5428
Web: www.nationalsintered.com
Newbrook Machines Inc 16 Mechanic St ....Silver Creek NY 14136 716-934-2644
Web: excelco.net
NobelClad 5405 Spine Rd.......................... Boulder CO 80301 303-665-5700 604-1897
NASDAQ: BOOM ■ *TF General:* 800-821-2666 ■ *Web:* www.dynamicmaterials.com
Nor-Cal Metal Fabricators 1121 Third St ....Oakland CA 94607 510-836-1451 208-2838
Web: www.nc-mf.com

Company / Address	City	State	Zip	Phone	Fax
Progressive Tool & Manufacturing Co					
290 Fifth St NE	Pine Island	MN	55963	507-356-8345	356-4557
Web: www.ptmmn.com					
Pulley-Kellam Company Inc 245 Erie St	Huntington	IN	46750	260-356-6326	356-1928
Quaker City Plating (QCP) PO Box 2406	Whittier	CA	90610	562-945-3721	945-9932
Web: www.quakercityplating.com					
Right Mfg 7949 Stromesa Ct Ste G	San Diego	CA	92126	858-566-7002	566-7623
Web: www.rightmfg.com					
Rose Metal Products Inc 1955 E Div St	Springfield	MO	65803	417-865-1676	865-7673
Web: www.rosemetalproducts.com					
Sommer Metalcraft Corp					
315 Poston Dr PO Box 688	Crawfordsville	IN	47933	765-362-6201	359-4202
TF: 888-876-6637 ■ *Web:* www.sommermetalcraft.com					
Southwire Company Machinery Div					
One Southwire Dr	Carrollton	GA	30119	770-832-4242	832-5228
TF: 800-444-1700 ■ *Web:* www.southwire.com					
TPI Powder Metallurgy Inc					
12030 Beaver Rd	Saint Charles	MI	48655	989-865-9921	865-9924
Web: www.tpipm.com					
Uni-Form Components Co 10703 Sheldon Rd	Houston	TX	77044	281-456-9310	456-0245
Web: www.uniformcomponents.com					
Unifab Corp 5260 Lovers Ln	Portage	MI	49002	269-382-2803	382-2825
TF General: 800-648-9569 ■ *Web:* www.unifabcorp.com					
Unique Aluminum Extrusion LLC					
333 Cedar Ave	Middlesex	NJ	08846	732-271-1160	
Weldments Inc 10720 N Second St	MACHESNEY PARK	IL	61115	815-633-3393	633-2524
Web: weldmentsinc.com					
White River Distributors Inc 720 Ramsey	Batesville	AR	72501	870-793-2374	793-8230
TF: 800-548-7219 ■ *Web:* www.lpgbobtails.com					
Wire Products Manufacturing Corp					
106 N Genesee St	Merrill	WI	54452	715-536-7144	

486 METAL FORGINGS

Company / Address	City	State	Zip	Phone	Fax
A & A Global Industries Inc					
17 Stenersen Ln	Cockeysville	MD	21030	410-252-1020	
Web: aaglobal.com					
Advanced Forming Technology Inc					
7040 Weld County Rd 20	Longmont	CO	80504	303-833-6000	
Web: aftmim.com/					
Advanced Metal Components Inc					
720 Empire Expy	Swainsboro	GA	30401	478-237-8994	
Web: www.amcinc.net					
Ajax Rolled Ring & Machine Inc 500 Wallace Way	York	SC	29745	803-684-3133	
TF: 800-727-6333 ■ *Web:* www.ajaxring.com					
Alcoa Wheel Products International					
1600 Harvard Ave	Cleveland	OH	44105	216-641-3600	641-4032
TF: 800-242-9898 ■ *Web:* www.alcoa.com					
Alken-Ziegler Inc 25575 Brest Rd	Taylor	MI	48180	734-946-4444	
Aluminum Precision Products Inc					
3333 W Warner St	Santa Ana	CA	92704	714-546-8125	540-8662
TF: 800-411-8983 ■ *Web:* www.aluminumprecision.com					
Ameri-Forge Group Inc 13770 Industrial Rd	Houston	TX	77015	713-393-4200	455-8366
Web: www.ameriforge.com					
AMSTED Industries Inc					
180 N Stetson St Ste 1800	Chicago	IL	60601	312-645-1700	819-8494*
**Fax:* Hum Res ■ *Web:* www.amsted.com					
Anchor-Harvey Components LLC 600 W Lamm Rd	Freeport	IL	61032	815-235-4400	
TF: 888-367-4464 ■ *Web:* www.anchorharvey.com					
ATI Ladish Company Inc					
5481 S Packard Ave PO Box 8902	Cudahy	WI	53110	414-747-2611	747-3540
Web: www.atimetals.com					
Bachman Machine Company Inc 4321 N Broadway	St Louis	MO	63147	314-231-4221	
Web: www.bachmanmachine.com					
Ball Chain Mfg Company Inc					
741 S Fulton Ave	Mount Vernon	NY	10550	914-664-7500	664-7460
Web: www.ballchain.com					
Batesville Tool & Die Inc					
177 Six Pine Ranch Rd	Batesville	IN	47006	812-934-5616	
Web: btdinc.com					
Berkeley Forge & Tool Inc 1331 E Shore Hwy	Berkeley	CA	94710	510-526-5034	525-9014
Web: www.berkforge.com					
Berkshire Manufactured Products Inc					
116 Parker St	Newburyport	MA	01950	978-462-8161	
Web: www.berkshiremfp.com					
Bharat Forge America 2807 S ML King Jr Blvd	Lansing	MI	48910	517-393-5300	393-6256
Bobby Rahal Automotive Group 10701 Perry Hwy	Wexford	PA	15090	724-935-9300	
Web: www.bobbyrahal.com					
Bomco Inc 125 Gloucester Ave	Gloucester	MA	01930	978-283-9000	
Web: www.bomco.com					
Brainerd Industries Inc 680 Precision Ct	Miamisburg	OH	45342	937-228-0488	
TF: 800-790-0430 ■ *Web:* www.brainerdindustries.com					
Braxton Mfg Company Inc 858 Echo Lk Rd	Watertown	CT	06795	860-274-6781	
Web: www.braxtonmfg.com					
Brunk Industries Inc 1225 Sage St	Lake Geneva	WI	53147	262-248-8873	
Web: www.brunkindustries.com					
Buchanan Metal Forming Inc (BMF)					
103 W Smith St	Buchanan	MI	49107	269-695-3836	695-3830
Web: www.bmfcorp.com					
Bula Forge & Machine Inc 3001 W 121st St	Cleveland	OH	44111	216-252-7600	
Web: www.bulaforge.com					
Canton Drop Forge Inc 4575 Southway St SW	Canton	OH	44706	330-477-4511	477-2046
Web: www.cantondropforge.com					
Carlton Forge Works Inc 7743 E Adams St	Paramount	CA	90723	562-633-1131	531-8896
Web: carltonforgeworks.com					
CB Kaupp & Sons Inc 6-10 Newark Way	Maplewood	NJ	07040	973-761-4000	
Web: kaupp-kihm.com					
Century Metal Spinning Company Inc					
430 Meyer Rd	Bensenville	IL	60106	630-595-3900	
Web: www.centurymetalspinning.com					
Cleveland Die & Manufacturing Co					
20303 First Ave	Middleburg Heights	OH	44130	440-243-3404	
Web: www.clevelanddie.com					
Clifford-Jacobs Forging Co					
2410 N Fifth St PO Box 830	Champaign	IL	61822	217-352-5172	352-4629
Web: www.clifford-jacobs.com					
Coining Technologies Inc 400 Kuller Rd	Clifton	NJ	07011	973-253-0500	
Web: www.coining.com					
Consolidated Industries Inc 677 Mixville Rd	Cheshire	CT	06410	203-272-5371	272-5672
Web: www.forgemetal.com					
Continental Forge Company Inc					
412 E El Segundo Blvd	Compton	CA	90222	310-603-1014	
Web: www.cforge.com					
Cornell Forge Co 6666 W 66th St	Chicago	IL	60638	708-458-1582	728-9883
Web: www.cornellforge.com					
Corry Forge Co 441 E Main St	Corry	PA	16407	814-664-9664	664-9452
Web: www.ellwoodgroup.com					
Coulter Forge Technology Inc 1494 67th St	Emeryville	CA	94608	510-420-3500	420-3555
Web: www.coulter-forge.com					
DeKalb Forge Co 1832 Pleasant St	DeKalb	IL	60115	815-758-6400	756-6958
Web: www.dekalbforge.com					
Doncasters Storms Forge Div					
160 Cottage St	Springfield	MA	01104	413-785-1801	785-5680
Web: doncasters.com					
Dowding Industries Inc 449 Marilin St	Eaton Rapids	MI	48827	517-663-5455	
Web: www.dowdingindustries.com					
E m J d Corp 4590 S Windermere St	Englewood	CO	80110	303-761-5236	
Web: emjd.com					
Ellwood City Forge 800 Commercial Ave	Ellwood City	PA	16117	724-752-0055	752-3449
TF: 800-843-0166 ■ *Web:* www.ellwoodcityforge.com					
Erie Forge & Steel Inc 1341 W 16th St	Erie	PA	16502	814-452-2300	
Web: www.whemco.com/erie_forge_and_steel.aspx					
Eyelet Crafters Inc 2712 S Main St	Waterbury	CT	06706	203-757-9221	
Web: www.eyeletcrafters.com					
Fansteel Inc 1746 Commerce Rd	Creston	IA	50801	641-782-8521	
Web: www.fansteel.com					
Federal Flange 4014 Pinemont St	Houston	TX	77018	713-681-0606	681-3005
TF: 800-231-0150 ■ *Web:* www.federalflange.com					
Ferguson Perforating & Wire Co					
130 Ernest St	Providence	RI	02905	401-941-8876	
TF: 800-341-9800 ■ *Web:* www.fergusonperf.com					
Fine Line Production 2221 Regal Pkwy	Euless	TX	76040	817-267-6750	267-6787
TF: 800-887-5625 ■ *Web:* www.finelineproduction.com					
Foremost Mfg Company Inc 941 Ball Ave	Union	NJ	07083	908-687-4646	
Web: www.foremost-mfg.com					
Forged Components Inc 14527 Smith Rd	Humble	TX	77396	281-441-4088	441-8899
Web: forgedcomponents.com					
Forged Products Inc (FPI)					
6505 N Houston Rosslyn Rd	Houston	TX	77091	713-462-3416	460-9404
TF: 800-876-3416 ■ *Web:* www.fpitx.com					
Forged Vessel Connections Inc 2525 DeSoto St	Houston	TX	77091	713-688-9705	688-7954
TF Cust Svc: 800-231-2701 ■ *Web:* www.forgedvesselconn.com					
Frontier Metal Stamping Inc 3764 Puritan Way	Erie	CO	80516	303-458-5129	
TF: 888-316-1266 ■ *Web:* www.frontiermetal.com					
GB Manufacturing Co 1120 E Main St	Delta	OH	43515	419-822-5323	
Web: www.gbmfg.com					
Green Bay Drop Forge 1341 State St	Green Bay	WI	54304	920-432-6401	432-0859
TF: 800-824-4896 ■ *Web:* www.greenbaydropforge.com					
H & L Tooth Company Inc 10055 E 56 St N	Tulsa	OK	74117	918-272-0951	272-0163
TF: 800-458-6684 ■ *Web:* www.hltooth.com					
Hammond & Irving Inc 254 N St	Auburn	NY	13021	315-253-6265	253-3136
Web: www.hammond-irving.com					
Hardware & Forging Co 3270 E 79th St	Cleveland	OH	44104	216-641-5200	641-0829
Web: www.clevelandhardware.com					
HHI Group Holdings LLC 2727 W 14 Mile Rd	Royal Oak	MI	48073	248-284-2900	284-2901
Web: hhiholdings.net					
Hirschvogel Inc 2230 S Third St	Columbus	OH	43207	614-445-6060	445-7335
Web: hirschvogel.com					
Hughes Parker Industries LLC					
1604 Mahr Ave	Lawrenceburg	TN	38464	931-762-9403	
Web: www.hughesparker.com					
Hydroform USA Inc 2848 E 208th St	Long Beach	CA	90810	310-632-6353	
Web: www.hydroforming.net					
Ice Industries Inc 3810 Herr Rd	Sylvania	OH	43560	419-842-3600	
Web: www.iceindustries.com					
Independent Forge Co 692 N Batavia St	Orange	CA	92868	714-997-7337	997-7546
Web: www.independentforge.com					
J & E Earl Manufacturing Co					
7925 215th St W	Lakeville	MN	55044	952-469-3933	
Web: www.jecompanies.com					
JD Norman Industries Inc 787 W Belden Ave	Addison	IL	60101	630-458-3700	
Web: www.jdnorman.com					
Jervis B. Webb Co					
34375 W 12 Mile Rd	Farmington Hills	MI	48331	248-553-1000	553-1228
Web: daifukuna.com					
Jorgensen Forge Corp 8531 E Marginal Way S	Tukwila	WA	98108	206-762-1100	
TF: 800-231-5382 ■ *Web:* www.jorgensenforge.com					
KAPCO Inc 1000 Badger Cir	Grafton	WI	53024	262-377-6500	
Web: www.kapcoinc.com					
Kerkau Manufacturing Co					
1321 S Valley Ctr Dr	Bay City	MI	48706	989-686-0350	686-0399
TF: 800-248-5060 ■ *Web:* www.kerkau.com					
Keystone Forging Co					
215 Duke St PO Box 269	Northumberland	PA	17857	570-473-3524	473-7273
Web: www.keystoneforging.com					
KomTeK Technologies 40 Rockdale St	Worcester	MA	01606	508-853-4500	853-2753
TF: 800-669-4500 ■ *Web:* www.komtektech.com					
Kreider Corp 2000 S Yellow Springs St	Springfield	OH	45506	937-325-8787	
Web: www.kreidercorp.com					
Kropp Forge 5301 W Roosevelt Rd	Cicero	IL	60804	708-652-6691	652-9144*
**Fax:* Sales ■ *Web:* www.kroppforge.com					

Company	City	State	Zip	Phone	Fax
L H Thomson Company Inc, The 7800 NE Industrial Blvd	Macon	GA	31216	478-788-5052	
Web: www.lhthomson.com					
Lakeview Forge Co 1725 Pittsburgh Ave	Erie	PA	16505	814-454-4518	455-5875
Web: lakeviewforge.com					
Larsen Mfg LLC 1201 Allanson Rd	Mundelein	IL	60060	847-970-9600	
Web: www.larsenmfg.net					
Lefere Forge & Machine Co 665 Hupp Ave	Jackson	MI	49203	517-784-7109	784-0929
Web: www.lefereforge.com					
Lehigh Heavy Forge Corp 275 Emery St	Bethlehem	PA	18015	610-332-8100	332-8101
Web: www.lhforge.com					
Lenape Forged Products Corp 1334 Lenape Rd	West Chester	PA	19382	610-793-5090	793-3070
Web: www.lenapeforge.com					
Liberty Forge Inc PO Box 1210	Liberty	TX	77575	936-336-5785	336-2740
TF: 800-231-2377 ■ *Web:* www.libertyforgeinc.com					
Machine Specialty & Manufacturing Inc 215 Rousseau Rd	Youngsville	LA	70592	337-837-0020	837-0062
TF: 800-256-1292 ■ *Web:* www.machine-specialty.com					
McKenzie Valve & Machining Co 145 Airport Rd	McKenzie	TN	38201	731-352-5027	352-3029
Web: www.mckenzievalve.com					
McWilliams Forge Company Inc 387 Franklin Ave	Rockaway	NJ	07866	973-627-0200	625-9316
Web: www.mcwilliamsforge.com					
Meadville Forging Co 15309 Baldwin St PO Box 459	Meadville	PA	16335	814-332-8200	333-4657
Web: www.meadforge.com					
Mercer Forge Corp 200 Brown St	Mercer	PA	16137	724-662-2750	662 5642
TF: 800-558-5075					
Metal Forming & Coining Corp (MFC) 1007 Illinois Ave	Maumee	OH	43537	419-893-8748	893-6828
Web: www.mfccorp.com					
Metal Spinners Inc 800 Growth Pkwy	Angola	IN	46703	260-665-2192	
Web: www.metalspinners.com					
Metalist International Inc 1159 S Pennsylvania Ave	Lansing	MI	48912	517-371-2940	371-3027
Web: www.metalist.com					
Mid-West Forge Corp 17301 St Clair Ave	Cleveland	OH	44110	216-481-3030	481-7288
Web: www.mid-westforge.com					
Millennium Forge Inc 990 W Ormsby Ave	Louisville	KY	40210	502-635-3350	635-3028
Web: www.millenniumforge.com					
MMD Equipment 121 High Hill Rd	Swedesboro	NJ	08085	856-467-3200	467-5235
TF: 800-433-1382 ■ *Web:* www.mmdequipment.com					
Modern Drop Forge Co 13810 S Western Ave	Blue Island	IL	60406	708-388-1806	597-3633
Web: www.modernforge.com					
Moline Forge Inc 4101 Fourth Ave	Moline	IL	61265	309-762-5506	762-5508
Web: www.molineforge.com					
MOLY-COP Canada 250 Andover Crescent	Kamloops	BC	V2C6X2	250-573-7770	
Web: scaw.co.za					
National Flange & Fitting Co 4420 Creekmont Dr	Houston	TX	77091	713-688-2515	688-0205
Nissin Precision North America Inc 375 Union Rd	Eagle wood	OH	45322	937-836-1910	832-1270
Web: www.epinei.com					
Norforge & Machining Inc 195 N Dean St	Bushnell	IL	61422	309-772-3124	
TF: 800-839-3706 ■ *Web:* bushnell.illinois.gov					
Ohio Star Forge Co (OSF) 4000 Mahoning Ave NW	Warren	OH	44480	330-847-6360	847-6368
Web: www.ohiostar.com					
Ohio Valley Manufacturing Inc 1501 Harrington Memorial Rd	Mansfield	OH	44903	419-522-5818	
Web: www.ohiovalleymfg.com					
Omni Manufacturing Inc 901 Mckinley Rd	Saint Marys	OH	45885	419-394-7424	
Web: www.omnimfg.com					
Orchid International Group Inc 94 Belinda Pkwy Ste 450	Mount Juliet	TN	37122	615-754-6600	
Web: www.orchidinternational.com					
Pacific Forge Inc 10641 Etiwanda Ave	Fontana	CA	92337	909-390-0701	390-0708
Web: www.pacificforge.com					
Parish International Inc PO Box 468	Hempstead	TX	77445	979-826-8222	826-8224
Web: www.parishforge.com					
Performance Stamping Company Inc 20 Lk Marian Rd	Carpentersville	IL	60110	847-426-2233	
Web: www.performancestamping.com					
Phoenix Forging Company Inc 800 Front St	Catasauqua	PA	18032	610-264-2861	266-0530
TF: 800-444-3674 ■ *Web:* www.phoenixforge.com					
Pinnacle Precision Sheet Metal Corp 5410 E La Palma Ave	Anaheim	CA	92807	714-777-3129	
Web: www.pinnacleprecisionsheetmetal.com					
Pinnacle Precision Technologies LLC 2607 Eaton Ln	Racine	WI	53404	262-632-2232	
Portland Forge 250 E Lafayette St	Portland	IN	47371	260-726-8121	726-8021*
**Fax Area Code:* 219 ■ *Web:* www.atimetals.com					
Powers & Sons LLC 44700 Helm St	Plymouth	MI	48170	734-354-6575	254-9517
Web: www.powersandsonsllc.com					
Precision Die & Stamping Inc 1704 W 10th St	Tempe	AZ	85281	480-967-2038	
Web: www.precisiondie.com					
Precision Drawn Metals Inc 1345 Plainfield Ave	Janesville	WI	53545	608-755-1495	
Web: www.drawnmetals.com					
Precision Metal Products Inc 850 W Bradley Ave	El Cajon	CA	92020	619-448-2711	448-2005
Web: www.pmp-elcajon.com					
Premier Pan Company Inc 33 Mcgovern Blvd Ste 2	Crescent	PA	15046	724-457-4220	
Web: www.prestigehomes.com					
Presrite Corp 3665 E 78th St	Cleveland	OH	44105	216-441-5990	441-2644
Web: www.presrite.com					
Quality Filters Inc 7215 Jackson Rd	Ann Arbor	MI	48103	734-668-0211	
Web: qualityfiltersinc.com					
Quick Way Stampings Inc of Texas 915 Stanley Dr	Euless	TX	76040	817-267-1515	
Web: www.quick-way.com					
Rago & Son Inc 1029 51st Ave	Oakland	CA	94601	510-536-5700	
Web: www.rago-son.com					
Ralco Industries Inc 2720 Auburn Ct	Auburn Hills	MI	48326	248-853-3200	
Web: www.ralcoind.com					
Randall Bearings Inc 1046 Greenlawn Ave PO Box 1258	Lima	OH	45802	419-223-1075	228-0200
TF: 800-626-7071 ■ *Web:* www.randallbearings.com					
Riley Gear Corp One Precision Dr	St. Augustine	FL	32092	904-829-5652	
Web: www.rileygear.com					
Ritatsu Manufacturing Inc 700 Old Liberty Church Rd	Beaver Dam	KY	42320	270-730-7010	
Royal Die & Stamping Co 125 Mercedes Dr	Carol Stream	IL	60188	630-766-2685	
Web: www.royaldie.com					
Saint Croix Forge Inc 5195 Scandia Trl	Forest Lake	MN	55025	651-464-8967	464-8213
TF: 866-668-7642 ■ *Web:* www.stcroixforge.com					
Scot Forge Co 8001 Winn Rd PO Box 8	Spring Grove	IL	60081	847-587-1000	587-2000
TF: 800-435-6621 ■ *Web:* www.scotforge.com					
Standard Steel LLC 500 N Walnut St	Burnham	PA	17009	717-248-4911	248-8050
Web: www.standardsteel.com					
Steel Industries Inc (SII) 12600 Beech-Daly Rd	Redford Township	MI	48239	877-783-3599	534-2165*
**Fax Area Code:* 313 ■ *Web:* www.steelindustriesinc.com					
T & W Forge Inc 970 East 64th Street	Cleveland	OH	44103	216-881-8600	821-7309*
**Fax Area Code:* 330 ■ *Web:* www.twforge.com					
T&C Stamping Inc 1403 Freeman Ave	Athens	AL	35613	256-233-7383	
Web: www.tandcstamping.com					
Talan Products Inc 18800 Cochran Ave	Cleveland	OH	44110	216-458-0170	
TF: 877-419-2805 ■ *Web:* www.talanproducts.com					
Texas Metal Works Inc 13770 Industrial Rd	Houston	TX	77015	713-393-4200	
Web: afglobalcorp.com/texmet					
TFO Tech Company Ltd 221 State St	Jeffersonville	OH	43128	740-426-6381	426-6511
Thermal Structures Inc (TSI) 2362 Railroad St	Corona	CA	92880	951-736-9911	736-1064
Web: www.thermalstructures.com					
Thoro'Bred Inc 5020 E La Palma Ave	Anaheim	CA	92807	714-779-2581	420-7040*
**Fax Area Code:* 765 ■ *TF:* 877-585-5152 ■ *Web:* www.horseshoes.com					
ThyssenKrupp Crankshaft Company LLC 1000 Lynch Rd	Danville	IL	61834	217-431-0060	431-8934
Web: www.thyssenkrupp-forginggroup.com					
Titan Tool & Die Ltd 2801 Howard Ave	Windsor	ON	N8X3Y1	519-966-1234	
Web: www.titantool.ca					
Toledo Metal Spinning Co 1819 Clinton St	Toledo	OH	43607	419-535-5931	
Web: www.toledometalspinning.com					
Toner Machining Technologies Inc 212 E Fleming Dr	Morganton	NC	28655	828-432-8007	
Web: www.tonermachining.com					
Trenton Forging Co 5523 Hoover St	Trenton	MI	48183	734-675-1620	675-4839
Web: www.trentonforging.com					
Trinity Forge Inc 947 Trinity Dr	Mansfield	TX	76063	817-473-1515	473-6743
Web: www.trinityforge.com					
Truelove & Maclean Inc 57 Callender Rd	Watertown	CT	06795	860-274-9600	
Web: www.trueloveandmaclean.com					
Turbine Engine Components Technologies Corp (TECT) 1211 Old Albany Rd	Thomasville	GA	31792	229-228-2600	
Web: www.tectcorp.com					
Unit Drop Forge Company Inc 1903 S 62nd St PO Box 340350	West Allis	WI	53219	414-545-3000	545-6318
Web: www.unitforgings.com					
United Brass Manufacturers Inc 35030 GoddaRd Rd PO Box 74095	Romulus	MI	48174	734-941-0700	941-0640
Web: unitedbrass.com					
Van-Rob Inc 200 Vandorf Sideroad	Aurora	ON	L4G0A2	905-727-8585	
Web: www.van-rob.com					
VH Blackinton & Company Inc 221 John L Dietsch Blvd	Attleboro Falls	MA	02763	508-699-4436	
Web: www.blackinton.com					
Vulcan Spring & Manufacturing Co 501 Schoolhouse Rd	Telford	PA	18969	215-721-1721	
Web: www.vulcanspring.com					
Walker Forge Inc 222 E Erie St Ste 300	Milwaukee	WI	53202	414-223-2000	223-2019
Web: www.walkerforge.com					
Weber Metals Inc 16706 Garfield Ave PO Box 318	Paramount	CA	90723	562-602-0260	602-0468
Web: webermetals.com					
Western Forge & Flange Co 687 County Rd 2201	Cleveland	TX	77327	281-727-7060	727-7060
TF: 800-352-6433 ■ *Web:* www.western-forge.com					
Wilton Precision Steel Co 320 W First St	Wilton	IA	52778	563-732-3363	732-3365
Web: www.wps01.com					
Wozniak Industries Inc Two Mid America Plz Ste 706	Oakbrook Terrace	IL	60181	630-954-3400	954-3605
Web: www.wozniakindustries.com					
Wozniak Industries Inc Commercial Forged Products Div 5757 W 65th St	Bedford Park	IL	60638	708-458-1220	458-9346
TF: 800-637-2695 ■ *Web:* www.commercialforged.com					
Wrought Washer Manufacturing Inc 2100 S Bay St	Milwaukee	WI	53207	414-744-0771	
TF: 800-558-5217 ■ *Web:* www.wroughtwasher.com					
Wyman-Gordon Forgings (Cleveland) Inc 3097 E 61st St	Cleveland	OH	44127	216-341-0085	
Web: www.dropdies.com					
Young Manufacturing Inc 2331 N 42nd St	Grand Forks	ND	58203	701-772-5541	
TF: 800-451-9884 ■ *Web:* www.youngmfg.com					

487 METAL HEAT TREATING

Company	City	State	Zip	Phone	Fax
Aberfoyle Metal Treaters Ltd 18 Kerr Cres	Guelph	ON	N0B2J0	519-763-1120	763-1121
Web: www.aberfoyle-mt.com					
Advanced Heat Treat Corp 2825 MidPort Blvd	Waterloo	IA	50703	319-232-5221	
Web: ahtweb.com					

Phone *Fax*

Aerocraft Heat Treating Co Inc
15701 Minnesota Ave. .... Paramount CA 90723 562-674-2400 633-0364
Web: www.aerocraft-ht.com

Ajax Metal Processing Inc 4651 Bellevue St. .... Detroit MI 48207 313-267-2100 267-2110
Web: www.ajaxmetal.com

Akron Steel Treating Co 336 Morgan Ave .... Akron OH 44311 330-773-8211
Web: www.akronsteeltreating.com

Alfe Heat Treating Inc
6920 Pointe Inverness Way Ste 140 .... Fort Wayne IN 46804 260-747-9422
Web: www.al-fe.com

Bluewater Thermal Solutions
201 Brookfield Pwy Ste 102 .... Greenville SC 29607 864-990-0050 990-0056
TF: 877-990-0050 ■ *Web:* www.bluewaterthermal.com

Byron Products Inc 3781 Port Union Rd. .... Fairfield OH 45014 513-870-9111
Web: www.byronproducts.com

Chem-plate Industries Inc
1800 Touhy Ave .... Elk Grove Village IL 60007 847-640-1600 640-1699
Web: www.chemplateindustries.com

Chicago Flame Hardening Company Inc
5200 Railroad Ave. .... East Chicago IN 46312 219-397-6475
Web: www.cflame.com

Commercial Steel Treating Corp
31440 Stephenson Hwy .... Madison Heights MI 48071 248-588-3300 588-3534
Web: www.commercialsteel.com

Curtiss-Wright Corp
10 Waterview Blvd 2nd Fl. .... Parsippany NJ 07054 973-541-3700 541-3699
NYSE: CW ■ *TF:* 855-449-0995 ■ *Web:* www.curtisswright.com

East Lind Heat Treat Inc
32045 Dequindre Rd. .... Madison Heights MI 48071 248-585-1415
Web: www.eastlind.com

Euclid Heat Treating Co 1340 E 222nd St .... Euclid OH 44117 216-481-8444
Web: www.euclidheattreating.com

Fisher-Barton Inc 1040 S 12th St. .... Watertown WI 53094 920-261-0131 261-4549

Flame Metals Processing Corp
12450 Ironwood Cir .... Rogers MN 55374 763-428-2596 428-3689
Web: flamemetals.com

FPM LLC 1501 S Lively Blvd .... Elk Grove Village IL 60007 847-228-2525 228-5912
TF: 877-437-6432 ■ *Web:* www.fpmht.com

Gibraltar Industries Inc 3556 Lakeshore Rd .... Buffalo NY 14219 716-826-6500 826-1589*
NASDAQ: ROCK ■ **Fax:* Sales ■ *TF:* 800-247-8368 ■ *Web:* www.gibraltar1.com

H & S Heat Treating Co 133 S St N. .... Port Robinson ON L0S1K0 905-384-9355
Web: www.hsheat.com

HI TecMetal Group Inc 1101 E 55th St .... Cleveland OH 44103 216-881-8100 426-6690
TF: 877-484-2867 ■ *Web:* www.htg.cc

Hudapack Metal Treating Inc 979 Koopman Ln .... Elkhorn WI 53121 262-723-3345
Web: www.hudapack.com

Industrial Steel Treating Inc 613 Carroll St .... Jackson MI 49202 800-253-9534 550-7045*
**Fax Area Code:* 866 ■ *TF:* 800-253-9534 ■ *Web:* www.indstl.com

Kowalski Heat Treating Co 3611 Detroit Ave .... Cleveland OH 44113 216-631-4411
Web: www.khtheat.com

Maxco Inc 1005 Charlevoix Dr Ste 100. .... Grand Ledge MI 48837 517-627-1734 627-4951

Metal Improvement Company LLC
80 Rt 4 E Ste 310 .... Paramus NJ 07652 201-843-7800 843-3460
Web: www.metalimprovement.com

Metals Technology Corp 120 N Schmale Rd .... Carol Stream IL 60188 630-221-2500
Web: metalstechnology.com

Miller Consolidated Industries Inc
2221 Arbor Blvd .... Dayton OH 45439 937-294-2681
Web: www.millerconsolidated.com

Modern Industries Inc 613 W 11th St .... Erie PA 16501 814-455-8061 453-4382
Web: modernind.com

Nitrex Metal Inc 3474 Poirier Blvd .... Saint-Laurent QC H4R2J5 514-335-7191 335-4160
Web: www.nitrex.com

Opticote Inc 10455 Seymour .... Franklin Park IL 60131 847-678-8900
Web: www.opticote.com

Pacific Metallurgical Inc 925 Fifth Ave S .... Kent WA 98032 253-854-4241
Web: www.pacmet.com

Paulo Products Company Inc 5711 W Park Ave .... St. Louis MO 63110 314-647-7500
Web: www.americanbrazing.com

Pennsylvania Metallurgical Inc
315 Columbia St. .... Bethlehem PA 18015 610-691-1313
Web: www.pmiheattreat.com

Precision Heat Treating Corp
2711 Adams Ctr Rd .... Fort Wayne IN 46803 260-749-5125
Web: www.phtc.net

Rex Heat Treat 951 W Eigth St PO Box 270 .... Lansdale PA 19446 215-855-1131 855-2028
TF: 800-220-4739 ■ *Web:* www.rexht.com

Riverdale Plating & Heat Treating Inc
680 W 134th St. .... Riverdale IL 60827 708-849-2050
Web: www.rpht.com

RMT Woodworth Inc 45755 Five Mile Rd .... Plymouth MI 48170 734-254-0566
Web: www.rmtwoodworth.com

Robert Wooler Co 1755 Susquehanna Rd .... Dresher PA 19025 215-542-7600 542-0250
Web: www.robertwooler.com

Solar Atmospheres Inc 1969 Clearview Rd .... Souderton PA 18964 215-721-1502
Web: www.solaratm.com

Specialty Heat Treat Holland
3700 Eastern Ave Se .... Grand Rapids MI 49508 616-245-0465
Web: www.specialtyheat.com

Specialty Steel Treating Inc
34501 Commerce Rd .... Fraser MI 48026 586-293-5355 293-5390
Web: sst.net/

Stahl Specialty Co 11 E Pacific PO Box 6 .... Kingsville MO 64061 816-597-3322 597-3485
TF: 800-821-7852 ■ *Web:* www.stahlspecialty.com

Super Steel Treating Inc 6227 Rinke .... Warren MI 48091 586-755-9140
Web: www.supersteeltreating.com

TC Industries Inc 3703 S Rt 31 .... Crystal Lake IL 60012 815-459-2400 459-3303
Web: www.tcindustries.com

Texas Heat Treating Inc 155 Texas Ave .... Round Rock TX 78664 512-255-5884 255-8464
Web: www.texasheattreating.com

Texas Stress Inc 1304 Underwood Rd .... La Porte TX 77571 281-930-0897 930-0992
Web: www.texasstress.com

Phone *Fax*

Thermal-vac Technology Inc 1221 W Struck Ave. .... Orange CA 92867 714-997-2601
Web: www.thermal-vac.com

Thortex Inc 15045 N.E. Mason St. .... Portland OR 97230 503-654-5726
Web: www.thortexinc.com

Tri-City Heat Treat Co 2020 Fifth St .... Rock Island IL 61201 309-786-2689 786-2691
Web: www.tcht.com

Wall Colmonoy Corp 101 W Girard Ave. .... Madison Heights MI 48071 248-585-6400 585-7960
Web: www.wallcolmonoy.com

Ward Aluminum Casting Co 642 Growth Ave. .... Fort Wayne IN 46808 260-426-8700 420-1919
Web: www.wardcorp.com

488 METAL INDUSTRIES (MISC)

SEE ALSO Foundries - Investment p. 2327; Foundries - Iron & Steel p. 2328; Foundries - Nonferrous (Castings) p. 2329; Metal Heat Treating p. 2743; Metal Tube & Pipe p. 2748; Steel - Mfr p. 3197; Wire & Cable p. 3297

Phone *Fax*

Alcoa Inc 390 Park Ave PO Box 8001 .... New York NY 10022 412-553-4545 459-2500*
**Fax Area Code:* 563 ■ *TF:* 800-523-9596 ■ *Web:* www.alcoa.com

Alcoa Primary Metals
900 S Gay St Riverview Twr Ste 1100 .... Knoxville TN 37902 865-594-4700 594-4790*
**Fax:* Sales ■ *TF:* 800-852-0238 ■ *Web:* www.alcoa.com

Allegheny Technologies Inc
1000 Six PPG Pl. .... Pittsburgh PA 15222 412-394-2800 394-3034*
NYSE: ATI ■ **Fax:* Hum Res ■ *TF Sales:* 800-258-3586 ■ *Web:* www.atimetals.com

Allvac Inc 2020 Ashcraft Ave PO Box 5030 .... Monroe NC 28110 704-289-4511 289-4018*
**Fax:* Sales ■ *TF:* 800-841-5491 ■ *Web:* www.atimetals.com

Altech LLC 242 America Pl .... Jeffersonville IN 47130 812-282-8256 280-6070
TF: 800-264-8256 ■ *Web:* www.altecextrusions.com

AMETEK Specialty Metal Products
21 Toelles Rd .... Wallingford CT 06492 203-265-6731 294-0196
Web: www.ametekmetals.com

Ampco Metal Inc
1117 E Algonquin Rd .... Arlington Heights IL 60005 847-437-6000 437-6008
TF: 800-844-6008 ■ *Web:* www.ampcometal.com

Anaheim Extrusion Company Inc
1330 N Kraemer Blvd PO Box 6380 .... Anaheim CA 92806 714-630-3111 630-0443
TF: 800-660-3318 ■ *Web:* www.anaheimextrude.com

Arvinyl Metal Laminates Corp
233 N Sherman Ave .... Corona CA 92882 800-278-4695 371-7118*
**Fax Area Code:* 951 ■ *TF:* 800-278-4695 ■ *Web:* www.arvinyl.com

Audubon Metals LLC 3055 Ohio Dr .... Henderson KY 42420 270-830-6622 830-9987
Web: www.audubonmetals.com

Big River Zinc Corp 2401 Mississippi Ave. .... Sauget IL 62201 618-274-5000
TF: 800-274-4002 ■ *Web:* www.bigriverzinc.com

Bolton Metal Products Co 2042 Axemann Rd .... Bellefonte PA 16823 814-355-6217 355-6219
Web: www.boltonmetalproducts.com

Bonnell Aluminum 25 Bonnell St. .... Newnan GA 30263 770-253-2020 254-7711
Web: www.bonlalum.com

Broco Inc 10868 Bell Ct .... Rancho Cucamonga CA 91730 909-483-3222 483-3233
TF: 800-845-7259 ■ *Web:* www.broco-rankin.com

Bunting Magnetics Co 500 S Spencer Ave. .... Newton KS 67114 316-284-2020 283-4975
TF: 800-835-2526 ■ *Web:* buntingmagnetics.com

Cabot Supermetals
1095 Windward Ridge Pkwy Ste 200 .... Alpharetta GA 30005 610-367-1500 297-1498*
**Fax Area Code:* 678 ■ *Web:* www.cabot-corp.com

Cannon Muskegon Corp
2875 Lincoln St PO Box 506 .... Muskegon MI 49441 231-755-1681 755-4975
TF: 800-253-0371 ■ *Web:* www.c-mgroup.com

Cardinal Aluminum Co 6910 Preston Hwy .... Louisville KY 40219 502-969-9302 969-6910*
**Fax Area Code:* 800 ■ *TF Cust Svc:* 800-398-7833 ■ *Web:* cardinalaluminum.com/

Century Aluminum Co
2511 Garden Rd Ste 200 Bldg A .... Monterey CA 93940 831-642-9300
NASDAQ: CENX ■ *Web:* www.centuryaluminum.com

Century Aluminum of Kentucky
1627 SR 271 N PO Box 500 .... Hawesville KY 42348 270-685-2493 852-2886
Web: centuryaluminum.com

Certified Alloy Products Inc
3245 Cherry Ave PO Box 90 .... Long Beach CA 90801 562-595-6621 427-8667
Web: doncasters.com

Chase Brass & Copper Co
14212 County Rd M 50 PO Box 152 .... Montpelier OH 43543 419-485-3193 485-5945*
**Fax:* Mail Rm ■ *TF:* 800-537-4291 ■ *Web:* www.chasebrass.com

Chicago Extruded Metals Co (CXM) 1601 S 54th Ave .... Cicero IL 60804 800-323-8102 780-3479*
**Fax Area Code:* 708 ■ *TF Cust Svc:* 800-323-8102 ■ *Web:* www.cxm.com

Colonial Metals Co 217 Linden St PO Box 311 .... Columbia PA 17512 717-684-2311 684-9555
Web: www.colonialmetalsco.com

Columbia Falls Aluminum Co
2000 Alluminum Dr .... Columbia Falls MT 59912 406-892-8400
Web: www.cfaluminum.com

Cookson Electronics Assembly Materials
300 Atrium Dr. .... Somerset NJ 08873 201-434-6778 434-7508
Web: alpha.alent.com

Croft LLC 107 Oliver Emmerich Dr. .... McComb MS 39648 601-684-6121
TF: 800-437-8421 ■ *Web:* www.croftllc.com

Curtis Steel Company LLC (CSC)
6504 Hurst St PO Box 7469 .... Houston TX 77008 713-861-4621 861-9718
TF: 800-749-4621 ■ *Web:* www.curtissteelco.com

Custom Aluminum Products Inc 414 Div St. .... South Elgin IL 60177 847-717-5000 741-2266
TF: 800-745-6333 ■ *Web:* www.custom-aluminum.com

Deringer-Ney Inc 616 Atrium Dr Ste 100 .... Vernon Hills IL 60061 847-566-4100 367-6029
Web: www.deringerney.com

Doe Run Co 1801 Pk 270 Dr Ste 300 .... Saint Louis MO 63146 314-453-7100 453-7177
TF: 800-356-3786 ■ *Web:* www.doerun.com

Dynamet Inc 195 Museum Rd .... Washington PA 15301 724-228-1000 229-4195
TF: 800-237-9655 ■ *Web:* www.cartech.com

Eastern Alloys Inc
11 Henry Henning Dr PO Box 317 .... Maybrook NY 12543 845-427-2151 427-5185
Web: www.eazall.com

Company	City	State	ZIP	Phone	Fax
Elmet Technologies Inc 1560 Lisbon St. TF: 800-343-8008 ■ Web: www.elmettechnologies.com	Lewiston	ME	04240	207-333-6100	786-8924
Empire Resources Inc 2115 Linwood Ave. NYSE: ERS ■ Web: www.empireresources.com	Fort Lee	NJ	07024	201-944-2200	944-2226
Flat Rock Metal Inc (FRM) 26601 W Huron River Dr PO Box 1090. Web: www.frm.com	Flat Rock	MI	48134	734-782-4454	782-5640
General Extrusions Inc 4040 Lk Pk Rd. Web: www.genext.com	Youngstown	OH	44512	330-783-0270	788-1250
Glines & Rhodes Inc 189 E St PO Box 2285. TF: 800-343-1196 ■ Web: www.glinesandrhodes.com	Attleboro	MA	02703	508-226-2000	226-7136
Globe Metallurgical Inc County Rd 32 PO Box 157. Web: www.glbsm.com/globemetallurgical	Beverly	OH	45715	740-984-2361	984-8691
H Kramer & Co 1345 W 21st St. TF: 800-621-2305 ■ Web: hkramer.com	Chicago	IL	60608	312-226-6600	226-4713
Handy & Harman 1133 Westchester Ave Ste N222. Web: www.handyharman.com	White Plains	NY	10604	914-461-1300	
Haynes International Inc 1020 W Pk Ave PO Box 9013. NASDAQ: HAYN ■ TF: 800-354-0806 ■ Web: www.haynesintl.com	Kokomo	IN	46904	765-456-6000	456-6905
HC Starck Inc 45 Industrial Pl. Web: www.hcstarck.com	Newton	MA	02461	617-630-5800	
Hoeganaes Corp 1001 Taylors Ln. *Fax: Hum Res ■ Web: www.gkn.com	Cinnaminson	NJ	08077	856-829-2220	786-2574*
Hoover & Strong Inc 10700 Trade Rd. TF Cust Svc: 800-759-9997 ■ Web: www.hooverandstrong.com	North Chesterfield	VA	23236	800-759-9997	616-9997
Hoover Precision Products Inc 2200 Pendley Rd. Web: www.hooverprecision.com	Cumming	GA	30041	770-889-9223	889-0828
Hussey Copper Ltd 100 Washington St. TF: 800-733-8866 ■ Web: www.husseycopper.com	Leetsdale	PA	15056	724-251-4200	251-4243
Industrial Tectonics Inc 7222 Huron River Dr. TF: 800-482-2255 ■ Web: www.itiball.com	Dexter	MI	48130	734-426-4681	426-4701
Johnson Matthey Inc 435 Devon Pk Dr Ste 600. Web: www.matthey.com	Wayne	PA	19087	610-971-3000	971-3191
JW Aluminum 435 Old Mt Holly Rd. TF Sales: 877-586-5314 ■ Web: www.jwaluminum.com	Mount Holly	SC	29445	877-586-5314	
Kaiser Aluminum Corp 27422 Portola Pkwy Ste 200. TF Sales: 800-873-2011 ■ Web: www.kaiseraluminum.com	Foothill Ranch	CA	92610	949-614-1740	614-1930
Keystone Powdered Metal Co 251 State St. Web: www.keystonepm.com	Saint Marys	PA	15857	814-781-1591	781-7648
Light Metals Corp 2740 Prairie St SW. TF: 888-363-8257 ■ Web: www.light-metals.com	Wyoming	MI	49509	616-538-3030	538-2713
Linemaster Switch Corp 29 Plaine Hill Rd. *Fax Area Code: 800 ■ TF: 800-974-3668 ■ Web: www.linemaster.com	Woodstock	CT	06281	860-974-1000	974-3668*
Loxcreen Co Inc, The 1630 Old Dunbar Rd PO Box 4004. TF: 800-330-5699 ■ Web: www.loxcreen.com	West Columbia	SC	29172	803-822-8200	822-8547
Lucas-Milhaupt Inc 5656 S Pennsylvania Ave. TF: 800-558-3856 ■ Web: www.lucasmilhaupt.com	Cudahy	WI	53110	414-769-6000	769-1093
Luvata Appleton LLC 553 Carter Ct. TF: 866-488-0217 ■ Web: www.luvata.com	Kimberly	WI	54136	920-749-3820	749-3850
Luvata Ohio Inc 1376 Pittsburgh Dr. Web: www.luvata.com	Delaware	OH	43015	740-363-1981	363-3847
Magnat-Fairview Inc 1102 Sheridan St. *Fax Area Code: 405 ■ TF: 800-636-3433 ■ Web: www.magnatfairview.com	Chicopee	MA	01022	413-593-5742	755-8425*
Magnetech Industrial Services Inc 800 Nave Rd SE. TF General: 800-837-1614 ■ Web: www.magnetech.com	Massillon	OH	44646	330-830-3500	830-3520
Magnode Corp 400 E State St. Web: www.magnode.com	Trenton	OH	45067	513-988-6351	988-6357
Magotteaux Inc 725 Cool Springs Blvd Ste 200. Web: www.magotteaux.com	Franklin	TN	37067	615-385-3055	297-6743
Maurice Pincoffs Company Inc 1235 N Loop W Ste 510 PO Box 920919. Web: www.pincoffs.com	Houston	TX	77292	713-681-5461	681-8521
Memry Corp Three Berkshire Blvd. TF: 866-466-3679 ■ Web: www.memry.com	Bethel	CT	06801	203-739-1100	798-6606
Metallurgical Products Co 810 Lincoln Ave PO Box 598. Web: www.metprodco.com	West Chester	PA	19381	610-696-6770	430-8431
Metglas Inc 440 Allied Dr. TF: 800-581-7654 ■ Web: www.metglas.com	Conway	SC	29526	843-349-7319	349-6815
Micro Surface Engr Inc 1550 E Slauson Ave. TF: 800-322-5832 ■ Web: www.precisionballs.com	Los Angeles	CA	90011	323-582-7348	582-0934
Midland Industries Inc 1424 N Halsted St. TF: 800-662-8228 ■ Web: www.zincbig.com	Chicago	IL	60642	312-664-7300	664-7371
Mueller Brass Co 2199 Lapeer Ave. *Fax Area Code: 616 ■ TF: 800-553-3336 ■ Web: muellerindustriesipd.com	Port Huron	MI	48060	810-987-7770	794-1214*
Mueller Industries Inc 8285 Tournament Dr Ste 150. NYSE: MLI ■ TF: 800-348-8464 ■ Web: www.muellerindustries.com	Memphis	TN	38125	901-753-3200	753-3251
NetShape Technologies Inc 31005 Solon Rd. TF: 866-429-5724 ■ Web: www.netshapetech.com	Solon	OH	44139	440-248-5456	248-5807
New England Miniature Ball Corp 163 Greenwood Rd W PO Box 585. Web: www.nemb.com	Norfolk	CT	06058	860-542-5543	542-5058
NN Inc 2000 Waters Edge Dr Bldg 3 Ste 12. NASDAQ: NNBR ■ TF: 877-888-0002 ■ Web: nninc.com	Johnson City	TN	37604	423-743-9151	743-8870
Noranda Aluminum Inc 801 Crescent Ctr Dr Ste 600. TF: 800-325-8112 ■ Web: www.norandaaluminum.com	Franklin	TN	37067	615-771-5700	771-5701
Norandal USA Inc 400 Bill Brooks Dr. Web: norandaaluminum.com	Huntingdon	TN	38344	731-986-5011	986-2739
Novelis North America 3560 Lenox Rd Ste 2000. *Fax Area Code: 440 ■ Web: www.novelis.com	Atlanta	GA	30326	404-760-4000	423-6601*
Nyrstar Clarksville 1800 Zinc Plant Rd PO Box 1104. Web: www.nyrstar.com	Clarksville	TN	37041	931-552-4200	552-0471
Olin Brass 305 Lewis & Clark Blvd. Web: www.olinbrass.com	East Alton	IL	62024	502-873-3000	
Patrick Industries Inc Patrick Metals Div 5020 Lincolnway E. TF: 800-922-9692 ■ Web: www.patrickmetals.com	Mishawaka	IN	46544	574-255-9692	256-6577
Penn Aluminum International Inc 1117 N Second St PO Box 490. TF All: 800-445-7366 ■ Web: www.pennaluminum.com	Murphysboro	IL	62966	618-684-2146	
Precision Engineered Products LLC 262 Broad St. Web: www.polymet.com	North Attleboro	MA	02760	508-695-7700	695-7700
Profile Extrusion Co 100 Anderson Rd. Web: profilecustomextrusions.com/	Rome	GA	30161	706-234-7558	234-7649
Revere Copper Products Inc One Revere Pk. *Fax: Sales ■ TF: 800-448-1776 ■ Web: www.reverecopper.com	Rome	NY	13440	315-338-2022	338-2224*
Ross Metals Corp 27 W 47th St. *Fax Area Code: 212 ■ TF: 800-334-7191 ■ Web: www.rossmetals.com	New York	NY	10036	800-334-7191	768-3018*
RSR Corp 2777 Stemmons Fwy Ste 1800. Web: rsrcorp.com	Dallas	TX	75207	214-631-6070	631-6146
Sandvik Special Metals LLC 235407 E SR 397. Web: www.smt.sandvik.com	Kennewick	WA	99337	509-586-4131	582-3552
Sipi Metals Corp 1720 N Elston Ave. Web: www.sipimetals.com	Chicago	IL	60642	773-276-0070	276-7014
Southwire Co 1 Southwire Dr. TF: 800-444-1700 ■ Web: www.southwire.com	Carrollton	GA	30119	770-832-4242	832-4406
Special Metals Corp 4317 Middle Settlement Rd. *Fax: Sales ■ TF: 800-334-8351 ■ Web: www.specialmetals.com	New Hartford	NY	13413	315-798-2900	798-2016*
Spectro Alloys Corp 13220 Doyle Path. Web: www.spectroalloys.com	Rosemount	MN	55068	651-437-2815	438-3714
Taber Extrusions LP 915 S Elmira Ave. TF: 800-563-6853 ■ Web: www.taberextrusions.com	Russellville	AR	72802	479-968-1021	968-8645
Titanium Metals Corp (TIMET) 224 Vly Creek Blvd Ste 200. NYSE: TIE ■ *Fax Area Code: 972 ■ TF: 800-753-1550 ■ Web: www.timet.com	Exton	PA	19341	610-968-1300	934-5345*
Tower Extrusions Ltd 1003 Hwy 79 S PO Box 218. Web: www.towerextrusion.com	Olney	TX	76374	940-564-5681	564-5033
Tree Island Industries 3933 Boundary Rd PO Box 50. TF: 800-663-0955 ■ Web: www.treeisland.com	Richmond	BC	V6V1T8	604-524-3744	524-2362
US Bronze Powders Inc 408 Rt 202 N. TF General: 800-544-0186 ■ Web: www.usbronzepowders.com	Flemington	NJ	08822	908-782-5454	782-3489
US Magnesium LLC 238 North 2200 West. Web: www.usmagnesium.com	Salt Lake City	UT	84116	801-532-2043	534-1407
Valimet Inc PO Box 31690. Web: www.valimet.com	Stockton	CA	95213	209-444-1600	982-1365
Valmont Industries Inc One Valmont Plz. NYSE: VMI ■ TF: 800-825-6668 ■ Web: www.valmont.com	Omaha	NE	68154	402-963-1000	
Victory White Metal Co 6100 Roland Ave. TF: 800-635-5050 ■ Web: www.victorywhitemetal.com	Cleveland	OH	44127	216-271-1400	271-6430
Wah Chang 1600 Old Salem Rd NE. TF: 888-926-4211 ■ Web: www.atimetals.com	Albany	OR	97321	541-926-4211	967-6994
Xyron Inc 8465 N 90th St Ste 6. TF: 800-793-3523 ■ Web: www.xyron.com	Scottsdale	AZ	85258	480-443-9419	443-0118

489 METAL PRODUCTS - HOUSEHOLD

Company	City	State	ZIP	Phone	Fax
Acme International Enterprises Inc 400 Lyster Ave. Web: acmeusa.com/	Saddle Brook	NJ	07663	973-416-0400	416-0499
All-Clad Metalcrafters LLC 424 Morganza Rd. TF Cust Svc: 800-255-2523 ■ Web: all-clad.com	Canonsburg	PA	15317	724-745-8300	746-5035
Calphalon Corp PO Box 583. *Fax Area Code: 419 ■ *Fax: Sales ■ TF: 800-809-7267 ■ Web: www.calphalon.com	Toledo	OH	43697	800-809-7267	666-2859*
G & S Metal Products Company Inc 3330 E 79th St. Web: www.gsmetal.com	Cleveland	OH	44127	216-441-0700	441-0736
Kitchen-Quip Inc 405 E Marion St. Web: www.kqcasting.com	Waterloo	IN	46793	260-837-8311	837-7919
Le Creuset of America Inc 114 Bob Gifford Blvd. TF: 877-418-5547 ■ Web: cookware.lecreuset.com	Early Branch	SC	29916	803-943-4308	943-4510
Lifetime Brands Inc 1000 Steward Ave. NASDAQ: LCUT ■ TF: 800-252-3390 ■ Web: www.lifetimebrands.com	Garden City	NY	11530	516-683-6000	683-6116
Lifetime Brands Inc Farberware Div 1000 Stewart Ave. TF: 800-999-2811 ■ Web: www.lifetimebrands.com	Garden City	NY	11530	516-683-6000	555-0101
Lifetime Brands Inc Hoffritz Div 1000 Stewart Ave. TF: 800-252-3390 ■ Web: www.lifetimebrands.com	Garden City	NY	11530	516-683-6000	555-0101
ME Heuck Co 1600 Beech St. *Fax Area Code: 513 ■ TF Cust Svc: 866-634-3825 ■ Web: www.heuck.com	Terre Haute	IN	47804	812-238-5000	573-9919*
Meyer Corp 1 Meyer Pl. *Fax: PR ■ TF Cust Svc: 800-888-3883 ■ Web: www.meyer.com	Vallejo	CA	94590	707-551-2800	551-2953*
Nordic Ware 5005 Hwy 7. TF: 877-466-7342 ■ Web: www.nordicware.com	Minneapolis	MN	55416	952-920-2888	924-8561
Norpro,Inc 2215 Merrill Creek Pkwy. Web: www.wholesale.norpro.com	Everett	WA	98203	425-261-1000	
Regal Ware Inc 1675 Reigle Dr. Web: www.regalware.com	Kewaskum	WI	53040	262-626-2121	626-8565
Rena Ware International Inc 15885 NE 28th St. Web: www.renaware.com	Bellevue	WA	98008	425-881-6171	882-7500
Saladmaster Inc 230 Westway Pl Ste 101. TF: 800-765-5795 ■ Web: www.saladmaster.com	Arlington	TX	76018	817-633-3555	633-5544

Company	City	State	Zip	Phone	Fax
Whitesell Corp 2703 Avalon Ave	Muscle Shoals	AL	35661	256-248-8500	248-8585*
*Fax: Hum Res ■ *TF General:* 800-826-3317 ■ *Web:* www.whitesellcorp.com					
Wilton Armetale Co PO Box 600	Mount Joy	PA	17552	800-779-4586	653-6573*
*Fax Area Code: 717 ■ *TF:* 800-779-4586 ■ *Web:* www.armetale.com					
Wilton Industries Inc 2240 W 75th St	Woodridge	IL	60517	630-963-7100	963-7196*
*Fax: Sales ■ *TF:* 800-794-5866 ■ *Web:* www.wilton.com					

490 METAL PRODUCTS (MISC)

Company	City	State	Zip	Phone	Fax
Accuride International Inc 12311 Shoemaker Ave	Santa Fe Springs	CA	90670	562-903-0200	903-0208
Web: www.accuride.com					
Aerodyne Alloys LLC 350 Pleasant Vly Rd	South Windsor	CT	06074	860-289-6011	289-2841
TF: 800-243-4344 ■ *Web:* www.aerodynealloys.com					
Alexandria Extrusion Co 401 County Rd 22 NW	Alexandria	MN	56308	320-763-6537	763-9250
TF: 800-568-6601 ■ *Web:* alexandriaindustries.com					
Aluchem Inc One Landy Ln	Cincinnati	OH	45215	513-733-8519	733-0608
TF: 800-336-8519 ■ *Web:* www.aluchem.com					
Aluminum Ladder Co 1430 W Darlington St	Florence	SC	29501	843-662-2595	661-0972
TF: 800-752-2526 ■ *Web:* www.aluminumladder.com					
Amatom Electronic Hardware LLC Five Pasco Hill Rd	Cromwell	CT	06416	860-828-0847	828-0381
TF: 800-243-6032 ■ *Web:* www.amatom.com					
Arland Tool & Manufacturing Inc PO Box 207	Sturbridge	MA	01566	508-347-3368	347-9397
Web: www.arland.com					
Bead Industries Inc 11 Cascade Blvd	Milford	CT	06460	203-301-0270	301-0280
TF: 800-297-4851 ■ *Web:* www.beadindustries.com					
BEMSCO Inc 1193 South 400 West	Salt Lake City	UT	84101	801-487-7455	
Web: www.bemsco.com					
Bobrick Washroom Equipment Inc 11611 Hart St	North Hollywood	CA	91605	818-764-1000	765-2700
Web: www.bobrick.com					
Carolina Carports Inc 187 Cardinal Ridge Trl	Dobson	NC	27017	800-670-4262	
TF: 800-670-4262 ■ *Web:* www.carolinacarportsinc.com					
Ditto Sales Inc 2332 Cathy Ln	Jasper	IN	47546	812-482-3043	482-9318
Web: www.dittosales.com					
Flinchbaugh Engineering Inc 4387 Run Way	York	PA	17406	717-755-1900	840-3217
TF: 866-967-5334 ■ *Web:* www.flinchbaughengineering.com					
General Magnaplate Corp 1331 Us Rt 1	Linden	NJ	07036	908-862-6200	
TF: 800-441-6173 ■ *Web:* www.magnaplate.com					
Gonzalez 29401 Stephenson Hwy	Madison Heights	MI	48071	248-548-6010	548-3160
Web: www.gonzalez-group.com					
J.a. Reinhardt & Co Inc Spruce Cabin Rd	Mountainhome	PA	18342	570-595-7491	595-3551
Web: jareinhardt.bethermalandpower.com					
Lechler Inc 445 Kautz Rd	Saint Charles	IL	60174	630-377-6611	444-7069*
*Fax Area Code: 800 ■ *TF Cust Svc:* 800-777-2926 ■ *Web:* www.lechlerusa.com					
Liberty Safe & Security Products Inc 1199 W Utah Ave	Payson	UT	84651	801-925-1000	465-2712
TF: 800-247-5625 ■ *Web:* www.libertysafe.com					
Magnetic Instrumentation Inc 8431 Castlewood Dr	Indianapolis	IN	46250	317-842-7500	849-7600
Web: www.maginst.com					
Metalworking Group Inc 9070 Pippin Rd	Cincinnati	OH	45251	513-521-4114	521-2816
TF: 800-476-9409 ■ *Web:* www.metalworkinggroup.com					
Metco Industries Inc 1241 Brusselles St	St Mary	PA	15857	814-781-3630	
Web: www.metcopm.com					
Muza Metal Products Corp 606 E Murdock Ave	Oshkosh	WI	54901	920-236-3535	236-3520
Web: www.muzametal.com					
Palmer International Inc PO Box 315	Skippack	PA	19474	610-584-4241	584-4870
Web: palmerint.com					
Polar Ware Co 502 Hwy 67	Kiel	WI	53042	800-237-3655	894-2532*
*Fax Area Code: 920 ■ *TF Cust Svc:* 800-237-3655 ■ *Web:* www.polarware.com					
Powdermet Inc 24112 Rockwell Dr	Euclid	OH	44117	216-404-0053	
Web: www.powdermetinc.com					
Precision Valve Corp 800 Westchester Ave	Rye Brook	NY	10573	914-969-6500	
TF: 866-686-8464 ■ *Web:* www.precisionglobal.com					
Spirol International Corp 30 Rock Ave	Danielson	CT	06239	860-774-8571	774-2048
Web: www.spirol.com					
Spraying Systems Co PO Box 7900	Wheaton	IL	60189	630-665-5000	260-0842
Web: www.spray.com					
Tooling & Equipment International Corp 12550 Tech Ctr Dr	Livonia	MI	48150	734-522-1422	522-1780
Web: www.teintl.net					
Trinity Industries Inc Head Div 11765 Hwy 6 S	Navasota	TX	77868	936-825-6581	
Web: www.trinityheads.com					
TST Inc 11601 Etiwanda Ave	Fontana	CA	92337	951-685-2155	685-7806
Web: www.tst-inc.com					
Viking Materials Inc 3225 Como Ave SE	Minneapolis	MN	55414	612-617-5800	623-9070
TF General: 800-682-3942 ■ *Web:* www.vikingmaterials.com					
Visual Planning Corp 71 Meadowbank Dr	Ottawa	NY	12919	613-563-8727	563-8730
TF: 888-884-5444 ■ *Web:* www.visualplanning.com					

491 METAL STAMPINGS

SEE ALSO Closures - Metal or Plastics p. 1952; Electronic Enclosures p. 2236; Metal Stampings - Automotive p. 2747

Company	City	State	Zip	Phone	Fax
Accurate Perforating Co 3636 S Kedzie Ave	Chicago	IL	60632	773-254-3232	254-9453
TF: 800-621-0273 ■ *Web:* www.accurateperforating.com					
Acme Metal Cap Inc Co 33-53 62nd St	Woodside	NY	11377	718-335-3000	335-3037
TF: 800-338-3581 ■ *Web:* www.acmepans.com					
Admiral Craft Equipment Corp 940 S Oyster Bay Rd	Hicksville	NY	11801	516-433-3535	447-7751*
*Fax Area Code: 800 ■ *TF:* 800-223-7750 ■ *Web:* www.admiralcraft.com					
AK Stamping Inc 1159 US Rt 22	Mountainside	NJ	07092	908-232-7300	232-5202
Web: www.akstamping.com					
Albest Metal Stamping Corp One Kent Ave	Brooklyn	NY	11211	718-388-6000	388-0404
Web: www.albest.com					
Alinabal Inc 28 Woodmont Rd	Milford	CT	06460	203-877-3241	874-5063
Web: www.alinabal.com					
All New Stamping Co 10801 Lower Azusa Rd	El Monte	CA	91731	800-877-7775	877-8121
TF: 800-877-7775 ■ *Web:* www.allnewstamping.com					
American Metalcraft Inc 2074 George St	Melrose Park	IL	60160	708-345-1177	345-5758
TF: 800-333-9133 ■ *Web:* www.amnow.com					
American Products LLC 597 Evergreen Rd	Strafford	MO	65757	417-736-2135	736-2662
TF: 855-736-2135 ■ *Web:* www.amprod.us					
American Trim 1005 W Grand Ave	Lima	OH	45801	419-228-1145	996-4850
Web: www.amtrim.com					
APG Cash Drawer LLC 5250 Industrial Blvd NE	Minneapolis	MN	55421	763-571-5000	571-5771
Web: cashdrawer.com					
Aranda Tooling Inc 15301 Springdale St	Huntington Beach	CA	92649	714-379-6565	379-6570
Web: www.arandatooling.com					
Argo Products Co 3500 Goodfellow Blvd	Saint Louis	MO	63120	314-385-1803	385-1808
Web: www.argoproducts.com					
Arrow Tru-Line Inc 2211 S Defiance St	Archbold	OH	43502	419-446-2785	445-2068
TF: 877-285-7253 ■ *Web:* www.arrowtruline.com					
Arvin Sango Inc 2905 Wilson Ave	Madison	IN	47250	812-265-2888	273-8339
Web: www.arvinsango.com					
Assurance Manufacturing Co 9010 Evergreen Blvd	Coon Rapids	MN	55433	763-780-4252	780-8847
Web: www.assurancemfg.com					
Ataco Steel Products Corp PO Box 270	Cedarburg	WI	53012	262-377-3000	377-3452
TF: 800-536-4822 ■ *Web:* www.atacosteel.com					
Atlantic Tool & Die Co (ATD) 19963 Progress Dr	Strongsville	OH	44149	440-238-6931	238-2210
Web: www.atlantictool.com					
Bazz Houston Co 12700 Western Ave	Garden Grove	CA	92841	714-898-2666	898-1389
TF: 800-385-9608 ■ *Web:* www.bazz-houston.com					
Behrens Manufacturing Co 1250 E Sanborn St	Winona	MN	55987	507-454-4664	452-2106
Web: www.behrensmfg.com					
Bermo Inc 4501 Ball Rd NE	Circle Pines	MN	55014	763-786-7676	785-2159
Web: www.bermo.com					
Beta Shim Co 11 Progress Dr	Shelton	CT	06484	203-926-1150	929-5509
Web: www.betashim.com					
Bopp-Busch Mfg Co 545 E Huron Rd	Au Gres	MI	48703	989-876-7121	876-6555
Web: www.boppbusch.com					
Btd Mfg Inc 1111 13th Ave SE	Detroit Lakes	MN	56501	866-562-3986	
TF: 866-562-3986 ■ *Web:* www.btdmfg.com					
Capitol Stampings Corp 2700 W N Ave	Milwaukee	WI	53208	414-372-3500	372-3535
Web: www.capitolstampings.com					
Clairon Metals Corp 11194 Alcovy Rd	Covington	GA	30014	770-786-9681	786-4183
Web: www.claironmetals.com					
Clow Stamping Co 23103 County Rd 3	Merrifield	MN	56465	218-765-3111	765-3904
Web: www.clowstamping.com					
Cly-Del Mfg Co 151 Sharon Rd	Waterbury	CT	06705	203-574-2100	
Crest Manufacturing Co Five Hood Dr	Lincoln	RI	02865	401-333-1350	333-0821
Web: www.crestmfg.com					
Custom Stamping & Manufacturing Inc 1340 SE Ninth Ave PO Box 14340	Portland	OR	97293	503-238-3700	238-3742
Web: www.customstampingmfg.com					
Danco Precision Inc Wheatland & Mellon Sts	Phoenixville	PA	19460	610-933-8981	935-2011
Web: www.dancoprecision.com					
Danville Metal Stamping Company Inc 20 Oakwood Ave	Danville	IL	61832	217-446-0647	446-0647
Web: www.danvillemetal.com					
Dayton Rogers Manufacturing Co 8401 W 35 W Service Dr	Minneapolis	MN	55449	763-784-7714	784-7714
TF: 800-677-8881 ■ *Web:* www.daytonrogers.com					
Defiance Metal Products 21 Seneca St	Defiance	OH	43512	419-784-5332	782-0148
Web: www.defiancemetal.com					
Delta Consolidated Industries Inc 4800 Krueger Dr	Jonesboro	AR	72401	870-935-3711	935-4994
TF: 800-643-0084 ■ *Web:* www.deltastorage.com					
Diamond Manufacturing Co 243 W Eigth St	Wyoming	PA	18644	570-693-0300	693-3500
TF: 800-233-9601 ■ *Web:* www.diamondman.com					
Diamond Perforated Metals Inc 7300 W Sunnyview Ave	Visalia	CA	93291	559-651-1889	651-1815
TF: 800-642-4334 ■ *Web:* www.diamondperf.com					
DORMA Architectural Hardware DORMA Dr Drawer AC	Reamstown	PA	17567	717-336-3881	336-2106
TF: 800-523-8483 ■ *Web:* www.dorma.com					
Dove Die & Stamping Co 15665 Brookpark Rd	Cleveland	OH	44142	216-267-3720	267-7250
Web: www.dovedie.com					
Dubuque Stamping & Manufacturing Inc 3190 Jackson St	Dubuque	IA	52001	563-583-5716	556-8729
Web: www.dbqstamp.com					
Dudek & Bock Spring Mfg Co 5100 W Roosevelt Rd	Chicago	IL	60644	773-379-4100	379-4108
Web: www.dudek-bock.com					
DureX Inc Five Stahuber Ave	Union	NJ	07083	908-688-0800	688-0718
Web: www.durexinc.com					
E S Investments LLC 14055 US Hwy 19 N	Clearwater	FL	33764	727-536-8822	536-6667
Web: www.sunmicrostamping.com					
East Moline Metal Products Co 1201 Seventh St	East Moline	IL	61244	309-752-1350	752-1380
TF Sales: 800-325-4151 ■ *Web:* www.emmetal.com					
Elmira Stamping & Mfg Corp 1704 Cedar St	Elmira	NY	14904	607-734-2058	732-0573
Web: www.elmirastamping.com					
Fraen Corp 80 Newcrossing Rd	Reading	MA	01867	781-205-5300	942-2426
TF: 800-370-0078 ■ *Web:* www.fraen.com					
Fuller Box Co 150 Chestnut St	North Attleboro	MA	02760	508-695-2525	695-2187
Web: www.fullerbox.com					

Company	City	State	ZIP	Phone	Fax
Fulton Industries Inc 135 E Linfoot St PO Box 377 *TF:* 800-537-5012 ■ *Web:* www.fultonindoh.com	Wauseon	OH	43567	419-335-3015	335-3215
Gasser & Sons Inc 440 Moreland Rd *Web:* www.gasser.com	Commack	NY	11725	631-543-6600	543-6649
Genesee Group Inc 1470 Ave T *Web:* www.geneseegroup.com	Grand Prairie	TX	75050	972-623-2004	623-0404
GMP Metal Products Inc 3883 Delor St *TF:* 800-325-9808 ■ *Web:* www.gmpmetal.com	Saint Louis	MO	63116	314-481-0300	481-1379
Gr Spring & Stamping Inc 706 Bond Ave **Fax Area Code:* 614 ■ *Web:* www.grs-s.com	Grand Rapids	MI	49503	616-453-4491	453-0951*
Griffiths Corp 2717 Niagara Ln N *Web:* www.griffithscorp.com	Minneapolis	MN	55447	763-557-8935	
Guarantee Specialties Inc 9401 Carr Ave	Cleveland	OH	44108	216-451-9744	
Hamrock Inc 12521 Los Nietos Rd *Web:* www.hamrock.com	Santa Fe Springs	CA	90670	562-944-0255	944-5676
Hannibal Industries Inc 3851 S Santa Fe Ave *TF:* 888-246-7074 ■ *Web:* www.hannibalindustries.com	Los Angeles	CA	90058	323-588-4261	589-5640
Harvey Vogel Manufacturing Co 425 Weir Dr *Web:* www.harveyvogel.com	Woodbury	MN	55125	651-739-7373	739-8666
Hendrick Manufacturing Co One Seventh Ave **Fax Area Code:* 570 ■ **Fax:* Sales ■ *TF Cust Svc:* 800-225-7373 ■ *Web:* www.hendrickmfg.com	Carbondale	PA	18407	800-225-7373	282-1506*
Heyco Products 1800 Industrial Way N *TF:* 800-526-4182 ■ *Web:* www.heyco.com	Toms River	NJ	08755	732-286-1800	244-8843
Hobson & Motzer Inc 30 Air Line Dr PO Box 427 *TF:* 800-476-5111 ■ *Web:* www.hobsonmotzer.com	Durham	CT	06422	860-349-1756	349-3602
HPL Stampings Inc 425 Enterprise Pkwy *TF:* 800-927-0397 ■ *Web:* www.hplstampings.com	Lake Zurich	IL	60047	847-540-1400	540-1422
HTT Inc. 1828 Oakland Ave *TF:* 866-270-4710 ■ *Web:* www.eclipsemfg.com	Sheboygan	WI	53081	920-457-2311	453-5301
Innovative Stamping Corp 2068 E Gladwick St *TF:* 800-400-0047 ■ *Web:* www.innovative-sys.com	Compton	CA	90220	310-537-6996	537-0312
Jagemann Stamping Co 5757 W Custer St PO Box 217 *TF:* 888-337-7853 ■ *Web:* www.jagemann.com	Manitowoc	WI	54221	920-682-4633	682-6002
Ken-Tron Manufacturing Inc PO Box 21250 *TF:* 800-872-9336 ■ *Web:* www.ken-tron.com	Owensboro	KY	42304	270-684-0431	684-0435
Kennedy Manufacturing Co 1260 Industrial Dr *TF:* 800-413-8665 ■ *Web:* www.kennedymfg.com	Van Wert	OH	45891	419-238-2442	238-5644
Kerns Manufacturing Corp 37-14 29th St *Web:* www.kernsmfg.com	Long Island City	NY	11101	718-784-4044	786-0534
Keystone Friction Hinge Co 520 Matthews Blvd *Web:* kfhinge.com	South Williamsport	PA	17702	570-323-9479	326-0217
Kickhaefer Mfg Co (KMC) 1221 S Pk St PO Box 348 *TF:* 800-822-6080 ■ *Web:* www.kmcstampings.com	Port Washington	WI	53074	262-377-5030	284-9774
Knaack Manufacturing Co 420 E Terra Cotta Ave *TF:* 800-456-7865 ■ *Web:* www.knaack.com	Crystal Lake	IL	60014	815-459-6020	459-9097
Kromet International Inc 200 Sheldon Dr *Web:* www.kromet.com	Cambridge	ON	N1R7K1	519-623-2511	624-9729
L H Carbide Corp 4420 Clubview Dr *Web:* www.lhindustries.com	Fort Wayne	IN	46804	260-432-5563	432-2503
Lacey Mfg Company Inc 1146 Barnum Ave *Web:* www.laceymfg.com	Bridgeport	CT	06610	203-336-0121	336-1774
Larson Tool & Stamping Co 90 Olive St *Web:* www.larsontool.com	Attleboro	MA	02703	508-222-0897	226-7407
Macon Resources Inc 2121 Hubbard Ave *Web:* www.maconresources.org	Decatur	IL	62526	217-875-1910	875-8899
Mass Precision Sheetmetal Inc 2110 Oakland Rd *Web:* www.massprecision.com	San Jose	CA	95131	408-954-0200	954-0288
McAlpin Industries Inc 255 Hollenbeck St *Web:* www.mcalpin-ind.com	Rochester	NY	14621	585-266-3060	266-8091
Meriden Manufacturing Inc PO Box 694 *Web:* www.meridenmfg.com	Meriden	CT	06450	203-237-7481	235-3146
Metal Box International 11600 W King St *TF General:* 800-622-2697 ■ *Web:* edsal.com	Franklin Park	IL	60131	847-455-8500	455-6030
Metal ComponentsLLC 3281 Roger B Chaffee Memorial Blvd SE *Web:* metalcompinc.com	Grand Rapids	MI	49548	616-252-1900	252-1970
Metal Flow Corp 11694 James St *Web:* www.metalflow.com	Holland	MI	49424	616-392-7976	392-5814
Micro Stamping Corp 140 Belmont Dr *Web:* www.microstamping.com	Somerset	NJ	08873	732-302-0800	302-0436
MIDLAND STAMPING & FABRICATING 9521 W Ainslie St *Web:* shalestamping.com/	Schiller Park	IL	60176	847-678-7573	
Midwest Wire Products LLC 649 S Lansing Ave PO Box 770 *TF:* 800-445-0225 ■ *Web:* www.wireforming.com	Sturgeon Bay	WI	54235	920-743-6591	743-3777
MJ Celco Inc 3900 Wesley Terr *Web:* www.mjcelco.com	Schiller Park	IL	60176	847-671-1900	671-1978
New Standard Corp 74 Commerce Way *Web:* www.newstandard.com	York	PA	17406	717-757-9450	757-2312
Niles Mfg & Finishing Inc 465 Walnut St *Web:* www.nilesmfg.com	Niles	OH	44446	330-544-0402	544-8018
Northern Stamping Corp 6600 Chapek Pkwy *Web:* northernstamping.com	Cleveland	OH	44125	216-883-8888	883-8237
Okay Industries Inc 200 Ellis St *Web:* www.okayind.com	New Britain	CT	06051	860-225-8707	225-7047
P & G Steel Products Company Inc 54 Gruner Rd *Web:* www.pgsteel.com	Buffalo	NY	14227	716-896-7900	896-4129
Pax Machine Works Inc PO Box 338 *Web:* www.paxmachine.com	Celina	OH	45822	419-586-2337	586-7123
Penn United Technology Inc 799 N Pike Rd *TF:* 866-572-7537 ■ *Web:* www.pennunited.com	Cabot	PA	16023	724-352-1507	352-4970
PEP Wauconda 821 W Algonquin *Web:* www.pepwauconda.com	Algonquin	IL	60102	847-658-4588	
Perfection Spring & Stamping Corp 1449 E Algonquin Rd *Web:* www.pss-corp.com	Mount Prospect	IL	60056	847-437-3900	437-1322
Plainfield Cos 24035 Riverwalk Ct *Web:* www.plainfieldprecision.com	Plainfield	IL	60544	815-436-5671	439-2970
Precision Resource 25 Forest Pkwy *Web:* www.precisionresource.com	Shelton	CT	06484	203-925-0012	926-9010
Prestige Stamping Inc 23513 Groesbeck Hwy *Web:* www.prestigestamping.com	Warren	MI	48089	586-773-2700	773-2700
Quaker Mfg Corp PO Box 449 *Web:* www.quakermfg.com	Salem	OH	44460	330-332-4631	332-1519
Quality Perforating Inc 166 Dundaff St *TF:* 800-872-7373 ■ *Web:* www.qualityperf.com	Carbondale	PA	18407	570-282-4344	282-4627
Quality Tool & Stamping Company Inc 2642 Mcilwraith St *Web:* www.qtstamping.com	Muskegon	MI	49444	231-733-2538	733-0983
Ramcel Engineering Co 2926 MacArthur Blvd *Web:* www.ramcel.com	Northbrook	IL	60062	847-272-6980	272-7196
RES Mfg Company Inc 7801 N 73rd St *TF:* 800-334-8044 ■ *Web:* www.resmfg.com	Milwaukee	WI	53223	414-354-4530	354-9027
Rockford Toolcraft Inc 766 Research Pkwy *Web:* www.rockfordtoolcraft.com	Rockford	IL	61109	815-398-5507	398-0132
Saunders Manufacturing Co 65 Nickerson Hill Rd *TF:* 800-341-4674 ■ *Web:* www.saunders-usa.com	Readfield	ME	04355	207-685-9860	685-9918
Slidematic Products Co 4520 W Addison St *Web:* www.slidematicproducts.com	Chicago	IL	60641	773-545-4213	545-0797
Small Parts Inc 600 Humphrey St PO Box 23 *Web:* www.smallpartsinc.com	Logansport	IN	46947	574-753-6323	753-6660
Sons Tool Inc 460 Thompson Rd *Web:* www.sonstool.com	Woodville	WI	54028	715-698-2471	698-2335
Spindustries LLC 1301 La Salle St *Web:* www.lgspin.com	Lake Geneva	WI	53147	262-248-6601	248-1277
Stack-On Products Co 1360 N Old Rand Rd *TF:* 800-323-9601 ■ *Web:* www.stack-on.com	Wauconda	IL	60084	847-526-1611	526-6599
Stamtex Metal Stampings 112 Erie St *Web:* www.stamtexmp.com	Niles	OH	44446	330-652-2558	652-7369
Stanley Spring & Stamping Corp 5050 W Foster Ave *Web:* www.stanleyspring.com	Chicago	IL	60630	773-777-2600	777-3894
Steel City Corp 190 N Meridian Rd *TF:* 800-321-0350 ■ *Web:* www.scity.com	Youngstown	OH	44501	330-792-7663	797-2947
Stewart EFI LLC 45 Old Waterbury Rd *TF:* 800-393-5387 ■ *Web:* www.stewartefi.com	Thomaston	CT	06787	860-283-8213	283-5610
T & D Metal Products Co 602 E Walnut St *TF:* 800-634-7267 ■ *Web:* www.tdmetal.com	Watseka	IL	60970	815-432-4938	432-6271
Taylor Metal Products Co 700 Springmill St *Web:* www.tmpind.com	Mansfield	OH	44903	419-522-3471	525-2948
Tech-Etch Inc 45 Aldrin Rd *Web:* www.tech-etch.com	Plymouth	MA	02360	508-747-0300	746-9639
Trans-Matic Manufacturing Co 300 E 48th St *Web:* www.transmatic.com	Holland	MI	49423	616-820-2500	820-2702
Trident Precision Manufacturing Inc 734 Salt Rd *Web:* www.tridentprecision.com	Webster	NY	14580	585-265-2010	265-2386
Triton Industries Inc 1020 N Kolmar Ave *Web:* www.tritonindustries.com	Chicago	IL	60651	773-384-3700	384-8748
Waterloo Industries Inc 139 W Forest Hill Ave **Fax Area Code:* 414 ■ **Fax:* Cust Svc ■ *TF Cust Svc:* 800-558-5528 ■ *Web:* www.waterlooindustries.com	Oak Creek	WI	53154	800-558-5528	766-6388*
Weiss-Aug Company Inc 220 Merry Ln *Web:* www.weiss-aug.com	East Hanover	NJ	07936	973-887-7600	887-8109
Winzeler Stamping Co 910 E Main St *Web:* www.winzelerstamping.com	Montpelier	OH	43543	419-485-3147	485-5039
WLS Stamping Co 3292 E 80th St *Web:* www.wlsstamping.com	Cleveland	OH	44104	216-271-5100	341-3203
Wolverine Metal Stamping Inc 3600 Tennis Ct *Web:* www.wms-inc.com	Saint Joseph	MI	49085	269-429-6600	429-6657
Wozniak Industries Inc Two Mid America Plz Ste 706 *Web:* www.wozniakindustries.com	Oakbrook Terrace	IL	60181	630-954-3400	954-3605
Wrico Stamping Co 2727 Niagara Ln N *Web:* www.wrico-net.com	Minneapolis	MN	55447	763-559-2288	553-7976

492 METAL STAMPINGS - AUTOMOTIVE

SEE ALSO Automotive Parts & Supplies - Mfr p. 1839

Company	City	State	ZIP	Phone	Fax
Ada Metal Products Inc 7120 Capitol Dr *Web:* www.adametal.com	Lincolnwood	IL	60712	847-673-1190	673-4860
Advance Engineering Co 7505 Baron Dr *TF:* 800-497-6388 ■ *Web:* www.adveng.net	Canton	MI	48187	313-537-3500	537-7389
AJ Rose Manufacturing Co 38000 Chester Rd *Web:* www.ajrose.com	Avon	OH	44011	440-934-7700	934-2802
American Metal & Plastics Inc 450 32nd St SW *TF:* 800-382-0067 ■ *Web:* www.ampi-gr.com	Grand Rapids	MI	49548	616-452-6061	452-3835
AMG Industries Inc 200 Commerce Dr **Fax:* Mail Rm ■ *Web:* www.amgindustries.com	Mount Vernon	OH	43050	740-397-4044	397-3092*
Automotive Engineered Products Inc 7149 Mission Gorge Rd **Fax Area Code:* 909 ■ *Web:* www.jbaheaders.com	San Diego	CA	92120	619-229-7797	599-6424*
Burkland Inc 6520 S State Rd *Web:* burklandinc.com	Goodrich	MI	48438	810-636-2233	636-7525
C Cowles & Co Inc 83 Water St *TF:* 800-624-4483 ■ *Web:* www.ccowles.com	New Haven	CT	06511	203-865-3117	773-1019
Center Mfg Inc 990 84th St *Web:* www.mecinc.com	Byron Center	MI	49315	920-387-4500	

Phone | Fax

Clark Metal Products Co 100 Serrell Dr .... Blairsville PA 15717 724-459-7550 459-0207
Web: www.clark-metal.com

Concord Tool & Mfg 118 N Groesbeck Hwy ...... Mount Clemens MI 48043 586-465-6537 465-7301
Web: www.concordtool.com

Cooper-Standard Automotive Inc
39550 Orchard Hill Pl Dr .... Novi MI 48375 248-596-5900 596-6540*
*Fax: Hum Res ■ Web: www.cooperstandard.com

Decoma International Inc
Magna Exteriors & Interiors 50 Casmir Ct .... Concord ON L4K4J5 905-669-2888 528-6450*
*Fax Area Code: 248 ■ TF: 888-348-2398 ■ Web: www.magna.com

Dixien 5286 Cir Dr .... Lake City GA 30260 404-366-7427
Web: www.dixien.com

Fisher Corp 1625 W Maple Rd .... Troy MI 48084 248-280-0808 280-0725
Web: www.fisherco.com

Gaffoglio Family Metalcrafters Inc
11161 Slater Ave. .... Fountain Valley CA 92708 714-444-2000
Web: www.metalcrafters.com

Genco Stamping & Manufacturing Co
2001 Genco Dr .... Cookeville TN 38506 931-528-5574 528-8379
Web: gencostamping.com

GHSP Co 1250 S Beechtree St .... Grand Haven MI 49417 616-842-5500 842-7230
Web: www.ghsp.com

Grant Industries Inc 33415 Groesbeck Hwy .... Fraser MI 48026 586-293-9200 293-9346
Web: www.grantgrp.com

Hamlin Newco LLC 2741 Wingate Ave .... Akron OH 44314 330-753-7791 753-5577
Web: www.hnmetalstamping.com

Hatch Stamping Co 635 E Industrial Dr .... Chelsea MI 48118 734-475-8628 475-6255
Web: www.hatchstamping.com

Hines Group Inc, The 5680 Old Hwy 54 E .... Philpot KY 42366 270-729-4242
Web: www.thehinesgroup.com

Honda Precision Parts of Georgia LLC
550 Honda Pkwy .... Tallapoosa GA 30176 770-574-3400
Web: www.cevalogistics.com

Industrial Components Inc
IC Assemblies Inc 2250 NW 102nd Ave. .... Miami FL 33172 305-477-0387 594-7332
Web: www.icassemblies.com

ITW Drawform 500 Fairview Rd .... Zeeland MI 49464 616-772-1910 772-9572
Web: www.drawform.com

ITW Highland 1240 Wolcott St PO Box 1858 .... Waterbury CT 06722 203-574-3200 754-4019
Web: www.itwhighland.com

Lake Air 7709 Winpark Dr .... Minneapolis MN 55427 763-546-0994 546-4469
TF: 888-785-2422 ■ Web: www.lakeairmetals.com

LMC Industries Inc 100 Manufacturers Dr .... Arnold MO 63010 636-282-8080 282-7114
Web: www.lmcindustries.com

Logghe Stamping Co 16711 E 13-Mile Rd .... Fraser MI 48026 586-293-2250

Marquette Tool & Die Co
3185 S KingsHwy Blvd .... Saint Louis MO 63139 314-771-8509 771-7964
Web: www.marquettetool.com

Matcor Automotive 401 S Steele St .... Ionia MI 48846 616-527-4050

McKechnie Vehicle Components (MVC)
27087 Gratiot Ave Fl 2 .... Roseville MI 48066 586-491-2600
Web: www.mvcusa.com

Means Industries Inc 3715 E Washington Rd. .... Saginaw MI 48601 989-754-1433 754-1103
Web: www.meansindustries.com

Midway Products Group Inc 1 Lyman E Hoyt Dr .... Monroe MI 48161 734-241-7242 384-0811*
*Fax: Sales ■ Web: www.midwayproducts.com

Modineer Co 2190 Industrial Dr PO Box 640 .... Niles MI 49120 269-683-2550 683-0750
Web: www.modineer.com

Moroso Performance Products Inc
80 Carter Dr .... Guilford CT 06437 203-453-6571 453-6906*
*Fax: Cust Svc ■ Web: www.moroso.com

ODM Tool & Manufacturing Co 9550 Joliet Rd .... McCook IL 60525 708-485-6130 485-6540
Web: www.odmtool.com

Ogihara America Corp 1480 W McPherson Pk Dr .... Howell MI 48843 517-548-4900 548-6036
Web: www.ogihara.com

Oshkosh Specialty Vehicles LLC
12770 44th St N .... Clearwater FL 33762 727-573-0400
Web: www.oshkoshsv.com

Philippi-Hagenbuch Inc 7424 W Plank Rd .... Peoria IL 61604 309-697-9200 697-2400
TF: 800-447-6464 ■ Web: www.philsystems.com

Pk USA Inc 600 W Northridge Dr .... Shelbyville IN 46176 317-395-5500 395-5501
Web: www.pkusa.com

Polar ware
W140 N8700 Lilly Rd PO Box 366 .... Menomonee Falls WI 53052 262-251-8800 251-8804
Web: polarware.com/polarware.htm

Pridgeon & Clay Inc
50 Cottage Grove St SW .... Grand Rapids MI 49507 616-241-5675 241-1799
Web: pridgeonandclay.com

Radar Industries 27101 Grosbeck Hwy .... Warren MI 48089 800-779-0301 758-6445*
*Fax Area Code: 586 ■ TF: 800-779-0301 ■ Web: www.radarind.com

Riviera Tool Co 5460 Executive Pkwy SE .... Grand Rapids MI 49512 616-698-2100 698-2470
OTC: RIVT ■ Web: www.rivieratool.com

Shiloh Industries Corp 880 Steel Dr .... Valley City OH 44280 330-558-2600
Web: www.shiloh.com

Spartanburg Steel Products Inc
1290 New Cut Rd PO Box 6428 .... Spartanburg SC 29304 864-585-5211 583-5641
TF: 888-974-7500 ■ Web: www.ssprod.com

Steel Parts Corp 801 Berryman Pk .... Tipton IN 46072 765-675-2191 675-4232
Web: steelparts.com

Stewart EFI LLC 45 Old Waterbury Rd .... Thomaston CT 06787 860-283-8213 283-5610
TF: 800-393-5387 ■ Web: www.stewartefi.com

Syracuse Stamping Co 1054 S Clinton St .... Syracuse NY 13202 315-476-5306 474-8876
TF: 800-581-5555 ■ Web: www.syraco.com

Thiel Tool & Engineering Company Inc
4622 Bulwer Ave PO Box 470007 .... Saint Louis MO 63147 314-241-6121 241-7857
Web: www.thieltool.com

Thomas Engineering Co 7024 Northland Dr. .... Minneapolis MN 55428 763-533-1501 533-8091
Web: www.thomasengineering.com

Tinnerman Palnut Engineered Products (Canada) Corp
686 Parkdale Ave N. .... Hamilton ON L8H5Z4 905-549-4661
Web: www.tinnermanpalnut.com

Troy Design & Manufacturing Co (TDM)
12675 Berwyn. .... Redford MI 48239 313-592-2300
Web: www.troydm.com

TYG Holding USA Inc 1800 N McDonald St. .... Mckinney TX 75071 972-542-1889
Web: www.tygus.com

United Metal Products Corp 8101 Lyndon St .... Detroit MI 48238 313-933-8750 933-1001
Web: www.unitedmetalproducts.com

Varbros LLC 16025 Brookpark Rd PO Box 42127 .... Cleveland OH 44142 216-267-5200 267-5205
Web: www.varbroscorp.com

Versatube Corp 4755 Rochester Rd. .... Troy MI 48085 248-689-7373 689-8293
Web: www.versatubecorp.com

VIA Motors Inc 165 Mtn Way Dr. .... Orem UT 84058 801-764-9333
Web: www.viamotors.com

Wellington Industries Inc
39555 S I-94 Service Dr. .... Belleville MI 48111 734-942-1060 942-9430
Web: www.wellingtonind.com

Wisconsin Metal Products Co 1807 DeKovin Ave .... Racine WI 53403 262-633-6301 633-8962
Web: www.wmpco.com

493 METAL TUBE & PIPE

Phone | Fax

Advanced Fabrication Services Inc 420 Oak St ...... Lemoyne PA 17043 717-763-0286
Web: www.afsenergy.com

AK Tube LLC 30400 E Broadway .... Walbridge OH 43465 419-661-4150 661-4380
TF: 800-955-8031 ■ Web: www.aktube.com

American Cast Iron Pipe Co (ACIPCO)
1501 31st Ave N .... Birmingham AL 35207 205-325-7701
TF: 800-442-2347 ■ Web: www.american-usa.com

ArcelorMittal Laplace LLC 138 Hwy 3217 .... Laplace LA 70068 985-652-4900

Atlas Tube 1855 E 122nd St .... Chicago IL 60633 773-646-4500 646-6128
TF: 800-733-5683 ■ Web: www.atlastube.com

Atlas Tubular LP 1710 S Hwy 77 .... Robstown TX 78380 361-387-7505 387-4613
Web: www.atlastubular.com

Berg Steel Pipe Corp 5315 W 19th St. .... Panama City FL 32401 850-769-2273 763-9683
Web: www.bergpipe.com

Bristol Metals LP 390 Bristol Metals Rd .... Bristol TN 37620 423-989-4700
Web: www.brismet.com

Bull Moose Tube Co
1819 Clarkson Rd Ste 100 .... Chesterfield MO 63017 636-537-2600 537-5848*
*Fax: Sales ■ TF: 800-325-4467 ■ Web: www.bullmoosetube.com

California Steel & Tube
16049 Stephens St .... City of Industry CA 91745 626-968-5511 369-9660
TF: 800-338-8823 ■ Web: californiasteelandtube.com

Canerector Inc 1 Sparks Ave. .... North York ON M2H2W1 416-225-6240
Web: www.canerector.com

Cardinal Mfg Company Inc
225 Eiler Ave PO Box 14127. .... Louisville KY 40214 502-363-2661
Web: www.cardinalmfg.com

Cerro Flow Products Inc PO Box 66800 .... Saint Louis MO 63166 618-337-6000 337-6958
TF: 888-237-7611 ■ Web: www.cerroflow.com

Charlotte Pipe & Foundry Co
2109 Randolph Rd .... Charlotte NC 28207 704-372-5030 348-6450
TF: 800-438-6091 ■ Web: www.charlottepipe.com

Clark Precision Machined Components LLC
320 Fourth St .... Blawnox PA 15238 412-828-1210
Web: www.clarkprecision.com

CTP Corp 3750 Shelby St. .... Indianapolis IN 46227 317-787-1322
Web: www.tubeproc.com/ctp-corporation

Davis Wire Corp 5555 Irwindale Ave .... Irwindale CA 91706 626-969-7651
Web: www.daviswire.com

Dixie Pipe Sales Inc
2407 Broiller PO Box 300650. .... Houston TX 77054 713-796-2021 799-8628
TF: 800-733-3494 ■ Web: www.dixiepipe.com

Earle M Jorgensen Co 10650 S Alameda St .... Lynwood CA 90262 323-567-1122 736-6168*
*Fax Area Code: 610 ■ TF Sales: 800-336-5365 ■ Web: www.emjmetals.com

Energy Alloys LLC 350 Glenborough Ste 300 .... Houston TX 77067 832-601-5800 601-5801
TF: 866-448-9831 ■ Web: www.ealloys.com

Felker Bros Corp 22 N Chestnut Ave .... Marshfield WI 54449 715-384-3121 387-6837
TF: 800-826-2304 ■ Web: www.felkerbrothers.com

Hanna Steel Corp
3812 Commerce Ave PO Box 558. .... Fairfield AL 35064 205-780-1111 783-8368
TF: 800-633-8252 ■ Web: www.hannasteel.com

Hannibal Industries Inc
3851 S Santa Fe Ave. .... Los Angeles CA 90058 323-588-4261 589-5640
TF: 888-246-7074 ■ Web: www.hannibalindustries.com

Hofmann Industries Inc
3145 Shillington Rd .... Sinking Spring PA 19608 610-678-8051 670-2221
Web: www.hofmann.com

Hydro Aluminum North America
999 Corporate Blvd Ste 100 .... Linthicum MD 21090 888-935-5752 487-8053*
*Fax Area Code: 410 ■ TF: 888-935-5752 ■ Web: www.hydro.com

International Metal Hose Co 520 Goodrich Rd .... Bellevue OH 44811 419-483-7690 483-8225
TF: 800-458-6855 ■ Web: www.metalhose.com

J D Rush C Inc 5900 E Lerdo Hwy .... Shafter CA 93263 661-392-1900 399-2728
TF: 800-537-6284 ■ Web: www.jdrush.com

Jackson Tube Service Inc 8210 Industry Pk Dr. .... Piqua OH 45356 937-773-8550 773-8806
TF: 800-543-8910 ■ Web: www.jackson-tube.com

Leavitt Tube 1717 W 115th St .... Chicago IL 60643 773-239-7700 239-1023
TF: 800-532-8488 ■ Web: www.leavitt-tube.com

LeFiell Manufacturing Co
13700 Firestone Blvd .... Santa Fe Springs CA 90670 562-921-3411 921-5480
TF: 800-451-5971 ■ Web: www.lefiell.com

Lock Joint Tube Inc 515 W Ireland Rd. .... South Bend IN 46614 574-299-5326 299-3464*
*Fax: Sales ■ TF: 800-257-6859 ■ Web: www.ljtube.com

Marcegaglia USA Inc 1001 E Waterfront Dr. .... Munhall PA 15120 412-462-2185 462-6059
Web: www.marcegaglia.com

Marlin Steel Wire Products
2640 Merchant Dr. .... Baltimore MD 21230 410-644-7456
Web: www.marlinwire.com

Company	City	State	ZIP	Phone	Fax
Mercury Tube Products 3211 W Bear Creek Dr	Englewood	CO	80110	303-761-1835	781-7307
Web: merctube.com/					
Morris Coupling Co 2240 W 15th St	Erie	PA	16505	814-459-1741	453-5155
TF: 800-426-1579 ■ *Web:* www.morriscoupling.com					
National Metalwares Inc 900 N Russell Ave	Aurora	IL	60506	630-892-9000	892-2573
Web: www.nationalmetalwares.com					
Naylor Pipe Co 1230 E 92nd St	Chicago	IL	60619	773-721-9400	721-9494
Web: www.naylorpipe.com					
Northwest Pipe Co 12005 N Burgard	Portland	OR	97203	503-285-1400	978-2561
NASDAQ: NWPX ■ *TF:* 800-824-9824 ■ *Web:* www.nwpipe.com					
Outokumpu Stainless Pipe Inc 1101 N Main St	Wildwood	FL	34785	352-748-1313	416-7473*
**Fax Area Code:* 800 ■ *TF:* 800-731-7473 ■ *Web:* www.outokumpu.com					
Parmatech Corp 2221 Pine View Way	Petaluma	CA	94954	707-778-2266	
Web: atwcompanies.com/parmatech					
Pipe Fabricating & Supply Co 1235 N Kraemer Blvd	Anaheim	CA	92806	714-630-5200	630-1277
Web: www.pipefab.com					
Plymouth Tube Co 29 W 150 Warrenville Rd	Warrenville	IL	60555	630-393-3550	393-3551
TF Mktg: 800-323-9506 ■ *Web:* www.plymouth.com					
Porter's Group LLC 1111 Oates Rd	Bessemer City	NC	28016	704-864-1313	
Web: www.portersfab.com					
PTC Alliance Copperleaf Corporate Ctr 6051 Wallace Rd Ext Ste 200	Wexford	PA	15090	412-299-7900	299-2619
Web: www.ptcalliance.com					
Quality Edge Inc 2712 Walkent Dr NW	Walker	MI	49544	888-784-0878	
Web: www.qualityedge.com					
Salem Tube Inc 951 Fourth St	Greenville	PA	16125	724-646-4301	646-4311
Web: www.salemtube.com					
Small Tube Products Company Inc PO Box 1017	Duncansville	PA	16635	814-695-4491	695-4304
TF: 800-458-3493 ■ *Web:* www.smalltubeproducts.com					
Southland Tube Inc 3525 Richard Arrington Blvd N	Birmingham	AL	35234	205-251-1884	251-1553
TF: 800-543-9024 ■ *Web:* www.southlandtube.com					
Stupp Corp 12555 Ronaldson Rd	Baton Rouge	LA	70807	225-775-8800	775-7610
TF: 800-535-9999 ■ *Web:* www.stuppcorp.com					
Superior Tube Co 3900 Germantown Pk	Collegeville	PA	19426	610-489-5200	489-5252
Web: www.superiortube.com					
Swepco Tube Corp 1 Clifton Blvd	Clifton	NJ	07015	973-778-3000	778-9289
Web: www.swepcotube.com					
Synalloy Corp 775 Spartan Blvd Ste 102 PO Box 5627	Spartanburg	SC	29304	864-585-3605	596-1501
NASDAQ: SYNL ■ *TF Orders:* 800-937-5449 ■ *Web:* www.synalloy.com					
Tex-Tube Co 1503 N Post Oak Rd	Houston	TX	77055	713-686-4351	681-5256
TF: 800-839-7473 ■ *Web:* www.tex-tube.com					
Troxel Co Hwy 57	Moscow	TN	38057	901-877-6875	877-6942
Web: www.troxel.com					
Tube Methods Inc PO Box 460	Bridgeport	PA	19405	610-279-7700	277-2005
Web: www.tubemethods.com					
Tube Processing Corp 604 E Le Grande Ave	Indianapolis	IN	46203	317-787-1321	786-3074
TF: 800-295-4119 ■ *Web:* www.tubeproc.com					
Unison LLC 7575 Baymeadows Way	Jacksonville	FL	32256	904-739-4000	739-4093
Web: www.unisonindustries.com					
Valmont Industries Inc One Valmont Plz	Omaha	NE	68154	402-963-1000	
NYSE: VMI ■ *TF:* 800-825-6668 ■ *Web:* www.valmont.com					
Van Leeuwen Pipe & Tube Inc 2875 64th Ave	Edmonton	AB	T6P1R1	780-469-7410	466-5970
Web: www.vanleeuwen.com					
Webco Industries Inc 9101 W 21st St PO Box 100	Sand Springs	OK	74063	918-245-2211	245-0306
OTC: WEBC ■ *Web:* www.webcoindustries.com					
Welded Tubes Inc 135 Penniman Rd	Orwell	OH	44076	440-437-5144	437-5180
Web: www.weldedtubes.com					
Western Pneumatic Tube LLC 835 Sixth St S	Kirkland	WA	98033	425-822-8271	828-6669
Web: www.wptube.com					
Western Tube & Conduit Corp 2001 E Dominguez St	Long Beach	CA	90810	310-537-6300	604-9785
Web: www.westerntube.com					
Wheatland Tube Co 700 S Dock St	Sharon	PA	16146	800-257-8182	
TF: 800-257-8182 ■ *Web:* www.wheatland.com					
Wieland Metals Inc 567 Northgate Pkwy	Wheeling	IL	60090	847-537-3990	537-4085
Web: www.wielandus.com					
World Resources Co 1600 Anderson Rd	Mclean	VA	22102	703-734-9800	
Web: www.worldresourcescompany.com					
Wytech Industries Inc 960 E Hazelwood Ave	Rahway	NJ	07065	732-396-3900	
Web: www.wytech.com					
Yarde Metals Inc 45 Newell St	Southington	CT	06489	860-406-6061	406-6040
TF: 800-444-9494 ■ *Web:* www.yarde.com					

494 METAL WORK - ARCHITECTURAL & ORNAMENTAL

Company	City	State	ZIP	Phone	Fax
Airolite Company LLC PO Box 410	Schofield	WI	54476	715-841-8757	841-8773
Web: www.airolite.com					
Alabama Metal Industries Corp (AMICO) 3245 Fayette Ave	Birmingham	AL	35208	205-787-2611	780-7838*
**Fax:* Sales ■ *TF:* 800-366-2642 ■ *Web:* www.amico-online.com					
Alpha Tech Inc 388 Cane Creek Rd	Fletcher	NC	28732	828-684-9709	
Web: www.alpha.com					
Alvarado Mfg Company Inc 12660 Colony St	Chino	CA	91710	909-591-8431	628-1403
TF: 800-423-4143 ■ *Web:* www.alvaradomfg.com					
American Stair Corp Inc 642 Forestwood Dr	Romeoville	IL	60446	800-872-7824	372-3684*
**Fax Area Code:* 815 ■ *TF:* 800-872-7824 ■ *Web:* www.americanstair.com					
Ameristar Fence Products Inc 1555 N Mingo Rd	Tulsa	OK	74116	918-835-0898	
TF: 888-333-3422 ■ *Web:* www.ameristarfence.com					
Armstrong Bros Holding Company Inc 8530 M 60	Union City	MI	49094	517-741-4471	
ATAS International Inc 6612 Snowdrift Rd	Allentown	PA	18106	610-395-8445	395-9342
TF: 800-468-1441 ■ *Web:* www.atas.com					
Bedford Machine & Tool Inc 2103 John Williams Blvd	Bedford	IN	47421	812-275-1948	
TF: 800-264-1948 ■ *Web:* www.bedfordmachine.com					
Bil-Jax Inc 125 Taylor Pkwy	Archbold	OH	43502	419-445-8915	445-0367
TF: 800-537-0540 ■ *Web:* www.biljax.com					
Bradley Pulverizer Company Inc 123 S Third St	Allentown	PA	18105	610-434-5191	
Web: www.bradleypulverizer.com					
Brand Energy & Infrastructure Services Inc 1325 Cobb International Dr Ste A-1	Kennesaw	GA	30152	678-285-1400	514-0285*
**Fax Area Code:* 770 ■ *TF:* 855-746-4477 ■ *Web:* www.beis.com					
Cherokee Metals Company Inc 5883 Glenridge Dr NE	Atlanta	GA	30328	770-449-1444	559-4933
Chicago Metallic Corp 4849 S Austin Ave	Chicago	IL	60638	708-563-4600	222-3744*
**Fax Area Code:* 800 ■ *TF:* 800-323-7164 ■ *Web:* www.chicago-metallic.com					
Construction Specialties Inc Three Werner Way	Lebanon	NJ	08833	908-236-0800	236-0801
TF: 800-972-7214 ■ *Web:* c-sgroup.com					
Duvinage Corp 60 W Oak Ridge Dr	Hagerstown	MD	21740	301-733-8255	791-7240
TF: 800-541-2645 ■ *Web:* www.duvinage.com					
Fisher & Ludlow Tru-Weld Grating 2000 Corporate Dr Ste 400	Wexford	PA	15090	724-934-5320	934-5348
TF: 800-334-2047 ■ *Web:* www.fisherludlow.com					
Goldline International Inc 1601 Cloverfield Blvd 100 S Tower	Santa Monica	CA	90404	310-587-1423	319-0265
TF: 877-376-2646 ■ *Web:* goldline.com					
Hafele America Company Inc 3901 Cheyenne Dr	Archdale	NC	27263	336-889-2322	325-6197*
**Fax Area Code:* 800 ■ *TF Cust Svc:* 800-423-3531 ■ *Web:* www.hafele.com					
Hapco Inc 26252 Hillman Hwy	Abingdon	VA	24210	276-628-7171	623-2594
TF: 800-368-7171 ■ *Web:* www.hapco.com					
IKG Industries 1514 S Sheldon Rd	Channelview	TX	77530	281-452-6637	378-3987*
**Fax Area Code:* 713 ■ *Web:* www.harscoikg.com					
Irvine Access Floors Inc 9425 Washington Blvd	Laurel	MD	20723	301-617-9333	617-9907
TF: 888-458-6339 ■ *Web:* www.irvineaccessfloors.com					
Jackburn Manufacturing Inc 438 Church St	Girard	PA	16417	814-774-3573	774-2854
Web: www.jackburn.com					
Jerith Mfg Company Inc 14400 McNulty Rd	Philadelphia	PA	19154	215-676-4068	676-9756
TF: 800-344-2242 ■ *Web:* www.jerith.com					
King Architectural Metals Inc PO Box 271169	Dallas	TX	75227	800-542-2379	388-1048*
**Fax Area Code:* 214 ■ *TF:* 800-542-2379 ■ *Web:* kingmetals.com					
Lapmaster International LLC 501 W Algonquin Rd	Mount Prospect	IL	60056	224-659-7101	
TF: 877-352-8637 ■ *Web:* www.lapmaster.com					
Lawrence Metal Products Inc 260 Spur Dr S PO Box 400	Bay Shore	NY	11706	800-441-0019	666-0336*
**Fax Area Code:* 631 ■ *TF:* 800-441-0019 ■ *Web:* www.tensator.com					
Livers Bronze Co 4621 E 75th Terr	Kansas City	MO	64132	816-300-2828	300-0864
Web: www.liversbronze.com					
MC Machinery Systems Inc 1500 Michael Dr	Wood Dale	IL	60191	630-860-4210	
Web: www.mcmachinery.com					
McGregor Industries Inc 46 Line St	Dunmore	PA	18512	570-343-2436	343-4915
Web: www.mcgregorindustries.com					
Milgo Industrial Inc 68 Lombardi St	Brooklyn	NY	11222	718-388-6476	963-0614
Web: www.milgo-bufkin.com					
MiTek Canada Inc 100 Industrial Rd	Bradford	ON	L3Z3G7	905-952-2900	952-2901
Web: www.mitek.ca					
NSK America Corp 1800 Global Pkwy	Hoffman Estates	IL	60192	847-843-7664	
Web: www.nskamericacorp.com					
Overly Manufacturing Co 574 W Otterman St	Greensburg	PA	15601	724-834-7300	830-2871
TF: 800-979-7300 ■ *Web:* www.overly.com					
Quickmill Inc 760 Rye St	Peterborough	ON	K9J6W9	705-745-2961	745-8130
Web: www.quickmill.com					
Spider Staging Corp 365 Upland Dr	Tukwila	WA	98188	206-575-6445	575-6240
TF: 877-774-3370 ■ *Web:* www.spiderstaging.com					
Steel Ceilings Inc 451 E Coshocton St	Johnstown	OH	43031	740-967-1063	967-1478
TF: 800-848-0496 ■ *Web:* www.steelceilings.com					
Superior Aluminum Products Inc 555 E Main St PO Box 430	Russia	OH	45363	937-526-4065	526-3904
TF: 800-548-8656 ■ *Web:* www.superioraluminum.com					
Swanton Welding & Machining Co 407 Broadway Ave	Swanton	OH	43558	419-826-4816	826-0489
Web: www.swantonweld.com					
T Tech Inc 510 Guthridge Ct	Norcross	GA	30092	770-455-0676	
Web: t-techtools.com/store/					
Tate Access Floors Inc 7510 Montevideo Rd	Jessup	MD	20794	410-799-4200	799-4207
TF: 800-231-7788 ■ *Web:* tateinc.com					
Thyssenkrupp Krause Inc 901 Doris Rd	Auburn Hills	MI	48326	248-340-8000	
Universal Builders Supply Inc (UBS) 27 Horton Ave	New Rochelle	NY	10801	914-699-2400	699-2609
Web: www.ubs1.com					
US Equipment Co 20580 Hoover Rd	Detroit	MI	48205	313-526-8300	
Web: www.usequipment.com					
VELUX America Inc 450 Old BrickyaRd Rd	Greenwood	SC	29648	864-941-4700	943-2631
TF: 866-358-3589 ■ *Web:* www.veluxusa.com					
Vicwest Corp 1296 S Service Rd W	Oakville	ON	L6L5T7	905-825-2252	825-2272
TF: 800-265-6583 ■ *Web:* www.vicwest.com					
Withers Tool Die & Mfg 1238 Veterans Memorial Hwy SE	Mableton	GA	30126	770-948-2544	
Web: www.witherstool.com					
Wolf Robotics LLC 4600 Innovation Dr	Fort Collins	CO	80525	970-225-7600	
TF: 866-965-3911 ■ *Web:* www.wolfrobotics.com					
Wooster Products Inc 1000 Spruce St PO Box 6005	Wooster	OH	44691	330-264-2844	262-4151
TF: 800-321-4936 ■ *Web:* www.wooster-products.com					

495 METALS SERVICE CENTERS

Company	City	State	ZIP	Phone	Fax
101 Pipe & Casing Inc 30101 Agoura Ct Ste 201	Agoura Hills	CA	91301	818-707-9101	
Web: www.101pipe.com					

Company	City	State	ZIP	Phone	Fax
A & B Aluminum & Brass Foundry 11165 Denton Dr *Web:* www.abfoundryonline.com	Dallas	TX	75229	972-247-3579	247-4981
A & D Constructors Inc 707 Schrader Dr *Web:* www.adconstructors.com	Evansville	IN	47712	812-428-3708	
A F K Corp 300 Pacific St *Web:* www.afkfoundry.com	Ripon	WI	54971	920-748-2265	
A&B Process Systems Corp 201 S Wisconsin Ave *Web:* www.abprocess.com	Stratford	WI	54484	715-687-4332	
A-588 & A-572 Steel Co, The 133 Sebago Lk Dr *Web:* www.a588a572steel.com	Sewickley	PA	15143	412-366-1980	366-3780
Abbott Ball Company Inc 19 Railroad Pl *Web:* www.abbottball.com	West Hartford	CT	06133	860-236-5901	
ABC Metals Inc 500 W Clinton St **Fax Area Code:* 574 ■ *TF:* 800-238-8470 ■ *Web:* www.abcmetals.com	Logansport	IN	46947	800-238-8470	753-6110*
Ability Metal Co 1355 Greenleaf Ave *Web:* abilitymetal.com	Elk Grove Village	IL	60007	847-437-7040	
Abt Foam LLC 259 Murdock Rd *Web:* www.abtdrains.com	Troutman	NC	28166	704-528-9806	
Accent Packaging Inc 10131 FM 2920 Rd *Web:* www.accentwire.com	Tomball	TX	77375	281-251-3700	
Accurate Alloys Inc 5455 Irwindale Ave *TF:* 800-842-2222 ■ *Web:* www.accuratealloys.com	Irwindale	CA	91706	626-338-4012	337-8393
Acid Piping Technology Inc 2890 Arnold Tenbrook Rd *Web:* www.acidpiping.com	Arnold	MO	63010	636-296-4668	
Acier Picard Inc 3000 Rue De L' Etchemin *TF:* 888-834-0646 ■ *Web:* www.acierpicard.com	Levis	QC	G6W7X6	418-834-8300	
Acme Metals & Steel Supply Inc 14930 S San Pedro St *Web:* www.acmemetalsonline.com	Gardena	CA	90248	310-329-2263	
Acme-Monaco Corp 75 Winchell Dr *Web:* www.acmemonaco.com	New Britain	CT	06052	860-224-1349	
Action Stainless & Alloys Inc 1505 Halsey Way *TF:* 800-749-2523 ■ *Web:* www.actionstainless.com	Carrollton	TX	75007	972-466-1500	466-0909
ACuPowder International LLC 901 Lehigh Ave *Web:* www.acupowder.com	Union	NJ	07083	908-851-4500	
Advanced Laser Machining Inc 600 Cashman Dr *Web:* www.laser27.com	Chippewa Falls	WI	54729	715-720-8093	
Advanced Support Products Inc 24227 Fm 2978 Rd *Web:* www.aspbase.com	Tomball	TX	77375	281-357-1277	357-0577
Advanced Technology Inc 6106 W Market St *Web:* www.advtechnology.com	Greensboro	NC	27409	336-668-0488	
AEB International Inc 654 Madison Ave Ste 1809 *Web:* aebint.com	New York	NY	10065	212-752-4647	
Aerex Industries Inc 3504 Industrial 27th St *Web:* www.aerexglobal.com	Ft Pierce	FL	34946	772-461-0004	
Aerospace Alloys Inc 11 Britton Dr *Web:* aalloys.com	Bloomfield	CT	06002	860-882-0019	
Akers National Roll Co 400 Railroad Ave *Web:* www.akersrolls.com	Avonmore	PA	15618	724-697-4533	
Aladdin Steel Inc PO Box 89 *TF:* 800-637-4455 ■ *Web:* www.aladdinsteel.com	Gillespie	IL	62033	217-839-2121	839-3823
Alaskan Copper & Brass Co 3223 Sixth Ave S *TF:* 800-552-7661 ■ *Web:* www.alascop.com	Seattle	WA	98134	206-623-5800	382-7335
Alcast Foundry Inc 2910 Fisk Ln *Web:* alcast.com	Redondo Beach	CA	90278	310-542-3581	
Alexandria Industries 401 County Rd 22 NW *Web:* www.alexandriaindustries.com	Alexandria	MN	56308	320-763-6537	
Alfiniti Inc 1152 rue Manic *Web:* www.alfiniti.com	Chicoutimi	QC	G7K1A2	418-696-2545	
All American Grating Inc 3001 Grand Ave *Web:* www.aagrating.com	Pittsburgh	PA	15225	412-771-6970	
All Foils Inc 16100 Imperial Pkwy *TF:* 800-521-0054 ■ *Web:* www.allfoils.com	Strongsville	OH	44149	440-572-3645	378-0161
All Metals Industries Inc PO Box 807 *TF:* 800-654-6043 ■ *Web:* www.allmetind.com	Belmont	NH	03220	603-267-7023	267-7025
All Star Metals LLC 101 Box Car Rd *Web:* www.allstarmetals.com	Brownsville	TX	78521	956-838-2110	
All State Fabricators Corp 1485 Elmwood Ave *Web:* www.emiindustries.com	Cranston	RI	02910	401-785-3900	
Alliance Corp 2395 Meadowpine Blvd *Web:* www.alliancecorporation.ca	Mississauga	ON	L5N7W6	905-821-4797	
Allied Metals Corp 1750 Stephenson Hwy *Web:* www.alliedmet.com	Troy	MI	48083	248-680-2400	
Allied Sinterings Inc 29 Briar Ridge Rd *TF:* 877-875-0464 ■ *Web:* alliedsinterings.com	Danbury	CT	06810	877-875-0464	
Alloy Surfaces Company Inc 121 N Commerce Dr Chester Township *Web:* www.alloysurfaces.com	Chester Township	PA	19014	610-497-7979	
Almet Inc 300 Hartzell Rd *Web:* www.almetinc.com	New Haven	IN	46774	260-493-1556	
Almetals Inc 51035 Grand River Ave *Web:* www.almetals.com	Wixom	MI	48393	248-348-7722	
Alro Steel Corp 3100 E High St *TF:* 800-877-2576 ■ *Web:* www.alro.com	Jackson	MI	49204	517-787-5500	787-6390
Alstate Steel Inc 203 Murry Rd Se *Web:* www.alstatesteel.com	Albuquerque	NM	87105	505-877-5454	
Alton Steel Inc Five Cut St *Web:* www.altonsteel.com	Alton	IL	62002	618-463-4490	
Alu-Bra Foundry Inc 630 E Green St *Web:* alubra.com	Bensenville	IL	60106	630-766-3112	
Alum-alloy Company Inc 603 S Hope Ave *Web:* www.webstercorp.com	Ontario	CA	91761	909-986-0410	
Alumawall Inc 1701 S Seventh St Ste 9 *Web:* www.alumawall.com	San Jose	CA	95112	408-292-6353	
Aluminum & Stainless Inc PO Box 3484 *TF:* 800-252-9074 ■ *Web:* www.aluminumandstainless.com	Lafayette	LA	70502	337-837-4381	837-5439
Aluminum Distributing 2930 Sw Second Ave *Web:* www.adimetal.com	Fort Lauderdale	FL	33315	954-523-6474	
Aluminum Extruded Shapes Inc 10549 Reading Rd *Web:* www.alum-ext.com	Cincinnati	OH	45241	513-563-2205	
Aluminum Extrusions Inc 140 Matthews Dr	Senatobia	MS	38668	662-562-6663	
Aluminum Resources Inc 789 Swan Dr *Web:* www.aluminumresources.com	Smyrna	TN	37167	615-355-6500	
Aluminum Service Inc Fl 1701 Blount Rd Bldg B *Web:* www.asibp.com	Pompano Beach	FL	33069	954-979-6774	
American Aluminum Extrusion Company LLC 1 Saint Lawrence Ave *Web:* www.americanaluminum.com	Beloit	WI	53511	608-361-1800	
American Bin & Conveyor Inc 221 Front St *Web:* www.americanconveyor.com	Burlington	WI	53105	262-763-0123	
American Chrome Co 518 W Crossroads Pkwy *Web:* www.americanchrome.com	Bolingbrook	IL	60440	630-685-2200	
American Douglas Metals Inc 783 Thorpe Rd *TF:* 800-428-0023 ■ *Web:* www.americandouglasmetals.com	Orlando	FL	32024	407-855-6590	857-3290
American Foundry Group Inc 14602 S Grant *Web:* www.americanfoundry.com	Bixby	OK	74008	918-366-4401	
American Steel & Aluminum Company Inc 3545 E Main St *Web:* www.asafab.com	Grand Prairie	TX	75050	972-264-1533	
American Steel Corp 4884 S Desert View Dr *Web:* www.americansteelcorporation.com	Apache Junction	AZ	85220	480-474-0100	
American Steel Products Inc 5620 Ne 65th Ave *Web:* www.americansteelonline.com	Portland	OR	97218	503-288-8420	
American Strip Steel Inc 901 Coopertown Rd **Fax Area Code:* 908 ■ *TF:* 800-526-1216 ■ *Web:* www.americanstrip.com	Delanco	NJ	08075	800-526-1216	412-1442*
AmeriFab Inc 3501 E Ninth St *Web:* www.amerifabinc.com	Indianapolis	IN	46201	317-231-0100	
Ameriflex Inc 2390 Railroad St *Web:* www.ameriflex.com	Corona	CA	92880	951-737-5557	
Ameritube Master Distribution LLC 1000 N Hwy 77 *Web:* www.ameritube.com	Hillsboro	TX	76645	254-580-9888	
AMI Metals Inc 1738 General George Patton Dr *TF:* 800-727-1903 ■ *Web:* www.amimetals.com	Brentwood	TN	37027	615-377-0400	377-0103
AmRod Corp 60 Pennsylvania Ave *Web:* www.amrod.com	Kearny	NJ	07032	973-344-3806	
Amsco Steel Co PO Box 11037 *TF:* 800-772-2743 ■ *Web:* www.amscosteel.com	Fort Worth	TX	76110	817-926-3355	923-2860
Amstek Metal LLC 2408 W Mcdonough *Web:* www.amstekmetal.com	Joliet	IL	60436	815-725-2520	
Amthor Steel 1717 Gaskell Ave *Web:* www.amthorsteel.com	Erie	PA	16503	814-452-4700	
Anel Corp 3244 Hwy 51 *Web:* www.anelcorp.com	Winona	MS	38967	662-283-1540	
Angstrom Sciences Inc 40 S Linden St *Web:* www.angstromsciences.com	Duquesne	PA	15110	412-469-8466	
Apel Steel Corp 2345 Second Ave NW *Web:* www.apelsteel.net	Cullman	AL	35058	256-739-6280	
Apex Spring & Stamping Corp 11420 First Ave NW *Web:* www.apexspring.com	Grand Rapids	MI	49534	616-453-5463	
Applied Laser Technologies 8404 Venture Cir *Web:* www.aplaser.com	Schofield	WI	54476	715-359-3002	
Arbon Steel & Service Co Inc 2355 Bond St *Web:* www.arbonsteel.com	University Park	IL	60484	708-534-6800	534-6826
ArcelorMittal Burns Harbor LLC 250 W US Hwy 12 *Web:* www.arcelormittal.com	Burns Harbor	IN	46304	219-787-2120	
Aristo Cast Inc 7400 Research Dr *Web:* www.aristo-cast.com	Almont	MI	48003	810-798-2900	
Ark Technologies Inc 3655 Ohio Ave *Web:* www.arktechno.com	Saint Charles	IL	60174	630-377-8855	
Arkansas Steel Associates LLC 2803 Van Dyke Rd *Web:* www.arkansassteel.com	Newport	AR	72112	870-523-3693	
Arnold Steel Company Inc 79 Randolph Rd *Web:* www.arnoldsteel.com	Howell	NJ	07731	732-363-1079	
Art Iron Inc 860 Curtis St *TF:* 800-472-1113 ■ *Web:* www.artiron.com	Toledo	OH	43609	419-241-1261	725-2027
Artistica Metal Designs Inc 3200 Golf Course Dr *Web:* artisticahome.com/	Ventura	CA	93003	805-850-1100	
ASA Alloys Inc 81 Steinway Blvd *Web:* www.asaalloys.com	Etobicoke	ON	M9W6H6	416-213-0000	213-9507
Astralloy Steel Products Inc 1550 Red Hollow Rd *Web:* www.astralloy.com	Birmingham	AL	35215	205-853-0300	
Astro Shapes Inc 65 Main St *Web:* www.astroshapes.com	Struthers	OH	44471	330-755-1414	
Atlantic Cordage Corp 35 Mileed Way *Web:* www.atlantic-group.com	Avenel	NJ	07001	732-574-0700	
Atlas Bronze 445 Bunting Ave *Web:* www.atlasbronze.com	Trenton	NJ	08611	609-599-1402	
Atlas Steel Products Co 7990 Bavaria Rd *TF:* 800-444-1682 ■ *Web:* www.atlassteel.com	Twinsburg	OH	44087	330-425-1600	425-1611
ATW Companies Inc 55 Service Ave *Web:* www.atwcompanies.com	Warwick	RI	02886	401-244-1002	

Company	City	State	ZIP	Phone	Fax
Aviotrade Inc 10850 NW 21st St Ste 230 & 240 *Web:* www.aviotrade.com	Miami	FL	33172	305-717-5000	
B E Peterson Inc 40 Murphy Dr Avon Industrial Pk *Web:* www.bepeterson.com	Avon	MA	02322	508-436-7900	
B&S Aircraft Alloys Inc 10 Aerial Way *Web:* www.bsaa.com	Syosset	NY	11791	516-681-2400	
Baldwin Intl 30403 Bruce Industrial Pkwy *Web:* www.baldwininternational.com	Solon	OH	44139	440-248-9500	
Bapko Metal Fabricators Inc 838 N Cypress St *Web:* www.bapko.com	Orange	CA	92867	714-639-9380	
Basic Metals Inc W180 Nn11819 River Ln *TF:* 800-989-1996 ■ *Web:* www.basicmetals.com	Germantown	WI	53022	262-255-9034	255-9073
BC Wire Rope & Rigging 2720 E Regal Park Dr *Web:* www.bcwirerope.com	Anaheim	CA	92806	714-666-8000	
Beaver Steel Services Inc 1200 Arch St *Web:* www.beaversteel.com	Carnegie	PA	15106	412-429-8860	
Beck Aluminum Corp 300 Allen Bradley Dr *Web:* www.beckaluminum.com	Mayfield Heights	OH	44124	216-861-4455	
Bee Steel Inc 2090 Celebration Dr Ste 209 *Web:* www.beesteelinc.com	Grand Rapids	MI	49525	616-363-6694	
Behringer Corp 17 Ridge Rd *Web:* www.behringersystems.com	Branchville	NJ	07826	973-948-0226	
Bell Foundry Co 5310 Southern Ave *Web:* www.bfco.com	Southgate	CA	90280	323-564-5701	
Belmont Metals Inc 330 Belmont Ave *Web:* www.belmontmetals.com	Brooklyn	NY	11207	718-342-4900	
Benner Metals Corp 1220 S State College Blvd *Web:* www.bennermetals.com	Fullerton	CA	92831	714-879-6477	
Berg Steel Corp 4306 Normandy Ct *Web:* www.bergsteel.com	Royal Oak	MI	48073	248-549-6066	549-1374
Bergkamp Inc 3040 Emulsion Dr *Web:* www.bergkampinc.com	Salina	KS	67401	785-825-1375	
Berlin Metals LLC 3200 Sheffield Ave *TF:* 800-754-8867 ■ *Web:* www.berlinmetals.com	Hammond	IN	46327	219-933-0111	933-0692
Berntsen Brass & Aluminum Foundry Inc 2334 Pennsylvania Ave *Web:* www.berntsen-foundry.com	Madison	WI	53704	608-249-9233	
Berry Metal Co 2408 Evans City Rd *Web:* www.berrymetal.com	Harmony	PA	16037	724-452-8040	
Betz Industries Inc 2121 Bristol Ave NW *Web:* www.betzindustries.com	Grand Rapids	MI	49504	616-453-4429	
Blackburn's Fabrication Inc 2467 Jackson Pk *Web:* blackburnsfab.com	Columbus	OH	43223	614-875-0784	
Blattner Steel Company Inc 2100 Rust Ave *Web:* www.blattnersteel.com	Cape Girardeau	MO	63703	573-339-1129	
Bluescope Steel Americas LLC 111 W Ocean Blvd Ste 1370 *Web:* www.bhpsteel.com	Long Beach	CA	90802	562-491-1441	
BMG Metals Inc 950 Masonic Ln *TF:* 800-552-1510 ■ *Web:* www.bmgmetals.com	Richmond	VA	23231	804-226-1024	222-3693
Boardman Inc 1135 S McKinley Ave *Web:* www.boardmaninc.com	Oklahoma City	OK	73108	405-634-5434	
Bobco Metals Co 2000 S Alameda St *TF:* 877-952-6226 ■ *Web:* bobcometal.com	Los Angeles	CA	90058	877-952-6226	
Bodine Aluminum Inc 2100 Walton Rd *Web:* www.bodinealuminum.com	St. Louis	MO	63114	314-423-8200	
Bohler-Uddeholm North America 2505 Millenium Dr *TF:* 800-638-2520 ■ *Web:* www.bucorp.com	Elgin	IL	60124	630-883-3100	883-3101
Bolduc Leroux Inc 3365 des Entreprises Blvd *Web:* www.bolducleroux.ca	Terrebonne	QC	J6X4J9	450-477-3413	
Bowers Manufacturing Co 6565 S Sprinkle Rd *Web:* www.bowers-mfg.com	Portage	MI	49002	269-323-2565	
Briteline Extrusions Inc 575 Beech Hill Rd *Web:* www.briteline.net	Summerville	SC	29485	843-873-4410	
Brodhead Steel Products Co 143 S Linden Ave *Web:* www.brodheadsteel.com	South San Francisco	CA	94080	650-871-8251	
Brown-Strauss Steel 2495 Uravan St *TF Sales:* 800-677-2778 ■ *Web:* www.brown-strauss.com	Aurora	CO	80011	303-371-2200	375-8122
BRT Extrusions Inc 1818 N Main St *Web:* www.brtextrusions.com	Niles	OH	44446	330-544-0244	
C & K Johnson Industries Inc 1061 Samoa Blvd *Web:* www.ckjohnsonind.com	Arcata	CA	95521	707-822-7687	
California Steel Services Inc 1212 S Mtn View Ave *Web:* www.calsteel.com	San Bernardino	CA	92408	909-796-2222	
Camalloy Inc 1960 N Main St *Web:* www.camalloy.com	Washington	PA	15301	724-222-2022	
Cambridge Street Metal Corp (CSM) 82 Stevens St *TF:* 800-254-7580 ■ *Web:* www.csmetal.net	East Taunton	MA	02718	508-822-2278	822-4667
Canada Pipe Company Ltd 1757 Burlington St E PO Box 2849 *Web:* www.canadapipe.com	Hamilton	ON	L8N3R5	905-547-3251	
Capitol Steel & Iron LLC 1726 S Agnew *Web:* www.capitol-steel.com	Oklahoma City	OK	73108	405-632-7710	
Carfaro Inc 2075 E State St *Web:* www.carfaro.com	Trenton	NJ	08619	609-890-6600	
Carley Foundry Inc 8301 Coral Sea St Ne *Web:* www.carleyfoundry.com	Blaine	MN	55449	763-780-5123	
Central Metal Fabricators Inc 900 Sw 70th Ave *Web:* www.centralmetalfab.com	Miami	FL	33144	305-261-6262	
Central Metals Inc 1054 S Second St *Web:* www.centralmetals.com	Camden	NJ	08103	856-963-5844	
Central States Industrial Supply Inc 8720 S 137th Cir *Web:* www.centralstatesgroup.com	Omaha	NE	68138	402-894-1003	
Century Foundry Inc 339 W Hovey Ave *Web:* www.centuryfoundry.com	Muskegon	MI	49444	231-733-1572	
CERTEX USA Inc 1721 W Culver St *Web:* www.certex.com	Phoenix	AZ	85007	602-271-9048	
CFC Canadoil Inc 8000 Market St Ste 100 *Web:* www.cfcfittings.com	Houston	TX	77029	713-676-0077	
Charleston Aluminum LLC 480 Frontage Rd *Web:* www.charlestonaluminum.com	Gaston	SC	29053	803-939-4600	
Charter Steel Trading Company Inc 4401 W Roosevelt Rd *Web:* www.chartersteeltrading.com	Chicago	IL	60624	773-522-3100	
Chatham Steel Corp 501 W Boundary St *TF:* 800-800-1337 ■ *Web:* www.chathamsteel.com	Savannah	GA	31401	912-233-5751	944-0236
Cherokee Steel Supply 196 Leroy Anderson Dr *Web:* www.cherokeesteel.com	Monroe	GA	30655	770-207-4621	
Chicago Tube & Iron Co One Chicago Tube Dr *TF Cust Svc:* 800-972-0217 ■ *Web:* www.chicagotube.com	Romeoville	IL	60446	815-834-2500	588-3958
Chickasaw Distributors Inc 800 Bering Dr Ste 330 *Web:* www.chickasawdistributors.com	Houston	TX	77057	713-974-2905	974-3109
City Pipe & Supply Corp PO Box 2112 *TF:* 844-307-4044 ■ *Web:* www.citypipe.com	Odessa	TX	79760	432-332-1541	333-2300
Classic Sheet Metal Inc 1065 Sesame St *Web:* www.classic-sheet-metal.com	Franklin Park	IL	60131	630-694-0300	
Clayton Metals Inc 546 Clayton Ct *Fax Area Code: 630 ■ *TF:* 800-323-7628 ■ *Web:* www.claytonmetals.com	Wood Dale	IL	60191	800-323-7628	860-1053*
Cleveland Steel Container Corp 1840 Enterprise Pkwy *Web:* www.cscpails.com	Twinsburg	OH	44087	330-405-3000	
CMC Rebar 4846 Singleton Blvd *Web:* www.cmc.com	Dallas	TX	75212	214-428-2861	
Coast Aluminum & Architectural Inc 30551 Huntwood Ave *Web:* www.coastaluminum.com	Hayward	CA	94544	510-441-6600	
Coastal Corrosion Control Surveys LLC 10172 Mammoth Ave *Web:* www.coastalcorrosion.com	Baton Rouge	LA	70814	225-275-6131	
Coilplus Ohio Inc 4801 Gateway Blvd *Web:* coilplusohio.com	Springfield	OH	45502	937-322-4455	
Coilplus Pennsylvania Inc 5135 Bleigh St *Web:* www.coilplus.com	Philadelphia	PA	19136	215-331-5200	331-9538
Col Pump Company Inc 131 E Railroad St *Web:* www.col-pump.net	Columbiana	OH	44408	330-482-1029	
Colby Metal Inc 701 Industrial Dr *Web:* www.colbymetal.com	Colby	WI	54421	715-223-2334	
Collins & Hermann Inc 1215 Dunn Rd *Web:* www.collinsandhermann.com	St. Louis	MO	63138	314-869-8000	
Columbia Pipe & Supply Co 1120 W Pershing Rd *TF:* 888-429-4635 ■ *Web:* www.columbiapipe.com	Chicago	IL	60609	773-927-6600	927-8415
Columbia Steel Inc 2175 N Linden Ave *Web:* www.columbiasteelinc.com	Rialto	CA	92377	909-874-8840	
Columbus Pipe & Equipment Co 773 E Markison Ave *Web:* www.columbuspipe.com	Columbus	OH	43207	614-444-7871	
Conestoga Supply Corp 11011 Sheldon Rd *Fax Area Code: 281 ■ *Web:* www.conestogasupply.com	Houston	TX	77044	832-391-9431	456-7574*
Connect-Air International Inc 4240 'B' St NW *Web:* www.connect-air.com	Auburn	WA	98001	253-813-5599	
Connector Specialists Inc 175 James Dr E *Web:* www.connectorspecialists.com	St Rose	LA	70087	504-469-1659	
Consolidated Pipe & Supply Inc 1205 Hilltop Pkwy *TF Sales:* 800-467-7261 ■ *Web:* www.consolidatedpipe.com	Birmingham	AL	35204	205-323-7261	251-7838
Consolidated Steel Services Inc 632 Glendale Vly Blvd *TF:* 800-237-8783 ■ *Web:* www.csteel.com	Fallentimber	PA	16639	814-944-5890	943-8278
Constellium Automotive USA LLC 46555 Magellan Dr *Web:* www.constellium.com	Novi	MI	48377	248-668-3200	
Consumers Pipe & Supply Co 5832 E 61st St *TF:* 800-338-7473 ■ *Web:* www.consumerspipe.com	Los Angeles	CA	90040	323-685-6870	724-3781
Continental Casting LLC 801 Second St *Web:* www.continentalcasting.com	Monroe City	MO	63456	573-735-4577	
Contractors Steel Co 36555 Amrhein Rd *Fax: Sales ■ *TF:* 800-521-3946 ■ *Web:* www.contractorssteel.com	Livonia	MI	48150	734-464-4000	452-3939*
CORPAC Steel Products Corp 20803 Biscayne Blvd Ste 502 *Web:* www.corpacsteel.com	Miami	FL	33180	305-918-0540	
Couturier Iron Craft Inc 5050 W River Dr Ne *Web:* www.couturierironcraft.com	Comstock Park	MI	49321	616-784-6780	
Crestwood Tubulars Inc 9962 Lin-Ferry Dr Ste 207 *Web:* www.crestwoodtubulars.com	St. Louis	MO	63123	314-842-8604	
Crown Extrusions Inc 122 Columbia Court N *Web:* www.crownextrusions.com	Chaska	MN	55318	952-448-3533	
CSC Inc 1109 Court St *Web:* www.medfab.com	Medford	OR	97501	541-779-1970	
Cullman Casting Corp 251 County Rd 490 *Web:* www.cullmancasting.com	Cullman	AL	35055	256-735-0900	
Cumberland Steel Div 4919 Grant Ave *Web:* www.cumberlandind.com	Cleveland	OH	44125	216-441-1800	
Damascus Steel Casting Co Blockhouse Rd Run Extn *TF:* 800-920-2210 ■ *Web:* www.damascussteel.com	New Brighton	PA	15066	724-846-2770	

Company	City	State	ZIP	Phone	Fax
Dameron Alloy Foundries Inc 927 S Santa Fe Ave *Web:* www.dameron.net	Compton	CA	90224	310-631-5165	
Decker Steel & Supply Inc 4500 Train Ave *TF:* 800-321-6100 ■ *Web:* www.deckersteel.com	Cleveland	OH	44102	216-281-7900	281-1441
Delta Metals Company Inc 1388 N Seventh St *Web:* www.delta-metals.com	Memphis	TN	38107	901-525-5000	575-3322
DenCol 4630 Washington St *Web:* www.dencol.com	Denver	CO	80216	303-295-1683	295-1689
Dennis Steel Inc 1105 Leander Dr *Web:* www.dennissteel.com	Leander	TX	78641	512-259-4001	259-1070
Doherty Steel Inc 21110 W 311th St *Web:* www.dohertysteel.com	Paola	KS	66071	913-557-9200	
Domtech Inc 40 East Davis St *Web:* www.domtech.net	Trenton	ON	K8V6S4	613-394-4884	394-0108
Double Eagle Steel Coating Co 3000 Miller Rd *Web:* www.descc.com	Dearborn	MI	48120	313-203-9800	
Dubose National Energy Services Inc PO Box 499 *TF:* 800-590-2150 ■ *Web:* www.dubosenes.com	Clinton	NC	28329	910-590-2151	590-3444
Duhig & Company Inc 5071 Telegraph Rd *Web:* www.duhig.com	Los Angeles	CA	90022	323-263-7161	263-7161
DW Clark Inc 692 N Bedford St *Web:* www.dwclark.com	East Bridgewater	MA	02333	508-378-4014	
E-J Enterprises Inc 7280 Baltimore Annapolis Blvd	Glen Burnie	MD	21061	410-625-8200	
Eagle Stainless Tube & Fabrication Inc 10 Discovery Way *Web:* www.eagletube.com	Franklin	MA	02038	508-528-8650	
Eagle Steel Products Inc 3420 Collins Ln *Web:* www.eaglesteelproducts.com	Louisville	KY	40245	502-241-6004	
East Coast Metal Distributors Inc 1313 S Briggs Ave *Web:* www.ecmdi.com	Durham	NC	27703	919-598-5030	598-1404
East Coast Metals 171 Ruth Rd *Web:* eastcoastmetals.com	Harleysville	PA	19438	215-256-9550	
Eastern Metal Supply Inc 3600 23rd Ave S *Web:* www.easternmetal.com	Lake Worth	FL	33461	561-533-6061	
Eaton Fabricating CoInc 1009 McAlpin Ct *Web:* www.eatonfabricating.com	Grafton	OH	44044	440-926-3121	
Eaton Steel Corp 10221 Capital Ave *TF:* 800-527-3851 ■ *Web:* www.eatonsteel.com	Oak Park	MI	48237	248-398-3434	398-3434
Ed Fagan Inc 769 Susquehanna Ave *TF:* 800-335-6827 ■ *Web:* www.edfagan.com	Franklin Lakes	NJ	07417	201-891-4003	891-3207
Edwards Steel Structural Div 1777 Mckinley Ave	Columbus	OH	43222	614-274-6800	
Effort Foundry Inc 6980 Chrisphalt Dr *Web:* www.effortfoundry.com	Bath	PA	18014	610-837-1837	
Electrosteel USA LLC 270 Doug Baker Blvd *Web:* www.electrosteelusa.com	Birmingham	AL	35242	205-516-8154	
Engineered Building Products Inc 18 Southwood Dr *Web:* www.ebpfab.com	Bloomfield	CT	06002	860-243-1110	
Erickson Metals Corp 25 Knotter Dr *Web:* www.ericksonmetals.com	Cheshire	CT	06410	203-272-2918	
Erie Steel Treating Inc 5540 Jackman Rd *Web:* www.erie.com	Toledo	OH	43613	419-478-3743	
Everglades Steel Corp 5901 NW 74th Ave *Web:* www.evergladessteel.com	Miami	FL	33166	305-591-9460	
Exploreco International LLC 11930 S Sam Houston Parkway East *Web:* www.exploreco.com	Houston	TX	77089	713-796-6000	
Express Contracting 420 Milam *Web:* www.expressmetalwork.com	San Antonio	TX	78202	210-337-2260	
Extruded Aluminum Corp 7200 Industrial Dr *Web:* www.extrudedaluminum.com	Belding	MI	48809	616-794-0300	
Extrudex Aluminum Ltd 411 Chrislea Rd *Web:* www.extrudex.com	Woodbridge	ON	L4L8N4	416-745-4444	
F M C of Plymouth Ohio Inc 500 Donnenwirth Dr *Web:* www.fetzermfg.com	Plymouth	OH	44865	419-687-8237	
FabArc Steel Supply Inc 111 Meadow Ln *Web:* www.fabarc.com	Oxford	AL	36203	256-831-8770	
Fairmount Foundry Inc 25 Second Ave *Web:* fairmountfdry.com	Woonsocket	RI	02895	401-769-1585	
Farwest Steel Corp 2000 Henderson Ave **Fax:* Hum Res ■ *Web:* www.farweststeel.com	Eugene	OR	97403	541-686-2000	681-7250*
Fay Industries Inc 17200 Foltz Pkwy *Web:* www.fayindustries.com	Strongsville	OH	44149	440-572-5030	
Federal Steel Supply Inc 747 Goddard Ave PO Box 840 *Web:* www.fedsteel.com	Chesterfield	MO	63005	636-537-2393	
Fehr Bros Industries Inc 895 Kings Hwy *Web:* endurancehardware.com	Saugerties	NY	12477	845-246-9525	
Feralloy Corp 8755 W Higgins Rd Ste 970 *Web:* www.feralloy.com	Chicago	IL	60631	773-380-1500	380-1535
Field System Machining Inc 720 Schneider Dr *Web:* www.fieldsystems.com	South Elgin	IL	60177	847-468-1313	
Flack Steel Ltd 425 W Lakeside Ave Ste 200 *Web:* www.flacksteel.com	Cleveland	OH	44113	216-456-0700	
Fotofabrication Corp 3758 W Belmont Ave *Web:* www.fotofab.com	Chicago	IL	60618	773-463-6211	
Fox Valley Spring Company Inc N915 Craftsmen Dr *Web:* www.foxvalleyspring.com	Greenville	WI	54942	920-757-7777	
Francis Manufacturing Co 2200 Russia Versailles Rd *Web:* www.francismanufacturing.com	Russia	OH	45363	937-526-4551	
Frontier Aluminum Corp 2480 Railroad St *Web:* www.frontier-aluminum.com	Corona	CA	92880	951-735-1770	
Frontier Steel Company Inc 4990 Grand Ave *Web:* www.frontiersteel.com	Pittsburgh	PA	15225	412-865-4444	865-0030
Fry Steel Company Inc 13325 Molette St *Web:* www.frysteel.com	Santa Fe Springs	CA	90670	562-802-2721	
G & L Manufacturing Inc 1975 Fisk Rd *Web:* www.glmanufacturing.com	Cookeville	TN	38506	931-528-1732	
G B C Inc 190 S Union Blvd *Web:* www.gbcinc.com	Lakewood	CO	80228	303-988-6450	
Galesburg Castings Inc 940 Ave C St *Web:* www.galesburgcastings.com	Galesburg	IL	61401	309-343-6178	
Garston Sign & Screen Printing 570 Tolland St *Web:* www.garston.com	East Hartford	CT	06108	860-289-3040	
Gayle Manufacturing Company Inc 1455 E Kentucky Ave *Web:* www.gaylemfg.com	Woodland	CA	95776	530-662-0284	
GB Tubulars Inc 1444 Blalock Rd *Web:* www.gbtubulars.com	Houston	TX	77055	713-465-3585	
General Steel Inc PO Box 1503 *TF:* 800-476-2794 ■ *Web:* www.steeldeal.com	Macon	GA	31202	478-746-2794	745-8136
Genesis Products Inc 2608 Almac Ct *Web:* www.genesisproductsinc.com	Elkhart	IN	46514	574-266-8292	
George Industries Inc One S Page St *Web:* www.georgeindustries.com	Endicott	NY	13760	607-748-3371	
Gerber Metal Supply Co 2 Boundary Rd **Fax Area Code:* 905 ■ *Web:* www.gerbermetal.com	Somerville	NJ	08876	908-823-9150	823-9160*
Gibbs Wire & Steel Company Inc Metals Dr PO Box 520 *TF:* 800-800-4422 ■ *Web:* www.gibbswire.com	Southington	CT	06489	860-621-0121	628-7780
Gilchrist Metal Fabricating Company Inc 18 Park Ave *Web:* www.gmfco.com	Hudson	NH	03051	603-889-2600	
Girard Machine Company Inc 700 Dot St *Web:* www.girardmachine.com	Girard	OH	44420	330-545-9731	
Glidewell Specialties Foundry Company Inc 600 Foundry Rd *Web:* www.glidewell-foundry.com	Calera	AL	35040	205-668-1881	
Global Brass & Copper Inc 475 N Martingale Rd Ste 1050 *Web:* www.gbcmetals.com	Schaumburg	IL	60173	847-240-4700	
Globe Iron Foundry Inc 5649 E Randolph St *Web:* www.globeiron.com	Commerce	CA	90040	323-723-8983	
GlobeNet Metals LLC 33755 N Scottsdale Rd Ste 110 *Web:* www.globenetmetals.com	Scottsdale	AZ	85266	480-575-3221	
Golden Aluminum Inc 1405 E 14th St *Web:* goldenaluminum.com	Fort Lupton	CO	80621	303-659-9767	
Gordon Aluminum Industries Inc 1000 Mason St *Web:* www.gordonaluminum.com	Schofield	WI	54476	715-359-6101	
Granite Industries Inc 595 E Lugbill Rd *Web:* www.graniteind.com	Archbold	OH	43502	419-445-4733	
Graphicast Inc 36 Knight St *Web:* www.graphicast.com	Jaffrey	NH	03452	603-532-4481	
Greenpoint Metals Inc 301 Shotwell Dr *Web:* www.greenpointmetals.com	Franklin	OH	45005	937-743-4075	
Griggs Steel Company Inc 1200 Souter Dr *Web:* www.griggssteel.com	Troy	MI	48083	248-298-0540	
H5 Colo 12712 Park Central Dr Ste 200 *Web:* www.h5colo.com	Dallas	TX	75251	469-533-0270	
Hanna Steel Corp 3812 Commerce Ave PO Box 558 *TF:* 800-633-8252 ■ *Web:* www.hannasteel.com	Fairfield	AL	35064	205-780-1111	783-8368
Hansen Architectural Systems 5500 Se Alexander St *Web:* aluminumrailing.com	Hillsboro	OR	97123	503-356-0959	
Harbor Steel & Supply Corp 1115 E Broadway *Web:* www.harborsteel.com	Muskegon	MI	49444	231-739-7152	
Hardwire LLC 1947 Clarke Ave *Web:* www.hardwirellc.com	Pocomoke City	MD	21851	410-957-3669	
Hascall Steel Co 4165 Spartan Industrial Dr *Web:* www.hascallsteel.com	Grandville	MI	49418	616-531-8600	
Haven Steel Products Inc 13206 S Willison Rd *Web:* www.havensteel.com	Haven	KS	67543	620-465-2573	
Hawk Steel Industries Inc 4010 S Eden Rd *Web:* www.hawksteel.com	Kennedale	TX	76060	817-483-7511	516-0200
Helfrich Bros Boiler Works Inc 39 Merrimack St *Web:* www.hbbwinc.com	Lawrence	MA	01843	978-683-7244	
Howard Precision Metals Inc PO Box 240127 *TF:* 800-444-0311 ■ *Web:* www.howardprecision.com	Milwaukee	WI	53224	414-355-9611	355-2637
Hugo Neu Corp 120 Fifth Ave Ste 600 *Web:* www.hugoneu.com	New York	NY	10011	646-467-6700	
Hynes Industries 3760 Oakwood **Fax Area Code:* 330 ■ *TF:* 800-321-9257 ■ *Web:* www.hynesindustries.com	Youngstown	OH	44515	800-321-9257	799-9098*
Hyprescon Inc 699 Boul Industriel *Web:* www.hyprescon.com	Saint-eustache	QC	J7R6C3	450-623-2200	
Hytech Spring & Machine Corp 950 Lincoln Pkwy *Web:* www.hytechspring.com	Plainwell	MI	49080	269-685-1768	
Ideal Manufacturing Inc 2011 Harnish Blvd *Web:* www.idealmfginc.com	Billings	MT	59101	406-656-4360	
IMS Buhrke-Olson 511 W Algonquin Rd *Web:* www.buhrke.com	Arlington Heights	IL	60005	847-981-7550	
Independence Tube Corp 6226 W 74th St *Web:* www.independencetube.com	Chicago	IL	60638	708-496-0380	
Industrial Door Contractors Inc 820 Mayberry Springs Rd *Web:* www.hangardoor.com	Columbia	TN	38401	931-380-0463	

Company	City	State	Zip	Phone	Fax
Industrial Material Corp 7701 Harborside Dr *Web:* www.industrialmaterial.com	Galveston	TX	77554	409-744-4538	744-1844
International Mold Steel Inc 6796 Powerline Dr *Web:* www.imsteel.com	Florence	KY	41042	859-342-6000	
Iowa Spring Manufacturing & Sales Co 2112 Greene St *Web:* www.iowaspring.com	Adel	IA	50003	515-993-4791	
Ironco Enterprises LLC 1025 E Broadway Rd *Web:* www.ironco.net	Phoenix	AZ	85040	602-243-5750	
J & E Earll Manufacturing 4500 Vly Industrial Blvd S *Web:* www.nybo.com	Shakopee	MN	55379	952-445-4500	
J Rubin & Company Inc 305 Peoples Ave *Web:* rockfordconsulting.com	Rockford	IL	61104	815-964-9471	
JDH Pacific Inc 15301 S Blackburn Ave *TF:* 800-818-9335 ■ *Web:* www.jdhpacific.com	Norwalk	CA	90650	562-926-8088	926-8066
John Sakash Company Inc 700 Walnut St *Web:* www.johnsakash.com	Elmhurst	IL	60126	630-833-3940	
JT Fennell Company Inc 1104 N Front St	Chillicothe	IL	61523	309-274-2145	
Kaiser Aluminum Canada Ltd 3021 Gore Rd *Web:* www.kaiseral.com	London	ON	N5V5A9	519-457-3610	
Kansas City Structural Steel Inc 3801 Raytown Rd *Web:* www.kcstructuralsteel.com	Kansas City	MO	64129	816-924-0977	
Kasco Fab Inc 4529 S Chestnut Ave	Fresno	CA	93725	559-442-1018	
Kemeny Overseas Products Corp The Civic Opera Bldg 20 N Wacker Dr Ste 1028 *Web:* www.kemenyoverseas.com	Chicago	IL	60606	312-857-0844	
Ken-Mac Metals Inc 17901 Englewood Dr *TF:* 800-831-9503 ■ *Web:* www.tkmna.com	Cleveland	OH	44130	440-234-7500	234-4459
Kenwal Steel Corp 8223 W Warren Ave *Web:* www.kenwal.com	Dearborn	MI	48126	313-739-1000	739-1001
Key Bellevilles Inc 100 Key Ln *Web:* www.keybellevilles.com	Leechburg	PA	15656	724-295-5111	
Keystone Profiles Ltd 220 Seventh Ave *Web:* www.keystoneprofiles.com	Beaver Falls	PA	15010	724-506-1500	
KGS Steel Inc 3725 Pine Ln *TF:* 800-533-3846 ■ *Web:* www.kgssteel.com	Bessemer	AL	35022	205-425-0800	
Kirsh Foundry Inc 125 Rowell St *Web:* www.kirshfoundry.com	Beaver Dam	WI	53916	920-887-0395	
Kivort Steel 380 Hudson River Rd *TF:* 800-462-2616 ■ *Web:* www.kivortsteel.com	Waterford	NY	12188	518-590-7233	235-2042
Klein Steel Service 105 Vanguarden Pkwy *TF Cust Svc:* 800-477-6789 ■ *Web:* www.kleinsteel.com	Rochester	NY	14606	585-328-4000	328-0470
KobeWieland Copper Products LLC 3990 US 311 Hwy N *Web:* www.wielandcopper.com	Pine Hall	NC	27042	336-445-4500	
Kovatch Castings Inc 3743 Tabs Dr *Web:* www.kovatchcastings.com	Uniontown	OH	44685	330-896-9944	
Kreher Steel Company LLC 1550 N 25th Ave **Fax Area Code:* 708 ■ *TF:* 800-323-0745 ■ *Web:* www.kreher.com	Melrose Park	IL	60160	800-323-0745	345-8293*
L Smith Cooper International Inc 2867 Vail Ave *Web:* www.smithcooper.com	Commerce	CA	90040	323-890-4455	890-4456
Laclede Chain Manufacturing Company LLC 1549 Fenpark Dr *Web:* www.lacledechain.com	Fenton	MO	63026	636-680-2320	
Laibe Corp 1414 Bates St *Web:* www.laibecorp.com	Indianapolis	IN	46201	317-231-2250	
Landmann Wire Rope Products Inc 1818 Gilbreth Rd Ste 148 *Web:* www.landmannwire.com	Burlingame	CA	94010	650-777-4210	
Lane Steel Co Inc 4 River Rd *Web:* www.lanesteel.com	McKees Rocks	PA	15136	412-777-1700	777-1709
Lapham-Hickey Steel Corp 5500 W 73rd St *TF:* 800-323-8443 ■ *Web:* www.lapham-hickey.com	Chicago	IL	60638	708-496-6111	496-8504
Latrobe Specialty Steel Co 2626 Ligonier St **Fax Area Code:* 302 ■ *Web:* www.cartech.com	Latrobe	PA	15650	724-537-7711	636-5454*
Lawler Foundry Corp 4908 Powell Ave S *Web:* www.lawlerfoundry.com	Birmingham	AL	35222	205-595-0596	
Lee Steel Corp 45525 Grand River Ave *Web:* www.leesteelcorp.com	Novi	MI	48374	313-925-2100	
LeMar Industries Corp 2070 NE 60th Ave *Web:* www.lemarindustries.com	Des Moines	IA	50313	515-266-7264	
Lexington Steel Corp 5443 W 70th Pl *Web:* www.lexsteel.com	Bedford Park	IL	60638	708-594-9200	594-5233
Liberty Casting Company LLC 550 S Liberty Rd *Web:* www.libertycasting.com	Delaware	OH	43015	740-363-1941	
Lindquist Steels Inc 1050 Woodend Rd **Fax Area Code:* 203 ■ *TF:* 800-243-9637 ■ *Web:* www.lindquiststeels.com	Stratford	CT	06615	800-243-9637	386-0132*
Lite Metals Co 700 N Walnut St *Web:* www.litemetals.com	Ravenna	OH	44266	330-296-6110	
Littell LLC 1211 Tower Rd *Web:* www.littell.com	Schaumburg	IL	60173	630-622-4700	
Livingston Pipe & Tube Inc 1612 Rt 4 N PO Box 300 *TF:* 800-548-7473 ■ *Web:* www.livingstonpipeandtube.com	Staunton	IL	62088	618-635-8700	635-8720
LMS Reinforcing Steel Group Inc 6320 148th St *Web:* www.lmsgroup.ca	Surrey	BC	V3S3C4	604-598-9930	
Loeffel Steel Products PO Box 2100 *Web:* www.loeffelsteel.com	Barrington	IL	60011	847-382-6770	382-2487
Loveman Steel Corp 5455 Perkins Rd **Fax Area Code:* 440 ■ *TF:* 800-568-3626 ■ *Web:* www.lovemansteel.com	Bedford Heights	OH	44146	800-568-3626	232-0914*
M C Steel Inc 2 Braco International Blvd *Web:* www.mcsteel.com	Wilder	Ky	41076	859-781-8600	
Maas-Hansen Steel Corp 2435 E 37th St PO Box 58364 **Fax Area Code:* 325 ■ *TF:* 800-647-8335 ■ *Web:* www.maashansen.com	Vernon	CA	90058	323-586-0171	586-0171*

Company	City	State	Zip	Phone	Fax
Mac Metal Sales Inc 1650 W Hwy 80 *Web:* www.macmetalsales.com	Somerset	KY	42503	606-678-8331	
Macomb Group Inc, The 6600 E 15 Mile Rd *Web:* www.macombgroup.com	Sterling Heights	MI	48312	586-274-4100	
Magic Steel Sales LLC 4242 Clay Ave SW *Web:* www.magicsteelsales.com	Grand Rapids	MI	49548	616-532-4071	
Main Steel Polishing Company Inc Two Hance Ave *Web:* www.mainsteel.com	Tinton Falls	NJ	07724	732-345-7310	
Majestic Steel USA 5300 Majestic Pkwy *TF:* 800-321-5590 ■ *Web:* www.majesticsteel.com	Cleveland	OH	44146	440-786-2666	786-0576
Mandel Metals Inc 11400 W Addison Ave *Web:* www.mandelmetals.com	Franklin Park	IL	60131	847-455-6606	
Manzi Metals Inc 15293 Flight Path Dr *Web:* www.manzimetals.com	Brooksville	FL	34604	352-799-8211	
Marchant Schmidt Inc 24 W Larsen Dr *Web:* www.marchantschmidt.net	Fond Du Lac	WI	54937	920-921-4760	
Marks Metal Technology Inc 10300 Se Jennifer St *Web:* www.marksmetal.com	Clackamas	OR	97015	503-656-0901	
Marmon/Keystone Corp PO Box 992 *TF:* 800-544-1748 ■ *Web:* www.marmonkeystone.com	Butler	PA	16003	724-283-3000	283-0558
Maruichi American Corp 11529 Greenstone Ave *Web:* www.macsfs.com	Santa Fe Springs	CA	90670	562-903-8600	
Masterloy Products Ltd 5663 Doncaster Rd *Web:* www.masterloy.com	Ottawa	ON	K1G3N4	613-822-1010	
Matenaer Corp 810 Schoenhaar Dr *TF:* 800-254-0873 ■ *Web:* www.matenaer.com	West Bend	WI	53090	262-338-0700	338-3491
Mattsco Supply Co 1111 N 161st E Ave *Web:* www.mattsco.org	Tulsa	OK	74116	918-836-0451	
Maumee Valley Fabricators 4801 Bennett Rd *Web:* www.maumeevalleyfab.com	Toledo	OH	43612	419-476-1411	
Mazel & Company Inc 4300 W Ferdinand St *TF:* 800-525-4023 ■ *Web:* www.mazelandco.com	Chicago	IL	60624	773-533-1600	533-9490
McLanahan Corp 200 Wall St *Web:* www.mclanahan.com	Hollidaysburg	PA	16648	814-695-9807	
McNichols Co 9401 Corporate Lake Dr **Fax Area Code:* 813 ■ *TF:* 877-884-4653 ■ *Web:* www.mcnichols.com	Tampa	FL	33634	877-884-4653	243-1888*
Mead Metals Inc 555 Cardigan Rd *Web:* www.meadmetals.com	St. Paul	MN	55126	651-484-1400	
Medcast Inc 596 E 200 N *Web:* www.medcast-inc.com	Warsaw	IN	46582	574-269-6142	
Medley Steel & Supply Inc 9925 Nw 116th Way *Web:* www.medleysteel.com	Medley	FL	33178	305-863-7480	
Meloon Foundries Inc 1841 Lemoyne Ave *Web:* www.meloon.com	Syracuse	NY	13208	315-454-3231	
Mercer Metals 9208 Chancellor Row *Web:* www.mercermetals.com	Dallas	TX	75247	972-790-1576	
Merfish Pipe & Supply Co PO Box 15879 *TF:* 800-869-5731 ■ *Web:* www.merfish.com	Houston	TX	77220	713-869-5731	867-0738
Merit USA 620 Clark Ave **Fax Area Code:* 925 ■ *TF:* 800-445-6374 ■ *Web:* www.meritsteel.com	Pittsburg	CA	94565	800-445-6374	427-6427*
Metal & Wire Products Co 1065 Salem Pkwy *Web:* www.metalandwire.com	Salem	OH	44460	330-332-9448	
Metal Supermarkets IP Inc 520 Abilene Dr Second Fl *TF:* 866-867-9344 ■ *Web:* www.metalsupermarkets.com	Mississauga	ON	L5T2H7	905-362-8226	
Metalcraft of Mayville Inc 1000 Metalcraft Dr *Web:* www.mtlcraft.com	Mayville	WI	53050	920-387-3150	
Metals Supply Company Ltd 5311 Clinton Dr *Web:* deltasteel.com	Houston	TX	77020	713-330-8080	
Metaltech Service Center Inc 9915 Monroe *Web:* www.metaltechsc.com	Houston	TX	77075	713-991-5100	
Metrolina Steel Inc 2601 Westinghouse Blvd *TF:* 800-849-7935 ■ *Web:* www.metrolinasteel.com	Charlotte	NC	28273	704-598-7007	897-2173
Metropolitan Alloys Corp 17385 Ryan Rd *Web:* www.metroalloys.com	Detroit	MI	48212	313-366-4443	366-9698
Michigan Extruded Aluminum Corp 205 Watts Rd *Web:* www.extrude.net	Jackson	MI	49203	517-764-5400	
Mid City Steel Fabricating Inc 115 Buchner Pl *Web:* www.mid-citysteel.com	La Crosse	WI	54603	608-782-0770	
Mid South Steel Inc 15 Welborn St *Web:* www.midsouthsteelinc.com	Pelham	AL	35124	205-663-1750	
Miller J Walter Company Brass Foundry 411 E Chestnut St *Web:* www.jwaltermiller.com	Lancaster	PA	17602	717-392-7428	
Miller Metals Service Corp 2400 Bond St *Web:* www.millermetals.com	University Park	IL	60484	708-534-7200	534-7211
Miller Technical Services Inc 7444 Haggerty Rd *Web:* www.mtsmedicalmfg.com	Canton	MI	48187	734-738-1970	
Minmetals Inc 1200 Harbor Blvd Eighth Fl *Web:* www.minmetalsusa.com	Weehawken	NJ	07086	201-809-1898	
Mitsubishi International Corp 655 Third Ave *Web:* www.mitsubishicorp.com	New York	NY	10017	212-605-2000	
Morris Bean & Co 777 E Hyde Rd *Web:* www.morrisbean.com	Yellow Springs	OH	45387	937-767-7301	
Motion Dynamics Corp 5625 Airline Rd *Web:* www.motiondc.com	Fruitport	MI	49415	231-865-7400	
Mountain States Steel Inc 325 S Geneva Rd *Web:* www.mssteel.com	Lindon	UT	84042	801-785-5085	
Mueller Metals LLC 2152 Schwartz Rd *Web:* www.muellermetals.com	San Angelo	TX	76904	325-651-9558	
MultAlloy Inc 8511 Monroe St *TF:* 800-568-9551 ■ *Web:* www.multalloy.com	Houston	TX	77061	800-568-9551	
Murphy & Nolan Inc 340 Peat St PO Box 6689 *TF:* 800-836-6385 ■ *Web:* www.murphynolan.com	Syracuse	NY	13217	315-474-8203	474-8208

Company	City	State	ZIP	Phone	Fax
Myers & Company Architectural Metals 555 Basalt Ave *Web:* www.myersandco.com	Basalt	CO	81621	970-927-4761	
Napco Steel Inc 1800 Arthur Dr. *TF:* 800-292-8010 ■ *Web:* www.napcosteel.com	West Chicago	IL	60185	630-293-1900	293-0881
National Bronze & Metals Inc 2929 W 12th St *Web:* www.nbmmetals.com	Houston	TX	77008	713-869-9600	869-0883
National Copper & Smelting Company Inc 3333 Stanwood Blvd. *Web:* www.nationaltube.com	Huntsville	AL	35811	256-859-4510	
National Electronic Alloys Inc Three Fir Ct *Web:* www.nealloys.com	Oakland	NJ	07436	201-337-9400	337-9698
National Material LP 1965 Pratt Blvd. *Web:* www.nmlp.com	Elk Grove Village	IL	60007	847-284-8464	806-4722
National Specialty Alloys LLC 18250 Keith Harrow Blvd *TF General:* 800-847-5653 ■ *Web:* www.nsalloys.com	Houston	TX	77084	281-345-2115	345-1133
National Tube Supply Co 925 Central Ave *TF:* 800-229-6872 ■ *Web:* www.nationaltubesupply.com	University Park	IL	60466	708-534-2700	534-0200
Nelsen Steel & Wire LP 9400 W Belmont Ave *Web:* www.nelsensteel.com	Franklin Park	IL	60131	847-671-9700	
New Process Steel Corp 5800 Westview Dr *TF:* 800-392-4989 ■ *Web:* www.nps.cc/?pgid=home	Houston	TX	77055	713-686-9631	686-5358
Nikkei MC Aluminum America Inc 6875 S Inwood Dr. *Web:* www.nmaluminum.net	Columbus	IN	47201	812-342-1141	
Nippon Steel USA Inc 1251 Ave of the Americas 34th Fl	New York	NY	10020	212-486-7150	593-3049
NMI Industrial Holdings Inc 8503 Weyand Ave *Web:* www.nmiindustrial.com	Sacramento	CA	95828	916-635-7030	
Noble Steel Inc 1741 W Lincoln St *Web:* www.noblesteelinc.com	Phoenix	AZ	85007	602-257-8822	
North American Steel Co 18300 Miles Ave *TF:* 800-321-9310 ■ *Web:* www.northamerican-steel.com	Cleveland	OH	44128	216-475-7300	475-6143
North Shore Steel 1566 Miles St *TF:* 877-453-3533 ■ *Web:* www.nssco.com	Houston	TX	77015	713-453-3533	671-5500
North Star BlueScope Steel LLC 6767 County Rd *Fax Area Code: 888 ■ *Web:* www.northstarbluescope.com	Delta	OH	43515	419-822-2210	822-2113*
Northeast Air Solutions Inc 3 Lopez Rd *Web:* www.air-eng.com	Wilmington	MA	01887	978-988-2000	988-2200
Northern Metal Fab Inc 510 Vandeberg St *Web:* www.nmfinc.com	Baldwin	WI	54002	715-684-3535	
Northwest Aluminum Specialties Inc 2929 W Second St *Web:* www.nwaluminum.com	The Dalles	OR	97058	541-296-6161	
Northwest Grating Products Inc 9230 Fourth Ave S *Web:* www.network1000.com	Seattle	WA	98108	206-767-3000	
Nucor Steel Marion Inc 912 Cheney Ave *Web:* www.nucorhighway.com	Marion	OH	43302	740-383-4011	
Nucor Steel Memphis Inc 3601 Paul R Lowry Rd *TF:* 888-682-6786 ■ *Web:* www.nucorbar.com	Memphis	TN	38109	888-682-6786	
O'neal Flat Rolled Metals 1229 S Fulton Ave *TF:* 800-336-3365 ■ *Web:* www.ofrmetals.com	Brighton	CO	80601	303-654-0300	
O'Neal Steel Inc 744 41st St N *Fax: Sales ■ *TF:* 800-861-8272 ■ *Web:* www.onealsteel.com	Birmingham	AL	35222	205-599-8000	599-8037*
Oberdorfer LLC 6259 Thompson Rd *Web:* www.oberdorferllc.com	Syracuse	NY	13206	315-437-7588	
Ohio Valley Aluminum Company LLC 1100 Brooks Industrial Rd *Web:* www.ovaco.com	Shelbyville	KY	40065	502-633-2783	
Olympic Foundry Inc 5200 Airport Way S *Web:* www.olympicfoundry.com	Seattle	WA	98108	206-764-6200	
Olympic Steel Inc 5096 Richmond Rd *NASDAQ: ZEUS* ■ *Fax: Sales ■ *TF:* 800-321-6290 ■ *Web:* www.olysteel.com	Bedford Heights	OH	44146	216-292-3800	292-3974*
Omega Steel Co 3460 Hollenberg Dr *Web:* www.assetcontrols.com	Bridgeton	MO	63044	314-209-0992	
OnlineMetals.com 1138 W Ewing *TF:* 800-533-6350 ■ *Web:* www.onlinemetals.com	Seattle	WA	98119	800-533-6350	
Orlando Spring Corp 11131 Winners Cir *Web:* www.orlandospring.com	Los Alamitos	CA	90720	562-594-8411	
Oshkosh Coil Spring Inc 3575 N Main St *Web:* www.oshkoshcoilspring.com	Oshkosh	WI	54901	920-235-7620	
Overseas Development Corp 953 Washington Blvd *Web:* www.overseasdevelopment.com	Stamford	CT	06901	203-964-0111	964-4929
Owen Industries Inc 501 Ave H *TF:* 800-831-9252 ■ *Web:* www.owenind.com	Carter Lake	IA	51510	712-347-5500	347-6166
P & W Industries LLC 68668 Hwy 59 *Web:* www.pandwindustries.com	Mandeville	LA	70470	985-892-2461	
PA Inc 6626 Gulf Fwy *Web:* www.painc.com	Houston	TX	77087	713-570-4900	
Pacesetter Steel Service Inc 1045 Big Shanty Rd *Fax Area Code: 678 ■ *TF:* 800-749-6505 ■ *Web:* www.teampacesetter.com	Kennesaw	GA	30144	770-919-8000	581-8880*
Pacific Alloy Castings Company Inc 5900 E Firestone Blvd *Web:* www.pacificalloy.com	South Gate	CA	90280	562-928-1387	
Pacific Industrial Development Corp 4788 Runway Blvd *Web:* www.pidc.com	Ann Arbor	MI	48108	734-930-9292	
Pacific Steel & Recycling 1401 Third St NW *TF:* 800-889-6264 ■ *Web:* pacific-steel.com	Great Falls	MT	59404	406-771-7222	453-4269
Packaging Inc 6775 Shady Oak Rd *Web:* www.packinc.com	Eden Prairie	MN	55344	952-935-3421	
Paco Steel & Engineering Corp 19818 S Alameda St *Web:* www.pacosteel.com	Rancho Dominguez	CA	90221	310-537-6375	
Palmer Manufacturing 18 N Bechtle Ave *Web:* www.palmermfg.com	Springfield	OH	45504	937-323-6339	
Paragon Steel Enterprises LLC 4211 County Rd 61 *TF:* 800-411-5677 ■ *Web:* www.pstparagonsteel.com	Butler	IN	46721	260-868-1100	868-1101
Parker Steel Co PO Box 2883 *TF:* 800-333-4140 ■ *Web:* www.metricmetal.com	Toledo	OH	43606	419-473-2481	471-2655
PC Campana Inc 1374 E 28th St *Web:* www.pccampana.com	Lorain	OH	44055	440-246-6500	
Peerless Steel Corp 2450 Austin *TF:* 800-482-3947 ■ *Web:* www.peerlesssteel.com	Troy	MI	48083	248-528-3200	528-9144
Pelco Structural LLC 1501 Industrial Blvd *Web:* www.pelcostructural.com	Claremore	OK	74017	918-283-4004	
Penn Mar Castings Inc 500 Broadway *Web:* www.pennmarcastings.com	Hanover	PA	17331	717-632-4165	
Pennex Aluminum Company LLC 50 Community St PO Box 1004 *Web:* www.pennexaluminum.com	Wellsville	PA	17365	717-432-9647	
Pennfab Inc 1431 Ford Rd *Web:* www.pennfab.com	Bensalem	PA	19020	215-245-1577	
Pentz Design Pattern & Foundry 14823 Main St Ne *Web:* www.pentzcastsolutions.com	Duvall	WA	98019	425-788-6490	
Perforated Tubes Inc 4850 Fulton St E *Web:* www.perforatedtubes.com	Ada	MI	49301	616-942-4550	
Peridot Corp 1072 Serpentine Ln *Web:* www.peridotcorp.com	Pleasanton	CA	94566	925-461-8830	
Peterson Steel Corp 61 W Mountain St *TF:* 800-325-3245 ■ *Web:* www.petersonsteel.com	Worcester	MA	01606	508-853-3630	853-7485
Phillips & Johnston Inc 21w179 Hill Ave *TF:* 877-411-8823 ■ *Web:* www.phillips-johnston.com	Glen Ellyn	IL	60137	630-469-8150	469-8048
Phoenix Electronic Enterprises Inc 131 Tillson Ave EXT *Web:* www.phoenixmfg.com	Highland	NY	12528	845-691-7700	691-7759
Phoenix Metals Co 4685 Buford Hwy *TF:* 800-241-2290 ■ *Web:* www.phoenixmetals.net	Norcross	GA	30071	770-447-4211	246-8166
Phoenix Tube Company Inc 1185 Win Dr *Web:* www.phoenixtube.com	Bethlehem	PA	18017	610-865-5337	
Pier Foundry & Pattern Shop Inc 51 State St *Web:* www.pierfoundry.com	Saint Paul	MN	55107	651-222-4461	
Pierce Aluminum 34 Forge Pkwy *Web:* www.piercealuminum.com	Franklin	MA	02038	508-541-7007	541-6077
Pioneer Steel Corp 7447 Intervale St *TF:* 800-999-9440 ■ *Web:* pioneersteel.us/	Detroit	MI	48238	313-933-9400	933-1621
Plymouth Foundry Inc 523 W Harrison St *Web:* www.plymouthfoundry.com	Plymouth	IN	46563	574-936-2106	
Polymet Alloys Inc 1701 Providence Pk Ste 100 *Web:* www.polymetalloys.com	Birmingham	AL	35242	205-981-2200	
Portland Products Inc 271 Morse Dr *Web:* www.portlandproducts.com	Portland	MI	48875	517-647-4191	
Posner Industries Inc 8641 Edgeworth Dr *TF:* 888-767-6377 ■ *Web:* www.posners.com	Capitol Heights	MD	20743	301-350-1000	350-1050
Precision Metal Services Inc 418 Stump Rd *Web:* www.precisionmetalservices.com	Montgomeryville	PA	18936	215-661-0225	
Precision Steel Manufacturing Corp 1723 Seibel Dr Ne *Web:* precisionsteelmfg.com	Roanoke	VA	24012	540-985-8963	
Precision Steel Warehouse Inc 3500 Wolf Rd *TF:* 800-323-0740 ■ *Web:* www.precisionsteel.com	Franklin Park	IL	60131	847-455-7000	455-1341
Precision Tube Company Inc 287 Wissahickon Ave *Web:* www.precisiontube.com	North Wales	PA	19454	215-699-5801	
Premier Aluminum LLC 3633 S Memorial Dr *Web:* www.premieraluminum.com	Racine	WI	53403	262-554-2100	
Prince & Izant Co 12999 Plz Dr *Web:* www.princeizant.com	Cleveland	OH	44130	216-362-7000	
PRL Aluminum 14760 Don Julian Rd *Web:* www.prlaluminum.com	City Of Industry	CA	91746	626-968-7507	
Pro Company Sound Inc 225 Parsons St *Web:* www.procosound.com	Kalamazoo	MI	49007	269-388-9675	
Process Sensors Corp 113 Cedar St *Web:* www.processsensors.com	Milford	MA	01757	508-473-9901	
Quality Manufacturing Corp 4300 Nw Urbandale Dr *Web:* qualitymfgcorp.com	Urbandale	IA	50322	515-331-4300	
Quality Metals Inc 2575 Doswell Ave *Web:* www.qualitymetalsinc.com	St Paul	MN	55108	651-645-5875	
R&S Steel Co 3811 Joliet St *Web:* www.rssteel.com	Denver	CO	80239	303-321-9660	
Rancocas Metals Corp 35 Indel Ave *TF:* 800-762-6382 ■ *Web:* www.rancocasmetals.com	Rancocas	NJ	08073	609-267-4120	267-5690
Randall Metals Corp 2483 Greenleaf Ave *Web:* www.randallmetals.com	Elk Grove Village	IL	60007	847-952-9690	
Ranger Steel Supply Corp 1225 N Loop W Ste 650 *Web:* www.rangersteel.com	Houston	TX	77008	713-633-1306	
Rangers Die Casting Co 10828 S Alameda St *Web:* www.rangersdiecasting.com	Lynwood	CA	90262	310-764-1800	
Ratner Steel Supply Company Inc 2500 W County Rd B *Web:* www.ratnersteel.com	Roseville	MN	55113	651-631-8515	
Rayco Industries Inc 1502 Valley Rd *Web:* www.raycoindustries.com	Richmond	VA	23222	804-321-7111	
Redline Industries Inc 8401 Mosley Rd *Web:* www.redlineindustries.com	Houston	TX	77075	713-946-5355	946-0747

Company	City	State	ZIP	Phone	Fax
Reliance Steel & Aluminum Co 350 S Grand Ave Ste 5100 *NYSE: RS* ■ *Web:* www.rsac.com	Los Angeles	CA	90071	213-687-7700	687-8792
Remelt Sources Inc 27151 Tungsten Rd *Web:* www.remeltsources.com	Cleveland	OH	44132	216-289-4555	289-0939
Rigidized Metals Corp 658 Ohio St *Web:* www.rigidized.com	Buffalo	NY	14203	716-849-4760	
Rj Torching Inc 5061 Energy Dr *Web:* www.rjtorching.com	Flint	MI	48505	810-785-9759	
RMD Instruments LLC 44 Hunt St *Web:* rmdinc.com	Watertown	MA	02472	617-668-6900	
Robert-James Sales Inc 2585 Walden Ave *Web:* www.rjsales.com	Buffalo	NY	14225	716-651-6000	
Rochester Aluminum Smelting Canada Ltd 31-35 Freshway Dr *Web:* www.rochesteraluminum.com	Concord	ON	L4K1R9	905-669-1222	
Rockingham Steel Inc 2565 John Wayland Hwy *Web:* www.rockinghamsteel.com	Harrisonburg	VA	22803	540-433-3000	
Rolled Alloys Inc 125 W Sterns Rd *TF:* 800-521-0332 ■ *Web:* www.rolledalloys.com	Temperance	MI	48182	734-847-0561	847-6917
Rolled Steel Products Corp 2187 Garfield Ave *TF:* 800-400-7833 ■ *Web:* www.rolledsteel.com	Los Angeles	CA	90040	323-723-8836	888-9866
Ross Aluminum Castings LLC 815 N Oak Ave *Web:* www.rossal.com	Sidney	OH	45365	937-492-4134	
Ross Casting & Innovation LLC 402 S Kuther Rd PO Box 89 *Web:* www.rciwheels.com	Sidney	OH	45365	937-497-4500	
Roton Products Inc 660 E Elliott Ave *Web:* www.roton.com	Saint Louis	MO	63122	314-821-4400	
Rowe Foundry Inc 147 W Cumberland St PO Box 130 *Web:* www.rowefoundry.com	Martinsville	IL	62442	217-382-4135	
Russel Metals Inc 6600 Financial Dr *TSE: RUS* ■ *TF:* 800-268-0750 ■ *Web:* www.russelmetals.com	Mississauga	ON	L5N7J6	905-819-7777	819-7409
Russellville Steel Company Inc PO Box 1538 *Web:* www.rsvlsteel.com	Russellville	AR	72811	479-968-2211	968-3486
Ryerson Inc 227 W Monroe St *Web:* www.ryerson.com	Chicago	IL	60606	312-292-5000	
S & S Steel Services Inc 444 E 29th St *Web:* www.sssteelservices.com	Anderson	IN	46016	765-622-4545	622-4556
Sabel Steel Industries Inc 749 N Ct St *Web:* www.sabelsteel.com	Montgomery	AL	36104	334-265-6771	264-3692
Sager Metal Strip Company LLC 100 Boone Dr *Web:* www.sagermetal.com	Michigan City	IN	46360	219-874-3609	
Saginaw Pipe Company Inc 1980 Hwy 31 S PO Box 8 **Fax Area Code: 717* ■ *TF:* 800-433-1374 ■ *Web:* www.saginawpipe.com	Saginaw	AL	35137	205-664-3670	838-8069*
Salit Steel Ltd 7771 Stanley Ave *Web:* www.salitsteel.com	Niagara Falls	ON	L2E6V6	905-354-5691	
Salzgitter Mannesmann International (USA) Inc 1770 St James Pl Ste 500 *Web:* www.salzgitter-usa.com	Houston	TX	77056	713-386-7900	
Sandvik Process Systems LLC 21 Campus Rd *Web:* www.processsystems.sandvik.com	Totowa	NJ	07512	973-790-1600	
SB International Inc 3626 N Hall St Ste 910 *Web:* sbisteel.com	Dallas	TX	75219	214-526-4423	526-1503
Scandic Spring Inc 700 Montague St *Web:* www.scandic.com	San Leandro	CA	94577	510-352-3700	
Searing Industries Inc 8901 Arrow Route *Web:* www.searingindustries.com	Rancho Cucamonga	CA	91730	909-948-3030	
Seneca Foundry Inc 240 Mackinlay Kantor Dr *Web:* www.senecafoundry.com	Webster City	IA	50595	515-832-1722	
Service Steel Aerospace Corp 4609 70th St E *TF:* 800-426-9794 ■ *Web:* www.ssa-corp.com	Fife	WA	98424	800-426-9794	
Service Steel Inc 5555 N Ch Ave Ste 2B7	Portland	OR	97217	503-224-9500	
SH Enterprises Inc 4000 Central Dr *Web:* www.shenter.com	Wausau	WI	54401	715-848-1200	
Shamrock Steel Sales Inc 238 W County Rd S *TF:* 800-299-2317 ■ *Web:* www.shamrocksteelsales.com	Odessa	TX	79763	432-337-2317	337-5049
Shannon Precision Fastener LLC 31600 Stephenson Hwy *Web:* www.shannonpf.com	Madison Heights	MI	48071	248-589-9670	
Sheffield Metals International Inc 5467 Evergreen Pkwy *Web:* www.sheffieldmetals.com	Sheffield Village	OH	44054	440-934-8500	
Shultz Steel Company Inc 5321 Firestone Blvd *Web:* www.shultzsteel.com	South Gate	CA	90280	323-564-3281	
Sibel Ayse Halac Iron Works Inc 21675 Ashgrove Ct *Web:* www.sahalac.com	Sterling	VA	20166	703-406-4766	
Sierra Aluminum Co 2345 Fleetwood Dr *Web:* www.sierraaluminum.com	Riverside	CA	92509	951-781-7800	
Sim-Tex LP 20880 FM 362 Rd *Web:* www.sim-tex.com	Waller	TX	77484	713-450-3940	
Siskin Steel & Supply Co Inc 1901 Riverfront Pkwy *TF:* 800-756-3671 ■ *Web:* www.siskin.com	Chattanooga	TN	37408	423-756-3671	756-3671
Skol Manufacturing Co 4444 N Ravenswood Ave *Web:* skolmfg.com	Chicago	IL	60640	773-878-5959	
Skyline Steel LLC Eight Woodhollow Rd Ste 102 *TF:* 866-875-9546 ■ *Web:* www.skylinesteel.com	Parsippany	NJ	07054	866-875-9546	
SMC Metal Fabricators Inc 2100 S Oakwood Rd *Web:* www.smcmetal.com	Oshkosh	WI	54904	920-426-6080	
Smithahn Company Inc 836 E N St *Web:* smithahn.com	Bethlehem	PA	18017	610-866-4461	
Soleno Inc 1160 Rt 133 CP 837 *Web:* www.soleno.com	Saint-jean-sur-richelieu	QC	J2X4J5	450-347-7855	
Solidiform Inc 3928 Lawnwood St *Web:* www.solidiform.com	Fort Worth	TX	76111	817-831-2626	831-8258
Solon Manufacturing Co 425 Center St *Web:* www.solonmfg.com	Chardon	OH	44024	440-286-7149	
South st Paul Steel Supply Company Inc 200 Hardman Ave N *Web:* sspss.com	South Saint Paul	MN	55075	651-451-6666	
Southern Copper & Supply Company Inc 875 Yeager Pkwy *Web:* www.southerncopper.com	Pelham	AL	35124	205-664-9440	
Southern Precision Spring Company Inc 2200 Old Steele Creek Rd *Web:* www.spspring.com	Charlotte	NC	28208	704-392-4393	
Southern Tank & Manufacturing Inc 1501 Haynes Ave *Web:* www.southerntank.net	Owensboro	KY	42303	270-684-2321	
Southern Wire Corp 8045 Metro Rd *Web:* www.southernwire.com	Olive Branch	MS	38654	662-890-4873	
Southwest Metalsmiths Inc 5026 E Beverly Rd *Web:* www.swmetalsmiths.com	Phoenix	AZ	85044	602-438-8577	
Southwest Steel Casting Co 600 Foundry Dr *Web:* www.swscc.com	Longview	TX	75604	903-759-3946	759-3224
Southwestern Suppliers Inc 6815 E 14th Ave *Web:* www.sowes.com	Tampa	FL	33619	813-626-2193	628-0511
Special Metals Inc 6406 S Eastern Ave *Web:* www.specialmetalsinc.com	Oklahoma City	OK	73129	405-677-7700	
Specialty Metals Corp 8300 S 206th St *Web:* www.specialtymetalscorp.com	Kent	WA	98032	253-398-1730	
Specialty Pipe & Tube Inc PO Box 516 *TF:* 800-842-5839 ■ *Web:* www.specialtypipe.com	Mineral Ridge	OH	44440	330-505-8262	505-8260
Spectra Aluminum Products Inc 95 Reagens Industrial Pkwy *Web:* www.spectraaluminum.com	Bradford	ON	L3Z2A4	905-778-8093	
St Louis Cold Drawn Inc 1060 Pershall Rd *Web:* www.stlcd.com	St. Louis	MO	63137	314-867-4301	
St Marys Foundry 409 E S St *Web:* www.stmfoundry.com	Saint Marys	OH	45885	419-394-3346	
St. Louis Pipe & Supply Inc 17740 Edison Ave *Web:* www.stlpipesupply.com	Chesterfield	MO	63005	636-391-2500	
Standard Wire & Steel Works 16255 Vincennes Ave *Web:* www.standardwiresteel.com	South Holland	IL	60473	708-333-8300	
State Pipe & Supply Inc 9615 S Norwalk Blvd *TF:* 800-733-6410 ■ *Web:* www.statepipe.com	Santa Fe Springs	CA	90670	562-695-5555	692-1054
State Steel Supply Co 214 Court St *Web:* www.statesteel.com	Sioux City	IA	51101	712-277-4000	
Staub Metals Corp 7747 E Rosecrans Ave *TF:* 800-447-8282 ■ *Web:* www.staubmetals.com	Paramount	CA	90723	562-602-2200	633-1456
Steal Network LLC 2181 California Ave Ste 400 *Web:* www.stealnetwork.com	Salt Lake City	UT	84104	801-210-0304	
Steel & Pipe Supply Co 555 Poyntz Ave *TF:* 800-521-2345 ■ *Web:* www.spsci.com	Manhattan	KS	66502	785-587-5100	587-5174
Steel Edge Inc (SEI) 716 W Mesquite Ave *Web:* www.steeledgeinc.com	Las Vegas	NV	89106	702-386-0023	
Steel LLC 405 N Clarendon Ave *Web:* www.steelincga.com	Scottdale	GA	30079	404-292-7373	
Steel Supply Co, The 5101 Newport Dr *TF:* 800-323-7571 ■ *Web:* www.steelsupply.com	Rolling Meadows	IL	60008	800-323-7571	828-1553
Steel Technologies Inc 15415 Shelbyville Rd *Web:* www.steeltechnologies.com	Louisville	KY	40245	502-245-2110	
Steel Unlimited Inc 456 W Valley Blvd *Web:* www.steelunlimited.com	Rialto	CA	92376	909-873-1222	
Steel Warehouse Company Inc 2722 W Tucker Dr *TF:* 800-348-2529 ■ *Web:* www.steelwarehouse.com	South Bend	IN	46619	574-236-5100	236-5154
Steel Works LLC, The 1020 Niedringhaus Ave *Web:* www.tsw.com	Granite City	IL	62040	618-452-2833	
Steelhead Partners LLC 333 - 108th Ave NE Ste 2010 *Web:* www.steelheadpartners.com	Bellevue	WA	98004	425-974-3788	
Steelways Inc 401 S Water St *Web:* www.steelwaysinc.com	Newburgh	NY	12553	845-562-0860	
Sterling Pipe & Tube Inc 5335 Enterprise Blvd *Web:* www.sterlingpipeandtube.com	Toledo	OH	43612	419-729-9756	
Steven F O'Donnell Inc 6724 Binder Ln *Web:* www.stevenfodonnellinc.com	Elkridge	MD	21075	410-796-7968	
Steward Steel Inc 1219 E US Hwy 62 PO Box 551 *Web:* www.stewardsteel.com	Sikeston	MO	63801	573-471-2121	471-2336
Stewart Amos Steel Inc 4400 Paxton St *Web:* www.stewart-amos.com	Harrisburg	PA	17111	717-564-3931	
Stripco Inc 56598 Magnetic Dr *Web:* www.stripco.com	Mishawaka	IN	46545	574-256-7800	
Structurlam Products Ltd 2176 Government St *Web:* www.structurlam.com	Penticton	BC	V2A8B5	250-492-8912	
Sunbelt Metals & Manufacturing Inc 920 S Bradshaw Rd *Web:* www.sunbeltmetals.com	Apopka	FL	32703	407-889-8960	
Supra Alloys Inc 351 Cortez Cir *TF:* 800-647-8772 ■ *Web:* www.supraalloys.com	Camarillo	CA	93012	805-388-2138	987-6492
Sylvania Steel Corp 4169 Holland Sylvania Rd *TF General:* 800-435-0986 ■ *Web:* www.sylvaniasteel.com	Toledo	OH	43623	419-885-3838	882-7270
T&B Tube Co 15525 S LaSalle St *Web:* www.tbtube.com	South Holland	IL	60473	708-333-1282	

Company	City	State	ZIP	Phone	Fax
Taco Metals Inc 50 NE 179th St *Web:* www.tacometals.com	Miami	FL	33162	305-652-8566	770-2387
Tarrier Steel Company Inc, The 1379 S 22nd St *Web:* www.tarrier.com	Columbus	OH	43206	614-444-4000	
Tata Steel International (Americas) Inc 475 N Martingale Rd Ste 400 *Web:* www.tatasteelamericas.com	Schaumburg	IL	60173	847-619-0400	
Tate Ornamental Inc 411 Industrial Dr *Web:* www.tateornamental.com	White House	TN	37188	615-672-0348	
Tazewell Machine Works Inc 2015 S Second St *Web:* www.tazewellmachine.com	Pekin	IL	61554	309-347-3181	
TCI Aluminum/North Inc 2353 Davis Ave *TF:* 800-824-6197 ■ *Web:* www.tcialuminum.com	Hayward	CA	94545	510-786-3750	786-3302
Tenenbaum Recycling Group 4500 W Bethany Rd *Web:* www.trg.net	North Little Rock	AR	72117	501-945-0881	945-3865
Terra Nova Steel & Iron (Ontario) Inc 3595 Hawkestone Rd *Web:* www.terranovasteel.ca	Mississauga	ON	L5C2V1	905-273-3872	273-6553
Texas Pipe & Supply Co Inc 2330 Holmes Rd *TF:* 800-233-8736 ■ *Web:* www.texaspipe.com	Houston	TX	77051	713-799-9235	799-8701
Texas Steel Processing Inc 5480 Windfern Rd *Web:* www.txstl.com	Houston	TX	77041	281-822-3200	
Thermo Vac Inc 201 W Oakwood Rd *Web:* www.thermovac.com	Oxford	MI	48371	248-969-0300	
Thompson Aluminum Casting Co 5161 Canal Rd *Web:* www.thompsoncasting.com	Cleveland	OH	44125	216-206-2781	
Three D Metals Inc 5462 Innovation Dr *Web:* www.threedmetals.com	Valley City	OH	44280	330-220-0451	
ThyssenKrupp Materials NA 22355 W 11 Mile Rd *TF:* 800-926-2600 ■ *Web:* www.tkmna.com	Southfield	MI	48033	248-233-5600	233-5600
Thyssenkrupp Steel North America Inc 22355 W Eleven Mile Rd *Web:* www.tksna.com	Southfield	MI	48033	248-233-5614	
Tioga Pipe Supply Company Inc 2450 Wheatsheaf Ln *TF:* 800-523-3678 ■ *Web:* www.tiogapipe.com	Philadelphia	PA	19137	215-831-0700	533-1645
Titan Steel Corp 2500-B Broening Hwy *Web:* www.titansteel.com	Baltimore	MD	21224	410-631-5200	631-5220
Tollman Spring Company Inc 91 Enterprise Dr *Web:* www.tollmanspring.com	Bristol	CT	06010	860-583-1326	
Tomson Steel Co (Inc) PO Box 940 **Fax Area Code:* 513 ■ *TF:* 800-837-3001 ■ *Web:* www.tomsonsteel.com	Middletown	OH	45042	800-837-3001	420-8610*
Tooling Technology LLC 100 Enterprise Dr *Web:* www.toolingtechgroup.com	Fort Loramie	OH	45845	937-295-3672	
Torrance Casting Inc 3131 Commerce St *Web:* www.torrancecasting.com	La Crosse	WI	54603	608-781-0600	
Totten Tubes Inc 500 Danlee St *Web:* www.tottentubes.com	Azusa	CA	91702	626-812-0220	812-0113
Town & Country Industries 400 W Mcnab Rd *Web:* www.tc-alum.com	Fort Lauderdale	FL	33309	954-970-9999	
Toyota Tsusho America Inc 805 Third Ave 16th Fl **Fax Area Code:* 502 ■ *TF:* 800-883-0100 ■ *Web:* www.taiamerica.com	New York	NY	10022	212-355-3600	868-3355*
Trans World Alloys Co 249 E Gardena Blvd *Web:* www.twalloys.com	Gardena	CA	90248	310-217-8777	
Tri Star Metals LLC 375 Village Dr *Web:* www.tristarmetals.com	Carol Stream	IL	60188	630-462-7600	
Tri-State Ironworks Inc 175 W Bodley Ave *Web:* www.tristateironworks.com	Memphis	TN	38109	901-942-1461	
Tri-Wire Engineering Solutions Inc 890 East St *Web:* www.triwire.net	Tewksbury	MA	01876	978-640-6899	
Trident Steel Corp 12825 Flushing Meadows Dr Ste 110 *Web:* www.tridentsteel.com	St. Louis	MO	63131	314-822-0500	
Triple-S Steel Supply LLC PO Box 21119 *TF:* 800-231-1034 ■ *Web:* www.sss-steel.com	Houston	TX	77226	713-697-7105	
Tristate Wire Rope Supply Inc 5246 Wooster Pk *Web:* tswr.com	Cincinnati	OH	45226	513-871-8656	
Tubetech North America Inc 900 East Taggart St *Web:* www.tubetechnorthamerica.com	East Palestine	OH	44413	330-426-9476	
Tubular Steel Inc 1031 Executive Pkwy Dr *TF:* 800-388-7491 ■ *Web:* www.tubularsteel.com	Saint Louis	MO	63141	314-851-9200	851-9336
Turret Steel Industries Inc 105 Pine St *TF:* 800-245-4800 ■ *Web:* www.turretsteel.com	Imperial	PA	15126	724-218-1014	218-1195
TW Metals Inc PO Box 644 *Web:* www.twmetals.com	Exton	PA	19341	610-458-1300	458-1399
Two Rivers Enterprises 490 River St W *Web:* www.stainlesskings.com	Holdingford	MN	56340	320-746-3156	746-3158
Ulbrich of Illinois Inc 12340 S Laramie Ave *Web:* www.astroplastics.com	Alsip	IL	60803	708-489-9500	
United Alloy Inc 4100 Kennedy Rd *Web:* www.unitedalloy.com	Janesville	WI	53545	608-758-4717	
United Aluminum Corp 100 United Dr *Web:* www.unitedaluminum.com	North Haven	CT	06473	203-239-5881	
United States Brass & Copper Co Inc 1401 Brook Dr *TF:* 800-821-2854 ■ *Web:* www.usbrassandcopper.com	Downers Grove	IL	60515	630-629-9340	629-9350
United Steel Inc 164 School St *Web:* www.unitedsteel.com	East Hartford	CT	06108	860-289-2323	
Universal Metals LLC 805 Chicago St *Web:* www.umimetals.com	Toledo	OH	43611	419-726-0850	
Universal Steel America Houston Inc 1230 E Richey Rd *Web:* www.universalsteelamerica.com	Houston	TX	77073	281-821-7400	
Universal Steel Co 6600 Grant Ave *TF:* 800-669-2645 ■ *Web:* www.univsteel.com	Cleveland	OH	44105	216-883-4972	341-0421
US Metals Inc 19102 Gundle Rd *Web:* www.tgrexotics.com	Houston	TX	77073	281-443-7473	443-6748
Usemco 1602 Rezin Rd *Web:* www.usemco.com	Tomah	WI	54660	608-372-5911	
Valiant Steel & Equipment Inc 6455 Old Peachtree Rd *TF:* 800-939-9905 ■ *Web:* www.valiantsteel.com	Norcross	GA	30071	770-417-1235	417-1669
Venture Steel Inc 60 Disco Rd *Web:* www.venturesteel.com	Etobicoke	ON	M9W1L8	416-798-9396	
Viking Materials Inc 3225 Como Ave SE *TF General:* 800-682-3942 ■ *Web:* www.vikingmaterials.com	Minneapolis	MN	55414	612-617-5800	623-9070
Vista Metals Inc 65 Ballou Blvd *TF:* 800-431-4113 ■ *Web:* www.vismet.com	Bristol	RI	02809	401-253-1772	
Vita Needle Co 919 Great Plain Ave *Web:* www.vitaneedle.com	Needham	MA	02492	781-444-1780	
Vital Link Inc 914 Bartlett Rd *Web:* www.vitallinkinc.com	Sealy	TX	77474	979-885-4181	
Waconia Manufacturing Inc 33 E Eigth St *Web:* www.waconiamfg.com	Waconia	MN	55387	952-442-4450	
Warren Steel Holdings LLC 4000 Mahoning Ave *Web:* www.warrensteelholdings.com	Warren	OH	44483	330-847-0487	
Waukegan Steel LLC 1201 Belvidere Rd *Web:* www.waukegansteel.com	Waukegan	IL	60085	847-662-2810	
WCJ - Pilgrim Wire LLC 4180 N Port Washington Rd *Web:* www.wcjwire.com	Glendale	WI	53212	414-291-9566	
Weber Specialties Co 15230 S Us 131 *Web:* www.weberspecialties.com	Schoolcraft	MI	49087	269-679-5160	
West Central Steel Inc 110 19th St NW PO Box 1178 *TF:* 800-992-8853 ■ *Web:* www.wcsteel.com	Willmar	MN	56201	320-235-4070	235-1816
Westfield Steel Inc 530 State Rd 32 W **Fax Area Code:* 317 ■ *Web:* www.westfieldsteel.com	Westfield	IN	46074	800-622-4984	896-5343*
White Aluminum Products LLC 2101 US Hwy 441 *Web:* www.whitealuminum.com	Leesburg	FL	34748	888-474-5884	
White Star Steel Inc 2200 Harbor Blvd *Web:* www.whitestarsteel.com	Houston	TX	77220	713-675-6501	
Whitefab Inc 724 Ave W *Web:* www.whitefab.com	Birmingham	AL	35214	205-791-2011	
Whitley Steel Company Inc 610 Us Hwy 301 S *Web:* www.whitleysteel.com	Jacksonville	FL	32234	904-289-7471	
Willbanks Metals Inc 1155 NE 28th St *TF:* 800-772-2352 ■ *Web:* www.willbanksmetals.com	Fort Worth	TX	76106	817-625-6161	625-8487
Willerding Welding Company Inc 1270 W Terra Ln *Web:* www.willerding.com	O'Fallon	MO	63366	636-272-2366	
Williams Metals & Welding Alloys Inc 125 Strafford Ave Ste 108 *Web:* www.wmwa.net	Wayne	PA	19087	610-225-0105	
Winchester Metals Inc 195 Ebert Rd *Web:* www.steelsupplier.com	Winchester	VA	22603	540-667-9000	
Winter F W Inc & Co 550 Delaware Ave *Web:* www.fwwinter.com	Camden	NJ	08102	856-963-7490	
Wire Rope Industries Ltd 5501 Trans-Canada Hwy *Web:* www.wirerope.com	Pointe-claire	QC	H9R1B7	514-697-9711	
Wiscolift Inc W6396 Speciality Dr *Web:* www.wiscolift.com	Greenville	WI	54942	920-757-8832	
Wisconsin Steel & Tube Corp 1555 N Mayfair Rd *TF:* 800-279-8335 ■ *Web:* www.wisteeltube.com	Milwaukee	WI	53226	414-453-4441	453-0789
WMK & Co 415 Albert St *Web:* www.wmkco.com	Billings	MT	59101	406-256-3200	
Wrisco Industries Inc 355 Hiatt Dr Ste B *TF:* 800-627-2646 ■ *Web:* www.wrisco.com	Palm Beach Gardens	FL	33418	561-626-5700	627-3574

496 METALWORKING DEVICES & ACCESSORIES

SEE ALSO Machine Tools - Metal Cutting Types p. 2684; Machine Tools - Metal Forming Types p. 2685; Tool & Die Shops p. 3238

Company	City	State	ZIP	Phone	Fax
Acme Industrial Co 441 Maple Ave *TF:* 800-323-5582 ■ *Web:* www.acmeindustrial.com	Carpentersville	IL	60110	847-428-3911	428-1820
Advanced Machine & Engineering Co 2500 Latham St *TF:* 800-225-4263 ■ *Web:* www.ame.com	Rockford	IL	61103	815-962-6076	962-6483
AG Davis Gage & Engineering Co 6533 Sims Dr *Web:* www.agdavis-aagage.com	Sterling Heights	MI	48313	586-977-9000	977-9190
Alcon Tool Co 565 Crosier St *Web:* www.alcontool.com	Akron	OH	44311	330-773-9171	773-8042
Allied Machine & Engineering Corp 120 Deeds Dr *TF:* 800-321-5537 ■ *Web:* www.alliedmachine.com	Dover	OH	44622	330-343-4283	343-4781
American Broach & Machine Co 575 S Mansfield *Web:* www.americanbroach.com	Ypsilanti	MI	48197	734-961-0300	961-9999
American Cutting Edge Inc 480 Congress Pk Dr **Fax Area Code:* 937 ■ *TF General:* 800-543-6860 ■ *Web:* www.cbmfg.com	Centerville	OH	45459	888-252-3372	866-6844*
American Drill Bushings Co (ADB) 5740 Hunt Rd *TF:* 800-423-4425 ■ *Web:* www.americandrillbushing.com	Valdosta	GA	31606	229-253-8928	253-8929
Apex Broach & Machine Co 22862 Hoover Rd *Web:* www.apbsi.com	Warren	MI	48089	586-758-2626	758-2627
ASKO Inc 501 W Seventh Ave *TF:* 800-321-1310 ■ *Web:* www.askoinc.com	Homestead	PA	15120	412-461-4110	461-5400
ATI Metal Working Products 1 Teledyne Pl **Fax Area Code:* 800 ■ **Fax:* Sales ■ *TF:* 888-926-4211 ■ *Web:* www.atimetals.com	La Vergne	TN	37086	615-641-4200	223-2219*

Company	City	State	Zip	Phone	Fax
Balax Inc PO Box 96	North Lake	WI	53064	262-966-2355	966-1028
Web: www.balax.com					
Besly Cutting Tools Inc 16200 Woodmint Ln	South Beloit	IL	61080	815-389-2231	389-1339
TF: 800-435-2965 ■ *Web:* www.besly.com					
Big Kaiser Precision Tooling Inc 641 Fargo Ave	Elk Grove Village	IL	60007	847-228-7660	228-0881
TF: 888-866-5776 ■ *Web:* www.bigkaiser.com					
Boley Tool & Machine Works Inc 1044 Spring Bay Rd	East Peoria	IL	61611	309-694-2722	694-7879
Web: boleytool.com/					
Buck Chuck Co 2155 Traversefield Dr	Traverse City	MI	49686	800-228-2825	947-4953*
**Fax Area Code:* 231 ■ *TF:* 800-228-2825 ■ *Web:* www.buckchuckusa.com					
Carbro Corp 15724 Condon Ave PO Box 278	Lawndale	CA	90260	310-643-8400	643-9703
TF: 888-738-4400 ■ *Web:* www.carbrocorp.com					
Carl Zeiss Industrial Metrology 6250 Sycamore Ln N	Maple Grove	MN	55369	763-744-2400	
TF: 800-752-6181 ■ *Web:* corporate.zeiss.com					
Cincinnati Gilbert Machine Tool Company LLC 3366 Beekman St	Cincinnati	OH	45223	513-541-4815	541-4885
Web: www.cincinnatigilbert.com					
CJT Koolcarb Inc 494 Mission St	Carol Stream	IL	60188	630-690-5933	690-6355
TF: 800-323-2299 ■ *Web:* www.cjtkoolcarb.com					
Cline Tool & Service Co PO Box 866	Newton	IA	50208	641-792-7081	792-0309
TF: 866-561-3022 ■ *Web:* www.clinetool.com					
Cole Carbide Industries Inc 4930 S Lapeer Rd	Orion Twp	MI	48359	586-757-8700	757-8701
Web: www.colecarbide.com					
Deltronic Corp 3900 W Segerstrom Ave	Santa Ana	CA	92704	714-545-5800	545-9548
TF: 800-451-6922 ■ *Web:* www.deltronic.com					
Detroit Edge Tool Co 6570 E Nevada St	Detroit	MI	48234	313-366-4120	366-1890
TF: 800-404-2038 ■ *Web:* www.detroitedge.com					
Dundick Corp 4616 W 20th St	Cicero	IL	60804	708-656-6363	656-2359
Web: www.dundick.com					
Edmunds Gages 45 Spring Ln	Farmington	CT	06032	860-677-2813	677-4243
TF: 800-878-1622 ■ *Web:* www.edmundsgages.com					
Enmark Tool & Gage Co Inc 18100 Cross Dr	Fraser	MI	48026	586-293-2797	293-1037
Web: www.enmarktool.com					
Forkardt 2155 Traverse Field Dr	Traverse City	MI	49686	231-995-8300	995-8361
TF: 800-544-3823 ■ *Web:* www.forkardt.us					
Fullerton Tool Company Inc 121 Perry St	Saginaw	MI	48602	989-799-4550	792-3335
TF: 855-722-7243 ■ *Web:* www.fullertontool.com					
Gaiser Tool Co 4544 McGrath St	Ventura	CA	93003	805-644-5583	644-2013
Web: www.gaisertool.com					
Garr Tool Co 7800 N Alger Rd	Alma	MI	48801	989-463-6171	463-3609
TF: 800-248-9003 ■ *Web:* www.garrtool.com					
General Broach Co 307 Salisbury St	Morenci	MI	49256	517-458-7555	458-6821
Web: www.generalbroach.com					
General Cutting Tools 6440 N Ridgeway Ave	Lincolnwood	IL	60712	847-677-8770	677-8786
Web: www.generalcuttingtools.com					
Gilman USA 1230 Cheyenne Ave PO Box 5	Grafton	WI	53024	262-377-2434	377-9438
TF: 800-445-6267 ■ *Web:* gilmanprecision.com/					
Glassline Corp PO Box 147	Perrysburg	OH	43552	419-666-5942	666-1549
Web: www.glassline.com					
Glastonbury Southern Gage 46 Industrial Pk Rd	Erin	TN	37061	931-289-4243	242-7142*
**Fax Area Code:* 800 ■ *TF:* 800-251-4243 ■ *Web:* www.gsgage.com					
Gleason Cutting Tools Corp 1351 Windsor Rd	Loves Park	IL	61111	815-877-8900	877-0264
Web: www.gleason.com					
Goss & DeLeeuw Machine Co 100 Harding St	Kensington	CT	06037	860-828-4121	828-8132
Web: goss-deleeuw.com					
Guhring Inc 1445 Commerce Ave	Brookfield	WI	53045	262-784-6730	784-9096
TF: 800-776-6170 ■ *Web:* www.guhring.com					
Hanlo Gages & Engineering Co 34403 Glendale	Livonia	MI	48150	734-422-4224	422-2244
Web: www.hanlogages.com					
Hannibal Carbide Tool Inc 5000 Paris Gravel Rd	Hannibal	MO	63401	573-221-2775	221-1140
TF: 800-451-9436 ■ *Web:* www.hannibalcarbide.com					
Hardinge Inc 1 Hardinge Dr	Elmira	NY	14902	607-734-2281	
NASDAQ: HDNG ■ *TF:* 800-843-8801 ■ *Web:* www.hardinge.com					
Hayden Twist Drill & Tool Company Inc 22822 Globe St	Warren	MI	48089	586-754-7700	754-3312
TF: 800-521-1780 ■ *Web:* www.haydendrills.com					
Heidenhain Corp 333 E State Pkwy	Schaumburg	IL	60173	847-490-1191	490-3931
Web: www.heidenhain.com					
High Tech Tool Inc 7803 S Loop E	Houston	TX	77012	713-641-2303	641-6664
Web: www.hightechtool.com					
Hoppe Technologies Inc 107 First Ave	Chicopee	MA	01020	413-592-9213	592-4688
Web: www.hoppetech.com					
Hougen Manufacturing Inc 3001 Hougen Dr	Swartz Creek	MI	48473	810-635-7111	635-8277
TF Orders: 800-426-7818 ■ *Web:* www.hougen.com					
Huron Machine Products Inc 228 SW 21st Terr	Fort Lauderdale	FL	33312	800-327-8186	583-2154*
**Fax Area Code:* 954 ■ **Fax:* Sales ■ *TF:* 800-327-8186 ■ *Web:* www.huronmachine.com					
Husqvarna Construction Products 17400 W 119th St	Olathe	KS	66061	800-288-5040	825-0028
TF: 800-288-5040 ■ *Web:* www.husqvarna.com					
Industrial Tools Inc (ITI) 1111 S Rose Ave	Oxnard	CA	93033	805-483-1111	483-6302
TF: 800-266-5561 ■ *Web:* www.iti-abrasives.com					
Iowa Precision Industries Inc 5480 Sixth St SW	Cedar Rapids	IA	52404	319-364-9181	364-3436
Web: mestekmachinery.com//					
Jasco Tools Inc 1390 Mt Read Blvd PO Box 60497	Rochester	NY	14606	585-254-7000	254-2655
TF: 800-724-5497 ■ *Web:* www.jascotools.com					
Jergens Inc 15700 S Waterloo Rd	Cleveland	OH	44110	877-486-1454	481-6193*
**Fax Area Code:* 216 ■ *TF:* 800-537-4367 ■ *Web:* www.jergensinc.com					
Kennametal Inc 1600 Technology Way PO Box 231	Latrobe	PA	15650	724-539-5000	539-8787
NYSE: KMT ■ *TF Cust Svc:* 800-446-7738 ■ *Web:* www.kennametal.com					
KEO Cutters Inc 25040 Easy St	Warren	MI	48089	586-771-2050	771-2062
TF: 888-390-2050 ■ *Web:* www.keocutters.com					
Lancaster Knives Inc 165 Ct St	Lancaster	NY	14086	716-683-5050	683-5068
TF: 800-869-9666 ■ *Web:* www.lancasterknives.com					
Lovejoy Tool Company Inc 133 Main St	Springfield	VT	05156	802-885-2194	885-9511
TF: 800-843-8376 ■ *Web:* www.lovejoytool.com					
Madison Cutting Tools Inc 485 Narragansett Pk Dr	Pawtucket	RI	02861	401-729-0400	333-4011
Web: www.madisontools.com					
Melin Tool Co 5565 Venture Dr Unit C	Cleveland	OH	44130	216-362-4230	521-1558*
**Fax Area Code:* 800 ■ *TF:* 800-521-1078 ■ *Web:* www.endmill.com					
Micro 100 Tool Corp 1410 E Pine Ave	Meridian	ID	83642	208-888-7310	888-2106
TF: 800-421-8065 ■ *Web:* www.micro100.com					
Micro-vu Corp 7909 Conde Ln	Windsor	CA	95492	707-838-6272	838-3985
Web: www.microvu.com					
NED Corp 31 Town Forest Rd	Oxford	MA	01540	800-343-6086	799-2796*
**Fax Area Code:* 508 ■ *TF:* 800-343-6086 ■ *Web:* www.nedkut.com					
Niagara Cutter Inc 200 John James Audubon Pkwy	Amherst	NY	14228	716-689-8400	689-8485
TF: 888-689-8400 ■ *Web:* www.niagaracutter.com					
North American Tool Corp 215 Elmwood Ave	South Beloit	IL	61080	815-389-2300	872-3299*
**Fax Area Code:* 800 ■ *TF:* 800-872-8277 ■ *Web:* www.natool.com					
Onsrud Cutter LP 800 Liberty Dr	Libertyville	IL	60048	847-362-1560	362-5028
TF: 800-234-1560 ■ *Web:* www.onsrud.com					
OSG Tap & Die Inc 676 E Fullerton Ave	Glendale Heights	IL	60139	630-790-1400	790-1477
TF: 800-837-2223 ■ *Web:* www.osgtool.com					
Phillips Corp 7390 Coca Cola Dr	Hanover	MD	21076	410-564-2929	564-2949
TF: 800-878-4242 ■ *Web:* www.phillipscorp.com					
Powers Fasteners Inc Two Powers Ln	Brewster	NY	10509	914-235-6300	576-6483
TF: 800-524-3244 ■ *Web:* www.powers.com					
Precision Grinding & Manufacturing Corp 1305 Emerson St	Rochester	NY	14606	585-458-4300	458-7281
Web: www.pgmcorp.com					
Precitech Precision Inc 44 Blackbrook Rd	Keene	NH	03431	603-357-2511	358-6174
Web: www.precitech.com					
Products Engineering Corp 2645 Maricopa St	Torrance	CA	90503	310-787-4500	787-4501
Web: www.productsengineering.com					
Regal-Beloit Corp 200 State St	Beloit	WI	53511	608-364-8800	364-8818
NYSE: RBC ■ *TF:* 800-672-6495 ■ *Web:* www.regalbeloit.com					
Reiff & Nestor Co 50 Reiff St PO Box 147	Lykens	PA	17048	717-453-7113	453-7555
TF: 800-521-3422 ■ *Web:* www.rntap.com					
Royal Machine & Tool Corp Four Willowbrook Dr	Berlin	CT	06037	860-828-6555	828-1591
Web: www.royalworkholding.com					
S-T Industries Inc 301 Armstrong Blvd N	Saint James	MN	56081	507-375-3211	375-4503
TF: 800-326-2039 ■ *Web:* www.stindustries.com					
Scotchman Industries Inc 180 E Hwy 14	Philip	SD	57567	605-859-2542	859-2499
TF: 800-843-8844 ■ *Web:* www.scotchman.com					
Scully Jones Seibert Corp 1901 S Rockwell St	Chicago	IL	60608	800-752-8665	
Seco Tools 2805 Bellingham Dr	Troy	MI	48083	248-528-5200	528-5600*
**Fax:* Cust Svc ■ *Web:* www.secotools.com					
Somma Tool Company Inc 109 Scott Rd	Waterbury	CT	06705	203-753-2114	756-5489
Web: www.sommatool.com					
Spiralock Corp 25235 Dequindre Rd	Madison Heights	MI	48071	248-543-7800	543-1403
TF: 800-521-2688 ■ *Web:* www.stanleyengineeredfastening.com					
Star Cutter Co 23461 Industrial Pk Dr	Farmington	MI	48335	248-474-8200	474-9518
TF: 877-635-3488 ■ *Web:* www.starcutter.com					
Starrett Webber Gage Div 24500 Detroit Rd	Cleveland	OH	44145	440-835-0001	892-9555
TF: 800-255-3924 ■ *Web:* www.starrett-webber.com					
Stilson Products 15935 Sturgeon St	Roseville	MI	48066	586-778-1100	778-4660
TF: 888-400-5978 ■ *Web:* www.stilsonproducts.com					
Strong Tool Co 1251 E 286th St	Cleveland	OH	44132	216-289-2450	
Web: mdm.com					
Tapmatic Corp 802 S Clearwater Loop	Post Falls	ID	83854	208-773-8048	773-3021
TF General: 800-854-6019 ■ *Web:* www.tapmatic.com					
Thread Check Inc 390 Oser Ave	Hauppauge	NY	11788	631-231-1515	231-1625
TF: 800-767-7633 ■ *Web:* www.threadcheck.com					
TM Smith Tool International Corp 360 Hubbard Ave	Mount Clemens	MI	48043	586-468-1465	468-7190
TF: 800-521-4894 ■ *Web:* www.tmsmith.com					
United Drill Bushing Corp 12200 Woodruff Ave	Downey	CA	90241	562-803-1521	486-3465*
**Fax Area Code:* 800 ■ *TF:* 800-486-3466 ■ *Web:* www.ucc-udb.com					
US Drill Head Co 5298 River Rd	Cincinnati	OH	45233	513-941-0300	941-9110
Web: usdrilhead.com/					
Utica Enterprises Co 13231 23-Mile Rd	Shelby Township	MI	48315	586-726-4300	726-4316
Viking Drill & Tool Inc 355 State St	Saint Paul	MN	55107	651-227-8911	227-1793
TF: 800-328-4655 ■ *Web:* www.vikingdrill.com					
Vulcan Tool Co 730 Lorraine Ave	Dayton	OH	45410	937-253-6194	253-1062
Web: www.vulcancut.com					
Walker Magnetics Group Inc 20 Rockdale St	Worcester	MA	01606	508-853-3232	852-8649
TF: 800-962-4638 ■ *Web:* www.walkermagnet.com					
Walter USA Inc N22 W23855 Ridgeview Pkwy W	Waukesha	WI	53188	800-945-5554	347-2501*
**Fax Area Code:* 262 ■ *TF:* 800-945-5554 ■ *Web:* www.walter-tools.com					
Zagar Inc 24000 Lakeland Blvd	Cleveland	OH	44132	216-731-0500	731-8591
Web: www.zagar.com					
Zenith Cutter Co 5200 Zenith Pkwy	Loves Park	IL	61111	815-282-5200	282-5232
TF: 800-223-5202 ■ *Web:* zenithcutter.com					

497 METALWORKING MACHINERY

SEE ALSO Rolling Mill Machinery p. 3129

Company	City	State	Zip	Phone	Fax
ADS Machinery Corp 1201 Vine Ave NE	Warren	OH	44483	330-399-3601	399-1190
Web: www.adsmachinery.com					
Armstrong Mfg Co 2700 SE Tacoma St	Portland	OR	97202	503-228-8381	228-8384
TF: 800-426-6226 ■ *Web:* www.armstrongblue.com					
Artos Engineering Co 21605 Gateway Ct	Brookfield	WI	53045	262-252-4545	252-4544
Web: www.artosengineering.com					
ATD Engineering & Machine LLC 533 N Ct St	Au Gres	MI	48703	989-876-7161	876-7162
Web: www.atdemllc.com					

				Phone	Fax
Bachi Co 1201 Ardmore Ave *Web:* www.bachiwinder.com	Itasca	IL	60143	630-773-5600	773-5621
Balance Technology Inc 7035 Jomar Dr *Web:* www.balancetechnology.com	Whitmore Lake	MI	48189	734-769-2100	769-2542
Bartell Machinery Systems LLC 6321 Elmer Hill Rd *TF:* 800-537-8473 ■ *Web:* www.bartellmachinery.com	Rome	NY	13440	315-336-7600	336-0947
Belvac Production Machinery Inc 237 Graves Mill Rd *TF:* 800-423-5822 ■ *Web:* www.belvac.com	Lynchburg	VA	24502	434-239-0358	239-1964
Delta Brands Inc (DBI) 2204 Century Ctr Blvd *Web:* www.dbimfg.com	Irving	TX	75062	972-438-7150	579-0100
Eagle Technologies Group 9850 Red Arrow Hwy *Web:* www.eagletechnologies.com	Bridgman	MI	49106	269-465-6986	465-6952
Eubanks Engineering Co 3022 Inland Empire Blvd *TF:* 800-729-4208 ■ *Web:* www.eubanks.com	Ontario	CA	91764	909-483-2456	483-2498
FANTA Equipment Co 6521 Storer Ave *Web:* www.fantaequip.com	Cleveland	OH	44102	216-281-1515	281-7755
Hogan Manufacturing Inc (HMI) PO Box 398 *Web:* www.hoganmfg.com	Escalon	CA	95320	209-838-7323	838-7329
J.R. Automation Technologies LLC 13365 Tyler St *Web:* www.jrautomation.com	Holland	MI	49424	616-399-2168	399-5593
Merrill Tool & Machine Co Inc 21659 Gratiot Rd *Web:* www.merrilltool.com	Merrill	MI	48637	989-643-7981	643-7975
Pannier Corp 207 Sandusky St *TF:* 877-726-6437 ■ *Web:* www.pannier.com	Pittsburgh	PA	15212	412-323-4900	323-4962
Pines Technology 30505 Clemens Rd *TF:* 800-207-2840 ■ *Web:* www.pinestech.com	Westlake	OH	44145	440-835-5553	835-5556
Precision Strip Inc 86 S Ohio St PO Box 104 *Web:* www.precision-strip.com	Minster	OH	45865	419-501-1347	
Red Bud Industries 200 B & E Industrial Dr *TF Cust Svc:* 800-851-4612 ■ *Web:* www.redbudindustries.com	Red Bud	IL	62278	618-282-3801	282-6718
Rowe Machinery & Automation Inc 76 Hinckley Rd *TF:* 800-247-2645 ■ *Web:* www.runwithrowe.com	Clinton	ME	04927	207-426-2351	426-7453
Superior Machine Company of South Carolina Inc 692 N Cashua Dr *Web:* www.smco.net	Florence	SC	29502	843-687-9305	
Sweed Machinery Inc 653 Second Ave PO Box 228 *TF Sales:* 800-888-1352 ■ *Web:* www.sweed.com	Gold Hill	OR	97525	541-855-1512	855-1165
Tridan International Inc 130 N Jackson St PO Box 537 *Web:* www.tridan.com	Danville	IL	61834	217-443-3592	443-3894
West Bond Inc 1551 S Harris Ct *Web:* www.westbond.com	Anaheim	CA	92806	714-978-1551	978-0431

498 METERS & OTHER COUNTING DEVICES

				Phone	Fax
AMETEK Inc Dixson Div 287 27 Rd *TF:* 888-302-0639 ■ *Web:* www.ametekvis.com	Grand Junction	CO	81503	970-242-8863	245-6267
AMETEK Sensor Technology Drexelbrook Div 205 Keith Valley Rd *TF Cust Svc:* 800-553-9092 ■ *Web:* www.drexelbrook.com	Horsham	PA	19044	215-674-1234	674-2731
Auto Meter Products Inc 413 W Elm St *TF:* 866-248-6356 ■ *Web:* www.autometer.com	Sycamore	IL	60178	815-895-8141	895-6786
Badger Meter Inc 4545 W Brown Deer Rd *NYSE: BMI* ■ *TF:* 800-876-3837 ■ *Web:* www.badgermeter.com	Milwaukee	WI	53223	414-355-0400	
Beede Electrical Instrument Co 88 Village St *Web:* www.beede.com	Penacook	NH	03303	603-753-6362	753-6201
Clark-Reliance Corp 16633 Foltz Pkwy *TF:* 800-238-4027 ■ *Web:* www.clarkreliance.com	Strongsville	OH	44149	440-572-1500	572-1500
Danaher Controls 1675 Delany Rd *TF:* 800-873-8731 ■ *Web:* www.danaherspecialtyproducts.com	Gurnee	IL	60031	847-662-2666	662-4150
Duncan Solutions Inc 633 W Wisconsin Ave Ste 1600 *TF:* 888-993-8622 ■ *Web:* www.duncanindustries.com	Milwaukee	WI	53203	888-993-8622	
Electro-Sensors Inc 6111 Blue Cir Dr *NASDAQ: ELSE* ■ *TF:* 800-328-6170 ■ *Web:* www.electro-sensors.com	Minnetonka	MN	55343	952-930-0100	930-0130
Elster American Meter Co 2221 Industrial Rd *TF:* 800-461-4076 ■ *Web:* www.elster-americanmeter.com	Nebraska City	NE	68410	402-873-8200	873-7616
Engineering Measurements Co (EMCO) 1150 Northpoint Blvd Ste C **Fax Area Code:* 803 ■ *TF:* 800-575-0394 ■ *Web:* www.spiraxsarco.com	Blythewood	SC	29016	800-575-0394	714-2222*
Eugene Ernst Products Company Inc PO Box 925 **Fax Area Code:* 888 ■ *TF:* 800-992-2843 ■ *Web:* www.ernstflow.com	Farmingdale	NJ	07727	732-938-5641	992-2843*
Greenwald Industries 212 Middlesex Ave *TF:* 800-221-0982 ■ *Web:* www.greenwaldindustries.com	Chester	CT	06412	860-526-0800	526-4205
Isspro Inc 2515 NE Riverside Way *TF:* 888-447-7776 ■ *Web:* www.issproinc.com	Portland	OR	97211	503-528-3400	249-2999
Laser Technology Inc 7070 S Tucson Way *TF:* 800-280-6113 ■ *Web:* www.lasertech.com	Englewood	CO	80112	303-649-1000	649-9710
Max Machinery Inc 33A Healdsburg Ave *Web:* www.maxmachinery.com	Healdsburg	CA	95448	707-433-2662	433-1818
Maxima Technologies Stewart Warner 1811 Rohrerstown Rd *TF:* 800-676-1837 ■ *Web:* www.maximatecc.com	Lancaster	PA	17601	717-581-1000	569-7247
PMP Corp 25 Security Dr *TF Cust Svc:* 800-243-6628 ■ *Web:* www.pmp-corp.com	Avon	CT	06001	860-677-9656	674-0196
POM Inc 200 S Elmira Ave PO Box 430 *TF:* 800-331-7275 ■ *Web:* www.pom.com	Russellville	AR	72802	479-968-2880	968-2840
Schlumberger Ltd 5599 San Felipe Ste 100 *NYSE: SLB* ■ *Web:* www.slb.com	Houston	TX	77056	713-513-2000	513-2006
Sparling Instruments Company Inc 4097 N Temple City Blvd *TF Sales:* 800-800-3569 ■ *Web:* www.sparlinginstruments.com	El Monte	CA	91731	626-444-0571	444-2314
Teleflex Morse Marine Products 640 N Lewis Rd *Web:* www.tfxmarine.com	Limerick	PA	19468	610-495-7011	495-7470
Thomas G Faria Corp 385 Norwich-New London Tpke *TF:* 800-473-2742 ■ *Web:* www.faria-instruments.com	Uncasville	CT	06382	860-848-9271	848-2704

499 MICROGRAPHICS PRODUCTS & SERVICES

				Phone	Fax
Anacomp Inc 15378 Ave of Science *OTC: ANMP* ■ *Web:* www.anacomp.com	San Diego	CA	92128	858-716-3400	
BMI Imaging Systems 1115 E Arques Ave *TF:* 800-359-3456 ■ *Web:* www.bmiimaging.com	Sunnyvale	CA	94085	408-736-7444	736-4397
Comgraphics Inc 329 W 18th St 10th Fl *Web:* ww3.cgichicago.com	Chicago	IL	60616	312-226-0900	226-9411
Comstor Productivity Ctr Inc 2219 N Dickey Rd *TF:* 800-776-2451 ■ *Web:* www.comstorinc.com	Spokane	WA	99212	509-534-5080	536-0281
DPF Data Services Group Inc 1990 Swarthmore Ave *TF:* 800-431-4416 ■ *Web:* www.dpfdata.com	Lakewood	NJ	08701	732-370-8840	370-1751
DST Output 5220 Robert J Mathews Pkwy *TF:* 800-441-7587 ■ *Web:* dstsystems.com	El Dorado Hills	CA	95762	916-939-4960	
Eye Communication Systems Inc 455 E Industrial Dr *TF:* 800-558-2153 ■ *Web:* www.eyecom.com	Hartland	WI	53029	262-367-1360	367-1362
HF Group Inc 203 W Artesia Blvd *TF:* 800-421-5000 ■ *Web:* www.hf76.com	Compton	CA	90220	310-605-0755	608-1181
Indus International Inc 340 S Oak St PO Box 890 *TF:* 800-843-9377 ■ *Web:* www.indususa.com	West Salem	WI	54669	608-786-0300	786-0786
Micro Com Systems Ltd 27 E Seventh Ave *Web:* www.microcomsys.com	Vancouver	BC	V5T1M4	604-872-6771	
microMEDIA Imaging Systems Inc 1979 Marcus Ave *Web:* www.imagingservices.com	Lake Success	NY	11042	516-355-0300	355-0316

500 MILITARY BASES

SEE ALSO Coast Guard Installations p. 1958

500-1 Air Force Bases

				Phone	Fax
Altus Air Force Base 305 E Ave *Web:* www.altus.af.mil	Altus Afb	OK	73523	580-482-8100	481-5966
Arnold Air Force Base 100 Kindel Dr Ste B-213 *Web:* www.arnold.af.mil	Arnold	TN	37389	931-454-3000	454-6086
Barksdale Air Force Base Second Bomb Wing Public Affairs *Web:* www.barksdale.af.mil	Barksdale AFB	LA	71110	318-456-3066	
Bolling Air Force Base (BAFB) 20 MacDill Blvd Ste 220 *Web:* www.cnic.navy.mil/regions/ndw/installations/jbab.html	Washington	DC	20032	202-404-3281	
Cannon Air Force Base 110 E Sextant Ave Ste 1150 **Fax Area Code:* 505 ■ *TF:* 877-283-3858 ■ *Web:* www.cannon.af.mil	Cannon AFB	NM	88103	575-784-4131	784-2338*
Columbus Air Force Base 555 Seventh St *Web:* www.columbus.af.mil	Columbus AFB	MS	39710	662-434-7068	434-7009
Davis-Monthan Air Force Base 5275 E Granite St *Web:* www.dm.af.mil	Davis-Monthan AFB	AZ	85707	520-228-3204	228-5299
Dover Air Force Base 201 Eagle Way *Web:* www.dover.af.mil	Dover AFB	DE	19902	302-677-3372	677-2901
Edwards Air Force Base 305 E Popson Ave *Web:* www.edwards.af.mil	Edwards AFB	CA	93524	661-277-1110	277-2732
Eglin Air Force Base Eglin Blvd *Web:* www.eglin.af.mil	Eglin AFB	FL	32542	850-882-1113	
Eielson Air Force Base 354 Broadway St Unit 2B *TF:* 800-538-6647 ■ *Web:* www.eielson.af.mil	Eielson AFB	AK	99702	907-377-1110	377-1606
Ellsworth Air Force Base 1958 Scott Dr *Web:* www.ellsworth.af.mil	Ellsworth AFB	SD	57706	605-385-5056	385-4668
Fairchild Air Force Base 100 W Ent St Ste 155 *Web:* www.fairchild.af.mil	Fairchild AFB	WA	99011	509-247-1212	247-5640
Goodfellow Air Force Base 351 Kearney Blvd *Web:* www.goodfellow.af.mil	Goodfellow AFB	TX	76908	325-654-3877	654-5414
Grand Forks Air Force Base 344 Sixth Ave Grand Forks AFB *Web:* grandforks.af.mil	Grand Forks	ND	58205	701-747-3000	
Hanscom Air Force Base Hanscom Dr *Web:* www.hanscom.af.mil	Lincoln	MA	01742	781-377-4441	
Hill Air Force Base 7285 Fourth St Bldg 180 Ste 109 *Web:* www.hill.af.mil	Hill AFB	UT	84056	801-777-5201	
Kirtland Air Force Base 2000 Wyoming Blvd SE Ste A-1 *TF:* 877-246-1453 ■ *Web:* www.kirtland.af.mil	Kirtland AFB	NM	87117	505-846-5991	
Langley Air Force Base 49 Spruce St PO Box 1000 **Fax:* Library ■ *Web:* www.jble.af.mil	Langley AFB	VA	23665	757-764-1110	764-3315*

				Phone	Fax
Laughlin Air Force Base 561 Liberty Dr Ste 3 *TF:* 866-966-1020 ■ *Web:* www.laughlin.af.mil	Laughlin AFB	TX	78843	830-298-5988	298-5047
Little Rock Air Force Base 1250 Thomas Ave *TF:* 800-557-6815 ■ *Web:* www.littlerock.af.mil	Little Rock AFB	AR	72099	501-987-1110	987-6978
Los Angeles Air Force Base 483 N Aviation Blvd Los Angeles AFB *Web:* www.losangeles.af.mil	El Segundo	CA	90245	310-653-1110	
Luke Air Force Base 14185 W Falcon St *TF:* 800-321-1080 ■ *Web:* www.luke.af.mil	Luke AFB	AZ	85309	623-856-5853	856-6013
Malmstrom Air Force Base 7410 Flightline Dr Bldg 300 *TF:* 866-731-4633 ■ *Web:* www.malmstrom.af.mil	Malmstrom AFB	MT	59402	406-731-1110	731-4048
Maxwell Air Force Base 55 Le May Plaza S *TF:* 877-353-6807 ■ *Web:* www.maxwell.af.mil	Maxwell AFB	AL	36112	334-953-2014	953-3379
McConnell Air Force Base 57837 Coffeyville St Ste 271 *TF:* 877-272-7337 ■ *Web:* www.mcconnell.af.mil	McConnell AFB	KS	67221	316-759-6100	759-3148
McGuire Air Force Base 2901 Falcon Ln Rm 235 *Web:* www.jointbasemdl.af.mil	Joint Base McGuire-Dix-Lakehurst	NJ	08641	609-754-2104	754-6999
Minot Air Force Base 201 Summit Dr *Web:* www.minot.af.mil	Minot AFB	ND	58705	701-723-6212	723-6534
Moody Air Force Base 4343 George St Bldg 904 *Web:* www.moody.af.mil	Moody AFB	GA	31699	229-257-3395	257-4804
Mountain Home Air Force Base 366 Gunfighter Ave Ste 314 *TF:* 855-366-0140 ■ *Web:* www.mountainhome.af.mil	Mountain Home AFB	ID	83648	208-828-6800	828-4205
Nellis Air Force Base 4430 Grissom Ave Ste 107 *Web:* www.nellis.af.mil	Nellis AFB	NV	89191	702-652-2750	652-9838
Offutt Air Force Base 906 Sac Blvd Ste 1 *Web:* www.offutt.af.mil	Offutt AFB	NE	68113	402-294-1110	294-7172
Patrick Air Force Base 1201 Edward H White Ste C-129 *Web:* www.patrick.af.mil	Patrick AFB	FL	32925	321-494-5933	494-7302
Scott Air Force Base 101 Heritage Dr Rm128 *Web:* www.scott.af.mil	Scott AFB	IL	62225	618-256-1110	
Seymour Johnson Air Force Base 1510 Wright Bros Ave *TF:* 800-525-0102 ■ *Web:* www.seymourjohnson.af.mil	Seymour Johnson AFB	NC	27531	919-722-0027	722-0007
Shaw Air Force Base 517 Lance Ave Ste 106 *TF:* 800-235-7776 ■ *Web:* www.shaw.af.mil	Shaw AFB	SC	29152	803-895-2019	895-2028
Sheppard Air Force Base 419 G Ave Ste 3 *TF:* 877-676-1847 ■ *Web:* www.sheppard.af.mil	Sheppard AFB	TX	76311	940-676-2511	676-4245
Tinker Air Force Base 3001 Staff Dr Ste 1AG85A *Web:* www.tinker.af.mil	Tinker AFB	OK	73145	405-739-2026	739-2882
Tyndall Air Force Base 445 Suwannee Rd 101 *TF:* 800-356-5273 ■ *Web:* www.tyndall.af.mil	Tyndall AFB	FL	32403	850-283-1110	283-3225
Vance Air Force Base 246 Brown Pkwy *TF:* 866-966-1020 ■ *Web:* vance.af.mil	Vance AFB	OK	73705	580-213-7476	213-6376
Vandenberg Air Force Base 706 Washington Ave Bldg 10122 *Web:* www.vandenberg.af.mil	Vandenberg	CA	93437	805-606-3595	606-8303
Whiteman Air Force Base 1081 Arnold Ave Bldg 59 Ste 104 *TF:* 866-363-8667 ■ *Web:* www.whiteman.af.mil	Whiteman AFB	MO	65305	660-687-6123	687-7948
Wright-Patterson Air Force Base 5030 Patterson Pkwy *Web:* www.wpafb.af.mil	Wright-Patterson AFB	OH	45433	937-257-1110	

500-2 Army Bases

				Phone	Fax
Fort AP Hill 18436 Fourth St *Web:* www.army.mil	Fort AP Hill	VA	22427	804-633-8120	633-8105
Fort Benning 6460Way Ave *Web:* www.benning.army.mil	Fort Benning	GA	31905	706-545-2218	545-1604
Fort Campbell Michigan Ave *Web:* www.campbell.army.mil/pages/camphome.aspx	Fort Campbell	KY	42223	270-798-2151	798-6247
Fort Detrick 810 Schreider St *Web:* www.detrick.army.mil	Frederick	MD	21702	301-619-7613	
Fort Gordon 201 Third Ave *Web:* www.gordon.army.mil	Fort Gordon	GA	30905	706-791-0110	791-2061
Fort Hamilton 113 Schum Ave Bldg 113 *Web:* www.hamilton.army.mil	Brooklyn	NY	11252	718-630-4101	630-4717
Fort Hood 761st Tank Battalion Ave Bldg 1001 Rm W105 *Web:* www.hood.army.mil	Fort Hood	TX	76544	254-287-1110	288-2750
Fort Huachuca Smith St Bldg 50010 *Web:* www.huachuca.army.mil	Fort Huachuca	AZ	85613	520-533-7111	533-5008
Fort Jackson 5450 Strom Thurmond Blvd 1011 Columbia *Web:* jackson.armylive.dodlive.mil/	Fort Jackson	SC	29207	803-751-7511	
Fort Knox PO Box 995 *Web:* www.knox.army.mil	Fort Knox	KY	40121	502-624-4985	
Fort Leavenworth 881 Mcclellan Ave *Web:* usacac.army.mil	Fort Leavenworth	KS	66027	913-758-3646	684-3624
Fort Lee 500 Lee Ave *Web:* www.lee.army.mil	Fort Lee	VA	23801	804-765-3000	734-4659
Fort Leonard Wood Bldg 744 *TF:* 800-350-7746 ■ *Web:* www.wood.army.mil	Fort Leonard Wood	MO	65473	573-596-0131	563-4012
Fort Meade 4550 Parade Field Ln Rm 102 *TF:* 877-372-3337 ■ *Web:* www.ftmeade.army.mil	Fort Meade	MD	20755	301-677-1361	677-1305
Fort Polk 2030 14th St *TF:* 800-752-4658 ■ *Web:* www.jrtc-polk.army.mil	Fort Polk	LA	71459	337-531-2911	531-6014
Fort Richardson Richardson Dr Bldg 600 *TF:* 800-984-1517 ■ *Web:* www.usarak.army.mil/main	Fort Richardson	AK	99505	907-384-0763	384-2060
Fort Riley 405 Pershing Ct *TF:* 800-273-8255 ■ *Web:* www.riley.army.mil	Fort Riley	KS	66442	785-239-2022	239-2592
Fort Sam Houston 3630 Stanley Rd *Web:* www.cs.amedd.army.mil	Fort Sam Houston	TX	78234	210-221-8580	
Fort Story 2600 Tarawa Ct *Web:* www.cnic.navy.mil	Norfolk	VA	23521	757-462-8425	
Fort Wainwright 1047-1 Marks Rd Ste 5900 *Web:* www.wainwright.army.mil	Fort Wainwright	AK	99703	907-353-6701	353-6711
Joint Base Myer 204 Lee Ave Bldg 59 *Web:* www.army.mil	Fort Myer	VA	22211	703-696-0584	696-2678
U.S Army Avitation center of Excellence & Fort Rucker 453 Novosel St Bldg 131 *Web:* www-rucker.army.mil	Fort Rucker	AL	36362	334-255-3400	255-1004

500-3 Marine Corps Bases

				Phone	Fax
Marine Corps Air Station Beaufort PO Box 55001 *Web:* www.beaufort.marines.mil	Beaufort	SC	29904	843-228-7121	228-6005
Marine Corps Air Station Yuma Shaw Ave Bldg 980 *Web:* mcasyuma.marines.mil	Yuma	AZ	85369	928-269-2252	269-3282
Marine Corps Base Hawaii PO Box 63002 *Web:* www.mcbhawaii.marines.mil	Kaneohe Bay	HI	96863	808-257-8840	257-2511
Marine Corps Base Quantico 3250 Catlin Ave *Web:* www.quantico.marines.mil	Quantico	VA	22134	703-784-2121	
Marine Corps Recruit Depot San Diego 1600 Henderson Ave *Web:* mcrdsd.marines.mil	San Diego	CA	92145	619-524-8727	
MCRD Parris Island 283 Blvd de France *Web:* mcrdpi.marines.mil	Parris Island	SC	29905	843-228-2111	228-2122

500-4 Naval Installations

				Phone	Fax
Naval Air Station Fallon 4755 Pasture Rd Bldg 309 *Web:* www.cnic.navy.mil	Fallon	NV	89496	775-426-3333	
Naval Air Station Jacksonville 6801 Roosevelt Blvd *TF:* 800-849-6024 ■ *Web:* www.cnic.navy.mil/jacksonville	Jacksonville	FL	32212	904-542-2338	
Naval Air Station Joint Reserve Base Fort Worth 1510 Chennault Ave *Web:* www.cnic.navy.mil/fortworth	Fort Worth	TX	76113	817-782-5000	
Naval Air Station Joint Reserve Base New Orleans 301 Russell Ave *TF:* 800-729-7327 ■ *Web:* www.cnic.navy.mil	New Orleans	LA	70143	504-678-3254	678-9595
Naval Air Station Key West PO Box 9001 *Web:* www.cnic.navy.mil/keywest	Key West	FL	33040	305-293-2425	
Naval Air Station Kingsville 554 Mccain St *Web:* www.cnic.navy.mil/kingsville	Kingsville	TX	78363	361-516-6146	516-6875
Naval Air Station Lemoore 700 Avenger *Web:* www.cnic.navy.mil/Lemoore	Lemoore	CA	93246	559-998-3300	998-3395
Naval Air Station Meridian 200 Rosenbaum Ave *Web:* cnic.navy.mil	Meridian	MS	39309	601-679-2211	
Naval Air Station North Island PO Box 357033 *Web:* www.cnic.navy.mil	San Diego	CA	92135	619-545-9589	545-6260
Naval Air Station Oceana 1750 Tomcat Blvd *Web:* www.cnic.navy.mil/oceana	Virginia Beach	VA	23460	757-433-3131	
Naval Air Station Patuxent River 22268 Cedar Point Road Bldg 409 *TF:* 877-995-5247 ■ *Web:* cnic.navy.mil/patuxent	Patuxent River	MD	20670	301-342-3000	
Naval Air Station Pensacola 190 Radford Blvd *Web:* navy-lodge.com	Pensacola	FL	32508	850-452-4785	
Naval Air Station Whiting Field 7550 USS Essex St *Web:* www.cnic.navy.mil	Milton	FL	32570	850-623-7341	
Naval Air Station Willow Grove PO Box 21 *Web:* www.cnic.navy.mil	Willow Grove	PA	19090	215-443-1000	443-6017
Naval Base Kitsap 120 S Dewey St *Web:* www.cnic.navy.mil	Bremerton	WA	98314	360-627-4024	
Naval Base San Diego 3455 Senn Rd *TF:* 877-995-5247 ■ *Web:* www.cnic.navy.mil/sandiego	San Diego	CA	92136	619-556-1011	
Naval Station Everett 2000 W Marine View Dr *Web:* www.cnic.navy.mil	Everett	WA	98207	425-304-3366	304-3096
Naval Station Great Lakes 2601E Paul Jones St *Web:* www.cnic.navy.mil	Great Lakes	IL	60088	847-688-3500	
Naval Station Mayport PO Box 280032 *TF:* 800-872-7245 ■ *Web:* www.cnic.navy.mil/mayport	Mayport	FL	32228	904-270-5401	270-5064
Naval Station Newport 690 Peary St *Web:* www.cnic.navy.mil/newport	Newport	RI	02841	401-841-3456	841-2265
Naval Station Pearl Harbor 4827 Bougainville Dr *Web:* www.cnic.navy.mil	Honolulu	HI	96818	808-474-1999	
Naval Support Activity 58 Bennion Rd *Web:* www.usna.edu	Annapolis	MD	21402	410-293-1000	293-3133
U.S. Fleet Forces Command 1562 Mitscher Ave Ste 250 *TF:* 800-473-3549 ■ *Web:* public.navy.mil	Norfolk	VA	23551	757-836-3630	836-3603

501 MILITARY SERVICE ACADEMIES

Company / Address	City	State	Zip	Phone	Fax
Royal Military College of Canada Stn Forces PO Box 17000. Web: www.rmc.ca	Kingston	ON	K7K7B4	613-541-6000	541-6599
US Air Force Academy (USAFA) 2304 Cadet Dr Ste 2300. *TF:* 800-443-9266 ■ *Web:* www.usafa.af.mil	Air Force Academy	CO	80840	719-333-1110	333-3644
US Military Academy Admissions Bldg 606 Third Fl. *Web:* www.usma.edu	West Point	NY	10996	845-938-4041	938-8121
US Naval Academy 121 Blake Rd. **Fax:* Admissions ■ *TF Admissions:* 888-249-7707 ■ *Web:* www.usna.edu	Annapolis	MD	21402	410-293-1000	293-4348*

502 MILLWORK

SEE ALSO Lumber & Building Supplies p. 2108; Doors & Windows - Wood p. 2205; Home Improvement Centers p. 2475; Shutters - Window (All Types) p. 3173

Company / Address	City	State	Zip	Phone	Fax
A & L Handles Inc 244 Shoemaker Rd. *Web:* www.alhandles.com	Pottstown	PA	19464	610-323-1516	
Accent' Windows Inc 14175 E 42nd Ave. *TF:* 888-284-3948 ■ *Web:* www.accentwindows.com	Denver	CO	80239	303-420-2002	
Alfab Inc 220 Boll Weevil Cir E. *Web:* www.alfabinc.com	Enterprise	AL	36330	334-347-9516	
Allegheny Millwork PBT 104 Commerce Blvd. *Web:* www.alleghenymillwork.com	Lawrence	PA	15055	724-873-8700	
Allen Millwork Inc 6969 Fern Loop PO Box 6480. *TF:* 800-551-8737 ■ *Web:* homedesigncentershreveport.com	Shreveport	LA	71105	318-629-5300	629-5301
ALLSCO Building Products Ltd 70 Rideout St. *Web:* www.allsco.com	Moncton	NB	E1E1E2	506-853-8080	853-9344
American Millwork Corp 4840 Beck Dr. *Web:* www.americanmillwork.com	Elkhart	IN	46516	574-295-4158	293-5378
Anderson Wood Products Co 1381 Beech St. *TF:* 800-825-5591 ■ *Web:* www.andersonwood.com	Louisville	KY	40211	502-778-5591	778-5599
Anlin Industries 1665 Tollhouse Rd. *TF:* 800-287-7996 ■ *Web:* www.anlin.com	Clovis	CA	93611	559-322-1531	322-1532
Annandale Millwork Allied Systems 220 Arbor Ct. *Web:* amcasc.com	Winchester	VA	22602	540-665-9600	
Appalachian Wood Products Inc 171 Loop Rd. *Web:* www.appwood.com	Clearfield	PA	16830	814-765-2003	765-4751
Arcways Inc 1076 Ehlers Rd. *Web:* www.arcways.com	Neenah	WI	54956	920-725-2667	
Bay Industries Inc 2929 Walker Dr. *Web:* www.bayindustries.com	Green Bay	WI	54308	920-406-4000	
Black Millwork Company Inc 220 W Crescent Ave. *Web:* www.blackmillwork.com	Allendale	NJ	07401	201-934-0100	
Boiseries Raymond Inc 11880, 56e Ave. *Web:* www.boiseriesraymond.com	Montreal	QC	H1E2L6	514-494-1141	494-9666
Bright Wood Corp 335 NW Hess St PO Box 828. *Web:* www.brightwood.com	Madras	OR	97741	541-475-2243	475-7086
Brochsteins Inc 11530 Main St. *Web:* www.brochsteins.com	Houston	TX	77025	713-666-2881	
Brockway-Smith Co (BWAY) 146 Dascomb Rd. **Fax Area Code:* 732 ■ *TF:* 800-225-7912 ■ *Web:* www.brosco.com	Andover	MA	01810	978-475-7100	826-0606*
Buffelen Woodworking Co 1901 Taylor Way. *Web:* www.buffelendoor.com	Tacoma	WA	98421	253-627-1191	
Cain Millwork Inc One Cain Pkwy. *Web:* www.cainmillwork.com	Rochelle	IL	61068	815-561-9700	
Canamould Extrusions Inc 101a Roytec Rd. *Web:* www.canamould.com	Woodbridge	ON	L4L8A9	905-264-4436	
Carter-Lee ProBuild 1717 W Washington St. *Web:* probuildindy.com	Indianapolis	IN	46222	317-639-5431	639-6982
Cascade Wood Products Inc PO Box 2429. *TF:* 800-423-3311 ■ *Web:* www.cascadewood.com	White City	OR	97503	541-826-2911	826-3985
Causeway Lumber Co 3318 SW Second Ave. *TF:* 800-375-5050 ■ *Web:* www.causewaylumber.com	Fort Lauderdale	FL	33315	954-763-1224	467-2389
Centennial Windows Ltd 687 Sovereign Rd. *Web:* www.centennialwindows.com	London	ON	N5V4K8	519-451-0508	
Central Woodwork Inc 870 Keough Rd. *TF:* 800-788-3775 ■ *Web:* www.centralwoodwork.com	Collierville	TN	38017	901-363-4141	542-6187
City Thermo Pane Ltd 420 Industrielle St. *Web:* www.citythermopane.com	Beresford	NB	E8K2C2	506-542-1130	542-1139
Columbia Woodworking Inc 935 Brentwood Rd NE. *Web:* cwwcorp.com	Washington	DC	20018	202-526-2387	526-5163
Commercial & Architectural Products Inc PO Box 250. *TF:* 800-377-1221 ■ *Web:* www.marlite.com	Dover	OH	44622	330-343-6621	343-7296
Conforce International Inc 51A Caldari Rd Second Fl. *Web:* conforceinternational.com	Concord	ON	L4K4G3	416-234-0266	
Contact Industries Inc 9200 SE Sunnybrook Blvd Ste 200. *TF:* 800-547-1038 ■ *Web:* www.contactind.com	Clackamas	OR	97015	503-228-7361	221-1340
Cox Interior Inc 1751 Old Columbia Rd. **Fax Area Code:* 270 ■ *TF:* 800-733-1751 ■ *Web:* www.coxinterior.com	Campbellsville	KY	42718	800-733-1751	465-7977*
CW Ohio Inc 1209 Maple Ave. *Web:* www.cwohio.com	Conneaut	OH	44030	440-593-5800	593-4545
Dashwood Industries Ltd 69323 Richmond St. *Web:* www.dashwood.com	Centralia	ON	N0M1K0	519-228-6624	228-2083
Delden Manufacturing Company Inc 3530 N Kimball Dr. *Web:* www.deldenmfg.com	Kansas City	MO	64161	816-413-1600	
DeLeers Millwork Inc 1735 Sal St. *Web:* www.deleersmillwork.com	Green Bay	WI	54302	920-593-7979	465-8835
Dorris Lumber & Moulding Co, The 2601 Redding Ave. *Web:* www.dorrismoulding.com	Sacramento	CA	95820	916-452-7531	
Dubois Wood Products Inc 707 E Sixth St PO Box 386. *Web:* www.duboiswood.com	Huntingburg	IN	47542	812-683-3613	683-3847
Durawood Products Inc 18 Industrial Way. *Web:* www.durawood.com	Denver	PA	17517	717-336-0220	
Eastern Millwork Co 3222 Oley Tpke Rd PO Box 4128	Reading	PA	19606	610-779-3550	779-1241
Faubion Associates Inc 1000 Forest Ave. *Web:* www.faubionassoc.com	Dallas	TX	75315	214-565-1000	
Fenetres Lapco Inc 12995 Rue Du Parc. *Web:* www.lapcoinc.com	Mirabel	QC	J7J1P3	450-971-0432	
Four C's Holdings Ltd 330 Mackenzie Blvd. *Web:* www.casman.ca	Fort Mcmurray	AB	T9H4C4	780-791-9283	
Giffin Interior & Fixture Inc 500 Scott Dr. *Web:* giffininterior.com	Bridgeville	PA	15017	412-221-1166	221-3745
Global Window Solutions 128 Industrial Park Rd. *Web:* www.globalwindows.ca	Richibucto	NB	E4W4A4	506-523-4900	
Graves Lumber Co 1315 S Cleveland-Massillon Rd. *TF:* 877-500-5515 ■ *Web:* www.graveslumber.com	Copley	OH	44321	330-666-1115	666-1377
Great Lakes Woodworking Co 11345 Mound Rd. *Web:* www.g-l-w.com	Detroit	MI	48212	313-892-8500	
Havco Wood Products LLC 3200 E Outer Rd. *Web:* www.havco.com	Scott City	MO	63780	573-334-6024	
HB&G Inc PO Box 589. *TF:* 800-264-4424 ■ *Web:* www.hbgcolumns.com	Troy	AL	36081	334-566-5000	566-4629
Herrick & White Ltd Three Flat St. *Web:* herrick-white.com	Cumberland	RI	02864	401-658-0440	
Hoff Cos Inc 1840 N Lakes Ave. *Web:* www.hoffcompanies.com	Meridian	ID	83646	208-884-2002	884-1115
Hollywood Woodwork Inc 2951 Pembroke Rd. *Web:* www.hollywoodwoodwork.com	Hollywood	FL	33020	954-920-5009	374-0876
Horner Millwork Corp 1255 Grand Army Hwy. *TF:* 800-543-5403 ■ *Web:* www.hornermillwork.com	Somerset	MA	02726	508-679-6479	
Huttig Bldg Products Inc (HBP) 555 Maryville University Dr Ste 400. *OTC: HBPI* ■ *TF:* 800-325-4466 ■ *Web:* www.huttig.com	Saint Louis	MO	63141	314-216-2600	216-2601
Imperial Woodworking Co 310 N Woodwork Ln. *Web:* www.imperialwoodworking.com	Palatine	IL	60067	847-358-6920	358-0905
Inline Fibreglass Ltd 30 Constellation Ct. *Web:* www.inlinefiberglass.com	Toronto	ON	M9W1K1	416-679-1171	679-1150
J C Millwork Inc 2013 County Rd 561. *Web:* www.jcmillwork.com	Princeton	TX	75407	972-734-3375	
Jeld-Wen Inc PO Box 1329. *TF:* 800-535-3936 ■ *Web:* www.jeld-wen.com	Klamath Falls	OR	97601	800-535-3936	
Koshii Maxelum America Inc 12 Van Kleeck Dr. *Web:* www.kmamax.com	Poughkeepsie	NY	12602	845-471-0500	
Lafayette Wood-Works Inc 3004 Cameron St. *TF:* 800-960-3311 ■ *Web:* www.lafwoodworks.com	Lafayette	LA	70506	337-233-5250	233-1147
Laflamme Doors & Windows Corp 39 Industrielle. *TF:* 800-463-1922 ■ *Web:* www.laflamme.com	St. Apollinaire	QC	G0S2E0	800-463-1922	
LJ Smith Co 35280 Scio-Bowerston Rd. *Web:* www.ljsmith.net	Bowerston	OH	44695	740-269-2221	269-9047
Long Island Fireproof Door Inc 1105 Clintonville St. *Web:* lifd.com	Whitestone	NY	11357	718-767-8800	
Loudoun Stairs Inc 341 N Maple Ave. *Web:* www.loudounstairs.com	Purcellville	VA	20132	703-478-8800	
Louisiana-Pacific Corp 414 Union St Ste 2000. *NYSE: LPX* ■ *TF:* 888-820-0325 ■ *Web:* www.lpcorp.com	Nashville	TN	37219	615-986-5600	986-5666
Mann & Parker Lumber Company Inc, The 335 N Constitution Ave. *TF:* 800-632-9098 ■ *Web:* m-pgoldbrand.com	New Freedom	PA	17349	717-235-4834	235-5547
MCD Innovations 3303 N MCDonald St. *Web:* www.mcdinnovations.com	Mckinney	TX	75071	972-548-1850	
Menzner Lumber & Supply Co PO Box 217. **Fax Area Code:* 715 ■ *TF:* 800-257-1284 ■ *Web:* www.menznerhardwoods.com	Marathon	WI	54448	800-257-1284	443-3798*
Michbi Doors Inc 75 Emjay Blvd. *Web:* www.michbidoors.com	Brentwood	NY	11717	631-231-9050	
Middlebury Hardwood Products Inc 101 Joan Dr PO Box 1429. *Web:* mhpi.us	Middlebury	IN	46540	574-825-9524	
Milliken Millwork Inc 6361 Sterling Dr N. *TF:* 800-686-9218 ■ *Web:* www.millikenmillwork.com	Sterling Heights	MI	48312	586-264-0950	264-5430
Mission Bell Manufacturing Inc 16100 Jacqueline Ct. *Web:* www.missionbell.com	Morgan Hill	CA	95037	408-778-2036	
Monarch Industries Inc 99 Main St. *Web:* www.monarchinc.com	Warren	RI	02885	401-247-5200	
Nana Wall Systems Inc 707 Redwood Hwy. *Web:* www.nanawall.com	Mill Valley	CA	94941	415-383-3148	
New England Garage Door 15 Campanelli Cir. *TF:* 800-676-7734 ■ *Web:* www.wayne-dalton.com	Canton	MA	02021	781-821-2737	
Nickell Moulding Company Inc 3015 Mobile Dr. *Web:* www.nickellmoulding.com	Elkhart	IN	46514	574-264-3129	
Northside Cabinets Inc 301 Millstone Dr. *Web:* www.northsidecabinets.com	Hillsborough	NC	27278	919-732-6100	
Ohline Corp 1930 W 139th St	Gardena	CA	90249	310-327-4630	

	City	State	Zip	Phone	Fax
Paltech Enterprises Inc 2560 Bing Miller Ln *Web:* www.paltech-entrps.com	Urbana	IA	52345	319-443-2700	
Parenti & Raffaelli Ltd 215 Prospect Ave E *Web:* www.parentiwoodwork.com	Mount Prospect	IL	60056	847-253-5550	253-6055
PGM Products LLC 1 Commerce Dr **Fax Area Code:* 846	Barrington	NJ	08007	856-546-0704	546-0539*
Polaris Technologies Inc 500 Victoria Rd *TF:* 800-783-2179 ■ *Web:* www.polaristechnologies.com	Austintown	OH	44515	800-783-2179	
Quanex Building Products 2270 Woodale Dr *TF:* 800-233-4383 ■ *Web:* www.quanex.com	Mounds View	MN	55112	763-231-4000	
R Value Inc 2267 N Interstate Ave *Web:* www.indowwindows.com	Portland	OR	97227	503-284-2260	
Randall Bros Inc 665 Marietta St NW *TF Cust Svc:* 800-476-4539 ■ *Web:* www.randallbrothers.com	Atlanta	GA	30313	404-892-6666	875-6102
Raynor Garage Doors 1101 E River Rd **Fax:* Cust Svc ■ *TF:* 800-472-9667 ■ *Web:* www.raynor.com	Dixon	IL	61021	815-288-1431	288-3720*
Reeb Millwork Corp 7475 Henry Clay Blvd *Web:* reeb.com	Liverpool	NY	13088	315-451-6699	
Royal Cup Coffee and Tea 3201 Wellington Ct Ste 104 *Web:* www.royalcup.com	Raleigh	NC	27615	919-855-8988	
Ruffin & Payne Inc 4200 Vawter Ave PO Box 27286 *Web:* www.ruffin-payne.com	Richmond	VA	23261	804-329-2691	321-4940
Sensitile Systems LLC 1735 Holmes Rd *Web:* www.sensitile.com	Ypsilanti	MI	48197	313-872-6314	
Shanahan's LP 8400-124 St *Web:* www.shanahans.com	Surrey	BC	V3W6K1	604-591-5111	
Shaw/Stewart Lumber Co 645 Johnson St NE *Web:* www.shawstewartlumberco.com	Minneapolis	MN	55413	612-378-1520	
Shuster's Bldg Components 2920 Clay Pk **Fax Area Code:* 800 ■ *TF:* 800-676-0640 ■ *Web:* www.shusters.com	Irwin	PA	15642	724-446-7000	676-0640*
Sierra Pacific Industries 19794 Riverside Ave *Web:* spi-ind.com	Anderson	CA	96007	530-378-8000	378-8109
Somerset Door & Column Co 174 Sagamore St *TF:* 800-242-7916 ■ *Web:* doorandcolumn.com	Somerset	PA	15501	814-444-9427	443-1658
Southern Staircase Inc 6025 Shiloh Rd Ste E *TF:* 800-874-8408 ■ *Web:* www.southernstaircase.com	Alpharetta	GA	30005	770-888-7333	888-7344
Southern Woodsmith Inc 40 Monroe Dr *Web:* www.southernwoodsmith.com	Pelham	AL	35124	205-663-5299	
Standard Lumber Co 1912 Lehigh Ave *Web:* standardlumberco.com	Glenview	IL	60026	847-729-7800	729-8500
Stephenson Millwork Company Inc 210 Harper St NE *Web:* www.stephensonmillwork.com	Wilson	NC	27893	252-237-1141	237-4377
Sundt Construction 2620 S 55th St *TF:* 800-280-3000 ■ *Web:* www.sundt.com	Tempe	AZ	85282	480-293-3000	
Sunrise Mfg. Inc 2665 Mercantile Dr *Web:* www.sunrisemfg.com	Rancho Cordova	CA	95742	916-635-6262	
Taney Corp 5130 Allendale Ln *Web:* www.taneystair.com	Taneytown	MD	21787	410-756-6671	756-4103
Taylor Bros Inc 905 Graves Mill Rd *Web:* www.taylorbrothers.com	Lynchburg	VA	24502	434-237-8100	237-4227
THV Compozit Windows & Doors 5611 FERN VALLEY Rd *Web:* www.thv.com	Louisville	KY	40228	502-968-2020	
Tru Tech Corp 20 Vaughan Vly Blvd *Web:* www.trutech.ca	Vaughan	ON	L4H0B1	905-856-0096	
Washington Woodworking Company Inc 2010 Beaver Rd *Web:* www.washingtonwoodworking.com	Landover	MD	20785	301-341-2500	341-2512
Weaber Inc 1231 Mount Wilson Rd *Web:* www.weaberlumber.com	Lebanon	PA	17042	717-867-2212	
Werzalit of America Inc 40 Holly Ave *TF:* 800-999-3730 ■ *Web:* www.werzalitusa.com	Bradford	PA	16701	814-362-3881	362-4237
Western Millwork Inc 2940 W Willetta St *Web:* www.westernmillworkaz.com	Phoenix	AZ	85009	602-233-1921	278-7101
Windebank Woodwork & Design Ltd 538 Culduthel Rd *Web:* www.windebank.ca	Victoria	BC	V8Z1G1	250-380-1416	
Woodfold Manufacturing Inc 1811 18th Ave PO Box 346 *Web:* www.woodfold.com	Forest Grove	OR	97116	503-357-7181	357-7185
Woodgrain Millworks Inc 300 NW 16th St PO Box 566 *TF:* 800-452-3801 ■ *Web:* www.woodgrain.com	Fruitland	ID	83619	208-452-3801	452-3800
Woodharbor Doors & Cabinetry Inc 3277 Ninth St SW *TF:* 866-219-9786 ■ *Web:* www.woodharbor.com	Mason City	IA	50401	641-423-0444	423-0345
Young Mfg Company Inc 521 S Main St PO Box 167 *TF:* 800-545-6595 ■ *Web:* youngmanufacturing.com	Beaver Dam	KY	42320	270-274-3306	274-9522

503 MINERAL PRODUCTS - NONMETALLIC

SEE ALSO Insulation & Acoustical Products p. 2566

	City	State	Zip	Phone	Fax
Asbury Graphite Mills Inc 405 Old Main St *Web:* asbury.com	Asbury	NJ	08802	908-537-2155	537-2908
Astro Met Inc 9974 Springfield Pk *Web:* www.astromet.com	Cincinnati	OH	45215	513-772-1242	772-9080
Big River Industries Inc 900 Ashwood Pkwy Ste 500 **Fax Area Code:* 877 ■ *TF:* 800-342-5483 ■ *Web:* www.bigriverindustries.com	Atlanta	GA	30338	770-640-3008	838-7839*
Brubaker-Mann Inc 36011 Soap Mine Rd *Web:* brubakermann.com	Barstow	CA	92311	760-256-2520	256-0127
Buffalo Crushed Stone Co Inc 2544 Clinton St *TF:* 800-543-3860 ■ *Web:* buffalocrushedstone.com	Buffalo	NY	14224	716-826-7310	826-1342
Burgess Pigment Company Inc 525 Beck Blvd PO Box 349 *TF:* 800-841-8999 ■ *Web:* www.burgesspigment.com	Sandersville	GA	31082	478-552-2544	552-4274
Ceradyne Inc 3169 Redhill Ave *NYSE: MMM* ■ **Fax:* Sales ■ *TF:* 877-992-7749 ■ *Web:* solutions.3m.com/	Costa Mesa	CA	92626	714-549-0421	549-5787*
Christy Refractories Co 4641 McRee Ave *Web:* www.christyco.com	Saint Louis	MO	63110	314-773-7500	773-8371
Consolidated Ceramic Products Inc 838 Cherry St *Web:* www.ccpi-inc.com	Blanchester	OH	45107	937-783-2476	783-2539
Continental Mineral Processing Corp 11817 Mosteller Rd PO Box 62005 *Web:* www.continentalmineral.com	Cincinnati	OH	45262	513-771-7190	771-9153
Crystex Composites LLC 125 Clifton Blvd *TF:* 800-638-8235 ■ *Web:* www.crystexllc.com	Clifton	NJ	07011	973-779-8866	779-2013
Dicaliter / Dicaperlr Minerals, Inc 1 Bala Ave Ste 310 *Web:* dicalite.com	Bala Cynwyd	PA	19004	610-660-8820	660-8817
Dri-Rite Co 11600 S Ave O PO Box 170319 *Web:* www.dririte.com	Chicago	IL	60617	773-409-4127	221-2909
Eagle-Picher Minerals Inc 9785 Gateway Dr Ste 1000 PO Box 12130 *TF Cust Svc:* 800-228-3865 ■ *Web:* www.epminerals.com	Reno	NV	89521	775-824-7600	824-7601
Ferro Corp Electronic Materials Div 4150 E 56th St *Web:* ferro.com	Cleveland	OH	44105	216-641-8580	
Graphel Corp 6115 Centre Pk Dr PO Box 369 *TF:* 800-255-1104 ■ *Web:* www.graphel.com	West Chester	OH	45071	513-779-6166	779-3057
Graphite Metallizing Corp 1050 Nepperhan Ave *Web:* www.graphalloy.com	Yonkers	NY	10703	914-968-8400	968-8468
Graphite Sales Inc 16710 W Pk Cir Dr *TF:* 800-321-4147 ■ *Web:* www.graphitesales.com	Chagrin Falls	OH	44023	440-543-8221	543-5183
Hill & Griffith Co 1085 Summer St *TF:* 800-543-0425 ■ *Web:* www.hillandgriffith.com	Cincinnati	OH	45204	513-921-1075	244-4199
Hydraulic Press Brick Co 5505 W 74th St *Web:* www.hpbhaydite.com	Indianapolis	IN	46268	317-290-1140	290-1071
JS McCormick Co 503 Hegner Way *Web:* www.jsmccormick.com	Sewickley	PA	15143	412-749-8222	749-2766
Kocour Co 4800 S St Louis Ave *Web:* www.kocour.net	Chicago	IL	60632	773-847-1111	847-3399
La Habra Products Inc 4125 E La Palma Ave Ste 250 *TF:* 866-516-0061 ■ *Web:* www.lahabrastucco.com	Anaheim	CA	92807	714-778-2266	774-2079
Merlex Stucco Co 2911 N Orange-Olive Rd *Web:* www.merlex.com	Orange	CA	92865	714-637-1700	637-4865
Miller & Co LLC 9700 W Higgins Rd Ste 1000 *TF:* 800-727-9847 ■ *Web:* www.millerandco.com	Rosemont	IL	60018	847-696-2400	696-2419
Miller Studio 734 Fair Ave NW *Web:* miller-studio.com	New Philadelphia	OH	44663	330-339-1100	
Mission Stucco Company Inc 7751 70th St *Web:* missionstucco.net	Paramount	CA	90723	562-634-1400	634-4440
Multicoat Corp 23331 Antonio Pkwy *TF:* 877-685-8426 ■ *Web:* www.multicoat.com	Rancho Santa Margarita	CA	92688	949-888-7100	888-2555
NYCO Minerals Inc 803 Mtn View Dr *Web:* sandb.com/our-brands/nyco/	Willsboro	NY	12996	518-963-4262	963-1110
Oil-Dri Corp of America 410 N Michigan Ave Ste 400 *NYSE: ODC* ■ *TF:* 800-645-3747 ■ *Web:* www.oildri.com	Chicago	IL	60611	312-321-1515	321-1271
Sacramento Stucco Co 1550 PkwyBlvd *Web:* www.westernblended.com	West Sacramento	CA	95691	916-372-7442	372-4836
San Jose Delta Assoc Inc 482 Sapena Ct *Web:* www.sanjosedelta.com	Santa Clara	CA	95054	408-727-1448	727-6019
Schundler Co 150 Whitman Ave *Web:* www.schundler.com	Edison	NJ	08817	732-287-2244	287-4185
Silbrico Corp 6300 River Rd *TF:* 800-323-4287 ■ *Web:* www.silbrico.com	Hodgkins	IL	60525	708-354-3350	354-6698
US Diamond Wheel Co 101 Kendall Pt Dr **Fax Area Code:* 630 ■ *TF:* 800-223-0457 ■ *Web:* www.radiac.com	Oswego	IL	60543	800-851-1095	898-1796*
USG Corp 550 W Adams St *NYSE: USG* ■ *TF:* 800-874-4968 ■ *Web:* www.usg.com	Chicago	IL	60661	312-436-4000	672-4093
Von Roll Isola USA 200 Von Roll Dr **Fax:* Cust Svc ■ *TF:* 800-654-7652 ■ *Web:* www.vonroll.com	Schenectady	NY	12306	518-344-7100	344-7288*
Winter Bros Material Co 13098 Gravois Rd *Web:* www.winterbrothersmaterial.com	Saint Louis	MO	63127	314-843-1400	843-1403
Ziegler Chemical & Mineral Corp 366 N Broadway Ste 210 *Web:* www.zieglerchemical.com	Jericho	NY	11753	516-681-9600	

504 MINING - COAL

	City	State	Zip	Phone	Fax
Allen Guthrie Mchugh & Thomas Pllc 500 Lee St E Ste 800	Charleston	WV	25301	304-345-7250	
Alliance Resource Partners LP 1717 S Boulder Ave Ste 400 *NASDAQ: ARLP* ■ *Web:* www.arlp.com	Tulsa	OK	74119	918-295-7600	295-7358
Alpha Natural Resources Inc 1 Alpha Pl PO Box 16429 *OTC: ANR* ■ *TF:* 866-322-5742 ■ *Web:* www.alphanr.com	Bristol	VA	24209	276-619-4410	623-2853
Amerikohl Mining Inc 202 Sunset Dr *Web:* www.amerikohl.com	Butler	PA	16001	724-282-2339	282-3226
Amira International 15005 E Layton Pl *Web:* amira.com.au	Aurora	CO	80015	303-400-3982	
Arch Materials LLC 4438 SR- 276 *Web:* archmaterials.com	Batavia	OH	45103	513-724-7625	
Argus Energy LLC 3026 Big Sandy Rd *Web:* www.argusenergy.com	Kenova	WV	25530	304-453-6140	
BNI Coal Ltd 1637 Burnt Boat Dr PO Box 897 *Web:* www.bnicoal.com	Bismarck	ND	58503	701-222-8828	222-1547

	City	State	ZIP	Phone	Fax
C & K Coal Co 1062 E Main St PO Box 69	Clarion	PA	16214	814-226-6911	226-9517
CanAm Coal Corp 1201-5th St SW Ste 202 *Web:* www.canamcoal.com	Calgary	AB	T2R0Y6	403-262-3797	
Cline Mining Corp Heritage Bldg 181 Bay St Brookfield Pl Third Fl *Web:* www.clinemining.com	Toronto	ON	M5J2T3	416-504-7600	
Cloud Peak Energy Inc (RTEA) 505 S Gillette Ave PO Box 3009 **Fax Area Code:* 303 ■ *TF:* 866-470-4300 ■ *Web:* www.cloudpeakenergy.com/	Gillette	WY	82717	307-687-6000	262-0604*
Colombia Energy Resources Inc One Embarcadero Ctr Ste 500	San Francisco	CA	94111	415-460-1165	
Coteau Properties Co 204 County Rd 15 *Web:* www.nacoal.com	Beulah	ND	58523	701-873-2281	873-7226
DH Blattner & Sons Inc 392 County Rd 50 *TF:* 800-877-2866 ■ *Web:* www.dhblattner.com	Avon	MN	56310	320-356-7351	356-7392
Drummond Co Inc PO Box 10246 *Web:* www.drummondco.com	Birmingham	AL	35202	205-945-6300	945-6557
East Fairfield Coal Co (EFCC) 10900 S Ave PO Box 217 *Web:* www.eastfairfieldcoal.com	North Lima	OH	44452	330-549-2165	
Emerald Intarnational Corp 6895 Burlington Pk *Web:* www.emeraldcoal.com	Florence	KY	41042	859-525-2522	525-4052
Hepburnia Coal Co PO Box I	Grampian	PA	16838	814-236-0473	236-1624
Holmes Limestone Co 4255 SR 39 *Web:* holmeslimestone.com	Millersburg	OH	44654	330-893-2721	893-2941
James River Coal Co 901 E Byrd St Ste 1600 *Web:* www.jamesrivercoal.com	Richmond	VA	23219	804-780-3000	780-0643
Jim Walter Resources Inc 16243 Hwy 216 *Web:* www.walterenergy.com	Brookwood	AL	35444	205-554-6150	554-6150
JM Huber Corp 499 Thornall St 8th Fl **Fax:* Hum Res ■ *TF:* 877-418-0038 ■ *Web:* www.huber.com	Edison	NJ	08837	732-549-8600	549-2239*
Knight Hawk Coal LLC 500 Cutler-Trico Rd *TF:* 855-611-2625 ■ *Web:* www.knighthawkcoal.com	Percy	IL	62272	618-426-3662	
Lee Ranch Coal Co PO Box 757	Grants	NM	87020	505-285-4651	
Natural Resource Partners LP 601 Jefferson St Ste 3600 *NYSE: NRP* ■ *TF:* 888-334-7102 ■ *Web:* www.nrplp.com	Houston	TX	77002	713-751-7507	751-7563
North American Coal Corp 5340 Legacy Dr Bldg I Ste 300 *Web:* www.nacoal.com	Plano	TX	75024	972-448-5400	
Ohio River Collieries Co 70245 Bannock Uniontown Rd	Bannock	OH	43972	740-968-3582	
Ohio Valley Coal Co 56854 Pleasant Ridge Rd	Alledonia	OH	43902	740-926-1351	926-1615
Pacific Coal Resources Ltd 333 Bay St Ste 1100 *Web:* www.pacificcoal.ca	Toronto	ON	M5H2R2	416-360-8725	
Peabody Energy Corp 701 Market St Ste 700 *NYSE: BTU* ■ *Web:* www.peabodyenergy.com	Saint Louis	MO	63101	314-342-3400	
Reading Anthracite Co 200 Mahantongo St PO Box 1200 *Web:* www.readinganthracite.com	Pottsville	PA	17901	570-622-5150	
RG Johnson Company Inc 25 S College St *Web:* rgjohnsoninc.com	Washington	PA	15301	724-222-6810	222-6815
Rhino Resource Partners LP 424 Lewis Hargett Cir Ste 250 *Web:* www.rhinolp.com	Lexington	KY	40503	859-389-6500	
S&B Industrial Minerals North America Inc 920 Cassatt Rd Ste 205	Berwyn	PA	19312	610-647-1123	
SABIA Inc 10911 Technology Pl *Web:* www.sabiainc.com	San Diego	CA	92127	858-217-2200	
Sharpe Resources Corp 3258 Mob Neck Rd *Web:* www.sharperesourcescorporation.com	Heathsville	VA	22473	804-580-8107	
STEWART MATERIALSÿ 13525 Indrio Rd *Web:* stewartmining.com	Fort Pierce	FL	34945	772-464-4499	
TECO Coal Corp 200 Allison Blvd *Web:* www.tecocoal.com	Corbin	KY	40701	606-523-4444	
Thunder Basin Coal Co PO Box 406 *Web:* www.archcoal.com	Wright	WY	82732	307-939-1300	464-2313
Usibelli Coal Mine Inc 100 River Rd PO Box 1000 *Web:* www.usibelli.com	Healy	AK	99743	907-683-2226	683-2253
Western Energy Co 138 Rosebud Ln PO Box 99 *Web:* westmoreland.com	Colstrip	MT	59323	406-748-5100	748-5181
Westmoreland Coal Co 9540 S Maroon Cir Ste 200 *NASDAQ: WLB* ■ **Fax Area Code:* 307 ■ *TF:* 855-922-6463 ■ *Web:* www.westmoreland.com	Englewood	CO	80112	719-442-2600	877-9089*
Westmoreland Resource Partners LP 41 S High St *Web:* oxfordresources.com	Columbus	OH	43215	614-643-0337	
Westmoreland Resources Inc 100 Sarpy Creek Rd PO Box 449 *Web:* westmoreland.com/location/absaloka-mine-montana/	Hardin	MT	59034	406-342-5201	342-5401

505 MINING - METALS

	City	State	ZIP	Phone	Fax
Agnico-Eagle Mines Ltd 145 King St E Ste 500 *NYSE: AEM* ■ *TF:* 888-822-6714 ■ *Web:* www.agnicoeagle.com	Toronto	ON	M5C2Y7	416-947-1212	367-4681
B2 Gold Corp 595 Burrard St Ste 3100 PO Box 49143 *TF:* 800-316-8855 ■ *Web:* www.b2gold.com	Vancouver	BC	V7X1J1	604-681-8371	681-6209
Badger Mining Corp 409 S Church St PO Box 328 *TF:* 800-932-7263 ■ *Web:* www.badgerminingcorp.com	Berlin	WI	54923	920-361-2388	361-2826
Barrick Gold Corp TD Canada Trust Tower 161 Bay St PO Box 212 *NYSE: ABX* ■ *TF:* 800-720-7415 ■ *Web:* www.barrick.com	Toronto	ON	M5J2S1	416-861-9911	861-2492
Barrick Goldstrike Mines Inc PO Box 29 *Web:* www.barrick.com	Elko	NV	89803	416-861-9911	
BCM Resources Corp 1040 W Georgia St Ste 480 *Web:* www.bcmresources.com	Vancouver	BC	V6E4H1	604-646-0144	
Callinan Royalties Corp 555 West Hastings St Ste 1110 *Web:* www.callinan.com	Vancouver	BC	V6B4N4	877-576-2209	
Cameco Corp 2121 11th St W *NYSE: CCO* ■ *Web:* www.cameco.com	Saskatoon	SK	S7M1J3	306-956-6200	956-6201
Chaparral Gold Corp 7950 E Acoma Dr Ste 211 *TSE: IMZ* ■ *Web:* chaparralgold.com	Scottsdale	AZ	85260	480-483-9932	483-9926
Claude Resources Inc 224 Fourth Ave S Ste 200 *TSE: CRJ* ■ *Web:* www.clauderesources.com	Saskatoon	SK	S7K5M5	306-668-7505	668-7500
Cliffs Natural Resources 200 Public Sq Ste 3300 *Web:* www.cliffsnaturalresources.com	Cleveland	OH	44114	216-694-5700	
Climax Molybdenum Co PO Box 220 **Fax:* Hum Res ■ *Web:* www.climaxmolybdenum.com	Fort Madison	IA	52627	602-366-8100	366-7318*
Corriente Resources Inc 5811 Cooney Rd Unit S209 *Web:* www.corriente.com	Richmond	BC	V6X3M1	604-282-7212	282-7568
Crown Gold Corp 970 Caughlin Crossing Ste 100 *TSE: CWM* ■ *Web:* www.crowngoldcorp.com	Reno	NV	89519	775-284-7200	
Crystallex International Corp Eight King St E Ste 1201 *TF:* 800-738-1577 ■ *Web:* www.crystallex.com	Toronto	ON	M5C1B5	416-203-2448	203-0099
Eldorado Gold Corp 550 Burrard St Ste 1188 *NYSE: ELD* ■ *TF:* 888-353-8166 ■ *Web:* www.eldoradogold.com	Vanouver	BC	V6C2B5	604-687-4018	687-4026
First Quantum Minerals Ltd 543 Granville St 8th Fl *TSE: FM* ■ *TF:* 888-688-6577 ■ *Web:* www.first-quantum.com	Vancouver	BC	V6C1X8	604-688-6577	688-3818
General Moly Inc 1726 Cole Blvd Ste 115 *Web:* www.generalmoly.com	Lakewood	CO	80401	303-928-8599	
Gold Reserve Inc 926 W Sprague Ave Ste 200 *TSE: GRZ* ■ *TF:* 800-625-9550 ■ *Web:* www.goldreserveinc.com	Spokane	WA	99201	509-623-1500	623-1634
Goldcorp Inc 666 Burrard St Ste 3400 *NYSE: G* ■ *TF:* 800-567-6223 ■ *Web:* www.goldcorp.com	Vancouver	BC	V6C2X8	604-696-3000	696-3001
Golden Star Resources Ltd 10901 W Toller Dr Ste 300 *NYSE: GSS* ■ *TF:* 800-553-8436 ■ *Web:* www.gsr.com	Littleton	CO	80127	303-830-9000	830-9094
Goldfield Corp 1684 W Hibiscus Blvd *NYSE: GV* ■ *Web:* www.goldfieldcorp.com	Melbourne	FL	32901	321-724-1700	724-1163
Hecla Mining Co 800 W Pender St Ste 970 *NYSE: HL* ■ *Web:* hecla-mining.com	Vancouver	BC	V6C2V6	604-682-6201	682-6215
Hibbing Taconite Co 4950 County Rd 5 N *Web:* cliffsnaturalresources.com	Hibbing	MN	55746	218-262-5950	
IAMGOLD Corp 401 Bay St Ste 3200 PO Box 153 *TSE: IMG* ■ *TF:* 888-464-9999 ■ *Web:* www.iamgold.com	Toronto	ON	M5H2Y4	416-360-4710	360-4750
IBC Advanced Alloys Corp 570 Granville St Ste 1200 *TF:* 800-373-3251 ■ *Web:* www.ibcadvancedalloys.com	Vancouver	BC	V6C3P1	604-685-6263	
Imperial Metals Corp 580 Hornby St Ste 200 *TSE: III* ■ *Web:* www.imperialmetals.com	Vancouver	BC	V6C3B6	604-669-8959	687-4030
Ivanhoe Mines Ltd 654-999 Canada Pl *Web:* www.ivanhoemines.com	Vancouver	BC	V6C3E1	604-688-6630	682-2060
Kennecott Uranium Co NW Of Rawlins	Rawlins	WY	82301	307-328-1476	
Kimber Resources Inc 800 W Pender St Ste 220 *Web:* invecture.com/	Vancouver	BC	V6C2V6	604-669-2251	
Kinross Gold Corp 25 York St 17th Fl *NYSE: KGC* ■ *TF:* 866-561-3636 ■ *Web:* www.kinross.com	Toronto	ON	M5J2V5	416-365-5123	363-6622
Kinross Gold USA Inc 5370 Kietzke Ln Ste 102 *Web:* kinross.com	Reno	NV	89511	775-829-1000	
Materion Corp 6070 Parkland Blvd *NYSE: MTRN* ■ *TF:* 800-321-2076 ■ *Web:* www.materion.com	Mayfield Heights	OH	44124	216-486-4200	383-4091
Meridian Gold Co 9670 Gateway Dr Ste 200 **Fax Area Code:* 888 ■ *TF:* 888-231-8191 ■ *Web:* yamana.com	Reno	NV	89521	775-850-3777	249-6189*
Mines Management Inc 905 W Riverside Ave Ste 311 *NYSE: MGN* ■ *Web:* www.minesmanagement.com	Spokane	WA	99201	509-838-6050	838-0486
Molycorp Inc 67750 Bailey Rd *Web:* www.molycorp.com	Mountain Pass	CA	92366	760-856-2201	856-2253
NA Degerstrom Inc 3303 N Sullivan Rd *Web:* www.nadinc.com	Spokane	WA	99216	509-928-3333	927-2010
New Gold Inc 666 Burrard St Ste 3110 *NYSE: NGD* ■ *Web:* www.newgoldinc.com	Vancouver	BC	V6C2X8	604-696-4100	696-4110
Newmont Mining Corp 6363 S Fiddler's Green Cir Ste 800 *NYSE: NEM* ■ *Web:* www.newmont.com	Greenwood Village	CO	80111	303-863-7414	837-5837
NMC Resource Corp 1111 Melville St Ste 1100 *Web:* www.nmcresource.com	Vancouver	BC	V6E3V6	604-643-1730	
Nord Resources Corp 1 W Wetmore Rd Ste 203 *Web:* www.nordresources.com	Tucson	AZ	85705	520-292-0266	292-0268
North American Palladium Ltd 200 Bay St Ste 2350 *TSE: PDL* ■ *Web:* www.napalladium.com	Toronto	ON	M5J2J2	416-360-7590	360-7709
North American Tungsten Corp Ltd 1188 W Georgia St Ste 1640 *Web:* www.natungsten.com	Vancouver	BC	V6E4A2	604-684-5300	
Northgate Minerals Corp 110 Yonge St Ste 1601 *CVE: NXG* ■ **Fax Area Code:* 416 ■ *Web:* www.auricogold.com	Toronto	ON	M5C1T4	647-260-8880	363-6392*
NovaGold Resources Inc 200 Grandville St Ste 2300 PO Box 24 *NYSE: NG* ■ *TF:* 866-699-6227 ■ *Web:* www.novagold.com	Vancouver	BC	V6C1S4	604-669-6227	669-6272
Optex Systems Holdings Inc 1420 Presidential Dr *OTC: OPXS* ■ *Web:* www.optexsys.com	Richardson	TX	75081	972-644-0722	234-3544
Pacific Rim Mining Corp 625 Howe St Ste 1050 *OTC: PFRMF* ■ *TF:* 888-775-7097 ■ *Web:* oceanagold.com/	Vancouver	BC	V6C2T6	604-689-1976	

	City	St	Zip	Phone	Fax
Pan American Silver Corp 625 Howe St Ste 1500 *TSE:* PAA ■ *Web:* www.panamericansilver.com	Vancouver	BC	V6C2T6	604-684-1175	684-0147
QIT-Fer et Titane Inc 1625 Marie-Victorin Rd *Web:* www.rtft.com	Sorel-Tracy	QC	J3R1M6	450-746-3000	746-4438
Roca Mines Inc 1122 Mainland St Ste 490 *Web:* www.rocamines.com	Vancouver	BC	V6B5L1	604-684-2900	
Royal Gold Inc 1660 Wynkoop St Ste 1000 *NASDAQ:* RGLD ■ *Web:* www.royalgold.com	Denver	CO	80202	303-573-1660	595-9385
Rubicon Minerals Corp 800 W Pender St Ste 1540 *NYSE:* RBY ■ *TF:* 866-365-4706 ■ *Web:* www.rubiconminerals.com	Vancouver	BC	V6C2V6	604-623-3333	
Seabridge Gold Inc 106 Front St E Ste 400 *TSE:* SEA ■ *Web:* www.seabridgegold.net	Toronto	ON	M5A1E1	416-367-9292	367-2711
Sherritt International Corp 1133 Yonge St *TSE:* S ■ *TF:* 800-704-6698 ■ *Web:* www.sherritt.com	Toronto	ON	M4T2Y7	416-924-4551	924-5015
Silver Standard Resources Inc 999 W Hastings St Ste 1180 *TSE:* SSO ■ *TF:* 888-338-0046 ■ *Web:* www.silverstandard.com	Vancouver	BC	V6C2W2	604-689-3846	689-3847
Stillwater Mining Co 1321 Discovery Dr *NYSE:* SWC ■ *Web:* www.stillwatermining.com	Billings	MT	59102	406-373-8700	373-8701
Stratcor Inc 1180 Omega Dr Ste 1180 *TF:* 800-573-6052 ■ *Web:* www.evrazstratcor.com	Pittsburgh	PA	15205	412-787-4500	787-5030
Sunridge International 16857 Saguaro Blvd	Fountain Hills	AZ	85268	480-837-6165	
Teck Cominco American Inc 501 N Riverpoint Blvd Ste 300 *TF:* 888-767-7718 ■ *Web:* www.teck.com	Spokane	WA	99202	509-747-6111	747-6111
Umetco Minerals Corp 2754 Compass Dr	Grand Junction	CO	81506	970-245-3700	
Uranium Resources Inc 405 State Hwy 121 Bypass A-110 *NASDAQ:* URRE ■ *Web:* www.uraniumresources.com	Lewisville	TX	75067	972-219-3330	
US Energy Corp 877 N Eigth W *NASDAQ:* USEG ■ *TF:* 800-776-9271 ■ *Web:* www.usnrg.com	Riverton	WY	82501	307-856-9271	857-3050
Vale 200 Bay St Ste 1600 PO Box 70 *Web:* www.nickel.vale.com	Toronto	ON	M5J2K2	416-361-7511	361-7781
Vista Gold Corp 7961 Shaffer Pkwy Ste 5 *NYSE:* VGZ ■ *Web:* www.vistagold.com	Littleton	CO	80127	720-981-1185	981-1186
Western Copper Corp 1111 W Georgia St Ste 2050 *TF:* 888-966-9995 ■ *Web:* westerncopperandgold.com	Vancouver	BC	V6E4M3	604-684-9497	669-2926
Western Nuclear Inc 2801 Youngfield St Ste 340	Golden	CO	80401	303-274-1767	
Wharf Resources USA Inc 10928 Wharf Rd *TF:* 800-567-6223 ■ *Web:* goldcorp.com	Lead	SD	57754	605-584-1441	584-4188
Woulfe Mining Corp 837 W Hastings St Ste 408 *Web:* www.woulfemining.com	Vancouver	BC	V6C3N6	604-684-6264	

506 MINING - MINERALS

506-1 Chemical & Fertilizer Minerals Mining

	City	St	Zip	Phone	Fax
American Borate Corp 5700 Cleveland St Ste 420 *TF:* 800-486-1072 ■ *Web:* www.americanborate.com	Virginia Beach	VA	23462	757-490-2242	490-1548
New Riverside Ochre Co 75 Old River Rd SE *TF Orders:* 800-248-0176 ■ *Web:* www.nroonline.com	Cartersville	GA	30121	770-382-4568	
Potash Corp 1101 Skokie Blvd *TF:* 800-667-0403 ■ *Web:* www.potashcorp.com	Northbrook	IL	60062	847-849-4200	849-4695
Searles Valley Minerals 9401 Indian Creek Pkwy Ste 1000 *TF:* 800-637-2775 ■ *Web:* www.svminerals.com	Overland Park	KS	66210	913-344-9500	344-9602
Solvay Chemicals Inc 3333 Richmond Ave *TF:* 800-765-8292 ■ *Web:* www.solvaychemicals.us	Houston	TX	77098	713-525-6800	525-7805
United Salt Corp 4800 San Felipe St *TF:* 800-554-8658 ■ *Web:* www.unitedsalt.com	Houston	TX	77056	713-877-2600	877-2609

506-2 Clay, Ceramic, Refractory Minerals Mining

	City	St	Zip	Phone	Fax
AMCOL International Corp 2870 Forbs Ave *NYSE:* ACO ■ **Fax Area Code:* 610 ■ *TF General:* 800-962-8586 ■ *Web:* www.amcol.com	Hoffman Estates	IL	60192	847-851-1500	250-3325*
Black Hills Bentonite LLC PO Box 9 *TF Orders:* 800-788-9443 ■ *Web:* www.bhbentonite.com	Mills	WY	82644	307-265-3740	235-8511
Dixie Clay Co 305 Dixie Clay Rd **Fax Area Code:* 205	Bath	SC	29816	803-593-2592	759-2606*
HC Spinks Clay Company Inc 275 Carothers Loop PO Box 820 *Web:* www.spinksclay.com	Paris	TN	38242	731-642-5414	642-5493
Holmes Limestone Co 4255 SR 39 *Web:* holmeslimestone.com	Millersburg	OH	44654	330-893-2721	893-2941
I-Minerals Inc 880 - 580 Hornby St *Web:* www.imineralsinc.com	Vancouver	BC	V6C3B6	604-303-6573	
Imerys USA Inc 100 Mansell Ct E Ste 300 *TF:* 800-374-3224 ■ *Web:* www.imerys-paper.com	Roswell	GA	30076	770-645-3300	645-3384
Kyanite Mining Corp 30 Willis Mtn Ln *Web:* www.kyanite.com	Dillwyn	VA	23936	434-983-2085	983-5178
Milwhite Inc 5487 S Padre Island Hwy *TF:* 800-442-0082 ■ *Web:* www.milwhite.com	Brownsville	TX	78521	956-547-1970	547-1999
Riverside Clay Co Inc 201 Truss Ferry Rd *TF:* 800-924-0637 ■ *Web:* riversiderefractories.com	Pell City	AL	35128	205-338-3366	338-7456
Riverside Refractories Inc 201 Truss Ferry Rd *TF:* 800-924-0637 ■ *Web:* www.riversiderefractories.com	Pell City	AL	35128	205-338-3366	338-7456
RT Vanderbilt Company Inc 30 Winfield St *TF Cust Svc:* 800-243-6064 ■ *Web:* www.rtvanderbilt.com	Norwalk	CT	06855	203-853-1400	853-1452
Thiele Kaolin Co PO Box 1056 **Fax:* Mail Rm ■ *Web:* www.thielekaolin.com	Sandersville	GA	31082	478-552-3951	552-4105*
US Silica Co 106 Sand Mine Rd PO Box 187 *TF:* 800-243-7500 ■ *Web:* www.ussilica.com	Berkeley Springs	WV	25411	304-258-2500	258-8295
Wyo-Ben Inc 1345 Discovery Dr *TF Cust Svc:* 800-548-7055 ■ *Web:* www.wyoben.com	Billings	MT	59102	406-652-6351	656-0748

506-3 Minerals Mining (Misc)

	City	St	Zip	Phone	Fax
Harborlite 130 Castilian Dr *TF:* 800-893-4445 ■ *Web:* www.worldminerals.com	Santa Barbara	CA	93117	805-562-0200	
ILC Resources 3301 106th Cir *TF:* 800-247-2133 ■ *Web:* www.ilcresources.com	Urbandale	IA	50322	515-243-8106	244-3200
Mountain Province Diamonds Inc 161 Bay St Ste 2315 *TSE:* MPV ■ *Web:* www.mountainprovince.com	Toronto	ON	M5J2S1	416-361-3562	603-8565
RT Vanderbilt Company Inc 30 Winfield St *TF Cust Svc:* 800-243-6064 ■ *Web:* www.rtvanderbilt.com	Norwalk	CT	06855	203-853-1400	853-1452
Stornoway Diamond Corp 980 W First St Ste 118 *TSE:* SWY ■ *TF:* 877-331-2232 ■ *Web:* www.stornowaydiamonds.com	N.Vancouver	BC	V7P3N4	604-983-7750	987-7107
Vanderbilt Minerals Corp 30 Winfield St *TF:* 800-243-6064 ■ *Web:* www.rtvanderbilt.com	Norwalk	CT	06855	203 853 1400	853 1452
WGI Heavy Minerals Inc 810 E Sherman Ave *TSE:* WG ■ *TF:* 888-542-7638 ■ *Web:* www.wgiheavyminerals.com	Coeur d'Alene	ID	83814	208-666-6000	666-4000

506-4 Sand & Gravel Pits

	City	St	Zip	Phone	Fax
Best Sand Corp 11830 Ravenna Rd PO Box 87 *TF:* 800-237-4986 ■ *Web:* www.fairmountminerals.com	Chardon	OH	44024	440-285-3132	285-4109
Brox Industries Inc 1471 Methuen St *Web:* www.broxindustries.com	Dracut	MA	01826	978-454-9105	805-9720
Edward C Levy Co 9300 Dix Ave **Fax:* Sales ■ *TF:* 877-938-0007 ■ *Web:* www.edwclevy.com	Dearborn	MI	48120	313-843-7200	849-9441*
Elmer Larson LLC 21218 Airport Rd	Sycamore	IL	60178	815-895-4837	895-4437
ER Jahna Industries Inc 202 E Stuart Ave *Web:* www.jahna.com	Lake Wales	FL	33853	863-676-9431	676-5137
Fisher Sand & Gravel Co 3948 First ST SW *TF:* 800-932-8740 ■ *Web:* www.fisherind.com	Underwood	ND	58576	701-442-5600	456-9168
Hills Materials Co 3975 Sturgis Rd PO Box 2320 *TF:* 800-325-7056 ■ *Web:* www.hillsmaterials.com	Rapid City	SD	57709	605-394-3300	341-3446
Hilltop Basic Resources Inc One W Fourth St Ste 1100 *Web:* www.hilltopbasicresources.com	Cincinnati	OH	45202	513-651-5000	684-8222
Janesville Sand & Gravel Co (JSG) 1110 Harding St *TF:* 800-955-7702 ■ *Web:* www.jsandg.com	Janesville	WI	53547	608-754-7701	
Lafarge North America Inc 12950 Worldgate Dr Ste 600 *Web:* www.lafarge-na.com	Herndon	VA	20170	703-480-3600	480-3899
LG Everist Inc 300 S Phillips Ave Ste 200 *TF:* 800-843-7992 ■ *Web:* www.lgeverist.com	Sioux Falls	SD	57117	605-334-5000	334-3656
Mark Sand & Gravel Co 525 Kennedy Pk Rd PO Box 458 *TF:* 800-427-8316 ■ *Web:* www.marksandgravel.com	Fergus Falls	MN	56537	218-736-7523	736-2647
Martin Marietta Materials Inc 2710 Wycliff Rd *NYSE:* MLM ■ *Web:* www.martinmarietta.com	Raleigh	NC	27607	919-781-4550	
Miles Sand & Gravel Company Inc 400 Valley Ave NE *Web:* www.milessandandgravel.com	Puyallup	WA	98372	253-833-3705	833-3746
Pete Lien & Sons Inc 3401 Universal Dr PO Box 440 *Web:* www.petelien.com	Rapid City	SD	57702	605-342-7224	342-6979
Pike Industries Inc 3 Eastgate Pk Rd *TF:* 800-283-0803 ■ *Web:* pikeindustries.com	Belmont	NH	03220	603-527-5100	527-5101
Pounding Mill Quarry Corp 171 St Clair S Crossing *TF:* 888-661-7625 ■ *Web:* www.pmqc.com	Bluefield	VA	24605	276-326-1145	322-6805
Rogers Group Inc 421 Great Cir Rd *Web:* www.rogersgroupincint.com	Nashville	TN	37228	615-242-0585	
Standard Sand & Silica Co 1850 US Highway 17 92 N	Davenport	FL	33837	863-422-7100	421-7349
Tower Rock Stone Co 19829 Lower Frenchman Rd PO Box 111	Sainte Genevieve	MO	63670	573-883-7415	883-3067
Unimin Corp 258 Elm St *TF:* 800-223-2236 ■ *Web:* www.unimin.com	New Canaan	CT	06840	203-966-8880	966-3453
US Silica Co 106 Sand Mine Rd PO Box 187 *TF:* 800-243-7500 ■ *Web:* www.ussilica.com	Berkeley Springs	WV	25411	304-258-2500	258-8295
Wendling Quarries Inc 2647 225th St PO Box 230 *Web:* www.wendlingquarries.com	De Witt	IA	52742	563-659-9181	659-3393
Westroc Inc 670 West 220 South *Web:* www.westrocinc.com	Pleasant Grove	UT	84062	801-785-5600	785-7408
Whibco Inc 87 E Commerce St *Web:* www.whibco.com	Bridgeton	NJ	08302	856-455-9200	455-9009

506-5 Stone Quarries - Crushed & Broken Stone

Company	City	State	Zip	Phone	Fax
Aggregate Industries Management Inc 7529 Standish Pl *Web:* www.aggregate-us.com	Rockville	MD	20855	301-284-3600	284-3645
Anderson Columbia Co Inc 871 NW Guerdon St PO Box 1829 *Web:* www.andersoncolumbia.com	Lake City	FL	32056	386-752-7585	755-5430
Ararat Rock Products Co 525 Quarry Rd	Mount Airy	NC	27030	336-786-4693	786-2189
Braen Stone Co 400 Central Ave PO Box 8310 *Web:* braenstone.com	Haledon	NJ	07508	973-595-6250	595-7087
Brox Industries Inc 1471 Methuen St *Web:* www.broxindustries.com	Dracut	MA	01826	978-454-9105	805-9720
Cessford Construction Co 3808 Old Hwy 61 *Web:* www.omgmidwest.com	Burlington	IA	52601	319-753-2297	753-0926
Eastern Industries Inc 4401 Camp Meeting Rd Ste 200 *Web:* www.eastern-ind.com	Center Valley	PA	18034	610-866-0932	867-1886
Edward C Levy Co 9300 Dix Ave **Fax:* Sales ■ *TF:* 877-938-0007 ■ *Web:* www.edwclevy.com	Dearborn	MI	48120	313-843-7200	849-9441*
ER Jahna Industries Inc 202 E Stuart Ave *Web:* www.jahna.com	Lake Wales	FL	33853	863-676-9431	676-5137
Hanson Aggregates North America 300 E John Carpenter Fwy Ste 500 *Web:* lehighhanson.com	Irving	TX	75062	972-653-5500	653-5580
Harney Rock & Paving Co 457 S Date Ave *TF:* 888-298-2681 ■ *Web:* www.harneyrock.com	Burns	OR	97720	541-573-7855	573-3532
HB Mellot Estate Inc 100 Mellott Dr Ste 100 *Web:* www.mellottcompany.com	Warfordsburg	PA	17267	301-678-2050	678-2051
Hills Materials Co 3975 Sturgis Rd PO Box 2320 *TF:* 800-325-7056 ■ *Web:* www.hillsmaterials.com	Rapid City	SD	57709	605-394-3300	341-3446
Hunt Midwest Enterprises Inc 8300 NE Underground Dr *TF:* 800-551-6877 ■ *Web:* www.huntmidwest.com	Kansas City	MO	64161	816-455-2500	
Hunt Midwest Mining Inc 8300 NE Underground Dr *TF:* 800-551-6877 ■ *Web:* www.huntmidwest.com	Kansas City	MO	64161	816-455-2500	455-4462
JF Shea Company Inc Redding Div 17400 Clear Creek Rd *Web:* www.jfshea.com	Redding	CA	96001	530-246-4292	246-0554
Lafarge North America Inc 12950 Worldgate Dr Ste 600 *Web:* www.lafarge-na.com	Herndon	VA	20170	703-480-3600	480-3899
LG Everist Inc 300 S Phillips Ave Ste 200 *TF:* 800-843-7992 ■ *Web:* www.lgeverist.com	Sioux Falls	SD	57117	605-334-5000	334-3656
Martin Marietta Materials Inc 2710 Wycliff Rd *NYSE: MLM* ■ *Web:* www.martinmarietta.com	Raleigh	NC	27607	919-781-4550	
Meckley's Limestone Products Inc 1543 State Rt 225 *Web:* www.meckleys.com	Herndon	PA	17830	570-758-3011	758-2400
Meshberger Bros Stone Corp 6311 W St Rd 218	Bluffton	IN	46714	260-334-5311	334-5353
Midwest Minerals Inc 709 N Locust St PO Box 412 *Web:* www.midwestminerals.com	Pittsburg	KS	66762	620-231-8120	235-0840
Mulzer Crushed Stone Inc 534 Mozart St PO Box 249 *Web:* www.mulzer.com	Tell City	IN	47586	812-547-7921	547-6757
New Enterprise Stone & Lime Company Inc (NESL) 3912 Brumbaugh Rd PO Box 77 *Web:* www.nesl.com	New Enterprise	PA	16664	814-766-2211	766-4400
NR Hamm Quarry Inc 609 Perry Pl	Perry	KS	66073	785-597-5111	597-5117
Pennsy Supply Inc 1001 Paxton St *Web:* www.pennsysupply.com	Harrisburg	PA	17104	717-233-4511	238-7312
Pike Industries Inc 3 Eastgate Pk Rd *TF:* 800-283-0803 ■ *Web:* pikeindustries.com	Belmont	NH	03220	603-527-5100	527-5101
Pounding Mill Quarry Corp 171 St Clair S Crossing *TF:* 888-661-7625 ■ *Web:* www.pmqc.com	Bluefield	VA	24605	276-326-1145	322-6805
Rogers Group Inc 421 Great Cir Rd *Web:* www.rogersgroupincint.com	Nashville	TN	37228	615-242-0585	
Stoneco Inc 7555 Whiteford Rd *Web:* stoneco.net	Ottawa Lake	MI	49267	734-856-2257	854-2607
Syar Industries Inc 2301 Napa Vallejo Hwy *Web:* syar.com	Napa	CA	94558	707-252-8711	224-5932
Texas Crushed Stone Co 5300 S IH-35 PO Box 1000 *TF:* 800-772-8272 ■ *Web:* www.texascrushedstoneco.com	Georgetown	TX	78627	512-930-0106	244-6055
Tilcon NY Inc 162 Old Mill Rd *TF:* 800-872-7762 ■ *Web:* www.tilconny.com	West Nyack	NY	10994	845-358-4500	
Tower Rock Stone Co 19829 Lower Frenchman Rd PO Box 111	Sainte Genevieve	MO	63670	573-883-7415	883-3067
Trap Rock Industries Inc 460 River Rd *Web:* www.traprock.com	Kingston	NJ	08528	609-924-0300	497-0135
Valley Quarries Inc 297 Quarry Rd PO Box J *Web:* www.valleyquarries.com	Chambersburg	PA	17201	717-267-2244	267-2521
Vulcan Materials Co 1200 Urban Ctr Dr PO Box 385014 *NYSE: VMC* ■ *TF:* 800-615-4331 ■ *Web:* www.vulcanmaterials.com	Birmingham	AL	35238	205-298-3000	298-2942
Vulcan Materials Company Western Div 3200 San Fernando Rd *NYSE: VMC* ■ *TF:* 800-615-4331 ■ *Web:* www.vulcanmaterials.com	Los Angeles	CA	90065	323-258-2777	258-1583
Wendling Quarries Inc 2647 225th St PO Box 230 *Web:* www.wendlingquarries.com	De Witt	IA	52742	563-659-9181	659-3393
Wyroc Inc 2142 Industrial Ct *Web:* www.wyroc.com	Vista	CA	92081	760-727-0878	727-9238

506-6 Stone Quarries - Dimension Stone

Company	City	State	Zip	Phone	Fax
American Clay Enterprises LLC 2418 Second St SW *TF:* 866-404-1634 ■ *Web:* www.americanclay.com	Albuquerque	NM	87102	505-243-5300	
Eden Stone Company Inc W4520 Lime Rd *Web:* edenstone.net	Eden	WI	53019	920-477-2521	477-4700
Fletcher Granite Company Inc 534 Groton Rd *TF:* 800-253-8168 ■ *Web:* www.fletchergranite.com	Westford	MA	01886	978-251-4031	251-8773
Inter-Rock Minerals Inc 20 Toronto St 12th Fl *Web:* inter-rockminerals.net	Toronto	ON	M5C2B8	416-367-3003	
Liter's Quarry Inc 5918 Haunz Ln *Web:* www.litersinc.com	Louisville	KY	40241	502-241-7637	241-9410
LW Rozzo Inc 17200 Pines Blvd	Pembroke Pines	FL	33029	954-435-8501	436-6243
Oldcastle Materials Inc 900 Ashwood Pkwy Ste 700 *Web:* www.apac.com	Atlanta	GA	30338	770-522-5600	522-5608
Pounding Mill Quarry Corp 171 St Clair S Crossing *TF:* 888-661-7625 ■ *Web:* www.pmqc.com	Bluefield	VA	24605	276-326-1145	322-6805
Swenson Granite Co LLC 369 N State St *Web:* www.swensongranite.com	Concord	NH	03301	603-672-7827	227-9541
Tower Rock Stone Co 19829 Lower Frenchman Rd PO Box 111	Sainte Genevieve	MO	63670	573-883-7415	883-3067
Wendling Quarries Inc 2647 225th St PO Box 230 *Web:* www.wendlingquarries.com	De Witt	IA	52742	563-659-9181	659-3393

507 MISSILES, SPACE VEHICLES, PARTS

SEE ALSO Weapons & Ordnance (Military) p. 3295

Company	City	State	Zip	Phone	Fax
Advanced Thermal Sciences Corp 3355 E La Palma Ave *Web:* www.atschiller.com	Anaheim	CA	92806	714-688-4200	
Aerojet PO Box 13222 *Web:* www.rocket.com	Sacramento	CA	95813	916-355-4000	351-8667
Aerojet Redmond Rocket Ctr 11411 139th Pl NE **Fax:* Mail Rm ■ *Web:* www.rocket.com	Redmond	WA	98052	425-885-5000	882-5804*
Alliant Techsystems Inc (ATK) 7480 Flying Cloud Dr *NYSE: ATK* ■ *Web:* www.atk.com	Minneapolis	MN	55344	952-351-3000	351-3009
Applied Aerospace Structures Corp (AASC) 3437 S Airport Way PO Box 6189 *Web:* www.aascworld.com	Stockton	CA	95206	209-982-0160	983-3375
Astrotech Corp 401 Congress Ave Ste 1650 *NASDAQ: ASTC* ■ *Web:* www.astrotechcorp.com	Austin	TX	78701	512-485-9530	485-9531
Boeing Co, The 100 N Riverside Plz *NYSE: BA* ■ *Web:* www.boeing.com	Chicago	IL	60606	312-544-2000	
Esterline Mason 13955 Balboa Blvd **Fax:* Sales ■ *TF:* 800-232-7700 ■ *Web:* www.esterline.com	Sylmar	CA	91342	818-361-3366	365-6809*
Hamilton Sundstrand Corp One Hamilton Rd *Web:* utcaerospacesystems.com	Windsor Locks	CT	06096	860-654-6000	654-4741
Hi-Shear Technology Corp (HSTC) 24225 Garnier St *TF Mktg:* 800-733-0321 ■ *Web:* www.hstc.com	Torrance	CA	90505	310-784-2100	325-5354
HITCO Carbon Composites Inc 1600 W 135th St *TF:* 800-421-5444 ■ *Web:* www.hitco.com	Gardena	CA	90249	310-527-0700	970-5468
International Launch Services (ILS) 1875 Explorer St Ste 700 *TF:* 800-852-4980 ■ *Web:* www.ilslaunch.com	Reston	VA	20190	571-633-7400	633-7500
Kratos Defense & Security Solutions, Inc. 3061 Industry Dr **Fax:* Sales ■ *Web:* kratosepd.com/page/moved/herley	Lancaster	PA	17603	717-397-2777	397-7079*
L'Garde Inc 15181 Woodlawn Ave *Web:* www.lgarde.com	Tustin	CA	92780	714-259-0771	259-7822
Leading Technology Composites Inc 2626 W May *Web:* www.ltc-ltc.com	Wichita	KS	67213	316-944-0011	
Lockheed Martin Corp 6801 Rockledge Dr *NYSE: LMT* ■ *TF:* 866-562-2363 ■ *Web:* www.lockheedmartin.com	Bethesda	MD	20817	301-897-6000	897-6083
Lockheed Martin Space Systems Co Michoud Operations 13800 Old Gentilly Rd **Fax Area Code:* 613 ■ *TF:* 866-562-2363	New Orleans	LA	70129	504-257-3311	688-0702*
Novatronics Inc 677 Erie St *Web:* www.novatronics.com	Stratford	ON	N5A6V6	519-271-3880	
Paragon Space Development Corp 3481 E Michigan St *Web:* www.paragonsdc.com	Tucson	AZ	85714	520-903-1000	
Qualitor Inc 24800 Denso Dr Ste 255 *Web:* www.qualitorinc.com	Southfield	MI	48033	248-204-8600	204-8619
Reinhold Industries Inc 12827 E Imperial Hwy *Web:* www.reinhold-ind.com	Santa Fe Springs	CA	90670	562-944-3281	944-7238
Sea Launch Company LLC 2700 Nimitz Rd *Web:* www.sea-launch.com	Long Beach	CA	90802	562-951-7000	
Space Vector Corp 9223 Deering Ave *Web:* www.spacevector.com	Chatsworth	CA	91311	818-734-2600	428-6249
Westar Aerospace & Defense Group Inc *QinetiQ North America Inc* Four Research Pk Dr *Web:* www.westardisplaytechnologies.com	Saint Charles	MO	63304	636-300-5000	300-5105

508 MOBILE HOMES & BUILDINGS

				Phone	Fax
American Homestar Corp 2450 S Shore Blvd Ste 300 *Fax: Acctg ■ TF: 800-313-5570 ■ Web: www.americanhomestar.com	League City	TX	77573	281-334-9700	334-6320*
Baker Storey McDonald Properties Inc 3001 Armory Dr Ste 250 Web: www.bsmproperties.com	Nashville	TN	37204	615-373-9511	
Cavalier Home Builders LLC 32 Wilson Blvd Ste 100	Addison	AL	35540	256-747-1575	747-2344
Cavalier Homes Inc 32 Wilson Blvd Ste 100 TF: 800-743-2284 ■ Web: cavalierhomebuilders.net	Addison	AL	35540	800-743-2284	
Cavco Industries Inc 1001 N Central Ave Eighth Fl NASDAQ: CVCO ■ TF: 800-790-9111 ■ Web: www.cavco.com	Phoenix	AZ	85004	602-256-6263	256-6189
Champion Enterprises Management Co 755 W Big Beaver Rd Ste 1000 Web: www.championhomes.com	Troy	MI	48084	910-814-4256	
Chariot Eagle Inc 931 NW 37th Ave Web: www.charioteagle.com	Ocala	FL	34475	352-629-7007	629-6920
Chief Custom Homes 111 Grant St PO Box 127 Web: bonnavilla.com/	Aurora	NE	68818	402-694-5250	694-5873
Commodore Corp 1423 Lincolnway E Web: www.commodorehomes.com	Goshen	IN	46526	574-533-7100	534-2716
Deer Valley Homebuilders Inc 205 Carriage St Web: www.deervalleyhb.com	Guin	AL	35563	205-468-8400	
Destiny Industries LLC 250 R W Bryant Rd TF: 866-782-6600 ■ Web: www.destinyhomebuilders.com	Moultrie	GA	31788	866-782-6600	
DHS Systems LLC 33 Kings Hwy Web: www.drash.com	Orangeburg	NY	10962	845-359-6066	365-2114
Fleetwood Homes of Idaho Inc 2611 E Comstock Ave *Fax: Sales ■ TF: 800-334-8958 ■ Web: fleetwoodhomes.com	Nampa	ID	83687	208-466-2438	467-1616*
Fleetwood Homes of Virginia Inc 90 Weaver St Web: www.fleetwoodhomes.com	Rocky Mount	VA	24151	540-483-5171	483-3517
Franklin Homes Inc 10655 Hwy 43 *Fax Area Code: 256 ■ TF: 800-332-4511 ■ Web: www.franklinhomesusa.com	Russellville	AL	35653	800-332-4511	331-2203*
Fuqua Homes Inc 7100 S Cooper St	Arlington	TX	76001	817-465-3211	465-5125
Giles Industries Inc 405 S Broad St TF: 800-844-4537 ■ Web: www.gilesindustries.com	New Tazewell	TN	37825	423-626-7243	626-7243
Homark Company Inc 100 Third St PO Box 309 Web: www.detroiter.com	Red Lake Falls	MN	56750	218-253-2777	253-2116
Hometown America LLC 150 N Wacker Dr Ste 2800 TF: 888-735-4310 ■ Web: www.hometownamerica.com	Chicago	IL	60606	312-604-7500	604-7501
Horton Homes Inc 101 Industrial Blvd TF: 800-657-4000 ■ Web: www.hortonhomes.com	Eatonton	GA	31024	706-485-8506	485-4446
Jacobsen Homes 600 Packard Ct TF: 800-843-1559 ■ Web: www.jachomes.com	Safety Harbor	FL	34695	727-726-1138	
Liberty Homes Inc 1101 Eisenhower Dr N OTC: LIBHA ■ Web: www.libertyhomesinc.com	Goshen	IN	46526	574-533-0431	533-0438
Little Valley Homes Inc 45225 Grand River Ave Web: www.lvhomes.net	Novi	MI	48375	248-349-2500	
Luxury Retreats International Inc 5530 St Patrick St Ste 2210 TF: 877-993-0100 ■ Web: www.luxuryretreats.com	Montreal	QC	H4E1A8	514-393-8844	
Manufactured Housing Enterprises Inc 09302 St Rt 6 Rt 6 TF: 800-821-0220 ■ Web: www.mheinc.com	Bryan	OH	43506	419-636-4511	636-4322
Mark Line Industries Inc 51687 County Rd 133 PO Box 277 Web: www.marklineindustries.com	Bristol	IN	46507	574-825-5851	825-9139
McGrath RentCorp 5700 Las Positas Rd NASDAQ: MGRC ■ TF: 800-962-4284 ■ Web: www.mgrc.com	Livermore	CA	94551	925-606-9200	453-3200
Meridian Mobile Home Park Spaces & Rentals 1801 Meridian St Ofc 18	Nashville	TN	37207	615-227-1159	
Mobile/Modular Express Inc 1301 Trimble Rd *Fax: Sales ■ Web: www.mobilemodular.com	Edgewood	MD	21040	410-676-3700	676-7288*
Moduline Industries Canada Ltd 1421 Brier Park Crescent NW Web: www.moduline.ca	Medicine Hat	AB	T1C1T8	403-527-1555	
Nashua Homes of Idaho Inc PO Box 170008 TF: 855-766-0222 ■ Web: www.nashuahomesofidaho.com	Boise	ID	83717	208-345-0222	345-1144
Nobility Homes Inc 3741 SW Seventh St OTC: NOBH ■ TF: 800-476-6624 ■ Web: www.nobilityhomes.com	Ocala	FL	34474	352-732-5157	732-4203
Pacific Mobile Structures Inc 1554 Bishop Rd Web: www.pacificmobile.com	Chehalis	WA	98532	360-748-0121	
R-Anell Custom Homes Inc 235 Anthony Grave Rd TF Cust Svc: 800-951-5511 ■ Web: www.r-anell.com	Crouse	NC	28033	704-483-5511	483-5674
Ritz-Craft Corp of Pennsylvania Inc 15 Industrial Pk Rd TF: 800-326-9836 ■ Web: www.ritz-craft.com	Mifflinburg	PA	17844	570-966-1053	966-9248
River Birch Homes Inc 400 River Birch Dr TF: 888-760-3314 ■ Web: www.riverbirchhomes.com	Hackleburg	AL	35564	205-935-1997	935-3578
Satellite Industries Inc 2530 Xenium Ln N TF: 800-328-3332 ■ Web: www.satelliteindustries.com	Minneapolis	MN	55441	800-328-3332	328-3334
Skyline Corp 2520 By-Pass Rd NYSE: SKY ■ TF: 800-348-7469 ■ Web: www.skylinecorp.com	Elkhart	IN	46514	574-294-6521	295-8601
VFP Inc 1701 Midland Rd PO Box 1809 Web: www.vfpinc.com	Salem	VA	24153	540-977-0500	977-5555
Virginia Homes Manufacturing Corp 142 Virginia Homes Ln PO Box 410 Web: www.virginiahomesmfg.com	Boydton	VA	23917	434-738-6107	738-6926
Wick Buildings 405 Walter Rd *Fax Area Code: 608 ■ TF: 855-438-9425 ■ Web: www.wickbuildings.com	Mazomanie	WI	53560	855-438-9425	795-2534*

509 MODELING AGENCIES

SEE ALSO Modeling Schools p. 2765; Talent Agencies p. 3203

				Phone	Fax
Click Model Management 129 W 27th St PH *Fax: Resv ■ Web: www.clickmodel.com	New York	NY	10001	212-206-1717	206-6228*
DNA Model Management Inc 555 W 25th St Web: www.dnamodels.com	New York	NY	10001	212-226-0080	226-7711
Ford Models Inc 111 Fifth Ave 9th Fl Web: models.fordmodels.com	New York	NY	10003	212-219-6500	966-5028
IMG Models 304 Pk Ave S PH N Web: www.imgmodels.com	New York	NY	10010	212-253-8884	253-8883
LA Models 7700 Sunset Blvd Web: www.latalent.com	Los Angeles	CA	90046	323-436-7700	436-7755
Marilyn Model Agency 300 Park Ave S 2nd Fl Web: www.marilynagency.com	New York	NY	10010	212-260-6500	
Next Model Management 15 Watts St Sixth Fl Web: www.nextmanagement.com	New York	NY	10013	212-925-5100	925-5931
San Diego Model Management 438 Camino del Rio S Ste 116 Web: www.sdmodel.com	San Diego	CA	92108	619-296-1018	296-3422
Wilhelmina Models Inc 300 Pk Ave S Web: www.wilhelmina.com	New York	NY	10010	212-473-0700	473-3223
Women Management 199 Lafayette St 7th Fl TF: 800-838-3006 ■ Web: www.womenmanagement.com	New York	NY	10012	212-334-7480	334-7492

510 MODELING SCHOOLS

				Phone	Fax
Abaris Training Resources Inc 5401 Longley Ln Ste 49 Web: www.abaris.com	Reno	NV	89511	775-827-6568	
Ambiance Models & Talent Inc 1096 Dayton Blvd Web: www.ambiancemodels.com	Chattanooga	TN	37405	423-265-2121	
Auburn Career Center 8140 Auburn Rd Web: www.auburncc.org	Painesville	OH	44077	440-357-7542	
Barbizon International LLC 3111 N University Dr Ste 1002 Web: www.barbizonmodeling.com	Coral Springs	FL	33065	954-345-4140	
Canadian Valley Technology Center 6505 E Us Hwy 66 Web: www.cvtech.edu	El Reno	OK	73036	405-262-2629	
Celt Inc 3462 Clemmons Rd Web: www.celt-inc.com	Clemmons	NC	27012	336-712-9906	
Cpr Savers & First Aid Supply 3666 N Miller Rd Web: www.cpr-savers.com	Scottsdale	AZ	85251	480-946-0971	
District 1199 C Training & Upgrade Fund 100 S Broad St Web: www.1199ctraining.org	Philadelphia	PA	19110	215-568-2220	
ECPI College of Technology 5555 Greenwich Rd Web: www.ecpi.edu	Virginia Beach	VA	23462	757-490-9090	
Frederick Taylor University 346 Rheem Blvd Ste 203 TF: 800-988-4622 ■ Web: www.ftu.edu	Moraga	CA	94556	800-988-4622	
Horizon Wellness Group 20 Jerusalem Ave Third Fl Web: www.horizonhealthfairs.com	Hicksville	NY	11801	516-326-2020	
Informa 75 W St Web: informatp.com	Walpole	MA	02081	508-668-0288	
Institute-study of Knowledge 323 Harvard Ave Web: iskme.org	Half Moon Bay	CA	94019	650-728-3322	
Jack b Keenan Inc 1820 Georgetta Dr Web: www.jackbkeenan.com	San Jose	CA	95125	408-448-4686	
Masterdrive 15659 E Hinsdale Dr Web: www.masterdrive.com	Centennial	CO	80112	303-627-4447	
Mayo-Hill School of Modeling 7887 San Felipe St Ste 127 Web: www.mayohill.com	Houston	TX	77063	713-789-7340	789-6163
MCN Healthcare Inc 1777 S Harrison St Ste 405 Web: www.mcnhealthcare.com	Denver	CO	80210	303-762-0778	
Mercy College of Ohio 2221 Madison Ave Web: www.mercycollege.edu	Toledo	OH	43604	419-251-1313	
Mid-atlantic Clearing House Association Inc, The 1344 Ashton Rd Ste 202 Web: www.macha.org	Hanover	MD	21076	410-859-0090	
Modern American Safety Training-mast 841 Alton Ave Web: www.mastohio.com	Columbus	OH	43219	614-252-0565	
National Massage Therapy Institute LLC 10050 Roosevelt Blvd Ste 8 Web: www.nmti.edu	Philadelphia	PA	19116	215-969-0320	
Northern Alberta Institute of Technology 11762 106 St NW Web: www.nait.ca	Edmonton	AB	T5G2R1	780-471-7400	
Pc Professor Computer Training & Repair 7056 Beracasa Way Web: www.pcprofessor.com	Boca Raton	FL	33433	561-750-7879	
Pima Medical Institute 3350 E Grant Rd Ste 200 Web: www.pmi.edu	Tucson	AZ	85716	520-326-1600	
Portage Lakes Career Center 4401 Shriver Rd Web: plcc.edu	Uniontown	OH	44685	330-896-8200	
Poynter Institute for Media Studies Inc, The 801 Third St South Web: www.poynter.org	St. Petersburg	FL	33701	727-821-9494	

Phone | Fax

Regional Occupational Programs
300 Dana St .... Fort Bragg CA 95437 707-964-9000
Web: mcoe.us

Rhino Medical Staffing
2000 E Lamar Blvd Ste 250 .... Arlington TX 76006 817-795-2295
Web: www.rhinomedical.com

Southern Financial Exchange
1340 Poydras St Ste 2010 .... New Orleans LA 70112 504-525-6779
Web: www.sfe.org

Southwest Applied Technology College
510 West 800 South .... Cedar City UT 84720 435-586-2899
Web: www.swatc.edu

St Luke's College 2720 Pierce St .... Sioux City IA 51104 712-279-3149
Web: www.stlukescollege.edu

St. Lawrence-Lewis BOCES 40 W Main St .... Canton NY 13617 315-386-4504
Web: www.sllboces.org

TechSherpas Inc 5404 Cypress Ctr Dr Ste 125 .... Tampa FL 33609 813-287-8876
Web: www.techsherpas.com

Villaris Martial Arts 196 Boston Tpke .... Shrewsbury MA 01545 508-752-0091
Web: www.villaristudios.com

511 MOPS, SPONGES, WIPING CLOTHS

SEE ALSO Brushes & Brooms p. 1887; Cleaning Products p. 1950

Phone | Fax

A&B Wiper Supply Inc 5601 Paschall Ave .... Philadelphia PA 19143 215-482-6100 482-6190
TF: 800-333-7247 ■ *Web:* www.bestrags.com

Abco Cleaning Products 6800 NW 36th Ave .... Miami FL 33147 305-694-2226 694-0451
TF: 888-694-2226 ■ *Web:* www.abcoproducts.com

Acme Sponge & Chamois Company Inc
855 Pine St .... Tarpon Springs FL 34689 727-937-3222 942-3064
Web: www.acmesponge.com

Bro-Tex Inc 800 Hampden Ave .... Saint Paul MN 55114 651-645-5721 646-1876
TF: 800-328-2282 ■ *Web:* www.brotex.com

Butler Home Products LLC
237 Cedar Hill St .... Marlborough MA 01752 508-597-8000 597-8010
TF: 888-318-8521 ■ *Web:* www.cleanerhomeliving.com

Cadie Products Corp 151 E 11th St .... Paterson NJ 07524 973-278-8300 278-0303
Web: www.cadie.com

Colman Wolf Sanitary Supply Co
15201 E 11-Mile Rd .... Roseville MI 48066 586-779-5500 779-5505
Web: www.theprofgroup.com

Continental Manufacturing Co
305 Rock Industrial Pk Dr .... Bridgeton MO 63044 314-656-4301 770-9938
TF: 800-325-1051 ■ *Web:* www.continentalcommercialproducts.com

Disco Inc 1895 Brannan Rd .... McDonough GA 30253 770-474-7575 327-5492*
**Fax Area Code:* 800 ■ *TF:* 800-325-1051 ■ *Web:* www.katyindustries.com

Ettore Products Co 2100 N Loop Rd .... Alameda CA 94502 510-748-4130 748-4146
TF: 800-438-8673 ■ *Web:* www.ettore.com

Golden Star Inc
4770 N Belleview Ave Ste 209 .... Kansas City MO 64116 816-842-0233 842-1129
TF: 800-821-2792 ■ *Web:* www.goldenstar.com

Houston Wiper & Mill Supply Co 1234 Kress St .... Houston TX 77020 713-672-0571 673-7637
Web: www.houstonwiperandmill.com

KLEEN-TEX Industries Inc
101 N Greenwood St Ste C .... LaGrange GA 30240 706-882-0111 298-8336*
**Fax Area Code:* 678 ■ *Web:* www.kleen-tex.com

L C Industries 1 Signature Dr .... Hazlehurst MS 39083 601-894-1771
TF: 877-524-4722 ■ *Web:* www.buylci.com

Southern Wipers 100 Fairview Rd .... Asheville NC 28803 704-377-3448

Tranzonic Cos
26301 Curtiss Wright Pkwy Ste 200 .... Cleveland OH 44143 216-535-4300 831-5647
TF: 800-553-7979 ■ *Web:* www.tranzonic.com

United Textile Company Inc 751-143rd Ave .... San Leandro CA 94578 510-276-2288 278-1981
TF General: 800-233-0077 ■ *Web:* unitedtextileinc.com

Wipe-Tex International Corp 110 E 153rd St .... Bronx NY 10451 718-665-0787 665-0787
TF: 800-643-9607 ■ *Web:* www.wipe-tex.com

512 MORTGAGE LENDERS & LOAN BROKERS

SEE ALSO Banks - Commercial & Savings p. 1848

Phone | Fax

21st Mortgage Corp 620 Market St Ste 100 .... Knoxville TN 37902 865-292-2120
Web: www.21stmortgage.com

AAA Financial Corp
4613 N University Dr .... Coral Springs FL 33065 954-344-2530 344-0257
TF: 800-881-2530 ■ *Web:* www.aaafinancial.com

Advantage Mortgage Group Inc, The
4835 E Cactus Rd Ste 150 .... Scottsdale AZ 85254 602-953-6500
Web: www.tamg.biz

AMS Servicing LLC 3374 Walden Ave Ste 120 .... Depew NY 14043 866-919-5608
TF: 866-919-5608 ■ *Web:* www.ams-servicing.com

Ascentium Capital LLC 23970 Hwy 59 N .... Kingwood TX 77339 866-722-8500
TF: 866-722-8500 ■ *Web:* www.ascentiumcapital.com

BRT Realty Trust 60 Cutter Mill Rd Ste 303 .... Great Neck NY 11021 516-466-3100 466-3132
NYSE: BRT ■ *TF:* 800-450-5816 ■ *Web:* www.brtrealty.com

Canada Deposit Insurance Corp
50 O'Connor St 17th Fl .... Ottawa ON K1P6L2 613-996-2081
Web: www.cdic.ca

Canada Mortgage & Housing Corp
700 Montreal Rd .... Ottawa ON K1A0P7 613-748-2000
Web: www.cmhc.ca

CapitalSource Inc 5404 Wisconsin Ave .... Chevy Chase MD 20815 866-590-1566
NYSE: CSE ■ *Web:* www.capitalsource.com

Central Mortgage Co 801 John Barrow Ste 1 .... Little Rock AR 72205 501-716-5600
Web: www.baanthai.com

CFS Mortgage Corp 7720 N 16th St Ste 325 .... Phoenix AZ 85020 602-241-9875
Web: www.cfs-mortgage.com

Phone | Fax

CitiMortgage Inc 1000 Technology Dr .... O'Fallon MO 63368 800-283-7918
TF Cust Svc: 800-283-7918 ■ *Web:* www.citimortgage.com

CMLS Financial Ltd
Oceanic Plz Bldg
Ste 2110 - 1066 W Hastings St .... Vancouver BC V6E3X2 604-687-2118
Web: m.cmls.ca

Community Preservation Corp, The (CPC)
28 E 28th St 9Fl .... New York NY 10016 212-869-5300 683-0694
Web: www.communityp.com

Danburg Management Corp
7700 Congress Ave Ste 3100 .... Boca Raton FL 33487 561-997-5777
Web: www.danburg.com

Dominion Capital Inc 120 Tredegar St .... Richmond VA 23219 804-819-2000
Web: dom.com

Dominion Lending Centres Inc
2215 Coquitlam Ave .... Port Coquitlam BC V3B1J6 866-928-6810
TF: 866-928-6810 ■ *Web:* www.dominionlending.ca

Eastern Light Capital Inc
100 Pine St Ste 560 .... San Francisco CA 94111 415-693-9500
OTC: ELCI

EPIC Processing Ltd 2919 Valmont Rd Ste 206 .... Boulder CO 80301 303-440-8617

EverHome Mortgage Co 301 W Bay St .... Jacksonville FL 32202 800-669-9721 281-6380*
**Fax Area Code:* 904 ■ **Fax:* Cust Svc ■ *TF Cust Svc:* 800-669-9721 ■ *Web:* www.everhomemortgage.com

Extraco Technology 1704 N Valley Mills Dr .... Waco TX 76710 254-761-2300 761-2489
Web: www.extracomortgage.com

Fannie Mae 3900 Wisconsin Ave NW .... Washington DC 20016 202-752-7000 752-5980
OTC: FNMA ■ *TF:* 800-732-6643 ■ *Web:* www.fanniemae.com

Fin-West Group 1131 W Sixth St .... Ontario CA 91762 909-595-1996 595-7430
OTC: FMOR

Financial Fedcorp Inc 6305 Humphreys Blvd .... Memphis TN 38120 901-756-2848 747-4009
Web: www.finfedmem.com

First Eastern Mortgage Corp
100 Brickstone Sq .... Andover MA 01810 978-749-3100 749-3148
TF: 800-777-2240 ■ *Web:* www.firsteastern.com

First Equity Mortgage Bankers
9300 S Dadeland Blvd Ste 500 .... Miami FL 33156 305-666-3333 666-3181
TF: 800-973-3654 ■ *Web:* www.fembi.com

First Financial Services Inc (FFSI)
6230 Fairview Rd Ste 450 .... Charlotte NC 28210 866-506-9090 365-3098*
**Fax Area Code:* 704 ■ *Web:* www.ffsmortgage.com

Forest City Residential Management Inc
50 Public Sq Ste 1515 .... Cleveland OH 44113 216-416-3906
TF: 800-750-0750 ■
Web: www.forestcity.net/company/people/residential/pages/default.aspx

Freddie Mac 8200 Jones Branch Dr .... McLean VA 22102 703-903-2000 903-2759
TF: 800-424-5401 ■ *Web:* www.freddiemac.com
North Central Region 333 W Wacker Dr Ste 2500 .... Chicago IL 60606 312-407-7400 407-7398
TF: 800-373-3343 ■ *Web:* www.freddiemac.com
Northeast Region 8200 Jones Branch Dr .... McLean VA 22102 703-903-2000 903-2759
TF: 800-373-3343 ■ *Web:* www.freddiemac.com
Southeast/Southwest Region
2300 Windy Ridge Pkwy Ste 200N .... Atlanta GA 30339 770-857-8800 857-8805
TF: 800-373-3343 ■ *Web:* www.freddiemac.com

George Mason Mortgage Corp
4100 Monu Crnr Dr Ste 100 .... Fairfax VA 22030 703-273-2600 934-9122
TF: 800-867-6859 ■ *Web:* www.gmmllc.com

Government National Mortgage Assn
451 Seventh St SW Ste B-133 .... Washington DC 20410 202-708-1535
Web: www.ginniemae.gov

Green Tree Servicing LLC 345 St Peter St .... Saint Paul MN 55102 800-423-9527
TF: 800-643-0202 ■ *Web:* www.gtservicing.com

Guild Mortgage Co
5898 Copley Dr Fourth & Fifth Fl .... San Diego CA 92111 800-365-4441
TF: 800-365-4441 ■ *Web:* www.guildmortgage.com

HomeSteps 500 Plano Pkwy .... Carrollton TX 75010 800-972-7555
TF: 800-972-7555 ■ *Web:* www.homesteps.com

HSBC Bank USA 2929 Walden Ave .... Depew NY 14043 800-338-4626 826-1874*
**Fax Area Code:* 817 ■ *TF:* 800-338-4626 ■ *Web:* www.us.hsbc.com

Huntington Mortgage Co
7575 Huntington Pk Dr .... Columbus OH 43235 614-480-6505 480-6880*
**Fax:* Cust Svc ■ *TF:* 800-323-4695 ■ *Web:* huntington.com

Inland Mortgage Corp 2901 Butterfield Rd .... Oak Brook IL 60523 630-218-8000
TF: 800-826-8228 ■ *Web:* www.inlandgroup.com

Intervest Mortgage Investment Co
180 Grand Ave Ste 1400 .... Oakland CA 94612 510-622-8500
Web: www.intervestcref.com

JI Kislak Inc 7900 Miami Lakes Dr W .... Miami Lakes FL 33016 305-364-4100
Web: www.kislak.com

Legg Mason Real Estate Investors Inc
350 S Beverly Dr Ste 300 .... Beverly Hills CA 90212 310-234-2100 234-2150
Web: www.lmrei.com

LendingTree Inc 11115 Rushmore Dr .... Charlotte NC 28277 704-541-5351 541-1824
TF: 800-555-8733 ■ *Web:* www.lendingtree.com

Lion Inc 4700 42nd Ave SW Ste 430 .... Seattle WA 98116 206-577-1440 577-1441
TF: 800-546-6463 ■ *Web:* www.lioninc.com

loanDepot 26642 Towne Centre Dr .... Foothill Ranch CA 92610 888-337-6888
TF: 888-337-6888 ■ *Web:* www.loandepot.com

Midland Mortgage Co PO Box 26648 .... Oklahoma City OK 73126 800-654-4566 767-5500*
**Fax Area Code:* 405 ■ **Fax:* Cust Svc ■ *TF:* 800-654-4566 ■ *Web:* www.mymidlandmortgage.com

MMA Capital Management LLC (MuniMae)
621 E Pratt St Ste 600 .... Baltimore MD 21202 443-263-2900
OTC: MMAB ■ *TF:* 855-650-6932 ■ *Web:* www.munimae.com

Mortgage Investors Group
8320 E Walker Springs Ln .... Knoxville TN 37923 865-691-8910 691-7714
TF: 800-489-8910 ■ *Web:* www.migonline.com

Mortgage Resources Inc (MRI)
425 S Woods Mill Rd Ste 100 .... Chesterfield MO 63017 314-576-5577 576-6071
TF: 800-965-9910 ■ *Web:* www.mortgageresources.com

Mortgage Returns 1335 Strassner Dr .... St. Louis MO 63144 314-989-9100
Web: www.web.mortgagereturns.com

Mortgagebot LLC 1000 W Donges Bay Rd Ste 200 .... Mequon WI 53092 262-292-0843
Web: www.mortgagebot.com

				Phone	Fax
National Rural Utilities Co-op Finance Corp 2201 Co-op Way *TF:* 800-424-2954 ■ *Web:* www.nrucfc.coop	Herndon	VA	20171	703-709-6700	
Obsidian Mortgage Corp 35 Grand Marshall Dr *Web:* www.obsidianmortgages.com	Toronto	ON	M1B5W9	416-283-2377	
One Reverse Mortgage LLC 9740 Scranton Rd Ste 300 *Web:* www.onereversemortgage.com	San Diego	CA	92121	858-455-9120	
Origen Financial Inc 27777 Franklin Rd Ste 1700 *OTC: ORGN* ■ *Web:* www.origenfinancial.com	Southfield	MI	48034	248-746-7000	746-7094
Payscape Advisors 729 Lambert Dr Ne *Web:* www.payscapeadvisors.com	Atlanta	GA	30324	404-350-6565	
PHH Mortgage Corp 3000 Leadenhall Rd *TF:* 800-210-8849 ■ *Web:* www.phhmortgagesolutions.com/	Mount Laurel	NJ	08054	800-210-8849	
Pinnacle Mortgage Group Inc 3605 S Teller St *Web:* www.pinnacle-mortgage.com	Lakewood	CO	80235	303-716-9000	
Platinum Bank 802 W Lumsden Rd *Web:* www.platinumbank.com	Brandon	FL	33511	813-655-1234	
Plaza Home Mortgage Inc 5090 Shoreham Pl Ste 206 *TF:* 866-260-2529 ■ *Web:* www.plazahomemortgage.com	San Diego	CA	92122	858-346-1208	677-6741
Portland Housing Center Inc 3233 Ne Sandy Blvd *Web:* www.portlandhousingcenter.org	Portland	OR	97232	503-282-7744	
R-B Financial-mortgages Inc 44028 Mound Rd Ste 3 *TF General:* 800-566-4663 ■ *Web:* www.rbfinancial.com	Sterling Heights	MI	48314	586-254-8435	254-8438
Redwood Trust Inc One Belvedere Pl Ste 300 *NYSE: RWT* ■ *TF:* 866-269-4976 ■ *Web:* www.redwoodtrust.com	Mill Valley	CA	94941	415-389-7373	381-1773
Regions Mortgage Inc 215 Forrest St *TF:* 800-986-2462 ■ *Web:* www.regions.com	Hattiesburg	MS	39401	800-986-2462	
Residential Mortgage LLC 100 Calais Dr *TF:* 888-357-2707 ■ *Web:* www.residentialmtg.com	Anchorage	AK	99503	907-222-8800	222-8801
Ringler Assoc Inc 27422 Aliso Creek Rd Ste 200 *Web:* www.ringlerassociates.com	Aliso Viejo	CA	92656	949-296-9000	
Safeguard Properties Inc 7887 Safeguard Cir *TF:* 800-852-8306 ■ *Web:* www.safeguardproperties.com	Valley View	OH	44125	216-739-2900	
Softgate Systems Inc 330 Passaic Ave Ste 1 *Web:* www.softgatesystems.com	Fairfield	NJ	07004	973-830-1575	
Sterling Centrecorp Inc 7827 W Flagler St Ste 305 *Web:* www.sterlingorganization.com	Miami	FL	33144	305-261-8773	
Street Capital Financial Corp One Yonge St Ste 2401 *Web:* www.streetcapital.ca	Toronto	ON	M5E1E5	647-259-7873	
SunTrust Mortgage Inc 1001 Semmes Ave **Fax Area Code:* 804 ■ **Fax:* Mktg ■ *TF:* 800-634-7928 ■ *Web:* www.suntrustmortgage.com	Richmond	VA	23224	800-634-7928	291-0495*
Top Flite Financial Inc 123 E Grand River Ave *Web:* www.teamtopflite.com	Williamston	MI	48895	517-655-2140	
Truwest Credit Union PO Box 3489 *TF:* 855-878-9378 ■ *Web:* www.truwest.org	Scottsdale	AZ	85271	480-441-5900	
Universal American Mortgage Co 700 NW 107th Ave 3rd Fl **Fax Area Code:* 866 ■ *TF:* 800-741-8262 ■ *Web:* www.uamc.com	Miami	FL	33172	800-741-8262	837-0427*
Universal Lending Corp (ULC) 6775 E Evans Ave **Fax Area Code:* 303 ■ *TF:* 800-758-4063 ■ *Web:* ulc.com	Denver	CO	80224	800-758-4063	756-2156*
Valley Bank 36 Church Ave SW PO Box 2740 *Web:* www.myvalleybank.com	Roanoke	VA	24001	540-769-8577	342-4514
Vanderbilt Mortgage & Finance Inc 500 Alcoa Trl **Fax Area Code:* 865 ■ *TF:* 800-970-7250 ■ *Web:* www.vmf.com	Maryville	TN	37804	800-970-7250	380-3418*
Velocity Trade 99 Yorkville Ave Ste 210 *Web:* velocitytrade.com	Toronto	ON	M5R3K5	416-855-2800	
Verico Capital Mortgages Inc 106-18 Deakin St *Web:* www.capitalmortgages.com	Ottawa	ON	K2E8B7	613-228-3888	
Vestin Group Inc 8880 W Sunset Rd # 200 *Web:* www.vestinmortgage.com	Las Vegas	NV	89148	702-227-0965	227-5247
Wells Fargo Home Mortgage 2840 Ingersoll Ave **Fax Area Code:* 877 ■ *TF:* 800-869-3557 ■ *Web:* www.wellsfargo.com/mortgage	Des Moines	IA	50312	515-237-5196	302-0366*

513 MORTUARY, CREMATORY, CEMETERY PRODUCTS & SERVICES

				Phone	Fax
AJ Desmond & Sons Funeral Directors 2600 Crooks Rd *TF:* 800-210-7135 ■ *Web:* www.desmondfuneralhome.com	Troy	MI	48084	248-362-2500	362-0190
Baue Funeral Homes 620 Jefferson St **Fax Area Code:* 636 ■ *TF:* 888-724-0073 ■ *Web:* baue.com	Saint Charles	MO	63301	888-724-0073	946-3084*
Bradford-O'Keefe Funeral Homes Inc 675 E Howard Ave *Web:* www.bradfordokeefe.com	Biloxi	MS	39530	228-374-5650	435-3638
Carriage Services Inc 3040 Post Oak Blvd Ste 300 *NYSE: CSV* ■ *TF:* 866-332-8400 ■ *Web:* www.carriageservices.com	Houston	TX	77056	713-332-8400	332-8401
Church & Chapel Metal Arts Inc 2616 W Grand Ave *TF:* 800-992-1234 ■ *Web:* www.church-chapel.com	Chicago	IL	60612	800-992-1234	626-3299
Dignity Memorial 1929 Allen Pkwy *TF:* 800-894-2024 ■ *Web:* www.dignitymemorial.com	Houston	TX	77019	713-522-5141	
Forest Lawn Memorial-Parks & Mortuaries 1712 S Glendale Ave **Fax:* Cust Svc ■ *TF:* 800-204-3131 ■ *Web:* www.forestlawn.com	Glendale	CA	91205	323-254-3131	551-5071*
Hillside Cemetery Assn 1401 Woodland Ave *Web:* hillsidecemetery.com	Scotch Plains	NJ	07076	908-756-1729	
Inglewood Park Cemetery Inc 720 E Florence Ave *Web:* www.inglewoodparkcemetery.org	Inglewood	CA	90301	310-412-6500	
Kensico Cemetery Inc, The 273 Lakeview Ave *Web:* www.kensico.org	Valhalla	NY	10595	914-949-0347	
Midwest Memorial Group LLC 31300 Southfield Rd Ste 1 *Web:* midwestmemorialgroup.com	Beverly Hills	MI	48025	248-290-0338	
Mount Sinai Memorial Park 5950 Forest Lawn Dr *Web:* www.mt-sinai.com	Los Angeles	CA	90068	323-469-6000	
Neptune Society 4312 Woodman Ave Third Fl *TF:* 888-637-8863 ■ *Web:* www.neptunesociety.com	Sherman Oaks	CA	91423	888-637-8863	
Palm Mortuary Inc 1325 N Main St *Web:* www.palmmortuary.com	Las Vegas	NV	89101	702-464-8300	464-8394
Rabenhorst Funeral Home Inc PO Box 2666 *Web:* www.rabenhorst.com	Baton Rouge	LA	70821	225-383-6831	336-3374
Service Corp International 1929 Allen Pkwy *NYSE: SCI* ■ *Web:* www.sci-corp.com	Houston	TX	77019	713-522-5141	
Skyview Memorial Lawn 200 Rollingwood Dr *Web:* www.skyviewmemorial.com	Vallejo	CA	94591	707-644-7474	
Spring Grove Cemetery 4521 Spring Grove Ave *TF:* 888-853-2230 ■ *Web:* www.springgrove.org	Cincinnati	OH	45232	513-681-7526	853-6802
Stewart Enterprises Inc 1333 S Clearview Pkwy *NASDAQ: STEI* ■ *TF:* 877-239-3264 ■ *Web:* sci-corp.com/scicorp/home.aspx	New Orleans	LA	70121	713-522-5141	
StoneMor Partners LP 311 Veterans Hwy *NYSE: STON* ■ *Web:* stonemor.com	Levittown	PA	19056	215-826-2800	
Tucson Cemetery Assn 3015 N Oracle Rd *Web:* evergreenmortuary-cemetery.com	Tucson	AZ	85705	520-888-7470	
Union Cemetery 2505 Minnehaha Ave E *Web:* unioncemeterymn.org	Maplewood	MN	55119	651-739-0466	
Wilson Financial Group Inc 15915 Katy Fwy Ste 500	Houston	TX	77094	281-579-2760	579-9089
Woodlawn Cemetery Inc, The Webster Ave & E 233rd St *Web:* www.thewoodlawncemetery.org	Bronx	NY	10470	718-920-0500	

514 MOTION PICTURE DISTRIBUTION & RELATED SERVICES

				Phone	Fax
Anchor Bay Entertainment Inc 1699 Stutz Dr *Web:* www.anchorbayentertainment.com	Troy	MI	48084	248-816-0909	
Baker & Taylor Inc 2550 W Tyvola Rd Ste 300 **Fax Area Code:* 704 ■ *TF:* 800-775-1800 ■ *Web:* www.btol.com	Charlotte	NC	28217	800-775-1800	998-3316*
Bridgestone Multimedia Group Inc 300 N McKemy Ave **Fax Area Code:* 602 ■ *Web:* gobmg.com	Chandler	AZ	85226	480-940-5777	438-2702*
Buena Vista Home Entertainment Inc (BVHE) 500 S Buena Vista St *Web:* www.bvhe.com	Burbank	CA	91521	818-560-1000	
Carsey-Werner LLC 16027 Ventura Blvd Ste 600 *Web:* www.carseywerner.com	Encino	CA	91436	818-464-9600	
Crown Media Holdings Inc 12700 Ventura Blvd Ste 200 *NASDAQ: CRWN* ■ *TF:* 800-479-7328 ■ *Web:* www.hallmarkchannel.com	Studio City	CA	91604	818-755-2400	755-2461
Current House Productions LLC 3860 Via Del Rey *Web:* chpadvertising.com	Bonita Springs	FL	34134	239-676-7658	
Desert Island Films Inc 30 Portico Wy **Fax Area Code:* 978 ■ *Web:* www.desertislandfilms.com	Plymouth	MA	02360	774-773-9223	254-5135*
Echo Bridge Entertainment LLC 3089 Airport Rd *Web:* www.ebhe.com	La Crosse	WI	54603	608-784-6620	
Extreme Reach Inc 75 2nd Ave Ste 720 *NASDAQ: DGIT* ■ **Fax Area Code:* 877 ■ *TF:* 888-326-8733 ■ *Web:* extremereach.com	Needham	MA	02494	781-577-2016	302-8633*
Facets Multimedia Inc 1517 W Fullerton Ave *TF Cust Svc:* 800-331-6197 ■ *Web:* www.facets.org	Chicago	IL	60614	773-281-9075	929-5437
First Run Features 630 Ninth Ave Ste 1213 *TF:* 800-229-8575 ■ *Web:* www.firstrunfeatures.com	New York	NY	10036	212-243-0600	989-7649
Image Entertainment 20525 Nordhoff St Ste 200 *OTC: DISK* ■ *Web:* www.image-entertainment.com	Chatsworth	CA	91311	818-407-9100	
Ingram Entertainment Inc 2 Ingram Blvd **Fax Area Code:* 818 ■ *TF:* 800-621-1333 ■ *Web:* www.ingramentertainment.com	La Vergne	TN	37089	615-287-4000	866-0226*
Insight Media 2162 Broadway *TF:* 800-233-9910 ■ *Web:* www.insight-media.com	New York	NY	10024	212-721-6316	799-5309
Kino International Corp 333 W 39th St Rm 503 *TF:* 800-562-3330 ■ *Web:* www.kinolorber.com	New York	NY	10018	212-629-6880	714-0871
Kultur International Films Ltd PO Box 755 *TF:* 888-329-2580 ■ *Web:* kulturvideo.com/	Forked River	NJ	08731	888-329-2580	
Lifesize Entertainment & Releasing 194 Elmwood Dr Ste 2 *Web:* www.lifesizeentertainment.com	Parsippany	NJ	07054	973-884-4884	
MPI Media Group 16101 108th Ave *TF:* 800-323-0442 ■ *Web:* www.mpimedia.com	Orland Park	IL	60467	708-460-0555	460-0175
Native Grounds Nursery & Garden Center 1172A S Mt Shasta Blvd *Web:* nativegrounds.org	Mount Shasta	CA	96067	530-926-0555	
Paramount Home Entertainment 5555 Melrose Ave *Web:* paramount.com	Los Angeles	CA	90038	323-956-5000	
Paramount Pictures Corp 5555 Melrose Ave *Web:* www.paramount.com	Los Angeles	CA	90038	323-956-5000	956-0121
Sony Pictures Classics 550 Madison Ave 8th Fl *Web:* sonypictures.com	New York	NY	10022	212-833-8833	833-8570

				Phone	Fax
Sony Pictures Entertainment Inc 10202 W Washington Blvd *TF:* 855-327-7669 ■ *Web:* www.sonypictures.com	Culver City	CA	90232	310-244-4000	840-8888
Sony Pictures Home Entertainment 10202 W Washington Blvd *Web:* www.sonypictures.com/spe	Culver City	CA	90232	310-244-4000	244-2626
Todd Street Productions 111 Eighth Ave Fl 16 *Web:* www.toddstreet.com	New York	NY	10011	212-966-5900	
Twentieth Century Fox Home Entertainment Inc 2121 Ave of the Stars Suite 100 **Fax Area Code:* 888 ■ *TF:* 877-369-7867 ■ *Web:* www.foxconnect.com	Los Angeles	CA	90067	310-369-3900	443-4369*
Universal Studios Home Entertainment 10 Universal City Plaza *Web:* www.universalstudiosentertainment.com	Universal City	CA	91608	818-777-1000	
Video Data Bank 112 S Michigan Ave *Web:* www.vdb.org	Chicago	IL	60603	312-345-3550	541-8073
Warner Bros Domestic Television Distribution 4000 Warner Blvd *Web:* warnerbros.com	Burbank	CA	91522	818-954-6000	
Warner Bros Entertainment Inc 4000 Warner Blvd *TF:* 800-778-7879 ■ *Web:* www.warnerbros.com	Burbank	CA	91522	818-954-1853	954-3817
WRS Motion Picture & Video Laboratory 213 Tech Rd *Web:* www.wrslabs.com	Pittsburgh	PA	15205	412-937-1200	922-1200

515 MOTION PICTURE PRE- & POST-PRODUCTION SERVICES

				Phone	Fax
Alpha Cine Labs 9800 40th Ave S	Seattle	WA	98118	206-682-8230	682-6649
American Media International LLC 2609 Tucker St *Web:* ami-media.com	Burlington	NC	27215	336-229-5554	228-1409
Ascent Media Group Inc 520 Broadway 5th Fl *Web:* ascentcapitalgroupinc.com	Santa Monica	CA	90401	310-434-7000	434-7007
Beyond Pix Studios 950 Battery St Third Fl *Web:* main.beyondpix.com	San Francisco	CA	94111	415-434-1027	434-1032
Broadway Video Inc 1619 Broadway *Web:* www.broadwayvideo.com	New York	NY	10019	212-265-7600	713-1535
Cafefx 1130 E Clark Ave	Santa Maria	CA	93455	805-922-9479	
Cinema Libre Studio 120 S Victory Blvd First Fl *Web:* www.cinemalibrestudio.com	Burbank	CA	91502	818-588-3033	349-9922
Crossman Post Production LLC 35 Lone Hollow *TF:* 888-553-1958 ■ *Web:* www.crossmanpost.com	Sandy	UT	84092	801-553-1958	553-0953
Downstream 1624 NW Johnson St *Web:* www.downstream.com	Portland	OR	97209	503-226-1944	226-1283
Edit Bay 571 N Poplar Ste I *Web:* www.theeditbay.com	Orange	CA	92868	714-978-7878	978-7858
Elastic Creative 550 Bryant St *Web:* www.elasticcreative.com	San Francisco	CA	94107	415-495-5595	543-8370
Elevation 905 Bernina Ave *Web:* thisiselevation.com	Atlanta	GA	30307	404-221-1705	
Encore Hollywood 6344 Fountain Ave *Web:* www.encorepost.com	Hollywood	CA	90028	323-466-7663	467-5539
Film Technology Company Inc 726 N Cole Ave *Web:* www.film-tech.com	Hollywood	CA	90038	323-464-3456	464-7439
Filmworks/Astro Lab 61 W Erie St *Web:* www.filmworkersastro.com	Chicago	IL	60654	312-280-5500	
FOX Studios 10201 W Pico Blvd *Web:* www.foxstudios.com	Los Angeles	CA	90035	310-369-1000	203-1558
Go Edit Inc 5614 Cahuenga Blvd *TF:* 800-833-9200 ■ *Web:* www.goedit.tv	North Hollywood	CA	91601	818-284-6260	985-6260
HDMG Corp 555 First Ave NE *Web:* www.hdmg.com	Minneapolis	MN	55413	612-224-9500	224-9515
Henninger Media Services Inc 2601a Wilson Blvd *Web:* www.henninger.com	Arlington	VA	22201	703-243-3444	243-5697
Level 3 Post 2901 W Alameda Ave *Web:* www.level3post.com	Burbank	CA	91505	818-840-7200	840-7801
Mad House 240 Madison Ave 14th Fl *Web:* www.madhousenyc.com	New York	NY	10016	212-867-1515	697-7168
Modern Videofilm Inc 2300 Empire Ave **Fax Area Code:* 323 ■ *Web:* www.mvfinc.com	Burbank	CA	91504	818-840-1700	203-3057*
Point.360 2701 Media Center Dr *NASDAQ: PTSX* ■ *Web:* www.point360.com	Los Angeles	CA	90065	818-565-1400	847-2503
Post Modern Co 2734 Walnut St *Web:* www.postmodernco.com	Denver	CO	80205	303-539-7001	539-7002
Post Modern Group LLC 2941 Alton Pkwy *Web:* www.postmoderngroup.com	Irvine	CA	92606	949-608-8700	608-8729
Postworks New York 100 Ave of the Americas 10th Fl *Web:* postworks.com/	New York	NY	10013	212-894-4000	941-0439
Raleigh Studios Worldwide 5300 Melrose Ave *TF:* 888-960-3456 ■ *Web:* www.raleighstudios.com	Hollywood	CA	90038	323-466-3111	871-5600
Rhythm & Hues Inc 2100 E Grand Ave *Web:* www.rhythm.com	El Segundo	CA	90245	310-448-7500	448-7600
RPG Productions 632 S Glenwood Pl *Web:* www.rpgproductions.com	Burbank	CA	91506	818-848-0240	848-2257
Technicolor Complete Post Inc 6040 Sunset Blvd *Web:* www.technicolor.com	Hollywood	CA	90028	323-817-6600	
Technicolor USA Inc 10330 N Meridian St *Web:* www.technicolor.com	Indianapolis	IN	46290	317-587-3000	
Victory Studios 2247 15th Ave W *Web:* www.victorystudios.com	Seattle	WA	98119	206-282-1776	282-3535
Video Post & Transfer Inc 2727 Inwood Rd *Web:* www.videopost.com	Dallas	TX	75235	214-350-2676	352-1427

				Phone	Fax
WRS Motion Picture & Video Laboratory 213 Tech Rd *Web:* www.wrslabs.com	Pittsburgh	PA	15205	412-937-1200	922-1200

516 MOTION PICTURE PRODUCTION - SPECIAL INTEREST

SEE ALSO Animation Companies p. 1743; Motion Picture & Television Production p. 2768

				Phone	Fax
Active Parenting Publishers 1955 Vaughn Rd Ste 108 *TF:* 800-825-0060 ■ *Web:* www.activeparenting.com	Kennesaw	GA	30144	770-429-0565	429-0334
American Educational Products Inc 401 Hickory St PO Box 2121 *TF:* 800-289-9299 ■ *Web:* www.amep.com	Fort Collins	CO	80522	970-484-7445	484-1198
Broadview Media Inc 4455 W 77th St **Fax Area Code:* 952 ■ *Web:* www.broadviewmedia.com	Edina	MN	55435	612-280-6947	835-0971*
Classic Worldwide Productions 5001 E Royalton Rd *Web:* classicworldwide.com	Cleveland	OH	44147	440-838-5377	
Coastal Training Technologies Corp 500 Studio Dr *TF:* 866-333-6888 ■ *Web:* www.coastal.com	Virginia Beach	VA	23452	757-498-9014	498-3657
CRM Learning 2218 Faraday Ave Ste 110 *TF:* 800-421-0833 ■ *Web:* www.crmlearning.com	Carlsbad	CA	92008	760-431-9800	931-5792
Gail & Rice Productions Inc 30700 Northwestern Hwy *Web:* www.gail-rice.com	Farmington Hills	MI	48334	248-799-5000	799-5001
Hammond Communications Group Inc 173 Trade St *TF:* 888-424-1878 ■ *Web:* www.hammondcg.com	Lexington	KY	40511	859-254-1878	254-4290
IMS Productions 4555 W 16th St *Web:* www.imsproductionstv.com	Indianapolis	IN	46222	317-492-8770	492-8746
Intaglio LLC 5809 Cross Roads Commerce Pkwy Ste 200 *TF:* 800-632-9153 ■ *Web:* www.intaglioav.com	Grand Rapids	MI	49519	616-243-3300	243-0923
Iris Films 2600 Tenth St Ste 413 *Web:* www.irisfilms.org	Berkeley	CA	94710	510-845-5415	841-3336
Keystone Learning Systems LLC 6030 Daybreak Cir Ste A150 116 **Fax Area Code:* 866 ■ *TF:* 800-949-5590 ■ *Web:* www.keystonelearning.com	Clarksville	MD	21029	410-800-4000	422-7015*
Kultur International Films Ltd PO Box 755 *TF:* 888-329-2580 ■ *Web:* kulturvideo.com/	Forked River	NJ	08731	888-329-2580	
Learning Communications LLC 5520 Trabuco Rd **Fax Area Code:* 949 ■ *TF:* 800-622-3610 ■ *Web:* www.learncom.com	Irvine	CA	92620	800-622-3610	727-4323*
Marcus Productions Inc 3107 Stirling Rd Ste 204 *Web:* www.marcusproductions.com	Fort Lauderdale	FL	33312	954-965-5295	
Medcom Trainex 6060 Phyllis Dr **Fax Area Code:* 714 ■ *TF Cust Svc:* 800-877-1443 ■ *Web:* www.medcomrn.com	Cypress	CA	90630	800-877-1443	898-4852*
National Film Board of Canada Stn Centre-Ville PO Box 6100 *Web:* www.nfb.ca	Montreal	QC	H3C3H5	514-283-9000	283-7564
New Amsterdam Entertainment Inc 1133 Ave of the Americas Ste 1621 *Web:* www.newamsterdamnyc.com	New York	NY	10036	212-922-1930	922-0674
Nightingale-Conant Corp 6245 W Howard St **Fax Area Code:* 847 ■ *TF Cust Svc:* 800-557-1660 ■ *Web:* www.nightingale.com	Niles	IL	60714	800-557-1660	647-5989*
PADI Americas 30151 Tomas St **Fax Area Code:* 800 ■ *TF:* 888-725-4801 ■ *Web:* kaptest.com	Rancho Santa Margarita	CA	92688	949-858-7234	878-4364*
Zelo Productions Inc Three S Newton St **Fax Area Code:* 781 ■ *Web:* www.zeloproductions.com	Denver	CO	80219	303-936-8995	623-7996*

517 MOTION PICTURE & TELEVISION PRODUCTION

SEE ALSO Animation Companies p. 1743; Motion Picture Production - Special Interest p. 2768

				Phone	Fax
3 Ball Entertainment 3650 Redondo Beach Ave *Web:* www.3ballproductions.com	Redondo Beach	CA	90278	424-236-7500	
3Play Media Inc 125 CambridgePark Dr *Web:* www.3playmedia.com	Cambridge	MA	02140	617-764-5189	
495 Productions Inc 4222 W Burbank Blvd Second Fl *Web:* www.495productions.com	Burbank	CA	91505	818-840-2750	
9 Story Entertainment Inc 23 Fraser Ave *Web:* www.9story.com	Toronto	ON	M6K1Y7	416-530-9900	
@radical.media 435 Hudson St Sixth Fl *Web:* www.radicalmedia.com	New York	NY	10014	212-462-1500	462-1600
ACT Video Productions Inc 5009 Pacific Hwy East Ste 10-O *Web:* www.actvp.com	Fife	WA	98424	253-926-2440	926-1130
Acutrack Inc 350 Sonic Ave *Web:* www.acutrack.com	Livermore	CA	94551	925-579-5000	
Adconion Media Group Ltd 950 Tower Ln *TF:* 800-542-2811 ■ *Web:* amobee.com	Santa Monica	CA	94404	650-802-8871	
Adm Productions Inc 40 Seaview Blvd *TF:* 800-236-3425 ■ *Web:* www.admpro.com	Port Washington	NY	11050	516-484-6900	621-2531
Affiliated Media Inc 445 E Ohio St Ste 305 *Web:* www.affiliatedmedia.net	Chicago	IL	60611	312-670-7200	
Alcon Entertainment LLC 10390 Santa Monica Blvd Ste 250 *Web:* www.alconent.com	Los Angeles	CA	90025	310-789-3040	
Alliance Tickets Inc 5178 S Broadway	Englewood	CO	80113	303-781-2220	
American Zoetrope 916 Kearny St *Web:* www.zoetrope.com	San Francisco	CA	94133	415-788-7500	989-7910

Company / Address	City	State	Zip	Phone	Fax
Animated Story Boards Ltd 1001 Ave of the Americas 24 fl *Web:* www.animatedstoryboards.com	New York	NY	10018	212-595-0400	
Ann Coppel Productions LLC PO Box 17144 *Web:* www.anncoppelproductions.com	Seattle	WA	98127	206-282-7720	
Anonymous Content LLC 3532 Hayden Ave *Web:* www.anonymouscontent.com	Culver City	CA	90232	310-558-3667	
Apostle Pictures 568 Broadway Ste 601 *Web:* www.apostlenyc.com	New York	NY	10012	212-541-4323	541-4330
Arcadia Entertainment Inc 6454 Quinpool Rd Ste 301 *Web:* www.arcadiatv.com	Halifax	NS	B3L1A9	902-446-3414	
Ascendant Pictures 406 Wilshire Blvd *Web:* www.ascendantpictures.com	Santa Monica	CA	90401	310-288-4600	
Associated Television International 4401 Wilshire Blvd *Web:* www.associatedtelevision.com	Los Angeles	CA	90010	323-556-5600	556-5610
Asylum, The 72 E Palm Ave *Web:* www.theasylum.cc	Burbank	CA	91502	323-850-1214	
Attraction Media Inc 5455 de Gaspe Ave Ste 805 *Web:* www.attractionmedia.ca	Montreal	QC	H2T3B3	514-846-1222	
Audio General Inc (AGI) 1680 Republic Rd *Web:* www.audiogeneral.com	Huntingdon Valley	PA	19006	267-288-0300	288-0301
Audio Video Systems Inc 14120 Sullyfield Cir *Web:* www.avsinc.net	Chantilly	VA	20151	703-263-1002	263-0722
Auritt Communications 555 Eigth Ave Rm 709 *Web:* auritt.com	New York	NY	10018	212-302-6230	
Aurora Pictures Inc 5249 Chicago Ave *Web:* www.aurorapictures.com	Minneapolis	MN	55417	612-821-6490	
Auryn Inc 6033 W Century Blvd Ste 808 *Web:* www.auryn.com	Los Angeles	CA	90045	310-649-4278	
Automated Media Services Corp 110 Commerce Dr *Web:* www.3gtv.com	Allendale	NJ	07401	201-934-6666	
Avalanche Creative Svcs Inc 135 W 29th St *Web:* www.avalanchecreative.tv	New York	NY	10001	212-206-9335	
Avatar Studios Inc 2675 Scott Ave Ste G *Web:* www.avatar-studios.com	Saint Louis	MO	63103	314-533-2242	533-3349
B-Reel 401 Broadway 24th Fl *Web:* www.b-reel.com	New York	NY	10013	212-966-6186	
Badiyan Inc 720 W 94th St *Web:* www.badiyan.com	Minneapolis	MN	55420	952-888-5507	
Banyan Communications Inc 3569 New Town Lk Dr *Web:* www.banyancom.com	Saint Charles	MO	63301	636-946-3456	
Bardel Entertainment Inc 548 Beatty St *Web:* bardel.ca	Vancouver	BC	V6B2L3	604-669-5589	669-9079
Bent Image Lab LLC 2729 SE Division St *Web:* bentimagelab.com	Portland	OR	97202	503-228-6206	
Best Buys Direct Inc 1044 State Rt 23 Ste 310 *Web:* www.bestbuysdirect.com	Wayne	NJ	07470	973-628-8100	
Big Deahl Productions Inc 1450 N Dayton St *Web:* www.bigdeahl.com	Chicago	IL	60642	312-573-0733	
Big Foot Productions Inc 3709 36th Ave *Web:* www.bigfootnyc.com	Long Island City	NY	11101	718-729-1900	729-8638
Bioquant Image Analysis Corp 5611 Ohio Ave *TF:* 800-221-0549 ■ *Web:* www.bioquant.com	Nashville	TN	37209	615-350-7866	
Booth Production Services Inc 5768 Remington Dr *Web:* www.boothproductionservices.com	Winston Salem	NC	27104	336-766-1961	
BRC Imagination Arts 2711 Winona Ave *Web:* www.brcweb.com	Burbank	CA	91504	818-841-8084	841-4996
Brightlight Pictures Inc 2400 Boundary Rd The Bridge Studios *Web:* www.brightlightpictures.com	Burnaby	BC	V5M3Z3	604-628-3000	
Broadcast Sports Inc 7455 Race Rd *Web:* broadcastsportsinc.com	Hanover	MD	21076	410-564-2600	
Brooksfilms Ltd 9336 W Washington Blvd	Culver City	CA	90232	310-202-3292	202-3225
Bruno White Entertainment Inc 9460 Delegates Dr Ste 101 *Web:* www.brunowhite.com	Orlando	FL	32837	407-352-5555	
Bullfrog Films Inc 372 Dautrich Rd *TF:* 800-543-3764 ■ *Web:* www.bullfrogfilms.com	Reading	PA	19606	610-779-8226	
Bunim/Murray Productions 6007 Sepulveda Blvd *Web:* www.bunim-murray.com	Van Nuys	CA	91411	818-756-5100	
Camelot Entertainment Group 300 Spectrum Center Dr Ste 400 *Web:* www.camelotfilms.com	Irvine	CA	92618	949-754-3030	
Campos Creative Works 1715 14th St *Web:* www.ccwla.com	Santa Monica	CA	90404	310-453-1511	
CAV Distributing Corp 253 Utah Ave *Web:* www.cavd.com	South San Francisco	CA	94080	650-588-2228	
CBS News 524 W 57th St *Web:* www.cbsnews.com	New York	NY	10019	212-975-3247	
CBS Studio Ctr 4024 Radford Ave **Fax:* Mail Rm ■ *Web:* www.cbssc.com	Studio City	CA	91604	818-655-5000	655-5409*
CBS Television Distribution 2450 Colorado Ave Ste 500E *Web:* www.cbstvd.com	Santa Monica	CA	90404	310-264-3300	264-3301
Center City Film & Video 1503 Walnut St *Web:* www.ccfv.com	Philadelphia	PA	19102	215-568-4134	568-6011
CenterStaging Corp 3407 Winona Ave *Web:* www.centerstaging.com	Burbank	CA	91504	818-559-4333	
Cev Multimedia Ltd 1020 SE Loop 289 *TF:* 877-610-5017 ■ *Web:* www.cevmultimedia.com	Lubbock	TX	79404	806-745-8820	
CGI Communications Inc 130 E Main St Ste 800 *TF:* 800-398-3029 ■ *Web:* www.cgicommunications.com	Rochester	NY	14604	585-427-0020	
Chainsaw Inc 940 N Orange Dr Second Fl *Web:* www.chainsawedit.com	Hollywood	CA	90038	323-785-1550	
Checchi Capital Advisors LLC 190 N Canon Dr Ste 402 *Web:* www.goodnewschannel.net	Beverly Hills	CA	90210	310-432-0010	
Chelsea Pictures Inc 33 Bond St Unit 1 *Web:* www.chelsea.com	New York	NY	10012	212-431-3434	
Cinecraft Productions Inc 2515 Franklin Blvd *Web:* www.cinecraft.com	Cleveland	OH	44113	216-781-2300	
Cineflix Media Inc 3510 Saint Laurent Blvd Ste 202 *Web:* www.cineflix.com	Montreal	QC	H2X2V2	514-278-3140	
Cinemavault Releasing Inc 175 Bloor St E S Tower Ste 1011 *Web:* www.cinemavault.com	Toronto	ON	M4W3R8	416-363-6060	
Cinemotion Inc 9062 General Dr *Web:* cinemotioninc.com	Plymouth	MI	48170	734-454-4433	
Cinespace Film Studios 30 Booth Ave Ste 100 *Web:* www.cinespace.com	Toronto	ON	M4M2M2	416-406-4000	
Cinetel Films 8255 W Sunset Blvd *Web:* cinetelfilms.com	West Hollywood	CA	90046	323-654-4000	
Cintrex Audio Visual 656 Axminister Dr *TF:* 800-325-9541 ■ *Web:* www.cintrexav.com	Fenton	MO	63026	636-343-0178	
CloverLeaf Digital LLC 20 Jay St Ste 213 *Web:* www.cloverleafdigital.com	Brooklyn	NY	11201	718-438-6448	
Collective Digital Studio LLC 8383 Wilshire Blvd Ste 1050 *Web:* www.collectivedigitalstudio.com	Beverly Hills	CA	90211	323-370-1500	
Columbia TriStar Motion Picture Group 10202 W Washington Blvd **Fax:* Mail Rm ■ *TF:* 855-327-7669 ■ *Web:* www.sonypictures.com/movies	Culver City	CA	90232	310-244-4000	840-8888*
Communca Inc 31 N Erie St *Web:* www.communica-usa.com	Toledo	OH	43604	419-244-7766	
Compass Rose Media LLC 105 Locust St *Web:* www.compassrosemedia.com	Santa Cruz	CA	95060	831-457-3533	
Concept Art House Inc 785 Market St Ste 1100 *Web:* www.conceptarthouse.com	San Francisco	CA	94103	415-707-1500	
Concepts Tv Production 328 W Main St *Web:* www.conceptstv.com	Boonton	NJ	07005	973-331-1500	
Contecture International Ltd 18006 Skypark Cir Ste 210 *Web:* www.contextureintl.com	Irvine	CA	92614	949-250-0811	
Contrast Creative 2598 Highstone Rd *Web:* www.contrastcreative.com	Cary	NC	27519	919-469-9151	
Cosmic Pictures Inc 1345 Major St *Web:* cosmicpictures.com	Salt Lake City	UT	84115	801-463-3880	
Cox Matthews & Associates Inc 10520 Warwick Ave Ste B-8 *Web:* www.diverseeducation.com	Fairfax	VA	22030	703-385-2981	
Creation Ground Media 999 Clark Ave *Web:* www.creationgroundmedia.com	Mountain View	CA	94040	650-947-7779	
Creative Film Management 430 W 14th St Fl 4 *Web:* www.crmmgt.com	New York	NY	10014	212-685-6070	
Crosswater Digital Media LLC 695 Delaware Ave *Web:* www.crosswater.net	Buffalo	NY	14209	716-884-8486	
Culver Studios 9336 W Washington Blvd *Web:* www.theculverstudios.com	Culver City	CA	90232	310-202-1234	
Curtis 1105 Western Ave *Web:* www.curtisinc.com	Cincinnati	OH	45203	513-621-8895	
Danetracks Inc 7356 Santa Monica Blvd *Web:* www.danetracks.com	West Hollywood	CA	90046	323-512-8160	
Davenport Theatrical Enterprises Inc 250 W 49th St Ste 301 *Web:* www.davenporttheatrical.com	New York	NY	10019	212-874-5348	
David Naylor & Assoc Inc 6535 Santa Monica Blvd *Web:* www.dnala.com	Los Angeles	CA	90038	323-463-2826	463-2535
Deluxe Digital Media Management Inc 29125 Ave Paine *Web:* www.bydeluxe.com	Valencia	CA	91355	661-702-5000	
Destination Cinema Inc 4155 Harrison Blvd Ste 201 *Web:* www.destinationcinema.com	Ogden	UT	84403	801-392-5881	
Devlin Video International LLC 1501 Broadway Ste 408 *Web:* www.devlinvideo.com	New York	NY	10036	212-391-1313	
Dick Clark Productions Inc (DCP) 2900 Olympic Blvd *Web:* www.dickclark.com	Santa Monica	CA	90404	310-255-4600	
Digital Domain Productions Inc 300 Rose Ave *Web:* www.digitaldomain.com	Venice	CA	90291	310-314-2800	
Digital FX Inc 6010 Perkins Rd Ste B *Web:* www.digitalfx.tv	Baton Rouge	LA	70808	225-763-6010	
Digital Outpost 2772 Loker Ave W *Web:* www.digitaloutpost.com	Carlsbad	CA	92010	760-431-3575	
Dillon Video & Film Productions Inc 2330 Ne Eigth Rd *Web:* www.dillonvideo.com	Ocala	FL	34470	352-620-0686	
Double r Productions LLC 1621 Connecticut Ave Nw Ste 4 *Web:* www.doublerproductions.com	Washington	DC	20009	202-797-7777	
Downtown Digital Post 401 E Jefferson St *Web:* www.downtowndigitalpost.com	Phoenix	AZ	85004	602-462-6464	
Dreamworks Animation LLC 1000 Flower St *Web:* www.dreamworks.com	Glendale	CA	91201	818-695-5000	
Drury Design Dynamics Inc 49 W 27th St *Web:* www.drurydesign.com	New York	NY	10001	212-213-4600	

Company	City	State	Zip	Phone	Fax
Dufferin Gate Productions Inc 20 Butterick Rd *Web:* www.dufferingate.com	Toronto	ON	M8W3Z8	416-252-9998	
E-n-g Mobile Systems Inc-broadcast & Mobilab Divs 2245 Via De Mercados *Web:* www.e-n-g.com	Concord	CA	94520	925-798-4060	
Eastco Multi Media Solutions Inc 3646 California Rd *TF:* 800-365-8273 ■ *Web:* www.eastcomultimedia.com	Orchard Park	NY	14127	716-662-0536	
Edmonds Entertainment 1635 N Cahuenga Blvd Fifth Fl *Web:* www.edmondsent.com	Los Angeles	CA	90028	323-860-1520	
Edward R Pressman Film Corp 9469 Jefferson Blvd Ste 119 *Web:* www.pressman.com	Los Angeles	CA	90232	310-450-9692	450-9705
EFILM LLC 1146 N Las Palmas Ave *Web:* www.efilm.com	Hollywood	CA	90038	323-463-7041	
Element Productions Inc 316 Stuart St Fourth Fl *Web:* elementproductions.com	Boston	MA	02116	617-779-8808	
Elephant Productions Inc 3404 Guadalupe St *Web:* www.changs.com	Austin	TX	78705	512-302-3130	
Emerging Pictures 49 W 27th St 8th Fl *Web:* www.emergingpictures.com	New York	NY	10019	212-245-6767	
Endemol USA Inc 9255 Sunset Blvd Ste 1100 *Web:* www.endemolusa.tv	Los Angeles	CA	90069	310-860-9914	
Entertainment Studios Inc 1925 Century Park E Ste 1025 *Web:* www.es.tv	Los Angeles	CA	90067	310-277-3500	
EUE/Screen Gems Studios 603 Greenwich St *Web:* euescreengems.com	New York	NY	10014	212-450-1600	867-4503
Event Producers Inc 5724 Salmen St *Web:* eventproducers.com	New Orleans	LA	70123	504-466-4066	
Evil Eye Pictures LLC 665 Third St Ste 503 *Web:* evileyepictures.com	San Francisco	CA	94107	415-777-0666	
Exodus Film Group Inc 1255 Electric Ave *Web:* www.exodusfilmgroup.com	Venice	CA	90291	310-684-3155	
F & F Productions LLC 14333 Myerlake Cir *Web:* fandfhd.tv	Clearwater	FL	33760	727-530-5000	535-6547
FDC Graphics Films Inc 3820 William Richardson Dr *Web:* www.fdcfilms.com	South Bend	IN	46628	574-273-4400	
Fenton Communications Inc 1010 Vermont Ave NW Ste 1100 *Web:* www.fenton.com	Washington	DC	20005	202-822-5200	
Film Workers Club 1006 17th Ave S *Web:* www.filmworkers.com	Nashville	TN	37212	615-322-9337	
First Generation Productions 410 Allentown Dr *Web:* www.firstgencom.com	Allentown	PA	18109	610-437-4300	
Focus Features 65 Bleeker St 3rd Fl **Fax Area Code:* 818 ■ *Web:* www.focusfeatures.com	New York	NY	10012	212-539-4000	866-4579*
Focus Features LLC 1540 2nd St Ste 200 *Web:* www.filminfocus.com	Santa Monica	CA	90401	818-777-8738	
Fortis Films 8581 Santa Monica Blvd Ste 1	West Hollywood	CA	90069	310-659-4533	659-4373
Forward Entertainment 9255 Sunset Blvd Ste 805	Los Angeles	CA	90069	310-278-6700	278-6770
Fox Searchlight Pictures 10201 W Pico Blvd Bldg 38 *Web:* www.foxsearchlight.com	Los Angeles	CA	90035	310-369-6000	
Frantic Films Corp 70 Arthur St Ste 300 *Web:* www.franticfilms.com	Winnipeg	MB	R3B1G7	204-949-0070	
Fresh Air Media 2015 Airpark Ct Ste 20 *Web:* freshairmedia.com	Auburn	CA	95602	530-888-7676	
Fujisankei Communications International Inc 150 E 52nd St 34th Fl *Web:* www.fci-ny.com	New York	NY	10022	212-753-8100	688-0392
FUNimation Entertainment Ltd 1200 Lakeside Pkwy Bldg 1 *Web:* www.funimation.com	Flower Mound	TX	75028	972-355-7300	
Game Creek Video LLC 23 Executive Dr *Web:* www.gamecreekvideo.com	Hudson	NH	03051	603-882-5222	
Garden State Studios 1325 Us Hwy 206	Skillman	NJ	08558	609-688-1004	
Genesis Communications Inc 900 Technology Pkwy Ste 300 *Web:* www.phantomefx.com	Cedar Falls	IA	50613	319-266-3656	
Geomedia Inc 4242 Medical Dr Ste 4200 *Web:* www.geomedia.com	San Antonio	TX	78229	210-614-5900	614-5922
Global Digital Media Xchange Inc 5432 W 102nd St	Los Angeles	CA	90045	818-972-0200	
Grace Creek Media Inc 100 Cathedral St Ste 9 *Web:* pub1.andyswebtools.com	Annapolis	MD	21401	410-280-8528	
Gracie Films 10201 W Pico Blvd Bldg 41/42 *Web:* www.graciefilms.com	Los Angeles	CA	90064	310-369-7222	
Grb Entertainment Inc 13400 Riverside Dr Ste 300 *Web:* grbtv.com/	Sherman Oaks	CA	91423	818-728-7600	
Greibok Designs LLC Three E Read St *Web:* www.greibo.com	Baltimore	MD	21202	410-244-8861	
Gurney Productions Inc 8929 S Sepulveda Blvd Ste 510 *Web:* www.gurneyproductions.com	Los Angeles	CA	90045	310-645-1499	
Guru Studio 500-110 Spadina Ave *Web:* www.gurustudio.com	Toronto	ON	M5V2K4	416-599-4878	
Guthy-Renker Corp 41550 Eclectic St Ste 200 *Web:* www.guthy-renker.com	Palm Desert	CA	92260	760-773-9022	773-9016
Half Yard Productions LLC 4922 Fairmont Ave Ste 300 *Web:* www.halfyardproductions.com	Bethesda	MD	20814	240-223-3400	
Harmony Gold Music Inc 7655 W Sunset Blvd *Web:* www.harmonygold.com	Los Angeles	CA	90046	323-851-4900	
Harpo Films Inc 345 N Maple Dr Ste 315 **Fax Area Code:* 312	Beverly Hills	CA	90210	310-278-5559	633-1976*
Harpo Productions Inc 110 N Carpenter *Web:* www.oprah.com	Chicago	IL	60607	312-633-1000	633-1976
Hearst Entertainment & Syndication Group 300 W 57th St *Web:* hearst.com/entertainment	New York	NY	10019	212-969-7553	
Hello World Communications 118 W 22nd St Fl 2 *Web:* www.hwc.tv	New York	NY	10011	212-243-8800	
Hendlin Visual Communications Inc 129 N Second St Ste 101 *Web:* hendin.com	Minneapolis	MN	55401	612-338-1663	
High Speed Productions Inc 1303 Underwood Ave *TF:* 888-520-9099 ■ *Web:* www.juxtapoz.com	San Francisco	CA	94124	415-822-3083	
Hillmann & Carr Inc 2233 Wisconsin Ave Nw Ste 425 *Web:* www.hillmanncarr.com	Washington	DC	20007	202-342-0001	
Hopsports Inc 24715 Ave Rockefeller *Web:* www.hopsports.com	Valencia	CA	91355	661-702-8946	
Horizons Video & Film Inc 4000 Horizons Dr *Web:* www.horizonscompanies.com	Columbus	OH	43220	614-481-7200	
Ian Ryan & Assoc Inc 1400 E Touhy Ave Ste 220 *Web:* www.ianryan.com	Des Plaines	IL	60018	847-803-2050	
Icon Productions 808 Wilshire Blvd *Web:* www.iconmovies.us	Santa Monica	CA	90401	310-434-7300	
ICV Digital Media 3908 Valley Ave Ste A *Web:* www.icvdm.com	Pleasanton	CA	94566	925-426-8230	
Image Recordings 4736 Penn Ave Ste 200 *Web:* www.aspstation.net	Pittsburgh	PA	15224	412-362-4050	
Imagina US 7291 NW 74th St *Web:* www.imaginaus.com	Miami	FL	33166	305-777-1900	
Imaginary Forces LLC 2254 S Sepulveda Blvd *Web:* www.imaginaryforces.com	Los Angeles	CA	90064	323-957-6868	
Imagine Entertainment Inc 9465 Wilshire Blvd *Web:* www.imagine-entertainment.com	Beverly Hills	CA	90212	310-858-2000	
iNDELIBLE Media Corp 535 Eighth Ave 16th Fl	New York	NY	10018	212-629-0802	
Infinitude Creative Group LP 1820 Preston Park Blvd Ste 2100 *Web:* www.nfinitude.com	Plano	TX	75093	972-867-6800	
Inhance Digital Corp 8057 Beverly Blvd Ste 200 *Web:* inhance.com	Los Angeles	CA	90048	323-297-7700	
Interface Media Group Inc 1233 20th St NW *Web:* www.interfacemedia.com	Washington	DC	20036	202-861-0500	
Island Co 312 Clematis St Ste 401 *Web:* www.islandcompany.com	West Palm Beach	FL	33401	561-833-8110	
Jerry Bruckheimer Films 1631 Tenth St *Web:* www.jbfilms.com	Santa Monica	CA	90404	310-664-6260	664-6261
Jerry Weintraub Productions 4000 Warner Blvd Bungalow 1	Burbank	CA	91522	818-954-2500	954-1399
Jon Voight Entertainment 10203 Santa Monica Blvd 5th Fl *Web:* www.crystalsky.com	Los Angeles	CA	90067	310-843-0223	553-9895
Jones Film & Video 916 W Sixth St *Web:* www.jonesinc.com	Little Rock	AR	72201	501-372-1981	
Jones Mobile Television 5200 Northshore Dr Ste F *Web:* jmtv.com	North Little Rock	AR	72118	501-376-1993	
Joseph Productions Inc 34525 Glendale St *Web:* www.jpitel.com	Livonia	MI	48150	734-266-0500	
JPL Integrated Communictions Inc 471 Jplwick Dr *Web:* www.jplcreative.com	Harrisburg	PA	17111	717-558-8048	
Just for Laughs Inc 2101 St-Laurent Blvd *Web:* www.hahaha.com	Montreal	QC	H2X2T5	514-845-3155	845-4140
Kantola Productions LLC 55 Sunnyside Ave *Web:* www.kantola.com	Mill Valley	CA	94941	415-381-9363	
Kartemquin Films Ltd 1901 W Wellington Ave *Web:* www.kartemquin.com	Chicago	IL	60657	773-472-4366	472-3348
Kennetic Productions Inc 5 W. Forsyth St Ste 200 *Web:* www.kenneticproductions.com	Jacksonville	FL	32202	904-464-0041	
Kenwood 75 Varney Pl *Web:* www.kenwoodgroup.com	San Francisco	CA	94107	415-957-5333	
Key Brand Entertainment Inc 1619 Broadway Ninth Fl *Web:* kbeinc.net	New York	NY	10019	917-421-5400	
Knock Inc 1315 Glenwood Ave *Web:* www.knockinc.com	Minneapolis	MN	55405	612-333-6511	
Lakeshore Entertainment Corp 9268 W Third St *Web:* www.lakeshoreentertainment.com	Beverly Hills	CA	90210	310-867-8000	
Lederle Machine Co 830 Jefferson St *Web:* www.lederle.com	Pacific	MO	63069	636-271-7200	
Limelight Communications Inc 2812 Roesh Way *Web:* www.limelight.com	Vienna	VA	22181	703-242-4596	
Line Plot Productions LLC 146 Mt Auburn St *Web:* www.lineplot.com	Cambridge	MA	02138	617-864-8300	
Lions Gate Entertainment Corp Lions Gate Television Div 2700 Colorado Ave Ste 200 *TF:* 800-322-2885 ■ *Web:* www.lionsgate.com	Santa Monica	CA	90404	310-449-9200	255-3870
Lions Gate Entertainment Inc 2700 Colorado Ave Ste 200 *Web:* www.lionsgate.com	ÿSanta Monica	CA	90404	310-449-9200	255-3870

Company / Address	City	State	Zip	Phone	Fax
Lions Gate Television Inc 2700 Colorado Ave Ste 200	Santa Monica	CA	90404	310-449-9200	
Web: www.lionsgatefilms.com					
Little Earth Productions 2400 Josephine St Ste 1	Pittsburgh	PA	15203	412-471-0909	
Web: www.littlearth.com					
Logan Media Services LLC 1515 Elm Hill Pk Ste 205	Nashville	TN	37210	615-361-8100	
Web: www.loganmediaservices.com					
London Broadcasting Co Inc 5052 Addison Cir	Addison	TX	75001	214-730-0151	
Web: www.londonbroadcastingcompany.com					
Lucasfilm Ltd PO Box 29901	San Francisco	CA	94129	415-623-1000	
Web: www.lucasfilm.com					
MacNeil Lehrer Productions LLC 2700 Quincy St Ste 250	Arlington	VA	22206	703-998-2170	
Web: www.macneil-lehrer.com					
Magno Sound Inc 729 Seventh Ave Fl 2	New York	NY	10019	212-302-2505	
Web: www.magnosound.com					
Maitland Primrose Group Inc 7220 N 16th St Ste A100	Phoenix	AZ	85020	602-944-0046	
Web: www.maitlandprimrose.com					
Mandalay Pictures 4751 Wilshire Blvd Third Fl	Los Angeles	CA	90010	323-549-4300	549-9824
Web: www.mandalay.com					
Mars Hill Productions Inc 4711 Lexington Blvd.	Missouri City	TX	77459	281-403-1463	403-4463
Web: www.mars-hill.org					
Maslow Media Group Inc, The 2233 Wisconsin Ave NW Ste 400	Washington	DC	20007	202-965-1100	
Web: www.maslowmedia.com					
McHenry Creative Services Inc 345 Main St	Harleysville	PA	19438	215-513-0251	
Web: www.mchenrycreative.com					
Media Imagery 7905 Browning Rd Ste 218	Pennsauken	NJ	08109	856-317-0990	
Web: www.mediaimagery.com					
Media Services Ltd 2510 W Dunlap Ave Ste 250	Phoenix	AZ	85021	602-674-5800	
Web: www.msgl.com					
Meditech Communications Inc 533 Phalen Blvd	Saint Paul	MN	55130	651-636-7350	
Web: www.gomeditech.com					
Memocast 1801 Bush St	San Francisco	CA	94109	415-673-5122	
Web: www.memocast.com					
Metro Teleproductions Inc 1400 E W Hwy Apt 628	Silver Spring	MD	20910	301-608-9077	
Web: www.mtitv.com					
Metro-Goldwyn-Mayer Studios Inc (MGM) 245 N Beverly Dr	Beverly Hills	CA	90210	310-586-8674	586-8670*
**Fax:* Mktg ■ *Web:* www.mgm.com					
MG Studios Inc 2005 Tree Fork Ln Ste 113	Longwood	FL	32750	407-679-9291	
Web: www.mg-studios.com					
Mills James Inc 3545 Fishinger Blvd.	Columbus	OH	43026	614-777-9933	
Web: www.mjp.com					
Minds Eye Entertainment Ltd 480 Henderson Dr	Regina	SK	S4N6E3	306-359-7618	
Web: www.mindseyepictures.com					
MIRA Mobile Television Inc 25749 SW Canyon Creek Rd Ste 100	Wilsonville	OR	97070	503-464-0900	
Mirage Productions Inc 111 Spring St	Newton	NJ	07860	973-300-9477	
Web: www.mirageproductions.com					
Miramax Film NY LLC 2540 Colorado Ave Ste 100E	Santa Monica	CA	90404	310-409-4321	
Web: www.miramax.com					
MMG Corporate Communication Inc 515 W Loveland Ave	Loveland	OH	45140	513-677-8787	
Web: www.mmgonline.com					
Mort Crim Communications Inc 155 W Congress Ste 501	Detroit	MI	48226	313-481-4700	
Web: www.mortcrim.com					
MPCA 10635 Santa Monica Blvd	Los Angeles	CA	90025	310-319-9500	319-9501
Web: mpcafilm.com					
Mr Mudd 5225 Wilshire Blvd Ste 604	Los Angeles	CA	90036	323-932-5656	932-5666
Web: mrmudd.com					
Muse Entertainment Enterprises Inc 3451 Rue St-Jacques	Montreal	QC	H4C1H1	514-866-6873	
Web: www.muse.ca					
My Eye Media LLC 3515 W Pacific Ave	Burbank	CA	91505	818-559-7200	
Web: myeyemedia.com					
NAMCO BANDAI Holdings (USA) Inc 5551 Katella Ave	Cypress	CA	90630	714-816-9500	
Web: www.namcobandai.com					
Nancy Glass Productions Inc 211 Rock Hill Rd Ste 201	Bala Cynwyd	PA	19004	610-668-1668	
Web: www.nancyglassproductions.com					
Nash Entertainment 1438 N Gower St Ste 35	Los Angeles	CA	90028	323-993-7384	
Web: www.nashentertainment.com					
National Media Services Inc 613 N Commerce Ave	Front Royal	VA	22630	540-635-4181	
Web: www.nationalmediaservices.com					
NBA Entertainment 450 Harmon Meadow Blvd.	Secaucus	NJ	07094	201-865-1500	865-2626*
**Fax:* Mail Rm ■ *TF:* 866-648-4668 ■ *Web:* nba.com					
Nelvana Ltd Corus Quay 25 Dockside Dr	Toronto	ON	M5A0B5	416-479-7000	
Web: www.nelvana.com					
Nerd Corps Entertainment Inc 1256 E Sixth Ave Level 3	Vancouver	BC	V5T1E7	604-484-0266	
Web: www.nerdcorps.com					
Net Element International Inc 1450 S Miami Ave	Miami	FL	33130	787-993-9650	
Web: www.netelement.com					
New Horizons Picture Corp 11600 San Vicente Blvd	Los Angeles	CA	90049	310-820-6733	
Web: www.newhorizonspictures.com					
New Perspective Productions 2949 Smallman St	Pittsburgh	PA	15201	412-681-1600	
Web: www.new-perspective.com					
NFL Films Inc One Nfl Plz	Mt Laurel	NJ	08054	856-222-3500	
Web: www.nflfilms.com					
Nikitova LLC 203 N Lasalle Ste 2100	Chicago	IL	60601	773-913-8015	
Web: www.nikitova.com					
North by Northwest Productions 601 W Broad St	Boise	ID	83702	208-345-7870	
Web: www.nxnw.net					
NTV International Corp 645 Fifth Ave Ste 303	New York	NY	10022	212-660-6900	660-6998
Web: www.ntvic.com					
Nu Image Inc 6423 Wilshire Blvd	Los Angeles	CA	90048	310-388-6900	
Web: www.millenniumfilms.com					
Omnifilm Entertainment Ltd 111 Water St	Vancouver	BC	V6B1A7	604-681-6543	
Web: www.omnifilm.com					
On-line Video Design Inc 710 Acacia Ave	Melbourne	FL	32904	321-676-5677	
Web: www.onlinevid.com					
Original Productions Inc 308 W Verdugo Ave	Burbank	CA	91502	818-295-6966	
Web: www.amygdalamusic.com					
Orion Multimedia 10397 W Centennial Rd	Littleton	CO	80127	720-891-4839	
Overbrook Entertainment Inc 10202 W Washington Blvd Fourth Fl	Culver City	CA	90232	310-432-2400	432-2401
Pacific Title Archives 10717 Vanowen St	North Hollywood	CA	91605	818-760-4223	
TF: 800-968-9111 ■ *Web:* www.pacifictitlearchives.com					
Paradise Fx 6711 Valjean Ave Ste A	Van Nuys	CA	91406	818-785-3100	
Web: www.paradisefx.com					
Paramount Pictures Corp 5555 Melrose Ave	Los Angeles	CA	90038	323-956-5000	956-0121
Web: www.paramount.com					
Participant Media LLC 331 Foothill Rd Third Fl	Beverly Hills	CA	90210	310-550-5100	
Web: www.participantmedia.com					
PayReel Inc 24928 Genesee Trl Rd.	Golden	CO	80401	303-526-4900	
TF: 800-352-7397 ■ *Web:* www.payreel.com					
PDC Productions 3217 N Flood Ave.	Norman	OK	73069	405-360-5130	
Web: www.pdcproductions.com					
People Productions Video Services Inc 1737 15th St Ste 200	Boulder	CO	80302	303-449-6086	
Web: www.peopleproductions.com					
Phoenix Pictures Inc 10203 W Washington Blvd Ste 400	Los Angeles	CA	90067	424-298-2788	298-2588
Web: www.phoenixpictures.com					
Pivot Point International Inc 1560 Sherman Ave Ste 700	Evanston	IL	60201	847-866-0500	
Web: www.pivot-point.com					
Pix System LLC 455 Market St Ste 900	San Francisco	CA	94105	415-357-9720	
Web: www.pixsystem.com					
Post Modern Inc 100 Ross St Lbby 3	Pittsburgh	PA	15219	412-391-6635	
Web: www.postmodern-pgh.com					
Pot o Gold Multi-cinema Productions Inc 2201 Rogero Rd	Jacksonville	FL	32211	904-744-7478	
Web: www.pogusa.com					
PRG Nocturne Productions Inc 300 Harvestore Dr.	Dekalb	IL	60115	815-756-9600	
Web: www.trichromes.com					
Producers Management Television Pmtv 681 Moore Rd Ste 100	King Of Prussia	PA	19406	610-768-1770	
Web: pmtv.com					
Production Masters Inc 202 Fifth Ave The Buhl Bldg	Pittsburgh	PA	15222	412-281-8500	
Raleigh Studios 1600 Rosecrans Ave	Manhattan Beach	CA	90266	310-727-2700	727-2710
Web: www.raleighstudios.com					
Reaction Audio Visual - Dallas LLC 9951 Muirlands Blvd	Irvine	CA	92618	949-600-8235	
Web: reactionav.com					
Red Hour Films 629 N La Brea Ave	Los Angeles	CA	90036	323-602-5000	602-5001
Reel FX Inc 301 N Crowdus St	Dallas	TX	75226	214-979-0961	
Web: www.reelfx.com					
Regency Enterprises 10201 W Pico Blvd Bldg 12	Los Angeles	CA	90035	310-369-8300	969-0470
Web: www.newregency.com					
Regent Entertainment Partnership LP 8411 Preston Rd Ste 650	Dallas	TX	75225	214-373-3434	
Web: www.regententertainment.com					
Renegade Productions Inc 10950 Gilroy Rd Ste J	Hunt Valley	MD	21031	410-667-1400	
Web: www.getrenegade.com					
Resolution Digital Studios 2226 W Walnut St	Chicago	IL	60612	312-846-4226	
Web: www.rdschicago.com					
Revelations Entertainment Inc 1221 Second St Fourth Fl	Santa Monica	CA	90401	310-394-3131	
Web: revelationsent.com					
Revision3 Corp 2415 Third St Ste 232	San Francisco	CA	94107	415-734-3500	
Web: www.revision3.com					
Revolution Studios 2900 Olympic Blvd	Santa Monica	CA	90404	310-255-7000	255-7001
Web: www.revolutionstudios.com					
RGB Group Inc 4141 N Miami Ave Ste 210	Miami	FL	33127	305-573-1672	
Web: www.rgbgroup.com					
Richter Studios 1143 W Rundell Pl	Chicago	IL	60607	312-861-9999	
Web: www.richterstudios.com					
Ring of Fire Studios LLC 1538 20th St	Santa Monica	CA	90404	310-966-5055	
Web: www.ringoffire.com					
RKO Pictures Inc 2034 Broadway	Santa Monica	CA	90404	310-277-0707	
Web: www.rko.com					
Rodgers & Hammerstein Organization, The 229 W 28th St 11th Fl	New York	NY	10001	212-541-6600	
Web: www.rnh.com					
Roush Media 84 E Santa Anita Ave	Burbank	CA	91502	818-559-8648	
Web: www.roush-media.com					
Samson Technologies Inc 45 Gilpin Ave	Hauppauge	NY	11788	631-784-2200	
Web: www.samsontech.com					
Samuel Goldwyn Films LLC 9570 W Pico Blvd Ste 400	Los Angeles	CA	90035	310-860-3100	860-3195
Web: www.samuelgoldwynfilms.com					
Scanline Vfx La Inc 12950 Culver Blvd	Los Angeles	CA	90066	310-827-1555	
Web: scanlinevfx.com					

Name / Address	City	State	Zip	Phone	Fax
Scope Seven Inc 2201 Park Pl Ste 100	El Segundo	CA	90245	310-220-3939	
Web: zoodigital.com//					
Scott Powers Productions Inc 135 W 29th St Rm 404	New York	NY	10001	212-242-4700	
Web: www.scottpowers.com					
Script to Screen Productions 200 N Tustin Ave Ste 200	Santa Ana	CA	92705	714-558-3971	
Web: www.scripttoscreen.com					
Section 8 Post Production Facility LLC 23716 Woodward Ave.	Pleasant Ridge	MI	48069	248-546-2714	
Web: www.section8.com					
Sesame Workshop One Lincoln Plz.	New York	NY	10023	212-595-3456	875-7359
Web: www.sesameworkshop.org					
Shaftesbury Films Inc 163 Queen St E Ste 100	Toronto	ON	M5A1S1	416-363-1411	
Web: www.shaftesbury.ca					
Shooters International Inc 63 Berkeley St	Toronto	ON	M5A2W5	416-862-1959	
Web: www.shootersfilm.com					
Sky High Entertainment 777 Blvd Lebourgneuf Ste 160	Quebec	QC	G2J1C3	418-682-1443	
Web: www.shemovie.com					
Skylight Studios Video Prodctns 109 Squirrel Ln.	Levittown	NY	11756	516-579-0245	
Smithgroup Communications Inc 267 SE 33rd Ave.	Portland	OR	97214	503-239-4215	
Web: smithgrp.com					
Smp Communications Corp 7626 E Greenway Rd Ste 100	Scottsdale	AZ	85260	480-905-4100	
Web: smpcom.com					
Snitily Carr Inc 300 S 68th St Pl Ste 200	Lincoln	NE	68510	402-489-2121	
Web: www.snitilycarr.com					
Sonar Entertainment 423 W 55th St 12th Fl	New York	NY	10019	212-977-9001	977-9049
Web: sonarent.com					
Sonic Pool Inc 6860 Lexington Ave	Los Angeles	CA	90038	323-460-4649	
Web: www.sonicpool.com					
Sony Pictures Entertainment Inc 10202 W Washington Blvd	Culver City	CA	90232	310-244-4000	840-8888
TF: 855-327-7669 ■ *Web:* www.sonypictures.com					
Sony Pictures Imageworks Inc 9050 W Washington Blvd	Culver City	CA	90232	310-840-8000	
Web: www.imageworks.com					
Sony Pictures Television 10202 W Washington Blvd	Culver City	CA	90232	310-244-4000	244-1874
TF: 888-476-6972 ■ *Web:* www.sonypictures.com					
Sony Wonder 550 Madison Ave	New York	NY	10022	212-833-8100	
Web: www.sonywondertechlab.com					
Spark Unlimited Inc 15000 Ventura Blvd Ste 202	Sherman Oaks	CA	91403	818-788-1005	
Web: www.sparkunlimited.com					
Spyglass Entertainment 245 N Beverly Dr	Beverly Hills	CA	90210	310-443-5800	443-5912
Web: www.spyglassent.com					
StagePost Full Screen Spectrum Media 255 French Landing Dr.	Nashville	TN	37228	615-248-1978	
Web: www.stagepost.com					
Stonemar Capital LLC 32 Union Sq E 11th Fl	New York	NY	10003	212-324-8306	
Web: www.stonemarproperties.com					
Strategic Media Services Inc 1911 North Ft Myer Dr Ste 400	Arlington	VA	20009	202-337-5700	
Web: www.strategicmediaservices.com					
Stu Segall Productions Inc 4705 Ruffin Rd	San Diego	CA	92123	858-974-8988	
Web: www.stusegall.com					
Summit Entertainment LLC 1630 Stewart St Ste 120	Santa Monica	CA	90404	310-309-8400	
Web: www.summit-ent.com					
Sundance Institute 1825 Three Kings Dr	Park City	UT	84060	801-328-3456	
Web: www.sundance.org					
Sunrise Communications 621 Newport Ave.	Westmont	IL	60559	630-570-5700	
Web: www.suncom.us					
Sunset Gower Studios 1438 N Gower St.	Hollywood	CA	90028	323-467-1001	
Web: www.sgsandsbs.com					
Swank Motion Pictures Inc 10795 Watson Rd	St Louis	MO	63127	314-984-6000	
TF: 888-248-8757 ■ *Web:* www.swank.com					
Team People LLC 125 N Washington St.	Falls Church	VA	22046	202-587-4111	
Web: www.teampeople.tv					
Three Leaf Productions 940 Science Blvd Ste C	Gahanna	OH	43230	614-626-4941	
Web: www.three-leaf.com					
Threshold Entertainment Inc 1649 11th St.	Santa Monica	CA	90404	310-452-8899	
Web: www.thethreshold.com					
Total Media Group Inc 432 N Canal St Ste 12	South San Francisco	CA	94080	650-583-8236	
Web: www.totalmediagroup.com					
Touchstone Pictures 500 S Buena Vista St	Burbank	CA	91521	818-560-3300	
Web: www.thewaltdisneycompany.com					
Touchstone Television Production LLC 500 S Buena Vista St	Burbank	CA	91521	818-560-5300	
Web: www.disneyworld.disney.go.com					
Trailblazer Studios Nc Inc 1610 Midtown Pl.	Raleigh	NC	27609	919-645-6600	
Web: videofonics.com					
Tribeca Productions 375 Greenwich St 8th Fl	New York	NY	10013	212-941-4000	941-3997
Web: www.tribecafilm.com					
Troupe Modern Media Design & Production, The Three Industrial Dr	Windham	NH	03087	603-893-4554	
Web: www.thetroupe.com					
True Blue Productions S Brand Blvd	Los Angeles	CA	90029	323-661-9191	
Two Cats Media Ltd 20 W 22nd St Ste 605	New York	NY	10010	212-929-2085	
Web: www.twocatstv.com					
Two Little Hands Productions 870 E N Union Ave	Midvale	UT	84047	801-676-4441	676-4441
Web: www.signingtime.com					
Uber Content 1040 N Las Palmas Ave Bldg 7n.	Los Angeles	CA	90038	323-860-8686	
Web: www.ubercontent.com					
Ultimatte Corp 20945 Plummer St	Chatsworth	CA	91311	818-993-8007	
Web: www.ultimatte.com					
Ultra Stereo Labs Inc 181 Bonetti Dr	San Luis Obispo	CA	93401	805-549-0161	
Web: www.uslinc.com					
Union Editorial LLC 12200 W Olympic Blvd Ste 140	Los Angeles	CA	90064	310-481-2200	
Web: www.unioneditorial.com					
Universal Image Production Inc 20750 Civic Ctr Dr Ste 100	Southfield	MI	48076	248-357-2247	
Web: www.universalimages.com					
Universal Studios Inc 100 Universal City Plaza	Universal City	CA	91608	800-864-8377	866-3600*
**Fax Area Code:* 818 ■ *Web:* www.universalstudios.com					
Ventana Productions 1819 L St Nw Ste 100w	Washington	DC	20036	202-785-5112	
Web: www.ventanadc.com					
Versabar Inc 1111 Engineers Rd	Belle Chasse	LA	70037	504-392-3200	
Web: www.vbar.com					
Viacom Entertainment Group 1515 Broadway	New York	NY	10036	212-258-6000	
Web: www.viacom.com					
Video Symphony Entertraining Inc 266 E Magnolia Blvd	Burbank	CA	91502	818-557-6500	
TF: 888-370-7589 ■ *Web:* www.vs.edu					
Videobred Inc 1000 Hamilton Ave	Louisville	KY	40204	502-584-5787	
Web: www.videobred.com					
Vision Global AR Ltee 80, Queen St Ste 301	Montreal	QC	H3C2N5	514-879-0020	
TF: 800-667-7690					
Vista Electronics Inc 27525 Newhall Ranch Rd	Valencia	CA	91355	661-294-9820	
Web: vistaelectronics.com					
Vista Productions Inc 1804 Anaconda Rd	Harrisonville	MO	64701	816-380-7750	
Web: www.vistaprod.com					
Visual Communications Group Inc 5721 Arapahoe Ave Ste 2a	Boulder	CO	80303	303-413-0878	
Web: visualcomgroup.com					
Visual Eyes Medical Media 31320 Via Colinas Ste 118	Westlake Village	CA	91362	818-707-9922	
Web: www.visualeyes.com					
Walden Media LLC 1888 Century Pk E	Los Angeles	CA	90067	310-887-1000	
Web: www.walden.com					
Warner Bros Entertainment Inc 4000 Warner Blvd.	Burbank	CA	91522	818-954-1853	954-3817
TF: 800-778-7879 ■ *Web:* www.warnerbros.com					
Warner Bros Television Production Inc 4000 Warner Blvd.	Burbank	CA	91522	818-954-1853	
Web: www2.warnerbros.com					
Warner Home Video 4000 Warner Blvd Bldg 168	Burbank	CA	91522	866-373-4389	
Web: www.wbshop.com					
WatchMojo Inc 5413 Saint Laurent St Ste 200	Montreal	QC	H2T1S5	514-448-1631	
Web: www.watchmojo.com					
Weinstein Company LLC, The 345 Hudson St	New York	NY	10014	646-862-3400	
Web: www.weinsteinco.com					
Western Creative Inc 26135 Plymouth Rd Ste 200	Redford	MI	48239	313-937-1000	
Web: www.westerncreative.com					
Wildbrain 660 Alabama St	San Francisco	CA	94110	415-553-8000	
Web: www.wildbrain.com					
Winkler Films Inc 190 N Canon Dr Ste 500	Beverly Hills	CA	90210	310-858-5780	
Working Title Films 9720 Wilshire Blvd Fourth Fl	Beverly Hills	CA	90212	310-777-3100	777-5243
Web: www.workingtitlefilms.com					
Worktank Enterprises 3131 We Ste 510	Seattle	WA	98121	206-529-3833	
Web: www.worktankseattle.com					
Zeitbyte LLC 32 W 22nd St Sixth Fl	New York	NY	10010	212-989-4800	
Web: www.zeitbyte.com					
Zoic Inc 3582 Eastham Dr	Culver City	CA	90232	310-838-0770	
Web: www.zoicstudios.com					
ZONE3 Inc 1055 Rene-Levesque Blvd E Ninth Fl	Montreal	QC	H2L4S5	514-284-5555	
Web: www.zone3.ca					

MOTION PICTURE THEATERS

SEE Theaters - Motion Picture p. 3230

518 MOTOR SPEEDWAYS

Name / Address	City	State	Zip	Phone	Fax
Ace Speedway 3401 Altamahaw Race Track Rd	Altamahaw	NC	27244	336-585-1200	585-1209
Web: www.acespeedway.com					
Antioch Speedway 1201 W Tenth St	Antioch	CA	94509	925-779-9220	779-9213
Web: www.antiochspeedway.com					
Atco Raceway 1000 Jackson Rd	Atco	NJ	08004	856-768-2167	753-9604
Web: www.atcoraceway.com					
Atlanta Dragway 500 E Ridgeway Rd.	Commerce	GA	30529	706-335-2301	
Web: www.atlantadragway.com					
Atlanta Motor Speedway PO Box 500	Hampton	GA	30228	770-946-4211	946-3928
TF: 877-926-7849 ■ *Web:* www.atlantamotorspeedway.com					
Auto Club Speedway 9300 Cherry Ave	Fontana	CA	92335	909-429-5000	429-5500
TF: 800-944-7223 ■ *Web:* autoclubspeedway.com					
Bandimere Speedway 3051 S Rooney Rd	Morrison	CO	80465	303-697-6001	697-0815
TF: 800-664-8946 ■ *Web:* www.bandimere.com					
Bloomington Speedway 5185 S Fairfax Rd	Bloomington	IN	47401	812-824-8753	824-7400
Web: www.bloomingtonspeedway.com					
Brainerd International Raceway 5523 Birchdale Rd	Brainerd	MN	56401	218-824-7223	824-7240
TF: 866-444-4455 ■ *Web:* www.brainerdraceway.com					
Bristol Motor Speedway 151 Speedway Blvd.	Bristol	TN	37620	423-989-6933	764-1646
TF: 866-415-4158 ■ *Web:* www.bristolmotorspeedway.com					
Carolina Dragway 302 Dragstrip Rd	Jackson	SC	29803	803-471-2285	266-4651
Web: www.houseofhook.com					

				Phone	Fax
Chicagoland Speedway 500 Speedway Blvd *Web:* www.chicagolandspeedway.com	Joliet	IL	60433	815-722-5500	727-7895
Colorado National Speedway 4281 Graden Blvd *Web:* www.coloradospeedway.com	Dacono	CO	80514	303-665-4173	828-2403
Columbus Motor Speedway Inc 1841 Williams Rd *Web:* www.columbusspeedway.com	Columbus	OH	43207	614-491-1047	491-6010
Concord Speedway 7940 US Hwy 601 *Web:* www.concordspeedway.net	South Concord	NC	28025	704-782-4221	782-4420
Corpus Christi Speedway 241 Flato Rd *Web:* www.ccspeedway.org	Corpus Christi	TX	78405	361-289-8847	
Darlington Raceway 1301 Harry Bird Hwy *Fax Area Code: 843 ■ *TF:* 866-459-7223 ■ *Web:* www.darlingtonraceway.com	Darlington	SC	29532	866-459-7223	395-8920*
Daytona International Speedway 1801 W International Speedway Blvd *Web:* www.daytonainternationalspeedway.com	Daytona Beach	FL	32114	386-254-2700	257-0281
Dubuque Fairgrounds Speedway 14569 Old Hwy Rd *Web:* www.dbqfair.com	Dubuque	IA	52002	563-588-1406	744-3598
Eagle Raceway 617 S 238th St *Web:* eagleraceway.com	Eagle	NE	68347	402-238-2595	238-3768
El Paso Speedway Park 3590 W Picacho *Web:* www.epspeedwaypark.com	Las Cruces	TX	88007	915-791-8749	
Elko Speedway 26350 France Ave *Web:* www.goelkospeedway.com	Elko	MN	55020	952-461-7223	
Evergreen Speedway 14405 179th Ave SE Bldg 305 *Web:* www.evergreenspeedway.com	Monroe	WA	98272	360-805-6100	805-6110
Florence Motor Speedway 836 E Smith St *Web:* www.florencemotorspeedway.com	Timmonsville	SC	29161	843-346-7711	
Gainesville Raceway 11211 N County Rd 225 *Web:* www.autoplusraceway.com	Gainesville	FL	32609	352-377-0046	371-4212
Grandview Speedway 43 Passmore Rd *Web:* www.grandviewspeedway.com	Bechtelsville	PA	19505	610-754-7688	754-6303
Hamilton County Speedway 1200 Bluff St *Web:* www.hamiltoncospeedway.com	Webster City	IA	50595	515-832-1443	832-6972
Heart O' Texas Speedway 784 N McLennan Dr *Web:* www.heartotexspeedway.com	Elm Mott	TX	76640	254-829-2294	776-1576
Heartland Park Topeka 7530 SW Topeka Blvd *TF:* 800-437-2237 ■ *Web:* www.hpt.com	Topeka	KS	66619	785-862-4781	862-2016
Hickory Motor Speedway 3130 Hwy 70 SE *TF:* 800-843-8725 ■ *Web:* www.hickorymotorspeedway.com	Newton	NC	28658	828-464-3655	465-5017
Holland NASCAR Motorsports Complex 11586 Holland Glenwood Rd *TF:* 866-655-0257 ■ *Web:* www.hollandspeedway.com	Holland	NY	14080	716-537-2272	537-9749
Homestead-Miami Speedway One Speedway Blvd *Web:* www.homesteadmiamispeedway.com	Homestead	FL	33035	305-230-5000	230-5140
Houston Motorsports Park 11620 N Lk Houston Pkwy *Web:* www.houstonmotorsportspark.com	Houston	TX	77044	281-458-1972	458-2836
Houston Raceway Park 2525 FM 565 S *Web:* www.royalpurpleraceway.com	Baytown	TX	77523	281-383-2666	383-3777
Kalamazoo Speedway 7656 Ravine Rd *Web:* www.kalamazoospeedway.com	Kalamazoo	MI	49009	269-349-3978	692-2848
Kentucky Speedway 1 Speedway Blvd *TF Resv:* 888-652-7223 ■ *Web:* www.kentuckyspeedway.com	Sparta	KY	41086	859-567-3400	647-4307
Kil-Kare Speedway 1166 Dayton-Xenia Rd *Web:* www.kilkare.com	Xenia	OH	45385	937-429-2961	426-5049
Lacrosse Fairgrounds Speedway N 4985 County Hwy M PO Box 853 *Web:* www.lacrossespeedway.com	West Salem	WI	54669	608-786-1525	786-1524
Langley Speedway 11 Dale Lemonds Dr *Web:* www.langley-speedway.com	Hampton	VA	23666	757-865-7223	865-1147
Las Vegas Motor Speedway 7000 Las Vegas Blvd N *TF:* 800-644-4444 ■ *Web:* www.lvms.com	Las Vegas	NV	89115	702-644-4444	632-8091
Lime Rock Park 60 White Hollow Rd *TF:* 800-722-3577 ■ *Web:* limerock.com	Lakeville	CT	06039	860-435-5000	435-5010
Los Angeles County Fairplex 1101 W McKinley Ave *TF:* 877-859-9909 ■ *Web:* www.fairplex.com	Pomona	CA	91768	909-623-3111	865-3602
Magic Valley Speedway 04N 150W Jerome *Web:* www.magicvalleyspeedway.com	Jerome	ID	83338	208-734-3700	324-9616
Mansfield Motorsports Speedway 100 Crall Rd *Web:* www.mansfield-speedway.com	Mansfield	OH	44903	419-524-0183	
Maple Grove Raceway 30 Stauffer Pk Ln *TF:* 877-814-2538 ■ *Web:* www.maplegroveraceway.com	Mohnton	PA	19540	610-856-7812	856-1601
Marion County International Raceway 2303 Richwood-LaRue Rd *Web:* www.mcir.com	La Rue	OH	43332	740-499-3666	499-2185
Martinsville Speedway 340 Speedway Rd *Fax Area Code: 276 ■ *Web:* www.martinsvillespeedway.com	Martinsville	VA	24112	877-722-3859	956-2820*
Michigan International Speedway 12626 US 12 *TF:* 800-354-1010 ■ *Web:* www.mispeedway.com	Brooklyn	MI	49230	517-592-6666	592-3848
Mid-Ohio Sports Car Course 7721 Steam Corners Rd PO Box 3108 *TF:* 800-643-6446 ■ *Web:* www.midohio.com	Lexington	OH	44904	419-884-4000	884-0042
Midway Speedway 22301 Hwy B *Web:* www.lebanonmidwayspeedway.com	Lebanon	MO	65536	417-588-4430	
Monett Speedway 685 Chapell Dr *Web:* www.monettspeedway.net	Monett	MO	65708	417-236-0600	
Motordrome Speedway 164 Motordrome Rd *Web:* www.motordrome.com	Smithton	PA	15479	724-872-7555	872-7695
Myrtle Beach Speedway 455 Hospitality Ln *Web:* www.myrtlebeachspeedway.com	Myrtle Beach	SC	29579	843-236-0500	236-0525
National Orange Show Events Center 689 SE St *Web:* www.nosevents.com	San Bernardino	CA	92408	909-888-6788	
New York International Raceway Park 2011 New Rd PO Box 296 *Web:* www.nyirp.com	Leicester	NY	14481	585-382-3030	382-9061
Ocean Speedway Inc 8070 Soquel Dr Ste 120 *TF:* 800-925-9925 ■ *Web:* oceanspeedway.com	Aptos	CA	95003	831-662-9466	688-0708
Oglethorpe Speedway Park 200 Jesup Rd PO Box 687 *Web:* www.ospracing.net	Pooler	GA	31322	912-964-8200	964-9501
Old Bridge Township Raceway Park 230 Pension Rd *Web:* www.etownraceway.com	Englishtown	NJ	07726	732-446-7800	446-1373
Oxford Plains Speedway 877 Main St PO Box 208 *Web:* www.oxfordplains.com	Oxford	ME	04270	207-539-8865	539-8860
Peoria Speedway 3520 W Farmington Rd *Web:* www.peoriaspeedway.com	Peoria	IL	61604	309-357-3339	486-3620
Pocono Raceway Long Pond Rd PO Box 500 *TF:* 800-722-3929 ■ *Web:* www.poconoraceway.com	Long Pond	PA	18334	570-646-2300	646-2010
Proctor Speedway 800 N Boundary Ave *Web:* www.proctorspeedway.com	Proctor	MN	55810	218-624-0606	
Quincy Raceways 8000 Broadway St *Web:* www.quincyraceways.com	Quincy	IL	62305	217-224-3843	224-3859
Riverhead Raceway PO Box 148 *Web:* www.riverheadraceway.com	Lindenhurst	NY	11757	631-842-7223	789-1160
Road America N 7390 Hwy 67 *TF:* 800-365-7223 ■ *Web:* www.roadamerica.com	Elkhart Lake	WI	53020	920-892-4576	892-4550
Road Atlanta Raceway 5300 Winder Hwy *TF:* 800-849-7223 ■ *Web:* www.roadatlanta.com	Braselton	GA	30517	770-967-6143	967-2668
Rockingham Dragway 2153 Hwy US 1 N PO Box 70 *Web:* www.rockinghamdragway.com	Rockingham	NC	28379	910-582-3400	582-8667
Sandusky Speedway 614 W Perkins Ave *Web:* www.sanduskyspeedway.com	Sandusky	OH	44870	419-625-4084	625-8110
Saugus Speedway 22500 Soledad Canyon Rd *Web:* www.saugusspeedway.com	Saugus	CA	91350	661-259-3886	259-8534
Sebring International Raceway 113 Midway Dr *TF:* 800-626-7223 ■ *Web:* www.sebringraceway.com	Sebring	FL	33870	863-655-1442	655-1777
Sonoma Raceway Hwy S 37 & 121 *TF:* 800-870-7223 ■ *Web:* www.racesonoma.com	Sonoma	CA	95476	707-938-8448	938-8430
South Boston Speedway 1188 James D Hagood Hwy PO Box 1066 *TF:* 877-440-1540 ■ *Web:* www.southbostonspeedway.com	South Boston	VA	24592	434-572-4947	575-8992
South Sound Speedway 3730 183rd Ave SW *Web:* www.southsoundspeedway.com	Rochester	WA	98579	360-858-1464	273-8113
Stafford Motor Speedway 55 W St PO Box 105 *Web:* staffordmotorspeedway.com	Stafford Springs	CT	06076	860-684-2783	684-6236
Summit Motorsports Park 1300 Ohio 18 *TF:* 800-729-6455 ■ *Web:* www.summitmotorsportspark.com	Norwalk	OH	44857	419-668-5555	663-0502
Texas Motorplex 7500 W Hwy 287 *TF:* 800-668-6775 ■ *Web:* www.texasmotorplex.com	Ennis	TX	75119	972-878-2641	878-1848
Thompson Speedway 205 E Thompson Rd PO Box 278 *Web:* www.thompsonspeedway.com	Thompson	CT	06277	860-923-2280	923-2398
Viking Speedway Inc PO Box 462 *Web:* www.vikingspeedway.net	Alexandria	MN	56308	320-760-9614	
Volusia Speedway Park 1500 W State Rd *Fax Area Code: 352 ■ *TF:* 800-275-4279 ■ *Web:* bubbaracewaypark.com/	De Leon Springs	FL	32130	386-985-4402	622-3126*
Watkins Glen International Inc 2790 CR 16 *Web:* www.theglen.com	Watkins Glen	NY	14891	607-535-2486	535-8918
Winchester Speedway 2656 W State Rd 32 PO Box 31 *Web:* www.winchesterspeedway.com	Winchester	IN	47394	765-584-9701	584-8111

519 MOTOR VEHICLES - COMMERCIAL & SPECIAL PURPOSE

SEE ALSO Campers, Travel Trailers, Motor Homes p. 1899; All-Terrain Vehicles p. 1740; Motorcycles & Motorcycle Parts & Accessories p. 2776; Automobiles - Mfr p. 1838; Snowmobiles p. 3176; Weapons & Ordnance (Military) p. 3295

				Phone	Fax
A.r.e. Inc PO Box 1100 *Web:* www.4are.com	Massillon	OH	44648	330-481-1333	730-4545
Accubuilt Inc 2550 Central Pt Pkwy *Web:* www.accubuilt.com	Lima	OH	45804	419-222-1501	222-4450
Allied Body Works Inc 625 S 96th St *TF General:* 800-733-7450 ■ *Web:* www.alliedbody.com	Seattle	WA	98108	206-763-7811	763-8836
Altec Industries Inc 210 Inverness Ctr Dr *Web:* altec.com	Birmingham	AL	35242	205-991-7733	408-8601
American LaFrance Corp 1090 Newtonway	Summerville	SC	29483	843-486-7400	
Art Moehn 2200 Seymour Rd *Fax Area Code: 517 ■ *Web:* artmoehn.com	Jackson	MI	49201	866-495-5942	787-6137*
Auto Crane Co PO Box 580697 *TF:* 888-848-5445 ■ *Web:* www.autocrane.com	Tulsa	OK	74158	918-836-0463	834-5979
Auto Truck Inc 1420 Brewster Creek Blvd *TF:* 877-284-4440 ■ *Web:* www.autotruck.com	Bartlett	IL	60103	630-860-5600	860-5631
Bianchi Motors Inc 8430 Peach St PO Box 3086 *TF:* 866-979-8132 ■ *Web:* www.bianchihonda.com	Erie	PA	16509	866-979-8132	
Blue Bird Corp 402 Blue Bird Blvd *Web:* www.blue-bird.com	Fort Valley	GA	31030	478-825-2021	822-2457
Bob Ross Dealerships, The 85 Loop Rd *Web:* www.bobrossauto.com	Centerville	OH	45459	937-401-2037	428-4083
Bobcat Co 250 E Beaton Dr *Web:* www.bobcat.com	West Fargo	ND	58078	701-241-8700	241-8704
Bristol-Donald Company Inc 50 Roanoke Ave *Web:* www.bristoldonald.com	Newark	NJ	07105	973-589-2640	589-2610
Brumbaugh Body Co One Jennifer Rd	Duncansville	PA	16635	814-696-9552	
Carnegie Body Co 9500 Brookpark Rd *TF:* 800-362-1989 ■ *Web:* carnegiefederalbody.com	Cleveland	OH	44129	216-749-5000	749-5740
Champion Bus Inc 331 Graham Rd *Fax: Mktg ■ *TF:* 800-776-4943 ■ *Web:* www.championbus.com	Imlay City	MI	48444	810-724-6474	724-1844*
Coach & Equipment Manufacturing Corp 130 Horizon Pk Dr PO Box 36 *TF:* 800-724-8464 ■ *Web:* www.coachandequipment.com	Penn Yan	NY	14527	800-724-8464	

	City	State	ZIP	Phone	Fax
Columbia ParCar Corp 1115 Commercial Ave *TF:* 800-222-4653 ■ *Web:* www.parcar.com	Reedsburg	WI	53959	608-524-8888	524-8380
Courtesy Chevrolet Ctr 750 Camino Del Rio N *Web:* www.courtesysandiego.com	San Diego	CA	92108	619-297-4321	
Crane Carrier Co 1925 N Sheridan Rd *Web:* www.cranecarrier.com	Tulsa	OK	74115	918-836-1651	832-7348
Curtis Industries LLC 111 Higgins St **Fax Area Code:* 508 ■ *TF:* 800-343-7676 ■ *Web:* curtisindustries.net	Worcester	MA	01606	800-343-7676	854-3377*
Dealers Truck Equipment Co 2460 Midway St *TF:* 800-259-7569 ■ *Web:* www.dealerstruck.com	Shreveport	LA	71108	318-635-7567	525-0903
Delphi Body Works Inc 313 S Washington St PO Box 30 *Web:* www.delphibodyworks.com	Delphi	IN	46923	765-564-2212	564-4255
Delta-Waseca 5200 Willson Rd *Web:* www.deltawaseca.com	Minneapolis	MN	55424	952-922-5569	922-1195
Diamond Coach Corp 2300 W Fourth St PO Box 489 *TF:* 800-442-4645 ■ *Web:* www.diamondcoach.com	Oswego	KS	67356	620-795-2191	795-2191
Dick Gores Rv World 14590 Duval Pl W *TF:* 800-635-7008 ■ *Web:* www.dickgoresrvworld.com	Jacksonville	FL	32218	904-741-5100	741-6682
Douglass Truck Bodies Inc 231 21st St *TF:* 800-635-7641 ■ *Web:* www.douglasstruckbodies.com	Bakersfield	CA	93301	661-327-0258	327-3894
E-ONE Inc 1601 SW 37th Ave *Web:* www.e-one.com	Ocala	FL	34474	352-237-1122	237-1151
E-Z-GO 1451 Marvin Griffin Rd *TF:* 800-241-5855 ■ *Web:* www.ezgo.com	Augusta	GA	30906	800-241-5855	
Ebus Inc 9250 Washburn Rd *Web:* www.ebus.com	Downey	CA	90242	562-904-3474	904-3468
Electric Golf Car Co 3190-B Orange Grove Ave *Web:* www.electricgolfcarcompany.com	North Highlands	CA	95660	916-773-2244	488-8857
Elgin Sweeper Co 1300 W Bartlett Rd *Web:* www.elginsweeper.com	Elgin	IL	60120	847-741-5370	742-3035
Elliott Machine Works Inc 1351 Freese Works Pl *Web:* www.elliottmachine.com	Galion	OH	44833	419-468-4709	468-4642
Erie Vehicle Co 60 E 51st St *Web:* erievehicle.com	Chicago	IL	60615	773-536-6300	536-5779
Fisher Engineering 50 Gordon Dr PO Box 529 **Fax Area Code:* 866 ■ **Fax:* Hum Res ■ *Web:* www.fisherplows.com	Rockland	ME	04841	207-701-4200	816-7256*
Fleet Engineers Inc 1800 E Keating Ave *TF Cust Svc:* 800-333-7890 ■ *Web:* www.fleetengineers.com	Muskegon	MI	49442	231-777-2537	777-2720
Fleet Equipment Corp 567 Commerce St *TF:* 800-631-0873 ■ *Web:* www.fectrucks.com	Franklin Lakes	NJ	07417	201-337-3294	337-3294
Fontaine Modification Co 9827 Mt Holly Rd *TF:* 800-366-8246 ■ *Web:* fontainemodification.com/	Charlotte	NC	28214	704-391-1355	391-1671
Fontaine Truck Equipment Co 7574 Commerce Cir *TF:* 800-874-9780 ■ *Web:* www.fontaine.com	Trussville	AL	35173	205-661-4900	655-9982
Ford of Ocala Inc 2816 NW Pine Ave *TF:* 888-255-1788 ■ *Web:* www.fordofocala.com	Ocala	FL	34475	352-732-4800	629-2666
Frank J Zamboni & Company Inc 15714 Colorado Ave *Web:* www.zamboni.com	Paramount	CA	90723	562-633-0751	633-9365
Gary Mathews Motors Inc 1100 Ashland City Rd *Web:* www.garymathewsmotors.com	Clarksville	TN	37040	931-552-7100	572-3163
General Body Manufacturing Co 7110 Jensen Dr *TF:* 800-395-8585 ■ *Web:* www.generalbody.com	Houston	TX	77093	713-692-5177	692-0700
General Motors Corp (GMC) 100 Renaissance Ctr *NYSE:* GM ■ *Web:* www.gm.com	Detroit	MI	48265	313-556-5000	
George Heiser Body Company Inc 11210 Tukwila International Blvd	Seattle	WA	98168	206-622-7985	622-7135
Gillig Corp 25800 Clawiter Rd *TF:* 800-735-1500 ■ *Web:* www.gillig.com	Hayward	CA	94545	510-785-1500	785-6819
Gowans-Knight Co Inc 49 Knight St *TF:* 800-352-4871 ■ *Web:* www.gowansknight.com	Watertown	CT	06795	860-274-8801	274-7937
Graham Cadillac 1515 W Fourth St **Fax Area Code:* 419 ■ *TF:* 866-472-4261 ■ *Web:* www.grahamautomall.com	Mansfield	OH	44906	866-472-4261	529-1859*
Hackney & Sons Inc 911 W 5th St PO Box 880 *TF:* 800-763-0700 ■ *Web:* www.hackneyandsons.com	Washington	NC	27889	252-946-6521	975-8340
Heil Environmental Ltd 2030 Hamilton Pl Blvd Ste 200 *TF:* 866-367-4345 ■ *Web:* www.heil.com	Chattanooga	TN	37421	423-899-9100	
Hercules Manufacturing Co 800 Bob Posey St *TF:* 800-633-3031 ■ *Web:* www.herculesvanbodies.com	Henderson	KY	42420	270-826-9501	826-0439
Hi-Lex America Inc 5200 Wayne Rd *Web:* www.hi-lex.com	Battle Creek	MI	49037	269-968-0781	968-0885
HME Inc 1950 Byron Ctr Ave *Web:* www.firetrucks.com	Wyoming	MI	49519	616-534-1463	534-1967
Holiday Automotive 321 N Rolling Meadows Dr *Web:* www.holidayautomotive.com	Fond Du Lac	WI	54937	920-921-8898	923-8454
Honda of Tiffany Springs 9200 NW Prairie View Rd *Web:* www.hondaoftiffanysprings.com	Kansas City	MO	64153	816-452-7000	452-2651
IC Bus LLC 4201 Winfield Rd *TF:* 800-892-7761 ■ *Web:* www.icbus.com	Warrenville	IL	60555	630-753-5000	
Johnson Refrigerated Truck Bodies 215 E Allen St *TF Sales:* 800-922-8360 ■ *Web:* www.johnsontruckbodies.com	Rice Lake	WI	54868	715-234-7071	234-4628
Joyce Koons Buick Gmc 10660 Automotive Dr *TF:* 866-224-9293 ■ *Web:* joycekoonsbuickgmc.com	Manassas	VA	20109	703-368-9100	366-1070
Kann Manufacturing Corp PO Box 400 *Web:* www.kannmfg.com	Guttenberg	IA	52052	563-252-2035	252-3069
Kassbohrer All Terrain Vehicles Inc 8850 Double Diamond Pkwy *Web:* www.pistenbullyusa.com	Reno	NV	89521	775-857-5000	857-5010
Kenworth Truck Co 10630 NE 38th Pl *Web:* www.kenworth.com	Kirkland	WA	98033	425-828-5000	828-5070
Kesler-Schaefer Auto Auction Inc 5333 W 46th St PO Box 53203 *Web:* www.ksaa1.com	Indianapolis	IN	46254	317-297-2300	297-6234
Keystone Chevrolet Inc 8700 Charles Page Blvd *Web:* www.keystonechevrolet.com	Sand Springs	OK	74063	918-245-2201	245-5820
Kidron Inc 13442 Emerson Rd *TF:* 800-321-5421 ■ *Web:* www.kidron.com	Kidron	OH	44636	330-857-3011	857-8451
KME Fire Apparatus 68 Sicker Rd *Web:* www.kovatch.com	Latham	NY	12110	518-785-0900	785-1794
Knapheide Mfg Co 1848 Westphalia Strasse PO Box 7140 *TF:* 855-264-4300 ■ *Web:* www.knapheide.com	Quincy	IL	62305	217-222-7131	222-5939
Labrie Environmental Group 175 du Pont *TF:* 800-463-6638 ■ *Web:* www.labriegroup.com	Saint-Nicolas	QC	G7A2T3	418-831-8250	831-5255
Laird Noller Ford Inc 2245 SW Topeka Blvd *Web:* www.nollerford-topeka.com	Topeka	KS	66611	785-235-9211	232-7766
Landmark Ford Inc 12000 SW 66th Ave PO Box 23970 *Web:* www.landmarkford.com	Tigard	OR	97223	503-639-1131	598-8350
Leson Chevrolet Co Inc 1501 Westbank Express *TF:* 877-496-2420 ■ *Web:* lesonauto.com	Harvey	LA	70058	504-366-4381	362-2135
Liberty Toyota Scion 4397 Rt 130 S *TF:* 888-809-7798 ■ *Web:* www.libertytoyota.com	Burlington	NJ	08016	609-386-6300	386-6203
Libertyville Chevrolet Inc 1001 S Milwaukee Ave *Web:* www.libertyvillechevrolet.com	Libertyville	IL	60048	847-362-1400	
Lodal Inc 620 N Hooper St PO Box 2315 **Fax:* Orders ■ *TF:* 800-435-3500 ■ *Web:* www.lodal.com	Kingsford	MI	49802	906-779-1700	779-1160*
Loren Berg Chevrolet Inc 2700 Portland Rd *Web:* www.lorenbergchevrolet.com	Newberg	OR	97132	503-476-3309	537-0747
Loren Hyundai Inc 1620 Waukegan Rd **Fax Area Code:* 847 ■ *Web:* www.lorenautogroup.com	Glenview	IL	60025	224-766-7189	724-8429*
Lumberton Honda Mitsubishi Inc 301 Wintergreen Dr *Web:* www.lumbertonhonda.com	Lumberton	NC	28358	910-739-9871	739-5214
Luther Brookdale Chevrolet 6701 Brooklyn Blvd *TF:* 800-716-1271 ■ *Web:* lutherbrookdalechev.com	Brooklyn Center	MN	55429	800-716-1271	
LZ Truck Equipment Inc 1881 Rice St *TF:* 800-247-1082 ■ *Web:* www.lztruckequipment.com	Saint Paul	MN	55113	651-488-2571	488-9857
M K Smith Chevrolet 12845 Central Ave PO Box 455	Chino	CA	91710	909-628-8961	628-6637
M. H. Eby Inc PO Box 127 *TF:* 800-292-4752 ■ *Web:* www.mheby.com	Blue Ball	PA	17506	717-354-4971	355-2114
Maple Shade Mazda 2921 Rt 73 S *Web:* www.msmazda.com	Maple Shade	NJ	08052	856-667-8004	667-8710
Marion Body Works Inc 211 W Ramsdell St PO Box 500 *Web:* www.marionbody.com	Marion	WI	54950	715-754-5261	754-5776
Martin Chevrolet 23505 Hawthorne Blvd *Web:* www.martinchevrolet.com	Torrance	CA	90505	310-378-0211	
Martin Chevrolet Sales Inc 8800 Gratiot Rd *Web:* martincars.com	Saginaw	MI	48609	989-607-0584	781-1722
Matt Castrucci Auto Mall of Dayton 3013 Mall Pk Dr *TF:* 855-204-5293 ■ *Web:* www.mattcastrucciautomall.com	Dayton	OH	45459	513-248-3431	
Matthews-Hargreaves Chevrolet Co 2000 E12 Mile Rd **Fax:* Purchasing ■ *Web:* www.mhchevy.com	Royal Oak	MI	48067	248-398-8800	548-4952*
Mayflower Vehicle System 55 N Garfield St	Norwalk	OH	44857	419-668-8132	
Mc Dermott Auto Group 655 Main St *Web:* mcdermottauto.com	East Haven	CT	06512	203-466-1000	466-1999
Mc-Coy-Mills 700 W Commonwealth **Fax Area Code:* 714 ■ *TF Sales:* 888-640-9266 ■ *Web:* www.mccoymillsford.com	Fullerton	CA	92832	888-434-3145	992-4744*
McClinton Chevrolet Co 712 Liberty St *Web:* mcclintonchevrolet.com	Parkersburg	WV	26101	304-699-2478	485-8197
McCluskey Chevrolet Inc 9673 Kings Automall Dr *Web:* www.mccluskeychevrolet.com	Cincinnati	OH	45249	513-761-1111	679-9130
McDaniel Motor Co 1111 Mt Vernon Ave *TF:* 888-350-3802 ■ *Web:* mcdanieltoyota.com	Marion	OH	43302	740-389-2355	389-6646
McGuire Cadillac Inc 910 Rt 1 N **Fax Area Code:* 732 ■ *TF:* 866-552-4208 ■ *Web:* www.mcguirecadillac.com	Woodbridge	NJ	07095	866-552-4208	326-0385*
McLaughlin Body Co 2430 River Dr *Web:* www.mclbody.com	Moline	IL	61265	309-762-7755	762-7807
McNeilus Cos Inc 524 County Rd 34 E PO Box 70 *TF:* 800-265-1098 ■ *Web:* www.mcneiluscompanies.com	Dodge Center	MN	55927	507-374-6321	374-6394
Medical Coaches Inc 399 County Hwy 58 *TF:* 800-432-1339 ■ *Web:* www.medcoach.com	Oneonta	NY	13820	607-432-1333	432-8190
Mel Rapton Inc 3630 Fulton Ave *Web:* www.melraptonhonda.com	Sacramento	CA	95821	916-482-5400	488-8739
Mercedes-Benz Of Cincinnati 8727 Montgomery Rd *Web:* cincybenz.com	Cincinnati	OH	45236	513-984-9000	984-9468
Metro Truck Body Inc 1201 W Jon St *Web:* www.metrotruckbody.com	Torrance	CA	90502	310-532-5570	532-0754
Meyer Truck Equipment 196 W State Rd 56 *Web:* www.meyertruckeq.com	Jasper	IN	47546	812-695-3451	695-3397
Mickey Truck Bodies Inc 1305 Trinity Ave PO Box 2044 *TF:* 800-334-9061 ■ *Web:* www.mickeybody.com	High Point	NC	27261	336-882-6806	889-6712
Mike Castrucci Ford Sales Inc 1020 SR- 28 *TF:* 855-971-6897 ■ *Web:* www.mikecastruccifordmilford.com	Milford	OH	45150	513-831-7010	831-4474
Momentum Bmw Ltd 10002 SW Fwy **Fax Area Code:* 713 ■ *TF:* 800-731-8114 ■ *Web:* momentumbmw.net	Houston	TX	77074	800-731-8114	596-3210*
Monroe Truck Equipment Inc 1051 W Seventh St *TF:* 800-356-8134 ■ *Web:* www.monroetruck.com	Monroe	WI	53566	608-328-8127	328-4278
Morgan Corp 111 Morgan Way PO Box 588 *TF:* 800-666-7426 ■ *Web:* www.morgancorp.com	Morgantown	PA	19543	610-286-5025	286-2226
Morgan Olson Corp 1801 S Nottawa Rd *TF:* 800-233-4823 ■ *Web:* www.morganolson.com	Sturgis	MI	49091	800-233-4823	624-9005
Morse Operations Inc 3790 W Blue Herron Blvd *TF:* 800-755-2593 ■ *Web:* www.edmorsehonda.com	Riviera Beach	FL	33404	800-755-2593	

Company	City	State	Zip	Phone	Fax
Motor Coach Industries International Co 1700 E Golf Rd Ste 300 *TF:* 800-743-3624 ■ *Web:* www.mcicoach.com	Schaumburg	IL	60173	847-285-2000	285-2066
Murrays Ford Inc 3007 Blinker Pkwy *TF:* 800-371-6601 ■ *Web:* www.murraysford.net	Du Bois	PA	15801	814-371-6600	
Nacarato GMC Truck Inc 519 New Paul Rd **Fax:* Acctg ■ *Web:* www.nacaratotrucks.com	La Vergne	TN	37086	615-259-9500	793-6665*
Nash Chevrolet Co 630 Scenic Hwy **Fax Area Code:* 770 ■ *Web:* nashchevy.com	Lawrenceville	GA	30046	678-317-2797	822-6668*
Noble Ford Mercury Inc 2406 N Jefferson Way *Web:* www.nobleford.com	Indianola	IA	50125	515-961-8151	961-2413
North Florida Lincoln Mercury 4620 Southside Blvd *TF:* 888-579-9646 ■ *Web:* northfloridalincoln.com	Jacksonville	FL	32216	888-579-9646	
O'Daniel Motor Sales Inc 5611 Illinois Rd *Web:* www.odanielauto.com	Fort Wayne	IN	46804	260-435-5300	435-5467
Obs Inc 1324 WTuscarawas St PO Box 6210 *TF:* 800-362-9592 ■ *Web:* www.obsinc.net	Canton	OH	44706	330-453-3725	580-2429
Olathe Toyota 685 N Rawhide *Web:* www.olathetoyota.com	Olathe	KS	66061	913-780-9919	780-9614
Omaha Standard Inc 3501 S 11th St Ste 1 *TF:* 800-279-2201 ■ *Web:* www.palfinger.com	Council Bluffs	IA	51501	712-328-7444	328-8383
Oshkosh Truck Corp 2307 Oregon St *TF:* 800-392-9921 ■ *Web:* www.oshkoshdefense.com	Oshkosh	WI	54903	920-235-9150	233-9540
PACCAR Inc 777 106th Ave NE *NASDAQ: PCAR* ■ *Web:* www.paccar.com	Bellevue	WA	98004	425-468-7400	468-8216
PACCAR Inc International Div 777 106th Ave NE 12th Fl *Web:* www.paccar.com	Bellevue	WA	98004	425-468-7400	468-8216
Papa's Dodge Inc 585 E Main St *Web:* www.papasjeep.com	New Britain	CT	06051	860-225-8751	
Parkhurst Manufacturing Co 18999 Hwy Y *TF:* 800-821-7380 ■ *Web:* www.parkhurstmfg.com	Sedalia	MO	65301	660-826-8685	
Parkway Chevrolet Inc 25500 Tomball Pkwy *Web:* www.parkwaychevrolet.com	Tomball	TX	77375	281-351-8211	357-3435
Patriot Buick GMC 4600 E Central Texas Expy *Web:* patriotcars.com	Killeen	TX	76543	254-690-7000	690-7701
Performance Chevrolet Inc 4811 Madison Ave *Web:* www.performancechevy.com	Sacramento	CA	95841	916-331-6777	332-9719
Peterbilt Motors Co 1700 Woodbrook St **Fax:* Hum Res ■ *Web:* www.peterbilt.com	Denton	TX	76205	940-591-4000	591-4260*
Pierce Mfg Inc 2600 American Dr *TF Cust Svc:* 888-974-3723 ■ *Web:* www.piercemfg.com	Appleton	WI	54914	920-832-3000	832-3353
Pohanka of Salisbury 2007 N Salisbury Blvd *Web:* www.pohankaofsalisbury.com	Salisbury	MD	21801	410-749-2301	749-7704
Porter Truck Sales LP 135 McCarty St *TF:* 800-956-2408 ■ *Web:* www.portertrk.com	Houston	TX	77029	713-672-2400	672-7343
Powers-Swain Chevrolet Inc 4709 Bragg Blvd *Web:* pschevy.com	Fayetteville	NC	28303	910-864-9500	868-6159
Prevost Car Inc 35 boul Gagnon *Web:* www.prevostcar.com	Sainte-Claire	QC	G0R2V0	418-883-3391	883-4157
Progressive Chevrolet Co 8000 Hills & Dales Rd PO Box 997 *Web:* www.progressivechevrolet.com	Massillon	OH	44646	330-833-8564	
Quad-City Peterbilt Inc 8100 N Fairmount St **Fax Area Code:* 563 ■ *TF:* 866-601-8607 ■ *Web:* www.quadcitypeterbilt.com	Davenport	IA	52806	866-601-8607	391-0195*
R & B Car Company Inc 3811 S Michigan St *Web:* www.rbcarcompany.com	South Bend	IN	46614	574-299-4838	
R & S/Godwin Truck Body Co LLC 5168 S US Hwy 23 PO Box 420 *TF:* 800-826-7413 ■ *Web:* www.rstruckbody.com	Ivel	KY	41642	606-874-2151	874-9136
R&H Motor Cars Ltd 9727 Reisterstown Rd *Web:* mercedesbenzofowingsmills.com/	Owings Mills	MD	21117	410-363-3900	363-3987
Rapid Chevrolet Company Inc 2090 Deadwood Ave PO Box 1765 *TF:* 800-456-2105 ■ *Web:* www.rapidchevrolet.com	Rapid City	SD	57702	605-343-1282	343-5458
Rdk Truck Sales Inc 3214 E Adamo Dr *TF:* 877-735-4636 ■ *Web:* www.rdk.com	Tampa	FL	33605	813-241-0711	241-0414
Reading Truck Body Inc 201 Hancock Blvd **Fax Area Code:* 610 ■ *TF All:* 800-458-2226 ■ *Web:* www.readingbody.com	Reading	PA	19611	800-458-2226	775-3261*
Reed Lallier Chevrolet Inc 4500 Raeford Rd *Web:* reedlallier.com	Fayetteville	NC	28304	910-426-2000	
Ressler Motor Co 8474 Huffine Ln *Web:* www.resslermotors.com	Bozeman	MT	59718	406-587-5501	
RIHM Motor Co 2108 University Ave W *Web:* www.rihmkenworth.com	Saint Paul	MN	55114	651-646-7833	646-0630
RKI Inc 2301 Central Pkwy *TF:* 800-346-8988 ■ *Web:* www.rki-us.com	Houston	TX	77092	713-688-4414	688-8982
Rochester-Syracuse Auto Auction 1826 State Rt 414 PO Box 129 *Web:* www.rsautoauction.com	Waterloo	NY	13165	315-539-5006	539-9508
Rocket Supply Corp 404 N Rt 115 PO Box 98 *TF:* 800-252-6871 ■ *Web:* www.rocketsupply.com	Roberts	IL	60962	800-252-6871	
Rush Truck Center - Lubbock 4515 Ave A *Web:* rushtruckcenters.com	Lubbock	TX	79404	806-747-2579	747-4171
Rydell Chevrolet Inc 1325 E San Marnan Dr *TF:* 866-697-5167 ■ *Web:* chevynorthridge.com	Waterloo	IA	50702	319-234-4601	
Saf-T-Cab Inc PO Box 2587 *TF:* 800-344-7491 ■ *Web:* www.saftcab.com	Fresno	CA	93745	559-268-5541	268-5822
Salvage Direct Inc 42336 Gilbert Dr *Web:* salvagedirect.com	Titusville	PA	16354	814-827-0300	
Sanborn Chevrolet Inc 1210 S Cherokee Ln *Web:* www.sanbornchevrolet.com	Lodi	CA	95240	209-642-4954	368-1849
Sanders Ford Inc 1135 Lejeune Blvd *TF General:* 888-897-8527 ■ *Web:* sandersfordsales.com	Jacksonville	NC	28540	910-455-1911	478-4277
Scania USA Inc 121 Interpark Blvd Ste 601 *TF:* 800-272-2642 ■ *Web:* www.scania.com	San Antonio	TX	78216	210-403-0007	403-0211
Scelzi Equipment Inc 1030 W Gladstone St *TF:* 866-972-3594 ■ *Web:* www.seinc.com	Azusa	CA	91702	626-334-0573	334-2753
Schetky Northwest Sales Inc 8430 NE Killingsworth St *TF:* 800-255-8341 ■ *Web:* www.schetkynw.com	Portland	OR	97220	503-287-4141	287-2931
Seagrave Fire Apparatus LLC 105 E 12th St *Web:* www.seagrave.com	Clintonville	WI	54929	715-823-2141	823-5768
Segway Inc 14 Technology Dr *TF:* 866-473-4929 ■ *Web:* www.segway.com	Bedford	NH	03110	603-222-6000	222-6001
Shealy's Truck Ctr Inc 1340 Bluff Rd *TF:* 800-951-8580 ■ *Web:* www.shealytruck.com	Columbia	SC	29201	803-771-0176	771-4879
Skaug Truck Body Works Inc 1404 First St	San Fernando	CA	91340	818-365-9123	365-6634
Smith-Cairns Ford 900 Central Pk Ave *Web:* www.smithcairns.com	Yonkers	NY	10704	914-377-8100	377-8118
Snethkamp Chrysler Dodge Jeep Ram 11600 Telegraph Rd *TF:* 888-455-6146 ■ *Web:* www.snethkampchryslerjeep.net	Redford	MI	48239	313-255-2700	
Somerset Welding & Steel Inc 10558 Somerset Pk *TF:* 800-777-2671 ■ *Web:* www.jjbodies.com	Somerset	PA	15501	814-444-3400	443-2621
Southern Connecticut Freightliner 15 E Industrial Rd *Web:* www.netruck.com	Branford	CT	06405	203-481-0373	481-3780
Spartan Motors Inc 1541 Reynolds Rd *NASDAQ: SPAR* ■ *TF:* 800-937-5449 ■ *Web:* www.spartanmotors.com	Charlotte	MI	48813	517-543-6400	
STAHL/A Scott Fetzer Co 3201 W Old Lincoln Way *TF:* 800-277-8245 ■ *Web:* www.stahltruckbodies.com	Wooster	OH	44691	330-264-7441	264-3319
Stanford Carr Development LLC 1100 Alakea St 27th Fl *Web:* www.stanfordcarr.com	Honolulu	HI	96813	808-537-5220	537-1801
Steelweld Equipment Company Inc 235 N Service Rd W	Saint Clair	MO	63077	636-629-3704	629-3734
Sterling McCall Ford 6445 SW Fwy *Web:* www.sterlingmccallford.com	Houston	TX	77074	281-588-5000	779-7907
Sterling Truck Corp 12120 Telegraph Rd **Fax Area Code:* 313 ■ *TF Cust Svc:* 800-385-4357 ■ *Web:* www.sterlingtrucks.com	Redford Township	MI	48239	800-785-4357	592-4246*
Steve Hopkins Inc 2499 Auto Mall Pkwy *TF:* 877-873-3913 ■ *Web:* www.hopkinsautogroup.com	Fairfield	CA	94533	707-427-1000	
Steve Landers Toyota 10825 Colonel Glenn Rd *TF:* 888-314-4350 ■ *Web:* www.landerstoyota.com	Little Rock	AR	72204	501-568-5800	
Stewart Cadillac LP 2520 Main St **Fax Area Code:* 713 ■ *Web:* stewartcadillac.com	Houston	TX	77002	832-369-8318	874-0982*
Sunbury Motor Co 943 N Fourth St *Web:* www.sunburymotors.com	Sunbury	PA	17801	570-286-7746	286-9389
Superior Auto Sales Inc 5201 Camp Rd *Web:* www.sascars.com	Hamburg	NY	14075	716-649-6695	
Superior Motors Inc 282 John C Calhoun Dr *Web:* www.superiormotors.com	Orangeburg	SC	29115	803-531-6161	533-7806
Superior Trailer Sales Co 501 Hwy 80 *TF:* 800-637-0324 ■ *Web:* www.stsco.com	Sunnyvale	TX	75182	972-226-3893	226-3899
Sutphen Corp PO Box 158 *TF:* 800-726-7030 ■ *Web:* www.sutphen.com	Amlin	OH	43002	614-889-1005	889-0874
Svi Inc 440 Mark Leany Dr *Web:* www.specialtyvehicles.com	Henderson	NV	89011	702-567-5256	567-3020
Sweeney Buick 7997 Market St **Fax Area Code:* 330 ■ *TF:* 877-360-4928 ■ *Web:* sweeneycars.com	Youngstown	OH	44512	877-360-4928	726-0557*
Ten-8 Fire Equipment Inc 2904 59th Ave Dr E *TF:* 877-989-7660 ■ *Web:* www.ten8fire.com	Bradenton	FL	34203	941-756-7779	756-2598
Thomas Built Buses Inc 1408 Courtesy Rd *Web:* www.thomasbus.com	High Point	NC	27260	336-889-4871	881-6509
Thomson-Macconnell Cadillac Inc 2820 Gilbert Ave **Fax Area Code:* 513 ■ *TF:* 877-472-0738 ■ *Web:* thomsonmacconnell.com	Cincinnati	OH	45206	877-472-0738	221-5774*
Thor Industries Inc 419 W Pike St *NYSE: THO* ■ **Fax Area Code:* 877 ■ *Web:* thorindustries.com	Jackson Center	OH	45334	937-596-6111	596-6111*
Tipton Motors Inc 3840 N Expy *Web:* www.tiptonmotors.com	Brownsville	TX	78526	956-350-5600	
Tom Nehl Truck Co 417 S Edgewood Ave *Web:* www.tomnehl.com	Jacksonville	FL	32254	904-389-3653	384-2467
Tom Roush Inc 525 W David Brown Dr *TF:* 877-349-0851 ■ *Web:* www.tomroush.com	Westfield	IN	46074	317-896-5561	896-2427
Town & Country Chrysler Inc 27490 SW 95th Ave *Web:* www.cjdwilsonville.com	Wilsonville	OR	97070	503-659-0570	
Trailercraft Inc 1301 E 64th Ave *TF:* 800-478-3238 ■ *Web:* www.trailercraft.com	Anchorage	AK	99518	907-563-3238	561-4995
Truck Utilities Inc 2370 English St *TF:* 800-869-1075 ■ *Web:* www.truckutilities.com	Saint Paul	MN	55109	651-484-3305	484-0076
Trucks only 550 S Country Club Dr *Web:* www.trucksonlysales.com	Mesa	AZ	85210	480-844-7071	844-7488
Tymco Inc 225 E Industrial Blvd PO Box 2368 *TF:* 800-258-9626 ■ *Web:* www.tymco.com	Waco	TX	76703	254-799-5546	799-2722
Unicell Body Co 571 Howard St *TF Cust Svc:* 800-628-8914 ■ *Web:* www.unicell.com	Buffalo	NY	14206	716-853-8628	843-8638
United Ford Parts & Distribtion Ctr Inc 12007 E 61st St *Web:* www.unitedford.com	Broken Arrow	OK	74012	918-317-6800	
Universal Ford Sales Inc 10751 W Broad St *Web:* www.richmondford.com	Glen Allen	VA	23060	804-273-9700	273-1591
Valley Chevrolet Inc 601 Kidder St *Web:* valleychevrolet.com	Wilkes Barre	PA	18702	570-821-2772	823-9639
Viking-Cives USA 14331 Mill St *Web:* www.vikingcives.com	Harrisville	NY	13648	315-543-2321	543-2366
Vista-pro Automotive LLC 15 Century Blvd Ste 600 *TF:* 888-250-2676 ■ *Web:* www.vistaproauto.com	Nashville	TN	37214	615-622-2200	622-2302

Company	City	State	Zip	Phone	Fax
Volvo Construction Equipment of North America Inc 312 Volvo Way *Web:* www.volvoce.com	Shippensburg	PA	17257	717-532-9181	
Volvo Group North America Inc 2900 K St NW Ste 401 *Web:* www.volvo.com	Washington	DC	20007	202-661-4770	
Volvo Honolulu 704 Ala Moana Blvd *TF:* 888-892-2456 ■ *Web:* www.volvohonolulu.com	Honolulu	HI	96813	888-892-2456	
Volvo Trucks North America Inc 7900 National Service Rd PO Box 26115 *Web:* www.volvotrucks.com	Greensboro	NC	27402	336-393-2000	393-2362
Walton Motors Inc 205 E Pawnee Dr *Web:* www.waltonmotorsinc.com	Savannah	MO	64485	816-324-3141	
Weld-Built Body Co Inc 276 Long Island Ave *Web:* www.weldbuilt.com	Wyandanch	NY	11798	631-643-9700	491-4728
Wendle Motors Inc 9000 N Div **Fax Area Code:* 509 ■ *TF:* 888-685-7177 ■ *Web:* www.wendle.com	Spokane	WA	99218	888-685-7177	468-4056*
Wentworth Chevytown 107 SE Grand Ave *Web:* www.wentworthchevrolet.com	Portland	OR	97214	503-200-2482	234-3370
Wheeled Coach Industries Inc 2737 Forsyth Rd *TF:* 800-342-0720 ■ *Web:* www.wheeledcoach.com	Winter Park	FL	32792	407-677-7777	679-1337
Wichita Kenworth Inc 5115 N Broadway *TF:* 800-825-5558 ■ *Web:* www.wichitakenworth.com	Wichita	KS	67219	316-838-0867	838-4845
Woburn Foreign Motors Inc 80-82 Olympia Ave *Web:* www.wfab.com	Woburn	MA	01801	781-935-3040	938-0225
World Wide Motors Inc 3900 E 96th St *Web:* www.wwmotors.mercedesdealer.com	Indianapolis	IN	46240	317-580-6800	
Yamaha Golf Cars of California Inc 5717 Brisa St *Web:* www.yamahagolfcarsofca.com	Livermore	CA	94550	925-371-5350	371-5311
Yark Automotive Group Inc 6019 W Central Ave **Fax Area Code:* 419 ■ *TF:* 866-390-8894 ■ *Web:* www.yarkauto.com	Toledo	OH	43615	866-390-8894	842-7788*

520 MOTORCYCLES & MOTORCYCLE PARTS & ACCESSORIES

Company	City	State	Zip	Phone	Fax
American Honda Motor Company Inc 1919 Torrance Blvd *TF:* 800-999-1009 ■ *Web:* www.honda.com	Torrance	CA	90501	310-783-3170	
American Suzuki Motor Corp 3251 Imperial Hwy *Web:* www.suzuki.com	Brea	CA	92821	714-996-7040	524-2512
Andrews Products Inc 431 Kingston Ct *Web:* www.andrewsproducts.com	Mount Prospect	IL	60056	847-759-0190	759-0848
City Cycle Inc 2222 Cantrell Rd *Web:* www.competitivecyclist.com	Little Rock	AR	72202	501-663-8796	
Compositech Inc 5315 Walt Pl *Web:* www.zipp.com	Speedway	IN	46254	317-481-1120	
Corbin 2360 Technology Pkwy *TF:* 800-538-7035 ■ *Web:* www.corbin.com	Hollister	CA	95023	831-634-1100	634-1059
Cycle Shack Inc 1104 San Mateo Ave *Web:* www.cycle-shack.com	South San Francisco	CA	94080	650-583-7014	583-9154
Edelbrock Corp 2700 California St *TF:* 800-739-3737 ■ *Web:* www.edelbrock.com	Torrance	CA	90503	310-781-2222	320-1187
ElliptiGO Inc 722 Genevieve St Ste O *Web:* www.elliptigo.com	Solana Beach	CA	92075	858-876-8677	
Fulmer Co 122 Gayoso Ave *TF:* 800-467-2400 ■ *Web:* www.fulmerhelmets.com	Memphis	TN	38103	901-525-5711	525-7993
Harley-Davidson Inc 3700 W Juneau Ave *NYSE: HOG* ■ **Fax:* Hum Res ■ *Web:* harley-davidson.com	Milwaukee	WI	53208	414-342-4680	343-4621*
Hed Cycling Products 1735 Terrace Dr *Web:* www.hedcycling.com	Roseville	MN	55113	651-653-0202	
Jenson USA Inc 1615 Eastridge Ave *Web:* www.jensonusa.com	Riverside	CA	92507	909-947-9036	
Kawasaki Motors Corp USA PO Box 25252 *Web:* www.kawasaki.com	Santa Ana	CA	92799	949-770-0400	460-5600
Lehman Trikes Inc 125 Industrial Dr *CVE: LHT* ■ *TF:* 888-394-3357 ■ *Web:* www.lehmantrikes.com	Spearfish	SD	57783	605-642-2111	642-1184
Mag-Knight 18121 117th St SE *Web:* www.mag-knight.com	Snohomish	WA	98290	360-805-0100	805-0811
Motovan Corp 1391 Guy Lussac *Web:* www.motovan.com	Boucherville	QC	J4B7K1	450-449-3903	449-7773
National Cycle Inc 2200 Maywood Dr *TF:* 877-972-7336 ■ *Web:* www.nationalcycle.com	Maywood	IL	60153	708-343-0400	343-0625
Persons Majestic Mfg Co PO Box 370 *TF:* 800-772-2453 ■ *Web:* www.permaco.com	Huron	OH	44839	419-433-9057	433-0182
Polaris Industries Inc 2100 Hwy 55 *NYSE: PII* ■ *Web:* www.polaris.com	Medina	MN	55340	763-542-0500	542-0599
Powroll Motor Performance PO Box 920 *Web:* www.powroll.com	Redmond	OR	97756	541-923-1290	923-5637
Rivco Products Inc 440 S Pine St *TF:* 888-801-8222 ■ *Web:* www.rivcoproducts.com	Burlington	WI	53105	262-763-8222	763-8949
Rolf Prima Inc 780 Bailey Hill Rd Ste 2 *Web:* www.rolfprima.com	Eugene	OR	97402	541-868-1715	
World Bicycle Relief 1333 N Kingsbury Ave Fourth Fl *Web:* www.worldbicyclerelief.org	Chicago	IL	60642	312-664-8800	
Yamaha Motor Corp USA 6555 Katella Ave *TF Cust Svc:* 800-656-7695 ■ *Web:* www.yamaha-motor.com	Cypress	CA	90630	800-656-7695	

MOTORS - FLUID POWER

SEE Pumps & Motors - Fluid Power p. 2995

521 MOTORS (ELECTRIC) & GENERATORS

SEE ALSO Automotive Parts & Supplies - Mfr p. 1839

Company	City	State	Zip	Phone	Fax
ADS/Transicoil Nine Iron Bridge Dr *TF:* 800-323-7115 ■ *Web:* www.adstcoil.com	Collegeville	PA	19426	484-902-1100	902-1150
Advanced Motors & Drives Inc 6268 E Molloy Rd	East Syracuse	NY	13057	315-434-9303	
Advanced Power & Controls LLC 605 E Alton Ave Ste A *Web:* www.advancedpowercontrols.com	Santa Ana	CA	92705	714-540-9010	540-5313
Advantage Manufacturing Inc 624 S B St Ste B *Web:* www.electricmotors.com	Tustin	CA	92780	714-505-1166	
Aerotech Inc 101 Zeta Dr *TF:* 888-492-8950 ■ *Web:* www.aerotech.com	Pittsburgh	PA	15238	412-967-6440	967-6870
Alliance Winding Equipment Inc 3939 Vanguard Dr *Web:* www.alliance-winding.com	Fort Wayne	IN	46809	260-478-2200	
Alltrax Inc 1111 Cheney Creek Rd *Web:* www.alltraxinc.com	Grants Pass	OR	97527	541-476-3565	
AMETEK Lamb Electric 100 E Erie St *Web:* www.ametektip.com	Kent	OH	44240	330-673-3451	673-8994
AMK Drives & Controls Inc 5631 S Laburnum Ave *Web:* amk-antriebe.de/en/	Richmond	VA	23231	804-222-0323	222-0339
AO Smith Corp 11270 W Pk Pl Ste 170 PO Box 245008 *NYSE: AOS* ■ *TF:* 800-359-4065 ■ *Web:* www.aosmith.com	Milwaukee	WI	53224	414-359-4000	359-4180
AO Smith Electrical Products Co 531 N Fourth St *TF:* 800-543-9450 ■ *Web:* www.centuryelectricmotor.com	Tipp City	OH	45371	937-667-2431	667-5030
Arco Electric Products Corp 2325 E Michigan Rd *TF:* 800-428-4370 ■ *Web:* www.arco-electric.com	Shelbyville	IN	46176	317-398-9713	398-2655
Arkansas General Industries Inc 102 Miller St PO Box 260 *Web:* www.argenind.com	Bald Knob	AR	72010	501-724-3227	724-5915
ASMO North America LLC 470 Crawford Rd *Web:* www.asmo-na.com	Statesville	NC	28625	704-878-6663	
Aura Systems Inc 1310 E Grand Ave *OTC: AUSI* ■ *TF:* 800-909-2872 ■ *Web:* www.aurasystems.com	El Segundo	CA	90245	310-643-5300	643-7457
Autotrol Corp 365 E Prairie St PO Box 557 *TF:* 800-228-6207 ■ *Web:* www.autotrol.com	Crystal Lake	IL	60039	815-459-3080	459-3227
Aveox Inc 2265A Ward Ave *Web:* www.aveox.com	Simi Valley	CA	93065	805-915-0200	
Baldor Electric Co 5711 RS Boreham Jr St PO Box 2400 *Web:* www.baldor.com	Fort Smith	AR	72901	479-646-4711	648-5792
Barta - Schoenewald Inc 3805 Calle Tecate *Web:* www.a-m-c.com	Camarillo	CA	93012	805-389-1935	389-1165
Bluffton Motor Works LLC 410 E Spring St *TF:* 800-579-8527 ■ *Web:* www.blmworks.com	Bluffton	IN	46714	260-827-2200	
Blutek Power Inc 300-1 SR- 17 S Ste B2 *Web:* www.blutekpower.com	Lodi	NJ	07644	973-594-1800	
Bodine Electric Co 201 Northfield Rd *TF:* 800-726-3463 ■ *Web:* www.bodine-electric.com	Northfield	IL	60093	773-478-3515	478-3232
Bosch Rexroth Corp 5150 Prairie Stone Pkwy *TF:* 800-860-1055 ■ *Web:* www.boschrexroth-us.com	Hoffman Estates	IL	60192	847-645-3600	645-6201
Buehler Motor Inc 860 Aviation Pkwy Ste 300 *Web:* www.buehlermotor.com	Morrisville	NC	27560	919-380-3333	380-3256
CALEX Manufacturing Co 2401 Stanwell Dr *TF:* 800-542-3355 ■ *Web:* www.calex.com	Concord	CA	94520	925-687-4411	687-3333
Calnetix Technologies LLC 16323 Shoemaker Ave *Web:* www.calnetix.com	Cerritos	CA	90703	562-293-1660	
Cambridge Pro Fab Inc 470 Franklin Blvd *Web:* www.cambridgeprofab.com	Cambridge	ON	N1R8G6	519-740-6033	
Composite Motors Acquisition Inc 15460 Aviation Loop Dr *Web:* compositemotors.com	Brooksville	FL	34604	352-799-2599	
Continental Electric Motors Inc 23 Sebago St *TF:* 800-335-6718 ■ *Web:* www.cecoinc.com	Clifton	NJ	07013	800-335-6718	
Curtis H Stout Inc 5110 Hollywood Ave *Web:* www.colinx.com	Shreveport	LA	71109	318-636-7777	
Custom Sensors & Technologies (CST) 14401 Princeton Ave *Web:* www.cstsensors.com	Moorpark	CA	93021	805-552-3599	
DA-TECH Corp 141 Railroad Dr *Web:* swemco.com/	Ivyland	PA	18974	215-322-9410	
Data Electronic Devices Inc 32 NW Dr *Web:* www.dataed.com	Salem	NH	03079	603-893-2047	893-2956
Direct Drive Systems Inc 621 Burning Tree Rd *Web:* www.directdrivesystems.net	Fullerton	CA	92833	714-872-5500	
Dumore Corp 1030 Veterans St **Fax Area Code:* 800 ■ *TF:* 888-467-8288 ■ *Web:* www.dumorecorp.com	Mauston	WI	53948	608-847-6420	338-6673*
EAD Motors Inc 1 Progress Dr *Web:* www.electrocraft.com	Dover	NH	03820	603-742-3330	742-3330
eCycle Inc 4700 N Fifth St *Web:* www.ecycle.com	Temple	PA	19560	610-939-0480	
Electric Apparatus Co 409 Roosevelt St *Web:* www.elecapp.net	Howell	MI	48843	517-546-0520	546-0547

Company	City	State	ZIP	Phone	Fax
Electric Machinery Company Inc 800 Central Ave NE *Web:* www.electricmachinery.com	Minneapolis	MN	55413	612-378-8000	
Electric Motor & Contracting Co Inc 3703 Cook Blvd *Web:* www.emc-co.com	Chesapeake	VA	23323	757-487-2121	487-5983
Electric Motors & Specialties Inc 701 W King St PO Box 180 *Web:* www.emsmotors.com	Garrett	IN	46738	260-357-4141	357-3888
Electro Sales Inc 100 Fellsway W	Somerville	MA	02145	617-666-0500	628-2800
Elwood Corp High Performance Motors Group 2701 N Green Bay Rd **Fax Area Code:* 414 ■ *TF:* 800-558-9489 ■ *Web:* www.elwood.com	Racine	WI	53404	262-637-6591	764-4298*
Emoteq Corp 10002 E 43rd St S *TF Sales:* 800-221-7572 ■ *Web:* www.emoteq.com	Tulsa	OK	74146	918-627-1845	660-0207
ENER-G Rudox 765 State Rt 17 *Web:* www.rudox.com	Carlstadt	NJ	07072	201-438-0111	438-3403
Engine Power Source Inc 348 Bryant Blvd *TF:* 800-374-7522 ■ *Web:* www.enginepowersource.com	Rock Hill	SC	29732	704-944-1999	
Everson Tesla Inc 615 Daniel's Rd *Web:* www.eversontesla.com	Nazareth	PA	18064	610-746-1520	746-1520
Fader Agencies 83 Shore Rd	Dartmouth	NS	B3A1A5	902-466-2333	
Faradyne Motors Inc 2077 Division St *Web:* www.faradynemotors.com	Palmyra	NY	14522	315-502-0125	
Five Star Electric of Houston Inc 19424 Pk Row Ste 100 *TF:* 888-492-7090 ■ *Web:* vfd.com	Houston	TX	77084	281-492-7090	
FLANDERS Inc 8101 Baumgart Rd PO Box 23130 *TF:* 855-875-5888 ■ *Web:* www.flandersinc.com	Evansville	IN	47724	812-867-7421	
Franklin Electric Co Inc 9255 Coverdale Rd *NASDAQ: FELE* ■ *TF:* 800-962-3787 ■ *Web:* www.franklin-electric.com	Fort Wayne	IN	46809	260-824-2900	824-2909
Gamesa Wind US LLC 2050 Cabot Blvd W *Web:* www.gamesacorp.com	Langhorne	PA	19047	215-710-3100	
Generac Power Systems Inc PO Box 8 *TF:* 888-436-3722 ■ *Web:* www.generac.com	Waukesha	WI	53187	262-544-4811	544-4851
Gillette Generators Inc 1340 Wade Dr *Web:* www.gillettegenerators.com	Elkhart	IN	46514	574-264-9639	
Glentek Inc 208 Standard St *TF:* 877-470-6742 ■ *Web:* www.glentek.com	El Segundo	CA	90245	310-322-3026	322-7709
Hankscraft Inc 300 Wengel Dr *Web:* www.hankscraft.com	Reedsburg	WI	53959	608-524-4341	524-4342
Hannon Co, The 1605 Waynesburg Dr SE *Web:* www.hanco.com	Canton	OH	44707	330-456-4728	456-3323
Hansen Corp 901 S First St *Web:* www.hansen-motor.com	Princeton	IN	47670	812-385-3415	385-3013
Hansome Energy Systems Inc 365 Dalziel Rd	Linden	NJ	07036	908-862-9044	862-8195
Himoinsa Power Systems Inc 16002 W 110th St *Web:* www.hipowersystems.com	Lenexa	KS	66219	913-495-5557	
Hostvedt Pavoni Inc 30 S Pine St *Web:* www.hpisales.com	Doylestown	PA	18901	215-489-7300	
Hyundai Ideal Electric Co 330 E First St *Web:* www.idealelectricco.com	Mansfield	OH	44902	419-522-3611	
Imperial Electric Co 1503 Exeter Rd *Web:* www.imperialelectric.com	Akron	OH	44306	330-734-3600	734-3601
Joliet Equipment Corp One Doris Ave *TF:* 800-435-9350 ■ *Web:* www.joliet-equipment.com	Joliet	IL	60433	815-727-6606	727-6626
Joy Global 4400 West National Ave *Web:* www.letourneau-inc.com	Milwaukee	WI	53214	414-671-4400	671-7604
Kencoil Inc 2805 Engineers Rd *Web:* www.kencoil.com	Belle Chasse	LA	70037	504-394-4010	
Kinetek Inc 1751 Lk Cook Rd ArborLake Ctr Ste 550 *Web:* www.kinetekinc.com	Deerfield	IL	60015	847-267-4473	945-9645
Kirkwood Industries Inc 1239 Rockside Rd *TF:* 800-262-2266 ■ *Web:* www.kirkwood-ind.com	Cleveland	OH	44134	216-267-6200	351-3141
Kollmorgen Corp 203A W Rock Rd *Web:* www.kollmorgen.com	Radford	VA	24141	540-633-3545	731-5647
Kraft Power Corp 199 Wildwood Ave *TF:* 800-969-6121 ■ *Web:* www.kraftpower.com	Woburn	MA	01801	781-938-9100	933-7812
Kurz Electric Solutions Inc 1325 McMahon Dr *TF:* 800-776-3629 ■ *Web:* www.kurz.com	Neenah	WI	54956	920-886-8200	886-8201
Leeson Electric Corp 2100 Washington St *Web:* www.leeson.com	Grafton	WI	53024	262-377-8810	
Lexel Corp 532 Broadhollow Rd Ste 125 *Web:* www.lexel.com	Melville	NY	11747	631-501-0700	501-1930
Louis Allis Co 645 Lester Doss Rd *Web:* louisallis.com	Warrior	AL	35180	205-590-2986	590-1571
Mabuchi Motor America Corp 3001 W Big Beaver Rd Ste 328 *Web:* www.mabuchi-motor.co.jp	Troy	MI	48084	248-816-3100	816-3242
Mamco Corp 8630 Industrial Dr *Web:* www.mamcomotors.com	Franksville	WI	53126	262-886-9069	886-4639
Marathon Electric Inc 100 E Randolf St PO Box 8003 *Web:* www.marathonelectric.com	Wausau	WI	54402	715-675-3311	675-8051
Martindale Electric Co 1375 Hird Ave *TF:* 800-344-9191 ■ *Web:* www.martindaleco.com	Lakewood	OH	44107	216-521-8567	521-9476
McMillan Electric Co 400 Best Rd *Web:* www.mcmillanelectric.com	Woodville	WI	54028	715-698-2488	698-2297
Merkle-Korff Industries Inc 25 NW Pt Blvd Ste 900 *Web:* www.merkle-korff.com	Elk Grove Village	IL	60007	847-439-3760	439-3963
Minarik Corp 905 E Thompson Ave **Fax Area Code:* 815 ■ *Web:* www.minarik.com	Glendale	CA	91201	818-637-7550	624-6960*
Mobile Electric Power Solutions Inc 2714 W Kingsley Rd *Web:* www.meps.com	Garland	TX	75041	972-864-1015	
Molon Motor & Coil Corp 300 N Ridge Ave *TF:* 800-526-6867 ■ *Web:* www.molon.com	Arlington Heights	IL	60005	847-253-6000	259-5491
Morrill Motors Inc 229 S Main Ave **Fax Area Code:* 423 ■ *TF:* 888-743-7001 ■ *Web:* www.morrillmotors.com	Erwin	TN	37650	888-743-7001	735-0117*
Motor Appliance Corp 555 Spirit of St Louis Blvd *TF:* 800-622-3406 ■ *Web:* www.macmc.com	Saint Louis	MO	63005	636-532-3406	532-4609
Motor Products Owosso Corp 201 S Delaney Rd **Fax Area Code:* 989 ■ *TF:* 800-248-3841 ■ *Web:* www.motorproducts.net	Owosso	MI	48867	800-248-3841	723-6035*
Motor Specialty Inc 2801-17 Lathrop Ave PO Box 081278 *Web:* www.motorspecialty.com	Racine	WI	53408	262-632-2794	632-8899
MTU Onsite Energy Corp 100 Power Dr **Fax:* Sales ■ *TF:* 800-325-5450 ■ *Web:* www.mtuonsiteenergy.com	Mankato	MN	56001	507-625-7973	625-2968*
NetGain Motors Inc 800 S State St Ste 4 *Web:* www.go-ev.com	Lockport	IL	60441	630-243-9100	
Nidec America Corp 50 Braintree Hill Pk Ste 110 *Web:* www.nidec.com	Braintree	MA	02184	781-848-0970	380-3634
Nidec Motor Corp 8050 W Florissant Ave *TF:* 888-637-7333 ■ *Web:* www.usmotors.com	Saint Louis	MO	63136	888-637-7333	
Northern Lights Inc 4420 14th Ave N.W. *Web:* www.lugger.com	Seattle	WA	98107	206-789-3880	
Ohio Electric Motors Inc 30 Paint Fork Rd PO Box 168 *Web:* www.ohioelectricmotors.com	Barnardsville	NC	28709	828-626-2901	626-2155
On Site Energy Company Inc 40 Charlotte Ave *Web:* www.onsite-energy.com	Hicksville	NY	11802	516-937-1500	
Peerless Electric Co 1401 W Market St *Web:* www.peerlesselectric.com	Warren	OH	44485	330-399-3651	
PennEngineering & Manufacturing Corp 5190 Old Easton Rd *TF:* 800-237-4736 ■ *Web:* www.penn-eng.com	Danboro	PA	18916	215-766-8853	766-3680
Petrotech Inc 151 Brookhollow Esplanade *TF:* 800-486-8850 ■ *Web:* www.petrotechinc.com	New Orleans	LA	70123	504-620-6600	
Phoenix Electric Manufacturing Co 3625 N Halsted St *Web:* www.phoenixelectric.com	Chicago	IL	60613	773-477-8855	
Phytron Inc 600 Blair Pk Rd Ste 220 *Web:* www.phytron.com	Williston	VT	05495	802-872-1600	872-0311
Piller Inc 45 Turner Rd **Fax Area Code:* 845 ■ *TF:* 800-597-6937 ■ *Web:* www.piller.com	Middletown	NY	10941	800-597-6937	692-0295*
Polyspede Electronics Company Inc 6770 Twin Hills Ave *TF:* 888-476-5944 ■ *Web:* www.polyspede.com	Dallas	TX	75231	214-363-7245	363-7245
Prestolite Electric Holding Inc 46200 Port St *Web:* www.prestolite.com	Plymouth	MI	48170	734-582-7200	
ProVision solar Inc 69 Railroad Ave Ste A-7 *Web:* www.provisiontechnologies.com	Hilo	HI	96720	808-969-3281	934-7462
RAE Corp 4615 Prime Pkwy *TF:* 800-323-7049 ■ *Web:* www.raemotors.com	McHenry	IL	60050	815-385-3500	344-1580
Reuland Electric Co 17969 E Railroad St *Web:* www.reuland.com	Industry	CA	91748	626-854-5193	
Robin America Inc 905 Telser Rd *Web:* subarupower.com/	Lake Zurich	IL	60047	847-540-7300	
Rotating Right Inc 6120 Davies Rd NW	Edmonton	AB	T6E4M9	780-485-2010	
Sacramento Computer Power Inc 829 W Stadium Ln *Web:* www.sacpower.com	Sacramento	CA	95834	916-923-2772	
Sag Harbor Industries Inc 1668 Sag Harbor Tpke *TF:* 800-724-5952 ■ *Web:* www.sagharborind.com	Sag Harbor	NY	11963	631-725-0440	725-4234
Shinano Kenshi Corp 5737 Mesmer Ave *TF:* 800-755-0752 ■ *Web:* www.shinano.com	Culver City	CA	90230	818-889-5028	991-6439
SIAG Aerisyn LLC 959 Windtower Dr *Web:* www.siag.de	Chattanooga	TN	37402	423-648-3884	
Siemens Power Generation 4400 N Alafaya Trl **Fax:* Hum Res ■ *Web:* www.energy.siemens.com	Orlando	FL	32826	407-736-4197	736-5009*
Skurka Aerospace Inc 4600 Calle Bolero PO Box 2869 *Web:* www.skurka-aero.com	Camarillo	CA	93011	805-484-8884	482-7771
SL-Montevideo Technology Inc 2002 Black Oak Ave *Web:* www.slmti.com	Montevideo	MN	56265	320-269-6562	269-7662
Specialty Motors Inc 25060 Ave Tibbitts *TF:* 800-232-2612 ■ *Web:* www.specialtymotors.com	Valencia	CA	91355	661-257-7388	257-7389
Stauffer Diesel Inc 34 Stauffer Ln *Web:* www.staufferdiesel.com	Ephrata	PA	17522	717-738-2500	
Stella Maris LLC 930 W Pont des Mouton *Web:* www.stellamarisllc.com	Lafayette	LA	70507	337-504-5128	
Sterling Electric Inc 7997 Allison Ave *TF Cust Svc:* 800-654-6220 ■ *Web:* www.sterlingelectric.com	Indianapolis	IN	46268	317-872-0471	872-0907
Stimple & Ward Co 3400 Babcock Blvd *TF:* 800-792-6457 ■ *Web:* www.swcoils.com	Pittsburgh	PA	15237	412-364-5200	364-5299
Swiger Coils Systems Inc 4677 Mfg Rd *TF:* 800-321-3310 ■ *Web:* www.swigercoil.com	Cleveland	OH	44135	216-362-7500	362-1496
Tampa Armature Works Inc 6312 78th St *TF:* 866-465-8905 ■ *Web:* www.tawinc.com	Riverview	FL	33578	813-621-5661	
Toledo Commutator 1101 S Chestnut St *Web:* toledocommutator.com	Owosso	MI	48867	989-725-8192	725-5930
Toshiba International Corp 13131 W Little York Rd *TF:* 800-231-1412 ■ *Web:* www.toshiba.com	Houston	TX	77041	713-466-0277	896-5240
TPS Houston Group LLC 7101 John Ralston Rd *Web:* www.tpshoustongroup.com	Houston	TX	77044	281-459-2435	
Tramco Services Inc 141 Campbell's Creek Rd *Web:* www.tramcoservices.com	Charleston	WV	25306	304-235-5370	
Tri State G & T Association 30739 Dd Rd *Web:* www.tristategt.org	Nucla	CO	81424	970-864-7316	
Trinity Racing 9242 Hyssop Dr *Web:* www.trinityracing.com	Rancho Cucamonga	CA	91730	877-327-8697	

Phone *Fax*

Umicore Technical Materials North America Inc
Nine Pruyn's Island Dr . . . Glens Falls NY 12801 518-792-7700
Web: www.umicore.com

Unico Inc 3725 Nicholson Rd . . . Franksville WI 53126 262-886-5678 504-7396
Web: www.unicous.com

Unitron LP 10925 Miller Rd PO Box 38902 . . . Dallas TX 75238 214-340-8600 341-2099
TF: 800-527-1279 ■ *Web:* www.unitronlp.com

UQM Technologies Inc 4120 Specialty Pl . . . Longmont CO 80504 303-682-4900 682-4901
NYSE: UQM ■ *Web:* www.uqm.com

Vicor Corp 25 Frontage Rd . . . Andover MA 01810 978-470-2900 475-6715
NASDAQ: VICR ■ *TF:* 800-869-5300 ■ *Web:* www.vicorpower.com

VLSI Standards Inc Five Technology Dr . . . Milpitas CA 95035 408-428-1800
Web: www.vlsistandards.com

Wabtec Railway Electronics
21200 Dorsey Mill Rd . . . Germantown MD 20876 301-515-2000 515-2100
Web: www.wabtec.com

Ward Leonard Electric Company Inc
401 Watertown Rd . . . Thomaston CT 06787 860-283-5801 283-5777
Web: www.wardleonard.com

Wenthe-Davidson Engineering Co
16300 W Rogers Dr PO Box 510286 . . . New Berlin WI 53151 262-782-1550 782-2020
Web: www.wenthe-davidson.com

Wolverine Power Systems Inc 3229 80th Ave . . . Zeeland MI 49464 616-879-0040 879-0045
TF: 800-485-8068 ■ *Web:* www.wolverinepower.com

Yamaha Motor Corp USA 6555 Katella Ave . . . Cypress CA 90630 800-656-7695
TF Cust Svc: 800-656-7695 ■ *Web:* www.yamaha-motor.com

Yaskawa America Inc 2121 Norman Dr S . . . Waukegan IL 60085 847-887-7000 887-7310*
**Fax:* Mktg ■ *TF:* 800-927-5292 ■ *Web:* www.yaskawa.com

522 MOVING COMPANIES

SEE ALSO Trucking Companies p. 3260
Companies that have the moving of household belongings as their primary business.

Phone *Fax*

A Colonial Moving & Storage Co
17 Mercer St . . . Hackensack NJ 07601 201-343-5777 343-1934
Web: www.colonialmoving.com

Ace World Wide Moving 1900 E College Ave . . . Cudahy WI 53110 414-764-1000 764-1650
TF: 800-558-3980 ■ *Web:* www.aceworldwide.com

Air Van Moving Group
2340 130th Ave NE Ste 201 . . . Bellevue WA 98005 425-629-4101 629-4120
TF: 800-989-8905 ■ *Web:* www.airvanmoving.com

Allied International NA Inc 700 Oakmont Ln . . . Westmont IL 60559 630-570-3500 570-3496
TF: 800-444-6787 ■ *Web:* www.allied.com

American Red Ball International
9750 Third Ave NE Ste 200 . . . Seattle WA 98115 206-526-1730 526-2967
TF: 800-669-6424 ■ *Web:* americanredball.com

American Red Ball Transit Company Inc
PO Box 1127 . . . Indianapolis IN 46206 800-733-8139
TF: 800-733-8139 ■ *Web:* www.redball.com

Andrews Van Lines Inc 310 S Seventh St . . . Norfolk NE 68701 402-371-5440 371-1349
TF Cust Svc: 800-228-8146 ■ *Web:* www.andrewsvanlines.com

Arnoff Moving & Storage Inc
1282 Dutchess Tpke . . . Poughkeepsie NY 12603 845-471-1504 452-3606
TF: 800-633-6683 ■ *Web:* www.arnoff.com

Atlantic Relocation Systems Inc
1314 Chattahoochee Ave NW . . . Atlanta GA 30318 404-351-5311 350-6530
TF Cust Svc: 800-241-1140 ■ *Web:* www.atlanticrelocation.com

Atlas Van Lines Inc 1212 St George Rd . . . Evansville IN 47711 812-424-2222 421-7129*
**Fax:* Cust Svc ■ *TF:* 800-638-9797 ■ *Web:* www.atlasvanlines.com

Bekins Van Lines LLC 8010 Castleton Rd . . . Indianapolis IN 46250 800-456-8092 570-4635*
**Fax Area Code:* 317 ■ *TF:* 800-456-8092 ■ *Web:* www.bekins.com

Berger Transfer & Storage Inc
2950 Long Lk Rd . . . Saint Paul MN 55113 877-268-2101 639-2277*
**Fax Area Code:* 651 ■ *TF:* 877-268-2101 ■ *Web:* www.berger-transfer.com

Beverly Hills Transfer & Storage Co
15500 S Main St . . . Gardena CA 90248 800-999-7114
TF: 800-999-7114 ■ *Web:* www.beverlyhillstransfer.com

Bohrens Moving & Storage Inc
Three Applegate Dr . . . Robbinsville NJ 08691 609-208-1470 208-1471
TF: 800-326-4736 ■ *Web:* www.bohrensmoving.com

Buehler Moving & Storage 3899 Jackson St . . . Denver CO 80205 303-388-4000 388-0296
TF: 800-234-6683 ■ *Web:* www.buehlercompanies.com

Callan & Woodworth Moving & Storage
900 Hwy 212 . . . Michigan City IN 46360 269-447-1578 872-0776*
**Fax Area Code:* 219 ■ *TF:* 800-584-0551 ■ *Web:* www.callanmoving.com

Cartwright Cos, The 11901 Cartwright Ave . . . Grandview MO 64030 800-821-2334 442-6360*
**Fax Area Code:* 816 ■ *TF:* 800-821-2334 ■ *Web:* www.cartwrightcompanies.com

Castine Moving & Storage 1235 Chestnut St . . . Athol MA 01331 978-249-9105 249-5337
TF: 800-225-8068 ■ *Web:* www.castinemovers.com

Coast to Coast Moving & Storage Co
136 41st St . . . Brooklyn NY 11232 718-443-5800
TF: 800-872-6683 ■ *Web:* www.ctcvanlines.com

Cook Moving Systems Inc 1845 Dale Rd . . . Buffalo NY 14225 800-828-7144 893-0500*
**Fax Area Code:* 716 ■ *TF:* 800-828-7144 ■ *Web:* www.cookmoving.com

Corrigan Moving Systems
23923 Research Dr . . . Farmington Hills MI 48335 800-267-7442 471-3746*
**Fax Area Code:* 248 ■ *TF:* 800-267-7442 ■ *Web:* www.corriganmoving.com

Davidson Transfer & Storage Co
1701 Florida Ave NW . . . Washington DC 20009 202-234-5600 520-3420*
**Fax Area Code:* 415 ■ *TF:* 800-736-6825 ■ *Web:* www.secor-group.com

East Side Moving & Storage
4836 SE Powell Blvd . . . Portland OR 97206 503-777-4181 775-8443
TF: 800-547-4600 ■ *Web:* www.move-northwest.com

Graebel Van Lines Inc 16346 Airport Cir . . . Aurora CO 80011 303-214-6683
TF: 800-568-0031 ■ *Web:* www.graebel.com

Hartford Despatch Moving & Storage Inc
225 Prospect St . . . East Hartford CT 06108 860-578-2600

Hilford Moving & Storage 1595 Arundell Ave . . . Ventura CA 93003 805-642-0221 654-8402
TF: 800-739-6683 ■ *Web:* www.hilford.com

Hollister Moving & Storage 1650 Lana Way . . . Hollister CA 95023 831-637-6250 636-5029
Web: hollistermovers.com

Phone *Fax*

I-Go Van & Storage 9820 S 142nd St . . . Omaha NE 68138 402-891-1222 891-6762
TF: 800-228-9276 ■ *Web:* www.igovanandstorage.com

Johnson Storage & Moving Co 221 Broadway . . . Denver CO 80202 303-778-6683 698-0512
TF: 800-289-6683 ■ *Web:* www.johnsonstorage.com

King Relocation Services
13535 Larwin Cir . . . Santa Fe Springs CA 90670 800-854-3679
TF: 800-854-3679 ■ *Web:* www.kingcompaniesusa.com

Lido Van & Storage Co Inc
2152 Alton Pkwy Ste N . . . Irvine CA 92606 949-863-9000 221-3479*
**Fax Area Code:* 323 ■ *TF:* 800-339-5436 ■ *Web:* www.lidomoving.com

Mayflower Transit LLC 1 Mayflower Dr . . . Fenton MO 63026 636-305-4000 349-2764
TF: 800-325-3924 ■ *Web:* www.mayflower.com/moving

McCollister's Transportation Group Inc
1800 Rt 130 N PO Box 9 . . . Burlington NJ 08016 609-386-0600 386-5608
TF: 800-257-9595 ■ *Web:* www.mccollisters.com

National Van Lines Inc 2800 W Roosevelt Rd . . . Broadview IL 60155 708-450-2900 450-9320*
**Fax:* Cust Svc ■ *TF:* 877-590-2810 ■ *Web:* www.nationalvanlines.com

Nationwide Van Lines Inc 1421 NW 65th Ave . . . Plantation FL 33313 954-585-3945 585-3970
TF: 800-310-0056 ■ *Web:* www.nationwidevanlines.com

Nelson Westerberg Inc
1500 Arthur Ave Ste 200 . . . Elk Grove Village IL 60007 847-437-2080 437-2199
TF: 800-245-2080 ■ *Web:* www.nelsonwesterberg.com

NorthStar Moving Corp 9120 Mason Ave . . . Chatsworth CA 91311 818-727-0128 727-7527
TF: 800-275-7767 ■ *Web:* www.northstarmoving.com

Palmer Moving & Storage 24660 Dequindre Rd . . . Warren MI 48091 586-436-3804 834-3414
TF: 800-521-3954 ■ *Web:* www.palmermoving.com

Paxton Van Lines Inc 5300 Port Royal Rd . . . Springfield VA 22151 703-321-7600 321-7729
TF: 800-336-4536 ■ *Web:* www.paxton.com

Pickens-Kane Moving Co 410 N Milwaukee Ave . . . Chicago IL 60610 312-942-0330 243-3287
TF: 888-871-9998 ■ *Web:* www.pickenskane.com

S & M Moving Systems Inc
12128 Burke St . . . Santa Fe Springs CA 90670 562-567-2100 693-5690
TF: 800-528-4561 ■ *Web:* www.smmoving.com

Security Storage Co 1701 Florida Ave NW . . . Washington DC 20009 202-234-5600 234-3513
TF: 800-736-6825 ■ *Web:* www.secor-group.com

Smith Dray Line 320 Frontage Rd . . . Greenville SC 29611 866-642-6389 269-3023*
**Fax Area Code:* 864 ■ *TF:* 866-642-6389 ■ *Web:* www.smithdray.com

Starving Students Moving & Storage Co
1850 Sawtelle Blvd Ste 300 . . . Los Angeles CA 90025 888-931-6683 825-1145*
**Fax Area Code:* 800 ■ *TF:* 888-931-6683 ■ *Web:* www.ssmovers.com

Stevens Worldwide Van Lines 527 W Morley Dr . . . Saginaw MI 48601 800-678-3836 755-3000*
**Fax Area Code:* 989 ■ *TF:* 888-860-4566 ■ *Web:* www.stevensworldwide.com

Suddath Cos 815 S Main St . . . Jacksonville FL 32207 904-352-2577 858-1208*
**Fax:* Hum Res ■ *TF:* 800-395-7100 ■ *Web:* www.suddath.com

Truckin Movers Corp 1031 Harvest St . . . Durham NC 27704 919-682-2300 688-2264
TF: 800-334-1651 ■ *Web:* www.truckinmovers.com

Two Guys Relocation Systems Inc
3571 Pacific Hwy . . . San Diego CA 92101 619-296-7995 296-7704
Web: www.twomenwillmoveyou.com

Two Men & A Truck International Inc
3400 Belle Chase Way . . . Lansing MI 48911 517-394-7210 394-7432
TF: 800-345-1070 ■ *Web:* www.twomenandatruck.com

United Van Lines Inc 1 United Dr . . . St. Louis MO 63026 636-343-3900 349-8794
TF: 877-740-3040 ■ *Web:* www.unitedvanlines.com

Von Paris Enterprises Inc 8691 Larkin Rd . . . Savage MD 20763 410-888-8500 888-9062
TF: 800-866-6355 ■ *Web:* www.vonparis.com

Wald Relocation Services Ltd
8708 W Little York Rd Ste 190 . . . Houston TX 77040 713-512-4800 512-4881
TF: 800-527-1408 ■ *Web:* www.waldrelocation.com

Wheaton Van Lines Inc 8010 Castleton Rd . . . Indianapolis IN 46250 317-849-7900 570-4635*
**Fax:* Cust Svc ■ *TF:* 800-932-7799 ■ *Web:* www.wheatonworldwide.com

523 MUSEUMS

SEE ALSO Museums - Children's p. 2801; Museums & Halls of Fame - Sports p. 2803
Listings for museums are organized alphabetically within state and province groupings. (Canadian provinces are interfiled among the US states, in alphabetical order.)

Alabama

Phone *Fax*

Alabama Constitution Village
109 Gates Ave . . . Huntsville AL 35801 256-564-8100 564-8151
TF: 800-678-1819 ■ *Web:* earlyworks.com

Alabama Dept of Archives & History
624 Washington Ave PO Box 300100 . . . Montgomery AL 36104 334-242-4435 240-3433
Web: www.archives.state.al.us

Alabama Jazz Hall of Fame 1631 Fourth Ave . . . Birmingham AL 35203 205-254-2731 254-2785
Web: www.jazzhall.com

Alabama Museum of Natural History
PO Box 870340 . . . Tuscaloosa AL 35487 205-348-7550 348-9292
Web: www.amnh.ua.edu

American Sport Art Museum & Archives
one Academy Dr . . . Daphne AL 36526 251-626-3303 621-2527
Web: www.asama.org

Barber Vintage Motorsports Museum
6030 Barber Motorsports Pkwy . . . Leeds AL 35094 205-699-7275 702-8700
Web: www.barbermuseum.org

Bessemer Hall of History 1905 Alabama Ave . . . Bessemer AL 35020 205-426-1633
Web: www.bhamrails.info

Birmingham Civil Rights Institute
520 16th St N . . . Birmingham AL 35203 205-328-9696 323-5219
TF: 866-328-9696 ■ *Web:* www.bcri.org

Birmingham Museum of Art 2000 Eigth Ave N . . . Birmingham AL 35203 205-254-2565
Web: www.artsbma.org

Bragg-Mitchell Mansion 1906 Springhill Ave . . . Mobile AL 36607 251-471-6364 478-3800
Web: www.braggmitchellmansion.com

Burritt on the Mountain 3101 Burritt Dr . . . Huntsville AL 35801 256-536-2882 532-1784
Web: www.burrittonthemountain.com

City of Birmingham, Alabama
331 Cotton Ave SW . . . Birmingham AL 35211 205-780-5656
Web: www.informationbirmingham.com

Museum	City	State	ZIP	Phone	Fax
Huntsville Museum of Art 300 Church St SW *TF:* 800-786-9095 ■ *Web:* www.hsvmuseum.org	Huntsville	AL	35801	256-535-4350	532-1743
Jasmine Hill Gardens & Outdoor Museum 3001 Jasmine Hill Rd *Web:* www.jasminehill.org	Wetumpka	AL	36093	334-567-6463	
Kentuck Museum 503 Main Ave *Web:* kentuck.org	Northport	AL	35476	205-758-1257	758-1258
McWane Science Center 200 19th St N *TF:* 877-462-9263 ■ *Web:* www.mcwane.org	Birmingham	AL	35203	205-714-8300	714-8400
Mobile Museum of Art 4850 Museum Dr *Web:* www.mobilemuseumofart.com	Mobile	AL	36608	251-208-5200	208-5201
Montgomery Museum of Fine Arts One Museum Dr PO Box 230819 *Web:* www.mmfa.org	Montgomery	AL	36117	334-240-4333	240-4384
North Alabama Railroad Museum 694 Chase Rd *Web:* www.northalabamarailroadmuseum.com	Huntsville	AL	35815	256-851-6276	
Phoenix Fire Museum 203 S Claiborne St *Web:* www.museumofmobile.com	Mobile	AL	36602	251-208-7569	
Richards-DAR House Museum 256 N Joachim St *Web:* www.richardsdarhouse.com	Mobile	AL	36603	251-208-7320	
Sloss Furnaces National Historic Landmark 20 32nd St N *Web:* www.slossfurnaces.com	Birmingham	AL	35222	205-324-1911	324-6758
Southern Museum of Flight 4343 73rd St N *Web:* www.southernmuseumofflight.org	Birmingham	AL	35206	205-833-8226	836-2439
Weeden House Museum 300 Gates Ave SE *Web:* www.weedenhousemuseum.com	Huntsville	AL	35801	256-536-7718	
White House of the Confederacy 644 Washington St *Web:* firstwhitehouse.org	Montgomery	AL	36130	334-242-1861	

Alaska

Museum	City	State	ZIP	Phone	Fax
Alaska Aviation Heritage Museum 4721 Aircraft Dr *Web:* alaskaairmuseum.org	Anchorage	AK	99502	907-248-5325	
Alaska Native Heritage Ctr 8800 Heritage Ctr Dr *TF:* 800-315-6608 ■ *Web:* www.alaskanative.net	Anchorage	AK	99504	907-330-8000	330-8030
Alaska State Museum 395 Whittier St *TF:* 800-440-2919 ■ *Web:* museums.alaska.gov	Juneau	AK	99801	907-465-2901	465-2976
Anchorage Museum of History & Art 625 C St *Web:* www.anchoragemuseum.org	Anchorage	AK	99501	907-929-9200	929-9290
Baranov Museum, The 101 Marine Way *Web:* www.baranovmuseum.org	Kodiak	AK	99615	907-486-5920	486-3166
Fraternal Order of Alaska State Troopers Museum 245 W Fifth Ave *TF:* 800-770-5050 ■ *Web:* www.alaskatroopermuseum.com	Anchorage	AK	99501	907-279-5050	279-5054
Imaginarium Science Discovery Ctr 737 W Fifth Ave Ste G *Web:* www.visit-ketchikan.com	Anchorage	AK	99501	907-276-3179	
Juneau-Douglas City Museum 114 W Fourth St *Web:* www.juneau.lib.ak.us	Juneau	AK	99801	907-586-3572	586-3203
Oscar Anderson House Museum 420 M St Elderberry Pk	Anchorage	AK	99501	907-274-2336	
Sheldon Jackson Museum 104 College Dr *TF:* 800-587-0430 ■ *Web:* museums.alaska.gov	Sitka	AK	99835	907-747-8981	747-3004
Tongass Historical Museum 629 Dock St *Web:* ketchikanmuseums.com	Ketchikan	AK	99901	907-225-5900	225-5602
University of Alaska Museum of the North 907 Yukon Dr *TF:* 866-478-2721 ■ *Web:* www.uaf.edu/museum	Fairbanks	AK	99775	907-474-7505	474-5469

Alberta

Museum	City	Prov	Postal Code	Phone	Fax
Aero Space Museum of Calgary 4629 McCall Way NE *Web:* www.asmac.ab.ca	Calgary	AB	T2E7H1	403-250-3752	250-8399
Alberta Aviation Museum 11410 Kingsway Ave *Web:* www.albertaaviationmuseum.com	Edmonton	AB	T5G0X4	780-451-1175	451-1607
Glenbow Museum 130-9 Ave SE *Web:* www.glenbow.org	Calgary	AB	T2G0P3	403-268-4100	265-9769
Reynolds-Alberta Museum 6426 40 Ave PO Box 6360 *TF:* 800-661-4726 ■ *Web:* www.history.alberta.ca/reynolds	Wetaskiwin	AB	T9A2G1	780-361-1351	361-1239
Royal Alberta Museum 102nd Ave Ste 12845 *Web:* www.royalalbertamuseum.ca	Edmonton	AB	T5N0M6	780-453-9100	454-6629
Royal Tyrrell Museum of Palaeontology Hwy 838 Midland Provincial Pk *TF:* 888-440-4240 ■ *Web:* www.tyrrellmuseum.com	Drumheller	AB	T0J0Y0	403-823-7707	823-7131
TELUS World of Science 11211 142nd St *Web:* telusworldofscienceedmonton.ca/	Edmonton	AB	T5M4A1	780-451-3344	455-5882

Arizona

Museum	City	State	ZIP	Phone	Fax
390th Memorial Museum 6000 E Valencia Rd *TF:* 800-639-4992 ■ *Web:* 390th.org	Tucson	AZ	85706	520-574-0287	574-3030
Arizona Doll & Toy Museum 5847 W Myrtle Ave	Glendalemaricopa	AZ	85301	623-939-6186	
Arizona Historical Society Museum 1300 N College Ave *TF:* 800-249-7737 ■ *Web:* www.arizonahistoricalsociety.org	Tempe	AZ	85281	480-929-0292	967-5450
Arizona Historical Society Pioneer Museum 2340 N Ft Valley Rd *Web:* www.arizonahistoricalsociety.org	Flagstaff	AZ	86001	928-774-6272	774-1596
Arizona Science Ctr 600 E Washington St *Web:* www.azscience.org	Phoenix	AZ	85004	602-716-2000	716-2099
Arizona State Capitol Museum 1700 W Washington St *TF:* 800-228-4710 ■ *Web:* azlibrary.gov/azcm	Phoenix	AZ	85007	602-542-4675	256-7985
Arizona State Museum 1013 E University Blvd University of Arizona *Web:* www.statemuseum.arizona.edu	Tucson	AZ	85721	520-621-6302	626-6761
Arizona State University Art Museum 10th St & Mill Ave Nelson Fine Arts Ctr Arizona State University *TF:* 855-278-5080 ■ *Web:* www.asuartmuseum.asu.edu	Tempe	AZ	85287	480-965-2787	965-5254
Arizona State University Museum of Anthropology Anthropology Bldg PO Box 872402 *Web:* www.shesc.asu.edu	Tempe	AZ	85287	480-965-6213	965-7671
Arizona Wing Commemorative Air Force Museum 2017 N Greenfield Rd Falcon Field *Web:* azcaf.org	Mesa	AZ	85215	480-924-1940	981-1954
Center for Creative Photography 1030 N Olive Rd *TF:* 888-472-4732 ■ *Web:* www.creativephotography.org	Tucson	AZ	85721	520-621-7968	621-9444
DeGrazia Gallery in the Sun 6300 N Swan Rd *TF:* 800-545-2185 ■ *Web:* www.degrazia.org	Tucson	AZ	85718	520-299-9191	299-1381
Flandrau Science Ctr & Planetarium 1601 E University Blvd *Web:* www.flandrau.org	Tucson	AZ	85719	520-621-4516	621-8451
Fort Lowell Museum 2900 N Craycroft Rd *Web:* arizonahistoricalsociety.org	Tucson	AZ	85712	520-885-3832	
Grand Canyon National Park Museum Collection Grand Canyon National Pk 2C Albright Ave *Web:* www.nps.gov	Grand Canyon	AZ	86023	928-638-7769	
Hall of Flame Museum of Firefighting 6101 E Van Buren St *Web:* www.hallofflame.org	Phoenix	AZ	85008	602-275-3473	275-0896
Heard Museum 2301 N Central Ave *Web:* www.heard.org	Phoenix	AZ	85004	602-252-8840	252-9757
International Wildlife Museum 4800 W Gates Pass Rd *Web:* www.thewildlifemuseum.org	Tucson	AZ	85745	520-629-0100	618-3561
Mesa Historical Museum 2345 N Horne St PO Box 582 *Web:* www.mesamuseum.org	Mesa	AZ	85211	480-835-7358	
Meteor Crater & Museum of Astrogeology Exit 233 Off I-40 Meteor Crater Rd **Fax Area Code:* 928 ■ *TF:* 800-289-5898 ■ *Web:* www.meteorcrater.com	Winslow	AZ	86047	800-289-5898	289-2598*
Museum of Northern Arizona 3101 N Ft Valley Rd *TF:* 800-423-1069 ■ *Web:* www.musnaz.org	Flagstaff	AZ	86001	928-774-5211	774-1229
Old Pueblo Archaeology Ctr 2201 W 44th St *Web:* www.oldpueblo.org	Tucson	AZ	85713	520-798-1201	798-1966
Petersen House Museum 1414 W Southern Ave *Web:* www.tempe.gov/museum	Tempe	AZ	85282	480-350-5100	350-5150
Phoenix Art Museum 1625 N Central Ave *Web:* www.phxart.org	Phoenix	AZ	85004	602-257-1222	253-8662
Phoenix Police Museum 17 S Second Ave *Web:* www.phoenixpolicemuseum.com	Phoenix	AZ	85003	602-534-7278	
Pima Air & Space Museum 6000 E Valencia Rd *Web:* www.pimaair.org	Tucson	AZ	85706	520-574-0462	574-9238
Pioneer Arizona Living History Museum 3901 W Pioneer Rd *Web:* www.pioneeraz.org	Phoenix	AZ	85086	623-465-1052	465-0683
Pueblo Grande Museum & Archaeological Park 4619 E Washington St *TF:* 877-706-4408 ■ *Web:* www.phoenix.gov/recreation/arts/museums/pueblo	Phoenix	AZ	85034	602-495-0901	495-5645
Rosson House Historic Museum 113 N Sixth St *Web:* www.rossonhousemuseum.org	Phoenix	AZ	85004	602-262-5070	
Scottsdale Historical Museum 7333 E Scottsdale Mall *Web:* www.scottsdalemuseum.com	Scottsdale	AZ	85251	480-945-4499	970-3251
Scottsdale Museum of Contemporary Art (SMOCA) 7374 E Second St *Web:* www.smoca.org	Scottsdale	AZ	85251	480-874-4666	
Shemer Arts Ctr & Museum Assn Inc (SACAMA) 5005 E Camelback Rd *Web:* www.shemerartcenter.org	Phoenix	AZ	85018	602-262-4727	262-1605
Tempe Historical Museum 809 E Southern Ave *Web:* www.tempe.gov/museum	Tempe	AZ	85282	480-350-5100	350-5150
University of Arizona Museum of Art 1031 N Olive Rd University of Arizona *Web:* artmuseum.arizona.edu	Tucson	AZ	85721	520-621-7567	621-8770

Arkansas

Museum	City	State	ZIP	Phone	Fax
Arkansas Arts Ctr 501 E Ninth St *TF:* 800-264-2787 ■ *Web:* www.arkarts.com	Little Rock	AR	72202	501-372-4000	375-8053
Arkansas Museum of Science & History *Museum of Discovery* 500 President Clinton Ave Ste 150 *TF:* 800-880-6475 ■ *Web:* museumofdiscovery.org	Little Rock	AR	72201	501-396-7050	396-7054
Arkansas State University Museum PO Box 490 *TF:* 800-342-2923 ■ *Web:* www.astate.edu/museum	State University	AR	72467	870-972-2074	972-2793
Fort Smith Museum of History 320 Rogers Ave *Web:* www.fortsmithmuseum.org	Fort Smith	AR	72901	479-783-7841	
Fort Smith Trolley Museum 100 S Fourth St *Web:* www.fstm.org	Fort Smith	AR	72901	479-783-0205	782-0649
Historic Arkansas Museum 200 E Third St *Web:* www.historicarkansas.org	Little Rock	AR	72201	501-324-9351	324-9345
Josephine Tussaud Wax Museum 250 Central Ave *Web:* www.rideaduck.com	Hot Springs	AR	71901	501-623-5836	

Phone Fax

MacArthur Museum of Arkansas Military History
503 E Ninth St .... Little Rock AR 72202 501-376-4602 376-4593
Web: arkmilitaryheritage.com

Mid-America Science Museum
500 Mid-America Blvd .... Hot Springs AR 71913 501-767-3461 767-1170
Web: www.midamericamuseum.org

Museum of Discovery
500 President Clinton Ave Ste 150 .... Little Rock AR 72201 501-396-7050 396-7054
TF: 800-880-6475 ■ *Web:* museumofdiscovery.org

Old State House Museum 300 W Markham St .... Little Rock AR 72201 501-324-9685 324-9688
Web: www.oldstatehouse.com

Terry House Community Gallery
9th & Commerce / MacArthur Park
PO Box 2137 .... Little Rock AR 72203 501-372-4000 975-5950
Web: www.arkarts.com

British Columbia

Phone Fax

Canadian Museum of Flight
5333 216th St Hngr 3 .... Langley BC V2Y2N3 604-532-0035 532-0056
Web: www.canadianflight.org

Canadian Museum of Rail Travel
57 Van Horne St S PO Box 400 .... Cranbrook BC V1C1Y7 250-489-3918 489-5744
Web: www.crowsnest.bc.ca/cmrt

Comox Air Force Museum
19 Wing Military Row PO Box 1000 Stn Forces .... Comex BC V0R2K0 250-339-8162 339-8162
Web: www.comoxairforcemuseum.ca

Museum of Vancouver
1100 Chestnut St Vanier Pk .... Vancouver BC V6J3J9 604-736-4431 736-5417
Web: www.museumofvancouver.ca

Royal British Columbia Museum (RBCM)
675 Belleville St .... Victoria BC V8W9W2 250-356-7226 387-5674
TF: 888-447-7977 ■ *Web:* www.royalbcmuseum.bc.ca

University of British Columbia Museum of Anthropology
6393 NW Marine Dr .... Vancouver BC V6T1Z2 604-822-5087 822-2974
Web: www.moa.ubc.ca

California

Phone Fax

African American Historical & Cultural Museum of San Joaquin Valley
1857 Fulton St .... Fresno CA 93721 559-268-7102
Web: aahcmsjv.org

African American Museum & Library in Oakland
659 14th St .... Oakland CA 94612 510-637-0200 637-0204
Web: oaklandlibrary.org/locations/african-american-museum-library-oakland

Agua Caliente Cultural Museum
219 S Palm Canyon Dr .... Palm Springs CA 92262 760-778-1079 320-0350
Web: www.accmuseum.org

Ainsley House 300 Grant St .... Campbell CA 95008 408-866-2119 866-2795
Web: www.campbellmuseums.org

Alice Arts Ctr 1428 Alice St .... Oakland CA 94612 510-238-7526
Web: mccatheater.com

Ardenwood Historic Farm 34600 Ardenwood Blvd .... Fremont CA 94555 510-544-2797 796-0231
TF: 888-327-2757 ■ *Web:* www.ebparks.org

Asian Art Museum
200 Larkin St Civic Ctr Plz .... San Francisco CA 94102 415-581-3500 581-4700
Web: www.asianart.org

Autry National Ctr Museum of the American West
4700 Western Heritage Way .... Los Angeles CA 90027 323-667-2000 660-5721
Web: theautry.org

Bakersfield Museum of Art 1930 R St .... Bakersfield CA 93301 661-323-7219 323-7266
Web: www.bmoa.org

Banning Museum, The 401 E 'M' St .... Wilmington CA 90744 310-548-7777 548-2644
Web: banningmuseum.org

Berkeley Art Museum & Pacific Film Archive
2626 Bancroft Way Ste 2250 .... Berkeley CA 94720 510-642-0808 642-4889
Web: www.bampfa.berkeley.edu

Bonita Museum & Cultural Center
4355 Bonita Rd .... Bonita CA 91902 619-267-5141 267-2143
Web: www.bonitacalifornia.org

Bowers Museum of Cultural Art
2002 N Main St .... Santa Ana CA 92706 714-567-3600 567-3603
Web: www.bowers.org

Brand Library & Art Ctr 1601 W Mountain St .... Glendale CA 91201 818-548-2051
Web: ci.glendale.ca.us/library/

Buena Vista Museum of Natural History
2018 Chester Ave .... Bakersfield CA 93301 661-324-6350 324-7522
Web: www.sharktoothhill.org

Burning Man 1900 Third St .... San Francisco CA 94158 415-865-3800
Web: www.burningman.com

Cabot's Pueblo Museum
67-616 E Desert View Ave .... Desert Hot Springs CA 92240 760-329-7610 329-2738
Web: www.cabotsmuseum.org

California Academy of Sciences
55 Music Concourse Dr Golden Gate Pk .... San Francisco CA 94103 415-321-8000 321-8610
Web: www.calacademy.org

California African American Museum
600 State Dr Exposition Pk .... Los Angeles CA 90037 213-744-7432 744-2050
Web: www.caamuseum.org

California Living Museum (CALM)
10500 Alfred Harrell Hwy .... Bakersfield CA 93306 661-872-2256 872-2205
Web: www.calmzoo.org

California Military Museum 1119 Second St .... Sacramento CA 95814 916-442-2883
Web: www.militarymuseum.org

California Museum for History Women & the Arts
1020 'O' St .... Sacramento CA 95814 916-653-7524 653-0314
Web: www.californiamuseum.org

California Museum of Photography
3824 Main St .... Riverside CA 92501 951-827-4787 827-4797
Web: artsblock.ucr.edu

Phone Fax

California Science Ctr 700 State Dr .... Los Angeles CA 90037 213-744-7400
Web: californiasciencecenter.org

California State Archives 1020 'O' St .... Sacramento CA 95814 916-653-7715 653-7134
TF: 800-633-5155 ■ *Web:* www.sos.ca.gov

California State Railroad Museum
125 "I" St 111 'I' St .... Sacramento CA 95814 916-323-9280 327-5655
TF: 866-240-4655 ■ *Web:* www.csrmf.org

Campbell Historical Museum 51 N Central Ave .... Campbell CA 95008 408-866-2757 866-2795
Web: www.campbellmuseums.org

Carnegie Art Museum 424 S 'C' St .... Oxnard CA 93030 805-385-8158 483-3654
Web: www.carnegieam.org

Cartoon Art Museum 655 Mission St .... San Francisco CA 94105 415-227-8666 243-8666
Web: www.cartoonart.org

Center for Beethoven Studies & Museum
150 E San Fernando St
Dr MLK Jr Library Fifth Fl .... San Jose CA 95112 408-808-2058 808-2060
Web: www.sjsu.edu

Chabot Space & Science Ctr
10000 Skyline Blvd .... Oakland CA 94619 510-336-7300 336-7491
Web: www.chabotspace.org

Chula Vista Heritage Museum
360 Third Ave .... Chula Vista CA 91910 619-427-8092
Web: www.chulavistaca.gov

Clarke Historical Museum 240 E St .... Eureka CA 95501 707-443-1947 443-0290
Web: www.clarkemuseum.org

Coachella Valley History Museum
82-616 Miles Ave PO Box 595 .... Indio CA 92201 760-342-6651 863-5232
Web: www.cvhm.org

Colton Hall Museum
570 Pacific St Monterey City Hall .... Monterey CA 93940 831-646-5648 646-3917
Web: www.monterey.org/museum

Computer History Museum, The
1401 N Shoreline Blvd .... Mountain View CA 94043 650-810-1010
Web: www.computerhistory.org

County of San Bernardino
2024 Orange Tree Ln .... Redlands CA 92374 909-307-2669 307-0539
Web: sbcounty.gov

Crocker Art Museum 216 'O' St .... Sacramento CA 95814 916-808-7000
Web: www.crockerartmuseum.org

Crown Point Press 20 Hawthorne St .... San Francisco CA 94105 415-974-6273 495-4220
Web: www.crownpoint.com

de Saisset Museum at Santa Clara University
500 El Camino Real .... Santa Clara CA 95053 408-554-4528 554-7840
TF: 866-554-6800 ■ *Web:* www.scu.edu/deSaisset

Death Valley Museum
Death Vly National Pk PO Box 579 .... Death Valley CA 92328 760-786-2331 786-3283
Web: www.nps.gov/deva

Discovery Science Ctr 2500 N Main St .... Santa Ana CA 92705 714-542-2823 542-2828
Web: www.discoverycube.org

Dr Willella Howe-Waffle House & Medical Museum
120 Civic Ctr Dr .... Santa Ana CA 92701 714-547-9645
Web: www.santaanahistory.com

Euphrat Museum of Art
21250 Stevens Creek Blvd .... Cupertino CA 95014 408-864-5464
Web: www.deanza.edu

Exploratorium, The 3601 Lyon St .... San Francisco CA 94123 415-561-0360 561-0370
TF: 800-232-9698 ■ *Web:* www.exploratorium.edu

Firehouse Museum 1572 Columbia St .... San Diego CA 92101 619-232-3473
Web: sandiegofirehousemuseum.com

Flying Leatherneck Aviation Museum
Anderson Ave MCAS Miramar .... San Diego CA 92145 858-693-1723 693-0037
TF: 877-359-8762 ■ *Web:* www.flyingleathernecks.org

Forest Lawn Museum 1712 S Glendale Ave .... Glendale CA 91205 800-204-3131
TF: 800-204-3131 ■ *Web:* www.forestlawn.com

Fort MacArthur Museum 3601 S Gaffey St .... San Pedro CA 90731 310-548-2631 241-0847
TF: 800-232-5505 ■ *Web:* www.ftmac.org

Fresno Art Museum (FAM) 2233 N First St .... Fresno CA 93703 559-441-4221 441-4227
Web: www.fresnoartmuseum.org

George C Page Museum at La Brea Tar Pits
5801 Wilshire Blvd .... Los Angeles CA 90036 323-857-6300 933-3974
Web: www.tarpits.org

Grier-Musser Museum 403 S Bonnie Brae St .... Los Angeles CA 90057 213-413-1814
Web: griermussermuseum.org

Haggin Museum, The 1201 N Pershing Ave .... Stockton CA 95203 209-940-6300 462-1404
Web: www.hagginmuseum.org

Hellenic Heritage Museum 1650 Senter Rd .... San Jose CA 95112 408-247-4685
Web: hhisj.org

Heritage Museum of Orange County, The
3101 W Harvard St .... Santa Ana CA 92704 714-540-0404 540-1932
Web: heritagemuseumoc.org

Heritage of the Americas Museum
12110 Cuyamaca College Dr W .... El Cajon CA 92019 619-670-5194 670-5198
TF: 800-234-1597 ■ *Web:* www.cuyamaca.net

Heritage Square Museum 3800 Homer St .... Los Angeles CA 90031 323-225-2700 225-2725
TF: 800-375-1771 ■ *Web:* www.heritagesquare.org

Hiller Aviation Museum 601 Skyway Rd .... San Carlos CA 94070 650-654-0200
Web: hiller.org

Historical Glass Museum 1157 Orange St .... Redlands CA 92374 909-798-0868
Web: historicalglassmuseum.com

Hobby City Doll & Toy Museum
1238 S Beach Blvd .... Anaheim CA 92804 714-527-2323 236-9762

Hollywood Museum 1660 N Highland Ave .... Hollywood CA 90028 323-464-7776 464-3777
Web: www.thehollywoodmuseum.com

Hollywood Wax Museum 6767 Hollywood Blvd .... Hollywood CA 90028 323-462-5991 462-3953
TF: 800-214-3661 ■ *Web:* www.hollywoodwaxmuseum.com

Intel Museum 2200 Mission College Blvd .... Santa Clara CA 95052 408-765-0503
TF: 800-628-8686 ■ *Web:* www.intel.in

International Surfing Museum
411 Olive Ave .... Huntington Beach CA 92648 714-960-3483 960-1434
Web: www.surfingmuseum.org

J Paul Getty Museum 1200 Getty Ctr Dr .... Los Angeles CA 90049 310-440-7300 440-7720*
**Fax:* Hum Res ■ *Web:* www.getty.edu

Museum	City	State	ZIP	Phone	Fax
Japanese American National Museum 369 E First St *TF:* 800-461-5266 ■ *Web:* www.janm.org	Los Angeles	CA	90012	213-625-0414	625-0414
Japanese-American Museum 535 N Fifth St *Web:* www.jamsj.org	San Jose	CA	95112	408-294-3138	294-1657
Jensen-Alvarado Historic Ranch & Museum 4307 Briggs St *Web:* rivcoparks.org	Riverside	CA	92509	951-369-6055	369-1153
Judah L Magnes Museum 2911 Russell St *Web:* www.magnes.org	Berkeley	CA	94705	510-549-6950	
Junipero Serra Museum 2727 Presidio Dr *Web:* www.sandiegohistory.org	San Diego	CA	92103	619-297-3258	
Kearney Mansion Museum 7160 W Kearney Blvd *Web:* www.valleyhistory.org	Fresno	CA	93706	559-441-0862	441-1372
Kern County Museum 3801 Chester Ave *Web:* www.kcmuseum.org	Bakersfield	CA	93301	661-852-0401	
Kern Valley Museum 49 Big Blue Rd PO Box 651 *Web:* kernvalleymuseum.org	Kernville	CA	93238	760-376-6683	
Legion of Honor Museum 100 34th Ave Lincoln Pk *Web:* legionofhonor.famsf.org	San Francisco	CA	94121	415-750-3600	
Legion of Valor Museum 2425 Fresno St at O St Ste 103 *Web:* www.legionofvalor.com	Fresno	CA	93721	559-498-0510	
Lindsay Wildlife Museum 1931 First Ave *Web:* www.wildlife-museum.org	Walnut Creek	CA	94597	925-627-2920	
Long Beach Museum of Art 2300 E Ocean Blvd *Web:* www.lbma.org	Long Beach	CA	90803	562-439-2119	439-3587
Los Angeles County Museum of Art 5905 Wilshire Blvd *Web:* www.lacma.org	Los Angeles	CA	90036	323-857-6000	857-6212
Lux Art Institute 1550 S El Camino Real *Web:* www.luxartinstitute.org	Encinitas	CA	92024	760-436-6611	
March Field Air Museum 22550 Van Buren Blvd *Web:* www.marchfield.org	Riverside	CA	92518	951-902-5949	697-6605
Maritime Museum of San Diego 1492 N Harbor Dr *Web:* www.sdmaritime.org	San Diego	CA	92101	619-234-9153	234-8345
McClellan Aviation Museum 3200 Freedom Pk Dr *Web:* www.aerospaceca.org	McClellan	CA	95652	916-643-3192	643-0389
McHenry Museum 1402 'I' St *Web:* www.mchenrymuseum.org	Modesto	CA	95354	209-577-5235	
Merritt Museum of Anthropology 12500 Campus Dr *Web:* merritt.edu	Oakland	CA	94619	510-531-4911	436-2405
Meux Home Museum 1007 R St *Web:* www.meux.mus.ca.us	Fresno	CA	93721	559-233-8007	233-2331
Mexican Museum Fort Mason Ctr 2 Marina Blvd Bldg D *Web:* www.mexicanmuseum.org	San Francisco	CA	94123	415-202-9700	
Mills College Art Museum 5000 MacArthur Blvd *Web:* mcam.mills.edu	Oakland	CA	94613	510-430-2164	430-3168
Mingei International Museum of Folk Art 1439 El Prado *Web:* www.mingei.org	San Diego	CA	92101	619-239-0003	239-0605
Minter Field Air Museum 401 Vultee St PO Box 445 *Web:* www.minterfieldairmuseum.com	Shafter	CA	93263	661-393-0291	393-3296
Mission Basilica San Diego de Alcala 10818 San Diego Mission Rd *Web:* www.missionsandiego.com	San Diego	CA	92108	619-283-7319	283-7762
Mission Inn Museum 3696 Main St *Web:* www.missioninnmuseum.com	Riverside	CA	92501	951-788-9556	341-6574
Monterey Maritime & History Museum Five Custom House Plz *Web:* museumofmonterey.org	Monterey	CA	93940	831-372-2608	655-3054
Monterey Museum of Art 559 Pacific St *Web:* www.montereyart.org	Monterey	CA	93940	831-372-5477	372-5680
Museo Italo-Americano Fort Mason Ctr Bldg C *Web:* www.museoitaloamericano.org	San Francisco	CA	94123	415-673-2200	673-2292
Museum of Contemporary Art San Diego 700 Prospect St *Web:* www.mcasd.org	La Jolla	CA	92037	858-454-3541	
Museum of History & Art 1100 Orange Ave *TF:* 866-599-7242 ■ *Web:* www.coronadohistory.org	Coronado	CA	92118	619-435-7242	435-8504
Museum of Jurassic Technology 9341 Venice Blvd *Web:* www.mjt.org	Culver City	CA	90232	310-836-6131	287-2267
Museum of Latin American Art 628 Alamitos Ave *Web:* molaa.org/	Long Beach	CA	90802	562-437-1689	437-7043
Museum of Local History 190 Anza St *Web:* www.museumoflocalhistory.org	Fremont	CA	94539	510-623-7907	
Museum of Making Music 5790 Armada Dr *TF:* 877-551-9976 ■ *Web:* www.museumofmakingmusic.org	Carlsbad	CA	92008	760-438-5996	438-8964
Museum of Neon Art 501 W Olympic Blvd Ste 101 *Web:* www.neonmona.org	Los Angeles	CA	90015	213-489-9918	
Museum of Photographic Arts 1649 El Prado *Web:* www.mopa.org	San Diego	CA	92101	619-238-7559	238-8777
Museum of San Diego History 1649 El Prado Balboa Pk *Web:* www.sandiegohistory.org	San Diego	CA	92101	619-232-6203	232-6297
Museum of Tolerance 9786 W Pico Blvd *TF:* 800-900-9036 ■ *Web:* www.wiesenthal.com	Los Angeles	CA	90035	310-553-8403	772-7655
National Steinbeck Ctr One Main St *Web:* www.steinbeck.org	Salinas	CA	93901	831-796-3833	796-3828
Natural History Museum of Los Angeles County 900 Exposition Blvd *Web:* www.nhm.org	Los Angeles	CA	90007	213-763-3466	746-2999
Newland House Museum 19820 Beach Blvd *Web:* www.hbsurfcity.com/history/newland.htm	Huntington Beach	CA	92648	714-962-5777	
Norton Simon Museum 411 W Colorado Blvd *Web:* nortonsimon.org	Pasadena	CA	91105	626-449-6840	796-4978
Oakland Aviation Museum 8252 Earhart Rd *Web:* www.oaklandaviationmuseum.org	Oakland	CA	94621	510-638-7100	
Oakland Museum of California 1000 Oak St *TF General:* 888-625-6873 ■ *Web:* www.museumca.org	Oakland	CA	94607	510-238-2200	238-2258
Orange County Museum of Art Newport Beach 850 San Clemente Dr *Web:* www.ocma.net	Newport Beach	CA	92660	949-759-1122	759-5623
Orange County Museum of Art South Coast Plaza 850 San Clemente Dr Third Fl *Web:* www.ocma.net	Newport Beach	CA	92660	949-759-1122	759-5623
Pacific Asia Museum 46 N Los Robles Ave *Web:* www.pacificasiamuseum.org	Pasadena	CA	91101	626-449-2742	449-2754
Pacific Grove Museum of Natural History 165 Forest Ave *Web:* www.pgmuseum.org	Pacific Grove	CA	93950	831-648-5716	372-3256
Pacific Southwest Railway Museum 4695 Nebo Dr *Web:* www.psrm.org	La Mesa	CA	91941	619-465-7776	
Paley Ctr for Media, The 465 N Beverly Dr *Web:* www.paleycenter.org	Beverly Hills	CA	90210	310-786-1000	786-1086
Palm Springs Air Museum 745 N Gene Autry Trl *Web:* palmspringsairmuseum.org	Palm Springs	CA	92262	760-778-6262	320-2548
Palm Springs Art Museum 101 Museum Dr *Web:* www.psmuseum.org	Palm Springs	CA	92262	760-322-4800	327-5069
Pardee Home Museum 672 11th St *Web:* www.pardeehome.org	Oakland	CA	94607	510-444-2187	444-7120
Petersen Automotive Museum 6060 Wilshire Blvd **Fax:* Admin ■ *TF:* 800-546-7866 ■ *Web:* www.petersen.org	Los Angeles	CA	90036	323-930-2277	930-6642*
Planes of Fame Air Museum 7000 Merrill Ave #17 *Web:* www.planesoffame.org	Chino	CA	91710	909-597-3722	597-4755
Rancho Los Alamitos Historic Ranch & Gardens 6400 E Bixby Hill Rd *Web:* www.rancholosalamitos.com	Long Beach	CA	90815	562-431-3541	430-9694
Rancho Los Cerritos Historic Ranch 4600 Virginia Rd *Web:* www.rancholoscerritos.org	Long Beach	CA	90807	562-570-1755	570-1893
Randall Museum 199 Museum Way *TF:* 866-807-7148 ■ *Web:* www.randallmuseum.org	San Francisco	CA	94114	415-554-9600	554-9609
Reuben H Fleet Science Ctr 1875 El Prado *Web:* www.rhfleet.org	San Diego	CA	92101	619-238-1233	685-5771
Richard Nixon Foundation, The 18001 Yorba Linda Blvd *Web:* www.nixonfoundation.org	Yorba Linda	CA	92886	714-993-5075	528-0544
Riverside Art Museum 3425 Mission Inn Ave *Web:* www.riversideartmuseum.org	Riverside	CA	92501	951-684-7111	684-7332
Riverside Metropolitan Museum 3580 Mission Inn Ave *Web:* www.riversideca.gov/museum	Riverside	CA	92501	951-826-5273	369-4970
Robert V Fullerton Art Museum 5500 University Pkwy California State University *Web:* raffma.csusb.edu	San Bernardino	CA	92407	909-537-7373	537-7068
Ronald Reagan Presidential Library & Museum 40 Presidential Dr *TF:* 800-410-8354 ■ *Web:* www.reagan.utexas.edu	Simi Valley	CA	93065	805-577-4000	577-4074
Rosicrucian Egyptian Museum & Planetarium 1342 Naglee Ave Rosicrucian Pk *Web:* www.rosicrucian.org	San Jose	CA	95191	408-947-3600	947-3677
San Diego Air & Space Museum 2001 Pan American Plz Balboa Pk *Web:* sandiegoairandspace.org	San Diego	CA	92101	619-234-8291	233-4526
San Diego Aircraft Carrier Museum 910 N Harbor Dr Navy Pier *Web:* www.midway.org	San Diego	CA	92101	619-544-9600	544-9188
San Diego Archaeological Ctr 16666 San Pasqual Vly Rd *Web:* www.sandiegoarchaeology.org	Escondido	CA	92027	760-291-0370	291-0371
San Diego Automotive Museum 2080 Pan American Plz Balboa Pk *Web:* www.sdautomuseum.org	San Diego	CA	92101	619-231-2886	231-9869
San Diego Hall of Champions Sports Museum 2131 Pan American Plz Balboa Pk *Web:* www.sdhoc.com	San Diego	CA	92101	619-234-2544	234-4543
San Diego Model Railroad Museum 1649 El Prado Balboa Pk *Web:* www.sdmodelrailroadm.com	San Diego	CA	92101	619-696-0199	696-0239
San Diego Museum of Art 1450 El Prado Balboa Pk PO Box 122107 *Web:* www.sdmart.org	San Diego	CA	92101	619-232-7931	232-9367
San Diego Museum of Man 1350 El Prado Balboa Pk *Web:* www.museumofman.org	San Diego	CA	92101	619-239-2001	239-2749
San Diego Natural History Museum 1788 El Prado PO Box 121390 *Web:* www.sdnhm.org	San Diego	CA	92101	619-232-3821	232-0248
San Francisco Fire Dept Museum 655 Presidio Ave *Web:* guardiansofthecity.org	San Francisco	CA	94115	415-563-4630	
San Francisco Museum of Modern Art 151 Third St *TF:* 800-792-0754 ■ *Web:* www.sfmoma.org	San Francisco	CA	94103	415-357-4000	357-4037

Name / Address	City	State	ZIP	Phone	Fax
San Joaquin County Historical Society & Museum 11793 N Micke Grove Rd *Web:* www.sanjoaquinhistory.org	Lodi	CA	95240	209-331-2055	331-2057
San Jose Museum of Art 110 S Market St *Web:* www.sjmusart.org	San Jose	CA	95113	408-271-6840	294-2977
San Jose Museum of Quilts & Textiles 520 S First St *Web:* www.sjquiltmuseum.org	San Jose	CA	95113	408-971-0323	971-7226
Santa Barbara Museum of Art 1130 State St *Web:* www.sbmuseart.org	Santa Barbara	CA	93101	805-963-4364	966-6840
Santa Barbara Museum of Natural History 2559 Puesta Del Sol Rd *Web:* www.sbnature.org	Santa Barbara	CA	93105	805-682-4711	569-3170
Santa Monica Museum of Art 2525 Michigan Ave Ste G1 *Web:* www.smmoa.org	Santa Monica	CA	90404	310-586-6488	
Seabee Museum 99 23rd Ave *Web:* www.seabeehf.org	Port Hueneme	CA	93043	805-982-5167	
Seymour Pioneer Museum Society of California Pioneers 300 Fourth St *Web:* www.californiapioneers.org	San Francisco	CA	94107	415-957-1849	957-9858
Sherman Indian Museum 9010 Magnolia Ave *Web:* www.shermanindianmuseum.org	Riverside	CA	92503	951-276-6719	276-6336
Southwest Museum 234 Museum Dr *Web:* theautry.org	Los Angeles	CA	90065	323-221-2164	
Stanley Ranch Museum 12174 S Euclid St PO Box 4297 *Web:* www.ci.garden-grove.ca.us	Garden Grove	CA	92840	714-530-8871	534-2611
Tech Museum of Innovation 201 S Market St *TF:* 800-660-4287 ■ *Web:* www.thetech.org	San Jose	CA	95113	408-294-8324	279-7167
Timken Museum of Art 1500 El Prado Balboa Pk *Web:* www.timkenmuseum.org	San Diego	CA	92101	619-239-5548	531-9640
Triton Museum of Art 1505 Warburton Ave *Web:* www.tritonmuseum.org	Santa Clara	CA	95050	408-247-3754	247-3796
Turtle Bay Exploration Park 840 Auditorium Dr *TF:* 800-887-8532 ■ *Web:* www.turtlebay.org	Redding	CA	96001	530-243-8850	243-8898
UCLA Fowler Museum of Cultural History University of California 308 Charles E Young Dr *Web:* www.fowler.ucla.edu	Los Angeles	CA	90095	310-825-4361	206-7007
UCLA Hammer Museum 10899 Wilshire Blvd *Web:* www.hammer.ucla.edu	Los Angeles	CA	90024	310-443-7000	443-7099
University Art Museum 1250 N Bellflower Blvd *Web:* www.csulb.edu	Long Beach	CA	90840	562-985-5761	985-7602
USC Fisher Museum of Art 823 Exposition Blvd University Pk *Web:* www.usc.edu	Los Angeles	CA	90089	213-740-4561	740-7676
USS Hornet Museum 707 W Hornet Ave Pier 3 *Web:* www.uss-hornet.org	Alameda	CA	94501	510-521-8448	749-3699
Ventura County Maritime Museum 3900 Bluefin Cir *Web:* channelislandsmaritimemuseum.org	Oxnard	CA	93035	805-984-6260	984-5970
Ventura County Museum of History & Art 100 E Main St *Web:* www.venturamuseum.org	Ventura	CA	93001	805-653-0323	653-5267
Veterans Museum & Memorial Ctr 2115 Pk Blvd *Web:* www.veteranmuseum.org	San Diego	CA	92101	619-239-2300	239-7445
Walt Disney Family Museum LLC, The 104 Montgomery St *Web:* www.waltdisney.org	San Francisco	CA	94129	415-345-6800	
Wells Fargo History Museum 420 Montgomery St *Web:* www.wellsfargohistory.com	San Francisco	CA	94163	415-396-2619	975-7430
Whaley House Museum 2476 San Diego Ave *Web:* www.whaleyhouse.org	San Diego	CA	92110	619-297-7511	291-3576
William S Hart Museum 24151 Newhall Ave *Web:* www.hartmuseum.org	Newhall	CA	91321	661-254-4584	
Wings of History Air Museum 12777 Murphy Ave PO Box 495 *Web:* www.wingsofhistory.org	San Martin	CA	95046	408-683-2290	683-2291
Yerba Buena Ctr for the Arts (YBCA) 701 Mission St Fl 3 *Web:* www.ybca.org	San Francisco	CA	94103	415-978-2787	978-9635

Colorado

Name / Address	City	State	ZIP	Phone	Fax
Aspen Art Museum 590 N Mill St *Web:* aspenartmuseum.org	Aspen	CO	81611	970-925-8050	925-8054
Aurora History Museum 15051 E Alameda Pkwy *Web:* www.auroragov.org	Aurora	CO	80012	303-739-6660	739-6657
Boulder History Museum 1206 Euclid Ave *Web:* www.boulderhistory.org	Boulder	CO	80302	303-449-3464	938-8322
Boulder Museum of Contemporary Art 1750 13th St *Web:* www.bmoca.org	Boulder	CO	80302	303-443-2122	447-1633
Buffalo Bill Memorial Museum 987 1/2 Lookout Mtn Rd *Web:* www.buffalobill.org	Golden	CO	80401	303-526-0744	526-0197
Byers-Evans House Museum 1310 Bannock St *Web:* www.historycolorado.org	Denver	CO	80204	303-620-4933	620-4795
Center of Southwest Studies 1000 Rim Dr *Web:* swcenter.fortlewis.edu	Durango	CO	81301	970-247-7456	247-7422
Colorado Railroad Museum 17155 W 44th Ave *TF:* 800-365-6263 ■ *Web:* coloradorailroadmuseum.org	Golden	CO	80403	303-279-4591	279-4229
Colorado Springs Fine Arts Ctr 30 W Dale St *Web:* colorado.com	Colorado Springs	CO	80903	719-634-5581	634-0570
Colorado Springs Pioneers Museum 215 S Tejon St *Web:* www.springsgov.com	Colorado Springs	CO	80903	719-385-5990	385-5645
Denver Art Museum 100 W 14th Ave Pkwy *Web:* www.denverartmuseum.org	Denver	CO	80204	720-865-5000	913-0001
Denver Firefighters Museum 1326 Tremont Pl *Web:* www.denverfirefightersmuseum.org	Denver	CO	80204	303-892-1436	892-1436
Denver Museum of Miniatures Dolls & Toys 1880 Gaylord St *Web:* dmmdt.org	Denver	CO	80206	303-322-1053	
Denver Museum of Nature & Science 2001 Colorado Blvd *Web:* www.dmns.org	Denver	CO	80205	303-370-6000	331-6492
Forney Museum of Transportation 4303 Brighton Blvd *Web:* www.forneymuseum.org	Denver	CO	80216	303-297-1113	287-3113
Fort Collins Museum 200 Matthews St *Web:* www.fcgov.com	Fort Collins	CO	80524	970-221-6738	416-2236
Fort Collins Museum of Contemporary Art 201 S College Ave *Web:* ftcma.org	Fort Collins	CO	80524	970-482-2787	482-0804
Fort Collins Museum of Discovery 408 Mason Ct *Web:* www.fcmdsc.org	Fort Collins	CO	80524	970-221-6738	416-2236
Ghost Town Museum 400 S 21st St *Web:* www.ghosttownmuseum.com	Colorado Springs	CO	80904	719-634-0696	
History Colorado Ctr 1200 Broadway *Web:* www.historycolorado.org/adult-visitors/museums-and-historic-sites	Denver	CO	80203	303-447-8679	
Leanin' Tree Museum of Western Art 6055 Longbow Dr *TF:* 800-525-0656 ■ *Web:* www.leanintree.com	Boulder	CO	80301	303-530-1442	530-5124
Manitou Cliff Dwellings Museum 10 Cliff Rd *TF:* 800-354-9971 ■ *Web:* www.cliffdwellingsmuseum.com	Manitou Springs	CO	80829	719-685-5242	685-1562
McAllister House Museum 423 N Cascade Ave *Web:* www.mcallisterhouse.org	Colorado Springs	CO	80903	719-635-7925	
Miramont Castle Museum 9 Capitol Hill Ave *TF:* 888-685-1011 ■ *Web:* www.miramontcastle.org	Manitou Springs	CO	80829	719-685-1011	685-1985
Mizel Museum of Judaica 400 S Kearney St *Web:* www.mizelmuseum.org	Denver	CO	80224	303-394-9993	394-1119
Molly Brown House 1340 Pennsylvania St *Web:* www.mollybrown.org	Denver	CO	80203	303-832-4092	832-2340
Museo de las Americas 861 Santa Fe Dr *Web:* www.museo.org	Denver	CO	80204	303-571-4401	607-9761
Museum of Contemporary Art Denver 1485 Delgany *Web:* mcadenver.org	Denver	CO	80202	303-298-7554	298-7553
Museum of Outdoor Arts 1000 Englewood Pkwy Ste 2-230 *Web:* www.artcom.com/museums/nv/mr/80111.htm	Englewood	CO	80110	303-806-0444	806-0504
Rocky Mountain Motorcycle Museum & Hall of Fame 5867 N Nevada Ave *Web:* www.themotorcyclemuseum.com	Colorado Springs	CO	80918	719-487-8005	487-8005
Rocky Mountain Quilt Museum 1111 Washington Ave *Web:* www.rmqm.org	Golden	CO	80401	303-277-0377	215-1636
State Historical Society of Colorado 1560 Broadway Ste 400 *Web:* www.historycolorado.org	Denver	CO	80202	303-447-8679	
University of Colorado Museum of Natural History 1030 Broadway St *Web:* cumuseum.colorado.edu	Boulder	CO	80309	303-492-6892	492-4195
Vance Kirkland Museum 1311 Pearl St *Web:* www.kirklandmuseum.org	Denver	CO	80203	303-832-8576	832-8404
Western Museum of Mining & Industry 225 N Gate Blvd *TF:* 800-752-6558 ■ *Web:* www.wmmi.org	Colorado Springs	CO	80921	719-488-0880	488-9261
Wings Over the Rockies Air & Space Museum 7711 E Academy Blvd *Web:* www.wingsmuseum.org	Denver	CO	80230	303-360-5360	360-5328

Connecticut

Name / Address	City	State	ZIP	Phone	Fax
American Clock & Watch Museum 100 Maple St *Web:* www.clockmuseum.org	Bristol	CT	06010	860-583-6070	583-1862
Barnum Museum 820 Main St *Web:* www.barnum-museum.org	Bridgeport	CT	06604	203-331-1104	331-0079
Bruce Museum of Arts & Science One Museum Dr *Web:* www.brucemuseum.org	Greenwich	CT	06830	203-869-0376	869-0963
Connecticut Audubon Society Birdcraft Museum & Sanctuary 314 Unquowa Rd *Web:* www.ctaudubon.org	Fairfield	CT	06824	203-259-0416	259-1344
Connecticut Historical Society Museum One Elizabeth St *Web:* www.chs.org	Hartford	CT	06105	860-236-5621	236-2664
Connecticut Science Center Inc 250 Columbus Blvd *Web:* www.ctsciencecenter.org	Hartford	CT	06103	860-727-0457	
Connecticut State Museum of Natural History 2019 Hillside Rd *Web:* www.mnh.uconn.edu	Storrs	CT	06268	860-486-4460	486-0827
Discovery Museum & Planetarium 4450 Pk Ave *Web:* www.discoverymuseum.org	Bridgeport	CT	06604	203-372-3521	374-1929
Eli Whitney Museum 915 Whitney Ave *Web:* www.eliwhitney.org	Hamden	CT	06517	203-777-1833	777-1229

	City	State	Zip	Phone	Fax
Ethnic Heritage Ctr 270 Fitch St Southern Connecticut State University *Web:* www.southernct.edu	New Haven	CT	06515	203-392-6126	392-5140
Fairfield Museum & History Ctr 370 Beach Rd *Web:* www.fairfieldhistoricalsociety.org	Fairfield	CT	06824	203-259-1598	255-2716
Henry Whitfield State Museum 248 Old Whitfield St *Web:* www.cultureandtourism.org	Guilford	CT	06437	203-453-2457	453-7544
Hill-Stead Museum 35 Mountain Rd *Web:* www.hillstead.org	Farmington	CT	06032	860-677-4787	677-0174
Housatonic Museum of Art Housatonic Community College 900 Lafayette Blvd *Web:* www.hcc.commnet.edu	Bridgeport	CT	06604	203-332-5000	332-5123
Institute for American Indian Studies, The 38 Curtis Rd PO Box 1260 *Web:* www.iaismuseum.org	Washington	CT	06793	860-868-0518	868-1649
Knights of Columbus Museum One State St *Web:* kofcmuseum.org/km/en/	New Haven	CT	06511	203-865-0400	773-3000
Lock Museum of America 230 Main St Rt 6 PO Box 104 *Web:* lockmuseumofamerica.org	Terryville	CT	06786	860-589-6359	
Lockwood-Mathews Mansion Museum 295 W Ave *Web:* www.ohwy.com	Norwalk	CT	06850	203-838-9799	838-1434
Lyman Allyn Art Museum 625 Williams St *Web:* www.lymanallyn.org	New London	CT	06320	860-443-2545	442-1280
Mark Twain House & Museum 351 Farmington Ave *Web:* www.marktwainhouse.org	Hartford	CT	06105	860-247-0998	278-8148
Mattatuck Museum of the Mattatuck Historical Society 144 W Main St *Web:* www.mattatuckmuseum.org	Waterbury	CT	06702	203-753-0381	756-6283
Mike's Famous Harley-Davidson of Groton 951 Bank St *TF:* 800-326-6874 ■ *Web:* www.mikesfamous.com	New London	CT	06320	860-574-9200	445-4513
Mystic Seaport -- The Museum of America & the Sea 75 Greenmanville Ave PO Box 6000 *TF:* 888-973-2767 ■ *Web:* www.mysticseaport.org	Mystic	CT	06355	860-572-0711	572-5395
New Britain Museum of American Art 56 Lexington St *Web:* www.nbmaa.org	New Britain	CT	06052	860-229-0257	229-3445
Noah Webster House 227 S Main St *Web:* www.noahwebsterhouse.org	West Hartford	CT	06107	860-521-5362	521-4036
Shore Line Trolley Museum 17 River St *Web:* www.bera.org	East Haven	CT	06512	203-467-6927	467-7635
Slater Memorial Museum 108 Crescent St *Web:* slatermuseum.org	Norwich	CT	06360	860-887-2506	885-0379
Stamford Historical Society Museum 1508 High Ridge Rd *Web:* www.stamfordhistory.org	Stamford	CT	06903	203-329-1183	322-1607
Stamford Museum & Nature Ctr 39 Scofieldtown Rd *Web:* www.stamfordmuseum.org	Stamford	CT	06903	203-322-1646	322-0408
Wadsworth Atheneum Museum of Art 600 Main St *Web:* thewadsworth.org/	Hartford	CT	06103	860-278-2670	
Yale Ctr for British Art 1080 Chapel St PO Box 208280 *TF:* 877-274-8278 ■ *Web:* britishart.yale.edu	New Haven	CT	06510	203-432-2800	432-9695
Yale Peabody Museum of Natural History 170 Whitney Ave Yale University *Web:* www.peabody.yale.edu	New Haven	CT	06511	203-432-3759	432-9816
Yale University Art Gallery 1111 Chapel St *Web:* www.yale.edu	New Haven	CT	06520	203-432-0600	432-7159
Yale University Collection of Musical Instruments 15 Hillhouse Ave *Web:* www.yale.edu	New Haven	CT	06511	203-432-0822	432-8342

Delaware

	City	State	Zip	Phone	Fax
Barratt's Chapel & Museum 6362 Bay Rd *Web:* www.barrattschapel.org	Frederica	DE	19946	302-335-5544	
Delaware Agricultural Museum & Village 866 N DuPont Hwy *Web:* www.agriculturalmuseum.org	Dover	DE	19901	302-734-1618	734-0457
Delaware Art Museum 2301 Kentmere Pkwy *TF:* 800-272-8258 ■ *Web:* www.delart.org	Wilmington	DE	19806	302-571-9590	571-0220
Delaware History Museum 504 N Market St *Web:* dehistory.org/	Wilmington	DE	19801	302-656-0637	655-7844
Delaware Museum of Natural History 4840 Kennett Pk *Web:* www.delmnh.org	Wilmington	DE	19807	302-658-9111	658-2610
Hagley Museum & Library 298 Buck Rd E *Web:* www.hagley.org	Greenville	DE	19807	302-658-2400	658-0568
Harrington Museum 108 Fleming St	Harrington	DE	19952	302-398-3698	
Indian River Lifesaving Station Museum 25039 Costal Hwy *TF:* 877-987-2757 ■ *Web:* www.destateparks.com	Rehoboth Beach	DE	19971	302-227-6991	227-6438
Johnson Victrola Museum 375 S New St *Web:* history.delaware.gov	Dover	DE	19901	302-744-5055	
Kalmar Nyckel Foundation 1124 E Seventh St *Web:* www.kalmarnyckel.org	Wilmington	DE	19801	302-429-7447	429-0350
Lewes Historical Society 110 Shipcarpenter St *Web:* www.historiclewes.org	Lewes	DE	19958	302-645-7670	645-2375
Old Swedes Church & Hendrickson House Museum 606 Church St *Web:* www.oldswedes.org	Wilmington	DE	19801	302-652-5629	652-8615
Sewell C Biggs Museum of American Art 406 Federal St *Web:* www.biggsmuseum.org	Dover	DE	19901	302-674-2111	674-5133
Taylor & Messick Inc 325 Walt Messick Rd *TF:* 800-237-1272 ■ *Web:* taylormessick.com	Harrington	DE	19952	302-398-3729	398-4732
Winterthur Museum & Country Estate 5105 Kennett Pk *TF:* 800-448-3883 ■ *Web:* www.winterthur.org	Winterthur	DE	19735	302-888-4600	888-4880

District of Columbia

	City	State	Zip	Phone	Fax
African-American Civil War Memorial & Museum 1200 U St NW *Web:* www.afroamcivilwar.org	Washington	DC	20001	202-667-2667	667-6771
B'nai B'rith Klutznick National Jewish Museum 1120 20th St NW *Web:* www.bnaibrith.org	Washington	DC	20036	202-857-6600	857-6601
Cathedral Church of Saint Peter & Saint Paul 3101 Wisconsin Ave NW *TF:* 800-622-6304 ■ *Web:* www.nationalcathedral.org	Washington	DC	20016	202-537-6200	364-6600
DAR Museum 1776 D St NW *Web:* www.dar.org/museum	Washington	DC	20006	202-879-3241	628-0820
Decatur House Museum 1610 H St NW *Web:* www.whitehousehistory.org	Washington	DC	20006	202-842-0917	842-0030
Dumbarton Oaks 1703 32nd St NW *Web:* www.doaks.org	Washington	DC	20007	202-339-6400	339-6400
Frederick Douglass Museum & Hall of Fame for Caring Americans 320 A St NE *Web:* www.caringinstitute.org	Washington	DC	20002	202-547-4273	
Freer and Sackler Galleries (Smithsonian Institution) 1050 Independence Ave SW PO Box 37012 *Web:* www.asia.si.edu	Washington	DC	20013	202-633-1000	357-4911
Freer Gallery of Art / Arthur M. Sackler Gallery 1050 Independence Ave SW PO Box 37012 *Web:* www.asia.si.edu	Washington	DC	20013	202-633-1000	357-4911
Hillwood Estate Museum & Gardens 4155 Linnean Ave NW *Web:* www.hillwoodmuseum.org	Washington	DC	20008	202-686-5807	966-7846
Hirshhorn Museum & Sculpture Garden (Smithsonian Institution) 700 Independence Ave *Web:* www.hirshhorn.si.edu	Washington	DC	20560	202-633-1000	786-2682
Historical Society of Washington DC 801 K St NW Historical Society of Washington DC *Web:* www.historydc.org	Washington	DC	20001	202-249-3955	417-3823
International Spy Museum 800 F St NW *Web:* www.spymuseum.org	Washington	DC	20004	202-393-7798	393-7797
Kreeger Museum, The 2401 Foxhall Rd NW *Web:* www.kreegermuseum.org	Washington	DC	20007	202-338-3552	337-3051
Lillian & Albert Small Jewish Museum 701 Third St NW *Web:* www.loc.gov/rr/main/religion/jhw.html	Washington	DC	20001	202-789-0900	789-0485
Marian Koshland Science Museum Sixth & E Sts NW *TF:* 888-567-4526 ■ *Web:* www.koshland-science-museum.org	Washington	DC	20001	202-334-1201	334-1548
National Air & Space Museum (Smithsonian Institution) Independence Ave & Sixth St SW *Web:* airandspace.si.edu	Washington	DC	20560	202-633-1000	
National Bldg Museum 401 F St NW *Web:* www.nbm.org	Washington	DC	20001	202-272-2448	272-2564
National Children's Museum 145 Fleet St Ste 202 *Web:* www.ccm.org	National Harbor	MD	20745	301-392-2400	
National Gallery of Art Sixth St & Constitution Ave NW *Web:* www.nga.gov	Washington	DC	20565	202-737-4215	842-2356
National Geographic Society Explorers Hall 1145 17th St NW **Fax Area Code: 202* ■ *TF:* 800-647-5463 ■ *Web:* www.nationalgeographic.com	Washington	DC	20036	800-647-5463	429-5709*
National Ladies Auxiliary Jewish War Veterans of USA Inc 1811 R St Nw *Web:* www.jwv.org	Washington	DC	20009	202-667-9061	
National Museum of African Art (Smithsonian Institution) 950 Independence Ave SW MRC 708 *Web:* africa.si.edu	Washington	DC	20560	202-633-4600	357-4879
National Museum of American History (Smithsonian Institution) (NMAH) 14th St & Constitution Ave NW *Web:* americanhistory.si.edu	Washington	DC	20560	202-633-1000	
National Museum of American Jewish Military History (JWV-NMI) 1811 R St NW *Web:* www.nmajmh.org	Washington	DC	20009	202-265-6280	462-3192
National Museum of Natural History (Smithsonian Institution) 10th St & Constitution Ave NW *TF:* 866-868-7774 ■ *Web:* www.mnh.si.edu	Washington	DC	20560	202-633-1000	357-4779
National Museum of the American Indian (Smithsonian Institution) 4th St & Independence Ave SW *Web:* www.nmai.si.edu	Washington	DC	20560	202-633-1000	
National Museum of Women in the Arts 1250 New York Ave NW *TF:* 866-875-4627 ■ *Web:* www.nmwa.org	Washington	DC	20005	202-783-5000	393-3234
National Postal Museum (Smithsonian Institution) Two Massachusetts Ave NE *Web:* www.postalmuseum.si.edu	Washington	DC	20002	202-633-5555	633-9393
Navy Museum 805 Kidder Breese St SE Washington Navy Yard *Web:* www.history.navy.mil	Washington	DC	20374	202-433-4882	433-8200
Newseum Inc 555 Pennsylvania Ave Nw *Web:* www.newseum.org	Washington	DC	20001	202-292-6100	
Phillips Collection 1600 21st St NW *Web:* www.phillipscollection.org	Washington	DC	20009	202-387-2151	387-2436

				Phone	Fax
Renwick Gallery of the Smithsonian American Art Museum 1661 Pennsylvania Ave NW *Web:* americanart.si.edu/renwick	Washington	DC	20006	202-633-7970	786-2810
Smithsonian Institution SI Bldg Rm 153 MRC 010 PO Box 37012 *Web:* www.si.edu	Washington	DC	20013	202-633-1000	
Textile Museum, The 2320 S St NW *Web:* museum.gwu.edu/	Washington	DC	20008	202-667-0441	483-0994
US Holocaust Memorial Museum 100 Raoul Wallenburg Pl SW *Web:* www.ushmm.org	Washington	DC	20024	202-488-0400	488-2613
Woodrow Wilson House Museum 2340 S St NW *Web:* www.woodrowwilsonhouse.org	Washington	DC	20008	202-387-4062	483-1466

Florida

				Phone	Fax
African American Museum of the Arts 325 S Clara Ave *Web:* www.africanamericanmuseumdeland.org	DeLand	FL	32721	386-736-4004	736-4088
Amelia Island Museum of History 233 S Third St *Web:* ameliamuseum.org	Fernandina Beach	FL	32034	904-261-7378	261-9701
American Police Hall of Fame & Museum 6350 Horizon Dr *Web:* www.aphf.org	Titusville	FL	32780	321-264-0911	264-0033
Audubon House & Tropical Garden 250 Whitehead St *Web:* www.audubonhouse.com	Key West	FL	33040	305-294-2116	
Bailey Matthews Shell Museum 3075 Sanibel-Captiva Rd PO Box 1580 *TF:* 888-679-6450 ■ *Web:* www.shellmuseum.org	Sanibel	FL	33957	239-395-2233	395-6706
Black Archives Research Ctr & Museum 445 Gamble St Rm 207 *Web:* cis.famu.edu	Tallahassee	FL	32307	850-599-3020	
Boca Raton Museum of Art 501 Plaza Real Mizner Pk *TF:* 888-472-4732 ■ *Web:* www.bocamuseum.org	Boca Raton	FL	33432	561-392-2500	391-6410
Bonnet House Museum & Garden 900 N Birch Rd *Web:* www.bonnethouse.org	Fort Lauderdale	FL	33304	954-563-5393	561-4174
Broward County Historical Commission 151 SW Second St *TF:* 866-682-2258 ■ *Web:* www.broward.org	Fort Lauderdale	FL	33301	954-765-4670	765-4437
Charles Hosmer Morse Museum of American Art 445 N Pk Ave *Web:* www.morsemuseum.org	Winter Park	FL	32789	407-645-5311	647-1284
Collier County Museum 3331 Tamiami Trl E *Web:* www.colliermuseums.com	Naples	FL	34112	239-252-8476	
Colonial Spanish Quarter Museum 33 St George St *Web:* colonialquarter.com	Saint Augustine	FL	32084	904-825-6830	825-6874
Cornell Fine Arts Museum 1000 Holt Ave *Web:* www.rollins.edu/cfam	Winter Park	FL	32789	407-646-2526	646-2524
Crowley Museum & Nature Ctr 16405 Myakka Rd *Web:* www.crowleymuseumnaturectr.org	Sarasota	FL	34240	941-322-1000	322-1000
Cummer Museum of Art & Gardens 829 Riverside Ave *Web:* www.cummer.org	Jacksonville	FL	32204	904-356-6857	353-4101
Florida Agricultural Museum 7900 Old Kings Rd *Web:* www.myagmuseum.com	Palm Coast	FL	32137	386-446-7630	446-7631
Florida Heritage Museum 167 San Marco Ave *TF:* 800-268-7252 ■ *Web:* www.amtrakvacations.com	Saint Augustine	FL	32084	904-829-9729	
Florida Holocaust Museum 55 Fifth St S *TF:* 800-388-4069 ■ *Web:* www.flholocaustmuseum.org	Saint Petersburg	FL	33701	727-820-0100	821-8435
Florida International Museum 244 Second Ave N St Petersburg College Downtown Ctr *Web:* www.floridamuseum.org	Saint Petersburg	FL	33701	727-341-7900	341-7908
Florida Museum of Natural History Museum Rd & Newell Dr PO Box 117800 *Web:* www.flmnh.ufl.edu	Gainesville	FL	32611	352-392-1721	392-8783
Florida State University Museum of Fine Arts 530 W Call St Fine Arts Bldg *Web:* www.mofa.fsu.edu	Tallahassee	FL	32306	850-644-6836	644-7229
Fort East Martello Museum 3501 S Roosevelt Blvd *Web:* kwahs.com	Key West	FL	33040	305-296-3913	296-6206
Fort Lauderdale Antique Car Museum 1527 SW First Ave *Web:* www.antiquecarmuseum.org	Fort Lauderdale	FL	33315	954-779-7300	779-2501
Fort Lauderdale Historical Society 219 SW Second Ave *Web:* fortlauderdalehistorycenter.org	Fort Lauderdale	FL	33301	954-463-4431	523-6228
Fort Lauderdale Museum of Art One E Las Olas Blvd *Web:* www.moafl.org	Fort Lauderdale	FL	33301	954-525-5500	524-6011
Frost Art Museum at Florida International University 10975 SW 17th St *Web:* thefrost.fiu.edu	Miami	FL	33199	305-348-2890	348-2762
Gillespie Museum of Minerals 421 N Woodland Blvd Unit 8403 *TF:* 800-688-0101 ■ *Web:* www.stetson.edu	DeLand	FL	32723	386-822-7330	822-7328
Goodwood Museum & Gardens 1600 Miccosukee Rd *Web:* www.goodwoodmuseum.org	Tallahassee	FL	32308	850-877-4202	877-3090
Gulf Beaches Historical Museum 115 Tenth Ave *Web:* gulfbeachesmuseum.com	Saint Pete Beach	FL	33706	727-552-1610	363-6704
Halifax Historical Museum 252 S Beach St *Web:* www.halifaxhistorical.org	Daytona Beach	FL	32114	386-255-6976	255-7605
Harry S Truman's Little White House Museum 111 Front St Truman Annex *TF:* 800-435-7352 ■ *Web:* www.trumanlittlewhitehouse.com	Key West	FL	33040	305-294-9911	294-9988
Henry B Plant Museum 401 W Kennedy Blvd *Web:* www.plantmuseum.com	Tampa	FL	33606	813-254-1891	258-7272
Henry Morrison Flagler Museum One Whitehall Way *Web:* www.flaglermuseum.us	Palm Beach	FL	33480	561-655-2833	655-2826
Historical Museum of Southern Florida 101 W Flagler St *Web:* www.historical-museum.org	Miami	FL	33130	305-375-1492	375-1609
Historical Society of Palm Beach County, The 300 N Dixie Hwy Ste 471 *Web:* www.historicalsocietypbc.org	West Palm Beach	FL	33401	561-832-4164	
Indian Temple Mound Museum 107 Miracle Strip Pkwy SW *TF:* 866-847-1301 ■ *Web:* www.fwb.org	Fort Walton Beach	FL	32548	850-833-9500	833-9640
Jacksonville Maritime Museum 2 Independent Dr Ste 162 *Web:* www.jacksonvillemaritimeheritagecenter.org	Jacksonville	FL	32202	904-355-1101	355-1106
Jacksonville Museum of Modern Art 333 N Laura St *Web:* www.mocajacksonville.org	Jacksonville	FL	32202	904-366-6911	366-6901
Jewish Museum of Florida 301 Washington Ave *Web:* jmof.fiu.edu	Miami Beach	FL	33139	305-672-5044	672-5933
John & Mable Ringling Museum of Art 5401 Bay Shore Rd *Web:* www.ringling.org	Sarasota	FL	34243	941-359-5700	358-3177
John G Riley Ctr/Museum of African American History & Culture 419 E Jefferson St *Web:* www.rileymuseum.org	Tallahassee	FL	32301	850-681-7881	681-7000
Key West Art & Historical Society 281 Front St *Web:* www.kwahs.com	Key West	FL	33040	305-295-6616	295-6649
Key West Lighthouse & Keepers Quarters Museum 938 Whitehead St *Web:* www.kwahs.org	Key West	FL	33040	305-294-0012	294-0012
Kingsley Plantation 11676 Palmetto Ave *TF:* 877-874-2478 ■ *Web:* www.nps.gov/timu	Jacksonville	FL	32226	904-251-3537	251-3577
Knott House Museum 301 E Pk Ave *Web:* museumoffloridahistory.com	Tallahassee	FL	32301	850-922-2459	413-7261
Lightner Museum, The 75 King St PO Box 334 *Web:* www.lightnermuseum.org	Saint Augustine	FL	32084	904-824-2874	824-2712
Lowe Art Museum University of Miami 1301 Stanford Dr *Web:* www6.miami.edu/lowe/	Coral Gables	FL	33124	305-284-3535	284-2024
Loxahatchee River Historical Museum 500 Captian Armours Way Burt Reynolds Pk *TF:* 800-435-7352 ■ *Web:* jupiterlighthouse.org	Jupiter	FL	33469	561-747-8380	575-3292
Mel Fisher Maritime Museum 200 Greene St *Web:* www.melfisher.org	Key West	FL	33040	305-294-2633	294-5671
Mennello Museum of American Folk Art 900 E Princeton St *Web:* www.mennellomuseum.com	Orlando	FL	32803	407-246-4278	246-4329
Miami Museum of Science & Planetarium 3280 S Miami Ave *Web:* www.miamisci.org	Miami	FL	33129	305-646-4200	646-4300
Morikami Museum & Japanese Gardens 4000 Morikami Pk Rd *Web:* www.morikami.org	Delray Beach	FL	33446	561-495-0233	499-2557
Museum of Arts & Sciences 352 S Nova Rd *Web:* www.moas.org	Daytona Beach	FL	32114	386-255-0285	255-5040
Museum of Contemporary Art Inc 770 NE 125th St Joan Lehman Bldg *Web:* www.mocanomi.org	North Miami	FL	33161	305-893-6211	
Museum of Fine Arts 255 Beach Dr NE *Web:* www.fine-arts.org	Saint Petersburg	FL	33701	727-896-2667	894-4638
Museum of Florida History 500 S Bronough St RA Gray Bldg *Web:* www.museumoffloridahistory.com	Tallahassee	FL	32399	850-245-6400	245-6433
Museum of Science & History of Jacksonville 1025 Museum Cir *Web:* www.themosh.org	Jacksonville	FL	32207	904-396-6674	
Museum of Southern History 4304 Herschel St *Web:* www.scv-kirby-smith.org	Jacksonville	FL	32210	904-388-3574	
Museum of the Americas (MoA) 2500 NW 79th Ave Ste 104 *Web:* www.museumamericas.org	Doral	FL	33122	305-599-8089	
Museum of the Everglades 105 W Broadway PO Box 8 *Web:* colliermuseums.com	Everglades City	FL	34139	239-695-0008	695-0036
My Jewish Discovery Place Children's Museum 6501 W Sunrise Blvd *Web:* www.sorefjcc.org	Plantation	FL	33313	954-792-6700	792-4839
Naples Museum of Art 5833 Pelican Bay Blvd *TF:* 800-597-1900 ■ *Web:* artisnaples.org	Naples	FL	34108	239-597-1111	597-8163
National Museum of Naval Aviation 1750 Radford Blvd Ste C *TF General:* 800-247-6289 ■ *Web:* www.navalaviationmuseum.org	Pensacola	FL	32508	850-452-3604	452-3296
Norton Museum of Art 1451 S Olive Ave *Web:* www.norton.org	West Palm Beach	FL	33401	561-832-5196	659-4689
Old Dillard Museum 1009 NW Fourth St *Web:* www.browardschools.com	Fort Lauderdale	FL	33311	754-322-8828	
Old Florida Museum 259 San Marco Ave *TF:* 800-813-3208 ■ *Web:* www.oldfloridamuseum.com	Saint Augustine	FL	32084	904-824-8874	

				Phone	Fax
Orange County Regional History Ctr 65 E Central Blvd *TF:* 800-965-2030 ■ *Web:* www.thehistorycenter.org	Orlando	FL	32801	407-836-8500	836-8550
Orlando Museum of Art 2416 N Mills Ave *TF:* 800-435-7352 ■ *Web:* www.omart.org	Orlando	FL	32803	407-896-4231	896-9920
Orlando Science Ctr 777 E Princeton St *TF:* 888-672-4386 ■ *Web:* www.osc.org	Orlando	FL	32803	407-514-2000	514-2277
Ormond Memorial Art Museum & Gardens 78 E Granada Blvd *Web:* www.ormondartmuseum.org	Ormond Beach	FL	32176	386-676-3347	676-3244
Palm Beach Photographic Centre 415 Clematis St *Web:* www.workshop.org	West Palm Beach	FL	33401	561-253-2600	
Pensacola Museum of Art 407 S Jefferson St *Web:* www.pensacolamuseum.org	Pensacola	FL	32502	850-432-6247	469-1532
Perez Art Museum Miami 101 W Flagler St *Web:* www.pamm.org	Miami	FL	33130	305-375-3000	375-1725
Pinellas County Heritage Village 11909 125th St N *Web:* www.pinellascounty.org	Largo	FL	33774	727-582-2123	582-2455
Pro Clear Aquatic Systems Inc 2959 Mercury Rd *Web:* www.pro-clear.com	Jacksonville	FL	32207	904-448-6800	
Ripley's Believe It or Not! Orlando Odditorium 8201 International Dr *Web:* www.ripleys.com	Orlando	FL	32819	407-345-0501	345-0803
Ritz Theatre & La Villa Museum 829 N Davis St *Web:* www.ritzjacksonville.com	Jacksonville	FL	32202	904-632-5555	632-5553
Saint Augustine Lighthouse & Museum 81 Lighthouse Ave *Web:* www.staugustinelighthouse.com	Saint Augustine	FL	32080	904-829-0745	808-1248
Saint Petersburg Museum of History (SPMOH) 335 Second Ave NE	Saint Petersburg	FL	33701	727-894-1052	525-8689
South Florida Museum 201 Tenth St W *Web:* www.southfloridamuseum.org	Bradenton	FL	34205	941-746-4131	747-2556
South Florida Science Museum 4801 Dreher Trail N *Web:* www.sfsciencecenter.org	West Palm Beach	FL	33405	561-832-1988	833-0551
Southeast Museum of Photography 1200 W International Speedway Blvd Bldg 100 Daytona Beach Community College *Web:* www.smponline.org	Daytona Beach	FL	32114	386-506-4475	506-4487
Stranahan House Museum Inc 335 SE Sixth Ave *TF:* 800-435-7352 ■ *Web:* www.stranahanhouse.org	Fort Lauderdale	FL	33301	954-524-4736	525-2838
Tallahassee Antique Car Museum 6800 Mahan Dr *Web:* www.tacm.com	Tallahassee	FL	32308	850-942-0137	576-8500
Tallahassee Museum of History & Natural Science 3945 Museum Dr *Web:* www.tallahasseemuseum.org	Tallahassee	FL	32310	850-576-1636	574-8243
Tampa Bay History Ctr 801 Old Water St *TF:* 800-352-3671 ■ *Web:* www.tampabayhistorycenter.org	Tampa	FL	33602	813-228-0097	223-7021
Tampa Museum of Art 120 W Gasparilla Plaza *TF:* 866-790-4111 ■ *Web:* www.tampagov.net	Tampa	FL	33602	813-274-8130	274-8732
University Galleries 400 SW 13th St Fine Arts Bldg B PO Box 115803 *TF:* 800-745-3000 ■ *Web:* www.arts.ufl.edu	Gainesville	FL	32611	352-273-3000	846-0266
Vizcaya Museum & Gardens 3251 S Miami Ave *Web:* vizcaya.org	Miami	FL	33129	305-250-9133	285-2004
Wolfsonian Museum 1001 Washington Ave	Miami Beach	FL	33139	305-531-1001	531-2133
Ximenez-Fatio House Museum 20 Aviles St *Web:* www.ximenezfatiohouse.org	Saint Augustine	FL	32084	904-829-3575	829-3445
Ybor City Museum State Park 1818 Ninth Ave *Web:* www.floridastateparks.org	Tampa	FL	33605	813-247-6323	

Georgia

				Phone	Fax
African-American Panoramic Experience Museum 135 Auburn Ave NE *Web:* www.apexmuseum.org	Atlanta	GA	30303	404-523-2739	523-3248
Atlanta History Ctr 130 W Paces Ferry Rd *Web:* www.atlantahistorycenter.com	Atlanta	GA	30305	404-814-4000	814-2041
Augusta Museum of History 560 Reynolds St *Web:* www.augustamuseum.org	Augusta	GA	30901	706-722-8454	724-5192
Coca-Cola Space Science Ctr 701 Front Ave *Web:* www.ccssc.org	Columbus	GA	31901	706-649-1470	649-1478
Columbus Museum 1251 Wynnton Rd *Web:* www.columbusmuseum.com	Columbus	GA	31906	706-748-2562	748-2570
Davenport House Museum 324 E State St *Web:* www.davenporthousemuseum.org	Savannah	GA	31401	912-236-8097	233-7938
Fernbank Science Ctr 156 Heaton Pk Dr NE *Web:* fernbank.edu	Atlanta	GA	30307	678-874-7102	874-7110
Georgia Museum of Art 90 Carlton St University of Georgia *Web:* www.uga.edu	Athens	GA	30602	706-542-4662	542-1051
Gertrude Herbert Institute of Art 506 Telfair St *Web:* www.ghia.org	Augusta	GA	30901	706-722-5495	722-3670
Goethe Institut Atlanta/German Cultural Ctr 1197 Peachtree St NE *TF:* 888-446-3843 ■ *Web:* www.goethe.de	Atlanta	GA	30361	404-892-2388	892-3832
High Museum of Art 1280 Peachtree St NE *Web:* www.high.org	Atlanta	GA	30309	404-733-4400	733-4502
Jimmy Carter Library & Museum 441 Freedom Pkwy *Web:* www.jimmycarterlibrary.gov	Atlanta	GA	30307	404-865-7100	865-7102
Lucy Craft Laney Museum 1116 Phillips St *Web:* www.lucycraftlaneymuseum.com	Augusta	GA	30901	706-724-3576	724-3576
Michael C Carlos Museum 571 S Kilgo St *Web:* www.carlos.emory.edu	Atlanta	GA	30322	404-727-4282	727-4292
Mighty Eighth Air Force Museum 175 Bourne Ave *Web:* www.mightyeighth.org	Pooler	GA	31322	912-748-8888	748-0209
Morris Museum of Art 1 Tenth St *Web:* www.themorris.org	Augusta	GA	30901	706-724-7501	724-7612
Museum of Aviation PO Box 2469 *Web:* www.museumofaviation.org	Warner Robins	GA	31099	478-926-2791	
Museum of Design Atlanta 285 Peachtree Ctr Ave *Web:* www.museumofdesign.org	Atlanta	GA	30303	404-979-6455	521-9311
National Infantry Museum 1775 Legacy Way *Web:* www.nationalinfantrymuseum.org	Columbus	GA	31903	706-685-5800	545-5158
National Museum of Patriotism 1927 Piedmont Cir *Web:* foundationofpatriotism.org	Atlanta	GA	30324	404-875-0691	
Oak Hill & Martha Berry Museum 2277 Martha Berry Hwy NW PO Box 490189 *Web:* www.berry.edu	Mount Berry	GA	30149	706-291-1883	802-0902
Oglethorpe University Museum of Art 4484 Peachtree Rd NE *Web:* museum.oglethorpe.edu	Atlanta	GA	30319	404-364-8555	364-8556
Port Columbus National Civil War Naval Museum 1002 Victory Dr *Web:* www.portcolumbus.org	Port Columbus	GA	31901	706-327-9798	324-7225
Robert C Williams American Museum of Papermaking 500 Tenth St NW *TF:* 800-558-6611 ■ *Web:* www.ipst.gatech.edu	Atlanta	GA	30318	404-894-7840	894-4778
Savannah History Museum 303 ML King Jr Blvd *Web:* www.chsgeorgia.org	Savannah	GA	31401	912-651-6840	651-6971
Ships of the Sea Maritime Museum 41 Martin Luther King Junior Blvd *Web:* www.shipsofthesea.org	Savannah	GA	31401	912-232-1511	234-7363
Telfair Museum of Art 121 Barnard St *Web:* telfair.org	Savannah	GA	31401	912-790-8800	
Tubman African American Museum 340 Walnut St *Web:* www.tubmanmuseum.com	Macon	GA	31201	478-743-8544	743-9063
Tybee Island Lighthouse & Museum 30 Meddin Dr *Web:* www.tybeelighthouse.org	Tybee Island	GA	31328	912-786-5801	786-6538
Westville 1850's Village 9294 Singer Pond Rd PO Box 1850 *TF:* 888-733-1850 ■ *Web:* www.westville.org	Lumpkin	GA	31815	229-838-6310	838-4000
William Breman Jewish Heritage Museum 1440 Spring St NW **Fax Area Code:* 404 ■ *Web:* www.thebreman.org	Atlanta	GA	30309	678-222-3700	881-4009*
World of Coca-Cola Atlanta 121 Baker St NW *TF:* 888-855-5701 ■ *Web:* www.worldofcoca-cola.com	Atlanta	GA	30313	404-676-5151	586-6299
Wren's Nest, The 1050 Ralph David Abernathy Blvd SW *Web:* wrensnest.org	Atlanta	GA	30310	404-753-7735	753-8535

Hawaii

				Phone	Fax
Bishop Museum 1525 Bernice St **Fax:* Hum Res ■ *Web:* www.bishopmuseum.org	Honolulu	HI	96817	808-847-3511	848-4146*
Hawaii's Plantation Village (HPV) 94-695 Waipahu St *Web:* www.hawaiiplantationvillage.org	Waipahu	HI	96797	808-677-0110	676-6727
Honolulu Academy of Arts 900 S Beretania St *TF:* 866-385-3849 ■ *Web:* honolulumuseum.org	Honolulu	HI	96814	808-532-8700	532-8787
Japanese Cultural Ctr of Hawaii 2454 S Beretania St *Web:* www.jcch.com	Honolulu	HI	96826	808-945-7633	944-1123
King Kamehameha V - Judiciary History Ctr 417 S King St *Web:* jhchawaii.net	Honolulu	HI	96813	808-539-4999	539-4996
Lyman Museum & Mission House 276 Haili St *Web:* www.lymanmuseum.org	Hilo	HI	96720	808-935-5021	969-7685
Mission Houses Museum 553 S King St *Web:* www.missionhouses.org	Honolulu	HI	96813	808-447-3910	545-2280
Pacific Aviation Museum Pearl Harbor 319 Lexington Blvd *Web:* www.pacificaviationmuseum.org	Honolulu	HI	96818	808-441-1017	
Polynesian Cultural Ctr 55-370 Kamehameha Hwy *TF:* 800-367-7060 ■ *Web:* www.polynesia.com	Laie	HI	96762	808-293-3005	293-3027
Tropic Lightning Museum Schofield Barracks Bldg 361 Waianae Ave *Web:* www.25idl.army.mil	Honolulu	HI	96857	808-655-0438	655-8301
US Army Museum of Hawaii PO Box 8064 *Web:* www.hiarmymuseumsoc.org	Honolulu	HI	96830	808-438-2821	941-3617
USS Bowfin Submarine Museum & Park 11 Arizona Memorial Dr *Web:* www.bowfin.org	Honolulu	HI	96818	808-423-1341	422-5201

Idaho

				Phone	Fax
Basque Museum & Cultural Ctr 611 W Grove St *Web:* www.basquemuseum.com	Boise	ID	83702	208-343-2671	336-4801
Boise Art Museum 670 Julia Davis Dr *Web:* www.boiseartmuseum.org	Boise	ID	83702	208-345-8330	345-2247
Discovery Ctr of Idaho (DCI) 131 Myrtle St *Web:* www.dcidaho.com	Boise	ID	83702	208-343-9895	343-0105
Idaho Black History Museum 508 Julia Davis Dr *Web:* www.ibhm.org	Boise	ID	83702	208-433-0017	
Idaho Historical Museum 610 N Julia Davis Dr *Web:* history.idaho.gov	Boise	ID	83702	208-334-2120	334-4059
Idaho Military History Museum 4692 W Harvard St *Web:* museum.mil.idaho.gov	Boise	ID	83705	208-272-4841	

	City	State	ZIP	Phone	Fax
Museum of North Idaho 115 NW Blvd PO Box 812 *Web:* www.museumni.org	Coeur d'Alene	ID	83816	208-664-3448	664-3448
Nez Perce County Historical Society & Museum 0306 Third St *Web:* npchistsoc.org	Lewiston	ID	83501	208-743-2535	
Warhawk Air Museum 201 Municipal Dr *Web:* www.warhawkairmuseum.org	Nampa	ID	83687	208-465-6446	465-6232

Illinois

	City	State	ZIP	Phone	Fax
Abraham Lincoln Presidential Library & Museum 112 N Sixth St *TF:* 800-610-2094 ■ *Web:* www.alplm.org	Springfield	IL	62701	217-557-6250	
African American Museum Hall of Fame 309 Du Sable St *Web:* aahfmpeoria.org	Peoria	IL	61605	309-673-2206	
Art Institute of Chicago 111 S Michigan Ave *Web:* www.artic.edu	Chicago	IL	60603	312-443-3600	
Balzekas Museum of Lithuanian Culture 6500 S Pulaski Rd *Web:* www.balzekasmuseum.org	Chicago	IL	60629	773-582-6500	582-5133
Burpee Museum of Natural History 737 N Main St *Web:* www.burpee.org	Rockford	IL	61103	815-965-3433	965-2703
Chanute Air Museum 1011 Pacesetter Dr *Web:* www.aeromuseum.org	Rantoul	IL	61866	217-893-1613	892-5774
Chicago History Museum 1601 N Clark St *Web:* www.chicagohs.org	Chicago	IL	60614	312-642-4600	266-2077
Clarke House Museum 1827 S Indiana Ave *Web:* www.cityofchicago.org	Chicago	IL	60616	312-326-1480	745-0077
Daughters of Union Veterans of the Civil War 503 S Walnut St PO Box 211 *Web:* www.duvcw.org	Springfield	IL	62704	217-544-0616	
DuSable Museum of African American History 740 E 56th Pl *Web:* www.dusablemuseum.org	Chicago	IL	60637	773-947-0600	947-0716
Erlander Home Museum 404 S Third St *Web:* www.swedishhistorical.org	Rockford	IL	61104	815-963-5559	963-5559
Ernest Hemingway Museum 200 N Oak Pk Ave *Web:* www.ehfop.org	Oak Park	IL	60302	708-524-5383	
Ethnic Heritage Museum 1129 S Main St *Web:* ethnicheritagemuseum.org	Rockford	IL	61101	815-962-7402	
Field Museum, The 1400 S Lk Shore Dr *Web:* www.fieldmuseum.org	Chicago	IL	60605	312-922-9410	
Frank Lloyd Wright Home & Studio 951 Chicago Ave *Web:* flwright.org	Oak Park	IL	60302	708-848-1976	848-1248
Glessner House Museum 1800 S Prairie Ave *TF:* 800-657-0687 ■ *Web:* www.glessnerhouse.org	Chicago	IL	60616	312-326-1480	326-1397
Hellenic Museum & Cultural Ctr 333 S Halsted Ave *Web:* www.nationalhellenicmuseum.org	Chicago	IL	60661	312-655-1234	655-1221
Illinois State Military Museum 1301 N MacArthur Blvd Ste 30 *TF:* 800-732-8868 ■ *Web:* www.il.ngb.army.mil	Springfield	IL	62702	217-761-3910	761-3709
Illinois State Museum 502 S Spring St *Web:* www.museum.state.il.us	Springfield	IL	62706	217-782-7386	782-1254
International Museum of Surgical Science 1524 N Lk Shore Dr *Web:* www.imss.org	Chicago	IL	60610	312-642-6502	642-9516
Intuit The Center for Intuitive & Outsider 756 N Milwaukee Ave *Web:* www.art.org	Chicago	IL	60642	312-243-9088	
ISM Dickson Mounds Museum 10956 N Dickson Mounds Rd *Web:* www.museum.state.il.us/ismsites/dickson	Lewistown	IL	61542	309-547-3721	547-3189
Krannert Art Museum & Kinkead Pavilion 500 E Peabody Dr *Web:* www.kam.uiuc.edu	Champaign	IL	61820	217-333-1861	333-0883
Lincoln's New Salem State Historic Site 15588 History Ln *Web:* www.lincolnsnewsalem.com	Petersburg	IL	62675	217-632-4000	632-4010
Lizzadro Museum of Lapidary Art 220 Cottage Hill Ave Wilder Pk *Web:* www.lizzadromuseum.org	Elmhurst	IL	60126	630-833-1616	833-1225
Midway Village Museum 6799 Guilford Rd *Web:* www.midwayvillage.com	Rockford	IL	61107	815-397-9112	397-9156
Museum of Contemporary Art 220 E Chicago Ave *Web:* www.mcachicago.org	Chicago	IL	60611	312-280-2660	397-4095
Museum of Contemporary Photography 600 S Michigan Ave Columbia College *Web:* www.mocp.org	Chicago	IL	60605	312-663-5554	369-8067
Museum of Science & Industry 5700 S Lk Shore Dr *TF:* 800-468-6674 ■ *Web:* www.msichicago.org	Chicago	IL	60637	773-684-1414	684-7141
Museum of the Grand Prairie 600 N Lombard St PO Box 1040 *Web:* www.museumofthegrandprairie.org	Mahomet	IL	61853	217-586-3360	586-5724
National Museum of Mexican Art 1852 W 19th St *Web:* www.nationalmuseumofmexicanart.org	Chicago	IL	60608	312-738-1503	738-9740
National Museum of Surveying 521 E Washington St PO Box 522 *Web:* www.surveyhistory.org	Springfield	IL	62701	217-523-3130	
Oriental Institute Museum 1155 E 58th St University of Chicago *TF:* 800-791-9354 ■ *Web:* www.oi.uchicago.edu	Chicago	IL	60637	773-702-9514	702-9853
Peggy Notebaert Nature Museum 2430 N Cannon Dr *Web:* www.naturemuseum.org	Chicago	IL	60614	773-755-5100	755-5199
Peoria Riverfront Museum 222 SW Washington St *Web:* www.peoriariverfrontmuseum.org	Peoria	IL	61602	309-686-7000	
Polish Museum of America (PMA) 984 N Milwaukee Ave *TF:* 800-535-2071 ■ *Web:* www.polishmuseumofamerica.org	Chicago	IL	60642	773-384-3352	384-3799
Quincy Museum 1601 Maine St *Web:* www.thequincymuseum.com	Quincy	IL	62301	217-224-7669	224-9323
Rockford Art Museum 711 N Main St *TF:* 800-521-0849 ■ *Web:* www.rockfordartmuseum.org	Rockford	IL	61103	815-968-2787	316-2179
Sousa Archives & Ctr for American Music (SACAM) 1103 S Sixth St 236 Harding Band Bldg *Web:* www.library.illinois.edu	Champaign	IL	61820	217-244-9309	244-8695
Spertus Museum 610 S Michigan Ave *Web:* www.spertus.edu	Chicago	IL	60605	312-322-1700	922-6406
Spurlock Museum *University of Illinois at Urbana* 600 S Gregory St *Web:* www.spurlock.illinois.edu	Urbana	IL	61801	217-333-2360	244-9419
Swedish American Museum 5211 N Clark St *Web:* www.swedishamericanmuseum.org	Chicago	IL	60640	773-728-8111	728-8870
Tinker Swiss Cottage Museum 411 Kent St *Web:* www.tinkercottage.com	Rockford	IL	61102	815-964-2424	964-2466
Ukrainian National Museum 2249 W Superior St *Web:* www.ukrainiannationalmuseum.org	Chicago	IL	60612	312-421-8020	

Indiana

	City	State	ZIP	Phone	Fax
Auburn Cord Duesenberg Museum 1600 S Wayne St *Web:* www.automobilemuseum.org	Auburn	IN	46706	260-925-1444	925-6266
Children's Museum of Indianapolis 3000 N Meridian St *Web:* www.childrensmuseum.org	Indianapolis	IN	46208	317-334-3322	920-2001
Conner Prairie Living History Museum 13400 Allisonville Rd *TF:* 800-966-1836 ■ *Web:* www.connerprairie.org	Fishers	IN	46038	317-776-6000	776-6014
Dan Quayle Ctr 815 Warren St PO Box 856 *Web:* www.quaylemuseum.org	Huntington	IN	46750	260-356-6356	
Eiteljorg Museum of American Indians & Western Art 500 W Washington St *Web:* www.eiteljorg.org	Indianapolis	IN	46204	317-636-9378	275-1400
Evansville Museum of Arts History & Science 411 SE Riverside Dr *Web:* www.emuseum.org	Evansville	IN	47713	812-425-2406	421-7509
Firefighters' Museum 226 W Washington Blvd *Web:* fortwaynefiremuseum.com	Fort Wayne	IN	46802	260-426-0051	
Fort Wayne Museum of Art 311 E Main St *Web:* www.fwmoa.org	Fort Wayne	IN	46802	260-422-6467	422-1374
Freetown Village Living History Museum PO Box 1041 *Web:* www.freetown.org	Indianapolis	IN	46206	317-631-1870	631-0224
History Ctr 302 E Berry St *Web:* www.fwhistorycenter.com	Fort Wayne	IN	46802	260-426-2882	424-4419
Indiana Medical History Museum 3045 W Vermont St *Web:* imhm.org	Indianapolis	IN	46222	317-635-7329	635-7349
Indiana State Museum 650 W Washington St *Web:* www.in.gov	Indianapolis	IN	46204	317-232-1637	
Indiana University Art Museum 1133 E Seventh St *Web:* www.indiana.edu	Bloomington	IN	47405	812-855-5445	855-1023
Indianapolis Motor Speedway & Hall of Fame Museum 4790 W 16th St *Web:* www.indianapolismotorspeedway.com	Indianapolis	IN	46222	317-492-6747	492-6571
Indianapolis Museum of Art 4000 Michigan Rd *Web:* www.imamuseum.org	Indianapolis	IN	46208	317-923-1331	931-1978
James Whitcomb Riley Museum Home 528 Lockerbie St *Web:* www.rileykids.org	Indianapolis	IN	46202	317-631-5885	
Macedonian Tribune Museum 124 W Wayne St Ste 204 *Web:* www.macedonian.org	Fort Wayne	IN	46802	260-422-5900	422-1348
Mathers Museum of World Cultures 416 N Indiana Ave *Web:* indiana.edu	Bloomington	IN	47408	812-855-6873	855-0205
Monroe County History Ctr 202 E Sixth St *Web:* monroehistory.org	Bloomington	IN	47408	812-332-2517	355-5593
Northern Indiana Ctr for History 808 W Washington St *Web:* www.centerforhistory.org	South Bend	IN	46601	574-235-9664	235-9059
Reitz Home Museum 224 SE First St *Web:* reitzhome.com	Evansville	IN	47706	812-426-1871	426-2179
Science Central 1950 N Clinton St *TF:* 866-776-2673 ■ *Web:* www.sciencecentral.org	Fort Wayne	IN	46805	260-424-2400	422-2899
Snite Museum of Art University of Notre Dame *Web:* www.nd.edu/~sniteart	Notre Dame	IN	46556	574-631-5466	631-8501
South Bend Museum of Art (SBM) 120 S St Joseph St *Web:* www.southbendart.org	South Bend	IN	46601	574-235-9102	235-5782
Studebaker National Museum 201 Chapin St *TF:* 888-391-5600 ■ *Web:* www.studebakermuseum.org	South Bend	IN	46601	574-235-9714	235-5522
Swope Art Museum 25 S Seventh St *Web:* www.swope.org	Terre Haute	IN	47807	812-238-1676	238-1677
Wylie House Museum 307 E Second St *Web:* www.indiana.edu	Bloomington	IN	47401	812-855-6224	

Iowa

Name / Address	City	State	ZIP	Phone	Fax
African American Historical Museum & Cultural Ctr of Iowa 55 12th Ave SE *TF:* 877-526-1863 ■ *Web:* www.blackiowa.org	Cedar Rapids	IA	52406	319-862-2101	862-2105
Cedar Rapids Museum of Art 410 Third Ave SE *Web:* www.crma.org	Cedar Rapids	IA	52401	319-366-7503	366-4111
Coe College Permanent Collection of Art 1220 First Ave NE *TF:* 800-273-8255 ■ *Web:* www.public.coe.edu	Cedar Rapids	IA	52402	319-399-8500	399-8019
Des Moines Art Ctr 4700 Grand Ave *Web:* www.desmoinesartcenter.org	Des Moines	IA	50312	515-277-4405	271-0357
Dubuque Museum of Art 701 Locust St *Web:* www.dbqart.com	Dubuque	IA	52001	563-557-1851	557-7826
Duffy's Collectible Cars 1195 Boyson Rd *TF:* 877-670-3937 ■ *Web:* www.duffys.com	Hiawatha	IA	52233	319-364-7000	
Figge Art Museum 225 W Second St *Web:* www.figgeartmuseum.org	Davenport	IA	52801	563-326-7804	326-7876
Granger House Museum 970 Tenth St *Web:* grangerhousemuseum.org	Marion	IA	52302	319-377-6672	
Herbert Hoover Presidential Library & Museum 210 Parkside Dr *Web:* www.hoover.archives.gov	West Branch	IA	52358	319-643-5301	643-6045
Hoyt Sherman Place 1501 Woodland Ave *Web:* www.hoytsherman.org	Des Moines	IA	50309	515-244-0507	237-3582
Iowa Gold Star Military Museum 7105 NW 70th Ave *Web:* www.iowanationalguard.com	Johnston	IA	50131	515-252-4531	727-3107
Iowa Masonic Library & Museum 813 First Ave SE *Web:* www.gl-iowa.org	Cedar Rapids	IA	52402	319-365-1438	
John Wayne Birthplace 216 S Second St *Web:* johnwaynebirthplace.museum	Winterset	IA	50273	515-462-1044	462-3289
Living History Farms 2600 111th St *Web:* www.lhf.org	Urbandale	IA	50322	515-278-5286	278-9808
National Balloon Museum 1601 N Jefferson Way PO Box 149 *Web:* www.nationalballoonmuseum.com	Indianola	IA	50125	515-961-3714	
National Czech & Slovak Museum & Library 87 16th Ave SW *Web:* www.ncsml.org	Cedar Rapids	IA	52404	319-362-8500	363-2209
National Farm Toy Museum 1110 16th Ave SE *TF:* 877-475-2727 ■ *Web:* www.nationalfarmtoymuseum.com	Dyersville	IA	52040	563-875-2727	
National Mississippi River Museum & Aquarium 350 E Third St *TF:* 800-226-3369 ■ *Web:* www.mississippirivermuseum.com	Dubuque	IA	52001	563-557-9545	583-1241
Pella Historical Village 507 Franklin St *Web:* pellahistorical.org	Pella	IA	50219	641-628-4311	628-9192
Science Ctr of Iowa 401 W Martin Luther King Jr Pkwy *Web:* www.sciowa.org	Des Moines	IA	50309	515-274-6868	274-3404
Sioux City Art Ctr 225 Nebraska St *Web:* siouxcityartcenter.org	Sioux City	IA	51101	712-279-6272	255-2921
Sioux City Public Museum 2901 Jackson St *Web:* www.sioux-city.org	Sioux City	IA	51104	712-279-6174	252-5615
State Historical Society of Iowa 600 E Locust St *Web:* www.iowahistory.org	Des Moines	IA	50319	515-281-5111	242-6498
University Museum 3219 Hudson Rd University of Northern Iowa *TF:* 800-772-2736 ■ *Web:* www.uni.edu/museum	Cedar Falls	IA	50614	319-273-2188	273-6924
University of Iowa Museum of Art 1375 Hwy 1 W 1840 Studio Arts Bldg *Web:* uima.uiowa.edu	Iowa City	IA	52242	319-335-1727	335-3677

Kansas

Name / Address	City	State	ZIP	Phone	Fax
Boot Hill Museum 500 W Wyatt Earp Blvd *Web:* www.boothill.org	Dodge City	KS	67801	620-227-8188	
Combat Air Museum 7016 SE Forbes Ave Forbes Field *Web:* www.combatairmuseum.org	Topeka	KS	66619	785-862-3303	862-3304
Dwight D Eisenhower Presidential Library & Museum 200 SE Fourth St *TF:* 877-746-4453 ■ *Web:* www.eisenhower.utexas.edu	Abilene	KS	67410	785-263-6700	263-6715
Great Plains Transportation Museum 700 E Douglas St *Web:* www.gptm.us	Wichita	KS	67202	316-263-0944	
Indian Ctr Museum *Mid America All Indian Ctr* 650 N Seneca St *Web:* theindiancenter.org	Wichita	KS	67203	316-350-3340	
Kansas African American Museum 601 N Water St *Web:* tkaamuseum.org	Wichita	KS	67203	316-262-7651	265-6953
Kansas Aviation Museum 3350 S George Washington Blvd *Web:* www.kansasaviationmuseum.org	Wichita	KS	67210	316-683-9242	683-0573
Kansas Museum of History 6425 SW Sixth St *TF:* 888-537-1222 ■ *Web:* www.kshs.org	Topeka	KS	66615	785-272-8681	272-8682
Lowell D Holmes Museum of Anthropology 114 Neff Hall Wichita State University *Web:* webs.wichita.edu/anthropology	Wichita	KS	67260	316-978-3195	978-3351
Mulvane Art Museum 1700 SW Jewell Ave *Web:* www.washburn.edu	Topeka	KS	66621	785-670-1124	
Museum of World Treasures 835 E First St *Web:* www.worldtreasures.org	Wichita	KS	67202	316-263-1311	263-1495
National Agricultural Ctr & Hall of Fame 630 Hall of Fame Dr *Web:* www.aghalloffame.com	Bonner Springs	KS	66012	913-721-1075	721-1202
Old Cowtown Museum 1865 W Museum Blvd *Web:* www.oldcowtown.org	Wichita	KS	67203	316-219-1871	
Santa Fe Trail Ctr 1349 K-156 Hwy *Web:* www.santafetrailcenter.org	Larned	KS	67550	620-285-2054	285-7491
Spencer Museum of Art 1301 Mississippi St University of Kansas *Web:* www.spencerart.ku.edu	Lawrence	KS	66045	785-864-4710	864-3112
Strawberry Hill Museum & Cultural Ctr 720 N Fourth St *Web:* www.strawberryhillmuseum.org	Kansas City	KS	66101	913-371-3264	
Ulrich Museum of Art 1845 Fairmount St Wichita State University *Web:* wichita.edu/	Wichita	KS	67260	316-978-3664	978-3898
Wichita Art Museum 1400 W Museum Blvd *Web:* www.wichitaartmuseum.org	Wichita	KS	67203	316-268-4921	268-4980
Wichita-Sedgwick County Historical Museum 204 S Main St *Web:* www.wichitahistory.org	Wichita	KS	67202	316-265-9314	265-9319

Kentucky

Name / Address	City	State	ZIP	Phone	Fax
American Saddlebred Museum 4083 Iron Works Pkwy *TF:* 800-829-4438 ■ *Web:* www.asbmuseum.org	Lexington	KY	40511	859-259-2746	255-4909
Aviation Museum of Kentucky 4020 Airport Rd *Web:* www.aviationky.org	Lexington	KY	40510	859-231-1219	381-8739
Bluegrass Scenic Railroad & Museum 175 Beasley Rd Woodford County Pk *Web:* www.bgrm.org	Versailles	KY	40383	859-873-2476	873-0408
Conrad Caldwell House Museum, The 1402 St James Ct *Web:* www.conrad-caldwell.org	Louisville	KY	40208	502-636-5023	
Farmington Historic Plantation 3033 BaRdstown Rd	Louisville	KY	40205	502-452-9920	456-1976
Filson Historical Society Museum 1310 S Third St *Web:* www.filsonhistorical.org	Louisville	KY	40208	502-635-5083	635-5086
Frazier International History Museum 829 W Main St *Web:* www.frazierarmsmuseum.org	Louisville	KY	40202	502-753-5663	412-8148
Headley-Whitney Museum 4435 Old Frankfort Pike *TF:* 800-310-5085 ■ *Web:* www.headley-whitney.org	Lexington	KY	40510	859-255-6653	255-8375
International Museum of the Horse 4089 Iron Works Pkwy *TF:* 800-678-8813 ■ *Web:* www.imh.org	Lexington	KY	40511	859-259-4232	
John James Audubon Museum 3100 Hwy 41 N	Henderson	KY	42419	270-826-2247	
Kentucky Derby Museum 704 Central Ave *TF:* 800-273-3729 ■ *Web:* www.derbymuseum.org	Louisville	KY	40208	502-637-1111	636-5855
Kentucky Historical Society 100 W Broadway *Web:* history.ky.gov	Frankfort	KY	40601	502-564-1792	
Kentucky Military History Museum 125 E Main St *Web:* www.history.ky.gov	Frankfort	KY	40601	502-564-3265	
Louisville Science Ctr 727 W Main St *TF:* 800-591-2203 ■ *Web:* www.kysciencecenter.org	Louisville	KY	40202	502-561-6100	561-6145
Muhammad Ali Ctr 144 N Sixth St *Web:* www.alicenter.org	Louisville	KY	40202	502-584-9254	589-4905
Museum of The American Quilters Society Inc 215 Jefferson St *Web:* www.quiltmuseum.org	Paducah	KY	42001	270-442-8856	
National Corvette Museum 350 Corvette Dr *TF:* 800-538-3883 ■ *Web:* www.corvettemuseum.org	Bowling Green	KY	42101	270-781-7973	781-5286
Old State Capitol Museum 300 W Broadway St *Web:* history.ky.gov	Frankfort	KY	40601	502-564-2301	564-4701
Shaker Village of Pleasant Hill 3501 Lexington Rd *TF:* 800-734-5611 ■ *Web:* www.shakervillageky.org	Harrodsburg	KY	40330	859-734-5411	734-5411
Speed Art Museum, The 2035 S Third St *Web:* changingspeed.org	Louisville	KY	40208	502-634-2700	
Thomas Edison House 729-731 E Washington St	Louisville	KY	40202	502-585-5247	585-5231
University of Kentucky Art Museum Rose St & Euclid Ave *Web:* www.uky.edu/artmuseum	Lexington	KY	40506	859-257-5716	323-1994
University of Kentucky Museum of Anthropology 211 Lafferty Hall *Web:* anthropology.as.uky.edu	Lexington	KY	40506	859-257-2710	323-1968

Louisiana

Name / Address	City	State	ZIP	Phone	Fax
8th Air Force Museum 88 Shreveport Rd *Web:* barksdaleglobalpowermuseum.com	Bossier City	LA	71110	318-752-0055	
Alexandre Mouton House/Lafayette Museum 1122 Lafayette St	Lafayette	LA	70501	337-234-2208	234-2208
Cathedral of Saint John the Evangelist Museum 515 Cathedral St *Web:* www.saintjohncathedral.org/welcome.html	Lafayette	LA	70501	337-232-1322	232-1379
Confederate Museum 929 Camp St *Web:* www.confederatemuseum.com	New Orleans	LA	70130	504-523-4522	523-8595
Enchanted Mansion Doll Museum 190 Lee Dr *Web:* www.enchantedmansion.org	Baton Rouge	LA	70808	225-769-0005	766-6822
Gallier House Museum 1132 Royal St *Web:* www.hgghh.org	New Orleans	LA	70116	504-525-5661	568-9735

Museum	City	State	Zip	Phone	Fax
Grandmother's Buttons Museum 9814 Royal St *TF:* 800-580-6941 ■ *Web:* www.grandmothersbuttons.com	Saint Francisville	LA	70775	225-635-4107	635-6067
Historic New Orleans Collection 533 Royal St *Web:* www.hnoc.org	New Orleans	LA	70130	504-523-4662	598-7108
House of Broel's Historic Mansion & Dollhouse Museum 2220 St Charles Ave *TF:* 800-827-4325 ■ *Web:* www.houseofbroel.com	New Orleans	LA	70130	504-522-2220	524-6775
Imperial Calcasieu Museum 204 W Sallier St *Web:* www.imperialcalcasieumuseum.org	Lake Charles	LA	70601	337-439-3797	
Lafayette Museum 1122 Lafayette St *TF:* 800-346-1958 ■ *Web:* lafayettetravel.com	Lafayette	LA	70501	337-234-2208	234-2208
Longue Vue House & Gardens Seven Bamboo Rd *Web:* www.longuevue.com	New Orleans	LA	70124	504-488-5488	486-7015
Louisiana Art & Science Museum 100 S River Rd *Web:* www.lasm.org	Baton Rouge	LA	70802	225-344-5272	344-9477
Louisiana Naval War Memorial 305 S River Rd *Web:* www.usskidd.com	Baton Rouge	LA	70802	225-342-1942	342-2039
Louisiana State Museum 751 Chartres St *TF:* 800-568-6968 ■ *Web:* www.crt.state.la.us	New Orleans	LA	70116	504-568-6968	568-4995
Louisiana State University Museum of Art 100 Lafayette St *Web:* www.lsumoa.org	Baton Rouge	LA	70801	225-389-7200	389-7219
Magnolia Mound Plantation 2161 Nicholson Dr *Web:* brec.org	Baton Rouge	LA	70802	225-343-4955	343-6739
Meadows Museum of Art at Centenary College 2911 Centenary Blvd *TF:* 800-234-4448 ■ *Web:* www.centenary.edu/meadows	Shreveport	LA	71104	318-869-5169	869-5730
Musee Conti Historical Wax Museum of New Orleans 917 Rue Conti French Quarter *TF:* 800-233-5405 ■ *Web:* www.neworleanswaxmuseum.com	New Orleans	LA	70112	504-525-2605	566-7636
New Orleans Museum of Art One Collins Diboll Cir *Web:* www.noma.org	New Orleans	LA	70124	504-658-4100	658-4199
New Orleans Pharmacy Museum 514 Chartres St *Web:* www.pharmacymuseum.org	New Orleans	LA	70130	504-565-8027	
Nottoway Plantation 31025 Louisiana Hwy 1 *TF:* 866-527-6884 ■ *Web:* www.nottoway.com	White Castle	LA	70788	225-545-2730	545-8632
Ogden Museum of Southern Art 925 Camp St *Web:* www.ogdenmuseum.org	New Orleans	LA	70130	504-539-9600	539-9602
Old Arsenal Museum 900 State Capitol dr *Web:* www.sos.la.gov	Baton Rouge	LA	70802	225-342-0401	
Pitot House Museum 1440 Moss St *Web:* www.pitothouse.org	New Orleans	LA	70119	504-482-0312	482-0363
Plaquemine Lock State Historic Site 57730 Main St *TF:* 877-987-7158 ■ *Web:* crt.state.la.us	Plaquemine	LA	70764	225-687-7158	
RW Norton Art Gallery 4747 Creswell Ave *Web:* www.rwnaf.org	Shreveport	LA	71106	318-865-4201	869-0435
Sci-Port Discovery Ctr 820 Clyde Fant Pkwy *TF:* 877-724-7678 ■ *Web:* www.sciport.org	Shreveport	LA	71101	318-424-3466	222-5592
Southern University Museum of Art (SUSLA) 3050 Martin Luther King Jr Dr *TF:* 800-458-1472 ■ *Web:* www.susla.edu	Shreveport	LA	71107	318-670-6000	670-6457
Spring Street Historical Museum 525 Spring St *Web:* www.springstreetmuseum.com	Shreveport	LA	71101	318-424-0964	424-0964
Touchstone Wildlife & Art Museum 3386 Highway 80 *Web:* touchstonemuseum.com	Haughton	LA	71037	318-949-2323	
West Baton Rouge Museum 845 N Jefferson Ave *TF:* 888-881-6811 ■ *Web:* www.westbatonrougemuseum.com	Port Allen	LA	70767	225-336-2422	336-2448
West Feliciana Historical Society Museum 11757 Ferdinand St	Saint Francisville	LA	70775	225-635-6330	635-4626

Maine

Museum	City	State	Zip	Phone	Fax
Abbe Museum 26 Mt Desert St *Web:* www.abbemuseum.org	Bar Harbor	ME	04609	207-288-3519	288-8979
Bangor Museum & History Ctr 159 Union St *Web:* www.bangormuseum.org	Bangor	ME	04401	207-942-1900	942-1910
Bowdoin College Museum of Art 9400 College Stn *Web:* www.bowdoin.edu	Brunswick	ME	04011	207-725-3275	725-3762
Brick Store Museum 117 Main St *Web:* www.brickstoremuseum.org	Kennebunk	ME	04043	207-985-4802	985-6887
Colby College Museum of Art 5600 Mayflower Hill *Web:* www.colby.edu	Waterville	ME	04901	207-859-5600	859-5606
Cole Land Transportation Museum 405 Perry Rd *Web:* www.colemuseum.org	Bangor	ME	04401	207-990-3600	990-2653
Farnsworth Art Museum 16 Museum St *Web:* www.farnsworthmuseum.org	Rockland	ME	04841	207-596-6457	596-0509
Hudson Museum 5746 Collins Ctr for the Arts *Web:* www.umaine.edu/hudsonmuseum	Orono	ME	04469	207-581-1901	581-1950
Maine Historical Society 489 Congress St Maine Historical Society *Web:* mainehistory.org	Portland	ME	04101	207-774-1822	775-4301
Maine Maritime Museum 243 Washington St *Web:* mainemaritimemuseum.org/	Bath	ME	04530	207-443-1316	443-1665
Maine Narrow Gauge Railroad Museum 58 Fore St *Web:* www.mainenarrowgauge.org	Portland	ME	04101	207-828-0814	879-6132
Maine State Museum 83 State House Stn State House Complex *Web:* www.mainestatemuseum.org	Augusta	ME	04333	207-287-2301	287-6633
Museum at Portland Head Light 1000 Shore Rd *Web:* www.portlandheadlight.com/museum.html	Cape Elizabeth	ME	04107	207-799-2661	799-2800
Old Fort Western 16 Cony St *Web:* www.oldfortwestern.org	Augusta	ME	04330	207-626-2385	626-2304
Old Town Museum 353 Main St *Web:* www.old-town.org	Old Town	ME	04468	207-827-7256	
Penobscot Marine Museum Five Church St PO Box 498 *TF:* 800-268-8030 ■ *Web:* www.penobscotmarinemuseum.org	Searsport	ME	04974	207-548-2529	548-2520
Portland Fire Museum 157 Spring St *Web:* www.portlandfiremuseum.com	Portland	ME	04101	207-772-2040	
Portland Museum of Art Seven Congress Sq *Web:* www.portlandmuseum.org	Portland	ME	04101	207-775-6148	773-7324
State House One State House Stn *Web:* www.maine.gov	Augusta	ME	04333	207-287-3531	287-6548
Tate House Museum 1267 Westbrook St *Web:* www.tatehouse.org	Portland	ME	04102	207-774-6177	774-6198
University of Maine Museum of Art 40 Harlow St Norumbega Hall *Web:* www.umma.umaine.edu	Bangor	ME	04401	207-561-3350	561-3351

Manitoba

Museum	City	Province	Postal Code	Phone	Fax
Ivan Franko Museum 1040 - 555 Main St 595 Pritchard Ave *Web:* www.museumsmanitoba.com	Winnipeg	MB	R3B1C3	204-947-1782	942-3749
Living Prairie Museum 2795 Ness Ave *Web:* www.livingprairie.ca	Winnipeg	MB	R3J3S4	204-832-0167	986-4172
Manitoba Museum 190 Rupert Ave *Web:* www.manitobamuseum.ca/main	Winnipeg	MB	R3B0N2	204-956-2830	942-3679

Maryland

Museum	City	State	Zip	Phone	Fax
Accokeek Foundation 3400 Bryan Pt Rd *Web:* www.accokeek.org	Accokeek	MD	20607	301-283-2113	
American Visionary Art Museum 800 Key Hwy *Web:* www.avam.org	Baltimore	MD	21230	410-244-1900	244-5858
Annapolis Maritime Museum 723 Second St PO Box 3088 *Web:* www.amaritime.org	Annapolis	MD	21403	410-295-0104	295-3022
B & O Railroad Museum 901 W Pratt St *TF:* 800-228-3748 ■ *Web:* www.borail.org	Baltimore	MD	21223	410-752-2490	752-2499
Baltimore Museum of Art 10 Art Museum Dr *TF:* 800-735-2964 ■ *Web:* www.artbma.org	Baltimore	MD	21218	443-573-1700	573-1582
Baltimore Museum of Industry 1415 Key Hwy *Web:* www.thebmi.org	Baltimore	MD	21230	410-727-4808	727-4869
Baltimore Streetcar Museum 1901 Falls Rd *Web:* www.baltimoremd.com	Baltimore	MD	21211	410-547-0264	547-0264
Banneker-Douglas Museum 84 Franklin St *TF:* 877-634-6361 ■ *Web:* bdmuseum.maryland.gov	Annapolis	MD	21401	410-216-6180	974-2553
Calvert Marine Museum 14200 Solomons Island Rd PO Box 97 *TF:* 800-735-2258 ■ *Web:* www.calvertmarinemuseum.com	Solomons	MD	20688	410-326-2042	326-6691
Calvin B Taylor House Museum 208 N Main St *Web:* www.taylorhousemuseum.org	Berlin	MD	21811	410-641-1019	
Chesapeake Bay Maritime Museum 213 N Talbot St *Web:* www.cbmm.org	Saint Michaels	MD	21663	410-745-2916	745-6088
Fire Museum of Maryland 1301 York Rd *Web:* www.firemuseummd.org	Lutherville	MD	21093	410-321-7500	769-8433
Fort McHenry National Monument & Historic Shrine 2400 E Fort Ave *TF:* 866-945-7920 ■ *Web:* www.nps.gov	Baltimore	MD	21230	410-962-4290	962-2500
Hammond-Harwood House 19 Maryland Ave *Web:* www.hammondharwoodhouse.org	Annapolis	MD	21401	410-263-4683	267-6891
Historic Annapolis Foundation Museum 77 Main St *TF:* 800-603-4020 ■ *Web:* www.annapolis.org	Annapolis	MD	21401	410-268-5576	
Homewood Museum 3400 N Charles St Johns Hopkins University *Web:* www.museums.jhu.edu	Baltimore	MD	21218	410-516-5589	516-7859
Jewish Museum of Maryland 15 Lloyd St *TF All:* 800-235-4045 ■ *Web:* jewishmuseummd.org	Baltimore	MD	21202	410-732-6400	732-6451
Lacrosse Hall of Fame & Museum 113 W University Pkwy *TF:* 866-877-7550 ■ *Web:* www.uslacrosse.org	Baltimore	MD	21210	410-235-6882	366-6735
Lovely Lane Museum 2200 St Paul St *Web:* www.lovelylanemuseum.org	Baltimore	MD	21218	410-889-4458	889-1501
Maryland Historical Society Museum & Library 201 W Monument St *TF:* 800-537-5487 ■ *Web:* www.mdhs.org	Baltimore	MD	21201	410-685-3750	385-2105
Maryland Science Ctr 601 Light St *Web:* www.mdsci.org	Baltimore	MD	21230	410-685-2370	545-5974
Mount Clare Museum House 1500 Washington Blvd Carroll Pk *Web:* www.mountclare.org	Baltimore	MD	21230	410-837-3262	837-0251
National Great Blacks in Wax Museum 1601-03 E N Ave *Web:* www.ngbiwm.com	Baltimore	MD	21213	410-563-3404	563-7806
National Museum of Dentistry 31 S Greene St *TF:* 866-787-8637 ■ *Web:* www.dental.umaryland.edu	Baltimore	MD	21201	410-706-0600	706-8313

	City	State	Zip	Phone	Fax
National Museum of Health & Medicine 2500 Linden Ln *Web:* www.medicalmuseum.mil	Silver Spring	MD	20910	202-782-2200	
Ocean City Life-Saving Station Museum 813 S Atlantic Ave. *Web:* www.ocmuseum.org	Ocean City	MD	21842	410-289-4991	289-4991
Reginald F Lewis Museum of Maryland African American History & Culture 830 E Pratt St **Fax Area Code:* 410 ■ *Web:* www.africanamericanculture.org	Baltimore	MD	21202	443-263-1800	333-1138*
Star-Spangled Banner Flag House, The 844 E Pratt St *Web:* www.flaghouse.org	Baltimore	MD	21202	410-837-1793	
US Naval Academy Museum 118 Maryland Ave. *Web:* www.usna.edu	Annapolis	MD	21402	410-293-2108	293-5220
Walters Art Museum 600 N Charles St. *Web:* www.thewalters.org	Baltimore	MD	21201	410-547-9000	783-7969
Ward Museum of Wildfowl Art 909 S Schumaker Dr. *Web:* www.wardmuseum.org	Salisbury	MD	21804	410-742-4988	742-3107
Washington County Museum of Fine Arts 401 Museum Dr PO Box 423 *Web:* www.wcmfa.org	Hagerstown	MD	21741	301-739-5727	745-3741
Wheels of Yesterday Antique & Classic Cars Museum 12708 Ocean Gateway	Ocean City	MD	21842	410-213-7329	

Massachusetts

	City	State	Zip	Phone	Fax
American Jewish Historical Society 101 Newbury St *Web:* www.ajhs.org	Boston	MA	02116	617-226-1245	559-8881
American Textile History Museum 491 Dutton St *Web:* www.athm.org	Lowell	MA	01854	978-441-0400	441-1412
Cape Cod Maritime Museum 135 S St PO Box 443 *Web:* www.capecodmaritimemuseum.org	Hyannis	MA	02601	508-775-1723	775-1706
Cape Cod Museum of Natural History 869 Main St *Web:* www.ccmnh.org	Brewster	MA	02631	508-896-3867	896-8844
Childrens Discovery Museum, The 177 Main St. *Web:* www.discoverymuseums.org	Acton	MA	01720	978-264-4200	
Fogg Art Museum 32 Quincy St Harvard University *Web:* www.harvardartmuseums.org/art/fogg-museum	Cambridge	MA	02138	617-495-9400	
Fuller Craft Museum 455 Oak St *Web:* fullercraft.org	Brockton	MA	02301	508-588-6000	587-6191
Gibson House Museum 137 Beacon St. *Web:* www.thegibsonhouse.org	Boston	MA	02116	617-267-6338	267-6338
Harvard Museum of Natural History 26 Oxford St Harvard University *Web:* www.mcz.harvard.edu	Cambridge	MA	02138	617-495-5891	496-8308
Higgins Armory Museum 100 Barber Ave. *Web:* www.higgins.org	Worcester	MA	01606	508-853-6015	852-7697
Historic Deerfield PO Box 321 *Web:* www.historic-deerfield.org	Deerfield	MA	01342	413-774-5581	775-7220
Isabella Stewart Gardner Museum 280 Fenway *Web:* www.gardnermuseum.org	Boston	MA	02115	617-566-1401	
John F Kennedy Hyannis Museum 397 Main St. *Web:* jfkhyannismuseum.org	Hyannis	MA	02601	508-790-3077	790-1970
John F Kennedy Presidential Library & Museum Columbia Pt *TF:* 866-535-1960 ■ *Web:* www.jfklibrary.org	Boston	MA	02125	617-514-1600	514-1652
Martha's Vineyard Museum 59 School St PO Box 1310 *Web:* www.marthasvineyardhistory.org	Edgartown	MA	02539	508-627-4441	627-4436
Massachusetts Historical Society, The 1154 Boylston St *Web:* www.masshist.org	Boston	MA	02215	617-646-0500	
MIT Museum 265 Massachusetts Ave. *TF:* 800-228-9000 ■ *Web:* www.web.mit.edu	Cambridge	MA	02139	617-253-4444	253-8994
Museum of African American History 46 Joy St *Web:* www.afroammuseum.org	Boston	MA	02114	617-725-0022	720-5225
Museum of Fine Arts Boston 465 Huntington Ave *Web:* www.mfa.org	Boston	MA	02115	617-267-9300	
Museum of Science Science Pk *Web:* www.mos.org	Boston	MA	02114	617-723-2500	589-0454
Museum of the National Ctr of Afro-American Artists (NCAAA) 300 Walnut Ave. *Web:* www.ncaaa.org/museum.html	Roxbury	MA	02119	617-442-8614	
National Heritage Museum 33 Marrett Rd *Web:* www.nationalheritagemuseum.org	Lexington	MA	02421	781-861-6559	861-9846
New Bedford Whaling Museum 18 Johnny Cake Hill *Web:* www.whalingmuseum.org	New Bedford	MA	02740	508-997-0046	
Nichols House Museum 55 Mt Vernon St. *Web:* www.nicholshousemuseum.org	Boston	MA	02108	617-227-6993	723-8026
Old Sturbridge Village One Old Sturbridge Village Rd *Web:* www.osv.org	Sturbridge	MA	01566	508-347-3362	347-0375
Peabody Essex Museum 161 Essex St. *Web:* www.pem.org	Salem	MA	01970	978-745-1876	744-6776
Peabody Museum of Archaeology & Ethnology 11 Divinity Ave *Web:* www.peabody.harvard.edu	Cambridge	MA	02138	617-496-1027	495-7535
Pilgrim Hall Museum 75 Ct St *Web:* www.pilgrimhallmuseum.org	Plymouth	MA	02360	508-746-1620	
Plimoth Plantation 137 Warren Ave *Web:* www.plimoth.org	Plymouth	MA	02360	508-746-1622	
Revere Paul House 19 N Sq *Web:* www.paulreverehouse.org	Boston	MA	02113	617-523-2338	523-1775
Salem Witch Museum 19 1/2 Washington Sq N. *TF:* 800-392-6100 ■ *Web:* www.salemwitchmuseum.com	Salem	MA	01970	978-744-1692	
Sandwich Glass Museum 129 Main St PO Box 103 *Web:* www.sandwichglassmuseum.org	Sandwich	MA	02563	508-888-0251	888-4941
Springfield Museums 21 Edwards St *TF:* 800-625-7738 ■ *Web:* www.springfieldmuseums.org	Springfield	MA	01103	413-263-6800	263-6807
Sterling & Francine Clark Art Institute 225 S St **Fax:* PR ■ *Web:* www.clarkart.edu	Williamstown	MA	01267	413-458-2303	458-5902*
Storrowton Village Museum 1305 Memorial Ave Eastern States Exposition *Web:* www.thebige.com	West Springfield	MA	01089	413-205-5051	205-5054
Titanic Museum 208 Main St *Web:* www.titanic1.org	Indian Orchard	MA	01151	413-543-4770	583-3633
USS Constitution Museum PO Box 291812 *Web:* www.ussconstitutionmuseum.org	Boston	MA	02129	617-426-1812	242-0496
Whaling Museum 13 Broad St. *Web:* nha.org	Nantucket	MA	02554	508-228-1894	228-5618
Willard House & Clock Museum 11 Willard St. *Web:* www.willardhouse.org	North Grafton	MA	01536	508-839-3500	
Worcester Art Museum 55 Salisbury St *Web:* www.worcesterart.org	Worcester	MA	01609	508-799-4406	798-5646
Worcester Historical Museum 30 Elm St. *Web:* www.worcesterhistory.org	Worcester	MA	01609	508-753-8278	753-9070

Michigan

	City	State	Zip	Phone	Fax
Air Zoo, The 6151 Portage Rd *Web:* www.airzoo.org	Portage	MI	49002	269-382-6555	
Ann Arbor Hands-On Museum 220 E Ann St *Web:* www.aahom.org	Ann Arbor	MI	48104	734-995-5439	995-1188
Art Center Kalamazoo Inst 314 S Park St *Web:* www.kiarts.org	Kalamazoo	MI	49007	269-349-7775	
Automotive Hall of Fame 21400 Oakwood Blvd *Web:* www.automotivehalloffame.org	Dearborn	MI	48124	313-240-4000	240-8641
Charles H Wright Museum of African American History 315 E Warren Ave *Web:* thewright.org	Detroit	MI	48201	313-494-5800	494-5855
Cranbrook Art Museum 39221 Woodward Ave. *Web:* www.cranbrookart.edu/museum	Bloomfield Hills	MI	48303	248-645-3323	645-3324
Cranbrook Institute of Science 39221 Woodward Ave PO Box 801 *Web:* www.cranbrook.edu	Bloomfield Hills	MI	48303	248-645-3000	645-3050
Detroit Historical Museum 5401 Woodward Ave *Web:* www.detroithistorical.org	Detroit	MI	48202	313-833-1805	833-5342
Detroit Institute of Arts 5200 Woodward Ave *Web:* www.dia.org	Detroit	MI	48202	313-833-7900	
Dossin Great Lakes Museum 100 Strand Dr Belle Isle *Web:* www.detroithistorical.org	Detroit	MI	48207	313-833-5538	833-5342
Exhibit Museum of Natural History 1109 Geddes Ave *Web:* www.lsa.umich.edu	Ann Arbor	MI	48109	734-764-0478	647-2767
Flint Institute of Arts 1120 E Kearsley St *Web:* www.flintarts.org	Flint	MI	48503	810-234-1695	234-1692
Gallerie 454 15105 Kercheval Ave *Web:* www.gallerie454.com	Grosse Pointe Park	MI	48230	313-822-4454	822-3768
Gerald R Ford Museum 303 Pearl St NW *TF:* 800-888-9487 ■ *Web:* www.ford.utexas.edu	Grand Rapids	MI	49504	616-254-0400	254-0386
Grand Rapids Art Museum 101 Monroe Ctr. *TF:* 800-272-8258 ■ *Web:* www.artmuseumgr.org	Grand Rapids	MI	49503	616-831-1000	831-1001
Greenfield Village 20900 Oakwood Blvd **Fax:* Cust Svc ■ *TF:* 800-835-5237 ■ *Web:* thehenryford.org/village	Dearborn	MI	48124	313-271-1620	982-6225*
Henry Ford Museum 20900 Oakwood Blvd *TF:* 800-733-0345 ■ *Web:* thehenryford.org/	Dearborn	MI	48124	313-271-1620	982-6225
Historic Hack House Museum 775 County St. *Web:* www.michigan.org	Milan	MI	48160	734-439-7522	
Holocaust Memorial Ctr 28123 OrchaRd Lake Rd *TF:* 800-875-5275 ■ *Web:* www.holocaustcenter.org	Farmington Hills	MI	48334	248-553-2400	553-2433
Impression 5 Science Ctr 200 Museum Dr. *Web:* www.impression5.org	Lansing	MI	48933	517-485-8116	485-8125
International Institute of Metropolitan Detroit 111 E Kirby St. *Web:* www.iimd.org	Detroit	MI	48202	313-871-8600	871-1651
Kelsey Museum of Archaeology 434 S State St University of Michigan *TF:* 800-562-3559 ■ *Web:* www.lsa.umich.edu/kelsey	Ann Arbor	MI	48109	734-763-3559	763-8976
Kempf House Museum 312 S Div St. *Web:* www.kempfhousemuseum.org	Ann Arbor	MI	48104	734-994-4898	
Kingman Museum 175 Limit St. *Web:* www.kingmanmuseum.org	Battle Creek	MI	49037	269-965-5117	
Leslie Science & Nature Ctr 1831 Traver Rd. *Web:* lesliesnc.org	Ann Arbor	MI	48105	734-997-1553	997-1072
Manistee County Historical Museum 425 River St *Web:* www.manisteemuseum.org	Manistee	MI	49660	231-723-5531	
Michigan Historical Museum 702 W Kalamazoo St. *Web:* michigan.gov	Lansing	MI	48915	517-373-3559	241-3647
Michigan State University Museum W Cir Dr *Web:* museum.msu.edu	East Lansing	MI	48824	517-355-2370	432-2846
Michigan Women's Historical Ctr & Hall of Fame 213 W Main St. *Web:* www.michiganwomenshalloffame.org	Lansing	MI	48933	517-484-1880	372-0170
Midland Ctr for the Arts Inc 1801 W St Andrews Rd *Web:* www.mcfta.org	Midland	MI	48640	989-631-5930	631-7890

Phone Fax

Milford Historical Society
124 E Commerce St Ste 2 .... Milford MI 48381 248-685-7308
Web: www.milfordhistory.org

Monroe County Historical Museum
126 S Monroe St .... Monroe MI 48161 734-240-7780 240-7788
Web: co.monroe.mi.us

Montrose Historical & Telephone Pioneer Museum
144 E Hickory St .... Montrose MI 48457 810-639-6644
Web: montrosemuseum.com

Motown Museum 2648 W Grand Blvd .... Detroit MI 48208 313-875-2264 875-2267
Web: www.motownmuseum.org

Public Museum of Grand Rapids
272 Pearl St NW Van Andel Museum Ctr .... Grand Rapids MI 49504 616-456-3977 456-3873
Web: grpm.org

RE Olds Transportation Museum 240 Museum Dr .... Lansing MI 48933 517-372-0529 372-2901
Web: www.reoldsmuseum.org

Rosedale Products Inc
3730 W Liberty Rd PO Box 1085 .... Ann Arbor MI 48106 734-665-8201
Web: www.rosedaleproducts.com

Sloan Museum 1221 E Kearsley St .... Flint MI 48503 810-237-3450 237-3451
Web: 'www.sloanlongway.org

Tuskegee Airman Natl Historical Museum
6325 W Jefferson .... Detroit MI 48209 313-843-8849 595-6576*
**Fax Area Code:* 800 ■ *Web:* tuskegeeairmennationalmuseum.org

University of Michigan Museum of Art
525 S State St .... Ann Arbor MI 48109 734-764-0395 764-3731
Web: www.umma.umich.edu

Voigt House Victorian Museum
115 College Ave SE .... Grand Rapids MI 49504 616-929-1700
Web: grpm.org

Ypsilanti Historical Museum 220 N Huron St .... Ypsilanti MI 48197 734-482-4990
Web: www.ypsilantihistoricalsociety.org

Minnesota

Phone Fax

American Swedish Institute, The (ASI)
2600 Pk Ave .... Minneapolis MN 55407 612-871-4907 871-8682
Web: www.asimn.org

Bakken, The 3537 Zenith Ave S .... Minneapolis MN 55416 612-926-3878 927-7265
Web: www.thebakken.org

Bell Museum of Natural History
10 Church St SE .... Minneapolis MN 55455 612-624-7083 626-7704
Web: www.bellmuseum.umn.edu

Depot, The
Saint Louis County Heritage & Arts Ctr
506 W Michigan St .... Duluth MN 55802 218-727-8025
Web: www.duluthdepot.org

Fitger's Brewery Museum 600 E Superior St .... Duluth MN 55802 218-722-8826 722-8826
TF: 888-348-4377 ■ *Web:* www.fitgers.com

Gibbs Museum of Pioneer & Dakotah Life
2097 W Larpenteur Ave .... Saint Paul MN 55113 651-646-8629 659-0345
Web: www.rchs.com

Hennepin History Museum 2303 Third Ave S .... Minneapolis MN 55404 612-870-1329 870-1320
Web: www.hennepinhistory.org

Juxtaposition Arts Inc
2007 Emerson Ave N .... Minneapolis MN 55411 612-588-1148
Web: www.juxtaposition.org

Lake Superior Maritime Visitors Ctr
600 Lake Ave S .... Duluth MN 55802 218-727-2497 720-5270
Web: www.lsmma.com

Lake Superior Railroad Museum
506 W Michigan St .... Duluth MN 55802 218-727-8025 733-7596
Web: www.lsrm.org

Mill City Museum 704 S Second St .... Minneapolis MN 55401 612-341-7555
Web: www.millcitymuseum.org

Minneapolis Institute of Arts
2400 Third Ave S .... Minneapolis MN 55404 612-870-3000 870-3004
TF: 888-642-2787 ■ *Web:* new.artsmia.org

Minnesota Discovery Ctr 1005 Discovery Dr .... Chisholm MN 55719 218-254-7959 254-7971
TF: 800-372-6437 ■ *Web:* www.mndiscoverycenter.com

Minnesota Historical Society History Ctr Museum
345 Kellogg Blvd W .... Saint Paul MN 55102 651-259-3001 296-1004
TF: 800-657-3773 ■ *Web:* www.mnhs.org

Minnesota State University Moorhead Regional Science Ctr
1104 Seventh Ave S .... Moorhead MN 56563 218-477-2920 477-4372
TF: 800-593-7246 ■ *Web:* www.mnstate.edu/regsci

Minnesota Transportation Museum
193 E Pennsylvania Ave .... Saint Paul MN 55130 651-228-0263 293-0857
Web: www.mtmuseum.org

Minnesota Wing Commemorative Air Force Museum
310 Airport Rd
Hanger 3 Fleming Field .... South Saint Paul MN 55075 651-455-6942 455-2160
Web: www.cafmn.org

Museum of Russian Art 5500 Stevens Ave S .... Minneapolis MN 55419 612-821-9045 821-4392
Web: www.tmora.org

Pavek Museum of Broadcasting
3517 Raleigh Ave .... Saint Louis Park MN 55416 952-926-8198 929-6105
Web: www.pavekmuseum.org

Schubert Club Museum, The
75 W Fifth St 302 Landmark Ctr .... Saint Paul MN 55102 651-292-3267 292-4317
Web: www.schubert.org

Science Museum of Minnesota
120 W Kellogg Blvd .... Saint Paul MN 55102 651-221-9444 221-4777
TF: 800-221-9444 ■ *Web:* www.smm.org

Tweed Museum of Art 1201 ordean Ct .... Duluth MN 55812 218-726-8222 726-8503
TF: 866-999-6995 ■ *Web:* www.d.umn.edu/tma

Twin Cities Model Railroad Museum
1021 Bandana Blvd E Ste 222 .... Saint Paul MN 55108 651-647-9628
Web: www.tcmrm.org

Walker Art Ctr 1750 Hennepin Ave .... Minneapolis MN 55403 612-375-7600 375-7618
TF: 888-339-4496 ■ *Web:* www.walkerart.org

Phone Fax

Weisman Art Museum 333 E River Pkwy .... Minneapolis MN 55455 612-625-9494
Web: www.weisman.umn.edu

Mississippi

Phone Fax

Elvis Presley Birthplace & Museum
306 Elvis Presley Dr .... Tupelo MS 38804 662-841-1245
Web: www.elvispresleybirthplace.com

International Checker Hall of Fame
220 Lynn Ray Rd .... Petal MS 39465 601-582-7090
Web: nccheckers.org

International Museum of Muslim Cultures
201 E Pascagoula St Ste 102 .... Jackson MS 39201 601-960-0440 960-0316
Web: www.muslimmuseum.org

Landrum's Homestead & Village 1356 Hwy 15 S .... Laurel MS 39443 601-649-2546 428-1663
Web: landrums.com

Lauren Rogers Museum of Art 565 N Fifth Ave .... Laurel MS 39440 601-649-6374 649-6379
Web: www.lrma.org

Manship House Museum 420 E Fortification St .... Jackson MS 39202 601-961-4724
Web: mdah.state.ms.us

Mississippi Agriculture & Forestry Museum/National Agricultural Aviation Museum
1150 Lakeland Dr .... Jackson MS 39216 601-359-1100 982-4292
TF: 800-844-8687 ■ *Web:* www.mdac.state.ms.us

Mississippi Dept of Archives & History (MDAH)
200 N St .... Jackson MS 39201 601-576-6876 576-6964
Web: mdah.state.ms.us

Mississippi Museum of Art 380 S Lamar St .... Jackson MS 39201 601-960-1515 960-1505
Web: www.msmuseumart.org

Mississippi Museum of Natural Science
2148 Riverside Dr .... Jackson MS 39202 601-576-6000 354-7227
TF: 800-467-2757 ■ *Web:* www.mdwfp.com

Museum of the Southern Jewish Experience
PO Box 16528 .... Jackson MS 39236 601-362-6357 366-6293
Web: isjl.org/

Ohr-O'Keefe Museum of Art 386 Beach Blvd .... Biloxi MS 39530 228-374-5547 436-3641
Web: www.georgeohr.org

Old Capitol Museum 100 S State St .... Jackson MS 39201 601-576-6920 576-6981
Web: www.mdah.state.ms.us

Oren Dunn City Museum
689 Rutherford Rd PO Box 2674 .... Tupelo MS 38801 662-841-6438 841-6458
Web: www.orendunnmuseum.org

Smith Robertson Museum & Cultural Ctr
528 Bloom St .... Jackson MS 39202 601-960-1457
TF: 800-354-7695

Missouri

Phone Fax

Alexander Majors Historic House & Museum
8201 State Line Rd .... Kansas City MO 64114 816-333-5556
Web: wornallmajors.org

American Jazz Museum 1616 E 18th St .... Kansas City MO 64108 816-474-8463 474-0074
TF: 800-745-3000 ■ *Web:* americanjazzmuseum.org

American Kennel Club Museum of the Dog
1721 S Mason Rd .... Saint Louis MO 63131 314-821-3647 821-7381
Web: www.akc.org

American Royal Museum & Visitors Ctr
1701 American Royal Ct .... Kansas City MO 64102 816-221-9800 221-8189
TF General: 866-844-2295 ■ *Web:* www.americanroyal.com

Arabia Steamboat Museum 400 Grand Blvd .... Kansas City MO 64106 816-471-1856
Web: www.1856.com

Boone County Historical Society Museum
3801 Ponderosa St .... Columbia MO 65201 573-443-8936 875-5268
Web: boonehistory.org

Chatillon-DeMenil Mansion & Museum
3352 DeMenil Pl .... Saint Louis MO 63118 314-771-5828
Web: www.demenil.org

Cole County Historical Museum
109 Madison St .... Jefferson City MO 65101 573-635-1850
Web: www.colecohistsoc.org

Concordia Historical Institute
804 Seminary Pl .... Saint Louis MO 63105 314-505-7900 505-7901
Web: www.lutheranhistory.org

Contemporary Art Museum Saint Louis
3750 Washington Blvd .... Saint Louis MO 63108 314-535-4660 535-1226
Web: camstl.org

Dutton Family Theatre 3454 W 76 Country Blvd .... Branson MO 65616 417-332-2772 339-4900
TF: 888-388-8661 ■ *Web:* www.theduttons.com

Eugene Field House & Saint Louis Toy Museum
634 S Broadway .... Saint Louis MO 63102 314-421-4689 588-9496
Web: www.eugenefieldhouse.org

Harry S Truman Presidential Library & Museum
500 W Hwy 24 .... Independence MO 64050 816-268-8200 268-8295
TF: 800-833-1225 ■ *Web:* www.trumanlibrary.org

Historic Aircraft Restoration Museum
3127 Creve Coeur Mill Rd .... Saint Louis MO 63146 314-434-3368 878-6453
Web: www.historicaircraftrestorationmuseum.org

History Museum On The Square
205 Park Central E 4th Fl .... Springfield MO 65806 417-864-1976
Web: historymuseumonthesquare.org

John Wornall House Museum
6115 Wornall Rd .... Kansas City MO 64113 816-444-1858
Web: wornallhouse.org

Kemper Museum of Contemporary Art
4420 Warwick Blvd .... Kansas City MO 64111 816-753-5784 753-5806
Web: www.kemperart.org

Laumeier Sculpture Park & Museum
12580 Rott Rd .... Saint Louis MO 63127 314-615-5278 615-5283
Web: laumeiersculpturepark.org

				Phone	Fax
Laura Ingalls Wilder Museum & Home 3068 Hwy A	Mansfield	MO	65704	877-924-7126	924-8580*
*Fax Area Code: 417 ■ TF: 877-924-7126 ■ Web: www.lauraingallswilderhome.com					
Liberty Memorial Museum 100 W 26th St	Kansas City	MO	64108	816-784-1918	784-1929
Web: www.theworldwar.org					
Margaret Harwell Art Museum 421 N Main St	Poplar Bluff	MO	63901	573-686-8002	
Web: www.mham.org					
Miniature Museum of Greater Saint Louis 4746 Gravois	Saint Louis	MO	63116	314-832-7790	
Web: www.miniaturemuseum.org					
Missouri History Museum 5700 Lindell Blvd PO Box 11940	Saint Louis	MO	63112	314-746-4599	454-3162
Web: www.mohistory.org					
Missouri State Museum 201 W Capitol	Jefferson City	MO	65101	573-751-2854	526-2927
Web: mostateparks.com					
Missouri Veterinary Medical Foundation Museum 2500 Country Club Dr	Jefferson City	MO	65109	573-636-8612	659-7175
TF: 800-632-6900 ■ Web: movma.org					
Museum of Anthropology 104 Swallow Hall University of Missouri	Columbia	MO	65211	573-882-3573	884-3627
Web: anthromuseum.missouri.edu					
Museum of Art & Archaeology 1 Pickard Hall	Columbia	MO	65211	573-882-3591	884-4039
TF: 866-447-9821 ■ Web: maa.missouri.edu					
Museum of Contemporary Religious Art 221 N Grand Blvd	Saint Louis	MO	63103	314-977-7170	977-2999
TF: 800-442-1142 ■ Web: www.slu.edu					
Museum of Missouri Military History 2302 Militia Dr	Jefferson City	MO	65101	573-638-9603	638-9676
Web: www.moguard.com					
Museums at 18th & Vine 1616 E 18th St	Kansas City	MO	64108	816-474-8463	474-0074
TF: 800-734-3447 ■ Web: americanjazzmuseum.org					
National Airline History Museum 201 Lou Holland Dr Hngr 9	Kansas City	MO	64116	816-421-3401	421-3421
Web: www.airlinehistory.org					
National World War I Museum 100 W 26th St	Kansas City	MO	64108	816-784-1918	
Web: www.libertymemorialmuseum.org					
Nelson-Atkins Museum of Art 4525 Oak St	Kansas City	MO	64111	816-751-1278	561-4011
Web: www.nelson-atkins.org					
Pony Express National Museum 914 Penn St	Saint Joseph	MO	64503	816-279-5059	233-9370
TF: 800-530-5930 ■ Web: www.ponyexpress.org					
Ralph Foster Museum College of the Ozarks PO Box 17	Point Lookout	MO	65726	417-690-3407	335-2618
Web: www.rfostermuseum.com					
Roy Rogers-Dale Evans Museum 3950 Green Mtn Dr	Branson	MO	65616	417-339-1900	
Web: www.royrogers.com					
Saint Louis Art Museum One Fine Arts Dr	Saint Louis	MO	63110	314-721-0072	721-6172
Web: www.slam.org					
Saint Louis Science Ctr 5050 Oakland Ave	Saint Louis	MO	63110	314-289-4400	535-0104
TF: 800-456-4491 ■ Web: www.slsc.org					
Saint Louis University Museum of Art 3663 Lindell Blvd O'Donnell Hall	Saint Louis	MO	63103	314-977-3399	
Web: sluma.slu.edu					
Sappington House Museum 1015 S Sappington Rd	Crestwood	MO	63126	314-822-8171	
Web: sappingtonhouse.org					
Shoal Creek Living History Museum 7000 NE Barry Rd Hodge Pk	Kansas City	MO	64156	816-792-2655	
Web: www.kcmo.org					
Soldiers Memorial Military Museum 1315 Chestnut St	Saint Louis	MO	63103	314-622-4550	
Web: stlsoldiersmemorial.org					
Springfield Art Museum 1111 E Brookside Dr	Springfield	MO	65807	417-837-5700	837-5704
Web: sgfmuseum.org					
State Historical Society of Missouri, The 1020 Lowry St	Columbia	MO	65201	573-882-1187	884-4950
TF: 800-747-6366 ■ Web: shs.umsystem.edu					

Montana

				Phone	Fax
Children's Museum of Montana 22 Railroad Sq	Great Falls	MT	59401	406-452-6661	
Web: www.childrensmuseumofmontana.org					
CM Russell Museum 400 13th St N	Great Falls	MT	59401	406-727-8787	727-2402
Web: www.cmrussell.org					
Holter Museum of Art 12 E Lawrence St	Helena	MT	59601	406-442-6400	442-2404
Web: www.holtermuseum.org					
Malmstrom Air Force Base Museum & Air Park 341 Missile Wing/MU 21 77th St N Ste 144	Malmstrom AFB	MT	59402	406-731-2705	731-2769
Web: www.malmstrom.af.mil					
Montana Historical Society Museum 225 N Roberts St	Helena	MT	59620	406-444-2694	444-2696
TF: 800-243-9900 ■ Web: mhs.mt.gov/					
Museum of the Rockies 600 W Kagy Blvd Montana State University	Bozeman	MT	59717	406-994-1998	994-2682
Web: www.museumoftherockies.org					
Paris Gibson Square Museum of Art 1400 First Ave N	Great Falls	MT	59401	406-727-8255	727-8256
Web: www.the-square.org					
Peter Yegen Jr Yellowstone County Museum 1950 Terminal Cir	Billings	MT	59105	406-256-6811	254-6031
Web: www.pyjrycm.org					
World Museum of Mining 155 Museum Way PO Box 33	Butte	MT	59703	406-723-7211	723-7211
Web: www.miningmuseum.org					
Yellowstone Art Museum 401 N 27th St	Billings	MT	59101	406-256-6804	256-6817
Web: www.yellowstone.artmuseum.org					
Yellowstone Western Heritage Ctr 2822 Montana Ave	Billings	MT	59101	406-256-6809	256-6850
Web: www.ywhc.org					

Nebraska

				Phone	Fax
Bank of Florence Museum 8502 N 30th St	Omaha	NE	68112	402-496-9923	
Web: www.historicflorence.org/attractions.php					
Durham Museum 801 S Tenth St	Omaha	NE	68108	402-444-5071	444-5397
Web: www.durhammuseum.org					
El Museo Latino 4701 S 25th St	Omaha	NE	68107	402-731-1137	733-7012
Web: www.elmuseolatino.org					
Great Plains Art Museum 1155 Q St PO Box 880250	Lincoln	NE	68588	402-472-6220	472-0463
Web: www.unl.edu					
Joslyn Art Museum 2200 Dodge St	Omaha	NE	68102	402-342-3300	342-2376
Web: www.joslyn.org					
Museum of Nebraska History 15th & P St PO Box 82554	Lincoln	NE	68508	402-471-4754	471-3314
TF: 800-833-6747 ■ Web: www.nebraskahistory.org/sites/mnh					
National Museum of Roller Skating 4730 S St	Lincoln	NE	68506	402-483-7551	483-1465
Web: www.rollerskatingmuseum.com					
Nebraska Jewish Historical Museum 333 S 132nd St	Omaha	NE	68154	402-334-6441	
Sheldon Museum of Art PO Box 880300	Lincoln	NE	68588	402-472-2461	472-4258
Web: www.sheldonartmuseum.org					
Strategic Air & Space Museum 28210 W Pk Hwy	Ashland	NE	68003	402-944-3100	944-3160
TF: 800-358-5029 ■ Web: www.sasmuseum.com					
Stuhr Museum of the Prairie Pioneer 3133 W Hwy 34	Grand Island	NE	68801	308-385-5316	385-5028
Web: stuhrmuseum.org					
University of Nebraska State Museum 14Th & U	Lincoln	NE	68588	402-472-2642	472-8899
Web: museum.unl.edu					
University of Nebraska-Lincoln 1155 Q St Hewit Pl	Lincoln	NE	68588	402-472-5841	472-0463
Web: www.unl.edu					

Nevada

				Phone	Fax
Atomic Testing Museum 755 E Flamingo Rd	Las Vegas	NV	89119	702-794-5151	794-5155
Web: www.nationalatomictestingmuseum.org					
Boulder City/Hoover Dam Museum 1305 Arizona St	Boulder City	NV	89005	702-294-1988	294-4380
Web: www.bcmha.org					
Carson Valley Museum & Cultural Ctr 1477 old US Hwy 395 S	Gardnerville	NV	89410	775-782-2555	783-8802
Churchill County Museum & Archives 1050 S Maine St	Fallon	NV	89406	775-423-3677	423-3662
Web: www.ccmuseum.org					
Clark County Museum 1830 S Boulder Hwy	Henderson	NV	89002	702-455-7955	455-7948
Web: clarkcountynv.gov					
Guggenheim Hermitage Museum 3355 Las Vegas Blvd S Venetian Resort Hotel & Casino	Las Vegas	NV	89109	212-423-3575	414-2442*
*Fax Area Code: 702 ■ TF: 800-329-6109 ■ Web: guggenheim.org					
Las Vegas Natural History Museum 900 Las Vegas Blvd N	Las Vegas	NV	89101	702-384-3466	
Web: www.lvnhm.org					
Lost City Museum of Archeology PO Box 807	Overton	NV	89040	702-397-2193	397-8987
Web: museums.nevadaculture.org					
Marjorie Barrick Museum 4505 S Maryland Pkwy	Las Vegas	NV	89154	702-895-3381	895-5737
TF: 877-895-0334 ■ Web: barrickmuseum.unlv.edu					
National Automobile Museum 10 S Lake St	Reno	NV	89501	775-333-9300	333-9309
Web: www.automuseum.org					
Nevada Museum of Art 160 W Liberty St	Reno	NV	89501	775-329-3333	329-1541
Web: www.nevadaart.org					
Nevada State Museum 600 N Carson St	Carson City	NV	89701	775-687-4810	687-4168
Web: museums.nevadaculture.org					
Nevada State Railroad Museum 2180 S Carson St	Carson City	NV	89701	775-687-6953	687-8294
Web: www.nsrm-friends.org					
Northeastern Nevada Museum 1515 Idaho St	Elko	NV	89801	775-738-3418	778-9318
Web: www.museumelko.org					
Roberts House Museum 1207 N Carson St	Carson City	NV	89701	775-887-2174	
Sparks Heritage Museum 814 Victorian Ave	Sparks	NV	89431	775-355-1144	
Web: www.sparksmuseum.org					
Way It Was Museum 113 N St	Virginia City	NV	89440	775-847-0766	
Wilbur D May Museum 1595 N Sierra St	Reno	NV	89503	775-785-5961	785-4707
Web: www.washoecounty.us					

New Brunswick

				Phone	Fax
Kings Landing Historical Settlement 5804 Rt 102	Prince William	NB	E6K0A5	506-363-4999	363-4989
TF General: 888-666-5547 ■ Web: www.kingslanding.nb.ca					
New Brunswick Museum One Market Sq	Saint John	NB	E2L4Z6	506-643-2300	643-6081
TF: 888-268-9595 ■ Web: www.nbm-mnb.ca/index.php?option=com_content&view=article&id=121&itemid=316					
University of Moncton 18 Ave Antonine-Maillet	Moncton	NB	E1A3E9	506-858-4088	858-4043
Web: www.umoncton.ca					

New Hampshire

				Phone	Fax
Canterbury Shaker Village 288 Shaker Rd	Canterbury	NH	03224	603-783-9511	
Web: www.shakers.org					

Name / Address	City	State	Zip	Phone	Fax
Currier Museum of Art 150 Ash St *Web:* www.currier.org	Manchester	NH	03104	603-669-6144	669-7194
Lawrence L Lee Scouting Museum 571 Holt Ave *Web:* www.scoutingmuseum.org	Manchester	NH	03109	603-669-8919	625-2467
Mount Kearsarge Indian Museum 18 Highlawn Rd *Web:* www.indianmuseum.com	Warner	NH	03278	603-456-2600	456-3092
Museum of New Hampshire History Six Eagle Sq *Web:* www.nhhistory.org	Concord	NH	03301	603-228-6688	228-6308
New Hampshire Historical Society 30 Pk St *Web:* www.nhhistory.org	Concord	NH	03301	603-228-6688	224-0463
New Hampshire Institute of Art 148 Concord St *TF:* 866-241-4918 ■ *Web:* www.nhia.edu	Manchester	NH	03104	603-623-0313	647-0658
Seacoast Science Center Inc 570 Ocean Blvd *Web:* www.seacoastsciencecenter.org	Rye	NH	03870	603-436-8043	
SEE Science Ctr 200 Bedford St *Web:* www.see-sciencecenter.org	Manchester	NH	03101	603-669-0400	669-0400
Strawbery Banke Museum 14 Hancock St *Web:* www.strawberybanke.org	Portsmouth	NH	03801	603-433-1100	433-1129

New Jersey

Name / Address	City	State	Zip	Phone	Fax
Afro-American Historical Society Museum 1841 Kennedy Blvd *Web:* www.cityofjerseycity.org	Jersey City	NJ	07305	201-547-5262	547-5392
Aljira Ctr for Contemporary Arts 591 Broad St *Web:* www.aljira.org	Newark	NJ	07102	973-622-1600	622-6526
American Labor Museum/Botto House National Landmark 83 Norwood St *Web:* www.labormuseum.net	Haledon	NJ	07508	973-595-7953	595-7291
Atlantic County Historical Society Museum 907 Shore Rd *Web:* www.aclink.org	Somers Point	NJ	08244	609-927-5218	927-5218
Creative Glass Center of America 1501 Glasstown Rd *Web:* www.wheatonarts.org	Millville	NJ	08332	856-825-6800	
Jersey City Museum 350 Montgomery St *Web:* jerseycityonline.com	Jersey City	NJ	07302	201-413-0303	413-9922
Liberty Science Ctr Liberty State Pk 222 Jersey City Blvd *Web:* www.lsc.org	Jersey City	NJ	07305	201-200-1000	
Marine Mammal Stranding Ctr 3625 Brigantine Blvd *Web:* www.mmsc.org	Brigantine	NJ	08203	609-266-0538	266-6300
Mid Atlantic Center for The Arts 1048 Washington St *Web:* www.capemaymac.org	Cape May	NJ	08204	609-884-5404	
Montclair Art Museum Three S Mtn Ave *Web:* montclairartmuseum.org	Montclair	NJ	07042	973-746-5555	746-0536
Morris Museum Six Normandy Heights Rd *Web:* www.morrismuseum.org	Morristown	NJ	07960	973-971-3700	538-0154
New Jersey Historical Society Museum 52 Pk Pl *Web:* www.jerseyhistory.org	Newark	NJ	07102	973-596-8500	596-6957
New Jersey State Museum 205 W State St *Web:* www.state.nj.us/state/museum	Trenton	NJ	08625	609-292-6300	292-7636
Newark Museum 49 Washington St *TF:* 888-370-6765 ■ *Web:* www.newarkmuseum.org	Newark	NJ	07102	973-596-6550	642-0459
Noyes Museum of Art 733 Lily Lake Rd *TF:* 800-852-7899 ■ *Web:* www.noyesmuseum.org	Oceanville	NJ	08231	609-652-8848	652-6166
Old Barracks Museum 101 Barrack St *Web:* www.barracks.org	Trenton	NJ	08608	609-396-1776	777-4000
Paterson Museum 2 Market St Ste 102 *Web:* www.thepatersonmuseum.com	Paterson	NJ	07501	973-321-1260	881-3435
Trenton City Museum at Ellarslie Mansion PO Box 1034 *Web:* www.ellarslie.org	Trenton	NJ	08606	609-989-1191	989-3624

New Mexico

Name / Address	City	State	Zip	Phone	Fax
American International Rattlesnake Museum 202 San Felipe NW Ste A *Web:* www.rattlesnakes.com	Albuquerque	NM	87104	505-242-6569	242-6569
Bataan Memorial Museum 1050 Old Pecos Trl *Web:* bataanmuseum.com	Santa Fe	NM	87505	505-474-1670	474-1670
Bradbury Science Museum 1350 Central PO Box 1663 *Web:* www.lanl.gov	Los Alamos	NM	87545	505-667-4444	665-6932
El Rancho de las Golondrinas Museum 334 Los Pinos Rd *Web:* www.golondrinas.org	Santa Fe	NM	87507	505-471-2261	471-5623
Explora 1701 Mtn Rd NW *Web:* explora.us	Albuquerque	NM	87104	505-224-8300	224-8325
Georgia O'Keeffe Museum 217 Johnson St *Web:* www.okeeffemuseum.org	Santa Fe	NM	87501	505-946-1000	
Historical Lawmen Museum 845 Motel Blvd *Web:* donaanacounty.org	Las Cruces	NM	88007	575-525-1911	647-7800
Hubbard Museum of the American West 26301 Hwy 70 W PO Box 40 *Web:* hubbardmuseum.org	Ruidoso Downs	NM	88346	575-378-4142	378-4166
Indian Pueblo Cultural Ctr 2401 12th St NW *TF:* 866-855-7902 ■ *Web:* www.indianpueblo.org	Albuquerque	NM	87104	505-843-7270	842-6959
Institute of American Indian Arts Museum 108 Cathedral Pl *Web:* www.iaia.edu	Santa Fe	NM	87501	505-983-8900	983-1222
Las Cruces Museum of Natural History PO Box 20000 *Web:* www.las-cruces.org	Las Cruces	NM	88004	575-532-3372	532-3370
Los Alamos Historical Museum 1050 Bathtub Row PO Box 43 *Web:* www.losalamoshistory.org	Los Alamos	NM	87544	505-662-6272	662-6312
Maxwell Museum of Anthropology University of New Mexico *TF:* 855-227-6231 ■ *Web:* www.unm.edu	Albuquerque	NM	87131	505-277-4405	277-1547
Museum of Indian Arts & Culture 710 Camino Lejo PO Box 2087 *Web:* www.miaclab.org	Santa Fe	NM	87501	505-476-1250	476-1330
Museum of International Folk Art 706 Camino Lejo *TF:* 888-670-3655 ■ *Web:* www.internationalfolkart.org	Santa Fe	NM	87505	505-476-1200	476-1300
Museum of Spanish Colonial Arts 750 Camino Lejo *Web:* spanishcolonial.org/	Santa Fe	NM	87502	505-982-2226	982-4585
New Mexico Farm & Ranch Heritage Museum 4100 Dripping Springs Rd *Web:* www.nmfarmandranchmuseum.org	Las Cruces	NM	88011	575-522-4100	522-3085
New Mexico Holocaust & Intolerance Museum & Study Ctr 616 Central Ave SW *Web:* www.nmholocaustmuseum.org	Albuquerque	NM	87102	505-247-0606	
New Mexico Museum of Art 107 W Palace Ave *TF:* 877-567-7380 ■ *Web:* www.nmartmuseum.org	Santa Fe	NM	87501	505-476-5072	476-5076
New Mexico Museum of Natural History & Science 1801 Mtn Rd NW *Web:* www.nmnaturalhistory.org	Albuquerque	NM	87104	505-841-2800	841-2866
New Mexico Museum of Space History Top of Hwy 2001 *TF:* 877-333-6589 ■ *Web:* www.nmspacemuseum.org	Alamogordo	NM	88311	575-437-2840	434-2245
New Mexico State University Museum University Ave & Solano Dr Kent Hall PO Box 30001 MSC 3564 *Web:* univmuseum.nmsu.edu/	Las Cruces	NM	88001	575-646-3739	646-1419
Roswell Museum & Art Ctr 100 W 11th St **Fax Area Code:* 505 ■ *Web:* www.roswellmuseum.org	Roswell	NM	88201	575-624-6744	624-6765*
Space Murals Museum 12450 Hwy 70 E	Las Cruces	NM	88011	575-382-0977	
Telephone Pioneer Museum of New Mexico 110 Fourth St NW *Web:* www.museumsusa.org	Albuquerque	NM	87102	505-842-2937	
Tinkertown Museum PO Box 303 *Web:* www.tinkertown.com	Sandia Park	NM	87047	505-281-5233	
University of New Mexico Art Museum One University of New Mexico *Web:* unmartmuseum.org	Albuquerque	NM	87131	505-277-4001	277-7315
Wheelwright Museum of the American Indian 704 Camino Lejo *TF:* 800-607-4636 ■ *Web:* www.wheelwright.org	Santa Fe	NM	87505	505-982-4636	989-7386
White Sands Missile Range Museum & Missile Park US Hwy 70 *Web:* www.wsmr-history.org	White Sands	NM	88002	575-678-8824	678-2199

New York

Name / Address	City	State	Zip	Phone	Fax
Albany Institute of History & Art 125 Washington Ave *Web:* www.albanyinstitute.org	Albany	NY	12210	518-463-4478	462-1522
Albright-Knox Art Gallery 1285 Elmwood Ave *Web:* www.albrightknox.org	Buffalo	NY	14222	716-882-8700	882-1958
Alice Austen House Museum & Garden Two Hylan Blvd *Web:* www.aliceausten.8m.com	Staten Island	NY	10305	718-816-4506	815-3959
American Folk Art Museum 45 W 53rd St *Web:* www.folkartmuseum.org	New York	NY	10019	212-265-1040	265-2350
American Numismatic Society 75 Varick St 11th Fl *Web:* www.numismatics.org	New York	NY	10013	212-571-4470	571-4479
Amherst Museum 3755 Tonawanda Creek Rd *Web:* www.bnhv.org	Amherst	NY	14228	716-689-1440	689-1409
Bartow-Pell Mansion Museum 895 Shore Rd Pelham Bay Pk *Web:* www.bartowpellmansionmuseum.org	Bronx	NY	10464	718-885-1461	885-9164
Bear Mountain Trailside Museums & Zoo Bear Mtn State Pk Rt 9 W *Web:* www.trailsidezoo.org	Bear Mountain	NY	10911	845-786-2701	
Belenky Bros Inc 91 Grand St *Web:* belenky.com	New York	NY	10013	212-674-4242	
Bronx County Historical Society 3309 Bainbridge Ave *Web:* www.bronxhistoricalsociety.org	Bronx	NY	10467	718-881-8900	881-4827
Bronx Museum of the Arts 1040 Grand Concourse *Web:* www.bronxmuseum.org	Bronx	NY	10456	718-681-6000	681-6181
Brooklyn Historical Society 128 Pierrepont St *Web:* www.brooklynhistory.org	Brooklyn	NY	11201	718-222-4111	
Brooklyn Museum of Art 200 Eastern Pkwy *Web:* www.brooklynmuseum.org	Brooklyn	NY	11238	718-638-5000	501-6136
Buffalo Fire Historical Museum 1850 William St *Web:* bfhsmuseum.com	Buffalo	NY	14206	716-892-8400	
Buffalo Museum of Science 1020 Humboldt Pkwy *TF:* 866-291-6660 ■ *Web:* www.sciencebuff.org	Buffalo	NY	14211	716-896-5200	897-6723
Children's Museum of Science & Technology 250 Jordan Rd *Web:* www.cmost.org	Troy	NY	12180	518-235-2120	235-6836
Cloisters Museum Fort Tryon Pk *TF:* 800-662-3397 ■ *Web:* www.metmuseum.org	New York	NY	10040	212-923-3700	795-3640
Cooper-Hewitt National Design Museum (Smithsonian Institution) 2 E 91st St *Web:* www.cooperhewitt.org	New York	NY	10128	212-849-8400	849-8401
Corning Museum of Glass One Museum Way *TF Cust Svc:* 800-732-6845 ■ *Web:* www.cmog.org	Corning	NY	14830	607-937-5371	438-5410

Name / Address	City	State	Zip	Phone	Fax
Doyle New York 175 E 87th St *Web:* www.doylenewyork.com	New York	NY	10128	212-427-2730	369-0892
Dyckman Farmhouse Museum 4881 Broadway at 204th St *Web:* www.dyckmanfarmhouse.org	New York	NY	10034	212-304-9422	304-0635
Ellis Island National Museum of Immigration 17 Battery Pl Ste 210 *Web:* www.ellisisland.org	New York	NY	10004	212-561-4588	
Empire State Aerosciences Museum 250 Rudy Chase Dr *Web:* www.esam.org	Glenville	NY	12302	518-377-2191	377-1959
Empire State Plaza Art Collection Empire State Plz Curatorial & Services 41st Fl Corning Twr *TF:* 877-659-4377 ■ *Web:* www.ogs.ny.gov	Albany	NY	12242	518-474-3899	457-3081
Erie Canal Museum 318 Erie Blvd E *Web:* www.eriecanalmuseum.org	Syracuse	NY	13202	315-471-0593	471-7220
Everson Museum of Art 401 Harrison St *Web:* www.everson.org	Syracuse	NY	13202	315-474-6064	474-6943
Fasny Museum of Firefighting 117 Harry Howard Ave *Web:* www.fasnyfiremuseum.com	Hudson	NY	12534	518-822-1875	
Franklin D Roosevelt Presidential Library & Museum 4079 Albany Post Rd *TF:* 800-337-8474 ■ *Web:* www.fdrlibrary.marist.edu	Hyde Park	NY	12538	845-486-7770	486-1147
Frick Collection One E 70th St *Web:* www.frick.org	New York	NY	10021	212-288-0700	628-4417
Genesee Country Village & Museum 1410 Flint Hill Rd *Web:* www.gcv.org	Mumford	NY	14511	585-538-6822	538-6927
Harbor Defense Museum 230 Sheridan Loop *Web:* harbordefensemuseum.com	Brooklyn	NY	11252	718-630-4349	630-4888
Herbert F Johnson Museum of Art 114 Central Ave *Web:* www.museum.cornell.edu	Ithaca	NY	14853	607-255-6464	
Hudson River Museum 511 Warburton Ave *Web:* www.hrm.org	Yonkers	NY	10701	914-963-4550	963-8558
Hyde Collection 161 Warren St *Web:* www.hydecollection.org	Glens Falls	NY	12801	518-792-1761	792-9197
International Ctr of Photography 1133 Ave of the Americas *Web:* www.icp.org	New York	NY	10036	212-857-0000	768-4688
International Museum of Photography & Film at George Eastman House 900 E Ave *Web:* www.eastmanhouse.org	Rochester	NY	14607	585-271-3361	271-3970
Intrepid Sea-Air-Space Museum W 46th St & 12th Ave Pier 86 *TF:* 877-957-7447 ■ *Web:* www.intrepidmuseum.org	New York	NY	10036	212-245-0072	
Iron Island Museum 998 E Lovejoy St *Web:* www.ironislandmuseum.com	Buffalo	NY	14206	716-892-3084	
Iroquois Indian Museum 324 Caverns Rd PO Box 7 *Web:* www.iroquoismuseum.org	Howes Cave	NY	12092	518-296-8949	296-8955
Jacques Marchais Museum of Tibetan Art 338 Lighthouse Ave *Web:* www.tibetanmuseum.org	Staten Island	NY	10306	718-987-3500	351-0402
Jefferson County Historical Society 228 Washington St *Web:* jeffersoncountyhistory.org	Watertown	NY	13601	315-782-3491	782-2913
Jewish Museum 1109 Fifth Ave *Web:* www.thejewishmuseum.org	New York	NY	10128	212-423-3200	423-3232
Karpeles Manuscript Library 453 Porter Ave *Web:* www.rain.org/~karpeles	Buffalo	NY	14201	716-885-4139	
Katonah Museum of Art Inc 134 Jay St *Web:* www.katonahmuseum.org	Katonah	NY	10536	914-232-9555	
Long Island Museum of American Art History & Carriages 1200 Rt 25A *Web:* www.longislandmuseum.org	Stony Brook	NY	11790	631-751-0066	751-0353
Lower East Side Tenement Museum National Historic Site 108 Orchard St *Web:* www.tenement.org	New York	NY	10002	212-431-0233	431-0402
Madame Tussauds New York Inc 234 W 42nd St Times Sq *Web:* www.madametussauds.com	New York	NY	10036	212-512-9600	
Memorial Art Gallery of the University of Rochester 500 University Ave *Web:* www.mag.rochester.edu	Rochester	NY	14607	585-276-8900	
Metropolitan Museum of Art 1000 Fifth Ave *TF:* 800-468-7386 ■ *Web:* www.metmuseum.org	New York	NY	10028	212-879-5500	570-3979
Morris-Jumel Mansion 65 Jumel Terr at 160th St *Web:* www.morrisjumel.org	New York	NY	10032	212-923-8008	923-8947
Mount Vernon Hotel Museum & Garden 421 E 61st St *Web:* www.mvhm.org	New York	NY	10065	212-838-6878	838-7390
Munson-Williams-Proctor Arts Institute 310 Genesee St *Web:* www.mwpai.org	Utica	NY	13502	315-797-0000	797-5608
Museo del Barrio 1230 Fifth Ave *Web:* www.elmuseo.org	New York	NY	10029	212-831-7272	831-7927
Museum for African Art 36-01 43rd Ave *Web:* www.africanart.org	Long Island City	NY	11101	718-784-7700	784-7718
Museum of American Financial History 48 Wall St *Web:* www.moaf.org	New York	NY	10005	212-908-4110	908-4601
Museum of American Illustration 128 E 63rd St *Web:* www.societyillustrators.org	New York	NY	10065	212-838-2560	838-2561
Museum of Arts & Design Two Columbus Cir *Web:* madmuseum.org	New York	NY	10019	212-299-7777	
Museum of Jewish Heritage 36 Battery Pl Battery Pk City *Web:* www.mjhnyc.org	New York	NY	10280	212-968-1800	
Museum of Modern Art 11 W 53rd St *Web:* www.moma.org	New York	NY	10019	212-708-9400	
Museum of Science & Technology 500 S Franklin St *Web:* www.most.org	Syracuse	NY	13202	315-425-9068	425-9072
Museum of Sex 233 Fifth Ave Rm 3b *Web:* museumofsex.com	New York	NY	10016	212-689-6337	
Museum of the City of New York 1220 Fifth Ave *Web:* www.mcny.org	New York	NY	10029	212-534-1672	423-0758
Museum of the Moving Image 3601 35th Ave	New York	NY	11106	718-777-6800	784-4681
National Academy Museum of Art 1083 Fifth Ave *Web:* www.nationalacademy.org	New York	NY	10128	212-369-4880	360-6795
National Women's Hall of Fame 76 Fall St PO Box 335 *Web:* www.greatwomen.org	Seneca Falls	NY	13148	315-568-8060	568-2976
Neuberger Museum of Art 735 Anderson Hill Rd Purchase College SUNY *Web:* www.neuberger.org	Purchase	NY	10577	914-251-6100	251-6101
New Museum of Contemporary Art 235 Bowery *Web:* www.newmuseum.org	New York	NY	10002	212-219-1222	431-5328
New York City Fire Museum 278 Spring St *Web:* www.nycfiremuseum.org	New York	NY	10013	212-691-1303	352-3117
New York City Police Museum 100 Old Slip *Web:* www.nycpolicemuseum.org	New York	NY	10005	212-480-3100	480-9757
New York Hall of Science 47-01 111th St *Web:* www.nysci.org	Queens	NY	11368	718-699-0005	
New York Historical Society 170 Central Pk W *Web:* www.nyhistory.org	New York	NY	10024	212-873-3400	874-8706
New York State Museum 260 Madison Ave *Web:* www.nysm.nysed.gov	Albany	NY	12210	518-474-5877	486-3696
New York Transit Museum 130 Livingston St Fl 10 *Web:* mta.info/mta/museum	Brooklyn	NY	11201	718-694-1600	
Pedaling History Bicycle Museum 3943 N Buffalo Rd *Web:* www.pedalinghistory.com	Orchard Park	NY	14127	716-662-3853	662-4594
Pierpont Morgan Library 225 Madison Ave *Web:* www.themorgan.org	New York	NY	10016	212-685-0008	481-3484
Queens County Farm Museum 73-50 Little Neck Pkwy *Web:* www.queensfarm.org	Floral Park	NY	11004	718-347-3276	
Queens Museum of Art New York City Bldg *TF:* 866-867-9665 ■ *Web:* www.queensmuseum.org	Queens	NY	11368	718-592-9700	592-5778
Roberson Museum & Science Ctr 30 Front St *TF:* 888-269-5325 ■ *Web:* www.roberson.org	Binghamton	NY	13905	607-772-0660	771-8905
Rochester Museum & Science Ctr 657 E Ave *Web:* www.rmsc.org	Rochester	NY	14607	585-271-4320	271-0492
Sainte Marie among the Iroquois Museum 6680 Onondaga Lk Pkwy *Web:* ongov.net	Liverpool	NY	13088	315-453-6768	
Schenectady Museum & Suits-Bueche Planetarium 15 Nott Terr Heights *Web:* www.schenectadymuseum.org	Schenectady	NY	12308	518-382-7890	382-7893
Solomon R Guggenheim Museum 1071 Fifth Ave *TF:* 800-329-6109 ■ *Web:* www.guggenheim.org	New York	NY	10128	212-423-3500	423-3640
South Street Seaport Museum 12 Fulton St *Web:* www.southstreetseaportmuseum.org	New York	NY	10038	212-748-8600	
Staten Island Institute of Arts & Sciences 75 Stuyvesant Pl *Web:* statenislandmuseum.org	Staten Island	NY	10301	718-727-1135	273-5683
Steel Plant Museum 100 Lee St Heritage Discovery Ctr *Web:* steelplantmuseumwny.org	Buffalo	NY	14210	716-821-9361	827-1997
Strong - National Museum of Play One Manhattan Sq *Web:* www.museumofplay.org	Rochester	NY	14607	585-263-2700	263-2493
Studio Museum in Harlem 144 W 125th St *Web:* www.studiomuseuminharlem.org	New York	NY	10027	212-864-4500	864-4800
Suffolk County Historical Society 300 W Main St *Web:* suffolkcountyhistoricalsociety.org	Riverhead	NY	11901	631-727-2881	727-3467
Ten Broeck Mansion Nine Ten Broeck Pl *Web:* tenbroeckmansion.org	Albany	NY	12210	518-436-9826	436-1489
Theodore Roosevelt Inaugural National Historic Site 641 Delaware Ave *Web:* www.nps.gov/thri	Buffalo	NY	14202	716-884-0095	884-0330
Ukrainian Museum 222 E Sixth St *Web:* www.ukrainianmuseum.org	New York	NY	10003	212-228-0110	228-1947
Victorian Doll Museum 4332 Buffalo Rd *Web:* chilidollhospital.com	North Chili	NY	14514	585-247-0130	
Whitney Museum of American Art 945 Madison Ave *TF:* 800-944-8639 ■ *Web:* www.whitney.org	New York	NY	10021	212-570-3600	
Wildenstein & Co 19 E 64th St *Web:* www.wildenstein.com	New York	NY	10021	212-879-0500	
Yager Museum of Art & Culture, The Hartwick College PO Box 4020 *Web:* www.hartwick.edu/academics/museum	Oneonta	NY	13820	607-431-4000	431-4468
Yeshiva University Museum 15 W 16th St *Web:* www.yu.edu	New York	NY	10011	212-294-8330	294-8335

North Carolina

Phone | Fax

Antique Car Museum/Grovewood Gallery
111 Grovewood Rd. . . . . Asheville NC 28804 828-253-7651 254-2489
TF: 877-622-7238 ■ *Web:* www.grovewood.com

Artspace Inc 201 E Davie St Ste 101. . . . . Raleigh NC 27601 919-821-2787
Web: www.artspacenc.org

Asheville Art Museum
Two S Pack Sq PO Box 1717 . . . . . Asheville NC 28801 828-253-3227 257-4503
Web: ashevilleart.org

Backing Up Classics Auto Museum
4545 Concord Pkwy S . . . . . Concord NC 28027 704-788-9500
Web: www.backingupclassics.com

CAM Raleigh (CAM) 409 W Martin St . . . . . Raleigh NC 27603 919-261-5920 515-7330
Web: camraleigh.org

Charlotte Hawkins Brown Museum
6136 Burlington Rd PO Box B . . . . . Sedalia NC 27342 336-449-4846 449-0176
Web: www.nchistoricsites.org

Charlotte Museum of History & Hezekiah Alexander Homesite
3500 Shamrock Dr . . . . . Charlotte NC 28215 704-568-1774 566-1817
Web: www.charlottemuseum.org

Charlotte Nature Museum 1658 Sterling Rd. . . . . Charlotte NC 28209 704-372-6261
TF: 800-935-0553 ■ *Web:* www.charlottenaturemuseum.org

Charlotte Trolley Inc 2104 S Blvd . . . . . Charlotte NC 28203 704-375-0850
Web: charlottetrolley.org

Colburn Earth Science Museum Two S Pack Sq . . . . . Asheville NC 28801 828-254-7162 257-4505
Web: colburnmuseum.wordpress.com

EnergyExplorium 13339 Hagers Ferry Rd. . . . . Huntersville NC 28078 980-875-5600 875-5602*
**Fax Area Code: 704* ■ *TF:* 800-777-0003 ■ *Web:* m.duke-energy.com

Estes-Winn Memorial Automobile Museum
111 Grovewood Rd. . . . . Asheville NC 28804 828-253-7651 254-2489
TF: 877-622-7238 ■
Web: www.grovewood.com/about-us/estes-winn-antique-car-museum

Folk Art Ctr PO Box 9545 . . . . . Asheville NC 28815 828-298-7928 298-7962
TF: 888-672-7717 ■ *Web:* www.southernhighlandguild.org

Greensboro Science Center
4301 Lawndale Dr. . . . . Greensboro NC 27455 336-288-3769 288-2531
Web: www.greensboroscience.org

Greenville Museum of Art 802 S Evans St . . . . . Greenville NC 27834 252-758-1946 758-7989
Web: www.gmoa.org

International Civil Rights Ctr & Museum
134 S Elm St. . . . . Greensboro NC 27401 336-274-9199 274-6244
TF: 800-748-7116 ■ *Web:* www.sitinmovement.org

Joel Lane House Museum & Gardens
728 W Hargett St . . . . . Raleigh NC 27603 919-833-3431
Web: www.joellane.org

Levine Museum of the New South
200 E Seventh St . . . . . Charlotte NC 28202 704-333-1887 333-1896
Web: www.museumofthenewsouth.org

Marbles Kids Museum 201 E Hargett St. . . . . Raleigh NC 27601 919-834-4040 834-3516
TF: 800-745-3000 ■ *Web:* www.marbleskidsmuseum.org

Mint Museum of Art 2730 Randolph Rd . . . . . Charlotte NC 28207 704-337-2000 337-2101
Web: www.mintmuseum.org

Museum of Early Southern Decorative Arts (MESDA)
924 S Main St. . . . . Winston-Salem NC 27101 336-721-7360 721-7367
TF: 800-441-5303 ■ *Web:* www.mesda.org

Nasher Museum of Art at Duke University
2001 Campus Dr Duke University. . . . . Durham NC 27701 919-684-5135 681-8624
Web: www.duke.edu

New Hope Valley Railway PO Box 40. . . . . New Hill NC 27562 919-362-5416
Web: www.nhvry.org

North Carolina Central University Art Museum
1801 Fayetteville St . . . . . Durham NC 27707 919-530-6211 560-5649
TF: 877-667-7533 ■ *Web:* www.nccu.edu

North Carolina Museum of Art
2110 Blue Ridge Rd . . . . . Raleigh NC 27607 919-839-6262 733-8034
Web: www.ncartmuseum.org

North Carolina Museum of History
Five E Edenton St . . . . . Raleigh NC 27601 919-807-7900 733-8655
Web: www.ncdcr.gov

North Carolina Museum of Life & Science
433 Murray Ave . . . . . Durham NC 27704 919-220-5429 220-5575
Web: lifeandscience.org

North Carolina Museum of Natural Sciences
11 W Jones St . . . . . Raleigh NC 27601 919-733-7450 733-1573
Web: www.naturalsciences.org

Old Salem 600 S Main St. . . . . Winston-Salem NC 27101 336-721-7300 721-7335
TF: 800-441-5305 ■ *Web:* www.oldsalem.org

Raleigh City Museum
220 Fayetteville St Ste 100. . . . . Raleigh NC 27601 919-996-2220 832-3085
Web: www.cityofraleighmuseum.org/

Reynolda House Museum of American Art
2250 Reynolda Rd . . . . . Winston-Salem NC 27106 336-758-5150 758-5704
TF: 888-663-1149 ■ *Web:* www.reynoldahouse.org

Richard Petty Museum 142 W Academy St. . . . . Randleman NC 27317 336-495-1143 495-1543
Web: www.richardpettymotorsports.com

Schiele Museum of Natural History & James H Lynn Planetarium
1500 E Garrison Blvd . . . . . Gastonia NC 28054 704-866-6908 866-6041
Web: www.schielemuseum.org/planetarium.php

SciWorks Science Ctr & Environmental Park of Forsyth County
400 Hanes-Mill Rd . . . . . Winston-Salem NC 27105 336-767-6730 661-1777
Web: www.sciworks.org

Smith McDowell House Museum
283 Victoria Rd. . . . . Asheville NC 28803 828-253-9231 253-5518
Web: www.wnchistory.org

Weatherspoon Art Museum 500 Tate St. . . . . Greensboro NC 27402 336-334-5770 334-5907
TF: 877-862-4123 ■ *Web:* www.uncg.edu

North Dakota

Phone | Fax

Bonanzaville USA 1351 Main Ave W. . . . . West Fargo ND 58078 701-282-2822 282-7606
Web: www.bonanzaville.org

Fargo Air Museum 1609 19th Ave N . . . . . Fargo ND 58102 701-293-8043 293-8103
Web: www.fargoairmuseum.org

Myra Museum 2405 Belmont Rd . . . . . Grand Forks ND 58201 701-775-2216 775-0317
Web: www.grandforkshistory.com

North Dakota Game & Fish Dept
100 N Bismarck Expy . . . . . Bismarck ND 58501 701-328-6300 328-6352
TF: 800-406-6409 ■ *Web:* www.gf.nd.gov

North Dakota Museum of Art
261Centennial Dr S-7305. . . . . Grand Forks ND 58202 701-777-4195 777-4425
Web: www.ndmoa.com

Nova Scotia

Phone | Fax

Anne Murray Centre 36 Main St PO Box 610 . . . . . Springhill NS B0M1X0 902-597-8614 597-2001
Web: www.annemurraycentre.com

Black Cultural Centre for Nova Scotia
10 Cherry Brook Rd . . . . . Cherry Brook NS B2Z1A8 902-434-6223 434-2306
TF: 800-465-0767 ■ *Web:* web1.bccnsweb.com

Fisheries Museum of the Atlantic
68 Bluenose Dr PO Box 1363. . . . . Lunenburg NS B0J2C0 902-634-4794 634-8990
TF: 866-579-4909 ■ *Web:* museum.novascotia.ca/

Maritime Museum of the Atlantic
1675 Lower Water St. . . . . Halifax NS B3J1S3 902-424-7490 424-0612
Web: maritime.museum.gov.ns.ca

Nova Scotia Museum of Industry
147 N Foord St. . . . . Stellarton NS B0K1S0 902-755-5425 755-7045
Web: museumofindustry.novascotia.ca/

Nova Scotia Museum of Natural History
1747 Summer St. . . . . Halifax NS B3H3A6 902-424-7353 424-0560
Web: naturalhistory.novascotia.ca

Ohio

Phone | Fax

Akron Art Museum One S High St. . . . . Akron OH 44308 330-376-9185 376-1180
Web: www.akronartmuseum.org

Akron Police - Community Relations
217 S High St Rm 402 . . . . . Akron OH 44308 330-375-2390 375-2412
Web: akronohio.gov

Arms Family Museum of Local History
648 Wick Ave . . . . . Youngstown OH 44502 330-743-2589 743-7210
Web: www.mahoninghistory.org

Blair Museum of Lithopanes
Toledo Botanical Garden 5403 Elmer Dr. . . . . Toledo OH 43615 419-245-1356
Web: www.lithophanemuseum.org

Boonshoft Museum of Discovery
2600 DeWeese Pkwy. . . . . Dayton OH 45414 937-275-7431 275-5811
Web: www.boonshoftmuseum.org

Butler Institute of American Art
524 Wick Ave . . . . . Youngstown OH 44502 330-743-1711 743-9567
Web: www.butlerart.com

Carillon Historical Park 1000 Carillon Blvd . . . . . Dayton OH 45409 937-293-2841 293-5798
Web: www.daytonhistory.org

Century Village 14653 E Pk St . . . . . Burton OH 44021 440-834-1492 834-4012
Web: centuryvillagemuseum.org

Cincinnati Art Museum 953 Eden Pk Dr . . . . . Cincinnati OH 45202 513-721-2787
TF: 877-472-4226 ■ *Web:* www.cincinnatiartmuseum.org

Cincinnati History Museum
1301 Western Ave Cincinnati Museum Ctr. . . . . Cincinnati OH 45203 513-287-7000 287-7029
TF: 800-733-2077 ■ *Web:* www.cincymuseum.org

Cincinnati Reds Great American Ball Park
100 Joe Nuxhall Way . . . . . Cincinnati OH 45202 513-765-7000
Web: reds.mlb.com

Citizens Motorcar Company America's Packard Museum, The
420 S Ludlow St. . . . . Dayton OH 45402 937-226-1710 224-1918
Web: www.americaspackardmuseum.org

Cleveland Museum of Art 11150 E Blvd . . . . . Cleveland OH 44106 216-421-7340 707-6679
TF Sales: 800-469-4449 ■ *Web:* www.clevelandart.org

Cleveland Museum of Natural History
One Wade Oval Dr University Cir . . . . . Cleveland OH 44106 216-231-4600 231-5919
TF: 800-317-9155 ■ *Web:* www.cmnh.org

Columbus Museum of Art 480 E Broad St. . . . . Columbus OH 43215 614-221-6801 221-0226
Web: www.columbusmuseum.org

COSI Columbus 333 W Broad St. . . . . Columbus OH 43215 614-228-2674 228-6363
TF: 888-819-2674 ■ *Web:* www.cosi.org

COSI Toledo One Discovery Way. . . . . Toledo OH 43604 419-244-2674 255-2674
Web: imaginationstationtoledo.org

Crawford Auto-Aviation Museum 10825 E Blvd . . . . . Cleveland OH 44106 216-721-5722 721-0891
Web: wrhs.org

Dayton Art Institute 456 Belmonte Pk N. . . . . Dayton OH 45405 937-223-5277 223-3140
TF: 800-272-8258 ■ *Web:* www.daytonartinstitute.org

Dittrick Museum of Medical History
11000 Euclid Ave. . . . . Cleveland OH 44106 216-368-3648 368-0165
TF: 800-368-4723 ■ *Web:* www.cwru.edu

Dunham Tavern Museum 6709 Euclid Ave. . . . . Cleveland OH 44103 216-431-1060
Web: www.dunhamtavern.org

Great Lakes Science Ctr 601 Erieside Ave. . . . . Cleveland OH 44114 216-694-2000 696-2140
Web: www.greatscience.com

Hale Farm & Village 2686 Oakhill Rd PO Box 296 . . . . . Bath OH 44210 330-666-3711 666-9497
TF: 800-589-9703 ■ *Web:* www.wrhs.org

Harriet Beecher Stowe House
2950 Gilbert Ave. . . . . Cincinnati OH 45206 513-751-0651
Web: www.ohiohistory.org

Heritage Village Museum 11450 Lebanon Pk. . . . . Cincinnati OH 45241 513-563-9484 563-0914
Web: www.heritagevillagecincinnati.org

				Phone	Fax
Hower House 60 Fir Hill University of Akron *Web:* www3.uakron.edu/howerhse	Akron	OH	44325	330-972-6909	384-2635
International Women's Air & Space Museum 1501 N Marginal Rd Burke Lakefront Airport *TF:* 877-287-4752 ■ *Web:* www.iwasm.org	Cleveland	OH	44114	216-623-1111	623-1113
Invent Now, Inc 3701 Highland Park NW *Fax Area Code: 330 ■ *TF:* 800-968-4332 ■ *Web:* www.invent.org	North Canton	OH	44720	800-968-4332	762-6313*
Kelton House Museum & Garden 586 E Town St *Web:* www.keltonhouse.com	Columbus	OH	43215	614-464-2022	464-3346
Kent State University Museum PO Box 5190 *TF:* 800-988-5368 ■ *Web:* www.kent.edu	Kent	OH	44242	330-672-3450	672-3218
Krohn Conservatory 1501 Eden Pk Dr *Web:* www.cincinnatiparks.com	Cincinnati	OH	45202	513-421-5707	421-6007
Lake View Cemetery 12316 Euclid Ave *Web:* lakeviewcemetery.com	Cleveland	OH	44106	216-421-2665	421-2415
McDonough Museum of Art 525 Wick Ave *Web:* web.ysu.edu	Youngstown	OH	44502	330-941-1400	941-1492
Museum of Contemporary Art Cleveland 11400 Euclid Ave *Web:* www.mocacleveland.org	Cleveland	OH	44106	216-421-8671	421-0737
Museum of Natural History & Science 1301 Western Ave Cincinnati Museum Ctr *TF:* 800-733-2077 ■ *Web:* www.cincymuseum.org	Cincinnati	OH	45203	513-287-7000	287-7029
National Afro-American Museum & Cultural Ctr 1350 Brush Row Rd PO Box 578 *TF:* 800-752-2603 ■ *Web:* www.ohiohistory.org	Wilberforce	OH	45384	937-376-4944	376-2007
National Inventors Hall of Fame 3701 Highland Park NW Inventure Pl *Fax Area Code: 330 ■ *TF:* 800-968-4332 ■ *Web:* www.invent.org	North Canton	OH	44720	800-968-4332	762-6313*
National Museum of the United States Air Force 1100 Spaatz St Wright-Patterson Air Force Base *Web:* www.nationalmuseum.af.mil	Dayton	OH	45433	937-255-3284	255-3286
National Underground Railroad Freedom Ctr 50 E Freedom Way *Web:* www.freedomcenter.org	Cincinnati	OH	45202	513-333-7739	
Ohio Craft Museum 1665 W Fifth Ave *Web:* www.ohiocraft.org	Columbus	OH	43212	614-486-4402	486-7110
Ohio Historical Society 1982 Velma Ave *TF:* 800-686-6124 ■ *Web:* www.ohiohistory.org	Columbus	OH	43211	614-297-2300	
Patterson Homestead Historic House Museum Rental Facility 1815 Brown St *Web:* www.daytonhistory.org	Dayton	OH	45409	937-222-9724	222-0345
Rock & Roll Hall of Fame & Museum 1100 Rock & Roll Blvd *Web:* www.rockhall.com	Cleveland	OH	44114	216-781-7625	515-1283
Roscoe Village 600 N Whitewoman St *TF:* 800-877-1830 ■ *Web:* www.roscoevillage.com	Coshocton	OH	43812	740-622-7644	623-6555
Sauder Village 22611 SR 2 PO Box 235 *TF:* 800-590-9755 ■ *Web:* www.saudervillage.org	Archbold	OH	43502	419-446-2541	445-5251
Stan Hywet Hall & Gardens 714 N Portage Path *TF:* 888-836-5533 ■ *Web:* www.stanhywet.org	Akron	OH	44303	330-836-5533	
Taft Museum of Art, The 316 Pike St *Web:* www.taftmuseum.org	Cincinnati	OH	45202	513-241-0343	241-7762
Thurber House 77 Jefferson Ave *Web:* www.thurberhouse.org	Columbus	OH	43215	614-464-1032	280-3645
Toledo Firefighters Museum 918 Sylvania Ave *Web:* www.toledofiremuseum.com	Toledo	OH	43612	419-478-3473	
Toledo Museum of Art 2445 Monroe St *TF:* 800-644-6862 ■ *Web:* www.toledomuseum.org	Toledo	OH	43620	419-255-8000	255-5638
War Vet Museum 23 E Main St *Web:* warvetmuseum.org	Canfield	OH	44406	330-533-6311	533-6311
Western Reserve Historical Society Museum 10825 E Blvd *Fax: Library ■ *Web:* www.wrhs.org	Cleveland	OH	44106	216-721-5722	721-5702*
Wexner Ctr for the Arts 1871 N High St Ohio State University *Web:* www.wexarts.org	Columbus	OH	43210	614-292-0330	292-3369
Works, The 55 S First St *Web:* www.attheworks.org	Newark	OH	43055	740-349-9277	

Oklahoma

				Phone	Fax
45th Infantry Div Museum 2145 NE 36th St *Web:* www.45thdivisionmuseum.com	Oklahoma City	OK	73111	405-424-5313	424-3748
Cherokee Heritage Ctr & National Museum 21192 S Keeler Dr *TF:* 888-999-6007 ■ *Web:* www.cherokeeheritage.org	Park Hill	OK	74451	918-456-6007	
Elsing Museum 7777 S Lewis Ave *Web:* www.oru.edu	Tulsa	OK	74171	918-495-6262	
Five Civilized Tribes Museum 1101 Honor Heights Dr *Web:* www.fivetribes.org	Muskogee	OK	74401	918-683-1701	683-3070
Fred Jones Jr Museum of Art 555 Elm Ave University of Oklahoma *Web:* www.ou.edu	Norman	OK	73019	405-325-3272	325-7696
Gilcrease Museum 1400 N Gilcrease Museum Rd *TF:* 888-655-2278 ■ *Web:* gilcrease.utulsa.edu	Tulsa	OK	74127	918-596-2700	596-2770
Harn Homestead & 1889er Museum 1721 N Lincoln Blvd *Web:* www.harnhomestead.com	Oklahoma City	OK	73105	405-235-4058	235-4041
International Photography Hall of Fame & Museum 3415 Olive St *Web:* www.iphf.org	St Louis	MO	63103	405-424-4055	424-4058
JM Davis Arms & Historical Museum 330 N JM Davis Blvd *Web:* www.thegunmuseum.com	Claremore	OK	74017	918-341-5707	341-5771
National Cowboy & Western Heritage Museum 1700 NE 63rd St *Web:* www.nationalcowboymuseum.org	Oklahoma City	OK	73111	405-478-2250	478-4714
Oklahoma City Museum of Art 415 Couch Dr *TF:* 800-579-9278 ■ *Web:* www.okcmoa.com	Oklahoma City	OK	73102	405-236-3100	236-3122
Oklahoma City National Memorial & Memorial Ctr Museum 620 N Harvey Ave *TF:* 888-542-4673 ■ *Web:* www.oklahomacitynationalmemorial.org	Oklahoma City	OK	73102	405-235-3313	235-3315
Oklahoma Jazz Hall of Fame 111 E First St Upper Level *Web:* www.okjazz.org	Tulsa	OK	74103	918-281-8600	948-7737
Oklahoma Museum of History 800 Nazih Zuhdi Dr *Web:* www.okhistory.org	Oklahoma City	OK	73105	405-522-5248	522-5402
Oklahoma Museum of Natural History 2401 Chautaugua Ave *Web:* samnoblemuseum.ou.edu	Norman	OK	73072	405-325-4712	
Oklahoma Territorial Museum 406 E Oklahoma Ave *Web:* www.okterritorialmuseum.org	Guthrie	OK	73044	405-282-1889	
Philbrook Museum of Art & Gardens 2727 S Rockford Rd *Web:* www.philbrook.org	Tulsa	OK	74114	918-749-7941	743-4230
Science Museum Oklahoma 2100 NE 52nd St *TF:* 800-532-7652 ■ *Web:* sciencemuseumok.org	Oklahoma City	OK	73111	405-602-6664	602-3768
Sherwin Miller Museum of Jewish Art 2021 E 71st St *Web:* www.jewishmuseum.net	Tulsa	OK	74136	918-492-1818	492-1888
Tulsa Air & Space Museum 3624 N 74 E Ave *Web:* www.tulsaairandspacemuseum.org	Tulsa	OK	74115	918-834-9900	834-6723
Will Rogers Memorial Museum 1720 W Will Rogers Blvd *TF:* 800-324-9455 ■ *Web:* willrogers.com	Claremore	OK	74017	918-341-0719	343-8119
Woolaroc Ranch Museum & Wildlife Preserve 1925 Woolaroc Ranch Rd *TF:* 888-966-5276 ■ *Web:* www.woolaroc.org	Bartlesville	OK	74003	918-336-0307	336-0084
World Organization of China Painters Museum 2641 NW Tenth St *Web:* wocporg.com	Oklahoma City	OK	73107	405-521-1234	521-1265

Ontario

				Phone	Fax
ARTspace 165 King St W *Web:* www.artspacechathamkent.com	Chatham	ON	N7M1E4	519-352-1064	
Bytown Museum One Canal Ln PO Box 523 Stn B *Web:* www.bytownmuseum.com	Ottawa	ON	K1P5P6	613-234-4570	234-4846
Canada Agriculture Museum Prince of Wales Dr PO Box 9724 Stn T *TF:* 866-442-4416 ■ *Web:* cafmuseum.techno-science.ca	Ottawa	ON	K1G5A3	613-991-3044	993-7923
Canada Aviation Museum & Space Museum 11 Aviation Pkwy PO Box 9724 *Web:* aviation.technomuses.ca/mobile/index.html	Ottawa	ON	K1K4R3	613-993-2010	990-3655
Canada Science & Technology Museum 1867 St Laurent Blvd PO Box 9724 *TF:* 866-442-4416 ■ *Web:* www.sciencetech.technomuses.ca/english/index.cfm	Ottawa	ON	K1G5A3	613-991-3044	990-3654
Canadian Museum of Contemporary Photography 380 Sussex Dr PO Box 427 Stn A *TF:* 800-319-2787 ■ *Web:* www.gallery.ca	Ottawa	ON	K1N9N4	613-990-1985	993-4385
Canadian Museum of Nature 240 McLeod St *Fax: Mktg ■ *TF:* 800-263-4433 ■ *Web:* www.nature.ca	Ottawa	ON	K2P2R1	613-566-4700	364-4021*
Currency Museum of the Bank of Canada 245 Sparks St *TF Hotline:* 800-303-1282 ■ *Web:* www.currencymuseum.ca	Ottawa	ON	K1A0G9	613-782-8914	782-7761
Fort Henry National Historic Site PO Box 213 *TF Cust Svc:* 800-437-2233 ■ *Web:* www.forthenry.com	Kingston	ON	K7L4V8	613-542-7388	542-3054
Gardiner Museum 111 Queen's Pk *Web:* www.gardinermuseum.on.ca	Toronto	ON	M5S2C7	416-586-8080	586-8085
Guinness World Records Museum 4943 Clifton Hill *TF:* 866-656-0310 ■ *Web:* falls.com	Niagara Falls	ON	L2G3N5	905-357-4330	
Lithuanian Museum/Archives of Canada 2185 Stavebank Rd *Web:* www.klb.org	Mississauga	ON	L5C1T3	416-533-3292	
Mackenzie House Museum 82 Bond St *Web:* www.toronto.ca	Toronto	ON	M5B1X2	416-392-6915	392-0114
Movieland Wax Museum of the Stars 4848 Clifton Hill *Web:* www.cliftonhill.com/attractions/movieland-wax-museum-stars	Niagara Falls	ON	L2G3N4	905-358-3061	358-5738
Ontario Science Centre 770 Don Mills Rd *Web:* www.ontariosciencecentre.ca	Toronto	ON	M3C1T3	416-696-1000	696-3166
Presqu'ile Provincial Park 328 Presqu Pkwy *Web:* ontarioparks.com	Brighton	ON	K0K1H0	613-475-4324	
Royal Canadian Military Institute 426 University Ave *TF:* 800-585-1072 ■ *Web:* www.rcmi.org	Toronto	ON	M5G1S9	416-597-0286	597-6919
Royal Ontario Museum 100 Queen's Pk *Web:* www.rom.on.ca	Toronto	ON	M5S2C6	416-586-8000	586-5504
Scarborough Historical Museum 1007 Brimley Rd *Web:* toronto.ca	Toronto	ON	M1P3E8	416-338-8807	
Toronto Aerospace Museum 65 Carl Hall Rd PO Box 1 *TF:* 866-585-2227 ■ *Web:* www.casmuseum.org	Toronto	ON	M3K2E1	416-638-6078	638-5509
Toronto's First Post Office 260 Adelaide St E *Web:* www.townofyork.com	Toronto	ON	M5A1N1	416-865-1833	865-9414
York Museum 2694 Eglinton Ave W *Web:* www.toronto.ca	Toronto	ON	M5M1V1	416-394-2759	394-2803

Oregon

	City	State	ZIP	Phone	Fax
Antique Powerland Museum 3995 Brooklake Rd NE *Web:* www.antiquepowerland.com	Brooks	OR	97303	503-393-2424	393-2424
Bush House Museum 600 Mission St SE *Web:* www.oregonlink.com/bush_house	Salem	OR	97302	503-363-4714	
Columbia River Maritime Museum 1792 Marine Dr *Web:* www.crmm.org	Astoria	OR	97103	503-325-2323	325-2331
Hallie Ford Museum of Art 700 State St *TF:* 844-232-7228 ■ *Web:* willamette.edu/arts/hfma	Salem	OR	97301	503-370-6855	375-5458
High Desert Museum 59800 S Hwy 97 *TF:* 866-632-9992 ■ *Web:* www.highdesertmuseum.org	Bend	OR	97702	541-382-4754	382-5256
Jensen Arctic Museum 590 Church St W *Web:* wou.edu/president/advancement/jensen/	Monmouth	OR	97361	503-838-8468	838-8289
Jordan Schnitzer Museum of Art 1430 Johnson Ln *Web:* jsma.uoregon.edu	Eugene	OR	97403	541-346-3027	346-0976
Keizer Heritage Museum 980 Chemawa Rd NE *Web:* www.keizerheritage.org	Keizer	OR	97303	503-393-9660	393-0209
Marion County Historical Society Museum (MCHS) 260 12th St SE *Web:* www.marionhistory.org	Salem	OR	97301	503-364-2128	391-5356
Oregon Air & Space Museum 90377 Boeing Dr *Web:* oasm.info	Eugene	OR	97402	541-461-1101	461-1101
Oregon Historical Society 1200 SW Pk Ave *Web:* www.ohs.org	Portland	OR	97205	503-222-1741	221-2035
Oregon Maritime Ctr & Museum 115 SW Ash St Ste 400-C *Web:* www.oregonmaritimemuseum.org	Portland	OR	97204	503-224-7724	
Oregon Museum of Science & Industry 1945 SE Water Ave *TF:* 800-955-6674 ■ *Web:* www.omsi.edu	Portland	OR	97214	503-797-4000	797-4500
Portland Art Museum 1219 SW Pk Ave *Web:* www.portlandartmuseum.org	Portland	OR	97205	503-226-2811	226-4842
Springfield Museum 590 Main St	Springfield	OR	97477	541-726-2300	
Tillamook County Pioneer Museum 2106 Second St *Web:* www.tcpm.org	Tillamook	OR	97141	503-842-4553	842-4553
University of Oregon Museum of Natural & Cultural History 1680 E 15th Ave	Eugene	OR	97401	541-346-3024	346-5334

Pennsylvania

	City	State	ZIP	Phone	Fax
Academy of Natural Sciences Museum 1900 Benjamin Franklin Pkwy *Web:* www.ansp.org	Philadelphia	PA	19103	215-299-1000	299-1028
African-American Museum in Philadelphia 701 Arch St *Web:* www.aampmuseum.org	Philadelphia	PA	19106	215-574-0380	574-3110
Allentown Art Museum 31 N Fifth St *Web:* www.allentownartmuseum.org	Allentown	PA	18101	610-432-4333	434-7409
American Helicopter Museum & Education Ctr 1220 American Blvd W *Web:* www.americanhelicopter.museum	West Chester	PA	19380	610-436-9600	436-8642
American Swedish Historical Museum 1900 Pattison Ave *Web:* www.americanswedish.org	Philadelphia	PA	19145	215-389-1776	389-7701
Andy Warhol Museum 117 Sandusky St *Web:* www.warhol.org	Pittsburgh	PA	15212	412-237-8300	237-8340
Atwater Kent Museum 15 S Seventh St *Web:* www.philadelphiahistory.org	Philadelphia	PA	19106	215-685-4830	685-4837
Barnes Foundation 300 N Latch's Ln *Web:* www.barnesfoundation.org	Merion	PA	19066	610-667-0290	664-4026
Brandywine Conservancy Inc US Rt 1 *Web:* www.brandywineconservancy.org	Chadds Ford	PA	19317	610-388-2700	
Brandywine River Museum One Hoffman's Mill Rd PO Box 141 *Web:* www.brandywinemuseum.org	Chadds Ford	PA	19317	610-388-2700	388-1197
Carnegie Museum of Art 4400 Forbes Ave *Web:* www.cmoa.org	Pittsburgh	PA	15213	412-622-3131	622-3112
Carnegie Museum of Natural History 4400 Forbes Ave *Web:* www.carnegiemnh.org	Pittsburgh	PA	15213	412-622-3131	622-6258
Carnegie Science Ctr One Allegheny Ave *Web:* www.carnegiesciencecenter.org	Pittsburgh	PA	15212	412-237-3400	237-3375
Chester County Historical Society General Info Lin 225 N High St *Web:* www.chestercohistorical.org	West Chester	PA	19380	610-692-4800	
Da Vinci Discovery Ctr of Science & Technology 3145 Hamilton Blvd Bypass *Web:* www.davincisciencecenter.org	Allentown	PA	18103	484-664-1002	
Electric City Trolley Station & Museum 300 Cliff St *TF:* 800-732-0999 ■ *Web:* www.ectma.org	Scranton	PA	18503	570-963-6590	963-6447
Elfreth's Alley Museum 126 Elfreth's Alley *Web:* www.elfrethsalley.org	Philadelphia	PA	19106	215-574-0560	922-7869
Erie Art Museum 411 State St *Web:* www.erieartmuseum.org	Erie	PA	16501	814-459-5477	452-1744
Erie County History Ctr 419 State St Erie County Historical Society *Web:* www.eriecountyhistory.org	Erie	PA	16501	814-454-1813	454-6890
Everhart Museum 1901 Mulberry St *Web:* everhart-museum.org	Scranton	PA	18510	570-346-7186	346-0652
Fabric Workshop & Museum 1214 Arch St *Web:* www.fabricworkshopandmuseum.org	Philadelphia	PA	19107	215-561-8888	561-8887
Fort Pitt Museum 101 Commonwealth Pl *Web:* fortpittblockhouse.com	Pittsburgh	PA	15222	412-471-1764	281-1417
Franklin Institute Science Museum 222 N 20th St *TF:* 800-732-0999 ■ *Web:* www.fi.edu	Philadelphia	PA	19103	215-448-1200	448-1235
Frick Art & Historical Ctr 7227 Reynolds St *Web:* thefrickpittsburgh.org	Pittsburgh	PA	15208	412-371-0600	371-6140
Gettysburg Battle Theatre 571 Steinwehr Ave *Web:* www.gettysburgbattlefieldtours.com	Gettysburg	PA	17325	717-334-6100	
Gettysburg Heritage Center 297 Steinwehr Ave *TF General:* 800-887-7775 ■ *Web:* www.gettysburgmuseum.com	Gettysburg	PA	17325	717-334-6245	
Holocaust Museum & Resource Ctr 601 Jefferson Ave *Web:* www.jewishnepa.org	Scranton	PA	18510	570-961-2300	346-6147
Houdini Museum 1433 N Main Ave *Web:* www.houdini.org	Scranton	PA	18508	570-342-5555	
Independence Seaport Museum 211 S Columbus Blvd *Web:* www.phillyseaport.org	Philadelphia	PA	19106	215-413-8655	925-6713
Institute of Contemporary Art 118 S 36th St University of Pennsylvania *Web:* www.icaphila.org	Philadelphia	PA	19104	215-898-7108	898-5050
Kemerer Museum of Decorative Arts 427 N New St *Web:* historicbethlehem.org	Bethlehem	PA	18018	610-868-6868	
Lake Shore Railway Museum 31 Wall St Lake Shore Historical Society *TF:* 800-945-0340 ■ *Web:* lakeshorerailway.com	North East	PA	16428	814-725-1911	725-1911
Lehigh County Museum 432 W Walnut St *Web:* www.lchs.museum	Allentown	PA	18102	610-435-1074	
Mercer Museums 84 S Pine St *Web:* www.mercermuseum.org	Doylestown	PA	18901	215-345-0210	
Mummers Museum 1100 S Second St *Web:* www.mummersmuseum.com	Philadelphia	PA	19147	215-336-3050	389-5630
National Constitution Ctr 525 Arch St Independence Mall *TF:* 866-917-1787 ■ *Web:* www.constitutioncenter.org	Philadelphia	PA	19106	215-409-6600	409-6650
National Liberty Museum 321 Chestnut St *TF:* 800-732-0999 ■ *Web:* libertymuseum.org	Philadelphia	PA	19106	215-925-2800	925-3800
National Museum of American Jewish History 101 S Independence Mall E *Web:* www.nmajh.org	Philadelphia	PA	19106	215-923-3811	923-0763
National Watch & Clock Museum 514 Poplar St *TF:* 800-368-6511 ■ *Web:* www.nawcc.org	Columbia	PA	17512	717-684-8261	684-0878
North Museum of Natural History & Science 400 College Ave *TF:* 800-732-0999 ■ *Web:* www.northmuseum.org	Lancaster	PA	17603	717-291-3941	358-4504
Old Economy Village 270 16th St *Web:* www.oldeconomyvillage.org	Ambridge	PA	15003	724-266-4500	266-7506
Pennsylvania Academy of the Fine Arts Museum (PAFA) 118 N Broad St *TF:* 800-799-7233 ■ *Web:* pafa.org/1	Philadelphia	PA	19102	215-972-7600	569-0153
Pennsylvania Anthracite Heritage Museum RR1 Bald Mountain Rd *TF:* 800-732-0999 ■ *Web:* anthracitemuseum.org	Scranton	PA	18504	570-963-4804	963-4194
Philadelphia Museum of Art 2600 Benjamin Franklin Pkwy *TF:* 800-732-0999 ■ *Web:* www.philamuseum.org	Philadelphia	PA	19130	215-763-8100	236-4465
Photo Antiquities-Museum of Photographic History 531 E Ohio St *Web:* www.photoantiquities.org	Pittsburgh	PA	15212	412-231-7881	231-1217
Polish American Cultural Ctr Museum 308 Walnut St *Web:* www.polishamericancenter.org	Philadelphia	PA	19106	215-922-1700	922-1518
Reading Public Museum & Art Gallery 500 Museum Rd *Web:* readingpublicmuseum.org	Reading	PA	19611	610-371-5850	371-5632
Rosenbach Museum & Library 2008-2010 Delancey St *Web:* www.rosenbach.org	Philadelphia	PA	19103	215-732-1600	545-7529
Senator John Heinz Pittsburgh Regional History Ctr 1212 Smallman St *Web:* www.heinzhistorycenter.org	Pittsburgh	PA	15222	412-454-6000	454-6039
Shriver House Museum 309 Baltimore St *Web:* www.shriverhouse.org	Gettysburg	PA	17325	717-337-2800	
Soldier's National Museum 777 Baltimore St *Web:* gettysburgbattlefieldtours.com	Gettysburg	PA	17325	717-334-4890	
Soldiers & Sailors National Military Museum & Memorial 4141 Fifth Ave *Web:* www.soldiersandsailorshall.org	Pittsburgh	PA	15213	412-621-4253	683-9339
State Museum of Pennsylvania, The 300 N St *Web:* www.statemuseumpa.org	Harrisburg	PA	17120	717-787-4980	783-4558
Stenton Museum 4601 N 18th St *Web:* www.stenton.org	Philadelphia	PA	19140	215-329-7312	329-7312
University of Pennsylvania Museum of Archaeology & Anthropology 3260 S St *Web:* www.penn.museum	Philadelphia	PA	19104	215-898-4000	898-0657
Wagner Free Institute of Science 1700 W Montgomery Ave *Web:* www.pacscl.org	Philadelphia	PA	19121	215-763-6529	763-1299
Westmoreland Museum of American Art 221 N Main St *Web:* www.wmuseumaa.org	Greensburg	PA	15601	724-837-1500	
Whitaker Center for Science & Arts 225 Market St *Web:* www.whitakercenter.org	Harrisburg	PA	17101	717-214-2787	
Woodmere Art Museum 9201 Germantown Ave *Web:* www.woodmereartmuseum.org	Philadelphia	PA	19118	215-247-0476	247-2387

Prince Edward Island

Name / Address	City	State	Zip	Phone	Fax
Prince Edward Island Museum & Heritage Foundation 2 Kent St	Charlottetown	PE	C1A1M6	902-368-6600	831-7944

Quebec

Name / Address	City	State	Zip	Phone	Fax
Canadian Centre for Architecture 1920 Baile St *Web:* cca.qc.ca	Montreal	QC	H3H2S6	514-939-7000	939-7020
Canadian Museum of Civilization 100 Laurier St *TF:* 800-555-5621 ■ *Web:* historymuseum.ca/	Gatineau	QC	K1A0M8	819-776-7000	776-8300
Jules Saint-Michel Luthier - Economuseum of Violin-Making 57 Ontario St W *Web:* www.luthiersaintmichel.com	Montreal	QC	H2X1Y8	514-288-4343	288-9296
McCord Museum of Canadian History 690 Sherbrooke St W *Web:* www.mccord-museum.qc.ca/en	Montreal	QC	H3A1E9	514-398-7100	398-5045
Montreal Holocaust Memorial Centre 5151 Ch de la C(te-Sainte-Catherine *Web:* www.mhmc.ca	Montreal	QC	H3W1M6	514-345-2605	344-2651
Musee de la Civilisation 85 Rue Dalhousie St	Quebec	QC	G1K8R2	418-643-2158	
Musee Des Beaux-Arts De Montreal 1380 Rue Sherbrooke O *Web:* www.mbam.qc.ca	Montreal	QC	H3G1J5	514-285-1600	
Pointe-a-Calliere - The Montreal Museum of Archaeology & History 350 Royale Pl Angle Joint *Web:* www.pacmusee.qc.ca	Old Montreal	QC	H2Y3Y5	514-872-9150	872-9151
Richard Robitaille Fourrures 329 St Paul St	Quebec	QC	G1K3W8	418-692-9699	692-3646

Rhode Island

Name / Address	City	State	Zip	Phone	Fax
Artillery Company of Newport Military Museum 23 Clark St *Web:* www.newportartillery.org	Newport	RI	02840	401-846-8488	846-1649
Culinary Arts Museum at Johnson & Wales University 315 Harborside Blvd *Web:* www.culinary.org	Providence	RI	02905	401-598-2805	598-2807
Governor Henry Lippitt House Museum 199 Hope St *Web:* preserveri.org	Providence	RI	02906	401-453-0688	453-8221
Haffenreffer Museum of Anthropology 300 Tower St *Web:* www.brown.edu	Bristol	RI	02809	401-253-8388	253-1198
Museum of Newport History at the Brick Market 127 Thames St *Web:* newporthistory.org/	Newport	RI	02840	401-841-8770	846-1853
Museum of Yachting Fort Adams State Pk *Web:* www.iyrs.edu	Newport	RI	02840	401-848-5777	847-8320
National Museum of American Illustration 492 Bellevue Ave *Web:* www.americanillustration.org	Newport	RI	02840	401-851-8949	851-8974
Naval War College Museum 686 Cushing Rd *Web:* www.usnwc.edu	Newport	RI	02841	401-841-4052	841-7074
Newport Art Museum 76 Bellevue Ave *Web:* www.newportartmuseum.org	Newport	RI	02840	401-848-8200	848-8205
Newport Historical Society 82 Touro St *Web:* newporthistory.org/	Newport	RI	02840	401-846-0813	846-1853
Providence Athenaeum 251 Benefit St *Web:* www.providenceathenaeum.org	Providence	RI	02903	401-421-6970	421-2860
Providence Jewelry Museum Four Edward St *Web:* www.providencejewelrymuseum.com	Providence	RI	02904	401-274-0999	
Rhode Island Historical Society 110 Benevolent St *Web:* www.rihs.org	Providence	RI	02906	401-331-8575	351-0127
Rhode Island School of Design - Museum of Art 224 Benefit St *Web:* www.risdmuseum.org	Providence	RI	02903	401-454-6502	454-6556
Roger Williams Park 1000 Elmwood Ave	Providence	RI	02905	401-785-9450	941-5920
Thames & Kosmos LLC 301 Friendship St *Web:* www.thamesandkosmos.com	Providence	RI	02903	401-459-6787	
Warwick Museum of Art 3259 Post Rd *Web:* www.warwickmuseum.org	Warwick	RI	02886	401-737-0010	737-1796

Saskatchewan

Name / Address	City	State	Zip	Phone	Fax
Moose Jaw Museum & Art Gallery 461 Langdon Crescent Pk *Web:* www.mjmag.ca	Moose Jaw	SK	S6H0X6	306-692-4471	694-8016
Prince Albert Historical Museum 10 River St E *Web:* www.historypa.com	Prince Albert	SK	S6V8A9	306-764-2992	
RCMP Heritage Ctr 5907 Dewdney Ave *TF:* 866-567-7267 ■ *Web:* www.rcmpheritagecentre.com	Regina	SK	S4T0P4	306-522-7333	
Royal Saskatchewan Museum 2445 Albert St *Web:* www.royalsaskmuseum.ca	Regina	SK	S4P4W7	306-787-2815	787-2820
Western Development Museum 2610 Lorne Ave S *Web:* www.wdm.ca	Saskatoon	SK	S7J0S6	306-931-1910	934-0525

South Carolina

Name / Address	City	State	Zip	Phone	Fax
Avery Research Ctr for African-American History & Culture 125 Bull St *Web:* www.cofc.edu	Charleston	SC	29424	843-953-7609	953-7607
Bob Jones University Museum & Gallery Bob Jones University 1700 Wade Hampton Blvd *Web:* www.bjumg.org	Greenville	SC	29614	864-770-1331	770-1306
Cayce Historical Museum 1800 12th St *Web:* www.caycesc.net	Cayce	SC	29033	803-796-9020	796-9072
Charleston Museum 360 Meeting St *Web:* www.charlestonmuseum.org	Charleston	SC	29403	843-722-2996	722-1784
Citadel Archives & Museum 171 Moultrie St The Citadel *Web:* www.citadel.edu	Charleston	SC	29409	843-953-6846	953-6956
Columbia Museum of Art 1515 Main St *Web:* columbiamuseum.org	Columbia	SC	29201	803-799-2810	
Franklin G Burroughs-Simeon B Chapin Art Museum 3100 S Ocean Blvd *Web:* www.myrtlebeachartmuseum.org	Myrtle Beach	SC	29577	843-238-2510	238-2910
Gibbes Museum of Art 135 Meeting St *Web:* www.gibbesmuseum.org	Charleston	SC	29401	843-722-2706	720-1682
Greenville County Museum of Art 420 College St *Web:* www.gcma.org	Greenville	SC	29601	864-271-7570	271-7579
Karpeles Manuscript Library Museum 68 Spring St *Web:* www.rain.org	Charleston	SC	29403	843-853-4651	853-4651
Patriots Point Naval & Maritime Museum 40 Patriots Pt Rd *TF:* 800-248-3508 ■ *Web:* www.state.sc.us	Mount Pleasant	SC	29464	843-884-2727	881-4232
Ripley's Believe It or Not! Museum 901 N Ocean Blvd *Web:* www.ripleys.com	Myrtle Beach	SC	29577	843-448-2331	
Roper Mountain Science Ctr 402 Roper Mtn Rd *Web:* www.ropermountain.org	Greenville	SC	29615	864-355-8900	
South Carolina Civil War Museum 4857 Hwy 17 Bypass S *Web:* mbisr.com	Myrtle Beach	SC	29577	843-293-3377	
South Carolina Museum & Library of Confederate History 15 Boyce Ave *Web:* confederatemuseumandlibrary.org	Greenville	SC	29601	864-421-9039	
South Carolina State Museum 301 Gervais St Loading Zone D *Web:* www.museum.state.sc.us	Columbia	SC	29201	803-898-4921	898-4969
University of South Carolina McKissick Museum University of S Carolina 816 Bull St *TF:* 888-825-9711 ■ *Web:* artsandsciences.sc.edu	Columbia	SC	29208	803-777-7251	777-2829
US Army Basic Combat Training Museum 4442 Ft Jackson Blvd *Web:* goarmy.com	Columbia	SC	29209	803-751-7419	

South Dakota

Name / Address	City	State	Zip	Phone	Fax
1881 Custer CountyCourthouse Museum 411 Mt Rushmore Rd PO Box 826 *Web:* www.1881courthousemuseum.com	Custer	SD	57730	605-673-2443	673-2443
Adams Museum 54 Sherman St *Web:* deadwoodhistory.org	Deadwood	SD	57732	605-578-1714	
Center for Western Studies 2101 S Summit Ave Augustana College *TF:* 800-727-2844 ■ *Web:* www.augie.edu	Sioux Falls	SD	57197	605-274-4007	274-4999
Delbridge Museum of Natural History 805 S Kiwanis Ave *Web:* www.greatzoo.org	Sioux Falls	SD	57104	605-367-7003	367-8340
Fort Meade Museum Sheridan St Bldg 55 PO Box 164 *Web:* www.fortmeademuseum.org	Fort Meade	SD	57741	605-347-9822	
Journey Museum 222 New York St *TF:* 877-343-8220 ■ *Web:* www.journeymuseum.org	Rapid City	SD	57701	605-394-6923	394-6940
Museum of Geology 501 E St Joseph St S Dakota School of Mines & Technology *TF:* 800-544-8162 ■ *Web:* www.sdsmt.edu	Rapid City	SD	57701	605-394-2467	394-6131
Museum of South Dakota State Historical Society 900 Governors Dr Cultural Heritage Ctr *Web:* www.history.sd.gov	Pierre	SD	57501	605-773-3458	773-6041
National Museum of Woodcarving Hwy 16 W PO Box 747 *Web:* woodcarving.blackhills.com/	Custer	SD	57730	605-673-4404	
National Music Museum 414 E Clark St *TF:* 877-225-0027 ■ *Web:* orgs.usd.edu	Vermillion	SD	57069	605-677-5306	677-6995
National Presidential Wax Museum 609 Hwy 16A *Web:* www.blackhillsbadlands.com	Keystone	SD	57751	605-666-4455	
Old Courthouse Museum 200 W Sixth St *Web:* siouxlandmuseums.com	Sioux Falls	SD	57104	605-367-4210	367-6004
Pettigrew Home & Museum 131 N Duluth Ave *Web:* siouxlandmuseums.com	Sioux Falls	SD	57104	605-367-7097	
Sioux Empire Medical Museum 1305 W 18th St *Web:* www.sdmuseums.org	Sioux Falls	SD	57105	605-333-6397	
South Dakota Discovery Ctr & Aquarium 805 W Sioux Ave *Web:* sd-discovery.org	Pierre	SD	57501	605-224-8295	224-2865
South Dakota National Guard Museum 425 E Capitol Ave *Web:* www.mva.sd.gov/natl_guard_museum.html	Pierre	SD	57501	605-773-3269	

	City	State	Zip	Phone	Fax
Washington Pavilion of Arts & Science 301 S Main PO Box 984	Sioux Falls	SD	57104	605-367-6000	367-7399
TF: 877-927-4728 ■ *Web:* www.washingtonpavilion.org					

Tennessee

	City	State	Zip	Phone	Fax
Adventure Science Ctr 800 Ft Negley Blvd	Nashville	TN	37203	615-862-5160	862-5178
Web: www.adventuresci.com					
American Museum of Science & Energy 300 S Tulane Ave	Oak Ridge	TN	37830	865-576-3200	576-6024
Web: amse.org					
Art Museum of the University of Memphis 142 Communication & Fine Arts Bldg The University of Memphis	Memphis	TN	38152	901-678-2224	678-5118
Web: www.memphis.edu					
B Carroll Reece Museum PO Box 70660	Johnson City	TN	37614	423-439-4392	439-4283
TF: 855-590-3878 ■ *Web:* www.etsu.edu/reece					
Belle Meade Plantation 5025 Harding Pk	Nashville	TN	37205	615-356-0501	356-0501
TF: 800-270-3991 ■ *Web:* www.bellemeadeplantation.com					
Bessie Smith Cultural Ctr 200 E Martin Luther King Blvd	Chattanooga	TN	37403	423-266-8658	267-1076
Web: www.bessiesmithcc.org					
Center for Southern Folklore 119 S Main St	Memphis	TN	38103	901-525-3655	
Web: www.southernfolklore.com					
Chattanooga History Ctr 2 W Acquarium Way	Chattanooga	TN	37402	423-265-3247	
Web: chattanoogahistory.com/					
Country Music Hall of Fame & Museum 222 Fifth Ave S	Nashville	TN	37203	615-416-2001	255-2245
TF: 800-852-6437 ■ *Web:* countrymusichalloffame.org					
Dixon Gallery & Gardens 4339 Pk Ave	Memphis	TN	38117	901-761-5250	682-0943
Web: www.dixon.org					
Doak House Museum 690 Erwin Hwy	Greeneville	TN	37745	423-636-8554	
East Tennessee Historical Society 601 S Gay St PO Box 1629	Knoxville	TN	37901	865-215-8824	215-8819
Web: www.easttnhistory.org					
Farragut Folklife Museum 11408 Municipal Ctr Dr	Farragut	TN	37934	865-966-7057	675-2096
Web: www.townoffarragut.org					
Fire Museum of Memphis 118 Adams Ave	Memphis	TN	38103	901-320-5650	529-8422
Web: www.firemuseum.com					
Frank H McClung Museum 1327 Cir Pk Dr University of Tennessee	Knoxville	TN	37996	865-974-2144	974-3827
Web: mcclungmuseum.utk.edu					
Graceland (Elvis Presley Mansion) 3734 Elvis Presley Blvd	Memphis	TN	38116	901-332-3322	
TF: 800-238-2000 ■ *Web:* www.elvis.com/graceland					
Hermitage The (Home of Andrew Jackson) 4580 Rachel's Ln	Hermitage	TN	37076	615-889-2941	889-9289
Web: www.thehermitage.com					
Historic Jonesborough Visitors Ctr & Museum 117 Boone St	Jonesborough	TN	37659	423-753-1010	753-1020
TF: 866-401-4223 ■ *Web:* www.historicjonesborough.com					
Houston Museum of Decorative Arts 201 High St	Chattanooga	TN	37403	423-267-7176	
Web: thehoustonmuseum.com					
Hunter Museum of American Art 10 Bluff View St	Chattanooga	TN	37403	423-267-0968	267-9844
Web: www.huntermuseum.org					
International Board of Jewish Missions Inc 1928 Hamill Rd	Hixson	TN	37343	423-876-8150	876-8156
Web: tnguy.com					
International Towing & Recovery Hall of Fame & Museum 3315 Broad St	Chattanooga	TN	37408	423-267-3132	267-0867
Web: www.internationaltowingmuseum.org					
James White's Fort 205 E Hill Ave	Knoxville	TN	37915	865-525-6514	
Web: jameswhitesfort.org					
Knoxville Museum of Art 1050 World Fair Pk Dr	Knoxville	TN	37916	865-525-6101	546-3635
Web: www.knoxart.org					
Memphis Brooks Museum of Art 1934 Poplar Ave Overton Pk	Memphis	TN	38104	901-544-6200	725-4071
TF: 877-829-5500 ■ *Web:* www.brooksmuseum.org					
Memphis Cotton Exchange, The 65 Union Ave Mezzanine	Memphis	TN	38103	901-531-7826	
Web: www.memphiscottonmuseum.org					
Memphis Pink Palace Museum 3050 Central Ave	Memphis	TN	38111	901-320-6320	320-6391
Web: www.memphismuseums.org					
Memphis Rock 'n' Soul Museum 191 Beale St	Memphis	TN	38103	901-205-2533	205-2534
Web: www.memphisrocknsoul.org					
Mississippi River Museum 125 N Front St	Memphis	TN	38103	901-576-7241	576-6666
TF: 800-507-6507 ■ *Web:* www.mudisland.com					
Museum of Appalachia 2819 Andersonville Hwy	Clinton	TN	37716	865-494-7680	494-8957
Web: museumofappalachia.org					
National Civil Rights Museum 450 Mulberry St	Memphis	TN	38103	901-521-9699	521-9740
Web: www.civilrightsmuseum.org					
National Medal of Honor Museum of Military History PO Box 11467	Chattanooga	TN	37401	423-877-2525	
Web: www.mohm.org					
National Ornamental Metal Museum 374 Metal Museum Dr	Memphis	TN	38106	901-774-6380	774-6382
TF: 877-881-2326 ■ *Web:* www.metalmuseum.org					
Parthenon, The 2600 W End Ave Centennial Pk PO Box 196340	Nashville	TN	37203	615-862-8431	885-2265
Web: nashville.gov/parks-and-recreation/parthenon.aspx					
Rocky Mount Museum 200 Hyder Hill Rd PO Box 160	Piney Flats	TN	37686	423-538-7396	538-1086
TF: 888-538-1791 ■ *Web:* www.rockymountmuseum.com					
Slave Haven Underground Railroad Museum 826 N Second St	Memphis	TN	38173	901-527-3427	
Web: www.slavehavenundergroundrailroadmuseum.org					
Tennessee Agricultural Museum 440 Hogan Rd	Nashville	TN	37204	615-837-5197	837-5194
Web: www.picktnproducts.org					
Tennessee Sports Hall of Fame Museum 501 Broadway	Nashville	TN	37203	615-242-4750	242-4752
Web: www.tshf.net					
Tennessee State Museum 505 Deaderick St	Nashville	TN	37243	615-741-2692	741-7231
TF: 800-407-4324 ■ *Web:* www.tnmuseum.org					
Tennessee Valley Railroad Museum 4119 Cromwell Rd	Chattanooga	TN	37421	423-894-8028	894-8029
Web: www.tvrail.com					
Upper Room Chapel & Museum 1908 Grand Ave	Nashville	TN	37212	615-340-7200	340-7293
TF: 800-972-0433 ■ *Web:* www.upperroom.org					

Texas

	City	State	Zip	Phone	Fax
12th Armored Div Memorial Museum 1289 N Second St	Abilene	TX	79601	325-677-6515	
Web: www.12tharmoredmuseum.com					
African American Museum 3536 Grand Ave Fair Pk	Dallas	TX	75210	214-565-9026	421-8204
Web: www.aamdallas.org					
Alamo, The 300 Alamo Plz	San Antonio	TX	78205	210-225-1391	229-1343
Web: www.thealamo.org					
Amarillo Museum of Art 2200 S Van Buren St	Amarillo	TX	79109	806-371-5050	373-9235
Web: www.amarilloart.org					
American Airlines CR Smith Museum 4601 Hwy 360 at FAA Rd	Fort Worth	TX	76155	817-967-1560	967-5737
TF: 877-277-6484 ■ *Web:* www.crsmithmuseum.org					
American Wind Power Ctr 1701 Canyon Lk Dr	Lubbock	TX	79403	806-747-8734	740-0668
Web: www.windmill.com					
Amon Carter Museum 3501 Camp Bowie Blvd	Fort Worth	TX	76107	817-738-1933	377-8523
TF: 800-573-1933 ■ *Web:* www.cartermuseum.org					
Arlington Museum of Art 201 W Main St	Arlington	TX	76010	817-275-4600	860-4800
Web: www.arlingtonmuseum.org					
Asian Cultures Museum 1809 N Chaparral St	Corpus Christi	TX	78401	361-881-8827	882-5718
Web: www.asianculturesmuseum.org					
Austin Museum of Art Downtown 700 Congress Ave Ste 100	Austin	TX	78701	512-453-5312	
Web: thecontemporaryaustin.org					
Austin Museum of Art Laguna Gloria 3809 W 35th St	Austin	TX	78703	512-458-8191	458-1571
Web: thecontemporaryaustin.org					
Battleship Texas SHS San Jacinto Battleground State Historic Site 3523 Independence Pkwy	La Porte	TX	77571	281-479-2431	479-5618
Web: www.tpwd.state.tx.us					
Bayou Bend Collection & Gardens 6003 Memorial Dr at Westcott St PO Box 6826	Houston	TX	77007	713-639-7750	
Web: www.mfah.org/bayoubend					
Blanton Museum of Art One University Stn D1303 University of Texas at Austin	Austin	TX	78712	512-471-7324	471-7023
Web: blantonmuseum.org					
Bob Bullock Texas State History Museum 1800 N Congress Ave	Austin	TX	78701	512-936-8746	936-4699
TF: 866-369-7108 ■ *Web:* www.thestoryoftexas.com					
Buckhorn Saloon & Museum 318 E Houston St	San Antonio	TX	78205	210-247-4000	247-4020
Web: www.buckhornmuseum.com					
Buddy Holly Ctr 1801 Crickets Ave	Lubbock	TX	79401	806-767-2686	767-0732
Web: www.mylubbock.us/departmental-websites/departments/buddy-holly-center/home					
Buffalo Gap Historic Village 133 William St PO Box 818	Buffalo Gap	TX	79508	325-572-3365	572-5449
Web: buffalogap.com					
Cattle Raisers Museum 1600 Gendy St PO Box 868	Fort Worth	TX	76107	817-332-8551	336-2470
Web: www.cattleraisersmuseum.org					
Cavanaugh Flight Museum 4572 Claire Chennault Addison Airport	Addison	TX	75001	972-380-8800	248-0907
Web: www.cavanaughflightmuseum.com					
Center for Women & Their Work 1710 Lavaca St	Austin	TX	78701	512-477-1064	477-1090
Web: www.womenandtheirwork.org					
Contemporary Arts Museum 5216 Montrose Blvd	Houston	TX	77006	713-284-8250	284-8275
Web: www.camh.org					
Corpus Christi Museum of Science & History 1900 N Chaparral St	Corpus Christi	TX	78401	361-826-4667	
Web: ccmuseum.com					
Dallas Firefighters Museum One Parry Ave	Dallas	TX	75226	214-821-1500	821-1500
Web: dallasfiremuseum.com					
Dallas Heritage Village 1515 S Harwood	Dallas	TX	75215	214-421-5141	428-6351
Web: www.dallasheritagevillage.org					
Dallas Holocaust Museum 211 N Record St Ste 100	Dallas	TX	75202	214-741-7500	747-2270
Web: www.dallasholocaustmuseum.org					
Dallas Museum of Art 1717 N Harwood St	Dallas	TX	75201	214-922-1200	736-6767*
**Fax Area Code:* 212 ■ *Web:* dma.org					
El Paso Centennial Museum University & Wiggins University of Texas	El Paso	TX	79968	915-747-5565	747-5411
Web: admin.utep.edu					
El Paso Museum of Art One Art Festival Plz	El Paso	TX	79901	915-532-1707	532-1010
Web: www.elpasoartmuseum.org					
El Paso Museum of History 510 Santa Fe St	El Paso	TX	79901	915-351-3588	351-4345
Web: elpasotexas.gov					
Elisabet Ney Museum 304 E 44th St	Austin	TX	78751	512-458-2255	453-0638
TF: 800-680-7289 ■ *Web:* www.ci.austin.tx.us					
Fielder House Museum 1616 W Abram St	Arlington	TX	76013	817-460-4001	
Web: historicalarlington.org					
Fort Bend Museum 500 Houston St	Richmond	TX	77469	281-342-6478	342-2439
Web: www.fortbendmuseum.org					
Fort Worth Museum of Science & History 1600 Gendy St	Fort Worth	TX	76107	817-255-9300	732-7635
TF: 888-255-9300 ■ *Web:* www.fortworthmuseum.org					

				Phone	Fax
French Legation Museum 802 San Marcos St	Austin	TX	78702	512-472-8180	
Web: www.frenchlegationmuseum.org					
Frontiers of Flight Museum 6911 Lemon Ave	Dallas	TX	75209	214-350-1651	351-0101
Web: www.flightmuseum.com					
Garland Landmark Museum 200 Museum Plz Dr	Garland	TX	75040	972-205-2749	205-3634
Web: garlandhistorical.org					
George Bush Library & Museum					
1000 George Bush Dr W	College Station	TX	77845	979-691-4000	346-1699*
**Fax Area Code:* 214					
George Ranch Historical Park 10215 FM 762	Richmond	TX	77469	281-343-0218	343-9316
Web: www.georgeranch.org					
George Washington Carver Museum & Cultural Ctr					
1165 Angelina St	Austin	TX	78702	512-974-4926	974-3699
Web: austintexas.gov/search404					
Glass Mountain Optics Inc 9517 Mcneil Rd	Austin	TX	78758	512-339-7442	
Web: www.glassmountain.com					
Grace Museum 102 Cypress St	Abilene	TX	79601	325-673-4587	675-5993
Web: www.thegracemuseum.org					
Heard Natural Science Museum & Wildlife Sanctuary					
One Nature Pl	McKinney	TX	75069	972-562-5566	548-9119
Web: www.heardmuseum.org					
Heritage Farmstead Museum 1900 W 15th St	Plano	TX	75075	972-881-0140	422-6481
Web: heritagefarmstead.org					
Historic Brownsville Museum					
641 E Madison St	Brownsville	TX	78520	956-548-1313	548-1391
Web: mitteculturaldistrict.org					
Historic Fort Worth Inc 1110 Penn St	Fort Worth	TX	76102	817-332-5875	336-2346
Web: www.historicfortworth.org					
Holocaust Museum Houston 5401 Caroline St	Houston	TX	77004	713-942-8000	942-7953
Web: www.hmh.org					
Houston Fire Museum 2403 Milam St	Houston	TX	77006	713-524-2526	520-7566
Web: www.houstonfiremuseum.org					
Houston Maritime Museum 2204 Dorrington St	Houston	TX	77030	713-666-1910	
Web: www.houstonmaritimemuseum.org					
Houston Museum of Natural Science					
5555 Hermann Pk Dr	Houston	TX	77030	713-639-4629	
Web: www.hmns.org					
Institute of Texan Cultures					
801 E Durango Blvd	San Antonio	TX	78205	210-458-2300	458-2205
TF: 800-447-3372 ■ *Web:* www.texancultures.com					
International Museum of Cultures					
7500 W Camp Wisdom Rd	Dallas	TX	75236	972-708-7406	708-7341
Web: www.internationalmuseumofcultures.org					
Interurban Railway Museum 901 E 15th St	Plano	TX	75074	972-941-2117	941-2656
Web: www.plano.gov					
John E Conner Museum					
905 W Santa Gertrudis Ave					
700 University Blvd	Kingsville	TX	78363	361-593-2810	593-2112
TF: 800-726-8192 ■ *Web:* www.tamuk.edu/artsci/museum					
Kimbell Art Museum 3333 Camp Bowie Blvd	Fort Worth	TX	76107	817-332-8451	877-1264
Web: www.kimbellart.org					
Lawndale Art & Performance Ctr 4912 Main St	Houston	TX	77002	713-528-5858	528-4140
Web: lawndaleartcenter.org					
LBJ Library & Museum 2313 Red River St	Austin	TX	78705	512-721-0216	721-0170
TF: 800-874-6451 ■ *Web:* www.lbjlib.utexas.edu					
Log Cabin Village					
2100 Log Cabin Village Ln	Fort Worth	TX	76109	817-392-5881	
Web: www.logcabinvillage.org					
Lone Star Flight Museum 2002 Terminal Dr	Galveston	TX	77554	409-740-7722	740-7612
Web: www.lsfm.org					
Louis Tussaud's Plaza Wax Museum & Ripley's Believe It or Not! Museum					
301 Alamo Plz	San Antonio	TX	78205	210-224-9299	224-1516
Web: www.ripleys.com					
Meadows Museum					
5900 Bishop Blvd					
Southern Methodist University	Dallas	TX	75205	214-768-2516	768-1688
Web: www.meadowsmuseumdallas.org					
Menil Collection 1515 Sul Ross St	Houston	TX	77006	713-525-9400	525-9444
Web: www.menil.org					
Mexic-Arte Museum 419 Congress Ave	Austin	TX	78701	512-480-9373	480-8626
Web: www.mexic-artemuseum.org					
Modern Art Museum of Fort Worth					
3200 Darnell St	Fort Worth	TX	76107	817-738-9215	
TF: 866-824-5566 ■ *Web:* themodern.org					
Museum of Health & Medical Science					
1515 Hermann Dr	Houston	TX	77004	713-521-1515	526-1434
Web: www.mhms.org					
Museum of Nature & Science 2201 N Field St	Dallas	TX	75201	214-428-5555	428-2033
Web: www.perotmuseum.org					
Museum of Texas Tech University					
3301 Fourth St	Lubbock	TX	79409	806-742-2442	742-1136
Web: www.depts.ttu.edu/museumttu					
Museum of the American Railroad					
1105 Washington St Fair Pk	Dallas	TX	75315	214-428-0101	426-1937
Web: www.museumoftheamericanrailroad.org					
National Border Patrol Museum					
4315 Woodrow Bean TransMtn Rd	El Paso	TX	79924	915-759-6060	759-0992
TF: 877-276-8738 ■ *Web:* www.borderpatrolmuseum.com					
National Cowgirl Museum & Hall of Fame					
1720 Gendy St	Fort Worth	TX	76107	817-336-4475	336-2470
TF: 800-476-3263 ■ *Web:* www.cowgirl.net					
National Ctr for Children's Illustrated Literature Museum					
102 Cedar St	Abilene	TX	79601	325-673-4586	673-0085
Web: www.nccil.org					
National Museum of Funeral History					
415 Barren Springs Dr	Houston	TX	77090	281-876-3063	876-4403
Web: www.nmfh.org					
National Ranching Heritage Ctr					
3121 Fourth St	Lubbock	TX	79409	806-742-0498	742-0616
Web: www.depts.ttu.edu					
National Scouting Museum					
1329 W Walnut Hill Ln	Irving	TX	75038	972-580-2100	580-2020
TF: 800-303-3047 ■ *Web:* www.bsamuseum.org					
O Henry Home & Museum 409 E Fifth St	Austin	TX	78701	512-472-1903	
Web: www.ci.austin.tx.us					
Panhandle-Plains Historical Museum					
2503 Fourth Ave	Canyon	TX	79015	806-651-2244	651-2250
Web: www.panhandleplains.org					
River Legacy Park 701 NW Green Oaks Blvd	Arlington	TX	76006	817-860-6752	860-1595
Web: www.riverlegacy.org					
San Antonio Museum of Art					
200 W Jones Ave	San Antonio	TX	78215	210-978-8100	978-8134
Web: samuseum.org					
San Jacinto Museum of History					
One Monument Cir	La Porte	TX	77571	281-479-2421	479-2428
Web: www.sanjacinto-museum.org					
Science Spectrum-Omni Theater					
2579 S Loop 289	Lubbock	TX	79423	806-745-2525	745-1115
Web: sciencespectrum.org					
Sixth Floor Museum					
411 Elm St Ste 120 Dealey Plz	Dallas	TX	75202	214-747-6660	747-6662
TF: 888-485-4854 ■ *Web:* www.jfk.org					
South Texas Institute for the Arts					
1902 N Shoreline Blvd	Corpus Christi	TX	78401	361-825-3500	825-3520
Web: www.artmuseumofsouthtexas.org					
Space Ctr Houston 1601 Nasa Rd 1	Houston	TX	77058	281-244-2100	283-7724
Web: www.spacecenter.org					
Spanish Governor's Palace					
105 Plz de Armas	San Antonio	TX	78205	210-224-0601	
Web: spanishgovernorspalace.org					
Steves Homestead Museum					
509 King William St	San Antonio	TX	78204	210-225-5924	223-9014
TF: 800-523-5077 ■ *Web:* saconservation.org					
Stillman House & Museum					
1325 E Washington St	Brownsville	TX	78520	956-541-5560	541-5524
Web: www.brownsvillehistory.org					
Stockyards Museum					
131 E Exchange Ave Ste 113	Fort Worth	TX	76164	817-625-5082	
Web: stockyardsmuseum.org					
Texas Memorial Museum 2400 Trinity St	Austin	TX	78705	512-471-1604	471-4794
TF: 800-687-4132 ■ *Web:* www.utexas.edu					
Texas Military Forces Museum PO Box 5218	Austin	TX	78763	512-782-5659	782-6750
Web: www.texasmilitaryforcesmuseum.org					
Texas Transportation Museum					
11731 Wetmore Rd	San Antonio	TX	78247	210-490-3554	
Web: www.txtransportationmuseum.org					
Tyler Museum of Art 1300 S Mahon Ave	Tyler	TX	75701	903-595-1001	595-1055
Web: www.tylermuseum.org					
Umlauf Sculpture Garden & Museum					
605 Robert E Lee Rd	Austin	TX	78704	512-445-5582	445-5583
Web: www.umlaufsculpture.org					
USS Lexington Museum on the Bay					
2914 N Shoreline Blvd	Corpus Christi	TX	78402	361-888-4873	
TF: 800-523-9539 ■ *Web:* www.usslexington.com					
Vintage Flying Museum					
505 NW 38th St Hanger 33 S Meacham Field	Fort Worth	TX	76106	817-624-1935	485-4454
Web: www.vintageflyingmuseum.org					
Witte Museum 3801 Broadway St	San Antonio	TX	78209	210-357-1900	357-1882
Web: www.wittemuseum.org					

Utah

				Phone	Fax
Brigham Young University Museum of Peoples & Cultures					
100 East 700 North 105 Allen Hall	Provo	UT	84602	801-422-0020	422-0026
Web: mpc.byu.edu					
Chase Home Museum of Utah Folk Art					
617 East South Temple	Salt Lake City	UT	84102	801-533-5760	533-4202
Web: heritage.utah.gov					
Crandall Historical Printing Museum					
275 E Ctr St	Provo	UT	84606	801-377-7777	
Web: crandallmuseum.org					
Daughters of Utah Pioneers Museum					
300 N Main St	Salt Lake City	UT	84103	801-532-6479	532-4436
Web: www.dupinternational.org					
Fort Douglas Military Museum					
32 Potter St Ft Douglas	Salt Lake City	UT	84113	801-581-1710	581-9846
Web: www.fortdouglas.org					
Hill Aerospace Museum					
7961 WaRdleigh Rd Bldg 1955	Hill AFB	UT	84056	801-777-6818	775-3034
Web: hill.af.mil					
John Hutchings Museum of Natural History					
55 N Ctr St	Lehi	UT	84043	801-768-7180	
Web: www.hutchingsmuseum.org					
John M Browning Firearms Museum 2501 Wall Ave	Ogden	UT	84401	801-393-9886	
Web: theunionstation.org/museums-2/john-m-browning-firearms-museum/					
Monte L Bean Life Science Museum					
Brigham Young University 645 E 1430 N	Provo	UT	84602	801-422-5051	422-0093
Web: mlbean.byu.edu					
Museum of Church History & Art					
45 NW Temple St	Salt Lake City	UT	84150	801-240-3310	240-5342
Web: history.lds.org					
Museum of Utah Art & History					
825 North 300 West Ste W109	Salt Lake City	UT	84103	801-364-4080	364-3468
Web: www.muahnet.org					
Ogden Eccles Dinosaur Park 1544 E Pk Blvd	Ogden	UT	84401	801-393-3466	399-0895
Web: www.dinosaurpark.org					
Pioneer Memorial Museum 300 N Main St	Salt Lake City	UT	84103	801-532-6479	532-4436
Web: www.dupinternational.org					
Roy Historical Museum 5550 South 1700 West	Roy	UT	84067	801-776-3626	
Web: roy-historical-museum.placestars.com					
Springville Museum of Art					
126 East 400 South	Springville	UT	84663	801-489-2727	
Web: www.springville.org					
Union Station 2501 Wall Ave	Ogden	UT	84401	801-393-9886	
Web: theunionstation.org					

Phone Fax

Utah Museum of Fine Arts
410 Campus Ctr Dr University of Utah .... Salt Lake City UT 84112 801-581-7332 585-5198
Web: www.umfa.utah.edu

Utah Museum of Natural History, The
301 Wakara Way .... Salt Lake City UT 84108 801-581-4303 585-3684
Web: nhmu.utah.edu

Utah State Railroad Museum 2501 Wall Ave .... Ogden UT 84401 801-393-9886
Web: theunionstation.org

Wattis-Dumke Model Railroad Museum
2501 Wall Ave Union Stn .... Ogden UT 84401 801-393-9886
Web: theunionstation.org/museums-2/

Wheeler Historic Farm
6351 South 900 East .... Salt Lake City UT 84121 801-264-2241 264-2213
Web: www.wheelerfarm.com

Vermont

Phone Fax

Bennington Museum 75 Main St .... Bennington VT 05201 802-447-1571 442-8305
Web: www.bennington.com

Fairbanks Museum & Planetarium
1302 Main St .... Saint Johnsbury VT 05819 802-748-2372 748-1893
Web: www.fairbanksmuseum.org

Lake Champlain Maritime Museum
4472 Basin Harbor Rd .... Vergennes VT 05491 802-475-2022 475-2953
Web: www.lcmm.org

Robert Hull Fleming Museum
61 Colchester Ave University of Vermont .... Burlington VT 05405 802-656-0750 656-8059
TF: 888-382-1222 ■ *Web:* www.uvm.edu

Rokeby Museum 4334 Rt 7 .... Ferrisburg VT 05456 802-877-3406 877-3406
Web: www.rokeby.org

Shelburne Museum 5555 Shelburne Rd .... Shelburne VT 05482 802-985-3346 985-2331
Web: www.shelburnemuseum.org

Virginia

Phone Fax

Agecroft Hall 4305 Sulgrave Rd.................. Richmond VA 23221 804-353-4241 353-2151
Web: www.agecrofthall.com

Alexandria Archaeology Museum
105 N Union St Ste 327 .... Alexandria VA 22314 703-746-4399 838-6491
TF: 800-367-7623 ■ *Web:* www.alexandriava.gov/historic/archaeology

Alexandria Black History Museum
902 Wythe St .... Alexandria VA 22314 703-838-4356 706-3999
TF: 800-367-7623 ■ *Web:* www.alexandriava.gov/historic/blackhistory

Anderson Gallery 907 1/2 W Franklin St............ Richmond VA 23284 804-828-1522 828-8585
Web: www.vcu.edu

Arlington Historical Museum
1805 S Arlington Ridge Rd........................ Arlington VA 22202 703-942-9247
Web: www.arlingtonhistoricalsociety.org

Atlantic Wildfowl Heritage Museum
1113 Atlantic Ave .... Virginia Beach VA 23451 757-437-8432 437-9055
Web: www.awhm.org

Beth Ahabah Museum & Archives
1109 W Franklin St.............................. Richmond VA 23220 804-353-2668 358-3451
Web: www.bethahabah.org

Black History Museum & Cultural Ctr of Virginia
00 Clay St...................................... Richmond VA 23219 804-780-9093 780-9107
Web: www.blackhistorymuseum.org

Carlyle House Historic Park
121 N Fairfax St .... Alexandria VA 22314 703-549-2997 549-5738
Web: www.nvrpa.org

Chrysler Museum of Art 245 W Olney Rd .... Norfolk VA 23510 757-664-6200 664-6201
Web: www.chrysler.org

DeWitt Wallace Decorative Arts Museum
325 Francis St .... Williamsburg VA 23185 800-447-8679
TF: 800-447-8679 ■ *Web:* www.colonialwilliamsburg.com

Drug Enforcement Administration Museum & Visitors Ctr
700 Army Navy Dr .... Arlington VA 22202 202-307-3463 307-8956
Web: www.deamuseum.org

Edgar Allan Poe Museum 1914 E Main St.......... Richmond VA 23223 804-648-5523 648-8729
TF: 866-229-8580 ■ *Web:* www.poemuseum.org

Endview Plantation 362 Yorktown Rd........... Newport News VA 23603 757-887-1862 888-3369
Web: www.endview.org

Federal Reserve Money Museum 701 E Byrd St ..... Richmond VA 23219 804-697-8000
Web: www.richmondfed.org

Fort Ward Museum & Historic Site
4301 W Braddock Rd .... Alexandria VA 22304 703-838-4848 671-7350
TF: 800-468-8894 ■ *Web:* www.alexandriava.gov/FortWard

Gadsby's Tavern Museum Society
134 N Royal St .... Alexandria VA 22314 703-746-4242
Web: www.gadsbystavernmuseum.us

George C Marshall Foundation VMI Parade......... Lexington VA 24450 540-463-7103
Web: www.marshallfoundation.org

Hampton Roads Naval Museum
One Waterside Dr Ste 248.......................... Norfolk VA 23510 757-322-2987 445-1867
Web: www.hrnm.navy.mil

Henricus Historical Park Henricus Pk Rd .... Chester VA 23836 804-748-1613 706-1356
TF: 800-514-3849 ■ *Web:* www.henricus.org

Hermitage Foundation Museum 7637 N Shore Rd ..... Norfolk VA 23505 757-423-2052 423-2410
Web: www.thehermitagemuseum.org

History Museum & Historical Society of Western Virginia
One Market Sq Sq Bldg Ste 3 .... Roanoke VA 24011 540-342-5770 224-1256
Web: vahistorymuseum.org

Hunter House Victorian Museum
240 W Freemason St .... Norfolk VA 23510 757-623-9814
Web: www.hunterhousemuseum.org

Lee-Fendall House Museum 614 Oronoco St........ Alexandria VA 22314 703-548-1789
Web: www.leefendallhouse.org

Lyceum History Museum 201 S Washington St....... Alexandria VA 22314 703-838-4994 838-4997
Web: www.alexandriava.gov/lyceum

MacArthur Memorial Museum, The 198 Bank St ...... Norfolk VA 23510 757-441-2965 441-5389
Web: macarthurmemorial.org

Magnolia Grange & Museum
10201 Iron Bridge Rd PO Box 40 .... Chesterfield VA 23832 804-796-7121 777-9643
Web: www.chesterfieldhistory.com

Mariners' Museum 100 Museum Dr............ Newport News VA 23606 757-596-2222 591-7320
TF: 800-581-7245 ■ *Web:* marinersmuseum.org

Maymont 2201 Shields Dr .... Richmond VA 23220 804-358-7166 358-9994
Web: www.maymont.org

Moses Myers House 1 Memonrial Place............... Norfolk VA 23510 757-333-1086 664-6201
Web: www.chrysler.org

Muscarelle Museum of Art PO Box 8795......... Williamsburg VA 23187 757-221-2700 221-2711
Web: wm.edu/index.php

Museum of the Confederacy 1201 E Clay St .... Richmond VA 23219 804-649-1861 644-7150
Web: www.moc.org

National Firearms Museum
11250 Waples Mill Rd .... Fairfax VA 22030 703-267-1000 267-3913
Web: programs.nra.org

National Museum of the Marine Corps
18900 Jefferson Davis Hwy .... Triangle VA 22172 703-221-1581 221-2988
TF: 877-635-1775 ■ *Web:* www.usmcmuseum.org

NAUTICUS the National Maritime Ctr
One Waterside Dr .... Norfolk VA 23510 757-664-1000 623-1287
TF: 800-664-1080 ■ *Web:* www.nauticus.org

Newsome House Museum & Cultural Ctr
2803 Oak Ave .... Newport News VA 23607 757-247-2360 926-6754
TF: 888-493-7386 ■ *Web:* www.newsomehouse.org

Old City Cemetery Museums & Arboretum
401 Taylor St................................... Lynchburg VA 24501 434-847-1465 856-2004
Web: www.gravegarden.org

Old Coast Guard Station
2401 Atlantic Ave .... Virginia Beach VA 23451 757-422-1587 491-8609
Web: www.oldcoastguardstation.com

Old Guard Museum 201 Lee Ave Ft Myer............. Fort Myer VA 22211 703-696-6670 696-4256
Web: www.army.mil

Richmond National Battlefield Park
3215 E Broad St .... Richmond VA 23223 804-226-1981 771-8522
TF: 866-733-7768 ■ *Web:* www.nps.gov

Salem Museum 801 E Main St .... Salem VA 24153 540-389-6760 389-6760
TF: 888-827-2536 ■ *Web:* www.salemmuseum.org

Science Museum of Western Virginia
One Market Sq .... Roanoke VA 24011 540-342-5710 224-1240
Web: www.smwv.org

Sherwood Forest Plantation
14501 John Tyler Memorial Hwy .... Charles City VA 23030 804-829-5377
Web: www.sherwoodforest.org

Taubman Museum of Art 110 Salem Ave Se .... Roanoke VA 24011 540-342-5760 342-5798
Web: taubmanmuseum.org

US Army Transportation Museum
300 Washington Blvd .... Fort Eustis VA 23604 757-878-1115
Web: www.transchool.lee.army.mil/museum/transportation%20museum/museum.htm

Valentine, The 1015 E Clay St .... Richmond VA 23219 804-649-0711 643-3510
Web: www.richmondhistorycenter.com

Virginia Aquarium & Marine Science Ctr
717 General Booth Blvd .... Virginia Beach VA 23451 757-385-3474
Web: www.virginiaaquarium.com/pages/default.aspx

Virginia Aviation Museum 5701 Huntsman Rd .... Richmond VA 23250 804-236-3622 236-3623
Web: www.vam.smv.org

Virginia Historical Society Museum of Virginia History
428 N Blvd .... Richmond VA 23220 804-358-4901 355-2399
Web: www.vahistorical.org

Virginia Holocaust Museum 2000 E Cary St......... Richmond VA 23223 804-257-5400 257-4314
Web: www.va-holocaust.com

Virginia Living Museum
524 J Clyde Morris Blvd...................... Newport News VA 23601 757-595-1900 599-4897
Web: www.thevlm.org

Virginia Museum of Fine Arts 200 N Blvd .... Richmond VA 23220 804-340-1400 340-1548
Web: vmfa.museum/

Virginia Museum of Transportation
303 Norfolk Ave .... Roanoke VA 24016 540-342-5670 342-6898
Web: www.vmt.org

Virginia War Museum 9285 Warwick Blvd .... Newport News VA 23607 757-247-8523 247-8627
TF: 888-493-7386 ■ *Web:* www.warmuseum.org

Watermen's Museum 309 Water St .... Yorktown VA 23690 757-887-2641
Web: www.watermens.org

Wilton House Museum 215 S Wilton Rd............. Richmond VA 23226 804-282-5936 288-9805
Web: www.wiltonhousemuseum.org

Washington

Phone Fax

Bellevue Arts Museum 510 Bellevue Way NE .... Bellevue WA 98004 425-519-0770 637-1799
TF: 800-367-2648 ■ *Web:* www.bellevuearts.org

Bigelow House Museum 918 Glass Ave NE............ Olympia WA 98506 360-753-1215
Web: www.bigelowhouse.org

Burke Museum of Natural History & Culture
University of Washington
17th Ave NE & NE 45th St............................ Seattle WA 98195 206-543-5590 685-3039
Web: www.burkemuseum.org

Center for Wooden Boats 1010 Valley St.............. Seattle WA 98109 206-382-2628 382-2699
Web: www.cwb.org

Charles & Emma Frye Free Public Art Museum
704 Terry Ave .... Seattle WA 98104 206-622-9250
Web: www.fryemuseum.org

Clark County Historical Museum
1511 Main St .... Vancouver WA 98660 360-993-5679 993-5683
Web: cchmuseum.org

DuPont Historical Museum 207 Barksdale Ave......... Dupont WA 98327 253-964-2399 964-3554
Web: www.dupontmuseum.com

Fireworks Fine Crafts Gallery
3307 Utah Ave S.................................... Seattle WA 98134 206-682-8707 467-6366
TF: 800-505-8882 ■ *Web:* www.fireworksgallery.net

Name / Address	City	State	ZIP	Phone	Fax
Fort Lewis Military Museum PO Box 331001 *Web:* fortlewismuseum.com	Fort Lewis	WA	98433	253-967-7206	
Foss Waterway Seaport 705 Dock St *Web:* www.fosswaterwayseaport.org	Tacoma	WA	98402	253-272-2750	273-3023
Frye Art Museum 704 Terry Ave *Web:* www.fryeart.org	Seattle	WA	98104	206-622-9250	223-1701
Henderson House Museum 602 Deschutes Way *Web:* www.ci.tumwater.wa.us	Tumwater	WA	98501	360-754-4217	
Henry Art Gallery University of Washington 15th Ave NE & NE 41st St *Web:* www.henryart.org	Seattle	WA	98195	206-543-2281	685-3123
Jundt Art Museum 202 E Cataldo Ave *Web:* www.gonzaga.edu	Spokane	WA	99258	509-313-6611	313-5525
Lacey Museum 829 1/2 Lacey St SE *Web:* ci.lacey.wa.us	Lacey	WA	98503	360-438-0209	
Meeker Mansion 312 Spring St *Web:* www.meekermansion.org	Puyallup	WA	98372	253-848-1770	
Museum of Flight 9404 E Marginal Way S *TF:* 877-217-6379 ■ *Web:* www.museumofflight.org	Seattle	WA	98108	206-764-5700	764-5707
Museum of Glass 1801 Dock St *TF General:* 866-468-7386 ■ *Web:* www.museumofglass.org	Tacoma	WA	98402	253-284-4750	369-1769
Museum of History & Industry 2700 24th Ave E *Web:* www.mohai.org	Seattle	WA	98112	206-324-1126	324-1346
Nordic Heritage Museum 3014 NW 67th St *Web:* www.nordicmuseum.com	Seattle	WA	98117	206-789-5707	789-3271
Northwest Museum of Arts & Culture 2316 W First Ave *Web:* www.northwestmuseum.org	Spokane	WA	99201	509-456-3931	363-5303
Olympic Flight Museum 7637A Old Hwy 99 SE *Web:* www.olympicflightmuseum.com	Olympia	WA	98501	360-705-3925	236-9839
Pacific Science Ctr 200 Second Ave N *TF:* 800-664-8775 ■ *Web:* www.pacificsciencecenter.org	Seattle	WA	98109	206-443-2001	443-3631
Port Townsend Marine Science Ctr 532 Battery Way *TF:* 800-566-3932 ■ *Web:* www.ptmsc.org	Port Townsend	WA	98368	360-385-5582	385-7248
Seattle Art Museum 1300 First Ave *Web:* www.seattleartmuseum.org	Seattle	WA	98101	206-654-3100	654-3135
Seattle Asian Art Museum 1400 E Prospect St Volunteer Pk *Web:* www.seattleartmuseum.org	Seattle	WA	98112	206-654-3210	654-3191
Tacoma Art Museum 1701 Pacific Ave *Web:* www.tacomaartmuseum.org	Tacoma	WA	98402	253-272-4258	627-1898
Tenino Depot Museum 399 Pk Ave W *Web:* ci.tenino.wa.us	Tenino	WA	98589	360-264-4321	
Two Rivers Heritage Museum 001 Durgan St PO Box 204 *Web:* 2rhm.com	Washougal	WA	98671	360-835-8742	
Washington State Capital Museum 211 21st Ave SW *Web:* www.washingtonhistory.org	Olympia	WA	98501	360-753-2580	586-8322
Wing Luke Asian Museum 719 S King St *Web:* www.wingluke.org	Seattle	WA	98104	206-623-5124	623-4559
World Kite Museum & Hall of Fame 303 Sid Snyder Dr *Web:* www.worldkitemuseum.com	Long Beach	WA	98631	360-642-4020	642-4020

West Virginia

Name / Address	City	State	ZIP	Phone	Fax
Challenger Learning Ctr (CLC) 316 Washington Ave Wheeling Jesuit University *TF:* 800-624-6992 ■ *Web:* www.wju.edu/clc	Wheeling	WV	26003	304-243-2279	243-4397
Huntington Museum of Art Inc 2033 McCoy Rd *Web:* www.hmoa.org	Huntington	WV	25701	304-529-2701	529-7447
Kruger Street Toy & Train Museum 144 Kruger St *TF:* 877-242-8133 ■ *Web:* www.toyandtrain.com	Wheeling	WV	26003	304-242-8133	242-1925
Marks Toy Museum 915 Second St *Web:* www.marxtoymuseum.com	Moundsville	WV	26041	304-845-6022	
Museums of Oglebay Institute 1330 National Rd *TF:* 800-624-6988 ■ *Web:* www.oionline.com	Wheeling	WV	26003	304-242-7272	
West Virginia State Museum 1900 Kanawha Blvd E The Cultural Ctr *TF:* 800-120-4000 ■ *Web:* www.wvculture.org/museum	Charleston	WV	25305	304-558-0220	558-2779

Wisconsin

Name / Address	City	State	ZIP	Phone	Fax
Cedarburg Cultural Center W62 N546 Washington Ave *Web:* www.cedarburgculturalcenter.org	Cedarburg	WI	53012	262-375-3676	
Charles Allis Art Museum 1801 N Prospect Ave *Web:* www.cavtmuseums.org	Milwaukee	WI	53202	414-278-8295	
Chazen Museum of Art 800 University Ave University of Wisconsin *Web:* www.chazen.wisc.edu	Madison	WI	53706	608-263-2246	263-8188
Circus World Museum 550 Water St *TF:* 866-693-1500 ■ *Web:* circusworldbaraboo.org/	Baraboo	WI	53913	608-356-8341	356-1800
Discovery World 500 N Harbor Dr *Web:* www.discoveryworld.org	Milwaukee	WI	53202	414-765-9966	765-0311
EAA AirVenture Museum 3000 Poberezny Rd *TF:* 888-322-3229 ■ *Web:* eaa.org/en/eaa-museum	Oshkosh	WI	54902	920-426-4800	426-6560
Greene Memorial Museum 3209 N Maryland Ave Lapham Hall UWM Campus *Web:* www.uwm.edu	Milwaukee	WI	53211	414-229-4561	229-5452
Hazelwood Historic Home Museum 1008 S Monroe Ave *Web:* www.browncohistoricalsoc.org	Green Bay	WI	54301	920-437-1840	455-4518
John Michael Kohler Arts Center 608 New York Ave *Web:* www.jmkac.org	Sheboygan	WI	53081	920-458-6144	
Kenosha Public Museum 5500 First Ave *TF:* 888-258-9966 ■ *Web:* www.kenosha.org	Kenosha	WI	53140	262-653-4140	653-4437
Madison Geology Museum 1215 W Dayton St *Web:* www.geologymuseum.org	Madison	WI	53706	608-262-2399	262-0693
Milwaukee Art Museum 700 N Art Museum Dr *TF:* 888-322-3326 ■ *Web:* www.mam.org	Milwaukee	WI	53202	414-224-3200	271-7588
Milwaukee Public Museum 800 W Wells St *Web:* www.mpm.edu	Milwaukee	WI	53233	414-278-2700	319-4656
Mitchell Gallery of Flight 5300 S Howell Ave General Mitchell International Airport *Web:* www.mitchellgallery.org	Milwaukee	WI	53207	414-747-5300	747-4525
National Railroad Museum 2285 S Broadway St *TF:* 866-468-7630 ■ *Web:* www.nationalrrmuseum.org	Green Bay	WI	54304	920-437-7623	437-1291
Neville Public Museum of Brown County 210 Museum Pl *Web:* www.nevillepublicmuseum.org	Green Bay	WI	54303	920-448-4460	448-4458
Old World Wisconsin W372 S9727 Hwy 67 PO Box 69 *Web:* oldworldwisconsin.wisconsinhistory.org	Eagle	WI	53119	262-594-6301	594-6342
Oshkosh Public Museum 1331 Algoma Blvd *Web:* www.oshkoshmuseum.org	Oshkosh	WI	54901	920-236-5799	424-4738
Patrick & Beatrice Haggerty Museum of Art 13th & Clybourn Sts Marquette University *Web:* www.marquette.edu/haggerty	Milwaukee	WI	53201	414-288-7290	288-5415
Villa Terrace Decorative Arts Museum & Gardens 2220 N Terr Ave *Web:* www.villaterracemuseum.org	Milwaukee	WI	53202	414-271-3656	271-3986
Wisconsin Black Historical Society Museum 2620 W Ctr St *Web:* www.wbhsm.org	Milwaukee	WI	53206	414-372-7677	372-4888
Wisconsin Historical Museum 30 N Carroll St *TF:* 888-748-7479 ■ *Web:* historicalmuseum.wisconsinhistory.org	Madison	WI	53703	608-264-6555	264-6575
Wisconsin Maritime Museum 75 Maritime Dr *TF:* 866-724-2356 ■ *Web:* www.wisconsinmaritime.org	Manitowoc	WI	54220	920-684-0218	684-0219
Wisconsin State Fair Park 640 S 84th St *TF:* 800-884-3247 ■ *Web:* www.wistatefair.com	West Allis	WI	53214	414-266-7033	266-7007
Wisconsin Veterans Museum 30 W Mifflin St *Web:* www.wisvetsmuseum.com	Madison	WI	53703	608-264-6086	264-7615

Wyoming

Name / Address	City	State	ZIP	Phone	Fax
Buffalo Bill Historical Ctr 720 Sheridan Ave *Web:* centerofthewest.org	Cody	WY	82414	307-587-4771	587-5714
Cheyenne Depot Museum 121 W 15th St Ste 300 *TF:* 800-544-2151 ■ *Web:* www.cheyennedepotmuseum.org	Cheyenne	WY	82001	307-632-3905	632-0614
Cheyenne Frontier Days Old West Museum 4610 N Carey Ave PO Box 2720 *Web:* www.oldwestmuseum.org	Cheyenne	WY	82001	307-778-7290	778-7288
Fort Caspar Museum 4001 Fort Caspar Rd *TF:* 800-877-7353 ■ *Web:* www.casperwy.gov	Casper	WY	82604	307-235-8462	235-8464
Geological Museum 1000 E University Ave *TF:* 800-842-2776 ■ *Web:* www.uwyo.edu/geomuseum	Laramie	WY	82071	307-766-2646	766-6679
Jackson Hole Historical Society & Museum 105 Mercill *Web:* www.jacksonholehistory.org	Jackson	WY	83001	307-733-9605	739-9019
Laramie Plains Museum 603 E Ivinson St *Web:* www.laramiemuseum.org	Laramie	WY	82070	307-742-4448	
Museum of the Mountain Man 700 E Hennick St *TF:* 877-686-6266 ■ *Web:* www.pinedaleonline.com	Pinedale	WY	82941	307-367-4101	367-6768
National Museum of Wildlife Art 2820 Rungius Rd PO Box 6825 *TF:* 800-313-9553 ■ *Web:* www.wildlifeart.org	Jackson	WY	83002	307-733-5771	733-5787
Nelson Museum of the West 1714 Carey Ave *Web:* www.nelsonmuseum.com	Cheyenne	WY	82001	307-635-7670	778-3926
Nicolaysen Art Museum 400 E Collins Dr *Web:* www.thenic.org	Casper	WY	82601	307-235-5247	235-0923
Sweetwater County Historical Museum 3 E Flaming Gorge Way *Web:* www.sweetwatermuseum.org	Green River	WY	82935	307-872-6435	872-3234
Werner Wildlife Museum 405 E 15th St *Web:* caspercollege.edu	Casper	WY	82601	307-235-2108	
Wyoming Dinosaur Ctr 110 Carter Ranch Rd *Web:* www.wyodino.org	Thermopolis	WY	82443	307-864-2997	
Wyoming State Museum 2301 Central Ave *Web:* wyomuseum.state.wy.us	Cheyenne	WY	82002	307-777-7022	777-5375

Yukon

Name / Address	City	State	ZIP	Phone	Fax
MacBride Museum 1124 First Ave *Web:* www.macbridemuseum.com	Whitehorse	YT	Y1A1A4	867-667-2709	633-6607

524 MUSEUMS - CHILDREN'S

Children's museums are organized alphabetically by states.

Name / Address	City	State	ZIP	Phone	Fax
Children's Hands-On Museum 2213 University Blvd *Web:* www.chomonline.org	Tuscaloosa	AL	35401	205-349-4235	349-4276
EarlyWorks Children's Museum 404 Madison St *Web:* earlyworks.com	Huntsville	AL	35801	256-564-8100	564-8151

	City	State	Zip	Phone	Fax
Gulf Coast Exploreum Science Ctr 65 Government St *Web:* www.exploreum.com	Mobile	AL	36602	251-208-6873	208-6889
Sci-Quest Hands on Science Ctr 102-D Wynn Dr *Web:* www.sci-quest.org	Huntsville	AL	35805	256-837-0606	837-4536
Tucson Children's Museum 200 S Sixth Ave *Web:* childrensmuseumtucson.org	Tucson	AZ	85702	520-792-9985	792-0639
Bay Area Discovery Museum 557 McReynolds Rd *Web:* www.baykidsmuseum.org	Sausalito	CA	94965	415-339-3900	339-3905
Bowers Kidseum, The 1802 N Main St *Web:* bowers.org/index.php/visit/kidseum/about-kidseum	Santa Ana	CA	92706	714-480-1520	
Children's Discovery Museum of San Jose 180 Woz Way *Web:* www.cdm.org	San Jose	CA	95110	408-298-5437	298-6826
Children's Discovery Museum of the Desert 71701 Gerald Ford Dr *Web:* www.cdmod.org	Rancho Mirage	CA	92270	760-321-0602	321-1605
Children's Museum of Stockton 402 W Weber Ave *Web:* www.stocktongov.com	Stockton	CA	95202	209-465-4386	465-4394
Discovery Ctr (TDC) 1944 N Winery Ave *Web:* www.thediscoverycenter.net	Fresno	CA	93703	559-251-5533	251-5531
Discovery Museum Science & Space Ctr 3615 Auburn Blvd *Web:* www.thediscovery.org	Sacramento	CA	95821	916-485-8836	575-3925
Gull Wings Children's Museum 418 W Fourth St *Web:* www.gullwings.org	Oxnard	CA	93030	805-483-3005	483-3226
Lori Brock Children's Discovery Ctr 3801 Chester Ave	Bakersfield	CA	93301	661-852-5050	633-9829
Museum of Children's Art 538 Ninth St Ste 210 *Web:* www.mocha.org	Oakland	CA	94607	510-465-8770	465-0772
My Museum 425 Washington St *Web:* www.mymuseum.org	Monterey	CA	93940	831-649-6444	649-1304
Sacramento History Museum 101 'I' St *Web:* www.historicoldsac.org/museum/default.asp	Sacramento	CA	95814	916-808-7059	264-5100
Youth Science Institute 296 Garden Hill Dr *Web:* www.ysi-ca.org	Los Gatos	CA	95032	408-356-4945	358-3683
Children's Museum of Denver 2121 Children's Museum Dr *Web:* www.mychildsmuseum.org	Denver	CO	80211	303-433-7444	433-9520
Durango Discovery Museum 1333 Camino Del Rio *Web:* powsci.org/	Durango	CO	81301	970-259-9234	259-6320
Connecticut Children's Museum 22 Wall St *Web:* www.childrensbuilding.org	New Haven	CT	06511	203-562-5437	787-9414
Living Classrooms Foundation 515 M St SE Ste 222 *Web:* livingclassroomsdc.org	Washington	DC	20003	202-488-0627	
Children's Museum 498 Crawford Blvd *Web:* www.cmboca.org	Boca Raton	FL	33432	561-368-6875	395-7764
Children's Science Explorium 300 S Military Trl *Web:* www.scienceexplorium.org/	Boca Raton	FL	33486	561-347-3912	347-3910
G Wiz Hands on Science Museum 1001 Blvd of the Arts *Web:* www.gwiz.org	Sarasota	FL	34236	941-309-4949	906-7292
Great Explorations Children's Museum 1925 Fourth St N *Web:* www.greatexplorations.org	Saint Petersburg	FL	33704	727-821-8992	823-7287
Miami Children's Museum 980 MacArthur Cswy *Web:* www.miamichildrensmuseum.org	Miami	FL	33132	305-373-5437	373-5431
Young at Art Children's Museum 751 SW 121st Ave *TF:* 800-435-7352 ■ *Web:* www.youngatartmuseum.org	Davie	FL	33325	954-424-0085	473-8798
Imagine It! Children's Museum of Atlanta 275 Centennial Olympic Pk Dr NW *Web:* www.childrensmuseumatlanta.org	Atlanta	GA	30313	404-659-5437	223-3675
Hawaii Children's Discovery Ctr 111 Ohe St *Web:* www.discoverycenterhawaii.org	Honolulu	HI	96813	808-524-5437	524-5400
Bourbonnais Township Park District 459 Kennedy Dr *Web:* www.exploration-station.org	Bourbonnais	IL	60914	815-933-9905	
Chicago Children's Museum 700 E Grand Ave *Web:* chicagochildrensmuseum.org	Chicago	IL	60611	312-527-1000	527-9082
Discovery Ctr Museum 711 N Main St *Web:* www.discoverycentermuseum.org	Rockford	IL	61103	815-963-6769	968-0164
Orpheum Children's Science Museum 346 N Neil St *Web:* orpheumkids.net/	Champaign	IL	61820	217-352-5895	352-8610
Hannah Lindahl Children's Museum 1402 S Main St *Web:* www.hlcm.org	Mishawaka	IN	46544	574-254-4540	254-4585
HealthWorks! Kids' Museum 111 W Jefferson Blvd Ste 200 *Web:* www.healthworkskids.org	South Bend	IN	46601	574-647-5437	
Koch Family Children's Museum of Evansville 22 SE Fifth St *Web:* www.cmoekids.org	Evansville	IN	47708	812-464-2663	477-4339
Muncie Children's Museum 515 S High St *Web:* munciemuseum.com	Muncie	IN	47305	765-286-1660	286-1662
Exploration Place 300 N McLean Blvd *TF:* 877-904-1444 ■ *Web:* www.exploration.org	Wichita	KS	67203	316-660-0600	660-0670
Kansas Cosmosphere & Space Ctr 1100 N Plum St *TF:* 800-397-0330 ■ *Web:* www.cosmo.org	Hutchinson	KS	67501	620-662-2305	662-3693
Explorium of Lexington 440 W Short St *Web:* www.explorium.com	Lexington	KY	40507	859-258-3253	258-3255
Children's Museum of Acadiana 201 E Congress St *Web:* www.childrensmuseumofacadiana.com/home	Lafayette	LA	70501	337-232-8500	232-8167

	City	State	Zip	Phone	Fax
Children's Museum of Lake Charles 327 Broad St *Web:* www.swlakids.org	Lake Charles	LA	70601	337-433-9420	433-0144
Louisiana Children's Museum 420 Julia St *Web:* www.lcm.org	New Orleans	LA	70130	504-586-0725	529-3666
Children's Museum of Maine 142 Free St PO Box 4041 *Web:* www.kitetails.org	Portland	ME	04101	207-828-1234	828-5726
Chesapeake Children's Museum 25 Silopanna Rd *Web:* www.theccm.org	Annapolis	MD	21403	410-990-1993	990-1007
Port Discovery Children's Museum in Baltimore 35 Market Pl *Web:* www.portdiscovery.org	Baltimore	MD	21202	410-727-8120	727-3042
Boston Children's Museum 308 Congress St *Web:* www.bostonchildrensmuseum.org	Boston	MA	02210	617-426-6500	426-1944
Cape Cod Children's Museum 577 Great Neck Rd S *Web:* www.capecodchildrensmuseum.org	Mashpee	MA	02649	508-539-8788	539-3285
EcoTarium 222 Harrington Way *Web:* www.ecotarium.org	Worcester	MA	01604	508-929-2700	929-2701
Flint Children's Museum 1602 W University Ave *Web:* www.flintchildrensmuseum.org	Flint	MI	48504	810-767-5437	767-4936
Grand Rapids Children's Museum 11 Sheldon Ave NE *Web:* www.grcm.org	Grand Rapids	MI	49503	616-235-4726	235-4728
Minnesota Children's Museum 10 W Seventh St *Web:* www.mcm.org	Saint Paul	MN	55102	651-225-6000	225-6006
Lynn Meadows Discovery Ctr 246 Dolan Ave *Web:* www.lmdc.org	Gulfport	MS	39507	228-897-6039	248-0071
Discovery Ctr of Springfield 438 E St Louis St *TF:* 888-636-4395 ■ *Web:* www.discoverycenter.org	Springfield	MO	65806	417-862-9910	862-6898
Kaleidoscope 2500 Grand Blvd PO Box 419580 *Web:* hallmarkkaleidoscope.com	Kansas City	MO	64108	816-274-8301	
Magic House Saint Louis Children's Museum 516 S Kirkwood Rd *Web:* www.magichouse.org	Saint Louis	MO	63122	314-822-8900	822-8930
Lincoln Children's Museum 1420 P St *Web:* www.lincolnchildrensmuseum.org	Lincoln	NE	68508	402-477-4000	477-2004
Omaha Children's Museum 500 S 20th St *Web:* www.ocm.org	Omaha	NE	68102	402-342-6164	342-6165
Children's Museum of Northern Nevada 813 N Carson St *Web:* www.cmnn.org	Carson City	NV	89701	775-884-2226	884-2179
Lied Discovery Children's Museum 360 Promenade Pl *Web:* www.discoverykidslv.org	Las Vegas	NV	89106	702-382-3445	382-0592
Children's Museum of New Hampshire Six Washington St *Web:* www.childrens-museum.org	Dover	NH	03820	603-742-2002	834-6275
Santa Fe Children's Museum 1050 Old Pecos Trl *Web:* www.santafechildrensmuseum.org	Santa Fe	NM	87505	505-989-8359	989-7506
Brooklyn Children's Museum 145 Brooklyn Ave *Web:* www.brooklynkids.org	Brooklyn	NY	11213	718-735-4400	
Children's Museum of History Natural History Science & Technology 311 Main St *Web:* www.museum4kids.net	Utica	NY	13501	315-724-6129	724-6120
Children's Museum of Manhattan 212 W 83rd St *Web:* www.cmom.org	New York	NY	10024	212-721-1223	721-1127
Children's Museum of the Arts 103 Charlton St *Web:* www.cmany.org	New York	NY	10014	212-274-0986	274-1776
Discovery Ctr of the Southern Tier 60 Morgan Rd *Web:* www.thediscoverycenter.org	Binghamton	NY	13903	607-773-8661	773-8019
Explore & More-A Children's Museum 300 Gleed Ave *Web:* www.exploreandmore.org	East Aurora	NY	14052	716-655-5131	655-5466
Long Island Children's Museum 11 Davis Ave *Web:* www.licm.org	Garden City	NY	11530	516-224-5800	302-8188
Staten Island Children's Museum 1000 Richmond Terr at Snug Harbor *Web:* sichildrensmuseum.org	Staten Island	NY	10301	718-273-2060	273-2836
Discovery Place 301 N Tryon St *TF:* 800-935-0553 ■ *Web:* www.discoveryplace.org	Charlotte	NC	28202	704-372-6261	337-2670
Greensboro Children's Museum 220 N Church St *Web:* www.gcmuseum.com	Greensboro	NC	27401	336-574-2898	574-3810
Rocky Mount Children's Museum 270 Gay St *Web:* museum.imperialcentre.org	Rocky Mount	NC	27804	252-972-1167	
Yunker Farm Children's Museum 1201 28th Ave N *Web:* www.childrensmuseum-yunker.org	Fargo	ND	58102	701-232-6102	232-4605
Children's Museum of Cleveland 10730 Euclid Ave *Web:* www.clevelandchildrensmuseum.org	Cleveland	OH	44106	216-791-7114	791-8838
Cincinnati Fire Museum 315 W Court St Ste 1 *Web:* www.cincyfiremuseum.com	Cincinnati	OH	45202	513-621-5553	
Cinergy Children's Museum 1301 Western Ave Cincinnati Museum Ctr *TF:* 800-733-2077 ■ *Web:* www.cincymuseum.org	Cincinnati	OH	45203	513-287-7000	287-7079
AC Gilbert's Discovery Village 116 Marion St NE *Web:* www.acgilbert.org	Salem	OR	97301	503-371-3631	316-3485
Portland Children's Museum 4015 SW Canyon Rd *Web:* www.portlandcm.org	Portland	OR	97221	503-223-6500	223-6600

Phone Fax

Science Factory Children's Museum & Planetarium
2300 Leo Harris Pkwy. Eugene OR 97401 541-682-7888 484-9027
Web: www.sciencefactory.org

Children's Museum of Pittsburgh
10 Children's Way. Pittsburgh PA 15212 412-322-5058 322-4932
Web: www.pittsburghkids.org

ExpERIEnce Children's Museum 420 French St. Erie PA 16507 814-453-3743 459-9735
Web: www.eriechildrensmuseum.org

Explore & More Hands-On Children's Museum
20 E High St Gettysburg PA 17325 717-337-9151
Web: www.exploreandmore.com

Hands-On House Children's Museum of Lancaster
721 Landis Vly Rd Lancaster PA 17601 717-569-5437 581-9283
Web: www.handsonhouse.org

Please Touch Museum
Memorial Hall Fairmount Pk
4231 Ave of the Republic Philadelphia PA 19131 215-963-0667 581-3183
TF: 800-732-0999 ■ *Web:* www.pleasetouchmuseum.org

Providence Children's Museum 100 S St Providence RI 02903 401-273-5437 273-1004
Web: www.childrenmuseum.org

Children's Museum of South Carolina
2204 N Oak St Myrtle Beach SC 29577 843-946-9469 946-7011
Web: www.cmsckids.org

Children's Museum of the Lowcountry
25 Ann St Charleston SC 29403 843-853-8962 853-1042
Web: www.explorecml.org

EdVenture Children's Museum 211 Gervais St Columbia SC 29201 803-779-3100 779-3144
TF: 800-915-4522 ■ *Web:* www.edventure.org

Children's Museum of Memphis
2525 Central Ave Memphis TN 38104 901-458-2678 458-4033
Web: www.cmom.com

Children's Museum of Oak Ridge
461 W Outer Dr. Oak Ridge TN 37830 865-482-1074 481-4889
TF: 877-524-1223 ■ *Web:* www.childrensmuseumofoakridge.org

Creative Discovery Museum
321 Chestnut St Chattanooga TN 37402 423-756-2738 267-9344
Web: www.cdmfun.org

East Tennessee Discovery Ctr
516 N Beaman St Chilhowee Pk Knoxville TN 37914 865-594-1494 594-1469
Web: themuseknoxville.com

Hands On! Regional Museum 315 E Main St Johnson City TN 37601 423-434-4263 928-6915
Web: www.handsonmuseum.org

Austin Children's Museum 201 Colorado St Austin TX 78701 512-472-2499 472-2495
Web: thinkeryaustin.org

Children's Museum of Houston 1500 Binz St. Houston TX 77004 713-522-1138 522-5747
Web: www.cmhouston.org

Don Harrington Discovery Ctr 1200 Streit Dr Amarillo TX 79106 806-355-9547 355-5703
Web: www.dhdc.org

Grace Museum 102 Cypress St Abilene TX 79601 325-673-4587 675-5993
Web: www.thegracemuseum.org

Imaginarium of South Texas
5300 San Dario Ste 505 Laredo TX 78041 956-728-0404 725-7776
Web: www.imaginariumstx.org

San Antonio Children's Museum
305 E Houston St San Antonio TX 78205 210-212-4453 242-1313
Web: www.sakids.org

Science Place, The 2201 N Field St. Dallas TX 75201 214-428-5555 756-5916
Web: www.perotmuseum.org

Discovery Gateway 444 West 100 South Salt Lake City UT 84101 801-456-5437 456-5440
Web: www.discoverygateway.org

Treehouse Museum 347 22nd St Ogden UT 84401 801-394-9663 528-5128
Web: www.treehousemuseum.org

Children's Museum of Richmond
2626 W Broad St Richmond VA 23220 804-474-7000 474-7099
TF: 866-737-5965 ■ *Web:* c-mor.org

Children's Museum of Virginia 221 High St Portsmouth VA 23704 757-393-5258 393-8083
Web: www.childrensmuseumva.com

Virginia Discovery Museum
524 E Main St PO Box 1128 Charlottesville VA 22902 434-977-1025 977-9681
Web: www.vadm.org

Children's Museum of Tacoma 936 Broadway Tacoma WA 98402 253-627-6031 627-2436
Web: www.playtacoma.org

Children's Museum Seattle 305 Harrison St Seattle WA 98109 206-441-1768 448-0910
Web: www.thechildrensmuseum.org

Hands On Children's Museum
414 Jefferson Street NE Olympia WA 98501 360-956-0818 754-8626
Web: www.hocm.org

Betty Brinn Children's Museum
929 E Wisconsin Ave Milwaukee WI 53202 414-390-5437 291-0906
Web: www.bbcmkids.org

Madison Children's Museum 100 N Hamilton St Madison WI 53703 608-256-6445
Web: www.madisonchildrensmuseum.org

525 MUSEUMS & HALLS OF FAME - SPORTS

Phone Fax

1932 & 1980 Lake Placid Winter Olympic Museum
Olympic Ctr 2634 Main St Lake Placid NY 12946 518-523-1655 523-9275
TF: 800-462-6236 ■ *Web:* www.orda.org

Alabama Sports Hall of Fame
2150 Richard Arrington Junior Blvd Birmingham AL 35203 205-323-6665 252-2212
Web: www.ashof.org

Alberta Sports Hall of Fame & Museum
4200 Hwy 2 Ste 102 Red Deer AB T4N1E3 403-341-8614 341-8619
Web: www.albertasportshalloffame.com

American Museum of Fly Fishing
4104 Main Rd. Manchester VT 05254 802-362-3300 362-3308
TF: 800-333-1550 ■ *Web:* www.amff.com

American Water Ski Hall of Fame & Museum
1251 Holy Cow Rd Polk City FL 33868 863-324-2472 324-3996
TF: 800-533-2972 ■ *Web:* usawaterskifoundation.org/

Phone Fax

Arizona-Sonora Desert Museum Inc
2021 N Kinney Rd. Tucson AZ 85743 520-883-1380
Web: www.desertmuseum.org

Arthaus Foundation 3840 S Ridgewood Ave. Port Orange FL 32129 386-767-0076
Web: arthaus.org

Arts Club of Chicago, The 201 E Ontario St. Chicago IL 60611 312-787-3997
Web: artsclubchicago.org

Babe Ruth Birthplace Museum 216 Emory St Baltimore MD 21230 410-727-1539 727-1652
Web: baberuthmuseum.org

Baseball Hall of Fame 910 S 3rd St. Minneapolis MN 55415 612-375-9707
TF: 888-375-9707 ■ *Web:* www.domeplus.com

Baseball Reliquary PO Box 1850 Monrovia CA 91017 626-791-7647
Web: www.baseballreliquary.org

Billingsley House Museum
6900 Green Landing Rd Upper Marlboro MD 20772 301-627-0730
Web: pgparks.com

Bob Feller Museum 310 Mill St PO Box 95. Van Meter IA 50261 515-996-2806 996-2952
Web: www.bobfellermuseum.org

Bobby Riggs Tennis Museum 875 Santa Fe Dr Encinitas CA 92024 760-753-4705
Web: bobbyriggs.net

Boca Raton Historical Society & Museum
71 N Federal Hwy Boca Raton FL 33432 561-395-6766
Web: www.bocahistory.org

British Columbia Sports Hall of Fame & Museum
777 Pacific Blvd S Ste 200 Vancouver BC V6B4Y8 604-687-5520 687-5510
Web: www.bcsportshalloffame.com

Britto Central Inc 818 Lincoln Rd Miami FL 33139 305-531-8821
Web: www.britto.com

Brunswick Historical Society 605 Brunswick Rd. Troy NY 12180 518-279-4024
Web: townofbrunswick.org

Canada Olympic Hall of Fame & Museum
88 Canada Olympic Rd SW. Calgary AB T3B5R5 403-247-5452 286-7213
Web: www.winsport.ca

Canada's Sports Hall of Fame
169 Canada Olympic Rd SW. Calgary AB T3B6B7 403-776-1040
Web: www.sportshall.ca

Canadian Football Hall of Fame & Museum
58 Jackson St W. Hamilton ON L8P1L4 905-528-7566 528-9781
Web: www.cfhof.ca

Canadian Golf Hall of Fame & Museum
Glen Abbey Golf Course 1333 Dorval Dr Ste 1 Oakville ON L6M4X7 905-849-9700 845-7040
TF: 800-263-0009 ■ *Web:* golfcanada.ca

Carolina Raptor Center 6000 Sample Rd. Huntersville NC 28078 704-875-6521
Web: carolinaraptorcenter.org

Cheap Joe's Art Stuff Inc
374 Industrial Park Dr. Boone NC 28607 828-263-5472
Web: www.cheapjoes.com

Clyfford Still Museum 1250 Bannock St Denver CO 80204 720-354-4880
Web: www.clyffordstillmuseum.org

Colorado Sports Hall of Fame
1701 Mile High Stadium. Denver CO 80204 720-258-3888 244-1003*
**Fax Area Code:* 303 ■ *Web:* www.coloradosports.org

Craft Emergency Relief Fund 24 Elm St. Montpelier VT 05602 802-229-2306
Web: www.craftemergency.org

D Day Museum The National
945 Magazine St. New Orleans LA 70130 504-527-6012
Web: www.ddaymuseum.org

Delaware Sports Museum & Hall of Fame
801 Shipyard Dr. Wilmington DE 19801 302-425-3263 425-3713
Web: www.desports.org

Don Garlits Museums 13700 SW 16th Ave Ocala FL 34473 352-245-8661 245-6895
TF: 877-271-3278 ■ *Web:* www.garlits.com

Dr Pepper Museum & Free Enterprise Institute, The
300 S Fifth St Waco TX 76701 254-757-1025
Web: www.drpeppermuseum.com

Eastern Museum of Motor Racing
100 Baltimore Rd York Springs PA 17372 717-528-8279
Web: www.emmr.org

Elmhurst Art Museum 150 S Cottage Hill Ave Elmhurst IL 60126 630-834-0202
Web: elmhurstartmuseum.org

Fernbank Museum of Natural History
767 Clifton Rd NE. Atlanta GA 30307 404-929-6300
Web: www.fernbankmuseum.org

Florida Air Museum at Sun 'n Fun
4175 Medulla Rd Lakeland FL 33811 863-644-2431 648-9264
Web: www.sun-n-fun.org

Fox Cities Performing Arts Center
400 W College Ave Appleton WI 54911 920-730-3782
Web: foxcitiespac.com

Georgia Sports Hall of Fame
301 Cherry St PO Box 4644 Macon GA 31201 478-752-1585 752-1587
Web: georgiasportshalloffame.com/site

Green Bay Packers Hall of Fame
1265 Lombardi Ave. Green Bay WI 54304 920-569-7512 569-7122
TF: 888-442-7225 ■ *Web:* www.packers.com

Greyhound Hall of Fame 407 S Buckeye Ave. Abilene KS 67410 785-263-3000 263-2604
TF: 800-932-7881 ■ *Web:* www.greyhoundhalloffame.com

Harness Racing Museum & Hall of Fame
240 Main St Goshen NY 10924 845-294-6330 294-3463
TF: 877-800-8782 ■ *Web:* www.harnessmuseum.com

Hendrick Motorsports Museum
4400 Papa Joe Hendrick Blvd. Charlotte NC 28262 877-467-4890 455-0346*
**Fax Area Code:* 704 ■ *TF:* 877-467-4890 ■ *Web:* www.hendrickmotorsports.com

Hockey Hall of Fame 30 Yonge St Toronto ON M5E1X8 416-360-7735 360-1316
Web: www.hhof.com

Hyde Park Art Center 5020 S Cornell Ave. Chicago IL 60615 773-324-5520
Web: hydeparkart.org

IGFA Fishing Hall of Fame & Museum
300 Gulf Stream Way Dania Beach FL 33004 954-922-4212 924-4220
Web: www.igfa.org

Improv Asylum 216 Hanover St Boston MA 02113 617-263-6887
Web: www.improvasylum.com

Name / Address	City	State	Zip	Phone	Fax
Indiana Basketball Hall of Fame 408 Trojan Ln *Web:* www.hoopshall.com	New Castle	IN	47362	765-529-1891	529-0273
Indiana Football Hall of Fame 815 N A St PO Box 40 *Web:* www.indiana-football.org	Richmond	IN	47374	765-966-2235	966-5700
International Bowling Museum & Hall of Fame 621 Six Flags Dr *Web:* www.bowlingmuseum.com	Arlington	TX	76011	817-385-8215	385-8210
International Boxing Hall of Fame Museum One Hall of Fame Dr *Web:* www.ibhof.com	Canastota	NY	13032	315-697-7095	697-5356
International Gymnastics Hall of Fame & Museum 2100 NE 52nd St *Web:* www.ighof.com	Oklahoma City	OK	73111	405-602-6664	602-3768
International Jewish Sports Hall of Fame 7922 Turncrest Dr *Web:* www.jewishsports.net	Potomac	MD	20854	301-602-9953	765-9865
International Motorsports Hall of Fame & Museum 3198 Speedway Blvd *Web:* www.motorsportshalloffame.com	Talladega	AL	35160	256-362-5002	
International Snowmobile Hall of Fame 1521 N Railroad St *Web:* www.ishof.com	Eagle River	WI	54521	715-479-2186	
International Swimming Hall of Fame One Hall of Fame Dr *Web:* www.ishof.org	Fort Lauderdale	FL	33316	954-462-6536	525-4031
International Tennis Hall of Fame & Museum 194 Bellevue Ave *TF:* 800-745-3000 ■ *Web:* www.tennisfame.com	Newport	RI	02840	401-849-3990	
International Wrestling Institute & Museum 303 Jefferson St *Web:* www.nwhof.org	Waterloo	IA	50701	319-233-0745	233-3477
Ivan Allen Jr Braves Museum & Hall of Fame 755 Hank Aaron Dr SE *Web:* atlanta.braves.mlb.com	Atlanta	GA	30315	404-614-2310	
Jack Nicklaus Museum 2355 Olentangy River Rd *Web:* www.nicklausmuseum.org	Columbus	OH	43210	614-247-5959	247-5906
Kansas Sports Hall of Fame 515 S Wichita *Web:* www.kshof.org	Wichita	KS	67202	316-262-2038	263-2539
Krasl Art Center 707 Lake Blvd *Web:* krasl.org	Saint Joseph	MI	49085	269-983-0271	
Legends of the Game Baseball Museum 1000 Ballpark Way **Fax Area Code:* 817 ■ *Web:* texas.rangers.mlb.com	Arlington	TX	76011	866-274-9053	273-5093*
Louisiana Sports Hall of Fame 500 Front St *Web:* www.lasportshall.com	Natchitoches	LA	71457	318-238-4255	238-4258
Louisville Slugger Museum 800 W Main St *TF:* 877-775-8443 ■ *Web:* www.sluggermuseum.com	Louisville	KY	40202	502-585-5226	585-1179
Manitoba Sports Hall of Fame & Museum 145 Pacific Ave *Web:* www.halloffame.mb.ca	Winnipeg	MB	R3B2Z6	204-925-5736	925-5916
Milwaukee Jewish Federation Inc 1360 N Prospect Ave *Web:* milwaukeejewish.org	Milwaukee	WI	53202	414-390-5700	
Mississippi Sports Hall of Fame & Museum 1152 Lakeland Dr *TF:* 800-280-3263 ■ *Web:* www.msfame.com	Jackson	MS	39216	601-982-8264	982-4702
Missouri Sports Hall of Fame 3861 E Stan Musial Dr *TF:* 800-498-5678 ■ *Web:* www.mosportshalloffame.com	Springfield	MO	65809	417-889-3100	889-2761
Moncton Museum 20 Mountain Rd *Web:* www.moncton.ca	Moncton	NB	E1C2J8	506-856-4383	
Motorcycle Hall of Fame Museum 13515 Yarmouth Dr *TF:* 800-262-5646 ■ *Web:* www.americanmotorcyclist.com	Pickerington	OH	43147	614-856-2222	856-2221
Motorsports Hall of Fame of America (MSHFA) PO Box 194 *Web:* www.mshf.com	Novi	MI	48376	248-349-7223	
Naismith Memorial Basketball Hall of Fame 1000 W Columbus Ave *TF:* 877-446-6752 ■ *Web:* www.hoophall.com	Springfield	MA	01105	413-781-6500	781-1939
NASCAR Hall of Fame 400 E Martin Luther King Jr Blvd *Web:* www.nascarhall.com	Charlotte	NC	28202	704-654-4400	
National Baseball Hall of Fame & Museum 25 Main St *TF:* 888-425-5633 ■ *Web:* baseballhall.org	Cooperstown	NY	13326	607-547-7200	547-2044
National Fresh Water Fishing Hall of Fame 10360 Hall of Fame Dr PO Box 690 *TF:* 866-268-4333 ■ *Web:* www.freshwater-fishing.org	Hayward	WI	54843	715-634-4440	634-4440
National Italian American Sports Hall of Fame 1431 W Taylor St *Web:* www.niashf.org	Chicago	IL	60607	312-226-5566	226-5678
National Museum of Polo & Hall of Fame 9011 Lk Worth Rd *Web:* www.polomuseum.com	Lake Worth	FL	33467	561-969-3210	964-8299
National Museum of Racing & Hall of Fame 191 Union Ave *TF:* 800-562-5394 ■ *Web:* www.racingmuseum.org	Saratoga Springs	NY	12866	518-584-0400	584-4574
National Polish-American Sports Hall of Fame 11727 Gallagher St *Web:* www.polishsportshof.com	Hamtramck	MI	48212	313-407-3300	876-7724
National Soaring Museum 51 Soaring Hill Dr *Web:* www.soaringmuseum.org	Elmira	NY	14903	607-734-3128	732-6745
National Soccer Hall of Fame 1801 S. Prairie Ave. *Web:* www.ussoccer.com	Chicago	IL	60616	312-808-1300	808-1301
National Softball Hall of Fame & Museum 2801 NE 50th St *TF:* 800-654-8337 ■ *Web:* www.asasoftball.com	Oklahoma City	OK	73111	405-424-5266	424-3855
National Sportscasters & Sportswriters Hall of Fame (NSSA) 325 N Lee St PO Box 1545 *Web:* www.nssafame.com	Salisbury	NC	28145	704-633-4275	
National Sprint Car Hall of Fame & Museum One Sprint Capital Pl *TF:* 800-874-4488 ■ *Web:* www.sprintcarhof.com	Knoxville	IA	50138	641-842-6176	842-6177
National Wrestling Hall of Fame (NWHOF) 405 W Hall of Fame Ave *Web:* nwhof.org	Stillwater	OK	74075	405-377-5243	377-5244
Negro Leagues Baseball Museum 1616 E 18th St *TF:* 888-221-6526 ■ *Web:* www.nlbm.com	Kansas City	MO	64108	816-221-1920	221-8424
New Brunswick Sports Hall of Fame 503 Queen St PO Box 6000 *Web:* nbsportshalloffame.com/sports/default.aspx	Fredericton	NB	E3B5H1	506-453-3747	459-0481
Nolan Ryan Exhibit Ctr 2925 S Bypass 35 *Web:* www.nolanryanfoundation.org	Alvin	TX	77511	281-388-1134	388-1135
North Carolina Auto Racing Hall of Fame 119 Knob Hill Rd Lakeside Pk *Web:* www.ncarhof.com	Mooresville	NC	28117	704-663-5331	663-6949
North Carolina Sports Hall of Fame 5 E Edenton St NC Museum of History *TF:* 877-627-6724 ■ *Web:* www.ncdcr.gov	Raleigh	NC	27601	919-807-7900	733-8655
North Carolina Tennis Hall of Fame 2709 Henry St *Web:* www.nctennis.com	Greensboro	NC	27405	336-852-8577	852-7334
Northwestern Ontario Sports Hall of Fame 219 May St S *Web:* www.nwosportshalloffame.com	Thunder Bay	ON	P7E1B5	807-622-2852	622-2736
Oceanside Museum of Art 704 Pier View Way *Web:* www.oma-online.org	Oceanside	CA	92054	760-435-3720	
Oklahoma Sports Hall of Fame & Jim Thorpe Museum 4040 N Lincoln Blvd *Web:* www.jimthorpeassoc.org	Oklahoma City	OK	73105	405-427-1400	778-8144
Paul W Bryant Museum 300 Paul W Bryant Dr *TF General:* 866-772-2327 ■ *Web:* www.bryantmuseum.ua.edu	Tuscaloosa	AL	35487	205-348-4668	348-8883
Peter J McGovern Little League Baseball Museum 539 US Rt 15 Hwy PO Box 3485 *Web:* littleleague.org/learn/museum.htm	Williamsport	PA	17701	570-326-1921	326-1074
Philadelphia Sports Hall of Fame Foundation 2701 Grant Ave *Web:* www.phillyhall.org	Philadelphia	PA	19114	215-254-5049	
Pretend City, The Childrens Museum of Orange County 17752 Sky Park Cir Ste 280 *Web:* pretendcity.org	Irvine	CA	92614	949-428-3900	
Pro Football Hall of Fame 2121 George Halas Dr NW *Web:* www.profootballhof.com	Canton	OH	44708	330-456-8207	456-8175
ProRodeo Hall of Fame & Museum of the American Cowboy 101 ProRodeo Dr *Web:* www.prorodeo.org	Colorado Springs	CO	80919	719-528-4703	548-4874
Putnam Museum of History & Natural Science 1717 W 12th St *Web:* putnam.org	Davenport	IA	52804	563-324-1933	
Rose Bowl Hall of Fame 391 S Orange Grove Blvd *Web:* www.tournamentofroses.com	Pasadena	CA	91184	626-449-4100	449-9066
Rubin Museum, The 150 W 17th St *Web:* www.rubinmuseum.org	New York	NY	10011	212-620-5000	
Santa Maria Museum of Flight Inc 3015 Airpark Dr *Web:* www.smmof.org	Santa Maria	CA	93455	805-922-8758	
Saskatchewan Sports Hall of Fame & Museum 2205 Victoria Ave *Web:* www.sshfm.com	Regina	SK	S4P0S4	306-780-9232	780-9427
Shanaman Sports Museum of Tacoma 2727 E 'D' St Tacoma Dome **Fax Area Code:* 253 ■ *Web:* www.tacomasportsmuseum.com	Tacoma	WA	98421	206-627-5857	593-7620*
Sports Immortals Museum 6830 N Federal Hwy *Web:* www.sportsimmortals.com	Boca Raton	FL	33487	561-997-2575	997-6949
Sports Legends at Camden Yards 301 W Camden St *Web:* baberuthmuseum.org	Baltimore	MD	21201	410-727-1539	727-1652
Sports Museum, The 100 Legends Way *Web:* www.sportsmuseum.org	Boston	MA	02114	617-624-1234	
Stepping Stones Museum For Children Inc 303 W Ave *Web:* www.steppingstonesmuseum.org	Norwalk	CT	06850	203-899-0606	
Texas Sports Hall of Fame 1108 S University Parks Dr *TF:* 800-567-9561 ■ *Web:* www.tshof.org	Waco	TX	76706	254-756-1633	756-2384
Trapshooting Hall of Fame & Museum 601 W National Rd *Web:* www.traphof.org	Vandalia	OH	45377	937-660-5663	660-5664
U.S. National Ski Hall of Fame 610 Palms Ave *TF:* 800-648-0720 ■ *Web:* www.skihall.com	Ishpeming	MI	49849	906-485-6323	486-4570
University of Iowa Athletics Hall of Fame KHF Bldg 446 *TF:* 877-462-6342 ■ *Web:* www.hawkeyesports.com	Iowa City	IA	52242	319-384-1031	335-9726
Us Art Company Inc 66 Pacella Park Dr *Web:* www.usart.com	Randolph	MA	02368	781-986-6500	
Vancouver Art Gallery 750 Hornby St *Web:* vanartgallery.bc.ca	Vancouver	BC	V6Z2H7	604-662-4700	
Ventura County Arts Council 646 County Sq Dr Ste 154 *Web:* www.vcapcd.org	Ventura	CA	93003	805-658-2213	
Virginia Sports Hall of Fame (VSHFM) 206 High St *Web:* www.vshfm.com	Portsmouth	VA	23704	757-393-8031	393-8288
Volleyball Hall of Fame 444 Dwight St *Web:* www.volleyhall.org	Holyoke	MA	01040	413-536-0926	539-6673

	City	State	Zip	Phone	Fax
Washoe Tribe 919 Us Hwy 395 N *Web:* www.washoetribe.us	Gardnerville	NV	89410	775-265-4191	
Waterloo Regional Childrens Museum Studio 10 King St W *Web:* kitchener-ontario.cylex.ca	Kitchener	ON	N2G1A3	519-749-9387	
Women's Basketball Hall of Fame 700 Hall of Fame Dr *Web:* www.wbhof.com	Knoxville	TN	37915	865-633-9000	633-9294
World Figure Skating Museum & Hall of Fame 20 First St *Web:* www.worldskatingmuseum.org	Colorado Springs	CO	80906	719-635-5200	635-9548
Zeum 221 Fourth St *Web:* www.zeum.org	San Francisco	CA	94103	415-820-3320	

526 MUSIC DISTRIBUTORS

	City	State	Zip	Phone	Fax
A-r Editions Inc 8551 Research Way Ste 180 *TF:* 800-736-0070 ■ *Web:* www.areditions.com	Middleton	WI	53562	608-836-9000	831-8200
Allegro Corp 20048 NE San Rafael St **Fax:* Orders ■ *TF:* 800-288-2007 ■ *Web:* www.allegro-music.com	Portland	OR	97230	503-491-8480	491-8488*
Baker & Taylor Inc 2550 W Tyvola Rd Ste 300 **Fax Area Code:* 704 ■ *TF:* 800-775-1800 ■ *Web:* www.btol.com	Charlotte	NC	28217	800-775-1800	998-3316*
Caroline Distribution 150 Fifth Ave *Web:* www.caroline.com	New York	NY	10011	212-786-8100	643-5563
EMI Christian Music Group 101 Winners Cir *Web:* www.capitolchristianmusicgroup.com.	Brentwood	TN	37027	615-371-4300	371-4305
Gotham Distributing Corp 60 Portland Rd *TF:* 800-446-8426 ■ *Web:* oldies.com	Conshohocken	PA	19428	610-649-7650	649-0315
Inspired Studios 9920 Royal Cardigan Way *Web:* www.inspired-studios.com	West Palm Beach	FL	33411	561-333-9142	
Malaco Music Group Inc 3023 W Northside Dr *TF Cust Svc:* 800-272-7936 ■ *Web:* www.malaco.com	Jackson	MS	39213	601-982-4522	982-4528
Orchard Enterprises Inc 23 E 4th St 3rd Fl *Web:* www.theorchard.com	New York	NY	10003	212-201-9280	201-9203
RED Distribution 345 Hudson St 6th Fl *Web:* www.redmusic.com	New York	NY	10014	917-421-7601	
Select-O-Hits Inc 1981 Fletcher Creek Dr *TF:* 800-346-0723 ■ *Web:* www.selectohits.com	Memphis	TN	38133	901-388-1190	388-3002
Walt Disney Records 500 S Buena Vista St *Web:* www.disney.go.com/disneyrecords	Burbank	CA	91521	818-560-1000	

527 MUSIC PROGRAMMING SERVICES

	City	State	Zip	Phone	Fax
DMX Music Inc 1703 W Fifth St Ste 600 *TF:* 800-345-5000 ■ *Web:* www.dmx.com	Austin	TX	78703	512-380-8500	380-8501
Music Choice 110 Gibraltar Rd Ste 200 **Fax Area Code:* 215 ■ *Web:* www.musicchoice.com	Horsham	PA	19044	646-459-3357	784-5870*
Muzak LLC 3318 Lakemont Blvd **Fax Area Code:* 803 ■ *TF:* 888-689-2559 ■ *Web:* us.moodmedia.com/	Fort Mill	SC	29708	888-689-2559	396-3136*
PlayNetwork Inc 8727 148th Ave NE *TF Sales:* 888-964-8274 ■ *Web:* www.playnetwork.com	Redmond	WA	98052	425-497-8100	497-8181

528 MUSIC STORES

SEE ALSO Book, Music, Video Clubs p. 1877

	City	State	Zip	Phone	Fax
Amazon.com Inc 1200 12th Ave S Ste 1200 *NASDAQ: AMZN* ■ **Fax:* Hum Res ■ *TF Cust Svc:* 800-201-7575 ■ *Web:* www.amazon.com	Seattle	WA	98144	206-266-1000	266-7601*
Best Buy Company Inc 7601 Penn Ave S *NYSE: BBY* ■ **Fax:* Cust Svc ■ *TF:* 888-237-8289 ■ *Web:* www.bestbuy.com	Minneapolis	MN	55423	612-291-1000	292-2323*
CD Universe 101 N Plains Industrial Rd *TF:* 800-231-7937 ■ *Web:* www.cduniverse.com	Wallingford	CT	06492	203-294-1648	294-0391
CD Warehouse 900 N Broadway **Fax Area Code:* 405 ■ *TF:* 800-641-9394 ■ *Web:* cdwarehouse.com	Oklahoma City	OK	73102	919-577-6000	949-2566*
eMusic.com Inc 511 Avenue of the Americas *Web:* www.emusic.com	New York	NY	10011	212-201-9240	
FirstCom Music 1325 Capital Pkwy Ste 109 *TF Cust Svc:* 800-858-8880 ■ *Web:* www.firstcom.com	Carrollton	TX	75006	972-446-8742	242-6526
Global Electronic Music Marketplace PO Box 2186 *TF:* 800-207-4366 ■ *Web:* gemm.com	La Jolla	CA	92038	858-456-0894	
Hastings Entertainment Inc 3601 Plains Blvd *NASDAQ: HAST* ■ **Fax Area Code:* 806 ■ *TF Cust Svc:* 877-427-8464 ■ *Web:* www.gohastings.com	Amarillo	TX	79102	877-427-8464	351-2424*
Mississippi Music Inc 222 N Main St *TF:* 800-844-5821 ■ *Web:* www.mississippimusic.com	Hattiesburg	MS	39401	601-544-5821	544-5841
Newbury Comics Inc 5 Guest St *Web:* www.newbury.com	Brighton	MA	02135	617-254-1666	254-1085
Record Exchange, The 1105 W Idaho St *Web:* www.therecordexchange.com	Boise	ID	83702	208-344-8010	336-2660
Record Town Inc 38 Corporate Cir *Web:* www.twec.com	Albany	NY	12203	518-452-1242	
SightSound Technologies Inc 311 S Craig St Ste 205 *Web:* www.sightsound.com	Pittsburgh	PA	15213	412-621-6100	

529 MUSICAL INSTRUMENT STORES

	City	State	Zip	Phone	Fax
Al C Rinaldi Inc 1718 Chestnut St *Web:* www.chopinpiano.com	Philadelphia	PA	19103	215-568-7800	
Alamo Music Ctr 425 N Main Ave *TF:* 800-822-5010 ■ *Web:* www.alamomusic.com	San Antonio	TX	78205	210-224-1010	226-8742
American Musical Supply PO Box 152 *TF:* 800-458-4076 ■ *Web:* www.americanmusical.com	Spicer	MN	56288	320-796-2088	
Amro Music Stores 2918 Poplar Ave *TF General:* 800-626-2676 ■ *Web:* www.amromusic.com	Memphis	TN	38111	901-323-8888	325-6407
Annex Pro Inc 49 Dunlevy Ave Ste 220 *Web:* www.annexpro.com	Vancouver	BC	V6A3A3	604-682-6639	
Ardsley Musical Instrument Service Ltd 219 Sprain Rd *Web:* www.ardsleymusic.com	Scarsdale	NY	10583	914-693-6639	693-6974
Armadillo Enterprises Inc 4924 W Waters Ave *Web:* www.armadilloent.com	Tampa	FL	33634	813-600-3920	
Bananas at Large 1504 Fourth St *Web:* www.bananasmusic.com	San Rafael	CA	94901	415-457-7600	457-9148
Beatport LLC 2399 Blake St Ste 170 *Web:* www.beatport.com	Denver	CO	80205	720-974-9500	
Bodine's Pianos 9361 Penn Ave S	Bloomington	MN	55431	612-866-2025	866-0463
Brook Mays Music Co 8605 John Carpenter Fwy *TF Cust Svc:* 800-637-8966 ■ *Web:* www.brookmays.com	Dallas	TX	75247	214-631-0928	905-4964
Buddy Rogers Music Inc 6891 Simpson Ave *TF:* 800-536-2263 ■ *Web:* www.buddyrogers.com	Cincinnati	OH	45239	513-729-1950	728-6010
Casavant Freres Inc 900 rue Girouard est *Web:* www.casavant.ca	St. Hyacinthe	QC	J2S2Y2	450-773-5001	
Cascio Interstate Music 13819 W National Ave *TF:* 800-462-2263 ■ *Web:* www.interstatemusic.com	New Berlin	WI	53151	262-789-7600	786-6840
Chaney's Music Exchange 1501 N Main St *Web:* www.listentocds.com	Walnut Creek	CA	94596	925-933-6310	
Corner Music Inc 2705 12th Ave S *Web:* cornermusicnashville.com	Nashville	TN	37204	615-297-9559	
Cream City Music 12505 W Bluemound Rd *Web:* www.warpdrivemusic.com	Brookfield	WI	53005	262-860-1800	
Creative Allies Inc 9 W Walnut St Ste 3B *Web:* www.creativeallies.com	Asheville	NC	28801	828-252-6300	
Elderly Instruments 1100 N Washington Ave *TF:* 888-473-5810 ■ *Web:* www.elderly.com	Lansing	MI	48906	517-372-7890	372-5155
Evola Music Center Inc 12745 23 Mile Rd *Web:* www.evola.com	Shelby Township	MI	48315	586-726-6570	
First Act Inc 745 Boylston St *TF:* 888-551-1115 ■ *Web:* www.firstact.com	Boston	MA	02116	617-226-7888	226-7890
Fletcher Music Centers Inc 3966 Airway Cir *TF:* 800-258-1088 ■ *Web:* www.fletchermusic.com	Clearwater	FL	33762	727-571-1088	572-4405
Fodera Guitars Inc 68 34th St Ste 3 *Web:* www.fodera.com	Brooklyn	NY	11232	718-832-3455	
Foster Family Music Center LLC 2967 State St	Bettendorf	IA	52722	563-355-0647	
Foxes Music Co 416 S Washington St *TF:* 800-446-4414 ■ *Web:* www.foxesmusic.com	Falls Church	VA	22046	703-533-7393	536-2171
Front End Audio 728 S Edisto Ave *Web:* www.frontendaudio.com	Columbia	SC	29205	803-748-0914	
Georges Music Inc 912 Third St S *Web:* www.georgesmusic.com	Jacksonville Beach	FL	32250	904-270-2220	
Gigasonic 260 E Gish Rd *Web:* www.gigasonic.com	San Jose	CA	95112	408-573-1400	
Graves Piano & Organ Company Inc 5798 Karl Rd *TF:* 800-686-4322 ■ *Web:* www.gravespiano.com	Columbus	OH	43229	614-847-4322	847-0808
Gruhn Guitars 400 Broadway *Web:* www.gruhn.com	Nashville	TN	37203	615-256-2033	255-2021
Guitar Center Inc 5795 Lindero Canyon Rd *Web:* www.guitarcenter.com	Westlake Village	CA	91362	818-735-8800	
Heid Music Company Inc 308 East College Ave *Web:* www.heidmusic.com	Appleton	WI	54911	920-734-1969	
Hermes Trading Company Inc 830 N Cage Blvd *Web:* www.hermes-music.com	Pharr	TX	78577	956-781-8472	
International Violin Co Ltd 1421 Clarkview Rd *TF:* 800-542-3538 ■ *Web:* www.internationalviolin.com	Baltimore	MD	21209	410-832-2525	832-2528
John Keal Music Company Inc 819 Livingston Ave *Web:* www.johnkealmusic.com	Albany	NY	12206	518-482-4405	
JW Pepper & Son Inc 2480 Industrial Blvd *TF:* 800-345-6296 ■ *Web:* www.jwpepper.com	Paoli	PA	19301	610-648-0500	993-0563
Kanstul Musical Instruments Inc 1332 S Claudina St *Web:* www.kanstul.com	Anaheim	CA	92805	714-563-1000	
Leitz Music Company Inc 508 Harrison Ave *Web:* www.leitzmusic.com	Panama City	FL	32401	850-769-0111	
Lone Star Percussion 10611 Control Pl *Web:* www.lonestarpercussion.com	Dallas	TX	75238	214-340-0835	
Long & McQuade Musical Instruments 722 Rosebank Rd *Web:* www.long-mcquade.com	Pickering	ON	L1W4B2	905-837-9785	837-9786
Lpd Music International Corp 32575 Industrial Dr *Web:* www.lpdmusic.com	Madison Heights	MI	48071	248-585-9630	585-7360
Lynx Studio Technology Inc 1048 Irvine Ave *Web:* www.lynxstudio.com	Newport Beach	CA	92660	949-515-8265	
M Steinert & Sons Co 162 Boylston St *Web:* www.msteinert.com	Boston	MA	02116	617-426-1900	426-1905
Malmark Inc 5712 Easton Rd *Web:* www.malmark.com	Plumsteadville	PA	18949	215-766-7200	
Marshall Music Co 545 28th St Sw *Web:* www.marshallmusic.com	Wyoming	MI	49509	616-530-7700	
Moog Music Inc 160 Broadway St *Web:* www.moogmusic.com	Asheville	NC	28801	828-251-0090	
Mullen Guitar Company Inc 11906 County Rd Mm *Web:* www.mullenguitars.com	Flagler	CO	80815	970-664-2518	
Music & Arts Centers Inc 4626 Wedgewood Blvd **Fax Area Code:* 301 ■ **Fax:* Mktg ■ *TF:* 888-731-5396 ■ *Web:* www.musicarts.com	Frederick	MD	21703	888-731-5396	662-7753*

Name / Address	City	State	ZIP	Phone	Fax
Music Shoppe Inc, The 1540 E College Ave Ste 4 *Web:* www.themusicshoppe.com	Normal	IL	61761	309-452-7436	
Musician's Friend Inc PO Box 7479 *TF:* 800-391-8762 ■ *Web:* www.musiciansfriend.com	Westlake Village	CA	91359	801-501-8110	
Musiciansbuy.com Inc 7830 Byron Dr Ste 1 *TF:* 877-778-7845 ■ *Web:* www.musiciansbuy.com	West Palm Beach	FL	33404	561-842-7451	840-9032
Princeton University Store 36 University Pl *Web:* www.pustore.com	Princeton	NJ	08540	609-921-8500	
Quantum Audio Designs Inc 6408 State Hwy 77 *TF:* 888-545-4404 ■ *Web:* www.quested.com	Benton	MO	63736	573-545-4404	545-4411
Quinlan & Fabish Music Co 166 Shore Dr *Web:* www.qandf.com	Burr Ridge	IL	60527	630-654-4111	
Railroad Bazaar LLC 1207 Eidson St *Web:* www.railroadbazaar.com	Athens	AL	35611	256-232-5800	
Reverb Music LLC 3316 N Lincoln Ave *Web:* www.chicagomusicexchange.com	Chicago	IL	60657	773-525-7773	
Saga Musical Instruments Inc 137 Utah Ave *Web:* www.sagamusic.com	South San Francisco	CA	94080	650-588-5558	
Schmitt Music Co 2400 Fwy Blvd *Web:* www.schmittmusic.com	Brooklyn Center	MN	55430	763-566-4560	
Seattle Sport Sciences Inc 24066 NE 53rd Pl *Web:* www.seattlesportsciences.com	Redmond	WA	98053	425-939-0015	
Seymour Duncan Inc 5427 Hollister Ave. *Web:* www.seymourduncan.com	Santa Barbara	CA	93111	805-964-9610	
Sherman Clay & Company Inc 1111 Bayhill Dr Ste 450 *Web:* www.shermanclay.com	San Bruno	CA	94066	650-952-2300	
Stanton's Sheet Music 330 S Fourth St. *TF:* 800-426-8742 ■ *Web:* www.stantons.com	Columbus	OH	43215	614-224-4257	224-5929
Steve's Music 51 Rue Saint-antoine O *Web:* www.stevesmusic.com	Montreal	QC	H2Z1G9	514-878-2216	
Strait Music Co 2428 W Ben White Blvd *TF:* 800-725-8877 ■ *Web:* www.straitmusic.com	Austin	TX	78704	512-476-6927	476-6968
Stringworks 5733 W Packard St *Web:* www.stringworks.com	Appleton	WI	54913	920-830-4959	
Sweetwater Sound Inc 5501 US Hwy 30 W *TF:* 800-222-4700 ■ *Web:* www.sweetwater.com	Fort Wayne	IN	46818	260-432-8176	432-1758
Tom Lee Music Ltd 929 Granville St *Web:* www.tomleemusic.ca	Vancouver	BC	V6Z1L3	604-685-8471	
Washington Music Ctr 11151 Veirs Mill Rd *Web:* chucklevins.com	Wheaton	MD	20902	301-946-8808	946-0487
West Music Inc 1212 Fifth St PO Box 5521 *TF:* 800-373-2000 ■ *Web:* www.westmusic.com	Coralville	IA	52241	319-351-2000	351-0479
Woodwind & Brasswind 4004 Technology Dr *TF:* 800-348-5003 ■ *Web:* www.wwbw.com	South Bend	IN	46628	574-251-3500	
World Music Supply 2414 W Seventh St. *Web:* www.worldmusicsupply.com	Muncie	IN	47302	765-213-6085	

530 MUSICAL INSTRUMENTS

Name / Address	City	State	ZIP	Phone	Fax
Alembic Inc 3005 Wiljan Ct *TF:* 800-322-5893 ■ *Web:* www.alembic.com	Santa Rosa	CA	95407	707-523-2611	523-2935
Allen Organ Co 150 Locust St. *Web:* www.allenorgan.com	Macungie	PA	18062	610-966-2202	965-3098
ALLParts Music Corp 13027 Brittmoore Park Dr *Web:* www.allparts.com	Houston	TX	77041	713-466-6414	
AP International Enterprise Inc 3301 SR- 66 *Web:* www.apintl.com	Neptune	NJ	07753	732-918-7001	
Austin Organs Inc 156 Woodland St *Web:* www.austinorgans.com	Hartford	CT	06105	860-522-8293	524-9828
Avedis Zildjian Co 22 Longwater Dr *TF:* 800-229-8672 ■ *Web:* www.zildjian.com	Norwell	MA	02061	781-871-2200	871-3984
Beamz Interactive Inc 15354 N 83rd Way Ste 101 **Fax Area Code:* 877 ■ *Web:* thebeamz.com	Scottsdale	AZ	85260	480-424-2053	591-8899*
Bevin Bros 10 Bevin Rd PO Box 60 *Web:* www.bevinbells.com	East Hampton	CT	06424	860-267-4431	267-8557
Brannen Brothers-flutemakers Inc 58 Dragon Ct *Web:* brannenflutes.com	Woburn	MA	01801	781-935-9522	
Burkart-Phelan Inc 2 Shaker Rd Ste D-107 *TF:* 800-236-4343 ■ *Web:* www.burkart.com	Shirley	MA	01464	978-425-4500	425-9800
Carvin Corp 12340 World Trade Dr *TF:* 800-854-2235 ■ *Web:* www.carvinworld.com	San Diego	CA	92128	858-487-1600	521-6034
CF Martin & Company Inc 510 Sycamore St PO Box 329 *TF:* 888-433-9177 ■ *Web:* www.martinguitar.com	Nazareth	PA	18064	610-759-2837	759-5757
Chesbro Music Company Inc 327 Broadway St. *Web:* www.chesbromusic.com	Idaho Falls	ID	83402	208-522-8691	
Chime Master Systems PO Box 936 **Fax Area Code:* 740 ■ *TF:* 800-344-7464 ■ *Web:* www.chimemaster.com	Lancaster	OH	43130	800-344-7464	746-9566*
Conn-Selmer Inc 600 Industrial Pkwy *Web:* www.bachbrass.com	Elkhart	IN	46516	574-522-1675	
Daisy Rock Guitars 16320 Roscoe Blvd Ste 100 *TF:* 877-693-2479 ■ *Web:* www.daisyrock.com	Van Nuys	CA	91410	877-693-2479	
Davitt & Hanser Music Co 3015 Kustom Dr *TF:* 800-999-5558 ■ *Web:* www.hansermusicgroup.com	Hebron	KY	41048	859-817-7100	817-7150
Dean Markley Strings Inc 3350 Scott Blvd Bldg 45 *Web:* www.deanmarkley.com	Santa Clara	CA	95054	408-988-2456	
Deering Banjo Co 3733 Kenora Dr. *TF:* 800-845-7791 ■ *Web:* www.deeringbanjos.com	Spring Valley	CA	91977	619-464-8252	464-0833
Dunlop Manufacturing Inc 150 Industrial Way *Web:* www.jimdunlop.com	Benicia	CA	94510	707-745-2722	
E & O Mari Inc 256 Broadway *TF:* 800-750-3034 ■ *Web:* www.labella.com	Newburgh	NY	12550	845-562-4400	562-4491
Edwards Instrument Co 530 S Hwy H *TF:* 800-562-6838 ■ *Web:* www.edwards-instruments.com	Elkhorn	WI	53121	262-723-4221	723-4245
Ernie Ball 151 Suburban Rd *TF:* 866-823-2255 ■ *Web:* www.ernieball.com	San Luis Obispo	CA	93401	805-544-7726	544-3826
Fender Musical Instruments Corp 17600 N Perimeter Dr Ste 100 *TF Cust Svc:* 800-488-1818 ■ *Web:* www.fender.com	Scottsdale	AZ	85255	480-596-9690	596-1384
Gemeinhardt Company LLC 57882 State Rd 19 S *Web:* www.gemeinhardt.com	Elkhart	IN	46517	574-295-5280	
General Music Corp 1164 Tower Ln *TF:* 800-323-0280 ■ *Web:* generalmusic.us	Bensenville	IL	60106	630-766-8230	766-8281
George Heinl & Co 201 Church St. *Web:* www.georgeheinl.com	Toronto	ON	M5B1Y7	416-363-0093	
Getzen Company Inc 530 S Cty Hwy H PO Box 440 *TF:* 800-366-5584 ■ *Web:* www.getzen.com	Elkhorn	WI	53121	262-723-4221	723-4245
GHS Corp 2813 Wilber Ave. *TF:* 800-388-4447 ■ *Web:* www.ghsstrings.com	Battle Creek	MI	49037	800-388-4447	860-6913
Gibson Guitar Corp 309 Plus Pk Blvd *TF:* 800-444-2766 ■ *Web:* www2.gibson.com	Nashville	TN	37217	615-871-4500	884-7256
Gibson Piano Ventures Inc 309 Plus Pk Blvd *TF:* 800-444-2766 ■ *Web:* www.gibson.com	Nashville	TN	37217	615-871-4500	889-5509
Hammond Suzuki USA Inc 743 Annoreno Dr *TF:* 888-765-2900 ■ *Web:* www.hammondorganco.com	Addison	IL	60101	630-543-0277	543-0279
Hohner Inc 1000 Technology Pk Dr. *TF:* 800-446-6010 ■ *Web:* www.hohnerusa.com	Glen Allen	VA	23059	804-515-1900	515-0189
Hoshino USA Inc 1726 Winchester Rd *Web:* www.ibanez.com	Bensalem	PA	19020	215-638-8670	245-8583
J D'Addario & Company Inc 595 Smith St *TF:* 800-323-2746 ■ *Web:* www.daddario.com	Farmingdale	NY	11735	631-439-3300	439-3333
JD Calato Mfg Company Inc 4501 Hyde Pk Blvd *TF Cust Svc:* 800-358-4590 ■ *Web:* www.regaltip.com	Niagara Falls	NY	14305	716-285-3546	285-2710
Kawai America Corp PO Box 9045 *Web:* www.kawaius.com	Rancho Dominguez	CA	90224	310-631-1771	604-6913
Korg USA Inc 316 S Service Rd. *Web:* www.korg.com	Melville	NY	11747	631-390-6500	390-6501
La Bella Strings 256 Broadway *TF:* 800-750-3034 ■ *Web:* www.labella.com	Newburgh	NY	12550	845-562-4400	562-4491
Lindeblad Piano Restoration 101 Us 46 *TF:* 888-587-4266 ■ *Web:* www.lindebladpiano.com	Pine Brook	NJ	07058	888-587-4266	
Lowrey Organ Co 847 N Church Ct *TF:* 800-451-5940 ■ *Web:* www.lowrey.com	Elmhurst	IL	60126	800-451-5939	
Lyon & Healy Harps Inc 168 N Ogden Ave *TF:* 800-621-3881 ■ *Web:* www.lyonhealy.com	Chicago	IL	60607	312-786-1881	226-1502
Maas-Rowe Carillons Inc 2255 Meyers Ave **Fax Area Code:* 760 ■ *TF:* 800-854-2023 ■ *Web:* www.maasrowe.com	Escondido	CA	92029	800-854-2023	747-2677*
Manhasset Specialty Co 3505 Fruitvale Blvd *TF:* 800-795-0965 ■ *Web:* www.manhasset-specialty.com	Yakima	WA	98902	509-248-3810	248-3834
Marimba One Inc 901 O St Ste D *Web:* www.marimbaone.com	Arcata	CA	95521	707-822-9570	
Mason & Hamlin Piano Co 35 Duncan St *Web:* www.masonhamlin.com	Haverhill	MA	01830	978-374-8888	374-8080
Morley Pedals 325 Cary Pt Dr *TF:* 800-284-5172 ■ *Web:* www.morleypedals.com	Cary	IL	60013	847-639-4646	639-4723
Musicorp 2456 Remount Rd *TF:* 800-845-1922 ■ *Web:* kmcmusicorp.com	North Charleston	SC	29406	843-745-8501	
NATIVE INSTRUMENTS North America Inc 5631 A Hollywood Blvd *Web:* www.native-instruments.com	Los Angeles	CA	90028	323-467-5260	
Noble & Cooley Co 42 Water St. *Web:* www.noblecooley.com	Granville	MA	01034	413-357-6321	357-6314
Nothing Shocking LLC 513 S Dudley St *Web:* www.mojotone.com	Burgaw	NC	28425	910-259-7291	
Organ Supply Industries Inc 2320 W 50th St *TF:* 800-458-0289 ■ *Web:* www.organsupply.com	Erie	PA	16506	814-835-2244	838-0349
OS Kelly Co 318 E N St	Springfield	OH	45503	937-322-4921	322-1322
Paul Reed Smith Guitars (PRS) 380 Log Canoe Cir *Web:* www.prsguitars.com	Stevensville	MD	21666	410-643-9970	643-9980
PianoDisc 4111 N Fwy Blvd *TF:* 800-566-3472 ■ *Web:* www.pianodisc.com	Sacramento	CA	95834	916-567-9999	567-1941
Prestini Musical Instruments Inc 2020 N Aurora Dr *TF General:* 800-528-6569 ■ *Web:* www.prestiniusa.com	Nogales	AZ	85628	520-287-4931	287-4931
QRS Music Technologies 2011 Seward Ave *Web:* www.qrsmusic.com	Naples	FL	34109	239-597-5888	
Remo Inc 28101 Industry Dr *TF:* 800-525-5134 ■ *Web:* www.remo.com	Valencia	CA	91355	661-294-5600	294-5700
Reuter Organ Co 1220 Timberedge Rd. *Web:* www.reuterorgan.com	Lawrence	KS	66049	785-843-2622	843-3302
Rhythm Tech 29 Beechwood Ave *Web:* rhythmtech.com	New Rochelle	NY	10801	914-636-6900	
Rickenbacker International Corp 3895 S Main St. *Web:* www.rickenbacker.com	Santa Ana	CA	92707	714-545-5574	
Rodgers Instruments LLC 1300 NE 25th Ave *Web:* www.rodgersinstruments.com	Hillsboro	OR	97124	503-648-4181	681-0444
Roland Corp US 5100 S Eastern Ave. *Web:* www.rolandus.com	Los Angeles	CA	90040	323-890-3700	890-3701
Sabian Ltd 219 Main St. *Web:* www.sabian.com	Meductic	NB	E6H2L5	506-272-2019	272-2040
Saint Louis Music Inc 1400 Ferguson Ave *TF:* 800-727-4512 ■ *Web:* www.stlouismusic.com/	Saint Louis	MO	63133	314-727-4512	727-8929
Samick Music Corp 1329 Gateway Dr. *Web:* www.smcmusic.com	Gallatin	TN	37066	615-206-0077	
Schaff Piano Supply Co 451 Oakwood Rd *TF:* 800-747-4266 ■ *Web:* www.schaffpiano.com	Lake Zurich	IL	60047	847-438-4556	438-4615
Schecter Guitar Research Inc 1840 Valpreda St *Web:* www.schecterguitars.com	Burbank	CA	91504	818-846-2700	
Schulmerich Carillons Inc Carillon Hill *TF:* 800-772-3557 ■ *Web:* www.schulmerichbells.com	Sellersville	PA	18960	215-257-2771	257-1910

	City	State	Zip	Phone	Fax
Source Audio LLC 120 Cummings Park *Web:* www.sourceaudio.net	Woburn	MA	01801	781-932-8080	
Steinway & Sons 1 Steinway Pl *TF:* 800-783-4692 ■ *Web:* www.steinway.com	Long Island City	NY	11105	718-721-2600	932-4332
Steinway Musical Instruments Inc 800 S St Ste 305 *NYSE: LVB* ■ *Web:* steinway.com/steinway-musical-instruments/	Waltham	MA	02453	781-894-9770	894-9803
Suzuki Musical Instrument Corp PO Box 261030 *TF Cust Svc:* 800-854-1594 ■ *Web:* www.suzukimusic.com	San Diego	CA	92196	619-258-1896	873-1997
Taylor-Listug Inc 1980 Gillespie Way *Web:* www.taylorguitars.com	El Cajon	CA	92020	619-258-1207	258-1623
TC Electronic Inc 5706 Corsa Ave Ste 107 *Web:* www.tcelectronic.com	Westlake Village	CA	91362	818-665-4900	
Tonepros Sound Lab Intl 1449 E F St Ste 101en205 *Web:* www.tonepros.com	Oakdale	CA	95361	209-848-4966	
Ultimate Support Systems Inc 5836 Wright Dr **Fax Area Code:* 970 ■ *TF:* 800-525-5628 ■ *Web:* www.ultimatesupport.com	Loveland	CO	80538	800-525-5628	776-1941*
Verne Q Powell Flutes Inc One Clock Tower Pl Ste 300 *Web:* www.powellflutes.com	Maynard	MA	01754	978-461-6111	461-6155
Wenger Corp 555 Pk Dr PO Box 448 *TF:* 800-493-6437 ■ *Web:* www.wengercorp.com	Owatonna	MN	55060	507-455-4100	455-4258
Wicks Pipe Organ Co 1100 Fifth St *TF Cust Svc:* 877-654-2191 ■ *Web:* www.organ.wicks.com	Highland	IL	62249	618-654-2191	654-3770
Wm S Haynes Company Inc 68 Nonset Path *Web:* wmshaynes.com	Acton	MA	01720	978-268-0600	268-0601
Woodstock Percussion Inc 167 DuBois Rd *Web:* www.chimes.com	Shokan	NY	12481	845-657-6000	
Yamaha Corp of America 6600 Orangethorpe Ave **Fax:* Hum Res ■ *Web:* www.yamaha.com	Buena Park	CA	90620	714-522-9011	522-9235*

531 MUTUAL FUNDS

	City	State	Zip	Phone	Fax
32 Degrees Capital 650 635-8th Ave S W *Web:* www.32degrees.ca	Calgary	AB	T2P3M3	403-695-1074	
Academy Capital Management 500 N Vly Mills Dr Ste 200 *Web:* www.academycapitalmgmt.com	Waco	TX	76710	254-751-0555	
ACG Advisory Services Inc 1640 Huguenot Rd *Web:* www.acgworldwide.com	Midlothian	VA	23113	804-323-1886	
Advanced Pension Solutions Inc 6830 Commerce Court Dr *Web:* www.advpen.com	Blacklick	OH	43004	614-501-7790	
Aether Investment Partners LLC 1900 Sixteenth St Ste 825 *Web:* www.aetherip.com	Denver	CO	80202	720-961-4190	
Agilith Capital Inc Victory Bldg 80 Richmond St W Ste 203 *Web:* www.agilith.com	Toronto	ON	M5H2A4	416-915-0284	
Alberta Enterprise Corp 10830 Jasper Ave Ste 1100 *Web:* www.alberta-enterprise.ca	Edmonton	AB	T5J2B3	780-392-3901	
Albright Capital Management LLC 1101 New York Ave NW Ste 900 *Web:* www.albrightcapital.com	Washington	DC	20005	202-370-3500	
Alerus Retirement Solutions Two Pine Tree Dr Ste 400 *TF:* 800-795-2697 ■ *Web:* www.alerusretirementsolutions.com	Arden Hills	MN	55112	800-795-2697	
Alger Family of Funds PO Box 8480 *TF:* 800-992-3863 ■ *Web:* www.alger.com	Boston	MA	02266	800-992-3863	
Alta Capital Management LLC 6440 South Wasatch Blvd Ste 260 *Web:* www.atlacapital.net	Salt Lake City	UT	84121	801-274-6010	
Altavista Wealth Management Inc One Town Sq Blvd Ste 260 *Web:* www.altavistawealth.com	Asheville	NC	28803	828-684-2600	
American Century Proprietary Holdings Inc PO Box 419200 **Fax:* Cust Svc ■ *TF:* 800-345-2021 ■ *Web:* www.americancentury.com	Kansas City	MO	64141	816-531-5575	340-7962*
Aquila Group of Funds 380 Madison Ave Ste 2300 *TF:* 800-437-1020 ■ *Web:* www.aquilafunds.com	New York	NY	10017	212-697-6666	687-5373
Arizona State Retirement System 3300 N Central Ave *Web:* www.know-the-ada.com	Phoenix	AZ	85012	602-240-2000	
Artisan Funds PO Box 8412 *TF Cust Svc:* 800-344-1770 ■ *Web:* www.artisanfunds.com	Boston	MA	02266	800-344-1770	
Artisan Partners Limited Partnership 875 E Wisconsin Ave Ste 800 *Web:* www.artisanpartners.com	Milwaukee	WI	53202	414-390-6100	
Ascendant Advisors LLC Four Oaks Pl 1330 Post Oak Blvd Ste 1550 *TF:* 800-552-6010 ■ *Web:* www.ascendantadvisors.com	Houston	TX	77056	800-552-6010	
Ashkenazy Acquisition Corp 150 E 58th St 39th Fl *Web:* www.aacrealty.com	New York	NY	10155	212-213-4444	
Asia Pacific Capital 345 S Figueroa St Ste 100 *Web:* www.apccusa.com	Los Angeles	CA	90071	213-680-8811	
Asset Preservation Advisors Inc 3344 Peachtree Rd Ste 2050 *Web:* assetpreservationadvisors.com	Atlanta	GA	30326	404-261-1333	
Aston Funds PO Box 9765 *Web:* www.astonfunds.com	Providence	RI	02940	312-268-1400	
Augenblick & Company Pc 368 W Bridge St *Web:* augenblickpc.com	New Hope	PA	18938	215-862-9153	
Aurelius Capital Management LP 535 Madison Ave 22nd Fl *Web:* www.aurelius-capital.com	New York	NY	10022	646-445-6500	
Auven Therapeutics Management L.L.L.P 6501 Redhook Plz Ste 201 *Web:* www.auventx.com	Saint Thomas	VI	00802	340-779-6908	
Avrio Capital Inc Crowfoot W Business Centre #235 600 Crowfoot Crescent NW *Web:* www.avrioventures.com	Calgary	AB	T3G0B4	403-215-5492	
B.C. Advantage (VCC) Funds Ltd Ste 410 221 W Esplanade *Web:* www.bcadvantagefunds.com	North Vancouver	BC	V7M3J3	604-688-6877	
Barnes Investment Advisory Inc 7250 N 16th St Ste 412 *Web:* www.barnesinvest.com	Phoenix	AZ	85020	602-248-9099	
Baron Funds 767 Fifth Ave 49th Fl *TF:* 800-992-2766 ■ *Web:* www.baronfunds.com	New York	NY	10153	212-583-2000	583-2150
Barrantagh Investment Management Inc 100 Yonge St Ste 1700 *Web:* www.barrantagh.com	Toronto	ON	M5C2W1	416-868-6295	
Bastion Infrastructure Group 801 - 1 Richmond St W *Web:* www.bastionfunds.com	Toronto	ON	M5H3W4	416-583-2600	
BC Investment Management Corp 2940 Jutland Rd Sawmill Point *Web:* www.bcimc.com	Victoria	BC	V8T5K6	250-356-0263	
Billings Capital Management LLC 1001 Nineteenth St N 19th Fl *Web:* www.billingscap.com	Arlington	VA	22209	703-962-1871	
Bowen, Hanes & Company Inc The Forum 3290 Northside Pkwy Ste 880 *Web:* www.bowenhanes.com	Atlanta	GA	30327	404-995-0507	
Bridges Investment Counsel Inc 256 Durham Plz 8401 W Dodge Rd *Web:* www.bridgesfund.com	Omaha	NE	68114	402-397-4700	
Brookdale Group, The 3455 Peachtree Rd NE Ste 700 *Web:* www.brookdalegroup.com	Atlanta	GA	30326	404-364-8080	
Brotman Financial Group Inc 16 Greenmeadow Dr Ste 201 *Web:* www.brotmanfinancial.com	Timonium	MD	21093	410-252-4555	
Brownfields Capital LLC 1125 17th St Ste 2350 *Web:* brownfieldscapital.com	Denver	CO	80202	303-534-2100	
BTR Capital Management Inc 550 Kearny St Ste 510 *Web:* www.btrcap.com	San Francisco	CA	94108	415-989-0100	
C.A. Delaney Capital Management Ltd 66 Wellington St W Ste 4410 TD Bank Tower Toronto Dominion Ctr *Web:* www.delaneycapital.com	Toronto	ON	M5K1H1	416-361-0688	
C.S. McKee LP One Gateway Ctr Eighth Fl *Web:* www.csmckee.com	Pittsburgh	PA	15222	412-566-1234	
Cabot Wealth Management Inc 216 Essex St *Web:* www.ecabot.com	Salem	MA	01970	978-745-9233	
Calvert Investments Inc 4550 Montgomery Ave Ste 1000N *TF:* 800-368-2748 ■ *Web:* www.calvert.com	Bethesda	MD	20814	301-951-4800	654-7820
Castletop Capital 3600 N Capital of Texas Hwy Bldg B Ste 320 *Web:* www.castletopcapital.com	Austin	TX	78746	512-329-6600	
Celtic House Venture Partners Inc 80 Aberdeen St Ste 300 *Web:* www.celtic-house.com	Ottawa	ON	K1S5R5	613-569-7200	
Center Coast Capital Advisors LP 1600 Smith Ste 3800 *Web:* www.centercoastcap.com	Houston	TX	77002	713-759-1400	
Centre Lane Partners LLC One Grand Central Pl 60 E 42nd St Ste 1400 *Web:* www.centrelanepartners.com	New York	NY	10165	646-843-0710	
CGM Funds 38 Newbury St Ste 8 *TF:* 800-345-4048 ■ *Web:* www.cgmfunds.com	Boston	MA	02116	617-859-7714	859-7295
Chandler Asset Management Inc 6225 Lusk Blvd *Web:* www.chandlerasset.com	San Diego	CA	92121	858-546-3737	
Chicago Equity Partners LLC 180 N LaSalle St Ste 3800 *Web:* www.chicagoequity.com	Chicago	IL	60601	312-629-8200	
CIBC Mellon Global Securities Services Co 320 Bay St PO Box 1 *Web:* www.cibcmellon.com	Toronto	ON	M5H4A6	416-643-5000	
City of Austin Employees' Retirement System 418 E Highland Mall Blvd *Web:* www.coaers.org	Austin	TX	78752	512-458-2551	
Claremont Companies Inc One Lakeshore Center *Web:* www.claremontcorp.com	Bridgewater	MA	02324	508-279-4300	
Clipper Fund 2949 E Elvira Rd Ste 101 *TF:* 800-432-2504 ■ *Web:* www.clipperfund.com	Tucson	AZ	85756	800-432-2504	
Cobb Planning Group 1206 N Broadway *Web:* www.cobbplanninggroup.com	Santa Ana	CA	92701	714-550-7242	
Coe Capital Management LLC Nine Pkwy N Ste 325 *Web:* www.coecapital.com	Deerfield	IL	60015	847-597-1700	
Compass Capital Management Inc 400 Baker Bldg 706 Second Ave South *Web:* www.compasscap.com	Minneapolis	MN	55402	612-338-4051	
Congruent Investment Partners LLC 3131 McKinney Ave Ste 850 *Web:* www.congruentinv.com	Dallas	TX	75204	214-760-7411	
Connective Capital Management LLC 385 Homer Ave *Web:* www.connectivecapital.com	Palo Alto	CA	94301	650-321-4826	

Phone | Fax

Cordiant Capital Inc
Ste 2400 1010 Sherbrooke St W . . . Montreal QC H3A2R7 514-286-1142
Web: cordiantcap.com

CornerCap Investment Counsel Inc
1355 Peachtree St NE The Peachtree Ste 1700 . . . Atlanta GA 30309 404-870-0700
Web: www.cornercap.com

Covalent Partners LLC
Reservoir Woods 930 Winter St Ste 2800 . . . Waltham MA 02451 617-658-5500
Web: www.covalentpartnersllc.com

Cozad Asset Management Inc 2501 Galen Dr . . . Champaign IL 61821 217-356-8363
Web: www.cozadassetmgmt.com

Creststreet Asset Management Ltd
70 University Ave Ste 1450 . . . Toronto ON M5J2M4 416-864-6330
Web: www.creststreet.com

Crow Holdings Capital Partners LLC
3819 Maple Ave . . . Dallas TX 75219 214-661-8000
Web: www.crowholdingscapital.com

Curian Capital LLC 7601 Technology Way . . . Denver CO 80237 720-489-6400
Web: www.curian.com

Dalfen America Corp
Westmount 4444 rue Sainte-Catherine W
Ste 100 . . . Montreal QC H3Z1R2 514-938-1050
Web: www.dalfen.ca

Dancap Private Equity Inc 197 Sheppard Ave W . . . Toronto ON M2N1M9 416-590-9444
Web: www.dancap.ca

Davis Capital Partners LLC
Three Harbor Dr Ste 301 . . . Sausalito CA 94965 415-362-3600
Web: www.daviscapitalpartners.com

Davis Funds 2949 E Elvira Rd Ste 101 . . . Tucson AR 85756 800-279-0279 806-7601*
**Fax Area Code:* 520 ■ *TF:* 800-279-0279 ■ *Web:* www.davisfunds.com

del Rey Global Investors LLC
6701 Ctr Dr W Ste 655 . . . Los Angeles CA 90045 310-649-1233
Web: www.delreyglobal.com

Delafield Hambrecht Inc
1301 Second Ave Ste 2850 . . . Seattle WA 98101 206-254-4100
Web: www.delafieldhambrecht.com

Diamond Creek Capital
26 Orange Blossom Cir Ste10 . . . Ladera Ranch CA 92694 949-429-7707
Web: www.diamondcreekcap.com

Dixon Mitchell Investment Counsel Inc
Ste 1680 1055 W Hastings St . . . Vancouver BC V6E2E9 604-669-3136
Web: www.dixonmitchell.com

Dodge & Cox Funds 30 Dan Rd PO Box 8422 . . . Canton MA 02021 800-621-3979
TF: 800-621-3979 ■ *Web:* www.dodgeandcox.com

Domini Social Investments PO Box 9785 . . . Providence RI 02940 800-582-6757
TF: 800-582-6757 ■ *Web:* www.domini.com

Dos Rios Partners
205 Wild Basin Rd S Bldg 3 Ste 100 . . . Austin TX 78746 512-298-0801
Web: www.dosriospartners.com

Double Eagle Capital Management LP
909 Lk Carolyn Pkwy Ste 1825 . . . Irving TX 75039 972-869-6880
Web: www.doubleeaglecapital.com

Dreyfus Family of Funds PO Box 55299 . . . Boston MA 02205 800-843-5466
TF: 800-843-5466 ■ *Web:* public.dreyfus.com

Dts Financial Group 5401 Tech Cir Ste A . . . Moorpark CA 93021 805-532-9000
Web: www.dtsfinancial.com

Eaton Vance Mutual Funds Two International Pl . . . Boston MA 02110 617-482-8260
TF: 800-225-6265 ■ *Web:* www.eatonvance.com

Elmhurst Group, The One Bigelow Sq Ste 630 . . . Pittsburgh PA 15219 412-281-8731
Web: www.elmhurstgrp.com

Equity Investment Corp
3007 Piedmont Rd Ste 200 . . . Atlanta GA 30305 404-239-0111
Web: www.eicatlanta.com

Essex Financial Services Inc 176 Westbrook Rd . . . Essex CT 06426 860-767-4300
Web: www.essexfinancialservices.com

Ewing Morris & Company Investment Partners
1407 Yonge St Ste 500 . . . Toronto ON M4T1Y7 416-640-2791
Web: www.ewingmorris.com

Fascet LLC 224 W 30 St Ste 808 . . . New York NY 10001 212-448-9831
Web: fascet.com

Fengate Capital Management Ltd
5000 Yonge St Ste 1805 . . . Toronto ON M2N7E9 416-488-4184
Web: www.fengatecapital.com

Ferguson Wellman Capital Management Inc
888 S W Fifth Ave Ste 1200 . . . Portland OR 97204 503-226-1444
Web: www.fergusonwellman.com

Fidelity Advisor Funds PO Box 770002 . . . Cincinnati OH 45277 800-522-7297 321-7349*
**Fax Area Code:* 888 ■ **Fax:* Mktg ■ *TF:* 800-522-7297 ■ *Web:* www.advisor.fidelity.com

Fidelity Investment Funds PO Box 770001 . . . Cincinnati OH 45277 800-343-3548
TF: 800-343-3548 ■ *Web:* www.fidelity.com

Fidelity Investments Institutional Operations Company Inc
PO Box 770002 . . . Cincinnati OH 45277 877-208-0098
TF: 877-208-0098 ■ *Web:* www.fidelity.com

Fidelity Partnership 1995 483 Bay St Ste 200 . . . Toronto ON M5G2N7 416-307-5200
Web: www.fidelity.ca

First American Funds PO Box 701 . . . Milwaukee WI 53201 800-677-3863 666-6015*
**Fax Area Code:* 877 ■ *TF:* 800-677-3863 ■ *Web:* www.firstamericanfunds.com

First Green Partners
1550 Utica Ave S Ste 450 . . . Minneapolis MN 55416 952-288-2760
Web: www.firstgreenpartners.com

Fondaction
Bureau 103 2175 Blvd de Maisonneuve Est . . . Montreal QC H2K4S3 514-525-5505
Web: www.fondaction.com

Fort Pitt Capital Group Inc
680 Andersen Dr Foster Plz Ten . . . Pittsburgh PA 15220 412-921-1822
Web: www.fortpittcapital.com

Fulham & Company Inc 593 Washington St . . . Wellesley MA 02482 781-235-2266
Web: www.fulhamco.com

Galecki Financial Management Inc
7743 W Jefferson Blvd . . . Fort Wayne IN 46804 260-436-8525
Web: www.galecki.com

GAMCO Investors Inc One Corporate Ctr . . . Rye NY 10580 914-921-5100 921-5118
NYSE: GBL ■ *TF:* 800-422-3554 ■ *Web:* www.gabelli.com

Garrett Nagle & Company Inc
300 Unicorn Park Dr 19th Fl . . . Woburn MA 01801 617-737-9090
Web: www.garrettnagle.com

GeneChem 1 Westmount Sq Ste 800 . . . Montreal QC H3Z2P9 514-849-7696
Web: www.genechem.com

Geolo Capital
Pier 5 The Embarcadero Ste 102 . . . San Francisco CA 94111 415-694-5802
Web: www.geolo.com

Gestion Fonds Capital Culture Quebec Inc
485 McGill St Ste 900 . . . Montreal QC H2Y2H4 514-940-6820
Web: capitalculture.ca

Glenmede Funds 1650 Market St Ste 1200 . . . Philadelphia PA 19103 215-419-6000 419-6199
TF: 800-966-3200 ■ *Web:* www.glenmede.com

GMO Trust Funds 40 Rowes Wharf . . . Boston MA 02110 617-330-7500 261-0134
Web: www.gmo.com

Goldman Sachs 200 W St . . . New York NY 10282 212-902-1000
NYSE: GS ■ *TF:* 800-526-7384 ■ *Web:* www.goldmansachs.com

Greybrook Capital Inc 890 Yonge St Seventh Fl . . . Toronto ON M4W3P4 416-322-9700
Web: www.greybrook.com

Greystone Investment Management LLC
3805 Edwards Rd Ste 180 . . . Cincinnati OH 45209 513-731-8444
Web: www.greystoneinvestment.com

Gryphon Investment Counsel Inc
20 Bay St Ste 1905 . . . Toronto ON M5J2N8 416-364-2299
Web: www.gryphon.ca

Guild Investment Management Inc
12400 Wilshire Blvd Ste 1080 . . . Los Angeles CA 90025 310-826-8600
Web: www.guildinvestment.com

GWL Realty Advisors Inc
401 - Ninth Ave SW Ste 185 . . . Calgary AB T2P3C5 403-216-3985
Web: www.gwlrealtyadvisors.com

Hadley Capital
1200 Central Ave Ste 300 Chase Bank Bldg . . . Wilmette IL 60091 847-906-5300
Web: www.hadleycapital.com

Harbor Capital Management Inc
831 E Morehead St Ste 350 . . . Charlotte NC 28202 704-377-6945
Web: harborcapitalmgmt.com

Hartford Mutual Funds 30 Dan Rd Ste 55022 . . . Canton MA 02021 888-843-7824
TF: 888-843-7824 ■ *Web:* www.hartfordfunds.com

Harvest Capital Management Inc
114 N Main St Ste 301 . . . Concord NH 03301 603-224-6994
Web: www.harvestcap.com

HealthCap Partners LLC
5910 N Central Expy Ste 1000 . . . Dallas TX 75206 214-953-1722
Web: www.healthcappartners.com

Heartland Funds 789 N Water St Ste 500 . . . Milwaukee WI 53202 414-347-7777 347-1339
TF: 800-432-7856 ■ *Web:* www.heartlandfunds.com

Hokanson Associates Inc
201 Lomas Santa Fe Dr Ste 360 . . . Solana Beach CA 92075 858-755-8899
Web: www.hokansonassociates.com

Hotaling Investment Management LLC
100 W Lancaster Ave Ste 105 . . . Wayne PA 19087 610-688-0616
Web: www.hotalingllc.com

Huron Valley Financial Inc
2395 Oak Vly Dr Ste 200 . . . Ann Arbor MI 48103 734-669-8000
Web: www.huronvalleyfinancial.com

ICMARC 777 N Capitol St NE Ste 600 . . . Washington DC 20002 202-962-4600 962-4601
TF General: 800-669-7471 ■ *Web:* www.icmarc.org

iGan Partners Rowanwood Centre 1067 Yonge St . . . Toronto ON M4W2L2 416-925-2433
Web: www.iganpartners.com

Illumina Partners Inc 67 Yonge St Ste 600 . . . Toronto ON M5E1J8 416-861-1717
Web: www.illuminapartners.com

ING Funds 7337 E Doubletree Ranch Rd . . . Scottsdale AZ 85258 800-992-0180 477-2700*
**Fax Area Code:* 480 ■ *TF:* 800-992-0180 ■ *Web:* investments.voya.com/

Invenshure LLC 227 Colfax Ave N Ste 148 . . . Minneapolis MN 55405 612-520-7361
Web: invenshure.com

Invesco 11 Greenway Plaza Ste 100 . . . Houston TX 77046 713-626-1919 992-9890*
**Fax:* Mail Rm ■ *TF:* 800-959-4246 ■ *Web:* invesco.com/us

Invesco Trimark Ltd 5140 Yonge St Ste 800 . . . Toronto ON M2N6X7 416-590-9855
Web: www.invesco.ca

Iron Yard LLC, The 101 N Main St Ste 400 . . . Greenville SC 29601 864-252-6064
Web: theironyard.com

Ivy Funds 6300 Lamar Ave . . . Overland Park KS 66202 913-236-2000 236-2017
TF: 888-923-3355 ■ *Web:* www.ivyfunds.com

JAG Advisors 9841 Clayton Rd . . . Saint Louis MO 63124 314-997-1277
Web: www.jaglynn.com

JMT Consulting Group Inc
2200-2202 Route 22 . . . Patterson NY 12563 845-278-9262
Web: www.jmtconsulting.com

John Hancock Funds 101 Huntington Ave 10th Fl . . . Boston MA 02199 617-375-1500 375-6250
TF: 800-338-8080 ■ *Web:* www.jhinvestments.com

Klitzberg Associates Inc 600 Alexander Rd . . . Princeton NJ 08540 609-452-2888
Web: klitzbergfundsolutions.com

Kopp Funds 7701 France Ave S . . . Minneapolis MN 55435 952-841-0480

Laborers National Pension Fund
14140 Midway Rd Ste 200 . . . Dallas TX 75244 972-233-4458
Web: www.lnpf.org

Lazard Funds 30 Rockefeller Plz 57th Fl . . . New York NY 10112 800-823-6300
TF: 800-823-6300 ■ *Web:* lazardnet.com/us/mutual-funds/open-end-funds/

Leonis Partners 1409 Peachtree St Ste 210 . . . Atlanta GA 30309 404-347-3992
Web: www.leonispartners.com

Levy Affiliated Holdings LLC
201 Wilshire Blvd Second Fl . . . Santa Monica CA 90401 310-395-5200
Web: www.levyaffiliated.com

Liberty Funds Group Inc 4711 Lakeside Dr . . . Colleyville TX 76034 214-369-0500
Web: www.libfungrp.com

Lincluden Investment Management
1275 N Service Rd W Ste 607 . . . Oakville ON L6M3G4 905-825-9000
Web: www.lincluden.com

Loomis Sayles Funds One Financial Ctr . . . Boston MA 02111 617-482-2450
TF: 800-633-3330 ■ *Web:* www.loomissayles.com

	City	State	Zip	Phone	Fax
Lubitz Financial Group, The 9130 S Dadeland Blvd Ste 1625 *Web:* www.lubitzfinancial.com	Miami	FL	33156	305-670-4440	
Lynx Equity Ltd 692 Queen St E Ste 205 *Web:* www.lynxequity.com	Toronto	ON	M4M1G9	416-323-3512	
Mairs & Power Funds 332 Minnesota St Ste W-1520 *TF:* 800-304-7404 ■ *Web:* mairsandpower.com	Saint Paul	MN	55101	651-222-8478	222-8470
Manulife Mutual Funds 200 Bloor St E N Twr 3 *TF:* 888-588-7999 ■ *Web:* www.manulife.ca	Toronto	ON	M4W1E5	888-588-7999	
Market Street Trust Co 80 E Market St Ste 300 *Web:* www.marketstreettrust.com	Corning	NY	14830	607-962-6876	
Market Traders Institute 400 Colonial Ctr Pkwy Ste 350 *Web:* www.markettraders.com	Lake Mary	FL	32746	407-740-0900	
MASTER Teacher Inc, The 2600 Leadership Ln *TF:* 800-669-9633 ■ *Web:* www.masterteacher.com	Manhattan	KS	66505	800-669-9633	
Matan Companies LLLP 4600 Wedgewood Blvd Ste A *Web:* www.mataninc.com	Frederick	MD	21703	301-694-9200	
Mather Group LLC, The Oakbrook Ter Tower One Tower Ln Ste 1820 *Web:* www.themathergroup.com	Oakbrook Terrace	IL	60181	630-537-1080	
Mawer Investment Management Ltd 517 - 10th Ave S W Ste 600 *Web:* www.mawer.com	Calgary	AB	T2R0A8	403-262-4673	
Maxim Partners LLC 105 E First St Ste 203 *Web:* www.maximpartnersllc.com	Hinsdale	IL	60521	630-206-4040	
MBG Technologies Inc 1105 Pittsburgh St *Web:* mbgtech.com	Cheswick	PA	15204	724-274-7741	
McElvaine Investment Management Ltd Ste 219 2187 Oak Bay Ave *Web:* mcelvaine.com	Victoria	BC	V8R1G1	250-708-8345	
McLean & Partners Wealth Management Ltd 801 Tenth Ave S W *Web:* www.mcleanpartners.com	Calgary	AB	T2R0B4	403-234-0005	
MD Physician Services Inc 1870 Alta Vista Dr *Web:* mdm.ca	Ottawa	ON	K1G6R7	613-731-4552	
Missouri State Employees' Retirement System 907 Wildwood Dr *Web:* www.mosers.org	Jefferson City	MO	65109	573-632-6100	
MITIMCo Private Equity 238 Main St Ste 200 E48-200 *Web:* www.mitimco.org	Cambridge	MA	02142	617-253-4900	
Monetta Family of Mutual Funds 1776A S Naperville Rd Ste 100 *TF:* 800-241-9772 ■ *Web:* www.monetta.com	Wheaton	IL	60189	630-462-9800	462-9332
Montrusco Bolton Investments Inc 1501 McGill College Ave Ste 1200 *Web:* www.montruscobolton.com	Montreal	QC	H3A3M8	514-842-6464	
Morgan Meighen & Associates Ltd 10 Toronto St *Web:* www.mmainvestments.com	Toronto	ON	M5C2B7	416-366-2931	
Morgan Stanley Family of Funds 1585 Broadway *TF:* 800-223-2440 ■ *Web:* morganstanley.com	New York	NY	10036	212-761-4000	761-0086
Mraz, Amerine & Associates Inc 1120 13th St Ste K *Web:* www.mrazamerine.com	Modesto	CA	95354	209-593-5870	
Mutual Benefit Group 409 Penn St PO Box 577 *TF:* 800-283-3531 ■ *Web:* www.mutualbenefitgroup.com	Huntingdon	PA	16652	814-643-3000	643-7210
NDI Capital Inc 210-736 Granville St *Web:* ndicapital.com	Vancouver	BC	V6Z1G3	604-620-8424	
Neuberger Berman Funds PO Box 8403 *TF:* 800-877-9700 ■ *Web:* www.nb.com	Boston	MA	02266	212-476-8800	476-8848
New Mexico Educational Retirement Board 701 Camino de Los Marquez PO Box 26129 *Web:* www.nmerb.org	Santa Fe	NM	87502	505-827-8030	
Nicholas Family of Funds 700 N Water St Ste 1010 *TF:* 800-227-5987 ■ *Web:* www.nicholasfunds.com	Milwaukee	WI	53202	414-272-6133	
Nicola-Crosby Real Estate Asset Management Ltd 420-1508 W Broadway *Web:* www.nicolacrosby.com	Vancouver	BC	V6J1W8	778-383-6940	
Norris, Perne & French LLP 40 Pearl St N W Ste 300 *Web:* www.norrisperne.com	Grand Rapids	MI	49503	616-459-3421	
North Growth Management Ltd Ste 830 One Bentall Centre 505 Burrard St *Web:* www.northgrowth.com	Vancouver	BC	V7X1M4	604-688-5440	
North Sky Capital 33 S Sixth St Ste 4646 *Web:* www.northskycapital.com	Minneapolis	MN	55402	612-435-7150	
Northern Funds PO Box 75986 **Fax Area Code:* 312 ■ *TF:* 800-595-9111 ■ *Web:* www.northerntrust.com/wealth-management	Chicago	IL	60675	800-595-9111	557-0411*
Northern Institutional Funds 801 S Canal St C5S **Fax Area Code:* 312 ■ *TF:* 800-637-1380 ■ *Web:* www.northerntrust.com/asset-management	Chicago	IL	60607	800-637-1380	557-0411*
NorthSpring Capital Partners 100 Pinebush Rd *Web:* www.northspringcapitalpartners.com	Cambridge	ON	N1R8J8	519-721-7144	
Northstar Investment Advisors LLC 700 17th St Ste 2350 *Web:* www.northstarinvest.com	Denver	CO	80202	303-832-2300	
Nova Scotia Pension Agency Ste 400 Fourth Fl 1949 Upper Water St *Web:* www.novascotiapension.ca	Halifax	NS	B3J3N3	902-424-5070	
Novare Capital Management 521 E Morehead St The Morehead Bldg Ste 510 *Web:* www.novarecapital.com	Charlotte	NC	28202	704-334-3698	
Oak Assoc Funds PO Box 8233 *TF:* 888-462-5386 ■ *Web:* www.oakfunds.com	Denver	CO	80201	888-462-5386	
OakBrook Investments LLC 2300 Cabot Dr Ste 300 *Web:* www.oakbrookinvest.com	Lisle	IL	60532	630-271-0100	
Oakmark Family of Funds 330 W nineth St **Fax Area Code:* 312 ■ *TF:* 800-625-6275 ■ *Web:* www.oakmark.com	Kansas City	MO	64105	617-483-8327	621-0372*
Old Dominion Capital Management Inc 815 E Jefferson St *Web:* odcm.com	Charlottesville	VA	22902	434-977-1550	
OppenheimerFunds Inc 225 Liberty St *TF:* 800-525-7048 ■ *Web:* www.oppenheimerfunds.com	New York	NY	10281	800-525-7048	
Optimum Asset Management Inc 425 De Maisonneuve Blvd W Ste 1620 *Web:* www.optimumgestion.com	Montreal	QC	H3A3G5	514-288-7545	
Orinda Asset Management LLC Four Orinda Way Ste 150-A *Web:* orindamanagement.com	Orinda	CA	94563	925-253-1300	
Pasadena Capital Partners LLC PO Box 60786 *Web:* www.pasadenacapitalpartners.com	Pasadena	CA	91116	626-432-7070	
Pax World Fund Family 30 Penhallow St Ste 400 *TF:* 800-767-1729 ■ *Web:* www.paxworld.com	Portsmouth	NH	03801	603-431-8022	
Penfund Bay Adelaide Centre 333 Bay St Ste 610 *Web:* www.penfund.com	Toronto	ON	M5H2R2	416-865-0707	
Pension Corp Stn Prov Govt Po Box 9460 *Web:* www.pensionsbc.ca	Victoria	BC	V8W9V8	250-387-1002	
PFM Capital Inc 1925 Victoria Ave Second Fl *Web:* www.pfm.ca	Regina	SK	S4P0R3	306-791-4855	
Phillips, Hager & North Investment Management Ltd 200 Burrard St 20th Fl *Web:* www.phn.com	Vancouver	BC	V6C3N5	604-408-6100	
PIMCO Institutional Funds PO Box 219024 **Fax Area Code:* 816 ■ *TF:* 800-927-4648 ■ *Web:* www.investments.pimco.com	Kansas City	MO	64121	800-927-4648	421-2861*
Pioneer Funds 60 State St **Fax:* Mail Rm ■ *TF:* 800-225-6292 ■ *Web:* pioneerfunds.com	Boston	MA	02109	617-742-7825	422-4265*
Polar Securities Inc 401 Bay St Ste 1900 PO Box 19 *Web:* www.polarsec.com	Toronto	ON	M5H2Y4	416-367-4364	
Poplar Forest Capital LLC 70 S Lk Ave Ste 930 *Web:* www.poplarforestllc.com	Pasadena	CA	91101	626-304-6000	
Prado Group Inc, The 150 Post St Ste 320 *Web:* www.pradogroup.com	San Francisco	CA	94108	415-395-0880	
Presima Inc 1000 Jean-Paul-Riopelle Pl Montreal Herald Bldg Fourth Fl *Web:* www.presima.com	Montreal	QC	H2Z2B6	514-673-1375	
Primevest Capital Corp 400 Burrard St Ste 1730 *Web:* www.primevestcapital.ca	Vancouver	BC	V6C3A6	604-630-7011	
Priviti Capital Corp 850 444 Fifth Ave S W *Web:* www.priviticapital.com	Calgary	AB	T2P2T8	403-263-9943	
Pro-Financial Asset Management Inc 5090 Oribtor Dr Unit 3 *Web:* www.pro-financial.ca	Mississauga	ON	L4W5B5	905-815-6900	
Punch & Associates Inc 3601 W 76th St Ste 225 *Web:* punchinvest.com	Edina	MN	55435	952-224-4350	
Putnam Family of Funds PO Box 41203 *TF:* 800-225-1581 ■ *Web:* www.putnam.com	Providence	RI	02940	800-225-1581	250-8411
Qwest Investment Management Corp Ste 310 650 W Georgia St PO Box 11549 *Web:* www.qwestfunds.com	Vancouver	BC	V6B4N7	604-601-5804	
R. G. Niederhoffer Capital Management Inc 1700 Broadway 39th Fl *Web:* www.niederhoffer.com	New York	NY	10019	212-245-0400	
Rainier Investment Management Mutual Funds 601 Union St Ste 2801 **Fax Area Code:* 206 ■ *TF:* 800-536-4640 ■ *Web:* www.rainierfunds.com	Seattle	WA	98101	800-536-4640	464-0616*
Raven Capital Management LLC 110 Greene St Ste 1102 *Web:* ravencm.com	New York	NY	10012	212-966-7926	
Raymond Martin Co 4709 Bluebonnet Blvd Ste A *Web:* www.raymondmartin.com	Baton Rouge	LA	70809	225-291-9300	
Redwood Asset Management Inc Richmond Adelaide Centre 120 Adelaide St W Ste 2400 *Web:* www.redwoodasset.com	Toronto	ON	M5H1T1	416-368-8898	
RidgeWorth Funds 50 Hurt Plaza Ste 1400 *TF:* 866-595-2470 ■ *Web:* www.ridgeworth.com	Atlanta	GA	30305	866-595-2470	
Ross Smith Asset Management Inc 601 10th Ave S W Ste 155 *TF:* 888-494-6893 ■ *Web:* www.rsam.ca	Calgary	AB	T2R0B2	888-494-6893	
Roxbury Capital Management LLC 6001 Shady Oak Rd Ste 120 *Web:* www.roxcap.com	Minnetonka	MN	55343	952-230-6140	
Rydex Funds 805 King Farm Blvd Ste 600 **Fax:* Admin ■ *TF Cust Svc:* 800-820-0888 ■ *Web:* guggenheiminvestments.com	Rockville	MD	20850	301-296-5100	296-5107*
Sandstone Asset Management Inc 115 101 - Sixth St SW *Web:* www.sandstoneam.com	Calgary	AB	T2P5K7	403-218-6125	
Sayer Energy Advisors 1620 540 - Fifth Ave SW *Web:* www.sayeradvisors.com	Calgary	AB	T2P0M2	403-266-6133	
Scholtz & Company LLC 32 Haviland St Ste 3 *Web:* www.scholtzandco.com	Norwalk	CT	06854	203-714-9900	
School Employees Retirement System of Ohio 300 E Broad St Ste 100 *Web:* www.ohsers.org	Columbus	OH	43215	614-222-5853	

Company / Address	City	State	Zip	Phone	Fax
Schwartz Investment Counsel Inc					
801 W Ann Arbor Trl Ste 244	Plymouth	MI	48170	734-455-7777	
Web: www.schwartzinvest.com					
Seabury Venture Partners					
345 Lorton Ave Ste 401	Burlingame	CA	94010	650-373-1030	
Web: seaburypartners.com					
SEAMARK Asset Management Ltd					
1801 Hollis St Ste 810	Halifax	NS	B3J3N4	902-423-9367	
Web: www.seamark.ca					
Security Funds One Security Benefit Pl	Topeka	KS	66636	785-438-3000	438-5177
TF: 800-888-2461 ■ *Web:* www.securitybenefit.com					
SEI One Freedom Vly Dr	Oaks	PA	19456	610-676-1000	
NASDAQ: SEIC ■ *TF:* 800-342-5734 ■ *Web:* www.seic.com					
Selected Funds PO Box 8243	Boston	MA	02266	800-243-1575	
TF: 800-243-1575 ■ *Web:* www.selectedfunds.com					
Sensato Investors LLC					
One Sansome St Ste 3430	San Francisco	CA	94104	415-391-4600	
Web: www.sensatoinvestors.com					
Sentry Investments Inc					
Commerce Court W 199 Bay St Ste 2700					
PO Box 108	Toronto	ON	M5L1E2	416-861-8729	
Web: www.sentry.ca					
Sequoia Fund Inc 767 Fifth Ave Ste 4701	New York	NY	10153	212-832-5280	832-5298
TF: 800-686-6884 ■ *Web:* www.sequoiafund.com					
Sheridan Legacy Group					
400 N Michigan Ave Ste 900	Chicago	IL	60611	312-212-3237	
Web: www.sheridanlegacy.com					
Shore Capital Partners LLC					
One E Wacker Dr Ste 400	Chicago	IL	60601	312-348-7580	
Web: www.shorecp.com					
Signal Hill Equity Partners					
Two Carlton St Ste 1700	Toronto	ON	M5B1J3	416-847-1502	
Web: www.signalhillequity.com					
Silver Companies 1001 E Telecom Dr	Boca Raton	FL	33431	561-981-5252	
Web: www.silvercompanies.com					
Skyline Asset Management LP					
120 S Lasalle St Ste 1320	Chicago	IL	60603	312-913-0900	
Web: www.skylinelp.com					
Slate Properties Inc 200 Front St W Ste 2400	Toronto	ON	M5V3K2	416-644-4264	
Web: www.slateproperties.ca					
Sound Shore Fund 3435 Stelzer Rd	Columbus	OH	43219	800-754-8758	343-5884*
**Fax Area Code:* 866 ■ *TF:* 800-754-8758 ■ *Web:* www.soundshorefund.com					
Southpaw Asset Management LP					
Two W Greenwich Office Park	Greenwich	CT	06831	203-862-6200	
Web: www.southpawassetmanagement.com					
Southridge LLC 90 Grove St Ste 206	Ridgefield	CT	06877	203-431-8300	
Web: www.southridge.com					
SpringBank TechVentures					
160 MacLaurin Dr Ste #1	Calgary	AB	T3Z3S4	403-685-8001	
Web: www.sbtechventures.com					
Sprott Inc					
200 Bay St Ste 2700 Royal Bank Plz S Twr	Toronto	ON	M5J2J1	416-362-7172	
Web: www.sprottinc.com					
SSgA Funds One Lincoln St	Boston	MA	02111	617-786-3000	664-6011
TF: 800-997-7327 ■ *Web:* www.ssgafunds.com					
State Farm Mutual Funds PO Box 219548	Kansas City	MO	64121	800-447-4930	
TF: 800-447-4930 ■ *Web:* www.statefarm.com/mutual/mutual.htm					
State Teachers Retirement System of Ohio					
275 E Broad St	Columbus	OH	43215	888-227-7877	
TF: 888-227-7877 ■ *Web:* www.strsoh.org					
Steadyhand Investment Funds Limited Partnership					
1747 W Third Ave	Vancouver	BC	V6J1K7	888-888-3147	
TF: 888-888-3147 ■ *Web:* www.steadyhand.com					
Steele Capital Management Inc					
788 Main St #200	Dubuque	IA	52001	563-588-2097	
Web: www.steelecapital.com					
Sterling Bay Companies LLC					
1040 W Randolph St	Chicago	IL	60607	312-466-4100	
Web: www.sterlingbay.com					
Stewart & Patten Company LLC					
One Post St Ste 850	San Francisco	CA	94104	415-421-4932	
Web: www.stewartandpatten.com					
Strategic Global Advisors LLC					
100 Bayview Cir Ste 650	Newport Beach	CA	92660	949-706-2640	
Web: www.sgadvisors.com					
SW Capital Partners					
Ste 1800 Scotia Centre 700 - Second St SW	Calgary	AB	T2P2W1	403-261-4239	
Web: www.swenergycap.com					
T Rowe Price Mutual Funds 100 E Pratt St	Baltimore	MD	21202	410-345-2000	539-4425
TF: 800-638-5660 ■ *Web:* corporate.troweprice.com					
Tandem 1250 Rene Levesque Blvd W 38th Fl	Montreal	QC	H3B4W8	514-510-8900	
Web: www.tandemexpansion.com					
Tannor Capital Management LLC					
150 Grand St Ste 401	White Plains	NY	10601	914-509-5000	
Web: www.tannorpartners.com					
TCW Group Inc 865 S Figueroa St Ste 1800	Los Angeles	CA	90017	213-244-0000	
TF: 800-386-3829 ■ *Web:* www.tcw.com					
Tepper Holdings Inc					
225 E Beaver Creek Rd Ste 201	Richmond Hill	ON	L4B3P4	905-889-0663	
Web: www.tepperholdings.com					
Terracap Group 100 Sheppard Ave E Ste 502	Toronto	ON	M2N6N5	416-222-9345	
Web: www.terracap.ca					
Teucrium Trading LLC 232 Hidden Lk Rd	Brattleboro	VT	05301	802-257-1617	
Web: www.teucrium.com					
TFS Capital LLC 10 N High St Ste 500	West Chester	PA	19380	888-837-4446	
TF: 888-837-4446 ■ *Web:* www.tfscapital.com					
TGV Partners 23 Corporate Plz Ste 215	Newport Beach	CA	92660	949-284-1114	
Web: www.tgvpartners.com					
Third Avenue Funds 622 Third Ave 32nd Fl	New York	NY	10017	212-888-5222	
Web: www.thirdavenuefunds.com					
Thornburg Investment Management Funds					
2300 N Ridgetop Rd	Santa Fe	NM	87506	505-984-0200	984-8973
TF: 800-533-9337 ■ *Web:* www.thornburginvestments.com					
Tillar-Wenstrup Advisors LLC					
1065 E Centerville Sta Rd	Centerville	OH	45459	937-428-9700	
Web: twadvisors.com					
Torray Fund 7501 Wisconsin Ave Ste 750 W	Bethesda	MD	20814	301-493-4600	530-0642
TF: 800-443-3036 ■ *Web:* www.torray.com					
Trade Street Residential					
19950 W Country Club Dr Ste 801	Aventura	FL	33180	786-248-5200	
Web: www.tradestreetresidential.com					
TransLink Capital 228 Hamilton Ave Ste 210	Palo Alto	CA	94301	650-330-7353	
Web: www.translinkcapital.com					
Trez Capital Limited Partnership					
1550 - 1185 W Georgia St	Vancouver	BC	V6E4E6	416-350-1299	
Web: www.trezcapital.com					
TriLinc Global LLC					
1230 Rosecrans Ave Ste 605	Manhattan Beach	CA	90266	310-997-0580	
Web: www.trilincglobal.com					
Trillium Asset Management LLC					
Two Financial Ctr 60 S St Ste 1100	Boston	MA	02111	617-423-6655	
Web: www.trilliuminvest.com					
Trinity Fiduciary Partners LLC					
106 Decker Court Ste 226	Irving	TX	75062	877-334-1283	
TF: 877-334-1283 ■ *Web:* www.trinityfiduciary.com					
Turtle Creek Asset Management					
Four King St W Ste 1300	Toronto	ON	M5H1B6	416-363-7400	
Web: www.turtlecreek.ca					
TVV Capital 201 Fourth Ave N Ste 1250	Nashville	TN	37219	615-256-8061	
Web: tvvcapital.com					
TWIN Capital Management Inc					
3244 Washington Rd Ste 202	Mcmurray	PA	15317	724-942-2000	
Web: www.twincapital.com					
Ulland Investment Advisors					
4550 IDS Ctr Eighty S Eighth St	Minneapolis	MN	55402	612-312-1400	
Web: www.ullandinvestment.com					
Upton Financial Group Inc					
131 Stony Cir Ste 500	Santa Rosa	CA	95401	707-523-9651	
Web: www.uptonco.com					
Valiant Trust Co 310 - 606 Fourth St SW	Calgary	AB	T2P1T1	403-233-2801	
Web: www.valianttrust.com					
Vaughan Nelson Investment Management LP					
600 Travis St Ste 6300	Houston	TX	77002	713-224-2545	
Web: www.vaughannelson.com					
Vested Business Brokers Inc					
50 Karl Ave # 102	Smithtown	NY	11787	631-265-7300	
Web: www.vestedbb.com					
Victory Funds 4900 Tiedeman Rd PO Box 182593	Brooklyn	OH	44144	800-539-3863	
TF: 800-539-3863 ■ *Web:* www.vcm.com					
Vigilant Capital Management LLC					
Two City Ctr Fourth Fl	Portland	ME	04101	207-523-1110	
Web: www.vigilantcap.com					
Vision Capital Management Inc					
One SW Columbia Ste 915	Portland	OR	97258	503-221-5656	
Web: www.vcmi.net					
Wealthsimple Financial Inc					
372 Richmond St W Ste 120	Toronto	ON	M5V1X6	647-350-7675	
Web: www.wealthsimple.com					
Weaver C. Barksdale & Associates Inc					
One Burton Hills Blvd Ste 100	Nashville	TN	37215	615-665-1085	
Web: www.wcbarksdale.com					
Welch & Forbes LLC					
45 School St Fifth Fl Old City Hall	Boston	MA	02108	617-523-1635	
Web: www.welchforbes.com					
Welch Group LLC, The					
3940 Montclair Rd Fifth Fl	Birmingham	AL	35213	205-879-5001	
Web: www.welchgroup.com					
Wesley Clover Corp 390 March Rd	Kanata	ON	K2K2W7	613-271-6305	
Web: www.wesleyclover.com					
Westcap Management Ltd 830 410 22nd St E	Saskatoon	SK	S7K5T6	306-652-5557	
Web: www.westcapmgt.ca					
Westwood Trust					
1125 S 103rd St Ste 250 One Pacific Pl	Omaha	NE	68124	402-393-1300	
Web: www.mccarthyadvisors.com					
Wharton Equity Partners LLC					
505 Park Ave 18th Fl	New York	NY	10022	212-570-5959	
Web: www.whartonequity.com					
Wheelock Partners LLC 213 School St Ste 301	Gardner	MA	01440	978-632-9800	
Web: www.wheelockpartners.com					
White Elm Capital LLC					
537 Steamboat Rd Ste 300	Greenwich	CT	06830	203-742-6000	
Web: www.whiteelmgroup.com					
White Oak Partners LLC					
5150 E Dublin Granville Rd Ste One	Westerville	OH	43081	614-855-1155	
Web: www.whiteoakpartners.com					
Whitecap Venture Partners					
22 St Clair Ave E Ste 1010	Toronto	ON	M4T2S3	416-961-5355	
Web: whitecastle.ca					
Wilshire Mutual Funds Inc PO Box 219512	Kansas City	MO	64121	888-200-6796	
TF: 888-200-6796 ■ *Web:* advisor.wilshire.com					
XPV Capital Corp 266 King St W Ste 403	Toronto	ON	M5V1H8	416-864-0475	
Web: www.xpvcapital.com					
Zynik Capital Corp					
1040 W Georgia St Grosvenor Bldg Ste 950	Vancouver	BC	V6E4H1	604-654-2555	
Web: www.zynik.com					

532 NAVIGATION & GUIDANCE INSTRUMENTS & SYSTEMS

Company / Address	City	State	Zip	Phone	Fax
AAI Corp 124 Industry Ln	Hunt Valley	MD	21030	410-666-1400	
Web: textronsystems.com/company-overview/rebrand					
Acutronic USA Inc 700 Waterfront Dr	Pittsburgh	PA	15222	412-926-1200	
Web: www.acutronic.com					

Company	City	State	ZIP	Phone	Fax
Adducent Technology Inc 230 Parque Margarita — *TF:* 800-648-0656 ■ *Web:* www.adducenttechnology.com	Rohnert Park	CA	94928	707-478-8136	
Aeroprobe Corp 2200 Kraft Dr Ste 1475 — *Web:* www.aeroprobe.com	Blacksburg	VA	24060	540-443-9215	
Allen Aircraft Products Inc 6168 Woodbine Ave — *Web:* www.allenaircraft.com	Ravenna	OH	44266	330-296-9621	
Alpine Electronics of America 19145 Gramercy Pl — **Fax:* Hum Res ■ *TF:* 800-257-4631 ■ *Web:* www.alpine-usa.com	Torrance	CA	90501	310-326-8000	320-5089*
American Reliance Inc (AMREL) 3445 Fletcher Ave — *Web:* www.amrel.com	El Monte	CA	91731	626-443-6818	443-8600
American Seal & Engineering Company Inc 295 Indian River Rd — *Web:* www.ameriseal.com	Orange	CT	06477	203-789-8819	
AMRO Fabrication Corp 1430 Adelia Ave — *Web:* www.amrofab.com	South El Monte	CA	91733	626-579-2200	
Apex Machine Tool Co 1790 New Britain Ave — *Web:* www.apexmachinetool.com	Farmington	CT	06032	860-677-2884	
Archangel Systems Inc 1635 Pumphrey Ave — *Web:* www.archangel.com	Auburn	AL	36832	334-826-8008	
Astronautics Corp of America 4115 N Teutonia Ave PO Box 523 — *Web:* www.astronautics.com	Milwaukee	WI	53201	414-449-4000	447-8231
Aviat Aircraft Inc 672 S Washington — *Web:* www.aviataircraft.com	Afton	WY	83110	307-885-3151	
Aviation Materials Management Inc 2581 Rulon White Blvd — *Web:* www.avmat.com	Ogden	UT	84404	801-782-8450	
Aviation Partners Inc 7213 Perimeter Rd S — *Web:* www.aviationpartners.com	Seattle	WA	98108	206-762-1171	
Avionics & Systems Integration Group LLC 10 Collins Industrial Pl Ste 3b — *Web:* asigllc.com	North Little Rock	AR	72113	501-771-9388	
Ball Aerospace & Technologies Corp 1600 Commerce St — **Fax:* Mail Rm ■ *Web:* www.ballaerospace.com	Boulder	CO	80301	303-939-4000	460-2315*
Ballard Technology Inc 11400 Airport Rd Ste 201 — *Web:* www.ballardtech.com	Everett	WA	98204	425-339-0281	
Baron Services Inc 4930 Research Dr — *Web:* www.baronservices.com	Huntsville	AL	35805	256-881-8811	
Bell Aerospace Services Inc 1305 Airport Fwy Ste 321	Bedford	TX	76021	817-278-0750	
Blue Ridge Optics LLC 118 Center St — *Web:* www.blueridgeoptics.com	Bedford	VA	24523	540-586-8526	
Boeing Phantom Works PO Box 2515 — *Web:* www.boeing.com	Seal Beach	CA	90740	562-797-2020	
Brek Manufacturing Co 1513 W 132nd St — *Web:* www.brek.aero	Gardena	CA	90249	310-329-7638	
Bright Lights USA Inc 145 Shreve Ave — *Web:* www.brightlightsusa.com	Barrington	NJ	08007	856-546-5656	
Butler National Corp 19920 W 161st St — *OTC: BUKS* ■ *TF:* 800-690-6903 ■ *Web:* www.butlernational.com	Olathe	KS	66062	913-780-9595	780-5088
C & D Zodiac Inc 5701 Bolsa Ave	Huntington Beach	CA	92647	714-934-0000	
Cicon Engineering 6633 Odessa Ave — *Web:* www.cicon.com	Van Nuys	CA	91406	818-909-6060	
CLC Networks 2275 Northwest Pkwy SE Ste 110 — *Web:* www.clcnetworks.com	Marietta	GA	30067	678-564-0522	
Cloud Cap Technology Inc 205 N Wasco Loop Ste 103 — *Web:* www.cloudcaptech.com	Hood River	OR	97031	541-387-2120	387-2030
CMI Inc 316 E Ninth St — *TF:* 866-835-0690 ■ *Web:* www.alcoholtest.com	Owensboro	KY	42303	270-685-6545	685-6678
Contract Fabrication & Design LLC 5427 Fm 546 — *Web:* cfdintl.com	Princeton	TX	75407	972-736-2260	
Cubic Corp 9333 Balboa Ave PO Box 85587 — *NYSE: CUB* ■ *TF:* 800-937-5449 ■ *Web:* www.cubic.com	San Diego	CA	92186	858-277-6780	505-1523
Cubic Defense Systems 9333 Balboa Ave — *TF:* 800-937-5449 ■ *Web:* www.cubic.com	San Diego	CA	92123	858-277-6780	505-1524
Cummins Aerospace 2200 E Orangethorpe Ave — *Web:* www.cumminsaerospace.com	Anaheim	CA	92806	714-879-2800	
Dean Baldwin Painting LP 2395 Bulverde Rd Ste 105 — *Web:* www.deanbaldwinpainting.com	Bulverde	TX	78163	830-438-5340	
Del Mar Avionics 1601 Alton Pkwy Ste C — *TF:* 800-854-0481 ■ *Web:* www.dma.com	Irvine	CA	92606	949-250-3200	261-0529
Deutsch Industrial Us 3850 Industrial Ave — *Web:* www.deutsch.net	Hemet	CA	92545	951-765-2250	765-2255
DRS C3 Systems LLC 400 Professional Dr — *TF:* 800-694-5005 ■ *Web:* www.drs.com	Gaithersburg	MD	20879	301-921-8100	921-8010
DRS Surveillance Support Systems Inc 6200 118th Ave — *Web:* www.drs.com	Largo	FL	33773	727-541-6681	
DRS Training & Control Systems 645 Anchors St NW — *TF:* 800-694-5005 ■ *Web:* www.drs.com	Fort Walton Beach	FL	32548	850-302-3000	302-3371
Dynalec Corp 87 W Main St — *Web:* www.dynalec.com	Sodus	NY	14551	315-483-6923	483-6656
Eaton Corp 1111 Superior Ave Eaton Ctr — *Web:* www.eaton.com	Cleveland	OH	44114	216-523-5000	
Esterline Technologies Corp 500 108th Ave NE Ste 1500 — *NYSE: ESL* ■ *Web:* www.esterline.com	Bellevue	WA	98004	425-453-9400	453-2916
EWR Weather Radar 336 Leffingwell Ave Ste 112 — *Web:* www.ewradar.com	Saint Louis	MO	63122	314-821-1022	
First Class Air Repair 15380 County Road 565A Ste G — *Web:* firstclassairrepair.com	Groveland	FL	34736	352-241-7684	
Flash Technology Corp 332 Nichol Mill Ln — *TF:* 888-313-5274 ■ *Web:* www.spx.com	Franklin	TN	37067	615-503-2000	261-2000
FLIR Systems Inc 27700-A SW Pkwy Ave — *NASDAQ: FLIR* ■ **Fax:* Sales ■ *TF:* 877-773-3547 ■ *Web:* www.flir.com	Wilsonville	OR	97070	503-498-3547	498-3904*
Forrest Machining Inc 27756 Ave Mentry — *Web:* www.forrestmachining.com	Valencia	CA	91355	661-257-0231	
Fortner Aerospace Manufacturing Inc 401 N Pleasant St — *Web:* syncaero.com	Prescott	AZ	86301	928-771-2434	
Frontier Electronic Systems Corp 4500 W Sixth Ave — **Fax:* Hum Res ■ *TF:* 800-677-1769 ■ *Web:* www.fescorp.com	Stillwater	OK	74074	405-624-1769	624-7898*
Gables Engineering Inc 247 Greco Ave — *Web:* www.gableseng.com	Coral Gables	FL	33146	305-774-4400	774-4465
Garmin Ltd 1200 E 151st St — *NASDAQ: GRMN* ■ *TF:* 888-442-7646 ■ *Web:* www.garmin.com	Olathe	KS	66062	913-397-8200	397-8282
GCE Industries Inc 1891 Nirvana Ave — *Web:* www.gceindustries.com	Chula Vista	CA	91911	619-421-1151	
GCM North American Aerospace LLC 21719 84th Ave S	Kent	WA	98032	253-872-7488	
GE Aviation Systems Div 3290 Patterson Ave SE — *Web:* www.geaviation.com	Grand Rapids	MI	49512	616-241-8274	
General Dynamics Advanced Information Systems 14700 Lee Rd Ste 600 — *Web:* www.gd-ais.com	Chantilly	VA	20151	703-263-2800	
General Dynamics C4 Systems 400 John Quincy Adams Rd Bldg 80 — **Fax Area Code:* 508 ■ *TF:* 877-449-0600 ■ *Web:* www.gdc4s.com	Taunton	MA	02780	877-449-0600	880-4800*
Goodrich Corp 2730 W Tyvola Rd 4 Coliseum Ctr — *NYSE: GR* ■ *TF:* 800-735-7899 ■ *Web:* utcaerospacesystems.com	Charlotte	NC	28217	704-423-7000	423-7002
GPS North America 406 Executive Dr — *Web:* gpsnorthamerica.com	Langhorne	PA	19047	215-497-0100	
Hampson Aerospace Inc 2700 112th St Ste 300	Grand Prairie	TX	75050	214-988-0630	
Innovative Configuration Inc 712 Via Palo Alto	Aptos	CA	95003	831-688-6917	
Innovative Solutions & Support Inc 720 Pennsylvania Dr — *NASDAQ: ISSC* ■ *TF:* 866-359-7876 ■ *Web:* www.innovative-ss.com	Exton	PA	19341	610-646-9800	646-0149
Interface Displays & Controls Inc 4630 N Ave — *Web:* www.interfacedisplays.com	Oceanside	CA	92056	760-945-0230	
Interstate Electronics Corp 602 E Vermont Ave PO Box 3117 — *TF:* 800-854-6979 ■ *Web:* www.l-3com.com	Anaheim	CA	92803	714-758-0500	758-4148
ITT Exelis Inc 1650 Tysons Blvd Ste 1700 — *Web:* exelisinc.com	McLean	VA	22102	703-790-6300	790-6360
ITT Industries Inc 1133 Westchester Ave — *NYSE: ITT* ■ *TF:* 800-254-2823 ■ *Web:* www.itt.com	White Plains	NY	10604	914-641-2000	696-2950
Jewell Instruments LLC 850 Perimeter Rd — *TF:* 800-227-5955 ■ *Web:* jewellinstruments.com	Manchester	NH	03103	603-669-6400	669-5962
Kearfott Guidance & Navigation Corp 1150 McBride Ave — *Web:* www.kearfott.com	Little Falls	NJ	07424	973-785-6000	785-6025
Kelly Manufacturing Co 555 S Topeka St — *Web:* www.kellymfg.com	Wichita	KS	67202	316-265-6868	265-6687
Kollsman Inc 220 Daniel Webster Hwy — *TF:* 800-772-9603 ■ *Web:* www.elbitsystems-us.com	Merrimack	NH	03054	603-889-2500	
Kor Electronics 10855 Business Ctr Dr — *Web:* www.mrcy.com	Cypress	CA	90630	714-898-8200	895-7526
KVH Industries Inc 50 Enterprise Ctr — *NASDAQ: KVHI* ■ *Web:* www.kvh.com	Middletown	RI	02842	401-847-3327	849-0045
L-3 Avionics Systems 5353 52nd St SE — **Fax:* Hum Res ■ *TF:* 800-253-9525 ■ *Web:* www.l-3avionics.com/	Grand Rapids	MI	49512	616-949-6600	285-4457*
L-3 Communications Corp Aviation Recorders Div 6000 Fruitville Rd — *TF:* 877-726-2228 ■ *Web:* www.l-3ar.com	Sarasota	FL	34232	941-371-0811	377-5598
L-3 Communications Corp Communication Systems East Div 1 Federal St — *TF:* 800-339-6197 ■ *Web:* www.l-3com.com/CS-East	Camden	NJ	08103	856-338-3000	338-6014
L-3 Communications Corp Randtron Antenna Systems Div 130 Constitution Dr — *TF Sales:* 866-900-7270 ■ *Web:* www.l-3com.com/randtron	Menlo Park	CA	94025	650-326-9500	326-1033
L-3 Communications Holdings Inc 640 North 2200 West PO Box 16850 — *Web:* www.l-3com.com/csw	Salt Lake City	UT	84116	801-594-2000	594-3572
L-3 Ocean Systems 15825 Roxford St — *Web:* www2.l3com.com	Sylmar	CA	91342	818-367-0111	
Laitram LLC 200 Laitram Ln — *TF:* 800-535-7631 ■ *Web:* www.laitram.com	Harahan	LA	70123	504-733-6000	733-2143
Liquid Measurement Systems 141 Morse Dr PO Box 2070 — *Web:* www.liquidmeasurement.com	Georgia	VT	05468	802-528-8100	528-8131
Lockheed Martin Canada 3001 Solandt Rd — *Web:* www.lockheedmartin.com/canada	Kanata	ON	K2K2M8	613-599-3270	599-3282
Lockheed Martin Corp 6801 Rockledge Dr — *NYSE: LMT* ■ *TF:* 866-562-2363 ■ *Web:* www.lockheedmartin.com	Bethesda	MD	20817	301-897-6000	897-6083
Lockheed Martin MS2 199 Borton Landing Rd — *Web:* lockheedmartin.com	Moorestown	NJ	08057	856-722-4100	
Lockheed Martin Sippican Seven Barnabas Rd — *Web:* www.sippican.com	Marion	MA	02738	508-748-1160	748-3626
Loral Space & Communications Ltd 600 Third Ave — *NASDAQ: LORL* ■ *Web:* www.loral.com	New York	NY	10016	212-697-1105	
Lowrance Electronics Inc 12000 E Skelly Dr — **Fax:* Hum Res ■ *TF:* 800-628-4487 ■ *Web:* www.lowrance.com	Tulsa	OK	74128	918-437-6881	234-1705*
Lycoming Engines 652 Oliver St — *TF:* 800-258-3279 ■ *Web:* www.lycoming.com	Williamsport	PA	17701	570-323-6181	
Mackay Communications Inc 3691 Trust Dr — *TF:* 877-462-2529 ■ *Web:* www.mackaycomm.com	Raleigh	NC	27616	919-850-3000	954-1707
Martin-Baker America Inc 423 Walters Ave — *Web:* www.martin-baker.com	Johnstown	PA	15904	814-262-9325	

				Phone	Fax
Maven Engineering Corp 15946 Derwood Rd .... Rockville *Web:* www.mavencorporation.com	MD	20855		301-519-3400	
Mikros Systems Corp 707 Alexander Rd Ste 208 PO Box 7189.............. Princeton *Web:* www.mikrossystems.com	NJ	08540		609-987-1513	
Morgan Aircraft LLC 220 S Business Park Dr Ste A6..................... Oostburg *Web:* morganaircraft.com	WI	53070		920-564-3900	
Nabtesco Aerospace Inc 17770 NE 78th Pl .... Redmond *Web:* www.nabtescoaero.com	WA	98052		425-602-8400	
NavCom Defense Electronics Inc 9129 Stellar Ct .... Corona *Web:* www.navcom.com	CA	92883		951-268-9230	
Navigation Solutions LLC 3314 N Central Expy Ste 210 .... Plano *Web:* www.navigationsolutions.com	TX	75074		972-633-2301	
NephroGenex Inc 79 Tw Alexander Dr 4401 Research Commons Bldg Ste 290 PO Box 14188 .... Research Triangle Park *Web:* www.nephrogenex.com	NC	27709		609-986-1780	
Newcon Optik 105 Sparks Ave..................... North York *TF:* 877-368-6666 ■ *Web:* www.newcon-optik.com	ON	M2H2S5		416-663-6963	663-9065
Northrop Grumman Corp 2980 Fairview Park Dr .... Falls Church *NYSE: NOC* ■ **Fax Area Code:* 310 ■ *Web:* www.northropgrumman.com	VA	22042		703-280-2900	201-3023*
Onboard Systems International 13915 NW Third Ct............................ Vancouver *TF:* 800-275-0883 ■ *Web:* www.onboardsystems.com	WA	98685		360-546-3072	
Orbit International Corp 80 Cabot Ct............. Hauppauge *NASDAQ: ORBT* ■ *Web:* www.orbitintl.com	NY	11788		631-435-8300	435-8458
Oregon Aero Inc 34020 Skyway Dr .... Scappoose *TF:* 800-888-6910 ■ *Web:* www.oregonaero.com	OR	97056		503-543-7399	
Parker Electronic Systems 300 Marcus Blvd .... Smithtown *Web:* www.parker.com	NY	11787		631-231-3737	434-8152
Pixel Velocity Inc 3917 Research Park Dr Ste B-1 .... Ann Arbor *Web:* www.pixel-velocity.com	MI	48108		734-213-3715	
Plures Technologies Inc 5297 Parkside Dr Ste 400 PO Box 24.............. Canandaigua	NY	14424		585-905-0554	
Pratt & Whitney AutoAir Inc 5640 Enterprise Dr................................ Lansing *Web:* www.autoair.com	MI	48911		517-393-4040	
Precision Aircraft Components Inc 2787 Armstrong Ln................................. Dayton	OH	45414		937-278-0264	278-4466
Professional Aircraft Accessories Inc 7035 Ctr Ln .... Titusville *Web:* www.gopaa.com	FL	32780		321-267-1040	269-0935
Proxy Technologies Inc 1840 Michael Faraday Dr Ste 220...................... Reston *Web:* www.proxyaviation.com	VA	20190		703-485-1035	
Q Holdings Inc 615 Arapeen Dr Ste 102 .... Salt Lake City *Web:* www.qthera.com	UT	84108		801-582-5400	
Quality Forming LLC 22906 Frampton Ave .... Torrance *Web:* www.qfinc.com	CA	90501		310-539-2855	
Radio Holland USA Inc 8943 Gulf Fwy .... Houston *Web:* imtech.com/en/imtechmarine-usa	TX	77017		713-941-2290	378-2101
Raymarine Inc 21 Manchester St................... Merrimack *TF:* 800-539-5539 ■ *Web:* www.raymarine.com	NH	03054		603-881-5200	864-4756
Raytheon Air Traffic Management Systems 870 Winter St .... Waltham *Web:* raytheon.com/capabilities/products/cnsatm	MA	02451		781-522-3000	522-5200
Raytheon Canada Ltd 360 Albert St Ste 1640 .... Ottawa *Web:* www.raytheon.ca	ON	K1R7X7		613-233-4121	233-1099
Raytheon Integrated Defense Systems 50 Apple Hill Dr .... Tewksbury *Web:* raytheon.com/ourcompany/businesses/	MA	01876		978-858-5000	
Raytheon Intelligence & Information Systems 1200 S Jupiter Rd.................................. Garland *TF:* 800-423-0210 ■ *Web:* raytheon.com/ourcompany/businesses/	TX	75042		972-205-5100	
Raytheon Network Centric Systems (NCS) 2501 W University Dr........................... McKinney *Web:* www.raytheon.com	TX	75071		781-522-3000	
Rockwell Collins Inc 400 Collins Rd NE .... Cedar Rapids *NYSE: COL* ■ **Fax:* PR ■ *TF:* 888-721-3094 ■ *Web:* www.rockwellcollins.com	IA	52498		319-295-1000	295-1542*
Rodale Electronics Inc 20 Oser Ave.............. Hauppauge *Web:* www.rodaleelectronics.com	NY	11788		631-231-0044	231-1345
Ross Laboratories Inc 3138 Fairview Ave E .... Seattle *Web:* www.rosslaboratories.com	WA	98102		206-324-3950	
Rostra Precision Controls Inc 2519 Dana Dr.................................. Laurinburg *TF Cust Svc:* 800-782-3379 ■ *Web:* www.rostra.com	NC	28352		910-276-4853	276-1354
Safe Flight Instrument Corp 20 New King St.............................. White Plains *Web:* www.safeflight.com	NY	10604		914-946-9500	946-7882
SELEX Inc 11300 W 89th St..................... Overland Park *TF:* 800-765-0861 ■ *Web:* us.selex-es.com/	KS	66214		913-495-2600	492-0870
Shadin LP 6831 Oxford St...................... St Louis Park *TF:* 800-328-0584 ■ *Web:* www.shadin.com	MN	55426		952-927-6500	
Solacom Technologies Inc 84 Jean-Proulx........... Gatineau *Web:* www.solacom.com	QC	J8Z1W1		613-693-0641	693-0642
Sonatech Inc 879 Ward Dr..................... Santa Barbara *Web:* channeltechgroup.com/products-and-services/systems/	CA	93111		805-683-1431	690-5388
Spectralux Corp 12335 134th Ct Ne .... Redmond *Web:* www.spectralux.com	WA	98052		425-285-3000	
Sperry Marine Northrop Grumman 1070 Seminole Trl............................ Charlottesville *Web:* www.sperrymarine.com	VA	22901		434-974-2000	974-2259
SSR Engineering 2556 W Woodland Dr .... Anaheim *Web:* www.ssreng.com	CA	92801		714-229-9020	
Stark Aerospace Inc 319 Charleigh D Ford Jr Dr .... Columbus *Web:* www.starkaerospace.com	MS	39701		662-798-4075	
Stewart Warner South Wind Corp 2495 Directors Row Ste F....................... Indianapolis *Web:* www.stewart-warner.com	IN	46241		317-486-2600	
Superior Air Parts Inc 621 S Royal Ln Ste 100 .... Coppell *TF:* 800-420-4727 ■ *Web:* www.superiorairparts.com	TX	75019		972-829-4600	829-4648
Systron Donner Inertial 355 Lennon Ln........... Walnut Creek *TF:* 866-234-4976 ■ *Web:* www.systron.com	CA	94598		925-979-4400	979-9827
Telair International 4175 Guardian St .... Simi Valley *Web:* www.telair.com	CA	93063		805-578-7301	578-7385
Teledyne Benthos Inc 49 Edgerton Dr .... North Falmouth *Web:* www.benthos.com	MA	02556		508-563-1000	563-6444
Teledyne Odom Hydrographic Systems Inc 1450 Seaboard Ave............................ Baton Rouge *Web:* www.odomhydrographic.com	LA	70810		225-769-3051	
Teledyne RD Instruments Inc 14020 Stowe Dr.......... Poway *Web:* www.rdinstruments.com	CA	92064		858-842-2600	
Textron Systems Corp 201 Lowell St .... Wilmington *Web:* textron.com	MA	01887		978-657-5111	657-6644
Thales ATM 23501 W 84th St...................... Shawnee *Web:* www.thalesgroup.com	KS	66227		913-422-2600	422-2917
Thales USA Inc 2733 S Crystal Dr Ste 1200........... Arlington *Web:* www.thalesgroup.com	VA	22202		703-838-9685	838-1688
Tideland Signal Corp PO Box 52430 .... Houston *Web:* www.tidelandsignal.com	TX	77052		713-681-6101	681-6233
Transbotics Corp 3400 Latrobe Dr .... Charlotte *OTC: TNSB* ■ *Web:* www.transbotics.com	NC	28211		704-362-1115	364-4039
Trimble Navigation Ltd 935 Stewart Dr .... Sunnyvale *NASDAQ: TRMB* ■ *TF:* 800-827-8000 ■ *Web:* www.trimble.com	CA	94085		408-481-8000	481-8585
Trutrak Flight Systems Inc 1500 S Old Missouri Rd.......................... Springdale *TF:* 866-878-8725 ■ *Web:* www.trutrakap.com	AR	72764		479-751-0250	
Tyonek Mfg Group Inc 229 Palmer Rd .... Madison *TF:* 877-258-6200 ■ *Web:* www.tyonek.com	AL	35758		256-258-6200	
Ultra Electronics 3Phoenix Inc 14585 Avion Pkwy Ste 200......................... Chantilly *Web:* www.3phoenix.com	VA	20151		703-956-6480	
Union Machine Company of Lynn Inc Six Federal Way .... Groveland *Web:* www.unionmachine.com	MA	01834		978-521-5100	
United Paradyne Corp 2415 Professional Pkwy .... Santa Maria *Web:* www.unitedparadyne.com	CA	93455		805-348-3155	
Van's Aircraft Inc 14401 Keil Rd Ne .... Aurora *Web:* www.vansaircraft.com	OR	97002		503-678-6545	
Vumii Inc 1100 Abernathy Rd 500 Northpark Town Ctr Ste 1100.. Atlanta *Web:* www.vumii.com	GA	30328		678-578-4700	
Wellbore Navigation Inc 15032 Red Hill Ave Ste D .... Tustin *Web:* www.welnavinc.com	CA	92780		714-259-7760	259-9257
Western Methods Machinery Corp 2344 Pullman St................................. Santa Ana	CA	92705		949-252-6600	
Whistler Group Inc 13016 N Walton Blvd........... Bentonville *TF Cust Svc:* 800-531-0004 ■ *Web:* www.whistlergroup.com	AR	72712		479-273-6012	273-3188
Wipaire Inc 1700 Henry Ave.................... South St Paul *TF:* 888-947-2473 ■ *Web:* www.wipaire.com	MN	55075		651-451-1205	
XATA Corp 965 Prairie Ctr Dr..................... Eden Prairie *TF:* 800-745-9282 ■ *Web:* xrscorp.com	MN	55344		952-707-5600	894-2463
Zonar Systems LLC 18200 Cascade Ave S............ Seattle *TF:* 877-843-3847 ■ *Web:* www.zonarsystems.com	WA	98188		206-878-2459	878-3082

533 NEWS SYNDICATES, SERVICES, BUREAUS

			Phone	Fax
AccountingWEB Inc PO Box 2252................ Westerville *TF:* 866-688-1678 ■ *Web:* www.accountingweb.com	OH	43086	866-688-1678	
AccuWeather Inc 385 Science Pk Rd............ State College *TF Sales:* 800-566-6606 ■ *Web:* www.accuweather.com	PA	16803	814-235-8650	238-1339
Aero-News Pob 9132 .... Winter Haven *Web:* www.aero-news.net	FL	33883	863-299-8680	
Africa News Service Inc 922 M St Se .... Washington *Web:* www.allafrica.com	DC	20003	202-546-0777	
Agence France-Presse (AFP) 1500 K St NW Ste 600 .... Washington *Web:* www.afp.com	DC	20005	202-289-0700	414-0525
Al-Wali Corp 401 Thornton Rd .... Lithia Springs *Web:* www.newleaf-dist.com	GA	30122	770-948-7845	
American Baptist News Service PO Box 851 .... Valley Forge *TF:* 800-222-3872 ■ *Web:* www.abc-usa.org	PA	19482	610-768-2000	
American Chiropractor, The 8619 NW 68Th St .... Miami *TF:* 888-369-1396 ■ *Web:* www.theamericanchiropractor.com	FL	33166	888-369-1396	
Anderson Merchandisers LP 421 SE 34th Ave......... Amarillo *Web:* www.amerch.com	TX	79103	806-376-6251	
Andrews McMeel Universal 1130 Walnut.......... Kansas City *TF:* 800-851-8923 ■ *Web:* www.amuniversal.com	MO	64106	816-581-7500	932-6684
Argus Interactive Agency Inc 217 N Main St Ste 200........................... Santa Ana *TF:* 866-595-9597 ■ *Web:* www.argusinteractive.com	CA	92701	866-595-9597	
Associated Press (AP) 450 W 33rd St .... New York *Web:* www.ap.org	NY	10001	212-621-1500	621-1679
Baptist Press 901 Commerce St .... Nashville *Web:* www.sbc.net	TN	37203	615-244-2355	782-8736
Bay News 1624 N Meadowcrest Blvd............... Crystal River *Web:* www.baynews9.com	FL	34429	352-563-2052	
Bloomberg LP 731 Lexington Ave .... New York *Web:* www.bloomberg.com	NY	10022	212-318-2000	893-5000
Bloomberg News 731 Lexington Ave.................. New York **Fax Area Code:* 917 ■ *Web:* www.bloomberg.com	NY	10022	212-318-2000	369-5000*

Name / Address	City	State	Zip	Phone	Fax
Brickyard VFX 2054 Broadway *Web:* www.brickyardvfx.com	Santa Monica	CA	90404	310-453-5722	
Business Wire 44 Montgomery St 39th Fl *Web:* www.businesswire.com	San Francisco	CA	94104	415-986-4422	788-5335
California Newspaper Service Bureau 915 E First St *Web:* dailyjournal.com	Los Angeles	CA	90012	213-229-5500	229-5481
Creators Syndicate Inc 5777 W Century Blvd Ste 700 *TF:* 877-563-4645 ■ *Web:* www.creators.com	Los Angeles	CA	90045	310-337-7003	337-7625
Crystal Pyramid Productions 7323 Rondel Ct *Web:* www.crystalpyramid.com	San Diego	CA	92119	619-644-3000	
Csrwire LLC 250 Albany St *Web:* csrwire.com	Springfield	MA	01105	413-733-5091	
Disaster News Network (DNN) PO Box 1746 *TF:* 888-384-3028 ■ *Web:* www.disasternews.net	Ellicott City	MD	21041	443-393-3330	420-0085
eDirectory 7004 Little River Tpke Ste O *Web:* www.edirectory.com	Annandale	VA	22003	703-914-0770	
Elias Sports Bureau Inc 500 Fifth Ave Ste 2140 *Web:* www.esb.com	New York	NY	10110	212-869-1530	354-0980
FADER Inc, The 71 W 23 St Fl 13 *Web:* www.thefader.com	New York	NY	10010	212-741-7100	
Federal Network Inc (FedNet) 122 C St NW Ste 520 *Web:* www.fednet.net	Washington	DC	20001	202-393-7300	393-5965
Federal News Services 1000 Vermont Ave NW Ste 500 *Web:* www.fednews.com	Washington	DC	20005	202-347-1400	393-4733
FurnitureDealer.net Inc PO Box 22251 *TF:* 866-387-6357 ■ *Web:* www.furnituredealer.net	Eagan	MN	55122	866-387-6357	
Gantec Publishing Solutions LLC 1111 N Plz Dr Ste 652 *Web:* www.gantecpublishing.com	Schaumburg	IL	60173	847-598-1144	
Gateway Newstands 240 Chrislea Rd *TF:* 800-942-5351 ■ *Web:* www.gatewaynewstands.com	Woodbridge	ON	L4L8V1	905-851-9652	
German Press Agency 529 14th St Nw Ste 969 *Web:* www.dpa.com	Washington	DC	20045	202-662-1220	
Hearst News Service 700 12th St NW Ste 1000 *Web:* www.hearst.com	Washington	DC	20005	202-263-6400	263-6441
Hispanic Link Inc 1420 N St NW	Washington	DC	20005	202-234-0280	
Hudson Group One Meadowlands Plz Ste 902 *Web:* www.hudsongroup.com	East Rutherford	NJ	07073	201-939-5050	
Inman News 1100 Marina Village Pkwy Ste 102 *TF:* 800-775-4662 ■ *Web:* www.inman.com	Alameda	CA	94501	510-658-9252	
Jewish Telegraphic Agency Inc 330 Seventh Ave 17th Fl *Web:* www.jta.org	New York	NY	10001	212-643-1890	643-8498
JM DigitalWorks 2460 Impala Dr *Web:* www.jmdigitalworks.com	Carlsbad	CA	92008	760-476-1783	
JUGGLE Magazine 3315 E Russell Rd #A4 203 *Web:* www.juggle.org	Las Vegas	NV	89120	702-798-0099	
Kagan 981 Calle Amanecer *Web:* www.kaganonline.com	San Clemente	CA	92673	949-369-6310	
Kansas Press Assn Inc 5423 SW Seventh St *Web:* www.kspress.com	Topeka	KS	66606	785-271-5304	271-7341
Kearney Hub 13 E 22Nd PO Box 1988 *Web:* www.kearneyhub.com	Kearney	NE	68847	308-237-2152	
King Features Syndicate Inc 300 W 57th St 15th Fl **Fax Area Code:* 646 ■ *TF:* 800-708-7311 ■ *Web:* www.kingfeatures.com	New York	NY	10019	212-969-7550	280-1550*
Lester Catalog Co 9850 Hillview Rd PO Box 1268 *Web:* www.lestercatalog.com	Newcastle	CA	95658	530-823-0963	
Levy Home Entertainment LLC 1420 Kensington Rd Ste 300 *Web:* www.readerlink.com	Oak Brook	IL	60523	708-547-4400	
Los Angeles Times-Washington Post News Service Inc 1150 15th St NW *TF:* 800-627-1150 ■ *Web:* www.washingtonpost.com	Washington	DC	20071	202-334-6000	
Mainebiz Two Cotton St Third Fl *Web:* www.mainebiz.biz	Portland	ME	04101	207-761-8379	
Majon International PO Box 6059 *Web:* www.majon.com	Los Osos	CA	93412	805-528-2100	
Market Wire Inc 100 N Sepulveda Blvd Ste 325 *TF General:* 800-774-9473 ■ *Web:* www.marketwired.com	El Segundo	CA	90245	310-765-3200	765-3297
Metro News Services 150 Dalton Dr *Web:* www.metro-news.com	Desoto	TX	75115	972-230-4277	
Microfinance Information Exchange Inc 1901 Pennsylvania Ave NW Ste 307 *Web:* www.mixmarket.org	Washington	DC	20006	202-659-9094	
New York Times News Service Div 620 Eigth Ave 9th Fl *TF:* 800-698-4637 ■ *Web:* www.nytimes.com	New York	NY	10018	212-556-7652	
NewRetirement LLC 1933 Davis St Ste 205 *TF:* 866-441-0246 ■ *Web:* www.newretirement.com	San Leandro	CA	94111	415-738-2435	
NY1 75 Ninth Ave *Web:* www.ny1.com	New York	NY	10011	212-379-3311	
Oversee.net 515 S Flower St Ste 4400 *Web:* www.oversee.net	Los Angeles	CA	90071	213-408-0080	
Pacific News Service 275 Ninth St *Web:* newamericamedia.org	San Francisco	CA	94103	415-503-4170	503-0970
Postmedia Network Inc 1450 Don Mills Rd *Web:* www.postmedia.com	Don Mills	ON	M3B3X7	416-383-2300	
PR Photos 4521 Pga Blvd *TF:* 866-551-7827 ■ *Web:* www.prphotos.com	Palm Beach Gardens	FL	33418	866-551-7827	
ProductionHUB 1806 Hammerlin Ave *Web:* www.productionhub.com	Winter Park	FL	32789	407-629-4122	
Religion News Service (RNS) 529 14th St NW Ste 425 *TF:* 800-767-6781 ■ *Web:* www.religionnews.com	Washington	DC	20045	202-463-8777	463-0033
SCB Marketing 5131 Industry Dr *Web:* scbmarketing.com	Melbourne	FL	32940	321-622-5986	
Scripps Howard News Service (SHNS) 1090 Vermont Ave NW Ste 1000	Washington	DC	20005	202-408-1484	408-2062
Shalom TV PO Box 1989 *Web:* www.shalomtv.com	Fort Lee	NJ	07024	201-242-9460	
Sofizar Inc 2850 Nantucket Ln *Web:* www.sofizar.com	Carlsbad	CA	92008	760-494-0692	
Softomate LLC 104 Sixth St Unit B *TF:* 877-243-8735 ■ *Web:* www.softomate.com	Lynden	WA	98264	877-243-8735	
Sports Network 2200 Byberry Rd Ste 200 *Web:* www.sportsnetwork.com	Hatboro	PA	19040	215-441-8444	441-9019
Stargate Digital 1001 El Centro St *Web:* www.stargatestudios.net	South Pasadena	CA	91030	626-403-8403	
Stephens Media Group Washington News Bureau 666 11th St NW Ste 535 *Web:* www.stephensmedia.com	Washington	DC	20001	202-783-1760	783-1955
Sticks 809 Central Ave Ste 315 *Web:* www.ssoutdooradventures.com	Fort Dodge	IA	50501	515-573-8898	
StoresOnline Inc 1303 North Research Way Buidling K *Web:* www.storesonline.com	Orem	UT	84097	801-434-8582	
Strategic News Service 38 Yew Ln *Web:* www.tapsns.com	Friday Harbor	WA	98250	360-378-1023	
Streetwise Reports LLC 101 Second St Ste 110 *Web:* www.theaureport.com	Petaluma	CA	94952	707-981-8999	
Talk Radio News Service 236 Massachusetts Ave NE Ste 306 *Web:* www.talkradionews.com	Washington	DC	20002	202-337-5322	337-1174
Tass News Agency 780 Third Ave Rm 1900	New York	NY	10017	212-245-4250	
Texas Fish & Game Magazine 1745 Greens Rd *Web:* www.fishgame.com	Houston	TX	77032	281-227-3001	
United Methodist News Service 810 12th Ave S *TF:* 800-251-8140 ■ *Web:* www.umcom.org	Nashville	TN	37203	615-742-5470	742-5125
United Press International (UPI) 1133 19th St NW *Web:* www.upi.com	Washington	DC	20036	202-898-8000	
Washington Post Writers Group 1150 15th St NW *TF:* 800-879-9794 ■ *Web:* syndication.washingtonpost.com	Washington	DC	20071	202-334-6375	334-5669
Website Magazine Inc 999 E Touhy Ave *Web:* www.websitemagazine.com	Des Plaines	IL	60018	773-628-2779	
Wireless Flash News Service PO Box 633030 *Web:* www.flashnews.com	San Diego	CA	92163	619-220-7191	
World Property Journal 1221 Brickell Ave Ste 900 *Web:* www.worldpropertychannel.com	Miami	FL	33131	305-375-9292	

534 NEWSLETTERS

534-1 Banking & Finance Newsletters

Name / Address	City	State	Zip	Phone	Fax
Banking Daily 1801 S Bell St *TF:* 800-372-1033 ■ *Web:* www.bna.com/banking-daily-p5439	Arlington	VA	22202	800-372-1033	
Bankruptcy Court Decisions 360 Hiatt Dr *TF:* 800-621-5463 ■ *Web:* www.lrp.com	Palm Beach Gardens	FL	33418	561-622-6520	622-2423
Best's Underwriting Newsletter Ambest Rd *Web:* www3.ambest.com/buglcem	Oldwick	NJ	08858	908-439-2200	
BestWeek Life/Health Newsletter Ambest Rd *Web:* www.ambest.com	Oldwick	NJ	08858	908-439-2200	439-3363
BestWeek Property/Casualty Newsletter Ambest Rd *Web:* www3.ambest.com/bestweek/bestweek.asp	Oldwick	NJ	08858	908-439-2200	
Commercial Lending Litigation News 360 Hiatt Dr *TF:* 800-621-5463 ■ *Web:* www.lrp.com	Palm Beach Gardens	FL	33418	561-622-6520	622-2423
Consumer Bankruptcy News 360 Hiatt Dr *TF:* 800-621-5463 ■ *Web:* www.lrp.com	Palm Beach Gardens	FL	33418	561-622-6520	622-2423
Credit Union Directors Newsletter 5710 Mineral Pt Rd **Fax:* Cust Svc ■ *TF:* 800-356-9655 ■ *Web:* www.cuna.org	Madison	WI	53705	608-231-4000	231-1869*
Credit Union Executive Newsletter 5710 Mineral Pt Rd *TF Circ:* 800-356-9655 ■ *Web:* www.cuna.org	Madison	WI	53705	608-231-4000	231-4370
Electronic Commerce & Law Report 1801 S Bell St *TF:* 800-372-1033 ■ *Web:* www.bna.com/electronic-commerce-law-p6796	Arlington	VA	22202	800-372-1033	
Forecaster Newsletter 19623 Ventura Blvd	Tarzana	CA	91356	818-345-4421	
International Business & Finance Daily 1801 S Bell St *TF:* 800-372-1033 ■ *Web:* www.bna.com/international-business-finance-p6707	Arlington	VA	22202	800-372-1033	
International Tax Monitor 1801 S Bell St *TF:* 800-372-1033 ■ *Web:* www.bna.com/international-tax-monitor-p9111	Arlington	VA	22202	800-372-1033	
Louisiana Banker PO Box 2871 *Web:* www.lba.org	Baton Rouge	LA	70821	225-387-3282	343-3159
Money Management Letter 225 Pk Ave S Seventh Fl *Web:* www.moneymanagementintelligence.com	New York	NY	10003	212-224-3300	224-3171
New York Banker 99 Pk Ave Fourth Fl **Fax:* PR ■ *Web:* www.nyba.com	New York	NY	10016	212-297-1600	297-1683*
Security Letter 166 E 96th St	New York	NY	10128	212-348-1553	

				Phone	Fax
Specialty Finance 212 Seventh St NE *Web:* www.snl.com	Charlottesville	VA	22902	434-977-1600	977-4466

534-2 Business & Professional Newsletters

				Phone	Fax
American Speaker PO Box 787 *TF:* 800-791-8699 ■ *Web:* www.americanspeaker.com	Williamsport	PA	17703	570-567-1982	
Antitrust & Trade Regulation Daily 1801 S Bell St. *TF:* 800-372-1033 ■ *Web:* www.bna.com/atrc/	Arlington	VA	22202	800-372-1033	
Authors Guild Bulletin 31 E 32nd St Seventh Fl *Web:* www.authorsguild.org	New York	NY	10016	212-563-5904	564-5363
CD Publications 8204 Fenton St. *TF:* 800-666-6380 ■ *Web:* cdpublications.com/pcodeprocess/pcodes.php?pc=pubs	Silver Spring	MD	20910	301-588-6380	588-6385
Corporate Writer & Editor 111 E Wacker Dr Ste 500 *TF:* 800-878-5331 ■ *Web:* www.ragan.com/main/home.aspx	Chicago	IL	60601	312-960-4140	
Customer Communicator, The (TCC) 712 Main St Ste 187B *TF:* 800-232-4317 ■ *Web:* www.customerservicegroup.com/the_customer_communicator.php	Boonton	NJ	07005	973-265-2300	402-6056
Daily Report for Executives 1801 S Bell St. *TF:* 800-372-1033 ■ *Web:* www.bna.com/daily-report-executives-p6093	Arlington	VA	22202	800-372-1033	
Daily Tax Report 1801 S Bell St. *TF:* 800-372-1033 ■ *Web:* www.bna.com/daily-tax-report-p7889	Arlington	VA	22202	800-372-1033	
Distribution Ctr Management (DCM) 712 Main St Ste 187B *TF:* 800-232-4317 ■ *Web:* www.distributiongroup.com/distribution_center_management.php	Boonton	NJ	07005	973-265-2300	402-6056
Downtown Idea Exchange (DIX) 712 Main St Ste 187B *TF:* 800-232-4317 ■ *Web:* www.downtowndevelopment.com/downtown_idea_exchange.php	Boonton	NJ	07005	973-265-2300	402-6056
Federal EEO Advisor 360 Hiatt Dr *TF:* 800-341-7874 ■ *Web:* www.lrp.com	Palm Beach Gardens	FL	33418	561-622-6520	622-2423
Government Employee Relations Report 1801 S Bell St. *TF:* 800-372-1033 ■ *Web:* www.bna.com/government-employee-relations-p5468	Arlington	VA	22202	800-372-1033	
Human Resources Report 1801 S Bell St. *TF:* 800-372-1033 ■ *Web:* www.bna.com/human-resources-report-p4458	Arlington	VA	22202	800-372-1033	
International Trade Reporter 1801 S Bell St. *TF:* 800-372-1033 ■ *Web:* www.bna.com/international-trade-reporter-p6101	Arlington	VA	22202	800-372-1033	
Journal of Employee Communication Management 316 N Michigan Ave Ste 400 *TF:* 800-878-5331 ■ *Web:* www.ragan.com/main/home.aspx	Chicago	IL	60601	312-960-4100	960-4106
Law Officer's Bulletin 610 Opperman Dr *TF:* 800-344-5008 ■ *Web:* legalsolutions.thomsonreuters.com	Eagan	MN	55123	651-687-7000	
LRP Publications 360 Hiatt Dr *Fax Area Code: 561 ■ *TF:* 800-341-7874 ■ *Web:* www.lrp.com	Palm Beach Gardens	FL	33418	800-341-7874	622-2423*
Manager's Intelligence Report (MIR) 316 N Michigan Ave Ste 400 *Fax Area Code: 312 ■ *TF:* 800-878-5331 ■ *Web:* www.managersintelligencereport.biz	Chicago	IL	60601	800-878-5331	861-3592*
Payroll Practitioner's Monthly Three Bethesda Metro Ctr Ste 250 *TF:* 800-372-1033 ■ *Web:* bna.com/ioma-site-m17179881473/	Bethesda	MD	20814	800-372-1033	253-0332
Ragan Communications Inc 316 N Michigan Ave Ste 400 *TF:* 800-878-5331 ■ *Web:* www.ragan.com/main/home.aspx	Chicago	IL	60601	312-960-4100	960-4106
Teamwork Newsletter 2222 Sedwick Dr *TF:* 800-223-8720 ■ *Web:* www.dartnellcorp.com	Durham	NC	27713	800-223-8720	508-2592
Working Together 360 Hiatt Dr *TF:* 800-621-5463 ■ *Web:* www.lrp.com	Palm Beach Gardens	FL	33418	561-622-6520	622-2423

534-3 Computer & Internet Newsletters

				Phone	Fax
Biotechnology Software 140 Huguenot St Third Fl *TF:* 800-654-3237 ■ *Web:* www.liebertpub.com	New Rochelle	NY	10801	914-740-2100	740-2109
Business Intelligence Advisor 37 Broadway Ste 1 *TF:* 800-964-5118 ■ *Web:* www.cutter.com	Arlington	MA	02474	781-648-8700	648-8707
Computer Economics Report, The 2082 Business Ctr Dr Ste 240 *TF:* 800-326-8100 ■ *Web:* www.computereconomics.com	Irvine	CA	92612	949-831-8700	442-7688
Cutter Consortium 37 Broadway Ste 1 *TF:* 800-964-5118 ■ *Web:* www.cutter.com	Arlington	MA	02474	781-648-8700	648-8707
Cutter IT Journal 37 Broadway Ste 1 *TF:* 800-964-5118 ■ *Web:* cutter.com/error404.html;jsessionid=00256af719f76acc1cf2ebc2a9ccd19f	Arlington	MA	02474	781-648-8700	648-8707
Electronic Information Report 60 Longridge Rd Ste 300 *Web:* simbainformation.com/	Stamford	CT	06902	203-325-8193	325-8915
Microprocessor Report 355 Chesley Ave *Fax Area Code: 650 ■ *Web:* www.linleygroup.com	Mountain View	CA	94040	408-270-3772	745-1490*
Network World Inc 492 Old Connecticut Path *Fax Area Code: 508 ■ *TF:* 800-622-1108 ■ *Web:* www.networkworld.com/newsletters/techexec/index.html	Framingham	MA	01701	800-622-1108	460-1192*
Technology News of America 123 Seventh Ave *Web:* www.tech-news.com	Brooklyn	NY	11215	718-369-7682	965-3039
Washington Internet Daily 2115 Ward Ct NW *TF:* 800-771-9202 ■ *Web:* www.warren-news.com	Washington	DC	20037	202-872-9200	293-3435

534-4 Education Newsletters

				Phone	Fax
Early Childhood Report 360 Hiatt Dr *TF:* 800-621-5463 ■ *Web:* www.lrp.com	Palm Beach Gardens	FL	33418	561-622-6520	622-2423
Education Grants Alert 360 Hiatt Dr *TF:* 800-621-5463 ■ *Web:* www.lrp.com	Palm Beach Gardens	FL	33418	561-622-6520	622-2423
Educational Research Newsletter PO Box 2347 *Fax Area Code: 815 ■ *TF:* 800-321-7471 ■ *Web:* www.ernweb.com	South Portland	ME	04116	207-632-1954	461-5647*
Electronic Education Report 60 Longridge Rd Ste 300 *Fax: Sales ■ *Web:* simbainformation.com/	Stamford	CT	06902	203-325-8193	325-8915*
Library of Congress Information Bulletin 101 Independence Ave SE *TF:* 888-371-5848 ■ *Web:* www.loc.gov/loc/lcib	Washington	DC	20540	202-707-2905	707-9199
New Jersey Law Journal 238 Mulberry St *Web:* www.law.com	Newark	NJ	07102	973-642-0075	642-0920
New York Education Law Report 360 Hiatt Dr *Fax: Edit ■ *TF:* 800-341-7874 ■ *Web:* www.lrp.com	Palm Beach	FL	33418	561-622-6520	622-1375*
School Law News 360 Hiatt Dr. *Fax Area Code: 561 ■ *TF:* 800-341-7874 ■ *Web:* www.lrp.com	Palm Beach Gardens	FL	33418	800-341-7874	622-2423*
Special Education Report 360 Hiatt Dr *TF Sales:* 800-621-5463 ■ *Web:* www.lrp.com	Palm Beach Gardens	FL	33418	561-622-6520	622-2423

534-5 Energy & Environmental Newsletters

				Phone	Fax
Chemical Regulation Reporter 1801 S Bell St. *TF:* 800-372-1033 ■ *Web:* www.bna.com/chemical-regulation-reporter-p4750	Arlington	VA	22202	800-372-1033	
Clean Air Report 1919 S Eads St Ste 201 *TF:* 800-424-9068 ■ *Web:* www.insideepa.com	Arlington	VA	22202	703-416-8516	416-8543
Coal Outlook 1200 G St NW Ste 1100 *TF:* 800-752-8878 ■ *Web:* www.platts.com	Washington	DC	20005	212-904-3070	904-4209
Daily Environment Report 1801 S Bell St *TF:* 800-372-1033 ■ *Web:* www.bna.com/daily-environment-report-p4751	Arlington	VA	22202	800-372-1033	
Electric Utility Week Two Penn Plz 25th Fl *TF:* 800-752-8878 ■ *Web:* www.platts.com	New York	NY	10121	212-904-3070	904-3738
Environment Reporter 1801 S Bell St *TF:* 800-372-1033 ■ *Web:* www.bna.com/environment-reporter-p4885	Arlington	VA	22202	800-372-1033	
Environmental Compliance Bulletin 1801 S Bell St. *TF:* 800-372-1033 ■ *Web:* www.bna.com/environmental-compliance-bulletin-p4886	Arlington	VA	22202	800-372-1033	
Gas Daily 1200 G St NW Ste 1000 *TF:* 800-752-8878 ■ *Web:* www.platts.com/products/gasdaily	Washington	DC	20005	202-383-2000	383-2024
Global Power Report Two Penn Plz 25th Fl *Fax Area Code: 212 ■ *TF:* 800-752-8878 ■ *Web:* www.platts.com	New York	NY	10121	800-752-8878	904-3738*
Inside Energy Two Penn Plz 25th Fl *Fax Area Code: 212 ■ *TF:* 800-752-8878 ■ *Web:* www.platts.com	New York	NY	10121	800-752-8878	904-2723*
Inside FERC Two Penn Plz 25th Fl *Fax Area Code: 212 ■ *TF:* 800-752-8878 ■ *Web:* www.platts.com	New York	NY	10121	800-752-8878	904-2723*
Inside FERC's Gas Market Report Two Penn Plz 25th Fl *TF:* 800-752-8878 ■ *Web:* www.platts.com	New York	NY	10121	212-904-3070	904-3738
Inside NRC Two Penn Plz 25th Fl *Fax Area Code: 212 ■ *TF:* 800-752-8878 ■ *Web:* www.platts.com	New York	NY	10121	800-752-8878	904-3738*
Megawatt Daily Two Penn Plz 25th Fl. *Fax Area Code: 800 ■ *Web:* platts.com/products/megawatt-daily	New York	NY	10121	212-904-3070	752-8878*
Northeast Power Report Two Penn Plz 25th Fl *Fax Area Code: 212 ■ *TF:* 800-752-8878 ■ *Web:* www.platts.com	New York	NY	10121	800-752-8878	904-2723*
NuclearFuel 1200 G St NW Ste 1000 *TF:* 800-228-9290 ■ *Web:* platts.com/products/nuclear-fuel	Washington	DC	20005	202-383-2000	383-2024
Nucleonics Week 2 Penn Plaza 25th Fl *TF:* 800-752-8878 ■ *Web:* platts.com/products/nucleonics-week	New York	NY	10121	212-904-3070	
Oil Price Information Service 3349 Hwy 138 Bldg D Ste D *TF Cust Svc:* 888-301-2645 ■ *Web:* www.opisnet.com	Wall	NJ	07719	732-901-8800	
OPIS 9737 Washingtonian Blvd Ste 100 *TF:* 888-301-2645 ■ *Web:* www.opisnet.com	Gaithersburg	MD	20878	301-287-2645	287-2820
Solid Waste Assn of North America (SWANA) 1100 Wayne Ave Ste 700 *TF:* 800-467-9262 ■ *Web:* swana.org	Silver Spring	MD	20910	301-585-2898	589-7068
State Environment Daily 1801 S Bell St. *TF:* 800-372-1033 ■ *Web:* www.bna.com/state-environment-daily-p4905	Arlington	VA	22202	800-372-1033	
Toxics Law Reporter 1801 S Bell St *TF:* 800-372-1033 ■ *Web:* www.bna.com/toxics-law-reporter-p5947	Arlington	VA	22202	800-372-1033	
Utility Environment Report Two Penn Plz 25th Fl *Fax Area Code: 212 ■ *TF:* 800-752-8878 ■ *Web:* www.platts.com	New York	NY	10121	800-752-8878	904-3738*
Water Tech Online 19 British American Blvd W. *Web:* www.watertechonline.com	Latham	NY	12110	518-783-1281	783-1386

534-6 General Interest Newsletters

				Phone	Fax
Bottom Line/Personal 281 Tresser Blvd Eighth Fl *Fax Area Code: 203 ■ *Fax: Edit ■ *TF Cust Svc:* 800-678-5835 ■ *Web:* blinepubs.com	Stamford	CT	06901	800-274-5611	967-3621*
FRM Weekly 54 Adams St.	Garden City	NY	11530	516-746-6700	294-8141
Kiplinger California Letter 1729 H St NW *TF:* 800-544-0155 ■ *Web:* www.kiplinger.com	Washington	DC	20006	202-887-6400	778-8976

	Phone	Fax
NRTA/AARP Bulletin 601 E St NW .... Washington DC 20049 *Fax: Hum Res ■ TF: 888-867-2277 ■ Web: aarp.org/about-aarp/nrta/	202-434-2277	434-2809*
Preferred Traveler 4501 Forbes Blvd .... Lanham MD 20706 *Fax Area Code: 781 ■ *Fax: Edit ■ Web: www.preferredtraveller.com	703-644-6844	849-2947*
Sotheby's Newsletter 1334 York Ave .... New York NY 10021 *Fax: Hum Res ■ Web: www.sothebys.com	212-606-7000	606-7107*

534-7 Government & Law Newsletters

	Phone	Fax
Alcoholic Beverage Control PO Box 27491 .... Richmond VA 23261 TF: 800-552-3200 ■ Web: www.abc.virginia.gov/enforce/offices.html	804-213-4565	213-4574
American Association for Justice 777 6th St NW Ste 200 .... Washington DC 20001 TF: 800-424-2727 ■ Web: www.justice.org	202-965-3500	625-7084
Bankruptcy Law Letter 610 Opperman Dr .... Eagan MN 55123 TF: 800-937-8529 ■ Web: legalsolutions.thomsonreuters.com	651-687-7000	687-8722
BD Week 9737 Washingtonian Blvd Ste 100 .... Gaithersburg MD 20878 *Fax Area Code: 301 ■ TF: 866-777-8567 ■ Web: iawatch.com	646-223-6771	287-2070*
Bioethics Legal Review 1617 JFK Blvd Ste 1750 .... Philadelphia PA 19103 TF: 877-256-2472 ■ Web: www.lawjournalnewsletters.com	215-557-2300	557-2301
Class Action Litigation Report 1801 S Bell St .... Arlington VA 22202 TF: 800-372-1033 ■ Web: www.bna.com/class-action-litigation-p5442	800-372-1033	
Community Development Digest 8204 Fenton St .... Silver Spring MD 20910 TF: 800-666-6380 ■ Web: www.cdpublications.com	301-588-6380	588-6385
Community Health Funding Week 8204 Fenton St .... Silver Spring MD 20910 TF: 800-666-6380 ■ Web: www.cdpublications.com	301-588-6380	588-0519
Computer Technology Law Report 1801 S Bell St .... Arlington VA 22202 TF: 800-372-1033 ■ Web: www.bna.com/computer-technology-law-p6795	800-372-1033	
Congress Daily 600 New Hampshire Ave The Watergate .... Washington DC 20037 TF: 800-424-2921 ■ Web: nationaljournal.com	202-266-7000	
Congressional Quarterly Budget Tracker 77 K St NE .... Washington DC 20002 TF: 800-432-2250 ■ Web: corporate.cqrollcall.com/products-services	202-650-6500	650-6740
Congressional Quarterly HealthBeat 77 K St NE .... Washington DC 20002 *Fax Area Code: 800 ■ TF: 800-432-2250 ■ Web: www.cq.com	202-650-6500	380-3810*
Congressional Quarterly House Action Reports 77 K St NE .... Washington DC 20002 *Fax Area Code: 800 ■ TF: 800-432-2250 ■ Web: www.cq.com	202-650-6500	380-3810*
Consumer Financial Services Law Report 360 Hiatt Dr .... Palm Beach Gardens FL 33418 TF: 800-621-5463 ■ Web: www.lrp.com	561-622-6520	622-2423
Corporate Compliance & Regulatory 1617 JFK Blvd Ste 1750 .... Philadelphia PA 19103 TF: 877-256-2472 ■ Web: www.lawjournalnewsletters.com	215-557-2300	557-2301
Criminal Law Reporter 1801 S Bell St .... Arlington VA 22202 TF: 800-372-1033 ■ Web: www.bna.com/criminal-law-reporter-p5446	800-372-1033	
Daily Labor Report 1801 S Bell St .... Arlington VA 22202 TF: 800-372-1033 ■ Web: www.bna.com/daily-labor-report-p5449	800-372-1033	
Development Director's Letter 8204 Fenton St .... Silver Spring MD 20910 TF: 800-666-6380 ■ Web: cdpublications.com/pcodeprocess/pcodes.php?pc=pubs	301-588-6380	588-6385
Disability Law Compliance Report 610 Opperman Dr .... Eagan MN 55123 TF Cust Svc: 800-328-4880 ■ Web: legalsolutions.thomsonreuters.com	651-687-7000	687-8722
e-Commerce Law & Strategy 1617 JFK Blvd Ste 1750 .... Philadelphia PA 19103 TF: 877-256-2472 ■ Web: www.lawjournalnewsletters.com	215-557-2300	557-2301
e-Discovery Law & Strategy 1617 JFK Blvd Ste 1750 .... Philadelphia PA 19103 TF: 877-256-2472 ■ Web: www.lawjournalnewsletters.com	215-557-2300	557-2301
Employment Discrimination Report 1801 S Bell St .... Arlington VA 22202 TF: 800-372-1033 ■ Web: www.bna.com/employment-discrimination-report-p5458	800-372-1033	
Expert Evidence Report 1801 S Bell St .... Arlington VA 22202 TF: 800-372-1033 ■ Web: www.bna.com/expert-evidence-report-p5463	800-372-1033	
Family Law Reporter 1801 S Bell St .... Arlington VA 22202 TF: 800-372-1033 ■ Web: www.bna.com/family-law-reporter-p6014	800-372-1033	
Federal Assistance Monitor 8204 Fenton St .... Silver Spring MD 20910 TF: 800-666-6380 ■ Web: www.cdpublications.com	301-588-6380	588-6385
Federal Contracts Report 1801 S Bell St .... Arlington VA 22202 TF: 800-372-1033 ■ Web: www.bna.com/federal-contracts-report-p6016	800-372-1033	
Franchising Business & Law Alert 1617 JFK Blvd Ste 1750 .... Philadelphia PA 19103 TF: 877-256-2472 ■ Web: www.lawjournalnewsletters.com	215-557-2300	557-2301
Health Care Fraud Report 1801 S Bell St .... Arlington VA 22202 TF: 800-372-1033 ■ Web: www.bna.com/health-care-fraud-p6025	800-372-1033	
Health Law Reporter 1801 S Bell St .... Arlington VA 22202 TF: 800-372-1033 ■ Web: www.bna.com/health-law-reporter-p6785	800-372-1033	
Homeland Security Funding Week 8204 Fenton St .... Silver Spring MD 20910 TF: 800-666-6380 ■ Web: www.cdpublications.com	301-588-6380	588-6385
Hospital Litigation Reporter 590 Dutch Vly Rd NE .... Atlanta GA 30324 TF: 800-926-7926 ■ Web: www.straffordpub.com	404-881-1141	881-0074
Hospitality Law 360 Hiatt Dr .... Palm Beach Gardens FL 33418 TF: 800-621-5463 ■ Web: www.lrp.com	561-622-6520	622-2423
Insurance Coverage Law Bulletin, The 1617 JFK Blvd Ste 1750 .... Philadelphia PA 19103 TF: 877-256-2472 ■ Web: www.lawjournalnewsletters.com	215-557-2300	557-2301
Internet Law & Strategy 1617 JFK Blvd Ste 1750 .... Philadelphia PA 19103 TF: 877-256-2472 ■ Web: www.lawjournalnewsletters.com	215-557-2300	557-2301
IRS Practice Adviser 1801 S Bell St .... Arlington VA 22202 TF: 800-372-1033 ■ Web: www.bna.com/irs-practice-adviser-p7876	800-372-1033	
Kiplinger Tax Letter 1729 H St NW .... Washington DC 20006 TF: 800-544-0155 ■ Web: www.kiplinger.com	202-887-6400	778-8976
Medical Research Law & Policy Report 1801 S Bell St .... Arlington VA 22202 TF: 800-372-1033 ■ Web: www.bna.com/medical-research-law-p6788	800-372-1033	
Medicare Compliance Alert 11300 Rockville Pk Ste 1100 .... Rockville MD 20852 TF: 800-929-4824 ■ Web: store.decisionhealth.com	301-287-2700	816-8945
Mergers & Acquisitions Law Report 1801 S Bell St .... Arlington VA 22202 TF: 800-372-1033 ■ Web: www.bna.com/mergers-acquisitions-law-p5940	800-372-1033	
Money & Politics Report 1801 S Bell St .... Arlington VA 22202 TF: 800-372-1033 ■ Web: www.bna.com/money-politics-report-p6103	800-372-1033	
Municipal Litigation Reporter 590 Dutch Vly Rd NE .... Atlanta GA 30324 TF: 800-926-7926 ■ Web: www.straffordpub.com	404-881-1141	881-0074
Patent Trademark & Copyright Law Daily 1801 S Bell St .... Arlington VA 22202 TF: 800-372-1033 ■ Web: www.bna.com/patent-trademark-copyright-daily-p5943	800-372-1033	
Pharmaceutical Law & Industry Report 1801 S Bell St .... Arlington VA 22202 TF: 800-372-1033 ■ Web: www.bna.com/pharmaceutical-law-industry-p6790	800-372-1033	
Privacy & Security Law Report 1801 S Bell St .... Arlington VA 22202 TF: 800-372-1033 ■ Web: www.bna.com/privacy-security-law-p6713	800-372-1033	
Private Security Case Law Reporter 590 Dutch Vly Rd NE PO Box 13729 .... Atlanta GA 30324 TF: 800-926-7926 ■ Web: www.straffordpub.com/products/psc	404-881-1141	881-0074
Real Estate Law Report 610 Opperman Dr .... Eagan MN 55123 *Fax Area Code: 800 ■ *Fax: Sales ■ TF Cust Svc: 800-328-4880 ■ Web: legalsolutions.thomsonreuters.com	651-687-7000	741-1414*
Roll Call 77 K St NE .... Washington DC 20002 TF: 800-432-2250 ■ Web: www.rollcall.com	202-650-6500	824-0475
Securities Law Daily 1801 S Bell St .... Arlington VA 22202 TF: 800-372-1033 ■ Web: www.bna.com/securities-law-daily-p5944	800-372-1033	
Securities Regulation & Law Report 1801 S Bell St .... Arlington VA 22202 TF: 800-372-1033 ■ Web: www.bna.com/securities-regulation-law-p5945	800-372-1033	
UCG Holdings 11300 Rockville Pike Ste 1100 .... Rockville MD 20852 TF: 800-929-4824 ■ Web: www.ucg.com	301-287-2700	816-8945
Virginia Dept of Taxation 1957 Westmoreland St PO Box 1115 .... Richmond VA 23230 TF: 800-828-1120 ■ Web: www.tax.virginia.gov	804-367-8037	254-6111
Washington International Business Report 818 Connecticut Ave NW 12th Fl .... Washington DC 20006 Web: www.ibgc.com	202-872-8181	872-8696
Workplace Law Report 1801 S Bell St .... Arlington VA 22202 TF: 800-372-1033 ■ Web: www.bna.com/workplace-law-report-p5953	800-372-1033	
World Securities Law Report 1801 S Bell St .... Arlington VA 22202 TF: 800-372-1033 ■ Web: www.bna.com	800-372-1033	

534-8 Health & Social Issues Newsletters

	Phone	Fax
Affordable Housing Update 8204 Fenton St .... Silver Spring MD 20910 TF: 800-666-6380 ■ Web: www.cdpublications.com	301-588-6380	588-6385
Aging News Alert 8204 Fenton St .... Silver Spring MD 20910 TF: 800-666-6380 ■ Web: cdpublications.com/pcodeprocess/pcodes.php?pc=pubs	301-588-6385	588-6385
AICR Newsletter 1759 R St NW .... Washington DC 20009 TF: 800-843-8114 ■ Web: www.aicr.org	202-328-7744	328-7226
American Parkinson's Disease Assn Newsletter 135 Parkinson Ave .... Staten Island NY 10305 TF: 800-223-2732 ■ Web: www.apdaparkinson.org	718-981-8001	981-4399
APCO Bulletin 351 N Williamson Blvd .... Daytona Beach FL 32114 TF: 888-272-6911 ■ Web: www.apcointl.org	386-322-2500	322-2501
Cancer Letter PO Box 9905 .... Washington DC 20016 TF: 800-513-7042 ■ Web: www.cancerletter.com	202-362-1809	379-1787
Cancer Letter Business & Regulatory Report PO Box 9905 .... Washington DC 20016 TF: 800-513-7042 ■ Web: www.cancerletter.com	202-362-1809	379-1787
Children & Youth Funding Report 8204 Fenton St .... Silver Spring MD 20910 TF: 800-666-6380 ■ Web: www.cdpublications.com/cyf	301-588-6380	588-6385
Congressional Quarterly HealthBeat 77 K St NE .... Washington DC 20002 *Fax Area Code: 800 ■ TF: 800-432-2250 ■ Web: www.cq.com	202-650-6500	380-3810*
Consumer Reports On Health 101 Truman Ave .... Yonkers NY 10703 TF: 800-234-1645 ■ Web: www.consumerreports.org	914-378-2000	378-2900
Dairy Council Digest 10255 W Higgins Rd Ste 900 .... Rosemont IL 60018 TF Cust Svc: 800-426-8271 ■ Web: www.nationaldairycouncil.org	847-803-2000	803-2077
Disability Funding Week 8204 Fenton St .... Silver Spring MD 20910 *Fax Area Code: 301 ■ TF: 800-666-6380 ■ Web: cdpublications.com/pcodeprocess/pcodes.php?pc=pubs	800-666-6380	588-6385*
Dr. Sinatra 95 Old Shoals Rd .... Arden NC 28704 TF: 800-304-1708 ■ Web: www.drsinatra.com	800-304-1708	
Environment of Care Leader 9737 Washintonian Blvd Ste 100 .... Gaithersburg MD 20878 TF Cust Svc: 800-929-4824 ■ Web: www.ucg.com	301-287-2700	287-2039
Harvard Men's Health Watch 10 Shattuck St .... Boston MA 02115 Web: www.health.harvard.edu	617-432-1370	
Harvard Women's Health Watch PO Box 9308 .... Big Sandy TX 75755 TF: 877-649-9457 ■ Web: www.health.harvard.edu	877-649-9457	

	City	State	Zip	Phone	Fax
Health After 50 500 Fifth Ave Ste 1900 *TF:* 800-829-0422 ■ *Web:* www.johnshopkinshealthalerts.com	New York	NY	10110	800-829-0422	
Health Care Daily Report 1801 S Bell St *TF:* 800-372-1033 ■ *Web:* www.bna.com/health-care-daily-p6781	Arlington	VA	22202	800-372-1033	
Health Care Policy Report 1801 S Bell St *TF:* 800-372-1033 ■ *Web:* www.bna.com/health-care-policy-p6782	Arlington	VA	22202	800-372-1033	
Health Law Week 590 Dutch Vly Rd NE *TF:* 800-926-7926 ■ *Web:* www.straffordpub.com	Atlanta	GA	30324	404-881-1141	881-0074
Healthcare Disparities Report 8204 Fenton St *TF:* 800-666-6380 ■ *Web:* www.cdpublications.com	Silver Spring	MD	20910	301-588-6385	588-6380
Home Health Line 11300 Rockville Pk Ste 1100 *TF:* 800-929-4824 ■ *Web:* www.ucg.com	Rockville	MD	20852	301-287-2700	816-8945
International Medical Device Regulatory Monitor 300 N Washington St Ste 200 *TF:* 888-838-5578 ■ *Web:* fdanews.com/publications/18	Falls Church	VA	22046	703-538-7600	538-7676
Mayo Clinic Health Letter 200 First St NW **Fax Area Code:* 507 ■ *Web:* store.mayoclinic.com	Rochester	MN	55905	800-291-1128	284-0252*
Mayo Clinic Women's Healthsource 200 First St SW **Fax Area Code:* 507 ■ *Web:* store.mayoclinic.com	Rochester	MN	55905	800-291-1128	284-0252*
Medicare Compliance Alert 11300 Rockville Pk Ste 1100 *TF:* 800-929-4824 ■ *Web:* store.decisionhealth.com	Rockville	MD	20852	301-287-2700	816-8945
Nutrition Action 1875 Connecticut Way NW Ste 300 *Web:* www.cspinet.org	Washington	DC	20009	202-332-9110	265-4954
OSHA Up-to-Date Newsletter 1121 Spring Lk Dr *TF Cust Svc:* 800-621-7615 ■ *Web:* www.nsc.org	Itasca	IL	60143	630-285-1121	285-1315

534-9 Investment Newsletters

	City	State	Zip	Phone	Fax
Bert Dohmen's Wellington Letter 1100 Glendon Ave Ste 1130 Westwood Ctr *Web:* dohmencapital.com	Los Angeles	CA	90024	310-208-6622	208-1038
Cabot Market Letter 176 N St PO Box 2049 *TF Orders:* 800-387-8588 ■ *Web:* www.cabot.net	Salem	MA	01970	978-745-5532	745-1283
Chartist Newsletter PO Box 758 *TF:* 800-942-4278 ■ *Web:* thechartist.com	Seal Beach	CA	90740	562-596-2385	
Commodity Research Bureau 330 S Wells St Ste 612 *TF:* 800-621-5271 ■ *Web:* www.crbtrader.com	Chicago	IL	60606	312-554-8456	939-4135
Dow Theory Forecasts 7412 Calumet Ave **Fax Area Code:* 219 ■ *TF:* 800-233-5922 ■ *Web:* www.dowtheory.com	Hammond	IN	46324	800-233-5922	931-6487*
DRIP Investor 7412 Calumet Ave *Web:* www.dripinvestor.com	Hammond	IN	46324	219-852-3200	931-6487
Elliott Wave Theorist 200 Main St *TF:* 800-336-1618 ■ *Web:* www.elliottwave.com	Gainesville	GA	30501	770-536-0309	536-2514
Fabian's Investment Resources 300 New Jersey Ave NW Ste 500 *TF:* 800-950-8765 ■ *Web:* www.fabian.com	Washington	DC	20001	267-295-8713	
Global Market Perspective PO Box 1618 *TF:* 800-336-1618 ■ *Web:* www.elliottwave.com/products/gmp	Gainesville	GA	30503	770-536-0309	536-2514
Gold Newsletter PO Box 84900 *TF:* 800-877-8847 ■ *Web:* jeffersoncompanies.com	Phoenix	AZ	85071	800-877-8847	
Growth Fund Guide 4020 Jackson Blvd *Web:* marketwatch.com	Rapid City	SD	57702	605-341-1971	
Investment Quality Trends (IQT) 2888 Loker Ave E Ste 116 **Fax Area Code:* 866 ■ *Web:* www.iqtrends.com	Carlsbad	CA	92010	858-459-3818	927-5251*
Option Advisor 5151 Pfeiffer Rd Ste 250 *TF:* 800-448-2080 ■ *Web:* www.schaeffersresearch.com	Cincinnati	OH	45242	513-589-3800	589-3810
Personal Finance Newsletter 7600A Leesburg Pk W Bldg Ste 300 *TF:* 800-832-2330 ■ *Web:* www.investingdaily.com	Falls Church	VA	22043	703-394-4931	905-8100
Peter Dag Portfolio Strategy & Management, The 65 Lk Front Dr *Web:* www.peterdag.com	Akron	OH	44319	330-644-2782	
Profitable Investing 9201 Corporate Blvd *TF:* 800-219-8592 ■ *Web:* www.profitableinvesting.investorplace.com	Rockville	MD	20850	301-250-2200	
Richard Young's Intelligence Report 700 Indian Springs Dr *TF Cust Svc:* 800-219-8592 ■ *Web:* intelligencereport.investorplace.com	Lancaster	PA	17601	800-219-8592	
Systems & Forecasts 150 Great Neck Rd Ste 301 *TF:* 800-982-4372 ■ *Web:* www.systemsandforecasts.com	Great Neck	NY	11021	516-829-6444	466-4676
Utility Forecaster 7600A Leesburg Pk W Bldg Ste 300 *TF:* 800-832-2330 ■ *Web:* www.investingdaily.com	Falls Church	VA	22043	703-394-4931	905-8100
Value Line 600 220 E 42nd St Sixth Fl *Web:* www.valueline.com	New York	NY	10017	212-907-1500	907-1922
Value Line Convertibles Survey 220 E 42nd St Sixth Fl *Web:* www.valueline.com	New York	NY	10017	212-907-1500	907-1922
Value Line Investment Survey 220 E 42nd St Sixth Fl *Web:* www.valueline.com	New York	NY	10017	212-907-1500	
Value Line Mutual Funds Survey 220 E 42nd St Sixth Fl *Web:* www.valueline.com	New York	NY	10017	212-907-1500	
Value Line Options Survey 485 Lexington Ave Ninth Fl *Web:* www.valueline.com	New York	NY	10017	212-907-1500	907-1922
Wall Street Letter 225 Pk Ave S Seventh Fl *Web:* www.wallstreetletter.com	New York	NY	10003	212-268-4910	224-3491

534-10 Marketing & Sales Newsletters

	City	State	Zip	Phone	Fax
Book Marketing Update P O Box 2887 *TF:* 888-468-7386 ■ *Web:* www.bookmarket.com	Taos	NM	87571	575-751-3398	751-3398
Downtown Promotion Reporter (DPR) 712 Main St Ste 187B *TF:* 800-232-4317 ■ *Web:* downtowndevelopment.com/downtown_promotion_reporter.php	Boonton	NJ	07005	973-265-2300	402-6056
Educational Marketer 60 Long Ridge Rd Ste 300 *Web:* educationalmarketer.net	Stamford	CT	06902	203-325-8193	325-8975
Marketing Library Services 143 Old Marlton Pk *TF:* 800-300-9868 ■ *Web:* www.infotoday.com/mls	Medford	NJ	08055	609-654-6266	654-4309
Sales Leader 2222 Sedwick Dr Ste 101 *TF:* 800-223-8720 ■ *Web:* www.dartnellcorp.com	Durham	NC	27713	800-223-8720	508-2592

534-11 Media & Communications Newsletters

	City	State	Zip	Phone	Fax
Book Publishing Report 60 Long Ridge Rd Ste 300 *Web:* www.bookpublishingreport.com	Stamford	CT	06902	203-325-8193	325-8915
Broadcasters Letter 1400 Independence Ave SW *Web:* www.usda.gov	Washington	DC	20250	202-720-4623	720-5773
Children's Book Insider 901 Columbia Rd *Web:* writeforkids.org	Fort Collins	CO	80525	970-495-0056	493-1810
Communications Daily 2115 Ward Ct NW *TF:* 800-771-9202 ■ *Web:* www.warren-news.com	Washington	DC	20037	202-872-9200	293-3435
First Draft 316 N Michigan Ave Ste 400 **Fax Area Code:* 312 ■ *TF:* 800-878-5331 ■ *Web:* www.ragan.com/main/home.aspx	Chicago	IL	60601	800-493-4867	960-4106*
Jack O'Dwyer's PR Newsletter 271 Madison Ave Ste 600 *Web:* www.odwyerpr.com	New York	NY	10016	212-679-2471	683-2750
Media Industry Newsletter (MIN) 110 William St 11th Fl *TF:* 888-707-5814 ■ *Web:* www.minonline.com	New York	NY	10038	212-621-4880	621-4879
Media Law Reporter 1801 S Bell St *TF:* 800-372-1033 ■ *Web:* www.bna.com/media-law-reporter-p5934	Arlington	VA	22202	800-372-1033	
Media Relations Report 316 N Michigan Ave Ste 400 *TF:* 800-878-5331 ■ *Web:* www.ragan.com	Chicago	IL	60601	312-960-4100	960-4106
Professional Publishing Report 60 Long Ridge Rd Ste 300 *Web:* simbainformation.com/	Stamford	CT	06902	203-325-8193	325-8915
Speechwriter's Newsletter 316 N Michigan Ave Ste 400 *TF:* 800-878-5331 ■ *Web:* www.ragan.com/main/home.aspx	Chicago	IL	60601	312-960-4100	960-4106
State Telephone Regulation Report 2115 Ward Ct NW *TF:* 800-771-9202 ■ *Web:* www.warren-news.com	Washington	DC	20037	202-872-9200	293-3435
Telecom AM 2115 Ward Ct NW *TF:* 800-771-9202 ■ *Web:* www.warren-news.com	Washington	DC	20037	202-872-9200	293-3435
Telecommunications Report 76 Ninth Ave Seventh Fl *Web:* www.aspenpublishers.com	New York	NY	10011	212-771-0600	
TR's Last-Mile Telecom Report 1333 H St NW Ste 100 *Web:* www.tr.com/newsletters/lmtr	Washington	DC	20005	202-312-6060	312-6111

534-12 Science & Technology Newsletters

	City	State	Zip	Phone	Fax
Flame Retardancy News 49 Walnut Pk Bldg 2 *TF:* 866-285-7215 ■ *Web:* www.bccresearch.com	Wellesley	MA	02481	781-489-7301	253-3933
Food Ingredient News 49 Walnut Pk Bldg 2 *TF:* 866-285-7215 ■ *Web:* www.bccresearch.com	Wellesley	MA	02481	781-489-7301	253-3933
Frost & Sullivan 7550 IH 10 W Ste 400 **Fax Area Code:* 888 ■ *TF:* 877-463-7678 ■ *Web:* www.frost.com	San Antonio	TX	78229	210-348-1000	690-3329*
Genetic Engineering News 140 Huguenot St 3rd Fl *TF:* 800-799-9436 ■ *Web:* www.genengnews.com	New Rochelle	NY	10801	914-740-2100	740-2101
Geophysical Research Letter 2000 Florida Ave NW *TF:* 800-966-2481 ■ *Web:* onlinelibrary.wiley.com	Washington	DC	20009	202-462-6900	328-0566
Physical Review Letters One Research Rd *Web:* aps.org	Ridge	NY	11961	631-591-4000	

534-13 Trade & Industry Newsletters

	City	State	Zip	Phone	Fax
AviationWeek 1200 G St NW Ste 900 **Fax Area Code:* 202 ■ *TF:* 800-525-5003 ■ *Web:* www.aviationweek.com/businessaviation.aspx	Washington	DC	20005	800-525-5003	383-2438*
Construction Claims Monthly 2222 Sedwick Dr *TF:* 800-223-8720 ■ *Web:* www.constructionclaimsmonthly.org	Durham	NC	27713	800-223-8720	508-2592
Construction Labor Report 1801 S Bell St *TF:* 800-372-1033 ■ *Web:* www.bna.com/construction-labor-report-p6002	Arlington	VA	22202	800-372-1033	
Cotton's Week 7193 Goodlett Farms Pkwy *TF:* 888-232-1738 ■ *Web:* www.cotton.org/news/cweek	Cordova	TN	38016	901-274-9030	725-0510
Cruise Industry News 441 Lexington Ave Ste 809 *TF:* 800-333-7300 ■ *Web:* www.cruiseindustrynews.com	New York	NY	10017	212-986-1025	986-1033
DealersEdge PO Box 606 *TF:* 800-321-5312 ■ *Web:* www.dealersedge.com	Barnegat Light	NJ	08006	609-879-4456	

Phone | Fax

Engineering Outlook
1308 W Green St 303 Engineering Hall ... Urbana IL 61801 217-333-2151 244-7705
Web: engineering.illinois.edu

Funeral Service Insider
3349 Hwy 138 Bldg D Ste D ... Wall NJ 07719 800-500-4585
TF: 800-500-4585 ■ *Web:* www.kates-boylston.com

Kiplinger Agriculture Letter 1729 H St NW ... Washington DC 20006 202-887-6400 778-8976
TF: 800-544-0155 ■ *Web:* www.kiplinger.com

Metals Week 2 Penn Plaza ... New York NY 10121 800-752-8878 *
**Fax:* Edit ■ *TF:* 800-752-8878 ■ *Web:* www.platts.com

National Farmers Union News (NFU)
20 F St NW Ste 300 ... Washington DC 20001 202-554-1600 554-1654
Web: www.nfu.org

PhotoSource 5106 Louetta Rd ... Spring TX 77379 281-370-2220
TF: 800-786-6277 ■ *Web:* www.photosource.com/cart/pl.php

Pro Farmer 6612 Chancellor Dr Ste 300 ... Cedar Falls IA 50613 319-277-1278 277-7982
TF Cust Svc: 800-772-0023 ■ *Web:* www.agweb.com

Questex LLC 275 Grove St Ste 2-130 ... Newton MA 02466 617-219-8300 219-8310
TF: 888-552-4346 ■ *Web:* www.questex.com

Shopping Centers Today
1221 Ave of the Americas ... New York NY 10020 646-728-3800 589-5555*
**Fax Area Code:* 212 ■ *TF:* 888-427-2885 ■ *Web:* www.icsc.org

Uniform Commercial Code Law Letter
610 Opperman Dr ... Eagan MN 55123 651-687-7000
TF Cust Svc: 800-328-4880 ■ *Web:* legalsolutions.thomsonreuters.com

Union Labor Report 1801 S Bell St ... Arlington VA 22202 800-372-1033
TF: 800-372-1033 ■ *Web:* www.bna.com/union-labor-report-p6722

Urban Transport News 65 E Wacker Pl Ste 400 ... Chicago IL 60601 312-782-3900 782-3901
Web: www.highbeam.com

US Rail News 65 E Wacker Pl Ste 400 ... Chicago IL 60601 312-782-3900 782-3901
Web: www.highbeam.com

Whitaker Newsletters Inc
14305 Shoreham Dr ... Silver Spring MD 20905 301-384-1573 879-8803
Web: www.bevnewsonline.com

535 NEWSPAPERS

SEE ALSO Newspaper Publishers p. 2988

535-1 Daily Newspapers - Canada

Phone | Fax

Calgary Herald
215-16th St SE PO Box 2400 Stn M ... Calgary AB T2E7P5 403-235-7100 235-7379
TF: 800-372-9219 ■ *Web:* www.calgaryherald.com

Calgary Sun 2615 12th St NE ... Calgary AB T2E7W9 403-410-1010 250-4176*
**Fax:* Edit ■ *TF:* 877-624-1463 ■ *Web:* www.calgarysun.com

Cape Breton Post 255 George St PO Box 1500 ... Sydney NS B1P6K6 902-564-5451 564-6280
Web: www.capebretonpost.com

Chatham Daily News 138 King St W ... Chatham ON N7M1E3 519-354-2000 436-0949
Web: www.chathamdailynews.ca

Chronicle Herald, The PO Box 610 ... Halifax NS B3J2T2 902-426-2811 426-1158
TF: 800-563-1187 ■ *Web:* thechronicleherald.ca

Chronicle-Journal, The
75 S Cumberland St ... Thunder Bay ON P7B1A3 807-343-6200 343-9409
Web: www.chroniclejournal.com

Cornwall Standard Freeholder, The
1150 Montreal Rd ... Cornwall ON K6H1E2 613-933-3160
Web: www.standard-freeholder.com

Daily Courier 550 Doyle Ave ... Kelowna BC V1Y7V1 250-762-4445 762-3866
Web: www.kelownadailycourier.ca

Edmonton Journal 10006 - 101 St ... Edmonton AB T5J2S6 780-429-5100 498-5696
TF: 800-232-9486 ■ *Web:* www.edmontonjournal.com

Edmonton Sun 4990 92nd Ave Ste 250 ... Edmonton AB T6B3A1 780-468-0100 468-0139
TF: 877-468-2401 ■ *Web:* www.edmontonsun.com

Expositor, The 195 Henry St Bldg 4 ... Brantford ON N3T5S8 519-756-2020 756-3285
Web: www.brantfordexpositor.ca

Globe & Mail Inc, The 444 Front St W ... Toronto ON M5V2S9 416-585-5000 585-5085
Web: www.theglobeandmail.com

Guardian, The 165 Prince St ... Charlottetown PE C1A4R7 902-629-6000 566-3808
Web: www.theguardian.pe.ca

Journal Le Droit 47 Clarence St ... Ottawa ON K1N9K1 613-562-0555 562-7553
TF: 800-267-6961 ■ *Web:* www.lapresse.ca

Kamloops Daily News 393 Seymour St ... Kamloops BC V2C6P6 250-372-2331 372-0823
Web: www.kamloopsnews.ca

Kenora Daily Miner & News
33 Main St S PO Box 1620 ... Kenora ON P9N3X7 807-468-5555 468-4318
Web: www.kenoradailyminerandnews.com

Kingston Whig-Standard, The
Six Cataraqui St ... Kingston ON K7L4Z7 613-544-5000 530-4122
Web: www.thewhig.com

L'Acadie-Nouvelle
476 Boul St-Pierre Ouest PO Box 5536 ... Caraquet NB E1W1B7 506-727-4444 727-7620
TF: 800-561-2255 ■ *Web:* www.acadienouvelle.com

La Tribune 1950 Rue Roy ... Sherbrooke QC J1K2X8 819-564-5450 564-5480
Web: www.lapresse.ca

Le Devoir 2050 Bleury St Ninth Fl ... Montreal QC H3A3M9 514-985-3333 985-3360
TF: 800-463-7559 ■ *Web:* www.ledevoir.com

Le Quotidien & Progres Dimanche
1051 boul Talbot ... Chicoutimi QC G7H5C1 418-545-4474
Web: www.lapresse.ca

Le Soleil 410 Charest Blvd E PO Box 1547 ... Quebec QC G1K8G3 418-686-3233
Web: www.lapresse.ca

Lethbridge Herald
504 - Seventh St S PO Box 670 ... Lethbridge AB T1J3Z7 403-328-4411 328-4536
Web: lethbridgeherald.com

London Free Press 369 York St PO Box 2280 ... London ON N6A4G1 519-679-1111 667-4528
TF: 866-541-6757 ■ *Web:* www.lfpress.com

National Post 1450 Don Mills Rd Ste 300 ... Toronto ON M3B3R5 416-383-2300 383-2305
TF: 800-267-6568 ■ *Web:* www.nationalpost.com

Phone | Fax

Niagara Falls Review 4801 Valley Way ... Niagara Falls ON L2E6T6 905-358-5711 356-0785
Web: www.niagarafallsreview.ca

Northern News
Eight Duncan Ave PO Box 1030 ... Kirkland Lake ON P2N3L4 705-567-5321 567-5377
Web: www.northernnews.ca

Nugget, The 259 Worthington St W ... North Bay ON P1B3B5 705-472-3200 472-1438
Web: www.nugget.ca

Ottawa Citizen 1101 Baxter Rd PO Box 5020 ... Ottawa ON K2C3M4 613-829-9100 726-1198
TF: 800-267-6100 ■ *Web:* www.ottawacitizen.com

Ottawa Sun PO Box 9729 ... Ottawa ON K1G5H7 613-739-7000 739-8041
TF: 877-624-1463 ■ *Web:* www.ottawasun.com

Owen Sound Sun Times 290 Ninth St E ... Owen Sound ON N4K5P2 519-376-2250 376-7190
Web: www.owensoundsuntimes.com

Prince George Citizen
150 Brunswick St PO Box 5700 ... Prince George BC V2L2B3 250-562-2441 562-7453
Web: www.princegeorgecitizen.com

Record, The 160 King St E ... Kitchener ON N2G4E5 519-894-2231 894-3829
TF: 800-265-8261 ■ *Web:* www.therecord.com

Red Deer Advocate 2950 Bremner Ave ... Red Deer AB T4R1M9 403-343-2400 341-6560
Web: www.reddeeradvocate.com

Regina Leader Post 1964 Pk St ... Regina SK S4P3G4 306-781-5211 565-2588
Web: www.leaderpost.com

Sault Star, The
145 Old Garden River Rd ... Sault Sainte Marie ON P6A5M5 705-759-3030 942-8690
Web: www.saultstar.com

Spectator, The 44 Frid St ... Hamilton ON L8N3G3 905-526-3333 526-1395
TF: 800-263-6902 ■ *Web:* www.thespec.com

Sudbury Star, The 33 MacKenzie St ... Sudbury ON P3C4Y1 705-674-5271 674-0624
Web: www.thesudburystar.com

Telegraph-Journal 210 Crown St PO Box 2350 ... Saint John NB E2L3V8 888-295-8665 645-3295*
**Fax Area Code:* 506 ■
Web: telegraphjournal.com/csp/cms/sites/tjonline/greatersj/index.csp

Thompson Citizen 141 Commercial Pl ... Thompson MB R8N1T1 204-677-4534 677-3681
Web: www.thompsoncitizen.net

Times Colonist 2621 Douglas St PO Box 300 ... Victoria BC V8T4M2 250-380-5211 380-5353
Web: www.timescolonist.com

Times-Transcript 939 Main St ... Moncton NB E1C8P3 506-859-4909
Web: www.telegraphjournal.com/times-transcript

Toronto Star One Yonge St ... Toronto ON M5E1E6 416-869-4949 869-4328*
**Fax:* News Rm ■ *TF:* 800-268-9756 ■ *Web:* www.thestar.com

Toronto Sun 333 King St E ... Toronto ON M5A3X5 416-947-2222 947-1664
TF: 888-786-7821 ■ *Web:* www.torontosun.com

Vancouver Province 200 Granville St Ste 1 ... Vancouver BC V6C3N3 604-605-2000 605-2720
Web: www.theprovince.com

Vancouver Sun 200 Granville St Ste 1 ... Vancouver BC V6C3N3 604-605-2000 605-2323*
**Fax:* News Rm ■ *Web:* www.vancouversun.com

Windsor Star, The 167 Ferry St ... Windsor ON N9A4M5 519-255-5711 255-5515
TF: 800-265-5647 ■ *Web:* www.windsorstar.com

Winnipeg Free Press 1355 Mountain Ave ... Winnipeg MB R2X3B6 204-697-7000 697-7412*
**Fax:* News Rm ■ *TF:* 800-542-8900 ■ *Web:* www.winnipegfreepress.com

Winnipeg Sun 1700 Church Ave ... Winnipeg MB R2X3A2 204-694-2022 694-2347*
**Fax:* News Rm ■ *Web:* www.winnipegsun.com

World Journal 2288 Clark Dr ... Vancouver BC V5N3G8 604-876-1338 876-9191
Web: worldjournal.com

535-2 Daily Newspapers - US

Listings here are organized by city names within state groupings. Most of the fax numbers given connect directly to the newsroom.

Alabama

Phone | Fax

Anniston Star 4305 McClellan Blvd PO Box 189 ... Anniston AL 36202 256-236-1551 241-1991
TF: 866-814-9253 ■ *Web:* www.annistonstar.com

Birmingham News 2201 Fourth Ave N ... Birmingham AL 35203 205-325-4444
TF: 800-283-4001 ■ *Web:* www.alabamamediagroup.com

Decatur Daily 201 First Ave SE ... Decatur AL 35601 256-353-4612 340-2392
TF: 888-353-4612 ■ *Web:* www.decaturdaily.com

Dothan Eagle PO Box 1968 ... Dothan AL 36302 334-792-3141 712-7979
TF: 800-811-1771 ■ *Web:* www.dothaneagle.com

Times Daily PO Box 797 ... Florence AL 35631 256-766-3434 740-4717
Web: www.timesdaily.com

Gadsden Times 401 Locust St ... Gadsden AL 35901 256-549-2000 549-2105
TF: 800-762-2464 ■ *Web:* www.gadsdentimes.com

Huntsville Times 2317 S Memorial Pkwy ... Huntsville AL 35801 256-532-4000 532-4420
TF: 800-239-5271 ■ *Web:* www.alabamamediagroup.com

Montgomery Advertiser 425 Molton St ... Montgomery AL 36104 334-262-1611 261-1521
TF: 877-424-0007 ■ *Web:* www.montgomeryadvertiser.com

Tuscaloosa News 315 28th Ave ... Tuscaloosa AL 35401 205-345-0505 722-0187
TF: 800-888-8639 ■ *Web:* www.tuscaloosanews.com

Alaska

Phone | Fax

Anchorage Daily News 1001 Northway Dr ... Anchorage AK 99508 907-257-4200 258-2157*
**Fax:* Edit ■ *TF:* 800-478-4200 ■ *Web:* www.adn.com

Fairbanks Daily News Miner
200 N Cushman St ... Fairbanks AK 99707 907-456-6661 452-7917
Web: www.newsminer.com

Juneau Empire 3100 Ch Dr ... Juneau AK 99801 907-586-3740 586-9097
Web: juneauempire.com

Arizona

Phone | Fax

Arizona Daily Sun 1751 S Thompson St ... Flagstaff AZ 86001 928-774-4545 774-4790
Web: www.azdailysun.com

East Valley Tribune 120 W First Ave ... Mesa AZ 85210 480-898-6500 898-6362
TF: 888-887-4286 ■ *Web:* www.eastvalleytribune.com

	City	State	ZIP	Phone	Fax
Arizona Republic 200 E Van Buren St **Fax:* News Rm ■ *TF:* 800-331-9303 ■ *Web:* www.azcentral.com/arizonarepublic	Phoenix	AZ	85004	602-444-8000	444-8044*
Scottsdale Tribune 6991 Camelback Rd. *Web:* www.eastvalleytribune.com	Scottsdale	AZ	85251	480-970-2330	970-2360
Daily News-Sun 10102 Santa Fe Dr *Web:* www.yourwestvalley.com	Sun City	AZ	85351	623-977-8351	876-3698
Arizona Daily Star 4850 S Pk Ave *TF:* 800-695-4492 ■ *Web:* tucson.com/	Tucson	AZ	85714	520-573-4343	573-4107
Yuma Daily Sun 2055 Arizona Ave *Web:* www.yumasun.com	Yuma	AZ	85364	928-783-3333	

Arkansas

	City	State	ZIP	Phone	Fax
Sentinel-Record 300 Spring St *Web:* www.hotsr.com	Hot Springs National Park	AR	71901	501-623-7711	623-8465
Jonesboro Sun 518 Carson St *TF:* 800-237-5341 ■ *Web:* www.jonesborosun.com	Jonesboro	AR	72401	870-935-5525	935-5823
Arkansas Democrat-Gazette 121 E Capital St *TF Cust Svc:* 800-482-1121 ■ *Web:* www.arkansasonline.com	Little Rock	AR	72203	501-378-3400	372-4765
Newport Daily Independent 2408 Hwy 367 N. *Web:* www.newportindependent.com	Newport	AR	72112	870-523-5855	523-6540
Pine Bluff Commercial 300 S Beech St *Web:* www.pbcommercial.com	Pine Bluff	AR	71601	870-534-3400	534-0113
Morning News of Northwest Arkansas 2560 N Lowell Rd. *Web:* www.nwaonline.com	Springdale	AR	72764	479-751-6200	872-5055

California

	City	State	ZIP	Phone	Fax
China Daily Press 2121 W Mission Rd *Web:* usqiaobao.com	Alhambra	CA	91803	626-281-8500	281-7900
Record-Gazette 218 N Murray St *Web:* www.recordgazette.net	Banning	CA	92220	951-849-4586	849-2437
El Mexicano 4045 Bonita Rd Ste 207 *Web:* www.medicis.tv	Bonita	CA	91902	619-267-6010	267-5965
Ventura County Star 550 Camarillo Ctr Dr *TF:* 800-221-7827 ■ *Web:* www.vcstar.com	Camarillo	CA	93010	805-437-0000	482-6167
Chico Enterprise Record 400 E Pk Ave PO Box 9 *TF:* 800-827-1421 ■ *Web:* www.chicoer.com	Chico	CA	95927	530-891-1234	342-3617
Daily Pilot 1375 Sunflower Ave. *Web:* www.dailypilot.com	Costa Mesa	CA	92626	714-966-4600	966-4679
Los Angeles Times Orange County 1375 W Sunflower Ave *Web:* www.reptiland.com	Costa Mesa	CA	92626	714-966-5600	966-7711
Davis Enterprise 315 G St *Web:* www.davisenterprise.com	Davis	CA	95616	530-756-0800	756-6707
Imperial Valley Press 205 N Eigth St. *Web:* www.ivpressonline.com	El Centro	CA	92243	760-337-3400	353-3003
Times-Standard 930 Sixth St *TF:* 800-514-0301 ■ *Web:* www.times-standard.com	Eureka	CA	95501	707-498-1817	441-0501
Daily Republic 1250 Texas St. *Web:* www.dailyrepublic.com	Fairfield	CA	94533	707-425-4646	425-5924
Fresno Bee 1626 E St *TF:* 800-877-3400 ■ *Web:* www.fresnobee.com	Fresno	CA	93786	559-441-6111	441-6436
Asbarez Armenian Daily 419 W Colorado St *Web:* www.asbarez.com	Glendale	CA	91204	818-500-9363	956-3230
Union, The 464 Sutton Way. *Web:* www.theunion.com	Grass Valley	CA	95945	530-273-9561	477-4292
Daily Review 22533 Foothill Blvd. *TF:* 800-595-9595 ■ *Web:* www.insidebayarea.com	Hayward	CA	94541	510-783-6111	293-2490
Lodi News-Sentinel 125 N Church St *TF:* 800-407-7653 ■ *Web:* www.lodinews.com	Lodi	CA	95240	209-369-2761	369-6706
Press-Telegram 300 Oceangate *Web:* www.presstelegram.com	Long Beach	CA	90844	562-435-1161	437-7892
Daily Commerce 915 E First St *Web:* www.dailyjournal.com	Los Angeles	CA	90012	213-229-5300	229-5481
Investor's Business Daily 12655 Beatrice St **Fax:* Cust Svc ■ *TF:* 800-831-2525 ■ *Web:* www.investors.com	Los Angeles	CA	90066	310-448-6000	577-7303*
La Opinion 700 S Flower St Ste 3000 *Web:* www.laopinion.com	Los Angeles	CA	90017	213-622-8332	896-2144
Los Angeles Times 202 W First St. *TF:* 800-528-4637 ■ *Web:* www.latimes.com	Los Angeles	CA	90012	213-237-5000	237-4712
Appeal-Democrat 1530 Ellis Lk Dr PO Box 431 **Fax:* News Rm ■ *TF:* 800-831-2345 ■ *Web:* www.appeal-democrat.com	Marysville	CA	95901	530-741-2345	749-8390*
Merced Sun-Star 3033 N G St. *Web:* www.mercedsunstar.com	Merced	CA	95340	209-722-1511	388-2460
Modesto Bee 1325 H St. *TF:* 800-776-4233 ■ *Web:* www.modbee.com	Modesto	CA	95354	209-578-2000	578-2207
Monterey County Herald Eight Upper Ragsdale Dr. *TF:* 800-688-1808 ■ *Web:* www.montereyherald.com	Monterey	CA	93940	831-372-3311	372-8401
Napa Valley Register 1615 Second St *Web:* www.napanews.com	Napa	CA	94559	707-226-3711	
Marin Independent Journal 150 Alameda Del Prado *TF:* 877-229-8655 ■ *Web:* www.marinij.com	Novato	CA	94949	415-883-8600	883-5458
Oakland Tribune 7677 Oakport St Ste 950. *Web:* www.insidebayarea.com	Oakland	CA	94621	510-208-6300	208-6477
Inland Valley Daily Bulletin 2041 E Fourth St. *Web:* www.dailybulletin.com	Ontario	CA	91764	909-987-6397	
Desert Sun 750 N Gene Autry Trl. *TF:* 800-233-3741 ■ *Web:* desertsun.com/	Palm Springs	CA	92263	760-322-8889	778-4654
Antelope Valley Press 37404 Sierra Hwy *TF:* 888-874-2527 ■ *Web:* www.avpress.com	Palmdale	CA	93550	661-273-2700	947-4870
Pasadena Star-News 911 E Colorado Blvd. *TF:* 800-788-1200 ■ *Web:* www.pasadenastarnews.com	Pasadena	CA	91106	626-578-6300	432-5248
Tri-Valley Herald 127 Spring St *Web:* www.contracostatimes.com	Pleasanton	CA	94566	925-935-2525	
Record Searchlight PO Box 492397 *TF:* 800-666-1331 ■ *Web:* www.redding.com	Redding	CA	96049	530-243-2424	225-8236
Press-Enterprise 3450 14th St. *TF:* 877-473-6397 ■ *Web:* www.pe.com	Riverside	CA	92501	951-684-1200	368-9023
Sacramento Bee PO Box 15779 *TF Cust Svc:* 800-284-3233 ■ *Web:* www.sacbee.com	Sacramento	CA	95852	916-321-1000	321-1109
Californian, The 123 W Alisal St *Web:* www.thecalifornian.com	Salinas	CA	93901	831-424-2221	754-4293
Sun, The 4030 N Georgia Blvd. *TF:* 800-922-0922 ■ *Web:* www.sbsun.com	San Bernardino	CA	92407	909-889-9666	885-8741
San Diego Daily Transcript 2131 Third Ave. **Fax:* Edit ■ *TF:* 800-697-6397 ■ *Web:* www.sddt.com	San Diego	CA	92101	619-232-4381	236-8126*
San Diego Union-Tribune 350 Camino De La Reina *TF:* 800-244-6397 ■ *Web:* www.utsandiego.com	San Diego	CA	92108	619-299-3131	293-1896
San Francisco Chronicle 901 Mission St. *TF:* 866-732-4766 ■ *Web:* www.sfgate.com	San Francisco	CA	94103	415-777-1111	896-1107
San Francisco Examiner 835 Market St Ste 550 *Web:* www.sfexaminer.com	San Francisco	CA	94103	415-359-2868	359-2766
Press-Enterprise, The 474 W Esplanade Ave. *Web:* www.pe.com	San Jacinto	CA	92583	951-763-3452	763-3450
San Jose Mercury News 750 Ridder Pk Dr. *Web:* www.mercurynews.com	San Jose	CA	95190	408-920-5000	288-8060
Tribune, The 3825 S Higuera St. *TF:* 800-477-8799 ■ *Web:* www.sanluisobispo.com	San Luis Obispo	CA	93401	805-781-7800	781-7905
San Mateo County Times 477 Ninth Ave Ste 110 *TF:* 800-870-6397 ■ *Web:* www.mercurynews.com/san-mateo-county	San Mateo	CA	94402	650-348-4321	348-4446
Orange County Register 625 N Grand Ave. *TF:* 877-469-7344 ■ *Web:* www.ocregister.com	Santa Ana	CA	92701	714-796-7000	796-5052
Santa Maria Times PO Box 400 *Web:* www.santamariatimes.com	Santa Maria	CA	93456	805-925-2691	928-5657
Press Democrat 427 Mendocino Ave. *TF:* 800-675-5056 ■ *Web:* www.pressdemo.com	Santa Rosa	CA	95401	707-546-2020	521-5330
Tahoe Daily Tribune 3079 Harrison Ave *Web:* www.tahoedailytribune.com	South Lake Tahoe	CA	96150	530-541-3880	541-0373
Daily Breeze 5215 Torrance Blvd **Fax:* Edit ■ *TF:* 800-356-7057 ■ *Web:* www.dailybreeze.com	Torrance	CA	90503	310-540-5511	540-6272*
Turlock Journal 138 S Center St *Web:* www.turlockjournal.com	Turlock	CA	95380	209-634-9141	632-8813
Reporter, The 916 Cotting Ln PO Box 1509 *Web:* www.thereporter.com	Vacaville	CA	95688	707-448-6401	447-8411
Vallejo Times Herald 440 Curtola Pkwy *TF:* 800-600-1141 ■ *Web:* www.timesheraldonline.com	Vallejo	CA	94590	707-644-1141	643-0128
Visalia Times-Delta 330 NW St PO Box 31 *Web:* www.visaliatimesdelta.com	Visalia	CA	93279	559-735-3200	735-3399
Contra Costa Times 2640 Shadelands Dr *Web:* www.contracostatimes.com	Walnut Creek	CA	94598	925-935-2525	943-8362
San Gabriel Valley Tribune 1210 N Azusa Canyon Rd *TF:* 800-788-1200 ■ *Web:* www.sgvtribune.com	West Covina	CA	91790	626-962-8811	338-9157
Nguoi Viet News 14771 Moran St *Web:* www.nguoi-viet.com	Westminster	CA	92683	714-892-9414	894-1381
Daily News of Los Angeles 21221 Oxnard St. *TF:* 800-559-1950 ■ *Web:* www.dailynews.com	Woodland Hills	CA	91367	818-713-3000	713-0058

Colorado

	City	State	ZIP	Phone	Fax
Aspen Times 310 E Main St *Web:* www.aspentimes.com	Aspen	CO	81611	970-925-3414	925-6240
Boulder Daily Camera 1048 Pearl St *TF:* 800-783-1202 ■ *Web:* www.dailycamera.com	Boulder	CO	80302	303-442-1202	449-9358
Colorado Daily 5450 Western Ave *Web:* www.coloradodaily.com	Boulder	CO	80301	303-473-1111	
Denver Post 101 W Colfax Ave. *TF:* 800-336-7678 ■ *Web:* www.denverpost.com	Denver	CO	80202	303-820-1010	820-1369
Durango Herald 1275 Main Ave. *TF:* 800-530-8318 ■ *Web:* www.durangoherald.com	Durango	CO	81301	970-247-3504	259-5011
Coloradoan, The 1300 Riverside Ave *TF:* 877-424-0063 ■ *Web:* www.coloradoan.com	Fort Collins	CO	80524	970-493-6397	224-7899
Greeley Tribune 501 Eigth Ave. *Web:* www.greeleytribune.com	Greeley	CO	80631	970-352-0211	356-5780
Gunnison Country Times 218 N Wisconsin St. *Web:* www.gunnisontimes.com	Gunnison	CO	81230	970-641-1414	641-6515
Daily Times-Call 350 Terry St *Web:* www.timescall.com	Longmont	CO	80501	303-776-2244	678-8615
Loveland Daily Reporter-Herald 201 E Fifth St *TF:* 800-244-5613 ■ *Web:* www.reporterherald.com	Loveland	CO	80537	970-669-5050	667-1111
Pueblo Chieftain 825 W Sixth St PO Box 440. *TF:* 800-279-6397 ■ *Web:* www.chieftain.com	Pueblo	CO	81003	719-544-3520	

Connecticut

	City	State	ZIP	Phone	Fax
Connecticut Post 410 State St *TF Edit:* 800-293-0795 ■ *Web:* www.ctpost.com	Bridgeport	CT	06604	203-333-0161	367-8158
News-Times 333 Main St. *Web:* www.newstimes.com	Danbury	CT	06810	203-744-5100	792-8730
Hartford Courant 285 Broad St *TF:* 800-524-4242 ■ *Web:* www.courant.com	Hartford	CT	06115	860-241-6200	520-6941

				Phone	Fax
Journal Inquirer 306 Progress Dr PO Box 510 *TF:* 800-237-3606 ■ *Web:* www.journalinquirer.com	Manchester	CT	06045	860-646-0500	646-9867
Record-Journal 11 Crown St *TF:* 800-228-6915 ■ *Web:* myrecordjournal.com	Meriden	CT	06450	203-235-1661	639-0210
Citizens News 71 Weid Dr *Web:* mycitizensnews.com	Naugatuck	CT	06770	203-729-2228	729-9099
New Britain Herald, The One Ct St Fourth Fl *Web:* www.newbritainherald.com	New Britain	CT	06051	860-225-4601	225-2611
New Haven Register 40 Sargent Dr *TF:* 800-925-2509 ■ *Web:* www.nhregister.com	New Haven	CT	06511	203-789-5200	865-7894
Hour, The 1 Selleck St *Web:* www.thehour.com	Norwalk	CT	06851	203-846-3281	
Norwich Bulletin 66 Franklin St *Web:* www.norwichbulletin.com	Norwich	CT	06360	860-887-9211	887-9666

Delaware

				Phone	Fax
Delaware State News 110 Galaxy Dr PO Box 737 *TF:* 800-282-8586 ■ *Web:* www.newszap.com	Dover	DE	19903	302-674-3600	741-8252

District of Columbia

				Phone	Fax
Washington Examiner 1015 15th St NW Ste 500 *Web:* www.examiner.com	Washington	DC	20005	202-903-2000	
Washington Post 1150 15th St NW *TF:* 800-627-1150 ■ *Web:* www.washingtonpost.com	Washington	DC	20071	202-334-6000	
Washington Times, The 3600 New York Ave NE *Web:* www.washingtontimes.com	Washington	DC	20002	202-636-3000	636-8906

Florida

				Phone	Fax
Citrus County Chronicle 1624 N Meadowcrest Blvd *Web:* www.chronicleonline.com	Crystal River	FL	34429	352-563-6363	563-3280
Daytona Beach News-Journal 901 Sixth St *Web:* www.news-journalonline.com	Daytona Beach	FL	32117	386-252-1511	258-8465
El Nuevo Herald 3511 NW 91st Ave *TF:* 800-437-2535 ■ *Web:* www.elnuevoherald.com	Doral	FL	33172	305-376-3535	376-2378
South Florida Sun-Sentinel 200 E Las Olas Blvd *TF Cust Svc:* 800-548-6397 ■ *Web:* www.sun-sentinel.com	Fort Lauderdale	FL	33301	954-356-4000	356-4559
Northwest Florida Daily News PO Box 2949 *TF:* 800-755-1185 ■ *Web:* www.nwfdailynews.com	Fort Walton Beach	FL	32549	850-863-1111	863-7834
Florida Times-Union One Riverside Ave *TF:* 800-472-6397 ■ *Web:* jacksonville.com	Jacksonville	FL	32202	904-359-4111	359-4478
Key West Citizen 3420 Northside Dr *Web:* www.keysnews.com	Key West	FL	33040	305-292-7777	292-3008
Ledger, The 300 W Lime St *TF:* 888-431-7323 ■ *Web:* www.theledger.com	Lakeland	FL	33815	863-802-7000	802-7809
Daily Commercial 212 E Main St *TF:* 866-273-2273 ■ *Web:* www.dailycommercial.com	Leesburg	FL	34748	352-365-8200	365-1951
Diario Las Americas 888 Brickell Ave 5th Fl *Web:* www.diariolasamericas.com	Miami	FL	33131	305-633-3341	
Naples Daily News 1075 Central Ave *TF:* 800-404-7343 ■ *Web:* www.naplesnews.com	Naples	FL	34102	239-262-3161	263-4816
Orlando Sentinel 633 N Orange Ave *TF:* 800-347-6868 ■ *Web:* www.orlandosentinel.com	Orlando	FL	32801	407-420-5000	420-5350
Port Saint Lucie News 760 NW Enterprise Dr *Web:* www.tcpalm.com	Port Saint Lucie	FL	34986	772-408-5300	408-5327
Seminole Herald PO Box 1667 *TF:* 800-955-8770 ■ *Web:* www.mysanfordherald.com	Sanford	FL	32772	407-322-2611	323-9408
Sarasota Herald-Tribune 1741 Main St *TF:* 866-284-7102 ■ *Web:* www.heraldtribune.com	Sarasota	FL	34236	941-953-7755	361-4800
Highlands Today 315 US Hwy 27 N *TF General:* 800-645-3423 ■ *Web:* www.highlandstoday.com	Sebring	FL	33870	863-386-5800	382-2509
Vero Beach Press-Journal PO Box 1268 *TF:* 866-894-9851 ■ *Web:* www.tcpalm.com	Vero Beach	FL	32961	772-562-2315	
Palm Beach Post 2751 S Dixie Hwy **Fax:* News Rm ■ *TF:* 800-432-7595 ■ *Web:* www.palmbeachpost.com	West Palm Beach	FL	33405	561-820-4100	820-4407*

Georgia

				Phone	Fax
Athens Banner-Herald One Press Pl *TF:* 800-533-4252 ■ *Web:* onlineathens.com	Athens	GA	30601	706-549-0123	208-2246
Atlanta Journal-Constitution 223 Perimeter Ctr Pkwy NE *Web:* www.ajc.com	Atlanta	GA	30346	404-526-5151	526-5746
Augusta Chronicle 725 Broad St **Fax:* News Rm ■ *TF:* 866-249-8223 ■ *Web:* chronicle.augusta.com	Augusta	GA	30901	706-724-0851	722-7403*
Brunswick News PO Box 1557 *Web:* www.thebrunswicknews.com	Brunswick	GA	31521	912-265-8320	280-0926
Columbus Ledger-Enquirer 17 W 12th St *TF:* 800-282-7859 ■ *Web:* www.ledger-enquirer.com	Columbus	GA	31901	706-324-5526	576-6290
Rockdale Citizen 969 S Main St NE *Web:* www.rockdalecitizen.com	Conyers	GA	30012	770-483-7108	483-5797
Gainesville Times 345 Green St NW *TF:* 800-395-5005 ■ *Web:* www.gainesvilletimes.com	Gainesville	GA	30501	770-532-1234	532-0457
Gwinnett Daily Post 725 Old Norcross Rd *Web:* www.gwinnettdailypost.com	Lawrenceville	GA	30045	770-963-9205	339-8081
Macon Telegraph 120 Broadway *TF:* 800-679-6397 ■ *Web:* www.macon.com	Macon	GA	31201	478-744-4200	744-4385
Marietta Daily Journal 580 Fairground St *Web:* www.mdjonline.com	Marietta	GA	30060	770-428-9411	428-7945
La Vision 2200 Norcross Pkwy *Web:* www.lavisionnewspaper.com	Norcross	GA	30071	770-963-7521	963-7218
Rome News-Tribune 305 E Sixth Ave PO Box 1633 *Web:* northwestgeorgianews.com/rome/	Rome	GA	30161	706-290-5252	
Savannah Morning News 1375 Chatham Pkwy *Web:* savannahnow.com	Savannah	GA	31405	912-236-9511	525-0795
Valdosta Daily Times PO Box 968 *TF:* 800-600-4838 ■ *Web:* www.valdostadailytimes.com	Valdosta	GA	31603	229-244-1880	244-2560

Hawaii

				Phone	Fax
Hawaii Tribune-Herald 355 Kinoole St *Web:* www.hawaiitribune-herald.com	Hilo	HI	96720	808-935-6621	961-3680
Honolulu Advertiser 500 Ala Moana Blvd *TF:* 877-233-1133 ■ *Web:* www.staradvertiser.com	Honolulu	HI	96813	808-529-4747	525-8037
Maui News 100 Mahalani St **Fax:* Edit ■ *TF:* 888-683-1115 ■ *Web:* www.mauinews.com	Wailuku	HI	96793	808-244-3981	242-9087*

Idaho

				Phone	Fax
Idaho Statesman PO Box 40 *TF:* 800-635-8934 ■ *Web:* www.idahostatesman.com	Boise	ID	83707	208-377-6400	377-6449
Coeur d'Alene Press 201 N Second St *Web:* www.cdapress.com	Coeur d'Alene	ID	83814	208-664-8176	664-0212
Post-Register PO Box 1800 *TF:* 800-574-6397 ■ *Web:* www.postregister.com	Idaho Falls	ID	83403	208-522-1800	529-9683
Lewiston Morning Tribune PO Box 957 *Web:* www.lmtribune.com	Lewiston	ID	83501	208-743-9411	746-1185
Idaho Press-Tribune 1618 N Midland Blvd *Web:* www.idahopress.com	Nampa	ID	83651	208-467-9251	467-9562
Idaho State Journal 305 S Arthur Ave *TF:* 800-669-9777 ■ *Web:* www.idahostatejournal.com	Pocatello	ID	83204	208-232-4161	233-8007

Illinois

				Phone	Fax
Telegraph, The PO Box 278 **Fax:* Edit ■ *TF:* 866-299-9256 ■ *Web:* www.thetelegraph.com	Alton	IL	62002	618-463-2500	463-2578*
Belleville News-Democrat 120 S Illinois St *TF:* 800-293-0795 ■ *Web:* www.bnd.com	Belleville	IL	62220	618-234-1000	236-9773
Pantagraph PO Box 2907 *TF:* 800-747-7323 ■ *Web:* www.pantagraph.com	Bloomington	IL	61702	309-829-9000	829-7000
Southern Illinoisan 710 N Illinois Ave PO Box 2108 *TF:* 800-228-0429 ■ *Web:* www.thesouthern.com	Carbondale	IL	62902	618-529-5454	457-2935
Centralia Sentinel 232 E Broadway *Web:* www.morningsentinel.com	Centralia	IL	62801	618-532-5604	532-1212
News Gazette 15 Main St *Web:* www.news-gazette.com	Champaign	IL	61824	217-351-5252	351-5374
Chicago Defender 4445 S King Dr *Web:* www.chicagodefender.com	Chicago	IL	60653	312-225-2400	225-6954
Chicago Sun-Times 350 N Orleans St *Web:* www.suntimes.com	Chicago	IL	60654	312-321-3000	321-3084
Chicago Tribune 435 N Michigan Ave *TF:* 800-874-2863 ■ *Web:* www.chicagotribune.com	Chicago	IL	60611	312-222-3232	222-2598
ViveloHoy 435 N Michigan Ave 12th Fl *Web:* www.vivelohoy.com	Chicago	IL	60611	312-527-8400	
Commercial-News 17 W N St **Fax:* News Rm ■ *TF:* 877-732-8258 ■ *Web:* www.commercial-news.com	Danville	IL	61832	217-446-1000	446-6648*
Herald & Review 601 E Williams St *TF:* 800-437-2533 ■ *Web:* www.herald-review.com	Decatur	IL	62523	217-429-5151	421-6913
Telegraph 113 S Peoria Ave *Web:* www.saukvalley.com	Dixon	IL	61021	815-284-2224	284-2078
Journal-Standard 27 S State Ave *TF:* 800-325-6397 ■ *Web:* www.journalstandard.com	Freeport	IL	61032	815-232-1171	232-0105
Register-Mail 140 S Prairie St PO Box 310 *TF:* 877-732-8258 ■ *Web:* www.register-mail.com	Galesburg	IL	61401	309-343-7181	
Daily Journal 8 Dearborn Sq *NASDAQ: DJCO* ■ *TF:* 866-299-9256 ■ *Web:* www.daily-journal.com	Kankakee	IL	60901	815-937-3300	937-3876
News-Tribune 426 Second St *TF:* 800-892-6452 ■ *Web:* www.newstrib.com	La Salle	IL	61301	815-223-3200	224-6443
Macomb Journal 203 N Randolph St **Fax Area Code:* 618 ■ *TF:* 800-747-5401 ■ *Web:* www.mcdonoughvoice.com	Macomb	IL	61455	309-833-2114	673-2110*
My Web Times 110 W Jefferson St *Web:* www.mywebtimes.com	Ottawa	IL	61350	815-433-2000	433-1639
Reporter 12247 S Harlem Ave *TF:* 800-633-4227 ■ *Web:* thereporteronline.net	Palos Heights	IL	60463	708-448-6161	448-4012
Pekin Daily Times PO Box 430 *Web:* www.pekintimes.com	Pekin	IL	61555	309-346-1111	346-9815
Peoria Journal Star One News Plz **Fax:* News Rm ■ *TF:* 800-225-5757 ■ *Web:* www.pjstar.com	Peoria	IL	61643	309-686-3000	686-3296*
Quincy Herald-Whig 130 S Fifth St *TF:* 800-373-9444 ■ *Web:* www.whig.com	Quincy	IL	62301	217-223-5100	221-3395
Rock Island Argus 1724 Fourth Ave *TF:* 800-660-2472 ■ *Web:* qconline.com	Rock Island	IL	61201	309-786-6441	786-7639
Rockford Register Star 99 E State St **Fax:* News Rm ■ *TF:* 800-383-7827 ■ *Web:* www.rrstar.com	Rockford	IL	61104	815-987-1200	987-1365*
Shelbyville Daily Union 100 W Main St *TF:* 800-772-1213 ■ *Web:* www.shelbyvilledailyunion.com	Shelbyville	IL	62565	217-774-2161	774-5732
State Journal-Register PO Box 219 *TF:* 800-397-6397 ■ *Web:* www.sj-r.com	Springfield	IL	62705	217-788-1300	788-1551
Daily Southtown 6901 W 159th St **Fax Area Code:* 312 ■ *Web:* southtownstar.suntimes.com	Tinley Park	IL	60477	708-633-6700	222-4674*

Indiana

Phone *Fax*

Herald Bulletin 1133 Jackson St .... Anderson IN 46016 765-622-1212 640-4815
TF: 800-750-5049 ■ *Web:* www.heraldbulletin.com
Herald-Republican 45 S Public Sq .... Angola IN 46703 260-665-3117 665-2322
Web: www.kpcnews.com
Times-Mail 813 16th St .... Bedford IN 47421 812-275-3355 277-3472
Web: www.tmnews.com
Republic, The 333 Second St .... Columbus IN 47201 812-372-7811 379-5711
TF: 800-876-7811 ■ *Web:* www.therepublic.com
Truth, The PO Box 487 .... Elkhart IN 46515 574-294-1661 294-3895
TF: 800-585-5416 ■ *Web:* www.elkharttruth.com
Evansville Courier & Press
300 E Walnut St .... Evansville IN 47713 812-424-7711 422-8196
TF: 800-288-3200 ■ *Web:* www.courierpress.com
Journal Gazette 600 W Main St.................. Fort Wayne IN 46802 260-461-8773 461-8648
TF: 888-966-4532 ■ *Web:* www.journalgazette.net
News-Sentinel 600 W Main St .... Fort Wayne IN 46802 260-461-8439 461-8817
TF: 800-444-3303 ■ *Web:* www.fortwayne.com/mld/newssentinel
Goshen News 114 S Main St PO Box 569 .... Goshen IN 46527 574-533-2151 534-8830
TF: 800-487-2151 ■ *Web:* www.goshennews.com
Indianapolis Star 307 N Pennsylvania St .... Indianapolis IN 46204 317-444-4000 444-6600
TF: 800-669-7827 ■ *Web:* www.indystar.com
Kokomo Tribune (KT) 300 N Union St PO Box 9014 ...... Kokomo IN 46901 765-459-3121 854-6733
TF: 800-382-0696 ■ *Web:* www.kokomotribune.com
Journal & Courier 217 N Sixth St .... Lafayette IN 47901 765-423-5511 420-5246
TF News Rm: 800-407-5813 ■ *Web:* www.jconline.com
Chronicle-Tribune 610 S Adams St................... Marion IN 46953 765-664-5111 668-4256
TF: 800-955-7888 ■ *Web:* www.chronicle-tribune.com
Muncie Star-Press 345 S High St...................... Muncie IN 47305 765-747-5700 213-5858
TF: 800-783-7827 ■ *Web:* www.thestarpress.com
Times, The 601 W 45th Ave .... Munster IN 46321 219-933-3200 933-3249
TF: 800-837-3232 ■ *Web:* www.nwitimes.com
Palladium-Item 1175 N a St...................... Richmond IN 47374 765-962-1575 973-4570
Web: www.pal-item.com
South Bend Tribune 225 W Colfax Ave .... South Bend IN 46626 574-235-6464 239-2642
TF: 800-220-7378 ■ *Web:* www.southbendtribune.com
Tribune-Star PO Box 149........................ Terre Haute IN 47808 812-231-4200 231-4321
TF: 800-783-8742 ■ *Web:* www.tribstar.com

Iowa

Phone *Fax*

Hawk Eye, The 800 S Main St PO Box 10 .... Burlington IA 52601 319-754-8461 754-6824
TF: 800-397-1708 ■ *Web:* www.thehawkeye.com
Gazette, The 501 Second Ave SE................. Cedar Rapids IA 52401 319-398-8333
TF: 800-397-8333 ■ *Web:* www.thegazette.com
Daily Nonpareil 535 W Broadway Ste 300 .... Council Bluffs IA 51503 712-328-1811 325-5776
TF: 800-283-1882 ■ *Web:* www.nonpareilonline.com
Quad-City Times 500 E Third St .... Davenport IA 52801 563-383-2200 383-2370
TF: 800-437-4641 ■ *Web:* www.qctimes.com
Des Moines Register 715 Locust St .... Des Moines IA 50309 515-284-8000 286-2504
TF: 800-247-5346 ■ *Web:* www.desmoinesregister.com
Telegraph Herald 801 Bluff St...................... Dubuque IA 52001 563-588-5611 588-5745*
**Fax:* Edit ■ *TF:* 800-553-4801 ■ *Web:* www.thonline.com
Messenger, The 713 Central Ave .... Fort Dodge IA 50501 515-573-2141 574-4529
TF: 800-622-6613 ■ *Web:* www.messengernews.net
Globe-Gazette
300 N Washington St PO Box 271 .... Mason City IA 50402 641-421-0500 421-7108
TF: 800-421-0546 ■ *Web:* www.globegazette.com
Ottumwa Courier 213 E Second St .... Ottumwa IA 52501 641-684-4611 684-7326*
**Fax:* News Rm ■ *TF:* 800-532-1504 ■ *Web:* www.ottumwacourier.com
Sioux City Journal 515 Pavonia St .... Sioux City IA 51101 712-293-4300 279-5059
TF: 800-397-3530 ■ *Web:* www.siouxcityjournal.com
Pilot Tribune PO Box 1187 .... Storm Lake IA 50588 712-732-3130 732-3152
TF: 800-447-1985 ■ *Web:* www.stormlakepilottribune.com
Waterloo Cedar Falls Courier PO Box 540........... Waterloo IA 50701 319-291-1421 291-2069
TF: 800-798-1730 ■ *Web:* www.wcfcourier.com

Kansas

Phone *Fax*

Goodland Star-News 1205 Main St.................. Goodland KS 67735 785-899-2338 899-6186
Web: www.nwkansas.com
Hiawatha World 607 Utah St........................ Hiawatha KS 66434 785-742-2111 742-2276
Web: cityofhiawatha.org
Hutchinson News 300 W Second St .... Hutchinson KS 67504 620-694-5700 662-4186
TF: 800-766-3311 ■ *Web:* www.hutchnews.com
Lawrence Journal-World 609 New Hampshire St ...... Lawrence KS 66044 785-843-1000 843-4512*
**Fax:* Edit ■ *TF:* 800-578-8748 ■ *Web:* www.ljworld.com
Norton Telegram 215 S Kansas St..................... Norton KS 67654 785-877-3361 877-3732
Web: www.nwkansas.com
Russell County News 958 Wichita Ave .... Russell KS 67665 785-483-2116 483-4012*
Salina Journal PO Box 740 .... Salina KS 67402 785-823-6363 827-6363
Web: www.salina.com
Topeka Capital-Journal 616 SE Jefferson St .... Topeka KS 66607 785-295-1111 295-1230
TF: 800-777-7171 ■ *Web:* cjonline.com
Wichita Eagle, The 825 E Douglas Ave .... Wichita KS 67202 316-268-6000 268-6627
TF: 800-200-8906 ■ *Web:* kansas.com/
Winfield Daily Courier PO Box 543 .... Winfield KS 67156 620-221-1050 221-1101
Web: www.winfieldcourier.com

Kentucky

Phone *Fax*

Times-Tribune, The 201 N Kentucky Ave.............. Corbin KY 40701 606-528-2464 528-1335
TF: 877-629-9722 ■ *Web:* thetimestribune.com
Kentucky Enquirer 226 Grandview Dr............... Covington KY 41017 859-578-5500 578-5565
Web: www.kentucky.gov

Phone *Fax*

News-Enterprise 408 W Dixie Ave .... Elizabethtown KY 42701 270-769-1200 769-6965
TF: 877-246-2322 ■ *Web:* www.thenewsenterprise.com
State Journal, The 1216 Wilkinson Blvd............. Frankfort KY 40601 502-227-4556 227-2831
TF: 800-621-3362 ■ *Web:* www.state-journal.com
Lexington Herald-Leader 100 Midland Ave.......... Lexington KY 40508 859-231-3100 231-3224
TF: 800-999-8881 ■ *Web:* www.kentucky.com
Courier-Journal
525 W Broadway PO Box 740031.................... Louisville KY 40201 502-582-4011 582-4200
TF: 800-765-4011 ■ *Web:* www.courier-journal.com
Messenger-Inquirer 1401 Fredrica St............. Owensboro KY 42301 270-926-0123 686-7868
Web: www.messenger-inquirer.com
Paducah Sun 408 Kentucky Ave..................... Paducah KY 42003 270-575-8600
Web: www.paducahsun.com

Louisiana

Phone *Fax*

Alexandria Daily Town Talk PO Box 7558 .... Alexandria LA 71306 318-487-6397 487-6488
TF: 800-523-8391 ■ *Web:* www.thetowntalk.com
Advocate, The 7290 Blue Bonnet Blvd .... Baton Rouge LA 70810 225-383-1111 388-0371
TF: 800-960-6397 ■ *Web:* theadvocate.com
Courier, The 3030 Barrow St .... Houma LA 70360 985-879-1557 857-2244
Web: www.houmatoday.com
Daily Advertiser, The 1100 Bertrand Dr .... Lafayette LA 70506 337-289-6300 289-6443*
**Fax:* Edit ■ *TF:* 888-522-6278 ■ *Web:* www.theadvertiser.com
American Press 4900 Hwy 90 E .... Lake Charles LA 70615 337-494-4080 494-4070
TF News Rm: 800-442-2511 ■ *Web:* www.americanpress.com
News-Star 411 N Fourth St.......................... Monroe LA 71201 318-322-5161 362-0273
TF: 800-259-7788 ■ *Web:* www.thenewsstar.com
Times-Picayune 3800 Howard Ave............... New Orleans LA 70125 504-826-3279 826-3007*
**Fax:* News Rm ■ *TF:* 800-925-0000 ■ *Web:* www.nola.com
Times 222 Lake St .... Shreveport LA 71101 318-459-3200 459-3301
TF: 800-551-8892 ■ *Web:* www.shreveporttimes.com

Maine

Phone *Fax*

Bangor Daily News 491 Main St PO Box 1329 .... Bangor ME 04402 207-990-8000 941-9476*
**Fax:* Edit ■ *TF:* 800-432-7964 ■ *Web:* www.bangordailynews.com
Sun-Journal PO Box 4400 .... Lewiston ME 04243 207-784-5411 777-3436
TF: 800-482-0759 ■ *Web:* www.sunjournal.com
Morning Sentinel 31 Front St .... Waterville ME 04901 207-873-3341 861-9191
TF: 800-287-1945 ■ *Web:* centralmaine.com/

Maryland

Phone *Fax*

Capital, The 2000 Capital Dr .... Annapolis MD 21401 410-268-5000 268-4643
Web: www.capitalgazette.com
Baltimore Sun 501 N Calvert St..................... Baltimore MD 21278 410-332-6000 332-6455
TF: 800-829-8000 ■ *Web:* www.baltimoresun.com
Cumberland Times-News 19 Baltimore St.......... Cumberland MD 21502 301-722-4600 722-5270
TF: 800-742-8149 ■ *Web:* www.times-news.com
Star Democrat 29088 Airpark Dr PO Box 600 .... Easton MD 21601 410-822-1500 770-4019
TF: 800-734-3158 ■ *Web:* www.stardem.com
Frederick News Post 200 E Patrick St .... Frederick MD 21701 301-662-1177
TF: 800-486-1177 ■ *Web:* www.fredericknewspost.com
Carroll County Times 201 Railroad Ave .... Westminster MD 21157 410-848-4400 857-8749*
**Fax:* Edit ■ *Web:* www.carrollcountytimes.com

Massachusetts

Phone *Fax*

Sun Chronicle PO Box 600 .... Attleboro MA 02703 508-222-7000 236-0462
Web: www.thesunchronicle.com
Boston Globe 135 Morrissey Blvd .... Boston MA 02125 617-929-2000 929-3192
Web: www.boston.com
Herald-News 207 Pocasset St .... Fall River MA 02722 508-676-8211 676-2566
Web: www.heraldnews.com
Sentinel & Enterprise PO Box 730.................. Fitchburg MA 01420 978-343-6911 342-1158
Web: www.sentinelandenterprise.com
MetroWest Daily News 33 New York Ave.......... Framingham MA 01701 508-626-4412 626-4400*
**Fax:* News Rm ■ *Web:* www.metrowestdailynews.com
Haverhill Gazette 181 Merrimack St................ Haverhill MA 01831 978-374-0321 556-3703
TF: 888-411-3245 ■ *Web:* www.hgazette.com
Cape Cod Times 319 Main St........................ Hyannis MA 02601 508-775-1200 771-3292*
**Fax:* Edit ■ *TF:* 800-451-7887 ■ *Web:* www.capecodonline.com
Daily Item, The 38 Exchange St PO Box 951 .... Lynn MA 01903 781-593-7700 598-2891
Web: www.itemlive.com
Malden Evening News 277 Commercial St............ Malden MA 02148 781-321-8000 321-8008
Web: maldennews.com
Eagle-Tribune 100 Tpke St .... North Andover MA 01845 978-946-2000 687-6045
Web: www.eagletribune.com
Daily Hampshire Gazette 115 Conz St............ NorthHampton MA 01060 413-584-5000 585-5299
Web: www.gazettenet.com
Berkshire Eagle 75 S Church St PO Box 1171 .... Pittsfield MA 01202 413-447-7311 499-3419
TF: 800-234-7404 ■ *Web:* www.berkshireeagle.com
Patriot Ledger
400 Crown Colony Dr PO Box 699159.................. Quincy MA 02269 617-786-7000 786-7025
TF: 888-782-2267 ■ *Web:* www.patriotledger.com

Michigan

Phone *Fax*

Daily Telegram 133 N Winter St....................... Adrian MI 49221 517-265-5111 263-4152
TF: 800-968-5111 ■ *Web:* www.lenconnect.com
Huron Daily Tribune 211 N Heisterman St............. Bad Axe MI 48413 989-269-6461 269-9435
Web: www.michiganthumb.com

Newspaper	City	State	ZIP	Phone	Fax
Battle Creek Enquirer 155 W Van Buren St *TF:* 800-333-4139 ■ *Web:* www.battlecreekenquirer.com	Battle Creek	MI	49017	269-964-7161	964-8242
Bay City Times 311 Fifth St **Fax:* Edit ■ *TF:* 800-727-7661 ■ *Web:* www.mlive.com	Bay City	MI	48708	989-895-8551	893-0649*
Detroit Free Press 615 W Lafayette Blvd. **Fax:* News Rm ■ *TF:* 800-395-3300 ■ *Web:* www.freep.com	Detroit	MI	48226	313-222-6400	222-5981*
Detroit News 615 W Lafayette Blvd. **Fax:* News Rm ■ *TF General:* 800-395-3300 ■ *Web:* www.detroitnews.com	Detroit	MI	48226	313-222-2300	222-2335*
Flint Journal 200 E First St *TF Circ:* 800-875-6200 ■ *Web:* www.mlive.com	Flint	MI	48502	810-766-6100	
Holland Sentinel 54 W Eigth St *TF:* 800-784-6776 ■ *Web:* www.hollandsentinel.com	Holland	MI	49423	616-392-2311	392-3526
Jackson Citizen Patriot 100 E Michigan Ave Ste 100 *TF:* 877-213-3754 ■ *Web:* experiencejackson.com	Jackson	MI	49201	877-213-3754	
Kalamazoo Gazette 401 S Burdick St. **Fax:* Edit ■ *TF:* 800-466-6397 ■ *Web:* www.mlive.com	Kalamazoo	MI	49007	269-345-3511	388-8447*
Lansing State Journal 120 E Lenawee St *TF:* 800-234-1719 ■ *Web:* www.lansingstatejournal.com	Lansing	MI	48919	517-377-1111	377-1298
Mining Journal PO Box 430 *Web:* www.miningjournal.net	Marquette	MI	49855	906-228-2500	228-2617
Midland Daily News 124 McDonald St *TF:* 877-411-2762 ■ *Web:* www.ourmidland.com	Midland	MI	48640	989-835-7171	835-6991
Monroe Evening News 20 W First St *Web:* www.monroenews.com	Monroe	MI	48161	734-242-1100	242-0937
Macomb Daily 100 Macomb Daily Dr **Fax:* Edit ■ *Web:* www.macombdaily.com	Mount Clemens	MI	48043	586-469-4510	469-2892*
Muskegon Chronicle 981 Third St *TF:* 800-783-3161 ■ *Web:* www.mlive.com	Muskegon	MI	49440	231-722-3161	722-2552
Saginaw News 203 S Washington Ave *TF:* 800-875-6397 ■ *Web:* www.mlive.com	Saginaw	MI	48607	989-752-7171	752-3115
Herald-Palladium 3450 Hollywood Rd PO Box 128 *TF:* 800-356-4262 ■ *Web:* www.heraldpalladium.com	Saint Joseph	MI	49085	269-429-2400	429-4398
Traverse City Record-Eagle PO Box 632 *Web:* www.record-eagle.com	Traverse City	MI	49685	231-946-2000	946-8632

Minnesota

Newspaper	City	State	ZIP	Phone	Fax
Duluth News-Tribune 424 W First St. *TF Circ:* 800-456-8080 ■ *Web:* www.duluthnewstribune.com	Duluth	MN	55802	218-723-5281	720-4120
Free Press 418 S Second St *TF:* 800-657-4662 ■ *Web:* www.mankatofreepress.com	Mankato	MN	56001	507-625-4451	388-4355
Star Tribune 425 Portland Ave *TF:* 800-827-8742 ■ *Web:* www.startribune.com	Minneapolis	MN	55488	612-673-4000	673-4359
Saint Cloud Times 3000 7th Street North PO Box 768 *TF:* 877-922-1274 ■ *Web:* www.sctimes.com	Saint Cloud	MN	56303	320-255-8700	255-8773
West Central Tribune PO Box 839 *TF:* 800-450-1150 ■ *Web:* www.wctrib.com	Willmar	MN	56201	320-235-1150	235-6769

Mississippi

Newspaper	City	State	ZIP	Phone	Fax
Delta Democrat Times 988 N Broadway St *TF:* 800-273-8255 ■ *Web:* www.ddtonline.com	Greenville	MS	38701	662-335-1155	335-2860
Hattiesburg American 825 N Main St **Fax:* News Rm ■ *TF:* 800-844-2637 ■ *Web:* www.hattiesburgamerican.com	Hattiesburg	MS	39401	601-582-4321	584-3130*
Clarion-Ledger, The 201 S Congress St *TF:* 877-850-5343 ■ *Web:* www.clarionledger.com	Jackson	MS	39201	601-961-7000	961-7211
Meridian Star, The PO Box 1591 *TF:* 800-232-2525 ■ *Web:* www.meridianstar.com	Meridian	MS	39302	601-693-1551	485-1275
Northeast Mississippi Daily Journal 1242 S Green St *TF:* 800-264-6397 ■ *Web:* www.djournal.com	Tupelo	MS	38804	662-842-2611	842-2233
Vicksburg Post 1601 N Frontage Rd Ste F *Web:* www.vicksburgpost.com	Vicksburg	MS	39180	601-636-4545	634-0897

Missouri

Newspaper	City	State	ZIP	Phone	Fax
Linn County Leader 107 N Main St PO Box 40 *Web:* www.linncountyleader.com	Brookfield	MO	64628	660-258-7237	258-7238
Southeast Missourian 301 Broadway St *TF:* 800-879-1210 ■ *Web:* www.semissourian.com	Cape Girardeau	MO	63701	573-335-6611	334-7288
Columbia Daily Tribune 101 N Fourth St *TF:* 800-333-6799 ■ *Web:* www.columbiatribune.com	Columbia	MO	65201	573-815-1700	815-1701
Columbia Missourian 221 S Eigth St **Fax:* News Rm ■ *Web:* columbiamissourian.com	Columbia	MO	65201	573-882-5700	882-5702*
Excelsior Springs Standard 417 S Thompson Ave *Web:* www.excelsiorspringsstandard.com	Excelsior Springs	MO	64024	816-637-6155	637-8411
Branson Daily News 200 Industrial Pk Dr *Web:* bransontrilakesnews.com	Hollister	MO	65672	417-334-3161	335-3933
Jefferson City News Tribune 210 Monroe St *TF:* 888-892-6333 ■ *Web:* www.newstribune.com	Jefferson City	MO	65101	573-636-3131	761-0235
Jefferson City Post-Tribune 210 Monroe St *Web:* www.newstribune.com	Jefferson City	MO	65101	573-636-3131	761-0235
Joplin Globe 117 E Fourth St *TF:* 800-444-8514 ■ *Web:* www.joplinglobe.com	Joplin	MO	64801	417-623-3480	623-8598
Kansas City Star 1729 Grand Ave **Fax Area Code:* 816 ■ *TF:* 877-962-7827 ■ *Web:* www.kansascity.com	Kansas City	MO	64108	877-962-7827	234-4926*
Daily American Republic 208 Poplar St PO Box 7 *TF:* 888-276-2242 ■ *Web:* darnews.com	Poplar Bluff	MO	63901	573-785-1414	785-2706
Springfield News Leader 651 N Boonville Ave *TF:* 800-695-2005 ■ *Web:* www.news-leader.com	Springfield	MO	65806	417-836-1100	837-1381

Montana

Newspaper	City	State	ZIP	Phone	Fax
Billings Gazette 401 N 28th St *TF:* 800-543-2505 ■ *Web:* www.billingsgazette.com	Billings	MT	59101	406-657-1200	657-1208
Montana Standard 25 W Granite St *TF:* 800-877-1074 ■ *Web:* www.mtstandard.com	Butte	MT	59701	406-496-5500	496-5551
Great Falls Tribune 205 River Dr S **Fax:* News Rm ■ *TF:* 800-438-6600 ■ *Web:* www.greatfallstribune.com	Great Falls	MT	59405	406-791-1444	791-1431*
Independent Record 317 Cruse Ave *TF:* 800-523-2272 ■ *Web:* www.helenair.com	Helena	MT	59601	406-447-4000	447-4052
Daily Inter Lake 727 E Idaho St *Web:* www.dailyinterlake.com	Kalispell	MT	59901	406-755-7000	752-6114
Missoulian PO Box 8029 *TF:* 800-366-7102 ■ *Web:* www.missoulian.com	Missoula	MT	59807	406-523-5200	523-5294

Nebraska

Newspaper	City	State	ZIP	Phone	Fax
Grand Island Independent 422 W First St *TF:* 800-658-3160 ■ *Web:* www.theindependent.com	Grand Island	NE	68801	308-382-1000	382-8129
Holdrege Daily Citizen 418 Garfield St PO Box 344	Holdrege	NE	68949	308-995-4441	995-5992
Lincoln Journal-Star 926 P St **Fax:* News Rm ■ *TF:* 800-742-7315 ■ *Web:* www.journalstar.com	Lincoln	NE	68508	402-475-4200	473-7291*
Norfolk Daily News PO Box 977 *TF:* 877-371-1020 ■ *Web:* www.norfolkdailynews.com	Norfolk	NE	68702	402-371-1020	371-5802
Omaha World-Herald 1314 Douglas St *TF:* 800-284-6397 ■ *Web:* www.omaha.com	Omaha	NE	68102	402-444-1000	345-0183

Nevada

Newspaper	City	State	ZIP	Phone	Fax
Nevada Appeal 580 Mallory Way *TF General:* 877-689-3249 ■ *Web:* www.nevadaappeal.com	Carson City	NV	89701	775-882-2111	423-9696
Las Vegas Sun 2360 Corporate Cir *Web:* www.lasvegassun.com	Henderson	NV	89074	702-385-3111	383-7264
Las Vegas Review-Journal 1111 W Bonanza Rd PO Box 70 *Web:* www.reviewjournal.com	Las Vegas	NV	89106	702-383-0211	383-4676
Reno Gazette-Journal PO Box 22000 *TF:* 800-648-5048 ■ *Web:* www.rgj.com	Reno	NV	89520	775-788-6200	788-6458

New Hampshire

Newspaper	City	State	ZIP	Phone	Fax
Concord Monitor One Monitor Dr PO Box 1177 *Web:* www.concordmonitor.com	Concord	NH	03302	603-224-5301	224-8120
Foster's Daily Democrat 150 Venture Dr *TF:* 800-660-8310 ■ *Web:* www.fosters.com	Dover	NH	03820	603-742-4455	749-7079
Union Leader 100 William Loeb Dr **Fax:* Edit ■ *TF:* 800-562-8218 ■ *Web:* www.unionleader.com	Manchester	NH	03109	603-668-4321	668-0382*
Valley News 24 Interchange Dr *TF:* 800-874-2226 ■ *Web:* www.vnews.com	West Lebanon	NH	03784	603-298-8711	298-0212

New Jersey

Newspaper	City	State	ZIP	Phone	Fax
Millville/Bridgeton News 100 E Commerce St *Web:* www.nj.com	Bridgeton	NJ	08302	856-451-1000	455-3098
Courier-Post 301 Cuthbert Blvd. *TF:* 800-677-6289 ■ *Web:* www.courierpostonline.com	Cherry Hill	NJ	08002	856-663-6000	663-2831
Jersey Journal 30 Journal Sq *Web:* www.jjournal.com	Jersey City	NJ	07306	201-653-1000	653-6615
Asbury Park Press 3601 Hwy 66 PO Box 1550 **Fax:* News Rm ■ *TF:* 800-883-7737 ■ *Web:* www.app.com	Neptune	NJ	07754	732-922-6000	643-4014*
Star-Ledger, The One Star Ledger Plz *TF:* 800-501-2100 ■ *Web:* www.nj.com	Newark	NJ	07102	973-877-4141	392-5845
New Jersey Herald Two Spring St *Web:* www.njherald.com	Newton	NJ	07860	973-383-1500	383-8477
Press of Atlantic City 11 Devins Ln *Web:* www.pressofatlanticcity.com	Pleasantville	NJ	08232	609-272-7000	272-7224
Home News Tribune 92 E Main St Ste 202 **Fax:* News Rm ■ *TF:* 800-627-4663 ■ *Web:* www.mycentraljersey.com	Somerville	NJ	08876	732-246-5500	565-7208*
Times of Trenton 500 Perry St *Web:* www.nj.com	Trenton	NJ	08618	609-989-7870	396-6563
Trentonian 600 Perry St *Web:* www.trentonian.com	Trenton	NJ	08618	609-989-7800	393-6072
Burlington County Times 4284 Rt 130 *Web:* www.phillyburbs.com	Willingboro	NJ	08046	609-871-8000	871-0490
Gloucester County Times 309 S Broad St *Web:* www.nj.com	Woodbury	NJ	08096	856-845-3300	845-5480
Herald News 1 Garret Mountain Plaza Ste 8 **Fax:* Edit ■ *Web:* www.northjersey.com	Woodland Park	NJ	07424	973-569-7000	569-7268*

New Mexico

Newspaper	City	State	ZIP	Phone	Fax
Albuquerque Journal 7777 Jefferson St NE *TF:* 800-990-5765 ■ *Web:* www.abqjournal.com	Albuquerque	NM	87109	505-823-7777	823-3994
Carlsbad Current-Argus 620 S Main St PO Box 1629 **Fax Area Code:* 505 ■ *Web:* www.currentargus.com	Carlsbad	NM	88221	575-887-5501	885-1066*
Daily Times 201 N Allen Ave *TF:* 877-599-3331 ■ *Web:* www.daily-times.com	Farmington	NM	87401	505-325-4545	564-4630

Phone Fax

Gallup Independent 500 N Ninth St Gallup NM 87301 505-863-6811 722-5750
Web: www.gallupindependent.com

Las Cruces Sun-News 256 W Las Cruces Ave Las Cruces NM 88005 575-541-5400 541-5498
TF: 877-827-7200 ■ *Web:* www.lcsun-news.com

Observer, The 1594 Sara Rd SE Ste D Rio Rancho NM 87124 505-892-8080 892-5719
Web: www.rrobserver.com

Santa Fe New Mexican, The
202 E Marcy St PO Box 2048 Santa Fe NM 87504 505-983-3303 986-9147*
**Fax:* News Rm ■ *Web:* www.santafenewmexican.com

New York

Phone Fax

Times Union 645 Albany Shaker Rd PO Box 15000 Albany NY 12212 518-454-5420 454-5628
TF: 877-263-7995 ■ *Web:* www.timesunion.com

Daily Challenge 1195 Atlantic Ave Brooklyn NY 11216 718-636-9500 857-9115
Web: www.challenge-group.com

Buffalo News One News Plz PO Box 100 Buffalo NY 14240 716-849-4444 856-5150
TF: 800-777-8640 ■ *Web:* buffalonews.com

Evening Observer 8-10 E Second St PO Box 391 Dunkirk NY 14048 716-366-3000 366-3005
TF: 800-836-0931 ■ *Web:* www.observertoday.com

Star-Gazette 201 Baldwin St Elmira NY 14902 607-734-5151 733-4408
TF: 800-836-8970 ■ *Web:* www.stargazette.com

Post-Star 76 Lawrence St Glens Falls NY 12801 518-792-3131 761-1255
TF: 800-724-2543 ■ *Web:* www.poststar.com

Register-Star 364 Warren St Hudson NY 12534 518-828-1616 828-9437
TF: 800-836-1616 ■ *Web:* www.registerstar.com

Ithaca Journal 123 W State St Ithaca NY 14850 607-272-2321
Web: www.ithacajournal.com

Post-Journal 15 W Second St Jamestown NY 14701 716-487-1111 664-5305
TF: 866-756-9600 ■ *Web:* www.post-journal.com

Daily Freeman 79 Hurley Ave Kingston NY 12401 845-331-5000 331-3557
Web: www.dailyfreeman.com

Newsday Inc 235 Pinelawn Rd Melville NY 11747 631-843-2700 843-5459*
**Fax:* News Rm ■ *TF:* 800-639-7329 ■ *Web:* www.newsday.com

Times Herald-Record
40 Mulberry St PO Box 2046 Middletown NY 10940 845-341-1100 343-2170
TF: 800-295-2181 ■ *Web:* www.recordonline.com

AM New York 330 W 34th St 17th Fl New York NY 10001 212-239-5555 239-2828
Web: www.amny.com

Financial Times 1330 Ave of the Americas New York NY 10019 212-641-6500 641-6479
TF: 800-628-8088 ■ *Web:* www.ft.com

International Herald Tribune 229 W 43rd St New York NY 10036 212-556-7707
Web: international.nytimes.com

New York Daily News 450 W 33rd St Third Fl New York NY 10001 212-210-2100 643-7831
TF: 800-692-6397 ■ *Web:* www.nydailynews.com

New York Post 1211 Ave of the Americas New York NY 10036 212-930-8000 930-8542
TF: 800-552-7678 ■ *Web:* www.nypost.com

New York Times 620 Eigth Ave New York NY 10018 212-556-1234 921-0385
Web: www.nytco.com

Niagara Gazette
310 Niagara St PO Box 549 Niagara Falls NY 14302 716-282-2311 286-3895
Web: www.niagara-gazette.com

Olean Times-Herald 639 Norton Dr Olean NY 14760 716-372-3121 373-6397*
**Fax:* News Rm ■ *TF:* 800-722-8812 ■ *Web:* www.oleantimesherald.com

Daily Star 102 Chestnut St PO Box 250 Oneonta NY 13820 607-432-1000 432-5707
TF: 800-721-1000 ■ *Web:* www.thedailystar.com

Press-Republican
170 Margaret St PO Box 459 Plattsburgh NY 12901 518-561-2300 561-3362
TF: 800-288-7323 ■ *Web:* www.pressrepublican.com

Poughkeepsie Journal 85 Civic Ctr Plz Poughkeepsie NY 12601 845-437-4800 437-4921
TF: 800-765-1120 ■ *Web:* www.poughkeepsiejournal.com

Democrat & Chronicle 55 Exchange Blvd Rochester NY 14614 585-232-7100 258-2237*
**Fax:* News Rm ■ *TF:* 800-790-9565 ■ *Web:* www.democratandchronicle.com

Rome Sentinel PO Box 471 Rome NY 13442 315-337-2480 339-6281
Web: romesentinel.com

Daily Gazette
2345 Maxon Rd Ext PO Box 1090 Schenectady NY 12301 518-374-4141 395-3072
TF: 800-262-2211 ■ *Web:* www.dailygazette.com

Staten Island Advance
950 FingerboaRd Rd Staten Island NY 10305 718-981-1234 981-5679
Web: www.silive.com

Post-Standard PO Box 4915 Syracuse NY 13221 315-470-0011 470-3081
TF: 866-447-3787 ■ *Web:* www.syracuse.com

Watertown Daily Times 260 Washington St Watertown NY 13601 315-782-1000 661-2523
TF: 800-642-6222 ■ *Web:* www.watertowndailytimes.com

North Carolina

Phone Fax

Courier-Tribune 500 Sunset Ave Asheboro NC 27203 336-625-2101 626-7074
TF: 800-488-0444 ■ *Web:* www.courier-tribune.com

Asheville Citizen Times 14 O'Henry Ave Asheville NC 28801 828-252-5622 251-0585
TF: 800-800-4204 ■ *Web:* www.citizen-times.com

Times-News PO Box 481 Burlington NC 27216 336-227-0131 229-2463
TF: 800-488-0085 ■ *Web:* www.thetimesnews.com

Charlotte Observer, The 600 S Tryon St Charlotte NC 28202 704-358-5000 358-5036
TF: 800-332-0686 ■ *Web:* www.charlotteobserver.com

Herald-Sun, The 2828 Pickett Rd Durham NC 27705 919-419-6500 968-4464
TF: 877-627-6724 ■ *Web:* www.heraldsun.com

Fayetteville Observer 458 Whitfield St Fayetteville NC 28306 910-323-4848 486-3545
TF: 800-345-9895 ■ *Web:* fayobserver.com

Gaston Gazette 1893 Remount Rd Gastonia NC 28054 704-869-1700 867-5751
TF: 800-527-5226 ■ *Web:* www.gastongazette.com

Goldsboro News-Argus PO Box 10629 Goldsboro NC 27532 919-778-2211 778-5408*
**Fax:* News Rm ■ *Web:* www.newsargus.com

News & Record 200 E Market St Greensboro NC 27401 336-373-7000 373-7382
TF: 800-553-6880 ■ *Web:* www.news-record.com

Hickory Daily Record 1100 Pk Pl Hickory NC 28602 828-322-4510 322-8439
TF: 800-849-8586 ■ *Web:* www.hickoryrecord.com

High Point Enterprise 210 Church Ave High Point NC 27262 336-888-3500
Web: www.hpenews.com

Daily News 724 Bell Fork Rd PO Box 196 Jacksonville NC 28541 910-353-1171 353-7316
TF: 800-659-2873 ■ *Web:* www.jdnews.com

Mount Airy News 319 N Renfro St Mount Airy NC 27030 336-786-4141 789-2816
Web: www.mtairynews.com

Sun Journal 3200 Wellons Blvd New Bern NC 28562 252-638-8101 638-4664
Web: www.newbernsj.com

News & Observer 215 S McDowell St Raleigh NC 27602 919-829-4500 829-4529
TF: 800-522-4205 ■ *Web:* www.newsobserver.com

Star-News PO Box 840 Wilmington NC 28402 910-343-2000 343-2227
TF: 800-272-1277 ■ *Web:* www.starnewsonline.com

Wilson Daily Times 2001 Downing St Wilson NC 27893 252-243-5151 243-2999
Web: www.wilsontimes.com

Winston-Salem Journal
418 N Marshall St Winston-Salem NC 27101 336-727-7211 727-7315
TF: 800-642-0925 ■ *Web:* www.journalnow.com

North Dakota

Phone Fax

Bismarck Tribune 707 E Front Ave Bismarck ND 58504 701-223-2500 223-2063*
**Fax:* Edit ■ *TF:* 866-476-5348 ■ *Web:* www.bismarcktribune.com

Forum, The 101 N Fifth St Fargo ND 58102 701-235-7311 241-5487
TF: 800-747-7311 ■ *Web:* www.inforum.com

Grand Forks Herald 375 Second Ave N Grand Forks ND 58203 701-780-1100 780-1123
Web: www.grandforksherald.com

Minot Daily News 301 Fourth St SE Mohall ND 58761 701-857-1900 857-1907
TF: 800-735-3119 ■ *Web:* www.minotdailynews.com

Ohio

Phone Fax

Star Beacon PO Box 2100 Ashtabula OH 44005 440-998-2323 998-7938
TF: 800-554-6768 ■ *Web:* www.starbeacon.com

Repository 500 Market Ave S Canton OH 44702 330-580-8300 454-5745*
**Fax:* News Rm ■ *Web:* www.cantonrep.com

Chillicothe Gazette 50 W Main St Chillicothe OH 45601 740-773-2111 772-9505
TF: 877-424-0215 ■ *Web:* www.chillicothegazette.com

Cincinnati Enquirer 312 Elm St Cincinnati OH 45202 513-721-2700 768-8340
TF: 800-876-4500 ■ *Web:* news.cincinnati.com

Kentucky Post 1720 Gilbert Ave Cincinnati OH 45202 513-721-9900
TF: 877-667-4265 ■ *Web:* www.wcpo.com

Plain Dealer 1801 Superior Ave Cleveland OH 44114 216-999-5000 999-6366
TF: 800-362-0727 ■ *Web:* www.cleveland.com

Columbus Dispatch 34 S Third St Columbus OH 43215 614-461-5000 461-7580*
**Fax:* News Rm ■ *TF:* 800-942-2745 ■ *Web:* www.dispatch.com

Dayton Daily News 1611 S Main St Dayton OH 45409 937-225-2000 225-2489
Web: www.daytondailynews.com

Crescent-News 624 W Second St PO Box 249 Defiance OH 43512 419-784-5441 784-1492
TF: 800-589-5441 ■ *Web:* www.crescent-news.com

Chronicle-Telegram 225 E Ave Elyria OH 44035 440-329-7000 329-7282
TF: 800-848-6397 ■ *Web:* chronicle.northcoastnow.com

Journal News 228 Ct St Hamilton OH 45011 513-863-8200 896-9489
Web: www.journal-news.com

Record-Courier 1050 W Main St PO Box 5199 Kent OH 44240 330-541-9400 296-2698
TF: 800-560-9657 ■ *Web:* www.recordpub.com

Lancaster Eagle-Gazette 138 W Chestnut St Lancaster OH 43130 740-654-1321 681-4505
TF: 877-513-7355 ■ *Web:* www.lancastereaglegazette.com

Lima News 3515 Elida Rd Lima OH 45807 419-223-1010 229-2926
TF: 800-686-9924 ■ *Web:* www.limaohio.com

Morning Journal 1657 Broadway Ave Lorain OH 44052 440-245-6901 245-6912
Web: www.morningjournal.com

News Journal 70 W Fourth St Mansfield OH 44903 419-522-3311 521-7415
TF: 800-472-5547 ■ *Web:* www.mansfieldnewsjournal.com

Marion Star, The 163 E Center St Marion OH 43302 740-387-0400 375-5188
TF: 877-987-2782 ■ *Web:* www.marionstar.com

Times Leader 200 S Fourth St Martins Ferry OH 43935 740-633-1131 633-1122
TF: 800-244-5671 ■ *Web:* www.timesleaderonline.com

Medina Gazette 885 W Liberty St Medina OH 44256 330-725-4166
TF: 800-633-4623 ■ *Web:* medinagazette.northcoastnow.com

Times Reporter 629 Wabash Ave NW New Philadelphia OH 44663 330-364-5577 364-8416
TF: 800-686-5577 ■ *Web:* www.timesreporter.com

Kroner Publications Inc 1123a W Pk Ave Niles OH 44446 330-544-5500 544-5511

Daily Sentinel 111 Ct St PO Box 729 Pomeroy OH 45769 740-992-2155 992-2157
Web: www.mydailysentinel.com

Portsmouth Daily Times PO Box 581 Portsmouth OH 45662 740-353-3101 353-4676
TF: 866-430-8358 ■ *Web:* www.portsmouth-dailytimes.com

Sandusky Register 314 W Market St Sandusky OH 44870 419-625-5500 625-3007
TF: 800-466-1243 ■ *Web:* www.sanduskyregister.com

Daily Globe 37 W Main St Shelby OH 44875 419-342-3261 342-4246
Web: www.sdgnewsgroup.com

Springfield News-Sun 202 N Limestone St Springfield OH 45503 937-328-0300 328-0328
TF: 800-441-6397 ■ *Web:* www.springfieldnewssun.com

Blade 541 N Superior St Toledo OH 43660 419-724-6000 724-6439
TF: 800-245-3317 ■ *Web:* www.toledoblade.com

Tribune Chronicle 240 Franklin St SE Warren OH 44482 330-841-1600 841-1717
TF: 888-550-8742 ■ *Web:* tribtoday.com/

Daily Record 212 E Liberty St PO Box 918 Wooster OH 44691 330-264-1125 264-3756
TF: 800-686-2958 ■ *Web:* www.the-daily-record.com

Vindicator, The
107 Vindicator Sq PO Box 780 Youngstown OH 44501 330-747-1471 747-6712
TF: 877-700-4647 ■ *Web:* www.vindy.com

Times Recorder 34 S Fourth St Zanesville OH 43701 740-452-4561 225-2610*
**Fax Area Code:* 202 ■ **Fax:* News Rm ■ *TF:* 844-265-6246 ■ *Web:* www.zanesvilletimesrecorder.com

Oklahoma

Phone Fax

Edmond Sun PO Box 2470 Edmond OK 73083 405-341-2121 340-7363
Web: www.edmondsun.com

	City	State	ZIP	Phone	Fax
Enid News & Eagle 227 W Broadway PO Box 3451 — TF: 800-299-6397 ■ Web: www.enidnews.com	Enid	OK	73701	580-548-8186	233-7645
Lawton Constitution 102 SW Third St PO Box 2069 — Web: www.swoknews.com	Lawton	OK	73502	580-353-0620	585-5140
Muskogee Daily Phoenix 214 Wall St — Web: www.muskogeephoenix.com	Muskogee	OK	74401	918-684-2828	684-2865
Norman Transcript 215 E Comanche St PO Box 1058 — Web: www.normantranscript.com	Norman	OK	73069	405-321-1800	366-3516
Journal Record Oklahoma City 101 N Robinson St Ste 101 — Web: www.journalrecord.com	Oklahoma City	OK	73102	405-235-3100	278-2890
Oklahoman, The 9000 N Broadway — TF: 800-375-6397 ■ Web: www.newsok.com	Oklahoma City	OK	73114	405-475-3311	475-3970
Tulsa World 315 S Boulder Ave — TF: 800-897-3557 ■ Web: www.tulsaworld.com	Tulsa	OK	74103	918-583-2161	581-8353
Wewoka Times PO Box 61 — Web: www.wewokatimes.com	Wewoka	OK	74884	405-257-3341	257-3342

Oregon

	City	State	ZIP	Phone	Fax
Albany Democrat-Herald 600 Lyons St SW PO Box 130 — TF: 877-634-2867 ■ Web: www.democratherald.com	Albany	OR	97321	541-926-2211	926-4799
Bulletin, The 1777 SW Chandler Ave — TF: 800-503-3933 ■ Web: www.bendbulletin.com	Bend	OR	97702	541-382-1811	385-5804
Register-Guard 3500 Chad Dr — Web: www.registerguard.com	Eugene	OR	97408	541-485-1234	683-7631
Medford Mail Tribune PO Box 1108 — TF: 800-452-4011 ■ Web: www.mailtribune.com	Medford	OR	97501	541-776-4411	858-5126
Daily Journal of Commerce 921 SW Washington St Ste 210 — *Fax: News Rm ■ Web: djcoregon.com	Portland	OR	97205	503-226-1311	802-7239*
Oregonian 1320 SW Broadway — TF News Rm: 800-723-3638 ■ Web: www.oregonlive.com	Portland	OR	97201	503-221-8100	227-5306
News-Review 345 NE Winchester St — *Fax: Edit ■ TF: 888-459-3830 ■ Web: www.nrtoday.com	Roseburg	OR	97470	541-672-3321	673-5994*
Statesman Journal 280 Church St NE — *Fax: News Rm ■ Web: www.statesmanjournal.com	Salem	OR	97301	503-399-6611	399-6706*

Pennsylvania

	City	State	ZIP	Phone	Fax
Morning Call PO Box 1260 — TF: 800-666-5492 ■ Web: www.mcall.com	Allentown	PA	18105	610-820-6500	820-6693
Altoona Mirror 301 Cayuga Ave — TF: 800-222-1962 ■ Web: www.altoonamirror.com	Altoona	PA	16602	814-946-7411	946-7540
Beaver County Times 400 Fair Ave — *Fax: Edit ■ Web: www.timesonline.com	Beaver	PA	15009	724-775-3200	775-4180*
Butler Eagle 114 W Diamond St — Web: www.butlereagle.com	Butler	PA	16001	724-282-8000	282-4180
Sentinel, The 457 E N St — TF: 800-829-5570 ■ Web: www.cumberlink.com	Carlisle	PA	17013	717-243-2611	243-3121
Public Opinion 77 N Third St — *Fax: News Rm ■ Web: www.publicopiniononline.com	Chambersburg	PA	17201	717-264-6161	264-0377*
Intelligencer, The 333 N Broad St — Web: www.phillyburbs.com	Doylestown	PA	18901	215-345-3000	345-3150
Express-Times 30 N Fourth St — TF: 800-360-3601 ■ Web: www.lehighvalleylive.com	Easton	PA	18042	610-258-7171	258-7130
Erie Times-News 205 W 12th St — TF: 800-352-0043 ■ Web: www.goerie.com	Erie	PA	16534	814-870-1600	870-1808
Gettysburg Times, The 1570 Fairfield Rd — Web: www.gettysburgtimes.com	Gettysburg	PA	17325	717-334-1131	334-4243
Tribune-Review 622 Cabin Hill Dr — Web: www.triblive.com	Greensburg	PA	15601	724-834-1151	838-5171
Evening Sun 135 Baltimore St PO Box 514 — TF: 800-877-3786 ■ Web: www.eveningsun.com	Hanover	PA	17331	717-637-3736	637-7730
Patriot-News 812 Market St — TF: 800-692-7207 ■ Web: www.pennlive.com	Harrisburg	PA	17101	717-255-8100	255-8456
Hazleton Standard Speaker 21 N Wyoming St — TF Cust Svc: 800-843-6680 ■ Web: www.standardspeaker.com	Hazleton	PA	18201	570-455-3636	455-4244
Wayne Independent 220 Eigth St — Web: www.wayneindependent.com	Honesdale	PA	18431	570-253-3055	253-5387
Indiana Gazette 899 Water St — Web: indianagazette.com	Indiana	PA	15701	724-465-5555	465-8267
Tribune-Democrat 425 Locust St — TF: 855-255-5975 ■ Web: tribdem.com/	Johnstown	PA	15907	814-532-5050	539-1409
Intelligencer Journal Eight W King St PO Box 1328 — TF: 800-809-4666 ■ Web: www.lancasteronline.com	Lancaster	PA	17603	717-291-8622	399-6507
Lancaster New Era Eight W King St PO Box 1328 — TF: 800-809-4666 ■ Web: www.lancasteronline.com	Lancaster	PA	17603	717-291-8733	399-6507
Lebanon Daily News 718 Poplar St — Web: www.ldnews.com	Lebanon	PA	17042	717-272-5611	274-1608
Meadville Tribune 947 Federal Ct — TF: 800-879-0006 ■ Web: www.meadvilletribune.com	Meadville	PA	16335	814-724-6370	724-8755
Valley Independent Eastgate 19 — Web: triblive.com	Monessen	PA	15062	724-684-5200	684-2602
Valley Mirror 3910 Main St	Munhall	PA	15120	412-462-0626	
New Castle News PO Box 60 — Web: www.ncnewsonline.com	New Castle	PA	16103	724-654-6651	654-5976
Times Herald PO Box 591 — Web: www.timesherald.com	Norristown	PA	19404	610-272-2500	272-0660
Philadelphia Daily News PO Box 8263 — Web: www.philly.com	Philadelphia	PA	19101	215-854-2000	854-5910
Philadelphia Inquirer 801 Market St Ste 300 PO Box 8263 — TF: 800-341-3413 ■ Web: philly.com/subscribe	Philadelphia	PA	19107	215-854-2000	
Pittsburgh Post-Gazette 34 Blvd of the Allies — Web: www.post-gazette.com	Pittsburgh	PA	15222	412-263-1100	391-8452
Pittsburgh Tribune-Review 503 Martindale St 3rd Fl — TF: 800-909-8742 ■ Web: triblive.com	Pittsburgh	PA	15212	412-321-6460	
Mercury, The 24 N Hanover St — Web: www.pottsmerc.com	Pottstown	PA	19464	610-323-3000	323-0682
Pottsville Republican 111 Mahantongo St — Web: www.pottsville.com	Pottsville	PA	17901	570-622-3456	628-6068
Delaware County Daily Times 500 Mildred Ave — Web: www.delcotimes.com	Primos	PA	19018	610-622-8800	622-8889
Scranton Times-Tribune 149 Penn Ave — TF: 800-228-4637 ■ Web: thetimes-tribune.com	Scranton	PA	18503	570-348-9100	348-9135
Herald, The 52 S Dock St — Web: www.sharonherald.com	Sharon	PA	16146	724-981-6100	981-5116
Centre Daily Times 3400 E College Ave — *Fax: News Rm ■ TF: 800-327-5500 ■ Web: www.centredaily.com	State College	PA	16801	814-238-5000	238-1811*
Pocono Record 511 Lenox St — *Fax: News Rm ■ TF: 800-530-6310 ■ Web: www.poconorecord.com	Stroudsburg	PA	18360	570-421-3000	421-6284*
Valley News Dispatch 210 Fourth Ave — *Fax Area Code: 724 ■ TF: 877-698-2553 ■ Web: triblive.com	Tarentum	PA	15084	800-909-8742	226-4677*
Herald-Standard Eight E Church St Ste 18 — TF: 800-342-8254 ■ Web: www.heraldstandard.com	Uniontown	PA	15401	724-439-7500	439-7559
Observer-Reporter 122 S Main St — *Fax: News Rm ■ TF: 800-222-6397 ■ Web: www.observer-reporter.com	Washington	PA	15301	724-222-2200	225-2077*
Daily Local News 250 N Bradford Ave — Web: www.dailylocal.com	West Chester	PA	19382	610-696-1775	430-1194
Citizens' Voice 75 N Washington St — *Fax: News Rm ■ Web: www.citizensvoice.com	Wilkes-Barre	PA	18711	570-821-2000	821-2247*
Times Leader, The 15 N Main St — *Fax: News Rm ■ TF: 800-427-8649 ■ Web: www.timesleader.com	Wilkes-Barre	PA	18711	570-829-7101	829-5537*
Williamsport Sun-Gazette 252 W Fourth St — TF: 800-339-0289 ■ Web: www.sungazette.com	Williamsport	PA	17701	570-326-1551	326-0314
York Daily Record (YDR) 1891 Loucks Rd — Web: www.ydr.com	York	PA	17408	717-771-2000	771-2009
York Dispatch 205 N George St — TF: 800-227-2345 ■ Web: www.yorkdispatch.com	York	PA	17401	717-854-1575	843-2814

Rhode Island

	City	State	ZIP	Phone	Fax
Newport Daily News 101 Malbone Rd — Web: www.newportri.com	Newport	RI	02840	401-849-3300	849-3306
Providence Journal 75 Fountain St — TF: 888-697-7656 ■ Web: www.providencejournal.com	Providence	RI	02902	401-277-7303	277-8175
Evening Call Publishing Co, The 75 Main St — Web: www.woonsocketcall.com	Woonsocket	RI	02895	401-762-3000	765-2834

South Carolina

	City	State	ZIP	Phone	Fax
Anderson Independent-Mail PO Box 2507 — TF: 800-859-6397 ■ Web: www.independentmail.com	Anderson	SC	29622	864-224-4321	260-1276
Island Packet 10 Buck Island Rd — TF: 877-706-8100 ■ Web: www.islandpacket.com	Bluffton	SC	29910	843-706-8100	706-3070
Post & Courier 134 Columbus St — *Fax: News Rm ■ Web: www.postandcourier.com	Charleston	SC	29403	843-577-7111	937-5579*
State, The 1401 Shop Rd — TF: 800-888-5353 ■ Web: www.thestate.com	Columbia	SC	29201	803-771-6161	771-8430
Morning News 310 S Dargan St — Web: www.scnow.com	Florence	SC	29506	843-317-6397	317-7292
Greenville News 305 S Main St — TF: 800-800-5116 ■ Web: www.greenvilleonline.com	Greenville	SC	29601	864-298-4100	298-4395
Index Journal 610 Phoenix St — Web: www.indexjournal.com	Greenwood	SC	29648	864-223-1411	223-7331
Sun News 914 Frontage Rd E — TF: 800-568-1800 ■ Web: www.myrtlebeachonline.com	Myrtle Beach	SC	29578	843-626-8555	626-0356
Spartanburg Herald-Journal 189 W Main St — TF: 800-922-4158 ■ Web: www.goupstate.com	Spartanburg	SC	29306	864-582-4511	594-6350
Item, The 20 N Magnolia St PO Box 1677 — Web: www.theitem.com	Sumter	SC	29151	803-774-1200	774-1210

South Dakota

	City	State	ZIP	Phone	Fax
Aberdeen American News 124 S Second St — TF: 800-925-4100 ■ Web: www.aberdeennews.com/mld/americannews	Aberdeen	SD	57402	605-225-4100	229-7532
Capital Journal 333 W Dakota Ave — TF: 800-537-0025 ■ Web: www.capjournal.com	Pierre	SD	57501	605-224-7301	224-9210
Rapid City Journal 507 Main St — TF: 800-843-2300 ■ Web: www.rapidcityjournal.com	Rapid City	SD	57701	605-394-8300	394-8463
Argus Leader 200 S Minnesota Ave — *Fax: Edit ■ TF: 800-530-6397 ■ Web: www.argusleader.com	Sioux Falls	SD	57104	605-331-2200	331-2294*
Black Hills Pioneer 315 Seaton Cir — Web: bhpioneer.com	Spearfish	SD	57783	605-642-2761	

Tennessee

	City	State	ZIP	Phone	Fax
Chattanooga Times Free Press 400 E 11th St — Web: www.timesfreepress.com	Chattanooga	TN	37403	423-756-6900	757-6383
Leaf-Chronicle PO Box 31029 — Web: www.theleafchronicle.com	Clarksville	TN	37040	931-552-1808	552-5859
Greeneville Sun 121 W Summer St — Web: www.greenevillesun.com	Greeneville	TN	37743	423-638-4181	638-7348
Jackson Sun 245 W LaFayette St — TF: 800-372-3922 ■ Web: www.jacksonsun.com	Jackson	TN	38301	731-427-3333	425-9639

Name / Address	City	State	ZIP	Phone	Fax
Johnson City Press 204 W Main St *Web:* www.johnsoncitypress.com	Johnson City	TN	37604	423-929-3111	929-7484
Kingsport Times-News 701 Lynn Garden Dr *TF:* 800-251-0328 ■ *Web:* www.timesnews.net	Kingsport	TN	37660	423-246-8121	392-1385
Knoxville News-Sentinel 2332 News Sentinel Dr **Fax:* Edit ■ *TF:* 800-237-5821 ■ *Web:* www.knoxnews.com	Knoxville	TN	37921	865-521-8181	342-8635*
Commercial Appeal 495 Union Ave *TF:* 800-444-6397 ■ *Web:* www.commercialappeal.com	Memphis	TN	38103	901-529-2345	529-2522
Citizen Tribune 1609 W First N St PO Box 625 *TF:* 800-624-0281 ■ *Web:* www.citizentribune.com	Morristown	TN	37815	423-581-5630	581-8863
Daily News Journal 224 N Walnut St *Web:* www.dnj.com	Murfreesboro	TN	37130	615-893-5860	893-4186
City Paper, The 210 12th Ave S Ste 100 *Web:* www.nashvillecitypaper.com	Nashville	TN	37203	615-244-7989	244-8578
Tennessean 1100 Broadway *TF:* 800-342-8237 ■ *Web:* www.tennessean.com	Nashville	TN	37203	615-259-8033	259-8093

Texas

Name / Address	City	State	ZIP	Phone	Fax
Abilene Reporter-News 101 Cypress St **Fax:* Edit ■ *TF:* 800-588-6397 ■ *Web:* www.reporternews.com	Abilene	TX	79601	325-673-4271	670-5242*
Amarillo Globe News PO Box 2091 *Web:* amarillo.com	Amarillo	TX	79166	806-376-4488	373-0810
Austin American-Statesman 305 S Congress Ave *TF:* 800-445-9898 ■ *Web:* www.statesman.com	Austin	TX	78704	512-445-3500	445-3679
Bay City Tribune 2901 16th St *TF:* 877-322-8228 ■ *Web:* www.baycitytribune.com	Bay City	TX	77414	979-245-5555	245-1537
Beaumont Enterprise 380 Main St *Web:* www.beaumontenterprise.com	Beaumont	TX	77701	409-838-2888	880-0757
Banner-Press PO Box 585 *Web:* www.brenhambanner.com	Brenham	TX	77834	979-836-7956	830-8577
Adpro International Advertising Co 1144 Lincoln St	Brownsville	TX	78521	956-542-5800	542-6023
Brownsville Herald, The 1135 E Van Buren St *TF:* 800-488-4301 ■ *Web:* www.brownsvilleherald.com	Brownsville	TX	78520	956-542-4301	542-0840
Bryan-College Station Eagle 1729 Briarcrest Dr *Web:* theeagle.com	Bryan	TX	77802	979-776-4444	776-8923
Brazosport Facts 720 S Main St *TF:* 800-864-8340 ■ *Web:* www.thefacts.com	Clute	TX	77531	979-265-7411	265-9052
Caller-Times 820 N Lower Broadway **Fax:* Edit ■ *TF:* 800-827-2011 ■ *Web:* www.caller.com	Corpus Christi	TX	78401	361-884-2011	886-3732*
Dallas Morning News 508 Young St *TF:* 800-431-0010 ■ *Web:* www.dallasnews.com	Dallas	TX	75202	214-977-8222	977-8319
Focus Daily News 1337 Marilyn Ave *Web:* www.focus-news.com	De Soto	TX	75115	972-223-9175	223-9202
Denton Record-Chronicle 314 E Hickory St *TF:* 800-275-1722 ■ *Web:* www.dentonrc.com	Denton	TX	76201	940-387-3811	566-6888
El Paso Times 300 N Campbell St Times Plz **Fax:* News Rm ■ *Web:* www.elpasotimes.com	El Paso	TX	79901	915-546-6100	546-6415*
Fort Worth Star-Telegram 808 Throckmorton St PO Box 1870 *Web:* www.dfw.com	Fort Worth	TX	76101	817-390-7761	390-7789
Galveston County Daily News 8522 Teichman Rd PO Box 628 *TF:* 800-561-3611 ■ *Web:* www.galvestondailynews.com	Galveston	TX	77553	409-683-5200	740-3421
Valley Morning Star PO Box 511 *TF:* 877-786-7612 ■ *Web:* www.valleymorningstar.com	Harlingen	TX	78551	956-430-6200	430-6233
Houston Chronicle 801 Texas Ave *TF:* 800-735-3800 ■ *Web:* www.chron.com	Houston	TX	77002	713-362-7171	362-6806
Killeen Daily Herald 1809 Florence Rd PO Box 1300 *Web:* www.kdhnews.com	Killeen	TX	76540	254-634-2125	200-7640
Laredo Morning Times 111 Esperanza Dr **Fax:* Edit ■ *TF:* 800-232-7907 ■ *Web:* www.lmtonline.com	Laredo	TX	78041	956-728-2500	724-3036*
Longview News-Journal 320 E Methvin St **Fax:* News Rm ■ *TF:* 800-825-9799 ■ *Web:* www.news-journal.com	Longview	TX	75601	903-757-3311	757-3742*
Lubbock Avalanche-Journal 710 Ave J *TF:* 800-692-4021 ■ *Web:* lubbockonline.com	Lubbock	TX	79401	806-762-8844	744-9603
Lufkin Daily News 300 Ellis Ave *TF:* 888-664-8792 ■ *Web:* www.lufkindailynews.com	Lufkin	TX	75904	936-632-6631	632-6655
Monitor, The 1400 E Nolana Loop *TF:* 800-366-4343 ■ *Web:* www.themonitor.com	McAllen	TX	78504	956-683-4000	683-4401
Midland Reporter-Telegram PO Box 1650 *TF:* 800-542-3952 ■ *Web:* mrt.com/	Midland	TX	79702	432-682-5311	570-7650
Odessa American PO Box 2952 *TF:* 800-592-4433 ■ *Web:* www.oaoa.com	Odessa	TX	79760	432-337-4661	333-7742
Pecos Enterprise PO Box 2057 *Web:* www.pecos.net	Pecos	TX	79772	432-445-5475	445-4321
Plano Star Courier 624 Crona Dr Ste 170 *Web:* starlocalmedia.com	Plano	TX	75074	972-398-4200	398-4270
Port Arthur News 3501 Turtle Creek Dr # 105 *Web:* www.panews.com	Port Arthur	TX	77642	409-729-6397	724-6840
Fort Bend Herald 1902 S Fourth St *Web:* www.fbherald.com	Rosenberg	TX	77471	281-342-4474	342-3219
San Angelo Standard-Times 34 W Harris Ave *TF:* 800-588-1884 ■ *Web:* www.gosanangelo.com	San Angelo	TX	76903	325-659-8200	659-8173
Metrocom Herald 17400 Judson Rd *Web:* www.primetimenewspapers.com	San Antonio	TX	78247	210-453-3300	828-3787
San Antonio Express-News Ave E & Third St *TF:* 800-555-1551 ■ *Web:* www.mysanantonio.com	San Antonio	TX	78205	210-250-3000	250-3105
Herald Democrat 603 S Sam Rayburn Fwy *TF:* 800-827-7183 ■ *Web:* www.heralddemocrat.com	Sherman	TX	75090	903-893-8181	868-1930
Texarkana Gazette 315 Pine St *TF General:* 866-747-7424 ■ *Web:* www.texarkanagazette.com	Texarkana	TX	75501	903-794-3311	794-3315
Tyler Morning Telegraph PO Box 2030 **Fax:* News Rm ■ *TF:* 800-772-1213 ■ *Web:* www.tylerpaper.com	Tyler	TX	75710	903-597-8111	595-0335*
Victoria Advocate PO Box 1518 **Fax:* News Rm ■ *TF:* 800-234-8108 ■ *Web:* www.victoriaadvocate.com	Victoria	TX	77902	361-575-1451	574-1220*
Waco Tribune-Herald 900 Franklin Ave *TF:* 800-678-8742 ■ *Web:* www.wacotrib.com	Waco	TX	76701	254-757-5757	757-0302
Times Record News PO Box 120 *TF:* 800-627-1646 ■ *Web:* www.timesrecordnews.com	Wichita Falls	TX	76307	940-767-8341	767-1741

Utah

Name / Address	City	State	ZIP	Phone	Fax
Herald Journal 75 W 300 N *TF:* 800-275-0423 ■ *Web:* www.hjnews.com	Logan	UT	84321	435-752-2121	753-6642
Standard-Examiner 332 Standard Way *TF:* 800-234-5505 ■ *Web:* www.standard.net	Ogden	UT	84404	801-625-4200	625-4299
Daily Herald 1555 N Freedom Blvd *TF:* 800-880-8075 ■ *Web:* www.heraldextra.com	Provo	UT	84604	801-373-5050	344-2985
Spectrum, The 275 E St George Blvd *Web:* www.thespectrum.com	Saint George	UT	84770	435-674-6200	674-6265
Deseret News 30 E 100 S Suite 400 PO Box 1257 *TF:* 800-999-7511 ■ *Web:* www.deseretnews.com	Salt Lake City	UT	84110	801-236-6000	237-2121
Salt Lake Tribune 90 South 400 West Ste 700 *Web:* www.sltrib.com	Salt Lake City	UT	84101	801-257-8742	257-8525

Vermont

Name / Address	City	State	ZIP	Phone	Fax
Burlington Free Press 100 Bank St *TF:* 800-427-3124 ■ *Web:* www.burlingtonfreepress.com	Burlington	VT	05401	802-863-3441	660-1802
Rutland Herald PO Box 668 **Fax Area Code:* 802 ■ *TF:* 800-498-4296 ■ *Web:* www.rutlandherald.com	Rutland	VT	05702	800-498-4296	747-6133*

Virginia

Name / Address	City	State	ZIP	Phone	Fax
Bristol Herald-Courier 320 Bob Morrison Blvd *TF:* 888-228-2098 ■ *Web:* www.tricities.com	Bristol	VA	24201	276-669-2181	669-3696
Free Lance Star 616 Amelia St **Fax:* News Rm ■ *TF:* 800-877-0500 ■ *Web:* www.fredericksburg.com	Fredericksburg	VA	22401	540-374-5000	373-8455*
Daily News-Record 231 S Liberty St *Web:* www.dnronline.com	Harrisonburg	VA	22801	540-574-6200	433-9112
News & Advance PO Box 10129 *TF:* 800-275-8830 ■ *Web:* www.newsadvance.com	Lynchburg	VA	24506	434-385-5555	385-5538
Martinsville Bulletin PO Box 3711 *TF:* 800-234-6575 ■ *Web:* www.martinsvillebulletin.com	Martinsville	VA	24115	276-638-8801	638-7409
Daily Press 7505 Warwick Blvd *Web:* www.dailypress.com	Newport News	VA	23607	757-247-4600	245-8618
Virginian-Pilot 150 W Bramelton Ave *TF:* 800-446-2004 ■ *Web:* www.hamptonroads.com	Norfolk	VA	23510	757-446-2000	446-2414
Progress-Index 15 Franklin St *Web:* www.progress-index.com	Petersburg	VA	23803	804-732-3456	732-8417
Roanoke Times 201 W Campbell Ave SW *TF:* 800-346-1234 ■ *Web:* www.roanoke.com	Roanoke	VA	24011	540-981-3340	981-3346
News Leader 11 N Central Ave *TF:* 800-793-2459 ■ *Web:* www.newsleader.com	Staunton	VA	24401	540-885-7281	885-1904
Winchester Star Two N Kent St *TF:* 800-296-8639 ■ *Web:* www.winchesterstar.com	Winchester	VA	22601	540-667-3200	667-1649

Washington

Name / Address	City	State	ZIP	Phone	Fax
Daily World 315 S Michigan St *TF:* 800-829-7880 ■ *Web:* www.thedailyworld.com	Aberdeen	WA	98520	360-532-4000	533-6039
Bellingham Herald 1155 N State St **Fax:* News Rm ■ *Web:* www.bellinghamherald.com	Bellingham	WA	98225	360-676-2600	756-2826*
Kitsap Sun PO Box 259 *TF:* 888-377-3711 ■ *Web:* www.kitsapsun.com	Bremerton	WA	98337	360-377-3711	415-2681
Tri-City Herald 333 W Canal Dr *TF:* 800-874-0445 ■ *Web:* www.tri-cityherald.com	Kennewick	WA	99336	509-582-1500	582-1510
Skagit Valley Herald 1000 E College Way PO Box 578 **Fax:* News Rm ■ *TF:* 800-683-3300 ■ *Web:* www.goskagit.com	Mount Vernon	WA	98273	360-424-3251	424-5300*
Olympian, The PO Box 407 **Fax:* News Rm ■ *Web:* www.theolympian.com	Olympia	WA	98507	360-754-5400	357-0202*
Peninsula Daily News 305 W First St PO Box 1330 *TF:* 800-826-7714 ■ *Web:* www.peninsuladailynews.com	Port Angeles	WA	98362	360-452-2345	417-3521
Seattle Daily Journal of Commerce PO Box 11050 *Web:* www.djc.com	Seattle	WA	98111	206-622-8272	622-8416
Seattle Post-Intelligencer 101 Elliott Ave W Second Fl *TF:* 800-542-0820 ■ *Web:* www.seattlepi.com	Seattle	WA	98119	206-448-8000	448-8166
Seattle Times 1120 John St *Web:* seattletimes.com	Seattle	WA	98109	206-464-2111	464-2261
News Tribune 1950 S State St *TF:* 800-388-8742 ■ *Web:* www.thenewstribune.com	Tacoma	WA	98405	253-597-8742	597-8274
Columbian 701 W Eigth St PO Box 180 *TF:* 800-743-3391 ■ *Web:* www.columbian.com	Vancouver	WA	98660	360-694-3391	699-6033
Wenatchee World 14 N Mission St *TF:* 800-572-4433 ■ *Web:* wenatcheeworld.com	Wenatchee	WA	98801	509-663-5161	665-1183
Yakima Herald-Republic PO Box 9668 *TF:* 800-343-2799 ■ *Web:* www.yakimaherald.com	Yakima	WA	98909	509-248-1251	577-7767

West Virginia

Name / Address	City	State	ZIP	Phone	Fax
Register-Herald 801 N Kanawha St *TF:* 800-950-0250 ■ *Web:* www.register-herald.com	Beckley	WV	25801	304-255-4400	255-4427

				Phone	Fax
Charleston Gazette 1001 Virginia St E *TF:* 800-982-6397 ■ *Web:* www.wvgazette.com	Charleston	WV	25301	304-348-5140	348-1233
Clarksburg Exponent Telegram 324 Hewes Ave *TF:* 800-982-6034 ■ *Web:* theet.com/	Clarksburg	WV	26301	304-626-1400	624-4188
Exponent Telegram 324 Hewes Ave *Fax Area Code:* 304 ■ *TF:* 800-982-6034 ■ *Web:* theet.com/	Clarksburg	WV	26301	800-982-6034	624-4188*
Herald-Dispatch 946 Fifth Ave *TF:* 800-444-2446 ■ *Web:* www.herald-dispatch.com	Huntington	WV	25701	304-526-4000	526-2857
Journal, The 207 W King St *Fax:* PR ■ *TF:* 800-448-1895 ■ *Web:* www.journal-news.net	Martinsburg	WV	25402	304-263-8931	267-2903*
Daily Athenaeum 284 Prospect St *Web:* www.thedaonline.com	Morgantown	WV	26505	304-293-4141	293-6857
Parkersburg News 519 Juliana St *Web:* www.newsandsentinel.com	Parkersburg	WV	26101	304-485-1891	485-5122
Wheeling News-Register 1500 Main St *Fax:* Edit ■ *Web:* theintelligencer.net/	Wheeling	WV	26003	304-233-0100	232-1399*

Wisconsin

				Phone	Fax
Beloit Daily News 149 State St *TF:* 800-356-3411 ■ *Web:* www.beloitdailynews.com	Beloit	WI	53511	608-365-8811	365-1420
Leader-Telegram 701 S Farwell St *Fax:* Edit ■ *TF:* 800-236-8808 ■ *Web:* www.leadertelegram.com	Eau Claire	WI	54701	715-833-9200	858-7308*
Action Reporter Media N6637 Rolling Meadows Dr PO Box 1955 *TF:* 800-261-5325 ■ *Web:* www.fdlreporter.com	Fond du Lac	WI	54936	920-922-4600	
Green Bay Press-Gazette PO Box 23430 *TF:* 800-289-8221 ■ *Web:* www.greenbaypressgazette.com	Green Bay	WI	54305	920-431-8400	431-8379
Janesville Gazette One S Parker Dr PO Box 5001 *Fax:* Edit ■ *TF:* 800-362-6712 ■ *Web:* www.gazetteextra.com	Janesville	WI	53547	608-754-3311	755-8349*
Kenosha News 5800 Seventh Ave *TF:* 800-292-2700 ■ *Web:* www.kenoshanews.com	Kenosha	WI	53140	262-657-1000	657-8455
La Crosse Tribune 401 N Third St *Fax:* Edit ■ *TF:* 800-262-0420 ■ *Web:* www.lacrossetribune.com	La Crosse	WI	54601	608-782-9710	782-9723*
Capital Times 1901 Fish Hatchery Rd *TF:* 800-362-8333 ■ *Web:* host.madison.com	Madison	WI	53713	608-252-6400	
Wisconsin State Journal 1901 Fish Hatchery Rd *TF:* 800-362-8333 ■ *Web:* host.madison.com	Madison	WI	53713	608-252-6200	252-6445
Herald Times Reporter 902 Franklin St *TF:* 800-783-7323 ■ *Web:* www.htrnews.com	Manitowoc	WI	54221	920-684-4433	686-2103
Milwaukee Journal Sentinel 333 W State St *TF:* 800-456-5943 ■ *Web:* www.jsonline.com	Milwaukee	WI	53201	414-224-2000	224-2047
Journal Times 212 Fourth St *Web:* www.journaltimes.com	Racine	WI	53403	262-634-3322	631-1780
Sheboygan Press 632 Center Ave PO Box 358 *TF:* 800-686-3900 ■ *Web:* www.sheboyganpress.com	Sheboygan	WI	53081	920-457-7711	457-3573
Waukesha County Freeman 801 N Barstow St PO Box 7 *TF:* 800-762-6219 ■ *Web:* www.gmtoday.com	Waukesha	WI	53187	262-542-2501	542-8259
Wausau Daily Herald 800 Scott St *TF:* 800-477-4838 ■ *Web:* www.wausaudailyherald.com	Wausau	WI	54403	715-842-2101	848-9361

Wyoming

				Phone	Fax
Star-Tribune 170 Star Ln *Web:* www.trib.com	Casper	WY	82604	307-266-0500	266-0568
Wyoming Tribune-Eagle 702 W Lincolnway *TF:* 800-561-6268 ■ *Web:* www.wyomingnews.com	Cheyenne	WY	82001	307-634-3361	633-3189

535-3 National Newspapers

				Phone	Fax
Advertising Age 711 Third Ave Ste 3 *Web:* www.adage.com	New York	NY	10017	212-210-0100	
Alameda Sun 3215 Encinal Ave Ste J *Web:* www.alamedasun.com	Alameda	CA	94501	510-263-1470	
Alberta Newsprint Company Ltd Whitecourt Plant Postal Bag 9000 10km W Hwy 43 *Web:* www.albertanewsprint.com	Whitecourt	AB	T7S1P9	780-778-7000	
All Island Media Inc One Rodeo Dr *Web:* www.lipennysaver.com	Edgewood	NY	11717	631-698-8400	
Alliance Publishing Company Inc 40 S Linden Ave *Web:* www.the-review.com	Alliance	OH	44601	330-821-1200	
American Town Network LLC 43 Ruane St *Web:* www.americantowns.com	Fairfield	CT	06824	203-256-3390	
American Waste Digest Corp 226 King St *Web:* www.americanwastedigest.com	Pottstown	PA	19464	610-326-9480	
Apologetics Press Inc Publshr 230 Landmark Dr *Web:* www.apologeticspress.org	Montgomery	AL	36117	334-272-8558	
Arizona Jewish Post 3822 E River Rd Ste 300 *Web:* www.jewishtucson.org	Tucson	AZ	85711	520-319-1112	
Atlanta Daily World Inc 3485 N Desert Dr Ste 2109 *Web:* www.atlantadailyworld.com	Atlanta	GA	30344	404-761-1114	761-1164
Auburn Journal Inc 1030 High St *Web:* www.auburnjournal.com	Auburn	CA	95603	530-885-5656	
Bay Area Reporter 395 Ninth St *Web:* www.ebar.com	San Francisco	CA	94103	415-861-5019	
Bay Citizen, The 126 Post St Ste 500 *Web:* www.baycitizen.org	San Francisco	CA	94108	415-821-8520	
Bedford Gazette 424 W Penn St *Web:* www.bedfordgazette.com	Bedford	PA	15522	814-623-1151	
BH Media Group Inc 1314 Douglas St Ste 1500 *Web:* bhmginc.com	Omaha	NE	68102	402-444-1493	
BlackBook Media Corp 29 E 19th St Fourth Fl *Web:* www.blackbookmag.com	New York	NY	10003	212-334-1800	
Boskage Commerce Publications Ltd 120 Cutler St *Web:* www.boskage.com	Allegan	MI	49010	269-673-7242	
Broadcaster Press Inc, The 201 W Cherry St *Web:* www.broadcasteronline.com	Vermillion	SD	57069	605-624-4429	
Bulletin Daily 211 N Main St *Web:* www.colfax.com	Colfax	WA	99111	509-397-3332	
BZ Media LLC Seven High St Ste 407 *Web:* www.bzmedia.com	Huntington	NY	11743	631-421-4158	
Cabinet Press Inc, The 17 Executive Dr *Web:* www.cabinet.com	Hudson	NH	03051	603-673-3100	
Canadian Press Ltd, The 36 King St E *Web:* www.thecanadianpress.com	Toronto	ON	M5C2L9	416-364-0321	
Capitol Hill Publishing Corp 1625 K St NW Ste 900 *Web:* www.thehill.com	Washington	DC	20006	202-628-8500	
Central Ohio Printing Co 30 S Oak St *Web:* www.madison-press.com	London	OH	43140	740-852-1616	
Challenge Graphics Corp 16611 Roscoe Pl *Web:* www.challenge-graphics.com	North Hills	CA	91343	818-892-0123	
Charleston Newspapers Ltd 1001 Virginia St E *Web:* www.cnpapers.com	Charleston	WV	25301	304-348-4848	
Cherokee Ledger News, The 103 E Main St *Web:* www.ledgernews.com	Woodstock	GA	30188	770-928-0706	
Chesterton Tribune 193 S Calumet Rd *Web:* www.chestertontribune.com	Chesterton	IN	46304	219-926-1131	
Christian Science Monitor 210 Massachusetts Ave *TF:* 800-453-3432 ■ *Web:* www.csmonitor.com	Boston	MA	02115	617-450-2000	450-7575
Circle Media Inc 5817 Old Leeds Rd *TF:* 800-356-9916 ■ *Web:* www.ncregister.com	Irondale	AL	35210	800-356-9916	
Clipper Magazine LLC 3708 Hempland Rd *Web:* www.clippermagazine.com	Mountville	PA	17554	717-569-5100	
Conway Daily Sun 64 Seavey St *Web:* badgerrealty.com	North Conway	NH	03860	603-356-3456	
Cookeville Newspapers Inc 1300 Neal St *Web:* www.herald-citizen.com	Cookeville	TN	38501	931-526-9715	
Covington Leader, The 2001 Hwy 51 S *Web:* www.covingtonleader.com	Covington	TN	38019	901-476-7116	
Cowles Publishing Co 999 W Riverside Ave *Web:* www.spokesman.com	Spokane	WA	99201	509-459-5000	
Crittenden Publishing Company Inc 1010 State Hwy 77 *Web:* www.theeveningtimes.com	Marion	AR	72364	870-735-2383	
CrossRoadsNews Inc 2346 Candler Rd *Web:* www.crossroadsnews.com	Decatur	GA	30032	404-284-1888	
Current Newspaper 6930 Carroll Ave Ste 350 *Web:* www.current.org	Takoma Park	MD	20912	301-270-7240	
Daily Californian 600 Eshleman Hall *Web:* www.dailycal.org	Berkeley	CA	94720	510-548-8300	
Daily Herald Co, The 1213 California St *Web:* www.heraldnet.com	Everett	WA	98201	425-339-3433	
Daily News Publishing Co 193 Jefferson Ave *Web:* www.memphisdailynews.com	Memphis	TN	38103	901-523-1561	
Daily Texan-student Newspaper 2500 Whitis Ave *Web:* www.dailytexanonline.com	Austin	TX	78712	512-471-4591	
Davis County Clipper Today 1370 South 500 West *Web:* www.spectrumpress.us	Woods Cross	UT	84010	801-295-2251	
Dispatch Publishing Company Inc, The 30 E First Ave *Web:* www.the-dispatch.com	Lexington	NC	27293	336-249-3981	
Dix Communications LLC 212 E Liberty St *Web:* www.dixcom.com	Wooster	OH	44691	330-264-1125	
Dover Publications Inc 31 E Second St *Web:* www.doverpublications.com	Mineola	NY	11501	516-294-7000	
Dowagiac 217 N Fourth St *Web:* www.leaderpub.com	Niles	MI	49120	269-683-2100	
Drummer & Wright Cnty Journal 108 Central Ave *Web:* www.thedrummer.com	Buffalo	MN	55313	763-682-1221	
Eagle Herald Publishing LLC 1809 Dunlap Ave *Web:* www.eagleherald.com	Marinette	WI	54143	715-735-6611	
Eagle Newspapers Inc 4901 Indian School Rd NE PO Box 12008 *Web:* www.eaglenewspapers.com	Salem	OR	97305	503-393-1774	
Easy-ad Inc 155 S Harvard St *Web:* www.easyadlive.com	Hemet	CA	92543	951-658-2244	
Edwards Publications Inc 125 Eagles Nest Dr St A *Web:* www.edwgroupinc.com	Seneca	SC	29678	864-882-3272	
El Observador Publications Inc 99 N First St Ste 100 *Web:* www.el-observador.com	San Jose	CA	95113	408-938-1700	
El Periodico u s a Inc 801 E Fir Ave *Web:* www.elperiodicousa.com	Mcallen	TX	78501	956-631-5628	
EO Media Group 211 SE Byers Ave *Web:* www.eastoregonian.com	Pendleton	OR	97801	541-276-2211	
Epoch Times Atlanta PO Box2041 *Web:* www.epochtimes.com	Suwanee	GA	30024	678-485-0136	
Fayette Daily News 210 Jeff Davis Pl *Web:* www.fayettedailynews.com	Fayetteville	GA	30214	770-461-6317	
Free Press Standard, The 43 E Main St *Web:* www.freepressstandard.com	Carrollton	OH	44615	330-627-5591	

Name / Address	City	State	Zip	Phone	Fax
Garavi Gujarat Publications 2020 Beaver Ruin Rd *Web:* www.amg.biz	Norcross	GA	30071	770-263-7728	
Genesee Valley Penny Saver Inc 1471 W Henrietta Rd *Web:* www.gvpennysaver.com	Avon	NY	14414	585-226-8111	
Gleim Publications Inc 4201 Nw 95th Blvd *Web:* www.gleim.com	Gainesville	FL	32606	352-375-0772	
Glendale Star 7122 N 59th Ave *Web:* www.glendalestar.com	Glendale	AZ	85301	623-842-6000	
Glennville Sentinel Inc, The 105 W Barnard St *Web:* www.glennvillesentinel.net	Glennville	GA	30427	912-654-2515	
Greenspun Media Group LLC, The 2360 Corporate Cir Third Fl *Web:* www.gmgvegas.com	Henderson	NV	89074	702-990-2550	
Hatchet Publications Inc 2140 G St Nw *Web:* www.gwhatchet.com	Washington	DC	20052	202-847-0400	
Havre Daily News 119 Second St *Web:* www.havredailynews.com	Havre	MT	59501	406-265-6795	
Heppner Gazette Times 188 Willow St *Web:* www.heppner.net	Heppner	OR	97836	541-676-9228	
High Country News 119 Grand Ave *Web:* www.hcn.org	Paonia	CO	81428	970-527-4898	
Highland Lakes Newspapers Inc 304 Gateway Loop *Web:* www.highlandernews.com	Marble Falls	TX	78654	830-693-4367	
Hill Times 69 Sparks St *Web:* www.hilltimes.com	Ottawa	ON	K1P5A5	613-232-5952	
Hood County News 1501 S Morgan St *Web:* www.hcnews.com	Granbury	TX	76048	817-573-7066	279-8371
Horizon Publications Inc 1120 N Carbon St Ste 100 *Web:* horizonpublicationsinc.com	Marion	IL	62959	618-993-1711	
Houston Newspapers- Herald & The Messenger 113 N Grand Ave *Web:* www.houstonherald.com	Houston	MO	65483	417-967-2000	
Improper Bostonian 142 Berkeley St Third Fl *Web:* www.improper.com	Boston	MA	02116	617-859-1400	
Indeco North America Inc 135 Research Dr *Web:* www.indeco-breakers.com	Milford	CT	06460	203-713-1030	
Jewish Press Inc 338 Third Ave *Web:* www.jewishpress.com	Brooklyn	NY	11215	718-330-1100	
Joongang Daily News California Inc 690 Wilshire Pl *Web:* www.koreadaily.com	Los Angeles	CA	90005	213-368-2500	
Kentucky New Era Inc PO Box 729 *Web:* www.kentuckynewera.com	Hopkinsville	KY	42241	270-886-4444	
Korea Times Los Angeles Inc, The 4525 Wilshire Blvd *Web:* www.koreatimes.com	Los Angeles	CA	90010	323-692-2000	
La Jolla Light Newspaper 565 Pearl St Ste 300 *Web:* www.lajollalight.com	La Jolla	CA	92037	858-459-4201	
Lafromboise Communications Inc 321 N Pearl St *Web:* www.chronline.com	Centralia	WA	98531	360-736-3311	
Lakeview Publishing of Elbow Lake Inc 35 Central Ave N *Web:* www.grantherald.com	Elbow Lake	MN	56531	218-685-5326	
Lawyers Weekly Inc 10 Milk St Ste 1000 *Web:* www.masslawyersweekly.com	Boston	MA	02108	617-451-7300	
Lebanon Publishing Company Inc 402 N Cumberland St *Web:* www.lebanondemocrat.com	Lebanon	TN	37087	615-444-3952	
Lewistown News-argus 521 W Main St *Web:* www.lewistownnews.com	Lewistown	MT	59457	406-535-3401	
Lompoc Record, The 115 N H St *Web:* www.lompocrecord.com	Lompoc	CA	93436	805-736-2313	
Long Island Business News Inc 2150 Smithtown Ave Ste 7 *Web:* www.libn.com	Ronkonkoma	NY	11779	631-737-1700	
Luso Americano Company Inc 66 Union St *Web:* www.lusoamericano.com	Newark	NJ	07105	973-344-3200	
Mader News Inc 913 Ruberta Ave *Web:* www.madernews.com	Glendale	CA	91201	818-551-5000	
Main Street Media Group LLC 6400 Monterey St *Web:* www.mainstreetmediagroup.com	Gilroy	CA	95020	408-842-6400	
Manufacturers' News Inc 1633 Central St *Web:* www.manufacturersnews.com	Evanston	IL	60201	847-864-7000	
MD Buyline Inc 5910 N Central Expy Ste 1800 *Web:* www.mdbuyline.com	Dallas	TX	75206	214-891-6700	
Metroland Media Group Ltd 3125 Wolfedale Rd *Web:* www.metroland.com	Mississauga	ON	L5C1W1	905-281-5656	281-5630
Mid Atlantic Printers Ltd 503 Third St *Web:* www.mapl.net	Altavista	VA	24517	434-369-6633	
Minnesota Womens Press Inc 771 Raymond Ave *Web:* www.womenspress.com	Saint Paul	MN	55114	651-646-3968	
Missouri Valley Times-enterprise Inc 501 E Erie St *Web:* www.dcpostgazette.com	Missouri Valley	IA	51555	712-642-2791	
Mobridge Tribune 1413 E Grand Xing *Web:* www.mobridgetribune.com	Mobridge	SD	57601	605-845-3646	
Montgomery Communications Inc 222 W Sixth St *Web:* www.dailyu.com	Junction City	KS	66441	785-762-5000	
Morris Herald-News 1804 N Division St *Web:* www.morrisdailyherald.com	Morris	IL	60450	815-942-3221	
Mountain Democrat 1360 Broadway *Web:* www.mtdemocrat.com	Placerville	CA	95667	530-622-1255	
N'digo Profiles 19 N Sangamon St *Web:* ndigo.com	Chicago	IL	60607	312-822-0202	
New Century Press Inc 310 First Ave *Web:* www.ncppub.com	Rock Rapids	IA	51246	712-472-2525	
News Examiner, The 847 Washington St *Web:* www.news-examiner.net	Montpelier	ID	83254	208-847-0552	
News-banner Publications Inc 125 N Johnson St *Web:* www.news-banner.com	Bluffton	IN	46714	260-824-0224	
Newspaper Services of America Inc 3025 Highland Pkwy Ste 700 *Web:* nsamedia.com	Downers Grove	IL	60515	630-729-7500	
Newsvine Inc 101 Elliott Ave W Ste 120 *Web:* www.newsvine.com	Seattle	WA	98119	206-529-4444	
Next Year's News One S Saint Clair St Ste 1b *Web:* www.nyninc.com	Toledo	OH	43604	419-241-3698	
Nittany Valley Offset Nittany Vly Offset 1015 Benner Pk *Web:* www.nittanyvalley.com	State College	PA	16801	814-238-3071	
Northern Michigan Review Inc 319 State St *Web:* www.petoskeynews.com	Petoskey	MI	49770	231-347-2544	
Oahu Publications Inc 500 Ala Moana Blvd Ste 7-500 *Web:* www.oahupublications.com	Honolulu	HI	96813	808-529-4700	
Ottawa Herald Inc 104 S Cedar St *Web:* www.ottawaherald.com	Ottawa	KS	66067	785-242-4700	
Outlook Publishing Inc 415 E Main PO Box 278 *Web:* www.laureloutlook.com	Laurel	MT	59044	406-628-4412	
Overton County News 415 W Main St *Web:* www.overtoncountynews.com	Livingston	TN	38570	931-823-6485	
Park Record PO Box 3688 *Web:* www.parkrecord.com	Park City	UT	84060	435-649-9014	
Pars International Corp 253 W 35th St Fl 7 *Web:* www.magreprints.com	New York	NY	10001	212-221-9595	
Payson Roundup Newspaper 708 N Beeline Hwy *Web:* www.paysonroundup.com	Payson	AZ	85541	928-474-5251	
Philadelphia Gay News 505 S Fourth St *Web:* www.epgn.com	Philadelphia	PA	19147	215-625-8501	
Pleasanton Weekly 5506 Sunol Blvd Ste 100 *Web:* www.pleasantonweekly.com	Pleasanton	CA	94566	925-600-0840	
Port Lavaca Wave 107 E Austin St *Web:* www.plwave.com	Port Lavaca	TX	77979	361-552-9788	
Quarasan Group Inc, The 405 W Superior St *Web:* www.quarasan.com	Chicago	IL	60654	312-981-2500	
Record Herald Publishing 30 Walnut St *Web:* www.therecordherald.com	Waynesboro	PA	17268	717-762-2151	
Richner Communications Inc Two Endo Blvd *Web:* www.liherald.com	Garden City	NY	11530	516-569-4000	
River Falls Journal 2815 Prairie Dr *Web:* www.rivertowns.net	River Falls	WI	54022	715-425-1561	
Robesonian, The 2175 N Roberts Ave *Web:* www.robesonian.com	Lumberton	NC	28358	910-739-4322	
Rubber & Plastics News 1725 Merriman Rd *Web:* www.rubbernews.com	Akron	OH	44313	330-836-9180	
San Diego Community Newspaper 4645 Cass St Fl 2 *Web:* www.sdnews.com	San Diego	CA	92109	858-270-3103	
Sand Mountain Reporter 1603 Progress Dr *Web:* www.sandmountainreporter.com	Albertville	AL	35950	256-840-2987	
Santa Cruz Sentinel Inc 207 Church St *Web:* www.santacruzsentinel.com	Santa Cruz	CA	95060	831-423-4242	
Santa Rosa Press Democrat Inc, The 427 Mendocino Ave PO Box 569 *Web:* www.pressdemocrat.com	Santa Rosa	CA	95402	707-526-8570	
Schurz Communications Inc 1301 E Douglas Rd *Web:* www.schurz.com	Mishawaka	IN	46545	574-247-7237	
Sentinel Power Services Inc 7517 E Pine St *Web:* www.sentinelpowerservices.com	Tulsa	OK	74115	918-359-0350	
Sentinel Systems Corp 1620 Kipling St *Web:* www.sentinelsystems.com	Lakewood	CO	80215	303-242-2000	
Sentinel Transportation LLC 3521 Silverside Rd Ste 2A *Web:* www.sentineltrans.com	Wilmington	DE	19810	302-477-1640	
Show-me Publishing Inc 2049 Wyandotte St *Web:* www.ingramsonline.com	Kansas City	MO	64108	816-842-9994	
Small Business Times 126 N Jefferson St Ste 403 *Web:* biztimes.com	Milwaukee	WI	53202	414-277-8181	
Smart Business Network Inc 835 Sharon Dr Ste 200 *Web:* www.sbnonline.com	Cleveland	OH	44145	440-250-7000	
Specht Newspapers Inc 203 Gleason St *Web:* www.nwlanews.com	Minden	LA	71055	318-377-1866	
Stanwood Camano News 9005 271st St Nw *Web:* www.scnews.com	Stanwood	WA	98292	360-629-2155	
State News 435 E Grand River Ave *Web:* statenews.com	East Lansing	MI	48823	517-432-3000	
Staunton Star Times 108 W Main St *Web:* www.stauntonstartimes.com	Staunton	IL	62088	618-635-2000	
Stockpickr LLC 14 Wall St Fl 15 *Web:* www.stockpickr.com	New York	NY	10005	212-321-5000	
Stone County Publishing Company Inc 104 W Main St *Web:* www.stonecountyleader.com	Mountain View	AR	72560	870-269-3841	
Straus News Inc 20 W Ave *Web:* www.strausnews.com	Chester	NY	10918	845-469-9000	
Swift Communications Inc 580 Mallory Way *Web:* www.swiftcom.com	Carson City	NV	89701	775-283-5500	
Synthesis 210 W Sixth St *Web:* www.synthesis.net	Chico	CA	95928	530-899-7708	

Phone Fax

Target Media Partners Inc 1800 N Highland Ave Ste 400 ... Los Angeles CA 90028 323-930-3123
Web: www.targetmediapartners.com

Times Record, The Three Business Pkwy ... Brunswick ME 04011 207-729-3311
Web: www.timesrecord.com

TimesLedger Newspapers, The 41-02 Bell Blvd Second Fl ... Bayside NY 11361 718-260-4545
Web: www.timesledger.com

Tomahawk Leader 315 W Wisconsin Ave ... Tomahawk WI 54487 715-453-2151
Web: www.tomahawkleader.com

Tracy Press Inc 131 W Tenth St ... Tracy CA 95376 209-835-3030
Web: www.tracypress.com

Tribune Inc 2012 Forest Ave ... Great Bend KS 67530 620-792-1211
Web: www.gbtribune.com

Tucson Shopper LLC 1861 W Grant Rd ... Tucson AZ 85745 520-622-0101

Tukwila Reporter, The 19426 68th Ave S Ste A ... Kent WA 98032 253-872-6600
Web: www.pnwlocalnews.com

Turley Publications Inc 24 Water St ... Palmer MA 01069 413-283-8393
Web: www.turley.com

USA Today 7950 Jones Branch Dr ... McLean VA 22108 703-854-3400
TF Cust Svc: 800-872-0001 ■ *Web:* www.usatoday.com

Vineyard Gazette Inc 34 S Summer St ... Edgartown MA 02539 508-627-4311
Web: www.mvgazette.com

Wall Street Journal, The 1211 Ave of the Americas ... New York NY 10036 212-416-2000
TF General: 800-568-7625 ■ *Web:* online.wsj.com/india

Washington Daily News, The 217 N Market St ... Washington NC 27889 252-946-2144
Web: www.wdnweb.com

Watertown Public Opinion 120 Third Ave Nw ... Watertown SD 57201 605-886-6901
Web: www.coteaushopper.com

Webster-Kirkwood Times Inc 122 W Lockwood Ave ... St. Louis MO 63119 314-968-2699
Web: www.websterkirkwoodtimes.com

Wednesday Journal 141 S Oak Park Ave Ste 3 ... Oak Park IL 60302 708-524-8300
Web: www.chicagoparent.com

Wehco Newspapers Inc 115 E Capitol Ave ... Little Rock AR 72201 501-378-3400
Web: www.arkansaonline.com

Western Producer Publications 2310 Millar Ave ... Saskatoon SK S7K2Y2 306-665-3500 665-4961
Web: www.producer.com

Wick Communications Co 5751 E Mayflower Ct ... Wasilla AK 99654 907-352-2277
Web: www.frontiersman.com

Wilson Post, The 216 Hartmann Dr ... Lebanon TN 37087 615-444-6008
Web: www.wilsonpost.com

Winneconne News 908 E Main St ... Winneconne WI 54986 920-582-4541
Web: www.rogerspublishing.com

World Publishing Co 14 N Mission St ... Wenatchee WA 98801 509-663-5161
Web: www.wenatcheeworld.com

535-4 Weekly Newspapers

Listings here are organized by city names within state groupings.

Alabama

Phone Fax

Birmingham Times 115 Third Ave W ... Birmingham AL 35204 205-251-5158 323-2294
TF: 866-456-4995 ■ *Web:* birminghamtimes.com

Over The Mountain Journal 2016 Columbiana Rd ... Birmingham AL 35216 205-823-9646 824-1246
Web: www.otmj.com

Shelby County Reporter 115 N Main St ... Columbiana AL 35051 205-669-3131 669-4217
Web: www.shelbycountyreporter.com

Courier Journal 1828 Darby Dr ... Florence AL 35630 256-764-4268 760-9618
Web: www.courierjournal.net

Greenville Advocate, The PO Box 507 ... Greenville AL 36037 334-382-3111 382-7104
Web: www.greenvilleadvocate.com

Hartselle Enquirer PO Box 929 ... Hartselle AL 35640 256-773-6566 773-1953
Web: www.hartselleenquirer.com

Montgomery Independent 141 Market Pl ... Montgomery AL 36117 334-265-7323 265-7320
Web: www.al.com

Alaska

Phone Fax

Anchorage Press 540 E Fifth Ave ... Anchorage AK 99501 907-561-7737 561-7777
Web: www.anchoragepress.com

Arizona

Phone Fax

Apache Junction Independent 850 S Ironwood Dr Ste 112 ... Apache Junction AZ 85220 480-982-7799 671-0016*
**Fax:* News Rm ■ *Web:* ajnews.com

West Valley View 200 W Wigwam Blvd ... Litchfield Park AZ 85323 623-535-8439 935-2103
Web: www.westvalleyview.com

Ahwatukee Foothills News 10631 S 51st St Ste 1 ... Phoenix AZ 85044 480-898-7900 893-1684*
**Fax:* News Rm ■ *Web:* www.ahwatukee.com

Sun Cities Independent 17220 N Boswell Blvd Ste 101 ... Sun City AZ 85373 623-972-6101 974-6004
Web: www.newszap.com

California

Phone Fax

Bakersfield News Observer 1219 20th St ... Bakersfield CA 93301 661-324-9466 324-9472

Beverly Hills Courier 8840 W Olympic Blvd ... Beverly Hills CA 90211 310-278-1322 271-5118
Web: www.bhcourier.com

Phone Fax

Chino Champion PO Box 607 ... Chino CA 91708 909-628-5501 590-1217
Web: www.championnewspapers.com

Rialto Record PO Box 110 ... Colton CA 92324 909-381-9898
Web: www.rialtorecord.com

Huntington Beach Independent 1375 Sunflower Ave ... Costa Mesa CA 92626 714-966-4600
Web: www.hbindependent.com

Elk Grove Citizen 8970 Elk Grove Blvd ... Elk Grove CA 95624 916-685-3945 686-6675
Web: www.egcitizen.com

Gardena Valley News 15005 S Vermont Ave ... Gardena CA 90247 310-329-6351 329-7501
TF: 800-329-6351 ■ *Web:* gvnoffset.com

Burbank Leader 111 W Wilson Ave ... Glendale CA 91203 818-637-3200 241-1975
Web: www.burbankleader.com

Hesperia Resorter PO Box 400937 ... Hesperia CA 92345 760-244-0021 244-6609
Web: www.valleywidenewspaper.com

Independent, The 2250 First St ... Livermore CA 94550 925-447-8700 447-0212
TF: 877-952-3588 ■ *Web:* www.independentnews.com

Los Altos Town Crier 138 Main St ... Los Altos CA 94022 650-948-9000 948-6647
Web: losaltosonline.com/

Los Angeles Downtown News 1264 W First St ... Los Angeles CA 90026 213-481-1448 250-4617
TF: 877-338-1010 ■ *Web:* www.ladowntownnews.com

Mammoth Times, The PO Box 3929 ... Mammoth Lakes CA 93546 760-934-3929 934-3951
TF: 800-427-7623 ■ *Web:* www.mammothtimes.com

Argonaut, The PO Box 11209 ... Marina del Rey CA 90295 310-822-1629 821-8029
Web: argonautnews.com

Milpitas Post 59 Marylinn Dr ... Milpitas CA 95035 408-262-2454 263-9710
TF: 800-870-6397 ■ *Web:* www.mercurynews.com

Bay Area Press 1520 Broadway ... Oakland CA 94612 510-835-2731 839-0164
Web: www.bayarearapidpress.com

Paradise Post 5399 Clark Rd ... Paradise CA 95969 530-877-4413 877-1326
TF: 855-857-7247 ■ *Web:* www.paradisepost.com

Paso Robles Press 829 10th St Ste B ... Paso Robles CA 93446 805-237-6060 237-6066
Web: www.pasoroblespress.com

Riverside County Record 4080 Lemon St ... Riverside CA 92501 951-955-1000 685-2961
Web: www.countyofriverside.us

Community Voice PO Box 2038 ... Rohnert Park CA 94927 707-584-2222 285-3226
Web: www.thecommunityvoice.com

Palos Verdes Peninsula News 609 Deep Valley Dr Ste 200 ... Rolling Hills Estates CA 90274 310-372-0388 372-6113
TF: 877-512-6397 ■ *Web:* www.pvnews.com

Cupertino Courier 1095 The Alameda ... San Jose CA 95126 408-200-1000 200-1013
Web: www.mercurynews.com

Sunnyvale Sun 1095 The Alameda ... San Jose CA 95126 408-200-1000 200-1013
Web: www.mercurynews.com

Sonoma Index-Tribune PO Box C ... Sonoma CA 95476 707-938-2111 938-1600
Web: www.sonomanews.com

Ceres Courier 138 S Center St ... Turlock CA 95380 209-537-5032 537-0543
Web: cerescourier.com

Glendora Highlander Press 1210 N Azusa Canyon Rd ... West Covina CA 91790 626-962-8811
Web: sgvtribune.com/highlanders

Colorado

Phone Fax

Aurora Sentinel 14305 E Alameda Ave Ste 200 ... Aurora CO 80012 303-750-7555 750-7699
TF: 855-269-4484 ■ *Web:* www.aurorasentinel.com

Eagle Valley Enterprise 108 W Second St ... Eagle CO 81631 970-328-6656 328-6393
Web: www.vaildaily.com

Connecticut

Phone Fax

Hartford News 563 Franklin Ave ... Hartford CT 06114 860-296-6128 296-3350

Bridgeport News 1000 Bridgeport Ave ... Shelton CT 06484 203-926-2080
TF Advestisement: 855-247-8573 ■ *Web:* thebridgeportnews.com

Milford Mirror 1000 Bridgeport Ave ... Shelton CT 06484 203-402-2315 926-2092
TF Advestisement: 800-372-2790 ■ *Web:* www.milfordmirror.com

Stratford Star 1000 Bridgeport Ave ... Shelton CT 06484 203-402-2319 926-2091
TF Advestisement: 800-372-2790 ■ *Web:* www.stratfordstar.com

Voices PO Box 383 ... Southbury CT 06488 203-262-6631 262-6665
Web: www.voicesnews.com

Reminder, The PO Box 210 ... Vernon CT 06066 860-875-3366 872-4614
TF: 888-456-2211 ■ *Web:* courant.com/reminder-news/

Westport Minuteman 1775 Post Rd E ... Westport CT 06880 203-752-2711
Web: minutemannewscenter.com

Delaware

Phone Fax

Dover Post 1196 S Little Creek Rd ... Dover DE 19901 302-678-3616 678-8291
TF: 800-942-1616 ■ *Web:* www.doverpost.com

Cape Gazette 17585 Nassau Commons Blvd PO Box 213 ... Lewes DE 19958 302-645-7700 645-1664
Web: capegazette.villagesoup.com

Dialog, The 1925 Delaware Ave ... Wilmington DE 19806 302-573-3109 573-6948
TF: 877-225-7870 ■ *Web:* www.cdow.org

Florida

Phone Fax

Bonita Banner PO Box 40 ... Bonita Springs FL 34133 239-213-6000 213-6088
Web: www.naplesnews.com

Hernando Today 15299 Cortez Blvd ... Brooksville FL 34613 352-544-5200 799-5246
Web: www.hernandotoday.com

Observer Newspaper 201 N Federal Hwy Ste 103 ... Deerfield Beach FL 33441 954-428-9045 428-9096
Web: observernewspaperonline.com

Clay Today 3513 US Hwy 17 ... Fleming Island FL 32003 904-264-3200 269-3285
TF: 888-434-9844 ■ *Web:* www.claytodayonline.com

				Phone	Fax
Osceola News-Gazette 108 Church St *Fax Area Code: 321 ■ TF: 800-281-5303 ■ Web: www.aroundosceola.com	Kissimmee	FL	34741	407-846-7600	402-2946*
Lake Worth Herald/Coastal Observer 130 S 'H' St Web: www.lwherald.com	Lake Worth	FL	33460	561-585-9387	585-5434
Longboat Observer 5570 Gulf of Mexico Dr PO Box 8100 Web: www.yourobserver.com	Longboat Key	FL	34228	941-383-5509	383-7193
Miami Today 710 Brickell Ave TF: 800-283-2707 ■ Web: www.miamitodaynews.com	Miami	FL	33131	305-358-2663	358-4811
Pelican Press 5011 Ocean Blvd Ste 206 Web: www.yourobserver.com	Sarasota	FL	34242	941-349-4949	346-7118
News-Sun 2227 US 27 S Web: www.newssun.com	Sebring	FL	33870	863-385-6155	385-1954
Kendall News Gazette 6796 SW 62nd Ave Web: www.communitynewspapers.com	South Miami	FL	33143	305-669-7355	661-0954
Carrollwood News 5625 W Waters Ave Ste G	Tampa	FL	33634	813-259-8295	249-5316
Daily Sun 1100 Main St TF: 800-726-6592 ■ Web: www.thevillagesdailysun.com	The Villages	FL	32159	352-753-1119	750-2381
Venice Gondolier Sun 200 E Venice Ave TF: 877-818-6204 ■ Web: www.venicegondoliersun.com	Venice	FL	34285	941-207-1000	629-2085

Georgia

				Phone	Fax
Revue & News, The 319 N Main St TF: 800-864-5960 ■ Web: www.northfulton.com	Alpharetta	GA	30004	770-442-3278	475-1216
Northside Neighbor & Sandy Springs Neighbor 5290 Roswell Rd NW Ste M Web: www.neighbornewspapers.com	Atlanta	GA	30342	404-256-3100	256-3292
Crier Newspapers LLC 5064 Nandina Ln Ste C Web: www.thecrier.net	Dunwoody	GA	30338	770-451-4147	451-4223
Clayton Neighbor 5442 Frontage Rd Ste 130 Web: www.neighbornewspapers.com	Forest Park	GA	30297	404-363-8484	363-0212
South Fulton Neighbor 5442 Frontage Rd Ste 130 Web: www.neighbornewspapers.com	Forest Park	GA	30297	404-363-8484	363-0212
Barrow County News 189 W Athens St Ste 22 Web: www.barrowcountynews.com	Winder	GA	30680	770-867-7557	867-1034

Illinois

				Phone	Fax
Times Record 219 S College Ave TF: 800-784-6776 ■ Web: www.aledotimesrecord.com	Aledo	IL	61231	309-582-5112	582-5319
Herald/Country Market 500 Brown Blvd Web: www.bbherald.com	Bourbonnais	IL	60914	815-933-1131	933-3785
Inside Publications 6221 N Clark St Second Fl Web: www.insideonline.com	Chicago	IL	60618	773-465-9700	465-9800
Granite City Journal Two Executive Dr TF: 800-766-3278 ■ Web: stltoday.com	Collinsville	IL	62234	618-877-7700	344-3831
Des Plaines Journal 622 Graceland Ave Web: www.journal-topics.com	Des Plaines	IL	60016	847-299-5511	298-8549
MySuburbanLife.com 1101 W 31st St Ste 100 Web: www.mysuburbanlife.com	Downers Grove	IL	60515	630-368-1100	969-0228
Galena Gazette 716 S Bench St TF: 800-373-6397 ■ Web: www.galenagazette.com	Galena	IL	61036	815-777-0019	777-3809
Lombardian 116 S Main St Web: lombardian.info	Lombard	IL	60148	630-627-7010	627-7027
Regional Publishing Corp, The 12243 S Harlem Ave Web: regionalpublishing.com	Palos Heights	IL	60463	708-448-4000	448-4012
Washington Courier 100 Ford Ln Web: www.courierpapers.com	Washington	IL	61571	309-444-3139	

Indiana

				Phone	Fax
Hendricks County Flyer 8109 Kingston St Ste 500 TF: 800-359-3747 ■ Web: www.flyergroup.com	Avon	IN	46123	317-272-5800	272-5887
Westside Community News 608 S Vine St	Indianapolis	IN	46241	317-241-7363	240-6397*
Papers, The 206 S Main St PO Box 188 TF: 800-733-4111 ■ Web: www.the-papers.com	Milford	IN	46542	574-658-4111	658-4701
Banner-Gazette 490 E State Rd 60 PO Box 38 TF: 800-889-3390 ■ Web: www.gbpnews.com	Pekin	IN	47165	812-967-3176	967-3194
Giveaway, The 183 E McClain St Web: www.gbpnews.com	Scottsburg	IN	47170	812-752-3171	

Kentucky

				Phone	Fax
West Kentucky News 1540 McCracken Blvd Web: www.ky-news.com	Paducah	KY	42001	270-442-7389	442-5220

Louisiana

				Phone	Fax
Bossier Press Tribune 4250 Viking Dr Web: www.bossierpress.com	Bossier City	LA	71111	318-747-7900	747-5298
Times of Acadiana 1100 Bertrand Dr TF: 877-289-2216 ■ Web: www.theadvertiser.com	Lafayette	LA	70506	337-289-6300	289-6443
Avoyelles Journal 105 N Main St TF: 800-565-4321 ■ Web: avoyellestoday.com	Marksville	LA	71351	318-253-5413	253-7223
Ouachita Citizen 1400 N Seventh St Web: hannapub.com/ouachitacitizen	West Monroe	LA	71291	318-322-3161	325-2285

Maine

				Phone	Fax
Coastal Journal 97 Commercial St Ste 3 TF: 800-649-6241 ■ Web: www.coastaljournal.com	Bath	ME	04530	207-443-6241	443-5605
Biddeford-Saco-OOB Courier 180 Main St Web: www.biddefordsacooobcourier.com	Biddeford	ME	04005	207-282-4337	282-4339
Forecaster, The 5 Fundy Rd Web: www.theforecaster.net	Falmouth	ME	04105	207-781-3661	781-2060

Maryland

				Phone	Fax
Maryland Gazette 2000 Capital Dr Web: www.capitalgazette.com	Annapolis	MD	21401	410-268-5000	268-4643
Baltimore Times 2513 N Charles St TF: 800-944-7403 ■ Web: baltimoretimes-online.com	Baltimore	MD	21218	410-366-3900	243-1627
Dundalk Eagle PO Box 8936 Web: www.dundalkeagle.com	Dundalk	MD	21222	410-288-6060	288-6963
Maryland Beachcomber 12417 Ocean Gateway Ste A-7 Web: www.mddcpress.com/	Ocean City	MD	21842	410-213-9442	213-9458

Michigan

				Phone	Fax
Camden Publications 331 E Bell St TF: 800-222-6336 ■ Web: www.farmersadvance.com	Camden	MI	49232	517-368-0365	368-5131
Cedar Springs Post 36 E Maple PO Box 370 TF: 888-937-4514 ■ Web: www.cedarspringspost.com	Cedar Springs	MI	49319	616-696-3655	696-9010
Dearborn Times-Herald 13730 Michigan Ave TF: 866-468-7630 ■ Web: downriversundaytimes.com	Dearborn	MI	48126	313-584-4000	584-1357
Grosse Pointe News 96 Kercheval Ave Web: www.grossepointenews.com	Grosse Pointe Farms	MI	48236	313-882-6900	882-1585
Ada/Cascade/Forest Hills Advance PO Box 9 Web: www.advancenewspapers.com	Jenison	MI	49429	616-669-2700	669-4848
Advance Newspaper PO Box 9 Web: www.advancenewspapers.com	Jenison	MI	49429	616-669-2700	669-4848
Grand Valley Advance PO Box 9 Web: www.advancenewspapers.com	Jenison	MI	49428	616-669-2700	669-4848
Walker/Westside Advance PO Box 9 Web: www.advancenewspapers.com	Jenison	MI	49429	616-669-2700	669-4848
Wyoming Advance PO Box 9 Web: www.advancenewspapers.com	Jenison	MI	49429	616-669-2700	669-4848
County Press PO Box 220 Web: thecountypress.mihomepaper.com	Lapeer	MI	48446	810-664-0811	664-5852
Observer & Eccentric, The 36251 Schoolcraft Rd Web: www.hometownlife.com	Livonia	MI	48150	734-591-2300	591-7279
Voice, The 51180 Bedford St TF: 800-561-2248 ■ Web: www.voicenews.com	New Baltimore	MI	48047	586-716-8100	716-8533
Advisor & Source Newspapers 48075 Van Dyke Ave Web: www.sourcenewspapers.com	Shelby Twp	MI	48317	586-731-1000	731-8172
Source Newspaper 51180 Bedford Dr Web: www.sourcenewspapers.com	Shelby Twp	MI	48047	586-716-8100	716-8533
News-Herald One Heritage Dr Ste 100 Web: www.thenewsherald.com	Southgate	MI	48195	734-246-0800	246-2727

Minnesota

				Phone	Fax
Proctor Journal 215 E Fifth St Web: www.proctorjournal.com	Duluth	MN	55805	218-624-3344	624-7037
Morrison County Record 216 SE First St TF: 888-637-2345 ■ Web: www.mcrecord.com	Little Falls	MN	56345	320-632-2345	632-2348
Southwest Journal 1115 Hennepin Ave S Web: southwestjournal.com/	Minneapolis	MN	55403	612-825-9205	825-0929
Plainview News 409 W Broadway	Plainview	MN	55964	507-534-3121	534-3920
Northern Watch PO Box 100 Web: www.trftimes.com	Thief River Falls	MN	56701	218-681-4450	681-4455

Missouri

				Phone	Fax
Bethany Republican-Clipper 202 N 16 St Web: www.bethanyclipper.com	Bethany	MO	64424	660-425-6325	425-3441
News Democrat Journal 14522 S Outer 40 Rd *Fax Area Code: 314 ■ Web: www.stltoday.com	Chesterfield	MO	63017	636-296-1800	657-3342*
Press Journal 14522 S Outer 40 Dr TF: 800-545-6953 ■ Web: www.stltoday.com	Chesterfield	MO	63017	314-821-1110	657-3342
Farmington Press 218 N Washington St PO Box 70 TF: 800-455-0206 ■ Web: dailyjournalonline.com	Farmington	MO	63640	573-756-8927	756-9160
Jefferson County Journal 1405 N Truman Blvd TF: 800-365-0820 ■ Web: www.stltoday.com	Festus	MO	63028	636-937-9811	931-2638
Liberty Tribune 104 N Main St Web: www.libertytribune.com	Liberty	MO	64068	816-781-4941	781-0909
Washington Missourian 14 W Main St PO Box 336 TF: 888-239-7701 ■ Web: www.emissourian.com	Washington	MO	63090	636-239-7701	239-0915

Montana

				Phone	Fax
Billings Times 2919 Montana Ave *Web:* billingstimes.net	Billings	MT	59101	406-245-4994	245-5115

Nebraska

				Phone	Fax
Bellevue Leader 604 Fort Crook Rd N *TF:* 800-284-6397 ■ *Web:* www.omaha.com	Bellevue	NE	68005	402-733-7300	733-9116
West Nebraska Register PO Box 608 *TF:* 800-652-2229 ■ *Web:* www.gidiocese.org	Grand Island	NE	68802	308-382-4660	382-6569

Nevada

				Phone	Fax
Ely Times 515 Murry St PO Box 150820 *Web:* www.elynews.com	Ely	NV	89315	775-289-4491	289-4566

New Jersey

				Phone	Fax
Suburbanite 210 Knickerbocker Rd Second Fl	Cresskill	NJ	07626	201-894-6700	568-4360
Twin-Boro News 210 Knickerbocker Rd *TF:* 888-473-2673	Cresskill	NJ	07626	201-894-6715	457-2520
Hunterdon County Democrat 8 Minneakoning Rd *TF:* 888-782-7533 ■ *Web:* www.nj.com	Flemington	NJ	08822	908-782-4747	782-6572
Hunterdon Observer Eight Minneakoning Rd *Web:* hcdemocrat.com	Flemington	NJ	08822	908-782-4747	
Central Record PO Box 1027 *Web:* southjerseylocalnews.com	Medford	NJ	08055	609-654-5000	654-8237
Reminder Newspaper Two W Vine St PO Box 1600 *Web:* reminderusa.net	Millville	NJ	08332	856-825-8811	825-0011
Town Topics 305 Witherspoon St *Web:* www.towntopics.com	Princeton	NJ	08542	609-924-2200	924-8818
Two River Times 46 Newman Springs Rd E *Web:* trtnj.com	Red Bank	NJ	07701	732-219-5788	747-7213
Cape May County Herald 1508 Rt 47	Rio Grande	NJ	08242	609-886-8600	886-1879
Community Life 372 Kinderkamack Rd	Westwood	NJ	07675	201-664-2501	664-1332

New Mexico

				Phone	Fax
Las Cruces Bulletin 840 N Telshor Blvd Ste E *Web:* www.lascrucesbulletin.com	Las Cruces	NM	88011	575-524-8061	526-4621

New York

				Phone	Fax
Queens Courier 38-15 Bell Blvd *TF:* 800-275-8777 ■ *Web:* www.queenscourier.com	Bayside	NY	11361	718-224-5863	224-5441
Chronicle, The 15 Ridge St *Web:* glensfallschronicle.com/	Glens Falls	NY	12801	518-792-1126	793-1587
Forum South 102-05 159th Ave *Web:* www.theforumnewsgroup.com	Howard Beach	NY	11414	718-845-3221	
New York Observer 915 Broadway Ninth Fl **Fax:* Edit ■ *Web:* www.observer.com	New York	NY	10010	212-755-2400	688-4889*
People's Weekly World 235 W 23rd St *Web:* www.peoplesworld.org	New York	NY	10011	212-924-2523	229-1713
Queens Tribune 150-50 14th Rd *Web:* www.queenstribune.com	New York	NY	11357	718-357-7400	357-9417
Villager, The 145 Sixth Ave First Fl *Web:* www.thevillager.com	New York	NY	10013	212-229-1890	229-2790
Our Town 36 Ridge St *Web:* ourtownnews.com	Pearl River	NY	10965	845-735-1342	620-9533
Times Newsweekly PO Box 860299 *Web:* www.timesnewsweekly.com	Ridgewood	NY	11386	718-821-7500	456-0120
Suburban News 1776 Hilton Palmar Corners Rd	Spencerport	NY	14559	585-352-3411	352-4811
Southern Duchess News 84 E Main St *Web:* sdutchessnews.com	Wappingers Falls	NY	12590	845-297-3723	297-6810

North Carolina

				Phone	Fax
Mountain Times PO Box 1815 *Web:* www.mountaintimes.com	Boone	NC	28607	828-264-6397	262-0282
Journal-Patriot PO Box 70 *TF:* 877-322-8228 ■ *Web:* journalpatriot.com	North Wilkesboro	NC	28659	336-838-4117	838-9864
Pilot, The PO Box 58 *Web:* www.thepilot.com	Southern Pines	NC	28388	910-692-7271	692-9382

North Dakota

				Phone	Fax
West Fargo Pioneer PO Box 457 *TF:* 888-382-1222 ■ *Web:* www.westfargopioneer.com	West Fargo	ND	58078	701-282-2443	282-9248
Plains Reporter PO Box 1447 *TF:* 800-950-2165 ■ *Web:* www.willistonherald.com	Williston	ND	58802	701-572-2165	572-9563

Ohio

				Phone	Fax
Sun Messenger 5510 Cloverleaf Pkwy *Web:* www.cleveland.com/sunmessenger	Cleveland	OH	44125	216-986-2600	
Sun Press 5510 Cloverleaf Pkwy *Web:* www.cleveland.com/sunpress	Cleveland	OH	44125	216-986-2600	
Rural-Urban Record 24487 Squire Rd	Columbia Station	OH	44028	440-236-8982	236-9198
Early Bird, The 5312 Sebring Warner Rd *TF:* 866-627-4557 ■ *Web:* earlybirdpaper.com	Greenville	OH	45331	937-548-3330	547-2292
Cuyahoga Falls News-Press 1050 W Main St PO Box 5199 *TF:* 800-560-9657 ■ *Web:* www.recordpub.com	Kent	OH	44240	330-541-9421	688-1588
Gateway News 1050 West Main St *TF:* 800-560-9657 ■ *Web:* www.recordpub.com	Kent	OH	44240	330-541-9400	296-2698
Today's Pulse 200 Harmon Ave *Web:* www.todayspulse.com	Lebanon	OH	45036	513-696-4520	932-6056
Delaware This Week 7801 N Central Dr *Web:* www.thisweeknews.com	Lewis Center	OH	43035	740-888-6100	888-6006
Dublin Villager 7801 N Central Dr *TF:* 866-790-4502 ■ *Web:* www.thisweeknews.com	Lewis Center	OH	43035	740-888-6100	888-6006
Hilliard This Week 7801 N Central Dr *TF:* 888-837-4342 ■ *Web:* www.thisweeknews.com	Lewis Center	OH	43035	740-888-6100	888-6006
Northland News 7801 N Central Dr PO Box 29912 *Web:* www.thisweeknews.com	Lewis Center	OH	43035	740-888-6000	888-6001
Reynoldsburg This Week 7801 N Central Dr *TF:* 888-837-4342 ■ *Web:* www.thisweeknews.com	Lewis Center	OH	43035	740 888 6100	888 6006
Southside This Week 7801 N Central Dr *Web:* www.thisweeknews.com	Lewis Center	OH	43035	740-888-6100	888-6006
This Week in Upper Arlington 7801 N Central Dr *Web:* www.thisweeknews.com	Lewis Center	OH	43035	740-888-6100	888-6006
ThisWeek Community Newspapers/Media 7801 N Central Dr PO Box 29912 **Fax:* Edit ■ *Web:* www.thisweeknews.com	Lewis Center	OH	43035	740-888-6000	888-6001*
Upper Arlington News 7801 N Central Dr PO Box 29912 **Fax:* Edit ■ *Web:* www.thisweeknews.com	Lewis Center	OH	43035	740-888-6000	888-6001*
Westerville This Week 7801 N Central Dr *TF:* 888-837-4342 ■ *Web:* www.thisweeknews.com	Lewis Center	OH	43035	740-888-6100	888-6006
Worthington This Week 7801 N Central Dr *Web:* www.thisweeknews.com	Lewis Center	OH	43035	740-888-6100	888-6006
Fairfield Echo 7320 Yankee Rd *Web:* www.todayspulse.com	Liberty Township	OH	45044	513-755-5060	483-5252
Pulse-Journal 7320 Yankee Rd *Web:* www.todayspulse.com	Liberty Township	OH	45044	513-755-5060	483-5252
Forest Hills Journal 394 WaRds Corner Rd Ste 170 **Fax Area Code:* 212 ■ *TF:* 888-894-2113 ■ *Web:* communitypress.cincinnati.com	Loveland	OH	45140	513-248-8600	688-7444*
Loveland Herald 394 WaRds Corner Rd Ste 170 *Web:* communitypress.cincinnati.com	Loveland	OH	45140	513-248-8600	248-1938
Suburban Press & Metro Press 1550 Woodville Rd *TF:* 800-300-6158 ■ *Web:* www.presspublications.com	Millbury	OH	43447	419-836-2221	836-1319
Beacon, The 205 SE Catawba Rd Ste G *Web:* www.thebeacon.net	Port Clinton	OH	43452	419-732-2154	734-5382
Budget, The 134 N Factory St PO Box 249 *Web:* www.thebudgetnewspaper.com	Sugarcreek	OH	44681	330-852-4634	852-4421
Boardman Town Crier 240 Franklin St SE *Web:* www.towncrieronline.com	Warren	OH	44483	330-629-6200	629-6210
Star-Republican 47 S S St	Wilmington	OH	45177	937-382-7796	382-4392

Oregon

				Phone	Fax
Hillsboro Argus 150 SE Third Ave *Web:* www.oregonlive.com	Hillsboro	OR	97123	503-648-1131	648-9191
Woodburn Independent 650 N First St *Web:* www.pamplinmedia.com	Woodburn	OR	97071	503-981-3441	981-1253

Pennsylvania

				Phone	Fax
Lancaster Farming PO Box 609 *Web:* www.lancasterfarming.com	Ephrata	PA	17522	717-626-1164	733-6058
Progress of Montgomery County PO Box 311 *Web:* www.montcopa.org	Norristown	PA	19044	610-278-3061	
Almanac, The 2600 Boyce Plz Rd Ste 142 **Fax:* Edit ■ *Web:* www.thealmanac.net	Pittsburgh	PA	15317	724-941-7725	941-8685*
Northeast Times 2512 Metropolitan Dr *TF:* 800-556-3655 ■ *Web:* www.northeasttimes.com	Trevose	PA	19053	215-355-9009	333-4508
York Sunday News 1891 Loucks Rd *TF:* 800-483-5517 ■ *Web:* www.ydr.com	York	PA	17408	717-767-6397	771-2009

Rhode Island

				Phone	Fax
Newport Mercury 101 Malbone Rd *Web:* www.newportri.com	Newport	RI	02840	401-380-2371	
Newport This Week 86 Broadway *Web:* www.newportchamber.com	Newport	RI	02840	401-847-7766	846-4974

South Carolina

				Phone	Fax
Bluffton Today 52 Persimmon St *TF:* 855-665-8549 ■ *Web:* blufftontoday.com	Bluffton	SC	29910	843-815-0800	815-0898

				Phone	Fax
Chronicle Independent 909 W Dekalb St. Camden *TF General:* 800-698-3514 ■ *Web:* www.chronicle-independent.com		SC	29020	803-432-6157	432-7609
Moultrie News 134 Columbus St. Charleston *Web:* www.moultrienews.com		SC	29403	843-849-1778	
Georgetown Times 615 Front St. Georgetown *TF:* 800-772-1213 ■ *Web:* gtowntimes.com		SC	29440	843-546-4148	264-5511
Myrtle Beach Herald 4761 US 501. Myrtle Beach		SC	29579	843-626-3131	
Star, The 106 E Buena Vista Ave North Augusta *TF:* 888-397-3742 ■ *Web:* www.northaugustastar.com		SC	29841	803-279-2793	278-4070

Tennessee

			Phone	Fax
Dickson Herald PO Box 387 Ashland City *Web:* www.tennessean.com	TN	37015	615-446-2811	446-5560
Farragutpress 11863 Kingston Pike Knoxville *Web:* www.farragutpress.com	TN	37934	865-675-6397	675-1675

Texas

			Phone	Fax
Preston Hollow People 750 N St Paul St Ste 2100 Dallas *Web:* www.prestonhollowpeople.com	TX	75201	214-739-2244	363-6948
Houston Forward Times PO Box 8346 Houston *Web:* forwardtimesonline.com	TX	77288	713-526-4727	526-3170
Leader Newspapers 3500 T C Jester Blvd PO Box 924487 Houston *Web:* theleadernews.com	TX	77292	713-686-8494	686-0970
Pearland Journal 650 FM 1959 Houston *Web:* www.yourhoustonnews.com/pearland	TX	77034	281-674-1340	922-4499
Humble Observer 907 E Main St Ste B Humble *Web:* www.yourhoustonnews.com	TX	77338	281-446-4438	964-4423
Hardin County News PO Box 8240 Lumberton *Web:* www.beaumontenterprise.com	TX	77657	409-755-4912	755-7731
Valley Town Crier 1811 N 23rd St McAllen *TF:* 800-285-5667 ■ *Web:* www.yourvalleyvoice.com	TX	78501	956-682-2423	630-6371

Utah

			Phone	Fax
Millard County Chronicle Progress 40 North 300 West Delta **Fax Area Code:* 775 ■ *Web:* millardccp.com	UT	84624	435-864-2400	514-2931*

Vermont

			Phone	Fax
World, The 403 US Rt 302-Berlin Barre *TF:* 800-639-9753 ■ *Web:* www.vt-world.com	VT	05641	802-479-2582	479-7916

Virginia

			Phone	Fax
Arlington Connection 1606 King St. Alexandria *Web:* www.connectionnewspapers.com	VA	22314	703-778-9410	706-3999
Loudoun Times-Mirror PO Box 359 Leesburg *TF:* 888-351-1660 ■ *Web:* www.northernvatimes.com	VA	20178	703-777-1111	771-0036
Mechanicsville Local 6400 Mechanicsville Tpke Mechanicsville *TF:* 800-468-3382 ■ *Web:* www.richmond.com	VA	23111	804-746-1235	730-0476
Fairfax County Times 1760 Reston Pkwy Ste 411 Reston *Web:* www.fairfaxtimes.com	VA	20190	703-437-5400	437-6019
Fauquier Times-Democrat 39 Culpeper St Warrenton *TF:* 888-351-1660 ■ *Web:* www.fauquier.com	VA	20186	540-347-4222	349-8676
Virginia Gazette 216 Ironbound Rd. Williamsburg *TF:* 800-944-6908 ■ *Web:* www.vagazette.com	VA	23188	757-220-1736	220-1665

Washington

			Phone	Fax
Reflector, The PO Box 2020 Battle Ground *Web:* www.thereflector.com	WA	98604	360-687-5151	687-5162
Dispatch, The PO Box 248 Eatonville *Web:* www.dispatchnews.com	WA	98328	360-832-4411	
Journal of the San Juan Islands PO Box 519 Friday Harbor *Web:* www.sanjuanjournal.com	WA	98250	360-378-5696	378-5128
Issaquah Press PO Box 1328 Issaquah *Web:* www.issaquahpress.com	WA	98027	425-392-6434	391-1541
Bothell/Kenmore Reporter 11630 Slater Ave NE Stes 8-9 Kirkland *Web:* www.bothell-reporter.com	WA	98034	425-483-3732	
Port Orchard Independent PO Box 27 Port Orchard *Web:* www.portorchardindependent.com	WA	98366	360-876-4414	876-4458
Capitol Hill Times 4000 Aurora Ave N Ste 100 Seattle *Web:* www.pacificpublishingcompany.com	WA	98103	206-461-1300	461-1285
Tribune Newspapers of Snohomish County 127 Ave C Ste B PO Box 499 Snohomish *TF:* 877-894-4663 ■ *Web:* www.snoho.com	WA	98291	360-568-4121	568-1484

West Virginia

			Phone	Fax
Coal Valley News 475 Main St. Madison *Web:* www.coalvalleynews.com	WV	25130	304-369-1165	369-1166

Wisconsin

			Phone	Fax
Country Today 701 S Farwell St Eau Claire *TF:* 800-236-4004 ■ *Web:* www.thecountrytoday.com	WI	54701	715-833-9270	858-7307
Foto News 807 E First St. Merrill *Web:* www.merrillfotonews.com	WI	54452	715-536-7121	539-3686
Milwaukee Courier 6310 N Port Washington Rd Milwaukee *Web:* milwaukeecourieronline.com	WI	53217	414-449-4860	906-5383

Wyoming

			Phone	Fax
Jackson Hole News & Guide 1225 Maple Way Jackson *Web:* jhnewsandguide.com	WY	83001	307-733-2047	733-2138

535-5 Weekly Newspapers - Alternative

			Phone	Fax
Ace Weekly 185 Jefferson Lexington *Web:* www.aceweekly.com	KY	40508	859-225-4889	226-0569
Alabama Rivers Alliance 2014 Sixth Ave N Birmingham *Web:* alabamarivers.org	AL	35203	205-322-6395	212-1005
Arkansas Times 201 E Markham Ste 200 Little Rock *Web:* www.arktimes.com	AR	72201	501-375-2985	375-3623
ArtVoice 810 Main St Buffalo *Web:* www.artvoice.com	NY	14202	716-881-6604	881-6682
Austin Chronicle PO Box 49066 Austin *TF:* 866-271-4900 ■ *Web:* www.austinchronicle.com	TX	78765	512-454-5766	458-6910
Baltimore City Paper 812 Pk Ave. Baltimore *Web:* citypaper.com	MD	21201	410-523-2300	523-2222
Boise Weekly 523 Broad St Boise *Web:* www.boiseweekly.com	ID	83702	208-344-2055	342-4733
Boston Phoenix, The 126 Brookline Ave. Boston **Fax:* Advertising ■ *Web:* thephoenix.com	MA	02215	617-536-5390	536-1463*
Bostons Weekly Dig 242 E Berkeley St Fifth Fl Boston *Web:* digboston.com	MA	02118	617-426-8942	426-8942
Boulder Weekly 690 S Lashley Ln. Boulder *Web:* boulderweekly.com	CO	80305	303-494-5511	494-2585
C-Ville Weekly 106 E Main St Charlottesville *Web:* www.c-ville.com	VA	22902	434-817-2749	817-2758
Charleston City Paper 1049 Morrison Dr # B. Charleston *Web:* www.charlestoncitypaper.com	SC	29403	843-577-5304	576-0380
Chicago Reader 11 E Illinois St. Chicago *TF:* 888-473-5362 ■ *Web:* www.chicagoreader.com	IL	60611	312-828-0350	828-9926
Chico News & Review 353 E Second St Chico *TF:* 866-703-3873 ■ *Web:* www.newsreview.com	CA	95928	530-894-2300	894-0143
Cincinnati CityBeat 811 Race St Cincinnati	OH	45202	513-665-4700	665-4368
City Newspaper 250 N Goodman St. Rochester *Web:* www.rochestercitynewspaper.com	NY	14607	585-244-3329	244-1126
City Pages 300 Third St PO Box 942 Wausau *Web:* www.thecitypages.com	WI	54402	715-845-5171	848-5887
Cityview 414 61st St Des Moines *Web:* www.dmcityview.com	IA	50312	515-953-4822	953-1394
Colorado Springs Independent 235 S Nevada Ave. Colorado Springs *Web:* www.csindy.com	CO	80903	719-577-4545	577-4107
Columbus Alive 34 S Third St Columbus *Web:* www.columbusalive.com	OH	43215	614-221-2449	461-8746
Creative Loafing Atlanta 384 Northyards Blvd Ste 600 Atlanta *TF:* 888-242-0208 ■ *Web:* clatl.com	GA	30313	404-688-5623	614-3599
Creative Loafing Tampa 1911 N 13th St Ste W200 Tampa *Web:* www.cltampa.com	FL	33605	813-739-4800	739-4801
Dallas Observer 2501 Oak Lawn Ave Ste 700 PO Box 190289 Dallas *Web:* www.dallasobserver.com	TX	75219	214-757-9000	757-8590
Dayton City Paper 126 N Main St Ste 240 Dayton *Web:* www.daytoncitypaper.com	OH	45402	937-222-8855	222-6113
East Bay Express 1335 Stanford Ave Ste 100 Emeryville *Web:* www.eastbayexpress.com	CA	94608	510-879-3700	879-3794
Eugene Weekly 1251 Lincoln St Eugene *TF:* 866-233-2250 ■ *Web:* www.eugeneweekly.com	OR	97401	541-484-0519	484-4044
Flagpole PO Box 1027 Athens *Web:* www.flagpole.com	GA	30603	706-549-9523	548-8981
Folio Weekly 9456 Philips Hwy Ste 11 Jacksonville *Web:* www.folioweekly.com	FL	32256	904-260-9770	260-9773
Fort Worth Weekly 3311 Hamilton Ave Fort Worth *Web:* www.fwweekly.com	TX	76107	817-321-9700	335-9575
Gambit Weekly 3923 Bienville St. New Orleans *Web:* www.bestofneworleans.com	LA	70119	504-486-5900	483-3116
Georgia Straight 1701 W Broadway Vancouver *Web:* www.straight.com	BC	V6J1Y3	604-730-7000	730-7010
Honolulu Weekly 1111 Ford St Mall Ste 214 Honolulu *Web:* www.honoluluweekly.com	HI	96813	808-528-1475	
Houston Press 1621 Milam St Ste 100 Houston *TF:* 877-926-8300 ■ *Web:* www.houstonpress.com	TX	77002	713-280-2400	280-2444
Independent Weekly PO Box 2690 Durham *Web:* www.indyweek.com	NC	27715	919-286-1972	286-4274
Isthmus Publishing Company Inc 101 King St. Madison *Web:* isthmus.com/	WI	53703	608-251-5627	251-2165
Ithaca Times 109 N Cayuga St. Ithaca *Web:* www.ithaca.com	NY	14850	607-277-7000	277-1012
LA Weekly 6715 Sunset Blvd Los Angeles **Fax Area Code:* 323 ■ *Web:* www.laweekly.com	CA	90028	806-884-4422	465-3220*
Long Island Press 575 Underhill Blvd Ste 210 Syosset *TF:* 800-545-6683 ■ *Web:* www.longislandpress.com	NY	11791	516-284-3300	284-3310

Name / Address	City	State	Zip	Phone	Fax
Louisville Eccentric Observer 640 S Fourth St Ste 100 *Web:* www.leoweekly.com	Louisville	KY	40202	502-895-9770	895-9779
Maui Time Weekly 33 N Market St Ste 201 *Web:* www.mauitime.com	Wailuku	HI	96793	808-244-0777	244-0446
Memphis Flyer 460 Tennessee St *TF:* 800-581-5156 ■ *Web:* www.memphisflyer.com	Memphis	TN	38103	901-521-9000	521-0129
Metro Pulse 602 S Gay St Ste Mezzanine *TF:* 800-686-4208 ■ *Web:* www.metropulse.com	Knoxville	TN	37902	865-522-5399	522-2955
Metro Santa Cruz 550 S First St *Web:* www.metroactive.com	San Jose	CA	95113	408-200-1300	
Metro Silicon Valley 550 S First St *Web:* www.metroactive.com	San Jose	CA	95113	408-298-8000	298-0602
Metro Times 733 St Antoine St *TF:* 866-501-3627 ■ *Web:* www.metrotimes.com	Detroit	MI	48226	313-961-4060	961-6598
Metroland 419 Madison Ave *Web:* www.metroland.net	Albany	NY	12210	518-463-2500	463-3712
Miami New Times 2800 Biscayne Blvd *Web:* www.miaminewtimes.com	Miami	FL	33137	305-576-8000	571-7677
Minneapolis/St. Paul City Pages 401 N Third St Ste 550 *TF:* 844-387-6962 ■ *Web:* www.citypages.com	Minneapolis	MN	55401	612-375-1015	372-3737
Missoula Independent 317 S Orange St *Web:* missoulanews.bigskypress.com	Missoula	MT	59801	406-543-6609	543-4367
Monday Magazine 818 Broughton St *Web:* www.mondaymag.com	Victoria	BC	V8W1E4	250-382-6188	381-2662
Monterey County Weekly 668 Williams Ave *Web:* www.montereycountyweekly.com	Seaside	CA	93955	831-394-5656	394-2909
Mountain Xpress 2 Wall St Ste 211 *Web:* www.mountainx.com	Asheville	NC	28801	828-251-1333	251-1311
Nashville Scene 210 12th Ave S Ste 100 *TF:* 800-577-3917 ■ *Web:* www.nashvillescene.com	Nashville	TN	37203	615-244-7989	244-8578
New City Communications 770 N Halsted St Ste 303 *Web:* newcity.com	Chicago	IL	60642	312-243-8786	
New Haven Advocate 900 Chapel St Ste 1100 *Web:* www.ct.com	New Haven	CT	06510	203-789-0010	787-1418
New Times Broward Palm Beach 16 NE Fourth St *Web:* www.browardpalmbeach.com	Fort Lauderdale	FL	33301	954-233-1600	233-1521
New York Press 333 Seventh Ave 14th Fl *Web:* www.nypress.com	New York	NY	10001	212-244-2282	244-9864
North Bay Bohemian 847 Fifth St *Web:* www.bohemian.com	Santa Rosa	CA	95404	707-527-1200	527-1288
NOW Magazine 189 Church St *Web:* www.nowtoronto.com	Toronto	ON	M5B1Y7	416-364-1300	364-1166
NUVO Newsweekly 3951 N Meridian St Ste 200 *Web:* www.nuvo.net	Indianapolis	IN	46208	317-254-2400	254-2405
OC Weekly 2975 Red Hill Ave Ste 150 *Web:* www.ocweekly.com	Costa Mesa	CA	92626	714-550-5900	550-5908
Oklahoma Gazette 3701 N Shartel Ave *Web:* okgazette.com	Oklahoma City	OK	73118	405-528-6000	528-4600
Orlando Weekly 1505 E Colonial Dr St Ste 200 *TF:* 800-474-7576 ■ *Web:* www.orlandoweekly.com	Orlando	FL	32803	407-377-0400	377-0420
Pacific Northwest Inlander 9 S Washington St *TF:* 888-431-9911 ■ *Web:* www.inlander.com	Spokane	WA	99201	509-325-0634	325-0638
Pacific Sun 1200 Fifth Ave Ste 200 *Web:* www.pacificsun.com	San Rafael	CA	94901	415-485-6700	485-6226
Palo Alto Weekly 450 Cambridge Ave *TF:* 800-766-4466 ■ *Web:* www.paloaltoonline.com/weekly	Palo Alto	CA	94306	650-326-8210	326-3928
Pasadena Weekly 50 S Delacey Ave Ste 200 *Web:* www.pasadenaweekly.com	Pasadena	CA	91105	626-584-1500	795-0149
Philadelphia City Paper 123 Chestnut St Third Fl *Web:* www.citypaper.net	Philadelphia	PA	19106	215-735-8444	
Phoenix New Times 1201 E Jefferson *Web:* www.phoenixnewtimes.com	Phoenix	AZ	85034	602-271-0040	340-8806
Pitch, The 1701 Main St *Web:* www.pitch.com	Kansas City	MO	64108	816-561-6061	756-0502
Pittsburgh City Paper 650 Smithfield St Ste 2200 *Web:* www.pghcitypaper.com	Pittsburgh	PA	15222	412-316-3342	316-3388
Portland Phoenix 16 York St Ste 102 *Web:* portland.thephoenix.com	Portland	ME	04101	207-773-8900	773-8905
Providence Phoenix 150 Chestnut St *Web:* providencephoenix.com	Providence	RI	02903	401-273-6397	273-0920
PW-Philadelphia Weekly 1500 Sansom St Third Fl *Web:* www.philadelphiaweekly.com	Philadelphia	PA	19102	215-563-7400	563-0620
Random Lengths News 1300 S Pacific Ave *Web:* www.randomlengthsnews.com	San Pedro	CA	90731	310-519-1442	832-1000
Reader, The 2314 M St PO Box 7360 *Web:* www.thereader.com	Omaha	NE	68107	402-341-7323	341-6967
Reno News & Review 708 N Ctr St *TF:* 866-703-3873 ■ *Web:* www.newsreview.com	Reno	NV	89501	916-498-1234	498-7910
Riverfront Times 6358 Delmar Blvd Ste 200 *Web:* www.riverfronttimes.com	Saint Louis	MO	63130	314-754-5966	754-5955
Sacramento News & Review 1124 Del Paso Blvd *Web:* www.newsreview.com	Sacramento	CA	95815	916-498-1234	498-7920
Salt Lake City Weekly 248 S Main St *Web:* cityweekly.net	Salt Lake City	UT	84101	801-575-7003	575-6106
San Antonio Current 915 Dallas St *Web:* sacurrent.com	San Antonio	TX	78215	210-227-0044	227-6611
San Francisco Bay Guardian 135 Mississippi St *Web:* www.sfbg.com	San Francisco	CA	94107	415-255-3100	437-3657
San Luis Obispo New Times 505 Higuera St *TF:* 800-546-4219 ■ *Web:* www.newtimesslo.com	San Luis Obispo	CA	93401	805-546-8208	546-8641
Santa Barbara Independent 122 W Figueroa St *Web:* www.independent.com	Santa Barbara	CA	93101	805-965-5205	965-5518
Santa Fe Reporter 132 E Marcy St *Web:* sfreporter.com	Santa Fe	NM	87501	505-988-5541	988-5348
Scene 1468 W Ninth St Ste 805 *TF:* 877-598-8703 ■ *Web:* www.clevescene.com	Cleveland	OH	44113	216-241-7550	802-7212
Seattle Weekly 1008 Western Ave Ste 300 *Web:* www.seattleweekly.com	Seattle	WA	98104	206-623-0500	467-4338
Seven Days 255 S Champlain St Ste 5 PO Box 1164 *Web:* www.7dvt.com	Burlington	VT	05401	802-864-5684	865-1015
SF Weekly 185 Berry St Lbby 4 Ste 3800 *Web:* www.sfweekly.com	San Francisco	CA	94107	415-536-8100	777-1839
Shepherd Express 207 E Buffalo St Ste 410 *Web:* expressmilwaukee.com	Milwaukee	WI	53202	414-276-2222	276-3312
Stranger, The 1535 11th Ave Third Fl *Web:* www.thestranger.com	Seattle	WA	98122	206-323-7101	323-7203
Style Weekly 1707 Summit Ave Ste 201 *Web:* www.styleweekly.com	Richmond	VA	23230	804-358-0825	358-9089
Syracuse New Times 1415 W Genesee St *TF:* 800-856-1900 ■ *Web:* syracusenewtimes.com	Syracuse	NY	13204	315-422-7011	422-1721
Tucson Weekly 3280 E Hemisphere Loop Ste 180 PO Box 27087 *Web:* www.tucsonweekly.com	Tucson	AZ	85706	520-294-1200	792-2096
Ventura County Reporter 700 E Main St *Web:* www.vcreporter.com	Ventura	CA	93001	805-648-2244	648-7801
Washington City Paper 2390 Champlain St NW *Web:* www.washingtoncitypaper.com	Washington	DC	20009	202-332-2100	332-8500
Weekly Alibi 2118 Central Ave SE PO Box 151 *Web:* www.alibi.com	Albuquerque	NM	87106	505-346-0660	256-9651
Westword 969 Broadway *Web:* www.westword.com	Denver	CO	80203	303-296-7744	296-5416
Willamette Week 2220 NW Quimby St *Web:* wweek.com	Portland	OR	97210	503-243-2122	243-1115

536 NURSES ASSOCIATIONS - STATE

SEE ALSO Health & Medical Professionals Associations p. 1796

Name / Address	City	State	Zip	Phone	Fax
Alabama State Nurses Assn (ASNA) 360 N Hull St *TF:* 800-270-2762 ■ *Web:* www.alabamanurses.org	Montgomery	AL	36104	334-262-8321	262-8578
Alaska Humanities Forum 161 E First Ave *Web:* www.akhf.org	Anchorage	AK	99501	907-272-3979	
Alaska Municipal League Joint Insurance Association 807 G St Ste 356 *Web:* www.amljia.org	Anchorage	AK	99501	907-258-2625	
Alaska Nurses Assn (AaNA) 3701 E Tudor Rd Ste 208 *Web:* www.aknurse.org	Anchorage	AK	99507	907-274-0827	272-0292
American Nurses Assn California (ANA\C) 1121 L St Ste 409 *Web:* www.anacalifornia.org	Sacramento	CA	95814	916-447-0225	442-4394
Arizona Nurses Assn (AzNA) 1850 E Southern Ave Ste 1 *Web:* www.aznurse.org	Tempe	AZ	85282	480-831-0404	839-4780
Arizona Osteopathic Medical Association 5150 N 16th St Ste A122 *Web:* az-osteo.org	Phoenix	AZ	85016	602-266-6699	
Arkansas Nurses Assn (ARNA) 1123 S University Ste 1015 *Web:* www.arna.org	Little Rock	AR	72204	501-244-2363	244-9903
Art Directors Club Inc 106 W 29th St *Web:* adcglobal.org	New York	NY	10001	212-643-1440	
B Oma Suburban Chicago 1515 E Woodfield Rd Ste 110 *Web:* www.bomasuburbanchicago.com	Schaumburg	IL	60173	847-995-0970	
Cai-clac 5355 Parkford Cir *Web:* caiclac.wordpress.com	Granite Bay	CA	95746	916-791-4750	
California Nurses Assn (CNA) 2000 Franklin St *Web:* www.nationalnursesunited.org	Oakland	CA	94612	510-273-2200	663-1625
Chester County Bar Association, The 15 W Gay St Second Fl *Web:* chescobar.org	West Chester	PA	19380	610-692-1889	
Colorado Nurses Assn (CNA) 2851 S. Parker Rd Ste 205 *Web:* coloradonurses.org/	Aurora	CO	80014	303-597-0128	757-8833
Connecticut Nurses Assn (CNA) 377 Research Pkwy Ste 2D *Web:* www.ctnurses.org	Meriden	CT	06450	203-238-1207	238-3437
Council of Ethical Organizations 214 S Payne St *Web:* www.medicarecompliance.com	Alexandria	VA	22314	703-683-7916	
Dallas County Medical Society 140 E 12th St *Web:* www.dallas-cms.org	Dallas	TX	75203	214-948-3622	
Delaware Nurses Assn (DNA) 4765 Ogletown-Stanton Rd Ste L10 *TF:* 800-626-4081 ■ *Web:* www.denurses.org	Newark	DE	19713	302-733-5880	
Diesel Technology Forum Inc 5291 Corporate Dr Ste 102 *Web:* dieselforum.org	Frederick	MD	21703	301-668-7230	
District of Columbia Nurses Assn (DCNA) 5100 Wisconsin Ave NW Ste 306 *Web:* www.dcna.org	Washington	DC	20016	202-244-2705	362-8285
Employers Group 1150 S Olive St Ste 2300 *Web:* www.employersgroup.com	Los Angeles	CA	90015	213-748-0421	
Federal Hearings & Appeals Services Inc 117 W Main St *Web:* fhas.com	Plymouth	PA	18651	570-779-5122	

Name / Address	City	State	Zip	Phone	Fax
Fine Book Club of Claifornia 312 Sutter St Ste 500 *Web:* www.bccbooks.org	San Francisco	CA	94108	415-781-7532	
Florida Nurses Assn (FNA) 1235 E Concord St PO Box 536985 *Web:* www.floridanurse.org	Orlando	FL	32853	407-896-3261	896-9042
Florida Osteopathic Medical Association District 3 Inc 2007 Apalachee Pkwy *Web:* www.fomadistrict2.com	Tallahassee	FL	32301	850-878-7364	
Georgia Avenue Rock Creek East Family Support Collaborative 1104 Allison St Nw *Web:* www.lssnca.org	Washington	DC	20011	202-722-1815	
Georgia Municipal Association 201 Pryor St SW *Web:* www.gmanet.com	Atlanta	GA	30303	404-688-0472	
Georgia Nurses Assn (GNA) 3032 Briarcliff Rd NE *TF:* 800-324-0462 ■ *Web:* www.georgianurses.org	Atlanta	GA	30329	404-325-5536	325-0407
Girls Inc of Alameda County 13666 E 14th St *Web:* www.girlsinc-alameda.org	San Leandro	CA	94578	510-357-5515	
Hawaii Nurses Assn (HNA) 949 Kapiolani Blvd Ste 107 *TF:* 800-617-2677 ■ *Web:* www.hawaiinurses.org	Honolulu	HI	96814	808-531-1628	524-2760
Hydrocephalus Association 870 Market St Ste 705 *Web:* www.hydroassoc.org	San Francisco	CA	94102	415-732-7040	
Iapp 170 Cider Hill Rd *Web:* privacyassociation.org	York	ME	03909	207-351-1500	
Ichp Building Company LLC 4055 N Perryville Rd *Web:* ichpnet.org	Loves Park	IL	61111	815-227-9292	
Idaho Nurses Assn (INA) 1850 E Southern Ave Ste 1 *TF:* 888-721-8904 ■ *Web:* www.idahonurses.org	Tempe	AZ	85224	404-760-2803	240-0998
Idaho Primary Care Association Inc 1087 W River St Ste 160 *Web:* www.idahopca.org	Boise	ID	83702	208-345-2335	
Illinois Alcoholism & Drug Dependence Assn 937 S Second St *Web:* iadda.org	Springfield	IL	62704	217-528-7335	
Illinois Health Care Association 1029 S Fourth St *Web:* www.ihca.com	Springfield	IL	62703	217-528-6455	
Illinois Nurses Assn (INA) 105 W Adams St Ste 2101 *Web:* www.illinoisnurses.com	Chicago	IL	60603	312-419-2900	419-2920
Illinois Principals Association 2940 Baker Dr *Web:* www.ilprincipals.org	Springfield	IL	62703	217-525-1383	
Indiana Association of School Principals Inc 11025 E 25th St *Web:* www.iasp.org	Indianapolis	IN	46229	317-891-9900	
Indiana State Nurses Assn (ISNA) 2915 N High School Rd *Web:* www.indiananurses.org	Indianapolis	IN	46224	317-299-4575	297-3525
Iowa Mortgage Association 8800 Nw 62nd Ave *Web:* www.iowama.org	Johnston	IA	50131	515-286-4352	
Iowa Nurses Assn (INA) 2400 86th St Ste 32 *Web:* www.iowanurses.org	Urbandale	IA	50322	515-225-0495	225-2201
Kansas Action for Children Inc 720 Sw Jackson St Ste 201 *Web:* www.kac.org	Topeka	KS	66603	785-232-0550	
Kansas State Nurses Assn (KSNA) 1109 SW Topeka Blvd *Web:* www.ksnurses.com	Topeka	KS	66612	785-233-8638	233-5222
Kentucky Bankers Association 600 W Main St Ste 400 *Web:* www.kybanks.com	Louisville	KY	40202	502-582-2453	
Kentucky Hospital Association 2501 Nelson Miller Pkwy Ste 200 *Web:* www.kyha.com	Louisville	KY	40223	502-426-6220	
Kfmc 2947 Sw Wanamaker Dr Ste A *Web:* www.kfmc.org	Topeka	KS	66614	785-273-2552	
Lake Mission Viejo Association 22555 Olympiad Rd *Web:* lakemissionviejo.org	Mission Viejo	CA	92692	949-770-1327	
League of Kansas Municipalities 300 Sw Eighth Ave Ste 100 *Web:* lkm.org	Topeka	KS	66603	785-354-9565	
Louisiana State Nurses Assn, The (LSNA) 5713 Superior Dr Ste A-6 *TF:* 800-457-6378 ■ *Web:* www.lsna.org	Baton Rouge	LA	70816	225-201-0993	201-0971
Maine Nurse Practitioners Association 11 Columbia St *Web:* www.mnpa.us	Augusta	ME	04330	207-621-0313	
Maine State Nurses Assn (MSNA) 160 Capitol St Ste 1 *Web:* www.nationalnursesunited.org	Augusta	ME	04330	207-622-1057	623-4072
Managed Funds Association 600 14th St NW Ste 900 *Web:* www.managedfunds.org	Washington	DC	20005	202-367-1140	
Maryland Municipal League Insurance Agency Inc 1212 W St Ste 100 *Web:* www.mdmunicipal.org	Annapolis	MD	21401	410-268-5514	
Maryland Nurses Assn (MNA) 21 Governor's Ct Ste 195 *Web:* www.marylandrn.org	Baltimore	MD	21244	410-944-5800	944-5802
Massachusetts Assn of Registered Nurses (MARN) PO Box 285 *Web:* anamass.org/?	Milton	MA	02186	617-990-2856	
Massachusetts Nurses Assn (MNA) 340 Tpke St *TF:* 800-882-2056 ■ *Web:* www.massnurses.org	Canton	MA	02021	781-821-4625	821-4445
MedReview Inc One Seaport Plz 199 Water St 27th Fl *Web:* www.medreview.us	New York	NY	10038	212-897-6000	
Mha an Association of Montana Health Care Providers 1720 Ninth Ave *Web:* mtha.org	Helena	MT	59601	406-442-1911	
Michigan Boating Industries Association 32398 5 Mile Rd *Web:* www.mbia.org	Livonia	MI	48154	734-261-0123	
Michigan Nurses Assn (MNA) 2310 Jolly Oak Rd *TF:* 888-646-8773 ■ *Web:* www.minurses.org	Okemos	MI	48864	517-349-5640	349-5818
Michigan Society of Association Executives 1350 Haslett Rd *Web:* www.msae.org	East Lansing	MI	48823	517-332-6723	
Microcredit Summit 440 First St Nw Ste 460 *Web:* www.microcreditsummit.org	Washington	DC	20001	202-637-9600	
Midwest Reliability Organization 380 Saint Peter St Ste 800 *Web:* www.midwestreliability.org	Saint Paul	MN	55102	651-855-1760	
Minnesota Nurses Assn (MNA) 345 Randolph Ave Ste 200 *TF:* 800-536-4662 ■ *Web:* www.mnnurses.org	Saint Paul	MN	55102	651-646-4807	647-5301
Mississippi Nurses Assn (MNA) 31 Woodgreen Pl *Web:* www.msnurses.org	Madison	MS	39110	601-898-0670	898-0190
Missouri Municipal League 1727 Southridge Dr *Web:* www.mocities.com	Jefferson City	MO	65109	573-635-9134	
Missouri Nurses Assn (MONA) 1904 Bubba Ln PO Box 105228 *Web:* www.missourinurses.org	Jefferson City	MO	65110	573-636-4623	636-9576
Montana Nurses Assn (MNA) 20 Old Montana State Hwy *Web:* www.mtnurses.org	Montana City	MT	59634	406-442-6710	442-1841
Multnomah Bar Association 620 Sw Fifth Ave Ste 1220 *Web:* mbabar.org	Portland	OR	97204	503-222-3275	
N J Coalition of Automotive Retailers 856 River Rd *Web:* www.njcar.org	Ewing	NJ	08628	609-883-5056	
Napaba 1612 K St Nw Ste 1400 *Web:* www.napaba.org	Washington	DC	20006	202-775-9555	
National Latino Education Institute 2011 W Pershing Rd *Web:* www.nlei.org	Chicago	IL	60609	773-247-0707	
Nebraska Nurses Assn (NNA) PO Box 3107 *TF:* 800-582-3014 ■ *Web:* www.nebraskanurses.org	Kearney	NE	68848	402-475-3859	474-6206
New Hampshire Nurses Assn (NHNA) 210 N State St Ste 1A *Web:* www.nhnurses.org	Concord	NH	03301	603-225-3783	228-6672
New Jersey State Nurses Assn (NJSNA) 1479 Pennington Rd *TF:* 888-876-5762 ■ *Web:* www.njsna.org	Trenton	NJ	08618	609-883-5335	883-5343
New York County Lawyers Association 14 Vesey St *Web:* www.nycla.org	New York	NY	10007	212-267-6646	
New York Professional Nurses Union (NYPNU) 1104 Lexington Ave Ste 2D *Web:* www.nypnu.org	New York	NY	10021	212-988-5565	
New York State Nurses Assn (NYSNA) 11 Cornell Rd *TF:* 800-724-6976 ■ *Web:* www.nysna.org	Latham	NY	12110	518-782-9400	782-9530
North Carolina Nurses Assn (NCNA) 103 Enterprise St PO Box 12025 *TF:* 800-626-2153 ■ *Web:* www.ncnurses.org	Raleigh	NC	27605	919-821-4250	829-5807
Ohio a C e p 3510 Snouffer Rd Ste 100 *Web:* www.ohacep.org	Columbus	OH	43235	614-792-6506	
Ohio Grantmakers Forum 37 W Broad St Ste 800 *Web:* www.philanthropyohio.org	Columbus	OH	43215	614-224-1344	
Ohio Nurses Assn (ONA) 4000 E Main St *Web:* www.ohnurses.org	Columbus	OH	43213	614-237-5414	237-6074
Ohio Poultry Association 5930 Sharon Woods Blvd *Web:* www.ohiopoultry.org	Columbus	OH	43229	614-882-6111	
Ohio Quarter Horse 101 Tawa Rd *Web:* oqha.com	Richwood	OH	43344	740-943-2346	
Oklahoma Nurses Assn (ONA) 6414 N Santa Fe Ave Ste A *Web:* clients.yourmembership.com/dns_error.asp?fqdn=www%2eoknurses%2ecom	Oklahoma City	OK	73116	405-840-3476	840-3013
Oregon Nurses Assn (ONA) 18765 SW Boones Ferry Rd *TF:* 800-634-3552 ■ *Web:* www.oregonrn.org	Tualatin	OR	97062	503-293-0011	293-0013
Oregon Society of CPAs 10206 SW Laurel St *Web:* www.orcpa.org	Beaverton	OR	97005	503-641-7200	
Pasadena Heritage 651 S Saint John Ave *Web:* pasadenaheritage.org	Pasadena	CA	91105	626-441-6333	
Pennsylvania Assn of Staff Nurses & Allied Professionals (PASNAP) One Fayette St Ste 475 *TF:* 800-500-7850 ■ *Web:* www.pennanurses.org	Conshohocken	PA	19428	610-567-2907	567-2915
Planetree Inc 130 Division St *Web:* planetree.org	Derby	CT	06418	203-732-1365	
Polaris Project PO Box 77892 *Web:* polarisproject.org	Washington	DC	20013	202-745-1001	
Public Company Accounting Oversight Board (PCAOB) 1666 K St NW *Web:* www.pcaobus.org	Washington	DC	20006	202-207-9100	
Red Hat Society Store 431 S Acacia Ave *Web:* www.redhatsociety.com	Fullerton	CA	92831	714-738-0001	
Rhode Island State Nurses Assn (RISNA) 150 Washington St Ste 415 *Web:* www.risna.org	Providence	RI	02903	401-331-5644	331-5646
San Jose Downtown Association 28 N First St Ste 1000 *Web:* www.sjdowntown.com	San Jose	CA	95113	408-279-1775	

Phone | Fax

Soaring Society of America Jack Gomez Blvd, Hobbs NM 88240, 575-392-1177
Web: www.ssa.org

South Carolina Education Association, The
421 Zimalcrest Dr, Columbia SC 29210, 803-772-6553
Web: www.thescea.org

South Carolina Nurses Assn (SCNA)
1821 Gadsden St, Columbia SC 29201, 803-252-4781, 779-3870
Web: www.scnurses.org

South Dakota Nurses Assn (SDNA) PO Box 1015, Pierre SD 57501, 605-945-4265, 425-3032*
**Fax Area Code:* 888 ■ *Web:* www.sdnursesassociation.org

Southeast Valley Regional Association of Realtors
1363 S Vineyard, Mesa AZ 85210, 480-833-7510
Web: www.sevrar.com

Tennessee Nurses Assn (TNA)
545 Mainstream Dr Ste 405, Nashville TN 37228, 615-254-0350, 254-0303
Web: www.tnaonline.org

Tennessee State Employees Association
627 Woodland St, Nashville TN 37206, 615-256-4533
Web: www.tseaonline.org

Texas Beef Council 8708 N Fm 620, Austin TX 78726, 512-335-2333
Web: www.txbeef.org

United Nurses & Allied Professionals
375 Branch Ave, Providence RI 02904, 401-831-3647
Web: www.unap.org

Utah Nurses Assn (UNA)
4505 S Wastch Blvd Ste 330B, Salt Lake City UT 84124, 801-272-4510
TF: 800-338-7657 ■ *Web:* www.utahnursesassociation.com

Van Alen Institute 30 W 22nd St Fl 6, New York NY 10010, 212-924-7000
Web: www.vanalen.org

Vermont State Nurses Assn (VSNA)
100 Dorset St Ste 13, South Burlington VT 05403, 802-651-8886, 651-8998
TF: 800-540-9390 ■ *Web:* www.vsna-inc.org

Virginia Nurses Assn (VNA)
7113 Three Chopt Rd Ste 204, Richmond VA 23226, 804-282-1808, 282-4916
Web: www.virginianurses.com

Washington State Nurses Assn (WSNA)
575 Andover Pk W Ste 101, Seattle WA 98188, 206-575-7979, 575-1908
TF: 800-231-8482 ■ *Web:* www.wsna.org

West Coast Conference
1111 Bayhill Dr Ste 405, San Bruno CA 94066, 650-873-8622
Web: wccsports.com

West Virginia Nurses Assn (WVNA)
1007 Bigley Ave Ste 308, Charleston WV 25302, 304-342-1169, 346-1861
TF: 800-400-1226 ■ *Web:* www.wvnurses.org

Western Institutional Review Board Inc
1019 39th Ave SE Ste 120, Puyallup WA 98374, 360-252-2500
Web: www.wirb.com

Wisconsin Nurses Assn (WNA) 6117 Monona Dr, Madison WI 53716, 608-221-0383, 221-2788
Web: www.wisconsinnurses.org

537 OFFICE & SCHOOL SUPPLIES

SEE ALSO Office Supply Stores p. 2833; Writing Paper p. 2854; Pens, Pencils, Parts p. 2899; Printing & Photocopying Supplies p. 2974

Phone | Fax

A & W Products Company Inc 14 Gardner St, Port Jervis NY 12771, 845-856-5156, 856-9772
Web: www.awproducts.com

Aakron Rule Corp PO Box 418, Akron NY 14001, 716-542-5483, 542-2205
Web: www.aakronline.com

Acroprint Time Recorder Co 5640 Departure Dr, Raleigh NC 27616, 919-872-5800, 850-0720
TF: 800-334-7190 ■ *Web:* acroprint.com

American Product Distributors Inc (APD)
8350 Arrowridge Blvd, Charlotte NC 28273, 704-522-9411
TF: 800-849-5842 ■ *Web:* www.americanproduct.com

American Solutions for Business
31 E Minnesota Ave PO Box 218, Glenwood MN 56334, 800-862-3690, 634-5265*
**Fax Area Code:* 320 ■ *TF:* 800-862-3690 ■ *Web:* home.americanbus.com

Arlington Industries Inc 1616 Lakeside Dr, Waukegan IL 60085, 847-689-2754, 689-1616
TF: 800-323-4147 ■ *Web:* www.arli.com

Aurora Corp of America 3500 Challenger St, Torrance CA 90503, 310-793-5650, 793-5658
TF: 800-327-8508 ■ *Web:* www.auroracorp.com

Avery Dennison Worldwide Office Products Div
207 Goode Ave, Glendale CA 91203, 626-304-2000, 848-2169*
**Fax Area Code:* 800 ■ *TF:* 800-462-8379 ■ *Web:* www.averydennison.com

Bartizan Corp 217 Riverdale Ave, Yonkers NY 10705, 914-965-7977, 965-7746
TF: 800-899-2278 ■ *Web:* www.bartizan.com

Baumgarten's 144 Ottley Dr, Atlanta GA 30324, 404-874-7675, 964-1279*
**Fax Area Code:* 480 ■ *TF:* 800-247-5547 ■ *Web:* www.b3.net

Business Stationery LLC 4944 Commerce Pkwy, Cleveland OH 44128, 216-514-1277
TF: 800-234-9954 ■ *Web:* www.bsiprint.com

C & S Sales Inc 12947 Chadron Ave, Hawthorne CA 90250, 310-538-1219, 538-2814
Web: www.cssales.com

C-Line Products Inc
1100 E Business Ctr Dr, Mount Prospect IL 60056, 847-827-6661, 827-3329
TF: 800-323-6084 ■ *Web:* www.c-lineproducts.com

Cardinal Office Products Inc 576 E Main St, Frankfort KY 40601, 502-875-3300, 539-4325*
**Fax Area Code:* 800 ■ *TF:* 800-589-5886 ■ *Web:* cardinaloffice.com

Case Logic Inc 6303 Dry Creek Pkwy, Longmont CO 80503, 303-652-1000
TF: 800-925-8111 ■ *Web:* www.caselogic.com

Champion Industries Inc
PO Box 2968 PO Box 2968, Huntington WV 25728, 304-528-2791, 528-2746
OTC: CHMP ■ *TF:* 800-624-3431 ■ *Web:* champion-industries.com

Dahle North America Inc
49 Vose Farm Rd Ste 110, Peterborough NH 03458, 603-924-0003, 924-1616
TF: 800-243-8145 ■ *Web:* www.dahle.com

Dart Manufacturing Co 3860 La Reunion Pkwy, Dallas TX 75212, 214-631-8024
Web: www.dartpromo.com

Deflect-O Corp 7035 E 86th St, Indianapolis IN 46250, 800-428-4328, 915-4456*
**Fax Area Code:* 317 ■ *TF:* 800-428-4328 ■ *Web:* www.deflecto.com

Phone | Fax

Douglas Stewart Co, The 2402 Advance Rd, Madison WI 53718, 608-221-1155, 221-5217
TF: 800-279-2795 ■ *Web:* www.dstewart.com

Eaton Office Supply Company Inc
180 John Glenn Dr, Buffalo NY 14228, 716-691-6100, 691-0074
TF: 800-365-3237 ■ *Web:* www.eatonofficesupply.com

GBS Corp 7233 Freedom Ave NW, North Canton OH 44720, 330-494-5330, 494-7075
TF: 800-552-2427 ■ *Web:* www.gbscorp.com

International Imaging Materials Inc
310 Commerce Dr, Amherst NY 14228, 716-691-6333, 691-3395
TF: 888-464-4625 ■ *Web:* www.iimak.com

Lakeshore Learning Materials
2695 E Dominguez St, Carson CA 90895, 800-778-4456, 537-5403
TF: 800-778-4456 ■ *Web:* www.lakeshorelearning.com

Lee Products Co 800 E 80th St, Bloomington MN 55420, 952-854-3544, 854-7177
TF: 800-989-3544 ■ *Web:* www.leeproducts.com

Magna Visual Inc 9400 Watson Rd, Saint Louis MO 63126, 800-843-3399, 843-0000*
**Fax Area Code:* 314 ■ *TF:* 800-843-3399 ■ *Web:* www.magnavisual.com

McGill Inc 131 E Prairie St PO Box 177, Marengo IL 60152, 815-568-7244, 568-6860
Web: www.mcgillinc.com

Millennium Marking Co
2600 Greenleaf Ave, Elk Grove Village IL 60007, 847-806-1750, 806-1751
Web: www.millmarking.com

Nina Enterprises 1350 S Leavitt St, Chicago IL 60608, 312-733-6400, 733-8356
TF: 800-886-8688 ■ *Web:* www.buddyproducts.com

PBS Supply Company Inc 7013 S 216th St, Kent WA 98032, 253-395-5550, 395-5575
TF: 877-727-7515 ■ *Web:* www.pbssupply.com

PerfectData Corp
1323 Conshohocken Rd, Plymouth Meeting PA 19462, 800-973-7332, 277-4390*
**Fax Area Code:* 610 ■ *TF:* 800-973-7332 ■ *Web:* www.perfectdata.com

Staples Business Advantage 500 Staples Dr, Framingham MA 01702, 877-826-7755
TF: 877-826-7755 ■ *Web:* www.staplesadvantage.com

TAB Products Co 605 Fourth St, Mayville WI 53050, 888-466-8228, 304-4947*
**Fax Area Code:* 800 ■ *TF:* 888-466-8228 ■ *Web:* www.tab.com

United Stationers Inc 1 PkwyN Blvd Ste 100, Deerfield IL 60015, 847-627-7000
TF: 855-275-6947 ■ *Web:* www.unitedstationers.com

United Stationers Supply Co (USSCO)
1 Pkwy N Blvd Ste 100 Ste 100, Deerfield IL 60015, 847-627-7000
Web: www.essendant.com

Van Ausdall & Farrar Inc 6430 E 75th St, Indianapolis IN 46250, 317-634-2913, 638-1843
TF: 800-467-7474 ■ *Web:* www.vanausdall.com

Weeks-Lerman Group 58-38 Page Pl, Maspeth NY 11378, 718-803-5000, 821-1515
TF: 800-544-5959 ■ *Web:* www.weekslerman.com

538 OFFICE SUPPLY STORES

Phone | Fax

AJ Stationers Inc 6675 Business Pkwy, Elkridge MD 21075, 410-360-4900, 360-4291

Artlite Office Supply Co
1860 Chshire Bridge Rd NE, Atlanta GA 30324, 404-875-7271, 875-2623
Web: www.artlite.net

Audit & Adjustment Company Inc
20700 44th Ave W Ste 100, Lynnwood WA 98036, 425-776-9797
TF: 800-526-1074 ■ *Web:* www.audit-adjustment.com

B J Bindery 833 S Grand Ave, Santa Ana CA 92705, 714-835-7342
Web: www.bjbindery.com

Belitec Inc 350 Rue Vachon, Trois-RiviŠres QC G8T8Y2, 819-373-3880
Web: www.belitec.ca

BenefitHelp Solutions Inc
10505 SE 17th Ave, Milwaukie OR 97222, 503-219-3679
TF: 888-398-8057 ■ *Web:* www.benefithelpsolutions.com

Benjamin Office Supply & Services Inc
760 E Gude Dr, Rockville MD 20850, 301-340-1384
Web: www.benjaminofficesupply.com

BNBS Inc 11600 Otter Creek S Rd, Mabelvale AR 72103, 501-224-1992
Web: www.bnbsinc.com

Brilliance Educator Supplies & Resources Inc
8679 Sudley Rd, Manassas VA 20110, 571-292-2331

Burkett's Office Supplies Inc
8520 Younger Creek Dr, Sacramento CA 95828, 916-387-8900, 381-3383
Web: www.burkettsoffice.com

Business Cards Tomorrow Inc
3000 NE 30th Pl Fifth Fl, Fort Lauderdale FL 33306, 954-563-1224
Web: www.bctonline.com

C M School Supply Inc 940 N Central Ave, Upland CA 91786, 909-982-9695
Web: www.cmschoolsupply.com

Cambridge Lasers Inc 853 Brown Rd, Fremont CA 94539, 510-651-0110
Web: www.cambridgelasers.com

Cash Control Business Systems
9101 Lackland Rd, Overland MO 63114, 314-427-6143
Web: www.cashcontrolbiz.com

Center Municipal Revenue Collection
PO Box 195387, San Juan PR 00926, 787-625-2746
Web: www.crimpr.net

Church & Stagg Office Supply Company Inc
3421 Sixth Ave, Birmingham AL 35222, 205-251-2951, 324-6874
TF: 800-239-5336 ■ *Web:* www.churchandstagg.com

Columbia Omnicorp 14 W 33rd St, New York NY 10001, 212-279-6161
Web: columbiaomni.com/

Computer Designs Inc 5235 W Coplay Rd, Whitehall PA 18052, 610-261-2100
Web: www.computer-designs.com

Conney Safety Products LLC 3202 Latham Dr, Madison WI 53744, 608-271-3300
Web: www.conney.com

Copy Products Inc 2103 W Vista St, Springfield MO 65807, 417-889-5665
Web: copyproductsinc.com

Create-a-card Inc 16 Brasswood Rd, Saint James NY 11780, 631-584-2273
Web: www.createacardinc.com

Danby Group LLP, The
3060-A Business Park Dr, Norcross GA 30071, 770-416-9844
Web: www.danbygroup.com

DBI Inc 912 E Michigan Ave, Lansing MI 48912, 517-485-3200, 485-3202
TF: 800-968-1324 ■ *Web:* www.dbiyes.com

Company / Address	City	State	Zip	Phone	Fax
Ddl Business Systems 5321 Mulberry St *Web:* www.ddlbusiness.com	Stephens City	VA	22655	540-869-7855	
Dick Blick Holdings Inc 1849 Green Bay Rd Ste 310 *Web:* dickblick.com	Highland Park	IL	60035	847-681-6800	
Discover Group Inc 2741 W 23rd St *TF:* 866-456-6555 ■ *Web:* www.discovergroup.net	Brooklyn	NY	11224	718-456-4500	
Dynetics Technical Services Inc 1002 Explorer Blvd *Web:* www.dts-dynetics.com	Huntsville	AL	35806	256-544-0764	
Eakes Office Plus 617 W Third St *TF:* 800-652-9396 ■ *Web:* www.eakes.com	Grand Island	NE	68801	308-382-8026	382-7401
Econ-o-copy Inc 4437 Trenton St Ste A *TF:* 877-256-0310 ■ *Web:* www.econ-o-copy.com	Metairie	LA	70006	504-457-0032	457-0114
Economy Office Supply Co 1725 Gardena Ave *Web:* www.economyofficesupply.com	Glendale	CA	91204	818-548-1525	
Egyptian Stationers Inc 129 W Main St *TF Cust Svc:* 800-642-3949 ■ *Web:* www.egyptian-stationers.com	Belleville	IL	62220	618-234-2323	234-0693
EIS Electro Imaging Systems 6553 Las Positas Rd *Web:* www.eisonline.net	Livermore	CA	94551	925-930-8696	
Envelopes Only Inc 2000 S Park Ave *Web:* envelopesonly.net	Streamwood	IL	60107	630-213-2500	
Envoy Plan Services Inc 901 Calle Amanecer Ste 200 *TF:* 800-248-8858 ■ *Web:* www.envoyplanservices.com	San Clemente	CA	92673	949-366-5070	
FASCore LLC 8515 E Orchard Rd *TF:* 800-232-0859 ■ *Web:* www.fascore.com	Greenwood Village	CO	80111	800-537-2033	
Firstline Business Systems Inc 2114 Main St 101 *Web:* firstline-online.com	Vancouver	WA	98660	360-695-3138	
Fisher Hawaii 450 Cooke St *Web:* www.fisherhawaii.biz	Honolulu	HI	96813	808-524-8770	524-8785
Friend's Professional Stationery Inc 1535 Lewis Ave *TF:* 800-323-4394 ■ *Web:* www.friendsstationery.com	Zion	IL	60099	800-323-4394	323-1535
GEMGroup LP 1200 Three Gateway Ctr *Web:* www.gemgrouplp.com	Pittsburgh	PA	15222	412-471-2885	
Gobin's Inc 615 N Santa Fe Ave *TF:* 800-425-2324 ■ *Web:* www.gobins.com	Pueblo	CO	81003	719-544-2324	544-2378
Guernsey Office Products 45070 Old Ox Rd *Web:* guernseyop.com	Dulles	VA	20166	703-968-8200	
Gulfland Office Supplies Inc 801 Brashear Ave *Web:* gulfandoffice.com	Morgan City	LA	70380	985-384-3250	
Halsey & Griffith Inc 1983 Tenth Ave N *Web:* www.halseygriffith.com	Lake Worth	FL	33461	561-820-8000	
High Technology Inc 109 Production Rd *Web:* www.htmed.com	Walpole	MA	02081	508-660-2221	
Hurst Group 257 E Short St *TF:* 800-926-4423 ■ *Web:* www.hurstgroup.net	Lexington	KY	40507	859-255-4422	255-4471
Infomax Office Systems Inc 1010 Illinois St *Web:* infomaxoffice.com	Des Moines	IA	50314	515-244-5203	
JL Darling LLC 2614 Pacific Hwy E *Web:* www.riteintherain.com	Tacoma	WA	98424	253-922-5000	
Keeton's Office & Art Supply Co 817 Manatee Ave W *Web:* www.keetonsonline.com	Bradenton	FL	34205	941-747-2995	
Kennedy Office Supply 4211-A Atlantic Ave *TF:* 800-733-9401 ■ *Web:* www.kennedyofficesupply.com	Raleigh	NC	27604	919-878-5400	790-9649
Kinloch Consulting Group Inc 25 Melville Park Rd Ste 260 *Web:* www.kinlochcg.com	Melville	NY	11747	631-773-6600	
Koch Bros 325 Grand Ave *TF:* 800-944-5624 ■ *Web:* www.kochbros.com	Des Moines	IA	50309	515-283-2451	243-3147
Kore Inc 355 Madison Ave *Web:* www.korecorp.com	Morristown	NJ	07960	973-883-0308	
Lafayette Copier Service & Sales 310 Farabee Dr *Web:* lafayettecopier.com	Lafayette	IN	47905	765-446-2230	
Lamination Depot Inc 1505 E McFadden Ave *Web:* www.laminationdepot.com	Santa Ana	CA	92705	714-954-0632	
Latta's School Supply 1502 Fourth Ave *TF:* 800-624-3501 ■ *Web:* www.lattas.com	Huntington	WV	25701	304-523-8400	525-5038
Louisiana Office Supply Co 7643 Florida Blvd *Web:* losco.com	Baton Rouge	LA	70806	225-927-1110	927-3085
Madden Communications Inc 901 Mittel Dr *Web:* www.madden.com	Wood Dale	IL	60191	630-787-2200	
Mallory Safety & Supply Inc 1040 Industrial Way PO Box 2068 *Web:* www.malloryco.com	Longview	WA	98632	360-636-5750	
Marimon Business Systems Inc 7300 N Gessner *Web:* www.marimoninc.com	Houston	TX	77040	713-856-2000	856-2001
Matik Inc 33 Brook St *Web:* www.matik.com	West Hartford	CT	06110	860-232-2323	
McCowan Design & Mfg Ltd 1760 Birchmount Rd *TF:* 888-782-5189 ■ *Web:* www.mccowan.ca	Toronto	ON	M1P2H7	416-291-7111	
MCR Technologies Six Greenwood St *Web:* www.mcrtechnologies.com	Wakefield	MA	01880	781-245-6644	
Meteorix Inc 260 Franklin St 11th Fl *Web:* www.meteorix.com	Boston	MA	02110	617-412-4333	
Metro Business Systems 2950 Kaverton Rd *Web:* www.mbs-copiers.com	District Heights	MD	20747	301-967-8758	
Mg Scientific Inc 8500 107th St *Web:* www.mgscientific.com	Pleasant Prairie	WI	53158	262-947-7000	
New World Imports Inc 160 Athens Way *Web:* www.newworldimports.com	Nashville	TN	37228	615-329-1906	
Newport Stationers Inc 17681 Mitchell N *Web:* www.newportstationers.com	Irvine	CA	92614	949-863-1200	852-8970
Nexus Office Systems Inc 898 Featherstone Rd *Web:* nexusofficesystems.com	Rockford	IL	61107	815-227-0170	
Northern Business Products Inc PO Box 16127 *TF:* 800-647-8775 ■ *Web:* www.nbpoffice.com	Duluth	MN	55816	218-726-0167	726-1023
NOVA Scientific Inc 10 Picker Rd *Web:* www.novascientific.com	Sturbridge	MA	01566	508-347-7679	
Novacopy Inc 5520 Shelby Oaks Dr *TF:* 800-264-0637 ■ *Web:* www.novacopy.net	Memphis	TN	38134	901-388-3399	432-2682
Oak Cliff Office Supply 1876 Lone Star Dr	Dallas	TX	75212	214-943-7421	
Office Depot Inc 2200 Old Germantown Rd *NASDAQ: ODP* ■ **Fax:* Hum Res ■ *TF:* 800-937-3600 ■ *Web:* www.officedepot.com	Delray Beach	FL	33445	561-438-4800	*
Office Resources Inc 374 Congress St *Web:* www.ori.com	Boston	MA	02210	617-423-9100	423-5590
Office Suppliers Inc 13621 Crayton Blvd *Web:* www.hyperspacellc.com	Hagerstown	MD	21742	301-797-3120	797-1504
Opus Framing Ltd 3445 Cornett Rd *TF:* 800-663-6953 ■ *Web:* www.opusframing.com	Vancouver	BC	V5M2H3	604-435-9991	
Paper Pigeon Inc 14701 SW 94 Ave *Web:* paperpigeonmiami.com	Miami	FL	33176	305-235-7887	
Patrick & Co 560 Market St *Web:* patrickandco.com	San Francisco	CA	94104	415-392-2640	591-0773
Phillips Group 501 Fulling Mill Rd *TF:* 800-538-7500 ■ *Web:* www.buyphillips.com	Middletown	PA	17057	717-944-0400	948-5297
Polack Corp, The 1400 Keystone Ave *Web:* www.polackcorp.com	Lansing	MI	48911	517-393-3440	
Prestige Graphics Inc 9630 Ridgehaven Ct Ste B *Web:* www.pgisd.com	San Diego	CA	92123	858-560-8213	
Printers & Stationers Inc 113 N Ct St *TF:* 800-624-5334 ■ *Web:* www.psi-online.net	Florence	AL	35630	256-764-8061	764-5024
Questa Engineering Corp 1010 Tenth St *Web:* www.questa.com	Golden	CO	80401	303-277-1629	
ShurTech Brands 32150 Just Imagine Dr *Web:* shurtech.com	Avon	OH	44011	440-937-7000	
Smith & Butterfield Co Inc 2800 Lynch Rd *TF:* 800-321-6543 ■ *Web:* www.smithbutterfield.com	Evansville	IN	47711	812-422-3261	429-0532
SpecialCare Hospital Management Corp 502 Earth City Plz Ste 311 *Web:* www.specialcarecorp.com	St Louis	MO	63045	314-770-2212	
Stationers Inc 1945 Fifth Ave *TF:* 800-862-7200 ■ *Web:* www.stationers-wv.com	Huntington	WV	25703	304-528-2780	528-2795
Supply Room Cos Inc 14140 N Washington Hwy *TF:* 800-849-7239 ■ *Web:* tsrcinc.net	Ashland	VA	23005	804-412-1200	412-1313
Tamarack Products Inc 1071 N Old Rand Rd *Web:* www.tamarackproducts.com	Wauconda	IL	60084	847-526-9333	
Techneal Inc 2100 S Reservoir St *Web:* www.techneal.com	Pomona	CA	91766	909-465-6325	
Thomas Lee Printing & Mailing Inc 3721 W 12th St	Erie	PA	16505	814-833-3233	
Total Merchant Concepts Inc 12300 NE Fourth Plain Rd A *Web:* www.totalmerchantconcepts.com	Vancouver	WA	98682	360-253-5934	
Triplett Office Essentials Corp 3553 109th St *TF:* 800-437-5034 ■ *Web:* www.tripletts.com	Urbandale	IA	50322	515-270-9150	270-9683
Unisource Canada Inc 50 E Wilmot St *Web:* www.unisource.ca	Richmond Hill	ON	L4B3Z3	905-771-4000	771-4219
Universal Bookbindery Inc 1200 N Colorado St *Web:* universalbookbindery.com	San Antonio	TX	78207	210-734-9502	
Valley Business Machines Inc 5825 Mayflower Ct *Web:* www.vbmalaska.com	Wasilla	AK	99654	907-376-5077	
Variant Microsystems 4128 Business Ctr Dr *Web:* www.variantusa.com	Fremont	CA	94538	510-440-2870	
Variety Office Products of Eau Claire Inc 145 N Clairemont Ave *Web:* varietyoffice.com	Eau Claire	WI	54703	715-834-6650	
Veritas Press 1250 Belle Meade Dr *Web:* www.veritaspress.com	Lancaster	PA	17601	717-519-1974	
WALZ Label & Mailing Systems 624 High Point Ln *Web:* walzeq.com	East Peoria	IL	61611	309-698-1500	
Wist Office Products Co 107 W Julie Dr *TF:* 800-999-9478 ■ *Web:* www.wist.com	Tempe	AZ	85283	480-921-2900	921-2121
Wrapmail Inc 305 S Andrews Ave Ste 601 *Web:* www.wrapmail.com	Fort Lauderdale	FL	33301	954-376-4750	
Xpedx Paper & Graphics 6285 Tri-Ridge Blvd *Web:* www.xpedx.com	Loveland	OH	45140	513-965-2900	
Zymo Research Corp 17062 Murphy Ave *Web:* www.zymoresearch.com	Irvine	CA	92614	949-679-1190	

539 OIL & GAS EXTRACTION

Company / Address	City	State	Zip	Phone	Fax
5J Oilfield Services LLC 4090 N Hwy 79 *Web:* www.5joilfield.net	Palestine	TX	75801	903-723-0253	
A H Belo Corp 508 Young St PO Box 224866 *NYSE: AHC* ■ *TF:* 800-230-1074 ■ *Web:* www.ahbelo.com	Dallas	TX	75202	214-977-8200	977-8201
ABARTA Oil & Gas Company Inc 200 Alpha Dr *Web:* www.abartaenergy.com	Pittsburgh	PA	15238	412-963-6443	
Abington Resources Ltd Ste 125A 1030 Denman St *Web:* www.abingtonresources.com	Vancouver	BC	V6G2M6	604-683-6657	
Abraxas Petroleum Corp 18803 Meisner Dr *NASDAQ: AXAS* ■ **Fax:* Acctg ■ *Web:* www.abraxaspetroleum.com	San Antonio	TX	78258	210-490-4788	490-8816*
Adams Resources & Energy Inc 4400 Post Oak Pkwy *NYSE: AE* ■ *Web:* www.adamsresources.com	Houston	TX	77027	713-881-3600	

				Phone	Fax
Aeropres Corp 1324 N Hearne Ave PO Box 78588 *Web:* www.aeropres.com	Shreveport	LA	71107	318-221-6282	
AES Safety Services 8588 Katy Fwy Ste 430 *Web:* www.aessafetyservices.com	Houston	TX	77024	979-505-0052	
Africa Fortesa Corp 7880 San Felipe St Ste 105 *Web:* www.fortesa.com	Houston	TX	77063	713-278-2727	
Africa Oil Corp 885 W Georgia St Ste 2000 *Web:* www.africaoilcorp.com	Vancouver	BC	V6C3E8	604-689-7842	
Allied-Horizontal Wireline Services LLC 15995 N Barker's Landing Ste 140 *Web:* alliedhorizontal.com	Houston	TX	77079	713-343-7280	
Alvopetro Energy Ltd Ste 1175 332 - 6 Ave SW *Web:* www.alvopetro.com	Calgary	AB	T2P0B2	587-794-4224	
America's Natural Gas Alliance 701 Eighth St NW Ste 800 *Web:* www.anga.us	Washington	DC	20001	202-789-2642	
American Eagle Energy Corp 2549 W Main St Ste 202 *Web:* www.americaneagleenergy.com	Littleton	CO	80120	303-385-1230	
AMERIgreen Energy Inc 1862 Charter Ln Ste 101 *Web:* www.amerigreen.com	Lancaster	PA	17601	717-945-1392	
Amerril Energy LLC 3721 Briarpark Dr Ste 155 *Web:* www.uskingking.com	Houston	TX	77042	713-660-1620	
Anadarko Petroleum Corp 1201 Lk Robbins Dr *NYSE: APC* ■ *TF:* 800-800-1101 ■ *Web:* www.anadarko.com	Spring	TX	77380	832-636-1000	
Angle Energy Inc Ste 700 324 - Eighth Ave SW *Web:* bellatrixexploration.com	Calgary	AB	T2P2Z2	403-263-4534	
Antrim Energy Inc 610-301 8 Ave SW *Web:* www.antrimenergy.com	Calgary	AB	T2P1C5	403-264-5111	
Apache Corp 2000 Post Oak Blvd Ste 100 *NYSE: APA* ■ *TF:* 800-272-2434 ■ *Web:* www.apachecorp.com	Houston	TX	77056	713-296-6000	296-6453
Applied LNG 31111 Agoura Rd Ste 208 *Web:* www.appliedlng.com	Westlake Village	CA	91361	818-450-3650	
Aramco Services Co 9009 W Loop S *TF:* 866-287-3592 ■ *Web:* www.aramcoservices.com	Houston	TX	77096	713-432-4000	432-4146
Arctic Hunter Energy Inc 1610 675 W Hastings St *Web:* www.arctichunter.com	Vancouver	BC	V6B1N2	604-681-3131	
Arete Industries Inc 7260 Osceola St *Web:* www.areteindustries.com	Westminster	CO	80030	303-427-8688	
Aruba Petroleum Inc 555 Republic Dr Ste 505 *Web:* www.arubapetroleum.com	Plano	TX	75074	972-312-9366	
Asean Energy Corp 409 Granville St Ste 400 *Web:* aseanenergycorp.com	Vancouver	BC	V6C1T2	604-608-1999	
ATP Oil & Gas Corp 4600 Post Oak Pl Ste 200 *OTC: ATPAQ*	Houston	TX	77027	713-622-3311	622-5101
Ballard Petroleum LLC 845 12th St W *Web:* www.ballardpetroleum.com	Billings	MT	59102	406-259-8790	
Barnwell Industries Inc 1100 Alakea St Ste 2900 *NYSE: BRN* ■ *Web:* www.brninc.com	Honolulu	HI	96813	808-531-8400	531-7181
Bayou State Oil Corp 1115 Hawn Ave	Shreveport	LA	71107	318-222-0737	222-0730
Baytex Energy Corp 2800 520 - Third Ave SW *Web:* www.baytexenergy.com	Calgary	AB	T2P0R3	587-952-3000	
Bently Nevada Inc 1631 Bently Pkwy South *Web:* www.bently.com	Minden	NV	89423	775-782-3611	
Berry Petroleum Co 1999 Broadway Ste 3700 *NYSE: BRY*	Denver	CO	80202	303-999-4400	999-4401
Beusa Energy Inc Four Waterway Sq Pl Ste 900 *Web:* www.beusaenergy.com	The Woodlands	TX	77380	281-296-1500	
BHP Billiton Petroleum (Americas) Inc 1360 Post Oak Blvd Ste 150 *Web:* www.bhpbilliton.com	Houston	TX	77056	713-961-8500	961-8400
Black Ridge Oil & Gas Inc Ste 310 10275 Wayzata Blvd *Web:* www.blackridgeoil.com	Minnetonka	MN	55305	952-426-1241	
Black Swan Energy Ltd Ste 1200 Bow Vly Sq III 255 - Fifth Ave SW *Web:* www.blackswanenergy.com	Calgary	AB	T2P3G6	403-930-4400	
BlackBrush Oil & Gas LP 18615 Tuscany Stone Ste 300 *Web:* www.blackbrushenergy.com	San Antonio	TX	78258	210-495-5577	
Blacksands Petroleum Inc Ste 410 25025 I-45 N *Web:* www.blacksandspetroleum.com	The Woodlands	TX	77380	713-554-4491	
Blaser Swisslube Inc 31 Hatfield Ln *Web:* www.blaser.com	Goshen	NY	10924	845-294-3200	
Blaze Energy Ltd 900 - Sixth Ave SW Ste 1010 *Web:* www.blazeenergy.com	Calgary	AB	T2P3K2	403-264-0877	
Blue Dolphin Energy Co 801 Travis St Ste 2100 *OTC: BDCO*	Houston	TX	77002	713-568-4725	227-7626
Bonterra Energy Corp Ste 901 1015 - Fourth St SW *Web:* www.bonterraenergy.com	Calgary	AB	T2R1J4	403-262-5307	
BP Canada Energy Co 240 Fourth Ave SW **Fax:* Mail Rm ■ *TF:* 877-833-1359 ■ *Web:* www.bp.com	Calgary	AB	T2P2H8	403-233-1359	233-1476*
BP Canada Energy Resources Co 240- Fourth Ave SW *Web:* www.bp.ca	Calgary	AB	T2P2H8	403-233-1313	
BP PLC 28100 Torch Pkwy *NYSE: BP* ■ *TF:* 877-638-5672 ■ *Web:* www.bp.com	Warrenville	IL	60555	630-420-5111	
BPZ Resources Inc 580 Westlake Park Blvd Ste 525 *Web:* www.bpzenergy.com	Houston	TX	77079	281-556-6200	
Breitling Energy Corp Ste 12000 1910 PACIFIC Ave *Web:* www.breitlingenergy.com	Dallas	TX	75201	214-716-2600	
Brenham Oil & Gas Corp 601 Cien Rd Ste 235 *Web:* www.brenhamoil.com	Kemah	TX	77565	281-334-9479	
Brigham Exploration Co 6300 Bridge Pt Pkwy Bldg 2 Ste 500 *NASDAQ: BEXP* ■ *Web:* www.statoil.com	Austin	TX	78730	512-427-3300	427-3400
BTA Oil Producers LLC 104 S Pecos *Web:* www.btaoil.com	Midland	TX	79701	432-682-3753	
Cabot Oil & Gas Corp 840 Gessner Rd Ste 1200 *NYSE: COG* ■ **Fax:* Hum Res ■ *TF:* 800-434-3985 ■ *Web:* cabotog.com	Houston	TX	77024	281-848-2799	589-4653*
Callon Petroleum Co 200 N Canal St *NYSE: CPE* ■ *TF:* 800-451-1294 ■ *Web:* www.callon.com	Natchez	MS	39120	601-442-1601	446-1410
Canadian Natural Resources Ltd (CNRL) 855 Second St SW Ste 2500 *NYSE: CNQ* ■ *TF:* 888-878-3700 ■ *Web:* www.cnrl.com	Calgary	AB	T2P4J8	403-517-6700	517-7350
Canamax Energy Ltd Ste 1820 715 - Fifth Ave SW *Web:* www.canamaxenergy.ca	Calgary	AB	T2P2X6	587-779-4259	
Cano Petroleum Inc 6500 N Belt Line Rd Ste 200 *OTC: CANOQ*	Irving	TX	75063	214-687-0030	
Capstone Natural Resources LLC 2250 E 73rd St *Web:* capstonenr.com	Tulsa	OK	74136	918-236-3800	
Caracal Energy Inc 555 - Fourth Ave SW Ste 2100 *Web:* www.glencore.com	Calgary	AB	T2P3E7	403-724-7200	
Carrizo Oil & Gas Inc 1000 Louisiana Ste 1500 *NASDAQ: CRZO* ■ *Web:* carrizo.com/	Houston	TX	77002	713-328-1000	328-1035
CASA Exploration LLC 1800 Post Oak Blvd Ste 380 *Web:* www.casaexploration.com	Houston	TX	77056	832-325-2300	
Case Pomeroy & Co Inc 529 Fifth Ave	New York	NY	10017	212-867-2211	682-2353
Casedhole Solutions Inc 940 Gateway Dr *Web:* www.casedhole-solutions.com	San Angelo	TX	76905	325-653-1750	
Caspian Energy Inc 410 396 11th Ave SW *Web:* www.caspianenergyinc.com	Calgary	AB	T2R0C5	403-252-2462	
Catalyst Energy Inc 424 S 27th St Ste 304 *Web:* www.catalystenergyinc.com	Pittsburgh	PA	15203	412-325-4350	
Caza Oil & Gas Inc Ste 200 10077 Grogan's Mill Rd *Web:* www.cazapetro.com	The Woodlands	TX	77380	281-363-4442	
Cenovus Energy Inc (USA) 2600 500 Centre St SE PO Box 766 *Web:* www.cenovus.com	Calgary	AB	T2P0M5	403-766-2000	
Century Wireline Services 1223 S 71st E Ave *Web:* www.centurywirelineservices.com	Tulsa	OK	74112	918-838-9811	
Cequence Energy Ltd Ste 3100 525 Eighth Ave SW *Web:* www.cequence-energy.com	Calgary	AB	T2P1G1	403-229-3050	
CGX Energy Inc 333 Bay St Ste 1100 *Web:* www.cgxenergy.com	Toronto	ON	M5H2R2	416-364-5569	
Chesapeake Energy Corp 6100 N Western Ave *NYSE: CHK* ■ *Web:* chk.com	Oklahoma City	OK	73118	405-848-3000	
Chevron Corp 6001 Bollinger Canyon Rd *NYSE: CVX* ■ **Fax Area Code:* 866 ■ *TF Cust Svc:* 800-243-8766 ■ *Web:* www.chevron.com	San Ramon	CA	94583	925-842-1000	420-0335*
Chuma Holdings Inc 350 N Glendale Ave Ste B 212 *Web:* chuma.us	Glendale	CA	91206	702-751-8455	
Cimmaron Field Services Inc 303 W Wall St Bank of America Tower Ste 600 *TF:* 877-944-2705 ■ *Web:* www.cimmaron.com	Midland	TX	79701	877-944-2705	
Circle Star Energy Corp 7065 Confederate Park Rd Ste 102 *Web:* www.circlestarenergy.com	Fort Worth	TX	76108	713-651-0060	
Citation Oil & Gas Corp 14077 Cutten Rd *Web:* www.cogc.com	Houston	TX	77069	281-891-1000	
Citizens Gas Fuel Co 127 N Main St *Web:* www.citizensgasfuel.com	Adrian	MI	49221	517-265-2144	
Clayton Williams Energy Inc 6 Desta Dr *NASDAQ: CWEI* ■ *Web:* www.claytonwilliams.com	Midland	TX	79705	432-682-6324	688-3247
ClearStream Energy Services LP 2112 Premier Way *Web:* www.clearstreamenergy.ca	Sherwood Park	AB	T8H2G4	780-410-9835	
Cobra Oil & Gas Corp 2201 Kell Blvd PO Box 8206 *Web:* www.cobraogc.com	Wichita Falls	TX	76308	940-716-5100	716-5190
Comstock Resources Inc 5300 Town & Country Blvd Ste 500 *NYSE: CRK* ■ *TF:* 800-877-1322 ■ *Web:* crkfrisco.com/	Frisco	TX	75034	972-668-8800	668-8812
Connacher Oil & Gas Ltd Ste 900 332-6 Ave SW *Web:* www.connacheroil.com	Calgary	AB	T2P0B2	403-538-6201	
ConocoPhillips 600 N Dairy Ashford Rd *NYSE: COP* ■ *Web:* www.conocophillips.com	Houston	TX	77079	281-293-1000	
ConocoPhillips Canada 401 Ninth Ave SW Ste 1600 *Web:* www.conocophillips.ca	Calgary	AB	T2P3C5	403-233-4000	233-5143
Contango Oil & Gas Co 3700 Buffalo Speedway Ste 960 *NYSE: MCF* ■ *Web:* www.contango.com	Houston	TX	77098	713-960-1901	960-1065
Cordillera Energy Partners III LLC 8450 E Crescent Pkwy Ste 400 *Web:* www.cordilleraep.com	Greenwood Village	CO	80111	303-290-0990	
Corridor Resources Inc 5475 Spring Garden Rd *Web:* www.corridor.ca	Halifax	NS	B3J3T2	902-429-4511	
Cortech Engineering Inc 22785 Savi Ranch Pkwy *Web:* cortecheng.com	Yorba Linda	CA	92887	714-779-0911	
Crawford Energy Inc 770 S Post Oak Ln Ste 520 *Web:* www.crawfordenergy.com	Houston	TX	77056	713-626-2637	
Crawley Petroleum Corp 105 N Hudson Ste 800 *Web:* www.crawleypetroleum.com	Oklahoma City	OK	73102	405-232-9700	
Crescent Point Energy Corp Ste 2000 585-8Th Ave Sw *Web:* www.crescentpointenergy.com	Calgary	AB	T2P1G1	403-693-0020	

	City	State	Zip	Phone	Fax
Crew Energy Inc 250 5 St SW Ste 800 *Web:* www.crewenergy.com	Calgary	AB	T2P0R4	403-266-2088	
Crimson Resource Management Corp 410 17th St Ste 1010 *Web:* www.crimsonrm.com	Denver	CO	80202	303-892-9333	
Crown Central Petroleum Corp One N Charles St **Fax:* Hum Res ■ *Web:* www.crowncentral.com	Baltimore	MD	21201	410-539-7400	659-4875*
Crude Energy LLC 1910 Pacific Ave Ste 7000 *Web:* www.crude.com	Dallas	TX	75201	214-716-2200	
CUB Energy Inc 5120 Woodway Dr Ste 10010 *Web:* www.cubenergyinc.com	Houston	TX	77056	713-677-0439	
Cubic Energy Inc 9870 PLANO Rd. *Web:* www.cubicenergyinc.com	Dallas	TX	75238	972-686-0369	
Culberson Construction Inc 4500 Colony Rd *Web:* www.ccincservices.com	Granbury	TX	76048	817-573-3079	
Curlew Lake Resources Inc 595 Howe St Ste 303 *Web:* www.curlew-lake.com	Vancouver	BC	V6C2T5	604-336-8613	
Cypress Hills Resource Corp Ste 1703 595 Burrard St *Web:* www.cypresshillsresource.com	Calgary	AB	V7X1J1	403-265-7663	
D d Dunlap Companies Inc 16897 Algonquin St Ste A *Web:* dddunlap.com	Huntington Beach	CA	92649	714-840-6460	
D.F. Industries (DFI) Inc 3403-74 Ave *Web:* www.dfi.ca	Edmonton	AB	T6B3B8	780-466-5237	
D.J. Simmons Inc 1009 Ridgeway Pl Ste 200 *Web:* www.djsimmons.com	Farmington	NM	87401	505-326-3753	
Daleco Resources Corp Fifth Fl 17 Wilmont Mews *Web:* www.dalecoresources.com	West Chester	PA	19382	610-429-0181	
DCOR LLC 290 Maple Court Ste 290 *Web:* www.dcorusa.com	Ventura	CA	93003	805-535-2000	
DCP Midstream Partners LP 370 17th St Ste 2775 *NYSE: DPM* ■ *Web:* dcppartners.com	Denver	CO	80202	303-633-2900	605-2225
Dejour Energy Inc 598-999 Canada Pl *Web:* www.dejour.com	Vancouver	BC	V6C3E1	604-638-5050	
Delmar Systems Inc 8114 W Hwy 90 *Web:* www.delmarus.com	Broussard	LA	70518	337-365-0180	
Delphi Energy Corp 300 500 - Fourth Ave SW *Web:* www.delphienergy.ca	Calgary	AB	T2P2V6	403-265-6171	
Delta Oil & Gas Inc 700 W Pender St Ste 604 *Web:* www.deltaoilandgas.com	Vancouver	BC	V6C1G8	604-602-1500	
Denbury Resources Inc 5320 Legacy Dr *NYSE: DNR* ■ *TF General:* 800-348-9030 ■ *Web:* www.denbury.com	Plano	TX	75024	972-673-2000	673-2430
Devon Energy Corp 20 N Broadway *NYSE: DVN* ■ *TF:* 877-860-5820 ■ *Web:* www.devonenergy.com	Oklahoma City	OK	73102	405-235-3611	
DHI Services Inc 33502 State Hwy 249 *Web:* www.dhiservices.com	Pinehurst	TX	77362	281-201-4141	
DKRW Advanced Fuels LLC 5444 Westheimer Ste 1560 *TF:* 855-876-4595 ■ *Web:* www.dkrwaf.com	Houston	TX	77056	855-876-4595	
Dorchester Minerals LP 3838 Oak Lawn Ave Ste 300 *NASDAQ: DMLP* ■ *Web:* www.dmlp.net	Dallas	TX	75219	214-559-0300	559-0301
Doxa Energy Ltd Ste 2080 777 Hornby St *Web:* www.doxaenergy.com	Vancouver	BC	V6Z1S4	604-662-3692	
Doyon Ltd One Doyon Pl Ste 300 *Web:* www.doyon.com	Fairbanks	AK	99701	907-459-2000	
Dugan Production Corp 709 E Murray Dr. *Web:* daily-times.com	Farmington	NM	87401	505-325-1821	327-4613
Dune Energy Inc Two Shell Plaza 811 Louisiana St Ste 2300 *Web:* www.duneenergy.com	Houston	TX	77002	713-229-6300	
E&B Natural Resources Management Corp 1600 Norris Rd *Web:* www.ebresources.com	Bakersfield	CA	93308	661-679-1700	
Eagle Energy Trust 500 4 Ave SW Ste 2710 *Web:* www.eagleenergytrust.com	Calgary	AB	T2P2V6	403-531-1575	
Eagle Ford Oil & Gas Corp 1110 Nasa Pkwy Ste 311 *Web:* www.efogc.com	Houston	TX	77058	281-383-9648	
Earthstone Energy Inc 633 17th St Ste 2320 *Web:* www.earthstoneenergy.com	Denver	CO	80202	303-296-3076	
EDCON-PRJ Inc 171 S Van Gordon St Ste E *Web:* edcon-prj.com	Denver	CO	80228	303-980-6556	
Elbow River Marketing Ltd 1500 335 Eighth Ave SW *Web:* www.elbowriver.com	Calgary	AB	T2P1C9	403-232-6868	
Elevation Resources LLC 200 N Loraine Ste 1010 *Web:* www.elevationres.com	Midland	TX	79701	432-686-7500	
Empire Energy Corporation International Level 3 65 Murray St Hobart Tasmania *Web:* www.empireenergy.com	Leawood	KS	66211	913-663-2310	
EnCana Corp 855 Second St SW Po Box 2850 *NYSE: ECA* ■ *TF:* 888-568-6322 ■ *Web:* www.encana.com	Calgary	AB	T2P2S5	403-645-2000	645-3400
Energy & Exploration Partners Inc 100 Throckmorton Two City Pl Ste 1700 *Web:* www.enxp.com	Fort Worth	TX	76102	817-789-6712	
Energy Water Solutions LLC 800 town and country blvd *Web:* www.energywatersolutions.com	Houston	TX	77024	713-722-0408	
Enhance Energy Inc 333 5 Ave SW Ste 900 *Web:* www.enhanceenergy.com	Calgary	AB	T2P3B6	403-984-0202	
Enhanced Oil Resources Inc One Riverway Ste 610 *Web:* www.enhancedoilres.com	Houston	TX	77056	832-485-8500	
Eni Petroleum Co 1200 Louisiana St Ste 1707 *Web:* eni.com	Houston	TX	77002	713-393-6100	
EOR Energy Services Inc 3950 Braxton Ste 100 *Web:* www.eorenergy.com	Houston	TX	77063	713-914-9300	
EQT Corp 625 Liberty Ave Ste 1700 *NYSE: EQT* ■ *TF:* 800-242-1776 ■ *Web:* www.eqt.com	Pittsburgh	PA	15222	412-553-5700	
ERHC Energy Inc Ste 1440 5444 Westheimer Rd *Web:* erhc.com	Houston	TX	77056	713-626-4700	
Extreme Plastics Plus Inc 148 Roush Cir *TF:* 866-408-2837 ■ *Web:* www.extremeplasticsplus.com	Fairmont	WV	26554	866-408-2837	
Exxon Mobil Corp 5959 Las Colinas Blvd *NYSE: XOM* ■ *TF:* 800-252-1800 ■ *Web:* www.exxonmobil.com	Irving	TX	75039	972-444-1000	444-1433
Fairborne Energy Ltd 3400-450 First St SW Ste 3400 *Web:* www.santoniaenergy.com	Calgary	AB	T2P5H1	403-290-7750	290-7724
FHG Inc 6809 Orchard Ridge Dr *Web:* www.fhg-inc.com	Charlotte	NC	28227	704-567-9548	
FieldPoint Petroleum Corp 1703 Edelweiss Dr Ste 301 *NYSE: FPP* ■ *Web:* www.fppcorp.com	Cedar Park	TX	78613	512-250-8692	335-1294
FLS Energy Inc 130 Roberts St *Web:* www.flsenergy.com	Asheville	NC	28801	828-350-3993	
Fortress Energy Inc Ste 802 322 11th Ave SW *Web:* www.fortressenergy.ca	Calgary	AB	T2R0C5	403-398-3345	
Future Acquisition Company LLC 1455 W Loop South *Web:* futurepetro.com	Houston	TX	77027	713-993-0774	
FX Energy Inc 3006 Highland Dr Ste 206 *Web:* www.fxenergy.com	Salt Lake City	UT	84106	801-486-5555	
Gasco Energy Inc 7979 E. Tufts Ave Suite 1150 *OTC: GSXN* ■ *Web:* www.gascoenergy.com	Denver	CO	80237	303-483-0044	483-0011
Gastar Exploration Ltd 1331 Lamar St Ste 1080 *NYSE: GST* ■ *Web:* www.gastar.com	Houston	TX	77010	713-739-1800	739-0458
Gear Energy Ltd 2600 500 - Fourth Ave SW *Web:* www.gearenergy.com	Calgary	AB	T2P2V6	403-538-8435	
Geoforce Inc 750 Canyon Dr Ste 140 *Web:* www.geoforce.com	Coppell	TX	75019	972-546-3878	
Geologic Data Systems Inc 2145 S Clermont St *Web:* www.geologicdata.com	Denver	CO	80222	303-837-1699	
GeoMark Research Ltd 218 Higgins St *Web:* www.geomarkresearch.com	Humble	TX	77338	832-644-1184	
GeoResources Inc 110 Cypress Stn Dr Ste 220 *NASDAQ: GEOI* ■ *TF:* 855-538-0599 ■ *Web:* www.halconresources.com	Williston	ND	58802	281-537-9920	537-8324
Gibson Energy Inc 440 - Second Ave SW Ste 1700 *Web:* www.gibsons.com	Calgary	AB	T2P5E9	403-206-4000	
GMX Resources Inc 9400 Bdwy Extension Hwy *NYSE: GMXRQ* ■ *TF:* 877-600-0711 ■ *Web:* www.gmxresources.com	Oklahoma City	OK	73114	405-600-0711	600-0600
Gran Tierra Energy Inc 200 150 13th Ave SW *Web:* www.grantierra.com	Calgary	AB	T2R0V2	403-265-3221	
Great Western Drilling Co Inc 700 W Louisiana St *Web:* www.gwdc.com	Midland	TX	79701	432-682-5241	684-3702
Grizzly Oil Sands ULC 605 - 5 Ave SW Fifth & Fifth Ste 2700 *Web:* www.grizzlyoilsands.com	Calgary	AB	T2P3H5	403-930-6450	
Gulfport Energy Corp 14313 N May Ave Ste 100 *Web:* www.gulfportenergy.com	Oklahoma City	OK	73134	405-848-8807	
GulfSlope Energy Inc Ste 800 2500 City W Blvd *Web:* www.gulfslope.com	Houston	TX	77042	281-918-4100	
Gullett & Associates Inc 7705 S Loop E *Web:* www.gulonline.com	Houston	TX	77012	713-644-3219	
Gunnison Energy Corp 1801 Broadway Ste 1200 *Web:* www.oxbow.com	Denver	CO	80202	303-296-4222	296-4555
Harken Energy Corp 180 State St Ste 200 *OTC: HKNI* ■ *Web:* www.hkninc.com	Southlake	TX	76092	817-424-2424	
Harvest Natural Resources Inc 1177 Enclave Pkwy Ste 300 *NYSE: HNR* ■ *Web:* www.harvestnr.com	Houston	TX	77077	281-899-5700	899-5702
Headington Oil Co 2711 N Haskell Ave Ste 2800 *Web:* www.headington.com	Dallas	TX	75204	214-696-0606	696-7746
Heavy Earth Resources Inc 1890 Bryant St Ste 316 *Web:* www.heavyearthresources.com	San Francisco	CA	94110	415-813-5079	
HG Energy LLC 5260 Dupont Rd *Web:* hgenergyllc.com	Parkersburg	WV	26101	304-420-1100	
Hibernia Management & Development Company Ltd 100 New Gower St Ste 1000 *Web:* www.hibernia.ca	St. John's	NL	A1C6K3	709-778-7000	
HLI Energy Services Inc 3600 W Hwy 67 *Web:* www.hlienergy.com	Cleburne	TX	76033	817-558-1018	
Hunt Oil Co 1900 N Akard St *Web:* www.huntoil.com	Dallas	TX	75201	214-978-8000	978-8888
Husky Energy Inc 707 Eigth Ave SW PO Box 6525 *TSE: HSE* ■ *TF:* 877-262-2111 ■ *Web:* www.huskyenergy.com	Calgary	AB	T2P3G7	403-298-6111	298-7464
Hyperdynamics Corp 12012 Wickchester Ln Ste 475 *OTC: HDYN* ■ *Web:* www.hyperdynamics.com	Houston	TX	77079	713-353-9400	353-9421
Imperium Renewables Inc 568 First Ave S Ste 600 *Web:* www.imperiumrenewables.com	Seattle	WA	98104	206-254-0203	
Iona Energy Inc The Grain Exchange Bldg Ste 310 815-1st St SW *Web:* www.ionaenergy.com	Calgary	AB	T2P1N3	587-889-8959	
J-W Operating Company Inc 15505 Wright Brothers Dr. *Web:* www.jwenergy.com	Addison	TX	75001	972-233-8191	
Japan Canada Oil Sands Ltd 639-5th Ave SW Standard Life Bldg Ste 2300 *Web:* www.jacos.com	Calgary	AB	T2P0M9	403-264-9046	
JBL Energy Partners LLC 23902 FM 2978 Ste B *Web:* www.jblenergypartners.com	Tomball	TX	77375	281-516-3137	

Phone / Fax

JC Fodale Energy Services LLC
6003 Financial Plz ..... Shreveport LA 71129 318-686-4070
Web: www.jcfodale.com

JM Huber Corp 499 Thornall St 8th Fl ..... Edison NJ 08837 732-549-8600 Fax: 549-2239*
**Fax:* Hum Res ■ *TF:* 877-418-0038 ■ *Web:* www.huber.com

JMA Energy Company LLC
1021 NW Grand Blvd ..... Oklahoma City OK 73118 405-947-4322
Web: www.jmaenergy.com

JP Oil Company LLC
1604 W Pinhook Rd Ste 300 ..... Lafayette LA 70508 337-234-1170
Web: www.jpoil.com

JPW Riggers Inc 6376 Thompson Rd ..... Syracuse NY 13206 315-432-1111
Web: www.jpwriggers.com

Junex Inc 2795 Laurier Blvd Ste 200 ..... Quebec QC G1V4M7 418-654-9661
Web: www.junex.ca

Kosmos Energy LLC 8176 Park Ln Ste 500 ..... Dallas TX 75231 214-445-9600
Web: www.kosmosenergy.com

Kraken Oil & Gas LLC 9821 Katy Fwy Ste 460 ..... Houston TX 77024 713-360-7705
Web: www.krakenoil.com

Lario Oil & Gas Co 301 S Market St ..... Wichita KS 67202 316-265-5611 Fax: 265-5610
Web: lariooil.com

Lenape Resources Inc 9489 Alexander Rd ..... Alexander NY 14005 585-344-1200 Fax: 344-3283
Web: www.lenaperesources.com

Limestone Exploration II LLC 1100 W Wall St ..... Midland TX 79701 432-687-4220
Web: www.limestone2.com

Loftin Equipment Company Inc 12 N 45th Ave ..... Phoenix AZ 85043 602-272-9466
Web: www.loftinequip.com

Lonestar Resources Inc 509 Pecan Ste 200 ..... Fort Worth TX 76102 817-921-1889
Web: lonestarresources.com

LPC Crude Oil Marketing LLC 408 W Wall ..... Midland TX 79701 432-682-8555
Web: lpccrude.com

Luca International Group LLC
39650 Liberty St Ste 410 ..... Fremont CA 94538 510-498-8829
Web: www.luca88.com

Lucas Energy Inc Ste 1550 3555 Timmons Ln ..... Houston TX 77027 713-528-1881
Web: www.lucasenergy.com

Mack Energy Co 1202 N Tenth St ..... Duncan OK 73533 580-252-5580
Web: www.mackenergy.com

Magellan Petroleum Corp
1775 Sherman St Ste 1950 ..... Denver CO 80203 720-484-2400
NASDAQ: MPET ■ *Web:* www.magellanpetroleum.com

Magnum Hunter Resources
120 Prosperous Pl Ste 201 ..... Lexington KY 40509 859-263-3948 Fax: 369-6992*
**Fax Area Code:* 832 ■ *TF:* 877-778-5463 ■ *Web:* www.magnumhunterresources.com

Mapan Energy Ltd 1910-605 5 Ave SW ..... Calgary AB T2P3H5 403-536-5770
Web: www.mapanenergy.com

Marathon Oil Corp 5555 San Felipe St ..... Houston TX 77056 713-629-6600 Fax: 296-2952
Web: www.marathonoil.com

Mart Resources Inc
310 1167 Kensington Crescent NW ..... Calgary AB T2N1X7 403-270-1841
Web: www.martresources.com

Matador Resources Co
5400 Lyndon B Johnson Fwy Ste 1500 ..... Dallas TX 75240 972-371-5200
Web: www.matadorresources.com

McCombs Energy Ltd 5599 San Felipe Ste 1200 ..... Houston TX 77056 713-621-0033
Web: www.mccombsenergy.com

MCW Energy Group Ltd 344 Mira Loma Ave ..... Glendale CA 91204 800-979-1897
TF: 800-979-1897 ■ *Web:* www.mcwenergygroup.com

MEG Energy Corp 1500 520 - 3 Ave SW ..... Calgary AB T2P0R3 403-770-0446
Web: www.megenergy.com

Merrion Oil & Gas 610 Reilly Ave ..... Farmington NM 87401 505-324-5300
Web: www.merrion.bz

Mexco Energy Corp
214 W Texas Ave Ste 1101 PO Box 10502 ..... Midland TX 79701 432-682-1119 Fax: 682-1123
NYSE: MXC ■ *Web:* www.mexcoenergy.com

Mid-Con Energy Partners LP
Ste 850 2431 E 61ST St ..... Tulsa OK 74136 918-743-7575
Web: www.midconenergypartners.com

Moncla Marine LLC 1023 E St Mary St ..... Lafayette LA 70505 337-456-8799
Web: www.moncla.com

Montana Exploration Corp
144 4 Ave SW Ste 2300 ..... Calgary AB T2P3N4 403-265-9091
Web: www.montanaexplorationcorp.com

MPX Geophysics Ltd Unit 14 25 Valleywood Dr ..... Markham ON L3R5L9 905-947-1782
Web: www.mpxgeophysics.com

New Source Energy Partners LP
914 N Broadway Ste 230 ..... Oklahoma City OK 73102 405-272-3028
Web: www.newsource.com

Newfield Exploration Co
363 N Sam Houston Pkwy E Ste 100 ..... Houston TX 77060 281-847-6000 Fax: 405-4242
NYSE: NFX ■ *TF:* 866-902-0562 ■ *Web:* newfield.com

Nexen Inc 801 Seventh Ave SW ..... Calgary AB T2P3P7 403-699-4000 Fax: 699-5800
NYSE: NXY ■ *Web:* nexencnoocltd.com/

Nexen Petroleum USA Inc
945 Bunker Hill Ste 1400 ..... Houston TX 77024 832-714-5000
Web: nexencnoocltd.com/

Niko Resources Ltd 400 Third Ave SW ..... Calgary AB T2P4H2 403-262-1020 Fax: 263-2686
TSE: NKO ■ *Web:* www.nikoresources.com

Nine Energy Service Inc
16945 Northchase Dr Ste 1600 ..... Houston TX 77060 281-730-5100
Web: nineenergyservice.com

Noble Energy Inc 100 Glenborough Dr Ste 100 ..... Houston TX 77067 281-872-3100 Fax: 872-3111
NYSE: NBL ■ *TF:* 800-220-5824 ■ *Web:* www.nobleenergyinc.com

North Atlantic Refining Ltd
One Refinery Rd PO Box 40 ..... Come By Chance NL A0B1N0 709-463-8811
Web: www.northatlantic.ca

Noveda Technologies Inc
1200 US Hwy 22 East Ste 2000 ..... Bridgewater NJ 08807 908-534-8855
Web: www.noveda.com

NuVista Energy Ltd 3500 700 - Second St SW ..... Calgary AB T2P2W2 403-538-8500
Web: www.nuvistaenergy.com

NW Natural 220 NW Second Ave PO Box 6017 ..... Portland OR 97209 503-226-4211 Fax: 273-4824*
**Fax:* Cust Svc ■ *TF:* 800-422-4012 ■ *Web:* www.nwnatural.com

O'Brien Energy Co
425 Ashley Ridge Blvd Ste 300 ..... Shreveport LA 71106 318-865-8568
Web: www.obrienenergyco.com

Occidental Oil & Gas Corp
5 Greenway Plaza Ste 110 ..... Houston TX 77046 713-215-7000 Fax: 215-7399
Web: www.oxy.com

Ohio Gas Co PO Box 528 ..... Bryan OH 43506 419-636-1117 Fax: 636-9837
TF: 800-331-7396 ■ *Web:* www.ohiogas.com

Okland Oil Co 110 N Robinson Ave ..... Oklahoma City OK 73102 405-236-3046
Web: www.oklandoil.com

Omimex Resources Inc 7950 John T White Rd ..... Fort Worth TX 76120 817-460-7777
Web: www.omimex.com

Omni Valve Company LLC 4520 Chandler Rd ..... Muskogee OK 74403 918-687-6100
Web: www.omnivalve.com

OriginClear Inc 5645 W Adams Blvd ..... Los Angeles CA 90016 323-939-6645
Web: www.originoil.com

Oryx Midstream Services LLC
4000 N Big Spring Ste 210 ..... Midland TX 79705 432-684-4272
Web: www.oryxmidstream.com

Oxbow Carbon & Minerals Inc
1601 Forum Pl Ste 1400 ..... West Palm Beach FL 33401 561-697-4300 Fax: 697-1876
Web: www.oxbow.com

Pantera Energy Co 817 S Polk St Ste 201 ..... Amarillo TX 79101 806-376-6625
Web: www.panteraenergy.com

Park Energy Services LLC
514 Colcord Dr ..... Oklahoma City OK 73102 405-896-3169
Web: www.parkenergyservices.com

Parsley Energy Inc 221 W Sixth St Ste 750 ..... Austin TX 78701 432-818-2100
Web: www.parsleyenergy.com

Pegasi Energy Resources Corp
218 N Broadway Ave Ste 204 ..... Tyler TX 75702 903-595-4139
Web: www.pegasienergy.com

Pemex Procurement International Inc
10344 sam houston park dr ..... Houston TX 77064 713-430-3100
Web: www.pemexprocurement.com

Penn Virginia Corp 100 Matsonford Rd Ste 200 ..... Radnor PA 19087 610-687-8900 Fax: 687-3688
NYSE: PVA ■ *TF:* 877-316-5288 ■ *Web:* www.pennvirginia.com

Penn West Petroleum Ltd Ninth Ave SW Ste 200 ..... Calgary AB T2P1K3 403-777-2500 Fax: 777-2699
TSE: PWT ■ *TF:* 866-693-2707 ■ *Web:* www.pennwest.com

Perpetual Energy Inc Ste 3200 -605 5 Ave SW ..... Calgary AB T2P3H5 403-269-4400
Web: www.perpetualenergyinc.com

Petro Vista Energy Corp
Ste 800 789 W Pender St ..... Vancouver BC V6C1H2 604-638-8067
Web: www.pvecorp.com

Petrobras USA 10350 Richmond Ave Ste 1400 ..... Houston TX 77042 713-808-2000
Web: www.petrobras.com

Petroglyph Energy Inc 960 Broadway Ave Ste 500 ..... Boise ID 83706 208-685-7600
Web: www.intermountainindustries.com

Petroleum Development Corp (PDC)
120 Genesis Blvd PO Box 26 ..... Bridgeport WV 26330 303-860-5800 Fax: 831-3988
NASDAQ: PDCE ■ *TF:* 800-624-3821 ■ *Web:* www.petd.com

Petrolia Inc 305 Charest Blvd E 10th Fl ..... Quebec QC G1K3H3 418-657-1966
Web: petrolia-inc.com

Petroplex Energy Inc
110 N Marienfeld St Ste 290 ..... Midland TX 79701 432-570-7030
Web: www.petroplex.net

PHX Energy Services Corp 1400-250 2 St SW ..... Calgary AB T2P0C1 403-543-4466
Web: www.phxtech.com

Pioneer Natural Resources Co
5205 N O'Connor Blvd Ste 200 ..... Irving TX 75039 972-444-9001 Fax: 969-3575
NYSE: PXD ■ *Web:* www.pxd.com

Pioneer Oil & Gas
Unit B 1206 W S Jordan Pkwy ..... South Jordan UT 84095 801-566-3000
Web: www.piol.com

Pioneer Petrotech Services Inc
Ste 1 1431-40 Ave NE ..... Calgary AB T2E8N6 403-282-7669
Web: www.pioneerps.com

Primexx Energy Partners Ltd
4849 Greenville Ave Two Energy Sq Ste 1600 ..... Dallas TX 75206 214-369-5909
Web: primexx.com

Questerre Energy Corp
1650 AMEC Place 801 Sixth Ave SW ..... Calgary AB T2P3W2 403-777-1185
Web: www.questerre.com

RAAM Global Energy Co
1537 Bull Lea Rd Ste 200 ..... Lexington KY 40511 859-253-1300
Web: www.raamglobal.com

Range Resources Corp
100 Throckmorton St Ste 1200 ..... Fort Worth TX 76102 817-870-2601 Fax: 869-9100
NYSE: RRC ■ *Web:* www.rangeresources.com

Redbud E&P Inc 16000 Stuebner Airline Ste 320 ..... Spring TX 77379 832-698-4234
Web: www.redbudinc.com

Regent Resources Ltd 1000 605 - Fifth Ave SW ..... Calgary AB T2P3H5 403-264-0018
Web: www.regentresources.com

Reserve Petroleum Co
Ste 300 6801 BROADWAY EXT ..... Oklahoma City OK 73116 405-848-7551
Web: www.reserve-petro.com

Resolute Energy Corp
1700 N Lincoln St Ste 2800 ..... Denver CO 80203 303-573-4886
Web: www.resoluteenergy.com

Rex Energy Corp 366 Walker Dr ..... State College PA 16801 814-278-7267
Web: www.rexenergycorp.com

Rice Energy Inc 400 Woodcliff Dr ..... Canonsburg PA 15317 724-746-6720
Web: www.riceenergy.com

Rife Resources Ltd 400 144 - Fourth Ave SW ..... Calgary AB T2P3N4 403-221-0800
Web: www.rife.com

Ring Energy Inc Ste 200 6555 S Lewis Ave ..... Tulsa OK 74136 918-499-3880
Web: ringenergy.com

Rio Bravo Oil Inc 2425 Fountainview Ste 300 ..... Houston TX 77057 281-724-3810
Web: www.riobravooil.com

RMP Energy Inc 1200-500 4 Ave SW ..... Calgary AB T2P2V6 403-930-6300
Web: www.rmpenergyinc.com

Rock Energy Inc 607 8 Ave SW Ste 800 ..... Calgary AB T2P0A7 403-218-4380
Web: www.rockenergy.ca

Phone Fax

Rockdale Resources Corp
710 N Post Oak Rd Ste 400 .... Houston TX 77024 832-941-0011
Web: www.rockdaleresources.com

Rooster Energy Ltd 16285 Park Ten Pl Ste 120 .... Houston TX 77084 832-772-6313
Web: www.roosterenergyltd.com

Royale Energy Inc 3777 WILLOW GLEN Dr .... El Cajon CA 92019 619-881-2800
Web: www.royl.com

RSP Permian Inc 3141 Hood St Ste 500 .... Dallas TX 75219 214-252-2728
Web: www.rsppermian.com

Saguaro Resources Ltd
3000 500 - Fourth Ave SW .... Calgary AB T2P2V6 403-453-3040
Web: saguaroresources.com

Sandridge Midstream Inc
1601 Northwest Expy Ste 1600 .... Oklahoma City OK 73118 405-753-5500
Web: www.sandridgeenergy.com

SeaBird Exploration Americas Inc
1155 N Dairy Ashford Ste 206 .... Houston TX 77079 281-556-1666
Web: www.sbexp.com

Seamar Holdings LLC 13715 N Promenade Blvd .... Stafford TX 77477 281-208-2522
Web: www.seamardivers.com

Sefton Resources Inc 2050 S Oneida St Ste 102 .... Denver CO 80224 303-759-2700
Web: www.seftonresources.com

Seismic Ventures LLC
4805 Westway Park Bouvelard Ste 100 .... Houston TX 77041 281-240-1234
Web: www.seismicventures.com

Seneca Resources Corp
1201 Louisiana St Ste 400 .... Houston TX 77002 713-654-2600 654-2654
TF: 800-365-3234 ■ *Web:* natfuel.com

Shell Canada Ltd 400 Fourth Ave SW .... Calgary AB T2P0J4 403-691-3111
Web: www.shell.ca

Shell Oil Co 910 Louisanna St .... Houston TX 77002 713-241-6161 241-2341
TF: 888-467-4355 ■ *Web:* www.shell.us

Shoal Point Energy Ltd
1060-1090 Georgia St W .... Vancouver BC V6E3V7 416-637-2181
Web: www.shoalpointenergy.com

Sinopec Daylight Energy Ltd
112-4th Ave SW Sun Life Plz E Tower Ste 2700 .... Calgary AB T2P0H3 403-266-6900
Web: www.sinopecdaylight.com

Slawson Cos Inc 727 N Waco St Ste 400 .... Wichita KS 67203 316-263-3201 268-0702
Web: www.slawsoncompanies.com

Snyder Brothers Inc One Glade Park Dr .... Kittanning PA 16201 724-548-8101
Web: www.snyderbrothersinc.com

Southwestern Energy Co
2350 N Sam Houston Pkwy E Ste 300 .... Houston TX 77032 832-796-1000 796-4818
NYSE: SWN ■ *TF:* 866-322-0801 ■ *Web:* www.swn.com

Spartan Energy Corp
Ste 500 850 - Second St SW .... Calgary AB T2P0R8 403-355-8920
Web: www.spartanenergy.ca

Spartan Offshore Drilling LLC
516 JF Smith Ave .... Slidell LA 70460 504-885-7449
Web: www.spartanoffshore.com

Special Energy Corp 4815 Perkins Rd .... Stillwater OK 74076 405-377-1177
Web: www.specialenergycorp.com

Spinnaker Exploration Co
1200 Smith St Ste 800 .... Houston TX 77002 713-759-1770
Web: www.subsea.org

Spyglass Resources Corp
Livingston Place 250 2 St SW Tower 1700 .... Calgary AB T2P0C1 403-303-8500
Web: www.spyglassresources.com

Starboard Resources Inc
300 E Sonterra Blvd Ste 1220 .... San Antonio TX 78258 210-999-5400
Web: www.starboardresources.com

Steelhead LNG Corp 650 - 669 Howe St .... Vancouver BC V6C0B4 604-235-3800
Web: www.steelheadlng.com

Stelbar Oil Corp Inc
1625 N Waterfront Pkwy Ste 200 .... Wichita KS 67206 316-264-8378

Stone Energy Corp 625 E Kaliste Saloom Rd .... Lafayette LA 70508 337-237-0410 521-2072
NYSE: SGY ■ *Web:* www.stoneenergy.com

Stonegate Production Company LLC
952 Echo Ln Ste 400 .... Houston TX 77024 713-600-8000
Web: www.stone-gate.net

Storm Resources Ltd 640 5 Ave SW Ste 200 .... Calgary AB T2P3G4 403-817-6145
Web: www.stormresourcesltd.com

Strad Energy Services Ltd
Ste 1200 440 - Second Ave SW .... Calgary AB T2P5E9 403-232-6900
Web: www.stradenergy.com

Strat Land Exploration Co
15 E Fifth St Ste 2020 .... Tulsa OK 74103 918-584-3844
Web: stratland.com

Strata Oil & Gas Inc
10010 - 98 St PO Box 7770 .... Peace River AB T8S1T3 403-237-5443
Web: www.strataoil.com

Strike Energy Services Inc
1300 505 - Third St SW .... Calgary AB T2P3E6 403-232-8448
Web: www.strikeenergy.com

Summit Midstream Partners LP
1790 Hughes Landing Blvd Ste 500 .... The Woodlands TX 77380 832-413-4770
Web: www.summitmidstream.com

Suncor Energy Inc 150 - 6 Ave SW PO Box 2844 .... Calgary AB T2P3E3 403-296-8000 296-3030
NYSE: SU ■ *TF:* 800-558-9071 ■ *Web:* www.suncor.com

Sunoco Inc 1735 Market St Ste LL .... Philadelphia PA 19103 215-977-3000 977-3409
NYSE: SUN ■ *TF:* 800-786-6261 ■ *Web:* www.sunocoinc.com

Sunshine Oilsands Ltd
Ste 1020 903 Eighth Ave SW .... Calgary AB T2P0P7 403-984-1450
Web: www.sunshineoilsands.com

Surge Energy Inc 2100 635 Eighth Ave SW .... Calgary AB T2P3M3 403-930-1010
Web: www.surgeenergy.ca

Swift Energy Co 16825 Northchase Dr Ste 400 .... Houston TX 77060 281-874-2700 874-2478*
NYSE: SFY ■ **Fax:* Hum Res ■ *TF:* 800-777-2412 ■ *Web:* www.swiftenergy.com

Sylios Corp
1717 Dr Martin Luther King Jr St N .... St. Petersburg FL 33704 727-482-1505
Web: www.sylios.com

Phone Fax

Syntroleum Corp 5416 S Yale Ave Ste 400 .... Tulsa OK 74135 918-592-7900 592-7979
NASDAQ: SYNM

Talisman Energy Inc 888 Third St SW Ste 2000 .... Calgary AB T2P5C5 403-237-1234 237-1902
NYSE: TLM ■ *Web:* www.talisman-energy.com

Tammany Oil & Gas LLC
20445 State Hwy 249 Ste 200 .... Houston TX 77070 281-517-0770
Web: www.tammanyoil.com

Tangle Creek Energy Ltd
715 Fifth Ave SW Ste 1400 .... Calgary AB T2P2X6 403-648-4900
Web: www.tanglecreekenergy.com

TanMar Companies LLC 711 S Chestnut .... Tomball TX 77375 281-591-6480
Web: www.tanmarcompanies.com

Tanos Exploration LLC
110 N College Ave Ste 1001 .... Tyler TX 75702 903-597-7667
Web: www.tanosexp.com

Taylor Energy Company LLC One Lee Cir .... New Orleans LA 70130 504-581-5491
Web: www.taylorenergy.com

Teine Energy Ltd 2300 520 - Third Ave SW .... Calgary AB T2P0R3 403-698-8300
Web: www.teine-energy.com

Tellus Operating Group LLC
602 Crescent Pl Ste 100 .... Ridgeland MS 39157 601-898-7444
Web: www.tellusoperating.com

Tengasco Inc 11121 Kingston Pk Ste E .... Knoxville TN 37934 865-675-1554 675-1621
NYSE: TGC ■ *TF:* 888-669-0684 ■ *Web:* www.tengasco.com

TerraSond Ltd 1617 S Industrial Way Ste 3 .... Palmer AK 99645 907-745-7215
Web: www.terrasond.com

Tervita Corp 500 140 - 10 Ave SE .... Calgary AB T2G0R1 403-233-7565
Web: www.tervita.com

Tesla Exploration Ltd 4500 8A St NE .... Calgary AB T2E4J7 403-216-0999
Web: www.teslaexploration.com

THUMS Long Beach Co 5 Greenway Plz Ste 110 .... Houston TX 77046 713-215-7000
Web: www.oxy.com

Titan Oil & Gas Services Inc
6809 King Ave W Bldg E .... Billings MT 59106 406-945-5036
Web: www.titanoilgas.com

Topaz Resources Inc 1012 N Masch Branch Rd .... Denton TX 76207 940-243-1122
Web: www.topazresourcesinc.com

Torchlight Energy Resources Inc
5700 W Plano Pkwy Ste 3600 .... Plano TX 75093 214-432-8002
Web: www.torchlightenergy.com

Total E&P Canada Ltd 240 - 4 Ave SW Ste 2900 .... Calgary AB T2P4H4 403-571-7599
Web: www.total-ep-canada.com

Trans Energy Inc 210 Second St PO Box 393 .... St. Marys WV 26170 304-684-7053
Web: transenergyinc.com

Ultra Petroleum Corp
400 N Sam Houston Pkwy E Ste 1200 .... Houston TX 77060 281-876-0120 876-2831
NYSE: UPL ■ *Web:* www.ultrapetroleum.com

Unit Corp 7130 S Lewis Ave Ste 1000 .... Tulsa OK 74136 918-493-7700 493-7711
NYSE: UNT ■ *TF:* 800-722-3612 ■ *Web:* www.unitcorp.com

United Hydrocarbon International Corp
308 - Fourth Ave SW Ste 2500 .... Calgary AB T2P0H7 403-774-9900
Web: www.unitedhydrocarbon.com

Unitex Oil & Gas LLC 310 W Wall Ste 503 .... Midland TX 79701 432-685-0014
Web: unitexoilandgas.com

Valence Operating Co
One Kingwood Pl 600 Rockmead Dr Ste 200 .... Kingwood TX 77339 281-359-3659
Web: www.valenceoperating.com

Valeura Energy Inc 1200-202 6 Ave SW .... Calgary AB T2P2R9 403-237-7102
Web: www.valeuraenergy.com

Value Creation Inc 1100 635 - Eighth Ave SW .... Calgary AB T2P3M3 403-539-4500
Web: www.vctek.com

Vangold Resources Ltd
7681 Prince Edward St .... Vancouver BC V5X3R4 604-684-1974
Web: www.vangold.ca

Vernon E. Faulconer Inc
1001 ESE Loop 323 Ste 160 .... Tyler TX 75701 903-581-4382
Web: www.vefinc.com

W & T Offshore Inc Nine Greenway Plz Ste 300 .... Houston TX 77046 713-626-8525 626-8527
Web: www.wtoffshore.com

Wagner & Brown Ltd 300 N Marienfeld St .... Midland TX 79701 432-682-7936 686-5928
Web: wbltd.com

Wagner Oil Co 500 Commerce St Ste 600 .... Fort Worth TX 76102 817-335-2222 334-0053
TF: 800-457-5332 ■ *Web:* www.wagneroil.com

Waldron Energy Corp 600-510 5 St SW .... Calgary AB T2P3S2 403-532-6700
Web: www.waldronenergy.ca

Ward Petroleum Corp 502 S Fillmore PO Box 1187 .... Enid OK 73702 580-234-3229 242-4334*
**Fax Area Code:* 405 ■ *Web:* www.wardpetroleum.com

Warpaint Resources LLC
1925 Cedar Springs Ste 103 .... Dallas TX 75201 469-250-7555
Web: www.warpaintresources.com

Warren Resources Inc
1114 Ave of the Americas 34th Fl .... New York NY 10036 212-697-9660 697-9466
NASDAQ: WRES ■ *TF:* 877-587-9494 ■ *Web:* www.warrenresources.com

Washakie Renewable Energy LLC
3950 South 700 East Ste 100 .... Salt Lake City UT 84107 801-327-8695
Web: wrebiofuels.com

Wayne Oil Company Inc
1301 Wayne Memorial Dr .... Goldsboro NC 27534 919-735-2021
Web: www.ballparkstores.com

Wenzlau Engineering Inc
1517 Fair Oaks Ave .... South Pasadena CA 91030 310-604-3400
Web: www.wenzlau.com

West Penn Energy Services LLC
4257 Gibsonia Rd .... Gibsonia PA 15044 724-444-0875
Web: www.westpenn-pa.com

Western Land Services Inc
1100 Conrad Industrial Dr .... Ludington MI 49431 231-843-8878
Web: westernls.com

Wexpro Co 333 S State St .... Salt Lake City UT 84145 801-324-2534 324-2637
Web: www.questar.com

Whitecap Resources Inc 500 222 Third Ave SW .... Calgary AB T2P0B4 403-266-0767
Web: www.wcap.ca

Company	City	State	Zip	Phone	Fax
Whiting Petroleum Corp 1700 Broadway Ste 2300 *NYSE: WLL* ■ *Web:* www.whiting.com	Denver	CO	80290	303-837-1661	861-4023
Wildcat Development Corp 230 Spring Hill Dr Ste 300 *Web:* wildcatdev.com	Spring	TX	77386	281-863-9370	
Wilshire Enterprises Inc 100 Eagle Rock Ave Ste 100 *OTC: WLSE* ■ *TF:* 888-697-3962 ■ *Web:* www.wilshireenterprisesinc.com	East Hanover	NJ	07936	973-585-7770	585-7771
Wood Group 17325 Park Row Ste 500 *Web:* www.woodgroup.com	Houston	TX	77084	281-828-3500	
XTO Energy Inc 810 Houston St *TF:* 800-299-2800 ■ *Web:* www.xtoenergy.com	Fort Worth	TX	76102	817-870-2800	870-1671
Yangarra Resources Ltd Ste 1530 715 - 5 Ave SW *Web:* www.yangarra.ca	Calgary	AB	T2P2X6	403-262-9558	
Yates Petroleum Corp 105 S Fourth St **Fax:* Hum Res ■ *Web:* www.yatespetroleum.com	Artesia	NM	88210	575-748-1471	748-4570*
Zargon Oil & Gas Ltd Ste 700 333 - Fifth Ave SW *Web:* www.zargon.ca	Calgary	AB	T2P3B6	403-264-9992	
ZaZa Energy Corp 1301 McKinney St Ste 3000 *NASDAQ: ZAZA* ■ *TF:* 866-266-2502 ■ *Web:* www.zazaenergy.com	Houston	TX	77010	713-595-1900	595-1919

540 OIL & GAS FIELD EQUIPMENT

Company	City	State	Zip	Phone	Fax
Abanaki Corp 17387 Munn Rd *Web:* www.abanaki.com	Chagrin Falls	OH	44023	440-543-7400	
Accumulators Inc 1175 Brittmoore Rd *Web:* www.accumulators.com	Houston	TX	77043	713-465-0202	
Alberta Oil Tool 9530 60th Ave *Web:* www.albertaoiltool.com	Edmonton	AB	T6E0C1	780-434-8566	436-4329
Alloy Carbide Co 7827 Ave H *Web:* www.alloycarbide.com	Houston	TX	77012	713-923-2700	923-4652
Baker Hughes Inc (BHI) 2929 Allen Pkwy Ste 1200 *NYSE: BHI* ■ *TF:* 800-229-7447 ■ *Web:* www.bakerhughes.com	Houston	TX	77019	713-439-8600	439-8699
Bolt Technology Corp Four Duke Pl *NASDAQ: BOLT* ■ *Web:* www.bolt-technology.com	Norwalk	CT	06854	203-853-0700	854-9601
BVM Corp 430 S Navajo St *Web:* www.bvmcorp.com	Denver	CO	80223	303-975-1402	
Cameron 1333 W Loop S Ste 1700 *NYSE: CAM* ■ *Web:* c-a-m.com	Houston	TX	77027	713-513-3300	513-3456
Carbo Ceramics Inc 575 N. Dairy Ashford Rd. Ste 300 *NYSE: CRR* ■ **Fax Area Code:* 972 ■ *TF:* 800-551-3247 ■ *Web:* www.carboceramics.com	Houston	TX	77079	281-921-6400	401-0705*
Cuming Corp 225 Bodwell St *TF:* 800-432-6464 ■ *Web:* www.cumingcorp.com	Avon	MA	02322	508-580-2660	580-0960
Dril-Quip Inc 13550 Hempstead Hwy *NYSE: DRQ* ■ *TF:* 877-316-2631 ■ *Web:* www.dril-quip.com	Houston	TX	77040	713-939-7711	939-8063
Drillers Service Inc 1792 Highland Ave NE PO Box 1407 *TF:* 800-334-2308 ■ *Web:* www.dsidsi.com	Hickory	NC	28601	828-322-1100	322-7436
En-fab Inc 3905 Jensen Dr *Web:* www.en-fabinc.com	Houston	TX	77026	713-225-4913	224-7937
FMC Technologies Inc 1803 Gears Rd *NYSE: FTI* ■ *TF:* 800-356-4898 ■ *Web:* www.fmctechnologies.com	Houston	TX	77067	281-591-4000	591-4102
Gearench Inc 4450 S Hwy 6 PO Box 192 *TF:* 800-221-1848 ■ *Web:* www.gearench.com	Clifton	TX	76634	254-675-8651	675-6100
GEFCO Inc (GEFCO) 2215 S Van Buren *TF:* 800-759-7441 ■ *Web:* www.gefco.com	Enid	OK	73703	580-234-4141	233-6807
Gulf Coast Manufacturing LLC 3622 W Main St *Web:* gulfcoastmfg.com	Gray	LA	70359	985-872-0187	
Gulf Island Fabrication Inc 567 Thompson Rd PO Box 310 *NASDAQ: GIFI* ■ *Web:* www.gulfisland.com	Houma	LA	70361	985-872-2100	876-5414
Halliburton Energy Services 10200 Bellaire Blvd *Web:* www.halliburton.com	Houston	TX	77072	281-871-4000	575-4032
Harbison-Fischer 901 N Crowley Rd *TF:* 800-364-7867 ■ *Web:* doverals.com/	Crowley	TX	76036	817-297-2211	297-4248
Kimray Inc 52 NW 42nd St *TF:* 866-586-7233 ■ *Web:* www.kimray.com	Oklahoma City	OK	73118	405-525-6601	525-7520
LDI Industries Inc 1864 Nage Ave PO Box 1810 *Web:* www.ldi-industries.com	Manitowoc	WI	54221	920-682-6877	684-7210
Lufkin Industries Inc 601 S Raguet St *NASDAQ: LUFK* ■ *Web:* www.lufkin.com	Lufkin	TX	75902	936-634-2211	637-5474
M & M Supply Co 909 W Peach Ave PO Box 548 *TF:* 800-424-9300 ■ *Web:* www.mmsupply.com	Duncan	OK	73534	580-252-7879	252-7708
Midwestern Manufacturing Company Inc 2119 S Union Ave *Web:* www.sidebooms.com	Tulsa	OK	74107	918-446-1587	
Morris Industries Inc 777 Rt 23 PO Box 278 *TF:* 800-835-0777 ■ *Web:* www.morrispipe.com	Pompton Plains	NJ	07444	973-835-6600	835-1245
Morrison Bros Co 570 E Seventh St *TF:* 800-553-4840 ■ *Web:* www.morbros.com	Dubuque	IA	52001	563-583-5701	583-5028
Natural Gas Services Group Inc (NGSG) 508 W Wall Ste 550 *NYSE: NGS* ■ *Web:* www.ngsgi.com	Midland	TX	79701	432-262-2700	262-2701
Norriseal 11122 W Little York Rd **Fax:* Sales ■ *Web:* www.norriseal.com	Houston	TX	77041	713-466-3552	896-7386*
NXT Energy Solutions Inc 505 Third St SW Ste 1400 *Web:* www.nxtenergy.com	Calgary	AB	T2P3E6	403-264-7020	
OTS International Inc 2615 Industrial Ln *Web:* otsintl.com	Conroe	TX	77301	936-539-0099	
Plant Process Equipment Inc 280 Reynolds Ave *Web:* www.plant-process.com	League City	TX	77573	281-333-7850	332-6280
Ruhrpumpen Inc 4501 S 86th E Ave *Web:* www.ruhrpumpen.com	Tulsa	OK	74145	918-627-8400	
Sandvik Mining & Construction USA LLC 13500 NW CR 235 *Web:* www.miningandconstruction.sandvik.com	Alachua	FL	32615	386-462-4100	462-5996
Schramm Inc 800 E Virginia Ave *TF:* 888-737-9438 ■ *Web:* www.schramminc.com	West Chester	PA	19380	610-696-2500	696-6950
ShawCor Ltd 25 Bethridge Rd *TSE: SCL/A* ■ *TF:* 800-668-4842 ■ *Web:* www.shawcor.com	Toronto	ON	M9W1M7	416-743-7111	743-7199
Southern Company Inc 3101 Carrier St *TF:* 800-264-7626 ■ *Web:* www.socomemphis.com	Memphis	TN	38116	901-345-2531	345-3555
Southtex Treaters LP 13405 Hwy 191 *Web:* www.southtex.com	Odessa	TX	79765	432-563-2766	563-1729
Southwest Oilfield Products Inc 10340 Wallisville Rd *Web:* www.swoil.com	Houston	TX	77013	713-675-7541	
Stewart & Stevenson LLC 1000 Louisiana St *Web:* www.stewartandstevenson.com	Houston	TX	77002	713-613-0633	751-2701
Stratco Inc 14821 N 73rd St *Web:* www.stratco.com	Scottsdale	AZ	85260	480-991-0450	991-0314
Stream-Flo Industries Ltd 4505 - 74 Ave *Web:* www.streamflo.com	Edmonton	AB	T6B2H5	780-468-6789	469-7724
Surface Equipment Corp 337 Cargill Rd *Web:* www.surfaceequip.com	Kilgore	TX	75662	903-984-0400	983-0018
Tam International Inc 4620 Southerland Rd *TF:* 800-462-7617 ■ *Web:* www.tamintl.com	Houston	TX	77092	713-462-7617	462-1536
Taylor Rigs LLC 6015 N Xanthus *Web:* www.taylorindustries.net	Tulsa	OK	74130	918-266-7301	
Titan Specialties Inc 11785 Hwy 152 *TF Sales:* 800-692-4486 ■ *Web:* hunting-intl.com/hunting-titan	Pampa	TX	79065	806-665-3781	669-6674
TIW Corp 12300 S Main St PO Box 35729 *Web:* www.tiwtools.com	Houston	TX	77035	713-729-2110	728-4767
Trendsetter Engineering Inc 10430 Rodgers Rd *Web:* www.trendsetterengineering.com	Houston	TX	77070	281-465-8858	
Weatherford Artificial Lift Systems 918 Hodgkins St *Web:* www.weatherford.com	Houston	TX	77032	281-449-1383	449-6235
Weatherford International Inc 515 Post Oak Blvd Ste 600 *NYSE: WFT* ■ **Fax:* Hum Res ■ *TF:* 866-398-0010 ■ *Web:* www.weatherford.com	Houston	TX	77027	713-693-4000	693-4270*
Weir Mesa 6510 N Golder Ave *Web:* www.weiroilandgas.com	Odessa	TX	79764	432-367-8606	
Winston F2S Corp 1604 Cherokee Trace *TF:* 800-527-8465 ■ *Web:* www.winstonf2s.com	White Oak	TX	75693	903-757-7341	759-6986

541 OIL & GAS FIELD EXPLORATION SERVICES

Company	City	State	Zip	Phone	Fax
Arctic Slope Regional Corp 1230 Agvik St PO Box 129 *TF:* 800-770-2772 ■ *Web:* www.asrc.com	Barrow	AK	99723	907-852-8633	852-5733
Arena Energy 4200 RES Forest Dr Ste 500 *Web:* www.arenaenergy.com	The Woodlands	TX	77381	281-681-9500	681-9503
Baker Hughes Inc Baker Atlas Div 2929 Allen Pkwy Ste 2100 *Web:* www.bakerhughes.com/bakeratlas	Houston	TX	77019	713-439-8600	
Baker Hughes INTEQ 17015 Aldine Westfield Rd *Web:* www.bakerhughes.com	Houston	TX	77073	713-625-4200	625-5200
Bill Barrett Corp 1099 18th St Ste 2300 *NYSE: BBG* ■ *TF:* 800-826-6762 ■ *Web:* www.billbarrettcorp.com	Denver	CO	80202	303-293-9100	291-0420
BP Prudhoe Bay Royalty Trust 101 Barclay St *NYSE: BPT*	New York	NY	10007	212-815-6908	
Breitburn Energy Partners LP 515 S Flower St Ste 4800 *NASDAQ: BBEP* ■ *TF:* 800-732-0330 ■ *Web:* www.breitburn.com	Los Angeles	CA	90071	213-225-5900	225-5916
CAMAC Inc 1330 Post Oak Blvd Ste 2200 *Web:* www.camacholdings.com	Houston	TX	77056	713-965-5100	965-5128
Central Resources Inc 1775 Sherman St Ste 2600 *Web:* www.centralresources.com	Denver	CO	80203	303-830-0100	830-9297
Chaparral Energy Inc 701 Cedar Lake Blvd *TF:* 866-478-8770 ■ *Web:* www.chaparralenergy.com	Oklahoma City	OK	73114	405-478-8770	
Concho Resources Inc 550 W Texas Ave Ste 100 *NYSE: CXO* ■ *Web:* www.conchoresources.com	Midland	TX	79701	432-683-7443	683-7441
ConocoPhillips 600 N Dairy Ashford Rd *NYSE: COP* ■ *Web:* www.conocophillips.com	Houston	TX	77079	281-293-1000	
Dawson Geophysical Co 508 W Wall St Ste 800 *NASDAQ: DWSN* ■ *TF:* 800-332-9766 ■ *Web:* www.dawson3d.com	Midland	TX	79701	432-684-3000	684-3030
Endeavour international corp 811 Main St Ste 2100 *OTC: ENDRQ* ■ *Web:* www.endeavourcorp.com	Houston	TX	77002	713-307-8700	
Energy XXI 1021 Main Ste 2626 *NASDAQ: EXXI* ■ *Web:* www.eplweb.com	Houston	TX	77002	504-569-1875	
EOG Resources Inc 1111 Bagby Sky Lobby 2 *NYSE: EOG* ■ *TF:* 877-363-3647 ■ *Web:* www.eogresources.com	Houston	TX	77002	713-651-7000	651-6995
Equal Energy Ltd 500 Fourth Ave SW *TF:* 877-263-0262 ■ *Web:* www.equalenergy.ca	Calgary	AB	T2P2V6	403-263-0262	294-1197
EXCO Resources Inc 12377 Merit Dr Ste 1700 *NYSE: XCO* ■ *TF:* 888-788-9449 ■ *Web:* www.excoresources.com	Dallas	TX	75251	214-368-2084	368-2087
Fidelity Exploration & Production Co 1801 California St Ste 2500 *TF:* 800-986-3133 ■ *Web:* www.fidelityepco.com	Denver	CO	80202	303-893-3133	893-1964
GeoGlobal Resources Inc (GGR) 625 Fourth Ave SW *OTC: GGLR* ■ *Web:* www.geoglobal.com	Calgary	AB	T2P0K2	403-777-9250	
Goodrich Petroleum Corp 333 Texas St Ste 1375 *Web:* www.goodrichpetroleum.com	Shreveport	LA	71101	318-429-1375	429-2296
Great White Energy Services 14201 Caliber Dr Ste 300	Oklahoma City	OK	73134	405-285-5812	

Company / Address	City	ST	ZIP	Phone	Fax
GulfMark Energy Inc 17 S Briar Hollow Ln Ste 100 *Web:* gulfmarkenergy.com	Houston	TX	77027	713-881-3603	
Halliburton Energy Services 10200 Bellaire Blvd *Web:* www.halliburton.com	Houston	TX	77072	281-871-4000	575-4032
Mustang Fuel Corp 9800 N Oklahoma Ave *TF:* 800-332-9400 ■ *Web:* www.mustangfuel.com	Oklahoma City	OK	73114	405-748-9400	748-9200
New Jersey Natural Gas Co 1415 Wyckoff Rd *TF:* 800-221-0051 ■ *Web:* www.njresources.com	Wall	NJ	07719	732-938-1480	938-3154
Northern Oil & Gas Inc 315 Manitoba Ave Ste 200 *NYSE: NOG* ■ *Web:* www.northernoil.com	Wayzata	MN	55391	952-476-9800	476-9801
Occidental International Corp 1717 Pennsylvania Ave NW Ste 400 *Web:* www.oxy.com	Washington	DC	20006	202-857-3000	857-3030
Panhandle Royalty Co 5400 N Grand Blvd Grand Ctr Bldg Ste 300 *TF:* 800-884-4225 ■ *Web:* www.panhandleoilandgas.com	Oklahoma City	OK	73112	405-948-1560	948-2038
Patterson-UTI Energy Inc 450 Gears Rd Ste 500 *NASDAQ: PTEN* ■ *TF:* 866-387-1933 ■ *Web:* www.patenergy.com	Houston	TX	77067	281-765-7100	765-7175
PetroQuest Energy Inc 400 E Kaliste Saloom Rd Ste 6000 *NYSE: PQ* ■ *Web:* www.petroquest.com	Lafayette	LA	70508	337-232-7028	232-0044
Power Service Products Inc PO Box 1089 *TF:* 800-643-9089 ■ *Web:* www.powerservice.com	Weatherford	TX	76086	817-599-9486	599-4893
Quicksilver Resources Inc 777 W Rosedale St Ste 300 *OTC: KWKAQ* ■ *TF:* 877-665-8600 ■ *Web:* www.qrinc.com	Fort Worth	TX	76104	817-665-5000	665-5014
Rosetta Resources Inc 717 Texas Ste 2800 *NASDAQ: ROSE* ■ *TF:* 800-526-2112 ■ *Web:* www.rosettaresources.com	Houston	TX	77002	713-335-4000	335-4197
Schlumberger Ltd 5599 San Felipe Ste 100 *NYSE: SLB* ■ *Web:* www.slb.com	Houston	TX	77056	713-513-2000	513-2006
Seitel Inc 10811 S Westview Cir Dr Bldg C Ste 100 *Web:* www.seitel.com	Houston	TX	77043	832-295-8300	295-8301
Slawson Cos Inc 727 N Waco St Ste 400 *Web:* www.slawsoncompanies.com	Wichita	KS	67203	316-263-3201	268-0702
Statoil Marketing & Trading 120 Long Ridge Rd Ste 3E01 *Web:* www.statoil.com	Stamford	CT	06902	203-978-6900	978-6952
Superior Energy Services Inc 601 Poydras St Ste 2400 *NYSE: SPN* ■ *TF:* 800-259-7774 ■ *Web:* www.superiorenergy.com	New Orleans	LA	70130	504-587-7374	362-1818
TGC Industries Inc 101 E Pk Blvd Ste 955 *NASDAQ: TGE* ■ *TF:* 800-223-7470 ■ *Web:* www.tgcseismic.com	Plano	TX	75074	972-881-1099	424-3943
Total E & P USA Inc 1201 Louisiana St Total Plaza Ste 1800 *Web:* www.total.com	Houston	TX	77002	713-647-4000	647-4030
TransGlobe Energy Corp 250 Fifth St SW Ste 2300 *TSE: TGL* ■ *Web:* www.trans-globe.com	Calgary	AB	T2P0R6	403-264-9888	770-8855
VAALCO Energy Inc 4600 Post Oak Pl Ste 309 *NYSE: EGY* ■ *Web:* www.vaalco.com	Houston	TX	77027	713-623-0801	623-0982
Veritas DGC Inc 10300 Townpark Dr *TF:* 800-344-4266 ■ *Web:* cgg.com	Houston	TX	77072	832-351-8300	351-8300
Walter Oil & Gas Corp 1100 Louisiana St Ste 200 *TF:* 888-756-7880 ■ *Web:* www.walteroil.com	Houston	TX	77002	713-659-1221	756-1155
WesternGeco 10001 Richmond Ave *Web:* www.slb.com	Houston	TX	77042	713-789-9600	789-0172
Zion Oil & Gas Inc 6510 Abrams Rd Ste 300 *Web:* www.zionoil.com	Dallas	TX	75231	214-221-4610	221-6510

542 OIL & GAS FIELD SERVICES

SEE ALSO Oil & Gas Field Exploration Services p. 2839

Company / Address	City	ST	ZIP	Phone	Fax
3es Innovation Inc Ste 400 227 - 11th Ave SW *Web:* 3esi.com	Calgary	AB	T2R1R9	403-270-3270	
4Refuel Canada Ltd 9440-202 St Ste 215 *Web:* 4refuel.com	Langley	BC	V1M4A6	604-513-0386	
Absolute Energy LLC 1372 State Line Rd *Web:* www.absenergy.org	St. Ansgar	IA	50472	641-326-2220	
AccessESP LLC 3656 Westchase Dr Ste 421 *Web:* www.accessesp.com	Houston	TX	77042	713-589-2599	
ACT Clean Technologies Inc 5412 Bolsa Ave Ste a *Web:* www.actcleantech.com	Huntington Beach	CA	92649	713-621-2737	
Advocate Media Inc 181 Brown's Point Rd *Web:* www.advocatemediainc.com	Pictou	NS	B0K1H0	902-485-1990	
AGI Industries Inc 2110 S W Evangeline Thruway *Web:* www.agiindustries.com	Lafayette	LA	70508	337-233-0626	
AKS Technologies Inc 1416 N Sam Houston Pkwy E Ste 140 *Web:* www.aks-technologies.com	Houston	TX	77032	281-987-2244	
Alaska Clean Seas Inc 4720 Business Park Blvd Ste G42 *Web:* www.alaskacleanseas.org	Anchorage	AK	99503	907-743-8989	
Alaska Interstate Construction LLC 301 W Northern Lights Blvd Ste 600 *Web:* www.aicllc.com	Anchorage	AK	99503	907-562-2792	
Alco Gas & Oil Production Equipment Ltd 5203 - 75th St *Web:* www.alcogasoil.com	Edmonton	AB	T6E5S5	780-465-9061	
Allamon Tool Company Inc 18935 Freeport Dr *TF:* 877-449-5433 ■ *Web:* www.allamontool.com	Montgomery	TX	77356	877-449-5433	
Americas Petrogas Inc 3911 Trasimene Cres SW *Web:* www.americaspetrogas.com	Calgary	AB	T3E7J6	403-685-1888	
Amplified Geochemical Imaging LLC 100 Chesapeake Blvd *Web:* www.agisurveys.net	Elkton	MD	21921	410-392-7600	
Apex Resources Inc 1705 Capital Of Texas Hwy S Ste 205 *Web:* apexr.com	Austin	TX	78746	512-328-0647	
Aqueos Corp 101 Millstone Rd *Web:* www.aqueossubsea.com	Broussard	LA	70518	337-714-0033	
ARC Pressure Data Inc 3718 Warschun Rd *Web:* www.arcpressure.com	Aubrey	TX	76277	940-565-8090	
Arcan Resources Ltd Ste 2200 -500 4 Ave SW *Web:* www.arcanres.com	Calgary	AB	T2P2V6	403-262-0321	
Argus Machine Company Ltd 5820 97th St NW *Web:* www.argusmachine.com	Edmonton	AB	T6E3J1	780-434-9451	
ASRC Energy Services Inc 3900 C St *Web:* www.asrcenergy.com	Anchorage	AK	99503	907-339-6200	
Atchafalaya Measurement Inc 124 Credit Dr *Web:* atchafalayameasurement.com	Scott	LA	70583	337-237-7675	
Atlanta Petroleum Equipment Co 4732 N Royal Atlanta Dr *Web:* www.atlantapetroleum.com	Tucker	GA	30084	770-491-6644	
AXH air-coolers LLC 2230 E 49th St *Web:* www.axh.com	Tulsa	OK	74105	918-712-8268	
Axon Pressure Products Inc 8909 Jackrabbit Rd *Web:* www.axonep.com	Houston	TX	77095	281-855-3200	
B & R Eckel's Transport Ltd 5514B - 50 Ave *Web:* www.breckels.com	Bonnyville	AB	T9N2K8	780-826-3889	
Badger Daylighting Corp 1300 E US Hwy 136 Ste E *Web:* badgerinc.com	Pittsboro	IN	46167	317-892-2666	
Baker Hughes Inc (BHI) 2929 Allen Pkwy Ste 1200 *NYSE: BHI* ■ *TF:* 800-229-7447 ■ *Web:* www.bakerhughes.com	Houston	TX	77019	713-439-8600	439-8699
Baker Hughes Inc Baker Atlas Div 2929 Allen Pkwy Ste 2100 *Web:* www.bakerhughes.com/bakeratlas	Houston	TX	77019	713-439-8600	
Basic Energy Services Inc 500 W Illinois Ste 800 Ste 800 *NYSE: BAS* ■ *Web:* www.basicenergyservices.com	Midland	TX	79701	432-620-5500	570-0437
Bayou Companies LLC, The 5200 Curtis Ln *Web:* www.bayoucompanies.com	New Iberia	LA	70560	337-369-3761	
Beckman Production Services Inc 3786 Beebe Rd *Web:* www.beckmanproduction.com	Kalkaska	MI	49646	231-258-9524	
Bell Geospace Inc 400 N Sam Houston Pkwy E Ste 325 *Web:* bellgeo.com	Houston	TX	77060	281-591-6900	
Bellatrix Exploration Ltd 1920 800 Fifth Ave Sw *Web:* www.bellatrixexploration.com	Calgary	AB	T2P3T6	403-266-8670	
Black Elk Energy LLC 11451 Katy Fwy Ste 500 *Web:* www.blackelkenergy.com	Houston	TX	77079	281-598-8600	
Blake International USA Rigs LLC 410 S Van Ave *Web:* www.blakeinternationalrigs.com	Houma	LA	70363	985-274-2200	
Blakely Construction Company Inc 1623 N Sooner Ave *Web:* www.blakelycc.com	Odessa	TX	79763	432-381-3540	
Blarney Castle Oil Co 12218 W St PO Box 246 *Web:* www.blarneycastleoil.com	Bear Lake	MI	49614	231-864-3111	
BlueStone Natural Resources LLC 2100 S Utica Ste 200 *Web:* www.bluestone-nr.com	Tulsa	OK	74114	918-392-9200	
Brady Oilfield Services LP Box 271 *Web:* www.brady.sk.ca	Midale	SK	S0C1S0	306-458-2344	
Brammer Engineering Inc 400 Texas St Bank One Bldg Ste 600 *Web:* www.brammer.com	Shreveport	LA	71101	318-429-2345	
Bronco Mfg LLC 4953 S 48th W Ave *Web:* www.broncomfg.com	Tulsa	OK	74107	918-446-7196	
Burbank Water & Power 164 W Magnolia Blvd *Web:* www.burbankwaterandpower.com	Burbank	CA	91502	818-238-3700	
C E Oil Tools & Supply Inc 104 Ridona St *Web:* www.ceoiltool.com	Lafayette	LA	70508	337-237-4941	
Cal Dive International Inc Ste 2200 2500 CityWest Blvd *Web:* www.caldive.com	Houston	TX	77042	713-361-2600	
Calfrac Well Services Ltd 411 8 Ave SW *Web:* www.calfrac.com	Calgary	AB	T2P1E3	403-266-6000	
Camex Equipment Sales & Rental Inc 1511 Sparrow Dr *Web:* www.camex.ca	Nisku	AB	T9E8H9	780-955-2770	
Camino Agave Inc RT3 Box 77A *Web:* www.caminoagave.com	Laredo	TX	78043	956-723-1701	
Canada Energy Partners Inc Ste 1680 Waterfront Centre 200 Burrard St *Web:* www.canadaenergypartners.com	Vancouver	BC	V6C3L6	604-909-1154	
Capitol Petroleum Equipment Inc 11319 Old Baltimore Pk *Web:* www.cpe123.com	Beltsville	MD	20705	301-931-9090	
Carbon Sciences Inc 5511C Ekwill St *Web:* www.carbonsciences.com	Santa Barbara	CA	93111	805-456-7000	
CarbonWrap Solutions LLC 2820 E Ft Lowell Rd *Web:* www.carbonwrapsolutions.com	Tucson	AZ	85716	520-292-3109	
Cel Oil Products Corp 5402 Dutton Ave *Web:* www.beequik.com	Charleston	SC	29406	843-744-2525	
Central Industries Inc 11438 Cronridge Dr Ste W *TF:* 800-304-8484 ■ *Web:* www.centralindustriesusa.com	Owings Mills	MD	21117	800-304-8484	932-1222
Chinn Exploration Co 4601 Mccann Rd *Web:* www.chinnexploration.com	Longview	TX	75605	903-663-4260	
Choice Exploration Inc 2221 Ave J *Web:* www.choiceexploration.com	Arlington	TX	76006	817-633-7777	

Company	City	State	ZIP	Phone	Fax
Cimarron Energy Inc 1012 24th Ave NW Ste 100 PO Box 722110	Norman	OK	73070	405-928-7373	
Web: www.cimarronenergy.com					
Cirm Corp 109 Long Hill Ter	New Haven	CT	06515	203-387-2068	
Web: www.cirmcorp.com					
City Water, Light & Power 800 E Monroe St Municipal Ctr E Fourth Fl	Springfield	IL	62757	217-789-2116	
Web: www.cwlp.com					
Coil Tubing Technology Holding Inc 19511 Wied Rd Ste E	Spring	TX	77388	281-651-0200	
Web: www.coiltubingtechnology.com					
Collarini Corp 11111 Richmond Ave Ste 126	Houston	TX	77082	504-887-7127	
Web: www.collarini.com					
Colloid Environmental Technologies Co (CETCO) 2870 Forbs Ave	Hoffman Estates	IL	60192	847-851-1899	527-9948*
**Fax Area Code:* 800 ■ *TF:* 800-527-9948 ■ *Web:* www.cetco.com					
Computer Modelling Group Ltd 200 1824 Crowchild Trl NW	Calgary	AB	T2M3Y7	403-531-1300	
Web: www.cmgl.ca					
Cordy Oilfield Services Inc 5366 55 St SE	Calgary	AB	T2C3G9	403-266-2067	
Web: www.cordy.ca					
Core Laboratories 6316 Windfern Rd	Houston	TX	77040	713-328-2673	328-2150
NYSE: CLB ■ *Web:* www.corelab.com					
Cougar Drilling Solutions Inc 7319 - 17 St	Edmonton	AB	T6P1P1	780-440-2400	
Web: www.cougards.com					
Cps Building Company Ltd 4327 Red Bank Rd	Cincinnati	OH	45227	513-271-9026	
Web: www.cpsconsult.com					
Crain Bros Inc 300 Rita Dr	Bell City	LA	70630	337-905-2411	905-2700
Web: www.crainbrothers.com					
Crest Resources Inc 15 E Fifth St Ste 3650	Tulsa	OK	74103	918-585-2900	
Web: crestnaturalresources.com					
Cross Group Inc, The 1950 S Van Ave	Houma	LA	70363	985-868-3906	
Web: www.thecrossgroup.com					
CSV Midstream Solutions Corp 521 - Third Ave SW Eau Claire Pl II Ste 800	Calgary	AB	T2P3T3	587-316-6900	
Web: www.csvmidstream.com					
CWC Energy Services Corp 255 - Fifth Ave SW Bow Vly Sq III Ste 755	Calgary	AB	T2P3G6	403-264-2177	
Web: www.cawsc.com					
Cypress Energy Partners LP 5727 S Lewis Ave Ste 500	Tulsa	OK	74105	918-748-3900	
Web: www.cypressenergy.com					
D & J Oil Company Inc 4720 W Garriott	Enid	OK	73706	580-242-3636	
Web: djoil.com					
Dalmac Oilfield Services Inc 4934 - 89 St	Edmonton	AB	T6E5K1	780-988-8510	
Web: www.dalmacenergy.com					
Danos & Curole Marine Contractors Inc 13083 Louisiana 308	Larose	LA	70373	985-693-3313	693-7342
TF: 800-487-5971 ■ *Web:* www.danos.com					
Datalog Technology Inc 10707 - 50th St SE	Calgary	AB	T2C3E5	403-243-2024	
Web: www.datalogtechnology.com					
Daybreak Oil & Gas Inc(NDA) 601 W Main Ave Ste 1012	Spokane	WA	99201	509-232-7674	
Web: www.daybreakoilandgas.com					
Deep Down Inc 8827 W Sam Houston Pkwy N Ste 100	Houston	TX	77040	281-517-5000	
Web: www.deepdowninc.com					
Delta Compression & Equipment LLC 160 James Ln	Krotz Springs	LA	70750	337-566-8888	
Web: www.deltacompression.com					
Delta SubSea LLC 550 Club Dr Ste 345	Montgomery	TX	77316	936-582-7237	
Web: www.deltasubsea-rov.com					
Derrick Equipment Co 15630 Export Plz Dr	Houston	TX	77032	281-590-3003	
Web: www.derrickequipment.com					
Desmarais Energy Corp 751-815 8 Ave SW	Calgary	AB	T2P3P2	403-265-8007	
Web: www.desmaraisenergy.com					
DEVIN International Inc 2545 SE Evangeline Thruway	Lafayette	LA	70508	337-233-3846	
Web: www.devindevin.com					
Dialog Wireline Services LLC 3100 Maverick Dr	Kilgore	TX	75662	903-988-2311	
Web: www.dialogwireline.com					
Diamond Oil Well Drilling Company Inc 2003 Commerce Dr	Midland	TX	79703	432-699-6132	
Web: www.dowdco.com					
Diamond Services Co 4220 Oklahoma Ave	Woodward	OK	73801	580-256-3385	256-9873
Web: diamond-services.com					
Diamond Services Corp 503 S DeGravelle Rd	Amelia	LA	70340	985-631-2187	631-2442
TF: 800-879-1162 ■ *Web:* www.dscgom.com					
Divergent Energy Services Corp 1170 800 - Sixth Ave SW	Calgary	AB	T2P3G3	403-543-0060	
Web: www.divergentenergyservices.com					
Downing Wellhead Equipment Inc 8528 S W Second St	Oklahoma City	OK	73128	405-789-8182	
Web: www.downingwell.com					
Drilltec Technologies Inc 10875 Kempwood Ste 2	Houston	TX	77043	713-895-9852	
Web: www.drilltec.com					
Duoline Technologies LP 250 W Bluebird Rd	Gilmer	TX	75645	903-734-1371	
Web: www.duoline.com					
Dwfritz Automation Inc 12100 SW Tualatin Rd	Tualatin	OR	97062	503-598-9393	
Web: dwfritz.com					
E. L. Farmer & Co 3800 E 42nd St Ste 417	Odessa	TX	79762	432-366-2010	
Web: www.elfarmer.com					
EagleClaw Midstream Services LLC 414 W Texas Ave Ste 315	Midland	TX	79701	432-789-1333	
Web: www.eagleclawmidstream.com					
Eaton Oil Tools Inc 118 Rue DuPain	Broussard	LA	70518	337-856-8820	
Web: www.eatonoiltools.com					
EFC Valve & Controls LLC 230 Progress Rd	Longview	TX	75604	903-759-0126	
Web: www.efcvalve.com					
Elastec Inc 1309 W Main	Carmi	IL	62821	618-382-2525	
Web: www.elastec.com					
Emerge Energy Services LP 1400 Civic Pl Ste 250	Southlake	TX	76092	817-488-7775	
Web: www.emergelp.com					
Emmart & Son Inc W H 305 Brick Kiln Rd	Winchester	VA	22601	540-662-8445	
Web: www.emmartoil.com					
Empirica 6741 Satsuma Dr	Houston	TX	77041	713-466-7400	
Web: www.empirica-logging.com					
EN Bisso & Son Inc 3939 N Causeway Blvd Ste 401	Metairie	LA	70002	504-828-3296	
Web: www.enbisso.com					
Epic Lift Systems LLC 14485 Hwy 377 South	Fort Worth	TX	76126	817-443-3500	
Web: www.epicliftsystems.com					
ERG Resources LLC Three Allen Ctr 333 Clay St Ste 4400	Houston	TX	77002	713-812-1800	
Web: www.energy-reserves.com					
ExPert E&P Consultants LLC 101 Ashland Way	Madisonville	LA	70447	985-801-4040	
Web: www.expertep.com					
Exterran Water Solutions Ltd 1721 27th Ave Noth E	Calgary	AB	T2E7E1	403-219-2210	
Web: www.exterranwatersolutions.com					
Failsafe Controls LLC 2712 Southwest Dr	New Iberia	LA	70560	337-365-2493	
Web: failsafecontrols.com					
Fairweather LLC 9525 King St	Anchorage	AK	99515	907-346-3247	349-1920
TF: 800-319-8802 ■ *Web:* www.fairweather.com					
Faith Mfg Company Inc 406 Atascocita Rd	Humble	TX	77396	281-441-9595	
Web: www.faithmfg.com					
Ferguson Beauregard Inc 2913 Specialty Dr	Tyler	TX	75707	903-561-4851	
Web: www.fergusonbeauregard.com					
FESCO Ltd 1000 Fesco Ave	Alice	TX	78332	361-661-7000	661-7000
TF: 800-375-3479 ■ *Web:* www.fescoinc.com					
Fire Creek Resources Ltd 206-11th Ave SE Main Fl	Calgary	AB	T2G0X8	403-234-9309	
Web: www.fire-creek.com					
Flow Petroleum Services Inc 209 Marcon Dr	Lafayette	LA	70507	337-593-9987	
Web: www.flowps.com					
Fluid Delivery Solutions LLC 6795 Corporation Pkwy Ste 200	Fort Worth	TX	76126	817-730-9761	
Web: www.fdsllc.com					
Fluid Systems Inc 16619 Aldine Westfield Rd	Houston	TX	77032	832-467-9898	467-9897
Web: www.fluidsystems.com					
Forent Energy Ltd Ste 200 340 - 12th Ave SW	Calgary	AB	T2R1L5	403-262-9444	
Web: www.forentenergy.com					
Fossil Creek Resources LLC 1521 N Cooper St Ste 650	Arlington	TX	76011	817-701-4970	
Web: www.fossilcreekres.com					
Freestone Resources Inc 325 N St Paul St Republic Ctr Ste 1350	Dallas	TX	75201	214-880-4870	
Web: www.freestoneresourcesinc.com					
Gas Field Specialists Inc 2107 SR- 44 S	Shinglehouse	PA	16748	814-698-2122	698-2124
Web: www.gfsinc.net					
Gas Liquids Engineering Ltd 2749-39th Ave NE Ste 300	Calgary	AB	T1Y4T8	403-250-2950	
Web: www.gasliquids.com					
Genco Energy Services Inc 1701 W Hwy 107	Mcallen	TX	78504	956-380-3710	
Web: www.genco.us					
Geophysical Pursuit Inc 3501 Allen Pkwy	Houston	TX	77019	713-529-3000	
Web: www.geopursuit.com					
Gilliam and Sons Inc 9831 Rosedale Hwy	Bakersfield	CA	93312	661-589-0913	
Web: www.gilliamandsons.com					
Global Industries Ltd 8000 Global Dr	Sulphur	LA	70665	337-583-5000	583-5100
TF: 800-525-3483 ■ *Web:* lake-charles.gopickle.com					
Globe Energy Services LLC 3204 W Hwy 180	Snyder	TX	79549	325-573-1310	
Web: globeenergyservices.com					
Gly-Tech Services Inc 2054 Paxton St	Harvey	LA	70058	504-348-8566	
Web: www.glytech.com					
Goldston Oil Corp 1819 Saint James Pl	Houston	TX	77056	713-355-3408	
Web: goldstonoil.com					
Gordon Petroleum Inc 950 Holmdel Rd	Holmdel	NJ	07733	732-946-6000	
Web: www.gordonpetroleum.com					
GOTCO International Inc 11410 Spring Cypress Rd	Tomball	TX	77375	281-376-3784	
Web: www.gotco-usa.com					
Grit Industries Inc 5508 59 Ave	Lloydminster	AB	T9V3A8	780-875-5577	
Web: www.gritindustries.com					
Gulf Offshore Logistics LLC 120 White Rose Dr	Raceland	LA	70394	866-532-1060	
TF: 866-532-1060 ■ *Web:* www.gulf-log.com					
Gulfmark Offshore Inc 842 W Sam Houston Pkwy N Ste 400	Houston	TX	77024	713-963-9522	664-5057*
NYSE: GLF ■ **Fax Area Code:* 281 ■ *Web:* www.gulfmark.com					
Guttman Group LLC, The 200 Speers St	Belle Vernon	PA	15012	724-483-3533	
Web: www.guttmangroup.com					
Guttmann & Blaevoet 2351 Powell St	San Francisco	CA	94133	415-625-0730	
Web: www.gb-eng.com					
Halliburton Energy Services 10200 Bellaire Blvd	Houston	TX	77072	281-871-4000	575-4032
Web: www.halliburton.com					
Hawk Rope Access Inc 124 Parker Ave	Rodeo	CA	94572	510-245-8728	
Web: www.ratsonline.com					
Hawkeye LLC 100 Marcus Blvd Ste 1	Hauppauge	NY	11788	631-447-3100	
Helix Energy Solutions Inc 400 N Sam Houston Pkwy E Ste 400	Houston	TX	77060	281-618-0400	618-0500
NYSE: HLX ■ *TF:* 888-345-2347 ■ *Web:* www.helixesg.com					
HII Technologies Inc 8588 Katy Fwy Ste 430	Houston	TX	77024	713-821-3157	
Web: www.hiitinc.com					
Hilliard Energy Inc 3001 W Loop 250 N Ste E103	Midland	TX	79705	432-683-9100	
Web: www.hilliardenergy.com					
HSE Integrated Ltd 630-6th Ave SW Ste 1000	Calgary	AB	T2P0S8	403-266-1833	
Web: www.hseintegrated.com					

				Phone	Fax
HTC Purenergy Inc 002 2305 Victoria Ave *Web:* www.htcenergy.com	Regina	SK	S4P0S7	306-352-6132	
I Reservoir Com Corp 1490 W Canal Court Ste 2000 *Web:* ireservoir.com	Littleton	CO	80120	303-713-1112	
Indel-Davis Inc 4401 S Jackson Ave *TF:* 800-331-6300 ■ *Web:* www.indel-davis.com	Tulsa	OK	74107	918-587-2151	446-1583
INOVA Geophysical Equipment Ltd 12200 Parc Crest Dr *Web:* www.inovageo.com	Stafford	TX	77477	281-568-2000	
Integrated Service Company LLC 1900 N 161st E Ave *Web:* www.inservusa.com	Tulsa	OK	74116	918-234-4150	
InterAct PMTI 4567 Telephone Rd Ste 203 *Web:* www.pacificmti.com	Ventura	CA	93003	805-658-5600	
JEBCO Seismic LP 2450 Fondren Rd Ste 112 *Web:* www.jebcoseis.com	Houston	TX	77063	713-975-0202	
Jetta Operating Company Inc 777 Taylor St Ft Worth Club Tower Ste P1 *Web:* www.jettaoperating.com	Fort Worth	TX	76102	817-335-1179	
Joining Technologies Inc 17 Connecticut S Dr *Web:* www.joiningtech.com	East Granby	CT	06026	860-653-0111	
Jones & Frank Corp 1330 St Mary's St Ste 210 *Web:* www.jones-frank.com	Raleigh	NC	27605	919-838-7555	
JW Williams Inc 2180 Renauna Ave	Casper	WY	82601	307-237-8345	
Kaiser-Francis Oil Co 6733 S Yale Ave *Web:* www.kfoc.net	Tulsa	OK	74136	918-494-0000	
Katalyst Data Management LLC 10311 Westpark Dr *Web:* www.katalystdm.com	Houston	TX	77042	281-529-3200	
Ketek Industries Ltd 20204 - 110 Ave NW *Web:* www.ketek.ca	Edmonton	AB	T5S1X8	780-447-5050	
Keystone Clearwater Solutions LLC 34 Northeast Dr *Web:* www.keystoneclear.com	Hershey	PA	17033	717-508-0550	
Klinge Corp 4075 E Market St *Web:* www.klingecorp.com	York	PA	17402	717-840-4500	
Koch Specialty Plant Services 12221 E Sam Houston Pkwy N *TF:* 800-765-9177 ■ *Web:* www.kochservices.com	Houston	TX	77044	713-427-7700	427-7747
LaBarge Coating LLC 8300 Eager Rd Ste 602 *Web:* www.labargecoating.com	Saint Louis	MO	63144	314-646-3400	
Lauren Concise 300 736-6 Ave SW *Web:* www.laurenconcise.com	Calgary	AB	T2P3T7	403-237-7160	
Leam Drilling Systems Inc 2027a Airport Rd *Web:* leam.net	Conroe	TX	77301	936-539-1315	
LH Gault & Son Inc 11 Ferry Ln W *Web:* www.gaultenergy.com	Westport	CT	06880	203-227-5181	
Lincoln Manufacturing Inc 31209 FM 2978 Rd *Web:* www.lincolnmanufacturing.com	Magnolia	TX	77354	281-252-9494	
Little Red Services Inc 3700 Centerpoint Dr Ste 1300 *Web:* www.littleredservices.com	Anchorage	AK	99503	907-349-2931	
Loadmaster Derrick & Equipment Inc 1084 Cruse Ave *Web:* www.loadmasterderrick.com	Broussard	LA	70518	337-837-5429	
Logan Industries International Corp Blasingame Rd *Web:* www.loganindustries.net	Hempstead	TX	77445	713-849-2979	
LoneStar West Inc RR 1 Box 1026 *Web:* www.lonestarwest.com	Sylvan Lake	AB	T4S1X6	403-887-2074	
M & M Pipeline Services LLC 274 Mount Moriah Rd *Web:* www.mmpipeline.com	Eupora	MS	39744	662-258-7101	
Mansfield Oil Co 1025 Airport Pkwy SW *TF:* 800-695-6626 ■ *Web:* www.mansfieldoil.com	Gainesville	GA	30501	800-695-6626	
Marksmen Energy Inc 368 Sunmills Dr SE *Web:* www.marksmen.ca	Calgary	AB	T2X3H6	403-265-7270	
Marmik Oil Co 200 N Jefferson Ave *Web:* www.marmikoil.com	El Dorado	AR	71730	870-862-8546	
Marquee Energy Ltd Ste 1700 500 4 Ave SW *Web:* www.marquee-energy.com	Calgary	AB	T2P2V6	403-384-0000	
Matrix Service Co 5100 E Skelly Dr 74135 *NASDAQ: MTRX* ■ **Fax Area Code:* 918 ■ *TF:* 866-367-6879 ■ *Web:* www.matrixservice.com	Tulsa	OK	74135	866-367-6879	838-8810*
MENA Hydrocarbons Inc 1000 Bow Vly Sq 2 205 - Fifth Ave SW *Web:* www.menahydrocarbons.com	Calgary	AB	T2P2V7	403-930-7500	
Meritage Midstream Services LLC 1331 Seventeenth St Ste 1100 *Web:* www.meritagemidstream.com	Denver	CO	80202	303-551-8150	
Merlin Petroleum Company Inc 235 Post Rd W *Web:* www.merlinpetroleum.com	Westport	CT	06880	203-227-3200	
Metro Fuel Oil Corp 500 Kingsland Ave *Web:* metroenergy.com	Brooklyn	NY	11222	718-383-1400	
MGS Services LLC 18775 N Frederick Ave Ste E *Web:* www.mgsservices.com	Gaithersburg	MD	20879	301-330-9793	
MIDCON Data Services Inc 13431 N Broadway Ext Ste 115 *Web:* www.midcondata.com	Oklahoma City	OK	73114	405-478-1234	
Milbar Hydro-Test Inc 651 Aero Dr *TF:* 800-259-8210 ■ *Web:* www.milbarhydro-test.com	Shreveport	LA	71107	318-227-8210	222-2558
MK Tech Solutions Inc 12843 Covey Ln *Web:* www.mktechsolutions.com	Houston	TX	77099	281-564-8851	
Mmi Services Inc 4042 Patton Way *Web:* www.mmi-services.com	Bakersfield	CA	93308	661-589-9366	
Mosaic Energy Ltd 606-4th St SW Ste 900 *Web:* mosaicenergy.ca	Calgary	AB	T2P1T1	403-699-7650	
Multi-Shot LLC 3335 Pollok Dr *Web:* msenergyservices.com	Conroe	TX	77303	936-442-2500	
Nabors Industries Ltd 515 W Greens Rd Ste 1200 *NYSE: NBR* ■ *Web:* www.nabors.com	Houston	TX	77067	281-874-0035	872-5205
Nabors Offshore Corp 515 W Greens Rd Ste 500 *Web:* www.nabors.com	Houston	TX	77067	281-874-0406	872-5205
NANA Regional Corporation Inc 1001 E Benson Blvd *Web:* www.nana.com	Kotzebue	AK	99752	907-442-3301	
Narragansett Bay Commission One Service Rd *Web:* www.narrabay.com	Providence	RI	02905	401-461-8848	
New Jersey Water Supply Authority Inc 1851 State Rt 31 *Web:* www.njwsa.org	Clinton	NJ	08809	908-638-6121	
New West Energy Services Inc Ste 500 435 - Fourth Ave SW *Web:* www.newwestenergyservices.com	Calgary	AB	T2P3A8	403-984-9798	
Newcomb Oil Co LLC 1360 E John Rowan Blvd *Web:* www.newcomboil.com	Bardstown	KY	40004	502-348-3961	348-6346
Newpark Mats & Integrated Services LLC 2700 Research Forest Dr Ste 100 **Fax Area Code:* 337 ■ *TF:* 877-628-7623 ■ *Web:* www.newpark.com	The Woodlands	TX	77381	281-362-6800	984-4445*
Northern Gulf Trading Group 164 St Francis St Ste 205 *Web:* www.ngtg.net	Mobile	AL	36602	251-432-0757	
NOW Inc 7402 N Eldridge Pkwy *Web:* www.distributionnow.com	Houston	TX	77041	281-823-4700	
Oceaneering International Inc 11911 FM 529 *NYSE: OII* ■ *TF:* 877-680-5478 ■ *Web:* www.oceaneering.com	Houston	TX	77041	713-329-4500	329-4951
Offshore Energy Services Inc 5900 US Hwy 90 E *Web:* www.offshoreenergyservices.com	Broussard	LA	70518	337-837-1024	
Offshore Specialty Fabricators LLC 115 Menard Rd *Web:* www.osf-llc.com	Houma	LA	70363	985-868-1438	
Oil States International Inc 333 Clay St Three Allen Ctr Ste 4620 *NYSE: OIS* ■ *Web:* www.oilstatesintl.com	Houston	TX	77002	713-652-0582	652-0499
Oil States Skagit SMATCO LLC 1180 Mulberry Rd *Web:* oilstates.com	Houma	LA	70363	985-868-0630	
One Earth Oil & Gas Inc 600-6th Ave SW Ste 320 *Web:* www.oneearthoilandgas.com	Calgary	AB	T2P0S5	403-984-3151	
OneSubsea LLC 4646 W Sam Houston Pkwy N *Web:* www.onesubsea.com	Houston	TX	77041	713-939-2211	
OPPORTUNE 1717 St. James Pl Ste 460 *Web:* www.ralphedavis.com	Houston	TX	77056	713-622-8955	
Pacific Paradym Energy Inc 1518-1030 Georgia St W *Web:* www.pacificparadym.com	Vancouver	BC	V6E2Y3	604-689-2646	
Painted Pony Petroleum Ltd Ste 1800 736 Sixth Ave SW *Web:* www.paintedpony.ca	Calgary	AB	T2P3T7	403-475-0440	
Pajak Engineering Ltd Ste 300 Iveagh House 707- Seventh Ave SW *Web:* www.pajakeng.com	Calgary	AB	T2P3H6	403-264-1197	
Palo Petroleum Inc 5944 Luther Ln Ste 900 *Web:* www.palopetro.com	Dallas	TX	75225	214-691-3676	
PanGeo Subsea Inc 277 Water St *Web:* www.pangeosubsea.com	St John's	NL	A1C6L3	709-739-8032	
Paragon Offshore PLC 3151 Briarpark Dr Ste 700 *Web:* www.paragonoffshore.com	Houston	TX	77042	832-783-4000	
Paramount Resources Ltd 4700 Bankers Hall W 888 Third St SW *Web:* www.paramountres.com	Calgary	AB	T2P5C5	403-290-3600	
Peak Completion Technologies Inc 7710 W Hwy 80 *Web:* peakcompletions.com	Midland	TX	79706	432-684-4155	
Peak Oilfield Services Co 2525 C St Ste 201 *Web:* www.peakalaska.com	Anchorage	AK	99503	907-263-7000	263-7070
Pentagon Optimization Services Inc 220 7700 - 76 St Close *Web:* www.pentagonoptimization.com	Red Deer	AB	T4P4G6	403-347-6277	
Petro-Techna International Ltd 28 Village Centre Pl *Web:* www.petro-techna.com	Mississauga	ON	L4Z1V9	905-277-5423	
Petroamerica Oil Corp Ste 200 903 Eighth AveSW *Web:* www.petroamericaoilcorp.com	Calgary	AB	T2P0P7	403-237-8300	
Petroleum Strategies Inc 303 W Wall St *Web:* www.petroleumstrategies.com	Midland	TX	79701	432-682-0292	
PetroMax Operating Company Inc 603 Main St Ste 201 *Web:* www.petromaxoperating.com	Garland	TX	75040	972-271-0999	
PetroSkills LLC 2930 S Yale Ave *Web:* www.petroskills.com	Tulsa	OK	74114	918-828-2500	
Pine Cliff Energy Ltd 850 1015-4th St SW *Web:* www.pinecliffenergy.com	Calgary	AB	T2R1J4	403-269-2289	
Pinnergy Ltd 111 Congress Ave Ste 2020 *Web:* www.pinnergy.com	Austin	TX	78701	512-343-8880	343-8885
Piper Valve Systems Inc 1020 E Grand Blvd *Web:* piper-oilfield.com	Oklahoma City	OK	73129	405-671-2000	
Platinum Control Technologies Corp 2822 W Fifth St *Web:* platinumcontrol.com	Fort Worth	TX	76107	817-529-6485	
Plump Engineering Inc 914 E Katella Ave *Web:* www.peica.com	Anaheim	CA	92805	714-385-1835	
PPV Inc 4927 NW Front Ave *Web:* www.ppvnw.com	Portland	OR	97210	503-261-9800	

Company / Address	City	State	ZIP	Phone	Fax
Premier Oilfield Equipment Co 2550 E Bijou *Web:* poequipment.com	Fort Morgan	CO	80701	970-542-1975	
Presco Inc 10200 Grogan's Mill Rd Ste 520 *Web:* www.prescocorp.com	The Woodlands	TX	77380	281-292-7792	
Pride International Inc 5847 San Felipe St Ste 3300 *TF:* 877-736-3772 ■ *Web:* rigzone.com	Houston	TX	77057	713-789-1400	789-1430
Prime Marine Services Inc 312 S Bernard Rd *Web:* www.primemarineinc.com	Broussard	LA	70518	337-837-6500	
Producers Service Corp 109 Graham St *Web:* www.producersservicecorp.com	Zanesville	OH	43701	740-454-6253	
Production Management Industries LLC 9761 Hwy 90 E *TF:* 888-229-3837 ■ *Web:* www.pmi.net	Morgan City	LA	70380	985-631-3837	631-0729
ProSep (USA) Inc 5353 W Sam Houston Pkwy N Ste 150 *Web:* prosep.com	Houston	TX	77041	281-504-2040	
Pumpco Energy Services Inc 117 Elm Grove Rd *Web:* www.pumpcoservices.com	Valley View	TX	76272	940-726-1800	
Pyramid Tubular Products LP Two Northpoint Dr Ste 610 *Web:* www.pyramidtubular.com	Houston	TX	77060	281-405-8090	
Questor Technology Inc 1121 940 - Sixth Ave SW *Web:* www.questortech.com	Calgary	AB	T2P3T1	403-571-1530	
Real Time Measurements Inc Bay 18 4750 106th Ave SE *Web:* www.rty.ca	Calgary	AB	T2C3G5	403-720-3444	
Reaveley Engineers & Associates Inc 675 East 500 South *Web:* www.reaveley.com	Salt Lake City	UT	84102	801-486-3883	
Reef Oil & Gas Partners LP 1901 N Central Expy Ste 300 *Web:* www.reefogc.com	Richardson	TX	75080	972-437-6792	
Regent Energy Group Ltd 3735 - 8 St *Web:* www.regentenergygroup.com	Nisku	AB	T9E8J8	780-955-4288	
RGL Reservoir Management Inc Ste 1110-700 Fourth Ave SW *Web:* www.gl-slotco.com	Calgary	AB	T2P3J4	403-261-1717	
Rig-Chem Inc 132 Thompson Rd *Web:* www.rigchem.com	Houma	LA	70363	985-873-7208	
Rising Star Services Inc 6106 Cargo Rd *Web:* www.risingstarservices.com	Odessa	TX	79762	432-617-0114	
Roberson Wireline Inc 314 SE Ninth Ave *Web:* robersonwireline.com	Perryton	TX	79070	806-435-3087	
Robert L. Bayless, Producer LLC 621 17th St Ste 2300 *Web:* www.rlbayless.com	Denver	CO	80293	303-296-9900	
RPC Inc 2801 Buford Hwy Ste 520 *NYSE: RES* ■ *TF:* 800-776-9437 ■ *Web:* www.rpc.net	Atlanta	GA	30324	404-321-2140	321-5483
S.S. Papadopulos & Associates Inc 7944 Wisconsin Ave *Web:* www.sspa.com	Bethesda	MD	20814	301-718-8900	
Saddle Butte Pipeline LLC 858 Main Ave Ste 301 *Web:* www.sbpipeline.com	Durango	CO	81301	970-375-3150	
SageRider Inc 3330 F County Rd 56 *Web:* www.sageriderinc.com	Rosharon	TX	77583	281-271-7095	
Sahara Energy Ltd Ste700 700 4 Ave SW *Web:* www.saharaenergyltd.com	Calgary	AB	T2P3J4	403-232-1359	
Salazar Service & Trucking Corp 1360 S US 385 *Web:* www.salazarservice.com	Andrews	TX	79714	432-523-9658	
Samson Resources Corp Samson Plz Two W Second St *Web:* www.samson.com	Tulsa	OK	74103	918-591-1791	
Schlumberger Wireline & Testing 210 Schlumberger Dr **Fax:* Hum Res ■ *Web:* www.slb.com	Sugar Land	TX	77478	281-285-4551	285-8970*
Schoeller-Bleckmann Energy Services LLC 712 Saint Etienne Rd *Web:* www.sbesllc.com	Broussard	LA	70518	337-837-2030	
SEC Energy Products & Services LP 9523 Fairbanks N *Web:* www.sec-ep.com	Houston	TX	77064	281-890-9977	
Seismic Source Co 9425 E Tower Rd *Web:* seismicsource.com	Ponca City	OK	74604	580-362-3402	
Shaw Pipeline Services Inc 4250 N Sam Houston Pkwy E Ste 180 *Web:* www.shawpipeline.com	Houston	TX	77032	832-601-0850	
Sklar Exploration Company LLC 401 Edwards St Ste 1601 *Web:* www.sklarexploration.com	Shreveport	LA	71101	318-227-8668	
Sound & Cellular Inc 824 W Yellowstone Hwy *Web:* www.soundandcellular.com	Casper	WY	82601	307-234-7256	
Southern Concrete Products Inc 266 E Church St *Web:* www.southernconcrete.com	Lexington	TN	38351	731-968-8394	
Spartek Systems Inc One Thevenaz Industrial Trl *Web:* www.sparteksystems.com	Sylvan Lake	AB	T4S2J6	403-887-2443	
Spatial Insights Inc 4938 Hampden Ln *Web:* www.spatialinsights.com	Bethesda	MD	20814	301-229-4413	
Stabil Drill Specialties LLC 110 Consolidate Dr *Web:* www.stabildrill.com	Lafayette	LA	70508	337-837-3001	
Stewart & Stevenson LLC 1000 Louisiana St *Web:* www.stewartandstevenson.com	Houston	TX	77002	713-613-0633	751-2701
Stokes & Spiehler Inc 110 Rue Jean Lafitte *Web:* www.stokesandspiehler.com	Lafayette	LA	70508	337-233-6871	
Stric-Lan Companies LLC 104 Sable St *Web:* www.striclan.com	Duson	LA	70529	337-984-7850	
Sub-Surface Tools LLC 1767 W Hwy 380 *Web:* www.subsurfacetools.com	Bridgeport	TX	76426	940-683-8283	
Superior Derrick Services LLC 4506 S Lewis St *Web:* www.superiorderrick.com	New Iberia	LA	70560	337-359-1955	
Supreme Oil Co 2109 W Monte Vista Rd **Fax Area Code:* 602 ■ *TF:* 800-752-7888 ■ *Web:* www.supremeoil.com	Phoenix	AZ	85009	800-752-7888	258-8801*
Surefire Industries LLC 1400 Brittmoore *Web:* surefireusa.com	Houston	TX	77043	713-481-9600	
T-3 Energy Services Inc 140 Cypress Stn Dr Ste 225 **Fax Area Code:* 281	Houston	TX	77090	713-996-4110	943-2042*
T-Rex Engineering & Construction LC 8100 Washington Ave Ste 200 *Web:* www.trexec.com	Houston	TX	77007	713-783-3363	
Talisman Energy USA Inc 337 Daniel Zenker Dr *Web:* www.talismanusa.com	Horseheads	NY	14845	607-562-4000	
Tana Exploration Company LLC 25025 I-45 N Ste 600 *Web:* www.tanaexp.com	The Woodlands	TX	77380	832-325-6000	
Team Inc 200 Hermann Dr *NYSE: TISI* ■ *TF:* 800-662-8326 ■ *Web:* www.teamindustrialservices.com	Alvin	TX	77511	281-331-6154	
Team Trident LLC 16300 Katy Fwy Ste 180 *Web:* www.teamtrident.com	Houston	TX	77094	281-600-1412	
TEC Well Service Inc 851 W Harrison Rd *Web:* www.tecwell.com	Longview	TX	75604	903-759-0082	
Terroco Industries Ltd Site 14 RR Ste 1 Box 10 *Web:* www.terroco.com	Red Deer	AB	T4N5E1	403-346-1171	
Testco 5403 Fm 715 *Web:* www.testco.com	Midland	TX	79706	432-683-2951	
Teton Buildings LLC 2701 Magnet St *Web:* tetonbuildings.com	Houston	TX	77054	713-351-6300	
Texas Electric Utility Construction Ltd 4613 Hwy 1417 N *Web:* www.texaselectric.com	Sherman	TX	75092	903-893-0949	
Thru Tubing Solutions Inc 11515 S Portland *Web:* www.thrutubing.com	Oklahoma City	OK	73170	405-692-1900	
Tiorco Inc 2452 S Trenton Way Ste M *TF:* 800-525-0578 ■ *Web:* www.tiorco.com	Denver	CO	80231	303-923-6440	923-6431
TK Stanley Inc 6739 Hwy 184 **Fax Area Code:* 601 ■ *TF:* 800-477-2855 ■ *Web:* dwservices.com	Waynesboro	MS	39367	800-477-2855	735-2857*
Tri-C Resources Inc 909 Wirt Rd *Web:* www.tricresources.com	Houston	TX	77024	713-685-3600	
Trican Well Service Ltd 645 Seventh Ave SW Ste 2900 *TSE: TCW* ■ *TF:* 877-587-4226 ■ *Web:* www.tricanwellservice.com	Calgary	AB	T2P4G8	403-266-0202	237-7716
United Hunter Oil & Gas Corp Ste 615 700 W Pender St *Web:* www.unitedhunteroil.com	Vancouver	BC	V6C1G8	832-487-0813	
Upham Oil & Gas Company LP 999 Energy Ave *Web:* www.uphamoilandgas.com	Mineral Wells	TX	76067	940-325-4491	
Valiant Corp 6555 Hawthorne Dr *Web:* www.valiantcorp.com	Windsor	ON	N8T3G6	519-974-5200	
Vector Seismic Data Processing Inc 1801 Broadway Ste 1150 *Web:* vector-seismic.com	Denver	CO	80202	303-571-1515	
Vidler Water Company Inc 3480 GS Richards Blvd Ste 101 *Web:* www.vidlerwater.com	Carson City	NV	89703	775-885-5000	
Viking Drilling LLC 3720 S Co Rd 1309 *Web:* www.viking-drilling.com	Odessa	TX	79765	432-550-0100	
Viking Oil Tools 25211 Grogans Mill Rd Ste 460 *Web:* www.vikingoiltools.com	The Woodlands	TX	77380	281-907-9676	
Ward Williston Oil Company Inc 36700 Woodward Ave Ste 101 *Web:* www.wardwilliston.com	Bloomfield Hills	MI	48304	248-594-6622	
Waschuk Pipe Line Construction Ltd #127-39015 Hwy 2A *Web:* www.waschukpipeline.com	Red Deer	AB	T4N2A3	403-346-1114	
Weatherford Completion Systems 11420 W Hwy 80 E *Web:* www.weatherford.com	Midland	TX	79711	432-563-7957	563-7956
Welker Inc 13839 W Bellfort *Web:* www.welker.com	Sugar Land	TX	77498	281-491-2331	
Well Power Inc 11111 Katy Fwy Ste 9 10 *Web:* www.wellpowerinc.com	Houston	TX	77079	713-973-5738	
Wet Tech Energy Inc 4598 Woodlawn Rd *Web:* www.wettechenergy.com	Maurice	LA	70555	337-893-9992	
White Oak Operating Company LLC 12941 N Fwy Ste 550 *Web:* www.whiteoakenergy.com	Houston	TX	77060	281-876-2025	
Wilbanks Energy Logistics 11246 Lovington Hwy Lovington Hwy PO Box 1390 *Web:* www.wilbankstrucking.com	Artesia	NM	88211	575-746-6318	
Wood Group PSN Inc 182 Equity Blvd *Web:* www.wgps.com	Houma	LA	70360	985-868-4116	
Woodside Energy (USA) Inc Sage Plz 5151 San Felipe St Ste 1200 *Web:* www.woodside.com.au	Houston	TX	77056	713-401-0000	
Yoho Resources Inc 500 521-3rd Ave SW *Web:* www.yohoresources.ca	Calgary	AB	T2P3T3	403-537-1771	
Yuba City Water Treatment Plant 701 Northgate Dr *Web:* www.yubacity.net	Yuba City	CA	95991	530-822-4636	

	City	State	Zip	Phone	Fax
Zedi Inc 902 11th Ave SW *Web:* www.zedi.ca	Calgary	AB	T2R0E7	403-444-1100	
Ziff Energy Group Ltd 6025-11th St SE Ste 180 *Web:* www.ziffenergy.com	Calgary	AB	T2H2Z2	403-265-0600	

543 OIL & GAS WELL DRILLING

	City	State	Zip	Phone	Fax
Aera Energy LLC 10000 Ming Ave *Web:* www.aeraenergy.com	Bakersfield	CA	93311	661-665-5000	
AKITA Drilling Ltd 311 - Sixth Ave SW Ste 900 *Web:* www.akita-drilling.com	Calgary	AB	T2P3H2	403-292-7979	
Apex Distribution Inc 407 - 2 St SW Ste 550 *Web:* www.apexdistribution.com	Calgary	AB	T2P2Y3	403-268-7333	
Atwood Oceanics Inc 15011 Katy Fwy Ste 800 *NYSE: ATW* ■ *Web:* www.atwd.com	Houston	TX	77094	281-749-7800	492-7871
Aztec Well Servicing Company Inc 300 Legion Rd PO Box 100 *Web:* www.aztecwell.com	Aztec	NM	87410	505-334-6194	
BCM Energy Partners Inc 5005 Riverway Ste 350 *Web:* www.bcmenergy.com	Houston	TX	77056	713-623-2003	
Berenergy Corp 1888 Sherman St	Denver	CO	80203	303-295-2323	
BICO Drilling Tools Inc 1604 Greens Rd *Web:* www.bicodrilling.com	Houston	TX	77032	281-590-6966	
Big 6 Drilling Co 7500 San Felipe St *Web:* www.big6drilling.com	Houston	TX	77063	713-783-2300	
Callon Petroleum Co 200 N Canal St *NYSE: CPE* ■ *TF:* 800-451-1294 ■ *Web:* www.callon.com	Natchez	MS	39120	601-442-1601	446-1410
Cambrian Management 2398 W 44th St *Web:* www.cambrianmanagement.com	Odessa	TX	79764	432-550-5245	
Cathedral Energy Services Ltd 6030 3 St SE *Web:* www.cathedralenergyservices.com	Calgary	AB	T2H1K2	403-265-2560	
Childress Directional Drilling 6429 cunningham rd *Web:* www.childressdrilling.com	Houston	TX	77041	713-466-7979	
Coast Oil Co 4250 Williams Rd *Web:* www.coastoil.com	San Jose	CA	95129	408-252-7720	
Crescent Directional Drilling LP 2040 Aldine Western Rd *Web:* crescentdirectional.com	Houston	TX	77038	281-668-9535	
Crescent Energy Services LLC 1304 Engineers Rd *Web:* crescentes.com	Belle Chasse	LA	70037	504-433-4188	
Cyclone Drilling Inc PO Box 908 *TF:* 800-318-3724 ■ *Web:* www.cyclonedrilling.com	Gillette	WY	82717	307-682-4161	682-3158
Dallas-Morris Drilling Inc 29 Morris Ln *Web:* www.dallas-morris.com	Bradford	PA	16701	814-362-6493	
Diamond Offshore Drilling Inc 15415 Katy Fwy *NYSE: DO* ■ *TF:* 800-848-1980 ■ *Web:* www.diamondoffshore.com	Houston	TX	77094	281-492-5300	492-5316
Doyon Drilling Inc 11500 C St Ste 200 *TF:* 800-478-9675 ■ *Web:* www.doyondrilling.com	Anchorage	AK	99515	907-563-5530	
Eagle Well Servicing Corp 8113-49 Ave Close *Web:* www.wesc.ca	Red Deer	AB	T4P2V5	403-346-7789	
Eastham Drilling Inc 4710 Bellaire Blvd Ste 350 *Web:* www.bigedrilling.com	Bellaire	TX	77401	713-661-6890	
Ensign Energy Services Inc 400 Fifth Ave SW Ste 1000 *TSE: ESI* ■ *Web:* www.ensignenergy.com	Calgary	AB	T2P0L6	403-262-1361	262-8215
Falcon Seaboard Resources Inc 109 N Post Oak Ln Ste 540 *Web:* www.falconseaboard.com	Houston	TX	77024	713-622-0055	
GEO Drilling Fluids Inc 1431 Union Ave *TF:* 800-438-7436 ■ *Web:* www.geodf.com	Bakersfield	CA	93305	661-325-5919	325-5648
Great White Pressure Control LLC 4500 SE 59th St *Web:* www.greatwhitepressurecontrol.com	Oklahoma City	OK	73135	405-605-2700	
Halliburton Energy Services 10200 Bellaire Blvd *Web:* www.halliburton.com	Houston	TX	77072	281-871-4000	575-4032
Helmerich & Payne Inc 1437 S Boulder Ave *NYSE: HP* ■ *TF:* 800-205-4913 ■ *Web:* www.hpinc.com	Tulsa	OK	74119	918-742-5531	
Hercules Offshore Inc 9 Greenway Plaza Ste 2200 *NASDAQ: HERO* ■ *TF:* 888-647-1715 ■ *Web:* www.herculesoffshore.com	Houston	TX	77046	713-350-5100	350-5105
Iron Horse Energy Services Inc 47 E Third Ave *Web:* www.ihes.ca	Dunmore	AB	T1B0J9	403-526-4600	
Jomax Drilling (1988) Ltd Calgary Pl II 355 - 4 Ave SW Ste 2020 *Web:* www.jomax.ca	Calgary	AB	T2P0J1	403-265-5312	
Justiss Oil Company Inc 1120 E Oak St *TF:* 800-256-2501 ■ *Web:* www.justissoil.com	Jena	LA	71342	318-992-4111	992-7201
Keen Energy Services LLC 4905 S Perkins Rd *Web:* www.keenenergyservices.com	Stillwater	OK	74074	405-743-2132	
Kenai Drilling Ltd 6430 Cat Canyon Rd *Web:* www.kenaidrilling.com	Santa Maria	CA	93454	805-937-7871	
Kicking Horse Energy Inc 1520-700 6 Ave SW *Web:* www.contactexp.com	Calgary	AB	T2P0T8	403-234-8663	
MATRRIX Energy Technologies 350 808 - Fourth Ave SW *Web:* www.matrrix.com	Calgary	AB	T2P3E8	403-984-5042	
Maverick Directional Services 25615 Oakhurst Dr *Web:* www.maverickdirectional.com	Spring	TX	77386	281-364-1212	
McClelland Oilfield Rentals Limited Patnership 8720-110 St *Web:* www.mcclellandoilfieldrentals.com	Grande Prairie	AB	T8V8K1	780-539-3656	
Nabors Alaska Drilling Inc 2525 C St Ste 200 *Web:* www.nabors.com	Anchorage	AK	99503	907-263-6000	563-3734
Nabors Drilling International Ltd 515 W Greens Rd Ste 1000 *TF:* 877-344-7529 ■ *Web:* nabors.com	Houston	TX	77067	281-874-0035	872-5205
Nabors Drilling USA Inc 515 W Greens Rd Ste 1000 *Web:* nabors.com	Houston	TX	77067	281-874-0035	872-5205
Nabors Industries Ltd 515 W Greens Rd Ste 1200 *NYSE: NBR* ■ *Web:* www.nabors.com	Houston	TX	77067	281-874-0035	872-5205
Nicklos Drilling Co 3355 W Alabama Ste 630 *Web:* www.nicklosdrilling.com	Houston	TX	77098	713-224-5959	
Noble Corp 13135 S Dairy Ashford Rd Ste 800 *NYSE: NE* ■ *TF:* 877-285-4162 ■ *Web:* www.noblecorp.com	Sugar Land	TX	77478	281-276-6100	491-2092
Omron Oilfield & Marine Inc 9510 N Houston Rosslyn Rd *Web:* www.oilfield.omron.com	Houston	TX	77088	713-849-1700	
Orion Drilling Company LLC 674 Flato Rd *Web:* www.oriondrilling.com	Corpus Christi	TX	78405	361-299-9800	
Parker Drilling Co 1401 Enclave Pkwy Ste 600 *NYSE: PKD* ■ *TF:* 800-468-9716 ■ *Web:* www.parkerdrilling.com	Houston	TX	77077	281-406-2000	406-2001
Patterson-UTI Energy Inc 450 Gears Rd Ste 500 *NASDAQ: PTEN* ■ *TF:* 866-387-1933 ■ *Web:* www.patenergy.com	Houston	TX	77067	281-765-7100	765-7175
Pioneer Drilling Co 1250 NE Loop 410 Ste 1000 *NASDAQ: PDCE* ■ *Web:* www.pioneerdrlg.com	San Antonio	TX	78209	210-828-7689	447-6080
ProPetro Services Inc 1706 S Midkiff Rd Bldg B PO Box 873 *Web:* www.propetroservices.com	Midland	TX	79701	432-688-0012	
Quail Tools LP 3713 Hwy 14 *Web:* www.quailtools.com	New Iberia	LA	70560	337-364-0407	
Range Resources Corp 100 Throckmorton St Ste 1200 *NYSE: RRC* ■ *Web:* www.rangeresources.com	Fort Worth	TX	76102	817-870-2601	869-9100
Reliance Well Service Inc 237 Hwy 79 S	Magnolia	AR	71753	870-234-2700	
Ringo Drilling I LP 104 Spinks Rd *Web:* www.ringodrilling.com	Tye	TX	79563	325-695-5600	695-5639
Rowan International Inc 2800 Post Oak Blvd Ste 5450 *TF:* 888-385-2663 ■ *Web:* www.rowancompanies.com	Houston	TX	77056	713-621-7800	
Scandrill Inc 11777 Katy Fwy Ste 470 *Web:* www.scandrill.com	Houston	TX	77079	281-496-5571	
Scientific Drilling Controls Inc 1100 Rankin Rd *Web:* www.scientificdrilling.com	Houston	TX	77073	281-443-3300	443-3311
Seadrill Americas Inc 11210 Equity Dr Ste 150 *Web:* www.seadrill.com	Houston	TX	77041	713-329-1150	
Seventy Seven Energy Inc 777 NW 63rd St *Web:* www.77nrg.com	Oklahoma City	OK	73116	405-608-7777	
SITE Ltd 120 Pembina Rd Ste 170 *Web:* www.siteenergy.com	Sherwood Park	AB	T8H0M2	780-400-7483	
SST Energy Corp 8901 W Yellowstone Hwy *Web:* www.sstenergy.com	Casper	WY	82604	307-235-3529	473-1650
Target Drilling Inc 1112 Glacier Dr *Web:* www.targetdrilling.com	Smithton	PA	15479	724-633-3927	
Texas Keystone Inc 560 Epsilon Dr *Web:* www.texaskeystone.com	Pittsburgh	PA	15238	412-434-5616	
Topco Oilsite Products Ltd Bay 5 3401 - 19 St NE *Web:* www.topcooilsite.com	Calgary	AB	T2E6S8	403-219-0255	
Total Energy Services Ltd 2550 300-5th Ave SW Ste 2550 *NYSE: TOT* ■ *TF:* 877-818-6825 ■ *Web:* www.totalenergy.ca	Calgary	AB	T2P3C4	403-216-3939	234-8731
Transocean Inc 4 Greenway Plaza *NYSE: RIG* ■ *TF:* 877-440-0173 ■ *Web:* www.deepwater.com	Houston	TX	77046	713-232-7500	232-7027
True Drilling LLC 455 N Poplar PO Box 2360 *Web:* truecos.com	Casper	WY	82602	307-237-9301	266-0373
U.S. Energy Development Corp 2350 N Forest Rd *Web:* usedc.com	Getzville	NY	14068	716-636-0401	
Union Drilling Inc 4055 International Plz Ste 610 *NASDAQ: UDRL* ■ *Web:* sidewinderdrilling.com	Fort Worth	TX	76109	817-735-8793	546-4368
Unit Corp 7130 S Lewis Ave Ste 1000 *NYSE: UNT* ■ *TF:* 800-722-3612 ■ *Web:* www.unitcorp.com	Tulsa	OK	74136	918-493-7700	493-7711
Vantage Drilling Co 777 Post Oak Blvd Ste 800 *NYSE: VTG* ■ *Web:* www.vantagedrilling.com	Houston	TX	77056	281-404-4700	404-4749
Veracity Energy Services Ltd 200 744 - Fourth Ave SW *Web:* www.veracityenergy.com	Calgary	AB	T2P3T4	403-537-1300	
Vermilion Energy Trust 3500 520 Third Ave SW *TSE: VET* ■ *TF:* 866-895-8101 ■ *Web:* www.vermilionenergy.com	Calgary	AB	T2P0R3	403-269-4884	476-8100
Victory Energy Corp 220 Airport Rd *Web:* www.victoryenergycorp.com	Indiana	PA	15701	724-349-6366	
Xtreme Drilling & Coil Services Corp 770 340 - 12th Ave SW *Web:* www.xtremecoildrilling.com	Calgary	AB	T2R1L5	403-262-9500	

544 OILS & GREASES - LUBRICATING

SEE ALSO Chemicals - Specialty p. 1944; Petroleum Refineries p. 2920

	City	State	Zip	Phone	Fax
Ackerman Oil Company Inc 2060 S Lube Way *Web:* www.ackoil.com	Jasper	IN	47546	812-482-6666	
Allied Sales Co 5005 E Seventh St *Web:* www.alliedsales.com	Austin	TX	78702	512-385-2167	385-0259

Phone Fax

American Lubrication Equipment Corp
11212A McCormick Rd PO Box 1350 Hunt Valley MD 21030 888-252-9300 759-2637*
*Fax Area Code: 800 ■ Web: americanlube.com

Amsoil Inc 925 Tower Ave Superior WI 54880 715-392-7101 392-5225
TF Sales: 800-777-7094 ■ Web: www.amsoil.com

Anderol Inc 215 Merry Ln PO Box 518 East Hanover NJ 07936 973-887-7410 887-8404
TF: 888-263-3765 ■ Web: www.anderol.com

Axel Plastics Research Laboratories Inc
5820 Broadway Woodside NY 11377 718-672-8300
Web: www.axelplastics.com

Battenfeld Grease & Oil Corp of New York
1174 Erie Ave PO Box 728 North Tonawanda NY 14120 716-695-2100 695-0367
Web: www.battenfeld-grease.com

Bel Ray Company Inc PO Box 526 Farmingdale NJ 07727 732-938-2421 938-4232
Web: www.belray.com

Benz Oil Inc 2724 W Hampton Ave Milwaukee WI 53209 414-442-2900 442-8388
Web: www.benzoil.com

BG Products Inc 740 S Wichita St Wichita KS 67213 316-265-2686 265-1082
TF: 800-961-6228 ■ Web: www.bgprod.com

Blachford Corp 401 Ctr Rd Frankfort IL 60423 905-823-3200 231-8321*
*Fax Area Code: 630 ■ TF: 800-435-5942 ■ Web: www.blachford.com

Bolton Oil Company Ltd
1316 54th St PO Box 3176 Lubbock TX 79412 806-747-1629
Web: www.boltonoil.com

BP Lubricants USA Inc 1500 Valley Rd Wayne NJ 07470 973-633-2200
TF: 800-333-3991 ■ Web: www.bp.com

Canada Forgings Inc 130 Hagar St Welland ON L3B5P8 905-735-1220
TF: 800-263-0440 ■ Web: www.canforge.com

Castrol Industrial North America Inc
150 W Warrenville Rd Naperville IL 60563 877-641-1600 648-9801
TF: 877-641-1600 ■ Web: www.castrol.com

Chem-Trend LP 1445 McPherson Pk Dr Howell MI 48843 517-546-4520
TF: 800-727-7730 ■ Web: www.chemtrend.com

Colorado Petroleum Products Co
4080 Globeville Rd Denver CO 80216 303-294-0302 294-9128
TF: 800-580-4080 ■ Web: www.colopetro.com

CRC Industries Inc 885 Louis Dr Warminster PA 18974 215-674-4300 674-2196
TF Cust Svc: 800-556-5074 ■ Web: www.crcindustries.com

D-A Lubricant Co 1340 W 29th St Indianapolis IN 46208 317-923-5321 923-3884*
*Fax: Cust Svc ■ TF: 800-645-5823 ■ Web: www.dalube.com

Delta Petroleum Co 10352 River Rd Saint Rose LA 70087 504-467-1399 467-1398
Web: www.deltacompanies.net

Elco Corp 1000 Belt Line St Cleveland OH 44109 216-749-2605 749-7462
TF: 800-321-0467 ■ Web: www.elcocorp.com

Fiske Bros Refining Co 129 Lockwood St Newark NJ 07105 973-589-9150 589-4432
TF: 800-733-4755 ■ Web: www.lubriplate.com

Fuchs Lubricants Canada Ltd Eastern Canada Div
405 Dobbie Dr PO Box 909 Cambridge ON N1R5X9 519-622-2040 622-2220
Web: www.fuchs.com

Fuchs Lubricants Co 17050 Lathrop Ave Harvey IL 60426 708-333-8900 333-9180
TF: 800-323-7755 ■ Web: www.fuchs.com

Hangsterfer's Laboratories Inc 175 Ogden Rd Mantua NJ 08051 856-468-0216 468-0200
TF: 800-433-5823 ■ Web: www.hangsterfers.com

Hercules Chemical Company Inc 111 S St Passaic NJ 07055 973-778-5000 777-4115
TF: 800-221-9330 ■ Web: www.oatey.com

Honstein Oil Co 11 Paseo Real Santa Fe NM 87507 505-471-1800
Web: www.honsteinoil.com

Houghton International Inc
945 Madison Ave PO Box 930 Valley Forge PA 19482 610-666-4000 666-0174
TF: 888-459-9844 ■ Web: www.houghtonintl.com

Hydrotex Inc 12920 Senlac D Ste 190 Farmers Branch TX 75234 800-527-9439 389-8526*
*Fax Area Code: 972 ■ TF: 800-527-9439 ■ Web: www.hydrotexlube.com

ITW Rocol North America 3650 W Lake Ave Glenview IL 60026 847-657-5278
TF: 800-452-5823 ■ Web: itwfluidsna.com/

Jackson Oil & Solvents Inc
1970 Kentucky Ave Indianapolis IN 46221 317-636-4421 685-2403
TF: 800-221-4603 ■ Web: www.jacksonoilsolvents.com

JD Streett & Company Inc
144 Weldon Pkwy Maryland Heights MO 63043 314-432-6600 432-4248
Web: www.jdstreett.com

Jet-Lube Inc 4849 Homestead Rd Ste 232 Houston TX 77226 713-670-5700 678-4604
TF: 800-538-5823 ■ Web: www.jetlube.com

Kluber Lubrication North America LP
32 Industrial Dr Londonderry NH 03053 603-647-4104 647-4106
TF: 800-447-2238 ■ Web: www.klueber.com

Leadership Performance Sustainability Laboratories
4647 Hugh Howell Rd Tucker GA 30084 800-241-8334 243-8899*
*Fax Area Code: 770 ■ TF: 800-241-8334 ■ Web: www.lpslabs.com

LiQuifix LLC 110 Lenox Ave Stamford CT 06906 203-653-4689
Web: www.liquifix.com

Lubri-Lab Inc 1540 de Coulomb Boucherville QC J4B8A3 450-449-1626 449-9174
Web: www.lubrilab.com

Lubricating Specialties Co
8015 Paramount Blvd Pico Rivera CA 90660 562-776-4000 776-4004
Web: www.lsc-online.com

Lubrication Engineers Inc 300 Bailey Ave Fort Worth TX 76107 817-834-6321 228-1142*
*Fax Area Code: 800 ■ *Fax: Sales ■ TF: 800-537-7683 ■ Web: www.lelubricants.com

Lubrication Technologies Inc
900 Mendelssohn Ave N Golden Valley MN 55427 763-545-0707 545-9256
TF: 800-328-5573 ■ Web: www.lube-tech.com

Lubrizol Corp 29400 Lakeland Blvd Wickliffe OH 44092 440-943-4200 943-5337
NYSE: LZ ■ TF: 800-380-5397 ■ Web: www.lubrizol.com

Master Chemical Corp 501 W Boundry St Perrysburg OH 43551 419-874-7902 874-0684
Web: www.masterchemical.com

Metalworking Lubricants Co
25 Silverdome Industrial Park Pontiac MI 48342 248-332-3500 332-4959
TF: 800-394-5494 ■ Web: www.metalworkinglubricants.com

Northland Products Co 1000 Rainbow Dr Waterloo IA 50701 319-234-5585 234-5580

Northtown Products Inc
5202 Argosy Ave Huntington Beach CA 92649 714-897-0700
Web: www.northtowncompany.com

Nye Lubricants Inc 12 Howland Rd Fairhaven MA 02719 508-996-6721 997-5285
Web: www.nyelubricants.com

Phone Fax

Oil Chem Inc 711 W 12th St Flint MI 48503 810-235-3040 238-5260
Web: www.oilcheminc.com

Oil Ctr Research LLC 106 Montrose Ave Lafayette LA 70503 337-993-3559 993-3149
TF: 800-256-8977 ■ Web: www.oilcenter.com

Orelube Corp, The 20 Sawgrass Dr Bellport NY 11713 631-205-9700 205-9797
TF: 800-645-9124 ■ Web: www.orelube.com

Perkins Oil Company Inc 4707 Pflaum Rd Madison WI 53718 608-221-4736
Web: perkinsoil.com

Primrose Oil Company Inc
11444 Benton Dr PO Box 29665 Dallas TX 75229 972-241-1100 241-4188
TF: 800-275-2772 ■ Web: www.primrose.com

Richards-Apex Inc 4202-24 Main St Philadelphia PA 19127 215-487-1100 487-3090
Web: www.richardsapex.com

Safariland LLC 13386 International Pkwy Jacksonville FL 32218 800-347-1200 741-5407*
*Fax Area Code: 904 ■ TF: 800-347-1200 ■ Web: www.break-free.com

Schaeffer Mfg Company Inc 102 Barton St Saint Louis MO 63104 314-865-4100 865-4107
TF Cust Svc: 800-325-9962 ■ Web: www.schaefferoil.com

Schultz Lubricants Inc
164 Shrewsbury St West Boylston MA 01583 508-835-4446
Web: www.schultzlubricants.com

Shell Lubricants PO Box 2463 909 Fannin St Houston TX 77252 713-241-6161
TF Cust Svc: 888-743-5586 ■ Web: www.shell.us

Smitty's Supply Inc
63399 Hwy 51 N PO Box 530 Roseland LA 70456 985-748-9687 748-3004
TF: 800-256-7575 ■ Web: www.smittysinc.net

Southwestern Petroleum Corp PO Box 961005 Fort Worth TX 76161 817-332-2336 877-4047
TF: 800-877-9372 ■ Web: www.swepcousa.com

Sun Drilling Products Corp
503 Main St PO Box 129 Belle Chasse LA 70037 504-393-2778 391-1383
TF: 800-962-6490 ■ Web: www.sundrilling.com

Texas Refinery Corp 840 N Main St Fort Worth TX 76164 817-332-1161 332-6110
TF: 800-827-0711 ■ Web: www.texasrefinery.com

Total Lubricants USA 5 N Stiles St Linden NJ 07036 908-862-9300 862-5374
TF: 800-323-3198 ■ Web: total-us.com

Tri Star Energy LLC 1740 Ed Temple Blvd Nashville TN 37208 615-313-3600
Web: dailys.com

Valvoline Co 3499 Blazer Pkwy PO Box 14000 Lexington KY 40509 859-357-7777 357-2686
TF: 800-832-6825 ■ Web: www.valvoline.com

WD-40 Co 1061 Cudahy Pl San Diego CA 92110 619-275-1400 275-5823
NASDAQ: WDFC ■ TF: 800-448-9340 ■ Web: www.wd40company.com

Westpower Equipment Ltd 4451-54 Ave S.E. Calgary AB T2C2A2 403-720-3300 236-9812
Web: www.westpower.ca

545 OPHTHALMIC GOODS

SEE ALSO Personal Protective Equipment & Clothing p. 2914

Phone Fax

Aearo Co 5457 W 79th St Indianapolis IN 46268 317-692-6666 692-6772
TF: 877-327-4332 ■ Web: earsc.com

Art Optical Contact Lens Inc
PO Box 1848 Grand Rapids MI 49501 616-453-1888 453-8702
Web: www.artoptical.com

Art-Craft Optical Company Inc
57 Goodway Dr S Rochester NY 14623 585-546-6640 546-5133
TF: 800-828-8288 ■ Web: www.artcraftoptical.com

Bausch & Lomb Inc 1400 N Goodman St Rochester NY 14609 585-338-6000 338-6896
TF: 800-553-5340 ■ Web: www.bausch.com

Bausch & Lomb Inc Vision Care Div
1400 Goodman St N Rochester NY 14609 585-338-6000
TF: 800-828-9030 ■ Web: www.bausch.com

Beitler-Mckee Optical Co 160 S 22nd St Pittsburgh PA 15203 412-481-4700
TF: 800-989-4700 ■ Web: beitlermckee.com

Bolle Inc 9200 Cody St Overland Park KS 66214 913-752-3400 752-3550
TF: 800-222-6553 ■ Web: www.bolle.com

Carskadden Optical Co 1525 Highpoint Ct Zanesville OH 43701 740-452-9306

CIBA Vision Corp 11460 Johns Creek Pkwy Duluth GA 30097 800-875-3001 415-4260*
*Fax Area Code: 678 ■ TF: 800-875-3001 ■ Web: www.cibavision.com

Conforma Laboratories Inc 4705 Colley Ave Norfolk VA 23508 757-321-0200 321-0201
TF: 800-426-1700 ■ Web: www.conforma.com

Cooper Cos Inc
6140 Stoneridge Mall Rd Ste 590 Pleasanton CA 94588 925-460-3600 460-3649
NYSE: COO ■ TF: 888-822-2660 ■ Web: www.coopercos.com

CooperVision Inc 370 Woodcliff Dr Ste 200 Fairport NY 14450 585-385-6810
TF: 800-538-7850 ■ Web: www.coopercos.com

Costa Del Mar 2361 Mason Ave Ste 100 Daytona Beach FL 32117 386-274-4000 274-4001
TF: 800-447-3700 ■ Web: www.costadelmar.com

Cumberland Optical Laboratory
806 Olympic St Nashville TN 37203 615-254-5868 254-5868

DAC Vision 3630 W Miller Ste 350 Garland TX 75041 972-677-2700 677-2800
TF: 800-800-1550 ■ Web: www.dacvision.com

Dakota Smith Signature Eyewear
498 N Oak St Inglewood CA 90302 310-330-2700 330-2748
TF: 800-765-3937 ■ Web: www.signatureeyewear.com

De'Vons Optics Inc 10823 Bell Ct Rancho Cucamonga CA 91730 909-466-4700 466-4703
Web: coppermax.com

Dispensers Optical Service Corp
1815 Plantside Dr
Bluegrass Industrial Park Louisville KY 40299 502-491-3440 491-3446

Duffens Langley Optical Co 8140 Marshall Dr Lenexa KS 66214 913-492-5379 888-5375*
*Fax Area Code: 800 ■ TF: 800-397-2020 ■ Web: www.duffens-optical.com

ER Precision Optical Corp 805 W Central Blvd Orlando FL 32805 407-292-5395
Web: www.eroptics.com

Essilor of America Inc 13515 N Stemmons Fwy Dallas TX 75234 214-496-4000
Web: www.essilorusa.com

Eye-Kraft Optical Inc 8 McLeland Rd Saint Cloud MN 56303 888-455-2022 950-7070*
*Fax Area Code: 800 ■ TF: 888-455-2022 ■ Web: www.eyekraft.com

Gargoyles Inc 500 George Washington Hwy Smithfield RI 02917 401-231-3800 356-4248*
*Fax Area Code: 800 ■ Web: gargoyleseyewear.com

Gentex Optics Inc 324 Main St Simpson PA 18407 570-282-3550 282-8555
TF: 800-736-0554 ■ Web: www.gentexcorp.com

Company	City	State	Zip	Phone	Fax
Homer Optical Company Inc 2401 Linden Ln *TF:* 800-627-2710 ■ *Web:* www.homeroptical.com	Silver Spring	MD	20910	301-585-9060	585-5934
Hoya Holdings Inc 3285 Scott Blvd *Web:* www.hoya.co.jp	Santa Clara	CA	95054	408-654-2300	
Icare Industries Inc 4399 35th St N *TF:* 877-422-7352 ■ *Web:* www.icarelabs.com	Saint Petersburg	FL	33714	727-526-0501	522-1408
IcareLabs 4399 35th St N **Fax Area Code:* 727 ■ *TF:* 877-422-7352 ■ *Web:* www.icarelabs.com	Saint Petersburg	FL	33714	877-422-7352	522-1408*
Instrument Technology Inc 33 Airport Rd *Web:* www.scopes.com	Westfield	MA	01085	413-562-3606	
Johnson & Johnson Vision Care Inc 7500 Centurion Pkwy *TF:* 800-843-2020 ■ *Web:* www.acuvueprofessional.com	Jacksonville	FL	32256	800-874-5278	
LBI Eyewear 20801 Nordhoff St *TF Cust Svc:* 800-423-5175 ■ *Web:* www.lbieyewear.com	Chatsworth	CA	91311	818-407-1890	407-1895
LensVector Inc 677 Palomar Ave *Web:* www.lensvector.com	Sunnyvale	CA	94085	408-542-0300	
Maui Jim Inc 721 Wainee St *TF:* 888-352-2001 ■ *Web:* www.mauijim.com	Lahaina	HI	96761	808-661-8841	661-0351
MEMS Optical Inc 205 Import Cir *Web:* www.memsoptical.com	Huntsville	AL	35806	256-859-1886	
Night Optics USA Inc 15182 Triton Ln Ste 101 *TF:* 800-306-4448 ■ *Web:* www.nightoptics.com	Huntington Beach	CA	92649	714-899-4475	
Oakley Inc 1 Icon **Fax Area Code:* 502 ■ **Fax:* Cust Svc ■ *TF Cust Svc:* 800-403-7449 ■ *Web:* www.oakley.com	Foothill Ranch	CA	92610	949-951-0991	368-2443*
Omega Optical 13515 N Stemmons Fwy **Fax Area Code:* 800 ■ *TF:* 800-366-6342 ■ *Web:* omega-dallas.com	Dallas	TX	75234	972-241-4141	877-0329*
Orange 21 Inc 2070 Las Palmas Dr *Web:* www.orangetwentyone.com	Carlsbad	CA	92009	760-804-8420	804-8421
Rosin Eyecare Ctr 6233 W Cermak Rd *Web:* www.rosineyecare.com	Berwyn	IL	60402	708-749-2020	749-7944
Serengeti Eyewear Inc 9200 Cody St *TF Cust Svc:* 800-423-3537 ■ *Web:* www.serengeti-eyewear.com	Overland Park	KS	66214	913-752-3400	752-3550
Sigma Corp of America 15 Fleetwood Ct *TF:* 800-896-6858 ■ *Web:* www.sigmaphoto.com	Ronkonkoma	NY	11779	631-585-1144	
Signature Eyewear Inc 498 N Oak St *OTC:* SEYE ■ *TF:* 800-765-3937 ■ *Web:* www.signatureeyewear.com	Inglewood	CA	90302	310-330-2700	330-2765
Southern Optical Company Inc 1909 N Church St *TF:* 800-888-8842 ■ *Web:* southern-optical.com	Greensboro	NC	27405	336-272-8146	273-6625
STAAR Surgical Co 1911 Walker Ave *NASDAQ:* STAA ■ **Fax:* Mktg ■ *TF:* 800-352-7842 ■ *Web:* www.staar.com	Monrovia	CA	91016	626-303-7902	303-2962*
Telops Inc 100-2600 St-Jean-Baptiste Ave *Web:* www.telops.com	Quebec City	QC	G2E6J5	418-864-7808	864-7843
Transitions Optical Inc 9251 Belcher Rd *TF:* 800-533-2081 ■ *Web:* www.transitions.com	Pinellas Park	FL	33782	727-545-0400	546-4732
US Vision Inc 1 Harmon Dr Glen Oaks Industrial Pk *TF:* 800-524-0789 ■ *Web:* www.usvision.com	Glendora	NJ	08029	856-228-1000	228-3339
Vision-Ease Lens Inc 7000 Sunwood Dr NW *TF Cust Svc:* 800-328-3449 ■ *Web:* www.vision-ease.com	Ramsey	MN	55303	320-251-8140	251-4312
Walman Optical Company Inc 801 12th Ave N *TF:* 800-873-9256 ■ *Web:* www.walman.com	Minneapolis	MN	55411	612-520-6000	520-6069
X-Cel Optical Company Inc 806 S Benton Dr **Fax Area Code:* 800 ■ *TF General:* 800-747-9235 ■ *Web:* www.x-celoptical.com	Sauk Rapids	MN	56379	320-251-8404	232-9235*
X-Ray Optical Systems Inc 15 Tech Valley Dr *Web:* www.xos.com	East Greenbush	NY	12061	518-880-1500	
Younger Optics 2925 California St *TF:* 800-366-5367 ■ *Web:* www.youngeroptics.com	Torrance	CA	90503	310-783-1533	783-6477

546 OPTICAL GOODS STORES

Company	City	State	Zip	Phone	Fax
Allegany Optical LLC 17301 Vly Mall Rd *Web:* www.alleganyoptical.com	Hagerstown	MD	21740	301-582-1771	
Art Partners LLC 284 S Sharon Amity Rd *Web:* www.bindersart.com	Charlotte	NC	28211	888-472-6866	
Aspen Optical Inc 1050 W Main St Ste 102 *Web:* www.aspenoptical.com	Mesa	AZ	85201	480-894-8770	
Atlantic Optical Company Inc 20801 Nordhoff St *Web:* www.ce-tru.com	Chatsworth	CA	91311	818-407-1890	
Barnett & Ramel Optical Co 7154 N 16th St *TF:* 800-228-9732 ■ *Web:* www.broptical.com	Omaha	NE	68112	800-228-9732	
BARSKA Optics 1721 Wright Ave *Web:* m.barska.com	La Verne	CA	91750	909-445-8168	
Beacon Advanced Eye Care Center 1320 Shelfer St *Web:* www.beaconvisioncenter.com	Leesburg	FL	34748	352-728-8318	
Carolina Eyecare Physicians 2060 Charlie Hall Blvd Ste 201 *Web:* www.carolinaeyecare.com	Charleston	SC	29414	843-722-2010	
CCHC Southern Gastroenterology Associates 3100 Wellons Blvd *Web:* www.cchealthcare.com	New Bern	NC	28562	252-634-9000	
Center for Behavioral Health Inc, The 175 Cedar Ln Ste A *Web:* www.njpsychologist.com	Teaneck	NJ	07666	201-692-9500	
Cliff Weil Inc 8043 Industrial Pk Rd *TF:* 800-446-9345 ■ *Web:* www.cliffweil.com	Mechanicsville	VA	23116	804-746-1321	746-2595
Co/op Optical Vision Designs 2424 E Eight-Mile *Web:* www.coopoptical.com	Detroit	MI	48234	313-366-5100	366-7313
Colonial Opticians 4942 St Elmo Ave *Web:* colonialopticians.com	Bethesda	MD	20814	301-657-3332	657-4092
Crown Vision Ctr 211 E Broadway *Web:* www.crownvisioncenter.com	Alton	IL	62002	618-462-9818	
Dakota Vision Center LLC 5012 S Bur Oak Pl *Web:* dakotavisioncenter.com	Sioux Falls	SD	57108	605-361-1680	
Debby Burk Optical Ltd Seven Overlook Ln *Web:* www.acmereadingglasses.com	Plainview	NY	11803	516-935-4584	
Designs for Vision Inc 760 Koehler Ave *Web:* www.designsforvision.com	Ronkonkoma	NY	11779	631-585-3300	
Doctors Vision Ctr 413 Mill St PO Box 7396 *TF:* 888-414-4442 ■ *Web:* www.doctorsvisioncenter.com	Rocky Mount	NC	27804	252-442-0802	442-2820
Dr Tavel Optical Group 2839 Lafayette Rd *Web:* www.drtavel.com	Indianapolis	IN	46222	317-924-1300	924-3741
Emerging Vision Inc 520 Eigth Ave 23rd Fl *Web:* www.emergingvision.com	New York	NY	10018	646-737-1500	
Empire Optical Inc 3238 E 21st St *Web:* empireoptical.com	Tulsa	OK	74114	918-744-8005	
Empire Vision Centers 2921 Erie Blvd E *TF:* 877-959-4160 ■ *Web:* visionworks.com/empire	Syracuse	NY	13224	315-446-5120	
Epic Labs Inc 95 Third St NE *Web:* www.epiclabs.com	Waite Park	MN	56387	320-656-1473	
Exact Eye Care 431 Pierce St *Web:* www.exacteyecare.com	Sioux City	IA	51101	712-252-4691	252-5339
Eye Glass World Inc 296 Grayson Hwy *TF:* 800-637-3597 ■ *Web:* www.eyeglassworld.com	Lawrenceville	GA	30046	800-637-3597	
Eye To Eye Vision Ctr 2255 Sewell Mill Rd Ste 310 *Web:* www.eyetoeyevisioncenter.com	Marietta	GA	30062	770-578-1900	578-6623
Eye-Mart Express Inc 13800 Senlac Dr Ste 200 **Fax Area Code:* 469 ■ *TF:* 888-372-2763 ■ *Web:* www.eyemartexpress.com	Dallas	TX	75234	972-488-2002	206-5194*
Eye-Mate Inc 77 N Centre Ave	Rockville Centre	NY	11570	516-678-9613	
Eyetique Corp 2242 Murray Ave *Web:* www.eyetique.com	Pittsburgh	PA	15217	412-422-5300	
For Eyes/Insight Optical 285 W 74th Pl *TF:* 877-688-9891 ■ *Web:* www.foreyes.com	Hialeah	FL	33014	305-557-9004	
General Vision Services LLC 520 Eigth Ave 9th Fl *TF:* 855-653-0586 ■ *Web:* www.generalvision.com	New York	NY	10018	212-729-5300	967-4781
Glasses Ltd 50 E Oak St Apt Bsmt *Web:* www.glasses.com	Chicago	IL	60611	312-944-6876	
H Rubin Vision Centers 7539 Garners Sperry Rd **Fax:* Cust Svc ■ *Web:* www.hrubinvision.com	Columbia	SC	29209	803-779-9313	779-9551*
Hart Specialties Inc 5000 New Horizons Blvd *Web:* www.newyorkeye.net	Amityville	NY	11701	631-226-5600	
Henry Ford OptimEyes 655 W 13-Mile Rd *TF:* 800-393-2273 ■ *Web:* henryford.com/homepage_optimeyes.cfm?id=51936	Madison Heights	MI	48071	248-588-9300	588-3355
Heritage Optical Center Inc 19010 Livernois Ave *Web:* www.heritageoptical.com	Detroit	MI	48221	313-863-9581	
Hi-tech Optical Inc 3139 Christy Way S *Web:* www.hi-techoptical.com	Saginaw	MI	48603	989-799-9390	
Horner Rausch Optical Super Store 968 Main St *Web:* hornerrauschoptical.com	Nashville	TN	37206	615-226-0251	226-8527
HOYA Optical Laboratories Inc 651 E Corporate Dr *Web:* www.hoyavision.com	Lewisville	TX	75057	972-221-4141	
I-MED Pharma Inc 1601 St. Regis Blvd *Web:* www.imedpharma.com	Dollard-des Ormeaux	QC	H9B3H7	514-685-8118	685-8998
INNOVA Medical Ophthalmics Inc 1430 Birchmount Rd *Web:* www.innovamed.com	Toronto	ON	M1P2E8	416-615-0185	
JAK Enterprises Inc 8309 N Knoxville Ave *TF:* 800-752-3295 ■ *Web:* www.bardoptical.com	Peoria	IL	61615	309-692-8222	
JC Penney Optical Co 821 N Central Expressway *TF:* 866-435-7111 ■ *Web:* www.jcpeyes.com	Plano	TX	75024	972-516-1393	
KBco The Polarized Lens Co 7328 S Revere Pkwy Unit 208 *Web:* www.kbco.net	Centennial	CO	80112	303-253-6600	
LensCrafters Inc 4000 Luxottica Pl *TF:* 877-753-6727 ■ *Web:* www.lenscrafters.com	Mason	OH	45040	513-765-4321	
Live Eyewear Inc 3490 Broad St *Web:* www.liveeyewear.com	San Luis Obispo	CA	93401	805-782-5070	
Lobob Laboratories Inc 1440 Atteberry Ln *Web:* lobob labs.com	San Jose	CA	95131	408-432-0580	
Lockport Optical 36 E Ave	Lockport	NY	14094	716-434-6900	434-8461
Magnifying Ctr 10086 W McNab Rd *TF:* 800-364-1612 ■ *Web:* www.magnifyingcenter.com	Tamarac	FL	33321	954-722-1580	
Malbar Vision Ctr 409 N 78th St *TF:* 800-701-3937 ■ *Web:* www.malbar.com	Omaha	NE	68114	402-391-6600	493-4041
Marco Ophthalmic Inc 11825 Central Pkwy *Web:* www.marco.com	Jacksonville	FL	32224	904-642-9330	
McLeod Optical Company Inc 50 Jefferson Park Rd *Web:* www.mcleodoptical.com	Warwick	RI	02888	401-467-3000	
Medical Associates Healthcare 911 Carter St Nw *Web:* www.mahealthcare.com	Elkader	IA	52043	563-245-1717	
Moscot Mobileyes Foundation Inc 118 Orchard St *Web:* www.moscot.com	New York	NY	10002	212-477-3796	
National Vision Inc 296 Grayson Hwy *TF Cust Svc:* 800-637-3597 ■ *Web:* www.nationalvision.com	Lawrenceville	GA	30045	770-822-3600	822-3601
Native Eyewear Inc 1444 Wazee St Ste 215 *Web:* www.nativeeyewear.com	Denver	CO	80202	215-938-6642	
Nea Optical LLC 1426 E Washington *Web:* neaoptical.com	Jonesboro	AR	72401	870-935-2179	

Phone Fax

Ophthalmic Consultants of Boston Inc
50 Staniford St Ste 600 .... Boston MA 02114 617-367-4800
Web: www.eyeboston.com

Opti Care Eye Health Center
87 Grandview Ave .... Waterbury CT 06708 203-574-2020 596-2230
TF: 800-334-3937 ■ *Web:* www.opticare.com

Optical Distributor Group LLC
Four Skyline Dr .... Hawthorne NY 10532 914-347-7400
Web: www.opticaldg.com

Optical Options
4620 J C Nichols Pkwy Ste 427 .... Kansas City MO 64112 816-561-4907
Web: www.cibiseyecare.com

Optovue Inc 2800 Bayview Dr .... Fremont CA 94538 510-623-8868
Web: www.optovue.com

Orb Optronix Inc 1003 Seventh Ave .... Kirkland WA 98033 425-605-8500
Web: www.orboptronix.com

Paris Miki Usa Inc 2863 152nd Ave Ne .... Redmond WA 98052 425-883-2464
Web: parismikiusa.com

Partec Inc 9301 Belmont Ave .... Franklin Park IL 60131 847-678-9520
Web: partec-inc.com

Pearle Vision Inc 4000 Luxottica Pl .... Mason OH 45040 513-765-4321 765-6388
Web: www.pearlevision.com

Polyvision Inc
9830 Norwalk Blvd Ste 174 .... Santa Fe Springs CA 90670 562-944-3924
Web: www.polycore-usa.com

Precision Tool Technologies Inc
309 13th Ave Nw .... Little Falls MN 56345 320-632-5320
Web: www.precisiontooltech.com

Premier Eyecare Group Inc
1524 Cedar Cliff Dr Ste 1 .... Camp Hill PA 17011 717-761-3077
Web: www.premiereyes.com

ProCare Vision Ctr Inc
1955 Newark-Granville Rd .... Granville OH 43023 740-587-3937 587-3589
Web: www.procarevisioncenters.com

Retina Consultants of Oklahoma
9913 S May Ave Ste C .... Oklahoma City OK 73159 405-691-0505
Web: retinaconsultantsoklahoma.com

Revision Military Ltd
Seven Corporate Dr .... Essex Junction VT 05452 802-879-7002
Web: www.revisionmilitary.com

Rite-Style Optical Co 12240 Emmet St .... Omaha NE 68164 402-492-8822 492-9414
TF: 800-373-3200 ■ *Web:* ritestyle.com

RJ Rippey Od Pa Dba Vision Vision Source
1635A S Voss Rd .... Houston TX 77057 713-954-2020

Rockwell Laser Industries Inc
7754 Camargo Rd Ste 3 .... Cincinnati OH 45243 513-271-1568
Web: www.rli.com

Rosin Eyecare Ctr 6233 W Cermak Rd .... Berwyn IL 60402 708-749-2020 749-7944
Web: www.rosineyecare.com

Rx Optical 1700 S Pk St .... Kalamazoo MI 49001 269-342-0003 342-4284
TF: 800-792-2737 ■ *Web:* www.rxoptical.com

Saint Charles Vision 8040 St Charles Ave .... New Orleans LA 70118 504-866-6311
Web: www.stcharlesvision.com

Singer Specs 211 W Lincoln Hwy .... Exton PA 19341 610-524-8886 524-7333
Web: singerspecs.net

Solar Bat Enterprises Inc
3628 E County Rd 600 N .... Brazil IN 47834 812-986-3551
Web: www.solarbat.com

SPY Inc 2070 Las Palmas Dr .... Carlsbad CA 92011 760-804-8420
Web: www.spyoptic.com

Sterling Optical 520 Eigth Ave 23rd Fl .... New York NY 10018 516-390-2117 390-2183
TF: 800-393-7789 ■ *Web:* www.sterlingoptical.com

Style Eyes Optics 824 W 18th St .... Costa Mesa CA 92627 949-548-5355
Web: www.styleeyes.com

SVS Vision 140 Macomb Pl .... Mount Clemens MI 48043 586-468-7612 468-7682
TF: 800-787-4600 ■ *Web:* www.svsvision.com

TearLab Corp 7360 Carroll Rd Ste 200 .... San Diego CA 92121 858-455-6006
Web: www.tearlab.com

Today's Vision 6970 FM 1960 W Ste A .... Houston TX 77069 281-469-2020 469-7531
Web: www.todaysvision.com

Tryiton Eyewear LLC 147 Post Rd E .... Westport CT 06880 203-544-0770
Web: www.eyeglasses.com

Union Eyecare Centers 4750 Beidler Rd .... Willoughby OH 44094 216-986-9700 986-1996
TF: 800-443-9699 ■ *Web:* www.unioneyecare.com

United Optical 2111 Van Deman St .... Baltimore MD 21224 888-267-8422
TF: 888-267-8422 ■ *Web:* www.united-optical.com

US Vision Inc
1 Harmon Dr Glen Oaks Industrial Pk .... Glendora NJ 08029 856-228-1000 228-3339
TF: 800-524-0789 ■ *Web:* www.usvision.com

Vision Care Associates
1120 E Washington St .... Grayslake IL 60030 847-223-2000
Web: www.visioncareclinic.com

VisionAid Inc 11 Kendrick Rd .... Wareham MA 02571 508-295-3300
Web: visionaidinc.com

Visionworks 854 Plaza Blvd .... Lancaster PA 17601 717-295-3111
Web: total-visioncare.com

Visionworks of America Inc
175 E Houston St .... San Antonio TX 78205 210-340-3531 524-6996
TF: 800-669-1183 ■ *Web:* www.visionworks.com

Vistar Eye Center Inc 707 S Jefferson St .... Roanoke VA 24016 540-855-5100
Web: www.vistareye.com

Vogue Optical Inc 20 Great George St .... Charlottetown PE C1A4J6 902-566-3326
Web: www.vogueoptical.com

Volk Optical Inc 7893 Enterprise Dr .... Mentor OH 44060 440-942-6161
Web: www.volk.com

Voorthuis Opticians Inc
3301 New Mexico Ave Nw Ste 119 .... Washington DC 20016 202-363-5087
Web: www.acebevdc.com

Vuzix Corp
2166 Brighton Henrietta Town Line Rd .... Rochester NY 14623 585-359-5900
Web: www.vuzix.com

Wiley X Inc 7800 Patterson Pass Rd .... Livermore CA 94550 925-243-9810
Web: www.wileyx.com

Phone Fax

Winchester Optical Company Inc 1935 Lake St .... Elmira NY 14901 607-734-4251
Web: www.winoptical.com

Wing Eyecare Inc 8740 Montgomery Rd Ste 1 .... Cincinnati OH 45236 513-791-2222
Web: www.wingeyecare.com

547 OPTICAL INSTRUMENTS & LENSES

SEE ALSO Laboratory Analytical Instruments p. 2617

Phone Fax

4D Technology Corp
3280 E Hemisphere Loop Ste 146 .... Tucson AZ 85706 520-294-5600
Web: www.4dtechnology.com

A C Tool Supply 5456 E Mcdowell Rd Ste 123 .... Mesa AZ 85215 480-968-6698
Web: www.aikencolon.com

Access Optics LLC 2001 N Willow Ave .... Broken Arrow OK 74012 918-294-1234
Web: www.accessoptics.com

Alcon Canada Inc 2665 Meadowpine Blvd .... Mississauga ON L5N8C7 905-826-6700
Web: www.alcon.ca

Allergan Inc 2525 Dupont Dr .... Irvine CA 92612 714-246-4500 246-6987*
NYSE: AGN ■ **Fax:* Mail Rm ■ *TF:* 800-347-4500 ■ *Web:* www.allergan.com

Altarum Institute 3520 Green Ct Ste 300 .... Ann Arbor MI 48105 734-302-4600
Web: www.altarum.org

American Polarizers Inc 141 S Seventh St .... Reading PA 19602 610-373-5177 373-2229
TF: 800-736-9031 ■ *Web:* www.apioptics.com

American Technology Network Corp
1341 San Mateo Ave .... South San Francisco CA 94080 650-875-0130
TF: 800-910-2862 ■ *Web:* www.atncorp.com

Applied Fiber Inc PO Box 1339 .... Leesburg GA 31763 229-759-8301 759-8333
TF: 800-226-5394 ■ *Web:* www.appliedfiber.com

Awareness Technology Inc PO Box 1679 .... Palm City FL 34991 772-283-6540 283-8020
Web: www.awaretech.com

B E Meyers & Co Inc 9461 Willows Rd NE .... Redmond WA 98052 425-881-6648 867-1759
TF: 800-327-5648 ■ *Web:* www.bemeyers.com

BAE Systems OASYS LLC 645 Harvey Rd Ste 9 .... Manchester NH 03103 603-232-8221
Web: hugedomains.com/domain_profile.cfm?d=oasystechnology&e=com

Beena Vision Systems Inc
600 Pinnacle Ct Ste 635 .... Norcross GA 30071 678-597-3156
Web: www.beenavision.com

Benz Research & Development Corp
6447 Parkland Dr .... Sarasota FL 34243 941-758-8256
Web: www.benzrd.com

Bond Optics LLC 76 Etna Rd PO Box 422 .... Lebanon NH 03766 603-448-2300 448-5489
Web: www.bondoptics.com

Bristol Instruments Inc
50 Victor Heights Pkwy .... Victor NY 14564 585-924-2620
Web: www.bristol-inst.com

Burris Company Inc 331 E Eigth St .... Greeley CO 80631 970-356-1670 356-8702
TF: 888-228-7747 ■ *Web:* www.burrisoptics.com

Bushnell Corp 9200 Cody St .... Overland Park KS 66214 913-752-3400 752-3550
TF: 800-423-3537 ■ *Web:* www.bushnell.com

Carl Zeiss Inc 1 Zeiss Dr .... Thornwood NY 10594 914-747-1800 681-7446
Web: corporate.zeiss.com

ChromaGen Vision LLC
326 W Cedar St Ste 1 .... Kennett Square PA 19348 855-473-2323
TF: 855-473-2323 ■ *Web:* www.ireadbetternow.com

Conoptics International Sales Corp
19 Eagle Rd .... Danbury CT 06810 203-743-3349 790-6145
TF: 800-748-3349 ■ *Web:* www.conoptics.com

CSC Laboratories Inc 180 Westgate Dr .... Watsonville CA 95076 831-763-6931
Web: www.csclabs.com

CST/Berger Corp 255 W Fleming St .... Watseka IL 60970 815-432-5237 913-0049*
**Fax Area Code:* 800 ■ *TF:* 800-435-1859 ■ *Web:* www.cstberger.us

Deltronic Corp 3900 W Segerstrom Ave .... Santa Ana CA 92704 714-545-5800 545-9548
TF: 800-451-6922 ■ *Web:* www.deltronic.com

Deltronic Crystal Industries Inc
64 Harding Ave .... Dover NJ 07801 973-328-7000
Web: www.deltroniccrystal.com

Direct Optical Research Co 8725 115th Ave .... Largo FL 33773 727-319-9000
Web: www.dorc.com

Directed Energy Solutions (DES)
890 Elkton Dr Ste 101 .... Colorado Springs CO 80907 719-593-7848 593-7846
Web: www.denergysolutions.com

Edmund Optics Inc 101 E Gloucester Pk .... Barrington NJ 08007 856-547-3488 573-6295
TF: 800-363-1992 ■ *Web:* edmundoptics.com

Elcan Optical Technologies 450 Leitz Rd .... Midland ON L4R5B8 705-526-5401
Web: www.elcan.com

Electro-optical Imaging Inc
4300 Fortune Pl Ste C .... West Melbourne FL 32904 321-435-8722
Web: www.eoimaging.com

Epilog Corp 16371 Table Mtn Pkwy .... Golden CO 80403 303-277-1188
Web: www.epiloglaser.com

Eschenbach Optik of America Inc
904 Ethan Allen Hwy .... Ridgefield CT 06877 203-438-7471
Web: www.eschenbach.com

Fosta-Tek Optics Inc 320 Hamilton St .... Leominster MA 01453 978-534-6511 537-2168
TF: 866-221-9157 ■ *Web:* www.fosta-tek.com

Fraser-Volpe Corp
Warminster Industrial Pk 1025 Thomas Dr .... Warminster PA 18974 215-675-5062

G-S Supplies 408 St Paul St .... Rochester NY 14605 585-295-0250 232-3866
TF: 800-295-3050 ■ *Web:* www.gssupplies.com

General Scientific Corp
1201 M St SE Ste 120 .... Washington DC 20003 202-547-4299 547-7550
Web: www.genscicorp.com

Gooch & Housego (Ohio) LLC 676 Alpha Dr .... Cleveland OH 44143 216-486-6100
Web: www.goochandhousego.com

Gould Technology LLC
1121 Benfield Blvd Stes J-P .... Millersville MD 21108 410-987-5600
Web: www.gouldfo.com

Hamilton Associates Inc
11403 Cronridge Dr .... Owings Mills MD 21117 410-363-9696
Web: www.atitest.com

				Phone	Fax
Hitachi High Technologies America Inc					
10 N Martingale Rd Ste 500	Schaumburg	IL	60173	847-273-4141	273-4407
Web: www.hitachi-hta.com					
II-VI Inc 375 Saxonburg Blvd	Saxonburg	PA	16056	724-352-4455	360-5848
NASDAQ: IIVI ■ *Web:* www.ii-vi.com					
Intevac Inc 3560 Bassett St	Santa Clara	CA	95054	408-986-9888	
NASDAQ: IVAC ■ *Web:* www.intevac.com					
ISP Optics Corp 50 S Buckhout St	Irvington	NY	10533	914-591-3070	
Web: www.ispoptics.com					
ITT Night Vision & Imaging					
7635 Plantation Rd	Roanoke	VA	24019	540-563-0371	362-4979
TF: 800-448-8678 ■ *Web:* www.nightvision.com					
Janos Technology LLC 55 Black Brook Rd	Keene	NH	03431	603-757-0070	365-4596*
**Fax Area Code:* 802 ■ *Web:* www.janostech.com					
JML Optical Industries Inc 820 Linden Ave	Rochester	NY	14625	585-248-8900	248-8924
Web: www.jmloptical.com					
Karl Storz Imaging Inc 175 Cremona Dr	Goleta	CA	93117	805-968-3568	
Web: www.optronics.com					
Kollmorgen Corp Electro-Optical Div					
50 Prince St	NorthHampton	MA	01060	413-586-2330	586-1324*
**Fax:* Sales ■ *TF:* 877-282-1168 ■ *Web:* www2.l-3com.com					
LaCroix Optical Company Inc 50 LaCroix Dr	Batesville	AR	72501	870-698-1881	
Web: www.lacroixoptical.com					
LaserMax Corp 3495 Winton Pl Bldg B	Rochester	NY	14623	585-272-5420	
Web: www.lasermax.com					
Latham & Phillips Ophthalmic Products Inc					
2300 Southwest Blvd	Grove City	OH	43123	614-871-6200	
Web: lpoproducts.com					
Leica Camera Inc One Pearl Ct Ste A	Allendale	NJ	07401	201-995-0051	
Web: www.leica-camera.com					
Lenstec Inc 1765 Commerce Ave N	St. Petersburg	FL	33716	727-571-2272	
Web: www.lenstec.com					
Lighthouse Imaging Corp 477 Congress St	Portland	ME	04101	207-253-5350	
Web: www.lighthouseoptics.com					
LightPath Technologies Inc					
2603 Challenger Tech Ct Ste 100	Orlando	FL	32826	407-382-4003	382-4007
NASDAQ: LPTH ■ *Web:* lightpath.com/					
Lincoln Laser Co 234 E Mohave St	Phoenix	AZ	85004	602-257-0407	257-0728
Web: www.lincolnlaser.com					
Luxury Optical Holdings Inc					
2651 N Crimson Canyon Dr Ste 200	Las Vegas	NV	89128	702-798-8638	
Web: www.loholdings.com					
Lyric Optical Company Wholsle					
3533 Cardiff Ave Ste 1	Cincinnati	OH	45209	513-321-2456	
Web: www.superoptical.com					
Meade Instruments Corp 27 Hubble	Irvine	CA	92618	949-451-1450	451-1460
NASDAQ: MEAD ■ *TF:* 800-626-3233 ■ *Web:* www.meade.com					
Microvision Inc 6222 185th Ave NE	Redmond	WA	98052	425-936-6847	882-6600
NASDAQ: MVIS ■ *TF:* 888-822-6847 ■ *Web:* www.microvision.com					
Mirrotek International LLC 90 Dayton Ave	Passaic	NJ	07055	973-472-1400	
TF: 888-659-3030 ■ *Web:* www.mirrotek.com					
MyEyeDr Inc 401 Maple Ave W	Vienna	VA	22180	703-938-5544	
Web: www.myeyedr.com					
MZA Associates Corp					
2021 Girard Blvd SE Ste 150	Albuquerque	NM	87106	505-245-9970	
Web: www.mza.com					
Neoptix Inc 1415 Frank-Carrel Ste 220	Quebec City	QC	G1N4N7	418-687-2500	
Web: www.neoptix.com					
Newport Corp 1791 Deere Ave	Irvine	CA	92606	949-863-3144	253-1680*
NASDAQ: NEWP ■ **Fax:* Sales ■ *TF Sales:* 800-222-6440 ■ *Web:* www.newport.com					
Nightforce Optics 336 Hazen Ln	Orofino	ID	83544	208-476-9814	
Web: www.nightforceoptics.com					
Obzerv Technologies Inc					
400 Jean-Lesage Ste 201	Quebec	QC	G1K8W1	418-524-3522	524-6745
Web: www.obzerv.com					
Ocean Optics Inc 830 Douglas Ave	Dunedin	FL	34698	727-733-2447	733-3962
Web: www.oceanoptics.com					
Opotek Inc 2233 Faraday Ave Ste E	Carlsbad	CA	92008	760-929-0770	
Web: www.opotek.com					
OPT-Sciences Corp 1912 Bannard St	Cinnaminson	NJ	08077	856-829-2800	
Web: www.optsciences.com					
Optek Systems Inc 12 Pilgrim Rd	Greenville	SC	29607	864-272-2640	
Web: www.opteksystems.com					
Optical Gaging Products Inc 850 Hudson Ave	Rochester	NY	14621	585-544-0450	544-4998
TF: 800-647-4243 ■ *Web:* www.ogpnet.com					
Optim LLC 64 Technology Park Rd	Sturbridge	MA	01566	508-347-5100	
Web: www.optimnet.com					
Optometrics Corp					
Eight Nemco Way Stony Brook Industrial Pk	Ayer	MA	01432	978-772-1700	
Web: www.optometrics.com					
Parker Hannifin Corp Daedal Div					
1140 Sandy Hill Rd	Irwin	PA	15642	724-861-8200	861-3300
TF: 800-245-6903 ■ *Web:* parker.com					
PerkinElmer Inc 940 Winter St	Waltham	MA	02451	203-925-4602	944-4904
NYSE: PKI ■ *Web:* www.perkinelmer.com					
Photon Technology International Inc					
300 Birmingham Rd PO Box 272	Birmingham	NJ	08011	609-894-4420	
Web: www.pti-nj.com					
ProPhotonix Inc 32 Hampshire Rd	Salem	NH	03079	603-893-8778	575-2420*
OTC: STKR ■ **Fax Area Code:* 781 ■ *TF:* 877-941-8631 ■ *Web:* www.prophotonix.com					
Quality Vision International Inc					
850 Hudson Ave	Rochester	NY	14621	585-544-0450	
Web: www.qvii.com					
Rancocas Nature Ctr 794 Rancocas Rd	Westampton	NJ	08060	609-261-2495	
Web: www.njaudubon.org					
Raytheon Canada Ltd 360 Albert St Ste 1640	Ottawa	ON	K1R7X7	613-233-4121	233-1099
Web: www.raytheon.ca					
Raytheon Network Centric Systems (NCS)					
2501 W University Dr	McKinney	TX	75071	781-522-3000	
Web: www.raytheon.com					
Reflex Photonics Inc					
1250 Oakmead Pkwy Ste 210	Sunnyvale	CA	94085	408-501-8886	
Web: www.reflexphotonics.com					
Reichert Inc 3362 Walden Ave	Depew	NY	14043	716-686-4500	
Web: www.reichert.com					
Research Electro-optics Inc					
5505 Airport Blvd	Boulder	CO	80301	303-938-1960	245-4396
Web: www.reoinc.com					
Research Frontiers Inc					
240 Crossways Park Dr	Woodbury	NY	11797	516-364-1902	
Web: www.smartglass.com					
Ross Optical Industries Inc					
1410 Gail Borden Pl	El Paso	TX	79935	915-595-5417	595-5466
TF: 800-880-5417 ■ *Web:* www.rossoptical.com					
RPC Photonics Inc 330 Clay Rd	Rochester	NY	14623	585-272-2840	
Web: www.rpcphotonics.com					
Schott North America Inc 555 Taxter Rd	Elmsford	NY	10523	914-831-2200	831-2201
TF: 877-261-2100 ■ *Web:* www.us.schott.com					
Science & Engineering Services (SESI)					
6992 Columbia Gateway Dr	Columbia	MD	21046	443-539-0139	539-1757
Web: www.sesi-md.com					
Seiko Optical Products of America Inc					
575 Corporate Dr	Mahwah	NJ	07430	201-529-9099	
Web: www.seikoeyewear.com					
Seiler Instrument & Mfg Company Inc					
3433 Tree Court Industrial Blvd	Saint Louis	MO	63122	314-968-2282	968-2637
TF: 800-489-2282 ■ *Web:* www.seilerinst.com					
Sellmark Corp 2201 Heritage Pkwy	Mansfield	TX	76063	817-225-0310	
Web: www.sellmark.net					
Servo Corp of America 123 Frost St	Westbury	NY	11590	516-938-9700	938-9644
Web: www.servo.com					
SheerVision Inc(NDA)					
4030 Palos Verdes Dr N Ste 104	Rolling Hills Estates	CA	90274	310-265-8918	
Web: www.sheervision.com					
Sorenson Media Inc 13961 Minuteman Dr Ste 100	Draper	UT	84020	801-501-8650	
TF: 888-767-3676 ■ *Web:* www.sorensonmedia.com					
Stevens Water Monitoring Systems					
12067 NE Glenn Widing Dr Ste 106	Portland	OR	97220	503-469-8000	469-8100
TF: 800-452-5272 ■ *Web:* www.stevenswater.com					
Suzo-Happ Group Inc 1743 Linneman Rd	Mount Prospect	IL	60056	847-593-6130	
Web: www.suzohapp.com					
Synergy International Optronics LLC					
101 Comac St	Ronkonkoma	NY	11779	631-277-0500	
Web: www.siollc.com					
Unilens Corp USA 10431 72td St N	Largo	FL	33777	727-544-2531	
Web: www.unilens.com					
Vectronix Inc					
19775 Belmont Executive Plz Ste 550	Ashburn	VA	20147	703-777-3900	
Web: www.vectronix.us					
Veeco Instruments Inc One Terminal Dr	Plainview	NY	11803	516-677-0200	714-1200
NASDAQ: VECO ■ *TF:* 888-248-3326 ■ *Web:* www.veeco.com					
Voxis Inc					
1160 Brickyard Cove Rd Ste 202	Point Richmond	CA	94801	510-232-8333	
Western Ophthalmics Corp					
19019 36th Ave W Ste G	Lynnwood	WA	98036	425-672-9332	423-4284*
**Fax Area Code:* 800 ■ *TF:* 800-426-9938 ■ *Web:* www.west-op.com					
Xenonics Holdings Inc 3186 Lionshead Ave	Carlsbad	CA	92010	760-477-8900	477-8897
OTC: XNNH ■ *Web:* www.xenonics.com					
Zygo Corp Laurel Brook Rd	Middlefield	CT	06455	860-347-8506	347-3968
NASDAQ: ZIGO ■ *TF:* 800-994-6669 ■ *Web:* www.zygo.com					

548 ORGAN & TISSUE BANKS

SEE ALSO Eye Banks p. 2280

				Phone	Fax
Alamo Tissue Service Ltd					
5844 Rocky Point Dr Ste 167	San Antonio	TX	78249	210-738-2663	732-4263
TF: 800-226-9091 ■ *Web:* www.alamotissueservice.com					
AlloSource 6278 S Troy Cir	Centennial	CO	80111	720-873-0213	873-0212
TF: 888-873-8330 ■ *Web:* www.allosource.org					
Bio-Tissue 7000 SW 97th Ave Ste 211	Miami	FL	33173	305-412-4430	412-4429
TF: 888-296-8858 ■ *Web:* www.biotissue.com					
Blood & Tissue Ctr of Central Texas					
4300 N Lamar Blvd	Austin	TX	78756	512-206-1266	458-3859
Web: www.bloodandtissue.org					
Bone Bank Allografts 4808 Research Dr	San Antonio	TX	78240	210-696-7616	696-7609
TF Sales: 800-397-0088 ■ *Web:* www.bonebank.com					
California Cryobank Inc					
11915 La Grange Ave	Los Angeles	CA	90025	310-443-5244	826-1605
TF: 866-927-9622 ■ *Web:* www.cryobank.com					
Community Tissue Services					
3573 Bristol Pike Ste 201	Bensalem	PA	19020	215-245-4506	
TF: 800-684-7783 ■ *Web:* www.communitytissue.org					
Comprehensive Tissue Ctr					
11402 University Ave Rm 7415	Edmonton	AB	T6G2J3	780-407-7510	407-7509
TF: 866-407-1970 ■ *Web:* albertahealthservices.ca/pagenotfound.htm					
Cryobiology Inc 4830D Knightsbridge Blvd	Columbus	OH	43214	614-451-4375	451-5284
TF: 800-359-4375 ■ *Web:* www.cryobio.com					
Cryogenic Laboratories Inc					
1944 Lexington Ave N	Roseville	MN	55113	651-489-8000	489-8989
TF: 800-466-2796 ■ *Web:* www.cryolab.com					
Donor Alliance Inc					
720 S Colorado Blvd Ste 800-N	Denver	CO	80246	303-329-4747	321-1183
TF: 888-868-4747 ■ *Web:* www.donoralliance.org					
Donor Awareness Coalition					
5323 Harry Hines Blvd MC 9074	Dallas	TX	75390	214-648-2609	648-2086
Donor Network West 1000 Broadway Ste 600	Oakland	CA	94607	510-444-8500	444-8501
Web: www.donornetworkwest.org					
Gift of Hope Organ & Tissue Donor Network					
425 Spring Lake Dr	Itasca	IL	60143	630-758-2600	
TF: 877-577-3747 ■ *Web:* www.giftofhope.org					
Gift of Life Donor Program					
401 N Third St	Philadelphia	PA	19123	215-557-8090	
TF: 800-543-6391 ■ *Web:* www.donors1.org					

Phone | Fax

Idant Laboratories 350 Fifth Ave Ste 7120 . . . . New York NY 10118 212-330-8500 330-8536
Web: www.idant.com

INDIANA DONOR NETWORK 3760 Guion Rd . . . . Indianapolis IN 46222 317-685-0389
TF: 888-275-4676 ■ *Web:* www.iopo.org

Kentucky Organ Donor Affiliates (KODA)
106 E Broadway . . . . Louisville KY 40202 502-581-9511 589-5157
TF: 800-525-3456 ■ *Web:* www.kyorgandonor.org

LifeBanc 4775 Richmond Rd Ste 350 . . . . Cleveland OH 44128 216-752-5433 751-4204
TF: 888-558-5433 ■ *Web:* www.lifebanc.org

LifeCell Corp One Millennium Way . . . . Branchburg NJ 08876 800-226-2714 947-1089*
**Fax Area Code:* 908 ■ *TF:* 800-226-2714 ■ *Web:* www.lifecell.com

Lifeline of Ohio 770 Kinnear Rd Ste 200 . . . . Columbus OH 43212 614-291-5667 291-0660
TF: 800-525-5667 ■ *Web:* www.lifelineofohio.org

LifeLink Tissue Bank 8510 Sunstate St . . . . Tampa FL 33634 813-886-8111 888-9419
TF: 800-683-2400 ■ *Web:* lifelinktb.org

LifeNet 1864 Concert Dr . . . . Virginia Beach VA 23453 757-464-4761 301-6582
TF: 800-847-7831 ■ *Web:* www.lifenethealth.org

LifeNet Health Northwest 501 SW 39th St . . . . Renton WA 98057 800-858-2282
TF: 800-858-2282 ■ *Web:* www.lnhnw.org

LifeShare Transplant Donor Services of Oklahoma
4705 NW Expy . . . . Oklahoma City OK 73132 405-840-5551 840-9748
TF: 888-580-5680 ■ *Web:* www.lifeshareoklahoma.org

Lifesharing Community Organ & Tissue Donation
3465 Camino del Rio S Ste 410 . . . . San Diego CA 92108 619-521-1983 521-2833
Web: www.lifesharing.org

Louisiana Organ Procurement Agency (LOPA)
3545 N I-10 Service Rd Ste 300 . . . . Metairie LA 70002 800-521-4483 837-3587*
**Fax Area Code:* 504 ■ *TF:* 800-521-4483 ■ *Web:* www.lopa.org

Mid-America Transplant Services (MTS)
1110 Highlands Plz Dr E Ste 100 . . . . Saint Louis MO 63110 314-735-8200
TF: 888-376-4854 ■ *Web:* www.mts-stl.org

Musculoskeletal Transplant Foundation
125 May St Ste 300 . . . . Edison NJ 08837 732-661-0202 661-2298
TF: 800-946-9008 ■ *Web:* www.mtf.org

Nevada Donor Network Inc 2061 E Sahara Ave . . . . Las Vegas NV 89104 702-796-9600 796-4225
TF: 855-683-6667 ■ *Web:* www.nvdonor.org

New England Organ Bank 60 First Ave . . . . Waltham MA 02451 617-244-8000 244-8755
TF: 800-446-6362 ■ *Web:* www.neob.org

New York Cryo 900 Northern Blvd Ste 230 . . . . Great Neck NY 11021 516-487-2700 487-2007
Web: www.newyorkcryo.com

OneLegacy Transplant Donor Network
221 S Figueroa St Ste 500 . . . . Los Angeles CA 90012 213-229-5600 229-5601
TF: 800-786-4077 ■ *Web:* www.onelegacy.org

Regional Tissue Bank QEII Health Sciences Centre
5788 University Ave Rm 431 MacKenzie Bldg . . . . Halifax NS B3H1V7 902-473-4171 473-2170
TF: 800-314-6515 ■ *Web:* www.cdha.nshealth.ca/regional-tissue-bank

Rocky Mountain Tissue Bank
2993 S Peoria St Ste 390 . . . . Aurora CO 80014 303-337-3330 337-9383
TF: 800-424-5169 ■ *Web:* www.rmtb.org

ScienceCare Inc 21410 N 19th Ave Ste 126 . . . . Phoenix AZ 85027 602-331-3641 331-4344
TF: 800-417-3747 ■ *Web:* www.sciencecare.com

Sierra Donor Services
1760 Creekside Oak Dr Ste 200 . . . . Sacramento CA 95833 916-567-1600
TF: 877-401-2546 ■ *Web:* sierradonor.org

South Texas Blood & Tissue Ctr
6211 IH-10 W . . . . San Antonio TX 78201 210-731-5555 731-5501
TF: 800-292-5534 ■ *Web:* southtexasblood.org

Southeast Tissue Alliance (SETA)
6241 NW 23rd St Ste 400 . . . . Gainesville FL 32653 352-248-2114 384-9323
TF: 866-432-1164 ■ *Web:* www.donorcare.org

Tennessee/DCI Donor Services 1600 Hayes St . . . . Nashville TN 37203 615-234-5251 234-5270
Web: www.donatelifetn.org

Wright Medical Technology Inc
5677 Airline Rd . . . . Arlington TN 38002 901-867-9971 867-9534*
**Fax:* Cust Svc ■ *TF:* 800-238-7188 ■ *Web:* www.wmt.com

549 PACKAGE DELIVERY SERVICES

Phone | Fax

Air T Inc 3524 Airport Rd . . . . Maiden NC 28650 828-464-8741 465-5281
NASDAQ: AIRT ■ *Web:* www.airt.net/mac

AirNet Systems Inc 7250 Star Check Dr . . . . Columbus OH 43217 614-409-4900
Web: www.airnet.com

Careful Courier Service Inc
2444 Old Middlefield Way . . . . Mountain View CA 94043 650-903-9393
Web: www.carefulcourier.com

Columbia Fruit Packers Inc
2575 Euclid Ave PO Box 920 . . . . Wenatchee WA 98801 509-662-7153 662-0933
Web: www.columbiafruit.com

Crosscountry Courier Inc PO Box 4030 . . . . Bismarck ND 58502 701-222-8498 223-5963
TF: 800-521-0287 ■ *Web:* www.crosscountrycourier.com

CS Logistics Inc 11001 W Mitchell St . . . . Milwaukee WI 53214 414-774-6322
Web: cslog.com

DHL Global Mail 2700 S Commerce Pkwy Ste 400 . . . . Weston FL 33331 954-903-6300
TF: 800-805-9306 ■ *Web:* us.dhlglobalmail.com

Dynamex Inc 5429 LBJ Fwy Ste 1000 . . . . Dallas TX 75240 214-560-9000 560-9349
TF Cust Svc: 888-478-1660 ■ *Web:* www.dynamex.com

Federal Express Europe Inc
3610 Hacks Cross Rd . . . . Memphis TN 38125 901-369-3600
TF: 800-463-3339 ■ *Web:* www.fedex.com

FedEx Custom Critical Inc 1475 Boettler Rd . . . . Uniontown OH 44685 234-310-4090
TF Cust Svc: 800-463-3339 ■ *Web:* www.customcritical.fedex.com

Financial Courier Service Inc
6099 Mt Moriah Ext Ste 13 . . . . Memphis TN 38115 901-761-4555 366-6165

Hot Shot Delivery Inc
747 N Shepherd Dr Ste 100 PO Box 701189 . . . . Houston TX 77007 713-869-5525 862-6354
TF: 866-261-3184 ■ *Web:* www.hotshot-delivery.com

Howard Ternes Packaging Co 12285 Dixie . . . . Redford MI 48239 313-531-5867 531-5868
Web: www.ternespackaging.com

Mass Bay Commuter Railroad Co 89 S St . . . . Boston MA 02111 617-222-8001

Phone | Fax

National Delivery Systems Inc
8700 Robert Fulton Dr . . . . Columbia MD 21046 410-312-4770
Web: www.national-delivery.com

Network Global Logistics (NGL)
320 Interlocken Pkwy Ste 100 . . . . Broomfield CO 80021 866-938-1870
TF: 866-938-1870 ■ *Web:* www.nglog.com

Newgistics Inc 2700 Via Fortuna Ste 300 . . . . Austin TX 78746 512-225-6000 225-6001
Web: newgistics.com

One Source Industries LLC 185 Technology Dr . . . . Irvine CA 92618 800-899-4990
TF: 800-899-4990 ■ *Web:* www.osicreative.com

Priority Express Courier Five Chelsea Pkwy . . . . Boothwyn PA 19061 610-364-3300 364-3310
TF: 800-526-4646 ■ *Web:* www.priorityexpress.com

Purolator Inc 5995 Avebury Rd . . . . Mississauga ON L5R3T8 905-712-8101
TF: 888-744-7123 ■ *Web:* www.purolator.com

Titan Trucks 306 Austin St . . . . Levelland TX 79336 806-894-4852 894-1365
Web: www.titanco.com

TNT USA Inc 68 S Service Rd . . . . Melville NY 11747 631-712-6700
Web: tnt.com

Tricor America Inc
717 Airport Blvd . . . . South San Francisco CA 94080 650-877-3650 583-3197
TF: 800-669-7874 ■ *Web:* www.tricor.com

Tyburn Railroad LLC 505 S Broad St . . . . Kennett Square PA 19348 610-925-0131
Web: www.tyburnrr.com

Unishippers Assn Inc
746 E Winchester Ste 200 . . . . Salt Lake City UT 84107 800-999-8721 487-7468*
**Fax Area Code:* 801 ■ *TF:* 800-999-8721 ■ *Web:* www.unishippers.com

United Parcel Service Inc (UPS)
55 Glenlake Pkwy NE . . . . Atlanta GA 30328 404-828-6000 828-6440
NYSE: UPS ■ *TF Cust Svc:* 800-742-5877 ■ *Web:* www.ups.com

United Shipping Solutions
6985 Union Pk Ctr Ste 565 . . . . Midvale UT 84047 801-352-0012 352-0339
Web: www.usshipit.com

Universal Express Inc 5295 Town Ctr Rd . . . . Boca Raton FL 33486 561-367-6177 367-6124
Web: www.usxp.com

Washington Express Service LLC
12240 Indian Creek Ct Ste 100 . . . . Beltsville MD 20705 301-210-0899 419-7075
TF: 800-939-5463 ■ *Web:* www.washingtonexpress.net

World Courier Inc 1313 Fourth Ave . . . . New Hyde Park NY 11040 516-354-2600 354-2637*
**Fax:* Cust Svc ■ *TF:* 800-221-6600 ■ *Web:* www.worldcourier.com

Worldwide Express 2828 Routh St Ste 400 . . . . Dallas TX 75201 214-720-2400 720-2446
TF: 800-758-7447 ■ *Web:* www.wwex.com

WPX Delivery Solutions
3320 W Valley Hwy N Ste 111 . . . . Auburn WA 98001 253-876-2760 876-2799
TF: 800-562-1091 ■ *Web:* www.wpx.com

Yamato Transport USA Inc 80 Seaview Dr . . . . Secaucus NJ 07094 201-583-9706 583-9703
Web: www.yamatoamerica.com

550 PACKAGING MACHINERY & EQUIPMENT

Phone | Fax

A-B-C Packaging Machine Corp
811 Live Oak St . . . . Tarpon Springs FL 34689 727-937-5144 938-1239
TF: 800-237-5975 ■ *Web:* www.abcpackaging.com

Accuplace 1800 Nw 69th Ave Ste 102 . . . . Plantation FL 33313 954-791-1500
Web: www.accuplace.com

Acraloc Corp 113 Flint Rd PO Box 4129 . . . . Oak Ridge TN 37830 865-483-1368 483-3500
Web: www.acraloc.com

ALine Systems Corp 13844 Struikman Rd . . . . Cerritos CA 90703 562-229-9727
Web: www.alinesys.com

AMS Filling Systems
2500 Chestnut Tree Rd . . . . Honey Brook PA 19344 610-942-4200
Web: www.amsfilling.com

ARPAC Group 9511 W River St . . . . Schiller Park IL 60176 847-678-9034 671-7006
TF: 800-496-7210 ■ *Web:* www.arpac.com

Automated Packaging Systems Inc
10175 Phillip Pkwy . . . . Streetsboro OH 44241 330-528-2000 342-2400
TF Sales: 800-527-0733 ■ *Web:* www.autobag.com

B & H Manufacturing Co 3461 Roeding Rd . . . . Ceres CA 95307 209-556-6160 537-6854
TF: 888-643-0444 ■ *Web:* www.bhlabeling.com

Barry-Wehmiller Cos Inc
8020 Forsyth Blvd . . . . Saint Louis MO 63105 314-862-8000 862-2744*
**Fax:* Sales ■ *TF:* 800-862-8020 ■ *Web:* www.barry-wehmiller.com

Barry-Wehmiller Cos Inc Accraply Div
3580 Holly Ln N . . . . Plymouth MN 55447 763-557-1313 519-9656
TF: 800-328-3997 ■ *Web:* www.accraply.com

Belco Packaging Systems Inc
910 S Mountain Ave . . . . Monrovia CA 91016 626-357-9566 359-3440
TF: 800-833-1833 ■ *Web:* www.belcopackaging.com

Bell-Mark Corp 331 Changebridge Rd . . . . Pine Brook NJ 07058 973-882-0202 808-4616
Web: www.bell-mark.com

Brenton LLC 4750 County Rd 13 NE . . . . Alexandria MN 56308 320-852-7705 852-7621
TF: 800-535-2730 ■ *Web:* www.brentonengineering.com

Butler Automatic Inc 41 Leona Dr . . . . Middleboro MA 02346 508-923-0544 923-0886
TF Cust Svc: 800-544-0070 ■ *Web:* www.butlerautomatic.com

Campbell Wrapper Corp 1415 Fortune Ave . . . . De Pere WI 54115 920-983-7100 983-7300*
**Fax:* Sales ■ *TF:* 800-727-4210 ■ *Web:* www.campbellwrapper.com

Corrugated Gear & Services Inc
100 Anderson Rd . . . . Alpharetta GA 30004 770-475-8929 442-3371
Web: www.corrugatedgear.com

Data Technology Inc 14225 Dayton Cir Ste 4 . . . . Omaha NE 68137 402-891-0711
TF General: 888-334-9300 ■ *Web:* drtinc.com

Delkor Systems Inc 8700 Rendova St NE . . . . Circle Pines MN 55014 763-783-0855 783-0875
TF: 800-328-5558 ■ *Web:* www.delkorsystems.com

Dynaric Inc 5740 Bayside Rd . . . . Virginia Beach VA 23455 800-526-0827
TF: 800-526-0827 ■ *Web:* www.dynaric.com

E-pak Machinery Inc 1535 S State Rd 39 . . . . La Porte IN 46350 219-393-5541 324-2884
TF: 800-328-0466 ■ *Web:* www.epakmachinery.com

EDL Packaging Systems 1260 Parkview Rd . . . . Green Bay WI 54304 920-336-7744
Web: www.edlpackaging.com

				Phone	Fax
Elliott Mfg Company Inc 2664 Cherry Ave PO Box 11277	Fresno	CA	93772	559-233-6235	233-6235
Web: www.elliott-mfg.com					
Elmar Worldwide Inc 200 Gould Ave PO Box 245	Depew	NY	14043	716-681-5650	681-5650
TF Cust Svc: 800-443-5468 ■ *Web:* www.elmarworldwide.com					
Exact Packaging Inc 1145 E Wellspring Rd	New Freedom	PA	17349	717-235-8345	
Web: www.epilabelers.com					
Fischbein Co 151 Walker Rd	Statesville	NC	28625	704-871-1159	872-3303
Web: www.fischbein.com					
Flexicon Corp 2400 Emrick Blvd	Bethlehem	PA	18020	610-814-2400	814-0600
TF: 888-353-9426 ■ *Web:* www.flexicon.com					
Fowler Products Co 150 Collins Industrial Blvd	Athens	GA	30601	706-549-3300	548-1278
Web: www.fowlerproducts.com					
Fox IV Technologies 6011 Enterprise Dr	Export	PA	15632	724-387-3500	
Web: www.foxiv.com					
Gottscho Printing Systems Inc 740 Veterans Cir	Warminster	PA	18974	267-387-3005	387-3015
Web: www.gottscho.com					
Hartness International Inc 1200 Garlington Rd PO Box 26509	Greenville	SC	29616	864-297-1200	288-5390
TF: 800-845-8791 ■ *Web:* www.hartness.com					
Heat Seal LLC 4580 E 71st St	Cleveland	OH	44125	216-341-2022	341-2163
TF: 800-342-6329 ■ *Web:* www.heatsealco.com					
Heisler Industries Inc 224 Passaic Ave	Fairfield	NJ	07004	973-227-6300	227-7627
Web: www.heislerind.com					
Hibar Systems Ltd 35 Pollard St	Richmond Hill	ON	L4B1A8	905-731-2400	731-6035
Web: www.hibar.com					
John R Nalbach Engineering Co 621 E Plainfield Rd	Countryside	IL	60525	708-579-9100	579-0122
Web: www.nalbach.com					
Kirk Rudy Inc 125 Lorraine Pkwy	Woodstock	GA	30188	770-427-4203	427-4036
TF: 800-897-1910 ■ *Web:* www.kirkrudy.com					
Kliklok-Woodman USA 5224 Snapfinger Woods Dr	Decatur	GA	30035	770-981-5200	987-7160
Web: www.kliklok.com					
Klikwood Corp 5224 Snapfinger Woods Dr	Decatur	GA	30035	770-981-5200	
Web: www.klikwood.com					
Kortec Inc 428 Newburyport Tpke	Rowley	MA	01969	978-238-7100	238-7171
Web: www.kortec.com					
Krones Inc 9600 S 58th St PO Box 321801	Franklin	WI	53132	414-409-4000	409-4100*
**Fax:* Cust Svc ■ *TF:* 800-752-3787 ■ *Web:* www.krones.com					
Label-Aire Inc 550 Burning Tree Rd	Fullerton	CA	92833	714-449-5155	526-0300
Web: www.label-aire.com					
Lantech Inc 11000 Bluegrass Pkwy	Louisville	KY	40299	502-815-9109	266-5031
TF: 800-866-0322 ■ *Web:* www.lantech.com					
Liquid Packaging Solutions 3999 E Hupp Rd Bldg R43	La Porte	IN	46350	219-393-3600	
Web: www.liquidpackagingsolution.com					
Loveshaw Corp 2206 Easton Tpke	South Canaan	PA	18459	570-937-4921	
TF Cust Svc: 800-747-1586 ■ *Web:* www.loveshaw.com					
Metro Machine & Engineering Corp 8001 Wallace Rd	Eden Prairie	MN	55344	952-937-2800	937-2374
Web: www.metromachine.com					
Mid-States Packaging Inc 12163 State Rte 274	Lewistown	OH	43333	937-843-3243	843-4378
Web: www.midstatespackaging.com					
Mooney General Paper Co 1451 Chestnut Ave PO Box 3800	Hillside	NJ	07205	973-926-3800	926-0425
TF: 800-882-8846 ■ *Web:* www.mooneygeneral.com					
MTS Medication Technologies Inc 2003 Gandy Blvd N	Saint Petersburg	FL	33702	800-845-0053	
TF General: 800-845-0053 ■ *Web:* www.mts-mt.com					
Muller Martini Mailroom Systems Inc 40 Rabro Dr	Hauppauge	NY	11788	631-582-4343	348-1961
TF: 800-331-5674 ■ *Web:* www.mullermartini.com/ms					
National Instrument LLC 4119 Fordleigh Rd	Baltimore	MD	21215	410-764-0900	764-7719
TF: 866-258-1914 ■ *Web:* www.filamatic.com					
New England Machinery Inc 2820 62nd Ave E	Bradenton	FL	34203	941-755-5550	751-6281
Web: www.neminc.com					
New Jersey Machine Inc 56 Etna Rd	Lebanon	NH	03766	603-448-0300	448-4810
TF Sales: 800-432-2990 ■ *Web:* www.njmpackaging.com					
New Way Packaging Machinery Inc 210 Bettner Ave	Hanover	PA	17331	717-637-2133	
TF: 844-801-3711					
Omega Design Corp 211 Philips Rd	Exton	PA	19341	610-363-6555	
Web: www.omegadesign.com					
Ossid Corp PO Drawer 1968 4000 College Rd	Rocky Mount	NC	27802	252-446-6177	442-7694
TF: 800-334-8369 ■ *Web:* www.ossid.com					
Package Machinery Co 380 Union St Ste 58	West Springfield	MA	01089	413-732-4000	732-1163
Web: www.packagemachinery.com					
Packaging Systems International Inc 4990 Acoma St	Denver	CO	80216	303-296-4445	298-1016
TF: 800-525-6110 ■ *Web:* www.pkgsys.com					
Pearson Packaging Systems 8120 W Sunset Hwy	Spokane	WA	99224	509-838-6226	747-8532
TF: 800-732-7766 ■ *Web:* www.pearsonpkg.com					
PMC Industries 275 Hudson St	Hackensack	NJ	07601	201-342-3684	342-3568
Web: www.pmc-industries.com					
PMI Cartoning Inc 850 Pratt Blvd	Elk Grove Village	IL	60007	847-437-1427	
Web: www.pmicartoning.com					
Pneumatic Scale Angelus 4485 Allen Rd	Stow	OH	44224	330-247-1800	928-7077
Web: www.psangelus.com					
Prodo-Pak Corp 77 Commerce St	Garfield	NJ	07026	973-777-7770	772-0471
Web: www.prodo-pak.com					
Qed Systems Inc 4646 N Witchduck Rd	Virginia Beach	VA	23455	757-490-5000	490-5027
Web: www.qedsysinc.com					
Quadrel Labeling Systems 7670 Jenther Dr	Mentor	OH	44060	440-602-4700	
Web: www.quadrel.com					
Raque Food Systems LLC PO Box 99594	Louisville	KY	40269	502-267-9641	267-2352
Web: www.raque.com					
Robert Bosch Corp Packaging Technology Div 2440 Summer Blvd	Raleigh	NC	27616	919-877-0886	877-0976
Web: www.boschpackaging.com					
Rollstock Inc 5720 Brighton Ave	Kansas City	MO	64130	616-570-0430	455-8469*
**Fax Area Code:* 816 ■ *TF:* 800-295-2949 ■ *Web:* www.rollstock.com					
Satake USA Inc 10905 Cash Rd	Stafford	TX	77477	281-276-3600	494-1427
Web: www.satake-usa.com					
Scandia Packaging Machinery Co 15 Industrial Rd	Fairfield	NJ	07004	973-473-6100	473-7226
Web: www.scandiapack.com					
Schneider Packaging Equipment Company Inc 5370 Guy Young Rd	Brewerton	NY	13029	315-676-3035	676-2875
Web: schneiderequip.com					
Shibuya Hoppmann Corp 13129 Airpark Dr Ste 120	Elkwood	VA	22718	540-829-2564	829-1726
TF Cust Svc: 800-368-3582 ■ *Web:* www.shibuyahoppmann.com					
Sidel Inc 5600 Sun Ct	Norcross	GA	30092	770-449-8058	447-0084
Web: www.sidel.com					
Speedline Technologies 16 Forge Pk	Franklin	MA	02038	508-520-0083	520-2288
Web: www.speedlinetech.com					
Standard Knapp Inc 63 Pickering St	Portland	CT	06480	860-342-1100	342-0782
TF Cust Svc: 800-628-9565 ■ *Web:* www.standard-knapp.com					
Stock America Inc 900 Cheyenne Ave Ste 700	Grafton	WI	53024	262-375-4100	
Web: www.stockamerica.com					
Stolle Machinery Co LLC 6949 S Potomac St	Centennial	CO	80112	303-708-9044	708-9045
TF: 800-433-8333 ■ *Web:* www.stollemachinery.com					
Summit Packaging Systems Inc 400 Gay St PO Box 5304	Manchester	NH	03103	603-669-5410	644-2594
Web: summitpackagingsystems.com					
SWF Cos 1949 E Manning Ave	Reedley	CA	93654	559-638-8484	638-7478
TF: 800-344-8951 ■ *Web:* www.swfcompanies.com					
Taylor Products Company Inc 2205 Jothi Ave	Parsons	KS	67357	620-421-5550	
Web: www.taylorproducts.com					
Thiele Technologies 315 27th Ave NE	Minneapolis	MN	55418	612-782-1200	782-1203
TF: 800-932-3647 ■ *Web:* www.thieletech.com					
Tri-Pak Machinery Inc 1102 N Commerce St	Harlingen	TX	78550	956-423-5140	423-9362
Web: www.tri-pakmachinery.com					
Triangle Package Machinery Co 6655 W Diversey Ave	Chicago	IL	60707	773-889-0200	889-4221
TF: 800-621-4170 ■ *Web:* www.trianglepackage.com					
U S Bottlers Machinery Co PO Box 7203	Charlotte	NC	28241	704-588-4750	588-3808
Web: www.usbottlers.com					
Universal Labeling Systems Inc 3501 Eigth Ave S	Saint Petersburg	FL	33711	727-327-2123	
Web: www.universal1.com					
US Digital Media Inc 1929 W Lone Cactus Dr	Phoenix	AZ	85027	623-587-4900	587-4920
TF: 877-992-3766 ■ *Web:* www.usdigitalmedia.com					
Weiler Engineering Inc 1395 Gateway Dr	Elgin	IL	60123	847-697-4900	697-4915
Web: www.weilerengineering.com					
Wulftec International Inc 209 Wulftec St	Ayer's Cliff	QC	J0B1C0	819-838-4232	838-5539
Web: www.wulftec.com					

551 PACKAGING MATERIALS & PRODUCTS - PAPER OR PLASTICS

SEE ALSO Coated & Laminated Paper p. 2853; Paper Converters p. 2854; Plastics Foam Products p. 2933; Bags - Paper p. 1846; Bags - Plastics p. 1846; Blister Packaging p. 1872

				Phone	Fax
Acme Paper & Supply Company Inc 8229 Sandy Ct PO Box 422	Savage	MD	20763	410-792-2333	792-2137
TF: 800-462-5812 ■ *Web:* www.acmepaper.com					
Adhesive Packaging Specialties Inc PO Box 31	Peabody	MA	01960	978-531-3300	532-8901
TF: 800-222-1117 ■ *Web:* www.adhesivepackaging.com					
Admiral Packaging Inc 10 Admiral St	Providence	RI	02908	401-274-7000	331-1910
TF: 800-556-6454 ■ *Web:* www.admiralpkg.com					
Advance Bag & Packaging Technologies 5720 Williams Lk Rd	Waterford	MI	48329	248-674-3126	674-2630
TF: 800-475-2247 ■ *Web:* www.advancepac.com					
Advanced Paper Forming 541 W Rincon St	Carona	CA	92880	951-738-1800	738-1234
Web: www.advancedpaper.com					
Alliance Rubber Co 210 Carpenter Dam Rd	Hot Springs	AR	71901	800-626-5940	262-3948*
**Fax Area Code:* 501 ■ *TF:* 800-626-5940 ■ *Web:* www.rubberband.com					
American Packaging Corp 777 Driving Pk Ave	Rochester	NY	14613	585-254-9500	254-5801
TF: 800-551-8801 ■ *Web:* www.ampkcorp.com					
American Packaging Corp Extrusion Div 777 Driving Pk Ave	Rochester	NY	14613	585-254-9500	254-5801
TF: 800-551-8801 ■ *Web:* www.ampkcorp.com					
Apco Extruders Inc 180 National Rd	Edison	NJ	08817	732-287-3000	287-1421
TF Orders: 800-942-8725					
Automated Packaging Systems Inc 10175 Phillip Pkwy	Streetsboro	OH	44241	330-528-2000	342-2400
TF Sales: 800-527-0733 ■ *Web:* www.autobag.com					
BagcraftPapercon 3900 W 43rd St	Chicago	IL	60632	773-254-8000	254-8204
TF: 800-621-8468 ■ *Web:* www.bagcraft.com					
Beaver Mfg Company Inc 12 Ed Needham Dr	Mansfield	GA	30055	770-786-1622	
Web: www.beaverloc.com					
Bedford Industries Inc 1659 Rowe Ave	Worthington	MN	56187	507-376-4136	376-6742
TF Cust Svc: 800-533-5314 ■ *Web:* bedford.com					
Bemis Co Inc Bemis Clysar Div 2451 Badger Ave	Oshkosh	WI	54903	920-303-7800	303-7820
TF: 888-425-9727 ■ *Web:* www.clysar.com					
Bemis Company Inc One Neenah Ctr Fourth Fl PO Box 669	Neenah	WI	54957	920-727-4100	
NYSE: BMS ■ *Web:* www.bemis.com					
Bemis Company Inc Paper Packaging Div 2445 Deer Pk Blvd	Omaha	NE	68105	800-541-4303	938-2609*
**Fax Area Code:* 402 ■ *TF:* 800-541-4303 ■ *Web:* www.bemispaper.com					
Bomarko Inc 1955 N Oak Rd	Plymouth	IN	46563	574-936-9901	936-5314
Web: www.bomarko.com					
BPM Inc 200 W Front St	Peshtigo	WI	54157	715-582-4551	582-4853
TF: 800-826-0494 ■ *Web:* www.bpmpaper.com					
Bryce Corp 4505 Old Lamar Ave PO Box 18338	Memphis	TN	38118	901-369-4400	369-4419*
**Fax:* Sales ■ *TF:* 800-238-7277 ■ *Web:* www.brycecorp.com					

Phone | Fax

Burrows Paper Corp Packaging Group
2000 Commerce Ctr Dr. . . . . Franklin OH 45005 937-746-1933 746-0344
TF: 800-732-1933 ■ *Web:* www.burrowspaper.com

Carton Service Inc First Quality Dr PO Box 702 . . . . . Shelby OH 44875 419-342-5010 342-4804
TF General: 800-533-7744 ■ *Web:* www.cartonservice.com

Catty Corp 6111 White Oaks Rd . . . . . Harvard IL 60033 815-943-2288 943-4473
Web: www.cattycorp.com

CCL Industries Inc
105 Gordon Baker Rd Ste 500 . . . . . Toronto ON M2H3P8 416-756-8500 756-8555
TSE: CCL/B ■ *Web:* www.cclind.com

Cello-Pack Corp 55 Innsbruck Dr . . . . . Cheektowaga NY 14227 716-668-3111 668-3816
TF: 800-778-3111 ■ *Web:* www.cello-pack.com

Charter Films Inc 1901 Winter St PO Box 277 . . . . . Superior WI 54880 715-395-8258 395-8259
TF: 877-411-3456 ■ *Web:* www.charternex.com

Clear Lam Packaging Inc
1950 Pratt Blvd. . . . . Elk Grove Village IL 60007 847-439-8570 439-8589
Web: www.clearlam.com

Command Plastic Corp 124 W Ave . . . . . Tallmadge OH 44278 330-434-3497 434-8316
TF: 800-321-8001 ■ *Web:* www.commandplastic.com

Consolidated Container Co (CCC)
3101 Towercreek Pkwy Ste 300 . . . . . Atlanta GA 30339 678-742-4600 742-4750
TF Sales: 888-831-2184 ■ *Web:* www.cccllc.com

Crawford Industries LLC
1414 Crawford Dr. . . . . Crawfordsville IN 47933 800-428-0840 962-3343
TF: 800-428-0840 ■ *Web:* www.crawford-industries.com

Crown Packaging Corp
17854 Chesterfld Airport Rd. . . . . Chesterfield MO 63005 636-681-8000 681-9600
TF: 800-883-9400 ■ *Web:* www.crownpack.com

Cryovac Food Packaging & Food Solutions
100 Rogers Bridge Rd. . . . . Duncan SC 29334 800-391-5645
TF: 800-391-5645 ■ *Web:* www.cryovac.com/en/default.aspx

Curwood Inc 2200 Badger Ave PO Box 2968 . . . . . Oshkosh WI 54903 920-303-7300 303-7309
TF: 800-544-4672 ■ *Web:* www.curwood.com

Dade Paper & Bag Co 9601 NW 112th Ave. . . . . Miami FL 33178 305-805-2600 883-9363
Web: www.dadepaper.com

DuPont Packaging & Industrial Polymers
Barley Mill Plaza 26-2122 PO Box 80026. . . . . Wilmington DE 19880 703-305-7666 892-7390*
**Fax Area Code:* 302 ■ *TF:* 800-438-7225 ■ *Web:* www.dupont.com

Exopack LLC 3070 Southport Rd PO Box 5687 . . . . . Spartanburg SC 29302 864-596-7140 596-7150
TF: 877-447-3539 ■ *Web:* www.exopack.com

Fibercel Packaging LLC
46 Brooklyn St PO Box 610 . . . . . Portville NY 14770 716-933-8703 933-6948
TF Sales: 800-545-8546 ■ *Web:* www.fibercel.com

Fibre Converters Inc PO Box 130. . . . . Constantine MI 49042 269-279-1700
Web: www.fibreconverters.com

Fisher Container Corp 1111 Busch Pkwy. . . . . Buffalo Grove IL 60089 847-541-0000 541-0075
TF: 800-837-2247 ■ *Web:* www.fishercontainer.com

Flextron Industries Inc 720 Mt Rd. . . . . Aston PA 19014 610-459-4600 459-5379
TF: 800-633-2181 ■ *Web:* www.flextronindustries.com

Flower City Tissue Mills Inc
700 Driving Pk Ave. . . . . Rochester NY 14613 585-458-9200 458-3812
TF: 800-595-2030 ■ *Web:* www.flowercitytissue.com

FPC Flexible Packaging Corp
1891 Eglinton Ave E . . . . . Toronto ON M1L2L7 416-288-3060 288-0808
TF: 888-288-7386 ■ *Web:* www.fpcflexible.com

Gateway Packaging Co
20 Central Industrial Dr
Northgate Industrial Pk. . . . . Granite City IL 62040 618-451-0010 876-4856
Web: www.gatewaypackaging.com

General Plastic Extrusions Inc
1238 Kasson Dr . . . . . Prescott WI 54021 715-262-3806 262-3836
TF: 800-532-3888 ■ *Web:* www.generalplastic.com

Genpak Corp 68 Warren St. . . . . Glens Falls NY 12801 518-798-9511
TF: 800-626-6695 ■ *Web:* www.genpak.com

Gift Wrap Co 338 Industrial Blvd. . . . . Midway GA 31320 800-443-4429
TF General: 800-443-4429 ■ *Web:* www.giftwrapcompany.com

Grayling Industries 1008 Branch Dr . . . . . Alpharetta GA 30004 770-751-9095 751-3710
TF: 800-635-1551 ■ *Web:* www.graylingindustries.com

Green Bay Packaging Inc 1700 Webster Ct. . . . . Green Bay WI 54302 920-433-5111
TF: 800-236-8400 ■ *Web:* www.gbp.com

HCP Packaging USA Inc 370 Monument Rd. . . . . Hinsdale NH 03451 603-256-3141 256-6979
Web: hcpackaging.com/

Huhtamaki Inc North America 9201 Packaging Dr. . . . . DeSoto KS 66018 913-583-3025 583-8756*
**Fax:* Hum Res ■ *TF:* 800-255-4243 ■ *Web:* www2.huhtamaki.com

Indiana Ribbon Inc 106 N Second St . . . . . Wolcott IN 47995 219-279-2112 279-3174*
**Fax Area Code:* 800 ■ *TF:* 800-531-3100 ■ *Web:* www.giftwrapgifts.com

Innovative Enterprises Inc
25 Town & Country Dr . . . . . Washington MO 63090 636-390-0300 390-4004
TF: 800-280-0300 ■ *Web:* www.innovative-1.com

International Paper Co 6400 Poplar Ave. . . . . Memphis TN 38197 901-419-9000
NYSE: IP ■ *TF Prod Info:* 800-223-1268 ■ *Web:* www.internationalpaper.com

ITW Hi-Cone 1140 W Bryn Mawr Ave . . . . . Itasca IL 60143 630-438-5300 438-5315
Web: www.itwhicone.com

Joshen Paper & Packaging Company Inc
5808 Grant Ave. . . . . Cleveland OH 44105 216-441-5600 441-7647
Web: www.joshen.com

LallyPak Inc 1209 Central Ave . . . . . Hillside NJ 07205 908-351-4141 351-4411
TF: 800-523-8484 ■ *Web:* www.lallypak.com

Laminations 3010 E Venture Dr. . . . . Appleton WI 54911 920-831-0596
TF: 800-925-2626 ■ *Web:* www.laminationsonline.com

Letica Corp 52585 Dequindre Rd PO Box 5005 . . . . . Rochester MI 48308 248-652-0557 608-2153
Web: www.letica.com

LPS Industries Inc 10 Caesar Pl . . . . . Moonachie NJ 07074 201-438-3515 643-0180*
**Fax Area Code:* 732 ■ *TF Sales:* 800-275-6577 ■ *Web:* www.lpsind.com

Multifilm Packaging Corp 1040 N McLean Blvd. . . . . Elgin IL 60123 847-695-7600 695-7645
TF: 800-837-9727 ■ *Web:* www.multifilm.com

Novacel 21 Third St. . . . . Palmer MA 01069 413-283-3468 283-3964
TF: 877-668-2235 ■ *Web:* www.novacelinc.com

Oracle Packaging 220 E Polo Rd . . . . . Winston-Salem NC 27105 336-777-5000 777-5440
Web: www.oraclepackaging.com

Overwraps Packaging LP 3950 La Reunion Pkwy. . . . . Dallas TX 75212 214-634-0427 634-9531
Web: www.overwraps.com

Phone | Fax

Packaging Concepts Inc
9832 Evergreen Indus Dr . . . . . Saint Louis MO 63123 314-329-9700 487-2666
Web: www.packagingconceptsinc.com

Pactiv Corp 1900 W Field Ct . . . . . Lake Forest IL 60045 847-482-2000 482-4738
TF: 888-828-2850 ■ *Web:* www.pactiv.com

Pak West Paper & Packaging
4042 W Garry Ave. . . . . Santa Ana CA 92704 714-557-7420
TF: 800-927-7299 ■ *Web:* www.pakwest.com

Perfecseal Inc 3500 N Main St PO Box 2968. . . . . Oshkosh WI 54903 920-303-7000 303-7002
TF: 888-871-8574 ■ *Web:* www.perfecseal.com

Pratt Industries USA 1800C Sarasota Pkwy . . . . . Conyers GA 30013 770-918-5678 918-5679
TF: 800-835-2088 ■ *Web:* www.prattindustries.com

Printpack Inc 2800 Overlook PkwyNE. . . . . Atlanta GA 30339 404-460-7000 460-7165
TF: 800-669-6820 ■ *Web:* www.printpack.com

Rexam Inc 4201 Congress St Ste 340. . . . . Charlotte NC 28209 704-551-1500 551-1572
TF: 800-944-2217 ■ *Web:* www.rexam.com

Robert Family Holdings Inc (RFH)
12430 Tesson Ferry Rd Ste 313 . . . . . Saint Louis MO 63128 636-305-2830 965-0309*
**Fax Area Code:* 314 ■ *Web:* www.rf-holdings.com

Robinson Industries Inc 3051 W Curtis Rd . . . . . Coleman MI 48618 989-465-6111 465-1217
TF: 877-465-4055 ■ *Web:* www.robinsonind.com

Rollprint Packaging Products Inc
320 S Stewart Ave. . . . . Addison IL 60101 630-628-1700 628-8510
TF: 800-276-7629 ■ *Web:* www.rollprint.com

Sabert Corp 2288 Main St Ext. . . . . Sayreville NJ 08872 800-722-3781 721-0622*
**Fax Area Code:* 732 ■ *TF:* 800-722-3781 ■ *Web:* www.sabert.com

Scholle Packaging Corporation 200 W N Ave . . . . . Northlake IL 60164 708-562-7290 723-6014*
**Fax Area Code:* 231 ■ *Web:* www.scholle.com

Sealed Air Corp Packaging Products Div
301 Mayhill St . . . . . Saddle Brook NJ 07663 201-712-7000 712-7070
Web: sealedair.com

SI Jacobson Mfg Co 1414 Jacobson Dr. . . . . Waukegan IL 60085 847-623-1414 623-2556
TF: 800-621-5492 ■ *Web:* www.sij.com

Silgan Holdings Inc Four Landmark Sq Ste 400 . . . . . Stamford CT 06901 203-975-7110 975-7902
NASDAQ: SLGN ■ *Web:* www.silganholdings.com

Southern Container Ltd
10410 Papalote St Ste 130. . . . . Houston TX 77041 713-466-5661 466-4223
Web: www.southerncontainer.com

Technimark Inc 180 Commerce Pl . . . . . Asheboro NC 27203 336-498-4171 498-5042
Web: www.technimark.com

Technipaq Inc 975 Lutter Dr . . . . . Crystal Lake IL 60014 815-477-1800 477-0777
Web: www.technipaq.com

Tegrant Corp 1401 Pleasant St. . . . . DeKalb IL 60115 815-756-8451
TF: 800-633-3962 ■ *Web:* www.tegrant.com

Trinity Packaging Corp 84 Business Pk Dr . . . . . Armonk NY 10504 914-273-4111 273-4715
Web: www.trinitypackaging.com

UFP Technologies Inc 172 E Main St . . . . . Georgetown MA 01833 978-352-2200
NASDAQ: UFPT ■ *TF:* 800-372-3172 ■ *Web:* www.ufpt.com

Unger Co 12401 Berea Rd . . . . . Cleveland OH 44111 216-252-1400 252-1427
TF: 800-321-1418 ■ *Web:* www.ungerco.com

Unicorr 455 Sackett Pt Rd . . . . . North Haven CT 06473 203-248-2161 248-0241
TF General: 800-877-6875 ■ *Web:* www.unicorr.com

Vision Plastics Inc 26000 SW Pkwy Ctr Dr. . . . . Wilsonville OR 97070 503-685-9000 685-9254
Web: www.visionplastics.com

Viskase Cos Inc 8205 S Cass Ste 115. . . . . Darien IL 60561 630-874-0700 874-0176
TF: 800-323-8562 ■ *Web:* www.viskase.com

Walter G. Anderson Inc 4535 Willow Dr . . . . . Hamel MN 55340 763-478-2133 478-6572
Web: www.wgacarton.com

Warp Bros Flex-O-Glass Inc
4647 W Augusta Blvd. . . . . Chicago IL 60651 773-261-5200 261-5204
TF: 800-621-3345 ■ *Web:* www.warpbros.com

Wausau Paper Corp 100 Paper Pl. . . . . Mosinee WI 54455 715-693-4470 692-2082
NYSE: WPP ■ *TF:* 800-723-0008 ■ *Web:* www.wausaupaper.com

Weyerhaeuser Co 33663 Weyerhaeuser Way S . . . . . Federal Way WA 98003 253-924-2345 924-2685
NYSE: WY ■ *TF:* 800-525-5440 ■ *Web:* www.weyerhaeuser.com

Winpak Ltd 100 Salteaux Crescent. . . . . Winnipeg MB R3J3T3 204-889-1015 888-7806
TSE: WPK ■ *TF:* 800-841-2600 ■ *Web:* www.winpak.com

WS Packaging Group Inc 2571 S. Hemlock Rd . . . . . Green Bay WI 54229 800-818-5481 866-6485*
**Fax Area Code:* 920 ■ *TF:* 800-236-3424 ■ *Web:* www.wspackaging.com

Wynalda Packaging 8221 Graphic Dr NE. . . . . Belmont MI 49306 616-866-1561 866-4316
TF General: 800-952-8668 ■ *Web:* www.wynalda.com

552 PACKING & CRATING

Phone | Fax

Allied Container Systems Inc
201 N Civic Dr Ste 180. . . . . Walnut Creek CA 94596 800-943-6510
TF: 800-943-6510 ■ *Web:* www.alliedcontainer.com

American Copak Corp 9175 Eton Ave . . . . . Chatsworth CA 91311 818-576-1000 882-1637
Web: www.americancopak.com

Bentley World Packaging Ltd
4080 N Port Washington Rd. . . . . Milwaukee WI 53212 414-967-8000 967-8001
Web: www.bentleywp.com

Cooke's Crating Inc 3124 E 11th St . . . . . Los Angeles CA 90023 323-268-5101 262-2001
Web: www.cookescrating.com

Craters & Freighters 331 Corporate Cir Ste J . . . . . Golden CO 80401 800-736-3335 399-9964*
**Fax Area Code:* 303 ■ *TF:* 800-736-3335 ■ *Web:* www.cratersandfreighters.com

ECI Technology Inc 60 Gordon Dr. . . . . Totowa NJ 07512 973-890-1114
Web: www.cvstechnology.com

Export Corp 6060 Whitmore Lk Rd . . . . . Brighton MI 48116 810-227-6153
Web: www.exportcorporation.com

Fapco Inc 216 Post Rd . . . . . Buchanan MI 49107 269-695-6889 695-5145
TF: 800-782-0167 ■ *Web:* www.fapcoinc.com

GJ Nikolas & Company Inc
2800 Washington Blvd . . . . . Bellwood IL 60104 708-544-0320
Web: www.finish1.com

Government Contracting Resources Inc
315 Page Rd # 7. . . . . Pinehurst NC 28374 910-215-1900
Web: www.gcrinc.net

Houston Crating Inc 18941 Aldine Westfield . . . . . Houston TX 77073 281-443-3222 443-3234
Web: www.houstoncrating.com

	City	State	Zip	Phone	Fax
Icepak Inc 909 S E Everett Mall Way Ste B220 *Web:* www.goicepak.com	Everett	WA	98208	425-293-0310	
Independent Packing Services Inc 7600-32nd Ave N *Web:* www.ipsipack.com	Crystal	MN	55427	763-425-7155	
Macmillan Piper Inc 1509 Taylor Way *Web:* www.macpiper.com	Tacoma	WA	98421	253-627-3767	
Navis Logistics Network 6551 S Revere Pkwy Ste 250 **Fax Area Code:* 303 ■ *TF:* 800-344-3528 ■ *Web:* www.gonavis.com	Centennial	CO	80111	800-344-3528	741-6653*
Navis Pack & Ship Centers 6551 S Revere Pkwy Ste 250 **Fax Area Code:* 303 ■ *TF:* 800-344-3528 ■ *Web:* www.gonavis.com	Centennial	CO	80111	800-344-3528	741-6653*
Packaging Services of Maryland Inc 16461 Elliott Pkwy *TF:* 800-223-6255 ■ *Web:* www.psimd.com	Williamsport	MD	21795	301-223-6200	223-8247
Rollins Moving & Storage Inc 1900 E Leffel Ln *Web:* www.rollins3pl.com	Springfield	OH	45505	937-325-2484	
Southern States Packaging Co PO Box 650 **Fax Area Code:* 864 ■ *TF:* 800-621-2051 ■ *Web:* www.sspc.biz	Spartanburg	SC	29304	800-621-2051	579-3932*
Strive Group, The 350 N Clark St Ste 300 *Web:* www.menashapackaging.com	Chicago	IL	60639	312-880-4620	
Suntreat Packing & Shipping Co 391 Oxford Ave *Web:* suntreat.com	Lindsay	CA	93247	559-562-4991	
Tech Packaging Inc 13241 Bartram Pk Blvd Ste 601 *TF:* 866-453-8324 ■ *Web:* www.techpackaging.net	Jacksonville	FL	32258	904-288-6403	
Trans-Pak Inc 520 Marburg Way *Web:* www.transpak.com	San Jose	CA	95133	408-254-0500	254-0551
Trans.NET Inc 710 NW Juniper St Ste 100 *Web:* www.transnetinc.com	Issaquah	WA	98027	425-557-0558	
Transaction Packing Inc 2928 Greens Rd Ste 100 *Web:* www.transactionpacking.com	Houston	TX	77032	281-443-0476	
Trident Crating & Services Inc 14320 InterDr E *Web:* www.tridentcrating.com	Houston	TX	77032	281-227-3999	
Trisept Solutions 777 W Glencoe Pl *Web:* www.triseptsolutions.com	Milwaukee	WI	53217	414-934-3900	934-3950
Tucson Container Corp 6601 S Palo Verde *Web:* www.tucsoncontainer.com	Tucson	AZ	85756	520-746-3171	
Unicep Packaging Inc 1702 Industrial Dr *TF:* 800-354-9396 ■ *Web:* www.unicep.com	Sandpoint	ID	83864	208-265-9696	265-4726
Venchurs Packaging 800 Liberty St *TF:* 855-264-4300 ■ *Web:* www.venchurs.com	Adrian	MI	49221	517-263-8937	265-7468
Walnut Industries Inc 1356 Adams Rd *Web:* www.ty-gard2000.com	Bensalem	PA	19020	215-638-7847	
Warren Industries Inc 3100 Mt Pleasant St *Web:* www.wrnind.com	Racine	WI	53404	262-639-7800	639-0920

553 PAINTS, VARNISHES, RELATED PRODUCTS

	City	State	Zip	Phone	Fax
Accurate Dispersions Inc 192 W 155th St *Web:* www.accurate-dispersions.com	South Holland	IL	60478	708-333-1337	
Aervoe Industries Inc PO Box 485 *TF:* 800-227-0196 ■ *Web:* www.aervoe.com	Gardnerville	NV	89410	775-783-3100	782-5687
Aexcel Corp 7373 Production Dr *Web:* www.aexcelcorp.com	Mentor	OH	44060	440-974-3800	974-3808
Akron Paint & Varnish Inc 1390 Firestone Pkwy *TF:* 800-772-3452 ■ *Web:* arcat.com	Akron	OH	44301	330-773-8911	773-1028
AkzoNobel Wood Finishes & Adhesives 2031 Nelson Miller Pkwy *Web:* www.akzonobel.com	Louisville	KY	40223	502-254-0470	
American Safety Technologies Inc 565 Eagle Rock Ave *TF:* 800-631-7841 ■ *Web:* www.astantislip.com	Roseland	NJ	07068	973-403-2600	403-1108
AP Nonweiler Co 3321 County Rd A PO Box 1007 *Web:* apnonweiler.com	Oshkosh	WI	54903	920-231-0850	231-8085
Behr Process Corp 3400 W Segerstrom Ave *TF:* 800-854-0133 ■ *Web:* www.behr.com	Santa Ana	CA	92704	714-545-7101	241-1002
Benjamin Moore & Co 101 Paragon Dr *TF:* 800-344-0400 ■ *Web:* www.benjaminmoore.com	Montvale	NJ	07645	201-573-9600	573-9046
Brewer Science Inc 2401 Brewer Dr *Web:* www.brewerscience.com	Rolla	MO	65401	573-364-0300	
Brewster WaLLPaper Corp 67 Pacella Park Dr *Web:* www.brewsterwallcovering.com	Randolph	MA	02368	781-963-4800	
BryCoat Inc 207 Vollmer Ave *TF:* 800-989-8788 ■ *Web:* www.brycoat.com	Oldsmar	FL	34677	727-490-1000	
C. E. Bradley Laboratories Inc PO Box 8238 *Web:* www.cebradley.com	Brattleboro	VT	05304	802-257-7971	257-7070
California Products Corp 150 Dascomb Rd **Fax Area Code:* 800 ■ *TF:* 800-225-1141 ■ *Web:* www.californiapaints.com	Andover	MA	01810	978-623-9980	533-6788*
Carboline Co 350 Hanley Industrial Ct *TF:* 800-848-4645 ■ *Web:* www.carboline.com	Saint Louis	MO	63144	314-644-1000	644-4617
Coating & Adhesive Corp (CAC) 1901 Popular St PO Box 1080 *TF:* 800-410-2999 ■ *Web:* www.cacoatings.com	Leland	NC	28451	910-371-3184	371-5580
Coatings Resource Corp 15541 Commerce Ln *Web:* www.coatingsresource.com	Huntington Beach	CA	92649	714-894-5252	893-2322
Color Putty Company Inc PO Box 738 *Web:* www.colorputty.com	Monroe	WI	53566	608-325-6033	325-6397
Color Wheel Paint Mfg Co Inc 2814 Silver Star Rd *TF:* 855-862-6639 ■ *Web:* brands.sherwin-williams.com/	Orlando	FL	32808	407-293-6810	293-0945
DAP Products Inc 2400 Boston St Ste 200 **Fax:* Cust Svc ■ *TF Cust Svc:* 800-543-3840 ■ *Web:* www.dap.com	Baltimore	MD	21224	410-675-2100	558-1068*
Davis Paint Company Inc 1311 Iron St PO Box 7589 *TF:* 800-821-2029 ■ *Web:* www.davispaint.com	North Kansas City	MO	64116	816-471-4447	471-1460
Day-Glo Color Corp 4515 St Clair Ave *TF:* 800-424-9300 ■ *Web:* www.dayglo.com	Cleveland	OH	44103	216-391-7070	391-7751
Diamond Vogel Paints 1110 Albany Pl SE PO Box 380 *Web:* www.vogelpaint.com	Orange City	IA	51041	712-737-8880	737-4998
Duckback Products 2644 Hegan Ln PO Box 980 **Fax Area Code:* 530 ■ *TF:* 800-825-5382 ■ *Web:* www.superdeck.com	Chico	CA	95927	800-825-5382	343-3283*
Dunn-Edwards Corp 4885 E 52nd Pl *TF:* 800-537-4098 ■ *Web:* www.dunnedwards.com	Los Angeles	CA	90058	323-771-3330	771-4440
DuPont Automotive 950 Stephenson Hwy PO Box 7013 *TF:* 800-533-1313 ■ *Web:* www.dupont.com	Troy	MI	48007	248-583-8000	
DuPont Performance Coatings 1007 Market St *TF:* 800-441-7515 ■ *Web:* www.dupont.com	Wilmington	DE	19898	302-774-1000	
EPKO Industries Inc 1200 Arthur Ave *Web:* www.epko.com	Elk Grove Village	IL	60007	847-437-4000	
Farrell-Calhoun Inc 221 E Carolina Ave *TF:* 888-832-7735 ■ *Web:* www.farrellcalhoun.com	Memphis	TN	38126	901-526-2211	774-4213
Ferro Corp 6060 Parkland Blvd **Fax Area Code:* 513 ■ *TF:* 800-321-3314 ■ *Web:* compositesworld.com	Mayfield Heights	IN	44124	216-875-5600	688-3201*
Ferro Corp Plastics Colorants Div Three Railroad Ave *TF:* 800-521-9094 ■ *Web:* www.ferro.com	Stryker	OH	43557	419-682-3311	682-4924
FinishMaster Inc 54 Monument Cir Eighth Fl *TF:* 888-311-3678 ■ *Web:* www.finishmaster.com	Indianapolis	IN	46204	317-237-3678	237-2150
Gallagher-Kaiser Corp 13710 Mt Elliott St *Web:* www.gkcorp.com	Detroit	MI	48212	313-368-3100	368-3109
Gemini Coatings Inc 421 SE 27th St *TF:* 800-262-5710 ■ *Web:* www.gemini-coatings.com	El Reno	OK	73036	405-262-5710	
Great Lake Woods Inc 3303 John F Donnelly Dr *Web:* www.greatlakewoods.com	Holland	MI	49424	616-399-3300	
Hallman Lindsay Paints Inc 1717 N Bristol St *Web:* www.hallmanlindsay.com	Sun Prairie	WI	53590	608-834-8844	837-1064
Harrison Paint Co 1329 Harrison Ave SW *TF:* 800-321-0680 ■ *Web:* www.harrisonpaint.com	Canton	OH	44706	330-455-5125	454-1750
HB Fuller Co 1200 Willow Lk Blvd PO Box 64683 *NYSE: FUL* ■ *TF:* 888-423-8553 ■ *Web:* www.hbfuller.com	Saint Paul	MN	55164	651-236-5900	236-5898
Hempel (USA) Inc 600 Conroe Park N Dr *Web:* www.hempel.com	Conroe	TX	77303	936-523-6000	
Hentzen Coatings Inc 6937 W Mill Rd *TF:* 800-236-6589 ■ *Web:* www.hentzen.com	Milwaukee	WI	53218	414-353-4200	353-0286
Hirshfield's Inc 725 Second Ave N *Web:* www.hirshfields.com	Minneapolis	MN	55405	612-377-3910	436-3384
Hudson Color Concentrates Inc 50 Francis St *Web:* www.hudsoncolor.com	Leominster	MA	01453	978-537-3538	
Insl-X Products Corp 101 Paragon Dr **Fax Area Code:* 888 ■ *TF Cust Svc:* 800-225-5554 ■ *Web:* www.insl-x.com	Montvale	NJ	07645	800-225-5554	248-2143*
Kalcor Coatings Company Inc 37721 Stevens Blvd *Web:* www.kalcor.com	Willoughby	OH	44094	440-946-4700	
Kelley Technical Coatings Inc 1445 S 15th St PO Box 3726 *Web:* www.smartsealco.com	Louisville	KY	40201	502-636-2561	
Kelly-Moore Paint Company Inc 987 Commercial St **Fax:* Hum Res ■ *TF:* 800-874-4436 ■ *Web:* www.kellymoore.com	San Carlos	CA	94070	650-592-8337	508-8563*
Kenyon Plastering Inc 4001 W Indian School Rd *TF:* 800-949-4319 ■ *Web:* www.kenyonweb.com	Phoenix	AZ	85019	602-233-1191	278-6801
KJ Quinn & Co Inc 34 Folly Mill Rd	Seabrook	NH	03874	603-474-5753	474-7122
Kop-Coat Inc 436 Seventh Ave 1850 Koppers Bldg *TF:* 800-221-4466 ■ *Web:* www.kop-coat.com	Pittsburgh	PA	15219	412-227-2426	227-2618
Lancaster Distributing Co 1310 Union St *TF General:* 800-845-8287 ■ *Web:* www.lancasterco.com	Spartanburg	SC	29302	864-583-3011	542-1315
Lansco Colors 1 Blue Hill Plaza 11th Fl PO Box 1685 *TF:* 800-526-2783 ■ *Web:* www.pigments.com	Pearl River	NY	10965	845-507-5942	735-2787
Magni Group Inc 390 Pk St *Web:* www.magnicoatings.com	Birmingham	MI	48009	248-647-4500	647-7506
Magni-Industries Inc 2771 Hammond St *Web:* www.magniindustries.com	Detroit	MI	48209	313-843-7855	842-6730
Mantros-Haeuser & Company Inc 1175 Post Rd E *TF General:* 800-344-4229 ■ *Web:* www.mantrose.com	Westport	CT	06880	203-454-1800	227-0558
Masterchem Industries LLC 3135 Old Hwy M **Fax Area Code:* 636 ■ *TF:* 866-774-6371 ■ *Web:* www.kilz.com	Imperial	MO	63052	866-774-6371	942-3663*
Michelman Inc 9080 Shell Rd *Web:* www.michelman.com	Cincinnati	OH	45236	513-793-7766	793-2504
Miller Paint Company Inc 12812 NE Whitaker Way *Web:* www.millerpaint.com	Portland	OR	97230	503-255-0190	255-0192
Minwax Co 10 Mountainview Rd **Fax Area Code:* 201 ■ *TF:* 800-523-9299 ■ *Web:* www.minwax.com	Upper Saddle River	NJ	07458	800-523-9299	818-7605*
Mobile Paint Manufacturing Co 4775 Hamilton Blvd *TF:* 800-621-6952 ■ *Web:* www.blpmobilepaint.com	Theodore	AL	36582	251-443-6110	408-0410
Morwear Manufacturing Inc 620 Lamar St *Web:* www.morwear.com	Los Angeles	CA	90031	323-222-7000	
Muralo Company Inc 148 E Fifth St *TF:* 800-631-3440 ■ *Web:* www.muralo.com	Bayonne	NJ	07002	201-437-0770	437-0664

Phone | Fax

Neogard Div Jones-blair Co
2728 Empire Central St. .... Dallas TX 75235 214-353-1600
TF: 800-492-9400 ■ Web: www.jones-blair.com

O'Leary Paint 300 E Oakland Ave. .... Lansing MI 48906 517-487-2066 487-1680
TF: 800-477-2066 ■ Web: www.olearypaint.com

Old Master Products Inc
7751 Hayvenhurst Ave .... Van Nuys CA 91406 818-785-8886

Painters Supply & Equipment Co 25195 Brest Rd. .... Taylor MI 48180 734-946-8119
TF: 800-589-8100 ■ Web: www.painters-supply.com

Parker Paint Mfg Co Inc 3003 S Tacoma Way .... Tacoma WA 98409 855-862-6639 473-0448*
*Fax Area Code: 253 ■ TF: 855-862-6639 ■ Web: brands.sherwin-williams.com/

Penn Color Inc 400 Old Dublin Pk .... Doylestown PA 18901 215-345-6550 345-0270
TF: 866-617-7366 ■ Web: www.penncolor.com

Pioneer Mfg 4529 Industrial Pkwy .... Cleveland OH 44135 216-671-5500 671-5502
TF: 800-877-1500 ■ Web: www.pioneerathletics.com

PPG Industries Inc 17451 Von Karman Ave. .... Irvine CA 92614 949-474-0400 474-7269
TF: 800-544-3338 ■ Web: www.ppgaerospace.com

Red Spot Paint & Varnish Co Inc
1107 E Louisiana St .... Evansville IN 47711 812-428-9100
TF: 877-777-4778 ■ Web: www.redspot.com

Republic Powdered Metals Inc 2628 Pearl Rd .... Medina OH 44256 800-382-1218 273-5061*
*Fax Area Code: 330 ■ TF: 800-382-1218 ■ Web: www.rpmrepublic.com

Rhino Linings Corp 9151 Rehco Rd. .... San Diego CA 92121 858-450-0441
Web: www.rhinolatino.com

Rodda Paint Co 6107 N Marine Dr. .... Portland OR 97203 503-521-4300 521-4400
Web: www.roddapaint.com

Roymal Inc Three Roymal Ln PO Box 658 .... Newport NH 03773 603-863-2410 863-9065
Web: www.roymalinc.com

RPM International Inc 2628 Pearl Rd. .... Medina OH 44256 330-273-5090 225-8743
NYSE: RPM ■ TF: 800-776-4488 ■ Web: www.rpminc.com

Rust-Oleum Corp 11 E Hawthorn Pkwy .... Vernon Hills IL 60061 847-367-7700
TF: 800-323-3584 ■ Web: www.rustoleum.com

Samuel Cabot Inc 100 Hale St. .... Newburyport MA 01950 978-465-1900
TF: 800-877-8246 ■ Web: www.cabotstain.com

Seymour of Sycamore Inc 917 Crosby Ave .... Sycamore IL 60178 815-895-9101 895-8475
TF: 800-435-4482 ■ Web: www.seymourpaint.com

Sheboygan Paint Company Inc
1439 N 25th St PO Box 417 .... Sheboygan WI 53082 920-458-2157 458-5620
TF: 800-773-7801 ■ Web: www.shebpaint.com

Sherwin-Williams Automotive Finishes
4440 Warrensville Ctr Rd .... Warrensville Heights OH 44128 216-332-8330
Web: sherwin-automotive.com

SP Kish Industries Inc 600 W Seminary St. .... Charlotte MI 48813 517-543-2650
Web: www.kishindustries.com

Sterling-Clark-Lurton Corp PO Box 130 .... Norwood MA 02062 781-762-5400 762-1095
TF: 800-225-9872 ■ Web: www.savogran.com

Talbot Industries Inc 5725 Howard Bush Dr. .... Neosho MO 64850 417-451-7440 451-7830

Textured Coatings Of America
2422 E 15th St .... Panama City FL 32405 850-769-0347 913-8619
TF: 800-454-0340 ■ Web: www.texcote.com

Tnemec Company Inc 6800 Corporate Dr. .... Kansas City MO 64120 816-483-3400 483-3969
TF: 800-863-6321 ■ Web: www.tnemec.com

Troy Corp 8 Vreeland Rd PO Box 955 .... Florham Park NJ 07932 973-443-4200 443-0258
TF: 800-448-2843 ■ Web: www.troycorp.com

United Gilsonite Laboratories Inc
1396 Jefferson Ave .... Scranton PA 18509 570-344-1202
Web: www.ugl.com

Valspar Refinish Inc 210 Crosby St .... Minneapolis MN 39466 800-845-2500 395-9129*
*Fax Area Code: 612 ■ TF Cust Svc: 800-844-3691 ■ Web: www.valsparrefinish.com

Vista Paint Corp 2020 E Orangethorpe Ave .... Fullerton CA 92831 714-680-3810 459-4708
Web: www.vistapaint.com

Whitmore Manufacturing Co PO Box 9300 .... Rockwall TX 75087 972-771-1000 722-2108
TF: 800-699-6318 ■ Web: www.whitmores.com

Willamette Valley Co 1075 Arrowsmith St. .... Eugene OR 97402 541-484-9621 345-7480
TF: 800-333-9826 ■ Web: www.wilvaco.com

WM Barr & Company Inc 2105 Ch Ave. .... Memphis TN 38109 901-775-0100 621-9508*
*Fax Area Code: 800 ■ TF: 800-238-2672 ■ Web: www.wmbarr.com

Wolf Gordon Inc 33-00 47th Ave .... Long Island City NY 11101 800-347-0550 361-1090*
*Fax Area Code: 718 ■ TF: 800-347-0550 ■ Web: www.wolfgordon.com

Yenkin-Majestic Paint Corp 1920 Leonard Ave. .... Columbus OH 43219 614-253-8511 253-6327
TF: 800-848-1898 ■ Web: www.yenkin-majestic.com

ZC&R Coatings for Optics Inc
1401 Abalone Ave. .... Torrance CA 90501 310-381-3060
Web: abrisatechnologies.com/redirect/

554 PALLETS & SKIDS

Phone | Fax

American Pallet Inc 1001 Knox Rd .... Oakdale CA 95361 209-847-6122 847-6154
Web: www.americanpallet.com

Anderson Forest Products Inc
1267 Old Edmonton Rd PO Box 520. .... Tompkinsville KY 42167 270-487-6778 487-8953
TF: 800-489-6778 ■ Web: www.afp-usa.com

Brunswick Box Company Inc
852 Planters Rd PO Box 7 .... Lawrenceville VA 23868 434-848-2222 848-3647

Clinch-Tite Corp 5264 Lake St PO Box 456 .... Sandy Lake PA 16145 724-376-7315 376-2785
TF General: 800-241-0900 ■ Web: www.clinchtite.com

Cutter Lumber Products (CLP)
10 Rickenbacker Cir .... Livermore CA 94551 925-443-5959 443-0648
Web: cutterlumber.com

Day Lumber Co 34 S Broad St. .... Westfield MA 01085 413-568-3511 568-6668
Web: www.daylumber.com

Delisa Pallet Corp 91-97 Blanchard St .... Newark NJ 07105 973-344-8600
Web: www.delisapallet.com

Eastern Wood Products Inc 2020 Mill Ln. .... Williamsport PA 17701 570-326-1946

Edwards Wood Products Inc
2215 Old Lawyers Rd PO Box 219 .... Marshville NC 28103 704-624-5098 624-6812
Web: www.ewpi.com

Hill Wood Products Inc 9483 Ashawa Rd .... Cook MN 55723 218-666-5933 666-5726
TF: 800-788-9689 ■ Web: www.hillwoodproducts.com

Phone | Fax

Hinchcliff Products Co
13477 Prospect Rd .... Strongsville OH 44149 440-238-5200 238-5202
Web: www.hinchcliffproducts.com

Hunter Woodworks Inc
21038 S Wilmington Ave PO Box 4937 .... Carson CA 90749 323-775-2544 775-2540
TF: 800-966-4751 ■ Web: www.hunterpallets.com

Ifco Systems 6829 Flintlock Rd .... Houston TX 77040 713-332-6200 286-2070*
*Fax Area Code: 813 ■ TF: 800-771-1148 ■ Web: www.ifco.com

Litco International Inc
one Litco Dr P.O. Box 150. .... Vienna OH 44473 330-539-5433 539-5388
Web: www.litco.com

Mountain Valley Farms & Lumber Inc
1240 Nawakwa Rd .... Biglerville PA 17307 717-677-6166 677-9283
Web: www.mtvalleyfarms.com

Nelson Co 2116 Sparrows Pt Rd .... Baltimore MD 21219 410-477-3000 388-0246
Web: www.nelsoncompany.com

Pallet Consultants Corp PO Box 1692. .... Pompano Beach FL 33061 954-946-2212
TF: 888-782-2909 ■ Web: www.palletconsultants.com

Pallet Masters Inc 655 E Florence Ave. .... Los Angeles CA 90001 323-758-6559 758-9600
TF: 800-675-2579 ■ Web: www.palletmasters.com

PalletOne Inc 1470 US Hwy 17 S .... Bartow FL 33830 863-533-1147 533-3065
TF: 800-771-1148 ■ Web: www.palletone.com

Potomac Supply Corp 1398 Kinsale Rd .... Kinsale VA 22488 804-472-2527 472-5058
TF Sales: 800-365-3900 ■ Web: www.potomacsupply.com

Precision Wood Products Inc
16363 NE Sandy Blvd PO Box 529 .... Portland OR 97230 503-285-0393 252-6046
Web: 360.columbian.com

Savanna Pallets Co
106 E First Ave PO Box 308 .... McGregor MN 55760 218-768-2077 768-3112
Web: www.savannapallets.com

Tasler Inc 1804 Tasler Dr .... Webster City IA 50595 515-832-5200 832-2721
TF: 800-482-7537 ■ Web: www.tasler.com

United Wholesale Lumber Co 8009 Doe Ave .... Visalia CA 93291 559-651-2037 651-0742
Web: www.uwlco.com

WNC Pallet & Forest Products Co Inc
1414 Smokey Pk Hwy. .... Candler NC 28715 828-667-5426 665-4759
Web: www.wncpallet.com

Wooden Pallets Gp LLC PO Box 555 .... Silsbee TX 77656 409-385-1234 385-6203
Web: www.woodenpalletsltd.com

Yoder Lumber Company Inc 4515 TR 367 .... Millersburg OH 44654 330-893-3131 893-3031
Web: www.yoderlumber.com

555 PAPER - MFR

SEE ALSO Packaging Materials & Products - Paper or Plastics p. 2850

555-1 Coated & Laminated Paper

Phone | Fax

Appleton Papers Inc
825 E Wisconsin Ave PO Box 359 .... Appleton WI 54912 920-734-9841
TF: 888-593-9546 ■ Web: www.appletonideas.com

Arkwright Inc 538 Main St. .... Fiskeville RI 02823 401-821-1000 826-3926
TF Cust Svc: 800-556-6866 ■ Web: sihlusa.com

Avery Dennison Worldwide Graphics Div
250 Chester St Bldg 8. .... Painesville OH 44077 440-358-3700 358-3665
TF: 800-443-9380 ■ Web: www.averygraphics.com

BPM Inc 200 W Front St .... Peshtigo WI 54157 715-582-4551 582-4853
TF: 800-826-0494 ■ Web: www.bpmpaper.com

Diversified Labeling Solutions
1285 Hamilton Pkwy. .... Itasca IL 60143 630-625-1225
TF: 800-397-3013 ■ Web: teamdls.com

Exopack Advanced Coatings 700 Crestdale St. .... Matthews NC 28105 704-847-9171 845-4307
Web: coverisadvancedcoatings.com/

Felix Schoeller North America Inc
179 County Route 2A Ste 2A .... Pulaski NY 13142 315-298-5133 298-3664
Web: www.schoeller.com

Fortifiber Building Systems Group
300 Industrial Dr. .... Fernley NV 89408 775-333-6400 333-6411
TF: 800-773-4777 ■ Web: www.fortifiber.com

French Paper Co 100 French St. .... Niles MI 49120 269-683-1100 683-3025
TF: 800-253-5952 ■ Web: www.frenchpaper.com

Horizon Paper Co Inc 1010 Washington Blvd. .... Stamford CT 06901 203-358-0855 358-0828
TF: 866-358-0855 ■ Web: www.horizonpaper.com

Lofton Label Inc 6290 Claude Way .... Inver Grove Heights MN 55076 651-552-6257 457-3709
TF: 877-447-8118 ■ Web: www.loftonlabel.com

Nashua Corp 11 Trafalgar Sq 2nd Fl .... Nashua NH 03063 603-880-2323 626-8415*
*Fax Area Code: 417 ■ TF: 800-430-7488 ■ Web: www.nashua.com

National/AZON 1148 Rochester Rd .... Troy MI 48083 800-325-5939 318-7323*
*Fax Area Code: 866 ■ TF: 800-325-5939 ■ Web: www.azon.com

Onyx Specialty Papers Inc 40 Willow St .... South Lee MA 01260 413-243-1231 243-4602
Web: onyxpapers.com

Sappi Fine Paper North America 255 State St .... Boston MA 02109 617-423-7300 423-5494*
*Fax: Mail Rm ■ Web: www.na.sappi.com

Shawsheen Rubber Company Inc PO Box 4296 .... Andover MA 01810 978-475-1710 475-8603
Web: www.shawsheencc.com

Technicote Westfield Inc 222 Mound Ave .... Miamisburg OH 45342 937-859-4448 859-9096
TF: 800-358-4448 ■ Web: www.technicote.com

TST/Impreso Inc 652 Southwestern Blvd. .... Coppell TX 75019 972-462-0100 562-5359*
*Fax Area Code: 800 ■ *Fax: Cust Svc ■ TF: 800-527-2878 ■ Web: www.tstimpreso.com

Wausau Paper Corp 100 Paper Pl. .... Mosinee WI 54455 715-693-4470 692-2082
NYSE: WPP ■ TF: 800-723-0008 ■ Web: www.wausaupaper.com

Wausau Paper Corp Specialty Paper Div
100 Paper Pl. .... Mosinee WI 54455 715-693-4470 692-2082
TF: 800-723-0008 ■ Web: www.wausaupaper.com

Wcp Solutions 6703 S 234th St Ste 120. .... Kent WA 98032 253-850-3560 852-9272
Web: wcpsolutions.com/index.php

555-2 Writing Paper

Phone *Fax*

Anna Griffin Inc 99 Armour Dr....................... Atlanta GA 30324 404-817-8170 817-0590
TF: 888-817-8170 ■ *Web:* www.annagriffin.com

Crane & Co Inc 30 S St............................ Dalton MA 01226 800-268-2281
TF Cust Svc: 800-268-2281 ■ *Web:* www.crane.com

Geographics 108 Main St Third Fl................... Norwalk CT 06851 800-436-4919 520-1955*
**Fax Area Code:* 866 ■ *TF:* 800-436-4919 ■ *Web:* www.geographics.com

Gordon Paper Company Inc PO Box 1806............ Norfolk VA 23501 757-464-3581 363-9355
TF: 800-457-7366 ■ *Web:* www.gordonpaper.com

Louisiana Assn For, The Blind, The
1750 Claiborne Ave............................ Shreveport LA 71103 318-635-6471 635-8902
TF: 877-913-6471 ■ *Web:* www.lablind.com

Mafcote Industries Inc 108 Main St................. Norwalk CT 06851 203-847-8500 849-9177
TF Cust Svc: 800-221-3056 ■ *Web:* www.mafcote.com

Mohawk Fine Papers Inc 465 Saratoga St............ Cohoes NY 12047 518-237-1740 237-7394
TF: 800-843-6455 ■ *Web:* www.mohawkconnects.com

Neenah Paper Inc
3460 Preston Ridge Rd Ste 600.................... Alpharetta GA 30005 678-566-6500
NYSE: NP ■ *Web:* www.neenah.com

Performance Office Papers
21565 Hamburg Ave.............................. Lakeville MN 55044 800-458-7189 488-5058
TF: 800-458-7189 ■ *Web:* www.perfpapers.com

Rytex Co 100 N Pk Ave............................... Peru IN 46970 800-277-5458 329-1669
TF: 800-277-5458 ■ *Web:* www.rytex.com

Schurman Fine Papers
500 Chadbourne Rd PO Box 6030................... Fairfield CA 94533 800-789-1649 428-0641*
**Fax Area Code:* 707 ■ *TF Sales:* 800-789-1649 ■ *Web:* www.papyrusonline.com

Southworth Co 265 Main St........................ Agawam MA 01001 413-789-1200 786-1529
TF: 800-225-1839 ■ *Web:* www.southworth.com

Specialty Loose Leaf Inc One Cabot St.............. Holyoke MA 01040 413-532-0106 887-0195
TF: 800-227-3623 ■ *Web:* www.specialtyll.com

Top Flight Inc 1300 Central Ave.................. Chattanooga TN 37408 423-266-8171 266-6857
TF: 800-777-3740 ■ *Web:* www.topflightpaper.com

Wausau Paper Corp 100 Paper Pl.................. Mosinee WI 54455 715-693-4470 692-2082
NYSE: WPP ■ *TF:* 800-723-0008 ■ *Web:* www.wausaupaper.com

Wausau Paper Corp Printing & Writing Paper Div
One Clark's Island................................. Wausau WI 54403 715-675-3361 675-8355
TF: 800-723-0008 ■ *Web:* www.wausaupaper.com

556 PAPER - WHOL

Phone *Fax*

2072906 Ontario Ltd 177 Crosby Ave........... Richmond Hill ON L4C2R3 905-883-4343
Web: plasticap.com

America Chung Nam Inc
1163 Fairway Dr............................ City of Industry CA 91789 909-839-8383 869-6310
Web: www.acni.net

Anchor Paper Company Inc 480 Broadway St.......... Saint Paul MN 55101 651-298-1311 298-0060
TF: 800-652-9755 ■ *Web:* www.anchorpaper.com

AT Clayton & Co Inc 300 Atlantic St................ Stamford CT 06901 203-658-1200 658-1201
TF: 800-282-5298 ■ *Web:* www.atclayton.com

Atlantic Packaging Co 806 N 23rd St............ Wilmington NC 28405 910-343-0624 763-5421
TF: 800-722-5841 ■ *Web:* www.atlanticpkg.com

Atlus USA Inc 199 Technology Dr...................... Irvine CA 92618 949-788-0455
Web: www.atlus.com

Brawner Paper Company Inc 5702 Armour Dr......... Houston TX 77020 713-675-6584
Web: www.brawnerpaper.com

Central Lewmar Paper Co
1200 Highland Dr Ste 1B....................... Westampton NJ 08060 609-518-9700 518-9736

CJ Duffey Paper Co 528 Washington Ave N......... Minneapolis MN 55401 612-338-8701 338-1320
TF: 800-752-8190 ■ *Web:* www.duffeypaper.com

Clampitt Paper Company of Dallas
9207 Ambassador Row................................ Dallas TX 75247 214-638-3300 634-7837
Web: www.clampitt.com

Clifford Paper Inc
600 E Crescent Ave...................... Upper Saddle River NJ 07458 201-934-5115 934-5188
Web: www.cliffordpaper.com

Cole Papers Inc 1300 N 38th St......................... Fargo ND 58102 701-282-5311 282-5513
TF: 800-800-8090 ■ *Web:* www.colepapers.com

Com-Pac International Inc
800 W Industrial Park Rd.......................... Carbondale IL 62901 618-529-2421
Web: com-pac.com

Dennis Paper Co 910 Acorn Dr...................... Nashville TN 37210 615-883-9010 885-2969
TF: 800-441-5684 ■ *Web:* www.dennispaper.com

Elof Hansson Pulp Inc 565 Taxter Rd............... Elmsford NY 10523 914-345-8380 345-8112
Web: www.elofhansson.com

Field Paper Co 3950 D St............................ Omaha NE 68107 402-733-3600 731-7113
TF: 800-969-3435 ■ *Web:* www.fieldpaper.com

Gould Paper Corp 11 Madison Ave 14th Fl............ New York NY 10010 212-301-0000 481-0067
TF: 800-275-4685 ■ *Web:* www.gouldpaper.com

Gpa Specialty Printable Sbstrt 8740 W 50th St........ McCook IL 60525 773-650-2020 395-3581*
**Fax Area Code:* 800 ■ *TF:* 800-395-9000 ■ *Web:* www.askgpa.com

GreenLine Paper Company Inc 631 S Pine St............ York PA 17403 717-845-8697 846-3806
TF: 800-641-1117 ■ *Web:* www.greenlinepaper.com

Hearn Paper Co 556 N Meridian Rd............... Youngstown OH 44509 330-792-6533 792-4762
TF: 800-225-2989 ■ *Web:* www.hearnpaper.com

Kelly Paper Co 288 Brea Canyon Rd..................... Walnut CA 91789 800-675-3559 859-8903*
**Fax Area Code:* 909 ■ *TF:* 800-675-3559 ■ *Web:* www.kellypaper.com

Lindenmeyr Book Publishing Papers
521 Fifth Ave 6th Fl.............................. New York NY 10175 212-551-3900 213-1457
TF: 800-221-3042 ■ *Web:* www.lindenmeyr.com

Lindenmeyr Central Three Manhattanville Rd.......... Purchase NY 10577 914-696-9300 696-9333
TF: 800-221-3042 ■ *Web:* www.lindenmeyr.com

Lindenmeyr Munroe 14 Research Pkwy.............. Wallingford CT 06492 800-842-8480 890-3115
TF: 800-842-8480 ■ *Web:* lindenmeyrmunroe.com

Lindenmeyr Munroe Central Central National-Gottesman Inc
Three Manhattanville Rd........................... Purchase NY 10577 914-696-9300 696-9333
Web: www.lindenmeyr.com

Phone *Fax*

Lindenmeyr Munroe Paper Corp
115 Moonachie Ave.............................. Moonachie NJ 07074 201-440-6491 440-6492
TF: 800-221-3042 ■ *Web:* www.lindenmeyr.com

Mac Papers 3300 Phillips Hwy PO Box 5369......... Jacksonville FL 32207 904-348-3300 348-3340
TF: 800-622-2968 ■ *Web:* www.macpapers.com

Marquardt & Co 161 Ave of the Americas............ New York NY 10013 212-645-7200 536-0282

Midland Paper 101 E Palatine Rd.................. Wheeling IL 60090 847-777-2700 777-2552
TF: 800-323-8522 ■ *Web:* www.midlandpaper.com

Millcraft Paper Co 6800 Grant Ave................ Cleveland OH 44105 216-441-5500 641-2610
TF: 800-860-2482 ■ *Web:* www.millcraft.com

Miller Supply Inc
29902 Avenida de las Banderas
.... Rancho Santa Margarita CA 92688 949-589-6033
Web: www.millersupplyinc.com

Morrisette Paper Company Inc
5925 Summit Ave PO Box 20768.............. Browns Summit NC 27214 336-375-1515 621-0751
TF: 800-822-8882 ■ *Web:* www.morrisettepaper.com

Murnane Paper Corp 345 Fischer Farm Rd............ Elmhurst IL 60126 630-530-8222 530-8325
TF: 855-632-8191 ■ *Web:* www.murnanepaper.com

Newell Paper Co 1212 Grand Ave PO Box 631......... Meridian MS 39301 601-693-1783 483-4900
TF: 800-844-8894 ■ *Web:* www.newellpaper.com

PaperDirect Inc 1005 E Woodmen Rd........ Colorado Springs CO 80920 800-272-7377 534-1741*
**Fax Area Code:* 719 ■ *TF:* 800-272-7377 ■ *Web:* www.paperdirect.com

Paterson Card & Paper Co PO Box 2286............ Paterson NJ 07501 973-278-2410 278-0677
Web: www.patersonpapers.com

Perez Trading Company Inc 3490 NW 125th St.......... Miami FL 33167 305-769-0761 681-7963
Web: www.pereztrading.com

Redd Paper Co 3851 Ctr Loop......................... Orlando FL 32808 407-299-6656 299-8142
TF: 800-961-6656 ■ *Web:* www.reddpaper.com

Rohn Industries Inc 862 Hersey St................... St. Paul MN 55114 651-647-1300
Web: rohnind.com

Roosevelt Paper Co One Roosevelt Dr............ Mount Laurel NJ 08054 856-303-4100 642-1949*
**Fax:* Sales ■ *TF:* 800-523-3470 ■ *Web:* www.rooseveltpaper.com

Spicers Paper Inc 12310 Slauson Ave......... Santa Fe Springs CA 90670 562-698-1199 945-2597
TF: 800-774-2377 ■ *Web:* www.spicers.com

Unisource Worldwide Inc
6600 Governors Lake Pkwy......................... Norcross GA 30071 770-447-9000 734-2000
TF: 800-864-7687 ■ *Web:* www.unisourceworldwide.com

White Paper Co 9990 River Way........................ Delta BC V4G1M9 604-951-3900 951-3944
TF: 888-840-7300 ■ *Web:* www.whitepaper.com

Wilcox Paper LLC 11100 Jefferson HWY N............ Champlin MN 55316 763-404-8400
Web: www.wilcoxpaper.com

557 PAPER CONVERTERS

Phone *Fax*

Ameri-Fax Corp 6520 W 20th Ave Ste 2............... Hialeah FL 33016 800-262-8214 824-1604*
**Fax Area Code:* 305 ■ *TF:* 800-262-8214 ■ *Web:* www.faxpaper.com

Artistry in Motion Inc 15101 Keswick St............ Van Nuys CA 91405 818-994-7388 994-7688
Web: www.artistryinmotion.com

Asian American Civic Association Inc
87 Tyler St Fl 5.................................... Boston MA 02111 617-426-9492
Web: www.aaca-boston.org

B & B Paper Converters Inc
12500 Elmwood Ave............................. Cleveland OH 44111 216-941-8100 941-8174
Web: bbpaper.com

BagcraftPapercon 3900 W 43rd St.................... Chicago IL 60632 773-254-8000 254-8204
TF: 800-621-8468 ■ *Web:* www.bagcraft.com

C-P Flexible Packaging 15 Grumbacher Rd............... York PA 17406 717-764-1193 764-2039
TF: 800-815-0667 ■ *Web:* www.cpconverters.com

Caraustar Industries Inc
5000 Austell-Powder Springs Rd Ste 300................ Austell GA 30106 770-948-3100
TF: 800-223-1373 ■ *Web:* www.caraustar.com

Case Paper Company Inc
500 Mamaroneck Ave Second Fl..................... Harrison NY 10528 914-899-3500 777-1028
TF: 800-222-2922 ■ *Web:* www.casepaper.com

Cindus Corp 515 Stn Ave.......................... Cincinnati OH 45215 800-543-4691 948-8805*
**Fax Area Code:* 513 ■ *TF:* 800-543-4691 ■ *Web:* www.cindus.com

Commercial Cutting & Graphics LLC
208 Central Ave.................................. Mansfield OH 44905 419-526-4800
Web: www.commercialcutting.com

Crusader Paper Company Inc 350 Holt Rd....... North Andover MA 01845 800-421-0007 794-1625*
**Fax Area Code:* 978 ■ *TF:* 800-421-0007 ■ *Web:* www.crusaderpaper.com

Damsky Paper Co 3501 First Ave N................ Birmingham AL 35222 205-521-9840 521-9840
Web: www.damskypaper.com

Fabricon Products 1721 W Pleasant Ave........... River Rouge MI 48218 313-841-8200 841-4819
TF: 800-676-9727 ■ *Web:* www.fabriconproducts.com

Gleason Industrial Products Inc
8575 Forest Home Ave Ste 100..................... Greenfield WI 53228 414-529-8357
Web: www.milwaukeehandtrucks.com

Graphic Converting LLC 877 N Larch Ave............ Elmhurst IL 60126 630-758-4100 833-1058
TF: 800-447-1935 ■ *Web:* www.graphicconverting.com

Great Southwest Paper Co
5707 Harvey Wilson Dr............................. Houston TX 77020 713-223-5050 223-3030
Web: www.gswpaper.com

Hampden Papers Inc 100 Water St PO Box 149......... Holyoke MA 01040 413-536-1000 532-9161
Web: www.hampdenpapers.com

Hazen Paper Co 240 S Water St PO Box 189............ Holyoke MA 01041 413-538-8204 533-1420
Web: www.hazen.com

International Converter Inc
17153 Industrial Hwy.............................. Caldwell OH 43724 740-732-5665 732-7515
TF: 800-848-6623 ■ *Web:* www.i-convert.com

Interstate Paper Supply Co Inc (IPSCO)
103 Good St PO Box 670............................ Roscoe PA 15477 724-938-2218 938-3415
Web: www.ipscoinc.com

Kanzaki Specialty Papers
1 Monarch Pl Ste 800............................ Springfield MA 01144 888-526-9254
TF: 888-526-9254 ■ *Web:* www.kanzakiusa.com

Lauterbach Group Inc W222 N5710 Miller Way.......... Sussex WI 53089 262-820-8130 820-1806
TF Sales: 800-841-7301 ■ *Web:* www.lauterbachgroup.com

Loyola Paper Co 951 W Lunt Ave.............. Elk Grove Village IL 60007 847-956-7770 956-6897

	City	State	ZIP	Phone	Fax
Mafcote Industries Inc 108 Main St *TF Cust Svc:* 800-221-3056 ■ *Web:* www.mafcote.com	Norwalk	CT	06851	203-847-8500	849-9177
Maritime Paper Products Ltd 25 Borden Ave Burnside Industrial Park *Web:* www.maritimepaper.com	Dartmouth	NS	B3B1C7	902-468-5353	
Max International Converters Inc 2360 Dairy Rd *TF:* 800-233-0222 ■ *Web:* www.maxintl.com	Lancaster	PA	17601	800-233-0222	
New Leaf Paper LLC 510 16th St Ste 520 *Web:* www.newleafpaper.com	Oakland	CA	94612	415-291-9210	
Newark Paperboard Products Inc 20 Jackson Dr *TF:* 800-777-7890 ■ *Web:* www.newarkgroup.com	Cranford	NJ	07016	908-276-4000	
Northeastern PA Carton & Finishing Co Inc 4820 Birney Ave US Rt 11 *Web:* www.nepacartons.com	Moosic	PA	18507	570-457-7711	457-3801
PAC Paper Inc 6416 NW Whitney Rd *TF:* 800-223-4981 ■ *Web:* www.pacpaperinc.com	Vancouver	WA	98665	360-695-7771	694-0943
Pacon Corp 2525 N Casaloma Dr **Fax Area Code:* 920 ■ *TF:* 800-333-2545 ■ *Web:* www.pacon.com	Appleton	WI	54912	800-333-2545	830-5099*
Paper Systems Inc 185 S Pioneer Blvd *TF:* 888-564-6774 ■ *Web:* www.papersystems.com	Springboro	OH	45066	937-746-6841	746-1089
PM Co 9220 Glades Dr *TF:* 800-327-4359 ■ *Web:* www.pmcompany.com	Fairfield	OH	45011	513-825-7626	825-2877
Port Townsend Paper Corp 100 Mill Rd *Web:* www.ptpc.com	Port Townsend	WA	98368	360-385-3170	
Protect-All Inc 109 Badger Pkwy *TF:* 888-432-8526 ■ *Web:* www.protect-all.com	Darien	WI	53114	888-432-8526	
Roselle Paper Company Inc 615 E First Ave *Web:* www.rosellepaper.com	Roselle	NJ	07203	908-245-6758	
Southeastern Paperboard Inc 100 S Harris Rd *Web:* www.southeasternpaperboard.com	Piedmont	SC	29673	864-277-7353	
Spectra-kote Corp 301 E Water St *Web:* www.spectra-kote.com	Gettysburg	PA	17325	717-334-3177	
Spinnaker Coating Inc 518 E Water St *TF:* 800-543-9452 ■ *Web:* spinnakercoating.com	Troy	OH	45373	937-332-6500	332-6518
SureVoid Products Inc 1895 W Dartmouth Ave *Web:* www.surevoid.com	Englewood	CO	80110	303-762-0324	
Texpack Inc 1001 Brickell Bay Dr *Web:* www.texpack.com	Miami	FL	33131	305-358-9696	
TimeMed Labeling Systems Inc 144 Tower Dr **Fax Area Code:* 800 ■ *TF Cust Svc:* 800-323-4840 ■ *Web:* www.pdchealthcare.com	Burr Ridge	IL	60527	630-986-1800	548-5359*
Tramont Corp 3701 N Humboldt Blvd *Web:* www.tramont.com	Milwaukee	WI	53212	414-967-8800	
Tufco Technologies Inc PO Box 23500 *NASDAQ: TFCO* ■ *TF:* 800-558-8145 ■ *Web:* www.tufco.com	Green Bay	WI	54305	920-336-0054	
Viking Paper Corp 5148 Stickney Ave *Web:* www.packpros.net	Toledo	OH	43612	419-729-4951	
Wedlock Paper Converters Ltd 2327 Stanfield Rd *Web:* www.wedlockpaper.com	Mississauga	ON	L4Y1R6	905-277-9461	272-1108
Western Robidoux Inc 4006 S 40th St *Web:* www.eyecandygraphicarts.com	Saint Joseph	MO	64503	816-279-1617	
Woodland Paper Inc 50785 Pontiac Trl *Web:* www.woodlandpaper.com	Wixom	MI	48393	248-926-5550	

558 PAPER FINISHERS (EMBOSSING, COATING, GILDING, STAMPING)

	City	State	ZIP	Phone	Fax
Colad Group 801 Exchange St *TF:* 800-950-1755 ■ *Web:* www.colad.com	Buffalo	NY	14210	716-961-1776	961-1753
Complemar Partners 500 Lee Rd Ste 200 *TF:* 800-388-7254 ■ *Web:* www.complemar.com	Rochester	NY	14606	585-647-5800	647-5800
Diecrafters Inc 1349 55th Ct *Web:* www.diecrafters.com	Cicero	IL	60804	708-656-3336	656-3386
Graphic Arts Finishers Inc 32 Cambridge St *Web:* graphicartsfinishers.com	Charlestown	MA	02129	617-241-9292	241-7326
Jen-Coat Inc 132 N Elm St **Fax:* Sales ■ *Web:* www.jencoat.com	Westfield	MA	01085	413-562-2315	*
Loroco Industries Inc 5000 Creek Rd *TF:* 800-215-9474 ■ *Web:* www.lorocoindustries.com	Cincinnati	OH	45242	513-891-9544	891-9549
Madison Cutting Die Inc 2547 Progress Rd *TF:* 800-395-9405 ■ *Web:* www.mcd.net	Madison	WI	53716	608-221-3422	223-6850
Markal Finishing Corp 400 Bostwick Ave *Web:* markalfinishing.com	Bridgeport	CT	06605	203-384-8219	336-1231
McGraphics Inc 601 Hagan St **Fax:* Orders ■ *TF:* 888-280-8200 ■ *Web:* www.mcgraphicsinc.com	Nashville	TN	37203	615-242-8779	254-3031*
Unifoil Corp 12 Daniel Rd *Web:* www.unifoil.com	Fairfield	NJ	07004	973-244-9900	244-5555
Walton Press (WP) 402 Mayfield Dr *TF:* 800-354-0235 ■ *Web:* www.waltonpress.com	Monroe	GA	30655	770-267-2596	267-9463

559 PAPER INDUSTRIES MACHINERY

	City	State	ZIP	Phone	Fax
ASC Machine Tools Inc 900 N Fancher Rd PO Box 11619 *Web:* www.ascmt.com	Spokane Valley	WA	99211	509-534-6600	536-7658
Baumfolder Corp 1660 Campbell Rd *TF:* 800-543-6107 ■ *Web:* www.baumfolder.com	Sidney	OH	45365	937-492-1281	492-7280
Black Clawson Converting Machinery Inc 46 N First St *Web:* www.davis-standard.com	Fulton	NY	13069	315-598-7121	593-0396
Cranston Machinery Company Inc 2251 SE Oak Grove Blvd *TF:* 800-547-1012 ■ *Web:* www.cranston-machinery.com	Oak Grove	OR	97267	503-654-7751	654-7751
Curt G Joa Inc 100 Crocker Ave PO Box 903 *Web:* www.joa.com	Sheboygan Falls	WI	53085	920-467-6136	467-2924
Double E Co 319 Manley St *Web:* www.doubleeusa.com	West Bridgewater	MA	02379	508-588-8099	580-2915
Entwistle Co Dietzco Div 6 Bigelow St *TF:* 800-445-8909 ■ *Web:* www.entwistleco.com	Hudson	MA	01749	508-481-4000	481-4004
Faustel Inc W 194 N 11301 McCormick Dr *Web:* www.faustel.com	Germantown	WI	53022	262-253-3333	253-3334
HG Weber & Company Inc 725 Fremont St *Web:* www.holwegweber.com	Kiel	WI	53042	920-894-2221	894-3786
Holyoke Machine Co 514 Main St PO Box 988 *Web:* www.holyokemachine.com	Holyoke	MA	01040	413-534-5612	532-9244
Kadant Black Clawson Inc 7312 Central Pk Blvd *Web:* www.kadant.com	Mason	OH	45040	513-229-8100	
Kadant Inc One Technology Pk Dr *NYSE: KAI* ■ *Web:* www.kadant.com	Westford	MA	01886	978-776-2000	635-1593
Kempsmith Machine Co 1819 S 71st St *Web:* www.kempsmith-dl.com	Milwaukee	WI	53214	414-256-8160	476-0564
Magna Machine Co 11180 Southland Rd *Web:* www.magna-machine.com	Cincinnati	OH	45240	513-851-6900	851-6904
MarquipWardUnited 1300 N Airport Rd *Web:* www.marquipwardunited.com	Phillips	wi	54555	715-339-2191	339-4469
Maxson Automatic Machinery Co 70 Airport Rd PO Box 1517 *Web:* www.maxsonautomatic.com	Westerly	RI	02891	401-596-0162	596-1050
Metso Paper USA Inc 25 Beloit St *Web:* www.metso.com	Aiken	SC	29805	803-293-2100	649-1036
Paco Winders Manufacturing Inc 2040 Bennett Rd *Web:* www.pacowinders.com	Philadelphia	PA	19116	215-673-6265	673-2027
Paper Machinery Corp 8900 W Bradley Rd PO Box 240100 *Web:* www.papermc.com	Milwaukee	WI	53224	414-354-8050	354-8614
Pemco Inc 3333 Crocker Ave *TF:* 888-310-1898 ■ *Web:* www.pemco-solutions.com	Sheboygan	WI	53082	920-458-2500	458-1265
Sandusky International Inc 615 W Market St *Web:* www.sanduskyintl.com	Sandusky	OH	44870	419-626-5340	626-8674
Voith Paper Inc 2200 N Roemer Rd PO Box 2337 *Web:* voith.com	Appleton	WI	54912	920-731-7724	997-9625
Zerand Corp 15800 W Overland Dr *Web:* cerutti.it	New Berlin	WI	53151	262-827-3800	827-3913

560 PAPER MILLS

SEE ALSO Paperboard Mills p. 2857; Pulp Mills p. 2994

	City	State	ZIP	Phone	Fax
AbitibiBowater Inc 1155 Metcalfe St Ste 800 *Web:* www.resolutefp.com	Montreal	QC	H3B5H2	514-875-2160	
Acupac Packaging Inc 55 Ramapo Vly Rd *Web:* www.acupac.com	Mahwah	NJ	07430	201-529-3434	
Advanced Poly Packaging Inc 1331 Emmitt Rd *Web:* www.advancedpoly.com	Akron	OH	44306	330-785-4000	
Ahlstrom Filtration LLC 122 W Butler St Mount Holly Springs plant *Web:* www.ahlstrom.com	Mount Holly Springs	PA	17065	717-486-3438	
Allen Packaging Co 1150 Valencia Ave *Web:* www.allenpkg.com	Tustin	CA	92780	714-259-0100	
Arjobex America Mill 10901 Westlake Dr *Web:* www.polyart.com	Charlotte	NC	28273	800-765-9278	
Armor Protective Packaging 951 Jones St *TF:* 800-365-1117 ■ *Web:* www.armorvci.com	Howell	MI	48843	517-546-1117	
Atlantic Tape Company Inc 611 Hwy 74 S Ste 300 *Web:* www.atlantictape.com	Peachtree City	GA	30269	770-461-3557	
Bag to Earth Inc 201 Richmond Blvd *Web:* bagtoearth.com	Napanee	ON	K7R3Z9	613-354-1330	354-1923
Bear Island Paper Company LLC 10026 Old Ridge Rd *Web:* www.paperage.com	Ashland	VA	23005	804-227-3394	
Boise Cascade LLC 1111 W Jefferson St Ste 300 *Web:* www.bc.com	Boise	ID	83702	208-384-6161	384-7189
BPM Inc 200 W Front St *TF:* 800-826-0494 ■ *Web:* www.bpmpaper.com	Peshtigo	WI	54157	715-582-4551	582-4853
Burrows Paper Corp 501 W Main St *TF:* 800-272-7122 ■ *Web:* www.burrowspaper.com	Little Falls	NY	13365	315-823-2300	823-3892
Buschman Corp 4100 Payne Ave Ste 1 *Web:* buschmancorp.com	Cleveland	OH	44103	216-431-6633	
Cad Store Inc, The 15353 N 91st Ave *Web:* thecadstore.com	Peoria	AZ	85381	623-931-7936	
Cases By Source Inc 215 Island Rd *Web:* www.casesbysource.com	Mahwah	NJ	07430	201-831-0005	
Catalyst Paper Corp 3600 Lysander Ln 2nd Fl *TSE: CTL* ■ *Web:* www.catalystpaper.com	Richmond	BC	V7B1C3	604-247-4400	247-0512
Cauthorne Paper Co 12124 S Washington Hwy *TF:* 800-552-3011 ■ *Web:* www.cauthornepaper.com	Ashland	VA	23005	804-798-6999	798-6466
Climax Manufacturing Co 7840 SR 26 *TF:* 800-225-4629 ■ *Web:* www.climaxpkg.com	Lowville	NY	13367	315-376-8000	376-2034
Conder Flag Co 4705 Dwight Evans Rd *Web:* www.allstarflags.com	Charlotte	NC	28217	704-529-1976	
Ecological Fibers Inc 40 Pioneer Dr *Web:* www.ecofibers.com	Lunenburg	MA	01462	978-537-0003	537-2238
Economy Paper Company of Rochester Inc 1175 E Main St *Web:* www.economypaper.com	Rochester	NY	14609	585-482-5340	
FF Soucy Inc 191 Delage *Web:* www.ffsoucy.com	Riviere Du Loup	QC	G5R3Z1	418-862-6941	867-1134
FiberMark North America, Inc. 161 Wellington Rd *TF Cust Svc:* 800-784-8558 ■ *Web:* www.fibermark.com	Brattleboro	VT	05302	802-257-0365	
Filtrona Greensboro Inc 303 Gallimore Dairy Rd *Web:* filtrona.com	Greensboro	NC	27409	336-605-0293	

Company	City	State	Zip	Phone	Fax
Finch Paper LLC One Glen St. *TF:* 800-833-9983 ■ *Web:* www.finchpaper.com	Glens Falls	NY	12801	518-793-2541	
Frankston Packaging 811 State Hwy 155 *Web:* frankstonpackaging.com	Frankston	TX	75763	903-876-0156	
Frontier Paper Inc 1848 Ship Ave. *Web:* www.frontierpaper.com	Anchorage	AK	99501	907-272-4000	
FutureMark Paper Co 13101 S Pulaski Rd *TF:* 866-580-8325 ■ *Web:* www.futuremarkpaper.com	Alsip	IL	60803	708-272-8700	
Gabriel Container Co 8844 S Millergrove Dr PO Box 3188 *Web:* www.gabrielcontainer.com	Santa Fe Springs	CA	90670	562-699-1051	699-3284
Glatfelter 96 S George St Ste 500 *Web:* www.glatfelter.com	York	PA	17401	717-225-4711	846-7208
Grays Harbor Paper LP 801 23rd St *Web:* www.ghpaper.com	Hoquiam	WA	98550	360-532-9600	
Green Field Paper Co 7196 Clairemont Mesa Blvd *TF:* 888-402-9979 ■ *Web:* www.greenfieldpaper.com	San Diego	CA	92111	858-565-2585	
Harvard Crimson Inc, The 14 Plympton St *Web:* thecrimson.com	Cambridge	MA	02138	617-576-6600	
Hollingsworth & Vose Co 112 Washington St *Web:* www.hollingsworth-vose.com	East Walpole	MA	02032	508-850-2000	668-3557
Inland Empire Paper Co 3320 N Argonne *TF:* 866-437-7711 ■ *Web:* www.iepco.com	Millwood	WA	99212	509-924-1911	927-8461
International Paper Co 6400 Poplar Ave. *NYSE:* IP ■ *TF Prod Info:* 800-223-1268 ■ *Web:* www.internationalpaper.com	Memphis	TN	38197	901-419-9000	
Interstate Paper LLC 2366 Interstate Rd. *Web:* www.interstatepaper.com	Riceboro	GA	31323	912-884-3371	
Interstate Resources Inc 1300 Wilson Blvd Ste 1075 *Web:* www.interstateresources.com	Arlington	VA	22209	703-243-3355	243-4681
Just Packaging 450 Oak Tree Ave Ste 1 *Web:* www.justpackaging.com	South Plainfield	NJ	07080	908-753-6700	
K D M Enterprise LLC 820 Commerce Pkwy *Web:* www.gokdm.com	Carpentersville	IL	60110	847-783-0333	
KAPS-ALL Packaging Systems Inc 200 Mill Rd. *Web:* www.kapsall.com	Riverhead	NY	11901	631-727-0300	
kapstone 5600 Virginia Ave PO Box 118005 *Web:* kapstonepaper.com	Charleston	SC	29423	843-745-3000	745-3067
KapStone Paper & Packaging Corp 1101 Skokie Blvd Ste 300 *NYSE:* KS ■ *Web:* www.kapstonepaper.com	Northbrook	IL	60062	847-239-8800	205-7551
KapStone Paper and Packaging Corp 300 Fibre Way PO Box 639 *Web:* www.longviewfibre.com	Longview	WA	98632	360-425-1550	230-5135
Katahdin Paper Co 50 Main St	East Millinocket	ME	04430	207-723-5131	723-2200
Keystone Adjustable Cap Co 1591 Hylton Rd Ste B *Web:* www.beringer.net	Pennsauken	NJ	08110	856-663-5740	
Kimberly-Clark Corp 351 Phelps Dr *NYSE:* KMB ■ *TF:* 888-525-8388 ■ *Web:* www.kimberly-clark.com	Irving	TX	75038	972-281-1200	281-1490
Kruger Inc 3285 Ch Bedford *Web:* www.kruger.com	Montreal	QC	H3S1G5	514-737-1131	343-3124
LBP Manufacturing Inc 1325 S Cicero Ave *Web:* www.lbpmfg.com	Cicero	IL	60804	708-652-5600	
M&A Advisor LLC, The 108-18 Queens Blvd Second Fl *Web:* www.maadvisor.com	Forest Hills	NY	11375	718-997-7900	
Madison Paper Industries Main St.	Madison	ME	04911	207-696-3307	696-1104
Marq Packaging Systems Inc 3801 W Washington Ave. *TF:* 800-998-4301 ■ *Web:* www.marq.net	Yakima	WA	98903	509-966-4300	
Maryland Paper Company LP 16144 Elliott Pkwy *Web:* www.marylandpaper.com	Williamsport	MD	21795	301-223-6550	223-7730
Menshen Packaging USA Inc 21 Industrial Pk *Web:* www.menshenusa.com	Waldwick	NJ	07463	201-445-7436	
Merchants Paper Co 4625 SE 24th Ave *Web:* merchantspaper.com	Portland	OR	97202	503-235-2171	
Mercury Paper Inc 495 Radio Sta Rd *Web:* www.mercurypaper.com	Strasburg	VA	22657	540-465-6900	
Metro Packaging & Imaging Inc 5 Haul Rd *Web:* metro-pi.com	Wayne	NJ	07470	973-709-9100	709-9477
Minas Basin Pulp & Power Co Ltd 53 Prince St PO Box 401 *Web:* www.minas.ns.ca	Hantsport	NS	B0P1P0	902-835-7100	
Monadnock Paper Mills Inc 117 Antrim Rd. **Fax:* Sales ■ *TF Orders:* 800-221-2159 ■ *Web:* www.mpm.com	Bennington	NH	03442	603-588-3311	588-3158*
Nelson Jit Packaging Supplies Inc 4022 W Turney Ave Ste 3 *Web:* www.nelsonjit.com	Phoenix	AZ	85019	623-939-3365	
Newton Falls Fine Paper Company LLC 875 County Rt 60 *Web:* www.newtonfallsfinepaper.com	Newton Falls	NY	13666	315-848-3321	
Norkol Inc & Converting 11650 W Grand Ave *Web:* www.norkol.com	Northlake	IL	60164	708-531-1000	531-0030
Oakland Packaging & Supply 3200 Regatta Blvd Ste F *Web:* www.oakpackaging.com	Richmond	CA	94804	510-307-4242	
Pac Tech USA - Packaging Technologies Inc 328 Martin Ave *Web:* www.pactech-usa.com	Santa Clara	CA	95050	408-588-1925	
Palmetto Infusion Services LLC 172 Mcswain Dr Ste A *Web:* www.palmettoinfusion.com	West Columbia	SC	29169	803-771-7740	
Plastiform Packaging Inc 114 Beach St. *Web:* www.plastiformpkg.com	Rockaway	NJ	07866	973-983-8900	
Potlatch Corp 601 W First Ave Ste 1600 *NASDAQ:* PCH ■ *Web:* www.potlatchcorp.com	Spokane	WA	99201	509-835-1500	835-1555
Pratt Industries USA 1800C Sarasota Pkwy *TF:* 800-835-2088 ■ *Web:* www.prattindustries.com	Conyers	GA	30013	770-918-5678	918-5679
Roll Bond Converting 12855 Vly Branch Ln *Web:* www.rbconverting.com	Dallas	TX	75234	972-239-0000	
Sabin Robbins Paper Co 9365 Allen Rd	West Chester	OH	45069	513-874-5270	874-0667
Sandusky Packaging Corp 2016 George St. *Web:* www.sanduskypackaging.com	Sandusky	OH	44870	419-626-8520	
Schweitzer-Mauduit International Inc 100 N Pt Ctr E Ste 600 *NYSE:* SWM ■ *TF:* 800-514-0186 ■ *Web:* www.swmintl.com	Alpharetta	GA	30022	770-569-4271	569-4275
Seaman Paper Co of Massachusetts 51 Main St *Web:* www.seamanpaper.com	Otter River	MA	01436	978-632-1513	632-6319
Sierra Converting Corp 1400 Kleppe Ln. *Web:* www.sierraconverting.com	Sparks	NV	89431	775-331-8221	
SP Newsprint Co 709 Papermill Rd **Fax Area Code:* 404	Dublin	GA	31027	478-272-1600	979-6615*
Spicers Canada Ltd 200 Galcat Dr *Web:* www.spicers.ca	Vaughan	ON	L4L0B9	905-265-5000	
Technocell Inc 3075 rue Bernier *Web:* www.felix-schoeller.com	Drummondville	QC	J2C6Y4	819-475-0066	
Telmark Packaging Corp 30 Freneau Ave *Web:* www.telmarkpkg.com	Matawan	NJ	07747	732-739-9100	
Twin Rivers Paper Company Inc 707 Sable Oaks Dr Ste 010 *Web:* www.twinriverspaper.com	South Portland	ME	04106	207-523-2350	
Verso Corp 6775 Lenox Ctr Ct Ste 400 *NYSE:* VRS ■ **Fax Area Code:* 901 ■ *TF:* 877-837-7606 ■ *Web:* www.versopaper.com	Memphis	TN	38115	877-837-7606	369-4174*
West Linn Paper Co 4800 Mill St *TF:* 800-989-3608 ■ *Web:* www.wlinpco.com	West Linn	OR	97068	503-557-6500	557-6616
Western Pulp Products Co 5025 SW Hout St *Web:* www.westernpulp.com	Corvallis	OR	97333	541-757-1151	
Willard Packaging Company Inc 18940 Woodfield Rd *Web:* www.willardpackaging.com	Gaithersburg	MD	20879	301-948-7700	
Woodland Pulp LLC 144 Main St	Baileyville	ME	04694	207-427-3311	
WR Rayson Company Inc 720 S Dickerson St *Web:* www.wrrayson.com	Burgaw	NC	28425	910-259-8100	
Xamax Industries Inc 63 Silvermine Rd *TF:* 888-926-2988 ■ *Web:* www.xamax.com	Seymour	CT	06483	203-888-7200	888-1002

561 PAPER PRODUCTS - SANITARY

Company	City	State	Zip	Phone	Fax
Aspen Products Inc 4231 Clary Blvd *Web:* www.aspenpro.com	Kansas City	MO	64130	816-921-0234	924-1488
Associated Hygienic Products LLC 3400 River Green Ct Ste 600 *TF General:* 800-757-0927 ■ *Web:* www.ahp-dsg.com	Duluth	GA	30096	770-497-9800	623-8887
Atlas Paper Mills LLC 3301 NW 107th St. *TF:* 800-562-2860 ■ *Web:* www.atlaspapermills.com	Miami	FL	33167	305-636-5740	
Bright of America Inc 300 Greenbrier Rd	Summersville	WV	26651	304-872-3000	872-3033
Erving Paper Mills 97 E Main St. *Web:* ervingpaper.com	Erving	MA	01344	413-422-2700	422-2710
Fempro I Inc 1330 Michaud St. *Web:* www.fempro.com	Drummondville	QC	J2C2Z5	819-475-8900	
Ferris Manufacturing Corp 16W300 83rd St. *Web:* www.polymem.com	Burr Ridge	IL	60527	630-887-9797	
Georgia-Pacific Corp 133 Peachtree St NE *Web:* www.gp.com	Atlanta	GA	30303	404-652-4000	
Hoffmaster 2920 N Main St *TF:* 800-327-9774 ■ *Web:* www.hoffmaster.com	Oshkosh	WI	54901	920-235-9330	235-1642
Kimberly-Clark Corp 351 Phelps Dr *NYSE:* KMB ■ *TF:* 888-525-8388 ■ *Web:* www.kimberly-clark.com	Irving	TX	75038	972-281-1200	281-1490
Kleen Test Products Inc 1611 Sunset Rd *Web:* www.kleentest.com	Port Washington	WI	53074	262-284-6600	284-6623
Nice-Pak Products Inc Two Nice-Pak Pk *TF:* 800-999-6423 ■ *Web:* www.nicepak.com	Orangeburg	NY	10962	845-365-1700	365-1717
Orchids Paper Products Co 4826 Hunt St. *NYSE:* TIS ■ *Web:* www.orchidspaper.com	Pryor	OK	74361	918-825-0616	825-0060
Personal Products Co One Johnson & Johnson Plaza *Web:* www.jnj.com/our_company/family_of_companies	New Brunswick	NJ	08933	732-524-0400	
Potlatch Corp 601 W First Ave Ste 1600 *NASDAQ:* PCH ■ *Web:* www.potlatchcorp.com	Spokane	WA	99201	509-835-1500	835-1555
Precision Paper Converters LLC 2600 Northridge Dr. *Web:* www.cornerstone-business.com	Kaukauna	WI	54130	920-462-0050	
Principle Business Enterprises Inc PO Box 129 *TF:* 800-467-3224 ■ *Web:* www.tranquilityproducts.com	Dunbridge	OH	43414	419-352-1551	352-8340
Roses Southwest Papers Inc 1701 Second St SW *Web:* www.rosessouthwest.com	Albuquerque	NM	87102	505-842-0134	242-0342
SCA Americas 2929 Arch St Ste 2600 *TF Cust Svc:* 800-328-9043 ■ *Web:* www.sca.com	Philadelphia	PA	19104	610-499-3700	499-3391
Tranzonic Cos 26301 Curtiss Wright Pkwy Ste 200 *TF:* 800-553-7979 ■ *Web:* www.tranzonic.com	Cleveland	OH	44143	216-535-4300	831-5647
Wausau Paper Corp 100 Paper Pl. *NYSE:* WPP ■ *TF:* 800-723-0008 ■ *Web:* www.wausaupaper.com	Mosinee	WI	54455	715-693-4470	692-2082

562 PAPER PRODUCTS - WHOL

Company	City	State	Zip	Phone	Fax
American Hotel Register Co 100 S Milwaukee Ave **Fax Area Code:* 800 ■ **Fax:* Sales ■ *TF:* 800-323-5686 ■ *Web:* www.americanhotel.com	Vernon Hills	IL	60061	847-743-3000	688-9108*

Company / Address	City	State	Zip	Phone	Fax
American Paper & Twine Co 7400 Cockrill Bend Blvd	Nashville	TN	37209	615-350-9000	413-5055*
*Fax Area Code: 877 ■ TF: 800-251-2437 ■ Web: shopapt.com					
Atlantic Paper & Twine Co Inc 85 York Ave	Pawtucket	RI	02904	401-725-0950	
TF: 800-613-0950 ■ Web: www.atlanticpaper.com					
BGR Inc 6392 Gano Rd	West Chester	OH	45069	513-755-7100	755-7855
TF: 800-628-9195 ■ Web: bgr.us					
Brame Specialty Company Inc PO Box 27	Durham	NC	27702	919-683-1331	682-6034
TF: 800-533-2041 ■ Web: www.brameco.com					
Butler-Dearden Paper Service Inc PO Box 1069	Boylston	MA	01505	508-869-9000	869-0211
TF: 800-634-7070 ■ Web: www.butlerdearden.com					
Central Paper Products Co Inc 350 Gay St Brown Ave Industrial Pk	Manchester	NH	03103	603-624-4065	624-8795
TF: 800-339-4065 ■ Web: www.centralpaper.com					
D-k Trading Corp PO Box E	Clarks Summit	PA	18411	570-586-9662	342-7511
Web: www.dk-t.com					
Dacotah Paper Co 3940 15th Ave NW	Fargo	ND	58102	701-281-1734	281-9799
TF: 800-270-6352 ■ Web: www.dacotahpaper.com					
Ernest Paper Products 5777 Smithway St	Commerce	CA	90040	800-233-7788	583-6561*
*Fax Area Code: 323 ■ TF: 800-233-7788 ■ Web: www.ernestpackaging.com					
Fleetwood-Signode 2222 Windsor Ct	Addison	IL	60101	630-268-9999	268-9919
TF: 800-862-7997 ■ Web: www.fleetsig.com					
Garland C Norris Co 1101 Terry Rd PO Box 28	Apex	NC	27502	919-387-1059	387-1325
TF: 800-331-8920 ■ Web: www.gcnorris.com					
Gem State Paper & Supply Co 1801 Highland Ave E	Twin Falls	ID	83303	208-733-6081	734-9870
TF: 800-727-2737 ■ Web: www.gemstatepaper.com					
George H Swatek Inc 1095 Edgewater Ave	Ridgefield	NJ	07657	201-941-2400	941-8681
Web: www.ghswatek.com					
H. T. Berry Co Inc PO Box B	Canton	MA	02021	781-828-6000	828-9788
TF: 800-736-2206 ■ Web: www.htberry.com					
Harder Corp 5301 Verona Rd	Madison	WI	53711	608-271-5127	271-4677
Web: www.hardercorp.com					
Hathaway Inc PO Box 1618	Waynesboro	VA	22980	540-949-8285	943-7619
Web: www.hathawaypaper.com					
Heartland Paper Co 808 W Cherokee St	Sioux Falls	SD	57104	605-336-1190	332-8378
TF Cust Svc: 800-843-7922 ■ Web: www.heartland-paper.com					
Johnston Paper Co 2 Eagle Dr	Auburn	NY	13021	315-253-8435	253-8744
TF: 800-800-7123 ■ Web: www.johnstonpaper.com					
Landsberg Orora 1640 S Greenwood Ave	Montebello	CA	90640	323-832-2000	
TF Cust Svc: 888-526-3723 ■ Web: www.landsberg.com					
Leonard Paper Co 725 N Haven St	Baltimore	MD	21205	800-327-5547	563-0249*
*Fax Area Code: 410 ■ TF Cust Svc: 800-327-5547 ■ Web: www.leonardpaper.com					
M Conley Co 1312 Fourth St SE	Canton	OH	44707	330-456-8243	588-2572*
*Fax: Cust Svc ■ TF: 800-362-6001 ■ Web: www.conleypackaging.com					
Mainland preparatory Academy 319 Newman Rd	La Marque	TX	77568	409-934-9100	934-9130
Web: www.mainpaperparty.com					
Max-Pak LLC 2808 New Tampa Hwy	Lakeland	FL	33815	863-682-0123	683-7895
Web: www.maxpak.cc					
Mayfield Paper Co 1115 S Hill St	San Angelo	TX	76903	325-653-1444	653-7031
TF: 800-725-1441 ■ Web: www.mayfieldpaper.com					
NAPCO 2400 Cantrell Rd Ste 116	Little Rock	AR	72202	501-374-5884	374-5129
National Paper & Sanitary Supply 2511 S 156th Cir	Omaha	NE	68130	402-330-5507	330-4109
TF: 800-647-2737 ■ Web: catalog.nationalew.com/catalog/					
Nichols Paper & Supply Company Inc PO Box 291	Muskegon	MI	49443	231-799-2120	777-8250
TF: 800-442-0213 ■ Web: www.enichols.com					
Pacific Packaging Products Inc 24 Industrial Way	Wilmington	MA	01887	978-657-9100	658-4933
TF: 800-777-0300 ■ Web: www.pacificpkg.com					
Packaging Distribution Services Inc (PDS) 2308 Sunset Rd	Des Moines	IA	50321	515-243-3156	243-1741
TF: 800-747-2699 ■ Web: www.pdspack.com					
Paper Products Company Inc 36 Terminal Way	Pittsburgh	PA	15219	412-481-6200	481-4787
Web: www.paperproducts-pgh.com					
Paterson Pacific Parchment Co 625 Greg St	Sparks	NV	89431	775-353-3000	456-8104*
*Fax Area Code: 800 ■ TF: 800-678-8104 ■ Web: www.patersonpaper.com					
Perez Trading Company Inc 3490 NW 125th St	Miami	FL	33167	305-769-0761	681-7963
Web: www.pereztrading.com					
Phillips Distribution Inc 3000 E Houston St Ste B	San Antonio	TX	78220	210-227-2397	222-0790*
*Fax Area Code: 361 ■ TF: 800-580-2397 ■ Web: www.phillipsdistribution.com					
Pollock Paper & Packaging One Pollock Pl	Grand Prairie	TX	75050	972-263-2126	262-4737
TF Cust Svc: 800-843-7320 ■ Web: www.pollockpaper.com					
S. Freedman & Sons Inc 3322 Pennsy Dr	Landover	MD	20785	301-322-5000	772-7563
TF: 800-545-7277 ■ Web: www.sfreedman.com					
Saint Louis Paper & Box Co 3843 Garfield Ave	Saint Louis	MO	63113	314-531-7900	531-0968
TF: 800-779-7901 ■ Web: www.stlpaper.com					
Schwarz 8338 Austin Ave	Morton Grove	IL	60053	800-323-4903	966-1271*
*Fax Area Code: 847 ■ TF: 800-323-4903 ■ Web: www.schwarz.com					
Shorr Packaging Inc 800 N Commerce St	Aurora	IL	60504	630-978-1000	978-1300
TF: 888-885-0055 ■ Web: www.shorr.com					
Snyder Paper Corp 250 26th St Dr SE	Hickory	NC	28602	828-328-2501	222-8562*
*Fax Area Code: 800 ■ TF: 800-222-8562 ■ Web: www.snyderpaper.com					
TSN Inc 4001 Salazar Way PO Box 679	Frederick	CO	80530	303-530-0600	530-1919
TF General: 888-997-5959 ■ Web: bunzldistribution.com					
Unisource Worldwide Inc 6600 Governors Lake Pkwy	Norcross	GA	30071	770-447-9000	734-2000
TF: 800-864-7687 ■ Web: www.unisourceworldwide.com					
Western Paper Distributors Inc PO Box 17425	Denver	CO	80217	303-371-6000	371-6111
Web: www.westernpaper.com					
xpedx 6285 Tri-Ridge Blvd	Loveland	OH	45140	513-965-2900	965-2849
Web: www.xpedx.com					

563 PAPERBOARD & CARDBOARD - DIE-CUT

Company / Address	City	State	Zip	Phone	Fax
Alvah Bushnell Co 519 E Chelten Ave	Philadelphia	PA	19144	215-842-9520	843-7725
TF: 800-255-7434 ■ Web: www.bushnellco.com					
Blanks/USA Inc 7700 68th Ave N #7	Minneapolis	MN	55428	800-328-7311	
TF: 800-328-7311 ■ Web: www.laserblanks.com					
Crescent Cardboard Company LLC 100 W Willow Rd	Wheeling	IL	60090	800-323-1055	537-7153*
*Fax Area Code: 847 ■ TF: 800-323-1055 ■ Web: www.crescentcardboard.com					
Demco Inc 4810 Forest Run Rd	Madison	WI	53704	608-241-1201	241-1799
TF Orders: 800-356-1200 ■ Web: www.demco.com					
GBS Filing Solutions 224 Morges Rd	Malvern	OH	44644	330-494-5330	444-9427*
*Fax Area Code: 800 ■ TF: 800-873-4427 ■ Web: www.gbscorp.com					
Tap Packaging Solutions 2160 Superior Ave	Cleveland	OH	44114	216-781-6000	771-2572
TF: 800-827-5679 ■ Web: www.tap-usa.com					
Topps Company Inc One Whitehall St	New York	NY	10004	212-376-0300	376-0573
TF: 800-489-9149 ■ Web: www.topps.com					
University Products Inc 517 Main St	Holyoke	MA	01040	413-532-3372	532-9281*
*Fax Area Code: 800 ■ TF: 800-628-1912 ■ Web: www.universityproducts.com					
Warren Industries Inc 3100 Mt Pleasant St	Racine	WI	53404	262-639-7800	639-0920
Web: www.wrnind.com					
Westcott Displays Inc 450 Amsterdam St	Detroit	MI	48202	313-872-1200	875-3295
Web: www.westcottdisplays.com					
Xertrex International Inc 1530 W Glenlake Ave	Itasca	IL	60143	630-773-4020	773-4696
TF: 800-822-2437 ■ Web: tabbies.com					
Xertrex International Inc Tabbies Div 1530 W Glenlake Ave	Itasca	IL	60143	630-773-4160	328-1722*
*Fax Area Code: 720 ■ TF: 800-822-2437 ■ Web: www.tabbies.com					

564 PAPERBOARD MILLS

SEE ALSO Paper Mills p. 2855; Pulp Mills p. 2994

Company / Address	City	State	Zip	Phone	Fax
Cascades Inc 404 Marie-Victorin Blvd	Kingsey Falls	QC	J0A1B0	819-363-5100	363-5155
TSE: CAS ■ TF: 800-361-4070 ■ Web: www.cascades.com					
Century Packaging Inc 42 Edgeboro Rd	East Brunswick	NJ	08816	732-249-6600	
Web: www.centurypackaginginc.com					
Combined Technologies Inc 13970 W Polo Trl Dr	Lake Forest	IL	60045	847-968-4855	
Web: ctipack.com					
DEX Products Inc 840 Eubanks Dr Ste A	Vacaville	CA	95688	707-451-7864	
Web: www.dexproducts.com					
FiberMark Inc 161 Wellington Rd	Brattleboro	VT	05301	802-257-0365	257-5907*
*Fax: Sales ■ Web: www.fibermark.com					
FiberMark North America, Inc. 161 Wellington Rd	Brattleboro	VT	05302	802-257-0365	
TF Cust Svc: 800-784-8558 ■ Web: www.fibermark.com					
Globe Die-Cutting Products Inc 76 Liberty St	Metuchen	NJ	08840	732-494-7744	
Web: www.globediecutting.com					
Green Bay Packaging Inc Mill Div 1700 N Webster Ct Box 19017	Green Bay	WI	54307	920-433-5111	433-5105
TF: 800-445-4269 ■ Web: www.gbp.com					
International Paper Co 6400 Poplar Ave	Memphis	TN	38197	901-419-9000	
NYSE: IP ■ TF Prod Info: 800-223-1268 ■ Web: www.internationalpaper.com					
Interpress Technologies Inc 1120 Del Paso Rd	Sacramento	CA	95834	916-929-9771	
Web: www.iptec.com					
KapStone Paper and Packaging Corp 300 Fibre Way PO Box 639	Longview	WA	98632	360-425-1550	230-5135
Web: www.longviewfibre.com					
Los Angeles Paper Box 6027 S Eastern Ave	Commerce	CA	90040	323-685-8900	
Web: www.lapb.com					
Lydall Inc One Colonial Rd	Manchester	CT	06042	860-646-1233	646-4917
NYSE: LDL ■ Web: www.lydall.com					
Newark Group 20 Jackson Dr	Cranford	NJ	07016	908-276-4000	276-9126
TF: 800-777-7890 ■ Web: www.newarkgroup.com					
Newman & Company Inc 6101 Tacony St	Philadelphia	PA	19135	215-333-8700	332-8586
TF: 800-523-3256 ■ Web: newmanpaperboard.com					
Norampac Industries Inc 4001 Packard Rd	Niagara Falls	NY	14303	716-285-3681	
Oji Intertech Inc 906 W Hanley Rd	North Manchester	IN	46962	260-982-1544	
Web: www.ojiintertech.com					
Packaging Corp of America 1955 W Field Ct	Lake Forest	IL	60045	800-456-4725	615-6379*
NYSE: PKG ■ *Fax Area Code: 847 ■ TF: 800-456-4725 ■ Web: www.packagingcorp.com					
Pactiv Corp 1900 W Field Ct	Lake Forest	IL	60045	847-482-2000	482-4738
TF: 888-828-2850 ■ Web: www.pactiv.com					
Paper Cut Inc, The 234 W Northland Ave	Appleton	WI	54911	920-954-6210	
Web: www.thepapercut.com					
PaperWorks Industries Inc 5000 Flat Rock Rd	Philadelphia	PA	19127	215-984-7000	
Web: www.paperworksindustries.com					
Potlatch Corp 601 W First Ave Ste 1600	Spokane	WA	99201	509-835-1500	835-1555
NASDAQ: PCH ■ Web: www.potlatchcorp.com					
Specialty Roll Products Inc 601 25th Ave	Meridian	MS	39301	601-693-1771	
Web: www.specialtyroll.com					
Superior Packaging Solutions 26858 Almond Ave	Redlands	CA	92374	800-680-2393	
TF: 800-680-2393 ■ Web: www.sps4pkg.com					
United States Box Corp 1296 Mccarter Hwy	Newark	NJ	07104	973-481-2000	
Web: www.usbox.com					
WinterBell Co 2018 Brevard Rd	High Point	NC	27263	336-887-2651	
Web: www.winterbell.com					

565 PARKING SERVICE

	City	State	Zip	Phone	Fax
Ace Parking Management Inc 645 Ash St *TF General:* 800-925-7275 ■ *Web:* www.aceparking.com	San Diego	CA	92101	619-233-6624	233-0741
Alco Parking Corp 501 Martindale St	Pittsburgh	PA	15212	412-323-4455	
Allpro Parking LLC 465 Main St Lafayette Court Bldg Ste 200Annex *Web:* www.allproparking.com	Buffalo	NY	14203	716-849-7275	
B & J Parking Lot Maintenance 12207 Inkster Rd *Web:* www.bandjmaint.com	Taylor	MI	48180	734-941-7570	
Baltimore County Revenue Authority 115 Towsontown Blvd E *TF:* 888-246-5384 ■ *Web:* www.baltimoregolfing.com	Baltimore	MD	21286	410-887-3127	296-7459
Classic Parking Inc 3208 Royal St *Web:* classicparking.com	Los Angeles	CA	90007	213-742-1238	
Colonial Parking Inc 1050 Thomas Jefferson St NW Ste 100 *TF:* 877-777-4778 ■ *Web:* www.ecolonial.com	Washington	DC	20007	202-295-8100	295-8111
Denison Parking 36 S Pennsylvania St Ste 200 *Web:* www.denisonparking.com	Indianapolis	IN	46204	317-633-4003	655-3101
Diamond Parking Inc 605 First Ave Ste 6000 *TF:* 800-340-7275 ■ *Web:* www.diamondparking.com	Seattle	WA	98104	206-284-3100	
Douglas Parking LLC 1721 Webster St *Web:* www.douglasparking.com	Oakland	CA	94612	510-444-7412	
Edison Properties LLC 100 Washington St *TF:* 888-727-5327 ■ *Web:* www.parkfast.com	Newark	NJ	07102	973-643-0895	643-2169
GGMC Parking LLC 1651 Third Ave *Web:* www.ggmcparking.com	New York	NY	10128	212-996-6363	
Imperial Parking Corp 601 W Cordova St Ste 300 *Web:* www.impark.com	Vancouver	BC	V6B1G1	604-681-7311	681-4098
Integrity Parking Systems LLC 9828 E Washington St *Web:* integrityparking.com	Chagrin Falls	OH	44023	440-543-4123	
InterPark 200 N LaSalle St Ste 1400 *Web:* www.interparkholdings.com	Chicago	IL	60601	312-935-2800	935-2999
Landmark Parking Inc 33 S Gay St *Web:* landmarkparking.com	Baltimore	MD	21202	410-837-5600	
Lanier Parking Solutions 233 Peachtree St NE *Web:* www.lanierparking.com	Atlanta	GA	30303	404-881-6076	881-6077
Loop Parking 1430 W Lake St *Web:* www.loopparking.com	Minneapolis	MN	55408	612-823-0527	
Miami Parking System 190 Ne Third St *Web:* miamiparking.com	Miami	FL	33132	305-373-6789	
Modern Parking Inc 1200 Wilshire Blvd Ste 300 *Web:* www.modernparking.com	Los Angeles	CA	90017	213-482-8400	
Park 'N Fly 2060 Mt Paran Rd Ste 207 **Fax Area Code:* 404 ■ **Fax:* Hum Res ■ *TF Cust Svc:* 800-325-4863 ■ *Web:* www.pnf.com	Atlanta	GA	30327	800-325-4863	264-1115*
Park To Fly Inc 7800 Narcoossee Rd *TF:* 888-851-8875 ■ *Web:* www.parktofly.com	Orlando	FL	32822	407-851-8875	851-8011
Parking Auth City of Rahway 67 Lewis St *Web:* www.rahwayparking.org	Rahway	NJ	07065	732-381-8778	
Parking Company of America (PCA) 11101 Lakewood Blvd *Web:* www.parkpca.com	Downey	CA	90241	562-862-2118	862-4409
Parking Company of America Inc 250 W Court St Ste 200E *Web:* www.thefastpark.com	Cincinnati	OH	45202	513-241-0415	
Parking Concepts Inc 12 Mauchly Bldg I *Web:* parkingconcepts.com	Irvine	CA	92618	949-753-7525	
Parking Management Inc 1725 Desales St NW Ste 300 *Web:* www.pmi-parking.com	Washington	DC	20036	202-785-9191	
Parking Panda Corp 3422 Fait Ave *TF:* 800-232-6415 ■ *Web:* www.parkingpanda.com	Baltimore	MD	21224	800-232-6415	
Parkway Corp 150 N Broad St *Web:* www.parkwaycorp.com	Philadelphia	PA	19102	215-575-4000	
Penn Parking Inc 7257 Pkwy Dr Ste 100 *Web:* pennparking.com	Hanover	MD	21076	410-782-9110	
PPS Parking Inc 1800 E Garry Ave Ste 107 *Web:* www.occruiser.com	Santa Ana	CA	92705	949-223-8707	
Quality IP LLC 145 S River St *Web:* www.qualityip.com	Kent	OH	44240	330-931-4141	
Republic Parking System 633 Chestnut St Ste 2000 *Web:* republicparking.com	Chattanooga	TN	37450	423-756-2771	265-5728
Robbins Parking Service Ltd 1102 Fort St *Web:* www.robbinsparking.com	Victoria	BC	V8V3K8	250-382-4411	380-7275
St. Louis Parking Company Inc 505 N Seventh St Ste 2405 *Web:* stlouisparking.com	Saint Louis	MO	63101	314-241-7777	
Standard Parking Corp 900 N Michigan Ave Ste 1600 **Fax:* Hum Res ■ *TF:* 888-700-7275 ■ *Web:* spplus.com/?ref=standard	Chicago	IL	60611	312-274-2000	640-6169*
USA Parking Systems Inc 1330 SE Fourth Ave Ste D *Web:* www.usaparking.net	Fort Lauderdale	FL	33316	954-524-6500	
Valet Parking Service 1335 S Flower St *Web:* www.valetparkingservice.com	Los Angeles	CA	90015	213-342-3388	222-0981

PARKS - AMUSEMENT

SEE Amusement Park Companies p. 1741; Amusement Parks p. 1742

566 PARKS - NATIONAL - CANADA

	City	State	Zip	Phone	Fax
Parks Canada 25-7-N Eddy St *TF:* 888-773-8888 ■ *Web:* www.pc.gc.ca/eng/index.aspx	Gatineau	QC	K1A0M5	613-860-1251	
Auyuittuq National Park PO Box 353 *Web:* www.pc.gc.ca	Pangnirtung	NU	X0A0R0	867-473-2500	473-8612
Banff National Park PO Box 900 *TF:* 877-737-3783 ■ *Web:* www.pc.gc.ca	Banff	AB	T1L1K2	403-762-1550	762-1551
Battle of the Windmill National Historic Site 370 Vankoughnet St *Web:* www.pc.gc.ca/eng/lhn-nhs/on/windmill/index.aspx	Prescott	ON	K0E1T0	613-925-2896	925-1536
Bellevue House National Historic Site 35 Centre St *Web:* www.pc.gc.ca/eng/lhn-nhs/on/bellevue/index.aspx	Kingston	ON	K7L4E5	613-545-8666	545-8721
Bethune Memorial House National Historic Site 235 John St N *Web:* www.pc.gc.ca/eng/lhn-nhs/on/bethune/index.aspx	Gravenhurst	ON	P1P1G4	705-687-4261	687-4935
Bois Blanc Island Lighthouse National Historic Site C/O Ft Malden Nhsc *Web:* www.pc.gc.ca/eng/lhn-nhs/on/boisblanc/index.aspx	Amherstburg	ON	N9V2Z2	519-736-5416	736-6603
Canso Islands National Historic Site 1465 Union St *Web:* www.pc.gc.ca/eng/lhn-nhs/ns/canso/index.aspx	Canso	NS	B0E1B0	902-366-3136	295-3496
Carleton Martello Tower National Historic Site 454 Whipple St *Web:* www.pc.gc.ca/eng/lhn-nhs/nb/carleton/index.aspx	Saint John	NB	E2M2R3	506-636-4011	636-4574
Fathom Five National Marine Park PO Box 189 *Web:* www.pc.gc.ca	Tobermory	ON	N0H2R0	519-596-2233	596-2298
Fort Langley National Historic Site 23433 Mavis Ave *Web:* www.pc.gc.ca/eng/lhn-nhs/bc/langley/index.aspx	Fort Langley	BC	V1M2R5	604-513-4777	513-4798
Fort Malden National Historic Site 100 Laird Ave *Web:* www.pc.gc.ca/eng/lhn-nhs/on/malden/index.aspx	Amherstburg	ON	N9V2Z2	519-736-5416	736-6603
Fort McNab National Historic Site C/O Halifax Citadel National Historic Site *Web:* www.pc.gc.ca/eng/lhn-nhs/ns/mcnab/contact.aspx	Halifax	NS	B3K5M7	902-426-5080	426-4228
Fort Rodd Hill National Historic Site 603 Ft Rodd Hill Rd *Web:* www.pc.gc.ca/eng/lhn-nhs/bc/fortroddhill/index.aspx	Victoria	BC	V9C2W8	250-478-5849	478-2816
Fort Wellington National Historic Site 370 Vankoughnet St *Web:* www.pc.gc.ca/eng/lhn-nhs/on/wellington/index.aspx	Prescott	ON	K0E1T0	613-925-2896	925-1536
Gwaii Haanas National Park Reserve &Haida Heritage Site PO Box 37 *Web:* www.pc.gc.ca	Queen Charlotte	BC	V0T1S0	250-559-8818	559-8366
HMCS Haida National Historic Site 57 Discovery Dr *Web:* www.pc.gc.ca/eng/lhn-nhs/on/haida/index.aspx	Hamilton	ON	L8L8K4	905-526-6742	526-9734
Inverarden House National Historic Site 370 Vankoughnet St *Web:* www.pc.gc.ca/eng/lhn-nhs/on/inverarden/index.aspx	Prescott	ON	K0E1T0	613-925-2896	925-1536
Kluane National Park & Reserve of Canada PO Box 5495 *TF:* 877-852-3100 ■ *Web:* www.pc.gc.ca	Haines Junction	YT	Y0B1L0	867-634-7250	634-7208
Laurier House National Historic Site 335 Laurier Ave E *Web:* www.pc.gc.ca/eng/lhn-nhs/on/laurier/index.aspx	Ottawa	ON	K1N6R4	613-992-8142	947-4851
Lower Fort Garry National Historic Site 5925 Hwy 9 *Web:* www.pc.gc.ca/eng/lhn-nhs/mb/fortgarry/index.aspx	Saint Andrews	MB	R1A4A8	204-785-6050	482-5887
Manoir-Papineau National Historic Site 500 Notre-Dame *Web:* www.pc.gc.ca/eng/lhn-nhs/qc/manoirpapineau/index.aspx	Montebello	QC	J0V1L0	819-423-6965	423-6455
Mingan Archipelago National Park Reserve of Canada 1340 de la Digue St *TF:* 877-737-3783 ■ *Web:* www.pc.gc.ca/pn-np/qc/mingan/index.aspx	Havre-Saint-Pierre	QC	G0G1P0	418-538-3331	538-3595
Mount Revelstoke National Park of Canada PO Box 350 *TF:* 866-787-6221 ■ *Web:* www.pc.gc.ca	Revelstoke	BC	V0E2S0	250-837-7500	837-7536
Point Pelee National Park of Canada 407 Monarch Ln RR 1 *TF:* 888-773-8888 ■ *Web:* www.pc.gc.ca/pn-np/on/pelee/index.aspx	Leamington	ON	N8H3V4	519-322-2365	322-1277
Prince Albert National Park of Canada Northern Prairies Field Unit PO Box 100 *TF Campground Resv:* 877-737-3783 ■ *Web:* www.pc.gc.ca/pn-np/sk/princealbert/index.aspx	Waskesiu Lake	SK	S0J2Y0	306-663-4522	
Prince Edward Island National Park of Canada 2 Palmers Ln *TF Campground Resv:* 800-663-7192 ■ *Web:* www.pc.gc.ca/eng/pn-np/pe/pei-ipe/natcul/natcul3.aspx	Charlottetown	PE	C1A5V8	902-672-6350	672-6370
Pukaskwa National Park of Canada PO Box 212 *Web:* www.pc.gc.ca	Heron Bay	ON	P0T1R0	807-229-0801	229-2097
Queenston Heights National Historic Site of Canada 26 Queen St *Web:* www.pc.gc.ca/eng/lhn-nhs/on/queenston/index.aspx	Niagara-On-The-Lake	ON	L0S1J0	905-468-4257	468-4638
Quttinirpaaq National Park PO Box 278 *Web:* www.pc.gc.ca/pn-np/nu/quttinirpaaq/contact.aspx	Iqaluit	NU	X0A0H0	867-975-4673	975-4674
Riding Mountain Park East Gate Registration Complex National Historic Site of Canada One Wasagaming Dr *Web:* www.pc.gc.ca/eng/lhn-nhs/mb/eastgate/index.aspx	Wasagaming	MB	R0J2H0	204-848-7275	848-2596
Riel House National Historic Site of Canada 330 River Rd **Fax Area Code:* 867 ■ *TF:* 877-852-3100	Winnipeg	MB	R2M3Z8	204-257-1783	252-3766*
Saguenay-Saint Lawrence Marine Park 182 Rue de l'Eglise PO Box 220 *Web:* pc.gc.ca/amnc%2dnmca/qc/saguenay/	Tadoussac	QC	G0T2A0	418-235-4703	235-4686

				Phone	Fax
Sault Ste Marie Canal National Historic Site of Canada One Canal Dr *Web:* www.pc.gc.ca/eng/lhn-nhs/on/ssmarie/index.aspx	Sault Sainte Marie	ON	P6A6W4	705-941-6262	941-6206
Sirmilik National Park PO Box 300 *Web:* www.pc.gc.ca	Pond Inlet	NU	X0A0S0	867-899-8092	899-8104
St Andrews Blockhouse National Historic Site of Canada 454 Whipple St *Web:* www.pc.gc.ca/eng/lhn-nhs/nb/standrews/index.aspx	Saint John	NB	E2M2R3	506-636-4011	636-4574
Thousand Islands National Park of Canada Two County Rd 5 *Web:* www.pc.gc.ca	Mallorytown	ON	K0E1R0	613-923-5261	923-1021
Tuktut Nogait National Park of Canada PO Box 91 *Web:* www.pc.gc.ca	Paulatuk	NT	X0E1N0	867-580-3233	580-3234
Wapusk National Park of Canada PO Box 127 *TF:* 888-773-8888 ■ *Web:* www.pc.gc.ca/pn-np/mb/wapusk/index.aspx	Churchill	MB	R0B0E0	204-675-8863	675-2026
Wood Buffalo National Park of Canada PO Box 750 *Web:* www.pc.gc.ca	Fort Smith	NT	X0E0P0	867-872-7900	872-3910

567 PARKS - NATIONAL - US

SEE ALSO Cemeteries - National p. 1908; Nature Centers, Parks, Other Natural Areas p. 1821; Parks - State p. 2865

				Phone	Fax
Alton Baker Park 1820 Roosevelt Blvd *Web:* www.ci.eugene.or.us	Eugene	OR	97402	541-682-4800	
City of Logan Recreation Center 195 South 100 West *Web:* loganutah.org	Logan	UT	84321	435-716-9250	
City of Piedmont Recreation Department 358 Hillside Ave *Web:* ci.piedmont.ca.us	Piedmont	CA	94611	510-420-3078	
City of Saskatoon Parks Branch 1101 Ave P N *Web:* www.city.saskatoon.sk.ca	Saskatoon	SK	S7K0J5	306-975-3300	
Cortlandt Recreation Dept One Heady St *Web:* www.townofcortlandt.com	Cortlandt Manor	NY	10567	914-734-1050	
Fresno Therapeutic Recreation 770 N San Pablo Ave *Web:* www.ci.fresno.ca.us	Fresno	CA	93728	559-488-3217	
Locust Shade Park 4701 Locust Shade Dr *Web:* www.pwcparks.org	Triangle	VA	22172	703-221-8579	
Metro Parks 1069 W Main St Unit A *Web:* www.metroparks.net	Westerville	OH	43081	614-891-0700	
Natural Lands Trust Inc 1031 Palmers Mill Rd *Web:* www.natlands.org	Media	PA	19063	610-353-5587	
Oxford Recreation Dept 6025 Fairfield Rd *Web:* www.cityofoxford.org	Oxford	OH	45056	513-523-6314	
Park Maintenance 20500 Madrona Ave *Web:* www.torrnet.com	Torrance	CA	90503	310-781-6901	
Reidsville Recreation Dept 200 N Franklin St *Web:* ci.reidsville.nc.us	Reidsville	NC	27320	336-349-1090	
Roar Foundation 6867 Soledad Canyon Rd *Web:* www.shambala.org	Acton	CA	93510	661-268-0380	
Rotary Park 350 Pageant Ln Ste 201 *Web:* www.montgomerycountytn.org	Clarksville	TN	37040	931-648-5732	
Sauk Rapids Recreation Program 901 First St S *Web:* www.isd47.org	Sauk Rapids	MN	56379	320-253-6631	
Tualatin Hills Aquatic Ctr 15707 Sw Walker Rd *Web:* www.thillsswimming.com	Beaverton	OR	97006	503-645-6433	
Wildplay Element Parks 485 Garbally Rd *Web:* www.wildplay.com	Victoria	BC	V8T2J9	250-595-2251	

Alabama

				Phone	Fax
Horseshoe Bend National Military Park 11288 Horseshoe Bend Rd *Web:* www.nps.gov	Daviston	AL	36256	256-234-7111	329-9905
Little River Canyon National Preserve 2141 Gault Ave N *Web:* www.nps.gov	Fort Payne	AL	35967	256-845-9605	997-9129
Russell Cave National Monument 3729 County Rd 98 *Web:* www.nps.gov/ruca	Bridgeport	AL	35740	256-495-2672	495-9220
Tuskegee Airmen National Historic Site 1616 Chappie James Ave *Web:* www.nps.gov	Tuskegee	AL	36083	334-724-0922	724-0952
Tuskegee Institute National Historic Site 1212 W Montgomery Rd *Web:* www.nps.gov/tuin	Tuskegee Institute	AL	36088	334-727-3200	727-1448

Alaska

				Phone	Fax
Alagnak Wild River PO Box 245 *Web:* www.nps.gov/alag	King Salmon	AK	99613	907-246-3305	246-2116
Aniakchak National Monument & Preserve PO Box 245 *Web:* www.nps.gov/ania	King Salmon	AK	99613	907-246-3305	246-2116
Cape Krusenstern National Monument PO Box 1029 *Web:* www.nps.gov/cakr	Kotzebue	AK	99752	907-442-3890	442-8316
Denali National Park & Preserve PO Box 9 *Web:* www.nps.gov	Denali Park	AK	99755	907-733-9119	683-9617
Gates of the Arctic National Park & Preserve 4175 Geist Rd *TF:* 866-869-6887 ■ *Web:* www.nps.gov/gaar	Fairbanks	AK	99709	907-457-5752	455-0601
Katmai National Park & Preserve King Salmon Mall PO Box 7 *Web:* www.nps.gov/katm	King Salmon	AK	99613	907-246-3305	246-2116
Klondike Gold Rush National Historical Park Second St & Broadway PO Box 517 *Web:* www.nps.gov/klgo	Skagway	AK	99840	907-983-2921	983-9249
Kobuk Valley National Park PO Box 1029 *Web:* www.nps.gov/kova	Kotzebue	AK	99752	907-442-3890	442-8316
Lake Clark National Park & Preserve 240 W Fifth Ave Ste 236 *Web:* www.nps.gov	Anchorage	AK	99501	907-644-3626	644-3810
National Park Service Regional Offices *Alaska Region* 240 W Fifth Ave Ste 114 *Web:* nps.gov	Anchorage	AK	99501	907-644-3510	644-3816
Noatak National Preserve PO Box 1029 *Web:* www.nps.gov/noat	Kotzebue	AK	99752	907-442-3890	442-8316
Sitka National Historical Park 106 Metlakatla St *Web:* www.nps.gov	Sitka	AK	99835	907-747-6281	747-5938
Wrangell-Saint Elias National Park & Preserve Mile 1068 Richardson Hwy PO Box 439 *Web:* www.nps.gov/wrst	Copper Center	AK	99573	907-822-5234	822-7216
Yukon-Charley Rivers National Preserve 4175 Geist Rd *Web:* www.nps.gov/yuch	Fairbanks	AK	99709	907-457-5752	455-0601

Arizona

				Phone	Fax
Canyon de Chelly National Monument PO Box 588 *Web:* www.nps.gov	Chinle	AZ	86503	928-674-5500	674-5507
Casa Grande Ruins National Monument 1100 W Ruins Dr *TF:* 877-642-4743 ■ *Web:* www.nps.gov	Coolidge	AZ	85128	520-723-3172	723-7209
Chiricahua National Monument 12856 E Rhyolite Creek Rd *Web:* www.nps.gov/chir	Willcox	AZ	85643	520-824-3560	824-3421
Coronado National Memorial 4101 E Montezuma Canyon Rd *Web:* www.nps.gov/coro	Hereford	AZ	85615	520-366-5515	366-5705
Fort Bowie National Historic Site 3203 S Old Ft Bowie Rd *Web:* www.nps.gov/fobo	Bowie	AZ	85605	520-847-2500	847-2221
Glen Canyon National Recreation Area 691 Scenic View Dr PO Box 1507 *Web:* www.nps.gov/glca	Page	AZ	86040	928-608-6200	608-6259
Grand Canyon National Park PO Box 129 **Fax:* Mail Rm ■ *Web:* www.nps.gov	Grand Canyon	AZ	86023	928-638-7888	638-7797*
Hohokam Pima National Monument c/o Casa Grande Ruins National Monument 1100 W Ruins Dr *Web:* www.nps.gov/pima	Coolidge	AZ	85228	520-723-3172	723-7209
Hubbell Trading Post National Historic Site 1/2 Mile W Hwy 191 on Hwy 264 PO Box 150 *Web:* www.nps.gov	Ganado	AZ	86505	928-755-3475	755-3405
Montezuma Castle National Monument 527 S Main St *Web:* www.nps.gov/moca	Camp Verde	AZ	86322	928-567-5276	567-3597
Navajo National Monument HC 71 PO Box 3 *Web:* www.nps.gov	Tonalea	AZ	86044	928-672-2700	672-2703
Petrified Forest National Park PO Box 2217 *Web:* www.nps.gov	Petrified Forest	AZ	86028	928-524-6228	524-3567
Pipe Spring National Monument 406 N Pipe Spring Rd HC 65 PO Box 5 *Web:* www.nps.gov/pisp	Fredonia	AZ	86022	928-643-7105	643-7583
Saguaro National Park 3693 S Old Spanish Trl *Web:* www.nps.gov	Tucson	AZ	85730	520-733-5100	733-5183
Tonto National Monument 26260 N Az Hwy 188 2 *Web:* www.nps.gov/tont	Roosevelt	AZ	85545	928-467-2241	467-2225
Tumacacori National Historical Park 1891 E Frontage Rd PO Box 8067 *Web:* www.nps.gov/tuma	Tumacacori	AZ	85640	520-398-2341	398-9271
Tuzigoot National Monument 527 S Main St *Web:* www.nps.gov/tuzi	Camp Verde	AZ	86322	928-634-5564	567-3597
Wupatki National Monument Flagstaff Area National Monuments 6400 N Hwy 89 *Web:* www.nps.gov/wupa	Flagstaff	AZ	86004	928-679-2365	679-2349

Arkansas

				Phone	Fax
Arkansas Post National Memorial 1741 Old Post Rd *Web:* www.nps.gov	Gillett	AR	72055	870-548-2207	548-2431
Buffalo National River 402 N Walnut St Ste 136 *Web:* www.nps.gov	Harrison	AR	72601	870-741-5443	741-7286
Fort Smith National Historic Site 301 Parker Ave *Web:* www.nps.gov	Fort Smith	AR	72901	479-783-3961	783-5307
Hot Springs National Park 101 Reserve St *Web:* www.nps.gov	Hot Springs	AR	71901	501-620-6715	620-6778
Little Rock Central High School National Historic Site 2120 W Daisy L Gatson Bates Dr *Web:* www.nps.gov	Little Rock	AR	72202	501-374-1957	376-4728

Phone Fax

Pea Ridge National Military Park
15930 Hwy 62 E .... Garfield AR 72732 479-451-8122 451-0219
Web: www.nps.gov

President William Jefferson Clinton Birthplace Home National Historic Site
117 S Hervey St .... Hope AR 71801 870-777-4455 777-4935
Web: www.nps.gov/wicl/index.htm

California

Phone Fax

Cabrillo National Monument
1800 Cabrillo Memorial Dr .... San Diego CA 92106 619-557-5450 226-6311
TF: 800-236-7916 ■ *Web:* www.nps.gov

Channel Islands National Park
1901 Spinnaker Dr .... Ventura CA 93001 805-658-5730 658-5799
Web: www.nps.gov

Death Valley National Park PO Box 579 .... Death Valley CA 92328 760-786-3200 786-3283
TF: 866-713-9688 ■ *Web:* www.nps.gov/deva

Devils Postpile National Monument
PO Box 3999 .... Mammoth Lakes CA 93546 760-934-2289 934-2289
Web: www.nps.gov/depo

Eugene O'Neill National Historic Site
1000 Kuss Rd .... Danville CA 94526 925-838-0249 396-3393*
**Fax Area Code:* 410 ■ *TF:* 866-945-7920 ■ *Web:* www.nps.gov

Fort Point National Historic Site
Fort Mason Bldg 201 .... San Francisco CA 94123 415-556-1693 561-4390
Web: www.nps.gov/fopo

Golden Gate National Recreation Area
Fort Mason Bldg 201 .... San Francisco CA 94123 415-561-4700 561-4750*
**Fax:* Hum Res ■ *Web:* www.nps.gov/goga

John Muir National Historic Site
4202 Alhambra Ave .... Martinez CA 94553 925-228-8860 228-8192
Web: www.nps.gov

Joshua Tree National Park
74485 National Pk Dr .... Twentynine Palms CA 92277 760-367-5500 367-6392
Web: www.nps.gov

Lassen Volcanic National Park
38050 Hwy 36 E PO Box 100 .... Mineral CA 96063 530-595-4480 595-3262
Web: www.nps.gov/lavo

Lava Beds National Monument
One Indian Well Headquarters .... Tulelake CA 96134 530-260-0537
Web: www.nps.gov/labe

Manzanar National Historic Site
5001 Hwy 395 PO Box 426 .... Independence CA 93526 760-878-2194 878-2949
Web: www.nps.gov/manz

Mojave National Preserve 2701 Barstow Rd .... Barstow CA 92311 760-252-6100 252-6174
Web: www.nps.gov/moja

Muir Woods National Monument
One Muir Woods Rd .... Mill Valley CA 94941 415-388-2596 389-6957
Web: www.nps.gov/muwo

Pinnacles National Monument 5000 Hwy 146 .... Paicines CA 95043 831-389-4485 389-4489
TF: 877-444-6777 ■ *Web:* www.nps.gov/pinn

Point Reyes National Seashore
1 Bear Valley Rd .... Point Reyes Station CA 94956 415-464-5100 663-8132
TF: 877-874-2478 ■ *Web:* www.nps.gov

Redwood National & State Parks
1111 Second St .... Crescent City CA 95531 707-465-7335 464-1812
Web: www.nps.gov/redw

Rosie the Riveter/World War II Home Front National Historical Park
1401 Marina Way S .... Richmond CA 94804 510-232-5050
Web: www.nps.gov

San Francisco Maritime National Historical Park
Lower Ft Mason Bldg E Rm 265 .... San Francisco CA 94123 415-561-7000 556-1624
Web: www.nps.gov/safr

Santa Monica Mountains National Recreation Area
401 W Hillcrest Dr .... Thousand Oaks CA 91360 805-370-2300 370-1851
TF: 888-275-8747 ■ *Web:* www.nps.gov/samo

Sequoia & Kings Canyon National Parks
47050 Generals Hwy .... Three Rivers CA 93271 559-565-3341 565-3730
Web: www.nps.gov/seki

Whiskeytown-Shasta-Trinity National Recreation Area
PO Box 188 .... Whiskeytown CA 96095 530-242-3400 246-5154
Web: www.nps.gov

Yosemite National Park
9039 Village Dr PO Box 577 .... Yosemite CA 95389 209-372-0200 379-1800
Web: www.nps.gov/yose

Colorado

Phone Fax

Bent's Old Fort National Historic Site
35110 Hwy 194 E .... La Junta CO 81050 719-383-5010 383-2129
Web: www.nps.gov/beol

Black Canyon of the Gunnison National Park
102 Elk Creek .... Gunnison CO 81230 970-641-2337 641-3127
Web: www.nps.gov/blca

Colorado National Monument 1750 Rim Rock Dr .... Fruita CO 81521 970-858-3617 858-0372
TF: 866-945-7920 ■ *Web:* www.nps.gov

Curecanti National Recreation Area
102 Elk Creek .... Gunnison CO 81230 970-641-2337 641-3127
TF: 866-713-9688 ■ *Web:* www.nps.gov/cure

Dinosaur National Monument 4545 E Hwy 40 .... Dinosaur CO 81610 970-374-3000 374-3003
Web: www.nps.gov/dino

Florissant Fossil Beds National Monument
PO Box 185 .... Florissant CO 80816 719-748-3253 748-3164
Web: www.nps.gov

Great Sand Dunes National Park & Preserve
11500 Hwy 150 .... Mosca CO 81146 719-378-6300 378-6310
Web: www.nps.gov/grsa

Hovenweep National Monument McElmo Rt .... Cortez CO 81321 970-562-4282 562-4283
Web: www.nps.gov/hove

National Park Service Regional Offices Intermountain Region
12795 W Alameda Pkwy .... Denver CO 80225 303-969-2500
Web: www.nps.gov

Rocky Mountain National Park 1000 Hwy 36 .... Estes Park CO 80517 970-586-1206 586-1256
Web: www.nps.gov

Sand Creek Massacre National Historic Site
910 Wansted .... Eads CO 81036 719-729-3003 438-5410
Web: www.nps.gov/sand

Yucca House National Monument
c/o Mesa Verde National Pk PO Box 8 .... Mesa Verde CO 81330 970-529-4465 529-4637
Web: www.nps.gov/yuho

Connecticut

Phone Fax

Weir Farm National Historic Site
735 Nod Hill Rd .... Wilton CT 06897 203-834-1896 834-2421
Web: www.nps.gov/wefa

District of Columbia

Phone Fax

Constitution Gardens 900 Ohio Dr SW .... Washington DC 20024 202-426-6841 724-0764
Web: www.nps.gov/coga

Ford's Theatre National Historic Site
511 Tenth St NW .... Washington DC 20004 202-233-0701 233-0706
Web: www.nps.gov/foth

Frederick Douglass National Historic Site
1900 Anacostia Dr SE .... Washington DC 20020 202-426-5961 426-0880
Web: www.nps.gov/frdo

Korean War Veterans Memorial
c/o National Capital Parks - Central
900 Ohio Dr SW .... Washington DC 20004 202-426-6841
Web: www.nps.gov/kowa

Mary McLeod Bethune Council House National Historic Site
1318 Vermont Ave NW .... Washington DC 20005 202-673-2402 673-2414
Web: www.nps.gov/mamc

National Mall
c/o National Capitol Parks - Central
900 Ohio Dr SW .... Washington DC 20024 202-426-6841 426-1835
Web: www.nps.gov/nama

National Park Service Regional Offices National Capital Region
1100 Ohio Dr SW .... Washington DC 20242 202-619-7000 619-7220
Web: www.nps.gov/ncro

Pennsylvania Avenue National Historic Site
c/o National Capitol Parks - Central
900 Ohio Dr SW .... Washington DC 20024 202-606-9686
Web: www.nps.gov/paav

Rock Creek Park 5200 Glover Rd NW .... Washington DC 20015 202-895-6000 895-6015
Web: www.nps.gov

Thomas Jefferson Memorial
c/o National Capital Parks - Central
900 Ohio Dr SW .... Washington DC 20024 202-426-6841 426-1835
Web: www.nps.gov/thje

Florida

Phone Fax

Big Cypress National Preserve
33100 Tamiami Trl E .... Ochopee FL 34141 239-695-2000 695-3901
Web: www.nps.gov

Biscayne National Park 9700 SW 328th St .... Homestead FL 33033 305-230-1144 230-1190
Web: www.nps.gov/bisc

Canaveral National Seashore
212 S Washington Ave .... Titusville FL 32796 321-267-1110 264-2906
Web: www.nps.gov/cana

Castillo de San Marcos National Monument
One S Castillo Dr .... Saint Augustine FL 32084 904-829-6506 823-9388
Web: www.nps.gov/casa

De Soto National Memorial
8300 Desoto Memorial Hwy .... Bradenton FL 34209 941-792-0458 792-5094
TF: 888-831-7526 ■ *Web:* www.nps.gov

Dry Tortugas National Park PO Box 6208 .... Key West FL 33041 305-242-7700 242-7711
Web: www.nps.gov/drto

Everglades National Park 40001 SR-9336 .... Homestead FL 33034 305-242-7700 242-7728
Web: www.nps.gov/ever

Fort Caroline National Memorial
12713 Ft Caroline Rd .... Jacksonville FL 32225 904-641-7155 641-3798
Web: www.nps.gov/foca

Fort Matanzas National Monument
8635 A1A S .... Saint Augustine FL 32080 904-471-0116 471-7605
Web: www.nps.gov/foma

Gulf Islands National Seashore (Florida)
1801 Gulf Breeze Pkwy .... Gulf Breeze FL 32563 850-934-2600 932-9654
Web: www.nps.gov

Timucuan Ecological & Historic Preserve
12713 Ft Caroline Rd .... Jacksonville FL 32225 904-641-7155 641-3798
Web: www.nps.gov/timu

Georgia

Phone Fax

Andersonville National Historic Site
496 Cemetery Rd .... Andersonville GA 31711 229-924-0343 924-1086
Web: www.nps.gov/ande

Chattahoochee River National Recreation Area
1978 Island Ford Pkwy .... Atlanta GA 30350 678-538-1200 399-8087*
**Fax Area Code:* 770 ■ *TF:* 877-874-2478 ■ *Web:* www.nps.gov/chat

Chickamauga & Chattanooga National Military Park
3370 Lafayette Rd PO Box 2128 .... Fort Oglethorpe GA 30742 706-866-9241 752-5215*
**Fax Area Code:* 423 ■ *Web:* www.nps.gov/chch

				Phone	Fax
Cumberland Island National Seashore 101 Wheeler St PO Box 806	Saint Marys	GA	31558	912-882-4336	673-7747
TF: 877-860-6787 ■ *Web:* www.nps.gov					
Fort Frederica National Monument 6515 Frederica Rd	Saint Simons Island	GA	31522	912-638-3639	634-5357
Web: www.nps.gov					
Fort Pulaski National Monument US Hwy 80 E	Savannah	GA	31410	912-786-5787	786-6023
Web: www.nps.gov					
Jimmy Carter National Historic Site 300 N Bond St	Plains	GA	31780	229-824-4104	824-3441
Web: www.nps.gov/jica					
Kennesaw Mountain National Battlefield Park 900 Kennesaw Mtn Dr	Kennesaw	GA	30152	770-427-4686	528-8398
Web: www.nps.gov					
Martin Luther King Jr National Historic Site 450 Auburn Ave NE	Atlanta	GA	30312	404-331-5190	730-3112
Web: www.nps.gov/malu					
Ocmulgee National Monument 1207 Emery Hwy	Macon	GA	31217	478-752-8257	752-8259
Web: www.nps.gov/ocmu					

Guam

				Phone	Fax
War in the Pacific National Historical Park 135 Murray Blvd Ste 100	Hagatna	GU	96910	671-477-7278	472-7281
Web: www.nps.gov/wapa					

Hawaii

				Phone	Fax
Haleakala National Park PO Box 369	Makawao	HI	96768	808-572-4400	572-1304
Web: www.nps.gov					
Hawaii Volcanoes National Park PO Box 52	Hawaii National Park	HI	96718	808-985-6000	985-6004
Web: www.nps.gov					
Kalaupapa National Historical Park PO Box 2222	Kalaupapa	HI	96742	808-567-6802	567-6729
Web: www.nps.gov					
Kaloko-Honokohau National Historical Park 73-4786 Kanalani St Ste 14	Kailua-Kona	HI	96740	808-329-6881	
Web: www.nps.gov					
Puukohola Heiau National Historic Site 62-3601 Kawaihae Rd	Kawaihae	HI	96743	808-882-7218	882-1215
Web: www.nps.gov					
USS Arizona Memorial One Arizona Memorial Pl	Honolulu	HI	96818	808-422-0561	483-8608
Web: www.nps.gov/usar					

Idaho

				Phone	Fax
City of Rocks National Reserve PO Box 169	Almo	ID	83312	208-824-5910	824-5563
Web: www.nps.gov/ciro					
Craters of the Moon National Monument & Preserve PO Box 29	Arco	ID	83213	208-527-1335	527-3073
Web: www.nps.gov/crmo					
Hagerman Fossil Beds National Monument 221 N State St PO Box 570	Hagerman	ID	83332	208-933-4100	837-4857
Web: www.nps.gov					
Minidoka National Historic Site PO Box 570	Hagerman	ID	83332	208-933-4127	837-4857
Web: www.nps.gov/miin					
Nez Perce National Historical Park 39063 US Hwy 95	Spalding	ID	83540	208-843-2261	843-7003
Web: www.nps.gov/nepe					

Illinois

				Phone	Fax
Lincoln Home National Historic Site 413 S Eigth St	Springfield	IL	62701	217-492-4241	492-4673
Web: www.nps.gov					

Indiana

				Phone	Fax
George Rogers Clark National Historical Park 401 S Second St	Vincennes	IN	47591	812-882-1776	882-7270
Web: www.nps.gov					
Indiana Dunes National Lakeshore 1100 N Mineral Springs Rd	Porter	IN	46304	219-395-1772	926-7561
Web: www.nps.gov/indu					
Lincoln Boyhood National Memorial 2916 E S St PO Box 1816	Lincoln City	IN	47552	812-937-4541	937-9929
Web: www.nps.gov/libo					

Iowa

				Phone	Fax
Effigy Mounds National Monument 151 Hwy 76	Harpers Ferry	IA	52146	563-873-3491	322-1704*
**Fax Area Code:* 800 ■ *Web:* www.nps.gov/efmo					
Herbert Hoover National Historic Site 110 Parkside Dr PO Box 607	West Branch	IA	52358	319-643-2541	643-7864
Web: www.nps.gov/heho					

Kansas

				Phone	Fax
Brown Vs Board of Education National Historic Site 1515 SE Monroe St	Topeka	KS	66612	785-354-4273	354-7213
Web: www.nps.gov					
Fort Larned National Historic Site 1767 Kansas Hwy 156	Larned	KS	67550	620-285-6911	285-3571
Web: www.nps.gov					
Fort Scott National Historic Site PO Box 918	Fort Scott	KS	66701	620-223-0310	223-0188
Web: www.nps.gov					
Nicodemus National Historic Site 510 Washington Ave B1	Bogue	KS	67625	785-839-4233	839-4325
Web: www.nps.gov					
Tallgrass Prairie National Preserve 226 Broadway PO Box 585	Cottonwood Falls	KS	66845	620-273-6034	273-6099
Web: www.nps.gov					

Kentucky

				Phone	Fax
Abraham Lincoln Birthplace National Historic Site 2995 Lincoln Farm Rd	Hodgenville	KY	42748	270-358-3137	358-3874
Web: www.nps.gov					
Cumberland Gap National Historical Park 91 Bartlett Pk Rd PO Box 1848	Middlesboro	KY	40965	606-248-2817	248-7276
TF: 888-831-7526 ■ *Web:* www.nps.gov/cuga					
Mammoth Cave National Park One Mammoth Cave Pkwy PO Box 7	Mammoth Cave	KY	42259	270-758-2180	758-2349
Web: www.nps.gov/maca					

Louisiana

				Phone	Fax
Cane River Creole National Historical Park 400 Rapides Dr	Natchitoches	LA	71457	318-356-8441	352-4549
Web: www.nps.gov/cari					
Jean Lafitte National Historical Park & Preserve 419 Decatur St	New Orleans	LA	70130	504-589-3882	589-3851
Web: www.nps.gov					
New Orleans Jazz National Historical Park 419 Decatur St	New Orleans	LA	70130	504-589-4806	589-3865
TF: 877-520-0677 ■ *Web:* www.nps.gov					
Poverty Point National Monument c/o Poverty Pt State Historic Site PO Box 276	Epps	LA	71237	318-926-5492	926-5366
TF: 888-926-5492 ■ *Web:* www.nps.gov					

Maine

				Phone	Fax
Acadia National Park 20 McFarland Hill Dr	Bar Harbor	ME	04609	207-288-3338	288-8813
Web: www.nps.gov					
Saint Croix Island International Historic Site PO Box 247	Calais	ME	04619	207-454-3871	288-8813
Web: www.nps.gov/sacr					

Maryland

				Phone	Fax
Antietam National Battlefield 5831 Dunker Church Rd PO Box 158	Sharpsburg	MD	21782	301-432-5124	432-4590
Web: www.nps.gov/anti					
Assateague Island National Seashore 7206 National Seashore Ln PO Box 38	Berlin	MD	21811	410-641-1441	
Web: www.nps.gov/asis					
Catoctin Mountain Park 6602 Foxville Rd	Thurmont	MD	21788	301-663-9330	
Web: www.nps.gov					
Chesapeake & Ohio Canal National Historical Park 1850 Dual Hwy Ste 100	Hagerstown	MD	21740	301-739-4200	739-5275
Web: www.nps.gov/choh					
Clara Barton National Historic Site 5801 Oxford Rd	Glen Echo	MD	20812	301-320-1410	
Web: www.nps.gov/clba					
Fort McHenry National Monument & Historic Shrine 2400 E Fort Ave	Baltimore	MD	21230	410-962-4290	962-2500
TF: 866-945-7920 ■ *Web:* www.nps.gov					
Fort Washington Park 13551 Ft Washington Rd	Fort Washington	MD	20744	301-763-4600	763-1389
Web: www.nps.gov					
Greenbelt Park 6565 Greenbelt Rd	Greenbelt	MD	20770	301-344-3948	344-1012
Web: www.nps.gov/gree					
Hampton National Historic Site 535 Hampton Ln	Towson	MD	21286	410-823-1309	823-8394
Web: www.nps.gov					
Monocacy National Battlefield 5201 Urbana Pk	Frederick	MD	21704	301-662-3515	662-3420
Web: www.nps.gov					
Piscataway Park c/o Ft Washington Pk 13551 Ft Washington Rd	Fort Washington	MD	20744	301-763-4600	763-1389
Web: www.nps.gov/pisc					
Thomas Stone National Historic Site 6655 Rose Hill Rd	Port Tobacco	MD	20677	301-392-1776	934-8793
Web: www.nps.gov					

Massachusetts

				Phone	Fax
Adams National Historical Park 135 Adams St	Quincy	MA	02169	617-773-1177	472-7562
Web: www.nps.gov					

				Phone	Fax
Boston African-American National Historic Site 14 Beacon St Ste 401	Boston	MA	02108	617-742-5415	720-0848
Web: www.nps.gov					
Boston Harbor Islands National Recreation Area 408 Atlantic Ave Ste 228	Boston	MA	02110	617-223-8666	223-8671
TF: 877-874-2478 ■ *Web:* www.nps.gov					
Boston National Historical Park Charlestown Navy Yard	Boston	MA	02129	617-242-5601	242-6006
Web: www.nps.gov/bost					
Frederick Law Olmsted National Historic Site 99 Warren St	Brookline	MA	02445	617-566-1689	232-4073
Web: www.nps.gov/frla					
John F Kennedy National Historic Site 83 Beals St	Brookline	MA	02446	617-566-7937	730-9884
Web: www.nps.gov/jofi					
Longfellow National Historic Site 105 Brattle St	Cambridge	MA	02138	617-876-4491	497-8718
Web: www.nps.gov/long					
Lowell National Historical Park 67 Kirk St	Lowell	MA	01852	978-970-5000	970-5085
Web: www.nps.gov					
Minute Man National Historical Park 174 Liberty St	Concord	MA	01742	978-369-6993	318-7800
Web: www.nps.gov					
New Bedford Whaling National Historical Park 33 William St	New Bedford	MA	02740	508-996-4095	984-1250
Web: www.nps.gov/nebe					
Salem Maritime National Historic Site 160 Derby St	Salem	MA	01970	978-740-1650	740-1654
Web: www.nps.gov/sama					
Saugus Iron Works National Historic Site 244 Central St	Saugus	MA	01906	781-233-0050	231-7345
Web: www.nps.gov					
Springfield Armory National Historic Site One Armory Sq Ste 2	Springfield	MA	01105	413-734-8551	747-8062
Web: www.nps.gov/spar					

Michigan

				Phone	Fax
Isle Royale National Park 800 E Lakeshore Dr	Houghton	MI	49931	906-482-0984	482-8753
Web: www.nps.gov					
Keweenaw National Historical Park 25970 Red Jacket Rd PO Box 471	Calumet	MI	49913	906-337-3168	337-3169
Web: www.nps.gov					
Pictured Rocks National Lakeshore N8391 Sandpoint Rd PO Box 40	Munising	MI	49862	906-387-2607	387-4025
Web: www.nps.gov					
Sleeping Bear Dunes National Lakeshore 9922 Front St	Empire	MI	49630	231-326-5134	326-5382
Web: www.nps.gov/slbe					

Minnesota

				Phone	Fax
Grand Portage National Monument PO Box 668	Grand Marais	MN	55604	218-387-2788	387-2790
Web: www.nps.gov					
Mississippi National River & Recreation Area 111 E Kellogg Blvd Ste 105	Saint Paul	MN	55101	651-290-4160	290-3214
Web: www.nps.gov/miss					
Voyageurs National Park 360 Hwy 11 E	International Falls	MN	56649	218-286-5258	285-7407
TF: 888-381-2873 ■ *Web:* www.nps.gov/voya					

Mississippi

				Phone	Fax
Brice's Crossroads National Battlefield Site 2680 Natchez Trace Pkwy	Tupelo	MS	38804	662-680-4025	680-4033
TF: 800-305-7417 ■ *Web:* www.nps.gov/brcr					
Gulf Islands National Seashore (Mississippi) 3500 Pk Rd	Ocean Springs	MS	39564	228-875-0823	875-2358
Web: www.nps.gov/guis					
Natchez National Historical Park One Melrose Montebello Pkwy	Natchez	MS	39120	601-446-5790	442-9516
Web: www.nps.gov/natc					
Natchez Trace National Scenic Trail 2680 Natchez Trace Pkwy	Tupelo	MS	38804	662-680-4025	680-4036
Web: www.nps.gov/natt					
Natchez Trace Parkway 2680 Natchez Trace Pkwy	Tupelo	MS	38804	662-680-4025	680-4036
TF: 800-305-7417 ■ *Web:* www.nps.gov/natr					
Tupelo National Battlefield 2680 Natchez Trace Pkwy	Tupelo	MS	38804	662-680-4025	680-4033
TF: 800-305-7417 ■ *Web:* www.nps.gov					
Vicksburg National Military Park 3201 Clay St	Vicksburg	MS	39183	601-636-0583	636-9497
Web: www.nps.gov/vick					

Missouri

				Phone	Fax
George Washington Carver National Monument 5646 Carver Rd	Diamond	MO	64840	417-325-4151	325-4231
Web: www.nps.gov					
Harry S Truman National Historic Site 223 N Main St	Independence	MO	64050	816-254-2720	254-4491
TF: 877-642-4743 ■ *Web:* www.nps.gov					
Jefferson National Expansion Memorial 11 N Fourth St	Saint Louis	MO	63102	314-655-1700	655-1641
TF: 855-733-4522 ■ *Web:* www.nps.gov/jeff					
Ozark National Scenic Riverways 404 Watercress Dr PO Box 490	Van Buren	MO	63965	573-323-4236	323-4140
TF: 877-444-6777 ■ *Web:* www.nps.gov/ozar					
Ulysses S Grant National Historic Site 7400 Grant Rd	Saint Louis	MO	63123	314-842-3298	842-1659
Web: www.nps.gov/ulsg					
Wilson's Creek National Battlefield 6424 W Farm Rd 182	Republic	MO	65738	417-732-2662	732-1167
Web: www.nps.gov					

Montana

				Phone	Fax
Big Hole National Battlefield 16425 Hwy 43 W	Wisdom	MT	59761	406-689-3155	689-3151
Web: www.nps.gov					
Bighorn Canyon National Recreation Area Five Ave B PO Box 7458	Fort Smith	MT	59035	406-666-2412	666-2415
Web: www.nps.gov/bica					
Glacier National Park PO Box 128	West Glacier	MT	59936	406-888-7800	888-7808
Web: www.nps.gov/glac					
Grant-Kohrs Ranch National Historic Site 266 Warren Ln	Deer Lodge	MT	59722	406-846-2070	846-3962
Web: www.nps.gov					
Little Bighorn Battlefield National Monument PO Box 39	Crow Agency	MT	59022	406-638-3214	638-2623
Web: www.nps.gov/libi					

Nebraska

				Phone	Fax
Agate Fossil Beds National Monument 301 River Rd	Harrison	NE	69346	308-668-2211	668-2318
Web: www.nps.gov					
Homestead National Monument of America 8523 W State Hwy 4	Beatrice	NE	68310	402-223-3514	228-4231
Web: www.nps.gov					
Niobrara National Scenic River 146 S Hall St PO Box 319	Valentine	NE	69201	402-376-1901	376-1949
Web: www.nps.gov/niob					

Nevada

				Phone	Fax
Great Basin National Park 100 Great Basin National Pk	Baker	NV	89311	775-234-7331	234-7269
Web: www.nps.gov/grba					
Lake Mead National Recreation Area 601 Nevada Hwy	Boulder City	NV	89005	702-293-8990	293-8936
Web: www.nps.gov					

New Hampshire

				Phone	Fax
Saint-Gaudens National Historic Site 139 St Gaudens Rd	Cornish	NH	03745	603-675-2175	675-2701
Web: www.nps.gov/saga					

New Jersey

				Phone	Fax
Morristown National Historical Park 30 Washington Pl	Morristown	NJ	07960	973-543-4030	451-9212
Web: www.nps.gov/morr					
Pinelands National Reserve 15 Springfield Rd	New Lisbon	NJ	08064	609-894-7300	894-7330
Web: www.nps.gov/pine					
Thomas Edison National Historic Site 211 Main St	West Orange	NJ	07052	973-736-0550	736-6567
Web: www.nps.gov/edis					

New Mexico

				Phone	Fax
Aztec Ruins National Monument 84 Ruins Rd 2900	Aztec	NM	87410	505-334-6174	334-6372
Web: www.nps.gov					
Capulin Volcano National Monument 46 Volcano Rd	Capulin	NM	88414	505-278-2201	278-2211
Web: www.nps.gov/cavo					
Chaco Culture National Historical Park PO Box 220	Nageezi	NM	87037	505-786-7014	786-7061
TF: 877-642-4743 ■ *Web:* www.nps.gov/chcu					
El Malpais National Monument 123 E Roosevelt Ave	Grants	NM	87020	505-285-4641	285-5661
Web: www.nps.gov					
El Morro National Monument HC 61 PO Box 43	Ramah	NM	87321	505-783-4226	783-4689
Web: www.nps.gov					
Fort Union National Monument PO Box 127	Watrous	NM	87753	505-425-8025	454-1155
Web: www.nps.gov					
Gila Cliff Dwellings National Monument HC 68 PO Box 100	Silver City	NM	88061	505-536-9461	536-9344
Web: www.nps.gov/gicl					
Pecos National Historical Park PO Box 418	Pecos	NM	87552	505-757-7200	757-7207
Web: www.nps.gov/peco					
White Sands National Monument PO Box 1086	Holloman AFB	NM	88330	505-679-2599	
Web: www.nps.gov/whsa					

New York

				Phone	Fax
African Burial Ground National Monument 290 Broadway First Fl *Web:* www.nps.gov/afbg	New York	NY	10007	212-637-2019	
Eleanor Roosevelt National Historic Site 4097 Albany Post Rd *TF:* 800-337-8474 ■ *Web:* www.nps.gov/elro	Hyde Park	NY	12538	845-229-9115	229-0739
Federal Hall National Memorial 26 Wall St *Web:* www.nps.gov/feha/index.htm	New York	NY	10005	212-825-6990	668-2899
Fire Island National Seashore 120 Laurel St *Web:* www.nps.gov/fiis	Patchogue	NY	11772	631-687-4750	289-4898
Gateway National Recreation Area 210 New York Ave *Web:* www.nps.gov/gate	Staten Island	NY	10305	718-354-4606	354-4605
General Grant National Memorial Riverside Dr & W 122nd St *Web:* www.nps.gov/gegr	New York	NY	10027	212-666-1640	932-9631
Hamilton Grange National Memorial (HAGR) 122 St Riverside Dr **Fax Area Code:* 646 ■ *Web:* www.nps.gov/hagr	New York	NY	10027	212-666-1640	548-5366*
Home of Franklin D Roosevelt National Historic Site 4097 Albany Post Rd *Web:* www.nps.gov/hofr	Hyde Park	NY	12538	845-229-9115	229-0739
Martin Van Buren National Historic Site 1013 Old Post Rd *Web:* www.nps.gov	Kinderhook	NY	12106	518-758-9689	758-6986
Sagamore Hill National Historic Site 20 Sagamore Hill Rd *Web:* www.nps.gov/sahi	Oyster Bay	NY	11771	516-922-4788	922-4792
Saint Paul's Church National Historic Site 897 S Columbus Ave *Web:* www.nps.gov	Mount Vernon	NY	10550	914-667-4116	667-3024
Saratoga National Historical Park 648 Rt 32 *Web:* www.nps.gov/sara	Stillwater	NY	12170	518-664-9821	664-3349
Statue of Liberty National Monument & Ellis Island Liberty Island *Web:* www.nps.gov/stli	New York	NY	10004	212-363-3200	
Theodore Roosevelt Birthplace National Historic Site 28 E 20th St *Web:* www.nps.gov/thrb	New York	NY	10003	212-260-1616	
Thomas Cole National Historic Site 218 Spring St *Web:* www.thomascole.org	Catskill	NY	12414	518-943-7465	943-0652
Vanderbilt Mansion National Historic Site 4097 Albany Post Rd *Web:* www.nps.gov/vama	Hyde Park	NY	12538	845-229-9115	229-0739
Women's Rights National Historical Park 136 Fall St *Web:* www.nps.gov/wori	Seneca Falls	NY	13148	315-568-2991	568-2141

North Carolina

				Phone	Fax
Cape Hatteras National Seashore 1401 National Pk Dr *Web:* www.nps.gov/caha	Manteo	NC	27954	252-473-2111	473-2595
Cape Lookout National Seashore 131 Charles St *Web:* www.nps.gov	Harkers Island	NC	28531	252-728-2250	728-2160
Carl Sandburg Home National Historic Site 81 Carl Sadburg Ln *TF:* 877-642-4743 ■ *Web:* www.nps.gov	Flat Rock	NC	28731	828-693-4178	693-4179
Fort Raleigh National Historic Site 1401 National Pk Dr *Web:* www.nps.gov	Manteo	NC	27954	252-473-5772	473-2595
Guilford Courthouse National Military Park 2332 New Garden Rd *Web:* www.nps.gov/guco	Greensboro	NC	27410	336-288-1776	282-2296
Moores Creek National Battlefield 40 Patriots Hall Dr *Web:* www.nps.gov	Currie	NC	28435	910-283-5591	283-5351

North Dakota

				Phone	Fax
Fort Union Trading Post National Historic Site 15550 Hwy 1804 *Web:* www.nps.gov	Williston	ND	58801	701-572-9083	572-7321
Knife River Indian Villages National Historic Site 564 County Rd 37 PO Box 9 *Web:* www.nps.gov	Stanton	ND	58571	701-745-3300	745-3708
Theodore Roosevelt National Park 315 Second Ave PO Box 7 *Web:* www.nps.gov/thro	Medora	ND	58645	701-623-4466	623-4840

Northern Mariana Islands

				Phone	Fax
American Memorial Park PO Box 5198-Chrb *Web:* www.nps.gov/amme	Saipan	MP	96950	670-234-7207	234-6698

Ohio

				Phone	Fax
Cuyahoga Valley National Park 15610 Vaughn Rd **Fax Area Code:* 440 ■ *TF:* 800-445-9667 ■ *Web:* www.nps.gov	Brecksville	OH	44141	216-524-1497	546-5989*
Dayton Aviation Heritage National Historical Park 16 S Williams St *Web:* www.nps.gov	Dayton	OH	45402	937-225-7705	222-4512
First Ladies National Historic Site 205 Market Ave S *Web:* www.nps.gov	Canton	OH	44702	330-452-0876	456-3414
Hopewell Culture National Historical Park 16062 SR-104 *Web:* www.nps.gov/hocu	Chillicothe	OH	45601	740-774-1126	774-1140
James A Garfield National Historic Site 8095 Mentor Ave *Web:* www.nps.gov/jaga	Mentor	OH	44060	440-255-8722	255-8545
Perry's Victory & International Peace Memorial 93 Delaware Ave PO Box 549 *Web:* www.nps.gov/pevi	Put-in-Bay	OH	43456	419-285-2184	285-2516
William Howard Taft National Historic Site 2038 Auburn Ave *Web:* www.nps.gov/wiho	Cincinnati	OH	45219	513-684-3262	684-3627

Oklahoma

				Phone	Fax
Chickasaw National Recreation Area 1008 W Second St *Web:* www.nps.gov	Sulphur	OK	73086	580-622-7234	622-6931
Washita Battlefield National Historic Site 18555 HWY 47A *Web:* www.nps.gov/waha	Cheyenne	OK	73628	580-497-2742	497-2712

Oregon

				Phone	Fax
Crater Lake National Park PO Box 7 *Web:* www.nps.gov	Crater Lake	OR	97604	541-594-3000	594-3010
John Day Fossil Beds National Monument 32651 Hwy 19 *Web:* www.nps.gov/joda	Kimberly	OR	97848	541-987-2333	987-2336
Oregon Caves National Monument 19000 Caves Hwy *TF:* 877-245-9022 ■ *Web:* www.nps.gov/orca	Cave Junction	OR	97523	541-592-2100	592-3981

Pennsylvania

				Phone	Fax
Allegheny Portage Railroad National Historic Site 110 Federal Pk Rd *Web:* www.nps.gov	Gallitzin	PA	16641	814-886-6150	884-0206
Delaware National Scenic River Delaware Water Gap National Recreation Area 1978 River Rd *Web:* www.nps.gov/dewa	Bushkill	PA	18324	570-426-2435	588-2402
Edgar Allan Poe National Historic Site 532 N Seventh St *Web:* www.nps.gov/edal	Philadelphia	PA	19123	215-597-8780	597-1901
Eisenhower National Historic Site 1195 Baltimore Pk Ste 100 *Web:* www.nps.gov	Gettysburg	PA	17325	717-338-9114	338-0821
Flight 93 National Memorial *National Park Service* PO Box 911 *Web:* www.nps.gov/flni/index.htm	Shanksville	PA	15560	814-893-6322	443-2180
Fort Necessity National Battlefield One Washington Pkwy *Web:* www.nps.gov	Farmington	PA	15437	724-329-5512	329-8682
Friendship Hill National Historic Site 223 New Geneva Rd *Web:* www.nps.gov/frhi	Point Marion	PA	15474	724-725-9190	725-1999
Gettysburg National Military Park 97 Taneytown Rd *Web:* www.nps.gov/gett	Gettysburg	PA	17325	717-334-1124	334-1891
Hopewell Furnace National Historic Site Two Mark Bird Ln *Web:* www.nps.gov	Elverson	PA	19520	610-582-8773	582-2768
Independence National Historical Park 143 S Third St *Web:* www.nps.gov/inde	Philadelphia	PA	19106	215-597-8787	861-4950
Johnstown Flood National Memorial 733 Lake Rd *Web:* www.nps.gov/jofl	South Fork	PA	15956	814-495-4643	495-7463
National Park Service Regional Offices NortheastRegion 200 Chestnut St Ste 3 *Web:* www.nps.gov	Philadelphia	PA	19106	215-597-7013	597-0815
Steamtown National Historic Site 150 S Washington Ave *TF:* 888-693-9391 ■ *Web:* www.nps.gov	Scranton	PA	18503	570-340-5200	340-5328
Upper Delaware Scenic & Recreation River 274 River Rd *Web:* www.nps.gov/upde	Beach Lake	PA	18405	570-729-7134	729-7148
Valley Forge National Historical Park 1400 N Outer Line Dr *Web:* www.nps.gov/vafo	King of Prussia	PA	19406	610-783-1077	783-1060

Puerto Rico

				Phone	Fax
San Juan National Historic Site 501 Norzagaray St *Web:* www.nps.gov/saju	San Juan	PR	00901	787-729-6960	289-7972

Rhode Island

	City	State	ZIP	Phone	Fax
Roger Williams National Memorial 282 N Main St *Web:* www.nps.gov/rowi	Providence	RI	02903	401-521-7266	521-7239

South Carolina

	City	State	ZIP	Phone	Fax
Charles Pinckney National Historic Site 1214 Middle St *Web:* www.nps.gov/chpi	Sullivans Island	SC	29482	843-881-5516	881-7070
Congaree National Park 100 National Pk Rd *Web:* www.nps.gov	Hopkins	SC	29061	803-776-4396	783-4241
Cowpens National Battlefield 4001 Chesnee Hwy PO Box 308 *Web:* www.nps.gov/cowp	Gaffney	SC	29341	864-461-2828	461-7795
Fort Sumter National Monument 1214 Middle St *Web:* www.nps.gov/fosu	Sullivans Island	SC	29482	843-883-3123	883-3910
Historic Camden Revolutionary War Site 222 Broad St *Web:* www.historic-camden.net	Camden	SC	29021	803-432-9841	432-3815
Kings Mountain National Military Park 2625 Pk Rd *Web:* www.nps.gov	Blacksburg	SC	29702	864-936-7921	936-9897
Ninety Six National Historic Site 1103 Hwy 248 PO Box 418 *Web:* www.nps.gov/nisi	Ninety Six	SC	29666	864-543-4068	543-2058

South Dakota

	City	State	ZIP	Phone	Fax
Badlands National Park 25216 Ben Reifel Rd PO Box 6 *Web:* www.nps.gov/badl	Interior	SD	57750	605-433-5361	433-5404
Jewel Cave National Monument 11149 US Hwy 16 Bldg B-12 *Web:* www.nps.gov	Custer	SD	57730	605-673-2288	673-3294
Minuteman Missile National Historic Site 21280 SD Hwy 240 *Web:* www.nps.gov	Philip	SD	57567	605-433-5552	433-5558
Missouri National Recreational River 508 E Second St *Web:* www.nps.gov/mnrr	Yankton	SD	57078	605-665-0209	665-4183
Mount Rushmore National Memorial 13000 Hwy 244 Bldg 31 Ste 1 *Web:* www.nps.gov	Keystone	SD	57751	605-574-2523	574-2307
Wind Cave National Park 26611 US Hwy 385 *Web:* www.nps.gov	Hot Springs	SD	57747	605-745-4600	745-4207

Tennessee

	City	State	ZIP	Phone	Fax
Big South Fork National River & Recreation Area 4564 Leatherwood Rd *Web:* www.nps.gov	Oneida	TN	37841	423-569-9778	569-5505
Fort Donelson National Battlefield PO Box 434 *Web:* www.nps.gov	Dover	TN	37058	931-232-5706	232-4085
Great Smoky Mountains National Park 107 Pk Headquarters Rd *Web:* www.nps.gov	Gatlinburg	TN	37738	865-436-1200	436-1220
Obed Wild & Scenic River 208 N Maiden St *Web:* www.nps.gov	Wartburg	TN	37887	423-346-6294	346-3362
Shiloh National Military Park 1055 Pittsburg Landing Rd *Web:* www.nps.gov/shil	Shiloh	TN	38376	731-689-5696	689-5450

Texas

	City	State	ZIP	Phone	Fax
Alibates Flint Quarries National Monument PO Box 1460 *Web:* www.nps.gov/alfl	Fritch	TX	79036	806-857-3151	857-2319
Amistad National Recreation Area 4121 Hwy 90 W *Web:* www.nps.gov	Del Rio	TX	78840	830-775-7491	778-9248
Big Bend National Park PO Box 129 *Web:* www.nps.gov/bibe	Big Bend National Park	TX	79834	432-477-2251	477-1175
Big Thicket National Preserve 6044 FM 420 *Web:* www.nps.gov/bith	Kountze	TX	77625	409-951-6700	951-6714
Chamizal National Memorial 800 S San Marcial St *TF:* 877-642-4743 ■ *Web:* www.nps.gov	El Paso	TX	79905	915-532-7273	532-7240
Fort Davis National Historic Site PO Box 1379 *Web:* www.nps.gov/foda	Fort Davis	TX	79734	432-426-3224	426-3122
Guadalupe Mountains National Park 400 Pine Canyon Rd *Web:* www.nps.gov	Salt Flat	TX	79847	915-828-3251	828-3269
Lake Meredith National Recreation Area 419 E Broadway *Web:* www.nps.gov/lamr	Fritch	TX	79036	806-857-3151	857-2319
Lyndon B. Johnson National Historical Park 100 Lady Bird Ln *Web:* www.nps.gov/lyjo	Johnson City	TX	78636	830-868-7128	868-7863
Padre Island National Seashore PO Box 181300 *Web:* www.nps.gov/pais	Corpus Christi	TX	78480	361-949-8068	949-8023
Rio Grande Wild & Scenic River PO Box 129 *Web:* www.nps.gov/rigr	Big Bend National Park	TX	79834	432-477-2251	477-1175
San Antonio Missions National Historical Park 2202 Roosevelt Ave *TF:* 866-945-7920 ■ *Web:* www.nps.gov/saan	San Antonio	TX	78210	210-534-8833	534-1106

Utah

	City	State	ZIP	Phone	Fax
Bryce Canyon National Park PO Box 640201 *Web:* www.nps.gov	Bryce Canyon	UT	84764	435-834-5322	834-4102
Canyonlands National Park 2282 SW Resource Blvd. *Web:* www.nps.gov/cany	Moab	UT	84532	435-719-2313	719-2300
Capitol Reef National Park 16 Scenic Dr *Web:* www.nps.gov	Torrey	UT	84775	435-425-3791	425-3026
Cedar Breaks National Monument 2390 W Hwy 56 Ste 11 *TF:* 877-642-4743 ■ *Web:* www.nps.gov	Cedar City	UT	84720	435-586-9451	586-3813
Golden Spike National Historic Site PO Box 897 *Web:* www.nps.gov/gosp	Brigham City	UT	84302	435-471-2209	471-2341
Natural Bridges National Monument HC 60 PO Box 1 *Web:* www.nps.gov/nabr	Lake Powell	UT	84533	435-692-1234	692-1111
Timpanogos Cave National Monument RR 3 PO Box 200 *Web:* www.nps.gov	American Fork	UT	84003	801-756-5239	756-5661
Zion National Park SR 9 *Web:* www.nps.gov/zion	Springdale	UT	84767	435-772-3256	772-3426

Vermont

	City	State	ZIP	Phone	Fax
Marsh-Billings-Rockefeller National Historical Park 54 Elm St *Web:* www.nps.gov	Woodstock	VT	05091	802-457-3368	457-3405

Virgin Islands

	City	State	ZIP	Phone	Fax
Buck Island Reef National Monument 2100 Church St Ste 100 *Web:* www.nps.gov/buis	Christiansted	VI	00820	340-773-1460	773-5995
Salt River Bay National Historical Park & Ecological Preserve c/o Christiansted National Historic Site 2100 Church St Ste 100 *Web:* www.nps.gov/sari	Christiansted	VI	00820	340-773-1460	773-5995

Virginia

	City	State	ZIP	Phone	Fax
Appomattox Court House National Historical Park Hwy 24 PO Box 218 *Web:* www.nps.gov/apco	Appomattox	VA	24522	434-352-8987	352-8330
Arlington House-Robert E Lee Memorial George Washington Memorial Pkwy Turkey Run Pk *Web:* www.nps.gov/arho	McLean	VA	22101	703-235-1530	235-1546
Booker T. Washington National Monument 12130 Booker T Washington Hwy *Web:* www.nps.gov/bowa	Hardy	VA	24101	540-721-2094	721-8311
Cedar Creek & Belle Grove National Historical Park 7718 1/2 Main St *Web:* www.nps.gov	Middletown	VA	22645	540-868-9176	869-4527
Colonial National Historical Park PO Box 210 *TF:* 866-945-7920 ■ *Web:* www.nps.gov/colo	Yorktown	VA	23690	757-898-3400	898-6346
Fredericksburg & Spotsylvania National Military Park 120 Chatham Ln *Web:* www.nps.gov/frsp	Fredericksburg	VA	22405	540-371-0802	371-1907
George Washington Birthplace National Monument 1732 Popes Creek Rd *Web:* www.nps.gov/gewa	Washington's Birthplace	VA	22443	804-224-1732	224-2142
George Washington Memorial Parkway Turkey Run Pk *Web:* www.nps.gov/gwmp	McLean	VA	22101	703-289-2500	289-2598
Lyndon Baines Johnson Memorial Grove on the Potomac Turkey Run Pk George Washington Memorial Pkwy *Web:* www.nps.gov/lyba	McLean	VA	22101	703-289-2500	289-2598
Maggie L Walker National Historic Site 600 N Second St *Web:* www.nps.gov/malw	Richmond	VA	23223	804-771-2017	771-2226
Petersburg National Battlefield 1539 Hickory Hill Rd *Web:* www.nps.gov/pete	Petersburg	VA	23803	804-732-3531	732-0835
Prince William Forest Park 18100 Pk Headquarters Rd *Web:* www.nps.gov	Triangle	VA	22172	703-221-7181	221-3258
Red Hill Patrick Henry National Memorial 1250 Red Hill Rd *TF:* 800-514-7463 ■ *Web:* www.redhill.org	Brookneal	VA	24528	434-376-2044	376-2647
Richmond National Battlefield Park 3215 E Broad St *TF:* 866-733-7768 ■ *Web:* www.nps.gov	Richmond	VA	23223	804-226-1981	771-8522
Shenandoah National Park 3655 US Hwy 211E *TF:* 800-732-0911 ■ *Web:* www.nps.gov/shen	Luray	VA	22835	540-999-3500	999-3601
Theodore Roosevelt Island Park c/o Turkey Run Pk George Washington Memorial Pkwy *Web:* www.nps.gov/this	McLean	VA	22101	703-289-2500	289-2598

	City	State	Zip	Phone	Fax
Wolf Trap National Park for the Performing Arts 1551 Trap Rd *Web:* www.nps.gov/wotr	Vienna	VA	22182	703-255-1800	255-1971

Washington

	City	State	Zip	Phone	Fax
Ebey's Landing National Historical Reserve 162 Cemetery Rd *Web:* www.nps.gov	Coupeville	WA	98239	360-678-6084	678-2246
Fort Vancouver National Historic Site 612 E Reserve St *TF:* 800-832-3599 ■ *Web:* www.nps.gov	Vancouver	WA	98661	360-816-6230	
Klondike Gold Rush National Historical Park - Seattle Unit 319 Second Ave S *Web:* www.nps.gov	Seattle	WA	98104	206-220-4240	
Lake Chelan National Recreation Area 810 State Rt 20 *Web:* www.nps.gov/lach	Sedro-Woolley	WA	98284	360-854-7200	856-1934
Lake Roosevelt National Recreation Area 1008 Crest Dr *Web:* www.nps.gov	Coulee Dam	WA	99116	509-633-9441	633-9332
Mount Rainier National Park 55210 238th Ave E *Web:* www.nps.gov/mora	Ashford	WA	98304	360-569-2211	569-6519
North Cascades National Park 810 SR 20 *Web:* www.nps.gov/noca	Sedro Woolley	WA	98284	360-856-5700	856-1934
Ross Lake National Recreation Area 810 State Rt 20 *Web:* www.nps.gov/rola	Sedro Woolley	WA	98284	360-854-7200	856-1934
San Juan Island National Historical Park 4668 Cattle Pt Rd PO Box 429 *Web:* www.nps.gov/sajh	Friday Harbor	WA	98250	360-378-2240	378-2615
Whitman Mission National Historic Site 328 Whitman Mission Rd *Web:* www.nps.gov	Walla Walla	WA	99362	509-522-6360	522-6355

West Virginia

	City	State	Zip	Phone	Fax
Appalachian National Scenic Trail PO Box 807 *Web:* www.nps.gov/appa	Harpers Ferry	WV	25425	304-535-6331	535-2667
Bluestone National Scenic River P O Box 246 PO Box 246 *Web:* www.nps.gov/blue	Glen Jean	WV	25846	304-465-0508	465-0591
Gauley River National Recreation Area 104 Main St PO Box 246 *Web:* www.nps.gov/gari	Glen Jean	WV	25846	304-465-0508	465-0591
Harpers Ferry National Historic Park PO Box 65 *Web:* www.nps.gov/hafe	Harpers Ferry	WV	25425	304-535-6029	535-6244
New River Gorge National River 104 Main St PO Box 246 *Web:* www.nps.gov/neri	Glen Jean	WV	25846	304-465-0508	465-0591
Potomac Heritage National Scenic Trail PO Box B *Web:* www.nps.gov/pohe	Harpers Ferry	WV	25425	304-535-4014	

Wisconsin

	City	State	Zip	Phone	Fax
Saint Croix National Scenic Riverway 401 N Hamilton St *Web:* www.nps.gov	Saint Croix Falls	WI	54024	715-483-3284	483-3288

Wyoming

	City	State	Zip	Phone	Fax
Devils Tower National Monument Hwy 110 Bldg 170 PO Box 10 *Web:* www.nps.gov/deto	Devils Tower	WY	82714	307-467-5283	467-5350
Fort Laramie National Historic Site 965 Grey Rocks Rd *Web:* www.nps.gov/fola	Fort Laramie	WY	82212	307-837-2221	837-2120
Fossil Butte National Monument PO Box 592 *Web:* www.nps.gov	Kemmerer	WY	83101	307-877-4455	877-4457
Grand Teton National Park Teton Pk Rd PO Box 170 *Web:* www.nps.gov/grte	Moose	WY	83012	307-739-3300	739-3438
John D. Rockefeller Jr Memorial Parkway PO Box 170 *Web:* www.nps.gov/jodr	Moose	WY	83012	307-739-3300	739-3438
Yellowstone National Park PO Box 168 **Fax:* Mail Rm ■ *Web:* www.nps.gov	Yellowstone National Park	WY	82190	307-344-7381	344-2323*

568 PARKS - STATE

SEE ALSO Nature Centers, Parks, Other Natural Areas p. 1821; Parks - National - Canada p. 2858; Parks - National - US p. 2859

Alabama

	City	State	Zip	Phone	Fax
Bladon Springs State Park 3921 Bladon Rd *TF:* 800-252-7275 ■ *Web:* www.alapark.com/parks	Bladon Springs	AL	36919	251-754-9207	754-9207
Blue Springs State Park 2595 Alabama 10 *Web:* www.alapark.com	Clio	AL	36017	334-397-4875	397-4875
Buck's Pocket State Park 393 County Rd 174 *TF:* 800-760-4089 ■ *Web:* www.alapark.com	Grove Oak	AL	35975	256-659-2000	659-2000
Cathedral Caverns State Park 637 Cave Rd *TF:* 800-252-7275 ■ *Web:* www.alapark.com	Woodville	AL	35776	256-728-8193	728-8193
Cheaha Resort State Park 19644 Hwy 281 *TF:* 800-610-5801 ■ *Web:* www.alapark.com	Delta	AL	36258	256-488-5111	488-5885
Chewacla State Park 124 Shell Toomer Pkwy *TF:* 800-252-7275 ■ *Web:* www.alapark.com	Auburn	AL	36830	334-887-5621	821-2439
Frank Jackson State Park 100 Jerry Adams Dr *TF:* 800-760-4089 ■ *Web:* www.alapark.com	Opp	AL	36467	334-493-6988	493-2478
Gulf State Park 20115 Alabama 135 *Web:* www.alapark.com	Gulf Shores	AL	36542	251-948-7275	948-7726
Joe Wheeler Resort State Park 4401 McLean Dr *Web:* www.alapark.com	Rogersville	AL	35652	256-247-5466	247-1449
Lake Lurleen State Park 13226 Lake Lurleen Rd *TF:* 800-760-4089 ■ *Web:* www.alapark.com	Coker	AL	35452	205-339-1558	339-8885
Lakepoint Resort State Park 104 Lakepoint Dr *TF:* 800-544-5253 ■ *Web:* www.alapark.com	Eufaula	AL	36027	334-687-8011	687-3273
Meaher State Park 5200 Battleship Pkwy *TF:* 800-252-7275 ■ *Web:* www.alapark.com	Spanish Fort	AL	36577	251-626-5529	626-5529
Monte Sano State Park 5105 Nolen Ave *TF:* 800-252-7275 ■ *Web:* www.alapark.com	Huntsville	AL	35801	256-534-3757	539-7069
Oak Mountain State Park 200 Terr Dr PO Box 278 *TF:* 800-252-7275 ■ *Web:* www.alapark.com	Pelham	AL	35124	205-620-2520	620-2531
Paul M. Grist State Park 1546 Grist Rd *TF:* 800-252-7275 ■ *Web:* www.alapark.com	Selma	AL	36701	334-872-5846	872-5846
Rickwood Caverns State Park 370 Rickwood Pk Rd *TF:* 800-252-7275 ■ *Web:* www.alapark.com	Warrior	AL	35180	205-647-9692	647-9692
Roland Cooper State Park 285 Deer Run Dr *TF:* 800-252-7275 ■ *Web:* www.alapark.com	Camden	AL	36726	334-682-4838	682-4050
Wind Creek State Park 4325 Al Hwy 128 *Web:* www.alapark.com	Alexander City	AL	35010	256-329-0845	234-4870

Alaska

	City	State	Zip	Phone	Fax
Big Delta State Historical Park c/o Northern Area Office 3700 Airport Way *Web:* www.dnr.alaska.gov/parks/units/deltajct/bigdelta.htm	Fairbanks	AK	99709	907-451-2695	
Birch Lake State Recreation Area c/o Northern Area Office 3700 Airport Way *Web:* www.dnr.alaska.gov/parks/units/birch.htm	Fairbanks	AK	99709	907-451-2695	
Blueberry Lake State Recreation Site 23 Richardson Hwy *Web:* dnr.alaska.gov/parks/aspunits/kenai/blueberrylksrs.htm	Valdez	AK	99686	907-269-8400	
Boswell Bay State Marine Park PO Box 1247 *Web:* dnr.alaska.gov/parks/units/pwssmp/smpcord.htm	Soldotna	AK	99669	907-262-5581	
Chena River State Recreation Area c/o Northern Area Office 3700 Airport Way *Web:* www.dnr.alaska.gov/parks/units/chena	Fairbanks	AK	99709	907-451-2705	
Chilkat Islands State Marine Park 550 W Seventh Ave Ste 1260 *Web:* dnr.alaska.gov/parks/units/haines.htm	Anchorage	AK	99501	907-269-8400	
Chilkoot Lake State Recreation Site 10 Mile Lutak Rd PO Box 111071 *Web:* www.dnr.alaska.gov/parks/aspunits/southeast/chilkootlksrs.htm	Juneau	AK	99811	907-465-4563	
Chugach State Park 18620 Seward Highway *TF:* 800-478-6196 ■ *Web:* dnr.alaska.gov	Anchorage	AK	99516	907-345-5014	345-6982
Clam Gulch State Recreation Area PO Box 1247 *Web:* dnr.alaska.gov/parks/units/clamglch.htm	Soldotna	AK	99669	907-262-5581	
Clearwater State Recreation Site 3700 Airport Way *Web:* www.dnr.alaska.gov/parks/units/deltajct/clearwtr.htm	Fairbanks	AK	99709	907-451-2695	
Crooked Creek State Recreation Site PO Box 1247 *Web:* dnr.alaska.gov/parks/units/kasilof.htm	Soldotna	AK	99669	907-262-5581	
Dall Bay State Marine Park 400 Willoughby Ave PO Box 111071 *Web:* www.dnr.alaska.gov/parks/aspunits/marinepark/dallbay.htm	Juneau	AK	99811	907-465-4563	
Decision Point State Marine Park 550 W Seventh Ave PO Box 1247 *Web:* dnr.alaska.gov/parks/units/pwssmp/smpwhit1.htm	Anchorage	AK	99501	907-269-8400	269-8901
Deep Creek State Recreation Area PO Box 1247 *Web:* dnr.alaska.gov/parks/units/deepck.htm	Soldotna	AK	99669	907-262-5581	
Delta State Recreation Site 3700 Airport Wy 3700 Airport Way *Web:* www.dnr.alaska.gov/parks/units/deltajct/deltasrs.htm	Fairbanks	AK	99709	907-451-2695	
Denali State Park 7278 E Bogard Rd *TF:* 800-478-6196 ■ *Web:* dnr.alaska.gov/parks/units/denali1.htm	Wasilla	AK	99654	907-745-3975	745-0938
Department of Natural Resources 550 W Seventh Ave Ste 1260 *Web:* dnr.alaska.gov/parks/units/haines.htm	Anchorage	AK	99501	907-269-8400	
Donnelly Creek State Recreation Site 3700 Airport Way *Web:* www.dnr.alaska.gov/parks/units/deltajct/donnelly.htm	Fairbanks	AK	99709	907-451-2695	
Driftwood Bay State Marine Park PO Box 1247 *Web:* dnr.alaska.gov/parks/units/pwssmp/smpsewd.htm	Soldotna	AK	99669	907-262-5581	
Eagle Beach State Recreation Area 400 Willoughby Ave Fourth Fl *Web:* www.dnr.alaska.gov/parks/aspunits/southeast/eaglebeachsra.htm	Juneau	AK	99811	907-465-4563	
Eagle Trail State Recreation Site c/o Northern Area Office 3700 Airport Way *Web:* www.dnr.alaska.gov/parks/aspunits/northern/eagletrailsrs.htm	Fairbanks	AK	99709	907-883-3686	
Entry Cove State Marine Park PO Box 1247 *Web:* dnr.alaska.gov/parks/units/pwssmp/smpwhit1.htm	Soldotna	AK	99669	907-262-5581	
Fielding Lake State Recreation Site 3700 Airport Way *Web:* www.dnr.alaska.gov/parks/units/deltajct/fielding.htm	Fairbanks	AK	99709	907-451-2695	

				Phone	Fax
Finger Lake State Recreation Area 7278 E Bogard Rd. *Web:* dnr.alaska.gov/parks/aspunits/matsu/fingerlksrs.htm	Wasilla	AK	99654	907-745-3975	
Funter Bay State Marine Park 400 Willoughby Ave PO Box 111071 *Web:* www.dnr.alaska.gov/parks/aspbro/charts/sejuneau.htm	Juneau	AK	99811	907-465-4563	
Granite Bay State Marine Park PO Box 1247 *Web:* dnr.alaska.gov/parks/units/pwssmp/smpwhit2.htm	Soldotna	AK	99669	907-262-5581	
Grindall Island State Marine Park 400 Willoughby Ave PO Box 111071 *Web:* www.dnr.alaska.gov/parks/aspunits/southeast/grindallimp.htm	Juneau	AK	99811	907-465-4563	
Harding Lake State Recreation Area c/o Northern Area Office 3700 Airport Way *Web:* www.dnr.alaska.gov/parks/units/harding.htm	Fairbanks	AK	99709	907-451-2695	
Horseshoe Bay State Marine Park PO Box 1247 *Web:* dnr.alaska.gov/parks/units/pwssmp/smpwhit2.htm	Soldotna	AK	99669	907-262-5581	
Kepler-Bradley Lakes State Recreation Area Mile 364 Glenn Hwy 7278 E Bogard Rd *Web:* dnr.alaska.gov/parks/aspunits/matsu/keplerbradlksra.htm	Palmer	AK	99645	907-317-9094	
King Mountain State Recreation Site Mile 76 Glenn Hwy 7278 E Bogard Rd *Web:* dnr.alaska.gov/parks/aspunits/matsu/kingmtnsrs.htm	Palmer	AK	99645	907-317-9094	
Lake Aleknagik State Recreation Site 550 W Seventh Ave Ste 1380 *Web:* www.dnr.alaska.gov/parks/aspunits/woodtik/lkaleknsrs.htm	Anchorage	AK	99501	907-842-2641	
Liberty Falls State Recreation Site Mile 23.5 Edgerton Hwy 7278 E Bogard Rd *Web:* dnr.alaska.gov/parks/aspunits/matsu/libertyflsrs.htm	Glennallen	AK	99588	907-823-2223	
Lower Chatanika River State Recreation Area c/o Northern Area Office 3700 Airport Way *Web:* www.dnr.alaska.gov/parks/aspunits/northern/lrchatrivsra.htm	Fairbanks	AK	99709	907-269-8400	
Matanuska Glacier State Recreation Site c/o Mat-Su/Copper Basin Area Office 7278 E Bogard Rd. *Web:* dnr.alaska.gov/parks/aspunits/matsu/matsuglsrs.htm	Wasilla	AK	99654	907-745-3975	
Moon Lake State Recreation Site c/o Northern Area Office 3700 Airport Way *Web:* www.dnr.alaska.gov/parks/aspunits/northern/moonlksrs.htm	Fairbanks	AK	99709	907-883-3686	
Mosquito Lake State Recreation Site 400 Willoughby Ave PO Box 111071 *Web:* www.dnr.alaska.gov/parks/aspunits/southeast/mosqlksrs.htm	Juneau	AK	99801	907-465-4563	
Nancy Lake State Recreation Area 7278 E Bogard Rd HC 32 PO Box 6706 *Web:* dnr.alaska.gov/parks/units/nancylk/nancylk.htm	Wasilla	AK	99654	907-745-3975	
Ninilchik State Recreation Area PO Box 1247 *Web:* dnr.alaska.gov/parks/units/nilchik.htm	Soldotna	AK	99669	907-262-5581	
Old Sitka State Historic Site PO Box 111071 *Web:* dnr.alaska.gov/parks/units/sitka.htm	Juneau	AK	99811	907-465-4563	
Oliver Inlet State Marine Park 400 Willoughby Ave PO Box 111071 *TF:* 855-277-4491 ■ *Web:* www.dnr.alaska.gov/parks	Juneau	AK	99801	907-465-4563	586-3113
Petroglyph Beach State Historic Site 400 Willoughby Ave PO Box 111071 *Web:* www.dnr.alaska.gov/parks/aspunits/southeast/wrangpetroshs.htm	Juneau	AK	11071	907-465-4563	
Portage Cove State Recreation Site 400 Willoughby Ave Fourth Fl PO Box 111071 *Web:* www.dnr.alaska.gov/parks/aspunits/southeast/portcovesrs.htm	Juneau	AK	99811	907-465-4563	
Quartz Lake State Recreation Area c/o Northern Area Office 3700 Airport Way *Web:* www.dnr.alaska.gov/parks/units/deltajct/quartz.htm	Fairbanks	AK	99709	907-451-2695	
Saint James Bay State Marine Park 400 Willoughby Ave Ste 500 *Web:* dnr.alaska.gov	Juneau	AK	99811	907-465-4563	586-3113
Salcha River State Recreation Site c/o Northern Area Office 3700 Airport Way *Web:* www.dnr.alaska.gov/parks/units/salcha.htm	Fairbanks	AK	99709	907-451-2695	
Security Bay State Marine Park PO Box 111071 *Web:* dnr.alaska.gov/parks/units/sitka.htm	Juneau	AK	99811	907-465-4563	
Shelter Island State Marine Park PO Box 111071 *Web:* dnr.alaska.gov/parks/cabins/south.htm	Juneau	AK	99811	907-465-4563	
Summit Lake State Recreation Site c/o Mat-Su/CB Area Office 7278 E Bogard Rd *Web:* dnr.alaska.gov/parks/units/summit.htm	Wasilla	AK	99654	907-745-3975	
Tok River State Recreation Site c/o Northern Area Office 3700 Airport Way *Web:* www.dnr.alaska.gov/parks/aspunits/northern/tokrvsrs.htm	Fairbanks	AK	99709	907-883-3686	
Totem Bight State Historical Park 400 Willoughby Ave PO Box 111071 *Web:* www.dnr.alaska.gov/parks/units/totembgh.htm	Juneau	AK	99811	907-465-4563	
Wickersham State Historic Site 400 Willoughby Ave Ste 500 PO Box 111071 *Web:* www.dnr.alaska.gov/parks/units/wickrshm.htm	Juneau	AK	99811	907-465-4563	
Willow Creek State Recreation Area 7278 E Bogard Rd. *Web:* dnr.alaska.gov/parks/aspunits/matsu/willowcksra.htm	Wasilla	AK	99654	907-745-3975	
Wood-Tikchik State Park 550 W Seventh Ave Ste 1390 *Web:* dnr.alaska.gov	Anchorage	AK	99510	907-269-8698	
Worthington Glacier State Recreation Site 287 Richardson Hwy. *Web:* dnr.alaska.gov/parks/aspunits/kenai/worthglsrs.htm	Soldotna	AK	99669	907-262-5581	

Arizona

				Phone	Fax
Boyce Thompson Arboretum State Park 37615 US Hwy 60. **Fax Area Code:* 684 ■ *TF:* 800-858-7378	Superior	AZ	85273	520-689-2811	699-5011*
Buckskin Mountain State Park 5476 Hwy 95	Parker	AZ	85344	928-667-3231	
Catalina State Park 11570 N Oracle Rd	Tucson	AZ	85737	520-628-5798	628-5797
Dead Horse Ranch State Park 675 Dead Horse Ranch Rd	Cottonwood	AZ	86326	928-634-5283	
Fool Hollow Lake Recreation Area 1500 N Fool Hollow Lk Rd	Show Low	AZ	85901	928-537-3680	
Homolovi Ruins State Park 87 N Rd *Web:* www.azstateparks.com	Winslow	AZ	86047	928-289-4106	289-2021
Jerome State Historic Park PO Box D *Web:* www.azstateparks.com	Jerome	AZ	86331	928-634-5381	
Kartchner Caverns State Park 2980 Arizona 90 *Web:* www.azstateparks.com	Benson	AZ	85602	520-586-2283	
Lake Havasu State Park 699 London Bridge Rd *Web:* golakehavasu.com	Lake Havasu City	AZ	86403	928-855-2784	453-9358
Lost Dutchman State Park 6109 N Apache Tr *Web:* azstateparks.com	Apache Junction	AZ	85219	480-982-4485	
Lyman Lake State Park 11 US 180. *Web:* www.azstateparks.com	Saint Johns	AZ	85936	928-337-4441	
Oracle State Park 3820 Wildlife Dr *Web:* azstateparks.com	Oracle	AZ	85623	520-896-2425	
Patagonia Lake State Park 400 Patagonia Lk Rd. *Web:* azstateparks.com	Patagonia	AZ	85624	520-287-6965	
Picacho Peak State Park 15520 Picacho Peak Rd *Web:* www.azstateparks.com	Picacho	AZ	85241	520-466-3183	
Red Rock State Park 4050 Red Rock Loop Rd *Web:* azstateparks.com	Sedona	AZ	86336	928-282-6907	282-5972
Riordan Mansion State Historic Park 409 W Riordan Rd	Flagstaff	AZ	86001	928-779-4395	556-0253
Roper Lake State Park 101 E Roper Lk Rd *Web:* azstateparks.itinio.com	Safford	AZ	85546	928-428-6760	428-7879
San Rafael Ranch State Park 2036 Duquesne Rd *Web:* azstateparks.com	Patagonia	AZ	85624	520-394-2447	
Slide Rock State Park 6871 N Hwy 89A *Web:* azpra.org	Sedona	AZ	86336	928-282-3034	
Tombstone Courthouse State Historic Park 223 E Toughnut St *Web:* azstateparks.com	Tombstone	AZ	85638	520-457-3311	
Tonto Natural Bridge State Park Hwy 87 N *Web:* www.azstateparks.com	Payson	AZ	85547	928-476-4202	476-2264
Tubac Presidio State Historic Park One Burruel St *Web:* azstateparks.com	Tubac	AZ	85646	520-398-2252	
Yuma Territorial Prison State Historic Park One Prison Hill Rd PO Box 10792 *Web:* azstateparks.com	Yuma	AZ	85364	928-783-4771	

Arkansas

				Phone	Fax
Arkansas Museum of Natural Resources 3853 Smackover Hwy *TF:* 888-287-2757 ■ *Web:* www.arkansasstateparks.com	Smackover	AR	71762	870-725-2877	725-2161
Arkansas Post Museum 5530 Hwy 165 S *Web:* www.arkansasstateparks.com	Gillett	AR	72055	870-548-2634	
Bull Shoals-White River State Park 129 Bull Shoals Pk *Web:* www.arkansasstateparks.com	Lakeview	AR	72642	870-431-5521	
Cane Creek State Park 50 State Pk Rd. *TF:* 888-287-2757 ■ *Web:* www.arkansasstateparks.com	Star City	AR	71667	870-628-4714	628-3611
Conway Cemetery State Park c/o Arkansas State Parks 1 Capitol Mall *TF:* 888-287-2757 ■ *Web:* www.arkansasstateparks.com/conwaycemetery	Little Rock	AR	72201	888-287-2757	
Cossatot River State Park-Natural Area 1980 Hwy 278 W *TF:* 877-665-6343 ■ *Web:* www.arkansasstateparks.com	Wickes	AR	71973	870-385-2201	385-7858
Crater of Diamonds State Park 209 State Pk Rd *Web:* www.craterofdiamondsstatepark.com	Murfreesboro	AR	71958	870-285-3113	
Crowley's Ridge State Park 2092 Hwy 168 N. *Web:* www.arkansasstateparks.com	Paragould	AR	72450	870-573-6751	
Daisy State Park 103 E Pk. *Web:* www.arkansasstateparks.com/daisy	Kirby	AR	71950	870-398-4487	
DeGray Lake Resort State Park 2027 State Pk Entrance Rd *Web:* www.degray.com	Bismarck	AR	71929	501-865-2801	
Delta Heritage Trail State Park PO Box 193 *Web:* www.arkansasstateparks.com	Watson	AR	71674	870-644-3474	
Devil's Den State Park 11333 W Arkansas Hwy 74. *TF:* 888-742-8701 ■ *Web:* www.arkansasstateparks.com	West Fork	AR	72774	479-761-3325	761-3676
Hampson Archeological Museum State Park PO Box 156 *TF:* 888-742-8701 ■ *Web:* www.arkansasstateparks.com	Wilson	AR	72395	870-655-8622	655-8061
Herman Davis State Park Corner of Ark 18 Baltimore St. *TF:* 888-287-2757 ■ *Web:* www.arkansasstateparks.com/hermandavis	Manila	AR	72201	888-287-2757	
Hobbs State Park-Conservation Area 21392 E Hwy 12 *Web:* www.arkansasstateparks.com	Rogers	AR	72756	479-789-2380	
Jacksonport State Park 1 Capitol Mall *Web:* www.arkansasstateparks.com	Newport	AR	72112	870-523-2143	523-4620
Lake Catherine State Park 1200 Catherine Pk Rd. *Web:* www.arkansasstateparks.com	Hot Springs	AR	71913	501-844-4176	844-4244
Lake Charles State Park 3705 Hwy 25 *Web:* www.arkansasstateparks.com/lakecharles	Powhatan	AR	72458	870-878-6595	
Lake Chicot State Park 2542 Hwy 257 *Web:* www.arkansasstateparks.com	Lake Village	AR	71653	870-265-5480	
Lake Dardanelle State Park 100 State Pk Dr. *Web:* www.arkansasstateparks.com	Russellville	AR	72802	479-967-5516	

				Phone	Fax
Lake Fort Smith State Park PO Box 4	Mountainburg	AR	72946	479-369-2469	
Web: www.arkansasstateparks.com					
Lake Frierson State Park 7904 Hwy	Jonesboro	AR	72401	870-932-2615	
Web: www.arkansasstateparks.com					
Lake Ouachita State Park 5451 Mtn Pine Rd	Mountain Pine	AR	71956	501-767-9366	
Web: www.arkansasstateparks.com					
Lake Poinsett State Park 5752 State Pk Ln	Harrisburg	AR	72432	870-578-2064	
Web: www.arkansasstateparks.com					
Logoly State Park PO Box 245	McNeil	AR	71752	870-695-3561	
Web: www.arkansasstateparks.com					
Lower White River Museum State Park 2009 Main St	Des Arc	AR	72040	870-256-3711	256-9202
Web: www.arkansasstateparks.com					
Mammoth Spring State Park PO Box 36	Mammoth Spring	AR	72554	870-625-7364	625-3255
Web: www.arkansasstateparks.com					
Millwood State Park 1564 Hwy 32 E	Ashdown	AR	71822	870-898-2800	898-2632
Web: www.arkansasstateparks.com					
Moro Bay State Park 6071 US Hwy 600	Jersey	AR	71651	870-463-8555	
TF: 888-742-8701 ■ *Web:* www.arkansasstateparks.com					
Mount Magazine State Park 16878 Hwy 309 S	Paris	AR	72855	479-963-8502	963-1031
Web: www.arkansasstateparks.com					
Mount Nebo State Park 16728 W State Hwy 155	Dardanelle	AR	72834	479-229-3655	
Web: www.arkansasstateparks.com					
Old Davidsonville State Park 7953 Hwy 166 S	Pocahontas	AR	72455	870-892-4708	
Web: www.arkansasstateparks.com					
Old Washington Historic State Park PO Box 129	Washington	AR	71862	870-983-2684	983-2736
Web: www.historicwashingtonstatepark.com					
Ozark Folk Ctr State Park 1032 Pk Ave	Mountain View	AR	72560	870-269-3851	269-2909
TF: 800-264-3655 ■ *Web:* www.ozarkfolkcenter.com					
Parkin Archeological State Park PO Box 1110	Parkin	AR	72373	870-755-2500	755-2676
Web: www.arkansasstateparks.com					
Petit Jean State Park 1285 Petit Jean Mtn Rd	Morrilton	AR	72110	501-727-5441	
Web: www.petitjeanstatepark.com					
Pinnacle Mountain State Park 11901 Pinnacle Vly Rd	Little Rock	AR	72223	501-868-5806	868-5018
Web: www.arkansasstateparks.com					
Plantation Agriculture Museum PO Box 87	Scott	AR	72142	501-961-1409	
Web: www.arkansasstateparks.com					
Prairie Grove Battlefield State Park 506 E Douglas St	Prairie Grove	AR	72753	479-846-2990	
Web: www.arkansasstateparks.com					
Queen Wilhelmina State Park 3877 Arkansas 88	Mena	AR	71953	479-394-2863	
Web: www.arkansasstateparks.com					
South Arkansas Arboretum PO Box 7010	El Dorado	AR	71731	888-287-2757	
TF: 888-287-2757 ■ *Web:* www.arkansasstateparks.com/southarkansasarboretum					
Toltec Mounds Archeological State Park 490 Toltec Mounds Rd	Scott	AR	72142	501-961-9442	961-9221
Web: www.arkansasstateparks.com					
Village Creek State Park 201 County Rd 754	Wynne	AR	72396	870-238-9406	238-9415
Web: www.arkansasstateparks.com					
White Oak Lake State Park 563 Hwy 387	Bluff City	AR	71722	870-685-2748	
Web: www.arkansasstateparks.com					
Withrow Springs State Park 33424 Spur 23	Huntsville	AR	72740	479-559-2593	
Web: www.arkansasstateparks.com					
Woolly Hollow State Park 82 Woolly Hollow Rd	Greenbrier	AR	72058	501-679-2098	
Web: www.arkansasstateparks.com					

California

				Phone	Fax
Ahjumawi Lava Springs State Park c/o Northern Buttes District Office 400 Glen Dr	Oroville	CA	95966	530-538-2200	
Web: www.parks.ca.gov/?page_id=464					
Antelope Valley Indian Museum State Historic Park Antelope Vly Fwy Ave M	Perris	CA	92571	661-946-3055	
Web: www.avim.parks.ca.gov					
Anza-Borrego Desert State Park 200 Palm Canyon Dr	Borrego Springs	CA	92004	760-767-5311	767-3427
Web: www.parks.ca.gov/?page_id=638					
Armstrong Redwoods State Reserve 17000 Armstrong Woods Rd	Guerneville	CA	95446	707-869-2015	869-5629
Web: www.parks.ca.gov/default.asp?page_id=450					
Asilomar State Beach & Conference Grounds 804 Crocker Ave 2211 Garden Rd	Pacific Grove	CA	93950	831-646-6440	
Web: www.parks.ca.gov/default.asp?page_id=566					
Auburn State Recreation Area 501 El Dorado St 7806 Folsom-Auburn Rd	Auburn	CA	95603	530-885-4527	
Web: www.parks.ca.gov/default.asp?page_id=502					
Austin Creek State Recreation Area 17000 Armstrong Woods Rd	Guerneville	CA	95446	707-869-2015	
Web: www.parks.ca.gov/default.asp?page_id=452					
Azalea State Reserve c/o N Coast Redwoods District Office PO Box 2006	Eureka	CA	95502	707-677-3132	
Web: www.parks.ca.gov/default.asp?page_id=420					
Benbow Lake State Recreation Area 1600 Hwy 101 PO Box 2006	Garberville	CA	95542	707-923-3238	
Web: www.parks.ca.gov/default.asp?page_id=426					
Benicia Capitol State Historic Park 115 W G St 845 Casa Grande Rd	Benicia	CA	94510	707-745-3385	
Web: www.parks.ca.gov/default.asp?page_id=475					
Benicia State Recreation Area One State Park Rd 845 Casa Grande Rd	Benicia	CA	94510	707-648-1911	
Web: www.parks.ca.gov/default.asp?page_id=476					
Bidwell-Sacramento River State Park 1416 Ninth St 400 Glen Dr	Sacramento	CA	95814	530-342-5185	
Web: www.parks.ca.gov/default.asp?page_id=463					
Big Basin Redwoods State Park 21600 Big Basin Way	Boulder Creek	CA	95006	831-338-8860	
Web: www.parks.ca.gov					
Bodie State Historic Park PO Box 515	Bridgeport	CA	93517	760-647-6445	
Web: www.parks.ca.gov					
Border Field State Park 301 Caspian Way 4477 Pacific Hwy	Imperial Beach	CA	91932	619-575-3613	
Web: www.parks.ca.gov/default.asp?page_id=664					
Bothe-Napa Valley State Park 3801 St Helena Hwy 845 Casa Grande Rd	Calistoga	CA	94515	707-942-4575	
Web: www.parks.ca.gov/default.asp?page_id=477					
Brannan Island State Recreation Area 17645 California 160 7806 Folsom-Auburn Rd	Rio Vista	CA	94571	916-777-7701	
Web: www.parks.ca.gov/default.asp?page_id=487					
Butano State Park 1500 Cloverdale Rd 303 Big Trees Pk Rd	Pescadero	CA	94060	650-879-2040	
Web: www.parks.ca.gov/default.asp?page_id=536					
Calaveras Big Trees State Park 1170 California 4 22708 Broadway St	Arnold	CA	95223	209-795-2334	
Web: www.parks.ca.gov/default.asp?page_id=551					
California State Mining & Mineral Museum 5005 Fairgrounds Rd	Mariposa	CA	95338	209-742-7625	966-3597
Web: www.parks.ca.gov/default.asp?page_id=588					
California State Railroad Museum 125 "I" St 111 'I' St	Sacramento	CA	95814	916-323-9280	327-5655
TF: 866-240-4655 ■ *Web:* www.csrmf.org					
Carlsbad State Beach c/o San Diego Coast District Office 4477 Pacific Hwy	San Diego	CA	92110	760-438-3143	
TF: 800-777-0369 ■ *Web:* www.parks.ca.gov/default.asp?page_id=653					
China Camp State Park 101 Peacock Gap Trl	San Rafael	CA	94901	415-456-0766	
Web: www.parks.ca.gov/default.asp?page_id=466					
Clay Pit State Vehicular Recreation Area 400 Glen Dr	Oroville	CA	95966	530-538-2200	
Web: www.parks.ca.gov					
Columbia State Historic Park 11255 Jackson St	Columbia	CA	95310	209-588-9128	
Web: www.parks.ca.gov					
Corona del Mar State Beach 3001 Ocean Blvd	Corona Del Mar	CA	92625	949-644-3151	
Web: www.parks.ca.gov/default.asp?page_id=652					
Crystal Cove State Park 8471 N Coast Hwy	Laguna Beach	CA	92651	949-494-3539	
Web: www.parks.ca.gov/default.asp?page_id=644					
Cuyamaca Rancho State Park 13652 Hwy 79	Julian	CA	92036	760-765-0755	765-3021
TF: 800-444-7275 ■ *Web:* www.parks.ca.gov/default.asp?page_id=667					
Del Norte Coast Redwoods State Park 1111 Second St	Crescent City	CA	95531	707-465-7335	
Web: www.parks.ca.gov/default.asp?page_id=414					
Delta Meadows 17645 State Hwy 160	Rio Vista	CA	94571	916-777-7701	
Web: www.parks.ca.gov/default.asp?page_id=492					
DL Bliss State Park c/o Sierra District Office PO Box 266	Tahoma	CA	96142	530-525-7277	
Web: www.parks.ca.gov/?page_id=505					
Dockweiler State Beach c/o Los Angeles County Dept of Beaches & Harbors 13837 Fiji Way	Marina del Rey	CA	90292	310-305-9503	
Web: www.parks.ca.gov					
Doheny State Beach 25300 Dana Pt Harbor Dr	Dana Point	CA	92629	949-496-6172	
Web: www.parks.ca.gov					
Donner Memorial State Park c/o Sierra District Office PO Box 266	Tahoma	CA	96142	530-582-7892	
Web: www.parks.ca.gov/default.asp?page_id=503					
Emerald Bay State Park c/o Sierra District Office PO Box 266	Tahoma	CA	96142	530-525-7277	
Web: www.parks.ca.gov/default.asp?page_id=506					
Empire Mine State Historic Park c/o Sierra District Office PO Box 266	Tahoma	CA	96142	530-273-8522	
Web: www.parks.ca.gov/default.asp?page_id=499					
Folsom Powerhouse State Historic Park 9980 Greenback Ln 7806 Folsom-Auburn Rd	Folsom	CA	95630	916-985-4843	
Web: www.parks.ca.gov					
Forest of Nisene Marks State Park c/o Santa Cruz District Office 303 Big Trees Pk Rd	Felton	CA	95018	831-763-7062	
Web: www.parks.ca.gov/?page_id=666					
Fort Humboldt State Historic Park c/o N Coast Redwoods District Office PO Box 2006	Eureka	CA	95502	707-445-6567	
Web: www.parks.ca.gov/default.asp?page_id=665					
Fort Ross State Historic Park 19005 Coast Hwy 1	Jenner	CA	95450	707-847-3286	
Web: www.parks.ca.gov/default.asp?page_id=449					
Fort Tejon State Historic Park c/o Central Valley District Office 22708 Broadway St	Columbia	CA	95310	209-536-5930	248-8373*
**Fax Area Code:* 661 ■ *Web:* www.parks.ca.gov/default.asp?page_id=585					
Governor's Mansion State Historic Park 1526 H St	Sacramento	CA	95814	916-323-3047	
Web: www.parks.ca.gov					
Half Moon Bay State Beach c/o San Mateo Coast Sector Office 95 Kelly Ave	Half Moon Bay	CA	94019	650-726-8819	726-8816
TF: 800-444-7275 ■ *Web:* www.parks.ca.gov					
Hearst San Simeon State Historical Monument 750 Hearst Castle Rd	San Simeon	CA	93452	805-927-2020	
TF: 800-444-4445 ■ *Web:* www.parks.ca.gov/default.asp?page_id=591					
Hendy Woods State Park c/o Mendocino District Office PO Box 440	Mendocino	CA	95460	707-895-3141	
Web: www.parks.ca.gov/default.asp?page_id=438					

Phone | Fax

Henry Cowell Redwoods State Park
c/o Santa Cruz District Office
303 Big Trees Pk Rd ... Felton CA 95018 831-335-4598
Web: www.parks.ca.gov/default.asp?page_id=546

Henry W. Coe State Park
c/o Monterey District Office 2211 Garden Rd ... Monterey CA 93940 408-779-2728
Web: www.parks.ca.gov/default.asp?page_id=561

Hollister Hills State Vehicular Recreation Area
7800 Cienega Rd ... Hollister CA 95023 831-637-8186
Web: www.parks.ca.gov

Humboldt Lagoons State Park
c/o N Coast Redwoods District Office
PO Box 2006 ... Eureka CA 95502 707-677-3132
Web: www.parks.ca.gov/default.asp?page_id=416

Humboldt Redwoods State Park
PO Box 100 PO Box 2006 ... Weott CA 95571 707-946-2409
Web: www.parks.ca.gov/default.asp?page_id=425

Hungry Valley State Vehicular Recreation Area
46001 Orwin Way ... Gorman CA 93243 661-248-7007
Web: www.parks.ca.gov

Huntington State Beach
21601 Pacific Coast Hwy
3030 Avenida del Presidente ... Huntington Beach CA 92646 714-536-1454
Web: www.parks.ca.gov/?page_id=643

Indian Grinding Rock State Historic Park
14881 Pine Grove-Volcano Rd ... Pine Grove CA 95665 209-296-7488
Web: www.parks.ca.gov/default.asp?page_id=553

Jack London State Historic Park
2400 London Ranch Rd 845 Casa Grande Rd ... Glen Ellen CA 95442 707-938-5216
Web: www.parks.ca.gov/default.asp?page_id=478

Julia Pfeiffer Burns State Park
Hwy 1 2211 Garden Rd ... Big Sur CA 93920 831-667-2315
Web: www.parks.ca.gov/default.asp?page_id=578

Kenneth Hahn State Recreation Area
c/o Angeles District Office
1925 Las Virgenes ... Calabasas CA 91302 323-298-3660
Web: www.parks.ca.gov/default.asp?page_id=612

Kings Beach State Recreation Area
c/o Sierra District Office PO Box 266 ... Tahoma CA 96142 530-546-4212
Web: www.parks.ca.gov/default.asp?page_id=511

Lake Oroville State Recreation Area
917 Kelly Ridge Rd ... Oroville CA 95966 530-538-2219
Web: www.parks.ca.gov/default.asp?page_id=462

Lake Perris State Recreation Area
17801 Lk Perris Dr ... Perris CA 92571 951-657-0676
Web: www.parks.ca.gov

Leland Stanford Mansion State Historic Park
800 N St ... Sacramento CA 95814 916-324-0575 324-5885

Leucadia State Beach 948 Neptune Ave ... Encinitas CA 92024 760-633-2740
Web: www.parks.ca.gov/default.asp?page_id=661

Lighthouse Field State Beach
West Cliff Dr ... Santa Cruz CA 95060 831-429-2850
Web: www.parks.ca.gov/default.asp?page_id=550

Limekiln State Park 1416 Ninth St ... Sacramento CA 94296 916-653-6995
Web: www.parks.ca.gov/default.asp?page_id=577

MacKerricher State Park
24100 MacKerricher Park Rd ... Fort Bragg CA 95437 707-964-9112
Web: www.parks.ca.gov/default.asp?page_id=436

Maillard Redwoods State Reserve PO Box 440 ... Mendocino CA 95460 707-937-5804
Web: www.parks.ca.gov/default.asp?page_id=439

Malibu Creek State Park
1925 Las Virgenes Rd ... Calabasas CA 91302 818-880-0367
Web: www.parks.ca.gov/default.asp?page_id=614

Malibu Lagoon State Beach
23200 Pacific Coast Hwy ... Malibu CA 90265 310-457-8143
Web: www.parks.ca.gov/default.asp?page_id=835

Marina State Beach
c/o Monterey District 2211 Garden Rd ... Monterey CA 93940 831-384-7695
Web: www.parks.ca.gov

Marshall Gold Discovery State Historic Park
310 Back St PO Box 265 ... Coloma CA 95613 530-622-3470
Web: www.parks.ca.gov/default.asp?page_id=484

McArthur-Burney Falls Memorial State Park
c/o Northern Buttes District Office
400 Glen Dr ... Oroville CA 95966 530-538-2200
Web: www.parks.ca.gov/?page_id=455

McConnell State Recreation Area
8810 McConnell Rd ... Ballico CA 95303 209-394-7755
Web: www.parks.ca.gov/default.asp?page_id=554

Mendocino Headlands State Park
8001 N Hwy 1 ... Little River CA 95456 707-937-5804
Web: www.parks.ca.gov/default.asp?page_id=442

Mendocino Woodlands State Park
39350 Little Lk Rd ... Mendocino CA 95460 707-937-5755
Web: www.parks.ca.gov

Millerton Lake State Recreation Area
5290 Millerton Rd ... Friant CA 93626 559-822-2332
Web: www.parks.ca.gov/default.asp?page_id=587

Mono Lake Tufa State Reserve PO Box 99 ... Lee Vining CA 93541 760-647-6331
Web: www.parks.ca.gov

Montara State Beach
c/o Santa Cruz District Office
303 Big Trees Pk Rd ... Felton CA 94018 650-726-8819
Web: www.parks.ca.gov/?page_id=532

Monterey State Beach
c/o Monterey District Office 2211 Garden Rd ... Monterey CA 93940 831-649-2836
Web: www.parks.ca.gov/default.asp?page_id=576

Monterey State Historic Park
20 Custom House Plz ... Monterey CA 93940 831-649-7118
Web: www.parks.ca.gov

Montgomery Woods State Reserve
c/o Mendocino District Office PO Box 440 ... Mendocino CA 95460 707-937-5804
Web: www.parks.ca.gov/default.asp?page_id=434

Morro Bay State Park
60 State Pk Rd Morro Bay State Pk Rd ... Morro Bay CA 93442 800-777-0369
TF: 800-777-0369 ■ *Web:* www.parks.ca.gov/?page_id=23793

Morro Strand State Beach
60 State Pk Rd Morro Bay State Pk Rd ... Morro Bay CA 93442 805-772-2560
Web: www.parks.ca.gov/?page_id=23793

Moss Landing State Beach
c/o Monterey District Office 2211 Garden Rd ... Monterey CA 93940 831-384-7695
Web: www.parks.ca.gov/default.asp?page_id=574

Natural Bridges State Beach
2531 W Cliff Dr ... Santa Cruz CA 95060 831-423-4609
Web: www.parks.ca.gov/default.asp?page_id=541

Ocotillo Wells State Vehicular Recreation Area
5172 Hwy 78 # 10 ... Borrego Springs CA 92004 760-767-1302
Web: www.parks.ca.gov

Old Town San Diego State Historic Park
4002 Wallace St ... San Diego CA 92110 619-220-5422 688-3229
TF: 800-777-0369 ■ *Web:* www.parks.ca.gov

Olompali State Historic Park PO Box 1016 ... Novato CA 94948 415-892-3383
Web: www.parks.ca.gov

Pacheco State Park
38787 Dinosaur Point Rd 22708 Broadway St ... Hollister CA 95023 209-826-6283
Web: www.parks.ca.gov/default.asp?page_id=560

Pacifica State Beach 1416 Ninth St ... Sacramento CA 95814 650-738-7381
Web: www.parks.ca.gov/default.asp?page_id=524

Palomar Mountain State Park
200 Palm Canyon Dr ... Borrego Springs CA 92004 760-742-3462
Web: www.parks.ca.gov/default.asp?page_id=637

Patrick's Point State Park
4150 Patrick's Pt Dr ... Trinidad CA 95570 707-677-3570
Web: www.parks.ca.gov

Pescadero State Beach
1416 Ninth St 303 Big Trees Pk Rd ... Sacramento CA 95814 916-653-6995
Web: www.parks.ca.gov/?page_id=522

Petaluma Adobe State Historic Park
3325 Old Adobe Rd ... Petaluma CA 94954 707-762-4871
Web: www.parks.ca.gov

Pfeiffer Big Sur State Park
c/o Monterey District Office 2211 Garden Rd ... Monterey CA 93940 831-667-2315
Web: parks.ca.gov/?page_id=570

Picacho State Recreation Area
1416 Ninth St PO Box 942896 ... Sacramento CA 95814 916-653-6995 654-6374
TF: 800-777-0369 ■ *Web:* www.parks.ca.gov

Pigeon Point Light Station State Historic Park
210 Pigeon Pt Rd ... Pescadero CA 94060 650-879-0633
Web: www.parks.ca.gov

Plumas-Eureka State Park 310 Johnsville Rd ... Blairsden CA 96103 530-836-2380
Web: www.parks.ca.gov

Point Dume State Beach
c/o Angeles District Office
1925 Las Virgenes ... Calabasas CA 91302 310-457-8143
Web: www.parks.ca.gov/default.asp?page_id=623

Point Sur State Historic Park
c/o Monterey District Office 2211 Garden Rd ... Monterey CA 93940 831-625-4419
Web: www.parks.ca.gov/default.asp?page_id=565

Pomponio State Beach
c/o Santa Cruz District Office
303 Big Trees Pk Rd ... Felton CA 95018 831-335-6318
Web: www.parks.ca.gov/?page_id=521

Portola Redwoods State Park
c/o Santa Cruz District Office
303 Big Trees Pk Rd ... Felton CA 95018 916-988-0205
Web: www.parks.ca.gov/default.asp?page_id=539

Prairie City State Vehicular Recreation Area
13300 White Rock Rd ... Rancho Cordova CA 95742 916-985-7378
Web: www.parks.ca.gov

Providence Mountains State Recreation Area
1416 Ninth St ... Sacramento CA 95814 800-777-0369
TF: 800-777-0369 ■ *Web:* www.parks.ca.gov/default.asp?page_id=615

Railtown 1897 State Historic Park
PO Box 1250 ... Jamestown CA 95327 209-984-3953
Web: www.railtown1897.org

Richardson Grove State Park
c/o N Coast Redwoods District Office
PO Box 2006 ... Eureka CA 95502 707-445-6547
Web: www.parks.ca.gov/default.asp?page_id=422

Robert H. Meyer Memorial State Beach
c/o Angeles District Office
1925 Las Virgenes Rd ... Calabasas CA 91302 310-457-8143
Web: www.parks.ca.gov/default.asp?page_id=633

Salt Point State Park 25050 Hwy 1 ... Jenner CA 95450 707-847-3221
Web: www.parks.ca.gov/default.asp?page_id=453

Salton Sea State Recreation Area
100-225 State Pk Rd ... North Shore CA 92254 760-393-3052
Web: www.parks.ca.gov/?page_id=639

Samuel P. Taylor State Park PO Box 251 ... Lagunitas CA 94938 415-488-9897
Web: www.parks.ca.gov

San Clemente State Beach
c/o Orange Coast District Office
3030 Avenida del Presidente ... San Clemente CA 92672 949-492-3156
Web: www.parks.ca.gov/default.asp?page_id=646

San Pasqual Battlefield State Historic Park
15808 San Pasqual Vly Rd ... Escondido CA 92027 760-737-2201
Web: www.parks.ca.gov

Santa Cruz Mission State Historic Park
c/o Santa Cruz District Office
303 Big Trees Pk Rd ... Felton CA 95060 831-425-5849 429-2870
Web: www.parks.ca.gov/default.asp?page_id=548

Santa Monica State Beach
c/o Angeles District Office
1925 Las Virgenes Rd ... Calabasas CA 91302 818-880-0363
Web: www.parks.ca.gov/default.asp?page_id=624

				Phone	Fax
Santa Susana Pass State Historic Park c/o Angeles District Office 1925 Las Virgenes Rd. *Web:* www.parks.ca.gov/default.asp?page_id=611	Calabasas	CA	91302	213-620-6152	
Shasta State Historic Park c/o Northern Buttes District Office 400 Glen Dr *Web:* www.parks.ca.gov/default.asp?page_id=456	Oroville	CA	95966	530-243-8194	
Silver Strand State Beach 5000 California 75 4477 Pacific Hwy *Web:* www.parks.ca.gov/default.asp?page_id=654	Coronado	CA	92118	619-435-5184	
Sinkyone Wilderness State Park PO Box 245 *Web:* www.parks.ca.gov	Whitethorn	CA	95489	707-986-7711	
Sonoma State Historic Park c/o Diablo Vista District Office 845 Casa Grande Rd. *Web:* www.parks.ca.gov	Petaluma	CA	94954	707-938-9560	
South Yuba River State Park 17660 Pleasant Vly Rd *Web:* www.parks.ca.gov	Penn Valley	CA	95946	530-432-2546	
Sutter's Fort State Historic Park 2701 L St *Web:* www.parks.ca.gov	Sacramento	CA	95816	916-445-4422	447-9318
Tolowa Dunes State Park 1375 Elk Vly Rd *Web:* www.parks.ca.gov	Crescent City	CA	95531	707-465-2145	
Tomales Bay State Park 1208 Pierce Pt Rd *Web:* www.parks.ca.gov/default.asp?page_id=470	Inverness	CA	94937	415-669-1140	
Topanga State Park 1925 Las Virgenes *Web:* www.parks.ca.gov/default.asp?page_id=629	Calabasas	CA	91302	818 880 0367	
Torrey Pines State Beach 4477 Pacific Hwy *Web:* www.parks.ca.gov/default.asp?page_id=658	San Diego	CA	92110	858-755-2063	
Torrey Pines State Reserve c/o San Diego Coast District 4477 Pacific Hwy *TF:* 866-240-4655 ■ *Web:* www.parks.ca.gov/?page_id=657	San Diego	CA	92110	858-755-2063	
Trinidad State Beach 4150 Patrick's Point Dr PO Box 2006 *Web:* www.parks.ca.gov/default.asp?page_id=418	Trinidad	CA	95570	707-677-3570	
Tule Elk State Reserve 8653 Station Rd. *Web:* www.parks.ca.gov/default.asp?page_id=584	Buttonwillow	CA	93206	661-764-6881	
Turlock Lake State Recreation Area 22600 Lake Rd *Web:* www.parks.ca.gov/default.asp?page_id=555	Columbia	CA	95310	209-874-2056	
Van Damme State Park 12301 N Hwy 1 PO Box 440 *Web:* www.parks.ca.gov/default.asp?page_id=433	Mendocino	CA	95460	707-937-5804	
Verdugo Mountains c/o Angeles District Office 1925 Las Virgenes *Web:* www.parks.ca.gov/default.asp?page_id=635	Calabasas	CA	91302	213-620-6152	
Watts Towers of Simon Rodia State Historic Park 1765 East 107th Street 1925 Las Virgenes *TF:* 866-240-4655 ■ *Web:* www.parks.ca.gov/default.asp?page_id=613	Calabasas	CA	91302	213-847-4646	
Will Rogers State Beach 1925 Las Virgenes *Web:* www.parks.ca.gov/default.asp?page_id=625	Calabasas	CA	91302	310-305-9503	
Will Rogers State Historic Park 1925 Las Virgenes *Web:* www.parks.ca.gov/default.asp?page_id=626	Calabasas	CA	91302	310-454-8212	

Colorado

				Phone	Fax
Arkansas Headwaters Recreation Area 307 W Sackett Ave *Web:* cpw.state.co.us	Salida	CO	81201	719-539-7289	
Barr Lake State Park 13401 Picadilly Rd *Web:* cpw.state.co.us	Brighton	CO	80603	303-659-6005	
Boyd Lake State Park 3720 N County Rd Ste 11-C *Web:* cpw.state.co.us	Loveland	CO	80539	970-669-1739	
Castlewood Canyon State Park 2989 S Hwy 83 *Web:* cpw.state.co.us	Franktown	CO	80116	303-688-5242	
Chatfield State Park 11500 N Roxborough Pk Rd *Web:* cpw.state.co.us	Littleton	CO	80125	303-791-7275	
Cherry Creek State Park 4201 S Parker Rd *TF:* 866-265-6447 ■ *Web:* cpw.state.co.us	Aurora	CO	80014	303-699-3860	699-3864
Cheyenne Mountain State Park 4255 Sinton Rd. *Web:* cpw.state.co.us	Colorado Springs	CO	80907	719-227-5256	
Crawford State Park 40468 Hwy 92 *Web:* cpw.state.co.us/placestogo/parks/crawford	Crawford	CO	81415	970-921-5721	
Eldorado Canyon State Park 9 Kneale Rd PO Box B *TF:* 866-265-6447 ■ *Web:* cpw.state.co.us	Eldorado Springs	CO	80025	303-494-3943	499-2729
Eleven Mile State Park 4229 County Rd 92 *Web:* cpw.state.co.us	Lake George	CO	80827	719-748-3401	
Golden Gate Canyon State Park 92 Crawford Gulch Rd *TF:* 866-265-6447 ■ *Web:* cpw.state.co.us	Golden	CO	80403	303-582-3707	582-3712
Harvey Gap State Park c/o Rifle Gap State Pk 5775 Hwy 325 *Web:* cpw.state.co.us	Rifle	CO	81650	970-625-1607	
Highline Lake State Park 1800 118 Rd *Web:* cpw.state.co.us	Loma	CO	81524	970-858-7208	
Jackson Lake State Park 26363 County Rd 3 *Web:* cpw.state.co.us	Orchard	CO	80649	970-645-2551	
James M. Robb - Colorado River State Park PO Box 700 *Web:* cpw.state.co.us	Clifton	CO	81520	970-434-3388	
Lake Pueblo State Park 640 Pueblo Reservoir Rd *Web:* cpw.state.co.us	Pueblo	CO	81005	719-561-9320	
Lathrop State Park 70 County Rd 502 *Web:* cpw.state.co.us	Walsenburg	CO	81089	719-738-2376	
Lory State Park 708 Lodgepole Dr. *Web:* cpw.state.co.us	Bellvue	CO	80512	970-493-1623	
Mancos State Park 42545 County Rd N *Web:* cpw.state.co.us	Mancos	CO	81328	970-533-7065	
Mueller State Park PO Box 39 *Web:* cpw.state.co.us	Divide	CO	80814	719-687-2366	
Navajo State Park PO Box 1697 *Web:* cpw.state.co.us	Arboles	CO	81121	970-883-2208	
North Sterling State Park 24005 County Rd 330 *Web:* cpw.state.co.us	Sterling	CO	80751	970-522-3657	
Paonia State Park PO Box 147 *Web:* cpw.state.co.us	Crawford	CO	81415	970-921-5721	
Pearl Lake State Park PO Box 750 *Web:* cpw.state.co.us	Clark	CO	80428	970-879-3922	
Ridgway State Park 28555 Hwy 550 *Web:* cpw.state.co.us	Ridgway	CO	81432	970-626-5822	
Rifle Falls State Park 5775 Hwy 325 *Web:* cpw.state.co.us	Rifle	CO	81650	970-625-1607	
Rifle Gap State Park 5775 Hwy 325 *Web:* cpw.state.co.us	Rifle	CO	81650	970-625-1607	
Roxborough State Park 4751 Roxborough Dr *Web:* cpw.state.co.us	Littleton	CO	80125	303-973-3959	
Saint Vrain State Park 3525 State Hwy 119 *Web:* cpw.state.co.us	Longmont	CO	80504	303-678-9402	
San Luis State Park & Wildlife Area PO Box 150 *Web:* cpw.state.co.us	Mosca	CO	81146	719-378-2020	
Stagecoach State Park 25500 County Rd 14 *Web:* cpw.state.co.us	Oak Creek	CO	80467	970-736-2436	
State Forest State Park 56750 Hwy 14 *TF:* 866-265-6447 ■ *Web:* cpw.state.co.us	Walden	CO	80480	970-723-8366	723-8325
Steamboat Lake State Park PO Box 750 *Web:* cpw.state.co.us	Clark	CO	80428	970-879-3922	
Sweitzer Lake State Park 1735 E Rd PO Box 173 *Web:* cpw.state.co.us	Delta	CO	81416	970-874-4258	
Sylvan Lake State Park 10200 Brush Creek Rd PO Box 1475 *Web:* cpw.state.co.us	Eagle	CO	81631	970-328-2021	
Trinidad Lake State Park 32610 State Hwy 12 *Web:* cpw.state.co.us	Trinidad	CO	81082	719-846-6951	
Vega State Park PO Box 186 *Web:* cpw.state.co.us	Collbran	CO	81624	970-487-3407	
Yampa River State Park 6185 W US Hwy 40 *Web:* cpw.state.co.us	Hayden	CO	81639	970-276-2061	

Connecticut

				Phone	Fax
Bigelow Hollow State Park & Nipmuck State Forest c/o Shenipsit State Forest 166 Chestnut Hill Rd *Web:* www.ct.gov	Stafford Springs	CT	06076	860-684-3430	
Black Rock State Park c/o Topsmead State Forest PO Box 1081 *Web:* www.ct.gov	Litchfield	CT	06759	860-567-5694	
Bluff Point State Park c/o Ft Trumbull State Pk 90 Walbach St *Web:* www.ct.gov	New London	CT	06320	860-444-7591	
Burr Pond State Park 384 Burr Mtn Rd. *Web:* www.ct.gov	Torrington	CT	06790	860-482-1817	
Chatfield Hollow State Park 381 Rt 80 *Web:* www.ct.gov	Killingworth	CT	06419	860-663-2030	
Cockaponset State Forest c/o Chatfield Hollow State Pk 381 Rt 80 *Web:* www.ct.gov	Killingworth	CT	06419	860-663-2030	
Connecticut Valley Railroad State Park 1 Railroad Ave PO Box 452 *TF:* 866-526-2014 ■ *Web:* www.essexsteamtrain.com	Essex	CT	06426	860-767-0103	767-0104
Day Pond State Park c/o Eastern District HQ 209 Hebron Rd. *Web:* www.ct.gov	Marlborough	CT	06447	860-295-9523	
Dennis Hill State Park c/o Burr Pond State Pk 385 Burr Mtn Rd *Web:* www.ct.gov	Torrington	CT	06790	860-482-1817	
Devil's Hopyard State Park 366 HopyaRd Rd. *Web:* www.ct.gov	East Haddam	CT	06423	860-526-2336	
Dinosaur State Park 400 W St *Web:* www.ct.gov	Rocky Hill	CT	06067	860-529-5816	257-1405
Fort Griswold Battlefield State Park c/o Ft Trumbull State Pk 90 Walbach St *Web:* www.ct.gov	New London	CT	06320	860-444-7591	
Fort Trumbull State Park 90 Walbach St *Web:* www.ct.gov/dep/cwp/view.asp?a=2716&q=325200	New London	CT	06320	860-444-7591	
Gay City State Park c/o Eastern District HQ 209 Hebron Rd. *Web:* www.ct.gov	Marlborough	CT	06447	860-649-6615	
Gillette Castle State Park 67 River Rd *Web:* www.ct.gov	East Haddam	CT	06423	860-526-2336	
Haley Farm State Park c/o Ft Trumbull State Pk 90 Walbach St *Web:* www.ct.gov	New London	CT	06320	860-444-7591	
Hammonasset Beach State Park 1288 Boston Post Rd PO Box 271 *Web:* www.ct.gov	Madison	CT	06443	203-245-2785	245-9201

				Phone	Fax
Haystack Mountain State Park c/o Burr Pond State Pk 385 Burr Mtn Rd *Web:* www.ct.gov	Torrington	CT	06790	860-482-1817	
Hopeville Pond State Park 193 Roode Rd *Web:* www.ct.gov	Jewett City	CT	06351	860-376-2920	
Housatonic Meadows State Park c/o Macedonia Brook State Pk 159 Macedonia Brook Rd *Web:* www.ct.gov	Kent	CT	06757	860-927-3238	
Hurd State Park c/o Gillette Castle State Pk 67 River Rd *Web:* www.ct.gov	East Haddam	CT	06423	860-526-2336	
Indian Well State Park c/o Osbornedale State Pk PO Box 113 *Web:* www.ct.gov	Derby	CT	06418	203-735-4311	
James L. Goodwin State Forest Goodwin Forest Conservation Education Ctr 23 Potter Rd *Web:* www.ct.gov	Hampton	CT	06226	860-455-9534	455-9857
John A. Minetto State Park c/o Burr Pond State Pk 385 Burr Mtn Rd *Web:* www.ct.gov	Torrington	CT	06790	860-482-1817	
Kent Falls State Park c/o Macedonia Brook State Pk 159 Macedonia Brook Rd *Web:* www.ct.gov	Kent	CT	06757	860-927-3238	
Kettletown State Park 1400 Georges Hill Rd *Web:* www.ct.gov	Southbury	CT	06488	203-264-5678	
Lake Waramaug State Park 30 Lk Waramaug Rd *Web:* www.ct.gov	New Preston	CT	06777	860-868-2592	
Macedonia Brook State Park 159 Macedonia Brook Rd *Web:* www.ct.gov	Kent	CT	06757	860-927-3238	
Mansfield Hollow State Park c/o Mashamoquet Brook State Pk RFD 1 147 Wolf Den Rd *Web:* www.ct.gov	Pomfret Center	CT	06259	860-928-6121	
Mashamoquet Brook State Park 147 Wolf Den Dr *Web:* www.ct.gov	Pomfret Center	CT	06259	860-928-6121	
Mohawk State Forest 20 Mohawk Mtn Rd *Web:* www.ct.gov	Goshen	CT	06756	860-491-3620	
Mount Tom State Park c/o Lk Waramaug State Pk 30 Lk Waramaug Rd *Web:* www.ct.gov	New Preston	CT	06777	860-868-2592	
Natchaug State Forest c/o Mashamoquet Brook State Pk RFD 1 Wolf Den Rd *Web:* www.ct.gov	Pomfret Center	CT	06259	860-928-6121	
Osbornedale State Park 555 Roosevelt Dr *Web:* www.ct.gov	Derby	CT	06418	203-735-4311	
Pachaug State Forest Rt 49 PO Box 5 *Web:* www.ct.gov	Voluntown	CT	06384	860-376-4075	
Penwood State Park 57 Gunn Mill Rd *Web:* www.ct.gov	Bloomfield	CT	06002	860-242-1158	
Putnam Memorial State Park 429 Black Rock Tpke *Web:* www.ct.gov	Redding	CT	06896	203-938-2285	
Quaddick State Park c/o Mashamoquet Brook State Pk 147 Wolf Den Dr *Web:* www.ct.gov	Pomfret Center	CT	06259	860-928-6121	
Rocky Neck State Park PO Box 676 *Web:* www.ct.gov	Niantic	CT	06357	860-739-5471	
Salmon River State Forest c/o Eastern District HQ 209 Hebron Rd *Web:* www.ct.gov	Marlborough	CT	06447	860-295-9523	
Selden Neck State Park c/o Gillette Castle State Pk 67 River Rd *Web:* www.ct.gov	East Haddam	CT	06423	860-526-2336	
Shenipsit State Forest 166 Chestnut Hill Rd Rt 190 *Web:* www.ct.gov/dep/cwp/view.asp?a=2716&q=332506	Stafford Springs	CT	06076	860-684-3430	684-4130
Sherwood Island State Park PO Box 188 *Web:* www.ct.gov	Greens Farms	CT	06838	203-226-6983	
Silver Sands State Park c/o Osbornedale State Pk PO Box 113 *Web:* www.ct.gov/dep/cwp/view.asp?a=2716&q=325262	Derby	CT	06418	203-735-4311	
Sleeping Giant State Park 200 Mt Carmel Ave *Web:* www.ct.gov	Hamden	CT	06518	203-789-7498	
Southford Falls State Park Quaker Farms Rd Rt 188 *Web:* www.ct.gov	Southbury	CT	06488	203-264-5169	
Squantz Pond State Park 178 Shortwoods Rd *Web:* www.ct.gov	New Fairfield	CT	06812	203-797-4165	
Stratton Brook State Park 57 Gun Mill Rd *Web:* www.ct.gov	Bloomfield	CT	06002	860-566-4840	
Talcott Mountain State Park c/o Penwood State Pk 57 Gunn Mill Rd *Web:* www.ct.gov	Bloomfield	CT	06002	860-242-1158	
Topsmead State Forest PO Box 1081 *Web:* www.ct.gov	Litchfield	CT	06759	860-567-5694	
Wadsworth Falls State Park c/o Chatfield Hollow State Pk 381 Rt 80 *Web:* www.ct.gov	Killingworth	CT	06419	860-663-2030	
West Rock Ridge State Park 200 Mt Carmel Ave c/o Sleeping Giant State Pk *Web:* www.ct.gov	Hamden	CT	06518	203-789-7498	
Wharton Brook State Park 200 Mt Carmel Ave c/o Sleeping Giant State Pk *Web:* www.ct.gov	Hamden	CT	06518	203-789-7498	

Delaware

				Phone	Fax
Bellevue State Park 800 Carr Rd *Web:* www.destateparks.com	Wilmington	DE	19809	302-761-6963	761-6951
Brandywine Creek State Park PO Box 3782 *Web:* www.destateparks.com	Greenville	DE	19807	302-577-3534	
Cape Henlopen State Park 42 Cape Henlopen Dr *Web:* www.destateparks.com	Lewes	DE	19958	302-645-8983	
Delaware Seashore State Park 130 Coastal Hwy *Web:* destateparks.com/park/delaware-seashore	Rehoboth Beach	DE	19971	302-227-2800	
Fenwick Island State Park 39415 Inlet Rd *Web:* www.destateparks.com/park/fenwick-island/index.asp	Rehoboth Beach	DE	19971	302-227-2800	227-7400
First State Heritage Park 102 S State St *Web:* www.destateparks.com/heritagepark	Dover	DE	19901	302-739-9194	739-6264
Fort Delaware State Park PO Box 170 *Web:* www.destateparks.com	Delaware City	DE	19706	302-834-7941	836-2539
Fort DuPont State Park 45 Clinton St *Web:* www.destateparks.com	Delaware City	DE	19706	302-834-7941	
Fox Point State Park c/o Bellevue State Pk 800 Carr Rd *Web:* www.destateparks.com/foxpt/foxpt.htm	Wilmington	DE	19809	302-761-6963	
Holts Landing State Park 89 Kings Hwy *Web:* www.destateparks.com	Dover	DE	19901	302-227-2800	
Killens Pond State Park 5025 Killens Pond Rd *Web:* www.destateparks.com	Felton	DE	19943	302-284-4526	284-4694
Lums Pond State Park 1068 Howell School Rd *Web:* www.destateparks.com	Bear	DE	19701	302-368-6989	
Trap Pond State Park 33587 Baldcypress Ln *Web:* www.destateparks.com	Laurel	DE	19956	302-875-5153	
White Clay Creek State Park 425 Wedgewood Rd *Web:* www.destateparks.com	Newark	DE	19711	302-368-6900	
Wilmington State Parks 1021 W 18th St *Web:* www.destateparks.com/wilmsp/wilmsp.htm	Wilmington	DE	19802	302-656-3665	577-7084

Florida

				Phone	Fax
Alafia River State Park 14326 S County Rd 39 *Web:* www.floridastateparks.org	Lithia	FL	33547	813-672-5320	
Alfred B. Maclay Gardens State Park 14326 S County Rd 39 *Web:* www.floridastateparks.org	Lithia	FL	33547	813-672-5320	
Amelia Island State Park 12157 Heckscher Dr *Web:* www.floridastateparks.org/ameliaisland	Jacksonville	FL	32226	904-251-2320	
Bahia Honda State Park 36850 Overseas Hwy *Web:* www.floridastateparks.org	Big Pine Key	FL	33043	305-872-2353	
Bald Point State Park 146 PO Box Cut *Web:* www.floridastateparks.org	Alligator Point	FL	32346	850-349-9146	
Barnacle Historic State Park, The 3485 Main Hwy *Web:* www.floridastateparks.org	Coconut Grove	FL	33133	305-442-6866	442-6872
Big Lagoon State Park 12301 Gulf Beach Hwy *Web:* www.floridastateparks.org/biglagoon	Pensacola	FL	32507	850-492-1595	492-4380
Big Shoals State Park PO Drawer G *Web:* www.floridastateparks.org	White Springs	FL	32096	386-397-4331	
Big Talbot Island State Park 12157 Heckscher Dr *Web:* www.floridastateparks.org/bigtalbotisland	Jacksonville	FL	32226	904-251-2320	
Bill Baggs Cape Florida State Park 1200 S Crandon Blvd *Web:* www.floridastateparks.org	Key Biscayne	FL	33149	305-361-5811	365-0003
Blackwater River State Park 7720 Deaton Bridge Rd *Web:* www.floridastateparks.org	Holt	FL	32564	850-983-5363	983-5364
Blue Spring State Park 2100 W French Ave *Web:* www.floridastateparks.org	Orange City	FL	32763	386-775-3663	
Bulow Creek State Park 3351 Old Dixie Hwy *Web:* www.floridastateparks.org/bulowcreek	Ormond Beach	FL	32174	386-676-4050	
Bulow Plantation Ruins Historic State Park 3501 Old Kings Rd *Web:* www.floridastateparks.org	Flagler Beach	FL	32136	386-517-2084	
Caladesi Island State Park One Cswy Blvd *Web:* www.floridastateparks.org/caladesiisland	Dunedin	FL	34698	727-469-5918	
Camp Helen State Park 23937 Panama City Beach Pkwy *Web:* www.floridastateparks.org	Panama City Beach	FL	32413	850-233-5059	236-3204
Cayo Costa State Park PO Box 1150 *Web:* www.floridastateparks.org/cayocosta	Boca Grande	FL	33921	941-964-0375	
Cedar Key Museum State Park 12231 SW 166 Ct *Web:* www.floridastateparks.org	Cedar Key	FL	32625	352-543-5350	
Collier-Seminole State Park 20200 E Tamiami Trl *Web:* www.floridastateparks.org/collierseminole	Naples	FL	34114	239-394-3397	394-5113
Constitution Convention Museum State Park 200 Allen Memorial Way *Web:* www.floridastateparks.org	Port Saint Joe	FL	32456	850-229-8029	
Crystal River Archaeological State Park 3400 N Museum Pointe *Web:* www.floridastateparks.org	Crystal River	FL	34428	352-795-3817	
Crystal River Preserve State Park 3266 N Sailboat Ave *TF:* 800-326-3521 ■ *Web:* www.floridastateparks.org/crystalriverpreserve	Crystal River	FL	34428	352-563-0450	563-0246
Dade Battlefield Historic State Park 7200 County Rd 603 S Battlefield Dr *Web:* www.floridastateparks.org	Bushnell	FL	33513	352-793-4781	

Name / Address	City	State	ZIP	Phone	Fax
Dagny Johnson Key Largo Hammock Botanical State Park					
905 County Rd	Key Largo	FL	33037	305-451-1202	
Web: www.floridastateparks.org/keylargohammock					
De Leon Springs State Park					
601 Ponce De Leon Blvd	De Leon Springs	FL	32130	386-985-4212	
Web: www.floridastateparks.org					
Deer Lake State Park 357 Main Pk Rd	Santa Rosa Beach	FL	32459	850-267-8300	231-1879
Web: www.floridastateparks.org/deerlake					
Delnor-Wiggins Pass State Park					
11135 Gulfshore Dr	Naples	FL	34108	239-597-6196	597-8223
Web: www.floridastateparks.org/delnorwiggins/default.cfm					
Devil's Millhopper Geological State Park					
4732 Millhopper Rd	Gainesville	FL	32653	352-955-2008	
Web: www.floridastateparks.org/devilsmillhopper					
Don Pedro Island State Park					
8450 Placida Rd PO Box 1150	Boca Grande	FL	33921	941-964-0375	
Web: www.floridastateparks.org/donpedroisland					
Dudley Farm Historic State Park					
18730 W Newberry Rd	Newberry	FL	32669	352-472-1142	
Web: www.floridastateparks.org					
Econfina River State Park					
4741 Econfina River Rd	Lamont	FL	32336	850-922-6007	
Web: www.floridastateparks.org					
Eden Gardens State Park					
181 Eden Gardens Rd	Santa Rosa Beach	FL	32459	850-267-8320	
Web: www.floridastateparks.org					
Edward Ball Wakulla Springs State Park					
465 Wakulla Park Dr	Wakulla Springs	FL	32327	850-561-7276	561-7251
Web: www.floridastateparks.org					
Egmont Key State Park one Cswy Blvd	Dunedin	FL	34698	727-893-2627	
Web: www.floridastateparks.org					
Fakahatchee Strand Preserve State Park					
137 Coastland Dr	Copeland	FL	34137	239-695-4593	
Web: www.floridastateparks.org					
Falling Waters State Park 1130 State Pk Rd	Chipley	FL	32428	850-638-6130	
Web: www.floridastateparks.org					
Fanning Springs State Park					
18020 NW Hwy 19	Fanning Springs	FL	32693	352-463-3420	463-3420
Web: www.floridastateparks.org					
Faver-Dykes State Park					
1000 Faver Dykes Rd	Saint Augustine	FL	32086	904-794-0997	446-6781*
*Fax Area Code: 386 ■ *Web:* www.floridastateparks.org					
Florida Caverns State Park 3345 Caverns Rd	Marianna	FL	32446	850-482-9598	
Web: www.floridastateparks.org					
Forest Capital Museum State Park					
204 Forest Pk Dr	Perry	FL	32348	850-584-3227	
Web: www.floridastateparks.org					
Fort Clinch State Park					
2601 Atlantic Ave	Fernandina Beach	FL	32034	904-277-7274	277-7225
Web: www.floridastateparks.org					
Fort Cooper State Park					
3100 S Old Floral City Rd	Inverness	FL	34450	352-726-0315	
Web: www.floridastateparks.org					
Fort George Island Cultural State Park					
12157 Heckscher Dr	Jacksonville	FL	32226	904-251-2320	
Web: www.floridastateparks.org/fortgeorgeisland					
Fort Mose Historic State Park					
15 Ft Mose Trl	Saint Augustine	FL	32084	904-823-2232	
Web: www.floridastateparks.org/fortmose					
Fort Pierce Inlet State Park					
905 Shorewinds Dr	Fort Pierce	FL	34949	772-468-3985	
Web: www.floridastateparks.org					
Fred Gannon Rocky Bayou State Park					
4281 E Hwy 20	Niceville	FL	32578	850-833-9144	
Web: www.floridastateparks.org					
Gamble Plantation Historic State Park					
3708 Patten Ave	Ellenton	FL	34222	941-723-4536	
Web: www.floridastateparks.org					
Gasparilla Island State Park					
880 Belche Rd	Boca Grande	FL	33921	941-964-0375	
Web: www.floridastateparks.org/gasparillaisland					
Grayton Beach State Park					
357 Main Pk Rd	Santa Rosa Beach	FL	32459	850-267-8300	
Web: www.floridastateparks.org/graytonbeach					
Henderson Beach State Park					
17000 Emerald Coast Pkwy	Destin	FL	32541	850-837-7550	
Web: www.floridastateparks.org					
Highlands Hammock State Park 5931 Hammock Rd	Sebring	FL	33872	863-386-6094	386-6095
Web: www.floridastateparks.org/highlandshammock					
Hillsborough River State Park					
15402 US 301 N	Thonotosassa	FL	33592	813-987-6771	
Web: www.floridastateparks.org					
Homosassa Springs Wildlife State Park					
4150 S Suncoast Blvd	Homosassa	FL	34446	352-628-5343	628-4243
Web: www.floridastateparks.org					
Hontoon Island State Park 2309 River Ridge Rd	DeLand	FL	32720	386-736-5309	
Web: www.floridastateparks.org					
Hugh Taylor Birch State Park					
3109 E Sunrise Blvd	Fort Lauderdale	FL	33304	954-564-4521	762-3737
Web: www.floridastateparks.org					
Ichetucknee Springs State Park					
12087 SW US Hwy 27	Fort White	FL	32038	850-245-2157	
Web: www.floridastateparks.org					
Indian Key Historic State Park					
US 1 Mile Marker 85 5	Islamorada	FL	33036	305-664-2540	
Web: www.floridastateparks.org/indiankey					
John D. MacArthur Beach State Park					
10900 SR 703 (A1A)	North Palm Beach	FL	33408	561-624-6950	
Web: www.floridastateparks.org					
John Gorrie Museum State Park					
PO Box 267	Apalachicola	FL	32320	850-653-9347	
Web: www.floridastateparks.org					
John U. Lloyd Beach State Park 6503 N Ocean Dr	Dania	FL	33004	954-923-2833	
Web: www.floridastateparks.org					
Kissimmee Prairie Preserve State Park					
33104 NW 192 Ave	Okeechobee	FL	34972	863-462-5360	
Web: www.floridastateparks.org					
Koreshan State Historic Site					
3800 Corkscrew Rd	Estero	FL	33928	239-992-0311	992-1607
Web: www.floridastateparks.org					
Lake Griffin State Park					
3089 US 441-27	Fruitland Park	FL	34731	352-360-6760	
Web: www.floridastateparks.org					
Lake Kissimmee State Park					
14248 Camp Mack Rd	Lake Wales	FL	33898	863-696-1112	
Web: www.floridastateparks.org					
Lake Louisa State Park 7305 US Hwy 27	Clermont	FL	34714	352-394-3969	
Web: www.floridastateparks.org					
Lake Manatee State Park 20007 Hwy 64 E	Bradenton	FL	34212	941-741-3028	
Web: www.floridastateparks.org					
Lignumvitae Key Botanical State Park					
Offshore Island	Islamorada	FL	33036	305-664-2540	
Web: www.floridastateparks.org/lignumvitaekey					
Little Manatee River State Park					
215 Lightfoot Rd	Wimauma	FL	33598	813-671-5005	
Web: www.floridastateparks.org					
Little Talbot Island State Park					
12157 Heckscher Dr	Jacksonville	FL	32226	904-251-2320	251-2325
TF: 800-326-3521 ■ *Web:* www.floridastateparks.org/littletalbotisland					
Long Key State Park PO Box 776	Long Key	FL	33001	305-664-4815	
Web: www.floridastateparks.org					
Lovers Key State Park					
8700 Estero Blvd	Fort Myers Beach	FL	33931	239-463-4588	463-8851
TF: 800-326-3521 ■ *Web:* www.floridastateparks.org					
Lower Wekiva River Preserve State Park					
1800 Wekiwa Cir	Apopka	FL	32712	407-884-2008	884-2039
TF: 800-326-3521 ■ *Web:* www.floridastateparks.org					
Manatee Springs State Park					
11650 NW 115th St	Chiefland	FL	32626	352-493-6072	
Web: www.floridastateparks.org					
Marjorie Kinnan Rawlings Historic State Park					
18700 S County Rd 325	Cross Creek	FL	32640	352-466-3672	
Web: www.floridastateparks.org					
Mike Roess Gold Head Branch State Park					
6239 SR 21	Keystone Heights	FL	32656	352-473-4701	
Web: www.floridastateparks.org					
Myakka River State Park 13208 SR 72	Sarasota	FL	34241	941-361-6511	361-6501
TF: 800-326-3521 ■ *Web:* www.floridastateparks.org					
Natural Bridge Battlefield Historic State Park					
7502 Natural Bridge Rd	Tallahassee	FL	32305	850-922-6007	488-0366
TF: 800-326-3521 ■ *Web:* www.floridastateparks.org/naturalbridge					
O'Leno State Park 410 SE Oleno Pk Rd	High Springs	FL	32643	386-454-1853	
Web: www.floridastateparks.org					
Ochlockonee River State Park					
429 State Pk Rd	Sopchoppy	FL	32358	850-962-2771	
Web: www.floridastateparks.org					
Oleta River State Park					
3400 NE 163rd St	North Miami Beach	FL	33160	305-919-1846	919-1845
TF: 800-326-3521 ■ *Web:* www.floridastateparks.org					
Orman House 177 Fifth St	Apalachicola	FL	32320	850-653-1209	
Web: www.floridastateparks.org/ormanhouse					
Oscar Scherer State Park 1843 S Tamiami Trail	Osprey	FL	34229	941-483-5956	480-3007
TF: 800-326-3521 ■ *Web:* www.floridastateparks.org					
Paynes Creek Historic State Park					
888 Lake Branch Rd	Bowling Green	FL	33834	863-375-4717	375-4510
TF: 800-326-3521 ■ *Web:* www.floridastateparks.org					
Paynes Prairie Preserve State Park					
100 Savannah Blvd	Micanopy	FL	32667	352-466-3397	
Web: www.floridastateparks.org					
Peacock Springs State Park					
Peacock Springs Rd	Luraville	FL	32038	386-776-2194	
Web: www.floridastateparks.org					
Perdido Key State Park					
15301 Perdido Key Dr	Pensacola	FL	32507	850-492-1595	492-4380
Web: www.floridastateparks.org/perdidokey					
Ponce de Leon Springs State Park					
2860 Ponce de Leon Springs Rd	Ponce de Leon	FL	32455	850-836-4281	
Web: www.floridastateparks.org					
Rainbow Springs State Park					
19158 SW 81st Pl Rd	Dunnellon	FL	34432	352-465-8555	
Web: www.floridastateparks.org					
Ravine Gardens State Park 1600 Twigg St	Palatka	FL	32177	386-329-3721	329-3718
TF: 800-326-3521 ■ *Web:* www.floridastateparks.org					
Rock Springs Run State Reserve 30601 CR 433	Sorrento	FL	32776	407-884-2008	884-2039
TF: 800-326-3521 ■ *Web:* www.floridastateparks.org/rockspringsrun					
Saint Andrews State Park					
4607 State Pk Ln	Panama City	FL	32408	850-233-5140	
Web: www.floridastateparks.org					
San Felasco Hammock Preserve State Park					
12720 NW 109 Ln	Alachua	FL	32615	386-462-7905	
Web: www.floridastateparks.org					
San Marcos de Apalache Historic State Park					
148 Old Ft Rd	Saint Marks	FL	32327	850-925-6216	
Web: www.floridastateparks.org					
San Pedro Underwater Archaeological Preserve State Park					
US 1	Islamorada	FL	33036	305-664-2540	
Web: www.floridastateparks.org/sanpedro					
Sebastian Inlet State Park					
9700 S A1A	Melbourne Beach	FL	32951	321-984-4852	
Web: www.floridastateparks.org					
Silver River State Park 1425 NE 58th Ave	Ocala	FL	34470	352-236-7148	236-7150
Web: www.floridastateparks.org					
Stephen Foster Folk Culture Ctr State Park					
11016 Lillian Saunders Dr	White Springs	FL	32096	386-397-2733	
Web: www.floridastateparks.org					

Phone Fax

Stump Pass Beach State Park
Barrier Islands State Parks PO Box 1150 Boca Grande FL 33921 941-964-0375 964-1154
Web: www.floridastateparks.org

Suwannee River State Park 3631 201st Path Live Oak FL 32060 386-362-2746
Web: www.floridastateparks.org

TH Stone Memorial Saint Joseph Peninsula State Park
8899 Cape San Blas Rd Port Saint Joe FL 32456 850-227-1327 227-1488
Web: www.floridastateparks.org

Three Rivers State Park
7908 Three Rivers Pk Rd Sneads FL 32460 850-482-9006
Web: www.floridastateparks.org

Tomoka State Park 2099 N Beach St Ormond Beach FL 32174 386-676-4050 676-4050
Web: www.floridastateparks.org/tomoka

Topsail Hill Preserve State Park
7525 W Scenic Hwy 30A Santa Rosa Beach FL 32459 850-245-2157
Web: www.floridastateparks.org

Torreya State Park 2576 NW Torreya Pk Rd Bristol FL 32321 850-643-2674
Web: www.floridastateparks.org

Troy Springs State Park
674 NE Troy Springs Rd Branford FL 32008 386-935-4835 935-4743
Web: www.floridastateparks.org/troyspring

Washington Oaks Gardens State Park
6400 N Oceanshore Blvd Palm Coast FL 32137 386-446-6780 446-6781
Web: www.floridastateparks.org

Wekiwa Springs State Park 1800 Wekiwa Cir Apopka FL 32712 407-884-2008 884-2039
Web: www.floridastateparks.org/wekiwasprings

Ybor City Museum State Park 1818 Ninth Ave Tampa FL 33605 813-247-6323
Web: www.floridastateparks.org

Georgia

Phone Fax

AH Stephens State Historic Park
456 Alexander St NW Crawfordville GA 30631 706-456-2602
Web: www.gastateparks.org

Amicalola Falls State Park & Lodge
418 Amicalola Falls State Pk Rd Dawsonville GA 30534 706-265-4703
Web: www.gastateparks.org

Black Rock Mountain State Park
3085 Black Rock Mtn Pkwy Mountain City GA 30562 706-746-2141
Web: www.gastateparks.org

Bobby Brown State Park
2509 Bobby Brown State Pk Rd Elberton GA 30635 706-213-2046
Web: www.gastateparks.org/info/bobbybrown

Chief Vann House State Historic Site
82 Georgia 225 Chatsworth GA 30705 706-695-2598
Web: www.gastateparks.org

Cloudland Canyon State Park
122 Cloudland Canyon Pk Rising Fawn GA 30738 706-657-4050
Web: www.gastateparks.org

Crooked River State Park
6222 Charlie Smith Sr Hwy Saint Mary's GA 31558 912-882-5256
Web: www.gastateparks.org

Dahlonega Gold Museum State Historic Site
One Public Sq Dahlonega GA 30533 706-864-2257
Web: www.gastateparks.org

Elijah Clark State Park
2959 McCormick Hwy Lincolnton GA 30817 706-359-3458
Web: www.gastateparks.org

Etowah Indian Mounds State Historic Site
813 Indian Mounds Rd SW Cartersville GA 30120 770-387-3747
Web: www.gastateparks.org

FD Roosevelt State Park
2970 GA Hwy 190 Pine Mountain GA 31822 706-663-4858 663-8906
TF: 800-864-7275 ■ *Web:* www.gastateparks.org

Fort King George State Historic Site
1600 Wayne St Darien GA 31305 912-437-4770
Web: www.gastateparks.org

Fort McAllister State Historic Park
3894 Ft McAllister Rd Richmond Hill GA 31324 912-727-2339 727-3614
TF: 800-864-7275 ■ *Web:* www.gastateparks.org

Fort Morris State Historic Site
2559 Ft Morris Rd Midway GA 31320 912-884-5999
Web: www.gastateparks.org

Fort Mountain State Park 181 Ft Mtn Pk Rd Chatsworth GA 30705 706-695-2621
Web: www.gastateparks.org

Fort Yargo State Park 210 S Broad St Winder GA 30680 770-867-3489
Web: www.gastateparks.org

General Coffee State Park 46 John Coffee Rd Nicholls GA 31554 912-384-7082
Web: www.gastateparks.org

George L. Smith State Park
371 Geo L Smith St Pk Rd Twin City GA 30471 478-763-2759
Web: www.gastateparks.org

George T. Bagby State Park & Lodge
330 Bagby Pkwy Fort Gaines GA 39851 229-768-2571
Web: www.gastateparks.org

Georgia Veterans State Park 2459 US 280 W Cordele GA 31015 229-276-2371
Web: www.gastateparks.org

Hamburg State Park 6071 Hamburg State Pk Rd Mitchell GA 30820 478-552-2393
Web: www.gastateparks.org

Hard Labor Creek State Park Knox Chapel Rd Rutledge GA 30663 706-557-3001
Web: www.gastateparks.org

Hart State Park 330 Hart Pk Rd Hartwell GA 30643 706-376-8756
Web: www.gastateparks.org

High Falls State Park 76 High Falls Pk Dr Jackson GA 30233 478-993-3053
Web: www.gastateparks.org

Hofwyl-Broadfield Plantation State Historic Site
5556 US Hwy 17 N Brunswick GA 31525 912-264-7333
Web: www.gastateparks.org

Indian Springs State Park 678 Lk Clark Rd Flovilla GA 30216 770-504-2277
Web: www.gastateparks.org

James H. Sloppy Floyd State Park
2800 Sloppy Floyd Lk Rd Summerville GA 30747 706-857-0826
Web: www.gastateparks.org

Jarrell Plantation State Historic Site
711 Jarrell Plantation Rd Juliette GA 31046 478-986-5172
Web: www.gastateparks.org

Jefferson Davis Memorial State Historic Site
338 Jeff Davis Pk Rd Fitzgerald GA 31750 229-831-2335
Web: www.gastateparks.org

John Tanner State Park
354 Tanner's Beach Rd Carrollton GA 30117 770-830-2222
Web: www.gastateparks.org

Kolomoki Mounds State Historic Park
205 Indian Mounds Rd Blakely GA 39823 229-724-2150
Web: www.gastateparks.org

Lapham-Patterson House State Historic Site
626 N Dawson St Thomasville GA 31792 229-225-4004
Web: www.gastateparks.org

Laura S. Walker State Park
5653 Laura Walker Rd Waycross GA 31503 912-287-4900
Web: www.gastateparks.org

Little Ocmulgee State Park & Lodge
PO Drawer 149 McRae GA 31055 229-868-7474
Web: www.gastateparks.org

Little White House State Historic Site
401 Little White House Rd Warm Springs GA 31830 706-655-5870 655-5872
TF: 800-864-7275 ■ *Web:* gastateparks.org/info/littlewhite

Magnolia Springs State Park
1053 Magnolia Springs Dr Millen GA 30442 478-982-1660
Web: www.gastateparks.org

Mistletoe State Park 3723 Mistletoe Rd Appling GA 30802 706-541-0321
Web: www.gastateparks.org

Moccasin Creek State Park 3655 Hwy 197 Clarkesville GA 30523 706-947-3194
Web: www.gastateparks.org

New Echota State Historic Site
1211 Chatsworth Hwy NE Calhoun GA 30701 706-624-1321
Web: www.gastateparks.org

Panola Mountain State Park
2600 Georgia 155 Stockbridge GA 30281 770-389-7801
Web: www.gastateparks.org

Pickett's Mill Battlefield State Historic Site
4432 Mt Tabor Church Rd Dallas GA 30157 770-443-7850
Web: www.gastateparks.org

Reed Bingham State Park 542 Reed Bingham Rd Adel GA 31620 229-896-3551
Web: www.gastateparks.org

Richard B. Russell State Park
2650 Russell State Pk Rd Elberton GA 30635 706-213-2045
Web: www.gastateparks.org

Robert Toombs House State Historic Site
216 E Robert Toombs Ave Washington GA 30673 706-678-2226
Web: www.gastateparks.org

Seminole State Park 7870 State Pk Dr Donalsonville GA 39845 229-861-3137
Web: www.gastateparks.org

Skidaway Island State Park 52 Diamond Cswy Savannah GA 31411 912-598-2300 598-2365
Web: www.gastateparks.org/info/skidaway

Smithgall Woods Conservation Area & Lodge
61 Tsalaki Trl Helen GA 30545 706-878-3087
Web: www.gastateparks.org/info/smithgall

Sprewell Bluff State Park
740 Sprewell Bluff Rd Thomaston GA 30286 706-646-6026
Web: www.gastateparks.org

Stephen C. Foster State Park 17515 Hwy 177 Fargo GA 31631 912-637-5274
Web: www.gastateparks.org

Sweetwater Creek State Park
1750 Mt Vernon Rd PO Box 816 Lithia Springs GA 30122 770-732-5871
Web: www.gastateparks.org/sweetwatercreek

Tallulah Gorge State Park
338 Jane Hurt Yarn Dr Tallulah Falls GA 30573 706-754-7970
Web: www.gastateparks.org

Traveler's Rest State Historic Site
4339 Riverdale Rd Toccoa GA 30577 706-886-2256
Web: www.gastateparks.org

Tugaloo State Park 1763 Tugaloo State Pk Rd Lavonia GA 30553 706-356-4362
Web: www.gastateparks.org

Unicoi State Park & Lodge 1788 Hwy 356 Rd Helen GA 30545 800-573-9659
TF: 800-573-9659 ■ *Web:* www.gastateparks.org/info/unicoi

Vogel State Park 7485 Vogel State Pk Rd Blairsville GA 30512 706-745-2628
Web: www.gastateparks.org

Watson Mill Bridge State Park
650 Watson Mill Rd Comer GA 30629 706-783-5349
Web: www.gastateparks.org

Wormsloe State Historic Site
7601 Skidaway Rd Savannah GA 31406 912-353-3023
Web: www.gastateparks.org/info/wormsloe

Hawaii

Phone Fax

Diamond Head State Monument PO Box 621 Honolulu HI 96809 808-587-0404 587-0390
Web: www.hawaii.gov

Haena State Park 3060 Eiwa St Ste 306 Lihue HI 96766 808-274-3444 274-3448
Web: www.hawaiistateparks.org

Halekii-Pihana Heiau State Monument
54 S High St Rm 101 Wailuku HI 96793 808-984-8109 984-8111
Web: www.hawaiistateparks.org

Hanauma Bay State Underwater Park
3949 Diamond Head Rd Honolulu HI 96816 808-587-0300
Web: www.hawaii.gov

Hapuna Beach State Recreation Area
75 Aupuni St Rm 204 PO Box 936 Hilo HI 96721 808-882-6206 961-9599
Web: www.hawaiistateparks.org

Name / Address	City	State	Zip	Phone	Fax
Hawaii Information Consortium (HIC) 201 Merchant St Ste 1805 *Web:* www.hawaii.gov	Honolulu	HI	96813	808-695-4620	695-4618
Hawaii State Parks Kalanimoku Bldg 1151 Punchbowl St Rm 310 *Web:* www.hawaiistateparks.org	Honolulu	HI	96813	808-587-0300	587-0311
Heeia State Park 46-465 Kamehameha Hwy *Web:* www.heeiastatepark.org	Kaneohe	HI	96744	808-235-6509	235-6519
Iao Valley State Monument 54 S High St Rm 101 *Web:* www.hawaiistateparks.org	Wailuku	HI	96793	808-984-8109	984-8111
Iolani Palace State Monument PO Box 621 *Web:* www.hawaiistateparks.org	Honolulu	HI	96809	808-587-0300	
Kaena Point State Park c/o Oahu District Office PO Box 621 *Web:* www.hawaiistateparks.org	Honolulu	HI	96809	808-587-0300	
Kahana Valley State Park 52-222 Kamehameha Hwy PO Box 621 *Web:* www.hawaiistateparks.org	Honolulu	HI	96809	808-587-0300	
Kalopa State Recreation Area 75 Aupuni St Rm 204 PO Box 936 *Web:* www.hawaii.gov	Hilo	HI	96721	808-961-9540	961-9599
Kaumahina State Wayside 54 S High St Rm 101 *Web:* www.hawaiistateparks.org	Wailuku	HI	96793	808-984-8109	984-8111
Keaiwa Heiau State Recreation Area 1151 Punchbowl St Rm 310 PO Box 621 *Web:* www.hawaii.gov	Honolulu	HI	96813	808-483-2511	
Kealakekua Bay State Historical Park PO Box 936 *Web:* www.hawaii.gov	Hilo	HI	96721	808-974-6200	
Kohala Historical Sites State Monument PO Box 936 *Web:* www.hawaiistateparks.org	Hilo	HI	96721	808-974-6200	
Kokee State Park 3060 Eiwa St Rm 306 *Web:* www.hawaiistateparks.org	Lihue	HI	96766	808-274-3444	
Kukaniloko Birthstones State Monument c/o Oahu District Office PO Box 621 *Web:* www.hawaiistateparks.org/parks/oahu/index.cfm?park_id=24	Honolulu	HI	96809	808-587-0300	
Laie Point State Wayside c/o Oahu District Office PO Box 621 *Web:* www.hawaiistateparks.org/parks/oahu/index.cfm?park_id=25	Honolulu	HI	96809	808-587-0300	
Lapakahi State Historical Park 75 Aupuni St Rm 204 PO Box 936 *Web:* www.hawaiistateparks.org	Hilo	HI	96721	808-327-4958	
Lava Tree State Monument 1151 Punchbowl St Rm 310 PO Box 621 *Web:* www.hawaiistateparks.org	Honolulu	HI	96813	808-587-0300	587-0311
Malaekahana State Recreation Area PO Box 621 *Web:* www.hawaiistateparks.org	Honolulu	HI	96809	808-587-0300	
Nuuanu Pali State Wayside PO Box 621 *Web:* www.hawaiistateparks.org	Honolulu	HI	96809	808-587-0300	
Old Kona Airport State Recreation Area 75 Aupuni St Rm 204 PO Box 936 *Web:* www.hawaiistateparks.org	Hilo	HI	96721	808-961-9540	961-9599
Pala'au State Park PO Box 621 *Web:* www.hawaiistateparks.org	Honolulu	HI	96809	808-587-0300	
Polihale State Park 3060 Eiwa St Ste 306 *Web:* www.hawaiistateparks.org	Lihue	HI	96766	808-274-3444	274-3448
Polipoli Spring State Recreation Area 54 S High St Rm 101 *Web:* www.hawaii.gov	Wailuku	HI	96793	808-984-8109	984-8111
Puaa Kaa State Wayside 54 S High St Rm 101 *Web:* www.hawaiistateparks.org	Wailuku	HI	96793	808-984-8109	984-8111
Puu o Mahuka Heiau State Monument 1151 Punchbowl St Rm 310 PO Box 621 *Web:* www.hawaii.gov	Honolulu	HI	96809	808-587-0300	587-0311
Puu Ualakaa State Wayside PO Box 621 *Web:* www.hawaiistateparks.org	Honolulu	HI	96809	808-587-0300	
Royal Mausoleum State Monument 2261 Nuuanu Ave *Web:* www.hawaiistateparks.org	Honolulu	HI	96817	808-587-0300	
Russian Fort Elizabeth State Historical Park 3060 Eiwa St Ste 306 *Web:* www.hawaiistateparks.org	Lihue	HI	96766	808-274-3444	274-3448
Sand Island State Recreation Area PO Box 621 *Web:* www.hawaiistateparks.org	Honolulu	HI	96809	808-832-3781	
Ulupo Heiau State Monument 1151 Punchbowl St PO Box 621 *Web:* www.hawaiistateparks.org	Honolulu	HI	96813	808-587-0300	587-0311
Waahila Ridge State Recreation Area 1151 Punchbowl St PO Box 621 *Web:* www.hawaii.gov	Honolulu	HI	96809	808-587-0300	587-0311
Wahiawa Freshwater State Recreation Area PO Box 621 *Web:* www.hawaiistateparks.org	Honolulu	HI	96809	808-622-6316	
Waianapanapa State Park 54 S High St Rm 101 *Web:* www.hawaiistateparks.org	Wailuku	HI	96793	808-984-8109	984-8111
Wailoa River State Recreation Area PO Box 936 *Web:* www.hawaiistateparks.org	Hilo	HI	96721	808-933-0416	
Wailua River State Park 3060 Eiwa St *Web:* www.hawaii.gov	Lihue	HI	96766	808-274-3444	
Wailua Valley State Wayside 54 S High St Rm 101 *Web:* www.hawaiistateparks.org	Wailuku	HI	96793	808-984-8109	984-8111
Waimea Canyon State Park 3060 Eiwa St Ste 306 *Web:* www.hawaii.gov	Lihue	HI	96766	808-274-3444	274-3448

Idaho

Name / Address	City	State	Zip	Phone	Fax
Bruneau Dunes State Park 27608 Sand Dunes Rd *Web:* www.parksandrecreation.idaho.gov	Mountain Home	ID	83647	208-366-7919	366-2844
Dworshak State Park PO Box 115 *Web:* www.visitidaho.org	Ahsahka	ID	83520	208-476-5994	
Eagle Island State Park 4000 W Hatchery Rd *Web:* www.visitidaho.org	Eagle	ID	83616	208-939-0696	939-0696
Farragut State Park 13550 E Hwy 54 *Web:* www.visitidaho.org	Athol	ID	83801	208-683-2425	683-7416
Hells Gate State Park 5100 Hells Gate Rd *Web:* www.idahoparks.org	Lewiston	ID	83501	208-799-5015	799-5187
Henrys Lake State Park 3917 E 5100 N *Web:* idahostateparks.reserveamerica.com	Island Park	ID	83429	208-558-7532	
Heyburn State Park 57 Chatcolet Rd *TF:* 866-634-3246 ■ *Web:* www.parksandrecreation.idaho.gov	Plummer	ID	83851	208-686-1308	
Lake Cascade State Park 970 Dam Rd *TF:* 866-634-3246 ■ *Web:* www.parksandrecreation.idaho.gov	Cascade	ID	83611	208-382-6544	382-4071
Lake Walcott State Park 959 E Minidoka Dam *Web:* www.parksandrecreation.idaho.gov	Rupert	ID	83350	208-436-1258	436-1268
Land of the Yankee Fork State Park PO Box 1086 *Web:* www.parksandrecreation.idaho.gov	Challis	ID	83226	208-879-5244	879-5243
Lucky Peak State Park 9725 E Hwy 21 *Web:* www.visitidaho.org	Boise	ID	83716	208-334-2432	
Massacre Rocks State Park 3592 N Pk Ln *Web:* parksandrecreation.idaho.gov	American Falls	ID	83211	208-548-2672	
McCroskey State Park 57 Chatcolet Rd *Web:* www.visitidaho.org/attraction/parks/mccroskey-state-park/	Plummer	ID	83851	208-686-1308	
Old Mission State Park 31732 S Mission Rd *Web:* parksandrecreation.idaho.gov	Cataldo	ID	83810	208-682-3814	682-4032
Ponderosa State Park 1920 N Davis Ave *Web:* www.idahoparks.org	McCall	ID	83638	208-634-2164	634-5370
Priest Lake State Park 314 Indian Creek Pk Rd *TF Resv:* 888-922-6743 ■ *Web:* www.visitidaho.org	Coolin	ID	83821	208-443-2200	443-3893
Round Lake State Park PO Box 170 *Web:* idahostateparks.reserveamerica.com	Sagle	ID	83860	208-263-3489	
Three Island Crossing State Park 1083 S Three Island Pk Dr *TF:* 866-634-3246 ■ *Web:* www.visitidaho.org/attraction/visitor-centers/three-island-crossing-state-park	Glenns Ferry	ID	83623	208-366-2394	366-7913
Winchester Lake State Park (IDPR) PO Box 186 *Web:* idahostateparks.reserveamerica.com	Winchester	ID	83555	208-924-7563	924-5941

Illinois

Name / Address	City	State	Zip	Phone	Fax
Anderson Lake Conservation Area 647 N State Hwy 100 *Web:* www.dnr.state.il.us	Astoria	IL	61501	309-759-4484	
Apple River Canyon State Park 8763 E Canyon Rd *Web:* www.dnr.state.il.us	Apple River	IL	61001	815-745-3302	
Argyle Lake State Park 640 Argyle Pk Rd *Web:* www.dnr.state.il.us	Colchester	IL	62326	309-776-3422	
Banner Marsh State Fish & Wildlife Area 19721 N US 24 *Web:* www.dnr.state.il.us/lands/landmgt/parks/r1/banner.htm	Canton	IL	61520	309-647-9184	
Beall Woods State Park 9285 Beall Woods Ave *Web:* www.dnr.state.il.us	Mount Carmel	IL	62863	618-298-2442	
Beaver Dam State Park 14548 Beaver Dam Ln *Web:* www.dnr.state.il.us	Plainview	IL	62685	217-854-8020	
Big Bend State Fish & Wildlife Area PO Box 181 *Web:* www.dnr.state.il.us/lands/landmgt/parks/r1/bigbend.htm	Prophetstown	IL	61277	815-537-2270	
Big River State Forest RR 1 PO Box 118 *Web:* www.dnr.state.il.us/lands/landmgt/parks/r1/bigriver.htm	Keithsburg	IL	61442	309-374-2496	
Buffalo Rock State Park & Effigy Tumuli 1300 N 27th Rd PO Box 2034 *Web:* www.dnr.state.il.us	Ottawa	IL	61350	815-433-2220	
Cache River State Natural Area 930 Sunflower Ln *Web:* www.dnr.state.il.us	Belknap	IL	62908	618-634-9678	
Cahokia Mounds State Historic Site 30 Ramey St *Web:* cahokiamounds.org	Collinsville	IL	62234	618-346-5160	346-5162
Carlyle Lake State Fish & Wildlife Area RR 2 *Web:* www.dnr.state.il.us	Vandalia	IL	62471	618-425-3533	
Castle Rock State Park 1365 W Castle Rd *Web:* www.dnr.state.il.us/lands/landmgt/parks/r1/castle.htm	Oregon	IL	61061	815-732-7329	
Cave-In-Rock State Park One New State Pk Rd PO Box 338 *Web:* www.dnr.state.il.us	Cave-In-Rock	IL	62919	618-289-4325	
Chain O'Lakes State Park 8916 Wilmot Rd *Web:* www.dnr.state.il.us	Spring Grove	IL	60081	847-587-5512	
Channahon State Park PO Box 54 *Web:* www.dnr.state.il.us	Channahon	IL	60410	815-467-4271	
Clinton Lake State Recreation Area RR 1 PO Box 4 *Web:* www.dnr.state.il.us	DeWitt	IL	61735	217-935-8722	
Coffeen Lake State Fish & Wildlife Area 15084 N Fourth Ave *Web:* www.dnr.state.il.us	Coffeen	IL	62017	217-537-3351	
Crawford County State Fish & Wildlife Area 12609 E 1700th Ave *Web:* www.dnr.state.il.us	Hutsonville	IL	62433	618-563-4405	
Des Plaines State Fish & Wildlife Area 24621 N River Rd *Web:* www.dnr.state.il.us	Wilmington	IL	60481	815-423-5326	
Donnelley/DePue State Fish & Wildlife Areas 1001 W Fourth St PO Box 52 *Web:* www.dnr.state.il.us	DePue	IL	61322	815-447-2353	

Name	City	State	ZIP	Phone	Fax
Eagle Creek State Recreation Area PO Box 16 *Web:* www.dnr.state.il.us	Findlay	IL	62534	217-756-8260	
Edward R. Madigan State Fish & Wildlife Area 1366 1010th Ave. *Web:* www.dnr.state.il.us	Lincoln	IL	62656	217-735-2424	
Eldon Hazlet State Recreation Area 20100 Hazlet Pk Rd *Web:* www.dnr.state.il.us/lands/landmgt/parks/r4/eldon.htm	Carlyle	IL	62231	618-594-3015	
Ferne Clyffe State Park PO Box 10 *Web:* www.dnr.state.il.us	Goreville	IL	62939	618-995-2411	
Fort Massac State Park 1308 E Fifth St *Web:* www.dnr.state.il.us	Metropolis	IL	62960	618-524-4712	
Fox Ridge State Park 18175 State Pk Rd *Web:* www.dnr.state.il.us	Charleston	IL	61920	217-345-6416	
Frank Holten State Recreation Area 4500 Pocket Rd *Web:* www.dnr.state.il.us	East Saint Louis	IL	62205	618-874-7920	
Franklin Creek State Natural Area 1872 Twist Rd *Web:* www.dnr.state.il.us	Franklin Grove	IL	61031	815-456-2878	
Fults Hill Prairie & Kidd Lake State Natural Areas c/o Randolph County State Recreation Area 4301 S Lk Dr *Web:* dnr.state.il.us/lands/landmgt/parks/r4/fhp.htm	Chester	IL	62233	618-826-2706	
Gebhard Woods State Park 401 Ottawa St PO Box 272 *Web:* www.dnr.state.il.us/lands/landmgt/parks/i&m/east/gebhard/park.htm	Morris	IL	60450	815-942-0796	
Giant City State Park 235 Giant City Rd *Web:* www.dnr.state.il.us	Makanda	IL	62958	618-457-4836	
Goose Lake Prairie State Natural Area 5010 N Jugtown Rd *Web:* www.dnr.state.il.us/lands/landmgt/parks/i&m/east/goose/home.htm	Morris	IL	60450	815-942-2899	
Green River State Wildlife Area 375 Game Rd *Web:* www.dnr.state.il.us	Harmon	IL	61042	815-379-2324	
Hamilton County State Fish & Wildlife Area RR 4 PO Box 242 *Web:* www.dnr.state.il.us	McLeansboro	IL	62859	618-773-4340	
Harry "Babe" Woodyard State Natural Area 19284 E 670 N *Web:* www.dnr.state.il.us	Georgetown	IL	61846	217-442-4915	
Heidecke Lake State Fish & Wildlife Area 5010 N Jugtown Rd *Web:* www.dnr.state.il.us	Morris	IL	60450	815-942-6352	
Henderson County Conservation Area PO Box 118 *Web:* www.dnr.state.il.us/lands/landmgt/parks/r1/henderso.htm	Keithsburg	IL	61442	309-374-2496	
Hennepin Canal Parkway State Park 16006 875 E St *Web:* www.dnr.state.il.us/lands/landmgt/parks/r1/hennpin.htm	Sheffield	IL	61361	815-454-2328	
Hidden Springs State Forest RR 1 PO Box 200 *Web:* www.dnr.state.il.us	Strasburg	IL	62465	217-644-3091	
Horseshoe Lake State Fish & Wildlife Area (Alexander County) 21204 Promised Land Rd *Web:* www.dnr.state.il.us	Miller City	IL	62962	618-776-5689	
Horseshoe Lake State Park (Madison County) 3321 Hwy 111 *Web:* www.dnr.state.il.us	Granite City	IL	62040	618-931-0270	
Illini State Park 2660 E 2350th Rd *Web:* www.dnr.state.il.us/lands/landmgt/parks/i&m/east/illini/park.htm	Marseilles	IL	61341	815-795-2448	
Illinois & Michigan Canal State Trail PO Box 272 *Web:* www.dnr.state.il.us/lands/landmgt/parks/i&m/main.htm	Morris	IL	60450	815-942-0796	942-9690
Illinois Beach State Park Lake Front *Web:* www.dnr.state.il.us	Zion	IL	60099	847-662-4811	662-6433
Illinois Caverns State Natural Area 10981 Conservation Rd *Web:* www.dnr.state.il.us	Baldwin	IL	62217	618-458-6699	
Iroquois County State Wildlife Area RR 1 2803 E 3300 N Rd *Web:* www.dnr.state.il.us	Beaverville	IL	60912	815-435-2218	
James Pate Philip State Park 2050 W Stearns Rd *Web:* www.dnr.state.il.us/lands/landmgt/parks/r2/jpatephillip.htm	Bartlett	IL	60103	847-608-3100	
Jim Edgar Panther Creek State Fish & Wildlife Area (JEPC) 10149 County Hwy 11 *Web:* www.dnr.state.il.us/lands/landmgt/parks/r4/jepc.htm	Chandlerville	IL	62627	217-452-7741	
Johnson-Sauk Trail State Park 28616 Sauk Trl Rd *Web:* www.dnr.state.il.us	Kewanee	IL	61443	309-853-5589	
Jubilee College State Park 13921 W Rt 150 *Web:* www.dnr.state.il.us	Brimfield	IL	61517	309-446-3758	446-3183
Kankakee River State Park 5314 W Rt 102 PO Box 37 *Web:* www.dnr.state.il.us	Bourbonnais	IL	60914	815-933-1383	
Kaskaskia River State Fish & Wildlife Area 10981 Conservation Rd *Web:* www.dnr.state.il.us/lands/landmgt/parks/r4/kaskas.htm	Baldwin	IL	62217	618-785-2555	
Kickapoo State Recreation Area 10906 Kickapoo Pk Rd *Web:* www.dnr.state.il.us/lands/landmgt/parks/r3/kickapoo.htm	Oakwood	IL	61858	217-442-4915	
Kinkaid Lake State Fish & Wildlife Area 52 Cinder Hill Dr *Web:* www.dnr.state.il.us/lands/landmgt/parks/r5/kinkaid.htm	Murphysboro	IL	62966	618-684-2867	
Lake Le-Aqua-Na State Recreation Area 8542 N Lk Rd *Web:* www.dnr.state.il.us	Lena	IL	61048	815-369-4282	
Lake Murphysboro State Park 52 Cinder Hill Dr *Web:* www.dnr.state.il.us/lands/landmgt/parks/r5/murphysb.htm	Murphysboro	IL	62966	618-684-2867	
LaSalle Lake State Fish & Wildlife Area 2660 E 2350th Rd *Web:* www.dnr.state.il.us	Marseilles	IL	61341	815-357-1608	
Lincoln Trail State Park 16985 E 1350th Rd *Web:* www.dnr.state.il.us	Marshall	IL	62441	217-826-2222	
Lowden State Park 1411 N River Rd *Web:* www.dnr.state.il.us/lands/landmgt/parks/r1/lowdensp.htm	Oregon	IL	61061	815-732-6828	
Lowden-Miller State Forest 1365 W Castle Rock Rd *Web:* www.dnr.state.il.us/lands/landmgt/parks/r1/lowdenmi.htm	Oregon	IL	61061	815-732-7329	
Mackinaw River State Fish & Wildlife Area 15470 Nelson Rd *Web:* www.dnr.state.il.us	Mackinaw	IL	61755	309-963-4969	
Marshall State Fish & Wildlife Area 236 State Rt 26 *Web:* www.dnr.state.il.us	Lacon	IL	61540	309-246-8351	
Matthiessen State Park PO Box 509 *Web:* www.dnr.state.il.us/lands/landmgt/parks/r1/mttindex.htm	Utica	IL	61373	815-667-4868	
Mautino State Fish & Wildlife Area 16006-875 E St *Web:* www.dnr.state.il.us/lands/landmgt/parks/r1/mautino.htm	Sheffield	IL	61361	815-454-2328	
Mazonia-Braidwood State Fish & Wildlife Areas PO Box 126 *Web:* www.dnr.state.il.us	Braceville	IL	60407	815-237-0063	
Mermet Lake State Fish & Wildlife Area 1812 Grinnell Rd *Web:* www.dnr.state.il.us	Belknap	IL	62908	618-524-5577	
Middle Fork State Fish & Wildlife Area 10906 Kickapoo Pk Rd *Web:* www.dnr.state.il.us/lands/landmgt/parks/r3/middle.htm	Oakwood	IL	61858	217-442-4915	
Mississippi Palisades State Park 16327A IL Rt 84 *Web:* www.dnr.state.il.us	Savanna	IL	61074	815-273-2731	
Mississippi River State Fish & Wildlife Area 17836 State Hwy 100 N *Web:* www.dnr.state.il.us/lands/landmgt/parks/r4/miss.htm	Grafton	IL	62037	618-376-3303	
Moraine Hills State Park 1510 S River Rd *Web:* www.dnr.state.il.us	McHenry	IL	60051	815-385-1624	
Moraine View State Recreation Area 27374 Moraine View Pk Rd *Web:* www.dnr.state.il.us	Le Roy	IL	61752	309-724-8032	
Morrison-Rockwood State Park 18750 Lake Rd *Web:* www.dnr.state.il.us	Morrison	IL	61270	815-772-4708	
Nauvoo State Park PO Box 426 *Web:* www.dnr.state.il.us	Nauvoo	IL	62354	217-453-2512	
Newton Lake State Fish & Wildlife Area 3490 E 500th Ave *Web:* www.dnr.state.il.us	Newton	IL	62448	618-783-3478	
Peabody River King State Fish & Wildlife Area 8900 Darmstadt Rd *Web:* www.dnr.state.il.us/lands/landmgt/parks/r4/peabody.htm	New Athens	IL	62264	618-475-9339	
Pere Marquette State Park 13112 Visitor Ctr Ln PO Box 158 *Web:* www.dnr.state.il.us/lands/landmgt/parks/r4/peremarq.htm	Grafton	IL	62037	618-786-3323	
Piney Creek Ravine State Natural Area 4301 N Lake Dr *Web:* www.dnr.state.il.us	Chester	IL	62233	618-826-2706	
Powerton Lake State Fish & Wildlife Area 7982 S Pk Rd *Web:* www.dnr.state.il.us/lands/landmgt/parks/r1/powerton.htm	Manito	IL	61546	309-968-7135	
Prophetstown State Recreation Area Riverside Dr PO Box 181 *Web:* www.dnr.state.il.us/lands/landmgt/parks/r1/prophet.htm	Prophetstown	IL	61277	815-537-2926	
Pyramid State Recreation Area 1562 Pyramid Pk Rd *Web:* www.dnr.state.il.us	Pinckneyville	IL	62274	618-357-2574	
Ramsey Lake State Recreation Area Ramsey Lk Rd PO Box 97 *Web:* www.dnr.state.il.us	Ramsey	IL	62080	618-423-2215	
Randolph County State Recreation Area 4301 S Lake Dr *Web:* www.dnr.state.il.us/lands/landmgt/parks/r4/rand.htm	Chester	IL	62233	618-826-2706	
Ray Norbut State Fish & Wildlife Area 46816 290th Ave *Web:* www.dnr.state.il.us	Griggsville	IL	62340	217-833-2811	
Red Hills State Park RR 2 PO Box 252A *Web:* www.dnr.state.il.us	Sumner	IL	62466	618-936-2469	
Rend Lake State Fish & Wildlife Area 10885 E Jefferson Rd *Web:* www.dnr.state.il.us	Bonnie	IL	62816	618-279-3110	
Rice Lake State Fish & Wildlife Area 19721 N US Hwy 24 *Web:* www.dnr.state.il.us/lands/landmgt/parks/r1/rice.htm	Canton	IL	61520	309-647-9184	
Rock Cut State Park 7318 Harlem Rd *Web:* www.dnr.state.il.us	Loves Park	IL	61111	815-885-3311	
Rock Island Trail State Park 311 E Williams St PO Box 64 *Web:* www.dnr.state.il.us	Wyoming	IL	61491	309-695-2228	
Saline County State Fish & Wildlife Area 85 Glen O Jones Rd *Web:* www.dnr.state.il.us	Equality	IL	62934	618-276-4405	
Sam Parr State Fish & Wildlife Area 13225 E State Hwy 33 *Web:* www.dnr.state.il.us	Newton	IL	62448	618-783-2661	
Sand Ridge State Forest PO Box 111 *Web:* www.dnr.state.il.us	Forest City	IL	61532	309-597-2212	
Sanganois State Fish & Wildlife Area 3594 County Rd 200 N *Web:* www.dnr.state.il.us/lands/landmgt/parks/r4/sangill.htm	Chandlerville	IL	62627	309-546-2628	
Sangchris Lake State Park 9898 Cascade Rd *Web:* www.dnr.state.il.us	Rochester	IL	62563	217-498-9208	
Shabbona Lake State Park 4201 Shabbona Grove Rd *Web:* www.dnr.state.il.us	Shabbona	IL	60550	815-824-2106	

				Phone	Fax
Shelbyville State Fish & Wildlife Area RR 1 PO Box 42A *Web:* www.dnr.state.il.us	Bethany	IL	61914	217-665-3112	
Siloam Springs State Park 938 E 3003rd Ln *Web:* www.dnr.state.il.us	Clayton	IL	62324	217-894-6205	
Silver Springs State Fish & Wildlife Area 13608 Fox Rd *Web:* www.dnr.state.il.us	Yorkville	IL	60560	630-553-6297	
South Shore State Park c/o Eldon Hazlet State Recreation Area 20100 Hazlet Pk Rd *Web:* www.dnr.state.il.us/lands/landmgt/parks/r4/sts.htm	Carlyle	IL	62231	618-594-3015	
Spitler Woods State Natural Area 705 Spitler Pk Dr *Web:* www.dnr.state.il.us/lands/landmgt/parks/r3/spitler.htm	Mount Zion	IL	62549	217-864-3121	
Spring Lake State Fish & Wildlife Area 7982 S Pk Rd *Web:* www.dnr.state.il.us/lands/landmgt/parks/r1/spl.htm	Manito	IL	61546	309-968-7135	
Starved Rock State Park PO Box 509 *Web:* www.dnr.state.il.us/lands/landmgt/parks/i&m/east/starve/park.htm	Utica	IL	61373	815-667-4726	
Stephen A. Forbes State Park 6924 Omega Rd *Web:* www.dnr.state.il.us	Kinmundy	IL	62854	618-547-3381	
Ten Mile Creek State Fish & Wildlife Area RR 1 PO Box 179 *Web:* www.dnr.state.il.us	McLeansboro	IL	62859	618-643-2862	
Trail of Tears State Forest 3240 State Forest Rd *Web:* www.dnr.state.il.us	Jonesboro	IL	62952	618-833-4910	
Tunnel Hill State Trail 302 E Vine St *Web:* www.dnr.state.il.us	Vienna	IL	62995	618-658-2168	
Turkey Bluffs State Fish & Wildlife Area 4301 S Lakeside Dr *Web:* dnr.state.il.us	Chester	IL	62233	618-826-2706	
Union County State Fish & Wildlife Area 2755 Refuge Rd *Web:* www.dnr.state.il.us	Jonesboro	IL	62952	618-833-5175	
Volo Bog State Natural Area 28478 W Brandenburg Rd *Web:* www.dnr.state.il.us	Ingleside	IL	60041	815-344-1294	
Walnut Point State Park 2331 E County Rd 370 N *Web:* www.dnr.state.il.us	Oakland	IL	61943	217-346-3336	
Washington County State Recreation Area 18500 Conservation Dr. *Web:* www.dnr.state.il.us	Nashville	IL	62263	618-327-3137	
Wayne Fitzgerrell State Recreation Area 11094 Ranger Rd *Web:* www.dnr.state.il.us	Whittington	IL	62897	618-629-2320	
Weinberg-King State Park PO Box 203 *Web:* www.dnr.state.il.us	Augusta	IL	62311	217-392-2345	
Weldon Springs State Park 1159 500 N RR 2 PO Box 87 *Web:* www.dnr.state.il.us	Clinton	IL	61727	217-935-2644	
White Pines Forest State Park 6712 W Pines Rd *Web:* www.dnr.state.il.us	Mount Morris	IL	61054	815-946-3717	
William W. Powers State Recreation Area 12949 S Ave O *Web:* www.dnr.state.il.us	Chicago	IL	60633	773-646-3270	
Wolf Creek State Park RR 1 PO Box 99 *Web:* www.dnr.state.il.us	Windsor	IL	61957	217-459-2831	

Indiana

				Phone	Fax
Brookville Lake PO Box 100 *Web:* www.in.gov	Brookville	IN	47012	765-647-2657	
Brown County State Park 1405 State Rd 46 W PO Box 608 *Web:* www.in.gov	Nashville	IN	47448	812-988-6406	
Cagles Mill Lake 1317 W Lieber Rd Ste 1 *Web:* www.in.gov	Cloverdale	IN	46120	765-795-4576	
Cecil M. Harden Lake 1588 S Raccoon Pkwy *Web:* www.in.gov	Rockville	IN	47872	765-344-1412	
Charlestown State Park 12500 Indiana 62 *Web:* www.in.gov	Charlestown	IN	47111	812-256-5600	
Clifty Falls State Park 1501 Green Rd *Web:* www.in.gov	Madison	IN	47250	812-273-8885	
Deam Lake State Recreation Area 1217 Deam Lk Rd *Web:* www.in.gov	Borden	IN	47106	812-246-5421	
Falls of the Ohio State Park 201 W Riverside Dr. *Web:* www.in.gov	Clarksville	IN	47129	812-280-9970	280-7110
Fort Harrison State Park 5753 Glenn Rd *Web:* www.in.gov	Indianapolis	IN	46216	317-591-0904	
Hardy Lake 4171 E Harrod Rd *Web:* www.in.gov	Scottsburg	IN	47170	812-794-3800	
Harmonie State Park 3451 Harmonie State Pk Rd *Web:* www.in.gov	New Harmony	IN	47631	812-682-4821	
Indiana Dunes State Park 1600 N 25 E *Web:* www.in.gov	Chesterton	IN	46304	219-926-1952	
J. Edward Roush Lake 517 N Warren Rd *Web:* www.in.gov	Huntington	IN	46750	260-468-2165	
Lincoln State Park Hwy 162 PO Box 216 *Web:* www.in.gov	Lincoln City	IN	47552	812-937-4710	
McCormick's Creek State Park 250 McCormick's Creek Rd *Web:* www.in.gov	Spencer	IN	47460	812-829-2235	
Mississinewa Lake 4673 S 625 E *Web:* www.in.gov	Peru	IN	46970	765-473-6528	
Monroe Lake 4850 S State Rd 446 *Web:* www.in.gov	Bloomington	IN	47401	812-837-9546	
Mounds State Park 4306 Mounds Rd *Web:* www.in.gov	Anderson	IN	46017	765-642-6627	
O'Bannon Woods State Park 7234 Old Forest Rd SW *Web:* www.in.gov	Corydon	IN	47112	812-738-8232	
Ouabache State Park 4930 E State Rd 201 *Web:* www.in.gov	Bluffton	IN	46714	260-824-0926	
Patoka Lake 3084 N DillaRd Rd *Web:* www.in.gov	Birdseye	IN	47513	812-685-2464	
Pokagon State Park 450 Ln 100 Lk James *Web:* in.gov/ai/errors/dnr_404.html	Angola	IN	46703	260-833-2012	
Potato Creek State Park 25601 State Rd 4 PO Box 908 *Web:* www.in.gov	North Liberty	IN	46554	574-656-8186	
Salamonie Lake 9214 Lost Bridge Rd W *Web:* www.in.gov	Andrews	IN	46702	260-468-2125	
Shakamak State Park 6265 W State Rd 48 *Web:* www.in.gov	Jasonville	IN	47438	812-665-2158	
Spring Mill State Park PO Box 376 *Web:* www.in.gov	Mitchell	IN	47446	812-849-4129	
Starve Hollow State Recreation Area 4345 S County Rd 275 W *Web:* www.in.gov	Vallonia	IN	47281	812-358-3464	
Summit Lake State Park 5993 N Messick Rd *Web:* www.in.gov	New Castle	IN	47362	765-766-5873	
Tippecanoe River State Park 4200 N US Hwy 35 *Web:* www.in.gov	Winamac	IN	46996	574-946-3213	
Turkey Run State Park 8121 Pk Rd *Web:* www.in.gov	Marshall	IN	47859	765-597-2635	
Versailles State Park US Hwy 50 PO Box 205 *Web:* www.in.gov	Versailles	IN	47042	812-689-6424	
White River State Park 801 W Washington St *TF:* 800-665-9056 ■ *Web:* www.in.gov	Indianapolis	IN	46204	317-233-2434	233-2367
Whitewater Memorial State Park 1418 S State Rd 101 *Web:* www.in.gov	Liberty	IN	47353	765-458-5565	

Iowa

				Phone	Fax
Backbone State Park 1282 120th St *Web:* www.iowadnr.gov	Strawberry Point	IA	52076	563-924-2000	
Beed's Lake State Park 1422 165th St Pk *Web:* www.iowadnr.gov	Hampton	IA	50441	641-456-2047	
Big Creek State Park 8794 NW 125th Ave *Web:* www.iowadnr.gov	Polk City	IA	50226	515-984-6473	984-9320
Black Hawk State Park 228 S Blossom *Web:* www.iowadnr.gov	Lake View	IA	51450	712-657-8712	657-2289
Brushy Creek State Recreation Area 2802 Brushy Creek Rd *Web:* www.iowadnr.gov	Lehigh	IA	50557	515-543-8298	843-8395
Cedar Rock 2611 Quasqueton Diagonal Blvd Buch Co Hwy W-35 *Web:* www.iowadnr.gov	Independence	IA	50644	319-934-3572	
Clear Lake State Park 2730 S Lakeview Dr *Web:* www.iowadnr.gov	Clear Lake	IA	50428	641-357-4212	357-4242
Dolliver Memorial State Park 2757 Dolliver Pk Ave *Web:* www.iowadnr.gov	Lehigh	IA	50557	515-359-2539	359-2542
Elinor Bedell State Park c/o Gull Pt State Pk 1500 Harpen St *Web:* www.iowabeautiful.com	Milford	IA	51351	712-330-5192	
Elk Rock State Park 811 146th Ave. *Web:* www.iowadnr.gov	Knoxville	IA	50138	641-842-6008	
Fort Atkinson State Preserve c/o Volga River State Recreation Area 10225 Ivy Rd *Web:* www.iowadnr.gov	Fayette	IA	52142	563-425-4161	
Fort Defiance State Park c/o Gull Pt State Pk 1500 Harpen St *Web:* www.iowadnr.gov	Milford	IA	51351	712-337-3211	
Geode State Park 3333 Racine Ave *Web:* www.iowadnr.gov	Danville	IA	52623	319-392-4601	
George Wyth State Park 3659 Wyth Rd *Web:* www.iowadnr.gov	Waterloo	IA	50703	319-232-5505	232-1508
Green Valley State Park 1480 130th St *Web:* www.iowadnr.gov	Creston	IA	50801	641-782-5131	782-8330
Gull Point State Park 1500 Harpen St *Web:* www.iowadnr.gov	Milford	IA	51351	712-337-3211	
Lake Ahquabi State Park 1650 118th Ave *Web:* www.iowadnr.gov	Indianola	IA	50125	515-961-7101	
Lake Anita State Park 55111 750th St *Web:* www.iowadnr.gov	Anita	IA	50020	712-762-3564	762-4352
Lake Darling State Park 111 Lk Darling Rd *Web:* www.iowadnr.gov	Brighton	IA	52540	319-694-2323	
Lake Keomah State Park 2720 Keomah Ln *Web:* www.iowadnr.gov	Oskaloosa	IA	52577	641-673-6975	673-0647
Lake Macbride State Park 3525 Hwy 382 NE *Web:* www.iowadnr.gov	Solon	IA	52333	319-624-2200	624-2188
Lake Manawa State Park 1100 S Shore Dr *Web:* www.iowadnr.gov	Council Bluffs	IA	51501	712-366-0220	366-0474
Lake of Three Fires State Park 2303 Lake Rd *Web:* www.iowadnr.gov	Bedford	IA	50833	712-523-2700	523-3104
Lake Wapello State Park 15248 Campground Rd *TF:* 866-495-4868 ■ *Web:* www.iowadnr.gov	Drakesville	IA	52552	641-722-3371	

Park	City	State	Zip	Phone	Fax
Ledges State Park 1515 P Ave *Web:* www.iowadnr.gov	Madrid	IA	50156	515-432-1852	
Maquoketa Caves State Park 10970 98th St *Web:* www.iowadnr.gov	Maquoketa	IA	52060	563-652-5833	652-0061
McIntosh Woods State Park 1200 E Lake St *Web:* www.iowadnr.gov	Ventura	IA	50482	641-829-3847	829-3841
Mines of Spain State Recreation Area 8991 Bellevue Heights *Web:* www.iowadnr.gov	Dubuque	IA	52003	563-556-0620	556-8474
Nine Eagles State Park RR 1 *Web:* www.iowadnr.gov	Davis City	IA	50065	641-442-2855	442-2856
Palisades-Kepler State Park 700 Kepler Dr *Web:* www.iowadnr.gov	Mount Vernon	IA	52314	319-895-6039	895-9660
Pikes Peak State Park 15316 Great River Rd *Web:* www.iowadnr.gov	McGregor	IA	52157	563-873-2341	873-3167
Pilot Knob State Park 2148 340th St *Web:* www.iowadnr.gov	Forest City	IA	50436	641-581-4835	
Pine Lake State Park 22620 County Hwy S56 *Web:* www.iowadnr.gov	Eldora	IA	50627	641-858-5832	858-5641
Pleasant Creek State Recreation Area 4530 McClintock Rd *Web:* www.iowadnr.gov	Palo	IA	52324	319-436-7716	436-7715
Prairie Rose State Park 680 Rd M47 *Web:* www.iowadnr.gov	Harlan	IA	51537	712-773-2701	773-2702
Preparation Canyon State Park 206 Polk St PO Box 158 *Web:* www.iowadnr.gov	Pisgah	IA	51564	712-423-2829	
Red Haw State Park 24550 US Hwy 34 *Web:* www.iowadnr.gov	Chariton	IA	50049	641-774-5632	774-8821
Rock Creek State Park 5627 Rock Creek E *Web:* www.iowadnr.gov	Kellogg	IA	50135	641-236-3722	236-5599
Shimek State Forest 33653 Rt J56 *Web:* www.iowadnr.gov	Farmington	IA	52626	319-878-3811	
Springbrook State Park 2437 160th Rd *Web:* www.iowadnr.gov	Guthrie Center	IA	50115	641-747-3591	747-8401
Stephens State Forest 1111 N Eigth St *Web:* www.iowadnr.gov	Chariton	IA	50049	641-774-4559	
Stone State Park 5001 Talbot Rd *Web:* www.iowadnr.gov	Sioux City	IA	51103	712-255-4698	
Union Grove State Park 1215 220th St *Web:* www.iowadnr.gov	Gladbrook	IA	50635	641-473-2556	473-3059
Viking Lake State Park 2780 Viking Lk Rd *Web:* www.iowadnr.gov	Stanton	IA	51573	712-829-2235	829-2842
Volga River State Recreation Area 10225 Ivy Rd *Web:* www.iowadnr.gov	Fayette	IA	52142	563-425-4161	425-3272
Walnut Woods State Park 3155 Walnut Woods Dr *Web:* www.iowadnr.gov	West Des Moines	IA	50265	515-285-4502	285-7476
Wapsipinicon State Park 21301 County Rd E34 *Web:* www.iowadnr.gov	Anamosa	IA	52205	319-462-2761	462-4878
Waubonsie State Park 2585 Waubonsie Pk Rd *Web:* www.iowadnr.gov	Hamburg	IA	51640	712-382-2786	382-9860
Wildcat Den State Park 1884 Wildcat Den Rd *Web:* www.iowadnr.gov	Muscatine	IA	52761	563-263-4337	264-8329
Wilson Island State Recreation Area 32801 Campground Ln *Web:* www.iowadnr.gov	Missouri Valley	IA	51555	712-642-2069	642-4390
Yellow River State Forest 729 State Forest Rd YRSF *Web:* www.iowadnr.gov	Harpers Ferry	IA	52146	563-586-2254	

Kansas

Park	City	State	Zip	Phone	Fax
Cedar Bluff State Park 32001 147 Hwy *Web:* kdwpt.state.ks.us	Ellis	KS	67637	785-726-3212	
Cheney State Park 16000 NE 50th St *Web:* kdwpt.state.ks.us	Cheney	KS	67025	316-542-3664	
Clinton State Park 798 N 1415 Rd *Web:* www.kdwpt.state.ks.us	Lawrence	KS	66049	785-842-8562	
Cross Timbers State Park 144 Hwy 105 *Web:* ksoutdoors.com/State-Parks/Locations/Cross-Timbers	Toronto	KS	66777	620-637-2213	
Eisenhower State Park 29810 S Fairlawn Rd *Web:* kdwpt.state.ks.us/	Osage City	KS	66523	785-528-4102	
El Dorado State Park 618 NE Bluestem Rd *Web:* www.kdwpt.state.ks.us	El Dorado	KS	67042	316-321-7180	
Elk City State Park 4825 Squaw Creek Rd *Web:* kdwpt.state.ks.us	Independence	KS	67301	620-331-6295	
Glen Elder State Park 2131 180 Rd *Web:* www.kdwpt.state.ks.us	Glen Elder	KS	67446	785-545-3345	
Hillsdale State Park 26001 W 255th St *Web:* www.kdwpt.state.ks.us	Paola	KS	66071	913-783-4507	
Kanopolis State Park 200 Horsethief Rd *Web:* www.kdwpt.state.ks.us	Marquette	KS	67464	785-546-2565	
Lake Scott State Park 520 W Scott Lk Dr *Web:* www.kansastravel.org	Scott City	KS	67871	620-872-2061	
Lovewell State Park 2446 250 Rd *Web:* ksoutdoors.com/State-Parks/Locations/Lovewell	Webber	KS	66970	785-753-4971	
Meade State Park 13051 V Rd *Web:* www.stateparks.com	Meade	KS	67864	620-873-2572	
Milford State Park 3612 State Pk Rd *Web:* ksoutdoors.com/State-Parks/Locations/Milford	Milford	KS	66514	785-238-3014	
Mushroom Rock State Park 200 Horsethief Rd *Web:* ksoutdoors.com/State-Parks/Locations/Mushroom-Rock	Marquette	KS	67464	785-546-2565	
Perry State Park 5441 Westlake Rd *Web:* ksoutdoors.com/State-Parks/Locations/Perry	Ozawkie	KS	66070	785-246-3449	246-0224
Pomona State Park 22900 S Hwy 368 *Web:* ksoutdoors.com/State-Parks/Locations/Pomona	Vassar	KS	66543	785-828-4933	
Prairie Spirit Trail 419 S Oak St *Web:* bikeprairiespirit.com	Garnett	KS	66032	785-448-6767	
Tuttle Creek State Park 5800-A River Pond Rd *Web:* ksoutdoors.com/State-Parks/Locations/Tuttle-Creek	Manhattan	KS	66502	785-539-7941	
Webster State Park 1210 Nine Rd *Web:* ksoutdoors.com/State-Parks/Locations/Webster	Stockton	KS	67669	785-425-6775	

Kentucky

Park	City	State	Zip	Phone	Fax
Ben Hawes State Park 400 Boothfield Rd *Web:* www.kentuckytourism.com/outdoor_adventure/attraction/ben-hawes-park/19	Owensboro	KY	42301	270-687-7137	687-7138
Big Bone Lick State Park 3380 Beaver Rd *Web:* www.parks.ky.gov	Union	KY	41091	859-384-3522	
Blue Licks Battlefield State Resort Park Hwy 68 *TF:* 800-443-7008 ■ *Web:* www.parks.ky.gov	Mount Olivet	KY	41064	800-443-7008	
Boone Station State Historic Site 240 Gentry Rd *Web:* www.parks.ky.gov	Lexington	KY	40502	859-527-3131	
Buckhorn Lake State Resort Park 4441 Kentucky Hwy 1833 *TF:* 800-325-0058 ■ *Web:* www.parks.ky.gov	Buckhorn	KY	41721	800-325-0058	
Carr Creek State Park Hwy 15 *Web:* www.parks.ky.gov	Sassafras	KY	41759	606-642-4050	
Columbus-Belmont State Park 350 Pk Rd *Web:* www.parks.ky.gov	Columbus	KY	42032	270-677-2327	
Constitution Square State Historic Site 134 S Second St *Web:* www.parks.ky.gov	Danville	KY	40422	859-239-7089	
Cumberland Falls State Resort Park 7351 Hwy 90 *TF:* 800-325-0063 ■ *Web:* www.parks.ky.gov	Corbin	KY	40701	800-325-0063	
Dr Thomas Walker State Historic Site 4929 KY 459 *Web:* www.parks.ky.gov	Barbourville	KY	40906	606-546-4400	
EP "Tom" Sawyer State Park 3000 Freys Hill Rd *Web:* www.parks.ky.gov	Louisville	KY	40241	502-429-7270	429-7273
Fishtrap Lake State Park 2204 Fishtrap Rd *Web:* www.parks.ky.gov/stateparks/ft	Shelbiana	KY	41562	606-437-7496	
Fort Boonesborough State Park 4375 Boonesborough Rd *Web:* www.parks.ky.gov	Richmond	KY	40475	859-527-3131	
General Burnside Island State Park 8801 S Hwy 27 *Web:* www.parks.ky.gov	Burnside	KY	42519	606-561-4104	
Grayson Lake State Park 314 Grayson Lk Pk Rd *Web:* www.parks.ky.gov	Olive Hill	KY	41164	606-474-9727	
Green River Lake State Park 179 Pk Office Rd *Web:* www.parks.ky.gov	Campbellsville	KY	42718	270-465-8255	
Jenny Wiley State Resort Park 75 Theatre Ct *TF:* 800-325-0142 ■ *Web:* www.parks.ky.gov	Prestonsburg	KY	41653	800-325-0142	
John James Audubon State Park 3100 US Hwy 41 N *Web:* www.parks.ky.gov	Henderson	KY	42419	270-826-2247	
Kenlake State Resort Park 542 Kenlake Rd *TF:* 800-325-0143 ■ *Web:* www.parks.ky.gov/findparks/resortparks/kl	Hardin	KY	42048	270-474-2211	
Kincaid Lake State Park 565 Kincaid Pk Rd *Web:* www.parks.ky.gov	Falmouth	KY	41040	859-654-3531	
Kingdom Come State Park 502 Pk Rd *Web:* www.parks.ky.gov	Cumberland	KY	40823	606-589-2479	
Lake Barkley State Resort Park 3500 State Pk Rd *TF:* 800-325-1708 ■ *Web:* parks.ky.gov/findparks/resortparks/lb	Cadiz	KY	42211	800-325-1708	
Levi Jackson State Park 998 Levi Jackson Mill Rd *Web:* www.parks.ky.gov	London	KY	40744	606-330-2130	
Lincoln Homestead State Park 5079 Lincoln Pk Rd *Web:* www.parks.ky.gov	Springfield	KY	40069	859-336-7461	
Mineral Mound State Park 48 Finch Ln *Web:* www.parks.ky.gov	Eddyville	KY	42038	270-388-3673	
My Old Kentucky Home State Park 501 E Stephen Foster Ave *Web:* www.parks.ky.gov	Bardstown	KY	40004	502-348-3502	
Natural Bridge State Resort Park 2135 Natural Bridge Rd *TF:* 800-325-1710 ■ *Web:* www.parks.ky.gov	Slade	KY	40376	800-325-1710	
Nolin Lake State Park PO Box 340 *Web:* www.parks.ky.gov	Bee Spring	KY	42207	270-286-4240	
Old Fort Harrod State Park 100 S College St *Web:* www.parks.ky.gov	Harrodsburg	KY	40330	859-734-3314	
Old Mulkey Meetinghouse State Historic Site 38 Old Mulkey Pk Rd *Web:* www.parks.ky.gov	Tompkinsville	KY	42167	270-487-8481	487-8481
Pennyrile Forest State Resort Park 20781 Pennyrile Lodge Rd *TF:* 800-325-1711 ■ *Web:* www.parks.ky.gov	Dawson Springs	KY	42408	800-325-1711	
Pine Mountain State Resort Park 1050 State Pk Rd *TF:* 800-325-1712 ■ *Web:* www.parks.ky.gov	Pineville	KY	40977	800-325-1712	
Rough River Dam State Resort Park 450 Lodge Rd *TF:* 800-325-1713 ■ *Web:* www.parks.ky.gov	Falls of Rough	KY	40119	800-325-1713	
Taylorsville Lake State Park 1320 Pk Rd *Web:* www.parks.ky.gov	Taylorsville	KY	40071	502-477-8713	
Waveland Museum State Historic Site 225 Waveland Museum Ln *Web:* www.parks.ky.gov	Lexington	KY	40514	859-272-3611	

	City	State	Zip	Phone	Fax
White Hall State Historic Site 500 White Hall Shrine Rd *Web:* www.parks.ky.gov	Richmond	KY	40475	859-623-9178	
Wickliffe Mounds State Historic Site 94 Green St *Web:* www.parks.ky.gov/parks/historicsites/wickliffe-mounds/default.aspx	Wickliffe	KY	42087	270-335-3681	
William Whitley House State Historic Site 625 William Whitley Rd *Web:* www.parks.ky.gov	Stanford	KY	40484	606-355-2881	
Yatesville Lake State Park PO Box 767 *Web:* www.parks.ky.gov	Louisa	KY	41230	606-673-1492	

Louisiana

	City	State	Zip	Phone	Fax
Bayou Segnette State Park 7777 Westbank Expy. *TF:* 888-677-2296 ■ *Web:* www.crt.state.la.us	Westwego	LA	70094	504-736-7140	436-4788
Centenary State Historic Site 3522 College St *TF:* 888-677-2364 ■ *Web:* www.crt.state.la.us	Jackson	LA	70748	225-634-7925	
Chemin-A-Haut State Park 14656 State Pk Rd. *TF:* 888-677-2436 ■ *Web:* www.crt.state.la.us	Bastrop	LA	71220	318-283-0812	
Chicot State Park 3469 Chicot Pk Rd *TF:* 888-677-2442 ■ *Web:* www.crt.state.la.us	Ville Platte	LA	70586	337-363-2403	
Cypremort Point State Park 306 Beach Ln *TF:* 888-867-4510 ■ *Web:* www.crt.state.la.us	Cypremort Point	LA	70538	337-867-4510	
Fairview-Riverside State Park 119 Fairview Dr *TF:* 888-677-3247 ■ *Web:* www.crt.state.la.us	Madisonville	LA	70447	985-845-3318	
Fontainebleau State Park 67825 US Hwy 190. *TF:* 888-677-3668 ■ *Web:* www.crt.state.la.us	Mandeville	LA	70448	985-624-4443	
Fort Jesup State Historic Site 32 Geoghagan Rd *TF:* 888-677-5378 ■ *Web:* www.crt.state.la.us	Many	LA	71449	318-256-4117	
Fort Saint Jean Baptiste State Historic Site 155 Jefferson St *TF:* 888-677-7853 ■ *Web:* www.crt.state.la.us	Natchitoches	LA	71457	318-357-3101	
Jimmie Davis State Park 1209 State Pk Rd *TF:* 888-677-2263 ■ *Web:* www.crt.state.la.us	Chatham	LA	71226	318-249-2595	
Lake Bistineau State Park 103 State Pk Rd. *TF:* 888-677-2478 ■ *Web:* www.crt.state.la.us	Doyline	LA	71023	318-745-3503	
Lake Bruin State Park 201 State Pk Rd *TF:* 888-677-2784 ■ *Web:* www.crt.state.la.us	Saint Joseph	LA	71366	318-766-3530	
Lake Claiborne State Park 225 State Pk Rd *TF:* 888-677-2524 ■ *Web:* www.crt.state.la.us	Homer	LA	71040	318-927-2976	
Lake D'Arbonne State Park 3628 Evergreen Rd *TF:* 888-677-5200 ■ *Web:* www.crt.state.la.us	Farmerville	LA	71241	318-368-2086	
Longfellow-Evangeline State Historic Site 1200 N Main St *TF:* 888-677-2900 ■ *Web:* www.crt.state.la.us	Saint Martinville	LA	70582	337-394-3754	
Los Adaes State Historic Site 6354 Hwy 485 *TF:* 888-677-5378 ■ *Web:* www.crt.state.la.us	Robeline	LA	71469	318-472-9449	
Louisiana State Arboretum 4213 Chicot Pk Rd *TF:* 888-677-6100 ■ *Web:* www.crt.state.la.us	Ville Platte	LA	70586	337-363-6289	
Mansfield State Historic Site 15149 Hwy 175 *TF:* 888-677-6267 ■ *Web:* www.crt.state.la.us	Mansfield	LA	71052	318-872-1474	
Marksville State Historic Site 837 ML King Dr *TF:* 888-253-8954 ■ *Web:* www.crt.state.la.us	Marksville	LA	71351	318-253-8954	
North Toledo Bend State Park 2907 N Toledo Pk Rd *TF:* 888-677-6400 ■ *Web:* www.crt.state.la.us	Zwolle	LA	71486	318-645-4715	
Palmetto Island State Park 19501 Pleasant Rd *TF:* 888-677-3668	Abbeville	LA	70510	337-893-3930	
Port Hudson State Historic Site 236 Hwy 61 *TF:* 888-677-3400 ■ *Web:* www.crt.state.la.us	Jackson	LA	70748	225-654-3775	654-4413
Poverty Point Reservoir State Park 1500 Poverty Pt Pkwy *TF:* 800-474-0392 ■ *Web:* www.crt.state.la.us	Delhi	LA	71232	318-878-7536	
Poverty Point State Historic Site 6859 Hwy 577 *TF:* 888-926-5492 ■ *Web:* www.crt.state.la.us	Pioneer	LA	71266	318-926-5492	
Rebel State Historic Site 1260 Hwy 1221 *TF:* 888-677-3600 ■ *Web:* www.crt.state.la.us	Marthaville	LA	71450	318-472-6255	
Saint Bernard State Park 501 St Bernard Pkwy *TF:* 888-677-7823 ■ *Web:* www.crt.state.la.us	Braithwaite	LA	70040	504-682-2101	
Sam Houston Jones State Park 107 Sutherland Rd *TF:* 888-677-7264 ■ *Web:* www.crt.state.la.us	Lake Charles	LA	70611	337-855-2665	
South Toledo Bend State Park 120 Bald Eaglel Rd *TF:* 888-398-4770 ■ *Web:* www.crt.state.la.us	Anacoco	LA	71403	337-286-9075	
Tickfaw State Park 27225 Patterson Rd. *TF:* 888-981-2020 ■ *Web:* www.crt.state.la.us	Springfield	LA	70462	225-294-5020	
Winter Quarters State Historic Site 4929 Hwy 608 *TF:* 888-677-9468 ■ *Web:* www.crt.state.la.us	Newellton	LA	71357	318-467-9750	

Maine

	City	State	Zip	Phone	Fax
Allagash Wilderness Waterway 106 Hogan Rd Ste 7 *Web:* www.maine.gov	Bangor	ME	04401	207-941-4014	
Aroostook State Park 87 State Pk Rd *Web:* www.maine.gov	Presque Isle	ME	04769	207-768-8341	
Baxter State Park 64 Balsam Dr *Web:* www.baxterstateparkauthority.com	Millinocket	ME	04462	207-723-5140	
Birch Point Beach State Park c/o Bureau of Parks & Lands 106 Hogan Rd. *Web:* maine.gov/dacf/mgs/index.shtml	Bangor	ME	04401	207-941-4014	
Bradbury Mountain State Park 528 Hallowell Rd *Web:* www.maine.gov	Pownal	ME	04069	207-688-4712	
Camden Hills State Park 280 Belfast Rd *Web:* www.maine.gov	Camden	ME	04843	207-236-3109	
Cobscook Bay State Park 40 S Edmunds Rd *Web:* www.maine.gov	Dennysville	ME	04628	207-726-4412	
Colonial Pemaquid State Historic Site Two Colonial Pemaquid Dr *Web:* www.maine.gov	New Harbor	ME	04554	207-677-2423	
Damariscotta Lake State Park Eight State Pk Rd *Web:* www.maine.gov	Jefferson	ME	04348	207-549-7600	
Ferry Beach State Park 95 Bayview Rd *Web:* www.maine.gov	Saco	ME	04072	207-283-0067	
Fort Edgecomb State Historic Site 66 Ft Rd *Web:* www.maine.gov	Edgecomb	ME	04556	207-882-7777	
Fort Halifax State on the Kennebec c/o Bureau of Parks & Lands 106 Hogan Rd. *Web:* maine.gov/dacf/parks/index.shtml	Bangor	ME	04401	207-941-4014	
Fort Kent State Historic Site 106 Hogan Rd *Web:* www.maine.gov/cgi-bin/online/doc/parksearch/index.pl	Bangor	ME	04401	207-941-4014	
Fort Knox State Historic Site 711 Ft Knox Rd *Web:* maine.gov/dacf/parks/index.shtml	Prospect	ME	04981	207-469-7719	
Fort McClary State Historic Site 28 Oldsfields Rd *Web:* maine.gov/dacf/parks/index.shtml	S. Berwick	ME	03908	207-384-5160	
Fort O'Brien State Historic Site 106 Hogan Rd *Web:* www.maine.gov/cgi-bin/online/doc/parksearch/index.pl	Bangor	ME	04401	207-941-4014	
Fort Point State Park c/o Bureau of Parks & Lands 106 Hogan Rd. *Web:* maine.gov/dacf/parks/index.shtml	Bangor	ME	04401	207-941-4014	
Fort Popham State Historic Site 10 Perkins Farm Ln *Web:* www.maine.gov	Phippsburg	ME	04562	207-389-1335	
Grafton Notch State Park 1941 Bear River Rd. *Web:* www.maine.gov	Newry	ME	04261	207-824-2912	
Holbrook Island Sanctuary PO Box 35 *Web:* www.maine.gov	Brooksville	ME	04617	207-326-4012	
John Paul Jones State Historic Site c/o Bureau of Parks & Lands *TF:* 800-452-1942 ■ *Web:* maine.gov/dacf/parks/index.shtml	Bangor	ME	04401	207-941-4014	941-4222
Katahdin Iron Works State Historic Site c/o Bureau of Parks & Lands 106 Hogan Rd. *Web:* maine.gov/dacf/mgs/index.shtml	Bangor	ME	04401	207-941-4014	
Lake Saint George State Park 278 Belfast Augusta Rd. *Web:* www.maine.gov	Liberty	ME	04949	207-589-4255	
Lamoine State Park 23 State Pk Rd *Web:* www.maine.gov	Lamoine	ME	04605	207-667-4778	
Lily Bay State Park 13 Myrle's Way *Web:* www.maine.gov	Greenville	ME	04441	207-695-2700	
Moose Point State Park 310 W Main St *Web:* www.maine.gov	Searsport	ME	04974	207-548-2882	
Mount Blue State Park Ctr Hill RR1 PO Box 610 *Web:* www.maine.gov	Weld	ME	04285	207-585-2261	
Peaks-Kenny State Park 401 State Pk Rd *Web:* www.maine.gov	Dover-Foxcroft	ME	04426	207-564-2003	
Popham Beach State Park 10 Perkins Farm Ln *Web:* www.maine.gov	Phippsburg	ME	04562	207-389-1335	
Quoddy Head State Park 973 S Lubec Rd *Web:* www.maine.gov	Lubec	ME	04652	207-733-0911	
Range Ponds State Park PO Box 475 *Web:* www.maine.gov	Poland Spring	ME	04274	207-998-4104	
Rangeley Lake State Park HC 32 PO Box 5000 *Web:* www.maine.gov	Rangeley	ME	04970	207-864-3858	
Reid State Park 375 Seguinland Rd. *Web:* www.maine.gov	Georgetown	ME	04548	207-371-2303	
Roque Bluffs State Park 145 Schoppee Pt Rd *Web:* www.maine.gov	Roque Bluffs	ME	04654	207-255-3475	
Sebago Lake State Park 11 Pk Access Rd. *Web:* www.maine.gov	Casco	ME	04055	207-693-6613	
Shackford Head State Park 106 Hogan Ave *Web:* www.maine.gov/cgi-bin/online/doc/parksearch/search_name.pl?state_park=68	Bangor	ME	04401	207-941-4014	
Swan Lake State Park 100 W Pk Ln *Web:* www.maine.gov	Swanville	ME	04915	207-525-4404	
Two Lights State Park Seven Tower Dr *Web:* www.maine.gov	Cape Elizabeth	ME	04107	207-799-5871	
Vaughan Woods State Park 28 Oldfields Rd. *Web:* www.maine.gov/cgi-bin/online/doc/parksearch/index.pl	South Berwick	ME	03908	207-287-3200	
Warren Island State Park PO Box 105 *Web:* www.maine.gov	Lincolnville	ME	04849	207-446-7090	
Whaleback Shell Midden State Historic Site PO Box 333 *Web:* www.maine.gov	Damariscotta	ME	04543	207-563-1393	
Wolfe's Neck Woods State Park 426 Wolfe's Neck Rd *Web:* www.maine.gov	Freeport	ME	04032	207-865-4465	

Maryland

				Phone	Fax
Assateague State Park 7307 Stephen Decatur Hwy *TF:* 888-432-2267 ■ *Web:* dnr2.maryland.gov/	Berlin	MD	21811	410-641-2120	641-3615
Big Run State Park c/o New Germany State Pk 10368 Savage River Rd *Web:* dnr2.maryland.gov/publiclands/pages/western/bigrun.aspx	Swanton	MD	21561	301-895-5453	
Calvert Cliffs State Park 10540 H. G. Trueman Road PO Box 1042 *Web:* dnr2.maryland.gov/publiclands/pages/southern/calvertcliffs.aspx	Lusby	MD	20657	301-743-7613	
Casselman River Bridge State Park 580 Taylor Ave Tawes State Ofc Bldg *TF:* 877-620-8367 ■ *Web:* dnr2.maryland.gov/	Annapolis	MD	21401	877-620-8367	
Cedarville State Forest 10201 Bee Oak Rd *Web:* dnr2.maryland.gov/	Brandywine	MD	20613	301-888-1410	
Choptank River Fishing Piers 29761 Bolingbroke Pt Dr *Web:* dnr2.maryland.gov/	Trappe	MD	21673	410-820-1668	
Cunningham Falls State Park 14039 Catoctin Hollow Rd *Web:* www.dnr.state.md.us/publiclands/western/cunningham.asp	Thurmont	MD	21788	301-271-7574	
Elk Neck State Park 4395 Turkey Pt Rd *Web:* dnr2.maryland.gov/	North East	MD	21901	410-287-5333	
Fair Hill Natural Resources Management Area 300 Tawes Dr *Web:* dnr2.maryland.gov/	Elkton	MD	21921	410-398-1246	
Fort Frederick State Park 11100 Ft Frederick Rd *Web:* dnr2.maryland.gov	Big Pool	MD	21711	301-842-2155	
Gambrill State Park 8602 Gambrill Pk Rd *TF:* 800-830-3974 ■ *Web:* www.dnr.state.md.us/publiclands/western/gambrill.asp	Frederick	MD	21702	301-271-7574	
Garrett State Forest 1431 Potomac Camp Rd *Web:* www.dnr.state.md.us/publiclands/western/garrettforest.asp	Oakland	MD	21550	301-334-2038	
Green Ridge State Forest 28700 Headquarters Dr NE *Web:* dnr2.maryland.gov/	Flintstone	MD	21530	301-478-3124	
Greenbrier State Park 21843 National Pk *Web:* dnr2.maryland.gov/	Boonsboro	MD	21713	301-791-4767	
Greenwell State Park 25450 Rosedale Manor Ln PO Box 198 *Web:* www.greenwellfoundation.org	Hollywood	MD	20636	301-373-9775	373-4735
Gunpowder Falls State Park 2813 Jerusalem Rd PO Box 480 *Web:* dnr2.maryland.gov/	Kingsville	MD	21087	410-592-2897	
Hart-Miller Island State Park c/o Gunpowder Falls State Pk 2813 Jerusalem Rd PO Box 480 *Web:* dnr2.maryland.gov/	Kingsville	MD	21087	410-592-2897	
Herrington Manor State Park 222 Herrington Ln *Web:* dnr.state.md.us	Oakland	MD	21550	301-334-9180	
Janes Island State Park 26280 Alfred Lawson Dr *TF:* 877-620-8367 ■ *Web:* dnr2.maryland.gov/	Crisfield	MD	21817	410-968-1565	968-2515
Martinak State Park 137 Deep Shore Rd *Web:* dnr2.maryland.gov/	Denton	MD	21629	410-820-1668	
Merkle Wildlife Sanctuary 580 Taylor Ave *TF:* 877-620-8367 ■ *Web:* dnr2.maryland.gov/	Annapolis	MD	21401	877-620-8367	
Monocacy River Natural Resources Management Area c/o Seneca Creek State Pk 11950 Clopper Rd *Web:* dnr2.maryland.gov/	Gaithersburg	MD	20878	301-924-2127	
Morgan Run Natural Environment Area Benros Ln *TF:* 800-830-3974 ■ *Web:* www.dnr.state.md.us/publiclands/central/morganrun.asp	Eldersburg	MD	21784	410-461-5005	
New Germany State Park 349 Headquarters Ln *TF:* 800-830-3974 ■ *Web:* www.dnr.state.md.us/publiclands/western/newgermany.asp	Grantsville	MD	21536	301-895-5453	
Patapsco Valley State Park 8020 Baltimore National Pk *Web:* dnr2.maryland.gov/	Ellicott City	MD	21043	410-461-5005	
Patuxent River State Park c/o Seneca Creek State Pk 11950 Clopper Rd *Web:* www.dnr.state.md.us/publiclands/central/patuxentriver.asp	Gaithersburg	MD	20878	301-924-2127	
Pocomoke River State Park 3461 Worcester Hwy *TF:* 877-620-8367 ■ *Web:* dnr2.maryland.gov/	Snow Hill	MD	21863	410-632-2566	632-2914
Pocomoke State Forest 580 Taylor Ave *TF:* 877-620-8367 ■ *Web:* dnr2.maryland.gov/	Annapolis	MD	21401	877-620-8367	
Point Lookout State Park 11175 Pt Lookout Rd *Web:* dnr2.maryland.gov/	Scotland	MD	20687	301-872-5688	872-5084
Potomac-Garrett State Forest 1431 Potomac Camp Rd *Web:* dnr2.maryland.gov/	Oakland	MD	21550	301-334-2038	
Rocks State Park 3318 Rocks Chrome Hill Rd *Web:* dnr.state.md.us	Jarrettsville	MD	21084	410-557-7994	
Rocky Gap State Park 12500 Pleasant Vly Rd *Web:* www.dnr.state.md.us/publiclands/western/rockygap.asp	Flintstone	MD	21530	301-722-1480	
Rosaryville State Park 7805 W Marlton Ave *Web:* www.dnr.state.md.us/publiclands/southern/rosaryville.asp	Upper Marlboro	MD	20735	301-856-9656	
Saint Mary's River State Park c/o Pt Lookout State Pk 11175 Pt Lookout Rd *TF:* 800-830-3974 ■ *Web:* www.dnr.state.md.us/publiclands/southern/stmarysriver.asp	Scotland	MD	20687	301-872-5688	
Sandy Point State Park 1100 E College Pkwy *TF:* 877-620-8836 ■ *Web:* dnr2.maryland.gov/	Annapolis	MD	21409	410-974-2149	974-2647
Sassafras Natural Resources Management Area 13070 Crouse Mill Rd *Web:* www.dnr.state.md.us/publiclands/eastern/sassafras.asp	Queen Anne	MD	21657	410-820-1668	
Seneca Creek State Park 11950 Clopper Rd *Web:* dnr2.maryland.gov/	Gaithersburg	MD	20878	301-924-2127	
Smallwood State Park 2750 Sweden Pt Rd *Web:* dnr.state.md.us	Marbury	MD	20658	301-743-7613	
Soldiers Delight Natural Environment Area 5100 Deer Park Rd *TF:* 800-830-3974 ■ *Web:* www.dnr.state.md.us/publiclands/central/soldiersdelight.asp	Owings Mills	MD	21117	410-461-5005	
Somers Cove Marina 715 Broadway PO Box 67 *TF:* 800-967-3474 ■ *Web:* dnr2.maryland.gov/	Crisfield	MD	21817	410-968-0925	968-1408
South Mountain State Park c/o S Mtn Recreation Area 21843 National Pk *Web:* www.dnr.state.md.us/publiclands/western/southmountain.asp	Boonsboro	MD	21713	301-791-4767	
Swallow Falls State Park c/o Herrington Manor State Pk 222 Herrington Ln *Web:* www.dnr.state.md.us/publiclands/western/swallowfalls.asp	Oakland	MD	21550	301-387-6938	
Tuckahoe State Park 13070 Crouse Mill Rd *Web:* dnr2.maryland.gov/	Queen Anne	MD	21657	410-820-1668	
Washington Monument State Park c/o Greenbrier State Pk 6620 Zittlestown Rd *Web:* www.dnr.state.md.us/publiclands/western/washington.asp	Middletown	MD	21769	301-791-4767	
Wye Island Natural Resources Management Area 632 Wye Island Rd *Web:* dnr2.maryland.gov/	Queenstown	MD	21658	410-827-7577	
Wye Oak State Park c/o Tuckahoe State Pk 13070 Crouse Mill Rd *Web:* www.dnr.state.md.us/publiclands/eastern/wyeoak.asp	Queen Anne	MD	21657	410-820-1668	
Youghiogheny River Natural Resources Management Area c/o Deep Creek Lake State Pk 898 State Pk Rd *TF:* 877-620-8367 ■ *Web:* dnr2.maryland.gov/	Swanton	MD	21561	301-387-5563	387-4462

Massachusetts

				Phone	Fax
Ames Nowell State Park Linwood St *Web:* www.mass.gov	Abington	MA	02351	781-857-1336	
Beartown State Forest 69 Blue Hill Rd *Web:* www.mass.gov/eea/agencies/dcr/massparks/regionwest/beartownstateforest.html	Monterey	MA	01245	413-528-0904	
Blackstone River & Canal Heritage State Park 287 Oak St *Web:* www.mass.gov	Uxbridge	MA	01569	508-278-7604	
Blue Hills Reservation 695 Hillside St *Web:* www.mass.gov/dcr/parks/metroboston/blue.htm	Milton	MA	02186	617-698-1802	
Borderland State Park Massapoag Ave *Web:* www.mass.gov	North Easton	MA	02356	508-238-6566	
Brimfield State Forest 86 Dearth Hill Rd *Web:* www.mass.gov	Brimfield	MA	01010	413-267-9687	
Chicopee Memorial State Park 570 Burnett Rd *Web:* www.mass.gov	Chicopee Falls	MA	01020	413-594-9416	
Clarksburg State Park 1199 Middle Rd *Web:* www.mass.gov	Clarksburg	MA	01247	413-664-8345	
Connecticut River Greenway State Park 136 Damon Rd *Web:* mass.gov	NorthHampton	MA	01060	413-586-8706	
DAR State Forest 78 Cape St Rt 112	Goshen	MA	01032	413-268-7098	
Demarest Lloyd State Park 115 Barneys Joy Rd *Web:* www.mass.gov	Dartmouth	MA	02748	508-636-3298	
Dighton Rock State Park Bay View Ave *Web:* www.mass.gov	Berkley	MA	02779	508-822-7537	
Douglas State Forest 107 Wallum Lk Rd *Web:* www.mass.gov	Douglas	MA	01516	508-476-7872	
Dunn State Park Rt 101 *Web:* www.mass.gov/dcr/parks/central/dunn.htm	Gardner	MA	01440	978-632-7897	
Ellisville Harbor State Park 198 Purgatory Rd *Web:* www.mass.gov	Sutton	MA	01590	508-234-3733	
Erving State Forest 200 E Main St Rt 2A *Web:* www.mass.gov	Erving	MA	01344	978-544-3939	
F. Gilbert Hills State Forest 45 Mill St *Web:* www.mass.gov	Foxboro	MA	02035	508-543-5850	
Fall River Heritage State Park Davol St *Web:* www.mass.gov	Fall River	MA	02720	508-675-5759	
Fort Phoenix State Reservation Green St	Fairhaven	MA	02719	508-992-4524	
Freetown-Fall River State Forest 110 Slab Bridge Rd *Web:* www.mass.gov	Assonet	MA	02702	508-644-5522	
Gardner Heritage State Park (GHSP) 26 Lake St *Web:* www.mass.gov/dcr/parks/central/ghsp.htm	Gardner	MA	01440	978-632-7897	
Granville State Forest 323 W Hartland Rd *Web:* www.mass.gov	Granville	MA	01034	413-357-6611	
Great Brook Farm State Park 984 Lowell Rd PO Box 0829 *Web:* www.mass.gov	Carlisle	MA	01741	978-369-6312	
Halibut Point State Park Gott Ave *Web:* www.mass.gov	Rockport	MA	01966	978-546-2997	
Hampton Ponds State Park 1048 N Rd *Web:* www.mass.gov	Westfield	MA	01085	413-532-3985	533-1837

	City	State	ZIP	Phone	Fax
Harold Parker State Forest					
305 Middleton Rd	North Andover	MA	01845	978-686-3391	
Web: www.mass.gov					
Holyoke Heritage State Park 221 Appleton St	Holyoke	MA	01040	413-534-1723	
Web: mass.gov					
Hopkinton State Park 71 Cedar St	Hopkinton	MA	01748	508-435-4303	
Web: www.mass.gov					
Horseneck Beach State Reservation					
Five John Reed Rd	Westport	MA	02791	508-636-8816	
Web: www.mass.gov					
JA Skinner State Park PO Box 91	Hadley	MA	01035	413-586-0350	
Web: www.mass.gov					
Lake Wyola State Park 94 Lk View Rd	Shutesbury	MA	01072	413-367-0317	
Web: www.mass.gov					
Lawrence Heritage State Park One Jackson St	Lawrence	MA	01840	978-794-1655	
Web: www.mass.gov					
Leominster State Forest					
90 Fitchburg Rd Rt 31	Westminster	MA	01473	978-874-2303	
Web: www.mass.gov					
Lowell Heritage State Park 160 Pawtucket Blvd	Lowell	MA	01854	978-458-8750	
Massasoit State Park Middleboro Ave	East Taunton	MA	02718	508-822-7405	
Web: www.mass.gov					
Maudslay State Park 74 Curzon Mill Rd	Newburyport	MA	01950	978-465-7223	
Web: www.mass.gov					
Mohawk Trail State Forest					
175 Mohawk Trl/ Rt 2 PO Box 7	Charlemont	MA	01339	413-339-5504	
Moore State Park Mill St	Paxton	MA	01612	508-792-3969	
Web: www.mass.gov					
Mount Everett State Reservation					
c/o Rd 3 E St	Mount Washington	MA	01258	413-528-0330	
Mount Grace State Forest Winchester Rd	Warwick	MA	01378	978-544-3939	
Web: www.mass.gov					
Mount Greylock State Reservation					
30 Rockwell Rd	Lanesborough	MA	01237	413-499-4262	
Web: www.mass.gov					
Mount Sugarloaf State Reservation					
300 Sugarloaf St	South Deerfield	MA	01373	413-665-2928	
Web: www.mass.gov					
Mount Tom State Reservation 125 Resv Rd	Holyoke	MA	01040	413-534-1186	
Web: mass.gov					
Mount Washington State Forest					
Rd 3 E St	Mount Washington	MA	01258	413-528-0330	
Myles Standish Monument State Reservation					
Crescent St Duxbury	Duxbury	MA	02332	508-747-5360	
Web: www.mass.gov					
Myles Standish State Forest					
Cranberry Rd	South Carver	MA	02366	508-866-2526	
Web: www.mass.gov					
Natural Bridge State Park					
McCauley Rd off Rte 8 PO Box 1757	North Adams	MA	01247	413-663-6392	
Web: www.mass.gov					
Nickerson State Park 3488 Main St Rt 151	Brewster	MA	02631	508-896-3491	
Web: mass.gov					
October Mountain State Forest 317 Woodland Rd	Lee	MA	01238	413-243-1778	
Web: www.mass.gov					
Otter River State Forest					
86 Winchendon Rd	Baldwinville	MA	01436	978-939-8962	
Web: www.mass.gov/dcr/parks/central/ottr.htm					
Pittsfield State Forest 1041 Cascade St	Pittsfield	MA	01201	413-442-8992	
Web: www.mass.gov/dcr/parks/western/pitt.htm					
Purgatory Chasm State Reservation					
Purgatory Rd	Sutton	MA	01590	508-234-3733	
Web: www.mass.gov					
Quinsigamond State Park 10 Lake Ave N	Worcester	MA	01612	508-755-6880	755-5347
Web: www.mass.gov					
Robinson State Park 428 N St PO Box 42	Feeding Hills	MA	01030	413-786-2877	
Web: www.mass.gov					
Roland C. Nickerson State Park					
c/o Nickerson State Pk 3488 Main St	Brewster	MA	02631	508-896-3491	
Rutland State Park Two Crawford Rd	Rutland	MA	01543	508-886-6333	
Web: www.mass.gov					
Salisbury Beach State Reservation					
Beach Rd Rt 1A	Salisbury	MA	01952	978-462-4481	
Savoy Mountain State Forest					
260 Central Shaft Rd	Florida	MA	01247	413-663-8469	
Web: www.mass.gov					
Schooner Ernestina					
New Bedford State Pier	New Bedford	MA	02741	508-992-4900	
Web: ernestina.org					
Scusset Beach State Reservation					
20 Scusset Beach Rd	Sandwich	MA	02563	508-888-0859	
Web: www.mass.gov					
South Cape Beach State Park Great Oak Rd	Mashpee	MA	02649	508-457-0495	
Web: www.mass.gov					
Spencer State Forest Howe Pond Rd	Spencer	MA	01562	508-886-6333	
Web: www.mass.gov					
Streeter Point Recreation Area					
Six Ster Pt Ave	Sturbridge	MA	01566	508-347-9316	
Web: www.mass.gov/dcr/parks/central/stpt.htm					
Tolland State Forest					
410 Tolland Rd PO Box 342	East Otis	MA	01029	413-269-6002	
Web: www.mass.gov					
Upton State Forest 205 Westboro Rd	Upton	MA	01568	508-278-6486	
Web: www.mass.gov					
Wachusett Mountain State Reservation					
345 Mountain Rd	Princeton	MA	01541	978-464-2987	
Web: www.mass.gov					
Walden Pond State Reservation 915 Walden St	Concord	MA	01742	978-369-3254	
Web: www.mass.gov					
Watson Pond State Park Bay Rd	Taunton	MA	02780	508-884-8280	
Web: www.mass.gov					
Wells State Park 159 Walker Pond Rd	Sturbridge	MA	01566	508-347-9257	
Web: www.mass.gov/dcr/parks/central/well.htm					
Wendell State Forest Montague Rd	Wendell	MA	01379	413-659-3797	
Web: www.mass.gov					
Western Gateway Heritage State Park					
115 State St Ste 4	North Adams	MA	01247	413-663-6312	
Web: www.mass.gov					
Willard Brook State Forest 595 Main St	Townsend	MA	01474	978-597-8802	
Web: www.mass.gov					
Wompatuck State Park 204 Union St	Hingham	MA	02043	781-749-7160	
Web: www.mass.gov					

Michigan

	City	State	ZIP	Phone	Fax
Albert E. Sleeper State Park					
6573 State Pk Rd	Caseville	MI	48725	989-856-4411	856-3590
Web: www.michigan.org/property/albert-e-sleeper-state-park					
Algonac State Park 8732 River Rd	Marine City	MI	48039	810-765-5605	
Web: www.michigandnr.com					
Bald Mountain Recreation Area					
1330 E Greenshield Rd	Lake Orion	MI	48360	248-693-6767	
Web: www.michigandnr.com					
Baraga State Park 1300 US Hwy 41 S	Baraga	MI	49908	906-353-6558	
Web: www.michigandnr.com					
Bay City Recreation Area 3582 State Pk Dr	Bay City	MI	48706	989-684-3020	
Web: www.michigandnr.com					
Bewabic State Park 720 Idlewild Rd	Crystal Falls	MI	49920	906-875-3324	
Web: www.michigandnr.com					
Brighton Recreation Area 6360 Chilson Rd	Howell	MI	48843	810-229-6566	
Web: www.michigandnr.com					
Brimley State Park 9200 W 6-Mile Rd	Brimley	MI	49715	906-248-3422	
Web: www.michigandnr.com					
Burt Lake State Park 6635 State Pk Dr	Indian River	MI	49749	231-238-9392	
Web: www.michigandnr.com					
Charles Mears State Park 400 W Lowell St	Pentwater	MI	49449	231-869-2051	
Web: www.michigandnr.com					
Cheboygan State Park 4490 Beach Rd	Cheboygan	MI	49721	231-627-2811	
Web: www.michigandnr.com					
Coldwater Lake State Park Copeland Rd	Coldwater	MI	49036	517-780-7866	
Web: www.michigandnr.com					
Craig Lake State Park					
851 County Rd AKE PO Box 88	Champion	MI	49814	906-339-4461	
Web: michigandnr.com					
Dodge #4 State Park 4250 Pkwy Dr	Waterford	MI	48327	248-682-7323	
Web: www.michigandnr.com					
Duck Lake State Park 3560 Memorial Dr	North Muskegon	MI	49445	231-744-3480	
Web: www.michigandnr.com/parksandtrails/details.aspx?type=sprk&id=446					
Fayette Historic State Park 13700 1325 Ln	Garden	MI	49835	906-644-2603	
Web: www.michigandnr.com					
Fisherman's Island State Park					
Bells Bay Rd PO Box 456	Charlevoix	MI	49720	231-547-6641	
Web: www.michigandnr.com					
FJ McLain State Park 18350 Hwy M-203	Hancock	MI	49930	906-482-0278	
Web: www.michigandnr.com					
Fort Custer Recreation Area					
5163 Ft Custer Dr	Augusta	MI	49012	269-731-4200	
Web: www.michigandnr.com					
Fort Wilkins State Park					
15223 US Hwy 41	Copper Harbor	MI	49918	906-289-4215	
Web: www.michigandnr.com					
Grand Haven State Park 1001 S Harbor Ave	Grand Haven	MI	49417	616-847-1309	
Web: www.michigandnr.com					
Harrisville State Park					
248 State Pk Rd PO Box 326	Harrisville	MI	48740	989-724-5126	
Hartwick Pines State Park 4216 Ranger Rd	Grayling	MI	49738	989-348-7068	
Web: www.michigandnr.com					
Highland Recreation Area					
5200 E Highland Rd	White Lake	MI	48383	248-889-3750	
Web: www.michigandnr.com					
Historic Mill Creek Discovery Park					
9001 US-23 PO Box 370	Mackinac Island	MI	49701	231-436-4100	847-3815*
**Fax Area Code:* 906 ■ *Web:* mackinacparks.com/parks-and-attractions					
Holland State Park 2215 Ottawa Beach Rd	Holland	MI	49424	616-399-9390	
Web: www.michigandnr.com					
Holly Recreation Area 8100 Grange Hall Rd	Holly	MI	48442	248-634-8811	
Web: www.michigandnr.com					
Interlochen State Park M-137	Interlochen	MI	49643	231-276-9511	
Web: www.michigandnr.com					
Ionia Recreation Area 2880 W David Hwy	Ionia	MI	48846	616-527-3750	
Web: www.michigandnr.com					
Island Lake Recreation Area					
12950 E Grand River Rd	Brighton	MI	48116	810-229-7067	
Web: www.michigandnr.com					
JW Wells State Park N7670 Hwy M-35	Cedar River	MI	49887	906-863-9747	
Web: www.michigandnr.com					
Kal-Haven Trail State Park					
4143 10th St N Commission PO Box 156	Kalamazoo	MI	49009	269-674-8011	
Web: www.michigandnr.com/parksandtrails/Details.aspx?type=SPRK&id=463					
Lake Gogebic State Park					
N9995 State Hwy M-64	Marenisco	MI	49947	906-842-3341	
Web: www.michigandnr.com					
Lake Hudson Recreation Area 5505 Morey Hwy	Clayton	MI	49235	517-445-2265	
Web: www.michigandnr.com					
Lakelands Trail State Park					
8555 Silver Hill Rd 8555 Silver Hill Rt 1	Pinckney	MI	48169	734-426-4913	
Web: www.michigan.gov					
Lakeport State Park 7605 Lakeshore Rd	Saint Clair	MI	48059	810-327-6224	
Web: www.michigandnr.com					
Leelanau State Park					
15310 N Lighthouse Pt Rd	Northport	MI	49670	231-386-5422	
Web: www.michigandnr.com					
Ludington State Park PO Box 709	Ludington	MI	49431	231-843-2423	
Web: www.michigandnr.com					

Park	City	State	ZIP	Phone	Fax
Maybury State Park 20145 Beck Rd *Web:* www.michigandnr.com	Northville	MI	48167	248-349-8390	
Meridian-Baseline State Park 16345 McClure Rd *Web:* www.michigandnr.com/parksandtrails/details.aspx?type=sprk&id=471	Chelsea	MI	48118	734-475-8307	
Metamora-Hadley Recreation Area 3871 Herd Rd *Web:* www.michigandnr.com	Metamora	MI	48455	810-797-4439	
Muskallonge Lake State Park 30042 County Rd 407 *Web:* www.michigandnr.com	Newberry	MI	49868	906-658-3338	
Muskegon State Park 3560 Memorial Dr *Web:* www.michigandnr.com/parksandtrails/details.aspx?type=sprk&id=475	North Muskegon	MI	49445	231-744-3480	
Newaygo State Park 2793 Beech St *Web:* www.michigandnr.com	Newaygo	MI	49337	231-856-4452	
North Higgins Lake State Park 11747 N Higgins Lk Dr *Web:* www.michigandnr.com/parksandtrails/details.aspx?id=478&type=sprk	Roscommon	MI	48653	989-821-6125	
Orchard Beach State Park 2064 N Lakeshore Rd *Web:* www.michigandnr.com	Manistee	MI	49660	231-723-7422	
Ortonville Recreation Area 5779 Hadley Rd *Web:* www.michigandnr.com	Ortonville	MI	48462	810-797-4439	
Otsego Lake State Park 7136 Old 27 S *Web:* michigandnr.com	Gaylord	MI	49735	989-732-5485	
Petoskey State Park 2475 M-119 Hwy *Web:* www.michigandnr.com	Petoskey	MI	49712	231-347-2311	
PH Hoeft State Park 5001 US Hwy 23 N *Web:* www.michigandnr.com	Rogers City	MI	49779	989-734-2543	
Pinckney Recreation Area 8555 Silver Hill *Web:* michigandnr.com	Pinckney	MI	48169	734-426-4913	
PJ Hoffmaster State Park 6585 Lk Harbor Rd *Web:* www.michigandnr.com	Muskegon	MI	49441	231-798-3711	
Pontiac Lake Recreation Area 7800 Gale Rd *Web:* www.michigandnr.com/parksandtrails/details.aspx?id=485&type=sprk	Waterford	MI	48327	248-666-1020	
Porcupine Mountains Wilderness State Park 33303 Headquarters Rd *Web:* www.michigandnr.com	Ontonagon	MI	49953	906-885-5275	
Port Crescent State Park 1775 Port Austin Rd *Web:* www.michigandnr.com	Port Austin	MI	48467	989-738-8663	
Rifle River Recreation Area 2550 Rose City Rd *Web:* www.michigandnr.com	Lupton	MI	48635	989-473-2258	
Seven Lakes State Park 14390 Fish Lk Rd *Web:* www.michigandnr.com	Holly	MI	48442	248-634-7271	
Sleepy Hollow State Park 7835 E Price Rd *Web:* www.michigandnr.com	Laingsburg	MI	48848	517-651-6217	
South Higgins Lake State Park 106 State Pk Dr *Web:* www.michigandnr.com	Roscommon	MI	48653	989-821-6374	
Sterling State Park 2800 State Pk Rd *Web:* www.michigandnr.com	Monroe	MI	48162	734-289-2715	
Straits State Park 720 Church St *Web:* www.michigandnr.com	Saint Ignace	MI	49781	906-643-8620	
Tahquamenon Falls State Park 41382 W M-123 *Web:* www.michigandnr.com	Paradise	MI	49768	906-492-3415	
Tawas Point State Park 686 Tawas Beach Rd *Web:* www.michigandnr.com	East Tawas	MI	48730	989-362-5041	
Thompson's Harbor State Park c/o Cheboygan Field Office 120 A St PO Box 117 *Web:* www.michigan.gov	Cheboygan	MI	49721	231-627-9011	
Traverse City State Park 1132 US-31 N *Web:* www.michigandnr.com	Traverse City	MI	49686	231-922-5270	
Tri-Centennial State Park & Harbor 1900 Atwater St *Web:* www.michigandnr.com	Detroit	MI	48207	313-396-0217	
Van Buren State Park 23960 Ruggles Rd *Web:* michigandnr.com	South Haven	MI	49090	269-637-2788	
Van Buren Trail State Park 23960 Ruggles Rd *Web:* www.michigandnr.com	South Haven	MI	49090	269-637-2788	
Van Riper State Park 851 County Rd AKE PO Box 88 *Web:* www.michigandnr.com	Champion	MI	49814	906-339-4461	
Warren Dunes State Park 12032 Red Arrow Hwy *Web:* www.michigandnr.com	Sawyer	MI	49125	269-426-4013	
Waterloo Recreation Area 16345 McClure Rd *Web:* www.michigandnr.com	Chelsea	MI	48118	734-475-8307	
Wilderness State Park 903 Wilderness Pk Dr *Web:* www.michigandnr.com	Carp Lake	MI	49718	231-436-5381	
William Michell State Park Camp Grounds 6093 E M-115	Cadillac	MI	49601	231-775-7911	
William Mitchell State Park 6093 E M-115	Cadillac	MI	49601	231-775-7911	
Wilson State Park 910 N First St PO Box 333 *Web:* www.michigandnr.com	Harrison	MI	48625	989-539-3021	
WJ Hayes State Park 1220 Wampler's Lk Rd *Web:* www.michigandnr.com	Onsted	MI	49265	517-467-7401	
Yankee Springs Recreation Area 2104 S Briggs Rd *Web:* www.michigandnr.com	Middleville	MI	49333	269-795-9081	
Young State Park 02280 Boyne City Rd *Web:* www.michigandnr.com	Boyne City	MI	49712	231-582-7523	

Minnesota

Park	City	State	ZIP	Phone	Fax
Afton State Park 6959 Peller Ave S *TF:* 800-366-8917 ■ *Web:* www.dnr.state.mn.us	Hastings	MN	55033	651-436-5391	436-6912
Banning State Park 61101 Banning Pk Rd PO Box 643 *Web:* www.dnr.state.mn.us	Sandstone	MN	55072	320-245-2668	245-0251
Bear Head Lake State Park 9301 Bear Head State Pk Rd *Web:* www.dnr.state.mn.us	Ely	MN	55731	218-365-7229	365-7204
Beaver Creek Valley State Park 15954 County Rd 1 *Web:* www.dnr.state.mn.us	Caledonia	MN	55921	507-724-2107	724-2107
Big Bog State Recreation Area 55716 Hwy 72 NE *Web:* www.dnr.state.mn.us	Waskish	MN	56685	218-647-8592	647-8730
Big Stone Lake State Park 35889 Meadowbrook State Pk Rd *TF:* 888-646-6367 ■ *Web:* www.dnr.state.mn.us	Ortonville	MN	56278	320-839-3663	839-3676
Blue Mounds State Park 1410 161st St *TF:* 888-646-6367 ■ *Web:* www.dnr.state.mn.us	Luverne	MN	56156	507-283-1307	283-1306
Buffalo River State Park 155 S St Hwy 10 PO Box 352 *Web:* www.dnr.state.mn.us	Glyndon	MN	56547	218-498-2124	498-2583
Camden State Park 1897 County Rd *Web:* www.dnr.state.mn.us	Lynd	MN	56157	507-865-4530	865-4608
Carley State Park 19041 Hwy 74 *TF:* 888-646-6367 ■ *Web:* www.stateparks.com/carley.html	Altura	MN	55910	507-932-3007	
Cascade River State Park 3481 W Hwy 61 *Web:* www.dnr.state.mn.us	Lutsen	MN	55612	218-387-3053	387-3054
Charles A. Lindbergh State Park 1615 Lindbergh Dr S PO Box 364 *TF:* 888-646-6367 ■ *Web:* www.dnr.state.mn.us	Little Falls	MN	56345	320-616-2525	616-2526
Crow Wing State Park 3124 State Pk Rd *TF:* 888-646-6367 ■ *Web:* www.dnr.state.mn.us	Brainerd	MN	56401	218-825-3075	825-3077
Cuyuna Country State Recreation Area 307 Third St PO Box 404 *Web:* www.dnr.state.mn.us	Ironton	MN	56455	218-546-5926	546-7369
Father Hennepin State Park 41294 Father Hennepin Pk Rd PO Box 397 *TF:* 888-646-6367 ■ *Web:* www.dnr.state.mn.us	Isle	MN	56342	320-676-8763	676-3748
Flandrau State Park 1300 Summit Ave *Web:* www.dnr.state.mn.us	New Ulm	MN	56073	507-233-9800	
Forestville/Mystery Cave State Park 21071 County 118 *TF:* 888-646-6367 ■ *Web:* www.dnr.state.mn.us	Preston	MN	55965	507-352-5111	352-5113
Fort Ridgely State Park 72158 County Rd 30 *TF:* 888-646-6367 ■ *Web:* www.dnr.state.mn.us	Fairfax	MN	55332	507-426-7840	426-7112
Fort Snelling State Park 101 Snelling Lake Rd *TF:* 888-646-6367 ■ *Web:* www.dnr.state.mn.us	Saint Paul	MN	55111	612-725-2389	725-2391
Franz Jevne State Park State Hwy 11 3684 54th Ave NW *Web:* www.dnr.state.mn.us/state_parks/franz_jevne	Birchdale	MN	56629	218-783-6252	783-6253
Frontenac State Park 29223 County 28 Blvd *TF:* 888-646-6367 ■ *Web:* www.dnr.state.mn.us	Frontenac	MN	55026	651-345-3401	345-3694
Garden Island State Recreation Area c/o Zippel Bay State Pk 3684 54th Ave NW *Web:* www.dnr.state.mn.us/state_parks/garden_island	Williams	MN	56686	218-783-6252	783-6253
George H. Crosby Manitou State Park c/o Tettegouche State Pk 5702 Hwy 61 *TF:* 888-646-6367 ■ *Web:* www.dnr.state.mn.us/state_parks/george_crosby_manitou	Silver Bay	MN	55614	218-226-6365	226-6366
Glacial Lakes State Park 25022 County Rd 41 *TF:* 888-646-6367 ■ *Web:* www.dnr.state.mn.us	Starbuck	MN	56381	320-239-2860	239-4605
Glendalough State Park 25287 Whitetail Ln *Web:* www.dnr.state.mn.us/state_parks/glendalough/index.html	Battle Lake	MN	56515	218-864-0110	864-0587
Gooseberry Falls State Park 3206 Hwy 61 *TF:* 888-646-6367 ■ *Web:* www.dnr.state.mn.us/state_parks/gooseberry_falls	Two Harbors	MN	55616	218-834-3855	834-3787
Grand Portage State Park 9393 E Hwy 61 *TF:* 888-646-6367 ■ *Web:* www.dnr.state.mn.us	Grand Portage	MN	55605	218-475-2360	475-2365
Great River Bluffs State Park 43605 Kipp Dr *TF:* 888-646-6367 ■ *Web:* www.dnr.state.mn.us	Winona	MN	55987	507-643-6849	643-6849
Hayes Lake State Park 48990 County Rd 4 *Web:* www.dnr.state.mn.us/state_parks/hayes_lake	Roseau	MN	56751	218-425-7504	
Itasca State Park 36750 Main Pk Dr *Web:* www.dnr.state.mn.us	Park Rapids	MN	56470	218-266-2100	266-3942
Jay Cooke State Park 780 Hwy 210 *Web:* www.dnr.state.mn.us	Carlton	MN	55718	218-384-4610	384-4851
Judge CR Magney State Park 4051 E Hwy 61 *Web:* www.dnr.state.mn.us	Grand Marais	MN	55604	218-387-3039	
Kilen Woods State Park 50200 860th St *Web:* www.dnr.state.mn.us	Lakefield	MN	56150	507-831-2900	
Lac Qui Parle State Park 14047 20th St NW *Fax Area Code: 320 ■ *Web:* www.dnr.state.mn.us	St. Paul	MN	55155	651-296-6157	734-4452*
Lake Bemidji State Park 500 Lafayette Rd *Fax Area Code: 218 ■ *Web:* www.dnr.state.mn.us	St. Paul	MN	55155	651-296-6157	755-4073*
Lake Bronson State Park County Hwy 28 *Web:* www.dnr.state.mn.us	Lake Bronson	MN	56734	218-754-2200	754-6141
Lake Carlos State Park 2601 County Rd 38 NE *Web:* www.dnr.state.mn.us	Carlos	MN	56319	320-852-7200	852-7349
Lake Louise State Park c/o Forestville/Mystery Cave State Pk 21071 County Rd 118 *Web:* www.dnr.state.mn.us	Preston	MN	55965	507-352-5111	352-5113
Lake Maria State Park 11411 Clementa Ave NW *Web:* www.dnr.state.mn.us	Monticello	MN	55362	763-878-2325	878-2620
Lake Shetek State Park 163 State Pk Rd *Web:* www.dnr.state.mn.us	Currie	MN	56123	507-763-3256	763-3330
Maplewood State Park 39721 Pk Entrance Rd *Web:* www.dnr.state.mn.us	Pelican Rapids	MN	56572	218-863-8383	
McCarthy Beach State Park 7622 McCarthy Beach Rd *Web:* www.dnr.state.mn.us	Side Lake	MN	55781	218-254-7979	254-7980

				Phone	Fax
Mille Lacs Kathio State Park 15066 Kathio State Pk Rd *Web:* www.dnr.state.mn.us	Onamia	MN	56359	320-532-3523	532-3529
Minneopa State Park 54497 Gadwall Rd *Web:* www.dnr.state.mn.us	Mankato	MN	56001	507-389-5464	389-5174
Minnesota Valley State Recreation Area 19825 Park Blvd 101 Snelling Lk Rd *Web:* www.dnr.state.mn.us	Jordan	MN	55352	651-259-5774	
Monson Lake State Park 1690 15th St NE *Web:* www.dnr.state.mn.us	Sunburg	MN	56289	320-366-3797	
Moose Lake State Park 4252 County Rd 137 *Web:* www.dnr.state.mn.us	Moose Lake	MN	55767	218-485-5420	485-5422
Myre-Big Island State Park 19499 780th Ave. *TF:* 888-646-6367 ■ *Web:* www.dnr.state.mn.us	Albert Lea	MN	56007	507-379-3403	379-3405
Nerstrand-Big Woods State Park 9700 170th St E *Web:* www.dnr.state.mn.us	Nerstrand	MN	55053	507-333-4840	333-4852
Old Mill State Park 33489 240th Ave NW Rt 1 PO Box 43 *Web:* www.dnr.state.mn.us	Argyle	MN	56713	218-437-8174	437-8104
Red River State Recreation Area 515 Second St NW *Web:* www.dnr.state.mn.us	East Grand Forks	MN	56721	218-773-4950	773-4951
Rice Lake State Park 8485 Rose St *Web:* www.dnr.state.mn.us	Owatonna	MN	55060	507-455-5871	446-2326
Saint Croix State Park 30065 St Croix Pk Rd. *TF:* 888-646-6367 ■ *Web:* www.dnr.state.mn.us	Hinckley	MN	55037	320-384-6591	384-7070
Sakatah Lake State Park 50499 Sakatah Lake State Pk Rd. *TF:* 888-646-6367 ■ *Web:* www.dnr.state.mn.us	Waterville	MN	56096	507-362-4438	362-4558
Savanna Portage State Park 55626 Lake Pl. *TF:* 888-646-6367 ■ *Web:* www.dnr.state.mn.us	McGregor	MN	55760	218-426-3271	426-4437
Scenic State Park 56956 Scenic Hwy 7 *Web:* www.dnr.state.mn.us	Bigfork	MN	56628	218-743-3362	743-1362
Sibley State Park 800 Sibley Pk Rd. *TF:* 888-646-6367 ■ *Web:* www.dnr.state.mn.us	New London	MN	56273	320-354-2055	354-2372
Soudan Underground Mine State Park 1302 McKinley Park Rd *TF:* 888-646-6367 ■ *Web:* www.dnr.state.mn.us	Soudan	MN	55782	218-753-2245	753-2246
Split Rock Creek State Park 50th Ave. *TF:* 888-646-6367 ■ *Web:* www.dnr.state.mn.us	Jasper	MN	56144	507-348-7908	348-8940
Split Rock Lighthouse State Park 3755 Split Rock Lighthouse Rd *TF:* 800-366-8917 ■ *Web:* www.dnr.state.mn.us/state_parks/split_rock_lighthouse	Two Harbors	MN	55616	218-595-7625	226-6378
Temperance River State Park 7620 W Hwy 61 PO Box 33 *Web:* www.dnr.state.mn.us	Schroeder	MN	55613	218-663-7476	
Tettegouche State Park 5702 Hwy 61 *TF:* 800-366-8917 ■ *Web:* www.dnr.state.mn.us/state_parks/tettegouche	Silver Bay	MN	55614	218-226-6365	226-6366
Upper Sioux Agency State Park 5908 Hwy 67 *TF:* 800-366-8917 ■ *Web:* www.dnr.state.mn.us	Granite Falls	MN	56241	320-564-4777	564-4838
Whitewater State Park 19041 Hwy 74 *TF:* 800-366-8917 ■ *Web:* www.dnr.state.mn.us	Altura	MN	55910	507-932-3007	932-5938
Wild River State Park 39797 Pk Trl *Web:* www.dnr.state.mn.us	Center City	MN	55012	651-583-2125	583-3101
William O'Brien State Park 16821 O'Brien Trl N *Web:* www.dnr.state.mn.us	Marine-on-Saint Croix	MN	55047	651-433-0500	
Zippel Bay State Park 3684 54th Ave NW *Web:* www.dnr.state.mn.us/state_parks/zippel_bay	Williams	MN	56686	218-783-6252	783-6253

Mississippi

				Phone	Fax
Buccaneer State Park 1150 S Beach Blvd. *Web:* www.mdwfp.com	Waveland	MS	39576	228-467-3822	
Clarkco State Park 386 Clarkco Rd *Web:* www.mdwfp.com/parkview/parks.asp?id=4842	Quitman	MS	39355	601-776-6651	
Golden Memorial State Park 2104 Damascus Rd. *Web:* www.mdwfp.com/parkview/parks.asp?id=4843	Walnut Grove	MS	39189	601-253-2237	
Holmes County State Park 5369 State Pk Rd *Web:* www.mdwfp.com/parkview/parks.asp?id=3824	Durant	MS	39063	662-653-3351	
John W. Kyle State Park 4235 State Pk Rd *Web:* www.mdwfp.com	Sardis	MS	38666	662-487-1345	
JP Coleman State Park 613 County Rd 321 *Web:* www.mdwfp.com/parkview/parks.asp?id=1814	Iuka	MS	38852	662-423-6515	
Lake Lincoln State Park 2573 Sunset Dr. *Web:* reserveamerica.com	Wesson	MS	39191	601-643-9044	
Lake Lowndes State Park 3319 Lk Lowndes Rd *Web:* www.mdwfp.com	Columbus	MS	39702	662-328-2110	
LeFleur's Bluff State Park 2140 Riverside Dr. *TF:* 800-237-6278 ■ *Web:* www.mdwfp.com	Jackson	MS	39202	601-987-3923	354-6930
Legion State Park 635 Legion State Pk Rd *Web:* www.mdwfp.com	Louisville	MS	39339	662-773-8323	
Leroy Percy State Park PO Box 176. *Web:* www.mdwfp.com	Hollandale	MS	38748	662-827-5436	
Natchez State Park 230-B Wickcliff Rd *Web:* www.mdwfp.com	Natchez	MS	39120	601-442-2658	442-4148
Percy Quin State Park 2036 Percy Quin Dr *Web:* www.mdwfp.com/parkview/parks.asp?id=5847	McComb	MS	39648	601-684-3938	
Roosevelt State Park 2149 Hwy 13 S *Web:* www.mdwfp.com	Morton	MS	39117	601-732-6316	
Shepard State Park 1034 Graveline Rd. *Web:* www.mdwfp.com	Gautier	MS	39553	228-497-2244	
Tombigbee State Park 264 Cabin Dr. *TF:* 800-467-2757 ■ *Web:* www.mdwfp.com	Tupelo	MS	38804	662-842-7669	840-5594
Wall Doxey State Park 3946 Hwy 7 S. *Web:* www.mdwfp.com	Holly Springs	MS	38635	662-252-4231	

Missouri

				Phone	Fax
Arrow Rock State Historic Site PO Box 1. *Web:* www.mostateparks.com	Arrow Rock	MO	65320	660-837-3330	
Battle of Lexington State Historic Site 1101 Deleware *Web:* www.mostateparks.com	Lexington	MO	64067	660-259-4654	
Bennett Spring State Park 26250 Hwy 64A *Web:* www.mostateparks.com	Lebanon	MO	65536	417-532-4338	
Big Lake State Park 204 Lk Shore Dr *Web:* www.mostateparks.com	Craig	MO	64437	660-442-3770	
Big Oak Tree State Park 13640 S Hwy 102 *Web:* www.mostateparks.com	East Prairie	MO	63845	573-649-3149	
Bollinger Mill State Historic Site 113 Bollinger Mill Rd *Web:* www.mostateparks.com	Burfordville	MO	63739	573-243-4591	
Bothwell Lodge State Historic Site 19349 Bothwell State Pk Rd *Web:* www.mostateparks.com	Sedalia	MO	65301	660-827-0510	
Castlewood State Park 1401 Kiefer Creek Rd *Web:* www.mostateparks.com	Ballwin	MO	63021	636-227-4433	
Confederate Memorial State Historic Site 211 W First St. *Web:* www.mostateparks.com	Higginsville	MO	64037	660-584-2853	
Crowder State Park 76 Hwy 128. *Web:* www.mostateparks.com	Trenton	MO	64683	660-359-6473	
Cuivre River State Park 678 State Rt 147 *Web:* www.mostateparks.com	Troy	MO	63379	636-528-7247	
Dillard Mill State Historic Site 142 DillaRd Mill Rd *Web:* www.mostateparks.com	Davisville	MO	65456	573-244-3120	
Dr. Edmund A Babler Memorial State Park 800 Guy Pk Dr *Web:* www.mostateparks.com	Wildwood	MO	63005	636-458-3813	
Edward Ted & Pat Jones- Confluence Point State Park 1000 Riverlands Way *Web:* www.mostateparks.com/park/edward-ted-and-pat-jones-confluence-point-state-park	West Alton	MO	63386	636-899-1135	
Felix Valle House State Historic Site 198 Merchant St. *Web:* mostateparks.com/park/felixvallehousestatehistoricsite	Sainte Genevieve	MO	63670	573-883-7102	
Finger Lakes State Park 1505 E Peabody Rd *Web:* www.mostateparks.com	Columbia	MO	65202	573-443-5315	443-4999
Fort Davidson State Historic Site 118 E Maple *Web:* www.mostateparks.com/ftdavidson.htm	Pilot Knob	MO	63663	573-546-3454	
General John J. Pershing Boyhood Home State Historic Site 1100 Pershing Dr *Web:* www.mostateparks.com	Laclede	MO	64651	660-963-2525	
Governor Daniel Dunklin's Grave State Historic Site PO Box 176 2901 Hwy 61. *TF:* 800-334-6946 ■ *Web:* www.mostateparks.com	Jefferson City	MO	65102	800-334-6946	
Ha Ha Tonka State Park 1491 State Rd D *Web:* www.mostateparks.com	Camdenton	MO	65020	573-346-2986	
Harry S Truman Birthplace State Historic Site 1009 Truman St *Web:* www.mostateparks.com	Lamar	MO	64759	417-682-2279	
Harry S Truman State Park 28761 State Pk Rd *Web:* www.mostateparks.com	Warsaw	MO	65355	660-438-7711	
Hawn State Park 12096 Pk Dr. *Web:* www.mostateparks.com	Sainte Genevieve	MO	63670	573-883-3603	
Hunter-Dawson State Historic Site PO Box 308 *Web:* www.mostateparks.com	New Madrid	MO	63869	573-748-5340	
Iliniwek Village State Historic Site c/o Battle of Athens State Historic Site Rt 1 PO Box 26 *Web:* www.mostateparks.com	Revere	MO	63465	660-877-3871	
Jefferson Landing State Historic Site & Missouri State Museum 201 W Capitol First Fl State Capitol *Web:* mostateparks.com/park/missouristatemuseum	Jefferson City	MO	65101	573-751-2854	
Jewell Cemetery State Historic Site c/o Rock Bridge Memorial State Pk 5901 S Hwy 163 *Web:* www.mostateparks.com/jewellcem.htm	Columbia	MO	65203	573-449-7402	
Johnson's Shut-Ins State Park 148 Taum Sauk Trl *Web:* mostateparks.com/park/johnsons-shut-ins-state-park	Middlebrook	MO	63656	573-546-2450	
Knob Noster State Park 873 SE 10th *Web:* www.mostateparks.com	Knob Noster	MO	65336	660-563-2463	
Lake of the Ozarks State Park PO Box 170 *Web:* www.mostateparks.com	Kaiser	MO	65047	573-348-2694	
Lake Wappapello State Park Hwy 172 *Web:* www.mostateparks.com	Williamsville	MO	63967	573-297-3232	
Lewis & Clark State Park 801 Lk Crest Blvd *Web:* www.mostateparks.com	Rushville	MO	64484	816-579-5564	
Long Branch State Park 28615 Visitor Ctr Rd *Web:* www.mostateparks.com	Macon	MO	63552	660-773-5229	
Mark Twain Birthplace State Historic Site 37352 Shrine Rd. *Web:* mostateparks.com/park/mark-twain-birthplace-state-historic-site	Florida	MO	65283	573-565-3449	
Mark Twain State Park 20057 State Pk Rd. *Web:* www.mostateparks.com	Stoutsville	MO	65283	573-565-3440	
Mastodon State Historic Site 1050 Charles J Becker Dr *TF:* 800-334-6946 ■ *Web:* www.mostateparks.com	Imperial	MO	63052	636-464-2976	
Meramec State Park 115 Meramec Pk Dr *Web:* www.mostateparks.com	Sullivan	MO	63080	573-468-6072	
Missouri Mines State Historic Site 4000 Missouri 32 *Web:* www.mostateparks.com	Park Hills	MO	63601	573-431-6226	
Missouri State Parks PO Box 176 *TF:* 800-334-6946 ■ *Web:* www.mostateparks.com	Jefferson City	MO	65102	800-334-6946	

				Phone	Fax
Montauk State Park 345 County Rd 6670 *Web:* www.mostateparks.com	Salem	MO	65560	573-548-2201	
Nathan Boone Homestead State Historic Site 7850 N State Hwy V *Web:* www.mostateparks.com	Ash Grove	MO	65604	417-751-3266	
Onondaga Cave State Park 7556 Hwy H *Web:* www.mostateparks.com	Leasburg	MO	65535	573-245-6576	
Pershing State Park 29277 Hwy 130 *Web:* www.mostateparks.com	Laclede	MO	64651	660-963-2299	
Pomme de Terre State Park Hwy 64B *Web:* www.mostateparks.com/park/pomme-de-terre-state-park	Pittsburg	MO	65724	417-852-4291	
Prairie State Park 128 NW 150th Ln *Web:* www.mostateparks.com	Mindenmines	MO	64769	417-843-6711	
Roaring River State Park 12716 Farm Rd 2239 *Web:* mostateparks.com	Cassville	MO	65625	417-847-2539	
Robertsville State Park 900 State Pk Dr *Web:* www.mostateparks.com	Robertsville	MO	63077	636-257-3788	
Rock Bridge Memorial State Park 5901 S Hwy 163 *TF:* 800-334-6946 ■ *Web:* www.mostateparks.com	Columbia	MO	65203	573-449-7402	442-2249
Route 66 State Park 97 N Outer Rd Ste 1 *Web:* www.mostateparks.com	Eureka	MO	63025	636-938-7198	938-7804
Saint Francois State Park 8920 US Hwy 67 N *Web:* www.mostateparks.com	Bonne Terre	MO	63628	573-358-2173	
Saint Joe State Park 2800 Pimville Rd *Web:* www.mostateparks.com	Park Hills	MO	63601	573-431-1069	
Sam A. Baker State Park Rt 1 PO Box 18150 *Web:* www.mostateparks.com	Patterson	MO	63956	573-856-4411	
Sandy Creek Covered Bridge State Historic Site c/o Mastodon State Historic Site 1050 Museum Dr *Web:* www.mostateparks.com	Imperial	MO	63052	636-464-2976	
Scott Joplin House State Historic Site 2658 Delmar Blvd *Web:* www.mostateparks.com	Saint Louis	MO	63103	314-340-5790	340-5793
Stockton State Park 19100 S Hwy 215 *Web:* www.mostateparks.com	Dadeville	MO	65635	417-276-4259	
Taum Sauk Mountain State Park 148 Taum Sauk Trl *Web:* mostateparks.com/park/taum-sauk-mountain-state-park	Middlebrook	MO	63656	573-546-2450	
Thomas Hart Benton Home & Studio State Historic Site 3616 Belleview *Web:* www.mostateparks.com	Kansas City	MO	64111	816-931-5722	
Thousand Hills State Park 20431 State Hwy 157 *Web:* www.mostateparks.com	Kirksville	MO	63501	660-665-6995	
Trail of Tears State Park 429 Moccasin Springs *Web:* www.mostateparks.com	Jackson	MO	63755	573-290-5268	
Van Meter State Park 32146 N Hwy 122 *Web:* www.mostateparks.com	Miami	MO	65344	660-886-7537	
Wakonda State Park 32836 State Pk Rd *Web:* www.mostateparks.com	LaGrange	MO	63448	573-655-2280	
Wallace State Park 10621 NE Hwy 121 *Web:* www.mostateparks.com	Cameron	MO	64429	816-632-3745	
Washington State Park 13041 State Hwy 104 *Web:* www.mostateparks.com	DeSoto	MO	63020	636-586-2995	
Watkins Woolen Mill State Park & State Historic Site 26600 Pk Rd N *Web:* www.mostateparks.com	Lawson	MO	64062	816-580-3387	
Weston Bend State Park 16600 Hwy 45 N *Web:* www.mostateparks.com	Weston Bend	MO	64098	816-640-5443	

Montana

				Phone	Fax
Ackley Lake State Park 4600 Giant Springs Rd *Web:* www.fwp.mt.gov	Great Falls	MT	59405	406-454-5840	
Anaconda Smoke Stack State Park 3201 Spurgin Rd FWP Reg 2 Ofc *Web:* stateparks.mt.gov	Missoula	MT	59804	406-542-5500	
Bannack State Park 4200 Bannack Rd *TF:* 855-922-6768 ■ *Web:* www.bannack.org	Dillon	MT	59725	406-834-3413	834-3548
Beaverhead Rock State Park c/o Bannack State Pk 4200 Bannack Rd *Web:* stateparks.mt.gov	Dillon	MT	59725	406-834-3413	
Beavertail Hill State Park 3201 Spurgin Rd FWP Reg 2 Ofc *Web:* stateparks.mt.gov	Missoula	MT	59804	406-542-5500	
Big Arm State Park 490 N Meridian Rd *Web:* www.fwp.mt.gov	Kalispell	MT	59901	406-752-5501	
Black Sandy State Park 1420 E 6thAve PO Box 200701 *Web:* stateparks.mt.gov	Helena	MT	59620	406-444-2535	
Chief Plenty Coups State Park PO Box 100 *Web:* www.fwp.mt.gov	Pryor	MT	59066	406-252-1289	
Clark's Lookout State Park c/o Bannack State Pk 4200 Bannack Rd *Web:* stateparks.mt.gov	Dillon	MT	59725	406-834-3413	
Cooney State Park PO Box 254 *Web:* www.fwp.mt.gov	Joliet	MT	59041	406-445-2326	
Council Grove State Park 3201 Spurgin Rd FWP Reg 2 Ofc *Web:* stateparks.mt.gov	Missoula	MT	59804	406-542-5500	
Elkhorn State Park 1420 E 6thAve PO Box 200701 *Web:* stateparks.mt.gov	Helena	MT	59620	406-444-2535	
Finley Point State Park 490 N Meridian Rd *Web:* www.fwp.mt.gov	Kalispell	MT	59901	406-752-5501	
First Peoples Buffalo Jump State Park 342 Ulm Vaughn Rd *Web:* www.fwp.mt.gov	Ulm	MT	59485	406-866-2217	
Fort Owen State Park PO Box 995 *Web:* stateparks.mt.gov	Lolo	MT	59847	406-273-4253	
Frenchtown Pond State Park 3201 Spurgin Rd FWP Reg 2 Ofc *Web:* stateparks.mt.gov	Missoula	MT	59804	406-542-5500	
Giant Springs State Park 4600 Giant Springs Rd *TF:* 855-922-6768 ■ *Web:* www.fwp.mt.gov	Great Falls	MT	59405	406-454-5840	761-8477
Granite Ghost Town State Park 3201 Spurgin Rd *Web:* stateparks.mt.gov	Missoula	MT	59804	406-542-5500	
Greycliff Prairie Dog Town State Park 2300 Lk Elmo Dr *Web:* stateparks.mt.gov	Billings	MT	59105	406-247-2940	
Hell Creek State Park PO Box 1630 *Web:* fwp.mt.gov/	Miles City	MT	59301	406-557-2362	
Lake Elmo State Park 2300 Lk Elmo Dr *Web:* stateparks.mt.gov	Billings	MT	59105	406-247-2955	
Lake Mary Ronan State Park 490 N Meridian Rd *Web:* www.fwp.mt.gov	Kalispell	MT	59901	406-752-5501	
Lewis & Clark Caverns State Park PO Box 489 *Web:* stateparks.mt.gov	Whitehall	MT	59759	406-287-3541	
Lone Pine State Park 490 N Meridian *Web:* www.fwp.mt.gov	Kalispell	MT	59901	406-752-5501	
Lost Creek State Park 3201 Spurgin Rd *Web:* stateparks.mt.gov	Missoula	MT	59804	406-542-5500	
Madison Buffalo Jump State Park 1400 S 19th St *Web:* www.fwp.mt.gov	Bozeman	MT	59715	406-994-4042	
Makoshika State Park PO Box 1242 *Web:* www.fwp.mt.gov	Glendive	MT	59330	406-377-6256	
Medicine Rocks State Park PO Box 1630 *Web:* fwp.mt.gov/	Miles City	MT	59301	406-234-0926	
Missouri Headwaters State Park 1400 S 19th Ave *Web:* www.stateparks.mt.gov	Bozeman	MT	59715	406-994-4042	
Painted Rocks State Park 3201 Spurgin Rd *Web:* stateparks.mt.gov	Missoula	MT	59804	406-542-5500	
Pirogue Island State Park PO Box 1630 *Web:* fwp.mt.gov/	Miles City	MT	59301	406-234-0926	
Placid Lake State Park PO Box 136 *Web:* stateparks.mt.gov	Seeley Lake	MT	59868	406-677-6804	
Rosebud Battlefield State Park PO Box 1630 *Web:* fwp.mt.gov/	Miles City	MT	59301	406-757-2219	
Salmon Lake State Park PO Box 136 *Web:* stateparks.mt.gov	Seeley Lake	MT	59868	406-677-6804	
Sluice Boxes State Park 4600 Giant Springs Rd *Web:* www.fwp.mt.gov	Great Falls	MT	59406	406-454-5840	
Smith River State Park 4600 Giant Springs Rd *Web:* www.fwp.mt.gov	Great Falls	MT	59405	406-454-5840	
Spring Meadow Lake State Park 1420 E 6thAve PO Box 200701 *Web:* stateparks.mt.gov	Helena	MT	59620	406-444-2535	
Thompson Falls State Park 490 N Meridian Rd *Web:* www.fwp.mt.gov	Kalispell	MT	59901	406-752-5501	
Tongue River Reservoir State Park PO Box 1630 *Web:* fwp.mt.gov/	Miles City	MT	59301	406-757-2298	
Wayfarers State Park 490 N Meridian Rd *Web:* www.fwp.mt.gov	Kalispell	MT	59901	406-752-5501	
West Shore State Park 490 N Meridian Rd *Web:* www.fwp.mt.gov	Kalispell	MT	59901	406-752-5501	
Wild Horse Island State Park 490 N Meridian Rd *Web:* www.fwp.mt.gov	Kalispell	MT	59901	406-752-5501	
Yellow Bay State Park 490 N Meridian Rd *Web:* www.fwp.mt.gov	Kalispell	MT	59901	406-752-5501	

Nebraska

				Phone	Fax
Alexandria State Recreation Area 57426 710th Rd *Web:* outdoornebraska.ne.gov	Fairbury	NE	68352	402-729-5777	
Arbor Lodge State Historical Park PO Box 15 *Web:* outdoornebraska.ne.gov	Nebraska City	NE	68410	402-873-7222	
Arnold State Recreation Area HC 69 PO Box 117 *Web:* www.outdoornebraska.ne.gov/parks	Anselmo	NE	68813	308-749-2235	
Ash Hollow State Historical Park PO Box 70 *Web:* outdoornebraska.ne.gov	Lewellen	NE	69147	308-778-5651	
Ashfall Fossil Beds State Historical Park 86930 517th Ave *Web:* outdoornebraska.ne.gov	Royal	NE	68773	402-893-2000	
Atkinson Lake State Recreation Area PO Box 508 *Web:* outdoornebraska.ne.gov	Bassett	NE	68714	402-684-2921	
Blue River State Recreation Area 3019 Apple St *Web:* outdoornebraska.ne.gov	Lincoln	NE	68503	402-471-0641	
Bowring Ranch State Historical Park PO Box 38 *Web:* outdoornebraska.ne.gov	Merriman	NE	69218	308-684-3428	

Name / Address	City	State	Zip	Phone	Fax
Branched Oak State Recreation Area 12000 W Branched Oak Rd *Web:* outdoornebraska.ne.gov	Raymond	NE	68428	402-783-3400	
Buffalo Bill Ranch State Historical Park 2921 Scouts Rest Ranch Rd *Web:* outdoornebraska.ne.gov	North Platte	NE	69101	308-535-8035	
Calamus State Recreation Area HC 79 PO Box 20L *Web:* outdoornebraska.ne.gov	Burwell	NE	68823	308-346-5666	
Chadron State Park 15951 Hwy 385 *Web:* outdoornebraska.ne.gov	Chadron	NE	69337	308-432-6167	
Champion Mill State Historical Park 73122 338 Ave *Web:* outdoornebraska.ne.gov	Enders	NE	69027	308-737-6577	
Cheyenne State Recreation Area PO Box 944 *Web:* outdoornebraska.ne.gov	Grand Island	NE	68832	308-385-6210	
Conestoga State Recreation Area 3800 NW 105th St *Web:* outdoornebraska.ne.gov	Lincoln	NE	68524	402-796-2362	
Cottonwood Lake State Recreation Area PO Box 38 *Web:* outdoornebraska.ne.gov	Merriman	NE	69218	308-684-3428	
Crystal Lake State Recreation Area 7425 S US Hwy 281 *Web:* outdoornebraska.ne.gov	Doniphan	NE	68832	308-385-6210	
Dead Timber State Recreation Area 227 County Rd & 12 Blvd *Web:* outdoornebraska.ne.gov	Scribner	NE	68057	402-664-3597	
DLD State Recreation Area 7425 S US Hwy 281 *Web:* outdoornebraska.ne.gov	Doniphan	NE	68832	308-385-6211	
Enders Reservoir State Recreation Area 73122 338th Ave. *Web:* outdoornebraska.ne.gov	Enders	NE	69027	308-394-5118	
Eugene T Mahoney State Park 28500 W Pk Hwy *Web:* outdoornebraska.ne.gov	Ashland	NE	68003	402-944-2523	
Fort Atkinson State Historical Park PO Box 240 *TF:* 800-742-7627 ■ *Web:* outdoornebraska.ne.gov	Fort Calhoun	NE	68023	402-468-5611	468-5066
Fort Hartsuff State Historical Park RR 1 PO Box 37 *Web:* outdoornebraska.ne.gov	Burwell	NE	68823	308-346-4715	
Fort Kearny State Recreation Area c/o Ft Kearny State Historical Pk 1020 'V' Rd *Web:* outdoornebraska.ne.gov	Kearney	NE	68847	308-865-5305	
Fort Robinson State Park PO Box 392 *Web:* outdoornebraska.ne.gov	Crawford	NE	69339	308-665-2900	
Fremont Lakes State Recreation Area 2351 County Rd 18 *Web:* outdoornebraska.ne.gov	Ames	NE	68621	402-727-3290	
Game & Parks Commission 301 E State Farm Rd *Web:* www.outdoornebraska.ne.gov	North Platte	NE	69101	308-535-8025	
Indian Cave State Park 65296 720 Rd *Web:* outdoornebraska.ne.gov	Shubert	NE	68437	402-883-2575	
Keller Park State Recreation Area PO Box 508 *Web:* outdoornebraska.ne.gov	Bassett	NE	68714	402-684-2921	
Lake McConaughy State Recreation Area 1450 Hwy 61N *Web:* outdoornebraska.ne.gov	Ogallala	NE	69153	308-284-8800	
Lake Minatare State Recreation Area PO Box 188 *Web:* outdoornebraska.ne.gov	Minatare	NE	69356	308-783-2911	
Lake Ogallala State Recreation Area 1450 Hwy 61N *Web:* outdoornebraska.ne.gov	Ogallala	NE	69153	308-284-8800	
Lewis & Clark State Recreation Area 54731 897 Rd *Web:* outdoornebraska.ne.gov	Crofton	NE	68730	402-388-4169	
Long Lake State Recreation Area 524 Panzer St PO Box 508 *Web:* outdoornebraska.ne.gov	Bassett	NE	68714	402-684-2921	
Long Pine State Recreation Area 524 Panzer St PO Box 508 *Web:* outdoornebraska.ne.gov	Bassett	NE	68714	402-684-2921	
Louisville State Recreation Area 15810 Hwy 50 *Web:* outdoornebraska.ne.gov	Louisville	NE	68037	402-234-6855	
Medicine Creek State Recreation Area 40611 Rd 728 *Web:* outdoornebraska.ne.gov	Cambridge	NE	69022	308-697-4667	
Merritt Reservoir State Recreation Area 420 E First St *Web:* outdoornebraska.ne.gov	Valentine	NE	69201	402-376-3320	
Mormon Island State Recreation Area 7425 S Hwy 281 *Web:* outdoornebraska.ne.gov	Doniphan	NE	68832	308-385-6211	
Niobrara State Park 89261 522 Ave *Web:* outdoornebraska.ne.gov	Niobrara	NE	68760	402-857-3373	
North Loup State Recreation Area 7425 S US Hwy 281 *Web:* outdoornebraska.ne.gov	Doniphan	NE	68832	308-385-6211	
Oliver Reservoir State Recreation Area 210615 Hwy 71 *Web:* outdoornebraska.ne.gov	Gering	NE	69341	308-436-3777	
Pawnee State Recreation Area RR 4 PO Box 41B *Web:* outdoornebraska.ne.gov	Lincoln	NE	68524	402-796-2362	
Pelican Point State Recreation Area 640 County Rd 19 *Web:* outdoornebraska.ne.gov	Craig	NE	68019	402-374-1727	
Pibel Lake State Recreation Area HC 79 PO Box 20L *Web:* outdoornebraska.ne.gov	Burwell	NE	68823	308-346-5666	
Platte River State Park 14421 346th St. *Web:* outdoornebraska.ne.gov	Louisville	NE	68037	402-234-2217	
Ponca State Park 88090 Spur 26 E PO Box 688 *Web:* www.outdoornebraska.ne.gov/parks	Ponca	NE	68770	402-755-2284	
Riverview Marina State Recreation Area PO Box 15 *Web:* outdoornebraska.ne.gov	Nebraska City	NE	68410	402-873-7222	
Rock Creek Lake State Recreation Area 73122 338 Ave *Web:* outdoornebraska.ne.gov	Enders	NE	69027	308-394-5118	
Rock Creek Station State Historical Park 57426 710th Rd *Web:* outdoornebraska.ne.gov	Fairbury	NE	68352	402-729-5777	
Rock Creek Station State Recreation Area 57426 710th Rd *Web:* www.outdoornebraska.ne.gov/parks	Fairbury	NE	68352	402-729-5777	
Schramm Park State Recreation Area 15810 Hwy 50 *Web:* www.outdoornebraska.ne.gov/parks	Louisville	NE	68037	402-234-6855	
Sherman Reservoir State Recreation Area RR 2 PO Box 117 *Web:* outdoornebraska.ne.gov	Loup City	NE	68853	308-745-0230	
Smith Falls State Park HC 13 PO Box 25 *Web:* outdoornebraska.ne.gov	Valentine	NE	69201	402-376-1306	376-3558
Summit Lake State Recreation Area 640 County Rd 19 *Web:* outdoornebraska.ne.gov	Craig	NE	68019	402-374-1727	
Swanson Reservoir State Recreation Area RR 2 PO Box 20 *Web:* www.outdoornebraska.ne.gov/parks/guides/parksearch/showpark.asp?area_no=172	Stratton	NE	69043	308-737-6577	
Two Rivers State Recreation Area 27702 'F' St. *Web:* outdoornebraska.ne.gov	Waterloo	NE	68069	402-359-5165	
Verdon State Recreation Area RR 1 PO Box 30 *Web:* outdoornebraska.ne.gov	Shubert	NE	68437	402-883-2575	
Wagon Train State Recreation Area 3019 Apple St. *Web:* outdoornebraska.ne.gov	Lincoln	NE	68503	402-471-5566	
Walgren Lake State Recreation Area 15951 Hwy 385 *Web:* outdoornebraska.ne.gov	Chadron	NE	69337	308-432-6167	432-6102
War Axe State Recreation Area PO Box 427 *Web:* outdoornebraska.ne.gov	Gibbon	NE	68840	308-468-5700	
Wildcat Hills State Recreation Area 210615 Hwy 71 *Web:* outdoornebraska.ne.gov	Gering	NE	69341	308-436-3777	
Windmill State Recreation Area PO Box 427 *Web:* outdoornebraska.ne.gov	Gibbon	NE	68840	308-468-5700	

Nevada

Name / Address	City	State	Zip	Phone	Fax
Belmont Courthouse State Historic Site c/o Fallon Region Headquarters 16799 Lahontan Dam *Web:* parks.nv.gov/parks/belmont-courthouse/	Fallon	NV	89406	775-867-3001	
Berlin-Ichthyosaur State Park HC 61 PO Box 61200 *Web:* www.parks.nv.gov	Austin	NV	89310	775-964-2440	964-2012
Big Bend of the Colorado State Recreation Area PO Box 32850 *Web:* www.parks.nv.gov	Laughlin	NV	89028	702-298-1859	
Cathedral Gorge State Park PO Box 176 *Web:* www.parks.nv.gov	Panaca	NV	89042	775-728-4460	
Cave Lake State Park PO Box 151761 *Web:* parks.nv.gov/parks/cave-lake-state-park/	Ely	NV	89315	775-867-3001	
Dayton State Park PO Box 1478 *Web:* www.parks.nv.gov	Dayton	NV	89403	775-687-5678	
Echo Canyon State Park HC 74 PO Box 295 *Web:* www.parks.nv.gov	Pioche	NV	89043	775-962-5103	
Fort Churchill State Historic Park 10000 Hwy 95A *Web:* www.parks.nv.gov	Silver Springs	NV	89429	775-577-2345	
Kershaw-Ryan State Park PO Box 985 *Web:* parks.nv.gov/parks/kershaw-ryan-state-park/	Caliente	NV	89008	775-726-3564	726-3557
Lahontan State Recreation Area 16799 Lahontan Dam *Web:* www.parks.nv.gov	Fallon	NV	89406	775-577-2235	
Lake Tahoe Nevada State Park PO Box 8867 *Web:* www.parks.nv.gov	Incline Village	NV	89452	775-831-0494	831-2514
Mormon Station State Historic Park PO Box 302 *Web:* parks.nv.gov/parks/mormon-station-state-historic-park/	Genoa	NV	89411	775-782-2590	
Old Las Vegas Mormon Fort State Historic Park 500 E Washington Ave *Web:* www.parks.nv.gov	Las Vegas	NV	89101	702-486-3511	486-3734
Rye Patch State Recreation Area 2505 Rye Patch Reservoir Rd *Web:* www.parks.nv.gov	Lovelock	NV	89419	775-538-7321	
South Fork State Recreation Area 353 Lower S Fork Unit 8 *Web:* www.parks.nv.gov	Spring Creek	NV	89815	775-744-4346	
Spring Mountain Ranch State Park PO Box 124 *Web:* www.parks.nv.gov	Blue Diamond	NV	89004	702-875-4141	
Spring Valley State Park HC 74 PO Box 201 *Web:* www.parks.nv.gov	Pioche	NV	89043	775-962-5102	
Ward Charcoal Ovens State Historic Park PO Box 151761 *Web:* parks.nv.gov/parks/ward-charcoal-ovens-state-historic-park/	Ely	NV	89315	775-867-3001	
Washoe Lake State Park 4855 E Lk Blvd. *Web:* www.parks.nv.gov	Carson City	NV	89704	775-687-4319	

Phone Fax

Wild Horse State Recreation Area State Rte 225 .... Elko NV 89801 775-385-5939
Web: www.parks.nv.gov

New Hampshire

Phone Fax

Ahern State Park Right Way Path .... Laconia NH 03246 603-485-2034
Web: www.nhstateparks.org/explore/state-parks/ahern-state-park.aspx

Androscoggin Wayside Park 1607 Berlin Rd .... Errol NH 03579 603-538-6707
Web: www.nhstateparks.org/explore/state-parks/androscoggin-wayside-park.aspx

Annett Wayside Park Cathedral Rd.................... Rindge NH 03461 603-485-2034
Web: www.nhstateparks.org

Bear Brook State Park 157 Deerfield Rd .... Allenstown NH 03275 603-271-3556 271-3553
Web: www.nhstateparks.org

Cardigan State Park 658 Cardigan Mtn Rd .... Orange NH 03741 603-227-8745
Web: www.nhstateparks.org/explore/state-parks/cardigan-state-park.aspx

Chesterfield Gorge Natural Area
1823 Route 9 .... Chesterfield NH 03443 603-363-8373
Web: www.nhstateparks.org

Clough State Park 455 Clough Pk Rd.................. Weare NH 03281 603-529-7112
Web: www.nhstateparks.org/explore/state-parks/clough-state-park.aspx

Coleman State Park 1155 Diamond Pond Rd....... Stewartstown NH 03597 603-237-5382
Web: www.nhstateparks.org

Crawford Notch State Park Rt 302 .... Harts Location NH 03812 603-374-2272
Web: www.nhstateparks.org

Daniel Webster Birthplace 131 N Rd .... Franklin NH 03235 603-934-5057
Web: www.nhstateparks.org

Deer Mountain Campground 5309 N Main St .... Pittsburg NH 03592 603-538-6965
Web: www.nhstateparks.org/explore/state-parks/deer-mountain-campground.aspx

Dixville Notch State Park Rt 26 .... Dixville NH 03576 603-538-6707
Web: www.nhstateparks.org

Echo Lake State Park 60 Echo Lk Rd .... Conway NH 03818 603-356-2672
Web: www.nhstateparks.org/explore/state-parks/echo-lake-state-park.aspx

Endicott Rock 17 Endicott St........................ Laconia NH 03246 603-271-3556
Web: www.nhstateparks.org/explore/state-parks/endicott-rock.aspx

Forest Lake State Park 397 Forest Lk Rd .... Dalton NH 03598 603-466-3860
Web: www.nhstateparks.org/explore/state-parks/forest-lake-state-park.aspx

Fort Stark Historic Site Wildrose Ln .... New Castle NH 03854 603-436-1552
Web: www.nhstateparks.org

Franconia Notch State Park
Nine Franconia Notch Pkwy .... Franconia NH 03580 603-745-8391
Web: www.nhstateparks.org/explore/state-parks/franconia-notch-state-park.aspx

Governor Wentworth Historic Site Rt 109 .... Wolfeboro NH 03894 603-823-7722
Web: www.nhstateparks.org

Hampton Beach State Park Rt 1A.................. Hampton NH 03842 603-926-3784
Web: www.nhstateparks.org

Hannah Duston Memorial Exit 17 Off I-93 .... Boscawen NH 03303 603-271-3556
Web: www.nhstateparks.org

Jenness State Beach 2280 Ocean Blvd .... Rye NH 03870 603-436-1552
Web: www.nhstateparks.org/explore/state-parks/jenness-state-beach.aspx

John Wingate Weeks Historic Site
200 Weeks State Park Rd .... Lancaster NH 03584 603-788-4004
Web: www.nhstateparks.org/explore/state-parks/weeks-state-park.aspx

Kingston State Park 124 Main St.................... Kingston NH 03848 603-642-5471
Web: www.nhstateparks.org

Lake Francis State Park 439 River Rd............... Pittsburg NH 03592 603-538-6965
Web: www.nhstateparks.org/parkspages/lakefrancis/lakefrancis.html

Lake Tarleton State Park 949 Rt 25C .... Piermont NH 03779 603-823-7722
Web: www.nhstateparks.org

Madison Boulder Natural Area 473 Boulder Rd....... Madison NH 03849 603-227-8745
Web: www.nhstateparks.org/explore/state-parks/madison-boulder-natural-area.aspx

Milan Hill State Park 427 Milan Hill Rd................ Milan NH 03588 603-449-2429
Web: www.nhstateparks.org/parkspages/milanhill/milanhill.html

Miller State Park 13 Miller Park Rd .... Peterborough NH 03458 603-924-3672
Web: www.nhstateparks.org

Mollidgewock State Park 1437 Berlin Rd .... Errol NH 03579 603-482-3373
Web: www.nhstateparks.org/explore/state-parks/mollidgewock-state-park.aspx

Monadnock State Park 116 Poole Rd................. Jaffrey NH 03452 603-532-8862
Web: www.nhstateparks.org

Mount Sunapee State Park 1460 Rt 103............ Newbury NH 03255 603-763-5561
Web: www.nhstateparks.org/explore/state-parks/mount-sunapee-state-park.aspx

North Beach Rt 1A .... Hampton NH 03842 603-436-1552
Web: www.nhstateparks.org

North Hampton State Beach
27 Ocean Blvd .... North Hampton NH 03862 603-227-8722
Web: www.nhstateparks.org/explore/state-parks/north-hampton-state-beach.aspx

Northwood Meadows State Park
755 First NH Tpke.............................. Northwood NH 03261 603-485-1031
Web: www.nhstateparks.org/explore/state-parks/northwood-meadows-state-park.aspx

Odiorne Point State Park 570 Ocean Blvd............ Rye NH 03870 603-436-7406
Web: www.nhstateparks.org/explore/state-parks/odiorne-point-state-park.aspx

Pawtuckaway State Park 128 Mountain Rd........ Nottingham NH 03290 603-895-3031
Web: www.nhstateparks.org

Pillsbury State Park
100 Pillsbury State Park Rd .... Washington NH 03280 603-863-2860
Web: www.nhstateparks.org/explore/state-parks/pillsbury-state-park.aspx

Rhododendron State Park
424 Rockwood Pond Rd .... Fitzwilliam NH 03447 603-532-8862
Web: www.nhstateparks.org

Robert Frost Farm Historic Site
122 Rockingham Rd .... Derry NH 03038 603-432-3091
Web: www.nhstateparks.org

Rollins State Park 1066 Kearsarge Mtn Rd............. Warner NH 03278 603-456-3808
Web: www.nhstateparks.org

Rye Harbor State Park 1730 Ocean Blvd .... Rye NH 03870 603-227-8722
Web: www.nhstateparks.org/explore/state-parks/rye-harbor-state-park.aspx

Taylor Mill Historic Site Island Pond Rd .... Derry NH 03038 603-431-6774
Web: www.nhstateparks.org/explore/state-parks/taylor-mill-state-historic-site.aspx

Umbagog Lake State Park Rt 26................. Cambridge NH 03579 603-482-7795
Web: www.nhstateparks.org

Wallis Sands State Beach 1050 Ocean Blvd .... Rye NH 03870 603-436-9404
Web: www.nhstateparks.org/explore/state-parks/wallis-sands-state-beach.aspx

Phone Fax

Wellington State Park 614 W Shore Rd .... Bristol NH 03222 603-744-2197
Web: www.nhstateparks.org/explore/state-parks/wellington-state-park.aspx

Wentworth State Park
297 Governor Wentworth Hwy .... Wolfeboro NH 03894 603-569-3699
Web: www.nhstateparks.org

Wentworth-Coolidge Mansion Historic Site
375 Little Harbor Rd .... Portsmouth NH 03801 603-436-6607
Web: www.nhstateparks.org

White Lake State Park Rt 16 .... Tamworth NH 03886 603-323-7350
Web: www.nhstateparks.org

Winslow State Park Kearsarge Mtn Rd................. Wilmot NH 03287 603-526-6168
Web: www.nhstateparks.org/explore/state-parks/winslow-state-park.aspx

New Jersey

Phone Fax

Abram S. Hewitt State Forest
c/o Wawayanda State Pk 885 Warwick Tpke.............. Hewitt NJ 07421 973-853-4462
Web: www.njparksandforests.org/parks/abram.html

Allaire State Park PO Box 220 .... Farmingdale NJ 07727 732-938-2371
Web: www.njparksandforests.org

Allamuchy Mountain State Park
c/o Stephens State Pk
800 Willow Grove St............................ Hackettstown NJ 07840 908-852-3790
Web: www.njparksandforests.org

Barnegat Lighthouse State Park
PO Box 167 .... Barnegat Light NJ 08006 609-494-2016
Web: www.njparksandforests.org

Bass River State Forest 762 Stage Rd .... Tuckerton NJ 08087 609-296-1114
Web: www.njparksandforests.org

Batsto Village State Historic Site Rd 9........... Hammonton NJ 08037 609-561-0024
Web: www.njparksandforests.org/historic/index.html

Belleplain State Forest
County Rt 50 PO Box 450........................... Woodbine NJ 08270 609-861-2404
Web: www.njparksandforests.org/parks/belle.html

Boxwood Hall State Historic Site
1073 E Jersey St...................................... Elizabeth NJ 07201 908-282-7617
Web: www.state.nj.us/dep/parksandforests/historic

Brendan T. Byrne State Forest PO Box 215........ New Lisbon NJ 08064 609-726-1191
Web: www.njparksandforests.org/parks/byrne.html

Bull's Island Recreation Area
2185 Daniel Bray Hwy .... Stockton NJ 08559 609-397-2949
Web: www.njparksandforests.org

Cape May Point State Park PO Box 107........ Cape May Point NJ 08212 609-884-2159
Web: www.njparksandforests.org

Cheesequake State Park 300 Gordon Rd............ Matawan NJ 07747 732-566-2161
Web: www.njparksandforests.org

Corson's Inlet State Park
c/o Belleplain State Forest
County Rt 550 PO Box 450......................... Woodbine NJ 08270 609-861-2404
Web: www.njparksandforests.org/parks/corsons.html

Craig House State Historic Site
347 Freehold-Englishtown Rd .... Manalapan NJ 07726 732-462-9616
Web: www.njparksandforests.org/historic/index.html

Delaware & Raritan Canal State Park
145 Mapleton Rd .... Princeton NJ 08540 609-924-5705
Web: www.njparksandforests.org

Double Trouble State Park
581 Pinewald Keswick Rd........................... Bayville NJ 08721 732-341-6662
Web: www.state.nj.us

Farny State Park
c/o Ringwood State Pk 1304 Sloatsburg Rd........... Ringwood NJ 07456 973-962-7031
Web: www.njparksandforests.org/parks/farny.html

Fort Mott State Park 454 Ft Mott Rd .... Pennsville NJ 08070 856-935-3218
Web: www.njparksandforests.org

Grover Cleveland Birthplace State Historic Site
207 Bloomfield Ave................................ Caldwell NJ 07006 973-226-0001
Web: www.njparksandforests.org

Hacklebarney State Park
c/o Voorhees State Pk
119 Hacklebarney Rd .... Long Valley NJ 07853 908-638-6969
Web: www.njparksandforests.org

Hancock House State Historic Site
Three Front St PO Box 139.................. Hancock's Bridge NJ 08038 856-935-4373
Web: www.njparksandforests.org

Hermitage State Historic Site, The
335 N Franklin Tpke .... Ho-Ho-Kus NJ 07423 201-445-8311 445-0437
Web: www.thehermitage.org

High Point State Park 1480 Rt 23..................... Sussex NJ 07461 973-875-4800
Web: www.njparksandforests.org

Hopatcong State Park PO Box 8519 .... Landing NJ 07850 973-398-7010
Web: www.njparksandforests.org

Indian King Tavern State Historic Site
233 Kings Hwy................................. Haddonfield NJ 08033 856-429-6792
Web: www.njparksandforests.org

Island Beach State Park PO Box 37 .... Seaside Park NJ 08752 732-793-0506
Web: www.njparksandforests.org

Jenny Jump State Forest 330 State Pk Rd.............. Hope NJ 07844 908-459-4366
Web: www.njparksandforests.org

Kittatinny Valley State Park PO Box 621............ Andover NJ 07821 973-786-6445
Web: www.njparksandforests.org

Leonardo State Marina 102 Concord Ave .... Leonardo NJ 07737 732-291-1333
Web: www.state.nj.us/dep/parksandforests/parks/marinas.html

Liberty State Park 200Morris Pesin Dr............. Jersey City NJ 07305 201-915-3440 915-3408
Web: www.njparksandforests.org/parks/liberty.html

Long Pond Ironworks State Park
c/o Ringwood State Pk 1304 Sloatsburg Rd........... Ringwood NJ 07456 973-962-7031
Web: www.njparksandforests.org/parks/longpond.html

Monmouth Battlefield State Park
347 Freehold-Englishtown Rd .... Manalapan NJ 07726 732-462-9616
Web: www.njparksandforests.org/parks/monbat.html

Phone | Fax

Norvin Green State Forest
c/o Ringwood State Pk 1304 Sloatsburg Rd — Ringwood NJ 07456 973-962-7031
Web: www.njparksandforests.org/parks/norvin.html

Parvin State Park 701 Almond Rd — Pittsgrove NJ 08318 856-358-8616
Web: www.njparksandforests.org

Penn State Forest
c/o Bass River State Forest 762 Stage Rd — Tuckerton NJ 08087 609-296-1114
Web: www.njparksandforests.org

Princeton Battlefield State Park
500 Mercer Rd — Princeton NJ 08540 609-921-0074
Web: www.njparksandforests.org

Ramapo Mountain State Forest
c/o Ringwood State Pk 1304 Sloatsburg Rd — Ringwood NJ 07456 973-962-7031
Web: www.njparksandforests.org/parks/ramapo.html

Rancocas State Park
c/o Brendan T Byrne State Forest
PO Box 215 — New Lisbon NJ 08064 609-726-1191
Web: www.njparksandforests.org/parks/rancocas.html

Ringwood State Park 1304 Sloatsburg Rd — Ringwood NJ 07456 973-962-7031
Web: www.njparksandforests.org

Rockingham State Historic Site
84 Laurel Ave — Kingston NJ 08528 609-683-7132
Web: www.rockingham.net

Round Valley Recreation Area
1220 Lebanon-Stanton Rd — Lebanon NJ 08833 908-236-6355
Web: www.njparksandforests.org

Senator Frank S Farley State Marina
600 Huron Ave — Atlantic City NJ 08401 609-441-8482
Web: www.njparksandforests.org/parks/marinas.html#senator

Somers Mansion State Historic Site
1000 Shore Rd — Somers Point NJ 08244 609-927-2212
Web: www.njparksandforests.org

Spruce Run Recreation Area
68 Van Syckel's Rd — Clinton NJ 08809 908-638-8572
Web: www.njparksandforests.org

Stephens State Park 800 Willow Grove St — Hackettstown NJ 07840 908-852-3790
Web: www.njparksandforests.org

Steuben House State Historic Site
1209 Main St — River Edge NJ 07661 201-487-1739
Web: www.njparksandforests.org

Stokes State Forest One Coursen Rd — Branchville NJ 07826 973-948-3820
Web: www.njparksandforests.org

Swartswood State Park PO Box 123 — Swartswood NJ 07877 973-383-5230
Web: www.njparksandforests.org

Twin Lights State Historic Site
Lighthouse Rd — Highlands NJ 07732 732-872-1814
Web: www.twinlightslighthouse.com

Voorhees State Park 251 County Rd 513 — Glen Gardner NJ 08826 908-638-6969
Web: www.njparksandforests.org

Wallace House State Historic Site
71 Somerset St — Somerville NJ 08876 908-725-1015
Web: www.njparksandforests.org

Walt Whitman House State Historic Site
330 Mickle Blvd — Camden NJ 08103 800-843-6420
TF: 800-843-6420 ■ *Web:* www.njparksandforests.org

Washington Crossing State Park
355 Washington Crossing-Pennington Rd — Titusville NJ 08560 609-737-0623
Web: www.njparksandforests.org

Washington Rock State Park
355 Milltown Rd Morris Pesin Dr — Bridgewater NJ 08807 908-722-1200
Web: www.njparksandforests.org/parks/washrock.html

Wawayanda State Park 885 Warwick Tpke — Hewitt NJ 07421 973-853-4462
Web: www.njparksandforests.org/parks/wawayanda.html

Wharton State Forest 31 Batsto Rd — Hammonton NJ 08037 609-561-0024
Web: www.njparksandforests.org/parks/wharton.html

Worthington State Forest HC 62 PO Box 2 — Columbia NJ 07832 908-841-9575
Web: www.njparksandforests.org

New Mexico

Phone | Fax

Coyote Creek State Park
Hwy 434 Mile Marker 17 — Guadalupita NM 87722 575-387-2328
Web: www.emnrd.state.nm.us

Fenton Lake State Park 455 Fenton Lake — Jemez Springs NM 87025 575-829-3630

Hyde Memorial State Park 740 Hyde Pk Rd — Santa Fe NM 87501 505-983-7175

Oasis State Park 1891 Oasis Rd — Portales NM 88130 575-356-5331
Web: www.emnrd.state.nm.us

Oliver Lee Memorial State Park
409 Dog Canyon Rd — Alamogordo NM 88310 575-437-8284 439-1290*
**Fax Area Code:* 505 ■ *Web:* emnrd.state.nm.us

Rio Grande Nature Ctr State Park
2901 Candelaria Rd NW — Albuquerque NM 87107 505-344-7240 344-4505
Web: emnrd.state.nm.us

New York

Phone | Fax

Allan H. Treman State Marine Park
c/o Robert H Tremin State Pk
105 Enfield Falls Rd — Ithaca NY 14850 607-273-3440
Web: www.nysparks.com

Allegany State Park 2373 ASP Rt 1 Ste 3 — Salamanca NY 14779 716-354-9121
Web: nysparks.com

Battle Island State Park 2150 State Rt 48 — Fulton NY 13069 315-593-3408 593-3411
Web: nysparks.com

Bayswater Point State Park
1479 Point Breeze Pl 50-50 2nd St — Far Rockaway NY 11101 718-786-6385
Web: nysparks.com

Bear Mountain State Park
625 Broadway Adminstration Bldg Rt 9 W — Albany NY 12207 845-786-2701
Web: www.nysparks.com/parks/13/details.aspx

Beaver Island State Park
2136 W Oakfield Rd — Grand Island NY 14072 716-773-3271
Web: nysparks.com

Belmont Lake State Park PO Box 247 — Babylon NY 11702 631-667-5055
Web: nysparks.com

Bennington Battlefield State Historic Site
c/o Grafton Lakes State Pk PO Box 163 — Grafton NY 12082 518-686-7109 279-1902
TF: 800-456-2267 ■ *Web:* www.nysparks.com/sites/info.asp?siteID=3

Bethpage State Park Bethpage Pkwy — Farmingdale NY 11735 516-249-0701 753-0413
TF: 800-456-2267 ■ *Web:* nysparks.com

Big Six Mile Creek Marina State Park
c/o Beaver Island State Pk
2136 W Oakfield Rd — Grand Island NY 14072 716-773-3271
Web: nysparks.com

Blauvelt State Park
Palisades Interstate Park Commission
Adminstration Bldg Rt 9 W — Bear Mountain NY 10911 845-359-0544
Web: www.nysparks.com/parks/49/details.aspx

Bowman Lake State Park 745 Bliven Sherman Rd — Oxford NY 13830 607-334-2718
Web: nysparks.com

Buckhorn Island State Park
c/o Beaver Island State Pk
2136 W Oakfield Rd — Grand Island NY 14072 716-773-3271
Web: nysparks.com

Burnham Point State Park
340765 NYS Rt 12E — Cape Vincent NY 13618 315-654-2522
Web: www.nysparks.com

Buttermilk Falls State Park
c/o Robert H Tremin State Pk
105 Enfield Falls Rd — Ithaca NY 14850 607-273-5761
Web: nysparks.com

Caleb Smith State Park Preserve
581 W Jericho Tpke PO Box 963 — Smithtown NY 11787 631-265-1054
Web: nysparks.com

Canandaigua Lake State Marine Park
620 S Main St — Canandaigua NY 14424 315-789-2331
Web: www.nysparks.com/parks/3/details.aspx

Canoe-Picnic Point State Park
36661 Cedar Pt State Pk Dr — Clayton NY 13624 315-686-3048 408-1032*
**Fax Area Code:* 518 ■ *Web:* nysparks.com

Captree State Park PO Box 247 — Babylon NY 11702 631-669-0449
Web: nysparks.com

Caumsett State Historic Park
25 Lloyd Harbor Rd — Huntington NY 11743 631-423-1770 423-8645
Web: www.nysparks.com

Cayuga Lake State Park 2678 Lower Lk Rd — Seneca Falls NY 13148 315-568-5163 568-5336
Web: www.parks.ny.gov

Cedar Island State Park County Rt 93 — Hammond NY 13646 315-482-3331
Web: nysparks.com

Cedar Point State Park
36661 Cedar Pt State Pk Dr — Clayton NY 13624 315-654-2522 654-3332
Web: nysparks.com

Chenango Valley State Park
153 State Pk Rd — Chenango Forks NY 13746 607-648-5251
Web: nysparks.com

Cherry Plain State Park 26 State Pk Rd — Cherry Plain NY 12040 518-733-5400 733-0671
Web: nysparks.com

Chittenango Falls State Park
2300 Rathbun Rd — Cazenovia NY 13035 315-655-9620
Web: nysparks.com

Clarence Fahnestock State Park 1498 Rt 301 — Carmel NY 10512 845-225-7207 228-5804
Web: nysparks.com

Clark Reservation State Park
6105 E Seneca Tpke — Jamesville NY 13078 315-492-1590
Web: nysparks.com

Clay Pit Ponds State Park Preserve
83 Nielsen Ave — Staten Island NY 10309 718-967-1976 966-5294
Web: nysparks.com

Clermont State Historic Site
1 Clermont Ave — Germantown NY 12526 518-537-4240 537-6240
TF: 800-456-2267 ■ *Web:* www.nysparks.com

Clinton House State Historic Site
549 Main St PO Box 88 — Poughkeepsie NY 12602 845-471-1630
Web: nysparks.com

Cold Spring Harbor State Park
25 Lloyd Harbor Rd — Huntington NY 11743 631-423-1770
Web: www.nysparks.com

Coles Creek State Park Rt 37 — Waddington NY 13694 315-388-5636
Web: nysparks.com

Connetquot River State Park Preserve
PO Box 505 — Oakdale NY 11769 631-581-1005
Web: www.nysparks.com

Crailo State Historic Site
Nine 1/2 Riverside Ave — Rensselaer NY 12144 518-463-8738
Web: www.nysparks.com

Crown Point State Historic Site
21 Grandview Dr — Crown Point NY 12928 518-597-4666 597-3666
TF: 800-456-2267 ■ *Web:* www.nysparks.com

Cumberland Bay State Park
152 Cumberland Head Rd — Plattsburgh NY 12901 518-563-5240
Web: nysparks.com

Darien Lakes State Park
10289 Harlow Rd — Darien Center NY 14040 585-547-9242
Web: nysparks.com

Darwin Martin House State Historic Site
125 Jewett Pkwy — Buffalo NY 14214 716-856-3858 856-4009
Web: nysparks.com

Delta Lake State Park 8797 SR- 46 — Rome NY 13440 315-337-4670
Web: nysparks.com

Devil's Hole State Park
c/o Niagara Frontier Region
PO Box 1132 — Niagara Falls NY 14303 716-284-5778
Web: nysparks.com

				Phone	Fax
Dewolf Point State Park 45920 County Rt 191 *Web:* nysparks.com	Fineview	NY	13640	315-482-2012	
Earl W. Brydges Artpark State Park 450 S Fourth St *Web:* nysparks.com	Lewiston	NY	14092	716-754-7766	
Eel Weir State Park Rd 3 *Web:* nysparks.com	Ogdensburg	NY	13669	315-393-1138	
Empire-Fulton Ferry State Park 26 New Dock St *Web:* nysparks.com	Brooklyn	NY	11201	212-803-3822	
Evangola State Park 10191 Old Lk Shore Rd *Web:* nysparks.com	Irving	NY	14081	716-549-1802	
Fair Haven Beach State Park 14985 State Park Rd *TF General:* 800-456-2267 ■ *Web:* nysparks.com	Sterling	NY	13156	315-947-5205	
Fillmore Glen State Park 1686 St Rt 38 *TF:* 800-456-2267 ■ *Web:* nysparks.com	Moravia	NY	13118	315-497-0130	497-0128
Fort Montgomery State Historic Site 690 Route 9W PO Box 213 *Web:* www.nysparks.com/sites/info.asp?siteid=36	Fort Montgomery	NY	10922	845-446-2134	786-5367
Fort Niagara State Park 1 Scott Ave *Web:* www.nysparks.com/parks/175/details.aspx	Youngstown	NY	14174	716-745-7273	
Fort Ontario State Historic Site One E Fourth St *Web:* www.nysparks.com	Oswego	NY	13126	315-343-4711	343-1430
Four Mile Creek State Park 1055 Lake Rd *Web:* www.nysparks.com/parks/info.asp?parkid=110	Youngstown	NY	14174	716-745-3802	
Franklin D. Roosevelt State Park 2957 Crompond Rd *Web:* www.nysparks.com	Yorktown Heights	NY	10598	914-245-4434	
Ganondagan State Historic Site 1488 SR 444 *Web:* www.nysparks.com	Victor	NY	14564	585-924-5848	
Gantry Plaza State Park 4-09 47th Rd *Web:* www.nysparks.com	Long Island	NY	11101	718-786-6385	
Gilbert Lake State Park 18 CCC Rd *Web:* www.nysparks.com	Laurens	NY	13796	607-432-2114	
Glimmerglass State Park 1527 County Hwy 31 *Web:* www.nysparks.com/parks/info.asp?parkid=22	Cooperstown	NY	13326	607-547-8662	
Golden Hill State Park 9691 Lower Lake Rd *Web:* www.nysparks.com	Barker	NY	14012	716-795-3885	
Goosepond Mountain State Park 1198 New York 17M Adminstration Bldg Rt 9 W *Web:* www.nysparks.com/parks/55/details.aspx	Chester	NY	10918	845-786-2701	
Grant Cottage State Historic Site PO Box 2294 *Web:* www.nysparks.com	Wilton	NY	12831	518-587-8277	
Grass Point State Park 42247 Grassy Pt Rd *Web:* nysparks.com	Alexandria Bay	NY	13607	315-686-4472	
Green Lakes State Park 7900 Green Lakes Rd *Web:* www.nysparks.com	Fayetteville	NY	13066	315-637-6111	
Hamlin Beach State Park One Camp Rd *TF:* 800-456-2267 ■ *Web:* www.nysparks.com/parks/info.asp?parkid=6	Hamlin	NY	14464	585-964-2462	964-7821
Harriman State Park Palisades Pkwy Exit 17 *Web:* www.nysparks.com/parks/145/details.aspx	Bear Mountain	NY	10911	845-942-2560	
Heckscher State Park One Heckscher State Pkwy *Web:* www.nysparks.com	East Islip	NY	11730	631-581-2100	
Hempstead Lake State Park Lakeside Dr *Web:* www.nysparks.com	West Hempstead	NY	11552	516-766-1029	
Herkimer Home State Historic Site 200 SR- 169 *Web:* www.nysparks.com	Little Falls	NY	13365	315-823-0398	
High Tor State Park 415 S Mountain Rd *Web:* www.nysparks.com/parks/info.asp?parkid=58	New City	NY	10911	845-634-8074	
Highland Lakes State Park 55-223 Tamms Rd *Web:* www.nysparks.com/parks/5/details.aspx	Middletown	NY	10911	845-786-2701	
Higley Flow State Park 442 Cold Brook Dr *Web:* www.nysparks.com	Colton	NY	13625	315-262-2880	
Hither Hills State Park 164 Old Montauk Hwy *Web:* www.nysparks.com	Montauk	NY	11954	631-668-2554	
Hudson Highlands State Park Rt 9D *Web:* www.nysparks.com	Beacon	NY	10512	845-225-7207	
Hudson River Islands State Park Schodack Island State Pk *TF:* 800-456-2267 ■ *Web:* www.nysparks.com	Schodack Landing	NY	12156	518-732-0187	732-0263
Hyde Hall State Historic Site PO Box 721 *Fax Area Code: 607 ■ *Web:* www.nysparks.com/sites/info.asp?siteid=13	Cooperstown	NY	13326	518-486-1868	547-8462*
Irondequoit Bay State Marine Park c/o Hamlin Beach State Pk *Web:* www.nysparks.com/parks/info.asp?parkid=7	Hamlin	NY	14464	716-256-4951	
James Baird State Park 280 Club House Rd Ste 1 *Web:* www.nysparks.com	Pleasant Valley	NY	12569	845-452-1489	
John Boyd Thacher State Park 1 Hailes Cave Rd *TF:* 800-456-2267 ■ *Web:* www.nysparks.com	Voorheesville	NY	12186	518-872-1237	872-9133
John Brown Farm State Historic Site 115 John Brown Rd *Web:* www.nysparks.com	Lake Placid	NY	12946	518-523-3900	
John Burroughs Memorial State Historic Site c/o Mine Kill State Pk PO Box 923 Rt 30 *TF:* 800-456-2267 ■ *Web:* www.nysparks.com/sites/info.asp?siteID=15	North Blenheim	NY	12131	518-827-6111	827-6782
John Jay Homestead State Historic Site PO Box 832 *TF:* 800-456-2267 ■ *Web:* www.nysparks.com	Katonah	NY	10536	914-232-5651	232-8085
Johnson Hall State Historic Site 139 Hall Ave *Web:* www.nysparks.com	Johnstown	NY	12095	518-762-8712	762-2330
Jones Beach State Park PO Box 1000 *Web:* www.nysparks.com	Wantagh	NY	11793	516-785-1600	
Joseph Davis State Park 4143 Lower River Rd *Web:* www.nysparks.com	Lewiston	NY	14092	716-754-4596	
Keewaydin State Park 46165 NYS Rt 12 PO Box 247 *Web:* www.nysparks.com	Alexandria Bay	NY	13607	315-482-3331	
Keuka Lake State Park 3560 Pepper Rd *Web:* www.nysparks.com	Keuka Park	NY	14478	315-536-3666	
Knox's Headquarters State Historic Site PO Box 207 *Web:* www.nysparks.com	Vails Gate	NY	12584	845-561-5498	
Kring Point State Park 25950 Kring Pt Rd *Web:* www.nysparks.com	Redwood	NY	13679	315-482-2444	
Lake Erie State Park 5838 Route 5 *Web:* www.nysparks.com	Brocton	NY	14716	716-792-9214	
Lake Taghkanic State Park 1528 Rt 82 *Web:* www.nysparks.com	Ancram	NY	12502	518-851-3631	851-3633
Lakeside Beach State Park Rt 18 *Web:* www.nysparks.com/parks/info.asp?parkid=8	Waterport	NY	14571	585-682-4888	
Letchworth State Park One Letchworth State Pk *Web:* www.nysparks.com	Castile	NY	14427	585-493-3600	
Lodi Point State Marine Park c/o Sampson State Pk 6096 Rt 96A *Web:* www.nysparks.com/parks/info.asp?parkid=38	Romulus	NY	14541	315-585-6392	
Long Point State Park - Finger Lakes 2063 Lake Rd *Web:* www.nysparks.com	Aurora	NY	13026	315-497-0130	
Long Point State Park - Thousand Islands 7495 State Pk Rd *Web:* www.nysparks.com	Three Mile Bay	NY	13693	315-649-5258	
Long Point State Park on Lake Chautauqua 4459 Rt 430 *Web:* www.nysparks.com	Bemus Point	NY	14712	716-386-2722	
Lorenzo State Historic Site 17 Rippleton Rd *Web:* www.nysparks.com	Cazenovia	NY	13035	315-655-3200	655-4304
Macomb Reservation State Park 201 Campsite Rd *Web:* www.nysparks.com	Schuyler Falls	NY	12985	518-643-9952	
Margaret Lewis Norrie State Park 9 Old Post Rd PO Box 308 *Web:* nysparks.com	Staatsburg	NY	12580	845-889-4646	889-8321
Mark Twain State Park & Soaring Eagles Golf Course 201 Middle Rd *Web:* www.nysparks.com	Horseheads	NY	14845	607-739-0034	
Mary Island State Park c/o Cedar Pt State Pk 36661 Cedar Pt State Pk Dr *Web:* www.nysparks.com/parks/info.asp?parkid=150	Clayton	NY	13624	315-654-2522	
Mine Kill State Park PO Box 923 Rt 30 *Web:* www.nysparks.com/parks/info.asp?parkid=117	North Blenheim	NY	12131	518-827-6111	827-6782
Montauk Downs State Park 50 S Fairview Ave *Web:* www.nysparks.com/parks/info.asp?parkid=165	Montauk	NY	11954	631-668-3781	
Montauk Point State Park 2000 Montauk Hwy *Web:* www.nysparks.com/parks/info.asp?parkid=136	Montauk	NY	11954	631-668-3781	
Moreau Lake State Park 605 Old Saratoga Rd *Web:* www.nysparks.com	Gansevoort	NY	12831	518-793-0511	761-6843
New Windsor Cantonment State Historic Site 374 Temple Hill Rd Rt 300 *Web:* www.nysparks.com	Vails Gate	NY	12584	845-561-1765	
Niagara Falls State Park PO Box 1132 *Web:* www.nysparks.com/parks/info.asp?parkid=113	Niagara Falls	NY	14303	716-278-1796	
Nissequogue River State Park St Johnland Rd PO Box 639 *Web:* www.nysparks.com/parks/info.asp?parkid=79	Kings Park	NY	11754	631-269-4927	
Nyack Beach State Park 698 N Broadway *Web:* www.nysparks.com/parks/info.asp?parkid=62	Upper Nyack	NY	10960	845-358-1316	
Oak Orchard State Marine Park c/o Lakeside Beach State Pk Rt 18 *Web:* www.nysparks.com/parks/131/details.aspx	Carlton	NY	14571	585-682-4888	
Ogden Mills & Ruth Livingston Mills State Park Mills Mansion 1 Rd *Web:* www.nysparks.com/parks/info.asp?parkid=133	Staatsburg	NY	12580	845-889-4646	
Olana State Historic Site 5720 State Rt 9G *Web:* www.olana.org	Hudson	NY	12534	518-828-0135	828-6742
Old Croton Aqueduct State Historic Park 15 Walnut St *Web:* www.nysparks.com	Dobbs Ferry	NY	10522	914-693-5259	674-8529
Old Erie Canal State Historic Park Rd 2 *Web:* nysparks.com	Kirkville	NY	13082	315-687-7821	
Old Fort Niagara State Historic Site PO Box 169 *Web:* www.oldfortniagara.org	Youngstown	NY	14174	716-745-7611	745-9141
Oquaga Creek State Park 5995 County Rt 20 *Web:* www.nysparks.com	Bainbridge	NY	13733	607-467-4160	
Oriskany Battlefield State Historic Site 7801 State Rt 69 *Web:* www.nysparks.com/sites/info.asp?siteid=23	Oriskany	NY	13424	315-768-7224	377-3081
Peebles Island State Park One Delaware Ave PO Box 295 *Web:* www.nysparks.com/parks/111/details.aspx	Waterford	NY	12188	518-237-8643	
Philipse Manor Hall State Historic Site 29 Warburton Ave *Web:* philipsemanorhall.blogspot.in	Yonkers	NY	10701	914-965-4027	
Pinnacle State Park & Golf Course 1904 Pinnacle Rd *Web:* nysparks.com	Addison	NY	14801	607-359-2767	
Point Au Roche State Park 19 Camp Red Cloud Rd *Web:* www.nysparks.com	Plattsburgh	NY	12901	518-563-0369	

Name / Address	City	State	Zip	Phone	Fax
Reservoir State Park c/o Niagara Frontier Region PO Box 1132 *Web:* www.nysparks.com/parks/info.asp?parkid=112	Niagara Falls	NY	14303	716-284-4691	
Riverbank State Park 679 Riverside Dr *Web:* www.nysparks.com	New York	NY	10031	212-694-3600	
Robert H. Treman State Park 105 Enfield Falls Rd *Web:* www.nysparks.com	Ithaca	NY	14850	607-273-3440	
Robert Moses State Park - Long Island Robert Moses State Pkwy PO Box 247 *Web:* www.nysparks.com/parks/info.asp?parkid=45	Babylon	NY	11702	631-669-0449	
Robert Moses State Park - Thousand Islands 19 Robinson Bay Rd *Web:* www.nysparks.com	Massena	NY	13662	315-769-8663	
Roberto Clemente State Park 301 W Tremont Ave *Web:* nysparks.com	Bronx	NY	10453	718-299-8750	
Rockefeller State Park Preserve 125 Phelps Way *Web:* www.nysparks.com	Pleasantville	NY	10570	914-631-1470	
Rockland Lake State Park PO Box 217 *Web:* nysparks.com	Congers	NY	10920	845-268-3020	
Saint Lawrence State Park Golf Course 4955 State Hwy 37 *Web:* www.nysparks.com	Ogdensburg	NY	13669	315-393-2286	
Sampson State Park 6096 Rt 96A *Web:* www.nysparks.com/parks/info.asp?parkid=100	Romulus	NY	14541	315-585-6392	
Saratoga Spa State Park 19 Roosevelt Dr *Web:* nysparks.com/parks/saratogaspa/details.aspx	Saratoga Springs	NY	12866	518-584-2535	
Schodack Island State Park One Schodack Way PO Box 7 *Web:* www.nysparks.com/parks/info.asp?parkid=87	Schodack Landing	NY	12156	518-732-0187	
Schoharie Crossing State Historic Site 129 Schoharie St PO Box 140 *TF:* 800-456-2267 ■ *Web:* www.nysparks.com	Fort Hunter	NY	12069	518-829-7516	829-7491
Schuyler Mansion State Historic Site 32 Catherine St *TF:* 800-456-2267 ■ *Web:* nysparks.com	Albany	NY	12202	518-434-0834	434-3821
Selkirk Shores State Park 7101 State Rt 3 *Web:* www.nysparks.com	Pulaski	NY	13142	315-298-5737	
Senate House State Historic Site 296 Fair St *TF:* 800-456-2267 ■ *Web:* www.nysparks.com	Kingston	NY	12401	845-338-2786	334-8173
Seneca Lake State Park One Lakefront Dr *Web:* www.nysparks.com	Geneva	NY	14456	315-789-2331	
Shadmoor State Park 900 Montauk Hwy *Web:* nysparks.com	Montauk	NY	11954	631-668-3781	
Silver Lake State Park 156 Lakeshore Dr *Web:* www.nysparks.com	Castile	NY	14427	585-237-6629	
Southwick Beach State Park 8119 Southwicks Pl *Web:* www.nysparks.com	Henderson	NY	13650	315-846-5338	
Staatsburgh State Historic Site 75 Mills Mansion Rd *Web:* www.nysparks.com	Staatsburg	NY	12580	845-889-8851	889-8321
Sterling Forest State Park 116 Old Forge Rd *Web:* www.nysparks.com	Tuxedo	NY	10987	845-351-5907	
Steuben Memorial State Historic Site c/o Ft Stanwix National Monument 112 E Park St *Web:* www.nysparks.com	Rome	NY	13440	315-338-7730	
Stony Brook State Park 10820 Rt 36 S *Web:* www.nysparks.com/parks/118/details.aspx	Dansville	NY	14437	585-335-8111	
Stony Point Battlefield State Historic Site PO Box 182 *Web:* nysparks.com	Stony Point	NY	10980	845-786-2521	
Storm King State Park Palisades Interstate Park Commission *Web:* www.nysparks.com/parks/152/details.aspx	Bear Mountain	NY	10911	845-786-2701	
Sunken Meadow State Park Rt 25A *Web:* www.nysparks.com/parks/37/details.aspx	Kings Park	NY	11754	631-269-4333	
Taconic State Park - Copake Falls Area Route 344 *Web:* www.nysparks.com	Copake Falls	NY	12517	518-329-3993	
Taconic State Park - Rudd Pond Area 59 Rudd Pond Dr *Web:* www.nysparks.com	Millerton	NY	12546	518-789-3059	
Tallman Mountain State Park Rt 9 W *Web:* www.nysparks.com/parks/119/details.aspx	Sparkill	NY	10976	845-359-0544	
Taughannock Falls State Park 2221 Taughannock Rd *Web:* www.nysparks.com	Trumansburg	NY	14886	607-387-6739	
Thompson's Lake State Park 68 Thompson's Lk Rd *Web:* www.nysparks.com	East Berne	NY	12059	518-872-1674	872-9133
Valley Stream State Park PO Box 670 *Web:* www.nysparks.com	Valley Stream	NY	11580	516-825-4128	
Verona Beach State Park PO Box 245 *Web:* www.nysparks.com	Verona Beach	NY	13162	315-762-4463	
Walt Whitman Birthplace State Historic Site 246 Old Walt Whitman Rd *Web:* www.nysparks.com	Huntington Station	NY	11746	631-427-5240	427-5247
Washington's Headquarters State Historic Site PO Box 1783 *Web:* nysparks.com	Newburgh	NY	12551	845-562-1195	561-1789
Waterson Point State Park 44927 Cross Island Rd *Web:* www.nysparks.com	Fineview	NY	13640	315-482-2722	
Watkins Glen State Park PO Box 304 *Web:* www.nysparks.com	Watkins Glen	NY	14891	607-535-4511	
Wellesley Island State Park 44927 Cross Island Rd *Web:* www.nysparks.com	Fineview	NY	13640	315-482-2722	
Westcott Beach State Park Rt 3 *Web:* www.nysparks.com	Henderson	NY	13650	315-938-5083	
Whetstone Gulf State Park 6065 W Rd *Web:* www.nysparks.com	Lowville	NY	13367	315-376-6630	
Whirlpool State Park 3180 De Veaux Woods Dr PO Box 1132 *Web:* www.nysparks.com/parks/info.asp?parkid=29	Niagara Falls	NY	14303	716-284-5778	
Wildwood State Park N Wading River Rd PO Box 518 *Web:* www.nysparks.com	Wading River	NY	11792	631-929-4314	
Wilson-Tuscarora State Park 3371 Lake Rd *Web:* www.nysparks.com	Wilson	NY	14172	716-751-6361	
Woodlawn Beach State Park 3580 Lk Shore Rd *Web:* www.nysparks.com	Blasdell	NY	14219	716-826-1930	827-0293

North Carolina

Name / Address	City	State	Zip	Phone	Fax
Carolina Beach State Park 1010 State Pk Rd PO Box 475 *Web:* www.ncparks.gov	Carolina Beach	NC	28428	910-458-8206	
Cliffs of the Neuse State Park 240 Park Entrance Rd *Web:* www.ncparks.gov/visit/parks/clne/main.php	Seven Springs	NC	28578	919-778-6234	
Crowders Mountain State Park 522 Pk Office Ln *Web:* www.ncparks.gov	Kings Mountain	NC	28086	704-853-5375	853-5391
Eno River State Park 6101 Cole Mill Rd *Web:* www.ncparks.gov	Durham	NC	27705	919-383-1686	382-7378
Falls Lake State Recreation Area 13304 Creedmoor Rd *Web:* www.ncparks.gov	Wake Forest	NC	27587	919-676-1027	676-2954
Fort Fisher State Recreation Area 1000 Loggerhead Rd *Web:* www.ncparks.gov	Kure Beach	NC	28449	910-458-5798	458-3722
Goose Creek State Park 2190 Camp Leach Rd *TF:* 877-722-6762 ■ *Web:* www.ncparks.gov	Washington	NC	27889	252-923-2191	
Gorges State Park 976 Grassy Ridge Rd PO Box 100 *Web:* www.ncparks.gov	Sapphire	NC	28774	828-966-9099	
Hammocks Beach State Park 1572 Hammock Beach Rd *Web:* www.ncparks.gov	Swansboro	NC	28584	910-326-4881	326-2060
Jockey's Ridge State Park PO Box 592 *Web:* www.jockeysridgestatepark.com	Nags Head	NC	27959	252-441-7132	
Jones Lake State Park 4117 NC 242 Hwy *Web:* www.ncparks.gov	Elizabethtown	NC	28337	910-588-4550	
Jordan Lake State Recreation Area 280 State Pk Rd *TF:* 877-722-6762 ■ *Web:* www.ncparks.gov	Apex	NC	27523	919-362-0586	362-1621
Kerr Lake State Recreation Area 6254 Satterwhite Pt Rd *Web:* www.ncparks.gov	Henderson	NC	27537	252-456-2328	438-7582
Lake James State Park 6883 NC Hwy 126 PO Box 340 *Web:* www.ncparks.gov/visit/parks/laja/main.php	Nebo	NC	28761	828-584-7728	
Lake Norman State Park 159 Inland Sea Ln *Web:* ncparks.gov	Troutman	NC	28166	704-528-6350	528-5623
Lake Waccamaw State Park 1866 State Pk Dr *Web:* www.ncparks.gov	Lake Waccamaw	NC	28450	910-646-4748	
Lumber River State Park 2819 Princess Ann Rd *Web:* www.ncparks.gov/visit/parks/luri/main.php	Orrum	NC	28369	910-628-4564	
Medoc Mountain State Park 1541 Medoc State Pk Rd *Web:* www.ncparks.gov	Hollister	NC	27844	252-586-6588	
Morrow Mountain State Park 49104 Morrow Mtn Rd *Web:* www.ncparks.gov	Albemarle	NC	28001	704-982-4402	982-5323
Mount Jefferson State Natural Area 1481 Mt Jefferson State Park Rd *Web:* ncparks.gov	West Jefferson	NC	28694	336-246-9653	
Mount Mitchell State Park 2388 State Hwy 128 *Web:* www.ncparks.gov	Burnsville	NC	28714	828-675-4611	675-9655
New River State Park 358 New River State Park Rd *Web:* www.ncparks.gov/visit/parks/neri/main.php	Laurel Springs	NC	28644	336-982-2587	
Pettigrew State Park 2252 Lk Shore Rd *Web:* www.ncparks.gov/visit/parks/pett/main.php	Creswell	NC	27928	252-797-4475	
Pilot Mountain State Park 1792 Pilot Knob Pk Rd *Web:* www.ncparks.gov	Pinnacle	NC	27043	336-325-2355	
Raven Rock State Park 3009 Raven Rock Rd *Web:* www.ncparks.gov	Lillington	NC	27546	910-893-4888	
Singletary Lake State Park 6707 NC 53 Hwy E *Web:* www.ncparks.gov	Kelly	NC	28448	910-669-2928	
South Mountains State Park (SOMO) 3001 S Mtns State Pk Ave *Web:* www.ncparks.gov	Connelly Springs	NC	28612	828-433-4772	433-4778
Stone Mountain State Park 3042 Frank Pkwy *TF:* 877-722-6762 ■ *Web:* ncparks.gov	Roaring Gap	NC	28668	336-957-8185	957-3985
Weymouth Woods Sandhills Nature Preserve 1024 Ft Bragg Rd *Web:* www.ncparks.gov	Southern Pines	NC	28387	910-692-2167	
William B Umstead State Park 8801 Glenwood Ave *Web:* ncparks.gov	Raleigh	NC	27617	919-571-4170	

North Dakota

Phone *Fax*

Beaver Lake State Park 3850 70th St SE. . . . . Wishek ND 58495 701-452-2752
Web: www.ndparks.com

Black Tiger Bay State Recreation Area
152 S Duncan Dr . . . . Devils Lake ND 58301 701-766-4015
Web: www.ndparks.com

De Mores State Historic Site PO Box 106. . . . . Medora ND 58645 701-623-4355
Web: www.nd.gov

Double Ditch State Historic Site
N Dakota 1804 . . . . Bismarck ND 58503 701-328-2666 328-3710
Web: www.history.nd.gov/historicsites/doubleditch/index.html

Doyle Memorial State Park
5981 Walt Hjelle Pkwy . . . . Wishek ND 58495 701-452-2351
Web: www.ndparks.com/parks/doyle-memorial-state-park

Former Governors' Mansion State Historic Site
612 E Blvd Ave. . . . . Bismarck ND 58505 701-328-2666 328-3710
TF: 866-243-5352 ■ *Web:* www.nd.gov

Fort Abercrombie State Historic Site
PO Box 148 . . . . Abercrombie ND 58001 701-553-8513
Web: www.nd.gov

Fort Abraham Lincoln State Park
4480 Ft Lincoln Rd. . . . . Mandan ND 58554 701-667-6340 667-6349
Web: ndparks.com/parks/fort-abraham-lincoln-state-park

Fort Buford State Historic Site
15349 39th Ln NW. . . . . Williston ND 58801 701-572-9034
Web: www.nd.gov

Fort Ransom State Park
5981 Walt Hjelle Pkwy . . . . Fort Ransom ND 58033 701-973-4331 973-4151
Web: www.ndparks.com

Fort Stevenson State Park 1252A 41st St NW. . . . . Garrison ND 58540 701-337-5576 337-5313
Web: www.ndparks.com

Fort Totten State Historic Site
PO Box 224 . . . . Fort Totten ND 58335 701-766-4441
Web: www.nd.gov

Icelandic State Park 13571 Hwy 5 . . . . Cavalier ND 58220 701-265-4561 265-4443
Web: www.ndparks.com

Indian Hills State Recreation Area & Resort
7302 14th St NW . . . . Garrison ND 58763 701-743-4122
Web: www.ndparks.com

Lake Metigoshe State Park
Two Lk Metigoshe State Pk. . . . . Bottineau ND 58318 701-263-4651 263-4648
Web: www.ndparks.com

Mouse River State Forest 307 - First St E. . . . . Bottineau ND 58318 701-228-5422 228-5448
Web: www.ndsu.edu

Sully Creek State Recreation Area
c/o Ft Abraham Lincoln State Pk
4480 Ft Lincoln Rd. . . . . Mandan ND 58554 701-667-6340
Web: www.parkrec.nd.gov

Tetrault Woods State Forest
1037 Forestry Dr. . . . . Bottineau ND 58318 701-228-3700 228-5111
Web: www.ndsu.edu

Turtle River State Park 3084 Pk Ave . . . . Arvilla ND 58214 701-591-4445 594-2556
Web: www.ndparks.com

Whitestone Hill State Historic Site
C/O Dorene Brandeburger 8692 98th Ave. . . . . Monango ND 58436 701-349-4103
Web: history.nd.gov/historicsites/whitestone/index.html

Ohio

Phone *Fax*

Adams Lake State Park
c/o Shawnee State Pk 4404 State Rt 125 . . . . Portsmouth OH 45663 740-858-6652
Web: www.ohiodnr.com

Alum Creek State Park 3615 S Old State Rd . . . . Delaware OH 43015 740-548-4631
Web: alum-creek-state-park.org

Barkcamp State Park 65330 Barkcamp Rd . . . . Belmont OH 43718 740-484-4064
Web: www.ohiodnr.com

Beaver Creek State Park
12021 Echo Dell Rd . . . . East Liverpool OH 43920 330-385-3091
Web: www.ohiodnr.com

Blue Rock State Park 7924 Cutler Lk Rd . . . . Blue Rock OH 43720 740-674-4794
Web: www.ohiodnr.com/default.aspx?alias=www.ohiodnr.com/parks

Buck Creek State Park 1901 Buck Creek Ln . . . . Springfield OH 45502 937-322-5284
Web: www.ohiodnr.com

Buckeye Lake State Park
2905 Liebs Island Rd . . . . Millersport OH 43046 740-467-2690
Web: www.ohiodnr.com

Burr Oak State Park 10220 Burr Oak Lodge Rd. . . . . Glouster OH 45732 740-767-3570
Web: www.ohiodnr.com

Caesar Creek State Park
8570 E State Rt 73 . . . . Waynesville OH 45068 513-897-3055
Web: www.caesarcreekstatepark.com

Catawba Island State Park
4049 E Moores Dock Rd. . . . . Port Clinton OH 43452 419-797-4530
Web: www.ohiodnr.com

Cowan Lake State Park 1750 Osborn Rd. . . . . Wilmington OH 45177 937-382-1096
Web: www.ohiodnr.com

Crane Creek State Park 13531 SR- 2 . . . . Oak Harbor OH 43449 614-265-6561
Web: www.ohiodnr.com

Deer Creek State Park
20635 Waterloo Rd. . . . . Mount Sterling OH 43143 740-869-3124
Web: www.ohiodnr.com

Delaware State Park 5202 US Rt 23 N. . . . . Delaware OH 43015 740-548-4631
TF: 866-644-6727 ■ *Web:* www.dnr.state.oh.us

Dillon State Park 5265 Dillon Hills Dr. . . . . Nashport OH 43830 740-453-4377
Web: www.ohiodnr.com

East Fork State Park 3294 Elklick Rd . . . . Bethel OH 45106 513-734-4323
Web: www.ohiodnr.com

Phone *Fax*

East Harbor State Park
1169 N Buck Rd . . . . Lakeside-Marblehead OH 43440 419-734-4424
Web: eastharborstatepark.org

Findley State Park 25381 State Rt 58. . . . . Wellington OH 44090 440-647-4490
Web: www.ohiodnr.com

Forked Run State Park
63300 SR- 124 PO Box 127. . . . . Reedsville OH 45772 740-378-6206
Web: www.ohiodnr.com

Geneva State Park
4499 Pandanarum Rd PO Box 429. . . . . Geneva OH 44041 440-466-8400
Web: www.ohiodnr.com

Great Seal State Park 4908 Marietta Rd. . . . . Chillicothe OH 45601 740-663-2125
Web: www.ohiodnr.com

Guilford Lake State Park 6835 E Lake Rd . . . . Lisbon OH 44432 330-222-1712
Web: www.ohiodnr.com

Harrison Lake State Park
26246 Harrison Lk Rd. . . . . Fayette OH 43521 419-237-2593
Web: www.ohiodnr.com

Headlands Beach State Park
c/o Cleveland Lakefront State Pk
8701 Lakeshore Blvd NE. . . . . Cleveland OH 44108 216-881-8141
Web: www.dnr.state.oh.us

Hocking Hills State Park 19852 State Rt 664 S. . . . . Logan OH 43138 740-385-6842
Web: thehockinghills.org

Hueston Woods State Park
6301 Pk Office Rd. . . . . College Corner OH 45003 513-523-6347
Web: www.ohiodnr.com

Indian Lake State Park 12774 State Rt 235 N . . . . Lakeview OH 43331 937-843-2717
Web: www.ohiodnr.com

Jefferson Lake State Park
501 Township Rd 261A. . . . . Richmond OH 43944 740-765-4459
Web: www.ohiodnr.com

John Bryan State Park 3790 SR- 370. . . . . Yellow Springs OH 45387 937-767-1274
Web: www.ohiodnr.com

Kelleys Island State Park
c/o Catawba Island State Pk
920 Division St. . . . . Kelleys Island OH 43452 419-734-4424
Web: www.dnr.state.oh.us

Lake Hope State Park 27331 State Rt 278 . . . . McArthur OH 45651 740-596-4938
Web: dnr.state.oh.us

Lake Logan State Park
20160 State Rd 664 20160 State Rd 664 . . . . Logan OH 43138 740-385-6842
Web: www.dnr.state.oh.us

Lake Loramie State Park
4401 Ft Loramie Swanders Rd . . . . Minster OH 45865 937-295-2011
Web: www.ohiodnr.com

Lake Milton State Park
16801 Mahoning Ave . . . . Lake Milton OH 44429 330-654-4989
Web: www.ohiodnr.com

Lake White State Park 2767 SR- 551 . . . . Waverly OH 45690 740-493-2212
Web: www.ohiodnr.com

Malabar Farm State Park 4050 Bromfield Rd . . . . Lucas OH 44843 419-892-2784 892-3988
Web: www.ohiodnr.com

Marblehead Lighthouse State Park
110 Lighthouse Dr . . . . Marblehead OH 43440 419-734-4424
Web: www.dnr.state.oh.us

Mary Jane Thurston State Park
1466 State Rt 65. . . . . McClure OH 43534 419-832-7662
TF: 866-644-6727 ■ *Web:* www.dnr.state.oh.us

Maumee Bay State Park 1400 State Pk Rd . . . . Oregon OH 43618 419-836-7758 836-8711
Web: www.ohiodnr.com

Middle Bass Island State Park
1719 Fox Rd. . . . . Middle Bass Island OH 43446 419-285-0311
TF: 866-644-6727 ■ *Web:* parks.ohiodnr.gov

Mohican State Park 3116 SR- 3 . . . . Loudonville OH 44842 419-938-6222
Web: www.ohiodnr.com

Mosquito Lake State Park 1439 State Rt 305. . . . . Cortland OH 44410 330-637-2856
Web: www.ohiodnr.com

Mount Gilead State Park
4119 State Rt 95. . . . . Mount Gilead OH 43338 419-946-1961
Web: www.ohiodnr.com

Muskingum River State Park
1390 Ellis Dam Rd . . . . Zanesville OH 43701 740-453-4377
Web: www.ohiodnr.com

ODNR Oil & Gas Resources Management
7317 Warner Huffer Rd . . . . Circleville OH 43113 740-869-3124
Web: www.ohiodnr.com/parks/awmarion/tabid/712/Default.aspx

Ohio DNR 4860 E Pk Dr . . . . London OH 43140 937-322-5284
Web: www2.ohiodnr.com/oilgas/citizens/public-records-request

Paint Creek State Park 280 Taylor Rd . . . . Bainbridge OH 45612 937-981-7061
TF: 866-644-6727 ■ *Web:* www.dnr.state.oh.us

Pike Lake State Park 1847 Pike Lk Rd . . . . Bainbridge OH 45612 740-493-2212
Web: pikelakestatepark.com

Portage Lakes State Park 5031 Manchester Rd . . . . Akron OH 44319 330-644-2220 644-7550
Web: www.ohiodnr.com

Punderson State Park 11755 Kinsman Rd. . . . . Newbury OH 44065 440-564-5465
Web: www.dnr.state.oh.us

Pymatuning State Park PO Box 1000 . . . . Andover OH 44003 440-293-6030
Web: www.ohiodnr.com

Rocky Fork State Park 9800 N Shore Dr . . . . Hillsboro OH 45133 937-393-4284
Web: www.ohiodnr.com

Salt Fork State Park 14755 Cadiz Rd . . . . Lore City OH 43755 740-439-3521 432-1515
Web: www.ohiodnr.com

Scioto Trail State Park 144 Lake Rd . . . . Chillicothe OH 45601 866-644-6727
TF: 866-644-6727 ■ *Web:* parks.ohiodnr.gov

Stonelick State Park 2895 Lake Dr . . . . Pleasant Plain OH 45162 513-734-4323
Web: www.ohiodnr.com

Strouds Run State Park 2045 Morse Rd . . . . Columbus OH 43229 740-592-2302
Web: www.ohiodnr.com

Sycamore State Park 4675 N Diamond Mill Rd. . . . . Trotwood OH 45426 513-523-6347
Web: www.ohiodnr.com

				Phone	Fax
Tar Hollow State Park 16396 Tar Hollow Rd ... *Web:* www.ohiodnr.com	Laurelville	OH	43135	740-887-4818	
Tinkers Creek State Park 1230 Old Mill Rd 10303 Aurora Hudson Rd ... *Web:* www.dnr.state.oh.us	Aurora	OH	44202	440-564-2279	
West Branch State Park 5708 Esworthy Rd ... *Web:* www.ohiodnr.com	Ravenna	OH	44266	330-296-3239	
Wolf Run State Park 16170 Wolf Run Rd ... *Web:* www.ohiodnr.com	Caldwell	OH	43724	740-732-5035	

Oklahoma

				Phone	Fax
Adair State Park Hwy 51 & Hwy 59 ... *Web:* www.oklahomacampers.com	Stilwell	OK	74960	918-696-6613	
Alabaster Caverns State Park 217036 SH 50A ... *Web:* www.travelok.com	Freedom	OK	73842	580-621-3381	621-3572
Arrowhead State Park 3995 Main Pk Rd ... *Web:* www.travelok.com	Canadian	OK	74425	918-339-2204	339-7236
Beaver Dunes State Park Hwy 270 N Rt 1 PO Box 51 ... *Web:* www.travelok.com	Beaver	OK	73932	580-625-3373	625-3525
Beavers Bend Resort Park PO Box 10 ... *Web:* www.beaversbend.com	Broken Bow	OK	74728	580-494-6300	
Bernice State Park 901 State Pk Rd ... *Web:* www.travelok.com	Grove	OK	74344	918-786-9447	787-5634
Black Mesa State Park & Nature Preserve County Rd 325 ... *Web:* www.travelok.com	Kenton	OK	73946	580-426-2222	426-2405
Boggy Depot State Park 475 S Pk Ln ... *Web:* www.travelok.com	Atoka	OK	74525	580-889-5625	889-7868
Boiling Springs State Park 207697 Boiling Springs Rd ... *Web:* www.travelok.com	Woodward	OK	73801	580-256-7664	256-4338
Cherokee Landing State Park 28610 Pk 20 ... *Web:* www.travelok.com	Park Hill	OK	74451	918-457-5716	457-4871
Cherokee State Park N 4475 Rd ... *Web:* www.travelok.com	Langley	OK	74350	918-435-8066	
Clayton Lake State Park Hwy 271 ... *Web:* www.travelok.com	Clayton	OK	74536	918-569-7981	
Disney/Little Blue State Park Hwy 28 E ... *TF:* 800-622-6317 ■ *Web:* www.travelok.com	Disney	OK	74340	918-435-8066	435-2101
Dripping Springs State Park 16830 Dripping Springs Rd ... *TF:* 800-622-6317 ■ *Web:* www.travelok.com/listings/view.profile/id.2368	Okmulgee	OK	74447	918-756-5971	759-9933
Fort Cobb Lake State Park 27022 Copperhead Rd ... *TF:* 800-622-6317 ■ *Web:* www.travelok.com	Fort Cobb	OK	73038	405-643-2249	643-5167
Foss State Park 10252 Hwy 44 ... *TF:* 800-622-6317 ■ *Web:* www.travelok.com	Foss	OK	73647	580-592-4433	592-4701
Gloss Mountain State Park Hwy 412 ... *Web:* www.travelok.com/listings/view.profile/id.3030	Fairview	OK	73737	580-227-2512	227-2513
Great Plains State Park 22487 E 1566 Rd ... *TF:* 800-622-6317 ■ *Web:* www.travelok.com	Mountain Park	OK	73559	580-569-2032	569-2375
Great Salt Plains State Park Rt 1 PO Box 28 ... *Web:* www.travelok.com	Jet	OK	73749	580-626-4731	
Greenleaf State Park Hwy 10 S ... *Web:* www.travelok.com	Braggs	OK	74423	918-487-5196	487-5406
Heavener Runestone State Park 18365 Runestone Rd ... *Web:* travelok.com	Heavener	OK	74937	918-653-2241	
Honey Creek State Park 901 State Pk Rd ... *TF:* 800-622-6317 ■ *Web:* www.travelok.com	Grove	OK	74344	918-786-9447	787-5634
Keystone State Park 1926 S Hwy 151 ... *TF:* 800-654-8240 ■ *Web:* www.travelok.com/listings/view.profile/id.4163	Sand Springs	OK	74063	918-865-4991	865-2083
Lake Eufaula State Park HC 60 PO ... *Web:* www.travelok.com	Checotah	OK	74426	918-689-7337	
Lake Murray State Park 120 N Robinson Ave Sixth Fl ... *TF:* 800-652-6552 ■ *Web:* www.travelok.com	Oklahoma City	OK	73152	800-652-6552	
Lake Thunderbird State Park 13101 Alameda Dr ... *Web:* www.travelok.com	Norman	OK	73026	405-360-3572	366-8150
Lake Wister State Park 25567 US Hwy 270 ... *TF:* 800-622-6317 ■ *Web:* www.travelok.com	Wister	OK	74966	918-655-7212	655-7274
Little Sahara State Park 101 Main St ... *Web:* www.travelok.com	Waynoka	OK	73860	580-824-1471	824-1472
McGee Creek State Park 576-A S McGee Creek Dam Rd ... *Web:* www.travelok.com	Atoka	OK	74525	580-889-5822	889-7868
Okmulgee State Park 16830 Dripping Springs Rd ... *Web:* www.travelok.com/listings/view.profile/id.5520	Okmulgee	OK	74447	918-756-5971	759-9933
Osage Hills State Park 2131 Osage Hills State Pk Rd ... *TF:* 800-622-6317 ■ *Web:* www.travelok.com	Pawhuska	OK	74056	918-336-4141	337-2176
Raymond Gary State Park Hwy 70 ... *TF:* 800-622-6317 ■ *Web:* www.travelok.com	Fort Towson	OK	74735	580-873-2307	326-2305
Red Rock Canyon State Park Hwy 281 S ... *Web:* www.travelok.com	Hinton	OK	73047	405-542-6344	542-6342
Robbers Cave State Park Hwy 2 N ... *TF:* 800-654-8240 ■ *Web:* travelok.com	Wilburton	OK	74578	918-465-2565	465-5763
Sequoyah Bay State Park 6237 E 100th St N ... *TF:* 800-622-6317 ■ *Web:* www.travelok.com	Wagoner	OK	74467	918-683-0878	687-6797
Sequoyah State Park & Western Hills Guest Ranch 17131 Pk 10 ... *Web:* www.travelok.com	Hulbert	OK	74441	918-772-2046	772-3042
Snowdale State Park 501 S 439 ... *TF:* 800-622-6317 ■ *Web:* www.travelok.com	Salina	OK	74361	918-434-2651	435-2101
Southwestern Oklahoma State University (SWOSU) 100 Campus Dr ... *Web:* www.swosu.edu	Weatherford	OK	73096	580-772-6611	
Spavinaw State Park 555 S Main ... *TF:* 800-622-6317 ■ *Web:* www.travelok.com	Spavinaw	OK	74366	918-589-2651	435-2101
Talimena State Park 50884 US Hwy 271 ... *Web:* www.travelok.com	Talihina	OK	74571	918-567-2052	567-2052
Tenkiller State Park Eight Miles N of Gore or SH 100 ... *Web:* www.oklahomacampers.com	Vian	OK	74962	918-489-5641	
Twin Bridges State Park 14801 Hwy 137 S ... *TF:* 800-622-6317 ■ *Web:* www.travelok.com	Fairland	OK	74343	918-540-2545	540-2545
Wah-Sha-She State Park HC 75 Hwy 60 ... *TF:* 800-622-6317 ■ *Web:* www.travelok.com	Copan	OK	74022	918-532-4334	337-2176
Walnut Creek State Park 209th W Ave ... *Web:* www.travelok.com/listings/view.profile/id.8380	Prue	OK	74060	918-865-4991	865-2050

Oregon

				Phone	Fax
Alfred A. Loeb State Park 725 Summer St NE Ste C ... *TF:* 800-551-6949 ■ *Web:* oregonstateparks.org/index.cfm?do=parkpage.dsp_parkpage&parkid=51	Salem	OR	97301	503-986-0707	
Alsea Bay Historic Interpretive Ctr 725 Summer St NE Ste C ... *TF:* 800-551-6949 ■ *Web:* www.oregonstateparks.org	Salem	OR	97301	800-551-6949	
Beverly Beach State Park 198 NE 123rd St ... *Web:* www.oregonstateparks.org	Newport	OR	97365	800-452-5687	
Bob Straub State Park US 101 ... *TF:* 800-551-6949 ■ *Web:* www.oregonstateparks.org	Pacific City	OR	97135	800-551-6949	
Bonnie Lure State Recreation Area 11321 SW Terwilliger Blvd ... *TF:* 800-551-6949 ■ *Web:* www.oregonstateparks.org	Portland	OR	97219	800-551-6949	
Bridal Veil Falls State Scenic Viewpoint E Bridal Veil Rd PO Box 100 ... *TF:* 800-551-6949 ■ *Web:* www.oregonstateparks.org	Bridal Veil	OR	97010	800-551-6949	
Bullards Beach State Park PO Box 569 ... *Web:* oregonstateparks.org/index.cfm?do=parkpage.dsp_parkpage&parkid=50	Bandon	OR	97411	541-347-2209	
Cape Arago State Park Cape Arago Hwy ... *Web:* www.oregonstateparks.org	Coos Bay	OR	97420	541-888-3778	
Cape Blanco State Park 39745 S Hwy 101 ... *Web:* www.oregonstateparks.org	Port Orford	OR	97465	541-332-6774	
Cape Lookout State Park 13000 Whiskey Creek Rd W ... *Web:* oregonstateparks.org/index.cfm?do=parkpage.dsp_parkpage&parkid=134	Tillamook	OR	97141	503-842-4981	
Cascadia State Park 725 Summer St NE Ste C ... *Web:* www.oregonstateparks.org	Salem	OR	97301	503-986-0707	
Cline Falls State Scenic Viewpoint 62976 OB Riley Rd ... *TF:* 800-551-6949 ■ *Web:* www.oregonstateparks.org	Bend	OR	97701	800-551-6949	
Collier Memorial State Park 46000 Hwy 97 N ... *Web:* www.oregonstateparks.org	Chiloquin	OR	97624	541-783-2471	
Coquille Myrtle Grove State Natural Site PO Box 569 ... *TF:* 800-551-6949 ■ *Web:* www.oregonstateparks.org	Bandon	OR	97411	800-551-6949	
Cove Palisades State Park 7300 Jordan Rd ... *Web:* www.oregonstateparks.org	Culver	OR	97734	541-546-3412	
Crissey Field State Recreation Site 1655 Hwy 101 N ... *TF:* 800-551-6949 ■ *Web:* www.oregonstateparks.org	Brookings	OR	97415	541-469-2021	
D River State Recreation Site 1110 NW U.S. 101 198 NE 123rd St ... *TF:* 800-551-6949 ■ *Web:* www.oregonstateparks.org	Lincoln City	OR	97367	541-994-7341	
Dabney State Recreation Area 30701 Historic Columbia River Hwy PO Box 100 ... *TF:* 800-551-6949 ■ *Web:* www.oregonstateparks.org	Troutdale	OR	97060	503-695-2261	
Darlingtonia State Natural Site 84505 Hwy 101 S ... *TF:* 800-551-6949 ■ *Web:* www.oregonstateparks.org	Florence	OR	97439	541-997-3851	
Del Rey Beach State Recreation Site 100 Peter Iredale Rd ... *TF:* 800-551-6949 ■ *Web:* www.oregonstateparks.org	Hammond	OR	97121	800-551-6949	
Depoe Bay Whale Center *Oregon Parks and Recreation Department* 58 US-101 198 NE 123rd St ... *TF:* 800-551-6949 ■ *Web:* www.oregonstateparks.org	Depoe Bay	OR	97341	541-765-3304	
Deschutes River State Recreation Area 89600 Biggs-Rufus Hwy ... *Web:* oregonstateparks.org/index.cfm?do=parkpage.dsp_parkpage&parkid=29	Wasco	OR	97065	541-739-2322	
Detroit Lake State Recreation Area PO Box 549 ... *Web:* www.oregonstateparks.org	Detroit	OR	97342	503-854-3346	
Devil's Lake State Recreation Area 198 NE 123rd St ... *TF:* 800-551-6949 ■ *Web:* www.oregonstateparks.org	Newport	OR	97365	800-551-6949	
Devil's Punchbowl State Natural Area 198 NE 123rd St ... *TF:* 800-551-6949 ■ *Web:* www.oregonstateparks.org	Newport	OR	97365	800-551-6949	
Dexter State Recreation Site 725 Summer St NE Ste C ... *Web:* www.oregonstateparks.org	Salem	OR	97301	541-937-1173	
Driftwood Beach State Recreation Site 5580 S Coast Hwy ... *TF:* 800-551-6949 ■ *Web:* www.oregonstateparks.org	Newport	OR	97366	800-551-6949	
Ecola State Park 84318 Ecola State Park Rd PO Box 366 ... *Web:* www.oregonstateparks.org	Cannon Beach	OR	97110	503-436-2844	
Ellmaker State Wayside 198 NE 123rd St ... *TF:* 800-551-6949 ■ *Web:* www.oregonstateparks.org	Newport	OR	97365	800-551-6949	

Phone Fax

Emigrant Springs State Heritage Area
Old Oregon Trl Hwy PO Box 85 .... Meacham OR 97859 541-983-2277
Web: www.oregonstateparks.org

Fall Creek State Recreation Area
84610 Peninsula Rd PO Box 511 .... Fall Creek OR 97438 541-937-1173
Web: oregonstateparks.org/index.cfm?do=parkpage.dsp_parkpage&parkid=176

Farewell Bend State Recreation Area
23751 Old Hwy 30 .... Huntington OR 97907 541-869-2365
Web: www.oregonstateparks.org

Fogarty Creek State Recreation Area
5150 Oregon Coast Hwy 198 NE 123rd St .... Depoe Bay OR 97341 800-551-6949
TF: 800-551-6949 ■ *Web:* www.oregonstateparks.org

Fort Rock State Natural Area
c/o LaPine Management Unit
15800 State Recreation Rd .... Lake County OR 97739 800-551-6949
TF: 800-551-6949 ■ *Web:* www.oregonstateparks.org

Fort Stevens State Park 100 Peter Iredale Rd .... Hammond OR 97121 503-861-1671
Web: www.oregonstateparks.org

Gleneden Beach State Recreation Site
198 NE 123rd St .... Newport OR 97365 800-551-6949
TF: 800-551-6949 ■ *Web:* www.oregonstateparks.org

Golden & Silver Falls State Natural Area
89814 Cape Arago Hwy .... Coos Bay OR 97420 541-888-3778
Web: www.oregonstateparks.org

Government Island State Recreation Area
725 Summer St NE Ste C .... Salem OR 97301 800-551-6949
TF: 800-551-6949 ■ *Web:* www.oregonstateparks.org/park_250.php

Governor Patterson Memorial State Recreation Site
5580 S Coast Hwy 5580 S Coast Hwy .... Newport OR 97394 800-551-6949
TF: 800-551-6949 ■ *Web:* www.oregonstateparks.org

H. B. Van Duzer Forest State Scenic Corridor
198 NE 123rd St .... Newport OR 97365 800-551-6949
TF: 800-551-6949 ■ *Web:* www.oregonstateparks.org

Harris Beach State Park 1655 Hwy 101 N .... Brookings OR 97415 541-469-2021
Web: oregonstateparks.org/index.cfm?do=parkpage.dsp_parkpage&parkid=58

Heceta Head Lighthouse State Scenic Viewpoint
93111 Hwy 101 N .... Florence OR 97439 800-551-6949
TF: 800-551-6949 ■ *Web:* www.oregonstateparks.org

Hoffman Memorial State Wayside PO Box 569 .... Bandon OR 97411 800-551-6949
TF: 800-551-6949 ■ *Web:* www.oregonstateparks.org

Humbug Mountain State Park PO Box 1345 .... Port Orford OR 97465 541-332-6774
Web: www.oregonstateparks.org

Jasper State Recreation Site
725 Summer St NE Ste C .... Salem OR 97301 541-937-1173
Web: www.oregonstateparks.org

Joseph H. Stewart State Recreation Area
35251 Hwy 62 .... Trail OR 97541 541-560-3334
Web: www.oregonstateparks.org

Kam Wah Chung State Heritage Site (KWC)
725 Summer St NE Ste C .... Salem OR 97301 503-986-0707
TF: 800-551-6949 ■
Web: oregonstateparks.org/index.cfm?do=parkpage.dsp_parkpage&parkid=5

Koberg Beach State Recreation Site
725 Summer St NE Ste C .... Salem OR 97301 503-986-0707
TF: 800-551-6949 ■
Web: oregonstateparks.org/index.cfm?do=parkpage.dsp_parkpage&parkid=115

Lake Owyhee State Park 725 Summer St NE Ste C .... Salem OR 97301 503-986-0707
TF: 800-551-6949 ■
Web: oregonstateparks.org/index.cfm?do=parkpage.dsp_parkpage&parkid=10

LaPine State Park 15800 State Recreation Rd .... La Pine OR 97739 800-551-6949
TF: 800-551-6949 ■
Web: oregonstateparks.org/index.cfm?do=parkpage.dsp_parkpage&parkid=32

Lewis & Clark State Recreation Site
725 Summer St NE Ste C .... Salem OR 97301 503-986-0707
TF: 800-551-6949 ■
Web: oregonstateparks.org/index.cfm?do=parkpage.dsp_parkpage&parkid=116

Manhattan Beach State Recreation Site
725 Summer St NE Ste C .... Salem OR 97301 503-986-0707
TF: 800-551-6949 ■
Web: oregonstateparks.org/index.cfm?do=parkpage.dsp_parkpage&parkid=138

Milo McIver State Park 24101 SE Entrance Rd .... Estacada OR 97023 503-630-7150
Web: www.oregonstateparks.org

Minam State Recreation Area
72214 Marina Ln
c/o Wallowa Lk Management Unit .... Joseph OR 97846 800-551-6949
TF: 800-551-6949 ■ *Web:* www.oregonstateparks.org

Nehalem Bay State Park
9500 Sandpiper Ln PO Box 366 .... Nehalem OR 97131 503-368-5154
Web: www.oregonstateparks.org

Neskowin Beach State Recreation Site
198 NE 123rd St .... Newport OR 97365 800-551-6949
TF: 800-551-6949 ■ *Web:* www.oregonstateparks.org

North Santiam State Recreation Area
PO Box 549 .... Detroit OR 97342 800-551-6949
TF: 800-551-6949 ■ *Web:* www.oregonstateparks.org

OC&E Woods Line State Trail
46000 Hwy 97 N 46000 Hwy 97 N .... Chiloquin OR 97624 541-883-5558
TF: 800-551-6949 ■
Web: oregonstateparks.org/index.cfm?do=parkpage.dsp_parkpage&parkid=167

Oceanside Beach State Recreation Site
13000 Whiskey Creek Rd W .... Tillamook OR 97141 800-551-6949
TF: 800-551-6949 ■ *Web:* www.oregonstateparks.org

Ona Beach State Park 5580 S Coast Hwy .... Newport OR 97366 800-551-6949
TF: 800-551-6949 ■ *Web:* www.oregonstateparks.org

Ontario State Recreation Site
23751 Old Hwy 30 .... Huntington OR 97907 800-551-6949
TF: 800-551-6949 ■ *Web:* www.oregonstateparks.org

Otter Crest State Scenic Viewpoint
198 NE 123rd St .... Newport OR 97365 800-551-6949
TF: 800-551-6949 ■ *Web:* www.oregonstateparks.org

Otter Point State Recreation Site
PO Box 1345 .... Port Orford OR 97465 800-551-6949
TF: 800-551-6949 ■ *Web:* www.oregonstateparks.org

Paradise Point State Recreation Site
PO Box 1345 .... Port Orford OR 97465 800-551-6949
TF: 800-551-6949 ■ *Web:* www.oregonstateparks.org

Prineville Reservoir State Park
19020 SE Parkland Dr .... Prineville OR 97754 541-447-4363
Web: www.oregonstateparks.org

Saddle Mountain State Natural Area
9500 Sandpiper Ln c/o Nehalem Bay Management Unit
PO Box 366 .... Nehalem OR 97138 800-551-6949
TF: 800-551-6949 ■ *Web:* www.oregonstateparks.org

Seneca Fouts Memorial State Natural Area
Wygant Trail .... Hood River OR 97014 800-551-6949
TF: 800-551-6949 ■ *Web:* www.oregonstateparks.org

Shore Acres State Park 89039 Cape Arago Hwy .... Coos Bay OR 97420 541-888-3732
Web: www.oregonstateparks.org

Silver Falls State Park
20024 Silver Falls Hwy SE .... Sublimity OR 97385 503-873-8681 873-8925
Web: www.oregonstateparks.org

Smith Rock State Park
9241 NE Crooked River Dr .... Terrebonne OR 97760 541-548-7501
Web: www.oregonstateparks.org

South Beach State Park 5580 S Coast Hwy .... South Beach OR 97366 541-867-4715
TF: 800-452-5687 ■
Web: oregonstateparks.org/index.cfm?do=parkpage.dsp_parkpage&parkid=149

Starvation Creek State Park
Historic Columbia River Highway State Trail
.... Cascade Locks OR 97014 503-695-2261
Web: www.oregonstateparks.org

Stonefield Beach State Recreation Site
725 Summer St NE 84505 Hwy 101 S .... Salem OR 97301 800-551-6949
Web: www.oregonstateparks.org

Succor Creek State Natural Area
1298 Lk Owyhee Dam Rd .... Adrian OR 97901 800-551-6949
TF: 800-551-6949 ■ *Web:* www.oregonstateparks.org

Sunset Bay State Park 89814 Cape Arago Hwy .... Coos Bay OR 97420 541-888-3778
Web: www.oregonstateparks.org

Tokatee Klootchman State Natural Site
93111 Hwy 101 N .... Florence OR 97439 800-551-6949
TF: 800-551-6949 ■ *Web:* www.oregonstateparks.org

Touvelle State Recreation Site
8598 Table Rock Rd 3792 N River Rd .... Central Point OR 97502 541-983-2277
TF: 800-551-6949 ■ *Web:* www.oregonstateparks.org

Tryon Creek State Natural Area
11321 SW Terwilliger Blvd .... Portland OR 97219 503-636-9886
Web: www.oregonstateparks.org

Tub Springs State Wayside
12845 Green Springs Hwy 3792 N River Rd .... Ashland OR 97520 800-551-6949
TF: 800-551-6949 ■ *Web:* www.oregonstateparks.org

Tumalo State Park 62976 OB Riley Rd .... Bend OR 97701 541-382-3586
Web: www.oregonstateparks.org

Ukiah-Dale Forest State Scenic Corridor
Ukiah-Dale Forest State Scenic Corridor
PO Box 85 .... Ukiah OR 97880 541-983-2277
TF: 800-551-6949 ■ *Web:* www.oregonstateparks.org

Umpqua Lighthouse State Park
84505 Hwy 101 S .... Florence OR 97439 800-551-6949
TF: 800-551-6949 ■ *Web:* www.oregonstateparks.org

Unity Forest State Scenic Corridor
US-26 23751 Old Hwy 30 .... Ironside OR 97908 800-551-6949
TF: 800-551-6949 ■ *Web:* www.oregonstateparks.org

Unity Lake State Recreation Site
18998 OR-245 59500 Hwy 26/395 .... Unity OR 97884 541-932-4453
TF: 800-551-6949 ■ *Web:* www.oregonstateparks.org

W.B. Nelson State Recreation Site
5580 S Coast Hwy .... Newport OR 97366 800-551-6949
TF: 800-551-6949 ■ *Web:* www.oregonstateparks.org

Wallowa Lake State Park 72214 Marina Ln .... Joseph OR 97846 541-388-6055
Web: www.oregonstateparks.org

Willamette Stone State Heritage Site
11321 SW Terwilliger Blvd .... Portland OR 97219 800-551-6949
TF: 800-551-6949 ■ *Web:* www.oregonstateparks.org

William M. Tugman State Park 72549 Hwy 101 ...... Lakeside OR 97449 800-551-6949
TF: 800-551-6949 ■
Web: oregonstateparks.org/index.cfm?do=parkpage.dsp_parkpage&parkid=69

Winchuck State Recreation Site
1655 Hwy 101 N .... Brookings OR 97415 800-551-6949
TF: 800-551-6949 ■ *Web:* www.oregonstateparks.org

Wolf Creek Inn State Heritage Site
PO Box 6 .... Wolf Creek OR 97497 541-866-2474 866-2692
Web: www.oregonstateparks.org

Yachats Ocean Road State Natural Site
5580 S Coast Hwy .... Newport OR 97366 800-551-6949
TF: 800-551-6949 ■ *Web:* www.oregonstateparks.org

Pennsylvania

Phone Fax

Allegheny Islands State Park
c/o Point State Park .... Prospect PA 15222 412-565-2850
Web: www.dcnr.state.pa.us/stateparks/parks/alleghenyislands.aspx

Bald Eagle State Park 149 Main Pk Rd .... Howard PA 16841 814-625-2775
Web: www.dcnr.state.pa.us

Beltzville State Park 2950 Pohopoco Dr .... Lehighton PA 18235 610-377-0045
Web: www.dcnr.state.pa.us

Bendigo State Park 533 State Pk Rd .... Johnsonburg PA 15845 814-965-2646
Web: www.dcnr.state.pa.us

Benjamin Rush State Park
c/o Ft Washington State Pk .... Fort Washington PA 19034 215-591-5250
Web: www.dcnr.state.pa.us

Big Pocono State Park
c/o Tobyhanna State Pk PO Box 387 .... Tobyhanna PA 18466 570-894-8336
Web: www.dcnr.state.pa.us/stateparks/parks/bigpocono.aspx

				Phone	Fax
Big Spring State Park c/o Colonel Denning State Pk 1599 Doubling Gap Rd *Web:* www.dcnr.state.pa.us/stateparks/parks/bigspring.aspx	Newville	PA	17241	717-776-5272	
Black Moshannon State Park 4216 Beaver Rd *Web:* www.dcnr.state.pa.us	Philipsburg	PA	16866	814-342-5960	
Blue Knob State Park 124 Pk Rd *Web:* www.dcnr.state.pa.us	Imler	PA	16655	814-276-3576	
Buchanan's Birthplace State Park c/o Cowans Gap State Pk 6235 Aughwick Rd *Web:* www.dcnr.state.pa.us/stateparks/parks/buchanansbirthplace.aspx	Fort Loudon	PA	17224	717-485-3948	
Bucktail State Park c/o Region 1 Office *Web:* www.dcnr.state.pa.us	Emporium	PA	15834	814-486-3365	
Caledonia State Park 101 Pine Grove Rd *Web:* www.dcnr.state.pa.us/stateparks/parks/caledonia.aspx	Fayetteville	PA	17222	717-352-2161	352-7026
Canoe Creek State Park 205 Canoe Creek Rd *Web:* www.dcnr.state.pa.us	Hollidaysburg	PA	16648	814-695-6807	
Chapman State Park 4790 Chapman Dam Rd *Web:* www.dcnr.state.pa.us	Clarendon	PA	16313	814-723-0250	
Cherry Springs State Park c/o Lyman Run State Pk 454 Lyman Run Rd *Web:* www.dcnr.state.pa.us/stateparks/parks/cherrysprings.aspx	Galeton	PA	16922	814-435-5010	
Clear Creek State Park 38 Clear Creek State Pk Rd *Web:* www.dcnr.state.pa.us	Sigel	PA	15860	814-752-2368	
Codorus State Park 2600 Smith Stn Rd *Web:* www.dcnr.state.pa.us	Hanover	PA	17331	717-637-2816	637-4720
Colonel Denning State Park 1599 Doubling Gap Rd *Web:* www.dcnr.state.pa.us	Newville	PA	17241	717-776-5272	
Colton Point State Park c/o Leonard Harrison State Pk 4797 Rt 660 *Web:* www.dcnr.state.pa.us/stateparks/parks/coltonpoint.aspx	Wellsboro	PA	16901	570-724-3061	
Cook Forest State Park PO Box 120 *Web:* www.dcnr.state.pa.us	Cooksburg	PA	16217	814-744-8407	
Cowans Gap State Park 6235 Aughwick Rd *Web:* www.dcnr.state.pa.us/stateparks/parks/cowansgap.aspx	Fort Loudon	PA	17224	717-485-3948	
Delaware Canal State Park 11 Lodi Hill Rd *Web:* www.dcnr.state.pa.us	Upper Black Eddy	PA	18972	610-982-5560	
Denton Hill State Park c/o Lyman Run 454 Lyman Run Rd *Web:* www.dcnr.state.pa.us/stateparks/parks/dentonhill.aspx	Galeton	PA	16922	814-435-2115	
Elk State Park c/o Bendigo State Pk 533 State Pk Rd *Web:* www.dcnr.state.pa.us/stateparks/parks/elk.aspx	Johnsonburg	PA	15845	814-965-2646	
Evansburg State Park 851 May Hall Rd *Web:* www.dcnr.state.pa.us	Collegeville	PA	19426	610-409-1150	
Fort Washington State Park 500 Bethlehem Pk *Web:* www.dcnr.state.pa.us	Fort Washington	PA	19034	215-591-5250	
Fowlers Hollow State Park c/o Colonel Denning State Pk 1599 Doubling Gap Rd *Web:* www.dcnr.state.pa.us/stateparks/parks/fowlershollow.aspx	Newville	PA	17241	717-776-5272	
Frances Slocum State Park 565 Mt Olivet Rd *Web:* www.dcnr.state.pa.us/stateparks/parks/francesslocum.aspx	Wyoming	PA	18644	570-696-3525	
French Creek State Park 843 Pk Rd *Web:* www.dcnr.state.pa.us	Elverson	PA	19520	610-582-9680	
Gifford Pinchot State Park 2200 Rosstown Rd *Web:* www.dcnr.state.pa.us	Lewisberry	PA	17339	717-432-5011	
Gouldsboro State Park c/o Tobyhanna State Pk PO Box 387 *Web:* www.dcnr.state.pa.us/stateparks/parks/gouldsboro.aspx	Tobyhanna	PA	18466	570-894-8336	
Greenwood Furnace State Park 15795 Greenwood Rd *Web:* www.dcnr.state.pa.us	Huntingdon	PA	16652	814-667-1800	
Hickory Run State Park PO Box 81 *Web:* www.dcnr.state.pa.us/stateparks/parks/hickoryrun.aspx	White Haven	PA	18661	570-443-0400	
Hills Creek State Park 111 Spillway Rd *Web:* www.dcnr.state.pa.us	Wellsboro	PA	16901	570-724-4246	
Hyner Run State Park 86 Hyner Pk Rd *Web:* www.dcnr.state.pa.us/stateparks/parks/hynerrun.aspx	Hyner	PA	17738	570-923-6000	
Hyner View State Park c/o Hyner Run State Pk 86 Hyner Pk Rd *Web:* www.dcnr.state.pa.us/stateparks/parks/hynerview.aspx	Hyner	PA	17738	570-923-6000	
Jacobsburg Environmental Education Ctr 835 Jacobsburg Rd *Web:* www.dcnr.state.pa.us	Wind Gap	PA	18091	610-746-2801	
Jennings Environmental Education Ctr 2951 Prospect Rd *Web:* www.dcnr.state.pa.us	Slippery Rock	PA	16057	724-794-6011	
Joseph E. Ibberson Conservation Area c/o Little Buffalo State Pk 1579 State Pk Rd *Web:* www.dcnr.state.pa.us/stateparks/parks/josepheibberson.aspx	Newport	PA	17074	717-567-9255	
Kettle Creek State Park 97 Kettle Creek Pk Ln *Web:* www.dcnr.state.pa.us	Renovo	PA	17764	570-923-6004	
Kings Gap Environmental Education & Training Ctr 500 Kings Gap Rd *Web:* www.dcnr.state.pa.us	Carlisle	PA	17015	717-486-5031	
Kinzua Bridge State Park c/o Bendigo State Pk 533 State Pk Rd *Web:* www.dcnr.state.pa.us/stateparks/parks/kinzuabridge.aspx	Johnsonburg	PA	15845	814-965-2646	
Kooser State Park 943 Glades Pk *Web:* www.dcnr.state.pa.us	Somerset	PA	15501	814-445-8673	
Lackawanna State Park 1839 Abington Rd *Web:* www.dcnr.state.pa.us/stateparks/parks/lackawanna.aspx	North Abington Township	PA	18414	570-945-3239	
Laurel Hill State Park 1454 Laurel Hill Pk Rd *Web:* www.dcnr.state.pa.us	Somerset	PA	15501	814-445-7725	
Laurel Mountain State Park c/o Linn Run *Web:* www.dcnr.state.pa.us/stateparks/parks/laurelmountain.aspx	Rector	PA	15677	724-238-6623	
Laurel Ridge State Park 1117 Jim Mtn Rd *Web:* www.dcnr.state.pa.us	Rockwood	PA	15557	724-455-3744	
Laurel Summit State Park PO Box 50 *Web:* www.dcnr.state.pa.us/stateparks/parks/laurelsummit.aspx	Rector	PA	15677	724-238-6623	
Lehigh Gorge State Park RR 1 PO Box 81 *Web:* www.dcnr.state.pa.us/stateparks/parks/lehighgorge.aspx	White Haven	PA	18661	570-443-0400	
Leonard Harrison State Park 4797 Rt 660 *Web:* www.dcnr.state.pa.us/stateparks/parks/leonardharrison.aspx	Wellsboro	PA	16901	570-724-3061	
Linn Run State Park PO Box 50 *Web:* www.dcnr.state.pa.us	Rector	PA	15677	724-238-6623	
Little Buffalo State Park 1579 State Pk Rd *Web:* www.dcnr.state.pa.us	Newport	PA	17074	717-567-9255	
Little Pine State Park c/o Little Pine State Pk 4205 Little Pine Creek Rd *Web:* www.dcnr.state.pa.us/stateparks/parks/upperpinebottom.aspx	Waterville	PA	17776	570-753-6000	
Locust Lake State Park 687 Tuscarora Pk Rd *Web:* www.dcnr.state.pa.us/stateparks/parks/locustlake.aspx	Barnesville	PA	18214	570-467-2404	
Lyman Run State Park 454 Lyman Run Rd *Web:* www.dcnr.state.pa.us/stateparks/parks/lymanrun.aspx	Galeton	PA	16922	814-435-5010	
Marsh Creek State Park 675 Pk Rd *Web:* www.dcnr.state.pa.us	Downingtown	PA	19335	610-458-5119	
Maurice K. Goddard State Park 684 Lk Wilhelm Rd *Web:* www.dcnr.state.pa.us	Sandy Lake	PA	16145	724-253-4833	
McCalls Dam State Park 17215 Buffalo Rd *Web:* www.dcnr.state.pa.us/stateparks/parks/mccallsdam.aspx	Mifflinburg	PA	17844	570-966-1455	
Memorial Lake State Park 18 Boundary Rd *Web:* www.dcnr.state.pa.us/stateparks/parks/memoriallake.aspx	Grantville	PA	17028	717-865-6470	
Milton State Park Bridge Ave *Web:* www.dcnr.state.pa.us/stateparks/parks/milton.aspx	Sunbury	PA	17801	570-988-5557	
Mont Alto State Park 101 Pine Grove Rd *Web:* www.dcnr.state.pa.us/stateparks/parks/montalto.aspx	Fayetteville	PA	17222	717-352-2161	352-7026
Moraine State Park 225 Pleasant Vly Rd *Web:* www.dcnr.state.pa.us/stateparks/parks/moraine.aspx	Portersville	PA	16051	724-368-8811	
Mount Pisgah State Park 28 Entrance Rd *Web:* www.dcnr.state.pa.us/stateparks/parks/mtpisgah.aspx	Troy	PA	16947	570-297-2734	
Nescopeck State Park 1137 Honey Hole Rd RR 1 PO Box 81 *Web:* www.dcnr.state.pa.us/stateparks/parks/nescopeck.aspx	Drums	PA	18222	570-403-2006	
Neshaminy State Park 3401 State Rd *Web:* www.dcnr.state.pa.us	Bensalem	PA	19020	215-639-4538	
Nockamixon State Park 1542 Mtn View Dr *Web:* www.dcnr.state.pa.us	Quakertown	PA	18951	215-529-7300	
Nolde Forest Environmental Education Ctr 2910 New Holland Rd *Web:* www.dcnr.state.pa.us	Reading	PA	19607	610-796-3699	
Norristown Farm Park 2500 Upper Farm Rd *Web:* www.dcnr.state.pa.us	Norristown	PA	19403	610-270-0215	
Oil Creek State Park 305 State Pk Rd *Web:* www.dcnr.state.pa.us	Oil City	PA	16301	814-676-5915	
Ole Bull State Park 31 Valhella VW *Web:* www.dcnr.state.pa.us	Cross Fork	PA	17729	814-435-5000	
Parker Dam State Park 28 Fairview Rd *Web:* www.dcnr.state.pa.us/stateparks/parks/parkerdam.aspx	Penfield	PA	15849	814-765-0630	
Patterson State Park c/o Lyman Run 454 Lyman Run Rd *Web:* www.dcnr.state.pa.us/stateparks/parks/patterson.aspx	Galeton	PA	16922	814-435-5010	
Penn-Roosevelt State Park c/o Greenwood Furnace PO Box 118 *Web:* www.dcnr.state.pa.us/stateparks/parks/pennroosevelt.aspx	Huntingdon	PA	16652	814-667-1800	
Pine Grove Furnace State Park 1100 Pine Grove Rd *TF:* 888-727-2757 ■ *Web:* www.dcnr.state.pa.us	Gardners	PA	17324	717-486-7174	486-4961
Poe Paddy State Park c/o Reeds Gap *Web:* www.dcnr.state.pa.us/stateparks/parks/poepaddy.aspx	Milroy	PA	17063	717-667-3622	
Point State Park 101 Commonwealth Pl *Web:* www.dcnr.state.pa.us	Pittsburgh	PA	15222	412-471-0235	
Presque Isle State Park 301 Peninsula Dr Ste 1 *TF:* 888-727-2757 ■ *Web:* www.dcnr.state.pa.us	Erie	PA	16505	814-833-7424	833-0266
Prince Gallitzin State Park 966 Marina Rd *Web:* www.dcnr.state.pa.us	Patton	PA	16668	814-674-1000	
Promised Land State Park PO Box 96 *Web:* www.dcnr.state.pa.us	Greentown	PA	18426	570-676-3428	
Prompton State Park c/o Lackawanna *TF:* 888-727-2757 ■ *Web:* www.dcnr.state.pa.us/stateparks/parks/prompton.aspx	North Abington Township	PA	18414	570-945-3239	
Prouty Place State Park c/o Lyman Run State Pk 454 Lyman Run Rd *Web:* www.dcnr.state.pa.us/stateparks/parks/proutyplace.aspx	Galeton	PA	16922	814-435-5010	
R. B. Winter State Park 17215 Buffalo Rd *Web:* www.dcnr.state.pa.us/stateparks/parks/rbwinter.aspx	Mifflinburg	PA	17844	570-966-1455	
Raccoon Creek State Park 3000 State Rt 18 *Web:* www.dcnr.state.pa.us/stateparks/parks/raccooncreek.aspx	Hookstown	PA	15050	724-899-2200	
Ralph Stover State Park c/o Delaware Canal State Pk 11 Lodi Hill Rd *Web:* www.dcnr.state.pa.us	Upper Black Eddy	PA	18972	610-982-5560	
Ravensburg State Park c/o R B Winter State Pk 17215 Buffalo Rd *Web:* www.dcnr.state.pa.us/stateparks/parks/ravensburg.aspx	Mifflinburg	PA	17844	570-966-1455	
Reeds Gap State Park 1405 New Lancaster Vly Rd *Web:* www.dcnr.state.pa.us	Milroy	PA	17063	717-667-3622	
Ricketts Glen State Park 695 State Rt 487 *Web:* www.dcnr.state.pa.us/stateparks/parks/rickettsglen.aspx	Benton	PA	17814	570-477-5675	

				Phone	Fax
Ridley Creek State Park 1023 Sycamore Mills Rd. *Web:* www.dcnr.state.pa.us	Media	PA	19063	610-892-3900	
Ryerson Station State Park 361 Bristoria Rd *Web:* www.dcnr.state.pa.us	Wind Ridge	PA	15380	724-428-4254	
S. B. Elliott State Park c/o Parker Dam State Pk 28 Fairview Rd. *Web:* www.dcnr.state.pa.us/stateparks/parks/sbelliott.aspx	Penfield	PA	15849	814-765-0630	
Salt Springs State Park c/o Lackawanna *TF:* 888-727-2757 ■ *Web:* www.dcnr.state.pa.us/stateparks/parks/saltsprings.aspx	North Abington Twp	PA	18414	570-945-3239	
Samuel S. Lewis State Park c/o Gifford Pinchot State Pk 2200 Rosstown Rd *Web:* www.dcnr.state.pa.us	Lewisberry	PA	17339	717-432-5011	
Sand Bridge State Park c/o R B Winter State Pk 13180 Buffalo Rd *Web:* www.dcnr.state.pa.us/stateparks/parks/sandbridge.aspx	Mifflinburg	PA	17844	570-966-1455	
Shawnee State Park 132 State Pk Rd. *Web:* www.dcnr.state.pa.us	Schellsburg	PA	15559	814-733-4218	
Shikellamy State Park Bridge Ave. *Web:* www.dcnr.state.pa.us	Sunbury	PA	17801	570-988-5557	
Sinnemahoning State Park 8288 First Fork Rd *Web:* www.dcnr.state.pa.us	Austin	PA	16720	814-647-8401	
Sizerville State Park 199 E Cowley Run Rd. *Web:* www.dcnr.state.pa.us	Emporium	PA	15834	814-486-5605	
Susquehannock State Park 1880 Pk Dr. *Web:* www.dcnr.state.pa.us	Drumore	PA	17518	717-432-5011	
Tobyhanna State Park PO Box 387 *Web:* www.dcnr.state.pa.us	Tobyhanna	PA	18466	570-894-8336	
Tuscarora State Park 687 Tuscarora Pk Rd *Web:* www.dcnr.state.pa.us/stateparks/parks/tuscarora.aspx	Barnesville	PA	18214	570-467-2404	
Tyler State Park 101 Swamp Rd *Web:* www.dcnr.state.pa.us	Newtown	PA	18940	215-968-2021	
White Clay Creek Preserve PO Box 172 *Web:* www.dcnr.state.pa.us	Landenberg	PA	19350	610-274-2900	
Worlds End State Park 82 Cabin Bridge Rd *Web:* www.dcnr.state.pa.us/stateparks/parks/worldsend.aspx	Forksville	PA	18616	570-924-3287	
Yellow Creek State Park 170 Rt 259 Hwy *Web:* www.dcnr.state.pa.us	Penn Run	PA	15765	724-357-7913	

Rhode Island

				Phone	Fax
Charlestown Breachway Charlestown Beach Rd *Web:* riparks.com	Charlestown	RI	02813	401-364-7000	322-3083
Colt State Park Hope St. *Web:* www.riparks.com	Bristol	RI	02809	401-253-7482	253-6766
East Beach One Burlingame State Pk *Web:* www.riparks.com	Charlestown	RI	02813	401-322-0450	322-3083
East Matunuck State Beach 950 Succotash Rd. *Web:* www.riparks.com	South Kingstown	RI	02881	401-789-8585	
Fishermen's Memorial State Park 1011 Pt Judith Rd. *Web:* www.riparks.com	Narragansett	RI	02882	401-789-8374	
Fort Adams State Park Harrison Ave *Web:* www.riparks.com	Newport	RI	02840	401-847-2400	841-9821
Goddard Memorial State Park 1095 Ives Rd *Web:* riparks.com	Warwick	RI	02818	401-884-2010	885-7720
Lincoln Woods State Park Two Manchester Print Works Rd. *Web:* www.riparks.com	Lincoln	RI	02865	401-723-7892	724-7951
Roger W. Wheeler State Beach 100 Sand Hill Cove Rd *Web:* www.riparks.com	Narragansett	RI	02882	401-789-3563	
Snake Den State Park 2321 Hartford Ave. *Web:* www.riparks.com	Johnston	RI	02919	401-222-2632	
World War II Memorial State Park c/o Lincoln Woods State Pk 2 Manchester Print Works Rd. *Web:* www.riparks.com	Lincoln	RI	02865	401-762-9717	

South Carolina

				Phone	Fax
Aiken State Natural Area 1145 State Pk Rd. *Web:* www.southcarolinaparks.com	Windsor	SC	29856	803-649-2857	
Andrew Jackson State Park 196 Andrew Jackson Pk Rd *Web:* www.southcarolinaparks.com	Lancaster	SC	29720	803-285-3344	
Baker Creek State Park 863 Baker Creek Rd. *Web:* southcarolinaparks.com/bakercreek/default.aspx	McCormick	SC	29835	864-443-2457	
Barnwell State Park 223 State Pk Rd. *Web:* www.southcarolinaparks.com	Blackville	SC	29817	803-284-2212	
Caesars Head State Park 8155 Geer Hwy *TF:* 866-345-7275 ■ *Web:* www.southcarolinaparks.com	Cleveland	SC	29635	864-836-6115	836-3081
Calhoun Falls State Recreation Area 46 Maintenance Shop Rd *TF:* 866-345-7275 ■ *Web:* www.southcarolinaparks.com	Calhoun Falls	SC	29628	864-447-8267	447-8638
Charles Towne Landing State Historic Site 1500 Old Towne Rd. *TF:* 866-345-7275 ■ *Web:* www.southcarolinaparks.com	Charleston	SC	29407	843-852-4200	852-4205
Cheraw State Park 100 State Pk Rd *Web:* www.southcarolinaparks.com	Cheraw	SC	29520	843-537-9656	
Chester State Park 759 State Pk Dr *Web:* www.southcarolinaparks.com	Chester	SC	29706	803-385-2680	
Colleton State Park 147 Wayside Ln *Web:* www.southcarolinaparks.com	Canadys	SC	29433	843-538-8206	
Colonial Dorchester State Historic Site 300 State Pk Rd *Web:* www.southcarolinaparks.com	Summerville	SC	29485	843-873-1740	
Croft State Natural Area 450 Croft State Pk Rd *Web:* www.southcarolinaparks.com	Spartanburg	SC	29302	864-585-1283	
Devils Fork State Park 161 Holcombe Cir **Fax Area Code: 877 ■ *TF:* 866-345-7275 ■ *Web:* www.southcarolinaparks.com	Salem	SC	29676	864-944-2639	228-8527*
Dreher Island State Recreation Area 3677 State Pk Rd *TF:* 866-345-7275 ■ *Web:* www.southcarolinaparks.com	Prosperity	SC	29127	803-364-4152	364-0756
Edisto Beach State Park 8377 State Cabin Rd. *TF:* 800-315-3087 ■ *Web:* www.southcarolinaparks.com	Edisto Island	SC	29438	843-869-2756	869-4428
Givhans Ferry State Park 746 Givhans Ferry Rd *Web:* www.southcarolinaparks.com	Ridgeville	SC	29472	843-873-0692	
Goodale State Park 650 Pk Rd *Web:* www.southcarolinaparks.com	Camden	SC	29020	803-432-2772	
Hamilton Branch State Recreation Area 111 Campground Rd *Web:* www.southcarolinaparks.com	Plum Branch	SC	29845	864-333-2223	
Hampton Plantation State Historic Site 1950 Rutledge Rd. *TF:* 800-315-3087 ■ *Web:* www.southcarolinaparks.com	McClellanville	SC	29458	843-546-9361	527-4995
Hickory Knob State Resort Park 1591 Resort Dr *TF:* 800-491-1764 ■ *Web:* www.southcarolinaparks.com	McCormick	SC	29835	864-391-2450	391-5390
Hunting Island State Park 2555 Sea Island Pkwy. *TF:* 800-315-3087 ■ *Web:* www.southcarolinaparks.com	Hunting Island	SC	29920	843-838-2011	838-4263
Huntington Beach State Park 16148 Ocean Hwy. *TF:* 800-491-1764 ■ *Web:* www.southcarolinaparks.com	Murrells Inlet	SC	29576	843-237-4440	237-3387
Jones Gap State Park 303 Jones Gap Rd *Web:* www.southcarolinaparks.com	Marietta	SC	29661	864-836-3647	
Keowee-Toxaway State Natural Area 108 Residence Dr *Web:* www.southcarolinaparks.com	Sunset	SC	29685	864-868-2605	
Kings Mountain State Park 1277 Pk Rd *Web:* www.southcarolinaparks.com	Blacksburg	SC	29702	803-222-3209	222-6948
Lake Greenwood State Recreation Area 302 State Pk Rd *Web:* www.southcarolinaparks.com	Ninety Six	SC	29666	864-543-3535	
Lake Hartwell State Recreation Area 19138 S Hwy 11 Ste A *Web:* www.southcarolinaparks.com	Fair Play	SC	29643	864-972-3352	
Lake Warren State Park 1079 Lk Warren Rd *Web:* www.southcarolinaparks.com	Hampton	SC	29924	803-943-5051	
Lake Wateree State Recreation Area 881 State Pk Rd *Web:* www.southcarolinaparks.com	Winnsboro	SC	29180	803-482-6401	482-6126
Landsford Canal State Park 2051 Pk Dr. *Web:* www.southcarolinaparks.com	Catawba	SC	29704	803-789-5800	
Lee State Natural Area 487 Loop Rd *Web:* www.southcarolinaparks.com	Bishopville	SC	29010	803-428-5307	
Little Pee Dee State Park 1298 State Pk Rd *TF:* 800-491-1764 ■ *Web:* www.southcarolinaparks.com	Dillon	SC	29536	843-774-8872	
Musgrove Mill State Historic Site 398 State Pk Rd *Web:* www.southcarolinaparks.com	Clinton	SC	29325	864-938-0100	
Myrtle Beach State Park 4401 S Kings Hwy *Web:* www.southcarolinaparks.com	Myrtle Beach	SC	29575	843-238-5325	
Oconee State Park 624 State Pk Rd *Web:* www.southcarolinaparks.com	Mountain Rest	SC	29664	864-638-5353	638-8776
Oconee Station State Historic Site 500 Oconee Stn Rd. *Web:* www.southcarolinaparks.com	Walhalla	SC	29691	864-638-0079	
Paris Mountain State Park 2401 State Pk Rd *TF:* 866-345-7275 ■ *Web:* www.southcarolinaparks.com	Greenville	SC	29609	864-244-5565	
Poinsett State Park 6660 Poinsett Pk Rd *Web:* www.southcarolinaparks.com	Wedgefield	SC	29168	803-494-8177	
Redcliffe Plantation State Historic Site 181 Redcliffe Rd *Web:* www.southcarolinaparks.com	Beech Island	SC	29842	803-827-1473	
Rivers Bridge State Historic Site 325 State Pk Rd *Web:* www.southcarolinaparks.com	Ehrhardt	SC	29081	803-267-3675	
Rose Hill Plantation State Historic Site 2677 SaRdis Rd *Web:* www.southcarolinaparks.com	Union	SC	29379	864-427-5966	
Sadlers Creek State Park 940 Sadlers Creek Rd *Web:* www.southcarolinaparks.com	Anderson	SC	29626	864-226-8950	
Santee State Park 251 State Pk Rd *Web:* www.southcarolinaparks.com	Santee	SC	29142	803-854-2408	854-4834
Sesquicentennial State Park 9564 Two Notch Rd. *TF:* 888-245-9300 ■ *Web:* www.southcarolinaparks.com	Columbia	SC	29223	803-788-2706	788-4414
Table Rock State Park 158 E Ellison Ln. *Web:* www.southcarolinaparks.com	Pickens	SC	29671	864-878-9813	878-9077
Woods Bay State Natural Area 11020 Woods Bay Rd *Web:* www.southcarolinaparks.com	Olanta	SC	29114	843-659-4445	

South Dakota

				Phone	Fax
Adams Homestead & Nature Preserve 272 Westshore Dr. *Web:* gfp.sd.gov	McCook Lake	SD	57049	605-232-0873	

Phone | Fax

Bear Butte State Park 20250 Hwy 79 PO Box 688........Sturgis SD 57785 605-347-5240
Web: gfp.sd.gov/state-parks/directory/bear-butte

Beaver Creek Nature Area
20641 SD Hwy 1806 25495 485th Ave...............Fort Pierre SD 57532 605-223-7660 773-6245
TF: 800-710-2267 ■ *Web:* gfp.sd.gov

Big Sioux Recreation Area 410 Pk Ave..............Brandon SD 57005 605-582-7243
Web: gfp.sd.gov/state-parks/directory/big-sioux

Big Stone Island Nature Area
c/o Hartford Beach State Pk
13672 Hartford Beach Rd.......................... Corona SD 57227 605-432-6374
Web: gfp.sd.gov/state-parks/directory/big-stone

Burke Lake Recreation Area
523 E Capitol Ave 35316 SD Hwy 44....................Pierre SD 57501 605-223-7660
Web: www.gfp.sd.gov

Buryanek Recreation Area 27450 Buryanek Rd.........Burke SD 57523 605-337-2587
Web: www.gfp.sd.gov/state-parks/directory/buryanek

Chief White Crane Recreation Area
31323 Toe Rd...................................Yankton SD 57078 605-668-2985
Web: www.gfp.sd.gov/state-parks/directory/chief-white-crane

Custer State Park 13329 US Hwy 16A................. Custer SD 57730 605-255-4515 255-4460
Web: gfp.sd.gov

Farm Island Recreation Area
1301 Farm Island Rd...............................Pierre SD 57501 605-773-2885
Web: gfp.sd.gov

Fisher Grove State Park 17290 Fishers Ln.......... Frankfort SD 57440 605-472-1336
Web: gfp.sd.gov

Fort Sisseton State Historical Park
11907 434th Ave...............................Lake City SD 57247 605-448-5474
Web: gfp.sd.gov/state parks/directory/fort-sisseton

George S. Mickelson Trail 11361 Nevada Gulch Rd....... Lead SD 57754 605-584-3896
Web: gfp.sd.gov/state-parks/directory/mickelson-trail

Hartford Beach State Park
13672 Hartford Beach Rd.......................... Corona SD 57227 605-432-6374
Web: gfp.sd.gov/state-parks/directory/hartford-beach

Indian Creek Recreation Area
12905 288th Ave................................Mobridge SD 57601 605-845-7112
Web: www.gfp.sd.gov/state-parks/directory/indian-creek

Lake Alvin Recreation Area
c/o Newton Hills State Pk 27225 480th Ave..........Harrisburg SD 57032 605-987-2263
Web: gfp.sd.gov

Lake Cochrane Recreation Area 3454 Edgewater Dr.......Gary SD 57237 605-882-5200
Web: gfp.sd.gov/state-parks/directory/lake-cochrane

Lake Herman State Park 23409 State Pk Dr.......... Madison SD 57042 605-256-5003
Web: gfp.sd.gov

Lake Hiddenwood Recreation Area
c/o W Whitlock Recreation Area
16157A W Whitlock Rd..........................Gettysburg SD 57442 605-765-9410
Web: www.gfp.sd.gov

Lake Poinsett Recreation Area 46109 202nd St.........Bruce SD 57220 605-627-5441
Web: sd.gov

Lake Thompson Recreation Area
21176 Flood Club Rd.........................Lake Preston SD 57249 605-847-4893
Web: gfp.sd.gov

Lake Vermillion Recreation Area
26140 451st Ave................................Canistota SD 57012 605-296-3643

Lewis & Clark Recreation Area
43349 SD Hwy 52.................................Yankton SD 57078 605-668-2985
Web: lewisandclarkpark.com

Little Moreau Recreation Area
c/o Shadehill Recreation Area
19150 Summerville Rd...........................Shadehill SD 57653 605-374-5114
Web: gfp.sd.gov/state-parks/directory/little-moreau

Llewellyn Johns Recreation Area
c/o Shadehill Recreation Area
19150 Summerville Rd...........................Shadehill SD 57653 605-374-5114
Web: gfp.sd.gov

Mina Lake Recreation Area
c/o Richmond Lk Recreation Area 402 Park Ave............ Mina SD 57451 605-626-3488
Web: www.gfp.sd.gov

Newton Hills State Park 28767 482nd Ave............Canton SD 57013 605-987-2263
Web: gfp.sd.gov

North Point Recreation Area
38180 297th St.............................. Lake Andes SD 57356 605-487-7046
Web: www.gfp.sd.gov/state-parks/directory/north-point

North Wheeler Recreation Area
29084 N Wheeler Rd.............................. Geddes SD 57342 605-487-7046
Web: www.gfp.sd.gov/state-parks/directory/north-wheeler

Oahe Downstream Recreation Area
20439 Marina Loop Rd........................Fort Pierre SD 57532 605-223-7722
Web: www.gfp.sd.gov/state-parks/directory/oahe-downstream

Oakwood Lakes State Park 46109 202nd St............Bruce SD 57220 605-627-5441
Web: sd.gov

Okobojo Point Recreation Area
19425 Okobojo Pt Dr.........................Fort Pierre SD 57532 605-223-7722
Web: www.gfp.sd.gov/state-parks/directory/okobojo-point

Pease Creek Recreation Area 37270 293rd St......... Geddes SD 57342 605-487-7046
Web: www.gfp.sd.gov/state-parks/directory/pease-creek

Pickerel Lake Recreation Area
12980 446th Ave...............................Grenville SD 57239 605-486-4753
Web: gfp.sd.gov

Pierson Ranch Recreation Area 31144 Toe Rd........Yankton SD 57078 605-668-2985
Web: www.gfp.sd.gov/state-parks/directory/pierson-ranch

Platte Creek Recreation Area
c/o Snake Creek Recreation Area
35910 282nd St...................................Platte SD 57369 605-337-2587
Web: gfp.sd.gov

Roy Lake State Park 11545 Northside Dr............Lake City SD 57247 605-448-5701
Web: gfp.sd.gov

Sica Hollow State Park
44950 Park Rd 44950 Park Rd...................... Sisseton SD 57247 605-448-5701
Web: gfp.sd.gov

Snake Creek Recreation Area 35316 SD Hwy 44.........Platte SD 57369 605-337-2587
Web: gfp.sd.gov

Spirit Mound Historic Prairie
31148 SD Hwy 19..............................Vermillion SD 57069 605-987-2263
Web: www.gfp.sd.gov/state-parks/directory/spirit-mound

Spring Creek Recreation Area
c/o Oahe Downstream Recreation Area
20439 Marina Loop Rd.........................Fort Pierre SD 57532 605-223-7722
Web: www.gfp.sd.gov/state-parks/directory/spring-creek

Swan Creek Recreation Area
c/o W Whitlock Recreation Area
16157A W Whitlock Rd..........................Gettysburg SD 57442 605-765-9410
Web: www.gfp.sd.gov

West Bend Recreation Area 22154 Wt Bend Rd........ Harrold SD 57536 605-773-2885
Web: gfp.sd.gov

West Whitlock Recreation Area
16157A W Whitlock Rd..........................Gettysburg SD 57442 605-765-9410
Web: gfp.sd.gov

Tennessee

Phone | Fax

Bicentennial Capitol Mall State Park
600 James Robertson Pkwy........................Nashville TN 37243 615-741-5280
Web: www.state.tn.us

Big Cypress Tree State Park
295 Big Cypress Rd............................Greenfield TN 38230 731-235-2700
Web: www.state.tn.us

Big Hill Pond State Park
1435 John Howell Rd..........................Pocahontas TN 38061 731-645-7967
Web: www.state.tn.us

Big Ridge State Park 1015 Big Ridge Rd.......... Maynardville TN 37807 865-992-5523
Web: www.state.tn.us

Bledsoe Creek State Park 400 Zieglers Ft Rd.......... Gallatin TN 37066 615-452-3706
Web: www.state.tn.us

Booker T. Washington State Park
5801 Champion Rd........................... Chattanooga TN 37416 423-894-4955 855-7879
Web: www.state.tn.us

Burgess Falls State Natural Area
4000 Burgess Falls Dr............................. Sparta TN 38583 931-432-5312
Web: www.state.tn.us

Cedars of Lebanon State Park
328 Cedar Forest Rd............................ Lebanon TN 37087 615-443-2769 443-2793
TF: 800-342-3145 ■ *Web:* www.state.tn.us

Chickasaw State Park 20 Cabin Ln................Henderson TN 38340 731-989-5141
Web: www.state.tn.us

Cordell Hull Birthplace State Park
1300 Cordell Hull Memorial Dr...................Byrdstown TN 38549 931-864-3247 864-6389
Web: www.state.tn.us

Cove Lake State Park 110 Cove Lake Ln............ Caryville TN 37714 423-566-9701 566-9717
TF: 800-342-3145 ■ *Web:* www.state.tn.us

Cumberland Mountain State Park
24 Office Dr..................................... Crossville TN 38555 931-484-6138
Web: www.state.tn.us

David Crockett State Park
1400 W Gaines PO Box 398................... Lawrenceburg TN 38464 931-762-9408 766-0047
Web: www.state.tn.us

Davy Crockett Birthplace State Park
1245 Davy Crockett Pk Rd.......................Limestone TN 37681 423-257-2167 257-2430
TF: 800-342-3145 ■ *Web:* www.state.tn.us

Dunbar Cave State Natural Area
401 Dunbar Cave Rd............................Clarksville TN 37043 931-648-5526
Web: www.state.tn.us

Edgar Evins State Park
1630 Edgar Evins State Pk Rd.................... Silver Point TN 38582 931-858-2446
Web: www.state.tn.us

Fall Creek Falls State Resort Park
2009 Village Camp Rd Rt 3 PO Box 300...............Pikeville TN 37367 423-881-5298
Web: www.state.tn.us

Fort Loudoun State Historic Park
338 Ft Loudoun Rd...............................Vonore TN 37885 423-884-6217
Web: www.state.tn.us

Fort Pillow State Historic Park 3122 Pk Rd..........Henning TN 38041 731-738-5581 738-9117
TF: 800-342-3145 ■ *Web:* www.state.tn.us

Frozen Head State Natural Area
964 Flat Fork Rd...............................Wartburg TN 37887 423-346-3318 346-6629
TF: 800-342-3145 ■ *Web:* www.state.tn.us

Harrison Bay State Park
8411 Harrison Bay Rd........................... Harrison TN 37341 423-344-6214
Web: www.state.tn.us

Henry Horton State Resort Park
4358 Nashville Hwy............................ Chapel Hill TN 37034 931-364-2222
Web: www.state.tn.us

Indian Mountain State Park 143 State Pk Cir........... Jellico TN 37762 423-784-7958
Web: www.state.tn.us

Johnsonville State Historic Park
900 Nell Beard Rd......................... New Johnsonville TN 37134 931-535-2789 535-3776
Web: tnstateparks.com

Justin P. Wilson Cumberland Trail State Park
220 Pk Rd....................................... Caryville TN 38555 423-566-2229 566-2290
TF: 800-342-3145 ■ *Web:* www.state.tn.us

Meeman-Shelby Forest State Park
910 Riddick Rd................................. Millington TN 38053 901-876-5215 876-3217
Web: www.state.tn.us

Montgomery Bell State Resort Park
1020 Jackson Hill Rd..............................Burns TN 37029 615-797-9052
Web: www.state.tn.us

Mousetail Landing State Park
Three Campground Rd.............................Linden TN 37096 731-847-0841
Web: www.state.tn.us

Natchez Trace State Park
24845 Natchez Trace Rd........................Wildersville TN 38388 731-968-3742
Web: www.state.tn.us

Phone Fax

Nathan Bedford Forrest State Park
1825 Pilot Knob Rd .... Eva TN 38333 731-584-6356 584-1841
Web: www.state.tn.us

Norris Dam State Resort Park
125 Village Green Cir .... Lake City TN 37769 865-426-7461
Web: www.state.tn.us

Old Stone Fort State Archaeological Park
732 Stone Ft Dr .... Manchester TN 37355 931-723-5073
Web: www.state.tn.us

Panther Creek State Park
2010 Panther Creek Pk Rd .... Morristown TN 37814 423-587-7046 587-7047
Web: www.state.tn.us

Paris Landing State Park 16055 Hwy 79N .... Buchanan TN 38222 731-641-4465
Web: www.state.tn.us

Pickett State Park 4605 Pickett Pk Hwy .... Jamestown TN 38556 931-879-5821
Web: www.state.tn.us

Pickwick Landing State Resort Park
PO Box 15 .... Pickwick Dam TN 38365 731-689-3129
Web: www.state.tn.us

Pinson Mounds State Archaeological Park
460 Ozier Rd .... Pinson TN 38366 731-988-5614
Web: www.state.tn.us

Port Royal State Historic Park
3300 Old Clarksville Hwy .... Adams TN 37010 931-648-5526
Web: www.state.tn.us

Radnor Lake State Park 1160 Otter Creek Rd .... Nashville TN 37220 615-373-3467
Web: tnstateparks.com

Red Clay State Historic Park
1140 Red Clay Pk Rd .... Cleveland TN 37311 423-478-0339
Web: www.state.tn.us

Roan Mountain State Park 1015 Hwy 143 .... Roan Mountain TN 37687 423-772-0190
Web: www.state.tn.us

Rock Island State Park 82 Beach Rd .... Rock Island TN 38581 931-686-2471
Web: www.state.tn.us

Sergeant Alvin C. York State Historic Park
General Delivery Hwy 127 .... Pall Mall TN 38577 931-879-6456
Web: www.state.tn.us

South Cumberland Recreation Area
11745 US 41 .... Monteagle TN 37356 931-692-3887
Web: www.state.tn.us

Standing Stone State Park
1674 Standing Stone Pk Hwy .... Hilham TN 38568 931-823-6347
Web: www.state.tn.us

Sycamore Shoals State Historic Park
1651 W Elk Ave .... Elizabethton TN 37643 423-543-5808 543-0078
Web: www.state.tn.us

T. O. Fuller State Park 1500 Mitchell Rd .... Memphis TN 38109 901-543-7581 785-8485
Web: www.state.tn.us

Tims Ford State Park 570 Tims Ford Dr .... Winchester TN 37398 931-962-1183
Web: www.state.tn.us

Warriors' Path State Park PO Box 5026 .... Kingsport TN 37663 423-239-8531 239-4982
Web: www.state.tn.us

Texas

Phone Fax

Abilene State Park 150 Pk Rd 32 .... Tuscola TX 79562 325-572-3204 572-3008
Web: www.tpwd.state.tx.us

Admiral Nimitz State Historic Site
328 E Main St .... Fredericksburg TX 78624 830-997-4379
Web: www.thc.state.tx.us

Atlanta State Park 927 Pk Rd 42 .... Atlanta TX 75551 903-796-6476
Web: www.tpwd.state.tx.us

Balmorhea State Park PO Box 15 .... Toyahvale TX 79786 432-375-2370
Web: www.tpwd.state.tx.us

Barton Warnock Environmental Education Ctr
PO Box 375 HC 70 .... Terlingua TX 79852 432-424-3327
Web: www.tpwd.state.tx.us

Bastrop State Park 3005 Hwy 21 E .... Bastrop TX 78602 512-321-2101
Web: www.tpwd.state.tx.us

Bentsen-Rio Grande Valley State Park
2800 S Bensen Palm Dr .... Mission TX 78572 956-585-1107 584-9126
TF: 800-792-1112 ■ *Web:* www.theworldbirdingcenter.com

Big Bend Ranch State Park PO Box 2319 .... Presidio TX 79845 432-229-3416
Web: tpwd.state.tx.us/state-parks/big-bend-ranch

Blanco State Park PO Box 493 .... Blanco TX 78606 830-833-4333
Web: www.tpwd.state.tx.us

Bonham State Park 1363 State Pk 24 .... Bonham TX 75418 903-583-5022
Web: www.tpwd.state.tx.us

Brazos Bend State Park 21901 FM 762 .... Needville TX 77461 409-553-5101
Web: www.tpwd.state.tx.us

Buescher State Park PO Box 75 .... Smithville TX 78957 512-237-2241
Web: www.tpwd.state.tx.us

Caddo Lake State Park 245 Pk Rd 2 .... Karnack TX 75661 903-679-3351
Web: www.tpwd.state.tx.us

Caddoan Mounds State Historic Site
1649 Texas 21 .... Alto TX 75925 936-858-3218
Web: www.tpwd.state.tx.us

Caprock Canyons State Park & Trailway
850 Caprock Canyon Pk Rd .... Quitaque TX 79255 806-455-1492
Web: www.tpwd.state.tx.us

Casa Navarro State Historic Site
228 S Laredo St .... San Antonio TX 78207 210-226-4801 226-4801
Web: www.tpwd.state.tx.us

Cedar Hill State Park 1570 W FM 1382 .... Cedar Hill TX 75104 972-291-3900
Web: www.tpwd.state.tx.us

Choke Canyon State Park PO Box 2 .... Calliham TX 78007 361-786-3868
Web: www.tpwd.state.tx.us

Cleburne State Park 5800 Pk Rd 21 .... Cleburne TX 76031 817-645-4215
Web: tpwd.state.tx.us/state-parks/cleburne

Colorado Bend State Park 6031 Colorado Pk Rd .... Bend TX 76824 325-628-3240
Web: www.tpwd.state.tx.us

Phone Fax

Confederate Reunion Grounds State Historic Site
c/o Ft Parker State Pk 194 Pk Rd 28 .... Mexia TX 76667 254-562-5751
Web: tpwd.state.tx.us/spdest/parkinfo/former_tpwd_parks/

Cooper Lake State Park 1664 Farm Rd 1529 S .... Cooper TX 75432 903-395-3100
Web: www.tpwd.state.tx.us

Copper Breaks State Park 777 Pk Rd 62 .... Quanah TX 79252 940-839-4331
Web: www.tpwd.state.tx.us

Daingerfield State Park 455 Pk Rd 17 .... Daingerfield TX 75638 903-645-2921
Web: www.tpwd.state.tx.us

Davis Mountains State Park PO Box 1458 .... Fort Davis TX 79734 432-426-3337
Web: www.tpwd.state.tx.us

Devil's Sinkhole State Natural Area
101 N Sweeten St .... Rocksprings TX 78880 830-683-3762
Web: www.tpwd.state.tx.us

Devils River State Natural Area
HC 01 PO Box 513 .... Del Rio TX 78840 830-395-2133
Web: www.tpwd.state.tx.us

Eisenhower Birthplace State Historic Site
609 S Lamar Ave .... Denison TX 75021 903-465-8908
Web: www.tpwd.state.tx.us

Enchanted Rock State Natural Area
16710 Ranch Rd 965 .... Fredericksburg TX 78624 325-247-3903
Web: www.tpwd.state.tx.us

exas Parks and Wildlife Departmenty
1331 McKelligon Canyon Rd .... El Paso TX 79930 915-566-6441
Web: www.tpwd.state.tx.us

Fairfield Lake State Park
123 State Pk Rd 64 .... Fairfield TX 75840 903-389-4514
Web: tpwd.state.tx.us/state-parks/fairfield-lake

Falcon State Park PO Box 2 .... Falcon Heights TX 78545 956-848-5327
Web: www.tpwd.state.tx.us

Fannin Battleground State Historic Site
c/o Goliad State Pk 108 Pk Rd 6 .... Goliad TX 77963 361-645-3405
Web: www.tpwd.state.tx.us

Fanthorp Inn State Historic Site
579 Main St .... Anderson TX 77830 936-873-2633
Web: www.tpwd.state.tx.us

Fort Griffin State Park & Historic Site
1701 N US Hwy 283 .... Albany TX 76430 325-762-3592
Web: www.tpwd.state.tx.us

Fort Lancaster State Historic Site
PO Box 306 .... Sheffield TX 79781 432-836-4391
Web: www.tpwd.state.tx.us

Fort Leaton State Historic Site PO Box 2319 .... Presidio TX 79845 432-229-3613
Web: tpwd.state.tx.us/state-parks/fort-leaton

Fort McKavett State Historic Site
7066 FM 864 Rd .... Fort McKavett TX 76841 325-396-2358
Web: www.visitfortmckavett.com/index.aspx?page=9

Fort Parker State Park 194 Pk Rd 28 .... Mexia TX 76667 254-562-5751
Web: tpwd.state.tx.us/state-parks/fort-parker

Fort Richardson State Park Historic Site & Lost Creek Reservoir State Trailway
228 State Pk Rd 61 .... Jacksboro TX 76458 940-567-3506
Web: www.tpwd.state.tx.us

Galveston Island State Park
14901 Termini San Luis Pass Rd .... Galveston TX 77554 409-737-1222
Web: www.tpwd.state.tx.us

Goliad State Park 108 Pk Rd 6 .... Goliad TX 77963 361-645-3405
Web: www.tpwd.state.tx.us

Goose Island State Park 202 S Palmetto St .... Rockport TX 78382 361-729-2858
Web: www.tpwd.state.tx.us

Government Canyon State Natural Area
12861 Galm Rd .... San Antonio TX 78254 210-688-9055
Web: www.tpwd.state.tx.us

Guadalupe River State Park
3350 Pk Rd 31 .... Spring Branch TX 78070 830-438-2656
Web: www.tpwd.state.tx.us

Hill Country State Natural Area
10600 Bandera Creek Rd .... Bandera TX 78003 830-796-4413
Web: www.tpwd.state.tx.us

Honey Creek State Natural Area
c/o Guadalupe River State Pk
3350 Pk Rd 31 .... Spring Branch TX 78070 830-438-2656
Web: www.tpwd.state.tx.us

Hueco Tanks State Historic Site
6900 Hueco Tanks Rd Ste 1 .... El Paso TX 79938 915-857-1135 845-1794*
*Fax Area Code: 979 ■ *TF:* 800-792-1112 ■ *Web:* www.tpwd.state.tx.us

Huntsville State Park PO Box 508 .... Huntsville TX 77342 936-295-5644
Web: www.tpwd.state.tx.us

Inks Lake State Park 3630 Pk Rd 4 .... Burnet TX 78611 512-793-2223
Web: www.tpwd.state.tx.us

Kickapoo Cavern State Park
23 Miles N Ranch Rd .... Brackettville TX 78832 830-563-2342
Web: www.tpwd.state.tx.us

Lake Arrowhead State Park 229 Pk Rd 63 .... Wichita Falls TX 76310 940-528-2211
Web: tpwd.state.tx.us/state-parks/lake-arrowhead

Lake Bob Sandlin State Park
341 State Pk Rd 2117 .... Pittsburg TX 75686 903-572-5531
Web: www.tpwd.state.tx.us

Lake Brownwood State Park
200 Hwy Pk Rd 15 .... Lake Brownwood TX 76801 325-784-5223
Web: www.tpwd.state.tx.us

Lake Colorado City State Park
4582 FM 2836 .... Colorado City TX 79512 325-728-3931
Web: www.tpwd.state.tx.us

Lake Corpus Christi State Park 23194 Pk Rd 25 .... Mathis TX 78368 361-547-2635
Web: www.tpwd.state.tx.us

Lake Mineral Wells State Park & Trailway
100 Pk Rd 71 .... Mineral Wells TX 76067 940-328-1171
Web: www.tpwd.state.tx.us

Lake Somerville State Park 14222 Pk Rd 57 .... Somerville TX 77879 979-535-7763
Web: www.tpwd.state.tx.us

Lake Tawakoni State Park 10822 Fm 2475 .... Wills Point TX 75169 903-560-7123
Web: www.tpwd.state.tx.us

Phone | Fax

Lake Texana State Park 46 Pk Rd 1 .... Edna TX 77957 361-782-5718
Web: www.tpwd.state.tx.us

Lake Whitney State Park PO Box 1175 .... Whitney TX 76692 254-694-3793
Web: www.tpwd.state.tx.us

Landmark Inn State Historic Site
402 E Florence St .... Castroville TX 78009 830-931-2133
Web: www.tpwd.state.tx.us

Lipantitlan State Historic Site
c/o Lk Corpus Christi State Pk PO Box 1167 .... Mathis TX 78368 361-547-2635
Web: www.tpwd.state.tx.us

Lockhart State Park 4179 State Pk Rd .... Lockhart TX 78644 512-398-3479
Web: www.tpwd.state.tx.us

Longhorn Cavern State Park PO Box 732 .... Burnet TX 78611 830-598-2283
Web: www.tpwd.state.tx.us

Lost Maples State Natural Area
37221 FM 187 .... Vanderpool TX 78885 830-966-3413
Web: www.tpwd.state.tx.us

Lyndon B. Johnson State Park & Historic Site
PO Box 238 .... Stonewall TX 78671 830-644-2252
Web: www.tpwd.state.tx.us

Magoffin Home State Historic Site
1120 Magoffin Ave .... El Paso TX 79901 915-533-5147
Web: tpwd.state.tx.us/spdest/parkinfo/former_tpwd_parks/

Martin Creek Lake State Park 9515 CR 2181D .... Tatum TX 75691 903-836-4336
Web: www.tpwd.state.tx.us

Martin Dies Jr State Park 634 Private Rd 5025 .... Jasper TX 75951 409-384-5231
Web: www.tpwd.state.tx.us

Matagorda Island Wildlife Management Area
1700 Seventh St .... Bay City TX 77414 979-244-7670
Web: www.tpwd.state.tx.us

McKinney Falls State Park
5808 McKinney Falls Pkwy .... Austin TX 78744 512-243-1643 243-0536
Web: www.tpwd.state.tx.us

Meridian State Park 173 Pk Rd 7 .... Meridian TX 76665 254-435-2536
Web: www.tpwd.state.tx.us

Mission Tejas State Park
120 State Pk Rd 44 .... Grapeland TX 75844 936-687-2394
Web: www.tpwd.state.tx.us

Monahans Sandhills State Park PO Box 1738 ...... Monahans TX 79756 432-943-2092
Web: www.tpwd.state.tx.us

Monument Hill & Kreische Brewery State Historic Sites
414 State Loop 92 .... La Grange TX 78945 979-968-5658
Web: www.tpwd.state.tx.us

Mother Neff State Park 1680 Texas 236 Hwy .... Moody TX 76557 254-853-2389
Web: www.tpwd.state.tx.us

Mustang Island State Park
17047 State Hwy 361 .... Port Aransas TX 78373 361-749-5246 749-6455
Web: www.tpwd.state.tx.us

Palmetto State Park 78 Pk Rd 11 S .... Gonzales TX 78629 830-672-3266
Web: www.tpwd.state.tx.us

Palo Duro Canyon State Park 11450 Pk Rd 5 .... Canyon TX 79015 806-488-2227 488-2556
Web: www.tpwd.state.tx.us

Pedernales Falls State Park
2585 Pk Rd 6026 .... Johnson City TX 78636 830-868-7304
Web: www.tpwd.state.tx.us

Port Isabel Lighthouse State Historic Site
421 E Queen Isabella Blvd .... Port Isabel TX 78578 956-943-2262
Web: www.tpwd.state.tx.us

Possum Kingdom State Park PO Box 70 .... Caddo TX 76429 940-549-1803
Web: www.tpwd.state.tx.us

Purtis Creek State Park 14225 FM 316 .... Eustace TX 75124 903-425-2332
Web: www.tpwd.state.tx.us

Ray Roberts Lake State Park 100 PW 4137 .... Pilot Point TX 76258 940-686-2148
Web: www.tpwd.state.tx.us

Rusk/Palestine State Park One Hwy 84 W .... Rusk TX 75785 903-683-5126
Web: www.tpwd.state.tx.us

Sabine Pass Battleground State Park & Historic Site
c/o Sea Rim State Pk PO Box 1066 .... Sabine Pass TX 77655 409-971-2559
Web: tpwd.state.tx.us/spdest/parkinfo/former_tpwd_parks/

Sam Bell Maxey House State Historic Site
812 S Church St .... Paris TX 75460 903-785-5716
Web: www.tpwd.state.tx.us

San Angelo State Park
3900 Mercedes St Ste 2 .... San Angelo TX 76901 325-949-4757
Web: www.tpwd.state.tx.us

San Jacinto Battleground State Historic Site
3523 Battleground Rd .... La Porte TX 77571 281-479-2431 479-5618
Web: tpwd.state.tx.us/state-parks/san-jacinto-battleground

Sea Rim State Park PO Box 356 .... Sabine Pass TX 77655 409-971-2559
Web: tpwd.state.tx.us/state-parks/sea-rim

Sebastopol State Historic Site PO Box 900 .... Seguin TX 78156 830-379-4833
Web: www.tpwd.state.tx.us

Seminole Canyon State Park & Historic Site
PO Box 820 .... Comstock TX 78837 432-292-4464
Web: www.tpwd.state.tx.us

Sheldon Lake State Park & Environmental Learning Ctr
15315 Beaumont Hwy at Pk Rd 138 .... Houston TX 77049 281-456-2800
Web: www.tpwd.state.tx.us

South Llano River State Park
1927 Park Rd 73 .... Junction TX 76849 325-446-3994
Web: www.tpwd.state.tx.us

Starr Family State Historic Site
407 W Travis St .... Marshall TX 75670 903-935-3044
Web: www.tpwd.state.tx.us

Stephen F. Austin State Park & San Felipe State Historic Site
120 Main St .... San Felipe TX 77473 979-885-3613
Web: www.tpwd.state.tx.us

Texas State Railroad State Park PO Box 39 .... Rusk TX 75785 903-683-2561
Web: www.tpwd.state.tx.us

Varner-Hogg Plantation State Historic Site
1702 N 13th St .... West Columbia TX 77486 979-345-4656
Web: www.tpwd.state.tx.us

Washington-on-the-Brazos State Historic Site
PO Box 305 .... Washington TX 77880 936-878-2214
Web: www.tpwd.state.tx.us

Utah

Phone | Fax

Anasazi State Park Museum 460 North Hwy 12 .... Boulder UT 84716 435-335-7308
Web: www.stateparks.utah.gov

Antelope Island State Park
4528 West 1700 South .... Syracuse UT 84075 801-773-2941
Web: www.stateparks.utah.gov

Bear Lake State Park 1030 N Bear Lk Blvd .... Garden City UT 84028 435-946-3343
Web: www.stateparks.utah.gov

Camp Floyd/Stagecoach Inn State Park & Museum
18035 West 1540 North .... Fairfield UT 84013 801-768-8932
Web: www.stateparks.utah.gov

Coral Pink Sand Dunes State Park PO Box 95 .... Kanab UT 84741 435-648-2800
Web: www.stateparks.utah.gov

Dead Horse Point State Park State Route 313 .... Moab UT 84532 435-259-2614
Web: www.stateparks.utah.gov

East Canyon State Park 5535 South Hwy 66 .... Morgan UT 84050 801-829-6866
Web: www.stateparks.utah.gov

Edge of the Cedars State Park Museum
660 West 400 North .... Blanding UT 84511 435-678-2238
Web: stateparks.utah.gov

Escalante State Park 710 N Reservoir Rd .... Escalante UT 84726 435-826-4466
Web: www.stateparks.utah.gov

Fremont Indian State Park & Museum
3820 W Clear Creek Canyon Rd .... Sevier UT 84766 435-527-4631
Web: www.stateparks.utah.gov

Goblin Valley State Park PO Box 637 .... Green River UT 84525 435-275-4584
Web: www.utah.com

Goosenecks State Park PO Box 788 660 W 400 N ..... Blanding UT 84511 435-678-2238
Web: stateparks.utah.gov

Green River State Park PO Box 637 .... Green River UT 84525 435-564-3633
Web: www.utah.com

Gunlock State Park 4405 West 3600 South .... Hurricane UT 84737 435-680-0715
Web: www.stateparks.utah.gov

Historic Union Pacific Rail Trail State Park
PO Box 754 .... Park City UT 84060 435-649-6839
Web: www.stateparks.utah.gov

Huntington State Park PO Box 1343 .... Huntington UT 84528 435-687-2491
TF: 800-322-3770 ■ *Web:* stateparks.utah.gov

Hyrum State Park 405 West 300 South .... Hyrum UT 84319 435-245-6866
Web: www.stateparks.utah.gov

Iron Mission State Park 635 N Main St .... Cedar City UT 84720 435-586-9290
Web: www.stateparks.utah.gov

Jordanelle State Park SR 319 515 PO Box 4 .... Heber City UT 84032 435-649-9540
Web: www.stateparks.utah.gov

Millsite State Park
Ferron Canyon Rd PO Box 1343 .... Huntington UT 84528 435-384-2552
TF: 800-322-3770 ■ *Web:* stateparks.utah.gov

Otter Creek State Park 400 East SR 22 .... Antimony UT 84712 435-624-3268
Web: www.stateparks.utah.gov

Palisade State Park 2200 E Palisade Rd .... Sterling UT 84665 435-835-7275
Web: www.stateparks.utah.gov

Piute State Park PO Box 43 .... Antimony UT 84712 435-624-3268
Web: www.stateparks.utah.gov

Quail Creek State Park 472 North 5300 West .... Hurricane UT 84737 435-879-2378
Web: www.stateparks.utah.gov

Red Fleet State Park 8750 North Hwy 191 .... Vernal UT 84078 435-789-4432
TF: 800-322-3770 ■ *Web:* stateparks.utah.gov

Sand Hollow State Park
4405 West 3600 South .... Hurricane UT 84737 435-680-0715
Web: www.stateparks.utah.gov

Snow Canyon State Park 1002 Snow Canyon Dr .... Ivins UT 84738 435-628-2255
Web: www.stateparks.utah.gov

Starvation State Park
24220 W 7655 S State Park Rd .... Duchesne UT 84021 435-738-2326
Web: www.stateparks.utah.gov

Steinaker State Park 4335 N Hwy 191 .... Vernal UT 84078 435-789-4432 789-4475
TF: 800-322-3770 ■ *Web:* stateparks.utah.gov

Territorial Statehouse State Park
50 W Capitol Ave .... Fillmore UT 84631 435-743-5316
Web: www.stateparks.utah.gov

Utah Field House of Natural History State Park
496 E Main St .... Vernal UT 84078 435-789-3799
Web: stateparks.utah.gov

Utah Lake State Park 4400 W Ctr St .... Provo UT 84601 801-375-0731 373-4215
Web: www.stateparks.utah.gov

Wasatch Mountain State Park
1281 Warm Springs Rd .... Midway UT 84049 435-654-1791
Web: www.stateparks.utah.gov

Willard Bay State Park
900 West 650 North Ste A .... Willard UT 84340 435-734-9494 734-2659
TF: 800-322-3770 ■ *Web:* www.stateparks.utah.gov

Yuba State Park 12225 S Yuba Dam Rd .... Levan UT 84639 435-758-2611
Web: www.stateparks.utah.gov

Vermont

Phone | Fax

Alburg Dunes State Park 151 Coon Pt Rd .... Alburg VT 05440 802-796-4170
Web: www.vtstateparks.com

Allis State Park 284 Allis State Pk Rd .... Randolph VT 05060 802-276-3175
Web: www.vtstateparks.com

Ascutney State Park 1826 Black Mtn Rd .... Windsor VT 05089 802-674-2060
Web: www.vtstateparks.com

Big Deer State Park 1467 Boulder Beach Rd .... Groton VT 05046 802-584-3822
Web: www.vtstateparks.com/htm/bigdeer.cfm

Name / Address	City	State	Zip	Phone	Fax
Bomoseen State Park 22 Cedar Mtn Rd *Web:* www.vtstateparks.com	Fair Haven	VT	05743	802-265-4242	
Boulder Beach State Park 44 Stillwater Rd *Web:* www.vtstateparks.com	Groton	VT	05046	802-584-3823	
Branbury State Park 3570 Lk Dunmore Rd Rt 53 *Web:* www.vtstateparks.com	Brandon	VT	05733	802-247-5925	
Brighton State Park 102 State Pk Rd *Web:* www.vtstateparks.com	Island Pond	VT	05846	802-723-4360	
Button Bay State Park Five Button Bay State Pk Rd *Web:* www.vtstateparks.com	Vergennes	VT	05491	802-475-2377	
Camp Plymouth State Park 2008 Scout Camp Rd *Web:* www.vtstateparks.com	Ludlow	VT	05149	802-228-2025	
Coolidge State Park 855 Coolidge State Pk Rd *Web:* www.vtstateparks.com	Plymouth	VT	05056	802-672-3612	
Crystal Lake State Park 96 Bellwater Ave *Web:* www.vtstateparks.com	Barton	VT	05822	802-525-6205	
D.A.R. State Park 6750 VT Rt 17 W *Web:* www.vtstateparks.com	Addison	VT	05491	802-759-2354	
Elmore State Park 856 VT Rt 12 *Web:* www.vtstateparks.com	Lake Elmore	VT	05657	802-888-2982	
Emerald Lake State Park 65 Emerald Lk Ln *Web:* www.vtstateparks.com	East Dorset	VT	05253	802-362-1655	
Fort Dummer State Park 517 Old Guilford Rd *Web:* www.vtstateparks.com	Brattleboro	VT	05301	802-254-2610	
Gifford Woods State Park 34 Gifford Woods *Web:* www.vtstateparks.com	Killington	VT	05751	802-775-5354	
Grand Isle State Park 36 E Shore S *Web:* www.vtstateparks.com	Grand Isle	VT	05458	802-372-4300	
Green River Reservoir State Park 1393 Green River Dam Rd *Web:* www.vtstateparks.com	Hyde Park	VT	05655	802-888-1349	
Half Moon Pond State Park 1621 Black Pond Rd *Web:* www.vtstateparks.com/htm/halfmoon.cfm	Fair Haven	VT	05743	802-273-2848	
Jamaica State Park 48 Salmon Hole Ln *Web:* www.vtstateparks.com	Jamaica	VT	05343	802-874-4600	
Kill Kare State Park 2714 Hathaway Point Rd PO Box 123 *Web:* www.vtstateparks.com/htm/killkare.htm	Saint Albans Bay	VT	05481	802-524-6021	
Kingsland Bay State Park 787 Kingsland Bay State Pk Rd *Web:* www.vtstateparks.com	Ferrisburgh	VT	05456	802-877-3445	
Knight Island State Park 1 Knight Island PO Box 123 *Web:* www.vtstateparks.com/htm/knightisland.htm	North Hero	VT	05474	802-524-6353	
Lake Carmi State Park 460 Marsh Farm Rd *TF Resv:* 888-409-7579 ■ *Web:* www.vtstateparks.com	Enosburg Falls	VT	05450	802-933-8383	
Lake Saint Catherine State Park 3034 VT Rt 30 S *Web:* www.vtstateparks.com	Poultney	VT	05764	802-287-9158	
Lake Shaftsbury State Park 262 Shaftsbury State Pk Rd *Web:* www.vtstateparks.com	Shaftsbury	VT	05262	802-375-9978	
Little River State Park 3444 Little River Rd *Web:* www.vtstateparks.com	Waterbury	VT	05676	802-244-7103	
Maidstone State Park 4858 Maidstone Lk Rd *Web:* www.vtstateparks.com	Maidstone	VT	05905	802-676-3930	
Molly Stark State Park 705 Rt 9 E *Web:* www.vtstateparks.com	Wilmington	VT	05363	802-464-5460	
Mount Philo State Park 5425 Mt Philo Rd *Web:* www.vtstateparks.com	Charlotte	VT	05445	802-425-2390	
North Hero State Park 3803 Lakeview Dr *Web:* www.vtstateparks.com	North Hero	VT	05474	802-372-8727	
Quechee State Park 5800 Woodstock Rd *Web:* www.vtstateparks.com	Hartford	VT	05047	802-295-2990	
Ricker Pond State Park 18 Ricker Pond Camp Ground Rd *Web:* www.vtstateparks.com	Groton	VT	05046	802-584-3821	
Sand Bar State Park 1215 US Rt 2 *Web:* www.vtstateparks.com	Milton	VT	05468	802-893-2825	
Seyon Lodge State Park 2967 Seyon Pond Rd *Web:* www.vtstateparks.com/htm/seyon.htm	Groton	VT	05046	802-584-3829	
Smugglers Notch State Park 6443 Mountain Rd *Web:* www.vtstateparks.com	Stowe	VT	05672	802-253-4014	
Stillwater State Park 44 Stillwater Rd *Web:* www.vtstateparks.com	Groton	VT	05046	802-584-3822	
Thetford Hill State Park 622 Academy Rd *Web:* www.vtstateparks.com	Thetford	VT	05075	802-785-2266	
Townshend State Park 2755 State Forest Rd *Web:* www.vtstateparks.com	Townshend	VT	05353	802-365-7500	
Underhill State Park PO Box 249 *Web:* www.vtstateparks.com	Underhill Center	VT	05490	802-899-3022	
Waterbury Ctr State Park 177 Reservoir Rd *Web:* www.vtstateparks.com	Waterbury Center	VT	05677	802-244-1226	
Wilgus State Park PO Box 196 *Web:* www.vtstateparks.com	Ascutney	VT	05030	802-674-5422	
Woodford State Park 142 State Pk Rd *Web:* www.vtstateparks.com	Bennington	VT	05201	802-447-7169	

Virginia

Name / Address	City	State	Zip	Phone	Fax
Bear Creek Lake State Park 22 Bear Creek Lk Rd *TF:* 800-933-7275 ■ *Web:* dcr.virginia.gov/state-parks/bear-creek-lake.shtml	Cumberland	VA	23040	804-492-4410	
Belle Isle State Park 1632 Belle Isle Rd *Web:* www.dcr.state.va.us	Lancaster	VA	22503	804-462-5030	
Bethel Beach Natural Area Preserve 600 E Main St 24th Fl *Web:* www.dcr.virginia.gov/natural_heritage/natural_area_preserves/bethel.shtml	Richmond	VA	23219	804-786-7951	
Breaks Interstate Park 627 Commission Cir PO Box 100 *Web:* www.breakspark.com/	Breaks	VA	24607	276-865-4413	
Caledon State Park 11617 Caledon Rd *TF:* 800-933-7275 ■ *Web:* www.dcr.virginia.gov	King George	VA	22485	540-663-3861	
Chippokes Plantation State Park 695 Chippokes Pk Rd *Web:* www.dcr.state.va.us	Surry	VA	23883	757-294-3728	
Claytor Lake State Park 6620 Ben H Boden Dr *Web:* www.dcr.virginia.gov	Dublin	VA	24084	540-643-2500	
Douthat State Park 14239 Douthat State Pk Rd *TF General:* 800-933-7275 ■ *Web:* www.dcr.state.va.us	Millboro	VA	24460	540-862-8100	862-8104
Fairy Stone State Park 967 Fairystone Lk Dr *Web:* www.dcr.state.va.us	Stuart	VA	24171	276-930-2424	
False Cape State Park 4001 Sandpiper Rd *TF General:* 800-933-7275 ■ *Web:* www.dcr.state.va.us	Virginia Beach	VA	23456	757-426-7128	426-0055
George Washington's Grist Mill 5513 Mt Vernon Memorial Hwy *Web:* mountvernon.org	Mount Vernon	VA	22309	703-780-3383	
Holliday Lake State Park 2759 State Pk Rd *TF:* 800-933-7275 ■ *Web:* www.dcr.state.va.us	Appomattox	VA	24522	434-248-6308	
Hungry Mother State Park 2854 Pk Blvd *Web:* www.dcr.state.va.us	Marion	VA	24354	276-781-7400	
Kiptopeke State Park 3540 Kiptopeke Dr *Web:* www.dcr.state.va.us	Cape Charles	VA	23310	757-331-2267	
Lake Anna State Park 6800 Lawyers Rd *Web:* www.dcr.state.va.us	Spotsylvania	VA	22553	540-854-5503	
Leesylvania State Park 2001 Daniel K Ludwig Dr *Web:* www.dcr.state.va.us	Woodbridge	VA	22191	703-730-8205	
Mason Neck State Park 7301 High Pt Rd *Web:* www.dcr.state.va.us	Lorton	VA	22079	703-490-4979	
Natural Tunnel State Park 1420 Natural Tunnel Pkwy *Web:* www.dcr.state.va.us	Duffield	VA	24244	276-940-2674	
New River Trail State Park 176 Orphanage Dr *Web:* www.dcr.state.va.us	Foster Falls	VA	24360	276-699-6778	
Occoneechee State Park 1192 Occoneechee Pk Rd *TF:* 800-933-7275 ■ *Web:* dcr.virginia.gov	Clarksville	VA	23927	434-374-2210	374-9243
Pocahontas State Park 10301 State Pk Rd *TF:* 800-933-7275 ■ *Web:* www.dcr.virginia.gov	Chesterfield	VA	23832	804-796-4255	796-4004
Raymond R Andy Guest Jr Shenandoah River State Park 350 Daughter of Stars Dr *TF:* 800-933-7275 ■ *Web:* www.dcr.virginia.gov	Bentonville	VA	22610	540-622-6840	622-6841
Sailor's Creek Battlefield State Park 6541 Saylers Creek Rd *Web:* www.dcr.virginia.gov	Rice	VA	23966	804-561-7510	
Shot Tower Historical State Park 176 Orphanage Dr *Web:* www.dcr.virginia.gov	Foster Falls	VA	24360	276-699-6778	
Sky Meadows State Park 11012 Edmonds Ln *Web:* www.dcr.state.va.us	Delaplane	VA	20144	540-592-3556	
Staunton River State Park 1170 Staunton Tr *Web:* www.dcr.state.va.us	Scottsburg	VA	24589	434-572-4623	
Twin Lakes State Park 788 Twin Lakes Rd *TF:* 800-933-7275 ■ *Web:* www.dcr.virginia.gov	Green Bay	VA	23942	434-392-3435	
Wilderness Road State Park 8051 Wilderness Rd *Web:* www.friendsofwildernessroad.org	Ewing	VA	24248	276-445-3065	445-3066

Washington

Name / Address	City	State	Zip	Phone	Fax
Battle Ground Lake State Park 18002 NE 249th St *TF:* 888-226-7688 ■ *Web:* www.parks.wa.gov	Battle Ground	WA	98604	360-687-4621	
Bay View State Park 10901 Bay View-Edison Rd *Web:* www.parks.wa.gov	Mount Vernon	WA	98273	360-757-0227	
Beacon Rock State Park 34841 State Rd 14 *TF:* 888-226-7688 ■ *Web:* www.parks.wa.gov	Skamania	WA	98648	509-427-8265	427-8265
Belfair State Park 3151 NE State Rt 300 *Web:* www.parks.wa.gov	Belfair	WA	98528	360-275-0668	275-8734
Birch Bay State Park 5105 Helwig Rd *Web:* www.parks.wa.gov	Blaine	WA	98230	360-371-2800	371-0455
Bogachiel State Park 185983 Hwy 101 *Web:* www.parks.wa.gov	Forks	WA	98331	360-374-6356	
Bridle Trails State Park 5300 116th Ave. N.W 20606 SE 56th St *Web:* www.parks.wa.gov	Issaquah	WA	98027	425-455-7010	
Brooks Memorial State Park 2465 Hwy 97 *Web:* www.parks.wa.gov	Goldendale	WA	98620	509-773-4611	
Camano Island State Park 2269 S Lowell Pt Rd *Web:* parks.wa.gov	Camano Island	WA	98282	360-387-3031	
Cape Disappointment State Park PO Box 488 *Web:* capedisappointment.org	Ilwaco	WA	98624	360-642-3078	
Columbia Hills State Park PO Box 426 *Web:* www.parks.wa.gov	Dallesport	WA	98617	509-767-1159	
Conconully State Park 119 W Broadway Ave *Web:* www.parks.wa.gov	Conconully	WA	98819	509-826-7408	
Curlew Lake State Park 62 State Pk Rd *Web:* www.parks.wa.gov	Republic	WA	99166	509-775-3592	

Name / Address	City	State	Zip	Phone	Fax
Daroga State Park One S Daroga Pk Rd *Web:* www.parks.wa.gov	Orondo	WA	98843	509-664-6380	
Dash Point State Park 5700 SW Dash Pt Rd *TF:* 888-226-7688 ■ *Web:* www.parks.wa.gov	Federal Way	WA	98023	253-661-4955	
Deception Pass State Park 41229 Washington 20 *Web:* www.parks.wa.gov	Oak Harbor	WA	98277	360-675-2417	675-8991
Fay Bainbridge State Park 15446 Sunrise Dr NE *Web:* www.parks.wa.gov	Bainbridge Island	WA	98110	206-842-3931	
Federation Forest State Park 49201 SE Enumclaw Chinook Pass Rd *Web:* www.parks.wa.gov	Enumclaw	WA	98022	360-663-2207	
Fields Spring State Park 992 Pk Rd *Web:* www.parks.wa.gov	Anatone	WA	99401	509-256-3332	
Fort Casey State Park 1280 S Engle Rd *Web:* www.parks.wa.gov	Coupeville	WA	98239	360-678-4519	
Fort Columbia State Park PO Box 488 *Web:* www.parks.wa.gov	Chinook	WA	98614	360-642-3078	
Fort Ebey State Park 400 Hill Vly Dr *Web:* www.parks.wa.gov	Coupeville	WA	98239	360-678-4636	
Fort Flagler State Park 10541 Flagler Rd *Web:* www.parks.wa.gov	Nordland	WA	98358	360-385-1259	
Fort Simcoe State Park 5150 Ft Simcoe Rd *Web:* www.parks.wa.gov	White Swan	WA	98952	509-874-2372	
Fort Worden State Park 200 Battery Way *Web:* www.parks.wa.gov/fortworden	Port Townsend	WA	98368	360-344-4400	
Ginkgo Petrified Forest State Park 4511 Huntzinger Rd *Web:* www.parks.wa.gov	Vantage	WA	98950	509-856-2700	
Goldendale Observatory State Park 1602 Observatory Dr *Web:* www.parks.wa.gov	Goldendale	WA	98620	509-773-3141	
Hope Island State Park E 391 Wingert Rd *Web:* www.parks.wa.gov	Shelton	WA	98584	360-426-9226	
Ike Kinswa State Park 873 SR 122 *Web:* www.parks.wa.gov	Silver Creek	WA	98585	360-983-3402	
Illahee State Park 3540 NE Bahia Vista Dr *Web:* www.parks.wa.gov	Bremerton	WA	98310	360-478-6460	
Jarrell Cove State Park 391 E Wingert Rd *Web:* www.parks.wa.gov	Shelton	WA	98584	360-426-9226	
Kanaskat-Palmer State Park 32101 Kanaskat-Cumberland Rd *Web:* www.parks.wa.gov	Ravensdale	WA	98051	360-886-0148	
Kitsap Memorial State Park 202 NE Pk St *Web:* www.parks.wa.gov	Poulsbo	WA	98370	360-779-3205	
Kopachuck State Park 11101 56th St NW *Web:* www.parks.wa.gov	Gig Harbor	WA	98335	253-265-3606	
Lake Chelan State Park 7544 S Lakeshore Dr *Web:* www.parks.wa.gov	Chelan	WA	98816	509-687-3710	
Lake Easton State Park 150 Lk Easton State Pk Rd *Web:* www.parks.wa.gov	Easton	WA	98925	509-656-2230	
Lake Sammamish State Park 1111 Israel Rd SW *Web:* www.parks.wa.gov	Tumwater	WA	98504	425-455-7010	
Lake Sylvia State Park PO Box 701 *Web:* www.parks.wa.gov	Montesano	WA	98563	360-249-3621	
Lake Wenatchee State Park 21588 A Hwy 207 *Web:* www.parks.wa.gov	Leavenworth	WA	98826	509-763-3101	
Larrabee State Park 245 Chuckanut Dr *Web:* www.parks.wa.gov	Bellingham	WA	98226	360-676-2093	
Lewis & Clark Trail State Park 36149 Hwy 12 *Web:* www.parks.wa.gov	Dayton	WA	99328	509-337-6457	
Lime Kiln Point State Park 1567 Westside Rd *Web:* www.parks.wa.gov	Friday Harbor	WA	98250	360-378-2044	
Lincoln Rock State Park 13253 State Rt 2 *Web:* www.parks.wa.gov	East Wenatchee	WA	98802	509-884-8702	
Manchester State Park 7767 E Hilldale	Port Orchard	WA	98366	360-871-4065	
Maryhill State Park 50 Hwy 97	Goldendale	WA	98620	509-773-5007	
Millersylvania State Park 12245 Tilley Rd S *Web:* www.parks.wa.gov	Olympia	WA	98512	360-753-1519	664-2180
Moran State Park 3572 Olga Rd *Web:* www.parks.wa.gov	Eastsound	WA	98245	360-376-2326	
Nolte State Park 36921 Veazie Cumberland Rd *Web:* www.parks.wa.gov	Enumclaw	WA	98022	360-825-4646	
Ocean City State Park 148 State Rt 115 *Web:* www.parks.wa.gov	Hoquiam	WA	98550	360-289-3553	
Old Fort Townsend State Park 1370 Old Ft Townsend Rd *Web:* www.parks.wa.gov	Port Townsend	WA	98368	360-385-3595	
Olmstead Place State Park 921 N Ferguson Rd *Web:* www.parks.wa.gov	Ellensburg	WA	98926	509-925-1943	
Osoyoos Lake State Park 2207 Juniper *Web:* www.parks.wa.gov	Oroville	WA	98844	509-476-3321	
Pacific Pines State Park 25904 R St *Web:* www.stateparks.com	Ocean Park	WA	98640	360-902-8844	
Palouse Falls State Park 100 SW Main St PO Box 541 *Web:* www.parks.wa.gov	Washtucna	WA	99371	360-902-8844	
Paradise Point State Park 33914 NW Paradise Pk Rd *Web:* www.parks.wa.gov	Ridgefield	WA	98642	360-263-2350	
Peace Arch State Park PO Box 87 *Web:* www.parks.wa.gov	Blaine	WA	98230	360-332-8221	
Pearrygin Lake State Park 561 Bear Creek Rd *Web:* www.parks.wa.gov	Winthrop	WA	98862	509-996-2370	
Penrose Point State Park 321 158th KPS	Lakebay	WA	98349	253-884-2514	
Potholes State Park 6762 Hwy 262 SE *Web:* www.parks.wa.gov	Othello	WA	99344	509-346-2759	
Potlatch State Park 21020 N US Hwy 101 *Web:* www.parks.wa.gov	Shelton	WA	98584	360-877-5361	
Rainbow Falls State Park 4008 Washington 6 *Web:* www.parks.wa.gov	Chehalis	WA	98532	360-291-3767	291-3377
Rasar State Park 38730 Cape Horn Rd *Web:* www.parks.wa.gov	Concrete	WA	98237	360-826-3942	
Rockport State Park 51905 WA-20 *Web:* www.parks.wa.gov	Rockport	WA	98283	360-853-8461	
Sacajawea State Park 2503 Sacajawea Pk Rd *Web:* www.parks.wa.gov	Pasco	WA	99301	509-545-2361	
Saint Edward State Park 14445 Juanita Dr NE *Web:* www.parks.wa.gov	Kenmore	WA	98028	425-823-2992	
Saltwater State Park 25205 Eigth Pl S *Web:* www.parks.wa.gov	Des Moines	WA	98198	253-661-4956	
Scenic Beach State Park PO Box 7 *Web:* www.parks.wa.gov	Seabeck	WA	98380	360-830-5079	
Schafer State Park W 1365 Schafer Pk Rd *Web:* www.parks.wa.gov	Elma	WA	98541	360-482-3852	
Seaquest State Park 3030 Spirit Lk Hwy *Web:* www.parks.wa.gov	Castle Rock	WA	98611	360-274-8633	
Sequim Bay State Park 269035 Hwy 101 *Web:* www.parks.wa.gov	Sequim	WA	98382	360-683-4235	
Shine Tidelands State Park 202 NE Pk St *Web:* www.parks.wa.gov	Poulsbo	WA	98370	360-779-3205	
South Whidbey Island State Park 4128 Smugglers Cove Rd *Web:* www.parks.wa.gov	Freeland	WA	98249	360-331-4559	
Steamboat Rock State Park 51052 Washington 155 *Web:* www.parks.wa.gov	Electric City	WA	99123	509-633-1304	
Sun Lakes State Park 34875 Pk Ln Rd NE *Web:* www.parks.wa.gov	Coulee City	WA	99115	509-632-5583	
Tolmie State Park 7730 61st Ave NE *Web:* www.parks.wa.gov	Olympia	WA	98506	360-456-6464	459-0104
Twanoh State Park 12190 E Hwy 106 *Web:* www.parks.wa.gov	Union	WA	98592	360-275-2222	
Twenty-Five Mile Creek State Park 20530 S Lakeshore Rd *Web:* www.parks.wa.gov	Chelan	WA	98816	509-687-3710	
Twin Harbors Beach State Park Hwy 105	Westport	WA	98595	360-268-9717	
Wallace Falls State Park 14503 Wallace Lk Rd *Web:* www.parks.wa.gov	Gold Bar	WA	98251	360-793-0420	
Wenatchee Confluence State Park 333 Olds Stn Rd *Web:* www.parks.wa.gov	Wenatchee	WA	98801	509-664-6373	
Wenberg State Park 15430 E Lk Goodwin Rd	Stanwood	WA	98292	360-652-7417	
Yakima Sportsman State Park 904 Keys Rd *Web:* www.parks.wa.gov	Yakima	WA	98901	509-575-2774	

West Virginia

Name / Address	City	State	Zip	Phone	Fax
Babcock State Park 486 Babcock Rd *TF:* 800-225-5982 ■ *Web:* www.babcocksp.com	Clifftop	WV	25831	304-438-3004	
Beartown State Park HC 64 PO Box 189 *TF General:* 800-225-5982 ■ *Web:* www.beartownstatepark.com	Hillsboro	WV	24946	304-653-4254	653-4254
Beech Fork State Park 5601 Long Branch Rd *Web:* www.beechforksp.com	Barboursville	WV	25504	304-528-5794	
Blackwater Falls State Park PO Drawer 490 *Web:* www.blackwaterfalls.com	Davis	WV	26260	304-259-5216	
Blennerhassett Island Historical State Park 137 Juliana St *Web:* www.blennerhassettislandstatepark.com	Parkersburg	WV	26101	304-420-4800	
Bluestone State Park HC 78 PO Box 3 *Web:* www.bluestonesp.com	Hinton	WV	25951	304-466-2805	466-2813
Cabwaylingo State Forest 4279 Cabwaylingo Pk Rd *Web:* www.cabwaylingo.com	Dunlow	WV	25511	304-385-4255	
Cacapon Resort State Park 818 Cacapon Lodge Dr *Web:* www.cacaponresort.com	Berkeley Springs	WV	25411	304-258-1022	
Camp Creek State Forest 2390 Camp Creek Rd *TF:* 800-225-5982 ■ *Web:* www.campcreekstatepark.com	Camp Creek	WV	25820	304-425-9481	
Camp Creek State Park PO Box 119 *Web:* www.campcreekstatepark.com	Camp Creek	WV	25820	304-425-9481	
Canaan Valley Resort State Park 230 Main Lodge Rd *TF:* 800-622-4121 ■ *Web:* www.canaanresort.com	Davis	WV	26260	304-866-4121	866-2172
Carnifex Ferry Battlefield State Park 1194 Carnifex Ferry Rd *Web:* www.carnifexferrybattlefieldstatepark.com	Summersville	WV	26651	304-872-0825	
Cass Scenic Railroad State Park 242 Main St *Web:* www.cassrailroad.com	Cass	WV	24927	304-456-4300	
Cathedral State Park Rt 1 12 Cathedral Way *TF:* 800-225-5982 ■ *Web:* www.cathedralstatepark.com	Aurora	WV	26705	304-735-3771	
Cedar Creek State Park 2947 Cedar Creek Rd *Web:* www.cedarcreeksp.com	Glenville	WV	26351	304-462-7158	
Chief Logan State Park General Delivery *Web:* www.chiefloganstatepark.com	Logan	WV	25601	304-792-7125	
Coopers Rock State Forest 61 County Line Dr *TF:* 800-225-5982 ■ *Web:* www.coopersrockstateforest.com	Bruceton Mills	WV	26525	304-594-1561	
Droop Mountain Battlefield State Park 683 Droop Park Rd *Web:* www.droopmountainbattlefield.com	Hillsboro	WV	24946	304-653-4254	653-4254
Hawks Nest State Park PO Box 857 *Web:* www.hawksnestsp.com	Ansted	WV	25812	304-658-5212	658-4549

Name / Address	City	State	Zip	Phone	Fax
Holly River State Park PO Box 70 *Web:* www.hollyriver.com	Hacker Valley	WV	26222	304-493-6353	
Kanawha State Forest 7500 Kanawha State Forest Dr *Web:* www.kanawhastateforest.com	Charleston	WV	25314	304-558-3500	558-3508
Kumbrabow State Forest PO Box 65 *Web:* kumbrabow.com	Huttonsville	WV	26273	304-335-2219	
Laurel Lake Wildlife Management Area Hc 70 PO Box 626 *Web:* www.laurellakewma.com	Lenore	WV	25676	304-475-2823	
Little Beaver State Park 1402 Grandview Rd *Web:* www.littlebeaverstatepark.com	Beaver	WV	25813	304-763-2494	
Lost River State Park 321 Pk Dr *Web:* www.lostriversp.com	Mathias	WV	26812	304-897-5372	
Moncove Lake State Park Rt-4 PO Box 73-A *Web:* www.moncovelakestatepark.com	Gap Mills	WV	24941	304-772-3450	772-3450
North Bend Rail Trail Rt 1 PO Box 221 *TF:* 800-225-5982 ■ *Web:* www.wvparks.com	Cairo	WV	26337	304-643-2931	
North Bend State Park 202 N Bend Pk Rd *Web:* www.northbendsp.com	Cairo	WV	26337	304-643-2931	
Panther State Forest HC 63 PO Box Box 923 *TF:* 800-225-5982 ■ *Web:* www.pantherstateforest.com	Panther	WV	24872	304-938-2252	
Pinnacle Rock State Park PO Box 1 *Web:* www.pinnaclerockstatepark.com	Bramwell	WV	24715	304-248-8565	
Pipestem Resort State Park PO Box 150 *Web:* www.pipestemresort.com	Pipestem	WV	25979	304-466-1800	466-2803
Pricketts Fort State Park 106 Overfort Ln PO Box 403 *Web:* www.prickettsfortstatepark.com	Fairmont	WV	26554	304-363-3030	363-3857
Seneca State Forest 10135 Browns Creek Rd *Web:* www.senecastateforest.com	Dunmore	WV	24934	304-799-6213	799-6213
Tomlinson Run State Park PO Box 97 *Web:* www.tomlinsonrunsp.com	New Manchester	WV	26056	304-564-3651	
Tu-Endie-Wei State Park PO Box 486 *Web:* www.tu-endie-weistatepark.com	Point Pleasant	WV	25550	304-675-0869	
Twin Falls Resort State Park PO Box 667 Rt 97 *Web:* www.twinfallsresort.com	Mullens	WV	25882	304-294-4000	294-4000
Watters Smith Memorial State Park PO Box 296 *Web:* www.watterssmithstatepark.com	Lost Creek	WV	26385	304-745-3081	

Wisconsin

Name / Address	City	State	Zip	Phone	Fax
Amnicon Falls State Park 4279 County Hwy U *Web:* dnr.wi.gov/topic/parks/name/amnicon	South Range	WI	54874	715-398-3000	
Aztalan State Park 1213 S Main St *Web:* dnr.wi.gov	Lake Mills	WI	53551	920-648-8774	648-5166
Big Foot Beach State Park 1452 Wells St *TF:* 888-936-7463 ■ *Web:* www.dnr.wi.gov	Lake Geneva	WI	53147	262-248-2528	
Black River State Forest 101 S Webster St PO Box 7921 *TF:* 888-936-7463 ■ *Web:* dnr.wi.gov	Madison	WI	53707	608-266-2621	275-3338
Blue Mound State Park 4350 Mounds Pk Rd *Web:* dnr.wi.gov	Blue Mounds	WI	53517	608-437-5711	
Browntown-Cadiz Springs State Recreation Area N2241 Cadiz Springs Rd *Web:* www.cadizsprings.com	Browntown	WI	53522	608-527-2335	
Brule River State Forest 6250 S Ranger Rd *Web:* www.dnr.wi.gov	Brule	WI	54820	715-372-5678	372-4836
Brunet Island State Park 23125 255th St *Web:* dnr.wi.gov/newurl.html	Cornell	WI	54732	715-239-6888	
Buckhorn State Park W8450 Buckhorn Pk Ave *Web:* dnr.wi.gov/newurl.html	Necedah	WI	54646	608-565-2789	
Capital Springs 3101 Lk Farm Rd *Web:* friendsofcapitalsprings.org	Madison	WI	53711	608-224-3606	
Chippewa Moraine Ice Age State Recreation Area 13394 County Hwy M *Web:* dnr.wi.gov	New Auburn	WI	54757	715-967-2800	967-2801
Copper Falls State Park 36764 Copper Falls Rd *Web:* dnr.wi.gov	Mellen	WI	54546	715-274-5123	
Council Grounds State Park N1895 Council Grounds Dr *Web:* reserveamerica.com	Merrill	WI	54452	715-536-8773	536-6772
Devil's Lake State Park S5975 Pk Rd *Web:* dnr.wi.gov	Baraboo	WI	53913	608-356-8301	356-4281
Flambeau River State Forest W1613 County Rd *Web:* dnr.wi.gov	Winter	WI	54896	715-332-5271	
Governor Dodge State Park 4175 State Hwy 23 N *Web:* dnr.wi.gov/	Dodgeville	WI	53533	608-935-2315	
Governor Knowles State Forest 325 SR 70 *Web:* dnr.wi.gov/newurl.html	Grantsburg	WI	54840	715-463-2898	
Governor Nelson State Park 5140 County Hwy M *Web:* www.dnr.wi.gov	Waunakee	WI	53597	608-831-3005	
Governor Thompson State Park N10008 Paust Ln *Web:* www.dnr.wi.gov	Crivitz	WI	54114	715-757-3979	
Harrington Beach State Park 531 County Rd D *Web:* dnr.wi.gov	Belgium	WI	53004	262-285-3015	
Hartman Creek State Park N2480 Hartman Creek Rd *Web:* dnr.wi.gov	Waupaca	WI	54981	715-258-2372	
Havenwoods State Forest 6141 N Hopkins St *TF:* 888-936-7463 ■ *Web:* dnr.wi.gov	Milwaukee	WI	53209	414-527-0232	527-0761
Heritage Hill State Historical Park 2640 S Webster Ave *Web:* heritagehillgb.org	Green Bay	WI	54301	920-448-5150	
High Cliff State Park N7630 State Pk Rd *Web:* dnr.wi.gov/newurl.html	Sherwood	WI	54169	920-989-1106	
Hoffman Hills State Recreation Area 921 BrickyaRd Rd *Web:* www.dnr.wi.gov	Menomonie	WI	54751	715-232-1242	
Interstate State Park PO Box 703 *Web:* dnr.wi.gov	Saint Croix Falls	WI	54024	715-483-3747	
Kettle Moraine State Forest - Northern Unit N1765 Hwy G *Web:* www.dnr.wi.gov	Campbellsport	WI	53010	262-626-2116	
Kettle Moraine State Forest - Pike Lake Unit 3544 Kettle Moraine Rd *Web:* dnr.wi.gov	Hartford	WI	53027	262-670-3400	670-3411
Kettle Moraine State Forest Southern Unit S91 W39091 Hwy 59 *Web:* dnr.wi.gov/newurl.html	Eagle	WI	53119	262-594-6200	
Kettle Moraine State Forest-Lapham Peak Unit W329 N846 County Hwy C *Web:* dnr.wi.gov	Delafield	WI	53018	262-646-4421	
Kinnickinnic State Park W11983 820th Ave *Web:* dnr.wi.gov	River Falls	WI	54022	715-425-1129	425-0010
Kohler-Andrae State Park 1020 Beach Pk Ln *Web:* www.wiparks.net	Sheboygan	WI	53081	920-451-4080	451-4086
Lake Kegonsa State Park 2405 Door Creek Rd *TF General:* 888-947-2757 ■ *Web:* dnr.wi.gov	Stoughton	WI	53589	608-873-9695	873-0674
Lake Wissota State Park 18127 County Hwy O *TF:* 800-847-9367 ■ *Web:* dnr.wi.gov	Chippewa Falls	WI	54729	715-382-4574	382-5187
Lakeshore State Park 2300 N Martin Luther King Jr Dr *Web:* dnr.wi.gov	Milwaukee	WI	53212	414-263-8500	
Merrick State Park S2965 Sr 35 *Web:* dnr.wi.gov	Fountain City	WI	54629	608-687-4936	
Mirror Lake State Park E10320 Fern Dell Rd *Web:* dnr.wi.gov	Baraboo	WI	53913	608-254-2333	
Nelson Dewey State Park PO Box 658 *TF:* 888-936-7463 ■ *Web:* dnr.wi.gov	Cassville	WI	53806	608-725-5374	
New Glarus Woods State Park (NGWSP) W5446 County Hwy NN *Web:* dnr.wi.gov	New Glarus	WI	53574	608-527-2335	527-6435
Newport State Park 475 County Rd NP *TF:* 800-847-9367 ■ *Web:* dnr.wi.gov	Ellison Bay	WI	54210	920-854-2500	854-1914
Northern Highland - American Legion State Forest 4125 County Hwy M *TF:* 800-847-9367 ■ *Web:* dnr.wi.gov/	Boulder Junction	WI	54512	715-385-2727	385-2752
Pattison State Park 6294 S State Rd 35 *Web:* dnr.wi.gov/newurl.html	Superior	WI	54880	715-399-3111	
Peninsula State Park 9462 Shore Rd *Web:* www.dnr.wi.gov	Fish Creek	WI	54212	920-868-3258	
Perrot State Park W26247 Sullivan Rd *Web:* dnr.wi.gov	Trempealeau	WI	54661	608-534-6409	
Peshtigo River State Forest N10008 Paust Ln *Web:* dnr.wi.gov/newurl.html	Crivitz	WI	54114	715-757-3965	
Point Beach State Forest 9400 County Hwy O *Web:* dnr.wi.gov/newurl.html	Two Rivers	WI	54241	920-794-7480	
Potawatomi State Park 3740 County Rd PD *TF:* 800-847-9367 ■ *Web:* www.dnr.wi.gov	Sturgeon Bay	WI	54235	920-746-2890	746-2896
Richard Bong State Recreation Area 26313 Burlington Rd *Web:* dnr.wi.gov/newurl.html	Kansasville	WI	53139	262-878-5600	878-5615
Tower Hill State Park 5808 County Rd C *Web:* dnr.wi.gov	Spring Green	WI	53588	608-588-2116	
Whitefish Dunes State Park 3275 County Hwy WD *Web:* dnr.wi.gov	Sturgeon Bay	WI	54235	920-823-2400	823-2640
Wildcat Mountain State Park E13660 State Hwy 33 PO Box 99 *Web:* www.dnr.wi.gov	Ontario	WI	54651	608-337-4775	
Willow River State Park 1034 County Hwy A *TF:* 800-847-9367 ■ *Web:* dnr.wi.gov	Hudson	WI	54016	715-386-5931	386-0431
Wyalusing State Park 13081 State Pk Ln *Web:* www.wyalusing.org	Bagley	WI	53801	608-996-2261	996-2410
Yellowstone Lake State Park 8495 Lake Rd *Web:* www.dnr.wi.gov	Blanchardville	WI	53516	608-523-4427	

Wyoming

Name / Address	City	State	Zip	Phone	Fax
Bear River State Park 601 Bear River Dr	Evanston	WY	82930	307-789-6547	
Boysen State Park 15 Ash St	Shoshoni	WY	82649	307-876-2796	
Buffalo Bill State Park 47 Lakeside Rd	Cody	WY	82414	307-587-9227	
Connor Battlefield State Historic Site Hwy 14 *Web:* wyoparks.state.wy.us/site/siteinfo.aspx?siteid=15	Ranchester	WY	82842	307-684-7629	
Fort Bridger State Historic Site PO Box 35 *Web:* www.wyomingtourism.org	Fort Bridger	WY	82933	307-782-3842	
Fort Fetterman State Historic Site 752 Hwy 93	Douglas	WY	82633	307-358-2864	
Fort Fred Steele State Historic Site I-80 Exit 228 *Web:* wyoparks.state.wy.us	Sinclair	WY	82334	307-320-3013	
Fort Phil Kearny State Historic Site 528 Wagon Box Rd *Web:* wyoparks.state.wy.us	Story	WY	82842	307-684-7629	684-7967
Glendo State Park 397 Glendo Pk Rd *Web:* wyoparks.state.wy.us	Glendo	WY	82213	307-735-4433	
Guernsey State Park PO Box 429 *Web:* wyoparks.state.wy.us/site/siteinfo.aspx?siteid=7	Guernsey	WY	82214	307-836-2334	
Hawk Springs State Recreation Area 2301 Central Ave *Web:* wyoparks.state.wy.us/permits/index.aspx	Cheyenne	WY	82002	307-777-6323	

Phone Fax

Historic Governors' Mansion 300 E 21st St .... Cheyenne WY 82001 307-777-7878
Independence Rock State Historic Site
5611 High Plains Rd. .... Cheyenne WY 82007 307-777-7777
Web: www.wyomingtourism.org/overview/independence-rock-state-historic-site/3337
Keyhole State Park 22 Marina Rd. .... Moorcroft WY 82721 307-756-3596
Web: wyoparks.state.wy.us
Medicine Lodge State Archaeological Site
Hwy 31 .... Hyattville WY 82428 307-469-2234
Web: wyoparks.state.wy.us
Seminoe State Park Seminoe Dam Rt .... Sinclair WY 82334 307-320-3013
Web: wyoparks.state.wy.us
Trail End State Historic Site
400 Clarendon Ave .... Sheridan WY 82801 307-674-4589 672-1720
Web: www.trailend.org

569 PARTY GOODS

Phone Fax

Alin Party Supplies Co 4139 Woodruff Ave. .... Lakewood CA 90713 562-420-2489
Web: www.alinpartysupply.com
Amscan Inc 80 Grasslands Rd .... Elmsford NY 10523 914-345-2020 345-3884
TF: 800-444-8887 ■ *Web:* www.amscan.com
Balloons Everywhere Inc 16474 Greeno Rd .... Fairhope AL 36532 800-239-2000 210-2105*
**Fax Area Code:* 251 ■ *TF:* 800-239-2000 ■ *Web:* www.balloons.com
Beistle Co One Beistle Plz. .... Shippensburg PA 17257 717-532-2131 532-7789
Web: www.beistle.com
Designware Inc 54 Fieldstone-Bashan Dr .... East Haddam CT 06423 860-873-8938 873-9993
Web: www.designwareinc.com
iParty Corp 270 Bridge St Ste 301 .... Dedham MA 02026 781-329-3952
NYSE: IPT ■ *Web:* partycity.com/
Paper Shack & Party Store Inc, The
2430 E Texas St .... Bossier City LA 71111 318-746-4108
Web: www.papershackpartystore.com
Paper Store Inc 20 Main St .... Acton MA 01720 844-480-7100 263-2466*
**Fax Area Code:* 978 ■ *Web:* www.thepaperstore.com
Party City Corp 25 Green Pond Rd Ste 1 .... Rockaway NJ 07866 973-453-8600
TF: 800-727-8924 ■ *Web:* www.partycity.com
Party Fair Inc 4345 US Hwy 9 .... Freehold NJ 07728 732-780-1110 780-5174
Web: www.partyfair.com

570 PATTERNS - INDUSTRIAL

Phone Fax

Allen Pattern of Michigan
202 McGrath Pl .... Battle Creek MI 49014 269-963-4131 963-4327
Anderson Global Inc
500 W Sherman Blvd .... Muskegon Heights MI 49444 231-733-2164 733-1288
Web: www.andersonglobal.com
Central Pattern Co 8830 Pershall Rd .... Hazelwood MO 63042 314-524-3626 522-8399
Web: www.centralpattern.com
Cunningham Pattern & Engineering Inc
4399 US 31 N PO Box 854 .... Columbus IN 47201 812-379-9571 379-9574
Web: www.cpepattern.com
D & F Corp 42455 Merrill Rd .... Sterling Heights MI 48314 586-254-5300 254-5610
Web: clientinfo.com/d-f
Foley Pattern Company Inc
500 W 11th St PO Box 150 .... Auburn IN 46706 260-925-4113 925-4115
Freeman Mfg & Supply Co 1101 Moore Rd. .... Avon OH 44011 440-934-1902 934-7200
TF: 800-321-8511 ■ *Web:* www.freemansupply.com
General Pattern Company Inc 3075 84th Ln NE. .... Blaine MN 55449 763-780-3518 780-3770
Web: www.generalpattern.com
Gopher Pattern Works Inc
422 Roosevelt St NE .... Minneapolis MN 55413 612-331-5512 331-6513
Hub Pattern Corp 2113 Salem Ave. .... Roanoke VA 24016 540-342-3505 343-5337
TF: 800-482-3505 ■ *Web:* www.hubcorp.net
Kakivik Asset Management LLC
560 E 34th Ave Ste 200 .... Anchorage AK 99503 907-770-9400 770-9450
Web: www.kakivik.com
Production Pattern Co 560 Solon Rd .... Bedford OH 44146 440-439-3243 439-0918
Web: www.prodpatt.com
United Industries Inc 1901 Revere Beach Pkwy .... Everett MA 02149 617-387-9500 387-6331
Web: www.united-ind.com

571 PATTERNS - SEWING

Phone Fax

Bonfit America Inc 8460 Higuera St .... Culver City CA 90232 310-204-7880 204-7893
TF: 800-526-6348 ■ *Web:* www.bonfit.com
Kwik-Sew Pattern Co Inc
3000 N Washington Ave .... Minneapolis MN 55411 612-521-7651
Web: kwiksew.mccall.com
McCall Pattern Co 615 McCall Rd .... Manhattan KS 66502 800-255-2762 776-1471*
**Fax Area Code:* 785 ■ *TF:* 800-255-2762 ■ *Web:* www.mccall.com

572 PAWN SHOPS

Phone Fax

EZCORP Inc 1901 Capital Pkwy. .... Austin TX 78746 512-314-3400 314-3404
NASDAQ: EZPW ■ *TF:* 800-873-7296 ■ *Web:* www.ezcorp.com
Facekey Corp 900 NE Loop 410 Ste D401 .... San Antonio TX 78209 210-826-8811
Web: www.facekey.com
First Cash Financial Services Inc
690 E Lamar Blvd Ste 400 .... Arlington TX 76011 817-460-3947 461-7019
NASDAQ: FCFS ■ *Web:* ww2.firstcash.com
Maxium Financial Services Inc
30 Vogell Rd Ste 1 .... Richmond Hill ON L4B3K6 905-780-6150
Web: www.maxium.net

Phone Fax

Us Pawn & Auto Inc 821 Us Hwy 17 # 92 .... Longwood FL 32750 407-699-5885
Web: www.uspawnandauto.com

573 PAYROLL SERVICES

SEE ALSO Data Processing & Related Services p. 2187; Professional Employer Organizations (PEOs) p. 2975

Phone Fax

Advantage Payroll Services Inc
126 Merrow Rd PO Box 1330 .... Auburn ME 04211 207-784-0178 786-0490
TF Cust Svc: 800-876-0178 ■ *Web:* www.advantagepayroll.com
Automatic Data Processing Inc (ADP)
One ADP Blvd. .... Roseland NJ 07068 973-994-5000 974-5390
NASDAQ: ADP ■ *TF:* 800-225-5237 ■ *Web:* www.adp.com
Basic Pay LLC 231 W 29th St Ste 1207 .... New York NY 10001 212-684-8827 684-6036
Web: www.basicpay.biz
Celergo LLC 750 Estate Dr Ste 110 .... Deerfield IL 60015 847-512-2600
Web: www.celergo.com
CheckPoint HR 2035 Lincoln Hwy Ste 1080 .... Edison NJ 08817 732-287-8270 287-2297
TF: 800-385-0331 ■ *Web:* www.checkpointhr.com
Corporate Business Solutions LLC
229 Peachtree St NE 1520 International Tower
.... Atlanta GA 30303 404-521-6030
Web: www.cbshro.com
DLH Holdings Corp
1776 Peachtree St NW Ste 300S .... Atlanta GA 30309 770-554-3545
NASDAQ: DLHC ■ *TF:* 866-352-5304 ■ *Web:* www.dlhcorp.com
DSI Payroll Services 300 Atrium Dr .... Somerset NJ 08873 732-748-3200
Web: businessfinder.lehighvalleylive.com
Employers Resource Management Co
1301 S Vista Ave Ste 200 .... Boise ID 83705 208-376-3000 363-7356
TF: 800-574-4668 ■ *Web:* www.employersresource.com
Hiregenics 47742 Van Dyke Ave. .... Shelby Township MI 48317 866-315-5489
TF: 866-315-5489 ■ *Web:* www.hiregenics.com
Media Services
500 S Sepulveda Blvd 4th Fl. .... Los Angeles CA 90049 310-440-9600 472-9979
TF: 800-738-0409 ■ *Web:* www.media-services.com
Nexpay 5121 N Mccoll Rd .... Mcallen TX 78504 956-994-1800
Web: www.nexpay.us
Paychex Inc 911 Panorama Trl S .... Rochester NY 14625 585-385-6666 383-3449*
NASDAQ: PAYX ■ **Fax:* Hum Res ■ *TF:* 800-828-4411 ■ *Web:* www.paychex.com
Paychex Major Market Services
12647 Alcosta Blvd Ste 200 .... San Ramon CA 94583 925-242-0700
Web: www.paychex.com
PayData Payroll Services Inc
PO Box 706 .... Essex Junction VT 05453 802-655-6160
Web: www.paydata.com
Payday Payroll Services
6465 College Park Sq Ste 200 .... Virginia Beach VA 23464 757-523-0605
Web: www.paydaypayroll.com
Paypro Corp 450 Wireless Blvd .... Hauppauge NY 11788 631-777-1100
Web: www.payprocorp.com
Payroll Factory, The 18 E Lancaster Ave .... Malvern PA 19355 610-644-4569
Web: www.thepayrollfactory.com
Payroll Management Inc
348 Miracle Strip Pkwy Ste 39 .... Fort Walton Beach FL 32548 850-243-5604 243-5640
Web: www.pmipeo.com
SurePayroll 2350 Ravine Way Ste 100 .... Glenview IL 60025 847-676-8420
TF: 877-954-7873 ■ *Web:* www.surepayroll.com

574 PENS, PENCILS, PARTS

SEE ALSO Art Materials & Supplies - Mfr p. 1752; Office & School Supplies p. 2833

Phone Fax

Alvin & Company Inc 1335 Blue Hills Ave .... Bloomfield CT 06002 860-243-8991 777-2896*
**Fax Area Code:* 800 ■ *TF:* 800-444-2584 ■ *Web:* www.alvinco.com
BIC Corp 1 BIC Way Ste 1 .... Shelton CT 06484 203-783-2000 783-2081*
**Fax:* Hum Res ■ *Web:* www.bicworld.com
California Cedar Products Co
1340 N Washingtron St. .... Stockton CA 95203 209-944-5800 944-9072
Web: www.calcedar.com
Dixon Ticonderoga Co 195 International Pkwy .... Heathrow FL 32746 407-829-9000 232-9396*
**Fax Area Code:* 800 ■ **Fax:* Cust Svc ■ *TF:* 800-824-9430 ■ *Web:* www.dixonticonderoga.com
Dri Mark Products Inc
999 S Oyster Bay Rd Ste 312 .... Bethpage NY 11714 516-484-6200 484-6279
TF: 800-645-9118 ■ *Web:* www.drimark.com
Fisher Space Pen Co 711 Yucca St. .... Boulder City NV 89005 702-293-3011 293-6616
Web: www.spacepen.com
General Pencil Co Inc 3160 Bay Rd. .... Redwood City CA 94063 650-369-4889 369-7169
Web: www.generalpencil.com
Harcourt Pencil Co 7765 S 175 W .... Milroy IN 46156 765-629-2244 629-2218
TF: 800-428-6584 ■ *Web:* www.harcourtoutlines.com
Hartley-Racon 280 N Midland Ave Bldg C-1 .... Saddle Brook NJ 07663 201-703-0663 703-0733
Web: www.hartleyraconusa.com
Jensen's Inc 715 W Jackson St .... Shelbyville TN 37160 931-684-5021 685-9229
Web: jensensincorporated.com
Listo Pencil Corp 1925 Union St .... Alameda CA 94501 510-522-2910 522-3798
TF: 800-547-8648 ■ *Web:* www.listo.com
Mercury Pen Company Inc
245 Eastline Rd. .... Ballston Lake NY 12019 518-899-9653 899-9657
Web: www.mercurypen.com
Musgrave Pencil Company Inc 701 W Ln St .... Shelbyville TN 37160 931-684-3611 685-1049
TF: 800-736-2450 ■ *Web:* pencils.net
National Pen Corp (NPC)
12121 Scripps Summit Dr Ste 200 .... San Diego CA 92131 858-675-3000 675-0890
TF: 800-854-1000 ■ *Web:* www.pens.com
Newell Rubbermaid Inc Office Products Group
Three Glenlake Pkwy. .... Atlanta GA 30328 770-418-7000
Web: newellrubbermaid.com/pages/index.aspx?redirect=1

	City	State	ZIP	Phone	Fax
Pentel of America Ltd 2715 Columbia St. *Web:* www.pentel.com	Torrance	CA	90503	760-200-0547	200-0586

575 PERFORMING ARTS FACILITIES

SEE ALSO Convention Centers p. 2153; Stadiums & Arenas p. 3192; Theaters - Broadway p. 3234; Theaters - Resident p. 3235

Most of the fax numbers provided for these facilities are for the box office.

Alabama

	City	State	ZIP	Phone	Fax
Bama Theatre 600 Greensboro Ave *Web:* www.tuscarts.org	Tuscaloosa	AL	35401	205-758-5195	345-2787
Birmingham Festival Theater 1901 1/2 11th Ave S PO Box 55321 *Web:* www.bftonline.org	Birmingham	AL	35205	205-933-2383	
Birmingham-Jefferson Convention Complex 2100 Richard Arrington Jr Blvd N *Web:* www.bjcc.org	Birmingham	AL	35203	205-458-8400	328-8523
Davis Theatre for the Performing Arts 251 Montgomery St *Web:* trojan.troy.edu	Montgomery	AL	36104	334-241-9567	241-9756
Library Theatre 200 Municipal Dr *Web:* www.thelibrarytheatre.com	Hoover	AL	35216	205-444-7888	444-7894
Renaissance Theatre Inc 1214 Meridian St *Web:* www.renaissancetheatre.net	Huntsville	AL	35801	256-536-3117	
Von Braun Ctr 700 Monroe St *Web:* www.vonbrauncenter.com	Huntsville	AL	35801	256-533-1953	551-2203

Alaska

	City	State	ZIP	Phone	Fax
Alaska Ctr for the Performing Arts 621 W Sixth Ave *Web:* www.myalaskacenter.com	Anchorage	AK	99501	907-263-2900	263-2927

Arizona

	City	State	ZIP	Phone	Fax
Arizona State University's Kerr Cultural Ctr 6110 N Scottsdale Rd *Web:* www.asukerr.com	Scottsdale	AZ	85253	480-596-2660	483-9646
Celebrity Theatre 440 N 32nd St *Web:* celebritytheatre.com	Phoenix	AZ	85008	602-267-1600	267-4882
Chandler Ctr for the Arts 250 N Arizona Ave. *Web:* www.chandlercenter.org	Chandler	AZ	85225	480-782-2680	782-2684
Comerica Theatre 400 W Washington St *Web:* www.comericatheatre.com	Phoenix	AZ	85003	602-379-2800	379-2002
Grady Gammage Memorial Auditorium 1200 S Forest Ave. *Web:* www.asugammage.com	Tempe	AZ	85281	480-965-3434	965-3583
Herberger Theater Ctr 222 E Monroe St *Web:* www.herbergertheater.org	Phoenix	AZ	85004	602-254-7399	258-9521
Rialto, The 318 E Congress St *Web:* www.rialtotheatre.com	Tucson	AZ	85701	520-740-1000	
Scottsdale Ctr for the Performing Arts 7380 E Second St *TF:* 800-309-8532 ■ *Web:* www.scottsdaleperformingarts.org	Scottsdale	AZ	85251	480-994-2787	874-4699
Tucson Convention Ctr 260 S Church Ave *Web:* tucsonaz.gov/	Tucson	AZ	85701	520-791-4101	791-5572

Arkansas

	City	State	ZIP	Phone	Fax
Fort Smith Convention Ctr 55 S Seventh St *Web:* www.fortsmith.org	Fort Smith	AR	72901	479-788-8932	788-8930
Robinson Ctr 101 S. Spring St PO Box 3232 *TF:* 800-844-4781 ■ *Web:* www.littlerockmeetings.com	Little Rock	AR	72201	501-376-4781	376-7833

California

	City	State	ZIP	Phone	Fax
Alex Theatre 216 N Brand Blvd. *Web:* www.alextheatre.org	Glendale	CA	91203	818-243-7700	241-2089
Annenberg Theater 101 Museum Dr Palm Springs Art Museum *Web:* www.psmuseum.org	Palm Springs	CA	92262	760-325-4490	322-3246
B Street Theatre 2711 B St *Web:* www.bstreettheatre.org	Sacramento	CA	95816	916-443-5300	443-0874
Bayview Opera House 4705 Third St *Web:* www.bvoh.org	San Francisco	CA	94124	415-824-0386	824-7124
Bill Graham Civic Auditorium 99 Grove St. *Web:* billgrahamcivicauditorium.com	San Francisco	CA	94102	510-548-3010	
Bren Events Ctr 100 Bren Events Ctr *Web:* www.bren.uci.edu	Irvine	CA	92697	949-824-5050	824-5097
California Ctr for the Arts 340 N Escondido Blvd *TF:* 800-988-4253 ■ *Web:* www.artcenter.org	Escondido	CA	92025	760-839-4138	
California Theatre of Performing Arts 562 W Fourth St *TF:* 800-745-3000 ■ *Web:* www.californiatheatre.net	San Bernardino	CA	92401	909-885-5152	885-8948
Cerritos Ctr for the Performing Arts 12700 Ctr Ct Dr *TF:* 800-300-4345 ■ *Web:* www.cerritoscenter.com	Cerritos	CA	90703	562-916-8501	916-8514
EXIT Theatre 156 Eddy St *Web:* www.theexit.org	San Francisco	CA	94102	415-931-1094	931-2699
Fox Theater 2001 H St *TF:* 888-825-5484 ■ *Web:* www.foxtheateronline.com	Bakersfield	CA	93301	661-324-1369	324-1854
Fresno Convention Ctr 848 M St *Web:* www.fresnoconventioncenter.com	Fresno	CA	93721	559-445-8100	445-8110
Gary Soren Smith Ctr for the Fine & Performing Arts *Ohlone College* 43600 Mission Blvd *TF:* 800-309-2131 ■ *Web:* www.ohlone.edu/org/smithcenter	Fremont	CA	94539	510-659-6031	659-6188
Glendale Centre Theatre 324 N Orange St *Web:* www.glendalecentretheatre.com	Glendale	CA	91203	818-244-8481	244-5042
Good Company Players 928 E Olive Ave. *Web:* gcplayers.com	Fresno	CA	93728	559-266-0660	266-1342
Greek, Theatre, The 2700 N Vermont Ave *Web:* www.greektheatrela.com	Los Angeles	CA	90027	323-665-5857	666-8202
Hollywood Bowl 2301 N Highland Ave *TF:* 800-653-8000 ■ *Web:* www.hollywoodbowl.com	Hollywood	CA	90068	323-850-2000	850-2155
Irvine Barclay Theatre 4242 Campus Dr *Web:* www.thebarclay.org	Irvine	CA	92612	949-854-4646	854-8490
John Anson Ford Theatres 2580 Cahuenga Blvd E *TF:* 800-466-3876 ■ *Web:* www.fordamphitheatre.org	Hollywood	CA	90068	323-461-3673	871-5904
Long Beach Playhouse 5021 E Anaheim St *Web:* www.lbplayhouse.org	Long Beach	CA	90804	562-494-1014	961-8616
Luckman Fine Arts Complex 5151 State University Dr *Web:* www.luckmanarts.org	Los Angeles	CA	90032	323-343-6611	343-6423
Marines Memorial Theatre 609 Sutter St *Web:* marinesmemorialtheatre.com/	San Francisco	CA	94102	415-447-0188	441-3649
McCallum Theatre 73000 Fred Waring Dr *TF:* 866-889-2787 ■ *Web:* www.mccallumtheatre.com	Palm Desert	CA	92260	760-340-2787	779-9445
Monterey Peninsula College Theatre 980 Fremont St. *Web:* www.mpctheatreco.com	Monterey	CA	93940	831-646-4213	
Music Ctr of Los Angeles County 135 N Grand Ave. *Web:* www.musiccenter.org	Los Angeles	CA	90012	213-972-7211	972-7323
New Conservatory Theatre Centre 25 Van Ness Ave. *Web:* www.nctcsf.org	San Francisco	CA	94102	415-861-4914	861-6988
Oxnard Performing Arts & Convention Ctr (PACC) 800 Hobson Way *Web:* www.oxnardpacc.com	Oxnard	CA	93030	805-486-2424	483-7303
Palace of Fine Arts Theatre 3301 Lyon St *Web:* www.palaceoffinearts.org	San Francisco	CA	94123	415-567-6642	567-4062
Palm Canyon Theatre 538 N Palm Canyon Dr. *Web:* www.palmcanyontheatre.org	Palm Springs	CA	92262	760-323-5123	323-7365
Pantages Theatre 6233 Hollywood Blvd *Web:* www.pantages-theater.com	Hollywood	CA	90028	800-430-8903	
Pasadena Convention Center 300 E Green St *Web:* www.pasadenacenter.com	Pasadena	CA	91101	626-793-2122	
Redding Civic Auditorium 700 Auditorium Dr. *Web:* www.reddingcivic.com	Redding	CA	96001	530-229-0036	229-0062
Redlands Bowl 25 Grant St *Web:* www.redlandsbowl.org	Redlands	CA	92373	909-793-7316	
Richard & Karen Carpenter Performing Arts Ctr (CPAC) 6200 Atherton St. *Web:* www.carpenterarts.org	Long Beach	CA	90815	562-985-7000	985-7023
San Francisco War Memorial & Performing Arts Ctr (SFWMPAC) 401 Van Ness Ave Rm 110 *Web:* www.sfwmpac.org	San Francisco	CA	94102	415-621-6600	621-5091
San Jose Convention Center (SJC) 150 W San Carlos St *TF:* 800-726-5673 ■ *Web:* www.sanjose.org/plan-a-meeting-event/venues/convention-center	San Jose	CA	95110	408-792-4194	277-3535
San Jose Ctr for the Performing Arts 255 Almaden Blvd *TF:* 800-726-5673 ■ *Web:* www.sanjose.org	San Jose	CA	95113	408-792-4111	277-3535
San Manuel Amphitheater 2575 Glen Helen Pkwy *Web:* www.livenation.com	San Bernardino	CA	92407	909-880-6500	885-6563
Santa Cruz Civic Auditorium 307 Church St *Web:* www.cityofsantacruz.com	Santa Cruz	CA	95060	831-420-5240	420-5261
Segerstrom Center for the Arts (SCFTA) 600 Town Ctr Dr *Web:* www.scfta.org/home/default.aspx	Costa Mesa	CA	92626	714-556-2121	556-8984
Shoreline Amphitheatre One Amphitheatre Pkwy *Web:* theshorelineamphitheatre.com	Mountain View	CA	94043	650-967-3000	967-4994
Shrine Auditorium & Exposition Ctr 665 W Jefferson Blvd *Web:* www.shrineauditorium.com	Los Angeles	CA	90007	213-748-5116	742-9922
Sleep Train Amphitheatre 2677 Forty Mile Rd. *Web:* sleeptrainamphitheatre.net	Wheatland	CA	95692	530-743-5200	634-0157
Sleep Train Pavilion at Concord 2000 Kirker Pass Rd *Web:* www.livenation.com	Concord	CA	94521	925-676-8742	676-7262
State Theatre 1307 J St PO Box 1492 *Web:* www.thestate.org	Modesto	CA	95354	209-527-4697	
Sturges Ctr for the Fine Arts 780 NE St *Web:* www.sturgescenter.org	San Bernardino	CA	92410	909-384-5415	384-5449
Thousand Oaks Civic Arts Plaza 2100 Thousand Oaks Blvd *Web:* www.toaks.org/theatre	Thousand Oaks	CA	91362	805-449-2787	
Tower Theatre for the Performing Arts 815 E Olive Ave. *Web:* www.towertheatrefresno.com	Fresno	CA	93728	559-485-9050	
Walt Disney Concert Hall 111 S Grand Ave *Web:* laphil.com	Los Angeles	CA	90012	323-850-2000	
Warnors Ctr for the Performing Arts 1400 Fulton St *TF:* 800-320-1733 ■ *Web:* warnors.publishpath.com/	Fresno	CA	93721	559-264-2848	

	City	State	Zip	Phone	Fax
Wiltern Theatre 3790 Wilshire Blvd *TF:* 800-348-8499 ■ *Web:* www.wilterntheatertickets.com	Los Angeles	CA	90010	213-388-1400	

Colorado

	City	State	Zip	Phone	Fax
Arvada Ctr for the Arts & Humanities 6901 Wadsworth Blvd *Web:* www.arvadacenter.org	Arvada	CO	80003	720-898-7200	898-7204
Aurora Fox Arts Ctr 9900 E Colfax Ave *Web:* www.aurorafoxartscenter.org	Aurora	CO	80010	303-739-1970	739-1975
Denver Ctr for the Performing Arts 1101 13th St *TF:* 800-641-1222 ■ *Web:* www.denvercenter.org	Denver	CO	80204	303-893-4000	595-9634
Denver Performing Arts Complex 1245 Champa St 1St Fl *TF:* 800-745-3000 ■ *Web:* www.artscomplex.com	Denver	CO	80204	720-865-4220	865-4247
Macky Auditorium Concert Hall 285 UCB University Ave *Web:* www.colorado.edu	Boulder	CO	80309	303-492-8423	492-1651
Newman Ctr for the Performing Arts 2344 E Iliff Ave *Web:* www.newmancenterpresents.com	Denver	CO	80208	303-871-7720	871-6507
Pikes Peak Ctr 190 S Cascade Ave *TF:* 866-464-2626 ■ *Web:* www.pikespeakcenter.com	Colorado Springs	CO	80903	719-477-2100	477-2199
Red Rocks Amphitheater 18300 W Alameda Pkwy *Web:* www.redrocksonline.com	Morrison	CO	80465	720-865-2494	865-2467
Sangre de Cristo Arts & Conference Ctr 210 N Santa Fe Ave *Web:* www.sdc-arts.org	Pueblo	CO	81003	719-295-7200	295-7230
Wheeler Opera House 320 E Hyman St *TF:* 866-449-0464 ■ *Web:* www.wheeleroperahouse.com	Aspen	CO	81611	970-920-5770	920-5780

Connecticut

	City	State	Zip	Phone	Fax
Bushnell Ctr for the Performing Arts 166 Capitol Ave *TF:* 888-824-2874 ■ *Web:* www.bushnell.org	Hartford	CT	06106	860-987-6000	987-6070
Fairmount Theatre 33 Main St Annex	New Haven	CT	06512	203-467-3832	467-3832
Garde Arts Ctr 325 State St *Web:* www.gardearts.org	New London	CT	06320	860-444-7373	701-0189
John Lyman Ctr for the Performing Arts 501 Crescent St *Web:* tickets.southernct.edu	New Haven	CT	06515	203-392-6154	392-6158
Long Wharf Theatre 222 Sargent Dr *TF:* 800-782-8497 ■ *Web:* www.longwharf.org	New Haven	CT	06511	203-787-4282	776-2287
Norwalk Concert Hall 125 E Ave *TF:* 800-357-9577 ■ *Web:* www.norwalkct.org	Norwalk	CT	06851	203-854-7900	854-7939
Oakdale Theatre 95 S Tpke Rd *Web:* www.oakdale.com	Wallingford	CT	06492	203-269-8721	284-1816
Sacred Heart University Edgerton Ctr for Performing Arts 5151 Pk Ave *Web:* www.edgertoncenter.org	Fairfield	CT	06825	203-371-7908	365-4858
Shubert Theater 247 College St *TF:* 866-889-8061 ■ *Web:* www.shubert.com	New Haven	CT	06510	203-624-1825	789-2286
Stamford Ctr for the Arts 61 Atlantic St *Web:* scalive.org	Stamford	CT	06901	203-325-4466	358-2313
Sterling Farms Theatre Complex 1349 Newfield Ave *Web:* www.curtaincallinc.com	Stamford	CT	06905	203-329-8207	322-3656
TheaterWorks 233 Pearl St *Web:* www.theaterworkshartford.org	Hartford	CT	06103	860-527-7838	525-0758
Westport Country Playhouse 25 Powers Ct *TF:* 888-927-7529 ■ *Web:* www.westportplayhouse.org	Westport	CT	06880	203-227-4177	221-7482
XFINITY Theatreÿ 61 Savitt Way *Web:* www.comcasttheatre.net	Hartford	CT	06120	203-265-1501	

Delaware

	City	State	Zip	Phone	Fax
Christina Cultural Arts Ctr 705 N Market St *Web:* ccacde.org	Wilmington	DE	19801	302-652-0101	652-7480
DuPont Theatre 1007 N Market St *TF:* 800-338-0881 ■ *Web:* www.duponttheatre.com	Wilmington	DE	19801	302-656-4401	594-1437
Grand, The 818 N Market St *TF:* 800-374-7263 ■ *Web:* www.thegrandwilmington.org	Wilmington	DE	19801	302-658-7897	
Schwartz Ctr for the Arts 226 S State St *Web:* www.schwartzcenter.com	Dover	DE	19901	302-678-5152	678-1267

District of Columbia

	City	State	Zip	Phone	Fax
Arena Stage 1101 Sixth St SW *Web:* www.arenastage.org	Washington	DC	20024	202-554-9066	488-4056
Carter Barron Amphitheatre 4850 Colorado Ave NW *Web:* www.nps.gov/rocr/planyourvisit/cbarron.htm	Washington	DC	20008	202-426-0486	
DAR Constitution Hall 1776 D St NW *Web:* dar.org/constitution-hall	Washington	DC	20006	202-628-1776	
Discovery Theater 1100 Jefferson Dr SW *Web:* www.discoverytheater.org	Washington	DC	20560	202-633-8700	343-1073
John F Kennedy Ctr for the Performing Arts 2700 F St NW *TF:* 800-444-1324 ■ *Web:* www.kennedy-center.org	Washington	DC	20566	202-416-8000	416-8205
National Theatre 1321 Pennsylvania Ave NW *Web:* thenationaldc.org	Washington	DC	20004	202-628-6161	638-4830

Florida

	City	State	Zip	Phone	Fax
Adrienne Arsht Ctr for the Performing Arts of Miami-Dade County Inc 1300 Biscayne Blvd *TF:* 877-949-6722 ■ *Web:* www.arshtcenter.org	Miami	FL	33132	786-468-2000	468-2001
American Stage 163 Third St N *Web:* www.americanstage.org	Saint Petersburg	FL	33731	727-823-1600	821-2444
Barbara B Mann Performing Arts Hall 13350 FSW Pkwy *TF:* 800-440-7469 ■ *Web:* www.bbmannpah.com	Fort Myers	FL	33919	239-489-3033	481-4620
Broward Ctr for the Performing Arts 201 SW Fifth Ave *TF:* 877-311-7469 ■ *Web:* www.browardcenter.org	Fort Lauderdale	FL	33312	954-462-0222	462-3541
Coral Springs Ctr for the Arts 2855 Coral Springs Dr *Web:* www.coralspringscenterforthearts.com	Coral Springs	FL	33065	954-344-5990	344-5980
Curtis M Phillips Ctr for the Performing Arts 315 Hull Rd PO Box 112750 *TF:* 800-905-2787 ■ *Web:* www.performingarts.ufl.edu	Gainesville	FL	32611	352-392-1900	392-3775
David A. Straz Jr Ctr for, The Performing Arts, The 1010 N WC MacInnes Pl *TF:* 800-955-1045 ■ *Web:* www.strazcenter.org	Tampa	FL	33602	813-222-1000	222-1057
Florida Theatre 128 E Forsyth St Ste 300 *Web:* www.floridatheatre.com	Jacksonville	FL	32202	904-355-5661	358-1874
GableStage 1200 Anastasia Ave Biltmore Hotel *Web:* www.gablestage.org	Coral Gables	FL	33134	305-446-1116	445-8645
Jackie Gleason Theater of the Performing Arts 1700 Washington Ave *Web:* fillmoremb.com	Miami Beach	FL	33139	305-673-7300	
James L Knight International Ctr 400 SE Second Ave *Web:* www.jlkc.com	Miami	FL	33131	305-416-5970	350-7910
Lakeland Ctr 701 W Lime St *Web:* www.thelakelandcenter.com	Lakeland	FL	33815	863-834-8100	834-8101
Limelight Theatre 11 Old Mission Ave *Web:* www.limelight-theatre.org	Saint Augustine	FL	32084	904-825-1164	825-4662
Mahaffey Theater for the Performing Arts 400 First St S *TF:* 800-435-7352 ■ *Web:* www.themahaffey.com	Saint Petersburg	FL	33701	727-892-5798	892-5897
Marina Civic Ctr 8 Harrison Ave *Web:* www.marinaciviccenter.com	Panama City	FL	32401	850-763-4696	785-5165
Miami-Dade County Auditorium 2901 W Flagler St	Miami	FL	33135	305-547-5414	541-7782
North Miami Beach/Julius Littman Performing Arts Theater 17011 NE 19th Ave *Web:* www.littmantheater.com	North Miami Beach	FL	33162	305-787-6005	787-6040
Ocean Ctr 101 N Atlantic Ave *TF:* 800-858-6444 ■ *Web:* www.oceancenter.com	Daytona Beach	FL	32118	386-254-4500	254-4512
Old School Square Cultural Arts Ctr 51 N Swinton Ave *Web:* delraycenterforthearts.org	Delray Beach	FL	33444	561-243-7922	243-7018
Olympia Theaterÿÿÿ 174 E Flagler St *Web:* www.gusmancenter.org	Miami	FL	33131	305-374-2444	
Orlando Repertory Theatre 1001 E Princeton St *Web:* www.orlandorep.com	Orlando	FL	32803	407-896-7365	897-3284
Parker Playhouse 707 NE Eigth St **Fax:* Administration ■ *Web:* www.parkerplayhouse.com	Fort Lauderdale	FL	33304	954-462-0222	524-9952*
Peabody Auditorium 600 Auditorium Blvd *Web:* www.peabodyauditorium.org	Daytona Beach	FL	32118	386-671-3460	239-6435
Pensacola Civic Ctr 201 E Gregory St *Web:* www.pensacolabaycenter.com	Pensacola	FL	32502	850-432-0800	432-1707
Pensacola Cultural Ctr (PCC) 400 S Jefferson St *Web:* www.pensacolalittletheatre.com/pcc	Pensacola	FL	32502	850-434-0257	438-2787
Philharmonic Ctr for the Arts 5833 Pelican Bay Blvd *TF:* 800-597-1900 ■ *Web:* artisnaples.org	Naples	FL	34108	239-597-1111	597-8163
Plaza Live, The 425 N Bumby Ave *TF:* 877-435-9849 ■ *Web:* www.plazaliveorlando.com	Orlando	FL	32803	407-228-1220	
Pompano Beach Amphitheater 1801 NE Sixth St *Web:* livenation.com	Pompano Beach	FL	33060	954-946-2402	
Raymond F Kravis Ctr for the Performing Arts 701 Okeechobee Blvd **Fax:* Mktg ■ *TF:* 800-572-8471 ■ *Web:* www.kravis.org	West Palm Beach	FL	33401	561-832-7469	833-0691*
Red Barn Theatre 319 Duval St Rear *Web:* redbarntheatre.com	Key West	FL	33040	305-296-9911	
Ritz Theatre & La Villa Museum 829 N Davis St *Web:* www.ritzjacksonville.com	Jacksonville	FL	32202	904-632-5555	632-5553
Ruth Eckerd Hall 1111 McMullen Booth Rd *TF:* 800-875-8682 ■ *Web:* www.rutheckerdhall.com	Clearwater	FL	33759	727-791-7060	724-5976
Saenger Theatre 118 S Palafox Pl *Web:* www.pensacolasaenger.com	Pensacola	FL	32502	850-595-3880	595-3886
Sugden Community Theatre 701 Fifth Ave S *Web:* www.naplesplayers.org	Naples	FL	34102	239-263-7990	434-7772
Tampa Theater 711 N Franklin St PO Box 172188 *Web:* www.tampatheatre.org	Tampa	FL	33602	813-274-8286	274-8978
Tennessee Williams Theatre 5901 W College Rd	Key West	FL	33040	305-296-1520	292-3725
Theatre Tallahassee (TLT) 1861 Thomasville Rd *Web:* theatretallahassee.org	Tallahassee	FL	32303	850-224-4597	224-4464
University of West Florida Ctr for Fine & Performing Arts 11000 University Pkwy Bldg 82 *TF:* 800-263-1074 ■ *Web:* uwf.edu/cfpa	Pensacola	FL	32514	850-474-2000	857-6176
Van Wezel Performing Arts Ctr 777 N Tamiami Trl *TF:* 800-826-9303 ■ *Web:* www.vanwezel.org	Sarasota	FL	34236	941-953-3368	951-1449

				Phone	Fax
Waterfront Playhouse 312 Wall St *TF:* 800-435-7352 ■ *Web:* waterfrontplayhouse.org	Key West	FL	33040	305-294-5015	294-0398

Georgia

				Phone	Fax
14th Street Playhouse 1280 Peachtree St NE	Atlanta	GA	30309	404-733-4738	733-5356
Boisfeuillet Jones Atlanta Civic Ctr 395 Piedmont Ave *TF:* 877-430-7596	Atlanta	GA	30308	404-523-6275	
Douglass Theatre 355 ML King Jr Blvd *Web:* www.douglasstheatre.org	Macon	GA	31201	478-742-2000	742-0270
Fox Theatre 660 Peachtree St NE *TF:* 855-285-8499 ■ *Web:* www.foxtheatre.org	Atlanta	GA	30308	404-881-2100	872-2972
Georgia Mountains Ctr 301 Main St SW PO Box 2496 *Web:* www.gainesville.org	Gainesville	GA	30501	770-534-8420	
Grand Opera House 651 Mulberry St *Web:* www.thegrandmacon.com/	Macon	GA	31201	478-301-5470	
Macon City Auditorium 415 First St *TF:* 877-532-6144 ■ *Web:* www.maconcentreplex.com	Macon	GA	31201	478-751-9152	751-9154
Macon Little Theater 4220 Forsyth Rd *Web:* www.maconlittletheatre.org	Macon	GA	31210	478-477-3342	471-8711
Rialto Ctr for the Arts 80 Forsyth St NW PO Box 2627 *Web:* rialto.gsu.edu	Atlanta	GA	30303	404-413-9800	413-9801
Savannah Civic Ctr 301 W Oglethorp Ave *TF:* 800-337-1101 ■ *Web:* www.savannahga.gov	Savannah	GA	31401	912-651-6550	651-6552
Spivey Hall Clayton College & State University 2000 Clayton State Blvd *Web:* www.spiveyhall.org	Morrow	GA	30260	678-466-4200	466-4494
Springer Opera House 103 Tenth St *Web:* www.springeroperahouse.org	Columbus	GA	31901	706-327-3688	324-4461
Townsend Ctr for the Performing Arts 1601 Maple St *Web:* westga.edu/~tcpa	Carrollton	GA	30118	678-839-4722	839-4805
Woodruff Arts Ctr 1280 Peachtree St NE *Web:* www.woodruffcenter.org	Atlanta	GA	30309	404-733-4200	733-4281

Idaho

				Phone	Fax
Morrison Ctr for the Performing Arts 2201 Cesar Chavez Ln Boise State University *Web:* morrisoncenter.com	Boise	ID	83725	208-426-1609	426-3021

Illinois

				Phone	Fax
Apollo Theater 2540 N Lincoln Ave *Web:* www.apollochicago.com	Chicago	IL	60614	773-935-6100	935-6214
Auditorium Theatre 50 E Congress Pkwy *Web:* www.auditoriumtheatre.org	Chicago	IL	60605	312-341-2310	431-2360
Broadway In Chicago 24 W Randolph St *Web:* www.broadwayinchicago.com	Chicago	IL	60601	312-977-1700	977-0519
Chicago Shakespeare Theater 800 E Grand Ave Navy Pier *Web:* www.chicagoshakes.com	Chicago	IL	60611	312-595-5600	595-5644
Civic Opera House 20 N Wacker Dr *Web:* www.lyricopera.org	Chicago	IL	60606	312-332-2244	332-8120
Coronado Theatre 314 N Main St *Web:* www.coronadopac.org	Rockford	IL	61101	815-968-2722	968-1318
Goodman Theatre 170 N Dearborn St *Web:* www.goodmantheatre.org	Chicago	IL	60601	312-443-3811	443-3821
Krannert Ctr for the Performing Arts 500 S Goodwin Ave *TF:* 800-527-2849 ■ *Web:* www.krannertcenter.com	Urbana	IL	61801	217-333-6700	244-0810
Lifeline Theatre 6912 N Glenwood Ave *Web:* www.lifelinetheatre.com	Chicago	IL	60626	773-761-4477	761-4582
Marriott Theatre in Lincolnshire 10 Marriott Dr *Web:* www.marriotttheatre.com	Lincolnshire	IL	60069	847-634-0200	850-7736
North Shore Ctr for the Performing Arts in Skokie 9501 N Skokie Blvd *Web:* www.northshorecenter.org	Skokie	IL	60077	847-673-6300	679-3704
Paramount Theatre Eight E Galena Blvd Ste 230 *Web:* paramountaurora.com	Aurora	IL	60506	630-896-7676	892-1084
Parkland College Theatre 2400 W Bradley Ave *TF:* 800-346-8089 ■ *Web:* www.parkland.edu/theatre	Champaign	IL	61821	217-351-2528	373-3899
Peoria Civic Ctr 201 SW Jefferson Ave *Web:* peoriaciviccenter.com	Peoria	IL	61602	309-673-8900	673-9223
Rosemont Theatre 5400 N River Rd *Web:* rosemont.com/theatre/	Rosemont	IL	60018	847-671-5100	671-6405
Royal George Theatre Ctr 1641 N Halsted St *Web:* www.theroyalgeorgetheatre.com	Chicago	IL	60614	312-988-9105	
Springfield Theatre Centre 420 S Sixth St *Web:* springfieldtheatrecentre.com	Springfield	IL	62701	217-523-0878	
Station Theatre 223 N Broadway Ave *Web:* www.stationtheatre.com	Urbana	IL	61801	217-384-4000	
Steppenwolf Theatre 1650 N Halsted St *Web:* www.steppenwolf.org	Chicago	IL	60614	312-335-1650	335-0440
Symphony Ctr 220 S Michigan Ave **Fax:* Mktg ■ *TF Cust Svc:* 800-223-7114 ■ *Web:* www.cso.org	Chicago	IL	60604	312-294-3000	294-3035*
Virginia Theatre 203 W Pk Ave *Web:* www.thevirginia.org	Champaign	IL	61820	217-356-9053	356-5729

Indiana

				Phone	Fax
American Cabaret Theatre 121 Monument Cir Ste 516 *Web:* www.thecabaret.org	Indianapolis	IN	46204	317-275-1169	
Christel DeHaan Fine Arts Ctr 1400 E Hanna Ave University of Indianapolis *TF:* 800-232-8634 ■ *Web:* www.uindy.edu/arts	Indianapolis	IN	46227	317-788-3566	788-3383
Embassy Theatre 125 W Jefferson Blvd *Web:* fwembassytheatre.org	Fort Wayne	IN	46802	260-424-6287	
Evansville Auditorium & Convention Ctr 715 Locust St *TF:* 844-381-4751 ■ *Web:* centre.evansvillegis.com	Evansville	IN	47708	812-435-5770	435-5500
Evansville Civic Theatre 717 N Fulton St *Web:* www.evansvillecivictheatre.org	Evansville	IN	47710	812-425-2800	423-2636
Indiana University Auditorium 1211 E Seventh St *Web:* www.iuauditorium.com	Bloomington	IN	47405	812-855-1103	855-4244
Indianapolis Artsgarden Above the Intersection of Washington Illinois St *Web:* www.indyarts.org	Indianapolis	IN	46204	317-624-2563	624-2564
Madame Walker Theatre Ctr 617 Indiana Ave *Web:* thewalkertheatre.org	Indianapolis	IN	46202	317-236-2099	236-2097
Morris Performing Arts Ctr 211 N Michigan St *TF:* 800-537-6415 ■ *Web:* www.morriscenter.org	South Bend	IN	46601	574-235-9190	235-5945
Warren Performing Arts Ctr 9500 E 16th St *Web:* www.warrenpac.org	Indianapolis	IN	46229	317-532-6280	532-6440

Iowa

				Phone	Fax
Civic Ctr of Greater Des Moines 221 Walnut St *Web:* www.desmoinesperformingarts.org	Des Moines	IA	50309	515-246-2300	246-2305
RiverCenter Adler Theatre 136 E Third St *Web:* www.riverctr.com	Davenport	IA	52801	563-326-8500	326-8505

Kansas

				Phone	Fax
Century II Performing Arts & Convention Ctr 225 W Douglas Ave *Web:* www.century2.org	Wichita	KS	67202	316-264-9121	303-8688
Cricket Wireless Amphitheater 633 N 130th St *Web:* www.cricketwirelessamp.com	Bonner Springs	KS	66012	913-825-3400	
Orpheum Performing Arts Centre 200 N Broadway *Web:* www.wichitaorpheum.com	Wichita	KS	67202	316-263-0884	
Topeka Performing Arts Ctr 214 SE Eigth Ave *Web:* www.tpactix.org	Topeka	KS	66603	785-234-2787	234-2307
Wichita Community Theatre 258 N Fountain *Web:* wichitact.org	Wichita	KS	67208	316-686-1282	652-0531
Wichita Ctr for the Arts 9112 E Central Ave *Web:* www.wcfta.com	Wichita	KS	67206	316-634-2787	634-0593

Kentucky

				Phone	Fax
Kentucky Ctr for, The Performing Arts, The 501 W Main St *Web:* www.kentuckycenter.org	Louisville	KY	40202	502-562-0100	562-0150
Kentucky Theater 214 E Main St *Web:* www.kentuckytheater.com	Lexington	KY	40507	859-231-7924	
Lexington Opera House 401 W Short St *Web:* www.lexingtonoperahouse.com	Lexington	KY	40507	859-233-4567	253-2718
Louisville Palace Theatre 625 S Fourth St *Web:* www.louisvillepalace.com	Louisville	KY	40202	502-583-4555	

Louisiana

				Phone	Fax
Baton Rouge Little Theater 7155 Florida Blvd *Web:* theatrebr.org	Baton Rouge	LA	70806	225-924-6496	924-9972
Baton Rouge River Ctr 275 S River Rd *Web:* www.brrivercenter.com	Baton Rouge	LA	70802	225-389-3030	389-4954
Contemporary Arts Ctr 900 Camp St *TF:* 800-568-6968 ■ *Web:* www.cacno.org	New Orleans	LA	70130	504-528-3805	528-3828
East Bank Community Theatre 630 Barksdale Blvd *Web:* bossierarts.org	Bossier City	LA	71111	318-741-8310	
Heymann Performing Arts Ctr 1373 S College Rd *TF:* 800-745-3000 ■ *Web:* heymanncenter.com	Lafayette	LA	70503	337-291-5540	291-5580
Lake Charles Civic Ctr 900 Lakeshore Dr *TF:* 888-620-1749 ■ *Web:* www.cityoflakecharles.com	Lake Charles	LA	70601	337-491-1256	491-1534
Monroe Civic Ctr 401 Lea Joyner Expy *Web:* ci.monroe.la.us	Monroe	LA	71201	318-329-2225	329-2548
Preservation Hall 726 St Peter St *Web:* www.preservationhall.com	New Orleans	LA	70116	504-522-2841	558-9192
Strand Theatre 619 Louisiana Ave *TF:* 800-313-6373 ■ *Web:* www.thestrandtheatre.com	Shreveport	LA	71101	318-226-1481	424-5434

Maine

Facility	City	State	Zip	Phone	Fax
Cumberland County Civic Ctr One Civic Ctr Sq *Web:* www.thecivccenter.com	Portland	ME	04101	207-775-3481	828-8344
Merrill Auditorium 20 Myrtle St *Web:* tickets.porttix.com	Portland	ME	04101	207-842-0800	842-0810

Manitoba

Facility	City	State	Zip	Phone	Fax
Burton Cummings Theatre 364 Smith St *Web:* burtoncummingstheatre.ca	Winnipeg	MB	R3B2H2	204-956-5656	956-2581

Maryland

Facility	City	State	Zip	Phone	Fax
Annapolis Summer Garden Theatre 143 Compromise St *Web:* www.summergarden.com	Annapolis	MD	21401	410-268-9212	
Chesapeake Arts Ctr 194 Hammonds Ln *Web:* www.chesapeakearts.org	Brooklyn Park	MD	21225	410-636-6597	636-9653
Everyman Theatre 1727 N Charles St *Web:* www.everymantheatre.org	Baltimore	MD	21201	410-752-2208	752-5891
Gordon Ctr for Performing Arts 3506 Gwynnbrook Ave *Web:* www.jcc.org	Owings Mills	MD	21117	410-356-7469	356-7605
Joseph Meyerhoff Symphony Hall 1212 Cathedral St *TF:* 877-276-1444 ■ *Web:* www.bsomusic.org	Baltimore	MD	21201	410-783-8100	
Lyric Opera House 110 W Mt Royal Ave *TF:* 800-872-7245 ■ *Web:* www.lyricoperahouse.com	Baltimore	MD	21201	410-685-5086	332-8234
Maryland Hall for the Creative Arts 801 Chase St *TF:* 866-438-3808 ■ *Web:* www.marylandhall.org	Annapolis	MD	21401	410-263-5544	263-5114
Maryland Theatre 21 S Potomac St *Web:* www.mdtheatre.org	Hagerstown	MD	21740	301-790-3500	791-6114
Merriweather Post Pavilion (MPP) 10475 Little Patuxent Pkwy *Web:* www.merriweathermusic.com	Columbia	MD	21044	410-715-5550	715-5560
Recher, Theatre, The 512 York Rd *Web:* torrentnightclub.com	Towson	MD	21204	410-337-7178	321-8175

Massachusetts

Facility	City	State	Zip	Phone	Fax
Bank of America Pavilion 290 Northern Ave *Web:* bankofamericapavilion.net	Boston	MA	02210	617-728-1600	
Berklee Performance Ctr 136 Massachusetts Ave *TF:* 877-237-5533 ■ *Web:* www.berklee.edu	Boston	MA	02115	617-747-2261	375-9228
Boston Ctr for the Arts 539 Tremont St *Web:* www.bcaonline.org	Boston	MA	02116	617-426-5000	426-5336
Boston Symphony Hall 301 Massachusetts Ave *TF:* 888-266-1200 ■ *Web:* www.bso.org	Boston	MA	02115	617-266-1492	
Charles Playhouse 74 Warrenton St *Web:* www.blueman.com	Boston	MA	02116	617-426-6912	
Citi Performing Arts Ctr Wang Theatre 270 Tremont St *Web:* citicenter.org	Boston	MA	02116	800-982-2787	
Colonial Theatre 106 Boylston St *Web:* boston.broadway.com	Boston	MA	02116	617-482-9393	880-2449
Cutler Majestic Theatre at Emerson College 219 Tremont St *TF:* 888-627-7115 ■ *Web:* www.emerson.edu	Boston	MA	02116	617-824-8000	824-3209
Mechanics Hall 321 Main St *Web:* www.mechanicshall.org	Worcester	MA	01608	508-752-5608	754-8442
South Shore Music Circus 130 Sohier St *Web:* www.themusiccircus.org	Cohasset	MA	02025	781-383-9850	383-9804
Stuart Street Playhouse 200 Stuart St	Boston	MA	02116	617-457-2623	
Wang Theatre 270 Tremont St *Web:* citicenter.org	Boston	MA	02116	800-982-2787	
Wilbur Theatre 246 Tremont St *Web:* thewilbur.com	Boston	MA	02116*	617-248-9700	
Xfinity Center 885 S Main St	Mansfield	MA	02048	508-339-2331	339-0550

Michigan

Facility	City	State	Zip	Phone	Fax
Ann Arbor Civic Theatre 322 W Ann St *Web:* www.a2ct.org	Ann Arbor	MI	48104	734-971-0605	971-2769
Detroit Opera House 1526 Broadway *Web:* www.michiganopera.org	Detroit	MI	48226	313-961-3500	237-3412
Dow Event Ctr 303 Johnson St *Web:* www.doweventcenter.com	Saginaw	MI	48607	989-759-1320	759-1322
Fillmore Detroit, The 2115 Woodward Ave *Web:* thefillmoredetroit.com	Detroit	MI	48201	313-961-5451	965-2808
Fisher Theatre 3011 W Grand Blvd *Web:* www.broadwayindetroit.com	Detroit	MI	48202	313-872-1000	872-0632
Gem Theatre & Century Grille 333 Madison Ave *Web:* www.gemtheatre.com	Detroit	MI	48226	313-963-9800	963-0873
Grand Rapids Civic Theatre 30 N Div Ave *TF:* 866-455-4728 ■ *Web:* www.grct.org	Grand Rapids	MI	49503	616-222-6650	222-6660
Interlochen Ctr for the Arts 4000 Michigan 137 *Web:* www.interlochen.org	Interlochen	MI	49643	231-276-7200	276-7444
Kerrytown Concert House 415 N Fourth Ave *Web:* www.kerrytownconcerthouse.com	Ann Arbor	MI	48104	734-769-2999	
Majestic Theatre 4120 Woodward Ave *Web:* www.majesticdetroit.com	Detroit	MI	48201	313-833-9700	833-1213
Masonic Temple Theatre 500 Temple St *Web:* www.themasonic.com	Detroit	MI	48201	313-832-7100	832-2922
Michigan Theater 603 E Liberty St *TF:* 800-745-3000 ■ *Web:* www.michtheater.org	Ann Arbor	MI	48104	734-668-8397	668-7136
Midland Ctr for the Arts Inc 1801 W St Andrews Rd *Web:* www.mcfta.org	Midland	MI	48640	989-631-5930	631-7890
Music Hall Ctr for the Performing Arts 350 Madison *Web:* www.musichall.org	Detroit	MI	48226	313-887-8500	887-8502
Riverside Arts Ctr 76 N Huron St *Web:* www.riversidearts.org	Ypsilanti	MI	48197	734-480-2787	
Riverwalk Theatre 228 Museum Dr *Web:* www.riverwalktheatre.com	Lansing	MI	48933	517-482-5700	482-9812
University of Michigan - Flint Theater 303 E Kearsley St *Web:* www.umflint.edu/theatredance	Flint	MI	48502	810-762-3300	766-6630
Wharton Ctr for the Performing Arts Michigan State University *TF:* 800-942-7866 ■ *Web:* www.whartoncenter.com	East Lansing	MI	48824	517-432-2000	353-5329
Whiting Auditorium 1241 E Kearsley St *TF:* 888-823-6837 ■ *Web:* www.thewhiting.com	Flint	MI	48503	810-237-7333	237-7335

Minnesota

Facility	City	State	Zip	Phone	Fax
Duluth Playhouse 506 W Michigan St *Web:* www.duluthplayhouse.org	Duluth	MN	55802	218-733-7555	733-7554
Fitzgerald Theater 10 E Exchange St *Web:* fitzgeraldtheater.publicradio.org	Saint Paul	MN	55101	651-290-1200	290-1195
Great American History Theatre 30 E Tenth St *Web:* www.historytheatre.com	Saint Paul	MN	55101	651-292-4323	292-4322
Guthrie Theater 818 S Second St *TF Resv:* 877-447-8243 ■ *Web:* www.guthrietheater.org	Minneapolis	MN	55415	612-377-2224	225-6004
Hennepin State Theatre 615 Hennepin Ave Ste 140 *Web:* hennepintheatretrust.org	Minneapolis	MN	55403	612-455-9500	455-9502
Historic Orpheum Theatre 910 Hennepin Ave *Web:* www.hennepintheatretrust.org/our-theatres/orpheum-theatre	Minneapolis	MN	55403	612-339-7007	
Historic Pantages Theatre 710 Hennepin Ave *Web:* www.hennepintheatretrust.org	Minneapolis	MN	55403	612-339-7007	339-4146
Jungle Theater 2951 Lindale Ave S *Web:* www.jungletheater.com	Minneapolis	MN	55408	612-822-4002	822-9408
Macphail Center For Music - Minneapolis 501 S Second St *Web:* www.macphail.org	Minneapolis	MN	55401	612-321-0100	321-9740
Music Box Theatre 1407 Nicollet Ave *Web:* musicboxtheatre.org	Minneapolis	MN	55403	612-874-1100	874-8987
Orchestra Hall 1111 Nicollet Mall *TF:* 800-292-4141 ■ *Web:* www.minnesotaorchestra.org	Minneapolis	MN	55403	612-371-5600	
Ordway Ctr for the Performing Arts 345 Washington St *Web:* www.ordway.org	Saint Paul	MN	55102	651-282-3000	282-3160
Penumbra Theatre 270 Kent St *Web:* www.penumbratheatre.org	Saint Paul	MN	55102	651-224-3180	288-6789
Reif Ctr 720 NW Conifer Dr *Web:* www.reifcenter.org	Grand Rapids	MN	55744	218-327-5780	327-5798
Renegade Theatre Co 222 E Superior St *Web:* www.renegadetheatercompany.org	Duluth	MN	55802	218-722-6775	
Rochester Civic Theatre 20 Civic Ctr Dr SE *Web:* www.rochestercivictheatre.org	Rochester	MN	55904	507-282-8481	282-0608

Mississippi

Facility	City	State	Zip	Phone	Fax
Thalia Mara Hall 255 E Pascagoula St *Web:* www.thaliamara.org	Jackson	MS	39201	601-960-1537	960-1583
Tupelo Community Theatre 201 N Broadway PO Box 1094 *Web:* www.tctwebstage.com/lyric.htm	Tupelo	MS	38802	662-844-1935	844-2990

Missouri

Facility	City	State	Zip	Phone	Fax
Andy Williams Moon River Theatre 2500 Hwy 76 *TF:* 800-666-6094 ■ *Web:* www.andywilliamstheatre.com	Branson	MO	65616	417-334-1800	334-3200
Coterie, Theatre, The 2450 Grand Blvd Ste 144 *Web:* thecoterie.org	Kansas City	MO	64108	816-474-6785	474-7112
Folly Theater 1020 Central Ste 200 PO Box 26505 *Web:* follytheater.org	Kansas City	MO	64105	816-474-4444	842-8709
Gem Theater Cultural & Performing Arts Ctr 1615 E 18th St *Web:* americanjazzmuseum.com	Kansas City	MO	64108	816-474-6262	474-0074
Juanita K Hammons Hall for the Performing Arts 901 S National Ave *TF:* 888-476-7849 ■ *Web:* www.hammonshall.com	Springfield	MO	65897	417-836-6776	836-6891
Kansas City Music Hall 301 W 13th St *TF:* 800-821-7060 ■ *Web:* visitkc.com/convention-center/index.aspx	Kansas City	MO	64105	816-513-5000	513-5001
Legends Theater 1600 W Hwy 76 *Fax: Investor Rel ■ *TF:* 800-374-7469 ■ *Web:* www.legendsinconcert.com	Branson	MO	65616	417-339-3003	335-2768*
Maplewood Barn Community Theatre Maplewood Barn Community Theatre PO Box 1704 *Web:* www.maplewoodbarn.com	Columbia	MO	65205	573-227-2276	
Midland by AMC, The 1228 Main St *Web:* www.midlandkc.com	Kansas City	MO	64105	816-283-9900	

				Phone	Fax
Missouri Theatre Ctr for the Arts 203 S Ninth St *Web:* www.motheatre.org	Columbia	MO	65201	573-875-0600	
Powell Symphony Hall 718 N Grand Blvd. *TF:* 800-232-1880 ■ *Web:* www.stlsymphony.org	Saint Louis	MO	63103	314-533-2500	
Quality Hill Playhouse 303 W Tenth St. *Web:* www.qualityhillplayhouse.com	Kansas City	MO	64105	816-421-1700	221-6556
Shepherd of the Hills Homestead & Outdoor Theatre 5586 W Hwy 76 *TF:* 800-653-6288 ■ *Web:* theshepherdofthehills.com/	Branson	MO	65616	417-334-4191	334-4617
Stained Glass Theatre 1996 W Evangel *Web:* www.sgtheatre.com	Ozark	MO	65721	417-581-9192	
Starlight Theatre 4600 Starlight Rd Swope Pk *TF:* 800-776-1730 ■ *Web:* www.kcstarlight.com	Kansas City	MO	64132	816-363-7827	361-6398
Unicorn Theatre 3828 Main St *Web:* www.unicorntheatre.org	Kansas City	MO	64111	816-531-7529	531-0421
University of Missouri 129 Fine Arts Bldg *Web:* theatre.missouri.edu	Columbia	MO	65211	573-882-2021	
Verizon Wireless Amphitheater 14141 Riverport Dr *Web:* www.livenation.com	Maryland Heights	MO	63043	314-298-9944	291-4719

Montana

				Phone	Fax
Alberta Bair Theater for the Performing Arts 2722 Third Ave N Ste 200 PO Box 1556 *TF:* 877-321-2074 ■ *Web:* www.albertabairtheater.org	Billings	MT	59103	406-256-8915	256-5060
Billings Studio Theatre (BST) 1500 Rimrock Rd *Web:* www.billingsstudiotheatre.com	Billings	MT	59102	406-248-1141	
Grand Street Theater 325 N Pk Ave *Web:* www.grandstreettheatre.com	Helena	MT	59601	406-442-4270	447-1573
Helena Civic Ctr 340 Neill Ave. *Web:* www.helenaciviccenter.com	Helena	MT	59601	406-447-8481	447-8480

Nebraska

				Phone	Fax
Blue Barn Theatre 614 S 11th St *Web:* www.bluebarn.org	Omaha	NE	68102	402-345-1576	
Lied Ctr for Performing Arts 301 N 12th St *TF:* 800-432-3231 ■ *Web:* www.unl.edu	Lincoln	NE	68588	402-472-4700	472-2725
Lincoln Community Playhouse 2500 S 56th St *Web:* www.lincolnplayhouse.com	Lincoln	NE	68506	402-489-7529	489-1035
Omaha Community Playhouse 6915 Cass St *TF:* 888-782-4338 ■ *Web:* www.omahaplayhouse.com	Omaha	NE	68132	402-553-0800	553-6288
Pershing Ctr 226 Centennial Mall S	Lincoln	NE	68508	402-441-8744	441-7913

Nevada

				Phone	Fax
Artemus W Ham Concert Hall 4505 Maryland Pkwy *Web:* pac.unlv.edu	Las Vegas	NV	89154	702-895-2787	895-4714
Brewery Arts Ctr 449 W King St *Web:* www.breweryarts.org	Carson City	NV	89703	775-883-1976	883-1922

New Hampshire

				Phone	Fax
Capitol Ctr for the Arts 44 S Main St *Web:* www.ccanh.com	Concord	NH	03301	603-225-1111	224-3408
Hopkins Ctr for the Arts 6041 Wilson Hall *TF:* 800-451-4067 ■ *Web:* www.hop.dartmouth.edu	Hanover	NH	03755	603-646-2422	646-1375

New Jersey

				Phone	Fax
Count Basie Theatre 99 Monmouth St *Web:* www.countbasietheatre.org	Red Bank	NJ	07701	732-842-9000	842-9323
McCarter Theatre 91 University Pl *Web:* www.mccarter.org	Princeton	NJ	08540	609-258-6500	497-0369
New Jersey Performing Arts Ctr 1 Ctr St *TF:* 888-466-5722 ■ *Web:* www.njpac.org	Newark	NJ	07102	973-642-8989	648-6724
Newark Symphony Hall 1030 Broad St *Web:* www.newarksymphonyhall.org	Newark	NJ	07102	973-643-8014	
Patriots Theater Memorial Dr *TF:* 866-847-7682 ■ *Web:* www.state.nj.us	Trenton	NJ	08608	609-984-8484	777-0581
PNC Bank Art Ctr Exit 116 Garden State Pkwy *Web:* livenation.com/venues/16839?from_tm=true	Holmdel	NJ	07733	732-203-2500	335-8637
Stockton Performing Arts Ctr 101 Vera King Farris Dr *Web:* stocktonpac.org	Galloway	NJ	08205	609-652-9000	626-5523

New Mexico

				Phone	Fax
Adobe Theater Inc 9813 Fourth St NW PO Box 276 *Web:* www.adobetheater.org	Albuquerque	NM	87114	505-898-9222	
Albuquerque Little Theatre 224 San Pasquale SW *Web:* www.albuquerquelittletheatre.org	Albuquerque	NM	87104	505-242-4750	
Flickinger Ctr for Performing Arts 1110 New York Ave *Web:* www.flickingercenter.com	Alamogordo	NM	88310	575-437-2202	434-0067
Greer Garson Theatre Ctr 1600 St Michael's Dr College of Santa Fe *TF:* 800-456-2673 ■ *Web:* www.santafeuniversity.edu	Santa Fe	NM	87505	505-473-6011	
KiMo Theater 423 Central Ave NW *Web:* kimotickets.com	Albuquerque	NM	87102	505-768-3522	768-3542
Las Cruces Community Theatre 313 N Downtown Mall *Web:* www.lcctnm.org	Las Cruces	NM	88001	575-523-1200	
Lensic Performing Arts Ctr 211 W San Francisco St *Web:* www.lensic.org	Santa Fe	NM	87501	505-988-7050	988-4370
Popejoy Hall UNM Public Events Popejoy Hall UNM Ctr for the Arts MSC 04 2580 *Web:* www.popejoypresents.com	Albuquerque	NM	87131	505-277-3824	277-7353
Santa Fe Performing Arts 1050 Old Pecos Trail *Web:* www.sfperformingarts.org	Santa Fe	NM	87502	505-982-7992	
Santa Fe Playhouse 142 E DeVargas St *Web:* www.santafeplayhouse.org	Santa Fe	NM	87501	505-988-4262	

New York

				Phone	Fax
Alleyway Theatre One Curtain Up Alley *Web:* www.alleyway.com	Buffalo	NY	14202	716-852-2600	852-2266
Apollo Theatre 253 W 125th St *Web:* www.apollotheater.org	New York	NY	10027	212-531-5300	749-2743
Artpark 450 S Fourth St *TF:* 877-325-5787 ■ *Web:* www.artpark.net	Lewiston	NY	14092	716-754-9000	754-2741
Brooklyn Academy of Music (BAM) 30 Lafayette Ave *Web:* www.bam.org	Brooklyn	NY	11217	718-636-4100	636-4121
Brooklyn Ctr for the Performing Arts 2900 Campus Rd PO Box 100163 *Web:* www.brooklyncenter.com	Brooklyn	NY	11210	718-951-4600	951-4343
Carnegie Hall 881 Seventh Ave *TF:* 800-728-3843 ■ *Web:* www.carnegiehall.org	New York	NY	10019	212-247-7800	581-6539
Center for the Arts 103 Ctr for the Arts *TF:* 800-745-3000 ■ *Web:* www.ubcfa.org	Buffalo	NY	14260	716-645-2787	645-6973
Eastman Theatre 26 Gibbs St *Web:* www.esm.rochester.edu	Rochester	NY	14604	585-274-1110	274-1067
Egg, The Empire State Plz Concourse Level Performing Arts Ctr *Web:* www.theegg.org	Albany	NY	12220	518-473-1845	473-1848
Emelin Theater 153 Library Ln *Web:* www.emelin.org	Mamaroneck	NY	10543	914-698-0098	698-1404
Geva Theatre Ctr 75 Woodbury Blvd *Web:* www.gevatheatre.org	Rochester	NY	14607	585-232-1366	232-4031
Kavinoky Theatre 320 Porter Ave *Web:* www.kavinokytheatre.com	Buffalo	NY	14201	716-829-7668	829-7790
Kleinhans Music Hall 3 Symphony Cir *Web:* www.kleinhansbuffalo.org	Buffalo	NY	14201	716-883-3560	883-7430
Landmark Theatre 362 S Salina St *Web:* www.landmarktheatre.org	Syracuse	NY	13202	315-475-7980	475-7993
Lehman Ctr for the Performing Arts Inc 250 Bedford Pk Blvd W *Web:* www.lehmancenter.org	Bronx	NY	10468	718-960-8232	960-8233
Lucille Lortel Theatre 121 Christopher St *Web:* www.lortel.org	New York	NY	10014	212-924-2817	
Manhattan Ctr Studios 311 W 34th St *Web:* www.mcstudios.com	New York	NY	10001	212-279-7740	564-1072
Mid-Hudson Civic Ctr 14 Civic Ctr Plz *Web:* www.midhudsonciviccenter.org	Poughkeepsie	NY	12601	845-454-5800	
New York City Ctr 130 W 56th St *Web:* www.nycitycenter.org	New York	NY	10019	212-247-0430	246-9778
Paul Robeson Theatre *Theatre Alliance of Buffalo* 350 Masten Ave *Web:* www.theatreallianceofbuffalo.com	Buffalo	NY	14209	716-884-2013	885-2590
Performing Arts Ctr 735 Anderson Hill Rd *Web:* www.artscenter.org	Purchase	NY	10577	914-251-6200	251-6171
Performing Arts Ctr at Rockwell Hall 1300 Elmwood Ave Rockwell Hall Rm 210 *Web:* www.buffalostate.edu	Buffalo	NY	14222	716-878-3005	878-4234
Proctor's Theatre 432 State St *Web:* www.proctors.org	Schenectady	NY	12305	518-382-3884	346-2468
Public, Theater, The 425 Lafayette St *Web:* www.publictheater.org	New York	NY	10003	212-539-8500	539-8505
Radio City Music Hall 1260 Ave of the Americas *Web:* www.radiocity.com	New York	NY	10020	212-247-4777	
Saratoga Performing Arts Ctr (SPAC) 108 Ave of the Pines *Web:* www.spac.org	Saratoga Springs	NY	12866	518-584-9330	584-0809
Shea's Performing Arts Ctr 646 Main St *TF:* 866-341-5945 ■ *Web:* www.sheas.org	Buffalo	NY	14202	716-847-1410	847-1644
Snug Harbor Cultural Ctr 1000 Richmond Terr *Web:* www.snug-harbor.org	Staten Island	NY	10301	718-448-2500	815-0198
Stanley Ctr for the Arts 259 Genesee St *Web:* www.thestanley.org	Utica	NY	13501	315-724-1113	624-2926
Tarrytown Music Hall 13 Main St PO Box 686 *TF:* 877-840-0457 ■ *Web:* www.tarrytownmusichall.org	Tarrytown	NY	10591	914-631-3390	
TRIBECA Performing Arts Ctr 199 Chambers St *Web:* tickets.tribecapac.org	New York	NY	10007	212-220-1459	732-2482

North Carolina

				Phone	Fax
Actor's Theatre of Charlotte 650 E Stonewall St *Web:* www.atcharlotte.org	Charlotte	NC	28202	704-342-2251	342-1229
Asheville Community Theatre 35 E Walnut St *Web:* www.ashevilletheatre.org	Asheville	NC	28801	828-254-1320	252-4723

				Phone	Fax
Carolina Theatre 310 S Greene St *Web:* www.carolinatheatre.com	Greensboro	NC	27401	336-333-2600	333-2604
Carolina, Theatre of Durham, The 309 W Morgan St *Web:* www.carolinatheatre.org	Durham	NC	27701	919-560-3040	560-3065
Diana Wortham Theatre at Pack Place 2 S Pack Sq *TF:* 800-999-2160 ■ *Web:* www.dwtheatre.com	Asheville	NC	28801	828-257-4530	251-5652
Flat Rock Playhouse 2661 Greenville Hwy *Web:* www.flatrockplayhouse.org	Flat Rock	NC	28731	828-693-0731	693-6795
Greensboro Coliseum Complex 1921 W Lee St *Web:* www.greensborocoliseum.com	Greensboro	NC	27403	336-373-7400	373-2170
Theatre in the Park 107 Pullen Rd *Web:* www.theatreinthepark.com	Raleigh	NC	27607	919-831-6936	831-9475

North Dakota

				Phone	Fax
Chester Fritz Auditorium 3475 University Ave PO Box 9028 *TF:* 800-375-4068 ■ *Web:* und.edu	Grand Forks	ND	58202	701-777-3076	777-4710
Empire Arts Ctr 415 DeMers Ave *Web:* www.empireartscenter.com	Grand Forks	ND	58201	701-746-5500	746-0500
Fargo Theatre 314 Broadway N PO Box 2190 *Web:* www.fargotheatre.org	Fargo	ND	58102	701-239-8385	235-0893
Festival Concert Hall *North Dakota State University* PO Box 5691 *TF:* 800-726-1724 ■ *Web:* www.ndsu.edu	Fargo	ND	58105	701-231-7932	231-2085
Fire Hall Theatre 412 Second Ave N *Web:* ggfct.com	Grand Forks	ND	58203	701-746-0847	

Ohio

				Phone	Fax
Akron Civic Theatre 182 S Main St *Web:* www.akroncivic.com	Akron	OH	44308	330-535-3179	535-9828
Aronoff Ctr for the Arts 650 Walnut St *Web:* www.cincinnatiarts.org	Cincinnati	OH	45202	513-721-3344	977-4150
Blossom Music Ctr Tickets 1145 W Steels Corners Rd **Fax Area Code: 304* ■ *TF:* 800-745-3000 ■ *Web:* www.livenation.com	Cuyahoga Falls	OH	44223	330-920-8040	645-6660*
Cain Park Theatre 40 Severance Cir *Web:* cainpark.com	Cleveland Heights	OH	44118	216-371-3000	371-6995
Canton Palace Theatre 605 Market Ave N *Web:* www.cantonpalacetheatre.org	Canton	OH	44702	330-454-8172	454-8171
Cincinnati Music Hall 650 Walnut St *Web:* www.cincinnatiarts.org	Cincinnati	OH	45202	513-744-3344	744-3345
Cincinnati Playhouse in the Park 962 Mt Adams Cir PO Box 6537 *TF:* 800-582-3208 ■ *Web:* www.cincyplay.com	Cincinnati	OH	45202	513-345-2242	345-2250
Coach House Theatre 732 W Exchange St *Web:* www.coachhousetheatre.org	Akron	OH	44302	330-434-7741	
Dobama Theater 2340 Lee Rd *Web:* www.dobama.org	Cleveland Heights	OH	44118	216-932-6838	932-6838
Edward W Powers Auditorium 260 Federal Plz W *Web:* www.youngstownsymphony.com/symphony_center.html	Youngstown	OH	44503	330-744-4269	744-1441
EJ Thomas Performing Arts Hall 198 Hill St University of Akron *TF:* 800-745-3000 ■ *Web:* www.uaevents.com	Akron	OH	44325	330-972-7570	972-2700
Fraze Pavilion 695 Lincoln Pk Blvd *Web:* www.fraze.com	Dayton	OH	45429	937-296-3300	296-3302
Ohio Theatre 55 E State St *Web:* www.capa.com/columbus/venues/ohio_about.php	Columbus	OH	43215	614-469-1045	461-0429
Palace Theatre 34 W Broad St *Web:* www.capa.com/	Columbus	OH	43215	614-469-9850	
Playhouse Square 1501 Euclid Ave Ste 200 *TF:* 866-546-1353 ■ *Web:* www.playhousesquare.org	Cleveland	OH	44115	216-771-4444	771-0217
Riverbend Music Ctr 6295 Kellogg Ave *Web:* www.riverbend.org	Cincinnati	OH	45230	513-232-6220	
Severance Hall 11001 Euclid Ave *TF:* 800-686-1411 ■ *Web:* www.clevelandorchestra.com	Cleveland	OH	44106	216-231-7300	231-0202
Stambaugh Auditorium 1000 Fifth Ave *TF:* 866-516-2269 ■ *Web:* www.stambaughauditorium.com	Youngstown	OH	44504	330-747-5175	747-1981
Stranahan Theater 4645 Heatherdowns Blvd *TF:* 866-381-7469 ■ *Web:* www.stranahantheater.org	Toledo	OH	43614	419-381-8851	381-9525
Taft, Theatre, The 317 E Fifth St *Web:* www.tafttheatre.org	Cincinnati	OH	45202	513-232-6220	
Valentine, Theatre, The 410 Adams St *Web:* www.valentinetheatre.com	Toledo	OH	43604	419-242-3490	242-2791
Victoria Theatre 138 N Main St *TF:* 888-228-3630 ■ *Web:* www.victoriatheatre.com	Dayton	OH	45402	937-228-3630	449-5068
Weathervane Community Playhouse 1301 Weathervane Ln *Web:* www.weathervaneplayhouse.com	Akron	OH	44313	330-836-2626	873-2150
Youngstown Playhouse 600 Playhouse Ln PO Box 11108 *Web:* www.theyoungstownplayhouse.com	Youngstown	OH	44511	330-788-8739	

Oklahoma

				Phone	Fax
Civic Ctr Music Hall 201 N Walker St *Web:* www.okcciviccenter.org	Oklahoma City	OK	73102	405-297-2584	297-3890
Jewel Box Theatre 3700 N Walker Ave *Web:* www.jewelboxtheatre.org	Oklahoma City	OK	73118	405-521-1786	525-6562
Tulsa Performing Arts Ctr 110 E Second St *Web:* www.tulsapac.com	Tulsa	OK	74103	918-596-7122	596-7144

Ontario

				Phone	Fax
Centre in the Square 101 Queen St N *TF:* 800-265-8977 ■ *Web:* centreinthesquare.com	Kitchener	ON	N2H6P7	519-578-1570	
Massey Hall 178 Victoria St *Web:* www.masseyhall.com	Toronto	ON	M5B1T7	416-872-4255	

Oregon

				Phone	Fax
Florence Events Ctr 715 Quince St *TF:* 888-968-4086 ■ *Web:* www.ci.florence.or.us	Florence	OR	97439	541-997-1994	902-0991
Historic Elsinore Theatre (HET) 170 High St SE *Web:* www.elsinoretheatre.com	Salem	OR	97301	503-375-3574	375-0284
Hult Ctr for the Performing Arts One Eugene Ctr *Web:* www.hultcenter.org	Eugene	OR	97401	541-682-5087	682-5426
McDonald Theatre 1010 Willamette St *Web:* www.mcdonaldtheatre.com	Eugene	OR	97401	541-345-4442	762-8093
Pentacle Theater 324 52nd Ave NW *Web:* www.pentacletheatre.org	Salem	OR	97304	503-364-7200	362-6393
Portland Ctr for the Performing Arts 1111 SW Broadway *Web:* www.portland5.com	Portland	OR	97205	503-248-4335	274-7490
Woodmen of the World Hall 291 W Eigth Ave *Web:* www.wowhall.org	Eugene	OR	97401	541-687-2746	687-1664

Pennsylvania

				Phone	Fax
Academy of Music 1500 Walnut St *Web:* www.kimmelcenter.org	Philadelphia	PA	19102	215-790-5800	
Annenberg Ctr for the Performing Arts 3680 Walnut St *Web:* www.annenbergcenter.org	Philadelphia	PA	19104	215-898-3900	573-9568
Carnegie Music Hall 4400 Forbes Ave *Web:* carnegiemuseums.org	Pittsburgh	PA	15213	412-622-3131	
Civic Theatre of Allentown 527 N 19th St *Web:* www.civictheatre.com	Allentown	PA	18104	610-432-8943	432-7381
Eichelberger Performing Arts Ctr 195 Stock St Ste 203 *Web:* theeich.org	Hanover	PA	17331	717-632-9356	637-4504
Erie Playhouse 13 W Tenth St *Web:* www.erieplayhouse.org	Erie	PA	16501	814-454-2852	454-0601
Fulton Opera House Foundation 12 N Prince St PO Box 1865 *TF:* 888-480-1265 ■ *Web:* www.thefulton.org	Lancaster	PA	17603	717-397-7425	397-3780
Heinz Hall for the Performing Arts 600 Penn Ave *TF:* 800-743-8560 ■ *Web:* www.pittsburghsymphony.org	Pittsburgh	PA	15222	412-392-4900	392-3328
Kimmel Ctr for the Performing Arts 260 S Broad St Ste 901 *Web:* www.kimmelcenter.org	Philadelphia	PA	19102	215-790-5800	790-5801
Liacouras Ctr 1776 N Broad St *TF:* 800-298-4200 ■ *Web:* www.liacourascenter.com	Philadelphia	PA	19121	215-204-2400	204-2405
Mann Ctr for the Performing Arts 5201 Parkside Ave *Web:* www.manncenter.org	Philadelphia	PA	19131	215-546-7900	546-9524
Music Box Dinner Playhouse 196 Hughes St *Web:* www.musicbox.org	Swoyersville	PA	18704	570-283-2195	283-0751
Providence Playhouse 1256 Providence Rd *Web:* actorscircle.org	Scranton	PA	18508	570-342-9707	
Scranton Cultural Ctr 420 N Washington Ave *Web:* www.scrantonculturalcenter.org	Scranton	PA	18503	570-346-7369	346-7365
Society Hill Playhouse 507 S Eigth St *Web:* www.societyhillplayhouse.org	Philadelphia	PA	19147	215-923-0210	
Sovereign Performing Arts Ctr 136 N Sixth St *Web:* santander-arena.com	Reading	PA	19601	610-898-7299	898-7297
Walnut Street Theatre 825 Walnut St *Web:* www.walnutstreettheatre.org	Philadelphia	PA	19107	215-574-3550	
Warner Theatre 811 State St *TF:* 800-352-0050 ■ *Web:* www.erieevents.com	Erie	PA	16501	814-452-4857	455-9931
Wilma Theater 265 S Broad St *TF:* 800-732-0999 ■ *Web:* www.wilmatheater.org	Philadelphia	PA	19107	215-893-9456	893-0895

Rhode Island

				Phone	Fax
AS220 115 Empire St *Web:* www.as220.org	Providence	RI	02903	401-831-9327	454-7445
Providence Performing Arts Ctr 220 Weybosset St *Web:* www.ppacri.org	Providence	RI	02903	401-421-2997	351-7827
Veterans Memorial Auditorium One Ave of the Arts *Web:* thevetsri.com	Providence	RI	02903	401-222-1467	222-1466

South Carolina

				Phone	Fax
Alabama Theatre 4750 Hwy 17 S *TF:* 800-342-2262 ■ *Web:* www.alabama-theatre.com	North Myrtle Beach	SC	29582	843-272-1111	272-7748
Arts Ctr of Coastal Carolina 14 Shelter Cove Ln *TF:* 888-860-2787 ■ *Web:* www.artshhi.com	Hilton Head Island	SC	29928	843-686-3945	842-7877
Carolina Opry 8901 Hwy 17 N Ste A **Fax Area Code: 843* ■ *TF:* 800-843-6779 ■ *Web:* thecarolinaopry.com/	Myrtle Beach	SC	29572	800-843-6779	913-1442*

Facility	City	State	Zip	Phone	Fax
Gaillard Municipal Auditorium 77 Calhoun St	Charleston	SC	29401	843-577-7400	
Greenville Little Theatre 444 College St *Web:* www.greenvillelittletheatre.org	Greenville	SC	29601	864-233-6238	233-6237
Ira & Nancy Koger Ctr for the Arts 1051 Greene St *Web:* www.koger.sc.edu	Columbia	SC	29201	803-777-7500	777-9774
Palace, Theatre, The 1420 Celebrity Cir Broadway at the Beach *TF:* 888-841-2787 ■ *Web:* www.palacetheatremyrtlebeach.com	Myrtle Beach	SC	29577	843-448-9224	626-9659
Town Theatre 1012 Sumter St *Web:* www.towntheatre.com	Columbia	SC	29201	803-799-4764	799-6463
Township Auditorium 1703 Taylor St *Web:* www.thetownship.org	Columbia	SC	29201	803-576-2350	576-2359
Trustus Theatre 520 Lady St *Web:* www.trustus.org	Columbia	SC	29201	803-254-9732	771-9153
Warehouse Theatre 37 Augusta St *Web:* www.warehousetheatre.com	Greenville	SC	29601	864-235-6948	
Workshop Theatre 1136 Bull St *Web:* www.workshoptheatre.com	Columbia	SC	29211	803-799-4876	799-0227

South Dakota

Facility	City	State	Zip	Phone	Fax
Matthews Opera House 612 Main St *Web:* www.matthewsopera.com	Spearfish	SD	57783	605-642-7973	642-3477

Tennessee

Facility	City	State	Zip	Phone	Fax
Chattanooga Theatre Centre 400 River St *Web:* www.theatrecentre.com	Chattanooga	TN	37405	423-267-8534	664-1211
Circuit Playhouse, The 51 S Cooper St *TF:* 888-648-8154 ■ *Web:* www.playhouseonthesquare.org	Memphis	TN	38104	901-725-0776	726-5521
Clarence Brown Theatre *University of Tennessee* 206 McClung Tower *Web:* www.clarencebrowntheatre.com	Knoxville	TN	37996	865-974-5161	974-4867
Darkhorse Theater Ltd 4610 Charlotte Ave *Web:* darkhorsetheater.com	Nashville-Davidson	TN	37209	615-297-7113	665-3336
Germantown Performing Arts Centre (GPAC) 1801 Exeter Rd *Web:* www.gpacweb.com	Germantown	TN	38138	901-751-7500	751-7514
Grand Ole Opry 2804 Opryland Dr *Web:* www.opry.com	Nashville	TN	37214	615-871-6779	871-5719
Knoxville Civic Auditorium/Coliseum 500 Howard Baker Jr Ave *TF:* 877-995-9961 ■ *Web:* www.knoxvillecoliseum.com	Knoxville	TN	37915	865-215-8900	215-8989
Laurel Theatre 1538 Laurel Ave *Web:* www.jubileearts.org	Knoxville	TN	37916	865-522-5851	522-5386
Memphis Cook Convention Ctr 3205 Elvis Presley Blvd *Web:* www.memphistravel.com	Memphis	TN	38116	901-543-5333	
Nashville Municipal Auditorium 417 Fourth Ave N *Web:* www.nashville.gov	Nashville	TN	37201	615-862-6390	862-6394
Orpheum Theatre 203 S Main St *Web:* www.orpheum-memphis.com	Memphis	TN	38103	901-525-3000	526-5499
Ryman Auditorium 116 Fifth Ave N *TF:* 800-733-6779 ■ *Web:* www.ryman.com	Nashville	TN	37219	615-458-8700	458-8701
Soldiers & Sailors Memorial Auditorium 399 McCallie Ave *TF:* 800-772-1213 ■ *Web:* www.chattanooga.gov	Chattanooga	TN	37402	423-757-5156	757-5326
Tennessee Performing Arts Ctr 505 Deaderick St *TF:* 866-455-2823 ■ *Web:* www.tpac.org	Nashville	TN	37219	615-782-4000	782-4001
Texas Troubadour Theatre 2416 Music Valley Dr Ste 110 *Web:* etrecordshop.com	Nashville	TN	37214	615-889-2474	885-6949
Theatre Memphis 630 Perkins Ext *Web:* www.theatrememphis.org	Memphis	TN	38117	901-682-8323	763-4096
University of Tennessee Music Hall 1741 Volunteer Blvd *Web:* www.music.utk.edu	Knoxville	TN	37996	865-974-3241	974-1941

Texas

Facility	City	State	Zip	Phone	Fax
Abilene Civic Ctr 1100 N Sixth St *Web:* www.abilenetx.com	Abilene	TX	79601	325-676-6211	676-6343
Abilene Community Theatre (ACT) 809 Barrow *Web:* abilenecommunitytheatre.com	Abilene	TX	79605	325-673-6271	
Alley Theatre 615 Texas Ave *Web:* www.alleytheatre.org	Houston	TX	77002	713-220-5700	222-6542
Amarillo Civic Ctr 401 S Buchanan St *Web:* www.civicamarillo.com	Amarillo	TX	79101	806-378-4297	378-4234
American Bank Ctr 1901 N Shoreline Blvd *Web:* www.americanbankcenter.com	Corpus Christi	TX	78401	361-826-4700	826-4905
Arneson River Theatre 418 Villita St La Villita *Web:* www.lavillita.com/arneson/index.htm	San Antonio	TX	78205	210-207-8610	207-4390
Bass Performance Hall 4th & Calhoun Sts *TF:* 877-212-4280 ■ *Web:* www.basshall.com	Fort Worth	TX	76102	817-212-4200	810-9294
Camille Lightner Playhouse One Dean Porter Pk *Web:* camilleplayhouse.org	Brownsville	TX	78520	956-542-8900	
Carpenter Performance Hall 3333 N MacArthur Blvd *Web:* www.irvingartscenter.com	Irving	TX	75062	972-252-7558	
Casa Manana Theatre 3101 W Lancaster Ave *Web:* www.casamanana.org	Fort Worth	TX	76107	817-332-2272	332-5711
Circle Theatre 230 W Fourth St *Web:* www.circletheatre.com	Fort Worth	TX	76102	817-877-3040	877-3536
Creative Arts Theatre & School 602 E S St *Web:* www.creativearts.org	Arlington	TX	76010	817-861-2287	274-0793
Cynthia Woods Mitchell Pavilion 2005 Lk Robbins Dr *Web:* www.woodlandscenter.org	The Woodlands	TX	77380	281-363-3300	364-3011
El Paso Convention & Performing Arts Ctr One Civic Ctr Plz *TF:* 800-351-6024 ■ *Web:* www.visitelpaso.com	El Paso	TX	79901	915-534-0600	534-0687
Ensemble Theatre 3535 Main St *Web:* www.ensemblehouston.com	Houston	TX	77002	713-520-0055	520-1269
Grand 1894 Opera House 2020 Postoffice St *TF:* 800-821-1894 ■ *Web:* www.thegrand.com	Galveston	TX	77550	409-765-1894	763-1068
Harbor Playhouse One Bayfront Pk *Web:* www.harborplayhouse.com	Corpus Christi	TX	78401	361-882-5500	888-4779
Hobby Ctr for the Performing Arts 800 Bagby St Ste 300 *Web:* www.thehobbycenter.org	Houston	TX	77002	713-315-2400	315-2402
Irving Arts Center 3333 N MacArthur Blvd *Web:* www.irvingartscenter.com	Irving	TX	75062	972-252-7558	570-4962
Irving Arts Ctr 3333 N MacArthur Blvd *Web:* www.irvingartscenter.com	Irving	TX	75062	972-252-7558	570-4962
Jesse H Jones Hall for the Performing Arts 615 Louisiana St Ste 101 *Web:* www.houstontx.gov	Houston	TX	77002	713-227-3974	
Jubilee Theatre 506 Main St *Web:* www.jubileetheatre.org	Fort Worth	TX	76102	817-338-4204	338-4206
Lila Cockrell Theatre 200 E Market St *TF General:* 877-504-8895	San Antonio	TX	78205	210-207-8500	
Miller Outdoor Theatre 6000 Hermann Pk Dr **Fax Area Code:* 713 ■ *Web:* www.milleroutdoortheatre.com	Houston	TX	77030	281-823-9103	942-0863*
Morton H Meyerson Symphony Ctr 2301 Flora St *Web:* www.dallasculture.org	Dallas	TX	75201	214-670-3600	670-4334
Music Hall at Fair Park 909 First Ave *Web:* www.liveatthemusichall.com	Dallas	TX	75210	214-565-1116	565-0071
One World Theatre 7701 Bee Caves Rd *TF:* 888-616-0522 ■ *Web:* www.oneworldtheatre.org	Austin	TX	78746	512-330-9500	330-9600
Palace Arts Ctr 300 S Main St *Web:* www.grapevinetexasusa.com/Heritage/PalaceArtsCenter	Grapevine	TX	76051	817-410-3100	
Paramount, Theatre, The 713 Congress Ave *Web:* www.austintheatre.org	Austin	TX	78701	512-472-5470	472-5824
Patty Granville Performing Arts Ctr 300 N Fifth St *Web:* www.garlandarts.com	Garland	TX	75040	972-205-2000	205-2775
Perot Theatre 219 Main St *Web:* www.trahc.org	Texarkana	TX	75501	903-792-4992	793-8511
Rockport Ctr for the Arts 902 Navigation Cir *Web:* www.rockportartcenter.com	Rockport	TX	78382	361-729-5519	729-3551
Sammons Ctr for the Arts 3630 Harry Hines Blvd *Web:* www.sammonsartcenter.org	Dallas	TX	75219	214-520-7789	522-9174
San Antonio Municipal Auditorium 200 E Market St PO Box 1809 *TF:* 877-504-8895 ■ *Web:* www.sahbgcc.com	San Antonio	TX	78205	210-207-8500	223-1495
San Pedro Playhouse 800 W Ashby Pl PO Box 12356 *Web:* www.theplayhousesa.org	San Antonio	TX	78212	210-733-7258	734-2651
Theatre Three 2800 Routh St Ste 168 *Web:* www.theatre3dallas.com	Dallas	TX	75201	214-871-3300	871-3139
University of Texas at Austin Performing Arts Ctr E 23rd St & E Robert Dedman Dr *TF:* 800-687-6010 ■ *Web:* www.texasperformingarts.org	Austin	TX	78713	512-471-1444	471-4783
Wichita Falls CVB 1000 Fifth St **Fax Area Code:* 940 ■ *TF:* 800-799-6732 ■ *Web:* wichitafalls.org	Wichita Falls	TX	76301	800-799-6732	716-5509*
Williams Performing Arts Ctr *Abilene Christian University* 1600 Campus Ct *TF:* 800-460-6228 ■ *Web:* www.acu.edu/aboutacu/map_acu/pac.html	Abilene	TX	79601	325-674-2199	674-2369
Zachary Scott Theatre Ctr 1510 Toomey Rd *Web:* www.zachtheatre.org	Austin	TX	78704	512-476-0541	476-0314

Utah

Facility	City	State	Zip	Phone	Fax
Capitol Theatre 50 W 200 S *Web:* www.arttix.org	Salt Lake City	UT	84101	801-355-2787	
Hale Centre Theater 3333 S Decker Lake Dr *TF:* 877-829-5500 ■ *Web:* www.hct.org	West Valley City	UT	84119	801-984-9000	984-9009
Hale Ctr Theater Orem 225 West 400 North *Web:* www.haletheater.org	Orem	UT	84057	801-226-8600	852-3189
Off Broadway Theatre 272 S Main St *Web:* www.theobt.org	Salt Lake City	UT	84101	801-355-4628	
Salt Lake Community College Grand Theatre 1575 S State St *Web:* www.slcc.edu/the-grand	Salt Lake City	UT	84115	801-957-3322	
Terrace Plaza Playhouse 99 E 4700 S *Web:* www.terraceplayhouse.com	Ogden	UT	84405	801-393-0070	
Tuacahn Amphitheatre & Ctr for the Arts 1100 Tuacahn Dr *Web:* www.tuacahn.org	Ivins	UT	84738	435-652-3300	652-3227

Vermont

Facility	City	State	Zip	Phone	Fax
Barre Opera House Six N Main St PO Box 583 *Web:* www.barreoperahouse.org	Barre	VT	05641	802-476-8188	476-5648

				Phone	Fax
Flynn Ctr for the Performing Arts 153 Main St *Web:* www.flynncenter.org	Burlington	VT	05401	802-863-5966	863-8788

Virginia

				Phone	Fax
Generic Theater 215 St Paul's Blvd *Web:* www.generictheater.org	Norfolk	VA	23510	757-441-2160	441-2729
George Mason University's Ctr for the Arts George Mason University 4400 University Dr MS 2F5 *Web:* cfa.gmu.edu	Fairfax	VA	22030	703-993-8888	993-8650
Jefferson Ctr 541 Luck Ave Ste 221 *TF:* 866-345-2550 ■ *Web:* www.jeffcenter.org	Roanoke	VA	24016	540-343-2624	343-3744
Landmark Theater Six N Laurel St *Web:* altriatheater.com/	Richmond	VA	23220	804-592-3368	
Little Theatre of Alexandria 600 Wolfe St *Web:* www.thelittletheatre.com	Alexandria	VA	22314	703-683-5778	683-1378
Little Theatre of Norfolk 801 Claremont Ave *Web:* www.ltnonline.org	Norfolk	VA	23507	757-627-8551	
MetroStage 1201 N Royal St *Web:* www.metrostage.org	Alexandria	VA	22314	703-548-9044	548-9089
Mill Mountain Theatre One Market Sq Second Fl *Web:* www.millmountain.org	Roanoke	VA	24011	540-342-5740	
Peninsula Community Theatre 10251 Warwick Blvd PO Box 11056 *Web:* www.pctlive.org	Newport News	VA	23601	757-595-5728	596-7436
Roper Performing Arts Ctr 340 Granby St *Web:* www.tcc.edu/roper	Norfolk	VA	23510	757-822-1450	822-1451
Virginia Beach Convention Ctr 2101 Parks Ave Ste 500 *TF:* 800-700-7702 ■ *Web:* www.visitvirginiabeach.com	Virginia Beach	VA	23451	757-385-4700	437-4747
Willett Hall 3701 Willett Dr *Web:* www.willetthall.com	Portsmouth	VA	23707	757-393-5144	393-7324
Wolf Trap Foundation for the Performing Arts 1645 Trap Rd *TF:* 877-965-3872 ■ *Web:* www.wolftrap.org	Vienna	VA	22182	703-255-1900	255-4077
WSC Avant Bard 3700 S Four Mile Run *Web:* wscavantbard.org	Arlington	VA	22206	703-418-4808	

Washington

				Phone	Fax
A Contemporary Theatre (ACT) 700 Union St Kreielsheimer Pl *TF:* 888-584-4849 ■ *Web:* www.acttheatre.org	Seattle	WA	98101	206-292-7660	292-7670
Behnke Ctr for Contemporary Performance 100 W Roy St PO Box 19515 *Web:* www.ontheboards.org	Seattle	WA	98119	206-217-9886	217-9887
Broadway Ctr for the Performing Arts 901 Broadway *TF:* 800-291-7593 ■ *Web:* www.broadwaycenter.org	Tacoma	WA	98402	253-591-5890	591-2013
Pantages Theater 901 Broadway *TF:* 800-291-7593 ■ *Web:* www.broadwaycenter.org	Tacoma	WA	98402	253-591-5890	591-2013
Rialto Theater 310 S Ninth St *TF:* 800-291-7593 ■ *Web:* www.broadwaycenter.org	Tacoma	WA	98402	253-591-5890	591-2013
Seattle Ctr 305 Harrison St *Web:* www.seattlecenter.com	Seattle	WA	98109	206-684-7200	684-7342
Spokane Civic Theatre 1020 N Howard St *TF:* 800-325-7328 ■ *Web:* www.spokanecivictheatre.com	Spokane	WA	99201	509-325-1413	325-9287
Spokane Ctr 720 W Mallon Ave *Web:* www.spokanecenter.com	Spokane	WA	99201	509-279-7000	279-7050
Tacoma Little Theatre 210 N 'I' St *Web:* www.tacomalittletheatre.com	Tacoma	WA	98403	253-272-2281	
Washington Ctr for the Performing Arts 512 Washington St SE *Web:* www.washingtoncenter.org	Olympia	WA	98501	360-753-8586	754-1177

West Virginia

				Phone	Fax
Charleston Civic Ctr & Coliseum 200 Civic Ctr Dr *Web:* www.charlestonwvciviccenter.com	Charleston	WV	25301	304-345-1500	345-3492
Clay Ctr for the Arts & Sciences One Clay Sq *Web:* www.theclaycenter.org	Charleston	WV	25301	304-561-3570	561-3598
Oglebay Institute's Towngate Theatre 2118 Market St *Web:* www.oionline.com	Wheeling	WV	26003	304-233-0820	
Victoria Vaudeville Theater 1228 Market St *TF:* 800-505-7464 ■ *Web:* www.victoria-theater.com	Wheeling	WV	26003	304-233-7464	

Wisconsin

				Phone	Fax
American Players Theater 5950 Golf Course Rd PO Box 819 *Web:* www.americanplayers.org	Spring Green	WI	53588	608-588-7401	588-7085
Barrymore Theatre 2090 Atwood Ave *Web:* www.barrymorelive.com	Madison	WI	53704	608-241-8633	241-8861
Broom Street Theatre 1119 Williamson St *Web:* bstonline.org	Madison	WI	53703	608-244-8338	
Marcus Ctr for the Performing Arts 929 N Water St *TF:* 888-612-3500 ■ *Web:* www.marcuscenter.org	Milwaukee	WI	53202	414-273-7206	273-5480
Milwaukee Chamber Theatre 158 N Broadway Broadway Theatre Ctr *Web:* www.chamber-theatre.com	Milwaukee	WI	53202	414-276-8842	277-4477
Overture Ctr for the Arts 201 State St *Web:* overturecenter.com	Madison	WI	53703	608-258-4177	258-4971
Pabst Theater 144 E Wells St *TF:* 800-523-7117 ■ *Web:* www.pabsttheater.org	Milwaukee	WI	53202	414-286-3205	
Rave, The 2401 W Wisconsin Ave *Web:* www.therave.com	Milwaukee	WI	53233	414-342-7283	342-0359
Riverside Theatre 116 W Wisconsin Ave *Web:* www.pabsttheater.org	Milwaukee	WI	53203	414-286-3663	
Weidner Ctr for the Performing Arts 2420 Nicolet Dr University of Wisconsin at Green Bay *TF:* 800-895-0071 ■ *Web:* www.weidnercenter.com	Green Bay	WI	54311	920-465-2726	465-2619

Wyoming

				Phone	Fax
Cheyenne Civic Ctr 510 W 20th St *TF:* 877-691-2787 ■ *Web:* www.cheyennecity.org	Cheyenne	WY	82001	307-637-6364	637-6365
Cheyenne Little Theatre Players PO Box 20087 *Web:* www.cheyennelittletheatre.org	Cheyenne	WY	82003	307-638-6543	638-6430
Jackson Hole Playhouse 145 W Deloney Ave *Web:* jacksonholeplayhouse.com	Jackson	WY	83001	307-733-6994	
Stage III Community Theatre 900 N Ctr St *Web:* www.stageiiitheatre.org	Casper	WY	82601	307-234-0946	

576 PERFORMING ARTS ORGANIZATIONS

SEE ALSO Arts & Artists Organizations p. 1760

576-1 Dance Companies

				Phone	Fax
Abilene Ballet Theatre 1265 N Second St *Web:* www.abileneballettheatre.org	Abilene	TX	79601	325-675-0303	
Alabama Ballet 2726 First Ave S *Web:* www.alabamaballet.org	Birmingham	AL	35233	205-322-4300	322-4444
Alabama Dance Theatre 1018 Madison Ave *Web:* www.alabamadancetheatre.com	Montgomery	AL	36104	334-241-2590	241-2504
Alonzo King's LINES Contemporary Ballet 26 Seventh St *Web:* www.linesballet.org	San Francisco	CA	94102	415-863-3040	863-1180
Alvin Ailey American Dance Theater 405 W 55th St *Web:* www.alvinailey.org	New York	NY	10019	212-405-9000	405-9001
American Ballet Theatre (ABT) 890 Broadway 3rd Fl *Web:* www.abt.org	New York	NY	10003	212-477-3030	254-5938
American Repertory Ballet Seven Livingston Ave PO Box 250 *Web:* www.americanrepertoryballet.org	New Brunswick	NJ	08901	732-249-1254	249-8475
Ann Arbor Civic Ballet 3900 E Jackson *Web:* www.sylviastudio.com	Ann Arbor	MI	48103	734-668-8066	
Aspen Santa Fe Ballet 0245 Sage Way *TF:* 866-449-0464 ■ *Web:* www.aspensantafeballet.com	Aspen	CO	81611	970-925-7175	925-1127
Atlanta Ballet 1695 Marietta Blvd NW *Web:* www.atlantaballet.com	Atlanta	GA	30318	404-873-5811	874-7905
Augusta Ballet Inc 1301 Greene St Ste 204 *Web:* www.augustaballet.org	Augusta	GA	30901	706-261-0555	261-0551
Axis Dance Co 1428 Alice St Ste 200 *TF:* 800-838-3006 ■ *Web:* www.axisdance.org	Oakland	CA	94612	510-625-0110	625-0321
Ballet Arizona 3645 E Indian School Rd *Web:* www.balletaz.org	Phoenix	AZ	85018	602-381-0184	381-0189
Ballet Arkansas 1521 Merrill Dr *Web:* www.balletarkansas.org	Little Rock	AR	72211	501-223-5150	
Ballet Austin 501 W Third St *Web:* www.balletaustin.org	Austin	TX	78705	512-476-9051	472-3073
Ballet British Columbia 677 Davie St Sixth Fl *Web:* www.balletbc.com	Vancouver	BC	V6B2G6	604-732-5003	732-4417
Ballet Chicago 17 N State St Ste 1900 *Web:* www.balletchicago.org	Chicago	IL	60602	312-251-8838	251-8840
Ballet Hispanico of New York 167 W 89th St *Web:* www.ballethispanico.org	New York	NY	10024	212-362-6710	362-7809
Ballet Idaho 501 S Eigth St Ste A *Web:* www.balletidaho.org	Boise	ID	83702	208-343-0556	424-3129
Ballet Lubbock 5702 Genoa Ave Ste A9 *Web:* www.balletlubbock.org	Lubbock	TX	79424	806-785-3090	785-3309
Ballet Magnificat 5406 I-55 N *TF:* 866-617-3257 ■ *Web:* www.balletmagnificat.com	Jackson	MS	39211	601-977-1001	977-8948
Ballet Mississippi 201 E Pascagoula St Ste 106 PO Box 1787 *Web:* www.balletms.com	Jackson	MS	39215	601-960-1560	960-2135
Ballet Pacifica 9527 Garfield Ave *Web:* www.balletpacifica.org	Fountain Valley	CA	92708	714-962-5440	962-9383
Ballet Quad Cities 613 17th St *Web:* www.balletquadcities.com	Rock Island	IL	61201	309-786-3779	786-2677
Ballet Tech 890 Broadway Eighth Fl *Web:* www.ballettech.org	New York	NY	10003	212-777-7710	353-0936
Ballet Tennessee 3202 Kelly's Ferry Rd *Web:* www.ballettennessee.org	Chattanooga	TN	37419	423-821-2055	821-2156
Ballet Theatre of Maryland 801 Chase St Maryland Hall for the Creative Arts *Web:* www.balletmaryland.org	Annapolis	MD	21401	410-263-8289	626-1835
Ballet Theatre of New Mexico 6913 Natalie NE *Web:* www.btnm.org	Albuquerque	NM	87110	505-888-1054	
Ballet West 50 West 200 South *Web:* www.balletwest.org	Salt Lake City	UT	84101	801-323-6900	359-3504

Organization	City	State	ZIP	Phone	Fax
Ballet Western Reserve 218 W Boardman St Morley Ctr for the Arts. *Web:* www.balletwesternreserve.org	Youngstown	OH	44501	330-744-1934	744-2631
BalletMet Columbus 322 Mt Vernon Ave. *Web:* www.balletmet.org	Columbus	OH	43215	614-229-4860	229-4858
Baton Rouge Ballet Theatre 10745 Linkwood Ct PO Box 82288. *Web:* www.batonrougeballet.org	Baton Rouge	LA	70884	225-766-8379	
Bill T Jones/Arnie Zane Dance Co 219 W 19th St. *Web:* www.newyorklivearts.org	New York	NY	10011	212-691-6500	633-1974
Boston Ballet 19 Clarendon St. *Web:* www.bostonballet.org	Boston	MA	02116	617-695-6950	695-6995
Boulder Ballet 2590 Walnut St Ste 10. *Web:* www.boulderballet.org	Boulder	CO	80302	303-443-0028	441-5266
Buglisi Dance Theatre 229 W 42nd St Ste 502. *TF:* 800-754-0797 ■ *Web:* www.buglisi-foreman.org	New York	NY	10036	212-719-3301	719-3302
California Ballet Co (CBC) 4819 Ronson Ct. *Web:* www.californiaballet.org	San Diego	CA	92111	858-560-5676	560-0072
Canyon Concert Ballet 1031 Conifer St Ste 3. *Web:* www.ccballet.org	Fort Collins	CO	80524	970-472-4156	472-4158
Carolina Ballet Inc 3401-131 Atlantic Ave. *TF:* 800-841-2787 ■ *Web:* www.carolinaballet.com	Raleigh	NC	27604	919-719-0800	719-0910
Carolyn Dorfman Dance Co (CDDC) 2780 Morris Ave Ste 1-A. *Web:* www.cddc.info	Union	NJ	07083	908-687-8855	686-5245
Cassandra Ballet of Toledo 3157 Sylvania Ave. *Web:* cassandraballet.com	Toledo	OH	43613	419-475-0458	
Central West Ballet Co (CWB) 5039 Pendecost Dr Ste B2. *Web:* cwballet.org	Modesto	CA	95356	209-576-8957	576-1308
Charleston Ballet 822 Virginia St E. *Web:* www.thecharlestonballet.com	Charleston	WV	25301	304-342-6541	345-1134
Chitresh Das Dance Co 2325 Third St Ste 320. *Web:* www.kathak.org	San Francisco	CA	94107	415-333-9000	333-9029
Cincinnati Ballet 1555 Central Pkwy. *TF:* 800-745-3000 ■ *Web:* www.cballet.org	Cincinnati	OH	45214	513-621-5219	621-4844
Cleo Parker Robinson Dance 119 Pk Ave W. *Web:* www.cleoparkerdance.org	Denver	CO	80205	303-295-1759	295-1328
Collage Dance Theatre 2934 1/2 Beverly Glen Cir. **Fax Area Code:* 604 ■ *TF:* 866-300-4287	Los Angeles	CA	90077	818-784-8669	682-1715*
Colorado Ballet 1278 Lincoln St. *Web:* www.coloradoballet.org	Denver	CO	80203	303-837-8888	861-7174
Columbia City Ballet 1545 Main St. *Web:* www.columbiacityballet.com	Columbia	SC	29201	803-799-7605	799-7928
Connecticut Ballet 20 Acosta St. *Web:* www.connecticutballet.com	Stamford	CT	06902	203-964-1211	961-1928
Contemporary Dance Theatre 1805 Larch Ave. *Web:* www.cdt-dance.org	Cincinnati	OH	45224	513-591-1222	
Corpus Christi Ballet 1621 N Mesquite St. *Web:* www.corpuschristiballet.com	Corpus Christi	TX	78401	361-882-4588	881-9291
Dallas Black Dance Theatre 2700 Flora St. *Web:* www.dbdt.com	Dallas	TX	75201	214-871-2376	871-2842
Dance Theatre of Harlem Inc 466 W 152nd St. *TF:* 800-538-2538 ■ *Web:* www.dancetheatreofharlem.org	New York	NY	10031	212-690-2800	690-8736
Dayton Ballet 140 N Main St. *TF:* 800-745-3000 ■ *Web:* daytonperformingarts.org	Dayton	OH	45402	937-449-5060	223-9189
Dayton Contemporary Dance Co 840 Germantown St. *TF:* 888-228-3630 ■ *Web:* www.dcdc.org	Dayton	OH	45402	937-228-3232	223-6156
Doug Varone & Dancers 37 W 32nd St. *TF:* 800-366-2100 ■ *Web:* www.dougvaroneanddancers.org	New York	NY	10001	212-279-3344	279-3344
Ethnic Dance Theatre 3507 Clinton Ave S. *Web:* www.ethnicdancetheatre.com	Minneapolis	MN	55408	763-545-1333	
First State Ballet Theatre 818 N Market St. *Web:* www.firststateballet.com	Wilmington	DE	19801	302-658-7897	
Flamenco Vivo Carlota Santana 4 W 43rd St Ste 608. *Web:* flamenco-vivo.org	New York	NY	10036	212-736-4499	736-1326
Fort Wayne Ballet Inc 300 E Main St. *Web:* www.fortwayneballet.org	Fort Wayne	IN	46802	260-484-9646	484-9647
Fort Wayne Dance Collective 437 E Berry St. *Web:* www.fwdc.org	Fort Wayne	IN	46802	260-424-6574	424-2789
Garth Fagan Dance 50 Chestnut St. *Web:* www.garthfagandance.org	Rochester	NY	14604	585-454-3260	454-6191
Georgia Ballet 1255 Field Pkwy. *Web:* www.georgiaballet.org	Marietta	GA	30066	770-528-0881	528-0891
Grand Rapids Ballet Co 341 Ellsworth Ave SW. *Web:* www.grballet.com	Grand Rapids	MI	49503	616-454-4771	454-0672
Greater Lansing Ballet Co 2225 E Grand River Ave. *Web:* www.greaterlansingballet.org	Lansing	MI	48912	517-372-9887	372-9887
Hawaii State Ballet 1418 Kapiolani Blvd. *Web:* www.hawaiistateballet.com	Honolulu	HI	96814	808-947-2755	
Houston Ballet 601 Preston St. *TF:* 800-828-2787 ■ *Web:* www.houstonballet.org	Houston	TX	77002	713-523-6300	523-4038
HT Chen & Dancers 70 Mulberry St Second Fl. *Web:* www.chendancecenter.org	New York	NY	10013	212-349-0126	349-0494
Hubbard Street Dance Chicago 1147 W Jackson Blvd. *Web:* www.hubbardstreetdance.com	Chicago	IL	60607	312-850-9744	455-8240
Huntsville Ballet 800 Regal Dr SW. *Web:* www.communityballet.org	Huntsville	AL	35801	256-539-0961	539-1837
Inland Pacific Ballet 5050 Arrow Hwy. *Web:* www.ipballet.org	Montclair	CA	91763	909-482-1590	482-1589
James Sewell Ballet 528 Hennepin Ave Ste 215. *Web:* www.jsballet.org	Minneapolis	MN	55403	612-672-0480	
Joe Goode Performance Group (JGPG) 499 Alabama St Ste 150. *Web:* www.joegoode.org	San Francisco	CA	94110	415-561-6565	561-6562
Joffrey Ballet of Chicago 10 E Randolph St Ste 1300. *Web:* joffrey.org/	Chicago	IL	60601	312-739-0120	739-0119
John Jasperse Co 140 Second Ave Ste 501. *Web:* www.johnjasperse.org	New York	NY	10003	212-375-8283	
Jose Matteo's Ballet Theatre 400 Harvard St. *Web:* www.ballettheatre.org	Cambridge	MA	02138	617-354-7467	354-7856
Kelly-Strayhorn Theater 5941 Penn Ave. *Web:* www.kelly-strayhorn.org	Pittsburgh	PA	15206	412-363-3000	363-4320
Lar Lubovitch Dance Co 229 W 42nd St Eighth Fl. *Web:* www.lubovitch.org	New York	NY	10036	212-221-7909	221-7938
Lexington Ballet Co (LBC) 161 N Mill St. *Web:* www.lexingtonballet.org	Lexington	KY	40507	859-233-3925	
Limon Dance Co 307 W 38th St Ste 1105. *Web:* www.limon.org	New York	NY	10018	212-777-3353	777-4764
Liz Lerman Dance Exchange 7117 Maple Ave. *Web:* www.danceexchange.org	Takoma Park	MD	20912	301-270-6700	270-2626
Louisville Ballet 315 E Main St. *TF:* 800-775-7777 ■ *Web:* www.louisvilleballet.org	Louisville	KY	40202	502-583-3150	583-0006
Madison Ballet 160 Westgate Mall. *Web:* www.madisonballet.org	Madison	WI	53711	608-278-7990	278-7992
Maine State Ballet 348 US Rt 1. *Web:* www.mainestateballet.org	Falmouth	ME	04105	207-781-7672	781-3663
Mark Morris Dance Group 3 Lafayette Ave. *TF:* 800-957-1046 ■ *Web:* www.markmorrisdancegroup.org	Brooklyn	NY	11217	718-624-8400	624-8900
Merce Cunningham Dance Co 130 W 56TH St Ste 707. *Web:* www.mercecunningham.org	New York	NY	10019	212-255-8240	633-2453
Miami City Ballet 2200 Liberty Ave. *TF:* 877-929-7010 ■ *Web:* www.miamicityballet.org	Miami Beach	FL	33139	305-929-7000	929-7012
Milwaukee Ballet 504 W National Ave. *TF:* 888-612-3500 ■ *Web:* www.milwaukeeballet.org	Milwaukee	WI	53204	414-643-7677	649-4066
Minnesota Ballet 301 W First St Ste 800. *TF:* 800-627-3529 ■ *Web:* www.minnesotaballet.org	Duluth	MN	55802	218-529-3742	529-3744
Minnesota Dance Theatre 528 Hennepin Ave Sixth Fl. *Web:* www.mndance.org	Minneapolis	MN	55403	612-338-0627	338-5160
Montgomery Ballet 2101 E Blvd Ste 223. *Web:* www.montgomeryballet.org	Montgomery	AL	36117	334-409-0522	409-2311
Mordine & Company Dance Theatre 1016 N Dearborn Pkwy. *Web:* www.mordine.org	Chicago	IL	60610	312-654-9540	
Nashville Ballet 3630 Redmon St. *Web:* www.nashvilleballet.com	Nashville	TN	37209	615-297-2966	297-9972
National Ballet 1816 Margaret Ave. *Web:* www.nationalballet.com	Annapolis	MD	21401	301-218-9822	686-7040
National Ballet of Canada Walter Carsen Centre for the National Ballet of Canada 470 Queens Quay W. *Web:* national.ballet.ca	Toronto	ON	M5V3K4	416-345-9686	345-8323
Nevada Ballet Theatre 1651 Inner Cir. *Web:* www.nevadaballet.com	Las Vegas	NV	89134	702-243-2623	804-0365
New Haven Ballet 70 Audubon St. *Web:* www.newhavenballet.org	New Haven	CT	06510	203-782-9038	
New Jersey Ballet Co 15 Microlab Rd. *Web:* www.njballet.org	Livingston	NJ	07039	973-597-9600	597-9442
New York City Ballet Inc 20 Lincoln Ctr New York State Theatre. *Web:* www.nycballet.com	New York	NY	10023	212-870-5656	870-7791
New York Theatre Ballet 30 E 31st St. *Web:* www.nytb.org	New York	NY	10016	212-679-0401	679-8171
Northern Ballet Theatre 36 Arlington St. *Web:* nbtdc.com	Nashua	NH	03060	603-889-8406	
Northwest Florida Ballet 310 Perry Ave SE. *Web:* www.nfballet.org	Fort Walton Beach	FL	32548	850-664-7787	664-0130
Oakland Ballet Co 2201 Broadway Ste 206. *TF:* 866-711-6037 ■ *Web:* www.oaklandballet.org	Oakland	CA	94612	510-893-3132	
ODC/San Francisco 3153 17th St. *Web:* www.odcdance.org	San Francisco	CA	94110	415-863-6606	863-9833
Ohio Ballet 354 E Market St	Akron	OH	44325	330-972-7900	972-7902
Oklahoma City Ballet 7421 N Classen Blvd. *Web:* www.okcballet.com	Oklahoma City	OK	73116	405-843-9898	843-9894
Oregon Ballet Theatre 818 SE Sixth Ave. *Web:* www.obt.org	Portland	OR	97214	503-227-0977	227-4186
Pacific Northwest Ballet 301 Mercer St. *TF:* 800-225-7635 ■ *Web:* www.pnb.org	Seattle	WA	98109	206-441-2424	441-2420
Parsons Dance Co 229 W 42nd St 8th Fl. *Web:* www.parsonsdance.org	New York	NY	10036	212-869-9275	944-7417
Paul Taylor Dance Co 551 Grand St. *Web:* www.ptdc.org	New York	NY	10002	212-431-5562	966-5673
Peninsula Ballet Theatre 1880 S Grant St Ste 206. *Web:* www.peninsulaballet.org	San Mateo	CA	94402	650-342-3262	
Pennsylvania Ballet 1819 John F Kennedy Blvd. *TF:* 800-732-0999 ■ *Web:* www.paballet.org	Philadelphia	PA	19103	215-551-7000	551-7224
Pennsylvania Youth Ballet (PYB) 556 Main St. *Web:* www.bglv.org	Bethlehem	PA	18018	610-865-0353	
Peoria Ballet 809 W Detweiller Dr # C. *Web:* www.peoriaballet.com	Peoria	IL	61615	309-690-7990	690-7991
Philadelphia Dance Co Nine N Preston St Philadanco Way. *Web:* www.philadanco.org	Philadelphia	PA	19104	215-387-8200	387-8203

				Phone	Fax
Pittsburgh Ballet Theatre 2900 Liberty Ave *TF:* 800-441-1414 ■ *Web:* www.pbt.org	Pittsburgh	PA	15201	412-281-0360	281-9901
Repertory Dance Theatre 138 West 300 South *Web:* www.xmission.com/~rdt	Salt Lake City	UT	84101	801-534-1000	534-1110
Richmond Ballet 407 E Canal St First Fl *Web:* richmondballet.com	Richmond	VA	23219	804-344-0906	344-0901
Ririe-Woodbury Dance Co 138 West Broadway *Web:* www.ririewoodbury.com	Salt Lake City	UT	84101	801-297-4241	297-4235
Robinson Ballet 107 Union St *Web:* www.robinsonballet.org	Bangor	ME	04401	207-990-3140	
Rochester City Ballet 1326 University Ave *Web:* www.rochestercityballet.org	Rochester	NY	14607	585-461-5850	473-8847
Sacramento Ballet 1631 K St *TF:* 800-925-9989 ■ *Web:* sacballet.org	Sacramento	CA	95814	916-552-5800	552-5815
San Diego Ballet 2650 Truxtun Rd *Web:* sandiegoballetdancecompany.org	San Diego	CA	92106	619-294-7378	
San Francisco Ballet 455 Franklin St *TF:* 888-622-2108 ■ *Web:* www.sfballet.org	San Francisco	CA	94102	415-865-2000	861-2684
Sarasota Ballet of Florida 5555 N Tamiami Trail *Web:* www.sarasotaballet.org	Sarasota	FL	34243	941-359-0099	358-1504
State Ballet of Rhode Island, The 52 Sherman Ave PO Box 155 *Web:* www.stateballet.com	Lincoln	RI	02865	401-334-2560	334-0412
Stuart Pimsler Dance & Theater 528 Hennepin Ave S Ste 707 *Web:* www.stuartpimsler.com	Minneapolis	MN	55403	763-521-7738	
Texas Ballet Theater 1540 Mall Cir *Web:* www.texasballettheater.org	Fort Worth	TX	76116	817-763-0207	763-0624
Texas International Theatrical Arts Society (TITAS) 2100 Ross Ave Ste 650 *Web:* www.titas.org	Dallas	TX	75201	214-880-0202	
Trisha Brown Dance Co 341 W 38th St Ste 801 *Web:* www.trishabrowncompany.org	New York	NY	10018	212-977-5365	
Tulsa Ballet 1212 E 45th Pl *TF:* 800-722-9942 ■ *Web:* www.tulsaballet.org	Tulsa	OK	74105	918-749-6030	749-0532
Tupelo Ballet Co 775 Poplarville Dr *Web:* www.tupeloballet.com	Tupelo	MS	38801	662-844-1928	844-1951
Urban Bush Women 138 S Oxford St Ste 4B *Web:* www.urbanbushwomen.org	Brooklyn	NY	11217	718-398-4537	398-4783
Virginia Ballet Theatre 134 W Olney Rd *TF:* 866-892-6990 ■ *Web:* www.virginia.org	Norfolk	VA	23510	757-622-4822	622-7904
Washington Ballet 3515 Wisconsin Ave NW *Web:* www.washingtonballet.org	Washington	DC	20016	202-362-3606	362-1311
Zenon Dance Company & School 528 Hennepin Ave Ste 400 *Web:* www.zenondance.org	Minneapolis	MN	55403	612-338-1101	338-2479

576-2 Opera Companies

				Phone	Fax
Academy of Vocal Arts (AVA) 1920 Spruce St *Web:* www.avaopera.com	Philadelphia	PA	19103	215-735-1685	732-2189
Amarillo Opera 2223 S Van Buren St *Web:* www.amarilloopera.org	Amarillo	TX	79109	806-372-7464	372-7465
Anchorage Opera 1507 Spar Ave *Web:* www.anchorageopera.org	Anchorage	AK	99501	907-279-2557	279-7798
Annapolis Opera Inc 801 Chase St Maryland Hall for the Creative Arts *Web:* www.annapolisopera.org	Annapolis	MD	21401	410-267-8135	267-6440
Aspen Opera Theater 225 Music School Rd *Web:* www.aspenmusicfestival.com	Aspen	CO	81611	970-925-3254	925-3802
Augusta Opera 1215 Troupe St	Augusta	GA	30904	706-364-9114	
Austin Opera 3009 Industrial Terrace Ste 100 *Web:* austinlyricopera.org	Austin	TX	78758	512-472-5927	
Central City Opera 400 S Colorado Blvd Ste 530 *Web:* www.centralcityopera.org	Denver	CO	80246	303-292-6500	292-4958
Charleston Light Opera Guild 411 Tennessee Ave *Web:* charlestonwv.com	Charleston	WV	25302	304-343-2287	
Chicago Opera Theater 70 E Lake St Ste 815 *Web:* www.chicagooperatheater.org	Chicago	IL	60601	312-704-8420	704-8421
Cincinnati Opera 1243 Elm St *Web:* www.cincinnatiopera.org	Cincinnati	OH	45202	513-768-5500	768-5553
Dallas Opera 8350 N Central Expy Ste 210 *TF:* 888-353-4537 ■ *Web:* www.dallasopera.org	Dallas	TX	75206	214-443-1000	443-1060
Dayton Opera 126 N Main St Ste 210 *Web:* www.daytonperformingarts.org	Dayton	OH	45402	937-224-3521	223-9189
Des Moines Metro Opera 106 W Boston Ave *Web:* www.desmoinesmetroopera.org	Indianola	IA	50125	515-961-6221	961-6221
Fargo-Moorhead Opera Co 114 Broadway Ste S-1 *Web:* www.fmopera.org	Fargo	ND	58102	701-239-4558	476-1991
Florentine Opera Co 700 N Water St Ste 950 *TF:* 800-326-7372 ■ *Web:* www.florentineopera.org	Milwaukee	WI	53202	414-291-5700	291-5706
Florida Grand Opera 8390 NW 25th St *TF:* 800-741-1010 ■ *Web:* www.fgo.org	Miami	FL	33122	305-854-1643	856-1042
Fort Worth Opera 1300 Gendy St *TF:* 877-396-7372 ■ *Web:* www.fwopera.org	Fort Worth	TX	76107	817-731-0833	731-0835
Fresno Grand Opera 2405 Capitol St Ste 103 *Web:* www.fresnograndopera.org	Fresno	CA	93721	559-442-5699	442-5649
Glimmerglass Festival 7300 State Hwy 80 PO Box 191 *TF:* 866-568-2388 ■ *Web:* www.glimmerglass.org	Cooperstown	NY	13326	607-547-0700	547-6030
Hawaii Opera Theatre 848 S Beretania St Ste 301 *Web:* www.hawaiiopera.org	Honolulu	HI	96813	808-596-7372	596-0379
Houston Grand Opera 510 Preston St Ste 500 *TF:* 800-626-7372 ■ *Web:* www.houstongrandopera.org	Houston	TX	77002	713-546-0200	236-8121
Indianapolis Opera 250 E 38th St *Web:* www.indyopera.org	Indianapolis	IN	46205	317-283-3531	923-5611
Kentucky Opera Assn 323 W Broadway Ste 601 *TF:* 800-690-9236 ■ *Web:* www.kyopera.org	Louisville	KY	40202	502-584-4500	
Knoxville Opera Co 612 E Depot Ave *Web:* www.knoxvilleopera.com	Knoxville	TN	37917	865-524-0795	524-7384
Long Beach Opera 507 Pacific Ave *Web:* www.longbeachopera.org	Long Beach	CA	90802	562-432-5934	683-2109
Los Angeles Opera 135 N Grand Ave Ste 327 *Web:* laopera.org/	Los Angeles	CA	90012	213-972-7219	687-3490
Lyric Opera of Chicago 20 N Wacker Dr Civic Opera House Ste 860 *Web:* www.lyricopera.org	Chicago	IL	60606	312-332-2244	332-8120
Metropolitan Opera 65th St & Broadway *Web:* metopera.org/	New York	NY	10023	212-799-3100	870-7410
Michigan Opera Theatre 1526 Broadway *Web:* michiganopera.org	Detroit	MI	48226	313-961-3500	237-3412
Minnesota Opera 620 N First St *TF:* 800-676-6737 ■ *Web:* www.mnopera.org	Minneapolis	MN	55401	612-333-2700	333-0869
Mississippi Opera PO Box 1551 *Web:* www.msopera.org	Jackson	MS	39215	601-960-2300	960-1526
Mobile Opera Inc 257 Dauphin St *Web:* mobileopera.org	Mobile	AL	36602	251-432-6772	431-7613
Musical Theatre Southwest (MTS) 6320 Domingo Rd NE Ste B *Web:* www.musicaltheatresw.com	Albuquerque	NM	87108	505-265-9119	262-9319
Ohio Light Opera, The 1189 Beall Ave *Web:* www.ohiolightopera.org	Wooster	OH	44691	330-263-2345	263-2272
Opera Birmingham 3601 Sixth Ave S *Web:* www.operabirmingham.org	Birmingham	AL	35222	205-322-6737	322-6206
Opera Carolina 345 N College St Ste 409 *Web:* www.operacarolina.org	Charlotte	NC	28202	704-332-7177	332-6448
Opera Colorado 695 S Colorado Blvd Ste 20 *Web:* www.operacolorado.org	Denver	CO	80246	303-778-1500	778-0479
Opera Company of Brooklyn 33 Indian Rd Ste 1G *Web:* www.operabrooklyn.org	New York	NY	10034	212-567-3283	
Opera Company of North Carolina 612 Wade Ave Ste 100 *Web:* www.ncopera.org	Raleigh	NC	27605	919-792-3850	
Opera Company of Philadelphia 1420 Locust St Ste 210 *Web:* www.operaphila.org	Philadelphia	PA	19102	215-893-3600	893-7801
Opera Memphis 6745 Wolf River Pkwy *Web:* www.operamemphis.org	Memphis	TN	38120	901-257-3100	257-3109
Opera Omaha 1625 Farnam St Ste 100 *TF:* 877-346-7372 ■ *Web:* www.operaomaha.org	Omaha	NE	68102	402-346-4398	346-7323
Opera Roanoke 541 Luck Ave *Web:* www.operaroanoke.org	Roanoke	VA	24016	540-982-2742	982-3601
Opera San Jose 2149 Paragon Dr *TF:* 800-745-3000 ■ *Web:* operasj.org	San Jose	CA	95131	408-437-4450	437-4455
Opera Santa Barbara 1330 State St *Web:* www.operasb.com	Santa Barbara	CA	93101	805-898-3890	898-3892
Opera Theatre at Wildwood 20919 Denny Rd *Web:* www.wildwoodpark.org	Little Rock	AR	72223	501-821-7275	821-7280
OperaDelaware Four S Poplar St *Web:* www.operade.org	Wilmington	DE	19801	302-658-8063	658-4991
Palm Beach Opera 415 S Olive Ave *TF:* 800-435-7352 ■ *Web:* pbopera.org	West Palm Beach	FL	33401	561-833-7888	833-8294
Pensacola Opera 75 S Tarragona St PO Box 1790 *Web:* www.pensacolaopera.com	Pensacola	FL	32502	850-433-6737	433-1082
Pittsburgh Civic Light Opera 719 Liberty Ave *Web:* www.pittsburghclo.org	Pittsburgh	PA	15222	412-281-3973	281-5339
Pittsburgh Opera 2425 Liberty Ave *Web:* www.pittsburghopera.org	Pittsburgh	PA	15222	412-281-0912	281-4324
Pocket Opera 469 Bryant St *Web:* www.pocketopera.org	San Francisco	CA	94107	415-972-8930	348-0931
Portland Opera 211 SE Caruthers St *TF:* 866-739-6737 ■ *Web:* www.portlandopera.org	Portland	OR	97214	503-241-1407	241-4212
San Diego Opera 1200 Third Ave Civic Ctr Plz 18th Fl *Web:* www.sdopera.com	San Diego	CA	92101	619-232-7636	231-6915
San Francisco Opera 301 Van Ness Ave *Web:* www.sfopera.com	San Francisco	CA	94102	415-861-4008	
Santa Fe Opera, The 301 Opera Dr *TF:* 800-280-4654 ■ *Web:* www.santafeopera.org	Santa Fe	NM	87506	505-986-5900	986-5999
Sarasota Opera 61 N Pineapple Ave *TF:* 866-951-0111 ■ *Web:* www.sarasotaopera.org	Sarasota	FL	34236	941-366-8450	955-5571
Seattle Musical Theatre 7400 Sand Pt Way NE Ste 101-N *Web:* www.seattlemusicaltheatre.org	Seattle	WA	98115	206-363-2809	363-0702
Seattle Opera PO Box 9248 *TF Sales:* 800-426-1619 ■ *Web:* www.seattleopera.org	Seattle	WA	98109	206-389-7600	389-7651
Shreveport Opera 212 Texas St Ste 101 *Web:* www.shreveportopera.org	Shreveport	LA	71101	318-227-9503	227-9518
Skylight Opera Theatre 158 N Broadway *Web:* www.skylightmusictheatre.org	Milwaukee	WI	53202	414-291-7811	291-7815
Syracuse Opera 411 Montgomery St Ste 60 *Web:* www.syracuseopera.com	Syracuse	NY	13202	315-475-5915	475-6319
Tacoma Opera 1119 Pacific Ave *Web:* www.tacomaopera.com	Tacoma	WA	98402	253-627-7789	
Toledo Opera 425 Jefferson Ave Ste 601 *TF:* 866-860-9048 ■ *Web:* www.toledoopera.org	Toledo	OH	43604	419-255-7464	255-6344
Tri-Cities Opera 315 Clinton St *Web:* www.tricitiesopera.com	Binghamton	NY	13905	607-729-3444	797-6344
Tulsa Opera 1610 S Boulder Ave *TF:* 866-298-2530 ■ *Web:* www.tulsaopera.com	Tulsa	OK	74119	918-582-4035	592-0380

Organization	City	State	ZIP	Phone	Fax
Wichita Grand Opera 225 W Douglas Ave Century II Performing Arts Ctr *TF:* 855-755-7328 ■ *Web:* www.wichitagrandopera.org	Wichita	KS	67202	316-683-3444	263-2126

576-3 Orchestras

Organization	City	State	ZIP	Phone	Fax
Abilene Philharmonic Orchestra 401 Cypress St Ste 520 *Web:* www.abilenephilharmonic.org	Abilene	TX	79601	325-677-6710	677-1299
Acadiana Symphony Orchestra 412 Travis St *TF:* 800-259-8852 ■ *Web:* www.acadianasymphony.org	Lafayette	LA	70503	337-232-4277	237-4712
Alabama Symphony Orchestra 3621 Sixth Ave S *Web:* www.alabamasymphony.org	Birmingham	AL	35222	205-975-2787	251-6840
Albany Symphony Orchestra 308 Flint Ave PO Box 70065 *Web:* www.albanysymphony.org	Albany	GA	31708	229-430-8933	
Alexandria Symphony Orchestra 2121 Eisenhower Ave Ste 608 *Web:* www.alexsym.org	Alexandria	VA	22314	703-548-0885	548-0985
Allentown Symphony Orchestra 23 N Sixth St *Web:* www.allentownsymphony.org	Allentown	PA	18101	610-432-6715	432-6735
American Composers Orchestra 240 W 35th St Ste 405 *Web:* www.americancomposers.org	New York	NY	10001	212-977-8495	977-8995
American Symphony Orchestra 263 W 38 St 10th Fl *Web:* www.americansymphony.org	New York	NY	10018	212-868-9276	868-9277
Anchorage Symphony Orchestra 400 D St Ste 230 *Web:* www.anchoragesymphony.org	Anchorage	AK	99501	907-274-8668	272-7916
Anderson Symphony Orchestra (ASO) 1124 Meridian Plz PO Box 741 *Web:* www.andersonsymphony.org	Anderson	IN	46016	765-644-2111	644-7703
Ann Arbor Symphony Orchestra 220 E Huron St Ste 470 *Web:* www.a2so.com	Ann Arbor	MI	48104	734-994-4801	994-3949
Annapolis Symphony Orchestra 801 Chase St Maryland Hall *Web:* www.annapolissymphony.org	Annapolis	MD	21401	410-269-1132	263-0616
Arapahoe Philharmonic 2100 W Littleton Blvd Ste 250 *Web:* www.arapahoe-phil.org	Littleton	CO	80120	303-781-1892	
Arkansas Symphony Orchestra 2417 N Tyler St PO Box 7328 *Web:* www.arkansassymphony.org	Little Rock	AR	72217	501-666-1761	666-3193
Asheville Symphony Orchestra 87 Haywood St PO Box 2852 *Web:* www.ashevillesymphony.org	Asheville	NC	28802	828-254-7046	254-1761
Aspen Chamber Symphony 225 Music School Rd *Web:* www.aspenmusicfestival.com	Aspen	CO	81611	970-925-3254	925-3802
Atlanta Pops 1830 Briarcliff Cir NE *Web:* www.altieriandassociates.com	Atlanta	GA	30329	404-636-0020	636-0020
Atlanta Symphony Orchestra 1280 Peachtree St NE Ste 4074 *Web:* www.atlantasymphony.org	Atlanta	GA	30309	404-733-4900	733-4901
Aurora Symphony Orchestra PO Box 441481 *Web:* www.aurorasymphony.org	Aurora	CO	80044	303-873-6622	
Austin Chamber Music Ctr 3814 Medical Pkwy *Web:* www.austinchambermusic.org	Austin	TX	78756	512-454-7562	454-0029
Austin Civic Orchestra PO Box 27132 *Web:* www.austincivicorchestra.org	Austin	TX	78755	512-200-2261	
Austin Symphony Orchestra 1101 Red River St *TF:* 888-462-3787 ■ *Web:* www.austinsymphony.org	Austin	TX	78701	512-476-6064	476-6242
Bakersfield Symphony Orchestra 1328 34th St Ste A *Web:* www.bsonow.org	Bakersfield	CA	93301	661-323-7928	323-7331
Baltimore Symphony Orchestra 1212 Cathedral St *TF:* 877-276-1444 ■ *Web:* www.bsomusic.org	Baltimore	MD	21201	410-783-8100	783-8004
Bangor Symphony Orchestra PO Box 1441 *TF General:* 800-639-3221 ■ *Web:* www.bangorsymphony.org	Bangor	ME	04402	207-942-5555	990-1272
Berkeley Symphony Orchestra 1942 University Ave Ste 207 *Web:* www.berkeleysymphony.org	Berkeley	CA	94704	510-841-2800	841-5422
Billings Symphony 2721 Second Ave N *Web:* www.billingssymphony.org	Billings	MT	59101	406-252-3610	252-3353
Bismarck-Mandan Symphony Orchestra 215 N Sixth St *Web:* www.bismarckmandansymphony.org	Bismarck	ND	58501	701-258-8345	258-8345
Boise Philharmonic Assn Inc 516 S Ninth St *Web:* www.boisephilharmonic.org	Boise	ID	83702	208-344-7849	336-9078
Boston Modern Orchestra Project 376 Washington St *Web:* www.bmop.org	Malden	MA	02148	781-324-0397	
Boston Philharmonic Orchestra 295 Huntington Ave Ste 210 *Web:* www.bostonphil.org	Boston	MA	02115	617-236-0999	236-8613
Boston Pops 301 Massachusetts Ave Symphony Hall *TF:* 888-266-1200 ■ *Web:* www.bso.org	Boston	MA	02115	617-266-1492	638-9493
Boston Symphony Orchestra 301 Massachusetts Ave Symphony Hall *TF:* 888-266-1200 ■ *Web:* www.bso.org	Boston	MA	02115	617-266-1492	638-9367
Boulder Philharmonic Orchestra 2590 Wallnut St Ste 100 *Web:* www.boulderphil.org	Boulder	CO	80302	303-449-1343	443-9203
Brockton Symphony Orchestra 156 W Elm St *Web:* www.brocktonsymphony.org	Brockton	MA	02301	508-588-3841	
Buffalo Philharmonic Orchestra 499 Franklin St *Web:* www.bpo.org	Buffalo	NY	14202	716-885-0331	885-9372
Calgary Philharmonic Orchestra 205 Eigth Ave SE Second Fl *Web:* www.cpo-live.com	Calgary	AB	T2G0K9	403-571-0270	294-7424
California Philharmonic Orchestra 2700 E Foothill Blvd *Web:* calphil.com/home	Pasadena	CA	91107	626-300-8200	300-8010
Camellia Symphony Orchestra 1545 River Pk Dr Ste 506 *Web:* www.camelliasymphony.org	Sacramento	CA	95815	916-929-6655	929-4292
Canton Symphony Orchestra 1001 Market Ave N *Web:* www.cantonsymphony.org	Canton	OH	44702	330-452-3434	452-4429
Carson City Symphony PO Box 2001 PO Box 2001 *Web:* www.ccsymphony.com	Carson City	NV	89702	775-883-4154	883-4371
Chamber Orchestra of Philadelphia 1520 Locust St Ste 500 *TF:* 800-732-0999 ■ *Web:* www.chamberorchestra.org	Philadelphia	PA	19102	215-545-5451	545-3868
Champaign-Urbana Symphony Orchestra (CUSO) 701 Devonshire Dr Ste C-24 *Web:* www.cusymphony.org	Champaign	IL	61820	217-351-9139	398-0413
Charleston Symphony Orchestra 756 St Andrews Blvd *Web:* www.charlestonsymphony.com	Charleston	SC	29407	843-723-7528	722-3463
Chattanooga Symphony & Opera (CSO) 701 Broad St *Web:* chattanoogasymphony.org	Chattanooga	TN	37402	423-267-8583	265-6520
Cheyenne Symphony Orchestra (CSO) 1904 Thomes Ave *Web:* www.cheyennesymphony.org	Cheyenne	WY	82001	307-778-8561	634-7512
Chicago Sinfonietta 70 E Lake St Ste 226 *Web:* www.chicagosinfonietta.org	Chicago	IL	60601	312-236-3681	236-5429
Chicago Symphony Orchestra 220 S Michigan Ave *TF:* 800-223-7114 ■ *Web:* www.cso.org	Chicago	IL	60604	312-294-3000	294-3035
Cincinnati Symphony Orchestra 1241 Elm St Music Hall *Web:* www.cincinnatisymphony.org	Cincinnati	OH	45202	513-621-1919	744-3535
Civic Orchestra of Tucson (COT) PO Box 42764 *Web:* www.cotmusic.org	Tucson	AZ	85733	520-730-3371	
Cleveland Chamber Symphony, The (CCS) 11125 Magnolia Dr The Music School Settlement *Web:* www.clevelandchambersymphony.org	Cleveland	OH	44106	216-202-4227	
Cleveland Orchestra, The 11001 Euclid Ave Severance Hall *TF:* 800-686-1141 ■ *Web:* www.clevelandorchestra.com	Cleveland	OH	44106	216-231-1111	231-4029
Cleveland Pops Orchestra 24000 Mercantile Rd Ste 11 *Web:* www.clevelandpops.com	Cleveland	OH	44122	216-765-7677	765-1931
Colorado Springs Philharmonic PO Box 1266 *Web:* www.csphilharmonic.org	Colorado Springs	CO	80901	719-575-9632	575-9656
Colorado Symphony Orchestra 1000 14th St Unit 15 *TF:* 877-292-7979 ■ *Web:* www.coloradosymphony.org	Denver	CO	80202	303-623-7876	293-2649
Columbus Symphony Orchestra 55 E State St *TF:* 800-745-3000 ■ *Web:* www.columbussymphony.com	Columbus	OH	43215	614-228-9600	224-7273
Corpus Christi Symphony Orchestra 555 N Carancahua St Tower II Ste 410 Ste 410 *TF:* 877-286-6683 ■ *Web:* www.ccsymphony.org	Corpus Christi	TX	78401	361-883-6683	882-4132
Da Camera of Houston 1427 Branard St *TF:* 800-233-2226 ■ *Web:* www.dacamera.com	Houston	TX	77006	713-524-7601	524-4148
Dallas Symphony Orchestra 2301 Flora St Ste 300 *Web:* mydso.com/	Dallas	TX	75201	214-692-0203	692-5133
Dayton Philharmonic Orchestra 109 N Main St Ste 200 *Web:* daytonperformingarts.org	Dayton	OH	45402	937-224-3521	223-9189
Daytona Beach Symphony Society PO Box 2 *Web:* new.dbss.org	Daytona Beach	FL	32115	386-253-2901	253-5774
DeKalb Symphony Orchestra (DSO) PO Box 1313 *Web:* www.dekalbsymphony.org	Tucker	GA	30085	678-891-3565	891-3575
Delaware Symphony Orchestra 818 N Market St *Web:* www.desymphony.org	Wilmington	DE	19801	302-656-7442	656-7754
Des Moines Symphony 221 Walnut St *Web:* www.dmsymphony.org	Des Moines	IA	50309	515-280-4000	280-4005
Detroit Symphony Orchestra 3711 Woodward Ave *TF:* 800-434-6340 ■ *Web:* dso.org	Detroit	MI	48201	313-576-5111	576-5109
Dubuque Symphony Orchestra 2728 Asbury Rd Ste 900 *TF:* 866-803-9280 ■ *Web:* www.dubuquesymphony.org	Dubuque	IA	52001	563-557-1677	557-9841
Durham Symphony Orchestra PO Box 1993 *Web:* www.durhamsymphony.org	Durham	NC	27702	919-560-2736	
Eastern Connecticut Symphony Orchestra 289 State St *Web:* www.ectsymphony.com	New London	CT	06320	860-443-2876	444-7601
Edmonton Symphony Orchestra 9720 102nd Ave *TF:* 800-563-5081 ■ *Web:* www.edmontonsymphony.com	Edmonton	AB	T5J4B2	780-428-1108	425-0167
El Paso Symphony Orchestra One Civic Ctr Plz *Web:* www.epso.org	El Paso	TX	79901	915-532-3776	533-8162
Erie Philharmonic 609 Walnut St *Web:* www.eriephil.org	Erie	PA	16502	814-455-1375	455-1377
Eugene Symphony 115 W Eigth Ave Ste 115 *Web:* www.eugenesymphony.org	Eugene	OR	97401	541-687-9487	687-0527
Evansville Philharmonic Orchestra 401 SE Sixth St *Web:* evansvillephilharmonic.org	Evansville	IN	47708	812-425-5050	426-7008

Organization	City	State	ZIP	Phone	Fax
Fairbanks Symphony Orchestra 312 Tanana Dr *Web:* www.fairbankssymphony.org	Fairbanks	AK	99775	907-474-5733	
Fairfax Symphony Orchestra 3905 Railroad Ave Ste 202-N *Web:* www.fairfaxsymphony.org	Fairfax	VA	22030	703-563-1990	293-9349
Flagstaff Symphony Orchestra 113 E Aspen Ave # A *TF:* 888-520-7214 ■ *Web:* www.flagstaffsymphony.org	Flagstaff	AZ	86001	928-774-5107	774-5109
Fort Collins Symphony 214 S College Ave *Web:* www.fcsymphony.org	Fort Collins	CO	80524	970-482-4823	482-4858
Fort Worth Symphony Orchestra Assn 330 E Fourth St Ste 200 *Web:* www.fwsymphony.org	Fort Worth	TX	76102	817-665-6500	665-6600
Fresno Philharmonic 7170 N. Financial Dr Ste 135 *Web:* www.fresnophil.org	Fresno	CA	93711	559-261-0600	261-0700
Grand Rapids Symphony 300 Ottawa Ave NW Ste 100 *Web:* www.grsymphony.org	Grand Rapids	MI	49503	616-454-9451	454-7477
Grant Park Orchestra 205 E Randolph St *Web:* www.grantparkmusicfestival.com	Chicago	IL	60601	312-742-7638	742-7662
Greater Bridgeport Symphony (GBS) 446 University Ave *Web:* www.gbs.org	Bridgeport	CT	06604	203-576-0263	367-0064
Greater Trenton Symphony Orchestra 28 W State St Ste 202 *Web:* www.trentonsymphony.org	Trenton	NJ	08608	609-394-1338	
Green Bay Symphony Orchestra 2420 Nicolet Dr PO Box 222 *Web:* www.greenbaysymphony.org	Green Bay	WI	54311	920-435-3465	435-1427
Greensboro Symphony Orchestra 200 N Davie St Ste 301 *Web:* www.greensborosymphony.org	Greensboro	NC	27401	336-335-5456	335-5580
Greenville Symphony Orchestra 200 S Main St *Web:* www.greenvillesymphony.org	Greenville	SC	29601	864-232-0344	467-3113
Greenwich Symphony Orchestra PO Box 35 *Web:* www.greenwichsymphony.org	Greenwich	CT	06836	203-869-2664	
Handel & Haydn Society 300 Massachusetts Ave *Web:* www.handelandhaydn.org	Boston	MA	02115	617-262-1815	266-4217
Harrisburg Symphony Orchestra 800 Corporate Cir Ste 101 *Web:* www.harrisburgsymphony.org	Harrisburg	PA	17110	717-545-5527	545-6501
Houston Symphony Orchestra 615 Louisiana St Ste 102 *Web:* www.houstonsymphony.org	Houston	TX	77002	713-224-4240	222-7024
Huntsville Symphony Orchestra 700 Monroe St PO Box 2400 *Web:* www.hso.org	Huntsville	AL	35801	256-539-4818	539-4819
Idaho State Civic Symphony 921 S Eigth Ave S- 8099 Idaho State University Fine Arts Dept *Web:* www.thesymphony.us	Pocatello	ID	83209	208-234-1587	282-4884
Illinois Symphony Orchestera 524 E Capitol Ave *TF:* 800-401-7222 ■ *Web:* www.ilsymphony.org	Springfield	IL	62701	217-522-2838	522-7374
Indianapolis Symphony Orchestra 45 Monument Cir *TF:* 800-366-8457 ■ *Web:* www.indianapolissymphony.org	Indianapolis	IN	46204	317-262-1100	262-1159
Jacksonville Symphony Orchestra (JSO) 300 W Water St Ste 200 *TF:* 877-662-6731 ■ *Web:* www.jaxsymphony.org	Jacksonville	FL	32202	904-354-5479	354-9238
Johnson City Symphony Orchestra PO Box 533 *Web:* www.jcsymphony.com	Johnson City	TN	37605	423-926-8742	926-8979
Juneau Symphony Orchestra 522 W Tenth St PO Box 21236 *Web:* www.juneausymphony.org	Juneau	AK	99802	907-586-4676	463-2555
Kalamazoo Symphony Orchestra 359 S Kalamazoo Mall Ste 100 *Web:* www.kalamazoosymphony.com	Kalamazoo	MI	49007	269-349-7759	349-9229
Kansas City Symphony 1020 Central St Ste 300 *TF:* 877-829-5590 ■ *Web:* www.kcsymphony.org	Kansas City	MO	64105	816-471-1100	471-0976
Kennedy Ctr Opera House Orchestra John F Kennedy Ctr for the Performing Arts 2700 F St NW **Fax Area Code:* 202 ■ *TF:* 800-444-1324 ■ *Web:* www.kennedy-center.org	Washington	DC	20566	800-444-1324	416-8205*
Kentucky Symphony Orchestra 540 Linden Ave PO Box 72810 *Web:* www.kyso.org	Newport	KY	41072	859-431-6216	431-3097
Knoxville Symphony Orchestra 100 S Gay St Ste 302 *Web:* www.knoxvillesymphony.com	Knoxville	TN	37902	865-523-1178	546-3766
Lansing Symphony Orchestra (LSO) 501 S Capitol Ave Ste 400 *Web:* www.lansingsymphony.org	Lansing	MI	48933	517-487-5001	487-0210
Las Cruces Symphony Orchestra 1075 N Horseshoe Cir *Web:* www.lascrucessymphony.com	Las Cruces	NM	88003	575-646-3709	646-1086
Lexington Philharmonic 161 N Mill St *TF:* 888-494-4226 ■ *Web:* www.lexphil.org	Lexington	KY	40507	859-233-4226	233-7896
Lincoln Symphony Orchestra 233 S 13th St Ste 1702 *Web:* lincolnsymphony.org	Lincoln	NE	68508	402-476-2211	476-2236
Long Beach Symphony Orchestra (LBSO) 555 E Ocean Blvd Ste 106 *Web:* www.lbso.org	Long Beach	CA	90802	562-436-3203	491-3599
Long Island Baroque Ensemble 154 West 123rd St *Web:* www.longislandbaroqueensemble.com	New York	NY	10027	914-965-7926	
Long Island Philharmonic (LIP) One Huntington Quadrangle Ste 2C21 *Web:* www.liphilharmonic.org	Melville	NY	11747	631-293-2223	293-2655
Los Angeles Philharmonic Assn 151 S Grand Ave *Web:* www.laphil.com	Los Angeles	CA	90012	323-850-2000	
Louisiana Philharmonic Orchestra 1010 Common St Ste 2120 *Web:* www.lpomusic.com	New Orleans	LA	70112	504-523-6530	595-8468
Louisville Orchestra 323 W Broadway Ste 700 *Web:* www.louisvilleorchestra.org	Louisville	KY	40202	502-587-8681	589-7870
Macon Symphony Orchestra 400 Poplar St *Web:* www.maconsymphony.com	Macon	GA	31201	478-301-5300	301-5505
Madison Symphony Orchestra 201 State St *Web:* www.madisonsymphony.org	Madison	WI	53703	608-257-3734	280-6192
Manitoba Chamber Orchestra 393 Portage Ave Portage Pl Ste Y300 *Web:* www.themco.ca	Winnipeg	MB	R3B3H6	204-783-7377	783-7383
Marin Symphony 4340 Redwood Hwy Ste 409C *Web:* www.marinsymphony.org	San Rafael	CA	94903	415-479-8100	479-8110
Maryland Symphony Orchestra, The 30 W Washington St *Web:* www.marylandsymphony.org	Hagerstown	MD	21740	301-797-4000	797-2314
Massachusetts Symphony Orchestra 10 Tuckerman St W Side Sta Po Box 20070 *Web:* www.tuckermanhall.org/pops.html	Worcester	MA	01609	508-754-1234	752-3671
Memphis Symphony Orchestra 585 S Mendenhall Rd *Web:* www.memphissymphony.org	Memphis	TN	38117	901-537-2525	537-2550
Miami Symphony Orchestra, The (MISO) 10689 N Kendall Dr Ste 307 *Web:* www.miamisymphony.org	Miami	Fl	33176	305-275-5666	275-4363
Milwaukee Symphony Orchestra 929 N Water St Ste 700 *TF:* 888-367-8101 ■ *Web:* milwaukee.broadway.com	Milwaukee	WI	53202	414-220-8322	
Minnesota Orchestra 1111 Nicollet Mall Orchestra Hall *TF:* 800-292-4141 ■ *Web:* www.minnesotaorchestra.org	Minneapolis	MN	55403	612-371-5600	371-7170
Mississippi Symphony Orchestra 201 E Pascagoula St *Web:* www.msorchestra.com	Jackson	MS	39201	601-960-1565	960-1564
Mobile Symphony PO Box 3127 *Web:* www.mobilesymphony.org	Mobile	AL	36652	251-432-2010	432-6618
Modesto Symphony Orchestra 911 13th St *TF:* 877-488-3380 ■ *Web:* www.modestosymphony.org	Modesto	CA	95354	209-523-4156	523-0201
Muncie Symphony Orchestra 2000 W University Ave # Ac112 *Web:* www.munciesymphony.org	Muncie	IN	47306	765-285-5531	285-9128
Music of the Baroque 111 N Wabash Ave Ste 810 *Web:* www.baroque.org	Chicago	IL	60602	312-551-1414	551-1444
National Philharmonic 5301 Tuckerman Ln *Web:* www.nationalphilharmonic.org	North Bethesda	MD	20852	301-493-9283	493-9284
National Symphony Orchestra 2700 F St NW *TF:* 800-444-1324 ■ *Web:* www.kennedy-center.org/nso	Washington	DC	20566	202-416-8000	416-8105
New Hampshire Music Festival Orchestra 52 Symphony Ln *Web:* www.nhmf.org	Center Harbor	NH	03226	603-279-3300	
New Haven Symphony Orchestra 105 Ct St # 302 *Web:* www.newhavensymphony.org	New Haven	CT	06511	203-865-0831	865-0845
New Jersey Symphony Orchestra 60 Pk Pl *Web:* www.njsymphony.org	Newark	NJ	07102	973-624-3713	624-2115
New West Symphony 2100 E Thousand Oaks Blvd Ste D *Web:* www.newwestsymphony.org	Thousand Oaks	CA	91362	805-497-5800	497-5839
New World Symphony 500 17th St *TF:* 800-597-3331 ■ *Web:* www.nws.edu	Miami Beach	FL	33139	305-673-3330	673-6749
New York Philharmonic 10 Lincoln Ctr Plaza Avery Fisher Hall **Fax:* Mktg ■ *Web:* www.nyphil.org	New York	NY	10023	212-875-5900	875-5717*
New York Pops 333 W 52nd St Ste 600 *Web:* www.newyorkpops.org	New York	NY	10019	212-765-7677	315-3199
North Arkansas Symphony 605 W Dixon St *Web:* sonamusic.org	Fayetteville	AR	72701	479-521-4166	
North Carolina Symphony Two E S St Memorial Auditorium *Web:* www.ncsymphony.org	Raleigh	NC	27601	919-733-2750	733-9920
Northeastern Pennsylvania Philharmonic 4101 Birney Ave *Web:* www.nepaphil.org	Moosic	PA	18507	570-341-1568	941-0318
Oklahoma City Philharmonic 428 W California Ave Ste 210 *Web:* www.okcphilharmonic.org	Oklahoma City	OK	73102	405-232-7575	232-4353
Omaha Symphony 1605 Howard St *Web:* www.omahasymphony.org	Omaha	NE	68102	402-342-3836	342-3819
Opera Orchestra of New York, The 344 E 63rd St Ste B-1 *Web:* www.operaorchestrany.org	New York	NY	10065	212-906-9137	906-9021
Orchestra Iowa 119 Third Ave SE *Web:* artsiowa.com/orchestra/	Cedar Rapids	IA	52401	319-366-8206	366-5206
Orchestra New England PO Box 200123 *TF:* 800-595-4849 ■ *Web:* orchestranewengland.org	New Haven	CT	06520	203-777-4690	
Orchestre Metropolitain du Grand Montreal 486 St Catherine St W Ste 401 *Web:* www.orchestremetropolitain.com	Montreal	QC	H3B1A6	514-598-0870	840-9195
Orchestre Symphonique de Montreal 260 de Maisonneuve Blvd W Second Fl *TF:* 888-842-9951 ■ *Web:* www.osm.ca	Montreal	QC	H2X1Y9	514-842-9951	842-0728
Oregon Symphony Orchestra 921 SW Washington St Ste 200 *TF:* 800-228-7343 ■ *Web:* www.orsymphony.org	Portland	OR	97205	503-228-4294	228-4150
Orlando Philharmonic Orchestra 812 E Rollins St Ste 300 *Web:* www.orlandophil.org	Orlando	FL	32803	407-896-6700	896-5512

Organization	City	State	ZIP	Phone	Fax
Orpheus Chamber Orchestra 490 Riverside Dr 11th Fl *Web:* www.orpheusnyc.com	New York	NY	10027	212-896-1700	896-1717
Ottawa Symphony Orchestra (OSO) Two Daly Ave Ste 250 *Web:* www.ottawasymphony.com	Ottawa	ON	K1N6E2	613-231-7802	231-3610
Owensboro Symphony Orchestra 211 E Second St *Web:* www.owensborosymphony.org	Owensboro	KY	42303	270-684-0661	683-0740
Paducah Symphony Orchestra 760 Broadway *Web:* paducahsymphony.org	Paducah	KY	42001	270-444-0065	444-0456
Pensacola Symphony Orchestra 205 E Zaragossa St PO Box 1752 *Web:* www.pensacolasymphony.com	Pensacola	FL	32502	850-435-2533	444-9910
Peoria Symphony Orchestra 203 Harrison St *Web:* www.peoriasymphony.org	Peoria	IL	61602	309-671-1096	
Peter Nero & the Philly Pops 1518 Walnut St Ste 1706 *Web:* www.phillypops.com	Philadelphia	PA	19102	215-875-8004	893-1948
Philadelphia Orchestra 260 S Broad St Ste 1600 *Web:* www.philorch.org	Philadelphia	PA	19102	215-893-1955	
Philharmonia Baroque Orchestra 180 Redwood St Ste 200 *Web:* www.philharmonia.org	San Francisco	CA	94102	415-252-1288	252-1488
Phoenix Symphony One N First St Ste 200 *TF:* 800-776-9080 ■ *Web:* www.phoenixsymphony.org	Phoenix	AZ	85004	602-495-1117	253-1772
Pittsburgh Symphony Orchestra 600 Penn Ave Heinz Hall for the Performing Arts *TF:* 800-743-8560 ■ *Web:* www.pittsburghsymphony.org	Pittsburgh	PA	15222	412-566-7366	392-3311
Plano Symphony Orchestra 5236 Tennyson Pkwy Ste 200 *Web:* www.planosymphony.org	Plano	TX	75024	972-473-7262	473-4639
Portland Baroque Orchestra 1020 SW Taylor St Ste 200 *TF:* 800-494-8497 ■ *Web:* www.pbo.org	Portland	OR	97205	503-222-6000	226-6635
Portland Symphony Orchestra 50 Monument Sq Second Fl *Web:* www.portlandsymphony.org	Portland	ME	04101	207-773-6128	773-6089
ProMusica Chamber Orchestra 620 E Broad St Ste 300 *Web:* www.promusicacolumbus.org	Columbus	OH	43215	614-464-0066	464-4141
Raleigh Symphony Orchestra PO Box 25878 *Web:* raleighsymphony.org	Raleigh	NC	27611	919-546-9755	
Redlands Symphony 1200 E Colton Ave *Web:* www.redlandssymphony.com	Redlands	CA	92373	909-748-8018	335-5213
Reno Chamber Orchestra 925 Riverside Dr Ste 5 *Web:* www.renochamberorchestra.org	Reno	NV	89503	775-348-9413	348-0643
Reno Philharmonic Orchestra 925 Riverside Dr Ste 3 *Web:* www.renophil.com	Reno	NV	89503	775-323-6393	323-6711
Rhode Island Philharmonic Orchestra 667 Waterman Ave *Web:* www.ri-philharmonic.org	East Providence	RI	02914	401-248-7070	248-7071
Richmond Symphony Orchestra 380 Hubelchison Pkwy PO Box 982 *Web:* www.richmondsymphony.org	Richmond	IN	47375	765-966-5181	962-8447
Ridgefield Symphony Orchestra 90 E Ridge PO Box 289 *Web:* www.ridgefieldsymphony.org	Ridgefield	CT	06877	203-438-3889	438-0222
River City Brass Band Inc 500 Grant St Ste 2720 *TF:* 800-292-7222 ■ *Web:* www.rivercitybrass.org	Pittsburgh	PA	15219	412-434-7222	235-9015
Roanoke Symphony Orchestra 541 Luck Ave Ste 200 *Web:* www.rso.com	Roanoke	VA	24016	540-343-6221	343-0065
Rochester Orchestra & Chorale 400 S Broadway *Web:* www.rochestersymphony.org	Rochester	MN	55904	507-286-8742	280-4136
Rochester Philharmonic Orchestra 108 E Ave *Web:* www.rpo.org	Rochester	NY	14604	585-454-7311	325-4905
Rockford Symphony Orchestra 711 N Main St *Web:* www.rockfordsymphony.com	Rockford	IL	61103	815-965-0049	965-0642
Saint Louis Symphony Orchestra 718 N Grand Blvd *TF:* 800-232-1880 ■ *Web:* www.stlsymphony.org	Saint Louis	MO	63103	314-533-2500	286-4111
Saint Paul Chamber Orchestra 408 St Peter St Third Fl *Web:* www.thespco.org	Saint Paul	MN	55102	651-291-1144	292-3281
San Antonio Symphony 711 Navarro St Ste235 *Web:* sasymphony.org	San Antonio	TX	78205	210-554-1000	554-1008
San Diego Symphony Orchestra 1245 Seventh Ave *Web:* www.sandiegosymphony.org	San Diego	CA	92101	619-235-0804	231-8178
San Francisco Symphony 201 Van Ness Ave *Web:* www.sfsymphony.org	San Francisco	CA	94102	415-864-6000	
Santa Barbara Symphony 1330 State Street Ste 102 *Web:* www.thesymphony.org	Santa Barbara	CA	93101	805-898-9386	898-9326
Santa Cruz Symphony 307 Church St *Web:* www.santacruzsymphony.org	Santa Cruz	CA	95060	831-462-0553	426-1193
Santa Fe Symphony Orchestra & Chorus Inc 551 W Cordova Rd Ste D Ste D *TF:* 800-480-1319 ■ *Web:* www.santafesymphony.org	Santa Fe	NM	87505	505-983-3530	982-3888
Santa Rosa Symphony (SRS) 50 Santa Rosa Ave Ste 410 *Web:* www.santarosasymphony.com	Santa Rosa	CA	95404	707-546-8742	546-7284
Sarasota Orchestra 709 N Tamiami Trl *TF:* 866-508-0611 ■ *Web:* www.sarasotaorchestra.org	Sarasota	FL	34236	941-953-4252	953-3059
Scottsdale Symphony Orchestra 3127 N 81st Pl	Scottsdale	AZ	85251	480-945-8071	
Seattle Symphony 200 University St *Web:* www.seattlesymphony.org	Seattle	WA	98101	206-215-4700	215-4701
Shreveport Symphony Orchestra 619 Louisiana Ave Ste 400 *Web:* www.shreveportsymphony.com	Shreveport	LA	71101	318-222-7496	222-7490
Sioux City Symphony Orchestra 520 Pierce St PO Box 754 *Web:* www.siouxcitysymphony.org	Sioux City	IA	51101	712-277-2111	252-0224
South Bend Symphony Orchestra (SBSO) 127 N Michigan St *TF:* 800-537-6415 ■ *Web:* www.southbendsymphony.com	South Bend	IN	46601	574-232-6343	232-6627
South Carolina Philharmonic 721 Lady St *Web:* www.scphilharmonic.com	Columbia	SC	29201	803-771-7937	771-0268
South Dakota Symphony Orchestra 301 S Main Ave Fourth Fl *Web:* www.sdsymphony.org	Sioux Falls	SD	57104	605-335-7933	335-1958
Spokane Symphony PO Box 365 *TF:* 800-899-1482 ■ *Web:* www.spokanesymphony.org	Spokane	WA	99210	509-624-1200	252-2637
Springfield Symphony Orchestra 1350 Main St *Web:* www.springfieldsymphony.org	Springfield	MA	01103	413-733-0636	781-4129
Symphony Nova Scotia 6101 University Ave Dalhousie Arts Ctr *TF:* 800-874-1669 ■ *Web:* www.symphonynovascotia.ca	Halifax	NS	B3H4R2	902-494-3820	494-2883
Symphony of the Mountains 1200 E Ctr St *Web:* www.symphonyofthemountains.org	Kingsport	TN	37660	423-392-8423	392-8428
Symphony Orchestra Augusta 1301 Greene St Ste 200 *Web:* soaugusta.org	Augusta	GA	30901	706-826-4705	826-4735
Symphony Silicon Valley 345 S First St *Web:* www.symphonysiliconvalley.org	San Jose	CA	95113	408-286-2600	286-2600
Tacoma Symphony 901 Broadway Ste 600 *Web:* www.tacomasymphony.org	Tacoma	WA	98402	253-272-7264	274-8187
Tallahassee Symphony Orchestra 1020 E Lafayette St	Tallahassee	FL	32301	850-224-0461	
Thayer Symphony Orchestra 14 Monument Sq # 406 *Web:* www.thayersymphony.org	Leominster	MA	01453	978-466-1800	840-1000
Toledo Symphony 1838 Parkwood Ave *TF:* 800-348-1253 ■ *Web:* www.toledosymphony.com	Toledo	OH	43604	419-246-8000	321-6890
Topeka Symphony 2100 SE 29th St PO Box 2206 *Web:* www.topekasymphony.org	Topeka	KS	66601	785-232-2032	232-6204
Traverse Symphony Orchestra (TSO) 300 E Front St Ste 230 *Web:* www.traversesymphony.org	Traverse City	MI	49684	231-947-7120	947-8118
Tucson Symphony Orchestra 2175 N Sixth Ave *Web:* www.tucsonsymphony.org	Tucson	AZ	85705	520-792-9155	792-9314
Tupelo Symphony Orchestra 1800 W Main St PO Box 474 *Web:* nmsymphony.com	Tupelo	MS	38801	662-842-8433	842-9565
Tuscaloosa Symphony Orchestra PO Box 20001 *Web:* www.tsoonline.org	Tuscaloosa	AL	35402	205-752-5515	345-2787
Union League Club 65 W Jackson Blvd Ste 133	Chicago	IL	60604	312-427-7800	
Utah Symphony & Opera 123 W S Temple *Web:* utahagenda.com	Salt Lake City	UT	84101	801-533-6683	
Vermont Symphony Orchestra Two Church St Ste 19 *TF:* 800-876-9293 ■ *Web:* www.vso.org	Burlington	VT	05401	802-864-5741	864-5109
Virginia Symphony Orchestra 861 Glenrock Rd Ste 200 *TF:* 855-876-7677 ■ *Web:* www.virginiasymphony.org	Norfolk	VA	23502	757-466-3060	466-3046
Wallingford Symphony Orchestra PO Box 6023 *Web:* www.wallingfordsymphony.org	Wallingford	CT	06492	203-697-2261	
Washington Metropolitan Philharmonic Assn (WMPA) PO Box 120 *Web:* www.wmpamusic.org	Mount Vernon	VA	22121	703-799-8229	360-7391
Washington Symphony Orchestra (WSO) PO Box 178 *Web:* www.washsym.org	Washington	PA	15301	724-223-9796	
Waterbury Symphony Orchestra 110 Bank St *Web:* www.waterburysymphony.org	Waterbury	CT	06702	203-574-4283	756-3507
Waterloo-Cedar Falls Symphony Orchestra Gallagher-Bluedorn Performing Arts Ctr Ste 17 *Web:* wcfsymphony.org	Cedar Falls	IA	50614	319-273-3373	
Westchester Philharmonic 123 Main St Lobby Level *TF:* 800-553-0031 ■ *Web:* www.westchesterphil.org	White Plains	NY	10601	914-682-3707	682-3716
Western Piedmont Symphony 243 Third Ave NE Ste 1-N *Web:* www.wpsymphony.org	Hickory	NC	28601	828-324-8603	324-1301
Wheeling Symphony Orchestra 1025 Main St Ste 811 *TF:* 800-395-9241 ■ *Web:* wheelingsymphony.com	Wheeling	WV	26003	304-232-6191	232-6192
Wichita Symphony Orchestra (WSO) 225 W Douglas St Ste 207 *Web:* wichitasymphony.org	Wichita	KS	67202	316-267-5259	267-1937
Windsor Symphony Orchestra 487 Oullette Ave *Web:* www.windsorsymphony.com	Windsor	ON	N9A4J2	519-973-1238	973-0764
Winston-Salem Symphony 201 N Broad St Ste 200 *Web:* www.wssymphony.org	Winston-Salem	NC	27101	336-725-1035	725-3924
Wyoming Symphony Orchestra 225 S David Ste B *Web:* www.wyomingsymphony.org	Casper	WY	82601	307-266-1478	266-4522
Youngstown Symphony Orchestra 260 Federal Plz W *Web:* www.youngstownsymphony.com	Youngstown	OH	44503	330-744-4269	744-1441

576-4 Theater Companies

Organization	City	State	Zip	Phone	Fax
A Contemporary Theatre (ACT) 700 Union St Kreielsheimer Pl *TF:* 888-584-4849 ■ *Web:* www.acttheatre.org	Seattle	WA	98101	206-292-7660	292-7670
Actors Theatre of Louisville 316 W Main St *TF:* 800-428-5849 ■ *Web:* www.actorstheatre.org	Louisville	KY	40202	502-584-1205	561-3300
Alabama Shakespeare Festival One Festival Dr *TF:* 800-841-4273 ■ *Web:* www.asf.net	Montgomery	AL	36117	334-271-5300	271-5348
Alaska Junior Theater 430 W Seventh Ave Ste 30 *Web:* www.akjt.org	Anchorage	AK	99501	907-272-7546	272-3035
Alley Theatre 615 Texas Ave *Web:* www.alleytheatre.org	Houston	TX	77002	713-220-5700	222-6542
Alliance Theatre Co 1280 Peachtree St NE Woodruff Arts Ctr *Web:* www.alliancetheatre.org	Atlanta	GA	30309	404-733-4650	733-4625
American Conservatory Theater (ACT) 30 Grant Ave 6th Fl *Web:* www.act-sf.org	San Francisco	CA	94108	415-956-0816	749-2291
American Stage 163 Third St N *Web:* www.americanstage.org	Saint Petersburg	FL	33731	727-823-1600	821-2444
Arden Theatre Co 40 N Second St *Web:* www.ardentheatre.org	Philadelphia	PA	19106	215-922-8900	922-7011
Arena Stage 1101 Sixth St SW *Web:* www.arenastage.org	Washington	DC	20024	202-554-9066	488-4056
Arkansas Repertory Theatre 601 Main St PO Box 110 *Web:* www.therep.org	Little Rock	AR	72201	501-378-0445	378-0012
Artists Repertory Theatre 1516 SW Alder St *Web:* www.artistsrep.org	Portland	OR	97205	503-241-9807	241-8268
Augusta Players, The 1301 Greene St Ste 304 PO Box 2352 *Web:* augustaplayers.org	Augusta	GA	30901	706-826-4707	
Barter Theatre 127 W Main St *Web:* www.bartertheatre.com	Abingdon	VA	24210	276-628-3991	619-3335
Baton Rouge Little Theater 7155 Florida Blvd *Web:* theatrebr.org	Baton Rouge	LA	70806	225-924-6496	924-9972
Berkshire Theatre Festival 83 E Main St *Web:* www.berkshiretheatregroup.org	Stockbridge	MA	01262	413-298-5576	298-3368
Biloxi Little Theatre 220 Lee St *Web:* www.4blt.org	Biloxi	MS	39530	228-432-8543	392-7639
Birmingham Festival Theater 1901 1/2 11th Ave S PO Box 55321 *Web:* www.bftonline.org	Birmingham	AL	35205	205-933-2383	
Capital Repertory Theatre 432 State St *Web:* www.capitalrep.org	Schenectady	NY	12305	518-462-4531	881-1823
Casa Manana Theatre 3101 W Lancaster Ave *Web:* www.casamanana.org	Fort Worth	TX	76107	817-332-2272	332-5711
Center Stage 700 N Calvert St *Web:* www.centerstage.org	Baltimore	MD	21202	410-986-4000	539-3912
Center Theatre Group 601 W Temple St *Web:* centertheatregroup.org	Los Angeles	CA	90012	213-628-2772	972-7402
Children's Musical Theater San Jose (CMTS) 1401 Parkmoor Ave Ste 100 *Web:* www.cmtsj.org	San Jose	CA	95126	408-288-5437	
City Lights Theatre 529 S Second St *Web:* www.cltc.org	San Jose	CA	95112	408-295-4200	295-8318
City Theatre Co 1300 Bingham St *Web:* www.citytheatrecompany.org	Pittsburgh	PA	15203	412-431-4400	431-5535
Clarence Brown Theatre *University of Tennessee* 206 McClung Tower *Web:* www.clarencebrowntheatre.com	Knoxville	TN	37996	865-974-5161	974-4867
Cleveland Public Theatre 6415 Detroit Ave *Web:* www.cptonline.org	Cleveland	OH	44102	216-631-2727	631-2575
Corn Stock Theatre 1700 Pk Rd *TF:* 800-220-1185 ■ *Web:* www.cornstocktheatre.com	Peoria	IL	61604	309-676-2196	676-9036
Court Theatre 5535 S Ellis Ave *Web:* www.courttheatre.org	Chicago	IL	60637	773-702-7005	834-1897
Dallas Theater Ctr 3636 Turtle Creek Blvd *Web:* www.dallastheatercenter.org	Dallas	TX	75219	214-526-8210	521-7666
Downtown Cabaret Theatre 263 Golden Hill St *Web:* www.dtcab.com	Bridgeport	CT	06604	203-576-1636	576-1444
Ensemble Theatre of Cincinnati 1127 Vine St *Web:* www.cincyetc.com	Cincinnati	OH	45202	513-421-3555	562-4104
Erie Playhouse 13 W Tenth St *Web:* www.erieplayhouse.org	Erie	PA	16501	814-454-2852	454-0601
Evansville Civic Theatre 717 N Fulton St *Web:* www.evansvillecivictheatre.org	Evansville	IN	47710	812-425-2800	423-2636
Fairbanks Shakespeare Theatre PO Box 73447 *Web:* www.fstalaska.org	Fairbanks	AK	99707	907-457-7638	457-4511
Fargo-Moorhead Community Theatre 333 Fourth St S *Web:* www.fmct.org	Fargo	ND	58103	701-235-1901	235-2685
Fort Smith Little Theatre 401 N Sixth St *Web:* www.fslt.org	Fort Smith	AR	72913	479-783-2966	
Fort Wayne Civic Theater 303 E Main St *Web:* www.fwcivic.org	Fort Wayne	IN	46802	260-422-8641	422-6699
GableStage 1200 Anastasia Ave Biltmore Hotel *Web:* www.gablestage.org	Coral Gables	FL	33134	305-446-1116	445-8645
Garland Civic Theatre 108 N Sixth St *Web:* www.garlandcivictheatre.org	Garland	TX	75040	972-485-8884	
Geffen Playhouse 10886 Le Conte Ave *Web:* www.geffenplayhouse.com	Los Angeles	CA	90024	310-208-5454	208-8383
Generic Theater 215 St Paul's Blvd *Web:* www.generictheater.org	Norfolk	VA	23510	757-441-2160	441-2729
Geva Theatre Ctr 75 Woodbury Blvd *Web:* www.gevatheatre.org	Rochester	NY	14607	585-232-1366	232-4031
Goodman Theatre 170 N Dearborn St *Web:* www.goodmantheatre.org	Chicago	IL	60601	312-443-3811	443-3821
Goodspeed Musicals PO Box A *TF:* 800-262-8721 ■ *Web:* www.goodspeed.org	East Haddam	CT	06423	860-873-8664	873-2329
Great Lakes Theater Festival 1501 Euclid Ave Ste 300 *Web:* www.greatlakestheater.org	Cleveland	OH	44115	216-241-5490	241-6315
Guthrie Theater 818 S Second St *TF Resv:* 877-447-8243 ■ *Web:* www.guthrietheater.org	Minneapolis	MN	55415	612-377-2224	225-6004
Huntington Beach Playhouse (HBPH) 7111 Talbert Ave *Web:* www.hbplayhouse.com	Huntington Beach	CA	92648	714-375-0696	847-0457
Huntington Theatre Co 264 Huntington Ave Boston University Theatre *Web:* www.huntingtontheatre.org	Boston	MA	02115	617-266-7900	353-8300
Indiana Repertory Theatre Inc 140 W Washington St *Web:* www.irtlive.com	Indianapolis	IN	46204	317-635-5277	236-0767
International City Theatre 110 Pine Ave Ste 820 Ste 820 *Web:* www.ictlongbeach.org	Long Beach	CA	90802	562-495-4595	436-7895
Invisible Theatre 1400 N First Ave *Web:* www.invisibletheatre.com	Tucson	AZ	85719	520-882-9721	884-5410
Irish Classical Theatre 625 Main St *Web:* www.irishclassicaltheatre.com	Buffalo	NY	14203	716-853-4282	853-0592
Jubilee Theatre 506 Main St *Web:* www.jubileetheatre.org	Fort Worth	TX	76102	817-338-4204	338-4206
La Jolla Playhouse PO Box 12039 *Web:* www.lajollaplayhouse.com	La Jolla	CA	92039	858-550-1070	550-1075
Laguna Playhouse, The 606 Laguna Canyon Rd PO Box 1747 *Web:* www.lagunaplayhouse.com	Laguna Beach	CA	92651	949-497-2787	497-6948
Lincoln Ctr Theater 150 W 65th St **Fax Area Code: 212* ■ *Web:* www.lct.org	New York	NY	10023	800-432-7250	873-0761*
Little Theatre of Alexandria 600 Wolfe St *Web:* www.thelittletheatre.com	Alexandria	VA	22314	703-683-5778	683-1378
Lost Nation Theater 39 Main St *Web:* www.lostnationtheater.org	Montpelier	VT	05602	802-229-0492	223-9608
Lyric Theatre of Oklahoma 1727 NW 16th St *Web:* www.lyrictheatreokc.com	Oklahoma City	OK	73106	405-524-9312	524-9316
Maltz Jupiter Theatre 1001 E Indiantown Rd *TF:* 800-445-1666 ■ *Web:* www.jupitertheatre.org	Jupiter	FL	33477	561-743-2666	743-0107
Manhattan Theatre Club Inc 311 W 43rd St Eighth Fl *Web:* www.manhattantheatreclub.com	New York	NY	10036	212-399-3000	399-4329
McCarter Theatre 91 University Pl *Web:* www.mccarter.org	Princeton	NJ	08540	609-258-6500	497-0369
Merrimack Repertory Theatre 132 Warren St *Web:* www.mrt.org	Lowell	MA	01852	978-654-7550	654-7575
Milwaukee Repertory Theater 108 E Wells St *Web:* www.milwaukeerep.com	Milwaukee	WI	53202	414-224-1761	224-9097
Music Theatre of Wichita 225 W Douglas Ste 202 *Web:* www.mtwichita.org	Wichita	KS	67202	316-265-3253	265-8708
Nashville Repertory Theatre 161 Rains Ave *Web:* www.tennesseerep.org	Nashville	TN	37203	615-244-4878	349-3222
National Theatre of the Deaf (NTD) 139 N Main St *Web:* www.ntd.org	West Hartford	CT	06107	860-236-4193	236-4163
Nebraska Repertory Theatre 12th & R Sts 215 Temple Bldg *TF:* 800-432-3231 ■ *Web:* www.unl.edu	Lincoln	NE	68588	402-472-2072	472-9055
New Stage Theatre 1100 Carlisle St *Web:* www.newstagetheatre.com	Jackson	MS	39202	601-948-3531	948-3538
North Carolina Theatre One E S St Memorial Auditorium *Web:* www.nctheatre.com	Raleigh	NC	27601	919-831-6941	831-6951
Northlight Theatre 9501 Skokie Blvd *TF:* 800-356-9377 ■ *Web:* www.northlight.org	Skokie	IL	60077	847-673-6300	679-1879
Old Globe Theatre 1363 Old Globe Way *Web:* www.oldglobe.org	San Diego	CA	92101	619-231-1941	231-5879
Omaha Community Playhouse 6915 Cass St *TF:* 888-782-4338 ■ *Web:* www.omahaplayhouse.com	Omaha	NE	68132	402-553-0800	553-6288
Pacific Repertory Theater PO Box 222035 *TF:* 866-622-0709 ■ *Web:* www.pacrep.org	Carmel	CA	93922	831-622-0700	622-0703
Pasadena Playhouse, The 39 S El Molino Ave *TF:* 800-733-2767 ■ *Web:* www.pasadenaplayhouse.org	Pasadena	CA	91101	626-356-7529	204-7399
Penobscot Theatre Co 131 Main St *Web:* www.penobscottheatre.org	Bangor	ME	04401	207-942-3333	947-6678
Pensacola Little Theatre (PLT) 400 S Jefferson St Pensacola Cultural Ctr *Web:* www.pensacolalittletheatre.com	Pensacola	FL	32502	850-432-2042	438-2787
People's Light & Theatre Co 39 Conestoga Rd *TF:* 800-732-0999 ■ *Web:* www.peopleslight.org	Malvern	PA	19355	610-647-1900	640-9521
Perseverance Theatre 914 Third St *TF:* 855-462-8497 ■ *Web:* www.perseverancetheatre.org	Douglas	AK	99824	907-364-2421	364-2603
Pittsburgh Public Theater 621 Penn Ave *TF:* 800-732-0999 ■ *Web:* www.ppt.org	Pittsburgh	PA	15222	412-316-8200	316-8219
PlayMakers Repertory Co 150 Country Club Rd **Fax Area Code: 866* ■ *Web:* www.playmakersrep.org	Chapel Hill	NC	27599	919-962-7529	904-8396*
Portland Ctr Stage (PCS) 128 NW Eleventh Ave *Web:* www.pcs.org	Portland	OR	97209	503-445-3700	445-3701
Portland Stage Co PO Box 1458 *Web:* www.portlandstage.org	Portland	ME	04104	207-774-1043	774-0576
Prince Music Theater 1412 Chestnut St *Web:* www.princetheater.org	Philadelphia	PA	19102	267-239-2941	

Phone Fax

Public, Theater, The 425 Lafayette St ... New York NY 10003 212-539-8500 539-8505
Web: www.publictheater.org

Repertory Theatre of Saint Louis
130 Edgar Rd PO Box 191730 ... Saint Louis MO 63119 314-968-7340 968-9638
Web: www.repstl.org

Rochester Repertory Theatre Co
103 Seventh St NE ... Rochester MN 55906 507-289-1737
Web: www.rochesterrep.org

Roundabout Theatre Co 231 W 39th St Ste 1200 ... New York NY 10018 212-719-9393 869-8817
Web: www.roundabouttheatre.org

Sacramento Theatre Co 1419 H St ... Sacramento CA 95814 916-443-6722 446-4066
TF: 888-478-2849 ■ *Web:* www.sactheatre.org

San Diego Repertory Theatre 79 Horton Plz ... San Diego CA 92101 619-231-3586
Web: www.sdrep.org

San Jose Repertory Theatre
101 Paseo de San Antonio ... San Jose CA 95113 408-367-7255 367-7236

San Jose Stage Co 490 S First St ... San Jose CA 95113 408-283-7142 283-7146
Web: www.sanjose-stage.com

San Pedro Playhouse
800 W Ashby Pl PO Box 12356 ... San Antonio TX 78212 210-733-7258 734-2651
Web: www.theplayhousesa.org

Sandra Feinstein-Gamm Theatre
172 Exchange St ... Pawtucket RI 02860 401-723-4266 723-0440
Web: www.gammtheatre.org

Seattle Repertory Theatre (SRT)
155 Mercer St PO Box 900923 ... Seattle WA 98109 206-443-2210 443-2379
TF: 877-900-9285 ■ *Web:* www.seattlerep.org

Second City Chicago 1608 N Wells St ... Chicago IL 60614 312-664-4032 664-9837
Web: www.secondcity.com

Shakespeare Theatre 516 Eigth St SE ... Washington DC 20003 202-547-3230 547-0226
TF: 877-487-8849 ■ *Web:* www.shakespearetheatre.org

Signature Theatre 4200 Campbell Ave ... Arlington VA 22206 703-820-9771 820-7790
Web: www.signature-theatre.org

South Carolina Children's Theatre
153 Augusta St ... Greenville SC 29601 864-235-2885 235-0208
Web: www.scchildrenstheatre.org

South Coast Repertory 655 Town Ctr Dr ... Costa Mesa CA 92626 714-708-5500 708-5576
Web: www.scr.org

Springfield Little Theatre
311 E Walnut Ave ... Springfield MO 65806 417-869-1334 869-4047
Web: www.landerstheatre.org

Stage Coach Theatre 4802 W Emerald ... Boise ID 83706 208-342-2000
Web: www.stagecoachtheatre.com

Stages Repertory Theatre
3201 Allen Pkwy Ste 101 ... Houston TX 77019 713-527-0220 527-8669
Web: www.stagestheatre.com

Stockton Civic Theatre (SCT)
2312 Rose Marie Ln ... Stockton CA 95207 209-473-2400 473-1502
Web: www.sctlivetheatre.com

Swine Palace Productions
105 Music & Dramatic Arts Bldg
Dalrymple Dr LSU ... Baton Rouge LA 70803 225-578-3533
Web: swinepalace.wix.com/sp-test#!__find

Syracuse Stage 820 E Genesee St ... Syracuse NY 13210 315-443-4008 443-9846
Web: www.syracusestage.org

Tacoma Musical Playhouse 7116 Sixth Ave ... Tacoma WA 98406 253-565-6867 564-7863
Web: www.tmp.org

Tempe Little Theatre 132 E Sixth St ... Tempe AZ 85281 480-350-8388

Theater of the Stars 1100 Spring St Ste 301 ... Atlanta GA 30309 404-252-8960 252-1460

THEATERWORK PO Box 842 ... Santa Fe NM 87504 505-471-1799
Web: theaterwork.org

Theatre Arlington 305 W Main St ... Arlington TX 76010 817-275-7661 275-3370
Web: www.theatrearlington.org

Theatre Cedar Rapids 102 Third St SE ... Cedar Rapids IA 52401 319-366-8592 366-8593
Web: www.theatrecr.org

Theatre Charlotte 501 Queens Rd ... Charlotte NC 28207 704-376-3777 347-5216
Web: www.theatrecharlotte.org

Theatre For A New Audience
154 Christopher St Ste 3D ... New York NY 10014 212-229-2819 229-2911
TF: 866-811-4111 ■ *Web:* www.tfana.org

Theatre Harrisburg 513 Hurlock St ... Harrisburg PA 17110 717-232-5501 232-5912
Web: www.theatreharrisburg.com

Theatre IV 114 W Broad St ... Richmond VA 23220 804-783-1688 775-2325
TF: 800-235-8687 ■ *Web:* www.theatreiv.org

Theatre of Youth (TOY) 203 Allen St ... Buffalo NY 14201 716-884-4400 819-9653
Web: www.theatreofyouth.org

Theatre Tulsa 412 N Boston Ave ... Tulsa OK 74103 918-587-8402
Web: www.theatretulsa.org

Theatre Tuscaloosa
9500 Old Greensboro Rd Ste 135 ... Tuscaloosa AL 35405 205-391-2277 391-2329
Web: www.theatretusc.com

Theatre Under the Stars 800 Bagby St Ste 200 ... Houston TX 77002 713-558-2600 558-2650
Web: www.tuts.com

TheatreWorks 1100 Hamilton Ct ... Palo Alto CA 94301 650-463-1950 463-1963
Web: www.theatreworks.org

Tihati Productions Ltd
3615 Harding Ave Ste 507 ... Honolulu HI 96816 808-735-0292 735-9479
TF: 877-846-5554 ■ *Web:* www.tihati.com

Toledo Repertoire Theatre 16 Tenth St ... Toledo OH 43604 419-243-9277
Web: www.toledorep.org

Trinity Repertory Co 201 Washington St ... Providence RI 02903 401-521-1100 751-5577
Web: www.trinityrep.com

Tuscaloosa Children's Theatre
10889 Magnolia Ln ... Coaling AL 35453 205-462-0100

Unicorn Theatre 3828 Main St ... Kansas City MO 64111 816-531-7529 531-0421
Web: www.unicorntheatre.org

Warehouse Theatre 37 Augusta St ... Greenville SC 29601 864-235-6948
Web: www.warehousetheatre.com

West Virginia Public Theatre 111 High St ... Morgantown WV 26505 304-291-4117 291-4125
Web: www.wvpublictheatre.org

Phone Fax

Western Nevada Musical Theater Co
Western Nevada College
2201 W College Pkwy Cedar Bldg 113 ... Carson City NV 89703 775-445-4249 445-3154
Web: www.wnc.edu

Westport Community Theatre 110 Myrtle Ave ... Westport CT 06880 203-226-1983
Web: www.westportcommunitytheatre.com

Wild Swan Theater 6175 Jackson Rd Ste B ... Ann Arbor MI 48103 734-995-0530 668-7292
Web: www.wildswantheater.org

Wilma Theater 265 S Broad St ... Philadelphia PA 19107 215-893-9456 893-0895
TF: 800-732-0999 ■ *Web:* www.wilmatheater.org

Wilmington Drama League (WDL) 10 W Lea Blvd ... Wilmington DE 19802 302-764-1172 764-7904
Web: www.wilmingtondramaleague.org

Yale Repertory Theatre
1120 Chapel St PO Box 1257 ... New Haven CT 06505 203-432-1234 432-6423
TF: 800-973-2837 ■ *Web:* www.yalerep.org

577 PERFUMES

SEE ALSO Cosmetics, Skin Care, and Other Personal Care Products p. 2176

Phone Fax

Avon Products Inc 1345 Ave of the Americas ... New York NY 10017 212-282-7000 282-6035
NYSE: AVP ■ *TF Cust Svc:* 800-367-2866 ■ *Web:* www.avon.com

Bijan Boutique 420 N Rodeo Dr ... Beverly Hills CA 90210 310-273-6544 273-6535
Web: www.bijan.com

Chanel Inc 15 E 57th St ... New York NY 10022 212-355-5050 752-1851
TF: 800-550-0005 ■ *Web:* www.chanel.com

Coty & Lancaster Inc 350 Fifth Ave 17th Fl ... New York NY 10118 212-479-4300
Web: www.coty.com

Crabtree & Evelyn Ltd 102 Peake Brook Rd ... Woodstock CT 06281 860-928-2761 928-1296
TF: 800-272-2873 ■ *Web:* www.crabtree-evelyn.com

Eagle Marketing Inc Perfume Originals Products Div
2412 Sequoia Pk ... Yukon OK 73099 800-233-7424 354-7882*
**Fax Area Code:* 405 ■ *TF:* 800-233-7424 ■ *Web:* www.eimi.com

Elizabeth Arden Inc 2400 NE 145th Ave 2nd Fl ... Miramar FL 33027 954-364-6900 364-6910
NASDAQ: RDEN ■ *TF:* 800-326-7337 ■ *Web:* www.elizabetharden.com

Inter Parfums Inc 551 Fifth Ave Ste 1500 ... New York NY 10176 212-983-2640 983-4197
NASDAQ: IPAR ■ *Web:* www.interparfumsinc.com

Key West Aloe 13095 N Telecom Pkwy ... Tampa FL 33637 305-293-1885 363-1443*
**Fax Area Code:* 786 ■ *TF:* 800-445-2563 ■ *Web:* www.keywestaloe.com

Parfums de Coeur Ltd 85 Old Kings Hwy N ... Darien CT 06820 800-887-2738 655-3193*
**Fax Area Code:* 203 ■ *TF:* 800-887-2738 ■ *Web:* www.fragrancerebel.com

Parfums Givenchy LLC 19 E 57th St ... New York NY 10022 212-931-2600
Web: www.givenchybeauty.com

ULTA Beauty 1000 Remington Blvd Ste 120 ... Bolingbrook IL 60440 630-410-4800 226-8210
TF: 866-983-8582 ■ *Web:* www.ulta.com

578 PERSONAL EMERGENCY RESPONSE SYSTEMS

Phone Fax

AlertOne Services Inc
1000 Commerce Park Dr Ste 300 ... Williamsport PA 17701 866-581-4540 565-0635
TF Cust Svc: 866-581-4540 ■ *Web:* www.alert-1.com

Life Alert 16027 Ventura Blvd ... Encino CA 91436 818-700-7000
TF: 800-920-3410 ■ *Web:* www.lifealert.com

Life Technologies Corp 3175 Staley Rd ... Grand Island NY 14072 800-955-6288 331-2286
TF: 800-955-6288 ■ *Web:* www.lifetechnologies.com

LifeFone 16 Yellowstone Ave ... White Plains NY 10607 888-687-0451 686-0669*
**Fax Area Code:* 914 ■ *TF:* 888-687-0451 ■ *Web:* www.lifefone.com

579 PERSONAL PROTECTIVE EQUIPMENT & CLOTHING

SEE ALSO Medical Supplies - Mfr p. 2733; Safety Equipment - Mfr p. 3130; Safety Equipment - Whol p. 3131; Sporting Goods p. 3182

Phone Fax

Aearo Co 5457 W 79th St ... Indianapolis IN 46268 317-692-6666 692-6772
TF: 877-327-4332 ■ *Web:* earsc.com

AGO Industries Inc
500 Sovereign Rd PO Box 7132 ... London ON N6M1A6 519-452-3780 452-3053
Web: www.ago1.com

Airborne Systems Group 5800 Magnolia Ave ... Pennsauken NJ 08109 856-663-1275 663-3028
Web: www.airborne-sys.com/

Allen-Vanguard Corp 2400 St Laurent Blvd ... Ottawa ON K1G5B4 613-739-9646
TF: 800-644-9078 ■ *Web:* www.allenvanguard.com

Ansell Healthcare Inc 111 S Wood Ave Ste 200 ... Iselin NJ 08830 732-345-5400 219-5114
TF: 800-365-2282 ■ *Web:* www.ansell.com

Bell Sports Corp 6225 N St Hwy 161 Ste 300 ... Irving TX 75038 469-417-6600 492-1639
TF: 866-525-2357 ■ *Web:* bellsports.com

Biomarine Inc 456 Creamery Way ... Exton PA 19341 610-524-8800 524-8807
TF: 800-378-2287 ■ *Web:* www.neutronicsinc.com

Bullard Co 1898 Safety Way ... Cynthiana KY 41031 859-234-6611 234-4352
TF: 800-227-0423 ■ *Web:* www.bullard.com

Carleton Technologies Inc 10 Cobham Dr ... Orchard Park NY 14127 716-662-0006 662-0747
Web: resources.carltech.com

Choctaw-Kaul Distribution Co
3540 Vinewood Ave ... Detroit MI 48208 313-894-9494 894-7977
Web: www.choctawkaul.com

David Clark Company Inc 360 Franklin St ... Worcester MA 01615 508-751-5800 753-5827*
**Fax:* Sales ■ *TF Cust Svc:* 800-298-6235 ■ *Web:* www.davidclark.com

Desco Industries Inc 3651 Walnut Ave ... Chino CA 91710 909-627-8178 627-7449
Web: desco.descoindustries.com

Encon Safety Products Co
6825 W Sam Houston Pkwy N PO Box 3826 ... Houston TX 77041 713-466-1449 466-1703
TF: 800-283-6266 ■ *Web:* www.enconsafety.com

Essex PB&R Corp 8007 Chivvis Dr ... Saint Louis MO 63123 314-351-6116

Fibre-Metal 2000 Plainfield Pk PO Box 248 ... Cranston RI 02921 800-430-4110 572-6346
TF: 800-430-4110 ■ *Web:* www.honeywellsafety.com

Fire-End & Croker Corp
Seven Westchester Plz ... Elmsford NY 10523 914-592-3640 592-3892
TF: 800-759-3473 ■ *Web:* www.fire-end.com

				Phone	Fax
Galls Inc 2680 Palumbo Dr	Lexington	KY	40509	859-266-7227	
TF: 800-477-7766 ■ *Web:* www.galls.com					
General Econopak Inc 1725 N Sixth St	Philadelphia	PA	19122	215-763-8200	763-8118
TF: 888-871-8568 ■ *Web:* www.generaleconopak.com					
Gexco 3460 Vine St	Norco	CA	92860	951-735-4951	
Web: gexcoenterprises.com					
Globe Mfg Co 37 Loudon Rd PO Box 128	Pittsfield	NH	03263	603-435-8323	435-6388
TF: 800-232-8323 ■ *Web:* www.globeturnoutgear.com					
Graham Medical Products 2273 Larsen Rd	Green Bay	WI	54303	920-494-8701	*
**Fax:* Cust Svc ■ *TF Cust Svc:* 800-558-6765 ■ *Web:* www.grahammedical.com					
Handgards Inc 901 Hawkins Blvd	El Paso	TX	79915	800-351-8161	779-1312*
**Fax Area Code:* 915 ■ *TF:* 800-351-8161 ■ *Web:* www.handgards.com					
HeatMax Inc 513 Hill Rd PO Box 1191	Dalton	GA	30721	706-226-1800	
TF: 800-432-8629 ■ *Web:* www.heatmax.com					
Helmet House Inc					
26855 Malibu Hill Rd	Calabasas Hills	CA	91301	818-880-0000	
Web: www.helmethouse.com					
Honeywell Safety Products					
2000 Plainfield Pike	Cranston	RI	02921	401-943-4400	572-6346*
**Fax Area Code:* 800 ■ *TF Cust Svc:* 800-430-4110 ■ *Web:* honeywellsafety.com					
ILC Dover Inc One Moonwalker Rd	Frederica	DE	19946	302-335-3911	335-0762
TF: 800-631-9567 ■ *Web:* www.ilcdover.com					
Indiana Mills & Manufacturing Inc					
18881 US 31 N	Westfield	IN	46074	317-896-9531	896-2142
Web: www.imminet.com					
International Sew-Right Co					
6190 Don Murie St	Niagara Falls	ON	L2E6X8	905-374-3600	374-6121
Web: www.safetyclothing.com					
Kappler Inc 115 Grimes Dr PO Box 490	Guntersville	AL	35976	256-505-4005	505-4151
TF: 800-600-4019 ■ *Web:* www.kappler.com					
Lakeland Industries Inc 701-7 Koehler Ave	Ronkonkoma	NY	11779	631-981-9700	981-9751
NASDAQ: LAKE ■ *TF:* 800-645-9291 ■ *Web:* www.lakeland.com					
Landauer Inc Two Science Rd	Glenwood	IL	60425	708-755-7000	755-7016
NYSE: LDR ■ *TF:* 800-323-8830 ■ *Web:* www.landauer.com					
Little Rapids Corp 2273 Larsen Rd	Green Bay	WI	54303	920-496-3040	494-5340
TF: 800-496-3040 ■ *Web:* www.littlerapids.com					
Louis M Gerson Company Inc 15 Sproat St	Middleboro	MA	02346	508-947-4000	947-5442
TF: 800-225-8623 ■ *Web:* www.gersonco.com					
MCR Safety 5321 E Shelby Dr	Memphis	TN	38118	901-795-5810	999-3908*
**Fax Area Code:* 800 ■ **Fax:* Sales ■ *TF:* 800-955-6887 ■ *Web:* www.mcrsafety.com					
Medline Industries Inc 1 Medline Pl	Mundelein	IL	60060	847-949-5500	643-3295
TF Cust Svc: 800-351-1512 ■ *Web:* www.medline.com					
Miller Products Company Inc					
2511 S Tricenter Blvd	Durham	NC	27713	919-313-2100	313-2101
TF: 800-782-7437 ■ *Web:* www.millerproducts.com					
Moldex Metric Inc 10111 W Jefferson Blvd	Culver City	CA	90232	310-837-6500	837-9563*
**Fax:* Sales ■ *TF:* 800-421-0668 ■ *Web:* www.moldex.com					
MTS Safety Products Inc (MTS) PO Box 204	Golden	MS	38847	800-647-8168	329-9687
TF General: 800-647-8168 ■ *Web:* www.mts-safety.com					
National Safety Apparel Inc (NSA)					
3865 W 150th St	Cleveland	OH	44111	800-553-0672	941-1130*
**Fax Area Code:* 216 ■ *TF:* 800-553-0672 ■ *Web:* www.nsamfg.com					
Newtex Industries Inc 8050 Victor Mendon Rd	Victor	NY	14564	585-924-9135	924-4645
TF: 800-836-1001 ■ *Web:* www.newtex.com					
Performance Designs Inc					
1300 E International Speedway Blvd	DeLand	FL	32724	386-738-2224	734-8297
Web: www.performancedesigns.com					
Plastic Safety Systems Inc 2444 Baldwin Rd	Cleveland	OH	44104	800-662-6338	231-2702*
**Fax Area Code:* 216 ■ *TF:* 800-662-6338 ■ *Web:* www.plasticsafety.com					
PolyConversions Inc 505 Condit Dr	Rantoul	IL	61866	217-893-3330	893-3003
TF: 888-893-3330 ■ *Web:* www.polyconversions.com					
Precept Medical Products Inc					
370 Airport Rd PO Box 2400	Arden	NC	28704	828-681-0209	681-8626
TF: 800-851-4431 ■ *Web:* www.preceptmed.com					
Protech Armored Products					
13386 International Pkwy	Jacksonville	FL	32218	413-445-4000	445-4455
Web: protecharmored.com					
Right-Gard Corp 531 N Fourth St	Denver	PA	17517	717-336-7594	
Saf-T-Gard International Inc 205 Huehl Rd	Northbrook	IL	60062	847-291-1600	291-1610
TF: 800-548-4273 ■ *Web:* www.saftgard.com					
Safe-T-Gard Corp 12105 W Cedar Dr	Lakewood	CO	80228	303-763-8900	763-8071
TF Cust Svc: 800-356-9026 ■ *Web:* www.safetgard.com					
Scott Health & Safety					
4320 Goldmine Rd PO Box 569	Monroe	NC	28110	704-291-8300	291-8340
TF: 800-247-7257 ■ *Web:* www.scottsafety.com					
Seattle Manufacturing Corp					
6930 Salashan Pkwy	Ferndale	WA	98248	360-366-5534	366-5723
TF: 800-426-6251 ■ *Web:* www.smcgear.net					
Sellstrom Manufacturing Co					
2050 Hammond Dr	Schaumburg	IL	60173	847-358-2000	358-8564
TF: 800-323-7402 ■ *Web:* www.sellstrom.com					
Standard Textile Company Inc					
One Knollcrest Dr	Cincinnati	OH	45237	513-761-9255	761-0467
TF: 800-999-0400 ■ *Web:* www.standardtextile.com					
Steel Grip Inc 700 Garfield St PO Box 747	Danville	IL	61832	217-442-6240	442-9370
TF: 800-223-1595 ■ *Web:* www.steelgripinc.com					
Steele Inc 26112 Iowa Ave NE PO Box 7304	Kingston	WA	98346	360-297-4555	297-2816
TF: 888-783-3538 ■ *Web:* www.steelevest.com					
Steiner Industries 5801 N Tripp Ave	Chicago	IL	60646	773-588-3444	588-3450
TF: 800-621-4515 ■ *Web:* www.steinerindustries.com					
Stemaco Products Inc 2211 Ogden Rd	Rock Hill	SC	29730	803-328-2191	328-2808
Strong Enterprises Inc 11236 Satellite Blvd	Orlando	FL	32837	407-859-9317	850-6978
TF: 800-344-6319 ■ *Web:* www.strongparachutes.com					
Tingley Rubber Corp					
1551 S Washington Ave Ste 403 Ste 403	Piscataway	NJ	08854	800-631-5498	757-9239*
**Fax Area Code:* 866 ■ *TF Cust Svc:* 800-631-5498 ■ *Web:* www.tingleyrubber.com					
United Knitting LP 310 Industrial Dr SW	Cleveland	TN	37311	423-476-9163	476-1163
Web: www.unitedknitting.com					
United Pioneer Co 2777 Summer St Ste 206	Stamford	CT	06905	800-466-9823	466-9828
TF: 800-466-9823 ■ *Web:* www.b340.com					
Uvex Safety Inc 900 Douglas Pk	Smithfield	RI	02917	800-682-0839	322-1330
TF General: 800-682-0839 ■ *Web:* www.uvex.us					
White Knight Engineered Products					
9525 Monroe Rd Ste 100	Charlotte	NC	28270	704-542-6876	
TF: 888-743-4700 ■ *Web:* www.wkep.com					
Wolf X-Ray Corp 100 W Industry Ct	Deer Park	NY	11729	631-242-9729	925-5003
TF Cust Svc: 800-356-9729 ■ *Web:* www.wolfxray.com					

580 PEST CONTROL SERVICES

				Phone	Fax
A 1 Termite & Pest Control Inc					
2686 Morganton Blvd Sw	Lenoir	NC	28645	828-758-4312	
Web: www.a1termitepc.com					
Action Pest Control Inc					
2301 S Green River Rd	Evansville	IN	47715	812-477-5546	
Web: www.actionpest.com					
Al Hoffer's Pest Protection Inc					
12329 NW 35 St	Coral Springs	FL	33065	866-549-7987	
TF: 866-549-7987 ■ *Web:* alhoffer.com					
Allgood Services Inc 106 Roosevelt St	Dublin	GA	31021	478-272-6271	
Web: www.allgoodpestsolutions.com					
Antimite Associates Inc 5867 Pine Ave	Chino Hills	CA	91709	909-606-2300	
Web: www.antimitepestcontrol.com					
Bain Pest Control Service Inc					
1320 Middlesex St	Lowell	MA	01851	978-452-9621	
Web: bainpestcontrol.com					
Banks Pest Control Inc					
215 Golden State Ave	Bakersfield	CA	93301	661-323-7858	
Web: bankspest.com					
Bird Solutions International					
1338 N Melrose Dr Ste H	Vista	CA	92083	760-758-9747	
Web: www.birdsolutions.com					
Black Pest Prevention Inc					
605 Springbrook Rd	Charlotte	NC	28217	704-522-9222	
Web: www.blackpest.com					
Bright Pest Control Co 4340 Sanita Ct	Louisville	KY	40213	502-452-9600	
Web: brightpest.com					
Bug Off Exterminators Inc					
1064 NW 54th St	Fort Lauderdale	FL	33309	954-772-8338	
Web: bugoffexterminatorsflorida.com					
Bug-Out Service Inc					
5951 Arlington Expwy	Jacksonville	FL	32211	904-743-8272	
Web: bugoutservice.com					
Burns Pest Elimination Inc					
2620 W Grovers Ave	Phoenix	AZ	85053	602-971-4782	
Web: burnspestelimination.com					
Clean Master 2201 Park Ave	Chico	CA	95928	530-343-0123	
Web: www.onlyforpc.com					
Cook's Pest Control Inc 1741 Fifth Ave SE	Decatur	AL	35601	256-355-3285	
Web: www.cookspest.com					
Copesan Services Inc					
W175 N5711 Technology Dr	Menomonee Falls	WI	53051	800-267-3726	783-6267*
**Fax Area Code:* 262 ■ *TF:* 800-267-3726 ■ *Web:* www.copesan.com					
Craig Thomas Pest Control Inc					
1186 Route 9G	Hyde Park	NY	12538	845-229-6833	
Web: callcraig.com					
Crane Pest Control Inc 2700 Geary Blvd	San Francisco	CA	94118	415-922-1666	
Web: www.cranepestcontrol.com					
Dewey Services Inc 939 E Union St	Pasadena	CA	91106	626-568-9248	
Web: deweypest.com					
Dodson Bros Exterminating Company Inc					
3712 Campbell Ave	Lynchburg	VA	24501	434-847-9051	847-2034
Web: www.dodsonbros.com					
Eradico Services Inc 41169 Vincenti Ct	Novi	MI	48375	248-477-4800	
Web: www.eradicoservices.com					
Fischer Environmental Service Inc					
1980 Surgi Dr	Mandeville	LA	70448	800-391-2565	626-7450*
**Fax Area Code:* 985 ■ *TF:* 800-391-2565 ■ *Web:* www.fischerenv.com					
Florida Pest Control & Chemical Company Inc					
116 NW 16th Ave	Gainesville	FL	32601	352-376-2661	376-2791
Web: www.flapest.com					
Gilbert Industries Inc 5611 Krueger Dr	Jonesboro	AR	72401	870-932-6070	
Web: www.gilbertinc.com					
Green Lawn Fertilizing Inc					
1004 Saunders Ln	West Chester	PA	19380	610-524-2175	
Web: www.greenlawnfertilizing.com					
Havasu Pest Control Inc					
2716 Maricopa Ave	Lake Havasu City	AZ	86406	928-855-1054	855-3329
Home Paramount Pest Control Cos Inc					
PO Box 850	Forest Hill	MD	21050	410-510-0700	
TF: 888-888-4663 ■ *Web:* www.homeparamount.com					
Horizon Termite & Pest Control Corp					
45 Cross Ave	Midland Park	NJ	07432	201-447-2530	447-9541
TF: 888-612-2847 ■ *Web:* www.horizonpestcontrol.com					
Knockout Pest Control Inc 1009 Front St	Uniondale	NY	11553	516-489-7817	489-4348
TF: 800-244-7378 ■ *Web:* www.knockoutpest.com					
Lawn Doctor Inc 142 SR 34	Holmdel	NJ	07733	800-631-5660	
TF: 800-631-5660 ■ *Web:* www.lawndoctor.com					
Light Brigade Inc, The 837 Industry Dr	Tukwila	WA	98188	206-575-0404	
Web: www.lightbrigade.com					
Loyal Termite & Pest Control Company Inc					
2610 E Parham Rd	Richmond	VA	23228	804-737-7777	
Web: www.loyalpest.com					
Massey Services Inc 315 Groveland St E	Orlando	FL	32804	407-645-2500	802-3736*
**Fax:* Cust Svc ■ *TF:* 888-262-7739 ■ *Web:* www.masseyservices.com					
McCall Service Inc 2861 College St	Jacksonville	FL	32205	904-389-5561	389-3212
TF: 800-342-6948 ■ *Web:* www.mccallservice.com					
NaturaLawn of America Inc One E Church St	Frederick	MD	21701	301-694-5440	846-0320
TF: 800-989-5444 ■ *Web:* www.naturalawn.com					
Nutrilawn Inc 25-1040 Martin Grove Rd	Toronto	ON	M9W4W4	416-620-7100	620-7771
Web: www.nutrilawn.com					

Phone *Fax*

Ohio Exterminating Company Inc
1347 N High St. . . . . Columbus OH 43201 614-294-6311
Web: ohioexterminating.com

Oliver Exterminating Corp 658 NW 99th St. . . . . Miami FL 33150 305-758-1811
Web: guaranteepest.com

Orkin Exterminating Co Inc
2170 Piedmont Rd NE . . . . . Atlanta GA 30324 877-250-1652 265-0238*
**Fax Area Code:* 510 ■ **Fax:* Cust Svc ■ *TF:* 844-498-7458 ■ *Web:* www.orkin.com

PCO Services Corp 5840 Falbourne St. . . . . Mississauga ON L5R4B5 905-502-9700
Web: www.orkincanada.ca

Pest Fog Inc 1424 Bonita . . . . . Corpus Christi TX 78404 361-884-8214 884-5903
Web: pestfog.com

Pest Shield Pest Control Inc
15329 Tradesman . . . . . San Antonio TX 78249 210-525-8823
Web: www.sanantonio-pestcontrol.com

Pestmaster Services Inc 137 East S St. . . . . Bishop CA 93514 760-873-8100
Web: www.pestmaster.com

Plunkett's Pest Control 808 E Second St . . . . . Duluth MN 55805 218-723-8464
Web: www.plunketts.net

Presto-X Co 10421 Portal Rd Ste 101 . . . . . Gretna NE 68028 800-759-1942 554-1544*
**Fax Area Code:* 402 ■ *TF:* 800-759-1942 ■ *Web:* www.prestox.com

Railinc Corp 7001 Weston Pkwy Ste 200 . . . . . Cary NC 27513 919-651-5193
Web: www.railinc.com

Rollins Inc 2170 Piedmont Rd NE. . . . . Atlanta GA 30324 404-888-2000 888-2672*
NYSE: ROL ■ **Fax:* Hum Res ■ *Web:* www.rollins.com

Rottler Pest & Lawn Solutions
8625 St Charles Rock Rd . . . . . Saint Louis MO 63114 314-426-6100
Web: www.rottler.com

Sandwich Isle Pest Solutions Inc
96-1368 Waihona St. . . . . Pearl City HI 96782 808-456-7716
Web: www.sandwichisle.com

Schendel Pest Services 1035 SE Quincy St . . . . . Topeka KS 66612 785-232-9357 232-4165
TF: 800-591-7378 ■ *Web:* www.schendelpest.com

Scotts Lawn Service 14111 Scottslawn Rd. . . . . Marysville OH 43040 937-644-0011 578-5444
TF Cust Svc: 888-270-3714 ■ *Web:* www.scotts.com

Serfco Termite & Pest Control Inc
1701 S Walton Blvd . . . . . Bentonville AR 72712 479-273-2220

Skyline Pest Solutions Inc
1745 Pennsylvania Ave. . . . . Mcdonough GA 30253 678-432-5464
Web: www.skylinepest.com

Smithereen Exterminators Inc
7400 N Melvina Ave . . . . . Niles IL 60714 847-647-0010 647-0606
TF: 800-336-3500 ■ *Web:* smithereen.com

Sprague Pest Solutions Inc
2725 Pacific Ave Ste 200 . . . . . Tacoma WA 98402 253-272-4400
Web: www.spraguepest.com

Spring-Green Lawn Care Corp
11909 Spaulding School Dr. . . . . Plainfield IL 60585 815-436-8777 436-9056
TF: 800-435-4051 ■ *Web:* www.spring-green.com

Steritech Group Inc, The 7600 Little Ave . . . . . Charlotte NC 28226 704-544-1900
Web: www.steritech.com

Sure Thing Pest Control
11541 Goldcoast Dr . . . . . Cincinnati OH 45249 513-247-0030
Web: surethingpestcontrol.net

Terminix International Company LP
860 Ridge Lk Blvd . . . . . Memphis TN 38120 866-399-0453 363-8541*
**Fax Area Code:* 901 ■ **Fax:* Mktg ■ *TF:* 866-399-0453 ■ *Web:* www.terminix.com

Terminix Service Inc 3618 Fernandina Rd . . . . . Columbia SC 29202 803-772-1783
Web: www.terminixsvc.com

Tomlinson Bomberger Lawn Care & Landscaping Inc
3055 Yellow Goose Rd . . . . . Lancaster PA 17601 717-399-1991
Web: www.tbll.com

TruGreen ChemLawn 860 Ridge Lk Blvd. . . . . Memphis TN 38120 866-369-9539 681-1900*
**Fax Area Code:* 901 ■ *TF:* 866-369-9539 ■ *Web:* www.trugreen.com

Truly Nolen of America Inc
3636 E Speedway Blvd . . . . . Tucson AZ 85716 800-528-3442 322-4002*
**Fax Area Code:* 520 ■ *TF:* 800-468-7859 ■ *Web:* www.trulynolen.com

TruTech LLC PO Box 6849 . . . . . Marietta GA 30065 770-977-2034
Web: www.trutechinc.com

Turf Management Systems LLC PO Box 26389. . . . . Birmingham AL 35260 205-979-8604 979-6063
Web: www.turfmanagementsystems.com

Waltham Services Inc 817 Moody St. . . . . Waltham MA 02453 781-893-1810 893-7921
TF: 866-974-7378 ■ *Web:* www.walthamservices.com

Weed Man 2399 Royal Windsor Dr . . . . . Mississauga ON L5J1K9 905-823-8300
Web: www.weedmancanada.com

Western Exterminator Co 305 N Crescent Way. . . . . Anaheim CA 92801 714-517-9000
TF: 800-698-2440 ■ *Web:* www.westernexterminator.com

PESTICIDES

581 PET PRODUCTS

SEE ALSO Leather Goods - Personal p. 2640; Livestock & Poultry Feeds - Prepared p. 2672

Phone *Fax*

Ainsworth Pet Nutrition 18746 Mill St . . . . . Meadville PA 16335 814-724-7710 337-2743
Web: www.ainsworthpets.com

Amalgamated Dairies Ltd 79 Water St . . . . . Summerside PE C1N1A6 902-888-5088
Web: www.adl.ca

American Nutrition Inc 2813 Wall Ave . . . . . Ogden UT 84401 801-394-3477
Web: www.anibrands.com

Arctic Glacier Holdings Inc 625 Henry Ave. . . . . Winnipeg MB R3A0V1 204-772-2473
TF: 888-573-9237 ■ *Web:* www.arcticglacier.com

Bailey Farms LLC 549 Karem Dr . . . . . Marshall WI 53559 608-655-3439
TF: 800-655-1705 ■ *Web:* www.baileyfarmspets.com

Baker Boy Bake Shop Inc 170 Gta Dr . . . . . Dickinson ND 58601 701-225-4444
Web: www.bakerboy.com

BioZyme Inc 6010 Stockyards Expy . . . . . Saint Joseph MO 64504 816-238-3326 238-7549
TF: 800-821-3070 ■ *Web:* www.biozymeinc.com

Phone *Fax*

Church & Dwight Company Inc
469 N Harrison St. . . . . Princeton NJ 08543 609-683-5900
NYSE: CHD ■ *Web:* www.churchdwight.com

Clorox Co 1221 Broadway . . . . . Oakland CA 94612 510-271-7000 832-1463
NYSE: CLX ■ *TF Cust Svc:* 800-424-9300 ■ *Web:* www.thecloroxcompany.com

Companion Pets Inc (CPI)
2001 N Black Canyon Hwy . . . . . Phoenix AZ 85009 602-255-0166 255-0841
TF: 800-646-3611 ■ *Web:* www.cpipets.com

Doctors Foster & Smith Inc
2253 Air Pk Rd PO Box 100 . . . . . Rhinelander WI 54501 715-369-3305 562-7169*
**Fax Area Code:* 800 ■ **Fax:* Cust Svc ■ *TF:* 800-826-7206 ■ *Web:* www.drsfostersmith.com

Doskocil Mfg Company Inc PO Box 1246. . . . . Arlington TX 76004 877-738-6283
TF: 877-738-6283 ■ *Web:* www.petmate.com

Eagle Pack Pet Foods Inc 200 Ames Pond Dr. . . . . Tewksbury MA 01876 574-259-7834
TF: 800-255-5959 ■ *Web:* www.eaglepack.com

Efficas Inc 7007 Winchester Cir Ste 120 . . . . . Boulder CO 80301 303-381-2070
TF: 866-446-0388 ■ *Web:* www.efficas.com

FL Emmert Co Inc 2007 Dunlap St. . . . . Cincinnati OH 45214 513-721-5808 721-6087
TF: 800-441-3343 ■ *Web:* www.emmert.com

Hartz Mountain Corp, The 400 Plz Dr . . . . . Secaucus NJ 07094 800-275-1414 271-0164*
**Fax Area Code:* 201 ■ *TF:* 800-275-1414 ■ *Web:* www.hartz.com

Healthy Pet 6960 Salashan Pkwy. . . . . Ferndale WA 98248 360-734-7415 671-1588
TF: 800-242-2287 ■ *Web:* www.absorptioncorp.com

Heath Manufacturing Co 140 Mill St. . . . . Coopersville MI 49404 616-997-8181 997-9491
Web: www.heathmfg.com

Hi-Tek Rations Inc PO Box 1223. . . . . Dublin GA 31040 478-272-8826 275-7510
Web: www.hitekrations.com

Hill's Pet Nutrition Inc 400 SW Eigth St. . . . . Topeka KS 66603 785-354-8523 368-5786
TF General: 800-569-7913 ■ *Web:* www.hillspet.com

IAMS Co 3700 Ohio 65. . . . . Leipsic OH 45856 419-943-4267
TF Cust Svc: 800-675-3849 ■ *Web:* www.iams.com

Jeffers Inc 310 W Saunders Rd PO Box 100 . . . . . Dothan AL 36301 334-793-6257 793-5179
TF: 800-533-3377 ■ *Web:* www.jefferspet.com

John A Van Den Bosch Co 4511 Holland Ave. . . . . Holland MI 49424 800-968-6477
TF: 800-968-6477 ■ *Web:* www.vbosch.com

Joy Dog Food PO Box 305. . . . . Pinckneyville IL 62274 800-245-4125 357-3651*
**Fax Area Code:* 618 ■ *TF:* 800-245-4125 ■ *Web:* www.joypetfood.com

Kaytee Products Inc 521 Clay St . . . . . Chilton WI 53014 920-849-2321 849-7044
TF: 800-669-9580 ■ *Web:* www.kaytee.com

Lake Country Foods Inc 132 S Concord Rd . . . . . Oconomowoc WI 53066 262-567-5521
Web: www.lcfoods.com

Manna Pro Corp
707 Spirit 40 Pk Dr Ste 150 . . . . . Chesterfield MO 63005 800-690-9908
TF: 800-690-9908 ■ *Web:* www.mannapro.com

Mark Hershey Farms Inc 479 Horseshoe Pk . . . . . Lebanon PA 17042 717-867-4624 867-4313
TF: 888-801-3301 ■ *Web:* www.markhersheyfarms.com

Mars Snack Food 800 High St. . . . . Hackettstown NJ 07840 908-852-1000 850-2734
TF: 800-551-0895 ■ *Web:* www.mars.com

MIDWEST Homes for Pets
3142 S Cowan Rd PO Box 1031. . . . . Muncie IN 47302 765-289-3355 289-6524
TF: 800-428-8560 ■ *Web:* www.midwesthomes4pets.com

Moyer & Son Inc 113 E Reliance Rd . . . . . Souderton PA 18964 215-799-2000 721-2814
TF: 866-669-3747 ■ *Web:* www.emoyer.com

Multipet International Inc
265 W Commercial Ave . . . . . Moonachie NJ 07074 201-438-6600 438-2990
TF: 800-900-6738 ■ *Web:* www.multipet.com

Natural Life Pet Products Inc
205 E 29th St . . . . . Pittsburg KS 66762 620-230-0888 230-0403
TF: 800-367-2391 ■ *Web:* www.nlpp.com

Nealanders International Inc
6980 Creditview Rd . . . . . Mississauga ON L5N8E2 905-812-7300
TF: 800-263-1939 ■ *Web:* www.nealanders.com

Nestle Purina PetCare Co
801 Chouteau Ave. . . . . Saint Louis MO 63102 314-982-1000 982-3327
TF: 800-778-7462 ■ *Web:* www.purina.com

North States Industries Inc 1507 92nd Ln NE. . . . . Blaine MN 55449 763-486-1756 486-1763
TF: 800-848-8421 ■ *Web:* www.northstatesind.com

Orrco Inc 515 Collins Blvd PO Box 147 . . . . . Orrville OH 44667 330-683-5015 683-0738
TF: 800-321-3085 ■ *Web:* www.orrvillepet.com

Penn-Plax Inc 35 Marcus Blvd . . . . . Hauppauge NY 11788 631-273-3787 273-2196
TF: 800-645-6055 ■ *Web:* www.pennplax.com

Pet Food Express 500 85th Ave. . . . . oakland CA 94621 510-924-3300 346-7788
Web: www.petfoodexpress.com

Pet Safe International 10427 Electric Ave . . . . . Knoxville TN 37932 865-777-5404 777-5419
TF Cust Svc: 800-732-2677 ■ *Web:* petsafe.net/home

Pet Supermarket Inc 1100 International Pkwy . . . . . Sunrise FL 33323 954-351-0834 351-0897
TF: 866-434-1990 ■ *Web:* www.petsupermarket.com

Pet Supplies "Plus" Inc
17197 N Laurel Prk Dre Ste 402. . . . . Livonia MI 48152 734-793-6600 374-7900*
**Fax Area Code:* 248 ■ *Web:* www.petsuppliesplus.com

Pet Valu Canada Inc 225 Royal Crest Crt . . . . . Markham ON L3R9X6 905-946-1200
TF: 800-845-4759 ■ *Web:* www.petvalu.com

PETCO Animal Supplies Inc 9125 Rehco Rd . . . . . San Diego CA 92121 858-453-7845 784-3489
TF: 877-738-6742 ■ *Web:* www.petco.com

PetFoodDirect.com 189 Main St . . . . . Harleysville PA 19438 215-513-1999 894-5034*
**Fax Area Code:* 877 ■ *TF Cust Svc:* 877-738-3663 ■ *Web:* www.petfooddirect.com

Petland Discounts Inc 355 Crooked Hill Rd. . . . . Brentwood NY 11717 631-273-6363 273-6513
Web: www.petlanddiscounts.com

Petland Inc 250 Riverside St . . . . . Chillicothe OH 45601 740-775-2464 775-2575
TF: 800-221-5935 ■ *Web:* petland.com

PetMed Express Inc 1441 SW 29th Ave . . . . . Pompano Beach FL 33069 954-979-5995 971-0544
NASDAQ: PETS ■ *TF:* 800-738-6337 ■ *Web:* www.1800petmeds.com

PETsMART Inc 19601 N 27th Ave . . . . . Phoenix AZ 85027 623-580-6100 580-6502
NASDAQ: PETM ■ *TF Cust Svc:* 800-738-1385 ■ *Web:* www.petsmart.com

Pied Piper Mills Inc 423 E Lake Dr. . . . . Hamlin TX 79520 325-576-3684 576-3460
Web: www.piedpiperpetfood.net

Prevue Pet Products Inc 224 N Maplewood Ave. . . . . Chicago IL 60612 312-243-3624 243-3624
TF: 800-243-3624 ■ *Web:* prevuepet.com

Prince Corp 8351 County Rd H. . . . . Marshfield WI 54449 715-384-3105 387-6924
TF: 800-777-2486 ■ *Web:* www.prince-corp.com

Ralco Nutrition Inc 1600 Hahn Rd . . . . . Marshall MN 56258 800-533-5306 532-5740*
**Fax Area Code:* 507 ■ *TF:* 800-533-5306 ■ *Web:* www.ralconutrition.com

				Phone	Fax
Rich Products Corp One Robert Rich Way *Web:* www.byronsbbq.com	Buffalo	NY	14213	716-878-8000	
Rolf C. Hagen Corp 305 Forbes Blvd *TF Cust Svc:* 800-724-2436 ■ *Web:* www.hagen.com	Mansfield	MA	02048	508-339-9531	339-6973
Simmons Pet Foods Inc 316 N Hico *TF:* 866-463-6738 ■ *Web:* simmonspetfood.simmonsglobal.com	Siloam Springs	AR	72761	866-463-6738	
Star Milling Co 24067 Water St *TF:* 800-733-6455 ■ *Web:* www.starmilling.com	Perris	CA	92570	951-657-3143	657-3114
Sunshine Mills Inc 500 Sixth St SW *Fax: Sales ■ *TF:* 800-633-3349 ■ *Web:* www.sunshinemills.com	Red Bay	AL	35582	256-356-9541	356-8287*
Texas Farm Products Co 915 S Fredonia St *TF:* 800-392-3110 ■ *Web:* www.texasfarm.com	Nacogdoches	TX	75964	936-564-3711	560-8200
Triumph Pet Industries Inc 500 Sixth St SW *Fax Area Code: 800 ■ *TF:* 800-633-3349 ■ *Web:* triumphpetfood.com	Red Bay	AL	35582	256-356-9541	331-5140*
United Pacific Pet 12060 Cabernet Dr *TF:* 800-979-3333 ■ *Web:* www.uppet.com	Fontana	CA	92337	951-360-8550	360-8540
United Pharmacal Company of Missouri Inc 3705 Pear St *TF:* 800-254-8726 ■ *Web:* www.upco.com	Saint Joseph	MO	64503	816-233-8800	233-9696
Virbac Corp 3200 Meacham Blvd *Web:* www.virbac.com	Fort Worth	TX	76137	817-831-5030	831-8327
Wild Birds Unlimited Inc 11711 N College Ave Ste 146 *TF:* 800-326-4928 ■ *Web:* www.wbu.com	Carmel	IN	46032	317-571-7100	571-7110

582 PETROLEUM & PETROLEUM PRODUCTS - WHOL

				Phone	Fax
A & W Oil Company Inc 1101 N Liberty St *Web:* www.awoil.com	Waynesboro	GA	30830	706-554-2121	554-7825
A.R. Sandri Inc 400 Chapman St *Web:* www.sandri.com	Greenfield	MA	01301	413-772-2121	
Abercrombie Oil Company Inc PO Box 1422 *Web:* www.abercrombieoil.com	Danville	VA	24543	434-792-8022	793-0143
Adams Resources Inc 17 S Briar Hollow Ln *Web:* www.adamsresources.com	Houston	TX	77001	713-881-3600	
Adium Oil Company Inc 310 Blattner Dr	Avon	MN	56310	320-356-7350	
Advance Petroleum Distributing Company Inc 2451 Great SW Pkwy *Web:* www.advancefuel.com	Fort Worth	TX	76106	817-626-5458	624-3102
All Points Coop 120 Eigth St PO Box 80 *Web:* www.allpoints.coop	Gothenburg	NE	69138	308-537-7141	
Allen Oil Co 1215 Old Birmingham Hwy *Web:* www.allenoil.com	Sylacauga	AL	35150	256-245-5478	
Allied Oil & Supply Inc 2209 S 24th St *TF:* 800-333-3717 ■ *Web:* www.alliedoil.com	Omaha	NE	68108	402-344-4343	344-4360
Allied Propane Service Inc 5000 Seaport Ave *Web:* www.alliedpropaneservice.com	Richmond	CA	94804	510-237-7077	
Amber Resources LLC 1543 W 16th St *Web:* www.sawyerpetroleum.com	Long Beach	CA	90813	562-786-8180	
American Biodiesel Inc 171 Saxony Rd Ste 202 *Web:* www.communityfuels.com	Encinitas	CA	92023	760-942-9306	
AmeriGas Propane Inc PO Box 965 *Fax: Mktg ■ *Web:* www.amerigas.com	Valley Forge	PA	19482	610-337-7000	768-7647*
Aos Thermal Compounds LLC 22 Meridian Rd Ste 6 *Web:* www.aosco.com	Eatontown	NJ	07724	732-389-5514	
Apex Oil Company Inc 8235 Forsyth Blvd Ste 400 *Web:* www.apexoil.com	Clayton	MO	63105	314-889-9600	854-8539
Apex-Petroleum Corp 9500 Arena Dr Ste 360 *Web:* www.apexpetroleum.com	Upper Marlboro	MD	20744	301-773-9009	
Arkansas Valley Petroleum Inc 8336 E 73rd St Ste 100 *Web:* arkvalprop.com	Tulsa	OK	74133	918-252-0508	250-4921
Armada Oil & Gas Company Inc 13530 Michigan Ave Ste 400 *Web:* www.armadaoil.com	Dearborn	MI	48126	313-582-1777	
Arr-maz Custom Chemicals Inc 9189 stevedoring rd *Web:* m.arrmaz.com	Convent	LA	70723	225-562-3065	
Ascent Aviation Group Inc One Mill St *Web:* www.ascent1.com	Parish	NY	13131	315-625-7299	
Atlas Oil Co 24501 Ecorse Rd *TF:* 800-878-2000 ■ *Web:* www.atlasoil.com	Taylor	MI	48180	313-292-5500	731-0264
Bagwell Oil Company Inc PO Box 136 *Web:* www.bagwelloil.com	Onancock	VA	23417	757-787-3580	
Beach Oil Company Inc 631 US Hwy 76 PO Box 3010 *Web:* www.beachoil.com	Clarksville	TN	37041	931-358-9303	358-9331
Behnke Lubricants Inc W134N5373 Campbell Dr *Web:* www.jax.com	Menomonee Falls	WI	53051	262-781-8850	
Bell Gas Inc 1811 SE Main St	Roswell	NM	88203	575-622-1733	
Berry Oil 3193 Leigh Ave *Web:* www.berryoil.net	Tetonia	ID	83452	208-456-2271	456-2091
Big River Oil Company Inc 1920 Orchard Ave *Web:* www.bigriveroil.com	Hannibal	MO	63401	573-221-0226	
Blueox Corp 38 N Canal St *Web:* www.blueoxenergy.com	Oxford	NY	13830	607-843-2583	
Blythewood Oil Company Inc 4118 Us Hwy 21 S	Ridgeway	SC	29130	803-754-3319	
Boyett Petroleum 601 McHenry Ave *TF:* 800-545-9212 ■ *Web:* www.boyett.net	Modesto	CA	95350	209-577-6000	577-6040
BP Lubricants USA Inc 1500 Valley Rd *TF:* 800-333-3991 ■ *Web:* www.bp.com	Wayne	NJ	07470	973-633-2200	
Bradco Inc 107-11th Ave PO Box 997 *Web:* www.bradcoinc.com	Holbrook	AZ	86025	928-524-3976	
Bretthauer Oil Co 453 SW Washington St *TF:* 800-359-3113 ■ *Web:* www.bretthauer.com	Hillsboro	OR	97123	503-648-2531	

				Phone	Fax
Brewer Oil Co 2701 Candelaria NE *Web:* www.breweroil.com	Albuquerque	NM	87107	505-884-2040	
Brewer-Hendley Oil Co 207 N Forest Hills School Rd *Web:* brewerhendley.com/	Marshville	NC	28103	704-233-2600	
Broadus Oil Corp of Illinois 201 Dannys Dr Ste 5 *Web:* www.broadusoil.com	Streator	IL	61364	815-673-5515	
Burkett Oil Company Inc 6788 Best Friend Rd *Web:* www.burkettoil.com	Norcross	GA	30071	770-447-8030	
C & R Distributing Inc 8528 Alameda Ave *Web:* www.candrdistributing.com	El Paso	TX	79907	915-860-4205	
Campbell Oil Company Inc 611 Erie St S *TF:* 800-589-8555 ■ *Web:* campbelloil.com	Massillon	OH	44646	330-833-8555	833-1083
Canyon State Oil Company Inc 2640 N 31st Ave *Web:* www.canyonstateoil.com	Phoenix	AZ	85009	602-269-7981	
Cardwell Distributing Inc 8137 S State St *Web:* www.cardwelldist.com	Midvale	UT	84047	801-561-4251	
Cargill Energy PO Box 9300 *TF:* 800-227-4455 ■ *Web:* www.cargill.com	Minneapolis	MN	55440	952-742-7575	
Carson Oil Company Inc 3125 NW 35th Ave PO Box 10948 *TF:* 800-998-7767 ■ *Web:* www.carsonoil.com	Portland	OR	97296	503-224-8500	222-0186
Cavalier Energy Inc Five Ave SW Ste 2500-255 *Web:* cavalierenergy.com	Calgary	AB	T2P3G6	403-268-3940	
Center Oil Co 600 Mason Ridge Ctr Dr Second Fl *Web:* www.centeroil.com	Saint Louis	MO	63141	314-682-3500	682-3599
Champlain Oil Company Inc 45 San Remo Dr *Web:* www.champlainoil.com	South Burlington	VT	05403	802-864-5380	
Chemoil Corp 4 Embarcadero Ctr 34thFl *Web:* www.chemoil.com	San Francisco	CA	94111	415-268-2700	268-2701
Chronister Oil Co 2026 N Republic St	Springfield	IL	62702	217-523-5050	
Coen Oil Co 1045 W Chestnut St *Web:* www.coenoil.com	Washington	PA	15301	724-223-5515	
Colonial Group Inc 101 N Lathrop Ave *Web:* colonialgroupinc.com	Savannah	GA	31415	912-236-1331	235-3881
Condon Oil Co 126 E Jackson St *TF:* 800-452-1212 ■ *Web:* www.condoncompanies.com	Ripon	WI	54971	920-748-3186	748-3201
Consolidated Energy Co 910 Main St PO Box 317 *TF:* 800-338-3021 ■ *Web:* www.cecgas.com	Jesup	IA	50648	319-827-1211	827-3154
Consumers Petroleum of Ct 204 Spring Hill Rd *Web:* www.cameca.com	Trumbull	CT	06611	203-261-3123	
Cosby Oil Company Inc 12902 E Park St *Web:* www.cosbyoil.com	Santa Fe Springs	CA	90670	562-946-4404	
Crestwood Energy Partners LP 700 Louisiana St Ste 2060 *Web:* www.crestwoodlp.com	Houston	TX	77002	832-519-2200	
Crossamerica Partners LP 645 W Hamilton St Ste 500 *Web:* www.crossamericapartners.com	Allentown	PA	18101	610-625-8000	
Crossroads Fuel Service Inc 1441 Fentress Rd Ste G *Web:* www.crossroadsfuel.com	Chesapeake	VA	23322	757-482-2179	482-7849
CRS Reprocessing LLC 13551 Triton Park Blvd One Triton Office Park Ste 1200 *Web:* www.crs-reprocessing.com	Louisville	KY	40223	502-778-3600	
Crystal Flash Limited Partnership 1754 Alpine Ave NW *Web:* www.crystalflash.com	Grand Rapids	MI	49504	616-363-4851	
Davison Fuels Inc 8450 Tanner Williams Rd *Web:* www.davisonoil.com	Mobile	AL	36608	251-633-4444	
Dickey Transport 401 E Fourth St *TF:* 800-247-1081 ■ *Web:* dickeytransport.com	Packwood	IA	52580	319-695-3601	
Dion & Sons Inc 1543 W 16th St *Web:* www.dionandsons.com	Long Beach	CA	90813	562-432-3946	
District Petroleum Products Inc 1814 River Rd Ste 100 *Web:* hymiler.com	Huron	OH	44839	419-433-8373	433-9646
Dominion Aviation Services Inc 7511 Airfield Dr *Web:* dominionaviation.com	Richmond	VA	23237	804-271-7793	
Doss Aviation Inc 3670 Rebecca Ln *Web:* www.dossaviation.com	Colorado Springs	CO	80917	719-570-9804	
Drake Petroleum Co Inc 221 Quinebaug Rd PO Box 866 *TF:* 800-243-6366 ■ *Web:* www.drakepetro.com	North Grosvenordale	CT	06255	800-243-6366	
Duncan Oil Company Inc 849 Factory Rd *Web:* www.duncan-oil.com	Beavercreek	OH	45434	937-426-5945	
Dutch Oil Company Inc 730 Alabama St *Web:* www.dutchoil-victory.com	Columbus	MS	39702	662-327-5202	
Earhart Petroleum Inc 1494 Lytle Rd *TF:* 800-686-2928 ■ *Web:* www.earhartpetroleum.com	Troy	OH	45373	937-335-2928	
East River Energy Inc 401 Soundview Rd *Web:* www.eastriverenergy.com	Guilford	CT	06437	203-453-1200	
Eastern Oil Co 590 S Paddock St *Web:* www.easternoil.com	Pontiac	MI	48341	248-333-1333	
EEL River Fuels Inc 3371 N State St *Web:* www.erenergy.com	Ukiah	CA	95482	707-462-5554	
Englefield Oil Co 447 James Pkwy *TF Cust Svc:* 800-837-4458 ■ *Web:* www.englefieldoil.com	Heath	OH	43056	740-928-8215	928-1531
Evans Oil Company LLC 8450 Millhaven Rd	Monroe	LA	71203	318-345-1502	
Fannon Petroleum Services Inc 7755 Progress Ct *Web:* www.fannonpetroleum.com	Gainesville	VA	20155	703-468-2060	754-2590
Farm & Home Oil Co 3115 State Rd *Web:* www.suburbanpropane.com	Telford	PA	18969	800-776-7263	
Farmers Ranchers Coop 224 S Main St *Web:* www.farmersrancherscoop.com	Ainsworth	NE	69210	402-387-2811	

Company	City	State	ZIP	Phone	Fax
Fauser Energy Resources 106 Center St *Web:* www.fauserenergy.com	Elgin	IA	52141	563-426-5811	
Federated Co-ops Inc 502 S Second St *TF:* 800-638-8228 ■ *Web:* www.federatedcoops.com	Princeton	MN	55371	763-389-2582	
Felts Oil Sales Inc 2412 Cullen St *Web:* www.feltsoil.com	Fort Worth	TX	76107	817-336-7132	
Fleet Card Fuels Inc 4200 Buck Owens Blvd *Web:* fleetcardfuels.com	Bakersfield	CA	93380	661-321-9961	321-9125
Fleetwing Corp 742 S Combee Rd *Web:* www.fleetwingoil.com	Lakeland	FL	33801	863-665-7557	
Flint Hills Resources LP 4111 E 37th St N *Web:* www.fhr.com	Wichita	KS	67220	316-828-3477	828-4228
Foster Blue Water Oil LLC 36065 Water St *Web:* www.fosterbluewateroil.com	Richmond	MI	48062	586-727-3996	
Foster Fuels Inc 16720 Brookneal Hwy *Web:* www.fosterfuels.com	Brookneal	VA	24528	434-376-2322	
Fraley & Company Inc 6723 Hwy 160-491	Cortez	CO	81321	970-565-8538	565-8743
Fred Garrison Oil Co 1107 Walter Griffin St PO Box 100 *Web:* www.allstarfuel.com	Plainview	TX	79073	806-296-6353	
G & G Oil Company of Indiana Inc 220 E Centennial Ave *Web:* www.ggoil.com	Muncie	IN	47303	765-288-7795	
Galen e Wilson Petroleum Co 3057 Davenport Ave *Web:* gewilsonpetroleum.com	Saginaw	MI	48602	989-793-2181	
Gassco 7515 Lindsay Rd *TF:* 800-390-7837 ■ *Web:* gasscoinc.com	Bakersfield	CA	93313	661-832-7406	832-9795
Gate Petroleum Co 9540 San Jose Blvd PO Box 23627 *TF:* 866-571-1982 ■ *Web:* www.gatepetro.com	Jacksonville	FL	32241	904-737-7220	732-7660
Geer Tank Trucks Inc 1136 S Main St *Web:* hugedomains.com/domain_profile.cfm?d=geertanktrucks&e=com	Jacksboro	TX	76458	940-567-2677	
General Petroleum Inc 7404 Disalle Blvd *Web:* www.genpet.com	Fort Wayne	IN	46825	260-489-8504	
George E Warren Corp 3001 Ocean Dr Ste 203 *Web:* www.gewarren.com	Vero Beach	FL	32963	772-778-7100	778-7171
Giant Oil Inc 1806 N Franklin St *Web:* www.giantoil.com	Tampa	FL	33602	813-740-0422	
Glacial Lakes Energy LLC 301 20th Ave SE PO Box 933 *Web:* www.glaciallakesenergy.com	Watertown	SD	57201	605-882-8480	
Global Partners LP 800 S St Ste 200 *NYSE:* GLP ■ *TF:* 800-685-7222 ■ *Web:* www.globalp.com	Waltham	MA	02454	781-894-8800	398-4160
Great Plains Ethanol LLC 27716-462nd Ave *Web:* www.poetenergy.com	Chancellor	SD	57015	605-647-0040	
Gulf Oil LP 100 Crossing Blvd *TF:* 800-256-4853 ■ *Web:* www.gulfoil.com	Framingham	MA	01702	508-270-8300	
Gull Industries 3404 Fourth Ave S	Seattle	WA	98134	206-624-5900	
H.N. Funkhouser & Company Inc 2150 S Loudoun St *Web:* www.hnfunkhouser.com	Winchester	VA	22601	540-662-9000	
H.R. Lewis Petroleum Co 1432 Cleveland St *Web:* www.lewispetroleum.com	Jacksonville	FL	32209	904-356-0731	
Hagan Kennington Oil 9250 S Carolina 9	Nichols	SC	29581	843-392-1300	
HALCO Industries LLC 1015 Norcross Industrial Ct *Web:* www.halcolubricants.com	Norcross	GA	30071	770-840-3480	
Halron Lubricants Inc 1618 State St *Web:* www.halron.com	Green Bay	WI	54304	920-436-4000	
Harnois Groupe Petrolier Inc 80 Rt 158 *Web:* www.legroupeharnois.com	Saint Thomas	QC	J0K3L0	450-759-7979	
Hasco Oil Company Inc 2800 Temple Ave *Web:* www.hascooil.com	Long Beach	CA	90806	562-595-8491	
Hawaii Petroleum Inc 16 Railroad Ave Ste 202 *Web:* www.hawaiipetroleum.com	Hilo	HI	96720	808-969-1405	
Heartland Petroleum LLC 4001 E Fifth Ave *Web:* www.heartland-petroleum.com	Columbus	OH	43219	614-441-4001	
Herdrich Petroleum 210 E US 52 *Web:* herdrich.com	Rushville	IN	46173	765-932-3224	932-4622
Heritage Petroleum LLC 516 N Seventh Ave *Web:* www.heritageoil.com	Evansville	IN	47719	812-422-3251	
Hightowers Petroleum Co 3577 Commerce Dr *Web:* www.hightowerspetroleum.com	Franklin	OH	45005	513-423-4272	
Inlet Petroleum Co 459 W Bluff Dr *Web:* inletpetroleum.com	Anchorage	AK	99501	907-274-3835	
Inter City Oil Company Inc (ICO) 1921 S St *Web:* www.icofuel.com	Duluth	MN	55812	218-728-3641	
Intercontinental Fuels 17617 Aldine Westfield Rd *Web:* www.ifl-usa.com	Houston	TX	77073	281-821-2225	
Isgett Distributors Inc 51 Highland Ctr Blvd *Web:* www.isgettdistributors.com	Asheville	NC	28806	828-667-9846	
Isobunkers LLC c/o ISOindustries Inc 5353 E Princess Anne Rd Ste F *Web:* www.isoindustries.com	Norfolk	VA	23502	757-855-0900	855-6200
Jerry Brown Company Inc, The 2690 Prairie Rd *Web:* www.jbco.com	Eugene	OR	97402	541-688-8211	
JH Williams Oil Company Inc 1237 E Twiggs St *TF:* 800-683-0536 ■ *Web:* www.jhwoil.com	Tampa	FL	33602	813-228-7776	224-9413
JJ Powell Inc 109 W Presqueisle St *Web:* www.jjpowell.com	Philipsburg	PA	16866	814-342-3190	
Johnson Oil Co (JOC) 1113 E Sara DeWitt Dr *TF:* 800-284-2432 ■ *Web:* www.johnsonoilcompany.com	Gonzales	TX	78629	830-672-9574	672-6659
JP Energy Partners LP 600 Las Colinas Blvd E Ste 2000 *Web:* www.jpenergypartners.com	Irving	TX	75039	972-444-0300	
Kern Oil & Refining Co 7724 E Panama Ln *Web:* www.kernoil.com	Bakersfield	CA	93307	661-845-0761	
Kildair Service Ltee 92 Delangis Rd *Web:* www.kildair.com	St-paul De Joliette	QC	J0K3E0	450-756-8091	
Kimbro Oil Company Inc 2200 Clifton Ave *Web:* www.kimbrooil.com	Nashville	TN	37203	615-320-7484	
King Fuels Inc 14825 Willis St *Web:* www.king fuels.com	Houston	TX	77039	281-449-9975	
L. G. Jordan Oil Company Inc 314 N Hughes St *Web:* www.lgjordanoil.com	Apex	NC	27502	919-362-8388	
Laguna Development Corp Interstate 40 W Exit 140 14500 Central Ave SW *Web:* www.lagunadevcorp.com	Albuquerque	NM	87121	505-352-7866	
Lakeside Oil Company Inc 555 W Brown Deer Rd Ste 200 *Web:* lakesideoil.com	Milwaukee	WI	53217	414-540-4000	540-4100
Lane Supply Inc 120 Fairview *Web:* www.lanesupplyinc.com	Arlington	TX	76010	817-261-9116	275-1660
Lanman Oil Co Inc PO Box 108 *TF:* 800-677-2819 ■ *Web:* www.lanmanoil.com	Charleston	IL	61920	800-677-2819	
Lard Oil Company Inc 914 Florida Blvd SW *Web:* www.lardoil.com	Denham Springs	LA	70726	225-664-3311	
Leffler Energy Inc 15 Mt Joy St *Fax Area Code: 717 ■ *TF:* 800-984-1411 ■ *Web:* www.leffleenergy.com	Mount Joy	PA	17552	800-984-1411	653-2728*
Licking Valley Oil Inc PO Box 246 *TF:* 800-899-9449 ■ *Web:* www.lvoinc.com	Butler	KY	41006	859-472-7111	472-7112
Littlefield Oil Co 3403 Cavanaugh Rd *Web:* www.littlefieldcompanies.com	Fort Smith	AR	72908	479-646-0595	
LQM Petroleum Services Inc 80 Broadway *Web:* www.lqm.com	Cresskill	NJ	07626	201-871-9010	
LubriCorp LLC 2648 Byington Solway Rd *Web:* www.lubricorp.net	Knoxville	TN	37931	865-474-7400	
MacEwen Petroleum Inc 18 Adelaide St PO Box 100 *Web:* www.macewen.ca	Maxville	ON	K0C1T0	613-527-2100	
Main-Care Energy PO Box 11029 *Fax Area Code: 518 ■ *TF:* 800-542-5552 ■ *Web:* www.maincareenergy.com	Albany	NY	12211	800-542-5552	438-5991*
Maritime Energy Inc 234 Pk St PO Box 485 *TF:* 800-333-4489 ■ *Web:* www.maritimeenergy.com	Rockland	ME	04841	207-594-4487	594-1648
Martin Eagle Oil Company Inc 2700 James St *TF:* 800-316-6148 ■ *Web:* www.martineagle.com	Denton	TX	76205	940-383-2351	
Martin Midstream Partners LP 4200 Stone Rd *NASDAQ:* MMLP ■ *TF:* 800-256-6644 ■ *Web:* martinmidstream.com	Kilgore	TX	75662	903-983-6200	983-6215
Mc Glaughlin Oil Co, The 3750 E Livingston Ave *Web:* www.mcglaughlinoil.com	Columbus	OH	43227	614-231-2518	
McCall Oil & Chemical Corp 5480 NW Front Ave *Web:* www.mccalloil.com	Portland	OR	97210	503-221-6400	
McClure Oil Corp Junction of Hwys 35 and 37 PO Box 1750 *Web:* in.mcclureoil.net	Marion	IN	46952	765-674-9771	
McNeece Brothers Oil Company Inc 691 E Heil Ave *Web:* www.mcneecebros.com	El Centro	CA	92243	760-352-4721	
Merle Boes Inc 11372 E Lakewood Blvd *Web:* www.merleboes.com	Holland	MI	49424	616-392-7036	
Mid South Sales Inc 243 County Rd 414 *Web:* midsouthsales.com/index.php	Jonesboro	AR	72404	870-933-6457	933-0446
Mid-Atlantic Petroleum Properties LLC (MAPP) 12311 Middlebrook Rd	Germantown	MD	20874	301-972-4116	
Miller Oil Co 1000 E City Hall Ave *TF:* 800-333-4645 ■ *Web:* www.milleroil.com	Norfolk	VA	23504	757-623-6600	625-0528
Mitsubishi International Corp 655 Third Ave *Web:* www.mitsubishicorp.com	New York	NY	10017	212-605-2000	
Morgan Distributing Inc 3425 N 22nd St *Web:* www.mdilubes.com	Decatur	IL	62526	217-877-3570	
Mountain Empire Oil Co 282 Christian Church Rd *Web:* www.roadrunnermarkets.com	Johnson City	TN	37616	423-928-7241	
Mutual Oil Inc 863 Crescent St PO Box 250 *Web:* www.mutualoil.com	Brockton	MA	02303	508-583-5777	
MW Sewall & Co 259 Front St *Web:* hugedomains.com/domain_profile.cfm?d=clippermart&e=com	Bath	ME	04530	207-442-7994	
National Oil & Gas Inc 409 N Main St *TF:* 800-322-8454 ■ *Web:* natloil.com	Bluffton	IN	46714	260-824-2220	824-2223
Newport Capital Group LLC 12 Broad St Fifth Fl *Web:* www.newportcapitalgroup.com	Red Bank	NJ	07701	732-741-8400	
Nisbet Oil Co PO Box 35367 *Web:* www.nisbetoil.com	Charlotte	NC	28235	704-332-7755	377-1607
NOCO Energy Corp 2440 Sheridan Dr *TF:* 800-500-6626 ■ *Web:* www.noco.com	Tonawanda	NY	14150	716-833-6626	832-1312*
Northwest Fuel Systems Inc 115 Industry Ct *Web:* nwestco.com	Kalispell	MT	59901	406-755-4343	
Nuvera Fuel Cells 129 Concord Rd Bldg 1 *Web:* www.nuvera.com	Billerica	MA	01821	617-245-7500	245-7511
Offen Petroleum Inc 5100 E 78th Ave *Web:* www.offenpet.com	Commerce City	CO	80022	303-297-3835	
Oilmen's Equipment Corp 140 Cedar Springs Rd *Web:* www.oilmens.com	Spartanburg	SC	29302	864-573-9311	
On Site Gas Systems Inc 35 Budney Rd Budney Industrial Park *Web:* www.onsitegas.com	Newington	CT	06111	860-667-8888	
Orange Line Oil Company Inc 404 E Commercial St *TF:* 800-492-6864 ■ *Web:* www.orangelineoil.com	Pomona	CA	91767	909-623-0533	
Oscar W Larson Co 10100 Dixie Hwy *Web:* www.larsonco.com	Clarkston	MI	48348	248-620-0070	

Company	City	State	Zip	Phone	Fax
Panef Inc 5700 W Douglas Ave *Web:* www.panef.com	Milwaukee	WI	53218	414-464-7200	
Papco Inc 4920 Southern Blvd *Web:* www.papco.com	Virginia Beach	VA	23462	757-499-5977	
Parker Oil Company Inc PO Box 120 *Web:* www.parkeroilcompany.com	South Hill	VA	23970	434-447-3146	447-2646
Parker Oil Products Inc 508 California Parker PO Box 775 *Web:* www.parkeroilproducts.com	Parker	AZ	85344	928-669-2617	669-2120
Patten Energy Enterprises Inc 3437 S Main St *Web:* pattenenergy.com	Los Angeles	CA	90007	323-235-3500	
Peerless Distributing Co 21700 NW Hwy Ste 1160	Southfield	MI	48075	248-559-1800	559-1861
Petro Lock Inc 45315 N Trevor Ave *Web:* petrolock.com	Lancaster	CA	93534	661-948-6044	948-9524
PetroCard Systems Inc 730 Central Ave S *Web:* www.petrocard.com	Kent	WA	98032	253-852-2777	
Petroleum Products Corp 900 S Eisenhower Blvd *Web:* ppcterminals.com	Middletown	PA	17057	717-939-0466	939-0294
Petroleum Traders Corp 7120 Pointe Inverness Way *Web:* www.petroleumtraders.com	Fort Wayne	IN	46804	260-432-6622	
Petroleum Wholesale LP 8550 Technology Forest Pl *Web:* petroleumwholesale.com/	The Woodlands	TX	77381	281-681-1000	
PetroLiance LLC 739 N State St **Fax Area Code:* 847 ■ *TF:* 800-628-7231 ■ *Web:* www.petroliance.com	Elgin	IL	60123	877-738-7699	741-2590*
Pioneer Oil LLC 1728 Lampman Dr Ste A *Web:* www.pioneeroil-co.com	Billings	MT	59102	406-254-7071	254-2560
Pro Petroleum Inc 4985 N Sloan Ln *TF:* 877-791-4900 ■ *Web:* www.propetroleum.com	Las Vegas	NV	89115	877-791-4900	
Pure Energy Corp 61 S Paramus Rd *Web:* www.pure-energy.com	Paramus	NJ	07652	201-843-8100	
R K Allen Oil Inc 36002 AL Hwy 21 *TF:* 800-445-5823 ■ *Web:* www.rkallenoil.com	Talladega	AL	35161	256-362-4261	362-6792
R Kidd Fuels Corp 1172 Twinney Dr *TF:* 866-274-2315 ■ *Web:* www.kiddfuels.com	Newmarket	ON	L3Y9E2	866-274-2315	
Ramos Oil Company Inc 1515 S River Rd *TF Cust Svc:* 800-477-7266 ■ *Web:* www.ramosoil.com	West Sacramento	CA	95691	916-371-2570	371-0635
RE Carroll Inc 1570 N Olden Ave *Web:* www.recarroll.com	Trenton	NJ	08638	609-695-6211	
Reeder Distributors Inc 5450 Wilbarger St *TF:* 800-722-3103 ■ *Web:* www.reederdistributors.com	Fort Worth	TX	76119	817-429-5957	429-9052
Renkert Oil Inc 3817 Main St PO Box 246 *Web:* www.renkertoil.com	Morgantown	PA	19543	610-286-8012	
Rentech Inc 10877 Wilshire Blvd 10th Fl *NASDAQ: RTK* ■ *Web:* www.rentechinc.com	Los Angeles	CA	90024	310-571-9800	571-9799
Retif Oil & Fuel Inc 527 Destrehan Ave PO Box 52679 *TF:* 800-349-9000 ■ *Web:* www.retif.com	Harvey	LA	70058	504-349-9000	349-9009
Rex Oil Co Inc 814 & 1000 Lexington Ave **Fax Area Code:* 800 ■ *TF:* 800-843-0572 ■ *Web:* www.rexoil.com	Thomasville	NC	27360	336-472-3368	843-0572*
Rhinehart Oil Company Inc 585 E State Rd *Web:* www.rhinehartoil.com	American Fork	UT	84003	801-756-9681	
Rinehart Oil Inc 2401 N State St *Web:* www.rinehartoil.com	Ukiah	CA	95482	707-462-8811	
Risser Oil Corp 2865 Executive Dr *Web:* www.therissercompanies.com	Clearwater	FL	33762	727-573-4000	572-9075
Rite Way Oil & Gas Company Inc PO Box 27049 **Fax Area Code:* 800	Omaha	NE	68127	402-331-6400	279-6401*
RKA Petroleum Companies Inc 28340 Wick Rd *Web:* www.rkapetroleum.com	Romulus	MI	48174	734-946-2199	
Robert V. Jensen Inc 4029 S Maple Ave *Web:* www.rvjensen.com	Fresno	CA	93725	559-485-8210	
S.A. White Oil Company Inc 590 Atlanta St SE *Web:* www.sawhite.com	Marietta	GA	30060	770-427-1387	
San Luis Butane Distributors Inc PO Box 3068 *Web:* www.deltaliquidenergy.com	Paso Robles	CA	93447	805-239-0616	239-2607
Sapp Bros. Petroleum Inc 9915 S 148th St *Web:* www.sappbros.net	Omaha	NE	68138	402-895-2202	
Saracen Energy Partners LP 3033 W Alabama *Web:* www.saracenenergy.com	Houston	TX	77098	713-285-2900	
Senergy Petroleum LLC 622 S 56th Ave *TF:* 800-964-0076 ■ *Web:* www.brownevans.com	Phoenix	AZ	85043	602-272-6795	
Shoco Oil Inc 5135 E 74th Ave *Web:* www.shocooil.com	Commerce City	CO	80037	303-289-1677	
Sierra Energy 1020 Winding Creek Rd Ste 100 *TF:* 800-576-2264 ■ *Web:* www.sierraenergy.net	Roseville	CA	95678	916-218-1600	218-1680
Silco Oil Company Inc 181 E 56th Ave Ste 600	Denver	CO	80216	303-292-0500	293-8069
Silvas Oil Company Inc 3217 E Lorena Ave *Web:* www.silvasoil.com	Fresno	CA	93725	559-233-5171	
Sinclair Marketing 550 E S Temple St *TF:* 800-325-3265 ■ *Web:* www.sinclairoil.com	Salt Lake City	UT	84102	801-524-2700	524-2721
SNC-Lavalin Constructors Inc 19015 N Creek Pkwy Ste 300 *Web:* www.slthermal.com	Bothell	WA	98011	425-489-8000	
SoCo Group Inc, The 5962 Priestly Dr *Web:* www.thesocogroup.com	Carlsbad	CA	92008	760-804-8460	
South Central Oil Company Inc 2121 W Main St *Web:* www.southcentraloil.com	Albemarle	NC	28001	704-982-2173	982-6434
Southern Maryland Oil Co Inc (SMO) 109 N Maple Ave **Fax Area Code:* 301 ■ **Fax:* Cust Svc ■ *TF:* 888-222-3720 ■ *Web:* www.smoenergy.com	La Plata	MD	20646	888-222-3720	932-3718*
Spencer Cos Inc 120 Woodson St PO Box 18128 *TF:* 800-633-2910 ■ *Web:* www.spencercos.com	Huntsville	AL	35801	256-533-1150	535-2910
Sprague Energy 185 International Dr Ste 200 **Fax:* Hum Res ■ *TF:* 800-225-1560 ■ *Web:* www.spragueenergy.com	Portsmouth	NH	03801	603-431-1000	430-5320*
Stern Oil Company Inc PO Box 218 *TF:* 800-477-2744 ■ *Web:* www.sternoil.com	Freeman	SD	57029	605-925-7999	925-4367
Sturdy Oil Company Inc 1511 Abbott St *Web:* www.sturdyoil.com	Salinas	CA	93901	831-422-8801	
Sun Coast Resources Inc 6922 Cavalcade St *TF:* 800-677-3835 ■ *Web:* www.suncoastresources.com	Houston	TX	77028	713-429-8492	844-9699
Sundays Energy Inc 2637 27th Ave S *Web:* www.sundaysenergy.com	Minneapolis	MN	55406	612-605-1788	
Super-Lube Inc 1311 N Paul Russell Rd *Web:* www.superlube.com	Tallahassee	FL	32301	850-222-5823	222-5152
Tauber Oil Co 55 Waugh Dr # 700 *Web:* www.tauberoil.com	Houston	TX	77007	713-869-8700	869-8069
Taylor Enterprises Inc (TEI) 2586 Southport Rd *TF:* 800-922-3149 ■ *Web:* www.teifms.com	Spartanburg	SC	29302	864-573-9518	583-4150
Taylor Oil Company Inc 77 Second St 77 Second St *Web:* www.tayloroilco.com	Somerville	NJ	08876	908-725-7737	
Technical Gas Products Inc 66 Leonardo Dr *TF:* 800-847-0745 ■ *Web:* www.tgpoxygen.com	North Haven	CT	06473	800-847-0745	
Tesoro Corp 1225 17th Street *TF:* 800-299-0570 ■ *Web:* www.tsocorp.com	Denver	CO	80202	800-299-0570	
Tetco Inc 1100 NE Loop 410 Ste 900 *Web:* www.tetco.com	San Antonio	TX	78217	210-821-5900	826-3003
Tex Con Oil Co 1701 Grand Ave Pkwy Ste A *Web:* www.texconoil.com	Pflugerville	TX	78660	512-670-7401	
Texas Enterprises Inc 5005 E Seventh St *TF:* 800-545-4412 ■ *Web:* www.alliedsalesco.com	Austin	TX	78702	512-385-2167	
Texor Petroleum Company Inc 3340 S Harlem Ave *Web:* www.texor.com	Riverside	IL	60546	708-447-1999	
Time Oil Co 2737 W Commodore Way	Seattle	WA	98199	206-285-2400	286-4479
Titan Laboratories 1380 Zuni St PO Box 40567 **Fax Area Code:* 303 ■ *TF:* 800-848-4826 ■ *Web:* www.titanlab.com	Denver	CO	80204	800-848-4826	539-0158*
Total Airport Services Inc 1985 Yosemite Ave Ste 230 *Web:* www.totalairportservices.com	Simi Valley	CA	93063	805-522-3565	
Tower Oil & Technology Co 4300 S Tripp Ave *Web:* www.toweroil.com	Chicago	IL	60632	773-346-6873	
Tower Sales Inc 936 E Grand Ave PO Box 36 *TF:* 800-839-1849 ■ *Web:* myshipley.com	Tower City	PA	17980	717-647-2100	647-2664
Transglobal Gas & Oil Co 10904A Mcbride Ln	Knoxville	TN	37932	865-777-2162	
Tri-Con Inc 7076 W Port Arthur Rd *Web:* www.triconinc.org	Beaumont	TX	77705	409-835-2237	
Tropic Oil Company Inc 10002 NW 89th Ave *Web:* www.tropicoil.com	Miami	FL	33178	305-888-4611	
Truman Arnold Cos 701 S Robison Rd **Fax Area Code:* 806 ■ *Web:* www.tacair.com	Texarkana	TX	75501	903-794-3835	335-2612*
Tucker Oil Company Inc 910 Industrial Dr *Web:* www.tuckeroilcompany.com	Slaton	TX	79364	806-828-6277	
Tulco Oils Inc 5240 E Pine PO Box 582410 *TF:* 800-375-2347 ■ *Web:* www.tulco.com	Tulsa	OK	74115	918-838-3354	834-1263
Turner Gas Company Inc PO Box 26554 *TF:* 800-932-4277 ■ *Web:* www.turnergas.com	Salt Lake City	UT	84126	801-973-6886	973-6882
Tyree Oil Inc 1355 W First Ave *Web:* www.tyreeoil.com	Eugene	OR	97402	541-687-0076	
Ullman Oil Inc PO Box 23399 *TF:* 800-543-5195 ■ *Web:* www.ullmanoil.com	Chagrin Falls	OH	44023	440-543-5195	543-6549
Union Distributing Company of Tucson 4000 E Michigan St *Web:* www.uniondistributing.connekt2.com	Tucson	AZ	85714	520-571-7600	
US Oil Co Inc 425 Better Way **Fax:* Acctg ■ *Web:* www.usventure.com	Appleton	WI	54915	920-739-6101	788-0531*
Valor Oil 1200 Alsop Ln *TF:* 800-544-5823 ■ *Web:* www.valorllc.com	Owensboro	KY	42303	270-683-2461	684-6654
Van Manen Petroleum Group 0-305 Lk Michigan Dr NW *Web:* www.vanmanen.com	Grand Rapids	MI	49534	616-453-6344	
Varouh Oil Inc 970 Griswold Rd *Web:* www.varouhoil.com	Elyria	OH	44035	440-324-5025	
Venture Fuels LLC 3819 Creekside St *Web:* venturefuels.com	Holman	WI	54636	608-783-9516	
Vesco Oil Corp 16055 W 12-Mile Rd **Fax Area Code:* 248 ■ *TF:* 800-527-5358 ■ *Web:* www.vesco-oil.com	Southfield	MI	48076	800-527-5358	557-2236*
Veterans Oil Delivery 2070 Hwy 150 *Web:* www.veteransoilinc.com	Bessemer	AL	35022	205-424-4400	424-4448
Waguespack Oil Company Inc 1818 HWY 3185 PO Box 326 *Web:* www.wagoil.com	Thibodaux	LA	70302	985-447-3668	447-5730
Walthall Oil Company Inc 2510 Allen Rd *Web:* www.walthall-oil.com	Macon	GA	31216	478-781-1234	
Warex Terminals Corp One S Water St PO Box 488 *Web:* www.warex-terminals.com	Newburgh	NY	12550	845-561-4000	
Waring Oil Company LLC 431 Port Terminal Cir *Web:* www.waringoil.com	Vicksburg	MS	39183	601-636-1065	
Warren Oil Company Inc PO Box 1507 *TF:* 800-779-6456 ■ *Web:* www.warrenoil.com	Dunn	NC	28335	910-892-6456	892-4245
Wesson Inc PO Box 2127 *Web:* www.wessonenergy.com	Waterbury	CT	06722	203-756-7041	754-6664
West Penn Oil Company Inc 2305 Market St *Web:* www.westpenn.com	Warren	PA	16365	814-723-9000	
Western Petroleum Co 9531 W 78th St *TF:* 800-972-3835 ■ *Web:* www.westernpetro.com	Eden Prairie	MN	55344	952-941-9090	941-7470
Western States Petroleum Inc 450 S 15th Ave *TF:* 800-220-1353 ■ *Web:* www.westernstatespetroleum.com	Phoenix	AZ	85007	602-252-4011	

Phone | Fax

Williams Oil Company Inc 44 Reuter Blvd .... Towanda PA 18848 570-265-6673
Web: www.williamsoil.com

Willis Oil Company Inc 1403 N Expy Ste B .... Griffin GA 30223 770-227-5724
Web: www.mikam.com

Windward Petroleum Inc
1064 Goffs Falls Rd .... Manchester NH 03103 603-222-2900 622-0834
Web: www.ghberlinwindward.com

Woodfin Co
8180 Mechanicsville Turnpike .... Mechanicsville VA 23111 804-730-5000
Web: www.askwoodfin.com

Workman Oil Co 14680 Forest Rd .... Forest VA 24551 434-525-1615

World Fuel Services Corp
9800 NW 41st St Ste 400 .... Miami FL 33178 305-428-8000 392-5600
NYSE: INT ■ TF: 800-345-3818 ■ Web: www.wfscorp.com

Yorkston Oil Company Inc 2801 Roeder Ave .... Bellingham WA 98225 360-734-2201
Web: www.yorkstonoil.com

583 PETROLEUM REFINERIES

Phone | Fax

A H Belo Corp 508 Young St PO Box 224866 .... Dallas TX 75202 214-977-8200 977-8201
NYSE: AHC ■ TF: 800-230-1074 ■ Web: www.ahbelo.com

Allegheny Petroleum Products Co
999 Airbrake Ave .... Wilmerding PA 15148 412-829-1990
TF: 800-600-2900 ■ Web: www.oils.com

Alon USA Energy Inc 7616 LBJ Fwy Ste 300 .... Dallas TX 75251 972-367-3600 367-3728
NYSE: ALJ ■ Web: www.alonusa.com

Alpha Oil Inc 490 Garyray Dr .... Weston ON M9L1P8 416-745-6131
Web: www.alphaoil.ca

Aventine Renewable Energy Inc 1300 S Second St .... Pekin IL 61554 309-347-9200
Web: www.aventinerei.com

Balch Petroleum Contractors & Builders Inc
930 Ames Ave .... Milpitas CA 95035 408-942-8686
Web: www.balchpetroleum.com

Beroth Oil Co 20 W 32nd St .... Winston Salem NC 27105 336-757-7600
Web: www.berothoil.com

BioProcess Algae LLC 45 High Point Ave .... Portsmouth RI 02871 401-683-5400
Web: www.bioprocessalgae.com

Bootheel Petroleum Company Inc
623 N SR- 25 PO Box 187 .... Dexter MO 63841 573-624-4160 624-2439
Web: www.bootheelpetroleum.com

Boyer Petroleum Co 1817 Hull Ave .... Des Moines IA 50313 515-243-4450
Web: www.boyerpetroleum.com

BP Pipelines (North America) Inc
150 W Warrenville Rd .... Naperville IL 60563 630-536-2532
Web: www.bppipelines.com

BP PLC 28100 Torch Pkwy .... Warrenville IL 60555 630-420-5111
NYSE: BP ■ TF: 877-638-5672 ■ Web: www.bp.com

Calcasieu Refining Co
4359 W Tank Farm Rd .... Lake Charles LA 70605 337-478-2130
Web: www.calcasieurefining.com

Calumet Lubricants Co
2780 Waterfront Pkwy Dr E Ste 200 .... Indianapolis IN 46214 317-328-5660 328-2359
TF: 800-437-3188 ■ Web: www.calumetspecialty.com

Calumet Specialty Products Partners LP
2780 Waterfront Pkwy E Dr Ste 200 .... Indianapolis IN 46214 317-328-5660 328-5668
NASDAQ: CLMT ■ TF: 800-437-3188 ■ Web: www.calumetspecialty.com

Canwest Propane Ltd 1700 440 - Second Ave SW .... Calgary AB T2P5E9 403-206-4100
Web: www.canwestpropane.com

Chalmette Refining LLC
500 W Saint Bernard Hwy .... Chalmette LA 70043 504-281-1212
Web: www.chalmetterefining.com

Chevron Canada Ltd 1200 - 1050 W Pender St .... Vancouver BC V6E3T4 604-668-5300 668-5559
TF: 800-663-1650 ■ Web: www.chevron.ca

Chevron Corp 6001 Bollinger Canyon Rd .... San Ramon CA 94583 925-842-1000 420-0335*
NYSE: CVX ■ *Fax Area Code: 866 ■ TF Cust Svc: 800-243-8766 ■ Web: www.chevron.com

Chevron Global Marine Products LLC
1500 Louisiana Fourth Fl .... Houston TX 77002 914-285-7390
Web: www.chevronmarineproducts.com

CITGO Petroleum Corp 1293 Eldridge Pkwy .... Houston TX 77077 832-486-4700
TF: 800-424-9300 ■ Web: www.citgo.com

Clean Fuels Ohio 530 W Spring St Ste 250 .... Columbus OH 43215 614-884-7336
Web: cleanfuelsohio.org

Clipper Oil Co
2040 Harbor Island Dr Ste 203 .... San Diego CA 92101 619-692-9701
Web: www.clipperoil.com

Coffeyville Resources LLC
10 E Cambridge Cir Dr .... Kansas City KS 66103 913-982-0500 982-0505
Web: www.coffeyvillegroup.com

ConocoPhillips 600 N Dairy Ashford Rd .... Houston TX 77079 281-293-1000
NYSE: COP ■ Web: www.conocophillips.com

Cross Oil Refining & Marketing Inc
484 E Sixth St .... Smackover AR 71762 870-881-8700 864-8656
TF: 800-725-3066 ■ Web: www.crossoil.com

Crown Central Petroleum Corp
One N Charles St .... Baltimore MD 21201 410-539-7400 659-4875*
*Fax: Hum Res ■ Web: www.crowncentral.com

Custom Carbon Processing Inc
17310-106 Ave NW .... Edmonton AB T5S1H9 780-443-4237
Web: www.customcarbonprocessing.com

Delek Refining Ltd 425 McMurrey Dr .... Tyler TX 75702 903-579-3400 579-3499
Web: www.delekus.com/

East Kansas Agri-Energy LLC 1304 S Main .... Garnett KS 66032 785-448-2888
Web: www.ekaellc.com

Elementa Group Inc
509 Glendale Ave E Ste 302 .... Niagara-on-the-lake ON L0S1J0 905-687-1900
Web: www.elementagroup.com

Enjet Inc 5373 W Alabama Ste 502 .... Houston TX 77056 713-552-1559
Web: www.enjet.com

Ergon Refining 2611 Haining Rd .... Vicksburg MS 39183 601-933-3000 630-8311
TF: 877-888-9758 ■ Web: www.ergon.com

Exxon Mobil Corp 5959 Las Colinas Blvd .... Irving TX 75039 972-444-1000 444-1433
NYSE: XOM ■ TF: 800-252-1800 ■ Web: www.exxonmobil.com

Flint Hills Resources LP 4111 E 37th St N .... Wichita KS 67220 316-828-3477 828-4228
Web: www.fhr.com

Guardian Energy LLC 4745 380th Ave .... Janesville MN 56048 507-234-5000
Web: www.guardiannrg.com

Guardian Lima LLC 2485 Houx Pkwy .... Lima OH 45804 567-940-9500
Web: www.guardianlima.com

Harbert Management Corp
2100 Third Ave N Ste 600 .... Birmingham AL 35203 205-987-5500
Web: www.harbert.net

Hart Petroleum 323 Skidmores Rd .... Deer Park NY 11729 631-667-3200
Web: www.harthomecomfort.com

Heritage Gas Ltd
Park Pl 1 Brownlow Ave Ste 200 - 238 .... Dartmouth NS B3B1Y2 902-466-2003
Web: www.heritagegas.com

Hough Petroleum Corp 340 Fourth St .... Ewing NJ 08638 609-771-1022
Web: houghpetroleum.com

Hunt Oil Co 1900 N Akard St .... Dallas TX 75201 214-978-8000 978-8888
Web: www.huntoil.com

Hunt Refining Co
100 Towncenter Blvd Ste 300 .... Tuscaloosa AL 35406 205-391-3300 752-6480
Web: www.huntrefining.com

Imperial Oil Resources Ltd
237 Fourth Ave SW PO Box 2480 Stn M .... Calgary AB T2P3M9 800-567-3776 237-2072*
*Fax Area Code: 403 ■ TF: 800-567-3776 ■ Web: www.imperialoil.ca

Inspection Oilfield Services
2809 Youngsville Hwy 89 .... Youngsville LA 70592 337-856-9001
Web: www.iospci.com

Integro Earth Fuels Inc Six Celtic Dr Ste A2 .... Arden NC 28704 828-651-8988
Web: www.integrofuels.com

International Group Inc 85 Old Eagle School Rd .... Wayne PA 19087 610-687-9030 687-2792
TF: 800-852-6537 ■ Web: www.igiwax.com

J.E. DeWitt Inc 1903 N Durfee Ave South .... El Monte CA 91733 626-444-2691
Web: www.dewittpetroleum.com

Laredo Energy LP
840 W Sam Houston Pkwy N Ste 400 .... Houston TX 77024 713-600-6000
Web: www.laredoenergy.com

Midstream Energy Services LLC
Geophysical Resource Ctr 8801 S Yale Ave
Ste 350 .... Tulsa OK 74137 918-388-6900
Web: www.midstreamenergyllc.com

Montana Refining Co 1900 Tenth St NE .... Great Falls MT 59404 317-328-5660 328-2359
Web: calumetspecialty.com

Motiva Enterprises LLC 700 Milam St .... Houston TX 77002 713-277-8000 546-8500
TF: 877-668-4825 ■ Web: www.motivaenterprises.com

Murphy Oil Corp 200 Peach St .... El Dorado AR 71730 870-862-6411 875-7675
TF: 888-289-9314 ■ Web: www.murphyoilcorp.com

National Co-op Refinery Assn
2000 S Main St .... McPherson KS 67460 620-241-2340 241-5531
Web: www.ncrarefinery.com

Outrigger Energy LLC
1200 Seventeenth St Ste 900 .... Denver CO 80202 720-638-7312
Web: outriggerenergy.com

Paramount Petroleum Corp 14700 Downey Ave ...... Paramount CA 90723 562-531-2060 634-7057*
*Fax: Hum Res ■ Web: www.ppcla.com

Placid Refining Company LLC
1940 Louisiana Hwy 1 N .... Port Allen LA 70767 225-387-0278 346-7403
Web: www.placidrefining.com

Poet 4615 N Lewis Ave .... Sioux Falls SD 57104 605-965-2200
Web: poet.com

Poma Holding Company Inc
571 W Slover Ave .... Bloomington CA 92316 909-877-2441
Web: www.pomacos.com

Pri Mar Petroleum Inc 1207 Broad St .... Saint Joseph MI 49085 269-983-7314
Web: www.primarpetro.com

Rain CII Carbon LLC
2627 Chestnut Ridge Rd Ste 200 .... Kingwood TX 77339 281-318-2400
Web: www.raincii.com

RPMG Inc 1157 Vly Park Dr Ste 100 .... Shakopee MN 55379 952-465-3220
Web: www.rpmgllc.com

San Joaquin Refining Company Inc
3129 Standard St .... Bakersfield CA 93308 661-327-4257 327-3236
Web: www.sjr.com

SEMCO ENERGY Gas Co 1411 Third St Ste A .... Port Huron MI 48060 800-624-2019
TF: 800-624-2019 ■ Web: www.semcoenergygas.com

Sinclair Oil Corp PO Box 30825 .... Salt Lake City UT 84130 801-524-2700 524-2880
Web: www.sinclairoil.com

Source North America Corp 510 S Westgate .... Addison IL 60101 847-364-9000
Web: www.sourcena.com

Southland Oil Co 5170 Galaxie Dr .... Jackson MS 39206 601-981-4151
Web: petroleum-oil-wholesalers.cmac.ws

Star-seal 6596 New Peachtree Rd .... Atlanta GA 30340 770-455-6551
Web: www.herculessealcoat.com

Sunoco Inc 1735 Market St Ste LL .... Philadelphia PA 19103 215-977-3000 977-3409
NYSE: SUN ■ TF: 800-786-6261 ■ Web: www.sunocoinc.com

Supreme Petroleum Inc 1001 S Church St .... Smithfield VA 23430 757-357-9652
Web: www.supremepetro.com

Texas Oil & Chemical Co 7752 FM 418 .... Silsbee TX 77656 409-385-1400 385-2453

Tower Energy Group 1983 W 190th St .... Torrance CA 90504 310-538-8000
Web: www.towerenergy.com

Tristate Midstream LP
3311 N Interstate 35 Ste 120 .... Denton TX 76207 940-387-4955
Web: www.tsmidstream.com

United Refining Company Inc 15 Bradley St .... Warren PA 16365 814-723-1500 726-4709
Web: www.urc.com

US Energy Markets Inc
19046 Bruce B Down BLVD 56 .... Tampa FL 33647 813-438-3837
Web: www.usenergymarkets.com

US Oil & Refining Co 3001 Marshall Ave .... Tacoma WA 98421 253-383-1651 383-9970
Web: www.usor.com

Vp Racing Fuels Inc 7124 Richter Rd .... Elmendorf TX 78112 210-635-7744
Web: www.vpracingfuels.com

				Phone	Fax
Western Dubuque Biodiesel LLC 904 Jamesmeier Rd PO Box 82 *Web:* www.wdbiodiesel.net	Farley	IA	52046	563-744-3554	
Western Refining Inc 123 W Mills Ave. *NYSE: WNR* ■ *Web:* www.wnr.com	El Paso	TX	79905	915-534-1400	881-0002
WMPI Pty LLC 10 Gilberton Rd *Web:* www.ultracleanfuels.com	Gilberton	PA	17934	570-874-1602	
World Oil Co 9302 Garfield Ave.	South Gate	CA	90280	562-928-0100	928-3234

584 PETROLEUM STORAGE TERMINALS

				Phone	Fax
Allied Energy Company LLC 2700 Ishkooda Wenonah Rd *Web:* alliedenergycorp.com	Birmingham	AL	35211	205-925-6600	
Bayside Fuel Oil Depot Corp 1776 Shore Pkwy *Web:* www.baysidedepot.com	Brooklyn	NY	11214	718-372-9800	
Bennett Oil Co 810 E Sheldon St *Web:* www.bennettoil.com	Prescott	AZ	86301	928-445-1181	
Best-Wade Petroleum Inc 201 Dodge Dr *Web:* www.bestwade.com	Ripley	TN	38063	731-635-9661	
Bi-Petro Inc 3150 Executive Park Dr *Web:* www.bipetro.com	Springfield	IL	62794	217-535-0181	
Blaylock Oil Company Inc 724 S Flagler Ave *Web:* www.blaylockoil.com	Homestead	FL	33030	305-247-7249	
Bountyland Petroleum Inc 5038 S Hwy 11 *Web:* mybountyland.com	Westminster	SC	29693	864-647-7282	
Brabham Oil Company Inc 525 Midway St *Web:* www.brabhamoil.com	Bamberg	SC	29003	803-245-2471	
Buckley Oil Company Inc 1809 Rock Island St *Web:* www.buckleyoil.com	Dallas	TX	75207	214-421-4147	
C Steinweg Inc 1201 Wallace St *Web:* www.steinweg.com	Baltimore	MD	21230	410-752-8254	
C.K. Smith & Company Inc 99 Crescent St *Web:* www.cksmithcompany.com	Worcester	MA	01605	508-753-1475	
CarterEnergy Corp 6000 Metcalf Ave *Web:* www.carterenergy.com	Overland Park	KS	66202	913-643-2300	
Cary Oil Company Inc 110 Mackenan Dr PO Box 5189 *TF:* 800-227-9645 ■ *Web:* www.caryoil.com	Cary	NC	27511	919-462-1100	481-6862
Central Crude Inc 4187 Hwy 3059 PO Box 1863 *TF:* 800-245-8408 ■ *Web:* www.centralcrude.com	Lake Charles	LA	70602	337-436-1000	436-9602
Central Oil & Supply Corp 2300 Booth St *Web:* www.central-oil.com	Monroe	LA	71201	318-388-2602	
Childers Oil Co 51 Hwy 2034 *Web:* www.doublekwik.com	Whitesburg	KY	41858	606-633-2525	
CHS Inc 3520 E River Rd PO Box 6878 *TF:* 888-254-0632 ■ *Web:* www.greenway.coop	Rochester	MN	55903	507-289-4086	289-7653
Coleman Oil Co 335 Mill Rd *Web:* www.colemanoil.com	Lewiston	ID	83501	208-799-2000	
Connell Oil Inc 1015 N Oregon Ave PO Box 3998 *Web:* www.connelloil.com	Pasco	WA	99302	509-547-3326	
Conrad & Bischoff Inc 2251 N Holmes Ave *Web:* www.conradbischoff.com	Idaho Falls	ID	83401	208-522-4217	
Cross Petroleum Inc 6920 Lockheed Dr *Web:* www.crosspetroleum.com	Redding	CA	96002	530-221-2588	
Dooley's Petroleum Inc 304 Main Ave. *Web:* www.dooleypetro.com	Murdock	MN	56271	320-875-2641	
Douglass Distributing Co 325 E Forest Ave *Web:* www.douglassdist.com	Sherman	TX	75090	903-893-1181	
Finley Resources Inc 1308 Lake St *Web:* www.finleyresources.com	Fort Worth	TX	76102	817-336-1924	
G&B Oil Company Inc 667 N Bridge St *Web:* www.gbenergy.com	Elkin	NC	28621	336-835-3607	
GM Petroleum Distributors Inc 2100 First Ave S *Web:* www.gmpetroleum.com	Billings	MT	59101	406-252-4661	
Gresham Petroleum Co 415 Pershing Ave P O Box 690 *Web:* www.greshampetroleum.com	Indianola	MS	38751	662-884-5000	
Hampel Oil Distributors Inc 3727 S W St *Web:* www.hampeloil.com	Wichita	KS	67217	316-529-1162	
Harpel Oil Company Inc 5480 Brighton Blvd *Web:* www.harpeloil.com	Commerce City	CO	80022	303-294-0767	
HOC Industries Inc 3511 N Ohio St *Web:* www.hocindustries.com	Wichita	KS	67219	316-838-4663	
Houston Fuel Oil Terminal Co 16642 Jacintoport Blvd *Web:* www.hfotco.com	Houston	TX	77015	281-452-3390	452-6306
Houston-Pasadena Apache Oil Company LP 5136 Spencer Hwy *Web:* www.apacheoilcompany.com	Pasadena	TX	77505	281-487-5400	
Hurt Company Inc, The 3310 Alice St *Web:* www.hurtco.com	Houston	TX	77021	713-747-7411	
Jack Becker Distributors Inc 6800 Suemac Pl *TF:* 800-488-8411 ■ *Web:* www.jackbecker.com	Jacksonville	FL	32254	800-488-8411	
JBC Inc 1414 E 20th St Ste 6 *Web:* www.jbc1.com	Scottsbluff	NE	69361	308-635-0455	
Jernigan Oil Company Inc 415 E Main St PO Box 688 *Web:* www.jerniganoil.com	Ahoskie	NC	27910	252-332-2131	
Johnson Oil Company of Gaylord 507 S Otsego Ave *Web:* www.johnsonspropane.com	Gaylord	MI	49734	989-732-2451	
Jones Petroleum Company Inc 407 E Second St *Web:* www.jonespetroleum.com	Jackson	GA	30233	770-775-2386	
Kellerstrass Oil Co 1500 West 2550 South *Web:* kellerstrassoil.com	Ogden	UT	84401	801-392-9516	392-9589
Ken Bettridge Distributing Inc 386 North 100 West *Web:* www.kboil.net	Cedar City	UT	84721	435-586-2411	
Kentucky Oil & Refining Co 156 Kentucky Oil Village *Web:* www.teamkore.com	Betsy Layne	KY	41605	606-478-9501	
LBC Houston 11666 Port Rd *Web:* www.lbchouston.com	Seabrook	TX	77586	281-474-4433	291-3428
Lee Oil Company Inc 1655 Bypass 35 *Web:* www.leeoilalvin.com	Alvin	TX	77511	281-331-3445	
Link Energy LLC 2000 W Sam Houston Pkwy S *Web:* www.linkenergy.com	Houston	TX	77042	713-993-5000	
Lott Oil Company Inc 1855 Hwy 1 *Web:* www.lottoil.com	Natchitoches	LA	71457	318-352-2055	
Magellan Midstream Partners LP One Williams Ctr *NYSE: MMP* ■ **Fax:* Mail Rm ■ *TF:* 800-574-6671 ■ *Web:* www.magellanlp.com	Tulsa	OK	74172	918-574-7000	573-6714*
Magness Oil Co 167 Tucker Cemetary Rd *Web:* www.magnessoil.com	Gassville	AR	72635	870-425-4353	
Maples Gas Company Inc 101-65th Ave *Web:* www.maplesgas.com	Meridian	MS	39301	601-693-5115	
Max Arnold & Sons LLC 702 N Main St *Web:* www.maxfuel.net	Hopkinsville	KY	42240	270-885-8488	
Mccraw Oil Company Inc 2207 N Ctr St *Web:* www.mccrawoil.com	Bonham	TX	75418	903-583-7481	
McPherson Companies Inc, The 5051 Cardinal St *Web:* www.mcphersonoil.com	Trussville	AL	35173	205-661-4400	
MFA Oil Co One Ray Young Dr *Web:* www.mfaoil.com	Columbia	MO	65205	573-442-0171	
Mid-State Petroleum Inc 4192 Mendenhall Oaks Pkwy *Web:* www.mid-statepetroleum.com	High Point	NC	27265	336-841-3000	
Mid-Town Petroleum Inc 9707 S 76th Ave *Web:* www.midtownoil.com	Bridgeview	IL	60455	708-599-8700	
Molo Oil Company Inc 123 Southern Ave *Web:* www.molocompanies.com	Dubuque	IA	52003	563-557-7540	
Nittany Oil Company Inc 1540 Martin St *Web:* www.nittanyoil.com	State College	PA	16803	814-237-4859	
NuStar Terminal Canada Partnership 4090 Port Malcolm Rd	Point Tupper	NS	B9A1Z5	902-625-1711	625-3098
Oiltanking Houston LP 15602 Jacinto Port Blvd *Web:* www.oiltanking.com	Houston	TX	77015	281-457-7900	457-7991
Powell-Christensen Inc 501 E Wine Country Rd *Web:* www.repowell.net	Grandview	WA	98930	509-882-2115	
Pumpelly Oil Company LLC 1890 Swisco Rd PO Box 2059 *Web:* www.reladyne.com	Sulphur	LA	70664	337-625-1117	
Quarles Petroleum Inc 1701 Fall Hill Ave *Web:* www.quarlesinc.com	Fredericksburg	VA	22401	540-371-2400	
R.H. Smith Distributing Co 315 Wine Country Rd *Web:* www.rhsmith.com	Grandview	WA	98930	509-882-3377	
Scott Petroleum Corporation Inc 102 Main St *Web:* www.scottpetroleuminc.com	Itta Bena	MS	38941	662-254-9024	
Sweetwater Valley Oil Company Inc 1236 New Hwy 68 *Web:* www.sweetwatervalleyoil.com	Sweetwater	TN	37874	423-337-6671	
Thomas Petroleum LLC 9701 US Hwy 59 N *Web:* www.thomaspetro.com	Victoria	TX	77905	361-573-7662	
TransMontaigne Partners LP 1670 Broadway Ste 3100 *NYSE: TLP* ■ *Web:* www.transmontaignepartners.com	Denver	CO	80202	303-626-8200	626-8228
Victron Energy Inc 105 YMCA Dr *Web:* victrongroup.com	Waxahachie	TX	75165	469-517-2000	
Vital Records Inc PO Box 688 *Web:* www.vitalrecords.com	Flagtown	NJ	08821	908-369-6900	369-7319
W.H. Breshears Inc 720 B St *Web:* www.whbreshears.com	Modesto	CA	95354	209-522-7291	

585 PHARMACEUTICAL COMPANIES

SEE ALSO Diagnostic Products p. 2198; Medicinal Chemicals & Botanical Products p. 2736; Pharmaceutical Companies - Generic Drugs p. 2924; Pharmaceutical & Diagnostic Products - Veterinary p. 2924; Vitamins & Nutritional Supplements p. 3286; Biotechnology Companies p. 1869

				Phone	Fax
aaiPharma Inc 1726 N 23rd St **Fax Area Code:* 910 ■ *TF:* 800-575-4224 ■ *Web:* www.aaipharma.com	Wilmington	NC	28405	800-575-4224	815-2300*
Abbott Laboratories Pharmaceutical Products Div 100 Research Dr Bioresearch Ctr *TF:* 866-427-8477 ■ *Web:* www.abbott.com	Worcester	MA	01605	847-937-6100	
Accentia BioPharmaceuticals Inc 324 S Hyde Pk Ave Ste 350 *OTC: ABPI*	Tampa	FL	33606	813-864-2554	
Accucaps Industries Ltd 2125 Ambassador Dr *TF:* 800-665-7210 ■ *Web:* www.accucaps.com	Windsor	ON	N9C3R5	519-969-5404	250-3321
Advanced Life Sciences Inc 1440 Davey Rd *OTC: ADLS* ■ *Web:* www.advancedlifesciences.com	Woodridge	IL	60517	630-739-6744	739-6754
Allergan Inc 2525 Dupont Dr *NYSE: AGN* ■ **Fax:* Mail Rm ■ *TF:* 800-347-4500 ■ *Web:* www.allergan.com	Irvine	CA	92612	714-246-4500	246-6987*
Alva-Amco Pharmacal Cos Inc 7711 Merrimac Ave *TF:* 800-792-2582 ■ *Web:* www.alva-amco.com	Niles	IL	60714	847-663-0700	663-1400
Amneal Pharmaceuticals LLC 75 Adams Ave *NYSE: IPAH* ■ **Fax Area Code:* 908 ■ *TF:* 866-525-7270	Hauppauge	NY	11788	631-952-0214	947-4146*

Company / Address	City	State	Zip	Phone	Fax
Amphastar Pharmaceuticals Inc 11570 Sixth St	Rancho Cucamonga	CA	91730	909-980-9484	980-8296
TF: 800-423-4136 ■ *Web:* www.amphastar.com					
Amylin Pharmaceuticals Inc 9360 Towne Ctr Dr	San Diego	CA	92121	858-552-2200	552-2212
NASDAQ: AMLN ■ *Web:* www.bms.com					
Apotex Inc 150 Signet Dr	Toronto	ON	M9L1T9	416-749-9300	401-3849
TF: 800-268-4623 ■ *Web:* www.apotex.com					
Apothecus Pharmaceutical Corp 220 Townsend Sq	Oyster Bay	NY	11771	516-624-8200	624-8201
TF: 800-227-2393 ■ *Web:* www.apothecus.com					
AstraZeneca Canada Inc 1004 Middlegate Rd	Mississauga	ON	L4Y1M4	905-277-7111	270-3248
TF: 800-565-5877 ■ *Web:* www.astrazeneca.ca					
AstraZeneca Pharmaceuticals LP 1800 Concord Pk PO Box 15437	Wilmington	DE	19850	800-236-9933	
TF: 800-236-9933 ■ *Web:* www.astrazeneca-us.com					
Atossa Genetics Inc 2345 Eastlake Ave E Ste 201	Seattle	WA	98102	206-588-0256	
Web: www.atossagenetics.com					
AutoImmune Inc 1199 Madia St	Pasadena	CA	91103	626-792-1235	
OTC: AIMM ■ *Web:* www.autoimmuneinc.com					
Banner Pharmacaps Inc 4100 Mendenhall Oaks Pkwy	High Point	NC	27265	336-812-3442	812-8777
TF Cust Svc: 866-529-2922 ■ *Web:* www.patheon.com					
Bausch & Lomb Inc 1400 N Goodman St	Rochester	NY	14609	585-338-6000	338-6896
TF: 800-553-5340 ■ *Web:* www.bausch.com					
Bausch & Lomb Pharmaceuticals Inc 8500 Hidden River Pkwy	Tampa	FL	33637	800-553-5340	
TF Cust Svc: 800-323-0000 ■ *Web:* www.bausch.com					
Baxter International Inc One Baxter Pkwy	Deerfield	IL	60015	847-948-2000	948-3948
NYSE: BAX ■ *Web:* www.baxter.com					
Bayer Corp 36 Columbia Rd	Morristown	NJ	07960	973-254-5000	
Web: www.bayerus.com					
Bayer Inc 77 Belfield Rd	Toronto	ON	M9W1G6	416-248-0771	248-6762*
**Fax:* Hum Res ■ *TF:* 800-622-2937 ■ *Web:* www.bayer.ca					
Beluga Composites Corp 6830 du Parc Ave Ste 572	Montreal	QC	H3N1W7	514-278-7856	
Web: www.belugacorporation.com.					
Berlex Laboratories Inc Six W Belt	Wayne	NJ	07470	973-694-4100	
TF: 888-842-2937 ■ *Web:* www.berlex.com					
Biocare Medical LLC 4040 Pike Ln	Concord	CA	94520	925-603-8000	
Web: biocare.net					
BioSante Pharmaceuticals Inc 111 Barclay Blvd Ste 280	Lincolnshire	IL	60069	847-478-0500	478-9152
NASDAQ: BPAX ■ *Web:* www.biospace.com/					
BioSpecifics Technologies Corp 35 Wilbur St	Lynbrook	NY	11563	516-593-7000	593-7039
NASDAQ: BSTC ■ *Web:* www.biospecifics.com					
Blistex Inc 1800 Swift Dr	Oak Brook	IL	60523	800-837-1800	571-3437*
**Fax Area Code:* 630 ■ *TF Cust Svc:* 800-837-1800 ■ *Web:* www.blistex.com					
Boehringer Ingelheim Ltd 5180 S Service Rd	Burlington	ON	L7L5H4	905-639-0333	639-3769
TF: 800-263-9107 ■ *Web:* www.boehringer-ingelheim.com					
Boehringer Ingelheim Pharmaceuticals Inc 900 Ridgebury Rd	Ridgefield	CT	06877	203-798-9988	791-6234*
**Fax:* Cust Svc ■ *TF:* 800-243-0127 ■ *Web:* www.boehringer-ingelheim.com					
Botanical Laboratories Inc 1441 W Smith Rd	Ferndale	WA	98248	360-384-5656	384-1140
TF: 800-232-4005 ■ *Web:* www.wellesse.com					
Bracco Diagnostics Inc 107 College Rd E	Princeton	NJ	08540	609-514-2200	
Web: corporate.bracco.com					
Brioschi Inc 19-01 Pollitt Dr	Fair Lawn	NJ	07410	201-796-4226	
Bristol-Myers Squibb Canada Inc 2344 Alfred-Nobel Blvd Ste 300	Montreal	QC	H4S0A4	514-333-3200	335-4102
TF Cust Svc: 800-267-0005 ■ *Web:* www.bmscanada.ca					
Bristol-Myers Squibb Co 345 Pk Ave	New York	NY	10154	212-546-4000	546-4020
NYSE: BMY ■ *Web:* www.bms.com					
Cardiovascular Consultants Pc 4330 Wornall Rd Ste 2000	Kansas City	MO	64111	816-931-1883	
Web: saintlukeshealthsystem.org/					
Care-Tech Laboratories Inc 3224 S KingsHwy Blvd	Saint Louis	MO	63139	314-772-4610	772-4613
TF: 800-325-9681 ■ *Web:* www.caretechlabs.com					
Cary Pharmaceuticals Inc 9903 Windy Hollow Rd	Great Falls	VA	22066	703-759-7460	
Web: www.carypharma.com					
CB Fleet Co Inc 4615 Murray Pl	Lynchburg	VA	24502	434-528-4000	
TF: 866-255-6960 ■ *Web:* www.cbfleet.com					
Chattem Inc 1715 W 38th St PO Box 2219	Chattanooga	TN	37409	423-821-4571	821-0395
Web: www.chattem.com					
Chembio Diagnostics Inc 3661 Horseblock Rd	Medford	NY	11763	631-924-1135	924-2065
NASDAQ: CEMI ■ *TF:* 844-243-6246 ■ *Web:* www.chembio.com					
Cirrus Healthcare Products LLC 60 Main St PO Box 220	Cold Spring Harbor	NY	11724	631-692-7600	692-9844
Web: www.cirrushealthcare.com					
Coating Place Inc 200 Paoli St	Verona	WI	53593	608-845-9521	845-9526
Web: www.coatingplace.com					
Combe Inc 1101 Westchester Ave	White Plains	NY	10604	914-694-5454	
TF: 800-431-2610 ■ *Web:* www.combe.com					
Corium International Inc 4558 50th St SE	Grand Rapids	MI	49512	616-656-4563	
Web: www.coriumgroup.com					
Coty Inc Two Pk Ave 17th Fl	New York	NY	10016	212-479-4300	336-6064*
**Fax Area Code:* 866 ■ *Web:* www.coty.com					
Covalon Technologies Ltd 405 Britannia Rd E Ste 106	Mississauga	ON	L4Z3E6	905-568-8400	
Web: www.covalon.com					
Daiichi Sankyo Inc 2 Hilton Ct	Parsippany	NJ	07054	973-359-2600	944-2645
Web: www.dsi.com					
Darby Group Cos Inc 300 Jericho Quad	Jericho	NY	11753	516-683-1800	688-2880
TF: 888-683-5001 ■ *Web:* www.darbygroup.com					
Delavau LLC 10101 Roosevelt Blvd	Philadelphia	PA	19154	215-671-1400	671-1401
Web: www.delavau.com					
Dickinson Brands Inc 31 E High St	East Hampton	CT	06424	860-267-2279	
TF: 888-860-2279 ■ *Web:* dickinsonbrands.com					
Discharge Resource Group 400 Oyster Point Blvd Ste 440	South San Francisco	CA	94080	415-877-8111	
Web: drgstaffing.com					
DPT Laboratories Ltd 318 McCullough	San Antonio	TX	78215	210-476-8150	224-6505
TF: 866-225-5378 ■ *Web:* www.dptlabs.com					
Dr Reddy's Laboratories Inc 200 Summerset Corporate Blvd	Bridgewater	NJ	08807	908-203-4900	203-4940
NYSE: RDY ■ *Web:* www.drreddys.com					
Dynavax Technologies Corp 2929 Seventh St Ste 100	Berkeley	CA	94710	510-848-5100	848-1327
NASDAQ: DVAX ■ *TF:* 877-848-5100 ■ *Web:* www.dynavax.com					
Eco-Med Pharmaceuticals Inc 7050B Bramalea Rd Unit 58	Mississauga	ON	L5S1S9	905-405-1050	405-0775
Web: www.eco-med.com					
Edwards Lifesciences Corp One Edwards Way	Irvine	CA	92614	949-250-2500	250-2525*
NYSE: EW ■ **Fax:* Cust Svc ■ *TF:* 800-424-3278 ■ *Web:* www.edwards.com					
Eisai Inc 100 Tice Blvd	Woodcliff Lake	NJ	07677	201-692-1100	692-1804
TF: 866-613-4724 ■ *Web:* www.eisai.com					
Eli Lilly & Co Lilly Corporate Ctr	Indianapolis	IN	46285	317-276-2000	535-4615*
NYSE: LLY ■ **Fax Area Code:* 800 ■ **Fax:* Cust Svc ■ *TF Prod Info:* 800-545-5979 ■ *Web:* www.lilly.com					
Eli Lilly Canada Inc 3650 Danforth Ave	Toronto	ON	M1N2E8	416-694-3221	699-7252*
**Fax:* Hum Res ■ *TF:* 888-545-5972 ■ *Web:* www.lilly.ca					
Elona Bio Technologies Inc 1040 Sierra Dr Ste 1000	Greenwood	IN	46143	317-865-4770	
Web: elonabiotech.wordpress.com					
Endo Pharmaceuticals Holdings Inc 100 Endo Blvd	Chadds Ford	PA	19317	610-558-9800	558-8979
TF Cust Svc: 800-462-3636 ■ *Web:* www.endo.com					
First Priority Inc 1590 Todd Farm Dr	Elgin	IL	60123	847-289-1600	
TF: 800-650-4899 ■ *Web:* www.prioritycare.com					
Forest Pharmaceutical Inc 13600 Shoreline Dr	Earth City	MO	63045	314-493-7000	
TF: 800-678-1605 ■ *Web:* www.frx.com					
G & W Laboratories Inc 111 Coolidge St	South Plainfield	NJ	07080	908-753-2000	753-5174*
**Fax:* Sales ■ *TF:* 800-922-1038 ■ *Web:* www.gwlabs.com					
Galderma Laboratories Inc 14501 N Fwy	Fort Worth	TX	76177	817-961-5000	
TF: 866-735-4137 ■ *Web:* www.galderma.com					
Germiphene Corp 1379 Colborne St E PO Box 1748	Brantford	ON	N3T5M1	519-759-7100	759-1625
TF: 800-265-9931 ■ *Web:* www.germiphene.com					
GlaxoSmithKline Inc 7333 Mississauga Rd N	Mississauga	ON	L5N6L4	905-819-3000	819-3099
TF: 800-387-7374 ■ *Web:* www.gsk.ca					
GMP Laboratories of America Inc 2931 E La Jolla St	Anaheim	CA	92806	714-630-2467	237-1374
Web: www.gmplabs.com					
Goyescas Corp of Florida Inc PO Box 524207	Miami	FL	33152	305-591-1474	591-7446
Web: www.goyescasusa.com					
Halocarbon Products Corp PO Box 661	River Edge	NJ	07661	201-262-8899	262-0019
TF: 800-338-5803 ■ *Web:* www.halocarbon.com					
Halozyme Therapeutics Inc 11388 Sorrento Vly Rd	San Diego	CA	92121	858-794-8889	704-8311
NASDAQ: HALO ■ *Web:* www.halozyme.com					
Heron Therapeutics Inc 123 Saginaw Dr	Redwood City	CA	94063	650-366-2626	365-6490
OTC: HRTX ■ *Web:* www.appharma.com					
Hi-Tech Pharmacal Co Inc 369 Bayview Ave	Amityville	NY	11701	631-789-8228	943-3694*
NASDAQ: HITK ■ **Fax Area Code:* 800 ■ *TF:* 888-628-0581 ■ *Web:* www.hitechpharm.com					
Hoffmann-LaRoche Inc 340 Kingsland St	Nutley	NJ	07110	973-235-5000	777-3327
TF: 800-526-6367 ■ *Web:* www.roche.com					
Hope Pharmaceuticals Inc 16416 N 92nd St Ste 125	Scottsdale	AZ	85260	800-755-9595	607-1971*
**Fax Area Code:* 480 ■ *TF:* 800-755-9595 ■ *Web:* www.hopepharm.com					
Hospira Inc 275 N Field Dr	Lake Forest	IL	60045	224-212-2000	
NYSE: HSP ■ *TF:* 877-946-7747 ■ *Web:* www.hospira.com					
Humco Holding Group Inc 7400 Alumax Dr	Texarkana	TX	75501	903-334-6200	334-6300
TF: 800-662-3435 ■ *Web:* www.humco.com					
Immtech Pharmaceuticals One N End Ave	New York	NY	10282	212-791-2911	791-2917
TF: 877-898-8038 ■ *Web:* www.immtechpharma.com					
Infinity Pharmaceuticals Inc 780 Memorial Dr	Cambridge	MA	02139	617-453-1000	453-1001
NASDAQ: INFI ■ *Web:* www.infi.com					
InterMune Inc 3280 Bayshore Blvd	Brisbane	CA	94005	415-466-2200	466-2300
NASDAQ: ITMN ■ *TF:* 877-862-2292 ■ *Web:* www.intermune.com					
Jaapharm Canada Inc 510 Rowntree Dairy Rd Unit 4	Woodbridge	ON	L4L8H2	905-851-7885	856-5838
Web: www.jaapharm.com					
Janssen Healthcare Learning Ctr PO Box 200	Titusville	NJ	08560	800-526-7736	
TF: 800-526-7736 ■ *Web:* www.janssenpharmaceuticalsinc.com					
Janssen Pharmaceutica Inc 1125 Trenton-Harbourton Rd	Titusville	NJ	08560	609-730-2000	730-2323
TF: 800-526-7736 ■ *Web:* www.janssen.com					
Janssen-Ortho Inc 19 Green Belt Dr	Toronto	ON	M3C1L9	416-449-9444	449-2658
TF: 800-387-8781 ■ *Web:* janssen.ca					
Jazz Pharmaceuticals Inc 3180 Porter Dr	Palo Alto	CA	94304	650-496-3777	
TF: 866-997-3688 ■ *Web:* www.jazzpharma.com					
Juniper Pharmaceuticals Inc 354 Eisenhower Pkwy Plaza 1 2nd Fl	Livingston	NJ	07039	973-994-3999	994-3001
NASDAQ: CBRX ■ *TF:* 866-566-5636 ■ *Web:* www.columbialabs.com					
K P Pharmaceutical Technology Inc 1212 W Rappel Ave	Bloomington	IN	47404	812-330-8121	330-8363
Web: www.kppt.com					
Keryx Biopharmaceuticals Inc 750 Lexington Ave 20th Fl	New York	NY	10022	212-531-5965	531-5961
NASDAQ: KERX ■ *TF:* 800-903-0247 ■ *Web:* www.keryx.com					
King Bio Pharmaceuticals Inc Three Westside Dr	Asheville	NC	28806	828-255-0201	255-0940
TF: 800-543-3245 ■ *Web:* www.kingbio.com					

				Phone	Fax
Konsyl Pharmaceuticals Inc 8050 Industrial Pk Rd *TF:* 800-356-6795 ■ *Web:* www.konsyl.com	Easton	MD	21601	410-822-5192	820-7032
Kramer Laboratories Inc 8778 SW Eigth St *TF:* 800-824-4894 ■ *Web:* www.kramerlabs.com	Miami	FL	33174	305-223-1287	223-5510
Kyowa Hakko USA Inc 212 Carnegie Ctr Ste 101 *Web:* www.kyowa-kirin-pharma.com	Princeton	NJ	08540	609-919-1100	919-1111
LED Medical Diagnostics Inc 235-5589 Byrne Rd *Web:* www.leddental.com	Burnaby	BC	V5J3J1	604-434-4614	
Ligand Pharmaceuticals Inc 11085 N Torrey Pines Rd Ste 300 *NASDAQ: LGND* ■ *Web:* www.ligand.com	La Jolla	CA	92037	858-550-7500	550-7506
Major Pharmaceutical Co 31778 Enterprise Dr *TF:* 800-875-0123 ■ *Web:* www.majorpharmaceuticals.com	Livonia	MI	48150	734-743-6161	
McNeil Consumer & Specialty Pharmaceuticals 7050 Camp Hill Rd **Fax:* Cust Svc ■ *TF:* 800-962-5357 ■ *Web:* www.mcneil-consumer.com/	Fort Washington	PA	19034	215-273-7000	273-7000*
Medical Products Laboratories Inc 9990 Global Rd PO Box 14366 *TF:* 800-523-0191 ■ *Web:* www.mplusa.com	Philadelphia	PA	19115	215-677-2700	677-7736
Medicis Pharmaceutical Corp 7720 N Dobson Rd *TF Cust Svc:* 855-396-2084 ■ *Web:* valeant.com/operational-expertise/valeant-united-states	Scottsdale	AZ	85256	800-321-4576	
Medivation Inc 201 Spear St Third Fl *NASDAQ: MDVN* ■ *Web:* www.medivation.com	San Francisco	CA	94105	415-543-3470	543-3411
MedPointe Pharmaceuticals 265 Davidson Ave Ste 300 *Web:* meda.us/	Somerset	NJ	08873	732-564-2200	564-2434
Melaleuca Inc 3910 S Yellowstone Hwy **Fax Area Code:* 888 ■ *TF Sales:* 800-282-3000 ■ *Web:* www.melaleuca.com	Idaho Falls	ID	83402	208-522-0700	528-2090*
Mentholatum Company Inc 707 Sterling Dr *TF:* 800-688-7660 ■ *Web:* www.mentholatum.com	Orchard Park	NY	14127	716-677-2500	677-9528
Merck & Company Inc One Merck Dr PO Box 100 *NYSE: MRK* ■ *TF Cust Svc:* 800-672-6372 ■ *Web:* www.merck.com	Whitehouse Station	NJ	08889	908-423-1000	
Merial Canada Inc 20000 Clark Graham *Web:* www.merial.ca	Baie-d'urfe	QC	H9X4B6	514-457-1555	
Mikart Inc 1750 Chattahoochee Ave NW *TF:* 888-464-5278 ■ *Web:* www.mikart.com	Atlanta	GA	30318	404-351-4510	350-0432
Mission Pharmacal PO Box 786099 *TF:* 800-531-3333 ■ *Web:* missionpharmacal.com	San Antonio	TX	78278	210-696-8400	696-6010
Mueller Sports Medicine Inc One Quench Dr *Web:* www.muellersportsmed.com	Prairie Du Sac	WI	53578	608-643-8530	
Murty Pharmaceuticals Inc 518 Codell Dr *Web:* www.mpirx.com	Lexington	KY	40509	859-266-2446	
Mylan 2751 Napa Valley Corporate Dr *TF:* 800-527-4278 ■ *Web:* www.mylanspecialty.com	Napa	CA	94558	707-224-3200	
Mylan Pharmaceuticals Inc 781 Chestnut Ridge Rd **Fax Area Code:* 304 ■ *TF:* 800-796-9526 ■ *Web:* mylan.com/products	Morgantown	WV	26505	800-796-9526	598-5406*
NanoScreen LLC 917 Commerce Cir *Web:* www.nanoscreen.com	Hanahan	SC	29410	843-881-8841	
Nature's Value Inc 468 Mill Rd *Web:* www.naturesvalue.com	Coram	NY	11727	631-846-2500	846-2527
Navinta LLC 1499 Lower Ferry Rd *Web:* navinta.com	Ewing	NJ	08618	609-883-1135	
NBTY Manufacturing 901 E 233rd St *Web:* www.nbty.com/	Carson	CA	90745	310-835-8400	952-7760
Neos Therapeutics 2940 N Hwy 360 Ste 100 *TF:* 844-375-8324 ■ *Web:* www.neostx.com	Grand Prairie	TX	75050	972-408-1300	408-1143
NextPharma Technologies Inc 5340 Eastgate Mall *Web:* www.nextpharma.com	San Diego	CA	92121	858-450-3123	450-0785
Noramco Inc 1440 Olympic Dr *Web:* www.noramco.com	Athens	GA	30601	706-353-4400	353-3205
NovaDel Pharma Inc 1200 Rt 22 E Ste 2000 *Web:* www.novadel.com	Bridgewater	NJ	08807	908-203-4640	203-4744
Novartis Pharmaceuticals Canada Inc 385 boul Bouchard **Fax:* Cust Svc ■ *TF:* 800-465-2244 ■ *Web:* www.novartis.ca	Dorval	QC	H9S1A9	514-631-6775	631-1867*
Novartis Pharmaceuticals Co 10401 Cornhusker Hwy *TF:* 888-669-6682 ■ *Web:* www.us.novartis.com	Waverly	NE	68462	402-464-6311	
Novartis Pharmaceuticals Corp 1 Health Plaza **Fax Area Code:* 973 ■ *TF Cust Svc:* 888-669-6682 ■ *Web:* www.pharma.us.novartis.com	East Hanover	NJ	07936	862-778-8300	781-8265*
Noven Pharmaceuticals Inc 11960 SW 144th St *Web:* www.noven.com	Miami	FL	33186	305-253-5099	251-1887
Novo Nordisk of North America Inc 100 College Rd W *TF:* 800-727-6500 ■ *Web:* www.novonordisk-us.com	Princeton	NJ	08540	609-987-5800	987-5394
Novo Nordisk Pharmaceuticals Inc 800 Scudders Mill Rd *TF Cust Svc:* 800-727-6500 ■ *Web:* www.novonordisk-us.com	Princeton	NJ	08536	609-987-5800	987-5394
Numark Laboratories Inc 164 Northfield Ave **Fax Area Code:* 732 ■ *TF:* 800-338-8079 ■ *Web:* www.numarklabs.com	Edison	NJ	08837	800-338-8079	225-0066*
NutriCology Inc 2300 N Loop Rd *Web:* www.nutricology.com	Alameda	CA	94502	510-263-2000	263-2100
Odor Management Inc 18-6 E Dundee Rd Ste 101 *TF:* 800-662-6367 ■ *Web:* www.odormanagement.com	Barrington	IL	60010	847-304-9111	304-0989
Ono Pharma USA Inc 2000 Lenox Dr *Web:* www.ono.co.jp	Trenton	NJ	08648	609-219-1010	219-9229
Pain Therapeutics Inc 7801 N Capital of Texas Hwy Ste 260 *NASDAQ: PTIE* ■ *Web:* www.paintrials.com	Austin	TX	78731	512-501-2444	614-0414

				Phone	Fax
Particle Dynamics International LLC 2629 S Hanley Rd *TF:* 800-452-4682 ■ *Web:* pdhllc.com	Saint Louis	MO	63144	314-968-2376	781-3354
Pegasus Laboratories Inc 8809 Ely Rd *Web:* www.pegasuslabs.com	Pensacola	FL	32514	850-478-2770	478-5639
Pfizer Animal Health 5 Giralda Farms *Web:* www.zoetisus.com/	Madison	NJ	07940	888-963-8471	
Pfizer Canada Inc 17300 TransCanada Hwy *TF:* 800-463-6001 ■ *Web:* www.pfizer.ca	Kirkland	QC	H9J2M5	514-695-0500	426-6997
Pfizer Inc 235 E 42nd St *NYSE: PFE* ■ *TF:* 800-879-3477 ■ *Web:* www.pfizer.com	New York	NY	10017	212-733-2323	573-7851
Pfizer Inc Pharmaceuticals Group 235 E 42nd St *Web:* www.pfizer.com	New York	NY	10017	212-573-2323	
PharmAthene Inc One Pk Pl Ste 450 *Web:* www.pharmathene.com	Annapolis	MD	21401	410-269-2600	269-2601
Pharmos Corp 99 Wood Ave S Ste 302 *PINK: PARS* ■ *Web:* www.pharmoscorp.com	Iselin	NJ	08830	732-452-9556	
Procter & Gamble Pharmaceuticals Canada Inc PO Box 355 Stn A *TF:* 800-668-0150 ■ *Web:* www.pg.com/en_ca	Toronto	ON	M5W1C5	416-730-4711	
Procter & Gamble Pharmaceuticals Inc One Proctor & Gamble Plz *Web:* pg.com	Cincinnati	OH	45202	513-983-1100	
Prometheus Laboratories Inc 9410 Carroll Pk Dr **Fax Area Code:* 877 ■ *TF:* 888-892-8391 ■ *Web:* www.prometheuslabs.com	San Diego	CA	92121	888-892-8391	816-4019*
ProPhase Labs Inc 621 Shady Retreat Rd *NASDAQ: PRPH* ■ *TF:* 800-505-2653 ■ *Web:* www.prophaselabs.com	Doylestown	PA	18901	215-345-0919	
Protide Pharmaceuticals Inc 505 Oakwood Rd Ste 200 *TF:* 800-552-3569 ■ *Web:* www.protidepharma.com	Lake Zurich	IL	60047	847-726-3100	726-3110
Qal-Tek Associates LLC 3998 Commerce Cir *Web:* www.qaltek.com	Idaho Falls	ID	83401	208-523-5557	
QLT USA Inc 2579 Midpoint Dr **Fax Area Code:* 604 ■ *TF:* 800-901-5241 ■ *Web:* www.qltinc.com	Fort Collins	CO	80525	970-482-5868	707-7001*
Qualicaps Inc 6505 Franz Warner Pkwy *TF:* 800-227-7853 ■ *Web:* www.qualicaps.com	Whitsett	NC	27377	336-449-3900	449-3333
Qualitest Pharmaceuticals 130 Vintage Dr **Fax Area Code:* 256 ■ *TF:* 800-444-4011 ■ *Web:* www.qualitestrx.com	Huntsville	AL	35811	800-444-4011	859-4021*
Quatrx Pharmaceuticals Co 777 E Eisenhower Pkwy Ste 100 *Web:* www.quatrx.com	Ann Arbor	MI	48108	734-913-9900	913-0743
Quintiles Canada Inc 100 Alexis-Nihon Ste 800 *TF General:* 866-267-4479 ■ *Web:* www.quintiles.com	Saint Laurent	QC	H4M2P4	514-855-0888	
Quintiles Transnational Corp 4820 Emperor Blvd *TF:* 866-267-4479 ■ *Web:* www.quintiles.com	Durham	NC	27703	919-998-2000	998-2003
RegeneRx Biopharmaceuticals Inc 15245 Shady Grove Rd Ste 470 *OTC: RGRX* ■ *Web:* www.regenerx.com	Rockville	MD	20850	301-208-9191	208-9194
Regenesis Biomedical Inc 5301 N Pima Rd *Web:* www.regenesisbio.com	Scottsdale	AZ	85250	480-970-4970	
Regis Technologies Inc 8210 Austin Ave *TF:* 800-323-8144 ■ *Web:* www.registech.com	Morton Grove	IL	60053	847-967-6000	967-5876
Roche Carolina Inc 6173 E Old Marion Hwy *Web:* www.rochecarolina.com	Florence	SC	29506	843-629-4300	
Roxane Laboratories Inc 1809 Wilson Rd *TF Cust Svc:* 800-520-1631 ■ *Web:* www.roxane.com	Columbus	OH	43228	614-276-4000	308-3540
Rules-based Medicine Inc 3300 Duval Rd *TF:* 866-726-6277 ■ *Web:* rbm.myriad.com	Austin	TX	78759	512-835-8026	835-4687
Sagent Pharmaceuticals Inc 1901 N Roselle Rd *NASDAQ: SGNT* ■ *Web:* www.sagentpharma.com	Schaumburg	IL	60195	847-908-1600	908-1601
Salix Pharmaceuticals Inc 8510 Colonnade Ctr Dr *NASDAQ: SLXP* ■ *TF:* 800-508-0024 ■ *Web:* www.salix.com	Raleigh	NC	27615	919-862-1000	862-1095
SciClone Pharmaceuticals Inc 950 Tower Ln Ste 900 *NASDAQ: SCLN* ■ *TF:* 800-724-2566 ■ *Web:* www.sciclone.com	Foster City	CA	94404	650-358-3456	358-3469
Sigma-Tau Pharmaceutical Inc 9841 Washingtonian Blvd Ste 500 *TF:* 800-447-0169 ■ *Web:* www.sigmatau.com	Gaithersburg	MD	20878	301-948-1041	948-1862
Silipos Inc 7049 Williams Rd *TF:* 800-229-4404 ■ *Web:* www.silipos.com	Niagara Falls	NY	14304	716-283-0700	283-0600
SISU Inc 7635 N Fraser Way Ste 102 *Web:* www.sisu.com	Burnaby	BC	V5J0B8	604-420-6610	
Solvay America Inc 3333 Richmond Ave *TF General:* 800-365-6565 ■ *Web:* www.solvay.com	Houston	TX	77098	713-525-6000	525-7887
Sovereign Pharmaceuticals Ltd 7590 Sand St *TF:* 877-248-0228 ■ *Web:* www.sovpharm.com	Fort Worth	TX	76118	817-284-0429	284-0531
SSS Co 71 University Ave PO Box 4447 *TF:* 800-237-3843 ■ *Web:* www.ssspharmaceuticals.com	Atlanta	GA	30315	404-521-0857	880-0383
Sucampo Pharmaceuticals Inc 4520 East-West Hwy 3rd Fl Ste 300 *NASDAQ: SCMP* ■ *TF:* 800-332-1088 ■ *Web:* www.sucampo.com	Bethesda	MD	20814	301-961-3400	961-3440
Summa Information Systems Inc 111 E Fire Tower Rd	Winterville	NC	28590	252-756-6110	
Synta Pharmaceuticals Corp 45 Hartwell Ave *NASDAQ: SNTA* ■ *Web:* www.syntapharma.com	Lexington	MA	02421	781-274-8200	274-8228
Taisho Pharmaceutical California Inc 3878 W Carson St Ste 216 *Web:* lipovitan.com	Torrance	CA	90503	310-543-2035	543-9636
Tamir Biotechnology Inc 12625 High Bluff Dr Ste 113 *OTC: ACEL* ■ *Web:* www.alfacell.com	San Diego	CA	92130	732-823-1003	652-4575
Targacept Inc 100 N Main St Ste 1510 *NASDAQ: TRGT* ■ *Web:* www.targacept.com	Winston-Salem	NC	27101	336-480-2100	480-2107
Taro Pharmaceuticals Inc 130 E Dr *TF:* 800-268-1975 ■ *Web:* www.taro.ca	Brampton	ON	L6T1C1	905-791-8276	791-5008

Company / Address	City	State	Zip	Phone	Fax
Tower Laboratories Ltd PO Box 306 *Web:* www.towerlabs.com	Centerbrook	CT	06409	860-767-2127	767-2129
UCB Pharma Inc 1950 Lake Pk Dr **Fax:* Hum Res ■ *TF:* 800-477-7877 ■ *Web:* www.ucb.com	Smyrna	GA	30080	770-970-7500	970-8857*
Unipack Inc 3253 Old Frankstown Rd *Web:* www.unipackinc.com	Pittsburgh	PA	15239	724-733-7381	327-6265
Unipharm Inc 350 Fifth Ave Ste 6701 *Web:* www.unipharmus.com	New York	NY	10118	212-594-3260	594-3261
United Therapeutics Corp 1040 Spring St *NASDAQ: UTHR* ■ *TF:* 877-864-8437 ■ *Web:* www.unither.com	Silver Spring	MD	20910	301-608-9292	608-9291
Upsher-Smith Laboratories Inc 6701 Evenstad Dr *TF:* 800-654-2299 ■ *Web:* www.upsher-smith.com	Maple Grove	MN	55369	763-315-2000	315-2001
Vanda Pharmaceuticals Inc 2200 Pennsylvania Ave NW Ste 300E *NASDAQ: VNDA* ■ *Web:* www.vandapharmaceuticals.com	Washington	DC	20037	202-734-3400	296-1450
Vivus Inc 1172 Castro St *NASDAQ: VVUS* ■ *TF:* 888-367-6873 ■ *Web:* www.vivus.com	Mountain View	CA	94040	650-934-5200	934-5389
WF Young Inc 302 Benton Dr PO Box 1990 *TF:* 800-628-9653 ■ *Web:* www.absorbine.com	East Longmeadow	MA	01028	413-526-9999	526-8990
Wright Group, The 6428 Airport Rd **Fax Area Code:* 318 ■ *TF:* 800-201-3096 ■ *Web:* www.thewrightgroup.net	Crowley	LA	70526	337-783-3096	783-3802*
Zalicus Inc 245 First St Third Fl *NASDAQ: ZLCS*	Cambridge	MA	02142	617-301-7000	425-7010
ZLB Behring LLC 1020 First Ave PO Box 61501 *TF:* 800-683-1288 ■ *Web:* www.cslbehring.com	King of Prussia	PA	19406	610-878-4000	878-4009
Zogenix Inc 12400 High Bluff Dr Ste 650 *TF:* 866-964-3649 ■ *Web:* www.zogenix.com	San Diego	CA	92130	858-259-1165	259-1166

586 PHARMACEUTICAL COMPANIES - GENERIC DRUGS

SEE ALSO Diagnostic Products p. 2198; Medicinal Chemicals & Botanical Products p. 2736; Pharmaceutical Companies p. 2921; Pharmaceutical & Diagnostic Products - Veterinary p. 2924; Vitamins & Nutritional Supplements p. 3286; Biotechnology Companies p. 1869

Company / Address	City	State	Zip	Phone	Fax
Apotex Corp 2400 N Commerce Pkwy Ste 400 **Fax Area Code:* 800 ■ *TF:* 877-427-6839 ■ *Web:* www.apotex.com	Weston	FL	33326	877-427-6839	706-5576*
Biocept Inc 5810 Nancy Ridge Dr Ste 150 *Web:* www.biocept.com	San Diego	CA	92121	858-320-8200	
Biotools Inc 17546 Bee Line Hwy *Web:* www.btools.com	Jupiter	FL	33458	561-625-0133	
Capricorn Pharma Inc 6900 English Muffin Way	Frederick	MD	21703	301-696-8520	696-1424
Church & Dwight Canada Corp 635 Secretariat Ct *Web:* www.churchdwight.ca	Mississauga	ON	L5S2A5	905-696-6570	
Difusion Technologies Inc 111 Cooperative Way Ste 250 *Web:* www.difusiontech.com	Georgetown	TX	78626	512-863-7777	
E Fougera & Co 60 Baylis Rd *TF:* 800-645-9833 ■ *Web:* www.fougera.com	Melville	NY	11747	631-454-6996	756-7017
Ethex Corp One Corporate Woods Dr	Bridgeton	MO	63044	314-646-3750	
Glenwood LLC 111 Cedar Ln *TF:* 800-542-0772 ■ *Web:* www.glenwood-llc.com	Englewood	NJ	07631	201-569-0050	569-0250
Healthpoint 3909 Hulen St *TF Cust Svc:* 800-441-8227 ■ *Web:* www.smith-nephew.com	Fort Worth	TX	76107	817-900-4000	900-4100
Impax Laboratories Inc 3735 Castor Ave *NASDAQ: IPXL* ■ *TF:* 877-994-6729 ■ *Web:* www.impaxlabs.com	Philadelphia	PA	19124	215-613-2400	613-2406
Legacy Pharmaceutical Packaging LLC 13480 Lakefront Dr *Web:* legacypackaging.com	St. Louis	MO	63045	314-813-1555	
Letco Medical Inc 1316 Commerce Dr NW *Web:* www.letcomedical.com	Decatur	AL	35601	256-350-1297	
Martec USA LLC 1800 N Topping Ave	Kansas City	MO	64120	816-241-4144	
Merical Inc 233 E Bristol Ln *Web:* www.merical.com	Orange	CA	92865	714-238-7225	238-7249
Mericon Industries Inc 8819 N Pioneer Rd *TF:* 800-242-6464 ■ *Web:* www.mericon-industries.com	Peoria	IL	61615	309-693-2150	
Meta Pharmaceutical Services LLC 482 Norristown Rd Ste 200 *Web:* www.metapharm.net	Blue Bell	PA	19422	610-834-9988	
Morton Grove Pharmaceuticals Inc 6451 Main St **Fax Area Code:* 973 ■ *TF:* 800-346-6854 ■ *Web:* www.wockhardtusa.com	Morton Grove	IL	60053	847-967-5600	257-4978*
Mylan Pharmaceuticals ULC 85 Advance Rd *TF:* 800-575-1379 ■ *Web:* www.mylan.ca	Etobicoke	ON	M8Z2S6	416-236-2631	236-2940
Neostem Inc 420 Lexington Ave Ste 450 *NASDAQ: NBS* ■ **Fax Area Code:* 646 ■ *Web:* www.neostem.com	New York	NY	10170	212-584-4180	514-7787*
Nephron Pharmaceuticals Corp 4121 SW 34th St *TF:* 800-443-4313 ■ *Web:* www.nephronpharm.com	Orlando	FL	32811	407-999-2225	872-1733
Nexgen Pharma Inc 46 Corporate Pk Ste 100 *Web:* www.nexgenpharma.com	Irvine	CA	92606	949-863-0340	261-2928
Norman Noble Inc 5507 Avion Park Dr *Web:* www.normannoble.net	Highland Heights	OH	44143	216-761-5387	
NuCare Pharmaceuticals Inc 622 W Katella Ave *TF:* 888-482-9545 ■ *Web:* www.nucarerx.com	Orange	CA	92867	888-482-9545	
Osteohealth Co One Luitpold Dr *Web:* www.osteohealth.com	Shirley	NY	11967	631-924-4000	
Par Pharmaceutical Cos Inc 300 Tice Blvd *NYSE: PRX* ■ *TF:* 800-828-9393 ■ *Web:* www.parpharm.com	Woodcliff Lake	NJ	07677	201-802-4000	802-4600
Par Pharmaceutical Inc One Ram Ridge Rd *TF:* 800-828-9393 ■ *Web:* www.parpharm.com	Spring Valley	NY	10977	201-802-4000	802-4600
Payless Drug Stores Inc 16100 SW 72nd Ave PO Box 230969 *TF:* 800-330-3665 ■ *Web:* www.paylessdrug.com	Portland	OR	97224	503-626-9436	372-1792
Perrigo Co 515 Eastern Ave *NYSE: PRGO* ■ *TF:* 800-719-9260 ■ *Web:* www.perrigo.com	Allegan	MI	49010	269-673-8451	673-9128
Pharmaceutical Calibrations & Instrumentation LLC 8100 Brownleigh Dr Ste 100-A *TF:* 877-724-2257 ■ *Web:* www.pci-llc.com	Raleigh	NC	27617	877-724-2257	
Pharmanet Development Group Inc 504 Carnegie Ctr *Web:* www.inventivhealthclinical.com	Princeton	NJ	08540	609-951-6800	514-0390
Piedmont Pharmaceuticals LLC 204 Muirs Chapel Rd Ste 200 *Web:* www.piedmontpharma.com	Greensboro	NC	27410	336-544-0320	
Ranbaxy Pharmaceuticals Inc 600 College Rd E Ste 2100 *Web:* www.ranbaxy.com	Princeton	NJ	08540	609-720-9200	720-1155
Rowpar Pharmaceuticals Inc 16100 N Greenway Hayden Loop Ste 400 *Web:* www.closys.com	Scottsdale	AZ	85260	480-948-6997	
Sandoz Inc 506 Carnegie Ctr Ste 400 *Web:* www.us.sandoz.com	Princeton	NJ	08540	609-627-8500	627-8659
Sentry BioPharma Services Inc 4605 Decatur Blvd Ameriplex Park *Web:* www.sentrybps.com	Indianapolis	IN	46241	317-856-5889	
Skilled Care Pharmacy Inc 6175 Hl Tek Ct *TF:* 800-334-1624 ■ *Web:* www.skilledcare.com	Mason	OH	45040	513-459-7455	459-8278
Taro Pharmaceuticals USA Inc 3 Skyline Dr *TF:* 800-544-1449 ■ *Web:* www.tarousa.com	Hawthorne	NY	10532	914-345-9001	345-8727
Teva Animal Health Inc 3915 S 48th St Ter *Web:* www.tevaanimalhealth.com	St. Joseph	MO	64503	816-364-3777	
Teva Pharmaceutical USA 1090 Horsham Rd *NYSE: TEVA* ■ *TF:* 800-545-8800 ■ *Web:* www.tevagenerics.com	North Wales	PA	19454	215-591-3000	591-8600
Triumph Pharmaceuticals Inc 10403 Baur Blvd Ste A *Web:* www.smartmouth.com	St. Louis	MO	63132	314-995-3090	
TruTouch Technologies Inc 73 Carriage Way *TF:* 866-721-6221 ■ *Web:* www.trutouchtechnologies.com	Sudbury	MA	01776	866-721-6221	
UDL Laboratories Inc 1718 Northrock Ct **Fax Area Code:* 815 ■ *TF:* 800-435-5272 ■ *Web:* mylan.com/products	Rockford	IL	61103	800-848-0462	282-9391*
USL Pharma 301 S Cherokee St *TF:* 800-654-2299 ■ *Web:* www.upsher-smith.com	Denver	CO	80223	303-607-4500	607-4503
Vectech Pharmaceutical Consultants International Inc 5640 W Maple Rd Ste 312 *Web:* www.vpcint.com	West Bloomfield	MI	48322	248-538-5150	
West-Ward Pharmaceutical Corp 401 Industrial Way W *TF Cust Svc:* 800-631-2174	Eatontown	NJ	07724	732-542-1191	542-0940
X-Gen Pharmaceuticals Inc 300 Daniels Zenker Dr PO Box 445 **Fax Area Code:* 607 ■ *TF:* 866-390-4411 ■ *Web:* www.x-gen.us	Horseheads	NY	14845	866-390-4411	562-2760*
Xanodyne Pharmaceuticals Inc 1 Riverfront Pl	Newport	KY	41071	859-371-6383	371-6391

587 PHARMACEUTICAL & DIAGNOSTIC PRODUCTS - VETERINARY

Company / Address	City	State	Zip	Phone	Fax
Abbott Laboratories Animal Health Div 1401 Sheridan Rd *TF:* 888-299-7416 ■ *Web:* www.abbottanimalhealth.com	North Chicago	IL	60064	847-937-6100	938-0659
ABS Corp 7031 N 16th St *Web:* www.abs-corporation.com	Omaha	NE	68112	402-453-6970	453-1052
Addison Biological Laboratory Inc 507 N Cleveland Ave *TF:* 800-331-2530 ■ *Web:* www.addisonlabs.com	Fayette	MO	65248	660-248-2215	248-2554
Alltech Inc 3031 Catnip Hill Pike *TF:* 800-289-8324 ■ *Web:* www.alltech.com	Nicholasville	KY	40356	859-885-9613	887-3256
Bimeda-MTC Animal Health Inc 420 Beaverdale Rd *TF:* 888-524-6332 ■ *Web:* www.bimedamtc.com	Cambridge	ON	N3C2W4	519-654-8000	654-8001
Bio-Serv 3 Foster Lane Suite 201 *TF:* 800-996-9908 ■ *Web:* www.bio-serv.com	Flemington	NJ	08822	908-284-2155	284-4753
Biomune Co 8906 Rosehill Rd *Web:* ceva.us	Lenexa	KS	66215	913-894-0230	894-0236
Bioniche Life Sciences Inc. 231 Dundas St E *TSE: BNC* ■ *TF:* 800-265-5464 ■ *Web:* www.bionicheanimalhealth.com	Belleville	ON	K8N1E2	613-966-8058	
Biovet Inc 4375 Ave Beaudry *TF:* 888-824-6838 ■ *Web:* biovet.ca	Saint-Hyacinthe	QC	J2S8W2	450-771-7291	771-4158
Biovet USA Inc 9025 Penn Ave S Ste 100 **Fax Area Code:* 954 ■ *TF:* 877-824-6838 ■ *Web:* biovet.ca	Minneapolis	MN	55431	952-884-3113	884-3473*
Boehringer Ingelheim Vetmedica Inc 2621 N Belt Hwy **Fax:* Hum Res ■ *TF:* 800-821-7467 ■ *Web:* www.bi-vetmedica.com	Saint Joseph	MO	64506	816-233-2571	390-0605*
Central Coast Pharmacy 590 Main St Ste B	Templeton	CA	93465	805-434-5999	
Cut-Heal Animal Care Products Inc 923 S Cedar Hill Rd **Fax Area Code:* 240 ■ *TF:* 800-288-4325	Cedar Hill	TX	75104	972-293-9700	597-2157*
Darby Group Cos Inc 300 Jericho Quad *TF:* 888-683-5001 ■ *Web:* www.darbygroup.com	Jericho	NY	11753	516-683-1800	688-2880
Dawe's Laboratories 3355 N Arlington Heights Rd *Web:* dawesnutrition.com	Arlington Heights	IL	60004	847-577-2020	577-1898
Delmont Laboratories Inc 715 Harvard Ave PO Box 269 *TF:* 800-562-5541 ■ *Web:* www.delmont.com	Swarthmore	PA	19081	610-543-3365	543-6298
DMS Laboratories Inc Two Darts Mill Rd *TF:* 800-567-4367 ■ *Web:* www.rapidvet.com	Flemington	NJ	08822	908-782-3353	782-0832
Dominion Veterinary Laboratories Inc 1199 Sanford St *TF:* 800-465-7122 ■ *Web:* www.domvet.com	Winnipeg	MB	R3E3A1	204-589-7361	943-9612
Elanco Animal Health 2500 Innovation Way *TF:* 877-352-6261 ■ *Web:* www.elanco.com	Greenfield	IN	46140	317-276-2000	276-9434
Heska Corp 3760 Rocky Mtn Ave *NASDAQ: HSKA* ■ *TF:* 800-464-3752 ■ *Web:* www.heska.com	Loveland	CO	80538	970-493-7272	619-3005

				Phone	Fax
IMMVAC Inc 6080 Bass Ln. *TF:* 800-944-7563 ■ *Web:* www.immvac.com	Columbia	MO	65201	573-443-5363	874-7108
K & K Veterinary Supply Inc 675 E Laura Ln PO Box 1090 **Fax Area Code:* 470 ■ *Web:* www.kkvet.com	Tontitown	AR	72770	479-361-1516	361-1744*
King Bio Pharmaceuticals Inc Three Westside Dr. *TF:* 800-543-3245 ■ *Web:* www.kingbio.com	Asheville	NC	28806	828-255-0201	255-0940
Lake Immunogenics Inc 348 Berg Rd. **Fax Area Code:* 585 ■ *TF:* 800-648-9990 ■ *Web:* www.lakeimmunogenics.com	Ontario	NY	14519	800-648-9990	265-2306*
Lloyd Inc 604 W Thomas Ave PO Box 130. *TF:* 800-831-0004 ■ *Web:* www.lloydinc.com	Shenandoah	IA	51601	712-246-4000	246-5245
Luitpold Pharmaceuticals Inc One Luitpold Dr PO Box 9001 *TF:* 800-645-1706 ■ *Web:* www.luitpold.com	Shirley	NY	11967	631-924-4000	924-1731
Merial Ltd 3239 Satellite Blvd Bldg 500 *TF:* 888-637-4251 ■ *Web:* www.merial.com	Duluth	GA	30096	678-638-3000	
MVP Laboratories Inc 4805 G St *TF:* 800-856-4648 ■ *Web:* www.mvplabs.com	Omaha	NE	68117	402-331-5106	331-8776
MWI Veterinary Supply Inc 3041 W Pasadena Dr *NASDAQ: MWIV* ■ *Web:* www.mwivet.com	Boise	ID	83705	208-955-8930	955-8902
Novartis Animal Health US Inc 1447 140th St.	Larchwood	IA	51241	712-477-2811	
Nutra-Blend Inc 3200 Second St. **Fax Area Code:* 417 ■ *TF:* 800-657-5657 ■ *Web:* www.nutrablend.net	Neosho	MO	64850	800-657-5657	451-4515*
Pfizer Inc Animal Health Group 235 E 42nd St. *TF:* 800-879-3477 ■ *Web:* www.pfizer.com/ah	New York	NY	10017	212-573-2323	
ProtaTek International Inc 2635 University Ave W Ste 140 *Web:* www.protatek.com	Saint Paul	MN	55114	651-644-5391	644-6831
Renco Corp 116 Third Ave N. *TF:* 800-359-8181 ■ *Web:* www.rencocorp.com	Minneapolis	MN	55401	612-338-6124	333-9026
Texas Vet Lab Inc 1702 N Bell St **Fax Area Code:* 325 ■ *TF:* 800-284-8403 ■ *Web:* www.texasvetlab.com	San Angelo	TX	76903	800-284-8403	653-4501*
Veterinary Pharmacies of America Inc 2854 Antoine Dr *TF:* 877-838-7979 ■ *Web:* www.vetrxrx.com	Houston	TX	77092	877-838-7979	329-7979
Vetoquinol Canada Inc 2000 Ch Georges *TF:* 800-363-1700 ■ *Web:* www.vetoquinol.ca	Lavaltrie	QC	J5T3S5	450-586-2252	586-4649
XF Enterprises Inc 500 S Taylor Ste 301 PO Box 229. **Fax Area Code:* 620 ■ *Web:* www.xfent.com	Amarillo	TX	79101	806-367-5810	672-5564*

588 PHARMACY ASSOCIATIONS - STATE

SEE ALSO Health & Medical Professionals Associations p. 1796

				Phone	Fax
Alabama Pharmacy Assn 1211 Carmichael Way *TF General:* 800-529-7533 ■ *Web:* www.aparx.org	Montgomery	AL	36106	334-271-4222	271-5423
Alaska Pharmacist's Assn 203 W 15th Ave Ste 100 *TF:* 800-228-9290 ■ *Web:* www.alaskapharmacy.org	Anchorage	AK	99501	907-563-8880	563-7880
Arizona Pharmacy Assn 1845 E Southern Ave *Web:* www.azpharmacy.org	Tempe	AZ	85282	480-838-3385	838-3557
Arkansas Pharmacists Assn 417 S Victory St *Web:* www.arpharmacists.org	Little Rock	AR	72201	501-372-5250	372-0546
California Pharmacists Assn (CPhA) 4030 Lennane Dr *TF:* 866-365-7472 ■ *Web:* www.cpha.com	Sacramento	CA	95834	916-779-1400	779-1401
Colorado Pharmacists Society 6825 E Tennessee Ave Ste 440 *Web:* www.copharm.org	Denver	CO	80224	303-756-3069	756-3649
Connecticut Pharmacists Assn 35 Cold Spring Rd Ste 121 *Web:* www.ctpharmacists.org	Rocky Hill	CT	06067	860-563-4619	257-8241
Delaware Pharmacists Society 27 N Main St *Web:* www.dpsrx.org	Smyrna	DE	19977	302-659-3088	
Florida Pharmacy Assn 610 N Adams St *Web:* www.pharmview.com	Tallahassee	FL	32301	850-222-2400	561-6758
Georgia Pharmacy Assn (GPhA) 50 Lenox Pointe NE *Web:* www.gpha.org	Atlanta	GA	30324	404-231-5074	237-8435
Idaho State Pharmacy Assn (ISPA) 816 W Bannock St Ste 105 *Web:* www.idahopharmacists.com	Boise	ID	83702	208-870-8312	629-8485
Illinois Pharmacists Assn (IPhA) 204 W Cook St *Web:* www.ipha.org	Springfield	IL	62704	217-522-7300	522-7349
Indiana Pharmacists Alliance 729 N Pennsylvania St *TF:* 800-516-0313 ■ *Web:* netforum.avectra.com	Indianapolis	IN	46204	317-634-4968	632-1219
Iowa Pharmacy Assn 8515 Douglas Ave Ste 16 *TF:* 866-512-1800 ■ *Web:* www.iarx.org	Des Moines	IA	50322	515-270-0713	270-2979
Kansas Pharmacists Assn 1020 SW Fairlawn Rd *TF:* 888-792-6273 ■ *Web:* kansaspharmacy.org	Topeka	KS	66604	785-228-2327	
Kentucky Pharmacists Assn 1228 US 127 S *TF:* 800-922-1557 ■ *Web:* kphanet.org	Frankfort	KY	40601	502-227-2303	227-2258
Louisiana Pharmacists Assn 450 Laurel St Ste 1400 *TF:* 877-252-5100 ■ *Web:* www.louisianapharmacists.com	Baton Rouge	LA	70801	225-346-6883	344-1132
Maine Pharmacy Assn 127 Pleasant Hill Rd. *Web:* www.mparx.com	Scarborough	ME	04074	207-396-5340	396-5341
Maryland Pharmacists Assn 1800 Washington Blvd Ste 333 *TF:* 800-833-7587 ■ *Web:* www.marylandpharmacist.org	Baltimore	MD	21201	410-727-0746	727-2253
Massachusetts Pharmacists Assn 500 W Cummings Pk Ste 3475 *TF:* 888-772-7227 ■ *Web:* netforum.avectra.com	Woburn	MA	01801	781-933-1107	933-1109
Michigan Pharmacists Assn 815 N Washington Ave *TF:* 866-226-2952 ■ *Web:* www.michiganpharmacists.org	Lansing	MI	48906	517-484-1466	484-4893
Minnesota Pharmacists Assn (MPhA) 1935 W County Rd B2 *TF:* 800-451-8349 ■ *Web:* www.mpha.org	Roseville	MN	55113	651-697-1771	697-1776
Mississippi Pharmacists Assn 341 Edgewood Terr Dr *TF:* 800-421-2408 ■ *Web:* www.mspharm.org	Jackson	MS	39206	601-981-0416	981-0451
Missouri Pharmacy Assn 211 E Capitol Ave *Web:* www.morx.com	Jefferson City	MO	65101	573-636-7522	636-7485
Nebraska Pharmacists Assn 6221 S 58th St Ste A *TF:* 866-365-7472 ■ *Web:* www.npharm.org	Lincoln	NE	68516	402-420-1500	420-1406
New Jersey Pharmacists Assn 760 Alexander Rd PO Box 1 *Web:* njpharmacists.org	Princeton	NJ	08543	609-275-4246	275-4066
New Mexico Pharmacists Assn (NMPhA) 2716 San Pedro Dr NE # C *Web:* www.nm-pharmacy.com	Albuquerque	NM	87110	505-265-8729	255-8476
North Carolina Assn of Pharmacists 109 Church St *Web:* www.ncpharmacists.org	Chapel Hill	NC	27516	919-967-2237	968-9430
North Dakota Pharmacists Assn (NDPhA) 1641 Capitol Way *Web:* www.nodakpharmacy.net	Bismarck	ND	58501	701-258-4968	258-9312
Ohio Pharmacists Assn 2674 Federated Blvd *Web:* www.associationdatabase.com	Columbus	OH	43235	614-389-3236	389-4582
Oklahoma Pharmacists Assn 45 NE 52nd St *Web:* www.opha.com	Oklahoma City	OK	73105	405-528-3338	528-1417
Oregon State Pharmacy Assn (OSPA) 147 SE 102nd Ave *Web:* www.oregonpharmacy.org	Portland	OR	97216	503-582-9055	253-9172
Pennsylvania Pharmacists Assn 508 N Third St *Web:* www.papharmacists.com	Harrisburg	PA	17101	717-234-6151	236-1618
Pharmacists Society of the State of New York 210 Washington Ave Ext *Web:* www.pssny.org	Albany	NY	12203	518-869-6595	464-0618
Pharmacy Society of Wisconsin 701 Heartland Trl *Web:* www.pswi.org	Madison	WI	53717	608-827-9200	827-9292
South Carolina Pharmacy Assn 1350 Browning Rd *Web:* www.scrx.org	Columbia	SC	29210	803-354-9977	354-9207
South Dakota Pharmacists Assn PO Box 518 *Web:* www.sdpha.org	Pierre	SD	57501	605-224-2338	224-1280
Tennessee Pharmacists Assn 500 Church St Ste 650 *Web:* www.tnpharm.org	Nashville	TN	37219	615-256-3023	255-3528
Texas Pharmacy Assn 12007 Research Blvd Ste 201 *TF:* 800-505-5463 ■ *Web:* www.texaspharmacy.org	Austin	TX	78759	512-836-8350	836-0308
Washington State Pharmacy Assn 411 Williams Ave S. *TF:* 800-562-6000 ■ *Web:* www.wsparx.org	Renton	WA	98057	425-228-7171	277-3897
West Virginia Pharmacists Assn 2016 1/2 Kanawha Blvd E *Web:* wvpharmacy.org	Charleston	WV	25311	304-344-5302	344-5316
Wyoming Pharmacists Assn 150 Powell St *Web:* www.wpha.net	Green River	WY	82935	307-272-3361	

589 PHARMACY BENEFITS MANAGEMENT SERVICES

A pharmacy benefits management service (PBM) is a company that manages various pharmacy-related aspects of a health insurance plan, such as the assignment of pharmacy cards, claims filing and processing, formulary management, etc. For the most part, PBM clients are insurance companies, HMOs, or PPOs rather than individuals or pharmacies.

				Phone	Fax
Abtex Corp 89 Main St PO Box 188 *Web:* www.abtex.com	Dresden	NY	14441	315-536-7403	
BioScrip 10050 Crosstown Cir Ste 300 *NASDAQ: BIOS* ■ *TF:* 800-444-5951 ■ *Web:* www.bioscrip.com	Eden Prairie	MN	55344	800-444-5951	
Caremark Rx Inc PO Box 832407 *TF:* 877-460-7766 ■ *Web:* www.caremark.com	Richardson	TX	75083	877-460-7766	
CoreSource Inc 400 Field Dr. *TF:* 800-832-3332 ■ *Web:* www.coresource.com	Lake Forest	IL	60045	847-604-9200	615-3900
CuraScript Inc 6272 Lee Vista Blvd *TF:* 888-773-7376 ■ *Web:* www.curascript.com	Orlando	FL	32822	888-773-7376	773-7386
Cvs Caremark 695 George Washington Hwy *Web:* www.cvs.com	Lincoln	RI	02865	401-334-0069	
Health Smart Rx 1301 E Ninth St **Fax Area Code:* 216 ■ *TF:* 800-681-6912 ■ *Web:* www.healthsmart.com	Cleveland	OH	44114	800-681-6912	479-2015*
Maxor National Pharmacy Services Corp 320 S Polk St Ste 100 *TF:* 800-658-6146 ■ *Web:* www.maxor.com	Amarillo	TX	79101	806-324-5400	324-5495
Medco Health Solutions Inc 100 Parsons Pond Dr *NYSE: MHS* ■ *Web:* www.express-scripts.com	Franklin Lakes	NJ	07417	201-269-3400	269-1222
MedImpact Healthcare Systems Inc 10680 Treena St Ste 500 *TF:* 800-788-2949 ■ *Web:* www.medimpact.com	San Diego	CA	92131	858-566-2727	790-6454
Old Dominion Brush Co 5118 Glen Alden Dr *Web:* www.odbco.com	Richmond	VA	23231	804-226-4433	
Premier Paint Roller LLC 131-11 Atlantic Ave *Web:* www.premierpaintroller.com	Richmond Hill	NY	11418	718-441-7700	
Prescription Solutions 3515 Harbor Blvd *TF:* 800-788-4863 ■ *Web:* www.optumrx.com	Costa Mesa	CA	92626	800-788-4863	
Prime Therapeutics Inc 1305 Corporate Ctr Dr **Fax Area Code:* 651 ■ *TF:* 800-858-0723 ■ *Web:* www.primetherapeutics.com	Eagan	MN	55121	612-777-4000	286-4263*

Phone *Fax*

San Antonio Lighthouse for The Blind
2305 Roosevelt Ave ....San Antonio TX 78210 210-533-5195
Web: www.idworld.net

Schaefer Brush Manufacturing Company Inc
1101 S Prairie Ave .... Waukesha WI 53186 262-547-3500
Web: schaeferbrush.com

ScripNet 10050 Banburry Cross Dr Ste 290 .... Las Vegas NV 89144 702-248-2692 245-1745*
**Fax Area Code:* 888 ■ *TF:* 888-880-8562 ■ *Web:* www.scripnet.com

Script Care Inc 6380 Folsom Dr .... Beaumont TX 77706 800-880-9988 833-7435*
**Fax Area Code:* 409 ■ *TF:* 800-880-9988 ■ *Web:* www.scriptcare.com

ScriptSave 4911 E Broadway Blvd Ste 200...............Tucson AZ 85711 800-347-5985 888-8069*
**Fax Area Code:* 520 ■ *TF:* 800-347-5985 ■ *Web:* www.scriptsave.com

Serve You Custom Prescription Management
10201 Innovation Dr Ste 600 ....Milwaukee WI 53226 414-410-8100 410-8181
TF: 888-243-6890 ■ *Web:* www.serve-you-rx.com

Walgreens Health Services
1411 Lake Cook Rd ....Deerfield IL 60015 800-207-2568 374-2645*
**Fax Area Code:* 847 ■ *Web:* www.walgreenshealth.com

590 PHARMACY MANAGEMENT SERVICES

Companies that provide long-term care pharmacy services to individuals with special needs (e.g., chronic disease or advanced age); and those that provide pharmacy management services to hospitals or other institutions.

Phone *Fax*

Accredo Health Group Inc
1640 Century Ctr Pkwy.............................Memphis TN 38134 901-385-3688 385-3689
TF: 877-222-7336 ■ *Web:* www.accredo.com

Fisher Bio Svc Inc 14665 Rothgeb Dr................Rockville MD 20850 301-315-8460 838-9320
TF: 888-462-7246 ■ *Web:* www.fisherbioservices.com

McKesson Pharmaceutical One Post St......... San Francisco CA 94104 415-983-8300 983-7160
TF: 800-571-2889 ■ *Web:* www.mckesson.com

Omnicare Inc 201 E 4th St Ste 1900 .... Cincinnati OH 45202 800-990-6664 392-3333*
NYSE: OCR ■ **Fax Area Code:* 859 ■ *TF:* 800-342-5627 ■ *Web:* omnicare.com

Pharmacy Systems Inc
5050 Bradenton Ave PO Box 130 ....Dublin OH 43017 614-766-0101 766-4448
Web: www.pharmacysystems.com

591 PHOTO PROCESSING & STORAGE

Phone *Fax*

Advanced Photographic Solutions
1525 Hardeman Ln.............................. Cleveland TN 37312 423-479-5481
TF: 800-241-9234 ■ *Web:* www.advancedphoto.com

BCP International Ltd
1800 N Beauregard St Ste 350 ....Alexandria VA 22311 703-575-7300
Web: www.bcpiltd.com

Burrell Imaging 1311 Merrillville Rd .... Crown Point IN 46307 219-663-3210 662-0915
TF: 800-348-8732 ■ *Web:* www.burrellprolabs.com

Candid Color Systems Inc
1300 Metropolitan Ave...........................Oklahoma City OK 73108 405-947-8747 951-7353
TF: 800-336-4550 ■ *Web:* www.candid.com

Dale Laboratories 2960 Simms St.................Hollywood FL 33020 954-925-0103 922-3008
TF: 800-327-1776 ■ *Web:* www.dalelabs.com

District Photo Inc 10501 Rhode Island Ave ....Beltsville MD 20705 301-937-5300 937-5627
Web: www.districtphoto.com

dotPhoto Inc 939 Ridge Rd Second Fl....... Monmouth Junction NJ 08852 609-434-0340 434-0344
Web: www.dotphoto.com

Dreamstime LLC 1616 Wgate Cir ....Brentwood TN 37027 615-771-5611
Web: www.dreamstime.com

FLM Graphics 123 Lehigh Dr ....Fairfield NJ 07004 973-575-9450 575-6424
Web: www.flmgraphics.com

Graphic Systems Inc 2632 26th Ave S .... Minneapolis MN 55406 612-721-6100
Web: www.graphicsystems.com

H & H Color Lab Inc
8906 E 67th St PO Box 219080 ....Raytown MO 64133 816-358-6677 313-1480
TF: 800-821-1305 ■ *Web:* www.hhcolorlab.com

iMemories 9181 E Bell Rd .... Scottsdale AZ 85260 800-845-7986 767-2511*
**Fax Area Code:* 480 ■ *TF:* 800-845-7986 ■ *Web:* www.imemories.com

McKenna Pro Imaging 2800 Falls Ave...............Waterloo IA 50701 319-235-6265 235-1121
TF General: 800-238-3456 ■ *Web:* www.mckennapro.com

Meisel Visual Imaging 2019 McKenzie Dr........... Carrollton TX 75006 214-688-4950 688-4950
TF: 800-527-5186 ■ *Web:* www.meisel.com

Photo USA 2140 Colonial Ave.......................Roanoke VA 24015 540-344-0961 565-950*
**Fax Area Code:* 800 ■ *TF:* 888-234-6320 ■ *Web:* www.photousa.com

PNI Digital Media Inc
425 Carrall St Ste 590 ....Vancouver BC V6B6E3 604-893-8955 893-8966
TSE: PN ■ *Web:* www.pnidigitalmedia.com

Shutterfly.com 2800 Bridge Pkwy Ste 101........ Redwood City CA 94065 650-610-5200 654-1299
Web: www.shutterfly.com

Yahoo! Photos 701 First Ave ....Sunnyvale CA 94089 408-349-3300 349-3301
TF: 888-267-7574 ■ *Web:* www.flickr.com

592 PHOTOCOPYING EQUIPMENT & SUPPLIES

SEE ALSO Business Machines - Whol p. 1894

Phone *Fax*

Coast to Coast Business Equipment Inc
Eight Vanderbilt PO Box 57077 ....Irvine CA 92618 949-457-7300 457-7365
Web: www.ctcbe.com

Eastman Kodak Co 343 State St .... Rochester NY 14650 585-724-4000 724-0663
OTC: EKDKQ ■ *Web:* www.kodak.com

Imaging Supplies Company Inc
804 Woodland Ave.................................Sanford NC 27330 919-776-1152
Web: www.imagingsuppliesco.com

Konica Minolta Business Solutions USA Inc
100 Williams Dr...................................Ramsey NJ 07446 201-825-4000
Web: www.kmbs.konicaminolta.us

Phone *Fax*

Kyocera Mita Corp 225 Sand Rd PO Box 40008.........Fairfield NJ 07004 973-808-8444
Web: www.kyoceradocumentsolutions.com

Lasercycle USA Inc 528 S Taylor Ave................Louisville CO 80027 303-666-7776
Web: www.lasercycleusa.com

Masterfile Corp Three Concorde Gate Fourth Fl .... Toronto ON M3C3N7 416-929-3000
Web: www.masterfile.com

Northwest Print Strategies Inc
8175 Sw Nimbus Ave .... Beaverton OR 97008 503-641-5156
Web: www.nwpsi.com

Oce-USA Inc 5450 N Cumberland Ave Sixth Fl...........Chicago IL 60656 773-714-8500 693-7634
TF: 800-877-6232 ■ *Web:* csa.canon.com

Precision Printer Services Inc
9185 Portage Industrial Dr .... Portage MI 49024 269-384-5725
Web: www.precisionprinterservices.com

R & d Computers
6767 Peachtree Industrial Blvd Ste B ....Norcross GA 30092 770-416-0103
Web: www.randdcomp.com

Sharp Electronics Corp One Sharp Plz.................Mahwah NJ 07430 201-529-8200 529-8413
TF: 800-237-4277 ■ *Web:* www.sharpusa.com

Toshiba America Inc
1251 Ave of the Americas Ste 4100 ....New York NY 10020 212-596-0600 593-3875
TF: 800-457-7777 ■ *Web:* www.toshiba.com

Xerox Canada Ltd 5650 Yonge St ....North York ON M2M4G7 800-939-3769 733-6811*
**Fax Area Code:* 416 ■ *TF:* 800-939-3769 ■ *Web:* www.xerox.ca

Xerox Corp 45 Glover Ave PO Box 4505 ....Norwalk CT 06856 203-968-3000
NYSE: XRX ■ *TF:* 800-327-9753 ■ *Web:* www.xerox.com

593 PHOTOGRAPH STUDIOS - PORTRAIT

Phone *Fax*

Alderman Studios 325 Model Farm Rd..............High Point NC 27263 336-889-6121 889-7717
Web: aldermancompany.com

All-League Sports Photos & Lab Inc
27062 Burbank.............................Foothill Ranch CA 92610 949-598-9297
Web: www.allleaguesportsphotos.com

Andy Rice Photography 7226 Rue De Roark............ La Jolla CA 92037 858-459-8458
Web: www.andyricephoto.com

Artech Photography Studio 3404 Bath Rd............... Perry MI 48872 517-625-5177
Web: www.artechphoto.com

Bell Photographers 341 Garfield St................Idaho Falls ID 83401 208-524-4601
Web: www.bellphoto.com

Berliner Photography LLC
314 N La Brea Ave ....Los Angeles CA 90036 323-857-1282
Web: www.berlinerphotography.com

Bryn-Alan Studios Inc 502 W Grand Central Ave......... Tampa FL 33606 813-844-3383
Web: lifetouch.com

Cherry Hill Photo Enterprises Inc
4 East Stow Rd ....Marlton NJ 08053 800-969-2440
TF: 800-969-2440 ■ *Web:* www.cherryhillphoto.com

CPI Corp 1706 Washington Ave .... Saint Louis MO 63103 314-231-1575 791-1092*
OTC: CPIC ■ **Fax Area Code:* 800 ■ **Fax:* Hum Res ■ *TF:* 800-422-9410 ■ *Web:* www.cpicorp.com

CPI Daylighting Inc 28662 N Ballard Dr .... Lake Forest IL 60045 847-816-1060
Web: www.cpidaylighting.com

Event Photography Group Inc
245 Chesterfield Industrial Blvd ....Chesterfield MO 63005 636-536-3838
Web: www.eventphotographygroup.com

Forster Daniel Marine Photography
57 High St .... Jamestown RI 02835 401-423-1900
Web: www.yachtphoto.com

Fox Edward Photography 4900 N Milwaukee Ave ....Chicago IL 60630 773-736-0200
Web: www.edwardfox.com

Freed Photography Inc
4931 Cordell Ave Ste 101..........................Bethesda MD 20814 301-652-5452
Web: www.freedphoto.com

Freestyle Photo Biz 5124 Sunset Blvd..............Hollywood CA 90027 800-292-6137
TF: 800-292-6137 ■ *Web:* www.freestylephoto.biz

Freeze Frame LLC 4205 Vineland Rd Ste L-9 .... Orlando FL 32811 407-648-2111
Web: www.freezeframe.com

Gartner Studios Inc 220 Myrtle St E................. Stillwater MN 55082 651-351-7700 351-1408
Web: www.gartnerstudios.com

George STREET Photo & Video LLC
230 W Huron St Ste 3W...............................Chicago IL 60654 866-831-4103
TF: 866-831-4103 ■ *Web:* www.georgestreetphoto.com

Hallmark Institute of Photography
241 Millers Falls Rd .... Turners Falls MA 01376 413-863-2478
Web: www.hallmark.edu

Imaging Associates Inc 11110 Westlake Dr .... Charlotte NC 28273 704-522-8094
Web: www.imaginga.com

Jostens Inc 3601 Minnesota Ave Ste 400.......... Minneapolis MN 55435 952-830-3300 830-3293*
**Fax:* Hum Res ■ *TF:* 800-235-4774 ■ *Web:* www.jostens.com

Lafayette Frame Shop
651 Germantown Pk..........................Lafayette Hill PA 19444 610-629-0704
Web: www.lafayette.com

Lumedyne Technologies Inc
9275 Sky Park Ct Ste 100........................San Diego CA 92123 858-560-5208
Web: www.omegasensors.com

MarathonFoto 3490 Martin Hurst Rd .... Tallahassee FL 32312 972-330-7656
Web: www.marathonfoto.com

New England School of Photography
537 Commonwealth Ave............................Boston MA 02215 617-437-1868
Web: www.nesop.com

Olan Mills Inc 4325 Amnicola Hwy............... Chattanooga TN 37406 423-622-5141 629-8106
Web: www.olanmills.com

Peters Main Street Photography 314 N Main St....... London OH 43140 740-852-2731
Web: www.petersphotography.com

Portrait Express 441 N Water St .... Silverton OR 97381 503-873-6365
Web: www.portraitexpress.com

Portrait Innovations Inc
2016 Ayrsley Town Blvd Ste 200....................... Charlotte NC 28273 704-499-9300
Web: www.portraitinnovations.com

Name / Address	City	State	Zip	Phone	Fax
Portraits International 10835 Rockley Rd *Web:* www.portraitsinternational.com	Houston	TX	77099	281-879-8444	
Ripcho Studio 7630 Lorain Ave *Web:* www.ripchostudio.com	Cleveland	OH	44102	216-631-0664	
Shugart Studios Inc 812 College Ave	Levelland	TX	79336	806-897-1754	
Spark Studios LLC 10811 Washington Blvd 4th Fl *Web:* www.sparkstudios.com	Culver City	CA	90232	424-298-8950	
Visual Image Photography 11612 Becky Lee Trce *Web:* www.vipis.com	Huntley	IL	60142	847-515-2425	
Walters Photography 1013 Suffolk Dr *Web:* portalmedia.com	Janesville	WI	53546	608-752-8808	

594 PHOTOGRAPHIC EQUIPMENT & SUPPLIES

SEE ALSO Cameras & Related Supplies - Retail p. 1899

Name / Address	City	State	Zip	Phone	Fax
Advance Reproductions Corp 100 Flagship Dr *Web:* www.advancerepro.com	North Andover	MA	01845	978-685-2911	685-1771
Agfa Corp 611 River Dr *TF:* 888-274-8626 ■ *Web:* www.agfagraphics.com/gs/usa/en/internet/maings/	Elmwood Park	NJ	07407	201-440-2500	
Alan Gordon Enterprises Inc 5625 Melrose Ave *TF:* 800-825-6684 ■ *Web:* www.alangordon.com	Hollywood	CA	90038	323-466-3561	871-2193
Anton/Bauer Inc 14 Progress Dr *TF:* 800-422-3473 ■ *Web:* www.antonbauer.com	Shelton	CT	06484	203-929-1100	929-9935
Ballantyne Strong Inc 13710 FNB Pkwy *NYSE:* BTN ■ *TF General:* 800-424-1215 ■ *Web:* ballantynestrong.com	Omaha	NE	68154	800-424-1215	
Beta Screen Corp 707 Commercial Ave *TF:* 800-272-7336 ■ *Web:* www.betascreen.com	Carlstadt	NJ	07072	201-939-2400	939-7656
Carr Corp 1547 11th St *TF:* 800-952-2398 ■ *Web:* www.carrcorporation.com	Santa Monica	CA	90401	310-587-1113	395-9751
Casio Inc 570 Mt Pleasant Ave **Fax:* Hum Res ■ *TF Cust Svc:* 800-634-1895 ■ *Web:* www.casio.com	Dover	NJ	07801	973-361-5400	537-8964*
Ceiva Logic Inc 214 E Magnolia Blvd *TF Tech Supp:* 877-693-7263 ■ *Web:* www.ceiva.com	Burbank	CA	91502	818-562-1495	562-1491
Champion Photochemistry 7895 Tranmere Dr Unit 203 *Web:* www.championphotochemistry.com	Mississauga	ON	L5S1V9	905-670-7900	670-2581
Da-Lite Screen Company Inc 3100 N Detroit St *TF:* 800-622-3737 ■ *Web:* www.da-lite.com	Warsaw	IN	46581	574-267-8101	267-7804
Douthitt Corp 245 Adair St *TF:* 800-368-8448 ■ *Web:* www.douthittcorp.com	Detroit	MI	48207	313-259-1565	259-6806
Draper Shade & Screen Co 411 S Pearl St *TF:* 800-238-7999 ■ *Web:* www.draperinc.com	Spiceland	IN	47385	765-987-7999	987-7999
DRS Technologies Inc 138 Bauer Dr *Web:* www.drs.com	Oakland	NJ	07436	201-337-3800	337-2704
Dukane Communication Systems 2900 Dukane Dr *Web:* www.dukane.com	Saint Charles	IL	60174	630-584-2300	584-2300
Eastman Kodak Co 343 State St *OTC:* EKDKQ ■ *Web:* www.kodak.com	Rochester	NY	14650	585-724-4000	724-0663
Fuji Photo Film USA Inc 200 Summit Lake Dr **Fax Area Code:* 914 ■ *Web:* www.fujifilm.com	Valhalla	NY	10595	936-520-2720	789-8664*
Geosystems Inc 210 S Washington Ave *Web:* zippermast.com	Titusville	FL	32796	321-383-9585	747-0601
Identatronics Inc 165 N Lively Blvd *TF Cust Svc:* 800-323-5403 ■ *Web:* www.identatronics.com	Elk Grove Village	IL	60007	847-437-2654	437-2660
InFocus Corp 13190 SW 68th Pkwy Ste 200 *TF:* 877-388-8385 ■ *Web:* www.infocus.com	Portland	OR	97223	503-207-4700	207-1937
Integrated Design Tools Inc 1202 E Pk Ave *TF:* 800-462-4307 ■ *Web:* www.idtvision.com	Tallahassee	FL	32301	850-222-5939	222-4591
Matthews Studio Equipment Group 2405 W Empire Ave **Fax Area Code:* 323 ■ *TF:* 800-237-8263 ■ *Web:* www.msegrip.com	Burbank	CA	91504	818-843-6715	849-1525*
Mogg QuickSet 3650 Woodhead Dr *Web:* www.tripods.com	Northbrook	IL	60062	847-498-0700	498-1258
Mustek Inc 15271 Barranca Pkwy *TF:* 800-308-7226 ■ *Web:* www.mustek.com	Irvine	CA	92618	949-790-3800	247-8960
MVM Products LLC 940 Calle Amanecer Ste K *TF:* 888-246-5832 ■ *Web:* www.ink-jet.com	San Clemente	CA	92673	949-366-1470	498-2958
Navitar Inc 200 Commerce Dr *TF Cust Svc:* 800-828-6778 ■ *Web:* www.navitar.com	Rochester	NY	14623	585-359-4000	359-4999
Neumade Products Corp 30 Pecks Ln Ste 40	Newtown	CT	06470	203-270-1100	270-7778
Neumade Products Corp Xetron Theatre Products Div 30 Pecks Ln	Newtown	CT	06470	203-270-1100	270-7778
Nikon Inc 1300 Walt Whitman Rd *TF Cust Svc:* 800-645-6687 ■ *Web:* www.nikonusa.com	Melville	NY	11747	631-547-4200	547-0299
OConnor Engineering 2701 N Ontario St *Web:* www.ocon.com	Burbank	CA	91504	818-847-8666	847-1205
Panavision Inc 6219 DeSoto Ave *TF:* 800-260-1846 ■ *Web:* www.panavision.com	Woodland Hills	CA	91367	818-316-1000	316-1111
Peter Pepper Products Inc 17929 S Susana Rd *TF:* 800-496-0204 ■ *Web:* www.peterpepper.com	Compton	CA	90221	310-639-0390	639-6013
Phase One Inc 200 Broadhollow Rd Ste 312 *TF:* 888-742-7366 ■ *Web:* www.phaseone.com	Melville	NY	11747	631-757-0400	547-9898
Reprographics One Inc 36060 Industrial Rd **Fax Area Code:* 313 ■ *TF:* 800-333-2600 ■ *Web:* www.reprographicsone.com	Livonia	MI	48150	734-542-8800	441-4621*
Research Technology International Inc 4700 W Chase Ave *TF Sales:* 800-323-7520 ■ *Web:* www.rti-us.com	Lincolnwood	IL	60712	847-677-3000	677-1311
Sanyo Fisher Co 21605 Plummer St *Web:* us.sanyo.com	Chatsworth	CA	91311	818-998-7322	
Schneider Optics Century Div 7701 Haskell Ave *TF:* 800-228-1254 ■ *Web:* www.schneideroptics.com	Van Nuys	CA	91406	818-766-3715	505-9865
Sharp Electronics Corp One Sharp Plz *TF:* 800-237-4277 ■ *Web:* www.sharpusa.com	Mahwah	NJ	07430	201-529-8200	529-8413
Sony Corp of America 550 Madison Ave *TF:* 800-282-2848 ■ *Web:* www.sony.com	New York	NY	10022	212-833-6800	
Stewart Filmscreen Corp 1161 W Sepulveda Blvd *TF:* 800-762-4999 ■ *Web:* stewartfilmscreen.com	Torrance	CA	90502	310-784-5300	326-6870
Tamron USA Inc 10 Austin Blvd *TF General:* 800-827-8880 ■ *Web:* www.tamron.com/en	Commack	NY	11725	631-858-8400	543-5666
Tiffen Company LLC 90 Oser Ave *TF:* 800-645-2522 ■ *Web:* www.tiffen.com	Hauppauge	NY	11788	631-273-2500	273-2557
Toshiba America Inc 1251 Ave of the Americas Ste 4100 *TF:* 800-457-7777 ■ *Web:* www.toshiba.com	New York	NY	10020	212-596-0600	593-3875
Visual Departures Ltd 2001 W Main St Ste 195 **Fax Area Code:* 203 ■ *TF:* 800-628-2003 ■ *Web:* www.visualdepartures.com	Stamford	CT	06902	800-628-2003	487-0791*
Vivitar Corp 195 Carter Dr *TF:* 800-637-1090 ■ *Web:* www.vivitar.com	Edison	NJ	08817	732-248-1306	
Vutec Corp 11711 W Sample Rd *TF:* 800-770-4700 ■ *Web:* www.vutec.com	Coral Springs	FL	33065	954-545-9000	545-9011
Waterhouse Inc 670 Queen St Ste 200	Honolulu	HI	96813	808-592-4800	
Wein Products Inc 115 W 25th St *Web:* www.weinproducts.com	Los Angeles	CA	90007	213-749-6049	749-6250

595 PHOTOGRAPHY - COMMERCIAL

Name / Address	City	State	Zip	Phone	Fax
A M C Colorgrafix Inc 2085 Peck Rd *Web:* www.amc-color.com	El Monte	CA	91733	626-575-1788	
Albion Associates Inc 622 Southwest St *Web:* www.albionassociates.net	High Point	NC	27260	336-883-8028	
Image Craft LLC 3401 E Broadway Rd *Web:* www.imagecraft.com	Phoenix	AZ	85040	602-276-2082	
Image Inc 1100 S Lynndale Dr *Web:* www.imagestudios.com	Appleton	WI	54914	920-738-4080	738-4089
Irvin Simon Photographers Inc 146 Meacham Ave *Web:* www.irvinsimon.com	Elmont	NY	11003	516-437-4700	
Kinetic The Technology Agency 200 Distillery Commons Ste 200 *Web:* kinetic.thetechnologyagency.com/default.aspx	Louisville	KY	40206	502-719-9500	719-9509
Photocrazy Inc 509 Raindance St *Web:* www.photocrazy.com	Thousand Oaks	CA	91360	805-492-0562	
Scenic Prints Landscape Photos 536 Sweetwater St *Web:* www.scenicprints.com	Lander	WY	82520	307-332-1532	
Sharp Shooter Spectrum Ventures LLC 11901 W 48th Ave *Web:* www.sharpshots.com	Wheat Ridge	CO	80033	303-962-2345	
Shutterstock Inc 350 Fifth Ave Fl 21 *Web:* www.shutterstock.com	New York	NY	10118	646-419-4452	
Sport Graphics PO Box 95 **Fax Area Code:* 877 ■ *Web:* www.sportgraphics.com	Shrewsbury	MA	01545	508-925-0406	330-7774*
Studio 3 Inc 1316 Se 12th Ave *Web:* studio3.com	Portland	OR	97214	503-238-1748	
Universal Image PO Box 77090 *TF:* 800-553-5499 ■ *Web:* www.universalphoto.com	Winter Garden	FL	34787	407-352-5302	
Van Gogh School Photographers 401 Cornell Ave *Web:* vangoghschoolphotographers.com	Barrington	IL	60010	847-382-2282	
Wasatch Photonics 1305 North 1000 West Ste 120 *Web:* www.wasatchphotonics.com	Logan	UT	84321	435-752-4301	

596 PHOTOGRAPHY - STOCK

Name / Address	City	State	Zip	Phone	Fax
Alaska Stock Images 2505 Fairbanks St *TF:* 800-487-4285 ■ *Web:* www.alaskastock.com	Anchorage	AK	99503	907-276-1343	258-7848
Bygone Designs PO Box 229 *Web:* www.bygones.com	Newport	MN	55055	651-451-6737	
Corbis Corp 710 Second Ave Ste 200 *TF:* 800-260-0444 ■ *Web:* www.corbisimages.com	Seattle	WA	98104	206-373-6000	373-6100
Custom Medical Stock Photo Inc 3660 W Irving Pk Rd *TF:* 800-373-2677 ■ *Web:* www.cmsp.com	Chicago	IL	60618	773-267-3100	267-6071
Image Works PO Box 443 *TF:* 800-475-8801 ■ *Web:* www.theimageworks.com	Woodstock	NY	12498	845-679-8500	679-0606
ImageState New York 29 E 19th St Fourth Fl	New York	NY	10003	212-982-1915	
Mountain Light Photography Inc 106 S Main St *Web:* www.mountainlight.com	Bishop	CA	93514	760-873-7700	873-3980
Photo Researchers Inc 307 Fifth Ave Third Fl *TF:* 800-833-9033 ■ *Web:* www.sciencesource.com	New York	NY	10016	212-758-3420	355-0731
Photo Resource Hawaii 111 Hekili St Ste 241 *TF:* 888-599-7773 ■ *Web:* www.photoresourcehawaii.com	Kailua	HI	96734	808-599-7773	

597 PIECE GOODS & NOTIONS

SEE ALSO Fabric Stores p. 2281

Name / Address	City	State	Zip	Phone	Fax
A Meyers & Sons Corp 325 W 38th St	New York	NY	10018	212-279-6632	594-4093
Advanced Probing Systems Inc 2300 Central Ave *TF:* 800-631-0005 ■ *Web:* www.advancedprobing.com	Boulder	CO	80301	303-939-9384	
American Process Lettering Inc 30 Bunting Ln *Web:* amprosports.com	Primos	PA	19018	610-623-9000	

	City	State	Zip	Phone	Fax
Aplix Inc 12300 Steele Creek Rd	Charlotte	NC	28273	704-588-1920	588-1941
Web: www.aplix.com					
Associated Fabrics Corp					
15-01 Pollitt Dr Unit 7	Fair Lawn	NJ	07410	800-232-4077	710-3850*
**Fax Area Code:* 866 ■ *TF:* 800-232-4077 ■ *Web:* www.afc-fabrics.com					
B Berger Co 1380 Highland Rd	Macedonia	OH	44056	330-425-3838	425-9797
TF Cust Svc: 800-288-8400 ■ *Web:* duralee.com					
Baum Textile Mills Inc 812 Jersey Ave	Jersey City	NJ	07310	201-659-0444	659-9719
TF: 866-842-7631 ■ *Web:* www.baumtextile.com					
Bay Island Sportswear Inc					
225 By Pass 72 NW	Greenwood	SC	29649	864-229-1298	
Web: www.bayislandsportswear.com					
Blank Quilting Corp					
Blank Quilting 49 West 37th St 14th fl	New York	NY	10018	800-294-9495	679-4578*
**Fax Area Code:* 212 ■ *TF:* 800-294-9495 ■ *Web:* www.blankquilting.com					
Blumenthal Lansing Co					
30 Two Bridges Rd Ste 110	Fairfield	NJ	07004	201-935-6220	935-0055
TF: 800-448-9749 ■ *Web:* www.buttonlovers.com					
Bob Barker Company Inc PO Box 429	Fuquay Varina	NC	27526	919-552-3431	552-5097
TF: 800-334-9880 ■ *Web:* www.bobbarker.com					
Brookwood Cos Inc 25 W 45th St 11th Fl	New York	NY	10036	212-551-0100	472-0294*
**Fax Area Code:* 646 ■ *TF:* 800-426-5468 ■ *Web:* www.brookwoodcos.net					
Burch Fabrics Group 4200 Brockton Dr SE	Grand Rapids	MI	49512	616-698-2800	698-0011
TF: 800-841-8111 ■ *Web:* www.burchfabrics.com					
Criterion Thread Company Inc					
21744 98th Ave	Queens Village	NY	11429	718-464-4200	464-3594
TF General: 800-695-0080 ■ *Web:* www.cthread.com					
Custom Metal Crafters Inc					
815 N Mountain Rd	Newington	CT	06111	860-953-4210	953-1746
Web: www.custom-metal.com					
Design/Craft Fabrics Corp 2230 Ridge Dr	Glenview	IL	60025	847-904-7000	904-7102
Web: www.design-craft.com					
Douglass Industries Inc					
412 Boston Ave	Egg Harbor City	NJ	08215	609-965-6030	
Web: www.dougind.com					
Dunlap Industries Inc 123 State St	Dunlap	TN	37327	423-949-4021	949-3648
TF: 800-251-7214 ■ *Web:* www.dunlapworld.com					
Duralee Fabrics Ltd Inc 1775 Fifth Ave	Bay Shore	NY	11706	631-273-8800	275-3297*
**Fax Area Code:* 800 ■ **Fax:* Cust Svc ■ *TF Cust Svc:* 800-275-3872 ■ *Web:* www.duralee.com					
Eagle Button Co Inc 700 Broadway	Westwood	NJ	07675	201-652-4063	
Web: www.eaglebutton.com					
Edgar Fabrics Inc 50 Commerce Dr	Hauppauge	NY	11788	631-435-9116	435-9151
EE Schenck Co 6000 N Cutter Cir	Portland	OR	97217	503-284-4124	288-4475
TF: 800-433-0722 ■ *Web:* www.eeschenck.com					
Hanes Cos Inc 500 N McLin Creek Rd	Conover	NC	28613	828-464-4673	269-7787*
**Fax Area Code:* 602 ■ *TF:* 877-252-3052 ■ *Web:* www.hanesindustries.com					
Hoffman California Fabrics Inc					
25792 Obrero Dr	Mission Viejo	CA	92691	800-547-0100	770-4022*
**Fax Area Code:* 949 ■ *TF:* 800-547-0100 ■ *Web:* www.hoffmanfabrics.com					
Ideal Fastener Corp 603 W Industry Dr	Oxford	NC	27565	919-693-3115	693-3118
Web: www.idealfastener.com					
Jaftex Corp 49 W 37th St	New York	NY	10018	212-686-5194	545-0058
Janlynn Corp 2070 Westover Rd	Chicopee	MA	01022	413-206-0002	206-0060
TF: 800-445-5565 ■ *Web:* www.janlynn.com					
JHB International Inc 1955 S Quince St	Denver	CO	80231	303-751-8100	751-3131
TF: 800-525-9007 ■ *Web:* www.buttons.com					
Keyston Bros 2801 Academy Way Ste A	Sacramento	CA	95815	916-646-1834	646-6392
TF: 800-453-1112 ■ *Web:* www.keystonbros.com					
Lew Jan Textile Corp					
366 Veterans Memorial Hwy	Commack	NY	11725	800-899-0531	543-0561*
**Fax Area Code:* 631 ■ *Web:* www.lewjan.com					
Majilite Corp 1530 Broadway Rd	Dracut	MA	01826	978-441-6800	441-0835
Web: www.majilite.com					
Marcus Bros Textiles Inc					
980 Ave of the Americas	New York	NY	10018	212-354-8700	768-0799
TF: 800-548-8295 ■ *Web:* www.marcusbrothers.com					
McKee Surfaces PO Box 230	Muscatine	IA	52761	563-263-2421	264-5365
TF Cust Svc: 800-553-9662 ■ *Web:* www.mckeesurfaces.com					
Meow Inc 307 W 36th St 16th Fl	New York	NY	10018	888-485-6738	
Web: www.rebeccataylor.com					
Miami Corp, The 720 Anderson Ferry Rd	Cincinnati	OH	45238	513-451-6700	451-7998
TF: 800-543-0448 ■ *Web:* www.miamicorp.com					
Miroglio Textiles USA Inc					
1430 Broadway Sixth Fl	New York	NY	10018	212-382-2020	382-2609
Mon Cheri Bridals LLC 1018 Whitehead Rd Extn	Trenton	NJ	08638	609-530-1900	
Web: www.moncheribridals.com					
Pine Cone Hill Inc 125 Pecks Rd	Pittsfield	MA	01201	413-496-9700	629-2400
TF: 877-586-4771 ■ *Web:* pineconehill.annieselke.com/					
Prym-Dritz Corp 950 Brisack Rd	Spartanburg	SC	29303	864-576-5050	587-3352*
**Fax:* Cust Svc ■ *TF Cust Svc:* 800-255-7796 ■ *Web:* www.dritz.com					
Raytex Fabrics Inc 130 Crossways Pk Dr	Woodbury	NY	11797	516-584-1111	584-1034
Web: www.raytexindustries.com					
Richloom Fabrics Group 261 Fifth Ave	New York	NY	10016	212-685-5400	689-0230
Web: richloom.com					
Robert Allen Fabrics Inc 225 Foxboro Blvd	Foxboro	MA	02035	800-333-3777	332-8256*
**Fax:* Sales ■ *TF:* 800-333-3777 ■ *Web:* www.robertallendesign.com					
Robert Kaufman Company Inc PO Box 59266	Los Angeles	CA	90059	310-538-3482	538-9235
TF: 800-877-2066 ■ *Web:* www.robertkaufman.com					
Rockville Fabrics Corp					
99 W Hawthorne Ave	Valley Stream	NY	11580	516-561-9810	
Rome Fastener Corp 257 Depot Rd	Milford	CT	06460	203-874-6719	877-0201
Web: www.romefast.com					
Scher Fabrics Inc 450 Fashion Ave	New York	NY	10123	212-382-2266	
Schott International Inc 2850 Gilchrist Rd	Akron	OH	44305	330-794-2121	794-2122
TF: 877-661-2121 ■ *Web:* www.schotttextiles.com					
Scovill Fasteners Inc 1802 Scovill Dr	Clarkesville	GA	30523	706-754-1000	754-4000*
**Fax:* Cust Svc ■ *TF Cust Svc:* 888-726-8455 ■ *Web:* www.scovill.com					
Spradling International Inc					
200 Cahaba Vly Pkwy PO Box 1668	Pelham	AL	35124	205-985-4206	985-9176
TF: 800-333-0955 ■ *Web:* www.spradlingvinyl.com					
Sumersault ltd 17 Overlook Rd	Scarsdale	NY	10583	914-472-5778	
Web: www.sumersault.com					
Swimwear Anywhere Inc 85 Sherwood Ave	Farmingdale	NY	11735	631-420-1400	
Web: www.swimwearanywhere.com					
Tiger Button Company Inc					
307 W 38th St Fourth Fl	New York	NY	10018	212-594-0570	695-0265
TF: 800-223-2754 ■ *Web:* www.tigerbutton.com					
Tingue 535 N Midland Ave	Saddle Brook	NJ	07663	201-796-5233	
Web: www.tinguebrownco.com					
Transhield Inc 2932 Thorne Dr	Elkhart	IN	46514	574-266-4118	
TF: 888-731-7700 ■ *Web:* www.transhield-usa.com					
Trimtex Saint Louis Trimming Div					
400 Pk Ave	Williamsport	PA	17701	570-326-9135	326-4250
Web: www.trimtex.com					
Twin Dragon Marketing Inc					
14600 S Broadway St	Gardena	CA	90248	310-715-7070	
Web: www.twindragonmarketing.com					
United Notions Inc 13800 Hutton St	Dallas	TX	75234	972-484-8901	
TF: 800-527-9447 ■ *Web:* storefront.unitednotions.com					
US Button Corp 328 Kennedy Dr	Putnam	CT	06260	860-928-2707	928-2847
TF: 800-243-1842 ■ *Web:* www.usbutton.com					
Valley Forge Fabrics Inc					
2981 Gateway Dr	Pompano Beach	FL	33069	954-971-1776	968-1775
Web: www.valleyforge.com					
Velcro USA Inc 406 Brown Ave	Manchester	NH	03103	603-669-4880	669-9271
TF: 800-225-0180 ■ *Web:* www.velcro.com					
Waterbury Button Co 1855 Peck Ln	Cheshire	CT	06410	800-928-1812	
TF: 800-928-1812 ■ *Web:* www.waterburybutton.com					
Weber & Sons Button Company Inc					
1009 E Sixth St	Muscatine	IA	52761	563-263-9451	
World Emblem International Inc 1500 NE 131 St	Miami	FL	33161	305-772-0362	
Web: www.worldemblem.com					
YKK USA Inc 1251 Vly Brook Ave	Lyndhurst	NJ	07071	201-935-4200	964-0123
Web: www.ykkfastening.com					
Young Fashions Inc 10300 Perkins Rd	Baton Rouge	LA	70810	225-766-1010	
TF: 800-824-4154 ■ *Web:* www.youngfashions.com					
Zabin Industries Inc 3957 S Hill St	Los Angeles	CA	90037	213-749-1215	747-6162
Web: www.zabin.com					

598 PIPE & PIPE FITTINGS - METAL (FABRICATED)

SEE ALSO Metal Tube & Pipe p. 2748

	City	State	Zip	Phone	Fax
Ace Tube Bending 14 Journey	Aliso Viejo	CA	92656	949-362-2220	
Web: www.acetubebending.com					
Advanced Tubing Technology Inc					
150 Intercraft Dr	Statesville	NC	28625	704-924-7020	
Web: www.tubularproducts.com					
Airdrome Precision Components					
3251 E Airport Way	Long Beach	CA	90806	562-426-9411	492-6909
Web: airdrome.com					
Allegan Tubular Products Inc 1276 Lincoln Rd	Allegan	MI	49010	269-673-6636	673-2477
Web: www.allegantube.com					
Allied Chucker & Engineering Co					
3529 Scheele Dr	Jackson	MI	49202	517-787-1370	787-2878
Web: alliedchucker.com					
Alloy Stainless Products Co 611 Union Blvd	Totowa	NJ	07512	973-256-1616	256-5256
TF: 800-631-8372 ■ *Web:* www.alloystainless.com					
AY McDonald Manufacturing Co					
4800 Chavenelle Rd PO Box 508	Dubuque	IA	52002	563-583-7311	588-0720
TF Cust Svc: 800-292-2737 ■ *Web:* www.aymcdonald.com					
Beck Mfg 330 E Ninth St	Waynesboro	PA	17268	717-762-9141	762-9153
Web: www.beckmfg.com					
Bendco Inc 801 Houston Ave	Pasadena	TX	77502	713-473-1557	473-1882
Web: www.bendco.com					
BendTec Inc 366 Garfield Ave	Duluth	MN	55802	218-722-0205	
Web: www.bendtec.com					
Berkley Industries 9938 Pigeon Rd	Bay Port	MI	48720	989-656-2171	
Web: www.avci.net					
Betts Industries Inc 1800 Pennsylvania Ave W	Warren	PA	16365	814-723-1250	723-7030
Web: www.bettsind.com					
Campbell Manufacturing Inc					
127 E Spring St	Bechtelsville	PA	19505	610-367-2107	369-3580
TF: 800-523-0224 ■ *Web:* www.bakerwatersystems.com					
Carpenter Powder Products 600 Mayer St	Bridgeville	PA	15017	412-257-5102	257-5058
TF: 866-790-9092 ■ *Web:* www.cartech.com					
Cascade Waterworks Manufacturing					
1213 Badger St	Yorkville	IL	60560	630-553-0840	
Web: www.cascademfg.com					
Central Pipe Supply Inc 101 Ware Rd PO Box 5470	Pearl	MS	39288	601-939-3322	932-8944
TF: 800-844-7700 ■ *Web:* www.centralpipe.com					
Champion Mfg Industries Inc 6021 N Galena Rd	Peoria	IL	61614	309-685-1031	685-1088
TF: 800-452-7473 ■ *Web:* www.championmfg.com					
Classic Tube 80 Rotech Dr	Lancaster	NY	14086	716-759-1800	
Web: www.classictube.com					
Colonial Engineering Inc 6400 Corporate Ave	Portage	MI	49002	269-323-2495	323-0630
TF: 800-374-0234 ■ *Web:* www.colonialengineering.com					
Controls Southeast Inc PO Box 7500	Charlotte	NC	28241	704-588-3030	644-5100
Web: www.csiheat.com					
Core Pipe 170 Tubeway Dr	Carol Stream	IL	60188	630-690-7000	690-9701
Web: www.gerlin.com					
Custom Fab Inc 109 Fifth St	Orlando	FL	32824	407-859-3954	
Web: www.customfab.com					
Custom Pipe & Coupling Inc					
10560 Fern St PO Box 978	Stanton	CA	90680	714-761-8801	
Web: www.custompipe.com					
Douglas Bros 423 Riverside Industrial Pkwy	Portland	ME	04103	207-797-6771	797-8385
TF: 800-341-0926 ■ *Web:* www.douglasbrothers.com					
Elkhart Products Corp 1255 Oak St	Elkhart	IN	46514	574-264-3181	264-4835
TF: 800-284-4851 ■ *Web:* www.elkhartproducts.com					
Empire Industries Inc 180 Olcott St	Manchester	CT	06040	860-647-1431	647-1160
TF: 800-243-4844 ■ *Web:* www.empireindustries.com					

	City	State	ZIP	Phone	Fax
Ever Roll Specialties Co 3988 Lawrenceville Dr *Web:* www.ever-roll.com	Springfield	OH	45504	937-964-1302	
FabCorp Inc 6951 W Little York *Web:* www.fabcorp.com	Houston	TX	77040	713-466-3962	466-3470
Flotech Inc 3330 Evergreen Ave *Web:* www.flotechinc.com	Jacksonville	FL	32206	904-358-1849	
Fuller Industrial 65 Nelson Rd *Web:* www.fullerindustrial.com	Lively	ON	P3Y1P4	705-682-2777	682-4777
Future Pipe Industries Inc 11811-11812 Proctor Rd *Web:* www.futurepipe.com	Houston	TX	77038	281-847-2987	
General Plug & Mfg Co Inc 455 Main St *TF:* 800-289-7584 ■ *Web:* www.generalplug.com	Grafton	OH	44044	440-926-2411	926-3305
Griffin Pipe Products Co 1011 Warrenville Rd Ste 700 *Web:* uspipe.com	Lisle	IL	60532	630-719-6500	719-2252
H & H Tube & Manufacturing Co 579 Garfield Ave *Web:* www.h-htube.com	Vanderbilt	MI	49795	989-983-2800	
H-P Products Inc 512 W Gorgas St *TF:* 800-822-8356 ■ *Web:* www.h-pproducts.com	Louisville	OH	44641	330-875-5556	875-7584
Highfield Manufacturing Co 380 Mtn Grove St *Web:* www.highfield-mfg.com	Bridgeport	CT	06605	203-384-2281	368-3906
Houston Pipe Benders 14500 E Hardy Rd *Fax Area Code: 713 ■ *Web:* www.hpbenders.com	Houston	TX	77039	281-449-8241	449-3707*
Hydro Tube Enterprises Inc 137 Artino St *Web:* www.hydrotube.com	Oberlin	OH	44074	440-774-1022	774-1482
Ideal Welders Ltd 660 Caldew St *Web:* www.idealwelders.com	Delta	BC	V3M5S2	604-525-5558	525-5313
Industrial Manufacturing & Machining 5495 E 69th Ave *Web:* www.dualdraw.com	Commerce City	CO	80022	303-287-2125	
JB Smith Manufacturing Co 6618 Navigation Blvd *Web:* www.jbsmith.com	Houston	TX	77011	713-928-5711	928-5219
JD Squared Inc 2244 Eddie Williams Rd *Web:* www.jd2.com	Johnson City	TN	37601	423-979-0309	
Kelly Pipe Company LLC 11680 Bloomfield Ave *TF:* 800-305-3559 ■ *Web:* www.kellypipe.com	Santa Fe Springs	CA	90670	562-868-0456	863-4695
Kraftube Inc 925 E Church Ave *Web:* www.kraftube.com	Reed City	MI	49677	231-832-5562	832-2937
Long Island Pipe Supply Inc 586 Commercial Ave *Web:* www.lipipe.com	Garden City	NY	11530	516-222-8008	
McWane Inc 2900 Hwy 280 Ste 300 *TF:* 877-231-0904 ■ *Web:* www.mcwane.com	Birmingham	AL	35223	205-414-3100	414-3170
Merit Brass Co One Merit Dr *Web:* www.meritbrass.com	Cleveland	OH	44143	216-261-9800	
MicroGroup Inc Seven Industrial Pk Rd *TF:* 800-255-8823 ■ *Web:* www.microgroup.com	Medway	MA	02053	508-533-4925	533-5691
Mills Iron Works Inc 14834 Maple Ave *Fax Area Code: 310 ■ *TF:* 800-421-2281 ■ *Web:* www.millsiron.com	Gardena	CA	90248	323-321-6520	532-0476*
Milwaukee Valve Company Inc 16550 W Stratton Dr *TF:* 800-348-6544 ■ *Web:* www.milwaukeevalve.com	New Berlin	WI	53151	262-432-2800	432-2801
Morton Industries LLC 70 Commerce Dr *Web:* www.mortonwelding.com	Morton	IL	61550	309-263-2590	263-0862
National Excelsior Co 1999 N Ruby St *TF:* 855-373-9235 ■ *Web:* www.excelsiorhvac.com	Melrose Park	IL	60160	708-343-4225	681-0041
National Tube Form Inc 3405 Engle Rd *Web:* www.nationaltubeform.com	Fort Wayne	IN	46809	260-478-2363	478-1043
NIBCO Inc 1516 Middlebury St *TF:* 800-234-0227 ■ *Web:* www.nibco.com	Elkhart	IN	46515	574-295-3000	295-3307
Nor-Cal Products Inc 1967 S Oregon St *Fax: Sales ■ *TF:* 800-824-4166 ■ *Web:* www.n-c.com	Yreka	CA	96097	530-842-4457	842-9130*
Norca Corp 185 Great Neck Rd Fourth Fl *Web:* www.norcaprecision.com	Great Neck	NY	11022	516-466-9500	466-9588
Parker Hannifin Corp Brass Products Div 100 Parker Dr *TF:* 800-272-7537 ■ *Web:* www.parker.com	Otsego	MI	49078	269-694-9411	694-4614
Parker Hannifin Corp Instrumentation Products Div 1005 A Cleaner Way *Web:* www.parker.com	Huntsville	AL	35805	256-885-3800	885-3853
Penn Machine Co 106 Stn St *Fax Area Code: 610 ■ *TF:* 800-736-6872 ■ *Web:* www.pennusa.com	Johnstown	PA	15905	814-288-1547	497-3325*
Perma-Pipe Inc 7720 N Lehigh Ave *Web:* www.permapipe.com	Niles	IL	60714	847-966-2235	470-1204
Pevco Sys Intl Inc 1401 Tangier Dr *Web:* www.pevco.com	Baltimore	MD	21220	410-931-8800	
Pioneer Pipe Inc 2021 Hanna Rd *Web:* www.pioneerpipeinc.com	Marietta	OH	45750	740-376-2400	373-8964
Piping Technology & Products Inc 3701 Holmes Rd PO Box 34506 *TF:* 866-746-9172 ■ *Web:* www.pipingtech.com	Houston	TX	77051	713-422-2271	731-8640
Propipe Technologies Inc 1800 Clayton Ave	Middletown	OH	45042	513-424-5311	424-5095
R & B Wagner Inc PO Box 423 *TF:* 888-243-6914 ■ *Web:* www.wagnercompanies.com	Butler	WI	53007	414-214-0444	214-0450
Rado Enterprises 20 Industrial Dr *Web:* www.radoenterprises.com	Bloomsburg	PA	17815	570-759-0303	
Richards Industries Inc 3170 Wasson Rd *Fax: Sales ■ *TF Cust Svc:* 800-543-7311 ■ *Web:* www.richardsind.com	Cincinnati	OH	45209	513-533-5600	871-0105*
Robert Mitchell Inc 350 Decarie Blvd via St-Louis and Crevier St *Web:* www.robertmitchell.com	St-laurent	QC	H4L3K5	514-747-2471	
Romac Industries Inc 21919 20th Ave SE *TF:* 800-426-9341 ■ *Web:* www.romac.com	Bothell	WA	98021	425-951-6200	951-6201
Roscoe Moss Co 4360 Worth St *Web:* www.roscoemoss.com	Los Angeles	CA	90063	323-263-4111	263-4497
Rovanco Piping Systems Inc 20535 SE Frontage Rd *Web:* www.rovanco.com	Joliet	IL	60431	815-741-6700	741-4229
Shaw Group Inc, The 4171 Essen Ln *NYSE:* SHAW ■ *TF General:* 866-235-5687 ■ *Web:* www.shawgrp.com	Baton Rouge	LA	70809	832-513-1000	
Smart Pipe Company Inc 1319 West Sam Houston Pkwy Ste 100 *Web:* www.smart-pipe.com	Houston	TX	77043	281-945-5700	
Snap-Tite Inc 8325 Hessinger Dr *Web:* www.snap-tite.com	Erie	PA	16509	814-838-5700	833-0145
Spitzer Industries Inc 11250 Tanner Rd *Web:* www.spitzerind.com	Houston	TX	77041	713-466-1518	466-1950
Star Pipe LLC 4018 Westhollow Pkwy *TF:* 800-999-3009 ■ *Web:* www.starpipeproducts.com	Houston	TX	77082	281-558-3000	
Steico Industries Inc 1814 Ord Way *Web:* www.steicoindustries.com	Oceanside	CA	92056	760-438-8015	
Swagelok Co 29500 Solon Rd *Web:* www.swagelok.com	Solon	OH	44139	440-248-4600	349-5970
Synalloy Corp 775 Spartan Blvd Ste 102 PO Box 5627 *NASDAQ:* SYNL ■ *TF Orders:* 800-937-5449 ■ *Web:* www.synalloy.com	Spartanburg	SC	29304	864-585-3605	596-1501
Tate Andale Inc 1941 Lansdowne Rd *TF:* 800-296-8283 ■ *Web:* www.tateandale.com	Baltimore	MD	21227	410-247-8700	247-9672
Tennessee Tubebending Inc 5112 N National Dr *Web:* www.evertite.com	Knoxville	TN	37914	865-546-6511	
Texas Steel Conversion Inc 3101 Holmes Rd *Web:* www.texassteelconversion.com	Houston	TX	77051	713-733-6013	
Thermacor Process LP 1670 Hicks Field Rd E *Web:* www.thermacor.com	Fort Worth	TX	76179	817-847-7300	847-7222
Triangle Engineering Inc Six Industrial Way *Web:* www.trieng.com	Hanover	MA	02339	781-878-1500	
Triple d Bending 4707 Glenmore Trail Se *Web:* www.pipebending.com	Calgary	AB	T2C2R9	403-255-2944	253-3261
Troy Tube & Manufacturing Co 50100 E Russell Schmidt Blvd *Web:* www.troytube.com	Chesterfield	MI	48051	586-949-8700	
Tru Line Manufacturing Inc 3510 Central Pkwy Sw *Web:* www.trulinemfg.com	Decatur	AL	35603	256-350-1002	
Tru-Flex Metal Hose Corp 2391 S State Rd 263 PO Box 247 *TF:* 800-255-6291 ■ *Web:* www.tru-flex.com	West Lebanon	IN	47991	765-893-4403	893-4114
Tube Forgings of America Inc 5200 NW Front Ave *Web:* www.tubeforgings.com	Portland	OR	97210	503-241-0716	
Tube Processing Corp 604 E Le Grande Ave *TF:* 800-295-4119 ■ *Web:* www.tubeproc.com	Indianapolis	IN	46203	317-787-1321	786-3074
Tubular Fabricators Industry Inc 600 W Wythe St *Web:* www.tfihealthcare.com	Petersburg	VA	23803	804-733-4000	
Tylok International Inc 1061 E 260th St *Web:* www.tylok.com	Euclid	OH	44132	216-261-7310	
United Spiral Pipe LLC 900 E Third St *Web:* www.unitedspiralpipe.com	Pittsburg	CA	94565	925-526-3100	
Universal Tube Inc 2607 Bond St *TF:* 800-394-8823 ■ *Web:* www.universaltube.com	Rochester Hills	MI	48309	248-853-5100	853-7365
US Pipe & Foundry Co Two Chase Corporate Drive Suite 200 *Fax Area Code: 205 ■ *TF:* 866-347-7473 ■ *Web:* www.uspipe.com	Birmingham	AL	35244	866-347-7473	417-8411*
Vacco Industries Inc 10350 Vacco St *Web:* www.vacco.com	South El Monte	CA	91733	626-443-7121	442-6943
Victaulic Co 4901 Kesslersville Rd *TF Sales:* 800-742-5842 ■ *Web:* www.victaulic.com	Easton	PA	18040	610-559-3300	250-8817
Vulcan Industries Corp N113 W18830 Carnegie Dr *Web:* www.vulcancorp.com	Germantown	WI	53022	262-253-5420	
Watson McDaniel Co 428 Jones Blvd Limerick Airport Business Ctr *Web:* www.watsonmcdaniel.com	Pottstown	PA	19464	610-495-5131	495-5134
Webster Valve Co 583 S Main St	Franklin	NH	03235	603-934-5110	934-1390
Whitley Products Inc 493 S Circle Dr W	Warsaw	IN	46580	574-267-7114	
Woolf Aircraft Products Inc 6401 Cogswell Rd *Web:* www.woolfaircraft.com	Romulus	MI	48174	734-721-5330	721-3490
World Wide Fittings Inc 7501 N Natchez Ave *TF:* 800-393-9894 ■ *Web:* www.worldwidefittings.com	Niles	IL	60714	847-588-2200	588-2212

599 PIPE & PIPE FITTINGS - PLASTICS

	City	State	ZIP	Phone	Fax
Advanced Drainage Systems Inc 4640 Trueman Blvd *Fax Area Code: 614 ■ *TF:* 800-821-6710 ■ *Web:* www.ads-pipe.com	Hilliard	OH	43026	800-821-6710	658-0204*
Ameron International Corp 245 S Los Robles Ave *Web:* www.nov.com	Pasadena	CA	91101	626-683-4000	683-4060
Bakersfield Pipe & Supply Inc 3301 Zachary Ave *Web:* www.bakersfieldpipe.com	Shafter	CA	93263	661-589-9141	589-3739
CANTEX Inc 202 Progress Rd *Web:* www.cantexinc.com	Auburndale	FL	33823	817-215-7000	215-7001
CertainTeed Corp 750 E Swedesford Rd *TF Prod Info:* 800-782-8777 ■ *Web:* www.certainteed.com	Valley Forge	PA	19482	610-341-7000	341-7777
CertainTeed Corp Pipe & Plastics Div 750 E Swedesford Rd PO Box 860 *TF:* 800-274-8530 ■ *Web:* www.certainteed.com	Valley Forge	PA	19482	610-341-7000	341-7413
Charlotte Pipe & Foundry Company Plastics Div 4210 Old Charlotte Hwy PO Box 1339 *Web:* unioncountycoc.com	Monroe	NC	28111	704-289-2531	348-6406

	Phone	Fax
Chemtrol Div NIBCO Inc 1516 Middlebury St. . . . Elkhart IN 46516 *TF:* 800-234-0227 ■ *Web:* nibco.com/industrial-plastics/chemtrol/	574-295-3000	295-3307
Chevron Phillips Chemical Company Performance Pipe Div 5085 W Pk Blvd Ste 500. . . . Plano TX 75093 *TF:* 800-527-0662 ■ *Web:* www.performancepipe.com	972-599-6600	
Crane ChemPharma Resistoflex 1 Quality Way . . . . Marion NC 28752 *Web:* www.resistoflex.com	828-724-4000	
Cresline-West Inc 600 Crosspointe Blvd. . . . Evansville IN 47715 *Web:* www.cresline.com	812-428-9300	428-9353
Diamond Plastics Corp 1212 Johnstown Rd PO Box 1608 . . . . Grand Island NE 68802 *TF:* 800-782-7473 ■ *Web:* www.dpcpipe.com	308-384-4400	384-9345
Dura Plastics Products Inc 533 E Third St . . . . Beaumont CA 92223 *Web:* www.duraplastics.com	951-845-3161	845-7644
Endot Industries Inc 60 Green Pond Rd . . . . Rockaway NJ 07866 *TF:* 800-443-6368 ■ *Web:* www.endot.com	973-625-8500	625-4087
Excalibur Extrusions Inc 110 E Crowther Ave . . . . Placentia CA 92870 *TF:* 800-648-6804 ■ *Web:* www.excaliburextrusions.com	714-528-8834	524-7453
Fernco Inc 300 S Dayton St . . . . Davison MI 48423 *TF:* 800-521-1283 ■ *Web:* www.fernco.com	810-653-9626	653-8714
Fusibond Piping Systems Inc 2615 Curtiss St. . . . . Downers Grove IL 60515 *Web:* www.fusibond.com	630-969-4488	969-2355
Hancor Inc PO Box 1047. . . . . Findlay OH 45839 *TF:* 888-892-2694 ■ *Web:* www.hancor.com	419-422-6521	424-8300
Hobas Pipe USA LP 1413 E Richey Rd. . . . . Houston TX 77073 *TF:* 800-856-7473 ■ *Web:* www.hobaspipe.com	281-821-2200	821-7715
Isco Industries 926 Baxter Ave PO Box 4545. . . . . Louisville KY 40204 *TF:* 800-345-4726 ■ *Web:* www.isco-pipe.com	502-583-6591	238-8165
JM Manufacturing Company Inc 5200 West Century Blvd. . . . . Los Angeles CA 90045 *TF:* 800-621-4404 ■ *Web:* www.jmeagle.com	800-621-4404	
Lasco Fittings Inc 414 Morgan St PO Box 116 . . . . Brownsville TN 38012 *TF:* 800-776-2756 ■ *Web:* www.lascofittings.com	731-772-3180	772-0835
Maloney Technical Products 1300 E Berry St. . . . . Fort Worth TX 76119 *TF:* 800-231-7236 ■ *Web:* www.maloneytech.com	817-923-3344	923-1339
Mueller Plastics Corp 3070 E Cedar . . . . Ontario CA 91761 *TF:* 800-348-8464 ■ *Web:* www.muellerindustries.com	909-930-2060	930-2070
National Pipe & Plastics Inc 3421 Old Vestal Rd. . . . . Vestal NY 13850 **Fax Area Code:* 607 ■ *TF:* 800-836-4350 ■ *Web:* www.nationalpipe.com	800-836-4350	729-6130*
Nebraska Plastics Inc PO Box 45 . . . . Cozad NE 69130 *TF:* 800-445-2887 ■ *Web:* www.countryestate.com	308-784-2500	
North American Pipe Corp 2801 Post Oak Blvd Ste 600. . . . . Houston TX 77056 *TF:* 800-370-5247 ■ *Web:* www.northamericanpipe.com	713-840-7473	552-0087
Oil Creek Plastics Inc 45619 State Hwy 27 PO Box 385 . . . . Titusville PA 16354 *TF:* 800-537-3661 ■ *Web:* www.oilcreek.com	814-827-3661	827-9599
Silver-Line Plastics 900 Riverside Dr. . . . . Asheville NC 28804 *Web:* www.slpipe.com	828-252-8755	285-8901
Teel Plastics Inc 1060 Teel Ct . . . . Baraboo WI 53913 *Web:* www.teel.com	608-355-3080	355-3088
Texas United Pipe Inc 11627 N Houston Rosslyn Rd. . . . . Houston TX 77086 *TF Sales:* 800-966-8741 ■ *Web:* www.texasunitedpipe.com	281-448-3276	448-6983
Vinylplex Inc 1800 Atkinson Ave. . . . . Pittsburg KS 66762 *TF:* 877-779-7473 ■ *Web:* www.vinylplex.com/main.html	620-231-8290	232-8547
Vinyltech Corp 201 S 61st Ave . . . . Phoenix AZ 85043 *TF:* 800-255-3924 ■ *Web:* www.vtpipe.com	602-233-0071	272-4847
Winrock Enterprises 1501 N University Ave Ste 360. . . . . Little Rock AR 72207	501-663-5340	663-4456

600 PIPELINES (EXCEPT NATURAL GAS)

	Phone	Fax
Alyeska Pipeline Service Co *Alaska Corp, The* 3700 Centerpoint Dr PO Box 196660 . . . . Anchorage AK 99503	907-787-8700	787-8330
Belle Fourche Pipeline 455 N Poplar St . . . . Casper WY 82601 *Web:* truecos.com	307-237-9301	266-0252
BP Exploration (Alaska) Inc (BPXA) PO Box 196612 . . . . Anchorage AK 99519 *Web:* www.bp.com	907-561-5111	
BP PLC 28100 Torch Pkwy . . . . Warrenville IL 60555 *NYSE:* BP ■ *TF:* 877-638-5672 ■ *Web:* www.bp.com	630-420-5111	
Buckeye Partners LP Five Radnor Corporate Ctr 100 Matsonford Rd Ste 500 . . . . Radnor PA 19087 *NYSE:* BPL ■ *Web:* www.buckeye.com	484-232-4000	
Chevron Pipe Line Co 4800 Fournace Pl . . . . Bellaire TX 77401 *Web:* www.chevron.com/prodserv/cpl	713-000-1111	
CITGO Pipeline Co 1293 Eldridge Pkwy. . . . . Houston TX 77077 *Web:* www.citgo.com	832-486-4000	
Collins Pipeline Co 355 Mississippi 588 . . . . Collins MS 39428	601-765-6593	
Colonial Pipeline Co 1185 Sanctuary Pkwy Ste 100 . . . . Alpharetta GA 30009 *TF:* 800-275-3004 ■ *Web:* www.colpipe.com	678-762-2200	762-2883
Country Mark Co-op 1200 Refinery Rd. . . . . Mount Vernon IN 47620 **Fax Area Code:* 812 ■ *TF:* 800-832-5490 ■ *Web:* www.countrymark.com	800-832-5490	838-8196*
Enbridge Energy Partners LP 1100 Louisiana Ste 3300 . . . . Houston TX 77002 *NYSE:* EEP ■ **Fax Area Code:* 646 ■ *TF:* 800-481-2804 ■ *Web:* www.enbridgepartners.com	713-821-2000	834-8133*
ExxonMobil Pipeline Co 800 Bell St Rm 653A . . . . Houston TX 77002 *Web:* www.exxonmobilpipeline.com	713-656-6885	656-9586
Genesis Energy LP 919 Milam Ste 2100. . . . . Houston TX 77002 *NYSE:* GEL ■ *TF:* 800-284-3365 ■ *Web:* www.genesisenergy.com	713-860-2500	860-2640
Hess Co 420 Hook Rd . . . . Bayonne NJ 07002 **Fax:* Hum Res ■ *Web:* hess.com	201-437-1017	437-8845*
Imperial Oil Resources Ltd 237 Fourth Ave SW PO Box 2480 Stn M . . . . Calgary AB T2P3M9 **Fax Area Code:* 403 ■ *TF:* 800-567-3776 ■ *Web:* www.imperialoil.ca	800-567-3776	237-2072*
Jayhawk Pipeline LLC 2000 S Main St . . . . McPherson KS 67460 *Web:* www.jayhawkpl.com	620-241-9270	241-9215
Kinder Morgan Energy Partners LP 500 Dallas St Ste 1000. . . . . Houston TX 77002 *NYSE:* KMI ■ **Fax Area Code:* 403 ■ **Fax:* Hum Res ■ *TF:* 866-208-3372 ■ *Web:* www.kindermorgan.com	713-369-9000	514-6401*
Kinder Morgan Management LLC 500 Dallas St 1 Allen Ctr Ste 1000. . . . . Houston TX 77002 *NYSE:* KMI ■ *Web:* www.kindermorgan.com	713-369-9000	
Magellan Midstream Partners LP One Williams Ctr . . . . Tulsa OK 74172 *NYSE:* MMP ■ **Fax:* Mail Rm ■ *TF:* 800-574-6671 ■ *Web:* www.magellanlp.com	918-574-7000	573-6714*
Marathon Pipe Line LLC (MPL) 539 S Main St Rm 7614 . . . . Findlay OH 45840 *Web:* www.marathonpipeline.com	419-422-2121	425-7040
MarkWest Energy Partners LP 1515 Arapahoe St Tower 1 Ste 1600. . . . . Denver CO 80202 *NYSE:* MWE ■ *TF:* 800-730-8388 ■ *Web:* www.markwest.com	303-925-9200	290-8769
Pioneer Pipe Line Company Inc 245 East 1100 North. . . . . North Salt Lake UT 84054 *Web:* conocophillips.com	801-295-2325	
Plains All American Pipeline LP 333 Clay St Ste 1600 . . . . Houston TX 77002 *NYSE:* PAA ■ *TF Mktg:* 866-753-3619 ■ *Web:* www.plainsallamerican.com	713-646-4100	
Plantation Pipe Line Co 1100 Alderman Dr Ste 200. . . . . Alpharetta GA 30005 *Web:* www.kindermorgan.com	770-751-4000	751-4133
Precision Pipeline Solutions LLC 617 Little Britain Rd Ste 200. . . . . New Windsor NY 12553 *Web:* www.precisionpipelinesolutions.com	845-566-8332	
Sunoco Inc 1735 Market St Ste LL . . . . Philadelphia PA 19103 *NYSE:* SUN ■ *TF:* 800-786-6261 ■ *Web:* www.sunocoinc.com	215-977-3000	977-3409
Sunoco Logistics Partners LP 525 Fritztown Rd. . . . . Sinking Spring PA 19608 *NYSE:* SXL ■ *Web:* www.sunocologistics.com	610-670-3200	
Teppco Crude Oil LP 210 Pk Ave. . . . . Oklahoma City OK 73102	405-239-7191	
Valero LP PO Box 696000. . . . . San Antonio TX 78269 **Fax Area Code:* 210 ■ *TF:* 800-333-3377 ■ *Web:* www.valero.com	866-297-6093	370-2646*

601 PLANETARIUMS

	Phone	Fax
Abrams Planetarium Michigan State University. . . . . East Lansing MI 48824 *Web:* www.pa.msu.edu/abrams	517-355-4676	432-3838
Adler Planetarium & Astronomy Museum 1300 S Lk Shore Dr . . . . Chicago IL 60605 *Web:* www.adlerplanetarium.org	312-922-7827	
Andrus Planetarium 511 Warburton Ave Hudson River Museum . . . . Yonkers NY 10701 *Web:* www.hrm.org/planetarium.html	914-963-4550	963-8558
Arnim D Hummel Planetarium Eastern Kentucky University . . . . Richmond KY 40475 *Web:* www.planetarium.eku.edu	859-622-1547	622-6666
Bays Mountain Planetarium & Observatory 853 Bays Mtn Pk Rd. . . . . Kingsport TN 37660 *Web:* baysmountain.com	423-229-9447	224-2589
BCC Planetarium & Obersvatory 1519 Clearlake Rd . . . . Cocoa FL 32922 *Web:* www.easternflorida.edu	321-433-7373	
Berea College Weatherford Planetarium 101 Chestnut St . . . . Berea KY 40404 *TF:* 800-326-5948 ■ *Web:* berea.edu	859-985-3000	985-3351
Buehler Planetarium & Observatory (BC) 3501 SW Davie Rd . . . . Davie FL 33314 *Web:* www.broward.edu/locations/central/buehler.jsp	954-201-6681	475-2858
Casper Planetarium 904 N Poplar St . . . . Casper WY 82601 *Web:* casperplanetarium.com	307-577-0310	
Cernan Earth & Space Ctr 2000 N Fifth Ave Triton College . . . . River Grove IL 60171 *TF:* 800-972-7000 ■ *Web:* www.triton.edu	708-456-0300	583-3153
Charles Hayden Planetarium One Science Pk . . . . Boston MA 02114 *Web:* www.mos.org	617-723-2500	589-0362
Chesapeake Planetarium 312 Cedar Rd. . . . . Chesapeake VA 23322 *Web:* virginia.org	757-547-0153	547-0252
Christa McAuliffe Planetarium Two Institute Dr. . . . . Concord NH 03301 *Web:* www.starhop.com	603-271-7827	271-7832
Clark Planetarium 110 S 400 W . . . . Salt Lake City UT 84101 *Web:* www.clarkplanetarium.net	385-468-7827	
Community College of Southern Nevada Planetarium & Observatory 3200 E Cheyenne Ave. . . . . North Las Vegas NV 89030 *TF:* 800-630-7563 ■ *Web:* www.csn.edu/planetarium	702-651-4759	651-4825
Discovery Museum & Planetarium 4450 Pk Ave . . . . Bridgeport CT 06604 *Web:* www.discoverymuseum.org	203-372-3521	374-1929
Downing Planetarium 5320 N Maple Ave MS DP132 California State University Fresno. . . . . Fresno CA 93740 *Web:* www.downing-planetarium.org	559-278-4121	278-4070
Dreyfuss Planetarium 49 Washington St . . . . Newark NJ 07102 *TF:* 888-370-6765 ■ *Web:* www.newarkmuseum.org	973-596-6529	642-0459
Fiske Planetarium 2414 Regent Dr . . . . Boulder CO 80309 *Web:* www.colorado.edu	303-492-5002	492-1725
Flandrau Science Ctr & Planetarium 1601 E University Blvd . . . . Tucson AZ 85719 *Web:* www.flandrau.org	520-621-4516	621-8451

Name / Address	City	State	Zip	Phone	Fax
Fleischmann Planetarium & Science Ctr University of Nevada	Reno	NV	89557	775-784-4811	784-4822
Web: planetarium.unr.nevada.edu					
Gheens Science Hall & Rauch Planetarium Rauch Planetarium University of Louisville	Louisville	KY	40292	502-852-6664	852-0831
TF: 800-996-7566 ■ *Web:* louisville.edu/planetarium					
Hayden Planetarium 81st St & Central Pk W	New York	NY	10024	212-769-5606	769-5427
Web: www.amnh.org					
Hopkins Planetarium One Market Square SE	Roanoke	VA	24011	540-342-5710	224-1240
Web: www.smwv.org					
JI Holcomb Observatory & Planetarium 4600 Sunset Ave	Indianapolis	IN	46208	317-940-8333	
Web: www.butler.edu/holcomb-observatory					
John Deere Planetarium 820 38th St Augustana College	Rock Island	IL	61201	309-794-7327	794-7564
TF: 800-798-8100 ■ *Web:* augustana.edu					
Kenner Planetarium & MegaDome Cinema 2020 Fourth St Rivertown	Kenner	LA	70062	504-468-7231	
Web: www.kenner.la.us					
Kitt Peak National Observatory 950 N Cherry Ave	Tucson	AZ	85719	520-318-8600	318-8724
TF: 888-809-4012 ■ *Web:* www.noao.edu/kpno					
Lafayette Natural History Museum & Planetarium 433 Jefferson St	Lafayette	LA	70501	337-291-5544	291-5464
Web: www.lafayettesciencemuseum.org					
Lake Afton Public Observatory 1845 Fairmount	Wichita	KS	67260	316-978-7827	978-3350
Web: www.webs.wichita.edu/lapo					
Lick Observatory Mt Hamilton Rd	San Jose	CA	95140	408-274-5061	
Web: www.ucolick.org					
Lodestar Astronomy Ctr 1801 Mtn Rd NW	Albuquerque	NM	87104	505-841-2800	
Web: www.nmnaturalhistory.org					
Longway Planetarium 1310 E Kearsley St	Flint	MI	48503	810-237-3400	237-3417
Web: www.sloanlongway.org					
Lowell Observatory 1400 W Mars Hill Rd	Flagstaff	AZ	86001	928-774-3358	774-6296
Web: www.lowell.edu					
Maria Mitchell Assn 4 Vestal St	Nantucket	MA	02554	508-228-9273	
Web: www.mmo.org					
Maynard F Jordan Planetarium & Observatory 5781 Wingate Hall Maynard F Jordan Planetarium	Orono	ME	04469	207-581-1341	581-1314
Web: www.galaxymaine.com					
Montgomery City Planetarium 1010 Forest Ave	Montgomery	AL	36106	334-241-4799	241-2301
Moody Planetarium 3301 Fourth St Museum of Texas Tech University	Lubbock	TX	79409	806-742-2432	742-1136
Web: www.depts.ttu.edu/museumttu					
Morehead Planetarium 250 E Franklin St UNC Chapel Hill CB 3480	Chapel Hill	NC	27599	919-962-1236	962-1238
Web: www.moreheadplanetarium.org					
Mueller Planetarium University of Nebraska 210 Morrill Hall	Lincoln	NE	68588	402-472-2641	472-8899
Web: www.spacelaser.com					
Ott Planetarium 1551 Edvalson St	Ogden	UT	84408	801-626-6871	
Web: www.ottplanetarium.org					
Portland Observatory 138 Congress St	Portland	ME	04101	207-774-5561	774-2509
Web: www.portlandlandmarks.org/observatory.htm					
Roger B Chaffee Planetarium 272 Pearl St NW	Grand Rapids	MI	49504	616-456-3977	
Web: grpm.org/planetarium					
Rosicrucian Egyptian Museum & Planetarium 1342 Naglee Ave Rosicrucian Pk	San Jose	CA	95191	408-947-3600	947-3677
Web: www.rosicrucian.org					
Russell C Davis Planetarium 201 E Pascagoula St	Jackson	MS	39201	601-960-1550	
Web: thedavisplanetarium.com					
Saint Petersburg College (SPC) PO Box 13489	Saint Petersburg	FL	33710	727-341-4772	
Web: www.spcollege.edu					
Sanford Museum & Planetarium 117 E Willow St	Cherokee	IA	51012	712-225-3922	
Web: www.sanfordmuseum.org					
Science Factory Children's Museum & Planetarium 2300 Leo Harris Pkwy	Eugene	OR	97401	541-682-7888	484-9027
Web: www.sciencefactory.org					
Science Museum of Viriginia 2500 W Broad St	Richmond	VA	23220	804-864-1400	
Web: www.smv.org					
Science Place, The 2201 N Field St	Dallas	TX	75201	214-428-5555	756-5916
Web: www.perotmuseum.org					
Sharpe Planetarium 3050 Central Ave	Memphis	TN	38111	901-636-2362	320-6391
Web: www.memphismuseums.org					
South Florida Science Center and Aquarium 4801 Dreher Trail N	West Palm Beach	FL	33405	561-832-1988	833-0551
Web: www.sfsciencecenter.org					
Southworth Planetarium 96 Falmouth St	Portland	ME	04104	207-780-4249	780-4055
Web: www.usm.maine.edu					
Space Transit Planetarium 3280 S Miami Ave	Miami	FL	33129	305-646-4200	646-4200
TF: 866-268-0250 ■ *Web:* www.miamisci.org					
Strasenburgh Planetarium 657 E Ave Rochester Museum & Science Ctr	Rochester	NY	14607	585-271-4320	271-0492
Web: www.rmsc.org					
Tomchin Planetarium & Observatory 425 Hodges Hall	Morgantown	WV	26506	304-293-4961	
Web: planetarium.wvu.edu					
University of Toledo, The 2801 W Bancroft MS 218	Toledo	OH	43606	419-530-2650	530-5167
Web: www.utoledo.edu					
William M Staerkel Planetarium 2400 W Bradley Ave Parkland College	Champaign	IL	61821	217-351-2568	
Web: www.parkland.edu					

602 PLASTICS - LAMINATED - PLATE, SHEET, PROFILE SHAPES

Name / Address	City	State	Zip	Phone	Fax
AccuTrex Products Inc 112 Southpointe Blvd	Canonsburg	PA	15317	724-746-4300	
Web: www.accutrex.com					
American Renolit Corp 1207 E Lincolnway	LaPorte	IN	46350	219-324-6886	324-5332
Web: laminatefinder.com					
American Thermoplastic Extrusion Co 4851 NW 128th St Rd	Opa Locka	FL	33054	305-769-9566	769-1998
AMETEK Inc Westchester Plastics Div 42 Mountain Ave	Nesquehoning	PA	18240	570-645-6900	645-6959
Web: www.ametek-westchesterplas.com					
Applied Plastics Company Inc 7320 S Sixth St	Oak Creek	WI	53154	414-764-2900	764-8606
Web: www.appliedplasticsinc.com					
Bourne Industries Inc 491 S Comstock St	Corunna	MI	48817	989-743-3461	743-5481
Web: www.bourneindustries.com					
C-K Composites Inc 361 Bridgeport Rd	Mount Pleasant	PA	15666	724-547-4581	547-2890
Web: www.ckcomposites.com					
California Combining Corp 5607 S Santa Fe Ave	Los Angeles	CA	90058	323-589-5727	585-8078
Web: www.californiacombining.com					
Commodore Plastics LLC 26 Maple Ave	Bloomfield	NY	14469	585-657-7777	
Web: www.commodoresolutions.com					
Connecticut Laminating Company Inc 162 James St	New Haven	CT	06513	203-787-2184	787-4073
TF: 800-753-9119 ■ *Web:* www.ctlaminating.com					
Current Inc 30 Tyler St PO Box 120183	East Haven	CT	06512	203-469-1337	467-8435
TF: 877-436-6542 ■ *Web:* www.currentcomposites.com					
Custom Pultrusions Inc 1331 S Chillicothe Rd	Aurora	OH	44202	330-562-5201	
DuPont Surfaces 4417 Lancaster Pk CRP 728/3105	Wilmington	DE	19805	302-774-1000	
TF: 800-448-9835 ■ *Web:* www.dupont.com					
Fiberesin Industries Inc 37031 E Wisconsin Ave PO Box 88	Oconomowoc	WI	53066	262-567-4427	567-4814
Web: www.fiberesin.com					
Flexsystems USA Inc 727 W Main St	El Cajon	CA	92020	619-401-1858	
Web: www.flexsystems.com					
Formica Corp 10155 Reading Rd	Cincinnati	OH	45241	513-786-3400	
TF: 800-367-6422 ■ *Web:* www.formica.com					
Franklin Fibre-Lamitex Corp 903 E 13th St	Wilmington	DE	19802	302-652-3621	571-9754
TF: 800-233-9739 ■ *Web:* www.franklinfibre.com					
Hartson-kennedy Cabinet Top Company Inc 522 W 22nd St PO Box 3095	Marion	IN	46953	765-668-8144	662-3452
TF: 800-388-8144 ■ *Web:* www.hartson-kennedy.com					
Insulfab Plastics Inc 834 Hayne St	Spartanburg	SC	29301	864-582-7506	582-5215
TF: 800-845-7599 ■ *Web:* www.insulfab.com					
Insultab Inc 45 Industrial Pkwy	Woburn	MA	01801	781-935-0800	935-0879
TF Cust Svc: 800-468-4822 ■ *Web:* www.insultab.com					
Iten Industries 4602 Benefit Ave	Ashtabula	OH	44004	440-997-6134	992-4966
TF Orders: 800-227-4836 ■ *Web:* www.itenindustries.com					
Klockner Pentaplast of America Inc 3585 Klockner Rd PO Box 500	Gordonsville	VA	22942	540-832-1400	832-1405
Web: www.kpfilms.com					
Lakeland Plastics Inc (LP) 1550 McCormick Blvd	Mundelein	IL	60060	847-680-1550	680-1595
TF: 800-454-4006 ■ *Web:* www.lakelandplastics.com					
Lamart Corp 16 Richmond St	Clifton	NJ	07015	973-772-6262	772-3673
TF: 800-526-2799 ■ *Web:* www.lamartcorp.com					
Laminating Company of America 20322 Windrow Dr	Lake Forest	CA	92630	949-587-3300	454-0066
Web: www.lcoa.com					
Lamsco West Inc 24823 Anza Dr	Santa Clarita	CA	91355	661-295-8620	295-8626
Web: www.shimtechgroup.com					
LSI Corp of America Inc 2100 Xenium Ln N	Plymouth	MN	55441	763-559-4664	559-4395
Web: www.lsi-casework.com					
Madico Inc 64 Industrial Pkwy	Woburn	MA	01801	781-935-7850	935-6841
TF: 800-456-4331 ■ *Web:* www.madico.com					
Mantec Services Inc 4400 24th Ave W	Seattle	WA	98199	206-285-5656	
Web: www.mantecservicesinc.com					
Mar-Bal Inc 16930 Munn Rd	Chagrin Falls	OH	44023	440-543-7526	543-4374
Web: www.mar-bal.com					
Miniature Precision Components Inc 820 Wisconsin St	Walworth	WI	53184	262-275-5791	275-6346
Web: www.mpc-inc.com					
Olon Industries Inc 42 Armstrong Ave	Georgetown	ON	L7G4R9	905-877-7300	877-7383
TF: 800-387-2319 ■ *Web:* www.olon.ca					
Optical Filters 13447 S Mosiertown Rd Ste A	Meadville	PA	16335	814-333-2222	
Web: www.opticalfiltersusa.com					
Petro Plastics Company Inc 450 S Ave	Garwood	NJ	07027	908-789-1200	789-1381
TF: 800-486-4738 ■ *Web:* www.petroplastics.com					
Reef Industries Inc 9209 Almeda Genoa Rd	Houston	TX	77075	713-507-4200	507-4295
TF: 800-231-6074 ■ *Web:* www.reefindustries.com					
Rotuba Extruders Inc 1401 S Pk Ave	Linden	NJ	07036	908-486-1000	486-0874
Web: www.rotuba.com					
Rowmark Inc 2040 Industrial Dr	Findlay	OH	45840	419-425-2407	425-2927
TF: 800-243-3339 ■ *Web:* www.rowmark.com					
Sabin Corp 3800 Constitution Ave PO Box 788	Bloomington	IN	47403	812-339-2235	554-8335*
**Fax Area Code:* 800 ■ *TF:* 800-457-4500 ■ *Web:* www.cookgroup.com					
Schneller Inc 6019 Powdermille Rd	Kent	OH	44240	330-673-1400	676-7122
Web: www.schneller.com					
Spaulding Composites Co 55 Nadeau Dr	Rochester	NH	03867	603-332-0555	332-5357
TF: 800-801-0560 ■ *Web:* www.spauldingcom.com					
Techniform Industries Inc 2107 Hayes Ave	Fremont	OH	43420	419-332-8484	334-5222
TF: 800-691-2816 ■ *Web:* www.techniform-plastics.com					
V-T Industries Inc 1000 Industrial Pk	Holstein	IA	51025	712-368-4381	368-4111
TF: 800-827-1615 ■ *Web:* www.vtindustries.com					

	City	State	Zip	Phone	Fax
Wilmington Fibre Specialty Co					
700 Washington St	New Castle	DE	19720	302-328-7525	328-6630
TF: 800-220-5132 ■ *Web:* www.wilmfibre.com					
Wilsonart International Inc 2400 Wilson Pl	Temple	TX	76504	254-207-7000	207-2545
TF Cust Svc: 800-433-3222 ■ *Web:* www.wilsonart.com					

603 PLASTICS - UNSUPPORTED - FILM, SHEET, PROFILE SHAPES

SEE ALSO Blister Packaging p. 1872

	City	State	Zip	Phone	Fax
Advance Bag & Packaging Technologies					
5720 Williams Lk Rd	Waterford	MI	48329	248-674-3126	674-2630
TF: 800-475-2247 ■ *Web:* www.advancepac.com					
AEP Industries Inc 125 Phillips Ave	South Hackensack	NJ	07606	201-641-6600	807-2443
NASDAQ: AEPI ■ *TF:* 800-999-2374 ■ *Web:* www.aepinc.com					
Allen Extruders Inc 1305 Lincoln Ave	Holland	MI	49423	616-394-3810	394-0100
TF: 800-833-1305 ■ *Web:* www.allenx.com					
Alte-rego Corp 36 Tidemore Ave	Etobicoke	ON	M9W5H4	416-740-3397	
Web: www.alte-rego.com					
Anaheim Custom Extruders 4640 E La Palma Ave	Anaheim	CA	92807	714-693-8508	693-9531
TF Cust Svc: 800-229-2760 ■ *Web:* acextrusions.com					
Arlon Graphics 2811 S Harbor Blvd	Santa Ana	CA	92704	714-540-2811	329-2756*
**Fax Area Code:* 800 ■ *TF:* 800-232-7161 ■ *Web:* www.arlon.com					
Atlas Roofing Falcon Foam Div					
8240 Byron Ctr Rd SW	Byron Center	MI	49315	800-917-9138	878-9942*
**Fax Area Code:* 616 ■ *TF:* 800-917-9138 ■ *Web:* atlaseps.com					
Avery Dennison Engineered Films Div					
207 Goode Ave Bldg 18	Glendale	CA	91203	626-304-2000	358-4684*
**Fax Area Code:* 440 ■ *Web:* averydennison.com					
Avery Dennison Worldwide Graphics Div					
250 Chester St Bldg 8	Painesville	OH	44077	440-358-3700	358-3665
TF: 800-443-9380 ■ *Web:* www.averygraphics.com					
Bemis Company Inc					
One Neenah Ctr Fourth Fl PO Box 669	Neenah	WI	54957	920-727-4100	
NYSE: BMS ■ *Web:* www.bemis.com					
Bi-ax Intl Inc 596 Cedar Ave	Wingham	ON	N0G2W0	519-357-1818	
Web: www.biaxinc.com					
Bixby International Corp 1 Preble Rd	Newburyport	MA	01950	978-462-4100	465-5184
TF: 800-466-4102 ■ *Web:* www.bixbyintl.com					
Brandywine Investment Group Homalite Div					
11 Brookside Dr	Wilmington	DE	19804	302-652-3686	652-4578
TF: 800-346-7802 ■ *Web:* www.homalite.com					
Catalina Graphic Films Inc					
27001 Agoura Rd Ste 100	Calabasas Hills	CA	91301	818-880-8060	880-1144
TF: 800-333-3136 ■ *Web:* www.catalinagraphicfilms.com					
Celgard LLC 13800 S Lakes Dr	Charlotte	NC	28273	704-588-5310	
Web: www.celgard.com					
Clopay Plastic Products Co 8585 Duke Blvd	Mason	OH	45040	513-770-4800	
TF: 800-282-2260 ■ *Web:* www.clopayplastics.com					
Coburn Co, The 834 E Milwaukee St	Whitewater	WI	53190	262-473-2822	473-3522
Web: coburn.com					
Crown Plastics Co 116 May Dr	Harrison	OH	45030	513-367-0238	
Web: www.crownplastics.com					
CUE Inc 11 Leonberg Rd	Cranberry Township	PA	16066	724-772-5225	772-5280
TF: 800-283-4621 ■ *Web:* www.cue-inc.com					
Daliah Plastics Corp 134 W Wainman Ave	Asheboro	NC	27203	336-629-0551	
Web: www.daliahplastics.com					
Dielectrics Industries Inc 300 Burnett Rd	Chicopee	MA	01020	413-594-8111	594-2343
TF: 800-472-7286 ■ *Web:* www.dielectrics.com					
Dunmore Corp 145 Wharton Rd	Bristol	PA	19007	215-781-8895	781-9293
TF: 800-444-0242 ■ *Web:* www.dunmore.com					
E S Robbins Corp 2802 Avalon Ave	Muscle Shoals	AL	35661	256-248-2400	248-2410
TF: 866-934-6018 ■ *Web:* www.esrobbins.com					
Enflo Corp 315 Lake Ave	Bristol	CT	06010	860-589-0014	589-7179
TF: 888-887-4093 ■ *Web:* www.enflo.com					
FLEXcon Company Inc					
One Flexcon Industrial Pk	Spencer	MA	01562	508-885-8200	885-8400
Web: www.flexcon.com					
Gary Plastic Packaging Corp 1340 Viele Ave	Bronx	NY	10474	718-893-2200	378-2141
TF: 800-221-8150 ■ *Web:* www.plasticboxes.com					
General Formulations Inc 309 S Union St	Sparta	MI	49345	616-887-7387	887-0537
TF: 800-253-3664 ■ *Web:* www.generalformulations.com					
Glasforms Inc 1226 Lincoln Ave	San Jose	CA	95125	408-297-9300	297-0601
TF: 888-297-3800 ■ *Web:* www.glassforms.com					
GSE Lining Technology Inc 19103 Gundle Rd	Houston	TX	77073	281-443-8564	875-6010
TF: 800-435-2008 ■ *Web:* www.gseworld.com					
i2M Inc					
755 Oak Hill Rd Crestwood Industrial Park	Mountain Top	PA	18707	570-474-6741	
Web: www.hpg-intl.com					
ILPEA Industries Inc 745 S Gardner St	Scottsburg	IN	47170	812-752-2526	752-3563
Web: www.ilpeaindustries.com					
Kama Corp 600 Dietrich Ave	Hazleton	PA	18201	412-553-4545	
TF: 888-252-6212 ■ *Web:* www.alcoa.com/kama					
Kayline Processing Inc 31 Coates St	Trenton	NJ	08611	609-695-1449	989-1094
TF Sales: 800-367-5546 ■ *Web:* www.kayline.com					
Kendall Packaging Corp					
10200 N Port Washington Rd	Mequon	WI	53092	262-404-1200	404-1221
TF: 800-237-0951 ■ *Web:* www.kendallpkg.com					
Kepner Plastics Fabricators Inc					
3131 Lomita Blvd	Torrance	CA	90505	310-325-3162	326-8560
Web: www.kepnerplastics.com					
Kimoto Tech Inc PO Box 1783	Cedartown	GA	30125	770-748-2643	748-2648
TF: 888-546-6861 ■ *Web:* www.kimototech.com					
Lavanture Products Co 22825 Gallatin Way	Elkhart	IN	46514	574-264-0658	264-6601
TF: 800-348-7625 ■ *Web:* www.lavanture.com					
Louisiana Plastic Industries Inc					
501 Downing Pines Rd	West Monroe	LA	71292	318-388-4562	387-5642
Web: laplastic.com					
Major Prime Plastics Inc					
649 N Ardmore Ave	Villa Park	IL	60181	630-834-9400	
Web: majorprime.com					
McNeel International Corp 5401 W Kennedy Blvd	Tampa	FL	33609	813-286-8680	286-1535
Mississippi Polymers Inc 2733 S Harper Rd	Corinth	MS	38834	662-287-1401	
Web: www.mississippipolymers.com					
Mitsubishi Polyester Film LLC 2001 Hood Rd	Greer	SC	29650	864-879-5000	879-5006*
**Fax:* Mktg ■ *TF:* 800-334-1934 ■ *Web:* www.m-petfilm.com					
MPI Technologies 37 E St	Winchester	MA	01890	781-729-8300	729-9093
TF: 888-674-8088 ■ *Web:* www.mpirelease.com					
Natvar 8720 US Hwy 70 W	Clayton	NC	27520	919-553-4151	553-4156
TF: 800-395-6288 ■ *Web:* natvar.tekni-plex.com					
New Hampshire Plastics Inc					
One Bouchard St	Manchester	NH	03103	603-669-8523	622-4888
TF: 800-258-3036 ■ *Web:* www.nhplastics.com					
Northland Plastics Inc					
1420 S 16th St PO Box 290	Sheboygan	WI	53081	800-776-7163	458-4881*
**Fax Area Code:* 920 ■ *TF:* 800-776-7163 ■ *Web:* www.northlandplastics.com					
O'Sullivan Films Inc 1944 Valley Ave	Winchester	VA	22601	540-667-6666	
Web: www.osul.com					
Orcon Corp 1570 Atlantic St	Union City	CA	94587	510-489-8100	489-6436
TF General: 800-227-0505 ■ *Web:* www.orcon-aerospace.com					
Pacur LLC 3555 Moser St	Oshkosh	WI	54901	920-236-2888	
Web: www.pacur.com					
Paragon Films Inc 3500 W Tacoma	Broken Arrow	OK	74012	918-250-3456	355-3456
Web: www.paragon-films.com					
Penn Fibre Plastics 2434 Bristol Rd	Bensalem	PA	19020	800-662-7366	702-9552*
**Fax Area Code:* 215 ■ *TF Cust Svc:* 800-662-7366 ■ *Web:* www.pennfibre.com					
Performance Coating International					
600 Murray St	Bangor	PA	18013	610-588-7900	588-7901
Web: pcoatingsintl.com					
Performance Materials Corp					
1150 Calle Suerte	Camarillo	CA	93012	805-482-1722	482-8776
Web: tencate.com/amer/industrial-composites/default.aspx					
Petoskey Plastics Inc One Petoskey St	Petoskey	MI	49770	231-347-2602	347-2878
TF: 800-999-6556 ■ *Web:* www.petoskeyplastics.com					
Pexco LLC 2500 Northwinds Pkwy Ste 472	Alpharetta	GA	30009	404-564-8560	564-8579
Web: www.pexco.com					
Phoenix Films Inc PO Box 3816	Clearwater	FL	33767	727-446-0300	
Web: www.phoenixfilms.com					
Pinnacle Films Inc 10701-A S Commerce Blvd	Charlotte	NC	28273	704-504-3200	
Web: www.pinnaclefilms.com					
Plaskolite Inc 1770 Joyce Ave	Columbus	OH	43219	614-294-3281	297-7287
TF: 800-848-9124 ■ *Web:* www.plaskolite.com					
Polyethics Industries Inc					
625 Harvie Settlement Rd	Orillia	ON	L3V7Y7	705-329-2266	
Web: polyethics.com					
Polyfil 74 Green Pond Rd	Rockaway	NJ	07866	973-627-4070	
Web: www.polyfilcorp.com					
Polyvinyl Films Inc PO Box 753	Sutton	MA	01590	508-865-3558	865-1562
TF: 800-343-6134 ■ *Web:* www.stretchtite.com					
Primex Plastics Corp 1235 N 'F' St	Richmond	IN	47374	765-966-7774	935-1083
TF: 800-222-5116 ■ *Web:* www.primexplastics.com					
Prinsco Inc 108 W Hwy 7 PO Box 265	Prinsburg	MN	56281	320-978-4116	978-8602
TF: 800-992-1725 ■ *Web:* www.prinsco.com					
Raven Industries Inc 205 E Sixth St	Sioux Falls	SD	57104	605-336-2750	335-0268
NASDAQ: RAVN ■ *TF:* 800-243-5435 ■ *Web:* www.ravenind.com					
Republic Plastics 27095 S Republic Rd	San Manuel	AZ	85631	520-385-2212	
Web: www.republicplastics.com					
Ross & Roberts Inc 1299 W Broad St	Stratford	CT	06615	203-378-9363	377-8841
Sancap Liner Technology Inc					
16125 Armour St NE	Alliance	OH	44601	330-821-1166	
Web: www.sancapliner.com					
Sheffield Plastics Inc 119 Salisbury Rd	Sheffield	MA	01257	413-229-8711	229-8717
TF Cust Svc: 800-254-1707 ■ *Web:* www.sheffieldplasticsinc.com					
Shepherd CE Company Inc 2221 Canada Dry St	Houston	TX	77023	713-924-4300	928-2324
TF: 800-324-6733 ■ *Web:* www.ceshepherd.com					
Shield Pack LLC 411 Downing Pines Rd	West Monroe	LA	71292	318-387-4743	325-4800
TF: 800-551-5185 ■ *Web:* www.shieldpack.com					
Sigma Plastics Group					
Page & Schuyler Aves Bldg 5	Lyndhurst	NJ	07071	201-507-9100	507-0447
Web: www.sigmaplastics.com					
Sinclair & Rush Inc 123 Manufacturers Dr	Arnold	MO	63010	636-282-6800	282-6888
Web: www.sinclair-rush.com					
SLM Manufacturing Corp 215 Davidson Ave	Somerset	NJ	08873	732-469-7500	469-5546
TF: 800-526-3708 ■ *Web:* www.slmcorp.com					
Soliant LLC 1872 Hwy 9 Bypass	Lancaster	SC	29720	803-285-9401	313-8227
TF: 800-288-9401 ■ *Web:* www.paintfilm.com					
Southern Film Extruders Inc					
2319 English Rd	High Point	NC	27262	336-885-8091	885-1221
TF: 800-334-6101 ■ *Web:* www.southernfilm.com					
Summit Plastics Inc 107 S Laurel St	Summit	MS	39666	601-276-7500	276-2400
TF: 800-790-7117 ■ *Web:* www.summitplastics.us					
Sunlite Plastics Inc					
W 194 N 11340 McCormick Dr	Germantown	WI	53022	262-253-0600	253-0601
Web: www.sunliteplastics.com					
Tee Group Films 605 N Main St	Ladd	IL	61329	815-894-2331	894-3387
Web: www.tee-group.com					
Thermoplastic Processes Inc 1268 Valley Rd	Stirling	NJ	07980	908-561-3000	753-6749
TF: 888-554-6400 ■ *Web:* www.thermoplasticprocesses.com					
Tredegar Corp Film Products Div					
1100 Boulders Pkwy	Richmond	VA	23225	804-330-1000	
TF: 855-330-1001 ■ *Web:* www.tredegarfilms.com					
Tri-Seal International Inc					
900 Bradley Hill Rd	Blauvelt	NY	10913	845-353-3300	353-3376
Web: www.tekni-plex.com					
Valley Decorating Co 2829 E Hamilton Ave	Fresno	CA	93721	559-495-1100	
Web: www.pomponcentral.com					
VCF Films Inc 1100 Sutton Ave	Howell	MI	48843	888-905-7680	546-2984*
**Fax Area Code:* 517 ■ *TF:* 888-905-7680 ■ *Web:* vcffilms.com					
Vinylex Corp 2636 Byington Rd	Knoxville	TN	37931	865-690-2211	691-6273*
**Fax:* Cust Svc ■ *Web:* www.vinylex.com					
VPI Corp 3123 S Ninth St	Sheboygan	WI	53081	920-458-4664	458-1368
TF Orders: 800-874-4240 ■ *Web:* www.vpicorp.com					

				Phone	Fax
Watersaver Company Inc 5870 E 56th Ave	Commerce City	CO	80022	303-289-1818	287-3136
TF: 800-525-2424 ■ *Web:* www.watersaver.com					
Zippertubing Co 7150 W Erie St	Chandler	AZ	85226	480-285-3990	285-3997
TF: 855-289-1874 ■ *Web:* www.zippertubing.com					

604 PLASTICS FOAM PRODUCTS

				Phone	Fax
A-Z Sponge & Foam Products Ltd 811 Cundy Ave Annacis Island	Delta	BC	V3M5P6	604-525-1665	525-1081
Web: www.a-zfoam.com					
Ace Packaging Ltd 7190 Torbram Rd	Mississauga	ON	L4T3L7	905-677-4141	
Web: www.acepackaging.ca					
ACH Foam Technologies LLC 5250 Sherman St	Denver	CO	80216	303-297-3844	
Web: www.achfoam.com					
Advanced Polymer Technology Corp 109 Conica Ln	Harmony	PA	16037	724-452-1330	
Web: www.advpolytech.com					
Aero Plastics Inc 91 Citation Dr	Concord	ON	L4K2Y8	905-738-9010	738-9175
Web: www.aeroplastics.ca					
AGC Chemicals Americas Inc 55 E Uwchlan Ave Ste 201	Exton	PA	19341	610-423-4300	
Web: www.agcchem.com					
Airdex International Inc 8975 S Pecos Rd Ste 7A	Henderson	NV	89074	702-270-6004	
Web: www.airdex.com					
Allied Aerofoam Products LLC 216 Kelsey Ln	Tampa	FL	33619	813-626-0090	569-0629
TF: 800-338-9140 ■ *Web:* www.alliedaerofoam.com					
Alpla Inc 289 Hwy 155 S	Mcdonough	GA	30253	770-914-1407	
Web: www.alpla.com					
Amatech Inc 1460 Grimm Dr	Erie	PA	16501	814-452-0010	
Web: www.amatechinc.com					
Amcor Ltd 935 Technology Dr Ste 100	Ann Arbor	MI	48108	734-428-9741	
Web: www.amcor.com					
American Excelsior Co 850 Ave H E PO Box 5067	Arlington	TX	76005	800-777-7645	649-7816*
**Fax Area Code:* 817 ■ *TF:* 800-777-7645 ■ *Web:* www.americanexcelsior.com					
American Gilsonite Co 29950 South Bonanza Hwy	Bonanza	UT	84008	435-789-1921	
Web: www.americangilsonite.com					
Anchor Packaging Inc 13515 Barrett Pkwy Dr	Saint Louis	MO	63021	314-822-7800	
Web: www.anchorpackaging.com					
Aragon Elastomers LLC 740 S Pierce Ave	Louisville	CO	80027	303-666-9519	
Web: www.aragonelastomers.com					
ArncoPathway 5141 Firestone Pl	South Gate	CA	90280	323-249-7500	
Web: www.arnconet.com					
Astrofoam Molding Company Inc 4117 Calle Tesoro	Camarillo	CA	93012	805-482-7276	482-6599
Web: www.astrofoam.com					
Balcan Plastics Ltd 9340 Meaux St	Saint Leonard	QC	H1R3H2	514-326-0200	326-4565
Web: www.balcan.com					
Barger Packaging Inc 2901 Oakland Ave	Elkhart	IN	46517	888-525-2845	
TF: 888-525-2845 ■ *Web:* www.bargerpkg.com					
Belle-Pak Packaging Inc 7465 Birchmount Rd	Markham	ON	L3R5X9	905-475-5151	475-9295
Web: www.belle-pak.com					
Big 3 Packaging LLC 4201 Torresdale Ave	Philadelphia	PA	19124	215-743-4201	
Web: big3packaging.com					
Boltaron Performance Products LLC One General St	Newcomerstown	OH	43832	740-498-5900	
Web: www.boltaron.com					
Bontex Inc 12918 Whitehorse Ln	St. Louis	MO	63131	314-965-8059	261-3784*
OTC: BOTX ■ **Fax Area Code:* 540 ■ *Web:* www.bontex.com					
Brushfoil LLC One Shoreline Dr Unit 6	Guilford	CT	06437	203-453-7403	
Web: www.brushfoil.com					
Bulldog Bag Ltd 13631 Vulcan Way	Richmond	BC	V6V1K4	604-273-8021	273-9927
Web: www.bulldogbag.com					
Carpenter Co 5016 Monument Ave	Richmond	VA	23230	804-359-0800	353-0694
TF: 800-288-3830 ■ *Web:* www.carpenter.com					
CDF Corp 77 Industrial Park Rd	Plymouth	MA	02360	508-747-5858	
Web: www.cdf1.com					
Cellofoam North America Inc 1917 Rockdale Industrial Blvd	Conyers	GA	30012	770-929-3688	929-3608
TF: 800-241-3634 ■ *Web:* www.cellofoam.com					
Cellox Corp 1200 Industrial St	Reedsburg	WI	53959	608-524-2316	524-2362
Web: www.cellox.com					
Chestnut Ridge Foam Inc PO Box 781	Latrobe	PA	15650	724-537-9000	537-9003
TF Cust Svc: 800-234-2734 ■ *Web:* www.chestnutridgefoam.com					
CKS Packaging Inc 445 Great SW Pkwy	Atlanta	GA	30336	404-691-8900	
Web: www.ckspackaging.com					
Clark Foam Products Corp 655 Remington Blvd	Bolingbrook	IL	60440	630-226-5900	226-5959
TF: 888-284-2290 ■ *Web:* www.clarkfoam.net					
Classic Packaging Co 5570 Bethania Rd	Pfafftown	NC	27040	336-922-4224	
Web: www.classicpackaging.com					
Clayton Corp 866 Horan Dr	Fenton	MO	63026	636-349-5333	349-5335
TF Cust Svc: 800-729-8220 ■ *Web:* www.claytoncorp.com					
Clear-Vu Products Inc 29 New York Ave	Westbury	NY	11590	516-333-8880	
Web: www.clear-vu.com					
ClingZ Inc 541 Laser Rd NE	Rio Rancho	NM	87124	505-892-2500	
Web: www.clingz.com					
Conglom Inc 2600 Marie-Curie Ave	St. Laurent	QC	H4S2C3	514-333-6666	
Web: www.conglom.com					
Creative Foam Corp 300 N Alloy Dr	Fenton	MI	48430	810-629-4149	629-7368
TF: 800-529-4149 ■ *Web:* www.creativefoam.com					
Crest Foam Industries Inc 100 Carol Pl	Moonachie	NJ	07074	201-807-0809	807-1113
Web: www.inoacusa.com					
CSP Technologies 960 W Veterans Blvd	Auburn	AL	36832	334-887-8300	
Web: www.csptechnologies.com					
Custom Pack Inc 662 Exton Cmns	Exton	PA	19341	610-321-2525	321-2526
TF: 800-722-7005 ■ *Web:* www.custompackinc.com					
Cyclics Corp 2135 Technology Dr	Schenectady	NY	12308	518-881-1440	881-1439
Web: www.cyclics.com					
Dart Container Corp 500 Hogsback Rd	Mason	MI	48854	800-248-5960	676-3883*
**Fax Area Code:* 517 ■ *TF:* 800-248-5960 ■ *Web:* www.dartcontainer.com					
Deltapac Packaging Inc 8200 de l'Industrie St.	Anjou	QC	H1J1S7	514-352-5546	352-5703
Web: www.deltapac.ca					
Diversified Plastics Corp 120 W Mount Vernon St	Nixa	MO	65714	417-725-2622	
Web: www.dpcap.com					
Dow Chemical Company, The 1881 W Oak Pkwy	Marietta	GA	30062	770-428-2684	428-9431
TF: 800-331-6451 ■ *Web:* www.dow.com					
Edge-Sweets Co 2887 Three-Mile Rd NW	Grand Rapids	MI	49534	616-453-5458	453-5458
Web: www.edge-sweets.com					
Eldon James Corp 10325 E 47th Ave	Denver	CO	80238	970-667-2728	
Web: www.eldonjames.com					
Elliott Company of Indianapolis Inc 9200 Zionsville Rd	Indianapolis	IN	46268	317-291-1213	291-1213
TF Orders: 800-545-1213 ■ *Web:* www.elliottfoam.com					
Enduro Composites Inc 16602 Central Green Blvd Ste 204	Houston	TX	77032	713-358-4000	358-4100
Web: www.endurocomposites.com					
Evergreen Plastics Inc 202 Watertower Dr	Clyde	OH	43410	419-547-1400	
Web: www.evergreenplastics.com					
Federal Foam Technologies Inc 600 Wisconsin Dr	New Richmond	WI	54017	715-246-9500	246-9500
TF: 800-898-9559 ■ *Web:* www.federalfoam.com					
Federal Plastics Manufacturing Ltd 5100 Fisher St	St-laurent	QC	H4T1J5	514-342-5411	342-3744
Web: www.fedplast.com					
Filmtech Corp 2121 31st St SW	Allentown	PA	18103	610-709-9999	
Web: www.filmtech-corp.com					
Flexible Packaging Company Inc PO Box 4321	Bayamon	PR	00958	787-622-7225	622-7245
Web: www.flepak.com					
Flexpak Corp 3720 W Washington St	Phoenix	AZ	85009	602-269-7648	269-7640
Web: www.flexpakcorp.com					
FLEXSTAR Packaging Inc 13320 River Rd	Richmond	BC	V6V1W7	604-273-9277	
Web: www.flexstar.ca					
Flextron Industries Inc 720 Mt Rd	Aston	PA	19014	610-459-4600	459-5379
TF: 800-633-2181 ■ *Web:* www.flextronindustries.com					
FM Corp 3535 Hudson Rd	Rogers	AR	72756	479-636-3540	631-2392
Web: www.fmcorp.com					
Foam Fabricators Inc 950 Progress Blvd	New Albany	IN	47150	812-948-1696	948-2450
Web: www.foamfabricatorsinc.com					
Foam Molders & Specialty Corp 20004 State Rd	Cerritos	CA	90703	800-378-8987	924-2168*
**Fax Area Code:* 562 ■ *TF:* 800-378-8987 ■ *Web:* www.foammolders.com					
Foam Products Corp 350 Beamer Rd	Calhoun	GA	30701	706-629-1256	
Web: www.foamproducts.com					
Foam Rubber Products Inc 2000 Troy Ave	New Castle	IN	47362	765-521-2000	521-2759
Web: www.foamrubberllc.com					
Fomo Products Inc 2775 Barber Rd	Norton	OH	44203	330-753-4585	753-9566*
**Fax:* Cust Svc ■ *TF:* 800-321-5585 ■ *Web:* www.fomo.com					
Free Flow Packaging International Inc 1090 Mills Way	Redwood City	CA	94063	650-261-5300	361-1713
TF: 800-866-9946 ■ *Web:* www.fpintl.com					
FRX Polymers Inc 200 Turnpike Rd	Chelmsford	MA	01824	978-244-9500	
Web: www.frxpolymers.com					
Future Foam Inc 1610 Ave N Council Bluffs	Council Bluffs	IA	51501	712-323-9122	
TF: 800-733-8061 ■ *Web:* www.futurefoam.com					
FXI 1400 N Providence Rd	Media	PA	19063	610-744-2300	
TF: 800-355-3626 ■ *Web:* fxi.com					
G & T Industries Inc 1001 76th St SW	Byron Center	MI	49315	800-968-6035	583-1524*
**Fax Area Code:* 616 ■ *TF:* 800-968-6035 ■ *Web:* www.gtindustries.com					
Gaco Western Inc 200 W Mercer St Ste 202	Seattle	WA	98119	206-575-0450	575-0587
TF: 800-456-4226 ■ *Web:* www.gaco.com					
General Foam Plastics Corp 3321 E Princess Anne Rd	Norfolk	VA	23502	757-857-0153	857-0033
Web: www.genfoam.com					
General Plastics Mfg Co 4910 S Burlington Way	Tacoma	WA	98409	253-473-5000	473-5104
TF: 800-806-6051 ■ *Web:* www.generalplastics.com					
Gracious Living Innovations Inc 151 Courtney Park Drive W	Mississauga	ON	L5W1Y5	905-795-5505	795-5523
Web: www.glinnov.com					
Green-Tek Inc 3708 Enterprise Dr	Janesville	WI	53546	608-754-7336	
Web: www.green-tek.com					
Guardian Packaging Inc 3615 Security St	Garland	TX	75042	214-349-1500	349-1584
TF: 800-259-1502 ■ *Web:* www.guardianpackaging.com					
Gunther Mele Ltd 30 Craig St	Brantford	ON	N3R7J1	519-756-4330	
Web: www.gunthermele.com					
Hermann Companies Inc 7701 Forsyth Blvd Ste 1000	St. Louis	MO	63105	314-863-9200	
Web: www.hermanncompanies.com					
Hibco Plastics Inc 1820 Us 601 Hwy	Yadkinville	NC	27055	336-463-2391	463-5591
TF: 800-849-8683 ■ *Web:* www.hibco.com					
Houston Foam Plastics Inc 2019 Brooks St	Houston	TX	77026	713-224-3484	224-5511
Web: www.houstonfoam.com					
Inland Plastics Inc 201 Center St	Rosedale	AB	T0J2V0	403-823-6252	
Web: www.inlandplastics.com					
Innovative Plastics Corp 400 Rt 303	Orangeburg	NY	10962	845-359-7500	359-0237
Web: innovative-plastics.com					
Intertrade Industries Ltd 15632 Commerce Ln	Huntington Beach	CA	92649	714-894-5566	894-3927
TF: 800-944-9277 ■ *Web:* www.intertradeindustries.com					
ISO Poly Films Inc 101 ISO Pkwy	Gray Court	SC	29645	864-876-4300	
Web: www.isopoly.com					
ITW Minigrip Inc 8125 Cobb Ctr Dr	Kennesaw	GA	30152	770-422-4187	
Web: www.minigrip.com					
ITW-GaleWrap 1320 Leslie Dr	Douglasville	GA	30134	866-425-3727	
TF: 866-425-3727 ■ *Web:* www.galewrap.com					
Jif-Pak Manufacturing Inc 1451 Engineer St	Vista	CA	92081	760-597-2665	
Web: www.jifpak.com					

				Phone	Fax
Keyes Packaging Group Inc 3715 State Hwy	Wenatchee	WA	98807	509-663-8537	
Web: www.keyespackaging.com					
KNF Flexpak Corp 734 W Penn Pk.	Tamaqua	PA	18252	570-386-3550	
Web: www.knfcorporation.com					
Lantec Products Inc 5302 Derry Ave Ste G	Agoura Hills	CA	91301	818-707-2285	
Web: www.lantecp.com					
Lomont Molding Imt 1516 E Mapleleaf Dr.	Mount Pleasant	IA	52641	319-385-1528	
Web: www.lomontimt.com					
Lucent Polymers Inc 1700 Lynch Rd	Evansville	IN	47711	812-421-2216	
Web: www.lucentpolymers.com					
MBA Polymers Inc 500 W Ohio Ave.	Richmond	CA	94804	510-231-9031	
Web: www.mbapolymers.com					
MDL Doors Inc 42918-B Cranbrook Rd.	Brussels	ON	N0G1H0	519-887-6974	
Web: www.mdldoors.com					
MedPlast Inc 405 W Geneva Dr.	Tempe	AZ	85282	480-553-6400	
Web: medplastgroup.com					
Mg International Inc 90 International Pkwy	Dallas	GA	30157	770-505-0004	664-6577*
**Fax Area Code: 786*					
Minnesota Diversified Products Inc 9091 County Rd 50.	Rockford	MN	55373	763-477-5854	477-5863
Web: www.diversifoam.com					
Modern Plastics Inc 88 Long Hill Cross Rd	Shelton	CT	06484	203-333-3128	
Web: www.modernplastics.com					
Monarch Plastics Inc 1205 65th St	Kenosha	WI	53143	262-652-4444	
Web: www.monarch-plastics.com					
MonoSol LLC 707 E 80th Pl Ste 301	Merrillville	IN	46410	219-762-3165	
Web: www.monosol.com					
Mossberg Industries Inc 204 N Second St	Garrett	IN	46738	260-357-5141	357-5144
Web: mossbergind.com/					
Munot Plastics Inc 2935 W 17th St	Erie	PA	16505	814-838-7721	833-2095
Web: www.munotplastics.com					
NACO Industries Inc 395 West 1400 North	Logan	UT	84341	435-753-8020	
Web: www.herndon-assoc.com					
Nan Ya Plastics Corporation America Nine Peach Tree Hill Rd	Livingston	NJ	07039	973-992-2090	
Web: www.npcam.com					
NAP Windows & Doors Ltd 2150 Enterprise Way	Kelowna	BC	V1Y6H7	250-762-5343	
Web: www.napwindows.com					
Newmar Window Manufacturing Inc 7630 Airport Rd	Mississauga	ON	L4T4G6	905-672-1233	
Web: www.newmar.com					
Noltex LLC 3930 Ventura Dr Ste 355	Arlington Heights	IL	60004	847-255-1211	
Web: www.soarus.com					
North Carolina Foam Industries Inc 1515 Carter St	Mount Airy	NC	27030	336-789-9161	789-9586
TF: 800-346-8229 ■ *Web:* www.ncfi.com					
Northern Pipe Products Inc 1302 39th St N	Fargo	ND	58102	701-282-7655	
Web: www.northernpipe.com					
Pacific Packaging Products Inc 24 Industrial Way	Wilmington	MA	01887	978-657-9100	658-4933
TF: 800-777-0300 ■ *Web:* www.pacificpkg.com					
Pacon Inc 4249 N Puente Ave.	Baldwin Park	CA	91706	626-814-4654	
Web: www.paconinc.com					
Palmetto Industries International Inc 6001 Horizon W Pkwy	Grovetown	GA	30813	706-737-7999	
Web: www.palmetto-industries.com					
Peel Plastic Products Ltd 49 Rutherford Rd S.	Brampton	ON	L6W3J3	905-456-3660	456-0870
Web: www.peelplastics.com					
Peninsula Packaging Company LLC 1030 N Anderson Rd	Exeter	CA	93221	559-594-6813	
Web: www.penpack.net					
Perfect Turf Inc 622 Sandpebble Dr	Schaumburg	IL	60193	888-796-8873	
TF: 888-796-8873 ■ *Web:* www.perfectturfinc.com					
Pinova Holdings Inc 2801 Cook St.	Brunswick	GA	31520	888-807-2958	
TF: 888-807-2958 ■ *Web:* www.pinovaholdings.com					
Plastic & Steel Supply Company Inc 50 Tannery Rd Readington Industrial Ctr Bldg 3.	Branchburg	NJ	08876	908-534-6111	
Web: www.pep-plastic.com					
Plastic Container Corp 2508 N Oak St.	Urbana	IL	61802	217-352-2722	
Web: www.netpcc.com					
Plastipak Industries Inc 150 Industriel Blvd	Boucherville	QC	J4B2X3	450-650-2200	650-2201
Web: www.plastipak.ca					
Plastomer Corp 37819 Schoolcraft Rd	Livonia	MI	48150	734-464-0700	464-4792
Web: www.plastomer.com					
Plastube Inc 590 Simonds S	Granby	QC	J2J1E1	450-378-2633	
Web: www.plastube.com					
PMC Biogenix Inc 1231 Pope St	Memphis	TN	38108	901-325-4930	
Web: www.pmcbiogenix.com					
PMC Global Inc 12243 Branford St.	Sun Valley	CA	91352	818-896-1101	686-2531
Web: www.pmcglobalinc.com					
Poly Foam Inc 116 Pine St S	Lester Prairie	MN	55354	320-395-2551	395-2702
TF: 844-446-4339 ■ *Web:* www.polyfoaminc.com					
Poly Molding LLC 96 Fourth Ave	Haskell	NJ	07420	973-835-7161	835-2438
TF: 800-229-7161 ■ *Web:* polymoldingllc.com					
Polycel Structural Foam Inc 68 County Line Rd	Somerville	NJ	08876	908-722-5254	722-7457
Web: www.polycel.com					
Polymer Industries LLC 10526 Alabama Hwy 40 PO Box 32	Henagar	AL	35978	256-657-5197	
Web: www.polymerindustries.com					
Precision Products Group Inc 9207 51st Ave.	College Park	MD	20740	301-474-3100	
Web: www.ppgintl.com					
Prestige Fabricators Inc 2206 Dumont St.	Asheboro	NC	27204	336-672-3383	
Web: www.prestigefab.com					
Pretium Packaging LLC 15450 S Outer Forty Dr Ste 120	Chesterfield	MO	63017	314-727-8200	
Web: www.pretiumpkg.com					
Professional Plastics Inc 1810 E Valencia Dr.	Fullerton	CA	92831	714-446-6500	
Web: www.professionalplastics.com					
Prolamina Corp 840 S Waukegan Rd Ste 208	Lake Forest	IL	60045	847-604-5900	
Web: www.prolamina.com					
Radva Corp 604 17th St PO Box 2900	Radford	VA	24143	540-731-3731	
NYSE: RDVA ■ *Web:* www.radva.com					
Republic Packaging Corp 9160 S Green St.	Chicago	IL	60620	773-233-6530	233-6005
Web: www.repco.com					
Resilux America LLC 265 John Brooks Rd	Pendergrass	GA	30567	706-693-7110	
Web: www.uniqueplastics.com					
Retail Resource Group International LLC 226 New Gate Loop	Lake Mary	FL	32746	407-878-6650	
Web: www.rrgtravelmugs.com					
Richards Packaging Inc 2321 NE Argyle St Ste D.	Portland	OR	97211	503-290-0000	
Web: www.richardspackaging.com					
RL Adams Plastics Inc 5955 Crossroads Commerce	Wyoming	MI	49519	616-261-4400	249-8955
TF: 800-968-2241 ■ *Web:* www.adamsplasticsinc.com					
Robbie Manufacturing Inc 10810 Mid America Ave	Lenexa	KS	66219	913-492-3400	492-1543
TF: 800-255-6328 ■ *Web:* www.robbieflexibles.com					
Roberts PolyPro Inc 5416 Wyoming Ave	Charlotte	NC	28273	704-588-1794	
Web: www.robertspolypro.com					
Rogers Foam Corp 20 Vernon St	Somerville	MA	02145	617-623-3010	629-2585
Web: rogersfoam.com					
Rubberlite Inc 2501 Guyan Ave.	Huntington	WV	25703	304-525-3116	523-4316
Web: www.rubberlite.com					
Safas Corp Two Ackerman Ave	Clifton	NJ	07011	973-772-5252	
Web: www.safascorp.com					
SBA Materials Inc 9430-H San Mateo Blvd NE	Albuquerque	NM	87113	505-924-2807	
Web: www.sbamaterials.com					
Sekisui Voltek LLC 100 Shepard St.	Lawrence	MA	01843	978-685-2557	685-9861
TF: 800-225-0668 ■ *Web:* www.sekisuivoltek.com					
Sertapak Packaging Corp 1039 Dundas St.	Woodstock	ON	N4S0B1	519-539-3330	
Web: www.sertapak.com					
Shawnee Chemical Company Inc 136 Main St Ste 300.	Princeton	NJ	08540	609-799-3930	
Web: www.shawchem.com					
Sigma Stretch Film Corp Page & Schuyler Aves Bldg 8	Lyndhurst	NJ	07071	201-507-9100	
Web: www.sigmastretchtools.com					
SimPak International LLC 2107 Production Dr	Louisville	KY	40299	502-671-8250	
Web: www.simpakinternational.com					
Sonoco One N Second St.	Hartsville	SC	29550	800-377-2692	
NYSE: SON ■ *TF:* 800-377-2692 ■ *Web:* www.sonoco.com					
Sonoma Graphic Products Inc 961 Stockton Ave	San Jose	CA	95110	408-294-2072	
Web: www.sgpweb.com					
Spectratek Technologies Inc 5405 Jandy Pl.	Los Angeles	CA	90066	310-822-2400	822-2660
Web: www.spectratek.net					
Spectrum Bags Inc 12850 Midway Pl.	Cerritos	CA	90703	562-623-2555	
Web: www.spectrumbags.com					
Stone Plastics & Manufacturing Inc 8245 Riley St	Zeeland	MI	49464	616-748-9740	
Web: www.stoneplasticsmfg.com					
Storopack Inc 12007 S Woodruff Ave	Downey	CA	90241	562-803-5582	803-4462
TF: 800-829-1491 ■ *Web:* www.storopack.us					
StyroChem Canada Ltee 19250 Clark Graham	Baie Durfe	QC	H9X3R8	514-457-3226	457-4390
Web: www.styrochem.com					
Styrotek Inc 545 Rd 176	Delano	CA	93215	661-725-4957	725-7064
Web: www.styrotek.com					
Sufix USA Inc 651 Brigham Rd Ste D	Greensboro	NC	27409	336-605-1950	
Web: www.sufix.com					
SupplyOne Corp 20 N Waterloo Rd Ste 200	Devon	PA	19333	484-582-5005	
Web: supplyone.com					
Syfan USA Corp 1522 Twin Bridges Rd.	Everetts	NC	27825	252-792-2547	
Web: www.syfanusa.com					
T-H Marine Supplies Inc 200 Finney Dr	Huntsville	AL	35824	256-772-0164	
Web: www.thmarine.com					
TCP Reliable Inc 551 Raritan Ctr Pkwy	Edison	NJ	08837	732-346-9200	
Web: www.tcpreliable.com					
Therma Foam Inc 8910 Oak Grove Rd.	Fort Worth	TX	76140	817-624-7204	
Web: www.thermafoam.com					
ThermoSafe Brands 3930 N Ventura Dr Ste 450.	Arlington Heights	IL	60004	847-398-0110	398-0653
TF: 800-323-7442 ■ *Web:* www.thermosafe.com					
ThermoServ 3901 Pipestone Rd.	Dallas	TX	75212	214-631-0307	631-0566
TF: 800-635-5559 ■ *Web:* www.thermoserv.com					
TMP Technologies Inc 1200 Northland Ave	Buffalo	NY	14215	716-895-6100	
Web: www.tmptech.com					
TO Plastics Inc 830 County Rd 75 PO Box 37	Clearwater	MN	55320	320-558-2407	
Web: www.toplastics.com					
Topp Industries Inc 420 N State Rd 25 PO Box 420.	Rochester	IN	46975	574-223-3681	223-6106
TF: 800-354-4534 ■ *Web:* www.toppindustries.com					
UFP Technologies Inc 172 E Main St	Georgetown	MA	01833	978-352-2200	
NASDAQ: UFPT ■ *TF:* 800-372-3172 ■ *Web:* www.ufpt.com					
Unique Fabricating Inc 800 Standard Pkwy.	Auburn Hills	MI	48326	248-853-2333	853-7720
Web: www.uniquefab.com					
Universal Protective Packaging Inc 61 Texaco Rd	Mechanicsburg	PA	17050	717-766-1578	
Web: www.uppi.com					
Visual Magnetics LP One Emerson St	Mendon	MA	01756	508-381-2400	
Web: www.visualmagnetics.com					
Wellman Plastics Recycling LLC 520 Kingsburg Hwy	Johnsonville	SC	29555	843-386-2011	
Web: www.wellmanplastics.com					

Company / Address	City	State	Zip	Phone	Fax
Western Concord Manufacturing Ltd 880 Cliveden Ave	Vancouver	BC	V3M5R5	604-525-1061	
Web: www.westernconcord.com					
WinCup 4640 Lewis Rd	Stone Mountain	GA	30083	770-938-5281	
TF: 800-292-2877 ■ *Web:* www.wincup.com					
Woodbridge Foam Corp 4240 Sherwoodtowne Blvd	Mississauga	ON	L4Z2G6	905-896-3626	896-9262
Web: www.woodbridgegroup.com					
Zurn Pex Inc 1900 W Hively Ave	Elkhart	IN	46517	574-294-7541	
Web: www.zurnpex.com					

605 PLASTICS MACHINING & FORMING

SEE ALSO Plastics Molding - Custom p. 2936

Company / Address	City	State	Zip	Phone	Fax
Akra Plastic Products Inc 1504 E Cedar St	Ontario	CA	91761	909-930-1999	930-1948
Web: akraplastics.com					
Bardes Plastics Inc 5225 W Clinton Ave	Milwaukee	WI	53223	800-558-5161	354-6331*
**Fax Area Code:* 414 ■ *TF Cust Svc:* 800-558-5161 ■ *Web:* www.bardesplastics.com					
Comco Plastics Inc 98-31 Jamaica Ave	Woodhaven	NY	11421	718-849-9000	441-5361
Web: www.comcoplastics.com					
Conroy & Knowlton Inc 320 S Montebello Blvd	Montebello	CA	90640	323-665-5288	722-4670
Web: www.conroyknowlton.com					
East Jordan Plastics Inc PO Box 575	East Jordan	MI	49727	800-353-1190	536-7090*
**Fax Area Code:* 231 ■ *Web:* www.eastjordanplastics.com					
Empire West Inc 9270 Graton Rd PO Box 511	Graton	CA	95444	707-823-1190	823-8531
TF: 800-521-4261 ■ *Web:* www.empirewest.com					
Engineered Plastics Inc 211 Chase St	Gibsonville	NC	27249	336-449-4121	449-6352
TF: 800-711-1740 ■ *Web:* www.engplas.com					
Fabri-Form Co 200 S Friendship Dr	New Concord	OH	43762	740-826-5000	826-5001
TF: 800-837-2574 ■ *Web:* portal.pendaform.com/					
Fabri-Kal Corp 600 Plastics Pl	Kalamazoo	MI	49001	269-385-5050	385-0197
TF: 800-888-5054 ■ *Web:* www.fabri-kal.com					
FNW Industrial Plastics Inc 12500 Jefferson Ave PO Box 2778	Newport News	VA	23602	757-874-7795	989-2501
TF: 800-721-2590 ■ *Web:* www.ferguson.com					
Formall Inc 3908 Fountain Vly Dr	Knoxville	TN	37918	865-922-7514	922-3941
TF: 800-643-3676 ■ *Web:* www.formall.com					
Gage Industries Inc 6710 McEwan Rd	Lake Oswego	OR	97035	503-639-2177	
Gregstrom Corp 64 Holton St	Woburn	MA	01801	781-935-6600	935-4905
Web: www.gregstrom.com					
Harvel Plastics Inc 300 Kuebler Rd	Easton	PA	18040	610-252-7355	253-4436
Web: www.harvel.com					
Inline Plastics Corp 42 Canal St	Shelton	CT	06484	203-924-2015	924-0370
TF: 800-826-5567 ■ *Web:* www.inlineplastics.com					
Innovize Inc 500 Oak Grove Pkwy	Saint Paul	MN	55127	877-605-6580	490-1651*
**Fax Area Code:* 651 ■ *TF:* 877-605-6580 ■ *Web:* www.innovize.com					
Jamestown Plastics Inc 8806 Highland Ave	Brocton	NY	14716	716-792-4144	792-4154
Web: www.jamestownplastics.com					
Kal Plastics 2050 E 48th St	Los Angeles	CA	90058	323-581-6194	581-1805
Web: www.kal-plastics.com					
Lamar Plastic Packaging Ltd 216 N Main St	Freeport	NY	11520	516-378-2500	378-6192
Web: lamarplastics.net					
Mack Prototype Inc 424 Main St	Gardner	MA	01440	978-632-3700	632-3777
Web: www.mackprototype.com					
McNeal Enterprises Inc 2031 Ringwood Ave	San Jose	CA	95131	408-922-7290	922-7299
TF: 800-562-6325 ■ *Web:* www.mcnealplasticmachining.com					
Meyer Plastics Inc 5167 E 65th St	Indianapolis	IN	46220	317-259-4131	252-4687
TF: 800-968-4131 ■ *Web:* www.meyerplastics.com					
Morgan Hill Plastics Inc 640 E Dunne Ave	Morgan Hill	CA	95037	408-779-2118	779-0322
Web: morganhillplastics.net					
New Concept Mfg LLC 320 Busser Rd PO Box 297	Emigsville	PA	17318	717-741-0840	741-4301
Web: www.newconcepttech.com					
Paradise Plastics 1200 W Dr Martin Luther King Jr Blvd	Plant City	FL	33563	813-752-1155	754-3168
Web: www.paradiseplastics.com					
Perkasie Industries Corp PO Box 179	Perkasie	PA	18944	215-257-6581	453-1703
TF Sales: 800-523-6747 ■ *Web:* perkasie.cylex-usa.com					
Placon Corp 6096 McKee Rd	Madison	WI	53719	608-271-5634	271-3162
TF: 800-541-1535 ■ *Web:* www.placon.com					
Polygon Co 103 Industrial Pk Dr PO Box 176	Walkerton	IN	46574	574-586-3145	586-7336
TF: 800-918-9261 ■ *Web:* www.polygoncomposites.com					
Precision Molding Inc 5500 Roberts Matthews Hwy	Sparta	TN	38583	931-738-8376	738-8429
Web: www.precision-molding.com					
Prent Corp 2225 Kennedy Rd	Janesville	WI	53545	608-754-0276	754-2410
Web: www.prent.com					
Productive Plastics Inc 103 W Pk Dr	Mount Laurel	NJ	08054	856-778-4300	234-3310
Web: www.productiveplastics.com					
PSC Manufacturinf Inc 312 Brokaw Rd	Santa Clara	CA	95050	408-988-5115	
Quadrant Engineering Plastic Products USA 2120 Fairmont Ave PO Box 14235	Reading	PA	19612	610-320-6600	320-6638
TF: 800-366-0300 ■ *Web:* www.quadrantplastics.com					
Ray Products Company Inc 1700 Chablis Ave	Ontario	CA	91761	909-390-9906	390-9984
TF: 800-423-7859 ■ *Web:* rayplastics.com					
Ronningen Research & Development Co 6700 E 'YZ' Ave	Vicksburg	MI	49097	269-649-0520	649-0526
Web: www.ronningenresearch.com					
Soroc Products Inc Plastics Div 4349 S Dort Hwy	Burton	MI	48529	810-743-2660	743-5922
Web: www.sorocproducts.com					
Spaulding Composites Company Fab Div 55 Nadeau Dr	Rochester	NH	03867	603-332-0555	332-5357
TF: 800-801-0560 ■ *Web:* www.spauldingcom.com					
Speck Plastics Inc PO Box 421	Nazareth	PA	18064	610-759-1807	759-3916
Stewart Industries Inc 16 S Idaho St	Seattle	WA	98134	206-652-9110	660-0421*
**Fax Area Code:* 269					
Sur-Flo Plastics & Engineering Inc 24358 Groesbeck Hwy	Warren	MI	48089	586-773-0400	773-8946
Web: www.sur-flo.com					
Teak Isle Manufacturing Inc 401 Capitol Ct PO Box 417	Ocoee	FL	34761	407-656-8885	656-2344
Web: www.teakisle.com					
Thermo-Fab Corp 76 Walker Rd	Shirley	MA	01464	978-425-2311	425-2305
Web: www.thermofab.com					
Total Plastics Inc 3316 Pagosa Ct	Indianapolis	IN	46226	317-543-3540	543-3553
TF: 800-382-4635 ■ *Web:* www.totalplastics.com					
Tri-Town Precision Plastics Inc 12 Bridge St	Deep River	CT	06417	860-526-3200	526-4848
Underwood Mold Co Inc 104 Dixie Dr PO Box 1607	Woodstock	GA	30189	770-926-2465	926-6565
Web: www.underwoodmoldco.com					
Western Fibre Products Inc 10924 Vulcan St	South Gate	CA	90280	562-861-6665	862-9692

606 PLASTICS MATERIALS - WHOL

Company / Address	City	State	Zip	Phone	Fax
A Daigger & Company Inc 620 Lakeview Pkwy	Vernon Hills	IL	60061	847-816-5060	320-7200*
**Fax Area Code:* 800 ■ *TF:* 800-621-7193 ■ *Web:* www.daigger.com					
Aetna Plastics Corp 1702 St Clair Ave	Cleveland	OH	44114	216-781-4421	781-4474
TF: 800-634-3074 ■ *Web:* www.aetnaplastics.com					
AIN Plastics Inc 1750 E Heights Dr	Madison Heights	MI	48071	248-356-4000	542-3920
TF Cust Svc: 877-246-7700 ■ *Web:* www.tkmna.com					
All American Containers Inc 9330 NW 110th Ave	Miami	FL	33178	305-887-0797	888-4133
Web: www.americancontainers.com					
Allpak Co 1010 Lake St	Oak Park	IL	60301	708-383-7200	
Aztec Supply 954 N Batavia St	Orange	CA	92867	714-771-6580	771-3013
TF: 800-836-3210 ■ *Web:* www.aztecblaze.com					
B. Schoenberg & Company Inc 345 Kear St	Yorktown	NY	10598	914-962-1200	
Web: www.bschoenberg.info					
Bamberger Polymers Inc Two Jericho Plz Ste 109	Jericho	NY	11753	516-622-3600	622-3610
TF: 800-888-8959 ■ *Web:* www.bambergerpolymers.com					
Buckley Industries Inc 1850 E 53rd St N	Wichita	KS	67219	316-744-7587	744-8463
TF: 800-835-2779 ■ *Web:* www.buckleyind.com					
Calsak Corp 1411 West 190th St Suite 400	Gardena	CA	90248	310-719-9500	719-1300
TF: 888-663-6005 ■ *Web:* www.calsak.com					
Cope Plastics Inc 4441 Industrial Dr	Godfrey	IL	62002	618-466-0221	466-7975*
**Fax:* Acctg ■ *TF:* 800-851-5510 ■ *Web:* www.copeplastics.com					
Delta Polymers Midwest Inc 6685 Sterling Dr N	Sterling Heights	MI	48312	586-795-2900	
Web: www.deltapoly.com					
E Hofmann Plastics 51 Centennial Rd	Orangeville	ON	L9W3R1	519-943-5055	
Web: www.hofmannplastics.com					
El Mar Plastics Inc 109 W 134th St	Los Angeles	CA	90061	310-436-6444	436-6445
TF: 800-255-5210 ■ *Web:* www.elmarplastics.com					
Faith Group Company Inc 195 Route 9 Ste 205	Manalapan	NJ	07726	732-431-1326	
Web: www.faith-group.com					
Golden Eagle Extrusions Inc 1762 State Rt 131	Milford	OH	45150	513-248-8292	
Web: www.goldeneagleextrusions.com					
Gvd Corp 45 Spinelli Pl	Cambridge	MA	02138	617-661-0060	
Web: www.gvdcorp.com					
H Muehlstein & Company Inc 10 Westport Rd	Wilton	CT	06897	203-855-6000	855-6221
TF: 800-257-3746 ■ *Web:* www.muehlstein.com					
H Sattler Plastics Co Inc 5410 W Roosevelt Rd	Chicago	IL	60644	312-733-2900	
Laird Plastics Inc 6800 Broken Sound Pkwy Ste 150	Boca Raton	FL	33487	561-443-9100	443-9108
TF: 800-243-9696 ■ *Web:* www.lairdplastics.com					
M Holland Co 400 Skokie Blvd Ste 600	Northbrook	IL	60062	847-272-7370	
TF: 800-872-7370 ■ *Web:* www.m-holland.com					
Maine Plastics Inc 1817 Kenosha Rd	Zion	IL	60099	847-379-9100	
Web: www.maineplastics.com					
Momentum Technologies Inc (MTI) 1507 Boettler Rd	Uniontown	OH	44685	330-896-5900	896-9943
TF: 800-720-0261 ■ *Web:* www.momentumtech.net					
Multi-Plastics Inc 7770 N Central Dr	Lewis Center	OH	43035	740-548-4894	548-5177
Web: www.multi-plastics.com					
Nytef Plastics Ltd Inc 6643 42nd Terr N	West Palm Beach	FL	33407	561-840-9499	638-7674*
**Fax Area Code:* 215 ■ *TF:* 800-646-9833 ■ *Web:* www.nytefplastics.com					
Orange County Industrial Plastics Inc 4811 E La Palma Ave	Anaheim	CA	92807	714-632-9450	630-6489
TF: 800-974-6247 ■ *Web:* www.ocip.com					
Pilcher Hamilton Corp 6845 Kingery Hwy	Willowbrook	IL	60527	630-655-8100	655-9948
Web: www.pilcherhamilton.com					
Plastic Film Corporation of America Inc 1287 Naperville Dr	Romeoville	IL	60446	630-887-0800	
Web: www.plasticfilmcorporation.com					
Plastics International Inc 7600 Anagram Dr	Eden Prairie	MN	55344	952-934-2303	
Web: www.plasticsintl.com					
Port Plastics Inc 15325 Fairfield Ranch Rd Ste 150	Chino Hills	CA	91709	480-813-6118	597-0116*
**Fax Area Code:* 909 ■ *TF:* 800-800-0039 ■ *Web:* www.portplastics.com					
Primepak Co 133 Cedar Ln	Teaneck	NJ	07666	201-836-5060	
Web: www.primepakcompany.com					
Regal Plastic Supply Co 111 E Tenth Ave	North Kansas City	MO	64116	816-421-6290	421-8206
TF: 800-627-2102 ■ *Web:* www.regalplastic.com					
Ryan Herco Products Corp 3010 N San Fernando Blvd	Burbank	CA	91504	818-841-1141	973-2600
TF: 800-848-1141 ■ *Web:* www.ryanherco.com					

	City	State	Zip	Phone	Fax
San Diego Plastics Inc 2220 Mckinley Ave *Web:* www.sdplastics.com	National City	CA	91950	619-477-4855	
Seelye Plastics Inc 9700 Newton Ave S **Fax Area Code:* 952 ■ **Fax:* Sales ■ *TF:* 800-328-2728 ■ *Web:* seelyeplastics.com	Bloomington	MN	55431	800-328-2728	881-3503*
Sekisui America Corp 333 Meadowlands Pkwy 4th Fl *TF General:* 866-260-5851 ■ *Web:* www.sekisui-corp.com	Secaucus	NJ	07094	201-423-7960	423-7979
Superior Oil Co Inc 1402 N Capitol Ave Ste 100 *TF:* 800-553-5480 ■ *Web:* www.superioroil.com	Indianapolis	IN	46202	317-781-4400	781-4401
Targun Plastics Co 899 Skokie Blvd *Web:* www.targunplastic.com	Northbrook	IL	60062	847-509-9355	509-9359
Tekra Corp 16700 W Lincoln Ave *TF:* 800-448-3572 ■ *Web:* www.tekra.com	New Berlin	WI	53151	262-784-5533	797-3276

607 PLASTICS MOLDING - CUSTOM

	City	State	Zip	Phone	Fax
Akron Porcelain & Plastics Co 2739 Cory Ave PO Box 15157 *TF:* 800-737-9664 ■ *Web:* www.akronporcelain.com	Akron	OH	44314	330-745-2159	745-6688
Aline Components Inc 1830 Tomlinson Rd PO Box 263 *Web:* www.alinecomponents.com	Kulpsville	PA	19443	215-368-0300	361-1400
Alladin Plastics Inc 140 Industrial Dr *TF:* 877-536-4693 ■ *Web:* www.alladinplasticsline.com	Surgoinsville	TN	37873	423-345-2351	
AMA Plastics Inc 1100 Citrus St *Web:* amaplastics.com	Riverside	CA	92507	951-734-5600	734-5666
American Metal & Plastics Inc 450 32nd St SW *TF:* 800-382-0067 ■ *Web:* www.ampi-gr.com	Grand Rapids	MI	49548	616-452-6061	452-3835
American Plastic Molding Corp 965 S Elm St *TF:* 877-527-8427 ■ *Web:* www.apmc.com	Scottsburg	IN	47170	812-752-7000	752-5155
American Plastics Group Inc 715 W Pk Rd *Web:* www.americanplasticsgroup.com	Union	MO	63084	636-583-2583	
American Urethane Inc 1905 Betson Ct *Web:* www.americanurethane.com	Odenton	MD	21113	410-672-2100	672-2191
AMS Plastics Inc 1530 Hilton Head Rd Ste 205 *Web:* www.amsplastics.com	El Cajon	CA	92019	619-713-2000	713-2975
Apollo Plastics Corp 5333 N Elston Ave *Web:* spcmfg.com	Chicago	IL	60630	773-282-9222	282-2763
Arrowhead Plastic Engineering Inc 2909 S Hoyt Ave *Web:* www.arrowheadinc.com	Muncie	IN	47302	765-286-0533	286-1681
ASK Plastics Inc 9750 Ashton Rd *Web:* www.askplastics.com	Philadelphia	PA	19114	215-969-0800	969-2164
Bekum America Corp 1140 W Grand River Ave PO Box 567 *Web:* www.bekumamerica.com	Williamston	MI	48895	517-655-4331	655-4121
Berry Plastics 44 Oneil St	EastHampton	MA	01027	413-527-1250	
Berry Plastics Corp 101 Oakley St *TF:* 877-662-3779 ■ *Web:* www.berryplastics.com	Evansville	IN	47710	812-424-2904	424-0128
C & J Industries 760 Water St *Web:* www.cjindustries.com	Meadville	PA	16335	814-724-4950	724-4959
C Brewer Co 3630 E Miraloma Ave *Web:* www.cbrewer.com	Anaheim	CA	92806	714-630-6810	630-5527
Capsonic Group 495 Renner Dr *Web:* www.capsonic.com	Elgin	IL	60123	847-888-7300	888-7543
Centro Inc 950 N Bend Dr *Web:* www.centroinc.com	North Liberty	IA	52317	319-626-3200	626-3203
Commercial Plastics Co (CPC) 800 Allanson Rd *Web:* www.ecommercialplastics.com	Mundelein	IL	60060	847-566-1700	566-4737
Confer Plastics Inc (CPI) 97 Witmer Rd *TF:* 800-635-3213 ■ *Web:* www.conferplastics.com	North Tonawanda	NY	14120	716-693-2056	694-3102
Connor Corp 10633 Coldwater Rd Ste 200 *Web:* www.connorcorp.com	Fort Wayne	IN	46845	260-424-1601	
Core Molding Technologies Inc (CMT) 800 Manor Pk Dr *NYSE: CMT* ■ *Web:* www.coremt.com	Columbus	OH	43228	614-870-5000	870-5051
Cosmo Corp 30201 Aurora Rd *Web:* www.cosmocorp.com	Cleveland	OH	44139	440-498-7500	498-7515
Curtil 12 Betnr Industrial Dr *Web:* www.curtil.com	Pittsfield	MA	01201	413-443-4481	
Cuyahoga Molded Plastics Corp 1265 Babbitt Rd *TF:* 800-805-9549 ■ *Web:* www.cuyahogaplastics.com	Cleveland	OH	44132	216-261-2744	261-3537
D & M Plastic Corp 150 French Rd PO Box 158 *Web:* www.dmplastics.com	Burlington	IL	60109	847-683-2054	683-2731
D-M-E Co 29111 Stephenson Hwy *TF:* 800-626-6653 ■ *Web:* www.dme.net	Madison Heights	MI	48071	248-398-6000	544-5705
Design & Molding Services Inc 25 Howard St	Piscataway	NJ	08854	732-752-0300	752-9672
Dickten Masch Plastics LLC N44 W33341 Watertown Plank Rd *Web:* www.dicktenplastics.com	Nashotah	WI	53058	262-369-5555	367-5630
Diemolding Corp 125 Rasbach St *Web:* www.diemolding.com	Canastota	NY	13032	315-697-2221	697-2221
Double H Plastics Inc 50 W St Rd *TF:* 800-523-3932 ■ *Web:* www.doublehplastics.com	Warminster	PA	18974	215-674-4100	674-5469
EFP Corp 223 Middleton Run Rd *TF:* 800-205-8537 ■ *Web:* www.efpcorp.com	Elkhart	IN	46516	574-295-4690	295-6512
Eifel Mold & Engineering 31071 Fraser Dr *Web:* eifelmoldandengineering.com/	Fraser	MI	48026	586-296-9640	296-7280
Elgin Molded Plastics 909 Grace St **Fax Area Code:* 800 ■ *TF:* 800-548-5483 ■ *Web:* www.elginmolded.com	Elgin	IL	60120	847-931-2455	524-0087*
Engineered Plastic Components 53150 N Main St *Web:* www.alcoa.com	Mattawan	MI	49071	269-668-3397	
Ensinger Putnam Precision Molding 11 Danco Rd *TF:* 800-752-7865 ■ *Web:* www.putnamprecisionmolding.com	Putnam	CT	06260	860-928-7911	928-2229
Evco Plastics 100 W N St PO Box 497 *TF:* 800-507-6000 ■ *Web:* www.evcoplastics.com	DeForest	WI	53532	800-507-6000	251-0822
Falcon Plastics Inc 1313 Western Ave *Web:* falconplastics.com	Brookings	SD	57006	605-696-2500	696-2585
Fawn Industries Inc 1920 Greenspring Dr Ste 140 *Web:* fawnplastics.com	Timonium	MD	21093	410-308-9200	308-9202
Filtertek Inc 11411 Price Rd *TF:* 800-248-2461 ■ *Web:* www.filtertek.com	Hebron	IL	60034	815-648-1001	648-2929
Flambeau Inc 15981 Valplast Rd *TF:* 800-457-5252 ■ *Web:* www.flambeau.com	Middlefield	OH	44062	440-632-1631	632-1581
FPI Thermoplastic Technologies 520 Speedwell Ave Ste 116 *Web:* www.njmep.org	Morris Plains	NJ	07950	973-998-9801	
Green Tokai Company Ltd 55 Robert Wright Dr *Web:* www.greentokai.com	Brookville	OH	45309	937-833-5444	833-2087
Gruber Systems Inc 25636 Ave Stanford *TF:* 800-257-4070 ■ *Web:* www.gruber-systems.com	Valencia	CA	91355	661-257-4060	257-4791
GW Plastics Inc 239 Pleasant St *Web:* www.gwplastics.com	Bethel	VT	05032	802-234-9941	234-9940
Hoffer Plastics Corp 500 N Collins St *Web:* www.hofferplastics.com	South Elgin	IL	60177	847-741-5740	741-3086
Industrial Molding Corp 616 E Slaton Rd *Web:* www.indmolding.com	Lubbock	TX	79404	806-474-1000	474-1168
Innovative Injection Technologies Inc 2360 Grand Ave *Web:* www.i2-tech.com	West Des Moines	IA	50265	515-225-6707	225-9673
Intec Group Inc 666 S Vermont St *Web:* www.intecgrp.com	Palatine	IL	60067	847-358-0088	358-4391
Ironwood Industries Inc 115 S Bradley Rd *Web:* www.ironind.com	Libertyville	IL	60048	847-362-8681	362-9190
Jones & Vining Inc 1115 W Chestnut St *Web:* www.jonesandvining.com	Brockton	MA	02301	508-232-7470	232-7477
Jordan Specialty Plastics Inc 1751 Lake Cook Rd	Deerfield	IL	60015	847-945-5591	945-5698
Juno Inc 1100 McKinley St *Web:* www.junoinc.com	Anoka	MN	55303	763-553-1312	553-1360
Kennerley Spratling Inc 2116 Farallon Dr *Web:* ksplastic.com	San Leandro	CA	94577	510-351-8230	352-9240
KI Industries Inc 5540 McDermott Dr *Web:* www.kiindustries.com	Berkeley	IL	60163	708-449-1990	449-1997
Kurz-Kasch Inc 511 Byers Rd *TF:* 888-587-9527 ■ *Web:* www.kurz-kasch.com	Miamisburg	OH	45342	937-299-0990	299-9292
Lacks Enterprises 5460 Cascade Rd SE *Web:* www.lacksenterprises.com	Grand Rapids	MI	49546	616-949-6570	285-2367
Lakeland Tool & Engineering Inc 2939 Sixth Ave	Anoka	MN	55303	763-422-8866	422-8867
Lehigh Valley Plastics Inc 187 N Commerce Way *TF:* 800-354-5344 ■ *Web:* www.lehighvalleyplastics.com	Bethlehem	PA	18017	484-893-5500	893-5511
Lenco Inc - PMC 10240 Deer Pk Rd PO Box 590 *Web:* www.lencopmc.com	Waverly	NE	68462	402-786-2000	786-2096
Leon Plastics Inc 4901 Clay Ave SW *Web:* www.leonplastics.com	Grand Rapids	MI	49548	616-531-7970	531-3393
LMC Industries Inc 100 Manufacturers Dr *Web:* www.lmcindustries.com	Arnold	MO	63010	636-282-8080	282-7114
M & Q Plastic Products Inc 1120 Welsh Rd Ste 170 **Fax Area Code:* 570 ■ *TF:* 800-600-3068 ■ *Web:* www.mqplastics.com/	North Wales	PA	19454	267-498-4000	385-4954*
Mack Molding Company Inc 608 Warm Brook Rd **Fax:* Hum Res ■ *Web:* www.mack.com	Arlington	VT	05250	802-375-2511	375-0792*
Makray Manufacturing Co 4400 N Harlem Ave *Web:* www.makray.com	Norridge	IL	60706	708-456-7100	456-7178
Mar-Lee Cos 55 Marshall St *Web:* www.mar-leecompanies.com	Leominster	MA	01453	978-534-8305	534-0472
Master Molded Products Corp 1000 Davis Rd *Web:* www.mastermolded.com	Elgin	IL	60123	847-695-9700	695-9707
Midwest Plastic Components 7309 W 27th St *Web:* spectrumplasticsgroup.com	Minneapolis	MN	55426	952-929-3312	929-8404
Miner Elastomer Products Corp 1200 E State St *Web:* www.minerelastomer.com	Geneva	IL	60134	630-232-3000	232-3172
Minnesota Rubber & Plastics 1100 Xenium Ln N *Web:* www.mnrubber.com	Minneapolis	MN	55441	952-927-1400	927-1470
Molded Fiber Glass Cos 2925 MFG Pl PO Box 675 *TF:* 800-860-0196 ■ *Web:* www.moldedfiberglass.com	Ashtabula	OH	44005	440-997-5851	994-5162
Molding Corp of America 10349 Norris Ave *TF:* 800-423-2747 ■ *Web:* www.moldingcorp.com	Pacoima	CA	91331	818-890-7877	890-7885
Mullinix Packages Inc 3511 Engle Rd *Web:* www.mullinixpackages.com	Fort Wayne	IN	46809	260-747-3149	747-1598
MXL Industries Inc 1764 Rohrerstown Rd *TF:* 800-233-0159 ■ *Web:* www.mxl-industries.com	Lancaster	PA	17601	717-569-8711	569-8716
Nyloncraft Inc 616 W McKinley Ave *Web:* www.nyloncraft.com	Mishawaka	IN	46545	574-256-1521	255-3278
NYX Inc 36111 Schoolcraft Rd *Web:* www.nyxinc.com	Livonia	MI	48150	734-462-2385	464-4830
Plaspros Inc 1143 Ridgeview Dr *TF:* 800-752-7776 ■ *Web:* www.plaspros.com	McHenry	IL	60050	815-430-2300	430-2260
Plastech Corp 920 S Field Ave *Web:* www.plastechcorporation.com	Rush City	MN	55069	651-407-5700	407-5495
Plastek Group 2425 W 23rd St *Web:* www.plastekgroup.com	Erie	PA	16506	814-878-4400	878-4529
Plastic Components Inc N 116 W 18271 Morse Dr *TF:* 877-253-1496 ■ *Web:* www.plasticcomponents.com	Germantown	WI	53022	877-253-1496	253-1497

Company	City	State	ZIP	Phone	Fax
Plastic Design International Inc 111 Industrial Pk Rd *Web:* www.plasticdesign.com	Middletown	CT	06457	860-632-2001	632-1776
Plastic Molded Concepts Inc PO Box 490 *Web:* www.pmcplastics.com	Eagle	WI	53119	262-594-5050	594-5075
Plastic Moldings Company LLC 2181 Grand Ave *Web:* www.pmcsmartsolutions.com	Cincinnati	OH	45214	513-921-5040	921-5883
Plastic Products Company Inc 30355 Akerson St *Web:* www.plasticproductsco.com	Lindstrom	MN	55045	651-257-5980	257-9774
Plastic-Plate Inc 5460 Cascade Rd SE *Web:* www.lacksenterprises.com/	Grand Rapids	MI	49546	616-949-6570	285-2367
Plastics Group Inc 7409 S Quincy St *Web:* www.theplasticsgroup.net	Willowbrook	IL	60527	630-325-1210	325-1393
Plastics Molding Company Inc 4211 N Broadway *Web:* plasticsmoldingco.com	Saint Louis	MO	63147	314-241-2479	241-3757
Polymer Corp 180 Pleasant St *Web:* www.polymerdesign.com	Rockland	MA	02370	781-871-4606	871-5460
Port Erie Plastics Inc 909 Troupe Rd *Web:* www.porterie.com	Harborcreek	PA	16421	814-899-7602	899-7854
Precision Plastics Inc 900 W Connexion Way *Web:* www.pplastic.com	Columbia City	IN	46725	260-244-6114	244-5995
Premix Inc US Rt 20 PO Box 281 *Web:* www.premix.com	North Kingsville	OH	44068	440-224-2181	224-2766
Product Miniature Co 627 Capitol Dr *Web:* www.pmplastic.com	Pewaukee	WI	53072	262-691-1700	691-4405
Proper Mold & Engineering Inc 13870 E 11-Mile Rd *Web:* propertooling.com	Warren	MI	48089	586-779-8787	779-4530
PTA Corp 148 Christian St *Web:* www.ptaplastics.com	Oxford	CT	06478	203-888-0585	888-1757
Quality Mold Inc 2200 Massillon Rd *Web:* www.qualitymold.com	Akron	OH	44312	330-645-6653	645-2493
R & R Technologies LLC 7560 E County Line Rd *Web:* www.rrtech.com	Edinburgh	IN	46124	812-526-2655	526-9294
Recto Molded Products Inc (RMP) 4425 Appleton St *Web:* www.rectomolded.com	Cincinnati	OH	45209	513-871-5544	871-8495
REO Plastics Inc 11850 93rd Ave N *Web:* www.reoplastics.com	Maple Grove	MN	55369	763-425-4171	425-0735
Rodgard 92 Msgr Valente Dr *Web:* www.rodgard.com	Buffalo	NY	14206	716-823-1411	852-7690
Royal Plastics Inc 9410 Pineneedle Dr *Web:* www.royalplastics.com	Mentor	OH	44060	440-352-1357	352-6681
Sabin Corp 3800 Constitution Ave PO Box 788 **Fax Area Code:* 800 ■ *TF:* 800-457-4500 ■ *Web:* www.cookgroup.com	Bloomington	IN	47403	812-339-2235	554-8335*
Sajar Plastics Inc 15285 S State Ave PO Box 37 *Web:* www.sajarplastics.com	Middlefield	OH	44062	440-632-5203	632-1848
Seitz LLC 212 Industrial Ln *TF:* 800-261-2011 ■ *Web:* www.seitzllc.com	Torrington	CT	06790	860-489-0476	482-6616
Steere Enterprises Inc 285 Commerce St *TF:* 800-875-4926 ■ *Web:* www.steere.com	Tallmadge	OH	44278	330-633-4926	633-3921
Stelrema Corp 4055 E 250 N *Web:* gettig.com	Knox	IN	46534	574-772-2103	
Sturgis Molded Products Co 1950 Clark St *Web:* www.smpco.com	Sturgis	MI	49091	269-651-9381	651-4072
Tech Group Inc, The 14677 N 74th St *Web:* westpharma.com/en/techgroup/pages/tech-group.aspx	Scottsdale	AZ	85260	480-281-4500	
Tech II Inc 1765 W County Line Rd PO Box 1468 *Web:* www.techii.com	Springfield	OH	45502	937-969-7000	
Thermotech Co 1302 S Fifth St *Web:* www.thermotech.com	Hopkins	MN	55343	952-933-9400	933-9412
Tigerpoly Manufacturing Inc 6231 Enterprise Pkwy *Web:* www.tigerpoly.com	Grove City	OH	43123	614-871-0045	871-2576
Toledo Molding & Die Inc Four E Laskey Rd *Web:* www.tmdinc.com	Toledo	OH	43612	419-476-0581	476-6053
Tri-Star Plastics Inc 1915 E Via Burton *Web:* www.tri-starplastics.com	Anaheim	CA	92806	714-533-7360	533-4383
Tricon Industries Inc Electromechanical Div 2325 Wisconsin Ave *Web:* industrialinterface.com	Downers Grove	IL	60515	630-964-2330	964-5179
Trimold LLC 200 Pittsburgh Rd	Circleville	OH	43113	740-474-7591	
Tuthill Corp Plastics Group 2050 Sunnydale Blvd *TF:* 800-634-2695 ■ *Web:* www.tuthill.com	Clearwater	FL	33765	727-446-8593	446-8595
United Plastics Group Inc (UPG) 405 W Geneva Dr *Web:* www.upgintl.com	Tempe	AZ	85282	480-553-6400	
Universal Plastic Mold Inc 13245 Los Angeles St **Fax Area Code:* 626 ■ *TF:* 888-893-1587 ■ *Web:* www.upminc.com	Baldwin Park	CA	91706	888-893-1587	960-7166*
ValTech LLC 1667 Emerson St *Web:* www.thevaltechgroup.com	Rochester	NY	14606	585-647-2300	647-6123
Vaupell Inc 1144 NW 53rd St *Web:* www.vaupell.com	Seattle	WA	98107	206-784-9050	784-9708
Venture Plastics Inc 4000 Warren Rd PO Box 249 *Web:* www.ventureplastics.com	Newton Falls	OH	44444	330-872-5774	872-3597
W-L Molding Co, The 8212 Shaver Rd *Web:* www.wlmolding.com	Portage	MI	49024	269-327-3075	323-8416
Westlake Plastics Co PO Box 127 *TF:* 800-999-1700 ■ *Web:* www.westlakeplastics.com	Lenni	PA	19052	610-459-1000	459-1084
Winzeler Gear Inc 7355 W Wilson Ave *Web:* www.winzelergear.com	Harwood Heights	IL	60706	708-867-7971	867-7974
WM Plastics Inc 5151 Bolger Ct *Web:* www.wmplastics.com	McHenry	IL	60050	815-578-8888	578-8818

608 PLASTICS & OTHER SYNTHETIC MATERIALS

608-1 Synthetic Fibers & Filaments

Company	City	State	ZIP	Phone	Fax
Buckeye Technologies Inc 1001 Tillman St *NYSE: BKI*	Memphis	TN	38112	901-320-8100	320-8204
Color-Fi Inc 320 Neeley St *TF:* 800-843-6382 ■ *Web:* www.colorfi.com	Sumter	SC	29150	803-436-4200	436-4220
Consolidated Fibers 8100 S Blvd **Fax Area Code:* 704 ■ *TF:* 800-243-8621 ■ *Web:* www.consolidatedfibers.com	Charlotte	NC	28273	800-243-8621	554-7782*
Deltech Corp 11911 Scenic Hwy *TF:* 800-424-9300 ■ *Web:* www.deltechcorp.com	Baton Rouge	LA	70807	225-775-0150	358-3149
DuPont Advanced Fibers Systems 5401 Jefferson Davis Hwy *TF:* 800-441-7515 ■ *Web:* www.dupont.com	Richmond	VA	23234	804-383-2000	
Fairfield Processing Corp 88 Rose Hill Ave *TF:* 800-980-8000 ■ *Web:* www.fairfieldworld.com	Danbury	CT	06810	203-744-2090	792-9710
Hexcel Corp 281 Tresser Blvd 16th Fl *NYSE: HXL* ■ *TF:* 800-444-3923 ■ *Web:* www.hexcel.com	Stamford	CT	06901	800-688-7734	
Honeywell Specialty Materials 101 Columbia Rd *TF:* 800-222-0094 ■ *Web:* www.honeywell-additives.com	Morristown	NJ	07962	973-455-2145	455-6154
International Fiber Corp 50 Bridge St *TF:* 888-698-1936 ■ *Web:* www.ifcfiber.com	North Tonawanda	NY	14120	716-693-4040	693-3528
InterTech Group Inc 4838 Jenkins Ave *Web:* www.theintertechgroup.com	North Charleston	SC	29405	843-744-5174	747-4092
INVISTA 4123 E 37th St N *TF:* 877-446-8478 ■ *Web:* www.invista.com	Wichita	KS	67220	316-828-1000	
Nylon Corp of America 333 Sundial Ave *TF:* 800-851-2001 ■ *Web:* www.nycoa.net	Manchester	NH	03103	603-627-5150	627-5154
Performance Fibers 13620 Reese Blvd *Web:* www.performancefibers.com	Huntersville	NC	28078	704-912-3700	
RadiciSpandex Corp 3145 NW Blvd *Web:* www.radicigroup.com	Gastonia	NC	28052	704-864-5495	
Stein Fibers Ltd Four Computer Dr W Ste 200 *Web:* www.steinfibers.com	Albany	NY	12205	518-489-5700	489-5713
TenCate Grass North America 1131 Broadway St *TF:* 800-251-1033 ■ *Web:* www.tencate.com	Dayton	TN	37321	423-775-0792	775-4460
Toray Industries America Inc 461 Fifth Ave Ninth Fl *Web:* www.toray.com	New York	NY	10017	212-697-8150	972-4279
United Plastic Fabricating Inc 165 Flagship Dr *TF:* 800-638-8265 ■ *Web:* www.unitedplastic.com	North Andover	MA	01845	800-638-8265	966-4520
Waltrich Plastic Corp 3005 Airport Rd PO Box D *Web:* www.waltrich.com	Walthourville	GA	31333	912-368-9341	369-3544

608-2 Synthetic Resins & Plastics Materials

Company	City	State	ZIP	Phone	Fax
A Schulman Inc 3550 W Market St *NASDAQ: SHLM* ■ *TF:* 800-547-3746 ■ *Web:* www.aschulman.com	Akron	OH	44333	330-666-3751	668-7204
Acton Technologies Inc 100 Thompson St *Web:* www.actontech.com	Pittston	PA	18640	570-654-0612	
Advanced Laser Materials LLC 3115 Lucius Mccelvey *Web:* www.alm-llc.com	Temple	TX	76504	254-773-3080	
Akcros Chemicals America 500 Jersey Ave *TF Cust Svc:* 800-500-7890 ■ *Web:* www.akcros.com	New Brunswick	NJ	08901	732-220-6882	247-2287
Alloy Polymers Inc (AP) 3310 Deepwater Terminal Rd *Web:* www.alloypolymers.com	Richmond	VA	23234	804-232-8000	230-0386
AlphaGary Corp 170 Pioneer Dr *TF:* 800-232-9741 ■ *Web:* www.alphagary.com	Leominster	MA	01453	978-537-8071	
American Stainless & Supply LLC 815 State Rd *Web:* americanstainlessandsupply.com	Cheraw	SC	29520	843-537-5231	
AOC LLC 955 Tennessee 57 *Web:* www.aoc-resins.com	Collierville	TN	38017	901-854-2800	854-1183
Asahi Kasei America Inc 800 Third Ave 30rd Fl *Web:* www.ak-america.com	New York	NY	10022	212-371-9900	371-9050
Asahi Kasei Plastics North America Inc 900 E Van Riper Rd *TF Cust Svc:* 800-993-5382 ■ *Web:* www.asahikaseiplastics.com	Fowlerville	MI	48836	517-223-2000	223-2002
Bayer Inc 77 Belfield Rd **Fax:* Hum Res ■ *TF:* 800-622-2937 ■ *Web:* www.bayer.ca	Toronto	ON	M9W1G6	416-248-0771	248-6762*
Bayer MaterialScience LLC 100 Bayer Rd *TF:* 800-662-2927 ■ *Web:* www.polymers-usa.bayer.com	Pittsburgh	PA	15205	412-777-2000	
Cambridge Resources Corp 960 Alabama Ave *Web:* www.cambridgeresources.com	Brooklyn	NY	11207	718-927-0009	
Canplas Industries Ltd 500 Veterans Dr *TF:* 800-461-1771 ■ *Web:* www.canplas.com	Barrie	ON	L4M4V3	705-726-3361	
Capital Resin Corp 324 Dering Ave *Web:* www.capitalresin.com	Columbus	OH	43207	614-445-7177	445-7290
Cartec International Inc 106 Powder Mill Rd *TF:* 800-821-4434 ■ *Web:* www.cartec.com	Canton	CT	06019	860-693-9395	
CL Hauthaway & Sons Corp 638 Summer St *Web:* www.hauthaway.com	Lynn	MA	01905	781-592-6444	599-9565
ConsumerMetrics Inc 2299 Perimeter Park Dr *Web:* www.cmiresearch.com	Atlanta	GA	30341	678-805-4000	
Crossfield Products Corp 3000 E Harcourt St *Web:* www.crossfieldproducts.com	Rancho Dominguez	CA	90221	310-886-9100	886-9119

Company	City	State	ZIP	Phone	Fax
Cytec Engineered Materials 2085 E Technology Cir Ste 300 — *Web:* www.cytec.com	Tempe	AZ	85284	480-730-2000	730-2088
Daikin America Inc 20 Olympic Dr — *TF Cust Svc:* 800-365-9570 ■ *Web:* www.daikin-america.com	Orangeburg	NY	10962	845-365-9500	365-9515
Dow Chemical Co 2030 Dow Ctr — *NYSE: DOW* ■ *TF Cust Svc:* 800-422-8193 ■ *Web:* www.dow.com	Midland	MI	48674	989-636-1463	636-1830
Dow Chemical Co, The 100 Independence Mall W — *Web:* www.dow.com	Philadelphia	PA	19106	215-592-3000	
DSM Engineering Plastics Inc 2267 W Mill Rd — **Fax:* Cust Svc ■ *TF:* 800-333-4237 ■ *Web:* www.dsm.com	Evansville	IN	47720	812-435-7500	435-7702*
DSM NeoResins Inc 730 Main St — *Web:* dsm.com	Wilmington	MA	01887	978-658-6600	
DuPont Engineering Polymers Lancaster Pike Rt 141, Barley Mill Plz Bldg 22 — *TF:* 800-441-7515 ■ *Web:* www.dupont.com	Wilmington	DE	19805	302-999-4592	
Eastman Chemical Co 200 S Wilcox Dr — *NYSE: EMN* ■ **Fax:* Mktg ■ *TF Cust Svc:* 800-327-8626 ■ *Web:* www.eastman.com	Kingsport	TN	37660	423-229-2000	229-1194*
Elster Perfection Corp 436 N Eagle St — *Web:* www.elster-perfection.com	Geneva	OH	44041	440-415-1600	
Engineered Polymer Solutions Inc 1400 N State St — **Fax Area Code:* 815 ■ *TF:* 800-654-4242 ■ *Web:* www.eps-materials.com	Marengo	IL	60152	800-654-4242	568-4145*
Essco Inc 1933 Highland Rd — *TF:* 800-321-2664 ■ *Web:* www.essco.net	Twinsburg	OH	44087	216-524-4141	
Esterline Technologies Corp 500 108th Ave NE Ste 1500 — *NYSE: ESL* ■ *Web:* www.esterline.com	Bellevue	WA	98004	425-453-9400	453-2916
ExxonMobil Chemical Co 13501 Katy Fwy — *Web:* www.exxonmobilchemical.com	Houston	TX	77079	281-870-6000	
Fabick Inc 4118 Robertson Rd — *Web:* www.fabick.com	Madison	WI	53714	608-242-1100	
Ferro Corp Filled & Reinforced Plastics Div 5001 O'Hara Dr — *Web:* www.ferro.com	Evansville	IN	47711	812-423-5218	423-5218
Formosa Plastics Corp USA Nine Peach Tree Hill Rd — **Fax:* Hum Res ■ *Web:* www.fpcusa.com	Livingston	NJ	07039	973-992-2090	716-7456*
Gallagher Corp 3908 Morrison Dr — *TF:* 800-524-8597 ■ *Web:* www.gallaghercorp.com	Gurnee	IL	60031	847-249-3440	249-3473
Goldsmith & Eggleton Inc 300 First St — *TF:* 800-321-0954 ■ *Web:* www.goldsmith-eggleton.com	Wadsworth	OH	44281	330-336-6616	334-4709
Heritage Plastics Inc 1002 Hunt St — *TF:* 800-245-4623 ■ *Web:* www.heritage-plastics.com	Picayune	MS	39466	601-798-8663	798-1946
Hexion Specialty Chemicals Inc 180 E Broad St — *Web:* www.momentive.com	Columbus	OH	43215	614-225-4000	
Huntsman Corp 500 Huntsman Way — *NYSE: HUN* ■ *TF:* 888-490-8484 ■ *Web:* www.huntsman.com	Salt Lake City	UT	84108	801-584-5700	584-5781
Indelco Plastics Corp 6530 Cambridge St — *TF:* 800-486-6456 ■ *Web:* www.indelco.com	Minneapolis	MN	55426	952-925-5075	
Industrial Dielectrics Inc 407 S Seventh St PO Box 357 — *Web:* www.idicomposites.com	Noblesville	IN	46061	317-773-1766	773-3877
Interplastic Corp 1225 Wolters Blvd — *TF:* 800-736-5497 ■ *Web:* www.interplastic.com	Saint Paul	MN	55110	651-481-6860	481-9836
Isotron Corp 1443 N Northlake Way Ste 101 — *Web:* www.isotron.net	Seattle	WA	98103	206-547-1196	
Kraton Performance Polymers Inc 15710 John F Kennedy Blvd Ste 300 — *NYSE: KRA* ■ *TF:* 800-457-2866 ■ *Web:* www.kraton.com	Houston	TX	77032	281-504-4950	504-4743
Landec Corp 3603 Haven Ave — *NASDAQ: LNDC* ■ *Web:* www.landec.com	Menlo Park	CA	94025	650-306-1650	368-9818
Lewcott Corp 86 Providence Rd — *TF Sales:* 800-225-7725 ■ *Web:* barrday.com	Millbury	MA	01527	508-865-1791	865-0302
Lord Corp 111 Lord Dr — *TF:* 877-275-5673 ■ *Web:* www.lord.com	Cary	NC	27511	919-468-5979	
Marval Industries Inc 315 Hoyt Ave — *Web:* www.marvalindustries.com	Mamaroneck	NY	10543	914-381-2400	381-2259
Michael Day Enterprises Inc PO Box 151 — *Web:* www.mdayinc.com	Wadsworth	OH	44282	330-335-5100	335-0905
Minova USA Inc 150 Carley Ct — *TF:* 800-626-2948 ■ *Web:* www.minovausa.com	Georgetown	KY	40324	502-863-6800	863-6805
Mitsui Chemicals America Inc 800 Westchester Ave — **Fax:* PR ■ *TF:* 800-972-7252 ■ *Web:* www.mitsuichemicals.com	Rye Brook	NY	10573	914-701-5245	253-0790*
Modern Dispersions Inc 78 Marguerite Ave — *Web:* www.moderndispersions.com	Leominster	MA	01453	978-534-3370	537-6065
MRC Polymers Inc 3307 S Lawndale Ave — *Web:* www.mrcpolymers.com	Chicago	IL	60623	773-890-9000	890-9007
Neville Chemical Co 2800 Neville Rd — *TF Cust Svc:* 877-704-4200 ■ *Web:* www.nevchem.com	Pittsburgh	PA	15225	412-331-4200	771-0226
NOVA Chemicals Corp 1000 Seventh Ave SW PO Box 2518 — *TF:* 866-289-6682 ■ *Web:* www.novachem.com	Calgary	AB	T2P5C6	403-750-3600	269-7410
Orion Enterprises Inc 2850 Fairfax Trafficway — *Web:* www.orionfittings.com	Kansas City	KS	66115	913-342-1653	
Osterman & Company Inc 726 S Main St — *Web:* www.osterman-co.com	Cheshire	CT	06410	203-272-2233	
Parker Hannifin Corp Chomerics Div 77 Dragon Ct — *Web:* www.parker.com	Woburn	MA	01801	781-935-4850	933-4318
Perstorp Polyols Inc 600 Matzinger Rd — *TF Cust Svc:* 800-537-0280 ■ *Web:* www.perstorp.com	Toledo	OH	43612	419-729-5448	729-3291
Plastics Color & Compounding Inc 14201 Paxton Ave — *TF:* 800-922-9936 ■ *Web:* www.plasticscolor.com	Calumet City	IL	60409	800-922-9936	
Plastics Engineering Company Inc 3518 Lk Shore Rd — *Web:* www.plenco.com	Sheboygan	WI	53083	920-458-2121	458-1923
Plextronics Inc 2180 William Pitt Way — *Web:* www.plextronics.com	Pittsburgh	PA	15238	412-423-2030	
PolyOne Corp 33587 Walker Rd — *NYSE: POL* ■ *TF:* 866-765-9663 ■ *Web:* www.polyone.com	Avon Lake	OH	44012	440-930-1000	930-3064
PSC Fabricating Co 1100 W Market St — *Web:* www.pscfabricating.com	Louisville	KY	40203	502-625-7700	625-7837
Reichhold Inc 2400 Ellis Rd — *TF:* 800-448-3482 ■ *Web:* www.reichhold.com	Durham	NC	27703	919-990-7500	990-7711
Resinall Corp PO Box 195 — *TF:* 800-421-0561 ■ *Web:* www.resinall.com	Severn	NC	27877	800-421-0561	
Revstone Industries LLC 2250 Thunderstick Dr Ste 1203	Lexington	KY	40505	859-294-5590	
RheTech Inc 1500 E N Territorial Rd — *TF:* 800-869-1230 ■ *Web:* www.rhetech.com	Whitmore Lake	MI	48189	734-769-0585	769-3565
Rimtec Corp 1702 Beverly Rd — *Web:* www.rimtec.com	Burlington	NJ	08016	609-387-0011	387-1436
Rogers Corp One Technology Dr — *TF:* 800-227-6437 ■ *Web:* www.rogerscorp.com	Rogers	CT	06263	860-774-9605	779-5509
RTP Co 580 E Front St — **Fax:* Hum Res ■ *TF:* 800-433-4787 ■ *Web:* www.rtpcompany.com	Winona	MN	55987	507-454-6900	454-2041*
Rubicon Inc 9156 Hwy 75 PO Box 517 — *Web:* www.huntsman.com	Geismar	LA	70734	225-673-6141	673-6442
Rutland Plastic Technologies 10021 Rodney St — *TF:* 800-438-5134 ■ *Web:* www.rutlandinc.com	Pineville	NC	28134	704-553-0046	552-6589
S & E Specialty Polymers LLC 140 Leominster-Shirley Rd — *Web:* sespoly.com	Lunenburg	MA	01462	978-537-8261	537-5310
Sartomer Co 502 Thomas Jones Way — *TF:* 800-345-8247 ■ *Web:* www.sartomer.com	Exton	PA	19341	610-363-4100	363-4140
Scientific Polymer Products Inc 6265 Dean Pkwy — *Web:* www.scientificpolymer.com	Ontario	NY	14519	585-265-0413	265-1390
Shintech Inc Three Greenway Plz Ste 1150 — *Web:* www.shintechinc.com	Houston	TX	77046	713-965-0713	965-0629
Shuman Plastics Inc 35 Neoga St — *Web:* www.shuman-plastics.com	Depew	NY	14043	716-685-2121	685-3236
SI Group Inc 2750 Balltown Rd — *Web:* www.siigroup.com	Schenectady	NY	12301	518-347-4200	346-6908
Sterling Fibers Inc 5005 Sterling Way — *TF Cust Svc:* 800-342-3779 ■ *Web:* www.sterlingfibers.com	Pace	FL	32571	850-994-5311	994-2579
Tahoma Rubber & Plastics Inc 255 Wooster Rd N — *Web:* www.tahomarubberplastics.com	Barberton	OH	44203	330-745-9016	745-4886
Talco Plastics Inc 1000 W Rincon St — *Web:* www.talcoplastics.com	Corona	CA	92880	951-531-2000	531-2058
Teijin Kasei America Inc 5555 Triangle Pkwy Ste 275 — *Web:* www.teijinkasei.com	Norcross	GA	30092	770-346-8949	346-7610
Texon USA Inc 1190 Huntington Rd — *Web:* www.texon.com	Russell	MA	01071	413-862-3652	
Thermoclad Co 361 W 11th St — *Web:* www.protechpowder.com	Erie	PA	16501	814-456-1243	459-2853
Ticona LLC 8040 Dixie Hwy — **Fax:* Sales ■ *TF:* 800-833-4882 ■ *Web:* www.celanese.com	Florence	KY	41042	859-372-3244	372-3125*
Tube-Mac Industries Ltd 853 Arvin Ave — *TF:* 877-643-8823 ■ *Web:* www.tube-mac.com	Stoney Creek	ON	L8E5N8	905-643-8823	
Vi-Chem Corp 55 Cottage Grove St SW — *TF:* 800-477-8501 ■ *Web:* www.vichem.com	Grand Rapids	MI	49507	616-247-8501	247-8703
Westlake Chemical Corp 2801 Post Oak Blvd Ste 600 — *NYSE: WLK* ■ *TF:* 888-953-3623 ■ *Web:* www.westlakechemical.com	Houston	TX	77056	713-960-9111	963-1562
WTE Corp Seven Alfred Cir — *Web:* www.wte.com	Bedford	MA	01730	781-275-6400	275-8612

608-3 Synthetic Rubber

Company	City	State	ZIP	Phone	Fax
AirBoss of America Corp Rubber Compounding 101 Glasgow St — *Web:* www.airbossrubbercompounding.com	Kitchener	ON	N2G4X8	519-576-5565	576-1315
Akrochem Corp 255 Fountain St — *TF:* 800-321-2260 ■ *Web:* www.akrochem.com	Akron	OH	44304	330-535-2100	535-8947
Bryant Rubber Corp 1112 Lomita Blvd — *Web:* www.bryantrubber.com	Harbor City	CA	90710	310-530-2530	530-9143
Goodyear Tire & Rubber Co 200 Innovation Way — *NASDAQ: GT* ■ **Fax:* Cust Svc ■ *TF Cust Svc:* 800-321-2136 ■ *Web:* www.goodyear.com	Akron	OH	44316	330-796-2121	796-2222*
Lanxess Corp 111 RIDC Pk W Dr — *TF:* 800-526-9377 ■ *Web:* www.lanxess.com	Pittsburgh	PA	15275	412-809-1000	
Midwest Elastomers Inc 700 Industrial Dr PO Box 412 — *TF:* 800-786-3539 ■ *Web:* www.midwestelastomers.com	Wapakoneta	OH	45895	419-738-8844	738-4411
Preferred Rubber Compounding Corp 1020 Lambert St — *Web:* preferredperforms.com	Barberton	OH	44203	330-798-4790	798-4795
R & S Processing Company Inc 15712 Illinois Ave PO Box 2037 — *Web:* rsprocessing.com	Paramount	CA	90723	562-531-1403	531-4318
Teknor Apex Co 505 Central Ave — *TF:* 800-556-3864 ■ *Web:* www.teknorapex.com	Pawtucket	RI	02861	401-725-8000	725-8095
Textile Rubber & Chemical Company Inc 1300 Tiarco Dr SW — *TF:* 800-727-8453 ■ *Web:* www.trcc.com	Dalton	GA	30721	706-277-1300	277-3738

609 PLASTICS PRODUCTS - FIBERGLASS REINFORCED

				Phone	Fax
Crane Composites Inc 23525 W Eames St *Fax: Hum Res ■ *TF:* 800-435-0080 ■ *Web:* www.cranecomposites.com	Channahon	IL	60410	815-467-8600	467-8666*
Ershigs Inc 742 Marine Dr *Web:* www.ershigs.com	Bellingham	WA	98225	360-733-2620	733-2628
Fibergrate Composite Structures Inc 5151 Beltline Rd Ste 700 *TF:* 800-527-4043 ■ *Web:* www.fibergrate.com	Dallas	TX	75254	972-250-1633	250-1530
Formed Fiber Technologies Inc 125 Allied Rd PO Box 1300 *Web:* www.formedfiber.com	Auburn	ME	04211	207-784-1118	784-1137
Glastic Corp 4321 Glenridge Rd *TF:* 800-360-1319 ■ *Web:* www.glastic.com	Cleveland	OH	44121	216-486-0100	486-1091
GMI Composites Inc 1355 W Sherman Blvd *TF:* 800-330-4045 ■ *Web:* www.gmicomposites.com	Muskegon	MI	49441	231-755-1611	755-1613
Haysite Reinforced Plastics 5599 Perry Hwy *Web:* www.haysite.com	Erie	PA	16509	814-868-3691	864-7803
McClarin Plastics Inc 15 Industrial Dr *TF:* 800-233-3189 ■ *Web:* www.mcclarinplastics.com	Hanover	PA	17331	717-637-2241	637-2091
Peterson Products Inc 1325 Old County Rd *Web:* www.petersonproducts.com	Belmont	CA	94002	650-591-7311	591-7498
Red Ewald Inc 2669 US 181 *TF:* 800-242-3524 ■ *Web:* www.redewald.com	Karnes City	TX	78118	830-780-3304	780-4272
Strongwell 400 Commonwealth Ave *Web:* www.strongwell.com	Bristol	VA	24201	276-645-8000	645-8132

610 PLASTICS PRODUCTS - HOUSEHOLD

				Phone	Fax
AFP Industries Inc 7900 Whitepine Rd *Web:* www.afpind.com	Richmond	VA	23237	804-275-1436	
Available Plastics Inc 5020 Beechmont Dr *Web:* www.apiplastics.com	Huntsville	AL	35811	256-859-4957	
Ayanna Plastics & Engineering 4701 110th Ave N *Web:* www.ayannaplastics.com	Clearwater	FL	33762	727-561-4329	
Blue Diamond Industries LLC 3399 Tates Creek Dr Ste 110 *Web:* www.bdiky.com	Lexington	KY	40502	859-224-0415	
Bow Plastics Ltd 5700 Cote de Liesse *Web:* www.bow-group.com	Montreal	QC	H4T1B1	514-735-5671	
Eagle Affiliates Inc 1000 S Second St *Fax: Hum Res ■ *TF:* 800-237-9255	Plainfield	NJ	07063	908-757-4464	*
GT Water Products Inc 5239 N Commerce Ave *TF:* 800-862-5647 ■ *Web:* www.gtwaterproducts.com	Moorpark	CA	93021	805-529-2900	529-4558
Home Products International Inc 4501 W 47th St *TF:* 800-327-3534 ■ *Web:* www.homzproducts.com	Chicago	IL	60632	773-890-1010	890-0523
Igloo Products Corp 777 Igloo Rd *TF:* 800-364-5566 ■ *Web:* www.igloocoolers.com	Katy	TX	77494	713-584-6800	584-6108
Iris USA Inc 11111 80th Ave *TF:* 800-320-4747 ■ *Web:* www.irisusainc.com	Pleasant Prairie	WI	53158	262-612-1000	612-1010
King Plastics Inc 840 N Elm St *Web:* www.kingplastics.com	Orange	CA	92867	714-997-7540	997-0491
Kraftware Corp 270 Cox St *Fax Area Code: 908 ■ *TF Cust Svc:* 800-221-1728 ■ *Web:* www.kraftwarecorp.com	Roselle	NJ	07203	800-221-1728	259-8885*
Mainetti USA 300 Mac Ln *Fax Area Code: 732 ■ *Web:* www.mainetti.com	Keasbey	NJ	08832	201-215-2900	738-7210*
Maryland Plastics Inc 251 E Central Ave *TF Cust Svc:* 800-544-5582 ■ *Web:* www.marylandplastics.com	Federalsburg	MD	21632	410-754-5566	754-8882
Prolon Inc 305 Industrial Ave *Fax Area Code: 888 ■ *TF:* 800-628-7749 ■ *Web:* www.prolon.biz	Port Gibson	MS	39150	601-437-4211	480-9828*
Silestone 2245 Texas Dr Ste 600 *Web:* www.silestoneusa.com	Sugar Land	TX	77479	281-494-7277	
Sterilite Corp PO Box 524 *Fax Area Code: 978 ■ *TF:* 800-225-1046 ■ *Web:* www.sterilite.com	Townsend	MA	01469	800-225-1046	597-1195*
TAP Plastics Inc 6475 Sierra Ln *TF:* 800-894-0827 ■ *Web:* www.tapplastics.com	Dublin	CA	94568	925-829-4889	
Thermos Co 475 N Martingale Rd Ste 1100 *TF:* 800-243-0745 ■ *Web:* www.thermos.com	Schaumburg	IL	60173	847-439-7821	593-5570
Tupperware Corp 14901 S Orange Blossom Trail *NYSE: TUP* ■ *TF Cust Svc:* 800-468-9716 ■ *Web:* ir.tupperwarebrands.com	Orlando	FL	32837	407-826-5050	847-1897
US Acrylic Inc 1320 Harris Rd *Web:* www.usacrylic.com	Libertyville	IL	60048	847-837-4800	837-1955

611 PLASTICS PRODUCTS (MISC)

				Phone	Fax
7-sigma Inc 2843 26th Ave S *TF:* 888-722-8396 ■ *Web:* www.7-sigma.com	Minneapolis	MN	55406	612-722-5358	
Accent Plastics Inc 1925 Elise Cir *Web:* www.accentplastics.com	Corona	CA	92879	951-273-7777	
ACCS Enterprises Inc 539 Sawgrass Corporate Pkwy *Web:* www.headsuponline.com	Sunrise	FL	33325	954-472-3300	
Accudyn Products Inc 2400 Yoder Dr *Web:* www.accudyn.com	Erie	PA	16506	814-833-7615	
Aco Polymer Products Inc 12080 Ravenna Rd *Web:* acousa.com	Chardon	OH	44024	440-285-7000	
Acry Fab Inc 584 Progress Way *TF:* 800-747-2279 ■ *Web:* vollrath.com	Sun Prairie	WI	53590	608-837-0045	837-1031
Acrylic Plastic Products Company Inc 4815 Hwy 80 W *Web:* acrylic1plasticproducts.com	Jackson	MS	39209	601-922-2651	
Adapt Plastics Inc 7949 Forest Hills Rd *Web:* adaptplastics.com	Loves Park	IL	61111	815-633-9263	
Advanced Fiberglass Technologies Inc 4400 Commerce Dr *Web:* www.ecccorrosion.com	Wisconsin Rapids	WI	54494	715-421-2060	
Agape Plastics Inc 11474 First Ave NW *Web:* www.agapeplastics.com	Grand Rapids	MI	49534	616-735-4091	735-4392
Aigner Index Inc 23 Mac Arthur Ave *TF:* 800-242-3919 ■ *Web:* www.aignerlabelholder.com	New Windsor	NY	12553	845-562-4510	562-2638
Ajax United Patterns & Molds Inc 34585 Seventh St *Web:* www.ajaxmfg.com	Union City	CA	94587	510-476-8000	476-8001
Albar Industries Inc 780 Whitney Dr *Web:* www.albar.com	Lapeer	MI	48446	810-667-0150	
Alco Plastics Inc 160 E Pond Dr *Web:* www.alcoplastics.com	Romeo	MI	48065	586-752-4527	
Alfred Manufacturing Co 4398 Elati St *Web:* alfredmfg.com	Denver	CO	80216	303-433-6385	
All Plastics Molding Inc 15700 Midway Rd *Web:* www.all-plastics.com	Addison	TX	75001	972-239-2686	
All States Inc 602 N 12th St *TF Cust Svc:* 800-621-5837 ■ *Web:* cable-ties.com	Saint Charles	IL	60174	773-728-0525	728-6410
Allied Plastic Supply LLC 1544 Valwood Pkwy *Web:* www.alliedplastic.org	Carrollton	TX	75006	972-241-0762	
ALP Lighting Components Inc 6333 Gross Point Rd *Web:* alplighting.com	Niles	IL	60714	773-774-9550	774-9331
American Window & Glass Inc 2715 Lynch Rd *Web:* www.americanwindowandglass.com	Evansville	IN	47711	812-464-9400	464-3131
Amerimade Technology Inc 449 Mtn Vista Pkwy *TF:* 800-938-3824 ■ *Web:* www.amerimade.com	Livermore	CA	94551	925-243-9090	243-9266
Armstrong Systems & Consulting 5101 Tremont Ave Ste A	Davenport	IA	52807	563-386-9090	391-2237
Ashland Hardware Systems 790 W Commercial Ave *Fax Area Code: 800 ■ *Web:* www.ashlandhardware.com	Lowell	IN	46356	219-696-5950	626-1758*
Automation Plastics Corp 150 Lena Dr *Web:* www.automationplastics.com	Aurora	OH	44202	330-562-5148	
Avery Dennison Fastener Div 224 Industrial Rd *TF:* 800-225-5913 ■ *Web:* www.fastener.averydennison.com	Fitchburg	MA	01420	800-225-5913	848-2169
Axion International Holdings Inc 4005 All American Way *Web:* www.axionintl.com	Zanesville	OH	43701	740-452-2500	452-5488
AXYS Technologies Inc 2045 Mills Rd *TF:* 877-792-7878 ■ *Web:* www.axystechnologies.com	Sidney	BC	V8L5X2	250-655-5850	655-5856
Bay Polymer Corp 44530 S Grimmer Blvd *Web:* www.baypolymer.com	Fremont	CA	94538	510-490-1791	490-5914
Bemis Manufacturing Co 300 Mill St *TF:* 800-558-7651 ■ *Web:* www.bemismfg.com	Sheboygan Falls	WI	53085	920-467-4621	467-8573
Bentonville Plastics Inc 607 SW A St *Web:* www.bentonvilleplastics.com	Bentonville	AR	72712	479-273-7272	
Blackmore Company Inc 10800 Blackmore Ave *TF:* 800-874-8660 ■ *Web:* www.blackmoreco.com	Belleville	MI	48111	734-483-8661	483-5454
Blow Molded Products Inc 4720 Felspar St *Web:* www.blowmoldedproducts.com	Riverside	CA	92509	951-360-6055	
Blue Star Plastics Inc 801 Nandino Blvd *Web:* www.bluestarplastics.com	Lexington	KY	40511	859-255-0714	
Bowman Mfg Company Inc 17301 51st Ave Ne *Web:* www.bowmandispensers.com	Arlington	WA	98223	360-435-5005	
Burco Molding Inc 15015 Herriman Blvd *TF:* 888-883-6656 ■ *Web:* www.burco-molding.com	Noblesville	IN	46060	317-773-5699	
C. L. Smith Co 1311 S 39th St *TF:* 800-264-1202 ■ *Web:* www.clsmith.com	Saint Louis	MO	63110	314-771-1202	771-3351
Cashmere Molding 20004 144th Ave Ne *Web:* www.cashmeremolding.com	Woodinville	WA	98072	425-485-6515	
Century Manufacturing Inc 3351 N Webb Rd *Web:* www.centurymfg.com	Wichita	KS	67226	316-636-5423	
Charter Plastics 221 S Perry St *Web:* www.charterplastics.com	Titusville	PA	16354	814-827-9665	
CMI Plastics Inc 222 Pepsi Way *Web:* www.cmiplastics.com	Ayden	NC	28513	252-746-2171	
Coeur Inc 209 Creekside Dr *Web:* coeurinc.com	Washington	NC	27889	252-946-1963	
Concept Plastics Inc (CPI) PO Box 847 *Web:* www.cpico.com	High Point	NC	27261	336-889-2001	889-5752
Cool Polymers Inc 51 Circuit Dr *Web:* www.coolpolymers.com	North Kingstown	RI	02852	401-739-7602	
Coverbind Corp 3200 Corporate Dr *TF:* 800-366-6060 ■ *Web:* www.coverbind.com	Wilmington	NC	28405	910-799-4116	799-3935
Craftech EDM Corp 2941 E La Jolla St *Web:* www.craftechcorp.com	Anaheim	CA	92806	714-630-8117	630-7959
Criterion Technologies Inc 101 Mcintosh Pkwy *Web:* criteriondomes.com	Thomaston	GA	30286	706-647-5082	
Crystal-Like Plastics 2547 N Ontario St *Fax Area Code: 818 ■ *TF:* 800-554-6091 ■ *Web:* www.crystal-likeplastics.com	Burbank	CA	91504	323-849-1735	846-0877*
Curbell Inc Seven Cobham Dr *Web:* www.curbell.com	Orchard Park	NY	14127	716-667-3377	
Custom Accents 1940 Lunt Ave *TF:* 888-553-6789 ■ *Web:* www.customaccents.com	Elk Grove Village	IL	60007	847-640-4725	572-0674
Danner Manufacturing Inc 160 Oval Dr *Web:* www.dannermfg.com	Islandia	NY	11749	631-234-5261	
Daramic Inc 5525 US Hwy 60 E *Web:* www.daramic.com	Owensboro	KY	42303	270-683-1561	686-9226
Dealernet Inc 608 Matthews Mint Hill Rd Ste E *Web:* www.dealernetinc.com	Matthews	NC	28105	704-321-3215	
DelStar Technologies Inc 220 E St Elmo Rd *TF:* 800-521-6713 ■ *Web:* www.delstarinc.com	Austin	TX	78745	512-447-7000	447-7444
Delta Pacific Products Inc 33170 Central Ave *Web:* www.deltapacificinc.com	Union City	CA	94587	510-487-4411	

	City	State	Zip	Phone	Fax
Den Hartog Industries Inc 4010 Hospers Dr S PO Box 425 *TF:* 800-342-3408 ■ *Web:* www.denhartogindustries.com	Hospers	IA	51238	712-752-8432	752-8222
DK Manufacturing Lancaster Inc 2118 Commerce St *Web:* dkmanufacturing.com	Lancaster	OH	43130	740-654-5566	
Dreco Inc 7887 Root Rd *Web:* www.drecoinc.com	North Ridgeville	OH	44039	440-327-6021	
Durabac Inc 22 ch Milton *Web:* www.durabac.ca	Granby	QC	J2J0P2	450-378-1723	
Duron Plastics Ltd 965 Wilson Ave	Kitchener	ON	N2C1J1	519-884-8011	
Dutchland Plastics Corp 54 Enterprise Ct *Web:* www.dutchlandplastics.com	Oostburg	WI	53070	920-564-3633	564-3337
Dynamic Plastics Inc 29831 Commerce Blvd *Web:* www.dynamicplastics.com	Chesterfield	MI	48051	586-749-6100	
E & O Tool & Plastics Inc 19178 Industrial Blvd NW *Web:* www.eoplastics.com	Elk River	MN	55330	763-441-6100	441-6452
Easyturf 2750 La Mirada Dr *Web:* www.easyturf.com	Vista	CA	92081	760-789-7772	
Egli Machine Company Inc 240 State Hwy 7 *Web:* www.eglimachine.com	Sidney	NY	13838	607-563-3021	
Eimo Americas 14320 Portage Rd *Web:* www.eimo.com	Vicksburg	MI	49097	269-649-0545	
Engineered Polymers Corp (EPC) 1020 Maple Ave E *TF:* 800-388-2155 ■ *Web:* www.epcmolding.com	Mora	MN	55051	320-679-3232	679-2323
Enor Corp 245 Livingston St *TF:* 800-977-6427 ■ *Web:* www.enor.com	Northvale	NJ	07647	201-750-1680	
Exotic Automation & Supply Inc 34700 Grand River Ave *Web:* www.exoticautomation.com	Farmington Hills	MI	48335	248-477-2122	477-0427
Fabricated Extrusion Company LLC 2331 Hoover Ave *Web:* www.fabexco.com	Modesto	CA	95354	209-529-9200	
Fiber Pad Inc 17260 E Young St *Web:* www.fiberpad.com	Tulsa	OK	74116	918-438-7430	
Fiberglass Specialties Inc PO Box 1340 *TF:* 800-527-1459 ■ *Web:* www.fsiweb.com	Henderson	TX	75653	903-657-6522	657-2318
First American Plastic Molding Enterprise Two Choctaw Trl *Web:* www.firstamericanplastic.com	Ocean Springs	MS	39564	228-872-4635	
Flagship Converters Inc 205 Shelter Rock Rd *Web:* www.flagshipconverters.com	Danbury	CT	06810	203-792-0034	797-0410
Form Plastics Co 3825 Stern Ave *Web:* www.formplastics.com	Saint Charles	IL	60174	630-443-1400	
Fox Lite Inc 8300 Dayton Rd *Web:* www.foxlite.com	Fairborn	OH	45324	937-864-1966	864-7010
Freetech Plastics Inc 2211 Warm Springs Ct *Web:* freetechplastics.com	Fremont	CA	94539	510-651-9996	
Fusion Optix Inc 19 Wheeling Ave *TF:* 866-506-8300 ■ *Web:* www.fusionoptix.com	Woburn	MA	01801	781-995-0805	
Garner Industries Inc 7201 N 98th St PO Box 29709 *TF:* 800-228-0275 ■ *Web:* www.garnerindustries.com	Lincoln	NE	68507	402-434-9100	434-9133
Gavco Plastics 9840 S 219th E Ave *Web:* www.gavcoplastics.com	Broken Arrow	OK	74014	918-455-7888	
Genova Products Inc 7034 E Court St *TF:* 800-521-7488 ■ *Web:* www.genovaproducts.com	Davison	MI	48423	810-744-4500	
GenPore 1136 Morgantown Rd PO Box 380 *TF:* 800-654-4391 ■ *Web:* www.genpore.com	Reading	PA	19607	610-374-5171	374-4990
Geonautics Manufacturing Inc 506 Merrimac St *Web:* www.geonauticsmfg.com	Newburyport	MA	01950	978-462-7161	
Gessner Products Company Inc 241 N Main St *Web:* gessnerproducts.com	Ambler	PA	19002	215-646-7667	
Glasteel-stabilit America Inc 285 Industrial Dr *TF:* 800-238-5546 ■ *Web:* www.glasteel.com	Moscow	TN	38057	901-877-3010	
GPK Products Inc 1601 43rd St NW *TF:* 800-437-4670 ■ *Web:* www.gpk-fargo.com	Fargo	ND	58102	701-277-3225	277-9286
GWI Inc Eight Pomerleau St *Web:* www.gwi.net	Biddeford	ME	04005	207-286-8686	
H.Q.C Inc 230 Kendall Pt Dr *Web:* www.hqcinc.com	Oswego	IL	60543	630-820-5550	820-5549
Habasit America 805 Satellite Blvd **Fax Area Code:* 678 ■ *TF:* 800-458-6431 ■ *Web:* www.habasit.com	Suwanee	GA	30024	800-458-6431	288-3651*
Hackney Ladish Inc 400 E Willow *Web:* www.hackney.com	Enid	OK	73701	580-237-4212	
Hanscom Inc 331 Market St *TF:* 877-725-6788 ■ *Web:* www.hanscominc.com	Warren	RI	02885	401-247-1999	247-4575
Hansen Plastic Corp 1270 Abbott Dr *Web:* www.hansenplastics.com	Elgin	IL	60123	847-741-4510	
Harbec Plastics Inc 369 SR- 104 *TF:* 888-521-4416 ■ *Web:* www.harbec.com	Ontario	NY	14519	585-265-0010	265-1306
Henry Plastic Molding Inc 41703 Albrae St *Web:* www.henryplastic.com	Fremont	CA	94538	510-490-7993	490-3548
Hicks Plastics Company Inc 51308 Industrial Dr *Web:* www.hicksplastics.com	Macomb	MI	48042	586-786-5640	
Hilco Technologies Inc 4172 Danvers Ct SE *Web:* www.hilcotech.com	Grand Rapids	MI	49512	616-957-1081	
Hycomp Inc 17960 Englewood Dr Ste A *Web:* hycompinc.com	Cleveland	OH	44130	440-234-2002	
Hygolet Inc 349 SE Second Ave *TF:* 800-494-6538 ■ *Web:* www.hygolet.com	Deerfield Beach	FL	33441	954-481-8601	481-8669
Ideal Pet Products Inc 24735 Ave Rockefeller *Web:* www.idealpetproducts.com	Valencia	CA	91355	661-294-2266	
Imark Molding Inc 104 Park Ave *Web:* www.imarkmolding.com	Woodville	WI	54028	715-698-3144	
Integrity Rotational Molding LLC 701 Carr Road Ste 101 *Web:* www.integrityrotational.com	Plainfield	IN	46168	317-837-1101	
Ironwood Plastics Inc 1235 Wall St *Web:* www.ironwood.com	Ironwood	MI	49938	906-932-5025	
Jacobson Plastics 1401 Freeman Ave *Web:* www.jacobsonplastics.com	Long Beach	CA	90804	562-433-4911	
Jatco Inc 725 Zwissig Way *Web:* www.jatco.com	Union City	CA	94587	510-487-0888	487-1880
Jentec Engineering Co 2820 E Coronado St	Anaheim	CA	92806	714-632-6762	
Kalwall Corp 1111 Candia Rd *TF:* 800-258-9777 ■ *Web:* www.kalwall.com	Manchester	NH	03109	603-627-3861	627-7905
Kelcourt Plastics Inc 1000 Calle Recodo *Web:* www.kelcourt.com	San Clemente	CA	92673	949-361-0774	
King Plastic Corp 1100 N Toledo Blade Blvd *TF:* 800-780-5502 ■ *Web:* www.kingplastic.com	North Port	FL	34288	941-493-5502	497-3274
Kleiss Gears 390 Industrial Ave *Web:* www.kleissgears.com	Grantsburg	WI	54840	715-463-5995	
Lakeside Plastics Inc 450 W 33rd Ave PO Box 2384 *Web:* www.lakesideplastics.net	Oshkosh	WI	54903	920-235-3620	235-6545
Lamcraft Partition Company Inc 1231 County Rd 4781	Boyd	TX	76023	940-433-5857	
Lamvin Inc 4675 N Ave *TF:* 800-446-6329 ■ *Web:* www.lamvin.com	Oceanside	CA	92056	760-806-6400	806-3200
Landmark Plastic Corp 1331 Kelly Ave *TF:* 800-242-1183 ■ *Web:* www.landmarkplastic.com	Akron	OH	44306	330-785-2200	785-9200
LCS Precision Molding Inc 119 S Second St *Web:* www.lcsplastics.com	Waterville	MN	56096	507-362-8685	
Leaktite Corp 40 Francis St *TF:* 800-392-0039 ■ *Web:* www.leaktite.com	Leominster	MA	01453	978-537-8000	534-3539
LHR Services & Equipment Inc lc-disc 4200 Fm 1128 Rd *Web:* lhrservices.com	Pearland	TX	77584	713-943-2324	
Little Kids Inc 225 Chapman St Ste 202 *TF:* 800-545-5437 ■ *Web:* www.littlekidsinc.com	Providence	RI	02905	401-454-7600	
LSP Products Group Inc 3689 Arrowhead Dr *TF:* 800-854-3215 ■ *Web:* www.lspproducts.com	Carson City	NV	89706	800-854-3215	243-1777
Magic Plastics Inc 25215 Ave Stanford *TF:* 800-369-0303 ■ *Web:* www.magicplastics.com	Valencia	CA	91355	661-257-4485	
Majors Plastics Inc 10117 I St *Web:* www.majorsplastics.com	Omaha	NE	68127	402-331-1660	331-9041
Mariplast North America Inc 365 Business Pkwy *Web:* mariplast.com	Greer	SC	29651	864-989-0560	989-0561
Masonry Technology Inc 24235 Electric St *Web:* iqpowertools.com/product-category/tec-connect/	Cresco	IA	52136	563-547-1122	
Mastercraft Mold Inc 3301 W Vernon Ave *TF:* 800-628-1672 ■ *Web:* www.mastercraft-companies.com	Phoenix	AZ	85009	602-484-4520	
Matlab Inc 1112 Nc Hwy 49 S *Web:* www.matlabinc.com	Asheboro	NC	27205	336-629-4161	
Matrix Iv Inc 610 E Judd St *Web:* www.matrixiv.com	Woodstock	IL	60098	815-338-4500	
Mauser USA LLC 35 Cotters Ln *Web:* mausergroup.com	Brunswick	IL	60440	732-353-7100	651-9777
Mc Pherson Plastics Inc PO Box 58 *Web:* www.mcpherson-plastics.com	Otsego	MI	49078	269-694-9487	694-6662
MedGyn Products Inc 100 W Industrial Rd *Web:* www.medgyn.com	Addison	IL	60101	630-627-4105	
Merrick Engineering Inc 1275 Quarry St *Web:* www.merrickengineering.com	Corona	CA	92879	951-737-6040	
Micro Plastics Inc 11 Industry Ln Hwy 178 N PO Box 149 *TF:* 800-466-1467 ■ *Web:* secure.microplastics.com	Flippin	AR	72634	870-453-2261	453-8676
Microdyne Plastics Inc 1901 E Cooley Dr *Web:* www.microdyneplastics.com	Colton	CA	92324	909-503-4010	503-4011
Middlefield Plastics Inc PO Box 708 *Web:* www.middlefieldplastics.com	Middlefield	OH	44062	440-834-4638	834-1247
MOCAP Inc 409 Parkway Dr *TF:* 800-633-6775 ■ *Web:* www.mocap.com	Park Hills	MO	63601	314-543-4000	543-4111
Mold-masters Ltd 41 Todd Rd *Web:* moldmasters.com	Georgetown	ON	L7G4R8	905-702-8955	
Mold-Rite Plastics LLC 1 Plant St PO Box 160 *TF:* 800-432-5277 ■ *Web:* www.mrpcap.com	Plattsburgh	NY	12901	518-561-1812	561-0017
Moldamatic LLC 29 Noeland Ave *Web:* www.moldamatic.com	Penndel	PA	19047	215-757-4819	
Molded Devices Inc 6918 Ed Perkic St *Web:* moldeddevices.com	Riverside	CA	92504	951-509-6918	
Mylan Technologies Inc 1000 Mylan Blvd *TF:* 800-294-1322 ■ *Web:* mylan.com/products/packaging-and-delivery-systems/	Canonsburg	PA	15317	724-514-1800	
N-k Mfg Technologies 1134 Freeman Ave SW *Web:* www.nkmfgtech.com	Grand Rapids	MI	49503	616-248-3200	
Neil Enterprises Inc 450 E Bunker Ct *TF:* 800-621-5584 ■ *Web:* www.neilenterprises.com	Vernon Hills	IL	60061	847-549-7627	
New Boston Rtm Inc 19155 Shook Rd *Web:* www.newbostonrtm.com	New Boston	MI	48164	734-753-9956	753-9221
Nishiba Industries Corp 2360 Marconi Ct *Web:* www.nishiba.com	San Diego	CA	92154	619-661-8866	482-1585
Nissen Chemitec America 350 E High St *Web:* nissenchemitec.com	London	OH	43140	740-852-3200	852-4547
Nordson MEDICAL 3325 S Timberline Rd *TF:* 888-404-5837 ■ *Web:* www.valueplastics.com	Fort Collins	CO	80525	970-267-5200	223-0953
Octex Corp 901 Sarasota Ctr Blvd *Web:* octexllc.com	Sarasota	FL	34240	941-371-6767	
Pac Tec 12365 Haynes St *TF:* 877-554-2544 ■ *Web:* www.pactecinc.com	Clinton	LA	70722	225-683-8602	
Paktech 1680 Irving Rd *Web:* www.paktech-opi.com	Eugene	OR	97402	541-461-5000	

Company	City	State	ZIP	Phone	Fax
Pelham Plastics Inc 42 Dick Tracy Dr *Web:* www.pelhamplastics.com	Pelham	NH	03076	603-886-7226	
PI Inc 213 Dennis St *TF:* 800-894-4876 ■ *Web:* www.pi-inc.com	Athens	TN	37303	423-745-6213	745-7852
Pinnacle Plastic Products 513 Napoleon Rd *Web:* pinnacleplasticproducts.com	Bowling Green	OH	43402	419-352-8688	
Piolax Corp 139 Etowah Industrial Ct *Web:* www.piolaxusa.com	Canton	GA	30114	770-479-2227	479-2399
Plastics Plus Technology Inc 1495 Research Dr *Web:* www.plasticsplus.com	Redlands	CA	92374	909-747-0555	
Plastikon Industries Inc 688 Sandoval Way *TF:* 800-370-0858 ■ *Web:* www.plastikon.com	Hayward	CA	94544	510-400-1010	400-1133
Plastiques Milsi Inc Les 2412 Rue De La Province *Web:* plastiquesmilsi.com	Longueuil	QC	J4G1G1	450-463-4568	
Plastpro Inc 5200 W Century Blvd 9F *TF:* 800-779-0561 ■ *Web:* www.plastproinc.com	Los Angeles	CA	90045	310-693-8600	693-8620
Pleiger Plastics Co PO Box 1271 *TF:* 800-753-4437 ■ *Web:* www.pleiger.com	Washington	PA	15301	724-228-2244	228-2253
Plitek LLC 69 Rawls Rd *TF:* 800-966-1250 ■ *Web:* www.plitek.com	Des Plaines	IL	60018	800-966-1250	
Ply Gem Holdings Inc 5020 Weston Pkwy Ste 400 *Web:* www.plygem.com	Cary	NC	27513	919-677-4019	
PMC Group Inc 1288 Rt 73 S Pmc Group Bldg Ste 401 *Web:* www.pmc-group.com	Mount Laurel	NJ	08054	856-533-1866	
Polymer Conversions Inc 5732 Big Tree Rd	Orchard Park	NY	14127	716-662-8550	
Polymos Inc 3333 Rue F-X-Tessier	Vaudreuil-Dorion	QC	J7V5V5	450-424-5333	
Polytec Products Corp 1190 Obrien Dr *Web:* polytecproducts.com	Menlo Park	CA	94025	650-322-7555	
Polyvel Inc 100 Ninth St *Web:* www.polyvel.com	Hammonton	NJ	08037	609-567-0080	
Porex Technologies Corp 500 Bohannon Rd *TF Cust Svc:* 800-241-0195 ■ *Web:* www.porex.com	Fairburn	GA	30213	770-964-1421	969-0954
Precision Southeast Inc 4900 Hwy 501 PO Box 50610 *Web:* www.precisionsoutheast.com	Myrtle Beach	SC	29579	843-347-4218	
Precision Thermoplastic Components Inc PO Box 1296 *TF:* 800-860-4505 ■ *Web:* www.ptclima.com	Lima	OH	45802	419-227-4500	
Preferred Plastics Inc 800 E Bridge St *Web:* www.preferredplastics.net	Plainwell	MI	49080	269-685-5873	685-1148
Preproduction Plastics Inc 210 Teller St *Web:* ppiplastics.com	Corona	CA	92879	951-340-9680	
Prism Plastics Inc 1544 Hwy 65 *TF:* 877-246-7535 ■ *Web:* www.prismplasticsinc.com	New Richmond	WI	54017	715-246-7535	246-5661
Pure-logic Industries Inc 1730 W Sunrise Blvd Ste A102 *Web:* www.purelogicind.com	Gilbert	AZ	85233	480-892-9395	
Questech Corp 92 Park St *Web:* www.questech.com	Rutland	VT	05701	802-773-1228	
Randall Mfg LLC 722 Church Rd *Web:* www.randallmfg.com	Elmhurst	IL	60126	630-782-0001	
Rayner Covering Systems Inc 665 Schneider Dr *TF:* 800-648-0757 ■ *Web:* www.raynercovering.com	South Elgin	IL	60177	847-695-2264	695-2363
Regency Plastics Company Ltd 50 Brisbane Rd *Web:* www.regencyplastics.com	North York	ON	M3J2K2	416-661-3000	
Rest-a-phone Corp 2801 NW Lower River Rd Ste A *Web:* www.abcplas.com	Vancouver	WA	98660	503-235-6778	
RGE USA Inc 365 Oliver Cromwell Dr *Web:* www.rgegroup.com	Newport	TN	37821	423-625-4909	
Richards & Richards 1741 Elm Hill Pk *Web:* www.richardsandrichards.com	Nashville	TN	37210	615-242-9600	
Rieke Corp 500 W Seventh St *Web:* www.riekepackaging.com	Auburn	IN	46706	260-925-3700	
Riverdale Color Manufacturing Inc One Walnut St *Web:* www.riverdalecolor.com	Perth Amboy	NJ	08861	732-376-9300	
RL Hudson & Co 2000 W Tacoma *Web:* www.rlhudson.com	Broken Arrow	OK	74012	918-259-6600	
Ro Mai Industries 1605 Enterprise Pkwy *Web:* www.rmihardware.com	Twinsburg	OH	44087	330-425-9090	
Rogan Corp 3455 Woodhead Dr *TF:* 800-584-5662 ■ *Web:* www.rogancorp.com	Northbrook	IL	60062	847-498-2300	498-2334
Rohrer Corp 717 Seville Rd PO Box 1009 *TF:* 800-243-6640 ■ *Web:* www.rohrer.com	Wadsworth	OH	44282	330-335-1541	336-5147
Rolco Inc 336 E Industrial St *Web:* www.rolcoinc.com	Kasota	MN	56050	507-931-4525	
Rolenn Mfg 2065 Roberta St *Web:* www.rolenn.com	Riverside	CA	92507	951-682-1185	
Roncelli Plastics Inc 330 W Duarte Rd *Web:* www.roncelli.com	Monrovia	CA	91016	626-359-2551	
Rubbermaid Commercial Products (RCP) 3124 Valley Ave *TF:* 800-347-9800 ■ *Web:* www.rubbermaidcommercial.com	Winchester	VA	22601	540-667-8700	542-8770
Safety Technology International Inc 2306 Airport Rd *TF:* 800-888-4784 ■ *Web:* www.sti-usa.com	Waterford	MI	48327	248-673-9898	
Sare Plastics 14600 Commerce St Ne *Web:* www.sareplastics.com	Alliance	OH	44601	330-821-4299	
Semco Plastic Co 5301 Old Baumgartner Rd *Web:* www.semcoplastics.com	Saint Louis	MO	63129	314-487-4557	487-4724
Seville Flexpack Corp 9905 S Ridgeview Dr *Web:* sevilleflexpack.com	Oak Creek	WI	53154	414-761-2751	761-3140
Shakespeare Monofilaments & Specialty Polymers 6111 Shakespeare Rd *TF:* 800-845-2110 ■ *Web:* www.shakespearemonofilaments.com	Columbia	SC	29223	803-754-7011	786-2568
Signature Cards LP 1299 Commerce Dr Ste B *Web:* www.signaturecard.net	Richardson	TX	75081	972-783-7600	783-1670
Simonton Windows Inc 5300 Briscoe Rd PO Box 1646 *Web:* www.simonton.com	Parkersburg	WV	26102	304-428-8261	
Smith McDonald Corp 1270 Niagara St *TF:* 800-753-8548 ■ *Web:* www.smithmcdonald.com	Buffalo	NY	14213	716-684-7200	684-2053
Spears Manufacturing Co PO Box 9203 *TF:* 800-862-1499 ■ *Web:* www.spearsmfg.com	Sylmar	CA	91392	818-364-1611	367-3014
Spencer Plastics Inc 4811 Industrial Dr *Web:* www.spencerplastics.com	Mesick	MI	49668	231-885-1443	
Spilltech Environmental Inc 1627 Odonoghue St *TF:* 800-228-3877 ■ *Web:* www.spilltech.com	Mobile	AL	36615	800-228-3877	
Spiratex Company Inc 1916 Frenchtown Ctr Dr *Web:* www.spiratex.com	Monroe	MI	48162	734-289-4800	
Stack Plastics 3525 Haven Ave *Web:* www.stackplastics.com	Menlo Park	CA	94025	650-361-8600	
Stanridge Color Corp P.O Box 1086 *Web:* www.standridgecolor.com	Social Circle	GA	30025	770-464-3362	464-2202
Stant Corp 1620 Columbia Ave *TF:* 800-822-3121 ■ *Web:* www.stant.com	Connersville	IN	47331	765-825-3121	825-2875
Star Die Molding Inc 2741 Katherine Way *Web:* www.stardie.com	Elk Grove Village	IL	60007	847-766-7952	
Steinwall Inc 1759 116th Ave NW *TF:* 800-229-9199 ■ *Web:* www.steinwall.com	Coon Rapids	MN	55448	763-767-7060	767-7061
Sueba USA 8235 El Rio St *Web:* www.s-h-m.com	Houston	TX	77054	713-747-7333	
Sunrise Windows Ltd. LLC 200 Enterprise Dr *Web:* www.sunrisewindows.com	Temperance	MI	48182	734-847-8778	847-7758
Syndicate Sales Inc PO Box 756 *TF:* 800-428-0515 ■ *Web:* www.syndicatesales.com	Kokomo	IN	46903	765-457-7277	454-2316
Syracuse Plastics LLC 7400 Morgan Rd *Web:* www.syracuseplastics.com	Liverpool	NY	13090	315-637-9881	637-9260
Tearepair Inc 2200 Knight Rd *Web:* tear-aid.com	Land O Lakes	FL	34639	813-948-6898	
Tech Nh Inc Eight Continental Blvd *Web:* www.technh.com	Merrimack	NH	03054	603-424-4404	
Techmer PM LLC One Quality Cir *Web:* www.techmerpm.com	Clinton	TN	37716	865-457-6700	
Technetics Group 3125 Damon Way *TF:* 800-618-4701 ■ *Web:* www.techneticsgroup.com	Burbank	CA	91505	818-841-9667	841-8057
Tecstar Manufacturing Co W190N11701 Moldmakers Way *Web:* www.mgstech.com	Germantown	WI	53022	262-250-2950	
Tessy Plastics Corp 488 Rt 5 W *Web:* www.tessy.com	Elbridge	NY	13060	315-689-3924	689-2027
Thermal Plastic Design Inc 1116 E Pine St *Web:* www.tdimolding.com	St Croix Falls	WI	54024	715-483-1841	
Thermo-tech Plastics Ltd 2299 Drew Rd *Web:* thermotechplastics.com	Mississauga	ON	L5S1A3	905-678-9448	
Thombert Inc 316 E Seventh St N *TF:* 800-433-3572 ■ *Web:* www.thombert.com	Newton	IA	50208	800-433-3572	433-3517
TMI LLC 5350 Campbells Run Rd *TF:* 800-888-9750 ■ *Web:* www.tmi-pvc.com	Pittsburgh	PA	15205	412-787-9750	
Totex Manufacturing Inc 2927 Lomita Blvd *Web:* www.batterytechnologies.com	Torrance	CA	90505	310-326-2028	
Transparent Container Company Inc 625 Thomas Dr **Fax Area Code:* 630 ■ *Web:* www.transparentcontainer.com	Bensenville	IL	60106	708-449-8520	860-3651*
Triad Products Co 1801 W 'B' St *TF General:* 888-253-4227 ■ *Web:* www.triadproducts.net	Hastings	NE	68901	402-462-2181	462-2246
Trippnt Inc 8830 NE 108th St *Web:* www.trippnt.com	Kansas City	MO	64157	816-792-2604	
Triwood Corp of Georgia Inc 124 Austin Rd *Web:* triwood.com	Americus	GA	31719	229-928-2233	
TSE Industries Inc 4370 112th Terr N *TF:* 800-237-7634 ■ *Web:* www.tse-industries.com	Clearwater	FL	33762	727-573-7676	572-0487
U S Farathane Corp 38000 Mound Rd *Web:* www.usfarathane.com	Sterling Heights	MI	48310	586-978-2800	268-5542
Ultra-Poly Corp 102 Demi Rd PO Box 330 *TF:* 800-932-0619 ■ *Web:* www.ultra-poly.com	Portland	PA	18351	570-897-7500	
Unette Corp 1578 Sussex Tpke Bldg Ste 5 *Web:* www.unette.com	Randolph	NJ	07869	973-328-6800	584-4794
Univenture Inc 13311 Industrial Pkwy **Fax Area Code:* 937 ■ *TF:* 800-992-8262 ■ *Web:* www.univenture.com	Marysville	OH	43040	800-992-8262	645-4700*
Vantage Plastics 1415 W Cedar St *Web:* www.vantageplastics.com	Standish	MI	48658	989-846-1029	846-0939
Ven-Tel Plastics Corp 11311 74th St N *Web:* www.ventelplastics.com	Largo	FL	33773	727-546-7470	546-7480
Ventana USA 6001 Enterprise Dr *Web:* www.ventana-usa.com	Export	PA	15632	724-325-3400	
Ventra Plastics - Russellville 140 Progress Dr	Russellville	KY	42276	270-726-4767	
Viking Plastics Inc One Viking St *Web:* www.vikingplastics.com	Corry	PA	16407	814-664-8671	
Vinyl Window Technologies Inc PO Box 588 *Web:* www.viwintech.com	Paducah	KY	42002	270-442-7870	
Vitec LLC 2627 Clark St *Web:* www.vitec-usa.com	Detroit	MI	48210	313-297-6676	843-1298
Viwinco Inc PO Box 499 *Web:* www.viwinco.com	Morgantown	PA	19543	610-286-8884	286-8877
Viziflex Seels Inc 406 N Midland Ave **Fax Area Code:* 201 ■ *TF:* 800-627-7752 ■ *Web:* www.viziflex.com	Saddle Brook	NJ	07663	800-627-7752	487-3266*
Watertown Plastics 830 Echo Lk Rd *Web:* www.watertownplastics.com	Watertown	CT	06795	860-274-7535	
Wausaukee Composites Inc 837 Cedar St *Web:* www.wauscomp.com	Wausaukee	WI	54177	715-856-6321	856-5567
Weener Plastics Inc 2201 Stantonsburg Rd SE *Web:* wppg.co.uk	Wilson	NC	27893	252-206-1400	

Phone | Fax

Westec Plastics Corp 6757 A Las Positas Rd .... Livermore CA 94551 925-454-3400
Web: www.westecplastics.com

Williamston Products Inc (WPI)
845 Progress Ct .... Williamston MI 48895 517-655-2131 655-2607
Web: www.wpius.com

WinDoor Inc 7500 Amsterdam Dr. .... Orlando FL 32832 407-481-8400
Web: www.windoorinc.com

Window Factory Inc, The 7550 Miramar Rd .... San Diego CA 92126 888-318-2951
Web: www.windowfactory.com

World Class Plastics Inc 7695 SR- 708 .... Russells Point OH 43348 937-843-4927 843-4934
TF: 800-954-3140 ■ *Web:* www.worldclassplastics.com

Worldwide Dispensers USA 78 2nd Ave S. .... Lester Prairie MN 55354 320-395-2553 395-2656
Web: dssmith.com

Wren Assoc Ltd 124 Wren Pkwy. .... Jefferson City MO 65109 573-893-2249
Web: www.wrensolutions.com

Yeti Coolers 3411 Hidalgo St .... Austin TX 78702 512-394-9384
TF: 888-872-0227 ■ *Web:* www.yeticoolers.com

Zadro Products Inc 5422 Argosy Ave .... Huntington Beach CA 92649 714-892-9200
TF: 800-468-4348 ■ *Web:* www.zadroinc.com

ZAGG Inc 3855 South 500 West Ste J .... Salt Lake City UT 84115 801-263-0699
TF: 800-700-9244 ■ *Web:* www.zagg.com

612 PLUMBING FIXTURES & FITTINGS - METAL

Phone | Fax

Accurate Partitions Corp
8000 Joliet Rd PO Box 287 .... McCook IL 60525 708-442-6800 442-7439
Web: www.accuratepartitions.com

Acorn Engineering Co
15125 Proctor Ave PO Box 3527 .... City of Industry CA 91744 626-336-4561 961-2200
TF: 800-488-8999 ■ *Web:* www.acorneng.com

American Brass Manufacturing Co
5000 Superior Ave .... Cleveland OH 44103 216-431-6565 431-9420
TF: 800-431-6440 ■ *Web:* www.americanbrass.com

American Specialties Inc (ASI)
441 Saw Mill River Rd .... Yonkers NY 10701 914-476-9000 476-0688
Web: www.americanspecialties.com

Ames Fire & Waterworks
1427 N Market Blvd Ste 9 .... Sacramento CA 95834 916-928-0123 928-9333
Web: www.amesfirewater.com

Anderson Copper & Brass Co
4325 Frontage Rd .... Oak Forest IL 60452 708-535-9030 535-9038
TF: 800-323-5284 ■ *Web:* andersonfittings.com

Barclay Products Ltd 4000 Porett Dr Ste B .... Gurnee IL 60031 847-244-1234
Web: www.barclayproducts.com

Bathcraft Inc 1610 James P Rodgers Dr .... Valdosta GA 31601 229-333-0805
Web: www.bathcraft.com

Bootz Industries PO Box 18010 .... Evansville IN 47719 812-423-5401 429-2254
Web: www.bootz.com

Bradley Corp
W 142 N 9101 Fountain Blvd .... Menomonee Falls WI 53051 262-251-6000 251-5817
TF: 800-272-3539 ■ *Web:* www.bradleycorp.com

Brass-Craft Manufacturing Co
39600 Orchard Hill Pl .... Novi MI 48375 248-305-6000 305-6012*
**Fax:* Sales ■ *Web:* www.brasscraft.com

Brasstech Inc 2001 Carnegie Ave .... Santa Ana CA 92705 949-417-5207 417-5208
Web: www.brasstech.com

Central Brass Mfg Company Inc
2950 E 55th St .... Cleveland OH 44127 216-883-0220 883-0875
TF: 800-321-8630 ■ *Web:* www.centralbrass.com

Champion-Arrowhead LLC 5147 Alhambra Ave ..... Los Angeles CA 90032 323-221-9137 221-2579
TF: 800-332-4267 ■ *Web:* www.arrowheadbrass.com

Chicago Faucets A Geberit Co
2100 S Clearwater Dr .... Des Plaines IL 60018 847-803-5000 298-3101*
**Fax:* Sales ■ *TF:* 800-323-5060 ■ *Web:* www.chicagofaucets.com

Elias Industries Inc 605 Epsilon Dr. .... Pittsburgh PA 15238 412-782-4300
Web: tapcogenuinepartscenter.com

Eljer Inc 1 Centennial Ave .... Piscataway NJ 08855 800-442-1902
TF: 800-442-1902 ■ *Web:* www.eljer.com

Elkay Manufacturing Co 2222 Camden Ct. .... Oak Brook IL 60523 630-574-8484 574-5012
Web: www.elkay.com

Fisher Manufacturing Co PO Box 60 .... Tulare CA 93275 800-421-6162 832-8238
TF: 800-421-6162 ■ *Web:* www.fisher-mfg.com

Fluidmaster Inc
30800 Rancho Viejo Rd .... San Juan Capistrano CA 92675 949-728-2000 728-2205
TF: 800-631-2011 ■ *Web:* www.fluidmaster.com

Fortune Brands Home & Hardware Inc
520 Lk Cook Rd .... Deerfield IL 60015 847-484-4400
Web: www.fortunebrands.com

Gerber Plumbing Fixtures LLC
2500 International Pkwy .... Woodridge IL 60517 888-648-6466 636-2021*
**Fax Area Code:* 514 ■ *TF:* 888-648-6466 ■ *Web:* www.gerberonline.com

Global Partitions 2171 Liberty Hill Rd. .... Eastanollee GA 30538 706-827-2700 827-2710
Web: www.globalpartitions.com

Grohe America Inc 241 Covington Dr .... Bloomingdale IL 60108 630-582-7711 582-7722
TF: 800-444-7643 ■ *Web:* www.grohe.com

Hansgrohe Inc 1490 Bluegrass Lakes Pkwy. .... Alpharetta GA 30004 770-360-9880 360-9887
TF: 800-334-0455 ■ *Web:* www.hansgrohe-usa.com

In-Sink-Erator 4700 21st St .... Racine WI 53406 262-554-5432
TF: 800-558-5712 ■ *Web:* www.insinkerator.com

Josam Co 525 W US Hwy 20 .... Michigan City IN 46360 219-872-5531 627-0008*
**Fax Area Code:* 800 ■ *TF:* 800-365-6726 ■ *Web:* www.josam.com

Keeney Manufacturing Co 1170 Main St .... Newington CT 06111 860-666-3342 665-0374*
**Fax:* Cust Svc ■ *TF Cust Svc:* 800-243-0526 ■ *Web:* www.keeneymfg.com

Kohler Plumbing North America 444 Highland Dr .... Kohler WI 53044 920-457-4441 459-1826*
**Fax:* Sales ■ *TF:* 800-456-4537 ■ *Web:* www.us.kohler.com

LDR Industries Inc 600 N Kilbourn Ave .... Chicago IL 60624 773-265-3000 265-3130
TF: 800-545-5230 ■ *Web:* www.ldrind.com

Masco Corp 21001 Van Born Rd. .... Taylor MI 48180 313-274-7400 792-4177
NYSE: MAS ■ *TF:* 888-627-6397 ■ *Web:* www.masco.com

Phone | Fax

Microphor Inc 452 E Hill Rd .... Willits CA 95490 707-459-5563 459-6617
TF Orders: 800-358-8280 ■ *Web:* www.microphor.com

Moen Inc 25300 Al Moen Dr .... North Olmsted OH 44070 440-962-2000 848-6636*
**Fax Area Code:* 800 ■ **Fax:* Hum Res ■ *TF Cust Svc:* 800-289-6636 ■ *Web:* www.moen.com

Moen Inc CSI Bath Accessories Div
25300 Al Moen Dr .... North Olmsted OH 44070 440-962-2000 962-2145
TF: 800-289-6636 ■ *Web:* www.moen.com

NAPAC Inc 229 Southbridge St .... Worcester MA 01608 508-363-4411
Web: www.napacinc.com

Norman Supply Co 825 SW Fifth St .... Oklahoma City OK 73109 405-235-9511
Web: www.morsco.com

Oatey Co 4700 W 160th St. .... Cleveland OH 44135 216-267-7100 321-9535*
**Fax Area Code:* 800 ■ *TF Cust Svc:* 800-321-9532 ■ *Web:* www.oatey.com

Pan-Pacific Plumbing Co
18250 Euclid St .... Fountain Valley CA 92708 949-474-9170 474-9180
Web: ppmechanical.com

Price Pfister Inc 19701 Da Vinci St. .... Lake Forest CA 92610 949-672-4000 672-4000
TF: 800-732-8238 ■ *Web:* www.pfisterfaucets.com

Quality Metal Finishing Company Inc
421 N Walnut St .... Byron IL 61010 815-234-2711 234-2243
Web: www.qmfco.com

SH Leggitt Co 1000 Civic Ctr Loop .... San Marcos TX 78666 512-396-2257 396-3064
Web: shleggitt.com

Sloan Valve Co 10500 Seymour Ave .... Franklin Park IL 60131 847-671-4300 671-6944
TF: 800-982-5839 ■ *Web:* www.sloanvalve.com

Speakman Co 400 Anchor Mill Rd .... New Castle DE 19720 800-537-2107 977-2747
TF: 800-537-2107 ■ *Web:* www.speakmancompany.com

Starline Manufacturing Company Inc
6060 W Douglas Ave .... Milwaukee WI 53218 414-358-4060

Sterling Plumbing 444 Highland Dr .... Kohler WI 53044 920-457-4441
TF Cust Svc: 888-783-7546 ■ *Web:* www.sterlingplumbing.com

Symmons Industries Inc 31 Brooks Dr .... Braintree MA 02184 781-848-2250 843-3849
TF: 800-796-6667 ■ *Web:* www.symmons.com

T & S Brass & Bronze Works Inc
PO Box 1088 .... Travelers Rest SC 29690 864-834-4102 834-3518
TF Cust Svc: 800-476-4103 ■ *Web:* www.tsbrass.com

Water Pik Inc 1730 E Prospect Rd .... Fort Collins CO 80553 800-525-2774
TF: 800-525-2774 ■ *Web:* www.waterpik.com

Water Saver Faucet Co 701 W Erie St 2nd Fl .... Chicago IL 60654 312-666-5500 666-5501
TF Parts: 800-973-7278 ■ *Web:* www.wsflab.com

Waterworks Operating Company LLC
60 Backus Ave .... Danbury CT 06810 203-546-6000
TF: 800-899-6757 ■ *Web:* www.waterworks.com

William Steinen Manufacturing Co
29 E Halsey Rd .... Parsippany NJ 07054 973-887-6400 887-4632
Web: www.steinen.com

Woodford Manufacturing Co
2121 Waynoka Rd .... Colorado Springs CO 80915 800-621-6032 574-7699*
**Fax Area Code:* 719 ■ *TF Sales:* 800-621-6032 ■ *Web:* www.woodfordmfg.com

613 PLUMBING FIXTURES & FITTINGS - PLASTICS

Phone | Fax

1st Mechanical 1295 Bluegrass Lakes Pkwy .... Alpharetta GA 30004 770-346-0792
Web: www.1stmech.com

A & A Industrial Piping Inc Six Gardner Rd .... Fairfield NJ 07004 973-882-2622
Web: www.a-agroup.com

A & R Mechanical Contractors Inc
11244 E 55th Pl .... Tulsa OK 74146 918-250-6500
Web: www.aandrmechanical.com

A T Klemens & Son Inc 814 12th St N. .... Great Falls MT 59401 406-452-9541
Web: www.atklemens.com

A-account Plumbing & Drain Cleaning LLC
5128 S Eastern Ave. .... Oklahoma City OK 73129 405-672-5754

AAA Refrigeration Service Inc 1804 Nereid Ave. .... Bronx NY 10466 718-324-2231
Web: www.aaarefrig.com

Able Plumbing Inc 2336 Bob Boozer Dr .... Omaha NE 68130 402-334-8887

Absocold Corp PO Box 1545 .... Richmond IN 47375 765-935-7501 935-3450
TF: 800-843-3714 ■ *Web:* www.absocold.com

Accurate Heating & Cooling 3001 River Rd .... Chillicothe OH 45601 740-775-5005
Web: accuratehvac.com

Accurate Plumbing 7595 Fishel Dr S .... Dublin OH 43016 614-526-0131
Web: plumbingrepairandservices.com

Accutrans Inc 2740 Indiana Ave Ste 100 .... Kenner LA 70062 504-469-0500
Web: accutransinc.com

ACE Duraflo Pipe Restoration Inc
3122 W Alpine Ave .... Santa Ana CA 92704 714-564-7600
Web: www.restoremypipes.com

Ace-Atlas Corp 5214 Flushing Ave .... Maspeth NY 11378 718-497-3003
Web: www.ace-atlas.com

Acker & Sons Inc 10516 Summit Ave .... Kensington MD 20895 301-897-0700
Web: ackerandsonsinc.com

Acorn Industrial Inc 7311 Acc Blvd .... Raleigh NC 27617 919-256-6500
Web: www.acornindustrial.com

Action Air Conditioning & Htg 3506 Ave S. .... Galveston TX 77550 409-765-8026

Adams Electric & Plumbing LLC 606 N Main St. .... Pratt KS 67124 620-672-7279
Web: adamsep.com

Aero Automatic Sprinkler Co
21605 N Central Ave. .... Phoenix AZ 85024 623-580-7800
Web: www.aerofire.com

Aero Energy 230 Lincoln Way E .... New Oxford PA 17350 717-624-4311
Web: www.aeroenergy.com

Afrl Hea 6030 S Kent Bldg 570 .... Mesa AZ 85212 480-988-2040

Agco Inc 2782 Simpson Cir. .... Norcross GA 30071 770-447-6990

Aiello Home Services Inc
600 Old County Cir. .... Windsor Locks CT 06096 860-292-2600
Web: www.aiellohomeservices.com

AJ Demor & Sons Inc 2150 Eldo Rd .... Monroeville PA 15146 412-242-6125
Web: www.ajdemor.com

Phone Fax

Ajax Santa Barbara Refrigeration & Heating
401 E Montecito St .... Santa Barbara CA 93101 805-963-1322
Web: ajaxrefrigerationandac.com

Alex Mccoy Plumbing 160 Binnington Crt .... Kingston ON K7M8N1 613-546-6846
Web: amph.ca

All-Temp Refrigeration Services Inc
271 Hwy 1085 .... Madisonville LA 70447 888-626-1277
TF: 888-626-1277 ■ *Web:* www.alltempinc.com

All-Tex Pipe & Supply Inc 9743 Brockbank .... Dallas TX 75220 214-350-5886
Web: www.alltexsupply.com

Allan Automatic Sprinkler Corp of so Cal
3233 Enterprise St .... Brea CA 92821 714-993-9500
Web: www.allansocal.com

Allied Blower & Sheet Metal 1350 Polson Dr .... Vernon BC V1T8H2 250-503-2533
Web: www.alliedblower.com

Alpha Energy Solutions Inc
7200 Distribution Dr .... Louisville KY 40258 502-968-0121
Web: www.alphamechanicalservice.com/

Alpha Mechanical Heating & Air Condi
4885 Greencraig Ln .... San Diego CA 92123 858-278-3500
Web: alphamech.com/

Alpine Plumbing Inc
14580 W Greenfield Ave .... Brookfield WI 53005 262-797-4120
Web: www.alpineplumbinginc.com

Amason & Assoc Inc
1820 Rice Mine Rd N Ste 100 .... Tuscaloosa AL 35406 205-345-9626
Web: www.amason-associates.com

American Air Distributing Inc
830 S Bolmar St .... West Chester PA 19382 610-918-7090
Web: aa.com

American Fire Protection 4019 E Summit Ln .... Nampa ID 83687 208-463-0209
Web: www.firesafetyboise.com

American Moistening Company Inc
10402 Rodney St .... Pineville NC 28134 704-889-7281
Web: www.amco.com

AMI Mechanical Inc 12141 Pennsylvania St .... Thornton CO 80241 303-280-1401
Web: www.amimechanical.com

Ampam Ldi Mechanical Inc
10920 Pump House Rd .... Annapolis Jct MD 20701 301-497-6500

Answer Heating & Cooling Inc
8490 Midland Rd .... Freeland MI 48623 989-695-9461
Web: www.answerheating.com

Apex Mechanical Systems Inc 7440 Trade St .... San Diego CA 92121 858-536-8700
Web: www.apexmech.com

Apex Piping Systems Inc 302 Falco Dr .... Wilmington DE 19804 302-995-6136
TF: 888-995-2739 ■ *Web:* www.apexpiping.com

Applied Mechanical Systems Inc
5598 Wolf Creek Pk .... Dayton OH 45426 937-854-3073
TF: 888-854-3073 ■ *Web:* www.appliedmechanicalsys.com

Aqua Bath Company Inc 921 Cherokee Ave .... Nashville TN 37207 615-227-0017
TF: 800-232-2284 ■ *Web:* www.aquabath.com

Aqua-Chem Inc
3001 E Governor John Sevier Hwy .... Knoxville TN 37914 865-544-2065
Web: www.aqua-chem.com

Arete Development Inc 20 Industrial Rd .... Fairfield NJ 07004 973-244-0037

Arneg Canada Inc 18 Rue Richelieu .... Lacolle QC J0J1J0 450-246-3837 246-2368
Web: arneg.ca

Arneg LLC 750 Old Hargrave Rd .... Lexington NC 27295 336-956-5300
Web: www.arnegusa.com

Astro Mechanical Contractors Inc
603 S Marshall Ave .... El Cajon CA 92020 619-442-9686
Web: astro-mech.com

Atlas Butler Heating & Cooling
619 Reynolds Ave .... Columbus OH 43201 614-294-8600
Web: www.atlasbutler.com

Atlas Sheet Metal Inc 19 Musick .... Irvine CA 92618 949-600-8787
Web: atlassheetmetal.com

Aurora Contractors Inc 100 Raynor Ave .... Ronkonkoma NY 11779 631-981-3785
TF: 866-423-2197 ■ *Web:* www.auroracontractors.com

Automatic Fire Protection Inc
4582 Old Christoval Rd .... San Angelo TX 76904 325-651-9000 651-9003
Web: www.automaticfireprotection.com

Automatic Fire Sprinkler Inc
7272 Mars Dr .... Huntington Beach CA 92647 714-841-2066
TF: 800-436-2066 ■ *Web:* www.afsfire.com

Automatic Sprinkler of Texas Inc
1147 S Cedar Ridge Dr .... Duncanville TX 75137 972-298-2772
Web: www.autosprinkleroftx.com

B & B Trade Distribution Centre 675 York St .... London ON N5W2S6 519-679-1770
TF: 800-265-0382 ■ *Web:* bbtrade.ca/

B Z Plumbing Company Inc 1901 Aviation Blvd .... Lincoln CA 95648 916-645-1600

Baker Septic Installations
7740 S George Blvd .... Sebring FL 33875 863-385-0917
Web: bakersepticfl.net

Ball Heating & Air 8332 W Oaklawn Rd .... Biloxi MS 39532 228-392-5432
Web: www.callballthatsall.com

Basic Plumbing Inc 1409 Mechanical Blvd .... Garner NC 27529 919-662-1082
Web: www.basicplumbinginc.com

Beaudin Le Prohon Inc 6171 Boul Bourque .... Sherbrooke QC J1N1H2 819-563-2454
Web: www.leprohon.com

Bel-Aire Mechanical Inc 4201 N 47th Ave .... Phoenix AZ 85031 623-846-8600
Web: belairemechanical.com

Belding Tank Technologies Inc
200 N Gooding St PO Box 160 .... Belding MI 48809 616-794-1130 794-3666
TF: 800-253-4252 ■ *Web:* www.beldingtank.com

Bell Pipe & Supply 215 E Ball Rd .... Anaheim CA 92805 714-772-3200
Web: www.bellpipe.com

Bell Products Inc 722 Soscol Ave .... Napa CA 94559 707-255-1811
Web: www.bellproducts.com

Benjamin Manufacturing
3215 S Sweetwater Rd .... Lithia Springs GA 30122 770-941-1433
Web: www.benjaminmfg.com

Phone Fax

BERG Chilling Systems Inc 51 Nantucket Blvd .... Toronto ON M1P2N5 416-755-2221
Web: www.berg-group.com

Bernsohn & Fetner LLC 625 W 51st St .... New York NY 10019 212-315-4330
Web: bfbuilding.com

Best Plumbing Tile & Stone 49 Rt 138 .... Somers NY 10589 914-232-2020
Web: www.bestplg.com

BG National Plumbing & Heating
200 Montrose Rd .... Westbury NY 11590 516-334-8282
Web: www.bgnational.com

BIOgroupUSA Inc 1059 Broadwy Ste F .... Dunedin FL 34698 727-789-1646
Web: www.biobagusa.com

Blauch Bros Inc 911 Chicago Ave .... Harrisonburg VA 22802 540-434-2589
TF: 888-881-3939 ■ *Web:* blauchbrothers.com

Blue Mountain Air Inc 707 Aldridge Rd .... Vacaville CA 95688 800-889-2085
Web: www.bluemountainair.net

Blue Sky Energy Inc 2598 Fortune Way Ste K .... Vista CA 92081 760-597-1642
Web: www.blueskyenergyinc.com

Boda Plumbing Inc 1909 Tower Industrial Dr .... Monroe NC 28110 704-291-9097
Web: www.bodaplumbing.com

Boland 30 W Watkins Mill Rd .... Gaithersburg MD 20878 240-306-3000
Web: www.boland.com

Boykin Contracting Inc 167 Lott Ct .... West Columbia SC 29169 803-926-4930
Web: www.boykinusa.com

Brennan J m Inc 2101 W Saint Paul Ave .... Milwaukee WI 53233 414-342-3829
Web: www.jmbrennan.com

Broadway Mechanical 873 81st Ave .... Oakland CA 94621 510-746-4000
TF: 800-862-4930 ■ *Web:* www.broadwaymechanical.com

Brower Mechanical Inc 4060 Alvis Ct .... Rocklin CA 95677 916-624-0808
TF: 800-360-9276 ■ *Web:* www.browermechanical.com

C & C Boiler Sales & Service Inc
3401 Rotary Dr .... Charlotte NC 28269 704-597-0003
Web: www.ccboiler.com

C H Garmong & Son Inc 3050 Poplar St .... Terre Haute IN 47803 812-234-3714
TF: 800-894-2962 ■ *Web:* www.garmong.net

Cambridgeport Air Systems Eight Fanaras Dr .... Salisbury MA 01952 978-465-8481
TF: 877-648-2872 ■ *Web:* www.cambridgeport.net

Can-am Plumbing Inc 151 Wyoming St .... Pleasanton CA 94566 925-846-1833
TF: 800-786-9797 ■ *Web:* www.canamplumbing.com

Can-Eng Furnaces International Ltd
6800 Montrose Rd PO Box 628 .... Niagara Falls ON L2E6V5 905-356-1327
Web: www.can-eng.com

Canyon Air Service Inc 416 S Vermont Ave .... Glendora CA 91741 626-339-3777
Web: canyonair.com

Carlo Doria Plbg & Htg Plumbr
23 Waterhouse Rd .... Cape Elizabeth ME 04107 207-799-0066

Carrier Interamerica 3450 NW 115th Ave .... Miami FL 33178 305-590-1000
Web: www.carriercca.com

Casto Technical Services Inc
540 Leon Sullivan Way .... Charleston WV 25301 304-346-0549
Web: castotech.com

Catalina Mechanical Contracting Inc
2702 S Alvernon Way .... Tucson AZ 85713 520-745-3000
Web: www.btucson.com

Cecchin Plumbing & Heating Inc
4N275 Cavalry Dr .... Bloomingdale IL 60108 630-529-4046
Web: cecchin-inc.com

Century Mechanical Contractors Inc
3008 Wichita Ct .... Fort Worth TX 76140 817-293-3803
Web: www.centurymech.com

Certified Plumbing of Brevard
1401 Pennykamp St Ne .... Palm Bay FL 32907 321-676-0812
Web: www.certpah.com

Cfi Mechanical Inc 6109 Brittmoore Rd .... Houston TX 77041 832-467-8200 467-8203
Web: cfimechanical.com

CJ Erickson Plumbing Co 4141 W 124th Pl .... Alsip IL 60803 708-371-4900
Web: www.cjerickson.com

Clarke & Rush Mechanical Inc
4411 Auburn Blvd .... Sacramento CA 95841 916-609-2665
Web: clarke-rush.com

Claybar Constracting Inc 424 Macnab St .... Dundas ON L9H2L3 905-627-8000
TF: 866-801-9305 ■ *Web:* www.claybar.ca

ClimateCraft Inc 518 N Indiana Ave .... Oklahoma City OK 73106 405-415-9230
Web: www.climatecraft.com

CMS Mechanical Services Inc
609 Technology Cir Ste A .... Windsor CO 80550 970-686-6800
Web: mechanicalservicesco.com/

Cole Industrial Inc 5924 203rd St SW .... Lynnwood WA 98036 425-774-6602
Web: www.coleindust.com

Colite International Ltd
Five Technology Cir .... Columbia SC 29203 803-926-7926
Web: www.colite.com

Combined Refrigeration Resources Inc
1118 First St .... Humble TX 77338 281-540-7552
Web: www.combinedrefrigeration.com

Comprehensive Energy Services Inc
777 Bennett Dr .... Longwood FL 32750 407-682-1313
Web: www.cesmechanical.com

Computerworks Technologies
711 S Victory Blvd .... Burbank CA 91502 818-244-4484
Web: www.computerworkstech.com

Concepts Av Integration 3712 S 132nd St .... Omaha NE 68144 402-298-5011
Web: www.conceptsav.com

Continental Fire Sprinkler Co 4518 S 133rd St .... Omaha NE 68137 402-330-5170
TF: 800-543-5170 ■ *Web:* www.continental-fire.com

Convoy Servicing Company Inc 3323 Jane Ln .... Dallas TX 75247 214-638-3050
Web: www.convoyservicing.com

Conway Services LLC 6426 Summer Gale .... Memphis TN 38134 901-384-3511
Web: www.conwayservices.net

Cool Check Air Conditioning
4-25 Coronet Rd .... Etobicoke ON M8Z2L8 416-236-1000
Web: coolcheck.ca

Couts Heating & Cooling Inc 1693 Rimpau Ave .... Corona CA 92881 951-278-5560
Web: www.couts.com

Phone | Fax

Cregger Company Inc 629 12th St Extn .... West Columbia SC 29169 803-791-5195
Web: www.creggercompany.com
Crosby-brownlie Inc 100 Nassau St .... Rochester NY 14605 585-325-1290
Web: crosbybrownlie.com
Crossland Mechanical Inc
237 W 37th St Rm 400 ....New York NY 10018 212-719-5330
Web: www.crosslandmech.com
Custom Air 6384 Tower Ln .... Sarasota FL 34240 941-371-0833
Web: www.customairinc.com
D V Brown & Assoc Inc 567 Vickers St Ste 2 ....Tonawanda NY 14150 716-695-5533
Web: www.dvbrown.com
D'Onofrio General Contractors Corp
202 28th St.................................... Brooklyn NY 11232 718-832-5700
Web: donofrio.biz
D'vontz 7208 E 38th St .... Tulsa OK 74145 918-622-3600
TF: 877-322-3600 ■ *Web:* www.dvontz.com
Dacon Corp 16 Huron Dr............................ Natick MA 01760 508-651-3600
Web: www.dacon1.com
Dallago Corp 2411 E Aztec Ave........................ Gallup NM 87301 505-722-6638 863-9433
Danamark Watercare Ltd 2-90 Walker Dr............Brampton ON L6T4H6 888-326-2627
Web: danamark.com
David Boland Inc
219 Indian River Ave Ste 201 .... Titusville FL 32796 321-269-1345
Web: www.dboland.com
DCM Manufacturing Inc 4540 W 160th St........... Cleveland OH 44135 216-265-8006
Web: www.dcm-mfg.com
Delhur Industries Inc
4333 Tumwater Truck Rte .... Port Angeles WA 98363 360-457-1133
Web: delhur.com
DeVincenzi Metal Products Inc
1655 Rollins Rd .... Burlingame CA 94010 650-692-5800
Web: www.devmetal.com
Devore & Johnson Inc 176 Forest Pkwy............ Forest Park GA 30297 404-366-4243
Web: devoreandjohnson.com
Dispensing Dynamics International
1020 Bixby Dr.............................. City of Industry CA 91745 626-961-3691 330-5266
TF: 800-888-3698 ■ *Web:* www.dispensingdynamics.com
Dominion Energy Management 11250 Hopson Rd ..... Ashland VA 23005 804-798-3189
Web: www.demiva.com
Dominion Mechanical Contractors Inc
12329 Braddock Rd .... Fairfax VA 22030 703-992-9588
Web: dominion-mechanical.com
Donner Plumbing & Heating Inc
107 Candelaria Rd NW .... Albuquerque NM 87107 505-884-1017
Web: donnerplumbing.com
Dornbracht Americas Inc
1700 Executive Dr S Ste 600 .... Duluth GA 30096 800-774-1181
TF: 800-774-1181 ■ *Web:* www.dornbracht.com
Douglas Orr Plumbing Inc
301 Flagler Dr.............................Miami Springs FL 33166 305-887-1687
Web: www.orrplumbing.com
dPoint Technologies Inc 1275 Venables St.......... Vancouver BC V6A2E4 604-488-1132
Web: www.dpoint.ca
DRM LLC 520 Crews St .... Lawrenceburg TN 38464 931-766-4500
Web: www.drmcontrols.com
Duffey Southeast Inc 627 Minuet Ln Ste D .... Charlotte NC 28217 704-527-3612
Web: duffeyinc.com
Eastway Supplies Inc 1561 Alum Creek Dr .... Columbus OH 43209 614-252-0974
Web: www.eastwaysupplies.com
ECSM Utility Contractors Inc
1200 Walnut Bottom Rd Ste 101...................... Carlisle PA 17015 717-258-8001
Web: ecsminc.com
Eddie Johnson Private Contractor
5005 Creston St .... Hyattsville MD 20781 301-772-0466
Edward B O'reilly & Assoc Inc
30 W Highland Ave........................... Philadelphia PA 19118 215-242-8100
Web: www.eboreilly.com
Effective Solar Products LLC
601 Crescent Ave .... Lockport LA 70374 985-532-0800
TF: 888-824-0090 ■ *Web:* www.effectivesolar.com
Elmbrook Management Co 1908 12th Ave NW Ste E ... Ardmore OK 73401 580-226-3055
Web: www.elmbrookhomes.com
Enagic USA Inc 4115 Spencer St.....................Torrance CA 90503 310-542-7700
Web: www.enagic.com
Enerco 750 Third Ave 9th Fl ....New York NY 10017 212-572-0783
Web: www.ener.co
Energy Air Inc 5401 Energy Air Ct.................... Orlando FL 32810 407-886-3729
Web: www.energyair.com
Energy Inspectors 8515 Edna Ave.................. Las Vegas NV 89117 702-365-8080
Web: www.energyinspectors.com
Equiptec Mechanical Inc
523 Capitola Ave Ste B.............................Capitola CA 95010 831-462-9511
Ez-flo International Inc 2750 E Mission Blvd .... Ontario CA 91761 909-947-5256 827-3012*
**Fax Area Code: 866 ■ Web:* www.ez-flo.net
F & G Mechanical Corp 348 New County Rd ....Secaucus NJ 07094 201-864-3580
Web: www.fgmech.com
Falasca Mechanical Inc 3329 N Mill Rd............ Vineland NJ 08360 856-794-2010
Web: www.falascamechanical.com
Federal Heating & Engineering Company Inc
160 Cross St................................. Winchester MA 01890 781-245-0185
Ferguson Enterprises Inc 57-22 49th St............ Maspeth NY 11378 718-937-9500
Web: ferguson.com/davis-and-warshow
Ferrandino & Son Inc 71 Carolyn Blvd............ Farmingdale NY 11735 516-735-0097
TF: 866-571-4609 ■ *Web:* www.ferrandinoandson.com
Finken Plumbing Heating & Cooling
628 19th Ave NE............................. Saint Joseph MN 56374 320-258-2005 258-2006
TF: 877-346-5367 ■ *Web:* www.finkens.com
Fire Fighter Sales & Service Co
791 Commonwealth Dr.......................... Warrendale PA 15086 724-720-6000 287-4926
TF: 888-412-3473 ■ *Web:* www.firefighter-pgh.com
Fitzgerald Electro-mechanical Company Inc
Six S Linden Ave Ste 4 ....South San Francisco CA 94080 650-589-9935
Web: www.fitzgeraldemco.com

Phone | Fax

Florestone Products Company Inc
2851 Falcon Dr.. Madera CA 93637 559-661-4171 661-2070
TF: 800-446-8827 ■ *Web:* www.florestone.com
Florida Cooling Supply Inc
1954 Carroll St.................................Clearwater FL 33765 727-449-1230
Web: www.flcoolingsupply.com
Florida Industrial Products Inc 1602 N 39th St......... Tampa FL 33605 813-247-5356
Web: www.fiponline.com
Florida Mechanical LLC 3615 Fiscal Ct...........Riviera Beach FL 33404 561-863-3606
Web: www.flamech.com
Fluid Conditioning Products Inc
Kleine & Warwick Sts................................ Lititz PA 17543 717-627-1550
Web: www.fcp-filters.com
Food Service Technologies Inc
5256 Eisenhower Ave............................Alexandria VA 22304 703-354-3835
Web: www.mytech24.com
Ford Meter Box Company Inc, The
775 Manchester Ave PO Box 443.......................Wabash IN 46992 260-563-3171
Web: www.fordmeterbox.com
Freedom Fire Pro LLC 811 Lester Ln ....Rogers AR 72756 479-631-6363
Web: www.freefirepro.com
Freeland Contracting 2100 Integrity Dr S .... Columbus OH 43209 614-443-2718
Web: freelandcontracting.com
Freitag Weinhardt Inc 5900 N 13th St............. Terre Haute IN 47805 812-466-9861
Web: www.freitaginc.com
Fresh Meadow Mechanical Corp
65-01 Fresh Meadow Ln.......................Fresh Meadows NY 11365 718-961-6634
Web: www.fmmcorp.com
Frigel North America Inc
150 Prairie Lk Rd .... East Dundee IL 60118 847-540-0160
Web: www.frigel.com
Frontier Mechanical Inc
2771 W Mansfield Ave ....Englewood CO 80110 303-806-5400
Web: www.frontiermechanicalinc.com
Fujitsu General America Inc 353 Rt 46 W ....Fairfield NJ 07004 973-575-0380
TF: 888-888-3424 ■ *Web:* www.fujitsugeneral.com
Galapagos Partners LP 55 Waugh Dr Ste 1130.........Houston TX 77007 713-803-4326
Web: www.gplp.com
Garden City Plumbing & Heating Inc
4025 Flynn Ln .... Missoula MT 59808 406-728-5550
Web: www.gardencityplumbing.com
Gateway Pacific Contractors Inc
8055 Freeport Blvd.............................Sacramento CA 95832 916-665-4100
Web: www.chinachef.com
GEM Technologies Inc 2033 Castaic Ln............. Knoxville TN 37932 865-560-9434
Web: www.gemserve.com
Gemini Industries Inc
200 Wheeler Rd N Tower......................... Burlington MA 01803 781-203-0100
Web: www.gemini-ind.com
Gilbert Plumbing Co 254 S Mesa Dr................... Mesa AZ 85210 480-834-1188
Web: gilbertplumbingllc.com
Gill Mike Pluming & Heating 46 Temi Rd .... Hudson MA 01749 978-568-8086
Web: mikegillplumbing.com
Greenberry Industrial
2273 NW Professional Dr......................... Corvallis OR 97330 541-757-8458
Web: www.greenberry.com
Groeniger & Company Inc
27750 Industrial Blvd .... Hayward CA 94545 510-786-3333
Web: www.groeniger.com
Groth Gates Heating & Sheet Metal Inc
2614 SE Hwy 101...............................Lincoln City OR 97367 541-994-2631
Web: www.grothgates.com
Guaranteed Industries Ltd 5420 Rue Pare .... Montreal QC H4P1R3 514-342-3400
Web: www.guaranteedindustries.com
Gulf Breeze News Inc
913 Gulf Breeze Pkwy Ste 35 .... Gulf Breeze FL 32561 850-932-8986
Web: news.gulfbreezenews.com
Haller Enterprises Inc 212 Bucky Dr .... Lititz PA 17543 717-625-1500
Web: www.hallerent.com
Halvorson Trane 2220 Nw 108Th St .... Clive IA 50325 515-270-0004
Web: www.halvorsontrane.com
Hansen Mechanical Contractors Inc
4580 W Post Rd .... Las Vegas NV 89118 702-361-5111
Web: www.hansenmechanical.com
Harrison Orr Air Conditioning LLC
4100 N Walnut ....Oklahoma City OK 73105 405-528-3333
Web: www.harrisonorr.com
HBD Industries Inc 5200 Upper Metro Pl Ste 110 .... Dublin OH 43017 614-526-7000
Web: www.hbdindustries.com
Healy Systems Inc 3760 Marsh Rd .... Madison WI 53718 608-838-8786
Web: www.franklinfueling.com
Heat Transfer Products Group LLC
201 Thomas French Dr..........................Scottsboro AL 35769 256-259-7400
Web: www.htpgusa.com
HelioPower Inc 25767 Jefferson Ave..................Murrieta CA 92562 951-677-7755
Web: www.heliopower.com
Herrman & Goetz Inc 225 S Lafayette Blvd.......... South Bend IN 46601 574-282-2596
Web: www.hgservices.com
High Tech Fire Protection Company Inc
84 Hackett Mills Rd ....Poland ME 04274 207-998-2551
Hospitality Investments LP
16114 E Indiana Ave Ste 200 .... Spokane Valley WA 99216 509-928-3736
Web: www.hospitalityassociates.com
Housh-the Home Energy Experts
225 American Way .... Monroe OH 45050 513-793-6374
Web: www.houshhomeenergy.com
HPI LLC 15503 W Hardy Rd ....Houston TX 77060 713-457-7500
Web: www.hpi-llc.com
Hussung Mechanical Contractors
6913 Enterprise Dr Ste B ....Louisville KY 40214 502-375-3500
Web: www.hussung.com

Company / Address	City	State	Zip	Phone	Fax
Illingworth Engineering Co 6855 Phillips Pkwy Dr S *Web:* boiler.publishpath.com/	Jacksonville	FL	32256	904-262-4700	
IMA LIFE North America Inc 2175 Military Rd *Web:* www.ima.it	Tonawanda	NY	14150	716-695-6354	
Imperial Manufacturing Group Inc 40 Industrial Park St *Web:* www.imperialgroup.ca	Richibucto	NB	E4W4A4	506-523-9117	
Imperial Mechanical Inc 30685 Solon Industrial Pkwy *Web:* www..imperialhvac.com	Solon	OH	44139	440-498-1788	
Industrial Ventilation Inc W6395 Speciality Dr *Web:* www.ivinc.com	Greenville	WI	54942	920-757-6001	
Infinity Contractors International Ltd 2563 E Loop 820 N *Web:* www.infinitycontractors.com	Fort Worth	TX	76118	817-838-8700	
Ingenuity Ieq 3600 Centennial Dr *TF:* 800-669-9726 ■ *Web:* www.ingenuityieq.com	Midland	MI	48642	989-496-2233	
IO Environmental & Infrastructure Inc 2840 Adams Ave Ste 301 *Web:* ioenvironmental.com	San Diego	CA	92116	619-280-3278	
Iron City Pipe & Supply 330 E Broadway St *Web:* ironcitypipe.com	Jackson	OH	45640	740-286-8080	
J C Wilkins Plumbing Company Inc 840 Massengill Pond Rd	Angier	NC	27501	919-639-6201	
J Lorber Company Inc 2659 Bristol Pk *Web:* www.jlorber.com	Bensalem	PA	19020	215-638-2300	
James Lane Air Conditioning Company Inc 5024 Old Jacksboro Hwy *Web:* www.jameslane.com	Wichita Falls	TX	76302	940-766-0244	
Jem Group LLC 509 N Second St *Web:* www.jemgroup.net	Harrisburg	PA	17101	717-238-7709	
Jestar Plumbing & Heating 23130 Ridge Rd	Germantown	MD	20876	301-353-1841	
Jet Industries Inc 1935 Silverton Rd NE PO Box 7362 *TF:* 800-659-0620 ■ *Web:* www.jetindustries.net	Salem	OR	97303	503-363-2334	
Johnson & Jordan Inc 18 Mussey Rd *Web:* johnsonandjordan.net	Scarborough	ME	04074	207-883-8345	
Johnson March Systems Inc 220 Railroad Dr *Web:* www.johnsonmarch.com	Ivyland	PA	18974	215-364-2500	
Jones Stephens Corp 3249 Moody Pkwy *Web:* www.jonesstephens.com	Moody	AL	35004	205-640-7200	
K & s Air Conditioning Inc 143 E Meats Ave *Web:* www.kandsair.com	Orange	CA	92865	714-685-0077	
K Bell Plumbing & Heating Inc 3476 West 4600 South *Web:* kbellplumbingandfire.com	West Haven	UT	84401	801-731-6886	
Kansas Building Systems Inc 1701 SW 41st St *Web:* kbsci.com	Topeka	KS	66609	785-266-4222	
Kazal Fire Protection Inc 3499 E 34th St *Web:* kazalfire.com	Tucson	AZ	85713	520-323-1518	
Kbaer Design Center 1020 Michigan Ave *Web:* dmplbg.com	Sheboygan	WI	53081	920-452-9666	
Kiewit Energy Co 10740 N Gessner Rd Ste 400 *Web:* kiewit.com	Houston	TX	77064	281-517-8900	517-8910
Kinetics Mechanical Service Inc 6691 Brisa St *TF:* 866-567-7378 ■ *Web:* www.kms-inc.com	Livermore	CA	94550	925-245-6200	
KITCO Fiber Optics Inc 5269 Cleveland St *TF:* 866-643-5220 ■ *Web:* www.kitcofo.com	Virginia Beach	VA	23462	757-518-8100	
Kliemann Bros Heating & Air Conditioning Inc 4703 116th St E *Web:* kliemannbros.com	Tacoma	WA	98446	253-537-0655	
Kohler Canada Company Hytec Plumbing Products Div 4150 Spallumcheen Dr *TF:* 800-871-8311 ■ *Web:* www.hytec.ca	Armstrong	BC	V0E1B6	250-546-3067	546-3170
Konarka Technologies Inc 116 John St Third Fl Ste 12 *Web:* www.konarkatech.com	Lowell	MA	01852	978-569-1400	
Krystal Klear Water Systems 10502 W 150th St *Web:* krystalklearh2o.com	Overland Park	KS	66221	913-897-6571	
Kuck Mechanical Contractors Inc 395 W 67th St PO Box 388 *Web:* www.kuckmechanical.com	Loveland	CO	80538	970-461-3553	
Kysor Warren Corp 5201 Transport Blvd *Web:* www.kysorwarren.com	Columbus	GA	31907	706-568-1514	
L B Plastics Inc PO Box 907 *TF:* 800-752-7739 ■ *Web:* www.lbplastics.com	Mooresville	NC	28115	704-663-1543	664-2989
Lawrence Green Fire Protection 18323 Weaver St	Detroit	MI	48228	313-835-5800	
Leduc & Dexter Inc 2833A Dowd Dr PO Box 11157 *Web:* www.ldplumb.com	Santa Rosa	CA	95406	707-575-1500	
Lescure Company Inc 3667 Mt Diablo Blvd PO Box 968 *Web:* www.lescurecompany.com	Lafayette	CA	94549	925-283-2528	
Little Caesars Pizza 2524 Third Line *Web:* littlecaesars.ca	Oakville	ON	L6M4Y7	905-825-0199	
Lochard Inc 903 Wapakoneta Ave *Web:* www.lochard-inc.com	Sidney	OH	45365	937-492-8811	
Louden Tunneling Company Inc 103 Shaw Rd	Sterling	VA	20166	703-450-5656	
Love Heating & Air Conditioning Inc 4115 E 10th St *Web:* love-hvac.com	Indianapolis	IN	46201	317-353-2141	
Luminalt Energy Corp 1320 Potrero Ave *Web:* www.luminalt.com	San Francisco	CA	94110	415-641-4000	
Lunseth Plumbing & Heating Co 1710 N Washington St *Web:* www.dakotafire.com	Grand Forks	ND	58203	701-772-6631	
Luppen & Hawley Inc 7400 14th Ave *Web:* www.luppenandhawleyinc.com	Sacramento	CA	95820	916-456-7831	
Lute Plumbing Supply Inc 3920 US Hwy 23 *Web:* www.lutesupply.com	Portsmouth	OH	45662	740-353-7638	
M Davis & Sons Inc 19 Germay Dr *Web:* www.mdavisinc.com	Wilmington	DE	19804	302-998-3385	
M&M Refrigeration Inc 412 Railroad Ave *Web:* www.mmrefrigeration.com	Federalsburg	MD	21632	410-754-8005	
Maax Corp 160 St Joseph Blvd *TF:* 888-957-7816 ■ *Web:* www.maax.com	Lachine	QC	H8S2L3	877-438-6229	
Maax Spas (Arizona) Inc 25605 S Arizona Ave *Web:* www.colemanspas.com	Chandler	AZ	85248	480-895-0598	
Madison Mechanical Inc 1539 Fannie Dorsey Rd *Web:* www.madisonmechanical.net	Sykesville	MD	21784	410-461-7301	
Maintenx 2202 N Howard Ave *TF:* 855-751-0075 ■ *Web:* www.mainten-x.com	Tampa	FL	33607	813-254-1656	915-5582
Mallick Plumbing & Heating 8010 Cessna Ave *Web:* www.mallickplumbing.com	Gaithersburg	MD	20879	301-840-5860	
Mark Harris Plumbing Company Inc 1830 Gillespie Way Ste 104 *Web:* mhp-co.com	El Cajon	CA	92020	619-596-9470	
Marquee Fire Protection 710 W Stadium Ln *Web:* www.marqueefire.com	Sacramento	CA	95834	916-641-7997	
Marvin Groves Electric Company Inc 506 Seventh St *Web:* www.marvingroveselectric.com	Wichita Falls	TX	76301	940-767-2711	
Matco-Norca Inc Rt 22 *TF:* 800-431-2082 ■ *Web:* www.matco-norca.com	Brewster	NY	10509	845-278-7570	
Matherly Mechanical Contractors LLC 1520 Ocama Blvd PO Box 30889 *Web:* www.matherlymech.com	Midwest City	OK	73140	405-737-3488	
Matthews Mfg 41 Branch St *Web:* www.matthewsmfg.net	Saint Louis	MO	63147	314-231-4900	
Mckenneys Air Conditioning Inc 2323 R St *Web:* mckenneysair.com	Bakersfield	CA	93301	661-327-4037	
McLain Plumbing & Electrical Service Inc 107 Magnolia St *Web:* www.mclaininc.com	Philadelphia	MS	39350	601-656-6333	
Mechanical Design Systems Inc 6302 Aaron Ln *Web:* www.mds-hvac.com	Clinton	MD	20735	301-877-9600	
Mechanical Services Inc 400 Presumpscot St *Web:* www.mechanicalservices.com	Portland	ME	04103	207-774-1531	
Mechanical Systems of Dayton 4401 Springfield St *Web:* www.msdinc.net	Dayton	OH	45431	937-254-3235	
Meckley Services Inc 5701 General Washington Dr Ste O *TF:* 877-632-5539 ■ *Web:* www.meckleyservices.com	Alexandria	VA	22312	703-333-2040	
Meier Supply Company Inc 530 Bloomingburg Rd *TF:* 800-418-3216 ■ *Web:* www.meiersupply.com	Middletown	NY	10940	845-733-5666	
Mesa Mechanical Inc 3514 Pinemont Dr *Web:* www.mesamechanical.com	Houston	TX	77018	713-681-5300	681-6675
Metro Hvac Mechanical Contractor Inc 7802 Norris Fwy	Knoxville	TN	37938	865-922-5912	
Metro Mechanical Contractors Inc 1200 SW 24th St	Newcastle	OK	73065	405-387-3930	
MG Mechanical Contracting Inc 1513 Lamb Rd *Web:* www.mgmechanical.com	Woodstock	IL	60098	815-334-9450	
Michels Plumbing & Heating 36352 Priestap St	Richmond	MI	48062	586-727-4636	
Miller Bonded Inc 4538 Mcleod Rd Ne *Web:* millerbonded.com	Albuquerque	NM	87109	505-881-0220	
Modern Controls Inc Seven Bellecor Dr *Web:* www.moderncontrols.com	New Castle	DE	19720	302-325-6800	
Mohr Power Solar Inc 1452 Pomona Rd *TF:* 800-637-6527 ■ *Web:* www.mohrpower.com	Corona	CA	92882	951-736-2000	
Monona Plumbing & Fire Protection Inc 3126 Watford Way *Web:* www.mononapfp.com	Madison	WI	53713	608-273-4556	
Monroe Energy Complex 208 Cherry Hill Rd	Monroe	GA	30656	770-207-5456	
Moss & Assoc 3019 SW 27th Ave Ste 202 *Web:* mosscm.com	Ocala	FL	34471	352-291-2940	
Mtech Mechanical Technologies Group Inc 12300 Pecos St *Web:* www.mtechg.com	Westminster	CO	80234	303-650-4000	
Nading Mechanical Inc 11673 N County Rd 775 E *Web:* nadingmechanicalinc.com	Hope	IN	47246	812-546-6111	
Nailor Industries Inc 98 Toryork Rd *Web:* www.map-hvac.com	Toronto	ON	M9L1X6	416-744-3300	744-3360
National Meter & Automation 7220 S Fraser St *TF:* 877-212-8340 ■ *Web:* www.nmaai.com	Centennial	CO	80112	303-339-9100	649-1017
National Office Systems Inc 7621 Rickenbacker Dr Ste 400 *Web:* nosinc.com	Gaithersburg	MD	20879	301-840-6264	
Neese Jones Heating & Air Conditioning I 1120 Alpha Dr *Web:* www.neesejones.com	Alpharetta	GA	30004	678-392-3381	
Nelson's Plumbing & Electric Inc 25269 Us Hwy 12 *Web:* nelsonsplumbingandelectric.com	Tomah	WI	54660	608-372-5469	
New Generation Mechanical 1133 Empire Central Dr *TF:* 877-235-5898 ■ *Web:* www.newgenm.com	Dallas	TX	75247	972-830-9900	830-9993
NextEnergy Inc 35 Earl Martin Dr **Fax Area Code: 877* ■ *Web:* www.nextenergy.ca	Elmira	ON	N3B3L4	519-669-2707	684-3112*
North South Supply Inc 686 Third Pl *Web:* www.northsouth.net	Vero Beach	FL	32962	772-569-3810	
Noveo Technologies Inc 9655 A Ignace St *TF:* 877-314-2044 ■ *Web:* www.noveo.ca	Brossard	QC	J4Y2P3	450-444-2044	

Company / Address	City	State	Zip	Phone	Fax
Nupla Corp 11912 Sheldon St	Sun Valley	CA	91352	818-768-6800	546-8752*
*Fax Area Code: 800 ■ *TF:* 800-872-7661 ■ *Web:* www.nuplacorp.com					
O&M Industries Inc 5901 Ericson Way	Arcata	CA	95521	707-822-8800	
Web: www.omindustries.com					
Ontario Refrigeration Service 635 S Mountain Ave	Ontario	CA	91762	909-984-2771	
Web: www.ontariorefrigeration.com					
Oswald Company Inc 8549 Montgomery Rd Ste 3	Cincinnati	OH	45236	513-793-8080	
Web: www.oswaldco.com					
OZZ Corp 20 Floral Pkwy	Concord	ON	L4K4R1	905-669-6223	
Web: www.ozzcorp.com					
Padgett Business Services LLC 140 Mtn Brook Dr	Canton	GA	30115	770-345-6100	
Web: www.padgettservices.com					
Palmer-christiansen Company Inc 2510 South West Temple	Salt Lake City	UT	84115	801-466-1679	
Web: palmerchris.com					
Parris & Assoc Inc 480 Turnpike St Ste 1	South Easton	MA	02375	508-230-0255	
Web: www.parrisandassociates.com					
Patriot Fire Protection Inc 2707 70th Ave E	Fife	WA	98424	253-926-2290	
Web: www.patriotfire.com					
Pedal Valves Inc 13625 River Rd	Luling	LA	70070	985-785-9997	
Web: pedalvalve.com					
Perfection Group Inc 2649 Commerce Blvd	Cincinnati	OH	45241	513-772-7545	
Web: perfectiongroup.com					
Performance Pulsation Control Inc 1325 19th St Ste 2b	Plano	TX	75074	972-633-8600	
Web: www.performancepulsation.com					
Performance Water Products Inc 6902 Aragon Cir	Buena Park	CA	90620	714-736-0137	
Web: www.pwqa.org					
Phybridge Inc 3495 Laird Rd Ste 12	Mississauga	ON	L5L5S5	905-901-3633	
TF: 888-901-3633 ■ *Web:* www.phybridge.com					
Pilot Contracting Corp 1452 Donaldson Hwy	Erlanger	KY	41018	859-525-8585	
Web: www.pilotbuilds.com					
Plumbing Concepts Inc 22951 La Palma Ave	Yorba Linda	CA	92887	714-694-1509	
Web: www.plumbingconcepts.com					
Pmc Mechanical Contractors Inc 15 S Ridge Ave	Ambler	PA	19002	215-628-3806	
Web: mcaepa.org					
PolyJohn Enterprises Corp 2500 Gaspar Ave	Whiting	IN	46394	219-659-1152	
Web: www.polyjohn.com					
Prier Products Inc 4515 E 139th St	Grandview	MO	64030	816-763-4100	
Web: www.prier.com					
Progressive Plumbing Inc 1064 W Hwy 50	Clermont	FL	34711	352-394-7171	
Web: progressiveplumbing.com					
PSF Mechanical Inc 9322 14th Ave S	Seattle	WA	98108	206-764-9663	
Web: www.psfmech.com					
Pumping Solutions Inc 2850 W 139th St Ste A	Blue Island	IL	60406	708-272-1800	272-1825
Web: www.pump.ws					
Pyron Solar Inc 1216 Liberty Way Ste A	Vista	CA	92081	760-599-5100	
Web: www.pyronsolar.com					
Quality Sprinkler Company Inc 10301 Old Concord Rd	Charlotte	NC	28213	704-549-8220	
Web: www.qualitysprinkler.com					
R J Lanthier Company Inc 485 Corporate Dr	Escondido	CA	92029	760-738-9798	
Web: www.rjlincco.com					
Rabe Environmental Systems Inc 2300 W 23 St	Erie	PA	16506	814-456-5374	
Web: www.rabehvac.com					
RASIRC Inc 7815 Silverton Ave	San Diego	CA	92126	858-259-1220	
Web: www.rasirc.com					
RCR Plumbing & Mechanical Inc 12620 Magnolia Ave	Riverside	CA	92503	951-371-5000	
Web: www.ampam.com					
Regency Fire Protection Inc 6925 Farmdale Ave	North Hollywood	CA	91605	818-982-0126	
Web: www.regencyfire.com					
Reliance Heating & Air Conditioning Inc 1694 Hwy 138 Ne	Conyers	GA	30013	770-483-3850	
Web: www.reliance-hvac.com					
Remtec International 1100 Haskins Rd	Bowling Green	OH	43402	419-867-8990	
Web: www.remtec.net					
Resin Systems Corp 62 Rt 101a Ste 1	Amherst	NH	03031	603-673-1234	673-4512
Web: www.resinsystems.com					
Rex Pipe & Supply Co 10311 Berea Rd	Cleveland	OH	44102	216-651-1900	
Web: www.rexpipe.com					
RF Macdonald Co 25920 Eden Landing Rd	Hayward	CA	94545	510-784-0110	
Web: www.rfmacdonald.com					
Richter & Ratner Contracting Corp 5505 Flushing Ave	Maspeth	NY	11378	718-497-1600	
Web: www.richterratner.com					
Rim Country Mechanical Inc 261 N Eighth St	Show Low	AZ	85901	928-537-1803	
Web: rimcountrymechanical.com					
RoboVent Products Group Inc 37900 Mound Rd	Sterling Heights	MI	48310	586-698-1800	
Web: www.robovent.com					
Rock City Mechanical Company LLC 2715 Grandview Ave	Nashville	TN	37211	615-251-3045	
Web: www.rcm-nashville.com					
Rohde Bros Inc W5745 Woodchuck Ln	Plymouth	WI	53073	920-893-5905	
Web: rohdebros.com					
Rolac Contracting Inc 1800 Valley St	Minot	ND	58701	701-839-6525	
Web: www.rolac-nd.com					
Rose Leonard & Sons Inc 212 Decatur St	Doylestown	PA	18901	215-345-9263	
Rowland Constructors 14811 N Kierland Blvd Ste 800	Scottsdale	AZ	85254	480-477-8300	
Web: www.rowlandconstructioncompany.com					
RS Harritan & Company Inc 3280 Formex Rd	Richmond	VA	23224	804-275-7821	
Web: www.rsharritan.com					
Ryan FireProtection Inc 9740 E 148th St	Noblesville	IN	46060	317-770-7100	
Web: www.indianasubcontractors.org					
S r C Refrigeration 6615 19 Mile Rd	Sterling Heights	MI	48314	586-254-0610	
Web: www.srcrefrigeration.com					
Salof Refrigeration Company Inc 1150 Schwab Rd	New Braunfels	TX	78132	830-625-1613	
Samuel t Wood Co 2704 Cedar Dr	Riva	MD	21140	410-798-7440	
Schuylerville Central School District 14-18 Spring St	Schuylerville	NY	12871	518-695-3255	
Web: www.schuylervilleschools.org					
SCI Infrastructure LLC 2825 S 154th St	Seatac,	WA	98188	206-242-0633	242-0792
TF: 800-255-0633 ■ *Web:* www.sciinfrastructure.com/					
Service Roundtable 131 W Main St	Lewisville	TX	75057	817-416-0978	
Web: www.serviceroundtable.com					
Shank Constructors Inc 3501 85Th Ave N	Minneapolis	MN	55443	763-424-8300	
Web: www.shankconstructors.com					
Shoffner Mechanical Industrial & Service Company Inc 3600 Papermill Dr	Knoxville	TN	37909	865-523-1129	
Web: skmes.com					
Solar Electric Systems 742 Hampshire Rd Ste A	Westlake Village	CA	91361	805-497-9808	
Web: www.solarelectricalsystems.com					
Solar Light Co Inc 100 E Glenside Ave	Glenside	PA	19038	215-517-8700	517-8747
Web: www.solarlight.com					
Solar Store LLC, The 2833 N Country Club Rd	Tucson	AZ	85716	520-322-5180	
Web: www.solarstore.com					
Spangler & Boyer Mechanical 5175 Commerce Dr	York	PA	17408	717-792-8854	
Web: www.spanglerboyer.com					
SSW Mechanical Inc Air Cond 670 S Oleander Rd	Palm Springs	CA	92264	760-325-6007	
Web: www.sswmechanical.com					
Standard Heating & Air Conditioning 1082 Payne Ave	Saint Paul	MN	55130	651-772-2449	
Web: www.standardheating.com					
Star Services 4663 Halls Mill Rd	Mobile	AL	36693	251-661-4050	
Web: www.star-service.com					
State Supply Co 597 Seventh St E	Saint Paul	MN	55130	651-774-5985	
TF: 877-775-7705 ■ *Web:* www.statesupply.com					
Stillwell Hansen Inc Three Fernwood Ave	Edison	NJ	08837	732-225-7474	
Web: www.stillwell-hansen.com					
Stouffer Mechanical Contractor LLC 2185 Carbaugh Ave	Chambersburg	PA	17201	717-262-0078	
Web: stouffermechanical.com					
Stutman Contracting Inc 22 Sutton Ave	Oxford	MA	01540	508-987-9472	
Web: stutmancontracting.com					
Summit Energy 4370 Dominion St	Burnaby	BC	V5G4L7	604-451-4466	
Sunforce Products Inc 9015 Ch Avon	Montreal-Ouest	QC	H4X2G8	514-989-2100	
Web: sunforceproducts.com					
Sunland Fire Protection Inc 1218 Elon Pl	High Point	NC	27263	336-886-7027	
Web: www.sunlandfire.com					
Sunstore Solar Energy Solutions 3090 S Hwy 14	Greer	SC	29650	864-297-6776	
TF: 800-571-8310 ■ *Web:* www.sunstoresolar.com					
Superior Alarms 600 Ash Ave	Mcallen	TX	78501	956-682-6005	630-2434
Web: www.superioralarms.com					
Superior Group Inc, The 8861 Elim St	Anchorage	AK	99507	907-349-6572	
Web: www.superiorpnh.com					
Suttles Plumbing & Mechanical Corp 21541 Nordhoff St Ste C	Chatsworth	CA	91311	818-718-9779	
Web: www.suttlesplumbing.com					
Syntrol Plumbing Heating Adn Air Inc 2120 March Rd	Roseville	CA	95747	916-772-5813	
Web: syntrol.net					
Tekmar Control Systems Ltd 5100 Silver Star Rd	Vernon	BC	V1B3K4	250-545-7749	545-0650
Web: www.tekmarcontrols.com					
Tezel & Cotter Air Conditioning Co 2730 Castroville Rd	San Antonio	TX	78237	210-734-5156	
Web: www.tezelandcotter.com					
Therma-Stor LLC 4201 Lien Rd	Madison	WI	53704	608-237-8400	
Web: www.thermastor.com					
Thermal Services Inc 13330 I St	Omaha	NE	68137	402-397-8100	
Web: www.thermalservices.com					
Thetford Corp 7101 Jackson Ave PO Box 1285	Ann Arbor	MI	48106	734-769-6000	769-2023
TF: 800-521-3032 ■ *Web:* www.thetford.com					
Thetford Corp Recreational Vehicle Group 2901 E Bristol St Ste B	Elkhart	IN	46514	574-266-7980	266-7984
TF: 800-831-1076 ■ *Web:* www.rvbusiness.com					
Thomas Partitions & Specialties Inc 4031 Verdugo Rd	Los Angeles	CA	90065	323-256-8666	
Thompson Industrial Services LLC 104 N Main	Sumter	SC	29150	803-773-8005	
TF: 800-849-8040 ■ *Web:* www.thompsonindustrialservices.com					
Tidewater Heating & Air Conditioning 150 Southern Blvd	Wilmington	NC	28401	910-343-1234	
Web: tidewaterac.com					
Tolin Mechanical Systems Co 12005 E 45th Ave	Denver	CO	80239	303-455-2825	
Web: www.tolin.com					
Total Energy Control Systems Inc 47-25 34th St Ste 4	Long Island City	NY	11101	718-247-2100	
Web: tecsystemsnyc.com					
Total Maintenance Solutions 3540 Rutherford Rd	Taylors	SC	29687	864-268-2891	
Web: www.tmssouth.com					
Total Plumbing Inc 12300 Pecos St	Westminster	CO	80234	303-393-7271	
Web: www.totalplbg.com					
Tri-state Fabricators Inc 1146 Ferris Rd	Amelia	OH	45102	513-752-5005	
TF: 888-523-1488 ■ *Web:* www.tristatefabricators.com					
Tri-state Home Services 1560 Tilco Dr Ste F	Frederick	MD	21704	301-624-5970	
Web: tri-statehomeservices.com					
Trilogy Plumbing Inc 184 E Liberty Ave	Anaheim	CA	92801	714-888-8575	
Web: www.cadlot.com					
Tru Flow Plumbing & Mechanical Inc 27893 Lenox Ave	Madison Heights	MI	48071	248-398-3560	
Tudi Mechanical Systems of Tampa Inc 343 Munson Ave	Mc Kees Rocks	PA	15136	412-771-4100	
TF: 877-367-8834 ■ *Web:* www.tudi.com					

	City	State	Zip	Phone	Fax
Tustin Mechanical Services Lehigh Valley LLC 2555 Industry Ln Ste B *Web:* www.tustinmechanical.com	Norristown	PA	19403	610-539-8200	
TWC Services Inc 2601 Bell Ave *Web:* www.twcservices.com	Des Moines	IA	50321	515-284-1911	
Tweet-Garot Mechanical Inc 2545 Larsen Rd *Web:* www.tweetgarot.com	Green Bay	WI	54307	920-498-0400	
Universal Air Conditioner Inc 1441 Heritage Pkwy *Web:* www.uacparts.com	Mansfield	TX	76063	817-740-3900	
Upchurch Plumbing Inc 2606 Baldwin Rd *Web:* www.upchurchplumbing.com	Greenwood	MS	38930	662-453-6860	
Velocity Futures LLC 5373 W Alabama St Ste 600 *Web:* www.velocityfutures.com	Houston	TX	77056	713-490-7600	
Ventrol Air Handling Systems Inc 9100 Rue Du Parcours *Web:* www.ventrol.com	Montreal	QC	H1J2Z1	514-354-7776	
Venture Mechanical Inc 2222 Century Cir *Web:* www.venturemech.com	Irving	TX	75062	972-871-1300	871-1301
Verigent LLC 149 Plantation Ridge Dr Ste 100 *TF:* 877-637-6422 ■ *Web:* www.verigent.com	Mooresville	NC	28117	704-658-3271	
Victory Energy Operations LLC 10701 E 126th St N *Web:* www.victoryenergyinc.com	Collinsville	OK	74021	918-274-0023	
Victory Heating & Air Conditioning Company Inc 115 Mendon St *Web:* www.victoryhvac.com	Bellingham	MA	02019	508-966-9858	
Vinotemp International Corp 16782 Von Karman Ave Ste 15 *Web:* www.vinotemp.com	Irvine	CA	92606	310-886-3332	
W O Blackstone & Company Inc 1841 Shop Rd *Web:* www.woblackstone.com	Columbia	SC	29202	803-252-8222	
Weldon Mechanical Corp 3428 W Pioneer Pkwy *Web:* www.weldon-contractors.com	Pantego	TX	76013	817-460-1111	460-3111
Westbrook Service Corp 1411 S Orange Blossom Trl *Web:* www.westbrookfl.com	Orlando	FL	32805	407-841-3310	
William Gotelli Plumbing Inc 21 Lovell Ave *Web:* www.gotelliplumbing.com	San Rafael	CA	94901	415-457-1145	
Winger Contracting Co 918 Hayne St *Web:* www.wingermechanical.com	Ottumwa	IA	52501	641-682-3407	
Wisco Supply Inc 815 S Saint Vrain St *TF:* 800-947-2689 ■ *Web:* www.wiscosupply.com	El Paso	TX	79901	915-544-8294	533-1804
Worly Plumbing Supply Inc 54 E Harrison St *Web:* worly.com	Delaware	OH	43015	740-363-1151	
WW Gay Fire & Integrated Systems Inc 522 Stockton St *Web:* www.wwgfp.com	Jacksonville	FL	32204	904-387-7973	
XL Technology Systems Inc 401 VFW Dr *Web:* www.xl-technology.com	Rockland	MA	02370	781-982-1220	
York Mahoning Mechanical Contrs Inc 724 Canfield Rd *Web:* yorkmahoning.com	Youngstown	OH	44511	330-788-7011	
Zampell Cos Nine Stanley Tucker Dr *TF:* 877-926-7355 ■ *Web:* www.zampell.com	Newburyport	MA	01950	978-465-0055	
Zehnder America Inc 540 Portsmouth Ave *TF:* 888-778-6701 ■ *Web:* www.zehnderamerica.com	Greenland	NH	03840	603-422-6700	
Zone Mechanical Inc 12539 Holiday Dr Ste A *Web:* www.zonemechanical.com	Alsip	IL	60803	708-388-1370	

614 PLUMBING FIXTURES & FITTINGS - VITREOUS CHINA & EARTHENWARE

	City	State	Zip	Phone	Fax
American Standard Cos Inc Bath & Kitchen Products Div One Centennial Ave PO Box 6820 *TF:* 800-442-1902 ■ *Web:* www.americanstandard-us.com	Piscataway	NJ	08855	800-442-1902	
Briggs Plumbing Products 300 Eagle Rd *TF:* 800-888-4458 ■ *Web:* www.briggsplumbing.com	Goose Creek	SC	29445	800-888-4458	627-4449
Eljer Inc 1 Centennial Ave *TF:* 800-442-1902 ■ *Web:* www.eljer.com	Piscataway	NJ	08855	800-442-1902	
Gerber Plumbing Fixtures LLC 2500 International Pkwy **Fax Area Code:* 514 ■ *TF:* 888-648-6466 ■ *Web:* www.gerberonline.com	Woodridge	IL	60517	888-648-6466	636-2021*
Kohler Plumbing North America 444 Highland Dr **Fax:* Sales ■ *TF:* 800-456-4537 ■ *Web:* www.us.kohler.com	Kohler	WI	53044	920-457-4441	459-1826*
Mansfield Plumbing Products Inc 150 E First St *TF:* 877-850-3060 ■ *Web:* www.mansfieldplumbing.com	Perrysville	OH	44864	419-938-5211	938-6234
Microphor Inc 452 E Hill Rd *TF Orders:* 800-358-8280 ■ *Web:* www.microphor.com	Willits	CA	95490	707-459-5563	459-6617
Norman Supply Co 825 SW Fifth St *Web:* www.morsco.com	Oklahoma City	OK	73109	405-235-9511	
Peerless Pottery Inc 319 S Fifth St **Fax Area Code:* 812 ■ *TF:* 800-457-5765 ■ *Web:* www.peerlesspottery.com	Rockport	IN	47635	800-457-5785	649-6429*
Sterling Plumbing 444 Highland Dr *TF Cust Svc:* 888-783-7546 ■ *Web:* www.sterlingplumbing.com	Kohler	WI	53044	920-457-4441	
Sunrise Specialty Co 930 98th Ave *TF:* 800-444-4280 ■ *Web:* www.sunrisespecialty.com	Oakland	CA	94603	510-729-7277	729-7270
Toto USA Inc 1155 Southern Rd **Fax:* Cust Svc ■ *TF:* 888-295-8134 ■ *Web:* www.totousa.com	Morrow	GA	30260	770-282-8686	282-8701*

615 PLUMBING, HEATING, AIR CONDITIONING EQUIPMENT & SUPPLIES - WHOL

SEE ALSO Refrigeration Equipment - Whol p. 3048

	City	State	Zip	Phone	Fax
A & B Pipe & Supply Inc 6500 Nw 37th Ave *Web:* www.abpipe.com	Miami	FL	33147	305-691-5000	
Aaron & Company Inc PO Box 8310 *TF:* 800-734-4822 ■ *Web:* www.aaronco.com	Piscataway	NJ	08855	732-752-8200	
AB Young Cos Inc 15305 Stony Creek Way *TF:* 800-886-7001 ■ *Web:* www.abyoung.com	Noblesville	IN	46060	317-565-5000	
ACR Group Inc 3200 Wilcrest Dr Ste 440 *Web:* www.acrgroup.com	Houston	TX	77042	713-780-8532	780-4067
Active Plumbing Supply Co 216 Richmond St *Web:* www.activeplumbing.com	Painesville	OH	44077	440-352-4411	352-0096
ADCO Companies LTD 3657 Pine Ln *Web:* www.adcoboiler.com	Bessemer	AL	35022	205-428-2326	
Advanced Modern Technologies Corp 6409 Independence Ave *Web:* www.amtcorporation.com	Woodland Hills	CA	91367	818-883-2682	
Advanced Solar Products Inc 270 S Main St Ste 203 *Web:* www.advancedsolarproducts.com	Flemington	NJ	08822	908-751-5818	
Air Monitor Corp 1050 Hopper Ave *TF:* 800-247-3569 ■ *Web:* www.airmonitor.com	Santa Rosa	CA	95403	707-544-2706	526-9970
Air Purchases Inc 24 Blanchard Rd *Web:* www.airpurchases.com	Burlington	MA	01803	781-273-2050	
Alltek Energy Systems 58 Hudson River Rd *Web:* www.alltekenergy.com	Waterford	NY	12188	518-238-2600	
Altmas Products 1201 Francisco St *Web:* www.altmansproducts.com	Torrance	CA	90502	310-559-4093	
American Backflow Specialties 3940 Home Ave *Web:* www.americanbackflow.com	San Diego	CA	92105	619-527-2525	
American Faucet & Coating Corp 3280 Corporate Vw *Web:* www.sigmafaucet.com	Vista	CA	92081	760-598-5895	
American Granby Inc 7652 Morgan Rd **Fax:* Acctg ■ *TF:* 800-776-2266 ■ *Web:* www.americangranby.com	Liverpool	NY	13090	315-451-1100	451-1876*
American Pipe & Supply Company Inc 4100 Eastlake Blvd *Web:* www.americanpipe-mt.com	Birmingham	AL	35217	205-252-9460	
Anderson Tube Company Inc 1400 Fairgrounds Rd *Web:* www.atube.com	Hatfield	PA	19440	215-855-0118	
Applied Membranes Inc 2325 Cousteau Ct *TF:* 800-321-9321 ■ *Web:* www.appliedmembranes.com	Vista	CA	92081	760-727-3711	727-4427
Applied Thermal Systems 8401 73rd Ave N Ste 74 *Web:* www.apptherm.com	Brooklyn Park	MN	55428	763-535-5545	
Arctic Combustion Ltd 2283 Argentia Rd Unit 25 *Web:* www.arctic-combustion.com	Mississauga	ON	L5N5Z2	905-858-4604	
Arizona Partsmaster Inc 7125 W Sherman St PO Box 23169 *TF:* 888-924-7278 ■ *Web:* www.azpartsmaster.com	Phoenix	AZ	85043	602-233-3580	233-3607
Arizona Wholesale Supply Co 2020 E University Dr *TF:* 866-977-6849 ■ *Web:* www.arizonawholesalesupply.com	Phoenix	AZ	85034	602-258-7901	258-8335
Atlas Heating & Vent Company Ltd 340 Roebling Rd *Web:* www.atlasheat.com	South San Francisco	CA	94080	650-873-7000	266-8079
Auburn Supply Co 3850 W 167th St *Web:* www.auburnsupply.com	Markham	IL	60428	708-596-9800	596-0981
BA Robinson Company Ltd 619 Berry St *Web:* www.barobinson.com	Winnipeg	MB	R3H0S2	204-784-0150	
Badger Plug Company Inc N1045 Technical Dr PO Box 199 *Web:* www.badgerplug.com	Greenville	WI	54942	920-757-7300	
Baker Distributing Co PO Box 2954 Ste 100 **Fax Area Code:* 904 ■ *TF:* 800-217-4698 ■ *Web:* www.bakerdist.com	Jacksonville	FL	32203	800-217-4698	407-8440*
Bardon Supplies Ltd 405 College St East PO Box 1023 *Web:* www.bardonsupplies.com	Belleville	ON	K8N4Z6	613-966-5643	
Barnett Inc 801 W Bay St *TF:* 888-803-4467 ■ *Web:* www.e-barnett.com	Jacksonville	FL	32204	904-384-6530	
Bartle & Gibson Company Ltd 13475 Ft Rd NW *Web:* www.bartlegibson.com	Edmonton	AB	T5A1C6	780-472-2850	
Barton Supply Inc 1260 Marlkress Rd *Web:* bartonsupply.com	Cherry Hill	NJ	08003	856-429-6500	
Bascom-turner Instrument 111 Downey St *Web:* www.bascomturner.com	Norwood	MA	02062	781-769-9660	
Bay Associates Group Inc 1432 Front Ave *Web:* www.bayassociates.com	Lutherville	MD	21093	410-825-6616	
Be-Cool Inc 310 Woodside Ave *Web:* www.becool.com	Essexville	MI	48732	989-895-9699	
Behler-Young Co 4900 Clyde Pk SW *Web:* www.behler-young.com	Grand Rapids	MI	49509	616-531-3400	531-1453
Best Plumbing Specialties 3039 Ventrie Ct *TF:* 800-448-6710 ■ *Web:* www.bestplumbingonline.com	Myersville	MD	21773	800-448-6710	
Bestwill Corp 439 Wald *Web:* bestwillcorp.com	Irvine	CA	92618	949-502-5700	
Biolonix Inc 4603 Triangle St *Web:* www.bioionix.com	Mcfarland	WI	53558	608-838-0300	
BJW Berghorst & Sons 11430 James St Ste A *Web:* www.berghorst.com	Holland	MI	49424	616-772-2114	
Blackman Plumbing Supply Company Inc 3480 Sunrise Hwy *Web:* www.blackman.com	Wantagh	NY	11793	516-785-6000	

Phone | Fax

Bob J Johnson & Associates Inc
16420 W Hardy Rd Ste 100 ... Houston TX 77060 281-873-5555
Web: www.bjja.com

Brock-McVey Co 1100 Brock-McVey Dr ... Lexington KY 40509 859-255-1412
Web: www.brockmcvey.com

Broedell Plumbing Supply Inc
1601 Commerce Ln ... Jupiter FL 33458 561-747-8000 743-4644
TF: 888-328-2383 ■ *Web:* www.broedell.com

Bruce Supply Corp 8805 18th Ave ... Brooklyn NY 11214 718-259-4900 256-5082
Web: www.brucesupplyplumbing.com

Buss Mechanical Services Inc 4471 Henry St ... Boise ID 83709 208-562-0600
Web: bussmechanical.com

Butcher Distributors Inc 101 Boyce Rd ... Broussard LA 70518 337-837-2088 837-2069
TF: 800-960-0008 ■ *Web:* www.butcherdistributors.com

Caroplast Inc PO Box 668405 ... Charlotte NC 28266 704-394-4191
TF: 800-327-5797 ■ *Web:* www.caroplast.com

Caylor Industrial Sales Inc PO Box 4659 ... Dalton GA 30721 706-226-3198 278-4104
Web: www.caylorindustrial.com

Central Arizona Supply 208 S Country Club Dr ... Mesa AZ 85210 480-834-5817
Web: www.centralazsupply.com

Champions Pipe & Supply Inc
2 NorthPoint Dr Ste 800 ... Houston TX 77060 713-468-6555 468-7936
Web: www.championspipe.com

City Plumbing & Electric Supply Co
730 EE Butler Pkwy ... Gainesville GA 30501 770-532-4123
Web: www.cpesupply.com

City Supply Corp 2326 Bell Ave ... Des Moines IA 50321 515-288-3211
Web: www.citysupplycorp.com

Clement Support Services Inc
480 Vandell Way ... Campbell CA 95008 408-227-1171
Web: www.clementsupport.com

Cleveland Plumbing Supply Company Inc
143 E Washington St ... Chagrin Falls OH 44022 440-247-2555 247-2116
TF: 800-331-1078 ■ *Web:* www.clevelandplumbing.com

Coastal Plumbing Supply Company Inc
480 Bay St ... Staten Island NY 10304 718-447-2692
Web: www.coastalplumbingsupply.com

Coburn Supply Company Inc 390 Pk St Ste 100 ... Beaumont TX 77701 409-838-6363 838-1920
TF: 800-832-8492 ■ *Web:* www.coburns.com

Comfort Products Distributing LLC 13202 I St ... Omaha NE 68137 402-334-7777
Web: www.comfortproducts.com

Connor Co 2800 N E Adams ... Peoria IL 61603 309-688-1068
Web: www.connorco.com

Consolidated Supply Co 7337 SW Kable Ln ... Tigard OR 97224 503-620-7050 684-3254
TF: 800-929-5810 ■ *Web:* www.consolidatedsupply.com

Corr Tech Inc 4545 Homestead Rd ... Houston TX 77028 713-674-7887 674-0840
Web: www.corr-tech.com

Crawford Supply Co 8150 Lehigh Ave ... Morton Grove IL 60053 847-967-1414
Web: www.crawfordsupply.com

Cunningham Supply Inc 674 Oakwood Ave ... West Hartford CT 06110 860-953-2101
Web: www.cunninghamsupply.com

D-S Pipe & Supply Company Inc
1301 Wicomico St Ste 3 ... Baltimore MD 21230 410-539-8000
Web: www.dspipe.com

Dana Kepner Company Inc 700 Alcott St ... Denver CO 80204 303-623-6161 623-1667
Web: www.danakepner.com

Dawson Co 1681 W Second St ... Pomona CA 91766 626-797-9710
Web: www.dawsonco.com

Delta T Inc 8323 Loch Lomond Dr ... Pico Rivera CA 90660 800-928-5828
TF: 800-928-5828 ■ *Web:* www.deltat.com

Desco Plumbing & Heating Supply Inc
65 Worcester Rd ... Etobicoke ON M9W5N7 416-213-1555
Web: www.desco.ca

Desert Pipe & Supply 75200 Merle Dr ... Palm Desert CA 92211 760-340-6322
Web: www.desertpipe.com

Downeast Energy Corp 18 Spring St ... Brunswick ME 04011 207-729-9921
Web: www.downeastenergy.com

Duncan Supply Company Inc
910 N Illinois St ... Indianapolis IN 46204 317-634-1335 264-6689
TF: 800-382-5528 ■ *Web:* www.duncansupply.com

Duravit USA Inc 2205 Northmont Pkwy Ste 200 ... Duluth GA 30096 770-931-3575
Web: www.duravit.com

Dutton-Lainson Co 451 W Second St ... Hastings NE 68901 402-462-4141
Web: www.dutton-lainson.com

East Coast Metal Distributors, Inc
1313 South Briggs Ave ... Durham NC 27703 844-227-9531 598-1404*
**Fax Area Code:* 919 ■ *Web:* www.ecmdi.com

Eastern Pennsylvania Supply Co
700 Scott St ... Wilkes-Barre PA 18705 570-823-1181 824-2514
TF: 800-432-8075 ■ *Web:* www.easternpenn.com

El Mustee & Sons Inc 5431 W 164th St ... Brook Park OH 44142 216-267-3100
Web: www.mustee.com

EMCO Corp 1108 Dundas St ... London ON N5W3A7 519-453-9600 645-2465
Web: www.emcoltd.com

Emerson-Swan Inc 300 Pond St ... Randolph MA 02368 781-986-2000 986-2028
TF: 800-346-9219 ■ *Web:* www.emersonswan.com

Engineering & Equipment Company Inc
910 N Washington St ... Albany GA 31701 229-435-5601
Web: www.engineeringandequipmentcoalbany.com

EPSCO International & Companies Inc
717 Georgia Ave ... Deer Park TX 77536 281-476-8100
Web: www.epscointl.com

ETNA Supply Company Inc 529 32nd St ... Grand Rapids MI 49548 616-241-5414
Web: www.etnasupply.com

Everett J Prescott Inc 32 Prescott St ... Gardiner ME 04345 207-582-1851 582-5637
TF: 800-357-2447 ■ *Web:* www.ejprescott.com

First Supply LLC 6800 Gisholt Dr ... Madison WI 53713 608-222-7799 223-6621
TF: 800-236-9795 ■ *Web:* www.1supply.com

Flynn Burner Corp 425 Fifth Ave ... New Rochelle NY 10801 914-636-1320
Web: www.flynnburner.com

Four Seasons Inc 1801 Waters Ridge Dr ... Lewisville TX 75057 972-316-8100 316-8213
TF: 800-433-7508 ■ *Web:* www.4s.com

Fresno Distributing Company Inc
2055 E McKinley Ave ... Fresno CA 93703 559-442-8800 264-3809
TF: 800-655-2542 ■ *Web:* www.fresnod.com

Frontier Supply Inc 981 Van Horn Rd ... Fairbanks AK 99701 907-374-3500 374-3570
TF: 800-478-7867 ■ *Web:* www.frontierplumbing.com

Fujikin of America Inc
4677 Old Ironsides Dr ... Santa Clara CA 95054 408-980-8269 980-0572
Web: www.fujikin.com

Gateway Supply Company Inc 1312 Hamrick St ... Columbia SC 29202 803-771-7160 376-5600
TF: 800-922-5312 ■ *Web:* www.gatewaysupply.net

General Plumbing Supply Company Inc
1530 San Luis Rd PO Box 4666 ... Walnut Creek CA 94597 925-939-4622 939-1548
Web: www.generalplumbingsupply.com

Gensco Inc 4402 20th St E ... Tacoma WA 98424 253-620-8203 926-2073
TF: 877-620-8203 ■ *Web:* www.gensco.com

Goodin Co 2700 N Second St ... Minneapolis MN 55411 612-588-7811 588-7820
TF: 800-328-8433 ■ *Web:* www.goodinco.com

Granite Group Wholesalers LLC 6 Storrs St ... Concord NH 03301 603-224-1901 224-4125
TF: 800-258-3690 ■ *Web:* www.thegranitegroup.com

Great Western Supply Inc 2626 Industrial Dr ... Ogden UT 84401 801-621-5412
Web: www.gwsupply.com

Greengate Power Corp
Ste 710 407 - Second St SW ... Calgary AB T2P2Y3 403-514-0556
Web: www.greengatepower.com

Greenscape Pump Services Inc
1425 Whitlock Ln Ste 108 ... Carrollton TX 75006 972-446-0037
Web: www.greenscapepump.com

Groupe Deschenes Inc 3901 Jarry St E Ste 250 ... Montreal QC H1Z2G1 514-253-3110
Web: www.groupedeschenes.com

Gulf Coast Paper Company Inc
3705 Houston Hwy ... Victoria TX 77901 361-576-1237
Web: www.gulfcoastpaper.com

GW Berkheimer Company Inc 6000 Southport Rd ... Portage IN 46368 219-764-5200 764-5203
Web: www.gwberkheimer.com

Habegger Corp 4995 Winton Rd ... Cincinnati OH 45232 309-793-4328 681-9892*
**Fax Area Code:* 513 ■ *Web:* www.habeggercorp.com

Hahn Supply Inc 2101 Main St ... Lewiston ID 83501 208-743-1577
Web: www.hahnsupply.com

Hajoca Corp 127 Coulter Ave ... Ardmore PA 19003 610-649-1430 884-2455*
**Fax Area Code:* 505 ■ *TF:* 888-328-2383 ■ *Web:* www.hajoca.com

Hajoca Corp Keenan Supply Div
1341 Philadelphia St ... Pomona CA 91766 909-613-1363 613-1173
TF: 800-332-0366 ■ *Web:* www.hajoca.com

Harri Plumbing & Heating Inc 809 W 12th St ... Juneau AK 99801 907-586-3190
TF: 800-478-3190 ■ *Web:* www.harriplumbing.com

Harry Cooper Supply Company Inc
605 N Sherman Pkwy ... Springfield MO 65802 417-865-8392 873-9146
TF: 800-426-6737 ■ *Web:* www.harrycooper.com

Heat Transfer Sales of the Carolinas Inc
4101 Beechwood Dr ... Greensboro NC 27410 336-294-3838
Web: www.heattransfersales.com

Henry Quentzel Plumbing Supply Co
379 Throop Ave ... Brooklyn NY 11221 718-455-6600
Web: www.quentzel.com

Hercules Industries Inc 1310 W Evans Ave ... Denver CO 80223 303-937-1000 937-0903
TF: 800-356-5350 ■ *Web:* www.herculesindustries.com

Hinkle Metals & Supply Company Inc
3300 11th Ave N ... Birmingham AL 35234 205-326-3300
Web: hinklemetals.com

Hot Water Products Inc 7254 N Teutonia Ave ... Milwaukee WI 53209 414-434-1371
Web: www.hotwaterproducts.com

Hubbard Pipe & Supply Inc
463 Robeson St ... Fayetteville NC 28301 910-484-0187
Web: hubbardpipeandsupply.com

Hugh M Cunningham Inc 13755 Benchmark Dr ... Dallas TX 75234 972-888-3800
Web: hughcunningham.com

Hughes Supply Inc 600 Ferguson Dr ... Orlando FL 32805 407-843-9100
Web: www.hughessupply.com

Hydro-flo Products Inc 3655 N 124th St ... Brookfield WI 53005 262-781-2810
Web: www.hydro-flo.com

I D Booth Inc PO Box 579 ... Elmira NY 14902 607-733-9121 733-9111
TF: 888-432-6684 ■ *Web:* www.idbooth.com

Ideal Supply Company Inc
2935 S Highland Dr ... Las Vegas NV 89109 702-731-3445
Web: www.idealsupplylv.com

ILLCO Inc 535 S River St ... Aurora IL 60506 630-892-7904 892-0318
Web: www.illco.com

Indeck Keystone Energy LLC
5340 Fryling Rd Ste 200 ... Erie PA 16510 814-452-6421
Web: www.indeck-keystone.com

Independent Pipe & Supply Corp Whitman Rd ... Canton MA 02021 781-828-8500
Web: www.indpipe.com

Industrial Pipe & Supply Company Inc
1779 Martin Luther King Junior Blvd ... Gainesville GA 30501 770-536-0517
Web: www.industrialpipega.com

Irr Supply Centers Inc
908 Niagara Falls Blvd ... North Tonawanda NY 14120 716-692-1600 692-1611
Web: www.irrsupply.com

J & B Supply Inc 4915 S Zero St ... Fort Smith AR 72903 479-649-4915 649-4911
Web: www.jandbsupply.com

JE Sawyer & Company Inc 64 Glen St ... Glens Falls NY 12801 800-724-3983
TF: 800-724-3983 ■ *Web:* www.jesawyer.com

JH Larson Co 10200 51st Ave N ... Plymouth MN 55442 763-545-1717 545-1144
TF: 800-292-7970 ■ *Web:* www.jhlarson.com

John M Frey Co Inc 2735 62nd St Ct ... Bettendorf IA 52722 563-332-9200 332-9880
TF: 800-397-3739 ■ *Web:* www.jmfcompany.com

Johnson Supply Inc 10151 Stella Link Rd ... Houston TX 77025 713-830-2499 662-5519
TF: 800-833-5455 ■ *Web:* www.johnsonsupply.com

Johnson's Boiler & Control Inc
2440 S Gearhart Ave ... Fresno CA 93725 559-237-7772
Web: www.johnsonsboiler.com

	City	State	Zip	Phone	Fax
Just Manufacturing Company Inc 9233 King St. *Web:* www.justmfg.com	Franklin Park	IL	60131	847-678-5151	
Keeling Co PO Box 15310. *Web:* www.keelingcompany.com	North Little Rock	AR	72231	501-945-4511	
Keidel Supply Co 1150 Tennessee Ave *Web:* www.keidel.com	Cincinnati	OH	45229	513-351-1600	351-9649
Keller Supply Company Inc 3209 17th Ave W **Fax:* Acctg ■ *TF:* 800-285-3302 ■ *Web:* www.kellersupply.com	Seattle	WA	98119	206-285-3300	283-8668*
Kelly's Pipe & Supply Co Inc 2124 Industrial Rd *TF:* 888-382-4957 ■ *Web:* www.kellyspipe.com	Las Vegas	NV	89102	888-382-4957	382-4879
Kent Supply Co 50 Jon Barrett Rd. *Web:* www.kentsupply.com	Patterson	NY	12563	845-878-6940	
Kleen Air Service Corp 5354 N Northwest Hwy *Web:* www.kleenair.com	Chicago	IL	60630	773-631-0007	
Koch Air LLC 1900 W Lloyd Expy PO Box 1167 *TF:* 877-456-2422 ■ *Web:* www.kochair.com	Evansville	IN	47712	812-962-5200	962-5306
Larsen Supply Company Inc 12055 E Slauson Ave PO Box 4388 *Web:* www.lasco.net	Santa Fe Springs	CA	90670	562-698-0731	
LDK Solar Tech USA Inc 1290 Oakmead Pkwy Ste 306 *Web:* www.ldksolar.com	Sunnyvale	CA	94085	408-245-0858	
Lee Supply Corp 6610 Guion Rd. *TF:* 800-873-1103 ■ *Web:* leesupplycorp.com	Indianapolis	IN	46268	317-290-2500	290-2512
Lemna Corporation Inc 2445 Park Ave. *Web:* www.lemna.com	Minneapolis	MN	55404	612-253-2000	
Longley Supply Company Inc 2018 Oleander Dr *Web:* longleysupplycompany.com	Wilmington	NC	28403	910-762-7793	762-9178
M & A Supply Company Inc 1540 Amherst Rd *Web:* www.masupplycompany.com	Knoxville	TN	37909	865-584-0510	
Mark's Plumbing Parts 3312 Ramona Dr *Web:* www.markspp.com	Fort Worth	TX	76116	817-731-6211	
Martz Supply Co 5330 Pecos St. *Web:* www.martzsupply.com	Denver	CO	80221	303-421-6665	
Masters' Supply Inc 4505 Bishop Ln *Web:* www.masterssupply.net	Louisville	KY	40218	800-388-6353	
May Supply Company Inc 1775 Erickson Ave *Web:* www.maysupply.com	Harrisonburg	VA	22801	540-433-2611	
McCain Engineering Inc 2002 Mccain Pkwy *Web:* www.mccainengineering.com	Pelham	AL	35124	205-663-0123	
McGuire Manufacturing 60 Grandview Ct. *Web:* www.mcguiremfg.com	Cheshire	CT	06410	203-699-1801	
Mdm Supply Inc PO Box 6018 *TF:* 800-949-0005 ■ *Web:* www.mdmsupply.com	Helena	MT	59604	406-443-4012	442-4536
Mid-Lakes Distributing Inc 1029 W Adams St *TF:* 888-733-2700 ■ *Web:* www.mid-lakes.com	Chicago	IL	60607	312-733-1033	733-1721
Mid-States Supply Co 1716 Guinotte Ave *TF:* 800-825-1410 ■ *Web:* www.midcoonline.com	Kansas City	MO	64120	816-842-4290	842-3630
Minvalco Inc 3340 Gorham Ave. *Web:* minvalco.com	Minneapolis	MN	55426	952-920-0131	
Mirixa Corp 11600 Sunrise Vly Dr Ste 100 *Web:* www.mirixa.com	Reston	VA	20191	703-683-1955	
Moore Supply Co 200 N Loop 336 W. *Web:* www.mooresupply.com	Conroe	TX	77301	936-756-4445	441-8468
Morley-Murphy Co 200 S Washington St Ste 305 *TF:* 877-499-3171 ■ *Web:* www.morley-murphycompany.com	Green Bay	WI	54301	920-499-3171	499-9409
Morrison Supply Company Inc 311 E Vickery Blvd *Web:* www.morsco.com	Fort Worth	TX	76104	817-336-0451	338-1612
Morrow Control & Supply Co 810 Marion Motley Ave Ne *Web:* www.morrowcontrol.com	Canton	OH	44705	330-452-9791	
Mountain States Pipe & Supply Co 111 W Las Vegas St *TF:* 800-777-7173 ■ *Web:* www.msps.com	Colorado Springs	CO	80903	719-634-5555	634-5551
Mountain States Supply Inc 184 West 3300 South *Web:* www.mountainlandsupply.com	Salt Lake City	UT	84115	801-484-8885	
Mountain Supply Co 2101 Mullan Rd. *Web:* www.mountainsupply.com	Missoula	MT	59808	406-543-8255	
Mountainland Supply Co 1505 West 130 South *Web:* www.mtncom.net	Orem	UT	84058	801-224-6050	224-6058
Murray Supply Co (MSC) 102 W Third St *TF:* 800-926-0457 ■ *Web:* www.murraysupply.com	Winston Salem	NC	27101	336-765-9480	245-0686
N & S Supply of Fishkill Inc 205 Old Rt 9 *Web:* www.nssupply.com	Fishkill	NY	12524	845-896-6291	
NanOasis Technologies Inc 4677 Meade St Ste 210 *Web:* www.nanoasisinc.com	Richmond	CA	94804	510-215-0186	
New York Replacement Parts Corp 19 School St *TF:* 800-228-4718 ■ *Web:* www.nyrpcorp.com	Yonkers	NY	10701	914-965-0122	965-3147
Newton Distributing Company Inc 966 Watertown St *Web:* newtondistributing.com	Newton	MA	02465	617-969-4002	
Next Generation Energy LLC 75 Waneka Pkwy *Web:* www.ngeus.com	Lafayette	CO	80026	303-665-2000	
Nexus Valve Inc 9982 E 121st St *Web:* www.nexusvalve.com	Fishers	IN	46037	317-257-6050	
Niagara Conservation Corp 45 Horsehill Rd. *Web:* www.niagaraconservation.com	Cedar Knolls	NJ	07927	973-829-0800	
Northeastern Supply Co Inc 8323 Pulaski Hwy **Fax:* Sales ■ *Web:* northeastern.com	Baltimore	MD	21237	410-574-0010	574-3315*
Northwest Pipe Fittings Inc 33 S Eigth St W *TF:* 800-937-4737 ■ *Web:* www.northwestpipe.net	Billings	MT	59101	406-252-0142	248-8072
O'Connor Sales Inc 16107 Piuma Ave *Web:* www.oconnorsales.net	Cerritos	CA	90703	562-403-3848	403-3858
Pasco Specialty & Manufacturing Inc 11156 Wright Rd *Web:* www.pascospecialty.com	Lynwood	CA	90262	310-537-7782	
Pbbs Equipment Corp N59W16500 Greenway Cir *Web:* www.pbbs.com	Menomonee Falls	WI	53051	262-252-7575	
Peabody Supply Co Inc PO Box 669 *TF:* 800-445-5816 ■ *Web:* www.peabodysupply.com	Peabody	MA	01960	978-532-2200	532-1463
Pepco Sales of Dallas Inc 11310 Gemini Ln. *Web:* www.pepcosales.com	Dallas	TX	75229	972-823-8700	
Performance Engineering Group Inc 32995 Industrial Rd *Web:* www.performanceengineering.com	Livonia	MI	48150	734-266-5300	
Perry Supply Company Inc 2625 Vassar NE. *Web:* www.perrysupply.net	Albuquerque	NM	87107	505-884-6972	
PHD Manufacturing Inc 44018 Columbiana-Waterford Rd *Web:* www.phd-mfg.com	Columbiana	OH	44408	330-482-9256	
Pipeline Supply Inc 620-16th Ave S *Web:* www.pipeline-supply.com	Hopkins	MN	55343	952-935-0445	
Platsky Company Inc 298 Montrose Rd *Web:* www.platsky.com	Westbury	NY	11590	516-333-9292	
Plumb Supply Co 1622 NE 51st Ave. *TF:* 800-483-9511 ■ *Web:* www.plumbsupply.com	Des Moines	IA	50313	515-262-9511	262-9790
Plumbers Supply Co 1000 E Main St *TF:* 800-626-5133 ■ *Web:* www.plumbers-supply-co.com	Louisville	KY	40206	502-582-2261	585-5521
Plumbing Distributors Inc 1025 Old Norcross Rd *TF:* 800-262-9231 ■ *Web:* relyonpdi.com	Lawrenceville	GA	30046	770-963-9231	
Plymouth Technology Inc 2925 Waterview Dr *Web:* www.plymouthtechnology.com	Rochester Hills	MI	48309	248-537-0081	
Porter Pipe & Supply Co 303 S Rohlwing Rd. *Web:* www.porterpipe.com	Addison	IL	60101	630-543-8145	543-6830
PrairieCoast Equipment 15102 101 St *Web:* www.prairiecoastequipment.com	Grande Prairie	AB	T8V0P7	780-532-8402	
Prima Supply Inc 649 Anita St Ste A1 *Web:* primasupply.com	Chula Vista	CA	91911	619-429-5202	
Proctor Sales Inc 20715 50th Ave W *Web:* www.proctorsales.com	Lynnwood	WA	98036	425-774-1441	
Ramapo Wholesalers Inc 54B Kennedy Dr *Web:* ramapowholesalers.com	Spring Valley	NY	10977	845-425-8400	
Rampart Supply Inc 1801 N Union Blvd *Web:* www.rampartsupply.com	Colorado Springs	CO	80909	719-482-7333	
Redlon & Johnson 172 St John St Ste 174 *TF:* 800-905-5250 ■ *Web:* www.redlon-johnson.com	Portland	ME	04102	207-773-4755	772-2957
Reeves-Wiedeman Co Inc 14861 W 100th St *TF:* 800-365-0024 ■ *Web:* rwco.com	Lenexa	KS	66215	913-492-7100	492-6962
Refrigeration Sales Corp 9450 Allen Dr Ste A *TF:* 866-894-8200 ■ *Web:* www.refrigerationsales.net	Valley View	OH	44125	216-881-7800	
Republic Plumbing Supply Company Inc 890 Providence Hwy **Fax Area Code:* 781 ■ *TF:* 800-696-3900 ■ *Web:* www.republicsupplyco.com	Norwood	MA	02062	800-696-3900	769-7842*
Res-Kem Corp Two New Rd Ste 123 *Web:* www.reskem.com	Aston	PA	19014	610-358-0717	
Roberts-Hamilton 6601 Pkwy Cir Ste A *TF:* 800-888-2222 ■ *Web:* www.robertshamilton.com	Brooklyn Center	MN	55430	763-315-0100	315-0199
Robertson Heating Supply Co 2155 W Main St *TF:* 800-433-9532 ■ *Web:* www.robertsonheatingsupply.com	Alliance	OH	44601	330-821-9180	821-8251
Robertson Supply Inc PO Box 1366 *Web:* www.robertsonsupply.com	Nampa	ID	83653	208-466-8907	466-8900
ROHL LLC Three Parker *Web:* www.rohlhome.com	Irvine	CA	92618	714-557-1933	
Ruehlen Supply Company Inc 491 Corban Ave Se *Web:* www.ruehlensupply.com	Concord	NC	28025	704-788-2180	
Rundle-Spence Manufacturing Co PO Box 510008 *TF:* 800-783-6060 ■ *Web:* www.rundle-spence.com	New Berlin	WI	53151	262-782-3000	782-5078
Samon's Tiger Stores Inc 2511 Monroe NE. *Web:* www.samons.biz	Albuquerque	NM	87110	505-884-4615	884-1725
San Jose Boiler Works Inc 610 Stockton Ave *Web:* www.sanjoseboiler.com	San Jose	CA	95126	408-295-5235	
Schumacher & Seiler Inc 9044 Frederick Rd *Web:* www.schumacherseiler.com	Ellicott City	MD	21042	410-465-7000	
Security Supply Corp 196 Maple Ave *TF:* 800-333-2226 ■ *Web:* www.secsupply.com	Selkirk	NY	12158	518-767-2226	767-2065
Sexauer Ltd 3-6990 Creditview Rd *Web:* www.sexauer.com	Mississauga	ON	L5N8R9	905-821-8292	
Shane Group Inc PO Box 765 *Web:* www.shanegroup.com	Hillsdale	MI	49242	517-439-4316	439-9159
Shore Distributors Inc 807 Brown St *Web:* www.shoredist.com	Salisbury	MD	21804	410-749-3121	
Sid Harvey Industries Inc 605 Locust St *Web:* www.sidharvey.com	Garden City	NY	11530	516-745-9200	222-9027
Sioux Chief Manufacturing Company Inc 24110 S Peculiar Dr *Web:* www.siouxchief.com	Peculiar	MO	64078	816-779-6104	
Smardan-Hatcher Company Inc 810 East Mason St *Web:* www.smardan.com	Santa Barbara	CA	93103	805-963-8991	
Solar Energy Systems LLC 1205 Manhattan Ave Ste 1210 *Web:* www.solaresystems.com	Brooklyn	NY	11222	718-389-1545	
SPS Cos Inc 6363 Minnesota 7 *Web:* www.spscompanies.com	Minneapolis	MN	55416	952-929-1377	929-1862
Standard Air & Lite Corp 2406 Woodmere Dr *TF:* 800-472-2458 ■ *Web:* www.stdair.com	Pittsburgh	PA	15205	412-920-6505	
Sunbelt Marketing Investment Corp 3255 S Sweetwater Rd *Web:* www.sunbeltmarketing.com	Lithia Springs	GA	30122	770-739-3740	

Phone | Fax

Superlon Plastic Pipe Co 2116 Taylor Way........... Tacoma WA 98421 253-383-5877
Web: www.superlon.com
Swan Corp, The 515 Olive St Ste 900 .... St. Louis MO 63101 314-231-8148
Web: www.swanstone.com
TBA LLC 6700 Enterprise Dr........................Louisville KY 40214 502-367-0222 361-0715
TF: 800-626-3525 ■ *Web:* www.cmiproduct.com
Temperature Equipment Corp
17725 Volbrecht Rd .... Lansing IL 60438 708-418-0900 418-5100
Web: www.tecmungo.com
Temperature Systems Inc 5001 Voges Rd .... Madison WI 53718 608-271-7500 274-1609
TF: 800-366-0930 ■ *Web:* www.tsihvac.com
Therm Air Sales Corp 1413 41st Stn.................... Fargo ND 58102 701-282-9500
Web: www.thermairsales.com
Thermal Corp 1264 Slaughter Rd.................... Madison AL 35758 256-837-1122 837-0265
TF: 800-633-2962 ■ *Web:* www.thermalcorp.com
TW Smith Co 1200 Campbell Ave .... San Jose CA 95126 408-249-9880
Web: www.kbshowplace.com
US Airconditioning Distributors
16900 Chestnut St............................ City of Industry CA 91748 626-854-4500 854-4690*
**Fax:* Sales ■ *TF:* 800-937-7222 ■ *Web:* www.us-ac.com
US Supply Company Inc
50 Portland Rd......................... West Conshohocken PA 19428 610-828-5600
Web: www.ussupply.com
V P Supply Corp PO Box 23868 .... Rochester NY 14692 585-272-0110 272-0547
Web: www.vpsupply.com
Vamac Inc 4201 Jacque St............................ Richmond VA 23230 804-353-7811 358-7855
TF: 800-768-2622 ■ *Web:* www.vamac.com
W C Rouse & Son Inc 110 Longale Rd............. Greensboro NC 27409 336-299-3035
Web: www.wcrouse.com
WA Roosevelt Co 2727 Commerce St .... La Crosse WI 54603 608-781-2000 781-8372
TF: 800-279-2726 ■ *Web:* www.waroosevelt.com
Ward Manufacturing LLC 117 Gulick St............ Blossburg PA 16912 570-638-2131
Web: www.wardmfg.com
Waxman Industries Inc
24460 Aurora Rd ....Bedford Heights OH 44146 440-439-1830 439-8678*
OTC: WXMN ■ **Fax:* Cust Svc ■ *TF:* 800-201-7298 ■ *Web:* www.waxman.com
Wayne Pipe & Supply Inc
6040 Innovation Blvd .... Fort Wayne IN 46818 260-423-9577
Web: www.waynepipe.com
Webber Supply Inc 32 Thatcher St ....Bangor ME 04401 207-942-7361
Web: www.webbersupply.com
Webstone Company Inc One Appian Way .... Worcester MA 01610 508-438-0131
Web: www.webstonevalves.com
Wellness Enterprises LLC
418 SW 140th Terrace...............................Newberry FL 32669 352-333-0480
Web: www.naturallyfiltered.com
Western Nevada Supply Co 950 S Rock Blvd .... Sparks NV 89431 775-359-5800 359-4649
TF: 800-648-1230 ■ *Web:* www.wns1.com
Wholesale Specialties Inc 4800 E 48th Ave............Denver CO 80216 303-296-2212
Web: www.wholesalespecialties.com
Wholesale Supply Group Inc 885 Keith St NW....... Cleveland TN 37311 423-478-1191 478-5120
Web: www.wsgwww.com
Wilkinson Supply Co 3300 Bush St .... Raleigh NC 27609 919-834-0395
Web: www.wilkinsonsupplyco.com
Willoughby Industries Inc
2210 W Morris St....................................Indianapolis IN 46221 317-638-2381
Web: www.willoughby-ind.com
WinWholesale Inc 3110 Kettering Blvd ....Dayton OH 45439 937-294-6878 293-9591
Web: winwholesale.com
Wolff Bros Supply Inc 6078 Wolff Rd................. Medina OH 44256 330-725-3451
Web: www.wolffbros.com
Wolverine Brass Inc 2951 Hwy 501 East .... Conway SC 29526 843-347-3121 945-9292*
**Fax Area Code:* 800 ■ *Web:* www.wolverinebrass.com
Woodhill Supply Inc 4665 Beidler Rd............... Willoughby OH 44094 440-269-1100 269-1027
TF: 800-362-6111 ■ *Web:* www.woodhillsupply.com
Yorkshire Supply Inc 8205 Centreville Rd .... Manassas VA 20111 703-368-9226
Web: www.yorkshiresupply.com
Zurier Company of San Francisco Inc
6147 Industrial Way Ste A .... Livermore CA 94551 925-449-5858
Web: zurier.com

616 PLYWOOD & VENEERS

SEE ALSO Lumber & Building Supplies p. 2108; Home Improvement Centers p. 2475

Phone | Fax

Aetna Plywood Inc 1401 St Charles Rd..............Maywood IL 60153 708-343-1515 343-1616
Web: www.aetnaplywood.com
Amos-Hill Assoc Inc 112 Shelby Ave PO Box 7 .... Edinburgh IN 46124 812-526-2671 526-5865
Web: www.amoshill.com
Anderson Hardwood Floors PO Box 1155............ Clinton SC 29325 864-833-6250 833-6664
Web: www.andersonfloors.com
Atlantic Veneer Corp
2457 Lennoxville Rd PO Box 660.....................Beaufort NC 28516 252-728-3169 728-4906
Web: www.moehringgroup.com
Bacon Veneer Co 6951 High Grove Blvd............Burr Ridge IL 60527 630-323-1414 323-1499
TF: 800-443-7995 ■ *Web:* www.baconveneer.com
Barmon Door & Plywood Inc
2508 Hartford Dr...............................Lake Stevens WA 98258 425-334-1222 335-0404
Buffalo Veneer & Plywood Company Inc
501 Sixth Ave NE ....Buffalo MN 55313 763-682-1822 682-9769
Web: www.buffaloveneerandplywood.com
California Panel & Veneer Co
14055 Artesia Blvd ....Cerritos CA 90703 562-926-5834 926-3139
TF: 800-451-1745 ■ *Web:* www.calpanel.com
Capital Veneer Works Inc
2550 Jackson Ferry Rd........................ Montgomery AL 36104 334-264-1401 264-6923
Web: capitalmat.com
Capitol Plywood Inc 160 Commerce Cir............ Sacramento CA 95815 916-922-8861 922-0775
TF: 800-326-1505 ■ *Web:* www.capitolplywood.com

Phone | Fax

Columbia Forest Products Inc
7900 Triad Ctr Dr Ste 200........................ Greensboro NC 27409 336-291-5905
TF: 800-637-1609 ■ *Web:* www.columbiaforestproducts.com
Columbia Forest Products Inc Columbia Plywood Div
7900 Triad Ctr Dr Ste 200..........................Greensboro NC 27409 800-637-1609
TF: 800-637-1609 ■ *Web:* columbiaforestproducts.com
Columbia Panel Manufacturing Co
100 Giles St ....High Point NC 27263 336-861-4100
Constantine's Wood Ctr
1040 E Oakland Pk Blvd......................Fort Lauderdale FL 33334 954-561-1716 565-8149
TF: 800-443-9667 ■ *Web:* www.constantines.com
Cummings Veneers Inc 601 E Fourth St ....New Albany IN 47150 812-944-2269 944-0212
Darlington Veneer Company Inc
225 Fourth St ....Darlington SC 29532 843-393-3861 393-8243
TF: 800-845-2388 ■ *Web:* www.darlingtonveneer.com
David R Webb Company Inc
206 S Holland St PO Box 8........................ Edinburgh IN 46124 812-526-2601 526-5842
Web: www.davidrwebb.com
Davis Wood Products Inc PO Box 604................ Hudson NC 28638 828-728-8444 728-4601
Web: www.daviswoodproducts.com
Eggers Industries Inc One Eggers Dr...............Two Rivers WI 54241 920-793-1351 793-2958
Web: www.eggersindustries.com
Fiber-Tech Industries Inc
2000 Kenskill Ave................... Washington Court House OH 43160 740-335-9400 335-4843
TF: 800-879-4377 ■ *Web:* fiber-tech.net
Flexible Materials Inc 1202 Port Rd ....Jeffersonville IN 47130 812-280-7000 280-7001
TF: 800-244-6492 ■ *Web:* www.flexwood.com
Freeman Corp, The
415 Magnolia St PO Box 96 .... Winchester KY 40392 859-744-4311 744-4363
Web: www.freemancorp.com
Freres Lumber Company Inc PO Box 276..............Lyons OR 97358 503-859-2121 859-2112
Web: www.fereslumber.com
G-L Veneer Co Inc 2224 E Slauson Ave .... Huntington Park CA 90255 323-582-5203 582-9681
TF: 800-588-5003 ■ *Web:* www.glveneer.com
Hambro Forest Products Inc
445 Elk Valley Rd ....Crescent City CA 95531 707-464-6131 464-9375
Harbor Sales 1000 Harbor Ct .... Sudlersville MD 21668 800-345-1712 868-9257
TF: 800-345-1712 ■ *Web:* www.harborsales.net
Hartzell Veneer Products
282 Industrial Dr PO Box 706....................... Hillsdale MI 49242 517-437-3117
Web: www.theveneershop.com
Hasty Plywood Co 100 N Austin St .... Maxton NC 28364 910-844-5267
Web: www.hasply.com
Hood Cos Inc 623 N Main St Ste 300 .... Hattiesburg MS 39401 601-582-4486
Web: www.hoodcompanies.com
Hood Industries Inc
15 Professional Pkwy # 8.......................... Hattiesburg MS 39402 601-264-2559 296-4755
Web: www.hoodindustries.com
Hoquiam Plywood Company Inc 1000 Woodlawn Rd... Hoquiam WA 98550 360-533-3060 532-6980
Inland Plywood Co 375 N Cass Ave .... Pontiac MI 48342 248-334-4706 338-7407
TF: 800-521-4355 ■ *Web:* www.inlandplywood.com
Louisiana-Pacific Corp
414 Union St Ste 2000.............................Nashville TN 37219 615-986-5600 986-5666
NYSE: LPX ■ *TF:* 888-820-0325 ■ *Web:* www.lpcorp.com
Marion Plywood Corp
222 S Parkview Ave PO Box 497 ....Marion WI 54950 715-754-5231 754-2582
Web: www.marionplywood.com
Murphy Hardwood Plywood 2350 Prairie Rd.......... Eugene OR 97402 541-461-4545 461-4547
TF: 888-461-4545 ■ *Web:* www.murphyplywood.com
Murphy Plywood Co 2350 Prairie Rd .... Eugene OR 97402 541-461-4545 461-4547
TF: 888-461-4545 ■ *Web:* www.murphyplywood.com
Norbord Inc One Toronto St Ste 600............... Toronto ON M5C2W4 416-365-0705 365-3292
TSE: NBD ■ *TF:* 888-667-2673 ■ *Web:* www.norbord.com
North American Plywood Corp
12343 Hawkins St...........................Santa Fe Springs CA 90670 562-941-7575
TF Sales: 800-421-1372 ■ *Web:* naply.com
Pasquier Panel Products Inc
1510 Puyallup St PO Box 1170 .... Sumner WA 98390 253-863-6323 891-7993
Web: www.pasquierpanel.com
Pavco Industries Inc PO Box 612................ Pascagoula MS 39568 228-762-3172 762-3170
Web: www.pavcoind.com
Phillips Plywood Company Inc
13599 Desmond St.................................... Pacoima CA 91331 818-897-7736 897-6571
TF Cust Svc: 800-649-6410 ■ *Web:* www.phillipsplywood.com
Plywood Supply Inc 7036 NE 175th St .... Kenmore WA 98028 425-485-8585 485-6195
TF: 888-774-9663 ■ *Web:* www.plywoodsupply.com
Potlatch Corp 601 W First Ave Ste 1600 .... Spokane WA 99201 509-835-1500 835-1555
NASDAQ: PCH ■ *Web:* www.potlatchcorp.com
Potlatch Corp Wood Products Div
805 Mill Rd PO Box 1388.......................... Lewiston ID 83501 509-835-1500 799-1918*
**Fax Area Code:* 208 ■ *Web:* www.potlatchcorp.com
Robert Weed Plywood Corp
705 Maple St PO Box 487 .... Bristol IN 46507 574-848-4408 848-5679
Web: www.robertweedplywood.com
Roseburg Forest Products Co PO Box 1088 ....Roseburg OR 97470 541-679-3311
TF: 800-245-1115 ■ *Web:* www.roseburg.com
SDS Lumber Co PO Box 266 ....Bingen WA 98605 509-493-2155 493-2535
Web: sdslumber.com
South Coast Lumber Co
885 Railroad Ave PO Box 670...................... Brookings OR 97415 541-469-2136 469-3487
Web: www.socomi.com
States Industries Inc PO Box 7037 .... Eugene OR 97401 541-688-7871
TF: 800-626-1981 ■ *Web:* www.statesind.com
StemWood Corp 2710 Grant Line Rd..............New Albany IN 47150 812-945-6646 945-7549
Web: www.stemwood.com
Stimson Lumber Co 520 SW Yamhill St Ste 700.........Portland OR 97204 503-222-1676 222-2682
TF: 800-445-9758 ■ *Web:* www.stimsonlumber.com
Stoll Brother True Value Lumber 509 S E St ....Odon IN 47562 812-636-4053 636-8025
Web: truevalue.com
Texas Plywood & Lumber Co Inc
1001 E Ave K ....Grand Prairie TX 75050 972-262-1331 642-2225
Web: www.texasplywood.com

	Phone	Fax
Trimac Panel Products 5201 SW Westgate Dr Ste 200 . . . . . Portland OR 97221 *TF General:* 800-237-8765 ■ *Web:* www.trimacpanel.com	503-297-1826	297-9049
United Plywood & Lumber Inc 1640 Mims Ave SW . . . . . Birmingham AL 35211 *TF:* 800-272-6486 ■ *Web:* www.unitedplywoods.com	205-925-7601	923-9511
Wavell-Huber Wood Products Inc 180 North 170 West . . . . . North Salt Lake UT 84054 *Web:* www.wavell-huber.com	801-936-6080	936-6078
Wisconsin Veneer & Plywood Inc Railroad St PO Box 140 . . . . . Mattoon WI 54450 *Web:* www.bessegroup.com/public/companies/wi_veneer.php	715-489-3611	489-3268

617 POINT-OF-SALE (POS) & POINT-OF-INFORMATION (POI) SYSTEMS

	Phone	Fax
3M Digital Signage 600 Ericksen Ave NE Ste 200 . . . . . Bainbridge Island WA 98110 *TF:* 888-460-8866 ■ *Web:* www.3mdigitalsignage.com	206-855-2000	855-4930
Checkpoint Systems Inc 101 Wolf Dr . . . . . Thorofare NJ 08086 *NYSE: CKP* ■ *TF:* 800-257-5540 ■ *Web:* www.checkpointsystems.com	856-848-1800	848-0937
Comtrex Systems Corp 1247 N Church St Ste 7 . . . . . Moorestown NJ 08057 *Web:* comtrex.co.uk	856-778-0090	778-9322
Datalogic Scanning 959 Terry St . . . . . Eugene OR 97402 *TF:* 800-695-5700 ■ *Web:* www.datalogic.com	541-683-5700	345-7140
Kiosk Information Systems Inc (KIS) 346 S Arthur Ave. . . . . . Louisville CO 80027 *TF General:* 800-509-5471 ■ *Web:* www.kis-kiosk.com	303-466-5471	466-6730
Micros Systems Inc 7031 Columbia Gateway Dr . . . . . Columbia MD 21046 *NASDAQ: MCRS* ■ *TF:* 800-937-2211 ■ *Web:* www.micros.com	443-285-6000	
MTI Inc 1050 NW 229th Ave . . . . . Hillsboro OR 97124 *TF:* 800-426-6844 ■ *Web:* www.mti-interactive.com	503-648-6500	648-7500
NextG Networks Inc 890 Tasman Dr . . . . . Milpitas CA 95035 *Web:* www.crowncastle.com	877-486-9377	
PAR Technology Corp 8383 Seneca Tpke . . . . . New Hartford NY 13413 *NYSE: PAR* ■ *TF:* 800-448-6505 ■ *Web:* www.partech.com	315-738-0600	738-0562
SeePoint Technology LLC 2619 Manhattan Beach Blvd. . . . . . Redondo Beach CA 90278 *TF:* 888-587-1777 ■ *Web:* www.seepoint.com	310-725-9660	535-9234
TouchSystems Corp 220 Tradesmen Dr . . . . . Hutto TX 78634 *TF:* 800-320-5944 ■ *Web:* www.touchsystems.com	512-846-2424	846-2425
UTC RETAIL Inc 100 Rawson Rd . . . . . Victor NY 14564 **Fax Area Code: 585* ■ *TF:* 800-349-0546 ■ *Web:* www.utcretail.com	800-349-0546	924-1434*
VeriFone Inc 2099 Gateway Pl Ste 600 . . . . . San Jose CA 95110 *NYSE: PAY* ■ *TF:* 800-837-4366 ■ *Web:* www.verifone.co.in	408-232-7800	232-7811
VeriFone Systems Inc 2099 Gateway Pl Ste 600 . . . . . San Jose CA 95110 *NYSE: PAY* ■ *TF:* 800-837-4366 ■ *Web:* www.verifone.co.in	408-232-7800	232-7811

618 POLITICAL ACTION COMMITTEES

SEE ALSO Civic & Political Organizations p. 1765

	Phone	Fax
A Jewish Voice for Peace Inc 1611 Telegraph Ave Ste 550 . . . . . Oakland CA 94612 *Web:* www.jvp.org	510-465-1777	
Action Committee for Rural Electrification (ACRE) 4301 Wilson Blvd . . . . . Arlington VA 22203 *Web:* www.nreca.coop	703-907-5500	907-5516
AFL-CIO Committee on Political Education 815 16th St NW . . . . . Washington DC 20006 **Fax Area Code: 202* ■ *Web:* www.aflcio.org	855-712-8441	637-5058*
American Academy of Ophthalmology PAC Governmental Affairs Div 20 F St NW Ste 400 . . . . . Washington DC 20001 *TF:* 866-561-8558 ■ *Web:* www.aao.org	202-737-6662	737-7061
American Academy of Physician Assistants (AAPA) 2318 Mill Rd Ste 1300 . . . . . Alexandria VA 22314 *Web:* www.aapa.org	703-836-2272	684-1924
American Apparel & Footwear Assn PAC 1601 N Kent St Ste 1200 . . . . . Arlington VA 22209 *TF:* 800-520-2262 ■ *Web:* www.wewear.org	703-524-1864	522-6741
American Assn for Justice PAC 777 Sixth St NW Ste 200 . . . . . Washington DC 20001 *Web:* www.justice.org	202-965-3500	
American Assn of Nurse Anesthetists PAC (AANAPAC) 222 S Prospect Ave. . . . . . Park Ridge IL 60068 *TF:* 855-526-2262	847-692-2051	692-7082
American Assn of Orthodontists PAC 401 N Lindbergh Blvd. . . . . . Saint Louis MO 63141 *TF:* 800-424-2841 ■ *Web:* www.aaoinfo.org	314-993-1700	997-1745
American Bakers Assn PAC 1300 'I' St NW Ste 700-W . . . . . Washington DC 20005 *Web:* americanbakers.org	202-789-0300	898-1164
American Bankers Assn PAC (ABAPAC) 1120 Connecticut Ave NW . . . . . Washington DC 20036 **Fax Area Code: 202* ■ *TF:* 800-226-5377 ■ *Web:* www.aba.com/default.htm	800-226-5377	663-7544*
American Beverage Assn PAC 1101 16th St NW . . . . . Washington DC 20036 *Web:* www.ameribev.org	202-463-6732	463-8178
American Chiropractic Assn PAC (ACA-PAC) 1701 Clarendon Blvd . . . . . Arlington VA 22209 *TF:* 800-986-4636 ■ *Web:* www.acatoday.org	703-276-8800	243-2593
American Family Life Assurance Co PAC (AFLAC PAC) 1932 Wynnton Rd Ste 300 . . . . . Columbus GA 31999 *NYSE: AFL* ■ **Fax Area Code: 877* ■ *TF Cust Svc:* 800-992-3522 ■ *Web:* www.aflac.com	706-323-3431	442-3522*
American Frozen Food Institute (AFFI) 2000 Corporate Ridge Blvd Ste 1000 . . . . . McLean VA 22102 *Web:* www.affi.org	703-821-0770	821-1350
American Health Care Assn PAC 1201 L St NW . . . . . Washington DC 20005 *Web:* ahcancal.org	202-842-4444	842-3860
American Hospital Assn PAC (AHAPAC) 325 Seventh St NW . . . . . Washington DC 20004 *TF:* 800-424-4301 ■ *Web:* aha.org	202-638-1100	626-2345
American Insurance Assn PAC 1130 Connecticut Ave NW Ste 1000 . . . . . Washington DC 20036 *Web:* www.aiadc.org	202-828-7100	293-1219
American Iron & Steel Institute PAC 1140 Connecticut Ave NW Ste 705 . . . . . Washington DC 20036 *Web:* www.steel.org	202-452-7100	463-6573
American Medical Assn PAC 25 Massachusetts Ave NW # 600 . . . . . Washington DC 20001 *Web:* ama-assn.org	202-789-7400	789-7485
American Motorcyclist Assn 101 Constitution Ave NW Ste 800W . . . . . Washington DC 20001 *TF:* 888-985-6090 ■ *Web:* www.americanmotorcyclist.com	202-742-4301	742-4304
American Moving & Storage Assn PAC 1611 Duke St . . . . . Alexandria VA 22314 *TF:* 888-849-2672 ■ *Web:* www.promover.org	703-683-7410	683-7527
American Nurses Assn PAC (ANA PAC) 8515 Georgia Ave Ste 400 . . . . . Silver Spring MD 20910 *TF:* 800-274-4262 ■ *Web:* www.nursingworld.org	301-628-5000	628-5001
American Pharmacists Assn PAC 2215 Constitution Ave NW . . . . . Washington DC 20037 *TF:* 800-237-2742 ■ *Web:* www.pharmacist.com	202-628-4410	783-2351
American Postal Workers Union PAC (COPA) 1300 L St NW . . . . . Washington DC 20005 *Web:* apwu.org	202-842-4200	842-4283
American Society of Travel Agents PAC 1101 King St Ste 490 . . . . . Alexandria VA 22314 *TF:* 800-275-2782 ■ *Web:* www.asta.org	703-739-2782	838-8467
American Sportfishing Assnn PAC (ASA PAC) 225 Reinekers Ln Ste 420 . . . . . Alexandria VA 22314 *Web:* www.asafishing.org	703-519-9691	519-1872
American Supply Assn PAC (ASA PAC) 1200 N Arlington Heights Rd Ste 150 . . . . . Itasca IL 60143 **Fax Area Code: 312* ■ *Web:* www.asa.net	630-467-0000	464-0091*
American Veterinary Medical Assn PAC (AVMA) 1910 Sunderland Pl NW . . . . . Washington DC 20036 *TF:* 800-321-1473 ■ *Web:* www.avma.org	202-789-0007	842-4360
ArchiPAC 1735 New York Ave NW . . . . . Washington DC 20006 *Web:* archipac.org	202-626-7300	626-7426
Associated General Contractors PAC 2300 Wilson Blvd Ste 400 . . . . . Arlington VA 22201 *TF:* 800-242-1767 ■ *Web:* www.agc.org/cs/about_agc/recognition_programs/agc_pac_donor_recognition	703-548-3118	548-3119
Association of Home Appliance Manufacturers PAC (AHAM PAC) 1111 19th St NW Ste 402 . . . . . Washington DC 20036 *Web:* aham.org	202-872-5955	872-9354
Burlington Northern Santa Fe Corp (BNSF) 500 New Jersey Ave NW Ste 550 . . . . . Washington DC 20001 *TF:* 800-964-9386 ■ *Web:* www.bnsf.com	202-347-8662	347-8675
Business-Industry Political Action Committee (BIPAC) 888 16th St NW Ste 305 . . . . . Washington DC 20006 *Web:* www.bipac.org	202-833-1880	833-2338
BUSPAC 700 13th St NW Ste 575 . . . . . Washington DC 20005 *TF:* 800-283-2877 ■ *Web:* buses.org	202-842-1645	842-0850
Campaign for Working Families (CWF) PO Box 1222 . . . . . Arlington VA 22116 *Web:* www.cwfpac.com	703-671-8800	
Caterpillar Inc Employees PAC 100 NE Adams St . . . . . Peoria IL 61629 **Fax Area Code: 309* ■ *Web:* caterpillar.com	888-614-4328	675-1753*
Coca-Cola Nonpartisan Committee for Good Government PO Box 1734 . . . . . Atlanta GA 30301 *TF:* 800-438-2653 ■ *Web:* www.coca-colacompany.com	800-438-2653	
College of American Pathologists PAC 1350 I St NW Ste 590 . . . . . Washington DC 20005 *TF:* 800-392-9994 ■ *Web:* www.cap.org	202-354-7100	354-7155
Consumer Specialty Products Assn PAC 1667 K St NW Ste 300 . . . . . Washington DC 20006 *Web:* www.cspa.org	202-872-8110	223-2636
Cosmetic Toiletry & Fragrance Assn PAC (CTFA PAC) 1101 17th St NW Ste 300 . . . . . Washington DC 20036 *Web:* cir-safety.org	202-331-1770	331-1969
Credit Union Legislative Action Council of CUNA (CULCAC) 601 Pennsylvania Ave NW S Bldg Ste 600 . . . . . Washington DC 20004 *Web:* cuna.org	202-638-5777	638-7734
Dairy Farmers of America PAC 10220 N Ambassador Dr Northpointe Twr . . . . . Kansas City MO 64153 *TF:* 888-332-6455 ■ *Web:* www.dfamilk.com	816-801-6455	801-6456
DGA-PAC 7920 W Sunset Blvd. . . . . . Los Angeles CA 90046 *TF:* 800-421-4173 ■ *Web:* www.dga.org	310-289-2000	289-2029
Electric Power Supply Assn PAC (EPSA PAC) 1401 New York Ave NW 11th Fl . . . . . Washington DC 20005	202-628-8200	628-8260
ESOP Assn PAC 1726 M St NW Ste 501 . . . . . Washington DC 20036 *TF:* 866-366-3832 ■ *Web:* www.esopassociation.org	202-293-2971	293-7568
FedEx Corp Government Affairs 942 S Shady Grove Rd . . . . . Memphis TN 38120 *Web:* www.fedex.com	901-818-7500	
Food Marketing Institute PAC (FoodPAC) 2345 Crystal Dr Ste 800 . . . . . Arlington VA 22202 *Web:* www.fmi.org	202-220-0600	429-4519
FRAN-PAC 1501 K St Ste 350 . . . . . Washington DC 20005 *TF:* 800-543-1038 ■ *Web:* www.franchise.org	202-628-8000	628-0812
Friends Committee on National Legislation (FCNL) 245 Second St NE . . . . . Washington DC 20002 *TF:* 800-630-1330 ■ *Web:* www.fcnl.org	202-547-6000	547-6019
GASPAC 400 N Capitol St NW . . . . . Washington DC 20001 *Web:* www.aga.org	202-824-7000	824-7115

Organization / Address	City	State	ZIP	Phone	Fax
General Dynamics Corp PAC 2941 Fairview Pk Dr *Web:* generaldynamics.com	Falls Church	VA	22042	703-876-3000	876-3125
General Electric Company PAC 1299 Pennsylvania Ave NW Ste 900	Washington	DC	20004	202-637-4000	637-4006
GOPAC 1101 16th St NW *Web:* www.gopac.org	Washington	DC	20036	202-464-5170	
HotelPAC 1201 New York Ave NW Ste 600 *Web:* www.ahla.com/default.aspx	Washington	DC	20005	202-289-3100	289-3185
Human Rights Campaign PAC (HRCPAC) 1640 Rhode Island Ave NW *TF:* 800-777-4723 ■ *Web:* www.hrc.org	Washington	DC	20036	202-628-4160	347-5323
IAFF 1750 New York Ave NW Ste 300 *Web:* www.iaff.org	Washington	DC	20006	202-737-8484	737-8418
IATSE PAC 1430 Broadway 20th Fl *TF:* 844-422-9273 ■ *Web:* iatse.net/	New York	NY	10018	212-730-1770	730-7809
Ice Cream Milk & Cheese PAC 1250 H St NW Ste 900 *Web:* www.idfa.org	Washington	DC	20005	202-737-4332	331-7820
Independent Action Inc 1619 13th St NW *Web:* www.independentaction.org	Washington	DC	20009	202-783-2900	
Independent Community Bankers of America PAC 1615 L St Ste 900 *TF:* 800-422-8439 ■ *Web:* icba.org	Washington	DC	20036	202-659-8111	659-3604
Independent Insurance Agents & Brokers of America PAC (INSURPAC) 412 First St SE Ste 300 *Web:* independentagent.com	Washington	DC	20003	202-863-7000	863-7015
International Chiropractors Assn PAC (ICA) 6400 Arlington Blvd Ste 800 *TF:* 800-423-4690 ■ *Web:* www.chiropractic.org	Falls Church	VA	22042	703-528-5000	528-5023
Iowa State Association of Counties 5500 Westown Pkwy 5500 Westown Pkwy *Web:* www.iowacounties.org	West Des Moines	IA	50266	515-244-7181	
Ironworkers Political Action League 1750 New York Ave NW Ste 400 *TF:* 800-368-0105 ■ *Web:* ironworkers.org/get-organized/politicalaction.aspx	Washington	DC	20006	202-383-4800	638-4856
Magazine Publishers of AmNAerica PAC 1211 Connecticut Ave NW Ste 610 *Web:* magazine.org	Washington	DC	20036	202-296-7277	296-0343
Maine People's Alliance 27 State St Ste 44 *Web:* mainepeoplesalliance.org	Bangor	ME	04401	207-990-0672	
Manufactured Housing Institute PAC (MHI PAC) 1655 N Ft Myer Dr Ste 104 *TF:* 800-505-5500 ■ *Web:* www.manufacturedhousing.org	Arlington	VA	22209	703-558-0400	558-0401
MassMutual PAC 1295 State St *TF:* 800-272-2216 ■ *Web:* www.massmutual.com/pac	Springfield	MA	01111	413-788-8411	744-6005
Mechanical Contractors Assn of America PAC 1385 Piccard Dr *TF:* 877-457-6482 ■ *Web:* www.mcaa.org	Rockville	MD	20850	301-869-5800	990-9690
MinePAC 101 Constitution Ave NW Ste 500 E *Web:* nma.org	Washington	DC	20001	202-463-2625	463-2666
Mortgage Bankers Assn PAC (MORPAC) 1717 Rhode Island Ave NW 5th Fl *Web:* www.morpac.org	Washington	DC	20036	202-557-2700	721-0249
Motion Picture Assn of America PAC 1600 'I' St NW **Fax Area Code:* 818 ■ *Web:* mpaa.org	Washington	DC	20006	202-293-1966	382-1799*
Motorola PAC 600 N US Hwy 45 **Fax Area Code:* 202 ■ *Web:* motorola-mobility-en-in.custhelp.com	Libertyville	IL	60048	800-102-2344	842-3578*
NA for Home Care & Hospice PAC (NAHC PAC) 228 Seventh St SE *Web:* www.nahc.org/home.html	Washington	DC	20003	202-547-7424	547-3540
NA of Chain Drug Stores PAC (NACDS PAC) 413 N Lee St	Alexandria	VA	22314	703-549-3001	836-4869
NA of Dental Plans PAC 12700 Pk Central Dr Ste 400 *Web:* www.nadp.org	Dallas	TX	75251	972-458-6998	458-2258
NA of Home Builders PAC 1201 15th St NW *TF:* 800-368-5242 ■ *Web:* www.nahb.org	Washington	DC	20005	202-266-8200	266-8400
NA of Insurance & Financial Advisors PAC 2901 Telestar Ct *Web:* www.naifa.org/advocacy/ifapac	Falls Church	VA	22042	703-770-8100	770-8151
NA of Retired Federal Employees 606 N Washington St *TF:* 800-627-3394 ■ *Web:* www.narfe.org	Alexandria	VA	22314	703-838-7760	838-7785
NAADAC PAC 901 N Washington St Ste 600 *TF:* 800-377-1136 ■ *Web:* www.naadac.org	Alexandria	VA	22314	703-741-7686	741-7698
NARAL Pro-Choice America PAC 1156 15th St NW Ste 700 *Web:* www.prochoiceamerica.org/elections	Washington	DC	20005	202-973-3000	973-3096
NASBIC PAC 1100 H St NW Ste 610 *TF:* 800-471-6153 ■ *Web:* www.sbia.org	Washington	DC	20005	202-628-5055	628-5080
National Air Traffic Controllers Assn PAC (NATCA PAC) 1325 Massachusetts Ave NW *TF:* 800-266-0895 ■ *Web:* www.natca.org	Washington	DC	20005	202-628-5451	628-5767
National Beer Wholesalers Assn PAC (NBWA PAC) 1101 King St Ste 600 *Web:* nbwa.org	Alexandria	VA	22314	703-683-4300	683-8965
National Cable & Telecommunications Assn PAC (Cable PAC) 25 Massachusetts Ave NW *Web:* www.ncta.com	Washington	DC	20001	202-222-2300	222-2517
National Cattlemen's Beef Assn PAC 1301 Pennsylvania Ave NW Ste 300 *Web:* beef.org	Washington	DC	20004	202-347-0228	638-0607
National Confectioners Assn PAC (NCA) 8320 Old Courthouse Rd Ste 300 *TF:* 800-433-1200 ■ *Web:* www.candyusa.com	Vienna	VA	22182	703-790-5750	790-5752
National Court Reporters Assn PAC 8224 Old Courthouse Rd *TF:* 800-272-6272 ■ *Web:* www.ncra.org	Vienna	VA	22182	703-556-6272	556-6291
National Fisheries Institute PAC 7918 Jones Branch Dr Ste 700 *Web:* www.aboutseafood.com	McLean	VA	22102	703-752-8880	752-7583
National Funeral Directors Assn PAC 13625 Bishop S Dr *TF:* 800-228-6332 ■ *Web:* nfda.org	Brookfield	WI	53005	262-789-1880	789-6977
National Grain & Feed Assn PAC 1250 'I' St NW Ste 1003 *Web:* www.ngfa.org	Washington	DC	20005	202-289-0873	289-5388
National Ground Water Assn PAC 601 Dempsey Rd *TF:* 800-551-7379 ■ *Web:* www.ngwa.org	Westerville	OH	43081	614-898-7791	898-7786
National Milk Producers Federation PAC (NMPF PAC) 2101 Wilson Blvd Ste 400 *Web:* nmpf.org	Arlington	VA	22201	703-243-6111	841-9328
National Multi Housing Council PAC 1850 M St NW Ste 540 *TF:* 866-987-7367 ■ *Web:* www.nmhc.org	Washington	DC	20036	202-974-2300	775-0112
National Organization for Women PAC (NOWPAC) 1100 H St NW Ste 300 *Web:* nowpac.org/	Washington	DC	20005	202-628-8669	785-8576
National Pork Producers Council PAC 122 C St NW Ste 875 *TF:* 800-392-5705 ■ *Web:* www.nppc.org	Washington	DC	20001	202-347-3600	347-5265
National Propane Gas Assn PAC (NPGAPAC) 1899 L St NW Ste 350 *TF:* 888-445-1404 ■ *Web:* www.npga.org/i4a/pages/index.cfm?pageid=1707	Washington	DC	20036	202-466-7200	466-7205
National Restaurant Assn PAC 2055 L St NW Ste 700 *TF:* 888-804-0001 ■ *Web:* www.restaurant.org	Washington	DC	20036	202-331-5900	
National Right to Life PAC 512 Tenth St NW *Web:* www.nrlc.org	Washington	DC	20004	202-626-8800	393-5433
National Roofing Contractors Assn PAC (NRCAPAC) 324 Fourth St NE *Web:* nrca.net	Washington	DC	20002	202-546-7584	546-9289
National Stone Sand & Gravel Assn PAC 1605 King St *TF:* 866-722-6959 ■ *Web:* nssga.org	Alexandria	VA	22314	703-525-8788	525-7782
National Sunflower Assn PAC 2401 46th Ave SE Ste 206 *TF:* 888-718-7033 ■ *Web:* www.sunflowernsa.com	Mandan	ND	58554	701-328-5100	328-5101
National Turkey Federation PAC 1225 New York Ave NW Ste 400 *Web:* eatturkey.com	Washington	DC	20005	202-898-0100	898-0203
National Venture Capital Assn (NVCA) 1655 N Ft Myer Dr Ste 850 *Web:* www.nvca.org	Arlington	VA	22209	703-524-2549	524-3940
NATSO PAC 1737 King St Ste 200 *Web:* natso.com	Alexandria	VA	22314	703-549-2100	684-4525
NCFC Co-op PAC 50 F St NW Ste 900 *Web:* www.ncfc.org	Washington	DC	20001	202-626-8700	626-8722
NEA Fund for Children & Public Education 1201 16th St NW *Web:* www.neafund.org	Washington	DC	20036	202-833-4000	822-7974
North American Meat Institute (AMIPAC) 1150 Connecticut Ave NW *Web:* www.meatami.com	Washington	DC	20036	202-587-4200	587-4300
NRA Institute for Legislative Action 11250 Waples Mill Rd **Fax Area Code:* 703 ■ *TF:* 800-392-8683 ■ *Web:* www.nraila.org	Fairfax	VA	22030	800-392-8683	267-3918*
Nuclear Energy Institute Federal PAC 1776 I St NW Ste 400 *Web:* www.nei.org	Washington	DC	20006	202-739-8000	785-4019
Ontario Pc Party 19 Duncan St *Web:* www.ontariopc.com	Toronto	ON	M5H3H1	416-861-9593	
Outdoor Adv Assn of America Inc (OAAA) 1850 M St NW Ste 1040 *TF:* 800-537-0983 ■ *Web:* www.oaaa.org	Washington	DC	20036	202-833-5566	833-1522
Outdoor Amusement Business Assn PAC (OABA-PAC) 1035 S Semoran Blvd Ste 1045A *Web:* www.oaba.org	Winter Park	FL	32792	407-681-9444	681-9445
Petroleum Marketers Assn of America's Small Business Community 1901 N Fort Myer Dr Ste 500 *TF:* 888-372-7341 ■ *Web:* epa.gov	Arlington	VA	22209	703-351-8000	351-9160
Planned Parenthood Action Fund Inc 1110 Vermont Ave NW *TF:* 800-430-4907 ■ *Web:* www.plannedparenthoodaction.org	Washington	DC	20005	202-973-4800	296-3242
Print PAC 601 13th St NW Ste 800 *Web:* www.printpaconline.org	Washington	DC	20005	202-730-7970	730-7987
REITPAC 1875 'I' St NW Ste 600 *TF:* 800-362-7348 ■ *Web:* www.reit.com	Washington	DC	20006	202-739-9400	739-9401
Society of American Florists PAC 1601 Duke St *TF:* 800-336-4743 ■ *Web:* www.safnow.org	Alexandria	VA	22314	703-836-8700	836-8705
Title Industry PAC (TIPAC) 1828 L St NW Ste 705 *TF:* 800-787-2582 ■ *Web:* www.alta.org	Washington	DC	20036	202-296-3671	223-5843
Truck PAC 430 First St SE Second Fl *Web:* www.truckline.com	Washington	DC	20003	202-544-6245	675-6568
Wine & Spirits Wholesalers of America PAC 805 15th St NW Ste 430 *Web:* www.wswa.org	Washington	DC	20005	202-371-9792	789-2405

POLITICAL LEADERS

SEE US Senators, Representatives, Delegates p. 2428; Governors - State p. 2437

619 POLITICAL PARTIES (MAJOR)

SEE ALSO Civic & Political Organizations p. 1765

				Phone	Fax
Communist Party USA 235 W 23rd St Eighth Fl. Web: www.cpusa.org	New York	NY	10011	212-989-4994	229-1713
Democratic National Committee 430 S Capitol St SE Web: www.democrats.org	Washington	DC	20003	202-863-8000	
Democratic Socialists of America 75 Maiden Ln Ste 505 Web: www.dsausa.org	New York	NY	10038	212-727-8610	
Libertarian Party 2600 Virginia Ave NW Ste 200 TF: 800-353-2887 ■ Web: www.lp.org	Washington	DC	20037	202-333-0008	333-0072
Republican National Committee (RNC) 310 First St SE TF: 800-445-5768 ■ Web: www.gop.com	Washington	DC	20003	202-863-8500	
Socialist Labor Party of America PO Box 218 Web: www.slp.org	Mountain View	CA	94042	408-280-7266	280-6964

619-1 Democratic State Committees

				Phone	Fax
Alabama Democratic Party 501 Adams Ave Web: aladems.org	Montgomery	AL	36104	334-262-2221	262 6474
Alaska Democratic Party 2602 Fairbanks St Web: www.alaskademocrats.org	Anchorage	AK	99503	907-258-3050	258-1626
Arkansas Democratic Party 1300 W Capitol Ave Web: www.arkdems.org	Little Rock	AR	72201	501-374-2361	376-8409
California Democratic Party 1401 21st St Ste 200 Web: www.cadem.org	Sacramento	CA	95811	916-442-5707	
Colorado Democratic Party 789 Sherman St Web: www.coloradodems.org	Denver	CO	80204	303-623-4762	623-2443
Connecticut Democratic Party 30 Arbor St Web: www.ctdems.org	Hartford	CT	06106	860-560-1775	387-0147
Delaware Democratic Party 19 E Commons Blvd Second Fl Web: www.deldems.org	New Castle	DE	19720	302-328-9036	328-9386
Florida Democratic Party 214 S Bronough St TF: 855-352-7233 ■ Web: www.floridadems.org	Tallahassee	FL	32301	850-222-3411	222-0916
Hawaii Democratic Party 1050 Ala Moana Blvd Ste D-26 Web: www.hawaiidemocrats.org	Honolulu	HI	96814	808-596-2980	596-2985
Idaho Democratic Party 943 W Overland Rd TF: 800-626-0471 ■ Web: idahodems.org	Meridian	ID	83642	208-336-1815	336-1817
Indiana Democratic Party 115 W Washington St Ste 1165 TF: 800-223-3387 ■ Web: www.indems.org	Indianapolis	IN	46204	317-231-7100	231-7129
Iowa Democratic Party 5661 Fleur Dr Web: www.iowademocrats.org	Des Moines	IA	50321	515-244-7292	244-5051
Kansas Democratic Party 700 SW Jackson St Ste 706 TF: 888-573-3547 ■ Web: www.ksdp.org	Topeka	KS	66603	785-234-0425	234-8420
Kentucky Democratic Party 190 Democrat Dr Web: www.kydemocrat.com	Frankfort	KY	40601	502-695-4828	695-7629
Louisiana Democratic Party 701 Government St Web: louisianademocrats.org	Baton Rouge	LA	70802	225-336-4155	336-0046
Maine Democratic Party PO Box 5258 Web: www.mainedems.org	Augusta	ME	04332	207-622-6233	622-2657
Massachusetts Democratic Party 77 Summer St 10th Fl Web: www.massdems.org	Boston	MA	02110	617-939-0800	426-5126
Michigan Democratic Party 606 Townsend St Web: www.michigandems.com	Lansing	MI	48933	517-371-5410	371-2056
Missouri Democratic Party PO Box 719 Web: www.missouridems.org	Jefferson City	MO	65102	573-636-5241	634-4259
Montana Democratic Party PO Box 802 Web: www.montanademocrats.org	Helena	MT	59624	406-442-9520	442-9534
New Hampshire Democratic Party 105 N State St Web: nhdp.org	Concord	NH	03301	603-225-6899	
New Jersey Democratic State Committee 196 W State St Web: www.njdems.org	Trenton	NJ	08608	609-392-3367	396-4778
New Mexico Democratic Party (DPNM) 8214 Second St NW ste A TF: 800-624-2457 ■ Web: www.nmdemocrats.org	Albuquerque	NM	87114	505-830-3650	830-3645
North Carolina Democratic Party 220 Hillsborough St TF: 800-229-3367 ■ Web: www.ncdp.org	Raleigh	NC	27603	919-821-2777	821-4778
North Dakota Democratic Party 1902 E Divide Ave Web: www.demnpl.com	Bismarck	ND	58501	701-255-0460	255-7823
Ohio Democratic Party 340 E Fulton St Web: www.ohiodems.org	Columbus	OH	43215	614-221-6563	221-0721
Oklahoma Democratic Party 4100 N Lincoln Blvd Web: www.okdemocrats.org	Oklahoma City	OK	73105	405-427-3366	
Oregon Democratic Party 232 NE Ninth Ave Web: www.dpo.org	Portland	OR	97232	503-224-8200	224-5335
Pennsylvania Democratic Party 300 N Second St 8th Fl TF: 800-437-7439 ■ Web: www.padems.com	Harrisburg	PA	17101	717-920-8470	901-7829
Rhode Island Democratic Party 151 Broadway Ste 310 Web: www.ridemocrats.org	Providence	RI	02903	401-272-3367	272-3368
South Carolina Democratic Party PO Box 5965 TF: 800-841-1817 ■ Web: www.scdp.org	Columbia	SC	29250	803-799-7798	765-1692
South Dakota Democratic Party 335 N Main Ave Ste 200 Web: www.sddp.org	Sioux Falls	SD	57104	605-271-5405	
Tennessee Democratic Party 1900 Church St Ste 203 Web: www.tndp.org	Nashville	TN	37203	615-327-9779	327-9759
Texas Democratic Party 505 W 12th St Ste 200 Web: www.txdemocrats.org	Austin	TX	78701	512-478-9800	480-2500
Virginia Democratic Party 1710 E Franklin St Second Fl TF: 800-322-1144 ■ Web: www.vademocrats.org	Richmond	VA	23223	804-644-1966	343-3642
Washington Democratic Party PO Box 4027 Web: www.wa-democrats.org	Seattle	WA	98194	206-583-0664	583-0301
West Virginia Democratic Party 717 Lee St Ste 214 Web: www.wvdemocrats.com	Charleston	WV	25301	304-342-8121	342-8122
Wisconsin Democratic Party 110 King St Ste 203 Web: www.wisdems.org	Madison	WI	53703	608-255-5172	255-8919

619-2 Republican State Committees

				Phone	Fax
Alabama Republican Party 3505 Lorna Rd Ste 219 TF: 800-274-8683 ■ Web: www.algop.org	Birmingham	AL	35216	205-212-5900	212-5910
Alaska Republican Party 1001 W Fireweed Ln Web: www.alaskarepublicans.com	Anchorage	AK	99503	907-276-4467	276-0425
Arizona Republican Party 3501 N 24th St Web: www.azgop.org	Phoenix	AZ	85016	602-957-7770	224-0932
California Republican Party 1903 W Magnolia Blvd Web: www.cagop.org	Burbank	CA	91506	818-841-5210	841-6668
Colorado Republican Party 5950 S Willow Dr Ste 210 Web: www.cologop.org	Greenwood Village	CO	80111	303-758-3333	
Connecticut Republican Party 31 Pratt St Fourth Fl Web: www.ctgop.org	Hartford	CT	06103	860-422-8211	422-8175
Georgia Republican Party 3110 Maple Dr Ste 200-E Web: www.gagop.org	Atlanta	GA	30305	404-257-5559	257-0779
Hawaii Republican Party 725 Kapiolani Blvd Ste C105 Web: www.gophawaii.com	Honolulu	HI	96813	808-593-8180	593-7742
Idaho Republican State Committee 802 W Bannock Lowr Plz 103 PO Box 2267 Web: www.idgop.org	Boise	ID	83702	208-343-6405	343-6414
Indiana Republican Party 47 S Meridian St Ste 200 TF: 800-466-1087 ■ Web: www.indgop.org	Indianapolis	IN	46204	317-635-7561	632-8510
Iowa Republican Party 621 E Ninth St Web: www.iowagop.org	Des Moines	IA	50309	515-282-8105	282-9019
Kansas Republican Party 2605 SW 21st St PO Box 4157 Web: www.ksgop.org	Topeka	KS	66604	785-234-3456	228-0353
Kentucky Republican Party PO Box 1068 Web: www.rpk.org	Frankfort	KY	40602	502-875-5130	223-5625
Louisiana Republican Party 530 Lk Land Rd Web: www.lagop.com	Baton Rouge	LA	70802	225-389-4495	389-4493
Maine Republican Party Nine Higgins St Web: www.mainegop.com	Augusta	ME	04330	207-622-6247	623-5322
Maryland Republican Party 95 Cathedral St Web: www.mdgop.org	Annapolis	MD	21401	410-263-2125	
Massachusetts Republican State Committee 85 Merrimac St Ste 400 Web: www.massgop.com	Boston	MA	02114	617-523-5005	523-6311
Michigan Republican State Committee 520 Seymour Ave Web: www.migop.org	Lansing	MI	48933	517-487-5413	487-0090
Minnesota Republican Party 2200 E Franklin Ave Ste 201 Web: www.mngop.com	Minneapolis	MN	55404	651-222-0022	224-4122
Mississippi Republican Party 415 Yazoo St PO Box 60 Web: www.msgop.org	Jackson	MS	39201	601-948-5191	354-0972
Montana Republican Party 1005 Partridge Pl Web: www.mtgop.org	Helena	MT	59602	406-442-6469	
Nebraska Republican Party 1610 N St Web: nadc.nebraska.gov	Lincoln	NE	68508	402-475-2122	475-3541
Nevada Republican Party 6330 McLeod Dr Ste 1 Web: www.nevadagop.org	Las Vegas	NV	89120	702-258-9182	258-9186
New Hampshire Republican State Committee 10 Water St Web: www.nhgop.org	Concord	NH	03301	603-225-9341	225-7498
New Mexico Republican Party (RPNM) 5150-A San Francisco Rd NE PO Box 94083 Web: www.gopnm.org	Albuquerque	NM	87109	505-298-3662	292-0755
New York Republican State Committee 315 State St Web: www.nygop.org	Albany	NY	12210	518-462-2601	449-7443
North Carolina Republican Party PO Box 12905 Web: www.ncgop.org	Raleigh	NC	27605	919-828-6423	899-3815
Ohio Republican Party 211 S Fifth St Web: www.ohiogop.org	Columbus	OH	43215	614-228-2481	228-1093

				Phone	Fax
Oklahoma Republican State Committee 4031 N Lincoln Blvd *Web:* www.okgop.com	Oklahoma City	OK	73105	405-528-3501	521-9531
Pennsylvania Republican State Committee 112 State St *Web:* www.pagop.org	Harrisburg	PA	17101	717-234-4901	231-3828
South Carolina Republican Party, The 1913 Marion St *Web:* www.scgop.com	Columbia	SC	29201	803-988-8440	988-8444
South Dakota Republican State Central Committee PO Box 1099 *Web:* www.southdakotagop.com	Pierre	SD	57501	605-224-7347	224-7349
Tennessee Republican Party 2424 21st Ave Ste 200 *Web:* www.tngop.org	Nashville	TN	37212	615-269-4260	269-4261
Texas Republican Party 1108 Lavaca Ste 500 *TF:* 800-525-5555 ■ *Web:* www.texasgop.org	Austin	TX	78701	512-477-9821	480-0709
Utah Republican Party 117 E S Temple St *Web:* utgop.org	Salt Lake City	UT	84111	801-533-9777	533-0327
Virginia Republican Party 115 E Grace St *Web:* www.rpv.org	Richmond	VA	23219	804-780-0111	343-1060
West Virginia Republican State Committee PO Box 2711 *Web:* www.wvgop.org	Charleston	WV	25330	304-768-0493	768-6083
Wisconsin Republican Party 148 E Johnson St *Web:* www.wisgop.org	Madison	WI	53703	608-257-4765	257-4141
Wyoming Republican Party 1821 Carey Ave PO Box 984 *TF:* 800-424-9530 ■ *Web:* www.wygop.org	Casper	WY	82003	307-234-9166	

620 PORTALS - VOICE

Voice portals permit users to access web-based messaging as well as various types of Internet information (e.g., weather, stock quotes, driving directions, etc.) via the telephone (wired or wireless).

				Phone	Fax
GoSolo Technologies Inc 5410 Mariner St Ste 175 *TF:* 866-246-7656 ■ *Web:* www.teamgosolo.com	Tampa	FL	33609	866-246-7656	
InternetSpeech.com 6980 Santa Teresa Blvd Ste 201 *Web:* www.internetspeech.com	San Jose	CA	95119	408-360-7730	360-7726
Tellme Networks Inc 1310 Villa St *Web:* www.bing.com	Mountain View	CA	94041	650-930-9000	930-9101

621 PORTS & PORT AUTHORITIES

SEE ALSO Cruise Lines p. 2183; Airports p. 1737

				Phone	Fax
Alabama State Port Authority PO Box 1588 *Web:* www.asdd.com	Mobile	AL	36633	251-441-7200	441-7216
Bradford Licensing Associates Seven Oak Pl Ste 1 *Web:* www.bradfordlicensing.com	Montclair	NJ	07042	973-509-0200	
Cleveland-Cuyahoga County Port Authority 1375 E Ninth St Ste 2300 *Web:* portofcleveland.com	Cleveland	OH	44114	216-241-8004	241-8016
Delaware River Port Authority one Port Center 2 Riverside Dr PO Box 1949 **Fax:* Hum Res ■ *Web:* www.drpa.org	Camden	NJ	08101	856-968-2000	968-2242*
Detroit-Wayne County Port Authority 130 E Atwater St *Web:* www.portdetroit.com	Detroit	MI	48226	313-259-5091	259-5093
Eastport Port Authority 3 Madison St *Web:* www.portofeastport.org	Eastport	ME	04631	207-853-4614	853-9584
Erie-Western Pennsylvania Port Authority 208 E Bayfront Pkwy Ste 201 *Web:* www.porterie.org	Erie	PA	16507	814-455-7557	455-8070
Georgia Ports Authority PO Box 2406 *TF:* 800-342-8012 ■ *Web:* www.gaports.com	Savannah	GA	31402	912-964-3811	964-3921
Greater Lafourche Port Commission PO Box 490 *Web:* www.portfourchon.com	Galliano	LA	70354	985-632-6701	632-6703
Halifax Port Authority 1215 Marginal Rd PO Box 336 *Web:* www.portofhalifax.ca	Halifax	NS	B3J2P6	902-426-8222	426-7335
Hamilton Port Authority 605 James St N 6th Fl *TF:* 800-263-2131 ■ *Web:* www.hamiltonport.ca	Hamilton	ON	L8L1K1	905-525-4330	528-6554
Hawaii Dept of Transportation Harbors Div 79 S Nimitz Hwy *Web:* www.hawaii.gov	Honolulu	HI	96813	808-587-1927	587-1928
Humboldt Bay Harbor District 601 Startare Dr *Web:* www.portofhumboldtbay.org	Eureka	CA	95501	707-443-0801	443-0800
Illinois International Port District 3600 E 95th St *TF:* 800-843-7678 ■ *Web:* iipd.com	Chicago	IL	60617	773-646-4400	221-7678
Indiana Port Commission 150 W Market St Ste 100 *TF:* 800-232-7678 ■ *Web:* www.portsofindiana.com	Indianapolis	IN	46204	317-232-9200	232-0137
International Port of Dutch Harbor PO Box 610 *TF:* 800-526-6731 ■ *Web:* ci.unalaska.ak.us/	Unalaska	AK	99685	907-581-1251	
Juneau Harbor 155 S Seward St *Web:* www.juneau.org/harbors	Juneau	AK	99801	907-586-5255	586-2507
Ketchikan Ports & Harbors Dept 2933 Tongass Ave *Web:* www.city.ketchikan.ak.us	Ketchikan	AK	99901	907-228-5632	247-3610
Kodiak Port & Harbor 403 Marine Way *TF:* 800-563-4254 ■ *Web:* city.kodiak.ak.us	Kodiak	AK	99615	907-486-8080	486-8090
Manatee County Port Authority 300 Tampa Bay Way *Web:* www.portmanatee.com	Palmetto	FL	34221	941-722-6621	729-1463
Massachusetts Port Authority One Harborside Dr Ste 200S *Web:* www.massport.com	East Boston	MA	02128	617-568-7300	
Mississippi State Port Authority at Gulfport 2510 14th St Ste 1450 *TF:* 877-881-4367 ■ *Web:* www.shipmspa.com	Gulfport	MS	39501	228-865-4300	865-4335
Montreal Port Authority Port of Montreal Bldg 2100 Pierre-Dupuy Ave Wing 1 *Web:* www.port-montreal.com	Montreal	QC	H3C3R5	514-283-7011	283-0829
Nanaimo Port Authority 104 Front St PO Box 131 *Web:* www.npa.ca	Nanaimo	BC	V9R5H7	250-753-4146	753-4899
New Bedford Harbor Development Commission 52 Fisherman S Wharf PO Box 50899 *Web:* www.portofnewbedford.org	New Bedford	MA	02745	508-961-3000	979-1517
New Hampshire State Port Authority 555 Market St *Web:* www.portsmouthnh.com	Portsmouth	NH	03801	603-436-8500	436-2780
North Carolina State Ports Authority 2202 Burnett Blvd PO Box 9002 *TF:* 800-334-0682 ■ *Web:* www.ncports.com	Wilmington	NC	28402	910-763-1621	
Ogdensburg Bridge & Port Authority 1 Bridge Plaza *Web:* www.ogdensport.com	Ogdensburg	NY	13669	315-393-4080	393-7068
Oregon International Port of Coos Bay 125 Central Ave Ste 300 PO Box 1215 *TF:* 800-463-3339 ■ *Web:* www.portofcoosbay.com	Coos Bay	OR	97420	541-267-7678	269-1475
Oshawa Harbour Commission 1050 Farewell Ave *Web:* portofoshawa.ca	Oshawa	ON	L1H6N6	905-576-0400	576-5701
Philadelphia Regional Port Authority 3460 N Delaware Ave 2nd Fl *TF:* 800-449-7575 ■ *Web:* www.philaport.com	Philadelphia	PA	19134	215-426-2600	426-6800
Port Alberni Port Authority 2750 Harbour Rd *Web:* portalberniportauthority.ca	Port Alberni	BC	V9Y7X2	250-723-5312	723-1114
Port Authority of New York/New Jersey 225 Pk Ave S 15th Fl *Web:* www.panynj.gov	New York	NY	10003	212-435-7000	
Port Canaveral 445 Challanger Rd *TF:* 888-767-8226 ■ *Web:* www.portcanaveral.com	Cape Canaveral	FL	32920	321-783-7831	784-6223
Port Everglades 1850 Eller Dr *Web:* www.porteverglades.org	Fort Lauderdale	FL	33316	954-523-3404	525-1910
Port Freeport PO Box 615 *TF:* 800-362-5743 ■ *Web:* www.portfreeport.com	Freeport	TX	77542	979-233-2667	233-5625
Port Metro Vancouver 100 The Pt 999 Canada Pl **Fax Area Code:* 866 ■ *Web:* www.portmetrovancouver.com	Vancouver	BC	V6C3T4	604-665-9000	284-4271*
Port of Albany *Albany Port District Commission* 106 Smith Blvd *Web:* www.portofalbany.us	Albany	NY	12202	518-463-8763	463-8767
Port of Anacortes 100 Commercial Ave *Web:* www.portofanacortes.com	Anacortes	WA	98221	360-293-3134	293-9608
Port of Anchorage 2000 Anchorage Port Rd *TF:* 877-650-8400 ■ *Web:* www.muni.org	Anchorage	AK	99501	907-343-6200	277-5636
Port of Astoria 422 Gateway Ave *TF:* 800-860-4093 ■ *Web:* www.portofastoria.com	Astoria	OR	97103	503-325-4521	325-4525
Port of Baltimore *Maryland Port Administration* 401 E Pratt St *TF General:* 800-638-7519 ■ *Web:* www.mpa.maryland.gov	Baltimore	MD	21202	800-638-7519	
Port of Beaumont 1225 Main St *Web:* www.portofbeaumont.com	Beaumont	TX	77701	409-835-5367	832-9592
Port of Bellingham 1801 Roeder Ave *Web:* www.portofbellingham.com	Bellingham	WA	98225	360-676-2500	671-6411
Port of Brownsville 1000 Foust Rd *TF:* 800-378-5395 ■ *Web:* www.portofbrownsville.com	Brownsville	TX	78521	956-831-4592	831-5006
Port of Burns Harbor 6625 S Boundary Dr *Web:* www.portsofindiana.com	Portage	IN	46368	219-787-8636	787-8842
Port of Corpus Christi 222 Power St *TF:* 800-580-7110 ■ *Web:* www.portofcorpuschristi.com	Corpus Christi	TX	78401	361-882-5633	882-7110
Port of Duluth *Duluth Seaway Port Authority* 1200 Port Terminal Dr *TF:* 800-232-0703 ■ *Web:* www.duluthport.com	Duluth	MN	55802	218-727-8525	727-6888
Port of Everett 2911 Bond St Ste 202 *TF:* 800-729-7678 ■ *Web:* www.portofeverett.com	Everett	WA	98201	425-259-3164	252-7366
Port of Galveston 123 25th St *Web:* www.portofgalveston.com	Galveston	TX	77550	409-765-9321	766-6107
Port of Grays Harbor 111 S Wooding St *Web:* www.portofgraysharbor.com	Aberdeen	WA	98520	360-533-9528	533-9505
Port of Greater Baton Rouge *Greater Baton Rouge Port Commission* 2425 Ernest Wilson Dr PO Box 380 *Web:* www.portgbr.com	Port Allen	LA	70767	225-342-1660	342-1666
Port of Homer 4350 Homer Spit Rd *Web:* www.cityofhomer-ak.gov	Homer	AK	99603	907-235-3160	235-3152
Port of Houston 111 E Loop N *Web:* www.portofhouston.com	Houston	TX	77029	713-670-2400	671-0359
Port of Iberia 4611 S Lewis St PO Box 9986 *Web:* www.portofiberia.com	New Iberia	LA	70562	337-364-1065	364-3136
Port of Jacksonville *Jacksonville Port Authority* 2831 Talleyrand Ave PO Box 3005 *Web:* www.jaxport.com	Jacksonville	FL	32206	904-357-3000	357-3060
Port of Lake Charles 150 Marine St *TF:* 800-845-7678 ■ *Web:* www.portlc.com	Lake Charles	LA	70601	337-439-3661	493-3523
Port of Long Beach 925 Harbor Plz *Web:* www.polb.com	Long Beach	CA	90801	562-437-0041	901-1725

				Phone	Fax
Port of Longview 10 Port Way *Web:* www.portoflongview.com	Longview	WA	98632	360-425-3305	425-8650
Port of Los Angeles 425 S Palos Verdes St **Fax:* Hum Res ■ *Web:* www.portoflosangeles.org	San Pedro	CA	90731	310-732-7678	831-0439*
Port of Miami 1015 N America Way *Web:* www.miamidade.gov	Miami	FL	33132	305-371-7678	347-4843
Port of Milwaukee 2323 S Lincoln Memorial Dr *TF:* 800-367-5690 ■ *Web:* city.milwaukee.gov/port	Milwaukee	WI	53207	414-286-3511	286-8506
Port of Mobile *Alabama State Docks Dept* 250 N Water St *Web:* www.asdd.com	Mobile	AL	36602	251-441-7203	441-7216
Port of Monroe *Monroe Port Commission* 2929 E Front St PO Box 585 *Web:* www.portofmonroe.com	Monroe	MI	48161	734-241-6480	241-0813
Port of New London *Connecticut Bureau of Aviation & Ports* State Pier *Web:* www.ct.gov/	New London	CT	06320	860-443-3856	
Port of New Orleans 1350 Port of New Orleans Pl *TF:* 800-776-6652 ■ *Web:* www.portno.com	New Orleans	LA	70130	504-522-2551	524-4156
Port of Newport 600 SE Bay Blvd *Web:* www.portofnewport.com	Newport	OR	97365	541-265-7758	265-4235
Port of Nome 307 Belmont St *Web:* www.nomealaska.org	Nome	AK	99762	907-443-6619	443-5473
Port of Oakland 530 Water St *Web:* www.portoakland.com	Oakland	CA	94607	510-627-1100	
Port of Olympia 915 Washington St NE *Web:* www.portolympia.com	Olympia	WA	98501	360-528-8000	528-8090
Port of Orange *Orange County Navigation Port District* 1201 Childers Rd *TF:* 800-368-3749 ■ *Web:* www.portoforange.com	Orange	TX	77630	409-883-4363	883-5607
Port of Oswego Authority One E Second St PO Box 387 *Web:* www.portoswego.com	Oswego	NY	13126	315-343-4503	343-5498
Port of Palm Beach 1 E 11th St Ste 400 *TF:* 877-377-1737 ■ *Web:* www.portofpalmbeach.com	Riviera Beach	FL	33404	561-842-4201	842-4240
Port of Pascagoula *Jackson County Port Authority* 3033 Pascagoula St *Web:* www.portofpascagoula.com	Pascagoula	MS	39567	228-762-4041	762-7476
Port of Pensacola 700 S Barracks St *TF:* 800-711-1712 ■ *Web:* www.portofpensacola.com	Pensacola	FL	32502	850-436-5070	436-5076
Port of Pittsburgh 425 Sixth Ave Ste 2990 *Web:* www.port.pittsburgh.pa.us	Pittsburgh	PA	15219	412-201-7330	201-7337
Port of Port Angeles 338 W First St PO Box 1350 *Web:* www.portofpa.com	Port Angeles	WA	98362	360-457-8527	452-3959
Port of Port Arthur 221 Houston Ave *Web:* www.portofportarthur.com	Port Arthur	TX	77640	409-983-2011	983-7572
Port of Port Lavaca-Point Comfort *Calhoun Port Authority* PO Box 397 *TF:* 800-933-3643 ■ *Web:* www.calhounport.com	Point Comfort	TX	77978	361-987-2813	987-2189
Port of Portland 389 Congress St *Web:* portlandmaine.gov	Portland	ME	04101	207-874-8892	874-8473
Port of Redwood City 675 Seaport Blvd *Web:* www.redwoodcityport.com	Redwood City	CA	94063	650-306-4150	369-7636
Port of Richmond Commission 900 E Broad St *TF:* 800-467-4943 ■ *Web:* richmondgov.com	Richmond	VA	23219	804-646-6335	646-5789
Port of Sacramento 1110 W Capitol Ave *Web:* www.cityofwestsacramento.org	West Sacramento	CA	95691	916-371-8000	372-4802
Port of Saint Helens 100 E St *Web:* www.portsh.org	Columbia City	OR	97018	503-397-2888	397-6924
Port of San Diego 3165 Pacific Hwy *TF:* 800-854-2757 ■ *Web:* www.portofsandiego.org	San Diego	CA	92101	619-686-6200	686-6400
Port of San Francisco Pier 1 The Embarcadero *TF:* 800-479-5314 ■ *Web:* www.sfport.com	San Francisco	CA	94111	415-274-0400	732-0400
Port of Seattle PO Box 1209 *TF:* 800-426-7817 ■ *Web:* www.portseattle.org	Seattle	WA	98111	206-728-3000	728-3280
Port of Sept-Iles 1 Quai Mgr-Blanche *Web:* www.portsi.com	Sept-Iles	QC	G4R5P3	418-968-1231	962-4445
Port of Seward PO Box 167 *TF:* 855-445-7131 ■ *Web:* www.cityofseward.net	Seward	AK	99664	907-224-3138	224-7187
Port of South Louisiana 171 Belle Terre Blvd PO Box 909 **Fax Area Code:* 504 ■ *TF:* 866-536-8300 ■ *Web:* www.portsl.com	LaPlace	LA	70068	985-652-9278	568-6270*
Port of Stockton 2201 W Washington St *TF:* 800-344-3213 ■ *Web:* www.portofstockton.com	Stockton	CA	95203	209-946-0246	465-7244
Port of Tacoma One Sitcum Way *Web:* www.portoftacoma.com	Tacoma	WA	98421	253-383-5841	593-4570
Port of Valdez 412 Ferry Terminal Way *Web:* www.ci.valdez.ak.us	Valdez	AK	99686	907-835-4564	835-4479
Port of Vancouver 3103 NW Lower River Rd *TF:* 800-475-8012 ■ *Web:* www.portvanusa.com	Vancouver	WA	98660	360-693-3611	735-1565
Port of Wilmington One Hausel Rd *Web:* www.portofwilmington.com	Wilmington	DE	19801	302-472-7678	472-7740
Port Panama City 5321 W Hwy 98 *Web:* www.portpanamacityusa.com	Panama City	FL	32401	850-767-3220	767-3235
Prince Rupert Port Authority 200-215 Cow Bay Rd *Web:* www.rupertport.com	Prince Rupert	BC	V8J1A2	250-627-8899	627-8980
Quebec Port Authority 150 Dalhousie St PO Box 80 Stn Haute-Ville *Web:* www.portquebec.ca	Quebec	QC	G1R4M8	418-648-3640	648-4160
Saguenay Port Authority 6600 Quai-Marcel-Dionne Rd *Web:* www.portsaguenay.ca	La Baie	QC	G7B3N9	418-697-0250	697-0243
Saint John Port Authority 111 Water St *Web:* www.sjport.com	Saint John	NB	E2L0B1	506-636-4869	636-4443
Sitka Harbor 617 Katlian St *TF:* 866-948-8683 ■ *Web:* cityofsitka.com	Sitka	AK	99835	907-747-3439	747-6278
South Carolina State Ports Authority 176 Concord St *TF:* 800-845-7106 ■ *Web:* www.scspa.com	Charleston	SC	29401	843-723-8651	577-8710
South Jersey Port Corp Second & Beckett St *Web:* www.southjerseyport.com	Camden	NJ	08103	856-757-4969	757-4903
Tampa Port Authority 1101 Channelside Dr *TF:* 800-741-2297 ■ *Web:* www.tampaport.com	Tampa	FL	33602	813-905-7678	905-5109
Thunder Bay Port Authority 100 Main St *Web:* www.portofthunderbay.com	Thunder Bay	ON	P7B6R9	807-345-6400	345-9058
Toledo-Lucas County Port Authority 1 Maritime Plaza *TF:* 800-969-4700 ■ *Web:* www.toledoportauthority.org	Toledo	OH	43604	419-243-8251	243-1835
Toronto Port Authority 60 Harbour St *Web:* www.torontoport.com	Toronto	ON	M5J1B7	416-863-2000	863-0495
Trois-Rivieres Port Authority 1545 Du Fleuve St Ste 300 *Web:* www.porttr.com	Trois-Rivieres	QC	G9A6K4	819-378-2887	378-2487
Virginia Port Authority 101 W Main St *Web:* www.portofvirginia.com	Norfolk	VA	23510	757-683-8000	683-8500
Waukegan Port District 55 S Harbor Pl PO Box 620 *Web:* www.waukeganport.com	Waukegan	IL	60085	847-244-3133	244-1348
Windsor Port Authority 251 Goyeau St Ste 502 *Web:* www.portwindsor.com	Windsor	ON	N9A6V2	519-258-5741	258-5905
Wrangell Harbor PO Box 531 *TF:* 800-347-4462 ■ *Web:* www.wrangell.com	Wrangell	AK	99929	907-874-3736	874-3197

622 POULTRY PROCESSING

SEE ALSO Meat Packing Plants p. 2723

				Phone	Fax
Allen Family Foods Inc 126 N Shipley St *Web:* allenharimllc.com/index.cfm	Seaford	DE	19973	302-629-9163	629-0514
American Dehydrated Foods Inc 3801 E Sunshine *TF:* 800-456-3447 ■ *Web:* www.adf.com/	Springfield	MO	65809	417-881-7755	881-4963
Amick Farms Inc 2079 Batesburg Hwy **Fax:* Sales ■ *TF:* 800-926-4257 ■ *Web:* www.amickfarms.com	Batesburg	SC	29006	803-532-1400	*
Barber's Poultry Inc 810 E 50th Ave *Web:* www.barberspoultry.com	Denver	CO	80216	303-466-7338	466-6960
Bell & Evans 154 W Main St PO Box 39 *Web:* www.bellandevans.com	Fredericksburg	PA	17026	717-865-6626	865-7046
Brakebush Bros Inc N4993 Sixth Dr *TF:* 800-933-2121 ■ *Web:* www.brakebush.com	Westfield	WI	53964	608-296-2121	296-3192
Brown Produce Co Hwy 37 PO Box 265	Farina	IL	62838	618-245-3301	
Butterfield Foods Co 225 Hubbard Ave **Fax Area Code:* 317	Butterfield	MN	56120	507-956-5103	776-4784*
Cargill Inc North America 15407 McGinty Rd *Web:* cargill.com	Wayzata	MN	55391	952-742-7575	
Case Farms Inc 121 Rand St *Web:* casefarms.com	Morganton	NC	28655	828-438-6900	437-5205
Claxton Poultry Farms 8816 Hway 301 PO Box 428 *TF:* 888-739-3181 ■ *Web:* www.claxtonpoultry.com	Claxton	GA	30417	912-739-3181	
Culver Duck Farms Inc PO Box 910 *TF:* 800-825-9225 ■ *Web:* www.culverduck.com	Middlebury	IN	46540	574-825-9537	825-2613
Echo Lake Farm Produce Co PO Box 279 *Web:* www.echolakefoods.com	Burlington	WI	53105	800-888-3447	
Empire Kosher Poultry Inc 247 Empire Dr *Web:* www.empirekosher.com	Mifflintown	PA	17059	717-436-7055	
Far Best Foods Inc 4689 S 400 W PO Box 480 *Web:* www.farbestfoods.com	Huntingburg	IN	47542	812-683-4200	683-4226
Fieldale Farms Corp 555 Broiler Blvd *TF:* 800-241-5400 ■ *Web:* www.fieldale.com	Baldwin	GA	30511	706-778-5100	778-3767
Foster Farms Inc 1000 Davis St PO Box 457 **Fax Area Code:* 209 ■ *TF:* 800-255-7227 ■ *Web:* www.fosterfarms.com	Livingston	CA	95334	800-255-7227	394-6362*
Georges Inc 402 W Robinson Ave *Web:* georgesinc.com	Springdale	AR	72764	479-927-7000	
Henningsen Foods Inc 14334 Industrial Rd *Web:* www.henningsenfoods.com	Omaha	NE	68144	402-330-2500	330-0875
Holmes Foods Inc 101 S Liberty Ave *Web:* holmesfoods.com	Nixon	TX	78140	830-582-1551	582-1090
House of Raeford Farms Inc 520 E Central Ave *TF:* 800-888-7539 ■ *Web:* www.houseofraeford.com	Raeford	NC	28376	910-875-5161	875-8300
ISE America Inc PO Box 267 *Web:* www.iseamerica.com	Galena	MD	21635	410-755-6300	755-6367
Jennie-O Turkey Store 2505 Willmar Ave SW *TF:* 800-621-3505 ■ *Web:* www.jennieo.com	Willmar	MN	56201	800-621-3505	
Keystone Foods LLC 300 Bar Harbor Dr Ste 600 5 Tower Bridge *Web:* www.keystonefoods.com	West Conshohocken	PA	19428	610-667-6700	667-1460
Koch Foods Inc 1300 Higgins Rd Ste 100 *TF:* 800-837-2778 ■ *Web:* www.kochfoods.com	Park Ridge	IL	60068	847-384-5940	384-5961
Mar-Jac Poultry Inc 1020 Aviation Blvd PO Box 1017 *Web:* www.marjacpoultry.com	Gainesville	GA	30501	770-531-5007	531-5049
Marshall Durbin Co 2830 Commerce Blvd *TF Sales:* 800-245-8204 ■ *Web:* www.marshalldurbin.com	Birmingham	AL	35210	205-380-3251	
Michael Foods Inc 301 Carlson Pkwy Ste 400 *TF:* 800-328-5474 ■ *Web:* www.michaelfoods.com	Minnetonka	MN	55305	952-258-4000	258-4911
Mid-valley Distributors Inc 3886 E Jensen Ave *Web:* www.midvalleydist.com	Fresno	CA	93725	559-485-2660	
Mountaire Farms 17269 NC Hwy 71 N **Fax Area Code:* 302 ■ **Fax:* Hum Res ■ *TF:* 877-887-1490 ■ *Web:* www.mountaire.com	Lumber Bridge	NC	28357	910-843-5942	732-6723*

				Phone	Fax
OK Foods Inc PO Box 1787	Fort Smith	AR	72902	800-635-9441	784-1338*
*Fax Area Code: 501 ■ TF: 800-635-9441 ■ Web: www.tenderbird.com					
Olymel LP 2200 Pratte Ave Pratte	Saint-Hyacinthe	QC	J2S4B6	450-771-0400	645-2869
TF: 800-361-7990 ■ Web: www.olymel.com					
PECO Foods Inc 3701 Kauloosa Ave	Tuscaloosa	AL	35401	205-345-3955	343-2401
Web: www.pecofoods.com					
Pennfield Corp 2260 Erin Ct PO Box 4366	Lancaster	PA	17601	717-299-2561	295-8766
Perdue Farms Inc 31149 Old Ocean City Rd	Salisbury	MD	21804	410-543-3000	543-3532
TF: 800-473-7383 ■ Web: www.perdue.com					
Pilgrim's Corp 1770 Promontory Cir	Greeley	CO	80634	800-321-1470	
NASDAQ: PPC ■ TF: 800-321-1470 ■ Web: www.pilgrimspride.com					
Randall Foods Inc 4408 Bandini Blvd	Vernon	CA	90058	323-261-6565	
Web: randallfoods.com					
Simmons Foods Inc 601 N Hico St	Siloam Springs	AR	72761	479-524-8151	
Web: simfoods.simmonsglobal.com					
Sonstegard Foods Co 1911 W 57th St Ste 102	Sioux Falls	SD	57108	800-533-3184	
TF: 800-533-3184 ■ Web: www.sonstegard.com					
Stevens Sausage Company Inc 3411 Stevens Sausage Rd	Smithfield	NC	27577	919-934-3159	
Web: www.stevens-sausage.com					
Tip Top Poultry Inc 327 Wallace Rd	Marietta	GA	30062	770-973-8070	973-6897
TF: 800-241-5230 ■ Web: tiptoppoultry.com					
Turkey Valley Farms 112 S Sixth St PO Box 200	Marshall	MN	56258	507-337-3100	337-3009
Web: www.turkeyvalleyfarms.com					
Tyson Foods Inc 2210 W Oaklawn Dr PO Box 2020	Springdale	AR	72762	479-290-4000	
NYSE: TSN ■ TF: 800-643-3410 ■ Web: www.tyson.com					
Valley Fresh Inc 3600 E Linwood Ave	Turlock	CA	95380	209-669-5600	
TF: 800-523-4635					
Wayne Farms Enterprises LLC 1020 County Rd 114	Jack	AL	36346	334-897-3435	897-1000
TF: 800-241-3110 ■ Web: waynefarms.com					
West Liberty Foods LLC 228 W Second St	West Liberty	IA	52776	319-627-6000	627-6334
TF: 888-511-4500 ■ Web: www.wlfoods.com					

623 POWER TRANSMISSION EQUIPMENT - MECHANICAL

SEE ALSO Bearings - Ball & Roller p. 1860

				Phone	Fax
Adams Co 8040 Chavenelle Rd	Dubuque	IA	52002	563-583-3591	583-8048
Web: www.theadamscompany.com					
Allied-Locke Industries 1088 Corregidor Rd	Dixon	IL	61021	815-288-1471	288-7945
TF: 800-435-7752 ■ Web: www.alliedlocke.com					
American Metal Bearing Co 7191 Acacia Ave	Garden Grove	CA	92841	714-892-5527	898-3217
TF: 800-888-3048 ■ Web: www.ambco.net					
Ameridrives Couplings 1802 Pittsburgh Ave PO Box 4000	Erie	PA	16512	814-480-5000	453-5891
TF: 800-352-0141 ■ Web: www.ameridrives.com					
AmeriDrives International 1802 Pittsburgh Ave	Erie	PA	16502	814-480-5000	453-5891
TF: 800-352-0141 ■ Web: www.ameridrives.com					
Barden Corp 200 Pk Ave	Danbury	CT	06810	203-744-2211	744-3756
TF: 800-243-1060 ■ Web: www.bardenbearings.com					
Beemer Precision Inc 230 New York Dr PO Box 3080	Fort Washington	PA	19034	215-646-8440	283-3397
TF: 800-836-2340 ■ Web: www.oilite.com					
Bird Precision One Spruce St PO Box 540569	Waltham	MA	02454	781-894-0160	894-6308
TF Cust Svc: 800-454-7369 ■ Web: www.birdprecision.com					
Bishop-Wisecarver Corp 2104 Martin Way	Pittsburg	CA	94565	925-439-8272	439-5931
TF: 888-580-8272 ■ Web: www.bwc.com					
Buckeye Power Sales Company Inc 6850 Commerce Ct Dr PO Box 489	Blacklick	OH	43004	614-861-6000	861-2291
TF: 800-523-3587 ■ Web: www.buckeyepowersales.com					
Cablecraft Motion Controls LLC 2110 Summit St	New Haven	IN	46774	260-749-5105	493-2387
Web: www.cablecraft.com/					
Cangro Industries Long Island Transmission Co 495 Smith St	Farmingdale	NY	11735	631-454-9000	454-9155
TF: 800-422-9210 ■ Web: www.cangroindustries.com					
Capitol Stampings Corp 2700 W N Ave	Milwaukee	WI	53208	414-372-3500	372-3535
Web: www.capitolstampings.com					
Carlyle Johnson Machine Co (CJM) 291 Boston Tpke	Bolton	CT	06043	860-643-1531	646-2645
TF: 888-629-4867 ■ Web: www.cjmco.com					
Certified Power Inc 970 Campus Dr	Mundelein	IL	60060	847-573-3800	573-3832
TF: 888-905-7411 ■ Web: www.certifiedpower.com					
Deublin Co 2050 Norman Dr W	Waukegan	IL	60085	847-689-8600	689-8690
Web: www.deublin.com					
Diamond Chain Co 402 Kentucky Ave	Indianapolis	IN	46225	317-638-6431	638-6431
TF Cust Svc: 800-872-4246 ■ Web: www.diamondchain.com					
Don Dye Company Inc 524 NW 20th Ave PO Box 107	Kingman	KS	67068	620-532-3131	532-2141
Web: dondyeco.com					
Eaton Corp 1111 Superior Ave Eaton Ctr	Cleveland	OH	44114	216-523-5000	
Web: www.eaton.com					
EC Styberg Engineering Company Inc 1600 Gold St PO Box 788	Racine	WI	53401	262-637-9301	637-1319
Web: www.styberg.com					
Elliott Manufacturing Inc 11 Beckwith Ave	Binghamton	NY	13901	607-772-0404	772-0431
Web: www.elliottmfg.com					
Entek International LLC 250 N Hansard Ave PO Box 127	Lebanon	OR	97355	541-259-3901	259-3932
Web: entek.com/lead-acid/					
Force Control Industries Inc 3660 Dixie Hwy	Fairfield	OH	45014	513-868-0900	868-2105
TF: 800-829-3244 ■ Web: www.forcecontrol.com					
General Bearing Corp 44 High St	West Nyack	NY	10994	845-358-6000	358-6277
TF Sales: 800-431-1766 ■ Web: www.generalbearing.com					
GGB North America 700 Mid Atlantic Pkwy PO Box 189	Thorofare	NJ	08086	856-848-3200	848-5115*
*Fax: Sales ■ TF: 888-840-2349 ■ Web: www.ggbearings.com					
GKN Rockford Inc 1200 Windsor Rd	Loves Park	IL	61111	815-633-7460	633-1311
Web: www.gkn.com					
Hebeler Corp 2000 Military Rd	Tonawanda	NY	14150	716-873-9300	873-7538
TF: 800-486-4709 ■ Web: www.hebeler.com					
Helical Products Co Inc 901 W McCoy Ln	Santa Maria	CA	93455	805-928-3851	928-2369
TF: 877-353-9873 ■ Web: www.heli-cal.com					
Hilliard Corp 100 W Fourth St	Elmira	NY	14902	607-733-7121	733-3009
Web: www.hilliardcorp.com					
Horton Inc 2565 Walnut St	Saint Paul	MN	55113	651-361-6400	
TF: 800-621-1320 ■ Web: www.hortonww.com					
Iberdrola Renewables Inc 1125 NW Couch Ste 700	Portland	OR	97209	503-796-7000	796-6901
Web: www.iberdrolarenewables.us					
Industrial Clutch 1701-3 Pearl St	Waukesha	WI	53186	262-547-3357	547-2949
Web: www.indclutch.com					
John Deere Coffeyville Works Inc 2624 N US Hwy	Coffeyville	KS	67337	800-844-1337	251-3262*
*Fax Area Code: 620 ■ Web: www.deere.com					
Kamatics Corp 1330 Blue Hills Ave	Bloomfield	CT	06002	860-243-9704	243-7993
TF: 866-540-5760 ■ Web: www.kaman.com					
Kingsbury Inc 10385 Drummond Rd	Philadelphia	PA	19154	215-824-4000	824-4999
TF Sales: 866-581-5464 ■ Web: www.kingsbury.com					
Linn Gear Co 100 N Eigth St PO Box 397	Lebanon	OR	97355	541-259-1211	259-1299
TF: 800-547-2471 ■ Web: www.linngear.com					
Lovejoy Inc 2655 Wisconsin Ave	Downers Grove	IL	60515	630-852-0500	
Web: www.lovejoy-inc.com					
Magtrol Inc 70 Gardenville Pkwy W	Buffalo	NY	14224	716-668-5555	668-8705
TF: 800-828-7844 ■ Web: www.magtrol.com					
Marland Clutch 485 S Frontage Rd Ste 330	Burr Ridge	IL	60527	800-216-3515	216-3001*
*Fax Area Code: 877 ■ TF: 800-216-3515 ■ Web: www.marland.com					
Martin Sprocket & Gear Inc 3100 Sprocket Dr PO Box 91588	Arlington	TX	76015	817-258-3000	258-3333
Web: www.martinsprocket.com					
Maurey Manufacturing Corp 410 Industrial Pk Rd	Holly Springs	MS	38635	800-284-2161	252-6364*
*Fax Area Code: 662 ■ TF: 800-284-2161 ■ Web: www.maurey.com					
Metallized Carbon Corp 19 S Water St	Ossining	NY	10562	914-941-3738	941-4050
Web: www.metcar.com					
Midwest Control Products Corp 590 E Main St	Bushnell	IL	61422	309-772-3163	772-2266
Web: www.midwestcontrol.com					
Nook Industries 4950 E 49th St	Cleveland	OH	44125	216-271-7900	271-7020
TF: 800-321-7800 ■ Web: www.nookindustries.com					
North American Clutch Corp 4360 N Green Bay Ave	Milwaukee	WI	53209	414-267-4000	267-4024
Web: www.noramclutch.com					
NSK Corp 4200 Goss Rd	Ann Arbor	MI	48105	800-675-9930	913-7102*
*Fax Area Code: 734 ■ TF: 888-446-5675 ■ Web: www.nskamericas.com					
NTN Bearing Corp of America 1600 E Bishop Ct	Mount Prospect	IL	60056	847-298-7500	699-9744
TF: 800-323-2358 ■ Web: www.ntnamericas.com					
OPW Engineered Systems 2726 Henkle Dr	Lebanon	OH	45036	513-932-9114	932-9845*
*Fax: Cust Svc ■ TF Cust Svc: 800-547-9393 ■ Web: www.opw-es.com					
Ormat Technologies Inc 6225 Neil Rd Ste 300	Reno	NV	89511	775-356-9029	356-9039
NYSE: ORA ■ Web: www.ormat.com					
Peer Bearing Co 2200 Norman Dr S	Waukegan	IL	60085	847-578-1000	578-1200*
*Fax: Orders ■ TF: 800-433-7337 ■ Web: www.peerbearing.com					
Pic Design Corp 86 Benson Rd PO Box 1004	Middlebury	CT	06762	203-758-8272	758-8271
TF: 800-243-6125 ■ Web: www.pic-design.com					
Ramsey Products Corp 3701 Performance Rd PO Box 668827	Charlotte	NC	28266	704-394-0322	394-9134
Web: www.ramseychain.com					
RBC Bearings Inc 3131 W Segerstrom Ave PO Box 1953	Santa Ana	CA	92704	714-546-3131	545-9885
TF: 866-722-2376 ■ Web: www.rbcbearings.com					
Real Goods Solar 833 W S Boulder Rd	Louisville	CO	80027	888-567-6527	
NASDAQ: RSGE ■ TF: 888-567-6527 ■ Web: rgsenergy.com/					
Reell Precision Manufacturing Corp 1259 Willow Lk Blvd	Saint Paul	MN	55110	651-484-2447	484-3867
Web: www.reell.com					
Regal-Beloit Corp 200 State St	Beloit	WI	53511	608-364-8800	364-8818
NYSE: RBC ■ TF: 800-672-6495 ■ Web: www.regalbeloit.com					
Renold Ajax Inc 100 Bourne St	Westfield	NY	14787	716-326-3121	326-6121
TF: 800-251-9012 ■ Web: www.renold.com					
Rollease Inc 200 Harvard Ave	Stamford	CT	06902	203-964-1573	358-5865
Web: www.rollease.com					
Schaeffler Group USA Inc 308 Springhill Farm Rd	Fort Mill	SC	29715	803-548-8500	548-8599
TF: 800-361-5841 ■ Web: www.schaeffler.us					
Siemens Power Transmission & Distribution Inc 7000 Siemens Rd	Wendell	NC	27591	919-365-2200	
Web: siemens.com					
Solaria Corp 6200 Paseo Padre Pkwy	Fremont	CA	94555	510-270-2500	793-8388
Web: www.solaria.com					
Solomon Corp 103 W Main PO Box 245	Solomon	KS	67480	785-655-2191	655-2502
TF: 800-234-2867 ■ Web: www.solomoncorp.com					
Speed Selector Inc 17050 Munn Rd	Chagrin Falls	OH	44023	440-543-8233	543-8527
Web: speedselector.com					
SS White Technologies Inc 151 Old New Brunswick Rd	Piscataway	NJ	08854	732-752-8300	752-8315
Web: www.sswt.com					
Stock Drive Products/Sterling Instrument 2101 Jericho Tpke	New Hyde Park	NY	11040	516-328-3300	326-8827
TF: 800-737-7436 ■ Web: www.sdp-si.com					
TB Wood's Inc 440 N Fifth Ave	Chambersburg	PA	17201	717-264-7161	264-6420
TF: 888-829-6637 ■ Web: www.tbwoods.com					
Twin Disc Inc 1328 Racine St	Racine	WI	53403	262-638-4000	
NASDAQ: TWIN ■ Web: www.twindisc.com					
Universal Bearings Inc 431 N Birkey St	Bremen	IN	46506	574-546-2261	546-5085
Web: www.univbrg.com					
US Tsubaki Inc 301 E Marquardt Dr	Wheeling	IL	60090	847-459-9500	459-9515
TF: 800-323-7790 ■ Web: www.ustsubaki.com					
Warner Electric 449 Gardner St	South Beloit	IL	61080	815-389-3771	
TF: 800-825-6544 ■ Web: www.warnernet.com					

				Phone	Fax
Waukesha Bearings Corp W 231 N 2811 Roundy Cir E Ste 200 *TF:* 888-832-3517 ■ *Web:* www.waukbearing.com	Pewaukee	WI	53072	262-506-3000	506-3001
Wheeler Industries 7261 Investment Dr *Web:* www.wheelerfluidfilmbearings.com	North Charleston	SC	29418	843-552-1251	552-4790
Whittet-Higgins Co 33 Higginson Ave PO Box 8 *Web:* www.whittet-higgins.com	Central Falls	RI	02863	401-728-0700	728-0703
Zero-Max Inc 13200 Sixth Ave N *TF:* 800-533-1731 ■ *Web:* www.zero-max.com	Plymouth	MN	55441	763-546-4300	546-8260

624 PRECISION MACHINED PRODUCTS

SEE ALSO Aircraft Parts & Auxiliary Equipment p. 1733; Machine Shops p. 2680

				Phone	Fax
A-1 Production Inc 5809 E Leighty Rd *Web:* www.a1production.com	Kendallville	IN	46755	260-347-0960	347-4727
Abbott Interfast Corp 190 Abbott Dr *TF:* 800-877-0789 ■ *Web:* www.abbott-interfast.com	Wheeling	IL	60090	847-459-6200	459-4076
Accellent Inc 200 W Seventh Ave *Web:* www.accellent.com/aboutus	Collegeville	PA	19426	610-489-0300	489-1150
Adept Fasteners Inc 28709 Industry Dr *Web:* www.adeptfasteners.com	Valencia	CA	91355	661-257-6600	
Afco Products Inc 2074 S Mannheim Rd *Web:* www.afco-products.com	Des Plaines	IL	60018	847-299-1055	299-8455
Air-Matic Products Company Inc 22218 Telegraph Rd *Web:* www.air-matic.com	Southfield	MI	48033	248-356-4200	356-0738
Alco Manufacturing Corp 10584 Middle Ave *Web:* www.alcomfgcorp.com	Elyria	OH	44035	440-458-5165	458-6821
Alger Mfg Company Inc 724 S Bon View Ave *TF:* 800-854-9833 ■ *Web:* www.alger1.com	Ontario	CA	91761	909-986-4591	983-3351
Allan Tool & Machine Company Inc 1822 E Maple Rd *Web:* allantool.com	Troy	MI	48083	248-585-2910	585-7728
Allied Screw Products Inc 815 E Lowell Ave *Web:* www.aspi-nc.com	Mishawaka	IN	46545	574-255-4718	255-4173
Allmetal Screw Products Corp 94 E Jefryn Blvd Ste A *Web:* www.allmetalcorp.com	Deer Park	NY	11729	631-243-5200	243-5307
Alpha Grainger Manufacturing Inc 20 Discovery Way *Web:* www.agmi.com	Franklin	MA	02038	508-520-4005	520-4185
American Products Company Inc 610 Rahway Ave *Web:* www.amerprod.com	Union	NJ	07083	908-687-4100	687-0037
American Turned Products Inc 7626 Klier Dr *Web:* www.atpteam.com	Fairview	PA	16415	814-474-4200	474-4718
Amsco-Wire Products Co 610 Grand Ave	Ridgefield	NJ	07657	201-945-5618	
Amtec Precision Products Inc 1355 Holmes Rd *Web:* www.amtecprecision.com	Elgin	IL	60123	847-695-8030	695-8295
Anchor Coupling Inc 5520 13th St *Web:* www.anchorcoupling.com	Menominee	MI	49858	906-863-2671	863-3242
Anderson Automatics Inc 6401 Welcome Ave N *Web:* www.andersonautomatics.com	Minneapolis	MN	55429	763-533-2206	533-0320
Anderson Precision Inc 20 Livingston Ave *Web:* www.andersonprecision.com	Jamestown	NY	14701	716-484-1148	484-7779
Anoplate Inc 459 Pulaski St 475 *Web:* anoplate.com	Syracuse	NY	13204	315-471-6143	471-7132
Ashley Ward Inc 7490 Easy St *Web:* www.ashleyward.com	Mason	OH	45040	513-398-1414	398-1125
Astro Seal Inc 827 Palmyrita Ave # B *Web:* www.astroseal.com	Riverside	CA	92507	951-787-6670	787-6677
ATEC Inc 12600 Executive Dr *Web:* www.atec.com	Stafford	TX	77477	281-276-2700	240-2682
Athanor Group Inc 921 E California Ave	Ontario	CA	91761	909-467-1205	467-1208
Auer Precision Inc 1050 W Birchwood Ave *Web:* www.auerprecision.com	Mesa	AZ	85210	480-834-4637	964-8237
Automatic Machine Products Co (AMP) 400 Constitution Dr *Web:* www.ampcomp.com	Taunton	MA	02780	508-822-4226	822-4476
Automatic Products Corp 2735 Forest Ln *Web:* www.ap-corp.com	Garland	TX	75042	972-272-6422	494-0533
Avanti Engineering Inc 200 W Lake Dr *Web:* www.avantiengineering.com	Glendale Heights	IL	60139	630-260-1333	260-1762
Barber-Nichols Inc 6325 W 55th Ave *Web:* www.barber-nichols.com	Arvada	CO	80002	303-421-8111	420-4679
Bay Swiss Mfg Company Inc Five Airpark Vista Blvd *TF:* 800-247-3207 ■ *Web:* www.bayswiss.com	Dayton	NV	89403	775-246-7100	246-7104
Berkley Screw Machine Products Inc 2100 Royce Haley Dr *Web:* berkleyscrew.com	Rochester Hills	MI	48309	248-853-0044	853-1532
Berkshire Industries Inc 109 Apremont Way *Web:* www.berkshireindustries.com	Westfield	MA	01085	413-568-8676	562-0061
Betar Inc 1524 Millstone River Rd *Web:* www.betar.net	Hillsborough	NJ	08844	908-359-4200	359-1010
Betty Machine Co 324 Freehill Rd *Web:* www.bettymachine.com	Hendersonville	TN	37075	615-826-6004	826-6262
Biddle Precision Components Inc 701 S Main St *TF:* 800-428-4387 ■ *Web:* www.emcprecision.com	Sheridan	IN	46069	317-758-4451	758-5260
Birken Manufacturing Co Three Old Windsor Rd *Web:* www.birken.net	Bloomfield	CT	06002	860-242-2211	242-2749
Blackhawk Machine Products Inc Six Industrial Dr *Web:* www.blackhawk-machine.com	Smithfield	RI	02917	401-232-7563	232-0770
Boker's Inc 3104 Snelling Ave *TF:* 800-927-4377 ■ *Web:* www.bokers.com	Minneapolis	MN	55406	612-729-9365	
Bracalente Mfg Group 20 W Creamery Rd PO Box 570 *Web:* www.bracalente.com	Trumbauersville	PA	18970	215-536-3077	536-4844
Burgess-Norton Manufacturing Co 737 Peyton St **Fax:* Hum Res ■ *Web:* www.burgessnorton.com	Geneva	IL	60134	630-232-4100	232-3700*
Camcraft Inc 1080 Muirfield Dr *Web:* www.camcraft.com	Hanover Park	IL	60133	630-582-6000	582-6019
Cass Screw Machine Products Co 4800 N Lilac Dr *Web:* www.csmp.com	Brooklyn Center	MN	55429	763-535-0501	535-9238
CE Holden Inc 938 Rt 910 *Web:* www.ceholden.com	Cheswick	PA	15024	412-767-5050	767-9922
Celina Aluminum Precision Technology Inc (CAPT) 7059 Staeger Rd *Web:* www.capt-celina.com	Celina	OH	45822	419-586-2278	586-6474
Charleston Metal Products Inc 350 Grant St *Web:* www.charlestonmetal.com	Waterloo	IN	46793	260-837-8211	837-8101
Cherry Aerospace LLC 1224 E Warner Ave *Web:* www.cherryaerospace.com	Santa Ana	CA	92705	714-545-5511	
CNW Inc 4710 Madison Rd	Cincinnati	OH	45227	513-321-2775	321-2618
Cole Screw Machine Products Inc 88 Great Hill Rd PO Box 1007 *Web:* colescrew.com	Naugatuck	CT	06770	203-723-1418	723-1252
Contour Tool Inc 38830 Taylor Pkwy *Web:* contourprecisionmilling.com/	North Ridgeville	OH	44039	440-365-7333	365-7335
Corlett-Turner Co 2500 104th Ave *Web:* www.corlett.com	Zeeland	MI	49464	616-772-9082	
Cox Manufacturing Co 5500 N Loop 1604 E *TF:* 800-900-7981 ■ *Web:* www.coxmanufacturing.com	San Antonio	TX	78247	210-657-7731	657-2345
CPI Aerostructures Inc 91 Heartland Blvd *NYSE: CVU* ■ *Web:* www.cpiaero.com	Edgewood	NY	11717	631-586-5200	586-5840
Curtis Screw Company Inc 50 Thielman Dr *TF:* 800-914-6276 ■ *Web:* www.curtisscrew.com	Buffalo	NY	14206	716-898-7800	898-7880
Dabko Industries Inc 50 Emmett St *Web:* www.rgdtech.com	Bristol	CT	06010	860-589-0756	585-0874
Davies Molding LLC 350 Kehoe Blvd *TF:* 800-554-9208 ■ *Web:* www.daviesmolding.com	Carol Stream	IL	60188	630-510-8188	510-9944
DCG Precision Mfg Nine Trowbridge Dr *Web:* www.dcgprecision.com	Bethel	CT	06801	203-743-5525	791-1737
Delo Screw Products Co 700 London Rd *Web:* www.deloscrew.com	Delaware	OH	43015	740-363-1971	363-0042
Devon Precision Industries Inc 251 Munson Rd *Web:* www.devonprecision.com	Wolcott	CT	06716	203-879-1437	879-5556
Dirksen Screw Products Co 14490 23-Mile Rd *Web:* www.dirksenscrew.com	Shelby Township	MI	48315	586-247-5400	247-9507
Diversified Machine Inc 28059 Ctr Oaks Ct	Wixom	MI	48393	248-277-4400	277-4399
Dow Screw Products 3810 Paule Ave	Saint Louis	MO	63125	314-638-5100	638-4838
Duffin Manufacturing Co 316 Warden Ave PO Box 4036 *Web:* www.duffinmfg.com	Elyria	OH	44036	440-323-4681	323-7389
DuPage Machine Products Inc 311 Longview Dr	Bloomingdale	IL	60108	630-690-5400	690-5504
Efficient Machine Products 12133 Alameda Dr *Web:* www.efficientm.com	Strongsville	OH	44149	440-268-0205	268-0215
EJ Basler Co 9511 Ainslie St *Web:* www.ejbasler.com	Schiller Park	IL	60176	847-678-8880	678-8896
Elyria Mfg Corp 145 Northrup St PO Box 479 *TF:* 866-365-4171 ■ *Web:* www.emcprecision.com	Elyria	OH	44035	440-365-4171	365-4000
Enoch Manufacturing Co 14242 SE 82nd Dr PO Box 98 *TF:* 888-659-2660 ■ *Web:* enochmachining.com/	Clackamas	OR	97015	503-659-2660	659-4439
Fairchild Auto-mated Parts Inc 10 White St *TF:* 800-927-2545 ■ *Web:* www.fairchildparts.com	Winsted	CT	06098	860-379-2725	379-5340
Farrar Corp 142 W Burns St *Web:* www.farrarusa.com	Norwich	KS	67118	620-478-2212	478-2200
FC Phillips Inc 471 Washington St *Web:* www.fcphillips.com	Stoughton	MA	02072	781-344-9400	344-3440
FCI Inc 4661 Giles Rd *TF:* 800-321-1032 ■ *Web:* www.fci-usa.com	Cleveland	OH	44135	216-251-5200	251-5206
Federal Screw Works 20229 Nine-Mile Rd *OTC: FSCR* ■ *Web:* www.federalscrew.com	Saint Clair Shores	MI	48080	586-443-4200	443-4210
Fischer Special Manufacturing Co 1188 Industrial Rd *Web:* www.fischerspecial.com	Cold Spring	KY	41076	859-781-1400	781-4702
Form Cut Industries Inc 197 Mt Pleasant Ave *Web:* www.formcut.com	Newark	NJ	07104	973-483-5154	483-4512
Fraen Machining Corp 324 New Boston St *Web:* www.swisstronics.com	Woburn	MA	01801	781-205-5400	205-5472
Gates Albert Inc 3434 Union St *TF:* 800-937-9311 ■ *Web:* www.gatesalbert.com	North Chili	NY	14514	585-594-9401	594-4305
General Automotive Mfg LLC 5215 W Airways Ave *Web:* www.gamfg.com	Franklin	WI	53132	414-423-6400	423-6415
General Engineering Works 1515 W Wrightwood Ct *Web:* www.gewinc.com	Addison	IL	60101	630-543-8000	543-8005
Grand Traverse Machine (GTM) 1247 Boon St *Web:* www.gtmachine.com	Traverse City	MI	49686	231-946-8006	946-6606
Greystone of Lincoln Inc 7 Wellington Rd *TF:* 800-446-1761 ■ *Web:* greyst.com	Lincoln	RI	02865	401-333-0444	334-5745
Griner Engineering Inc 2500 N Curry Pk *Web:* www.griner.com	Bloomington	IN	47404	812-332-2220	332-2229
H & H Swiss Screw Machine Products Company Inc 1478 Chestnut Ave **Fax Area Code:* 908 ■ *TF:* 800-826-9985 ■ *Web:* www.hhswiss.com	Hillside	NJ	07205	800-826-9985	688-3503*

Company	City	State	ZIP	Phone	Fax
H & L Tool Company Inc 32701 Dequindre Rd. *Web:* www.hltool.com	Madison Heights	MI	48071	248-585-7474	585-5774
Hadady Corp 510 W 172nd St. *Web:* hadadycorp.com	South Holland	IL	60473	708-596-5168	596-7563
Hall Industries Inc 514 Mecklem Ln *Web:* hallindustries.com	Ellwood City	PA	16117	724-752-2000	758-1558
Herker Industries Inc N57 W13760 Carmen Ave. *Web:* www.herker.com	Menomonee Falls	WI	53051	262-781-8270	781-0931
High Precision Inc 375 Morse St. *Web:* www.highprecisioninc.com	Hamden	CT	06517	203-777-5395	773-1976
Highland Machine 700 Fifth St *Web:* www.highlandmachine.com	Highland	IL	62249	618-654-2103	654-8016
Horizon Mfg Industries Inc 11417 Cyrus Way Ste 1 *Web:* www.horizonman.com	Mukilteo	WA	98275	425-493-1220	493-0042
Horspool & Romine Manufacturing Inc 5850 Marshall St **Fax Area Code: 510* ■ *TF:* 800-446-2263 ■ *Web:* www.horspool.com	Oakland	CA	94608	800-446-2263	652-3455*
Huron Automatic Screw Co PO Box 610068 *TF:* 800-500-4000 ■ *Web:* www.huronauto.com	Port Huron	MI	48061	810-364-6636	364-6639
Huron Inc 6554 Lakeshore Rd *Web:* huroninc.com	Lexington	MI	48450	810-359-5344	359-7521
Hyland Screw Machine Products 1900 Kuntz Rd. **Fax Area Code: 937* ■ *TF:* 866-863-7282 ■ *Web:* www.hylandmach.com	Dayton	OH	45404	866-863-7282	233-7067*
Insaco Inc 1365 Canary Rd. *Web:* www.insaco.com	Quakertown	PA	18951	215-536-3500	536-7750
Intat Precision Inc 2148 N State Rd 3 PO Box 488 *Web:* www.intat.com	Rushville	IN	46173	765-932-5323	932-3032
Iseli Co 402 N Main St *Web:* iseli.com	Walworth	WI	53184	262-275-2108	275-6094
J T M Technologies Inc 204 Industrial Ct *TF:* 877-586-8324 ■ *Web:* www.jtmtechnologies.com	Wylie	TX	75098	972-429-6575	635-6905
Jay Sons Screw Machine Products Inc 197 Burritt St PO Box 674 *Web:* www.jaysons.com	Milldale	CT	06467	860-621-0141	621-0142
Jessen Mfg Company Inc 1409 W Beardsley Ave PO Box 1729 *Web:* www.jessenmfg.com	Elkhart	IN	46515	574-295-3836	522-2962
Kaddis Mfg Corp 293 Patriot Wy PO Box 92985 *Web:* www.kaddis.com	Rochester	NY	14692	585-464-9000	464-0008
Kenlee Precision Corp 1701 Inverness Ave *TF:* 800-969-5278 ■ *Web:* www.kenlee.com	Baltimore	MD	21230	410-525-3800	646-3278
Kerr Lakeside Inc 26841 Tungsten Rd *TF:* 800-487-5377 ■ *Web:* www.kerrlakeside.com	Euclid	OH	44132	216-261-2100	261-9798
Keystone Engineering 6310 Sidney St. *Web:* www.keystoneeng.com	Houston	TX	77021	713-747-1478	
Komet Of America Inc 2050 Mitchell Blvd **Fax Area Code: 800* ■ *TF:* 800-865-6638 ■ *Web:* www.komet.com	Schaumburg	IL	60193	847-923-8400	865-6638*
Lakeshore Automatic Products Inc 1865 Industrial Pk Dr *Web:* www.lakeshore-automatic.com	Grand Haven	MI	49417	616-846-5090	846-0790
Liberty Brass Turning Company Inc 38-01 Queens Blvd *TF:* 800-345-5939 ■ *Web:* www.libertybrass.com	Long Island City	NY	11101	718-784-2911	784-2038
Machine Specialties Inc (MSI) 6511 Franz Warner Pkwy *Web:* www.machspec.com	Whitsett	NC	27377	336-603-1919	303-1920
Maddox Foundry & Machine Works Inc 13370 SW 170th St *Web:* www.maddoxfoundry.com	Archer	FL	32618	352-495-2121	495-3962
Mantel Machine Products Inc W141 N9350 Fountain Blvd *Web:* www.mantelmachine.com	Menomonee Falls	WI	53051	262-255-6780	255-9724
Manth-Brownell Inc 1120 Fyler Rd *Web:* www.manth.com	Kirkville	NY	13082	315-687-7263	687-6856
MarathonNorco Aerospace Inc 8301 Imperial Dr *Web:* www.mnaerospace.com	Waco	TX	76712	254-776-0650	776-6558
Marox Corp 373 Whitney Ave *Web:* www.marox.com	Holyoke	MA	01040	413-536-1300	534-1829
Meaden Precision Machined Products Co 16W210 83rd St *Web:* www.meaden.com	Burr Ridge	IL	60527	630-655-0888	655-3012
Mennie's Machine Co (MMC) Rt 71 & Mennie Dr PO Box 110 *Web:* www.mennies.com	Mark	IL	61340	815-339-2226	339-6550
Metric Machining Co 1425 S Vineyard Ave *TF:* 800-937-9311 ■ *Web:* www.metricorp.com	Ontario	CA	91761	909-947-9222	923-1796
Micor Industries Inc 1314 A State Docks Rd *Web:* www.micorind.com	Decatur	AL	35601	256-560-0770	
Micro-Matics Corp 8050 Ranchers Rd. *Web:* www.micro-matics.com	Minneapolis	MN	55432	763-780-2700	780-2706
Microbest Inc 670 Captain Neville Dr *Web:* www.microbest.com	Waterbury	CT	06705	203-597-0355	597-0655
Midwest Screw Products Inc 34700 Lakeland Blvd *Web:* www.midwestllc.com	Eastlake	OH	44095	440-951-2333	951-2336
Mitchel & Scott Machine Co 1841 Ludlow Ave *Web:* www.mitsco.com	Indianapolis	IN	46201	317-639-5331	684-8245
Modern Machine & Engineering Corp 9380 Winnetka Ave N *Web:* www.mmeincmn.com	Brooklyn Park	MN	55445	612-781-3347	781-0030
Mold-Masters Injectioneering LLC 103 Peyerk Ct Ste E *TF:* 800-387-2483 ■ *Web:* www.moldmasters.com	Romeo	MI	48065	586-752-6551	752-6552
MSK Precision Products Inc 10101 NW 67th St *TF:* 800-992-5018 ■ *Web:* www.mskprecision.com	Tamarac	FL	33321	954-776-0770	776-3780
Multimatic Products Inc 390 Oser Ave *TF:* 800-767-7633 ■ *Web:* www.multimaticproducts.com	Hauppauge	NY	11788	631-231-1515	231-1625
National Technologies Inc 7641 S Tenth St *Web:* www.nationaltechnologies.com	Oak Creek	WI	53154	414-571-1000	571-1010
New Castle Industries Inc 1399 Countyline Rd *TF:* 800-897-2830	New Castle	PA	16101	724-656-5620	656-5620
Northern Screw Machine Company Inc 300 Atwater St	Saint Paul	MN	55117	651-488-2568	
Northwest Swiss-Matic Inc 8400 89th Ave N *Web:* www.nwswissmatic.com	Minneapolis	MN	55445	763-544-4222	544-6873
Ntn-bower Corp 707 Bower Rd *Web:* www.ntnbower.com	Macomb	IL	61455	309-837-0440	837-0438
Ohio Screw Products Inc 818 Lowell St *Web:* www.ohioscrew.com	Elyria	OH	44035	440-322-6341	322-0750
Omni-Lite Industries Canada Inc 17210 Edwards Rd *TF:* 800-577-6664 ■ *Web:* www.omni-lite.com	Cerritos	CA	90703	562-404-8510	
P&R Fasteners Inc 325 Pierce St *Web:* www.prfasteners.com	Somerset	NJ	08873	732-302-3600	
Pacific Aerospace & Electronics Inc 434 Olds Stn Rd *Web:* www.pacaero.com	Wenatchee	WA	98801	509-667-9600	667-5311
Pacific Rim Manufacturing Inc 5456 SE International Way Willard - Quality Focal *Web:* www.pacificrimmfg.com	Milwaukie	OR	97222	503-654-9543	654-8050
Palladin Precision Products Inc 57 Bristol St *Web:* www.palladin.com	Waterbury	CT	06708	203-574-0246	756-9478
Paul R Briles Inc 1700 W 132nd St *Web:* www.pbfasteners.com	Gardena	CA	90249	310-323-6222	
Peerless Screw Products Corp 286 Sandbank Rd	Cheshire	CT	06410	203-272-6413	271-2269
Peterson Tool Company Inc 739 Fesslers Ln PO Box 100830 *Web:* www.petersontool.com	Nashville	TN	37224	615-242-7341	242-7362
Pohlman Inc 140 Long Rd *Web:* www.pohlman.com	Chesterfield	MO	63005	636-537-1909	537-1930
Powin Corp 20550 SW 115th Ave *Web:* www.powin.com	Tualatin	OR	97062	503-598-6659	598-3941
Precision Machine Works Inc 2024 Puyallup Ave *Web:* www.cadenceaerospace.com	Tacoma	WA	98421	253-272-5119	272-6921
Precision Metal Products Co 353 Garden Ave PO Box 1047 *Web:* www.pmpc1.com	Holland	MI	49422	616-392-3109	392-3100
Precision Plus Inc 840 Kootman Ln PO Box 168 *Web:* www.preplus.com	Elkhorn	WI	53121	262-743-1700	743-1701
Precision Screw Machine Products Inc 20 Gooch St *Web:* www.psmp.com	Biddeford	ME	04005	207-283-0121	283-4824
Precisionform Inc 148 W Airport Rd *TF:* 800-233-3821 ■ *Web:* www.precisionform.com	Lititz	PA	17543	717-560-7610	569-4792
Prime Engineered Components 1012 Buckingham St PO Box 359 *Web:* www.primeeci.com	Watertown	CT	06795	860-274-6773	274-7939
Production Products Co 6176 E Molloy Rd *TF:* 800-800-6652 ■ *Web:* www.ppc-online.com	East Syracuse	NY	13057	315-431-7200	431-7201
Quality Control Corp (QCC) 7315 W Wilson Ave *Web:* www.qccorp.com	Howard Heights	IL	60706	708-867-5400	887-5009
Rable Machine Inc 30 Paragon Pkwy PO Box 1583 *Web:* www.rablemachineinc.com	Mansfield	OH	44901	419-525-2255	525-2371
RB Royal Industries Inc 1350 S Hickory St PO Box 1168 *TF:* 800-892-1550 ■ *Web:* www.rbroyal.com	Fond du Lac	WI	54936	920-921-1550	921-4713
Rima Mfg Co 3850 Munson Hwy *Web:* www.rimamfg.com	Hudson	MI	49247	517-448-8921	448-7142
Robert A Main & Sons Inc 555 Goffle Rd *Web:* www.ramsco-inc.com	Wyckoff	NJ	07481	201-447-3700	447-0302
Roberts Automatic Products Inc 880 Lake Dr *TF:* 800-879-9837 ■ *Web:* www.robertsautomatic.com	Chanhassen	MN	55317	952-949-1000	949-9240
Rollin J Lobaugh Inc 240 Ryan Way *Web:* www.rjlobaugh.com	South San Francisco	CA	94080	650-583-9682	583-0445
Royal Screw Machine Products Co 409 LAKE AVENUE	Bristol	CT	06010	860-845-8567	845-8789
RW Screw Products Inc 999 Oberlin Rd SW *TF:* 866-797-2739 ■ *Web:* rwscrew.com	Massillon	OH	44647	330-837-9211	837-9223
Selflock Screw Products Co Inc 461 E Brighton Ave *Web:* www.selflockscrew.com	Syracuse	NY	13210	315-541-4464	475-1093
Senior Aerospace Jet Products 9106 Balboa Ave *Web:* www.seniorplc.com/aerospace/company.cfm/9	San Diego	CA	92123	858-430-2203	278-8768
SFS intec Inc Spring St & Van Reed Rd *TF:* 800-234-4533 ■ *Web:* www.sfsintecusa.com	Wyomissing	PA	19610	610-376-5751	
Skyway Precision Inc 41225 Plymouth Rd *Web:* www.skywayprecision.com	Plymouth	MI	48170	734-454-3550	455-9659
Smith & Richardson Manufacturing Co PO Box 589 *TF:* 800-426-0876 ■ *Web:* www.smithandrichardson.com	Geneva	IL	60134	630-232-2581	232-2610
Smithfield Manufacturing Inc 237 Kraft St	Clarksville	TN	37040	931-552-4327	648-4460
Sorenson Engineering Inc 32032 Dunlap Blvd *Web:* www.sorensoneng.com	Yucaipa	CA	92399	909-795-2434	795-7190
Specialty Screw Machine Products Inc 1028 Dillerville Rd PO Box 4185 *Web:* www.ssmp-online.com	Lancaster	PA	17604	717-397-2867	397-5912

	City	State	ZIP	Phone	Fax
Sperry Automatics Company Inc 1372 New Haven Rd PO Box 717	Naugatuck	CT	06770	203-729-4589	729-7787
Web: www.sperryautomatics.com					
Stadco Corp 1931 N Broadway	Los Angeles	CA	90031	323-227-8888	222-0053
Web: www.stadco.com					
Standby Screw Machine Products Company Inc 1122 W Bagley Rd	Berea	OH	44017	440-243-8200	243-8310
Web: standbyscrew.com					
Sumitomo Metal Industries Ltd 1815 Sandusky St.	Fostoria	OH	44830	419-436-4499	435-3881
TF: 866-877-2020 ■ *Web:* sumitomocanada.com					
Superior Products Inc 3786 Ridge Rd	Cleveland	OH	44144	216-651-9400	651-4071
TF: 800-651-9490 ■ *Web:* www.superiorprod.com					
Supreme Machined Products Company Inc 18686 172nd Ave	Spring Lake	MI	49456	616-842-6550	842-4481
Web: www.supreme1.com					
Supreme-Lake Manufacturing Inc 455 Atwater St PO Box 19	Plantsville	CT	06479	860-621-8911	628-9746
Web: www.supremelake.com					
T & L Automatics Inc 770 Emerson St	Rochester	NY	14613	585-647-3717	647-1126
Web: www.tandlautomatics.com					
Talladega Machinery & Supply Co Inc 301 N Johnson Ave PO Box 736	Talladega	AL	35161	256-362-4124	761-2579
TF Cust Svc: 800-289-8672 ■ *Web:* www.tmsco.com					
Tamer Industries 185 Riverside Ave	Somerset	MA	02725	508-677-0900	677-3037
Web: www.tamerind.com					
Tanko Screw Products Corp 515 Thomas Dr.	Bensenville	IL	60106	630-787-0504	787-0507
Web: ldredmer.com					
Taylor Metalworks Inc 3925 California Rd	Orchard Park	NY	14127	716-662-3113	662-1096
Web: www.taylorcnc.com					
Thorrez Industries Inc 4909 W Michigan Ave	Jackson	MI	49201	517-750-3160	750-1792
Web: www.thorrez.com					
Tompkins Products Inc 1040 W Grand Blvd	Detroit	MI	48208	313-894-2222	894-2901
Web: www.tompkinsproducts.com					
Torco Inc 1330 Old 41 Hwy NW	Marietta	GA	30060	770-427-3704	426-9369
Web: www.torcoinc.com					
Trace-A-Matic Inc (T-A-M) 1570 Commerce Ave	Brookfield	WI	53045	262-797-7300	797-9434
TF: 877-375-0217 ■ *Web:* www.traceamatic.com					
Tri Tool Inc 3041 Sunrise Blvd	Rancho Cordova	CA	95742	916-288-6100	288-6160
TF: 800-345-5015 ■ *Web:* www.tritool.com					
Triumph Components 203 N Johnson Ave	El Cajon	CA	92020	619-440-2504	440-2509
Web: www.triumphgroup.com					
Triumph Corp 2130 S Industrial Pk Ave	Tempe	AZ	85282	480-967-3337	921-0446
Web: www.triumphcorp.com					
V-S Industries Inc 900 Chaddick Dr.	Wheeling	IL	60090	847-520-1800	520-0269
Vallorbs Jewel Co 2599 Old Philadelphia Pk	Bird-in-Hand	PA	17505	717-392-3978	392-8947
Web: vallorbs.com					
Vanamatic Co 701 Ambrose Dr	Delphos	OH	45833	419-692-6085	692-3260
Web: www.vanamatic.com					
Willie Washer Manufacturing Corp 2101 Greenleaf Ave	Elk Grove Village	IL	60007	847-956-1344	
Web: www.williewasher.com					
Winslow Automatic Inc 23 St Clair Ave	New Britain	CT	06051	860-225-6321	224-1733
Web: winslowautomatics.com					
Xaloy Inc 1399 Countyline Rd	New Castle	PA	16101	800-897-2830	656-5620*
**Fax Area Code:* 724 ■ *TF:* 800-897-2830 ■ *Web:* www.xaloy.com					
Yoder 4899 Commerce Pkwy	Cleveland	OH	44128	216-292-4460	831-7948
TF: 800-631-0520 ■ *Web:* yodermfg.com					

625 PREPARATORY SCHOOLS - BOARDING

SEE ALSO Preparatory Schools - Non-boarding p. 2962

Schools listed here are independent, college-preparatory schools that provide housing facilities for students and teachers. All are members of The Association of Boarding Schools (TABS), and many are considered to be among the top prep schools in the United States.

	City	State	ZIP	Phone	Fax
Academie Ste Cecile International School (ASCIS) 925 Cousineau Rd	Windsor	ON	N9G1V8	519-969-1291	969-7953
Web: stececile.ca					
Admiral Farragut Academy 501 Pk St N	Saint Petersburg	FL	33710	727-384-5500	347-5160
Web: www.farragut.org					
Albert College 160 Dundas St W	Belleville	ON	K8P1A6	613-968-5726	968-9651
Web: www.albertcollege.ca					
American Boychoir School 19 Lambert Dr	Princeton	NJ	08540	609-924-5858	924-5812
TF: 888-269-2464 ■ *Web:* www.americanboychoir.org					
Andrews Osborne Academy 38588 Mentor Ave	Willoughby	OH	44094	440-942-3600	954-5020
TF: 800-753-4683 ■ *Web:* www.andrewsosborne.org					
Annie Wright School 827 N Tacoma Ave	Tacoma	WA	98403	253-272-2216	572-3616
Web: aw.org					
Appleby College 540 Lakeshore Rd W	Oakville	ON	L6K3P1	905-845-4681	845-9505
Web: www.appleby.on.ca					
Army & Navy Academy 2605 Carlsbad Blvd PO Box 3000	Carlsbad	CA	92018	760-729-2385	434-5948
TF: 888-762-2338 ■ *Web:* www.armyandnavyacademy.org					
Asheville School 360 Asheville School Rd	Asheville	NC	28806	828-254-6345	252-8666
Web: www.ashevilleschool.org					
Athenian School 2100 Mt Diablo Scenic Blvd	Danville	CA	94506	925-837-5375	831-1120
Web: www.athenian.org					
Avon Old Farms School 500 Old Farms Rd	Avon	CT	06001	860-404-4100	675-6051
TF: 800-464-2866 ■ *Web:* www.avonoldfarms.com					
Balmoral Hall School 630 Westminster Ave	Winnipeg	MB	R3C3S1	204-784-1600	774-5534
Web: www.balmoralhall.com					
Bement School 94 Main St	Deerfield	MA	01342	413-774-7061	774-7863
TF: 877-405-3949 ■ *Web:* www.bement.org					
Ben Lippen School 7401 Monticello Rd	Columbia	SC	29203	803-786-7200	744-1387
TF: 800-777-2227 ■ *Web:* www.benlippen.com					
Berkshire School 245 N Undermountain Rd	Sheffield	MA	01257	413-229-8511	229-1016
TF: 866-738-5500 ■ *Web:* www.berkshireschool.org					
Bishop Strachan School 298 Lonsdale Rd	Toronto	ON	M4V1X2	416-483-4325	481-5632
Web: www.bss.on.ca					
Bishop's College School 80 Moulton Hill Rd PO Box 5001	Lennoxville	QC	J1M1Z8	819-566-0227	822-8917
Web: www.bishopscollegeschool.com					
Blair Academy Two Pk St PO Box 600	Blairstown	NJ	07825	908-362-6121	362-7975
Web: www.blair.edu					
Blue Ridge School 273 Mayo Dr	Saint George	VA	22935	434-985-2811	
Web: blueridgeschool.com					
Boarding Schools Start Class 154 S Mountain Rd	Northfield	MA	01360	413-498-2906	
Web: boarding-schools.findthebest.com					
Bolles School 7400 San Jose Blvd	Jacksonville	FL	32217	904-733-9292	739-9929
Web: www.bolles.org					
Brandon Hall School 1701 Brandon Hall Dr	Atlanta	GA	30350	770-394-8177	868-1444*
**Fax Area Code:* 678 ■ *Web:* www.brandonhall.org					
Branksome Hall 10 Elm Ave	Toronto	ON	M4W1N4	416-920-9741	920-5390
Web: www.branksome.on.ca					
Brehm Preparatory School 1245 E Grand Ave	Carbondale	IL	62901	618-457-0371	529-1248
Web: www.brehm.org					
Brentwood College School 2735 Mt Baker Rd	Mill Bay	BC	V0R2P1	250-743-5521	743-2911
Web: www.brentwood.bc.ca					
Brewster Academy 80 Academy Dr.	Wolfeboro	NH	03894	603-569-7200	569-7272
TF: 800-842-9961 ■ *Web:* www.brewsteracademy.org					
Bridgton Academy PO Box 292	North Bridgton	ME	04057	207-647-3322	647-8513
Web: www.bridgtonacademy.org					
Brooks School 1160 Great Pond Rd	North Andover	MA	01845	978-725-6300	725-6298
Web: www.brooksschool.org					
Cambridge School of Weston 45 Georgian Rd	Weston	MA	02493	781-642-8650	398-8344
Web: www.csw.org					
Canterbury School 101 Aspetuck Ave	New Milford	CT	06776	860-210-3800	350-1120
Web: www.cbury.org					
Canyonville Christian Academy 250 E First St PO Box 1100	Canyonville	OR	97417	541-839-4401	839-6228
Web: www.canyonville.net					
Cardigan Mountain School 62 Alumni Dr	Canaan	NH	03741	603-523-4321	523-3565
Web: www.cardigan.org					
Carson Long Military Institute 200 N Carlisle St PO Box 98	New Bloomfield	PA	17068	717-582-2121	582-8763
Web: www.carsonlong.org					
Cate School 1960 Cate Mesa Rd	Carpinteria	CA	93013	805-684-4127	684-8940
Web: www.cate.org					
CFS the School at Church Farm PO Box 2000	Paoli	PA	19301	610-363-7500	280-6746
TF: 800-439-4745 ■ *Web:* www.gocfs.net					
Chaminade College Preparatory School 425 S Lindbergh Blvd	Saint Louis	MO	63131	314-993-4400	993-5732
TF: 877-378-6847 ■ *Web:* chaminade-stl.org					
Chatham Hall 800 Chatham Hall Cir	Chatham	VA	24531	434-432-2941	432-2405
Web: www.chathamhall.org					
Cheshire Academy 10 Main St	Cheshire	CT	06410	203-272-5396	250-7209
Web: www.cheshireacademy.org					
Choate Rosemary Hall 333 Christian St	Wallingford	CT	06492	203-697-2239	697-2629
Web: www.choate.edu					
Christ School 500 Christ School Rd	Arden	NC	28704	828-684-6232	684-4869
TF: 800-422-3212 ■ *Web:* www.christschool.org					
Christchurch School 49 Seahorse Ln	Christchurch	VA	23031	804-758-2306	758-0721
TF: 800-296-2306 ■ *Web:* www.christchurchschool.org					
Colorado Rocky Mountain School 1493 County Rd 106	Carbondale	CO	81623	970-963-2562	963-9865
Web: www.crms.org					
Concord Academy 166 Main St	Concord	MA	01742	978-402-2200	402-2210
Web: www.concordacademy.org					
Cotter High School 1115 W Broadway	Winona	MN	55987	507-453-5000	
Web: www.cotterschools.org					
Cranbrook Schools 39221 Woodward Ave	Bloomfield Hills	MI	48304	248-645-3610	645-3025
Web: www.schools.cranbrook.edu					
Culver Academies 1300 Academy Rd	Culver	IN	46511	574-842-7000	842-8066
TF: 800-528-5837 ■ *Web:* www.culver.org					
Cushing Academy 39 School St PO Box 8000	Ashburnham	MA	01430	978-827-7000	827-6253
Web: www.cushing.org					
Dana Hall School 45 Dana Rd PO Box 9010	Wellesley	MA	02482	781-235-3010	235-0577
Web: www.danahall.org					
Darlington School 1014 Cave Spring Rd	Rome	GA	30161	706-235-6051	232-3600
TF: 800-368-4437 ■ *Web:* www.darlingtonschool.org					
Darrow School 110 Darrow Rd	New Lebanon	NY	12125	518-794-6000	794-7065
TF: 877-432-7769 ■ *Web:* www.darrowschool.org					
Deerfield Academy Seven Boyden Ln	Deerfield	MA	01342	413-772-0241	772-1100
Web: www.deerfield.edu					
Devereux Glenholme School 81 Sabbaday Ln	Washington	CT	06793	860-868-7377	868-7894
Web: www.theglenholmeschool.org					
Dublin School 18 Lehmann Way PO Box 522	Dublin	NH	03444	603-563-8584	563-8671
Web: www.dublinschool.org					
Dunn School 2555 Hwy 154 PO Box 98	Los Olivos	CA	93441	805-688-6471	686-9715
TF: 800-287-9197 ■ *Web:* www.dunnschool.org					
Eagle Hill School 242 Old Petersham Rd PO Box 116	Hardwick	MA	01037	413-477-6000	477-6837
Web: www.ehs1.org					
Eaglebrook School 271 Pine Nook Rd	Deerfield	MA	01342	413-774-9111	774-9119
Web: www.eaglebrook.org					
Emma Willard School 285 Pawling Ave	Troy	NY	12180	518-833-1300	833-1805
Web: www.emmawillard.org					
Episcopal High School 1200 N Quaker Ln	Alexandria	VA	22302	703-933-4062	933-3016
TF: 877-933-4347 ■ *Web:* www.episcopalhighschool.org					
Ethel Walker School 230 Bushy Hill Rd	Simsbury	CT	06070	860-408-4200	408-4201
Web: www.ethelwalker.org					
Fay School 48 Main St	Southborough	MA	01772	508-485-0100	481-7872
TF: 800-933-2925 ■ *Web:* www.fayschool.org					
Fessenden School 250 Waltham St	West Newton	MA	02465	617-630-2300	630-2303
Web: www.fessenden.org					

				Phone	Fax
Flintridge Sacred Heart Academy 440 St Katherine Dr *Fax: Admissions ■ Web: www.fsha.org	La Canada	CA	91011	626-685-8333	685-8520*
Forman School 12 Norfolk Rd PO Box 80 Web: www.formanschool.org	Litchfield	CT	06759	860-567-1802	567-3501
Fountain Valley School of Colorado 6155 Fountain Vly School Rd Web: www.fvs.edu	Colorado Springs	CO	80911	719-390-7035	390-7762
Fox River Country Day School 1600 Dundee Ave Web: www.frcds.org	Elgin	IL	60120	847-888-7910	
Foxcroft School 22407 Foxhound Ln TF: 800-858-2364 ■ Web: www.foxcroft.org	Middleburg	VA	20117	540-687-5555	687-3627
Fryeburg Academy 745 Main St TF: 877-935-2013 ■ Web: www.fryeburgacademy.org	Fryeburg	ME	04037	207-935-2013	935-5013
Garrison Forest School 300 Garrison Forest Rd Web: www.gfs.org	Owings Mills	MD	21117	410-363-1500	
George School 1690 Newtown-Langhorne Rd TF: 888-804-1300 ■ Web: www.georgeschool.org	Newtown	PA	18940	215-579-6547	579-6549
Georgetown Preparatory School 10900 Rockville Pk Web: www.gprep.org	North Bethesda	MD	20852	301-493-5000	493-6128
Gilmour Academy 34001 Cedar Rd TF: 800-533-5140 ■ Web: www.gilmour.org	Gates Mills	OH	44040	440-442-1104	473-8010
Girard College 2101 S College Ave Ste 311 Web: www.girardcollege.com	Philadelphia	PA	19121	215-787-2600	787-4457
Gould Academy PO Box 860 Web: www.gouldacademy.org	Bethel	ME	04217	207-824-7777	824-2926
Governor Dummer Academy One Elm St Web: www.thegovernorsacademy.org	Byfield	MA	01922	978-499-3120	462-1278
Gow School 2491 Emery Rd PO Box 85 Web: www.gow.org	South Wales	NY	14139	716-652-3450	652-3457
Grand River Academy 3042 College St PO Box 222 Web: www.grandriver.org	Austinburg	OH	44010	440-275-2811	275-1825
Greenwood School 14 Greenwood Ln TF: 800-380-9218 ■ Web: greenwood.org	Putney	VT	05346	802-387-4545	387-5396
Grier School Rt 453 PO Box 308 Web: www.grier.org	Tyrone	PA	16686	814-684-3000	684-2177
Groton School 282 Farmers Row PO Box 991 Web: www.groton.org	Groton	MA	01450	978-448-3363	448-3100
Gunnery, The 99 Green Hill Rd Web: portal.gunnery.org	Washington	CT	06793	860-868-7334	868-1614
Hackley School 293 Benedict Ave Web: www.hackleyschool.org	Tarrytown	NY	10591	914-631-0128	
Hampshire Country School 28 Patey Cir Web: www.hampshirecountryschool.org	Rindge	NH	03461	603-899-3325	899-6521
Hargrave Military Academy (HMA) 200 Military Dr TF: 800-432-2480 ■ Web: www.hargrave.edu	Chatham	VA	24531	434-432-2481	432-3129
Harvey School 260 Jay St Web: www.harveyschool.org	Katonah	NY	10536	914-232-3161	232-6034
Havergal College 1451 Ave Rd Web: www.havergal.on.ca	Toronto	ON	M5N2H9	416-483-3519	483-6796
Hawaii Preparatory Academy 65-1692 Kohala Mountain Rd TF: 800-644-4481 ■ Web: www.hpa.edu	Kamuela	HI	96743	808-881-4007	881-4045
Hebron Academy Rt 119 PO Box 309 TF: 888-432-7664 ■ Web: www.hebronacademy.org	Hebron	ME	04238	207-966-2100	966-1111
High Mowing School 222 Isaac Frye Hwy Web: www.highmowing.org	Wilton	NH	03086	603-654-2391	654-6588
Hill School 717 E High St TF: 877-651-2800 ■ Web: www.thehill.org	Pottstown	PA	19464	610-326-1000	705-1753
Hillside School 404 Robin Hill Rd TF: 800-344-8328 ■ Web: www.hillsideschool.net	Marlborough	MA	01752	508-485-2824	485-4420
Hockaday School 11600 Welch Rd Web: www.hockaday100.org	Dallas	TX	75229	214-363-6311	373-0520
Holderness School Chapel Ln PO Box 1879 TF: 877-262-1492 ■ Web: www.holderness.org	Plymouth	NH	03264	603-536-1747	536-2125
Hoosac School 14 Pine Vly Rd Web: www.hoosac.com	Hoosick	NY	12089	518-686-7331	686-3370
Hotchkiss School 11 Interlaken Rd PO Box 800 Web: www.hotchkiss.org	Lakeville	CT	06039	860-435-3102	435-0042
Houghton Academy 9790 Thayer St Web: www.houghtonacademy.org	Houghton	NY	14744	585-567-8115	567-8048
Howe Military School PO Box 240 TF: 888-462-4693 ■ Web: howemilitary.org	Howe	IN	46746	260-562-2131	562-3678
Hun School of Princeton 176 Edgerstoune Rd Web: www.hunschool.org	Princeton	NJ	08540	609-921-7600	279-9398
Hyde School 616 High St Web: www.hyde.edu	Bath	ME	04530	207-443-5584	442-9346
Idyllwild Arts Academy 52500 Temecula Rd PO Box 38 Web: www.idyllwildarts.org	Idyllwild	CA	92549	951-659-2171	659-2058
Incarnate Word High School 727 E Hildebrand Ave Web: www.incarnatewordhs.org	San Antonio	TX	78212	210-829-3100	829-3101
Indian Mountain School 211 Indian Mtn Rd Web: www.indianmountain.org	Lakeville	CT	06039	860-435-0871	435-0641
Indian Springs School 190 Woodward Dr TF General: 888-843-9477 ■ Web: www.indiansprings.org	Pelham	AL	35124	205-988-3350	988-3797
Kent School PO Box 2006 TF: 800-538-5368 ■ Web: www.kent-school.edu	Kent	CT	06757	860-927-6111	927-6109
Kents Hill School Rt 17 PO Box 257 Web: www.kentshill.org	Kents Hill	ME	04349	207-685-4914	685-9529
Kildonan School 425 Morse Hill Rd Web: www.kildonan.org	Amenia	NY	12501	845-373-8111	373-2004
Kimball Union Academy 64 Main St Web: www.kua.org	Meriden	NH	03770	603-469-2000	469-2040
Kiski School 1888 Brett Ln TF: 877-547-5448 ■ Web: www.kiski.org	Saltsburg	PA	15681	724-639-3586	639-8596
Knox School 541 E Long Beach Rd Web: www.knoxschool.org	Saint James	NY	11780	631-686-1600	686-1650
La Lumiere School 6801 N Wilhelm Rd Web: www.lalumiere.org	La Porte	IN	46350	219-326-7450	325-3185
Lake Forest Academy 1500 W Kennedy Rd Web: www.lfanet.org	Lake Forest	IL	60045	847-234-3210	615-3202
Lakefield College School 4391 County Rd 29	Lakefield	ON	K0L2H0	705-652-3324	652-6320
Landmark School 429 Hale St PO Box 227 Web: www.landmarkschool.org	Prides Crossing	MA	01965	978-236-3010	927-7268
Lawrence Academy Powderhouse Rd PO Box 992 TF: 800-977-4698 ■ Web: www.lacademy.edu	Groton	MA	01450	978-448-6535	448-9208
Lawrenceville School 2500 Main St PO Box 6008 TF: 800-735-2030 ■ Web: www.lawrenceville.org	Lawrenceville	NJ	08648	609-896-0400	895-2217
Leelanau School One Old Homestead Rd Web: www.leelanau.org	Glen Arbor	MI	49636	231-334-5800	334-5898
Linden Hall School for Girls 212 E Main St TF: 800-258-5778 ■ Web: www.lindenhall.org	Lititz	PA	17543	717-626-8512	627-1384
Linsly School 60 Knox Ln Web: www.linsly.org	Wheeling	WV	26003	304-233-3260	234-4614
Loomis Chaffee School Four Batchelder Rd Web: www.loomischaffee.org	Windsor	CT	06095	860-687-6400	298-8756
Lowell Whiteman School 42605 RCR 36 Web: www.lws.edu	Steamboat Springs	CO	80487	970-879-1350	879-0506
MacDuffie School 66 School St TF: 877-477-6217 ■ Web: macduffie.org	Granby	MA	01033	413-255-0000	467-1607
Madeira School 8328 Georgetown Pk Web: www.madeira.org	McLean	VA	22102	703-556-8200	
Maine Central Institute 295 MAIN ST Web: www.mci-school.org	Pittsfield	ME	04967	207-487-3355	487-3512
Marianapolis Preparatory School 26 Chase Rd PO Box 304 Web: www.marianapolis.org	Thompson	CT	06277	860-923-9565	923-3730
Marvelwood School 476 Skiff Mountain Rd TF: 800-440-9107 ■ Web: marvelwood.org	Kent	CT	06757	860-927-0047	927-0021
Massanutten Military Academy 614 S Main St TF: 877-466-6222 ■ Web: www.militaryschool.com	Woodstock	VA	22664	540-459-2167	459-5421
Masters School, The 49 Clinton Ave Web: www.mastersny.org	Dobbs Ferry	NY	10522	914-479-6400	693-1230
Maur Hill-Mount Academy 1000 Green St Web: www.maurhillmountacademy.com	Atchison	KS	66002	913-367-5482	367-5096
McCallie School 500 Dodds Ave TF: 800-234-2163 ■ Web: www.mccallie.org	Chattanooga	TN	37404	423-624-8300	493-5426
Mercersburg Academy 300 E Seminary St TF: 800-588-2550 ■ Web: www.mercersburg.edu	Mercersburg	PA	17236	717-328-6173	328-6319
Mid-Pacific Institute 2445 Kaala St Web: www.midpac.edu	Honolulu	HI	96822	808-973-5000	973-5099
Middlesex School 1400 Lowell Rd Web: www.mxschool.edu	Concord	MA	01742	978-369-2550	287-4759
Midland School 5100 Figueroa Mtn Rd PO Box 8 Web: www.midland-school.org	Los Olivos	CA	93441	805-688-5114	686-2470
Millbrook School 131 Millbrook School Rd Web: www.millbrook.org	Millbrook	NY	12545	845-677-8261	677-1265
Miller School 1000 Samuel Miller Loop Web: millerschoolofalbemarle.org	Charlottesville	VA	22903	434-823-4805	823-6617
Milton Academy 170 Centre St TF: 866-645-8661 ■ Web: www.milton.edu	Milton	MA	02186	617-898-1798	898-1701
Milton Hershey School PO Box 830 TF: 800-322-3248 ■ Web: www.mhs-pa.org	Hershey	PA	17033	717-520-2100	520-2117
Miss Hall's School 492 Holmes Rd Web: www.misshalls.org	Pittsfield	MA	01201	413-443-6401	448-2994
Miss Porter's School 60 Main St Web: www.missporters.org	Farmington	CT	06032	860-409-3530	409-3531
Monte Vista Christian School Two School Way Web: www.mvcs.org	Watsonville	CA	95076	831-722-8178	722-6003
Montverde Academy 17235 Seventh St Web: www.montverde.org	Montverde	FL	34756	407-469-2561	469-3711
National Sports Academy 821 Mirror Lk Dr Web: www.nationalsportsacademy.com	Lake Placid	NY	12946	518-523-3460	523-3488
New Hampton School 70 Main St PO Box 579 Web: www.newhampton.org	New Hampton	NH	03256	603-677-3400	677-3481
New York Military Academy 78 Academy Ave TF: 888-275-6962 ■ Web: www.nyma.org	Cornwall On Hudson	NY	12520	845-534-3710	534-7699
North Country School 4382 Cascade Rd Web: www.nct.org	Lake Placid	NY	12946	518-523-9329	523-4858
Northfield Mount Hermon School 206 Main St TF: 866-664-4483 ■ Web: www.nmhschool.org	Northfield	MA	01360	413-498-3227	498-3152
Northwest School 1415 Summit Ave TF: 800-426-7127 ■ Web: www.northwestschool.org	Seattle	WA	98122	206-682-7309	328-1776
Northwood School PO Box 1070 Web: www.northwoodschool.com	Lake Placid	NY	12946	518-523-3382	523-3405
Oak Grove School 220 W Lomita Ave Web: oakgroveschool.org	Ojai	CA	93023	805-646-8236	646-6509
Oak Hill Academy 2635 Oak Hill Rd Web: www.oak-hill.net	Mouth of Wilson	VA	24363	276-579-2619	579-4722
Oakwood Friends School 22 Spackenkill Rd TF: 800-843-3341 ■ Web: www.oakwoodfriends.org	Poughkeepsie	NY	12603	845-462-4200	462-4251
Ojai Valley School 723 El Paseo Rd Web: www.ovs.org	Ojai	CA	93023	805-646-1423	646-0362
Oldfields School 1500 Glencoe Rd TF: 800-767-0700 ■ Web: www.oldfieldsschool.org	Glencoe	MD	21152	410-472-4800	472-6839
Olney Friends School 61830 Sandy Ridge Rd TF: 800-303-4291 ■ Web: www.olneyfriends.org	Barnesville	OH	43713	740-425-3655	425-3202

School	City	State	Zip	Phone	Fax
Oregon Episcopal School 6300 SW Nicol Rd *Web:* www.oes.edu	Portland	OR	97223	503-246-7771	768-3140
Orme School HC 63 PO Box 3040 *Web:* www.ormeschool.org	Mayer	AZ	86333	928-632-7601	632-7601
Oxford Academy 1393 Boston Post Rd *Web:* www.oxfordacademy.net	Westbrook	CT	06498	860-399-6247	399-6805
Peddie School 201 S Main St *Web:* www.peddie.org	Hightstown	NJ	08520	609-944-7500	944-7901
Pennington School 112 W Delaware Ave *Web:* www.pennington.org	Pennington	NJ	08534	609-737-1838	730-1405
Perkiomen School 200 Seminary St PO Box 130 *TF:* 866-966-9998 ■ *Web:* www.perkiomen.org	Pennsburg	PA	18073	215-679-9511	679-1146
Phelps School 583 Sugartown Rd *TF:* 800-344-8328 ■ *Web:* www.thephelpsschool.org	Malvern	PA	19355	610-644-1754	644-6679
Phillips Academy 180 Main St *TF:* 877-445-5477 ■ *Web:* www.andover.edu	Andover	MA	01810	978-749-4000	749-4068
Phillips Exeter Academy 20 Main St *TF:* 800-245-2525 ■ *Web:* www.exeter.edu	Exeter	NH	03833	603-772-4311	777-4399
Pickering College 16945 Bayview Ave *Web:* www.pickeringcollege.on.ca	Newmarket	ON	L3Y4X2	905-895-1700	895-9076
Piney Woods School 5096 Hwy 49 S PO Box 69 *Web:* www.pineywoods.org	Piney Woods	MS	39148	601-845-2214	845-2604
Pomfret School 398 Pomfret St PO Box 128 *Web:* www.pomfretschool.org	Pomfret	CT	06258	860-963-6100	963-2042
Portsmouth Abbey School 285 Cory's Ln *Web:* www.portsmouthabbey.org	Portsmouth	RI	02871	401-683-2000	683-6766
Proctor Academy 204 Main St PO Box 500 *TF:* 800-626-4907 ■ *Web:* www.proctoracademy.org	Andover	NH	03216	603-735-6000	735-6284
Purnell School 51 Pottersville Rd PO Box 500 *TF:* 800-228-9290 ■ *Web:* www.purnell.org	Pottersville	NJ	07979	908-439-2154	439-4088
Putney School 418 Houghton Brook Rd *TF:* 800-999-9080 ■ *Web:* www.putneyschool.org	Putney	VT	05346	802-387-5566	387-6278
Rabun Gap-Nacoochee School 339 Nacoochee Dr *TF:* 800-543-7467 ■ *Web:* www.rabungap.org	Rabun Gap	GA	30568	706-746-7467	746-2594
Randolph-Macon Academy 200 Academy Dr. *TF:* 800-272-1172 ■ *Web:* www.rma.edu	Front Royal	VA	22630	540-636-5200	636-5419
Rectory School 528 Pomfret St PO Box 68 *Web:* www.rectoryschool.org	Pomfret	CT	06258	860-928-7759	928-4961
Ridley College Two Ridley Rd PO Box 3013 *Web:* www.ridley.on.ca	Saint Catharines	ON	L2R7C3	905-684-1889	684-8875
Riverside Military Academy 2001 Riverside Dr. **Fax Area Code:* 678 ■ *TF:* 800-462-2338 ■ *Web:* www.riversidemilitary.com	Gainesville	GA	30501	770-532-6251	291-3364*
Rock Point School One Rock Pt Rd *Web:* www.rockpointschool.org	Burlington	VT	05408	802-863-1104	863-6628
Rosseau Lake College 1967 Bright St *Web:* www.rosseaulakecollege.com	Rosseau	ON	P0C1J0	705-732-4351	732-6319
Rumsey Hall School 201 Romford Rd *Web:* www.rumseyhall.org	Washington Depot	CT	06794	860-868-0535	868-7907
Saint Andrew's College 15800 Yonge St *TF:* 877-378-1899 ■ *Web:* www.sac.on.ca	Aurora	ON	L4G3H7	905-727-3178	727-9032
Saint Andrew's School 63 Federal Rd *Web:* www.standrews-ri.org	Barrington	RI	02806	401-246-1230	246-0510
Saint Andrew's-Sewanee School 290 QuintaRd Rd *Web:* www.sasweb.org	Sewanee	TN	37375	931-598-5651	598-0039
Saint Anne's-Belfield School 2132 Ivy Rd *Web:* www.stab.org	Charlottesville	VA	22903	434-296-5106	979-1486
Saint Anthony's Catholic High School 3200 McCullough Ave *Web:* www.sachs.org	San Antonio	TX	78212	210-832-5600	832-5633
Saint Bernard Preparatory School 1600 St Bernard Dr SE *TF:* 800-722-0999 ■ *Web:* www.stbernardprep.com	Cullman	AL	35055	256-739-6682	734-2925
Saint Catherine's School 6001 Grove Ave *TF:* 800-648-4982 ■ *Web:* www.st.catherines.org	Richmond	VA	23226	804-288-2804	285-8169
Saint James School 17641 College Rd *Web:* www.stjames.edu	Saint James	MD	21740	301-733-9330	739-1310
Saint John's Northwestern Military Academy 1101 N Genesee St *TF:* 800-752-2338 ■ *Web:* www.sjnma.org	Delafield	WI	53018	262-646-7115	646-7128
Saint John's Preparatory School 1857 Watertower Rd PO Box 4000 *TF:* 800-525-7737 ■ *Web:* www.sjprep.net	Collegeville	MN	56321	320-363-3321	363-3322
Saint John's-Ravenscourt School 400 S Dr *TF:* 800-437-0040 ■ *Web:* www.sjr.mb.ca	Winnipeg	MB	R3T3K5	204-477-2400	477-2429
Saint Mark's School 25 Marlborough Rd *Web:* www.stmarksschool.org	Southborough	MA	01772	508-786-6000	786-6120
Saint Mary's School 900 Hillsborough St *TF:* 800-948-2557 ■ *Web:* www.sms.edu	Raleigh	NC	27603	919-424-4000	424-4122
Saint Michael's University School 3400 Richmond Rd *TF:* 800-661-5199 ■ *Web:* www.smus.ca	Victoria	BC	V8P4P5	250-592-2411	592-2812
Saint Paul's School 325 Pleasant St *Web:* www.sps.edu	Concord	NH	03301	603-229-4600	
Saint Stanislaus College 304 S Beach Blvd *Web:* www.ststan.com	Bay Saint Louis	MS	39520	228-467-9057	466-2972
Saint Stephen's Episcopal School 6500 St Stephen's Dr *Web:* www.sstx.org	Austin	TX	78746	512-327-1213	327-6771
Saint Thomas Choir School 202 W 58th St *Web:* www.choirschool.org	New York	NY	10019	212-247-3311	247-3393
Saint Timothy's School 8400 Greenspring Ave *Web:* www.stt.org	Stevenson	MD	21153	410-486-7400	486-1167
Salem Academy (SA) 942 Lancaster Dr NE *Web:* www.salemacademy.org	Salem	OR	97301	503-378-1219	

School	City	State	Zip	Phone	Fax
Salisbury School 251 Canaan Rd *Web:* www.salisburyschool.org	Salisbury	CT	06068	860-435-5732	435-5750
San Domenico School 1500 Butterfield Rd *Web:* www.sandomenico.org	San Anselmo	CA	94960	415-258-1905	258-1906
San Marcos Academy 2801 Ranch to Market 12 *TF Admissions:* 800-428-5120 ■ *Web:* www.smabears.org	San Marcos	TX	78666	512-353-2400	753-8031
Sandy Spring Friends School 16923 Norwood Rd. *Web:* www.ssfs.org	Sandy Spring	MD	20860	301-774-7455	924-1115
Santa Catalina School 1500 Mark Thomas Dr *Web:* www.santacatalina.org	Monterey	CA	93940	831-655-9300	655-7535
Scattergood Friends School 1951 Delta Ave *TF:* 888-737-4636 ■ *Web:* www.scattergood.org	West Branch	IA	52358	319-643-7628	643-7638
Shady Side Academy 423 Fox Chapel Rd *Web:* www.shadysideacademy.org	Pittsburgh	PA	15238	412-968-3000	968-3213
Shattuck-Saint Mary's School 1000 Shumway Ave PO Box 218 *TF:* 800-421-2724 ■ *Web:* www.s-sm.org	Faribault	MN	55021	507-333-1616	333-1661
Shawnigan Lake School (SLS) 1975 Renfrew Rd *Web:* www.shawnigan.ca	Shawnigan Lake	BC	V0R2W1	250-743-5516	743-6200
Solebury School 6832 Phillips Mill Rd *TF:* 800-675-6900 ■ *Web:* www.solebury.org	New Hope	PA	18938	215-862-5261	862-3366
South Kent School 40 Bulls Bridge Rd **Fax Area Code:* 888 ■ *Web:* www.southkentschool.org	South Kent	CT	06785	860-927-3539	803-0040*
Southwestern Academy 2800 Monterey Rd *Web:* www.southwesternacademy.edu	San Marino	CA	91108	626-799-5010	799-0407
Stanstead College 450 Dufferin St *Web:* www.stansteadcollege.com	Stanstead	QC	J0B3E0	819-876-2223	876-5891
Stevenson School 3152 Forest Lk Rd *Web:* www.stevensonschool.org	Pebble Beach	CA	93953	831-625-8300	625-5208
Stoneleigh-Burnham School 574 BernaRdston Rd. *Web:* www.sbschool.org	Greenfield	MA	01301	413-774-2711	772-2602
Stony Brook School One Chapman Pkwy *Web:* www.stonybrookschool.org	Stony Brook	NY	11790	631-751-1800	751-4211
Storm King School 314 Mountain Rd *TF:* 800-225-9144 ■ *Web:* www.sks.org	Cornwall On Hudson	NY	12520	845-534-9860	534-9860
Stuart Hall School 235 W Frederick St PO Box 210 *TF:* 888-306-8926 ■ *Web:* www.stuarthallschool.org	Staunton	VA	24402	540-885-0356	886-2275
Subiaco Academy 405 N Subiaco Ave. *Web:* www.subi.org	Subiaco	AR	72865	479-934-1000	934-1033
Suffield Academy 185 N Main St PO Box 999 *Web:* www.suffieldacademy.org	Suffield	CT	06078	860-668-7315	668-2966
Tabor Academy 66 Spring St *Web:* www.taboracademy.org	Marion	MA	02738	508-748-2000	748-0353
Taft School 110 Woodbury Rd *Web:* www.taftschool.org	Watertown	CT	06795	860-945-7777	945-7808
Tallulah Falls School 201 Campus Dr PO Box 10 *Web:* www.tallulahfalls.org	Tallulah Falls	GA	30573	706-754-0400	754-3595
Texas Military Institute (TMI) 20955 W Tejas Trail *Web:* www.tmi-sa.com/	San Antonio	TX	78257	210-698-7171	698-0715
Thacher School 5025 Thacher Rd *Web:* www.thacher.org	Ojai	CA	93023	805-640-3210	640-1033
Thomas Jefferson School 4100 S Lindbergh Blvd *Web:* www.tjs.org	Saint Louis	MO	63127	314-843-4151	843-3527
Thomas More Prep-Marian 1701 Hall St. *Web:* www.tmp-m.org	Hays	KS	67601	785-625-6577	625-3912
Tilton School 30 School St. *Web:* www.tiltonschool.org	Tilton	NH	03276	603-286-4342	286-1705
Trafalgar Castle School 401 Reynolds St *Web:* www.castle-ed.com	Whitby	ON	L1N3W9	905-668-3358	668-4136
Trinity College School 55 Deblaquire St N *Web:* www.tcs.on.ca	Port Hope	ON	L1A4K7	905-885-4565	885-7444
Trinity-Pawling School 700 Rt 22 *Web:* www.trinitypawling.org	Pawling	NY	12564	845-855-3100	855-3816
Universal Ballet Academy 4301 Harewood Rd NE *Web:* universalballet.com	Washington	DC	20017	202-832-1087	526-4274
Upper Canada College 200 Lonsdale Rd *Web:* www.ucc.on.ca	Toronto	ON	M4V1W6	416-488-1125	484-8611
Valley Forge Military Academy & College 1001 Eagle Rd **Fax:* Admissions ■ *TF:* 800-234-8362 ■ *Web:* www.vfmac.edu	Wayne	PA	19087	610-989-1300	688-1545*
Vanguard School 22000 US Hwy 27 *Web:* www.vanguardschool.org	Lake Wales	FL	33859	863-676-6091	676-8297
Verde Valley School 3511 Verde Vly School Rd *Web:* www.vvsaz.org	Sedona	AZ	86351	928-284-2272	284-0432
Vermont Academy PO Box 500 *TF:* 800-698-8867 ■ *Web:* www.vermontacademy.org	Saxtons River	VT	05154	802-869-6229	869-6242
Villanova Preparatory School 12096 N Ventura Ave *Web:* www.villanovaprep.org	Ojai	CA	93023	805-646-1464	646-4430
Virginia Episcopal School 400 VES Rd PO Box 408 *TF:* 800-937-3582 ■ *Web:* www.ves.org	Lynchburg	VA	24503	434-385-3607	385-3603
Wasatch Academy 120 South 100 West *TF:* 800-634-4690 ■ *Web:* www.wasatchacademy.org	Mount Pleasant	UT	84647	435-462-1400	462-3380
Washington Academy 66 High St *Web:* www.washingtonacademy.org	East Machias	ME	04630	207-255-8301	255-8303
Wayland Academy 101 N University Ave. *TF:* 800-860-7725 ■ *Web:* www.wayland.org	Beaver Dam	WI	53916	920-885-3373	887-3373
Webb School PO Box 488 *TF:* 888-733-9322 ■ *Web:* www.thewebbschool.com	Bell Buckle	TN	37020	931-389-9322	389-6657
Webb Schools 1175 W Baseline Rd *Web:* www.webb.org	Claremont	CA	91711	909-482-5214	621-4582

	City	State	Zip	Phone	Fax
West Nottingham Academy 1079 Firetower Rd *TF:* 866-381-3684 ■ *Web:* www.wna.org	Colora	MD	21917	410-658-5556	658-9264
Western Reserve Academy 115 College St *TF:* 877-486-2048 ■ *Web:* www.wra.net	Hudson	OH	44236	330-650-9717	650-9722
Westminster School 995 Hopmeadow St *Web:* www.westminster-school.org	Simsbury	CT	06070	860-408-3060	408-3042
Westover School PO Box 847 *Web:* www.westoverschool.org	Middlebury	CT	06762	203-758-2423	577-4588
Westtown School PO Box 1799 *Web:* www.westtown.edu	Westtown	PA	19395	610-399-0123	399-3760
White Mountain School 371 W Farm Rd *Web:* www.whitemountain.org	Bethlehem	NH	03574	603-444-2928	444-5568
Wilbraham & Monson Academy 423 Main St *Web:* wma.us	Wilbraham	MA	01095	413-596-6811	596-2448
Williston Northampton School 19 Payson Ave *Web:* www.williston.com	EastHampton	MA	01027	413-529-3241	527-9494
Winchendon School 172 Ash St *Web:* winchendon.org	Winchendon	MA	01475	978-297-4476	297-0911
Wolfeboro Camp School 93 Camp School Rd *Web:* www.wolfeboro.org	Wolfeboro	NH	03894	603-569-3451	569-4080
Woodhall School 58 Harrison Ln PO Box 550 *Web:* www.woodhallschool.org	Bethlehem	CT	06751	203-266-7788	266-5896
Woodlands Academy of the Sacred Heart 760 E Westleigh Rd *TF:* 888-234-3080 ■ *Web:* www.woodlandsacademy.org	Lake Forest	IL	60045	847-234-4300	234-4348
Woodside Priory School 302 Portola Rd *Web:* www.prioryca.org	Portola Valley	CA	94028	650-851-8221	851-2839
Worcester Academy 81 Providence St *TF:* 800-235-6426 ■ *Web:* www.worcesteracademy.org	Worcester	MA	01604	508-754-5302	752-2382
Wyoming Seminary 201 N Sprague Ave *TF:* 877-996-7361 ■ *Web:* www.wyomingseminary.org	Kingston	PA	18704	570-270-2160	270-2191

626 PREPARATORY SCHOOLS - NON-BOARDING

SEE ALSO Preparatory Schools - Boarding p. 2959

The schools listed here are among the leading private elementary and secondary schools in the U.S. None of these schools are boarding schools.

	City	State	Zip	Phone	Fax
Albuquerque Academy 6400 Wyoming Blvd NE *Web:* www.aa.edu	Albuquerque	NM	87109	505-828-3200	828-3320
Blake School 110 Blake Rd S *Web:* www.blakeschool.org	Hopkins	MN	55343	952-988-3405	988-3455
Brearley School 610 E 83rd St *Web:* www.brearley.org	New York	NY	10028	212-744-8582	472-8020
Chapin School 100 E End Ave *Web:* www.chapin.edu	New York	NY	10028	212-744-2335	
Glen Mills Schools PO Box 5001 *Web:* www.glenmillsschool.org	Concordville	PA	19331	610-459-8100	558-1493
Iolani School 563 Kamoku St *TF:* 888-879-8970 ■ *Web:* www.iolani.org	Honolulu	HI	96826	808-949-5355	943-2297
Kinkaid School, The 201 Kinkaid School Dr *Web:* www.kinkaid.org	Houston	TX	77024	713-782-1640	782-3543
Latin School of Chicago 59 W N Blvd *Web:* www.latinschool.org	Chicago	IL	60610	312-582-6000	
Mary Institute & Saint Louis Country Day School 101 N Warson Rd *Web:* www.micds.org	Saint Louis	MO	63124	314-993-5100	
National Cathedral School 3609 Woodley Rd NW *Web:* www.ncs.cathedral.org	Washington	DC	20016	202-537-6339	537-5743
North Shore Country Day School 310 Green Bay Rd *Web:* www.nscds.org	Winnetka	IL	60093	847-446-0674	446-0675
Orchard School 615 W 64th St *Web:* www.orchard.org	Indianapolis	IN	46260	317-251-9253	254-8454
Punahou School 1601 Punahou St *Web:* www.punahou.edu	Honolulu	HI	96822	808-944-5711	944-5779
Roxbury Latin School 101 St Theresa Ave *Web:* www.roxburylatin.org	West Roxbury	MA	02132	617-325-4920	325-3585
Saint Albans School 3001 Wisconsin Ave NW	Washington	DC	20016	202-537-6435	537-5613
Saint Stephen's & Saint Agnes School 1000 St Stephen's Rd *Web:* www.sssas.org	Alexandria	VA	22304	703-751-2700	683-5930
Sidwell Friends School 3825 Wisconsin Ave NW *Web:* www.sidwell.edu	Washington	DC	20016	202-537-8100	537-8138
University School Hunting Vly Campus 2785 SOM Ctr Rd *Web:* www.us.edu	Hunting Valley	OH	44022	216-831-2200	292-7810
University School of Milwaukee 2100 W Fairy Chasm Rd *Web:* www.usm.k12.wi.us	Milwaukee	WI	53217	414-352-6000	352-8076
Westminster Schools 1424 W Paces Ferry Rd NW *Web:* www.westminster.net	Atlanta	GA	30327	404-355-8673	355-6606

627 PRESS CLIPPING SERVICES

	City	State	Zip	Phone	Fax
3i People Inc 5755 N Point Pkwy Ste 9 *Web:* www.3ipeople.com	Alpharetta	GA	30022	404-636-2397	
ActioNet Inc 2600 Park Tower Dr Ste 1000 *Web:* www.actionet.com	Vienna	VA	22180	703-204-0090	
Acumera Inc 3112 Windsor Rd Ste A-512 *Web:* www.acumera.net	Austin	TX	78703	512-473-2290	
Alta Associates Inc Eight Bartles Corner Rd Ste 21 *Web:* www.altaassociates.com	Flemington	NJ	08822	908-806-8442	
Antiok Holdings Inc 34 Shining Willow Way # 132 *Web:* www.antiok.com	La Plata	MD	20646	301-743-2100	
Art Resource Inc 536 Broadway Fifth Fl *Web:* www.artres.com	New York	NY	10012	212-505-8700	
Attendee Management Inc 15572 Ranch Rd 12 Ste 1 *Web:* attendeenet.com	Wimberley	TX	78676	512-847-5174	
BC Public School Employers' Association 106-1525 W Eighth Ave *Web:* www.bcpsea.bc.ca	Vancouver	BC	V6J1T5	604-730-4507	
BurrellesLuce 30 B Vreeland Rd PO Box 674 *TF:* 800-631-1160 ■ *Web:* www.burrellesluce.com	Florham Park	NJ	07932	973-992-6600	992-7675
Cision US Inc 130 East Randolph St 7th Fl **Fax:* Cust Svc ■ *Web:* www.cision.com	Chicago	IL	60601	312-922-2400	*
CoakleyTech LLC 4000 W Burnham St *Web:* www.coakleytech.com	Milwaukee	WI	53215	414-389-1900	
Colorado Press Clipping Service 1336 Glenarm Pl *Web:* www.coloradopressassociation.com	Denver	CO	80204	303-571-5117	571-1803
CompetitivEdge 196 S Main St	Colchester	CT	06415	860-537-6731	
Datatech Labs 8000 e quincy ave *Web:* www.datatechlab.com	Denver	CO	80237	303-770-3282	
DocuData Solutions LLC 7777 John Carpenter Fwy *Web:* www.docudatasolutions.com	Dallas	TX	75247	214-678-9898	
Edifice Information Management Systems Inc Six Upper Pond Rd *Web:* www.edificeinfo.com	Parsippany	NJ	07054	973-616-2929	
Excet 8001 Braddock Rd Ste 303 *Web:* www.excetinc.com	Springfield	VA	22151	703-635-7089	
Florida Newsclips LLC PO Box 2190 **Fax Area Code:* 727 ■ *TF:* 800-442-0332 ■ *Web:* www.newsclipsonweb.com	Palm Harbor	FL	34682	800-442-0332	736-5005*
FlyData Inc 1043 N Shoreline Blvd Ste 200 *TF:* 855-427-9787 ■ *Web:* www.flydata.com	Mountain View	CA	94043	855-427-9787	
Imagewerks Marketing 3758 Dunlap St N *Web:* www.iwmarketing.com	Arden Hills	MN	55112	651-770-1319	
INFINITT North America Inc 755 Memorial Pkwy Hillcrest Professional Plz Ste 304 *Web:* www.infinittna.com	Phillipsburg	NJ	08865	908-387-6960	
InfySource Ltd 8345 NW 66th St *TF:* 800-275-7503 ■ *Web:* www.infy-source.com	Miami	FL	33166	800-275-7503	
Insight Investments Corp 611 Anton Blvd Ste 700 *Web:* www.insightinvestments.com	Costa Mesa	CA	92626	714-939-2300	
IT Direct LLC 67 Prospect Ave Ste 202 *Web:* www.gettingyouconnected.com	West Hartford	CT	06106	860-656-9110	
Itm Marketing Inc 470 Downtowner Plz *Web:* www.itmmarketing.com	Coshocton	OH	43812	740-295-3575	
Kentucky Press Assn 101 Consumer Ln *TF Cust Svc:* 800-264-5721 ■ *Web:* www.kypress.com	Frankfort	KY	40601	502-223-8821	226-3867
Knowledge Mosaic Inc 3450 16th Ave W Ste 301 *Web:* www.knowledgemosaic.com	Seattle	WA	98119	206-525-8395	
Landis Computer 1120 Division Hwy *Web:* landiscomputer.com	Ephrata	PA	17522	717-733-0793	
LCS Technologies Inc 11230 Gold Express Dr Ste 310-140 *TF:* 855-277-5527 ■ *Web:* www.lcs-technologies-inc.com	Gold River	CA	95670	855-277-5527	
Link Solutions Inc 12007 Sunrise Vly Dr Ste 280 *Web:* www.linksol-inc.com	Reston	VA	20191	703-707-6256	
Magnolia Clipping Service 298 Commerce Pk Dr Ste A *Web:* www.magnoliaclips.com	Ridgeland	MS	39157	601-856-0911	856-3340
MedValue Offshore Solutions Inc 1415 W 22nd St Tower Fl Regency Towers *Web:* www.medvaluebpo.com	Oak Brook	IL	60523	630-299-7370	
Mindgruve Inc 1018 Eight Ave *Web:* mindgruve.com	San Diego	CA	92101	619-757-1325	
MX Logic LLC 9781 S Meridian Blvd Ste 400 *Web:* www.mxlogic.com	Englewood	CO	80112	720-895-5700	
New York State Clipping Service 200 Central Pk Ave N	Hartsdale	NY	10530	914-948-2525	948-3534
OCZ Storage Solutions Inc 6373 San Ignacio Ave *Web:* ocz.com	San Jose	CA	95119	408-733-8400	
Oklahoma Press Service Inc 3601 N Lincoln Blvd *Web:* www.okpress.com	Oklahoma City	OK	73105	405-524-4421	524-2201
Plexent 16479 Dallas Pkwy Ste 140 *Web:* www.plexent.com	Addison	TX	75001	972-381-0077	
Pulse Seismic Inc Ste 2400 639 Fifth Ave SW *Web:* www.pulseseismic.com	Calgary	AB	T2P0M9	403-237-5559	
Senture LLC 460 Industrial Blvd *Web:* www.senture.com	London	KY	40741	606-877-6670	
SightLine Systems Corp 11130 Fairfax Blvd Ste 200 *Web:* www.sightlinesystems.com	Fairfax	VA	22030	703-563-3000	
SIX Financial Information USA Inc One Omega Dr River Bend Centre Bldg 3 *Web:* www.six-group.com	Stamford	CT	06907	203-353-8100	
SMS proTECH 1089 Fairington Dr *Web:* perryprotech.com	Sidney	OH	45365	937-498-7080	
South Carolina Press Services Inc 106 Outlet Pointe Blvd PO Box 11429 *TF:* 888-727-7377 ■ *Web:* www.scpress.org	Columbia	SC	29210	803-750-9561	551-0903
South Dakota Newspaper Services 1125 32nd Ave Ste 202 *TF:* 800-658-3697 ■ *Web:* www.sdna.com	Brookings	SD	57006	605-692-4300	692-6388

	City	State	ZIP	Phone	Fax
Ssf Conference Catering LLC 255 S Airport Blvd *Web:* ssfconf.com	South San Francisco	CA	94080	650-877-8787	
Talton Communications Inc 910 Ravenwood Dr *Web:* www.taltoncommunications.com	Selma	AL	36701	334-877-0704	
Thrive Networks Inc 655 Andover St Fl 3 *Web:* www.thrivenetworks.com	Lawrence	MA	01843	978-461-3999	
United Data Technologies Inc 8825 NW 21st Terrace *Web:* udtonline.com	Doral	FL	33172	305-882-0435	
Vigilant Technologies LLC 3290 W Big Beaver Rd Ste 310 *Web:* www.vigt.com	Troy	MI	48084	248-614-2500	
Virginia Press Services Inc 11529 Nuckols Rd *TF:* 800-849-8717 ■ *Web:* www.vpa.net	Glen Allen	VA	23059	804-521-7570	521-7590
West Virginia Press Association 3422 Pennsylvania Ave *TF:* 800-235-6881 ■ *Web:* www.wvpress.org	Charleston	WV	25302	304-342-6908	343-5879
WorkSmart Inc 100 Meredith Dr Ste 200 *Web:* www.worksmart.com	Durham	NC	27713	919-484-1010	
Xylo Technologies Inc 2434 Superior Dr NW Ste 105 *Web:* www.xylotechnologies.com	Rochester	MN	55901	507-289-9956	

628 PRINTED CIRCUIT BOARDS

SEE ALSO Electronic Components & Accessories - Mfr p. 2232; Semiconductors & Related Devices p. 3166

	City	State	ZIP	Phone	Fax
3Dlabs Inc Ltd 1901 McCarthy Blvd *TF:* 800-464-3348 ■ *Web:* www.3dlabs.com	Milpitas	CA	95035	408-530-4700	
A Star Electric Co 200 Seegers Ave *Web:* www.astareg.com	Elk Grove Village	IL	60007	847-439-4122	
Abelconn LLC 9210 Science Ctr Dr *TF:* 800-526-2828 ■ *Web:* www.abelconn.com	New Hope	MN	55428	763-533-3533	536-0349
Acromag Inc 30765 S Wixom Rd *TF:* 877-295-7092 ■ *Web:* www.acromag.com	Wixom	MI	48393	248-624-1541	624-9234
Advanced Circuits Inc 21101 E 32nd Pkwy **Fax Area Code:* 888 ■ *TF:* 800-979-4722 ■ *Web:* www.4pcb.com	Aurora	CO	80011	303-576-6610	224-3291*
Aimtron Corp 1448 Yorkshire Dr *Web:* www.aimtronrcorporation.com	Streamwood	IL	60107	630-372-7500	
AMDTechnologies Inc One Commerce Vly Dr E *Web:* www.amd.com	Markham	ON	L3T7X6	905-882-2600	882-2620
American Board Assembly Inc 5456 Endeavour Ct *Web:* www.americanboard.com	Moorpark	CA	93021	805-523-0274	523-1185
Amitron Inc 2001 Landmeier Rd *Web:* www.amitroncorp.com	Elk Grove Village	IL	60007	847-290-9800	290-9823
Ansen Corp 100 Chimney Pt Dr *Web:* www.ansencorp.com	Ogdensburg	NY	13669	315-393-3573	393-7638
Antex Electronics Corp 19160 Van Ness Ave *Web:* www.antex.com	Torrance	CA	90501	310-532-3092	532-8509
Arc-tronics Inc 1150 Pagni Dr *Web:* www.arc-tronics.com	Elk Grove Village	IL	60007	847-437-0211	437-0181
ASUSTeK Computer International 800 Corporate Way *Web:* www.asus.com	Fremont	CA	94539	510-739-3777	608-4555
Benchmark Electronics Inc 3000 Technology Dr *NYSE: BHE* ■ *Web:* www.bench.com	Angleton	TX	77515	979-849-6550	848-5271
Bicom Inc 755 Main St *Web:* www.bicominc.com	Monroe	CT	06468	203-268-4484	
Bourns Inc 1200 Columbia Ave *TF:* 877-426-8767 ■ *Web:* www.bourns.com	Riverside	CA	92507	951-781-5690	781-5006
Cal Quality Electronics 2700 S Fairview St *Web:* www.calquality.com	Santa Ana	CA	92704	714-545-8886	545-4975
Centon Electronics Inc 15 Argonaut **Fax Area Code:* 948 ■ *TF:* 800-836-1986 ■ *Web:* www.centon.com	Aliso Viejo	CA	92656	949-855-9111	586-8778*
Circuit Express Inc 229 S Clark Dr **Fax Area Code:* 480 ■ *Web:* www.4pcb.com	Tempe	AZ	85281	800-979-4722	966-5896*
CM Solutions Inc 2674 S Harper Rd *Web:* www.cm-solutions.biz	Corinth	MS	38834	662-287-8810	
Compunetics Inc 700 Seco Rd *Web:* www.compunetics.com	Monroeville	PA	15146	412-373-8110	373-8060
Computer Modules Inc 11409 W Bernardo Ct *Web:* www.dveo.com	San Diego	CA	92127	858-613-1818	613-1815
Creative Labs Inc 1901 McCarthy Blvd *TF Cust Svc:* 800-998-1000 ■ *Web:* www.us.creative.com	Milpitas	CA	95035	408-428-6600	428-6611
Crucial Technology 3475 E Commercial Ct *TF:* 800-336-8915 ■ *Web:* www.crucial.com	Meridian	ID	83642	208-363-5790	363-5501
CyOptics Inc 350 W Trimble Rd Bldg 90 **Fax Area Code:* 484 ■ *Web:* www.avagotech.com	San Jose	PA	18031	408-435-7400	397-3592*
Data Translation Inc 100 Locke Dr *OTC: DATX* ■ *TF:* 800-525-8528 ■ *Web:* www.datatranslation.com	Marlborough	MA	01752	508-481-3700	481-3700
Dataram Corp 777 Alexander Rd Ste 100 *NASDAQ: DRAM* ■ *TF:* 800-328-2726 ■ *Web:* www.dataram.com	Princeton	NJ	08540	609-799-0071	799-6734
DCX-CHOL Enterprises Inc 12831 S Figueroa St *Web:* www.dcxchol.com	Los Angeles	CA	90061	310-516-1692	
DDi Corp 1220 Simon Cir *NASDAQ: TTMI* ■ *Web:* www.viasystems.com	Anaheim	CA	92806	714-688-7200	688-7500
Diversified Technology Inc 476 Highland Colony Pkwy *Web:* www.dtims.com	Ridgeland	MS	39157	601-856-4121	
DIVSYS International LLC 8110 Zionsville Rd *Web:* www.divsys.com	Indianapolis	IN	46268	317-405-9427	
DRS Laurel Technologies 246 Airport Rd *Web:* www.drs.com	Johnstown	PA	15904	814-534-8900	534-8815
Dynaco Corp 3020 S Pk Dr *Web:* www.dynacocorp.com	Tempe	AZ	85282	602-437-8003	437-8015
Dynatem Inc 23263 Madero Ste C *TF:* 800-543-3830 ■ *Web:* www.dynatem.com	Mission Viejo	CA	92691	949-855-3235	770-3481
EDGE Tech Corp 655 Leffingwell Ave *Web:* www.edgetechcorp.com	Saint Louis	MO	63122	314-856-4042	
EI Microcircuits Inc 1651 Pohl Rd *Web:* www.eimicro.com	Mankato	MN	56001	507-345-5786	345-7559
Electropac Company Inc 252 Willow St *Web:* www.electropac.com	Manchester	NH	03103	603-622-3711	622-3711
Epec LLC 174 Duchaine Blvd *Web:* www.epecpcb.com	New Bedford	MA	02745	508-995-5171	
Federal Electronics Inc 75 Stamp Farm Rd *Web:* www.federalelec.com	Cranston	RI	02921	401-944-6200	946-6280
Flex Technologies 5479 Gundy Dr PO Box 400 *Web:* www.flextechnologies.com	Midvale	OH	44653	740-922-5992	922-4416
GE Fanuc Embedded Systems Inc 7401 Snaproll NE *TF:* 888-790-1820 ■ *Web:* www.geautomation.com	Albuquerque	NM	87109	505-875-0600	
Gigabyte Technology Inc 17358 Railroad St *Web:* gigabyte.com/	City of Industry	CA	91748	626-854-9338	854-9339
GoldenRAM Computer Products 13 Whatney *TF:* 800-222-8861 ■ *Web:* www.goldenram.com	Irvine	CA	92618	949-460-9000	460-7600
Hauppauge Computer Works Inc 91 Cabot Ct *TF:* 800-443-6284 ■ *Web:* www.hauppauge.com	Hauppauge	NY	11788	631-434-1600	434-3198
Hauppauge Digital Inc 91 Cabot Ct *OTC: HAUP* ■ *TF:* 800-443-6284 ■ *Web:* www.hauppauge.com	Hauppauge	NY	11788	631-434-1600	434-3198
Holaday Circuits Inc 11126 Bren Rd W *Web:* www.holaday.com	Hopkins	MN	55343	952-933-3303	
I-Bus Corp 3350 Scott Blvd Bldg 54 *Web:* www.ibus.com	Santa Clara	CA	95054	408-450-7880	450-7881
IEC Electronics Corp 105 Norton St *NYSE: IEC* ■ *Web:* www.iec-electronics.com	Newark	NY	14513	315-331-7742	331-3547
Intel Corp 2200 Mission College Blvd *NASDAQ: INTC* ■ *TF Cust Svc:* 800-628-8686 ■ *Web:* www.intel.in	Santa Clara	CA	95052	408-765-8080	
IXI Technology 23231 La Palma Ave *Web:* www.sabtech.com	Yorba Linda	CA	92887	714-692-3800	692-3838
Jabil Circuit Inc 10560 ML King St N *NYSE: JBL* ■ *TF:* 877-217-6328 ■ *Web:* www.jabil.com	Saint Petersburg	FL	33716	727-577-9749	231-3945
Joule Technologies Inc 4167 W Orleans St *Web:* www.jouletechnologies.com	Mchenry	IL	60050	815-759-0600	
KCA Electronics Inc 223 N Crescent Way *Web:* www.kcamerica.com	Anaheim	CA	92801	714-239-2433	
Killdeer Mountain Manufacturing Inc (KMM) 233 Rodeo Dr PO Box 450 *Web:* www.kmmnet.com	Killdeer	ND	58640	701-764-5651	764-5427
Kimball Electronics 13700 Reptron Blvd *TF:* 800-903-8328	Tampa	FL	33626	813-854-2000	
Kimball Electronics Group 1038 E 15th St **Fax:* Sales ■ *TF:* 800-482-1616 ■ *Web:* www.kegroup.com	Jasper	IN	47549	812-634-4200	634-4330*
Leadtek Research Inc 910 Auburn Ct *Web:* www.leadtek.com	Fremont	CA	94538	510-490-8076	490-7759
Leda Corp 7080 Kearny Dr *Web:* www.ledacorp.net	Huntington Beach	CA	92648	714-841-7821	842-3683
Libra Industries Inc 7770 Div Dr *TF:* 800-825-1674 ■ *Web:* www.libraind.com	Mentor	OH	44060	440-974-7770	974-7779
Lone Star Circuits 901 Hensley Ln *TF:* 800-303-9266 ■ *Web:* lscpcbs.com	Wylie	TX	75098	214-291-1427	
M-Wave Inc 1300 Norwood Ave *Web:* www.mwav.com	Itasca	IL	60143	630-562-5550	
Macrolink Inc 1500 N Kellogg Dr *Web:* www.macrolink.com	Anaheim	CA	92807	714-777-8800	777-8807
Masterwork Electronics Inc 630 Martin Ave *Web:* www.masterworkelectronics.com	Rohnert Park	CA	94928	707-588-9906	588-9908
McDonald Technologies International Inc 2310 McDaniel Dr *Web:* www.mcdonald-tech.com	Carrollton	TX	75006	972-421-4100	241-2643
Micro Industries Corp 8399 Green Meadow Dr N *TF:* 800-722-1842 ■ *Web:* www.microindustries.com	Westerville	OH	43081	740-548-7878	548-6184
Micro-Star Int'l Co.,Ltd 901 Canada Ct *Web:* msicomputer.com	Cityofindustry	CA	91748	626-913-0828	913-0818
Microboard Processing Inc 36 Cogwheel Ln *Web:* www.microboard.com	Seymour	CT	06483	203-881-4300	881-4302
Micron Technology Inc 8000 S Federal Way *NASDAQ: MU* ■ *TF:* 888-363-2589 ■ *Web:* www.micron.com	Boise	ID	83707	208-368-4000	368-4617
Micron Technology Inc SpecTek Div 8000 S Federal Way PO Box 6 *Web:* www.spectek.com	Boise	ID	83707	208-363-5716	
MIKTAM Technologies Americas Inc 2362 Qume Dr Ste B *Web:* www.miktamusa.com	San Jose	CA	95131	408-392-0668	
Modular Components National Inc 105 E Jarrettsville Rd PO Box 453 *Web:* www.modularcomp.com	Forest Hill	MD	21050	410-879-6553	838-7629
Mti Electronics Inc W133 N5139 Campbell Dr *Web:* www.mtielectronics.com	Menomonee Falls	WI	53051	262-783-6080	783-4959
Natel Engineering Co Inc 9340 Owensmouth Ave *TF:* 800-590-5774 ■ *Web:* www.natelems.com	Chatsworth	CA	91311	818-734-6500	734-6530
National Semiconductor Corp 2900 Semiconductor Dr *Web:* www.ti.com	Santa Clara	CA	95051	408-721-5000	739-9803
National Technology Inc 1101 Carnegie St *Web:* www.nationaltech.com	Rolling Meadows	IL	60008	847-506-1300	506-1340
NVIDIA Corp 2701 San Tomas Expy *NASDAQ: NVDA* ■ *Web:* www.nvidia.com	Santa Clara	CA	95050	408-486-2000	486-2200

				Phone	Fax
Oncore Mfg Services LLC 225 Carando Dr *Web:* www.oncorems.com	Springfield	MA	01104	413-736-2121	736-6373
Osi Electronics Inc 2385 Pleasant Valley Rd *Web:* www.osielectronics.com	Camarillo	CA	93012	805-499-6877	499-4072
Parallax Inc 599 Menlo Dr Ste 100 *TF:* 888-512-1024 ■ *Web:* www.parallax.com	Rocklin	CA	95765	916-624-8333	624-8003
Park Electrochemical Corp 48 S Service Rd Ste 300 *NYSE: PKE* ■ *Web:* www.parkelectro.com	Melville	NY	11747	631-465-3600	465-3100
Parlex Corp One Parlex Pl *Web:* www.parlex.com	Methuen	MA	01844	978-685-4341	
Pentek Inc One Pk Way **Fax:* Acctg ■ *Web:* www.pentek.com	Upper Saddle River	NJ	07458	201-818-5900	818-5692*
Pioneer Circuits Inc (PCI) 3000 S Shannon St *Web:* www.pioneercircuits.com	Santa Ana	CA	92704	714-641-3132	641-3120
Plexus Corp One Plexus Way PO Box 156 *NASDAQ: PLXS* ■ *Web:* www.plexus.com	Neenah	WI	54957	920-722-3451	751-5395
PNC Inc 115 E Centre St *Web:* www.pnconline.com	Nutley	NJ	07110	973-284-1600	284-1925
Printed Circuits Assembly Corp 13221 SE 26th St Ste E *Web:* www.pcacorporation.com	Bellevue	WA	98005	425-644-7754	644-6430
Progress Instruments Inc 807 NW Commerce Dr *Web:* www.progressthermal.com	Lees Summit	MO	64086	816-524-4442	
Projects Unlimited Inc 6300 Sand Lk Rd *Web:* www.pui.com	Dayton	OH	45414	937-918-2200	
Promise Technology Inc 580 Cottonwood Dr *TF Sales:* 800-888-0245 ■ *Web:* www.promise.com	Milpitas	CA	95035	408-228-1400	228-1100
Q-flex Inc 1301 E Hunter Ave *Web:* qflexinc.com	Santa Ana	CA	92705	714-664-0101	
Qual-pro Corp 18510 S Figueroa St *Web:* www.qual-pro.com	Gardena	CA	90248	310-329-7535	
Quality Circuits Inc 1102 Progress Dr *Web:* www.qciusa.com	Fergus Falls	MN	56537	218-739-9707	739-9705
Quality Systems Integrated Corp 6720 Cobra Way *Web:* www.qsic.com	San Diego	CA	92121	858-587-9797	
Quatech Inc 5675 Hudson Industrial Pkwy *TF:* 800-553-1170 ■ *Web:* bb-elec.com	Hudson	OH	44236	330-655-9000	655-9010
RadiSys Corp 5445 NE Dawson Creek Dr *NASDAQ: RSYS* ■ *TF:* 800-950-0044 ■ *Web:* www.radisys.com	Hillsboro	OR	97124	503-615-1100	615-1115
Riverside Electronics Ltd One Riverside Dr *Web:* riversideelectronics.com/	Lewiston	MN	55952	507-523-3220	523-2831
SAE Circuits Colorado Inc 4820 N 63rd St *TF:* 800-234-9001 ■ *Web:* www.saecircuits.com	Boulder	CO	80301	303-530-1900	530-0210
Sanmina-SCI Corp 2700 N First St *NASDAQ: SANM* ■ *Web:* www.sanmina-sci.com	San Jose	CA	95134	408-964-3500	964-3440
Saturn Electronics & Engineering Inc 2120 Austin Ave *Web:* www.saturnee.com	Rochester Hills	MI	48309	248-853-5724	299-8514
Saturn Electronics Corp 28450 Northline Rd *Web:* www.saturnelectronics.com	Romulus	MI	48174	734-941-8100	941-3707
Siemens Mfg Company Inc 410 W Washington St *Web:* www.siemensmfg.com	Freeburg	IL	62243	618-539-3000	539-6172
Sigma Designs Inc 1778 Mcarthy Blvd *NASDAQ: SIGM* ■ *Web:* www.sigmadesigns.com	Milpitas	CA	95035	408-262-9003	957-9740
SigmaTron International Inc 2201 Landmeier Rd *NASDAQ: SGMA* ■ **Fax:* Hum Res ■ *TF:* 800-700-9095 ■ *Web:* www.sigmatronintl.com	Elk Grove Village	IL	60007	847-956-8000	956-9410*
SIIG Inc 6078 Stewart Ave *Web:* www.siig.com	Fremont	CA	94538	510-657-8688	657-5962
Sopark Corp 3300 S Pk Ave *TF:* 866-576-7275 ■ *Web:* www.sopark.com	Buffalo	NY	14218	716-822-0434	822-5062
Spectrum Signal Processing by Vecima 2700 Production Way Ste 300 *TF:* 800-663-8986 ■ *Web:* www.spectrumsignal.com	Burnaby	BC	V5A4X1	604-676-6700	421-1764
Suntron Corp 2401 W Grandview Rd *TF:* 800-690-6903 ■ *Web:* www.bench.com	Phoenix	AZ	85023	602-298-4939	282-8794
Supermicro Computer Inc (SMCI) 980 Rock Ave *NASDAQ: SMCI* ■ *Web:* www.supermicro.com.tw	San Jose	CA	95131	408-503-8000	503-8008
TechWorks 4030 W Braker Ln *TF Cust Svc:* 800-688-7466 ■ *Web:* techwrks.com	Austin	TX	78759	512-794-8533	794-8520
Tekram USA 14228 Albers Way Ste B *Web:* www.tekram.com	Brea	CA	91710	909-606-1111	597-3713
TTM Technologies Inc 1665 Scenic Ave Ste 250 *Web:* www.ttmtechnologies.com	Costa Mesa	CA	92626	714-327-3000	
TYAN Computer Corp USA 3288 Laurelview Ct *Web:* www.tyan.com	Fremont	CA	94538	510-651-8868	651-7688
Unicircuit Inc 8192 Southpark Ln *TF:* 800-648-6449 ■ *Web:* www.anaren.com	Littleton	CO	80120	303-730-0505	730-0606
Unigen Corp 45388 Warm Springs Blvd *TF:* 800-826-0808 ■ *Web:* www.unigen.com	Fremont	CA	94539	510-668-2088	668-4889
Universal Scientific of Illinois Inc 2101 Arthur Ave *Web:* www.usipcb.com	Elk Grove Village	IL	60007	847-228-6464	228-0523
Viasystems Group Inc 101 S Hanley Rd Ste 400 *Web:* www.viasystems.com	Saint Louis	MO	63105	314-727-2087	746-2233
VM Services Inc 6701 Mowry Ave	Newark	CA	94560	510-744-3720	744-3730
Voyetra Turtle Beach Inc 150 Clearbrook Rd Ste 162 *Web:* www.turtlebeach.com	Elmsford	NY	10523	914-345-2255	345-2266
Westak Inc 1225 Elko Dr *TF:* 800-387-3766 ■ *Web:* www.westak.com	Sunnyvale	CA	94089	408-734-8686	734-3592
Western Electronics LLC 1550 S Tech Ln **Fax Area Code:* 303 ■ *TF:* 888-857-5775 ■ *Web:* www.westernelectronics.com	Meridian	ID	83642	208-955-9700	465-9798*
Wintec Industries Inc 675 Sycamore Dr *TF:* 866-989-4683 ■ *Web:* www.wintecindustries.com	Milpitas	CA	95035	408-856-0500	856-0501
Yun Industrial Company Ltd 161 Selandia Ln *Web:* www.yic-assm.com	Carson	CA	90746	310-715-1898	532-8128
ZTEST Electronics Inc 523 Mcnicoll Ave *TF:* 866-393-4891 ■ *Web:* www.ztest.com	North York	ON	M2H2C9	416-297-5155	

629 PRINTING COMPANIES - BOOK PRINTERS

				Phone	Fax
Ace Group Inc, The 149 W 27th St	New York	NY	10001	212-255-7846	
Adair Printing Technologies 7850 Second St *TF:* 800-637-5025 ■ *Web:* adairgraphic.com	Dexter	MI	48130	734-426-2822	426-4360
B Squared Inc 104 W 29th St Seventh Fl *Web:* www.bsqu.com	New York	NY	10001	212-777-2044	
Bang Printing Inc 3323 Oak St *TF:* 800-328-0450 ■ *Web:* www.bangprinting.com	Brainerd	MN	56401	218-829-2877	829-7145
Berryville Graphics 25 Jack Enders Blvd *Web:* www.beprintersamerica.com	Berryville	VA	22611	540-955-2750	955-2633
BOLT Solutions Inc 90 Park Ave Ste 1700 *TF:* 888-608-4646 ■ *Web:* boltinc.com	New York	NY	10016	212-608-4646	
Bradford & Bigelow Inc Three Perkins Way *Web:* www.bradford-bigelow.com	Newburyport	MA	01950	978-904-3100	
Calendar Holdings LLC 6411 Burleson Rd *Web:* calendarholdings.com/index.asp	Austin	TX	78744	512-386-7220	369-6192
CJK 3962 Virginia Ave *TF:* 800-598-7808 ■ *Web:* www.cjkusa.com	Cincinnati	OH	45227	513-271-6035	271-6082
Claitor's Law Books & Publishing PO Box 261333 *TF:* 800-274-1403 ■ *Web:* www.claitors.com	Baton Rouge	LA	70826	225-344-0476	344-0480
Command Financial Press Corp 345 Hudson St 15th Fl *Web:* www.commandfinancial.com	New York	NY	10013	212-274-0070	
Command Web Offset Inc 100 Castle Rd *Web:* www.commandweb.com	Secaucus	NJ	07094	201-863-8100	863-5443
Consolidated Printers Inc 2630 Eigth St *Web:* www.consoprinters.com	Berkeley	CA	94710	510-843-8524	486-0580
Cookbook Publishers Inc 9825 Widmer Rd *TF:* 800-227-7282 ■ *Web:* www.cookbookpublishers.com	Lenexa	KS	66215	913-492-5900	492-5947
Courier Corp 15 Wellman Ave *NASDAQ: CRRC* ■ *Web:* www.courier.com	North Chelmsford	MA	01863	978-251-6000	251-6000
CRW Graphics Inc 9100 Pennsauken Hwy *Web:* www.crwgraphics.com	Pennsauken	NJ	08110	856-662-9111	
Cushing-Malloy Inc 1350 N Main St *TF:* 888-295-7244 ■ *Web:* www.cushing-malloy.com	Ann Arbor	MI	48104	734-663-8554	663-5731
Darby Printing Co 6215 Purdue Dr	Atlanta	GA	30336	404-344-2665	346-3332
E & M Bindery Inc 11 Peekay Dr *TF:* 800-736-2463 ■ *Web:* www.embindery.com	Clifton	NJ	07014	973-777-9300	
Edwards Bros Inc 2500 S State St **Fax:* Cust Svc ■ *Web:* www.edwardsbrothersmalloy.com	Ann Arbor	MI	48104	734-769-1000	913-1338*
Friesens Corp One Printers Way *Web:* www.friesens.com	Altona	MB	R0G0B0	204-324-6401	324-1333
Garlich Printing Co 525 Rudder Rd *TF:* 800-276-2622 ■ *Web:* www.garlich.com	Fenton	MO	63026	636-349-8000	
Geyer Printing Company Inc 55 38th St *Web:* www.geyerprinting.com	Pittsburgh	PA	15201	412-682-3633	
Gospel Publishing House 1445 N Boonville Ave *TF Orders:* 800-641-4310 ■ *Web:* www.gospelpublishing.com	Springfield	MO	65802	417-862-2781	862-8558
Griffin Publishing Group 18022 Cowan	Irvine	CA	92614	949-263-3733	
Hagadone Printing Company Inc 274 Puuhale Rd *Web:* www.hagadoneprinting.com	Honolulu	HI	96819	808-847-5310	
Hamilton Printing Co Inc 22 Hamilton Way	CastletononHudson	NY	12033	518-732-4491	
Heritage Auctions Inc 3500 Maple Ave 17th Fl *Web:* www.ha.com	Dallas	TX	75219	214-528-3500	443-8407
Houchen Bindery LTD 340 First St *TF:* 800-869-0420 ■ *Web:* www.houchenbindery.com	Utica	NE	68456	402-534-2261	
Joe Christensen Inc 1540 Adams St *TF:* 800-228-5030 ■ *Web:* jci.mightydrake.com	Lincoln	NE	68521	402-476-7535	476-3094
John Henry Co 5800 W Grand River Ave **Fax Area Code:* 800 ■ *TF:* 800-748-0517 ■ *Web:* www.jhc.com	Lansing	MI	48906	517-323-9000	968-5646*
Jostens Inc 3601 Minnesota Ave Ste 400 **Fax:* Hum Res ■ *TF:* 800-235-4774 ■ *Web:* www.jostens.com	Minneapolis	MN	55435	952-830-3300	830-3293*
Lehigh Phoenix 18249 Phoenix Dr *TF General:* 800-632-4111 ■ *Web:* www.phoenixcolor.com	Hagerstown	MD	21742	301-733-0018	
Library Reproduction Service 14214 S Figueroa St *TF:* 800-255-5002 ■ *Web:* www.largeprintschoolbooks.com	Los Angeles	CA	90061	310-354-2610	354-2601
Malloy Inc 5411 Jackson Rd PO Box 1124 *Web:* www.edwardsbrothersmalloy.com	Ann Arbor	MI	48103	734-665-6113	665-2326
Maple-Vail Book Mfg Group 480 Willow Springs Ln *Web:* www.maple-vail.com	York	PA	17406	717-764-5911	764-4702
McAdams Graphics Inc 7200 S First St *Web:* www.mcadamsgraphics.com	Oak Creek	WI	53154	414-768-8080	768-8099
MCB Printing Inc 230 Walnut Hill Ln *Web:* www.mcbprinting.com	Havertown	PA	19083	610-446-6011	446-6013
McNaughton & Gunn Inc 960 Woodland Dr **Fax Area Code:* 800 ■ *Web:* www.mcnaughton-gunn.com	Saline	MI	48176	734-429-5411	677-2665*
Moran Printing Inc 5425 Florida Blvd *TF:* 800-211-8335 ■ *Web:* www.moranprinting.com	Baton Rouge	LA	70806	225-923-2550	
Mossberg & Company Inc 301 E Sample St *TF:* 800-428-3340 ■ *Web:* www.mossbergco.com	South Bend	IN	46601	574-289-9253	
New Video Group Inc 902 Broadway Ninth Fl *Web:* newvideo.com	New York	NY	10010	212-206-8600	
Offset Paperback Manufacturers Inc 101 Memorial Hwy *Web:* www.beprintersamerica.com	Dallas	PA	18612	570-675-5261	675-8714
Omaha Printing Co 4700 F St *Web:* www.omahaprint.com	Omaha	NE	68117	402-734-4400	

				Phone	Fax
Packaging Printing Specialists Inc 3915 Stern Ave *Web:* www.ppsofil.com	St Charles	IL	60174	630-513-8060	
Page Litho Inc 6445 E Vernor Hwy	Detroit	MI	48207	313-921-6880	921-6771
Plunkett Research Ltd Po Drawer 541737 *Web:* www.plunkettresearch.com	Houston	TX	77254	713-932-0000	
Print Communications Inc 2457 E Washington St	Indianapolis	IN	46201	317-266-8208	
Publishers Press Inc 100 Frank E Simon Ave *TF:* 800-627-5801 ■ *Web:* www.pubpress.com	Shepherdsville	KY	40165	502-955-6526	543-8808
Rose Printing Company Inc 2503 Jackson Bluff Rd *TF:* 800-227-3725 ■ *Web:* www.roseprinting.com	Tallahassee	FL	32304	850-576-4151	
RR Donnelley 111 S Wacker Dr **Fax Area Code:* 925 ■ *TF:* 800-742-4455 ■ *Web:* www.rrdonnelley.com	Chicago	IL	60606	800-742-4455	951-1355*
Sheridan Group 11311 McCormick Rd Ste 260 *TF:* 800-352-2210 ■ *Web:* www.sheridan.com	Hunt Valley	MD	21031	410-785-7277	785-7217
Smith-Edwards-Dunlap Co 2867 E Allegheny Ave *TF:* 800-829-0020 ■ *Web:* www.sed.com	Philadelphia	PA	19134	215-425-8800	425-9110
Southwest Publishing & Mailing Corp 2600 NW Topeka Blvd *Web:* www.swpks.com	Topeka	KS	66617	785-233-5662	
Thomson-Shore Inc 7300 W Joy Rd **Fax Area Code:* 800 ■ *Web:* www.thomsonshore.com	Dexter	MI	48130	734-426-3939	706-4545*
Tweddle Litho Co 24700 Maplehurst Dr *Web:* www.tweddle.com	Clinton Township	MI	48036	586-307-3700	307-3708
Typecraft Wood & Jones Inc 2040 E Walnut St *Web:* www.typecraft.com	Pasadena	CA	91107	626-795-8093	795-2423
United Graphics Inc 2916 Marshall Ave *Web:* www.unitedgraphicsinc.com	Mattoon	IL	61938	217-235-7161	234-6274
United Record Pressing LLC 453 Chestnut St *TF:* 866-407-3165 ■ *Web:* www.urpressing.com	Nashville	TN	37203	615-259-9396	
Versa Press Inc 1465 Springbay Rd **Fax Area Code:* 309 ■ *TF:* 800-447-7829 ■ *Web:* www.versapress.com	East Peoria	IL	61611	800-447-7829	822-8141*
Vicks Lithograph & Printing Co 5166 Commercial Dr PO Box 270 *Web:* www.vicks.biz	Yorkville	NY	13495	315-736-9344	736-1901
Victor Graphics Inc 1211 Bernard Dr *TF:* 800-899-8303 ■ *Web:* www.victorgraphics.com	Baltimore	MD	21223	410-233-8300	233-8304
Webcrafters Inc 2211 Fordem Ave *Web:* www.webcrafters-inc.com	Madison	WI	53704	608-244-3561	244-5120
Whitehall Printing Co 4244 Corporate Sq **Fax Area Code:* 239 ■ *TF:* 800-321-9290 ■ *Web:* www.whitehallprinting.com	Naples	FL	34104	800-321-9290	643-6439*
Worzalla Publishing Co 3535 Jefferson St PO Box 307 *Web:* www.worzalla.com	Stevens Point	WI	54481	715-344-9600	344-2578
Wright Color Graphics 9051 Sunland Blvd *TF:* 877-246-8877 ■ *Web:* www.wrightcolor.com	Sun Valley	CA	91352	818-246-8877	246-8984

630 PRINTING COMPANIES - COMMERCIAL PRINTERS

				Phone	Fax
1 to 1 Printers LLC 15031 Woodham Dr Ste 370 *Web:* www.1to1printers.com	Houston	TX	77073	281-821-4400	
11 X 17 Inc 2034 N *Web:* www.11x17.com	Jacksonville	TX	75766	903-541-0100	
3e Marketing Communications 3933 N Ventura Dr *Web:* www.3elitho.com	Arlington Heights	IL	60004	847-398-8677	
4over Inc 5900 San Fernando Rd *TF:* 877-782-2737 ■ *Web:* www.4over.com	Glendale	CA	91202	877-782-2737	
518 Prints LLC 1548 Burden Lk Rd Ste 4 *Web:* www.518prints.com	Averill Park	NY	12018	518-674-5346	
A & a Printing Inc 320 Queen Anne Ave N *Web:* aaprinting.com	Seattle	WA	98109	206-285-1700	
A & m Printing 3589 Nevada St *Web:* www.anmprinting.com	Pleasanton	CA	94566	925-484-3690	
A Better Image Printing 1709 Legion Rd *Web:* www.abetterimageprinting.com	Chapel Hill	NC	27517	919-967-0319	
A&B Printing & Mailing 2908 S Highland Dr Ste B *Web:* www.abprint.com	Las Vegas	NV	89109	702-731-5888	
A&h Lithoprint Inc 2540 S 27th Ave *Web:* www.ahlithoprint.com	Broadview	IL	60155	708-345-1196	
A. Carlisle & Company of Nevada Inc 1080 Bible Way *Web:* acarlisle.com	Reno	NV	89502	775-323-5163	
A.E. Litho Offset Printers Inc 450 Broad St *Web:* aelitho.com	Beverly	NJ	08010	609-239-0700	
Abb Enterprise Inc 1010 E 18th St *Web:* www.abblabels.com	Los Angeles	CA	90021	213-748-7480	
Abbott Printing Company Inc 110 Atlantic Dr *Web:* www.abbottcg.com	Maitland	FL	32751	407-831-2999	
Ability Building Center Inc 1911 14th St NW *Web:* www.abcinc.org	Rochester	MN	55903	507-281-6262	
Accent InterMedia LLC 300 Missouri Ave Ste 300 *Web:* www.accentintermedia.com	Jeffersonville	IN	47130	812-206-2475	
Accu-Label Inc 2021 Research Dr *Web:* www.acculabel.com	Fort Wayne	IN	46808	260-482-5223	
Acculink 1055 Greenville Blvd Sw *Web:* www.acculink.com	Greenville	NC	27834	252-321-5805	
Accuprint Inc 2414 Palumbo Dr *Web:* www.accuprint.us	Lexington	KY	40509	859-268-8844	
Ace Reprographic Service Inc 74 E 30th St *Web:* www.acereprographics.com	Paterson	NJ	07514	973-684-5945	
Adams McClure LP 1245 S Inca St *Web:* www.adamsmcclure.com	Denver	CO	80223	303-777-1984	
Adcraft Products Company Inc 1230 S Sherman St *Web:* www.adcraftproducts.com	Anaheim	CA	92805	714-776-1230	
Adp Media Group LLC 7700 Camp Bowie W Blvd Ste B *Web:* www.adpmediagroup.com	Fort Worth	TX	76116	817-244-2740	
Advance Printing & Graphics 1349 Delashmut Ave *Web:* www.advancecolumbus.com	Columbus	OH	43212	614-299-9770	
AGS Custom Graphics Inc 8107 Bavaria Rd *Web:* www.agscustomgraphics.com	Macedonia	OH	44056	330-963-7770	
Air Waves Inc 7787 Graphics Way *Web:* www.airwavesinc.com	Lewis Center	OH	43035	740-548-1200	
Aj Images Inc 259 E First Ave *Web:* ajimages.com	Roselle	NJ	07203	908-241-6900	
Aka Printing & Mailing Inc 44 Joseph Mills Dr *Web:* akaprintingandmailing.com	Fredericksburg	VA	22408	540-373-1111	
Alcom Printing Group Inc 140 Christopher Ln *Web:* www.alcomprinting.com	Harleysville	PA	19438	215-513-1600	
Aldine Inc 150 Varick St Fl 6 *Web:* aldine.com	New York	NY	10013	212-226-2870	
All About Packaging Inc 2200 W Everett St *Web:* www.aapack.com	Appleton	WI	54912	920-830-2700	
All-Pro Printing 11626 Prosperous Dr *Web:* www.allproprinting.com	Odessa	FL	33556	727-375-1502	
Allegra Digital Imaging 1302 Anderson Rd *Web:* www.allegratroywest.com	Clawson	MI	48017	248-655-0444	
Allied Photocopy Inc 1821 University Dr NW *Web:* alliedphotocopy.com	Huntsville	AL	35801	256-539-2973	
Allied Printing Services Inc One Allied Way *Web:* www.alliedprinting.com	Manchester	CT	06045	860-643-1101	
AlphaGraphics Inc 215 S State St Ste 320 *TF:* 800-955-6246 ■ *Web:* www.alphagraphics.com	Salt Lake City	UT	84111	801-595-7270	595-7271
Alpine Packaging Inc 4000 Crooked Run Rd *Web:* www.alpinepackaging.com	North Versailles	PA	15137	412-664-4000	
ALTA Systems Inc 6825 NW 18th Dr *Web:* altainc.com	Gainesville	FL	32653	352-372-2534	
Alwan Printing 7549 W 99th Pl *Web:* alwanprinting.com	Bridgeview	IL	60455	708-430-5620	
Ambrose Printing Co 210 Cumberland Bend *Web:* www.ambroseprint.com	Nashville	TN	37228	615-256-1151	
American Banknote Corp 2200 Fletcher Ave *Web:* www.abnote.com	Fort Lee	NJ	07024	201-592-3400	224-2762
American Spirit Graphics Corp 801 SE Ninth St *Web:* www.asgc.com	Minneapolis	MN	55414	612-623-3333	623-9314
Americas Printer Comm 6910 Aragon Cir Ste B *Web:* www.americasprinter.com	Buena Park	CA	90620	714-521-1100	
Americor Press 880 Louis Dr *Web:* www.americorpress.com	Warminster	PA	18974	215-259-1600	
Amidon Graphics 1966 Benson Ave *TF:* 800-328-6502 ■ *Web:* www.amidongraphics.com	Saint Paul	MN	55116	651-690-2401	690-4009
Ampco Manufacturers Inc #101 - 9 Burbidge St *Web:* www.ampcomfg.com	Coquitlam	BC	V3K7B2	604-472-3800	
Anderson Printing & Mailing 139 S Mechanic St *Web:* www.printanderson.com	Jackson	MI	49201	517-787-4562	
Angel Printing & Reproduction Inc 1400 W 57th St *Web:* www.angelprinting.com	Cleveland	OH	44102	216-631-5225	
Angstrom Graphics 2025 McKinley St *TF:* 800-634-1262 ■ *Web:* www.angstromgraphics.com	Hollywood	FL	33020	954-920-7300	
Angstrom Graphics Inc 4437 E 49th St *TF:* 800-634-1262 ■ *Web:* www.angstromgraphics.com	Cleveland	OH	44125	216-271-5300	271-7650
Annan & Bird Lithographers Ltd 1060 Tristar Dr *Web:* www.annan-bird.com	Mississauga	ON	L5T1H9	905-670-0604	
Another Printer Inc 10 Bush River Ct *Web:* anotherprinterinc.com	Columbia	SC	29210	803-798-1380	
ANRO Inc 931 S Matlack St *Web:* www.anro.com	West Chester	PA	19382	610-687-1200	
Apollo Graphics 5104 NE Oregon St *Web:* www.apollographicsprinting.com	Portland	OR	97213	503-288-9191	
Arandell Inc N 82 W 13118 Leon Rd *TF:* 800-558-8724 ■ *Web:* www.arandell.com	Menomonee Falls	WI	53051	262-255-4400	253-3166
Arbor Press LLC 4303 Normandy Ct *Web:* www.arboroakland.com	Royal Oak	MI	48073	248-549-0150	
Arcade Marketing Inc 1700 Broadway Ste 2500 *Web:* www.arcadeinc.com	New York	NY	10019	212-541-2600	489-3026
Ares Printing & Packaging Corp 63 Flushing Ave Unit 224 *Web:* www.aresny.com	Brooklyn	NY	11205	718-858-8760	
Argosy Publishing Inc 109 Oak St *Web:* www.argosypublishing.com	Newton	MA	02464	617-527-9999	
Arkansas Graphics Inc 800 S Gaines St *Web:* www.arkansasgraphics.com	Little Rock	AR	72201	501-376-8436	
Asap Printing Corp 643 Billinis Rd *Web:* www.asapprintingcorp.com	Salt Lake City	UT	84119	801-263-2727	
Aspen Graphics Inc 4795 Oakland St *Web:* www.aspengraphics.net	Denver	CO	80239	303-371-2345	
Astley Gilbert Ltd 42 Carnforth Rd *Web:* www.astleygilbert.com	Toronto	ON	M4A2K7	416-288-8666	

Company	City	State	Zip	Phone	Fax
Auburn Printers Inc 13020 Earhart Ave. Web: www.auburnprinters.com	Auburn	CA	95602	530-885-9674	
Aus-Tex Printing & Mailing 2431 Forbes Dr. Web: www.austex.com	Austin	TX	78754	512-476-7581	
Austin Business Printing 404 W Powell Ln. Web: www.abpcreative.com	Austin	TX	78753	512-836-6902	
Autumn Press Inc 945 Camelia St. Web: www.autumnpress.com	Berkeley	CA	94710	510-654-4545	
B & B Express Printing Inc 7519 W Kennewick Ave A. Web: www.bbprinting.com	Kennewick	WA	99336	509-783-7383	
B & D Litho of Arizona 3820 N 38th Ave. Web: www.bndlithoaz.com	Phoenix	AZ	85019	602-269-2526	
B & G House of Printing Inc 1825 W 169th St Ste A. Web: bgprinting.com	Gardena	CA	90247	310-532-1533	
B H G Inc PO Box 309. TF: 800-658-3485 ■ Web: www.bhgnews.com	Garrison	ND	58540	701-463-2201	
B-W Graphics Inc 101 Westview St. Web: www.bwgraphics.com	Versailles	MO	65084	573-378-6363	
Badger Press Inc 100 E Blackhawk Dr. Web: www.badgerpress.com	Fort Atkinson	WI	53538	920-563-5144	
Balmar Inc 2818 Fallfax Dr. Web: www.balmar.com	Falls Church	VA	22042	703-289-9000	
Barker Blue Digital Imaging Inc 363 N Amphlett Blvd. Web: www.barkerblue.com	San Mateo	CA	94401	650-696-2100	
Basin Printing 1437 E Second Ave. Web: www.basinprinting.com	Durango	CO	81301	970-247-5212	
Bassett Printing Corp 3321 Fairystone Park Hwy. TF: 800-336-5102 ■ Web: www.bassettprinting.com	Bassett	VA	24055	800-336-5102	
Bay State Envelope Inc 440 Chauncy St. Web: www.baystateenvelope.com	Mansfield	MA	02048	508-337-8900	
BCW Diversified 514 E 31st St. Web: www.bcwpages.com	Anderson	IN	46016	765-644-2033	
Beckmanxmo 376 Morrison Rd. TF: 800-864-2232 ■ Web: beckmanxmo.com	Columbus	OH	43213	614-864-2232	864-3305
Bel Aire Displays 506 W Ohio Ave. Web: www.belairedisplays.com	Richmond	CA	94804	510-439-4300	
Berney Office Solutions LLC 10690 John Knight Close. Web: www.berney.com	Montgomery	AL	36117	334-271-4750	
Bertek Systems Inc 133 Bryce Blvd. Web: www.berteksystems.com	Fairfax	VT	05454	802-752-3170	
Best Press Inc 4201 Airborn Dr. Web: www.bestpress.com	Addison	TX	75001	972-930-1000	
Better Label & Products Inc 3333 Empire Blvd SW. Web: www.betterlabel.com	Atlanta	GA	30354	404-763-8440	
BFC Forms Service Inc 1051 N Kirk Rd. TF: 800-774-6840 ■ Web: www.bfcprint.com	Batavia	IL	60510	630-879-9240	
Bfi Print Communications Holding Co 602 Bedford St. Web: www.bfiprint.com	Whitman	MA	02382	781-447-1199	
BFS Business Printing Inc 76 South St. Web: www.bfsprinters.com	Boston	MA	02111	617-482-7770	
Bibbero Systems Inc 1300 N McDowell Blvd. TF: 800-242-2376 ■ Web: www.bibbero.com	Petaluma	CA	94954	707-778-3131	778-0824
Biz Print 600 W Front St. Web: bizprint.com	Boise	ID	83702	208-338-9746	
Blue Dog Printing & Design 1039 Andrew Dr. Web: getbluedog.com	West Chester	PA	19380	610-430-7992	
Blue Ocean Press Inc 6299 NW 27th Way. Web: www.blueoceanpress.com	Fort Lauderdale	FL	33309	954-973-1819	
Blue Tape Inc 16101 College Oak. Web: www.blue-tape.com	San Antonio	TX	78249	210-222-0580	
Bolder Graphics 5375 50 St Se. Web: www.boldergraphics.com	Calgary	AB	T2C3W1	403-299-9400	
Bolger LLC 3301 Como Ave SE. TF: 866-264-3287 ■ Web: www.bolgerinc.com	Minneapolis	MN	55414	651-645-6311	645-1750
Bonanza Press Inc 19860 141st Pl NE. Web: www.bonanzapress.com	Woodinville	WA	98072	425-486-3399	
Bond Printing Company Inc 104 Plain St. Web: www.bondprinting.com	Hanover	MA	02339	781-871-3990	
Boone Printing & Graphics Inc 70 S Kellogg Ave. Web: boonegraphics.net	Goleta	CA	93117	805-683-2349	
BOPI 1705 S Veterans Pkwy. Web: www.bopi.com	Bloomington	IL	61701	309-662-3395	
Bounty Print Ltd 6359 Bayne St. Web: www.bountyprint.com	Halifax	NS	B3K2V6	902-453-0300	
Bourne Brothers Printing Company Inc 5276 Hwy 42. Web: www.bournebrothers.com	Hattiesburg	MS	39401	601-582-1808	
Br Printers Inc 10154 toebben dr. Web: www.brprinters.com	Independence	KY	41051	859-292-1700	
Bradley Graphic Solutions Inc 941 Mill Rd. Web: bradleygraphics.net	Bensalem	PA	19020	215-638-8771	
Breakaway Press Inc 9620 Topanga Canyon Pl. Web: www.breakawaypress.com	Chatsworth	CA	91311	818-727-7388	
Brenneman Printing Inc 1909 Olde Homestead Ln. Web: www.brenprint.com	Lancaster	PA	17601	717-299-2847	
Brenner Printing Inc 1234 Triplett St. Web: www.brennerprinting.com	San Antonio	TX	78216	210-349-4024	
Briabe Mobile 1800 B-C Abbot Kinney Blvd. Web: www.briabemobile.com	Venice	CA	90291	310-694-3283	
Brimar Industries Inc 64 Outwater Ln. Web: www.brimar-online.com	Garfield	NJ	07026	973-340-7889	
Brodock Press Inc 502 Court St. Web: www.brodock.com	Utica	NY	13502	315-735-9577	
Buffalo Printing Co 2620/30 Elmwood Ave. Web: www.buffaloprinting.com	Kenmore	NY	14217	716-877-9444	
Burns Printing Inc 6131 Industrial Heights Dr. Web: www.burnsmp.com	Knoxville	TN	37909	865-584-2265	
Burton & Mayer Inc W140 N9000 Lilly Rd. TF: 800-236-1770 ■ Web: www.burtonmayer.com	Menomonee Falls	WI	53051	262-781-0770	781-9598
Business Wise Inc 6190 Powers Ferry Rd Nw. Web: www.businesswise.com	Atlanta	GA	30339	770-956-1955	
Butler Color Press Inc 119 Bonnie Dr. Web: www.butlercp.com	Butler	PA	16002	724-283-9132	
C & E Specialities 2530 Laude Dr. Web: www.cespecialties.com	Rockford	IL	61109	815-229-9230	
C Commerce Register in 190 Godwin Ave. Web: comreginc.com	Midland Park	NJ	07432	201-445-3000	
C r & a Custom Inc 312 W Pico Blvd. Web: www.cracustom.com	Los Angeles	CA	90015	213-749-4440	
Caddy Printing & Graphics Inc 13701 Neutron Rd. Web: www.caddyprinting.com	Dallas	TX	75244	972-991-1770	
Calev Print Media LLC 333 S Miami Ave. Web: www.cpmprint.com	Miami	FL	33130	305-672-2900	
Campbell Printing Co 2017 Cleveland Hwy. Web: www.campbellprintingco.com	Dalton	GA	30721	706-259-3344	
Canaan Printing Inc 4820 Jefferson Davis Hwy. Web: www.canaanprinting.net	Richmond	VA	23234	804-271-4820	
Canadian Bank Note Company Ltd (CBNC) 145 Richmond Rd. Web: www.cbnco.com	Ottawa	ON	K1Z1A1	613-722-3421	722-2548
Canfield & Tack Inc 925 Exchange St. TF General: 800-836-0861 ■ Web: www.canfieldtack.com	Rochester	NY	14608	585-235-7710	235-4166
Capital Imaging Inc 2521 E Michigan Ave. Web: www.capital-imaging.com	Lansing	MI	48912	517-482-2292	
Capital Mailing Services Inc 2424 Del Monte St. Web: capitalmail.net	West Sacramento	CA	95691	916-256-4670	
Capital Printing Corp 420 South Ave. Web: www.capitalprintingcorp.com	Middlesex	NJ	08846	732-560-1515	
Capitol Press 5306 Beethoven St. Web: www.capitolpress.com	Los Angeles	CA	90066	310-577-6606	
Carded Graphics LLC Green Hills Industrial Park 2 Industry Way. Web: www.cardedgraphics.com	Staunton	VA	24401	540-248-5566	
Carlith LLC 250 Carpenter Blvd. Web: www.carlith.com	Carpentersville	IL	60110	847-426-3488	
Carter Composition Corp 2007 N Hamilton St. Web: www.carterprinting.com	Richmond	VA	23230	804-359-9206	
Castle-Pierce Printing Co 2247 Ryf Rd. Web: www.castlepierce.com	Oshkosh	WI	54903	920-235-2020	
Cathedral Corp 632 Ellsworth Rd Griffis Technology Park. Web: www.cathedralcorporation.com	Rome	NY	13441	315-338-0021	
Cavanaugh Press Inc 8960 Yellow Brick Rd. Web: www.cavanaughpress.com	Baltimore	MD	21237	410-391-1900	
Ceci New York 130 W 23rd St Fl 2. Web: cecinewyork.com	New York	NY	10011	212-989-0695	
Century Marketing Solutions LLC 3000 Cameron St. TF: 800-256-6000 ■ Web: www.centurymarketingsolutions.com	Monroe	LA	71201	800-256-6000	
Cenveo Inc 201 Broad St 1 Canterberry Green. NYSE: CVO ■ Web: www.cenveo.com	Stamford	CT	06901	203-595-3000	595-3070
Cereus Graphics Printing Co 2950-2 E Broadway Rd. Web: cereusgraphics.com	Phoenix	AZ	85040	602-445-0681	
Challenge Printing Co, The Two Bridewell Pl. TF: 800-654-1234 ■ Web: www.challengeprintingco.com	Clifton	NJ	07014	973-471-4700	471-5211
Champion Graphics 3901 Virginia Ave. Web: champion-graphics.com	Cincinnati	OH	45227	513-271-3800	271-5963
Champion Industries Inc PO Box 2968 PO Box 2968. OTC: CHMP ■ TF: 800-624-3431 ■ Web: champion-industries.com	Huntington	WV	25728	304-528-2791	528-2746
Chippewa Graphics Inc 8801 Bass Lk Rd. Web: www.chippewagraphics.com	Minneapolis	MN	55428	763-536-9889	
Circle Graphics LLC 120 Ninth Ave. Web: www.circlegraphicsonline.com	Longmont	CO	80501	303-532-2370	
City Printing Company Inc 122 Oak Hill Ave. Web: www.cityprinting.com	Youngstown	OH	44502	330-747-5691	
Clear Image Printing Inc 731 W Wilson Ave. Web: clearimageprinting.com	Glendale	CA	91203	818-547-4684	
Clearpath Capital Partners 222 Front St Third Fl. Web: clearpathcapital.com	San Francisco	CA	94111	415-682-6900	
Click2mail 3103 10th St N Ste 201. Web: click2mail.com	Arlington	VA	22201	703-521-9029	
Clintrak Clinical Labeling Services LLC 2800 Veterans Hwy. Web: www.clintrak.com	Bohemia	NY	11716	631-467-3900	
Coastal Printing Inc of Sarasota 1730 Independence Blvd Ste 34234. Web: www.coastalprint.com	Sarasota	FL	34234	941-351-1515	
Coastal Tag & Label Inc 13233 Barton Cir. Web: www.coastaltag.com	Santa Fe Springs	CA	90670	562-946-4318	
Cober Evolving Solutions 1351 Strasburg Rd. Web: www.cobersolutions.com	Kitchener	ON	N2R1H2	519-745-7136	
Colonial Press Inc, The 10607 Harrison St. Web: www.thecolonialpress.net	La Vista	NE	68128	402-593-0580	

Company	City	State	ZIP	Phone	Fax
Color Ink Inc W250 N6681 Hwy 164 PO Box 360 *Web:* www.colorink.com	Sussex	WI	53089	262-246-5000	
Color West Inc 2228 N Hollywood Way *Web:* www.colorwestprinting.com	Burbank	CA	91505	818-840-8881	
ColorCraft of Virginia Inc 22645 Sally Ride Dr *Web:* www.colorcraft-va.com	Sterling	VA	20164	703-709-2270	
ColorDynamics 200 E Bethany Dr *TF:* 800-445-0017 ■ *Web:* www.colordynamics.com	Allen	TX	75002	972-390-6500	390-6588
ColorGraphics Inc 150 N Myers St *Web:* www.colorgraphics.com	Los Angeles	CA	90033	323-261-7171	261-7077
Colormark LC 1840 Hutton Dr Bldg 208 *Web:* www.colormark-lc.com	Carrollton	TX	75006	972-243-1919	
Colortech Graphics Inc 28700 Hayes Rd *Web:* www.colortechgraphics.com	Roseville	MI	48066	586-779-7800	
Commerce Printing Service 322 N 12th St *Web:* www.commerceprinting.com	Sacramento	CA	95814	916-442-8100	
Computype Inc 2285 W County Rd C *Web:* www.computype.com	St. Paul	MN	55113	651-633-0633	
Concord Litho Group 92 Old Tpke Rd *TF:* 800-258-3662 ■ *Web:* www.concordlitho.com	Concord	NH	03301	603-225-3328	225-6120
Conley Publishing Group Ltd 119 Monroe St	Beaver Dam	WI	53916	920-885-7800	887-0439
Consolidated Graphics Group Inc 1614 E 40th St *TF General:* 888-884-9191 ■ *Web:* csinc.com	Cleveland	OH	44103	216-881-9191	881-3442
Consolidated Graphics Inc 5858 Westheimer Rd Ste 200 *NYSE:* CGX	Houston	TX	77057	713-787-0977	787-5013
Content Management Corp 37900 Central Ct *Web:* www.cmcondemand.com	Newark	CA	94560	510-505-1100	
Continental Web Press Inc 1430 Industrial Dr *Web:* www.continentalweb.com	Itasca	IL	60143	630-773-1903	773-1903
Control Printing Group Inc 4212 S Hocker Dr Ste 150 *Web:* www.controlprinting.com	Independence	MO	64055	816-350-8100	
COP Communications Inc 620 W Elk Ave *Web:* www.copprints.com	Glendale	CA	91204	818-291-1100	291-1190
Copy Cat Printing 365 N Broadwell Ave *Web:* www.copycatprinting.com	Grand Island	NE	68803	308-384-8520	
Copy World 1728 Warwick Ave *Web:* copyworldri.com	Warwick	RI	02889	401-739-7400	
Coral Color Process Ltd 50 Mall Dr *Web:* www.coralcolor.com	Commack	NY	11725	631-543-5200	
Cosmos Communications Inc 11-05 44th Dr *TF:* 800-223-5751 ■ *Web:* www.cosmoscommunications.com	Long Island City	NY	11101	718-482-1800	482-1968
Courier Graphics Corp 2621 S 37th St *Web:* www.couriergraphics.com	Phoenix	AZ	85034	602-437-9700	
Courier Printing One Courier Pl *TF:* 800-467-0444 ■ *Web:* www.courierprinting.com	Smyrna	TN	37167	615-355-4000	
Cowan Graphics Inc 9253 48 St Nw *Web:* www.cowan.ca	Edmonton	AB	T6B2R9	780-577-5700	
Coyle Reproductions Inc 14949 Firestone Blvd *TF:* 866-269-5373 ■ *Web:* www.coylerepro.com	La Mirada	CA	90638	714-690-8200	690-8219
CPS Printing Inc 2304 Faraday Ave *Web:* www.cpsprinting.com	Carlsbad	CA	92008	760-438-9411	
Craft Originators Inc 41a Brockley Dr *Web:* www.craftoriginators.com	Hamilton	ON	L8E3C3	905-560-1337	
Craftsman Printing Inc 120 Citation Ct *Web:* craftsmanprintinginc.com	Birmingham	AL	35209	205-942-3939	
Crest Craft Co 3860 Virginia Ave *Web:* www.crestcraft.com	Cincinnati	OH	45227	513-271-4858	
Crossmark Graphics Inc 16100 W Overland Dr *Web:* www.crossmarkgraphicsinc.com	New Berlin	WI	53151	262-821-1343	
Cushing & Company Inc 420 W Huron St *Web:* www.cushingco.com	Chicago	IL	60654	312-266-8228	
Custom Cuts Printing Inc 805 E Broward Blvd Ste 301 *Web:* www.mdtdirect.com	Fort Lauderdale	FL	33301	954-764-2630	
Cyber Press 3380 Viso Ct *Web:* www.cyber-press.net	Santa Clara	CA	95054	408-970-9200	
Cyril Scott Company Inc, The 3950 State Rt 37 E *Web:* www.cyrilscott.com	Lancaster	OH	43130	740-654-2112	
D S L Adventures Inc 5692 Stewart Ave *Web:* www.dslprint.com	Fremont	CA	94538	510-353-7475	
Dahlstrom Display Inc 2875 S 25th Ave *Web:* dahlstromdisplay.com	Broadview	IL	60155	708-410-4500	
Daily Printing Inc 2333 Niagara Ln *Web:* www.dailyprinting.com	Plymouth	MN	55447	763-475-2333	
DALB Inc 73 Industrial Blvd *Web:* www.dalb.com	Kearneysville	WV	25430	304-725-0300	
Dan Dolan Printing Inc 2301 E Hennepin Ave *Web:* www.dolanprinting.com	Minneapolis	MN	55413	612-379-2311	
Daniels Business Services Inc 131 Sweeten Creek Rd *Web:* www.danielsgraphics.com	Asheville	NC	28803	828-277-8250	
Darwill Inc 11900 Roosevelt Rd *Web:* www.darwill.com	Hillside	IL	60162	708-236-4900	236-5820
Datamark Graphics Inc 603 W Bailey St *Web:* www.datamarkgraphics.com	Asheboro	NC	27203	336-629-5282	
David A Smith Printing Inc 742 S 22nd St *Web:* www.dasprint.com	Harrisburg	PA	17104	717-564-3719	
Davis Direct Inc 1241 Newell Pkwy *Web:* davisdirect.net	Montgomery	AL	36110	334-277-0878	
Deluxe Check Printing 1600 E Touhy Ave *Web:* www.deluxe.com	Des Plaines	IL	60018	847-635-7200	
Delzer Lithograph Co 510 S W Ave *Web:* www.delzer.com	Waukesha	WI	53186	262-522-2600	
Demand Printing Solutions Inc 3900 Rutledge Rd NE *Web:* www.dpsnm.com	Albuquerque	NM	87109	505-881-2927	
Design Label Manufacturing Inc Seven Capitol Dr *Web:* www.designlabel.com	East Lyme	CT	06333	860-739-6266	
DESIGNASHIRT.COM 905 N Scottsdale Rd *Web:* www.designashirt.com	Tempe	AZ	85281	480-966-3500	
Designers' Press Inc 6305 Chancellor Dr *Web:* www.designerspressinc.com	Orlando	FL	32809	407-843-3141	
DG3 North America Inc 100 Burma Rd *Web:* www.dg3.com	Jersey City	NJ	07305	201-793-5000	
Di Graphics Inc 4850 Ward Rd *Web:* www.digraphics.com	Wheat Ridge	CO	80033	303-425-0510	
Diamond Graphics Inc 14350 Azurite St NW *Web:* www.dgiusa.net	Ramsey	MN	55303	763-235-4141	
Diego & Son Printing Inc 2104 National Ave *Web:* www.diegoandsonprinting.com	San Diego	CA	92113	619-233-5373	
Direct Connection Printing & Mailing 1968 Yeager Ave *Web:* www.directconnectionmail.com	La Verne	CA	91750	909-392-2334	
Disc Graphics Inc 10 Gilpin Ave *Web:* www.discgraphics.com	Hauppauge	NY	11788	631-234-1400	234-1460
District Creative Printing Inc 6350 Fallard Dr *Web:* www.dcpprint.com	Upper Marlboro	MD	20772	301-868-8610	
Document Security Systems Inc 28 E Main St Ste 1525 *NYSE:* DSS ■ *TF:* 877-407-8031 ■ *Web:* www.dsssecure.com	Rochester	NY	14614	585-325-3610	325-2977
Docuplex Inc 725 E Bayley *Web:* www.docuplex.com	Wichita	KS	67211	316-262-2662	
DocuSource of North Carolina LLC 2800 Slater Rd *Web:* www.docusourceofnc.com	Morrisville	NC	27560	919-459-5900	
Docustar Inc 1325 Glendale Milford Rd *Web:* www.docustar.com	Cincinnati	OH	45215	513-772-5400	
Dolce Printing Inc 29 Brook Ave *Web:* www.dolceprint.com	Maywood	NJ	07607	201-843-0400	
Dolphin Shirt Co 757 Buckley Rd *Web:* www.dolphinshirt.com	San Luis Obispo	CA	93401	805-541-2566	
Dome Printing 340 Commerce Cir *Web:* www.domeprinting.com	Sacramento	CA	95815	916-923-3663	
Dominion Blue Digital Reprographics 99 Sixth Ave W *Web:* dominionblue.com	Vancouver	BC	V5Y1K2	604-681-7504	
Doodad Printing LLC 7990 Second Flags Dr *Web:* www.doodad.com	Austell	GA	30168	770-732-0321	
Doremus Financial Printing 225 Varick St Fifth Fl *Web:* www.doremusfp.com	New York	NY	10014	212-366-3800	
Dot Generation Inc 16 Dyke Ln *Web:* www.dotgeneration.com	Stamford	CT	06902	203-967-8112	
Dot Printer Inc, The 2424 Mcgaw Ave *Web:* www.dotprinter.com	Irvine	CA	92614	949-474-1100	
Double Quick Printing Services Inc 2180 S Colorado Blvd *Web:* www.dqprint.com	Denver	CO	80222	303-759-9999	
Dowling Graphics Inc 12920 Automobile Blvd *Web:* www.dowlinggraphics.com	Clearwater	FL	33762	727-573-5997	
Downeast Graphics & Printing Inc 477 Washington Jct Rd *Web:* www.downeastgraphics.com	Ellsworth	ME	04605	207-667-5582	
DPS Printing Service Inc 3500 S Blvd St 38c *Web:* www.dpsprinting.com	Edmond	OK	73013	405-340-0004	
Drew & Rogers Inc 30 Plymouth St *Web:* www.drewandrogers.com	Fairfield	NJ	07004	973-575-6210	
Drug Package Inc 901 Drug Package Ln *TF:* 800-325-6137 ■ *Web:* www.drugpackage.com	O'Fallon	MO	63366	800-325-6137	
Drummond Press Inc, The 2472 Dennis St *Web:* www.drummondpress.com	Jacksonville	FL	32204	904-354-2818	
DS Graphics Inc 120 Stedman St *Web:* www.dsgraphics.com	Lowell	MA	01851	978-970-1359	
Dsj Printing Inc 3103 Pico Blvd *Web:* www.dsjprinting.com	Santa Monica	CA	90405	310-828-8051	
Duncan Printing Co 619 S Fremont Ave Ste A *Web:* www.duncanprinting.com	Alhambra	CA	91803	626-281-2016	
Dupli Graphics Corp One Dupli Park Dr *TF:* 800-724-2477 ■ *Web:* www.duplionline.com	Syracuse	NY	13204	800-724-2477	
DuraColor 1840 Oakdale Ave **Fax Area Code:* 262 ■ *TF:* 877-899-7900 ■ *Web:* www.duracolor.net	Racine	WI	53406	877-899-7900	636-0040*
Dynamic Printing of Brandon Inc 2705 N Falkenburg Rd *Web:* www.dynamicprinting.net	Tampa	FL	33619	813-664-6880	
Eagle Flexible Packaging 1100 Kingsland Dr *Web:* www.eagleflexible.com	Batavia	IL	60510	630-406-1760	
Eagle:XM LLC 5105 E 41st Ave *Web:* www.eaglexm.com	Denver	CO	80216	303-320-5411	
Earl d Arnold Printing Co 630 Lunken Park Dr *Web:* www.arnoldprinting.com	Cincinnati	OH	45226	513-533-6900	
East Ridge Printing 1258 E Ridge Rd *Web:* www.eastridgeprint.com	Rochester	NY	14621	585-266-4911	
EBSCO Media 801 Fifth Ave S *Web:* www.ebscomedia.com	Birmingham	AL	35233	205-323-1508	
Eclipse Colour & Imaging Corp 875 Laurentian Dr *Web:* www.eclipseimaging.com	Burlington	ON	L7N3W7	905-634-1900	
Edison Lithograph & Printing Corp 3725 tonnelle ave *Web:* www.edisonlitho.com	North bergen	NJ	07047	201-902-9191	

Company	City	State	Zip	Phone	Fax
eDOC Communications 555 E Business Ctr Dr *Web:* www.edoccommunications.com	Mount Prospect	IL	60056	847-824-5610	
Edwards Graphic Arts Inc 2700 Bell Ave *Web:* www.ega.com	Des Moines	IA	50321	515-280-9765	
Edwards Label 2277 Knoll Dr *Web:* www.edwardslabel.com	Ventura	CA	93003	805-658-2626	
Egan Printing, Co 1245 Elati St *Web:* eganprinting.com	Denver	CO	80204	303-534-0171	
EGT Printing Solutions LLC 32031 Townley St *Web:* www.egprint.com	Madison Heights	MI	48071	248-583-2500	
Electric City Printing Co 730 Hampton Rd *Web:* www.ecprint.com	Williamston	SC	29697	864-224-6331	
Elk Grove Graphics Inc 1200 Chase Ave *Web:* elkgrovegraphics.com	Elk Grove Village	IL	60007	847-439-7834	
Elm Press 16 Tremco Dr *Web:* www.elmpress.com	Terryville	CT	06786	860-583-3600	
Embossed Graphics 1175 S Frontenac Rd *Web:* embossedgraphics.com	Aurora	IL	60504	630-236-4000	
Emerald City Graphics 23328 66th Ave S *TF General:* 877-631-5178 ■ *Web:* www.emeraldcg.com	Kent	WA	98032	253-520-2600	520-2607
Envelopes & Forms Inc 2505 Meadowbrook Pkwy *Web:* www.envelopesandforms.com	Duluth	GA	30096	770-449-1755	
Envelopes Etcetera Inc 69 Townsend St *Web:* envetc.com	Port Chester	NY	10573	914-937-6162	
EU Services 649 N Horners Ln *Web:* www.euservices.com	Rockville	MD	20850	301-424-3300	424-3696
Excelsior Printing Company Inc 60 Roberts Dr *Web:* www.excelsiorprinting.com	North Adams	MA	01247	413-663-3771	
Express Envelopes Unlimited 3799 N Alvin St *Web:* expressenvelopesunlimited.com	Appleton	WI	54913	920-997-0182	
Express Printing & Graphics Inc 1205 Alderwood Ave *Web:* expressprintingusa.com	Sunnyvale	CA	94089	408-400-0223	
Expresscopy.com 6623 NE 59th Pl *Web:* www.expresscopy.com	Portland	OR	97218	503-234-4880	
F&M Expressions Inc 211 Island Rd *Web:* www.fmexpressions.com	Mahwah	NJ	07430	201-512-3338	
Falcon Printing Inc 6360 Fulton St E *Web:* falconprintinginc.com	Ada	MI	49301	616-676-3737	
Fallbrook Printing Corp 504 E Alvarado St *Web:* www.fallbrookprinting.com	Fallbrook	CA	92028	760-731-2020	
FCL Graphics Inc 4600 N Olcott Ave *Web:* www.fclgraphics.com	Harwood Heights	IL	60706	708-867-5500	867-7768
FEY Printing Co 910 29th Ave N *Web:* feyprinting.com	Wisconsin Rapids	WI	54495	715-423-2400	
Fineline Printing Group 8081 Zionsville Rd *Web:* finelineprintinggroup.com	Indianapolis	IN	46268	317-872-4490	
Finlay Printing LLC 44 Tobey Rd *Web:* www.finlay.com	Bloomfield	CT	06002	860-242-2800	
Firehouse Image Center 2000 N Illinois St *Web:* onyx.fire-house.net	Indianapolis	IN	46202	317-236-1747	
Flagship Press Inc 150 Flagship Dr *TF:* 800-733-1520 ■ *Web:* www.flagshippress.com	North Andover	MA	01845	978-975-3100	975-0635
Flexo Impressions 8647 Eagle Creek Pkwy *Web:* www.flexoimpressions.com	Savage	MN	55378	952-884-9442	
Fort Dearborn Co 6035 W Gross Pt Rd *Web:* www.fortdearborn.com	Niles	IL	60714	773-774-4321	774-9105
Fort Orange Press Inc 11 Sand Creek Rd *Web:* www.fortorangepress.com	Albany	NY	12205	518-489-3233	
Foster Printing Service Inc 4295 Ohio St *Web:* www.fosterprinting.com	Michigan City	IN	46360	219-879-8366	
Fotoprint 975 Pandora Ave *Web:* www.fotoprint.ca	Victoria	BC	V8V3P4	250-382-8218	
Four Colour Print Group 2410 Frankfort Ave *Web:* www.fourcolour.com	Louisville	KY	40206	502-896-9644	
Foxfire Printing & Packaging Inc 750 Dawson Dr *Web:* www.foxfireprinting.com	Newark	DE	19713	302-368-9466	
FP Horak Co 401 Saginaw St *Web:* www.fphorak.com	Bay City	MI	48708	989-892-6505	
Fracture LLC 112 SW Sixth St *Web:* www.fractureme.com	Gainesville	FL	32601	352-234-3722	
Franklin Imaging LLC 500 Schrock Rd *Web:* www.franklinimaging.com	Columbus	OH	43229	614-885-6894	
Franzen Graphics Inc 5300 State Hwy 42 *Web:* www.franzenlitho.com	Sheboygan	WI	53083	920-565-4656	
Frederic Printing Co 14701 E 38th Ave *Web:* www.fredericprinting.com	Aurora	CO	80011	303-371-7990	
Freeport Press Inc 121 Main St *Web:* www.freeportpress.com	Freeport	OH	43973	740-658-4000	
Fricke-Parks Press Inc 33250 Transit Ave *Web:* www.fricke-parks.com	Union City	CA	94587	510-489-6543	
Fruitridge Printing & Lithograph Inc 3258 Stockton Blvd *Web:* www.fruitridgeprinting.com	Sacramento	CA	95820	916-452-9213	
Fry Communications Inc 800 W Church Rd *Web:* www.frycomm.com	Mechanicsburg	PA	17055	717-766-0211	
Fundcraft Publishing Inc PO Box 340 *TF:* 800-964-5715 ■ *Web:* www.fcpromotions.com	Collierville	TN	38027	901-853-7070	853-6196
G & a Label Inc 1601 Wyoming Ave *Web:* www.ganda-label.com	El Paso	TX	79902	915-544-1766	
Gallus Inc 2800 Black Lk Pl *Web:* www.gallus.org	Philadelphia	PA	19154	215-677-9600	
Gannett Offset 7950 Jones Branch Dr *TF:* 800-255-1457 ■ *Web:* www.gannett.com	McLean	VA	22107	703-750-8673	658-8359
Garlock Printing & Converting Corp 164 Fredette St *Web:* garlockprinting.com	Gardner	MA	01440	978-630-1028	
Garner Printing Co 1697 NE 53rd Ave *Web:* www.garnerprint.com	Des Moines	IA	50313	515-266-2171	
Garrett Printing & Graphics Inc 331 Riverside Ave *Web:* www.garrettprinting.us	Bristol	CT	06010	860-589-6710	
Garrity Print Solutions 109 Research Dr *Web:* www.garritysolutions.com	Harahan	LA	70123	504-733-9654	
Gasch Printing LLC 1780 Crossroads Dr *Web:* www.gaschprinting.com	Odenton	MD	21113	301-362-0700	
Gazette Publishing Inc 1114 Broadway *TF:* 800-567-8303 ■ *Web:* www.mnnews.com	Wheaton	MN	56296	320-563-8146	563-8147
GBF Inc 2427 Penny Rd *Web:* www.gbf-inc.com	High Point	NC	27265	336-665-0205	
General Financial Supply Inc 1235 N Ave *Web:* www.generalfinancialsupply.com	Nevada	IA	50201	515-382-3549	
General Press Corp 110 Allegheny Dr *Web:* www.generalpress.com	Natrona Heights	PA	15065	724-224-3500	
Genie Repros Inc 2211 Hamilton Ave *Web:* www.genierepros.com	Cleveland	OH	44114	216-696-6677	
George H. Dean Co 140 Campanelli Dr *Web:* www.ghdean.com	Braintree	MA	02184	781-356-4100	
George Schmitt & Company Inc 251 Boston Post Rd *Web:* www.georgeschmitt.com	Guilford	CT	06437	203-453-4334	
Georgia Printco 90 S Oak St *TF:* 866-572-0146 ■ *Web:* www.georgiaprintco.com	Lakeland	GA	31635	866-572-0146	
Gerald Printing Service Inc 105 Hunter Ct *Web:* www.geraldprinting.com	Bowling Green	KY	42103	270-781-4770	
Ginny's Printing 8410-B Tuscany Way *Web:* www.ginnysprinting.com	Austin	TX	78754	512-454-6874	453-2178
Global Group Inc 4901 N Beach St *Web:* www.xpressdocs.com	Fort Worth	TX	76137	817-831-2631	
Global Trim Sales Inc 22835 Savi Ranch Pkwy *Web:* globalspecialties.com	Yorba Linda	CA	92887	714-998-4400	
Goetz Printing Co, The 7939 Angus Ct *Web:* www.goetzprinting.com	Springfield	VA	22153	703-569-8232	
Golden Ink Litho & Design 7602 Vickers St *Web:* www.goldeninklitho.com	San Diego	CA	92111	858-541-2259	
Gooding Company Inc 5568 Davison Rd *Web:* www.theinsertoutsertexperts.com	Lockport	NY	14094	716-434-5501	
Goodway Print & Copy Inc 15121 Ventura Blvd *Web:* www.goodwayprintcopy.com	Sherman Oaks	CA	91403	818-783-5172	
Goodwin Graphics Inc 1410 Vinylex Dr *Web:* www.goodwingraphics.com	Carrollton	TX	75006	972-446-7313	
Grafico Inc 15320 Cornet Ave *Web:* www.grafico.com	Santa Fe Springs	CA	90670	562-921-6731	
Grafika Commercial Printing Inc 710 Johnston St *Web:* www.grafikaprint.com	Sinking Spring	PA	19608	610-678-8630	
Grand Central Graphics Inc 272 N 12th St *Web:* grandcentralgraphics.com	Milwaukee	WI	53233	414-273-7446	
Grandville Printing Company Inc 4719 Ivanrest Ave SW *Web:* www.gpco.com	Grandville	MI	49418	616-534-8647	
Graphcom Inc 1219 Chambersburg Rd *Web:* www.graphcom.com	Gettysburg	PA	17325	717-334-3107	
Graphcom LLC 1375 Highlands Ridge Rd SE *Web:* www.graphcomprints.com	Smyrna	GA	30082	404-355-3415	
Graphic Design Inc 315 Second St E PO Box 307 *Web:* www.gd-inc.com	Hastings	MN	55033	651-437-6459	
Graphic Resource Group Inc 1380 Hamel Rd *Web:* www.grg-inc.com	Medina	MN	55340	763-746-0400	
Graphic Technology of Maryland Inc 8620 Old Dorsey Run Rd *Web:* www.graphtec.com	Jessup	MD	20794	301-317-0100	
Graphics Plus Inc 1808 Ogden Ave *Web:* www.gpdelivers.com	Lisle	IL	60532	630-968-9073	
Graphics Type & Color Enterprises Inc 2300 NW Seventh Ave *Web:* www.clubflyers.com	Miami	FL	33127	305-591-7600	
Graphicworks 5611 Silverado Way # D *Web:* www.graphicworks.net	Anchorage	AK	99518	907-272-7400	
Graphtech 1310 Crooked Hill Rd *Web:* www.thinkgraphtech.com	Harrisburg	PA	17110	717-238-5751	
Greenway Print Solutions 5425 E Bell Rd #120 *Web:* www.greenwayforms.com	Scottsdale	AZ	85254	602-482-1100	
Greenwell Chisholm Printing Co 420 E Parrish Ave *Web:* www.gc1919.com	Owensboro	KY	42303	270-684-3267	
Grigg Graphic Services Inc 20982 Bridge St *Web:* www.grigg.com	Southfield	MI	48033	248-356-5005	
Grit Commercial Printing Inc 80 Choate Cir *Web:* www.gritprinting.com	Montoursville	PA	17754	570-368-8021	
Groupe Lelys Inc 3275 Ave Francis Hughes *Web:* www.lelys.com	Laval	QC	H7L5A5	450-662-7161	
Grove Printing Corp 4225 Howard Ave *Web:* www.groveprinting.com	Kensington	MD	20895	301-571-1024	
GSL Fine Lithographers 8386 Rovana Cir *Web:* www.gslitho.com	Sacramento	CA	95828	916-231-1410	
Guide, The 24904 Sussex Hwy *Web:* www.theguide.com	Seaford	DE	19973	302-629-5060	

Company	City	State	Zip	Phone	Fax
Guynes Printing Company of Texas Inc 927 Tony Lama *Web:* www.guynesprinting.com	El Paso	TX	79915	915-772-2211	
H&N Printing & Graphics Inc 1913 Greenspring Dr *Web:* www.hnprinting.com	Timonium	MD	21093	410-252-5300	
H&W Printing Inc 1724 Sands Pl. *Web:* www.hwprinting.com	Marietta	GA	30067	770-951-9800	
H.O.T. Printing & Graphics Inc 2595 Tracy Ct *Web:* www.h-o-tgraphics.com	Northwood	OH	43619	419-242-7000	
Haig's Quality Printing 6360 Sunset Corporate Dr *Web:* www.haigsprinting.com	Las Vegas	NV	89120	702-966-1000	
Hall Letter Shop Inc 5200 Rosedale Hwy *Web:* www.hallprintmail.com	Bakersfield	CA	93308	661-327-3228	
Hammer Packaging Corp 200 Lucius Gordon Dr. *Web:* www.hammerpackaging.com	Rochester	NY	14692	585-424-3880	
Hampton Paper & Transfer Printing Inc 2230 Eddie Williams Rd *Web:* www.hamptonprints.com	Johnson City	TN	37601	423-928-7247	
Handbill Printers Inc 820 E Parkridge Ave *Web:* www.handbillprinters.com	Corona	CA	92879	951-547-5910	
Hanes Erie Inc 7601 Klier Dr S. *Web:* www.haneserie.com	Fairview	PA	16415	814-474-1999	
Harman Press Inc, The 6840 Vineland Ave *Web:* www.harmanpress.com	North Hollywood	CA	91605	818-432-0570	
Harmony Press 717 W Berwick St *Web:* www.harmonypress.com	Easton	PA	18042	610-559-9800	
Harper Engraving & Printing Co 2626 Fisher Rd. *Web:* www.harperengraving.com	Columbus	OH	43204	614-276-0700	
Hart Industries Inc 11412 Cronridge Dr *Web:* hartind.com	Owings Mills	MD	21117	410-581-1900	
Harty Press Inc, The PO Box 324 *TF:* 800-654-0562 ■ *Web:* www.hartynet.com	New Haven	CT	06513	203-562-5112	782-9168
Hazard Communication Systems LLC 190 Old Milford Rd. *Web:* www.clarionsafety.com	Milford	PA	18337	570-296-5686	
HBP Inc 952 Frederick St *Web:* www.hbp.com	Hagerstown	MD	21740	301-733-2000	
Hennegan Co 7455 Empire Dr *Web:* www.hennegan.com	Florence	KY	41042	859-282-3600	
Henry Wurst Inc 1331 Saline St. *Web:* www.henrywurst.com	North Kansas City	MO	64116	816-842-3113	
Heuss Printing Inc 903 N Second St. *Web:* www.heuss.com	Ames	IA	50010	515-232-6710	
Heyrman Printing LLC 2083 Holmgren Way *Web:* heyrman.com	Green Bay	WI	54304	920-499-4815	
Hickory Printing Group Inc 725 Reese Dr SW. *TF:* 800-442-5679 ■ *Web:* www.hickoryprinting.com	Conover	NC	28613	828-465-3431	465-2517
Holmes W & Sons Printing Inc 401 E Columbia St *Web:* www.holmesprinting.com	Springfield	OH	45503	937-325-1509	
Hooven-Dayton Corp 511 Byers Rd *Web:* www.hoovendayton.com	Miamisburg	OH	45342	937-233-4473	
Hopkins Printing Inc 2246 CityGate Dr. *Web:* www.hopkinsprinting.com	Columbus	OH	43219	614-509-1080	
Horseheads Printing 2077 Grand Central Ave *Web:* horseheadsprinting.com	Horseheads	NY	14845	607-796-2681	
Horton & Horton Printing Co 12412 Sardis Rd. *Web:* hortonandhorton.com	Mabelvale	AR	72103	501-455-3168	
Ideal Jacobs Corp 515 Valley St *Web:* idealjacobs.com	Maplewood	NJ	07040	973-275-5100	
imageMEDIA Inc 425 E Spruce *Web:* www.imagemedia.com	St Tarpon Springs	FL	34689	727-772-8889	
Imagine! Print Solutions Inc 1000 Vly Park Dr *Web:* www.imagineps.com	Minneapolis	MN	55379	952-903-4400	
Immedia Inc 3311 Broadway St NE *Web:* www.immediaretail.com	Minneapolis	MN	55413	612-524-3400	
Indexx Inc 303 Haywood Rd *Web:* www.indexx.com	Greenville	SC	29607	864-234-1024	
Infovine Inc 1100 W 23rd St Ste 100 *Web:* www.infovine.com	Houston	TX	77008	713-223-9994	
Ink Spot Inc, The 40 Oval Rd Ste 2 *Web:* theinkspot.com	Quincy	MA	02170	617-773-7605	
Inkjet International Ltd 4443 Simonton Rd. *Web:* www.inkjetintl.com	Dallas	TX	75244	972-991-4577	
Inkstone Printing Inc 129 Liberty St *Web:* www.inkstone.com	Brockton	MA	02301	508-587-5200	
Inland Arts & Graphics Inc 14440 Edison Dr *Web:* inlandgraphics.com	New Lenox	IL	60451	815-485-4050	
Inland Printing Co 2009 W Ave South. *Web:* www.inlandlabel.com	La Crosse	WI	54601	608-788-5800	
Inovar Packaging Group LLC 602 Magic Mile. *Web:* www.inovarpkg.com	Arlington	TX	76011	817-277-6666	
Instant Sign Center 4431 Government Blvd *Web:* www.instantsigncenter.com	Mobile	AL	36693	251-666-9567	
Integra Graphix 160 Koser Rd *Web:* www.yourvisitorguide.com	Lititz	PA	17543	717-626-7895	
IntegraColor 3210 Innovative Way. *TF:* 800-933-9511 ■ *Web:* www.integracolor.com	Mesquite	TX	75149	972-289-0705	285-4881
Intelligencer Printing Co 330 Eden Rd. **Fax Area Code:* 877 ■ *TF:* 800-233-0107 ■ *Web:* www.intellprinting.com	Lancaster	PA	17601	800-233-0107	834-1443*
Interprint Inc 12350 US Hwy 19 N *Web:* www.printerusa.com	Clearwater	FL	33764	727-531-8957	
Interprint LLC 7111 Hayvenhurst Ave. *TF:* 800-926-9873 ■ *Web:* www.interprintusa.com	Van Nuys	CA	91406	818-989-3600	989-4600
Ironwood Lithographers Inc 455 S 52nd St *Web:* www.ironwoodlitho.com	Tempe	AZ	85281	480-829-7700	
Issgr Inc 6611 Portwest Dr Ste 190 *Web:* www.imageset.com	Houston	TX	77024	713-869-7700	
Itp of Usa Inc 520 E Bainbridge St *Web:* www.continentalpress.com	Elizabethtown	PA	17022	717-367-3670	
J & A Printing Inc PO Box 457 *TF:* 800-793-1781 ■ *Web:* www.japrinting.com	Hiawatha	IA	52233	319-393-1781	
J L i Marketing & Printing 18d Home News Row *Web:* jlisigns.com	New Brunswick	NJ	08901	732-828-8877	
J. J. Collins' Sons Inc 7125 Janes Ave Ste 200 *Web:* www.jjcollins.com	Woodridge	IL	60517	630-960-2525	
J.B. Kenehan LLC W238 N1700 Rockwood Dr. *Web:* www.jbkenehan.com	Waukesha	WI	53188	262-523-8400	
J.S. McCarthy Printers Inc 15 Darin Dr. *Web:* www.jsmccarthy.com	Augusta	ME	04330	207-622-6241	
Jaco-Bryant Printing LLC 4783 Hickory Hill Rd *Web:* www.jaco-bryant.com	Memphis	TN	38141	901-546-9600	
Jacob North Companies 3721 W Mathis St *Web:* www.jacobnorth.com	Lincoln	NE	68524	402-470-5335	
Jakprints Inc 3133 Chester Ave. *Web:* www.jakprints.com	Cleveland	OH	44114	216-622-6360	
James Allyn Printing Inc 6575 Trinity Ct Ste B *Web:* www.jamesallyn.com	Dublin	CA	94568	925-828-5530	
James Mulligan Printing Corp 1808 Washington Ave. *Web:* mobile.weprint.com	St. Louis	MO	63103	314-621-0875	
Jarvis Press Inc, The 9112 Viscount Row *Web:* www.jarvispress.com	Dallas	TX	75247	214-637-2340	
Jena Communications 125 Stokes Ave. *Web:* www.downtownstroud.com	Stroudsburg	PA	18360	570-476-6900	
Jessen Press Inc 3982 Alabama Ave S *Web:* www.jessenpress.com	Minneapolis	MN	55416	952-929-0346	
John Manlove Marketing & Communications 5125 Preston Ave *Web:* johnmanlove.com	Pasadena	TX	77505	281-487-6767	
John Roberts Co 9687 E River Rd *TF:* 800-551-1534 ■ *Web:* www.johnroberts.com	Coon Rapids	MN	55433	763-755-5500	754-4400
JohnsByrne Co 6701 W Oakton St. *Web:* www.johnsbyrne.com	Niles	IL	60714	847-583-3100	
Johnson Litho Graphics of Eau Claire Ltd 2219 Galloway St. *Web:* www.johnsonlitho.com	Eau Claire	WI	54703	715-832-3211	
Johnson Press of America Inc 800 N Court St. *Web:* jpapontiac.com	Pontiac	IL	61764	815-844-5161	
Jones Printing Service Inc 931 Ventures Way. *Web:* www.jones-printing.com	Chesapeake	VA	23320	757-436-3331	
K&M Printing Company Inc 1410 N Meacham Rd *Web:* www.kmprinting.com	Schaumburg	IL	60173	847-884-1100	
Karol Media Hanover Industrial Estates 375 Stewart Rd *Web:* www.karolmedia.com	Wilkes-barre	PA	18706	570-822-8899	
Kay Toledo Tag Inc PO Box 5038. *TF:* 800-822-8247 ■ *Web:* www.kaytag.com	Toledo	OH	43612	419-729-5479	729-0315
Keiger Printing Co 3735 Kimwell Dr *Web:* keiger.com	Winston Salem	NC	27103	336-760-0099	
Keller Crescent Co Inc 6454 Saguaro Ct **Fax:* Cust Svc ■ *Web:* www.kellercrescent.com	Indianapolis	IN	46268	812-464-2461	426-7601*
Kelly Press Inc 1701 Cabin Branch Dr. *Web:* www.thekellycompanies.com	Cheverly	MD	20785	301-386-2800	
Kempenfelt Group Inc 84 Saunders Rd *Web:* www.kempenfeltgroup.com	Barrie	ON	L4N9A8	705-722-4437	
Kenny The Printer 17931 Sky Park Cir Ste C *Web:* www.kennytheprinter.com	Irvine	CA	92614	949-250-3212	
Kenwel Printers Inc 4272 Indianola Ave. *Web:* kenwel.com	Columbus	OH	43214	614-261-1011	
Kenyon Press Inc One Kenyon Press Dr PO Box 710 *Web:* www.kenyonpress.net	Sherburne	NY	13460	607-674-9066	
Keys Printing Co 1004 Keys Dr *Web:* www.keysprinting.com	Greenville	SC	29615	864-288-6560	
Kingery Printing Co 3012 S Banker PO Box 727 *Web:* www.kingeryprinting.com	Effingham	IL	62401	217-347-5151	
Kirkwood Printing Company Inc 904 Main St *Web:* www.kirkwoodprinting.com	Wilmington	MA	01887	978-658-4200	658-5547
Kiwi Coders Corp 265 Messner Dr. *Web:* www.kiwicoders.com	Wheeling	IL	60090	847-541-4511	
Knepper Press Corp 2251 Sweeney Dr *Web:* www.knepperpress.com	Clinton	PA	15026	724-899-4200	899-1331
Knight Printing LLC 16 South 16th St. *Web:* www.knightprinting.com	Fargo	ND	58103	701-235-1121	
Knight-Abbey Commercial Prntrs 315 Caillavet St *Web:* www.knightabbey.com	Biloxi	MS	39530	228-374-3298	
Knox Services 2250 Fourth Ave *Web:* www.knoxservices.com	San Diego	CA	92101	619-233-9700	
Kolossos Printing Inc 2055 W Stadium Blvd *Web:* kolossosprinting.com	Ann Arbor	MI	48103	734-994-5400	
Koza Inc 2910 S Main St *Web:* www.kozas.com	Pearland	TX	77581	281-485-1462	
Kreate & Print Inc 14 Central St *Web:* www.kreateandprint.com	Norwood	MA	02062	781-255-0505	
Kwik Kopy Corp 12715 Telge Rd *Web:* www.iced.net	Cypress	TX	77429	281-256-4100	

Company / Address	City	State	Zip	Phone	Fax
Kwik Kopy Printing Canada Corp 1550-16th Ave Bldg D	Richmond Hill	ON	L4B3K9	416-798-7007	
Web: www.kkpcanada.ca					
I'Usine Tactic Inc 127e rue E Ste 2030	Saint George	QC	G5Y2W8	418-227-4279	
Web: www.samplingproduct.com					
La Crosse Graphics Inc 3025 East Ave S	La Crosse	WI	54601	608-788-2500	
Web: www.lacrossegraphics.com					
Label Impression Inc 1831 W Sequoia Ave	Orange	CA	92868	714-634-3466	
Web: www.labelimpressions.com					
Label Printers Lp, The 1710 N Landmark Rd	Aurora	IL	60506	630-897-6970	
Web: www.thelabelprinters.com					
Label Systems Inc 4111 Lindbergh Dr	Addison	TX	75001	972-387-4512	
Web: www.labelsystemsinc.com					
Label Technology Inc 2050 Wardrobe Ave	Merced	CA	95341	209-384-1000	
Web: www.labeltech.com					
Label Works 2025 Lookout Dr	North Mankato	MN	56002	800-522-3558	
TF: 800-522-3558 ■ *Web:* www.labelworks.com					
Lake County Press Inc 98 Noll St	Waukegan	IL	60085	847-336-4333	336-5846
Web: www.lakecountypress.com					
Lake Erie Graphics Inc 5372 W 130th St	Brook Park	OH	44142	216-265-7575	
Web: www.lakeeriegraphics.com					
Lake Printing Company Inc 6815 Hwy 54	Osage Beach	MO	65065	573-346-0600	
Web: www.lakeprinting.com					
Lane Press Inc 87 Meadowland Dr PO Box 130	Burlington	VT	05402	802-863-5555	264-1485
TF: 800-733-3740 ■ *Web:* www.lanepress.com					
Laser Image Inc 2451 N Stemmons Fwy	Dallas	TX	75207	214-267-1313	
Web: www.laserimagedallas.com					
Laser Imaging Systems Inc 120 N St	York	PA	17403	717-718-1300	
Web: www.laserlis.com					
Laser Print Plus Inc 1261 First St S Ext	Columbia	SC	29209	803-695-7090	
Web: www.laserprintplus.com					
Laser Reproductions Inc 950E Taylor Sta Rd	Gahanna	OH	43230	614-552-6905	
Web: www.laserrepro.com					
Lasting Impressions Inc 7406 43rd Ave NE	Marysville	WA	98270	360-659-1255	
Web: www.lastingimp.com					
Lawrence Printing Co 400 Stribling Ave PO Box 886	Greenwood	MS	38935	662-453-6301	
Web: www.laprico.com					
LCI Graphics Inc 1515 Broad St	Bloomfield	NJ	07003	973-893-2913	
Web: www.lcigraphics.com					
Leader Printing Co 214 S Egan Ave	Madison	SD	57042	605-256-4444	
Web: madisondailyleader.com					
Lee Printing Company Inc 3904 Leeland St	Houston	TX	77003	713-227-5566	
Web: www.leeprintingco.com					
Lellyett & Rogers Services Company LLC 1717 Lebanon Pk	Nashville	TN	37210	615-316-0780	
Web: www.lrprint.com					
Lester Lithograph Inc 1128 N Gilbert St	Anaheim	CA	92801	714-491-3981	
Web: www.lesterlitho.com					
Lew A. Cummings Company Inc Four Peters Brook Dr	Hooksett	NH	03106	800-647-0035	
TF: 800-647-0035 ■ *Web:* www.cummingsprinting.com					
Lewisburg Printing Inc 135 Legion Ave	Lewisburg	TN	37091	931-359-1526	
Web: www.lewisburgprinting.com					
Linemark Printing Inc 501 Prince Georges Blvd	Upper Marlboro	MD	20774	301-925-9000	
Web: www.linemark.com					
Litho-Krome Co 5700 Old Brim Dr	Midland	GA	31820	706-562-7900	
TF: 800-572-8028 ■ *Web:* www.lithokrome.com					
LithoFlexo Grafics Inc 2400 South 600 West	Salt Lake City	UT	84115	801-484-8503	
Web: lithoflexo.com					
Lithographix Inc 12250 Crenshaw Blvd	Hawthorne	CA	90250	323-770-1000	706-6574*
**Fax Area Code:* 310 ■ *TF General:* 800-848-2449 ■ *Web:* www.lithographix.com					
Lithtex Northwest LLC 3550 Meridian St Ste 6	Bellingham	WA	98225	360-676-1977	
Web: www.lithtexnw.com					
Lithtex Printing Solutions Inc 6770 NW Century Blvd	Hillsboro	OR	97124	503-641-5367	
Web: www.lithtex.com					
Litigation Solution Inc, The 901 Main St Ste C121	Dallas	TX	75202	214-939-9700	
Web: www.xitsolution.com					
Livewire Printing Co 310 Second St PO Box 208	Jackson	MN	56143	507-847-3771	847-5822
Web: www.livewireprinting.com					
LMI Packaging Solutions Inc 8911 102nd St	Pleasant Prairie	WI	53158	262-947-3300	
Web: www.lmipackaging.com					
LogoNation Inc 128 Overhill Dr Ste 102	Mooresville	NC	28117	704-799-0612	
Web: www.logonation.com					
Lowen Corp PO Box 1528	Hutchinson	KS	67504	620-663-2161	663-1429
TF: 800-835-2365 ■ *Web:* www.lowen.com					
Lti Printing Inc 518 N Centerville Rd	Sturgis	MI	49091	269-651-7574	
Web: www.ltiprinting.com					
Lynn Blueprint & Supply Company Inc 328 Old Vine St	Lexington	KY	40507	859-255-1021	
Web: www.lynnimaging.com					
Lynx Group Inc 2746 Front St NE	Salem	OR	97301	503-588-9339	
Web: www.lynxgroup.com					
M & R Sales & Service Inc 1n 372 Main St	Glen Ellyn	IL	60137	630-858-6101	858-6134
TF: 800-736-6431 ■ *Web:* www.mrprint.com					
M&D Printing 515 University Ave	Henry	IL	61537	309-364-3957	
Web: www.mdprint.com					
M. Lee Smith Publishers LLC PO Box 5094	Brentwood	TN	37024	615-373-7517	373-5183
TF: 800-274-6774 ■ *Web:* www.mleesmith.com					
Magna IV 2401 Commercial Ln	Little Rock	AR	72206	501-376-2397	
Web: www.magna4.com					
Mahaffey's Quality Printing Inc 355 W Pearl St	Jackson	MS	39203	601-353-9663	
Web: quality-printing.com					
Mail Communications Group LLC 4100 121st St	Des Moines	IA	50323	515-727-7700	
Web: www.mailcommunicationsgroup.com					
Mail Handling Inc 7550 Corporate Way	Eden Prairie	MN	55344	952-975-5000	
Web: mailhandling.com					
Mail Stream Inc 125 Mason Cir Ste K	Concord	CA	94520	925-676-6711	
Web: mail-stream.net					
Mainline Printing Inc 3500 SW Topeka Blvd	Topeka	KS	66611	785-233-2338	
Web: www.mainlineprinting.com					
Marathon Press Inc 1500 Sq Turn Blvd	Norfolk	NE	68701	402-371-5040	
Web: www.marathonpress.com					
Marfield Corporate Stationery 1225 E Crosby Rd Ste B1	Carrollton	TX	75006	972-245-9122	
Web: www.marfield.com					
Marina Graphic Center 12901 Cerise Ave	Hawthorne	CA	90250	310-970-1777	
Web: marinagraphics.com					
Martino-White Printing 543 N Central Ave	Hapeville	GA	30354	404-768-8708	
Web: www.martinowhite.com					
Master Graphics LLC 1100 S Main St	Rochelle	IL	61068	815-562-5800	562-6600
Web: www.mg-printing.com					
Master Print Inc 8401 Terminal Rd	Newington	VA	22122	703-550-9555	550-9673
Web: www.master-print.com					
MATLET Group LLC 60 Delta Dr	Pawtucket	RI	02860	401-834-3007	
Web: www.thematletgroup.com					
Matrix Imaging Solutions Inc 6341 Inducon Dr	Sanborn	NY	14132	716-504-9700	
Web: www.matriximaging.com					
Mc Carty Printing Corp 246 E Seventh St	Erie	PA	16503	814-454-6337	
Web: www.mccartyprinting.com					
McCallum Printing Group Inc 11755 108 Ave Northwest	Edmonton	AB	T5H1B8	780-455-8885	
Web: www.mcprint.ca					
Mccormick Armstrong Company Inc 1501 E Douglas	Wichita	KS	67211	316-264-1363	
Web: www.mcaprint.com					
McKay Press Inc 7600 W Wackerly Rd	Midland	MI	48642	989-631-2360	
Web: mckaypress.com					
Medical Legal Reproductions Inc 4940 Disston St Ste 3	Philadelphia	PA	19135	215-335-3212	
Web: www.medleg.com					
Mehle Printing Co 2250 Craig Dr	Oxnard	CA	93036	805-485-3175	
Web: www.mehleprinting.com					
Menzies Printers Ltd 9917 A - 97th Ave	Grande Prairie	AB	T8V0N2	780-532-8730	
Web: www.menziesprinters.com					
Mercersburg Printing 9964 Buchanan Trl W	Mercersburg	PA	17236	717-328-3902	
Web: www.mercersburg.net					
Mercury Press Inc 1910 S Nicklas St	Oklahoma City	OK	73128	405-682-3468	
Web: www.mercurypressinc.com					
Meredith-Webb Printing Company Inc 334 N Main St	Burlington	NC	27217	336-228-8378	
Web: www.meredithwebb.com					
Meridian Graphics Inc 2652 Dow Ave	Tustin	CA	92780	949-833-3500	
Web: www.mglitho.com					
Merrill Corp 1 Merrill Cir	Saint Paul	MN	55108	651-646-4501	646-5332
TF: 800-688-4400 ■ *Web:* www.merrillcorp.com					
Meteor Photo & Imaging Inc 750 Letica Dr	Rochester	MI	48307	248-583-3090	
Web: www.meteorprint.com					
Metro Web Corp 5901 Tonnelle Ave	North Bergen	NJ	07047	201-553-0700	
Web: www.metrowebnj.com					
Meyers Printing Cos Inc, The 7277 Boone Ave N	Minneapolis	MN	55428	763-533-9730	531-5771
TF: 800-927-9709 ■ *Web:* www.meyers.com					
MicroPRINT 335 Bear Hill Rd	Waltham	MA	02451	781-890-7500	
Web: www.mprint.com					
Midland Information Resources Co 5440 Corporate Pk Dr	Davenport	IA	52807	563-359-3696	359-1333
TF: 800-232-3696 ■ *Web:* elandersamericas.com/pages/redirect.aspx					
Midtown Printing LLC 2115 59th St	St. Louis	MO	63110	314-781-6505	
Web: www.modernlitho.com					
Migu Press Inc 260 Ivyland Rd	Warminster	PA	18974	215-957-9763	
Web: www.migupress.com					
Millet the Printer Inc 1000 S Ervay St	Dallas	TX	75201	214-741-3602	
Web: www.milletttheprinter.com					
Mines Press Inc, The 231 Croton Ave	Cortlandt Manor	NY	10567	914-788-1800	
Web: www.minespress.com					
Minuteman Press International Inc 61 Executive Blvd	Farmingdale	NY	11735	631-249-1370	249-5618
TF: 800-645-3006 ■ *Web:* www.minutemanpress.com					
Mm & t Packaging Co 5485 Tomken Rd	Mississauga	ON	L4W3Y3	905-625-1010	
Web: www.mmt.ca					
Modern Press Inc One Colonie St	Albany	NY	12207	518-434-2921	
Web: www.modernpress.com					
Modern Print Shop 508 Cortlandt St	Houston	TX	77007	713-861-7262	
Web: modernprintshop.com					
Modern Way Printing & Fulfillment 8817 Production Ln	Ooltewah	TN	37363	423-238-4500	
Web: www.modernwayco.com					
Mojave Copy & Printing Inc 12402 Industrial Blvd	Victorville	CA	92395	760-241-7898	
Web: www.mojavecopy.com					
Mold in Graphic Systems 999 Hwy 89	Clarkdale	AZ	86324	928-634-8838	
Web: www.moldingraphics.com					
Monarch Litho Inc 1501 Date St	Montebello	CA	90640	323-727-0300	720-1169
Web: www.monarchlitho.com					
Moquin Press Inc 555 Harbor Blvd	Belmont	CA	94002	650-592-0575	
Web: www.moquinpress.com					
Morgan Printing Inc 402 Hill Ave	Grafton	ND	58237	701-352-0640	
Web: www.morganprinting.com					
Morgantown Printing & Binding LLC 915 Greenbag Rd	Morgantown	WV	26508	304-292-3368	
Web: www.morgantownprinting.com					
Morris Printing Group 3212 Hwy 30 E	Kearney	NE	68847	308-236-7888	
Web: www.morriscookbooks.com					
Motivating Graphics Inc 3100 Eagle Pkwy	Fort Worth	TX	76177	817-491-4788	
Web: www.motivatinggraphics.com					

Company / Address	City	State	Zip	Phone	Fax
Mount Royal Printing Company Inc 6310 Blair Hill Ln *Web:* mtroyalprinting.com	Baltimore	MD	21209	410-296-1117	
MR Label Inc 5018 Gray Rd *Web:* www.mrlabelco.com	Cincinnati	OH	45232	513-681-2088	
MRI Flexible Packaging Co 122 Penns Trl *Web:* www.mriflex.com	Newtown	PA	18940	215-860-7676	
MT&L Card Products & Fulfillment Services 2911 Kraft Dr *Web:* www.mtlcard.com	Nashville	TN	37204	615-254-9471	
Multi-Craft Litho Inc 131 E Sixth St PO Box 72960 *Web:* www.multi-craft.com	Newport	KY	41072	859-581-2754	
Mv Printing Solutions Inc 23531 Ridge Rt Dr Ste A *Web:* mvprintsolutions.com	Laguna Hills	CA	92653	949-598-9610	
MWM Dexter Inc 107 Washington Ave *Web:* www.mwmdexter.com	Aurora	MO	65605	417-841-1040	
Nahan Printing Inc 7000 Saukview Dr PO Box 697 *Web:* www.nahan.com	Saint Cloud	MN	56302	320-251-7611	259-1378
Nameplate & Panel Technology 387 Gundersen Dr *Web:* www.nptec.com	Carol Stream	IL	60188	630-690-9360	
Napa Printing & Graphics Center Inc 630 Airpark Rd Ste D *Web:* www.napaprinting.com	Napa	CA	94558	707-257-6555	
National Graphics Inc 248 Branford Rd *Web:* natgraphics.com	North Branford	CT	06471	203-481-2351	
National Mail Graphics Corp 300 Old Mill Ln *Web:* www.nmgcorp.com	Exton	PA	19341	610-524-1600	524-7638
Nationwide Graphics Inc 2500 W Loop S Ste 500 *Web:* www.nwas-llc.com	Houston	TX	77027	713-961-4700	961-4701
NCL Graphic Specialties Inc N29 W 22960 Marjean Ln *Web:* nclgs.com/	Waukesha	WI	53186	262-832-6100	
ND Graphic Product Ltd 55 Interchange Way Unit 1 *Web:* www.ndgraphics.com	Concord	ON	L4K5W3	416-663-6416	
Nebraska Printing Company Inc 4411 W Tampa Bay Blvd *TF:* 800-683-2056 ■ *Web:* www.nebcofl.com	Tampa	FL	33614	813-873-7117	873-1193
Network Communications Inc Two Sun Ct NW Ste 300 *Web:* www.nci.com	Norcross	GA	30092	678-346-9300	
New Era Portfolio 2101 E St Elmo Rd Ste 110 *Web:* www.newerahd.com	Austin	TX	78744	512-928-3200	
New World Group Inc 500 County Ave *Web:* www.newworldgroup.com	Secaucus	NJ	07094	201-770-1404	
Newark Trade Digital Graphics 177 Oakwood Ave *Web:* www.newarktrade.com	Orange	NJ	07050	973-674-3727	
Neyenesch Printers Inc 2750 Kettner Blvd *Web:* www.neyenesch.com	San Diego	CA	92101	415-566-1599	
Nieman Printing Inc 10615 Newkirk St Ste 100 *Web:* niemanprinting.com	Dallas	TX	75220	972-506-7400	
North Toledo Graphics LLC 5225 Telegraph Rd *Web:* www.northtoledographics.com	Toledo	OH	43612	419-476-8808	
Northern Ohio Printing Inc 4721 Hinckley Indus Pkwy *Web:* www.nohioprint.com	Cleveland	OH	44109	216-398-0000	
Nowata Printing Co Po Box 472 *Web:* www.nowataprinting.com	Nowata	OK	74048	918-273-1950	
NPC Inc 13710 Dunnings Hwy *Web:* www.npcweb.com	Claysburg	PA	16625	814-239-8787	
Nta Graphics South Inc 501 Republic Cir *Web:* www.ntagraphics.com	Birmingham	AL	35214	205-798-2123	
Nutis Press Inc 3540 E Fulton St *Web:* www.nutispress.com	Columbus	OH	43227	614-237-8626	
O'Neil Printing Inc 366 N Second Ave *Web:* www.oneilprint.com	Phoenix	AZ	85003	602-258-7789	
Odyssey Digital Printing Inc 5301 S 125th E Ave *Web:* www.odysseyprint.com	Tulsa	OK	74146	918-660-0492	
Old Trail Printing Company Inc, The 100 Fornoff Rd *Web:* www.oldtrailprinting.com	Columbus	OH	43207	614-443-4852	
Oliver Printing Company Inc 1760 Enterprise Pkwy *Web:* www.oliverprinting.com	Twinsburg	OH	44087	330-425-7890	
Olympus Press Inc 3400 S 150th St *Web:* www.olympuspress.com	Seattle	WA	98188	206-242-2700	
Omega Printing Inc 201-207 Williams St *Web:* omegaprinting.com	Bensenville	IL	60106	630-595-6344	
Origen Partners Inc 2260 Defoor Hills Rd *Web:* www.origenpartners.com	Atlanta	GA	30318	404-355-8910	
Original Impressions LLC 12900 SW 89th Ct *Web:* www.originalimpressions.com	Miami	FL	33176	305-233-1322	
Outlook Group Corp 1180 American Dr PO Box 748 *Web:* www.outlookgroup.com	Neenah	WI	54956	920-727-7999	727-8529
Output Services Inc 6410 O'Dell Pl *Web:* www.outputservices.com	Boulder	CO	80301	303-530-3403	
P & P Press Inc 6513 N Galena Rd *Web:* pppress.com	Peoria	IL	61614	309-691-8511	
Pacific Color Graphics 440 Boulder Ct 100d *Web:* www.pacificcolor.com	Pleasanton	CA	94566	925-600-3006	
Packaging Products Corporation LLC 6820 Squibb Rd *Web:* www.packagingproductscorp.com	Mission	KS	66202	913-262-3033	
Page International Communications 2748 Bingle Rd *Web:* www.page-intl.com	Houston	TX	77055	713-464-8484	
Palm Printing 6001 Business Blvd *Web:* palmprinting.com	Sarasota	FL	34240	941-907-0090	
Palmas Printing Inc 200 East Dr *Web:* www.palmasprinting.com	Melbourne	FL	32904	321-984-4451	
Panel Prints Inc 1001 Moosic Rd *TF:* 800-557-2635 ■ *Web:* www.panelprints.com	Old Forge	PA	18518	570-457-8334	457-6440
Panoramic Press Inc 2920 N 35th St *Web:* panoramicpress.com	Phoenix	AZ	85018	602-955-2001	
Paradigm Imaging Group 1590 Metro Dr Ste 116 *Web:* www.paradigmimaging.com	Costa Mesa	CA	92626	714-432-7226	
Paragon Press Inc 2532 South 3270 West *Web:* www.paragonpress.com	Salt Lake City	UT	84119	801-978-3500	
Paravista Inc 1055 Centennial Ave *Web:* www.paravistainc.com	Piscataway	NJ	08854	732-752-1222	
Paris Art Label Company Inc 217 River Ave *Web:* www.parisartlabel.com	Patchogue	NY	11772	631-648-6200	
Park Printing Inc 2801 California St NE *Web:* www.parkprint.com	Minneapolis	MN	55418	612-789-4333	
Parris Printing 211 Whitsett Rd *Web:* www.parrisprinting.com	Nashville	TN	37210	615-832-7170	
Patson's Media Group 970 Stewart Dr *Web:* www.patsons.com	Sunnyvale	CA	94085	408-732-0911	
Pauler Communications Inc 7271 Engle Rd Ste 309 *Web:* townplanner.com	Cleveland	OH	44130	440-243-1229	
Pavsner Press Inc 9008 Yellow Brick Rd *Web:* www.pavsnerpress.com	Baltimore	MD	21237	410-687-7550	
Payne Printery Inc 3235 Memorial Hwy *Web:* www.payneinc.net	Dallas	PA	18612	570-675-1147	
Pazazz Printing Inc 5584 Cote-de-Liesse *Web:* www.pazazz.com	Montreal	QC	H4P1A9	514-856-3330	
PBM Graphics Inc 3700 S Miami Blvd *TF:* 800-849-8100 ■ *Web:* www.pbmgraphics.com	Durham	NC	27703	919-544-6222	544-6695
PCA LLC 15 W Aylesbury Rd *Web:* www.printpca.com	Timonium	MD	21093	410-561-5533	
PCH Litho Inc 1497 Poinsettia Ave 159 *Web:* pchlitho.com	Vista	CA	92081	760-798-1190	
PCI Group Inc 11632 Harrisburg Rd *Web:* www.pcigroup.com	Fort Mill	SC	29707	803-578-7700	
PDQ Print Center Inc 301 Mulberry St *Web:* www.pdqprint.com	Scranton	PA	18503	570-343-0414	
PDQ Printing Inc 3820 S Vly View Blvd *Web:* www.pdqvegas.com	Las Vegas	NV	89103	702-876-3235	
Peake DeLancey Printers LLC 2500 Schuster Dr *Web:* www.peakedelancey.com	Cheverly	MD	20781	301-341-4600	
Pel Hughes Printing Inc 3801 Toulouse St *Web:* www.pelhughes.com	New Orleans	LA	70119	504-486-8646	
Pemcor LLC 2100 State Rd *Web:* www.pemcor.com	Lancaster	PA	17601	717-898-1555	
Penmor Lithographers Inc Eight Lexington St *Web:* penmor.com	Lewiston	ME	04240	207-784-1341	
Perfect Image Inc 8505 Crown Crescent Ct *Web:* www.perfectimageprint.com	Charlotte	NC	28227	704-841-2464	
Perkinson Reprographics Inc 735 E Brill St *Web:* www.prigraphics.com	Phoenix	AZ	85006	602-393-3131	
Philipp Lithographing Co 1960 Wisconsin Ave PO Box 4 *Web:* www.philipplitho.com	Grafton	WI	53024	262-377-1100	
Phoenix Innovate Inc 1775 Bellingham *Web:* www.phoenixinnovate.com	Troy	MI	48083	248-457-9000	
Phoenix Lithographing Corp 11631 Caroline Rd *Web:* www.phoenixlitho.com	Philadelphia	PA	19154	215-698-9000	
Piccadilly Printing Co 32 E Piccadilly St *Web:* www.picprinting.com	Winchester	VA	22601	540-662-3804	
Pictorial Offset Corp 111 Amor Ave PO Box 157 *Web:* www.pictorialoffset.com	Carlstadt	NJ	07072	201-935-7100	935-3254
Piedmont Graphics Inc 6903 International Dr *Web:* www.piedmontgraphics.com	Greensboro	NC	27409	336-230-0040	
PIP Printing & Document Services Inc 26722 Plaza Dr Ste 200 *Web:* www.pip.com	Mission Viejo	CA	92691	949-348-5000	348-5066
Platon Digital Graphics 136 Oregon St *TF:* 800-499-0292 ■ *Web:* platongraphics.com	El Segundo	CA	90245	800-499-0292	
Plum Grove Inc 2160 Stoningtone Ave *Web:* www.plumgroveprinters.com	Hoffman Estates	IL	60169	847-882-4020	
Pma Inc 17128 Edwards Rd *Web:* www.printmgt.com	Cerritos	CA	90703	562-407-9977	
Pollock Printing Company Inc 928 Sixth Ave South *Web:* www.pollockprinting.com	Nashville	TN	37203	615-255-0526	
Polytype America Corp 10 Industrial Ave *Web:* www.wifag-polytype.com	Mahwah	NJ	07430	201-995-1000	995-1080
Premier Graphics LLC 860 Honeyspot Rd *Web:* www.premiergraphicsinc.com	Stratford	CT	06615	203-378-6200	
Premium Color Group LLC 95-B Industrial *Web:* www.premiumcolor.com	Clifton	NJ	07012	973-472-7007	
Prentice Products 4236 W Ferguson Rd *Web:* www.prenticeproducts.com	Fort Wayne	IN	46809	260-747-3195	
Print Art Inc 6726 Delilah Rd *Web:* www.print-art.net	Egg Harbor Township	NJ	08234	609-645-1940	
Print Basics Inc 1059 Sw 30th Ave *Web:* www.printbasics.com	Deerfield Beach	FL	33442	954-354-0700	
Print Direction Inc 1600 Indian Brook Way *TF:* 877-435-1672 ■ *Web:* www.printdirection.com	Norcross	GA	30093	770-446-6446	

Phone Fax

Print Fulfillment Services LLC
2929 Magazine St ... Louisville KY 40211 502-776-7704
Web: www.printfulfillmentservices.com

Print House, The 200 Maplewood St ... Malden MA 02148 781-324-4455
Web: www.printhouse.com

Print NW LLC 9914 32nd Ave S ... Tacoma WA 98499 253-284-2300
Web: www.printnw.net

Print Papa 1920 Lafayette St Ste L ... Santa Clara CA 95050 408-567-9553
Web: www.printpapa.com

Print Tech LLC 49 Fadem Rd ... Springfield NJ 07081 908-232-2287
Web: www.print-tech.com

Print Time Inc
8016 State Line Rd Ste 111 ... Shawnee Mission KS 66208 913-642-1700
Web: www.printtime.com

Print Works 3850 98 St Nw ... Edmonton AB T6E3L2 780-452-8921
Web: www.printworksprint.com

Printer Inc, The 1220 Thomas Beck Rd ... Des Moines IA 50315 515-288-7241 288-9234
Web: www.the-printer.com

Printing Control Services Inc
1011 Andover Park E ... Tukwila WA 98188 206-575-4114
Web: printingcontrol.com

Printing Images Inc 12266 Wilkins Ave A ... Rockville MD 20852 301-984-1140
Web: www.printingimages.com

Printing Methods Inc 1525 Emerson St ... Rochester NY 14606 585-458-2133
Web: www.printingmethods.com

Printing Partners Inc 929 W 16th St ... Indianapolis IN 46202 317-635-2282
Web: www.printingpartners.net

Printing Source Inc, The 2373 Ball Dr ... St. Louis MO 63146 314-373-7200
Web: www.theprintingsource.com

PrintingForLess.com Inc 100 PFL Way ... Livingston MT 59047 800-930-6040
TF: 800-930-6040 ■ Web: www.printingforless.com

PrintPlace.com 1130 Ave H E ... Arlington TX 76011 817-701-3555
Web: www.printplace.com

Printpoint Printing Inc 150 S Patterson Blvd ... Dayton OH 45402 937-223-9041
Web: www.printpointprinting.com

Printsouth Printing Inc
1114 Silstar Rd ... West Columbia SC 29170 803-796-2619
Web: www.printsouthprinting.com

Prisma Graphic Corp 2937 E Broadway Rd ... Phoenix AZ 85040 602-243-5777 268-4804
TF: 800-379-5777 ■ Web: www.prismagraphic.com

Pro Copy 5219 E Fowler Ave ... Tampa FL 33617 813-988-5900
Web: www.pro-copy.com

Pro-Graphics Communications Inc
5664 New Peachtree Rd ... Atlanta GA 30341 678-597-1050
Web: www.prographinc.com

Production Press Inc 307 E Morgan St ... Jacksonville IL 62650 217-243-3353 245-0400
TF: 800-231-3880 ■ Web: www.productionpress.com

ProForma 8800 E Pleasant Vly Rd ... Independence OH 44131 216-520-8400 520-8444
TF: 800-825-1525 ■ Web: www.proforma.com

Progress Printing Co 2677 Waterlick Rd ... Lynchburg VA 24502 800-572-7804 237-1618*
*Fax Area Code: 434 ■ TF: 800-572-7804 ■ Web: www.progressprintplus.com

Promatch Solutions LLC 2251 Arbor Blvd ... Dayton OH 45439 937-299-0185
Web: www.promatchsolutions.com

Prosource Fitness Equipment 6503 Hilburn Dr ... Raleigh NC 27613 919-781-8077
Web: prosourcefitness.com

PSPrint LLC 2861 Mandela Pkwy ... Oakland CA 94608 510-444-3933
Web: www.psprint.com

Pub Cite 191 Rue Theberge ... Delson QC J5B2J9 450-635-0635
Web: pubcite.com

Publication Printers Corp
2001 S Platte River Dr ... Denver CO 80223 303-936-0303 934-6712
TF: 888-824-0303 ■ Web: www.publicationprinters.com

Publishers Printing Co
100 Frank E Simon Ave ... Shepherdsville KY 40165 502-955-6526 955-5586
TF: 800-627-5801 ■ Web: www.pubpress.com

PXP Inc 2485 Merritt Dr ... Garland TX 75041 214-221-7669
Web: www.ponyprinting.com

Pyramid Checks & Printing Inc
208 Riverside Indus Pkwy ... Portland ME 04103 207-878-9832
Web: www.pyramidchecks-printing.com

Quad/Graphics Inc N63 W23075 Main St ... Sussex WI 53089 414-566-6000 566-4646*
NYSE: QUAD ■ *Fax: Hum Res ■ Web: www.qg.com

Quadriscan Inc 6600 Rue Saint-urbain ... Montreal QC H2S3G8 514-277-6022
Web: quadriscan.com

Quartier Printing Company Inc
5795 Bridge St E Syracuse ... Syracuse NY 13057 315-449-0900
Web: www.quartierprinting.com

Queen City Printers Inc 701 Pine St ... Burlington VT 05401 802-864-4566
Web: www.qcpinc.com

Questmark Information Management Inc
9440 Kirby Dr ... Houston TX 77054 713-662-9022
Web: questmark.net

Quick Color Solutions Inc 829 Knox Rd ... Mc Leansville NC 27301 336-698-0951
Web: www.quickcolorsolutions.com

Quick Tab Ii Inc 241 Heritage Dr ... Tiffin OH 44883 419-448-6622
Web: www.qt2.com

R.C. Brayshaw & Company Inc 45 Waterloo St ... Warner NH 03278 603-456-3101
Web: www.rcbrayshaw.com

R.R. Donnelley Seymour Inc 709 A Ave E ... Seymour IN 47274 812-523-1800
Web: www.rrd.com

Raff Printing Inc PO Box 42365 ... Pittsburgh PA 15203 412-431-4044
Web: www.raffprinting.com

Rainbow Graphics Inc 933 Tower Rd ... Mundelein IL 60060 847-824-9600
Web: www.rainbowgraphics.com

Raintree Graphics Inc 5921 Richard St ... Jacksonville FL 32216 904-396-1653
Web: www.raintreegraphics.com

Ramsbottom Printing Inc 135 Waldron Rd ... Fall River MA 02720 508-730-2220
Web: www.rpiprinting.net

Rand Graphics Inc 500 S Florence St ... Wichita KS 67209 316-942-1218
Web: www.randgraphics.com

Range Inc 1022 Madison St ... Brainerd MN 56401 218-829-5982
Web: www.rangeprinting.com

Rapid Press Printing & Copy Center Inc
608 Lake St S ... Forest Lake MN 55025 651-464-6200
Web: www.rapidpressprinting.com

Rapid Printers of Monterey 201 Foam St ... Monterey CA 93940 831-373-1822
Web: www.rapidprinters.com

Raven Printing 325 S Union ... Lakewood CO 80228 303-989-9888
Web: www.ravenprinting.com

Regal Press Inc, The 129 Guild St ... Norwood MA 02062 781-769-3900 769-7361
TF: 800-447-3425 ■ Web: www.regalpress.com

Reindl Printing Inc 1300 Johnson St ... Merrill WI 54452 715-536-9537
Web: www.reindlprinting.com

Reischling Press Inc 3325 S 116th St Ste 161 ... Seattle WA 98168 206-905-5999
Web: www.rpiprint.com

Reni Publishing Inc 150 Third St SW ... Winter Haven FL 33880 863-294-2812
Web: www.reni.net

Replico Corp 7700 Arroyo Cir ... Gilroy CA 95020 408-842-8600
Web: www.replicocorp.com

Rhino Print Solutions Inc 13880 Mayfield Pl ... Richmond BC V6V2E4 604-232-5600
Web: rhinoprintsolutions.com

Richmond Printing LLC 5825 Schumacher ... Houston TX 77057 713-952-0800
Web: www.richmondprinting.com

Rider Dickerson Inc 815 Twenty-Fifth Ave ... Bellwood IL 60104 312-427-2926
Web: www.riderdickerson.com

Riegel Printing Company Inc One Graphics Dr ... Ewing NJ 08628 609-771-0555
Web: www.riegelprintinginc.com

Ries Graphics Ltd 12727 W Custer Ave ... Butler WI 53007 262-781-5720
Web: www.riesgraphics.com

Rinaldi Printing Co 4514 E Adamo Dr ... Tampa FL 33605 813-247-3921
Web: www.rinaldiprinting.com

Rink Printing Company Inc 814 S Main St ... South Bend IN 46601 574-232-7935
Web: www.rinkprinting.com

RMF Printing Technologies Inc 50 Pearl St ... Lancaster NY 14086 716-683-7500
Web: www.rmfprinting.com

Roberts Printing Co 207 E Eighth St ... Georgetown TX 78626 512-863-2323
Web: www.robpri.com

Robyn Inc 7717 W Britton Rd ... Oklahoma City OK 73132 405-722-4600
Web: www.robynpromo.com

Rocket Imaging Inc 12365 Rhea Dr ... Plainfield IL 60585 815-577-6315
Web: www.rprgraphics.com

Rogers Printing Inc PO Box 215 ... Ravenna MI 49451 231-853-2244 853-6558
TF: 800-622-5591 ■ Web: www.rogersprinting.net

Rotary Multiforms Inc
1340 E 11 Mile Rd ... Madison Heights MI 48071 586-558-7960
Web: www.rmi-printing.com

Rotary Offset Press Inc 6600 S 231st St ... Kent WA 98032 253-813-9900
Web: www.rotaryoffsetpress.com

Royal Conservatory of Music The
273 Bloor St W ... Toronto ON M5S1W2 416-408-2824
Web: www.rcmusic.ca

Royle Printing Co 745 S Bird St ... Sun Prairie WI 53590 608-837-5161
Web: www.royle.com

RP Graphics Group Inc 5990 Falbourne St ... Mississauga ON L5R3S7 905-507-8782
Web: rpgraphics.com

Salem Printing Company Inc
5670 Shattalon Dr ... Winston-salem NC 27105 336-744-9990
Web: www.esalem.net

Salt Lake Mailing & Printing Inc
1841 S Pioneer Rd ... Salt Lake City UT 84104 801-974-7600
Web: www.saltlakemailing.com

San Diego Printers 9190 Camino Santa Fe ... San Diego CA 92121 858-684-5200
Web: www.sdprinters.com

Sandy Alexander Inc 200 Entin Rd ... Clifton NJ 07014 973-470-8100 470-9269
Web: www.sandyinc.com

Santa Fe Professional Duplicating Inc
1248 San Felipe Ave ... Santa Fe NM 87505 505-983-3101
Web: www.ptig.com

Sauers Group Inc, The
1585 Roadhaven Dr ... Stone Mountain GA 30083 770-621-8888
Web: www.sauersgroup.com

Schawk Inc 1695 S River Rd ... Des Plaines IL 60018 847-827-9494 827-1264
NYSE: SGK ■ TF: 800-621-1909 ■ Web: www.schawk.com

Schmidt Printing Inc 1101 Frontage Rd NW ... Byron MN 55920 507-775-6400 775-6655
Web: www.schmidt.com

Schumann Printers Inc 701 S Main St ... Fall River WI 53932 920-484-3348 484-3661
Web: www.spiweb.com

Screenco Enterprises Nine Bell Rd ... Selma AL 36701 334-872-0051
Web: www.screenco.biz

Sekuworks LLC 9487 Dry Fork Rd ... Harrison OH 45030 513-202-1210
Web: www.sekuworks.com

Sennett Security Products
4212A Technology Ct ... Chantilly VA 20151 703-803-8880 803-8880
Web: banknote.com

Senton Printing & Packaging Inc
1669 Oxford St E ... London ON N5V2Z5 519-455-5500
Web: www.senton.com

Service Litho-Print Inc 50 W Fernau Ave ... Oshkosh WI 54901 920-231-3060
Web: www.service-litho.com

Sewell Printing Service Inc
2697 Apple Vly Rd NE ... Atlanta GA 30319 404-237-2553
Web: www.sewellprinting.com

Sexton Printing Inc 250 Lothenbach Ave ... St. Paul MN 55118 651-457-9255
Web: www.sextonprinting.com

Sharprint Silkscreen & Graphics Inc
4200 W Wrightwood Ave ... Chicago IL 60639 773-862-9300
Web: www.sharprint.com

Shea Brothers Inc 65 Innerbelt Rd ... Somerville MA 02143 617-623-2001
Web: www.sheabrothers.com

Shelton-Turnbull Printers Inc
3403 W Seventh Ave ... Eugene OR 97402 541-687-1214
Web: www.stprint.com

Sheridan Group 11311 McCormick Rd Ste 260 ... Hunt Valley MD 21031 410-785-7277 785-7217
TF: 800-352-2210 ■ Web: www.sheridan.com

Company / Address	City	State	ZIP	Phone	Fax
Sigler Companies Inc 3100 S Riverside Dr PO Box 887	Ames	IA	50010	515-232-6997	
Web: www.sigler.com					
Sign-ups & Banners Corp 2764 W T C Jester Blvd	Houston	TX	77018	713-682-7979	
Web: www.signupsandbanners.com					
Signature Printing Inc Five Almeida Ave	East Providence	RI	02914	401-438-1200	
Web: www.signatureprinters.com					
Sinclair Printing Co 4005 Whiteside St	Los Angeles	CA	90063	323-264-4000	
Web: www.sinclairprinting.com					
Sir Speedy Inc 26722 Plaza Dr	Mission Viejo	CA	92691	949-348-5000	348-5066
TF: 800-854-8297 ■ *Web:* www.sirspeedy.com					
Skinner & Kennedy Co 9451 Natural Bridge Rd	Saint Louis	MO	63134	314-426-2800	
Web: www.skinnerkennedy.com					
Slate Group Inc 6024 45th St	Lubbock	TX	79407	806-794-7752	
Web: www.copycraft.com					
SMS Productions Inc 10555 Guilford Rd Ste 114	Jessup	MD	20794	301-953-0011	
Web: www.smsproductions.com					
Solar Communications Inc 1150 Frontenac Rd	Naperville	IL	60563	630-983-1400	
Web: www.solarcommunications.com					
Solisco Inc 120 10e Rue	Scott	QC	G0S3G0	418-387-8908	
Web: www.solisco.com					
Solo Printing Inc 7860 NW 66th St	Miami	FL	33166	305-594-8699	599-5245
TF: 800-325-0118 ■ *Web:* www.soloprinting.com					
SOS Printing Inc 8135 Ronson Rd	San Diego	CA	92111	858-292-1800	
Web: www.sosprint.com					
Southland Printing Company Inc 213 Airport Dr	Shreveport	LA	71107	318-221-8662	
Web: www.southlandprinting.com					
Southwest Offset Printing Company Inc 13650 Gramercy Pl	Gardena	CA	90249	310-323-0112	
Web: www.southwestoffset.com					
Sp Mount 1306 E 55th St	Cleveland	OH	44103	216-881-3316	
Web: www.spmount.com					
Spangler Graphics LLC 2930 S 44th St	Kansas City	KS	66106	913-722-4500	
Web: www.spanglergraphics.com					
Spartan Graphics Inc 200 Applewood Dr	Sparta	MI	49345	616-887-8243	
Web: spartangraphics.com					
Spartan Printing Inc 320 109th St	Arlington	TX	76011	817-640-6341	
Web: paramount-consulting.com					
Spectrum Litho 4300 Business Ctr Dr	Fremont	CA	94538	510-438-9192	
Web: www.spectrumlithograph.com					
Spectrum Printing Company LLC 4651 S Butterfield Dr	Tucson	AZ	85714	520-571-1114	
Web: www.spectrumprintingcompany.com					
Speedpro Imaging Inc 15333 N Pima Rd Ste 100	Scottsdale	AZ	85260	480-422-4022	
Web: speedproimaging.com					
Sport Graphics Inc 3423 Park Davis Cir	Indianapolis	IN	46235	317-899-7000	
Web: www.sportg.com					
Springdot Inc 2611 Colerain Ave	Cincinnati	OH	45214	513-542-4000	
Web: www.springdot.com					
Sprint Copy Center 175 N Main St	Sebastopol	CA	95472	707-823-3900	
Web: www.sprintcopycenter.net					
Sprint Quality Printing Inc 3609 Silverside Rd	Wilmington	DE	19810	302-478-0720	
Web: www.sprintqp.com					
Sprint-Denver Inc 4999 Kingston St	Denver	CO	80239	303-371-0566	371-2341
Web: www.sprintdenver.com					
Square 1 Art LLC 5470 Oakbrook Pkwy Ste E	Norcross	GA	30093	678-906-2291	
Web: www.square1art.com					
St Joseph Communications 50 MacIntosh Blvd	Concord	ON	L4K4P3	905-660-3111	669-1972
TF General: 877-660-3111 ■ *Web:* www.stjoseph.com					
Stafford Printing Co 2707 Jefferson Davis Hwy	Stafford	VA	22554	540-659-4554	
Web: staffordprinting.com					
State Port Pilot 114 E Moore St	Southport	NC	28461	910-457-4568	
Web: stateportpilot.com					
Stella Color Inc 620 S Dakota St	Seattle	WA	98108	206-223-2303	
Web: www.stellacolor.com					
Stellar Printing Inc 3838 Ninth St	Long Island City	NY	11101	718-361-1600	
Web: www.stellarprinting.com					
Steven Label Corp 11926 Burke St	Santa Fe Springs	CA	90670	562-698-9971	
Web: www.stevenlabel.com					
Stolze Printing 3435 Hollenberg Dr	Bridgeton	MO	63044	314-209-1997	
Web: www.stolze.com					
StorterChilds Printing Company Inc 1540 NE Waldo Rd	Gainesville	FL	32641	352-376-2658	
Web: www.storterchilds.com					
Strathmore Co 2000 Gary Ln	Geneva	IL	60134	630-232-9677	232-0198
Web: www.strath.com					
Streeter Printing Inc 9880 Via Pasar	San Diego	CA	92126	858-566-0866	
Web: www.streeterprinting.com					
Strine Printing Co Inc 30 Grumbacher Rd	York	PA	17406	717-767-6602	505-3227
Stuyvesant Press Inc 119 Coit St	Irvington	NJ	07111	973-399-3880	
Web: stuyvesantpress.com					
Success Printing & Mailing Inc Ten Pearl St	Norwalk	CT	06850	203-847-1112	
Web: www.successprint.com					
Suddekor LLC 240 Bowles Rd	Agawam	MA	01001	413-821-9000	
Web: www.suddekorllc.com					
Sun Graphics LLC 1818 Broadway	Parsons	KS	67357	620-421-6200	
Web: www.sun-graphics.com					
Sun Printing 1800 Grand Ave	Wausau	WI	54403	715-845-4911	
Web: www.sunprinting.com					
Sunbelt Printing & Graphics 1691 Sands Pl Ste E	Marietta	GA	30067	770-988-0812	
Web: www.sunbeltprinting.com					
Suncraft Technologies Inc 1301 Frontenac Rd	Naperville	IL	60563	630-369-7900	639-7070
Web: www.suncraft-tech.com					
Sunkist Graphics Inc 401 E Sunset Rd	Henderson	NV	89011	702-566-9008	
Web: www.sunkistgrfx.com					
Sunset Printing 4522 1/2 Rosemead Blvd	Pico Rivera	CA	90660	562-692-3950	
Web: sunset-printing.com					
Super Color Digital LLC 16761 Hale Ave	Irvine	CA	92606	949-622-0010	622-0050
TF: 800-979-4446 ■ *Web:* supercolor.com					
SureSource LLC 20 Constitution Blvd South	Shelton	CT	06484	203-922-7500	
Web: www.suresource.com					
Suttle-Straus Inc 1000 Uniek Dr PO Box 370	Waunakee	WI	53597	608-849-1000	
Web: www.suttle-straus.com					
Swift Mailing Services Inc 794 Haunted Ln	Bensalem	PA	19020	215-638-4122	
Web: www.swiftmailing.com					
Swift Print Communication 1248 Research Blvd	Saint Louis	MO	63132	314-991-4300	
Web: www.printcommunications.com					
Symphony Printing Company Inc 19 21 Brook St	Belleville	NJ	07109	973-751-5100	
Web: www.symphonyprinting.com					
T K Direct 1288 Barclay Blvd	Buffalo Grove	IL	60089	847-541-8800	
Web: tkdirect.com					
TanaSeybert LLC 350 Michele Pl	Carlstadt	NY	07072	212-453-9300	
Web: www.tanaseybert.com					
Tectonics Industries Inc 24680 Mound Rd	Warren	MI	48091	586-755-6522	
Web: www.tectonicsindustries.com					
Tenenz Inc 1100 E 80th St	Minneapolis	MN	55420	952-888-2712	
Web: www.tenenz.com					
Tepel Brothers Printing Co 1725 John R Rd	Troy	MI	48083	248-743-2903	
Web: tepelbrothers.com					
Teton Machine Co 1805 NE Tenth Ave	Payette	ID	83661	208-642-9344	
Web: www.tetonmachine.com					
Teuteberg Inc 12200 W Wirth St	Wauwatosa	WI	53222	414-257-4110	
Web: www.teuteberg.com					
Tewell Warren Printing Co 4710 Lipan St	Denver	CO	80211	303-458-8505	
Web: www.tewellwarren.com					
Tidewater Direct LLC 300 Tidewater Dr	Centreville	MD	21617	410-758-1500	
Web: www.tidewaterdirect.com					
Tiger Press Administration 155 Industrial Dr	Northampton	MA	01060	413-585-1616	
Web: www.tigerpress.com					
Times Printing Company Inc 100 Industrial Dr	Random Lake	WI	53075	920-994-4396	994-2059*
**Fax:* Cust Svc ■ *TF:* 800-236-4396 ■ *Web:* www.timesprintingco.com					
Tko Enterprises Inc 2751 Stafford Rd Ste A	Plainfield	IN	46168	317-271-1398	
Web: www.tkographix.com					
Toppan Printing Company America Inc 1100 Randolph Rd	Somerset	NJ	08873	732-469-8400	469-1868*
**Fax:* Sales ■ *Web:* www.ta.toppan.com					
Total Printing Systems 103 E Morgan St	Newton	IL	62448	618-783-3614	
Web: www.tps1.com					
Transfer Express Inc 7650 Tyler Blvd	Mentor	OH	44060	440-918-1900	
Web: www.transferexpress.com					
Tranter Graphics Inc 8094 N State Rd 13	Syracuse	IN	46567	574-834-2626	
Web: www.trantergraphics.com					
Travers Printing Inc 32 Mission St	Gardner	MA	01440	978-632-0530	
Web: www.traversprinting.com					
Trend Offset Printing Services Inc 3791 Catalina St	Los Alamitos	CA	90720	562-598-2446	430-2373*
**Fax:* Cust Svc ■ *Web:* www.trendoffset.com					
Tri-State Financial Press LLC 109 N Fifth St	Saddle Brook	NJ	07663	201-226-9220	
Web: www.tsfpress.com					
Tri-state Printing Inc 120 Bester St Ste 101	Hagerstown	MD	21740	301-733-9560	
Web: www.tristateprinting.net					
Tristar Web Graphics Inc 4010 Airline Dr	Houston	TX	77022	713-691-0005	
Web: www.tristarholdings.com					
Triune Color Corp 2605 N River Rd	Cinnaminson	NJ	08077	856-829-5600	
Web: www.triunecolor.com					
Trojan Press Inc 1635 Burlington St	Kansas City	MO	64116	816-221-6477	
Web: www.trojanpressinc.com					
Troyk Printing Corp 9980 S Oakwood Park Dr	Franklin	WI	53132	414-423-2200	
Web: www.troyk.com					
Tucker Printers Inc 270 Middle Rd	Henrietta	NY	14467	585-359-3030	
Web: www.tuckerprinters.com					
Tucker-Castleberry Printing Inc 3500 McCall Pl	Atlanta	GA	30340	770-454-1580	
Web: www.tuckercastleberry.com					
Tursso Companies Inc 223 Plato Blvd E	St. Paul	MN	55107	651-222-8445	
Web: www.tursso.com					
Tvp Color Graphics Inc 230 Roma Jean Pkwy	Streamwood	IL	60107	630-837-3600	
Web: www.thinkvariable.com					
Two b Printing Inc 625 Ne 42nd St	Oakland Park	FL	33334	954-566-4886	
Web: twobprinting.com					
Typecraft Press Inc 45 S 23rd St	Pittsburgh	PA	15203	412-488-1600	
Web: www.typecraftpress.com					
U B S Printing Group Inc 2577 Research Dr	Corona	CA	92882	951-273-7900	
Web: www.ubsprint.com					
Ultra Flex Packaging Corp 975 Essex St	Brooklyn	NY	11208	718-272-9100	
Web: www.ultraflex.com					
Ultra-Tech Printing Co 5851 Crossroads Commerce	Grand Rapids	MI	49519	616-249-0500	
Web: www.utprinting.com					
Uni-Graphic Inc 110 Commerce Way Ste 6	Woburn	MA	01801	781-231-7200	938-7727
Web: www.uni-graphic.com					
Unicom Graphics Ltd 4501 Manitoba Rd Se	Calgary	AB	T2G4B9	403-287-2020	
Web: www.unicomgraphics.com					
Unique Litho Inc Nine Inverness Dr E	Englewood	CO	80112	303-830-2999	
Web: www.uniquelitho.com					
United Reprographics LLC 1750 Fourth Ave S	Seattle	WA	98134	206-382-1177	
Web: www.unitedreprographics.com					
Universal Printing Co 1234 S Kings Hwy	Saint Louis	MO	63110	314-771-6900	771-7987
Web: www.universalprintingco.com					

	City	State	Zip	Phone	Fax
USS Corp 780 Frelinghuysen Ave *Web:* usscorp.com	Newark	NJ	07114	973-242-1110	
Ussery Printing Company Inc 3402 Century Cir *Web:* www.usseryprinting.com	Irving	TX	75062	972-438-8344	
Valassis Communications Inc 19975 Victor Pkwy *NYSE:* VCI ■ **Fax:* Hum Res ■ *TF:* 800-437-0479 ■ *Web:* www.valassis.com	Livonia	MI	48152	734-591-3000	591-4994*
Valley Offset Printing Inc 160 S Sheridan Ave *Web:* www.valleyoffset.com	Valley Center	KS	67147	316-755-0061	
Valley Printing Company Inc 3919 Vanderbilt Rd *Web:* valleyprinting.net	Birmingham	AL	35217	205-841-2746	
Vectra Visual 3950 Business Pk Dr *TF:* 800-862-2341 ■ *Web:* www.msbv.com	Columbus	OH	43204	614-351-6868	351-4569
Ventura Printing 1593 Palma Dr *Web:* www.v3corporation.com	Ventura	CA	93006	805-981-2600	
Victorystore.Com Inc 5200 SW 30Th St *TF:* 866-241-2295 ■ *Web:* www.victorystore.com	Davenport	IA	52802	866-241-2295	
Villanti & Sons, Printers Inc 15 Catamount Dr *Web:* www.villanti.com	Milton	VT	05468	802-864-0723	
Vision Envelope Inc 2451 Executive St *Web:* www.visionenvelope.com	Charlotte	NC	28208	704-392-9090	
Vision Graphics Inc 5610 Boeing Dr *Web:* www.visiongraphics-inc.com	Loveland	CO	80538	970-679-9000	
Visions Inc 8801 Wyoming Ave N *Web:* www.visionsfirst.com	Brooklyn Park	MN	55445	763-425-4251	
Vista Color Corp 1401 NW 78th Ave *Web:* www.vistacolor.com	Miami	FL	33126	305-635-2000	
Walter Snyder Printer Inc 691 River St *Web:* www.snyderprinter.com	Troy	NY	12180	518-272-8881	
Warren Printing & Mailing Inc 5000 Eagle Rock Blvd *Web:* print-mail.com	Los Angeles	CA	90041	323-258-2621	
Watermark Group Inc, The 4271 Gate Crst *Web:* www.thewatermarkgroup.com	San Antonio	TX	78217	210-599-0400	
Watson Label Products Corp 10616 Trenton Ave *TF:* 800-678-6715 ■ *Web:* www.wlp.com	Saint Louis	MO	63132	314-493-9300	493-9390
Watt Printing Co 4544 Hinckley Industrial Pkwy *Web:* www.wattprinters.com	Cleveland	OH	44109	216-398-2000	
We Print Today LLC 66 Summer St *Web:* www.weprinttoday.com	Kingston	MA	02364	781-585-6021	
Weatherall Printing Co 1349 Cliff Gookin Blvd *Web:* www.weatherallprinting.com	Tupelo	MS	38801	662-842-5284	
Web Offset Printing Company Inc 12198 44th St N *Web:* www.weboffsetprint.com	Clearwater	FL	33762	727-572-7488	
WebbMason Inc 10830 Gilroy Rd *Web:* www.webbmason.com	Hunt Valley	MD	21031	410-785-1111	
Weldon Williams & Lick Inc 711 N A St *TF:* 800-242-4995 ■ *Web:* www.wwlinc.com	Fort Smith	AR	72901	479-783-4113	783-7050
Wells Printing Company Inc 6030 Perimeter Pkwy *Web:* www.wellsprinting.com	Montgomery	AL	36116	334-281-3449	
Wendling Printing Co 111 Beech St *Web:* www.wendlingprinting.net	Newport	KY	41071	859-261-8300	
Wentworth Printing Corp 101 N 12th St *Web:* www.wentworthprinting.com	West Columbia	SC	29169	803-796-9990	
West Metro Printing Co 33100 Industrial Rd *Web:* www.westmetroprinting.com	Livonia	MI	48150	734-522-0410	
West Press Printing & Copying 1663 W Grant Rd *Web:* westpress.com	Tucson	AZ	85745	520-624-4939	
West-Camp Press Inc 39 Collegeview Rd *Web:* www.westcamp.com	Westerville	OH	43081	614-882-2378	
Western Pad 391 Thor Pl *Web:* www.westernpad.com	Brea	CA	92821	714-671-1900	
Westland Enterprises Inc 3621 Stewart Rd *Web:* www.westlandenterprises.com	Forestville	MD	20747	301-736-0600	
Westland Printers Inc 14880 Sweitzer Ln *Web:* www.westlandprinters.com	Laurel	MD	20707	301-384-7700	384-2616
Wetzel Brothers LLC 2401 E Edgerton *Web:* www.wetzelbrothers.com	Cudahy	WI	53110	414-271-5444	
Wildes-spirit Design & Printing 4321 Charles Crossing Dr *Web:* www.wildes-spirit.com	White Plains	MD	20695	301-870-4141	
William George Printing LLC 3469 Black and Decker Rd *Web:* m.wgprinting.com	Hope Mills	NC	28348	910-221-2700	
Williamson Printing Corp 6700 Denton Dr *Web:* www.twpc.com	Dallas	TX	75235	214-904-2100	
Wingate Packaging Inc 4347 Indeco Ct *Web:* www.wingate-packaging.com	Cincinnati	OH	45241	513-745-8600	
Winston Printing Company Inc 8095 N Point Blvd *Web:* www.winstonpackaging.com	Winston Salem	NC	27106	336-759-0051	
Wisconsin Web Offset LLC 21045 Enterprise Ave *Web:* wwoffset.com	Brookfield	WI	53045	262-395-2000	
Wizbang Solutions Inc 6747 E 50th Ave *Web:* www.wizbangsolutions.com	Commerce City	CO	80022	720-974-5623	
Wolf Printing 1200 Haines Rd *Web:* www.wolfprinting.com	York	PA	17402	717-755-1560	
Woolverton Printing Co 6714 Chancellor Dr *Web:* www.woolverton.com	Cedar Falls	IA	50613	319-277-2616	
Wright Printing Co 11616 I St *Web:* www.wright-print.com	Omaha	NE	68137	402-334-0788	
Xlibris Corp 1663 Liberty Dr Ste 200 *TF:* 888-795-4274 ■ *Web:* www.xlibris.com	Bloomington	IN	47403	888-795-4274	
Yellowdog Printing & Graphics LLC 490 S Santa Fe Dr Unit A *Web:* www.yellowdogprinting.com	Denver	CO	80223	303-765-2000	
Yoder & Armstrong Printing 627 E Baltimore Ave *Web:* yoderandarmstrong.com	Lansdowne	PA	19050	610-622-6118	
Yurchak Printing Inc 920 Links Ave *Web:* www.yurchak.com	Landisville	PA	17538	717-399-0209	
Z Three - Printing Co 902 W Main St *Web:* www.threez.com	Teutopolis	IL	62467	217-857-3153	857-3010
Zebra Graphics Inc 1611 Kentucky Ave *Web:* www.zebragraphics.com	Paducah	KY	42003	270-443-4771	
Zoo Printing Inc 4730 Eastern Ave *Web:* www.zooprinting.com	Bell	CA	90201	310-253-7751	

631 PRINTING & PHOTOCOPYING SUPPLIES

	City	State	Zip	Phone	Fax
Abco Distribution Inc 6282 Proprietors Rd *TF:* 800-821-9435 ■ *Web:* www.printingbyabco.com	Worthington	OH	43085	800-821-9435	
Anderson & Vreeland Inc Eight Evans St *Web:* andersonvreeland.com	Fairfield	NJ	07004	973-227-2270	
Art Lithocraft Co 219 W 18th St *Web:* www.artlithocraft.com	Kansas City	MO	64108	816-421-8335	
Balance Innovations LLC 11011 Eicher Dr *Web:* balanceinnovations.com	Lenexa	KS	66219	913-599-1177	
Buckeye Business Products Inc 3830 Kelley Ave **Fax Area Code:* 216 ■ *TF:* 800-837-4323 ■ *Web:* www.buckeyebusiness.com	Cleveland	OH	44114	800-837-4323	881-6105*
Chromaline Corp 4832 Grand Ave *TF:* 800-328-4261 ■ *Web:* www.chromaline.com	Duluth	MN	55807	218-628-2217	628-3245
Color Imaging Inc 4350 Peachtree Industrial Blvd Ste 100 **Fax Area Code:* 800 ■ *TF:* 800-783-1090 ■ *Web:* www.colorimaging.com	Norcross	GA	30071	770-840-1090	783-9010*
Convertech Inc 353 Richard Mine Rd *Web:* www.convertech.com	Wharton	NJ	07885	973-328-1850	
Drent Goebel North America Inc 2583 Chomedey Blvd *Web:* www.rdpmarathon.com	Laval	QC	H7T2R2	450-687-7262	
DuraLine Imaging Inc 110 Commercial Blvd *TF:* 866-359-2506 ■ *Web:* www.duralineimaging.com	Flat Rock	NC	28731	828-692-1301	
Equipements De Transformation Imac (E.T.I.) Inc 1490-H Nobel St *Web:* www.eticonverting.com	Boucherville	QC	J4B5H3	450-641-7900	
ExOne Co 127 Industry Blvd *Web:* www.exone.com	North Huntingdon	PA	15642	724-863-9663	
Glunz & Jensen K&F Inc 12633 Industrial Dr *Web:* www.glunz-jensen.com	Granger	IN	46530	574-272-9950	
Graphic Controls LLC 400 Exchange St *TF:* 800-669-1535 ■ *Web:* www.graphiccontrols.com	Buffalo	NY	14204	800-669-1535	347-2420
Hurst Chemical Co 2360 Eastman Ave Ste 108 *TF Cust Svc:* 800-723-2004 ■ *Web:* www.hurstchemical.com	Oxnard	CA	93030	800-723-2004	723-2005
Image One Corp 13201 Capital Ave *TF:* 800-799-5377 ■ *Web:* www.imageoneway.com	Oak Park	MI	48237	248-414-9955	414-9951
Ink Technology Corp 18320 Lanken Ave *TF:* 800-633-2826 ■ *Web:* www.inktechnology.com	Cleveland	OH	44119	216-486-6720	486-6003
IQinVision Inc 33122 Valle Rd *Web:* www.iqeye.com	San Juan Capistrano	CA	92675	949-369-8100	
ITW Coding Products 111 W Pk Dr *Web:* www.codingproducts.com	Kalkaska	MI	49646	231-258-5521	258-6120
Kase Equipment Corp 7400 Hub Pkwy *Web:* www.kaseequip.com	Valley View	OH	44125	216-642-9040	
Ko-Rec-Type Div Barouh Eaton Allen Corp 67 Kent Ave *Web:* www.korectype.com	Brooklyn	NY	11249	718-782-2601	
LexJet Corp 1680 Fruitville Rd 3rd Fl *TF:* 800-453-9538 ■ *Web:* www.lexjet.com	Sarasota	FL	34236	941-330-1210	330-1220
Light Impressions 2340 Brighton Henrietta Town Line Rd *TF:* 800-975-6429 ■ *Web:* www.lightimpressionsdirect.com	Rochester	NY	14623	800-975-6429	786-7939
Micro Solutions Enterprises (MSE) 8201 Woodley Ave *TF:* 800-673-4968 ■ *Web:* www.mse-usa.com	Van Nuys	CA	91406	818-407-7500	407-7575
NER Data Products Inc 307 S Delsea Dr **Fax Area Code:* 856 ■ *TF:* 888-637-3282 ■ *Web:* www.nerdata.com	Glassboro	NJ	08028	888-637-3282	881-5524*
Pad Print Machinery of Vermont Inc 201 Tennis Way *Web:* www.epsvt.com	East Dorset	VT	05253	802-362-0844	
Perfecopy Co 103 W 61st St	Westmont	IL	60559	630-769-9901	
Rayven Inc 431 Griggs St N *TF Cust Svc:* 800-878-3776 ■ *Web:* www.rayven.com	Saint Paul	MN	55104	651-642-1112	642-9497
Ricoh Printing Systems America Inc 2390 Ward Ave Ste A *Web:* www.rpsa.ricoh.com	Simi Valley	CA	93065	805-578-4000	578-4001
Rima Enterprises Inc 5340 Argosy Ave *Web:* www.rima-system.com	Huntington Beach	CA	92649	714-893-4534	
RVision Inc 2445 Fifth Ave Ste 450 *Web:* www.rvisionusa.com	San Diego	CA	92101	619-233-1403	
Spitz Inc 700 Brandywine Dr *Web:* www.spitzinc.com	Chadds Ford	PA	19317	610-459-5200	
Texas Lift-Off Correction Ribbon 1700 Surveyor Blvd Ste 110	Carrollton	TX	75006	972-416-8100	416-9690
Thistle Roller Company Inc 209 Van Norman Rd *Web:* thistleroller.com	Montebello	CA	90640	562-948-3705	
Tomoegawa USA Inc 742 Glenn Ave *Web:* www.tomoegawa.com	Wheeling	IL	60090	847-541-3001	459-7150

Phone Fax

Western Printing Machinery Co
9229 Ivanhoe Ave .... Schiller Park IL 60176 847-678-1740
Web: www.wpm.com

WNC Supply LLC 37841 N 16th St .... Phoenix AZ 85086 623-594-4602 594-3769
TF: 800-538-5108 ■ *Web:* www.westnc.com

Xenetech Usa Inc 12139 Airline Hwy .... Baton Rouge LA 70817 225-752-0225
Web: www.xenetech.com

632 PRINTING & PUBLISHING EQUIPMENT & SYSTEMS

SEE ALSO Printers p. 2013

Phone Fax

Apex Machine Co 3000 NE 12th Terr .... Fort Lauderdale FL 33334 954-566-1572 563-2844
Web: www.apexmachine.com

AWT World Trade Inc 4321 N Knox Ave .... Chicago IL 60641 773-777-7100 777-0909
Web: www.awt-gpi.com

Baldwin Technology Co Inc
2 Trap Falls Rd Ste 402 .... Shelton CT 06484 203-402-1000 402-5500
NYSE: BLD ■ *TF:* 800-728-5839 ■ *Web:* www.baldwintech.com

BMP America Inc 11625 Maple Ridge Rd .... Medina NY 14103 585-798-0950 798-4272
Web: www.bmpworldwide.com

Brackett Inc 451 Forbes Field Bldg 451 J Ste .... Topeka KS 66619 785-862-2205 862-1127
TF: 800-255-3506 ■ *Web:* www.brackett-inc.com

Brandtjen & Kluge Inc
539 Blanding Woods Rd..................... Saint Croix Falls WI 54024 715-483-3265 483-1640
TF: 800-826-7320 ■ *Web:* www.kluge.biz

Burgess Industries Inc (BII)
7500 Doone Ave N Ste 111..................... Brooklyn Park MN 55428 763-553-7800 553-9289
TF: 800-233-2589 ■ *Web:* www.burgessind.com

CODA Inc 30 Industrial Ave .... Mahwah NJ 07430 201-825-7400 825-8133
Web: www.codamount.com

Craftsmen Machinery Co
1257 Worcester Rd Unit 167..................... Framingham MA 01701 508-376-2001 376-2003
Web: www.craftsmenmachinery.com

Delphax Technologies Inc 6100 W 110th St .... Bloomington MN 55438 952-939-9000 939-1151*
OTC: DLPX ■ **Fax:* Cust Svc ■ *Web:* www.delphax.com

Goss International Americas Inc
121 Technology Dr .... Durham NH 03824 603-749-6600 750-6860
Web: www.gossinternational.com

Graphic Innovators Inc
855 Morse Ave .... Elk Grove Village IL 60007 847-718-1516 718-1517
Web: www.graphicinnovators.com

Gravograph-New Hermes Inc 2200 Northmont Pkwy..... Duluth GA 30096 770-623-0331 533-7637*
**Fax Area Code:* 800 ■ *TF:* 800-843-7637 ■ *Web:* www.gravograph.com

Heidelberg USA Inc 1000 Gutenberg Dr .... Kennesaw GA 30144 770-419-6500 419-6550
TF Cust Svc: 888-472-9655 ■ *Web:* www.us.heidelberg.com

LasscoWizer Inc 485 Hague St .... Rochester NY 14606 585-436-1934 464-8665
TF: 800-854-6595 ■ *Web:* www.lasscowizer.com

MAN Roland Inc 800 E Oak Hill Dr.................. Westmont IL 60559 630-920-2000
Web: manrolandsheetfed.com

Mark Andy Inc
18081 Chesterfield Airport Rd .... Chesterfield MO 63005 636-532-4433 532-4701*
**Fax:* Cust Svc ■ *TF:* 800-700-6275 ■ *Web:* www.markandy.com

Pamarco Global Graphics 235 E 11th Ave............ Roselle NJ 07203 908-241-1200 241-4237
TF: 800-526-2180 ■ *Web:* www.pamarcoglobal.com

Presstek Inc 55 Executive Dr.......................... Hudson NH 03051 603-595-7000 546-4234
NASDAQ: PRST ■ *TF:* 800-422-3616 ■ *Web:* www.presstek.com

Rosback Co 125 Hawthorne Ave.................. Saint Joseph MI 49085 269-983-2582 983-2516
TF: 800-542-2420 ■ *Web:* www.rosbackcompany.com

Stevens Technology LLC 5700 E Belknap St .... Fort Worth TX 76117 817-831-3500 759-4080
Web: www.stevenstechnology.com

Stolle Machinery Co LLC 6949 S Potomac St .... Centennial CO 80112 303-708-9044 708-9045
TF: 800-433-8333 ■ *Web:* www.stollemachinery.com

Xerox Corp 45 Glover Ave PO Box 4505 .... Norwalk CT 06856 203-968-3000
NYSE: XRX ■ *TF:* 800-327-9753 ■ *Web:* www.xerox.com

633 PRISON INDUSTRIES

Prison industries are programs established by federal and state governments that provide work for inmates while they are incarcerated as well as on-the-job training to help them become employable on release. At the same time, prison industries provide quality goods and services at competitive prices.

Phone Fax

Alabama Correctional Industries
1400 Lloyd St .... Montgomery AL 36107 334-261-3600 240-3162
TF: 800-224-7007 ■ *Web:* www.aci.alabama.gov

Arizona Correctional Industries
3701 W Cambridge Ave .... Phoenix AZ 85009 602-272-7600 255-3108
Web: aci.az.gov

Arkansas Correctional Industries (ACI)
2403 E Harding St .... Pine Bluff AR 71601 870-850-8431 850-8440
TF: 877-635-7213 ■ *Web:* www.acicatalog.com

Badger State Industries (BSI)
3099 E Washington Ave PO Box 8990 .... Madison WI 53708 608-240-5200 240-3320
TF: 800-862-1086 ■ *Web:* www.buybsi.com

California Prison Industry Authority
560 E Natoma St.. Folsom CA 95630 916-358-2733 358-2660*
**Fax:* Cust Svc ■ *Web:* www.pia.ca.gov

Cornhusker State Industries
800 Pioneers Blvd .... Lincoln NE 68502 402-471-4597 471-1236
TF: 800-348-7537 ■ *Web:* www.nebraska.gov

Correctional Enterprises of Connecticut
24 Wolcott Hill Rd.............................. Wethersfield CT 06109 860-263-6839 263-6838
TF: 800-842-1146 ■ *Web:* www.ct.gov

Delaware Correctional Industries 245 McKee Rd........ Dover DE 19904 302-739-5601 739-1608
Web: doc.delaware.gov

Federal Prison Industries Inc
320 First St NW .... Washington DC 20534 800-827-3168
TF: 800-827-3168 ■ *Web:* www.unicor.gov

Phone Fax

Georgia Correctional Industries
2984 Clifton Springs Rd .... Decatur GA 30034 404-244-5100 244-5141
TF: 800-282-7130 ■ *Web:* www.gci-ga.com

Idaho Correctional Industries
1301 N OrchaRd Rd Ste 110.......................... Boise ID 83705 208-577-5555 577-5545
Web: www.ci.idaho.gov

Iowa Prison Industries (IPI)
1445 E Grand Ave............................... Des Moines IA 50316 515-242-5770 242-5779
TF: 800-670-4537 ■ *Web:* www.iaprisonind.com

Kansas Correctional Industries PO Box 2 .... Lansing KS 66043 913-727-3249 727-2331
Web: kancorind.com

Kentucky Correctional Industries
1041 Leestown Rd .... Frankfort KY 40601 502-573-1040 573-1050
TF: 800-828-9524 ■ *Web:* www.kci.ky.gov

Louisiana Prison Enterprises
PO Box 94304 .... Baton Rouge LA 70804 225-342-6633 342-2022
Web: www.doc.louisiana.gov

Maryland Correctional Enterprises (MCE)
7275 Waterloo Rd................................... Jessup MD 20794 410-540-5454 540-5570
Web: mce.md.gov

Massachusetts Correctional Industries
1 Industries Dr Bldg A PO Box 188.................. Norfolk MA 02056 508-850-1070 850-1091
TF: 800-222-2211 ■ *Web:* www.mass.gov

Michigan State Industries 5656 S Cedar St........... Lansing MI 48909 517-373-4277 241-9063*
**Fax:* Hum Res ■ *Web:* www.michigan.gov

Mississippi Prison Industries Corp
663 N State St..................................... Jackson MS 39202 601-969-5750 969-5757
Web: www.mpic.net

Missouri Vocational Enterprises
1717 Industrial Dr PO Box 1898................. Jefferson City MO 65102 573-751-6663 751-9197
TF Sales: 800-392-8486 ■ *Web:* www.doc.mo.gov

New Hampshire Correctional Industries (NHCI)
105 Pleasant St PO Box 1806....................... Concord NH 03302 603-271-5600 271-5643
Web: www.nh.gov/nhdoc

New Jersey Bureau of State Use Industries
163 N Olden Ave PO Box 867........................ Trenton NJ 08625 800-321-6524 633-2495*
**Fax Area Code:* 609 ■ *TF:* 800-321-6524 ■ *Web:* www.state.nj.us/deptcor

New York Correctional Industries 550 Broadway........ Albany NY 12204 518-436-6321 436-6007
TF: 800-436-6321 ■ *Web:* www.corcraft.org

North Carolina Correction Enterprises
2020 Yonkers Rd .... Raleigh NC 27604 919-716-3600 716-3974
Web: www.doc.state.nc.us

Ohio Penal Industries (OPI) 1221 McKinley Ave ...... Columbus OH 43222 614-752-0287 752-0303
TF: 800-237-3454 ■ *Web:* www.opi.state.oh.us

Oklahoma Correctional Industries
3402 N Martin Luther King Ave.................. Oklahoma City OK 73111 405-425-7500 425-2838*
**Fax:* Cust Svc ■ *TF:* 800-522-3565 ■ *Web:* www.ocisales.com

PEN Products 2010 E New York St .... Indianapolis IN 46201 317-955-6800 234-7635
TF: 800-736-2550 ■ *Web:* www.in.gov

Pennsylvania Correctional Industries
PO Box 47 .... Camp Hill PA 17001 717-425-7292 425-7291
TF General: 877-673-3724 ■ *Web:* www.pci.state.pa.us

Prison Rehabilitative Industries & Diversified Enterprises Inc (PRIDE)
223 Morrison Rd Ste 200 .... Brandon FL 33511 813-324-8700 890-2132
TF: 877-283-6819 ■ *Web:* www.prideenterprises.org

Rhode Island Correctional Industries
40 Howard Ave .... Cranston RI 02920 401-462-2611

Rough Rider Industries 3303 E Main Ave............. Bismarck ND 58506 701-328-6161 328-6164
TF: 800-732-0557 ■ *Web:* www.roughriderindustries.com

Silver State Industries 3955 W Russell Rd .... Las Vegas NV 89118 702-682-3147 486-9908
Web: www.ssi.nv.gov

South Carolina Prison Industries
4444 Broad River Rd.............................. Columbia SC 29210 803-896-8516 896-2173*
**Fax:* Cust Svc ■ *Web:* www.doc.sc.gov

Tennessee Rehabilitative Initiative in Correction (TRICOR)
240 Great Cir Rd Ste 310 .... Nashville TN 37228 615-741-5705 741-2747
TF: 800-958-7426 ■ *Web:* www.tricor.org

Texas Correctional Industries PO Box 4013......... Huntsville TX 77342 936-437-6048 437-6040
Web: www.tci.tdcj.state.tx.us

Utah Correctional Industries
14072 S Pony Express Rd .... Draper UT 84020 801-576-7700 523-9753
Web: uci.utah.gov

Vermont Correctional Industries
103 S Main St.................................... Waterbury VT 05671 802-323-6214 241-1475
Web: www.vowp.com

Virginia Correctional Enterprises
8030 White Bark Terr .... Richmond VA 23237 804-743-4100 743-2206
Web: www.govce.net

Washington Correctional Industries
801 88th Ave SE .... Tumwater WA 98501 360-725-9100 753-0219
Web: www.washingtonci.com

West Virginia Correctional Industries
617 Leon Sullivan Way........................... Charleston WV 25301 304-558-6054 558-6056
TF: 800-525-5381 ■ *Web:* wvcorrectionalindustries.com

634 PROFESSIONAL EMPLOYER ORGANIZATIONS (PEOS)

Companies listed here contractually assume human resources responsibilities for client companies in exchange for a fee, thus allowing the client company to focus on its true company business. The PEO establishes and maintains an employer relationship with the workers assigned to its client companies, with the PEO and the client company each having specific rights and responsibilities toward the employees.

Phone Fax

A-1 Contract Staffing Inc 3829 Coconut Palm Dr .... Tampa FL 33619 813-620-1661
Web: www.a-1contractstaffing.com

AB Staffing Solutions LLC
2680 S Val Vista Dr Bldg 10 Ste 152 .... Gilbert AZ 85295 480-345-6668
Web: www.abstaffing.com

Abacus Corp 610 Gusryan St .... Baltimore MD 21224 410-633-1900
Web: www.abacuscorporation.com

Phone / Fax

Accion Labs US Inc 1121 Boyce Rd Ste 1400 .... Pittsburgh PA 15241 412-979-8111
Web: accionlabs.com

Accord Hum Res Inc 210 Pk Ave Ste 1200 .... Oklahoma City OK 73102 405-232-9888 232-9899

Adams Keegan Inc 6055 Primacy Pkwy Ste 300 .... Memphis TN 38119 901-683-5353 820-0472
TF: 800-621-1308 ■ *Web:* www.adamskeegan.com

ADP TotalSource Co 10200 Sunset Dr .... Miami FL 33173 305-630-1000
TF: 800-447-3237 ■ *Web:* www.adp.com

Advice Media LLC PO Box 982064 .... Park City UT 84098 800-260-9497
TF: 800-260-9497 ■ *Web:* advicemedia.com

Agile Frameworks LLC 1826 Buerkle Rd .... Saint Paul MN 55110 651-487-3245
Web: www.agileframeworks.com

Alcott Group 71 Executive Blvd .... Farmingdale NY 11735 631-420-0100 420-1894
TF: 888-425-2688 ■ *Web:* www.alcottgroup.com

Alithya Group Inc 2875 Laurier Blvd Ste 1250 .... Quebec QC G1V2M2 418-650-2866
Web: www.alithya.com

Allevity HR & Payroll 870 Manzanita Ct Ste A .... Chico CA 95926 530-345-2486 345-8486
TF: 800-447-8233 ■ *Web:* www.allevityhr.com

Allied Employer Group
4400 Buffalo Gap Rd Ste 4500 .... Abilene TX 79606 325-695-5822 692-9660
TF: 800-495-3836 ■ *Web:* www.coemployer.com

AlphaStaff Inc
800 Corporate Dr Ste 600 .... Fort Lauderdale FL 33334 954-267-1760 632-8090*
**Fax Area Code:* 866 ■ *TF:* 888-335-9545 ■ *Web:* www.alphastaff.com

ALTRES Inc 967 Kapiolani Blvd .... Honolulu HI 96814 808-591-4940 591-4914
TF: 888-425-8737 ■ *Web:* www.altres.com

Assent Consulting Inc 10054 Pasadena Ave .... Cupertino CA 95014 408-366-8820 610-3885*
**Fax Area Code:* 662 ■ *TF:* 800-747-0940 ■ *Web:* www.docsglobal.com

Axcet HR Solutions
Axet 8325 Lenexa Dr Ste 410 .... Lenexa KS 66214 913-383-2999 383-2949
TF: 800-801-7557 ■ *Web:* www.axcethr.com

Barrett Business Services Inc
8100 NE Pkwy Dr Ste 200 .... Vancouver WA 98662 360-828-0700 828-0701
NASDAQ: BBSI ■ *TF:* 800-494-5669 ■ *Web:* www.barrettbusiness.com

Bco Inc 799 Middlesex Tpke .... Billerica MA 01821 978-663-2525
Web: www.bco-inc.com

Beacon Hill Staffing Group LLC 152 Bowdoin St .... Boston MA 02108 617-326-4000 227-1220
Web: www.beaconhillstaffing.com

Bedroc Inc 3351 Aspen Grove Dr Ste 350 .... Franklin TN 37067 615-815-1785
Web: www.bedroc.com

Bettinger The Company Inc
42 S 15th St Ste 1210 .... Philadelphia PA 19102 215-564-0700
Web: www.bettingerco.com

BlueRange Technology Inc
2590 Sheridan Garden Dr .... Oakville ON L6J7R2 905-829-5333
Web: www.bluerangetech.com

Brandmovers Inc 590 Means St Ste 250 .... Atlanta GA 30318 888-463-4933
TF: 888-463-4933 ■ *Web:* www.brandmovers.com

Burnett Cos Consolidated Inc
9800 Richmond Ave Ste 800 .... Houston TX 77042 713-977-4777 977-7533
Web: www.burnettstaffing.com

Cardinal Path LLC 301 W Warner Rd Ste 136 .... Tempe AZ 85284 480-285-1622
Web: www.cardinalpath.com

Careers Express 234 Mall Blvd Ste 120 .... Kng Of Prussa PA 19406 610-768-1788
Web: careersexpress.com

Century II Staffing Inc
278 Franklin Rd Ste 350 .... Brentwood TN 37027 615-665-9060 665-1833
Web: www.centuryii.net

Chipton-ross Inc 343 Main St .... El Segundo CA 90245 310-414-7800 414-7808
TF: 800-927-9318 ■ *Web:* www.chiptonross.com

Co-Advantage Resources
111 W Jefferson St Ste 100 .... Orlando FL 32801 407-422-8448
TF: 800-868-1016 ■ *Web:* www.coadvantage.com

Cohen Brown Management Group
11835 Olympic Blvd Ste 920 .... Los Angeles CA 90064 310-966-1001
Web: www.cbmg.com

CrowdSource Solutions Inc 33 Bronze Pointe .... Swansea IL 62226 855-276-9376
TF: 855-276-9376 ■ *Web:* www.crowdsource.com

Cyber 360 Solutions Inc 607 N Ave Ste 15 .... Wakefield MA 01880 781-438-4380
Web: www.cyber360solutions.com

Datacore Consulting LLC
5755 Granger Rd Ste 777 .... Independence OH 44131 216-398-8499
Web: www.datacoreonline.com

DecisionHR Inc
100 Carillon Pkwy Ste 350 .... St. Petersburg FL 33716 727-572-7331
Web: www.decisionhr.com

Destiny Corp 2075 Silas Deane Hwy .... Rocky Hill CT 06067 860-721-1684
Web: www.destinycorp.com

Dismas Distribution Services LLC
6772 Kilowatt Cir .... Blacklick OH 43004 614-861-2525
Web: www.dismas.net

Diversified Hum Res Inc
3020 E Camelback Rd Ste 213 .... Phoenix AZ 85016 480-941-5588 553-4684*
**Fax Area Code:* 602 ■ *TF:* 888-870-5588 ■ *Web:* www.dhr.net

Doherty Employment Group 7625 Parklawn Ave .... Edina MN 55435 952-832-8383 356-1953
TF Sales: 888-297-0495 ■ *Web:* www.dohertyemployment.com

Einstein HR Inc 3805 Crestwood Pkwy Ste 100 .... Duluth GA 30096 770-962-1700
Web: www.einsteinhr.com

Employee & Family Resources Inc (EFR)
505 Fifth Ave Ste 600 .... Des Moines IA 50309 515-288-9020
Web: www.efr.org

Employee Management Services 435 Elm St .... Cincinnati OH 45202 513-651-3244 381-2764
TF: 888-651-1536 ■ *Web:* www.emshro.com

Employer's Hum Res Inc (EHRI)
75899 State Hwy 16 .... Wagoner OK 74467 918-485-9404 485-9317

Employers Choice Solutions Inc
22476 Sacramento Ave .... Port Charlotte FL 33954 941-627-0777
Web: www.employerchoice.com

EMPO Corp 3100 W Lk St Ste 100 .... Minneapolis MN 55416 612-285-8707
Web: www.empocorp.com

Endeavour Software Technologies Inc
8140 N Mopac Expy Westpark 1 Ste 220 .... Austin TX 78759 512-464-1218
Web: www.techendeavour.com

eSoftware Professionals Inc
10450 SW Nimbus Ave Ste B .... Portland OR 97223 503-608-3601
Web: www.esopro.com

Extensible Computing LLC
1254 Okeechobee Rd .... West Palm Beach FL 33401 561-835-8351
Web: www.slpowers.com

G4S PLC 1395 University Blvd .... Jupiter FL 33458 561-691-6669 691-6591*
**Fax:* Hum Res ■ *Web:* www.g4s.com

HR Affiliates 1930 Bishop Ln # 111 .... Louisville KY 40218 502-485-9675 485-1242
Web: www.hraffiliates.com

Human Capital
2055 Crooks Rd Lowr Level .... Rochester Hills MI 48309 888-736-9071
TF: 888-736-9071 ■ *Web:* www.human-capital.com

Human Resources Inc 2127 Espey Ct Ste 306 .... Crofton MD 21114 410-451-4202 451-4206
Web: www.hri-online.com

Iconma LLC 850 Stephenson Hwy Ste 612 .... Troy MI 48083 888-451-2519 489-8046*
**Fax Area Code:* 800 ■ *TF:* 888-451-2519 ■ *Web:* www.iconma.com

Ideaca Knowledge Services Ltd
36 York Mills Rd Ste 502 .... Toronto ON M2P2E9 416-961-4332
Web: www.ideaca.com

Identity Theft Resource Center
9672 Via Excelencia Ste 101 .... San Diego CA 92126 858-693-7935
Web: www.idtheftcenter.org

Inek Technologies LLC
9200 Indian Creek Pkwy Ste 187 .... Overland Park KS 66210 913-469-1066
Web: www.inekinfo.com

Innovate E-Commerce Inc 160 N Craig St .... Pittsburgh PA 15213 888-771-9606
TF: 888-771-9606 ■ *Web:* www.innovateec.com

Inspirage Inc 40 Lk Bellevue Dr Ste 100 .... Bellevue WA 98005 855-517-4250
TF: 855-517-4250 ■ *Web:* www.inspirage.com

Internet Solver Inc 11308 Aurora Ave .... Urbandale IA 50322 515-224-9229
Web: www.internetsolver.com

Irontouch Managed Services Inc 540 Dado St .... San Jose CA 95131 714-408-4700
Web: www.irontouchms.com

IT Staffing Inc
Five Bliss Court Ste 200 .... Woodcliff Lake NJ 07677 201-505-0493
Web: www.itstaffinc.com

Jackson Healthcare LLC
2655 Northwinds Pkwy .... Alpharetta GA 30009 770-643-5500
Web: www.jacksonhealthcare.com

JCS Consulting Group Inc
2775 Via De La Valle Ste 206 .... San Diego CA 92014 858-947-0101
Web: jcsconsulting.com

JTECH Networks LLC 540 Lk Ctr Pkwy Ste 208 .... Cumming GA 30040 770-889-8181
Web: www.jtechnetworks.com

Jvt Advisors
35 New England Business Ctr Dr Ste 210 .... Andover MA 01810 978-683-4555
Web: www.jvtadvisors.com

Key2 Consulting LLC
1000 Peachtree Industrial Blvd Ste 6-289 .... Suwanee GA 30024 770-402-6938
Web: www.key2consulting.com

Konrad Group Inc 445 King St W Third Fl .... Toronto ON M5V1K4 416-551-3684
Web: www.konradgroup.com

Laboratoires Bug-Tracker Inc
2030 Blvd Pie-IX Ste 208 .... Montreal QC H1V2C8 514-496-0093
Web: www.bug-tracker.com

Legacy Engineering LLC
18662 Macarthur Blvd Ste 457 .... Irvine CA 92612 949-794-5860 794-5866
Web: www.legacyeng.com

Lsg Solutions LLC 501 E 15th St Ste 200B .... Edmond OK 73013 405-285-2500
Web: www.lsgsolutions.com

Manpower Inc. 8170 W Sahara Ave Ste 207 .... Las Vegas NV 89101 702-363-2626 363-0461
Web: www.manpowerlv.com

Marvel Consultants Inc
28601 Chagrin Blvd Ste 210 .... Cleveland OH 44122 216-292-2855 292-7207
TF: 800-338-1257 ■ *Web:* www.marvelconsultants.com

Merit Resources Inc 4410 114th St .... Des Moines IA 50322 515-278-1931 727-1241
TF: 800-336-1931 ■ *Web:* www.meritresources.com

Miss Paige Ltd 8430 W Bryn Mawr Ste 625 .... Chicago IL 60631 773-693-0480 693-9071
Web: www.jobgiraffe.com

Mitchell Martin Inc 307 W 38th St Ste 1305 .... New York NY 10018 212-943-1404 355-0229*
**Fax Area Code:* 646 ■ *Web:* www.mitchellmartin.com

Modern Business Associates Inc
9455 Koger Blvd Ste 200 .... St. Petersburg FL 33702 727-563-1500
Web: www.mbahro.com

Moresource Inc 401 Vandiver Dr .... Columbia MO 65202 573-443-1234 441-1225
Web: www.moresource-inc.com

Mountain Ltd 19 Yarmouth Dr Ste 301 .... New Gloucester ME 04260 207-688-6200 688-6212
TF: 800-322-8627 ■ *Web:* www.mountainltd.com

Naviant Inc 201 Prairie Heights Dr .... Verona WI 53593 608-848-0900
Web: www.naviant-inc.com

NETSHARE Inc 359 Bel Marin Keys Ste 24 .... Novato CA 94949 415-883-1700
Web: netshare.com

Nexio Group Inc, The
2050 de Bleury St Ste 500 .... Montreal QC H3A2J5 514-798-3707
Web: www.nexio.com

Nomad Technology Group LLC
1315 Read St Unit C .... Evansville IN 47710 812-618-4032
Web: nomadtechgroup.com

NumbersOnly Inc
1520 State Hwy 130 N Ste 201 .... North Brunswick NJ 08902 732-940-0033
Web: www.numbersonly.com

Oasis Outsourcing 4511 Woodland Corporate Blvd .... Tampa FL 33614 813-864-8321 812-8424*
**Fax Area Code:* 888 ■ *TF:* 866-709-9401 ■ *Web:* www.oasisadvantage.com

Oasis Outsourcing Inc
2054 Vista Pkwy Ste 300 .... West Palm Beach FL 33411 888-627-4735 274-4419
TF General: 888-627-4735 ■ *Web:* www.oasisadvantage.com

OmniTI Computer Consulting Inc
11830 W Market Pl Ste F .... Fulton MD 20759 240-646-0770
Web: www.omniti.com

OneSource Virtual HR Inc
5601 N MacArthur Blvd Ste 100 .... Irving TX 75038 972-916-9847
Web: www.onesourcevhr.com

Phone Fax

Optimum Outsourcing LLC
1300 Quail st #202 ... Newport Beach CA 92660 949-610-7981
Web: www.optimumhr.net

Optimus Information Inc
120-1412 W Seventh Ave ... Vancouver BC V6H1C1 604-736-4600
Web: www.optimusinfo.com

Pay Plus Benefits Inc 1110 N Ctr Pkwy Ste B ... Kennewick WA 99336 509-735-1143 735-7668
TF: 888-531-5781 ■ *Web:* www.payplusbenefits.com

Pencom Systems Inc 152 Remsen St ... Brooklyn NY 11201 718-923-1111 923-6065
TF: 800-736-2664 ■ *Web:* www.pencom.com

People Lease Inc 689 Town Ctr Blvd Ste B ... Ridgeland MS 39157 601-987-3025 987-3029
TF: 800-723-3025 ■ *Web:* www.peoplelease.com

Personnel Management Inc PO Box 6657 ... Shreveport LA 71136 318-869-4555 841-4350
TF: 800-259-4126 ■ *Web:* www.pmiresource.com

PES Payroll Inc 4100 W Burbank Blvd ... Burbank CA 91505 818-729-0080
Web: www.pespayroll.com

Primary Staffing Inc 4247 S Kedzie Ave ... Chicago IL 60632 773-376-0486
Web: primary-staffing.net

Professional Group Plans Inc (PGP)
225 Wireless Blvd Ste 200 ... Hauppauge NY 11788 631-951-9200 951-9623
Web: www.pgpbenefits.com

Professional Staff Management Inc
6801 Lake Plaza Dr Suite D-405 ... Indianapolis IN 46220 317-816-7007 816-7005
TF: 800-967-5515 ■ *Web:* www.psmin.com

Progressive Employer Services
6407 Parkland Dr ... Sarasota FL 34243 941-925-2990 308-1789
TF: 888-925-2990 ■ *Web:* www.progressiveemployer.com

Qualified Resources International LLC
78 Kenwood St ... Cranston RI 02907 401-946-1002
TF: 866-421-9840 ■ *Web:* www.qristaffing.com

Quinn Communications LC 1155 Main St Ste 109 ... Jupiter FL 33458 561-622-7577
Web: www.quinncom.net

Radical Support 585 Colonial Park Dr Ste 201 ... Roswell GA 30075 770-542-0000
Web: www.radicalsupport.com

Randstad Canada Group
810 Boul De Maisonneuve Quest ... Montreal QC H3A3E6 514-350-0033
Web: www.randstad.ca

Rapidsoft Systems Inc
Seven Diamond Ct ... Princeton Junction NJ 08550 609-439-4775
Web: www.rapidsoftsystems.com

Recon Management Services Inc
3649 S Beglis Pkwy ... Sulphur LA 70665 337-583-4662 583-7565
TF: 888-301-4662 ■ *Web:* www.recon-group.com

Red Foundry Inc 1608 S Ashland Ave ... Chicago IL 60608 888-406-1099
TF: 888-406-1099 ■ *Web:* www.redfoundry.com

REMPREX LLC 7501 S Quincy St Ste 100 ... Willowbrook IL 60527 630-910-0600
Web: www.remprex.com

Reserves Network, The 22021 Brookpark Rd ... Cleveland OH 44126 440-779-6681
TF: 866-876-2020 ■ *Web:* www.trnstaffing.com

Resource Management Inc 281 Main St Ste 5 ... Fitchburg MA 01420 800-508-0048 343-0719*
**Fax Area Code:* 978 ■ *TF Cust Svc:* 800-508-0048 ■ *Web:* www.rmi-solutions.com

RKL eSolutions LLC 1800 Fruitville Pk ... Lancaster PA 17604 717-735-9109
Web: www.rklesolutions.com

RMPersonnel Inc 4707 Montana Ave ... El Paso TX 79903 915-565-7674 565-7687
TF: 866-333-7176 ■ *Web:* www.rmpersonnel.com

Slate Professional Resources Inc
800 W Main St Ste 204 ... Freehold NJ 07728 732-303-6329
Web: www.slateprofessional.com

SmartLink Internet Strategies Inc
8895 N Military Trl Ste B202 ... Palm Beach Gardens FL 33410 561-688-8155
Web: thinksmartlink.com

SourceGear LLC 115 N Neil St Ste 408 ... Champaign IL 61820 217-356-0105
Web: www.sourcegear.com

SPARK Experience Design LLC
7979 Old Georgetown Rd Ste 801 ... Bethesda MD 20814 301-294-3340
Web: sparkexperience.com

Spongelab Interactive Inc
662 King St W Ste 101 ... Toronto ON M5V1M7 416-703-9753
Web: www.spongelab.com

SPR Consulting
Sears Tower 233 S Wacker Dr Ste 3500 ... Chicago IL 60606 312-756-1760
Web: spr.com

Staff Management Inc 5919 Spring Creek Rd ... Rockford IL 61114 815-282-3900 282-0515*
**Fax:* Hum Res ■ *TF General:* 800-535-3518 ■ *Web:* www.staffmgmt.com

Staff One Inc 8111 LBJ Fwy ... Dallas TX 75251 800-771-7823 461-1141*
**Fax Area Code:* 214 ■ *TF:* 800-771-7823 ■ *Web:* www.staffone.com

Strom Aviation Inc 109 S Elm St ... Waconia MN 55387 952-544-3611 544-3948
Web: www.stromaviation.com

Summit Technical Services Inc
355 Centerville Rd ... Warwick RI 02886 401-736-8323 738-3341
TF: 800-643-7372 ■ *Web:* www.summit-technical.com

Sycara Inc 6263 N Scottsdale Rd Ste 180 ... Scottsdale AZ 85250 855-479-2272
TF: 855-479-2272 ■ *Web:* www.sycaralocal.com

Synygy Pte. Ltd 2501 Seaport Dr ... Chester PA 19013 610-494-3300
Web: www.synygy.com

T & t Staff Management Inc
511 Executive Ctr Blvd ... El Paso TX 79902 915-771-0393
Web: www.ttstaff.com

TekPartners 5810 Coral Ridge Dr Ste 250 ... Coral Springs FL 33076 954-656-8600 282-6070
Web: www.tekpartners.com

TeleSearch Staffing Solutions 251 Re 206 ... Flanders NJ 07836 973-927-7870 927-7880
TF: 800-499-8367 ■ *Web:* www.telesearch.com

THINKstrategies Inc 22 Park Ave ... Wellesley MA 02481 781-431-2690
Web: www.thinkstrategies.com

Tilson HR Inc 1530 American Way Ste 200 ... Greenwood IN 46143 317-885-3838 807-1039
TF: 800-276-3976 ■ *Web:* www.tilsonhr.com

Torry Harris Business Solutions Inc
536 Fayette St ... Perth Amboy NJ 08861 732-442-0049
Web: www.thbs.com

Training Assoc Corp, The 289 Tpke Rd ... Westborough MA 01581 508-890-8500 890-8658
TF: 800-241-8868 ■ *Web:* www.thetrainingassociates.com

Phone Fax

TriCore Solutions LLC
141 Longwater Dr Ste 100 ... Norwell MA 02061 617-774-5200
Web: www.tricoresolutions.com

TriNet Group Inc
1100 San Leandro Blvd Ste 300 ... San Leandro CA 94577 510-352-5000 352-6480
TF: 888-874-6388 ■ *Web:* www.trinet.com

Virsys12 LLC 5205 Maryland Way Ste 202 ... Brentwood TN 37027 615-800-6768
Web: virsys12.com

VJV IT 96 Linwood Plz ... Fort Lee NJ 07024 800-614-7561
TF: 800-614-7561 ■ *Web:* www.vjvit.com

Willmott & Associates Inc
922 Waltham St Ste 103 ... Lexington MA 02421 781-863-5400
Web: www.willmott.com

Winterhawk Consulting LLC
1643 Williamsburg Sq ... Lakeland FL 33803 813-731-9665
Web: winterhawkconsulting.com

635 PUBLIC BROADCASTING ORGANIZATIONS

SEE ALSO Radio Networks p. 3000; Television Networks - Broadcast p. 3212

Phone Fax

Alabama Educational Television Commission
2112 11th Ave S Ste 400 ... Birmingham AL 35205 205-328-8756 251-2192
TF: 800-239-5233 ■ *Web:* www.aptv.org

Alabama Public Television (APT)
2112 11th Ave S Ste 400 ... Birmingham AL 35205 205-328-8756 251-2192
TF: 800-239-5233 ■ *Web:* www.aptv.org

Alaska Public Broadcasting Inc (APBI)
135 Cordova St ... Anchorage AK 99501 907-277-6300 586-5692
Web: www.akpb.org

American Public Television (APT)
55 Summer St 4th Fl ... Boston MA 02110 617-338-4455 338-5369
Web: aptonline.org/aptweb.nsf/home?readform

Annenberg Media
1301 Pennsylvania Ave NW ste302 ... Washington DC 20004 800-532-7637 783-0333*
**Fax Area Code:* 202 ■ *TF:* 800-532-7637 ■ *Web:* www.learner.org

Arkansas Educational Television Network (AETN)
350 S Donaghey Ave ... Conway AR 72034 501-682-2386 682-4122
TF: 800-662-2386 ■ *Web:* www.aetn.org

Association of Independents in Radio (AIR)
42 Charles St 2nd Fl ... Dorchester MA 02122 617-825-4400
Web: www.airmedia.org

Association of Public Television Stations (APTS)
2100 Crystal Dr Ste 700 ... Arlington VA 22202 202-654-4200 654-4236
TF: 855-948-5853 ■ *Web:* www.apts.org

Blue Ridge Public Television 1215 McNeil Dr ... Roanoke VA 24015 540-344-0991 344-2148
TF: 888-332-7788 ■ *Web:* www.blueridgepbs.org

Boise State Radio 1910 University Dr ... Boise ID 83725 208-426-1000 344-6631
Web: boisestatepublicradio.org

California Public Radio
4100 Vachell Ln ... San Luis Obispo CA 93401 805-549-8855 781-3025
Web: www.kcbx.org

Capitol Steps Productions Inc
210 N Washington St ... Alexandria VA 22314 703-683-8330
TF: 800-733-7837 ■ *Web:* www.capsteps.com

Commonwealth Club of California
595 Market St Second Fl ... San Francisco CA 94105 415-597-6700 597-6729
TF: 800-933-7548 ■ *Web:* www.commonwealthclub.org

Commonwealth Public Broadcasting
23 Sesame St ... Richmond VA 23235 804-320-1301 320-8729
Web: www.ideastations.org

Connecticut Public Broadcasting Inc (CPBI)
1049 Asylum Ave ... Hartford CT 06105 860-278-5310 244-9624
TF: 800-683-2112 ■ *Web:* www.cpbn.org

Corporation for Public Broadcasting (CPB)
401 Ninth St NW ... Washington DC 20004 202-879-9600 879-9700
TF: 800-272-2190 ■ *Web:* www.cpb.org

East Tennessee Public Communications Corp
1611 E Magnolia Ave ... Knoxville TN 37917 865-595-0220 595-0300
TF: 844-686-2378 ■ *Web:* www.easttennesseepbs.org

Georgia Public Broadcasting (GPB)
260 14th St NW ... Atlanta GA 30318 800-222-6006
TF: 800-222-6006 ■ *Web:* www.gpb.org

GPB Education 260 14th St NW ... Atlanta GA 30318 404-685-2550 685-2556
TF: 888-501-8960 ■ *Web:* www.gpb.org

Hawaii Public Television 2350 Dole St ... Honolulu HI 96822 808-973-1000 973-1090
TF: 800-238-4847 ■ *Web:* www.pbshawaii.org

Idaho Public Television (IPTV) 1455 N Orchard St ... Boise ID 83706 208-373-7220 373-7245
TF: 800-543-6868 ■ *Web:* www.idptv.state.id.us

Independent Television Service (ITVS)
651 Brannan St Ste 410 ... San Francisco CA 94107 415-356-8383 356-8391
TF: 800-621-6196 ■ *Web:* www.itvs.org

Kentucky Educational Television (KET)
600 Cooper Dr ... Lexington KY 40502 859-258-7000 258-7399
TF: 800-432-0951 ■ *Web:* www.ket.org

KUAC FM/TV PO Box 755620 ... Fairbanks AK 99775 907-474-7491 474-5064
TF: 800-727-6543 ■ *Web:* kuac.org

Louisiana Public Broadcasting
7733 Perkins Rd ... Baton Rouge LA 70810 225-767-5660 767-4299
TF: 800-973-7246 ■ *Web:* lpb.org

Maine Public Broadcasting Network (MPBN)
65 Texas Ave ... Bangor ME 04401 207-941-1010 942-2857
TF: 800-884-1717 ■ *Web:* www.mpbn.net

Metropolitan Indianapolis Public Broadcasting Corp
1401 N Meridian St ... Indianapolis IN 46202 317-636-2020 633-7418
Web: www.wfyi.org

Michigan Public Media
535 W William St Ste 110 ... Ann Arbor MI 48103 734-764-9210 647-3348
Web: www.michiganradio.org

Minnesota Public Radio (MPR) 480 Cedar St ... Saint Paul MN 55101 651-290-1212
TF: 800-228-7123 ■ *Web:* minnesota.publicradio.org

	City	State	Zip	Phone	Fax
Mississippi Authority for Educational Television 3825 Ridgewood Rd *TF:* 800-850-4406 ■ *Web:* www.mpbonline.org	Jackson	MS	39211	601-432-6565	432-6311
Montana Public Radio 32 Campus Dr University of Montana *TF:* 800-325-1565 ■ *Web:* www.mtpr.org	Missoula	MT	59812	406-243-4931	243-3299
Montana Public Television 183 Visual Communications Bldg **Fax Area Code:* 406 ■ *TF:* 800-426-8243 ■ *Web:* www.montanapbs.org	Bozeman	MT	59717	866-832-0829	994-6545*
National Captioning Institute (NCI) 3725 Concorde Pkwy Ste 100 *TF:* 800-825-6758 ■ *Web:* www.ncicap.org	Chantilly	VA	20151	703-917-7600	917-9853
National Educational Telecommunications Assn (NETA) 939 S Stadium Rd *TF:* 866-270-5141 ■ *Web:* www.netaonline.org	Columbia	SC	29201	803-799-5517	771-4831
National Public Radio (NPR) 635 Massachusetts Ave NW *Web:* www.npr.org	Washington	DC	20001	202-513-3232	513-3329
Nebraska Educational Telecommunications (NET) 1800 N 33rd St **Fax Area Code:* 402 ■ *TF:* 800-868-1868 ■ *Web:* netdb.unl.edu	Lincoln	NE	68503	800-868-1868	472-1785*
New Hampshire Public Television (NHPTV) 268 Mast Rd *TF:* 800-639-8408 ■ *Web:* www.nhptv.org	Durham	NH	03824	603-868-1100	868-7552
NPR West 9909 Jefferson Blvd *Web:* www.npr.org	Culver City	CA	90232	310-815-4200	815-4329
Oregon Public Broadcasting Inc (OPB) 7140 SW Macadam Ave *Web:* www.opb.org	Portland	OR	97219	503-244-9900	293-1919
Prairie Public Broadcasting Inc 207 N Fifth St *TF:* 800-359-6900 ■ *Web:* www.prairiepublic.org	Fargo	ND	58102	701-241-6900	239-7650
Public Broadcasting Council of Central New York 506 Old Liverpool Rd PO Box 2400 *TF:* 800-451-9269 ■ *Web:* www.wcny.org	Syracuse	NY	13220	315-453-2424	451-8824
Public Broadcasting Northwest Pennsylvania 8425 Peach St *TF:* 800-727-8854 ■ *Web:* www.wqln.org	Erie	PA	16509	814-864-3001	864-4077
Public Broadcasting Service (PBS) 2100 Crystal Dr *Web:* www.pbs.org	Arlington	VA	22202	703-739-5000	739-0775
Radio Research Consortium Inc (RRC) PO Box 1309 *Web:* www.rrconline.org	Olney	MD	20830	301-774-6686	774-0976
Rhode Island PBS 50 Pk Ln *Web:* www.ripbs.org	Providence	RI	02907	401-222-3636	222-3407
Rocky Mountain Public Broadcasting Network (RMPB) 1089 Bannock St *TF:* 800-274-6666 ■ *Web:* www.rmpbs.org	Denver	CO	80204	303-892-6666	620-5600
Small Station Assn KRWG-TV PO Box 30001 MSCPB 22 *TF:* 877-308-2408 ■ *Web:* www.krwg.org	Las Cruces	NM	88003	575-646-2222	646-1974
Smoky Hills Public Television (SHPTV) 604 Elm St *TF:* 800-362-9347 ■ *Web:* www.shptv.org	Bunker Hill	KS	67626	785-483-6990	483-4605
South Carolina Educational Television Commission (ETV) 1101 George Rogers Blvd *Web:* www.scetv.org	Columbia	SC	29201	803-737-3200	737-3526
South Dakota Public Broadcasting (SDPB) 555 N Dakota St PO Box 5000 *TF:* 800-456-0766 ■ *Web:* www.sdpb.org	Vermillion	SD	57069	605-677-5861	677-5010
Station Resource Group (SRG) 6935 Laurel Ave Ste 202 *Web:* www.srg.org	Takoma Park	MD	20912	301-270-2617	270-2618
Texas Public Radio (TPR) 8401 Datapoint Dr Ste 800 *TF:* 800-622-8977 ■ *Web:* www.tpr.org	San Antonio	TX	78229	210-614-8977	614-8983
ThinkTV 110 S Jefferson St *TF:* 800-247-1614 ■ *Web:* www.thinktv.org	Dayton	OH	45402	937-220-1600	220-1642
TRAC Media Services 3961 E Speedway Blvd Ste 410 *TF:* 888-299-1866 ■ *Web:* www.tracmedia.org	Tucson	AZ	85712	520-299-1866	577-6077
Twin Cities Public Television Inc 172 E Fourth St *TF:* 866-229-1300 ■ *Web:* www.tpt.org	Saint Paul	MN	55101	651-222-1717	229-1282
University of North Carolina Ctr for Public Television (UNC-TV) 10 TW Alexander Dr PO Box 14900 *TF:* 800-906-5050 ■ *Web:* www.unctv.org	Research Triangle Park	NC	27709	919-549-7000	549-7201
Vermont Public Television (VPT) 204 Ethan Allen Ave *TF:* 800-639-7811 ■ *Web:* www.vpt.org	Colchester	VT	05446	802-655-4800	655-6593
WAMC/Northeast Public Radio 318 Central Ave *TF:* 800-323-9262 ■ *Web:* www.wamc.org	Albany	NY	12206	518-465-5233	432-6974
West Central Illinois Educational Telecommunications Corp PO Box 6248 *TF:* 800-232-3605 ■ *Web:* www.networkknowledge.tv	Springfield	IL	62708	217-483-7887	483-1112
WGBH Educational Foundation One Guest St Brighton Landing *Web:* www.wgbh.org	Boston	MA	02135	617-300-2000	300-1026
Wisconsin Educational Communications Board 3319 W Beltline Hwy *TF:* 800-422-9707 ■ *Web:* www.ecb.org	Madison	WI	53713	608-264-9600	264-9622
Wisconsin Public Radio (WPR) 821 University Ave **Fax Area Code:* 608 ■ *TF:* 800-747-7444 ■ *Web:* www.wpr.org	Madison	WI	53706	800-747-7444	263-9763*
Wisconsin Public Television (WPT) 821 University Ave *TF:* 800-422-9707 ■ *Web:* www.wpt.org	Madison	WI	53706	608-263-2121	263-9763
Wyoming Public Television 2660 Peck Ave *TF:* 800-495-9788 ■ *Web:* wyomingpbs.org/	Riverton	WY	82501	307-856-6944	856-3893

636 PUBLIC INTEREST RESEARCH GROUPS (PIRGS) - STATE

SEE ALSO Consumer Interest Organizations p. 1768

	City	State	Zip	Phone	Fax
Alaska Public Interest Research Group (AkPIRG) 737 W Fifth Ave # 206 *Web:* www.akpirg.org	Anchorage	AK	99501	907-278-3661	
California Public Interest Research Group (CAPIRG) 1107 Ninth St Ste 601 *Web:* www.calpirg.org	Sacramento	CA	95814	916-448-4516	
Colorado Public Interest Research Group (COPIRG) 1543 Wazee St Ste 330 *Web:* www.copirg.org	Denver	CO	80202	303-573-7474	
Connecticut Public Interest Research Group (CONNPIRG) 198 Pk Rd Second Fl *Web:* www.connpirg.org	West Hartford	CT	06119	860-233-7554	233-7574
Florida Public Interest Research Group 926 E Pk Ave *Web:* www.floridapirg.org	Tallahassee	FL	32301	850-224-3321	224-1310
Georgia Public Interest Research Group (PIRG) 817 W Peachtree St NW Ste 204 *Web:* www.georgiapirg.org	Atlanta	GA	30308	404-892-3405	
Iowa Public Interest Research Group 3209 Ingersoll Ave *Web:* www.iowapirg.org	Des Moines	IA	50312	515-282-4193	
Maryland Public Interest Research Group (MaryPIRG) 3121 St Paul St Ste 26 *Web:* www.marylandpirg.org	Baltimore	MD	21218	410-467-0439	366-2051
Massachusetts Public Interest Research Group (MASSPIRG) 44 Winter St Fourth Fl *Web:* www.masspirg.org	Boston	MA	02108	617-292-4800	292-4800
New Hampshire Public Interest Research Group (NHPIRG) 30 S Main St Ste 301-A *Web:* www.nhpirg.org	Concord	NH	03301	603-229-1343	
New Mexico Public Interest Research Group (NMPIRG) PO Box 40173 *Web:* www.nmpirg.org	Albuquerque	NM	87196	505-254-1244	
New York Public Interest Research Group (NYPIRG) Nine Murray St *Web:* www.nypirg.org	New York	NY	10007	212-349-6460	349-1366
North Carolina Public Interest Research Group (NCPIRG) 112 S Blount St *Web:* www.ncpirg.org	Raleigh	NC	27601	919-833-2070	839-0767
Oregon State Public Interest Research Group (OSPIRG) 1536 SE 11th Ave *Web:* www.ospirg.org	Portland	OR	97214	503-231-4181	231-4007
Pennsylvania Public Interest Research Group (PennPIRG) 1420 Walnut St Ste 650 *Web:* www.pennpirg.org	Philadelphia	PA	19102	215-732-3747	732-4599
Public Interest Research Group In Michigan (PIRGIM) 103 E Liberty St Ste 202 *Web:* www.pirgim.org	Ann Arbor	MI	48104	734-662-6597	662-8393
Rhode Island Public Interest Research Group (RIPIRG) Nine S Angell St Second Fl-A *Web:* www.ripirg.org	Providence	RI	02906	401-421-6578	
Texas Public Interest Research Group 815 Brazos Ste 600 *Web:* www.texpirg.org	Austin	TX	78701	512-479-7287	
US Public Interest Research Group (US PIRG) 218 D St SE *Web:* www.uspirg.org	Washington	DC	20003	202-546-9707	546-2461
Vermont Public Interest Research Group (VPIRG) 141 Main St Ste 6 *Web:* www.vpirg.org	Montpelier	VT	05602	802-223-5221	223-6855
Washington State Public Interest Research Group 1402 Third Ave Ste 715 *Web:* www.washpirg.org	Seattle	WA	98101	206-568-2854	
Wisconsin Public Interest Research Group (WISPIRG) 210 N Bassett St Ste 200 *Web:* www.wispirg.org	Madison	WI	53703	608-251-1918	287-0865

637 PUBLIC POLICY RESEARCH CENTERS

	City	State	Zip	Phone	Fax
A Alfred Taubman Ctr for State & Local Government Harvard Univ John F Kennedy School of Government 79 JFK St *Web:* www.hks.harvard.edu/centers/taubman	Cambridge	MA	02138	617-495-2199	496-1722
AARP Public Policy Institute 601 E St NW *TF:* 888-687-2277 ■ *Web:* aarp.org/research/ppi/	Washington	DC	20049	202-434-2277	434-7599
Acton Institute for the Study of Religion & Liberty 161 Ottawa Ave NW Ste 301 *TF:* 800-345-2286 ■ *Web:* www.acton.org	Grand Rapids	MI	49503	616-454-3080	454-9454
Allegheny Institute for Public Policy 305 Mt Lebanon Blvd Ste 208 *TF:* 800-242-2184 ■ *Web:* www.alleghenyinstitute.org	Pittsburgh	PA	15234	412-440-0079	440-0085
American Assembly 475 Riverside Dr Ste 456 *Web:* www.americanassembly.org	New York	NY	10115	212-870-3500	870-3555
American Enterprise Institute for Public Policy Research (AEI) 1150 17th St NW Ste 1100 *TF:* 800-862-5801 ■ *Web:* www.aei.org	Washington	DC	20036	202-862-5800	862-7177
Ashbrook Ctr 401 College Ave Ashland University *TF:* 877-289-5411 ■ *Web:* www.ashbrook.org	Ashland	OH	44805	419-289-5411	289-5425
Aspen Institute One DuPont Cir NW Ste 700 *Web:* www.aspeninstitute.org	Washington	DC	20036	202-736-5823	467-0790
Atlantic Council of the United States 1101 15th St NW 11th Fl *TF:* 800-311-9410 ■ *Web:* www.atlanticcouncil.org	Washington	DC	20005	202-463-7226	463-7241

Organization	City	State	Zip	Phone	Fax
Belfer Ctr for Science & International Affairs (BCSIA) Harvard Univ John F Kennedy School of Government 79 JFK St *Web:* belfercenter.ksg.harvard.edu	Cambridge	MA	02138	617-495-1400	495-8963
Benton Foundation 1625 K St NW 11th Fl *Web:* www.benton.org	Washington	DC	20006	202-638-5770	638-5771
Brookings Institution 1775 Massachusetts Ave NW *TF:* 800-275-1447 ■ *Web:* www.brookings.edu	Washington	DC	20036	202-797-6000	797-6004
Capital Research Ctr 1513 16th St NW *TF:* 800-459-3950 ■ *Web:* www.capitalresearch.org	Washington	DC	20036	202-483-6900	483-6902
Carnegie Council for Ethics in International Affairs (CCEIA) Merrill House 170 E 64th St *Web:* www.carnegiecouncil.org	New York	NY	10065	212-838-4120	752-2432
Carnegie Endowment for International Peace 1779 Massachusetts Ave NW *TF:* 877-866-3070 ■ *Web:* www.carnegieendowment.org	Washington	DC	20036	202-483-7600	483-1840
Carter Ctr One Copenhill Ave 453 Freedom Pkwy *TF:* 800-550-3560 ■ *Web:* www.cartercenter.org	Atlanta	GA	30307	404-420-5100	331-0283
Cascade Policy Institute 4850 SW Scholls Ferry Rd Ste 103 *Web:* www.cascadepolicy.org	Portland	OR	97225	503-242-0900	242-3822
Cato Institute 1000 Massachusetts Ave NW *Web:* www.cato.org	Washington	DC	20001	202-842-0200	842-3490
Center for American Progress 1333 H St NW 10th Fl *Web:* www.americanprogress.org	Washington	DC	20005	202-682-1611	682-1867
Center for Animals & Public Policy Tufts Univ School of Veterinary Medicine 200 Westboro Rd *TF:* 888-748-8387 ■ *Web:* vet.tufts.edu	North Grafton	MA	01536	508-839-7920	839-2953
Center for Cognitive Liberty & Ethics PO Box 73481 *Web:* www.cognitiveliberty.org	Davis	CA	95617	530-750-7912	
Center for Equal Opportunity (CEO) 14 Pidgeon Hill Dr Ste 500 *Web:* www.ceousa.org	Sterling	VA	20165	703-421-5443	421-6401
Center for Immigration Studies 1522 K St NW Ste 820 *Web:* www.cis.org	Washington	DC	20005	202-466-8185	466-8076
Center for International Development at Harvard University (CID) Harvard Univ John F Kennedy School of Government 1 Eliot St Bldg 79 JFK St *Web:* www.hks.harvard.edu/centers/cid	Cambridge	MA	02138	617-495-4112	496-8753
Center for International Private Enterprise 1155 15th St NW Ste 700 *Web:* www.cipe.org	Washington	DC	20005	202-721-9200	721-9250
Center for Law & Social Policy (CLASP) 1015 15th St NW Ste 400 *TF:* 800-821-4367 ■ *Web:* www.clasp.org	Washington	DC	20005	202-906-8000	842-2885
Center for Mathematical Studies in Economics & Management Sciences 580 Leverone Hall 2001 Sheridan Rd *Web:* www.kellogg.northwestern.edu/research/math	Evanston	IL	60208	847-491-3527	491-2530
Center for National Policy One Massachusetts Ave NW Ste 333 *Web:* cnponline.org	Washington	DC	20001	202-682-1800	682-1818
Center for Neighborhood Technology 2125 W N Ave *Web:* www.cnt.org	Chicago	IL	60647	773-278-4800	278-3840
Center for Policy Research Syracuse University 426 Eggers Hall *TF:* 800-325-3535 ■ *Web:* www.maxwell.syr.edu	Syracuse	NY	13244	315-443-3114	443-1081
Center for Public Integrity 910 17th St NW Seventh Fl *Web:* www.publicintegrity.org	Washington	DC	20006	202-466-1300	466-1101
Center for Public Leadership Harvard Univ John F Kennedy School of Government 79 JFK St *Web:* www.centerforpublicleadership.org	Cambridge	MA	02138	617-496-8866	496-3337
Center for Responsive Politics 1101 14th St NW Ste 1030 *Web:* www.opensecrets.org	Washington	DC	20005	202-857-0044	857-7809
Center for Security Policy 1920 L St NW *Web:* centerforsecuritypolicy.org	Washington	DC	20036	202-835-9077	835-9066
Center for Strategic & International Studies 1800 K St NW Ste 400 *Web:* www.csis.org	Washington	DC	20006	202-887-0200	775-3199
Center of the American Experiment (CAE) 12 S Sixth St 1024 Plymouth Bldg *TF:* 800-657-3717 ■ *Web:* www.americanexperiment.org	Minneapolis	MN	55402	612-338-3605	338-3621
Center on Budget & Policy Priorities 820 First St NE Ste 510 *Web:* www.cbpp.org	Washington	DC	20002	202-408-1080	408-1056
Century Foundation, The 1 Whitehall St 15th Fl *Web:* www.tcf.org	New York	NY	10004	212-535-4441	879-9197
Chicago Council on Global Affairs, The (CCGA) 332 S Michigan Ave Ste 1100 *Web:* www.thechicagocouncil.org	Chicago	IL	60604	312-726-3860	821-7555
Claremont Institute 937 W Foothill Blvd Ste E *Web:* www.claremont.org	Claremont	CA	91711	909-621-6825	626-8724
Committee for Economic Development (CED) 2000 L St NW Ste 700 *TF:* 800-676-7353 ■ *Web:* www.ced.org	Washington	DC	20036	202-296-5860	223-0776
Commonwealth Institute 186 Hampshire St *Web:* comw.org	Cambridge	MA	02139	617-547-4474	868-1267
Consortium for Policy Research in Education (CPRE) University of Pennsylvania 3440 Market St Ste 560 *Web:* www.cpre.org	Philadelphia	PA	19104	215-573-0700	573-7914
Discovery Institute 208 Columbia St *Web:* www.discovery.org	Seattle	WA	98104	206-292-0401	682-5320
Earth Policy Institute 1350 Connecticut Ave NW Ste 403 *Web:* www.earth-policy.org	Washington	DC	20036	202-496-9290	496-9325
EastWest Institute (EWI) One E 26th St 20th Fl *Web:* www.ewi.info	New York	NY	10010	212-824-4100	824-4149
Economic Policy Institute 1333 H St NW Ste 300 E Twr *Web:* www.epi.org	Washington	DC	20005	202-775-8810	775-0819
Economic Strategy Institute 3050 K St NW Ste 220 *Web:* www.econstrat.org	Washington	DC	20007	202-965-9484	965-1104
Employee Benefit Research Institute (EBRI) 1100 13th St NW Ste 878 *Web:* www.ebri.org	Washington	DC	20005	202-659-0670	775-6312
Employment Policies Institute 1090 Vermont Ave NW Ste 800 *Web:* www.epionline.org	Washington	DC	20005	202-463-7650	463-7107
Ethics & Public Policy Ctr 1730 M St NW *Web:* www.eppc.org	Washington	DC	20036	202-682-1200	408-0632
Faith & Reason Institute 1730 Rhode Island Ave NW Ste 212 *Web:* www.frinstitute.org	Washington	DC	20036	202-289-8775	393-7004
Food & Agricultural Policy Research Institute (FAPRI) Iowa State University 578 Heady Hall *Web:* www.fapri.iastate.edu	Ames	IA	50011	515-294-1183	294-6336
Foreign Policy Institute 1740 Massachusetts Ave NW Nitze Bldg *Web:* www.sais-jhu.edu	Washington	DC	20036	202-663-5600	663-5769
Foreign Policy Research Institute (FPRI) 1528 Walnut St Ste 610 *Web:* www.fpri.org	Philadelphia	PA	19102	215-732-3774	732-4401
Foundation for Economic Education (FEE) 30 S Broadway *TF:* 800-960-4333 ■ *Web:* www.fee.org	Irvington-on-Hudson	NY	10533	914-591-7230	591-8910
Free Congress Foundation 901 N Washington St Ste 206 *Web:* www.freecongress.org	Alexandria	VA	22314	703-837-0030	837-0031
George Mason School of Public Policy 4400 University Dr	Fairfax	VA	22030	703-993-1000	993-2284
Goldwater Institute 500 E Coronado Rd *Web:* www.goldwaterinstitute.org	Phoenix	AZ	85004	602-462-5000	256-7045
Hauser Ctr for Nonprofit Organizations Harvard Univ John F Kennedy School of Government 79 JFK St *Web:* www.hks.harvard.edu/hauser	Cambridge	MA	02138	617-496-5675	495-0996
Heartland Institute 19 S LaSalle St Ste 903 *Web:* www.heartland.org	Chicago	IL	60603	312-377-4000	377-5000
Heritage Foundation 214 Massachusetts Ave NE *TF:* 800-546-2843 ■ *Web:* www.heritage.org	Washington	DC	20002	202-546-4400	546-8328
Hoover Institution on War Revolution & Peace Stanford University 434 Galvez Mall *Web:* www.hoover.org	Stanford	CA	94305	650-723-1754	723-1687
Hudson Institute 1015 15th St NW Ste 600 *TF:* 888-554-1325 ■ *Web:* www.hudson.org	Washington	DC	20005	202-974-2400	974-2410
Independent Institute 100 Swan Way *TF:* 800-927-8733 ■ *Web:* www.independent.org	Oakland	CA	94621	510-632-1366	568-6040
Institute for Foreign Policy Analysis Inc 675 Massachusetts Ave 10th Fl *Web:* www.ifpa.org	Cambridge	MA	02139	617-492-2116	492-8242
Institute For Health Policy 3333 California St	San Francisco	CA	94118	415-476-4921	
Institute for Humane Studies 3301 N Fairfax Dr Ste 440 *TF:* 800-697-8799 ■ *Web:* www.theihs.org	Arlington	VA	22201	703-993-4880	993-4890
Institute for International Economics 1750 Massachusetts Ave NW *Web:* www.iie.com	Washington	DC	20036	202-328-9000	328-5432
Institute for Justice 901 N Glebe Rd Ste 900 *TF:* 888-322-6397 ■ *Web:* www.ij.org	Arlington	VA	22203	703-682-9320	682-9321
Institute for Philosophy & Public Policy Maryland School of Public Policy 3111 Van Munching Hall *Web:* www.msu.edu	College Park	MD	20742	301-405-4763	
Institute for Policy Studies (IPS) 1112 16th St NW Ste 600 *TF:* 877-564-6833 ■ *Web:* www.ips-dc.org	Washington	DC	20036	202-234-9382	387-7915
Institute for Research on the Economics of Taxation (IRET) 1710 Rhode Island Ave NW 11th Fl *Web:* www.iret.org	Washington	DC	20036	202-463-1400	463-6199
Institute for the North 1675 C St Ste 106 *Web:* www.institutenorth.org	Anchorage	AK	99501	907-786-6324	343-2466
Institute of Government & Public Affairs Univ of Illinois 1007 W Nevada St *TF:* 866-794-3340 ■ *Web:* igpa.uillinois.edu	Urbana	IL	61801	217-333-3340	244-4817
Institute of World Politics 1521 16th St NW *TF:* 888-566-9497 ■ *Web:* www.iwp.edu	Washington	DC	20036	202-462-2101	464-0335
Institute on Education & the Economy 525 W 120th St Ste 439 *Web:* www.tc.columbia.edu	New York	NY	10027	212-678-3091	678-3699
Inter-American Dialogue 1211 Connecticut Ave NW Ste 510 *Web:* www.thedialogue.org	Washington	DC	20036	202-822-9002	822-9553
International Ctr for Alcohol Policies (ICAP) 1519 New Hampshire Ave NW *Web:* www.icap.org	Washington	DC	20036	202-986-1159	986-2080
International Food Policy Research Institute (IFPRI) 2033 K St NW *Web:* www.ifpri.org	Washington	DC	20006	202-862-5600	467-4439

	Phone	Fax

Joan Shorenstein Ctr on the Press Politics & Public Policy
Harvard Univ John F Kennedy School of Government
79 John F Kennedy St. .... Cambridge MA 02138 617-495-8269 495-8696
Web: shorensteincenter.org

Joint Ctr for Housing Studies
1033 Massachusetts Ave .... Cambridge MA 02138 617-495-7908 496-9957
Web: www.jchs.harvard.edu

Levy Economics Institute of Bard College
Blithewood Rd Bard College .... Annandale-on-Hudson NY 12504 845-758-7700 758-1149
Web: www.levyinstitute.org

Malcolm Wiener Ctr for Social Policy
John F Kennedy School of Government Harvard University
79 John F Kennedy St. .... Cambridge MA 02138 617-496-4082 496-9053
TF: 866-845-6596 ■ *Web:* www.hks.harvard.edu

Manhattan Institute for Policy Research
52 Vanderbilt Ave Third Fl .... New York NY 10017 212-599-7000 599-3494
Web: www.manhattan-institute.org

Manpower Demonstration Research Corp
16 E 34th St 19th Fl .... New York NY 10016 212-532-3200 684-0832
TF: 800-221-3165 ■ *Web:* www.mdrc.org

Margaret Chase Smith Policy Ctr
University of Maine York Complex Ste 4 .... Orono ME 04469 207-581-1648 581-1266
TF: 877-486-2364 ■ *Web:* www.umaine.edu

Mathematica Inc PO Box 2393 .... Princeton NJ 08543 609-799-3535 799-0005
Web: www.mathematica-mpr.com

Mershon Ctr 1501 Neil Ave .... Columbus OH 43201 614-292-1681 292-2407
Web: www.mershoncenter.osu.edu

Milken Institute 1250 Fourth St .... Santa Monica CA 90401 310-570-4600 570-4601
Web: www.milkeninstitute.org

National Academy on an Aging Society
1220 L St NW Ste 901 .... Washington DC 20005 202-408-3375 842-1150
Web: www.agingsociety.org

National Ctr for Policy Analysis
12770 Coit Rd Ste 800 .... Dallas TX 75251 972-386-6272 386-0924
Web: www.ncpa.org

National Ctr for Public Policy Research (NCPPR)
501 Capitol Ct NE Ste 200 .... Washington DC 20002 202-543-4110 543-5975
Web: ncppr.org

National Ctr on Institutions & Alternatives
7222 Ambassador Rd .... Baltimore MD 21244 443-780-1300 597-9656*
**Fax Area Code:* 410 ■ *Web:* www.ncianet.org

Nelson A Rockefeller Institute of Government
411 State St .... Albany NY 12203 518-443-5522 443-5788
Web: www.rockinst.org

New America Foundation 1899 L St NW .... Washington DC 20036 202-986-2700 986-3696
Web: www.newamerica.net

Northeast-Midwest Institute (NMI)
50 F St NW Ste 950 .... Washington DC 20001 202-544-5200 544-0043
Web: www.nemw.org

Pacific Research Institute for Public Policy (PRI)
One Embarcadero Ctr .... San Francisco CA 94111 415-989-0833 989-2411
Web: www.pacificresearch.org

Panetta Institute for Public Policy, The
California State University Monterey Bay
100 Campus Ctr Bldg 86E .... Seaside CA 93955 831-582-4200 582-4082
Web: www.panettainstitute.org

Phoenix Ctr for Advanced Legal & Economic Public Policy Studies
5335 Wisconsin Ave NW Ste 440 .... Washington DC 20015 202-274-0235 244-8257
Web: www.phoenix-center.org

Princeton Institute for International & Regional Studies (PIIRS)
Princeton University Bendheim Hall .... Princeton NJ 08544 609-258-4852 258-3988
TF: 888-486-3339 ■ *Web:* www.princeton.edu/piirs

Progress & Freedom Foundation (PFF)
1444 Eye St NW Ste 500 .... Washington DC 20005 202-289-8928 289-6079
Web: www.pff.org

Progressive Policy Institute (PPI)
1101 14th St NW Ste 1250 .... Washington DC 20005 202-525-3926 525-3941
Web: progressivepolicy.org

Public Agenda Six E 39th St .... New York NY 10016 212-686-6610 889-3461
Web: www.publicagenda.org

RAND Corp 1776 Main St. .... Santa Monica CA 90401 310-393-0411 393-4818
TF: 877-584-8642 ■ *Web:* www.rand.org

Reason Public Policy Institute
3415 S Sepulveda Blvd Ste 400 .... Los Angeles CA 90034 310-391-2245 391-4395
TF: 888-732-7668 ■ *Web:* www.reason.org

Renewable Energy Policy Project (REPP)
1612 K St NW Ste 1200 .... Washington DC 20006 202-293-2898

Resources for the Future 1616 P St NW .... Washington DC 20036 202-328-5000 939-3460
Web: www.rff.org

Robert J Dole Institute of Politics
2350 Petefish Dr. .... Lawrence KS 66045 785-864-4900 864-1414
Web: www.doleinstitute.org

Rockford Institute 928 N Main St. .... Rockford IL 61103 815-964-5053 964-9403
TF: 800-383-0680 ■ *Web:* chroniclesmagazine.org

Schneider Institute for Health Policy
Brandeis University 415 S St .... Waltham MA 02454 781-736-3964
Web: sihp.brandeis.edu

Science & Environmental Policy Project
1600 S Eads St Ste 712-S .... Arlington VA 22202 212-664-4555
Web: www.sepp.org

Social Science Research Council (SSRC)
810 Seventh Ave. .... New York NY 10019 212-377-2700 377-2727
Web: www.ssrc.org

Tellus Institute 11 Arlington St .... Boston MA 02116 617-266-5400 266-8303
Web: www.tellus.org

Urban Institute 2100 M St NW. .... Washington DC 20037 202-833-7200 331-9747
Web: www.urban.org

Weatherhead Ctr for International Affairs
Harvard Univ 1737 Cambridge St. .... Cambridge MA 02138 617-495-4420 495-8292
Web: www.wcfia.harvard.edu

Weil Program on Collaborative Governance Ctr for Business & Government, The
Harvard Univ John F Kennedy School of Government
Weil Hall 79 JFK St. .... Cambridge MA 02138 617-496-0587 496-6104
Web: www.hks.harvard.edu/m-rcbg/wpcg

Winrock International 2101 Riverfront Dr .... Little Rock AR 72202 501-280-3000 280-3090
Web: www.winrock.org

Woodrow Wilson International Ctr for Scholars
One Woodrow Wilson Plz
1300 Pennsylvania Ave NW .... Washington DC 20004 202-691-4000 691-4001
Web: wilsoncenter.org

World Policy Institute (WPI)
220 Fifth Ave 9th Fl .... New York NY 10001 212-481-5005 481-5009
TF: 800-207-8354 ■ *Web:* www.worldpolicy.org

World Resources Institute (WRI)
10 G St NE Ste 800 .... Washington DC 20002 202-729-7600 729-7610
Web: www.wri.org

Worldwatch Institute
1776 Massachusetts Ave NW .... Washington DC 20036 202-452-1999 296-7365
TF: 877-539-9946 ■ *Web:* www.worldwatch.org

638 PUBLIC RECORDS SEARCH SERVICES

SEE ALSO Investigative Services p. 2590

	Phone	Fax

Accufax PO Box 35563 .... Tulsa OK 74153 800-256-8898 936-3027*
**Fax Area Code:* 866 ■ *TF:* 800-256-8898 ■ *Web:* www.accufax-us.com

All-Search & Inspection Inc
1108 E S Union Ave .... Midvale UT 84047 801-984-8160 984-8170
TF: 800-227-3152 ■ *Web:* www.all-search.com

American Driving Records Inc
2860 Gold Tailings Ct PO Box 1970 .... Rancho Cordova CA 95670 916-456-3200 456-3332
TF: 800-766-6877 ■ *Web:* www.adr-inc.com

AmRent 950 Threadneedle Ste 255 .... Houston TX 77079 713-266-1870 260-1290
TF: 800-324-4595 ■ *Web:* www.amrent.com

Applicant Insight Ltd
5396 School Rd PO Box 458 .... New Port Richey FL 34652 800-771-7703 890-6454
TF: 800-771-7703 ■ *Web:* applicantinsight.com

Apscreen Inc PO Box 80639 .... Rancho Santa Margarita CA 92688 949-646-4003 277-2733*
**Fax Area Code:* 888 ■ *TF:* 800-277-2733 ■ *Web:* www.apscreen.com

Background Bureau Inc
2019 Alexandria Pike .... Highland Heights KY 41076 859-781-3400 781-9540
TF: 800-854-3990 ■ *Web:* www.backgroundbureau.com

Background Information Services Inc
1800 30th St Ste 204 .... Boulder CO 80301 303-442-3960 442-1004
TF: 800-433-6010 ■ *Web:* www.bisi.com

Best Reports Inc PO Box 546 .... Richmond IL 60071 815-678-2703 839-7440
Web: www.bestreports.net

Capitol Lien Records & Research Inc
1010 N Dale St .... Saint Paul MN 55117 651-488-0100 488-0200
Web: www.capitollien.com

Capitol Services Inc 800 Brazos St Ste 400 .... Austin TX 78701 800-345-4647 432-3622
TF: 800-345-4647 ■ *Web:* www.capitolservices.com

CARCO Group Inc 5000 Corporate Ct. .... Holtsville NY 11742 631-862-9300 584-7094
TF: 800-645-4556 ■ *Web:* www.carcogroup.com

CCH Washington Service Bureau Inc
1015 15th St NW 10th Fl .... Washington DC 20005 202-312-6600 962-0152
TF: 800-955-5219 ■ *Web:* www.wsb.com

CDI Credit Inc
6160 Peachtree Dunwoody Rd NE Ste B-210 .... Atlanta GA 30328 770-350-5070 394-2197
TF: 800-633-3961 ■ *Web:* www.cdicredit.com

Charles Jones LLC PO Box 8488 .... Trenton NJ 08650 800-792-8888 883-0677
TF: 800-792-8888 ■ *Web:* www.charlesjones.com

Colby Attorneys Service Company Inc
111 Washington Ave Ste 703 .... Albany NY 12210 800-832-1220
TF: 800-832-1220 ■ *Web:* www.colbyservice.com

CoreLogic SafeRent 7300 Westmore Rd Ste 3 .... Rockville MD 20850 866-873-3651 715-1212*
**Fax Area Code:* 240 ■ *TF:* 866-873-3651 ■ *Web:* www.corelogic.com

CT Lien Solutions 2727 Allen Pkwy Ste 1000 .... Houston TX 77019 800-833-5778 850-5194*
**Fax Area Code:* 877 ■ *TF:* 800-833-5778 ■ *Web:* ctliensolutions.com

D+H CollateralGuard RC (CSRS)
4126 Norland Ave Ste 200 .... Burnaby BC V5G3S8 604-637-4000 637-4001
TF: 866-873-9780 ■ *Web:* www.csrs.ca

Doc-U-Search Inc 63 Pleasant St PO Box 777 .... Concord NH 03301 800-332-3034 224-2794*
**Fax Area Code:* 603 ■ *TF:* 800-332-3034 ■ *Web:* www.docusearchinc.com

Driving Records Facilities PO Box 1086 .... Glen Burnie MD 21061 800-772-5510 760-5837*
**Fax Area Code:* 410 ■ *TF:* 800-772-5510 ■ *Web:* www.dr-rec-fac.com

Edge Information Management Inc
1682 W Hibiscus Blvd .... Melbourne FL 32901 321-722-3343 780-3299*
**Fax Area Code:* 800 ■ *TF:* 800-725-3343 ■ *Web:* www.edgeinformation.com

Employment Screening Services Inc
627 E Sprague St Ste 100 .... Spokane WA 99202 509-624-3851 321-2905*
**Fax Area Code:* 800 ■ *TF:* 800-473-7778 ■ *Web:* www.employscreen.com

Explore Information Services LLC
2900 Lone Oak Pkwy Ste 140 PO Box 21636 .... St. Paul MN 55121 800-531-9125 681-4476*
**Fax Area Code:* 651 ■ *TF:* 800-531-9125 ■ *Web:* www.exploredata.com

Fidelifacts 42 Broadway Ste 1548 .... New York NY 10004 212-425-1520 248-5619
TF: 800-678-0007 ■ *Web:* www.fidelifacts.com

Government Liaison Services Inc (GLS)
200 N Glebe Rd Ste 321 .... Arlington VA 22203 703-524-8200 525-8451
TF: 800-642-6564 ■ *Web:* www.trademarkinfo.com

HireRight Inc 5151 California Ave .... Irvine CA 92617 949-428-5800 224-6020
TF: 800-400-2761 ■ *Web:* www.hireright.com

IMI Data Search Inc
275 E Hillcrest Dr Ste 102 .... Thousand Oaks CA 91360 805-495-1149 495-0310
TF: 800-860-7779 ■ *Web:* www.imidatasearch.com

Information Management Systems Inc
114 W Main St Ste 211 PO Box 2924 .... New Britain CT 06050 860-229-1119 225-5524
TF: 888-403-8347 ■ *Web:* www.imswebb.com

KnowX LLC 730 Peachtree St. .... Atlanta GA 30308 404-541-0220 541-0260
TF: 877-317-5000 ■ *Web:* www.knowx.com

Kress Employment Screening
320 Westcott St Ste 108 .... Houston TX 77007 713-880-3693 880-3694
TF: 888-636-3693 ■ *Web:* www.kressinc.com

Kroll Background America Inc
100 Centerview Dr Ste 300 .... Nashville TN 37214 615-320-9800 320-9916
TF: 800-697-7189 ■ *Web:* www.kroll.com

				Phone	Fax
Laborchex Co, The 2506 Lakeland Dr Ste 200	Jackson	MS	39232	601-664-6760	844-2722*
*Fax Area Code: 800 ■ TF: 800-880-0366 ■ Web: www.laborchex.com					
Legal Data Resources Inc 2816 W Summerdale Ave	Chicago	IL	60625	773-561-2468	561-2488
TF: 844-732-2437 ■ Web: www.ldrsearch.com					
LegalEase Inc 211 E 43rd St Ste 2203	New York	NY	10017	212-393-9070	580-4761*
*Fax Area Code: 888 ■ TF: 800-393-1277 ■ Web: www.legaleaseinc.com					
MLQ Attorney Services 2000 River Edge Pkwy Ste 885	Atlanta	GA	30328	770-984-7007	984-7049
TF: 800-446-8794 ■ Web: www.mlqattorneyservices.com					
OPENonline 1650 Lk Shore Dr Ste 350	Columbus	OH	43204	614-481-6999	481-6980
TF: 888-381-5656 ■ Web: www.openonline.com					
Orange Tree Employment Screening 7275 Ohms Ln	Minneapolis	MN	55439	952-941-9040	941-9041
TF: 800-886-4777 ■ Web: www.orangetreescreening.com					
Parasec Inc 2804 Gateway Oaks Dr Ste 200 PO Box 160568	Sacramento	CA	95833	800-533-7272	603-5868
TF General: 800-533-7272 ■ Web: www.parasec.com					
Penncorp Servicegroup Inc 600 N Second St Ste 401	Harrisburg	PA	17101	717-234-2300	264-1137*
*Fax Area Code: 800 ■ TF: 800-544-9050 ■ Web: www.penncorp.net/default/default.htm					
Property Owners Exchange Inc 6630 Baltimore National Pk Ste 208	Catonsville	MD	21228	410-719-0100	719-6715
TF: 800-869-3200 ■ Web: www.poeknows.com					
Questel Orbit 1725 Duke St Ste 625	Alexandria	VA	22314	703-519-1820	519-1821
TF: 800-456-7248 ■ Web: www.questel.orbit.com					
Quick Search 4155 Buena Vista	Dallas	TX	75204	214-358-2840	358-6057
Web: quicksius.com/					
Record Search America Inc 1201 N Liberty St	Boise	ID	83704	208-375-1906	
Rental Research Services Inc 7525 Mitchell Rd Ste 301	Eden Prairie	MN	55344	952-935-5700	935-9212
TF: 800-328-0333 ■ Web: www.rentalresearch.com					
Search Company International 1535 Grant St Ste 140	Denver	CO	80203	303-863-1800	863-7767
TF: 800-727-2120 ■ Web: www.searchcompanyintl.com					
Search Network Ltd 1503 42nd St Ste 210	West Des Moines	IA	50266	515-223-1153	223-2814
TF: 800-383-5050 ■ Web: www.searchnetworkltd.com					
SearchTec Inc 314 N 12th St Ste 100	Philadelphia	PA	19107	215-963-0888	851-8775
TF: 877-273-2724 ■ Web: www.searchtec.com					
Securitech Inc 8230 E Broadway Blvd Ste E-10	Tucson	AZ	85710	520-721-0305	721-7706
TF: 888-792-4473 ■ Web: www.hiresafe.com					
Superior Information Services Inc 300 Phillips Blvd Ste 500	Trenton	NJ	08618	609-883-7000	883-0677
TF: 800-792-8888 ■ Web: www.superiorinfo.com					
TABB Inc PO Box 10	Chester	NJ	07930	800-887-8222	879-8675*
*Fax Area Code: 908 ■ TF: 800-887-8222 ■ Web: www.tabb.net					
Thomson CompuMark 500 Victory Rd	North Quincy	MA	02171	617-479-1600	543-1983*
*Fax Area Code: 800 ■ TF: 800-692-8833 ■ Web: trademarks.thomsonreuters.com					
TML Information Services Inc 11655 Queens Blvd	Forest Hills	NY	11375	718-793-3737	544-2853
UCC Filing & Search Services Inc 1574 Village Sq Blvd Ste 100	Tallahassee	FL	32309	850-681-6528	681-6528
Unisearch Inc 1780 Barnes Blvd SW	Tumwater	WA	98512	360-956-9500	531-1717*
*Fax Area Code: 800 ■ TF: 800-722-0708 ■ Web: www.unisearch.com					
USIS 7799 Leesburg Pk Ste 1100-S	Falls Church	VA	22043	703-448-0178	
TF: 888-270-8978 ■ Web: www.usis.com					
Verified Credentials Inc 20890 Kenbridge Ct	Lakeville	MN	55044	952-985-7200	985-7218
TF: 800-473-4934 ■ Web: www.verifiedcredentials.com					
Westlaw Court Express 1100 13th St NW Ste 300	Washington	DC	20005	202-423-2163	
TF: 877-362-7387 ■ Web: www.courtexpress.westlaw.com					

639 PUBLIC RELATIONS FIRMS

SEE ALSO Advertising Agencies p. 1705

				Phone	Fax
5W Public Relations LLC 1166 Ave of the Americas Fourth Fl	New York	NY	10036	212-999-5585	
Web: www.5wpr.com					
A Larry Ross Communications Inc 4300 Marsh Ridge Rd Ste 114	Carrollton	TX	75010	972-267-1111	
Web: www.alarryross.com					
A&A Merchandising Ltd 3250 Lakeshore Blvd W	Toronto	ON	M8V1M1	416-503-3343	
Web: www.aamerch.com					
Abbi Agency Inc, The 275 Hill St Ste 250	Reno	NV	89501	775-323-2977	
Web: theabbiagency.com					
Ackermann Public Relations & Marketing 1111 Northshore Dr Ste N-400	Knoxville	TN	37919	865-584-0550	588-3009
TF General: 877-325-9453 ■ Web: www.ackermannpr.com					
Admarc Southwest Ltd 10 Desta Dr Ste 170LL	Midland	TX	79705	432-687-1127	
Web: admarc.com					
Advocacy Solutions LLC Four Richmond Sq Ste 300	Providence	RI	02906	401-831-3700	
Web: advocacysolutionsllc.com					
Advocal 1000 Q St	Sacramento	CA	95811	916-446-6161	
Web: www.advocal.com					
Alcalde & Fay 2111 Wilson Blvd Eighth Fl	Arlington	VA	22201	703-841-0626	
Web: www.alcalde-fay.com					
Allied Experiential 111 E 12 St Second Fl	New York	NY	10003	212-253-8777	
Web: www.grandcentralmarketing.com					
Andrea Obston Marketing Communications LLC Three Regency Dr	Bloomfield	CT	06002	860-243-1447	
Web: www.aomc.com					
Andrew Edson & Associates Inc 89 Bounty Ln	Jericho	NY	11753	516-931-0873	
Web: www.edsonpr.com					
Anne Klein & Assoc Inc 1000 Atrium Way Ste 102	Mount Laurel	NJ	08054	856-866-0411	
Web: www.akleinpr.com					
APCO Worldwide 700 12th St	Washington	DC	20005	202-778-1000	466-6002
Web: www.apcoworldwide.com					
Apex Group 1201 1201 K St Ste 750 St Ste 750	Sacramento	CA	95814	916-444-3116	
Web: theapexgroup.net					
Arment Dietrich Public Relations 506 N Clark St Ste 4n	Chicago	IL	60654	312-787-7249	
Web: www.armentdietrich.com					
Asher Agency Inc 535 W Wayne St	Fort Wayne	IN	46802	260-424-3373	
Web: www.asheragency.com					
B & B Media Group 109 S Main St	Corsicana	TX	75110	903-872-0517	872-0518
TF: 800-927-0517 ■ Web: www.tbbmedia.com					
BackBay Communications Inc 20 Park Plz Ste 801	Boston	MA	02116	617-556-9982	
Web: www.backbaycommunications.com					
Backbone Media LLC 65 N Fourth St Ste 1	Carbondale	CO	81623	970-963-4873	
Web: backbonemedia.com					
Baltz & Co 49 W 23rd St Fl 9	New York	NY	10010	212-982-8300	
Web: www.baltzco.com					
barry r. epstein associates Inc 11922 Waterwood Dr	Boca Raton	FL	33428	561-852-0000	
Web: www.publicrelations.nu					
Bender/Helper Impact (BHI) 11500 W Olympic Blvd Ste 655	Los Angeles	CA	90064	310-473-4147	478-4727
Web: www.bhimpact.com					
Bianchi PR Inc 888 W Big Beaver Rd Ste 777	Troy	MI	48084	248-269-1122	
Web: www.bianchipr.com					
Birch Tree Promotions Five tyng st	Newburyport	MA	01950	978-270-3852	
Web: www.birchtreepromotions.com					
Birnbach Communications Inc 20 Devereux St Ste 3A	Marblehead	MA	01945	781-639-6701	
Web: www.birnbachcom.com					
Bite 345 Spear St Ste 750	San Francisco	CA	94105	415-365-0222	365-0223
Web: www.biteglobal.com					
Blattel Communications 250 Montgomery St Ste 1200	San Francisco	CA	94104	415-397-4811	
Web: www.blattel.com					
BluePoint Venture Marketing 17 Draper Rd	Wayland	MA	01778	508-358-6371	
Web: www.bluepointmktg.com					
Boardroom Communications Inc Bank Of America Plaza 1776 N Pine Island Rd Ste 320	Fort Lauderdale	FL	33322	954-370-8999	
TF: 877-773-4761 ■ Web: www.boardroompr.com					
Boca Communications LLC 2159 Powell St	San Francisco	CA	94133	415-738-7718	
Web: www.bocacommunications.com					
Bolton-st Johns Inc 146 State St Ste 12	Albany	NY	12207	518-462-4620	
Web: www.boltonstjohns.com					
Bouvier Kelly Inc 212 S Elm St Ste 200	Greensboro	NC	27401	336-275-7000	
Web: www.bouvierkelly.com					
Brandon Assoc 29 Commonwealth Ave Ste 901	Boston	MA	02116	857-362-7360	
Web: www.brandonassociatesllc.com					
Bridge Global Strategies LLC 16 W 36th St Ste 1002	New York	NY	10018	212-583-1043	
Web: www.bridgeny.com					
Calhoun & Company Communications LLC 3275 Sacramento St	San Francisco	CA	94115	415-346-2929	
Web: calhounwine.com					
Campbell Marketing & Communications 3200 Greenfield St Ste 280	Dearborn	MI	48120	313-336-9000	
Web: www.pcgcampbell.com					
Carmichael Lynch Spong 110 N Fifth St	Minneapolis	MN	55403	612-334-6000	375-8501
Web: spongpr.com/					
Carol Fox & Associates 1412 W Belmont Ave	Chicago	IL	60657	773-327-3830	
Web: www.carolfoxassociates.com					
Carrot & Stick Inc 115 New St Ste A	Decatur	GA	30030	404-371-1891	
Web: www.carrotandstick.com					
Cary Francis Group Inc PO Box 321050	Franklin	WI	53132	414-304-6400	
Web: www.thecfg.com					
Casey Communications Inc 8301 Maryland Ave Ste 350	St. Louis	MO	63105	314-721-2828	
Web: www.caseycomm.com					
Cerrell Assoc Inc 320 N Larchmont Blvd	Los Angeles	CA	90004	323-466-3445	466-8653
Web: www.cerrell.com					
Chandler Chicco Agency 450 W 15th St Seventh Fl	New York	NY	10011	212-229-8400	229-8496
Web: www.ccapr.com					
Charles Ryan Assoc Inc 601 Morris St Ste 301	Charleston	WV	25301	877-342-0161	
TF: 877-342-0161 ■ Web: www.charlesryan.com					
Clockwork Marketing Services Inc 10245 Centurion Pkwy N Ste 315	Jacksonville	FL	32256	904-280-7960	
Web: www.clockworkmarketing.com					
Cohn & Wolfe 200 Fifth Ave	New York	NY	10010	212-798-9700	329-9900
Web: www.cohnwolfe.com					
Colehour & Cohen 615 Second Ave Ste 405	Seattle	WA	98104	206-262-0363	
Web: www.colehourcohen.com					
Compassionate Passages Inc 29869 White Hall Dr	Farmington Hills	MI	48331	248-592-9390	
Web: compassionatepassages.org					
Cone Inc 855 Boylston St	Boston	MA	02116	617-227-2111	227-2111
Web: www.conecomm.com					
Connect PR One Market St 36th Fl	San Francisco	CA	94105	415-222-9691	
TF: 800-455-8855 ■ Web: www.connectmarketing.com					
Connect Public Relations 80 East 100 North	Provo	UT	84606	801-373-7888	
Web: www.connectpr.com					
Coyne Public Relations LLC Five Wood Hollow Rd	Parsippany	NJ	07054	973-588-2000	
Web: www.coynepr.com					
Cramer-Krasselt 246 E Chicago St	Milwaukee	WI	53202	414-227-3500	
Web: www.c-k.com					
D Exposito & Partners LLC 875 Sixth Ave 25th Fl	New York	NY	10001	646-747-8800	
Web: www.newamericanagency.com					

Firm	City	State	ZIP	Phone	Fax
D.M. Reid Associates Ltd 50 Grove St Ste 227 — *Web:* www.dmreid.com	Salem	MA	01970	978-744-3818	
Dan Klores Communications Inc (DKC) 261 Fifth Ave. — *Web:* www.dkcnews.com	New York	NY	10016	212-685-4300	685-9024
Deardorff Associates 319 E Lea Blvd — *Web:* www.deardorffassociates.com	Wilmington	DE	19802	302-764-7573	
Dehart & Company Public Relations LLC 1375 Lenoir Rhyne Blvd Se Ste 109 — *Web:* www.dehartandcompany.com	Hickory	NC	28602	828-325-4966	
Dennis Garberg & Associates Inc 14001 Marshall Dr — *Web:* www.sunflowergroup.com	Lenexa	KS	66215	913-890-0900	
Deveney Communication Consulting LLC 2406 Chartres St. — *Web:* www.deveney.com	New Orleans	LA	70117	504-949-3999	
DeVries Public Relations 909 Third Ave. — *Web:* www.devriesglobal.com	New York	NY	10022	212-546-8500	
Digennaro Communications 18 W 21st St Sixth Fl — *Web:* www.digennaro-usa.com	New York City	NY	10010	212-966-9525	
Digiwaxx LLC 349 5th Ave 4th Fl — *Web:* www.digiwaxx.com	New York	NY	10016	212-665-8607	
Dittoe Public Relations Inc 2815 E 62nd St Ste 300 — *Web:* www.dittoepr.com	Indianapolis	IN	46220	317-202-2280	
Dix & Eaton Inc 200 Public Sq Ste 1400 — *Web:* www.dix-eaton.com	Cleveland	OH	44114	216-241-0405	
Dixon Schwabl Advertising 1595 Moseley Rd. — *Web:* dixonschwabl.com	Victor	NY	14564	585-383-0380	
DJ Case & Assoc Inc 317 E Jefferson Blvd — *Web:* www.djcase.com	Mishawaka	IN	46545	574-258-0100	
Dovetail Public Relations 15951 Los Gatos Blvd Ste 16 — *Web:* www.dovetailpr.com	Los Gatos	CA	95032	408-395-3600	
Downey Mcgrath Group Inc 1225 I St Nw Ste 600 — *Web:* dmggroup.com	Washington	DC	20005	202-789-1110	
Duffey Communications Inc 3379 Peachtree Rd NE Ste 300 — *Web:* www.duffey.com	Atlanta	GA	30326	404-266-2600	262-3198
DVL Public Relations & Adv 700 12th Ave S Ste 400 — *Web:* www.dvl.com	Nashville	TN	37203	615-244-1818	780-3396
E. Boineau & Co 128 Beaufain St — *Web:* www.eboineauandco.com	Charleston	SC	29401	843-723-1462	
Echo Media Group Inc 12711 Newport Ave Ste H — *Web:* www.echomediapr.com	Tustin	CA	92780	714-573-0899	
Edelman Public Relations Worldwide 200 E Randolph Dr 63rd Fl — *Web:* www.edelman.com	Chicago	IL	60601	312-240-3000	240-2900
Elasticity LLC 1008 Locust Ave Ste 300 — *Web:* goelastic.com	St. Louis	MO	63101	314-561-8253	
Entertainment Fusion Group Inc 8899 Beverly Blvd Ste 412 — *Web:* www.efgpr.com	Los Angeles	CA	90048	310-432-0020	
Epoch 5 Public Relations 755 New York Ave. — *Web:* www.epoch5.com	Huntington	NY	11743	631-427-1713	
Equals Three Communications 7910 Woodmont Ave Ste 200 — *Web:* www.equals3.com	Bethesda	MD	20814	301-656-3100	652-5264
Erwin-Penland Inc 125 E Broad St — *Web:* www.erwinpenland.com	Greenville	SC	29601	864-271-0500	
ES3 Inc 1625 Star Batt Dr — *Web:* site.es3.net	Rochester Hills	MI	48309	248-537-0110	
fama PR Inc Liberty Wharf 250 Northern Ave Ste 300 — *Web:* www.famapr.com	Boston	MA	02210	617-986-5002	
Feinstein Kean Healthcare 245 First St 14th Fl — *Web:* www.fkhealth.com	Cambridge	MA	02142	617-577-8110	
Fleishman-Hillard Inc 200 N Broadway — *Web:* www.fleishmanhillard.com	Saint Louis	MO	63102	314-982-1700	
Focus Media Inc 10 Matthews St. — *Web:* www.advertisingandpr.com	Goshen	NY	10924	845-294-3342	
Formula PR, Inc. - El Segundo 810 Parkview Dr N — *Web:* www.formulapr.com	El Segundo	CA	90245	310-578-7050	
Freeman Public Relations 16 Furler St. — *Web:* worldofchampagne.com	Totowa	NJ	07512	973-470-0400	
French West Vaughan 112 E Hargett St — *Web:* fwv-us.com	Raleigh	NC	27601	919-832-6300	832-8322
Fresh Ideas Group Inc 2400 Spruce St Ste 100 — *Web:* www.freshideasgroup.com	Boulder	CO	80302	303-449-2108	
Gelia, Wells & Mohr Inc 390 S Youngs Rd — *Web:* www.gelia.com	Williamsville	NY	14221	716-629-3200	
Gibbs & Soell, Inc. 60 E 42nd St Ste 44 — *Web:* www.gibbs-soell.com	New York	NY	10165	212-697-2600	697-2646
Giles Communications LLC 2975 Westchester Ave Ste 402 — *Web:* giles.com	Purchase	NY	10577	914-644-3500	
GMR Marketing LLC 5000 S Towne Dr — *Web:* www.gmrmarketing.com	New Berlin	WI	53151	262-786-5600	
Gordon C James Public Relations Inc 4715 N 32nd St Ste 104 — *Web:* www.gcjpr.com	Phoenix	AZ	85018	602-274-1988	
Griffin & Associates 119 Dartmouth Dr SE — *Web:* www.griffinassoc.com	Albuquerque	NM	87106	505-764-4444	
GS Schwartz & Company Inc 470 Pk Ave S 10th Fl — *Web:* www.schwartz.com	New York	NY	10016	212-725-4500	725-9188
Gulf Coast Tmc 7670 Hwy 10 — *Web:* www.gulfcoasttmc.com	Ethel	LA	70730	225-683-6636	
Hager Sharp Inc 1030 15th St NW Ste 600 E — *Web:* www.hagersharp.com	Washington	DC	20005	202-842-3600	
Halliburton Investor Relations 14651 Dallas Pkwy Ste 800 — *Web:* halliburtonir.com	Dallas	TX	75254	972-458-8000	
Harris, Deville & Associates Inc 521 Laurel St — *Web:* hdaissues.com	Baton Rouge	LA	70801	225-344-0381	
Hawthorn Group LC 625 Slaters Ln # 100 — *Web:* www.hawthorngroup.com	Alexandria	VA	22314	703-299-4499	299-4488
Highwire Public Relations Inc 727 sansome st — *Web:* www.highwirepr.com	San Francisco	CA	94111	415-963-4174	
Hill & Knowlton Inc 825 Third Ave — *Web:* www.hillandknowlton.com	New York	NY	10022	212-885-0300	885-0570
HLB Communications Inc 875 N Michigan Ave	Chicago	IL	60611	312-649-0371	
HMA Public Relations 3610 N 44th St Ste 110 — *Web:* hmapr.com	Phoenix	AZ	85018	602-957-8881	
Hubbell Group Inc, The 101 Derby St Ste 201 — *Web:* www.hubbellgroup.com	Hingham	MA	02043	781-878-8882	
Hunter Public Relations 41 Madison Ave 5th Fl — *TF:* 866-395-7710 ■ *Web:* www.hunterpr.com	New York	NY	10010	212-679-6600	679-6607
i.d.e.a. 444 W Beech St — *Web:* www.theideabrand.com	San Diego	CA	92101	619-295-8232	
Ink Inc 511 Delaware St Ste 200 — *Web:* www.inkincpr.com	Kansas City	MO	64105	816-753-6222	
InQuest Marketing Inc 9249 Ward Pkwy — *Web:* www.inquestmarketing.com	Kansas City	MO	64114	816-994-0994	
Interprose Inc 2635 Steeplechase Dr. — *Web:* www.interprosepr.com	Reston	VA	20191	703-860-0577	
J p r Communications 5950 Canoga Ave Ste 430 — *Web:* www.jprcom.com	Woodland Hills	CA	91367	818-884-8282	
J.C. Watts Companies 600 13th St Nw Ste 790 — *Web:* www.wattsconsultinggroup.com	Washington	DC	20005	202-207-2854	
Jasculca/Terman & Assoc (JTPR) 730 N Franklin Ste 510 — *Web:* www.jtpr.com	Chicago	IL	60654	312-337-7400	337-8189
Jones Agency, The 303 N Indian Canyon Dr — *Web:* www.jonesagency.com	Palm Springs	CA	92262	760-325-1437	
Jones Huyett Partners Inc 3200 SW Huntoon St. — *Web:* jhpadv.com	Topeka	KS	66604	785-228-0900	
KCSA Public Relations Worldwide 880 Third Ave # 6 — *Web:* www.kcsa.com	New York	NY	10022	212-682-6300	697-0910
Kemper Lesnik Communications 500 Skokie Blvd 4th Fl — *Web:* www.klc.com	Northbrook	IL	60062	847-850-1818	559-0406
Ketchum 1285 Ave of the Americas — *Web:* www.ketchum.com	New York	NY	10019	646-935-3900	935-4499
Kohnstamm Communications 400 Robert St N Ste 1450 — *Web:* kohnstamm.com	Saint Paul	MN	55101	651-228-9141	
Kurman Communications Inc 345 N Canal St Ste 1404 — *Web:* kurman.com	Chicago	IL	60606	312-651-9000	
LaForce & Stevens 41 E 11th St 6th Fl — *Web:* www.laforce-stevens.com	New York	NY	10003	212-242-9353	242-9565
Lanza Group LLC 1710 Defoor Ave NW Penthouse 2 — *Web:* www.lanzagroup.com	Atlanta	GA	30318	404-350-0200	
Laura Davidson Public Relations Inc 72 Madison Ave Fl 11 — *Web:* www.ldpr.com	New York	NY	10016	212-696-0660	
LeGrand Hart 1055 Auraria Pkwy Ste 200 — *Web:* www.legrandhart.com	Denver	CO	80204	303-298-8470	
Lenzi Martin Communications 701 Hayes Ave — *Web:* lenzimartin.com	Oak Park	IL	60302	708-848-8404	
LEVICK LLC 1900 M St NW Ste 400 — *Web:* levick.com	Washington	DC	20036	202-973-1300	
Linden Lab 945 Battery St — *Web:* www.lindenlab.com	San Francisco	CA	94111	415-243-9000	
Lois Paul & Partners (LPP) One Beacon St Second Fl — *Web:* www.lpp.com	Boston	MA	02108	617-986-5700	
Love Communications 546 South 200 West — *Web:* www.lovecomm.net	Salt Lake City	UT	84101	801-519-8880	
Lovio George Inc 681 W Forest Ave — *Web:* www.loviogeorgeinc.com	Detroit	MI	48201	313-832-2210	
Lukas Partners Inc 11915 P St Ste 100 — *Web:* www.lukaspartners.com	Omaha	NE	68137	402-895-2552	
M Booth & Assoc Inc 300 Pk Ave S 12th Fl — *Web:* www.mbooth.com	New York	NY	10010	212-481-7000	481-9440
Makovsky + Co 16 E 34th St — *Web:* www.makovsky.com	New York	NY	10016	212-508-9600	751-9710
Manning Selvage & Lee 1675 Broadway 14th Fl — *Web:* northamerica.mslgroup.com	New York	NY	10019	212-468-4200	
Manzella Marketing Group 80 Sonwil Dr — *Web:* promo.manzellamarketing.com	Buffalo	NY	14225	716-681-6565	
Marcus Group Inc, The 150 Clove Rd Ste 24 — *Web:* www.marcusgroup.com	Little Falls	NJ	07424	973-890-9590	
Martin Bontempo Matacera Bartlett Inc 212 W State St — *Web:* www.mbiglucksshaw.com	Trenton	NJ	08608	609-392-3100	
Marx Layne & Co 31420 NW Hwy — *Web:* www.marxlayne.com	Farmington Hills	MI	48334	248-855-6777	855-6719

Company	City	State	ZIP	Phone	Fax
Masto Public Relations Inc 1811 Western Ave *Web:* mastopr.com	Albany	NY	12203	518-786-6488	
Maximum Marketing Services Inc 833 W Jackson Blvd *Web:* www.maxmarketing.com	Chicago	IL	60607	312-226-4111	
McNeely Pigott & Fox 611 Commerce St Ste 2800 *TF:* 800-818-6953 ■ *Web:* www.mpf.com	Nashville	TN	37203	615-259-4000	259-4040
MCS Healthcare Public Relations 1420 US Hwy 206 Ste 100 *TF:* 888-652-8200 ■ *Web:* www.mcspr.com	Bedminster	NJ	07921	908-234-9900	470-4490
Mercury Public Affairs 137 Fifth Ave Third Fl *Web:* www.mercuryllc.com	New York	NY	10010	212-681-1380	
Merkle Group Inc 7001 Columbia Gateway Dr *Web:* www.merkleinc.com	Columbia	MD	21046	443-542-4000	542-4758
Metis Communications Inc 121 E Berkeley St *Web:* metiscomm.com	Boston	MA	02118	617-236-0500	
Milani Marketing & Public Relations LLC 714 Laurel Ave *Web:* www.milanimarketing.com	Burlingame	CA	94010	650-685-5565	
Mirrorball Group LLC 134 w 25th st *Web:* www.mirrorball.com	New York	NY	10001	212-604-9988	
Montesquieu Winery 8221 Arjons Dr *TF:* 800-860-2378 ■ *Web:* www.montesquieu.com	San Diego	CA	92126	800-860-2378	
Morgan & Myers N 16 W 23233 Stone Ridge Dr Ste 200 *Web:* www.morganmyers.com	Weukesha	WI	53188	262-650-7260	650-7261
MSR Communications 832 Sansome St Second Fl *Web:* www.msrcommunications.com	San Francisco	CA	94111	415-989-9000	
Multi Marketing Corp 2033 N Fine Ave *Web:* multimarketingcorp.com	Fresno	CA	93727	559-454-9400	
MurphyEpson Inc 151 E Nationwide Blvd *Web:* murphyepson.com	Columbus	OH	43215	614-221-2885	
Neibart Group 20 Jay St Ste 820 *Web:* www.neibartgroup.com	Brooklyn	NY	11201	718-875-2300	
NM Marketing Communications Inc 706 Waukegan Rd *Web:* www.nmmarketingbiz.com	Glenview	IL	60025	847-657-6011	
Nyhus Communications LLC 720 Third Ave Fl 12 *Web:* www.nyhus.com	Seattle	WA	98104	206-323-3733	
O'Malley Hansen Communications 180 N Wacker Dr Ste 400 *Web:* omalleyhansen.com	Chicago	IL	60606	312-377-0630	
O'reilly Public Relations 3403 10th St Ste 110 *Web:* www.oreillypr.com	Riverside	CA	92501	951-781-2240	
Ogilvy Public Relations Worldwide 636 11th Ave *Web:* www.ogilvypr.com	New York	NY	10036	212-880-5200	370-4636
Oliver Russell & Assoc Inc 217 S 11th St *Web:* www.oliverrussell.com	Boise	ID	83702	208-344-1734	344-1211
Otto Creative Marketing Inc 1611 Colley Ave *Web:* www.thinkotto.com	Norfolk	VA	23517	757-622-4050	
Pacifico Inc 1190 Coleman Ave Ste 110 *Web:* www.pacifico.com	San Jose	CA	95110	408-327-8888	
Padilla Speer Beardsley Inc 1101 W River Pkwy Ste 400 *Web:* padillacrt.com/	Minneapolis	MN	55415	612-455-1700	455-1060
PAN Communications 300 Brickstone Sq *Web:* www.pancommunications.com	Andover	MA	01810	617-502-4300	
Paul Werth Assoc Inc 10 N High St Ste300 *Web:* www.paulwerth.com	Columbus	OH	43215	614-224-8114	
Paul Wilmot Communications LLC 581 Sixth Ave Ste 2 Fl *Web:* www.paulwilmot.com	New York	NY	10001	212-206-7447	
PepperCom Inc 470 Pk Ave S 4th Fl N *Web:* www.peppercom.com	New York	NY	10016	212-931-6100	931-6159
Peritus Public Relations 200 S Fifth St Ste 700 N *Web:* www.perituspr.com	Louisville	KY	40202	502-585-3919	
Picture Marketing Inc 1202 Grant Ave Ste D *Web:* www.picturemarketing.com	Novato	CA	94945	949-623-9889	
Porter Novelli International 75 Varick St Sixth Fl *Web:* www.porternovelli.com	New York	NY	10013	212-601-8000	601-8101
Power PR 18103 Prairie Ave *Web:* www.powerpr.com	Torrance	CA	90504	310-787-1940	
Prism Public Affairs 1399 New York Ave NW Ste 550 *Web:* www.prismpublicaffairs.com	Washington	DC	20005	202-575-3800	
Pro Motion Inc 18405 Edison Ave *Web:* www.promotion1.com	Chesterfield	MO	63005	636-449-3162	
Prr (PRR) 1501 Fourth Ave Ste 550 *Web:* www.prrbiz.com	Seattle	WA	98101	206-623-0735	623-0731
Prx Inc 991 W Hedding St Ste 201 *Web:* www.prxdigital.com	San Jose	CA	95126	408-287-1700	
Public Conversations Project 46 Kondazian St *Web:* www.publicconversations.org	Watertown	MA	02472	617-923-1216	
Public Opinion Strategies LLC 214 N Fayette St *Web:* www.pos.org	Alexandria	VA	22314	703-836-7655	
Publicis Inc 7300 Lone Star Dr *Web:* publicisdallas.com	Plano	TX	75024	469-366-2550	
Pyramid Communications Inc 1932 First Ave Ste 507 *Web:* pyramidcommunications.com/	Seattle	WA	98101	206-374-7788	
Q Advertising & Public Relations 8080 W Sahara Ave Ste A *Web:* qapr.com	Las Vegas	NV	89117	702-256-5511	
Quest Corp of America Inc 3837 Northdale Blvd # 242 *Web:* qcausa.com	Tampa	FL	33624	813-926-2942	
R&J Public Relations LLC 1140 Route 22 E Ste 200 *Web:* www.randjpr.com	Bridgewater	NJ	08807	908-722-5757	
R&R Partners Inc 900 S Pavillion Ctr Dr *Web:* www.rrpartners.com	Las Vegas	NV	89144	702-228-0222	
Regan Communications Group Inc 106 Union Wharf *Web:* www.regancommunications.com	Boston	MA	02109	617-488-2800	
Rendon Group Inc 1875 Conn Ave NW *Web:* www.rendon.com	Washington	DC	20009	202-745-4900	745-0215
Revive Public Relations LLC 915 Saint Vincent Ave *Web:* www.thinkrevivehealth.com	Santa Barbara	CA	93101	805-617-2832	
RF|Binder Partners Inc 950 Third Ave Seventh Fl *Web:* www.rfbinder.com	New York	NY	10022	212-994-7600	
Richmond Public Relations 1411 Fourth Ave Ste 610 *Web:* www.richmondpr.com	Seattle	WA	98101	206-682-6979	
Richter7 280 South 400 West Ste 200 *Web:* www.richter7.com	Salt Lake City	UT	84101	801-521-2903	
Rinck Advertising Two Great Falls Plz Unit 8 Sixth Fl *Web:* www.rinckadvertising.com	Auburn	ME	04210	207-755-9470	
RMR Assoc Inc 5870 Hubbard Dr *Web:* www.rmr.com	Rockville	MD	20852	301-230-0045	230-0046
Rob Bailey Communications 310 State Rt 17 *Web:* rbcpr.com	Upper Saddle River	NJ	07458	201-760-0200	
Robin Leedy & Assoc Inc 118 N Bedford Rd Ste 302 *Web:* robinleedyassociates.com	Mount Kisco	NY	10549	914-241-0086	
Rogers Group, The 1875 Century Pk E Ste 200 *Web:* rogerspr.com	Los Angeles	CA	90067	310-552-6922	
Rosen Group LLC, The Thirty W 26 St Third Fl *Web:* rosengrouppr.com	New York	NY	10010	212-255-8455	
Rubin Communications Group Inc 4542 Bonney Rd Ste B *Web:* rubincommunications.com	Virginia Beach	VA	23462	757-456-5212	
Ruder Finn 301 E 57th St Fourth Fl *Web:* www.ruderfinn.com	New York	NY	10022	212-593-6400	
Rulmeca Corp 6508 Windmill Way Ste B *Web:* www.rulmecacorp.com	Wilmington	NC	28405	910-794-9294	
S&S Public Relations Inc One Northfield Plz Ste 400 **Fax Area Code:* 847 ■ *TF:* 800-287-2279 ■ *Web:* www.sspr.com	Northfield	IL	60093	800-287-2279	955-7720*
Salter Mitchell Inc 117 S Gadsden St *Web:* www.saltermitchell.com	Tallahassee	FL	32301	850-681-3200	
Schwartz Communications Inc 300 Fifth Ave *Web:* www.schwartzmsl.com	Waltham	MA	02451	781-684-0770	684-6500
Scorr Marketing 2201 Central Ave Ste A *Web:* www.scorrmarketing.com	Kearney	NE	68847	308-237-5567	
Scott Public Relations 21201 Victory Blvd Ste 235 *Web:* scottpublicrelations.com	Canoga Park	CA	91303	818-610-0270	
Seigenthaler Public Relations Inc 115 29th Ave South *Web:* www.seig-pr.com	Nashville	TN	37212	615-327-7999	
Seyferth & Associates Inc 40 Monroe Ctr NW *Web:* www.seyferthpr.com	Grand Rapids	MI	49503	616-776-3511	
Shank Public Relations Counselors Inc 2611 Waterfront Pkwy E Dr Ste 310 *Web:* shankpr.com	Indianapolis	IN	46214	317-293-5590	
Shannon Systems LLC 173 Spark St *Web:* www.b2bgateway.net	Brockton	MA	02302	508-894-2150	
Shelton Group 12400 Coit Rd Ste 650 *Web:* www.sheltongroup.com	Dallas	TX	75251	972-239-5119	
SHIFT Communications LLC 275 Washington St Ste 410 *TF:* 800-494-8477 ■ *Web:* www.shiftcomm.com	Newton	MA	02458	617-779-1800	779-1899
Sitrick & Co 1840 Century Pk E Ste 800 *TF:* 800-288-8809 ■ *Web:* www.sitrick.com	Los Angeles	CA	90067	310-788-2850	788-2855
Sloane & Co 7 Times Sq 17th Fl *Web:* www.sloanepr.com	New York	NY	10036	212-486-9500	486-9094
Smith Growth Partners Mill Centre Penthouse 3000 Chestnut Ave *Web:* www.smithgrowthpartners.com	Baltimore	MD	21211	410-235-7004	
Southard Communications Inc 515 W 20th St Sixth Fl *Web:* www.southardinc.com	New York	NY	10011	212-777-2220	993-5811
Spitfire Strategies LLC 1800 M St NW *Web:* spitfirestrategies.com	Washington	DC	20036	202-293-6200	
Stanton Public Relations & Marketing 880 Third Ave *Web:* www.stantonprm.com	New York	NY	10022	212-366-5300	
Storefront Political Media 250 Sutter St Ste 650 *Web:* www.storefrontpolitical.com	San Francisco	CA	94108	415-834-0501	
Strat@comm 1156 15th St NW Ste 800 *Web:* www.stratacomm.net	Washington	DC	20005	202-289-2001	
Sunshine Sachs & Associates 8409 santa monica blvd *Web:* www.sunshinesachs.com	West Hollywood	CA	90069	323-822-9300	
Taylor Global Inc 350 Fifth Ave *Web:* www.taylorstrategy.com	New York	NY	10118	212-714-1280	695-5685
Tech Image Ltd 330 N Wabash Ave Ste 1900 *Web:* www.techimage.com	Chicago	IL	60611	847-279-0022	

	City	State	Zip	Phone	Fax
Text 100 North America 100 Montgomery St 3rd Fl *Web:* www.text100.com	San Francisco	CA	94104	415-593-8400	593-8401
Thomas Boyd Communications 117 N Church St *Web:* thomasboyd.com	Moorestown	NJ	08057	856-642-6226	
Thomson Safaris 14 Mt Auburn St *TF:* 800-235-0289 ■ *Web:* www.thomsonsafaris.com	Watertown	MA	02472	617-923-0426	
Thorp & Co 150 Alhambra Cir Ste 900 Coral Gables *Web:* www.thorpco.com	Miami	FL	33134	305-446-2700	
Tierney Communications 200 S Broad St 10th Fl *Web:* www.hellotierney.com	Philadelphia	PA	19102	215-790-4100	790-4363
TransMedia Group Inc 240 W Palmetto Park Rd *Web:* www.transmediagroup.com	Boca Raton	FL	33432	561-750-9800	
TSG Consulting Ii LLC 118 Capitol St *Web:* tsgsolution.com	Charleston	WV	25301	304-345-1161	
Tunheim Partners 8009 34th Ave S Ste 1100 *Web:* www.tunheim.com	Minneapolis	MN	55425	952-851-1600	851-1610
Van Aartrijk Group Inc, The 7411 Alban Sta Ct Ste B265 *Web:* www.aartrijk.com	Springfield	VA	22150	703-912-7974	
Vest Adv Mktg & PR 3007 Sprowl Rd *Web:* www.vestadvertising.com	Louisville	KY	40299	502-267-5335	
Viviani Associates Public Relations 160 Littleton Rd Ste 311 *Web:* www.vivianipr.com	Parsippany	NJ	07054	973-968-7929	
Voce Communications Inc 298 S Sunnyvale Ave Ste 101 *Web:* www.vocecommunications.com	Sunnyvale	CA	94086	408-738-7840	
VPE Public Relations 1605 Hope St Ste 250 *Web:* vpe-pr.com	South Pasadena	CA	91030	626-403-3200	
W2O Group 60 Francisco St *Web:* www.w2ogroup.com	San Francisco	CA	94133	415-362-5018	
Wagstaff Worldwide Inc 6725 W Sunset Blvd Ste 590 *Web:* www.wagstaffworldwide.com	Los Angeles	CA	90028	323-871-1151	
Walt & Company Communications 2105 S Bascom Ave Ste 240 *Web:* www.walt.com	Campbell	CA	95008	408-369-7200	369-7201
Warschawski 1501 Sulgrave Ave Ste 350 *Web:* www.warschawski.com	Baltimore	MD	21209	410-367-2700	
Weber Shandwick Worldwide 909 Third Ave *Web:* www.webershandwick.com	New York	NY	10022	212-445-8000	
Weidert Group Inc 210 W College Ave *Web:* www.weidert.com	Appleton	WI	54911	920-731-2771	
Welcomm Inc 7975 Raytheon Rd Ste 340 *Web:* www.welcomm.com	San Diego	CA	92111	858-279-1611	
Widmeyer Communications 1129 20th St NW Ste 200 *Web:* www.widmeyer.com	Washington	DC	20036	202-667-0901	667-0902
ZAG Communications 4060D Peachtree Rd Ste 534 *Web:* www.zagcommunications.com	Atlanta	GA	30319	678-799-8279	
Zaiss & Co 11626 Nicholas St *Web:* www.zaissco.com	Omaha	NE	68154	402-964-9293	
Zapwater Communications Inc 118 N Peoria Fourth Fl *Web:* zapwater.com	Chicago	IL	60607	312-943-0333	
Zeno Group 44 E 30th St Ste 11 *Web:* www.zenogroup.com	New York	NY	10016	212-299-8888	
Zeppos & Associates Inc 400 E Mason St Ste 200 *Web:* www.zeppos.com	Milwaukee	WI	53202	414-276-6237	
Zimmerman Agency, The 1821 Miccosukee Commons *Web:* www.zimmerman.com	Tallahassee	FL	32308	850-668-2222	656-4622
Zone 5 25 Monroe St Ste 300 *Web:* www.zone5.com	Albany	NY	12210	518-242-7000	

PUBLICATIONS

SEE Magazines & Journals p. 2686; Newsletters p. 2813; Newspapers p. 2817

640 PUBLISHING COMPANIES

SEE ALSO Literary Agents p. 2671; Magazines & Journals p. 2686; Newsletters p. 2813; Newspapers p. 2817; Book Producers p. 1877

640-1 Atlas & Map Publishers

	City	State	Zip	Phone	Fax
DeLorme Two DeLorme Dr PO Box 298 **Fax Area Code:* 800 ■ *TF Sales:* 800-452-5931 ■ *Web:* www.delorme.com	Yarmouth	ME	04096	207-846-7000	561-5105*
MARCOA Publishing Inc 9955 Black Mtn Rd *TF:* 800-854-2935 ■ *Web:* www.marcoa.com	San Diego	CA	92126	858-695-9600	695-9641
Nystrom 4719 W 62nd St	Indianapolis	IN	46268	317-612-3901	329-3305
Rand McNally 9855 Woods Dr PO Box 7600 **Fax Area Code:* 540 ■ *TF:* 800-275-7263 ■ *Web:* www.randmcnally.com	Skokie	IL	60077	800-275-7263	891-7590*
Simon & Schuster Interactive 1230 Ave of the Americas *TF:* 800-223-2336 ■ *Web:* www.simonandschuster.biz	New York	NY	10020	212-698-7000	632-8099

640-2 Book Publishers

	City	State	Zip	Phone	Fax
ABC-CLIO Inc 130 Cremona Dr *TF:* 800-368-6868 ■ *Web:* www.abc-clio.com	Goleta	CA	93117	805-968-1911	685-9685
American Printing House for the Blind 1839 Frankfort Ave PO Box 6085 *TF:* 800-223-1839 ■ *Web:* www.aph.org	Louisville	KY	40206	502-895-2405	899-2274
Antique Collectors Club 116 Pleasant St *TF:* 800-254-4100 ■ *Web:* businessfinder.masslive.com	EastHampton	MA	01027	413-529-0861	
Applewood Books Inc 1 River Rd *TF General:* 800-277-5312 ■ *Web:* www.applewoodbooks.com	Carlisle	MA	01741	781-271-0055	
Atlantic Publishing Co 315 E Washington St **Fax Area Code:* 352 ■ *TF:* 800-814-1132 ■ *Web:* www.atlantic-pub.com	Starke	FL	32091	800-814-1132	622-1875*
Author House 1663 Liberty Dr Ste 200 *TF:* 888-728-8467 ■ *Web:* www.authorhouse.com	Bloomington	IN	47403	812-339-6000	339-6554
Avalon Travel Publishing 1700 Fourth St *Web:* www.avalontravelbooks.com	Berkeley	CA	94710	510-595-3664	595-4228
Aviation Supplies & Academics Inc 7005 132nd Pl Se *Web:* asa2fly.com	Newcastle	WA	98059	425-235-1500	
Barron's Educational Series Inc 250 Wireless Blvd *TF:* 800-645-3476 ■ *Web:* www.barronseduc.com	Hauppauge	NY	11788	631-434-3311	434-3723
Beacon Press Inc 24 Farnsworth St *Web:* www.beacon.org	Boston	MA	02210	617-742-2110	723-3097
Behrman House Inc 11 Edison Pl *Web:* behrmanhouse.com	Springfield	NJ	07081	973-379-7200	
Bertelsmann SE & Co 1745 Broadway *Web:* www.bertelsmann.com	New York	NY	10019	490-524-1800	
Black Classic Press PO Box 13414 *Web:* www.blackclassicbooks.com	Baltimore	MD	21203	410-242-6954	
BOA Editions Ltd 250 N Goodman St Ste 306 *Web:* www.boaeditions.org	Rochester	NY	14607	585-546-3410	546-3913
BRB Publications Inc PO Box 27869 **Fax Area Code:* 800 ■ *TF:* 800-929-3811 ■ *Web:* www.brbpub.com	Tempe	AZ	85285	480-829-7475	929-4981*
Brillacademic Publishers Inc 2 liberty Sq 11th Fl *TF:* 800-337-9255 ■ *Web:* www.brill.com	Boston	MA	02109	617-263-2323	263-2324
Browntrout Publishers Inc 201 Continental Blvd *TF:* 800-777-7812 ■ *Web:* www.browntrout.com	El Segundo	CA	90245	310-607-9010	607-9011
Bureau of National Affairs Inc 1801 S Bell St *TF:* 800-372-1033 ■ *Web:* www.bna.com	Arlington	VA	22202	703-341-3000	
Bureau of National Affairs Inc BNA Books Div 1801 S Bell St *TF Sales:* 800-372-1033 ■ *Web:* www.bna.com/bnabooks/	Arlington	VA	22202	703-341-3500	341-1610
Candlewick Press Inc 99 Dover St *Web:* www.candlewick.com	Somerville	MA	02144	617-661-3330	661-0565
Carroll Publishing Co 4701 Sangamore Rd Ste S-155 *TF:* 800-336-4240 ■ *Web:* www.carrollpublishing.com	Bethesda	MD	20816	301-263-9800	263-9801
Catholic News Publishing Company Inc 210 N Ave *Web:* catholicguides.com	New Rochelle	NY	10801	914-632-1220	
Cengage Learning PO Box 6904 *TF:* 800-354-9706 ■ *Web:* www.cengage.com/highered	Florence	KY	41022	800-354-9706	487-8488
Charles C Thomas Publisher 2600 S First St PO Box 19265 *TF Sales:* 800-258-8980 ■ *Web:* www.ccthomas.com	Springfield	IL	62704	217-789-8980	789-9130
Chelsea Green Publishing Co 85 N Main St *Web:* chelseagreen.com	White River Junction	VT	05001	802-295-6300	
Children's Press 557 Broadway *Web:* scholastic.co.in	New York	NY	10012	212-343-6100	
Chronicle Books 680 Second St *TF:* 800-722-6657 ■ *Web:* www.chroniclebooks.com	San Francisco	CA	94107	415-537-4200	537-4460
Clarion Books 215 Pk Ave S *Web:* www.hmhco.com	New York	NY	10003	212-420-5800	420-5855
Commemorative Brands Inc 7211 Cir S Rd **Fax Area Code:* 512 ■ *TF:* 800-225-3687 ■ *Web:* www.balfour.com	Austin	TX	78745	800-225-3687	443-5213*
Corwin Press Inc 2455 Teller Rd *TF Orders:* 800-233-9936 ■ *Web:* www.corwin.com	Thousand Oaks	CA	91320	805-499-9734	499-0871
CPP Inc 1055 Joaquin Rd Ste 200 *Web:* cpp.com	Mountain View	CA	94043	650-969-8901	
CRC Press LLC 6000 Broken Sound Pkwy NW Ste 300 **Fax Area Code:* 800 ■ **Fax:* Cust Svc ■ *TF Cust Svc:* 800-272-7737 ■ *Web:* www.crcpress.com	Boca Raton	FL	33487	561-994-0555	374-3401*
Creative Communications For The Parish Inc 1564 Fencorp Dr *TF:* 800-325-9414 ■ *Web:* www.creativecommunications.com	Fenton	MO	63026	636-305-9777	305-9333
Curriculum Assoc Inc 153 Rangeway Rd *TF:* 800-225-0248 ■ *Web:* www.curriculumassociates.com	North Billerica	MA	01862	800-225-0248	225-0248
D & B 103 JFK Pkwy *NYSE:* DNB ■ *TF:* 800-234-3867 ■ *Web:* www.dnb.com	Short Hills	NJ	07078	973-921-5500	921-5501
Dalmation Press 113 Seaboard Ln Ste C-250 **Fax Area Code:* 615 ■ *TF:* 800-815-8696 ■ *Web:* www.dalmatianpress.com	Franklin	TN	37067	800-815-8696	370-8034*
Dickinson Press Inc 5100 33rd St Se *Web:* dickinsonpress.com	Grand Rapids	MI	49512	616-957-5100	
Disney Consumer Products 500 S Buena Vista St **Fax Area Code:* 215 ■ **Fax:* Cust Svc ■ *TF PR:* 877-282-8322 ■ *Web:* thewaltdisneycompany.com	Burbank	CA	91521	818-560-1000	553-5402*
Disney Publishing Worldwide Inc 44 S Broadway	White Plains	NY	10601	914-288-4100	
Dolan Media Co 222 S Ninth St Ste 2300 *Web:* www.thedolancompany.com	Minneapolis	MN	55402	612-317-9420	321-0563
Donning Company Publishers 184 Business Pk Dr Ste 206 **Fax Area Code:* 757 ■ *TF:* 800-296-8572 ■ *Web:* www.donning.com	Virginia Beach	VA	23462	800-296-8572	497-2542*

Company	City	State	Zip	Phone	Fax
Dorling Kindersley Publishing 375 Hudson St *TF Cust Svc:* 800-631-8571 ■ *Web:* us.dk.com	New York	NY	10014	646-674-4047	674-4047
Educators Publishing Service Inc (EPS) 625 Mt Auburn St Third Fl PO Box 9031 *TF:* 800-225-5750 ■ *Web:* eps.schoolspecialty.com/	Cambridge	MA	02139	800-225-5750	
EMC-Paradigm Publishing Co 875 Montreal Way *Fax Area Code: 800 ■ *TF:* 800-328-1452 ■ *Web:* newmountainlearning.com	Saint Paul	MN	55102	651-290-2800	328-4564*
Encyclopaedia Britannica Inc 331 N La Salle St *Fax: PR ■ *TF:* 800-323-1229 ■ *Web:* www.britannica.com	Chicago	IL	60654	312-347-7159	294-2104*
Ethan Ellenberg Literary Agency 548 Broadway *Web:* ethanellenberg.com	New York	NY	10012	212-431-4554	
FA Davis Co 1915 Arch St *TF:* 800-323-3555 ■ *Web:* www.fadavis.com	Philadelphia	PA	19103	215-568-2270	568-5065
Feminist Press at the City University of New York 365 Fifth Ave Ste 5406 *TF:* 800-283-3572 ■ *Web:* www.feministpress.org	New York	NY	10016	212-817-7922	817-1593
Financial Publishing Co PO Box 570 *TF Cust Svc:* 800-433-0090 ■ *Web:* www.financial-publishing.com	South Bend	IN	46624	574-243-6040	243-6060
Forbes Inc 60 Fifth Ave *TF:* 800-295-0893 ■ *Web:* www.forbes.com	New York	NY	10011	212-620-2200	206-5534
Free Spirit Publishing Inc 217 Fifth Ave N Ste 200 *Web:* freespirit.com	Minneapolis	MN	55401	612-338-2068	
Gale Cengage Learning 27500 Drake Rd *Fax Area Code: 877 ■ *TF Cust Svc:* 800-877-4253 ■ *Web:* www.gale.cengage.com	Farmington Hills	MI	48331	248-699-4253	363-4253*
Glencoe/McGraw-Hill 8787 Orion Pl *TF:* 800-848-1567 ■ *Web:* www.glencoe.com	Columbus	OH	43240	800-848-1567	
Good Will Publishers Inc PO Box 269 *Web:* www.goodwillpublishers.com	Gastonia	NC	28052	704-865-1256	861-1085
Goodheart-Willcox Publisher 18604 W Creek Dr *Fax Area Code: 888 ■ *TF:* 800-323-0440 ■ *Web:* www.g-w.com	Tinley Park	IL	60477	708-687-5000	409-3900*
Government Research Service 1516 SW Boswell Ave *TF:* 800-346-6898 ■ *Web:* statelegislativesourcebook.com	Topeka	KS	66604	785-232-7720	232-1615
Grade Finders Inc PO Box 944 *TF:* 800-777-8074 ■ *Web:* www.gradefinders.com	Exton	PA	19341	610-524-7070	269-7077
Greenwood-Heinemann 361 Hanover St *TF:* 800-541-2086 ■ *Web:* www.heinemann.com	Portsmouth	NH	03801	603-431-7894	431-7840
Grey House Publishing 4919 Rt 22 PO Box 56 *TF:* 800-562-2139 ■ *Web:* www.greyhouse.com	Amenia	NY	12501	518-789-8700	789-0556
Grove/Atlantic Inc 841 Broadway 4th Fl *Fax Area Code: 212 ■ *Web:* www.groveatlantic.com	New York	NY	10003	781-314-0800	614-7886*
Hachette Book Group 237 Pk Ave *TF:* 800-759-0190 ■ *Web:* www.hachettebookgroup.com	New York	NY	10017	800-759-0190	331-1664
Haights Cross Communications 136 Madison Ave 8th Fl *Fax Area Code: 866 ■ *TF:* 800-338-6519 ■ *Web:* www.haightscross.com	New York	NY	10016	212-209-0500	805-5723*
Harlequin Enterprises Ltd 225 Duncan Mill Rd *TF:* 888-343-9777 ■ *Web:* www.harlequin.com	Don Mills	ON	M3B3K9	416-445-5860	445-8655
Harlequin-Silhouette Books 233 Broadway Ste 1001 *TF:* 800-873-8635 ■ *Web:* www.harlequin.com	New York	NY	10279	212-553-4200	227-8969
HarperCollins Publishers Inc 10 E 53rd St *TF:* 800-242-7737 ■ *Web:* www.harpercollins.com	New York	NY	10022	212-207-7000	207-6998
Harris Connect LLC 1511 Rt 22 Ste C-25 *Fax Area Code: 845 ■ *TF:* 800-516-4915 ■ *Web:* www.harrisconnect.com	Brewster	NY	10509	800-516-4915	940-0801*
Harry N Abrams Inc 115 W 18th St Sixth Fl *Web:* www.abramsbooks.com	New York	NY	10011	212-206-7715	519-1210
Health Communications Inc (HCI) 3201 SW 15th St *TF Cust Svc:* 800-441-5569 ■ *Web:* www.hcibooks.com	Deerfield Beach	FL	33442	954-360-0909	360-0034
Holtzbrinck Publishers 175 Fifth Ave *Fax Area Code: 212 ■ *TF:* 800-221-7945 ■ *Web:* macmillan.com	New York	NY	10010	646-307-5151	420-9314*
Houghton Mifflin Company School Div 222 Berkeley St *Web:* www.eduplace.com	Boston	MA	02116	617-351-3699	351-1100
Houghton Mifflin Company Trade & Reference Div 222 Berkeley St *Web:* www.houghtonmifflinbooks.com	Boston	MA	02116	617-351-5000	351-1100
Houghton Mifflin Harcourt 222 Berkeley St *TF:* 877-866-2586 ■ *Web:* www.hmhco.com	Boston	MA	02116	617-351-5000	351-1114
Human Kinetics 1607 N Market St *TF:* 800-747-4457 ■ *Web:* www.humankinetics.com	Champaign	IL	61820	217-351-5076	351-2674
HW Wilson Co 10 Estes St *TF:* 800-653-2726 ■ *Web:* www.ebscohost.com	Ipswich	MA	01938	978-356-6500	
Inner Traditions International one Pk Row *TF:* 800-246-8648 ■ *Web:* www.innertraditions.com	Rochester	VT	05767	802-767-3174	767-3726
Island Press 2000 M St NW Suite 650 *TF:* 800-621-2736 ■ *Web:* www.islandpress.org	Washington	DC	20036	202-232-7933	234-1328
iUniverse 1663 Liberty Dr *Fax Area Code: 812 ■ *TF:* 800-288-4677 ■ *Web:* www.iuniverse.com	Bloomington	IN	47403	800-288-4677	355-4085*
Jane's Information Group 110 N Royal St Ste 200 *TF:* 800-824-0768 ■ *Web:* www.janes.com	Alexandria	VA	22314	703-683-3700	836-0029
Jeppesen Sanderson Inc 55 Inverness Dr E *TF:* 800-621-5377 ■ *Web:* ww1.jeppesen.com	Englewood	CO	80112	303-799-9090	328-4153
John Wiley & Sons Inc 111 River St *NYSE: JW/A* ■ *TF Sales:* 800-225-5945 ■ *Web:* www.wiley.com	Hoboken	NJ	07030	201-748-6000	748-6088
Jossey-Bass & Pfeiffer 989 Market St 5th Fl *Fax Area Code: 415 ■ *Web:* wiley.com/wileycda/brand/id-17.html	San Francisco	CA	94103	317-572-3994	433-0499*
Judaica Press Inc 123 Ditmas Ave *TF:* 800-972-6201 ■ *Web:* www.judaicapress.com	Brooklyn	NY	11218	718-972-6200	972-6204
Kendall/Hunt Publishing Co 4050 Westmark Dr PO Box 1840 *Fax Area Code: 800 ■ *Fax: Cust Svc ■ *TF Cust Svc:* 800-228-0810 ■ *Web:* www.kendallhunt.com	Dubuque	IA	52002	563-589-1000	772-9165*
Kensington Publishing Corp 119 W 40th St *TF:* 800-221-2647 ■ *Web:* www.kensingtonbooks.com	New York	NY	10018	212-407-1500	935-0699
Key Curriculum Press 1150 65th St *Fax Area Code: 800 ■ *TF:* 800-338-3987 ■ *Web:* www.keycurriculum.com	Emeryville	CA	94608	510-595-7000	541-2442*
Lawyers Diary & Manual 240 Mulberry St PO Box 50 *Fax: Cust Svc ■ *TF:* 800-444-4041 ■ *Web:* www.lawdiary.com	Newark	NJ	07102	973-642-1440	642-4280*
Leadership Directories Inc 104 Fifth Ave 3rd Fl *TF:* 800-627-0311 ■ *Web:* www.leadershipdirectories.com	New York	NY	10011	212-627-4140	645-0931
Lerner Publishing Group 1251 Washington Ave N *TF:* 800-328-4929 ■ *Web:* www.lernerbooks.com	Minneapolis	MN	55401	800-328-4929	332-1132
LexisNexis Matthew Bender 744 Broad St *TF:* 800-252-9257 ■ *Web:* www.lexisnexis.com	Newark	NJ	07102	973-820-2000	
Lightning Source 1246 Heil Quaker Blvd *TF:* 800-509-4156 ■ *Web:* www.lightningsource.com	La Vergne	TN	37086	615-213-5815	213-4426
Linden Publishing 2006 S Mary St *TF Sales:* 800-345-4447 ■ *Web:* www.woodworkerslibrary.com	Fresno	CA	93721	559-233-6633	233-6933
Linguisystems Inc 3100 Fourth Ave *Web:* linguisystems.com	East Moline	IL	61244	309-755-2300	
Lippincott Williams & Wilkins 530 Walnut St *Web:* www.lww.com	Philadelphia	PA	19106	215-521-8300	521-8902
Little Brown & Co 237 Pk Ave *TF Cust Svc:* 800-759-0190 ■ *Web:* www.hachettebookgroup.com	New York	NY	10017	212-364-1100	
Llewellyn Worldwide Inc 2143 Wooddale Dr *TF:* 800-843-6666 ■ *Web:* www.llewellyn.com	Woodbury	MN	55125	651-291-1970	291-1908
Lonely Planet Publications 50 Linden St *TF:* 800-275-8555 ■ *Web:* www.lonelyplanet.com	Oakland	CA	94607	510-893-8555	893-8572
Marquis Who's Who 300 Connell Dr Ste 2000 *TF:* 800-473-7020 ■ *Web:* www.marquiswhoswho.com	Berkeley Heights	NJ	07922	908-673-1000	673-1189
McFarland & Company Inc 960 NC Hwy 88 W PO Box 611 *TF:* 800-253-2187 ■ *Web:* www.mcfarlandpub.com	Jefferson	NC	28640	336-246-4460	246-5018
McGraw-Hill Cos Inc 1221 Ave of the Americas *NYSE: MHFI* ■ *Web:* www.mcgraw-hill.com	New York	NY	10020	212-512-2000	
McGraw-Hill Higher Education Group 1333 Burr Ridge Pkwy *Fax Area Code: 614 ■ *TF:* 800-634-3963 ■ *Web:* www.mhhe.com	Burr Ridge	IL	60527	630-789-4000	755-5654*
McGraw-Hill Professional Publishing Group Two Penn Plz 11th Fl *Fax Area Code: 212 ■ *TF:* 877-833-5524 ■ *Web:* www.mhprofessional.com	New York	NY	10121	877-833-5524	904-4070*
Mel Bay Publications Inc Four Industrial Dr *TF:* 800-863-5229 ■ *Web:* www.melbay.com	Pacific	MO	63069	636-257-3970	257-5062
Meredith Corp 1716 Locust St *NYSE: MDP* ■ *Web:* www.meredith.com	Des Moines	IA	50309	515-284-3000	284-3806
Merriam-Webster Inc PO Box 281 *TF Cust Svc:* 800-828-1880 ■ *Web:* www.merriam-webster.com	Springfield	MA	01102	413-734-3134	731-5979
Microsoft Press one Microsoft Wy *TF Cust Svc:* 800-642-7676 ■ *Web:* www.microsoft.com/mspress	Redmond	WA	98052	425-882-8080	936-7329
Midwest Plan Service 122 Davidson Hall ISU *TF:* 800-562-3618 ■ *Web:* www-mwps.sws.iastate.edu	Ames	IA	50011	515-294-4337	294-9589
Mike Murach & Assoc Inc 4340 N Knoll *TF:* 800-221-5528 ■ *Web:* www.murach.com	Fresno	CA	93722	559-440-9071	440-0963
Moody's Corp 250 Greenwich St 7 World Trade Ctr *NYSE: MCO* ■ *Web:* www.moodys.com	New York	NY	10007	212-553-0300	
National Academy Press 500 Fifth St NW PO Box 285 *Fax: Sales ■ *TF:* 800-624-6242 ■ *Web:* www.nap.edu	Washington	DC	20055	202-334-3313	334-2451*
National Braille Press Inc 88 St Stephen St *TF:* 888-965-8965 ■ *Web:* www.nbp.org	Boston	MA	02115	617-266-6160	437-0456
National Register Publishing Co 430 Mountain Ave Suite 400 *Fax Area Code: 908 ■ *TF:* 800-473-7020 ■ *Web:* www.nationalregisterpub.com	New Providence	NJ	07974	800-473-7020	673-1189*
National Underwriter Co 5081 Olympic Blvd *Fax Area Code: 859 ■ *TF:* 800-543-0874 ■ *Web:* www.nationalunderwriter.com	Erlanger	KY	41018	800-543-0874	692-2175*
Nerdy Books 135 Main St *Web:* www.nerdybooks.com	Flemington	NJ	08822	908-788-4676	788-7097
New Generation Research Inc 225 Friend St Ste 801 *TF:* 800-468-3810 ■ *Web:* www.turnarounds.com	Boston	MA	02114	617-573-9550	573-9554
New Readers Press 1320 Jamesville Ave *Fax Area Code: 866 ■ *TF:* 800-448-8878 ■ *Web:* www.newreaderspress.com	Syracuse	NY	13210	315-422-9121	894-2100*
Newkirk Products Inc 15 Corporate Cir *TF:* 800-525-4237 ■ *Web:* www.newkirk.com	Albany	NY	12203	518-862-3200	862-3399
Nielsen Business Media *Nielsen Co, The* 770 Broadway *Web:* www.nielsen.com	New York	NY	10003	646-654-4500	
Nightingale-Conant Corp 6245 W Howard St *Fax Area Code: 847 ■ *TF Cust Svc:* 800-557-1660 ■ *Web:* www.nightingale.com	Niles	IL	60714	800-557-1660	647-5989*
No Starch Press Inc 38 Ringold St *TF:* 800-420-7240 ■ *Web:* www.nostarch.com	San Francisco	CA	94103	415-863-9900	863-9950
Nolo.com 950 Parker St *TF:* 800-728-3555 ■ *Web:* www.nolo.com	Berkeley	CA	94710	800-728-3555	645-0895
Omnigraphics Inc PO Box 31-1640 *TF:* 800-234-1340 ■ *Web:* www.omnigraphics.com	Detroit	MI	48231	800-234-1340	875-1340
Open Court Publishing Co 70 E Lake St Ste 800 *Fax Area Code: 312 ■ *TF:* 800-815-2280 ■ *Web:* www.opencourtbooks.com	Chicago	IL	60601	800-815-2280	701-1728*
Overlook Press 141 Wooster St *TF:* 800-527-9703 ■ *Web:* www.overlookpress.com	New York	NY	10012	212-673-2210	673-2296
Oxford University Press 198 Madison Ave *Fax Area Code: 919 ■ *TF Orders:* 800-445-9714	New York	NY	10016	212-726-6000	677-1303*
Pathway Press 1080 Montgomery Ave NE *Fax: Sales ■ *Web:* www.pathwaypress.org	Cleveland	TN	37311	423-478-6440	*
Pearson Education Inc One Lake St *TF Cust Svc:* 800-922-0579 ■ *Web:* www.pearsoned.com	Upper Saddle River	NJ	07458	201-236-6716	
Pearson Education School Div 1900 E Lk Ave Ofc Ste B-110A *Fax: Cust Svc ■ *TF:* 800-348-4474 ■ *Web:* www.pearsonschool.com	Glenview	IL	60025	800-348-4474	841-8939*

Phone Fax

Pencor Services Inc 613 Third St. . . . . Palmerton PA 18071 610-826-2552
Web: www.pencor.com

Penguin Group (USA) Inc 375 Hudson St. . . . . New York NY 10014 212-366-2000 366-2933
TF Sales: 800-847-5515 ■ *Web:* penguin.com/

Penguin Random House 1745 Broadway . . . . New York NY 10019 212-782-9000 782-5157
TF: 800-733-3000 ■ *Web:* www.randomhouse.com

Penguin Random House Inc
Bantam Dell Publishing Group
1745 Broadway 10th Fl . . . . New York NY 10019 212-782-9000
TF: 888-523-9292 ■ *Web:* www.penguinrandomhouse.com

Peoples Educational Holdings Inc
299 Market St. . . . . Saddle Brook NJ 07663 201-712-0090 712-0045
OTC: PEDH ■ *TF:* 800-822-1080 ■ *Web:* www.peopleseducation.com

Perseus Books Group, The 210 American Dr . . . . Jackson TN 38301 731-426-6061 351-5073*
**Fax Area Code:* 800 ■ *TF:* 800-343-4499 ■ *Web:* perseusbooksgroup.com/

Peter Lang Publishing Inc 29 Broadway . . . . New York NY 10006 212-647-7706 647-7707
Web: www.peterlang.com

Prentice-Hall Inc 1 Lake St . . . . Upper Saddle River NJ 07458 800-328-5999 236-3400*
**Fax Area Code:* 201 ■ *Web:* www.pearsoned.com/

Price Books & Forms Inc
531 E Sierra Madre Ave . . . . Glendora CA 91741 800-423-8961 768-2162*
**Fax Area Code:* 626 ■ *TF:* 800-423-8961 ■ *Web:* www.autopricebooks.com

PublicAffairs 250 W 57th St 15th Fl . . . . New York NY 10107 212-397-6666 340-8125
Web: www.publicaffairsbooks.com

Publications International Ltd
7373 N Cicero Ave . . . . Lincolnwood IL 60712 847-676-3470 676-3671
TF General: 800-777-5582 ■ *Web:* pilbooks.com

Quebecor Media Inc 612 Rue St Jacques . . . . Montreal QC H3C4M8 514-380-1999 985-8652
Web: www.quebecor.com

Rand McNally 9855 Woods Dr PO Box 7600 . . . . Skokie IL 60077 800-275-7263 891-7590*
**Fax Area Code:* 540 ■ *TF:* 800-275-7263 ■ *Web:* www.randmcnally.com

Regnery Publishing Inc
300 New Jersey Ave NW . . . . Washington DC 20001 202-216-0600 216-0612
TF: 888-219-4747 ■ *Web:* www.regnery.com

Rizzoli International Publications Inc
300 Pk Ave S 3rd Fl . . . . New York NY 10010 212-387-3400 387-3535
Web: www.rizzoliusa.com

Rosen Publishing Group Inc, The
29 E 21st St . . . . New York NY 10010 800-237-9932 436-4643*
**Fax Area Code:* 888 ■ *TF:* 800-237-9932 ■ *Web:* www.rosenpublishing.com

Rowman & Littlefield Publishers Inc
4501 Forbes Blvd Ste 200 . . . . Lanham MD 20706 301-459-3366 429-5748
TF: 800-462-6420 ■ *Web:* rowman.com

RR Bowker LLC 630 Central Ave . . . . New Providence NJ 07974 908-286-1090 219-0193*
**Fax:* Cust Svc ■ *TF:* 888-269-5372 ■ *Web:* www.bowker.co.uk

Sage Publications Inc 2455 Teller Rd. . . . . Thousand Oaks CA 91320 805-499-9774 499-0871
TF: 800-818-7243 ■ *Web:* www.sagepub.com

Sams Technical Publishing
9850 E 30th St . . . . Indianapolis IN 46229 800-428-7267 552-3910
TF Cust Svc: 800-428-7267 ■ *Web:* www.samswebsite.com

Santillana USA Publishing Co 2023 NW 84th Ave . . . . Doral FL 33122 305-591-9522 248-9518*
**Fax Area Code:* 888 ■ *TF:* 800-245-8584 ■ *Web:* www.santillanausa.com

School Annual Publishing Co
2568 Park Ctr Blvd Ste B . . . . State College PA 16801 800-436-6030 436-6048
TF: 800-436-6030 ■ *Web:* www.schoolannual.com

Simon & Schuster 1230 Ave of the Americas. . . . . New York NY 10020 212-698-7000
TF Cust Svc: 800-223-2336 ■ *Web:* www.simonandschuster.biz

Slack Inc 6900 Grove Rd. . . . . Thorofare NJ 08086 856-848-1000 848-6091
TF: 800-257-8290 ■ *Web:* www.slackinc.com

Sourcebooks Inc 1935 Brookdale Rd Ste 139. . . . . Naperville IL 60563 630-961-3900 961-2168
TF: 800-432-7444 ■ *Web:* www.sourcebooks.com

SRDS 1700 Higgins Rd . . . . Des Plaines IL 60018 847-375-5000 375-5001
TF: 800-851-7737 ■ *Web:* login.srds.com

Stackpole Books 5067 Ritter Rd . . . . Mechanicsburg PA 17055 717-796-0411 796-0412
TF Sales: 800-732-3669 ■ *Web:* www.stackpolebooks.com

Standard & Poor's Corp 55 Water St . . . . New York NY 10041 212-438-1000 438-2000
TF: 877-772-5436 ■ *Web:* www.standardandpoors.com

Sterling Publishing Company Inc
387 Pk Ave S Fifth Fl . . . . New York NY 10016 212-532-7160 213-2495
TF Cust Svc: 800-367-9692 ■ *Web:* www.sterlingpublishing.com

Storey Publishing LLC 210 Mass Moca Way . . . . North Adams MA 01247 413-346-2100 346-2199*
**Fax:* Edit ■ *TF:* 800-827-7444 ■ *Web:* www.storey.com

Sunset Publishing Corp 80 Willow Rd. . . . . Menlo Park CA 94025 650-321-3600 327-7537*
**Fax:* Edit ■ *TF:* 800-227-7346 ■ *Web:* www.sunset.com

Taylor & Francis Group 270 Madison Ave . . . . New York NY 10016 212-216-7855 643-1430
TF: 800-797-3803 ■ *Web:* www.taylorandfrancis.com

Technology Marketing Corp One Technology Plz. . . . . Norwalk CT 06854 203-852-6800 866-3326
TF Cust Svc: 800-243-6002 ■ *Web:* www.tmcnet.com

TFH Publications Inc One TFH Plz PO Box 427 . . . . Neptune NJ 07754 732-988-8400 988-5466
TF General: 800-631-2188 ■ *Web:* www.tfh.com

Thomas Publishing Co 5 Penn Plaza . . . . New York NY 10001 212-695-0500 290-7362
TF: 800-733-1127 ■ *Web:* www.thomaspublishing.com

Thorndike Press 10 Water St Ste 310. . . . . Waterville ME 04901 207-861-7500 861-7501*
**Fax:* Sales ■ *TF:* 800-223-1244 ■ *Web:* thorndike.gale.com

Torstar Corp 1 Yonge St Ste 600. . . . . Toronto ON M5E1P9 416-869-4010 869-4183
TSE: TS.B ■ *Web:* www.torstar.com

Townsend Press 439 Kelley Dr . . . . West Berlin NJ 08091 856-753-0554 225-8894*
**Fax Area Code:* 800 ■ *TF:* 800-772-6410 ■ *Web:* www.townsendpress.com

Triumph Learning 136 Madison Ave . . . . New York NY 10016 800-221-9372 805-5723*
**Fax Area Code:* 866 ■ **Fax:* Cust Svc ■ *TF:* 800-221-9372 ■ *Web:* www.triumphlearning.com

Tuttle Publishing
364 Innovation Dr
Airport Industrial Pk . . . . North Clarendon VT 05759 802-773-8930 329-8885*
**Fax Area Code:* 800 ■ *TF Sales:* 800-526-2778 ■ *Web:* www.tuttlepublishing.com

Unisystems Inc 155 E 55th St . . . . New York NY 10022 212-826-0850 759-9069
Web: www.modernpublishing.com

University Press of America
4501 Forbes Blvd Ste 200 . . . . Lanham MD 20706 301-459-3366 429-5746
TF: 800-462-6420 ■ *Web:* rowman.com

Vantage Press Inc 419 Pk Ave S 18th Fl. . . . . New York NY 10016 212-736-1767

Verso Books 20 Jay St Ste 1010. . . . . Brooklyn NY 11201 718-246-8160 246-8165
Web: www.versobooks.com

Walch Education 40 Walch Dr. . . . . Portland ME 04103 207-772-2846 772-3105
TF: 800-558-2846 ■ *Web:* www.walch.com

Walsworth Publishing Co 306 N Kansas Ave . . . . Marceline MO 64658 660-376-3543 258-7798*
**Fax:* Hum Res ■ *TF:* 800-972-4968 ■ *Web:* www.walsworthyearbooks.com

West Group 610 Opperman Dr. . . . . Eagan MN 55123 651-687-7000 687-7551
TF Cust Svc: 800-328-4880 ■ *Web:* legalsolutions.thomsonreuters.com

WH Freeman & Co 41 Madison Ave . . . . New York NY 10010 212-576-9400 689-2383
TF: 800-446-8923 ■ *Web:* www.whfreeman.com

Wheatmark Inc 1760 E River Rd Ste 145 . . . . Tucson AZ 85718 520-798-0888 798-3394
TF: 888-934-0888 ■ *Web:* www.wheatmark.com

Wilderness Press
c/o Keen Communications 2204 First Ave S
Ste 102. . . . . Birmingham AL 35233 800-443-7227 326-1012*
**Fax Area Code:* 205 ■ *TF:* 800-443-7227 ■ *Web:* www.wildernesspress.com

Wiley Publishing Inc 111 River St . . . . Hoboken NJ 07030 201-748-6000 748-6088
TF: 800-225-5945 ■ *Web:* as.wiley.com

William H Sadlier Inc Nine Pine St. . . . . New York NY 10005 800-221-5175 312-6080*
OTC: SADL ■ **Fax Area Code:* 212 ■ *TF:* 800-221-5175 ■ *Web:* www.sadlier.com

William Morrow & Co 10 E 53rd St. . . . . New York NY 10022 212-207-7000 207-7145*
**Fax:* Edit ■ *TF:* 800-242-7737 ■ *Web:* www.harpercollins.com

William S Hein & Company Inc 1285 Main St . . . . Buffalo NY 14209 716-882-2600 883-8100
TF: 800-828-7571 ■ *Web:* www.wshein.com

Wilshire Book Co 9731 Variel Ave. . . . . Chatsworth CA 91311 818-700-1522 700-1527
Web: www.mpowers.com

Wimmer Cookbooks 4650 Shelby Air Dr. . . . . Memphis TN 38118 901-362-8900 363-1771
Web: www.wimmerco.com

Workman Publishing 225 Varick St . . . . New York NY 10014 212-254-5900 254-8098
TF: 800-722-7202 ■ *Web:* www.workman.com

World Book Inc 233 N Michigan Ave Ste 2000 . . . . Chicago IL 60601 312-729-5800 729-5600
TF: 800-967-5325 ■ *Web:* www.worldbook.com

WW Norton & Company Inc
500 Fifth Ave Sixth Fl . . . . New York NY 10110 212-354-5500 869-0856
TF: 800-233-4830 ■ *Web:* books.wwnorton.com

Zaner-Bloser Inc 1201 Dublin Rd . . . . Columbus OH 43215 614-486-0221 487-2699
TF: 800-421-3018 ■ *Web:* www.zaner-bloser.com

Zebra Books
Kensington Publishing Corp 119 W 40th St . . . . New York NY 10018 212-407-1500
TF: 800-221-2647 ■ *Web:* www.kensingtonbooks.com

640-3 Book Publishers - Religious & Spiritual Books

Phone Fax

American Bible Society 1865 Broadway . . . . New York NY 10023 212-408-1200 408-1512
TF: 800-322-4253 ■ *Web:* www.americanbible.org

Augsburg Fortress Publishers
100 S Fifth St Ste 600. . . . . Minneapolis MN 55402 612-330-3300 330-3455
TF: 800-426-0115 ■ *Web:* www.augsburgfortress.org

Baker Book House Company Inc 6030 E Fulton St. . . . . Ada MI 49301 616-676-9185 676-9573
TF Orders: 800-877-2665 ■ *Web:* www.bakerpublishinggroup.com

Baker Book House Company Inc Revell Div
6030 E Fulton St. . . . . Ada MI 49301 616-676-9185 676-9573
TF Orders: 800-877-2665 ■ *Web:* bakerpublishinggroup.com

Bethany House Publishers
11400 Hampshire Ave S . . . . Bloomington MN 55438 616-676-9185 676-9573
TF: 800-328-6109 ■ *Web:* bakerpublishinggroup.com

Brethren Press 1451 Dundee Ave . . . . Elgin IL 60120 800-441-3712 667-8188
TF: 800-441-3712 ■ *Web:* www.brethrenpress.com

Broadman & Holman Publishers
127 Ninth Ave N MSN 114 . . . . Nashville TN 37234 800-448-8032 251-3914*
**Fax Area Code:* 615 ■ *TF:* 800-448-8032 ■ *Web:* www.bhpublishinggroup.com

Concordia Publishing House Inc
3558 S Jefferson Ave . . . . Saint Louis MO 63118 314-268-1000 268-1329
TF Cust Svc: 800-325-3040 ■ *Web:* www.cph.org

Cook Communications Ministries
4050 Lee Vance View . . . . Colorado Springs CO 80918 719-536-0100 536-3265
TF: 800-708-5550 ■ *Web:* www.davidccook.com

Deseret Book Co 57 W S Temple. . . . . Salt Lake City UT 84111 801-534-1515
TF: 800-453-4532 ■ *Web:* www.deseretbook.com

DeVore & Sons Inc 9020 E 35th St N . . . . Wichita KS 67226 316-267-3211
Web: www.devoreandsons.com

E-Church Depot 75 Utley Dr Ste 101 . . . . Camp Hill PA 17011 800-233-4443 761-7273*
**Fax Area Code:* 717 ■ *TF:* 800-233-4443 ■ *Web:* www.echurchdepot.com

Gospel Light Publications 1957 Eastman Ave. . . . . Ventura CA 93003 805-644-9721 650-8173*
**Fax:* Mktg ■ *TF:* 800-446-7735 ■ *Web:* www.gospellight.com

Hay House Inc PO Box 5100. . . . . Carlsbad CA 92018 760-431-7695 650-5115*
**Fax Area Code:* 800 ■ *TF:* 800-654-5126 ■ *Web:* www.hayhouse.com

Jewish Publication Society
2100 Arch St Second Fl . . . . Philadelphia PA 19103 215-832-0600 568-2017
TF: 800-234-3151 ■ *Web:* www.jewishpub.org

NavPress 351 Executive Dr . . . . Carol Stream CO 60188 855-277-9400 343-3902*
**Fax Area Code:* 800 ■ *TF:* 800-366-7788 ■ *Web:* www.navpress.com

New Leaf Publishing Group PO Box 726 . . . . Green Forest AR 72638 870-438-5288 438-5120
TF: 800-999-3777 ■ *Web:* www.nlpg.com

New World Library 14 Pamaron Way. . . . . Novato CA 94949 415-884-2100 884-2199
TF: 800-972-6657 ■ *Web:* www.newworldlibrary.com

Northwestern Publishing House
1250 N 113th St . . . . Milwaukee WI 53226 414-475-6600 475-7695
TF Orders: 800-662-6022 ■ *Web:* online.nph.net

Oregon Catholic Press (OCP) 5536 NE Hassalo St . . . . Portland OR 97213 503-281-1191 462-7329*
**Fax Area Code:* 800 ■ *TF:* 877-596-1653 ■ *Web:* www.ocp.org

Our Sunday Visitor Inc 200 Noll Plaza . . . . Huntington IN 46750 260-356-8400 356-8472
TF: 800-348-2440 ■ *Web:* www.osv.com

Pauline Books & Media 50 St Paul's Ave. . . . . Boston MA 02130 617-522-8911 524-8035
TF Sales: 800-876-4463 ■ *Web:* www.pauline.org

Review & Herald Publishing Assn
55 W Oak Ridge Dr . . . . Hagerstown MD 21740 301-393-3000 393-3209
TF: 800-456-3991 ■ *Web:* www.rhpa.org

Standard Publishing Co
8805 Governors Hill Dr Ste 400 . . . . Cincinnati OH 45249 513-931-4050 867-5751*
**Fax Area Code:* 877 ■ *TF Orders:* 800-543-1353 ■ *Web:* www.standardpub.com

	City	State	ZIP	Phone	Fax
Standex International Corp Consumer Group 11 Keewaydin Dr. *NYSE:* SXI ■ *TF:* 800-514-5275 ■ *Web:* www.standex.com	Salem	NH	03079	603-893-9701	893-7324
Thomas Nelson Inc 501 Nelson Pl PO Box 141000 *TF:* 800-251-4000 ■ *Web:* www.thomasnelson.com	Nashville	TN	37214	615-889-9000	889-5940
Tyndale House Publishers Inc 351 Executive Dr. *TF:* 800-323-9400 ■ *Web:* www.tyndale.com	Carol Stream	IL	60188	800-323-9400	684-0247
United Methodist Publishing House 201 Eigth Ave S *TF:* 800-672-1789 ■ *Web:* umph.org	Nashville	TN	37203	615-749-6000	
Whitaker House/Anchor Distributors 1030 Hunt Vly Cir. *TF General:* 800-444-4484 ■ *Web:* www.anchordistributors.com	New Kensington	PA	15068	724-334-7000	334-1200

640-4 Book Publishers - University Presses

	City	State	ZIP	Phone	Fax
Catholic University of America Press 620 Michigan Ave NE 240 Leahy Hall *TF:* 800-537-5487 ■ *Web:* www.cua.edu	Washington	DC	20064	202-319-5052	319-4985
Columbia University Press 61 W 62nd St 3rd Fl *TF:* 800-944-8648 ■ *Web:* www.columbia.edu	New York	NY	10023	212-459-0600	459-3677
Cornell University Press 750 Cascadilla St PO Box 6525 *TF Sales:* 800-666-2211 ■ *Web:* www.cornellpress.cornell.edu	Ithaca	NY	14850	607-277-2338	277-6292
Duke University Press 905 W Main St Ste 18-B **Fax Area Code:* 888 ■ **Fax:* Cust Svc ■ *TF Cust Svc:* 888-651-0122 ■ *Web:* www.dukeupress.edu	Durham	NC	27701	919-687-3600	651-0124*
Gallaudet University Press 800 Florida Ave NE *TF:* 800-621-2736 ■ *Web:* gupress.gallaudet.edu	Washington	DC	20002	202-651-5488	651-5489
Harvard Business School Publishing 60 Harvard Way **Fax Area Code:* 617 ■ *TF:* 800-795-5200 ■ *Web:* www.harvardbusiness.org	Boston	MA	02163	800-795-5200	783-7556*
Harvard University Press 79 Garden St **Fax Area Code:* 800 ■ *TF:* 800-405-1619 ■ *Web:* www.hup.harvard.edu	Cambridge	MA	02138	617-495-2600	406-9145*
Indiana University Press 601 N Morton St *TF:* 800-842-6796 ■ *Web:* www.iupress.indiana.edu	Bloomington	IN	47404	812-855-8817	855-8507
Johns Hopkins University Press 2715 N Charles St **Fax:* Orders ■ *TF Orders:* 800-537-5487 ■ *Web:* www.press.jhu.edu	Baltimore	MD	21218	410-516-6900	516-6998*
Michigan State University Press 1405 S Harrison Rd Ste 25 Manly Miles Bldg *Web:* msupress.org	East Lansing	MI	48823	517-355-9543	432-2611
MIT Press, The One Rogers St *Web:* www.mitpress.mit.edu	Cambridge	MA	02142	617-253-5646	253-1709
Naval Institute Press 291 Wood Rd *TF:* 800-233-8764 ■ *Web:* usni.org	Annapolis	MD	21402	410-268-6110	295-1049
Ohio State University Press 1070 Carmack Rd *Web:* www.ohiostatepress.org	Columbus	OH	43210	614-292-6930	292-2065
Ohio University Press 19 Cir Dr The Ridges *TF Sales:* 800-621-2736 ■ *Web:* www.ohioswallow.com	Athens	OH	45701	740-593-1154	593-4536
Oregon State University Press 121 The Vly Library *TF Orders:* 800-426-3797 ■ *Web:* www.oregonstate.edu	Corvallis	OR	97331	541-737-3166	737-3170
Pennsylvania State University Press 820 N University Dr USB1 Ste C *TF:* 800-326-9180 ■ *Web:* www.psupress.org	University Park	PA	16802	814-865-1327	863-1408
Princeton University Press 41 William St *TF:* 800-777-4726 ■ *Web:* www.press.princeton.edu	Princeton	NJ	08540	609-258-4900	258-6305
Purdue University Press 504 W State St Stewart Ctr 370 *TF Orders:* 800-247-6553 ■ *Web:* www.thepress.purdue.edu	West Lafayette	IN	47907	765-494-2038	496-2442
Rutgers University Press 106 Somerset St 3rd Fl *TF:* 800-272-6817 ■ *Web:* rutgerspress.rutgers.edu	New Brunswick	NJ	08901	732-745-4935	445-7039
Stanford University Press 1450 Page Mill Rd *TF:* 800-621-2736 ■ *Web:* www.sup.org	Palo Alto	CA	94304	650-723-9434	725-3457
State University of New York Press (SUNY) 22 Corporate Woods Blvd Third Fl *TF:* 866-430-7869 ■ *Web:* www.sunypress.edu	Albany	NY	12211	518-472-5000	472-5038
Temple University Press 1852 N 10th St USB 305 **Fax:* Edit ■ *TF:* 800-621-2736 ■ *Web:* www.temple.edu/tempress	Philadelphia	PA	19122	215-926-2140	204-4719*
Texas A & M University Press John H Lindsey Bldg 4354 TAMU *TF Orders:* 800-826-8911 ■ *Web:* www.tamu.edu	College Station	TX	77843	979-845-1436	847-8752
Texas Tech University Press 2903 Fourth St *TF:* 800-832-4042 ■ *Web:* ttupress.org	Lubbock	TX	79409	806-742-2982	742-2979
University of Alabama Press, The 200 Hackberry Ln Second Fl PO Box 870380 *TF Orders:* 800-621-2736 ■ *Web:* www.uapress.ua.edu	Tuscaloosa	AL	35487	205-348-5180	348-9201
University of Alaska Press 794 University Ave Ste 220 *TF:* 888-252-6657 ■ *Web:* www.uaf.edu	Fairbanks	AK	99709	907-474-5831	474-5502
University of Arizona Press, The 1510 E University Blvd PO Box 210055 *TF:* 800-426-3797 ■ *Web:* www.uapress.arizona.edu	Tucson	AZ	85721	520-621-1441	621-8899
University of Arkansas Press McIlroy House 105 McIlroy *TF:* 800-621-2736 ■ *Web:* www.uapress.com	Fayetteville	AR	72701	479-575-7258	575-6044
University of California Press 2120 Berkeley Way *TF:* 800-777-4726 ■ *Web:* www.ucpress.edu	Berkeley	CA	94704	510-642-4247	643-7127
University of Chicago Press 1427 E 60th St *TF Sales:* 800-621-2736 ■ *Web:* www.press.uchicago.edu	Chicago	IL	60637	773-702-7700	702-9756
University of Delaware Press 181 S College Ave Rm 200-A *Web:* www2.lib.udel.edu/udpress	Newark	DE	19717	302-831-1149	831-6549
University of Hawaii Press 2840 Kolowalu St **Fax Area Code:* 800 ■ *TF:* 888-847-7377 ■ *Web:* www.uhpress.hawaii.edu	Honolulu	HI	96822	808-956-8255	650-7811*
University of Illinois Press 1325 S Oak St *TF:* 866-244-0626 ■ *Web:* www.press.uillinois.edu	Champaign	IL	61820	217-333-0950	244-8082
University of Iowa Press 119 W Pk Rd 100 Kuhl House *TF:* 800-621-2736 ■ *Web:* www.uiowapress.org	Iowa City	IA	52242	319-335-2000	335-2055
University of Massachusetts Press PO Box 429 *TF:* 800-562-0112 ■ *Web:* www.umass.edu/umpress	Amherst	MA	01004	413-545-2217	545-1226
University of Michigan Press 839 Greene St *TF:* 866-804-0002 ■ *Web:* www.press.umich.edu	Ann Arbor	MI	48104	734-764-4388	615-1540
University of Minnesota Press 111 Third Ave S Ste 290 *Web:* www.upress.umn.edu	Minneapolis	MN	55401	612-627-1970	627-1980
University of Missouri Press 2910 LeMone Blvd *TF:* 800-621-2736 ■ *Web:* press.umsystem.edu	Columbia	MO	65201	573-882-7641	884-4498
University of Nebraska Press 1111 Lincoln Mall *TF Orders:* 800-755-1105 ■ *Web:* www.nebraskapress.unl.edu	Lincoln	NE	68508	402-472-3581	
University of Nevada Press Morrill Hall MS 0166 *Web:* www.nvbooks.nevada.edu	Reno	NV	89557	775-784-6573	784-6200
University of North Carolina Press 116 S Boundary St *TF:* 800-848-6224 ■ *Web:* www.uncpress.unc.edu	Chapel Hill	NC	27514	919-966-3561	966-3829
University of North Texas Press 1155 Union Cir Ste 311336 *TF:* 800-826-8911 ■ *Web:* untpress.unt.edu	Denton	TX	76203	940-565-2142	565-4590
University of Pennsylvania Press 3902 Spruce St *TF Cust Svc:* 800-537-5487 ■ *Web:* www.upenn.edu/pennpress	Philadelphia	PA	19104	215-898-6261	898-0404
University of Pittsburgh Press 3400 Forbes Ave 5th Fl *TF Sales:* 800-621-2736 ■ *Web:* www.upress.pitt.edu	Pittsburgh	PA	15261	412-383-2456	383-2466
University of South Carolina Press 1600 Hampton St Fifth Fl *TF Orders:* 800-768-2500 ■ *Web:* www.sc.edu/uscpress	Columbia	SC	29208	803-777-5243	777-0160
University of Tennessee Press 600 Henley St *Web:* utpress.org	Knoxville	TN	37902	865-974-3321	974-3724
University of Texas Press 2100 Comal St *TF Sales:* 800-252-3206 ■ *Web:* www.utexas.edu/utpress	Austin	TX	78722	512-471-7233	232-7178
University of Utah Press 295 South 1500 East Ste 5400 *TF:* 800-621-2736 ■ *Web:* www.uofupress.com	Salt Lake City	UT	84112	801-585-0082	581-3365
University of Virginia Press 210 Sprigg Ln PO Box 400318 *TF Orders:* 800-831-3406 ■ *Web:* www.upress.virginia.edu	Charlottesville	VA	22903	434-924-3469	982-2655
University of Washington Press 4333 Brooklyn Ave NE *TF:* 800-537-5487 ■ *Web:* www.washington.edu	Seattle	WA	98195	206-543-4050	543-3932
University of Wisconsin Press 1930 Monroe St Third Fl *Web:* www.wisc.edu	Madison	WI	53711	608-263-1110	263-1132
University Press of Colorado 5589 Arapahoe Ave Ste 206C *TF:* 800-621-2736 ■ *Web:* www.upcolorado.com	Boulder	CO	80303	720-406-8849	406-3443
University Press of Florida 15 NW 15th St *TF Sales:* 800-226-3822 ■ *Web:* www.upf.com	Gainesville	FL	32611	352-392-1351	392-7302
University Press of Kansas 2502 Westbrooke Cir *Web:* www.kansaspress.ku.edu	Lawrence	KS	66045	785-864-4154	864-4586
University Press of Kentucky 663 S Limestone St **Fax:* Mktg ■ *TF Sales:* 800-537-5487 ■ *Web:* www.kentuckypress.com	Lexington	KY	40508	859-257-8400	257-8481*
University Press of Mississippi 3825 Ridgewood Rd *TF:* 800-737-7788 ■ *Web:* www.upress.state.ms.us	Jackson	MS	39211	601-432-6205	432-6217
University Press of New England (UPNE) One Ct St Ste 250 *TF Orders:* 800-421-1561 ■ *Web:* www.upne.com	Lebanon	NH	03766	603-448-1533	448-9429
Vanderbilt University Press 2014 Broadway Ste 320 *TF:* 800-627-7377 ■ *Web:* vanderbilt.edu/university-press	Nashville	TN	37203	615-322-3585	343-8823
Wesleyan University Press 215 Long Ln *TF:* 800-421-1561 ■ *Web:* www.wesleyan.edu	Middletown	CT	06459	860-685-7711	685-7712
Yale University Press 302 Temple St *TF Sales:* 800-405-1619 ■ *Web:* www.yale.edu	New Haven	CT	06511	203-432-0960	432-0948
Yeshiva University Press 500 W 185th St *Web:* www.yu.edu	New York	NY	10033	212-960-5400	960-0043

640-5 Comic Book Publishers

	City	State	ZIP	Phone	Fax
Archie Comic Publications Inc 325 Fayette Ave *Web:* www.archiecomics.com	Mamaroneck	NY	10543	914-381-5155	381-4015
Dark Horse Comics Inc 10956 SE Main St *TF:* 800-862-0052 ■ *Web:* www.darkhorse.com	Milwaukie	OR	97222	503-652-8815	654-9440
DC Entertainment 1700 Broadway **Fax:* Mktg ■ *Web:* www.dccomics.com	New York	NY	10019	212-636-5400	636-5599*
Diamond Comic Distributors Inc 1966 Greenspring Dr Ste 300 *TF:* 800-452-6642 ■ *Web:* www.diamondcomics.com	Timonium	MD	21093	410-560-7100	560-7148
Fantagraphics Books 7563 Lk City Way NE *TF:* 800-657-1100 ■ *Web:* www.fantagraphics.com	Seattle	WA	98115	206-524-1967	524-2104
Viz Media 295 Bay St *Web:* www.viz.com	San Francisco	CA	94133	415-546-7073	546-7086

Phone Fax

640-6 Directory Publishers

Phone Fax

1-800 Attorney Lawyer Holdings LLC
2525 McKinnon Ave Ste 625 ..... Dallas TX 75201 800-288-6763
OTC: ATTY ■ *TF:* 800-288-6763 ■ *Web:* www.1800attorney.com

ASD Data Services LLC PO Box 1184 ..... Manchester TN 37349 877-742-7297
TF: 877-742-7297 ■ *Web:* www.asd.com

Bresser's Cross Index Directory Co
684 W Baltimore St ..... Detroit MI 48202 313-874-0570 874-3510
TF: 800-995-0570 ■ *Web:* www.bressers.com

BurrellesLuce
30 B Vreeland Rd PO Box 674 ..... Florham Park NJ 07932 973-992-6600 992-7675
TF: 800-631-1160 ■ *Web:* www.burrellesluce.com

Chain Store Guide
10117 Princess Palm Ave Ste 375 ..... Tampa FL 33610 800-927-9292 627-6888*
**Fax Area Code:* 813 ■ *TF:* 800-927-9292 ■ *Web:* www.chainstoreguide.com

Cincinnati Bell Directory (CBD)
312 Plum St Ste 600 ..... Cincinnati OH 45202 800-877-0475
Web: www.theberrycompany.com

Cision US Inc 130 East Randolph St 7th Fl ..... Chicago IL 60601 312-922-2400 *
**Fax:* Cust Svc ■ *Web:* www.cision.com

Cole Information Services 3401 NW 39th St ..... Lincoln NE 68524 402-555-5678
TF: 800-800-3271 ■ *Web:* www.coleinformation.com

Contractors Register Inc
800 E Main St PO Box 500 ..... Jefferson Valley NY 10535 800-431-2584 243-0287*
**Fax Area Code:* 914 ■ *TF:* 800-431-2584 ■ *Web:* www.thebluebook.com

DAG Media Inc 125-10 Queens Blvd Ste 14 ..... Kew Gardens NY 11415 718-263-8454 793-2522
TF: 800-261-2799 ■ *Web:* jewishyellow.com

Dataman Group Inc 22594 Lemon Tree Ln ..... Boca Raton FL 33428 561-451-9302
Web: datamangroup.com

Diamond Mktg Solutions Group Inc
280 Madsen Dr ..... Bloomingdale IL 60108 630-523-5250
Web: dmsolutions.com

Dickman Directories Inc
6145 Columbus Pk ..... Lewis Center OH 43035 740-548-6130 548-2217
TF: 877-836-4154 ■ *Web:* dickmandirectories.com

Downey Publishing Inc
2545 E Southlake Blvd ..... Southlake TX 76092 817-416-6661
Web: downeypublishing.com

Genesis Publisher Services
3310 Eagle Pk Dr NE Ste 200 ..... Grand Rapids MI 49525 616-831-2800 831-0831
TF: 800-828-1022 ■ *Web:* www.genesispubservices.com

Haines & Company Inc 8050 Freedom Ave ..... North Canton OH 44720 800-843-8452 494-3862*
**Fax Area Code:* 330 ■ *TF:* 800-843-8452 ■ *Web:* www.haines.com

HealthLeaders-InterStudy
One Vantage Way Ste B-300 ..... Nashville TN 37228 615-385-4131 385-4979
TF: 800-643-7600 ■ *Web:* www.hl-isy.com

Hoover's Inc 5800 Airport Blvd ..... Austin TX 78752 512-374-4500 374-4501
TF: 800-486-8666 ■ *Web:* www.hoovers.com

LexisNexis Martindale-Hubbell
121 Chanlon Rd ..... New Providence NJ 07974 800-526-4902 665-3593*
**Fax Area Code:* 908 ■ **Fax:* Sales ■ *TF:* 800-526-4902 ■ *Web:* www.martindale.com

Marc Publishing Co
600 Germantown Pk Ste B ..... Lafayette Hill PA 19444 610-834-8585 834-7707
TF: 800-432-5478 ■ *Web:* www.marcpub.com

RH Donnelley Corp 1001 Winstead Dr ..... Cary NC 27513 919-297-1600 297-1600
TF: 844-339-6334 ■ *Web:* dexmedia.com/?ref=do

Stewart Directories Inc
100 W Pennsylvania Ave PO Box 20250 ..... Towson MD 21204 800-311-0786 901-7570*
**Fax Area Code:* 443 ■ *TF:* 800-311-0786 ■ *Web:* www.stewartdirectories.com

University Directories 88 VilCom Cir ..... Chapel Hill NC 27514 800-743-5556 743-0009
TF: 800-743-5556 ■ *Web:* aroundcampusgroup.com/

Valley Yellow Pages 1850 N Gateway Blvd ..... Fresno CA 93727 559-251-8888 253-9729
TF: 800-350-8887 ■ *Web:* www.myyp.com

Van Dam Inc 127 W 27 St ..... New York NY 10011 212-929-0416
Web: vandam.com

World Chamber of Commerce Directory Inc
446 E 29th St ..... Loveland CO 80538 970-663-3231 663-6187
TF: 888-883-3231 ■ *Web:* www.chamberdirectoryonline.com

Yellow Book USA 398 RXR Plaza ..... Uniondale NY 11556 917-861-5858 *
**Fax:* Hum Res ■ *TF:* 877-237-6120 ■ *Web:* www.yellowbook.com

640-7 Music Publishers

Phone Fax

Carl Fischer Inc 65 Bleecker St 28th Fl ..... New York NY 10012 212-777-0900 477-6996
TF: 800-762-2328 ■ *Web:* www.carlfischer.com

G Schirmer Inc 257 Pk Ave S 20th Fl ..... New York NY 10010 212-254-2100 254-2013
Web: www.musicsalesclassical.com

Hal Leonard Corp 960 E Mark St ..... Winona MN 55987 507-454-2920 454-8334
TF: 800-321-3408 ■ *Web:* www.halleonard.com

Lorenz Corp 501 E Third St ..... Dayton OH 45402 937-228-6118 223-2042
TF: 800-444-1144 ■ *Web:* www.lorenz.com

Malaco Music Group Inc 3023 W Northside Dr ..... Jackson MS 39213 601-982-4522 982-4528
TF Cust Svc: 800-272-7936 ■ *Web:* www.malaco.com

Mel Bay Publications Inc Four Industrial Dr ..... Pacific MO 63069 636-257-3970 257-5062
TF: 800-863-5229 ■ *Web:* www.melbay.com

Sony/ATV Music Publishing LLC
550 Madison Ave 5th Fl ..... New York NY 10022 212-833-7730
Web: www.sonyatv.com/cookiepolicy.php?re=Lw==

Theodore Presser Co 588 N Gulph Rd ..... King of Prussia PA 19406 610-592-1222 592-1229
TF: 800-854-6764 ■ *Web:* www.presser.com

Universal Music Publishing
2100 Colorado Ave ..... Santa Monica CA 90404 310-235-4700 235-4900
Web: www.umusicpub.com

Warner/Chappell Music Inc
10585 Santa Monica Blvd ..... Los Angeles CA 90025 310-441-8600 441-8780
Web: www.warnerchappell.com

Phone Fax

640-8 Newspaper Publishers

Phone Fax

ABC Inc 77 W 66th St ..... New York NY 10023 212-456-7777 456-2795
Web: www.abc.go.com

Ada Evening News Corp PO Box 489 ..... Ada OK 74821 580-310-7500 332-8734
Web: theadanews.com

Afro-American Newspapers Co
2519 N Charles St ..... Baltimore MD 21218 410-554-8200 570-9297*
**Fax Area Code:* 877 ■ *TF:* 800-237-6892 ■ *Web:* www.afro.com

Alameda Times-Star 7677 Oakport St Ste 950 ..... Oakland CA 94604 510-208-6300
TF: 866-225-5277 ■ *Web:* alamedaca.gov

Albany Herald Publishing Company Inc
126 N Washington St ..... Albany GA 31702 229-888-9300 888-9357
TF: 800-234-3725 ■ *Web:* www.albanyherald.com

Albert Lea Tribune, The
808 W Front St PO Box 60 ..... Albert Lea MN 56007 507-373-1411 373-0333
TF: 800-657-4996 ■ *Web:* www.albertleatribune.com

Arizona Publishing Cos PO Box 1950 ..... Phoenix AZ 85001 602-444-8000
TF: 800-331-9303 ■ *Web:* www.azcentral.com

Athens Messenger, The 9300 Johnson Rd ..... Athens OH 45701 740-592-6612 592-4647
Web: www.athensohiotoday.com

Athens Newspaper Inc PO Box 912 ..... Athens GA 30603 706-549-0123 208-2246
Web: athensga.com

Auburn Publishers Inc 25 Dill St ..... Auburn NY 13021 315-253-5311 253-6031
TF: 800-878-5311 ■ *Web:* www.auburnpub.com

Austin Daily Herald Inc 310 NE Second St ..... Austin MN 55912 507-433-8851 437-8644
Web: www.austindailyherald.com

Berwick Offray PO Box 790 ..... Buffalo NY 14225 716-668-5223
Web: communitypapersofwny.com/

Bliss Communications Inc PO Box 5001 ..... Janesville WI 53547 608-754-3311 754-8038
TF: 800-362-6712 ■ *Web:* www.blissnet.net

BMH Books 1104 Kings Hwy PO Box 544 ..... Winona Lake IN 46590 800-348-2756 267-4745*
**Fax Area Code:* 574 ■ *TF:* 800-348-2756 ■ *Web:* www.bmhbooks.com

Boone Newspapers Inc
15222 Freeman's Bend Rd Northport
PO Box 2370 ..... Tuscaloosa AL 35403 205-330-4100 330-4140
Web: www.boonenewspapers.com

Booth Michigan 169 Monroe Ave Ste 100 ..... Grand Rapids MI 49503 800-878-1400
TF: 800-886-5529 ■ *Web:* www.boothnewspapers.com

Breese Publishing Co 8060 Old US Hwy 50 ..... Breese IL 62230 618-526-7211 526-2590
Web: www.breesepub.com

Breeze Newspaper 2510 Del Prado Blvd ..... Cape Coral FL 33904 239-574-1110 574-3403
Web: www.breezenewspapers.com

Brehm Communications Inc
16644 W Bernardo Dr # 300 ..... San Diego CA 92127 858-451-6200 451-3814
Web: www.brehmcommunications.com

Burlington Hawk Eye Co
800 S Main St PO Box 10 ..... Burlington IA 52601 319-754-8461 754-6824
TF: 800-397-1708 ■ *Web:* www.thehawkeye.com

Capital City Press Inc PO Box 588 ..... Baton Rouge LA 70821 225-383-1111 388-0397*
**Fax:* Hum Res ■ *Web:* theadvocate.com

Capital Gazette Communications LLC
2000 Capital Dr ..... Annapolis MD 21401 410-268-5000 280-5953
TF: 888-607-8365 ■ *Web:* www.capitalgazette.com

Capital Newspapers 1901 Fish Hatchery Rd ..... Madison WI 53713 920-887-0321 887-8790*
**Fax:* Cust Svc ■ *TF:* 888-798-4468 ■ *Web:* www.wiscnews.com

Casa Grande Valley Newspaper Inc
PO Box 15002 ..... Casa Grande AZ 85130 520-836-7461 836-0343
TF: 800-352-3796 ■ *Web:* www.trivalleycentral.com

Casiano Communications Inc
1700 Fernandez Juncos Ave PO Box 12130 ..... San Juan PR 00909 787-728-3000 268-1001
TF: 844-723-2351 ■ *Web:* www.casiano.com

Cheyenne Newspaper Inc 702 W Lincolnway ..... Cheyenne WY 82001 307-634-3361 633-3189
TF: 800-561-6268 ■ *Web:* www.wyomingnews.com

Christian Science Publishing Society
210 Massachusetts Ave P02-15 ..... Boston MA 02115 617-450-2000
TF: 800-456-2220 ■ *Web:* www.csmonitor.com

Citizen Publishing Company Inc 260 Tenth St ..... Windom MN 56101 507-831-3455 831-3740
Web: www.windomnews.com

Columbia Star PO Box 5955 ..... Columbia SC 29250 803-771-0219
Web: www.thecolumbiastar.com

Community Newspaper Co Inc 72 Cherry Hill Dr ..... Beverly MA 01915 978-739-1300 739-8501
TF: 800-281-6498 ■ *Web:* www.wickedlocal.com

Community Newspapers Inc 6605 SE Lake Rd ..... Portland OR 97222 503-684-0360 620-3433
Web: www.portlandtribune.com

Community Press Newspapers
394 Wards Corner Rd ..... Loveland OH 45140 513-242-4300 242-2649

Consolidated Publishing Co PO Box 189 ..... Anniston AL 36202 256-236-1551 241-1991
TF: 866-814-9253 ■ *Web:* www.annistonstar.com

Contra Costa Newspapers Inc 1700 Cavallo Rd ..... Antioch CA 94509 925-757-2525 706-2305
Web: www.contracostatimes.com

Coulter Press Inc 156 Church St ..... Clinton MA 01510 978-368-0176 368-1151

Cox Media Group 6205 Peachtree Dunwoody Rd ..... Atlanta GA 30328 678-645-0000 645-5002
Web: www.coxmediagroup.com

Daily Globe, The 118 E McLeod Ave PO Box 548 ..... Ironwood MI 49938 906-932-2211 932-4211
TF: 800-236-2887 ■ *Web:* www.yourdailyglobe.com

Daily Journal Corp 915 E First St ..... Los Angeles CA 90012 213-229-5300 229-5481
NASDAQ: DJCO ■ *Web:* www.dailyjournal.com

Daily Progress 685 W Rio Rd ..... Charlottesville VA 22902 434-978-7200 978-7252
TF: 866-469-4866 ■ *Web:* www.dailyprogress.com

Daily Record Inc Six Century Dr ..... Parsippany NJ 07054 973-428-6200 428-6666
Web: www.dailyrecord.com

Daily Record, The 11 E Saratoga St ..... Baltimore MD 21202 443-524-8100
Web: www.thedailyrecord.com

Day Publishing Co 47 Eugene O'Neill Dr ..... New London CT 06320 860-442-2200 442-5599
TF: 800-542-3354 ■ *Web:* www.theday.com

Dayton Newspapers Inc 116 S Main St ..... Dayton OH 45409 937-225-2000 225-2043*
**Fax:* Mktg ■ *Web:* www.daytondailynews.com

Delphos Herald Inc 405 N Main St ..... Delphos OH 45833 419-695-0015 692-7704
TF: 800-589-6950 ■ *Web:* www.delphosherald.com

				Phone	Fax
Denver Newspaper Agency 101 W Colfax Ave. *TF:* 800-336-7678 ■ *Web:* www.denverpost.com	Denver	CO	80202	303-954-1010	954-1010
Derrick Publishing Co 1510 W First St. *TF:* 800-352-1002 ■ *Web:* www.thederrick.com	Oil City	PA	16301	814-676-7444	677-8351
Desert Sun Publishing Co PO Box 2734 *TF Advertising:* 800-233-3741 ■ *Web:* desertsun.com/	Palm Springs	CA	92263	760-322-8889	322-8889
Detroit Legal News Co 1409 Allen Rd Ste B *TF:* 800-875-5275 ■ *Web:* www.legalnews.com	Troy	MI	48083	248-577-6100	577-6111
Diocese of Steubenville Catholic Charities PO Box 969 *Web:* www.diosteub.org	Steubenville	OH	43952	740-282-3631	282-3327
Dispatch Printing Co 34 S Third St *TF:* 800-282-0263 ■ *Web:* www.dispatch.com	Columbus	OH	43215	614-461-5000	461-5565
Dow Jones & Company Inc 1211 Ave of the Americas *Web:* www.dowjones.com	New York	NY	10281	212-416-2000	416-2658
Eagle Publishing Co 75 S Church St. *TF:* 800-245-0254 ■ *Web:* www.berkshireeagle.com	Pittsfield	MA	01201	413-447-7311	447-7311
East Hampton Star Inc, The 153 Main St PO Box 5002 *TF:* 800-968-7364 ■ *Web:* www.easthamptonstar.com	East Hampton	NY	11937	631-324-0002	324-7943
Eau Claire Press Co 701 S Farwell St *TF:* 800-236-8808 ■ *Web:* www.leadertelegram.com	Eau Claire	WI	54701	715-833-9200	833-9244
ECM Publishers Inc 4095 Coon Rapids Blvd. *Web:* www.ecm-inc.com	Coon Rapids	MN	55433	763-712-2400	
Edward A Sherman Publishing Co 101 Malbone Rd *TF:* 800-320-2378 ■ *Web:* www.newportri.com	Newport	RI	02840	401-849-3300	849-3306
EW Scripps Co 312 Walnut St Ste 2800 *NYSE: SSP* ■ **Fax:* Hum Res ■ *TF:* 800-888-3000 ■ *Web:* www.scripps.com	Cincinnati	OH	45202	513-977-3000	977-3800*
Express-News Corp PO Box 2171 *TF:* 800-555-1551 ■ *Web:* www.mysanantonio.com	San Antonio	TX	78297	210-250-3000	
Feather Publishing Co Inc 287 Lawrence St *TF:* 866-849-8390 ■ *Web:* www.plumasnews.com	Quincy	CA	95971	530-283-0800	283-3952
Findlay Publishing Co 701 W Sandusky St *Web:* www.thecourier.com	Findlay	OH	45840	419-422-5151	422-2937
Finger Lakes Times 218 Genesse St PO Box 393 *TF:* 800-388-6652 ■ *Web:* www.fltimes.com	Geneva	NY	14456	315-789-3333	789-4077
Flashes Publishers Inc 595 Jenner Dr *TF:* 800-968-4415 ■ *Web:* www.flashespublishers.com	Allegan	MI	49010	269-673-2141	673-4761
Fort Wayne Newspapers Inc 600 W Main St *TF:* 800-444-3303 ■ *Web:* www.fortwayne.com	Fort Wayne	IN	46802	260-461-8444	461-8899
Forum Communications Co 101 Fifth St N *TF:* 800-747-7311 ■ *Web:* www.forumcomm.com	Fargo	ND	58102	701-451-5629	241-5406
Forward Publishing 125 Maiden Ln *TF:* 800-266-0773 ■ *Web:* www.forward.com	New York	NY	10038	212-889-8200	447-6406
Frankfort Publishing Co LLC 1216 Wilkinson Blvd P.O. Box 368 *Web:* www.state-journal.com	Frankfort	KY	40601	502-227-4556	227-2831
Freedom Communications Inc 17666 Fitch *TF:* 866-262-7678 ■ *Web:* www.freedom.com	Irvine	CA	92614	949-253-2300	474-7675
Galesburg Printing & Publishing Co 140 S Prairie St *TF:* 800-733-2767 ■ *Web:* www.galesburg.com	Galesburg	IL	61401	309-343-7181	343-2382
GateHouse Media Inc 350 Willowbrook Office Pk *NYSE: GHSE* ■ *TF:* 866-487-9243 ■ *Web:* www.gatehousemedia.com	Fairport	NY	14450	585-598-0030	248-2631
Gateway Newspapers 610 Beatty Rd *Web:* triblive.com	Monroeville	PA	15146	412-856-7400	856-7954
Gazette Newspapers Inc 9030 Comprint Ct. **Fax:* Hum Res ■ *TF:* 888-670-7100 ■ *Web:* www.gazette.net	Gaithersburg	MD	20877	301-948-3120	670-7138*
George J Foster Co Inc 150 Venture Dr *TF:* 800-462-2265 ■ *Web:* www.fosters.com	Dover	NH	03820	603-742-4455	749-7079
Gilmer Mirror Co 214 E Marshall St *Web:* www.gilmermirror.com	Gilmer	TX	75644	903-843-2503	843-5123
Glastonbury Citizen Inc PO Box 373 *Web:* www.glcitizen.com	Glastonbury	CT	06033	860-633-4691	657-3258
Glendale News Press 221 N Brand Ave *Web:* www.glendalenewspress.com	Glendale	CA	91203	818-637-3200	241-1975
Grant County Journal 29 A St SW	Ephrata	WA	98823	509-754-4636	
Gray Television Inc 4370 Peachtree Rd NE *NYSE: GTN* ■ *Web:* www.gray.tv	Atlanta	GA	30319	404-504-9828	
Greater Media Inc 35 Braintree Hill Pk Ste 300 *Web:* www.greater-media.com	Braintree	MA	02184	781-348-8600	
Guard Publishing Co PO Box 10188 *Web:* www.registerguard.com	Eugene	OR	97440	541-485-1234	984-4699
Hastings & Sons Publishing 38 Exchange St *TF:* 877-226-4267 ■ *Web:* www.itemlive.com	Lynn	MA	01901	781-593-7700	598-2891
Hearst Corp 300 W 57th St *Web:* www.hearst.com	New York	NY	10019	212-649-2275	
Hearst Newspapers 300 W 57th St 41st Fl *Web:* www.hearst.com/newspapers	New York	NY	10019	212-649-2000	
Herald Publishing Co PO Box 153 *TF:* 888-421-1866 ■ *Web:* www.jhvonline.com	Houston	TX	77001	713-630-0391	630-0404
Herald-Mail Co, The 100 Summit Ave PO Box 439 *TF:* 800-626-6397 ■ *Web:* www.heraldmailmedia.com	Hagerstown	MD	21741	301-733-5131	714-0245
Herald-Star 401 Herald Sq *TF:* 800-526-7987 ■ *Web:* heraldstaronline.com/	Steubenville	OH	43952	740-283-4711	284-7355
Herald-Times Inc PO Box 909 *Web:* www.heraldtimesonline.com	Bloomington	IN	47402	812-332-4401	331-4285
Heritage Newspapers Inc One Heritage Pl Ste 100 *Web:* www.heritagenews.com	Southgate	MI	48195	734-246-0800	246-2727
Hersam Acorn Newspapers 16 Bailey Ave. *TF:* 800-372-2790 ■ *Web:* hersamacorn.com	Ridgefield	CT	06877	203-438-6544	438-3395
Hi-Desert Publishing Co 56445 29 Palms Hwy *Web:* www.hidesertstar.com	Yucca Valley	CA	92284	760-365-3315	365-2650
High Plains Publishers Inc 1500 W Wyatt Earp Blvd *TF:* 800-452-7171 ■ *Web:* hpj.com	Dodge City	KS	67801	620-227-7171	227-7173
Home News Enterprises 333 Second St **Fax Area Code:* 317 ■ *TF:* 800-876-7811 ■ *Web:* homenewsenterprises.com	Columbus	IN	47201	800-876-7811	736-2756*
Hubbard Publishing Co 127 E Chillicothe Ave PO Box 40 *TF:* 866-632-9992 ■ *Web:* www.examiner.org	Bellefontaine	OH	43311	937-592-3060	592-4463
Huse Publishing Co 525 Norfolk Ave PO Box 977 *TF:* 877-371-1020 ■ *Web:* www.norfolkdailynews.com	Norfolk	NE	68701	402-371-1020	371-5802
Hutchinson Leader Inc 36 Washington Ave W *Web:* www.hutchinsonleader.com	Hutchinson	MN	55350	320-587-5000	587-6104
Independent Publishing Co 1000 Williamston Rd *TF:* 800-859-6397 ■ *Web:* www.independentmail.com	Anderson	SC	29621	864-224-4321	260-1276
Indian Hill Journal 394 Wards Corner Ste 170	Loveland	OH	45140	513-248-8600	248-1938
Indiana Newspapers Inc 307 N Pennsylvania Pkwy *Web:* indystar.com	Indianapolis	IN	46206	317-444-5500	
Indiana Printing & Publishing Co 899 Water St PO Box 10 *Web:* www.indianagazette.com	Indiana	PA	15701	724-465-5555	465-8267
Isanti County News 234 S Main St *Web:* www.isanticountynews.com	Cambridge	MN	55008	763-689-1981	689-4372
Journal & Topics Newspapers 622 Graceland Ave *Web:* www.journal-topics.com	Des Plaines	IL	60016	847-299-5511	298-8549
Journal Communications Inc 333 W State St *NYSE: JRN* ■ *Web:* www.journalmediagroup.com	Milwaukee	WI	53201	414-224-2000	224-2469
Journal Graphics Inc 2840 NW 35th Ave Ste B *TF:* 888-609-6051 ■ *Web:* www.journalgraphics.com	Portland	OR	97210	503-790-9100	790-9043
Journal Publishing Co 1242 S Green St *TF:* 800-264-6397 ■ *Web:* djournal.com	Tupelo	MS	38804	662-842-2611	842-2233
Keene Publishing Corp PO Box 546 *TF:* 800-765-9994 ■ *Web:* www.sentinelsource.com	Keene	NH	03431	603-352-1234	352-0437
Knight Publishing Co 600 S Tryon St *TF:* 800-332-0686 ■ *Web:* www.charlotteobserver.com	Charlotte	NC	28202	704-358-5000	
Lake Charles American Press Inc PO Box 2893 *TF:* 800-737-2283 ■ *Web:* www.americanpress.com	Lake Charles	LA	70602	337-433-3000	494-4008
Lakeville Journal Co LLC 33 Bissell St PO Box 1688 *TF:* 800-553-2234 ■ *Web:* www.lakevillejournal.com	Lakeville	CT	06039	860-435-9873	435-4802
Lancaster Newspapers Inc Eight W King St PO Box 1328 *TF:* 800-809-4666 ■ *Web:* www.lancasteronline.com	Lancaster	PA	17603	717-291-8811	291-8728
Landmark Community Newspapers Inc 601 Taylorsville Rd *TF:* 800-939-9322 ■ *Web:* www.lcni.com	Shelbyville	KY	40065	502-633-4334	633-4447
Law Bulletin Publishing Co 415 N State St *Web:* www.lawbulletin.com	Chicago	IL	60654	312-644-7800	644-4255
Lawrence Daily Journal-World Co 609 New Hampshire St PO Box 888 *TF:* 800-578-8748 ■ *Web:* www2.ljworld.com	Lawrence	KS	66044	785-843-1000	843-4512
Leader Union, The 229 S Fifth St *Web:* www.leaderunion.com	Vandalia	IL	62471	618-283-3374	283-0977
Leaf Chronicle Co 200 Commerce St *Web:* www.theleafchronicle.com	Clarksville	TN	37040	931-552-1808	648-8001
Lee Enterprises Inc 201 N Harrison St Ste 600 *NYSE: LEE* ■ *Web:* www.lee.net	Davenport	IA	52801	563-383-2100	328-4331
Lee Publications Inc 6113 State Hwy 5 *Web:* www.leepub.com	Palatine Bridge	NY	13428	518-673-3237	673-3245
Livingston County Daily Press & Argus 323 E Grand River Ave **Fax Area Code:* 248 ■ *TF:* 888-999-1288 ■ *Web:* www.livingstondaily.com	Howell	MI	48843	517-548-2000	437-9460*
Lowell Sun Publishing Co 491 Dutton St **Fax:* Edit ■ *TF Cust Svc:* 800-359-1300 ■ *Web:* www.lowellsun.com	Lowell	MA	01854	978-458-7100	970-4600*
Madison Newspapers Inc 1901 Fish Hatchery Rd *TF Sales:* 800-252-7723 ■ *Web:* host.madison.com	Madison	WI	53713	608-252-6200	252-6119
Magic Valley Newspapers 132 Fairfield St W *TF:* 800-658-3883 ■ *Web:* www.magicvalley.com	Twin Falls	ID	83301	208-733-0931	734-5538
Manhattan Media LLC 79 Madison Ave 16th Fl *Web:* www.manhattanmedia.com	New York	NY	10016	212-268-8600	268-0503
Marshall Independent 508 W Main St PO Box 411 *TF:* 877-276-6070 ■ *Web:* www.marshallindependent.com	Marshall	MN	56258	507-537-1551	537-1557
Maverick Media Inc 123 W 17th St *Web:* www.ncnewspress.com	Syracuse	NE	68446	402-269-2135	269-2392
McClatchy Co 2100 Q St *NYSE: MNI* ■ *TF:* 866-807-2200 ■ *Web:* www.mcclatchy.com	Sacramento	CA	95816	916-321-1855	321-1869
McClatchy Newspapers 2100 Q St *TF:* 866-807-2200 ■ *Web:* www.mcclatchy.com	Sacramento	CA	95816	916-321-1000	321-1869
Media General Inc 333 E Franklin St *NYSE: MEG* ■ *Web:* www.media-general.com	Richmond	VA	23219	804-649-6000	
MediaNews Group Inc 101 W Colfax Ave. *Web:* digitalfirstmedia.com	Denver	CO	80202	303-954-6360	954-6320
Memphis Publishing Co 495 Union Ave *TF Cust Svc:* 800-444-6397 ■ *Web:* local.commercialappeal.com	Memphis	TN	38103	901-529-2666	
Meridian Star Inc 814 22nd Ave *TF Cust Svc:* 800-232-2525 ■ *Web:* www.meridianstar.com	Meridian	MS	39301	601-693-1551	485-1275
MetroActive Publishing Inc 550 S First St *Web:* www.metroactive.com	San Jose	CA	95113	408-298-8000	298-0602
Mid-America Publishing Corp 9 Second St NW *TF:* 800-558-1244 ■ *Web:* www.hamptonchronicle.com	Hampton	IA	50441	641-456-2585	456-2587
Milford Daily News Co 159 S Main St *TF:* 800-281-6498 ■ *Web:* www.milforddailynews.com	Milford	MA	01757	508-634-7522	634-7514
Mineral Daily News Tribune Inc 24 Armstrong St *Web:* www.newstribune.info	Keyser	WV	26726	304-788-3333	788-3398

Company / Address	City	State	ZIP	Phone	Fax
Minnesota Sun Publications					
4095 Coon Rapids Blvd	Coon Rapids	MN	55433	763-712-2400	
Web: www.ecm-inc.com					
Missouri Lawyers Media 319 N Fourth St	Saint Louis	MO	63102	314-421-1880	421-0436
TF: 800-635-5297 ■ *Web:* www.molawyersmedia.com					
Missourian Publishing Co 14 W Main St	Washington	MO	63090	636-239-7701	239-0915
TF: 888-239-7701 ■ *Web:* www.emissourian.com					
Moline Dispatch Publishing Co 1720 Fifth Ave	Moline	IL	61265	309-764-4344	797-0317
TF: 800-660-2472 ■ *Web:* qconline.com					
Morning Call Inc 101 N Sixth St	Allentown	PA	18101	610-820-6500	820-6693*
**Fax:* Mktg ■ *TF:* 800-666-5492 ■ *Web:* www.mcall.com					
Morris Communications Company LLC					
725 Broad St	Augusta	GA	30901	706-724-0851	828-3830
TF: 800-622-6358 ■ *Web:* www.morris.com					
Morris Multimedia Inc 27 Abercorn St	Savannah	GA	31401	912-233-1281	232-4639
Web: www.morrismultimedia.com					
Mountain Home News					
195 S Third E St PO Box 1330	Mountain Home	ID	83647	208-587-3331	587-9205
Web: www.mountainhomenews.com					
Natchez Newspapers Inc 503 N Canal St	Natchez	MS	39120	601-442-9101	442-7315
TF: 877-896-0974 ■ *Web:* www.natchezdemocrat.com					
Native American Times PO Box 411	Tahlequah	OK	74465	918-708-5838	431-0213
TF: 800-367-5390 ■ *Web:* www.nativetimes.com					
New Mexico Newspapers Inc PO Box 450	Farmington	NM	87499	505-325-4545	564-4630
TF: 866-272-3622 ■ *Web:* www.daily-times.com					
New York News LP 450 W 33rd St 3rd Fl	New York	NY	10001	212-210-2100	643-7831
Web: www.nydailynews.com					
News Publishing Co 305 E Sixth Ave PO Box 1633	Rome	GA	30161	706-290-5330	
Web: www.npco.com					
Newspapers of New England Inc PO Box 1177	Concord	NH	03302	603-224-5301	224-6949
Web: www.concordmonitor.com					
Northwest Herald Inc PO Box 250	Crystal Lake	IL	60039	815-459-4040	459-5640
TF: 800-589-8910 ■ *Web:* www.nwherald.com					
Northwest Publications 99 E State St	Rockford	IL	61104	815-987-1200	987-1365*
**Fax:* Edit ■ *Web:* www.rrstar.com					
Oakland Press 48 W Huron St	Pontiac	MI	48342	248-332-8181	
TF: 888-977-3677 ■ *Web:* www.theoaklandpress.com					
Observer & Eccentric Newspapers					
615 W Lafayette Second Level	Detroit	MI	48226	866-887-2737	
TF: 866-887-2737 ■ *Web:* www.hometownlife.com					
Observer Dispatch Inc 221 Oriskany Plz	Utica	NY	13501	315-797-9150	
Web: www.uticaod.com					
Observer Publishing Co 122 S Main St	Washington	PA	15301	724-222-2200	225-2077
TF: 800-222-6397 ■ *Web:* www.observer-reporter.com					
Ogden Newspapers Inc 1500 Main St	Wheeling	WV	26003	304-233-0100	233-2867
Web: www.oweb.com					
Ojai Valley News Inc 408 Bryant Cir # A	Ojai	CA	93023	805-646-1476	646-4281
Web: www.ojaivalleynews.com					
Oklahoma Publishing Co					
100 W Main Ste 100	Oklahoma City	OK	73102	405-475-3338	892-1342
Web: www.opubco.com					
Oshkosh Northwestern Co 224 State St	Oshkosh	WI	54901	920-235-7700	
TF: 800-924-6168 ■ *Web:* www.thenorthwestern.com					
Our Sunday Visitor Inc 200 Noll Plaza	Huntington	IN	46750	260-356-8400	356-8472
TF: 800-348-2440 ■ *Web:* www.osv.com					
Owatonna Peoples Press 135 W Pearl St	Owatonna	MN	55060	507-451-2840	444-2382
Web: www.southernminn.com					
Pacific Palisades Post Co					
839 Via de la Paz	Pacific Palisades	CA	90272	310-454-1321	454-1078
Web: palipost.com/					
Pacific Publishing Co					
636 Alaska St S PO Box 80156	Seattle	WA	98108	206-461-1300	
Web: www.pacificpublishingcompany.com					
Paddock Publications Inc					
155 E Algonquin Rd	Arlington Heights	IL	60005	847-427-4300	427-1301
Web: www.dailyherald.com					
Palm Beach Newspapers Inc					
PO Box 24700	West Palm Beach	FL	33416	561-820-4100	820-4407
TF: 800-432-7595 ■ *Web:* www.palmbeachpost.com					
Papers Inc 206 S Main St	Milford	IN	46542	574-658-4111	658-4701
TF: 800-733-4111 ■ *Web:* www.the-papers.com					
Pennysaver 26522 La Alameda	Mission Viejo	CA	92691	949-614-2600	
PG Publishing Co 34 Blvd of the Allies	Pittsburgh	PA	15222	412-263-1100	263-1703
TF Cust Svc: 800-228-6397 ■ *Web:* www.post-gazette.com					
Philadelphia Tribune Co 520 S 16th St	Philadelphia	PA	19146	215-893-4050	735-3612
Web: www.phillytrib.com					
Phoenix Media Communications Group					
126 Brookline Ave	Boston	MA	02215	617-536-5390	536-1463
TF: 888-536-7464 ■ *Web:* www.thephoenix.com					
Phoenix Newspapers Inc 200 E Van Buren St	Phoenix	AZ	85004	602-444-8000	444-8044
Web: azcentral.com					
Pioneer Newspapers Inc					
221 First Ave W Ste 405	Seattle	WA	98119	206-284-4424	
Web: pioneernewsgroup.com					
Pipestone Publishing Co PO Box 277	Pipestone	MN	56164	507-825-3333	825-2168
TF: 800-325-6440 ■ *Web:* www.pipestonestar.com					
Ponca City Publishing Inc PO Box 191	Ponca City	OK	74602	580-765-3311	762-6397
TF: 866-765-3311 ■ *Web:* www.poncacitynews.com					
Post Publishing Co 131 W Innes St	Salisbury	NC	28144	704-633-8950	639-0003
TF: 800-546-5664 ■ *Web:* www.salisburypost.com					
Press-Enterprise Co PO Box 792	Riverside	CA	92502	951-684-1200	368-9023
TF: 800-794-6397 ■ *Web:* www.pe.com					
Press-Enterprise Inc 3185 Lackawanna Ave	Bloomsburg	PA	17815	570-784-2121	784-9226
TF: 888-484-6345 ■ *Web:* www.pressenterprise.net					
Princeton Packet, The					
300 Witherspoon St PO Box 350	Princeton	NJ	08542	609-924-3244	921-2714
TF: 888-747-1122 ■ *Web:* centraljersey.com					
Progressive Communications Corp					
18 E Vine St PO Box 791	Mount Vernon	OH	43050	740-397-5333	397-1321
Web: www.mountvernonnews.com					
Progressive Publishing Co PO Box 291	Clearfield	PA	16830	814-765-5581	765-5165
Web: www.theprogressnews.com					
Quebecor Media Inc 612 Rue St Jacques	Montreal	QC	H3C4M8	514-380-1999	985-8652
Web: www.quebecor.com					
Quincy Newspapers Inc 130 S Fifth St	Quincy	IL	62301	217-223-5100	223-9757
TF: 800-373-9444 ■ *Web:* www.whig.com					
Recorder Publishing Co					
17 Morristown Rd	Bernardsville	NJ	07924	908-766-3900	
Reminder Press Inc 130 Old Town Rd PO Box 27	Vernon	CT	06066	860-875-3366	875-2089
TF: 888-456-2211 ■ *Web:* courant.com/reminder-news/					
Republican Co 1860 Main St	Springfield	MA	01103	413-788-1000	788-1301
TF: 800-828-5597 ■ *Web:* www.repub.com					
Republican-American Inc 389 Meadow St	Waterbury	CT	06702	203-574-3636	596-9277
TF: 800-992-3232 ■ *Web:* www.rep-am.com					
Richmond Times-Dispatch PO Box 85333	Richmond	VA	23293	804-649-6000	819-1216
TF: 800-468-3382 ■ *Web:* www.timesdispatch.com					
Rivertown Newspaper Group					
2760 N Service Dr PO Box 15	Red Wing	MN	55066	651-388-8235	388-3404
TF: 800-535-1660 ■ *Web:* www.republican-eagle.com					
Rock Valley Publishing LLC					
11512 N Second St	Machesney Park	IL	61115	815-877-4044	654-4857
Web: www.rvpublishing.com					
Rome Sentinel Co 333 W Dominick St	Rome	NY	13440	315-337-4000	339-6281
Web: www.romesentinel.com					
San Angelo Standard Times Inc PO Box 5111	San Angelo	TX	76902	325-653-1221	659-8173
TF: 800-588-1884 ■ *Web:* www.gosanangelo.com					
San Gabriel Valley Newspaper Group					
1210 N Azusa Canyon Rd	West Covina	CA	91790	626-962-8811	338-9157
Web: www.sgvn.com					
Santa Barbara News-Press Publishing Co					
715 Anacapa St	Santa Barbara	CA	93101	805-564-5200	966-6258
TF: 800-654-3292 ■ *Web:* www.newspress.com					
Scripps Howard Inc PO Box 5380	Cincinnati	OH	45202	513-977-3000	977-3721*
**Fax:* PR ■ *TF:* 800-888-3000 ■ *Web:* www.scripps.com					
Singapore Press Holdings					
529 14th St NW					
National Press Bldg Ste 916	Washington	DC	20045	202-662-8726	662-8729
Web: www.sph.com.sg					
Sonoma Index-Tribune Inc 117 W Napa St	Sonoma	CA	95476	707-938-2111	938-1600
Web: www.sonomanews.com					
Sound Publishing Inc 19351 8th Ave NE	Poulsbo	WA	98370	360-394-5800	394-5829
Web: www.soundpublishing.com					
Southern Connecticut Newspapers Inc					
9 Riverbend Dr S Bldg 9-A	Stamford	CT	06907	203-964-2200	964-2345
TF: 800-542-2517 ■ *Web:* www.stamfordadvocate.com					
Southern Newspapers Inc (SNI) 5701 Woodway Dr	Houston	TX	77057	713-266-5481	266-1847
Web: www.sninews.com					
Star News 296 Third Ave	Chula Vista	CA	91910	619-427-3000	426-6346
Web: www.thestarnews.com					
Star-News Newspapers PO Box 840	Wilmington	NC	28402	910-343-2000	343-2210
Web: www.starnewsonline.com					
Stephens Media Group 1111 W Bonanza Rd	Las Vegas	NV	89106	702-383-0211	
Web: www.stephensmedia.com					
Stonebridge Press Inc 25 Elm St	Southbridge	MA	01550	508-764-4325	764-8015
TF: 800-536-5836 ■ *Web:* www.stonebridgepress.com					
Suburban Life Publications					
1101 W 31st St Ste 100	Downers Grove	IL	60515	630-368-1100	969-0228
TF: 800-397-9397 ■ *Web:* www.mysuburbanlife.com					
Sun Newspapers 5510 Cloverleaf Pkwy	Cleveland	OH	44125	216-999-3900	
TF: 800-362-8008 ■ *Web:* www.neohiomediagroup.com					
Tacoma News Inc 1950 S State St	Tacoma	WA	98405	253-597-8742	597-8274
Web: www.thenewstribune.com					
TB Butler Publishing Co 410 W Erwin St	Tyler	TX	75702	903-597-8111	595-0335
TF: 800-333-9141 ■ *Web:* www.tylerpaper.com					
Tennessee Valley Printing Company Inc					
PO Box 2213	Decatur	AL	35609	256-353-4612	340-2392
TF: 888-353-4612 ■ *Web:* www.decaturdaily.com					
This Week Community Newspapers					
7801 N Central Dr PO Box 608	Lewis Center	OH	43035	740-888-6000	888-6006
Web: www.thisweeknews.com					
Times & News Publishing Co					
1570 Fairfield Rd PO Box 3669	Gettysburg	PA	17325	717-334-1131	334-4243
Web: www.gettysburgtimes.com					
Times Herald Inc 410 Markley St PO Box 591	Norristown	PA	19404	610-272-2500	272-0660
TF: 888-933-4233 ■ *Web:* www.timesherald.com					
Times News Publishing Co 707 S Main St	Burlington	NC	27215	336-227-0131	228-1889
TF: 800-488-0085 ■ *Web:* www.thetimesnews.com					
Times-Citizen Communications Inc					
406 Stevens St PO Box 640	Iowa Falls	IA	50126	641-648-2521	648-4765
TF: 800-798-2691 ■ *Web:* www.timescitizen.com					
Tribune Review Publishing Co					
622 Cabin Hill Dr	Greensburg	PA	15601	724-834-1151	838-5171
TF: 800-524-5700 ■ *Web:* classifieds.triblive.com					
Truth Publishing Company Inc 421 S Second St	Elkhart	IN	46516	574-294-1661	294-3895
TF: 800-585-5416 ■ *Web:* www.elkharttruth.com					
Warrick Publishing Inc					
204 W Locust St PO Box 266	Boonville	IN	47601	812-897-2330	897-3703
Web: www.tristate-media.com					
Western Communications Inc 1777 SW Chandler Ave	Bend	OR	97702	541-382-1811	383-0372
Web: www.bendbulletin.com					
Western States Weeklies Inc PO Box 600600	San Diego	CA	92160	619-280-2985	
TF: 800-628-9466 ■ *Web:* www.navydispatch.com					
Wick Communications Inc					
333 W Wilcox Dr Ste 302	Sierra Vista	AZ	85635	520-458-0200	458-6166
Web: www.wickcommunications.com					
William J Kline & Son Inc One Venner Rd	Amsterdam	NY	12010	518-843-1100	843-1338
TF: 800-453-6397 ■ *Web:* www.recordernews.com					
Wooster Republican Printing Co					
212 E Liberty St	Wooster	OH	44691	330-264-1125	264-3756
TF: 800-686-2958 ■ *Web:* www.the-daily-record.com					
Worcester Telegram & Gazette Inc					
20 Franklin St PO Box 15012	Worcester	MA	01615	508-793-9100	793-9313
TF: 800-678-6680 ■ *Web:* www.telegram.com					

Phone Fax

Yankton Press & Dakotan
319 Walnut St PO Box 56 Yankton SD 57078 605-665-7811 665-1721
TF: 800-743-2968 ■ *Web:* www.yankton.net
York Newspaper Co 1891 Loucks Rd. York PA 17408 717-767-6397 772-8284
TF: 800-559-3520 ■ *Web:* www.inyork.com
Your Houston News
523 N Sam Houston Pkwy E Ste 600 Houston TX 77060 281-668-1100
Web: www.yourhoustonnews.com

640-9 Periodicals Publishers

Phone Fax

1105 Media Inc 9201 Oakdale Ave Ste 101 Chatsworth CA 91311 818-814-5200 734-1522
Web: www.1105media.com
ABC Inc 77 W 66th St. New York NY 10023 212-456-7777 456-2795
Web: www.abc.go.com
Access Intelligence LLC
Four Choke Cherry Rd Second Fl. Rockville MD 20850 301-354-2000
TF: 800-777-5006 ■ *Web:* www.accessintel.com
ACTION On-Line Inc
Four S Central Ave Ste 1 Saint Louis MO 63105 314-726-4994
Web: actionol.com
Adler & Adler Publishers Inc
5530 Wisconsin Ave Ste 1460 Chevy Chase MD 20815 301-654-4271
Advanstar Communications Inc 131 W First St. Duluth MN 55802 218-740-7200
Web: ubmadvanstar.com
Advanstar Veterinary Healthcare Communications
8033 Flint St. Lenexa KS 66214 913-871-3800 871-3808
TF: 800-255-6864 ■ *Web:* advanstar.com
Advantage Business Media
100 Enterprise Dr Ste 600 PO Box 912. Rockaway NJ 07866 973-920-7000 920-7542*
**Fax:* Hum Res ■ *Web:* advantagemedia.com/
Advertising Specialties Institute 4800 St Rd. Trevose PA 19053 215-942-8600 953-3045
TF: 800-546-1350 ■ *Web:* www.asicentral.com
Advisor Media Inc 4849 Viewridge Ave. San Diego CA 92123 858-278-5600
Adweek Directories 770 Broadway New York NY 10003 646-654-5000
Web: www.adweek.com
Affinity Group Inc 2575 Vista Del Mar. Ventura CA 93001 805-667-4100 667-4298
Web: www.goodsamclub.com
AHC Media LLC
3525 Piedmont Rd NE Bldg 6 Ste 400 Atlanta GA 30305 404-262-5476 262-5560*
**Fax:* Cust Svc ■ *TF Cust Svc:* 800-688-2421 ■ *Web:* www.ahcmedia.com
Alexander Communications Group Inc
712 Main St Ste 187-B. Boonton NJ 07005 973-265-2300 402-6056
TF: 800-232-4317 ■ *Web:* www.alexcommgrp.com
American City Business Journals Inc
120 W Morehead St Ste 400. Charlotte NC 28202 704-973-1000 973-1001
Web: www.bizjournals.com
American Lawyer Media Inc (ALM)
120 Broadway Fifth Fl. New York NY 10271 212-457-9400 417-7705*
**Fax Area Code:* 646 ■ *TF:* 877-256-2472 ■ *Web:* www.alm.com
American Media Inc Four New York Plz. New York NY 10004 212-545-4800
Web: www.americanmediainc.com
American Psychiatric Publishing Inc
1000 Wilson Blvd Ste 1825 Arlington VA 22209 703-907-7322 907-1091
TF: 800-368-5777 ■ *Web:* www.appi.org
Amos Press Inc 911 S Vandemark Rd Sidney OH 45365 937-498-0850 498-0812
TF: 866-468-1622 ■ *Web:* www.amospress.com
Annual Reviews 4139 El Camino Way. Palo Alto CA 94303 650-493-4400 855-9815
TF: 800-523-8635 ■ *Web:* www.annualreviews.org
APN Media LLC PO Box 20113. New York NY 10023 212-581-3380 245-4226
TF: 800-470-7599 ■ *Web:* www.ohranger.com
Atlantic Information Services Inc
1100 17th St NW Ste 300. Washington DC 20036 202-775-9008 331-9542
TF: 800-521-4323 ■ *Web:* www.aishealth.com
Augsburg Fortress Publishers
100 S Fifth St Ste 600. Minneapolis MN 55402 612-330-3300 330-3455
TF: 800-426-0115 ■ *Web:* www.augsburgfortress.org
AVN Media Network Inc 9400 Penfield Ave Chatsworth CA 91311 818-718-5788
Web: www.avnmedianetwork.com
Bauer Publishing Co LP
270 Sylvan Ave. Englewood Cliffs NJ 07632 212-764-3344 569-5303*
**Fax Area Code:* 201 ■ *Web:* www.bauerpublishing.com
BCC Research LLC 49 Walnut Pk Bldg 2 Wellesley MA 02481 781-489-7301 489-7308
TF: 866-285-7215 ■ *Web:* www.bccresearch.com
Becker Communications
119 Merchant St Ste 300 Honolulu HI 96813 808-533-4165 537-4990
Web: www.beckercommunications.com
Bertelsmann SE & Co 1745 Broadway. New York NY 10019 490-524-1800
Web: www.bertelsmann.com
Bloomberg LP 731 Lexington Ave New York NY 10022 212-318-2000 893-5000
Web: www.bloomberg.com
Boardroom Inc 281 Tresser Blvd 8th Fl. Stamford CT 06901 800-274-5611 967-3086*
**Fax Area Code:* 203 ■ *TF:* 800-274-5611 ■ *Web:* blinepubs.com
Bobit Business Media 3520 Challenger St. Torrance CA 90503 310-533-2400 533-2500*
**Fax:* Hum Res ■ *TF:* 888-239-2455 ■ *Web:* www.bobit.com
Bureau of National Affairs Inc
1801 S Bell St. Arlington VA 22202 703-341-3000
TF: 800-372-1033 ■ *Web:* www.bna.com
Business & Legal Reports Inc (BLR)
141 Mill Rock Rd E. Old Saybrook CT 06475 860-510-0100 510-7225
TF: 800-727-5257 ■ *Web:* www.blr.com
Business News Publishing Co
2401 W Big Beaver Rd Ste 700. Troy MI 48084 248-362-3700 362-0317
TF: 800-837-7370 ■ *Web:* www.bnpmedia.com
Buyers Laboratory Inc 20 Railroad Ave Hackensack NJ 07601 201-488-0404 488-0461
TF: 800-578-5902 ■ *Web:* www.buyerslab.com
Cabot Heritage Corp 176 N St PO Box 2049. Salem MA 01970 978-745-5532 745-1283
TF: 800-654-1514 ■ *Web:* www.cabot.net

Phone Fax

Cambridge Whos Who Publishing Inc
498 Rexcorp Plz Fourth Fl Uniondale NY 11556 516-535-1515
Web: cambridgewhoswho.com
Card Player Media LLC
6940 O'Bannon Dr Ste 8. Las Vegas NV 89117 702-871-1720
Web: www.cardplayer.com
Challenge Publications Inc
9509 Vassar Ave Ste A Chatsworth CA 91311 818-700-6868 700-6282
TF: 800-562-9182 ■ *Web:* www.challengeweb.com
Christianity Today International
465 Gundersen Dr Carol Stream IL 60188 630-260-6200 260-0114
Web: www.christianitytoday.com
Cobblestone Publishing Co
30 Grove St Ste C. Peterborough NH 03458 603-924-7209 924-7380
TF: 800-821-0115 ■ *Web:* www.cobblestonepub.com
Coffey Communications Inc
1505 Business One Cir. Walla Walla WA 99362 509-525-0101
Web: coffeycomm.com
CollegeBound Network 1200 S Ave Ste 202. Staten Island NY 10314 718-761-4800 761-3300
Web: www.collegebound.net
Commodity Information Systems Inc
3030 NW Expy Ste 725. Oklahoma City OK 73112 405-604-8726 604-8726
TF: 800-231-0477 ■ *Web:* www.cis-okc.com
Computer Economics Inc
2082 Business Ctr Dr Ste 240 Irvine CA 92612 949-831-8700 442-7688
Web: www.computereconomics.com
Conde Nast Publications Inc Four Times Sq New York NY 10036 212-286-2860
TF: 800-897-8666 ■ *Web:* www.condenast.com
Consumers Digest Inc 520 Lk Cook Rd Ste 500 Deerfield IL 60015 847-607-3000
Web: consumersdigest.com
Consumers Union of US Inc 101 Truman Ave Yonkers NY 10703 914-378-2000
TF: 800-927-4357 ■ *Web:* www.consumersunion.org
Cook Communications Ministries
4050 Lee Vance View Colorado Springs CO 80918 719-536-0100 536-3265
TF: 800-708-5550 ■ *Web:* www.davidccook.com
Crain Communications Inc 1155 Gratiot Ave. Detroit MI 48207 313-446-6000 446-0361*
**Fax:* Hum Res ■ *TF:* 888-288-6954 ■ *Web:* www.crain.com
CRC Press LLC
6000 Broken Sound Pkwy NW Ste 300. Boca Raton FL 33487 561-994-0555 374-3401*
**Fax Area Code:* 800 ■ **Fax:* Cust Svc ■ *TF Cust Svc:* 800-272-7737 ■ *Web:* www.crcpress.com
Cutter Information Corp 37 Broadway Ste 1 Arlington MA 02474 781-648-8700 648-8707
TF: 800-964-5118 ■ *Web:* www.cutter.com
Cygnus Business Media Inc
1233 Janesville Ave Fort Atkinson WI 53538 631-845-2700 227-4245*
**Fax Area Code:* 203 ■ *TF:* 800-547-7377 ■ *Web:* www.cygnus.com
DataTrends Publications Inc PO Box 3221 Leesburg VA 20177 571-313-9916 771-9091*
**Fax Area Code:* 703 ■ *Web:* www.datatrendspublications.com
Deal LLC, The 20 Broad St New York NY 10005 212-313-9325 545-8442
TF Cust Svc: 888-667-3325 ■ *Web:* www.thedeal.com
Desert Homes Magazine
303 N Indian Canyon Dr PO Box 2724. Palm Springs CA 92262 760-325-2333
Web: www.palmspringslife.com
Desktop Engineering 1283 Main St PO Box 1039 Dublin NH 03444 603-563-1631 563-8192
Web: www.deskeng.com
Disney Consumer Products
500 S Buena Vista St Burbank CA 91521 818-560-1000 553-5402*
**Fax Area Code:* 215 ■ **Fax:* Cust Svc ■ *TF PR:* 877-282-8322 ■ *Web:* thewaltdisneycompany.com
Diversified Business Communications
121 Free St. Portland ME 04101 207-842-5500 842-5503
Web: divcom.com
Dupont Publishing Inc 3051 Tech Dr St Petersburg FL 33716 727-573-9339
Web: dupontregistry.com
E H Publishing Inc PO Box 989 Framingham MA 01701 508-663-1500 663-1599
Web: www.ehpub.com
Earl G Graves Ltd 130 Fifth Ave 10th Fl New York NY 10011 212-242-8000 886-9532
TF Cust Svc: 800-727-7777 ■ *Web:* www.blackenterprise.com
Economist Intelligence Unit
750 Third Ave 5th Fl. New York NY 10017 212-554-0600 586-1181
Web: www.eiu.com
Editorial Projects in Education
6935 Arlington Rd Ste 100. Bethesda MD 20814 301-280-3100 280-3200
Web: www.edweek.org
EGW.com Inc 4075 Papazian Way Fremont CA 94538 510-668-0268 668-0280
TF Cust Svc: 800-546-4754 ■ *Web:* www.egw.com
Elliott Wave International (EWI)
PO Box 1618 Gainesville GA 30503 770-536-0309 536-2514
TF Cust Svc: 800-336-1618 ■ *Web:* www.elliottwave.com
Elsevier Science Ltd 360 Pk Ave S. New York NY 10010 212-989-5800 633-3990
TF: 888-437-4636 ■ *Web:* www.elsevier.com
Emerging Portfolio Fund Research Inc
80 Sherman St Cambridge MA 02140 617-864-4999
Web: www.epfr.com
Energy Intelligence Group 5 E 37th St 5th Fl New York NY 10016 212-532-1112 532-4479
Web: www.energyintel.com
Entrepreneur Media Inc 2445 McCabe Way Ste 400 Irvine CA 92614 949-261-2325 261-7729
TF: 877-652-5295 ■ *Web:* www.entrepreneur.com
EPM Communications Inc 19 W 21st St Ste 303 New York NY 10010 212-941-0099 941-1622
TF: 888-852-9467 ■ *Web:* www.epmcom.com
Ernst Publishing Co LLC
one Commerce Plaza 99 Washington Ave Ste 309 Albany NY 12210 800-345-3822 252-0906
TF: 800-345-3822 ■ *Web:* www.ernstpublishing.com
Essence Communications Inc
135 W 50th St 4th Fl. New York NY 10020 800-274-9398 921-5173*
**Fax Area Code:* 212 ■ *TF Sales:* 800-274-9398 ■ *Web:* www.essence.com
Euromoney Institutional Investor PLC
225 Pk Ave S New York NY 10003 212-224-3300 224-3171
Web: www.institutionalinvestor.com
F+W, A Content + eCommerce Company
10151 Carver Rd Ste 200 Cincinnati OH 45236 513-531-2690 531-2690
TF Sales: 800-289-0963 ■ *Web:* www.fwcommunity.com
Forbes Inc 60 Fifth Ave New York NY 10011 212-620-2200 206-5534
TF: 800-295-0893 ■ *Web:* www.forbes.com

Company / Address	City	State	Zip	Phone	Fax
Forecast International 22 Commerce Rd *TF:* 800-451-4975 ■ *Web:* www.forecastinternational.com	Newtown	CT	06470	203-426-0800	426-1964
Forum Publishing Co 383 E Main St *TF:* 800-635-7654 ■ *Web:* www.forum123.com	Centerport	NY	11721	631-754-5000	754-0630
Gardner Publications Inc 6915 Valley Ave *TF:* 800-950-8020 ■ *Web:* www.gardnerweb.com	Cincinnati	OH	45244	513-527-8800	527-8801
Grace Communion International PO Box 5005 *TF:* 800-423-4444 ■ *Web:* www.gci.org	Glendora	CA	91740	626-650-2300	
Grand View Media Group Inc (GVMG) 200 Croft St Ste 1 *TF:* 888-431-2877 ■ *Web:* www.gvmg.com	Birmingham	AL	35242	205-408-3700	408-3797
Grandstand Publishing LLC 990 Grove St Ste 400 *Web:* baseballdigest.com	Evanston	IL	60201	847-491-6440	491-0459
Greater Washington Publishing Inc 1919 Gallows Rd Ste 200 *Web:* www.gwpi.net	Vienna	VA	22182	703-992-1100	893-8356
Gulf Publishing Company Inc Two Greenway Plz Ste 1020 *TF:* 800-231-6275 ■ *Web:* www.gulfpub.com	Houston	TX	77046	713-529-4301	520-4433
Hanley-Wood LLC 1 Thomas Cir NW Ste 600 *TF:* 800-227-8839 ■ *Web:* www.hanleywood.com	Washington	DC	20005	202-452-0800	785-1974
Hart Publications Inc 1616 S Voss Rd Ste 1000 *TF:* 800-874-2544 ■ *Web:* www.hartenergy.com	Houston	TX	77057	713-260-6400	840-8585
Hatton Brown Publishers Inc PO Box 2268 *TF:* 800-669-5613 ■ *Web:* www.hattonbrown.net	Montgomery	AL	36102	334-834-1170	
Health Forum 155 North Wacker Drive Suite 400 *TF:* 800-621-6902 ■ *Web:* healthforum.com	Chicago	IL	60606	312-422-2165	
Healthy Directions LLC 7811 Montrose Rd **Fax Area Code:* 301 ■ **Fax:* Hum Res ■ *TF:* 866-599-9491 ■ *Web:* www.healthydirections.com	Potomac	MD	20854	866-599-9491	251-3758*
Hearst Magazines Div 300 W 57th St *Web:* www.hearst.com	New York	NY	10019	212-649-2275	
Highlights for Children Inc 1800 Watermark Dr *TF Cust Svc:* 800-255-9517 ■ *Web:* www.highlights.com	Columbus	OH	43216	614-486-0631	324-1630
Hli Properties Inc PO Box 1052 *TF:* 800-247-2000 ■ *Web:* www.hlipublishing.com	Fort Dodge	IA	50501	515-955-1600	574-2125
Hobsons CollegeView 50 E Business Way Ste 300 *TF:* 800-927-8439 ■ *Web:* www.collegeview.com	Cincinnati	OH	45241	800-927-8439	891-8531
Homes & Land Magazine Affiliates LLC 1830 E Pk Ave *TF:* 800-277-7800 ■ *Web:* www.homesandland.com	Tallahassee	FL	32301	850-575-0189	574-2525
Honolulu Publishing Co Ltd 707 Richards St Ste PH3 *TF:* 800-272-5245 ■ *Web:* www.honolulupublishing.com	Honolulu	HI	96813	808-524-7400	531-2306
Horizon House Publications Inc (HHP) 685 Canton St *TF:* 800-225-9977 ■ *Web:* www.horizonhouse.com	Norwood	MA	02062	781-769-9750	762-9071
IEEE Computer Society Press 10662 Los Vaqueros Cir PO Box 3014 *TF:* 800-272-6657 ■ *Web:* computer.org/portal/web/cspress/home	Los Alamitos	CA	90720	714-821-8380	821-4010
Information Today Inc 143 Old Marlton Pike *TF:* 800-300-9868	Medford	NJ	08055	609-654-6266	654-4309
InfoWorld Media Group Inc 501 Second St Ste 120 *TF:* 800-227-8365 ■ *Web:* www.infoworld.com	San Francisco	CA	94107	415-243-0500	978-3120
Inside Washington Publishers 1919 S Eads St Ste 201 *TF:* 800-424-9068 ■ *Web:* www.iwpnews.com	Arlington	VA	22202	703-416-8500	416-8543
Institutional Investor Newsletters 225 Pk Ave S 8th Fl **Fax:* Cust Svc ■ *TF:* 800-437-9997 ■ *Web:* www.iinews.com	New York	NY	10003	212-224-3300	224-3491*
International Data Group Inc (IDG) 1 Exeter Plaza 15th Fl *TF Orders:* 800-343-4952 ■ *Web:* www.idg.com	Boston	MA	02116	617-534-1200	859-8642
Internet Business Network 303 Ross Dr *TF:* 866-497-6747 ■ *Web:* www.interbiznet.com	Mill Valley	CA	94941	415-377-2255	380-8245
JOC Group Inc 2 Penn Plaza E 975 Raymond Blvd **Fax Area Code:* 609 ■ **Fax:* Edit ■ *TF Cust Svc:* 800-223-0243 ■ *Web:* www.joc.com	Newark	NJ	07105	973-776-7824	759-7632*
Johnson Publishing Company Inc 200 S Michigan Ave *Web:* www.johnsonpublishing.com	Chicago	IL	60604	312-322-9200	
Jossey-Bass & Pfeiffer 989 Market St 5th Fl **Fax Area Code:* 415 ■ *Web:* wiley.com/wileycda/brand/id-17.html	San Francisco	CA	94103	317-572-3994	433-0499*
Journey Group Inc 418 Fourth St Ne *Web:* journeygroup.com	Charlottesville	VA	22902	434-961-2500	
JR O'Dwyer Co 271 Madison Ave Sixth Fl *TF:* 866-395-7710 ■ *Web:* www.odwyerpr.com	New York	NY	10016	212-679-2471	683-2750
Kiplinger Washington Editors Inc 1729 H St NW *TF:* 800-544-0155 ■ *Web:* www.kiplinger.com	Washington	DC	20006	202-887-6400	496-1817
Latin Press Inc 2455 SW 27th Ave *Web:* www.latinpressinc.com	Miami	FL	33145	305-285-3133	
Laurin Publishing Co Inc 100 West St *TF:* 877-422-7300 ■ *Web:* www.photonics.com	Pittsfield	MA	01202	413-499-0514	442-3180
Lawrence Ragan Communications Inc 111 E Wacker Dr Ste 500 **Fax Area Code:* 312 ■ *TF:* 800-878-5331 ■ *Web:* www.ragan.com	Chicago	IL	60601	800-493-4867	960-4106*
Lebhar-Friedman Inc 425 Pk Ave Sixth Fl *Web:* www.lf.com	New York	NY	10022	212-756-5000	
LFP Inc 8484 Wilshire Blvd Ste 900 *Web:* hustler.com	Beverly Hills	CA	90211	323-651-5400	651-3525
Lionheart Publishing Inc 506 Roswell St *Web:* lionhrtpub.com	Marietta	GA	30060	770-431-0867	
Lippincott Williams & Wilkins 530 Walnut St *Web:* www.lww.com	Philadelphia	PA	19106	215-521-8300	521-8902
Liturgical Publications Inc 2875 S James Dr *TF:* 800-876-4574 ■ *Web:* www.4lpi.com	New Berlin	WI	53151	262-785-1188	785-9567
MAC Publishing LLC 501 Second St *Web:* www.macworld.com	San Francisco	CA	94107	415-243-0505	
Mary Ann Liebert Publishers Inc 140 Huguenot St Third Fl *TF:* 800-654-3237 ■ *Web:* www.liebertpub.com	New Rochelle	NY	10801	914-740-2100	740-2101
McGraw-Hill Cos Inc 1221 Ave of the Americas *NYSE: MHFI* ■ *Web:* www.mcgraw-hill.com	New York	NY	10020	212-512-2000	
McKnight's Long-Term Care News One Northfield Plz Ste 521 *TF:* 800-558-1703 ■ *Web:* www.mcknights.com	Northfield	IL	60093	847-784-8706	784-9346
Media Business Corp 1810 Platte St *Web:* mediabiz.com	Denver	CO	80202	303-271-9960	
Meister Media Worldwide 37733 Euclid Ave *TF Orders:* 800-572-7740 ■ *Web:* www.meistermedia.com	Willoughby	OH	44094	440-942-2000	942-0662
Mercedes Distribution Center Inc Brooklyn Navy Yard 63 Flushing Ave Ste 340 *Web:* www.mdist.com	Brooklyn	NY	11205	718-534-3000	
Meredith Corp 1716 Locust St *NYSE: MDP* ■ *Web:* www.meredith.com	Des Moines	IA	50309	515-284-3000	284-3806
Mergent Inc 477 Madison Ave Ste 410 *TF:* 800-937-1398 ■ *Web:* www.mergent.com	New York	NY	10022	212-413-7700	413-7670
Merion Publications Inc 2900 Horizon Dr *TF:* 800-355-1088 ■ *Web:* www.advanceweb.com	King of Prussia	PA	19406	610-278-1400	278-1425
Miles Media Group Inc 6751 Professional Pkwy W Ste 200 *TF:* 877-342-2424 ■ *Web:* www.see-florida.com	Sarasota	FL	34240	941-342-2300	907-0300
Moody's Corp 250 Greenwich St 7 World Trade Ctr *NYSE: MCO* ■ *Web:* www.moodys.com	New York	NY	10007	212-553-0300	
National Braille Press Inc 88 St Stephen St *TF:* 888-965-8965 ■ *Web:* www.nbp.org	Boston	MA	02115	617-266-6160	437-0456
National Catholic Reporter Publishing Co 115 E Armour Blvd *TF:* 800-333-7373 ■ *Web:* www.ncronline.org	Kansas City	MO	64111	816-531-0538	968-2292
Natural Mktg Institute Inc, The 272 Ruth Rd *Web:* www.nmisolutions.com	Harleysville	PA	19438	215-513-7300	
Nelson Publishing 2500 Tamiami Trl N *TF:* 800-226-6113 ■ *Web:* www.nelsonpub.com	Nokomis	FL	34275	941-966-9521	966-2590
News Corp 1211 Ave of the Americas 2nd Fl *NASDAQ: NWSA* ■ *Web:* www.newscorp.com	New York	NY	10036	212-416-3400	
North American Publishing Co (NAPCO) 1500 Springarden St 12th Fl *TF:* 800-627-2689 ■ *Web:* www.napco.com	Philadelphia	PA	19130	215-238-5300	238-5457
Northstar Travel Media LLC 100 Lighting Way **Fax:* Hum Res ■ *TF:* 800-742-7076 ■ *Web:* www.northstartravelmedia.com	Secaucus	NJ	07094	201-902-2000	902-2045*
Our Sunday Visitor Inc 200 Noll Plaza *TF:* 800-348-2440 ■ *Web:* www.osv.com	Huntington	IN	46750	260-356-8400	356-8472
Pace Communications Inc 1301 Carolina St Ste 200 *Web:* www.paceco.com	Greensboro	NC	27401	336-378-6065	378-8273
Pacific Press 1350 N Kings Rd *TF Cust Svc:* 800-765-6955 ■ *Web:* www.pacificpress.com	Nampa	ID	83687	208-465-2500	465-2531
Paisano Publications LLC 28210 Dorothy Dr *TF:* 800-323-3484 ■ *Web:* www.paisanopub.com	Agoura Hills	CA	91301	818-889-8740	889-5214
Parade Publications Inc 711 Third Ave *Web:* parade.com/	New York	NY	10017	212-450-7000	450-7287
PC World Communications Inc 501 Second St *TF General:* 800-234-3498 ■ *Web:* www.pcworld.com	San Francisco	CA	94107	415-243-0505	
Penton Media Inc 1300 E Ninth St *Web:* www.penton.com	Cleveland	OH	44114	216-696-7000	696-1752
Photosource International 1910 35th Rd *TF:* 800-786-6277 ■ *Web:* www.photosource.com	Osceola	WI	54020	715-248-3800	
Platts Two Penn Plz 25th Fl *TF:* 800-752-8878 ■ *Web:* www.platts.com	New York	NY	10121	212-904-3070	
Pohly Co 867 Boylston St 5th Fl *TF:* 800-383-0888 ■ *Web:* www.pohlyco.com	Boston	MA	02116	617-451-1700	338-7767
Powersports Business Magazine 6420 Sycamore Ln N *Web:* www.powersportsbusiness.com	Maple Grove	MN	55369	763-383-4400	
PRIMEDIA Inc & Consumer Source Inc 3585 Engineering Dr Ste 100 *TF:* 800-216-1423 ■ *Web:* rentpath.com	Norcross	GA	30092	678-421-3000	
Professional Sports Publications 519 Eigth Ave 25th Fl *Web:* www.pspsports.com	New York	NY	10018	212-697-1460	
Progressive Impressions 1 Hardman Dr *TF:* 800-644-0444 ■ *Web:* www.whateverittakes.com	Bloomington	IL	61701	309-664-0444	662-2055
Publications & Communications Inc 13552 Hwy 183 N Ste A *TF:* 800-678-9724 ■ *Web:* www.pcinews.com	Austin	TX	78750	512-250-9023	331-3950
Publications International Ltd 7373 N Cicero Ave *TF General:* 800-777-5582 ■ *Web:* pilbooks.com	Lincolnwood	IL	60712	847-676-3470	676-3671
Publishing Group of America Media 341 Cool Springs Blvd Ste 400 *Web:* pgoamedia.com	Franklin	TN	37067	615-468-6000	468-6100
Putman Media Inc 555 W Pierce Rd **Fax:* Hum Res ■ *TF:* 866-666-6033 ■ *Web:* www.putman.net	Itasca	IL	60143	630-467-1301	467-0153*
Quebecor Media Inc 612 Rue St Jacques *Web:* www.quebecor.com	Montreal	QC	H3C4M8	514-380-1999	985-8652
Randall-Reilly Publishing Co 3200 Rice Mine Rd NE *TF Cust Svc:* 800-633-5953 ■ *Web:* randallreilly.com	Tuscaloosa	AL	35406	800-633-5953	
Reader's Digest Association Inc 44 S Bdwy *TF:* 800-457-4708 ■ *Web:* www.rda.com	White Plains	NY	10601	914-244-2293	

	City	State	ZIP	Phone	Fax
Renard Communications Inc					
197 Mountain Ave	Springfield	NJ	07081	973-912-8550	
Web: diversitycareers.com					
RentPath Inc 3585 Engineering Dr Ste 100	Norcross	GA	30092	678-421-3000	754-0100*
**Fax Area Code:* 212 ■ *TF:* 800-216-1423 ■ *Web:* rentpath.com					
Review & Herald Publishing Assn					
55 W Oak Ridge Dr	Hagerstown	MD	21740	301-393-3000	393-3209
TF: 800-456-3991 ■ *Web:* www.rhpa.org					
Sage Publications Inc 2455 Teller Rd	Thousand Oaks	CA	91320	805-499-9774	499-0871
TF: 800-818-7243 ■ *Web:* www.sagepub.com					
Saint Croix Press Inc					
1185 S Knowles Ave	New Richmond	WI	54017	715-246-5811	246-2486
TF: 800-826-6622 ■ *Web:* www.stcroixpress.com					
Sandhills Publishing 120 W Harvest Dr	Lincoln	NE	68521	402-479-2181	479-2195
TF: 800-331-1978 ■ *Web:* www.sandhills.com					
Schaeffer's Investment Research Inc					
5151 Pfeiffer Rd Ste 250	Cincinnati	OH	45242	513-589-3800	589-3810
TF: 800-448-2080 ■ *Web:* www.schaeffersresearch.com					
Scholastic Corp 557 Broadway	New York	NY	10012	212-343-6100	
TF Cust Svc: 800-724-6527 ■ *Web:* scholastic.co.in					
Simba Information 60 Long Ridge Rd Ste 300	Stamford	CT	06902	203-325-8193	325-8915
TF: 888-297-4622 ■ *Web:* simbainformation.com/					
Simmons-Boardman Publishing Corp					
55 Broad St 26th fl 12th Fl	New York	NY	10004	212-620-7200	633-1165
TF: 800-895-4389 ■ *Web:* www.simmonsboardman.com					
Singapore Press Holdings					
529 14th St NW					
National Press Bldg Ste 916	Washington	DC	20045	202-662-8726	662-8729
Web: www.sph.com.sg					
Sky Publishing Corp 90 Sherman St	Cambridge	MA	02140	617-864-7360	864-6117
TF: 800-253-0245 ■					
Web: skyandtelescope.com/a-brief-history-of-skytelescope					
Slack Inc 6900 Grove Rd	Thorofare	NJ	08086	856-848-1000	848-6091
TF: 800-257-8290 ■ *Web:* www.slackinc.com					
Smithsonian Institution Business Ventures Div					
600 Maryland Ave SW Ste 6000	Washington	DC	20024	202-633-6080	633-6093
TF: 800-521-5330 ■ *Web:* www.si.edu					
Source Media Inc One State St Plz 27th Fl	New York	NY	10004	212-803-8200	
TF: 800-221-1809 ■ *Web:* www.sourcemedia.com					
Stamats Communications Inc					
615 Fifth St SE	Cedar Rapids	IA	52401	319-364-6167	364-4278
TF: 800-553-8878 ■ *Web:* www.stamats.com					
Standard Publishing Co					
8805 Governors Hill Dr Ste 400	Cincinnati	OH	45249	513-931-4050	867-5751*
**Fax Area Code:* 877 ■ *TF Orders:* 800-543-1353 ■ *Web:* www.standardpub.com					
Strafford Publications Inc PO Box 13729	Atlanta	GA	30324	404-881-1141	881-0074
TF: 800-926-7926 ■ *Web:* www.straffordpub.com					
Strang Communications 600 Rinehart Rd	Lake Mary	FL	32746	407-333-0600	333-7100
Web: www.charismamedia.com					
Sunset Publishing Corp 80 Willow Rd	Menlo Park	CA	94025	650-321-3600	327-7537*
**Fax:* Edit ■ *TF:* 800-227-7346 ■ *Web:* www.sunset.com					
Sys-con Media Inc					
577 Chestnut Ridge Rd	Woodcliff Lake	NJ	07677	201-802-3000	782-9600*
**Fax:* Cust Svc ■ *Web:* www.sys-con.com					
Taunton Press Inc 63 S Main St PO Box 5506	Newtown	CT	06470	203-426-8171	426-3434
Web: www.taunton.com					
Tax Analysts 400 S Maple Ave	Falls Church	VA	22046	703-533-4400	
Web: taxanalysts.com					
Tax Management Inc 1801 S Bell St	Arlington	VA	22202	703-341-3000	
TF: 800-372-1033 ■ *Web:* www.bna.com					
Testa Communications					
25 Willowdale Ave	Port Washington	NY	11050	516-767-2500	767-9335
Web: www.testa.com					
Thompson Publishing Group Inc					
805 15th St NW Third Fl	Washington	DC	20005	202-872-4000	296-1091
TF Cust Svc: 800-677-3789 ■ *Web:* www.thompson.com					
Time Inc 1271 Ave of the Americas	New York	NY	10020	212-522-1212	522-4543
Web: www.timeinc.com					
Transcontinental Inc					
1100 Rene-Levesque Blvd W 24th Fl	Montreal	QC	H3B4X9	514-392-9000	
TF: 800-361-5479 ■ *Web:* tctranscontinental.com					
TransWorld Business					
2052 Corte Del Nogal Ste 100	Carlsbad	CA	92011	760-722-7777	722-0653
TF General: 800-788-7072 ■ *Web:* business.transworld.net					
Travelhost Inc 10701 N Stemmons Fwy	Dallas	TX	75220	972-556-0541	432-8729
TF: 800-527-1782 ■ *Web:* www.travelhost.com					
United Methodist Publishing House					
201 Eigth Ave S	Nashville	TN	37203	615-749-6000	
TF: 800-672-1789 ■ *Web:* umph.org					
University of Chicago Press Journals Div					
PO Box 37005	Chicago	IL	60637	773-702-7700	753-0811
TF: 877-705-1878 ■ *Web:* www.press.uchicago.edu					
Value Line Inc 220 E 42nd St	New York	NY	10017	212-907-1500	818-9747
NASDAQ: VALU ■ *TF Cust Svc:* 800-634-3583 ■ *Web:* www.valueline.com					
Vance Publishing Corp					
400 Knightsbridge Pkwy	Lincolnshire	IL	60069	847-634-2600	634-4379
TF: 800-621-2845 ■ *Web:* www.vancepublishing.com					
Vendome Group LLC 216 E 45th St Sixth Fl	New York	NY	10017	800-519-3692	228-1308*
**Fax Area Code:* 212 ■ *TF:* 800-519-3692 ■ *Web:* www.vendomegrp.com					
Virgo Publishing Inc					
3300 N Central Ave Ste 300	Phoenix	AZ	85012	480-990-1101	990-0819
Web: www.vpico.com					
Viz Media 295 Bay St	San Francisco	CA	94133	415-546-7073	546-7086
Web: www.viz.com					
Warren Communications News Inc					
2115 Ward Ct NW	Washington	DC	20037	202-872-9200	318-8350
TF: 800-771-9202 ■ *Web:* www.warren-news.com					
Watt Publishing Co 303 N Main St Ste 500	Rockford	IL	61101	815-734-4171	968-0941
Web: www.wattnet.com					
Weddings In Houston Lp 525 Arlington St	Houston	TX	77007	713-464-4321	464-2880
Web: weddingsinhouston.com					
West World Production Inc					
420 N Camden Dr	Beverly Hills	CA	90210	310-276-9500	
Web: www.wwpi.com					
Wright's Media 2407 Timberloch Pl Ste B	The Woodlands	TX	77380	281-419-5725	
Web: www.wrightsreprints.com					
Yankee Publishing Inc PO Box 520	Dublin	NH	03444	603-563-8111	563-8252
TF: 800-729-9265 ■ *Web:* yankeemagazine.com					
Ziff Davis Inc 28 E 28th St	New York	NY	10016	212-503-3500	
Web: www.ziffdavis.com					

640-10 Publishers (Misc)

	City	State	ZIP	Phone	Fax
Allrecipescom Inc 413 Pine St Ste 500	Seattle	WA	98101	206-292-3990	
Web: www.webconnoisseur.com					
AM Best Co Ambest Rd	Oldwick	NJ	08858	908-439-2200	439-3296
TF: 800-424-2378 ■ *Web:* www.ambest.com					
American Printing House for the Blind					
1839 Frankfort Ave PO Box 6085	Louisville	KY	40206	502-895-2405	899-2274
TF: 800-223-1839 ■ *Web:* www.aph.org					
Animax Interactive LLC 6627 Valjean Ave	Van Nuys	CA	91406	818-787-4444	
Web: www.animaxent.com					
Brodart Company Automation Div					
500 Arch St	Williamsport	PA	17701	570-326-2461	999-6799*
**Fax Area Code:* 800 ■ *TF:* 800-233-8467 ■ *Web:* www.brodart.com					
Casino City Inc 95 Wells Ave	Newton Centre	MA	02459	617-332-2850	
Web: www.casinocitypress.com					
Cathedral Press Inc 600 NE Sixth St	Long Prairie	MN	56347	320-732-6143	732-3457
TF Cust Svc: 800-874-8332 ■ *Web:* www.cathedralpress.com					
Cellfish Media Inc 468 Rue St-Jean Ste 200	Montreal	QC	H2Y2S1	514-288-5858	
Web: corp.bandsintown.com					
Chalk & Vermilion Fine Arts Inc					
55 Old Post Rd Ste 2	Greenwich	CT	06830	203-869-9500	869-9520
TF: 800-877-2250 ■ *Web:* www.chalk-vermilion.com					
Channing Bete Co One Community Pl	South Deerfield	MA	01373	413-665-7611	499-6464*
**Fax Area Code:* 800 ■ **Fax:* Cust Svc ■ *TF:* 800-477-4776 ■ *Web:* www.channing-bete.com					
Clement Communications Inc					
Three Creek Pkwy PO Box 2208	Boothwyn	PA	19061	610-459-4200	
TF: 800-253-6368 ■ *Web:* www.clement.com					
Coastal Training Technologies Corp					
500 Studio Dr	Virginia Beach	VA	23452	757-498-9014	498-3657
TF: 866-333-6888 ■ *Web:* www.coastal.com					
CSS Industries Inc					
1845 Walnut St Ste 800	Philadelphia	PA	19103	215-569-9900	569-9979
NYSE: CSS ■ *Web:* www.cssindustries.com					
Drivers License Guide Co					
1492 Oddstad Dr	Redwood City	CA	94063	650-369-4849	364-8740
TF: 800-227-8827 ■ *Web:* www.driverslicenseguide.com					
EBSCO Publishing Inc 10 Estes St	Ipswich	MA	01938	978-356-6500	356-6500
TF: 800-653-2726 ■ *Web:* www.ebscohost.com					
Encyclopedia Britannica Inc					
331 N Las Salle St	Chicago	IL	60654	312-347-7159	294-2104
TF Cust Svc: 800-323-1229 ■ *Web:* www.britannica.com					
Flyer.Com 201 Kelsey Ln	Tampa	FL	33619	813-626-9430	
Web: theflyer.com					
Force Mass Acceleration 20 W 22nd St Ste 601	New York	NY	10010	212-691-5000	
Forecast International 22 Commerce Rd	Newtown	CT	06470	203-426-0800	426-1964
TF: 800-451-4975 ■ *Web:* www.forecastinternational.com					
Genesis Press Inc 7112 Augusta Rd	Piedmont	SC	29673	864-552-2000	
Hadley House Co 4816 Nicollet Ave S	Minneapolis	MN	55419	800-423-5390	286-5815*
**Fax Area Code:* 320 ■ *TF:* 800-423-5390 ■ *Web:* www.hadleyhouse.com					
IDI Multimedia Inc					
7250 Heritage Village Plz Ste 201	Gainesville	VA	20155	703-753-2141	
Web: www.idimultimedia.com					
Imagination Publishing					
600 W Fulton St Ste 600	Chicago	IL	60661	312-887-1000	887-1003
TF: 800-482-0776 ■ *Web:* www.imaginepub.com					
InfoCommerce Group Inc					
2 Bala Plaza Ste 300	Bala Cynwyd	PA	19004	610-649-1200	471-0515
Web: www.infocommercegroup.com					
Innovative Integration Inc					
2390-A Ward Ave	Simi Valley	CA	93065	805-578-4260	
Web: www.innovative-dsp.com					
Interactive Data Corp 32 Crosby Dr	Bedford	MA	01730	781-687-8500	687-8005
TF: 800-228-9715 ■ *Web:* www.interactivedata.com					
Kongregate Inc 660 Mission St Ste 400	San Francisco	CA	94105	415-618-0087	
Web: www.kongregate.com					
Lifetouch Church Directories					
1371 Portland Way N	Galion	OH	44833	419-468-4739	
TF: 800-521-4611 ■ *Web:* www.lifetouch.com					
Majesco Entertainment Co 160 Raritan Ctr Pkwy	Edison	NJ	08837	732-225-8910	225-8408
NASDAQ: COOL ■ *Web:* www.majescoent.com					
Mergent FIS Inc 580 Kingsley Pk Dr	Fort Mill	SC	29715	800-342-5647	559-6945*
**Fax Area Code:* 704 ■ *TF:* 800-342-5647 ■ *Web:* www.mergent.com					
Microcomputer Applications Inc					
1025 W Seventh Ave	Denver	CO	80204	720-904-2252	
Web: www.keylok.com					
New York Graphic Society Ltd 129 Glover Ave	Norwalk	CT	06850	800-677-6947	846-4869*
**Fax Area Code:* 203 ■ *TF:* 800-677-6947 ■ *Web:* www.nygs.com					
O'neil & Assoc Inc 495 Byers Rd	Miamisburg	OH	45342	937-865-0800	865-5858
Web: www.oneil.com					
OAG Worldwide					
3025 Highland Pkwy Ste 200	Downers Grove	IL	60515	630-515-5300	515-3933
TF: 800-342-5624 ■ *Web:* www.oag.com					
OmniPrint Inc 9700 Philadelphia Ct	Lanham	MD	20706	301-731-7000	
OneSource Information Services Inc					
300 Baker Ave	Concord	MA	01742	978-318-4300	318-4690
TF: 800-433-0287 ■ *Web:* avention.com					
Post Asylum Inc 5642 Dyer St	Dallas	TX	75206	214-363-0162	363-8871
Web: www.postasylum.com					

Company	City	State	Zip	Phone	Fax
PRS Group Inc, The Heritage Landing Dr Ste E Syracuse *Web:* www.prsgroup.com	New York	NY	13057	315-431-0511	
Reactrix Systems Inc PO Box 878 *Web:* www.reactrix.com	Ramsey	NJ	07446	240-342-6346	
San Dieguito Printers 1880 Diamond St *TF:* 800-321-5794 ■ *Web:* www.sd-print.com	San Marcos	CA	92078	760-744-0910	744-5811
Semantic Research Inc 4922 N Harbor Dr *Web:* www.semanticresearch.com	San Diego	CA	92106	619-222-4050	
ServerBeach Ltd 8500 Vicar Dr Ste 500 *Web:* www.peer1.com	San Antonio	TX	78218	210-798-4400	
Somerset Fine Arts PO Box 869 *Fax Area Code: 713 ■ *TF Sales:* 800-444-2540 ■ *Web:* www.somersetfineart.com	Fulshear	TX	77441	800-444-2540	932-7861*
TechTarget 275 Grove St Ste 800 *TF:* 888-274-4111 ■ *Web:* www.techtarget.com	Newton	MA	02466	617-431-9200	431-9201
Thomson CenterWatch Inc 100 N Washington St Ste 301 *TF Cust Svc:* 800-765-9647 ■ *Web:* www.centerwatch.com	Boston	MA	02114	617-948-5100	948-5101
Washington Publishing Co 2107 Elliott Ave Ste 305 *Fax Area Code: 775 ■ *Web:* www.wpc-edi.com	Seattle	WA	98121	425-562-2245	239-2061*
Wonderlic Inc 400 Lakeview Pkwy Ste 200 *TF:* 877-605-9496 ■ *Web:* www.wonderlic.com	Vernon Hills	IL	60061	847-680-4900	680-9492
Xperts Inc 4701 Cox Rd Ste 135 *Web:* www.xperts.com	Glen Allen	VA	23060	804-290-4272	
Zagat Survey LLC 10 Columbus Cir Third Fl *Web:* www.zagat.com	New York	NY	10019	212-823-9335	977-6488

640-11 Technical Publishers

Company	City	State	Zip	Phone	Fax
Aircraft Technical Publishers 101 S Hill Dr *Fax: Sales ■ *TF:* 800-227-4610 ■ *Web:* www.atp.com	Brisbane	CA	94005	415-330-9500	468-1596*
American Chemical Society Publications 1155 16th St NW Publications Support Services	Washington	DC	20036	202-872-4600	872-6060
Applied Computer Research Inc (ACR) PO Box 41730 *Fax Area Code: 602 ■ *TF:* 800-234-2227 ■ *Web:* www.itmarketintelligence.com	Phoenix	AZ	85080	800-234-2227	548-4800*
Buyers Laboratory Inc 20 Railroad Ave *TF:* 800-578-5902 ■ *Web:* www.buyerslab.com	Hackensack	NJ	07601	201-488-0404	488-0461
Cambridge Information Group (CIG) 111 W 57th St *Web:* www.cambridgeinformationgroup.com	New York	NY	10019	212-897-6635	897-6640
Faulkner Information Services 7905 Browning Rd *TF:* 800-843-0460 ■ *Web:* www.faulkner.com	Pennsauken	NJ	08109	856-662-2070	662-0905
Health Forum 155 North Wacker Drive Suite 400 *TF:* 800-621-6902 ■ *Web:* healthforum.com	Chicago	IL	60606	312-422-2165	
Information Gatekeepers Inc (IGI) 1340 Soldiers Field Rd Ste 2 *TF:* 800-323-1088 ■ *Web:* www.igigroup.com	Brighton	MA	02135	617-782-5033	782-5735
JJ Keller & Assoc Inc 3003 Breezewood Ln PO Box 368 *Fax Area Code: 800 ■ *TF:* 800-558-5011 ■ *Web:* www.jjkeller.com	Neenah	WI	54957	920-722-2848	727-7516*
Ken Cook Co 9929 W Silver Springs Dr *Web:* www.kencook.com	Milwaukee	WI	53225	414-466-6060	466-9275
Mitchell 1 14145 Danielson St Ste A *Fax: Sales ■ *TF:* 888-724-6742 ■ *Web:* www.mitchell1.com	Poway	CA	92064	858-391-5000	746-8915*
Mitchell International Inc 6220 Greenwich Dr *TF:* 800-854-7030 ■ *Web:* www.mitchell.com	San Diego	CA	92122	858-578-6550	530-4632
O'Reilly & Assoc Inc 1005 Gravenstein Hwy N *TF:* 800-998-9938 ■ *Web:* www.oreilly.com	Sebastopol	CA	95472	707-829-0515	829-0104
TeleGeography Inc 1909 K St NW Ste 380 *Web:* www.telegeography.com	Washington	DC	20006	202-741-0020	741-0021
Thompson Publishing Group Inc 805 15th St NW Third Fl *TF Cust Svc:* 800-677-3789 ■ *Web:* www.thompson.com	Washington	DC	20005	202-872-4000	296-1091

641 PULP MILLS

SEE ALSO Paper Mills p. 2855; Paperboard Mills p. 2857

Company	City	State	Zip	Phone	Fax
Alabama River Pulp Company Inc Lena Landegger Hwy County Rd 39 *Web:* www.ariver.com	Perdue Hill	AL	36470	251-575-2000	
Alberta-Pacific Forest Industries Inc PO Box 8000 *TF:* 800-661-5210 ■ *Web:* www.alpac.ca	Boyle	AB	T0A0M0	780-525-8000	525-8028
Allied Paper Company LLC 5700 Plauche Ct *Web:* www.alliedpapercompany.com	New Orleans	LA	70123	504-733-5700	
Arizona Pacific Pulp & Paper Inc 3209 S 36th St *Web:* www.azpacificpaper.com	Phoenix	AZ	85040	602-220-9200	
AV Nackawic Inc 103 Pinder Rd *Web:* www.av-group.ca	Nackawic	NB	E6G1W4	506-575-3314	
Canadian Forest Products Ltd 5162 Northwood Pulp Mill Rd PO Box 9000 *Fax: Acctg ■ *Web:* www.canfor.com	Prince George	BC	V2L4W2	250-962-3500	962-3473*
Cheney Pulp & Paper Company Inc 1000 Anderson St *Web:* www.cheneypulp.com	Franklin	OH	45005	937-746-9991	
Cosmo Specialty Fibers Inc 1701 First St *Web:* www.cosmospecialtyfibers.com	Cosmopolis	WA	98537	360-500-4600	
Daishowa-Marubeni International Ltd 510 Burrard St Ste 700 *Web:* www.dmi.ca	Vancouver	BC	V6C3A8	604-684-4326	
Donco Paper Supply Co 2100 Losantiville Ave *Fax Area Code: 312	Cincinnati	OH	45237	513-731-0208	337-7891*
Fox Converting Inc 1250 Cornell Rd *Web:* www.foxconverting.com	Green Bay	WI	54313	920-434-5272	
Gateway Products Recycling Inc 4223 E 49th St *Web:* www.gatewayrecycle.com	Cleveland	OH	44125	216-341-8777	
International Paper Co 6400 Poplar Ave *NYSE: IP* ■ *TF Prod Info:* 800-223-1268 ■ *Web:* www.internationalpaper.com	Memphis	TN	38197	901-419-9000	
KapStone Paper and Packaging Corp 300 Fibre Way PO Box 639 *Web:* www.longviewfibre.com	Longview	WA	98632	360-425-1550	230-5135
Kimberly-Clark Corp 351 Phelps Dr *NYSE: KMB* ■ *TF:* 888-525-8388 ■ *Web:* www.kimberly-clark.com	Irving	TX	75038	972-281-1200	281-1490
Longhorn Recycling LP 5785 Fm 1346 *Web:* www.longhornrecycling.com	San Antonio	TX	78220	210-661-2341	
Nippon Paper Industries USA Co 1902 Marine Dr *Web:* npiusa.com	Port Angeles	WA	98363	360-457-4474	
Northern Pulp Nova Scotia Corp 260 Granton Abercrombie Branch Rd *Web:* www.northernpulp.ca	Abercrombie	NS	B2H5C6	902-752-8461	
Omaha Paper Co 6936 L St *Web:* www.omahapaper.com	Omaha	NE	68117	402-331-3243	
Parsons & Whittemore Inc 4 International Dr	Rye Brook	NY	10573	914-937-9009	937-2259
Potlatch Corp 601 W First Ave Ste 1600 *NASDAQ: PCH* ■ *Web:* www.potlatchcorp.com	Spokane	WA	99201	509-835-1500	835-1555
Southern Cellulose Products Inc 105 W 45th St	Chattanooga	TN	37410	423-821-1561	

642 PUMPS - MEASURING & DISPENSING

Company	City	State	Zip	Phone	Fax
AccuSport Inc 4310 Enterprise Dr Ste C *Web:* www.accusport.com	Winston-Salem	NC	27106	336-759-3300	
Alameda Applied Sciences Corp 3077 Teagarden St *Web:* www.aasc.net	San Leandro	CA	94577	510-483-4156	
American Sensor Technologies Inc 450 Clark Dr *Web:* www.astsensors.com	Mt Olive	NJ	07828	973-448-1901	
Apantec LLC 4500 N Cannon Ave *Web:* www.apantec.com	Lansdale	PA	19446	267-436-3991	
Apex Precision Technologies Inc 8824 Union Mills Dr *Web:* www.apexprecision.com	Camby	IN	46113	317-821-1000	
Assay Technology Inc 1382 Stealth St *TF:* 800-833-1258 ■ *Web:* www.assaytech.com	Livermore	CA	94551	925-461-8880	
ATC Inc 4037 Guion Ln *Web:* www.atcinc.net	Indianapolis	IN	46268	317-328-8492	
Belfort Instrument Co 727 S Wolfe St *Web:* www.belfortinstrument.com	Baltimore	MD	21231	410-342-2626	
Bennett Pump Co 1218 Pontaluna Rd *TF:* 800-235-7618 ■ *Web:* bennettpump.com	Spring Lake	MI	49456	231-798-1310	799-6202
Brooks Utility Products Group 23847 Industrial Park Dr *TF:* 888-687-3008 ■ *Web:* www.brooksutility.com	Farmington Hills	MI	48335	248-477-0250	
Bubble Technology Industries Inc 31278 Hwy 17 *Web:* www.bubbletech.ca	Chalk River	ON	K0J1J0	613-589-2456	
Chen Instrument Design Inc 4845 NW Camas Meadows Dr *Web:* www.cid-inc.com	Camas	WA	98607	360-833-8835	
ComSonics Electronic Mfg Services Inc 780 Keezletown Rd Ste 102 *Web:* www.cemsi.com	Weyers Cave	VA	24486	540-434-7500	
Controlled Access Inc 1515 W 130th St *TF:* 800-942-0829 ■ *Web:* www.controlledaccess.com	Hinckley	OH	44233	330-273-6185	
Daily Instruments Inc 5700 Hartsdale Dr *Web:* www.dailyinst.com	Houston	TX	77036	713-780-8600	
DICKEY-john Corp 5200 Dickey-John Rd *TF:* 800-637-2952 ■ *Web:* www.dickey-john.com	Auburn	IL	62615	217-438-3371	
Dyne Systems Company LLC W209N17391 Industrial Dr *Web:* www.dynesystems.com	Jackson	WI	53037	262-677-9300	
Echometer Co 5001 Ditto Ln *Web:* www.echometer.com	Wichita Falls	TX	76302	940-767-4334	
Electro Static Technology 31 Winterbrook Rd *TF:* 866-738-1857 ■ *Web:* www.est-static.com	Mechanic Falls	ME	04256	207-998-5140	
Ferro Solutions Inc Five Constitution Way *Web:* www.ferrosi.com	Woburn	MA	01801	781-935-7878	
Gagemaker LP 712 Southmore Ave *TF:* 800-767-7633 ■ *Web:* gagemaker.com	Pasadena	TX	77502	713-472-7360	472-7241
Gammex Inc 7600 Discovery Dr *TF:* 800-426-6391 ■ *Web:* www.gammex.com	Middleton	WI	53562	608-828-7000	
Gasboy International Inc 7300 W Friendly Ave *Fax Area Code: 800 ■ *Fax: Cust Svc ■ *TF Sales:* 800-444-5579 ■ *Web:* www.gasboy.com	Greensboro	NC	27420	336-547-5000	444-5569*
GEM Systems Inc 135 Spy Ct *Web:* www.gemsys.ca	Markham	ON	L3R5H6	905-752-2202	752-2205
Gerhart Systems & Controls Corp 754 Roble Rd Ste 140 *Web:* gerhart.com	Allentown	PA	18109	610-264-2800	
Gilbarco Inc 7300 W Friendly Ave *Fax: Mktg ■ *Web:* www.gilbarco.com	Greensboro	NC	27420	336-547-5000	547-5890*
Headwall Photonics Inc 601 River St *Web:* www.headwallphotonics.com	Fitchburg	MA	01420	978-353-4100	

Company	City	State	Zip	Phone	Fax
Intelametrix 6246 Preston Ave *Web:* www.intelametrix.com	Livermore	CA	94551	925-606-7044	
Kamp Synergy 9434 N 107th St *Web:* kampscada.com	Milwaukee	WI	53224	414-354-6700	
Krohne Inc Seven Dearborn Rd *Web:* www.krohne.com	Peabody	MA	01960	978-535-6060	
Medicomp Inc 7845 Ellis Rd *TF:* 800-234-3278 ■ *Web:* www.medicompinc.com	Melbourne	FL	32904	321-676-0010	
Mehta Tech Inc 208 N 12th Ave *Web:* www.mehtatech.com	Eldridge	IA	52748	563-285-9151	
Motion Analysis Corp 3617 Wwind Blvd *Web:* www.motionanalysis.com	Santa Rosa	CA	95403	707-579-6500	
Nicol Scales 7239 Envoy Ct *Web:* www.nicolscales.com	Dallas	TX	75247	214-428-8181	428-8127
O'Day Equipment Inc 1301 40th St NW *TF:* 800-654-6329 ■ *Web:* www.odayequipment.com	Fargo	ND	58102	701-282-9260	281-9770
Pacific Precision Laboratories Inc 20447 Nordhoff St *Web:* www.ppli.com	Chatsworth	CA	91311	818-700-8977	
Pajarito Scientific Security Corp 2532 Camino Entrada *Web:* www.pajaritoscientific.com	Santa Fe	NM	87507	505-424-6660	
Physical Acoustics Corp 195 Clarksville Rd *Web:* www.pacndt.com	Princeton Junction	NJ	08550	609-716-4000	
Pressco Technology Inc 29200 Aurora Rd *Web:* www.pressco.com	Cleveland	OH	44139	440-498-2600	
Refraction Technology Inc 1600 10th St Ste A *Web:* www.reftek.com	Plano	TX	75074	214-440-1265	
Rexon Components Inc 24500 Highpoint Rd *Web:* www.rexon.com	Beachwood	OH	44122	216-292-7373	
Rice Lake Weighing Systems Inc 230 W Coleman St *Web:* www.ricelakehockey.com	Rice Lake	WI	54868	800-472-6703	
Spectec Nine Polaris Way *Web:* www.spectecsensors.com	Emigrant	MT	59027	406-333-4967	
Standard Imaging Inc 3120 Deming Way *TF:* 800-261-4446 ■ *Web:* www.standardimaging.com	Middleton	WI	53562	608-831-0025	
Thermtrol Corp 8914 Pleasantwood Ave NW *Web:* www.thermtrol.com	North Canton	OH	44720	330-497-4148	
THK America Inc 200 E Commerce Dr *Web:* www.thk.com	Schaumburg	IL	60173	847-310-1111	
Thwing-Albert Instrument Company Inc 14 W Collings Ave *Web:* www.thwingalbert.com	West Berlin	NJ	08091	856-767-1000	
TSA Systems Ltd 14000 Mead St *Web:* www.tsasystems.com	Longmont	CO	80504	970-535-9949	
Tuthill Transfer Systems 8500 S Madison *Web:* www.tuthill.com	Burr Ridge	IL	60527	260-747-7529	747-3159
Vortek Instruments LLC 8475 W I25 Frontage Rd Ste 300 *Web:* vortekinst.com	Longmont	CO	80504	303-682-9999	
Xiris Automation Inc 1016 Sutton Dr Ste C5 *Web:* www.xiris.com	Burlington	ON	L7L6B8	905-331-6660	331-6661

643 PUMPS & MOTORS - FLUID POWER

Company	City	State	Zip	Phone	Fax
Applied Energy Company Inc (AEC) 1205 Venture Ct Ste 100 *TF:* 800-580-1171 ■ *Web:* www.appliedenergyco.com	Carrollton	TX	75006	214-355-4200	355-4201
Bosch Rexroth Corp 5150 Prairie Stone Pkwy *TF:* 800-860-1055 ■ *Web:* www.boschrexroth-us.com	Hoffman Estates	IL	60192	847-645-3600	645-6201
Bosch Rexroth Corp Piston Pump Div 8 Southchase Ct *TF:* 877-266-7811 ■ *Web:* boschrexroth.com	Fountain Inn	SC	29644	864-967-2777	967-8900
Cross Manufacturing Inc 11011 King St Ste 210 *Web:* www.crossmfg.com	Overland Park	KS	66210	913-451-1233	451-1235
Delta Power Co 4484 Boeing Dr *Web:* www.delta-power.com	Rockford	IL	61109	815-397-6628	397-2526
Dynex Rivett Inc 770 Capitol Dr *Web:* www.dynexhydraulics.com	Pewaukee	WI	53072	262-691-0300	691-0312
Fluid Metering Inc Five Aerial Way Ste 500 *TF:* 800-223-3388 ■ *Web:* fluidmetering.com	Syosset	NY	11791	516-922-6050	624-8261
Hydreco 1500 County Naple Blvd *Web:* www.hydreco.com	Charlotte	NC	28273	704-295-7575	295-7574
Jetstream of Houston LLP 4930 Cranswick *TF:* 800-231-8192 ■ *Web:* www.waterblast.com	Houston	TX	77041	713-462-7000	462-5387
Liquid Drive Corp 418 Hadley St *Web:* www.liquiddrive.com	Holly	MI	48442	248-634-5382	
Milton Roy USA 201 Ivyland Rd *Web:* www.miltonroy.com	Ivyland	PA	18974	215-441-0800	441-8620
Mte Hydraulics PO Box 5906 *Web:* www.mtehydraulics.com	Rockford	IL	61125	815-397-4701	399-5528
Oilgear Co 2300 S 51st St PO Box 343924 *Web:* www.oilgear.com	Milwaukee	WI	53219	414-327-1700	327-0532
Parker Hannifin Corp Hydraulic Pump/Motor Div 2745 Snapps Ferry Rd *Web:* www.parker.com	Greeneville	TN	37745	423-639-8151	787-2418
Parker Hannifin Corp Nichols Portland Div 2400 Congress St *Web:* parker.com	Portland	ME	04102	207-774-6121	774-3601
Permco Inc 1500 Frost Rd *TF:* 800-628-2801 ■ *Web:* www.permco.com	Streetsboro	OH	44241	330-626-2801	626-2805
Pnucor Inc 10525 Granite St Ste A *Web:* www.pnucor.com	Charlotte	NC	28273	704-588-3333	
Sauer-Danfoss 2800 E 13th St *NYSE: SHS* ■ *Web:* powersolutions.danfoss.com	Ames	IA	50010	515-239-6000	239-6318
SPX Fluid Power 5885 11th St *Web:* spx.com/en/hydraulic-technologies/	Rockford	IL	61109	815-874-5556	874-7853
TexLoc Ltd 4700 Lone Star Blvd *Web:* www.texloc.com	Fort Worth	TX	76106	817-625-5081	
TII Network Technologies Inc 141 Rodeo Dr *NASDAQ: TIII* ■ *TF:* 888-844-4720 ■ *Web:* tiitech.com/	Edgewood	NY	11717	631-789-5000	789-5063
Viking Pump Inc 406 State St *TF:* 800-123-1234 ■ *Web:* www.vikingpump.com	Cedar Falls	IA	50613	319-266-1741	273-8157
Voith Turbo Inc 25 Winship Rd *Web:* www.usa.voithturbo.com	York	PA	17406	717-767-3200	767-3210

644 PUMPS & PUMPING EQUIPMENT (GENERAL USE)

SEE ALSO Industrial Machinery, Equipment, & Supplies p. 2554

Company	City	State	Zip	Phone	Fax
Ace Pump and Supply 6013 Johnson St *Web:* acepumpandsupply.com	Hollywood	FL	33024	954-981-7424	
Ace Pump Corp PO Box 13187 *Web:* www.acepumps.com	Memphis	TN	38113	901-948-8514	774-6147
Acme Dynamics Inc 3608 Sydney Rd PO Box 1780 *TF:* 800-622-9355 ■ *Web:* www.acmedynamics.com	Plant City	FL	33566	813-752-3137	752-4580
Advanced Pressure Systems LP 701 S Persimmon St Ste 85 *Web:* www.advancedpressuresystems.com	Tomball	TX	77375	281-290-9950	
Aermotor Pumps Inc 293 Wright St *TF:* 800-230-1816 ■ *Web:* www.aermotor.com	Delavan	WI	53115	800-230-1816	230-1816
Air Systems International Inc 829 Juniper Crescent *TF:* 800-866-8100 ■ *Web:* www.airsystems.com	Chesapeake	VA	23320	757-424-3967	
American Machine & Tool Company Inc 400 Spring St *TF:* 888-268-7867 ■ *Web:* www.amtpump.com	Royersford	PA	19468	610-948-3800	948-5300
Amico Corp 85 Fulton Way *Web:* www.amico.com	Richmond Hill	ON	L4B2N4	905-764-0800	
Ampco Pumps Company Inc 2045 W Mill Rd *TF:* 800-737-8671 ■ *Web:* www.ampcopumps.com	Glendale	WI	53209	414-643-1852	
Aqua-Dyne Inc 3620 W 11th St *Web:* www.aqua-dyne.com	Houston	TX	77008	713-864-6929	864-0313
AR Wilfley & Sons Inc 7350 E Progress Pl Ste 200 *TF:* 800-525-9930 ■ *Web:* www.wilfley.com	Englewood	CO	80111	303-779-1777	779-1277
Armstrong International Inc 2081 SE Ocean Blvd 4th Fl *TF:* 866-738-5125 ■ *Web:* www.armstronginternational.com	Stuart	FL	34996	772-286-7175	286-1001
Armstrong Pumps Inc 93 E Ave *Web:* armstrongfluidtechnology.com	North Tonawanda	NY	14120	716-693-8813	
ASM Industries Inc Pacer Pumps Div 41 Industrial Cir *TF Cust Svc:* 800-233-3861 ■ *Web:* www.pacerpumps.com	Lancaster	PA	17601	717-656-2161	656-0477
Banjo Corp 150 Banjo Dr *Web:* www.banjocorp.com	Crawfordsville	IN	47933	765-362-7367	
Barker Air & Hydraulics Inc 1308 Miller Rd *Web:* www.barkerair.com	Greenville	SC	29607	864-288-3537	
Barney's Pumps Inc 2965 Barney's Pumps Pl *Web:* www.barneyspumps.com	Lakeland	FL	33812	863-665-8500	666-3858
Barrett Engineered Pumps Inc 1695 National Ave *Web:* www.barrettpump.com	San Diego	CA	92113	619-232-7867	
Bayou City Pump Inc 8139 Tidwell Rd PO Box 23342 *Web:* www.bayoucitypumps.com	Houston	TX	77028	713-631-6451	
Beckett Corp 3250 Skyway Cir N *TF:* 888-232-5388 ■ *Web:* www.beckettpumps.com	Irving	TX	75038	972-871-8000	871-8888
Berkeley Pumps 293 Wright St **Fax Area Code:* 800 ■ **Fax:* Cust Svc ■ *Web:* www.berkeleypumps.com	Delavan	WI	53115	262-728-5551	426-9446*
Blackmer 1809 Century Ave *TF:* 888-363-7886 ■ *Web:* www.psgdover.com	Grand Rapids	MI	49503	616-241-1611	241-3752
Buffalo Pumps Inc 874 Oliver St *Web:* www.buffalopumps.com	North Tonawanda	NY	14120	716-693-1850	693-6303
Busch Vacuum Technics Inc 1740 Lionel Bertrand *Web:* busch.ca	Boisbriand	QC	J7H1N7	450-435-6899	
Carver Pump Co 2415 Pk Ave *Web:* www.carverpump.com	Muscatine	IA	52761	563-263-3410	262-7688
Cascade Pump Co 10107 Norwalk Blvd *Web:* www.cascadepump.com	Santa Fe Springs	CA	90670	562-946-1414	941-3730
Cat Pumps 1681 94th Ln NE *Web:* www.catpumps.com	Minneapolis	MN	55449	763-780-5440	780-2958
CDS-John Blue Co 290 Pinehurst Dr *TF:* 800-253-2583 ■ *Web:* www.cds-johnblue.com	Huntsville	AL	35806	256-721-9090	
CIRCOR International Inc 30 Corporate Dr Ste 200 *NYSE: CIR* ■ *Web:* www.circor.com	Burlington	MA	01803	781-270-1200	270-1299
CLYDE UNION Pumps 4600 W Dickman Rd *TF:* 800-877-7867	Battle Creek	MI	49037	269-966-4600	962-5447
Coffin Turbo Pump Inc 326 S Dean St *TF:* 800-568-9798 ■ *Web:* www.coffinturbopump.com	Englewood	NJ	07631	201-568-2826	568-4716
Colfax Corp 8730 Stony Pt Pkwy Ste 150 *Web:* www.colfaxcorp.com	Richmond	VA	23235	804-560-4070	560-4076
Complete Pump Service 461 S Irmen Dr *Web:* www.completepump.com	Addison	IL	60101	630-628-1600	
Corken Inc 3805 NW 36th St *TF:* 800-631-4929 ■ *Web:* www.corken.com	Oklahoma City	OK	73112	405-946-5576	948-6664
Cornell Pump Co 16261 SE 130th Ave PO Box 6334 *Web:* www.cornellpump.com	Portland	OR	97228	503-653-0330	653-0338
Crane Co 100 First Stamford Pl Fourth Fl *NYSE: CR* ■ *Web:* www.craneco.com	Stamford	CT	06902	203-363-7300	363-7295

Company	City	State	ZIP	Phone	Fax
Crane Pumps & Systems 420 Third St *Web:* www.cranepumps.com	Piqua	OH	45356	937-773-2442	773-2238
CS & P Technologies LP 18119 Telge Rd **Fax Area Code:* 832 ■ *Web:* www.csphouston.com	Cypress	TX	77429	713-467-0869	464-2089*
Custom Cylinders Inc 700 Industrial Dr Ste I *Web:* www.customcylinders.com	Cary	IL	60013	847-516-6467	
DADCO Inc 43850 Plymouth Oaks Blvd *Web:* www.dadco.net	Plymouth	MI	48170	734-207-1100	
Discflo Corp 10850 Hartley Rd *Web:* www.discflo.com	Santee	CA	92071	619-596-3181	
Div 15 Sales Inc 12026 Roberts Rd *Web:* www.division-15.com	La Vista	NE	68128	402-597-6353	
Ebara international corp 350 Salomon Cir *Web:* www.ebaraintl.com	Sparks	NV	89434	775-356-2796	356-2884
Environment One Corp 2773 Balltown Rd *Web:* www.eone.com	Niskayuna	NY	12309	518-346-6161	
Estabrook Corp 700 W Bagley Rd *Web:* www.estabrookcorp.com	Berea	OH	44017	440-234-8566	
Evans-Hydro 18128 S Santa Fe Ave *TF:* 800-429-7867 ■ *Web:* evanshydro.com	Rancho Dominguez	CA	90221	310-608-5801	608-0685
F E Myers 1101 Myers Pkwy *Web:* www.femyers.com	Ashland	OH	44805	419-289-1144	
Flint & Walling Inc 95 N Oak St *TF Sales:* 800-345-9422 ■ *Web:* www.flintandwalling.com	Kendallville	IN	46755	260-347-1600	347-6664
Flowserve Corp 5215 N O'Connor Blvd Ste 2300 *NYSE:* FLS ■ *TF:* 800-350-1082 ■ *Web:* www.flowserve.com	Irving	TX	75039	972-443-6500	443-6800
Fluid Equipment Development Company LLC 800 Ternes Dr *Web:* www.fedco-usa.com	Monroe	MI	48162	734-241-3935	
Fluid Power Equipment Inc 6305 Cunningham Rd *Web:* www.fluidpowerequipment.com	Houston	TX	77041	713-466-8088	
FMG Enterprises Inc 1125 Memorex Dr *TF:* 800-327-6177 ■ *Web:* www.fmgvacpump.com	Santa Clara	CA	95050	408-982-0110	
Fortbrand Services Inc 50 Fairchild Ct *Web:* www.fortbrand.com	Plainview	NY	11803	516-576-3200	
Fristam Pumps USA LP 2410 Parview Rd *Web:* www.fristam.com	Middleton	WI	53562	608-831-5001	
Gardner Denver Thomas - Products Div 1419 Illinois Ave *Web:* www.gd-thomas.com	Sheboygan	WI	53081	920-457-4891	
GIW Industries Inc 5000 Wrightsboro Rd *TF:* 888-832-4449 ■ *Web:* www.ksb.com	Grovetown	GA	30813	706-863-1011	860-5897
Global Pump Company LLC 10162 E Coldwater Rd *Web:* www.globalpump.com	Davison	MI	48423	810-653-4828	
Godwin Pumps of America Inc 84 Floodgate Rd *Web:* www.godwinpumps.com	Bridgeport	NJ	08014	856-467-3636	
Gorman-Rupp Co 305 Bowman St PO Box 1217 *NYSE:* GRC ■ *Web:* www.gormanrupp.com	Mansfield	OH	44901	419-755-1011	755-1263
Gorman-Rupp Industries 180 Hines Ave *Web:* www.gripumps.com	Bellville	OH	44813	419-886-3001	886-2338
GPM Industries Inc 110 Gateway Dr *TF:* 888-476-7867 ■ *Web:* www.gpmind.com	Macon	GA	31210	478-471-7867	
Graco Inc 88 11th Ave NE PO Box 1441 *NYSE:* GGG ■ **Fax:* Hum Res ■ *TF Cust Svc:* 800-328-0211 ■ *Web:* www.graco.com	Minneapolis	MN	55413	612-623-6000	623-6777*
Graymills Corp 3705 N Lincoln Ave *TF:* 877-465-7867 ■ *Web:* www.graymills.com	Chicago	IL	60613	773-477-4100	477-4133
Great Plains Industries Inc 5252 E 36th St N *TF Sales:* 800-835-0113 ■ *Web:* www.gpi.net	Wichita	KS	67220	316-686-7361	686-6746
Grundfos Pumps Corp 17100 W 118th Terr *TF:* 800-345-4555 ■ *Web:* grundfos.com	Olathe	KS	66061	913-227-3400	227-3500
Gusher Pumps 115 Industrial Dr *Web:* www.gusher.com	Williamstown	KY	41097	859-824-3100	824-7248
Hale Products Inc 700 Spring Mill Ave **Fax:* Cust Svc ■ *TF:* 800-220-4253 ■ *Web:* www.haleproducts.com	Conshohocken	PA	19428	610-825-6300	825-6440*
Hammelmann Corp 600 Progress Rd *TF:* 800-783-4935 ■ *Web:* www.hammelmann.de	Dayton	OH	45449	937-859-8777	
Harben Inc 2010 Ronald Regan Blvd *TF:* 800-327-5387 ■ *Web:* www.harben.com	Cumming	GA	30041	770-889-9535	887-9411
Haskel International Inc 100 E Graham Pl **Fax:* Sales ■ *TF:* 800-743-2720 ■ *Web:* www.haskel.com	Burbank	CA	91502	818-843-4000	841-4291*
Hayward Tyler Inc 480 Roosevelt Hwy *Web:* www.haywardtyler.com	Colchester	VT	05446	802-655-4444	655-4682
Houston Grinding & Manufacturing Inc 3544 W 12th St	Houston	TX	77008	713-869-3573	
Hydromatic Pump Co 740 E Ninth St *TF:* 888-957-8677 ■ *Web:* www.hydromatic.com	Ashland	OH	44805	888-957-8677	
Hydromotion Inc 85 E Bridge St *Web:* www.hydromotion.com	Spring City	PA	19475	610-948-4150	
HydroPressure Cleaning Inc 413 Dawson Dr *Web:* www.hydropressure.com	Camarillo	CA	93012	800-934-2399	
Hypro 375 Fifth Ave NW **Fax:* Sales ■ *TF Cust Svc:* 800-424-9776 ■ *Web:* www.hypropumps.com	New Brighton	MN	55112	651-766-6300	766-6600*
IDEX Corp 1925 W Field Ct Ste 200 *NYSE:* IEX ■ *Web:* www.idexcorp.com	Lake Forest	IL	60045	847-498-7070	
Imo Pump 1710 Airport Rd **Fax:* Sales ■ *TF:* 800-405-0148 ■ *Web:* www.imo-pump.com	Monroe	NC	28110	704-289-6511	289-9273*
Ingersoll-Rand Co 800-E Beaty St *Web:* www.ingersollrand.com	Davidson	NC	28036	704-655-4000	
Integrated Flow Solutions LLC 6461 Reynolds Rd *TF:* 800-859-7867 ■ *Web:* www.ifsolutions.com	Tyler	TX	75708	903-595-6511	
ITT Corp 1133 Westchester Ave **Fax:* Mktg ■ *Web:* www.bellgossett.com	White Plains	NY	10604	914-641-2000	696-2950*
Iwaki America Inc Five Boynton Rd *Web:* www.walchem.com	Holliston	MA	01746	508-429-1110	429-7433
Jit Cylinders 2201 Hwy 31 SW *Web:* www.jitindustries.com	Hartselle	AL	35640	256-751-2548	751-2189
Kappe Associates Inc 100 Wormans Mill Ct *Web:* www.kappe-inc.com	Frederick	MD	21701	301-846-0200	
Kemlon Products & Development Co 1424 N Main St *Web:* www.kemlon.com	Pearland	TX	77581	281-997-3300	997-1300
Kerr Pump & Supply 12880 Cloverdale St *TF:* 800-482-8259 ■ *Web:* www.kerrpump.com	Oak Park	MI	48237	248-543-3880	543-3236
Kimray Inc 52 NW 42nd St *TF:* 866-586-7233 ■ *Web:* www.kimray.com	Oklahoma City	OK	73118	405-525-6601	525-7520
Koshin America Corp 1218 Remington Rd *Web:* koshinamerica.com	Schaumburg	IL	60173	847-310-0740	
Kraft Fluid Systems Inc 14300 Foltz Pkwy *TF:* 800-257-1155 ■ *Web:* www.kraftfluid.com	Strongsville	OH	44149	440-238-5545	238-5266
Lehigh Fluid Power Inc 1413 Rt 179 *TF:* 800-257-9515 ■ *Web:* www.lehighfluidpower.com	Lambertville	NJ	08530	800-257-9515	
LEWA Inc 132 Hopping Brook Rd *Web:* lewa-inc.com	Holliston	MA	01746	508-429-7403	
Liberty Pumps Inc 7000 Apple Tree Ave *TF:* 800-543-2550 ■ *Web:* www.libertypumps.com	Bergen	NY	14416	585-494-1817	
Liquiflo Equipment Co 443 N Ave *Web:* www.liquiflo.com	Garwood	NJ	07027	908-518-0777	518-1847
Madden Manufacturing Inc PO Box 387 **Fax:* Sales ■ *TF:* 800-369-6233 ■ *Web:* www.maddenmfg.com	Elkhart	IN	46515	574-295-4292	295-7562*
Magnatex Pumps Inc 709 N Nevada Ave Ste 208 *Web:* www.magnatexpumps.com	Colorado Springs	CO	80903	719-329-0777	
McNally Industries LLC 340 W Benson Ave *TF:* 800-366-1410 ■ *Web:* www.northern-pump.com	Grantsburg	WI	54840	715-463-8300	463-5261
Met-Pro Corp Fybroc Div 700 Emlen Way *TF:* 800-392-7621 ■ *Web:* www.mp-gps.com	Telford	PA	18969	215-723-8155	723-2197
Met-Pro Corp Sethco Div 800 Emlen Way *TF:* 800-645-0500 ■ *Web:* www.mp-gps.com	Telford	PA	18969	215-799-2577	799-0920
Micropump Inc 1402 NE 136th Ave *TF Sales:* 800-222-9565 ■ *Web:* www.micropump.com	Vancouver	WA	98684	360-253-2008	253-8294
Moyno Inc 1895 W Jefferson St **Fax:* Mktg ■ *TF:* 877-486-6966 ■ *Web:* www.moyno.com	Springfield	OH	45506	937-327-3111	327-3177*
MP Pumps Inc 34800 Bennett Dr *TF:* 800-563-8006 ■ *Web:* www.mppumps.com	Fraser	MI	48026	586-293-8240	293-8469
MWI Corp 33 N.W. 2nd St *Web:* www.mwicorp.com	Deerfield Beach	FL	33441	954-426-1500	426-1582
Nagle Pumps Inc 1249 Ctr Ave **Fax:* Sales ■ *Web:* www.naglepumps.com	Chicago Heights	IL	60411	708-754-2940	754-2944*
National Pump Company LLC 7706 N 71st Ave *TF:* 800-966-5240 ■ *Web:* www.nationalpumpcompany.com	Glendale	AZ	85303	623-979-3560	
Neptune Chemical Pump Co PO Box 247 *TF:* 800-255-4017 ■ *Web:* www.psgdover.com	Lansdale	PA	19446	215-699-8700	699-0370
Neptune-Benson Inc Six Jefferson Dr *TF:* 800-832-8002 ■ *Web:* www.neptunebenson.com	Coventry	RI	02816	401-821-2200	
NH Yates & Company Inc 117 Church Ln # C **Fax Area Code:* 888 ■ *TF:* 800-878-8181 ■ *Web:* www.nhyates.com	Cockeysville	MD	21030	800-878-8181	667-9201*
Nikkiso Pumps America Inc 3433 N Sam Houston Pkwy W Ste 400 *Web:* www.nikkisopumpsamerica.com	Houston	TX	77086	281-310-6747	
Odessa Pumps & Equipment Inc 3209 N County Rd W *Web:* www.odessapumps.com	Odessa	TX	79764	432-333-2817	333-2841
Oteco Inc PO Box 1849 *Web:* www.oteco.com	Houston	TX	77251	713-695-3693	695-3520
Packworld USA 539 S Main St Ste 1 *Web:* www.packworldusa.com	Nazareth	PA	18064	610-746-2765	
PACO Pumps Inc 902 Koomey Rd *Web:* www.paco-pumps.com	Brookshire	TX	77423	281-994-2700	
Paragon Products LLC 4475 Golden Foothill Pkwy *Web:* www.paragonproducts.net	El Dorado Hills	CA	95762	916-941-9717	
Patterson Pump Co 2129 Ayersville Rd *Web:* www.pattersonpumps.com	Toccoa	GA	30577	706-886-2101	886-0023
Peerless Pump Co 2005 ML King Jr St PO Box 7026 *TF:* 800-879-0182 ■ *Web:* www.peerlesspump.com	Indianapolis	IN	46207	317-925-9661	924-7388
Penn Air & Hydraulics Corp 1750 Industrial Hwy *Web:* www.pennair.com	York	PA	17402	717-840-8100	
Pentair Inc 5500 Wayzata Blvd Ste 800 *NYSE:* PNR ■ *Web:* www.pentair.com	Minneapolis	MN	55416	763-545-1730	656-5400
Pentair Water Pool & Spa 1620 Hawkins Ave *TF:* 800-831-7133 ■ *Web:* www.pentairpool.com	Sanford	NC	27330	800-831-7133	284-4151
Predator Systems Inc 600 PSI Dr *Web:* www.predatorsystemsinc.com	Boca Raton	FL	33431	561-394-9991	
Price Pump Co 21775 Eighth St E *Web:* www.pricepump.com	Sonoma	CA	95476	707-938-8441	
Procon Products 869 7 Oaks Blvd Ste 120 *Web:* www.proconpumps.com	Smyrna	TN	37167	615-355-8000	355-8001
Progressive Hydraulics Inc 350 N Midland Ave *Web:* www.phionline.com	Saddle Brook	NJ	07663	201-791-3400	
Pulsafeeder Inc 2883 Brighton-Henrietta Town Line Rd *Web:* www.pulsa.com	Rochester	NY	14623	585-292-8000	424-5619
Ramrod Industries LLC 800 S Monroe St *Web:* www.ramrodindustries.com	Spencer	WI	54479	715-659-4996	
Randolph Austin Company Inc 2119 FM 1626 PO Box 988 *Web:* www.randolphaustin.com	Manchaca	TX	78652	512-282-1590	
Rl Deppmann Co 20929 Bridge St *Web:* www.deppmann.com	Southfield	MI	48033	248-354-3710	
Roper Pump Co 3475 Old Maysville Rd *TF Sales:* 800-944-6769 ■ *Web:* www.roperpumps.com	Commerce	GA	30529	706-335-5551	335-5490
Roth Pump Co PO Box 4330 *TF:* 888-444-7684 ■ *Web:* www.rothpump.com	Rock Island	IL	61204	309-787-1791	787-5142
RS Corcoran Co 500 N Vine St *TF:* 800-637-1067 ■ *Web:* www.corcoranpumps.com	New Lenox	IL	60451	815-485-2156	485-2156
Scot Pump 6437 Pioneer Rd PO Box 286 *TF:* 888-835-0600 ■ *Web:* www.scotpump.com	Cedarburg	WI	53012	262-377-7000	377-7330
seepex Inc 511 Speedway Dr *Web:* www.seepex.com	Enon	OH	45323	937-864-7150	864-7157

Company	City	State	ZIP	Phone	Fax
Serfilco Ltd 2900 MacArthur Blvd *TF:* 800-323-5431 ■ *Web:* www.serfilco.com	Northbrook	IL	60062	847-559-1777	559-1141
Shanley Pump & Equipment Inc 2525 S Clearbrook Dr *Web:* www.shanleypump.com	Arlington Heights	IL	60005	847-439-9200	
Shippensburg Pump Company Inc PO Box 279 *Web:* www.shipcopumps.com	Shippensburg	PA	17257	717-532-7321	
SHURflo Pump Mfg Company Inc 5900 Katella Ave Ste A *TF:* 800-854-3218 ■ *Web:* www.shurflo.com	Cypress	CA	90630	562-795-5200	795-7554
SIHI Pumps Inc 303 Industrial Blvd *Web:* www.sihi-pumps.com	Grand Island	NY	14072	716-773-6450	773-2330
Simflo Pumps Inc 754 E Maley St PO Box 849 *Web:* www.simflo.com	Willcox	AZ	85644	520-384-2273	384-4042
Smith Pump Co Inc 301 M B Industrial *TF:* 800-299-8909 ■ *Web:* www.smithpump.com	Woodway	TX	76712	254-776-0377	776-0023
Standard Alloys & Mfg PO Box 969 *TF:* 800-231-8240 ■ *Web:* www.standardalloys.com	Port Arthur	TX	77640	409-983-3201	983-7837
Stansteel Asphalt Plant Products 12700 Shelbyville Rd *Web:* www.stansteel.com	Louisville	KY	40243	502-245-1977	
Sulzer Pumps (US) Inc 2800 NW Front Ave *Web:* www.sulzer.com	Portland	OR	97210	503-205-3600	226-5286
Syncroflo Inc 6700 Best Friend Rd *Web:* www.syncroflo.com	Norcross	GA	30071	770-447-4443	448-5120
Systecon Inc 6121 Schumacher Pk Dr *Web:* www.systecon.com	West Chester	OH	45069	513-777-7722	777-0259
TBK America Inc 3700 W Industries Rd *Web:* www.tbk-jp.com	Richmond	IN	47374	765-962-0147	
Textron Fluid & Power Inc 40 Westminster St *Web:* www.textron.com	Providence	RI	02903	401-421-2800	621-5045
Thompson Pump & Mfg Company Inc 4620 City Ctr Dr PO Box 291370 *TF:* 800-767-7310 ■ *Web:* www.thompsonpump.com	Port Orange	FL	32129	386-767-7310	761-0362
Thrush Company Inc Je Company Inc 340 W Eigth St *Web:* www.comteck.com	Peru	IN	46970	765-472-3351	
Townley Engineering & Manufacturing Company Inc 10551 SE 110th St Rd *Web:* www.townley.net	Candler	FL	32111	352-687-3001	
Tramco Pump Co 1500 W Adams St **Fax:* Sales ■ *Web:* www.tramcopump.com	Chicago	IL	60607	312-243-5800	243-0702*
TURBOCAM Inc 607 Calef Hwy *Web:* www.turbocam.com	Barrington	NH	03825	603-905-0200	
Tuthill Corp 8500 S Madison St *TF:* 800-634-2695 ■ *Web:* www.tuthill.com	Burr Ridge	IL	60527	630-382-4900	382-4999
Tuthill Pump Group 12500 S Pulaski Rd *Web:* www.tuthillpump.com	Alsip	IL	60803	708-389-2500	388-0869
Ultimate Washer Inc 711 Commerce Way Ste 1 *Web:* www.ultimatewasher.com	Jupiter	FL	33458	561-741-7022	
V&P Hydraulic Products LLC 1700 Pittsburgh Dr *Web:* www.vphyd.com	Delaware	OH	43015	740-203-3600	
Vanton Pump & Equipment Corp 201 Sweetland Ave *Web:* www.vanton.com	Hillside	NJ	07205	908-688-4216	686-9314
Vaughan Company Inc 364 Monte-Elma Rd *TF:* 888-249-2467 ■ *Web:* www.chopperpumps.com	Montesano	WA	98563	360-249-4042	249-6155
Veeder-Root Red Jacket Div 125 Powder Forest Dr PO Box 2003 *TF:* 800-873-3313 ■ *Web:* www.veeder.com	Simsbury	CT	06070	860-651-2700	651-7140
Viking Pump Inc 406 State St *TF:* 800-123-1234 ■ *Web:* www.vikingpump.com	Cedar Falls	IA	50613	319-266-1741	273-8157
Vogelsang USA 7966 State Rt 44 *Web:* vogelsangusa.com	Ravenna	OH	44266	330-296-3820	
Wanner Engineering Inc 1204 Chestnut Ave *Web:* www.wannereng.com	Minneapolis	MN	55403	612-332-5681	
Warren Pumps LLC 82 Bridges Ave *Web:* www.warrenpumps.com	Warren	MA	01083	413-436-7711	
Warren Rupp Inc 800 N Main St *Web:* www.warrenrupp.com	Mansfield	OH	44902	419-524-8388	522-7867
Wastecorp Inc PO Box 70 *TF:* 888-829-2783 ■ *Web:* www.wastecorp.com	Grand Island	NY	14072	888-829-2783	
Waterous Co 125 Hardman Ave *TF:* 800-488-1228 ■ *Web:* www.waterousco.com	South Saint Paul	MN	55075	651-450-5000	450-5090
Watson-Marlow Inc 37 Upton Technology Park *Web:* www.watson-marlow.com	Wilmington	MA	01887	978-658-6168	
Waukesha Cherry-Burrell Corp (WCB) 611 Sugar Creek Rd *TF:* 800-252-5200 ■ *Web:* www.spx.com	Delavan	WI	53115	262-728-1900	728-4904
Weil Pump Co W57 N14363 Doerr Wy PO Box 887 *Web:* www.weilpump.com	Cedarburg	WI	53012	262-377-1399	377-0515
Weir Floway Inc 2494 S Railroad Ave *Web:* weirminerals.com	Fresno	CA	93706	559-442-4000	
Weir Group, The 2701 S Stoughton Rd *Web:* weirminerals.com	Madison	WI	53716	608-221-2261	221-5807
Weir Minerals 225 N Cedar St *Web:* www.weirminerals.com	Hazleton	PA	18201	570-455-7711	459-2586
Wilden Pump & Engineering Co 22069 Van Buren St *Web:* www.psgdover.com	Grand Terrace	CA	92313	909-422-1730	783-3440
Yeomans Chicago Corp 3905 Enterprise Ct PO Box 6620 *Web:* www.yccpump.com	Aurora	IL	60504	630-236-5500	236-5511
Zoeller Co 3649 Kane Run Rd *OTC: ZOLR* ■ *TF:* 800-928-7867 ■ *Web:* www.zoeller.com	Louisville	KY	40211	502-778-2731	774-3624

645 RACING & RACETRACKS

SEE ALSO Motor Speedways p. 2772

Company	City	State	ZIP	Phone	Fax
Alameda County Fair Assn (ACFA) 4501 Pleasanton Ave *TF:* 800-874-9253 ■ *Web:* www.alamedacountyfair.com	Pleasanton	CA	94566	925-426-7600	426-7599
Arlington Park 2200 W Euclid Ave PO Box 7 *Web:* www.arlingtonpark.com	Arlington Heights	IL	60006	847-385-7500	385-7251
Atlantic City Racing Course (ACRC) 4501 Black Horse Pk *Web:* acracecourse.com	Mays Landing	NJ	08330	609-641-2190	
Balmoral Park 26435 S Dixie Hwy *Web:* www.balmoralpark.com	Crete	IL	60417	708-672-1414	672-5932
Batavia Downs 8315 Pk Rd *Web:* www.westernotb.com	Batavia	NY	14020	585-343-3750	343-7773
Belmont Park 2150 Hempstead Tpke *Web:* www.nyra.com	Elmont	NY	11003	516-488-6000	
Brainerd International Raceway 5523 Birchdale Rd *TF:* 866-444-4455 ■ *Web:* www.brainerdraceway.com	Brainerd	MN	56401	218-824-7223	824-7240
Buffalo Raceway 5600 McKinley Pkwy *Web:* www.buffaloraceway.com	Hamburg	NY	14075	716-649-1280	649-0033
Calder Casino & Race Course 21001 NW 27th Ave *TF:* 800-522-4700 ■ *Web:* www.calderracecourse.com	Miami	FL	33056	305-625-1311	620-2569
Calgary Exhibition & Stampede Ltd 1410 Olympic Way S E *Web:* www.calgarystampede.com	Calgary	AB	T2G2W1	403-261-0101	
Canterbury Park Holding Corp 1100 Canterbury Rd *NASDAQ: CPHC* ■ *TF:* 800-340-6361 ■ *Web:* www.canterburypark.com	Shakopee	MN	55379	952-445-7223	496-6400
Cassia County Fairgrounds 1101 Elba Ave *Web:* cassiacountyfair.com	Burley	ID	83318	208-678-9150	678-3612
Central Wyoming Fairgrounds 1700 Fairgrounds Rd *Web:* www.centralwyomingfair.com	Casper	WY	82604	307-235-5775	266-4224
Charlotte Motor Speedway 5555 Concord Pkwy S *TF:* 800-455-3267 ■ *Web:* www.charlottemotorspeedway.com	Concord	NC	28027	704-455-3200	455-2547
Churchill Downs Inc 700 Central Ave *NASDAQ: CHDN* ■ **Fax Area Code:* 212 ■ *TF:* 800-994-9909 ■ *Web:* www.churchilldowns.com	Louisville	KY	40208	502-636-4400	283-4901*
Colonial Downs 10515 Colonial Downs Pkwy **Fax:* PR ■ *TF:* 888-482-8722 ■ *Web:* www.colonialdowns.com	New Kent	VA	23124	804-966-7223	966-1565*
Columbus Races 822 15th St *Web:* www.agpark.com	Columbus	NE	68601	402-564-0133	564-0990
Dale Earnhardt Inc 1675 Dale Earnhardt Hwy 3 *Web:* www.daleearnhardtinc.com	Mooresville	NC	28115	704-662-8000	
Del Mar Thoroughbred Club 2260 Jimmy Durante Blvd *Web:* www.dmtc.com	Del Mar	CA	92014	858-755-1141	755-1141
Delaware North Cos Gaming & Entertainment 40 Fountain Plz *TF:* 800-828-7240 ■ *Web:* www.delawarenorth.com	Buffalo	NY	14202	716-858-5000	858-5926
Delaware Park Racetrack & Slots Casino 777 Delaware Pk Blvd **Fax:* Hum Res ■ *TF:* 800-417-5687 ■ *Web:* www.delawarepark.com	Wilmington	DE	19804	302-994-2521	993-8952*
Delaware Racing Assn 777 Delaware Pk Blvd *Web:* www.delawarepark.com	Wilmington	DE	19804	302-994-2521	994-3392
Delta Downs Racetrack 2717 Delta Downs Dr **Fax Area Code:* 337 ■ *TF:* 800-589-7441 ■ *Web:* www.deltadowns.com	Vinton	LA	70668	800-589-7441	589-2399*
Dover Downs Hotel & Casino 1131 N DuPont Hwy *NYSE: DDE* ■ *TF:* 800-711-5882 ■ *Web:* www.doverdowns.com	Dover	DE	19901	302-674-4600	
Dover International Speedway 1131 N DuPont Hwy PO Box 843 *TF:* 800-441-7223 ■ *Web:* www.doverspeedway.com	Dover	DE	19901	302-883-6500	672-0100
Dover Motorsports Inc 1131 N Dupont Hwy *NYSE: DVD* ■ *TF:* 800-441-7223 ■ *Web:* www.dovermotorsportsinc.com	Dover	DE	19901	302-883-6500	672-0100
DuQuoin State Fair 655 Executive Dr *Web:* www.agr.state.il.us/dq	Du Quoin	IL	62832	618-542-1515	542-1541
Elko County Fairgrounds PO Box 2067 *Web:* www.elkocountyfair.com	Elko	NV	89803	775-738-3616	778-3468
Ellis Park Race Course LLC 3300 US 41 *Web:* www.ellisparkracing.com	Henderson	KY	42420	812-425-1456	
Fair Grounds Race Course 1751 Gentilly Blvd *TF:* 800-262-7983 ■ *Web:* www.fairgroundsracecourse.com	New Orleans	LA	70119	504-944-5515	948-1160
Fair Meadows at Tulsa 4609 E 21st St *TF:* 877-781-2660 ■ *Web:* exposquare.com	Tulsa	OK	74114	918-743-7223	743-8053
Fairmount Park 9301 Collinsville Rd **Fax Area Code:* 314 ■ *Web:* www.fairmountpark.com	Collinsville	IL	62234	618-345-4300	436-1516*
Finger Lakes Gaming & Race Track 5857 Rt 96 *TF:* 877-846-7369 ■ *Web:* www.fingerlakesgaming.com	Farmington	NY	14425	585-924-3232	924-3967
Finger Lakes Racing Assn 5857 Rt 96 *Web:* www.fingerlakesgaming.com	Farmington	NY	14425	585-924-3232	924-3967
Flamboro Downs Ltd 967 Hwy 5 *Web:* www.flamborodowns.com	Hamilton	ON	L9H5E2	905-627-3561	
Fonner Park 700 E Stolley Pk Rd *Web:* www.fonnerpark.com	Grand Island	NE	68801	308-382-4515	384-2753
Fort Erie Race Track 230 Catherine St PO Box 1130 *TF:* 800-295-3770 ■ *Web:* www.forterieracing.com	Fort Erie	ON	L2A5N9	905-871-3200	994-3629
Freehold Raceway 130 Pk Ave *Web:* www.freeholdraceway.com	Freehold	NJ	07728	732-462-3800	462-2920
Fresno District Fair 1121 S Chance Ave *TF:* 866-275-3772 ■ *Web:* www.fresnofair.com	Fresno	CA	93702	559-650-3247	650-3226
Gillespie County Fairgrounds 530 Fair Dr PO Box 526 *TF:* 800-280-9531 ■ *Web:* gillespiefair.net	Fredericksburg	TX	78624	830-997-2359	997-4923

				Phone	Fax
Global Gaming Solutions LLC 210 N Broadway	Ada	OK	74820	580-559-0886	
Web: www.globalgamingsol.com					
Golden Gate Fields 1100 Eastshore Hwy	Berkeley	CA	94710	510-559-7300	559-7467
Web: www.goldengatefields.com					
Goshen Historic Track Inc 44 Pk Pl PO Box 192	Goshen	NY	10924	845-294-5333	294-3998
Web: www.goshenhistorictrack.com					
Grand Prix of Long Beach 3000 Pacific Ave	Long Beach	CA	90806	562-981-2600	
Web: www.gplb.com					
Grays Harbor Raceway 32 Elma McCleary Rd PO Box 768	Elma	WA	98541	360-482-4374	892-6582
TF: 800-667-7711 ■ *Web:* www.graysharborraceway.com					
Harrah's Louisiana Downs 8000 East Texas St	Bossier City	LA	71111	318-742-5555	
Web: www.harrahslouisianadowns.com					
Harrington Raceway 15 W Rider Rd	Harrington	DE	19952	302-398-7223	
TF: 888-887-5687 ■ *Web:* casino.harringtonraceway.com					
Hawthorne Race Course 3501 S Laramie Ave	Cicero	IL	60804	708-780-3700	780-3677
Web: www.hawthorneracecourse.com					
Hazel Park Raceway 1650 E 10 Mile Rd	Hazel Park	MI	48030	248-398-1000	398-5236
TF: 800-794-8001 ■ *Web:* www.hazelparkraceway.com					
Hollywood Casino at Charles Town Races 750 Hollywood Dr	Charles Town	WV	25414	304-725-7001	725-6979
TF: 800-795-7001 ■ *Web:* www.hollywoodcasinocharlestown.com					
Hollywood Casino at Penn National Race Course 777 Hollywood Blvd	Grantville	PA	17028	717-469-2211	
Web: www.hollywoodpnrc.com					
Hollywood Park Land Company LLC 1050 S Prairie Ave	Inglewood	CA	90301	310-419-1500	
Web: www.hollywoodpark.com					
Hoosier Park Racing & Casino 4500 Dan Patch Cir	Anderson	IN	46013	765-642-7223	608-2754
TF: 800-526-7223 ■ *Web:* www.hoosierpark.com					
Humboldt County Fair 1250 Fifth St	Ferndale	CA	95536	707-786-9511	786-9450
Web: www.humboldtcountyfair.org					
Illinois State Fairgrounds 801 E Sangamon Ave	Springfield	IL	62702	217-782-4231	524-6194
Web: www.agr.state.il.us					
Indiana State Fairgrounds 1202 E 38th St	Indianapolis	IN	46205	317-927-7500	927-7695
Web: www.in.gov					
Indianapolis Motor Speedway Corp 4790 W 16th St	Indianapolis	IN	46222	317-492-8500	
Web: indianapolismotorspeedway.com					
Iowa Speedway LLC 3333 Rusty Wallace Dr	Newton	IA	50208	641-791-8000	
Web: www.iowaspeedway.com					
Jacksonville Greyhound Racing Inc 455 Park Ave	Orange Park	FL	32073	904-646-0001	
Web: www.jaxkennel.com					
Jefferson County Kennel Club Inc 3079 N Jefferson St	Monticello	FL	32344	850-997-2561	
Web: www.jckcgreyhounds.com					
Jerome County Fairgrounds 200 N Fir St	Jerome	ID	83338	208-324-7209	324-7057
Web: www.jeromecountyfair.com					
Joe Gibbs Racing Inc 13415 Reese Blvd W	Huntersville	NC	28078	704-944-5000	
Web: www.joegibbsracing.com					
Josephine County Fairgrounds 1451 Fairgrounds Rd PO Box 672	Grants Pass	OR	97527	541-476-3215	476-1027
TF: 800-773-1162 ■ *Web:* www.co.josephine.or.us					
Kentucky Downs LLC 5629 Nashville Rd	Franklin	KY	42135	270-586-7778	
Web: www.kentuckydowns.com					
Kyle Busch Motorsports Inc 351 Mazeppa Rd	Mooresville	NC	28115	704-662-0000	
Web: www.kylebuschmotorsports.com					
Lake Erie Speedway 10700 Delmas Dr	North East	PA	16428	814-725-3303	725-3353
Web: www.lakeeriespeedway.com					
Laurel Park Rt 198 & Racetrack Rd PO Box 130	Laurel	MD	20724	301-725-0400	792-7775*
**Fax Area Code:* 410 ■ *TF:* 800-638-1859 ■ *Web:* www.laurelpark.com					
Lone Star Park at Grand Prairie 1000 Lone Star Pkwy	Grand Prairie	TX	75050	972-263-7223	237-5505
Web: www.lonestarpark.com					
Los Alamitos Race Course 4961 Katella Ave	Los Alamitos	CA	90720	714-820-2800	
Web: www.losalamitos.com/laqhr					
Los Angeles Turf Club Inc 285 W Huntington Dr	Arcadia	CA	91007	626-574-7223	446-1456
Maywood Park 8600 W N Ave	Melrose Park	IL	60160	708-343-4800	343-2564
Web: www.maywoodpark.com					
Meadowlands Racetrack 50 Rt 120	East Rutherford	NJ	07073	201-843-2446	
Web: www.meadowlandsracetrack.com					
Meadows Racetrack 210 Racetrack Rd	Washington	PA	15301	724-225-9300	
Web: www.meadowsgaming.com					
Melbourne Greyhound Park 1100 N Wickham Rd	Melbourne	FL	32935	321-259-9800	259-3437
Web: www.mgpark.com					
MetraPark PO Box 2514	Billings	MT	59103	406-256-2400	256-2479
TF: 800-366-8538 ■ *Web:* www.metrapark.com					
Mile High Racing & Entertainment/Mile High 10750 E Iliff Ave	Aurora	CO	80014	303-751-5918	289-1640
Web: www.mihiracing.com					
Mohave County Fair Assn 2600 Fairgrounds Blvd	Kingman	AZ	86401	928-753-2636	753-8383
Web: www.mcfairgrounds.org					
Monmouth Park Racetrack 175 Oceanport Ave	Oceanport	NJ	07757	732-222-5100	571-5226
Web: www.monmouthpark.com					
Montana State Fair 400 Third St NW	Great Falls	MT	59404	406-727-8900	452-8955
Web: www.montanastatefair.com					
Mystique Casino 1855 Greyhound Pk Dr	Dubuque	IA	52001	563-582-3647	
TF: 800-373-3647 ■ *Web:* www.mystiquedbq.com					
Naples/Fort Myers Greyhound Track 10601 Bonita Beach Rd	Bonita Springs	FL	34135	239-992-2411	947-9244
Web: www.naplesfortmyersdogs.com					
New Mexico State Fair 300 San Pedro NE	Albuquerque	NM	87108	505-222-9700	266-7784
Web: www.exponm.com					
New York Racing Assn (NYRA) 110-00 Rockaway Blvd PO Box 90	Jamaica	NY	11420	718-641-4700	
Web: www.nyra.com					
Northfield Park Associates LLC 10705 Northfield Rd PO Box 374	Northfield	OH	44067	330-467-4101	
Web: www.northfieldpark.com					
Northville Downs 301 S Ctr St	Northville	MI	48167	248-349-1000	348-8955
Web: www.northvilledowns.com					
Oaklawn Park 2705 Central Ave	Hot Springs	AR	71901	501-623-4411	624-4950
TF General: 800-625-5296 ■ *Web:* www.oaklawn.com					
Ocean Downs 10218 Racetrack Rd PO Box 11	Berlin	MD	21811	410-641-0600	641-2711
Web: www.oceandowns.com					
Ontario Lottery & Gaming Corp 70 Foster Dr Ste 800	Sault Ste. Marie	ON	P6A6V2	705-946-6464	
Web: www.olg.ca					
Panther Racing LLC 5101 Decatur Blvd Ste P	Indianapolis	IN	46241	317-856-9500	
Web: www.pantherracing.com					
Penn National Gaming Inc 825 Berkshire Blvd Ste 200	Wyomissing	PA	19610	877-565-2112	376-2842*
NASDAQ: PENN ■ **Fax Area Code:* 610 ■ *TF:* 877-565-2112 ■ *Web:* www.hollywoodpnrc.com					
Pensacola Greyhound Track 951 Dog Track Rd	Pensacola	FL	32506	850-455-8595	453-8883
TF: 800-345-3997 ■ *Web:* www.pensacolagreyhoundtrack.com					
Petaluma Fairgrounds Speedway 100 Fairgrounds Dr	Petaluma	CA	94952	707-763-7223	
Web: www.petaluma-speedway.com/					
Phoenix Greyhound Park 3801 E Washington St	Phoenix	AZ	85034	602-273-7181	273-6176
Web: www.phoenixgreyhoundpark.com					
Pinnacle Entertainment Inc 3980 Howard Hughes Pkwy	Las Vegas	NV	89169	702-541-7777	
NYSE: PNK ■ *TF:* 877-764-8750 ■ *Web:* www.pnkinc.com					
Pocatello Downs 10560 N Fairgrounds Rd	Pocatello	ID	83202	208-238-1721	
Web: theracingjournal.com					
Portland International Raceway 1940 N Victory Blvd	Portland	OR	97217	503-823-7223	823-5896
Web: www.portlandraceway.com					
Portland Meadows Horse Track 1001 N Schmeer Rd	Portland	OR	97217	503-285-9144	286-9763
Web: www.portlandmeadows.com					
Ravalli County Fair 100 Old Corvallis Rd	Hamilton	MT	59840	406-363-3411	375-9152
TF: 800-225-6779 ■ *Web:* ravalli.us					
Remington Park Race Track One Remington Pl	Oklahoma City	OK	73111	405-424-1000	425-3297
TF: 866-456-9880 ■ *Web:* www.remingtonpark.com					
Retama Park 1 Retama Pkwy	Selma	TX	78154	210-651-7000	651-7097
TF: 800-473-8262 ■ *Web:* www.retamapark.com					
Rockingham Park Rockingham Pk Blvd	Salem	NH	03079	603-898-2311	898-7163
Web: www.rockinghampark.com					
Sam Houston Race Park 7575 N Sam Houston Pkwy W	Houston	TX	77064	281-807-8700	807-8777
TF: 800-807-7223 ■ *Web:* www.shrp.com					
San Joaquin County Fairgrounds 1658 S Airport Way	Stockton	CA	95206	209-466-5041	466-5739
Web: www.sanjoaquinfair.com					
San Luis Rey Downs 5772 Camino Del Rey	Bonsall	CA	92003	760-414-3273	
Web: www.slrd.com					
Santa Anita Park 285 W Huntington Dr	Arcadia	CA	91007	626-574-7223	446-9565
Web: www.santaanita.com					
Santa Cruz County Fair & Rodeo 3142 Arizona 83 PO Box 85	Sonoita	AZ	85637	520-455-5553	455-5330
TF: 866-394-0121 ■ *Web:* sonoitafairgrounds.com					
Sarasota Kennel Club Inc 5400 Bradenton Rd	Sarasota	FL	34234	941-355-7744	
Web: www.sarasotakennelclub.com					
Saratoga Gaming & Raceway 342 Jefferson St PO Box 356	Saratoga Springs	NY	12866	518-584-2110	583-1269
Web: www.saratogacasino.com					
Saratoga Race Course 267 Union Ave	Saratoga Springs	NY	12866	718-641-4700	
Web: www.saratogaracetrack.com					
Scarborough Downs 90 Payne Rd	Scarborough	ME	04070	207-883-4331	883-2020
Web: www.scarboroughdowns.com					
Scioto Downs Inc 6000 S High St	Columbus	OH	43207	614-295-4700	
Web: www.sciotodowns.com					
Shoreline Star Greyhound Park & Entertainment Complex LLC 255 Kossuth St	Bridgeport	CT	06608	888-463-6446	
TF: 888-463-6446 ■ *Web:* www.shorelinestar.com					
Solano County Fair 900 Fairgrounds Dr	Vallejo	CA	94589	707-551-2000	642-7947
TF: 800-700-2482 ■ *Web:* www.scfair.com					
Sonoma County Fairgrounds 1350 Bennett Valley Rd	Santa Rosa	CA	95404	707-545-4200	573-9342
TF: 866-487-9243 ■ *Web:* www.sonomacountyfair.com					
Sports Car Racing Association of Monterey Peninsula 1021 Monterey Salinas Hwy	Salinas	CA	93908	831-242-8201	
Web: www.laguna-seca.com					
Sports Creek Raceway 4290 Morrish Rd	Swartz Creek	MI	48473	810-635-3333	635-9711
TF: 844-635-4708 ■ *Web:* www.sportscreek.com					
Stewart-haas Racing LLC 6001 Haas Way	Kannapolis	NC	28081	704-652-4227	
Web: stewarthaasracing.com					
Sunland Park Racetrack & Casino 1200 Futurity Dr	Sunland Park	NM	88063	575-874-5200	589-1518
TF: 800-572-1142 ■ *Web:* www.sunland-park.com					
Tampa Bay Downs Inc 11225 Racetrack Rd	Tampa	FL	33626	813-855-4401	854-3539
TF: 800-200-4434 ■ *Web:* www.tampabaydowns.com					
Tampa Greyhound Track 8300 N Nebraska Ave	Tampa	FL	33604	813-932-4313	932-5048
Web: www.tampadogs.com					
Team Rahal Inc 4601 Lyman Dr	Hilliard	OH	43026	614-529-7000	
Web: www.rahal.com					
Technicon Engineering Services Inc 4539 N Brawley Ave Ste 108	Fresno	CA	93722	559-276-9311	
Web: www.technicon.net					
Thistledown Racing Club Inc 21501 Emery Rd	Cleveland	OH	44128	216-662-8600	662-5339
TF: 866-503-3792 ■ *Web:* www.caesars.com					

	City	State	Zip	Phone	Fax
Tillamook County Fairgrounds 4603 E Third St PO Box 455 *Web:* www.tillamookfair.com	Tillamook	OR	97141	503-842-2272	842-3314
TrackMaster 2083 Old Middlefield Way Ste 206 *Web:* www.trackmaster.com	Mountain View	CA	94043	650-316-1020	
Turf Paradise Racetrack 1501 W Bell Rd *TF:* 800-639-8783 ■ *Web:* www.turfparadise.com	Phoenix	AZ	85023	602-942-1101	942-8659
Twin River Casino 100 Twin River Rd *TF:* 877-827-4837 ■ *Web:* www.twinriver.com	Lincoln	RI	02865	401-475-8505	
Walla Walla Racetrack 363 Orchard St *Web:* www.wallawallafairgrounds.com	Walla Walla	WA	99362	509-527-3247	527-3259
Western Montana Fair 1101 S Ave W *Web:* www.missoulafairgrounds.com	Missoula	MT	59801	406-721-3247	728-7479
Woodbine Entertainment Group Inc 555 Rexdale Blvd PO Box 156 *Web:* www.woodbineentertainment.com	Toronto	ON	M9W5L2	416-675-7223	
World Racing Group Inc 7575 D W Winds Blvd Ste D *Web:* www.worldracinggroup.com	Concord	NC	28027	704-795-7223	
Yonkers Raceway 810 Yonkers Ave *Web:* www.yonkersraceway.com	Yonkers	NY	10704	914-968-4200	457-2537
Yuma County Fair 2520 E 32nd St *Web:* www.yumafair.com	Yuma	AZ	85365	928-726-4420	344-3480

646 RADIO COMPANIES

	City	State	Zip	Phone	Fax
Artistic Media Partners Inc 5520 E 75th St *Web:* www.artisticradio.com	Indianapolis	IN	46250	317-594-0600	594-9567
Backyard Broadcasting 4237 Salisbury Rd Ste 225 *Web:* www.bybradio.com	Jacksonville	FL	32216	904-674-0260	854-4596
Beasley Broadcast Group Inc 3033 Riviera Dr Ste 200 *NASDAQ: BBGI* ■ *Web:* www.bbgi.com	Naples	FL	34103	239-263-5000	263-8191
Bi-Coastal Media LLC 140 N Main St *Web:* www.bicoastalmedia.com	Lakeport	CA	95453	707-263-6113	263-0939
Bible Broadcasting Network Inc 11530 Carmel Commons Blvd PO Box 7300 *TF:* 800-888-7077 ■ *Web:* www.bbnradio.org	Charlotte	NC	28226	704-523-5555	522-1967
Birach Broadcasting Corp Tower 14 Ste 1190 *Web:* www.birach.com	Southfield	MI	48075	248-557-3500	557-2950
Bliss Communications Inc PO Box 5001 *TF:* 800-362-6712 ■ *Web:* www.blissnet.net	Janesville	WI	53547	608-754-3311	754-8038
Bonneville International Corp 55 N 300 W *Web:* www.bonneville.com	Salt Lake City	UT	84101	801-575-7500	575-5820
Bott Radio Network 10550 Barkley St Ste 100 *TF:* 800-875-1903 ■ *Web:* www.bottradionetwork.com	Overland Park	KS	66212	913-642-7770	642-1319
Brazos Valley Radio 1240 E Villa Maria Rd *Web:* www.brazosradio.com	Bryan	TX	77802	979-776-1240	
Bristol Broadcasting Company Inc 901 E Valley Dr PO Box 1389 *Web:* www.bristolbroadcasting.com	Bristol	VA	24203	276-669-8112	669-0541
Buckley Broadcasting Corp 166 W Putnam Ave *Web:* www.buckleyradio.com	Greenwich	CT	06830	203-661-4307	622-7341
Canadian Broadcasting Corp (CBC) PO Box 3220 *Web:* www.cbc.radio-canada.ca	Ottawa	ON	K1Y1E4	514-597-6000	
Cherry Creek Radio 501 S Cherry St Ste 480 *Web:* www.cherrycreekradio.com	Denver	CO	80246	303-468-6500	468-6555
Crawford Broadcasting Co (CBC) 2821 S Parker Rd Ste 1205 *Web:* www.crawfordbroadcasting.com	Denver	CO	80014	303-433-5500	433-1555
Cromwell Group Inc 1824 Murfreesboro Rd Second Fl *Web:* www.cromwellradio.com	Nashville	TN	37217	615-361-7560	366-4313
Cumulus Media Inc 3280 Peachtree Rd Ste 2300 *NASDAQ: CMLS* ■ *Web:* www.cumulus.com	Atlanta	GA	30305	404-949-0700	949-0740
Curtis Media Group 3012 Highwoods Blvd Ste 200 *Web:* 96rockonline.com	Raleigh	NC	27604	919-790-9392	882-1746
Delmarva Broadcasting Co PO Box 7492 *Web:* www.radiocenter.com	Wilmington	DE	19803	302-478-2700	
Eagle Communications Inc 2703 Hall St Ste 15 Ste 15 *TF:* 877-613-2453 ■ *Web:* www.eaglecom.net	Hays	KS	67601	785-625-5910	625-8030
Eagle Radio Inc 2300 Hall *TF:* 877-613-2453 ■ *Web:* eaglecom.net	Hays	KS	67601	785-625-2578	
Educational Media Foundation 5700 W Oaks Blvd *TF General:* 800-525-5683 ■ *Web:* www.klove.com	Rocklin	CA	95765	916-251-1600	251-1650
Emmis Communications Corp 40 Monument Cir 1 Emmis Plz Ste 700 *NASDAQ: EMMS* ■ *Web:* www.emmis.com	Indianapolis	IN	46204	317-266-0100	631-3750
Entercom Communications Corp 401 City Ave Ste 809 *NYSE: ETM* ■ *TF:* 800-776-9437 ■ *Web:* www.entercom.com	Bala Cynwyd	PA	19004	610-660-5610	660-5620
Entravision Communications Corp 2425 Olympic Blvd Ste 6000 W *NYSE: EVC* ■ *Web:* www.entravision.com	Santa Monica	CA	90404	310-447-3870	447-3899
Family Radio 290 Hegenberger Rd **Fax Area Code:* 510 ■ *TF:* 800-543-1495 ■ *Web:* familyradio.org/	Oakland	CA	94621	800-543-1495	562-0749*
Far East Broadcasting Co Inc 15700 Imperial Hwy PO Box 1 *TF:* 800-523-3480 ■ *Web:* www.febc.org	La Mirada	CA	90638	800-523-3480	
Flinn Broadcasting 6080 Mt Moriah Rd Ext *Web:* www.flinn.com	Memphis	TN	38115	901-375-9324	375-0041
Forever Broadcasting One Forever Dr *Web:* www.foreverradio.com	Hollidaysburg	PA	16648	814-941-9800	943-2754
Galaxy Communications LP 235 Walton St *Web:* www.galaxycommunications.com	Syracuse	NY	13202	315-472-9111	472-1888
Georgia-Carolina Radiocasting Cos LLC 233 Big A Rd PO Box E *Web:* www.gacaradio.com	Toccoa	GA	30577	706-297-7264	297-7266
Great Scott Broadcasting 20200 DuPont Blvd *Web:* www.greatscottbroadcasting.com	Georgetown	DE	19947	302-856-2567	856-7633
Greater Media Inc 35 Braintree Hill Pk Ste 300 *Web:* www.greater-media.com	Braintree	MA	02184	781-348-8600	
Hall Communications Inc 404 W Lime St PO Box 2038 *Web:* www.hallradio.com	Lakeland	FL	33815	863-682-8184	
International Broadcasting Bureau 330 Independence Ave SW *Web:* www.bbg.gov	Washington	DC	20237	202-203-4000	203-4585
Journal Broadcast Group Inc 333 W State St *Web:* www.journalmediagroup.com	Milwaukee	WI	53203	414-224-2000	
Keymarket Communications LLC 123 Blaine Rd	Brownsville	PA	15417	724-938-2000	938-7824
KVOC 218 N Wolcott St	Casper	WY	82601	307-265-1984	
Liberman Broadcasting Inc 1845 W Empire Ave *Web:* www.lbimedia.com	Burbank	CA	91504	818-729-5300	567-1062
Lotus Communications Corp 3301 Barham Blvd Ste 200 *Web:* www.lotuscorp.com	Los Angeles	CA	90068	323-512-2225	512-2224
Mahaffey Enterprises 3327 E Ridgeview St	Springfield	MO	65804	417-883-9180	
Main Line 25 Penncraft Ave # 4 *Web:* mix95.com	Chambersburg	PA	17201	717-263-0813	263-9649
Maritime Broadcasting System (MBS) 5121 Sackville St Seventh Fl *Web:* www.mbsradio.com	Halifax	NS	B3J1K1	902-425-1225	423-2093
Mel Wheeler Inc 5009 S Hulen St Ste 107 *Web:* melwheelerinc.com	Fort Worth	TX	76132	817-294-7644	294-8519
Mid-America Radio Group Inc 60 N Wayne St PO Box 1970	Martinsville	IN	46151	765-349-1485	
Midwest Communications Inc 904 Grand Ave **Fax:* Hum Res ■ *TF:* 877-945-4236 ■ *Web:* www.mwcradio.com	Wausau	WI	54403	715-842-1437	842-7061*
Midwest Family Broadcasting 319 E Battlefield Ste B *Web:* www.mwfmarketing.fm	Springfield	MO	65807	417-886-5677	886-2155
Multicultural Radio Broadcasting 27 William St 11th Fl *Web:* www.mrbi.net	New York	NY	10005	212-966-1059	
Newcap Radio (NCC) 745 Windmill Rd *Web:* www.ncc.ca	Dartmouth	NS	B3B1C2	902-468-7557	468-7558
Newfoundland Capital Corp Ltd 745 Windmill Rd *TSE: NCC.A* ■ *Web:* www.ncc.ca	Dartmouth	NS	B3B1C2	902-468-7557	468-7558
NextMedia Group Inc 6312 S Fiddlers Green Cir Ste 205E	Greenwood Village	CO	80111	303-694-9118	694-4940
Northeast Broadcasting Corp 288 S River Rd	Bedford	NH	03110	603-668-6400	668-6470
Northern Star Broadcasting LLC 3250 Racquet Club Dr *TF:* 888-847-2346 ■ *Web:* www.nsbroadcasting.com	Traverse City	MI	49684	231-922-4981	922-3633
NRG Media 2875 Mt Vernon Rd SE *Web:* www.nrgmedia.com	Cedar Rapids	IA	52403	319-862-0300	286-9383
Pamal Broadcasting Ltd 6 Johnson Rd *Web:* www.pamal.com	Latham	NY	12110	518-786-6600	
Quantum Communications Corp 1266 E Main St Sixth Fl	Stamfort	CT	06902	203-388-0048	388-0054
Radio Training Network Inc 5015 S Florida Ave	Lakeland	FL	33813	863-644-3464	
Renda Broadcasting Corp 900 Parish St Fourth Fl *Web:* www.rendabroadcasting.com	Pittsburgh	PA	15220	412-875-1800	875-1801
Results Radio LLC 1355 N Dutton Ave Ste 225 **Fax Area Code:* 530	Santa Rosa	CA	95401	707-546-9185	244-9707*
Saga Communications Inc 73 Kercheval Ave *NYSE: SGA* ■ *TF:* 800-777-3674 ■ *Web:* sagacom.com	Grosse Pointe Farms	MI	48236	313-886-7070	886-7150
Salem Communications Corp 4880 Santa Rosa Rd *NASDAQ: SALM* ■ *Web:* www.salem.cc	Camarillo	CA	93012	805-987-0400	384-4505
Shamrock Communications Inc 149 Penn Ave *TF:* 800-228-4637 ■ *Web:* www.thetimes-tribune.com	Scranton	PA	18503	570-348-9100	348-9109
Simmons Media Group Inc 515 South 700 East *Web:* www.simmonsmedia.com	Salt Lake City	UT	84102	801-524-2600	521-9234
South Central Communications Corp PO Box 3848 *Web:* www.southcentralcommunications.net	Evansville	IN	47736	812-463-7950	463-7915
Spanish Broadcasting System Inc (SBS) 2601 S Bayshore Dr PH 2 *NASDAQ: SBSA* ■ *Web:* www.spanishbroadcasting.com	Coconut Grove	FL	33133	305-441-6901	446-5148
Tejas Broadcasting LLP 1733 S Brownlee Blvd	Corpus Christi	TX	78404	361-883-1600	883-9303
Telesouth Communications Inc 6311 Ridgewood Rd *TF:* 888-808-8637 ■ *Web:* www.telesouth.com	Jackson	MS	39211	601-957-1700	956-5228
Three Eagles Communications Co 3800 Cornhusker Hwy *Web:* www.threeeagles.com	Lincoln	NE	68504	402-466-1234	467-4095
Townsquare Media Inc 240 Greenwich Ave *Web:* www.townsquaremedia.com	Greenwich	CT	06830	203-861-0900	
Triad Broadcasting Company LLC 2511 Garden Rd Bldg A Ste 104	Monterey	CA	93940	831-655-6350	655-6355
VerStandig Broadcasting 10960 John Wayne Dr PO Box 788 *Web:* www.verstandig.com	Greencastle	PA	17225	717-597-9200	597-9210

				Phone	Fax
Waitt Corp LLC 1125 S 103rd St Ste 425 — *Web:* www.waittcompany.com	Omaha	NE	68124	402-697-8000	
Walt Disney Co 500 S Buena Vista St — *NYSE: DIS* ■ **Fax:* Mail Rm ■ *Web:* thewaltdisneycompany.com	Burbank	CA	91521	818-560-1000	553-7210*
West Virginia Radio Corp 1251 Earl L Core Rd — *Web:* wvaq.com	Morgantown	WV	26505	304-296-0029	296-3876
Withers Broadcasting Co PO Box 1508 — *TF:* 800-333-1577 ■ *Web:* www.mywithersradio.com/wmix	Mount Vernon	IL	62864	618-242-3500	242-2490
Zimmer Radio Group 3215 Lemone Industrial Blvd Ste 200 — *TF:* 800-455-1099 ■ *Web:* www.zimmercommunications.com	Columbia	MO	65201	573-875-1099	875-2439

647 RADIO NETWORKS

				Phone	Fax
American Family Association PO Drawer 2440 — *TF:* 800-326-4543 ■ *Web:* www.afa.net	Tupelo	MS	38803	662-844-5036	842-6791
BGC Partners Inc 499 Pk Ave — *NASDAQ: BGCP* ■ *Web:* www.bgcpartners.com	New York	NY	10022	646-346-7000	346-6919
Black Radio Network 166 Madison Ave — *TF:* 800-226-8276 ■ *Web:* www.blackradionetwork.com	New York	NY	10016	212-686-6850	686-7308
Bott Radio Network 10550 Barkley St Ste 100 — *TF:* 800-875-1903 ■ *Web:* www.bottradionetwork.com	Overland Park	KS	66212	913-642-7770	642-1319
CBC Radio Canada 181 Queen St PO Box 3220 — *Web:* www.cbc.ca	Ottawa	ON	K1P1K9	613-288-6000	
CBC Radio Two 181 Queen St PO Box 3220 Stn C — **Fax:* Mktg ■ *Web:* music.cbc.ca	Ottawa	ON	K1P1K9	613-288-6000	724-5112*
CBS Corp 51 W 52nd St — *NYSE: CBS* ■ *Web:* www.cbscorporation.com	New York	NY	10019	212-975-4321	975-4516
CBS Radio Network 524 W 57th St — *Web:* www.cbsnews.com	New York	NY	10019	212-975-3247	
CNN Radio Network 190 Marietta St NW — *Web:* www.cnnradio.com	Atlanta	GA	30303	404-827-2750	
Crystal Media Networks 7201 Wisconsin Ave Ste 780 — *Web:* www.crystalmedianetworks.com/	Bethesda	MD	20814	240-223-0846	
Dial Global Inc Candler Tower 220 W 42nd St — *Web:* www.westwoodone.com	New York	NY	10036	212-967-2888	
ESPN Radio Network 545 Middle St — *Web:* www.espn.go.com/espnradio	Bristol	CT	06010	860-766-2000	766-2213
Family Life Communications Inc PO Box 35300 — **Fax Area Code:* 520 ■ *TF:* 800-776-1070 ■ *Web:* www.myflr.org	Tucson	AZ	85740	800-776-1070	742-6979*
Far East Broadcasting Co Inc 15700 Imperial Hwy PO Box 1 — *TF:* 800-523-3480 ■ *Web:* www.febc.org	La Mirada	CA	90638	800-523-3480	
Hispanic Communications Network 50 F Street, NW 8th Floor — *Web:* www.hcnmedia.com	Washington	DC	20001	202-637-8800	
Jones International Ltd 9697 E Mineral Ave — *TF:* 800-525-7002 ■ *Web:* www.jones.com	Centennial	CO	80112	800-525-7002	
Learfield Communications Inc 505 Hobbs Rd — *Web:* www.learfield.com	Jefferson City	MO	65109	573-893-7200	893-2321
Moody Global Ministries 820 N La Salle Blvd — *Web:* moodyglobal.org	Chicago	IL	60610	312-329-4000	329-4468
Motor Racing Network (MRN) 555 MRN Dr — *Web:* motorracingnetwork.com	Concord	NC	28027	704-262-6700	262-6811
Pacifica Radio Foundation 1925 ML King Jr Way — *Web:* www.pacifica.org	Berkeley	CA	94704	510-849-2590	849-2617
Public Radio International (PRI) 401 Second Ave N Ste 500 — *Web:* www.pri.org	Minneapolis	MN	55401	612-338-5000	330-9222
Radio America 1100 N Glebe Rd Ste 900 — **Fax Area Code:* 571 ■ *TF:* 800-807-4703 ■ *Web:* www.radioamerica.org	Arlington	VA	22201	703-302-1000	480-4141*
Radio Free Asia 2025 M St NW Ste 300 — *Web:* www.rfa.org	Washington	DC	20036	202-530-4900	530-7794
Radio Free Europe/Radio Liberty (RFE/RL) 1201 Connecticut Ave NW 4th Fl — *Web:* www.rferl.org	Washington	DC	20036	202-457-6900	457-6992
Relevant Radio 1496 Bellevue St Ste 202 PO Box 10707 — *TF:* 877-291-0123 ■ *Web:* www.relevantradio.com	Green Bay	WI	54311	920-884-1460	884-3170
Salem Communications Corp 4880 Santa Rosa Rd — *NASDAQ: SALM* ■ *Web:* www.salem.cc	Camarillo	CA	93012	805-987-0400	384-4505
Salem Radio Network 6400 N Beltline Rd Ste 210 — *Web:* www.srnonline.com	Irving	TX	75063	972-831-1920	831-8626
SRN Broadcasting 307 E Washington	Lake Bluff	IL	60044	847-735-1995	
Tiger Financial News Network 601 Cleveland St Ste 618 — *TF:* 877-518-9190 ■ *Web:* www.tfnn.com	Clearwater	FL	33755	727-467-9190	443-0869
Trident Communications 31 Timber Ln	Hilton Head Island	SC	29926	843-837-4978	
Triton Media Group 15303 Ventura Blvd Ste 1500 — *Web:* www.tritonmedia.com	Sherman Oaks	CA	91403	310-575-9700	
United Stations Radio Network 1065 Ave of the Americas 3rd Fl — *TF:* 866-989-1975 ■ *Web:* www.unitedstations.com	New York	NY	10018	212-869-1111	869-1115
Voice of America Radio Network 330 Independence Ave SW — *Web:* www.voanews.com	Washington	DC	20237	202-203-4000	260-2579
Yesterday USA Radio Networks, The 2001 Plymouth Rock Dr — *TF:* 800-624-2272 ■ *Web:* www.yesterdayusa.com	Richardson	TX	75081	972-889-9872	889-2329

648 RADIO STATIONS

AAA	Adult Album Alternative	**NAC**	New Adult Contemporary
AC	Adult Contemporary	**Nost**	Nostalgia
Alt	Alternative	**NPR**	National Public Radio
CBC	Canadian Broadcasting Corp	**Oldies**	Oldies/80s
CHR	Contemporary Hit Radio	**Rel**	Religious
Clas	Classical	**Rock**	Rock
CR	Classic Rock	**Span**	Spanish
Ctry	Country	**Sports**	Sports
Ethnic	Multilingual	**Urban**	Urban
N/T	News/Talk	**Var**	Variety

SEE ALSO Internet Broadcasting p. 2588

				Phone	Fax
100.7 WLEV 2158 Ave C Ste 100 — *Web:* www.wlevradio.com	Bethlehem	PA	18017	610-266-7600	231-0400
102.9 The Whale 869 Blue Hills Ave — *Web:* drcfm.com	Bloomfield	CT	06002	860-243-1115	286-8257
92.5 FM WVNN 1717 Hwy 72 E — *Web:* www.wvnn.com	Athens	AL	35611	256-830-8300	232-6842
97.1 THE WAVE 919 Ellegood St PO Box 909 — *Web:* www.971thewave.com	Salisbury	MD	21801	410-219-3500	548-1543
97.3 NOW Milwaukee 12100 W Howard Ave — *Web:* www.973radionow.com	Greenfield	WI	53228	414-545-8900	327-3200
ALT 98.7 3400 W Olive Ave Ste 550 — *Web:* www.987fm.com	Burbank	CA	91505	818-559-2252	
ALT AZ 93.3 1167 W Javelina Ave — **Fax:* Sales ■ *Web:* www.kdkb.com	Mesa	AZ	85210	480-897-9300	*
AM 570 LA Sports 3400 W Olive Ave Ste 550 — *TF:* 866-987-2570 ■ *Web:* www.am570radio.com	Burbank	CA	91505	818-559-2252	
Bell media 1640 Ouellette Ave — *Web:* www.939theriverradio.com	Windsor	ON	N8X1L1	519-258-8888	258-0182
CBS Miami 194 NW 187th St — *Web:* www.wqam.com	Miami	FL	33169	305-654-1700	
CBS Radio 1271 Ave of the Americas Fl 44 — *Web:* www.cbsradio.com/	New York	NY	10020	248-855-5100	
CBV-FM 106.3 (CBC) PO Box 500 Stn A — *TF:* 866-306-4636 ■ *Web:* www.cbc.radio-canada.ca	Toronto	ON	M5W1E6	866-306-4636	
CHML 875 Main St W Ste 900 — *Web:* 900chml.com	Hamilton	ON	L8S4R1	905-521-9900	540-2452
CJXY-FM 107.9 (Rock) 875 Main St W Ste 900 — *Web:* www.y108.ca	Hamilton	ON	L8S4R1	905-521-9900	540-2452
CKLW-AM 800 (N/T) 1640 Ouellette Ave — *TF:* 800-263-2559 ■ *Web:* www.am800cklw.com	Windsor	ON	N8X1L1	519-258-8888	258-0182
Entercom Boston 20 Guest St Third Fl — *Web:* www.entercom.com	Brighton	MA	02135	617-779-5800	779-5375
Family Stations Inc 290 Hegenberger Rd — *TF:* 800-543-1495 ■ *Web:* familyradio.org/	Oakland	CA	94621	800-543-1495	
Fun 101.3 FM 1996 Auction Rd — *TF:* 877-870-5678 ■ *Web:* www.roseradio.com	Manheim	PA	17545	717-653-0800	653-0122
Go 96.3 420 N Fifth St Ste 150 — *Web:* www.ktwin.com	Minneapolis	MN	55401	612-659-4848	313-2795
Hot 103.1 1355 California St PO Box 968 — *Web:* www.hot103.fm	Las Cruces	NM	88001	575-525-9298	525-9419
KAAM-AM 770 (Nost) 3201 Royalty Row — *Web:* www.kaamradio.com	Irving	TX	75062	972-445-1700	438-6574
KABX-FM 97.5 (Oldies) 1020 W Main St — *TF:* 800-350-3777 ■ *Web:* www.975kabx.com	Merced	CA	95340	209-723-2191	205-1013
KACL-FM 98.7 (Oldies) 4303 Memorial Hwy — *Web:* www.cool987fm.com	Mandan	ND	58554	701-663-9898	663-8790
KADI-FM 99.5 (Rel) 5431 W Sunshine St — *Web:* www.99hitfm.com	Brookline Station	MO	65619	417-831-0995	831-4026
KAJN-FM 102.9 (Rel) 110 W Third St PO Box 1469 — *Web:* www.kajn.com	Crowley	LA	70527	337-783-1560	783-1674
KANU-FM 91.5 (NPR) 1120 W 11th St Kansas Public Radio — *TF:* 888-577-5268 ■ *Web:* www.kansaspublicradio.org	Lawrence	KS	66044	785-864-4530	864-5278
KBAQ-FM 89.5 (Clas) 2323 W 14th St — *Web:* www.kbaq.org	Tempe	AZ	85281	480-833-1122	774-8475
KBBY-FM 95.1 (AC) 1376 Walter St — *TF:* 888-288-9242 ■ *Web:* www.951kbby.com	Ventura	CA	93003	805-642-8595	
KBCO-FM 97.3 (AAA) 4695 S Monaco St Ste 315 — *Web:* www.kbco.com	Denver	CO	80237	303-444-5600	
KBHE-FM 89.3 (NPR) 555 N Dakota St PO Box 5000 — *TF:* 800-456-0766 ■ *Web:* www.sdpb.org	Vermillion	SD	57069	605-677-5861	677-5010
KBIA-FM 91.3 (NPR) 409 Jesse Hall — *TF:* 800-292-9136 ■ *Web:* www.kbia.org	Columbia	MO	65211	573-882-3431	882-2636
KBIG-FM 104.3 (AC) 3400 W Olive Ave Ste 550 — *TF:* 866-544-6936 ■ *Web:* www.1043myfm.com	Burbank	CA	91505	818-559-2252	955-8151
KBRG-FM 100.3 (Span AC) 750 Battery St Ste 200 — *TF:* 888-808-1003 ■ *Web:* 1003masvariedad.univision.com	San Francisco	CA	94111	415-989-5765	733-5766
KBUE-FM 105.5 (Span) 1845 Empire Ave — *Web:* aquisuena.estrellatv.com	Burbank	CA	91504	818-729-5300	
KBYZ-FM 96.5 (CR) 4303 Memorial Hwy — *TF:* 888-663-9650 ■ *Web:* www.965thefox.com	Mandan	ND	58554	701-663-9600	663-8790
KCAQ-FM 104.7 (CHR) 2284 S Victoria Ave Ste 2G — *Web:* www.q1047.com	Ventura	CA	93003	805-289-1400	644-7906
KCBI-FM 90.9 (Rel) 411 Ryan Plz Dr — *Web:* www.kcbi.org	Arlington	TX	76011	817-792-3800	
KCFR-FM 90.1 (NPR) 7409 S Alton Ct — *TF:* 800-722-4449 ■ *Web:* www.cpr.org	Centennial	CO	80112	303-871-9191	733-3319
KCFX-FM 101.1 (CR) 5800 Foxridge Dr Sixth Fl — *Web:* www.101thefox.net	Mission	KS	66202	913-514-3000	262-3946

Station / Address	City	State	ZIP	Phone	Fax
KCHZ-FM 95.7 (CHR) 5800 Foxridge Dr Fl 6 *Web:* www.957thevibe.com	Mission	KS	66202	913-514-3000	
KCLR-FM 99.3 (Ctry) 3215 Lemone Industrial Blvd Ste 200 *TF:* 800-455-5257 ■ *Web:* www.clear99.com	Columbia	MO	65201	573-875-1099	875-2439
KCLU-FM 88.3 (NPR) 60 W Olsen Rd Ste 4400 *Web:* www.kclu.org	Thousand Oaks	CA	91360	805-493-3900	
KCMO-AM 710 (N/T) 5800 Foxridge Dr Sixth Fl *Web:* www.kcmotalkradio.com	Mission	KS	66202	913-514-3000	262-3946
KCMO-FM 94.9 (Oldies) 5800 Foxridge Dr Sixth Fl *Web:* www.949kcmo.com	Mission	KS	66202	913-514-3000	262-3946
KCMQ-FM 96.7 (CR) 3215 Lemone Industrial Blvd Ste 200 *TF:* 800-455-1967 ■ *Web:* www.kcmq.com	Columbia	MO	65201	573-875-1099	
KCRW-FM 89.9 (NPR) 1900 Pico Blvd *TF:* 877-527-9227 ■ *Web:* www.kcrw.com	Santa Monica	CA	90405	310-450-5183	450-7172
KCSD-FM 90.9 (NPR) 555 N Dakota St PO Box 5000 *TF:* 800-456-0766 ■ *Web:* www.sdpb.org	Vermillion	SD	57069	605-677-5861	677-5010
KCSM-FM 91.1 (Jazz) 1700 W Hillsdale Blvd *Web:* www.kcsm.org	San Mateo	CA	94402	650-574-6586	524-6975
KCSP-AM 610 (Sports) 7000 Squibb Rd *Web:* 610sports.com/	Mission	KS	66202	913-744-3600	744-3700
KDB-FM 93.7 (Clas) 414 E Cota St *Web:* www.kdb.com	Santa Barbara	CA	93101	805-966-4131	966-4788
KDES-FM 98.5 (Soft AC) 2100 E Tahquitz Canyon Way *Web:* www.kdes.com	Palm Springs	CA	92262	760-325-2582	
KDON-FM 102.5 (CHR) 903 N Main St *TF:* 888-558-5366 ■ *Web:* www.kdon.com	Salinas	CA	93906	831-755-8181	755-8193
Keymarket Communications 56325 High Ridge Rd *Web:* www.wyjkfm.com	Bellaire	OH	43906	740-676-5661	676-2742
KEYY-AM 1450 (Rel) 307 S 1600 W *Web:* www.keyradio.org	Provo	UT	84601	801-374-5210	
KEZA-FM 107.9 (AC) 2049 E Joyce Blvd Ste 101 *Web:* www.magic1079.com	Fayetteville	AR	72703	479-582-1079	587-8255
KEZN-FM 103.1 (AC) 72-915 Parkview Dr	Palm Desert	CA	92260	760-340-9383	340-5756
KFAX-AM 1100 (Rel) 39138 Fremont Blvd *Web:* www.kfax.com	Fremont	CA	94538	510-713-1100	505-1448
KFI-AM 640 (N/T) 3400 W Olive Ave Ste 550 *Web:* www.kfiam640.com	Burbank	CA	91505	818-559-2252	
KFJM-FM 90.7 (AAA) 207 N Fifth St *TF:* 800-366-6888 ■ *Web:* www.prairiepublic.org	Fargo	ND	58102	701-241-6900	239-7650
KFRG-FM 95.1 (Ctry) 900 E Washington St Ste 315 *TF:* 888-431-3764 ■ *Web:* kfrog.cbslocal.com	Colton	CA	92324	909-825-9525	825-0441
KGNU-FM 88.5 (Var) 4700 Walnut St *TF:* 800-737-3030 ■ *Web:* www.kgnu.org	Boulder	CO	80301	303-449-4885	339-6340
KGOU-FM 106.3 (NPR) 860 Van Vleet Oval Rm 300 *TF:* 866-533-2470 ■ *Web:* www.kgou.org	Norman	OK	73019	405-325-3388	325-7129
KGPR-FM 89.9 (NPR) 2100 16th Ave S Rm G118 *Web:* www.kgpr.org	Great Falls	MT	59405	406-268-3739	268-3736
KGRT-FM 103.9 (Ctry) 1355 California St PO Box 968 *Web:* www.kgrt.com	Las Cruces	NM	88001	575-525-9298	525-9419
KGY-AM 1240 (AC) 1700 Marine Dr NE *Web:* www.kgyradio.com	Olympia	WA	98501	360-943-1240	352-1222
KGY-FM 96.9 (Ctry) 1700 Marine Dr NE *TF:* 855-549-1240 ■ *Web:* www.kgyradio.com	Olympia	WA	98501	360-943-1240	352-1222
KHAY-FM 100.7 (Ctry) 1376 Walter St *Web:* www.khay.com	Ventura	CA	93003	805-642-8595	656-5838
KHCC-FM 90.1 (NPR) 815 N Walnut St Ste 300 *TF:* 800-723-4657 ■ *Web:* www.radiokansas.org	Hutchinson	KS	67501	620-662-6646	
KHOZ-FM 102.9 (Ctry) 1111 Radio Ave *Web:* www.1029thez.com	Harrison	AR	72601	870-741-2301	741-3299
KIIS-FM 102.7 (CHR) 3400 W Olive Ave Ste 550 *Web:* www.kiisfm.com	Burbank	CA	91505	818-559-2252	729-2502
KIIX-AM 1410 (Sports) 4270 Byrd Dr *Web:* www.kiixcountry.com	Loveland	CO	80538	970-461-2560	461-0118
KIXI-AM 880 (Nost) 3650 131st Ave SE Ste 550 *TF:* 866-880-5494 ■ *Web:* www.kixi.com	Bellevue	WA	98006	425-562-8964	653-1088
KJJY-FM 92.5 (Ctry) 4143 109th St *Web:* 925nashicon.com	Urbandale	IA	50322	515-331-9200	331-9292
KJLH-FM 102.3 (Urban) 161 N La Brea Ave *Web:* www.kjlhradio.com	Inglewood	CA	90301	310-330-2200	330-5555
KJZZ-FM 91.5 (NPR) 2323 W 14th St *Web:* kjzz.org	Tempe	AZ	85281	480-834-5627	774-8475
KKRQ-FM 100.7 (CR) One Stephen Atkins Dr *Web:* www.kkrq.com	Iowa City	IA	52245	319-354-9500	354-9504
KLBB-AM 1220 (Nost) 104 N Main St *Web:* www.klbbradio.com	Stillwater	MN	55082	651-439-5006	439-5015
KLHT-AM 1040 (Rel) 98 - 1016 Komo Mai Dr *Web:* www.klight.org	Aiea	HI	96701	808-524-1040	487-1040
KLTY-FM 94.9 (Rel) 6400 N Beltline Rd Ste 120 *Web:* www.klty.com	Irving	TX	75063	972-870-9949	
KMBR-FM 95.5 (Rock) 750 Dewey Blvd Ste 1 *Web:* www.955kmbr.com	Butte	MT	59701	406-494-4442	494-6020
KMBZ-AM 980 (N/T) 7000 Squibb Rd *Web:* www.kmbz.com	Mission	KS	66202	913-744-3600	744-3700
KMFC-FM 92.1 (Rel) 1249 E Hwy 22 *Web:* www.kmfc.com	Centralia	MO	65240	573-682-5525	
KNDR-FM 104.7 (Rel) 1400 NE Third St *TF:* 800-767-5095 ■ *Web:* www.kndr.fm	Mandan	ND	58554	701-663-2345	663-2347
KNOW-FM 91.1 (NPR) 480 Cedar St *TF:* 800-228-7123 ■ *Web:* minnesota.publicradio.org	Saint Paul	MN	55101	651-290-1500	290-1295
KNOX-AM 1310 (N/T) 1185 Ninth St NE *Web:* www.knoxradio.com	Thompson	ND	58278	701-775-4611	772-0540
KNUS-AM 710 (N/T) 3131 S Vaughn Way Ste 601 *Web:* www.710knus.com	Aurora	CO	80014	303-750-5687	696-8063
KNWI-FM 107.1 (Rel) 3737 Woodland Ave Ste 300 *TF:* 800-701-3123 ■ *Web:* life1071.com	West Des Moines	IA	50266	515-327-1071	327-1073
KOCP-FM 95.9 (CR) 2284 S Victoria Ave Ste 2G *Web:* www.rewind959.com	Ventura	CA	93003	805-289-1400	
KOHL-FM 89.3 (CHR) 43600 Mission Blvd *Web:* www.kohlradio.com	Fremont	CA	94539	510-659-6221	659-6001
KOKZ-FM 105.7 (Oldies) 514 Jefferson St **Fax:* News Rm ■ *Web:* 1057kokz.com/	Waterloo	IA	50701	319-234-2200	233-4946*
KOLA-FM 99.9 (Clas) 1940 Orange Tree Ln Ste 200 *Web:* www.kolafm.com	Redlands	CA	92374	909-793-3554	793-7225
KOPN-FM 89.5 (Var) 915 E Broadway *TF:* 800-895-5676 ■ *Web:* www.kopn.org	Columbia	MO	65201	573-874-1139	499-1662
KOST-FM 103.5 (AC) 3400 W Olive Ave Ste 550 *Web:* www.kost1035.com	Burbank	CA	91505	818-559-2252	260-9961
KPAW-FM 107.9 (CR) 4270 Byrd Dr *Web:* www.1079thebear.com	Loveland	CO	80538	970-461-2560	461-0118
KPCC-FM 89.3 (NPR) 1570 E Colorado Blvd *Web:* www.scpr.org	Pasadena	CA	91106	626-585-7000	585-7916
KPIG-FM 107.5 (AAA) 1110 Main St Ste 16 *Web:* www.kpig.com	Watsonville	CA	95076	831-722-9000	722-7548
KPLU-FM 88.5 (NPR) 12180 Pk Ave S *TF:* 800-677-5758 ■ *Web:* www.kplu.org	Tacoma	WA	98447	253-535-7758	535-8332
KPUL-FM 99.5 (Rel) 33365 335th St *Web:* www.pulse995.com	Waukee	IA	50263	515-987-9995	987-9808
KPVU-FM 91.3 (NPR) Prairie View A & M University MS 1415 *TF:* 877-241-1752 ■ *Web:* pvamu.edu/auxiliaryservices/kpvu/	Prairie View	TX	77446	936-261-3750	261-3769
KQFX-FM 104.3 (Span) 3639 Wolflin Ave	Amarillo	TX	79102	806-355-1043	
KQKS-FM 107.5 (Urban) 7800 E OrchaRd Rd Ste 400 *Web:* www.ks1075.com	Greenwood Village	CO	80111	303-228-1075	
KQRC-FM 98.9 (Rock) 7000 Squibb Rd *Web:* www.989therock.com	Mission	KS	66202	913-744-3600	744-3700
KRBZ-FM 96.5 (Alt) 7000 Squibb Rd *Web:* www.965thebuzz.com	Mission	KS	66202	913-744-3600	744-3700
KRBZ-FM 96.5 (Clas) 7000 Squibb Rd *Web:* www.entercom.com	Mission	KS	66202	913-744-3600	
KRCD-FM 103.9 (Span) 655 N Central Ave Ste 2500 *TF:* 888-382-1222 ■ *Web:* masvariedadla.univision.com	Glendale	CA	91203	818-500-4500	500-4480
KRKS-FM 94.7 (Rel) 3131 S Vaughn Way Ste 601 *TF:* 888-346-4700 ■ *Web:* www.947krks.com	Aurora	CO	80014	303-750-5687	696-8063
KRMD-FM 101.1 (Ctry) 270 Plz Loop *Web:* www.krmd.com	Bossier City	LA	71111	318-549-8500	549-8505
KROX-AM 1260 (Var) 208 S Main St *TF:* 800-222-2537 ■ *Web:* www.kroxam.com	Crookston	MN	56716	218-281-1140	281-5036
KRWG-FM 90.7 (NPR) PO Box 3000 *Web:* krwg.org	Las Cruces	NM	88003	575-646-2222	646-1974
KSEA-FM 107.9 (Span) 608 E Boronda Rd Ste C *Web:* www.campesina.net	Salinas	CA	93906	831-754-1469	754-1563
KSKY-AM 660 (N/T) 6400 N Beltline Rd Ste 110 **Fax Area Code:* 214 ■ *Web:* www.660amtheanswer.com	Irving	TX	75063	972-870-9949	561-9662*
KSME-FM 96.1 (CHR) 4270 Byrd Dr *TF:* 877-498-9600 ■ *Web:* www.kissfmcolorado.com	Loveland	CO	80538	970-461-2560	461-0118
KTMY-FM 107.1 (N/T) 3415 University Ave *Web:* www.mytalk1071.com	St. Paul	MN	55114	651-642-4107	647-2904
KTOM-FM 92.7 (Ctry) 903 N Main St *TF General:* 800-660-5866 ■ *Web:* www.ktom.com	Salinas	CA	93906	831-755-8181	755-8193
KTSD-FM 91.1 (NPR) 555 N Dakota St PO Box 5000 *TF:* 800-456-0766 ■ *Web:* www.sdpb.org	Vermillion	SD	57069	605-677-5861	677-5010
KTXY-FM 106.9 (AC) 3215 Lemone Industrial Blvd Ste 200 *TF:* 800-500-9107 ■ *Web:* www.y107.com	Columbia	MO	65201	573-875-1099	
KUAD-FM 99.1 (Ctry) 600 Main St **Fax Area Code:* 970 ■ *TF:* 800-500-2599 ■ *Web:* www.k99.com	Windsor	CO	80550	800-500-2599	686-7491*
KUAF 91.3 Public Radio 9 S School Ave *TF:* 800-522-5823 ■ *Web:* www.kuaf.org	Fayetteville	AR	72701	479-575-2556	575-8440
KUCR-FM 88.3 (Var) UC Riverside *Web:* www.kucr.org	Riverside	CA	92521	951-827-3737	827-3240
KUDL-FM 98.1 (AC) 7000 Squibb Rd *Web:* www.kmbz.com	Mission	KS	66202	913-744-3600	
KUFM-FM 89.1 (NPR) 32 Campus Dr University of Montana *TF:* 800-325-1565 ■ *Web:* www.mtpr.net	Missoula	MT	59812	406-243-4931	243-3299
KUNA-FM 96.7 (Span) 42-650 Melanie Pl *Web:* www.kesq.com	Palm Desert	CA	92211	760-568-6830	568-3984
KUPD-FM 97.9 (Rock) 1900 W Carmen St *Web:* www.98kupd.com	Tempe	AZ	85283	480-838-0400	
KUSP-FM 88.9 (NPR) 203 Eigth Ave *TF:* 800-655-5877 ■ *Web:* www.kusp.org	Santa Cruz	CA	95062	831-476-2800	476-2802
KUWC-FM 91.3 (NPR) 1000 E University Ave *Web:* www.uwyo.edu	Laramie	WY	82071	307-766-1121	
KUWJ-FM 90.3 (NPR) 1000 E University Ave *Web:* www.wyomingpublicmedia.org	Laramie	WY	82071	307-766-4240	766-6184
KUWS-FM 91.3 (NPR) 1805 Catlin Ave *TF:* 800-300-8530 ■ *Web:* www.kuws.fm	Superior	WI	54880	715-394-8530	394-8404
KVLC-FM 101.1 (Oldies) 101 Perkins Dr *TF:* 877-527-1011 ■ *Web:* www.101gold.com	Las Cruces	NM	88005	575-527-1111	527-1100
KWWR-FM 95.7 (Ctry) 1705 E Liberty St *Web:* info.kwwr.com	Mexico	MO	65265	573-581-5500	581-1801
KWYR-FM 93.7 (AC) PO Box 491 *TF:* 800-388-5997 ■ *Web:* www.kwyr.com	Winner	SD	57580	605-842-3333	842-3875
KXFG-FM 92.9 (Ctry) 900 E Washington Ste 315 *TF:* 888-431-3764 ■ *Web:* kfrog.cbslocal.com	Colton	CA	92324	909-825-9525	
KXXO-FM 96.1 (AC) 119 NE Washington St *Web:* www.mixx96.com	Olympia	WA	98501	360-943-9937	352-3643

Station / Address	City	State	ZIP	Phone	Fax
KYCK-FM 97.1 (Ctry) 1185 Ninth St NE *Web:* www.97kyck.com	Thompson	ND	58278	701-775-4611	772-0540
KYGO-FM 98.5 (Ctry) 7800 E OrchaRd Rd Ste 400 *Web:* www.kygo.com	Greenwood Village	CO	80111	303-321-0950	
La Rockola 96.7FM 3101 W Fifth St *Web:* larockola967.estrellatv.com	Santa Ana	CA	92703	714-554-5000	554-9362
Magic 107.3 KMJK-FM 5800 Foxridge Dr Ste 600 *Web:* www.magic1073.com	Mission	KS	66202	816-576-7107	
NASH-FM 97.3 4143 109th St *Web:* www.nashfm973.com	Urbandale	IA	50322	515-331-9200	331-9292
NEW MOViN 92.5, The 3650 131st Ave SE Ste 550	Bellevue	WA	98006	425-653-9462	653-9464
Patriot AM 1150, The 3400 W Olive Ave Ste 550 *Web:* www.ktlkam1150.com	Burbank	CA	91505	818-559-2252	
Queen B 51 Means Dr	Platteville	WI	53818	608-349-2000	349-2002
Real 92.3 FM 3400 W Olive Blvd Ste 550 *Web:* www.hot923.com	Burbank	CA	91505	818-559-2252	
Star 92.9 265 Hegeman Ave *TF:* 866-865-7827 ■ *Web:* www.star929.com	Colchester	VT	05446	802-655-0093	655-0478
Super Talk 1270 4303 Memorial Hwy *TF:* 844-255-7886 ■ *Web:* www.supertalk1270.com	Mandan	ND	58554	701-663-1270	
Trending Radio 93.3 N 72 W 12922 Good Hope Rd *Web:* www.b933fm.com	Menomonee Falls	WI	53051	414-778-1933	771-3036
Triad's 105.7 Man Up, The 2-B PAI Pk *TF:* 800-950-2482 ■ *Web:* www.ihaveabuzz.com	Greensboro	NC	27409	336-822-2000	
WAAF-FM 107.3 (Rock) 20 Guest St Third Fl **Fax:* Mktg ■ *Web:* www.waaf.com	Brighton	MA	02135	617-779-5800	779-5447*
WAEB-AM 790 (N/T) 1541 Alta Dr Ste 400 *Web:* www.790waeb.com	Whitehall	PA	18052	610-434-1742	434-6288
WAEB-FM 104.1 (AC) 1541 Alta Dr 4th Fl *Web:* www.b104.com	Whitehall	PA	18052	610-434-1742	434-6288
WAFL-FM 97.7 (AC) 1666 Blairs Pond Rd *Web:* www.eagle977.com	Milford	DE	19963	302-422-7575	422-3069
WAJZ-FM 96.3 (Urban) Six Johnson Rd *Web:* www.jamz963.com	Latham	NY	12110	518-786-6600	786-6610
WAKB-FM 100.9 (Urban) 6025 Broadcast Dr *Web:* www.1009magic.com	North Augusta	SC	29841	803-279-2330	279-8149
WAKS-FM 96.5 (CHR) 6200 Oak Tree Blvd S Fourth Fl *Web:* www.kisscleveland.com	Independence	OH	44131	216-520-2600	524-2600
WALK-FM 97.5 (AC) 66 Colonial Dr *TF:* 877-263-7995 ■ *Web:* www.walkradio.com	Patchogue	NY	11772	631-475-5200	
WAPN-FM 91.5 (Rel) 1508 State Ave *Web:* www.wapn.net	Holly Hill	FL	32117	386-677-4272	
WAQY-FM 102.1 (CR) 45 Fisher Ave *Web:* www.rock102.com	East Longmeadow	MA	01028	413-525-4141	525-4334
WARF-AM 1350 (Sports) 7755 Freedom Ave *Web:* www.sportsradio1350.com	North Canton	OH	44720	330-836-4700	
WARO-FM 94.5 (CR) 2824 Palm Beach Blvd *Web:* www.classicrock945.com	Fort Myers	FL	33916	239-337-2346	332-0767
WASH-FM 97.1 (AC) 1801 Rockville Pk Fifth Fl *TF:* 866-927-4361 ■ *Web:* www.washfm.com	Rockville	MD	20852	240-747-2700	
WAVA-AM 780 (Rel) 1901 N Moore St Ste 200 **Fax Area Code:* 202 ■ *TF:* 888-976-6924 ■ *Web:* www.wava.com	Arlington	VA	22209	703-807-2266	342-3800*
WAVA-FM 105.1 (Rel) 1901 N Moore St Ste 200 *TF:* 888-293-9282 ■ *Web:* www.wava.com	Arlington	VA	22209	703-807-2266	807-2248
WAYJ-FM 88.7 (Rel) 1860 Boyscout Dr Ste 202	Fort Myers	FL	33907	239-936-1929	936-5433
WAYV-FM 95.1 (CHR) 8025 Black Horse Pike *Web:* www.951wayv.com	West Atlantic City	NJ	08232	609-484-8444	646-6331
WAYZ-FM 104.7 (Ctry) 10960 John Wayne Dr *TF:* 888-950-1047 ■ *Web:* www.wayz.com	Greencastle	PA	17225	717-597-9200	597-9210
WBAB-FM 102.3 (Rock) 555 Sunrise Hwy *Web:* www.wbab.com	West Babylon	NY	11704	631-587-1023	587-1282
WBACH 98 Main St	Ellsworth	ME	04605	207-667-9800	
WBAP-AM 820 (N/T) 3090 Olive St Ste 400 **Fax Area Code:* 817 ■ *Web:* www.wbap.com	Dallas	TX	75219	214-526-2400	695-0018*
WBBN-FM 95.9 (Ctry) 4580 Hwy 15 N PO Box 6408 *Web:* www.b95country.com	Laurel	MS	39441	601-649-0095	649-8199
WBCI-FM 105.9 (Rel) 122 Main St *Web:* lifechangingradio.com	Topsham	ME	04086	207-725-9224	725-2686
WBEN-AM 930 (N/T) 500 Corporate Pkwy Ste 200 *Web:* www.wben.com	Amherst	NY	14226	716-843-0600	832-3080
WBGG-FM 105.9 (CR) 7601 Riviera Blvd *Web:* www.big1059.com	Miramar	FL	33023	954-862-2000	862-4013
WBGO-FM 88.3 (Jazz) 54 Pk Pl *Web:* www.wbgo.org	Newark	NJ	07102	973-624-8880	824-8888
WBIG-FM 100.3 (Oldies) 1801 Rockville Pk Fifth Fl *TF:* 800-493-1003 ■ *Web:* www.wbig.com	Rockville	MD	20852	240-747-2700	
WBLI-FM 106.1 (CHR) 555 Sunrise Hwy *Web:* www.wbli.com	West Babylon	NY	11704	631-669-9254	587-1282
WBON-FM 98.5 (Span) 3075 Veterans Memorial Hwy Ste 201 *Web:* www.lafiestali.com	Ronkonkoma	NY	11779	631-648-2500	648-2510
WBRB-FM 101.3 (Ctry) 1065 Radio Pk Dr *TF:* 877-232-7121 ■ *Web:* www.1013thebear.com	Mount Clare	WV	26408	304-623-6546	
WBTT-FM 105.5 (Urban) 13320 Metro Pkwy Ste 1 *Web:* www.1055thebeat.com	Fort Myers	FL	33966	239-225-4300	225-4410
WBWB-FM 96.7 (CHR) 304 SR 446 PO Box 7797 *Web:* www.wbwb.com	Bloomington	IN	47401	812-336-8000	336-7000
WBYT-FM 100(Ctry) 237 W Edison Rd *Web:* www.b100.com	Mishawaka	IN	46545	574-258-5483	258-0930
WBZN-FM 107.3 (CHR) 49 Acme Rd PO Box 100 *Web:* z1073.com	Brewer	ME	04412	207-989-5631	989-5685
WBZO-FM 103.1 (Oldies) 234 Airport Plz Ste 5 *Web:* www.b103.com	Farmingdale	NY	11735	631-770-4200	
WCAR-AM 1090 (Rel) 32500 Pk Ln	Garden City	MI	48135	734-525-1111	
WCAT-FM 102.3 (Ctry) 728 N Hanover St *TF:* 800-932-0505 ■ *Web:* www.red1023.com	Carlisle	PA	17013	717-243-1200	243-0255
WCBK-FM 102.3 (Ctry) 1639 Burton Ln *Web:* www.wcbk.com	Martinsville	IN	46151	765-342-3394	342-5020
WCBM-AM 680 (N/T) 1726 Reisterstown Rd Ste 117 *Web:* www.wcbm.com	Pikesville	MD	21208	410-580-6800	580-6810
WCBN-FM 88.3 (Alt) University of Michigan 530 Student Activities Bldg *Web:* wcbn.org	Ann Arbor	MI	48109	734-763-3500	
WCKT-FM 107.1 (Ctry) 13320 Metro Pkwy Ste 1 **Fax:* Hum Res ■ *Web:* www.catcountry1071.com	Fort Myers	FL	33966	239-225-4300	225-4410*
WCLT-FM 100.3 (Ctry) PO Box 5150 *TF:* 800-837-9258 ■ *Web:* www.wclt.com	Newark	OH	43058	740-345-4004	345-5775
WCMR-AM 1270 (Rel) PO Box 307 *TF:* 800-522-9376 ■ *Web:* www.solidgospel1270.com	Elkhart	IN	46515	574-875-5166	875-6662
WCMS-FM 94.5 (Ctry) 103-D W Wood Hill Dr *Web:* www.wcms.com	Nags Head	NC	27959	252-480-4655	441-4827
WCNK-FM 98.7 (Ctry) 30336 Overseas Hwy *Web:* www.conchcountry.com	Big Pine Key	FL	33043	305-872-9100	872-1603
WCNY-FM 91.3 (NPR) 506 Old Liverpool Rd *TF:* 800-451-9269 ■ *Web:* www.wcny.org	Liverpool	NY	13088	315-453-2424	451-8824
WCPV-FM 101.3 (CR) 265 Hegeman Ave *Web:* www.1013espn.com	Colchester	VT	05446	802-655-0093	
WCQR-FM 88.3 (Rel) 2312 Oak St *TF:* 888-477-5676 ■ *Web:* www.wcqr.org	Gray	TN	37615	423-477-5676	477-7060
WCRZ-FM 107.9 (AC) 3338 E Bristol Rd *Web:* wcrz.com	Burton	MI	48529	810-743-1080	742-5170
WCSX-FM 94.7 (CR) One Radio Plz *Web:* www.wcsx.com	Ferndale	MI	48220	248-398-9470	
WCTL-FM 106.3 (Rel) 10912 Peach St *TF:* 800-568-8924 ■ *Web:* www.wctl.org	Waterford	PA	16441	814-796-6000	
WCTO-FM 96.1 (Ctry) 2158 Ave C Ste 100 *Web:* www.catcountry96.com	Bethlehem	PA	18017	610-266-7600	231-0400
WDAF-FM 106.5 (Ctry) 7000 Squibb Rd *Web:* www.1065thewolf.com	Mission	KS	66202	913-744-3600	443-3700
WDAI-FM 98.5 (Urban) 11640 Hwy 17 Bypass *Web:* www.985kissfm.net	Murrells Inlet	SC	29576	843-272-3000	
WDAS-FM 105.3 (Urban AC) 111 Presidential Blvd Ste 100 *TF:* 800-745-3000 ■ *Web:* www.wdasfm.com	Bala Cynwyd	PA	19004	610-784-3333	784-2098
WDEA-AM 1370 (Nost) 49 Acme Rd PO Box 100 *Web:* wdea.am	Brewer	ME	04412	207-989-5631	989-5685
WDEV-AM 550 (N/T) Nine Stowe St *Web:* www.wdevradio.com	Waterbury	VT	05676	802-244-7321	244-1771
WDEV-FM 96.1 (Clas) Nine Stowe St PO Box 550 *Web:* wdevradio.com	Waterbury	VT	05676	802-244-7321	244-1771
WDFN-AM 1130 (Sports) 27675 Halsted Rd *Web:* www.wdfn.com	Farmington Hills	MI	48331	248-324-5800	
WDIY-FM 88.1 (NPR) 301 Broadway Third Fl *Web:* www.wdiyfm.org	Bethlehem	PA	18015	610-694-8100	954-9474
WDJA-AM 1420 (N/T) 2710 W Atlantic Ave *TF:* 877-278-1420 ■ *Web:* www.universo1420.com	Delray Beach	FL	33445	561-278-1420	278-7515
WDRM-FM 102.1 (Ctry) 26869 Peoples Rd *TF:* 866-302-0102 ■ *Web:* www.wdrm.com	Madison	AL	35756	256-309-2400	350-2653
WDSD-FM 94.7 (Ctry) 920 W Basin Rd Ste 400 *Web:* www.wdsd.com	New Castle	DE	19720	302-395-9800	
WEDR-FM 99.1 (Urban) 2741 N 29th Ave *TF:* 800-843-2677 ■ *Web:* www.wedr.com	Hollywood	FL	33020	305-444-4404	444-4404
WEEI-AM 850 (Sports) 20 Guest St Third Fl *TF:* 888-525-0850 ■ *Web:* www.weei.com	Brighton	MA	02135	617-779-3500	779-3557
WEKU-FM 88.9 (Clas) 521 Lancaster Ave 102 Perkins Bldg-EKU **Fax Area Code:* 859 ■ *TF:* 800-621-8890 ■ *Web:* www.weku.fm	Richmond	KY	40475	800-621-8890	622-6276*
WELI-AM 960 (N/T) 495 Benham St *Web:* www.960weli.com	Hamden	CT	06514	203-281-9600	281-2795
WEMU-FM 89.1 (NPR) PO Box 980350 *TF:* 888-299-8910 ■ *Web:* www.wemu.org	Ypsilanti	MI	48198	734-487-2229	487-1015
WERU-FM 89.9 (Var) 1186 Acadia Hwy *TF:* 800-643-6273 ■ *Web:* www.weru.org	East Orland	ME	04431	207-469-6600	469-8961
WETA-FM 90.9 (NPR) 2775 S Quincy St *Web:* www.weta.org/fm	Arlington	VA	22206	703-998-2600	998-3401
WEVO-FM 89.1 (N/T) Two Pillsbury St Ste 600 *TF:* 800-639-4131 ■ *Web:* www.nhpr.org	Concord	NH	03301	603-228-8910	224-6052
WEZL-FM 103.5 (Ctry) 950 Houston Northcutt Blvd 2nd Fl *Web:* www.wezl.com	Mount Pleasant	SC	29464	843-884-2534	884-1218
WEZN-FM 99.9 (AC) 440 Wheelers Farm Rd Ste 302 *Web:* star999.com	Milford	CT	06461	203-783-8200	
WEZQ-FM 92.9 (AC) 49 Acme Rd PO Box 100 *Web:* 929theticket.com	Brewer	ME	04412	207-989-5631	989-5685
WFBY-FM 102.3 (CR) 1065 Radio Pk Dr **Fax:* News Rm ■ *Web:* www.wfby.com	Mount Clare	WV	26408	304-623-6546	623-6547*
WFCF-FM 88.5 (Var) Flagler College PO Box 1027 *TF:* 800-304-4208 ■ *Web:* www.flagler.edu	Saint Augustine	FL	32085	904-819-6449	826-0094
WFCR-FM 88.5 (NPR) University of Massachusetts 131 County Cir *Web:* nepr.net	Amherst	MA	01003	413-735-6600	732-7417
WFDM-FM 95.9 (N/T) 645 Industrial Dr *TF:* 800-278-9200 ■ *Web:* www.freedom95.us	Franklin	IN	46131	317-736-4040	736-4781
WFHB-FM 91.3 (Var) 108 W Fourth St *Web:* www.wfhb.org	Bloomington	IN	47404	812-323-1200	323-0320

	City	State	ZIP	Phone	Fax
WFHM-FM 95.5 (Rel) Four Summit Pk Dr Ste 150 *Web:* www.955thefish.com	Cleveland	OH	44131	216-901-0921	
WFHN-FM 107.1 (CHR) 22 Sconticut Neck Rd *TF:* 877-854-9467 ■ *Web:* www.fun107.com	Fairhaven	MA	02719	508-999-6690	999-1420
WFIU-FM 103.7 Indiana University 1229 E Seventh St *TF:* 877-285-9348 ■ *Web:* indianapublicmedia.org	Bloomington	IN	47405	812-855-1357	855-5600
WFLF-FM 540 (N/T) 2500 Maitland Ctr Pkwy Ste 401 *Web:* 1025wfla.com/	Maitland	FL	32751	407-916-7800	916-7406
WFLY-FM 92.3 (CHR) Six Johnson Rd *Web:* www.fly92.com	Latham	NY	12110	518-786-6600	786-6610
WFNT-AM 1470 (N/T) 3338 E Bristol Rd *Web:* wfnt.com	Burton	MI	48529	810-743-1080	742-5170
WFOY-AM 1240 (N/T) 567 Lewis Pt Rd Ext *Web:* www.1023newsradio.com	Saint Augustine	FL	32086	904-797-1955	
WFPG-FM 96.9 (AC) 950 Tilton Rd Ste 200 *TF:* 800-969-9374 ■ *Web:* www.literock969.com	Northfield	NJ	08225	609-645-9797	272-9224
WFRE-FM 99.9 (Ctry) 5966 Grove Hill Rd *TF:* 877-999-9373 ■ *Web:* www.wfre.com	Frederick	MD	21703	301-663-4181	682-8018
WFUV-FM 90.7 (Var) 441 E Fordham Rd Fordham University *TF:* 888-400-5520 ■ *Web:* www.wfuv.org	Bronx	NY	10458	718-817-4550	365-9815
WGAR-FM 99.5 (Ctry) 6200 Oak Tree Blvd S 4th Fl **Fax:* Sales ■ *TF:* 855-222-0995 ■ *Web:* www.wgar.com	Independence	OH	44131	216-520-2600	524-2600*
WGBG-FM 98.5 (CR) 20200 DuPont Blvd *TF:* 866-292-5483 ■ *Web:* www.bigclassicrock.com	Georgetown	DE	19947	302-856-2567	856-7633
WGCU-FM 90.1 (NPR) 10501 FGCU Blvd S *TF:* 888-824-0030 ■ *Web:* www.wgcu.org	Fort Myers	FL	33965	239-590-2300	590-2310
WGEZ-AM 1490 (Oldies) 622 Public Ave *Web:* www.1490trueoldies.com	Beloit	WI	53511	608-365-8865	365-8867
WGGY-FM 101.3 (Ctry) 305 Hwy 315 *Web:* www.froggy101.com	Pittston	PA	18640	570-883-1111	883-9851
WGMD-FM 92.7 (N/T) PO Box 530 *TF:* 800-518-9292 ■ *Web:* www.wgmd.com	Rehoboth Beach	DE	19971	302-945-2050	945-3781
WGNA-FM 107.7 (Ctry) 1241 Kings Rd *Web:* www.wgna.com	Schenectady	NY	12303	518-881-1515	881-1516
WGNE-FM 99.9 (Ctry) 6440 Atlantic Blvd *TF:* 888-725-2345 ■ *Web:* www.999gatorcountry.com	Jacksonville	FL	32211	904-727-9696	721-9322
WGPA-AM 1100 (Var) 528 N New St	Bethlehem	PA	18018	610-866-8074	866-9381
WGR-AM 550 (Sports) 500 Corporate Pkwy Ste 200 *Web:* www.wgr550.com	Amherst	NY	14226	716-843-0600	832-3080
WGTS-FM 91.9 (Rel) 7600 Flower Ave *TF:* 877-948-7919 ■ *Web:* www.wgts.org	Takoma Park	MD	20912	301-891-4200	270-9191
WGTY-FM 107.7 (Ctry) 1560 Fairfield Rd PO Box 3179 *TF:* 800-366-9489 ■ *Web:* www.wgty.com	Gettysburg	PA	17325	717-334-3101	334-5822
WGY-AM 810 (N/T) 1203 Troy-Schenectady Rd Ste 201 Riverhill Ctr *TF:* 800-825-5949 ■ *Web:* www.wgy.com	Latham	NY	12110	518-452-4800	452-4813
WHB-AM 810 (Sports) 6721 W 121st St *Web:* www.810whb.com	Overland Park	KS	66209	913-344-1500	344-1599
WHCC-FM 105.1 (Ctry) 304 State Rd 446 PO Box 7797 *Web:* www.whcc105.com	Bloomington	IN	47401	812-336-8000	336-7000
WHFS-AM 1580 (N/T) 4200 Parliament Pl Ste 300 *TF:* 888-432-1580 ■ *Web:* washington.cbslocal.com	Lanham	MD	20706	301-731-1580	
White River Broadcasting Station 3212 Washington St *Web:* www.wkkg.com	Columbus	IN	47203	812-372-4448	372-1061
WHLI-AM 1100 (Nost) 234 Airport Plz Ste 5 *Web:* www.whli.com	Farmingdale	NY	11735	631-770-4200	770-0101
WHQT-FM 105.1 (Urban) 2741 N 29th Ave **Fax Area Code:* 954 ■ *Web:* www.hot105fm.com	Hollywood	FL	33020	305-444-4404	847-3223*
WHRB-FM 95.3 (Var) 389 Harvard St *Web:* www.whrb.org	Cambridge	MA	02138	617-495-4818	
WHVR-AM 1280 (Ctry) 275 Radio Rd *Web:* thepeak985.com	Hanover	PA	17331	717-637-3831	637-9006
WHYI-FM 100.7 (CHR) 7601 Riviera Blvd *Web:* www.y100.com	Miramar	FL	33023	954-862-2000	862-4013
WICO-AM 1320 (N/T) 919 Ellegood St PO Box 909 *Web:* www.wicoam.com	Salisbury	MD	21801	410-219-3500	
WILK-AM 980 (N/T) 305 Hwy 315 *Web:* www.wilknewsradio.com	Pittston	PA	18640	570-883-9800	883-9851
WIOQ-FM 102.1 (CHR) 111 Presidential Blvd Ste 100 *TF:* 800-521-1021 ■ *Web:* www.q102.com	Bala Cynwyd	PA	19004	610-784-3333	
WISN-AM 1130 (N/T) 12100 W Howard Ave *Web:* www.newstalk1130.com	Greenfield	WI	53228	414-545-8900	546-9654
WJDA-AM 1300 (N/T) 90 Everett Ave *Web:* www.wjda1300am.com	Chelsea	MA	02150	617-884-4500	
WJIB-AM 740 (AC) 443 Concord Ave *Web:* wjib.org	Cambridge	MA	02138	617-868-7400	
WJKK-FM 98.7 (AC) 265 Highpoint Dr *Web:* www.mix987.com	Ridgeland	MS	39157	601-956-0102	978-3980
WJMH-FM 102.1 (Urban) 7819 National Service Rd Ste 401 *Web:* www.102jamz.com	Greensboro	NC	27409	336-605-5200	605-5221
WJMI-FM 99.7 (Urban) 731 S Pear OrchaRd Rd Ste 27 *Web:* www.wjmi.com	Ridgeland	MS	39157	601-957-1300	956-0516
WJMN-FM 94.5 (Urban) 10 Cabot Rd Ste 302 *Web:* www.jamn945.com	Medford	MA	02155	781-663-2500	290-0722
WJOY-AM 1230 (Nost) 70 Joy Dr *Web:* www.wjoy.com	South Burlington	VT	05403	802-658-1230	862-0786
WJPT-FM 106.3 (Nost) 20125 S Tamiami Trl *Web:* sunny1063.com/	Estero	FL	33928	239-495-2100	
WJQK-FM 99.3 (Rel) 425 Centerstone Ct *TF:* 866-931-9936 ■ *Web:* www.jq99.com	Zeeland	MI	49464	616-931-9930	931-1280
WJRR-FM 101.1 (Alt) 2500 Maitland Ctr Pkwy Ste 401 *Web:* www.wjrr.com	Maitland	FL	32751	407-916-7800	916-7406
WJYY-FM 105.5 (CHR) *NH1 Media Center* 4 Church St NH1 Media Ctr *Web:* wjyy.nh1media.com	Concord	NH	03301	603-230-9000	228-2030
WKAR-AM 870 (NPR) Michigan State University 283 Communications Arts & Sciences Bldg *Web:* www.wkar.org	East Lansing	MI	48824	517-432-9527	353-7124
WKAR-FM 90.5 (NPR) Michigan State University 283 Comm Arts & Sciences Bldg *Web:* www.wkar.org	East Lansing	MI	48824	517-432-9527	
WKCI-FM 101.3 (CHR) 495 Benham St *Web:* www.kc101.com	Hamden	CT	06514	203-281-9600	281-2795
WKCQ-FM 98.1 (Ctry) 2000 Whittier St *TF:* 800-262-0098 ■ *Web:* www.98fmkcq.com	Saginaw	MI	48601	989-752-8161	752-8102
WKDD-FM 98.1 (AC) 7755 Freedom Ave *TF:* 888-533-4582 ■ *Web:* www.wkdd.com	North Canton	OH	44720	330-836-4700	836-5321
WKGM-AM 940 (Rel) 13379 Great Spring Rd *Web:* reverbnation.com	Smithfield	VA	23430	757-357-9546	365-0412
WKKV-FM 100.7 (Urban) 12100 W Howard Ave *Web:* www.v100.com	Greenfield	WI	53228	414-321-1007	546-9654
WKPT-AM 1400 (Nost) 222 Commerce St *Web:* www.wkptam.com	Kingsport	TN	37660	423-246-9578	247-9836
WKQI-FM 95.5 (CHR) 27675 Halsted Rd *Web:* www.channel955.com	Farmington Hills	MI	48331	248-324-5800	
WKRR-FM 92.3 (CR) 192 E Lewis St *TF:* 800-762-5923 ■ *Web:* www.rock92.com	Greensboro	NC	27406	336-274-8042	274-5745
WKRZ-FM 98.5 (CHR) 305 Hwy 315 *Web:* www.985krz.com	Pittston	PA	18640	570-883-9850	883-9851
WKSE-FM 98.5 (CHR) 500 Corporate Pkwy Ste 200 *Web:* www.kiss985.com	Amherst	NY	14226	716-843-0600	832-3080
WKSU-FM 89.7 (NPR) 1613 E Summit St *TF:* 800-672-2132 ■ *Web:* www.wksu.org	Kent	OH	44242	330-672-3114	672-4107
WKTO-FM 88.9 (Rel) 900 Old Mission Rd *Web:* wkto.net	New Smyrna Beach	FL	32168	386-427-1095	
WKVV-FM 101.7 PO Box 2098 *TF:* 800-525-5683 ■ *Web:* www.klove.com	Omaha	NE	68103	800-525-5683	
WKZL-FM 107.5 (CHR) 192 E Lewis St *TF:* 800-682-1075 ■ *Web:* www.1075kzl.com	Greensboro	NC	27406	336-274-8042	274-5745
WKZW-FM 94.3 (AC) 4580 Hwy 15 N PO Box 6408 *Web:* www.kz94.com	Laurel	MS	39441	601-649-0095	649-8199
WLIF-FM 101.9 (AC) 1423 Clarkview Rd Ste 100 *Web:* todays1019.cbslocal.com/	Baltimore	MD	21209	410-825-1000	
WLLL-AM 930 (Rel) PO Box 11375 *TF Cust Svc:* 888-224-9809 ■ *Web:* www.wlllradio.com	Lynchburg	VA	24506	434-385-9555	385-6073
WLUM-FM 102.1 (Rock) N 72 W 12922 Good Hope Rd *Web:* www.fm1021milwaukee.com	Menomonee Falls	WI	53051	414-771-1021	771-3036
WLXC-FM 98.5 (Urban) 1801 Charleston Hwy Ste J *Web:* www.kiss-1031.com	Cayce	SC	29033	803-796-7600	
WLZX-FM 99.3 (Rock) 45 Fisher Ave *Web:* www.lazer993.com	East Longmeadow	MA	01028	413-525-4141	525-4334
WMAG-FM 99.5 (AC) 2-B PAI Pk *TF:* 866-415-4158 ■ *Web:* www.995wmag.com	Greensboro	NC	27409	336-822-2000	
WMBR-FM 88.1 (Var) Three Ames St *Web:* www.wmbr.org	Cambridge	MA	02142	617-253-4000	
WMBS-AM 590 (Oldies) 44 S Mt Vernon Ave *Web:* www.wmbs590.com	Uniontown	PA	15401	724-438-3900	438-2406
WMGC-FM 105.1 (AC) One Radio Plz *Web:* www.detroitsports1051.com	Ferndale	MI	48220	248-414-5600	542-8800
WMGE-FM 94.9 (Span CHR) 7601 Riviera Blvd *TF:* 877-599-2946 ■ *Web:* www.mega949.com	Miramar	FL	33023	954-862-2000	862-4015
WMGF-FM 107.7 (AC) 2500 Maitland Ctr Pkwy Ste 401 *Web:* www.magic107.com	Maitland	FL	32751	407-916-7800	916-7406
WMGK-FM 102.9 (CR) One Bala Plz Ste 339 *Web:* www.wmgk.com	Bala Cynwyd	PA	19004	610-667-8500	664-9610
WMGM-FM 103.7 (CR) 1601 New Rd *Web:* www.1037wmgm.com	Linwood	NJ	08221	609-653-1400	601-0450
WMID-AM 1340 (Nost) 8025 Black Horse Pk Ste 100 *Web:* www.classicoldieswmid.com	West Atlantic City	NJ	08232	609-484-8444	646-6331
WMIL-FM 106.1 (Ctry) 12100 W Howard Ave *Web:* www.fm106.com	Greenfield	WI	53228	414-545-8900	327-3200
WMIT-FM 106.9 (Rel) Three Porters Cove Rd *TF:* 800-330-9648 ■ *Web:* brb.org/	Asheville	NC	28805	828-285-8477	298-0117
WMJI-FM 105.7 (Oldies) 6200 Oak Tree Blvd Fourth Fl *Web:* www.wmji.com	Independence	OH	44131	216-520-2600	524-2600
WMMJ-FM 102.3 (Urban AC) 8515 Georgia Ave 9th Fl *Web:* mymajicdc.com	Silver Spring	MD	20910	301-306-1111	306-9540
WMMR-FM 93.3 (Rock) One Bala Plz Ste 424 *Web:* www.wmmr.com	Bala Cynwyd	PA	19004	610-771-0933	771-9610
WMPI-FM 105.3 (Ctry) 22 E McClain Ave *TF:* 800-441-1053 ■ *Web:* i1053country.com	Scottsburg	IN	47170	812-752-3688	752-2345
WMUM-FM 89.7 (NPR) 243 Carey Salem Rd *TF:* 800-222-4788 ■ *Web:* www.gpb.org/radio/stations/wmum	Cochran	GA	31014	478-301-5760	
WMXU-FM 106.1 (Urban) 200 Sixth St N Ste 205 *Web:* www.mymix1061.com	Columbus	MS	39701	662-327-1183	328-1122
WMYX-FM 99.1 (AC) 11800 W Grange Ave *Web:* www.991themix.com	Hales Corners	WI	53130	414-529-1250	529-2122
WMZQ-FM 98.7 (Ctry) 1801 Rockville Pk Fifth Fl *TF:* 800-505-0098 ■ *Web:* www.wmzq.com	Rockville	MD	20852	240-747-2700	

Phone *Fax*

WNCS-FM 104.7 (AAA) 169 River St. . . . . Montpelier VT 05602 802-223-2396 223-1520
Web: www.pointfm.com

WNCW-FM 88.7 (AAA) PO Box 804 . . . . . Spindale NC 28160 828-287-8000 287-8012
TF: 800-245-8870 ■ *Web:* www.wncw.org

WNIC-FM 100.3 (AC) 27675 Halsted Rd . . . . . Farmington Hills MI 48331 248-324-5800
Web: wnic.com/

WNIJ-FM 89.5 (NPR) 801 N First St . . . . . DeKalb IL 60115 815-753-9000 753-9938
Web: www.northernpublicradio.org

WNIU-FM 90.5 (Clas) 801 N First St. . . . . DeKalb IL 60115 815-753-9000 753-9938
Web: www.northernpublicradio.org

WNKU-FM 105.9 (Ctry)
301 Landrum Academic Ctr . . . . . Highland Heights KY 41099 859-572-6500
TF: 855-897-7897 ■ *Web:* www.wnku.org

WNOG-AM 1270 (N/T) 2824 Palm Beach Blvd. . . . . Fort Myers FL 33916 650-412-1910
Web: www.tunein.com/radio/WNOG-1270-s21511

WNOR-FM 98.7 (Rock)
870 Greenbrier Cir Ste 399. . . . . Chesapeake VA 23320 757-366-9900 366-0022
Web: www.fm99.com

WNSN-FM 101.5 (AC) 1301 E Douglas Rd . . . . . Mishawaka IN 46545 574-233-3141 239-4231
Web: www.sunny1015.com

WNST-AM 1570 (Sports) 1550 Hart Rd. . . . . Towson MD 21286 410-821-9678 828-4698
Web: www.wnst.net

WNUE-FM 98.1 (Span)
523 Douglas Ave. . . . . Altamonte Springs FL 32714 407-774-2626
Web: www.salsa981.com

WNWV-FM 107.3 (NAC)
6133 Rockside Rd Ste 102 . . . . . Independence OH 44131 216-828-1073
Web: 1073thewave.net

WODE-FM 99.9 107 Paxinosa Rd W. . . . . Easton PA 18040 610-258-6155 253-3384
TF: 800-733-2767 ■ *Web:* www.999thehawk.com

WOGG-FM 94.9 (Ctry) 123 Blaine Rd . . . . . Brownsville PA 15417 724-938-2000
TF: 866-983-9898 ■ *Web:* www.froggyland.com

WOGH-FM 103.5 (Ctry) 320 Market St . . . . . Steubenville OH 43952 740-283-4747 283-3655
Web: www.froggyland.com

WOGL-FM 98.1 (Oldies)
Two Bala Plz Ste 800 . . . . . Bala Cynwyd PA 19004 610-668-5998 668-5977
TF: 800-942-8998 ■ *Web:* wogl.cbslocal.com

WOKO-FM 98.9 (Ctry) 70 Joy Dr. . . . . South Burlington VT 05403 802-862-9890 862-0786
TF: 800-354-9890 ■ *Web:* www.woko.com

WOKQ-FM 97.5 (Ctry) 292 Middle Rd PO Box 576. . . . . Dover NH 03821 603-749-9750 749-1459
Web: www.wokq.com

WOKY-AM 920 (Oldies) 12100 W Howard Ave . . . . . Greenfield WI 53228 414-545-8900 546-9654
Web: www.thebig920.com

WOLC-FM 102.5 (Rel)
11890 Crisfield Ln PO Box 130 . . . . . Princess Anne MD 21853 410-543-9652 651-9652

WOLZ-FM 95.3 (AC) 13320 Metro Pkwy Ste 1. . . . . Fort Myers FL 33966 239-225-4300 225-4410
Web: www.953theriver.com

WOMC-FM 104.3 (Oldies)
2201 Woodward Heights. . . . . Ferndale MI 48220 248-327-2900 546-5446
Web: womc.cbslocal.com

Woodward Communications Inc 801 Bluff St . . . . . Dubuque IA 52001 800-553-4801 588-5739*
**Fax Area Code:* 563 ■ *TF:* 800-553-4801 ■ *Web:* www.wcinet.com

WOSM-FM 103.1 (Rel) 4720 Radio Rd. . . . . Ocean Springs MS 39564 228-432-1032 875-6461

WPCV-FM 97.5 (Ctry) 404 W Lime St. . . . . Lakeland FL 33815 863-682-8184 683-2409
TF: 800-227-9797 ■ *Web:* www.wpcv.com

WPGC-FM 95.5 (CHR) 4200 Parliament Pl Ste 300. . . . . Lanham MD 20706 877-955-5267 383-9497*
**Fax Area Code:* 646 ■ *TF:* 877-955-5267 ■ *Web:* wpgc.cbslocal.com

WPHI-FM 107.9 (Urban)
2 Bala Plaza Ste 700. . . . . Bala Cynwyd PA 19004 610-538-1100
Web: boomphilly.com

WPHT-AM 1210 (N/T) Two Bala Plz Ste 800 . . . . . Bala Cynwyd PA 19004 610-668-5800 668-5885
Web: philadelphia.cbslocal.com

WPLK-AM 800 (Nost) 1428 St Johns Ave . . . . . Palatka FL 32177 386-325-5800 328-8725
Web: www.wplk.com

WPLM-FM 99.1 (AC) 17 Columbus Rd . . . . . Plymouth MA 02360 508-746-1390 830-1128
TF: 877-327-9991 ■ *Web:* www.easy991.com

WPLR-FM 99.1 (Rock)
440 Wheelers Farm Rd Ste 302 . . . . . Milford CT 06461 203-783-8200 783-8399
Web: wplr.com

WPOR-FM 101.9 (Ctry) 420 Western Ave. . . . . South Portland ME 04106 207-774-4561 774-3788
Web: www.wpor.com

WPRO-FM 92.3 (CHR)
1502 Wampanoag Trl . . . . . East Providence RI 02915 401-433-4200
TF: 800-638-0092 ■ *Web:* www.92profm.com

WPST-FM 94.5 (AC) 619 Alexander Rd 3rd Fl. . . . . Princeton NJ 08540 609-419-0300 419-0143
TF: 800-248-9778 ■ *Web:* www.wpst.com

WPUR-FM 107.3 (Ctry) 950 Tilton Rd Ste 200. . . . . Northfield NJ 08225 609-645-9797 272-9228
Web: www.catcountry1073.com

WPWX-FM 92.3 (Urban) 6336 Calumet Ave. . . . . Hammond IN 46324 773-734-4455 933-0323*
**Fax Area Code:* 219 ■ *Web:* www.power92chicago.com

WQBK-FM 103.9 (Rock) 1241 Kings Rd. . . . . Schenectady NY 12303 518-881-1515 881-1516
Web: q103albany.com

WQCB-FM 106.5 (Ctry) 49 Acme Rd PO Box 100. . . . . Brewer ME 04412 207-989-5631 989-5685
Web: q1065.fm

WQFL-FM 100.9 (Rel) PO Box 2118. . . . . Omaha NE 68103 888-937-2471
TF: 888-937-2471 ■ *Web:* www.air1.com

WQLZ-FM 92.7 (Rock) PO Box 460. . . . . Springfield IL 62561 217-629-7077 629-7952
Web: www.wqlz.com

WQTX-FM 92.1 (Oldies) 2495 Cedar St . . . . . Holt MI 48842 517-699-0111 699-1880
Web: www.big921.com

WQUN-AM 1220 (Nost) 3085 Whitney Ave . . . . . Hamden CT 06518 203-582-8984 582-5372
TF: 800-462-1944 ■ *Web:* www.quinnipiac.edu

WRBR-FM 103.9 (Rock) 237 W Edison Rd. . . . . Mishawaka IN 46545 574-258-5483 258-0930
Web: www.wrbr.com

WRCH-FM 100.5 (AC) 10 Executive Dr . . . . . Farmington CT 06032 860-677-6700
TF: 800-530-1005 ■ *Web:* wrch.cbslocal.com

WRDW-FM 96.5 (Urban)
555 City Line Ave Ste 330 . . . . . Bala Cynwyd PA 19004 610-667-9000
TF: 866-811-4111 ■ *Web:* www.wired965.com

WRDX-FM 92.9 (CR) 920 W Basin Rd Ste 400 . . . . . New Castle DE 19720 302-395-9800 395-9808
Web: www.iheart.com

Phone *Fax*

WRFQ-FM 104.5 (CR)
950 Houston Northcutt Blvd 2nd Fl . . . . . Mount Pleasant SC 29464 843-884-2534 884-1218
Web: www.q1045.com

WRIT-FM 95.7 (CR) 12100 W Howard Ave . . . . . Greenfield WI 53228 414-545-8900 546-9654
Web: www.milwaukeeoldies.com

WRKO-AM 680 (N/T) 20 Guest St Third Fl. . . . . Brighton MA 02135 617-779-3400 779-5447
TF: 877-469-4322 ■ *Web:* www.wrko.com

WROW-AM 6 Johnson Rd . . . . . Latham NY 12110 518-786-6600
Web: www.albanymagic.com

WROW-AM 590 (N/T) Six Johnson Rd. . . . . Latham NY 12110 518-786-6600 786-6610
Web: albanymagic.com

WRVE-FM 99.5 (AC)
1203 Troy-Schenectady Rd Riverhill Ctr
Ste 201. . . . . Latham NY 12110 518-452-4800 452-4855
TF: 800-995-9783 ■ *Web:* www.995theriver.com

WRVM-FM 102.7 (Rel) PO Box 212. . . . . Suring WI 54174 920-842-2900
TF: 888-225-9786 ■ *Web:* www.wrvmradio.org/pages/?p=3

WRZK-FM 95.9 (Alt) 222 Commerce St. . . . . Kingsport TN 37660 423-246-9578 247-9836
Web: www.wrzk.com

WSAN-AM 1470 (Sports) 1541 Alta Dr Ste 400 . . . . . Whitehall PA 18052 610-434-1742 434-6288
Web: www.fox1470.com

WSBY-FM 98.9 (Urban AC) 351 Tilghman Rd . . . . . Salisbury MD 21804 410-742-1923 742-2329
Web: www.mymagic989.com

WSCI-FM 89.3 (NPR) 1101 George Rogers Blvd. . . . . Columbia SC 29201 803-737-3545 737-3552
Web: www.scetv.org

WSEN-FM 92.1 (CR)
8456 Smokey Hollow Rd PO Box 1050. . . . . Baldwinsville NY 13027 315-635-3971 635-3490
TF: 866-890-6453 ■ *Web:* www.wsenfm.com

WSGL-FM 104.7 (AC) 10915 K-Nine Dr . . . . . Bonita Springs FL 34135 239-495-8383 495-0883
Web: www.1047mixfm.com

WSHU-FM 91.1 (NPR) 5151 Pk Ave. . . . . Fairfield CT 06825 203-365-0425
TF: 800-937-6045 ■ *Web:* www.wshu.org

WSIC-AM 1400 (N/T) 1117 Radio Rd. . . . . Statesville NC 28677 704-872-6345 873-6921
Web: www.wsicweb.com

WSMK-FM 99.1 (Urban) 925 N Fifth St . . . . . Niles MI 49120 269-683-4343 683-7759
Web: www.wsmkradio.com

WSRS-FM 96.1 (AC) 96 Stereo Ln. . . . . Paxton MA 01612 508-757-9696 757-1779
Web: www.wsrs.com

WTAG-AM 580 (N/T) 96 Stereo Ln. . . . . Paxton MA 01612 508-795-0580 757-1779
Web: www.wtag.com

WTAK-FM 106.1 (CR) 26869 Peoples Rd . . . . . Madison AL 35756 256-309-2410 350-2653
Web: www.wtak.com

WTAM-AM 1100 (N/T)
6200 Oak Tree Blvd Fourth Fl . . . . . Independence OH 44131 216-520-2600 524-2600
Web: www.wtam.com

WTFM-FM 98.5 (AC) 222 Commerce St . . . . . Kingsport TN 37660 423-246-9578 247-9836
TF: 888-633-5452 ■ *Web:* www.wtfm.com

WTIC-AM 1080 (N/T) 10 Executive Dr . . . . . Farmington CT 06032 860-677-6700 284-9842
Web: connecticut.cbslocal.com

WTIX-FM 94.3 (Oldies)
4539 N I-10 Service Rd Third Fl. . . . . Metairie LA 70006 504-454-9000 454-9002
Web: www.wtixfm.com

WTLN-AM 950 (Rel) 1188 Lakeview Dr . . . . . Altamonte Springs FL 32714 407-682-9494 682-7005
Web: www.wtln.com

WTMD-FM 89.7 (AAA)
8000 York Rd Towson University . . . . . Towson MD 21252 410-704-8938
Web: wwwnew.towson.edu

WTPL-FM 107.7 (N/T) 501 S St Third Fl. . . . . Bow NH 03304 603-545-0777 545-0781
Web: www.wtplfm.com

WTRY-FM 98.3 (Oldies)
1203 Troy-Schenectady Rd
Ste 201 Riverhill Ctr . . . . . Latham NY 12110 518-452-4884 452-4855
Web: www.oldies983.com

WTSR-FM 91.3 (Alt)
College of New Jersey Kendall Hall PO Box 7718. . . . . Ewing NJ 08628 609-771-3200
Web: www.wtsr.org

WTSS-FM 102.5 (AC) 500 Corporate Pkwy Ste 200 . . . . . Amherst NY 14226 716-843-0600 832-3080
Web: www.mystar1025.com

WTSU-FM 89.9 (NPR) Troy University Wallace Hall. . . . . Troy AL 36082 800-800-6616 670-3934*
**Fax Area Code:* 334 ■ *TF:* 800-800-6616 ■ *Web:* www.troypublicradio.org

WTTH-FM 96.1 (Urban)
8025 Black Horse Pike Ste 100. . . . . West Atlantic City NJ 08232 609-484-8444 646-6331
Web: www.961wtth.com

WTTS-FM 92.3 (AAA) 400 One City Centre. . . . . Bloomington IN 47404 812-332-3366 331-4570
TF: 800-923-9887 ■ *Web:* www.wttsfm.com

WUFM-FM 88.7 (Rel) 116 County Line Rd W. . . . . Westerville OH 43082 877-272-3468 839-1329*
**Fax Area Code:* 614 ■ *Web:* www.radiou.com

WUMP-AM 730 (Sports)
3280 Peachtree Rd Ste 2300. . . . . Atlanta GA 30305 256-830-8300 232-6842
TF: 866-485-9867 ■ *Web:* www.730ump.com

WUNC-FM 91.5 (NPR)
120 Friday Center Dr PO Box 0915. . . . . Chapel Hill NC 27517 919-445-9150
TF: 800-962-9862 ■ *Web:* www.wunc.org

WUSJ-FM 96.3 (Ctry) 265 Highpoint Dr. . . . . Ridgeland MS 39157 601-956-0102 978-3980
Web: www.us963.com

WUSL-FM 99 (Urban)
111 Presidential Blvd Ste 100. . . . . Bala Cynwyd PA 19004 610-784-3333 784-2075
Web: www.power99.com

WVFJ-FM 93.3 (Rel) 1175 Senoia Rd . . . . . Tyrone GA 30290 770-487-4500
Web: georgia.thejoyfm.com

WVPE-FM 88.1 (NPR) 2424 California Rd. . . . . Elkhart IN 46514 574-262-5660 262-5700
TF: 888-399-9873 ■ *Web:* www.wvpe.org

WVPS-FM 107.9 (NPR) 365 Troy Ave . . . . . Colchester VT 05446 802-655-9451 655-2799
TF: 800-639-2192 ■ *Web:* www.vpr.net

WWBN-FM 101.5 (Rock) 3338 E Bristol Rd . . . . . Burton MI 48529 810-743-1080 742-5170
Web: banana1015.com

WWDC-FM 101.1 (Rock)
1801 Rockville Pk Fifth Fl. . . . . Rockville MD 20852 240-747-2701
TF: 866-913-2101 ■ *Web:* www.dc101.com

WWDE-FM 101.3 (AC)
236 Clearfield Ave Ste 206 . . . . . Virginia Beach VA 23462 757-497-2000 456-5458
Web: 2wd.com/

Station	City	State	Zip	Phone	Fax
WWFG-FM 99.9 (Ctry) 351 Tilghman Rd *TF:* 800-664-3764 ■ *Web:* www.froggy999.com/main.html	Salisbury	MD	21804	410-742-1923	742-2329
WWGR-FM 101.9 (Ctry) 10915 K-Nine Dr *TF:* 877-787-1019 ■ *Web:* www.gatorcountry1019.com	Bonita Springs	FL	34135	239-495-8383	495-0883
WWKA-FM 92.3 (Ctry) 4192 N John Young Pkwy *TF:* 866-438-0220 ■ *Web:* www.k923orlando.com	Orlando	FL	32804	407-298-9292	299-4947
WWKX-FM 106.3 (Urban) 1502 Wampanoag Trail *Web:* www.hot1063.com	East Providence	RI	02914	401-433-4200	
WWLI-FM 105.1 (AC) 1502 Wampanoag Trl *Web:* www.literock105fm.com	East Providence	RI	02915	401-433-4200	433-5967
WWMJ-FM 95.7 (CR) 49 Acme Rd PO Box 100 *Web:* i95rocks.com	Brewer	ME	04412	207-989-5631	989-5685
WWRV-AM 1330 (Span Rel) 419 Broadway *Web:* www.radiovision.net	Paterson	NJ	07501	973-881-8700	881-8324
WWTC-AM 1280 (N/T) 2110 Cliff Rd *Web:* www.am1280thepatriot.com	Eagan	MN	55122	651-405-8800	405-8222
WWUS-FM 104.1 (CR) 30336 Overseas Hwy *Web:* www.us1radio.com	Big Pine Key	FL	33043	305-872-9100	872-1603
WWWS-AM 1400 (Urban) 500 Corporate Pkwy Ste 200 *Web:* www.am1400solidgoldsoul.com	Amherst	NY	14226	716-843-0600	832-3080
WXBM-FM 102.7 (Ctry) 6085 Quintette Rd *TF:* 844-962-7436 ■ *Web:* www.wxbm.com	Pace	FL	32571	850-994-5357	478-3971
WXCY-FM 103.7 (Ctry) 707 Revolution St *Web:* www.wxcyfm.com	Havre de Grace	MD	21078	410-939-1100	939-1104
WXKB-FM 103.9 (CHR) 20125 S Tamiami Trl *Web:* www.b1039.com	Estero	FL	33928	239-495-2100	
WXKS-FM 107.9 (CHR) 10 Cabot Rd Ste 302 *Web:* www.kiss108.com	Medford	MA	02155	781-396-1430	290-0722
WXLY-FM 102.5 (Oldies) 950 Houston Northcutt Blvd Ste 201 *Web:* www.y1025.com	Mount Pleasant	SC	29464	843-884-2534	884-1218
WXRL-AM 1300 (Ctry) PO Box 170 PO Box 170 *Web:* www.wxrl.com	Lancaster	NY	14086	716-681-1313	681-7172
WXRR-FM 104.5 (Rock) 4580 Hwy 15 N *Web:* www.rock104fm.com	Laurel	MS	39443	601-649-0095	649-8199
WXRV-FM 92.5 (AAA) 30 How St *Web:* theriverboston.com	Haverhill	MA	01830	978-374-4733	373-8023
WXSS-FM 103.7 (CHR) 11800 W Grange Ave *Web:* www.1037kissfm.com	Hales Corners	WI	53130	414-529-1250	529-2122
WXTU-FM 92.5 (Ctry) 555 E City Ave Ste 330 *Web:* 925xtu.com/	Bala Cynwyd	PA	19004	610-667-9000	667-5978
WXXX-FM 95.5 (CHR) 118 Malletts Bay Ave *Web:* www.95triplex.com	Colchester	VT	05446	802-655-9550	655-1329
WYCB-AM 1340 (Rel) 8515 Georgia Ave Ninth Fl *Web:* myspiritdc.com	Silver Spring	MD	20910	301-306-1111	306-9540
WYCR-FM 98.5 (AC) 275 Radio Rd *Web:* thepeak985.com	Hanover	PA	17331	717-637-3831	637-9006
WYCS-FM 91.5 (Rel) 7330 George Washington Memorial Hwy Bldg J	Yorktown	VA	23692	757-886-7490	
WYGM-AM 740 (Span) 2500 Maitland Ctr Pkwy Ste 401 *TF:* 800-729-8255 ■ *Web:* www.740thegame.com	Maitland	FL	32751	407-916-7800	916-7406
WYJB-FM 95.5 (AC) Six Johnson Rd *Web:* www.b95.com	Latham	NY	12110	518-786-6600	786-6610
WYNZ-FM 100.9 (Oldies) 420 Western Ave *Web:* rewind1009.com	South Portland	ME	04106	207-774-4561	774-3788
WYUS-AM 930 (Span) 1666 Blairs Pond Rd *Web:* laexitosa.com	Milford	DE	19963	302-422-7575	422-3069
WZBA-FM 100.7 (CR) 11350 McCormick Rd Executive Plz 3 Ste 701	Hunt Valley	MD	21031	410-229-0105	771-1616
WZBC-FM 90.3 (Var) Boston College 107 McElroy Commons *Web:* www.wzbc.org	Chestnut Hill	MA	02467	617-552-3511	552-1738
WZBT-FM 91.1 (Alt) 300 N Washington St Gettysburg College *Web:* www.gettysburg.edu	Gettysburg	PA	17325	717-337-6300	
WZLX-FM 100.7 (CR) 83 Leo Birmingham Pkwy *Web:* wzlx.cbslocal.com	Brighton	MA	02135	617-746-5100	
WZMX-FM 93.7 (Urban) 10 Executive Dr *Web:* hot937.cbslocal.com	Farmington	CT	06032	860-677-6700	
WZXL-FM 100.7 (Rock) 8025 Black Horse Pk Ste 100 *Web:* www.wzxl.com	West Atlantic City	NJ	08232	609-484-8444	646-6331
WZZO-FM 95.1 (Rock) 1541 Alta Dr Ste 400 *Web:* www.951zzo.com	Whitehall	PA	18052	610-434-1742	434-6288
XLTN-FM 104.5 (Span AC) 2403 Hoover Ave *Web:* wp.1045radiolatina.com	National City	CA	91950	619-336-7800	420-1092
your network of praise PO Box 2426 *Web:* www.ynop.org	Havre	MT	59501	406-949-4308	265-8860

648-1 Abilene, TX

Station	City	State	Zip	Phone	Fax
KACU-FM 89.7 (NPR) 1925 Campus Ct *Web:* www.kacu.org	Abilene	TX	79699	325-674-2441	674-2417
KBCY-FM 99.7 (Ctry) 2525 S Danville Dr *Web:* www.kbcy.com	Abilene	TX	79605	325-793-9700	692-1576
KEAN-FM 105.1 (Ctry) 3911 S First St *TF:* 800-588-5326 ■ *Web:* www.keanradio.com	Abilene	TX	79605	325-676-5326	676-3851
KFGL-FM 100.7 (Oldies) 3911 S First St *Web:* koolfmabilene.com	Abilene	TX	79605	325-676-5100	676-3851
KGNZ-FM 88.1 (Rel) 542 Butternut St *TF:* 800-588-8801 ■ *Web:* www.kgnz.com	Abilene	TX	79602	325-673-3045	672-7938
KKHR-FM 106.3 (Span) 402 Cypress St *Web:* www.radioabilene.com	Abilene	TX	79601	325-672-5442	
KULL-FM 92.5 (Oldies) 3911 S First St *Web:* mix925abilene.com	Abilene	TX	79605	325-676-7711	676-3851

648-2 Akron, OH

Station	City	State	Zip	Phone	Fax
WAKR-AM 1590 (N/T) 1795 W Market St **Fax Area Code: 888* ■ *TF:* 888-723-9688 ■ *Web:* www.akronnewsnow.com	Akron	OH	44313	330-869-9800	826-0573*
WAPS-FM 91.3 (AAA) 65 Steiner Ave *TF:* 877-411-3662 ■ *Web:* www.913thesummit.com	Akron	OH	44301	330-761-3099	761-3103
WNIR-FM 100.1 (N/T) PO Box 2170 *Web:* www.wnir.com	Akron	OH	44309	330-673-2323	673-0301
WONE-FM 97.5 (Rock) 1795 W Market St *TF:* 888-588-8436 ■ *Web:* www.wone.net	Akron	OH	44313	330-869-9800	869-9750
WQMX-FM 94.9 1795 W Market St *TF:* 800-589-6499 ■ *Web:* www.wqmx.com	Akron	OH	44313	330-869-9800	864-6799
WZIP-FM 88.1 (Rock) 302 Buchtel Common *Web:* www.wzip.fm	Akron	OH	44325	330-972-7105	

648-3 Albany, NY

Station	City	State	Zip	Phone	Fax
WAMC-FM 90.3 (NPR) 318 Central Ave *TF:* 800-323-9262 ■ *Web:* www.wamc.org	Albany	NY	12206	518-465-5233	432-6974

648-4 Albuquerque, NM

Station	City	State	Zip	Phone	Fax
KANW-FM 89.1 (NPR) 2020 Coal Ave SE *Web:* www.kanw.com	Albuquerque	NM	87106	505-242-7163	
KHFM 95.5 4125 Carlisle Blvd NE	Albuquerque	NM	87107	505-878-0980	878-0098
KHFM-FM 95.5 (Clas) 4125 Carlisle Blvd NE *Web:* www.classicalkhfm.com	Albuquerque	NM	87107	505-878-0980	
KKSS-FM 97.3 (CHR) 8009 Marble Ave NE *Web:* www.mykiss973.com	Albuquerque	NM	87110	505-254-7110	254-7108
KMGA-FM 99.5 (AC) 500 Fourth St NW 5th Fl *Web:* www.995magicfm.com	Albuquerque	NM	87102	505-767-6700	767-9199
KNML-AM 610 (Sports) 500 Fourth St NW Fifth Fl *TF:* 888-922-0610 ■ *Web:* www.610thesportsanimal.com	Albuquerque	NM	87102	505-767-6700	767-6711
KUNM-FM 89.9 (NPR) 1University of New Mexico MSC 06 3520 *TF:* 877-277-4806 ■ *Web:* www.kunm.org	Albuquerque	NM	87131	505-277-4806	277-6393

648-5 Amarillo, TX

Station	City	State	Zip	Phone	Fax
KACV-FM 90 (Alt) PO Box 447 *TF:* 800-766-0176 ■ *Web:* www.kacvfm.org	Amarillo	TX	79178	800-766-0176	
KATP-FM 101.9 (Ctry) 6214 W 34th St *Web:* blakefm.com/help	Amarillo	TX	79109	806-355-9777	355-5832
KGNC-AM 710 (N/T) 3505 Olsen Blvd Ste 117 *TF:* 800-285-0710 ■ *Web:* www.kgncam.com	Amarillo	TX	79109	806-355-9801	354-8779
KGNC-FM 97.9 (Ctry) 3505 Olsen Blvd Ste 117 *TF:* 877-765-9790 ■ *Web:* www.kgncfm.com	Amarillo	TX	79109	806-355-9801	354-8779
KISS FM 96.9 6214 W 34th St *Web:* kissfm969.com	Amarillo	TX	79109	806-355-9777	355-5832
KMXJ-FM 94.1 (AC) 6214 W 34th St *Web:* www.mix941kmxj.com	Amarillo	TX	79109	806-355-9777	355-5832
KPRF-FM 98.7 (CHR) 6214 W 34th St *TF:* 866-930-5225 ■ *Web:* 987jackfm.com	Amarillo	TX	79109	806-355-9777	
KZRK-FM 107.9 (Rock) 301 S Polk St Ste 100 *Web:* www.amarillosrockstation.com	Amarillo	TX	79101	806-342-5200	342-5202

648-6 Anchorage, AK

Station	City	State	Zip	Phone	Fax
KASH-FM 107.5 (Ctry) 800 E Dimond Blvd Ste 3-370 *Web:* www.kashcountry1075.com	Anchorage	AK	99515	907-522-1515	743-5186
KATB-FM 89.3 (Rel) 6401 E Northern Lights Blvd *Web:* www.katb.org	Anchorage	AK	99504	907-333-5282	337-0003
KBBO-FM 92.1 (AC) 833 Gambell St *Web:* www.921bob.fm	Anchorage	AK	99501	907-344-4045	522-6053
KBFX-FM 100.5 (CR) 800 E Dimond Blvd Ste 3-370 *Web:* www.1005thefox.com	Anchorage	AK	99515	907-522-1515	743-5186
KBRJ-FM 104.1 (Ctry) 301 Arctic Slope Ave Ste 200 *Web:* www.kbrj.com	Anchorage	AK	99518	907-344-9622	349-3299
KEAG-FM 97.3 301 Arctic Slope Ave Ste 200 *Web:* www.kool973.com	Anchorage	AK	99518	907-344-9622	349-3299
KENI-AM 650 (N/T) 800 E Dimond Blvd Ste 3-370 *Web:* www.650keni.com	Anchorage	AK	99515	907-522-1515	743-5186
KFAT-FM 92.9 (Urban) 833 Gambell *Web:* 929kfat.com	Anchorage	AK	99501	907-344-4045	522-6053
KGOT-FM 101.3 (CHR) 800 E Dimond Blvd Ste 3-370 *Web:* www.kgot.com	Anchorage	AK	99515	907-522-1515	

	City	State	ZIP	Phone	Fax
KMXS-FM 103.1 (AC) 301 Arctic Slope Ave *Web:* www.kmxs.com	Anchorage	AK	99518	907-344-9622	344-1276
KNBA-FM 90.3 (NPR) 3600 San Geronimo Dr Ste 480 *TF:* 888-278-5622 ■ *Web:* www.knba.org	Anchorage	AK	99508	907-793-3500	793-3536
KSKA-FM 91.1 (NPR) 3877 University Dr *Web:* www.alaskapublic.org	Anchorage	AK	99508	907-550-8400	550-8403
KWHL-FM 106.5 (Rock) 301 Arctic Slope Ave *Web:* www.kwhl.com	Anchorage	AK	99518	907-344-9622	344-0742
KXLW-FM 96.3 (Rock) 833 Gambell St *Web:* www.963thewolf.com	Anchorage	AK	99501	907-344-4045	522-6053
KYMG-FM 98.9 (AC) 800 E Dimond Blvd Ste 3-370 *TF:* 877-868-8857 ■ *Web:* www.magic989fm.com	Anchorage	AK	99515	907-522-1515	743-5186
New Northwest Broadcasters 833 Gambell St *Fax Area Code: 206	Anchorage	AK	99501	907-344-4045	204-0214*

648-7 Ann Arbor, MI

	City	State	ZIP	Phone	Fax
WCBN-FM 88.3 (Alt) University of Michigan 530 Student Activities Bldg *Web:* wcbn.org	Ann Arbor	MI	48109	734-763-3500	
WTKA-AM 1050 (N/T) 1100 Victors Way Ste 100 *Web:* www.wtka.com	Ann Arbor	MI	48108	734-302-8100	213-7508
WUOM-FM 91.7 (NPR) 535 W William St Ste 110 *TF:* 888-258-9866 ■ *Web:* www.michiganradio.org	Ann Arbor	MI	48103	734-764-9210	647-3488
WWWW-FM 102.9 (Ctry) 1100 Victors Way Ste 100 *Web:* www.w4country.com	Ann Arbor	MI	48108	734-302-8100	213-7508

648-8 Annapolis, MD

	City	State	ZIP	Phone	Fax
WRNR-FM 103.1 112 Main St 3rd Fl *TF:* 877-762-1031 ■ *Web:* www.wrnr.com	Annapolis	MD	21401	410-626-0103	267-7634

648-9 Asheville, NC

	City	State	ZIP	Phone	Fax
News Radio 570 WWNC 13 Summerlin Rd *Web:* www.880therevolution.com	Asheville	NC	28806	828-257-2700	255-7850
WCQS-FM 88.1 (NPR) 73 Broadway *TF:* 866-448-3881 ■ *Web:* www.wcqs.org	Asheville	NC	28801	828-210-4800	210-4801
WISE-AM 1310 (Sports) 1190 Patton Ave *Web:* espnasheville.com	Asheville	NC	28806	828-259-9695	253-5619
WKJV-AM 1380 70 Adams Hill Rd *TF:* 800-809-9558 ■ *Web:* www.wkjv.com	Asheville	NC	28806	828-252-1380	259-9427
WKSF-FM 99.9 (Ctry) 13 Summerlin Rd *TF:* 800-303-5477 ■ *Web:* www.99kisscountry.com	Asheville	NC	28806	828-257-2700	255-7850
WSKY-AM 1230 (Rel) 40 Westgate Pkwy Ste 2 *Web:* www.wilkinsradio.com	Asheville	NC	28806	828-251-2000	
WWNC-AM 570 (N/T) 13 Summerlin Rd *Web:* www.wwnc.com	Asheville	NC	28806	828-257-2700	255-7850

648-10 Atlanta, GA

	City	State	ZIP	Phone	Fax
89.9 & 90.5 PO Box 929 *Web:* www.wper.org	Blacksburg	VA	24063	540-347-4825	
American General Media Corp 1400 Easton Dr Ste 144 *Web:* www.americangeneralmedia.com	Bakersfield	CA	93309	661-328-1410	
Apex Broadcasting Inc 2294 Clements Ferry Rd *Web:* www.apexbroadcasting.com	Charleston	SC	29492	843-972-1100	
Autonet Mobile Inc 1700 Montgomery St Ste 111 *Web:* www.autonetmobile.com	San Francisco	CA	94111	415-223-0316	
Centennial Broadcasting LLC 6201 Town Ctr Dr Ste 210 *Web:* www.centennialbroadcasting.com	Clemmons	NC	27012	336-766-2828	
Chicago Public Radio 848 E Grand Ave *Web:* www.chicagopublicradio.org	Chicago	IL	60611	312-948-4600	
Clarke Broadcasting Corp 342 S Washington St *Web:* www.kzsqfm.com	Sonora	CA	95370	209-533-1450	
Community Broadcasters LLC 199 Wealtha Ave *Web:* www.commbroadcasters.com	Watertown	NY	13601	315-782-1240	
Computer Furniture Outlet 256 E Jericho Tpke *Web:* www.computer-furniture.com	Mineola	NY	11501	516-747-4938	
Delmarva Broadcasting Company Inc 2727 Shipley Rd *Web:* www.delmarvabroadcasting.com	Wilmington	DE	19810	302-478-2700	
Elyria-Lorain Broadcasting Co 538 Broad St Fourth Fl *Web:* www.elbc.net	Elyria	OH	44035	440-322-3761	
Federated Media 421 S Second St *Web:* www.federatedmedia.com	Elkhart	IN	46516	574-295-2500	
HomeTown Daily News 202 Courtney St *Web:* www.hometowndailynews.com	Branson	MO	65616	417-334-6003	
JMP Media LLC 331 Fulton St Ste 1200 *Web:* www.jmpmedia.com	Peoria	IL	61602	309-637-3700	
Kidd Kraddick in The Morning 220 Las Colinas Blvd E Ste 210 *Web:* www.kiddlive.com	Irving	TX	75039	972-432-9094	
KRCB FM 5850 Labath Ave *Web:* www.krcb.org	Rohnert Park	CA	94928	707-584-2020	
Krvn Transmitter 73744 M Rd *Web:* www.krvn.com	Holdrege	NE	68949	308-995-5541	
Life Radio Ministries Inc 100 S Hill St Ste 100 *Web:* www.wmvv.com	Griffin	GA	30223	770-229-2020	
Majic 107.5 101 Marietta St 12th Fl *Web:* majicatl.com	Atlanta	GA	30303	404-765-9750	688-7686
Majic ATL 107.5|97.5 101 Marietta St 12th Fl *Web:* www.majicatl.com	Atlanta	GA	30303	404-765-9750	688-7686
Meyer Communications Inc 3000 E Chestnut Expy *Web:* radiospringfield.com	Springfield	MO	65802	417-862-3751	
My Praise ATL 102.5 101 Marietta St 12th Fl *Web:* mypraiseatl.com	Atlanta	GA	30303	404-765-9750	688-7686
Myat Inc 360 Franklin Tpke *Web:* www.myat.com	Mahwah	NJ	07430	201-684-0100	
Power 106 Radio 2600 W Olive Ave Ste 800 *Web:* www.power106.com	Burbank	CA	91505	818-953-4200	
Rock 100.5 780 Johnson Ferry Rd NE 5th Fl *Web:* www.99x.com	Atlanta	GA	30342	404-497-4700	
Rockville Community School Corp Rockville Jr-Sr High School 506 N Beadle St *Web:* www.rockville.k12.in.us	Rockville	IN	47872	765-569-5686	
Signalfire Wireless Telemetry Inc 43 Broad St *Web:* www.signal-fire.com	Hudson	MA	01749	978-212-2868	
Summit Handling Systems Inc 11 Defco Park Rd *Web:* www.summithandling.com	North Haven	CT	06473	203-239-5351	
WABE-FM 90.1 (NPR) 740 Bismark Rd NE *Web:* www.wabe.org	Atlanta	GA	30324	678-686-0321	686-0356
WACG-FM 90.7 (NPR) 2500 Walton Way *TF:* 800-222-4788 ■ *Web:* www.gpb.org	Atlanta	GA	30904	706-737-1661	
WALR-FM 104.1 (AC) 1601 W Peachtree St NE *Web:* www.kiss104fm.com	Atlanta	GA	30309	404-897-7500	897-6495
WAOK-AM 1380 (N/T) 1201 Peachtree St NE Ste 800 *Web:* atlanta.cbslocal.com	Atlanta	GA	30361	404-898-8900	898-8909
WAY Media Inc 1860 Boy Scout Dr Ste 202 *Web:* www.wayfm.com	Fort Myers	FL	33907	239-936-1929	
WCLK-FM 91.9 (Jazz) 111 James P Brawley Dr SW *TF:* 888-448-3925 ■ *Web:* www.wclk.com	Atlanta	GA	30314	404-880-8273	880-8869
WFSH-FM 104.7 (Rel) 2970 Peachtree Rd NW Ste 700 *Web:* www.thefishatlanta.com	Atlanta	GA	30305	404-995-7300	816-0748
WGRC FM Radio 101 Armory Blvd *Web:* www.wgrc.com	Lewisburg	PA	17837	570-523-1190	
WGST-AM 640 (N/T) 1819 Peachtree Rd NE Ste 700 *Web:* www.640wgst.com	Atlanta	GA	30309	404-875-8080	367-1057
WHTA-FM 107.9 (Urban) 101 Marietta St 12th Fl *Web:* hotspotatl.com	Atlanta	GA	30303	404-765-9750	688-7686
Wilks Broadcast Group LLC 6470 E Johns Crossing Ste 450 *Web:* www.wilksbroadcastgroup.com	Duluth	GA	30097	678-240-8976	
WIMI WJMS 222 S Lawrence St *Web:* www.wimifm.com	Ironwood	MI	49938	906-932-2411	
WJLF 2925 Nw 39th Ave *Web:* www.thejoyfm.com	Gainesville	FL	32605	352-371-1457	
World Christian Broadcasting Corp 605 Bradley Ct *Web:* www.worldchristian.org	Franklin	TN	37067	615-371-8707	
WRAS *Georgia State University* 33 Gilmer St MSC 2A1220 *Web:* www2.gsu.edu	Atlanta	GA	30303	404-651-3504	
WRFG-FM 89.3 (Var) 1083 Austin Ave NE *Web:* www.wrfg.org	Atlanta	GA	30307	404-523-3471	523-8990
WSB-AM 750 (N/T) 1601 W Peachtree St NE *Web:* www.wsbradio.com	Atlanta	GA	30309	404-897-7500	897-7363
WSB-FM 98.5 (AC) 1601 W Peachtree St NE *Web:* www.b985.com	Atlanta	GA	30309	404-897-7500	897-7363
WSRV-FM 97.1 (AC) 1601 W Peachtree St *Web:* www.971theriver.com	Atlanta	GA	30309	404-897-7500	897-7380
WUSF Public Broadcasting 4202 E Fowler Ave TVB100 *Web:* www.wusf.usf.edu	Tampa	FL	33620	813-974-8700	
WVEE-FM 103.3 (Urban) 1201 Peachtree St NE Ste 800 *Web:* v103.cbslocal.com	Atlanta	GA	30361	404-898-8900	898-8909
WZGC-FM 92.9 (CR) 1201 Peachtree St *Web:* atlanta.cbslocal.com/station/92-9-the-game/	Atlanta	GA	30361	404-898-8900	

648-11 Augusta, GA

	City	State	ZIP	Phone	Fax
WBBQ-FM 104.3 (AC) 2743 Perimeter Pkwy Bldg 100 Ste 300 *Web:* www.wbbq.com	Augusta	GA	30909	706-396-6000	396-6010
WCHZ-FM 95.1 (Rock) 4051 Jimmie Dyess Pkwy *Web:* www.95rock.com	Augusta	GA	30909	706-396-7000	396-7100
WEKL-FM 105.7 (CR) 2743 Perimeter Pkwy Bldg 100 Ste 300 *Web:* eagle102.com/	Augusta	GA	30909	706-396-6000	396-6010
WFAN-AM 66 (Rel) 345 Hudson St *Web:* newyork.cbslocal.com	New York	NY	10014	212-352-2409	
WGAC-AM 580 (N/T) 4051 Jimmie Dyess Pkwy *Web:* www.wgac.com	Augusta	GA	30909	706-396-7000	396-7100

	City	State	ZIP	Phone	Fax
WHHD-FM 98.3 (AC) 4051 Jimmie Dyess Pkwy *Web:* www.hd983.com	Augusta	GA	30909	706-396-7000	396-7100
WKXC-FM 99.5 (Ctry) 4051 Jimmie Dyess Pkwy *Web:* www.kicks99.com	Augusta	GA	30909	706-396-7000	396-7100
WPRW-FM 107.7 (Urban) 2743 Perimeter Pkwy Bldg 100 Ste 300 *TF:* 800-650-2876 ■ *Web:* www.power107.net	Augusta	GA	30909	706-396-6000	396-6010

648-13 Augusta, ME

	City	State	ZIP	Phone	Fax
WEBB-FM 98.5 (Ctry) 56 Western Ave Ste 13 *Web:* www.b985.fm	Augusta	ME	04330	207-623-4735	626-5948
WMME-FM 92.3 (CHR) 56 Western Ave Ste 13 *Web:* www.92moose.fm	Augusta	ME	04330	207-623-4735	626-5948

648-14 Austin, TX

	City	State	ZIP	Phone	Fax
KAMX-FM 94.7 (AC) 4301 Westbank Dr Bldg B Third Fl *Web:* www.mix947.com	Austin	TX	78746	512-327-9595	329-6288
KASE-FM 100.7 (Ctry) 3601 S Congress Ave Bldg F *Web:* www.kase101.com	Austin	TX	78704	512-684-7300	684-7441
KAZI-FM 88.7 (Var) 8906 Wall St Ste 203 *Web:* www.kazifm.org	Austin	TX	78754	512-836-9544	836-9563
KGSR-FM 93.3 (Urban) 8309 N IH-35 *Web:* www.kgsr.com	Austin	TX	78753	512-832-4000	832-4071
KHFI-FM 96.7 (CHR) 3601 S Congress Ave Bldg F *Web:* www.967kissfm.com	Austin	TX	78704	512-684-7300	684-7441
KJCE-AM 1370 (N/T) 4301 Westbank Dr *Web:* www.talkradio1370am.com	Austin	TX	78746	512-327-9595	329-6252
KKMJ-FM 95.5 (AC) 4301 Westbank Dr Bldg B Third Fl *Web:* www.majic.com	Austin	TX	78746	512-327-9595	329-6252
KLBJ-AM 590 (N/T) 8309 N IH-35 *Web:* www.newsradioklbj.com	Austin	TX	78753	512-832-4000	832-4081
KLBJ-FM 93.7 (Rock) 8309 N IH-35 *Web:* www.klbjfm.com	Austin	TX	78753	512-832-4000	832-4081
KPEZ-FM 102.3 (Rel) 3601 S Congress Ave Bldg F *Web:* www.thebeatatx.com	Austin	TX	78704	512-684-7300	
KROX-FM 101.5 (Alt) 8309 N IH-35 *Web:* www.101x.com	Austin	TX	78753	512-832-4000	832-4071
KUT-FM 90.5 (NPR) University of Texas 1 University Stn PO Box A-0704 *Web:* www.kut.org	Austin	TX	78712	512-471-1631	471-3700
KVET-AM 1300 (Sports) 3601 S Congress Ave Bldg F *Web:* www.am1300thezone.com	Austin	TX	78704	512-684-7300	684-7441

648-15 Bakersfield, CA

	City	State	ZIP	Phone	Fax
KBFP-FM 105.3 (Span) 1100 Mohawk St Ste 280 *Web:* www.iheart.com	Bakersfield	CA	93309	661-322-9929	
KDFO-FM 98.5 (CR) 1100 Mohawk St Ste 280 *Web:* www.985thefox.com	Bakersfield	CA	93309	661-322-9929	322-9239
Kelly 95.3 FM 3651 Pegasus Dr Ste 107 *Web:* www.klly.com	Bakersfield	CA	93308	661-393-1900	393-1915
KGFM-FM 101.5 (AC) 1400 Easton Dr Ste 144-B *Web:* www.kgfm.com	Bakersfield	CA	93309	661-328-1410	328-0873
KIWI-FM 102.9 (Span) 5100 Commerce Dr *Web:* www.radiolobo.com	Bakersfield	CA	93309	661-327-9711	327-0797
KKBB-FM 99.3 (Oldies) 3651 Pegasus Dr Ste 107 *TF:* 866-758-4696 ■ *Web:* www.groove993.com	Bakersfield	CA	93308	661-393-1900	393-1915
KMYX-FM 92.5 (Span) 6313 Schirra Ct *Web:* www.campesina925.com/	Bakersfield	CA	93313	661-837-0745	837-1612
KNZR-AM 1560 (N/T) 3651 Pegasus Dr Ste 107 *Web:* www.knzr.com	Bakersfield	CA	93308	661-393-1900	393-1915
KRAB-FM 106.1 (Rock) 1100 Mohawk St Ste 280 *Web:* www.krab.com	Bakersfield	CA	93309	661-322-9929	
KUZZ-FM 107.9 (Ctry) 3223 Sillect Ave *Web:* www.kuzzradio.com/home.shtml	Bakersfield	CA	93308	661-326-1011	328-7503
KVMX-FM 92.1 (Span CHR) 5100 Commerce Dr *Web:* www.maxfm921.com	Bakersfield	CA	93309	661-327-9711	327-0797

648-16 Baltimore, MD

	City	State	ZIP	Phone	Fax
WBAL-AM 1090 (N/T) 3800 Hooper Ave *Web:* www.wbal.com	Baltimore	MD	21211	410-467-3000	
WBJC-FM 91.5 (Clas) 6776 Reisterstown Rd Ste 202 *Web:* www.wbjc.com	Baltimore	MD	21215	410-580-5800	
WEAA-FM 88.9 (Jazz) 1700 E Cold Spring Ln *Web:* www.weaa.org	Baltimore	MD	21251	443-885-3564	885-8206
WERQ-FM 92.3 (Urban) 1705 Whitehead Rd *Web:* www.92q.com	Baltimore	MD	21207	410-481-9292	
WIYY-FM 97.9 (Rock) 3800 Hooper Ave *Web:* www.98online.com	Baltimore	MD	21211	410-889-0098	
WJZ-AM 1300 (N/T) 1423 Clarkview Rd Ste 100 *Web:* baltimore.cbslocal.com	Baltimore	MD	21209	410-481-1057	
WLIF-FM 101.9 (AC) 1423 Clarkview Rd Ste 100 *Web:* todays1019.cbslocal.com/	Baltimore	MD	21209	410-825-1000	
WPOC-FM 93.1 (Country) 711 W 40th St Ste 350 *TF:* 866-962-5487 ■ *Web:* www.wpoc.com	Baltimore	MD	21211	410-366-7600	235-3899
WQSR-FM 102.7 (Var) 711 W 40th St *TF:* 888-410-1027 ■ *Web:* www.1027jackfm.com	Baltimore	MD	21211	410-366-7600	
WRBS-FM 95.1 (Rel) 3500 Commerce Dr *TF:* 800-965-9324 ■ *Web:* www.951shinefm.com	Baltimore	MD	21227	410-247-4100	247-4533
WWMX-FM 106.5 (CHR) 1423 Clarkview Rd Ste 100 *Web:* mix1065fm.cbslocal.com	Baltimore	MD	21209	410-825-1000	821-8256
WYPR-FM 88.1 (NPR) 2216 N Charles St *TF:* 866-789-8627 ■ *Web:* www.wypr.org	Baltimore	MD	21218	410-235-1660	235-1161

648-17 Bangor, ME

	City	State	ZIP	Phone	Fax
WHCF-FM 88.5 (Rel) PO Box 5000 *TF:* 800-947-2577 ■ *Web:* www.whcffm.com	Bangor	ME	04402	207-947-2751	947-0010
WHSN-FM 89.3 (Alt) 1 College Cir *Web:* www.whsn-fm.com	Bangor	ME	04401	207-941-7116	947-3987
WMEH-FM 90.9 (NPR) 63 Texas Ave *TF:* 800-884-1717 ■ *Web:* www.mpbn.net	Bangor	ME	04401	207-941-1010	761-0318
WVOM-FM 101.3 (N/T) 184 Target Industrial Cir *Web:* www.wvomfm.com	Bangor	ME	04861	207-947-9100	
WVOM-FM 103.9 (N/T) 184 Target Industrial Cir *TF:* 800-966-1039 ■ *Web:* www.wvomfm.com	Bangor	ME	04401	207-947-9100	942-8039

648-18 Baton Rouge, LA

	City	State	ZIP	Phone	Fax
WBKL-FM 92.7 (Rel) PO Box 2098 *TF:* 800-525-5683 ■ *Web:* www.klove.com	Omaha	NE	68103	800-525-5683	
WDGL-FM 98.1 (CR) 929-B Government St *Web:* www.eagle981.com	Baton Rouge	LA	70802	225-388-9898	499-9800
WFMF-FM 102.5 (CHR) 5555 Hilton Ave Ste 500 *Web:* www.wfmf.com	Baton Rouge	LA	70808	225-231-1860	231-1879
WJBO-AM 1150 (N/T) 5555 Hilton Ave Ste 500 *Web:* www.wjbo.com	Baton Rouge	LA	70808	225-231-1860	231-1879
WRKF-FM 89.3 (NPR) 3050 Vly Creek Dr *Web:* www.wrkf.org	Baton Rouge	LA	70808	225-926-3050	926-3105
WSKR-AM 1210 (Sports) 5555 Hilton Ave Ste 500 *Web:* www.247comedy.com	Baton Rouge	LA	70808	225-499-1210	231-1879
WYNK-FM 101.5 (Ctry) 5555 Hilton Ave Ste 500 *Web:* www.wynkcountry.com	Baton Rouge	LA	70808	225-231-1860	231-1879

648-19 Billings, MT

	City	State	ZIP	Phone	Fax
KBLG-AM 910 (N/T) 2075 Central Ave *Web:* www.kblg910.com	Billings	MT	59102	406-248-7777	
KBUL-AM 970 (N/T) 27 N 27th St 23rd Fl *Web:* newstalk955.com	Billings	MT	59101	406-248-7827	252-9577
KCTR-FM 102.9 (Ctry) 27 N 27th St 23rd Fl *Web:* catcountry1029.com	Billings	MT	59101	406-248-7827	252-9577
KEMC-FM 91.7 (NPR) 1500 University Dr *TF:* 800-441-2941 ■ *Web:* www.yellowstonepublicradio.org	Billings	MT	59101	406-657-2941	657-2977
KEWF-FM Radio Billings, LLC 222 N 32nd St 10th Fl *Web:* www.985thewolf.com	Billings	MT	59101	406-238-1000	238-1038
KKBR-FM 97.1 (Oldies) 27 N 27th St 23rd Fl *Web:* popcrush971.com	Billings	MT	59101	406-245-9700	252-9577
KMHK-FM 103.7 (Var) 27 N 27th St 23rd Fl *Web:* kmhk.com	Billings	MT	59101	406-294-1037	252-9577
KRKX-FM 94.1 (CR) 2075 Central Ave *Web:* www.941ksky.com	Billings	MT	59102	406-248-7777	
KURL-AM 730 (Rel) 636 Haugen St *Web:* www.kurlradio.com	Billings	MT	59101	406-245-3121	245-0822

648-20 Birmingham, AL

	City	State	ZIP	Phone	Fax
WAPI-AM 1070 (N/T) 244 Goodwin Crest Dr Ste 300 *Web:* www.1070wapi.com	Birmingham	AL	35209	205-945-4646	
WBHK-FM 98.7 (Urban) 2700 Corporate Pkwy *Web:* 987kiss.com	Birmingham	AL	35242	205-322-2987	290-1061
WBHM-FM 90.3 (NPR) 650 11th St S *TF:* 800-444-9246 ■ *Web:* www.wbhm.org	Birmingham	AL	35233	205-934-2606	934-5075
WBPT-FM 106.9 (AC) 2700 Corporate Dr Ste 115 *Web:* birminghamseagle.com	Birmingham	AL	35242	205-916-1100	290-1061
WDXB-FM 102.5 (Ctry) 600 Beacon Pkwy W Ste 400 *TF:* 877-541-1966 ■ *Web:* www.1025thebull.com	Birmingham	AL	35209	205-439-9600	439-8390
WERC-AM 960 (N/T) 600 Beacon Pkwy W Ste 400 *Web:* www.wercfm.com	Birmingham	AL	35209	205-439-9600	439-8390

Station / Address	City	State	ZIP	Phone	Fax
WJLD-AM 1400 (Var) 1449 Spaulding Ishkooda Rd *Web:* wjldradio.com	Birmingham	AL	35211	205-942-1776	
WJSR-FM 91.1 (CR) Jefferson State Community College 2601 Carson Rd *TF:* 800-767-4984 ■ *Web:* www.angelfire.com/music2/wjsr	Birmingham	AL	35215	205-856-7702	815-8499
WMJJ-FM 96.5 (AC) 600 Beacon Pkwy W Ste 400 *Web:* www.magic96.com	Birmingham	AL	35209	205-439-9600	439-8390
WQEN-FM 103.7 (CHR) 600 Beacon Pkwy W Ste 400 *Web:* www.1037theq.com	Birmingham	AL	35209	205-439-9600	439-8390
WZZK-FM 104.7 (Ctry) 2700 Corporate Dr Ste 115 *Web:* wzzk.com	Birmingham	AL	35242	205-916-1100	290-1061

648-21 Bismarck, ND

Station / Address	City	State	ZIP	Phone	Fax
KKCT-FM 97.5 (CHR) 1830 N 11th St *Web:* www.hot975fm.com	Bismarck	ND	58501	701-250-6602	250-6632
KXMR-AM 710 (Sports) 3500 E Rosser Ave PO Box 2156 *TF:* 866-522-5710 ■ *Web:* am710thefan.com/main.html	Bismarck	ND	58501	701-255-1234	222-1131
KYYY-FM 92.9 (AC) 3500 E Rosser Ave. *TF:* 866-929-9393 ■ *Web:* www.y93.fm	Bismarck	ND	58501	701-255-1234	222-1131

648-22 Boise, ID

Station / Address	City	State	ZIP	Phone	Fax
KAWO-FM 104.3 (Ctry) 827 E Pk Blvd Ste 100 *Web:* www.wow1043.com	Boise	ID	83712	208-344-6363	
KBSX-FM 91.5 (NPR) 1910 University Dr *Web:* www.boisestatepublicradio.org	Boise	ID	83725	208-426-3663	344-6631
KBXL-FM 94.1 (Rel) 1440 S Weideman Ave *Web:* www.941thevoice.com	Boise	ID	83709	208-377-3790	377-3792
KIZN-FM 92.3 (Ctry) 1419 W Bannock St *Web:* www.kizn.com	Boise	ID	83702	208-336-3670	336-3734
KQXR-FM 100.3 (Rock) 5257 Fairview Ave Ste 260 *Web:* www.xrock.com	Boise	ID	83706	208-344-3511	947-6765
KTIK-AM 1350 (Sports) 1419 W Bannock St *Web:* www.ktik.com	Boise	ID	83702	208-336-3670	336-3734

648-23 Boston, MA

Station / Address	City	State	ZIP	Phone	Fax
WBCN-FM 104.1 (Alt) 83 Leo Birmingham Pkwy *Web:* wzlx.cbslocal.com	Boston	MA	02135	617-931-1234	746-1402
WBMX-FM 104.1 83 Leo M Birmingham Pkwy *Web:* mix1041.cbslocal.com	Boston	MA	02135	617-931-1234	
WBOS-FM 92.9 (AAA) 55 Morrissey Blvd *Web:* www.myradio929.com	Boston	MA	02125	617-822-9600	822-6759
WBUR-FM 90.9 (NPR) 890 Commonwealth Ave *TF:* 800-909-9287 ■ *Web:* www.wbur.org	Boston	MA	02215	617-353-0909	353-9380
WBZ-AM 1030 (N/T) 1170 Soldiers Field Rd *Web:* boston.cbslocal.com	Boston	MA	02134	617-787-7000	787-7060
WGBH-FM 89.7 (NPR) One Guest St *Web:* www.wgbh.org	Boston	MA	02135	617-300-2000	300-1026
WKLB-FM 102.5 (Ctry) 55 Morrissey Blvd **Fax:* News Rm ■ *TF:* 888-819-1025 ■ *Web:* www.wklb.com	Boston	MA	02125	617-822-9600	822-6659*
WMJX-FM 106.7 (CHR) 55 Morrissey Blvd *Web:* www.magic1067.com	Boston	MA	02125	617-822-9600	822-6559
WODS-FM 103.3 (Oldies) 83 Leo Birmingham Pkwy. *Web:* 1033ampradio.cbslocal.com	Brighton	MA	02135	617-787-7500	787-7523
WROR-FM 105.7 (Oldies) 55 Morrissey Blvd *Web:* www.wror.com	Boston	MA	02125	617-822-9600	822-6459
WUMB-FM 91.9 (Folk) 100 Morrissey Blvd *TF:* 800-573-2100 ■ *Web:* www.wumb.org	Boston	MA	02125	617-287-6900	287-6916

648-24 Branson, MO

Station / Address	City	State	ZIP	Phone	Fax
KLFC-FM 88.1 (Rel) 205 W Atlantic St *TF:* 877-410-8592 ■ *Web:* www.klfcradio.com	Branson	MO	65616	417-334-5532	335-2437

648-25 Buffalo, NY

Station / Address	City	State	ZIP	Phone	Fax
Mix 96 14 Lafayette Sq Ste 1200 *Web:* 961joyfm.com	Buffalo	NY	14203	716-852-7444	
WBFO-FM 88.7 (NPR) 3435 Main St 205 Allen Hall *Web:* news.wbfo.org	Buffalo	NY	14214	716-829-6000	829-2277
WBLK-FM 93.7 (Urban) 14 Lafayette Sq Ste 1300 *Web:* www.wblk.com	Buffalo	NY	14203	716-852-9393	852-9390
WBNY-FM 91.3 (Alt) 1300 Elmwood Ave *Web:* www.buffalostate.edu/wbny	Buffalo	NY	14222	716-878-5104	878-6600
WDCX-FM 99.5 (Rel) 625 Delaware Ave Ste 308 *TF:* 800-684-2848 ■ *Web:* www.wdcxradio.com	Buffalo	NY	14202	716-883-3010	883-3606
WEDG-FM 103.3 (Alt) 50 James E Casey Dr *Web:* www.wedg.com	Buffalo	NY	14206	716-881-4555	884-2931
WGRF-FM 96.9 (CR) 50 James E Casey Dr *Web:* www.97rock.com	Buffalo	NY	14206	716-881-4555	884-2931
WHTT-FM 104.1 (AC) 50 James E Casey Dr *Web:* www.whtt.com	Buffalo	NY	14206	716-881-4555	884-2931
WNED-AM 970 (NPR) 140 Lower Terr *Web:* www.wned.org	Buffalo	NY	14202	716-845-7000	845-7043
WYRK-FM 106.5 (Ctry) 14 Lafayette Sq Ste 1200 *Web:* www.wyrk.com	Buffalo	NY	14203	716-852-7444	

648-26 Burlington, VT

Station / Address	City	State	ZIP	Phone	Fax
WIZN-FM 106.7 (Rock) 255 S Champlain St *TF:* 888-873-9496 ■ *Web:* www.wizn.com	Burlington	VT	05401	802-860-2440	860-1818

648-27 Calgary, AB

Station / Address	City	State	ZIP	Phone	Fax
CBR-AM 1010 (N/T) 1724 Westmount Blvd NW **Fax:* News Rm ■ *Web:* cbc.ca/news/canada/calgary/	Calgary	AB	T2N3G7	403-521-6000	521-6262*
CHFM-FM 95.9 (AC) 2723 37th Ave NE Ste 240 *Web:* kiss959.com/	Calgary	AB	T1Y5R8	403-246-9696	
CHQR-AM 770 (N/T) 200 Barclay Parade SW Ste 170 *TF:* 800-563-7770 ■ *Web:* www.newstalk770.com	Calgary	AB	T2P4R5	403-716-6500	716-2111
CJAY-FM 92.1 (CR) 1110 Ctr St NE Ste 300 *Web:* www.cjay92.com	Calgary	AB	T2E2R2	403-240-5800	240-5801
CKMX-AM 1060 (Ctry) 1110 Ctr St NE Ste 300 *Web:* www.classiccountryam1060.com	Calgary	AB	T2E2R2	403-240-5800	240-5801

648-28 Casper, WY

Station / Address	City	State	ZIP	Phone	Fax
KHOC-FM 102.5 (AC) 218 N Wolcott St. *Web:* wyomingradio.com	Casper	WY	82601	307-265-1984	266-3295
KRVK-FM 107.9 (Rock) 150 N Nichols Ave *TF:* 800-442-2256 ■ *Web:* www.theriver1079.com	Casper	WY	82601	307-266-5252	235-9143
KTRS-FM 104.7 (CHR) 150 N Nichols Ave *TF:* 800-442-2256 ■ *Web:* www.kisscasper.com	Casper	WY	82601	307-266-5252	235-9143
KTWO-AM 1030 (Ctry) 150 N Nichols Ave *Web:* www.k2radio.com	Casper	WY	82601	307-266-5252	235-9143
KVOC-AM 1230 (Nost) 218 N Wolcott St.	Casper	WY	82601	307-265-1984	
KWYY-FM 95.5 (Ctry) 150 N Nichols Ave. *TF:* 800-339-4673 ■ *Web:* www.mycountry955.com	Casper	WY	82601	307-266-5252	235-9143

648-29 Cedar Rapids, IA

Station / Address	City	State	ZIP	Phone	Fax
KCCK-FM 88.3 (Jazz) 6301 Kirkwood Blvd SW *TF:* 800-373-5225 ■ *Web:* www.kcck.org	Cedar Rapids	IA	52404	319-398-5446	398-5492
KHAK-FM 98.1 (Ctry) 425 Second St SE Fourth Fl *Web:* www.khak.com	Cedar Rapids	IA	52401	319-365-9431	363-8062
KMRY-AM 1450 (Nost) 1957 Blairs Ferry Rd NE *Web:* www.kmryradio.com	Cedar Rapids	IA	52402	319-393-1450	393-1407
KZIA-FM 102.9 (CHR) 1110 26th Ave SW *Web:* www.kzia.com	Cedar Rapids	IA	52404	319-363-2061	363-2948
WMT-FM 96.5 (AC) 600 Old Marion Rd NE *TF:* 800-258-0096 ■ *Web:* www.965kisscountry.com	Cedar Rapids	IA	52402	319-395-0530	393-9600

648-30 Champaign, IL

Station / Address	City	State	ZIP	Phone	Fax
Rewind 92.5 2603 W Bradley Ave. *Web:* www.925thechief.com	Champaign	IL	61821	217-352-4141	352-1256
WBGL-FM 91.7 (Rel) 4101 Fieldstone Road PO Box 111 *TF Cust Svc:* 800-475-9245 ■ *Web:* www.wbgl.org	Champaign	IL	61822	217-359-8232	359-7374
WDWS-AM 1400 (N/T) 2301 S Neil St. *TF:* 800-223-9397 ■ *Web:* news-gazette.com/wdws	Champaign	IL	61820	217-351-5300	351-5385
WEFT-FM 90.1 (Var) 113 N Market St. *Web:* www.weft.org	Champaign	IL	61820	217-359-9338	
WGKC-FM 105.9 (CR) 4112 C Fieldstone Rd *Web:* www.wgkc.net	Champaign	IL	61822	217-367-1195	367-3291
WIXY-FM 100.3 (Ctry) 2603 W Bradley Ave *Web:* www.wixy.com	Champaign	IL	61821	217-352-4141	352-1256
WLRW-FM 94.5 (CHR) 2603 W Bradley Ave *Web:* www.mix945.com	Champaign	IL	61821	217-352-4141	352-1256
WPCD-FM 88.7 (Rock) 2400 W Bradley Ave. *Web:* wpcd.parkland.edu/	Champaign	IL	61821	217-373-3790	
WPGU-FM 107.1 (Alt) 512 E Green St Ste 107 *Web:* www.wpgu.com	Champaign	IL	61820	217-337-8382	337-8303

648-31 Charleston, SC

Station / Address	City	State	ZIP	Phone	Fax
WYBB-FM 98.1 (Alt) 59 Windermere Blvd *Web:* www.my98rock.com	Charleston	SC	29407	843-769-4799	

648-32 Charleston, WV

Station / Address	City	State	ZIP	Phone	Fax

				Phone	Fax
WCHS-AM 58 (N/T) 1111 Virginia St E *Web:* www.58wchs.com	Charleston	WV	25301	304-342-8131	344-4745
WKWS-FM 96.1 (Ctry) 1111 Virginia St E *Web:* www.961thewolf.com	Charleston	WV	25301	304-342-8131	344-4745
WQBE-FM 97.5 (Ctry) 817 Suncrest Pl *TF:* 800-222-3697 ■ *Web:* www.wqbe.com	Charleston	WV	25303	304-344-9700	342-3118
WVAF-FM 1111 Virginia St E *Web:* www.v100.fm	Charleston	WV	25301	304-342-8131	

648-33 Charlotte, NC

				Phone	Fax
WBAV-FM 101.9 (Urban AC) 1520 S Blvd Ste 300 *Web:* v1019.cbslocal.com	Charlotte	NC	28203	704-570-1019	227-8985
WBT-AM 1110 (N/T) One Julian Price Pl *Web:* www.wbt.com	Charlotte	NC	28208	704-374-3500	
WEND-FM 106.5 (Alt) 801 Wood Ridge Ctr Dr *TF:* 800-934-1065 ■ *Web:* www.1065.com	Charlotte	NC	28217	704-714-9444	
WFAE-FM 90.7 (NPR) 8801 JM Keynes Dr Ste 91 *TF Cust Svc:* 800-876-9323 ■ *Web:* www.wfae.org	Charlotte	NC	28262	704-549-9323	547-8851
WFNZ-AM 610 (Sports) 1520 S Blvd Ste 300 *TF:* 866-570-9610 ■ *Web:* charlotte.cbslocal.com	Charlotte	NC	28203	704-319-9369	
WKKT-FM 96.9 (Ctry) 801 Wood Ridge Ctr Dr *TF:* 877-903-7867 ■ *Web:* www.969thekat.com	Charlotte	NC	28217	704-714-9444	
WLNK-FM 107.9 (AC) One Julian Price Pl *Web:* www.1079thelink.com	Charlotte	NC	28208	704-374-3500	374-3889
WLYT-FM 102.9 (AC) 801 Wood Ridge Ctr Dr *Web:* www.1029thelake.com	Charlotte	NC	28217	704-714-9444	
WPEG-FM 97.9 (Urban) 1520 S Blvd Ste 300 *TF:* 800-525-0098 ■ *Web:* power98fm.cbslocal.com	Charlotte	NC	28203	704-342-2644	227-8985
WRFX-FM 99.7 (CR) 801 Wood Ridge Ctr Dr *TF:* 800-766-9970 ■ *Web:* www.wrfx.com	Charlotte	NC	28217	704-714-9444	

648-34 Chattanooga, TN

				Phone	Fax
107.9 Nash Icon 821 Pineville Rd *Web:* www.wogt.com	Chattanooga	TN	37405	423-756-6141	
WDEF-FM 92.3 (AC) 2615 S Broad St *Web:* www.sunny923.com	Chattanooga	TN	37408	423-321-6200	321-6270
WDOD-FM 96.5 (CHR) 2615 S Broad St *Web:* www.hits96.com	Chattanooga	TN	37408	423-321-6200	321-6270
WGOW-FM 102.3 (N/T) 821 Pineville Rd *Web:* www.wgow.com	Chattanooga	TN	37405	423-756-6141	266-3629
WSKZ-FM 106.5 (Rock) 821 Pineville Rd *Web:* www.wskz.com	Chattanooga	TN	37405	423-756-6141	266-3629
WUSY-FM 101 7413 Old Lee Hwy *Web:* www.us101country.com	Chattanooga	TN	37421	423-892-3333	899-7224
WUTC-FM 88.1 (NPR) 615 McCallie Ave 104 Cadek Hall Dept 1151 *TF:* 800-272-3900 ■ *Web:* www.wutc.org	Chattanooga	TN	37403	423-425-4756	425-2379

648-35 Cheyenne, WY

				Phone	Fax
KFBC-AM 1240 (N/T) 1806 Capitol Ave *Web:* www.kfbcradio.com	Cheyenne	WY	82001	307-634-4461	632-8586
KGAB-AM 650 (N/T) 1912 Capitol Ave Ste 300 *Web:* www.kgab.com	Cheyenne	WY	82001	307-632-4400	632-1818

648-36 Chicago, IL

				Phone	Fax
Chicago's wshe 100.3 130 E Randolph St 1 Prudential Plaza Ste 2780 *Web:* www.wilv.com	Chicago	IL	60601	312-297-5100	297-5155
WBBM-AM 780 (N/T) 180 N Stetson Ste 1100 *Web:* chicago.cbslocal.com	Chicago	IL	60601	312-297-7800	297-7822
WBBM-FM 96.3 (CHR) 180 N Stetson Ste 1100 Prudential Plz 2 *Web:* b96.cbslocal.com	Chicago	IL	60601	312-591-9696	297-7822
WBEZ-FM 91.5 (NPR) 848 E Grand Ave Navy Pier *Web:* www.wbez.org	Chicago	IL	60611	312-948-4600	
WDRV-FM 97.1 (CR) 875 N Michigan Ave Ste 1510 *Web:* www.wdrv.com	Chicago	IL	60611	312-274-9710	274-1304
WFMT-FM 98.7 (Clas) 5400 N St Louis Ave *Web:* www.wfmt.com	Chicago	IL	60625	773-279-2000	279-2199
WGCI-FM 107.5 (Urban) 233 N Michigan Ave Ste 2800 *Web:* www.wgci.com	Chicago	IL	60601	312-540-2000	
WGN Radio 720 (N/T) 435 N Michigan Ave *Web:* www.wgnradio.com	Chicago	IL	60611	312-222-4700	222-5165
WKSC-FM 103.5 (CHR) 233 N Michigan Ave Ste 2800 *Web:* www.1035kissfm.com	Chicago	IL	60601	312-540-2000	
WLEY-FM 107.9 (Span) 150 N Michigan Ave Ste 1040 **Fax:* PR ■ *Web:* www.laley1079.com	Chicago	IL	60601	312-920-9500	920-9515*
WLUP-FM 97.9 (CR) 222 Merchandise Mart Ste 230 *Web:* www.wlup.com	Chicago	IL	60654	312-245-1200	527-3620
WMBI-FM 90.1 (Rel) 820 N LaSalle Blvd *TF:* 877-376-2194 ■ *Web:* www.moodyradiochicago.fm	Chicago	IL	60610	312-329-4300	329-4468
WMVP-AM 1000 (Sports) 190 N State St 7th Fl **Fax:* Sales ■ *TF:* 800-438-3776 ■ *Web:* espn.go.com	Chicago	IL	60601	312-980-1000	980-1010*
WNUA-FM 95.5 (NAC) 233 N Michigan Ave Ste 2800 **Fax Area Code:* 210 ■ *Web:* www.955elpatron.com	Chicago	IL	60601	312-540-2000	832-3149*
WOJO-FM 105.1 (Span) 625 N Michigan Ave Ste 300 *Web:* 1051chicago.univision.com	Chicago	IL	60611	312-981-1800	312-1840
WTMX-FM 101.9 (AC) 130 E Randolph St Ste 2700 1 Prudential Plz *Web:* www.wtmx.com	Chicago	IL	60601	312-946-1019	946-4747
WUSN-FM 99.5 (Ctry) Two Prudential Plz Ste 1000 *Web:* us995.cbslocal.com	Chicago	IL	60601	312-649-0099	856-9586
WVAZ-FM 102.7 (Urban AC) 233 N Michigan Ave Ste 2800 *Web:* www.v103.com	Chicago	IL	60601	312-540-2000	938-4477
WVON-AM 1690 (N/T) 1000 E 87th St *Web:* www.wvon.com	Chicago	IL	60619	773-247-6200	

648-37 Cincinnati, OH

				Phone	Fax
WAKW-FM 93.3 (Rel) 6275 Collegevue Pl PO Box 24126 *TF:* 888-542-9393 ■ *Web:* www.mystar933.com	Cincinnati	OH	45224	513-542-9259	542-9333
WCKY-AM 1530 (N/T) 8044 Montgomery Rd Ste 650 *Web:* www.espn1530.com	Cincinnati	OH	45236	513-686-8300	
WCVX-AM 1050 (Rel) 635 W Seventh St Ste 400	Cincinnati	OH	45203	513-533-2500	
WGRR-FM 103.5 (Oldies) 4805 Montgomery Rd Ste 300 *Web:* www.wgrr.com	Cincinnati	OH	45212	513-241-9898	241-6689
WGUC-FM 90.9 (Clas) 1223 Central Pkwy *Web:* www.wguc.org	Cincinnati	OH	45214	513-241-8282	241-8456
WIZF-FM 101.1 (Urban) 705 Central Ave *TF:* 866-236-7588 ■ *Web:* wiznation.com	Cincinnati	OH	45202	513-679-6000	679-6014
WKFS-FM 107.1 (CHR) 8044 Montgomery Rd Ste 650 *Web:* www.kiss107.com	Cincinnati	OH	45236	513-686-8300	421-3299
WKRC-AM 550 (N/T) 8044 Montgomery Rd Ste 650 *Web:* www.55krc.com	Cincinnati	OH	45236	513-686-8300	651-2555
WLW-AM 700 (N/T) 8044 Montgomery Rd Ste 650 *Web:* www.700wlw.com	Cincinnati	OH	45236	513-686-8300	665-9700
WNNF-FM 94.1 (AC) 4805 Montgomery Rd Ste 300 *Web:* nashfm941.com/	Cincinnati	OH	45212	513-241-9898	241-6689
WRRM-FM 98.5 (AC) 4805 Montgomery Rd Ste 300 *Web:* www.warm98.com	Cincinnati	OH	45212	513-241-9898	241-6689
WUBE-FM 105.1 (Ctry) 2060 Reading Rd *Web:* b105.com	Cincinnati	OH	45202	513-699-5105	699-5000
WVXU-FM 91.7 (NPR) 1223 Central Pkwy *Web:* www.wvxu.org	Cincinnati	OH	45214	513-352-9170	241-8456

648-38 Cleveland, OH

				Phone	Fax
WCPN-FM 90.3 (NPR) 1375 Euclid Ave *Web:* www.wcpn.org	Cleveland	OH	44115	216-916-6100	
WENZ-FM 107.9 (Urban) 2510 St Clair Ave NE *TF:* 800-440-1079 ■ *Web:* zhiphopcleveland.com	Cleveland	OH	44114	216-579-1111	771-4164
WERE-AM 1490 (N/T) 2510 St Clair Ave NE *Web:* www.newstalkcleveland.com	Cleveland	OH	44114	216-579-1111	771-4164
WFHM-FM 95.5 (Rel) Four Summit Pk Dr Ste 150 *Web:* www.955thefish.com	Cleveland	OH	44131	216-901-0921	
WJMO-AM 1300 (Rel) 2510 St Clair Ave NE *Web:* www.praisecleveland.com	Cleveland	OH	44114	216-579-1111	771-4164
WKNR-AM 850 (Sports) 1301 E Ninth St Ste 252 *Web:* www.espncleveland.com	Cleveland	OH	44114	216-583-9901	583-9550
WMMS-FM 100.7 (Rock) 6200 Oak Tree Blvd S Fourth Fl *Web:* www.wmms.com	Cleveland	OH	44131	216-520-2600	901-8166
WNCX-FM 98.5 (CR) 1041 Huron Rd *Web:* wncx.cbslocal.com	Cleveland	OH	44115	216-861-0100	696-0385
WZAK-FM 93.1 (Urban) 2510 St Clair Ave NE *Web:* wzakcleveland.com	Cleveland	OH	44114	216-579-1111	771-4164

648-39 Colorado Springs, CO

				Phone	Fax
KBIQ-FM 102.7 (Rel) 7150 Campus Dr Ste 150 *Web:* www.kbiqradio.com	Colorado Springs	CO	80920	719-531-5438	531-5588
KCCY-FM 96.9 (Ctry) 2864 S Cir Dr Ste 300 *Web:* www.y969.com	Colorado Springs	CO	80906	719-540-9200	579-0882
KILO-FM 94.3 (Rock) 1805 E Cheyenne Rd *TF General:* 800-727-5456 ■ *Web:* kilo943.com	Colorado Springs	CO	80905	719-634-4896	634-5837
KKFM-FM 98.1 (CR) 6805 Corporate Dr Ste 130 *Web:* www.kkfm.com	Colorado Springs	CO	80919	719-593-2700	593-2727

Station	City	State	ZIP	Phone	Fax
KKLI-FM 106.3 (AC) 2864 S Cir Dr Ste 150 *Web:* www.klite1063.com	Colorado Springs	CO	80906	719-540-9200	579-0882
KKMG-FM 98.9 (CHR) 6805 Corporate Dr Ste 130 *Web:* www.989magicfm.com	Colorado Springs	CO	80919	719-593-2700	593-2727
KRCC-FM 91.5 (NPR) 912 N Weber St *TF:* 800-748-2727 ■ *Web:* www.krcc.org	Colorado Springs	CO	80903	719-473-4801	473-7863
KVOR-AM 740 (N/T) 6805 Corporate Dr Ste 130 *TF:* 800-232-6459 ■ *Web:* www.kvor.com	Colorado Springs	CO	80919	719-593-2700	540-0740
KVUU-FM 99.9 (AC) 2864 S Cir Dr Ste 300 *Web:* www.my999radio.com	Colorado Springs	CO	80906	719-540-9200	579-0882

648-40 Columbia, SC

Station	City	State	ZIP	Phone	Fax
WCOS-AM 1400 (Sports) 316 Greystone Blvd *Web:* www.foxsportsradio1400.com	Columbia	SC	29210	803-343-1100	748-9267
WCOS-FM 97.5 (Ctry) 316 Greystone Blvd *TF:* 800-570-9690 ■ *Web:* www.975wcos.com	Columbia	SC	29210	803-343-1100	748-9267
WEPR-FM 90.1 (NPR) 1101 George Rogers Blvd *Web:* www.scetv.org	Columbia	SC	29201	803-737-3545	737-3552
WFMV-FM 95.3 (Rel) 2440 Milwood Ave *Web:* columbiainspiration.com	Columbia	SC	29205	803-939-9530	939-9469
WHMC-FM 90.1 (NPR) 1101 George Rogers Blvd. *Web:* www.scetv.org	Columbia	SC	29201	803-737-3545	737-3552
WHXT-FM 103.9 (Urban) 1900 Pineview Rd. *TF:* 877-874-1039 ■ *Web:* www.hot1039fm.com	Columbia	SC	29209	803-695-8600	695-8605
WLTR-FM 91.3 (NPR) 1101 George Rogers Blvd. *Web:* www.scetv.org	Columbia	SC	29201	803-737-3545	737-3552
WLTY-FM 96.7 (AC) 316 Greystone Blvd *Web:* www.967stevefm.com	Columbia	SC	29210	803-343-1100	
WMFX-FM 102.3 (CR) 1900 Pineview Rd *Web:* fox1023.com/	Columbia	SC	29209	803-695-8600	695-8605
WNOK-FM 104.7 (CHR) 316 Greystone Blvd *Web:* www.wnok.com	Columbia	SC	29210	803-343-1100	
WVOC-AM 560 (N/T) 316 Greystone Blvd *Web:* www.wvoc.com	Columbia	SC	29210	803-343-1100	256-5255

648-41 Columbus, GA

Station	City	State	ZIP	Phone	Fax
WCGQ-FM 107.3 (AC) 1820 Wynnton Rd *Web:* www.q1073.com	Columbus	GA	31906	706-327-1217	596-4600
WDAK-AM 540 (N/T) 1501 13th Ave *Web:* www.newsradio540.com	Columbus	GA	31901	706-576-3000	576-3010
WKCN-FM 99.3 (Ctry) 1820 Wynnton Rd *TF:* 800-628-2866 ■ *Web:* www.kissin993.com	Columbus	GA	31906	706-327-1217	596-4600
WRCG-AM 1420 (N/T) 1820 Wynnton Rd *Web:* www.1069rocks.com	Columbus	GA	31906	706-327-1217	596-4600

648-42 Columbus, OH

Station	City	State	ZIP	Phone	Fax
WBNS-AM 1460 (Sports) 605 S Front St Ste 300 *Web:* www.971thefan.com	Columbus	OH	43215	614-460-3850	
WBNS-FM 97.1 (AC) 605 S Front St Ste 300 *TF:* 888-691-9710 ■ *Web:* www.971thefan.com	Columbus	OH	43215	614-460-3850	460-3757
WCBE-FM 90.5 (NPR) 540 Jack Gibbs Blvd *Web:* www.wcbe.org	Columbus	OH	43215	614-365-5555	365-5060
WCKX-FM 107.5 (Urban) 350 E First Ave Ste 100 *Web:* mycolumbuspower.com	Columbus	OH	43201	614-487-1444	487-5862
WCOL-FM 92.3 (Ctry) 2323 W Fifth Ave Ste 200 *TF:* 800-899-9265 ■ *Web:* www.wcol.com	Columbus	OH	43204	614-486-6101	487-2559
WLVQ-FM 96.3 (Rock) 2400 Corporate Exchange Dr Ste 200 *TF:* 877-736-9696 ■ *Web:* www.qfm96.com	Columbus	OH	43231	614-227-9696	
WMNI-AM 920 (Nost) 1458 Dublin Rd *Web:* www.wmni.com	Columbus	OH	43215	614-481-7800	
WNCI-FM 97.9 (CHR) 2323 W Fifth Ave Ste 200 *Web:* www.wnci.com	Columbus	OH	43204	614-486-6101	487-2559
WNND-FM 103.5 (NAC) 4401 Carriage Hill Ln *TF:* 877-984-8786 ■ *Web:* rewindcolumbus.com	Columbus	OH	43220	614-451-2191	451-1831
WOSU-AM 820 (NPR) 2400 Olentangy River Rd. *Web:* www.wosu.org	Columbus	OH	43210	614-292-9678	292-7625
WRKZ-FM 99.7 (Rock) 1458 Dublin Rd *Web:* www.theblitz.com	Columbus	OH	43215	614-481-7800	
WSNY-FM 94.7 (AC) 4401 Carriage Hill Ln *Web:* www.sunny95.com	Columbus	OH	43220	614-451-2191	451-1831
WTVN-AM 610 (N/T) 2323 W Fifth Ave Ste 200 *Web:* www.610wtvn.com	Columbus	OH	43204	614-486-6101	487-2559

648-43 Corpus Christi, TX

Station	City	State	ZIP	Phone	Fax
KEDT-FM 90.3 (NPR) 4455 S Padre Island Dr Ste 38 *TF:* 800-307-5338 ■ *Web:* www.kedt.org	Corpus Christi	TX	78411	361-855-2213	855-3877
KEYS-AM 1440 (N/T) 2117 Leopard St *Web:* www.1440keys.com	Corpus Christi	TX	78408	361-883-3516	882-9767
KFTX-FM 97.5 (Ctry) 1520 S Port Ave *TF:* 866-975-5389 ■ *Web:* www.kftx.com	Corpus Christi	TX	78405	361-883-5987	883-3648
KLUX-FM 89.5 (AC) 1200 Lantana St. *Web:* www.goccn.org	Corpus Christi	TX	78407	361-289-6437	289-1420
KMXR-FM 93.9 (Oldies) 501 Tupper Ln *Web:* www.939online.com	Corpus Christi	TX	78417	361-289-0111	
KNCN-FM 101.3 (Rock) 501 Tupper Ln *Web:* www.c101.com	Corpus Christi	TX	78417	361-289-0111	289-5035
KRYS-FM 99.1 (Ctry) 501 Tupper Ln. *Web:* www.k99country.com	Corpus Christi	TX	78417	361-289-0111	289-5035
KSAB-FM 99.9 (Span) 501 Tupper Ln *Web:* www.ksabfm.com	Corpus Christi	TX	78417	361-289-0111	289-5035
KZFM-FM 95.5 (CHR) 2117 Leopard St. *Web:* www.hotz95.com	Corpus Christi	TX	78408	361-883-3516	

648-44 Dallas/Fort Worth, TX

Station	City	State	ZIP	Phone	Fax
KBFB-FM 97.9 (Urban) 13331 Preston Rd Ste 1180 *TF:* 888-362-8683 ■ *Web:* thebeatdfw.com	Dallas	TX	75240	972-331-5400	331-5560
KDGE-FM 102.1 (Alt) 14001 N Dallas Pkwy Ste 300 *Web:* www.kdge.com	Dallas	TX	75240	214-866-8000	866-8008
KDMX-FM 102.9 (AC) 14001 N Dallas Pkwy Ste 300 *Web:* www.1029now.com	Dallas	TX	75240	214-866-8000	866-8008
KEGL-FM 97.1 (Rock) 14001 N Dallas Pkwy Ste 300 *Web:* www.kegl.com	Dallas	TX	75240	214-866-8000	866-8008
KERA-FM 90.1 (NPR) 3000 Harry Hines Blvd *TF:* 800-456-5372 ■ *Web:* www.kera.org	Dallas	TX	75201	214-871-1390	754-0635
KHKS-FM 106.1 (CHR) 14001 N Dallas Pkwy Ste 300 *Web:* www.1061kissfm.com	Dallas	TX	75240	214-866-8000	866-8008
KJKK-FM 100.3 (Var) 4131 N Central Expy Ste 1000 *Web:* jackontheweb.cbslocal.com	Dallas	TX	75204	214-525-7000	
KKDA-FM 104 621 NW Sixth St *Web:* www.myk104.com	Grand Prairie	TX	75050	972-263-9911	558-0010
KLUV-FM 98.7 (Oldies) 4131 N Central Expy Ste 1000 *TF:* 855-987-5588 ■ *Web:* kluv.cbslocal.com	Dallas	TX	75204	214-525-7000	
KMVK-FM 107.5 (Urban) 4131 N Central Expy Ste 1000 *Web:* lagrande1075.cbslocal.com	Dallas	TX	75204	214-525-7000	
KRLD-AM 1080 (N/T) 4131 N Central Expy Ste 100 *TF:* 800-289-1080 ■ *Web:* dfw.cbslocal.com	Dallas	TX	75204	214-525-7000	
KVIL-FM 103.7 (AC) 4131 N Central Expy Ste 1000 *TF:* 877-787-1037 ■ *Web:* kvil.cbslocal.com	Dallas	TX	75204	214-525-7000	
KXT-FM 91.7 (Rel) 3000 Harry Hines Blvd *Web:* kxt.org	Dallas	TX	75201	214-871-1390	754-0635
KZPS-FM 92.5 (CR) 14001 N Dallas Pkwy Ste 300 *Web:* www.lonestar925.com	Dallas	TX	75240	214-866-8000	866-8008
WRR-FM 101.1 (Clas) PO Box 159001 *Web:* www.wrr101.com	Dallas	TX	75315	214-670-8888	670-8394

648-45 Dayton, OH

Station	City	State	ZIP	Phone	Fax
WDHT-FM 102.9 (Urban) 717 E David Rd. *Web:* www.hot1029.com	Dayton	OH	45429	937-294-5858	297-5233
WDPR-FM 88.1 (Clas) 126 N Main St. *Web:* discoverclassical.org	Dayton	OH	45402	937-496-3850	496-3852
WFCJ-FM 93.7 (Rel) PO Box 937 *Web:* www.wfcj.com	Dayton	OH	45449	937-424-1640	866-2062
WHIO-AM 1290 (N/T) 1414 Wilmington Ave *Web:* www.whio.com	Dayton	OH	45420	937-259-2111	259-2168
WHKO-FM 99.1 (Ctry) 1611 S Main St *Web:* www.k99online.com	Dayton	OH	45409	937-259-2111	259-2168
WING-AM 1410 (Sports) 717 E David Rd *Web:* www.wingam.com	Dayton	OH	45429	937-294-5858	297-5233
WMMX-FM 107.7 (AC) 101 Pine St *Web:* www.mix1077.com	Dayton	OH	45402	937-224-1137	224-3667
WONE-AM 980 (Sports) 101 Pine St. *Web:* www.wone.com	Dayton	OH	45402	937-224-1137	224-5015
WROU-FM 92.1 (Urban AC) 717 E David Rd *Web:* www.921wrou.com	Dayton	OH	45429	937-294-5858	297-5233
WTUE-FM 104.7 (Rock) 101 Pine St *Web:* www.wtue.com	Dayton	OH	45402	937-224-1137	224-5015
WXEG-FM 103.9 (Alt) 101 Pine St *Web:* www.newrock1039.com	Dayton	OH	45402	937-224-1137	224-5015

648-46 Daytona Beach, FL

Station	City	State	ZIP	Phone	Fax
WVYB-FM 103.3 (CHR) 126 W International Speedway Blvd	Daytona Beach	FL	32114	386-257-6900	

648-47 Denver, CO

Station	City	State	ZIP	Phone	Fax
KBPI-FM 106.7 (Rock) 4695 S Monaco St *Web:* www.kbpi.com	Denver	CO	80237	303-713-8000	713-8743
KEZW-AM 1430 (Nost) 4700 S Syracuse St Ste 1050 *Web:* www.studio1430.com	Denver	CO	80237	303-967-2700	
KHOW-AM 630 (N/T) 4695 S Monaco St *Web:* www.khow.com	Denver	CO	80237	303-713-8000	
KIMN-FM 100.3 (AC) 720 S Colorado Blvd Ste 1200N *Web:* www.mix100.com	Denver	CO	80246	303-832-5665	

Station	City	State	ZIP	Phone	Fax
KKZN-AM 760 (N/T) 4695 S Monaco St *Web:* realtalk760.com/	Denver	CO	80237	303-713-8000	713-8424
KOA-AM 850 (N/T) 4695 S Monaco Ave *Web:* www.850koa.com	Denver	CO	80237	303-713-8000	713-8424
KOSI-FM 101(AC) 4700 S Syracuse Pkwy Ste 1050 *Web:* www.kosi101.com	Denver	CO	80237	303-967-2700	
KPTT-FM 95.7 (CHR) 4695 S Monaco St *Web:* www.957theparty.com	Denver	CO	80237	303-713-8000	713-8734
KTCL-FM 93.3 (Alt) 4695 S Monaco St Ste 1300 *Web:* www.area93.com	Denver	CO	80237	303-713-8000	713-8743
KUVO-FM 89.3 (Jazz) 2900 Welton St Ste 200 *TF:* 800-574-5886 ■ *Web:* www.kuvo.org	Denver	CO	80205	303-480-9272	291-0757
KWOF-FM 92.5 (Ctry) 720 S Colorado Blvd *Web:* www.925thewolf.com	Denver	CO	80246	303-832-5665	
KXKL-FM 105 (Oldies) 720 S Colorado Blvd Ste 1200 N *Web:* www.kool105.com	Denver	CO	80246	303-832-5665	832-7000

648-48 Des Moines, IA

Station	City	State	ZIP	Phone	Fax
KAZR-FM 103.3 (Rock) 1416 Locust St *Web:* www.lazer1033.com	Des Moines	IA	50309	515-280-1350	280-3011
KDRB-FM 100.3 (AC) 2141 Grand Ave *Web:* www.thebusfm.com	Des Moines	IA	50312	515-245-8900	245-8902
KIOA-FM 93.3 (Oldies) 1416 Locust St *TF:* 877-984-8786 ■ *Web:* www.kioa.com	Des Moines	IA	50309	515-280-1350	280-3011
KKDM-FM 107.5 (AC) 2141 Grand Ave *Web:* www.1075kissfm.com	Des Moines	IA	50312	515-245-8854	245-8902
KSTZ-FM 102.5 (AC) 1416 Locust St *Web:* www.star1025.com	Des Moines	IA	50309	515-280-1350	280-3011
MORE 104 KMYR 1416 Locust St *Web:* more104music.com/	Des Moines	IA	50309	515-280-1350	280-3011
WHO-AM 1040 (N/T) 2141 Grand Ave *Web:* www.whoradio.com	Des Moines	IA	50312	515-245-8900	245-8902

648-49 Detroit, MI

Station	City	State	ZIP	Phone	Fax
WDET-FM 101.9 (NPR) 4600 Cass Ave Wayne State University *Web:* wdet.org	Detroit	MI	48201	313-577-4146	577-1300
WDMK-FM 105.9 (Urban) 3250 Franklin St *Web:* www.kissdetroit.com	Detroit	MI	48207	313-259-2000	259-7011
WDRQ-FM 93.1 (Var) 3011 W Grand Blvd Fisher Bldg Ste 800 *Web:* nashfm931.com	Detroit	MI	48202	313-871-9300	
WDVD-FM 96.3 (AC) 3011 W Grand Blvd Fisher Bldg Ste 800 *Web:* www.963wdvd.com	Detroit	MI	48202	313-871-3030	
WGPR-FM 107.5 (Urban) 3146 E Jefferson Ave	Detroit	MI	48207	313-259-8862	259-6662
WJR-AM 760 (N/T) 3011 W Grand Blvd Ste 800 *Web:* www.wjr.com	Detroit	MI	48202	313-875-4440	875-9022
WMUZ-FM 103.5 (Rel) 12300 Radio Pl *Web:* www.wmuz.com	Detroit	MI	48228	313-272-3434	272-5045
WMXD-FM 92.3 (Urban) 27675 Halsted Rd Ste 633 **Fax Area Code:* 313 ■ *Web:* www.mix923fm.com	Farmington Hills	MI	48331	248-324-5800	965-3965*
WRIF-FM 101.1 (Rock) One Radio Plz Rd *Web:* www.wrif.com	Detroit	MI	48220	248-547-0101	542-8800

648-50 Dubuque, IA

Station	City	State	ZIP	Phone	Fax
WDBQ-AM 1490 (N/T) 5490 Saratoga Rd *Web:* www.wdbqam.com	Dubuque	IA	52002	563-557-1040	583-4535
WDBQ-FM 107.5 (Oldies) 5490 Saratoga Rd *Web:* www.myq1075.com	Dubuque	IA	52002	563-557-1040	583-4535
WJOD-FM 103.3 (Ctry) 5490 Saratoga Rd *Web:* www.103wjod.com	Dubuque	IA	52002	563-557-1040	583-4535

648-51 Duluth, MN

Station	City	State	ZIP	Phone	Fax
KBMX-FM 107.7 (AC) 14 E Central Entrance *Web:* www.mix108.com	Duluth	MN	55811	218-727-4500	727-9356
KDNW-FM 97.3 (Rel) 1101 E Central Entrance *Web:* life973.com	Duluth	MN	55811	218-722-6700	
KKCB-FM 105.1 (Ctry) 14 E Central Entrance *Web:* www.kkcb.com	Duluth	MN	55811	218-727-4500	727-9356
KLDJ-FM 101.7 (Oldies) 14 E Central Entrance *Web:* www.kool1017.com	Duluth	MN	55811	218-727-5665	727-9356
KTCO-FM 98.9 (Ctry) 715 E Central Entrance *Web:* katcountry989.com	Duluth	MN	55811	218-722-4321	722-5423
KUMD-FM 103.3 (Var) 1201 ordean Ct 130 Humanities Bldg Rm 130 *Web:* www.kumd.org	Duluth	MN	55812	218-726-7181	726-6571
WEBC-AM 560 (Sports) 14 E Central Entrance *Web:* www.webc560.com	Duluth	MN	55811	218-727-4500	727-9356
WSCN-FM 100.5 (NPR) 207 W Superior St Ste 224 *TF:* 800-228-7123 ■ *Web:* minnesota.publicradio.org	Duluth	MN	55802	218-722-9411	720-4900
WWJC-AM 850 (Rel) 1120 E McCuen St *Web:* www.wwjc.com	Duluth	MN	55808	218-626-2738	626-2585

648-52 Edmonton, AB

Station	City	Prov	Postal Code	Phone	Fax
CFBR-FM 100.3 (CR) 18520 Stony Plain Rd Ste 100 *Web:* www.thebearrocks.com	Edmonton	AB	T5S2E2	780-486-2800	489-6927
CHED-AM 630 (N/T) 5204 84th St *Web:* www.630ched.com	Edmonton	AB	T6E5N8	780-440-6300	469-5937
CHFA-AM 680 (CBC) 10062 102nd Ave 123 Edmonton City Ctr *Web:* www.radio-canada.ca	Edmonton	AB	T5J2Y8	780-468-7500	468-7849
K-97 8882 170th St 2394 W Edmonton Mall *Web:* www.k97.fm	Edmonton	AB	T5T4M2	780-437-4996	

648-53 El Paso, TX

Station	City	State	ZIP	Phone	Fax
KELP-AM 1590 (Rel) 6900 Commerce St *Web:* www.kelpradio.com	El Paso	TX	79915	915-779-0016	779-6641
KHEY-FM 96.3 (Ctry) 4045 N Mesa St *Web:* www.khey.com	El Paso	TX	79902	915-351-5400	351-3136
KINT-FM 93.9 (Span) 5426 N Mesa St *TF:* 866-560-5673 ■ *Web:* www.jose939.com	El Paso	TX	79912	915-581-1126	585-4611
KLAQ-FM 95.5 (Rock) 4180 N Mesa St *TF:* 877-566-8477 ■ *Web:* www.klaq.com	El Paso	TX	79902	915-880-4955	532-3334
KPRR-FM 102.1 (CHR) 4045 N Mesa St *Web:* www.kprr.com	El Paso	TX	79902	915-351-5400	351-3136
KROD-AM 600 (N/T) 4180 N Mesa St *Web:* www.krod.com	El Paso	TX	79902	915-880-5763	
KSII-FM 93.1 (AC) 4180 N Mesa St *Web:* kisselpaso.com	El Paso	TX	79902	915-544-9300	532-3334
KTEP-FM 88.5 (NPR) 500 W University Ave Cotton Memorial Bldg Rm 203 *Web:* www.ktep.org	El Paso	TX	79968	915-747-5152	880-5837
KTSM-AM 690 (N/T) 4045 N Mesa St *Web:* www.ktsmradio.com	El Paso	TX	79902	915-351-5400	351-3136
KTSM-FM 99.9 (AC) 4045 N Mesa St *Web:* www.sunny999fm.com	El Paso	TX	79902	915-351-5400	351-3136
Univision Radio 2211 E Missouri Ave Ste S-300	El Paso	TX	79903	915-544-9797	544-1247

648-54 Erie, PA

Station	City	State	ZIP	Phone	Fax
WFNN-AM 1330 (Sports) one Boston Store Pl *Web:* www.sportsradio1330.com	Erie	PA	16501	814-461-1000	
WJET-AM 1400 (N/T) one Boston Store Pl *Web:* www.jetradio1400.com	Erie	PA	16501	814-461-1000	
WQLN-FM 91.3 (NPR) 8425 Peach St *TF:* 800-727-8854 ■ *Web:* www.wqln.org	Erie	PA	16509	814-864-3001	864-4077
WRIE-AM 1260 (Sports) 471 Robison Rd *Web:* www.am1260thescore.com	Erie	PA	16509	814-868-5355	868-1876
WXKC-FM 99.9 (AC) 471 Robison Rd *Web:* www.classy100.com	Erie	PA	16509	814-868-5355	868-1876

648-55 Eugene, OR

Station	City	State	ZIP	Phone	Fax
KDUK-FM 104.7 (CHR) 1500 Valley River Dr Ste 350 *Web:* www.kduk.com	Eugene	OR	97401	541-284-3600	484-5769
KKNU-FM 93.3 (Ctry) 925 Country Club Rd Ste 200 *Web:* kknu.fm/	Eugene	OR	97401	541-484-9400	344-9424
KLCC-FM 89.7 (NPR) 4000 E 30th Ave *Web:* www.klcc.org	Eugene	OR	97401	541-463-6000	463-6046
KMGE-FM 94.5 (AC) 925 Country Club Rd Ste 200 *Web:* 945mixfm.com/	Eugene	OR	97401	541-484-9400	344-9424
KODZ-FM 99.1 (CR) 1500 Vly River Dr Ste 350 *Web:* www.kool991.com	Eugene	OR	97401	541-284-3600	484-5769
KUGN-AM 590 (N/T) 1200 Executive Pkwy Ste 440 *TF:* 800-590-5846 ■ *Web:* www.kugn.com	Eugene	OR	97401	541-284-8500	485-0969
KZEL-FM 96.1 (CR) 1200 Executive Pkwy Ste 440 *Web:* www.96kzel.com	Eugene	OR	97401	541-284-8500	

648-56 Evansville, IN

Station	City	State	ZIP	Phone	Fax
WABX-FM 107.5 (CR) 1162 Mt Auburn Rd *Web:* www.wabx.net	Evansville	IN	47720	812-424-8284	426-7928
WDKS-FM 106.1 (CHR) 117 SE Fifth St *TF:* 888-454-5477 ■ *Web:* 1061evansville.com	Evansville	IN	47708	812-425-4226	
WGBF-AM 1280 (N/T) 117 SE Fifth St *Web:* www.newstalk1280.com	Evansville	IN	47708	812-425-4226	
WGBF-FM 103.1 (Rock) 117 SE Fifth St *Web:* www.103gbfrocks.com	Evansville	IN	47708	812-425-4226	
WIKY-FM 104.1 (AC) 1162 Mt Auburn Rd *TF:* 800-454-9459 ■ *Web:* www.wiky.com	Evansville	IN	47720	812-424-8284	426-7928
WJLT-FM 105.3 (Oldies) 117 SE Fifth St *Web:* espnevansville.com/	Evansville	IN	47708	812-421-1117	
WKDQ-FM 99.5 (Ctry) 117 SE Fifth St *Web:* www.wkdq.com	Evansville	IN	47708	812-425-4226	
WNIN-FM 88.3 (NPR) 405 Carpenter St *TF:* 855-888-9646 ■ *Web:* www.wnin.org	Evansville	IN	47708	812-423-2973	428-7548

Station	City	State	Zip	Phone	Fax
WSTO-FM 96.1 (CHR) 1162 Mt Auburn Rd *TF:* 888-685-1961 ■ *Web:* www.wsto.com	Evansville	IN	47720	812-421-9696	426-7928

648-57 Fairbanks, AK

Station	City	State	Zip	Phone	Fax
KAKQ-FM 101.1 (AC) 546 Ninth Ave *Web:* www.101magic.com	Fairbanks	AK	99701	907-450-1000	457-2128
KCBF-AM 820 (Sports) 819 First Ave Ste A *Web:* www.820sports.com	Fairbanks	AK	99701	907-451-5910	451-5999
KFAR-AM 660 AM 819 First Ave Ste A *Web:* www.kfar660.com	Fairbanks	AK	99701	907-451-5910	451-5999
KFBX-AM 970 (N/T) 546 Ninth Ave *Web:* www.970kfbx.com	Fairbanks	AK	99701	907-450-1000	450-1092
KIAK-FM 102.5 (Ctry) 546 Ninth Ave *Web:* www.kiak.com	Fairbanks	AK	99701	907-450-1000	457-2128
KKED-FM 104.7 (Rock) 546 Ninth Ave *Web:* www.1047theedge.com	Fairbanks	AK	99701	907-450-1000	457-2128
KSUA-FM 91.5 (Alt) 307 Capital Dr *Web:* www.ksuaradio.com	Fairbanks	AK	99709	907-474-7054	
KUAC-FM 89.9 (NPR) 312 Tanana Dr Ste 202 PO Box 755620 *TF:* 800-727-6543 ■ *Web:* www.kuac.org	Fairbanks	AK	99775	907-474-7491	474-5064

648-58 Fargo, ND

Station	City	State	Zip	Phone	Fax
Big 98.7 2720 Seventh Ave S *Web:* www.big987.com	Fargo	ND	58103	701-237-4500	235-9082
KDSU-FM 91.9 (NPR) 207 Fifth St N *TF:* 800-359-6900 ■ *Web:* www.prairiepublic.org	Fargo	ND	58102	701-241-6900	239-7651
KFGO-AM 790 (N/T) 1020 25th St S *Web:* www.kfgo.com	Fargo	ND	58103	701-237-5346	
KFNW-FM 97.9 (Rel) 5702 52nd Ave S *Web:* www.life979.com	Fargo	ND	58104	701-282-5910	
KPFX-FM 107.9 (CR) 2720 Seventh Ave S *Web:* www.1079thefox.com	Fargo	ND	58103	701-237-4500	235-9082
KRWK-FM 101.9 (CR) 1020 25th St S *Web:* www.rock102online.com	Fargo	ND	58103	701-237-5346	235-4042
KVOX-FM 99.9 (Ctry) 1020 S 25th St *Web:* www.froggyweb.com	Fargo	ND	58103	701-237-5346	235-9082
Q105.1 Rocks 2720 Seventh Ave S *Web:* www.q1051rocks.com	Fargo	ND	58103	701-237-4500	
WDAY-AM 970 (N/T) 301 Eigth St S *Web:* www.wday.com	Fargo	ND	58103	701-237-6500	241-5373
WDAY-FM 93.7 (CHR) 1020 25th St S *TF:* 877-478-5437 ■ *Web:* www.y94.com	Fargo	ND	58103	701-237-5346	237-0980

648-59 Flagstaff, AZ

Station	City	State	Zip	Phone	Fax
KAFF-AM 930 (Ctry) 1117 W Rt 66 *Web:* kaff.gcmaz.com	Flagstaff	AZ	86001	928-774-5231	779-2988
KAFF-FM 92.9 (Ctry) 1117 W Rt 66 *Web:* kaff.gcmaz.com	Flagstaff	AZ	86001	928-774-5231	779-2988
KMGN-FM 93.9 (CR) 1117 W Rt 66 *Web:* 939themountain.gcmaz.com	Flagstaff	AZ	86001	928-774-5231	779-2988
KNAU-FM 88.7 (NPR) Bldg 83 ,515 E Pine Knoll Dr PO Box 5764 *TF:* 800-523-5628 ■ *Web:* www.knau.org	Flagstaff	AZ	86011	928-523-5628	523-7647
KSED-FM 107.5 (Ctry) 2409 N Fourth St Ste 101 *Web:* www.koltcountry.com	Flagstaff	AZ	86004	928-779-1177	774-5179

648-60 Flint, MI

Station	City	State	Zip	Phone	Fax
WDZZ-FM 92.7 (Urban) 6317 Taylor Dr *Web:* www.wdzz.com	Flint	MI	48507	810-238-7300	238-7310
WRSR-FM 103.9 (CR) G-4511 Miller Rd *Web:* www.classicfox.com	Flint	MI	48507	810-720-9510	720-9513
WWCK-FM 105.5 (CHR) 6317 Taylor Dr *Web:* www.wwck.com	Flint	MI	48507	810-238-7300	238-7310

648-61 Fort Smith, AR

Station	City	State	Zip	Phone	Fax
KBBQ-FM 102.7 (Urban) 3101 Free Ferry Rd Ste E *Web:* www.1027thevibe.com	Fort Smith	AR	72903	479-452-0681	452-0873
KKBD-FM 95.9 (CR) 311 Lexington Ave *TF:* 866-503-1398 ■ *Web:* www.bigdog959.com	Fort Smith	AR	72901	479-782-8888	785-5946
KMAG-FM 99.1 (Ctry) 311 Lexington Ave *Web:* www.kmag991.com	Fort Smith	AR	72901	479-782-8888	785-5946
KOMS-FM 107.3 (Ctry) 3101 Free Ferry Rd Ste E *Web:* bigcountry1073.com	Fort Smith	AR	72903	479-452-0681	452-0873
KTCS-FM 99.9 (Ctry) 5304 Hwy 45 E *Web:* www.ktcs.com	Fort Smith	AR	72916	479-646-6151	646-3509
KWHN-AM 1320 (N/T) 311 Lexington Ave *Web:* www.kwhn.com	Fort Smith	AR	72901	479-782-8888	785-5946
KZBB-FM 97.9 (CHR) 311 Lexington Ave *TF:* 866-503-1398 ■ *Web:* www.kzbb.com	Fort Smith	AR	72901	479-782-8888	785-5946
KZKZ-FM 106.3 (Rel) 6420 S Zero St *Web:* www.kzkzfm.com	Fort Smith	AR	72903	479-646-6700	646-1373

648-63 Fort Wayne, IN

Station	City	State	Zip	Phone	Fax
89.1 WBOI 3204 Clairmont Ct *TF General:* 800-471-9264 ■ *Web:* www.wbni.org	Fort Wayne	IN	46808	260-452-1189	
98.9 the Bear WBYR 1005 Production Rd *Web:* www.989thebear.com	Fort Wayne	IN	46808	260-471-5100	471-5224
WBCL-FM 90.3 (Rel) 1025 W Rudisill Blvd *Web:* www.wbcl.org	Fort Wayne	IN	46807	260-745-0576	456-2913
WFWI 92.3 the Fort 1005 Production Rd *Web:* wowo.com	Fort Wayne	IN	46808	260-471-5100	471-5224
WJFX-FM 107.9 (CHR) 2000 Lower Huntington Rd *Web:* www.hot1079online.com	Fort Wayne	IN	46819	260-747-1511	482-8655
WLDE-FM 101.7 (Oldies) 347 W Berry St Ste 600 *TF:* 888-450-1017 ■ *Web:* fun1017.com/	Fort Wayne	IN	46802	260-423-3676	422-5266
WMEE-FM 97.3 (AC) 2915 Maples Rd *Web:* www.wmee.com	Fort Wayne	IN	46816	260-447-5511	447-7546
WOWO-AM 1190 (N/T) 2915 Maples Rd *TF:* 800-333-1190 ■ *Web:* www.wowo.com	Fort Wayne	IN	46816	260-447-5511	447-7546

648-64 Fresno, CA

Station	City	State	Zip	Phone	Fax
KBOS-FM 94.9 (CHR) 83 E Shaw Ave Ste 150 *TF:* 877-565-9467 ■ *Web:* www.b95forlife.com	Fresno	CA	93710	559-230-4300	243-4301
KFRR-FM 104.1 (Rock) 1066 E Shaw Ave *Web:* newrock1041.fm	Fresno	CA	93710	559-230-0104	230-0177
KJWL-FM 99.3 (Nost) 1415 Fulton Ave *Web:* www.kjwl.com	Fresno	CA	93721	559-497-5118	497-9760
KMGV-FM 97.9 (Oldies) 1071 W Shaw Ave *Web:* www.mega979.com	Fresno	CA	93711	559-442-4850	490-4199
KMJ-AM 580 (N/T) 1071 W Shaw Ave *TF:* 800-776-5858 ■ *Web:* kmjnow.com/	Fresno	CA	93711	559-490-5800	490-5878
KMJ-FM 105.9 1071 W Shaw Ave *TF:* 800-491-1899 ■ *Web:* www.kmjnow.com	Fresno	CA	93711	559-490-5800	490-5878
KPRX-FM 89.1 (NPR) 3437 W Shaw Ave Ste 101 *TF:* 800-275-0764 ■ *Web:* www.kvpr.org	Fresno	CA	93711	559-275-0764	275-2202
KRZR-FM 103.7 (Rock) 83 E Shaw Ave Ste 150 *Web:* www.thebeat1037.com	Fresno	CA	93710	559-230-4300	243-4301
KSKS-FM 93.7 (Ctry) 1071 W Shaw Ave *TF:* 800-767-5477 ■ *Web:* www.ksks.com	Fresno	CA	93711	559-490-5800	490-5889
KSOF-FM 98.9 (AC) 83 E Shaw Ave Ste 150 *TF:* 800-423-5870 ■ *Web:* www.softrock989.com	Fresno	CA	93710	559-230-4300	243-4301
KVPR-FM 89.3 (NPR) 3437 W Shaw Ave Ste 101 *TF:* 800-275-0764 ■ *Web:* www.kvpr.org	Fresno	CA	93711	559-275-0764	275-2202
KWYE-FM 101.1 (CHR) 1071 W Shaw Ave *TF:* 800-345-9101 ■ *Web:* www.y101hits.com	Fresno	CA	93711	559-490-5800	

648-65 Grand Forks, ND

Station	City	State	Zip	Phone	Fax
KFJM-FM 90.7 (AAA) 207 N Fifth St *TF:* 800-366-6888 ■ *Web:* www.prairiepublic.org	Fargo	ND	58102	701-241-6900	239-7650
KJKJ-FM 107.5 (Rock) 505 University Ave *Web:* www.kjkj.com	Grand Forks	ND	58203	701-746-1417	746-1410
KQHT-FM 96.1 (CR) 505 University Ave *Web:* www.961thefox.com	Grand Forks	ND	58203	701-746-1417	746-1410
KZLT-FM 104.3 (AC) 1185 Ninth St NE PO Box 13638 *Web:* www.1043citiesfm.com/	Thompson	ND	58278	701-775-4611	772-0540

648-66 Grand Rapids, MI

Station	City	State	Zip	Phone	Fax
WBCT-FM 93.7 (Ctry) 77 Monroe Ctr St NW Ste 1000 *TF:* 800-633-9393 ■ *Web:* www.b93.com	Grand Rapids	MI	49503	616-459-1919	732-3330
WCSG-FM 91.3 (Rel) 1159 E Beltline Ave NE *TF:* 800-968-4543 ■ *Web:* www.wcsg.org	Grand Rapids	MI	49525	616-942-1500	942-7078
WFGR-FM 98.7 (Oldies) 50 Monroe Ave NW Ste 500 *Web:* www.wfgr.com	Grand Rapids	MI	49503	616-451-4800	451-0113
WGRD-FM 97.9 (Rock) 50 Monroe Ave NW Ste 500 *TF:* 800-947-3979 ■ *Web:* www.wgrd.com	Grand Rapids	MI	49503	616-451-4800	451-9595
WGVU-FM 88.5 (NPR) 301 W Fulton St *TF:* 800-442-2771 ■ *Web:* www.wgvu.org	Grand Rapids	MI	49504	616-331-6666	331-6625
Wlav 60 Monroe Ctr St NW 3rd Fl *Web:* wlav.com	Grand Rapids	MI	49503	616-774-8461	451-3299
WLHT-FM 95.7 (AC) 50 Monroe Ave NW Ste 500 *Web:* mychannel957.com	Grand Rapids	MI	49503	616-451-4800	451-0113
WOOD-AM 1300 (N/T) 77 Monroe Ctr St NW Ste 1000 *Web:* www.woodradio.com	Grand Rapids	MI	49503	616-459-1919	242-9373
WSNX-FM 104.5 (CHR) 77 Monroe Ctr St NW Ste 1000 *Web:* www.1045snx.com	Grand Rapids	MI	49503	616-459-1919	242-9373

648-67 Green Bay, WI

Station	City	State	Zip	Phone	Fax
WDUZ-AM 1400 (Sports) 810 Victoria St *TF:* 855-724-1075 ■ *Web:* www.thefan1075.com	Green Bay	WI	54302	920-468-4100	468-0250
WIXX-FM 101.1 (CHR) PO Box 23333 *Web:* www.wixx.com	Green Bay	WI	54305	920-435-3771	321-2300
WNCY-FM 100.3 (Ctry) PO Box 23333 *TF:* 800-359-1003 ■ *Web:* www.wncy.com	Green Bay	WI	54305	920-435-3771	321-2300
WOGB-FM 103.1 (AC) 810 Victoria St *Web:* www.wogb.fm	Green Bay	WI	54302	920-468-4100	468-0250
WPNE-FM 89.3 (NPR) 2420 Nicolet Dr *TF:* 800-654-6228 ■ *Web:* www.wpr.org	Green Bay	WI	54311	920-465-2444	465-2576
WQLH-FM 98.5 (AC) 810 Victoria St *TF:* 855-782-7985 ■ *Web:* www.star98.net	Green Bay	WI	54302	920-468-4100	468-0250

648-68 Greenville, SC

Station	City	State	Zip	Phone	Fax
106.3 WORD 25 Garlington Rd *Web:* www.1063word.com/	Greenville	SC	29615	864-271-9200	
92.5 WESC-FM 101 N Main St PO Box 100 *TF:* 800-248-0863 ■ *Web:* www.wescfm.com	Greenville	SC	29601	864-242-4660	271-3830
WFBC-FM 93.7 (CHR) 25 Garlington Rd *Web:* www.b937.com	Greenville	SC	29615	864-271-9200	242-1567
WJMZ-FM 107.3 (Urban) 220 N Main St Ste 402 *TF:* 800-767-1073 ■ *Web:* www.1073jamz.com	Greenville	SC	29601	864-235-1073	370-3403
WLFJ-FM 89.3 (Rel) 2420 Wade Hampton Blvd *TF:* 800-447-7234 ■ *Web:* www.hisradio.com	Greenville	SC	29615	864-292-6040	292-8428
WMUU-FM 94.5 (Var) 920 Wade Hampton Blvd *Web:* www.wmuu.com	Greenville	SC	29609	864-242-6240	370-3829
WMYI-FM 102.5 (AC) 101 N Main St Ste 1000 PO Box 100 *TF:* 800-248-0863 ■ *Web:* my1025.com/	Greenville	SC	29601	864-235-1025	271-3830
WROQ-FM 101.1 (CR) 25 Garlington Rd *TF:* 888-257-0058 ■ *Web:* classicrock1011.com/	Greenville	SC	29615	864-271-9200	242-1567
WSPA-FM 98.9 (AC) 25 Garlington Rd *Web:* www.magic989online.com	Greenville	SC	29615	864-271-9200	242-1567
WTPT-FM 93.3 (Rock) 25 Garlington Rd *TF:* 800-774-0093 ■ *Web:* 933theplanetrocks.com/	Greenville	SC	29615	864-271-9200	242-1567

648-69 Gulfport/Biloxi, MS

Station	City	State	Zip	Phone	Fax
WCPR-FM 97.9 (Rock) 1909 E Pass Rd Ste D-11 *Web:* www.979cprrocks.com	Gulfport	MS	39507	228-388-2001	896-9736
WGCM-FM 102.3 (Oldies) 10250 Lorraine Rd *Web:* www.coast102.com	Gulfport	MS	39503	228-896-5500	896-0458
WJZD-FM 94.5 (Urban) 10211 Southpark Dr *Web:* www.wjzd.com	Gulfport	MS	39503	228-896-5307	896-5703
WKNN-FM 99.1 (Ctry) 286 DeBuys Rd *Web:* www.k99fm.com	Biloxi	MS	39531	228-388-2323	388-2362
WMJY-FM 93.7 (AC) 286 DeBuys Rd *Web:* www.magic937.com	Biloxi	MS	39531	228-388-2323	388-2362
WQBB-FM 105.9 (CR) 1909 E Pass Rd Ste D-11 *Web:* www.bob1059.com	Gulfport	MS	39507	228-388-2001	896-9736
WXYK-FM 107.1 1909 E Pass Rd Ste D-11 *Web:* www.1071themonkey.net	Gulfport	MS	39507	228-388-1071	896-9736

648-70 Halifax, NS

Station	City	State	Zip	Phone	Fax
CFLT-FM 92.9 (Ctry) 6080 Young St Ninth Fl *Web:* 929jackfm.ca/	Halifax	NS	B3K5L2	902-493-7200	
CHAL-FM 89.9 (Oldies) 90 Lovett Lake Ct Ste 300 *Web:* 899thewave.fm	Halifax	NS	B3S0H6	902-422-1651	

648-71 Harrisburg, PA

Station	City	State	Zip	Phone	Fax
WHP-AM 580 (N/T) 600 Corporate Cir *TF:* 888-251-7797 ■ *Web:* www.whp580.com	Harrisburg	PA	17110	717-540-8800	671-9973
WITF-FM 89.5 (NPR) 4801 Lindle Rd *TF:* 800-366-9483 ■ *Web:* www.witf.org	Harrisburg	PA	17111	717-704-3000	704-3659
WNNK-FM 104.1 (AC) 2300 Vartan Way *Web:* www.wink104.com	Harrisburg	PA	17110	717-238-1041	234-4842
WRBT-FM 94.9 (Ctry) 600 Corporate Cir *TF:* 800-682-3047 ■ *Web:* www.bob949.com	Harrisburg	PA	17110	717-540-8800	540-9268
WRVV-FM 97.3 (AC) 600 Corporate Cir *Web:* www.theriver973.com	Harrisburg	PA	17110	717-540-8076	671-9973
WWKL-FM 92.1 (CHR) 2300 Vartan Way *Web:* www.hot935fm.com	Harrisburg	PA	17110	717-238-1041	234-4842

648-72 Hartford, CT

Station	City	State	Zip	Phone	Fax
ESPN Radio 1410 10 Columbus Blvd *Web:* www.foxsportsradio1410.com	Hartford	CT	06106	860-723-6000	723-6195
Kiss 95.7 10 Columbus Blvd *Web:* www.kiss957.com	Hartford	CT	06106	860-723-6000	723-6195
Marlin Broadcasting 1039 Asylum Ave *Web:* www.beethoven.com	Hartford	CT	06105	860-525-1069	246-9084
Rock 106.9 WCCC, The 1039 Asylum Ave *Web:* www.wccc.com	Hartford	CT	06105	860-525-1069	246-9084
WHCN-FM 105.9 (CR) 10 Columbus Blvd *Web:* www.theriver1059.com	Hartford	CT	06106	860-723-6000	
WPKT-FM 90.5 (NPR) 1049 Asylum Ave *Web:* www.wnpr.org	Hartford	CT	06105	860-278-5310	
WRTC-FM 89.3 (Var) Trinity College 300 Summit St *Web:* www.wrtcfm.com	Hartford	CT	06106	860-297-2439	297-5201
WWYZ-FM 92.5 (Ctry) 10 Columbus Blvd *Web:* www.country925.com	Hartford	CT	06106	860-723-6000	

648-73 Honolulu, HI

Station	City	State	Zip	Phone	Fax
KAIM-FM 95.5 (Rel) 1160 N King St Second Fl *Web:* www.thefishhawaii.com	Honolulu	HI	96817	808-533-0065	524-2104
KCCN-FM 100.3 (CHR) 900 Ft St Ste 700 *Web:* kccnfm100.com	Honolulu	HI	96813	808-275-1000	536-2528
KDDB-FM 102.7 (CHR) 1000 Bishop St Ste 200 *Web:* www.1027dabomb.net	Honolulu	HI	96813	808-947-1500	
KDNN-FM 98.5 (Island) 650 Iwilei Rd Ste 400 *Web:* www.island985.com	Honolulu	HI	96817	808-550-9200	
KHJZ-FM 93.9 (CHR) 650 Iwilei Rd Ste 400 *TF:* 800-745-3000 ■ *Web:* www.939jamz.com	Honolulu	HI	96817	808-550-9200	550-9288
KHPR-FM 88.1 (NPR) 738 Kaheka St Ste 101 *Web:* www.hawaiipublicradio.org	Honolulu	HI	96814	808-955-8821	946-3863
KHVH-AM 830 (N/T) 650 Iwilei Rd Ste 400 **Fax:* Sales ■ *TF:* 888-565-8383 ■ *Web:* www.khvhradio.com	Honolulu	HI	96817	808-550-9200	550-9288*
KINE-FM 105.1 (AC) 900 Ft St Ste 700 *Web:* hawaiian105.com	Honolulu	HI	96813	808-275-1000	536-2528
KKOL-FM 107.9 (Oldies) 1160 N King St Second Fl *Web:* www.oldies1079honolulu.com	Honolulu	HI	96817	808-533-0065	524-2104
KPOI-FM 105.9 (CR) 1000 Bishop St Ste 200 *Web:* www.kpoifm.com	Honolulu	HI	96813	808-947-1500	296-1059
KRTR-FM 96.3 (AC) 900 Ft St Ste 700 *Web:* krater963.com	Honolulu	HI	96813	808-275-1000	536-2528
KSSK-AM 590 (AC) 650 Iwilei Rd Ste 400 *Web:* www.ksskradio.com	Honolulu	HI	96817	808-550-9200	
KSSK-FM 92.3 (AC) 650 Iwilei Rd Ste 400 *Web:* www.ksskradio.com	Honolulu	HI	96817	808-550-9200	
KUCD-FM 101.9 (Alt) 650 Iwilei Rd Ste 400 **Fax:* Sales ■ *Web:* www.star1019.com	Honolulu	HI	96817	808-550-9200	550-9288*
KUMU-FM 94.7 (AC) 1000 Bishop St Ste 200 *Web:* www.kumu.com	Honolulu	HI	96813	808-947-1500	

648-74 Hot Springs, AR

Station	City	State	Zip	Phone	Fax
KHTH-FM 101.7 (AC) 1410 Neotomas Ave Ste 200 *Web:* hot1017.com/	Santa Rosa	CA	95405	707-543-0100	571-1097
KHTO-FM 96.7 125 Corporate Terr *TF:* 866-425-9600 ■ *Web:* www.myhotsprings.com	Hot Springs	AR	71913	501-525-9700	525-9739
KLAZ-FM 105.9 (CHR) 208 Buena Vista Rd *TF:* 800-621-3362 ■ *Web:* www.klaz.com	Hot Springs	AR	71913	501-525-4600	525-4344
KLXQ-FM 101.9 (CR) 125 Corporate Terr *Web:* www.myhotsprings.com	Hot Springs	AR	71913	501-525-9700	525-9739
KQUS-FM 97.5 (Ctry) 125 Corporate Terr *Web:* www.myhotsprings.com	Hot Springs	AR	71913	501-525-9700	525-9739

648-75 Houston, TX

Station	City	State	Zip	Phone	Fax
KAMA-FM 104.9 (Urban) 5100 SW Fwy *Web:* 1049tumusica.univision.com	Houston	TX	77056	713-965-2400	965-2401
KBXX-FM 97.9 (Urban) 24 Greenway Plaza Ste 900 *TF:* 888-407-4747 ■ *Web:* theboxhouston.com	Houston	TX	77046	713-623-2108	300-5751
KHMX-FM 96.5 (CHR) 24 Greenway Plz Ste 1900 *Web:* mix965houston.cbslocal.com	Houston	TX	77046	713-212-5965	
KKBQ-FM 92.9 (Ctry) 1990 Post Oak Blvd Ste 2300 *Web:* www.thenew93q.com	Houston	TX	77056	713-963-1200	993-9300
KKHT-FM 100.0 (Rel) 6161 Savoy Dr Ste 1200 *Web:* www.kkht.com	Houston	TX	77036	713-260-3600	
KKRW-FM 93.7 (CR) 2000 W Loop S Ste 300 *Web:* 937thebeathouston.com/	Houston	TX	77027	713-212-8000	212-8963
KLAT-AM 1010 (Span N/T) 5100 SW Fwy *TF:* 800-646-6779 ■ *Web:* corporate.univision.com	Houston	TX	77056	713-407-1415	407-1400
KMJQ Majic 102.1 24 24 Greenway Plaza Ste 900 *Web:* myhoustonmajic.com	Houston	TX	77046	713-623-2108	300-5764
KODA-FM 99.1 (AC) 2000 W Loop S Ste 300 *Web:* www.sunny99.com	Houston	TX	77027	713-212-8000	212-8963
KPRC-AM 950 (N/T) 2000 W Loop S Ste 300 *Web:* www.kprcradio.com	Houston	TX	77027	713-212-8000	212-8963
KRBE-FM 104.1 (CHR) 9801 Westheimer Rd Ste 700 *TF:* 888-955-2993 ■ *Web:* www.krbe.com	Houston	TX	77042	713-266-1000	954-2344
KSEV-AM 700 (N/T) 11451 Katy Fwy Ste 215 **Fax Area Code:* 832 ■ *Web:* www.ksevradio.com	Houston	TX	77079	281-588-4800	358-9556*
KTBZ-FM 94.5 (Alt) 2000 W Loop S Ste 300 *Web:* www.thebuzz.com	Houston	TX	77027	713-212-8000	212-8963
KTHT-FM 1990 Post Oak Blvd Ste 2300 *TF:* 877-745-6591 ■ *Web:* www.countrylegends971.com	Houston	TX	77056	713-963-1200	622-5457

	City	State	ZIP	Phone	Fax
KTRH-AM 740 (N/T) 2000 W Loop S Ste 300 *Web:* www.ktrh.com	Houston	TX	77027	713-212-8000	212-8958
KUHF-FM 88.7 (Clas) 4343 Elgin St 3rd Fl *TF:* 877-252-0436 ■ *Web:* www.kuhf.org	Houston	TX	77204	713-743-0887	743-0868
Rovi Corporation 1990 Post Oak Blvd Ste 2300 *Web:* www.houstonseagle.com	Houston	TX	77056	713-963-1200	622-5457

648-76 Huntsville, AL

	City	State	ZIP	Phone	Fax
Mix 96.9 8402 Memorial Pkwy SW *Web:* www.lite969.com	Huntsville	AL	35802	256-885-9797	885-9796
WEUP-FM 103.1 (Urban) 2609 Jordan Ln NW *Web:* www.103weup.com	Huntsville	AL	35816	256-837-9387	837-9404
WJOU-FM 90.1 (Rel) 7000 Adventist Blvd *Web:* www.wjou.org	Huntsville	AL	35896	256-722-9990	837-7918
WLOR-AM 1550 (Oldies) 1555 the Boardwalk Ste 1 *Web:* sunny981.com	Huntsville	AL	35816	256-536-1568	536-4416
WLRH-FM 89.3 (NPR) University of Alabama-Huntsville John Wright Dr *TF:* 800-239-9574 ■ *Web:* www.wlrh.org	Huntsville	AL	35899	256-895-9574	830-4577

648-77 Indianapolis, IN

	City	State	ZIP	Phone	Fax
93.9 The beat 6810 N Shadeland Ave *Web:* www.indysi94.com	Indianapolis	IN	46220	317-842-9550	921-1996
Country 97.1 HANK FM 40 Monument Cir Ste 600 *Web:* www.hankfm.com	Indianapolis	IN	46204	317-266-9700	684-2021
WFBQ-FM 94.7 (CR) 6161 Fall Creek Rd *Web:* www.q95.com	Indianapolis	IN	46220	317-257-7565	254-9619
WFMS-FM 95.5 (Ctry) 6810 N Shadeland Ave *Web:* www.wfms.com	Indianapolis	IN	46220	317-842-9550	577-3361
WFYI-FM 90.1 1630 N Meridian St *Web:* www.wfyi.org	Indianapolis	IN	46202	317-636-2020	283-6645
WHHH-FM 96.3 (CHR) 21 E St Joseph St *Web:* indyhiphop.com	Indianapolis	IN	46204	317-266-9600	328-3870
WIBC-FM 93.1 (N/T) 40 Monument Cir Ste 400 *TF:* 800-571-9422 ■ *Web:* www.wibc.com	Indianapolis	IN	46204	317-266-9422	684-2022
WJJK-FM 104.5 (CR) 6810 N Shadeland Ave *Web:* www.1045wjjk.com	Indianapolis	IN	46220	317-842-9550	577-3361
WNDE-AM 1260 (Sports) 6161 Fall Creek Rd *Web:* www.wnde.com	Indianapolis	IN	46220	317-257-7565	254-9619
WNTR-FM 107.9 (AC) 9245 N Meridian St Ste 300 *Web:* www.indysmix.com	Indianapolis	IN	46260	317-816-4000	816-4035
WTLC-AM 1310 (Rel) 21 E St Joseph St *Web:* praiseindy.com	Indianapolis	IN	46204	317-266-9600	328-3870
WXNT-AM 1430 (N/T) 9245 N Meridian St Ste 300 *Web:* www.cbssports1430.com	Indianapolis	IN	46260	317-218-2264	
WYXB-FM 105.7 (AC) 40 Monument Cir Ste 600 *Web:* www.b1057.com	Indianapolis	IN	46204	317-681-1057	684-2021
WZPL-FM 99.5 (AC) 9245 N Meridian St Ste 300 *Web:* www.wzpl.com	Indianapolis	IN	46260	317-816-4000	

648-78 Jackson, MS

	City	State	ZIP	Phone	Fax
WHLH-FM 95.5 (Rel) 1375 Beasley Rd *Web:* www.hallelujah955.com	Jackson	MS	39206	601-982-1062	362-1905
WJDX-AM 620 (Sports) 1375 Beasley Rd *Web:* www.wjdx.com	Jackson	MS	39206	601-982-1062	362-1905
WMAE-FM 89.5 (NPR) 3825 Ridgewood Rd *TF:* 800-850-4406 ■ *Web:* mpbonline.org	Jackson	MS	39211	601-432-6565	432-690
WMAH-FM 90.3 (NPR) 3825 Ridgewood Rd *Web:* www.mpbonline.org	Jackson	MS	39211	601-432-6565	432-6806
WMSI-FM 102.9 (Ctry) 1375 Beasley Rd *Web:* www.miss103.com	Jackson	MS	39206	601-982-1062	362-1905
WSTZ-FM 106.7 (CR) 1375 Beasley Rd *Web:* www.z106.com	Jackson	MS	39206	601-982-1062	362-1905

648-79 Jacksonville, FL

	City	State	ZIP	Phone	Fax
107.3 jack fm 11700 Central Pkwy **Fax:* Sales ■ *Web:* www.1073jack.com	Jacksonville	FL	32224	904-636-0507	*
Jacksonville's Country WQIK 99.1 11700 Central Pkwy **Fax:* Sales ■ *Web:* www.991wqik.com	Jacksonville	FL	32224	904-636-0507	*
V101.5 11700 Central Pkwy **Fax:* Sales ■ *Web:* www.v1015.com	Jacksonville	FL	32224	904-636-0507	*
WAPE-FM 95.1 (CHR) 8000 Belfort Pkwy Ste 100 *TF:* 800-475-9595 ■ *Web:* www.wape.com	Jacksonville	FL	32256	904-245-8500	245-8501
WCGL-AM 1360 (Rel) 3890 Dunn Ave Ste 804 *Web:* www.wcgl1360.com	Jacksonville	FL	32218	904-766-9955	765-9214
WEJZ-FM 96.1 (AC) 6440 Atlantic Blvd *Web:* www.wejz.com	Jacksonville	FL	32211	904-727-9696	721-9322
WFKS-FM 97.9 (CHR) 11700 Central Pkwy *Web:* 979kissfm.com/	Jacksonville	FL	32224	904-636-0507	
WJAX-AM 1220 (Nost) 5353 Arlington Expy *TF:* 800-331-0176 ■ *Web:* www.wktz.jones.edu	Jacksonville	FL	32211	904-371-1184	896-1669
WJBT-FM 93.3 (Urban) 11700 Central Pkwy **Fax:* Sales ■ *Web:* www.wjbt.com	Jacksonville	FL	32224	904-636-0507	636-7971*
WJCT-FM 89.9 100 Festival Pk Ave *Web:* www.wjct.org	Jacksonville	FL	32202	904-353-7770	
WJGL-FM 96.9 (CR) 8000 Belfort Pkwy *TF:* 800-438-1601 ■ *Web:* www.969theeagle.com	Jacksonville	FL	32256	904-245-8500	245-8501
WKTZ-FM 90.9 (AC) 5353 Arlington Expy *Web:* www.wktz.jones.edu	Jacksonville	FL	32211	904-371-1184	
WOKV-AM 690 (N/T) 8000 Belfort Pkwy Ste 100 *Web:* www.wokv.com	Jacksonville	FL	32256	904-245-8500	245-8501
WXXJ-FM 102.9 (AC) 8000 Belfort Pkwy *TF:* 800-460-6394 ■ *Web:* www.x1029.com	Jacksonville	FL	32256	904-245-8500	245-8501
WZNZ-AM 1460 (Rel) PO Box 51585 *Web:* www.qopradio.com	Jacksonville Beach	FL	32240	904-241-3311	

648-80 Jefferson City, MO

	City	State	ZIP	Phone	Fax
KLIK-AM 1240 (N/T) 1002 Diamond Ridge Ctr Ste 400 *Web:* www.klik1240.com	Jefferson City	MO	65109	573-893-5100	893-8330

648-81 Johnson City, TN

	City	State	ZIP	Phone	Fax
WETB-AM 790 (Rel) 231 Brandonwood Dr PO Box 4127	Johnson City	TN	37604	423-928-7131	928-8392
WETS-FM 89.5 (NPR) PO Box 70630 *TF:* 888-895-9387 ■ *Web:* etsu.edu/wets/	Johnson City	TN	37614	423-439-6440	439-6449

648-82 Juneau, AK

	City	State	ZIP	Phone	Fax
KTOO-FM 104.3 (NPR) 360 Egan Dr *Web:* www.ktoo.org	Juneau	AK	99801	907-586-1670	

648-83 Kansas City, KS & MO

	City	State	ZIP	Phone	Fax
KCKC-FM 102.1 (AC) 508 Westport Rd Ste 202 *Web:* kc1021.com	Kansas City	MO	64111	816-753-4000	
KCUR-FM 89.3 (NPR) 4825 Troost Ave Ste 202 *TF:* 855-778-5437 ■ *Web:* www.kcur.org	Kansas City	MO	64110	816-235-1551	235-2864
KFKF-FM 94.1 (Ctry) 508 Westport Rd Ste 202 *Web:* www.kfkf.com	Kansas City	MO	64111	816-753-4000	753-4045
KGGN-AM 890 (Rel) 1734 E 63rd St Ste 600 *TF:* 800-924-3177 ■ *Web:* www.kggnam.com	Kansas City	MO	64110	816-333-0092	363-8120
KKFI-FM 90.1 (Var) 3901 Main St Ste 203 *Web:* www.kkfi.org	Kansas City	MO	64111	816-931-3122	931-7078
KLJC-FM 88.5 (Rel) 15800 Calvary Rd *Web:* life885.com	Kansas City	MO	64147	816-331-8700	331-3497
KMXV-FM 93.3 (CHR) 508 Westport Rd Ste 202 *Web:* www.mix93.com	Kansas City	MO	64111	816-753-4000	753-4045
KPRS-FM 103.3 (Urban) 11131 Colorado Ave *TF:* 800-273-8255 ■ *Web:* www.kprs.com	Kansas City	MO	64137	816-763-2040	966-1055
KPRT-AM 1590 (Rel) 11131 Colorado Ave *Web:* www.kprt.com	Kansas City	MO	64137	816-763-2040	966-1055

648-84 Key West, FL

	City	State	ZIP	Phone	Fax
WAIL-FM 99.5 (Rock) 5450 MacDonald Ave Ste 10 *Web:* www.sun103.com	Key West	FL	33040	305-296-7511	296-0358
WEOW-FM 92.7 (CHR) 5450 MacDonald Ave Ste 10 *Web:* www.weow927.com	Key West	FL	33040	305-296-7511	296-0358
WIIS-FM 107.1 (Alt) 1075 Duval St Ste C17 *Web:* www.island107.com	Key West	FL	33040	305-292-1071	
WKWF-AM 1600 (Sports) 5450 MacDonald Ave Ste 10 *Web:* www.sportsradio1600.com	Key West	FL	33040	305-294-2523	

648-85 Knoxville, TN

	City	State	ZIP	Phone	Fax
NEWS TALK 98.7 4711 Old Kingston Pike **Fax:* News Rm ■ *Web:* www.newstalk987.com	Knoxville	TN	37919	865-588-6511	588-3725*
WCYQ-FM 93.1 (Oldies) 1533 Amherst Rd *Web:* www.q100country.com	Knoxville	TN	37909	865-824-1021	
WFIV-FM 105.3 (AAA) 517 Watt Rd *Web:* www.myi105.com	Knoxville	TN	37934	865-675-4105	
WIMZ-FM 103.5 (CR) 1100 Sharps Ridge Memorial Pk Dr *Web:* www.wimz.com	Knoxville	TN	37917	865-525-6000	

Station	City	State	Zip	Phone	Fax
WITA-AM 1490 (Rel) 2914 Sanderson Rd *Web:* www.1490wita.com	Knoxville	TN	37921	865-588-2974	
WIVK-FM 107.7 (Ctry) 4711 Old Kingston Pike *TF:* 877-995-9961 ■ *Web:* www.wivk.com	Knoxville	TN	37919	865-588-6511	588-3725
WJBZ-FM 96.3 (Rel) 7101 Chapman Hwy *Web:* www.praise963.com	Knoxville	TN	37920	865-577-4885	
WJXB-FM 97.5 (AC) 1100 Sharps Ridge Rd PO Box 27100 *Web:* www.b975.com	Knoxville	TN	37917	865-525-6000	525-2000
WUOT-FM 91.9 (NPR) 209 Communications Bldg University of Tennessee *TF:* 888-266-9868 ■ *Web:* www.wuot.org	Knoxville	TN	37996	865-974-5375	974-3941
WWST-FM 102.1 (CHR) 1533 Amherst Rd *Web:* www.star1021fm.com	Knoxville	TN	37909	865-824-1021	824-1880

648-86 Lafayette, LA

Station	City	State	Zip	Phone	Fax
KJCB-AM 770 (Urban) 604 St John St	Lafayette	LA	70501	337-233-4262	235-9681
KMDL-FM 97.3 (Ctry) 1749 Bertrand Dr *Web:* 973thedawg.com	Lafayette	LA	70506	337-233-6000	234-7360
KPEL-AM 1420 (Sports) 1749 Bertrand Dr *Web:* espn1420.com	Lafayette	LA	70506	337-233-6000	234-7360
KPEL-FM 105.1 (N/T) 1749 Bertrand Dr *Web:* www.kpel965.com	Lafayette	LA	70506	337-233-6000	
KRKA-FM 107.9 (Urban) 1749 Bertrand Dr. *Web:* 1079ishot.com	Lafayette	LA	70506	337-233-6000	234-7360
KRRQ-FM 95.5 (Urban) 202 Galbert Rd *Web:* www.krrq.com	Lafayette	LA	70506	337-232-1311	233-3779
KTDY-FM 99.9 (AC) 1749 Bertrand Dr *Web:* 999ktdy.com	Lafayette	LA	70506	337-233-6000	234-7360
KXKC-FM 99.1 (Ctry) 202 Galbert Rd *Web:* www.nashfm991.com	Lafayette	LA	70506	337-534-8700	233-3779

648-87 Lansing, MI

Station	City	State	Zip	Phone	Fax
WFMK-FM 99.1 (AC) 3420 Pine Tree Rd *Web:* www.99wfmk.com	Lansing	MI	48911	517-394-7272	394-3565
WHZZ-FM 101.7 (AC) 600 W Cavanaugh Rd *Web:* www.1017mikefm.com	Lansing	MI	48910	517-393-1320	393-0882
WITL-FM 100.7 (Ctry) 3420 Pine Tree Rd *Web:* www.witl.com	Lansing	MI	48911	517-394-7272	394-3565
WJIM-AM 1240 (N/T) 3420 Pine Tree Rd. **Fax:* News Rm ■ *Web:* www.wjimam.com	Lansing	MI	48911	517-394-7272	394-3565*
WJIM-FM 97.5 (CHR) 3420 Pine Tree Rd *Web:* www.975now.com	Lansing	MI	48911	517-394-7272	394-3565
WLNZ-FM 89.7 (Var) 400 N Capitol Ave Ste 001 *Web:* www.lcc.edu	Lansing	MI	48933	517-483-1710	483-1894
WMMQ-FM 94.9 (CR) 3420 Pine Tree Rd *Web:* www.wmmq.com	Lansing	MI	48911	517-394-7272	394-3565
WQHH-FM 96.5 (Urban) 600 W Cavanaugh *Web:* www.power965fm.com	Lansing	MI	48910	517-393-1320	393-0882
WVFN-AM 730 (Sports) 3420 Pine Tree Rd. *Web:* thegame730am.com	Lansing	MI	48911	517-394-7272	394-3565

648-88 Las Vegas, NV

Station	City	State	Zip	Phone	Fax
KCEP-FM 88.1 (Urban) 330 W Washington Ave *Web:* kcep.power88lv.com	Las Vegas	NV	89106	702-648-0104	647-0803
KDWN-AM 720 (N/T) 1455 E Tropicana Ave Ste 800 *TF:* 866-297-5303 ■ *Web:* www.kdwn.com	Las Vegas	NV	89119	702-730-0300	736-8447
KENO-AM 1460 (Sports) 8755 W Flamingo Rd. *Web:* wearelv.com	Las Vegas	NV	89147	702-876-1460	
KKLZ-FM 96.3 1455 E Tropicana Ave Ste 800 *Web:* www.963kklz.com	Las Vegas	NV	89119	702-730-0300	736-8447
KKVV-AM 1060 (Rel) 3185 S Highland Dr Ste 13 *Web:* www.kkvv.com	Las Vegas	NV	89109	702-731-5588	731-5851
KMXB-FM 94.1 (AC) 7255 S Tenaya Way Ste 100 *TF:* 866-438-0220 ■ *Web:* mix941fm.cbslocal.com	Las Vegas	NV	89113	702-257-9400	257-2936
KNPR-FM 89.5 (NPR) 1289 S Torrey Pines Dr. *TF:* 888-258-9895 ■ *Web:* www.knpr.org	Las Vegas	NV	89146	702-258-9895	258-5646
KOMP-FM 92.3 (Rock) 8755 W Flamingo Rd *Web:* www.komp.com	Las Vegas	NV	89147	702-876-3692	876-6685
KPLV-FM 93.1 (AC) 2880 Meade Ave Ste 250 *Web:* www.my931.com	Las Vegas	NV	89102	702-238-7300	732-4890
KSNE-FM 106.5 (AC) 2880 Meade Ave Ste 250 *Web:* www.sunny1065.com	Las Vegas	NV	89102	702-238-7300	732-4890
KVEG-FM 97.5 (Urban) 3999 Las Vegas Blvd S Ste K *Web:* www.kvegas.com	Las Vegas	NV	89119	702-736-6161	736-2986
KWNR-FM 95.5 (Ctry) 2880 Meade Ave Ste 250 *Web:* www.955thebull.com	Las Vegas	NV	89102	702-238-7300	732-4890
KXNT-AM 840 (N/T) 7255 S Tenaya Way Ste 100 *Web:* lasvegas.cbslocal.com	Las Vegas	NV	89113	702-889-7300	
KXTE-FM 107.5 (Alt) 7255 S Tenaya Way Ste 100 *Web:* x1075lasvegas.cbslocal.com	Las Vegas	NV	89113	702-257-1075	889-7555

648-89 Lexington/Frankfort, KY

Station	City	State	Zip	Phone	Fax
WBUL-FM 98.1 (Ctry) 2601 Nicholasville Rd *Web:* www.wbul.com	Lexington	KY	40503	859-422-1000	
WFKY-FM 104.9 (Cty) 115 W Main St *Web:* www.myfroggy1049.com	Frankfort	KY	40601	502-875-1130	875-1225
WGKS-FM 96.9 (AC) 401 W Main St Ste 301 *Web:* www.969kissfm.com	Lexington	KY	40507	859-233-1515	233-1517
WKYL-FM 102.1 (NAC) 102 Perkins Bldg 521 Lancaster Ave *TF:* 800-621-8890 ■ *Web:* www.weku.fm	Richmond	KY	40475	800-621-8890	
WLAP-AM 630 (N/T) 2601 Nicholasville Rd. *Web:* www.wlap.com	Lexington	KY	40503	859-422-1000	422-1038
WLKT-FM 104.5 (CHR) 2601 Nicholasville Rd *Web:* www.1045thecat.com	Lexington	KY	40503	859-422-1000	
WMXL-FM 94.5 (AC) 2601 Nicholasville Rd *Web:* www.mymix945.com	Lexington	KY	40503	859-422-1000	422-1038
WUKY-FM 91.3 (NPR) 340 McVey Hall University of Kentucky *Web:* wuky.org	Lexington	KY	40506	859-257-3221	257-6291
WWRW-FM 105.5 (Oldies) 2601 Nicholasville Rd. *Web:* www.rewind1055.com	Lexington	KY	40503	859-422-1000	

648-90 Lincoln, NE

Station	City	State	Zip	Phone	Fax
KBBK-FM 107.3 (AC) 4343 'O' St *Web:* www.b1073.com	Lincoln	NE	68510	402-475-4567	479-1411
KFGE-FM 98.1 (Ctry) 4343 'O' St *Web:* www.froggy981.com	Lincoln	NE	68510	402-475-4567	479-1411
KFRX-FM 106.3 (CHR) 3800 Cornhusker Hwy *TF:* 800-523-9101 ■ *Web:* www.kfrxfm.com	Lincoln	NE	68504	402-466-1234	467-4095
KIBZ-FM 104.1 (Rock) 3800 Cornhusker Hwy *Web:* www.kibz.com	Lincoln	NE	68504	402-466-1234	467-4095
KTGL-FM 92.9 (CR) 3800 Cornhusker Hwy *Web:* www.ktgl.com	Lincoln	NE	68504	402-466-1234	467-4095

648-91 Little Rock, AR

Station	City	State	Zip	Phone	Fax
KABF-FM 88.3 (Var) 2101 Main St # 200 **Fax Area Code:* 504 ■ *Web:* www.kabf.org	Little Rock	AR	72206	501-372-6119	376-3952*
KABZ-FM 103.7 (N/T) 2400 Cottondale Ln *TF:* 800-477-1037 ■ *Web:* www.1037thebuzz.com	Little Rock	AR	72202	501-661-1037	664-5871
KIPR-FM 92.3 (Urban) 700 Wellington Hills Rd *Web:* www.power923.com	Little Rock	AR	72211	501-401-0200	401-0366
KKPT-FM 94.1 (CR) 2400 Cottondale Ln. *TF:* 800-844-0094 ■ *Web:* www.point941.com	Little Rock	AR	72202	501-664-9410	664-5871
KLAL-FM 107.7 (CHR) 700 Wellington Hills Rd *Web:* www.alice1077.com	Little Rock	AR	72211	501-401-0200	
KMJX-FM 105.1 (CR) 10800 Colonel Glenn Rd *Web:* www.1051thewolf.com	Little Rock	AR	72204	501-217-5000	
KOKY-FM 102.1 (Urban) 700 Wellington Hills Rd *Web:* www.koky.com	Little Rock	AR	72211	501-401-0200	
KSSN-FM 95.7 (Ctry) 10800 Colonel Glenn Rd *Web:* www.kssn.com	Little Rock	AR	72204	501-217-5000	228-9547
KURB-FM 98.5 (AC) 700 Wellington Hills Rd *Web:* www.b98.com	Little Rock	AR	72211	501-401-0200	

648-92 Los Angeles, CA

Station	City	State	Zip	Phone	Fax
KABC-AM 790 (N/T) 3321 S La Cienega Blvd PO Box 790 *TF:* 800-222-5222 ■ *Web:* www.kabc.com	Los Angeles	CA	90016	310-840-4900	
KFWB-AM 980 (N/T) 5670 Wilshire Blvd Ste 200 *Web:* kfwbam.com	Los Angeles	CA	90036	855-962-3278	
KLAX-FM 97.9 (Span) 10281 W Pico Blvd *Web:* www.979laraza.com	Los Angeles	CA	90064	310-203-0900	843-4969
KLOS-FM 95.5 (CR) 3321 S La Cienega Blvd. *Web:* www.955klos.com	Los Angeles	CA	90016	310-840-4828	
KNX-AM 1070 (N/T) 5670 Wilshire Blvd Ste 200 *Web:* losangeles.cbslocal.com	Los Angeles	CA	90036	323-957-4524	964-8398
KROQ-FM 106.7 (Alt) 5901 Venice Blvd *TF:* 800-520-1067 ■ *Web:* kroq.cbslocal.com	Los Angeles	CA	90034	323-930-1067	
KRTH-FM 101.1 (Oldies) 5670 Wilshire Blvd Ste 200 *TF:* 800-232-5784 ■ *Web:* kearth101.cbslocal.com	Los Angeles	CA	90036	323-936-5784	933-6072
KSWD-FM 100.3 (Rock) 5900 Wilshire Blvd Ste 1900 *Web:* www.thesoundla.com	Los Angeles	CA	90036	323-634-1800	634-1888
KUSC-FM 91.5 (Clas) 1149 S Hill St Ste H100 PO Box 7913 *TF:* 877-587-2227 ■ *Web:* www.kusc.org	Los Angeles	CA	90015	213-225-7400	225-7410

648-93 Louisville, KY

Station	City	State	Zip	Phone	Fax
WAMZ-FM 97.5 (Ctry) 4000 Radio Dr. *Web:* www.wamz.com	Louisville	KY	40218	502-479-2222	479-2223
WDJX-FM 99.7 (CHR) 520 S Fourth Ave Second Fl *Web:* www.wdjx.com	Louisville	KY	40202	502-625-1220	625-1253
WFPK-FM 91.9 (AAA) 619 S Fourth St *Web:* www.wfpk.org	Louisville	KY	40202	502-814-6500	814-6599
WFPL-FM 89.3 (NPR) 619 S Fourth St *Web:* www.wfpl.org	Louisville	KY	40202	502-814-6500	814-6599
WGZB-FM 96.5 (Urban) 520 S Fourth Ave Second Fl *Web:* hiphopb965.com/	Louisville	KY	40202	502-625-1220	625-1253
WHAS-AM 840 (N/T) 4000 One Radio Dr *TF:* 800-444-8484 ■ *Web:* www.whas.com	Louisville	KY	40218	502-479-2222	479-2308
WLOU-AM 1350 (Rel) 2001 W Broadway *Web:* www.wlouonline.com	Louisville	KY	40203	502-776-1240	
WQNU-FM 103.1 (Ctry) 316 W. Main St *Web:* www.newcountryq1031.com	Louisville	KY	40202	502-636-5023	
WTMT-FM 105.9 (Span) 1190 Patton Ave *Web:* 1059themountain.com	Asheville	NC	28806	828-259-9695	253-5619
WVEZ-FM 106.9 (AC) 612 S 4th St *TF:* 866-566-2456 ■ *Web:* lite1069.com	Louisville	KY	40202	502-589-4800	589-1377
WXMA-FM 102.3 (AC) 520 S Fourth Ave Second Fl *Web:* www.themaxfm.com	Louisville	KY	40202	502-625-1220	625-1255

648-94 Lubbock, TX

Station	City	State	Zip	Phone	Fax
KFMX-FM 94.5 (Rock) 4413 82nd St Ste 300 *Web:* www.kfmx.com	Lubbock	TX	79424	806-798-7078	798-7052
KFYO-AM 790 (N/T) 4413 82nd St Ste 300 *Web:* www.kfyo.com	Lubbock	TX	79424	806-798-7078	798-7052
KLLL-FM 96.3 (Ctry) 33 Briercroft Office Pk *Web:* www.klll.com	Lubbock	TX	79412	806-762-3000	770-5363
KMMX-FM 100.3 (AC) 33 Briercroft Office Pk. *Web:* www.kmmx.com	Lubbock	TX	79412	806-762-3000	770-5363
KONE-FM 101.1 (Rock) 33 Briercroft Office Pk. *Web:* www.rock101.fm	Lubbock	TX	79412	806-762-3000	770-5363
KQBR-FM 99.5 (Ctry) 4413 82nd St Ste 300. *Web:* 995blakefm.com	Lubbock	TX	79424	806-798-7078	798-7052
KZII-FM 102.5 (CHR) 4413 82nd St Ste 300 *Web:* 1025kiss.com	Lubbock	TX	79424	806-798-7078	798-7052

648-95 Macon, GA

Station	City	State	Zip	Phone	Fax
Cumulus Broadcasting Inc 544 Mulberry St Fifth Fl	Macon	GA	31201	478-746-6286	749-1393
WDEN-FM 99.1 (Ctry) 544 Mulberry St Fifth Fl. *Web:* www.wden.com	Macon	GA	31201	478-746-6286	749-1393
WIBB-FM 97.9 (Urban) 7080 Industrial Hwy. *TF:* 800-813-8418 ■ *Web:* www.wibb.com	Macon	GA	31216	478-781-1063	781-6711
WLZN-FM 92.3 (Urban) 544 Mulberry St 5th Fl *Web:* www.blazin923.com	Macon	GA	31201	478-330-6162	749-1393
WMAC-AM 940 (N/T) 544 Mulberry St Fifth Fl *Web:* www.wmac-am.com	Macon	GA	31201	478-746-6286	749-1393
WMGB-FM 95.1 (CHR) 544 Mulberry St Fifth Fl *Web:* www.allthehitsb951.com	Macon	GA	31201	478-646-9510	749-1393
WRBV-FM 101.7 (Urban AC) 7080 Industrial Hwy *Web:* www.v1017.com	Macon	GA	31216	478-781-1063	781-6711

648-96 Madison, WI

Station	City	State	Zip	Phone	Fax
Triple M 105.5 fm 7601 Ganser Way *Web:* www.1055triplem.com	Madison	WI	53719	608-826-0077	826-1244
WERN-FM 88.7 (NPR) 821 University Ave. **Fax Area Code:* 608 ■ *TF:* 800-747-7444 ■ *Web:* www.wpr.org	Madison	WI	53706	800-747-7444	263-9763*
WHA-AM 970 (NPR) 821 University Ave. **Fax Area Code:* 608 ■ *TF:* 800-747-7444 ■ *Web:* www.wpr.org	Madison	WI	53706	800-747-7444	263-9763*
WHIT-AM 1550 (Nost) 730 Rayovac Dr *TF:* 800-422-7128 ■ *Web:* hankonline.net	Madison	WI	53711	608-273-1000	441-0098
WIBA-AM 1310 (N/T) 2651 S Fish Hatchery Rd. *Web:* www.wiba.com	Madison	WI	53711	608-274-5450	274-5521
WIBA-FM 101.5 (CR) 2651 S Fish Hatchery Rd. *Web:* www.wibafm.com	Madison	WI	53711	608-274-5450	274-5521
WJJO-FM 94.1 (Rock) 730 Rayovac Dr. *Web:* www.wjjo.com	Madison	WI	53711	608-321-0941	271-8182
WMAD-FM 96.3 (Ctry) 2651 S Fish Hatchery Rd *Web:* 963starcountry.com/	Madison	WI	53711	608-274-5450	274-5521
WMGN-FM 98.1 (AC) 730 Rayovac Dr. *Web:* www.magic98.com	Madison	WI	53711	608-273-1000	441-0098
WTSO-AM 1070 (Sports) 2651 S Fish Hatchery Rd *Web:* www.thebig1070.com	Madison	WI	53711	608-274-5450	274-5521
WWQM-FM 106.3 (Ctry) 730 Rayovac Dr. *Web:* www.q106.com	Madison	WI	53711	608-273-1000	271-8182
WXXM-FM 92.1 (N/T) 2651 S Fish Hatchery Rd *Web:* www.themic921.com	Madison	WI	53711	608-274-5450	274-5521
WZEE-FM 104.1 (CHR) 2651 S Fish Hatchery Rd *Web:* www.z104fm.com	Madison	WI	53711	608-274-5450	274-5521

648-97 Manchester, NH

Station	City	State	Zip	Phone	Fax
WFEA-AM 1370 (Nost) 500 Commercial St. *Web:* www.wfea1370.com	Manchester	NH	03101	603-669-5777	669-4641
WGIR-AM 610 (N/T) 195 McGregor St Ste 810 *Web:* www.nhnewsnetwork610.com	Manchester	NH	03102	603-625-6915	625-9255
WGIR-FM 101.1 (Rock) 195 McGregor St Ste 810 *Web:* www.iheart.com	Manchester	NH	03102	603-625-6915	625-9255
WMLL-FM 96.5 (CR) 500 Commercial St *TF:* 800-666-0957 ■ *Web:* 965themill.com	Manchester	NH	03101	603-669-5777	669-4641

648-98 Memphis, TN

Station	City	State	Zip	Phone	Fax
600 WREC 2650 Thousand Oaks Blvd Ste 4100 *TF:* 800-474-9732 ■ *Web:* www.600wrec.com	Memphis	TN	38118	901-259-1300	259-6456
K FM 97.1 2650 Thousand Oaks Blvd Ste 4100 *Web:* www.k97fm.com	Memphis	TN	38118	901-259-1300	259-6456
KWAM-AM 990 (N/T) 5495 Murray Rd *Web:* www.kwam990.com	Memphis	TN	38119	901-261-4200	261-4210
Rock 103 2650 Thousand Oaks Blvd Ste 4100 *TF:* 800-444-9347 ■ *Web:* www.rock103.com	Memphis	TN	38118	901-259-1300	259-6456
V101 2650 Thousand Oaks Blvd Ste 4100 *Web:* www.myv101.com/main.html	Memphis	TN	38118	901-259-1300	
WDIA-AM 1070 (Urban) 2650 Thousand Oaks Blvd Ste 4100. *TF:* 800-339-4673 ■ *Web:* www.mywdia.com	Memphis	TN	38118	901-259-1300	259-6456
WGKX-FM 105.9 (Ctry) 5629 Murray Rd *Web:* www.kix106.com	Memphis	TN	38119	901-682-1106	767-9531
WHAL-FM 95.7 (Rel) 2650 Thousand Oaks Blvd Ste 4100. *TF:* 888-302-6222 ■ *Web:* www.hallelujahfm.com	Memphis	TN	38118	901-259-1300	259-6456
WKIM-FM 98.9 (AC) 5629 Murray Rd *Web:* www.newstalkfm989.com	Memphis	TN	38119	901-682-1106	767-9531
WKNO-FM 91.1 (NPR) 900 Getwell Rd *TF:* 800-766-9566 ■ *Web:* www.wknofm.org	Memphis	TN	38111	901-325-6544	729-8176
WLOK-AM 1340 (Rel) 363 S Second St. *Web:* www.wlok.com	Memphis	TN	38103	901-527-9565	528-0335
WRBO-FM 103.5 (Oldies) 5629 Murray Rd *Web:* www.soulclassics.com	Memphis	TN	38119	901-682-1106	767-9531
WRVR-FM 104.5 (AC) 1835 Moriah Woods Blvd Bldg 1 *Web:* www.1045theriver.com	Memphis	TN	38117	901-384-5900	767-6076
WXMX-FM 98.1 (Rock) 5629 Murray Rd *Web:* www.981themax.com	Memphis	TN	38119	901-535-9898	767-9531

648-99 Miami/Fort Lauderdale, FL

Station	City	State	Zip	Phone	Fax
El ZOL 106.7 FM 7007 NW 77th Ave. *Web:* www.elzol.com	Miami	FL	33166	305-444-9292	883-7701
POWER 96 194 NW 187th St *Web:* www.power96.com	Miami	FL	33169	305-654-1700	654-1715
WDNA-FM 88.9 (Jazz) 2921 Coral Way. *TF:* 877-929-7001 ■ *Web:* www.wdna.org	Miami	FL	33145	305-662-8889	
WINZ-AM 940 (N/T) 7601 Riviera Blvd. *Web:* www.940winz.com	Miramar	FL	33023	954-862-2000	862-4013
WIOD-AM 610 (N/T) 7601 Riviera Blvd *Web:* www.wiod.com	Miramar	FL	33023	954-862-2000	
WKIS-FM 99.9 (Ctry) 194 NW 187th St. *TF:* 866-978-0800 ■ *Web:* www.wkis.com	Miami	FL	33169	305-654-1700	654-1715
WLRN-FM 91.3 (NPR) 172 NE 15th St. *Web:* www.wlrn.org	Miami	FL	33132	305-995-1717	995-2299
WLYF-FM 101.5 (AC) 20450 NW Second Ave **Fax Area Code:* 305 ■ *TF:* 877-790-1015 ■ *Web:* www.litemiami.com	Miami	FL	33169	877-790-1015	521-1414*
WMBM-AM 1490 (Rel) 13242 NW Seventh Ave *TF:* 800-721-9626 ■ *Web:* www.wmbm.com	North Miami	FL	33168	305-769-1100	769-9975
WMXJ-FM 102.7 (Oldies) 20450 NW Second Ave. *TF:* 800-924-1027 ■ *Web:* www.magicmiami.com	Miami	FL	33169	305-521-5100	521-1414
WSUA-AM 1260 (Span) 2100 Coral Way Ste 201 *TF:* 877-453-5437 ■ *Web:* www.caracol1260.com	Miami	FL	33145	305-285-1260	
Zeta 92.3 7007 NW 77th Ave. *Web:* www.clasica92fm.com	Miami	FL	33166	305-444-9292	

648-100 Milwaukee, WI

Station	City	State	Zip	Phone	Fax
94.5 KTI Country 720 E Capitol Dr. *Web:* www.945thelake.com	Milwaukee	WI	53212	414-332-9611	967-5266
WAUK-AM 540 (Sports) 310 W Wisconsin Ave Ste 100 *TF:* 800-990-3776 ■ *Web:* www.espnmilwaukee.com	Milwaukee	WI	53203	414-273-3776	291-3776
WHAD-FM 90.7 (NPR) 310 W Wisconsin Ave Ste 750-E *TF:* 800-486-8655 ■ *Web:* www.wpr.org	Milwaukee	WI	53203	414-227-2040	227-2043
WHQG-FM 102.9 (Rock) 5407 W McKinley Ave *TF:* 877-777-1029 ■ *Web:* www.1029thehog.com	Milwaukee	WI	53208	414-978-9000	978-9001
WJMR-FM 98.3 (Urban) 5407 W McKinley Ave *Web:* jammin983.com	Milwaukee	WI	53208	414-978-9000	978-9001
WJYI-AM 1340 (Rel) 5407 W McKinley Ave *Web:* www.joy1340.com	Milwaukee	WI	53208	414-978-9000	978-9001
WKLH-FM 96.5 (CR) 5407 W McKinley Ave *Web:* www.wklh.com	Milwaukee	WI	53208	414-978-9000	978-9001

Station	City	State	ZIP	Phone	Fax
WTMJ-AM 620 (N/T) 720 E Capitol Dr *Web:* www.620wtmj.com	Milwaukee	WI	53212	414-799-1620	967-5298
WUWM-FM 89.7 (NPR) 111 E Wisconsin Ave Ste 700 *TF:* 844-387-6926 ■ *Web:* www.wuwm.com	Milwaukee	WI	53202	414-227-3355	270-1297

648-101 Minneapolis/Saint Paul, MN

Station	City	State	ZIP	Phone	Fax
KDWB-FM 101.3 (CHR) 1600 Utica Ave S Ste 400 *Web:* www.kdwb.com	Minneapolis	MN	55416	952-417-3000	417-3001
KEEY-FM 102.1 (Ctry) 1600 Utica Ave S Ste 500 *Web:* www.k102.com	St. Louis Park	MN	55416	952-417-3000	417-3001
KFAN-AM 1130 (Sports) 1600 Utica Ave S Ste 400 *TF:* 800-320-5326 ■ *Web:* www.kfan.com	Minneapolis	MN	55416	952-417-3000	417-3001
KQQL-FM 107.9 (Oldies) 1600 Utica Ave S Ste 400 *TF:* 800-745-3000 ■ *Web:* www.kool108.com	Minneapolis	MN	55416	952-417-3000	417-3001
KQRS-FM 92.5 (CR) 2000 SE Elm St *Web:* www.92kqrs.com	Minneapolis	MN	55414	612-617-4000	676-9292
KSTP-AM 1500 (N/T) 3415 University Ave *TF:* 877-615-1500 ■ *Web:* www.1500espn.com	Saint Paul	MN	55114	651-646-8255	647-2904
KSTP-FM 94.5 (AC) 3415 University Ave *Web:* www.ks95.com	Minneapolis	MN	55414	651-642-4141	647-2904
KTCZ-FM 97.1 (AAA) 1600 Utica Ave S Ste 400 *Web:* www.cities97.com	Minneapolis	MN	55416	952-417-3000	417-3001
KXXR-FM 93.7 (Rock) 2000 SE Elm St *Web:* www.93x.com	Minneapolis	MN	55414	612-617-4000	676-8292
KZJK-FM 104.1 (Var) 625 Second Ave S *Web:* 1041jackfm.cbslocal.com	Minneapolis	MN	55402	612-370-0611	
WCCO-AM 830 (N/T) 625 Second Ave S Ste 200 *Web:* minnesota.cbslocal.com	Minneapolis	MN	55402	612-370-0611	
WLTE-FM 102.9 (AC) 625 Second Ave S Ste 200 *Web:* buzn1029.cbslocal.com	Minneapolis	MN	55402	612-370-0611	612-5653

648-102 Mobile, AL

Station	City	State	ZIP	Phone	Fax
WABB-FM 97.5 (CHR) 1551 Springhill Ave	Mobile	AL	36604	251-432-5572	
WBHY-FM 88.5 (Rel) PO Box 1328 *TF:* 888-473-8488 ■ *Web:* www.goforth.org	Mobile	AL	36633	251-473-8488	300-3149
WGOK-AM 900 (Rel) 2800 Dauphin St Ste 104 *Web:* www.gospel900.com	Mobile	AL	36606	251-652-2064	652-2007
WHIL-FM 91.3 (NPR) 166 Reese Phifer Hall PO Box 870150 *TF:* 800-654-4262 ■ *Web:* apr.org	Tuscaloosa	AL	35487	205-348-6644	
WMXC-FM 99.9 (AC) 555 Broadcast Dr Third Fl *Web:* www.litemix.com	Mobile	AL	36606	251-450-0100	479-3418
WNSP-FM 105.5 (Sports) 1100 Dauphin St Ste E *Web:* www.wnsp.com	Mobile	AL	36604	251-438-5460	438-5462
WNTM-AM 710 (N/T) 555 Broadcast Dr Third Fl *Web:* www.newsradio710.com	Mobile	AL	36606	251-450-0100	479-3418
WRKH-FM 96.1 (CR) 555 Broadcast Dr Third Fl *Web:* www.961therocket.com	Mobile	AL	36606	251-450-0100	479-3418

648-103 Modesto, CA

Station	City	State	ZIP	Phone	Fax
KFIV-AM 1360 (N/T) 2121 Lancey Dr *Web:* www.powertalk1360.com	Modesto	CA	95355	209-551-1306	551-1359
KMRQ-FM 96.7 (Rock) 2121 Lancey Dr *TF:* 800-505-3967 ■ *Web:* www.rock967.com	Modesto	CA	95355	209-866-6677	551-1359
KQOD-FM 100.1 (Oldies) 2121 Lancey Dr *TF:* 877-967-6342 ■ *Web:* mega100fm.com/	Modesto	CA	95355	209-551-1306	551-5319

648-104 Monterey, CA

Station	City	State	ZIP	Phone	Fax
KCDU-FM 101.7 (AC) 60 Garden Ct Ste 300 *Web:* www.1017thebeach.com	Monterey	CA	93940	831-658-5200	658-5299
KHIP-FM 104.3 (CR) 60 Garden Ct Ste 300 *TF:* 877-762-5104 ■ *Web:* www.thehippo.com	Monterey	CA	93940	831-658-5200	658-5299

648-105 Montgomery, AL

Station	City	State	ZIP	Phone	Fax
WBAM-FM 98.9 (Ctry) 4101-A Wall St *Web:* bamacountry.com	Montgomery	AL	36106	334-244-0961	279-9563
WHLW-FM 104.3 (Rel) 203 Gunn Rd *Web:* www.1043hallelujahfm.com	Montgomery	AL	36117	334-274-6464	274-6467
WQKS 4101-A Wall St *Web:* www.q961fm.com	Montgomery	AL	36106	334-244-0961	279-9563
WWMG-FM 97.1 (Urban) 203 Gunn Rd *Web:* www.mymagic97.com	Montgomery	AL	36117	334-274-6464	274-6467
WXFX-FM 95.1 (Rock) One Commerce St Ste 300 *Web:* www.wxfx.com	Montgomery	AL	36104	334-240-9274	240-9219
WZHT-FM 105.7 (Urban) 203 Gunn Rd *Web:* www.myhot105.com	Montgomery	AL	36117	334-274-6464	274-6467

648-106 Morgantown, WV

Station	City	State	ZIP	Phone	Fax
WAJR-AM 1440 (N/T) 1251 Earl L Core Rd *Web:* www.wajr.com	Morgantown	WV	26505	304-296-0029	296-3876
WCLG-FM 100.1 (Rock) PO Box 885 *Web:* www.wclg.com	Morgantown	WV	26507	304-292-2222	292-2224
WKKW-FM 97.9 (Ctry) 1251 Earl L Core Rd *Web:* www.wkkwfm.com	Morgantown	WV	26505	304-296-0029	
WVAQ-FM 101.9 (CHR) 1251 Earl L Core Rd *Web:* www.wvaq.com	Morgantown	WV	26505	304-296-0029	
WWVU-FM 91.7 (Var) PO Box 6446 *Web:* u92.wvu.edu	Morgantown	WV	26506	304-293-3329	293-7363

648-107 Myrtle Beach, SC

Station	City	State	ZIP	Phone	Fax
WEZV-FM 105.9 (AC) 3926 Wesley St Ste 301 *Web:* www.wezv.com	Myrtle Beach	SC	29579	843-903-9962	903-1797
WKZQ-FM 96.1 (Rock) 1016 Ocala St *Web:* www.wkzq.net	Myrtle Beach	SC	29577	843-448-1041	626-5988
WMYB-FM 92.1 (AC) 1016 Ocala St *Web:* www.star921.net	Myrtle Beach	SC	29577	843-448-1041	626-2508
WRNN-FM 99.5 (N/T) 1016 Ocala St *Web:* www.wrnn.net	Myrtle Beach	SC	29577	843-448-1041	626-5988
WYAV-FM 104.1 (CR) 1016 Ocala St *Web:* wave104.net	Myrtle Beach	SC	29577	843-448-1041	626-5988

648-108 Naples, FL

Station	City	State	ZIP	Phone	Fax
WAVV-FM 101.1 (AC) 11800 Tamiami Trl E *TF:* 866-310-9288 ■ *Web:* www.wavv101.com	Naples	FL	34113	239-775-9288	793-7000

648-109 Nashville, TN

Station	City	State	ZIP	Phone	Fax
BIG 98, The 55 Music Sq W *Web:* www.wsix.com	Nashville	TN	37203	615-664-2400	
SuperTalk 99.7 WTN 10 Music Cir E *TF:* 800-618-7445 ■ *Web:* www.997wtn.com	Nashville	TN	37203	615-321-1067	
WBUZ-FM 102.9 (Alt) 1824 Murfreesboro Rd *Web:* www.1029thebuzz.com	Nashville	TN	37217	615-399-1029	361-9873
WCJK-FM 96.3 (Var) 504 Rosedale Ave *Web:* www.963jackfm.com	Nashville	TN	37211	615-259-4567	259-4594
WENO-AM 760 (Rel) 545 Mainstream Dr Ste 106 *Web:* www.760thegospel.com	Nashville	TN	37228	615-742-6506	
WJXA-FM 92.9 (AC) 504 Rosedale Ave *Web:* www.mix929.com	Nashville	TN	37211	615-737-0929	259-4594
WLAC-AM 1510 (N/T) 55 Music Sq W *TF:* 800-688-9522 ■ *Web:* www.wlac.com	Nashville	TN	37203	615-664-2400	744-4743
WPLN-FM 90.3 (NPR) 630 Mainstream Dr *TF:* 877-760-2903 ■ *Web:* nashvillepublicradio.org	Nashville	TN	37228	615-760-2903	760-2904
WPRT-FM 102.5 (AC) 1824 Murfreesboro Rd *Web:* 1025thegame.com	Nashville	TN	37217	615-399-1029	361-9873
WRLT-FM 100.1 (AAA) 1310 Clinton St Ste 200 *Web:* lightning100.com	Nashville	TN	37203	615-242-5600	296-9039
WRVW-FM 107.5 (CHR) 55 Music Sq W *Web:* www.1075theriver.com	Nashville	TN	37203	615-664-2400	664-2434
WSM-AM 650 (Ctry) 2644 McGavock Pk *Web:* wsmonline.com	Nashville	TN	37214	615-737-9650	
WSM-FM 95.5 (Ctry) 10 Music Cir E *Web:* 955nashicon.com	Nashville	TN	37203	615-321-1067	
WUBT-FM 101.1 (Urban) 55 Music Sq W *Web:* www.1011thebeat.com	Nashville	TN	37203	615-664-2400	664-2406

648-110 New Haven, CT

Station	City	State	ZIP	Phone	Fax
WYBC-AM 1340 (Var) 142 Temple St Ste 203 *Web:* www.wybc.com	New Haven	CT	06510	203-776-4118	776-2446
WYBC-FM 94.3 (Urban) 440 Wheelers Farms Rd Ste 302 *Web:* www.943wybc.com	Milford	CT	06461	203-783-8200	783-8383

648-111 New Orleans, LA

Station	City	State	ZIP	Phone	Fax
KKND-FM 102.9 (Urban) 201 St Charles Ave Ste 201 *Web:* www.power1029.com	New Orleans	LA	70170	504-581-7002	566-4857
KMEZ-FM 106.7 (Oldies) 201 St Charles Ave Ste 201 *Web:* www.oldschool1067.com	New Orleans	LA	70170	504-581-7002	566-4857
WKBU-FM 95.7 (Rock) 400 Poydras St Ste 800 *Web:* www.bayou957.com	New Orleans	LA	70130	504-593-6376	593-2099
WLMG-FM 101.9 (AC) 400 Poydras St Ste 800 *Web:* www.magic1019.com	New Orleans	LA	70130	504-593-6376	593-2099
WNOE-FM 101.1 (Ctry) 929 Howard Ave *Web:* www.wnoe.com	New Orleans	LA	70113	504-679-7300	679-7345

Station / Address	City	State	Zip	Phone	Fax
WQUE-FM 93.3 (Urban) 929 Howard Ave *Web:* www.q93.com	New Orleans	LA	70113	504-679-7300	679-7345
WRKN-FM 92.3 (AC) 201 St Charles Ave Ste 201 *Web:* nashfm923.com.	New Orleans	LA	70170	504-581-7002	
WRNO-FM 99.5 (N/T) 929 Howard Ave *Web:* www.wrno.com	New Orleans	LA	70113	504-679-7300	679-7345
WSHO-AM 800 (Rel) 365 Canal St Ste 1175 *Web:* www.wsho.com	New Orleans	LA	70130	504-527-0800	527-0881
WWL-AM 870 (N/T) 400 Poydras St Ste 800 *Web:* www.wwl.com	New Orleans	LA	70130	504-593-6376	593-2099
WWL-FM 105.3 N/T) 400 Poydras St Ste 800 *Web:* www.wwl.com	New Orleans	LA	70130	504-593-6376	593-2099
WWNO-FM 89.9 (NPR) University of New Orleans Lake Frnt Campus *TF:* 800-286-7002 ■ *Web:* www.wwno.org	New Orleans	LA	70148	504-280-7000	280-6061
WWOZ-FM 90.7 (Var) 1008 N Peters St *Web:* www.wwoz.org	New Orleans	LA	70116	504-568-1239	558-9332
WYLD-AM 940 (Rel) 929 Howard Ave *TF:* 800-899-9265 ■ *Web:* www.am940.com	New Orleans	LA	70113	504-679-7300	679-7345
WYLD-FM 98.5 (Urban) 929 Howard Ave *Web:* www.wyldfm.com	New Orleans	LA	70113	504-679-7300	679-7345

648-112 New York, NY

Station / Address	City	State	Zip	Phone	Fax
WABC-AM 770 (N/T) 2 Penn Plaza 17th Fl *TF:* 800-848-9222 ■ *Web:* www.wabcradio.com	New York	NY	10121	212-613-3800	613-3837
WAXQ-FM 104.3 (CR) 32 Ave of the Americas *TF:* 888-872-1043 ■ *Web:* www.q1043.com	New York	NY	10013	212-377-7900	
WBBR-AM 1130 (N/T) 731 Lexington Ave *Web:* www.bloomberg.com/radio	New York	NY	10022	212-318-2000	940-1994
WCBS-AM 880 (N/T) 524 W 57th St 8th Fl *TF:* 800-242-6397 ■ *Web:* newyork.cbslocal.com	New York	NY	10019	212-975-4321	
WCBS-FM 101.1 (Oldies) 345 Hudson St 10th Fl *Web:* wcbsfm.cbslocal.com	New York	NY	10014	212-314-9200	
WHTZ-FM 100.3 (CHR) 32 Ave of the Americas *TF:* 800-242-0100 ■ *Web:* www.z100.com	New York	NY	10013	212-377-7900	226-4201
WINS-AM 1010 (N/T) 345 Hudson St *Web:* newyork.cbslocal.com	New York	NY	10014	212-315-7036	
WKTU-FM 103.5 (CHR) 32 Ave of the Americas *Web:* www.ktu.com	New York	NY	10013	212-377-7900	
WLTW-FM 106.7 (AC) 32 Ave of the Americas 2nd Fl *TF:* 800-222-1067 ■ *Web:* www.1067litefm.com	New York	NY	10013	212-377-7900	
WNYC-AM 820 (NPR) 160 Varick St Seventh Fl *Web:* www.wnyc.org	New York	NY	10013	646-829-4400	829-4171
WNYC-FM 93.9 (NPR) 160 Varick St Seventh Fl *Web:* www.wnyc.org	New York	NY	10013	646-829-4400	829-4171
WOR-AM 710 (N/T) 32 Ave of the Americas 3rd Fl *Web:* www.wor710.com	New York	NY	10013	212-377-7900	
WPAT-FM 93.1 (Span AC) 26 W 56th St *Web:* www.931amor.com	New York	NY	10019	212-541-9200	541-8535
WPLJ-FM 95.5 (AC) 2 Penn Plaza 17th Fl *Web:* www.plj.com	New York	NY	10121	212-613-8905	613-8956
WQHT-FM 97.1 (Urban) 395 Hudson St Seventh Fl *TF:* 800-223-9797 ■ *Web:* www.hot97.com	New York	NY	10014	212-229-9797	929-8559
WQXR-FM 96.3 (Clas) 160 Varick St Eighth Fl *Web:* www.wqxr.org	New York	NY	10013	646-829-4400	
WSKQ-FM 97.9 (Span) 26 W 56th St *Web:* www.lamega.com	New York	NY	10019	212-541-9200	541-8535
WWPR-FM 105.1 (Urban) 32 Ave of the Americas *TF:* 800-585-1051 ■ *Web:* www.power1051fm.com	New York	NY	10013	212-377-7900	

648-113 Norfolk/Virginia Beach, VA

Station / Address	City	State	Zip	Phone	Fax
92.1 The Beat 1003 Norfolk Sq *Web:* www.kissva.com	Norfolk	VA	23502	757-466-0009	
WGH 5589 Greenwich Rd Ste 200 *Web:* www.espnradio1310.com	Virginia Beach	VA	23462	757-671-1000	671-1010
WGH-FM 97.3 (Ctry) 5589 Greenwich Rd Ste 200 *Web:* www.eagle97.com	Virginia Beach	VA	23462	757-671-1000	671-1010
WHRO-FM 90.3 (Clas) 5200 Hampton Blvd *Web:* www.whro.org	Norfolk	VA	23508	757-889-9400	489-0007
WOWI-FM 102.9 (Urban) 1003 Norfolk Sq *Web:* www.103jamz.com	Norfolk	VA	23502	757-466-0009	
WPTE-FM 94.9 (AC) 236 Clearfield Ave Ste 206 *Web:* www.pointradio.com	Virginia Beach	VA	23462	757-497-2000	518-1721
WVBW-FM 92.9 (Oldies) 5589 Greenwich Rd Ste 200 *Web:* www.929thewave.com	Virginia Beach	VA	23462	757-671-1000	671-1010

648-114 Ocean City, MD

Station / Address	City	State	Zip	Phone	Fax
WOCM-FM 98.1 (AAA) Irie Radio 117 W 49th St *Web:* ocean98.com	Ocean City	MD	21842	410-723-3683	723-4347

648-115 Oklahoma City, OK

Station / Address	City	State	Zip	Phone	Fax
KATT-FM 100.5 (Rock) 4045 NW 64th St Ste 600 *Web:* www.katt.com	Oklahoma City	OK	73116	405-848-0100	843-5288
KJYO-FM 102.7 (CHR) 1900 NW Expy Ste 1000 *Web:* www.kj103fm.com	Oklahoma City	OK	73118	405-460-1027	
KMGL-FM 104.1 (AC) 400 E Britton Rd *Web:* www.magic104.com	Oklahoma City	OK	73114	405-478-5104	
KOMA-FM 92.5 (Oldies) 400 E Britton Rd *Web:* www.komaradio.com	Oklahoma City	OK	73114	405-478-5104	475-7021
KRXO-FM 107.7 (CR) 400 E Britton Rd *Web:* www.krxo.com	Oklahoma City	OK	73114	405-478-5104	
KTOK-AM 1000 (N/T) 1900 Northwest Expy Ste 1000 *Web:* www.ktok.com	Oklahoma City	OK	73118	405-840-5271	858-5333
KTST-FM 101.9 (Ctry) 50 Penn Pl NW Expy & Pennsylvania Ave Ste 1000 *Web:* www.thetwister.com	Oklahoma City	OK	73118	405-840-5271	858-5333
KYIS-FM 98.9 (AC) 4045 NW 64th St Ste 600 *Web:* www.kyis.com	Oklahoma City	OK	73116	405-848-0100	843-5288

648-116 Omaha, NE

Station / Address	City	State	Zip	Phone	Fax
KAT 103.7FM 5010 Underwood Ave *Web:* www.thekat.com	Omaha	NE	68132	402-561-2000	556-8937*
KFAB-AM 1110 (N/T) 5010 Underwood Ave *Web:* www.kfab.com	Omaha	NE	68132	402-561-2000	556-8937
KIOS-FM 91.5 (NPR) 3230 Burt St *Web:* www.kios.org	Omaha	NE	68131	402-557-2777	557-2559
KISS FM 96.1 5010 Underwood Ave *Web:* www.961kissonline.com	Omaha	NE	68132	402-558-9696	
KQCH-FM 94.1 (CHR) 5030 N 72nd St **Fax:* Sales ■ *Web:* www.channel941.com	Omaha	NE	68134	402-938-9400	592-9434*
KQKQ-FM 98.5 (CHR) 5011 Capitol Ave *Web:* pro.kqkq-fm.tritonflex.com	Omaha	NE	68132	402-342-2000	827-5293
Superhits 99.9 5010 Underwood Ave *Web:* www.kgor.com	Omaha	NE	68132	402-561-2000	556-8937
Z92 FM 10714 Mockingbird Dr *TF:* 800-955-9230 ■ *Web:* www.z92.com	Omaha	NE	68127	402-592-5300	

648-117 Orlando, FL

Station / Address	City	State	Zip	Phone	Fax
WCFB-FM 94.5 (AC) 4192 N John Young Pkwy *Web:* www.star945.com	Orlando	FL	32804	407-294-2945	297-7595
WDBO-AM 580 (N/T) 4192 N John Young Pkwy *Web:* www.news965.com	Orlando	FL	32804	321-281-2000	
WJHM-FM 102 (Urban) 1800 Pembrook Dr Ste 400 *TF:* 866-438-0220 ■ *Web:* 1019ampradio.cbslocal.com/	Orlando	FL	32810	407-919-1000	816-9070
WMMO-FM 98.9 (AC) 4192 N John Young Pkwy **Fax Area Code:* 407 ■ *Web:* www.wmmo.com	Orlando	FL	32804	321-281-2000	422-6538*
WOCL-FM 105.9 (Rock) 1800 Pembrook Dr Ste 400 *TF:* 877-919-1059 ■ *Web:* 1059sunnyfm.cbslocal.com	Orlando	FL	32810	407-919-1000	919-1190
WOMX-FM 105.1 (AC) 1800 Pembrook Dr Ste 400 *TF:* 877-919-1051 ■ *Web:* mix1051.cbslocal.com	Orlando	FL	32810	407-919-1000	919-1190
WPYO-FM 95.3 (CHR) 4192 N John Young Pkwy **Fax Area Code:* 407 ■ *Web:* www.power953.com	Orlando	FL	32804	321-281-2000	291-6912*
WUCF-FM 89.9 (Jazz) 12405 Aquarius Agora Dr Communication Bldg 75 Ste 130 *Web:* www.wucf.ucf.edu	Orlando	FL	32816	407-823-0899	
WWKA-FM 92.3 (Ctry) 4192 N John Young Pkwy *TF:* 866-438-0220 ■ *Web:* www.k923orlando.com	Orlando	FL	32804	407-298-9292	299-4947

648-118 Ottawa, ON

Station / Address	City	State	Zip	Phone	Fax
CFRA-AM 580 (N/T) 87 George St *Web:* www.cfra.com	Ottawa	ON	K1N9H7	613-789-2486	738-5024
CHEZ-FM 106.1 (CR) 2001 Thurston Dr *Web:* www.chez106.com	Ottawa	ON	K1G6C9	613-736-2001	736-2002
CIWW-AM 1310 (Oldies) 2001 Thurston Dr *Web:* www.1310news.com	Ottawa	ON	K1G6C9	613-736-2001	736-2002
Ottawa-AM 1200 (Sports) 87 George St *TF:* 877-670-1200 ■ *Web:* www.tsn1200.ca	Ottawa	ON	K1N9H7	613-789-2486	738-5024

648-119 Oxnard, CA

Station / Address	City	State	Zip	Phone	Fax
KDAR-FM 98.3 (Rel) 500 E Esplanade Dr *Web:* www.kdar.com	Oxnard	CA	93036	805-485-8881	
KMLA-FM 103.7 (Span) 355 So 'A' St Ste 103 *Web:* www.lam1037.com	Oxnard	CA	93030	805-385-5656	385-5690
KXLM-FM 102.9 (Span) 200 S Ste 400 *Web:* www.radiolazer.com	Oxnard	CA	93030	805-240-2070	240-5960

648-120 Palm Springs, CA

Station	City	State	Zip	Phone	Fax
Desert Radio Group 1321 N Gene Autry Trl	Palm Springs	CA	92262	760-322-7890	322-5493
Jammin-FM 99.5 (Alt) 75153 Merle Dr Ste G *Web:* www.jammin995fm.com	Palm Desert	CA	92211	760-568-4550	341-7600
KCLB-FM 93.7 (Rock) 1321 N Gene Autry Trl *Web:* 937kclb.com	Palm Springs	CA	92262	760-322-7890	322-5493
KKUU-FM 92.7 (CHR) 1321 N Gene Autry Trl *Web:* www.927kkuu.com	Palm Springs	CA	92262	760-322-7890	322-5493
KPLM-FM 106.1 (Ctry) 75153 Merle Dr Ste G *Web:* www.thebig106.com	Palm Desert	CA	92211	760-568-4550	341-7600
KPSI-AM 920 (N/T) 2100 Tahquitz Canyon Way *Web:* www.newstalk920.com	Palm Springs	CA	92262	760-325-2582	325-4693
KPSI-FM 100.5 (AC) 2100 Tahquitz Canyon Way *Web:* www.mix1005.fm	Palm Springs	CA	92262	760-325-2582	

648-121 Pensacola, FL

Station	City	State	Zip	Phone	Fax
WPCS-FM 89.5 (Rel) PO Box 18000 *TF:* 800-726-1191 ■ *Web:* www.rejoice.org	Pensacola	FL	32523	850-479-6570	
WPNN-AM 790 (N/T) 3801 N Pace Blvd *Web:* talk790.com	Pensacola	FL	32505	850-433-1141	433-1142
WUWF-FM 88.1 (NPR) 11000 University Pkwy *Web:* www.wuwf.org	Pensacola	FL	32514	850-474-2787	474-3283

648-122 Peoria, IL

Station	City	State	Zip	Phone	Fax
WCBU-FM 89.9 (NPR) 1501 W Bradley Ave *TF:* 888-488-9228 ■ *Web:* peoriapublicradio.org	Peoria	IL	61625	309-677-3690	677-3462
WCIC-FM 91.5 (Rel) 3902 W Baring Trace **Fax Area Code:* 309 ■ *TF:* 877-692-9242 ■ *Web:* www.wcicfm.org	Peoria	IL	61615	877-692-9242	692-9241*
WFYR-FM 97.3 (Ctry) 120 Eaton St *Web:* www.973nashfm.com	Peoria	IL	61603	309-673-0973	
WGLO-FM 95.5 (CR) 120 Eaton St *Web:* www.955glo.com	Peoria	IL	61603	309-676-9595	676-5000
WMBD-AM 1470 (N/T) 331 Fulton St Ste 1200 *Web:* www.1470wmbd.com	Peoria	IL	61602	309-637-3700	686-8655
WSWT-FM 106.9 (AC) 331 Fulton St Ste 1200 *TF:* 800-597-1069 ■ *Web:* www.literock107.com	Peoria	IL	61602	309-637-3700	686-8655
WXCL-FM 104.9 (Ctry) 331 Fulton St 12th Fl *Web:* www.1049thewolf.com	Peoria	IL	61602	309-637-3700	272-1476

648-123 Philadelphia, PA

Station	City	State	Zip	Phone	Fax
KYW-NEWSRADIO 1060 (N/T) 400 Market St 10th Fl *Web:* philadelphia.cbslocal.com	Philadelphia	PA	19106	215-238-1060	238-4657
WEMG-AM 1310 (Span) 1341 N Delaware Ave Ste 509	Philadelphia	PA	19125	215-426-1900	426-1550
WHYY-FM 90.9 (NPR) 150 N Sixth St *Web:* www.whyy.org	Philadelphia	PA	19106	215-351-1200	351-1211
WRTI-FM 90.1 (NPR) 1509 Cecil B Moore Ave 3rd Fl *TF:* 866-809-9784 ■ *Web:* www.wrti.org	Philadelphia	PA	19121	215-204-8405	204-7027
WXPN-FM 88.5 (AAA) 3025 Walnut St *Web:* www.xpn.org	Philadelphia	PA	19104	215-898-6677	898-0707

648-124 Phoenix, AZ

Station	City	State	Zip	Phone	Fax
KESZ-FM 99.9 (AC) 4686 E Van Buren St Ste 300 *Web:* www.kez999.com	Phoenix	AZ	85008	602-374-6000	
KGME-AM 910 (Sports) 4686 E Van Buren Ste 300 *Web:* www.foxsports910.com	Phoenix	AZ	85008	602-374-6000	
KHOT-FM 105.9 (Span) 4745 N Seventh St Ste 140 *Web:* lanueva1059.univision.com	Phoenix	AZ	85014	602-308-7900	308-7979
KMXP-FM 96.9 (AC) 4686 E Van Buren Ste 300 *Web:* www.mix969.com	Phoenix	AZ	85008	602-374-6000	
KNIX-FM 102.5 (Ctry) 4686 E Van Buren St Ste 300 *Web:* www.knixcountry.com	Phoenix	AZ	85008	602-374-6000	374-6035
KOOL-FM 94.5 (Oldies) 840 N Central Ave *TF:* 800-222-4357 ■ *Web:* kool.cbslocal.com	Phoenix	AZ	85004	602-260-9494	440-6530
KOY-AM 1230 (Nost) 4686 E Van Buren St Ste 300 *Web:* kfyi2.com/	Phoenix	AZ	85008	602-374-6000	
KSLX-FM 100.7 (CR) 4343 E Camelback Rd Ste 200 *Web:* kslx.com	Phoenix	AZ	85018	602-260-1007	
KTAR-FM 98.7 7740 N 16th St Ste 200 *Web:* ktar.com	Phoenix	AZ	85020	602-274-6200	
KZON-FM 101.5 (Urban) 840 N Central Ave *Web:* live1015phoenix.cbslocal.com	Phoenix	AZ	85004	602-452-1000	
KZZP-FM 104.7 (CHR) 4686 E Van Buren St Ste 300 *TF:* 877-541-1966 ■ *Web:* www.1047kissfm.com	Phoenix	AZ	85008	602-374-6000	374-6035

648-125 Pierre, SD

Station	City	State	Zip	Phone	Fax
KCCR-AM 1240 106 W Capitol Ave *Web:* www.todayskccr.com	Pierre	SD	57501	605-224-1240	945-4270
KMLO-FM 100.7 (Ctry) 214 W Pleasant Dr *TF:* 800-658-5439 ■ *Web:* www.drgnews.com	Pierre	SD	57501	605-224-8686	224-8984
KPLO-FM 94.5 (Ctry) 214 W Pleasant Dr *TF General:* 800-658-5439 ■ *Web:* www.drgnews.com	Pierre	SD	57501	605-224-8686	224-8984

648-126 Pittsburgh, PA

Station	City	State	Zip	Phone	Fax
KQV-AM 1410 (N/T) 650 Smithfield St Ste 620 Ctr City Towers *TF:* 800-289-2642 ■ *Web:* www.kqv.com	Pittsburgh	PA	15222	412-562-5900	562-5903
WBGG-AM 970 (Sports) 200 Fleet St Fourth Fl *Web:* www.970espn.com	Pittsburgh	PA	15220	412-937-1441	937-0323
WDSY-FM 107.9 (Ctry) 651 Holiday Dr Foster Plz Second Fl *Web:* y108.cbslocal.com	Pittsburgh	PA	15220	412-920-9400	920-9449
WDUQ-FM 90.5 (NPR) 67 Bedford Sq *Web:* www.wesa.fm	Pittsburgh	PA	15203	412-381-9131	
WDVE-FM 102.5 (Rock) 200 Fleet St *Web:* www.dve.com	Pittsburgh	PA	15220	412-937-1441	937-0323
WKST-FM 96.1 (CHR) 200 Fleet St Fourth Fl *Web:* www.961kiss.com	Pittsburgh	PA	15220	412-937-1441	937-0323
WLTJ-FM 92.9 (AC) 650 Smithfield St Ste 2200 *Web:* www.q929fm.com	Pittsburgh	PA	15222	412-316-3342	316-3388
WPGB-FM 104.7 (N/T) 200 Fleet St *Web:* big1047.com/	Pittsburgh	PA	15220	412-937-1441	937-0323
WQED-FM 89.3 (Clas) 4802 Fifth Ave *TF:* 800-876-1316 ■ *Web:* www.wqed.org	Pittsburgh	PA	15213	412-622-1436	622-7073
WSHH-FM 99.7 (AC) 900 Parish St Third Fl *Web:* www.wshh.com	Pittsburgh	PA	15220	412-875-9500	875-9474
WWSW-FM 94.5 (Oldies) 200 Fleet St 4th Fl *TF:* 800-653-2258 ■ *Web:* www.3wsradio.com	Pittsburgh	PA	15220	412-937-1441	937-0323
WXDX-FM 105.9 (Alt) 200 Fleet St Fourth Fl *Web:* www.1059thex.com	Pittsburgh	PA	15220	412-937-1441	937-0323
WZPT-FM 100.7 (AC) 651 Holiday Dr Second Fl *Web:* starpittsburgh.cbslocal.com	Pittsburgh	PA	15220	412-920-9400	920-9449

648-127 Pocatello, ID

Station	City	State	Zip	Phone	Fax
KISU-FM 91.1 (NPR) Idaho State University 921 S Eigth Ave PO Box 8014 *Web:* www.isu.edu/kisufm	Pocatello	ID	83209	208-282-3691	282-4600
KZBQ-FM 93.7 (Ctry) PO Box 97 *Web:* www.kzbq.com	Pocatello	ID	83204	208-234-1290	234-9451
Pacific Empire Radio Corp 403 Capital St *Web:* pacempire.com	Lewiston	ID	83501	208-743-6564	

648-128 Portland, ME

Station	City	State	Zip	Phone	Fax
WRED-FM 95.9 (Urban) 779 Warren Ave *Web:* atlanticcoastradio.com	Portland	ME	04103	207-773-9695	761-4406
WTHT-FM 99.9 (Ctry) 477 Congress St Third Fl Annex *Web:* wtht.nh1media.com	Portland	ME	04101	207-797-0780	797-0368

648-129 Portland/Salem, OR

Station	City	State	Zip	Phone	Fax
All Classical Portland 515 NE 15th Ave *TF:* 888-306-5277 ■ *Web:* www.allclassical.org	Portland	OR	97232	503-943-5828	802-9456
FM NEWS 101 KXL 1211 SW Fifth Ave *TF:* 877-733-1011 ■ *Web:* www.kxl.com	Portland	OR	97204	503-517-6000	417-7661
KBNP-AM 1410 (N/T) 278 SW Arthur St *Web:* www.kbnp.com	Portland	OR	97201	503-223-6769	223-4305
KBOO-FM 90.7 (Var) 20 SE Eigth Ave	Portland	OR	97214	503-231-8032	
KBZY-AM 1490 (AC) 2659 Commercial St SE Ste 204 *Web:* www.kbzy.com	Salem	OR	97302	503-362-1490	362-6545
KEX-AM 1190 (N/T) 13333 SW 68th Parkway Suite 310 *TF:* 888-457-4838 ■ *Web:* www.1190kex.com	Tigard	OR	97223	503-323-6400	323-6660
KFIS-FM 104.1 (Rel) 6400 SE Lk Rd Ste 350 *Web:* www.1041thefish.com	Portland	OR	97222	503-786-0600	786-1551
KGON-FM 92.3 (CR) 0700 SW Bancroft St *TF:* 800-222-9236 ■ *Web:* www.kgon.com	Portland	OR	97239	503-223-1441	223-6909
KINK-FM 101.9 (AAA) 1211 SW Fifth Ave *TF:* 877-567-5465 ■ *Web:* www.kink.fm	Portland	OR	97204	503-517-6000	517-6401
KKRZ-FM 100.3 (CHR) 13333 SW 68th Pkwy Ste 310 *TF:* 888-483-0100 ■ *Web:* www.z100portland.com	Tigard	OR	97223	503-460-0100	323-6660
KLTH-FM 106.7 (AC) 4949 SW Macadam Ave *Web:* 1067theeagle.com/	Portland	OR	97239	503-323-6400	323-6660

	City	State	ZIP	Phone	Fax
KNRK-FM 94.7 (Alt) 0700 SW Bancroft St *TF:* 800-777-0947 ■ *Web:* www.947.fm	Portland	OR	97239	503-733-5470	223-6909
KOPB-FM 91.5 (NPR) 7140 SW Macadam Ave *Web:* www.opb.org	Portland	OR	97219	503-293-1905	
KPDQ-FM 93.9 (Rel) 6400 SE Lake Rd Ste 350 *TF:* 800-845-2162 ■ *Web:* www.kpdq.com	Portland	OR	97222	503-786-0600	786-1551
KPOJ-AM 620 (N/T) 13333 SW 68th Pkwy Ste 310 *Web:* www.foxsportsradio620.com	Tigard	OR	97223	503-323-6400	323-6664
KWBY-AM 940 (Span) 1665 James St *Web:* lapantera940.com	Woodburn	OR	97071	503-981-9400	981-3561
KWJJ-FM 99.5 (Ctry) 0700 SW Bancroft St *TF:* 866-239-9653 ■ *Web:* www.thewolfonline.com	Portland	OR	97239	503-733-9653	223-6909
KXJM-FM 107.5 (AC) 13333 SW 68th Pkwy Ste 310 *TF:* 800-567-1075 ■ *Web:* jamn1075.com/	Portland	OR	97223	503-248-1075	
KYKN-AM 1430 (N/T) PO Box 1430 *Web:* www.kykn.com	Salem	OR	97308	503-390-3014	390-3728

648-130 Providence, RI

	City	State	ZIP	Phone	Fax
WBRU-FM 95.5 (Alt) 88 Benevolent St *Web:* www.wbru.com	Providence	RI	02906	401-272-9550	272-9278
WHJJ-AM 920 (N/T) 75 Oxford St Third Fl *Web:* www.920whjj.com	Providence	RI	02905	401-781-9979	781-9329
WHJY-FM 94.1 (Rock) 75 Oxford St Third Fl *Web:* www.94hjy.com	Providence	RI	02905	401-781-9979	781-9329
WRNI-AM 1290 (NPR) One Union Stn *Web:* ripr.org	Providence	RI	02903	401-351-2800	351-0246
WSNE-FM 93.3 (AC) 75 Oxford St Third Fl *Web:* www.coast933.com	Providence	RI	02905	401-781-9979	

648-131 Quebec City, QC

	City	State	ZIP	Phone	Fax
CBVE-FM 104.7 (CBC) PO Box 3220 Station C *Web:* www.cbc.radio-canada.ca	Ottawa	ON	K1Y1E4	418-654-1341	
Nrj 98.9 900 Dyouville First Fl	Quebec	QC	G1R3P7	418-687-9900	687-3106

648-132 Raleigh/Durham, NC

	City	State	ZIP	Phone	Fax
B93.9 new county 3100 Smoketree Ct 7th Fl *Web:* b939country.com/	Raleigh	NC	27604	919-878-1500	
WFXC-FM 107.1 (Urban AC) 8001-101 Creedmoor Rd *TF:* 800-467-3699 ■ *Web:* foxync.com	Raleigh	NC	27613	919-848-9736	848-4724
WFXK-FM 104.3 (Urban AC) 8001-101 Creedmoor Rd *TF:* 800-321-5975 ■ *Web:* foxync.com	Raleigh	NC	27613	919-848-9736	848-4724
WKIX-FM 102.9 (Oldies) 4601 6 Forks Rd Ste 520 *Web:* www.kix1029.com	Raleigh	NC	27609	919-875-9100	510-6990
WKNC-FM 88.1 (Rock) 343 Witherspoon Student Ctr NCSU PO Box 8607 *Web:* wknc.org	Raleigh	NC	27695	919-515-2401	
WNCU-FM 90.7 (NPR) PO Box 19875 *Web:* www.wncu.org	Durham	NC	27707	919-530-7445	530-5031
WNNL-FM 103.9 (Rel) 8001-101 Creedmoor Rd *TF:* 877-310-9665 ■ *Web:* www.thelightnc.com	Raleigh	NC	27613	919-848-9736	
WPTF-AM 680 (N/T) 3012 Highwoods Blvd Ste 201 *TF:* 800-662-7979 ■ *Web:* www.wptf.com	Raleigh	NC	27604	919-790-9392	790-8369
WQDR-FM 94.7 (Ctry) 3012 Highwoods Blvd Ste 201 *Web:* www.947qdr.com	Raleigh	NC	27604	919-876-6464	790-8893
WQOK-FM 97.5 (Urban) 8001-101 Creedmoor Rd *Web:* hiphopnc.com	Raleigh	NC	27613	919-863-4820	
WRAL-FM 101.5 (AC) 3100 Highwoods Blvd Ste 140 *TF:* 800-745-3000 ■ *Web:* www.wralfm.com	Raleigh	NC	27604	919-890-6101	890-6146
WRDU CLASSIC ROCK 100.7 3100 Smoketree Ct 7th Fl *Web:* www.wrdu.com	Raleigh	NC	27604	919-878-1500	876-8578
WRJD-AM 1410 (Rel) 707 Leon St *Web:* www.1410wrjd.com	Durham	NC	27704	919-220-3226	
WSHA-FM 88.9 (Jazz) 118 E S St *TF:* 800-241-0421 ■ *Web:* www.shawu.edu	Raleigh	NC	27601	919-546-8430	546-8315
WXDU-FM 88.7 (Alt) PO Box 90689 *Web:* www.wxdu.org	Durham	NC	27708	919-684-2957	684-3260

648-133 Rapid City, SD

	City	State	ZIP	Phone	Fax
KFXS-FM 100.3 (CR) 660 Flormann St Ste 100 *Web:* www.foxradio.com	Rapid City	SD	57701	605-394-4487	343-9012
KIMM-AM 1150 (Ctry) 11 Main St	Rapid City	SD	57701	605-342-1150	343-1096
KKMK-FM 93.9 (AC) 660 Flormann St Ste 100 *Web:* schurz.com/properties/radio/rushmore-media-company/	Rapid City	SD	57709	605-343-6161	343-9012
KLMP-FM 88.3 1853 Fountain Plz Dr *Web:* www.klmp.com	Rapid City	SD	57702	605-342-6822	342-0854
KOUT-FM 98.7 (Ctry) 660 Flormann St Ste 100 *Web:* www.katradio.com	Rapid City	SD	57701	605-343-6161	343-9012
KRCS-FM 93.1 (CHR) 660 Flormann St Ste 100 *Web:* www.hot931.com	Rapid City	SD	57701	605-343-6161	343-9012

648-134 Reno/Carson City, NV

	City	State	ZIP	Phone	Fax
KBUL-FM 98.1 (Ctry) 595 E Plumb Ln *Web:* www.kbul.com	Reno	NV	89502	775-789-6700	789-6767
KDOT-FM 104.5 (Rock) 2900 Sutro St *TF:* 800-227-1885 ■ *Web:* www.kdot.com	Reno	NV	89512	775-329-9261	323-1450
KLCA-FM 96.5 (Alt) 961 Matley Ln Ste 120 *Web:* www.alice965.com	Reno	NV	89502	775-829-1964	825-3183
KNIS-FM 91.3 (Rel) PO Box 21888 *TF:* 800-541-5647 ■ *Web:* www.pilgrimradio.com	Carson City	NV	89721	775-883-5647	
KODS-FM 103.7 (Oldies) 961 Matley Ln Ste 120 *TF:* 855-354-9111 ■ *Web:* www.river1037.com	Reno	NV	89502	775-829-1964	825-3183
KOZZ-FM 105.7 (CR) 2900 Sutro St *Web:* www.kozzradio.com	Reno	NV	89512	775-329-9261	323-1450
KRNO-FM 106.9 (AC) 961 Matley Ln Ste 120 *TF:* 888-505-1261 ■ *Web:* 1069morefm.com/	Reno	NV	89502	775-829-1964	825-3183
KUUB-FM 94.5 (Ctry) 2900 Sutro St *Web:* www.espn945.com	Reno	NV	89512	775-329-9261	323-1450

648-135 Richmond, VA

	City	State	ZIP	Phone	Fax
98.9 The Wolf 300 Arboretum Pl Ste 590 *Web:* www.931thewolf.com	Richmond	VA	23236	804-327-9902	
99.3/105.7 KISS FM 2809 Emerywood Pkwy Ste 300 *Web:* kissrichmond.com	Richmond	VA	23294	804-672-9299	
Cox Radio Inc 812 Moorefield Pk Dr Ste 300	Richmond	VA	23236	804-330-5700	862-3301
WBBT-FM 107.3 (Oldies) 300 Arboretum Pl Ste 590 *Web:* www.bigoldies1073.com	Richmond	VA	23236	804-327-9902	327-9911
WBTJ-FM 106.5 (Urban) 3245 Basie Rd *Web:* www.1065thebeat.com	Richmond	VA	23228	804-474-0000	474-0096
WCDX-FM 92.1 (Urban) 2809 Emerywood Pkwy Ste 300 *Web:* ipowerrichmond.com	Richmond	VA	23294	804-672-9299	672-9316
WLEE-AM 990 (N/T) 308 W Broad St *Web:* www.wlee990.am	Richmond	VA	23220	804-643-0990	
WRNL-AM 910 (Sports) 3245 Basie Rd *Web:* www.sportsradio910.com	Richmond	VA	23228	804-474-0000	474-0096
WRVA-AM 1140 (N/T) 3245 Basie Rd *Web:* www.1140wrva.com	Richmond	VA	23228	804-474-0000	474-0096
WRVQ-FM 94.5 (CHR) 3245 Basie Rd *Web:* www.q94radio.com	Richmond	VA	23228	804-474-0000	474-0096
WRXL-FM 102.1 (Rock) 3245 Basie Rd *Web:* www.xl102richmond.com	Richmond	VA	23228	804-474-0000	474-0096
WTVR-FM 98.1 (AC) 3245 Basie Rd *Web:* www.lite98.com	Richmond	VA	23228	804-474-0000	474-0096
WXGI-AM 950 (Sports) 701 German School Rd *Web:* www.espn950am.com	Richmond	VA	23225	804-233-7666	233-7681

648-136 Riverside/San Bernardino, CA

	City	State	ZIP	Phone	Fax
KCAL-FM 96.7 (Rock) 1940 Orange Tree Ln Ste 200 *Web:* www.kcalfm.com	Redlands	CA	92374	909-793-3554	798-6627
KCXX-FM 103.9 (Alt) 242 E Airport Dr Ste 106 *Web:* www.x1039.com	San Bernardino	CA	92408	909-890-5904	890-9035
KGGI-FM 99.1 (CHR) 2030 Iowa Ave Ste A **Fax:* Sales ■ *TF:* 866-991-5444 ■ *Web:* www.kggiradio.com	Riverside	CA	92507	951-684-1991	274-4949*
KPRO-AM 1570 (Rel) 7351 Lincoln Ave *Web:* kpro1570.com	Riverside	CA	92504	951-688-1570	688-7009
KSGN-FM 89.7 (Rel) 2048 Orange Tree Ln Ste 200 *TF:* 888-897-5746 ■ *Web:* www.ksgn.com	Redlands	CA	92374	909-583-2150	583-2170
KUCR-FM 88.3 (Var) UC Riverside *Web:* www.kucr.org	Riverside	CA	92521	951-827-3737	827-3240
KVCR-FM 91.9 (NPR) 701 S Mt Vernon Ave *TF:* 800-533-5827 ■ *Web:* www.kvcr.org	San Bernardino	CA	92410	909-384-4444	885-2116

648-137 Roanoke, VA

	City	State	ZIP	Phone	Fax
WFIR-AM 960 (N/T) 3934 Electric Rd SW *TF:* 800-367-7623 ■ *Web:* wfir960.com	Roanoke	VA	24018	540-345-1511	342-2270
WSLQ-FM 99.1 (AC) 3934 Electric Rd SW *Web:* www.q99fm.com	Roanoke	VA	24018	540-387-0234	342-2270
WSNV-FM 93.5 (AC) 3807 Brandon Ave Ste 2350 *Web:* www.sunny935.com	Roanoke	VA	24018	540-725-1220	725-1245
WVTF-FM 89.1 (NPR) 3520 Kingsbury Ln *TF:* 800-856-8900 ■ *Web:* www.wvtf.org	Roanoke	VA	24014	540-989-8900	776-2727
WXLK-FM 92.3 (CHR) 3934 Electric Rd SW *TF:* 800-468-9236 ■ *Web:* www.k92radio.com	Roanoke	VA	24018	540-774-9200	774-5667

648-138 Rochester, MN

	City	State	ZIP	Phone	Fax
KFSI-FM 92.9 (Rel) 4016 28th St SE *Web:* www.kfsi.org	Rochester	MN	55904	507-289-8585	529-4017

Station	City	State	ZIP	Phone	Fax
KLSE-FM 91.7 (Clas) 206 S Broadway Ste 735 — *TF:* 800-652-9700 ■ *Web:* minnesota.publicradio.org	Rochester	MN	55904	507-282-0910	282-2107
KRCH-FM 101.7 (CR) 1530 Greenview Dr SW Ste 200 — *Web:* www.laser1017.com	Rochester	MN	55902	507-288-3888	288-7815
KROC-AM 1340 (N/T) 122 SW Fourth St — *Web:* www.krocam.com/info/contact_us.php	Rochester	MN	55902	507-286-1010	286-9370
KWEB-AM 1270 (Sports) 1530 Greenview Dr SW Ste 200 — *TF:* 888-519-6683 ■ *Web:* www.fan1270.com	Rochester	MN	55902	507-288-3888	288-7815

648-139 Rochester, NY

Station	City	State	ZIP	Phone	Fax
WBEE-FM 92.5 (Ctry) 70 Commercial St — *Web:* www.wbee.com	Rochester	NY	14614	585-423-2900	423-2947
WBZA-FM 98.9 (CR) 70 Commercial St — *Web:* www.rochesterbuzz.com	Rochester	NY	14614	585-423-2900	423-2947
WCMF-FM 96.5 (CR) 70 Commercial St — *Web:* www.wcmf.com	Rochester	NY	14614	585-423-2900	399-5750
WDKX-FM 103.9 (Urban) 683 E Main St — *Web:* www.wdkx.com	Rochester	NY	14605	585-262-2050	262-2626
WDVI-FM 100.5 (AC) 100 Chestnut St 17th Fl — *Web:* www.mydrivefm.com	Rochester	NY	14604	585-454-4884	454-5081
WHAM-AM 1180 (N/T) 100 Chestnut St — *Web:* www.wham1180.com	Rochester	NY	14604	585-454-4884	454-5081
WKGS-FM 106.7 (CHR) HSBC Plz 100 Chestnut St 17th Fl — *Web:* www.kiss1067.com	Rochester	NY	14604	585-454-4884	454-5081
WPXY-FM 97.9 (CHR) 70 Commercial St — *Web:* www.98pxy.com	Rochester	NY	14614	585-423-2900	399-5750
WXXI-AM 1370 (NPR) PO Box 30021 — *Web:* interactive.wxxi.org	Rochester	NY	14603	585-325-7500	258-0339
WXXI-FM 91.5 (Clas) PO Box 30021 — *Web:* interactive.wxxi.org	Rochester	NY	14603	585-325-7500	258-0339
WZNE-FM 94.1 (Alt) 28 E Main St Eighth Fl — *Web:* www.thezone941.com	Rochester	NY	14614	585-399-5700	399-5750

648-140 Rockford, IL

Station	City	State	ZIP	Phone	Fax
WNTA-AM 1330 (N/T) 2830 Sandy Hollow Rd — *Web:* wnta.com	Rockford	IL	61109	815-874-7861	874-2202
WROK-AM 1440 (N/T) 3901 Brendenwood Rd — *Web:* www.1440wrok.com	Rockford	IL	61107	815-398-9765	484-2432

648-141 Sacramento, CA

Station	City	State	ZIP	Phone	Fax
Capital Public Radio Inc 7055 Folsom Blvd — *TF:* 877-480-5900 ■ *Web:* www.capradio.org	Sacramento	CA	95826	916-278-8900	278-8989
KCTC-AM 1320 (Sports) 5345 Madison Ave — *Web:* espn1320.net	Sacramento	CA	95841	916-334-7777	339-4591
KDND-FM 107.9 (CHR) 5345 Madison Ave — *Web:* www.endonline.com	Sacramento	CA	95841	916-334-7777	339-4591
KFBK-AM 1530 (N/T) 1545 River Park Dr Ste 500 — *Web:* www.kfbk.com	Sacramento	CA	95815	916-929-5325	
KFBK-FM 92.5 (AC) 1545 River Park Dr Ste 500 — *Web:* www.kfbk.com	Sacramento	CA	95815	916-929-5325	
KHHM-FM 103.4 (CHR) 1436 Auburn Blvd — *Web:* www.hot1035radio.com	Sacramento	CA	95815	916-646-4000	646-3237
KHTK-AM 1140 (Sports) 5244 Madison Ave — *TF:* 800-920-1140 ■ *Web:* sacramento.cbslocal.com	Sacramento	CA	95841	916-338-9200	338-9208
KKDO-FM 94.7 (NAC) 5345 Madison Ave — *Web:* www.radio947.net	Sacramento	CA	95841	916-334-7777	339-4591
KKFS-FM 103.9 (Rel) 1425 River Pk Dr Ste 520 — *Web:* www.1039thefish.com	Sacramento	CA	95815	916-924-0710	924-1587
KRXQ-FM 98.5 (Rock) 5345 Madison Ave — *Web:* www.krxq.net	Sacramento	CA	95841	916-334-7777	339-4591
KSEG-FM 96.9 (CR) 5345 Madison Ave — *Web:* www.eagle969.com	Sacramento	CA	95841	916-334-7777	339-4591
KTKZ-AM 1380 (N/T) 1425 River Pk Dr Ste 520 — *TF:* 888-923-1380 ■ *Web:* www.am1380theanswer.com	Sacramento	CA	95815	916-924-0710	924-1587
KXPR-FM 88.9 (Clas) 7055 Folsom Blvd — *TF:* 877-480-5900 ■ *Web:* www.capradio.org	Sacramento	CA	95826	916-278-8900	278-8989
KYMX-FM 96.1 (AC) 280 Commerce Cir — *Web:* kymx.cbslocal.com	Sacramento	CA	95815	916-923-6800	
KZZO-FM 100.5 (AC) 280 Commerce Cir — *Web:* now100fm.cbslocal.com	Sacramento	CA	95815	916-923-6800	927-6468

648-142 Saint Louis, MO

Station	City	State	ZIP	Phone	Fax
KEZK-FM 102.5 (AC) 3100 Market St — *Web:* fresh1025.cbslocal.com	Saint Louis	MO	63103	314-531-0000	
KPNT-FM 105.7 (Alt) 401 S 18th St — *Web:* 1057thepoint.com	Saint Louis	MO	63103	314-231-1057	621-3000
KTRS-AM 550 (N/T) 638 Westport Plaza — *TF:* 888-550-5877 ■ *Web:* www.ktrs.com	Saint Louis	MO	63146	314-453-5500	453-9704
KWMU-FM 90.7 (NPR) 3651 Olive St — *Web:* www.kwmu.org	Saint Louis	MO	63108	314-516-5968	
KYKY-FM Y98 (AC) 3100 Market St — *Web:* y98.cbslocal.com	Saint Louis	MO	63103	314-531-0000	531-9855
WEW-AM 770 (Var) 2740 Hampton Ave — *Web:* www.wewradio.com	Saint Louis	MO	63139	314-781-9397	781-8545

648-143 Salt Lake City, UT

Station	City	State	ZIP	Phone	Fax
KBEE-FM 98.7 (AC) 434 Bearcat Dr — *Web:* www.b987.com	Salt Lake City	UT	84115	801-485-6700	485-6611
KBZN-FM 97.9 (NAC) 257 East 200 South Ste 400 — *Web:* www.kbzn.com	Salt Lake City	UT	84111	801-364-9836	364-8068
KEGA-FM 101.5 (Ctry) 50 West Broadway Ste 200 — *TF:* 866-551-1015 ■ *Web:* www.1015theeagle.com	Salt Lake City	UT	84101	801-524-2600	364-1811
KJMY-FM 99.5 (Rock) 2801 S Decker Lk Dr — *Web:* www.my995fm.com	Salt Lake City	UT	84119	801-908-1300	908-1310
KLO-AM 1430 (N/T) 257 East 200 South Ste 400 — *TF:* 866-627-1430 ■ *Web:* www.kloradio.com	Salt Lake City	UT	84111	801-364-9836	
KNRS-AM 570 (N/T) 2801 S Decker Lk Dr — *Web:* www.knrs.com	Salt Lake City	UT	84119	801-908-1300	908-1310
KODJ-FM 94.1 (Oldies) 2801 S Decker Lk Dr — *Web:* www.oldies941.com	Salt Lake City	UT	84119	801-908-1300	908-1415
KOSY-FM 106.5 (AC) 2801 S Decker Lk Dr — *Web:* www.rock1065.com	Salt Lake City	UT	84119	801-908-1300	908-1310
KSL RADIO & TV 55 N 300 W — *Web:* www.ksl.com	Salt Lake City	UT	84101	801-575-5555	575-5561
KSL-AM 1160 (N/T) 55 N 300 W — *Web:* www.ksl.com	Salt Lake City	UT	84180	801-575-7600	575-5561
KSOP-AM 1370 (Ctry) 1285 West 2320 South — *Web:* www.cc1370.com	Salt Lake City	UT	84119	801-972-1043	974-0868
KSOP-FM 104.3 (Ctry) 1285 West 2320 South — *Web:* www.ksopcountry.com	West Valley City	UT	84119	801-972-1043	974-0868
KUBL-FM 93.3 (Ctry) 434 Bearcat Dr — *Web:* www.kbull93.com	Salt Lake City	UT	84115	801-485-6700	
KUER-FM 90.1 (NPR) 101 S Wasatch Dr — *TF:* 800-491-1148 ■ *Web:* www.kuer.org	Salt Lake City	UT	84112	801-581-6625	581-6758
KUUU-FM 92.5 (Urban) 515 South 700 East Ste 1-C — *Web:* www.u92online.com	Salt Lake City	UT	84102	801-524-2600	643-1811
KZHT-FM 97.1 (CHR) 2801 S Decker Lake Dr — *TF:* 800-888-8499 ■ *Web:* www.971zht.com	Salt Lake City	UT	84119	801-908-1300	908-1310
KZNS-AM 1280 (Sports) 301 W S Temple — *Web:* www.1280thezone.com	Salt Lake City	UT	84101	855-340-9663	

648-144 San Antonio, TX

Station	City	State	ZIP	Phone	Fax
930 AM The Answer 9601 McAllister Fwy Ste 1200 — *TF:* 866-308-8867 ■ *Web:* www.klup.com	San Antonio	TX	78216	210-344-8481	
KAJA-FM 97.3 (Ctry) 6222 NW IH-10 — *TF:* 800-707-5150 ■ *Web:* www.kj97.com	San Antonio	TX	78201	210-736-9700	735-8811
KCYY-FM 100.3 (Ctry) 8122 Datapoint Dr Ste 600 — *Web:* www.y100fm.com	San Antonio	TX	78229	210-615-5400	615-5331
KISS-FM 99.5 (Rock) 8122 Datapoint Dr Ste 600 — *TF:* 866-333-6747 ■ *Web:* www.kissrocks.com	San Antonio	TX	78229	210-615-5400	615-5331
KJXK-FM 102.7 (Var) 4050 Eisenhauer Rd — *Web:* jackfmsa.com	San Antonio	TX	78218	210-654-5100	855-5076
KKYX-AM 680 (Ctry) 8122 Datapoint Dr Ste 600 — *Web:* www.kkyx.com	San Antonio	TX	78229	210-615-5400	615-5330
KQXT-FM 101.9 (AC) 6222 NW IH-10 — *Web:* www.q1019.com	San Antonio	TX	78201	210-736-9700	735-8811
KROM-FM 92.9 (Span) 1777 NE Loop 410 Ste 400 — *TF:* 888-382-1222 ■ *Web:* 929sanantonio.univision.com/	San Antonio	TX	78217	210-821-6548	804-7820
KSLR-AM 630 (Rel) 9601 McAllister Fwy Ste 1200 — *TF:* 888-346-4700 ■ *Web:* www.kslr.com	San Antonio	TX	78216	210-344-8481	340-1213
KSTX-FM 89.1 (NPR) 8401 Datapoint Dr Ste 800 — *TF:* 800-622-8977 ■ *Web:* www.tpr.org	San Antonio	TX	78229	210-614-8977	614-8983
KTKR-AM 760 (Sports) 6222 NW IH-10 — *Web:* www.ticket760.com	San Antonio	TX	78201	210-736-9700	735-8811
KTKX-FM 106.7 (Urban) 8122 Datapoint Dr Ste 600 — *Web:* www.x1067fm.com	San Antonio	TX	78229	210-615-5400	615-5300
KTSA-AM 550 (N/T) 4050 Eisenhauer Rd — *TF:* 800-299-5872 ■ *Web:* www.ktsa.com	San Antonio	TX	78218	210-654-5100	
KXXM-FM 96.1 (CHR) 6222 NW IH-10 — *Web:* www.mix961.com	San Antonio	TX	78201	210-736-9700	735-8811
KZEP-FM 104.5 (CR) 6222 NW IH-10 — *Web:* www.kzep.com	San Antonio	TX	78201	210-736-9700	735-8811
WOAI-AM 1200 (N/T) 6222 NW IH-10 — *TF:* 800-707-5150 ■ *Web:* www.woai.com	San Antonio	TX	78201	210-736-9700	832-3149

648-145 San Diego, CA

Station	City	State	Zip	Phone	Fax
KFMB-AM 760 (N/T) 7677 Engineer Rd *TF:* 800-760-5362 ■ *Web:* www.760kfmb.com	San Diego	CA	92111	858-292-7600	279-7676
KFMB-FM 100.7 (AC) 7677 Engineer Rd. *Web:* www.sandiegojack.com	San Diego	CA	92111	858-571-8888	
KGB-FM 101.5 (CR) 9660 Granite Ridge Dr Ste 100 *Web:* www.101kgb.com	San Diego	CA	92123	858-292-2000	
KHTS-FM 93.3 (CHR) 9660 Granite Ridge Dr Ste 100 *Web:* www.channel933.com	San Diego	CA	92123	858-292-2000	294-2916
KIFM-FM 98.1 (NAC) 1615 Murray Canyon Rd Ste 710 *Web:* www.easy981.com	San Diego	CA	92108	619-291-9797	543-1353
KIOZ-FM 105.3 (Rock) 9660 Granite Ridge Dr Ste 100 *Web:* www.rock1053.com	San Diego	CA	92123	858-292-2000	522-5768
KLNV-FM 106.5 (Span) 600 W Broadway Ste 2150 *TF:* 800-879-4278 ■ *Web:* www.univision.com	San Diego	CA	92101	619-235-0600	744-4300
KMYI-FM 94.1 (AC) 9660 Granite Ridge Dr Ste 100 *Web:* www.star941fm.com	San Diego	CA	92123	858-292-2000	294-2916
KOGO-AM 600 (N/T) 9660 Granite Ridge Dr Ste 100 *Web:* www.kogo.com	San Diego	CA	92123	858-292-2000	715-3675
KOGO-FM 95.7 (Ctry) 9660 Granite Ridge Dr *Web:* www.kogo.com	San Diego	CA	92123	858-292-2000	
KPBS-FM 89.5 (NPR) San Diego State University 5200 Campanile Dr. *TF:* 888-399-5727 ■ *Web:* www.kpbs.org	San Diego	CA	92182	619-265-6438	594-3812
KSCF-FM 103.7 (N/T) 8033 Linda Vista Rd. *TF:* 888-388-1037 ■ *Web:* energy1037.cbslocal.com	San Diego	CA	92111	858-571-7600	571-0326
KSDS-FM 88.3 (Jazz) 1313 Pk Blvd *Web:* www.jazz88.org	San Diego	CA	92101	619-388-3037	388-3928
KSON-FM 97.3 (Ctry) 1615 Murray Canyon Rd Ste 710 *TF:* 800-988-4253 ■ *Web:* www.kson.com	San Diego	CA	92108	619-291-9797	543-1353
KYXY-FM 96.5 (AC) 8033 Linda Vista Rd *TF:* 888-560-9650 ■ *Web:* kyxy.cbslocal.com	San Diego	CA	92111	858-571-7600	571-0326
XEMO-AM 860 (Span) 5030 Camino de la Siesta Ste 403 *Web:* www.uniradio.com	San Diego	CA	92108	619-497-0600	497-1019
XHRM-FM 92.5 (Oldies) 6160 Cornerstone Ct E Ste 150 *Web:* www.magic925.com	San Diego	CA	92121	858-888-7000	
XHTZ-FM 90.3 (Urban) 6160 Cornerstone Ct E Ste 150 *Web:* www.z90.com	San Diego	CA	92121	858-888-7000	
XTRA-FM 91.1 (Alt) 6160 Cornerstone Ct E Ste 150 *Web:* www.91x.com	San Diego	CA	92121	858-888-7000	

648-146 San Francisco, CA

Station	City	State	Zip	Phone	Fax
KALW-FM 91.7 (NPR) 500 Mansell St. *Web:* www.kalw.org	San Francisco	CA	94134	415-841-4121	841-4125
KCBS-AM 740 (N/T) 865 Battery St Third Fl *Web:* sanfrancisco.cbslocal.com	San Francisco	CA	94111	415-765-8758	765-4146
KFOG-FM 104.5 (CH) 750 Battery St 3rd Fl. *Web:* www.kfog.com	San Francisco	CA	94111	415-995-6800	995-6829
KFRC-AM 15.50 (Oldies) 865 Battery St Second Fl	San Francisco	CA	94111	415-391-9970	765-4146
KGO-AM 810 (N/T) 55 Hawthorne St. *TF:* 855-847-7247 ■ *Web:* www.kgoradio.com	San Francisco	CA	94105	415-995-5721	995-7099
KIOI-FM 101.3 (AC) 340 Townsend St Fourth Fl. *TF:* 800-800-1013 ■ *Web:* www.1013.com	San Francisco	CA	94107	415-975-5555	538-1000
KISQ-FM 98.1 (Urban AC) 340 Townsend St Fourth Fl. *Web:* www.981kissfm.com	San Francisco	CA	94107	415-975-5555	
KITS-FM 105.3 (Alt) 865 Battery St. *TF:* 800-696-1053 ■ *Web:* live105.cbslocal.com	San Francisco	CA	94111	800-696-1053	
KKSF-FM 103.7 (NAC) 340 Townsend St Fourth Fl. *TF:* 866-900-1037 ■ *Web:* big1037fm.com/	San Francisco	CA	94107	415-975-5555	
KMEL-FM 106.1 (Urban) 340 Townsend St Fourth Fl. *Web:* www.kmel.com	San Francisco	CA	94107	415-975-5555	
KMVQ-FM 99.7 (AC) 865 Battery St *TF:* 888-456-9970 ■ *Web:* 997now.cbslocal.com	San Francisco	CA	94111	415-765-4112	765-4152
KOIT-FM 96.5 (AC) 201 Third St Ste 1200. *Web:* www.koit.com	San Francisco	CA	94103	415-777-0965	896-0965
KQED-FM 88.5 (NPR) 2601 Mariposa St. *TF:* 800-723-3566 ■ *Web:* www.kqed.org	San Francisco	CA	94110	415-864-2000	553-2183
KSAN-FM 107.7 (Alt) 750 Battery St 3rd Fl. **Fax Area Code:* 888 ■ *TF:* 888-303-2663 ■ *Web:* www.1077thebone.com	San Francisco	CA	94105	415-995-6800	709-2663*
KYLD-FM 94.9 (Urban) 340 Townsend St Ste 5101 *TF:* 888-333-9490 ■ *Web:* www.wild949.com	San Francisco	CA	94107	415-975-5555	538-1000

648-147 San Jose, CA

Station	City	State	Zip	Phone	Fax
98.5 KFOX 201 Third St Ste 1200 *TF:* 877-410-5369 ■ *Web:* www.kfox.com	San Francisco	CA	94103	877-410-5369	
KBAY-FM 94.5 (AC) 190 Pk Ctr Plz Ste 200. *TF:* 800-948-5229 ■ *Web:* www.kbay.com	San Jose	CA	95113	408-287-5775	293-3341
KRTY-FM 95.3 (Ctry) 750 Story Rd. *Web:* www.krty.com	San Jose	CA	95122	408-293-8030	
KXSC-FM 104.9 (Alt) PO Box 6375. *Web:* www.kdfc.com	Artesia	CA	90702	415-546-8710	

648-148 Santa Fe, NM

Station	City	State	Zip	Phone	Fax
KBAC-FM 98.1 (AAA) 2502 Camino Entrada Ste C *TF:* 888-321-5123 ■ *Web:* www.santafe.com	Santa Fe	NM	87507	505-988-5222	473-2667
KSWV-AM 810 (Span) 102 Taos St *TF:* 800-873-3372 ■ *Web:* santafenewmexican.com	Santa Fe	NM	87505	505-989-7441	
KTRC-AM 1260 (N/T) 2502 Camino Entrada Ste C *TF:* 888-321-5123 ■ *Web:* www.santafe.com/ktrc	Santa Fe	NM	87507	505-471-1067	473-2667

648-149 Savannah, GA

Station	City	State	Zip	Phone	Fax
WAEV-FM 97.3 (AC) 245 Alfred St *TF:* 800-543-3548 ■ *Web:* www.973kissfm.com	Savannah	GA	31408	912-964-7794	964-9414
WJCL-FM 96.5 (Ctry) 214 Television Cir. *Web:* www.nashfm965.com	Savannah	GA	31406	912-961-9000	961-7070
WLVH-FM 101.1 (Urban AC) 245 Alfred St. *Web:* www.love1011.com	Savannah	GA	31408	912-964-7794	964-9414
WQBT-FM 94.1 (Urban) 245 Alfred St. *Web:* www.941thebeat.com	Savannah	GA	31408	912-964-7794	964-9414
WRHQ-FM 105.3 (Rock) 1102 E 52nd St *Web:* www.wrhq.com	Savannah	GA	31404	912-234-1053	354-6600
WSOK-AM 1230 (Rel) 245 Alfred St *Web:* www.1230wsok.com	Savannah	GA	31408	912-964-7794	964-9414
WSVH-FM 91.1 (NPR) 13040 Abercorn St Ste 8 **Fax Area Code:* 404 ■ *TF:* 877-472-1227 ■ *Web:* gpb.org/savannah	Savannah	GA	31419	912-344-3565	362-4564*
WTKS-AM 1290 (N/T) 245 Alfred St. *TF:* 877-263-7995 ■ *Web:* www.newsradio1290wtks.com	Savannah	GA	31408	912-964-7794	964-9414
WYKZ-FM 98.7 (AC) 245 Alfred St. *TF:* 800-473-8546 ■ *Web:* www.987theriver.com	Savannah	GA	31408	912-964-7794	964-9414

648-150 Scranton, PA

Station	City	State	Zip	Phone	Fax
Wejl 149 Penn Ave *Web:* nepasespnradio.com	Scranton	PA	18503	570-346-6555	346-6038
WEZX-FM 106.9 (Rock) 149 Penn Ave. *Web:* www.rock107.com	Scranton	PA	18503	570-346-6555	346-6038
WVMW-FM 91.7 (Alt) 2300 Adams Ave *Web:* www.vmfm917.org	Scranton	PA	18509	570-348-6202	961-4769

648-151 Seattle/Tacoma, WA

Station	City	State	Zip	Phone	Fax
KBKS-FM 106.1 (CHR) 645 Elliott Ave W Ste 400 *TF:* 888-343-1061 ■ *Web:* www.kissfmseattle.com	Seattle	WA	98119	206-494-2000	
KCMS-FM 105.3 (Rel) 19319 Fremont Ave N *Web:* www.spirit1053.com	Shoreline	WA	98133	206-546-7350	289-7792
KHHO-AM 850 (Sports) 645 Elliott Ave W Ste 400. *TF:* 800-829-0950 ■ *Web:* www.sportsradiokjr.com	Seattle	WA	98119	206-494-2000	286-2376
KING-FM 98.1 (Clas) 10 Harrison St Ste 100 *Web:* www.king.org	Seattle	WA	98109	206-691-2981	691-2982
KIRO-FM 97.3 (N/T) 1820 Eastlake Ave E. *Web:* www.mynorthwest.com	Seattle	WA	98102	206-726-7000	726-5446
KISW-FM 99.9 (Rock) 1100 Olive Way Ste 1650 *Web:* www.kisw.com	Seattle	WA	98101	206-285-7625	215-9355
KJAQ-FM 96.5 (Var) 1000 Dexter Ave N Ste 100. *TF:* 866-416-5225 ■ *Web:* jackseattle.cbslocal.com	Seattle	WA	98109	206-805-1100	805-0932
KJR-AM 950 (Sports) 351 Elliott Ave W Ste 300. *TF:* 800-829-0950 ■ *Web:* www.sportsradiokjr.com	Seattle	WA	98119	206-494-2000	286-2376
KNDD-FM 107.7 (Alt) 1100 Olive Way Ste 1650 *Web:* www.1077theend.com	Seattle	WA	98101	206-622-3251	682-8349
KOMO-AM 1000 (N/T) 140 Fourth Ave N Ste 340 *TF:* 888-477-5666 ■ *Web:* www.komonews.com	Seattle	WA	98109	206-404-4000	404-3646
KPLZ-FM 101.5 (AC) 140 Fourth Ave N Ste 340 *TF:* 888-821-1015 ■ *Web:* www.star1015.com	Seattle	WA	98109	206-404-4000	404-1015
KPTK-AM 1090 (N/T) 1000 Dexter Ave N Ste 100 *Web:* seattle.cbslocal.com	Seattle	WA	98109	206-805-1100	805-0922
KUBE-FM 93.3 (AC) 351 Elliott Ave W Ste 300 *TF:* 877-933-9393 ■ *Web:* www.kube93.com	Seattle	WA	98119	206-494-2000	286-2376
KUOW-FM 94.9 (NPR) 4518 University Way NE Ste 310 *TF:* 800-289-5869 ■ *Web:* www.kuow.org	Seattle	WA	98105	206-543-2710	543-2720
KVI-AM 570 (N/T) 140 Fourth Ave N Ste 340. *Web:* www.kvi.com	Seattle	WA	98109	206-404-4000	404-3648
KZOK-FM 102.5 (CR) 1000 Dexter Ave N. *TF:* 800-252-1025 ■ *Web:* kzok.cbslocal.com	Seattle	WA	98109	206-421-1025	

648-152 Shreveport, LA

Station	City	State	Zip	Phone	Fax
KBTT-FM 103.7 (CHR) 208 N Thomas *Web:* kbtt.fm	Shreveport	LA	71137	318-222-3122	320-0102
KDAQ-FM 89.9 (NPR) One University Pl PO Box 5250 *TF:* 800-552-8502 ■ *Web:* www.redriverradio.org	Shreveport	LA	71115	318-797-5150	797-5265
KDKS-FM 102.1 (Urban) 208 N Thomas *Web:* www.kdks.fm	Shreveport	LA	71137	318-222-3122	320-0102
KLKL-FM 95.7 (Oldies) 208 N Thomas *Web:* www.klkl.fm	Shreveport	LA	71137	318-222-3122	
KRUF-FM 94.5 (CHR) 6341 W Port Ave *Web:* k945.com	Shreveport	LA	71129	318-688-1130	
KVKI-FM 96.5 (AC) 6341 W Port Ave *TF:* 800-487-1840 ■ *Web:* www.965kvki.com	Shreveport	LA	71129	318-688-1130	687-8574
KXKS-FM 93.7 (Ctry) 6341 W Port Ave *Web:* mykisscountry937.com	Shreveport	LA	71129	318-688-1130	

648-153 Sioux Falls, SD

Station	City	State	Zip	Phone	Fax
KELO-AM 1320 (N/T) 500 S Phillips Ave *Web:* kelo.com	Sioux Falls	SD	57104	605-336-1320	336-0415
KELO-FM 92.5 (AC) 500 S Phillips Ave *Web:* www.kelofm.com	Sioux Falls	SD	57104	605-331-5350	336-0415
KIKN-FM 100.5 (Ctry) 5100 S Tennis Ln *Web:* www.kikn.com	Sioux Falls	SD	57108	605-361-0300	339-2735
KKLS-FM 104.7 (CHR) 5100 S Tennis Ln *Web:* www.hot1047.com	Sioux Falls	SD	57108	605-361-0300	339-2735
KMXC-FM 97.3 (AC) 5100 S Tennis Ln *Web:* www.mix97-3.com	Sioux Falls	SD	57108	605-361-0300	339-2735
KNWC-AM 96.5 (Rel) 6300 S Tallgrass Ave *TF:* 888-569-5692 ■ *Web:* life965.fm	Sioux Falls	SD	57108	605-339-1270	339-1271
KRRO-FM 103.7 (Rock) 500 S Phillips Ave *TF:* 877-263-7995 ■ *Web:* www.krro.com	Sioux Falls	SD	57104	605-331-5350	336-0415
KRSD-FM 88.1 (Clas) 480 Cedar St *TF:* 800-228-7123 ■ *Web:* minnesota.publicradio.org	Saint Paul	MN	55101	651-290-1500	
KSOO-AM 1140 (N/T) 5100 S Tennis Ln *Web:* www.ksoo.com	Sioux Falls	SD	57108	605-361-0300	339-2735
KTWB-FM 101.9 (Ctry) 500 S Phillips Ave *TF:* 877-263-7995 ■ *Web:* www.ktwb.com	Sioux Falls	SD	57104	605-331-5350	336-0415
KXRB-AM 1000 (Ctry) 5100 S Tennis Ln *Web:* www.kxrb.com	Sioux Falls	SD	57108	605-361-0300	339-2735
KYBB-FM 102.7 (CR) 5100 S Tennis Ln *Web:* www.b1027.com	Sioux Falls	SD	57108	605-361-0300	339-2735

648-154 South Bend, IN

Station	City	State	Zip	Phone	Fax
WNDV-FM 92.9 (CHR) 3371 Cleveland Rd Ste 300 *TF:* 800-242-0100 ■ *Web:* www.u93.com	South Bend	IN	46628	574-273-9300	273-9090

648-155 Spokane, WA

Station	City	State	Zip	Phone	Fax
KBBD-FM 103.9 (AC) 1601 E 57th Ave *Web:* www.1039bobfm.com	Spokane	WA	99223	509-448-1000	448-7015
KDRK-FM 93.7 (Ctry) 1601 E 57th Ave *TF:* 877-871-6772 ■ *Web:* www.937thecat.com	Spokane	WA	99223	509-448-1000	448-7015
KGA-AM 1510 (N/T) 1601 E 57th Ave *Web:* www.1510kga.com	Spokane	WA	99223	509-448-1000	448-7015
KHTQ-FM 94 « (Rock) 500 W Boone Ave *Web:* www.rock945.com	Spokane	WA	99201	509-324-4200	352-0676
KISC-FM 98.1 (AC) 808 E Sprague Ave *Web:* www.kiss981.com	Spokane	WA	99202	509-242-2400	242-1160
KKZX-FM 98.9 (CR) 808 E Sprague Ave *Web:* www.989kkzx.com	Spokane	WA	99202	509-242-2400	242-1160
KPTQ-AM 1280 (N/T) 808 E Sprague Ave *Web:* www.1280foxsports.com	Spokane	WA	99202	509-242-2400	242-1160
KXLY-AM 920 (N/T) 500 W Boone Ave *Web:* www.kxly.com	Spokane	WA	99201	509-324-4200	325-0676
KZBD-FM 105.7 (Rock) 1601 E 57th Ave *Web:* www.now1057fm.com	Spokane	WA	99223	509-448-1000	448-7015
KZZU-FM 92.9 (CHR) 500 W Boone Ave *TF:* 866-845-0929 ■ *Web:* www.kzzu.com	Spokane	WA	99201	509-324-4200	325-7729
Spokane Public Radio 2319 N Monroe St *TF:* 800-328-5729 ■ *Web:* www.kpbx.org	Spokane	WA	99205	509-328-5729	328-5764

648-156 Springfield, IL

Station	City	State	Zip	Phone	Fax
WDBR-FM 103.7 (CHR) 3501 E Sangamon Ave *Web:* www.wdbr.com	Springfield	IL	62707	217-753-5400	753-7902
WFMB-AM 1450 (Sports) 3055 S Fourth St *Web:* www.sportsradio1450.com	Springfield	IL	62703	217-528-3033	528-5348
WFMB-FM 104.5 (Ctry) 3055 S Fourth St *Web:* www.wfmb.com	Springfield	IL	62703	217-528-3033	528-5348
WMAY-AM 970 (N/T) *Mid-West Family Broadcasting* 1510 N Third St *Web:* www.wmay.com	Riverton	IL	62561	217-629-7077	629-7952
WNNS-FM 98.7 (AC) PO Box 460 *Web:* www.wnns.com	Springfield	IL	62705	217-629-5483	629-7952
WQQL-FM 101.9 (Oldies) 3501 E Sangamon Ave *TF:* 877-984-8786 ■ *Web:* cool939.com	Springfield	IL	62707	217-753-5400	753-7902
WTAX-AM 1240 (N/T) 3501 E Sangamon Ave *Web:* www.wtax.com	Springfield	IL	62707	217-753-5400	753-7902
WUIS-FM 91.9 (NPR) University of Illinois at Springfield 1 University Plz WUIS-130 *Web:* www.wuis.org	Springfield	IL	62703	217-206-9847	206-6527
WXAJ-FM 99.7 (CHR) 3055 S Fourth St *Web:* www.997kissfm.com	Springfield	IL	62703	217-528-3033	528-5348
WYMG-FM 100.5 (CR) 3501 E Sangamon Ave *Web:* www.wymg.com	Springfield	IL	62707	217-753-5400	753-7902

648-157 Springfield, MA

Station	City	State	Zip	Phone	Fax
WHYN-AM 560 (N/T) 1331 Main St Fourth Fl *TF:* 800-345-9759 ■ *Web:* www.whyn.com	Springfield	MA	01103	413-781-1011	734-4434
WHYN-FM 93.1 (AC) 1331 Main St Fourth Fl *TF:* 888-293-9310 ■ *Web:* www.mix931.com	Springfield	MA	01103	413-781-1011	
WNNZ-AM 640 (NPR) 131 County Cir *Web:* nepr.net	Amherst	MA	01003	413-735-6600	
WSCB-FM 89.9 (Urban) 263 Alden St *TF:* 800-727-0504 ■ *Web:* www.springfieldcollege.edu	Springfield	MA	01109	413-748-3000	748-3473
WTCC-FM 90.7 (Var) One Armory Sq *Web:* www.wtccfm.org	Springfield	MA	01105	413-736-2781	755-6305

648-158 Springfield, MO

Station	City	State	Zip	Phone	Fax
KGBX-FM 105.9 (AC) 1856 S Glenstone Ave *TF:* 800-445-1059 ■ *Web:* www.kgbx.com	Springfield	MO	65804	417-890-5555	890-5050
KSMS-FM 90.5 (NPR) Missouri State University 901 S National Ave *TF:* 800-767-5768 ■ *Web:* www.ksmu.org	Springfield	MO	65804	417-836-5878	836-5889
KSMU-FM 91.1 (NPR) Missouri State University 901 S National Ave *TF:* 800-767-5768 ■ *Web:* www.ksmu.org	Springfield	MO	65897	417-836-5878	836-5889
KSPW-FM 96.5 (CHR) 2330 W Grand St *Web:* www.power965.com	Springfield	MO	65802	417-865-6614	865-9643
KSWF-FM 100.5 (Ctry) 1856 S Glenstone Ave *TF:* 844-289-7234 ■ *Web:* www.1005thewolf.com	Springfield	MO	65804	417-890-5555	
KTOZ-FM 95.5 (AC) 1856 S Glenstone Ave *TF:* 800-757-9550 ■ *Web:* www.alice955.com	Springfield	MO	65804	417-890-5555	890-5050
KTTS-FM 94.7 (Ctry) 2330 W Grand St *TF:* 855-574-2533 ■ *Web:* www.ktts.com	Springfield	MO	65802	417-865-6614	865-9643
KTXR-FM 101.3 (AC) 3000 E Chestnut Expy *TF General:* 855-586-8852 ■ *Web:* www.ktxrfm.com	Springfield	MO	65806	417-862-3751	869-7675

648-159 Stamford/Bridgeport, CT

Station	City	State	Zip	Phone	Fax
WEBE-FM 108 (AC) Two Lafayette Sq *TF:* 800-932-3108 ■ *Web:* www.webe108.com	Bridgeport	CT	06604	203-333-9108	384-0600
WICC-AM 600 (N/T) Two Lafayette Sq *Web:* www.wicc600.com	Bridgeport	CT	06604	203-333-9108	384-0600
WPKN-FM 89.5 (Var) 244 University Ave *Web:* www.wpkn.org	Bridgeport	CT	06604	203-331-9756	

648-160 Stockton, CA

Station	City	State	Zip	Phone	Fax
KSTN-AM 1420 (Oldies) 2171 Ralph Ave *Web:* www.valleyradio.org	Stockton	CA	95206	209-948-1420	
KWIN-FM 97.7 (CHR) 3136 Boeing Way Ste 125 *Web:* www.kwin.com	Stockton	CA	95206	209-476-1230	
KYCC-FM 90.1 (Rel) 9019 W Ln *TF:* 800-654-5254 ■ *Web:* www.kycc.org	Stockton	CA	95210	209-477-3690	477-2762

648-161 Syracuse, NY

Station	City	State	Zip	Phone	Fax
TK99 235 Walton St *Web:* tk99.net	Syracuse	NY	13202	315-472-9111	472-1888
WAER-FM 88.3 (Jazz) 795 Ostram Ave *Web:* www.waer.org	Syracuse	NY	13210	315-443-4021	
WAQX-FM 95.7 1064 James St *Web:* www.95x.com	Syracuse	NY	13203	315-472-0200	472-1146
WBBS-FM 104.7 (Ctry) 500 Plum St Ste 100 *Web:* www.b1047.net	Syracuse	NY	13204	315-472-9797	472-2323
WHEN-AM 620 (Sports) 500 Plum St Ste 400 *TF:* 800-582-7583 ■ *Web:* www.wsyr.com	Syracuse	NY	13204	315-472-9797	472-2323
WKRL-FM 100.9 (Alt) 235 Walton St *Web:* syracuse.krock.com	Syracuse	NY	13202	315-472-9111	472-1888
WNTQ-FM 93.1 1064 James St *Web:* www.93q.com	Syracuse	NY	13203	315-472-0200	478-5625
WSYR-AM 570 (N/T) 500 Plum St Ste 400 *Web:* www.wsyr.com	Syracuse	NY	13204	315-472-9797	472-2323
WYYY-FM 94.5 (AC) 500 Plum St Ste 400 *Web:* www.y94fm.com	Syracuse	NY	13204	315-472-9797	472-2323

648-162 Tallahassee, FL

Station	City	State	Zip	Phone	Fax
WBZE-FM 98.9 (AC) 3411 W Tharpe St *Web:* www.mystar98.com	Tallahassee	FL	32303	850-201-3000	201-2329
WFSQ-FM 91.5 (Clas) 1600 Red Barber Plaza *TF:* 866-321-9378 ■ *Web:* www.wfsu.org	Tallahassee	FL	32310	850-487-3086	487-2611
WFSU-FM 88.9 (NPR) 1600 Red Barber Plaza *TF:* 800-322-9378 ■ *Web:* www.wfsu.org	Tallahassee	FL	32310	850-487-3086	487-2611
WGLF-FM 104.1 (CR) 3411 W Tharpe St *Web:* www.gulf104.com	Tallahassee	FL	32303	850-201-3000	201-2329
WHTF-FM 104.9 (CHR) 3000 Olson Rd *Web:* www.hot1049.com	Tallahassee	FL	32308	850-386-8004	422-1897
WNLS-AM 1270 (Sports) 325 John Knox Rd Bldg G *Web:* www.1270theteam.com	Tallahassee	FL	32303	850-422-3107	383-0747
WTLY-FM 107.1 (AC) 325 John Knox Rd Bldg G *TF:* 855-274-2389 ■ *Web:* kissfm1071.com/	Tallahassee	FL	32303	850-422-3107	
WTNT-FM 94.9 (Ctry) 325 John Knox Rd Bldg G *Web:* www.949tnt.com	Tallahassee	FL	32303	850-422-3107	383-0747
WXSR-FM 101.5 (Alt) 325 John Knox Rd Bldg G *Web:* www.x1015.com	Tallahassee	FL	32303	850-422-3107	383-0747

648-163 Tampa/Saint Petersburg, FL

Station	City	State	Zip	Phone	Fax
Am860 The Answer 5211 W Laurel St Ste 101 *Web:* www.860wgul.com	Tampa	FL	33607	813-639-1903	639-1272
Cox Media Group Tampa 11300 Fourth St N Ste 300 *TF:* 888-723-9388 ■ *Web:* www.wduv.com	Saint Petersburg	FL	33716	727-579-2000	579-2271
Straight Way Radio LLC 407 N Howard Ave	Tampa	FL	33606	813-259-9867	
WDAE-AM 620 (Sports) 4002 W Gandy Blvd *TF:* 888-546-4620 ■ *Web:* www.620wdae.com	Tampa	FL	33611	813-832-1000	832-1090
WHPT-FM 102.5 (CR) 11300 Fourth St N Ste 300 *TF:* 800-771-1025 ■ *Web:* www.theboneonline.com	Saint Petersburg	FL	33716	727-579-2000	579-2271
WQYK-AM 1010 (Ctry) 9721 Executive Ctr Dr N Ste 200 *Web:* wqyk.cbslocal.com	Saint Petersburg	FL	33702	727-579-1925	
WQYK-FM 99.5 (Ctry) 9721 Executive Ctr Dr N Ste 200 *Web:* wqyk.cbslocal.com	Saint Petersburg	FL	33702	727-579-1925	
WRXB-AM 1590 (Urban) 3551 42nd Ave S Ste B-106 *Web:* www.wrxb.us	Saint Petersburg	FL	33711	727-865-1591	866-1728
WSJT-FM 94.1 (NAC) 1271 Avenue of Americas Ste 200 **Fax Area Code: 727* ■ *Web:* tampa.cbslocal.com	New York	NY	10020	212-649-9600	579-9250*
WSUN-FM 97.1 (Alt) 11300 Fourth St N Ste 300 *TF:* 877-327-9797 ■ *Web:* www.97xonline.com	Saint Petersburg	FL	33716	727-579-2000	579-2271
WTBN-AM 570 (Rel) 5211 W Laurel St Ste 101 *Web:* www.letstalkfaith.com	Tampa	FL	33607	813-639-1903	639-1272
WUSF-FM 89.7 (NPR) 4202 E Fowler Ave TVB 100 *TF:* 800-741-9090 ■ *Web:* wusf.usf.edu/radio	Tampa	FL	33620	813-974-8700	974-5016
WXGL-FM 107.3 (AC) 11300 Fourth St N Ste 300 *TF:* 800-242-1073 ■ *Web:* www.1073theeagle.com	Saint Petersburg	FL	33716	727-579-2000	578-0949
WXTB-FM 97.9 (Rock) 4002 W Gandy Blvd *Web:* www.98rock.com	Tampa	FL	33611	813-832-1000	831-3299

648-164 Toledo, OH

Station	City	State	Zip	Phone	Fax
WGTE-FM 91.3 (NPR) 1270 S Detroit Ave PO Box 30 *Web:* www.wgte.org	Toledo	OH	43614	419-380-4600	380-4710
WIOT-FM 104.7 (Rock) 125 S Superior St *Web:* www.wiot.com	Toledo	OH	43604	419-244-8321	244-7631
WRQN-FM 93.5 (Oldies) 3225 Arlington Ave *Web:* www.935wrqn.com	Toledo	OH	43614	419-725-5700	
WRVF-FM 101.5 (AC) 125 S Superior St *Web:* www.1015theriver.com	Toledo	OH	43604	419-244-8321	244-7631
WSPD-AM 1370 (N/T) 125 S Superior St *TF:* 800-745-3000 ■ *Web:* www.wspd.com	Toledo	OH	43604	419-244-8321	244-7631
WVKS-FM 92.5 (CHR) 125 S Superior St *Web:* www.925kissfm.com	Toledo	OH	43604	419-244-8321	244-7631
WXKR-FM 94.5 (CR) 3225 Arlington Ave *TF:* 866-240-9945 ■ *Web:* www.wxkr.com	Toledo	OH	43614	419-725-5700	725-5805

648-165 Topeka, KS

Station	City	State	Zip	Phone	Fax
KMAJ-AM 1440 (N/T) 825 S Kansas Ave Ste 100 *TF:* 877-297-1077 ■ *Web:* www.kmaj.com	Topeka	KS	66612	785-272-2122	272-6219
KMAJ-FM 107.7 (AC) 825 S Kansas Ave Ste 100 *TF:* 877-297-1077 ■ *Web:* www.kmaj.com	Topeka	KS	66612	785-272-2122	272-6219
KTPK-FM 106.9 (Ctry) 1210 SW Executive Dr *Web:* www.ktpk1069.com	Topeka	KS	66615	785-273-1069	273-0123
KWIC-FM 99.3 (Oldies) 825 S Kansas Ave Ste 100 *Web:* www.eagle993.com	Topeka	KS	66612	785-272-2122	272-6219
WIBW-AM 580 (N/T) 1210 SW Executive Dr PO Box 1818 *Web:* www.wibwnewsnow.com	Topeka	KS	66615	785-272-3456	228-7282
WIBW-FM 94.5 (Ctry) 1210 SW Executive Dr PO Box 1818 *Web:* www.94country.com	Topeka	KS	66601	785-272-3456	228-7282

648-166 Toronto, ON

Station	City	State	Zip	Phone	Fax
CFNY-FM 102.1 (Alt) 25 Dock Side Dr *Web:* www.edge.ca	Toronto	ON	M5A0B5	416-870-3343	847-3300
CHIN-AM 1540 (Ethnic) 622 College St Fourth Fl *Web:* www.chinradio.com	Toronto	ON	M6G1B6	416-531-9991	531-5274
CHIN-FM 100.7 (Ethnic) 622 College St Fourth Fl *Web:* www.chinradio.com	Toronto	ON	M6G1B6	416-531-9991	531-5274

648-167 Trenton, NJ

Station	City	State	Zip	Phone	Fax
NJTV 825 Eighth Avenue *TF:* 800-882-6622 ■ *Web:* www.njtvonline.org	New York	NY	10019	609-777-0031	
WIMG-AM 1300 (Rel) PO Box 9078 *Web:* www.wimg1300.com	Trenton	NJ	08650	609-695-1300	278-1588
WKXW-FM 101.5 (N/T) 109 Walters Ave *TF:* 800-800-7822 ■ *Web:* www.nj1015.com	Trenton	NJ	08638	609-359-5300	359-5301

648-168 Tucson, AZ

Station	City	State	Zip	Phone	Fax
KFMA-FM Radio 3871 N Commerce Dr *Web:* www.kfma.com	Tucson	AZ	85705	520-407-4500	407-4600
KHYT-FM 107.5 (CR) 575 W Roger Rd *Web:* www.khit1075.com	Tucson	AZ	85705	520-887-1000	887-6397
KIIM-FM 99.5 (Ctry) 575 W Roger Rd *Web:* www.kiimfm.com	Tucson	AZ	85705	520-880-5446	887-6397
KLPX-FM 96.1 (Rock) 3871 N Commerce Dr *Web:* www.klpx.com	Tucson	AZ	85705	520-407-4500	407-4600
KMXZ-FM 94.9 7280 E Rosewood *Web:* www.mixfm.com	Tucson	AZ	85710	520-722-5486	
KNST-AM 790 (N/T) 3202 N Oracle Rd *Web:* www.knst.com	Tucson	AZ	85705	520-618-2100	
KOHT-FM 98.3 (Urban) 3202 N Oracle Rd *Web:* www.hot983.com	Tucson	AZ	85705	520-618-2100	
KRQQ-FM 93.7 (CHR) 3202 N Oracle Rd *Web:* www.krq.com	Tucson	AZ	85705	520-618-2100	
KUAT-FM 90.5 (Clas) PO Box 210067 *Web:* radio.azpm.org/classical	Tucson	AZ	85719	520-621-5828	

648-169 Tulsa, OK

Station	City	State	Zip	Phone	Fax
92.9 BOB FM 4590 E 29th St Ste 711 *Web:* www.929bobfm.com	Tulsa	OK	74114	918-743-7814	
KFAQ-AM 1170 (N/T) 4590 E 29th St *Web:* www.1170kfaq.com	Tulsa	OK	74114	918-743-7814	743-7613
KHTT-FM 106.9 (CHR) 4590 E 29th St *Web:* www.khits.com	Tulsa	OK	74114	918-743-7814	
KJSR-FM 103.3 (CR) 7136 S Yale Ave Ste 500 *Web:* 1033theeagle.com/	Tulsa	OK	74136	918-493-3434	493-2376
KMOD-FM 97.5 (Rock) 2625 S Memorial Dr *Web:* www.kmod.com	Tulsa	OK	74129	918-388-5100	665-0555
KQLL-FM 106.1 (Oldies) 2625 S Memorial Dr *Web:* www.1061thetwister.com	Tulsa	OK	74129	918-388-5100	665-0555
KRAV-FM 96.5 (AC) 7136 S Yale Ave Ste 500 *Web:* www.mix96tulsa.com	Tulsa	OK	74136	918-491-9696	
KRMG-AM 740 (N/T) 7136 S Yale Ave Ste 500 *TF:* 855-297-9696 ■ *Web:* www.krmg.com	Tulsa	OK	74136	918-493-7400	493-2376
KTBT-FM 92.1 (Urban) 2625 S Memorial Dr *Web:* www.921thebeat.com	Tulsa	OK	74129	918-388-5100	665-0555
KTBZ-AM 1430 (Sports) 2625 S Memorial Dr *Web:* www.buzztulsa.com	Tulsa	OK	74129	918-388-5100	
KVOO-FM 98.5 (Ctry) 4590 E 29th St *Web:* www.kvoo.com	Tulsa	OK	74114	918-743-7814	743-7613
KWEN-FM 95.5 (Ctry) 7136 S Yale Ave Ste 500 *Web:* www.k95tulsa.com	Tulsa	OK	74136	918-493-7400	
KXOJ-FM 100.9 (Rel) 2448 E 81st St Ste 5500 *Web:* www.kxoj.com	Tulsa	OK	74137	918-492-2660	492-8840
Public Radio 89.5 800 Tucker Dr *TF:* 888-594-5947 ■ *Web:* www.kwgs.org	Tulsa	OK	74104	918-631-2577	631-3695

648-170 Tupelo, MS

Station	City	State	Zip	Phone	Fax
Miss 98 County 2214 S Gloster St *Web:* www.miss98.net	Tupelo	MS	38801	662-842-7658	
WSEL-FM 96.7 (Rel) Mississippi 6	Pontotoc	MS	38863	662-489-0297	
WWZD-FM 106.7 (Ctry) 5026 Cliff Gookin Blvd *Web:* www.wizard106.com	Tupelo	MS	38801	662-842-1067	844-2887

648-171 Tuscaloosa, AL

				Phone	Fax
WQZZ-FM 104.3 (Urban AC) 601 Greensboro Ave Ste 507	Tuscaloosa	AL	35401	205-345-4787	
WRTR-AM 105.9 (Sports) 3900 11th Ave S *Web:* www.talkradio1059.com	Tuscaloosa	AL	35401	205-344-4589	366-9774
WTBC-AM 1230 (N/T) 2110 McFarland Blvd E Ste C *TF:* 800-518-1977 ■ *Web:* www.wtbc1230.com	Tuscaloosa	AL	35404	205-758-5523	752-9696
WTSK-AM 790 (Rel) 142 Skyland Blvd *Web:* 790wtsk.com	Tuscaloosa	AL	35405	205-345-7200	349-1715
WTUG-FM 92.9 (Urban) 142 Skyland Blvd *Web:* www.wtug.com	Tuscaloosa	AL	35405	205-345-7200	349-1715
WTXT-FM 98.1 (Ctry) 3900 11th Ave S *Web:* www.98txt.com	Tuscaloosa	AL	35401	205-344-4589	366-9774
WUAL-FM 91.5 (NPR) 166 Reese Phifer Hall PO Box 870150 *TF:* 800-654-4262 ■ *Web:* www.apr.org	Tuscaloosa	AL	35487	205-348-6644	

648-172 Vancouver, BC

				Phone	Fax
CHQM-FM 103.5 (AC) 969 Robson St Ste 500 *Web:* www.qmfm.com	Vancouver	BC	V6Z1X5	604-871-9000	871-2901

648-173 Washington, DC

				Phone	Fax
WAMU-FM 88.5 (NPR) 4000 Brandywine St NW American University Radio *Web:* www.wamu.org	Washington	DC	20016	202-885-1200	
WHUR-FM 96.3 (Urban AC) 529 Bryant St NW *TF:* 877-550-0694 ■ *Web:* accessatlanta.com	Washington	DC	20059	202-806-3500	806-3522
WMAL-AM 630 (N/T) 4400 Jenifer St NW *Web:* wmal.com	Washington	DC	20015	202-686-3100	
WRQX-FM 107.3 (AC) 4400 Jenifer St NW Fourth Fl *Web:* 1073hits.com/	Washington	DC	20015	202-686-3100	686-3091
WTLP-FM 103.9 (N/T) 3400 Idaho Ave NW *Web:* www.wtop.com	Washington	DC	20016	202-895-5000	
WTOP-FM 103.5 (N/T) 3400 Idaho Ave NW *Web:* www.wtop.com	Washington	DC	20016	202-895-5000	

648-174 West Palm Beach, FL

				Phone	Fax
Sunny 107.9 Radio *Palm Beach Broadcasting* 701 Northpoint Pkwy Ste 500 *TF:* 800-919-1079 ■ *Web:* www.sunny1079.com	West Palm Beach	FL	33407	561-616-4777	
WBZT-AM 1230 (N/T) 3071 Continental Dr *Web:* www.wbzt.com	West Palm Beach	FL	33407	800-889-0267	
WJNO-AM 1290 (N/T) 3071 Continental Dr *Web:* www.wjno.com	West Palm Beach	FL	33407	561-616-6600	616-6677
WKGR-FM 98.7 (CR) 3071 Continental Dr *TF:* 877-541-1966 ■ *Web:* www.gaterrocks.com	West Palm Beach	FL	33407	561-616-6600	616-6677
WLDI-FM 95.5 (CHR) 3071 Continental Dr *Web:* www.wild955.com	West Palm Beach	FL	33407	561-616-6600	
WMBX-FM 102.3 (Urban) 701 Northpoint Pkwy Ste 500 **Fax Area Code:* 561 ■ *TF:* 800-969-1023 ■ *Web:* thex1023.com	West Palm Beach	FL	33407	800-969-1023	686-0157*
WOLL-FM 105.5 (AC) 3071 Continental Dr *TF:* 888-415-1055 ■ *Web:* www.1055online.com	West Palm Beach	FL	33407	561-616-6600	616-6677
WXEL-FM 90.7 (NPR) 3401 S Congress Ave *TF:* 800-915-9935 ■ *Web:* www.wxel.org	West Palm Beach	FL	33426	561-737-8000	369-3067

648-175 Wheeling, WV

				Phone	Fax
WEGW-FM 107.5 (Rock) 1015 Main St *Web:* www.eagle1075.com	Wheeling	WV	26003	304-232-1170	234-0041
WKWK-FM 97.3 (AC) 1015 Main St *Web:* www.mix973wheeling.com	Wheeling	WV	26003	304-232-1170	234-0041
WOVK-FM 98.7 (Ctry) 1015 Main St *Web:* www.wovk.com	Wheeling	WV	26003	304-232-1170	234-0041
WVKF-FM 95.7 (CHR) 1015 Main St *Web:* www.kisswheeling.com	Wheeling	WV	26003	304-232-1170	234-0036
WWVA-AM 1170 (N/T) 1015 Main St *Web:* www.newsradio1170.com	Wheeling	WV	26003	304-232-1170	234-0041

648-176 Wichita, KS

				Phone	Fax
KDGS-FM 93.9 (CHR) 2120 N Woodlawn St Ste 352 *Web:* www.power939.com	Wichita	KS	67208	316-685-2121	685-3408
KEYN-FM 103.7 (Oldies) 2120 N Woodlawn St Ste 352 *Web:* www.keyn.com	Wichita	KS	67208	316-436-1037	
KFBZ-FM 105.3 (AC) 2120 N Woodlawn St Ste 352 *Web:* www.1053thebuzz.com	Wichita	KS	67208	316-685-2121	685-1287
KFDI-FM 101.3 (Ctry) 4200 N Old Lawrence Rd *Web:* www.kfdi.com	Wichita	KS	67219	316-838-9141	838-3607
KFH-AM 1240 (N/T) 2120 N Woodlawn St Ste 352 *Web:* www.kfhradio.com	Wichita	KS	67208	316-685-2121	
KFTI-AM 1070 (Ctry) 4200 N Old Lawrence Rd *Web:* www.kfdi.com	Wichita	KS	67219	316-838-9141	838-3607
KICT-FM 95.1 (Rock) 4200 N Old Lawrence Rd *Web:* www.t95.com	Wichita	KS	67219	316-838-9141	838-3607
KMUW-FM 89.1 (NPR) 3317 E 17th St N *Web:* www.kmuw.org	Wichita	KS	67208	316-978-6789	978-3946
KNSS-AM 1330 (N/T) 2120 N Woodlawn St Ste 352 *Web:* www.knssradio.com	Wichita	KS	67208	316-685-2121	
KRBB-FM 97.9 (AC) 9323 E 37th St N *Web:* www.b98fm.com	Wichita	KS	67226	316-494-6600	494-6730
KTHR 9323 E 37th St N **Fax Area Code:* 306	Wichita	KS	67226	316-436-1073	873-2372*
KZCH-FM 96.3 (CHR) 9323 E 37th St N *TF:* 800-800-1013 ■ *Web:* www.channel963.com	Wichita	KS	67226	316-494-6600	494-6730
KZSN-FM 102.1 (Ctry) 9323 E 37th St N *TF:* 800-505-0098 ■ *Web:* www.1021thebull.com	Wichita	KS	67226	316-494-6600	494-6730

648-177 Wilmington/Dover, DE

				Phone	Fax
WDEL-AM 1150 (N/T) 2727 Shipley Rd *TF:* 800-544-1150 ■ *Web:* www.wdel.com	Wilmington	DE	19810	302-478-2700	478-0100
WDOV-AM 1410 (N/T) 1575 McKee Rd Ste 206 *Web:* www.wdov.com	Dover	DE	19904	302-395-9800	674-8621
WJBR-FM 99.5 (AC) 812 Philadelphia Pk *Web:* www.wjbr.com	Wilmington	DE	19809	302-765-1160	765-1192
WMPH-FM 91.7 (CHR) 5201 Washington St Ext *Web:* www.wmph.net	Wilmington	DE	19809	302-762-3671	
WSTW-FM 93.7 (CHR) 2727 Shipley Rd *TF:* 800-544-9370 ■ *Web:* www.wstw.com	Wilmington	DE	19810	302-478-2700	478-0100

648-178 Winnipeg, MB

				Phone	Fax
CBW-AM 990 (CBC) 541 Portage Ave *Web:* cbc.ca/news/canada/manitoba/	Winnipeg	MB	R3B2G1	204-788-3222	788-3227
CFQX-FM 104.1 (Ctry) 177 Lombard Ave Third Fl *Web:* www.qx104fm.com	Winnipeg	MB	R3B0W5	204-944-1031	989-5291
CITI-FM 92.1 (CR) 4-166 Osborne St *Web:* www.92citifm.ca	Winnipeg	MB	R3L1Y8	204-788-3400	788-3401
CJOB-AM 680 (N/T) 1440 Jack Blick Ave *Web:* www.cjob.com	Winnipeg	MB	R3G0L4	204-786-2471	783-4512
CKY-FM 102.3 (AC) 4-166 Osborne St *TF:* 877-413-7970 ■ *Web:* 1023clearfm.com/	Winnipeg	MB	R3L1Y8	204-788-3400	663-7309
Fab-FM 94.3 177 Lombard Ave *Web:* www.fab943.com	Winnipeg	MB	R3B0W5	204-944-1031	989-5291

648-179 Winston-Salem, NC

				Phone	Fax
WBFJ-FM 89.3 (Rel) 1249 Trade St *Web:* wbfj.fm	Winston-Salem	NC	27101	336-721-1560	777-1032
WFDD-FM 88.5 (NPR) 1834 Wake Forest Rd Ste 8850 *TF:* 800-262-8850 ■ *Web:* www.wfdd.org	Winston-Salem	NC	27109	336-758-8850	758-3083
WSJS-AM 600 (N/T) 875 W Fifth St *Web:* www.wsjs.com	Winston-Salem	NC	27101	336-777-3900	777-3915

648-180 Worcester, MA

				Phone	Fax
WCRN-AM 830 (N/T) 82 Franklin St *Web:* www.wcrnradio.com	Worcester	MA	01608	508-438-0965	
WCUW-FM 91.3 (Var) 910 Main St *Web:* www.wcuw.org	Worcester	MA	01610	508-753-1012	
WICN-FM 90.5 (NPR) 50 Portland St *Web:* www.wicn.org	Worcester	MA	01608	508-752-0700	752-7518
WORC-AM 1310 (Span) 122 Green St Ste 2L *Web:* www.megaworcester.com	Worcester	MA	01604	508-791-2111	
WVNE-AM 760 (Rel) 70 James St Ste 201 *Web:* lifechangingradio.com	Worcester	MA	01603	508-831-9863	831-7964
WWFX-FM 100.1 (CR) 250 Commercial St 5th Fl *Web:* www.pikefm.com	Worcester	MA	01608	508-752-1045	973-0824
WXLO-FM 104.5 (AC) 250 Commercial St *Web:* www.wxlo.com	Worcester	MA	01608	508-752-1045	793-0824

648-181 Youngstown, OH

				Phone	Fax
WBBW-AM 1240 (Sports) 4040 Simon Rd *Web:* www.wbbw.com	Youngstown	OH	44512	330-783-1000	
WYSU-FM 88.5 (Clas) Youngstown State University 1 University Plz *Web:* www.wysu.org	Youngstown	OH	44555	330-941-3363	941-1501

649 RADIO SYNDICATORS

Phone Fax

American Urban Radio Networks
960 Penn Ave Fourth Fl ... Pittsburgh PA 15222 412-456-4000 456-4040
TF: 800-456-4211 ■ *Web:* www.aurn.com

BGC Partners Inc 499 Pk Ave ... New York NY 10022 646-346-7000 346-6919
NASDAQ: BGCP ■ *Web:* www.bgcpartners.com

Car Clinic Productions 5675 N Davis Hwy ... Pensacola FL 32503 850-478-3139 477-0862
TF: 888-227-2546 ■ *Web:* www.carclinicnetwork.com

Crystal Media Networks
7201 Wisconsin Ave Ste 780 ... Bethesda MD 20814 240-223-0846
Web: www.crystalmedianetworks.com/

Lichtenstein Creative Media Inc
One Broadway 14th Fl ... Cambridge MA 02142 617-682-3700 682-3710
Web: www.lcmedia.com

Media Syndication Services
236 Massachusetts Ave NE Ste 303 ... Washington DC 20002 202-544-4457 546-8435
Web: buildbettermedia.com

MediaTracks Communications
2250 E Devon Ave Ste 151 ... Des Plaines IL 60018 847-299-9500 299-9501
Web: www.mediatracks.com

New Dimensions Radio Broadcasting Network
PO Box 7847 ... Santa Rosa CA 95407 707-468-5215
TF: 800-935-8273 ■ *Web:* www.newdimensions.org

North American Network Inc
5335 Wisconsin Ave NW ... Washington DC 20015 202-243-0592 243-0594
Web: www.radiospace.com

Premiere Radio Networks Inc
15260 Ventura Blvd Ste 400 ... Sherman Oaks CA 91403 818-377-5300 461-5490
TF All: 800-276-4431 ■ *Web:* www.premrad.com

Radio America 1100 N Glebe Rd Ste 900 ... Arlington VA 22201 703-302-1000 480-4141*
**Fax Area Code:* 571 ■ *TF:* 800-807-4703 ■ *Web:* www.radioamerica.org

Radio Express Inc
1415 W Magnolia Blvd Ste 201 ... Burbank CA 91506 818-295-5800 295-5801
Web: www.radioexpress.com

Salem Radio Network 6400 N Beltline Rd Ste 210 ... Irving TX 75063 972-831-1920 831-8626
Web: www.srnonline.com

Strand Media Group
3955 Hwy 17 Bypass Ste D PO Box 1389 ... Murrells Inlet SC 29576 843-626-8911 626-6452
TF: 877-844-1722 ■ *Web:* www.strandmedia.com

Syndicated Solutions Inc PO Box 1078 ... Ridgefield CT 06877 203-431-0790 431-0792
Web: www.syndicatedsolutions.com

Syndication Networks Corp
8700 Waukegan Rd Ste 250 ... Morton Grove IL 60053 847-583-9000 583-9025
TF: 800-743-1988 ■ *Web:* syndication.net

Talk Radio Network (TRN) PO Box 3755 ... Central Point OR 97502 888-383-3733 664-6250*
**Fax Area Code:* 541 ■ *TF:* 888-383-3733 ■ *Web:* www.trncorporate.com

TM Century Inc 2002 Academy Ln Ste 110 ... Dallas TX 75234 972-406-6800 406-6890
Web: www.tmstudios.com

Transmedia 719 Battery St ... San Francisco CA 94111 415-956-3118 956-2595
TF: 800-229-7234 ■ *Web:* www.transmediasf.com

WCLV 1375 Euclid Ave Idea Ctr ... Cleveland OH 44115 216-916-6301 916-6365
TF: 877-399-3307 ■ *Web:* www.wclv.com

WestStar Talk Radio Networks 2711 N 24th St ... Phoenix AZ 85008 602-381-8200 381-8221
Web: www.weststar.com

650 RADIO & TELEVISION BROADCASTING & COMMUNICATIONS

SEE ALSO Audio & Video Equipment p. 1825; Telecommunications Equipment & Systems p. 3206

Phone Fax

24eight LLC 711 Third Ave 11th Fl ... New York NY 10017 212-888-2248
Web: www.24eight.com

ACG Systems Inc 133 Defense Hwy Ste 206 ... Annapolis MD 21401 410-224-0224
Web: www.acgsys.com

Adrienne Electronics Corp
7225 Bermuda Rd Unit G ... Las Vegas NV 89119 702-896-1858
Web: www.adrielec.com

ADS-B Technologies LLC
900 Merrill Field Dr ... Anchorage AK 99501 907-258-2372
Web: www.ads-b.com

Advanced Media Technologies Inc
3150 SW 15th St ... Deerfield Beach FL 33442 954-427-5711
Web: www.amt.com

Advatech Pacific Inc
1711 W Greentree Dr Ste 112 ... Tempe AZ 85284 480-598-4005 598-6767
Web: www.advatechpacific.com

AeroSat Corp 62 Rt 101A Ste 2B ... Amherst NH 03031 603-879-0205
Web: www.aerosat.com

Aethercomm Inc 3205 Lionshead Ave ... Carlsbad CA 92010 760-208-6002
Web: www.aethercomm.com

AheadTek Inc 6410 Via Del Oro ... San Jose CA 95119 408-226-9991 226-9195
TF: 800-971-9191 ■ *Web:* www.aheadtek.com

Airbiquity Inc 1011 Western Ave Ste 600 ... Seattle WA 98104 206-219-2700 842-9259
TF: 888-334-7741 ■ *Web:* www.airbiquity.com

Alien Technology Corp
18220 Butterfield Blvd ... Morgan Hill CA 95037 408-782-3900 782-3910
Web: www.alientechnology.com

Aluma Tower Company Inc
1639 Old Dixie Hwy ... Vero Beach FL 32960 772-567-3423
Web: www.alumatower.com

Phone Fax

Ambrado Inc
1301 W President George Bush Hwy Ste 150 ... Richardson TX 75080 972-696-6800
Web: www.ambrado.com

Andersen Manufacturing Inc
3125 N Yellowstone Hwy ... Idaho Falls ID 83401 208-523-6460 523-6562
TF: 800-635-6106 ■ *Web:* andersenhitches.com

Antedo Inc PO Box 725 ... Cupertino CA 95015 408-253-1870
Web: www.antedo.com

Antenna Products Corp 101 SE 25th Ave ... Mineral Wells TX 76067 940-325-3301 325-0716
Web: www.antennaproducts.com

Antenna Technology Communications Inc
450 N McKemy Ave ... Chandler AZ 85226 480-844-8501
Web: www.atci.com

Antennas for Communications 2499 SW 60 Ave ... Ocala FL 34474 352-687-4121 687-1203
Web: www.afcsat.com

Apex Airtronics Inc 2465 Atlantic Ave ... Brooklyn NY 11207 718-485-8560 485-8564

AR Worldwide 160 Schoolhouse Rd ... Souderton PA 18964 215-723-8181 723-5688
Web: www.ar-worldwide.com

Arkansas Valley Communications
1201 E Eigth St ... Russellville AR 72801 479-968-1502
Web: www.avc-wireless.com

Arris 60 Decibel Rd ... State College PA 16801 814-238-2461 238-4065
TF: 800-233-2267 ■ *Web:* www.arrisi.com

Arris Group Inc 3871 Lakefield Dr ... Suwanee GA 30024 678-473-2000 473-8470
NASDAQ: ARRS ■ *TF:* 866-362-7747 ■ *Web:* www.arrisi.com

Artel Video Systems Corp 5B Lyberty Way ... Westford MA 01886 978-263-5775 263-9755
TF: 800-225-0228 ■ *Web:* www.artel.com

Ascom (US) Inc 598 Airport Blvd Ste 300 ... Morrisville NC 27560 919-234-2500
Web: www.ascom.us

Associated Industries
11347 Vanowen St ... North Hollywood CA 91605 818-760-1000 760-2142
Web: www.associated-ind.com

Atrex Inc 175 Industrial Loop S ... Orange Park FL 32073 904-264-9086 269-4916
TF: 800-874-4505 ■ *Web:* www.atrexinc.com

ATX Networks Corp 1-501 Clements Rd W ... Ajax ON L1S7H4 905-428-6068
Web: www.atxnetworks.com

Avi Systems Inc 9675 W 76th St Ste 200 ... Eden Prairie MN 55344 952-949-3700 949-6000
TF: 800-488-4954 ■ *Web:* www.avisystems.com

Avtech Corp 3400 Wallingford Ave N ... Seattle WA 98103 206-695-8000 695-8011
Web: www.avtcorp.com

Axcera Corp 103 Freedom Dr ... Lawrence PA 15055 724-873-8100 873-8105
TF: 800-215-2614 ■ *Web:* www.axcera.com

Ball Aerospace & Technologies Corp
1600 Commerce St ... Boulder CO 80301 303-939-4000 460-2315*
**Fax:* Mail Rm ■ *Web:* www.ballaerospace.com

Barker & Williamson 603 Cidco Rd ... Cocoa FL 32926 321-639-1510 445-6031
Web: www.bwantennas.com

Beacon Wireless Solutions Inc
206 Laird Dr Ste 207 ... Toronto ON M4G3W5 416-696-7555
Web: www.beaconwireless.net

Blonder Tongue Laboratories Inc
1 Jake Brown Rd ... Old Bridge NJ 08857 732-679-4000 679-4353
NYSE: BDR ■ *TF:* 877-407-8033 ■ *Web:* www.blondertongue.com

BridgeWave Communications Inc
3350 Thomas Rd ... Santa Clara CA 95054 408-567-6900
Web: www.bridgewave.com

Broad Reach Engineering Co
1113 Washington Ave Ste 200 ... Golden CO 80401 303-216-9777
Web: www.broadreachengineering.com

Broadcast Electronics Inc 4100 N 24th St ... Quincy IL 62305 217-224-9600 224-9607
Web: www.bdcast.com

Broadcast International Group
10458 Nw 31st Ter ... Doral FL 33172 305-599-2112
Web: www.bigmiami.com

Cabot Coach Builders Inc 99 Newark St ... Haverhill MA 01832 978-374-4530
Web: www.royalelimo.com

CalAmp Corp 1401 N Rice Ave ... Oxnard CA 93030 805-987-9000 419-8498
NASDAQ: CAMP ■ *Web:* www.calamp.com

Canyon State Wireless Eight Corral Rd ... Sierra Vista AZ 85635 520-458-4772
Web: www.canyonstatewireless.com

Cattron Group International
58 W Shenango St ... Sharpsville PA 16150 724-962-3571 962-4310
Web: www.cattron.com

Celerity Systems Inc
8401 Greensboro Dr Ste 500 ... McLean VA 22102 703-848-1900 848-2139
Web: www.celerity.com

Channell 26040 Ynez Rd ... Temecula CA 92591 951-719-2600 296-2322
OTC: CHNL ■ *Web:* www.channell.com

Chaparral Communications Inc
950 S Bascom Ave Ste 3111 ... San Jose CA 95128 408-294-2900 294-6969
Web: www.chaparral.net

Coaxial Dynamics
6800 Lake Abrams Dr ... Middleburg Heights OH 44130 440-243-1100 243-1101
TF: 800-262-9425 ■ *Web:* www.coaxial.com

Cobalt Digital Inc 2406 E University Ave Ste 4 ... Urbana IL 61802 217-344-1243
Web: www.cobaltdigital.com

Cobham 2121 Crystal City Dr Ste 625 ... Arlington VA 22202 703-414-5300
Web: www.cobham.com

Cobra Electronics Corp 6500 W Cortland St ... Chicago IL 60707 773-889-8870 889-8870
NASDAQ: COBR ■ *Web:* www.cobra.com

Cohu Inc 12367 Crosthwaite Cir ... Poway CA 92064 858-848-8100 848-8185
NASDAQ: COHU ■ *TF:* 800-685-5050 ■ *Web:* www.cohu.com

COMARK Communications 104 Feeding Hills Rd ... Southwick MA 01077 413-998-1100
TF: 800-288-8364 ■ *Web:* www.comarktv.com

Communications & Power Industries Inc Beverly Microwave Div (CPI-BMD)
150 Sohier Rd ... Beverly MA 01915 978-922-6000 922-2736
Web: cpii.com/division.cfm/8

Phone Fax

Comtech PST Corp 105 Baylis Rd .... Melville NY 11747 631-777-8900
Web: www.comtechpst.com

Comtech Systems Inc 2900 Titan Row Ste 142 .... Orlando FL 32809 407-854-1950 851-6960
Web: www.comtechsystems.com

Comtech Telecommunications Corp
68 S Service Rd Ste 230............................ Melville NY 11747 631-962-7000 962-7001
NASDAQ: CMTL ■ *Web:* www.comtechtel.com

Concurrent 4375 River Green Pkwy Ste 100 .... Duluth GA 30096 678-258-4000 258-4300
NASDAQ: CCUR ■ *TF:* 877-978-7363 ■ *Web:* www.ccur.com

Connecticut Radio Holding LLC
1208 Cromwell Ave Ste C......................... Rocky Hill CT 06067 860-563-4867
Web: connradio.com

Conolog Corp Five Columbia Rd .... Somerville NJ 08876 908-722-8081 722-8081
OTC: CNLG ■ *TF:* 800-526-3984 ■ *Web:* iniven.com

Continental Electronics Corp
4212 S Buckner Blvd .... Dallas TX 75227 214-381-7161 381-4949
TF: 800-733-5011 ■ *Web:* www.contelec.com

Control Dynamics Corp 960 Louis Dr............. Warminster PA 18974 215-956-0700
Web: www.controldynamics.us.com

Dage-MTI Inc 701 N Roeske Ave .... Michigan City IN 46360 219-872-5514 872-5559
Web: www.dagemti.com

Data Flow Systems Inc
605 N John Rodes Blvd .... Melbourne FL 32934 321-259-5009
Web: dataflowsys.com

Datron World Communications Inc
3030 Enterprise Ct .... Vista CA 92081 760-597-1500 597-1510
Web: www.dtwc.com

Dayton-Granger Inc 3299 SW Ninth Ave .... Fort Lauderdale FL 33315 954-463-3451 761-3172
Web: www.daytongranger.com

Destron Fearing 490 Villaume Ave .... South Saint Paul MN 55075 651-552-6300
TF: 800-328-0118 ■ *Web:* www.destronfearing.com

Diamond Antenna & Microwave Corp
59 Porter Rd .... Littleton MA 01460 978-486-0039 486-0079
Web: www.diamondantenna.com

Dielectric Communications Inc 22 Tower Rd .... Raymond ME 04071 207-655-8100
Web: www.dielectric.com

Digital Broadcast Inc 2731 NW 41 St Ste A.......... Gainesville FL 32606 352-377-8344
Web: www.digitalbcast.com

Digital Video Group Inc
8529 Meadowbridge Rd Ste 100................ Mechanicsville VA 23116 804-559-8850
Web: www.digitalvideogroup.com

Dnfcontrols 12843 Foothill Blvd Ste D .... Sylmar CA 91342 818-898-3380
Web: www.dnfcontrols.com

Eagle Comtronics Inc 7665 Henry Clay Blvd .... Liverpool NY 13088 315-622-3402 622-3800
TF: 800-448-7474 ■ *Web:* www.eaglecomtronics.com

Earmark LLC 1125 Dixwell Ave....................... Hamden CT 06514 203-777-2130 777-2886
Web: www.earmark.com

Earthwave Technologies Inc
710 E 64th St .... Indianapolis IN 46220 317-257-8740
Web: www.earthwavetech.com

Eco-Site Inc 1414 Raleigh Rd Ste 445 .... Chapel Hill NC 27517 919-636-6810
Web: eco-site.com

Edge Velocity Corp Three Bourbon St................ Peabody MA 01960 978-304-0142
Web: www.edgevelocity.com

EFJohnson Technologies 1440 Corporate Dr .... Irving TX 75038 972-819-0700 819-0639
TF: 800-328-3911 ■ *Web:* www.efjohnsontechnologies.com

Empower Rf Systems Inc 316 W Florence Ave .... Inglewood CA 90301 310-412-8100 412-9232
Web: www.empowerrf.com

Envivio Inc
400 Oyster Pt Blvd Ste 325............... South San Francisco CA 94080 650-243-2700 243-2750
Web: www.envivio.com

Etm Electromatic Inc 35451 Dumbarton Ct .... Newark CA 94560 510-797-1100 797-4358
TF: 800-883-4386 ■ *Web:* www.etm-inc.com

Eventide Inc One Alsan Way .... Little Ferry NJ 07643 201-641-1200
Web: www.eventide.com

F H Video Inc 6137 Geary Blvd Fl 2............... San Francisco CA 94121 415-221-6128
Web: www.fhvideo.com

Fidelity Technologies Corp 2501 Kutztown Rd......... Reading PA 19605 610-929-3330 929-1969
Web: www.fidelitytech.com

First Signal LLC
1750 Enterprise Way Se Ste 107...................... Marietta GA 30067 770-988-8744
Web: www.firstsignal.com

Fleet Safety Equipment Inc
1100 Hemlock St .... North Little Rock AR 72114 501-370-9500
Web: www.fleetsafety.com

GAI-Tronics Corp 400 E Wyomissing Ave .... Mohnton PA 19540 610-777-1374 775-6540
TF: 800-492-1212 ■ *Web:* www.gai-tronics.com

GCS Inc 7640 Omnitech Pl .... Victor NY 14564 585-742-9100
Web: www.globalcoms.com

General Dynamics SATCOM Technologies
1500 Prodelin Dr .... Newton NC 28658 828-464-4141 464-5725
TF: 888-874-7646 ■ *Web:* www.gdsatcom.com

Globecomm Systems Inc 45 Oser Ave............ Hauppauge NY 11788 631-231-9800 231-1557
NASDAQ: GCOM ■ *TF:* 866-499-0223 ■ *Web:* www.globecommsystems.com

GPSi LLC 25307 Dequindre Rd................ Madison Heights MI 48071 248-399-4731
Web: www.guidepointsystems.com

Guardian Mobility Corp 43 Auriga Dr .... Ottawa ON K2E7Y8 613-225-8885
Web: www.guardianmobility.com

HAL Communications Corp
1201 W Kenyon Rd PO Box 365....................... Urbana IL 61803 217-367-7373 367-1701
Web: www.halcomm.com

Harmonic Inc 4300 N First St....................... San Jose CA 95134 408-542-2500 542-2511
NASDAQ: HLIT ■ *TF:* 800-322-2885 ■ *Web:* www.harmonicinc.com

Harris Corp 1025 W NASA Blvd .... Melbourne FL 32919 321-727-9100
NYSE: HRS ■ *TF:* 800-442-7747 ■ *Web:* www.harris.com

Harris Corp Government Communication Systems Div
2400 Palm Bay Rd .... Palm Bay FL 32905 321-729-2289
Web: www.govcomm.harris.com

Harris Corp RF Communications Div
1680 University Ave............................ Rochester NY 14610 585-244-5830 242-4755
TF: 866-264-8040 ■ *Web:* rf.harris.com

Henschel Inc Nine Malcolm Hoyt Dr .... Newburyport MA 01950 978-462-2400
Web: www.l-3mps.com

Hitachi Kokusai Electric America Ltd
150 Crossways Pk Dr........................... Woodbury NY 11797 516-921-7200 496-3718
TF: 888-687-6877 ■ *Web:* www.hitachikokusai.us

Honeywell International Inc
101 Columbia Rd PO Box M6/LM .... Morristown NJ 07962 480-353-3020
NYSE: HON ■ *TF:* 877-841-2840 ■ *Web:* www.honeywell.com

iBiquity Digital Corp
65 Stanford Blvd Ste 202 .... Columbia MD 21045 410-872-1530
Web: www.ibiquity.com

ICOM America Inc 2380 116th Ave NE .... Bellevue WA 98004 425-454-8155 454-1509
TF: 800-872-4266 ■ *Web:* www.icomamerica.com

ID Systems Inc 123 Tice Blvd Ste 101 .... Woodcliff Lake NJ 07677 201-996-9000 996-9144
NASDAQ: IDSY ■ *TF:* 866-410-0152 ■ *Web:* www.id-systems.com

Ikegami Electronics USA Inc 37 Brook Ave .... Maywood NJ 07607 201-368-9171 569-1626
TF: 800-368-9171 ■ *Web:* www.ikegami.com

Imagine GPS Inc 6847 S Ea Ste 104 .... Las Vegas NV 89119 702-990-5600
Web: www.gpscity.com

Industrial Communications & Electronics Inc
40 Lone St .... Marshfield MA 02050 781-319-1100
Web: www.induscom.com

Information Station Specialists Inc
3368 88th Ave.................................... Zeeland MI 49464 616-772-2300
Web: www.theradiosource.com

Integral Systems Inc
6721 Columbia Gateway Dr .... Columbia MD 21046 443-539-5330
Web: www.integ.com

IONX LLC 515 S Franklin St .... West Chester PA 19382 484-653-2600
Web: www.ionxlive.com

IPMobileNet LLC 1221 E Dyer Rd Ste 250 .... Santa Ana CA 92705 714-434-6019
Web: www.ipmn.com

Iteris Inc 1700 Carnegie Ave Ste 100 .... Santa Ana CA 92705 949-270-9400 270-9401
NYSE: ITI ■ *Web:* www.iteris.com

ITT Exelis Inc 1650 Tysons Blvd Ste 1700 .... McLean VA 22102 703-790-6300 790-6360
Web: exelisinc.com

Jampro Antennas Inc 6340 Sky Creek Dr........... Sacramento CA 95828 916-383-1177 383-1182
Web: www.jampro.com

Jem Engineering LLC 8683 Cherry Ln.................. Laurel MD 20707 301-317-1070
Web: www.jemengineering.com

Kairos Autonomi Inc 508 West 8360 South .... Sandy UT 84070 801-255-2950
Web: www.kairosautonomi.com

Kenwood USA Corp 2201 E Dominguez St .... Long Beach CA 90810 310-639-9000
TF: 800-536-9663 ■ *Web:* www.kenwoodusa.com

Kintronic Laboratories Inc
144 Pleasant Grove Rd .... Bluff City TN 37618 423-878-3141
Web: www.kintronic.com

Klein Electronics Inc 349 N Vinewood St............ Escondido CA 92029 760-781-3220
Web: www.headsetusa.com

Knight Sky LLC 7470-F New Technology Way .... Frederick MD 21703 240-252-1950
Web: www.knight-sky.com

Kongsberg Maritime Inc
5373 W Sam Houston Pkwy N Ste 200................. Houston TX 77041 713-329-5580 329-5581
Web: www.km.kongsberg.com

KVH Industries Inc 50 Enterprise Ctr............... Middletown RI 02842 401-847-3327 849-0045
NASDAQ: KVHI ■ *Web:* www.kvh.com

Kyocera Communications Inc
9520 Towne Centre Dr .... San Diego CA 92121 858-882-1400
Web: www.kyoceramobile.com

L-3 Communications Corp
600 Third Ave 34-35 Fl.......................... New York NY 10016 212-697-1111 490-0731
NYSE: LLL ■ *TF:* 800-351-8483 ■ *Web:* www.l-3com.com

L-3 Communications ESSCO 90 Nemco Way .... Ayer MA 01432 978-568-5100 772-7581
TF: 877-282-1168 ■ *Web:* www.l-3com.com

L-3 Communications Telemetry East Div
1515 Grundy's Ln................................. Bristol PA 19007 267-545-7000 545-0100
Web: www.l-3com.com

L-3 Communications Telemetry West Div
9020 Balboa Ave............................... San Diego CA 92123 858-694-7500 694-7538
TF: 800-351-8483 ■ *Web:* www.l-3com.com/tw

Larcan Inc 228 Ambassador Dr................... Mississauga ON L5T2J2 905-564-9222 564-9244

Lightspeed Aviation Inc 6135 Jean Rd .... Lake Oswego OR 97035 503-968-3113
Web: www.lightspeedaviation.com

Logitek Electronic Systems Inc
5622 Edgemoor Dr .... Houston TX 77081 713-664-4470
Web: www.logitekaudio.com

MCL Inc 501 S Woodcreek Rd .... Bolingbrook IL 60440 630-759-9500 759-5018
TF Support: 800-743-4625 ■ *Web:* www.mcl.com

MDI Security Systems Inc
12500 Network Dr Ste 303 .... San Antonio TX 78249 210-477-5400 477-5401
TF: 866-435-7634 ■ *Web:* www.mdisecure.com

Mesh Dynamics Inc
2953 Bunker Hill Ln Ste 400....................... Santa Clara CA 95054 408-373-7700
Web: www.meshdynamics.com

Metropolitan Communications
309 Commerce Dr Ste 100 .... Exton PA 19341 610-363-5858
Web: www.mcsradio.com

MFJ Enterprises Inc 300 Industrial Pk Rd............ Starkville MS 39759 662-323-5869 323-6551
TF: 800-647-1800 ■ *Web:* www.mfjenterprises.com

Microphase Corp 587 Connecticut Ave............... Norwalk CT 06854 203-866-8000 866-6727
Web: www.microphase.com

Microwave Networks Inc
4000 Greenbriar Ste 100A .... Stafford TX 77477 281-263-6500 263-6400
Web: www.microwavenetworks.com

Midian Electronic Comm Systems 2302 E 22nd St...... Tucson AZ 85713 520-884-7981
Web: www.midians.com

Phone | Fax

Midland Instruments Ltd
20 Ed Connelly Dr Huronia Airport . . . . Tiny ON L0L2J0 705-527-4447 527-5557
Web: www.midlandinstruments.com

Millitech Inc 29 Industrial Dr E . . . . NorthHampton MA 01060 413-582-9620
Web: www.millitech.com

Minerva Networks Inc 2150 Gold St . . . . Santa Clara CA 95002 408-567-9400 567-0747
TF: 800-806-9594 ■ *Web:* www.minervanetworks.com

MiTAC Digital Corp 471 El Camino Real . . . . Santa Clara CA 95050 408-615-5100
Web: www.magellangps.com

Mitsubishi International Corp 655 Third Ave . . . . New York NY 10017 212-605-2000
Web: www.mitsubishicorp.com

Modular Communications Systems
13309 Saticoy St . . . . North Hollywood CA 91605 818-764-1333
Web: www.moducom.com

Morcom International Inc
3656 Centerview Dr Unit 1 . . . . Chantilly VA 20151 703-263-9305 263-9308
Web: www.morcom.com

Moseley Assoc Inc 82 Coromar Dr . . . . Santa Barbara CA 93117 805-968-9621 685-9638
Web: www.moseleysb.com

MTSI Inc 541 Sterling Dr . . . . Richardson TX 75081 972-669-0591
Web: www.mtsiinc.com

Nanowave Technologies Inc 425 Horner Ave . . . . Etobicoke ON M8W4W3 416-252-5602 252-7077
Web: www.nanowavetech.com

Nautel Ltd 10089 Peggy'S Cove Rd . . . . Hackett'S Cove NS B3Z3J4 902-823-3900
TF: 877-662-8835 ■ *Web:* www.nautel.com

Northway Communications Inc 105 E Oak St . . . . Wausau WI 54401 715-842-0841
Web: www.northwaycom.com

NSC Communications 6820 Power Line Dr . . . . Florence KY 41042 859-727-6640
Web: www.nsccom.com

Orbit/FR Inc 506 Prudential Rd . . . . Horsham PA 19044 215-674-5100 674-5108
OTC: ORFR ■ *Web:* www.orbitfr.com

ParkerVision Inc 7915 Baymeadows Way . . . . Jacksonville FL 32256 904-737-1367 731-0958
NASDAQ: PRKR ■ *TF:* 800-532-8034 ■ *Web:* www.parkervision.com

Pelco 3500 Pelco Way . . . . Clovis CA 93612 559-292-1981 348-1120
TF: 800-289-9100 ■ *Web:* www.pelco.com

Pico Macom Inc 8880 Rehco Rd . . . . San Diego CA 92121 858-546-5050 546-5051
TF: 800-421-6511 ■ *Web:* www.picomacom.com

PolarSat Inc 549 Meloche Ave . . . . Dorval QC H9P2W2 514-635-0040 635-0044
Web: www.polarsat.com

Powerwave Technologies Inc
1801 E St Andrew Pl . . . . Santa Ana CA 92705 714-466-1000 466-5800
NASDAQ: PWAV

PROCON Inc 2035 Lakeside Centre Way Ste 125 . . . . Knoxville TN 37922 865-694-2704
Web: fleet.mobilesecurezone.com

RA Miller Industries Inc
14500 168th Ave PO Box 858 . . . . Grand Haven MI 49417 616-842-9450 842-2771
TF: 888-845-9450 ■ *Web:* www.rami.com

Radio Communication Service 510 S Pike E . . . . Sumter SC 29150 803-773-9743
Web: www.radiocommsc.com

Radio Frequency Systems 200 Pondview Dr . . . . Meriden CT 06450 203-630-3311 634-2273
Web: www.rfsworld.com

Radio Holland USA Inc 8943 Gulf Fwy . . . . Houston TX 77017 713-941-2290 378-2101
Web: imtech.com/en/imtechmarine-usa

Radio North 2682 Garfield Rd N Ste 22 . . . . Traverse City MI 49686 231-929-2934
Web: msatc.com

Rantec Microwave Systems Inc
24003 Ventura Blvd . . . . Calabasas CA 91302 818-223-5000 223-5199
Web: www.rantecantennas.com

RELM Wireless Corp 7100 Technology Dr . . . . West Melbourne FL 32904 321-984-1414 676-4403
NYSE: RWC ■ *TF Cust Svc:* 800-648-0947 ■ *Web:* www.relm.com

REVL Communications & Systems
650 W 58th Ave Ste J . . . . Anchorage AK 99518 907-563-8302
Web: www.revlinc.net

RF Products Inc 1500 Davis St . . . . Camden NJ 08103 856-365-5500 342-9757
Web: www.rfproducts.com

Ritron Wireless Solutions 505 W Carmel Dr . . . . Carmel IN 46032 317-846-1201
Web: www.ritron.com

RL Drake Co 9900 Springboro Pike . . . . Miamisburg OH 45342 937-746-4556 806-1510
TF: 800-777-8876 ■ *Web:* www.rldrake.com

Rockwell Collins Inc 400 Collins Rd NE . . . . Cedar Rapids IA 52498 319-295-1000 295-1542*
NYSE: COL ■ **Fax:* PR ■ *TF:* 888-721-3094 ■ *Web:* www.rockwellcollins.com

Ruckus Wireless Inc 350 W JAVA Dr . . . . Sunnyvale CA 94089 650-265-4200
Web: www.ruckuswireless.com

SAT Corp 931 Benecia Ave . . . . Sunnyvale CA 94085 408-530-1020
Web: www.sat.com

Satcom Scientific Inc 5644 Commerce Dr . . . . Orlando FL 32839 407-856-1050 855-7640
Web: www.satcomscientific.com

SATCOM Technologies
1500 Prodelin Dr PO Box 850 . . . . Newton NC 28658 828-464-4141 464-4147
TF: 888-874-7646 ■ *Web:* www.gdsatcom.com/prodelin.php

Satellite Systems Corp 101 Malibu Dr . . . . Virginia Beach VA 23452 757-463-3553 463-3891
Web: www.satsyscorp.com

SEA Com Corp 7030 220th St SW . . . . Mountlake Terrace WA 98043 425-771-2182 771-2650
Web: www.seacomcorp.com

SeaChange International Inc 50 Nagog Pk . . . . Acton MA 01720 978-897-0100 897-0132
NASDAQ: SEAC ■ *TF:* 844-855-8324 ■ *Web:* www.schange.com

SeaSpace Corp 12120 Kear Pl . . . . Poway CA 92064 858-746-1100
Web: www.seaspace.com

Secure Communication Systems Inc
1740 E Wilshire Ave . . . . Santa Ana CA 92705 714-547-1174 547-1343
TF: 866-926-2940 ■ *Web:* www.securecomm.com

SEKAI Electronics Inc 14600 Industry Cir . . . . La Mirada CA 90638 714-736-4180
Web: www.sekai-electronics.com

Sensor Systems Inc 8929 Fullbright Ave . . . . Chatsworth CA 91311 818-341-5366 341-9059
Web: www.sensorantennas.com

Setcom Corp 3019 Alvin DeVane Blvd Ste 560 . . . . Austin TX 78741 650-965-8020
Web: www.setcomcorp.com

Shively Labs 188 Harrison Rd PO Box 389 . . . . Bridgton ME 04009 207-647-3327 647-8273
TF: 888-744-8359 ■ *Web:* www.shively.com

Sierra Video Systems Inc
104 New Mohawk Rd . . . . Nevada City CA 95959 530-478-1000
Web: www.sierravideo.com

Silynx Communications Inc
9901 Belward Campus Dr Ste 150 . . . . Rockville MD 20850 301-217-9223
Web: www.silynxcom.com

Simrex Corp 5490 Broadway St . . . . Lancaster NY 14086 480-926-6069
Web: www.simrex.com

Sirtrack Ltd 845 Pheasant Ln . . . . North Liberty IA 52317 319-665-2542
Web: www.sirtrack.com

Skitter Inc 3230 Peachtree Corners Cir Ste H . . . . Norcross GA 30092 678-894-8808
Web: www.skitter.tv

Skybox Imaging Inc
1061 Terra Bella Ave . . . . Mountain View CA 94043 650-316-6660
Web: www.skyboximaging.com

Sonetics Corp 7340 Sw Durham Rd . . . . Portland OR 97224 800-833-4558
TF: 800-833-4558 ■ *Web:* www.firecom.com

Space Micro Inc 10237 Flanders Ct . . . . San Diego CA 92121 858-332-0700
Web: www.spacemicro.com

Space Systems/Loral 3825 Fabian Way . . . . Palo Alto CA 94303 650-852-4000
TF: 800-332-6490 ■ *Web:* sslmda.com

Sunair Electronics LLC 3131 SW 42 St . . . . Fort Lauderdale FL 33312 954-400-5100
Web: www.sunairhf.com

Synergy Broadcast Systems 16115 Dooley Rd . . . . Addison TX 75001 972-980-6991

Tachyon Networks Inc
9339 Carroll Park Dr Ste 150 . . . . San Diego CA 92121 858-882-8100

Talk-a-phone Co 7530 N Natchez Ave . . . . Niles IL 60714 773-539-1100 539-1241
Web: www.talkaphone.com

Talon Communications Inc
7795 Arjons Dr Ste 201 . . . . San Diego CA 92126 858-653-0100
Web: www.taloncom.com

TCI International Inc 3541 Gateway Blvd . . . . Fremont CA 94538 510-687-6100 687-6101
TF: 800-827-2661 ■ *Web:* www.spx.com

Tecom Industries Inc
375 Conejo Ridge Ave . . . . Thousand Oaks CA 91361 805-267-0100 267-0181
TF: 866-840-8550 ■ *Web:* www.tecom-ind.com

Telemobile Inc 19840 Hamilton Ave . . . . Torrance CA 90502 310-538-5100 532-8526
Web: www.telemobile.com

Telepath Corp 49111 Milmont Dr . . . . Fremont CA 94538 510-656-5600
Web: www.telepathcorp.com

Telephonics Corp 815 Broad Hollow Rd . . . . Farmingdale NY 11735 631-755-7000 755-7200
TF: 877-517-2327 ■ *Web:* www.telephonics.com

Thales Communications Inc
22605 Gateway Ctr Dr . . . . Clarksburg MD 20871 240-864-7000 864-7920
TF: 800-258-4420 ■ *Web:* www.thalescomminc.com

TMC Design Corp 4325 Del Rey Blvd . . . . Las Cruces NM 88012 575-382-4600
Web: www.tmcdesign.com

TPL Communications
3370 San Fernando Rd Unit 206 . . . . Los Angeles CA 90065 323-256-3000 254-3210
TF: 800-447-6937 ■ *Web:* www.tplcom.com

Trak Com Wireless Inc 101-3780 14th Ave . . . . Markham ON L3R9Y5 905-474-9935 474-9938
Web: www.trakcom.com

Tridon Communications 10017 Queen St . . . . Fort Mcmurray AB T9H4Y9 780-791-1002
Web: www.tridon.com

Troll Systems Corp 24950 Anza Dr . . . . Valencia CA 91355 661-702-8900
Web: www.trollsystems.com

TVU networks Corp 1225 Pear Ave Ste 100 . . . . Mountain View CA 94043 650-969-6732
Web: tvupack.com

u-blox America Inc
1902 Campus Commons Dr Ste 310 . . . . Reston VA 20191 703-483-3180
Web: www.u-blox.com

UltiSat Inc
708 Quince Orchard Rd Ste 120 . . . . Gaithersburg MD 20878 240-243-5100
Web: www.ultisat.com

Ultra Electronics Flightline Systems Inc
7625 Omni Tech Pl . . . . Victor NY 14564 585-924-4000 742-5397
TF: 888-959-9001 ■ *Web:* www.ultra-fei.com

Ultra Electronics-DNE Technologies Inc
50 Barnes Pk N . . . . Wallingford CT 06492 203-265-7151 265-9101
TF: 800-370-4485 ■ *Web:* www.dnetech.com

Unique Broadband Systems Ltd
400 Spinnaker Way Unit 1 10 . . . . Vaughan ON L4K5Y9 905-669-8533
Web: www.uniquesys.com

Usglobalsat Inc 1308 John Reed Ct . . . . City Of Industry CA 91745 626-968-4145
Web: www.usglobalsat.com

Utah Scientific Inc
4750 Wiley Post Way Ste 150 . . . . Salt Lake City UT 84116 801-575-8801
Web: www.utsci.com

VehSmart Inc 12180 Ridgecrest Rd Ste 412 . . . . Victorville CA 92395 855-834-7627
TF: 855-834-7627 ■ *Web:* www.vehsmart.com

Verismo Networks Inc
5201 Great America Pkwy Ste 457 . . . . Santa Clara CA 95054 408-598-3661
Web: www.verismonetworks.com

Vicon Industries Inc 89 Arkay Dr . . . . Hauppauge NY 11788 631-952-2288 951-2288
NYSE: VII ■ *TF Sales:* 800-645-9116 ■ *Web:* www.vicon-security.com

Wegener 11350 Technology Cir . . . . Johns Creek GA 30097 770-814-4000 623-0698
OTC: WGNR ■ *Web:* www.wegener.com

Wilcom Inc 73 Daniel Webster Hwy PO Box 508 . . . . Belmont NH 03220 603-524-2622 524-3735
TF: 800-222-1898 ■ *Web:* www.wilcominc.com

Winegard Co 3000 Kirkwood St . . . . Burlington IA 52601 319-754-0600 754-0787
TF Cust Svc: 800-288-8094 ■ *Web:* www.winegard.com

Xcitex Inc 25 First St Ste 105 . . . . Cambridge MA 02141 617-225-0080
Web: www.xcitex.com

Zephyrus Electronics Ltd 168 S 122nd E Ave . . . . Tulsa OK 74128 918-437-3333
Web: www.big-z.com

Zetron Inc 12034 134th Ct NE . . . . Redmond WA 98052 425-820-6363 820-7031
Web: www.zetron.com

651 RAIL TRANSPORT SERVICES

SEE ALSO Logistics Services (Transportation & Warehousing) p. 2673

				Phone	Fax
Aberdeen & Rockfish Railroad Co 101 E Main St *TF:* 800-849-8985 ■ *Web:* www.aberdeen-rockfish.com	Aberdeen	NC	28315	910-944-2341	944-9738
Atlantic & Western Railway LP 136 S Steele St	Sanford	NC	27330	919-776-7521	774-4621
Bonneville Transloaders Inc (BTI) 642 S Federal Blvd *Web:* www.bonntran.com	Riverton	WY	82501	307-856-7480	856-4623
Buffalo & Pittsburgh Railroad Inc (BPRR) 1200-C Scottsville Rd Ste 200 **Fax Area Code:* 800 ■ *TF:* 800-603-3385 ■ *Web:* www.gwrr.com	Rochester	NY	14624	585-463-3307	477-4947*
Burlington Northern & Santa Fe Railway (BNSF) 2650 Lou Menk Dr **Fax Area Code:* 817 ■ *TF:* 800-795-2673 ■ *Web:* www.bnsf.com	Fort Worth	TX	76131	800-795-2673	352-7171*
Canadian National Railway Co 935 Rue de la Gauchetiere O *TSE: CNR* ■ *TF:* 888-668-4626 ■ *Web:* www.cn.ca	Montreal	QC	H3B2M9	888-888-5909	
Canadian Pacific Railway Co 401 9 Ave SW Ste 500 **Fax Area Code:* 800 ■ **Fax:* Hum Res ■ *TF:* 888-333-6370 ■ *Web:* www.cpr.ca	Calgary	AB	T2P4Z4	403-319-7000	704-3000*
Cedar Rapids & Iowa City Railway Co 2330 12th St SW *Web:* www.crandic.com	Cedar Rapids	IA	52404	319-786-3698	
CHEP USA 8517 S Pk Cir *TF Cust Svc:* 866-855-2437 ■ *Web:* www.chep.com	Orlando	FL	32819	407-370-2437	355-6211
Chicago Southshore & South Bend Railroad 505 N Carroll Ave *TF:* 800-356-2079 ■ *Web:* www.southshorefreight.com	Michigan City	IN	46360	219-874-9000	879-3754
Consolidated Rail Corp 1717 Arch St Ste 3210 *TF:* 800-272-0911 ■ *Web:* www.conrail.com	Philadelphia	PA	19103	215-209-2000	209-4819
CSX Transportation Inc 500 Water St *Web:* www.csx.com	Jacksonville	FL	32202	904-359-3100	
Dardanelle & Russellville Railroad Co 4416 S Arkansas Ave *TF:* 888-877-7267 ■ *Web:* up.com	Russellville	AR	72802	479-968-6455	968-2634
El Dorado & Wesson Railway Co 900 SW Ave	El Dorado	AR	71730	870-863-7100	863-7130
Genesee & Wyoming Inc 66 Field Pt Rd *NYSE: GWR* ■ *Web:* www.gwrr.com	Greenwich	CT	06830	203-629-3722	661-4106
Georgetown Railroad Co 5300 S IH-35 PO Box 529 *TF:* 888-456-6777	Georgetown	TX	78626	512-863-2538	
Illinois & Midland Railroad Inc 1500 N Grand Ave E *Web:* www.gwrr.com	Springfield	IL	62702	217-788-8601	788-8630
Iowa Interstate Railroad 5900 Sixth St SW *TF:* 800-321-3884 ■ *Web:* www.iaisrr.com	Cedar Rapids	IA	52404	319-298-5400	298-5454
Kansas City Southern Railway Co 427 W 12th St *TF:* 800-468-6527 ■ *Web:* www.kcsouthern.com	Kansas City	MO	64105	816-983-1303	
Lake State Railway Co 750 N Washington Ave *Web:* www.lsrc.com	Saginaw	MI	48607	989-393-9800	757-2134
Louisiana & Delta Railroad Inc (LDRR) 402 W Washington St *Web:* www.gwrr.com	New Iberia	LA	70560	337-364-9625	
McCloud Railway Co 801 Industrial Way	McCloud	CA	96057	530-964-2147	
Mississippi Export Railroad Co 4519 McInnis Ave *Web:* mserailroad.com	Moss Point	MS	39563	228-475-3322	475-3337
Modesto & Empire Traction Co 530 11th St *Web:* www.metrr.com	Modesto	CA	95354	209-524-4631	529-0336
Montana Rail Link Inc 101 International Way *TF:* 800-338-4750 ■ *Web:* www.montanarail.com	Missoula	MT	59808	406-523-1500	523-1493
Montreal Maine & Atlantic Railway Ltd 15 Iron Rd **Fax Area Code:* 207 ■ *TF:* 800-635-9449 ■ *Web:* cmqrailway.com	Hermon	ME	04401	800-222-1433	848-4232*
New England Central Railroad (NECR) 7411 Fullerton St Ste 300 *TF:* 877-777-4778 ■ *Web:* gwrr.com/pages/landing.html	Jacksonville	FL	32256	904-596-1045	
New York Susquehanna & Western Railway Corp (NYSW) One Railroad Ave *TF General:* 800-366-6979 ■ *Web:* www.nysw.com	Cooperstown	NY	13326	607-547-2555	547-9834
Norfolk Southern Railway Co Three Commercial Pl *TF:* 800-635-5768 ■ *Web:* www.nscorp.com	Norfolk	VA	23510	800-453-2530	
Paducah & Louisville Railway Inc 200 Clark St *Web:* www.palrr.com	Paducah	KY	42003	270-444-4300	
Pioneer Railcorp 1318 S Johanson Rd *OTC: PRRR* ■ *Web:* www.pioneer-railcorp.com	Peoria	IL	61607	309-697-1400	697-5387
Providence & Worcester Railroad Co 75 Hammond St *NASDAQ: PWX* ■ *TF:* 877-373-6374 ■ *Web:* www.pwrr.com	Worcester	MA	01610	508-755-4000	753-5548
Trans-Continental Systems Inc 10801 Evendale Dr *TF:* 800-525-8726 ■ *Web:* www.tcsohio.com	Cincinnati	OH	45241	513-769-4774	769-3215
Triple Crown Services 2720 Dupont Commerce Ct Ste 200 *TF:* 800-325-6510 ■ *Web:* www.triplecrownsvc.com	Fort Wayne	IN	46825	260-416-3600	416-3771
Union Pacific Railroad Co 1400 Douglas St **Fax Area Code:* 402 ■ *TF:* 888-870-8777 ■ *Web:* www.up.com	Omaha	NE	68179	888-870-8777	271-5572*
Union Railroad Co 1200 Penn Ave *Web:* www.tstarinc.com	Pittsburgh	PA	15222	412-433-7066	
Winston-Salem Southbound Railway Co 4550 Overdale Rd *TF:* 888-780-7245 ■ *Web:* www.ncrailways.org	Winston-Salem	NC	27107	336-788-9407	788-9085

652 RAIL TRAVEL

SEE ALSO Mass Transportation (Local & Suburban) p. 2719

				Phone	Fax
Buckingham Branch Railroad Co PO Box 336 *Web:* www.buckinghambranch.com	Dillwyn	VA	23936	434-983-3300	
Dakota Missouri Valley & Western Railroad Inc 3501 E Rosser Ave *Web:* www.dmvwrr.com	Bismarck	ND	58501	701-223-9282	
Dew Distribution Services Inc 2201 Touhy Ave *TF:* 800-837-3391 ■ *Web:* www.dewdist.com	Elk Grove Village	IL	60007	800-837-3391	
First Union Rail Corp One O'Hare Ctr 6250 River Rd Ste 5000 *Web:* www.firstunionrail.com	Rosemont	IL	60018	847-318-7575	
Grand Canyon Railway Inc 1201 W Rt 66 Ste 200 *Web:* www.thetrain.com	Flagstaff	AZ	86001	928-773-1976	
Idaho Northern & Pacific Railroad 119 N Commercial Ave *Web:* www.rgpc.com	Emmett	ID	83617	208-365-6353	
Indiana Rail Road Co, The 101 W Ohio St Ste 1600 *Web:* www.inrd.com	Indianapolis	IN	46204	317-262-5140	
Iowa Northern Railway Co 305 Second St SE Paramount Theatre Bldg Ste 400 *Web:* www.iowanorthern.com	Cedar Rapids	IA	52401	319-297-6000	
Louisville & Indiana Railroad Co 500 Willinger Ln *Web:* www.anacostia.com	Jeffersonville	IN	47130	812-288-0940	
National Railroad Passenger Corp 60 Massachusetts Ave NE *TF:* 800-872-7245 ■ *Web:* www.amtrak.com	Washington	DC	20002	202-906-3741	906-3285
Omega Rail Management 4721 Trousdale Dr Ste 206 *Web:* www.omegarail.com	Nashville	TN	37220	615-331-1900	
Pandrol Canada Ltd 6910 34th St *Web:* www.pandrolcanada.ca	Edmonton	AB	T6B2X2	780-413-4281	
Patriot Rail Company LLC 10060 Skinner Lk Dr *Web:* www.patriotrail.com	Jacksonville	FL	32246	904-423-2540	
Pinsly Railroad Company Inc 53 Southampton Rd *Web:* www.pinsly.com	Westfield	MA	01085	413-568-6426	
Shamokin Valley Railroad Co 356 Priestley Ave *Web:* www.nshr.com	Northumberland	PA	17857	570-473-7949	
Trinity Railway Express 1600 E Lancaster Ave *Web:* www.the-t.com	Fort Worth	TX	76102	817-215-8600	
Twin Cities & Western Railroad 2925 12th St E *Web:* www.tcwr.net	Glencoe	MN	55336	320-864-7200	
VIA Rail Canada Inc Three Pl Ville-Marie Ste 500 *TF:* 800-681-2561 ■ *Web:* www.viarail.ca	Montreal	QC	H3B2C9	514-871-6000	871-6104

653 RAILROAD EQUIPMENT - MFR

SEE ALSO Transportation Equipment & Supplies - Whol p. 3251

				Phone	Fax
A Stucki Co 2600 Neville Rd *TF:* 888-266-6630 ■ *Web:* www.stucki.com	Pittsburgh	PA	15225	412-771-7300	771-7308
Adams & Westlake Ltd 940 N Michigan St PO Box 4524 *Web:* www.adlake.com	Elkhart	IN	46514	574-264-1141	264-1146
Alco Ventures Inc 9747-199A St *Web:* www.probuiltrailings.com	Langley	BC	V1M2X7	604-888-7655	
American Motive Power Inc 9431 Foster Wheeler Rd *Web:* www.americanmotivepower.com	Dansville	NY	14437	585-335-3131	
American Railcar Industries Inc 100 Clark St *NASDAQ: ARII* ■ *TF:* 800-489-9888 ■ *Web:* www.americanrailcar.com	Saint Charles	MO	63301	636-940-6000	940-6030
AMSTED Industries Inc 180 N Stetson St Ste 1800 **Fax:* Hum Res ■ *Web:* www.amsted.com	Chicago	IL	60601	312-645-1700	819-8494*
Bombardier Transportation North America 1101 Parent St *Web:* www.bombardier.com	Saint-Bruno	QC	J3V6E6	450-441-2020	441-1515
CAD Railway Industries Ltd 155 boul. Montreal-Toronto (Hwy 2-20) *Web:* www.cadrail.ca	Lachine	QC	H8S1B4	514-634-3131	954-0431
CANAC Inc 6505 Trans-Canada Hwy Ste 405 *TF:* 800-588-4387 ■ *Web:* www.canac.com	St Laurent	QC	H4T1S3	514-734-4700	734-4850
Cando Contracting Ltd 740 Rosser Ave Fl 4 *Web:* www.candoltd.com	Brandon	MB	R7A0K9	204-725-2627	
Cardwell Westinghouse Co 8400 S Stewart Ave *Web:* www.wabtec.com	Chicago	IL	60620	773-483-7575	
Clark Filter Inc 3649 Hempland Rd *Web:* www.clarkfilter.com	Lancaster	PA	17601	717-285-5941	
Curran Group Inc 286 Memorial Ct *Web:* www.currangroup.com	Crystal Lake	IL	60014	815-455-5100	455-7894
Dayton-Phoenix Group Inc 1619 Kuntz Rd *TF:* 800-657-0707 ■ *Web:* www.dayton-phoenix.com	Dayton	OH	45404	937-496-3974	496-3969
Electro-Motive Diesel Inc 9301 W 55th St *TF:* 800-255-5355 ■ *Web:* www.emdiesels.com	La Grange	IL	60525	708-387-6000	387-6626
FreightCar America Inc 17 Johns St *NASDAQ: RAIL* ■ **Fax Area Code:* 814 ■ *TF:* 800-458-2235 ■ *Web:* www.freightcaramerica.com	Johnstown	PA	15901	800-458-2235	533-5010*

Phone | Fax

GE Aviation One Neumann Way. . . . . Cincinnati OH 45215 513-243-2000
Web: www.geaviation.com

GE Transportation Rail 2901 E Lake Rd . . . . Erie PA 16531 814-875-2234 875-3591*
**Fax:* Hum Res ■ *TF Prod Info:* 800-626-2000 ■ *Web:* www.getransportation.com

Graham-White Manufacturing Co
1242 Colorado St PO Box 1099 . . . . Salem VA 24153 540-387-5600 387-5697
Web: www.grahamwhite.com

Gray Mfg Industries LLC 6258 Icehouse Rd . . . . Hornell NY 14843 607-281-1325
Web: gmihornell.com

Greenbrier Co One Centerpointe Dr Ste 200 . . . . . . Lake Oswego OR 97035 503-684-7000 684-7553
NYSE: GBX ■ *TF:* 800-343-7188 ■ *Web:* www.gbrx.com

Harsco Rail (HTT) 2401 Edmund Rd PO Box 20 . . . West Columbia SC 29171 803-822-9160 822-8107
Web: www.harscorail.com

Holland Co 1000 Holland Dr. . . . . Crete IL 60417 708-672-2300 672-0119
TF: 800-899-7754 ■ *Web:* www.hollandco.com

Interstate Transport Inc
324 First Ave N. . . . . St Petersburg FL 33701 727-822-9999
TF: 866-281-1281 ■ *Web:* www.interstate-transport.com

Kasgro Rail Corp 121 Rundle Rd. . . . . New Castle PA 16102 724-658-9061
Web: www.kasgro.com

Kawasaki Rail Car Inc 29 Wells Ave Bldg 4. . . . . Yonkers NY 10701 914-376-4700
Web: www.kawasakirailcar.com

LB Foster Co 415 Holiday Dr. . . . . Pittsburgh PA 15220 800-255-4500 928-7891*
NASDAQ: FSTR ■ **Fax Area Code:* 412 ■ **Fax:* Sales ■ *TF:* 800-255-4500 ■ *Web:* www.lbfoster.com

Loram Maintenance of Way
3900 Arrowhead Dr PO Box 188. . . . . Hamel MN 55340 763-478-6014 478-6916
TF: 800-328-1466 ■ *Web:* www.loram.com

Miner Enterprises Inc
1200 E State St PO Box 471 . . . . Geneva IL 60134 630-232-3000 232-3055
TF: 888-822-5334 ■ *Web:* www.minerent.com

Motive Equipment Inc 8300 W Sleske Ct. . . . . Milwaukee WI 53223 414-446-3379
Web: www.motiveequipment.com

MotivePower 4600 Apple St . . . . Boise ID 83716 208-947-4800 947-4820
TF: 800-445-8667 ■ *Web:* www.motivepower-wabtec.com

National Railway Equipment Co (NREC)
14400 Robey Ave Ste 2. . . . . Dixmoor IL 60426 708-388-6002 388-2487
TF: 800-253-2905 ■ *Web:* www.nationalrailway.com

New York Air Brake Co 748 Starbuck Ave. . . . . Watertown NY 13601 315-786-5200 786-5675*
**Fax:* Sales ■ *TF:* 888-836-6922 ■ *Web:* www.nyab.com

Nolan Co 1016 Ninth St SW. . . . . Canton OH 44707 330-453-7922 453-7449
TF: 800-297-1383 ■ *Web:* www.nolancompany.com

Pacific Coast Container Inc
432 Estudillo Ave . . . . San Leandro CA 94577 510-346-6100
TF: 800-458-4788 ■ *Web:* www.pcclogistics.com

Plasser American Corp
2001 Myers Rd PO Box 5464. . . . . Chesapeake VA 23324 757-543-3526 494-7186
Web: www.plasseramerican.com

Portec Rail Products Inc
900 Old Freeport Rd. . . . . Pittsburgh PA 15238 412-782-6000 782-1037
Web: www.lbfoster-railtechnologies.com

Quantem Aviation Services Inc
175 Ammon Dr. . . . . Manchester NH 03103 603-647-1717
Web: qasllc.aero

Racine Railroad Products Inc
1524 Frederick St PO Box 044577. . . . . Racine WI 53404 262-637-9681 637-9069
Web: www.racinerailroad.com

Rail Car Service Co 584 Fairground Rd. . . . . Mercer PA 16137 724-662-3660
Web: www.parailcar.com

Salco Products Inc 1385 101st St Ste A. . . . . Lemont IL 60439 630-783-2570 783-2590
TF: 800-535-8990 ■ *Web:* www.salcoproducts.com

Siemens Mobility 7464 French Rd . . . . Sacramento CA 95828 916-681-3000
Web: usa.siemens.com/infrastructure-cities/us/en/

Southern Railway of British Columbia Ltd
2102 River Dr. . . . . New Westminster BC V3M6S3 604-521-1966
Web: www.sryraillink.com

Standard Car Truck Co 865 Busse Hwy . . . . Park Ridge IL 60068 847-692-6050
Web: www.sctco.com

Tealinc Ltd 1606 Rosebud Creek Rd. . . . . Forsyth MT 59327 406-347-5237
Web: www.tealinc.com

Trackmobile Inc 1602 Executive Dr . . . . LaGrange GA 30240 706-884-6651 884-0390
Web: www.trackmobile.com

Transco Railway Products Inc 820 Hopley Ave . . . . Bucyrus OH 44820 419-562-1031 562-3684
TF: 800-472-4592 ■ *Web:* www.transcorailway.com

Transportation Research Corp
4305 Business Dr. . . . . Cameron Park CA 95682 530-676-7770
Web: www.varnaproducts.com

Trinity Mining Service 109 48th St. . . . . Pittsburgh PA 15201 412-682-4700 682-4725
TF: 800-264-2583 ■ *Web:* www.trin-mine.com

Trinity Rail Group LLC 2525 N Stemmons Fwy. . . . . Dallas TX 75207 214-631-4420 589-8623
TF: 800-631-4420 ■ *Web:* www.trinityrail.com

Union Tank Car Co 175 W Jackson Blvd Ste 2100. . . . . . . Chicago IL 60604 312-431-3111 431-5125
TF: 866-535-7685 ■ *Web:* www.utlx.com

Vapor Bus International
1010 Johnson Dr . . . . Buffalo Grove IL 60089 847-777-6400 520-2222
TF: 866-375-4126 ■ *Web:* www.vapordoors.com

WABCO Freight Car Products Ltd
475 Seaman Dr. . . . . Stoney Creek ON L8E2R2 905-561-8700 561-8705
Web: www.wabtec.com

WABCO Locomotive Products
1001 Air Brake Ave. . . . . Wilmerding PA 15148 412-825-1000 825-1019
TF Cust Svc: 877-922-2627 ■ *Web:* www.wabtec.com

Wabtec Corp 1001 Air Brake Ave. . . . . Wilmerding PA 15148 412-825-1000 825-1019
NYSE: WAB ■ *TF Cust Svc:* 877-922-2627 ■ *Web:* www.wabtec.com

Wabtec Corp WABCO Transit Div PO Box 11 . . . . Spartanburg SC 29304 864-433-5900 433-0176
Web: www.wabtec.com

Watco Companies LLC 315 W Third St. . . . . Pittsburg KS 66762 620-231-2230 231-0812
TF: 866-386-9321 ■ *Web:* www.watcocompanies.com

Western Reman Industrial LLC 588 W Seventh St. . . . . Peru IN 46970 765-472-2002
Web: www.wriservices.com

654 RAILROAD SWITCHING & TERMINAL SERVICES

Phone | Fax

Belt Railway Co of Chicago
6900 S Central Ave. . . . . Bedford Park IL 60638 708-496-4000 496-3037
TF: 877-772-5772 ■ *Web:* www.beltrailway.com

Central California Traction Co
2201 W Washington St Ste 12 . . . . Stockton CA 95203 209-466-6927 466-1204
Web: www.cctrailroad.com

East Erie Commercial Railroad
1030 Lawrence Pkwy . . . . Erie PA 16511 814-875-5437

Indiana Harbor Belt Railroad Co
2721 161st St. . . . . Hammond IN 46323 219-989-4703 989-4707
Web: www.ihbrr.com

Minnesota Commercial Railway
508 Cleveland Ave N. . . . . Saint Paul MN 55114 651-646-2010 646-8337
Web: mnnr.net

OmniTRAX Inc 252 Clayton St Ste 400 . . . . Denver CO 80206 303-398-4500 398-4540
Web: www.omnitrax.com

Portland Terminal Railroad Co
3500 NW Yeon Ave. . . . . Portland OR 97210 503-241-9898 241-4494

Public Belt Railroad Commission
4822 Tchoupitulas St . . . . New Orleans LA 70115 504-896-7410 896-7452
TF Cust Svc: 800-524-3421 ■ *Web:* nopb.com

Rail Link Inc
13901 Sutton Pk Dr S Ste 125 . . . . Jacksonville FL 32224 904-223-1110 223-8710
TF: 877-777-4778 ■ *Web:* gwrr.com

Railserve Inc 1691 Phoenix Blvd Ste 110 . . . . Atlanta GA 30349 770-996-6838 996-6830
TF: 800-345-7245 ■ *Web:* www.railserveinc.com

Rescar Inc 1101 31st St Ste 250. . . . . Downers Grove IL 60515 630-963-1114 963-6342
TF: 800-851-5196 ■ *Web:* www.rescar.com

Roadrunner Transportation Systems Inc
4900 S Pennsylvania Ave . . . . Cudahy WI 53110 414-615-1500 615-1513
NYSE: RRTS ■ *TF:* 800-831-4394 ■ *Web:* www.rrts.com

Terminal Railroad Assn of Saint Louis
415 S 18th St Ste 200. . . . . Saint Louis MO 63103 314-231-5196
Web: www.terminalrailroad.com

Vermont Railway Inc One Railway Ln. . . . . Burlington VT 05401 802-658-2550
Web: www.vermontrailway.com

Wheeling & Lake Erie Railway Co
100 E First St . . . . Brewster OH 44613 330-767-3401
Web: www.wlerwy.com

655 REAL ESTATE AGENTS & BROKERS

Phone | Fax

33rd Co Inc 1800 Wooddale Dr Ste 100 . . . . Woodbury MN 55125 651-777-5500 777-5501
Web: www.33rdcompany.com

4-D Properties 2870 N Swan Rd. . . . . Tucson AZ 85712 520-325-9600

A J Clarke Real Estate Corp
1035 River Rd. . . . . New Milford NJ 07646 201-836-7464

A to b Realty 1500 E Hamilton Ave Ste 105 . . . . Campbell CA 95008 408-626-4800
Web: www.atobrealty.com

Access Property Management
Four Walter E Foran Blvd Ste 311. . . . . Flemington NJ 08822 908-806-2600
Web: www.accesspm.com

Ackman-Ziff Real estate Group LLC
110 E 42nd St. . . . . New York NY 10017 212-697-3333
Web: www.ackmanziff.com

Advenir Real Estate 17501 Biscayne Blvd . . . . Aventura FL 33160 305-948-3535
Web: advenir.net

Advisor Group Inc, The 3000 Mcknight E Dr . . . . Pittsburgh PA 15237 412-931-3900
Web: www.theadvisorgroup.com

Alain Pinel Realtors Inc
12772 Saratoga-Sunnyvale Rd . . . . Saratoga CA 95070 408-741-1111
Web: www.apr.com

Aldrich-Thomas Group Inc 18 N Third St . . . . Temple TX 76501 254-773-4901
Web: aldrich-thomas.com

Ale Solutions Inc
One Illinois St Ste 300 . . . . Saint Charles IL 60174 630-513-6434
Web: www.alesolutions.com

All Power Brokers Real Estate Inc
847 N Hwy 49/88 Ste 1. . . . . Jackson CA 95642 209-223-0237
Web: allpower.com

Allen Morris Co
121 Alhambra Plz Ste 1600 . . . . Coral Gables FL 33134 305-443-1000 443-1462
Web: www.allenmorris.com

Alterra Real Estate Advisors LLC
540 Officenter Pl Ste 260 . . . . Gahanna OH 43230 614-365-9000
Web: www.alterrare.com

America's Choice Home Loans LP
8584 Katy Fwy Ste 200. . . . . Houston TX 77024 713-463-6779
Web: www.achlonline.com

American Landmark Properties
8114 Lawndale Ave. . . . . Skokie IL 60076 847-568-0808
Web: www.americanlandmark.com

Amira Dba Rossum Realty Unlimited
3875 S Jones Blvd Ste 101. . . . . Las Vegas NV 89103 702-368-1850

Amtrust Realty Corp 250 Broadway Rm 3001. . . . . New York NY 10007 212-732-4776
Web: www.amtrustre.com

Anchor Realty Assoc Inc 1113 W Baker Rd Ste D . . . . Baytown TX 77521 281-427-4747
Web: har.com

Aquila Commercial LLC 1717 W Sixth St. . . . . Austin TX 78703 512-684-3800
Web: www.aquilacommercial.com

Arcadia Assn of Realtors Inc 601 S First Ave. . . . . Arcadia CA 91006 626-446-2115
Web: theaar.com

Aronov Realty 3500 Eastern Blvd. . . . . Montgomery AL 36116 334-277-1000 272-0747
Web: www.aronov.com

				Phone	Fax
Arthur J Rogers & Co 1559 Elmhurst Rd *Web:* www.arthurjrogers.com	Elk Grove Village	IL	60007	847-297-2200	
Ascent Real Estate 2900 N Park Way *Web:* ascentrealestate.net	San Diego	CA	92104	619-814-3420	
Assist-2-Sell Inc 1610 Meadow Wood Ln. *TF:* 800-528-7816 ■ *Web:* www.assist2sell.com	Reno	NV	89502	775-688-6060	823-8823
Atlanta Intown Real Estate Services 181 10th St Ne *Web:* www.atlantaintown.com	Atlanta	GA	30309	404-881-1810	
Atlantic & Pacific Management 11075 Carmel Mtn Rd Ste 200 *Web:* www.apmanagement.net	San Diego	CA	92129	858-672-3100	
Atlantic Realty Partners Inc 3378 Peachtree Rd *Web:* www.atlantic-realty.com	Atlanta	GA	30326	404-591-2900	
Bailey Properties 106 Aptos Beach Dr *Web:* www.baileyproperties.com	Aptos	CA	95003	831-688-7009	
Baird & Warner Inc 120 S LaSalle St Ste 2000 *Web:* www.bairdwarner.com	Chicago	IL	60603	312-368-1855	368-1490
Bald Head Island Rentals LLC 21 Keelson Row *Web:* www.baldheadislandrentals.com	Bald Head Island	NC	28461	910-457-1702	
Barletta & Assoc Inc 1313 Campbell Rd Ste F *Web:* www.barlettainc.com	Houston	TX	77055	713-464-7700	464-3696
Barrington Management Company Inc 376 Massachusetts Ave *Web:* www.barrington-mgmt.com	Arlington	MA	02474	781-648-9600	
Barshop & Oles Company Inc 801 Congress Ave Ste 300 *Web:* www.barshopoles.com	Auslin	TX	78701	512-477-1212	
Beach Realty & Construction 4826 N Croatan Hwy *TF:* 800-635-1559 ■ *Web:* www.beachrealtync.com	Kitty Hawk	NC	27949	252-261-3815	
Beatty Management Company Inc 6824 Elm St Ste 200 *Web:* www.beattycos.com	Mclean	VA	22101	703-821-0500	
Beco Management Inc 5410 Edson Ln Ste 200 *Web:* beconet.com/	Rockville	MD	20852	301-816-1500	816-1501
Beer-wells Real Estate Services Inc 11311 N Central Expy Ste 100 *Web:* beerwells.com	Dallas	TX	75243	214-750-5600	
Ben M Muller Realty Company Inc 1971 E Beltline Ave Ne Ste 240 *Web:* mullerrealty.com	Grand Rapids	MI	49525	616-456-7114	
Bently Holdings Corp 240 Stockton St Ste 200 *Web:* www.kamalaspa.com	San Francisco	CA	94108	415-288-0202	
Bergman Real Estate 3259 SR- 28 *Web:* adkreal.com	North Creek	NY	12853	518-251-2122	
Berkeley Hills Real Estate Inc 1714 Solano Ave *Web:* www.berkhills.com	Berkeley	CA	94707	510-524-9888	
Birtcher Anderson Realty Management 31910 Del Obispo Ste 100 *Web:* www.barealtyllc.com	San Juan Capistrano	CA	92675	949-545-0500	
Block Hawley Commercial Real Estate Services LLC 16253 Swingley Ridge Rd Ste 150 *Web:* blockhawley.com	Chesterfield	MO	63017	636-534-2900	
Blue Canoe Properties LLC 2120 16th Ave S	Birmingham	AL	35205	205-918-0921	
Bluestone & Hockley Real Estate Services 9320 SW Barbur Blvd Ste 300 *Web:* www.bluestonehockley.com	Portland	OR	97219	503-222-3800	
Bobeck Real Estate Company Inc 3333 W Hamilton Rd	Fort Wayne	IN	46814	260-432-1000	
Bosshardt Realty Services LLC 5542 NW 43rd St *TF:* 800-284-6110 ■ *Web:* www.bosshardtrealty.com	Gainesville	FL	32653	352-371-6100	
Boydell Development Co 743 Beaubien St	Detroit	MI	48226	313-964-0333	
Boys & Girls Club of Zionsville 1575 Mulberry st *Web:* www.bagcoz.org	Zionsville	IN	46077	317-873-6670	
Brack Capital Real Estate USA 885 Third Ave Ste no 2401 *Web:* www.brack-capital.com	New York	NY	10022	212-308-7200	
Bradford Allen 200 S Michigan Ave 18th Fl *Web:* www.bradfordallen.com	Chicago	IL	60604	312-994-5700	
Brady Sullivan Properties LLC 670 N Commercial St *Web:* www.bradysullivan.com	Manchester	NH	03101	603-622-6223	
Bray Real Estate 637 N Ave *TF:* 888-760-4251 ■ *Web:* www.brayandco.com	Grand Junction	CO	81501	970-242-8450	
Briarlane Rental Property Management Inc 85 Spy Ct Ste 100 *Web:* www.briarlane.ca	Markham	ON	L3R4Z4	905-944-9406	
Brookfield Residential Services Ltd 3190 Steeles Ave E Ste 200 *Web:* brookfieldcondominiums.com/	Markham	ON	L3R1G9	416-510-8700	
Brown Ken J Realtors 1618 S Western St	Amarillo	TX	79106	806-352-5617	
Brownstone Real Estate Co 1840 Fishburn Rd *TF:* 877-533-6222 ■ *Web:* www.brwnstone.com	Hershey	PA	17033	717-533-6222	
Bulfinch Cos Inc 250 First Ave Ste 200 *Web:* www.bulfinch.com	Needham Hgts	MA	02494	781-707-4000	
Bull Island Realty Inc 29 Holloway Rd *Web:* bullislandrealty.com	Poquoson	VA	23662	757-868-4663	
Burke & Assoc Professional Property Management 4974 N Fresno St Ste 106	Fresno	CA	93726	559-225-6075	
Burnac Corp 44 St Clair Ave W *Web:* www.burnac.com	Toronto	ON	M4V3C9	416-964-3600	
Bwb Properties Inc 1384 North 450 East	Orem	UT	84097	801-222-3600	
Cagan Management Group Inc 16554 Cagan Crossings Blvd Ste 4 *Web:* www.cagan.com	Clermont	FL	34714	352-242-2444	

				Phone	Fax
Cambria Pines Realty Inc 746-A Main St *Web:* cambriapinesrealty.com	Cambria	CA	93428	805-927-8616	
Cambridge Realty Capital LLC 125 S Wacker Dr Ste 1800 *Web:* www.cambridgecap.com	Chicago	IL	60606	312-357-1601	
Camelot Homes 6607 N Scottsdale Rd Ste H100 *Web:* www.camelothomes.com	Scottsdale	AZ	85250	480-367-4300	
Cardinal Management Group 3704 Golf Trl Ln *Web:* cardinalmanagementgroup.com	Fairfax	VA	22033	703-591-1818	
Cardinal Pacific Escrow Inc 6615 E Pacific Coast Hwy Ste 240 *Web:* www.cardinalpacific.com	Long Beach	CA	90803	562-493-9393	
Carlson Real Estate Company Inc 301 Carlson Pkwy Ste 100 *Web:* carlsonrealestate.biz	Minnetonka	MN	55305	952-404-5000	404-5001
Carolina Farms Real Estate 547 S Main St *TF:* 800-559-2113 ■ *Web:* www.carolinafarms.com	King	NC	27021	336-983-5263	
Carson Dunlop Home Inspections 407-120 Carlton St *Web:* www.carsondunlop.com	Toronto	ON	M5A4K2	416-964-9415	
Castrop Wolfe Development Co 5775 Perimeter Dr Ste 290 *Web:* www.cwbpm.com	Dublin	OH	43017	614-793-2244	
Ceis Review Inc Eight Tannery Ln *Web:* ceisreview.com	Camden	ME	04843	207-230-2515	
Center for Real Estate Education & Research 210 S Poplar St	New Washington	IN	47162	812-333-2299	
Central Management Inc (CMI) 820 Gessner Rd Ste 1525 *Web:* www.cmirealestate.com	Houston	TX	77024	713-961-9777	961-5730
Century 21 A Property Shoppe 2033 N Main St	Salinas	CA	93906	831-443-2121	
Century 21 Consolidated Real Estate 2820 Flamingo Rd *Web:* c21consolidated.com	Las Vegas	NV	89121	702-732-7282	
Century 21 Percy Fulton Ltd 2911 Kennedy Rd *Web:* www.century21toronto.com	Toronto	ON	M1V1S8	416-298-8200	
CENTURY 21 Sweyer & Assoc 1630 Military Cutoff Rd *TF:* 800-848-0021 ■ *Web:* www.century21sweyer.com	Wilmington	NC	28403	910-256-0021	
Champions Real Estate Group LLC 2323 S Voss Rd Ste 120 *Web:* creg1.com	Houston	TX	77057	713-785-6666	
Chandler Properties 2799 California St *Web:* chandlerproperties.com	San Francisco	CA	94115	415-921-5733	
Chapin Hall Center For Children 1313 E 60th St *Web:* www.chapinhall.org	Chicago	IL	60637	773-753-5900	
Charles Dunn Co Inc 800 W Sixth St Sixth Fl *Web:* www.charlesdunn.com	Los Angeles	CA	90017	213-683-0500	
Chris Smith Realty 306 Morris Ave *Web:* chrissmithrealty.com	Spring Lake	NJ	07762	732-449-3777	
Chromatin Inc 10 S Lasalle St Ste 2100 *Web:* www.chromatininc.com	Chicago	IL	60603	312-292-5400	
Cip Real Estate Property Services Inc 19762 Macarthur Blvd Ste 300 *Web:* www.ciprealestate.com	Irvine	CA	92612	949-474-7030	
Citi-Habitats Inc 250 Park Ave S 11th Fl *Web:* www.citi-habitats.com	New York	NY	10003	212-685-7777	
City Property Management Co 4645 E Cotton Gin Loop *Web:* cityproperty.com	Phoenix	AZ	85040	602-437-4777	
Cityfeetcom Inc 443 Park Ave S Ste 3A *Web:* www.cityfeet.com	New York	NY	10016	212-924-6450	
Claimsource One Services Group Inc 490 Sun Vly Dr Ste 103 *Web:* claimsourceone.com	Roswell	GA	30076	404-252-1771	
Clay Herman Realtor Inc 251 Park Rd Ste 710 *Web:* clayherman.com	Burlingame	CA	94010	650-342-1141	
Closing USA LLC 903 Elmgrove Rd *Web:* www.closingusa.com	Rochester	NY	14624	585-454-1730	
Cohen Financial LP 227 W Monroe St Ste 1000 *Web:* www.cohenfinancial.com	Chicago	IL	60606	312-346-5680	346-6669
Cohen-Esrey Real Estate Services LLC 6800 W 64th St *Web:* www.cohenesrey.com	Overland Park	KS	66202	913-671-3300	671-3301
Coldwell Banker Gundaker 2458 Old Dorsett Rd Ste 300 *TF:* 800-325-1978 ■ *Web:* www.cbgundaker.com	Maryland Heights	MO	63043	314-298-5000	
Coldwell Banker Honig-Bell 950 Essington Rd *Web:* www.cbhonig-bell.com	Joliet	IL	60435	815-744-1000	
Coldwell Banker Howard Perry & Walston 1001 Wade Ave *Web:* www.hpw.com	Raleigh	NC	27605	919-782-5600	
Coldwell Banker Platinum Partners 6349 Abercorn St *Web:* www.greatersavannah.com	Savannah	GA	31405	912-352-1222	
Coldwell Banker Residential Brokerage 600 Grant St Ste 925 *TF All:* 800-552-6787 ■ *Web:* www.coloradohomes.com	Denver	CO	80203	303-409-1500	409-6336
Coldwell Banker Residential Real Estate 5951 Cattleridge Ave *TF:* 888-937-6426 ■ *Web:* www.floridamoves.com	Sarasota	FL	34232	941-378-8211	
Coldwell Banker Schmidt Realtors 402 E Front St *Web:* www.cbgreatlakes.com	Traverse City	MI	49686	231-922-2350	
Coldwell Banker Select Professionals 1000 N Prince St *Web:* www.cbsp.com	Lancaster	PA	17603	717-569-0608	

	City	State	Zip	Phone	Fax
Collett & Assoc LLC 1111 Metropolitan Ave Ste 700 *Web:* www.collettassociates.com	Charlotte	NC	28204	704-206-8300	
Collier Enterprises Management Inc 2550 Goodlette Rd N Ste 100 *Web:* www.collierenterprises.com	Naples	FL	34103	239-261-4455	
Colliers International 601 Union St Ste 4800 *Web:* www.colliers.com	Seattle	WA	98101	206-695-4200	
Colliers Parrish International Inc One Almaden Blvd Ste 300 *Web:* www.collierssparrish.com	San Jose	CA	95113	408-282-4000	
Colliers Pinkard 7172 Columbia Gateway Dr Ste 400 *Web:* www.colliers.com/markets/baltimore	Columbia	MD	21046	443-297-9000	543-0191
Commercial Realty & Resources Corp 1415 Wyckoff Rd PO Box 1468 *Web:* njresources.com	Wall	NJ	07719	732-938-1111	938-6735
ConAm Management Corp 3990 Ruffin Rd Ste 100 *Web:* www.conam.com	San Diego	CA	92123	858-614-7200	
Conopco Realty & Development Inc 5448 Prairie Stone Pkwy Ste 250) *Web:* www.conopco.com	Hoffman Estates	IL	60192	847-645-5000	645-5050
Constable Commercial Real Estate Services 2845 Moorpark Ave Ste 112 *Web:* www.constablecommercial.com	San Jose	CA	95128	408-984-3700	
Conterra Ultra Broadband LLC 2101 Rexford Rd Ste 200E *TF:* 800-634-1374 ■ *Web:* www.conterra.com	Charlotte	NC	28211	704-936-1800	
Corcoran Group Inc, The 660 Madison Ave. *TF:* 800-544-4055 ■ *Web:* www.corcoran.com	New York	NY	10021	212-355-3550	
Core Partners LLC 320 Martin St Ste 140 *Web:* www.corepartners.net	Birmingham	MI	48009	248-399-9999	
Corus Realty Holdings Inc 6726 Curran St *Web:* www.corushome.com	Mclean	VA	22101	703-827-0075	
Costar Video Systems LLC 101 Wrangler Dr Ste 201 *Web:* www.costarvideo.com	Coppell	TX	75019	469-635-6800	446-8866
Crosspoint Realty Services Inc 260 California St Fl 4 *Web:* crosspointrealty.com	San Francisco	CA	94111	415-288-6888	
Crye-Leike Inc 6525 N Quail Hollow Rd **Fax Area Code:* 901 ■ *Web:* www.crye-leike.com	Memphis	TN	38120	866-310-3102	758-5641*
Cummings Properties LLC 200 W Cummings Pk *Web:* www.meadowsestates.com	Woburn	MA	01801	781-935-8000	
Cushman & Wakefield Inc 1290 Ave of the Americas *Web:* www.cushmanwakefield.com	New York	NY	10019	212-841-7500	841-7867
Cutten Realty Inc 2120 Campton Rd Ste C *Web:* cuttenrealty.com	Eureka	CA	95503	707-445-8811	
Dana B Kenyon Co 5772 Timuquana Rd *Web:* www.dbkenyon.com	Jacksonville	FL	32210	904-777-0833	
Dana Group, The 6892 S Yosemite Ct *Web:* www.danainvestments.com	Centennial	CO	80112	303-694-7100	
Daniel Gale Sotheby's International Realty 187 Park Ave. *Web:* www.danielgale.com	Huntington	NY	11743	631-427-6600	
Dart Appraisalcom 2600 W Big Beaver Rd Ste 100 *TF:* 888-327-8123 ■ *Web:* dartappraisal.com	Troy	MI	48084	888-327-8123	
Dartmouth Company Inc, The 351 Newbury St *Web:* www.dartco.com	Boston	MA	02115	617-262-6620	
Daum Commercial Real Estate Services 801 S Figueroa St Ste 600 *Web:* www.daumcommercial.com	Los Angeles	CA	90017	213-626-9101	
David Plunkett Realty LLC 8832 Riverside Dr *Web:* davidplunkettrealty.com	Parker	AZ	85344	928-667-1699	
Delois Smith All-Star Team Inc Four Willow Bend Dr Ste 2A *Web:* deloissmith.com	Hattiesburg	MS	39402	601-545-3900	
Delphi Business Properties Inc 7100 Hayvenhurst Ave Ste 211 *Web:* go2delphi.com	Van Nuys	CA	91406	818-780-7878	
DelShah Capital LLC 114 E 13th St. *Web:* www.delshah.com	New York	NY	10003	212-677-4506	
Development Planning & Financing Group Inc 27127 Calle Arroyo Ste 1910 *TF:* 800-535-5795 ■ *Web:* www.dpfg.com	San Juan Capistrano	CA	92675	949-388-9269	
DH Bader Management Services Inc 14435 Cherry Ln Ct Ste 210 *Web:* dhbader.com	Laurel	MD	20707	301-953-1955	
Diamond Realty Management Corp 790 Watervliet Shaker Rd Ste 2 *Web:* www.ambroselec.com	Latham	NY	12110	518-783-5000	
Discovery Green Conservancy 1500 Mckinney St *Web:* discoverygreen.com	Houston	TX	77010	713-400-7336	
DJM Capital Partners Inc 60 S Market St Ste 1120 *Web:* www.djmcapital.com	San Jose	CA	95113	408-271-0366	
Dominion First Realty Inc 2420 Maplewood Ave *Web:* www.dominionfirst.com	Richmond	VA	23220	804-359-9200	
Drake Commercial Lp 19310 Stone Oak Pkwy Ste 201 *Web:* drakecommercial.com	San Antonio	TX	78258	210-402-6363	
Eakin Partners LLC Roundabout Plz 1600 Division St Ste 600 *Web:* www.eakinpartners.com	Nashville	TN	37203	615-250-1800	
Eddy Group Ltd 660 St Anne St. *Web:* www.eddygroup.com	Bathurst	NB	E2A2N6	506-546-6631	
Edina Realty Inc 6800 France Ave S Ste 600 *Web:* www.edinarealty.com	Edina	MN	55435	952-928-5563	
Emerald Cos Inc 400 Travis St. *Web:* www.emeraldcompanies.com	Shreveport	LA	71101	318-425-7083	
Emil Anderson Construction (EAC) Inc 907 Ethel St *Web:* www.eac.bc.ca	Kelowna	BC	V1Y2W1	250-762-9999	762-6171
Engel Realty Company Inc 951 Eighteenth St S Ste 200 *Web:* www.engelrealty.com	Birmingham	AL	35201	205-939-6800	
Enpria Inc 10260 SW Greenburg Rd Ste 850	Portland	OR	97223	503-293-8444	
Equine Canada 2685 Queensview Dr *TF:* 866-282-8395 ■ *Web:* www.equinecanada.ca	Ottawa	ON	K2B8K2	613-248-3484	
ERA Grizzard Real Estate 1300 W N Blvd. *Web:* www.tomgrizzard.com	Leesburg	FL	34748	352-787-6966	
ERA Naper Realty Inc 865 N Columbia St. *Web:* www.eranaper.com	Naperville	IL	60563	630-961-1776	
ERA Wilder Realty 120A Columbia Ave PO Box 610 *TF:* 866-593-7653 ■ *Web:* erawilderrealty.com	Chapin	SC	29036	803-345-6713	772-9226
Etkin Equities LLC 200 Franklin Ctr 29100 NW Hwy *Web:* etkinllc.com	Southfield	MI	48034	248-358-0800	
Fc Tucker Company Inc 9279 N Meridian St Ste 100 *Web:* talktotucker.com	Indianapolis	IN	46260	317-571-2200	
Fimc Commercial Realty 1619 S Tyler St. *Web:* fimcrealty.com	Amarillo	TX	79102	806-358-7151	
Findwell 920 Dexter Ave N *Web:* www.findwell.com	Seattle	WA	98109	206-462-6200	
Firm Realty Inc 1930 Harrison St Ste 505 *Web:* www.firmrealty.com	Hollywood	FL	33020	954-926-2510	
Flans & Weiner Inc 16200 Ventura Blvd Ste 417 *Web:* flansweiner.com	Encino	CA	91436	818-501-4888	
Fortune Builders International 25082 Paseo Arboleda	Lake Forest	CA	92630	949-380-3080	
FPI Management Inc 800 Iron Pt Rd *Web:* www.fpimgt.com	Folsom	CA	95630	916-357-5300	357-5310
Fraser Forbes Co LLC 6862 Elm St Ste 620 *Web:* www.fraserforbes.com	Mclean	VA	22101	703-790-9400	
FREEMAN WEBB CO 3810 Bedford Ave Ste 300 *Web:* www.freemanwebb.com	Nashville	TN	37215	615-271-2700	
Frye Properties 300 W Freemason St *Web:* www.fryeproperties.com	Norfolk	VA	23510	757-627-1980	
Galman Group, The 261 Old York Rd Ofc	Jenkintown	PA	19046	215-886-2000	
Garden State Mltple Lsting Services 1719 SR- 10 Ste 223 *Web:* www.gsmls.com	Parsippany	NJ	07054	973-898-1900	
Gart Cos Inc, The 299 Milwaukee St Ste 500 *Web:* www.gartcompanies.com	Denver	CO	80206	303-333-1933	
GEM Technology International Corp 2800 Ponce De Leon Blvd Ste 1100 *Web:* www.gemtechnology.com	Coral Gables	FL	33134	305-447-1344	
Gerald A Teel Co 974 Campbell Rd Ste 204 *Web:* www.gateel.com	Houston	TX	77024	713-467-5858	467-0704
Glacier Real Estate Services Inc 444 NE Ravenna Blvd Ste 101 *Web:* www.glacierres.com	Seattle	WA	98115	206-985-8200	
Gorilla Capital Inc 1342 High St. *Web:* www.gorillacapital.com	Eugene	OR	97401	541-344-7867	
Gove Group Real Estate LLC 70 Portsmouth Ave *TF:* 866-778-6400 ■ *Web:* www.thegovegroup.com	Stratham	NH	03885	603-778-6400	
Greater Fort Worth Assn of Realtors Inc 2650 Parkview Dr *Web:* www.gfwar.org	Fort Worth	TX	76102	817-336-5165	
Green Acres of America LLC 615 Lindsay St	Chattanooga	TN	37403	423-756-4082	
Greg Malik Real Estate Group Inc 7450 Morro Rd *Web:* gregmalik.com	Atascadero	CA	93422	805-466-2540	
Gregg Distributors Ltd 16215-118 Ave. *Web:* www.greggdistributors.ca	Edmonton	AB	T5V1C7	780-447-3447	
Grubb Company Inc, The 1960 Mountain Blvd. *Web:* www.grubbco.com	Oakland	CA	94611	510-339-0400	
Guarantee Real Estate Corp 5380 N Fresno Ave Ste 103 *Web:* www.guarantee.com	Fresno	CA	93710	559-650-6088	
GVD Commercial Properties Inc 1915 E Katella Ave Ste A *Web:* www.gvdcommercialproperties.com	Orange	CA	92867	714-639-2131	
H Pearce Real Estate Co 393 State St *TF:* 800-373-3411 ■ *Web:* www.joelgalvin.com	North Haven	CT	06473	203-281-3400	
Habitat Company LLC, The 350 W Hubbard St Ste 500 *Web:* www.habitat.com	Chicago	IL	60610	312-527-5400	527-7440
Halstead Property LLC 770 Lexington Ave *Web:* www.halstead.com	New York	NY	10065	212-317-7800	
Hardin & Company Ltd 113 S 19th Ave Ste C *Web:* hardinre.com	Bozeman	MT	59718	406-587-1211	
Harold A Davison 1723 Claredon Ave NW	Canton	OH	44708	330-454-1244	
Harry B Lucas Co 2828 E Trinity Mills Rd *Web:* hblco.com	Carrollton	TX	75006	972-991-4567	
Hart Corp 900 Jaymor Rd. *TF:* 800-368-4278 ■ *Web:* www.hartcorp.com	SoutHampton	PA	18966	215-322-5100	322-5840
Hart Realty Advisers Inc One Mill Pond Ln *Web:* www.hartadvisers.com	Simsbury	CT	06070	860-651-4000	
Heartland Multiple Listing Service Inc 11150 Overbrook Rd Ste 125 *Web:* matrix.heartlandmls.com	Leawood	KS	66211	913-661-1600	
Heller Real Estate Group Inc, The 171 Saxony Rd Ste 205 *Web:* www.hellerthehomeseller.com	Encinitas	CA	92024	760-632-8408	
Help-U-Sell Real Estate 240 N Washington Blvd *Web:* www.helpusell.com	Sarasota	FL	34236	941-951-7707	
Henderson Properties Inc 919 Norland Rd *Web:* www.hendersonproperties.com	Charlotte	NC	28205	704-535-1122	

	City	State	Zip	Phone	Fax
Herbert K Horita Realty Inc 98-150 Kaonohi St Ste B128	Aiea	HI	96701	808-487-1561	
Web: www.hicentral.com					
Herbert Yentis & Company Inc 7300 City Line Ave	Philadelphia	PA	19151	215-878-7300	
Web: yentis.com					
Heritage Title Co Frost Bank Tower Ste 1500 401 Congress Ave	Austin	TX	78701	512-505-5000	505-5024
Web: reca.org/					
Herman & Kittle Properties Inc 500 E 96th St Ste 300	Indianapolis	IN	46240	317-846-3111	
Web: hermankittle.com					
Hill & Company Real Estate Inc 1880 Lombard St	San Francisco	CA	94123	415-921-6000	
Web: www.marinadistrictrealestate.com					
Hilliker Corp 2001 S Hanley Ste 300	St Louis	MO	63144	314-781-0001	
Web: www.hillikercorp.com					
Hoban & Assoc Dba Coast Real Estate Services 2829 Rucker Ave	Everett	WA	98201	425-339-3638	
TF: 800-339-3634 ■ *Web:* www.coastmgt.com					
HomeGain.com Inc 6001 Shellmound St Ste 550	Emeryville	CA	94608	510-655-0800	655-0848
TF: 888-542-0800 ■ *Web:* www.homegain.com					
HomeServices of America Inc 333 S Seventh St 27th Fl	Minneapolis	MN	55402	888-485-0018	336-5572*
*Fax Area Code: 612 ■ *TF:* 888-485-0018 ■ *Web:* www.homeservices.com					
HomeSmart International LLC 8388 E Hartford Dr Ste 100	Scottsdale	AZ	85255	602-230-7600	
Web: www.homesmartinternational.com					
Horah Group, The 351 Manville Rd Ste 105	Pleasantville	NY	10570	914-495-3200	
Web: www.horah.com					
Hospitality Real Estate Counselors 6400 S Fiddler'S Green Cir Ste 1730	Greenwood Village	CO	80111	303-267-0057	
Web: www.hrec.com					
Hotpadscom PO Box 53104	Washington	DC	20009	202-232-1581	
TF: 888-876-1992 ■ *Web:* hotpads.com					
Housing Resources Group 1651 Bellevue Ave	Seattle	WA	98122	206-623-0506	
Web: www.hrg.org					
Howes & Jefferies Realtors 345 Fifth Ave S	Clinton	IA	52732	563-242-3265	
Web: howesandjefferies.com					
Hughes Commercial Properties Inc 935 S Main St Ste 202	Greenville	NC	29603	864-233-0079	
Web: www.hughescommercial.com					
Hughes Marino Inc 1450 Front St	San Diego	CA	92101	619-238-2111	
Web: www.hughesmarino.com					
In-Rel Properties Inc 2328 10th Ave N Ste 401	Lake Worth	FL	33461	561-533-0344	
Web: in-rel.com					
Industrial Realty Group LLC 11100 Santa Monica Blvd Ste 850	Los Angeles	CA	90025	562-803-4761	
Web: www.industrialrealtygroup.com					
Inland Group Inc 2901 Butterfield Rd	Oak Brook	IL	60523	630-218-8000	218-4917
TF: 800-826-8228 ■ *Web:* www.inlandgroup.com					
Inland Real Estate Sales Inc 2901 Butterfield Rd	Oak Brook	IL	60523	630-218-8000	990-5350
TF: 800-828-8999 ■ *Web:* www.inlandgroup.com/ires					
Inspirato with American Express 1625 Wazee St Ste 400	Denver	CO	80202	303-586-7771	
Web: www.inspirato.com					
Institutional Real Estate Inc 2274 Camino Ramon	San Ramon	CA	94583	925-244-0500	
Web: www.irei.com					
Intereal Corp 520 Third St Ste 555	San Francisco	CA	94107	415-778-3900	
Iowa Realty Company Inc 3501 Westown Pkwy	West Des Moines	IA	50266	515-453-6222	453-5786
TF: 800-247-2430 ■ *Web:* www.iowarealty.com					
Irving A Miller Inc 2550 W Chester Pk	Broomall	PA	19008	610-356-1130	
J & s Management 702 Marshall St Ste 420	Redwood City	CA	94063	650-361-8350	
J Rockcliff Realtors 15 Railroad Ave	Danville	CA	94526	925-855-4000	
Web: www.rockcliff.com					
Jack Conway 137 Washington St	Norwell	MA	02061	781-871-0080	878-2632
TF: 800-283-1030 ■ *Web:* www.jackconway.com					
James R Mclauchlen Real Estate Inc 789 Hill St	Southampton	NY	11968	631-283-0448	
Web: mclauchlen.com					
Jameson Real Estate LLC 425 W N Ave	Chicago	IL	60610	312-751-0300	
TF: 888-751-4663 ■ *Web:* www.50eastchestnut.com					
Janet Mcafee Inc 9889 Clayton Rd	Saint Louis	MO	63124	314-997-4800	997-0647
TF: 888-991-4800 ■ *Web:* www.janetmcafee.com					
Javelina Partners 616 Texas St	Fort Worth	TX	76102	817-336-7109	
JB Goodwin Real Estate Company Inc 3933 Steck Ave Ste 110	Austin	TX	78759	512-502-7800	
Web: www.jbgoodwin.com					
Jersey Cape Realty Inc 739 Washington St	Cape May	NJ	08204	609-884-5800	
TF: 800-643-0043 ■ *Web:* www.jerseycaperealty.com					
JJ Clarke Enterprises Inc 2905 N Charles St	Baltimore	MD	21218	410-962-0241	
Web: jjclarkeenterprises.com					
JL Properties Inc 813 D St Ste 200	Anchorage	AK	99501	907-279-8068	
Web: www.jlproperties.com					
John C R Kelly Realty 3535 Blvd Of The Allies	Pittsburgh	PA	15213	412-683-7300	
Web: jcrkelly.com					
John d Miller Real Estate Investments LLC 1370 W SR- 89A Ste 17	Sedona	AZ	86336	928-204-9000	
Web: johndmiller.com					
John Daugherty Realtors 520 Post Oak Blvd Sixth Fl	Houston	TX	77027	713-626-3930	963-9588
TF: 800-231-2821 ■ *Web:* www.johndaugherty.com					
John Stewart Company Inc 1388 Sutter St Fl 11	San Francisco	CA	94109	415-345-4400	614-9175
Web: www.jsco.net					
Jones Lang LaSalle IP Inc 200 E Randolph Dr	Chicago	IL	60601	312-782-5800	
Web: www.jll.com					
Joseph P Day Realty Corp Nine E 40th St Eighth Fl	New York	NY	10016	212-889-7460	
Web: www.jpday.com					
Joyner Fine Properties (JFP) 2727 Enterprise Pkwy PO Box 31355	Richmond	VA	23294	804-270-9440	967-2770
TF: 800-446-3858 ■ *Web:* www.joynerfineproperties.com					
JR Realty 101 E Horizon Dr	Henderson	NV	89015	702-564-5142	
Web: century21jrrealty.com					
Kansas City Regional Assn of Realtors Inc, The 11150 Overbrook Rd Ste 100	Leawood	KS	66211	913-498-1100	
Web: www.kcrar.com					
Keefe Real Estate 1155 E Geneva St	Delavan	WI	53115	262-728-8757	
TF: 800-690-2292 ■ *Web:* www.keeferealestate.com					
Keegan & Coppin Company Inc 1355 N Dutton Ave	Santa Rosa	CA	95401	707-528-1400	
Web: www.keegancoppin.com					
Keller Williams Realty Inc 807 Las Cimas Pkwy Ste 200	Austin	TX	78746	512-327-3070	328-1433
Web: www.kw.com					
Kelly Waters Inc Five Clementine Pk	Dorchester Center	MA	02124	617-282-3620	
Web: kellywaters.com					
Kensington Realty Advisors Inc 100 N Riverside Plz Ste 2300	Chicago	IL	60606	312-993-7800	
Web: www.kra-net.com					
Keystone Property Group Inc One Presidential Blvd Ste 300	Bala Cynwyd	PA	19004	610-980-7000	
Web: www.keystonepropertygroup.com					
Kiemle & Hagood Co 601 W Main Ave Ste 400	Spokane	WA	99201	509-838-6541	458-4014
Web: www.khco.com					
Kindred Partners LLC 2755 Campus Dr Ste 220	San Mateo	CA	94403	650-573-5500	
Web: www.kindredpartners.com					
Kislak Company Inc, The 1000 Rt 9 N	Woodbridge	NJ	07095	732-750-3000	
Web: kislakrealty.com					
Kline Scott Visco Commercial Real Estate Inc 117 W Patrick St	Frederick	MD	21701	301-694-8444	
Web: klinescottvisco.com					
KW Property Management LLC 8200 NW 33rd St Ste 300	Miami	FL	33122	305-476-9188	
Web: kwpropertymanagement.com					
L a Tews Realty Inc 13011 Lazdins Cir	Cypress	TX	77429	281-807-3444	
Web: www.latews.com					
L b Property Management 4730 Woodman Ave Ste 200	Sherman Oaks	CA	91423	818-981-1802	
L Peres & Assoc Inc 525 River Rd	Edgewater	NJ	07020	201-943-7717	
Web: lperes.com					
Land Home Financial Services Inc 1355 Willow Way Ste 250	Concord	CA	94520	925-676-7038	
Web: lhfinancial.com					
Landmark Realty LLC 2205 Beckett St Ste A2	Bossier City	LA	71111	318-747-0052	
Web: www.landmarkrealty.org					
Landshark Inc PO Box 1791	Boulder	CO	80306	303-494-1229	
LANE4 Property Group Inc 4705 Central St	Kansas City	MO	64112	816-960-1444	
Web: www.lane4group.com					
Lang Realty 2901 Clint Moore Rd Ste 9	Boca Raton	FL	33496	561-998-0100	
Web: www.langrealty.com					
Latt Maxcy Corp 21299 Us Hwy 27	Lake Wales	FL	33859	863-679-6700	
Web: www.lattmaxcy.com					
Latter & Blum Inc 430 Notre Dame St	New Orleans	LA	70130	504-525-1311	569-9336
Web: www.latterblum.com					
Lawler-Wood LLC 1600 Riverview Tower	Knoxville	TN	37902	865-637-7777	
Web: www.lawlerwood.com					
LCB Assoc Inc 388 17th St Ste 200	Oakland	CA	94612	510-763-7016	
Web: www.lcbassociates.com					
Lechner Realty Group Inc 13421 Manchester Rd	Saint Louis	MO	63131	314-909-8100	909-8105
Web: www.lechnerrealty.com					
Lee & Assoc Commercial Real Estate Services Inc 13181 Crossroads Pkwy N Ste 300	City Of Industry	CA	91746	562-699-7500	
Web: www.lee-associates.com					
Leisure World of Maryland 3701 Rossmoor Blvd	Silver Spring	MD	20906	301-598-1000	
Web: www.lwmc.com					
Lereta LLC 1123 Parkview Dr	Covina	CA	91724	626-339-5221	
Web: www.lereta.com					
Lewis Group 2766 Degen Dr	Bonita	CA	91902	619-470-9110	
Web: www.mcmillinrealty.com					
LG2 Environmental Solutions Inc 88 Riberia St	St Augustine	FL	32084	904-824-8633	
TF: 800-435-0072 ■ *Web:* www.lg2es.com					
Lightstone Group, The 460 Pk Ave Ste 1300	New York	NY	10022	212-616-9969	
Web: www.lightstonegroup.com					
Lincoln Equities Group LLC One Meadowlands Plz Ste 803	East Rutherford	NJ	07073	201-460-3440	
Web: www.lincolnequities.com					
Lindy Property Management Co 207 Leedom St	Jenkintown	PA	19046	215-886-8030	
Web: www.lindyproperty.com					
Living Room Realtors Inc 1401 NE Alberta St	Portland	OR	97211	503-719-5588	
Web: www.livingroomre.com					
Loeb Properties Inc 825 Vly Brook Dr	Memphis	TN	38120	901-761-3333	
Web: www.loebproperties.com					
London Properties Ltd 6442 N Maroa Ave	Fresno	CA	93704	559-436-4000	
Web: www.londonproperties.com					
Long & Foster Realtors 14501 George Carter Way	Chantilly	VA	20151	703-653-8500	
TF: 800-237-8800 ■ *Web:* www.longandfoster.com					

Phone *Fax*

Loopnet Inc 2100 E Rt 66 .... Glendora CA 91740 626-803-5000
Web: loopnet.com
Losvet Company LLC
260 S Beverly Dr Ste 301 .... Beverly Hills CA 90212 310-273-5364
Lucas Ltd 1200 Wilshire Blvd Ste 208 .... Los Angeles CA 90017 213-240-5990
Macdonald Realty 203 5188 Wminster Hwy .... Richmond BC V7C5S7 604-279-9822
TF: 877-278-3888 ■ *Web:* www.macrealty.com
MacPherson's Property Management Inc
18551 Aurora Ave N Ste 301 .... Seattle WA 98133 206-542-6363 542-0783
TF: 800-962-6473 ■ *Web:* www.macphersons.com
Mad Inc Dba Century 21 Salvadori Realty
3500 N G St .... Merced CA 95340 209-383-6475
Web: c21salvadori.com
Major Properties Real Estate
1200 W Olympic Blvd .... Los Angeles CA 90015 213-747-4151 749-7972
Web: www.majorproperties.com
Mansermar Inc 2405 Satellite Blvd Ste 100 .... Duluth GA 30096 678-330-2000
Web: mansermar.com
Mar West Real Estate Inc
1049 Camino Del Mar Ste 12 .... Del Mar CA 92014 858-775-4917
Web: marwestre.com
Marcus & Assoc Inc 1045 Mapunapuna St .... Honolulu HI 96819 808-839-7446
Web: www.marcusrealty.com
Mason-McDuffie Real Estate Inc
5724 W Las Positas Blvd .... Pleasanton CA 94588 925-924-4600 924-1852
TF: 888-971-4636 ■ *Web:* www.bhghome.com/homepage.aspx
Massaro Properties LLC 120 Delta Dr .... Pittsburgh PA 15238 412-963-2800
Web: www.massaroproperties.com
Massey Knakal Realty Services Inc
275 Madison Ave Third Fl .... New York NY 10016 212-696-2500
Web: www.masseyknakal.com
Matrix Realty Group LLC 2066 Ridge Rd .... Homewood IL 60430 708-799-3600
Web: www.matrixrealtygroup.com
Mattson Resources Inc
7994 Swamp Flower Dr E .... Jacksonville FL 32244 904-772-6506
Max Hansen & Son Inc
200 Industrial Rd Ste 130 .... San Carlos CA 94070 650-595-5841
MCAP Service Corp 400-200 King St W .... Toronto ON M5H3T4 416-598-2665
TF: 800-387-4405 ■ *Web:* www.mcap.com
Mccaffery Interests Inc
875 N Michigan Ave Ste 1800 .... Chicago IL 60611 312-944-3777
Web: www.mccafferyinterests.com
Mccall & Almy Inc One Post Office Sq Ste 3740 .... Boston MA 02109 617-542-4141
Web: mccallalmy.com
McCann Realty Partners LLC
2520-B Gaskins Rd .... Richmond VA 23238 804-290-8870
Web: www.mrpapts.com
McEagle Properties LLC
1001 Boardwalk Springs Pl .... O'Fallon MO 63368 636-561-9300
Web: www.mc-eagle.com
Mcenearney Assoc Inc 109 S Pitt St .... Alexandria VA 22314 703-549-9292
TF: 877-624-9322 ■ *Web:* www.mcenearney.com
Mcwhirter Realty Partners LLC Formerly Mcwhirter Realty Corp
4045 Orchard Rd Bldg 400 .... Smyrna GA 30080 770-955-2000
Web: mcwhirterrealty.com
MD Atkinson Company Inc
1401 19th St Ste 400 .... Bakersfield CA 93301 661-334-4800
Web: www.mdatkinson.com
MD Management Inc 5201 Johnson Dr Ste 450 .... Mission KS 66205 913-831-2996
Web: www.mdmgt.com
Me Cos Inc 635 Brooksedge Blvd .... Westerville OH 43081 614-818-4900 818-4901
Web: www.mecompanies.com
Medve Group Inc 8390 Delmar Blvd Fl 1 .... Saint Louis MO 63124 314-569-0004
Web: www.medve.com
MEI Real Estate Services
5757 W Century Blvd Ste 605 .... Los Angeles CA 90045 310-258-0444
Web: www.meirealty.com
Menas Realty Co 4990 Mission Blvd .... San Diego CA 92109 619-276-5169
Web: www.menas.com
Merin Hunter Codman Inc
1601 Forum Pl Ste 200 .... West Palm Beach FL 33401 561-471-8000 471-9992
Web: www.mhcreal.com
Metcalfe Realty & Auction Company Inc
100 Castle Ridge Dr .... Edmonton KY 42129 270-432-7355
Web: metcalferealty.net
Mitsui Fudosan America Inc
1251 Ave of the Americas Ste 800 .... New York NY 10020 212-403-5600 403-5657
Web: www.mfamerica.com
Morrison Ekre & Bart Management Services Inc
1215 E Missouri Ave .... Phoenix AZ 85014 602-279-5515
Web: mebapts.com/
Morrow Realty Co Inc 809 22nd Ave .... Tuscaloosa AL 35401 205-759-5781
Web: www.morrowrealty.com/
Mountain Thunder Lodge 50 Mountain Dr .... Breckenridge CO 80424 970-547-5650
Web: breckresorts.com
Mytina Inc Dba Real Estate Mortgage Exchange
842 Foothill Blvd .... La Canada Flintridge CA 91011 818-507-0077
Nai Hunneman 303 Congress St .... Boston MA 02210 617-457-3400
Web: www.naihunneman.com
National Church Residences Inc
2335 N Bank Dr .... Columbus OH 43220 800-388-2151 451-0351*
**Fax Area Code:* 614 ■ *TF:* 800-388-2151 ■ *Web:* www.nationalchurchresidences.org
Nationwide Property & Appraisal Services LLC
10 Foster Ave Ste 3c .... Gibbsboro NJ 08026 856-258-6977
Web: onestopappraisals.com
Navarre Beach Realty 8305 Navarre Pkwy .... Navarre FL 32566 850-936-0700
Web: www.navarrebeachrealty.com
Nebo Agency Inc 197 East 100 North Ste 100 .... Payson UT 84651 801-465-2535
Net Lease Capital Advisors One Tara Blvd .... Nashua NH 03062 603-598-9500
Web: www.netleasecapital.com
New Bedford Management Corp
210 E 23rd St Ste 5 .... New York NY 10010 212-674-6123
Web: www.newbedfordmanagement.com

Phone *Fax*

Newland Communities LLC
9820 Towne Centre Dr Ste 100 .... San Diego CA 92121 858-455-7503
Web: www.newlandcommunities.com
Newmark Grubb Knight Frank 1800 Larimer St .... Denver CO 80202 303-892-1111
Web: newmarkkffr.com
Neyer Properties Inc 2135 Dana Ave Ste 200 .... Cincinnati OH 45207 513-563-7555
Web: www.neyer1.com
Nicholson Cos Inc, The 819 W Little Creek Rd .... Norfolk VA 23505 757-423-3281
Web: thenicholsoncompanies.com
Nicolson Porter & List
1300 W Higgins Rd Ste 104 .... Park Ridge IL 60068 847-698-7400
Web: nplchicago.com
North Orange County Escrow Corp
1370 Brea Blvd Ste 110 .... Fullerton CA 92835 714-526-5400 526-1744
Web: www.nocescrow.com/contact/
North Pacific Management 1905 SE 10th Ave .... Portland OR 97214 503-425-1500
Web: www.northp.com
NP Dodge Real Estate 8701 W Dodge Rd Ste 300 .... Omaha NE 68114 402-397-4900
TF: 800-642-5008 ■ *Web:* www.npdodge.com
NRC Realty & Capital Advisors LLC
363 W Erie St Ste 300 E .... Chicago IL 60654 312-278-6800
Web: www.nrc.com
O'Neill Properties Group LP
2701 Renaissance Blvd Fourth Fl .... King Of Prussia PA 19406 610-239-6100
Web: www.oneillproperties.com
Olive Real Estate Group
102 N Cascade Ave Ste 250 .... Colorado Springs CO 80903 719-598-3000 578-0089
Web: www.olivereg.com
Olmstead Properties Inc
575 Eighth Ave Rm 2400 .... New York NY 10018 212-564-6662
Web: olmsteadinc.com
Ontario Real Estate Assn 99 Duncan Mill Rd .... Don Mills ON M3B1Z2 416-445-9910
TF: 866-444-5557 ■ *Web:* www.orea.com
P J Morgan Real Estate Auctioneers
7801 Wakeley Plz .... Omaha NE 68114 402-397-7775
Web: www.pjmorgan.com
Pacific Coast Valuations
740 Corporate Ctr Dr Ste 200 .... Pomona CA 91768 909-623-4001
Web: www.pcvmurcor.com
Pacifica Hotel Co 1933 Cliff Dr Ste 1 .... Santa Barbara CA 93109 805-957-0095
Web: www.hcareers.com
Packard Cos, The 8775 Aero Dr Ste 335 .... San Diego CA 92123 858-277-4305
Web: www.packard-1.com
Pan Pacific Ocean Hotel Inc
243 Kearny St .... San Francisco CA 94108 415-433-0177
Paragon Management Company LLC
4370 La Jolla Village Dr Ste 640 .... San Diego CA 92122 858-535-9000
Web: www.paragoncompany.com
Paramount Property Management Inc
473 Broadway Ste 500 .... Bayonne NJ 07002 201-858-8500
Web: www.paramountassets.com
Park Regency Real Estate
10146 Balboa Blvd .... Granada Hills CA 91344 818-363-6116
Web: parkregency.com
Partners Trust Real Estate Brokerage & Acquisitions
9378 Wilshire Blvd Ste 200 .... Beverly Hills CA 90212 310-500-3900
Web: www.thepartnerstrust.com
Patterson-Schwartz & Assoc Inc
7234 Lancaster Pike Ste 100A .... Hockessin DE 19707 302-234-5270
TF: 877-456-4663 ■ *Web:* www.pattersonschwartz.com
Peabody Properties Inc 536 Granite St .... Braintree MA 02184 781-794-1000
Web: www.ayerlofts.com
Pegasus Residential LLC
1750 Founders Pkwy Ste 180 .... Alpharetta GA 30009 678-347-2802
Web: www.pegasusresidential.com
Pembroke Commercial Realty Corp
4460 Corporation Ln Ste 300 .... Virginia Bch VA 23462 757-490-3141
Web: www.pembrokerealty.com
Pendleton Manor 414 Summit Dr .... Greenville SC 29609 864-271-7562
Web: pendletonmanor.com
Penn-Florida Cos
1515 N Federal Hwy Ste 306 .... Boca Raton FL 33432 561-750-1030
Web: www.pennflorida.com
Perennial Mgmt Ltd 40 Aberdeen Ave .... St John'S NL A1A5T3 709-754-2057
Web: perennialmanagement.ca
Phillips Property Management
6106 Macarthur Blvd Ste 102 .... Bethesda MD 20816 301-320-0422 229-0937
Web: www.phillipspm.com
Phoenix Realty & Trust Co PO Box 87420 .... Phoenix AZ 85080 602-494-0202
Pierce-Eislen Inc
9200 E Pima Ctr Pkwy Ste 150 .... Scottsdale AZ 85258 480-663-1149
Web: pi-ei.com
PK Partners LLC
3610 River Crossing Pkwy .... Indianapolis IN 46240 317-817-8888
Web: pkpartners.com
Places Real Estate
400 Hibben St Ste 200 .... Mount Pleasant SC 29464 843-849-3636
Web: www.scplaces.com
Placitas Realty Inc 03 Homesteads Rd Ste A .... Placitas NM 87043 505-867-8000
PMCS-ICAP 829 W Genesee St .... Syracuse NY 13204 315-423-7962
Web: www.pmcs-icap.com
Preferred Properties of Venice Inc
325 W Venice Ave .... Venice FL 34285 941-485-9602 485-9604
TF: 877-640-7653 ■ *Web:* www.veniceflproperties.com
Premier Real Estate Management LLC
19105 W Capitol Dr Ste 200 .... Brookfield NY 53045 262-790-4560
Web: www.premierremgmt.com
Premier Realty Group Two N Sewalls Point Rd .... Stuart FL 34996 772-287-1777
TF: 800-915-8517 ■ *Web:* www.premierrealtygroup.com
Primera Partners LLC
111 Soledad St Ste 1250 .... San Antonio TX 78205 210-444-1400 444-1401
Web: primerapartners.com

				Phone	Fax
Principal Properties Inc 3295 W 4 Ave *Web:* principalproperties.com	Hialeah	FL	33012	305-883-7555	
Pyramid Brokerage Co 5786 Widewaters Pkwy *Web:* www.pyramidbrokerage.com	Syracuse	NY	13214	315-445-1030	
Quad Cities Realty 1053 Ripon Ave *Web:* qcrhomes.com	Lewiston	ID	83501	208-798-7798	
Ramsey-Shilling Commercial Real Estate Services Inc 6711 Forest Lawn Dr *Web:* www.ramsey-shilling.com	Los Angeles	CA	90068	323-851-6666	
Ray Stone Inc 550 Howe Ave Ste 200 *Web:* www.raystoneinc.com	Sacramento	CA	95825	916-649-7500	
Raymond Group Inc, The 8333 Greenway Blvd Ste 200 *Web:* www.raymondteam.com	Middleton	WI	53562	608-833-4100	
Re-Max Masters 108 Buchmans Close Cir *Web:* movesyracuse.com	Fayetteville	NY	13066	315-449-9944	
RE/MAX International Inc 5075 S Syracuse St *TF Cust Svc:* 800-525-7452 ■ *Web:* www.remax.com	Denver	CO	80237	303-770-5531	796-3599
RE/MAX of Western Canada Inc 1060 Manhattan Dr Ste 340 *TF:* 800-563-3622 ■ *Web:* www.remax.ca	Kelowna	BC	V1Y9X9	250-860-3628	860-7424
RE/MAX Ontario-Atlantic 7101 Syntex Dr *TF:* 888-542-2499 ■ *Web:* www.remax.ca	Mississauga	ON	L5N6H5	905-542-2400	542-3340
RE/MAX Quebec Inc 1500 Cunard St *TF:* 800-361-9325 ■ *Web:* www.remax-quebec.com	Laval	QC	H7S2B7	450-668-7743	668-2115
Real Estate Institute of Bc 1750 - 355 Burrard St *TF:* 800-667-2166 ■ *Web:* www.reibc.org	Vancouver	BC	V6C2G8	604-685-3702	
Real Estate One Inc 25800 NW Hwy Ste 100 *TF:* 800-521-0508 ■ *Web:* www.realestateone.com	Southfield	MI	48075	248 304 6700	263 5966
Real Living First Service Realty 13155 SW 42nd St Ste 200 *TF:* 800-899-8477 ■ *Web:* www.realliving.com	Miami	FL	33175	305-551-9400	551-4965
Real Living Inc 77 E Nationwide Blvd *TF:* 800-848-7400 ■ *Web:* www.realliving.com	Columbus	OH	43215	614-459-7400	457-6807
RealCapitalMarketscom LLC 5780 Fleet St Ste 130 *Web:* www.rcm1.com	Carlsbad	CA	92008	760-602-5080	
Realestateexpresscom 12977 N 40 Dr Ste 108 **Fax Area Code:* 314 ■ *TF:* 866-739-7277 ■ *Web:* www.realestateexpress.com	Saint Louis	MO	63141	866-739-7277	205-1613*
Reality Interactive 6121 Baker Rd Ste 115	Minnetonka	MN	55345	952-253-4700	
Realogy Corp 175 Park Ave *Web:* www.realogy.com	Madison	NJ	07940	973-407-2000	407-7779
Realty Executives International Inc 7600 N 16th St Ste 100 *TF:* 800-252-3366 ■ *Web:* www.realtyexecutives.com	Phoenix	AZ	85020	602-957-0747	224-5542
Realty Plus Chicago Inc 453 E 111th St Apt 16	Chicago	IL	60628	773-785-1400	
Reata Real Estate Services LP 1100 NE Loop 410 Ste 400 *Web:* www.reatarealestate.com	San Antonio	TX	78216	210-930-4111	
Rebman Properties Inc 1014 W Fairbanks Ave *Web:* www.rebmanproperties.com	Winter Park	FL	32789	407-875-8001	875-8004
Redstone Properties 1120 W SR- 89A Ste B2 *Web:* www.redstoneproperties.com	Sedona	AZ	86336	928-204-2500	
Redwood Adventure LLC 44075 Pipeline Plz Ste 225 *Web:* www.c21redwood.com	Ashburn	VA	20147	703-858-5676	
Reece & Nichols Realtors 11601 Granada *Web:* www.reeceandnichols.com	Leawood	KS	66211	913-945-3704	491-0930
Regional Group of Cos Inc, The 1737 Woodward Dr Second Fl *Web:* www.regionalgroup.com	Ottawa	ON	K2C0P9	613-230-2100	
Relocation Center Inc, The 1042 E Juneau Ave *TF:* 800-783-5337 ■ *Web:* www.trcgs.com	Milwaukee	WI	53202	414-226-4200	
Remax Villa Realtors 7505 Bergenline Ave *Web:* www.remax-villa.com	North Bergen	NJ	07047	201-868-3100	868-9440
RemoteReality Corp 100 Northfield Dr Ste 205 *Web:* www.remotereality.com	Windsor	CT	06095	508-870-1500	
Retail Planning Corp 35 Johnson Ferry Rd *Web:* www.retailplanningcorp.com	Marietta	GA	30068	770-956-8383	
Right at Home Properties PO Box 631154 *Web:* www.rightathomeproperties.com	Irving	TX	75063	972-333-4164	
RIS Media Inc 69 E Ave *Web:* www.rismedia.com	Norwalk	CT	06851	203-855-1234	
Ritchie Commercial 34 W Santa Clara St *Web:* www.ritchiecommercial.com	San Jose	CA	95113	408-971-2700	
Riverbay Corp 2049 Bartow Ave *Web:* www.riverbaycorp.com	Bronx	NY	10475	718-671-3050	
Rivercrest Realty Assoc 8816 Six Forks Rd Ste 201 *Web:* rivercrestrealty.com	Raleigh	NC	27615	919-846-4046	
RM Bradley One Financial Plz *Web:* www.servuscorp.com	Hartford	CT	06103	860-278-2040	
Roose & Ressler Lpa 243 E Liberty St Ste 230 *Web:* theohiodisabilitylawyers.com	Wooster	OH	44691	330-263-5333	
Rose Assoc Inc 200 Madison Ave *TF:* 888-475-8860 ■ *Web:* www.rosenyc.com	New York	NY	10016	212-210-6666	
Ross Realty Investments Inc 3325 S University Dr Ste 210 *TF:* 800-370-4202 ■ *Web:* www.ross-realty.com	Davie	FL	33328	954-452-5000	452-4700
Rothman Goodman Managmnt Corp 27236 Grand Central Pkwy	Floral Park	NY	11005	718-224-2880	
Rowell Auctions Inc 1303 Fourth St SW *Web:* rowellauctions.com	Moultrie	GA	31768	229-985-8388	
Rowley Properties Inc 1595 NW Gilman Blvd Ste 1 *Web:* www.rowleyproperties.com	Issaquah	WA	98027	425-392-6407	
Royal T Management 7419 N Cedar Ave Ste 102 *Web:* royaltmanagement.com	Fresno	CA	93720	559-447-9887	
Royco Inc The World Bldg 8121 Georgia Ave Ste 500	Silver Spring	MD	20910	301-608-2212	
Ruben Cos 600 Madison Ave *Web:* www.rubenco.com	New York	NY	10022	212-293-9400	
Russ Lyon Sotheby's International Realty 21040 N Pima Rd *Web:* www.russlyon.com	Scottsdale	AZ	85255	480-502-3500	
Russell & Jeffcoat Realtors Inc 1022 Calhoun St *Web:* www.russellandjeffcoat.com	Columbia	SC	29201	803-779-6000	
Sachse Real Estate Company Inc 315 S Beverly Dr Ste 415 *Web:* www.sachsere.com	Beverly Hills	CA	90212	310-284-7100	
Salisbury Management Inc 120 Shrewsbury St *Web:* www.salisburymanagement.com	Boylston	MA	01505	508-869-0764	
Sam Hatfield Realty Inc 4470 Mansford Rd *Web:* samhatfield.com	Winchester	TN	37398	931-968-0500	
Sandor Development Co 5725 N Scottsdale Rd Ste C-195 *Web:* sandordev.com	Scottsdale	AZ	85250	480-949-9011	
Sandy River Co 509 Forest Ave PO Box 110 *Web:* sandyrivercompany.com	Portland	ME	04112	207-879-5800	879-5810
Select Group Real Estate Inc 437 Century Park Dr Ste B *Web:* selectgroupre.com	Yuba City	CA	95991	530-237-1800	
Selective First Realty 4110 Main St *Web:* selectivefirstrealty.com	Flushing	NY	11355	718-461-2510	
Semonin Realtors 4967 US Hwy 42 Ste 200 *TF:* 800-548-1650 ■ *Web:* www.semonin.com	Louisville	KY	40222	502-425-4760	339-8950
Sereno Group Real Estate 369 S San Antonio Rd *Web:* www.serenogroup.com	Los Altos	CA	94022	650-947-2900	
Shannon Oaks 2228 Hwy 167 S	Sheridan	AR	72150	870-942-3907	
Sheldon Gross Realty Inc 80 Main St Fourth Fl *Web:* www.sheldongrossrealty.com	West Orange	NJ	07052	973-325-6200	
Shelter Canadian Properties Ltd 2600 Seven Evergreen Pl *Web:* www.scpl.com	Winnipeg	MB	R3L2T3	204-475-9090	
Shorewest Realtors Inc 17450 W N Ave *Web:* www.shorewest.com	Brookfield	WI	53008	262-827-4200	
Silicon Valley Assn of Realtors 19400 Stevens Creek Blvd Ste 100 *TF:* 877-699-6787 ■ *Web:* www.silvar.org	Cupertino	CA	95014	408-200-0100	200-0101
Situs Inc 4665 SW Fwy *Web:* www.situs.com	Houston	TX	77027	713-328-4403	355-5882
Skyline Properties South Inc 50 116th Ave SE Ste 120 *Web:* www.skylineproperties.com	Bellevue	WA	98004	425-455-2065	
Social Compact 113 S W St Third Fl *Web:* www.socialcompact.org	Alexandria	VA	22314	202-547-2581	
Solari Enterprises Inc 1572 N Main St *Web:* www.solari-ent.com	Orange	CA	92867	714-282-2520	
Solid Earth Inc 113 Clinton Ave W *Web:* www.solidearth.com	Huntsville	AL	35801	256-536-0606	
Sotheby's International Realty 38 E 61st St *TF:* 866-899-4747 ■ *Web:* www.sothebysrealty.com	New York	NY	10065	212-606-7660	606-4199
Southwest Management Group Inc 622 W Maple St Ste H	Farmington	NM	87401	505-327-3611	
Southwest Property Management Corp 1044 Castello Dr Ste 206 *Web:* www.southwestpropertymanagement.com	Naples	FL	34103	239-261-3440	
St Aubin Edwin & Co 4151 17 Mile Rd Ste A *Web:* www.michiganhousehunter.com	Sterling Heights	MI	48310	586-939-1400	
Stan Johnson Company Inc 6120 S Yale Ave Ste 813 *Web:* www.stanjohnsonco.com	Tulsa	OK	74136	918-494-2690	
Stan White Realty & Construction Inc 812 Ocean Trl *Web:* outerbanksrentals.com	Corolla	NC	27927	252-453-6131	
Steele Realty & Investment Company Inc 8900 Grant Line Rd *Web:* www.steelerealtyinc.com	Elk Grove	CA	95624	916-686-6500	686-8504
Stiles Realty Co 301 E Las Olas Blvd *Web:* www.stiles.com	Fort Lauderdale	FL	33301	954-627-9300	627-9305
Stout Management Co 10151 Park Run Dr *Web:* www.smc-lv.com	Las Vegas	NV	89145	702-227-0444	
StreamCo LLC 7130 Glen Forest Dr Ste 110 *Web:* www.streamco.net	Richmond	VA	23226	804-955-4397	
Strother Ventures II Inc 2929 Breezewood Ave Ste 200 *TF:* 855-753-6143 ■ *Web:* www.erastrother.com	Fayetteville	NC	28303	910-864-2327	
Studley Inc 399 Pk Ave 11th Fl *Web:* www.studley.com	New York	NY	10022	212-326-1000	326-1034
Stumbos & Company Real Estate 2251 Fair Oaks Blvd	Sacramento	CA	95825	916-646-4400	
Suburban Realty Inc 1055 Spring St *Web:* suburbanrealty.biz	Grafton	WI	53024	262-377-3060	
Sudberry Properties Inc 5465 Morehouse Dr Ste 260 *Web:* www.sudprop.com	San Diego	CA	92121	858-546-3000	
Summit Realty Group 111 Monument Cir Chase Tower Ste 4750 *Web:* www.summitrealtygroup.com	Indianapolis	IN	46204	317-713-2100	
Sun Realty Inc 1500 S Croatan Hwy PO Box 1630 *Web:* www.sunrealtync.com	Kill Devil Hills	NC	27948	252-441-7033	

				Phone	Fax
Surterre Properties Inc 1400 Newport Ctr Dr Ste 100 *Web:* www.surterreproperties.com	Newport Beach	CA	92660	949-717-7100	
Sutton Alliance LLC 515 Rockaway Ave *Web:* suttonalliance.com/progressive	Valley Stream	NY	11581	516-837-6100	
Tarbell Realtors 1403 N Tustin Ave Ste 380 *Web:* www.edwards.net	Santa Ana	CA	92705	714-972-0988	
Tarlton Properties Inc 955 Alma St *Web:* www.tarlton.com	Menlo Park	CA	94301	650-330-3600	
Taylor Morrison Inc 4900 N Scottsdale Rd Ste 2000 *Web:* www.taylormorrison.com	Scottsdale	AZ	85251	480-840-8100	344-7001
TCN Worldwide 400 Chisholm Pl Ste 104 *Web:* www.tcnworldwide.com	Plano	TX	75075	972-769-8701	
Terrance Company & f Wood 400 Mann St Ste 509	Crp Christi	TX	78401	361-888-8891	
Thalhimer Inc Morton G 11100 W Broad St *Web:* www.thalhimer.com	Glen Allen	VA	23060	804-648-5881	697-3479
Themlsonline Com Inc 11144 Commerce Ln N *Web:* www.themlsonline.com	Champlin	MN	55316	763-576-8286	
TheRedPincom Realty Inc 180 Bloor St W *Web:* www.theredpin.com	Toronto	ON	M5E1M2	416-800-0812	
THF Realty Inc 2127 Innerbelt Business Ctr Dr Ste 200 *Web:* www.thfrealty.com	St Louis	MO	63114	314-429-0900	
Tiempo Escrow Ii 18433 Amistad St *Web:* www.gotescrow.com	Fountain Valley	CA	92708	714-500-1500	
Tmmc 1404 Milbury St	Castle Rock	CO	80104	720-733-1369	
Tom J Keith & Assoc Inc 121 S Cool Spring St *Web:* www.keithvaluation.com	Fayetteville	NC	28301	910-323-3222	
Trammell Crow Co 2100 McKinney Ave Suite 800 *Web:* www.trammellcrow.com	Dallas	TX	75201	214-863-4101	863-4493
Travers Realty Corp 840 Newport Ctr Dr Ste 770 *Web:* www.traversrealty.com	Newport Beach	CA	92660	949-644-5900	
Tri Commercial Real Estate Services Inc 100 Pine St Ste 1000 *Web:* www.tricommercial.com	San Francisco	CA	94111	415-268-2200	268-2289
Tri Properties Inc 4309 Emperor Blvd Ste 110 *Web:* www.triprop.com	Durham	NC	27703	919-941-5745	
Tri-Land Kansas City Investors LLC One Wbrook Corporate Ctr Ste 520 *Web:* www.trilandproperties.com	Westchester	IL	60154	708-531-8210	
Trillium Residential LLC 230 W Fifth St *Web:* www.trilliumresidential.com	Tempe	AZ	85281	480-294-6300	294-6301
Trimark Properties LLC 321 SW 13th St *Web:* trimarkproperties.com	Gainesville	FL	32601	352-376-6223	
Trimont Real Estate Advisors Inc 3424 Peachtree Rd NE *Web:* www.trimontrea.com	Atlanta	GA	30326	404-420-5600	
Tvo North America 2500 Guerrero Dr	Carrollton	TX	75006	972-242-1517	
United Commercial Development Inc 7001 Preston Rd Ste 500 *Web:* www.ucdcorp.com	Dallas	TX	75205	214-224-4600	219-2080
United Country Real Estate Inc 2820 NW Barry Rd *TF:* 800-999-1020 ■ *Web:* www.unitedcountry.com	Kansas City	MO	64154	816-420-6200	
United Realty Group 8951 W Atlantic Blvd *Web:* urgfl.com	Coral Springs	FL	33071	954-670-5671	
Urdang Capital Management Inc 630 W Germantown Pk Ste 300 *Web:* centersquare.com/	Plymouth Mtng	PA	19462	610-834-9500	
US Residential Group LLC 6404 International Pkwy Ste 1010 *Web:* www.usrgroup.com	Plano	TX	75093	469-546-6400	
Vacation Palm Springs Real Estate Inc 1276 N Palm Canyon Dr Ste 211 *Web:* vacationpalmsprings.com	Palm Springs	CA	92262	760-778-7832	
Valuation Management Group LLC 1640 Powers Ferry Rd SE Bldg 100 *Web:* valuationmanagementgroup.com	Marietta	GA	30067	678-483-4420	
Victor International Corp 7640 Dixie Hwy Ste 100 *Web:* www.victorintl.com	Clarkston	MI	48346	248-364-2400	
Vintage Realty Co 330 Marshall St Ste 200 *Web:* www.vintagerealty.com	Shreveport	LA	71101	318-222-2244	
Virginia Cook Realtors LLC 5950 Sherry Ln Ste 110 *Web:* www.virginiacook.com	Dallas	TX	75225	214-696-8877	
Voit Real Estate Services Inc 101 Shipyard Way *Web:* www.voitco.com	Newport Beach	CA	92663	949-644-8648	
Walsh Property Management PO Box 2657 *Web:* www.walshpm.com	Castro Valley	CA	94546	510-888-8965	
Wangard Partners Inc 1200 N Mayfair Rd Ste 220 *Web:* www.wangard.com	Milwaukee	WI	53226	414-777-1200	
Waterfront Properties & Club Communities 825 Pkwy Ste 8 *Web:* www.waterfront-properties.com	Jupiter	FL	33477	561-746-7272	
Watson Realty Co 9101 Camino Media *TF:* 800-777-0646 ■ *Web:* www.watsonrealty.com	Bakersfield	CA	93311	661-327-5161	617-3707
Weichert Financial 6911 Laurel Bowie Rd Ste 100	Bowie	MD	20715	301-805-7788	
Weichert Realtors 1625 Rt 10 E *Web:* www.weichert.com	Morris Plains	NJ	07950	973-984-1400	984-4075
West Terrace Inc 1382 W Ninth St Ste 210 *Web:* yourerc.com/	Cleveland	OH	44113	216-696-4466	
WestCorp Management Group LLC 6655 S Eastern Ave *Web:* www.westcorpmg.com	Las Vegas	NV	89119	702-307-2881	
Westcorp Properties Inc 200 College Plz 8215 - 112 St *Web:* www.westcorp.net	Edmonton	AB	T6G2C8	780-431-3300	
Western Development Corp 1228 31st St NW Ste 200 *Web:* www.westdev.com	Washington	DC	20007	202-338-5200	333-0223
Westsiderentalscom 1020 Wilshire Blvd *Web:* www.westsiderentals.com	Santa Monica	CA	90401	310-395-7368	
Wilkinson & Assoc Real Estate Inc 8604 Cliff Cameron Dr Ste 110 *Web:* www.wilkinsonandassociates.com	Charlotte	NC	28269	704-393-0048	
William C Smith & Company Inc 1100 New Jersey Ave SE *Web:* www.wcsmith.com	Washington	DC	20003	202-371-1220	371-9410
William Douglas Management Inc 4523 Park Rd Ste 201 A *Web:* www.wmdouglas.com	Charlotte	NC	28209	704-347-8900	
Williams & Williams Real Estate Auction 7120 S Lewis Ave Ste 200 *TF:* 800-801-8003 ■ *Web:* www.williamsauction.com	Tulsa	OK	74136	918-250-2012	
Wilson Meany Sullivan LLC Four Embarcadero Ctr Ste 3330 *Web:* www.wmspartners.com	San Francisco	CA	94111	415-905-5300	
Wilson Realty Exchange Inc 16910 15th Ave Ne *Web:* wilsonrealtyexchange.com	Shoreline	WA	98155	206-367-0200	
Wilwat Properties Inc 1958 Monroe Dr Ne *Web:* www.wilwatproperties.com	Atlanta	GA	30324	404-872-8666	
Windsor Co Ltd 101 W Liberty St *Web:* www.windsorhouseinc.com	Girard	OH	44420	330-545-1550	545-2444
Winter Management Corp 730 Fifth Ave 12th Fl *Web:* winter.com/history/	New York	NY	10019	212-616-8900	616-8985
Wisconsin Management Co 2040 S Park St *Web:* wisconsinmanagement.com	Madison	WI	53713	608-258-2080	
Woodbury Corp 2733 E Parleys Way Ste 300 *Web:* www.woodburycorp.com	Salt Lake Cty	UT	84109	801-485-7770	485-0209
Woodfill & Pressler LLP 909 Fannin St 2 Houston Ctr Ste 1470	Houston	TX	77010	713-751-3080	
Youngwoo & Assoc LLC 435 Hudson St Fourth Fl *Web:* www.iyoungwoo.com	New York	NY	10014	212-477-8008	
Zalco Realty Inc 8701 Georgia Ave Ste 300 *Web:* www.gjainc.com	Silver Spring	MD	20910	301-495-6600	
Zara Realty Holding Corp 166-07 Hillside Ave *Web:* www.zararealty.com	Jamaica	NY	11432	718-291-3331	
ZipRealty Inc 2000 Powell St Ste 300 *NASDAQ: ZIPR* ■ *TF:* 800-225-5947 ■ *Web:* www.ziprealty.com	Emeryville	CA	94608	510-735-2600	735-2850
ZRS Management LLC 2001 Summit Park Dr Ste 300 *Web:* zrsmanagement.com	Orlando	FL	32810	407-644-6300	

656 REAL ESTATE DEVELOPERS

SEE ALSO Construction - Building Contractors - Non-Residential p. 2072; Construction - Building Contractors - Residential p. 2085

				Phone	Fax
A & B Properties Inc 822 Bishop St *Web:* www.abprop.com	Honolulu	HI	96813	808-525-6676	525-8447
AG Spanos Cos 10100 Trinity Pkwy Fifth Fl *Web:* www.agspanos.com	Stockton	CA	95219	209-478-7954	473-3703
Al Neyer Inc 302 W Third St Ste 800 *TF:* 877-271-6400 ■ *Web:* www.neyer.com	Cincinnati	OH	45202	513-271-6400	271-1350
Allen & O'Hara Inc PO Box 771889 Ste 300 *Web:* www.aoinc.com	Memphis	TN	38177	901-471-2080	471-2087
Alter Group 5500 W Howard St *TF:* 800-637-4842 ■ *Web:* www.altergroup.com	Skokie	IL	60077	847-676-4300	676-4302
Amerco Real Estate Co 2727 N Central Ave Ste 500 *TF General:* 800-528-0463 ■ *Web:* www.amercorealestate.com	Phoenix	AZ	85004	602-263-6555	277-5824
American West Homes 250 Pilot Rd Ste 140 *Web:* www.americanwesthomes.com	Las Vegas	NV	89119	702-736-6434	617-0281
AMLI Residential Properties Trust 200 W Monroe St Ste 2200 *Web:* www.amli.com	Chicago	IL	60606	312-283-4700	283-4720
AMREP Corp 300 Alexander Pk Ste 204 *NYSE: AXR* ■ *Web:* www.amrepcorp.com	Princeton	NJ	08540	609-716-8200	716-8255
AMREP Southwest Inc 333 New Mexico 528 Ste 400 *Web:* www.amrepsw.com	Rio Rancho	NM	87124	505-892-9200	
Asset Plus Co 675 Bering Dr Ste 200 *Web:* www.assetpluscorp.com	Houston	TX	77057	713-782-5800	268-5111
AV Homes Inc 8601 N Scottsdale Rd Ste 225 *NASDAQ: AVHI* ■ *TF:* 866-392-4286 ■ *Web:* www.avhomesinc.com	Scottsdale	AR	85283	480-214-7400	
Barone Galasso & Assoc Inc 710 W Ivy *Web:* www.baronegalasso.com	San Diego	CA	92101	619-232-2100	
Beazer Homes 9202 N Meridian St Ste 300 *Web:* www.beazer.com	Indianapolis	IN	46260	317-574-1950	846-0398
Beazer Homes USA Inc 1000 Abernathy Rd Ste 1200 *NYSE: BZH* ■ *Web:* www.beazer.com	Atlanta	GA	30328	770-829-3700	481-0431
Bellmont Cabinet Co 13610 52nd St E Ste 300 *Web:* bellmontcabinets.com	Sumner	WA	98390	253-321-3011	
Belz Enterprises 100 Peabody Pl Ste 1400 *Web:* www.belz.com	Memphis	TN	38103	901-767-4780	271-7238
BPG Properties Ltd 1500 Market St 3200 Ctr Sq W *Web:* www.equuspartners.com	Philadelphia	PA	19102	215-496-0400	496-0431
Brooks Resources Corp 409 NW Franklin Ave *TF:* 877-475-9779 ■ *Web:* brooks-resources.com	Bend	OR	97701	541-382-1662	385-3285

	City	State	ZIP	Phone	Fax
Brothers Property Corp Two Alhambra Plz Ste 1280 *Web:* www.brothersproperty.com	Coral Gables	FL	33134	305-285-1035	858-2733
Butler Real Estate 1540 Genessee St *Web:* www.butlermfg.com	Kansas City	MO	64102	816-968-3000	968-3720
Buzz Oates Construction LP 8615 Elder Creek Rd *Web:* www.buzzoates.com	Sacramento	CA	95828	916-379-3800	
Cadillac Fairview Ltd 20 Queen St W Fifth Fl *Web:* www.cadillacfairview.com	Toronto	ON	M5H3R4	416-598-8200	598-8578
Cafaro Co 2445 Belmont Ave *Web:* www.cafarocompany.com	Youngstown	OH	44504	330-747-2661	743-2902
California Pacific Homes 38 Executive Pk Ste 200 *Web:* www.calpacifichomes.com	Irvine	CA	92614	949-833-6000	833-6133
Cannon Instrument Co 2139 High Tech Rd *Web:* www.cannoninstrument.com	State College	PA	16803	814-353-8000	
Cappelli Enterprises Inc 115 E Stevens Ave *Web:* www.cappelli-inc.com	Valhalla	NY	10595	914-769-6500	747-9268
Carlisle Corp 263 Wagner Pl *Web:* www.carlislecorp.com	Memphis	TN	38103	901-526-5000	
Casden Properties LLC 9090 Wilshire Blvd	Beverly Hills	CA	90211	310-274-5553	276-6486
Castle & Cooke Inc 10900 Wilshire Blvd Ste 1600 *Web:* www.castlecooke.net	Los Angeles	CA	90024	310-208-3636	
CenterCal Properties LLC 7455 SW Bridgeport Rd Ste 205 *Web:* www.centercal.com	Tigard	OR	97224	503-968-8940	
CFC Inc 320 W Eigth St Ste 200 *Web:* www.cfcproperties.com	Bloomington	IN	47402	812-332-0053	333-4680
Chelsea Investment Corp 5993 Avenida Encinas Ste 101 *Web:* www.chelseainvestco.com	Carlsbad	CA	92008	760-456-6000	456-6001
Christopherson Homes Inc 1315 Airport Blvd *Web:* www.christophersonhomes.com	Santa Rosa	CA	95403	707-524-8222	360-6208
Comstock Holding Companies Inc 1886 Metro Ctr Dr 4th Fl *NASDAQ: CHCI* ■ *Web:* www.comstockhomebuilding.com	Reston	VA	20190	703-883-1700	760-1520
Connell Realty & Development Co 200 Connell Dr *TF:* 800-233-3240 ■ *Web:* www.connell-realestate.com	Berkeley Heights	NJ	07922	908-673-3700	673-3800
Conner Homes Co 846 108th Ave NE *Web:* www.connerhomes.com	Bellevue	WA	98004	425-455-9280	462-0426
Cooper Communities Inc 903 N 47th St *Web:* www.cooper-communities.com	Rogers	AR	72756	479-246-6500	
Corcoran Jennison Development Co 150 Mt Vernon St Bayside Ofc Ctr Ste 500 *Web:* www.corcoranjennison.com	Boston	MA	02125	617-822-7350	822-7352
Cornerstone Group 2100 Hollywood Blvd *TF:* 800-809-4099 ■ *Web:* www.theapartmentcorner.com	Hollywood	FL	33020	305-443-8288	
Coscan Homes LLC 5555 Ravenswood Rd	Fort Lauderdale	FL	33312	954-620-1000	
CountryTyme Inc 3451 Cincinnati-Zanesville Rd SW *TF:* 800-213-8365 ■ *Web:* www.countrytyme.com	Lancaster	OH	43130	740-475-6001	
Crescent Resources Inc 227 W Trade St Ste 1000 *Web:* crescentcommunities.com/	Charlotte	NC	28202	980-321-6000	
Cullinan Properties Ltd 2020 W War Memorial Dr Ste 103 *Web:* www.cullinanproperties.com	Peoria	IL	61614	309-999-1700	
Darling Homes 2500 Legacy Dr Ste 100 **Fax Area Code: 972* ■ *Web:* www.darlinghomes.com	Frisco	TX	75034	469-252-2200	624-4106*
David Weekley Homes Inc 1111 N Post Oak Rd *TF:* 800-390-6774 ■ *Web:* www.davidweekleyhomes.com	Houston	TX	77055	713-963-0500	963-0322
De Anza Land & Leisure Corp 1615 Cordova St	Los Angeles	CA	90007	323-734-9951	734-2531
Deltona Corp 8014 SW 135th St Rd *TF:* 800-935-6378 ■ *Web:* www.deltona.com	Ocala	FL	34473	352-347-2322	307-8103
Desert Mountain Properties LP 37700 Desert Mountain Pkwy *Web:* www.desertmountain.com	Scottsdale	AZ	85262	480-488-2998	
Development Services of America 16100 N 71st St Ste 520 *Web:* www.developmentservicesofamerica.com/corpcenterseattle.html	Scottsdale	AZ	85254	480-927-4892	
Dixon Builders & Developers Inc 8050 Beckett Crt D Ste 213 *Web:* www.dixonbuilders.com	West Chester	OH	45069	513-887-6400	887-6643
Dominion Homes Inc 4900 Tuttle Crossing Blvd *Web:* www.dominionhomes.com	Dublin	OH	43016	614-356-5000	
Donohoe Cos Inc 2101 Wisconsin Ave NW *Web:* www.donohoe.com	Washington	DC	20007	202-333-0880	342-3924
Double Diamond Co 5495 Belt Line Rd Suite 200 *TF:* 800-324-7438 ■ *Web:* www.ddresorts.com	Dallas	TX	75254	214-706-9801	706-9878
DR Horton Inc 301 Commerce St Ste 500 *NYSE: DHI* ■ *TF:* 800-846-7866 ■ *Web:* www.drhorton.com	Fort Worth	TX	76102	817-390-8200	
Duffel Financial & Construction Co 1430 Willow Pass Rd Ste 220	Concord	CA	94520	925-603-8444	603-8440
East West Partners Management Co 14700 Village Sq Pl *Web:* www.eastwestrealty.com	Midlothian	VA	23112	804-739-3800	
EJM Development Co 9061 Santa Monica Blvd *Web:* www.ejmdevelopment.com	Los Angeles	CA	90069	310-278-1830	278-2965
Elliott Homes 80 Iron Pt Cir Ste 110 *Web:* www.elliotthomes.com	Folsom	CA	95630	916-984-1300	984-1322
Embrey Partners Ltd 1020 NE Loop 410 Ste 700 *Web:* www.embreydc.com	San Antonio	TX	78209	210-824-6044	824-7656
Emmer Group 2801 SW Archer Rd *Web:* www.emmergroup.com	Gainesville	FL	32608	352-376-2444	376-2260
Epcon Communities Inc 500 Stonehenge Pkwy *Web:* epconcommunities.com	Dublin	OH	43017	614-761-1010	
Ergon Properties Inc PO Box 1639 *TF:* 800-824-2626 ■ *Web:* www.ergonproperties.com	Jackson	MS	39215	601-933-3174	
Fieldstone Homes Two Ada *TF:* 800-665-0661 ■ *Web:* www.fieldstone-homes.com	Irvine	CA	92618	949-790-5400	453-0944
First Hartford Corp 149 Colonial Rd *OTC: FHRT* ■ *TF:* 888-646-6555 ■ *Web:* www.firsthartford.com	Manchester	CT	06042	860-646-6555	646-8572
Flagship Properties Corp One Greenway Plz Ste 750 *Web:* flagshipco.com	Houston	TX	77046	713-623-6000	
Flournoy Development Co 900 Brookstone Ctr Pkwy *Web:* flournoycompanies.com/	Columbus	GA	31904	706-324-4000	324-4150
Forest City Commercial Group 50 Public Sq Ste 1515 *Web:* www.forestcity.net/company/people/commercial/pages/default.aspx	Cleveland	OH	44113	216-416-3906	
Forest City Enterprises Inc 50 Public Sq 1100 Terminal Twr *NYSE: FCEA* ■ *Web:* www.forestcity.net	Cleveland	OH	44113	216-736-7646	416-3916
Forest City Equity Services Inc 50 Public Sq Ste 1170 *Web:* www.forestcity.net/contact/pages/residential_development_inquiries.aspx	Cleveland	OH	44113	216-621-6060	
Forest City Land Group 50 Public Sq Ste 1515 *Web:* www.forestcity.net	Cleveland	OH	44113	216-416-3906	
Forest City Ratner Cos (FCRC) One MetroTech Ctr N *Web:* www.forestcity.net	Brooklyn	NY	11201	718-923-8400	
Forsberg Real Estate Co 2422 Jolly Rd Ste 200 *Web:* www.lansingrealestate.com	Okemos	MI	48864	517-349-9330	349-7131
Friendswood Development Co 11506 Island Manor St Ste 100	Pearland	TX	77584	281-875-1552	872-4207
Gambone Bros Development Co 1030 W Germantown Pk PO Box 287 *Web:* www.gambone.com	Fairview Village	PA	19409	610-539-4700	539-2020
Gatehouse Group Inc, The 120 Forbes Blvd Ste 180 *Web:* gatehousemgt.com	Mansfield	MA	02048	508-337-2500	
Gehan Homes 15725 N Dallas Pkwy Ste 300 *Web:* www.gehanhomes.com	Addison	TX	75001	972-383-4300	383-4399
Gentry Homes Ltd 560 N Nimitz Hwy **Fax: Sales* ■ *Web:* www.gentryhawaii.com	Honolulu	HI	96809	808-599-5558	599-8347*
Gilbane Inc Seven Jackson Walkway *TF:* 800-445-2263 ■ *Web:* www.gilbaneco.com	Providence	RI	02903	401-456-5890	456-5996
Ginsburg Development Cos LLC (GDC) 100 Summit Lk Dr *Web:* www.gdc-homes.com	Valhalla	NY	10595	914-747-3600	747-1608
GJ Grewe Inc 9109 Watson Rd *Web:* www.gjgrewe.com	Saint Louis	MO	63126	314-962-6300	
GL Homes of Florida Corp 1600 Sawgrass Corporate Pkwy Ste 400 *Web:* www.glhomes.com	Sunrise	FL	33323	954-753-1730	753-4509
Goldenberg Group Inc, The 630 Sentry Pkwy Ste 300 *Web:* www.goldenberggroup.com	Blue Bell	PA	19422	610-260-9600	
Goldrich & Kest Industries 5150 Overland Ave *Web:* www.gkind.com	Culver City	CA	90230	310-204-2050	204-1900
Grand Homes Inc 5150 Keller Springs Rd *Web:* www.grandhomes.com	Dallas	TX	75001	214-750-6528	750-6849
Greenwood Communities & Resorts Inc 104 Maxwell Ave *Web:* www.greenwoodcr.com	Greenwood	SC	29646	864-941-4044	
Haas & Haynie Corp 400 Oyster Pt Blvd Ste 123 *Web:* www.hh1898.com	South San Francisco	CA	94080	650-588-5600	873-9150
Hamilton Co, The 39 Brighton Ave *Web:* www.thehamiltoncompany.com	Allston	MA	02134	617-783-0039	783-0568
Hamilton Partners Inc 300 Park Blvd Ste 500 *Web:* www.hamiltonpartners.com	Itasca	IL	60143	630-250-9700	
Hamlet Homes 308 East 4500 South Ste 200 *Web:* www.hamlethomes.com	Salt Lake City	UT	84107	801-281-2223	281-2224
Harbour Homes LLC 1441 N 34th St Ste 200 *Web:* www.harbourhomes.com	Seattle	WA	98103	206-315-8130	315-8131
Harristown Development Corp 11 N 3rd St *Web:* strawberrysquare.com	Harrisburg	PA	17101	717-236-5061	236-8975
Hartz Construction Co Inc 9026 Heritage Pkwy *Web:* www.hartzhomes.com	Woodridge	IL	60517	630-228-3800	228-4910
Hartz Mountain Real Estate 400 Plz Dr *Web:* www.hartzmountain.com	Secaucus	NJ	07094	201-348-1200	348-4358
Hearn Co, The 875 N Michigan Ave Ste 4100 *Web:* www.hearncompany.com	Chicago	IL	60611	312-408-3000	408-3010
Hff Inc 301 Grant St Ste 600 *NYSE: HF* ■ *Web:* www.hfflp.com	Pittsburgh	PA	15219	412-281-8714	281-2792
Highland Homes 5601 Democracy Dr Ste 300 *Web:* www.highlandhomes.com	Dallas	TX	75024	972-789-3500	
Hills Communities Inc 4901 Hunt Rd *Web:* www.hillsinc.com	Cincinnati	OH	45242	513-984-0300	618-7681
Hilton New Orleans Riverside 2 Poydras St *Web:* hiltonneworleansriverside.com	New Orleans	LA	70130	504-561-0500	
Hines Interest LP 2800 Post Oak Blvd *TF:* 800-891-7017 ■ *Web:* www.hines.com	Houston	TX	77056	713-621-8000	966-2636
Hoffman Homes for Youth PO Box 4777 *Web:* www.hoffmanhomes.com	Gettysburg	PA	17325	717-359-7148	359-2600
Hofmann Co, The 1380 Galaxy Way *Web:* www.hofmannhomes.com	Concord	CA	94520	925-682-4830	682-4771
Holiday Builders Inc 2293 W Eau Gallie Blvd *TF:* 866-431-2533 ■ *Web:* www.holidaybuilders.com	Melbourne	FL	32935	321-610-5172	

Phone | Fax

Hunt Midwest Enterprises Inc
8300 NE Underground Dr .... Kansas City MO 64161 816-455-2500
TF: 800-551-6877 ■ *Web:* www.huntmidwest.com

Hunt Midwest Residential Development
8300 NE Underground Dr .... Kansas City MO 64161 816-455-2500 455-2890
TF: 800-551-6877 ■ *Web:* www.huntmidwest.com

IDI Group Cos 1700 N Moore St Ste 2020 .... Arlington VA 22209 703-558-7300 558-7377
Web: www.idigroup.com

Inland Real Estate Development Corp
2901 Butterfield Rd .... Oak Brook IL 60523 630-218-8000 990-5350
TF: 866-954-5692 ■ *Web:* www.inlandgroup.com

Instrument Development Corp Inc
820 Swan Dr .... Mukwonago WI 53149 262-363-7307
Web: www.idcwi.com

Intervest Construction Inc
2379 Beville Rd .... Daytona Beach FL 32119 855-215-297
Web: www.icihomes.com

Irvine Co 550 Newport Ctr Dr .... Newport Beach CA 92660 949-720-2000 720-2218*
**Fax:* Hum Res ■ *Web:* www.irvinecompany.com

Iskalo Development Corp
Harbinger Sq 5166 Main St .... Williamsville NY 14221 716-633-2096
Web: www.iskalo.com

Ivory Homes 970 E Woodoak Ln .... Salt Lake City UT 84117 888-455-5561 747-7090*
**Fax Area Code:* 801 ■ *Web:* www.ivoryhomes.com

JA Billipp Co 6925 Portwest Dr Ste 130 .... Houston TX 77024 713-426-5000
TF: 800-216-9013 ■ *Web:* www.jabillipp.com

JAIR LYNCH Development Partners
1508 U St NW .... Washington DC 20009 202-462-1092
Web: www.jairlynch.com

JJ Gumberg Company Inc 1051 Brinton Rd .... Pittsburgh PA 15221 412-244-4000 244-9133
Web: www.jjgumberg.com

JMC Communities
2201 Fourth St N Ste 200 .... Saint Petersburg FL 33704 727-823-0022 821-2007
TF: 800-741-4106 ■ *Web:* www.jmccommunities.com

John Buck Co One N Wacker Dr Ste 2400 .... Chicago IL 60606 312-993-9800 993-0857
Web: www.tjbc.com

John F Buchan Homes 2821 Northup Way Ste 100 .... Bellevue WA 98004 425-827-2266 827-0462
TF: 866-528-2426 ■ *Web:* www.buchan.com

John F Long Properties LLLP
5035 W Camelback Rd .... Phoenix AZ 85031 602-272-0421 846-7208*
**Fax Area Code:* 623 ■ *Web:* www.jflong.com

John Wieland Homes & Neighborhoods
4125 Atlanta Rd SE .... Smyrna GA 30080 770-996-2400 907-3481
TF: 800-376-4663 ■ *Web:* www.jwhomes.com

Jupiter Realty Corp 401 Michigan Ave Ste 1300 .... Chicago IL 60611 312-642-6000 642-2316
Web: www.jupiterrealty.com

Kaiser Ventures LLC
3633 Inland Empire Blvd Ste 480 .... Ontario CA 91764 909-483-8500

KB Home 10990 Wilshire Blvd Seventh Fl .... Los Angeles CA 90024 310-231-4000 231-4222
NYSE: KBH ■ *TF:* 800-304-0657 ■ *Web:* www.kbhome.com

Kettler 1751 Pinnacle Dr Ste 700 .... McLean VA 22102 703-641-9000 641-9630
Web: www.kettler.com

Keystone Builders Resource Group Inc
1207 Roseneath Rd Ste 200 .... Richmond VA 23230 804-354-8830 358-6976
Web: www.keybuild.com

Kravco Co 234 Mall Blvd .... King of Prussia PA 19406 610-854-2800 768-6444
Web: www.kravco.com

Lancia Homes 9430 Lima Rd Ste A .... Fort Wayne IN 46818 260-489-4433
Web: www.lanciahomes.com

LCOR Inc 850 Cassatt Rd Ste 300 .... Berwyn PA 19312 610-251-9110 408-4420
Web: www.lcor.com

LeCesse Development Corp
650 S Northlake Blvd Ste 450 .... Altamonte Springs FL 32701 407-645-5575 645-0553
Web: www.lecesse.com

Legacy Property Group LLC
300 Marietta St NW Ste 304 .... Atlanta GA 30313 404-222-9100 222-9090
Web: www.legacyproperty.com

Legend Homes Corp 12755 SW 69th Ave Ste 100 .... Portland OR 97223 503-620-8080 598-8900
TF: 888-782-7937 ■ *Web:* www.legendhomes.com

Lord Baltimore Properties
6225 Smith Ave Ste B100 .... Baltimore MD 21209 410-415-7638 580-9250
Web: www.lordbaltimoreprop.com

Lozier Homes Corp 1203 114th Ave SE .... Bellevue WA 98004 425-454-8690 646-8695

M/I Homes Inc Three Easton Oval .... Columbus OH 43219 614-418-8700 418-8080
NYSE: MHO ■ *TF:* 888-644-4111 ■ *Web:* www.mihomes.com

Magellan Development Group LLC
225 N Columbus Dr Ste 100 .... Chicago IL 60601 312-642-8869
Web: www.magellandevelopment.com

Maui Land & Pineapple Company Inc
120 Kane St PO Box 187 .... Kahului HI 96733 808-877-3351 871-0953
Web: www.mauiland.com

McGuyer Homebuilders Inc (MHI)
7676 Woodway Ste 104 .... Houston TX 77063 713-952-6767 952-5637
Web: www.mcguyerhomebuilders.com

McKee Group 940 W Sproul Rd Ste 301 .... Springfield PA 19064 610-604-9800
Web: www.mckeebuilders.com

McStain Neighborhoods 7100 N Broadway Ste 5-H .... Denver CO 80221 303-494-5900
Web: www.mcstain.com

Meritage Homes Corp
17851 N 85th St Ste 300 .... Scottsdale AZ 85255 480-515-8100
NYSE: MTH ■ *Web:* www.meritagehomes.com

Metro Development Group
2502 N Rocky Point Dr Ste 1050 .... Tampa FL 33607 813-288-8078
Web: mdgflorida.com

Mid-West Terminal Warehouse Company Inc
1700 Universal Ave .... Kansas City MO 64120 816-231-8811 231-0020
Web: www.mwtco.com

Miller & Smith Cos 8401 Greensboro Dr Ste 300 .... McLean VA 22102 703-821-2500
Web: www.millerandsmith.com

Mitchell Company Inc
41 W I-65 Service Rd N
Colonial Bank Ctr Third Fl .... Mobile AL 36608 251-380-2929 345-1264
Web: www.mitchellcompany.com

Mitsubishi Estate NY Inc
1221 Ave of the Americas 17th Fl .... New York NY 10020 212-698-2200 698-2211

Moceri Development Corp
3005 University Dr Ste 100 .... Auburn Hills MI 48326 248-340-9400 340-9401
Web: www.moceri.com

Morningside Equities Group Inc
223 W Erie St Third Fl .... Chicago IL 60654 312-280-7770
Web: www.morningsideusa.com

Narragansett Improvement Co
223 Allens Ave .... Providence RI 02903 401-331-7420 351-6444
Web: www.nicori.com

Newhall Land 25124 Springfield Ct Ste 300 .... Valencia CA 91355 661-255-4000 255-3960
Web: www.valencia.com

Newmark Knight Frank 125 Pk Ave .... New York NY 10017 212-372-2000 372-2426
Web: www.ngkf.com

Norwood Builders Inc 250 S NE Hwy Ste 300 .... Park Ridge IL 60068 847-655-7700 655-7701
Web: www.norwoodbuilders.com

NTS Development Co 10172 Linn Stn Rd .... Louisville KY 40223 502-426-4800 426-4994
Web: www.ntsdevelopment.com

NTS Realty Holdings LP 10172 Linn Stn Rd .... Louisville KY 40223 502-426-4800 426-4994
NYSE: NLP ■ *Web:* www.ntsdevelopment.com

Orleans Homebuilders Inc
3333 St Rd 1 Greenwood Sq Ste 101 .... Bensalem PA 19020 215-245-7500
Web: orleanshomes.com

Ovation Development Corp
6021 S Ft Apache Rd Ste 100 .... Las Vegas NV 89148 702-990-2390

Pacific American Group LLC
104 Caledonia St .... Sausalito CA 94965 415-331-3838
Web: www.pacamgroup.com

Paparone Corp 702 N White Horse Pk .... Stratford NJ 08084 856-784-0550 627-0650
Web: www.paparonenewhomes.com

Paramount Group Inc 1633 Broadway Ste 1801 .... New York NY 10019 212-237-3100 237-3197
Web: www.paramount-group.com

Peebles Corp, The 5937 Collins Ave .... Miami Beach FL 33140 305-993-5050 360-1764*
**Fax Area Code:* 786 ■ *Web:* www.peeblescorp.com

Picerne Real Estate Group
75 Lambert Lind Hwy .... Warwick RI 02886 401-732-3700 738-6452
Web: www.picerne.com

Pineloch Management Inc
102 W Pineloch Ave Ste 10 .... Orlando FL 32806 407-859-3550 650-0303
Web: www.pineloch.com

Pitcairn Properties Inc
165 Township Line Rd .... Jenkintown PA 19046 215-690-3000 690-3100
Web: www.pitcairnproperties.com

Pizzuti Inc 629 N High St Ste 500 .... Columbus OH 43215 614-280-4000 280-5000
Web: www.pizzuti.com

Polygon Northwest Co
11624 SE Fifth St Ste 200 .... Bellevue WA 98005 425-586-7700 688-0500
TF: 800-765-9466 ■ *Web:* www.polygonhomes.com

Porten Cos 333 NE Second St .... Delray Beach FL 33483 561-819-1109

Post Properties Inc
4401 Northside Pkwy Ste 800 .... Atlanta GA 30327 404-846-5000 846-6161*
NYSE: PPS ■ **Fax:* Hum Res ■ *Web:* www.postproperties.com

Prairie Management & Development Inc
333 N Michigan Ave Ste 1700 .... Chicago IL 60601 312-644-1055

Prestige Properties & Development Company Inc
546 Fifth Ave .... New York NY 10036 212-944-0444

Puget Western Inc 19515 N Creek Pkwy Ste 310 .... Bothell WA 98011 425-487-6550 487-6565
Web: pugetwestern.com

Quadrant Corp 14725 SE 36 St .... Bellevue WA 98006 425-455-2900 646-8300
Web: www.quadranthomes.com

Redd Brown & Williams
201 Bridge St PO Box 1720 .... Paintsville KY 41240 606-789-8119 789-5414
Web: www.rbandw.com

Related Group of Florida 315 S Biscayne Blvd .... Miami FL 33131 305-460-9900 460-9911
Web: www.relatedgroup.com

Related Midwest 350 W Hubbard St Ste 300 .... Chicago IL 60654 312-595-7400
Web: www.relatedmidwest.com

Republic Properties Corp
1280 MD Ave SW Ste 280 .... Washington DC 20024 202-552-5300 552-5320
Web: www.republicpropertiescorp.com

Richman Group of Cos 340 Pemberwick Rd .... Greenwich CT 06831 203-869-0900 869-1034
TF: 800-333-3509 ■ *Web:* www.therichmangroup.com

Richmond American Homes Inc 4350 S Monaco St .... Denver CO 80237 303-773-2727
TF: 888-402-4663 ■ *Web:* www.richmondamerican.com

Robson Communities 9532 E Riggs Rd .... Sun Lakes AZ 85248 800-732-9949 895-0136*
**Fax Area Code:* 480 ■ *TF:* 800-732-9949 ■ *Web:* www.robson.com

Ryland Group Inc, The
3011 Townsgate Rd Ste 200 .... Westlake Village CA 91361 805-367-3800
NYSE: RYL ■ *Web:* www.ryland.com

S & A Custom Built Homes
2121 Old Gatesburg Rd Ste 200 .... State College PA 16803 814-231-4780 272-8821
Web: www.sahomebuilder.com

Sabey Corp
12201 Tukwila International Blvd Fourth Fl .... Seattle WA 98168 206-281-8700 282-9951
Web: www.sabey.com

Schatten Properties Management Company Inc
1514 S St .... Nashville TN 37212 615-329-3011 327-2343
TF: 800-892-1315 ■ *Web:* www.schattenproperties.com

Schostak Bros & Company Inc
17800 Laurel Pk Dr N Ste 200C .... Livonia MI 48152 248-262-1000 262-1814
Web: www.schostak.com

Sea Pines Resort, The
32 Greenwood Dr .... Hilton Head Island SC 29928 843-785-3333
TF: 866-561-8802 ■ *Web:* www.seapines.com

Sea Trail Corp 75A Clubhouse Rd .... Sunset Beach NC 28468 910-287-1100
TF: 888-321-9076 ■ *Web:* www.seatrail.com

SEDA Construction Co
2120 Corporate Sq Blvd Ste 3 .... Jacksonville FL 32216 904-724-7800 727-9500
Web: www.sedaconstruction.com

Shea Homes Inc
8800 N Gainey Ctr Dr Ste 350 .... Scottsdale AZ 85258 480-348-6000
Web: m.sheahomes.com

Company / Address	City	State	Zip	Phone	Fax
Shelter Group, The 218 N Charles St Ste 220	Baltimore	MD	21201	410-962-0595	347-0587
Web: www.thesheltergroup.com					
Shodeen Inc 17 N First St	Geneva	IL	60134	630-232-8694	
Web: shodeen.com					
Silver Saddle Ranch & Club Inc					
20751 Aristotle Dr	California City	CA	93505	760-373-8617	
Web: www.silversaddleranch.com					
Simpson Housing LLLP (SHLP)					
8110 E Union Ave Ste 200	Denver	CO	80237	303-283-4100	
Web: www.simpsonhousing.com					
Singh Homes Inc					
7125 OrchaRd Lk Rd Ste 200	West Bloomfield	MI	48322	248-865-1600	865-1630
Web: www.singhweb.com					
Skanska USA Inc 1616 Whitestone Expy	Whitestone	NY	11356	718-767-2600	767-2663
Web: www.skanska.com					
South Shore Harbor Development Ltd					
2525 S Shore Blvd Ste 207	League City	TX	77573	281-334-7501	
Web: www.southshoreharbour.com					
Space Ctr Inc 2501 Rosegate	Saint Paul	MN	55113	651-604-4200	604-4222
Web: www.spacecenterinc.com					
Stanley Martin Cos					
11111 Sunset Hills Rd Ste 200	Reston	VA	20190	703-964-5000	715-8076
TF: 800-446-4807 ■ *Web:* www.stanleymartin.com					
Steiner & Assoc Inc 4016 Townsfair Way	Columbus	OH	43219	614-414-7300	414-7311
Web: www.steiner.com					
Stiles Corp 301 East Las Olas Blvd	Fort Lauderdale	FL	33301	954-627-9300	627-9288
Web: www.stiles.com					
Stratus Properties Inc 212 Lavaca St Ste 300	Austin	TX	78701	512-478-5788	478-6340
NYSE: STRS ■ *TF:* 800-690-0315 ■ *Web:* www.stratusproperties.com					
Sueba USA Corp 1800 W Loop S Ste 1300	Houston	TX	77027	713-961-3588	961-1343
Web: www.suebausa.com					
Susquehanna Real Estate					
140 E Market St PO Box 2026	York	PA	17401	717-848-5500	771-1430
Web: www.susquehanna-realestate.com					
TAK Construction 60 Walnut Ave Ste 400	Clark	NJ	07066	732-340-0700	340-0850
Web: www.takgroupinc.com					
TELACU 5400 E Olympic Blvd Third Fl	Los Angeles	CA	90022	323-721-1655	724-3372
Web: www.telacu.com					
Toll Bros Inc 250 Gibraltar Rd	Horsham	PA	19044	215-938-8000	938-8217*
NYSE: TOL ■ **Fax:* Mktg ■ *TF:* 855-897-8655 ■ *Web:* www.tollbrothers.com					
Trammell Crow Co 2100 McKinney Ave Suite 800	Dallas	TX	75201	214-863-4101	863-4493
Web: www.trammellcrow.com					
Trammell Crow Residential (TCR) 3819 Maple St	Dallas	TX	75219	770-801-1600	861-7622*
**Fax Area Code:* 614 ■ *Web:* www.tcresidential.com					
TransCon Builders Inc 25250 Rockside Rd	Cleveland	OH	44146	440-439-2100	439-6710
TF: 800-451-2608 ■ *Web:* www.transconbuilders.com					
TW Lewis 850 W Elliot Rd Ste 101	Tempe	AZ	85284	480-820-0807	820-1455
Web: www.twlewis.com					
Uniwell Corp 21172 Figueroa St	Carson	CA	90745	310-782-8888	
Victory Housing Inc					
5430 Grosvenor Ln Ste 210	Bethesda	MD	20814	301-493-6000	493-9788
Web: www.victoryhousing.org					
Village Builders 550 Greens Pkwy Ste 200	Houston	TX	77067	281-873-4663	877-1697
Web: www.lennar.com					
Village Green Cos 30833 NW Hwy	Farmington Hills	MI	48334	248-851-9600	851-6161
TF: 800-521-2220 ■ *Web:* www.villagegreen.com					
Villages of Lake Sumter Inc					
1000 Lk Sumter Landing	The Villages	FL	32162	352-753-2270	
TF: 800-245-1081 ■ *Web:* www.thevillages.com					
Vineland Construction Co 71 W Pk Ave	Vineland	NJ	08360	856-794-4500	794-4721
Web: www.vinelandconstruction.com					
Walt Disney Imagineering 500 S Vuenavista St	Burbank	CA	91521	407-939-2273	544-7995*
**Fax Area Code:* 818 ■ *Web:* disneyworld.disney.go.com					
Walton Associated Company Inc					
2001 Financial Way Ste 200	Glendora	CA	91741	626-963-8505	914-7016
Waters Mcpherson Mcneill Pc					
300 Lighting Way Seventh Fl PO Box 1560	Secaucus	NJ	07096	201-863-4400	863-2866
Web: www.lawwmm.com					
Watson Land Co 22010 S Wilmington Ave Ste 400	Carson	CA	90745	310-952-6400	522-8788
Web: www.watsonlandcompany.com					
Wave Crest Development Inc					
530 Chestnut St	Santa Cruz	CA	95060	831-423-2100	
Web: www.wavecrestdevelopment.com					
WCI Communities Inc					
24301 Walden Ctr Dr	Bonita Springs	FL	34134	239-498-8200	498-8278*
**Fax:* Hum Res ■ *TF:* 800-924-4005 ■ *Web:* www.wcicommunities.com					
Weiss Homes Inc 828 E Jefferson Blvd	South Bend	IN	46617	574-234-7373	
Western Golf Properties LLC					
One Spectrum Pointe Dr Ste 310	Lake Forest	CA	92630	949-417-3251	
Web: www.cacm.org					
Weyerhaeuser Co 33663 Weyerhaeuser Way S	Federal Way	WA	98003	253-924-2345	924-2685
NYSE: WY ■ *TF:* 800-525-5440 ■ *Web:* www.weyerhaeuser.com					
Willard Cos Inc, The					
75 Builders Pride Dr Ste 200	Hardy	VA	24101	540-721-5288	
Web: www.thewillardcompanies.com					
Wispark LLC 301 W Wisconsin Ave Ste 400	Milwaukee	WI	53203	414-274-4600	274-4640
Web: www.wispark.com					
Wooldridge Organization					
395 Taylor Blvd Ste 120	Pleasant Hill	CA	94523	925-680-7979	
Zaremba Group 14600 Detroit Ave	Cleveland	OH	44107	216-221-6600	221-9742
Web: www.zarembagroup.com					
Zicka Homes 7861 E Kemper Rd	Cincinnati	OH	45249	513-247-3500	247-3512
Web: www.zickahomes.com					

657 REAL ESTATE INVESTMENT TRUSTS (REITS)

Company / Address	City	State	Zip	Phone	Fax
Acadia Realty Trust					
1311 Mamaroneck Ave Ste 260	White Plains	NY	10605	914-288-8100	428-2380
NYSE: AKR ■ *TF:* 800-937-5449 ■ *Web:* www.acadiarealty.com					
Alexandria Real Estate Equities Inc					
385 E Colorado Blvd Ste 299	Pasadena	CA	91101	626-578-0777	578-0896
NYSE: ARE ■ *TF:* 800-776-9437 ■ *Web:* are.com					
American Campus Communities Inc					
12700 Hill Country Blvd Ste T-200	Austin	TX	78738	512-732-1000	732-2450
NYSE: ACC ■ *Web:* www.americancampus.com					
AMLI Residential 200 W Monroe St Ste 2200	Chicago	IL	60606	312-283-4700	283-4720
Web: www.amli.com					
Anworth Mortgage Asset Corp					
1299 Ocean Ave Second Fl	Santa Monica	CA	90401	310-255-4493	434-0070
NYSE: ANH ■ *Web:* www.anworth.com					
Apartment Investment & Management Co					
4582 S Ulster St Pkwy Ste 1100	Denver	CO	80237	303-691-4350	759-3226
NYSE: AIV ■ *TF General:* 888-789-8600 ■ *Web:* www.aimco.com					
Arbor Realty Trust Inc					
333 Earle Ovington Blvd Ste 900	Uniondale	NY	11553	800-272-6710	832-8045*
NYSE: ABR ■ **Fax Area Code:* 516 ■ *TF:* 800-272-6710 ■ *Web:* www.arborrealtytrust.com					
Ashford Hospitality Trust Inc					
14185 Dallas Pkwy Ste 1100	Dallas	TX	75254	972-490-9600	980-2705
NYSE: AHT ■ *Web:* www.ahtreit.com					
AutoStar 114 Ave of the Americas Ste 39	New York	NY	10036	212-930-9400	
TF: 800-288-6782 ■ *Web:* www.autostar.com					
Benchmark Group 4053 Maple Rd	Amherst	NY	14226	716-833-4986	833-2954
TF: 800-876-0160 ■ *Web:* www.benchmarkgrp.com					
BioMed Realty Trust Inc					
17190 Bernardo Ctr Dr	San Diego	CA	92128	858-485-9840	485-9843
NYSE: BMR ■ *Web:* www.biomedrealty.com					
BRT Realty Trust 60 Cutter Mill Rd Ste 303	Great Neck	NY	11021	516-466-3100	466-3132
NYSE: BRT ■ *TF:* 800-450-5816 ■ *Web:* www.brtrealty.com					
Camden Property Trust					
11 Greenway Plz Ste 2400	Houston	TX	77046	713-354-2500	354-2700*
NYSE: CPT ■ **Fax:* Mktg ■ *TF:* 800-922-6336 ■ *Web:* www.camdenliving.com					
Canadian Real Estate Investment Trust (CREIT)					
175 Bloor St E Ste 500	Toronto	ON	M4W3R8	416-628-7771	628-7777
TSE: REF.UN ■ *Web:* www.creit.ca					
Capital Automotive Real Estate Services Inc					
8270 Greensboro Dr Ste 950	McLean	VA	22102	703-288-3075	288-3375
TF: 877-422-7288 ■ *Web:* www.capitalautomotive.com					
CAPREIT 11200 Rockville Pk Ste 100	Rockville	MD	20852	301-231-8700	
Web: www.capreit.com					
Capstead Mortgage Corp					
8401 N Central Expy Ste 800	Dallas	TX	75225	214-874-2323	874-2398
NYSE: CMO ■ *TF:* 800-358-2323 ■ *Web:* www.capstead.com					
Cedar Shopping Centers Inc					
44 S Bayles Ave Ste 304	Port Washington	NY	11050	516-767-6492	767-6497
NYSE: CDR ■ *Web:* www.cedarrealtytrust.com					
Centro Properties Group					
One Fayette St Ste 200	Conshohocken	PA	19428	610-825-7100	834-8110
Chesapeake Lodging Trust (CLT)					
1997 Annapolis Exchange Pkwy Ste 410	Annapolis	MD	21401	800-698-2820	
NYSE: CHSP ■ *TF:* 800-698-2820 ■ *Web:* www.chesapeakelodgingtrust.com					
Choice Group 755 W Big Beaver Rd	Troy	MI	48084	248-362-4150	362-4154
Web: www.choiceproperties.com					
Colonial Properties Trust 6584 Poplar Ave	Memphis	TN	38138	866-620-1130	248-4188*
NYSE: CLP ■ **Fax Area Code:* 901 ■ *Web:* www.maac.com					
Commercial Properties Realty Trust					
402 N Fourth St	Baton Rouge	LA	70802	225-924-7206	924-1235
TF: 800-648-9064 ■ *Web:* www.cprt.com					
Corporate Office Properties Trust					
6711 Columbia Gateway Dr Ste 300	Columbia	MD	21046	443-285-5400	285-7650
NYSE: OFC ■ *Web:* www.copt.com					
Cousins Properties Inc					
191 Peachtree St NE Ste 500	Atlanta	GA	30303	404-407-1000	
NYSE: CUZ ■ *Web:* www.cousinsproperties.com					
DiamondRock Hospitality Co (DRHC)					
3 Bethesda Metro Ctr Ste 1500	Bethesda	MD	20814	240-744-1150	744-1199
NYSE: DRH ■ *TF:* 888-246-5941 ■ *Web:* www.drhc.com					
Digital Realty Trust Inc					
560 Mission St Ste 2900	San Francisco	CA	94105	415-738-6500	738-6501
NYSE: DLR ■ *Web:* www.digitalrealty.com					
Dividend Capital Trust 518 17th St Ste 1700	Denver	CO	80202	303-228-2200	228-0128
TF: 866-324-7348 ■ *Web:* www.dividendcapital.com					
Donahue Schriber Realty Group Inc					
200 E Baker St Ste 100	Costa Mesa	CA	92626	714-545-1400	545-4222
Web: www.donahueschriber.com					
Duke Realty Corp 600 E 96th St Ste 100	Indianapolis	IN	46240	317-808-6000	808-6794
NYSE: DRE-M.CL ■ *Web:* www.dukerealty.com					
Dupont Fabros Technology Inc					
1212 New York Ave NW Ste 900	Washington	DC	20005	202-728-0044	728-0220
NYSE: DFT ■ *Web:* www.dft.com					
Dynex Capital Inc 4991 Lk Brook Dr Ste 100	Glen Allen	VA	23060	804-217-5800	217-5860
NYSE: DX ■ *Web:* www.dynexcapital.com					
EastGroup Properties Inc					
190 E Capitol St Ste 400	Jackson	MS	39201	601-354-3555	352-1441
NYSE: EGP ■ *Web:* www.eastgroup.net					
ECC Capital Corp					
2600 E Coast Hwy Ste 250	Corona Del Mar	CA	92625	949-954-7060	
OTC: ECRO ■ *Web:* www.ecccapital.com					
Education Realty Trust Inc					
530 Oak Ct Dr Ste 300	Memphis	TN	38117	901-259-2500	259-2594
NYSE: EDR ■ *Web:* www.edrtrust.com					
Equity Office Properties Trust					
222 S Riverside Plaza Ste 2100	Chicago	IL	60606	312-466-3300	454-0332
Web: www.equityoffice.com					
Essex Property Trust Inc 925 E Meadow Dr	Palo Alto	CA	94303	650-494-3700	494-8743
NYSE: ESS ■ *Web:* essex.com/					
Federal Realty Investment Trust					
1626 E Jefferson St	Rockville	MD	20852	301-998-8100	998-3700
NYSE: FRT ■ *TF:* 800-658-8980 ■ *Web:* www.federalrealty.com					
FelCor Lodging Trust Inc					
545 E John Carpenter Fwy Ste 1300	Irving	TX	75062	972-444-4900	444-4949
NYSE: FCH ■ *Web:* www.felcor.com					

	Phone	Fax
First Industrial Realty Trust Inc 311 S Wacker Dr Ste 4000 .... Chicago IL 60606 *NYSE: FR* ■ *Web:* www.firstindustrial.com	312-344-4300	922-6320
First Potomac Realty Trust 7600 Wisconsin Ave 11th Fl....................... Bethesda MD 20814 *NYSE: FPO* ■ *Web:* www.first-potomac.com	301-986-9200	986-5554
First Real Estate Investment 505 Main St .... Hackensack NJ 07602 *Web:* freitnj.com	201-488-6400	487-1798
Franklin Street Properties Corp 401 Edgewater Pl Ste 200....................... Wakefield MA 01880 *NYSE: FSP* ■ *TF:* 877-686-9496 ■ *Web:* www.franklinstreetproperties.com	781-557-1300	
Gables Residential Trust 3399 Peachtree Rd NE Ste 600....................... Atlanta GA 30326 *Web:* www.gables.com	561-997-9700	
GE Capital Solutions Franchise Finance 8377 E Hartford Dr Ste 200....................... Scottsdale AZ 85255 *TF:* 866-438-4333 ■ *Web:* www.geffcenter.com	866-438-4333	
Ginkgo Residential LLC 301 S College St Ste 3850....................... Charlotte NC 28202 **Fax Area Code:* 412 ■ *Web:* ginkgores.com	704-944-0100	502-3933*
Gramercy Capital Corp 420 Lexington Ave .... New York NY 10170 *NYSE: GKK* ■ *Web:* www.gptreit.com	212-297-1000	297-1090
Health Care Property Investors Inc 1920 Main St Ste 1200............................. Irvine CA 92614 *TF:* 888-604-1990 ■ *Web:* www.hcpi.com	949-407-0700	407-0800
Health Care REIT Inc 4500 Dorr St.................... Toledo OH 43615 *NYSE: HCN* ■ *Web:* www.hcreit.com	419-247-2800	247-2826
Healthcare Realty Trust Inc 3310 W End Ave Ste 700 .... Nashville TN 37203 *NYSE: HR* ■ *Web:* www.healthcarerealty.com	615-269-8175	269-8260
Highwoods Properties Inc 3100 Smoketree Ct Ste 600 .... Raleigh NC 27604 *NYSE: HIW* ■ *TF:* 866-449-6637 ■ *Web:* www.highwoods.com	919-872-4924	876-2448
HMG/Courtland Properties Inc 1870 S Bayshore Dr .... Coconut Grove FL 33133 *AMEX: HMG* ■ *Web:* hmgcourtland.com	305-854-6803	856-7342
Home Properties Inc 850 Clinton Sq .... Rochester NY 14604 *NYSE: HME* ■ *Web:* www.homeproperties.com	585-546-4900	546-5433
Horizon Group Properties Inc 5000 Hakes Dr........ Muskegon MI 49441 *Web:* www.horizongroup.com	231-798-9100	798-5100
Host Hotels & Resorts Inc 6903 Rockledge Dr Ste 1500 .... Bethesda MD 20817 *NYSE: HST* ■ *Web:* www.hosthotels.com	240-744-1000	744-5125
Impac Mortgage Holdings Inc 19500 Jamboree Rd .... Irvine CA 92612 *NYSE: IMH* ■ *TF:* 800-597-4101 ■ *Web:* www.impaccompanies.com	949-475-3600	
Inland Real Estate Corp 2901 Butterfield Rd............................. Oak Brook IL 60523 *NYSE: IRC* ■ **Fax:* Investor Rel ■ *TF:* 888-331-4732 ■ *Web:* www.inlandrealestate.com	630-218-8000	218-7357*
Innkeepers USA Trust 340 Royal Poinciana Way Ste 306 .... Palm Beach FL 33480 *Web:* www.innkeepersusa.com	561-835-1800	835-0457
InnSuites Hospitality Trust 1625 E Northern Ave Ste 105 .... Phoenix AZ 85020 *NYSE: IHT* ■ *TF:* 800-842-4242 ■ *Web:* www.innsuitestrust.com	602-944-1500	678-0281
Investors Real Estate Trust 1400 31st Ave Ste 60............................... Minot ND 58701 *NYSE: IRET* ■ *TF:* 888-478-4738 ■ *Web:* iretapartments.com	701-837-4738	838-7785
iStar Financial Inc 1114 Ave of the Americas 39th Fl.................... New York NY 10036 *NYSE: STAR* ■ *TF:* 888-603-5847 ■ *Web:* www.istarfinancial.com	212-930-9400	
Kilroy Realty Corp 12200 W Olympic Blvd Ste 200 .... Los Angeles CA 90064 *NYSE: KRC* ■ *Web:* www.kilroyrealty.com	310-481-8400	481-6501
Kimco Realty Corp 3333 New Hyde Pk Rd .... New Hyde Park NY 11042 *NYSE: KIM* ■ *TF:* 800-645-6292 ■ *Web:* www.kimcorealty.com	516-869-9000	
Kite Realty Group Trust 30 S Meridian St Ste 1100......................... Indianapolis IN 46204 *NYSE: KRG* ■ *TF:* 888-577-5600 ■ *Web:* www.kiterealty.com	317-577-5600	577-5605
KKR Asset Management LLC 555 California St Ste 5000 .... San Francisco CA 94104 *Web:* kkr.com	415-315-3620	391-3077
LaSalle Hotel Properties Three Bethesda Metro Ctr Ste 1200 .... Bethesda MD 20814 *NYSE: LHO* ■ *Web:* www.lasallehotels.com	301-941-1500	941-1553
Lexington Corporate Properties Trust One Penn Plz Ste 4015........................... New York NY 10119 *TF:* 800-850-3948 ■ *Web:* www.lxp.com	212-692-7200	594-6600
Lexington Realty Trust Inc One Penn Plz Ste 4015........................... New York NY 10119 *Web:* www.lxp.com	212-692-7200	594-6600
Liberty Property Trust 500 Chesterfield Pkwy .... Malvern PA 19355 *NYSE: LPT* ■ *Web:* www.libertyproperty.com	610-648-1700	644-4129
LTC Properties Inc 2829 Townsgate Rd Ste 350.................. Westlake Village CA 91361 *NYSE: LTC* ■ *Web:* www.ltcproperties.com	805-981-8655	981-8663
Macerich Co, The 401 Wilshire Blvd Ste 700 .... Santa Monica CA 90401 *NYSE: MAC* ■ *TF:* 800-421-7237 ■ *Web:* www.macerich.com	310-394-6000	395-2791
Mack-Cali Realty Corp 343 Thornall St................ Edison NJ 08837 *NYSE: CLI* ■ *TF:* 800-317-4445 ■ *Web:* www.mack-cali.com	732-590-1000	205-8237
Madison Park Financial Corp 155 Grand Ave Ste 1025............................ Oakland CA 94612 *Web:* www.mpfcorp.com	510-452-2944	452-2973
Medical Properties Trust Inc 1000 Urban Ctr Dr Ste 501...................... Birmingham AL 35242 *NYSE: MPW* ■ *Web:* www.medicalpropertiestrust.com	205-969-3755	969-3756
Meredith Enterprises Inc 3000 Sand Hill Rd Bldg 2 Ste 120 .... Menlo Park CA 94025 *Web:* www.meredithreit.com	650-233-7140	233-7160
MFA Mortgage Investments Inc 350 Pk Ave 20th Fl............................... New York NY 10022 *Web:* www.mfafinancial.com	212-207-6400	207-6420
MHI Hospitality Corp 410 W Francis St Ste 201....................... Williamsburg VA 23185 *Web:* www.mhihospitality.com	757-229-5648	564-8801
Monmouth Real Estate Investment Corp (MREIC) 3499 Rt 9 N Ste 3C.............................. Freehold NJ 07728 *NASDAQ: MNR* ■ *Web:* www.mreic.com	732-577-9996	577-9981
MPG Office Trust Inc 355 S Grand Ave Ste 3300 .... Los Angeles CA 90071 *Web:* brookfieldofficeproperties.com	213-626-3300	687-4758
National Health Investors Inc 222 Robert Rose Dr .... Murfreesboro TN 37129 *NYSE: NHI* ■ *Web:* nhireit.com/	615-890-9100	
New York Mortgage Trust Inc (NYMT) 52 Vanderbilt Ave Ste 403......................... New York NY 10017 *NASDAQ: NYMT* ■ *TF:* 800-937-5449 ■ *Web:* www.nymtrust.com	212-792-0107	
Newcastle Investment Corp 1345 Ave of the Americas 46th Fl.................... New York NY 10105 *NYSE: NCT* ■ *Web:* www.newcastleinv.com	212-798-6100	
NorthStar Realty Finance Corp 399 Pk Ave 18th Fl.............................. New York NY 10022 *NYSE: NRF* ■ *Web:* www.nrfc.com	212-547-2600	547-2700
Novastar Financial Inc 2114 Central Ste 600 .... Kansas City MO 64108 *TF:* 800-591-1137 ■ *Web:* www.novationcompanies.com	816-237-7000	
One Liberty Properties Inc 60 Cutter Mill Rd Ste 303....................... Great Neck NY 11021 *NYSE: OLP* ■ *TF:* 800-937-5449 ■ *Web:* 1liberty.com	516-466-3100	466-3132
Parkway Properties Inc 188 E Capitol St Ste 1000.......................... Jackson MS 39201 *NYSE: PKY* ■ *TF:* 800-748-1667 ■ *Web:* www.pky.com	601-948-4091	949-4077
Pennsylvania Real Estate Investment Trust 200 S Broad St Third Fl .... Philadelphia PA 19102 *NYSE: PEI* ■ *TF:* 866-875-0700 ■ *Web:* www.preit.com	215-875-0700	546-7311
Plum Creek Timber Company Inc 601 Union St Ste 3100............................. Seattle WA 98101 *NYSE: PCL* ■ *TF:* 800-858-5347 ■ *Web:* www.plumcreek.com	206-467-3600	467-3795
PMC Commercial Trust 17950 Preston Rd Ste 600 .... Dallas TX 75252 *NASDAQ: CMCT* ■ *TF:* 800-486-3223 ■ *Web:* cimgroup.com/pmc/	972-349-3200	349-3265
Post Properties Inc 4401 Northside Pkwy Ste 800......................... Atlanta GA 30327 *NYSE: PPS* ■ **Fax:* Hum Res ■ *Web:* www.postproperties.com	404-846-5000	846-6161*
Premium Outlets 105 Eisenhower Pkwy .... Roseland NJ 07068 *Web:* www.premiumoutlets.com	973-228-6111	
ProLogis 4545 Airport Way .... Denver CO 80239 *NYSE: PLD* ■ *TF:* 800-566-2706 ■ *Web:* www.prologis.com	303-375-9292	567-5903
PS Business Parks Inc 701 Western Ave............. Glendale CA 91201 *NYSE: PSB* ■ *TF Cust Svc:* 888-299-3246 ■ *Web:* www.psbusinessparks.com	818-244-8080	242-0566
Public Storage Inc 701 Western Ave................. Glendale CA 91201 *NYSE: PSA* ■ **Fax:* Mail Rm ■ *TF Cust Svc:* 800-567-0759 ■ *Web:* www.publicstorage.com	818-244-8080	291-1015*
Ramco-Gershenson Properties Trust 31500 NW Hwy Ste 300 .... Farmington Hills MI 48334 *NYSE: RPT* ■ *Web:* www.ramcogershenson.com	248-350-9900	350-9925
Regency Centers One Independent Dr Ste 114...................... Jacksonville FL 32202 *NYSE: REG* ■ *TF:* 800-950-6333 ■ *Web:* regencycenters.com	904-598-7000	634-3428
Resource Capital Corp 712 Fifth Ave 12th Fl.......... New York NY 10019 *NYSE: RSO* ■ *Web:* www.resourcecapitalcorp.com	212-506-3899	245-6372
RioCan Real Estate Investment Trust 2300 Yonge St Ste 500 PO Box 2386.................. Toronto ON M4P1E4 *TSE: REI.UN.CA* ■ *TF:* 800-465-2733 ■ *Web:* www.riocan.com	416-866-3033	866-3020
Simon Property Group Inc 225 W Washington St........................... Indianapolis IN 46204 *NYSE: SPG* ■ **Fax:* Cust Svc ■ *Web:* www.simon.com	317-636-1600	263-7658*
SL Green Realty Corp 420 Lexington Ave .... New York NY 10170 *NYSE: SLG* ■ *Web:* www.slgreen.com	212-594-2700	216-1790
Strategic Hotels & Resorts 200 W Madison St Ste 1700.......................... Chicago IL 60606 *NYSE: BEE* ■ *Web:* www.strategichotels.com	312-658-5000	658-5799
Sun Communities Inc 27777 Franklin Rd Ste 200......................... Southfield MI 48034 *NYSE: SUI* ■ *Web:* www.suncommunities.com	248-208-2500	208-2640
Supertel Hospitality Inc 309 N Fifth St PO Box 1448 .... Norfolk NE 68701 *NASDAQ: SPPR* ■ *Web:* www.supertelinc.com	402-371-2520	
Tanger Factory Outlet Centers Inc 3200 Northline Ave Ste 360 .... Greensboro NC 27408 *NYSE: SKT* ■ *TF:* 800-720-6728 ■ *Web:* www.tangeroutlet.com	336-292-3010	852-2096
Taubman Centers Inc 200 E Long Lk Rd Ste 300 .... Bloomfield Hills MI 48303 *NYSE: TCO* ■ *TF:* 800-297-6003 ■ *Web:* www.taubman.com	248-258-6800	258-7683
Thayer Lodging Group 1997 Annapolis Exchange # 550 .... Annapolis MD 21401 *Web:* www.thayerlodging.com	410-268-0515	268-1582
Transcontinental Realty Investors Inc 1603 Lyndon B Johnson Fwy Ste 800.................. Dallas TX 75234 *NYSE: TCI* ■ *TF:* 800-400-6407 ■ *Web:* www.transconrealty-invest.com	469-522-4200	522-4299
United Mobile Homes Inc 3499 Rt 9 N Ste 3C......... Freehold NJ 07728 *NYSE: UMH* ■ *Web:* www.umh.com	732-577-9997	577-9980
Universal Health Realty Income Trust 367 S Gulph Rd .... KingofPrussia PA 19406 *NYSE: UHT* ■ *Web:* www.uhrit.com	610-265-0688	
Urstadt Biddle Properties Inc 321 Railroad Ave............................. Greenwich CT 06830 *NYSE: UBA* ■ *Web:* www.ubproperties.com	203-863-8200	861-6755
Ventas Inc 353 N Clark St Ste 3300................. Chicago IL 60654 *NYSE: VTR* ■ *TF:* 877-483-6827 ■ *Web:* www.ventasreit.com	877-483-6827	
Vornado Realty Trust 888 Seventh Ave.............. New York NY 10019 *NYSE: VNO* ■ *TF:* 800-294-1322 ■ *Web:* www.vno.com	212-894-7000	902-9316
Washington Real Estate Investment Trust (WRIT) 6110 Executive Blvd Ste 800 .... Rockville MD 20852 *NYSE: WRE* ■ *TF:* 800-565-9748 ■ *Web:* www.writ.com	301-984-9400	984-9610
Watson Land Co 22010 S Wilmington Ave Ste 400........ Carson CA 90745 *Web:* www.watsonlandcompany.com	310-952-6400	522-8788

Phone | Fax

Weingarten Realty Investors
2600 Citadel Plz Dr Ste 300 Houston TX 77008 713-866-6000 866-6049
NYSE: WRI ■ *TF:* 800-688-8865 ■ *Web:* www.weingarten.com

Westfield America Inc
2049 Century Park E Century City CA 90067 310-478-4456
Web: www.westfield.com

Winthrop Realty Trust 7 Bulfinch Pl Ste 500 Boston MA 02114 617-570-4614 570-4746
NYSE: FUR ■ *TF:* 800-622-6757 ■ *Web:* www.winthropreit.com

WP Carey & Company LLC
50 Rockefeller Plz Second Fl New York NY 10020 212-492-1100 492-8922
NYSE: WPC ■ *TF:* 800-972-2739 ■ *Web:* www.wpcarey.com

658 REAL ESTATE MANAGERS & OPERATORS

SEE ALSO Hotels & Hotel Companies p. 2530; Retirement Communities p. 3124

Phone | Fax

A&G Management Inc 7779 New York Ln Glen Burnie MD 21061 410-766-8900 766-6557
Web: aandgmanagement.com

Acadia Realty Trust
1311 Mamaroneck Ave Ste 260 White Plains NY 10605 914-288-8100 428-2380
NYSE: AKR ■ *TF:* 800-937-5449 ■ *Web:* www.acadiarealty.com

Agellan Capital Partners Inc
156 Front St W Ste 303 Toronto ON M5J2L6 416-593-6800
Web: www.agellancapital.com

Agree Realty Corp 70 E Long Lake Rd Farmington Hills MI 48334 248-737-4190
NYSE: ADC ■ *Web:* www.agreerealty.com

Alexander Summer LLC 205 Robin Rd Ste 120 Paramus NJ 07652 201-712-1000 712-1274
Web: alexandersummer.com

Alexander's Inc 210 Rt 4 E Paramus NJ 07652 201-587-8541 708-6214
NYSE: ALX ■ *Web:* www.alx-inc.com

Alexandria Real Estate Equities Inc
385 E Colorado Blvd Ste 299 Pasadena CA 91101 626-578-0777 578-0896
NYSE: ARE ■ *TF:* 800-776-9437 ■ *Web:* are.com

Allied Hotel Properties Inc
Ste 300 515 W Pender St Vancouver BC V6B6H5 604-669-5335
Web: www.alliedhotels.com

Allied Realty Co 20 26th St Huntington WV 25703 304-525-9125 697-5511
Web: alliedlogistics.com

American Assets Inc 11455 El Camino Real San Diego CA 92130 858-350-2600
Web: www.americanassetstrust.com

American Golf Corp 2951 28th St Santa Monica CA 90405 310-664-4000
TF: 800-238-7267 ■ *Web:* www.americangolf.com

American Motel Management
2200 Northlake Pkwy Ste 277 Tucker GA 30084 770-939-1801 939-1419
TF: 800-580-8258 ■ *Web:* www.americanmotelonline.com

American Realty Investors Inc
1800 Vly View Ln Ste 300 Dallas TX 75234 469-522-4200 522-4299
NYSE: ARL ■ *TF:* 800-400-6407 ■ *Web:* www.americanrealtyinvest.com

American Spectrum Realty Inc
2401 Fountain View Ste 510 Houston TX 77057 713-706-6200 706-6201
NYSE: AQQ ■ *TF:* 888-315-2776 ■ *Web:* www.americanspectrum.com

Apartment Investment & Management Co
4582 S Ulster St Pkwy Ste 1100 Denver CO 80237 303-691-4350 759-3226
NYSE: AIV ■ *TF General:* 888-789-8600 ■ *Web:* www.aimco.com

ARC Properties Inc 1401 Broad St Second Fl Clifton NJ 07013 973-249-1000 249-1001
Web: www.arcproperties.com

Archstone-Smith Trust
9200 E Panorama Cir Ste 400 Englewood CO 80112 303-708-5959 708-5999

Arden Realty Inc
11601 Wilshire Blvd Ste 400 Los Angeles CA 90025 310-966-2600 966-2699
Web: www.ardenrealty.com

Aronov Realty 3500 Eastern Blvd Montgomery AL 36116 334-277-1000 272-0747
Web: www.aronov.com

Associated Estates Realty Corp
One AEC Pkwy Richmond Heights OH 44143 216-261-5000 289-9600
NYSE: AEC ■ *TF:* 800-440-2372 ■ *Web:* www.associatedestates.com

Belz Enterprises 100 Peabody Pl Ste 1400 Memphis TN 38103 901-767-4780 271-7238
Web: www.belz.com

Berkshire Property Advisors LLC
1 Beacon St Ste 1550 Boston MA 02108 617-646-2300 646-2375
Web: www.berkshirecommunities.com

Berwind Natural Resources Corp
1500 Market St 3000 Ctr Sq W Philadelphia PA 19102 215-563-2800
Web: www.berwind.com

Blue Ridge Real Estate Co PO Box 707 Blakeslee PA 18610 570-443-8433 443-9544
OTC: BLRGZ ■ *Web:* www.bouldercreekresort.com

Bob Harris Oil Co 905 S Main St Cleburne TX 76033 817-558-0615

Boston Properties Inc 800 Boylston St Boston MA 02199 617-236-3300
NYSE: BXP ■ *Web:* www.bostonproperties.com

Boyle Investment Co 5900 Poplar Ave Ste 100 Memphis TN 38119 901-767-0100 766-4299
Web: www.boyle.com

Bozzuto Group 7850 Walker Dr Ste 400 Greenbelt MD 20770 301-220-0100 220-3738
TF General: 866-698-7513 ■ *Web:* www.bozzuto.com

Bradford Cos 9400 N Central Expy Ste 500 Dallas TX 75231 972-776-7000 776-7083
Web: www.bradford.com

Brandywine Realty Trust
555 E Lancaster Ave Ste 100 Radnor PA 19087 610-325-5600 325-5622
NYSE: BDN ■ *TF:* 866-426-5400 ■ *Web:* www.brandywinerealty.com

Brixmor Property Group
420 Lexington Ave Seventh Fl New York NY 10170 212-869-3000 869-8969
Web: brixmor.com

Broadstone Real Estate LLC 530 Clinton Sq Rochester NY 14604 585-287-6500
Web: www.broadstone.com

Brookfield Office Properties Canada
181 Bay St Ste 330 PO Box 770 Toronto ON M5J2T3 416-359-8555 359-8596
NYSE: BPO ■ *Web:* www.brookfieldofficepropertiescanada.com

Brookfield Properties Corp (BOP)
181 Bay St Ste 330 Toronto ON M5J2T3 416-369-2300 369-2301
NYSE: BPO ■ *TF:* 800-387-0825 ■ *Web:* www.brookfieldofficeproperties.com

Brooklyn Navy Yard Development Corp
63 Flushing Ave Bldg 292 Third Fl Brooklyn NY 11205 718-907-5900 643-9296
Web: brooklynnavyyard.org

Phone | Fax

BVT Equity Holdings Inc
400 Interstate N Pkwy Ste 700 Atlanta GA 30339 770-618-3500
Web: www.bvt.com

Cadillac Fairview Ltd 20 Queen St W Fifth Fl Toronto ON M5H3R4 416-598-8200 598-8578
Web: www.cadillacfairview.com

Calista Corp 301 Calista Ct Ste A Anchorage AK 99518 907-279-5516 272-5060
TF: 800-277-5516 ■ *Web:* www.calistacorp.com

Camden Property Trust
11 Greenway Plz Ste 2400 Houston TX 77046 713-354-2500 354-2700*
NYSE: CPT ■ **Fax:* Mktg ■ *TF:* 800-922-6336 ■ *Web:* www.camdenliving.com

CAPREIT 11200 Rockville Pk Ste 100 Rockville MD 20852 301-231-8700
Web: www.capreit.com

Capstone Real Estate Investments LLC
431 Office Park Dr Birmingham AL 35223 205-414-6400
Web: www.capstonecompanies.com

Carneghi-blum & Partners Inc
1602 The Alameda Ste 205 San Jose CA 95126 408-535-0900
Web: cbpappraisal.com

Casto Realty 191 W Nationwide Blvd Ste 200 Columbus OH 43215 614-228-5331 469-8376
Web: castolp.com

CBH Homes 1977 E Overland Rd Meridian ID 83642 208-288-5560
Web: www.cbhhomes.com

Cedar Shopping Centers Inc
44 S Bayles Ave Ste 304 Port Washington NY 11050 516-767-6492 767-6497
NYSE: CDR ■ *Web:* www.cedarrealtytrust.com

Cencor Realty Services Inc
3102 Maple Ave Ste 500 Dallas TX 75201 214-954-0300 953-0860
Web: www.weitzmangroup.com

CenterPoint Properties Trust 1808 Swift Dr Oak Brook IL 60523 630-586-8000 586-8010
Web: centerpoint.com/

Centro Properties Group
One Fayette St Ste 200 Conshohocken PA 19428 610-825-7100 834-8110

Charles E Lakin Enterprises
8990 W Dodge Rd Ste 225 Omaha NE 68114 402-393-5550

Chrisken Property Management LLC
345 N Canal St Ste 201 Chicago IL 60606 312-454-1626 454-1627
Web: www.chrisken.com

ClubCorp Inc 3030 Lyndon B Johnson Fwy Ste 600 Dallas TX 75234 972-243-6191 888-7555
TF: 800-433-5079 ■ *Web:* www.clubcorp.com

ClubLink Corp 15675 Dufferin St King City ON L7B1K5 905-841-3730 841-1134
TF: 800-661-1818 ■ *Web:* en.clublink.ca

Codding Enterprises
1400 Valley House Dr Ste 100 Rohnert Park CA 94928 707-795-3550 665-2882
Web: www.codding.com

Colonial Properties Trust 6584 Poplar Ave Memphis TN 38138 866-620-1130 248-4188*
NYSE: CLP ■ **Fax Area Code:* 901 ■ *Web:* www.maac.com

Combined Properties Inc 300 Commercial St Malden MA 02148 781-321-7800 321-5144
Web: www.combinedproperties.com

CommonWealth REIT
255 Washington St 2 Newton Pl Newton MA 02458 617-332-3990 332-2261
Web: www.cwhreit.com

Community Development Trust (CDT)
1350 Broadway Ste 700 New York NY 10018 212-271-5080 271-5079
Web: www.cdt.biz

Cornell & Assoc Inc 2633 E Lake Ave Ste 307 Seattle WA 98102 206-329-0085 329-4110
Web: www.cornellandassociates.com

Corporate Office Properties Trust
6711 Columbia Gateway Dr Ste 300 Columbia MD 21046 443-285-5400 285-7650
NYSE: OFC ■ *Web:* www.copt.com

Cousins Properties Inc
191 Peachtree St NE Ste 500 Atlanta GA 30303 404-407-1000
NYSE: CUZ ■ *Web:* www.cousinsproperties.com

Crescent Real Estate Equities Co
777 Main St Ste 2000 Fort Worth TX 76102 817-321-1566 321-2000
Web: www.crescent.com

Crombie REIT 115 King St Stellarton NS B0K1S0 902-755-8100 755-6477
Web: crombiereit.ca

Cushman & Wakefield Inc
1290 Ave of the Americas New York NY 10019 212-841-7500 841-7867
Web: www.cushmanwakefield.com

Daniel Corp 3660 Grandview Pkwy Birmingham AL 35243 205-443-4500
Web: www.danielcorp.com

Developers Diversified Realty Corp
3300 Enterprise Pkwy Beachwood OH 44122 216-755-5500 755-1500
NYSE: DDR ■ *TF:* 877-225-5337 ■ *Web:* ddr.com

Donahue Schriber Realty Group Inc
200 E Baker St Ste 100 Costa Mesa CA 92626 714-545-1400 545-4222
Web: www.donahueschriber.com

Douglas Allred Co
11452 El Camino Real Ste 200 San Diego CA 92130 858-793-0202 793-5363
Web: www.douglasallredco.com

Douglas Elliman Property Management
675 Third Ave Sixth Fl New York NY 10017 212-370-9200 455-4726
Web: www.ellimanpm.com

Draper & Kramer Inc 33 W Monroe 19th Fl Chicago IL 60603 312-346-8600 346-8600
Web: www.draperandkramer.com

Duke Realty Corp 600 E 96th St Ste 100 Indianapolis IN 46240 317-808-6000 808-6794
NYSE: DRE-M.CL ■ *Web:* www.dukerealty.com

E Ra The Masiello Group 486 W Main St Tilton NH 03276 603-286-3010
Web: www.masiello.com

EastGroup Properties Inc
190 E Capitol St Ste 400 Jackson MS 39201 601-354-3555 352-1441
NYSE: EGP ■ *Web:* www.eastgroup.net

Entertainment Properties Trust
909 Walnut Ste 200 Kansas City MO 64106 816-472-1700 472-5794
NYSE: EPR ■ *TF:* 888-377-7348 ■ *Web:* www.eprkc.com

Equity Lifestyle Properties Inc
Two N Riverside Plz Ste 800 Chicago IL 60606 312-279-1400 279-1710
NYSE: ELS ■ *TF:* 800-274-7314 ■ *Web:* www.equitylifestyle.com

Equity Office Properties Trust
222 S Riverside Plaza Ste 2100 Chicago IL 60606 312-466-3300 454-0332
Web: www.equityoffice.com

				Phone	Fax
Equity One Inc 1696 NE Miami Gardens Dr *NYSE: EQY* ■ *Web:* www.equityone.net	North Miami Beach	FL	33179	305-947-1664	947-1734
Equity Residential Two N Riverside Plz *NYSE: EQR* ■ *Web:* www.equityapartments.com	Chicago	IL	60606	312-474-1300	454-8703
Essex Property Trust Inc 925 E Meadow Dr *NYSE: ESS* ■ *Web:* essex.com/	Palo Alto	CA	94303	650-494-3700	494-8743
Eugene Burger Management Corp 6600 Hunter Dr *TF:* 800-788-0233 ■ *Web:* www.ebmc.com	Rohnert Park	CA	94928	707-584-5123	584-5124
Federal Realty Investment Trust 1626 E Jefferson St *NYSE: FRT* ■ *TF:* 800-658-8980 ■ *Web:* www.federalrealty.com	Rockville	MD	20852	301-998-8100	998-3700
FelCor Lodging Trust Inc 545 E John Carpenter Fwy Ste 1300 *NYSE: FCH* ■ *Web:* www.felcor.com	Irving	TX	75062	972-444-4900	444-4949
Festival Co 9841 Airport Blvd Ste 700 *Web:* www.festivalcos.com	Los Angeles	CA	90045	310-665-9600	665-9009
First Industrial Realty Trust Inc 311 S Wacker Dr Ste 4000 *NYSE: FR* ■ *Web:* www.firstindustrial.com	Chicago	IL	60606	312-344-4300	922-6320
First Real Estate Investment 505 Main St *Web:* freitnj.com	Hackensack	NJ	07602	201-488-6400	487-1798
First Realty Management Corp 151 Tremont St PH 1 *Web:* www.frmboston.com	Boston	MA	02111	617-423-7000	482-6617
First Republic Corp of America 302 Fifth Ave Ste 6 Ste 6 *NYSE: FRPC*	New York	NY	10001	212-279-6100	629-6848
FirstService Corp 1140 Bay St First Service Bldg Ste 4000 *TSE: FSV* ■ *Web:* www.firstservice.com	Toronto	ON	M5S2B4	416-960-9500	960-5333
Fisher Auction Company Inc 351 S Cypress Rd Ste 210 *Web:* www.fisherauction.com	Pompano Beach	FL	33060	954-942-0917	
Flatley Co, The 35 Braintree Hill Office Pk *Web:* www.flatleyco.com	Braintree	MA	02184	781-848-2000	849-4430
Forest City Residential Group 50 Public Sq Ste 1515 *Web:* www.forestcity.net	Cleveland	OH	44113	216-416-3906	
Freeport Ctr Assoc PO Box 160466 *Web:* www.freeportcenter.com	Clearfield	UT	84016	801-825-9741	825-3587
G&L Realty Corp 439 N Bedford Dr *Web:* www.glrealty.com	Beverly Hills	CA	90210	310-273-9930	248-2222
Gene B Glick Company Inc 8425 Woodfield Crossing Blvd *Web:* www.genebglick.com	Indianapolis	IN	46240	317-469-0400	
General Growth Properties Inc 110 N Wacker Dr *NYSE: GGP* ■ *TF:* 888-395-8037 ■ *Web:* www.ggp.com	Chicago	IL	60606	312-960-5000	960-5475
Ginkgo Residential LLC 301 S College St Ste 3850 **Fax Area Code: 412* ■ *Web:* ginkgores.com	Charlotte	NC	28202	704-944-0100	502-3933*
Goodale & Barbieri Co 818 W Riverside Ave Ste 300 *Web:* www.g-b.com	Spokane	WA	99201	509-459-6109	344-4939
Grady Management Inc 8630 Fenton St Ste 625 *TF:* 800-544-7239 ■ *Web:* www.gradymgt.com	Silver Spring	MD	20910	301-587-3330	
Graham Cos 6843 Main St *Web:* www.miamilakes.com	Miami Lakes	FL	33014	305-821-1130	557-0313
Great American Group Inc 21860 Burbank Blvd Ste 300 *OTC: GAMR* ■ *Web:* www.greatamerican.com	Woodland Hills	CA	91367	818-884-3737	884-2976
Gundaker Property Management 2458 Old Dorsett Rd Ste 100 *TF:* 800-325-1978 ■ *Web:* www.cbgundaker.com	Maryland Heights	MO	63043	314-298-5200	298-5096
Gyrodyne Company of America Inc One Flowerfield Ste 24 *NASDAQ: GYRO* ■ *Web:* www.gyrodyne.com	Saint James	NY	11780	631-584-5400	584-7075
H & R Retail Inc 2800 Quarry Lk Dr Ste 320 *Web:* www.hrretail.com	Baltimore	MD	21209	410-308-0800	486-2733
Hall Financial Group 6801 Gaylord Pkwy Ste 100 *Web:* www.hallfinancial.com	Frisco	TX	75034	972-377-1100	377-1170
Harrison & Lear Inc 2310 Tower Pl Ste 105 *Web:* www.harrison-lear.com	Hampton	VA	23666	757-825-9100	838-2574
Hawaii Reserves Inc 55-510 Kamehameha Hwy *Web:* www.hawaiireserves.com	Laie	HI	96762	808-293-9201	293-6456
Health Care Property Investors Inc 1920 Main St Ste 1200 *TF:* 888-604-1990 ■ *Web:* www.hcpi.com	Irvine	CA	92614	949-407-0700	407-0800
Health Care REIT Inc 4500 Dorr St *NYSE: HCN* ■ *Web:* www.hcreit.com	Toledo	OH	43615	419-247-2800	247-2826
Healthcare Realty Trust Inc 3310 W End Ave Ste 700 *NYSE: HR* ■ *Web:* www.healthcarerealty.com	Nashville	TN	37203	615-269-8175	269-8260
Heitman LLC 191 N Wacker Dr Ste 2500 *TF:* 800-225-5435 ■ *Web:* www.heitman.com	Chicago	IL	60606	312-855-5700	251-4807
Hemstreet Development Co 16100 NW Cornell Rd Ste 100 *Web:* www.hemstreet.com	Beaverton	OR	97006	503-531-4000	531-4001
Herb Redl Inc 80 Washington St Ste 100 *Web:* www.hredlproperties.com	Poughkeepsie	NY	12601	845-471-3388	471-3851
Hersha Hospitality Trust 510 Walnut St Ninth Fl *NYSE: HT* ■ *Web:* www.hersha.com	Philadelphia	PA	19106	215-238-1046	238-0157
Hickel Investment Co 939 W Fifth Ave *Web:* hickelinvestment.com	Anchorage	AK	99501	907-343-2400	
Highwoods Properties Inc 3100 Smoketree Ct Ste 600 *NYSE: HIW* ■ *TF:* 866-449-6637 ■ *Web:* www.highwoods.com	Raleigh	NC	27604	919-872-4924	876-2448
Holiday Retirement Corp 5885 Meadows Rd Ste 500 *TF:* 800-322-0999 ■ *Web:* www.holidaytouch.com	Lake Oswego	OR	97035	503-370-7070	
Holladay Corp 3400 Idaho Ave NW Ste 500 *Web:* holladaycorp.com	Washington	DC	20016	202-362-2400	
Home Properties Six Garrison View Rd *NYSE: HME* ■ *Web:* www.homeproperties.com	Owings Mills	MD	21117	410-356-3320	356-0324
Home Properties Inc 850 Clinton Sq *NYSE: HME* ■ *Web:* www.homeproperties.com	Rochester	NY	14604	585-546-4900	546-5433
Horizon Group Properties Inc 5000 Hakes Dr *Web:* www.horizongroup.com	Muskegon	MI	49441	231-798-9100	798-5100
Horning Bros 1350 Connecticut Ave NW Ste 800 *Web:* www.horningbrothers.com	Washington	DC	20036	202-659-0700	659-9489
Hospitality Properties Trust 255 Washington St *NYSE: HPT* ■ *Web:* www.hptreit.com	Newton	MA	02458	617-964-8389	969-5730
Hunt Midwest Enterprises Inc 8300 NE Underground Dr *TF:* 800-551-6877 ■ *Web:* www.huntmidwest.com	Kansas City	MO	64161	816-455-2500	
Imperial Realty Company Inc 4747 W Peterson Ave *Web:* www.imperial-realty.com	Chicago	IL	60646	773-736-4100	736-4541
Inland Group Inc 2901 Butterfield Rd *TF:* 800-826-8228 ■ *Web:* www.inlandgroup.com	Oak Brook	IL	60523	630-218-8000	218-4917
Inland Real Estate Corp 2901 Butterfield Rd *NYSE: IRC* ■ **Fax:* Investor Rel ■ *TF:* 888-331-4732 ■ *Web:* www.inlandrealestate.com	Oak Brook	IL	60523	630-218-8000	218-7357*
Irvine Company Apartment Communities 110 Innovation Dr *Web:* www.rental-living.com	Irvine	CA	92617	949-720-5600	720-5601
Jim Wilson & Assoc Inc 2660 Eastchase Ln Ste 100 *Web:* www.jwamalls.com	Montgomery	AL	36117	334-260-2500	260-2533
JJ Gumberg Company Inc 1051 Brinton Rd *Web:* www.jjgumberg.com	Pittsburgh	PA	15221	412-244-4000	244-9133
JMG Realty Inc 5605 Glenridge Dr Ste 1010 *Web:* www.jmgrealty.com	Atlanta	GA	30342	404-995-1111	995-1112
John F Long Properties LLLP 5035 W Camelback Rd **Fax Area Code: 623* ■ *Web:* www.jflong.com	Phoenix	AZ	85031	602-272-0421	846-7208*
Jonas Equities 725 Church Ave *Web:* www.jonasequities.com	Brooklyn	NY	11218	718-871-6020	871-4324
Jones Lang LaSalle Inc 200 E Randolph Dr *NYSE: JLL* ■ *Web:* www.jll.com	Chicago	IL	60601	312-782-5800	782-4339
Jones Lang LaSalle IP Inc 200 E Randolph Dr *Web:* www.jll.com	Chicago	IL	60601	312-782-5800	
JW Mays Inc Nine Bond St *NASDAQ: MAYS* ■ *Web:* www.jwmays.com	Brooklyn	NY	11201	718-624-7400	935-0378
Kilroy Realty Corp 12200 W Olympic Blvd Ste 200 *NYSE: KRC* ■ *Web:* www.kilroyrealty.com	Los Angeles	CA	90064	310-481-8400	481-6501
Kimco Realty Corp 3333 New Hyde Pk Rd *NYSE: KIM* ■ *TF:* 800-645-6292 ■ *Web:* www.kimcorealty.com	New Hyde Park	NY	11042	516-869-9000	
Kratsa Properties 1025 William Pitt Way *Web:* www.kratsaproperties.com	Pittsburgh	PA	15238	412-828-7711	828-9296
Kraus-Anderson Realty Co 4210 W Old Shakopee Rd *Web:* www.krausanderson.com	Bloomington	MN	55437	952-881-8166	881-8114
Kravco Co 234 Mall Blvd *Web:* www.kravco.com	King of Prussia	PA	19406	610-854-2800	768-6444
L & B Realty Advisors LLP 8750 N Central Expy Ste 800 *Web:* www.lbgroup.com	Dallas	TX	75231	214-989-0800	989-0600
Lexington Corporate Properties Trust One Penn Plz Ste 4015 *TF:* 800-850-3948 ■ *Web:* www.lxp.com	New York	NY	10119	212-692-7200	594-6600
Lexington Ctr Corp 430 W Vine St *Web:* www.lexingtoncenter.com	Lexington	KY	40507	859-233-4567	253-2718
Liberty Property Trust 500 Chesterfield Pkwy *NYSE: LPT* ■ *Web:* www.libertyproperty.com	Malvern	PA	19355	610-648-1700	644-4129
Lincoln Property Co 2000 McKinney Ave Ste 1000	Dallas	TX	75201	214-740-3300	740-3441
Lomax Cos, The 200 Highpoint Dr Ste 215 *Web:* www.thelomaxcos.com	Chalfont	PA	18914	215-822-1550	997-9582
Lone Oak Fund LLC 11611 San Vincente Blvd Ste 640 *Web:* www.loneoakfund.com	Los Angeles	CA	90049	310-826-2888	
Lowe Enterprises 11777 San Vicente Blvd Ste 900 *Web:* www.loweenterprises.com	Los Angeles	CA	90049	310-820-6661	207-1132
Macerich Co, The 401 Wilshire Blvd Ste 700 *NYSE: MAC* ■ *TF:* 800-421-7237 ■ *Web:* www.macerich.com	Santa Monica	CA	90401	310-394-6000	395-2791
Mack-Cali Realty Corp 343 Thornall St *NYSE: CLI* ■ *TF:* 800-317-4445 ■ *Web:* www.mack-cali.com	Edison	NJ	08837	732-590-1000	205-8237
Macklowe Properties Inc 767 Fifth Ave *Web:* www.macklowe.com	New York	NY	10153	212-265-5900	554-5893
Madison Marquette 909 Montgomery St Ste 200 **Fax Area Code: 202* ■ *Web:* www.madisonmarquette.com	San Francisco	CA	94133	415-277-6800	741-3801*
Madison Park Financial Corp 155 Grand Ave Ste 1025 *Web:* www.mpfcorp.com	Oakland	CA	94612	510-452-2944	452-2973
Madison Square Garden Corp Two Pennsylvania Plz 16th Fl **Fax:* Hum Res ■ *Web:* www.thegarden.com	New York	NY	10121	212-465-6000	465-6026*
Maier Siebel Baber 260 California Fifth Fl *Web:* www.msb-realestate.com	San Francisco	CA	94111	415-591-9900	
Majestic Realty Co 13191 Crossroads Pkwy N Sixth Fl *Web:* www.majesticrealty.com	City of Industry	CA	91746	562-692-9581	695-2329

				Phone	Fax
Maxus Realty Trust Inc 104 Armour Rd PO Box 34729	North Kansas City	MO	64116	816-303-4500	221-1829
OTC: MRTI ■ *Web:* www.mrti.com					
Mericle Commercial Real Estate Services 100 Baltimore Dr	Wilkes Barre	PA	18702	570-823-1100	823-0300
Web: www.mericle.com					
Merritt Properties LLC 2066 Lord Baltimore Dr	Baltimore	MD	21244	410-298-2600	298-9644
Web: www.merrittproperties.com					
Mid-America Apartment Communities Inc (MAAC) 6584 Poplar Ave Ste 300	Memphis	TN	38138	901-682-6600	682-6667
NYSE: MAA ■ *Web:* www.maac.com					
Mid-Atlantic PenFed Realty Berkshire Hathaway HomeServices (PCR) 3050 Chain Bridge Rd	Fairfax	VA	22030	703-691-7653	691-7662
TF: 800-550-2364 ■ *Web:* www.penfedrealty.com					
Miller Valentine Group 4000 Miller Valentine Ct	Dayton	OH	45439	937-293-0900	299-1564
TF: 877-684-7687 ■ *Web:* www.mvgse.com					
Monmouth Real Estate Investment Corp (MREIC) 3499 Rt 9 N Ste 3C	Freehold	NJ	07728	732-577-9996	577-9981
NASDAQ: MNR ■ *Web:* www.mreic.com					
MonteLago Village Resort 30 Strada di Villaggio	Henderson	NV	89011	702-564-4700	
Web: www.montelagovillage.com					
Moody Rambin Interests 3003 W Alabama St	Houston	TX	77098	713-271-5900	773-5555
Web: www.moodyrambin.com					
Mullan Enterprises Inc 2330 W Joppa Rd Ste 210	Luthvle Timon	MD	21093	410-494-9200	
Web: www.mullancontr.com					
National Realty & Development Corp 3 Manhattanville Rd	Purchase	NY	10577	914-694-4444	694-5448
TF: 800-932-7368 ■ *Web:* www.nrdc.com					
NDC LLC 6312 S 27th St Ste 202	Oak Creek	WI	53154	414-761-2040	761-3576
Web: www.ndcllc.com					
New England Development One Wells Ave	Newton	MA	02459	617-965-8700	243-7085
Web: www.nedevelopment.com					
Newcastle Investment Corp 1345 Ave of the Americas 46th Fl	New York	NY	10105	212-798-6100	
NYSE: NCT ■ *Web:* www.newcastleinv.com					
NorthMarq Capital Inc 3500 W American Blvd Ste 500	Bloomington	MN	55431	952-356-0100	
Web: www.northmarq.com					
NTS Realty Holdings LP 10172 Linn Stn Rd	Louisville	KY	40223	502-426-4800	426-4994
NYSE: NLP ■ *Web:* www.ntsdevelopment.com					
Omega Healthcare Investors Inc 200 International Cir Ste 3500	Hunt Valley	MD	21030	410-427-1700	
NYSE: OHI ■ *TF:* 877-511-2891 ■ *Web:* www.omegahealthcare.com					
One Liberty Properties Inc 60 Cutter Mill Rd Ste 303	Great Neck	NY	11021	516-466-3100	466-3132
NYSE: OLP ■ *TF:* 800-937-5449 ■ *Web:* 1liberty.com					
Oxford Development Co 301 Grant St	Pittsburgh	PA	15219	412-261-1500	642-7543
Web: www.oxford-pgh.com					
Oxford Properties Group Inc 130 Adelaide St W Oxford Tower Ste 1100	Toronto	ON	M5H3P5	416-865-8300	
Web: www.oxfordproperties.com					
Parkway Properties Inc 188 E Capitol St Ste 1000	Jackson	MS	39201	601-948-4091	949-4077
NYSE: PKY ■ *TF:* 800-748-1667 ■ *Web:* www.pky.com					
Patriot Properties Inc 123 Pleasant St	Marblehead	MA	01945	781-586-9670	
Web: www.patriotproperties.com					
Peek Properties 258 E Arapaho Rd 160	Richardson	TX	75081	972-783-6040	669-0586
Pennsylvania Real Estate Investment Trust 200 S Broad St Third Fl	Philadelphia	PA	19102	215-875-0700	546-7311
NYSE: PEI ■ *TF:* 866-875-0700 ■ *Web:* www.preit.com					
Perini Management Services Inc 73 Mt Wayte Ave	Framingham	MA	01701	508-628-2000	628-2357
Web: www.tutorperini.com					
Persis Corp 900 Ft St Mall Ste 1725	Honolulu	HI	96813	808-599-8000	526-4114
Web: www.persis.com					
Peterson Cos, The 12500 Fair Lakes Cir Ste 400	Fairfax	VA	22033	703-227-2000	631-6481
Web: www.petersoncos.com					
Picerne Real Estate Group 75 Lambert Lind Hwy	Warwick	RI	02886	401-732-3700	738-6452
Web: www.picerne.com					
PM Realty Group 1000 Main St Ste 2400	Houston	TX	77002	713-209-5800	209-5702*
**Fax:* Hum Res ■ *Web:* www.pmrg.com					
Portman Holdings LLC 303 Peachtree St NE Ste 575	Atlanta	GA	30303	404-614-5252	614-5400
Web: www.portmanholdings.com					
PRC Group 40 Monmouth Pk Hwy	West Long Branch	NJ	07764	732-222-2000	222-6410
Web: www.prcgroup.com					
Premium Outlets 105 Eisenhower Pkwy	Roseland	NJ	07068	973-228-6111	
Web: www.premiumoutlets.com					
Price Edwards & Co 210 Pk Ave Ste 1000	Oklahoma City	OK	73102	405-843-7474	236-1849
Web: www.priceedwards.com					
Prime Group Realty Trust 330 N Wabash Ave Ste 2800	Chicago	IL	60611	312-917-1300	917-1310
Web: www.rrpchicago.com					
Professional Community Management Inc 23726 Birtcher Dr	Lake Forest	CA	92630	800-369-7260	859-3729*
**Fax Area Code:* 949 ■ *TF:* 800-369-7260 ■ *Web:* www.associaonline.com					
ProLogis 4545 Airport Way	Denver	CO	80239	303-375-9292	567-5903
NYSE: PLD ■ *TF:* 800-566-2706 ■ *Web:* www.prologis.com					
PS Business Parks Inc 701 Western Ave	Glendale	CA	91201	818-244-8080	242-0566
NYSE: PSB ■ *TF Cust Svc:* 888-299-3246 ■ *Web:* www.psbusinessparks.com					
Pyramid Cos 4 Clinton Sq	Syracuse	NY	13202	315-422-7000	472-4035
Web: www.pyramidmg.com					
Ramco-Gershenson Properties Trust 31500 NW Hwy Ste 300	Farmington Hills	MI	48334	248-350-9900	350-9925
NYSE: RPT ■ *Web:* www.ramcogershenson.com					
RD Management LLC 810 Seventh Ave 10th Fl	New York	NY	10019	212-265-6600	459-9133
Web: www.rdmanagement.com					
Real Foundation Inc 13737 Noel Rd Ste 900	Dallas	TX	75240	214-292-7000	
Web: www.realfoundations.net					
Realty Income Corp 600 La Terraza Blvd	Escondido	CA	92025	760-741-2111	741-8674
NYSE: O ■ *TF:* 877-924-6266 ■ *Web:* www.realtyincome.com					
Regency Centers One Independent Dr Ste 114	Jacksonville	FL	32202	904-598-7000	634-3428
NYSE: REG ■ *TF:* 800-950-6333 ■ *Web:* regencycenters.com					
Richard E Jacobs Group Inc 25425 Ctr Ridge Rd	Cleveland	OH	44145	440-871-4800	808-6902
Web: www.rejacobsgroup.com					
Rochdale Village Inc 169-65 137th Ave	Jamaica	NY	11434	718-276-5700	723-0963
Web: rochdalevillage.com					
Rosen Assoc Management Corp 33 S Service Rd	Jericho	NY	11753	516-333-2000	333-7555
Web: www.rosenmgmt.com					
Rossmar & Graham Community Assn Management Co 9362 E Raintree Dr	Scottsdale	AZ	85260	480-551-4300	551-6000
Web: fsresidential.com					
Ruffin Cos 1522 S Florence St	Wichita	KS	67209	316-942-7940	942-0216
Web: www.ruffinco.com					
RXR REALTY 625 Rex Plz	Uniondale	NY	11556	516-506-6000	506-6800
Web: www.rxrrealty.com					
Sabey Corp 12201 Tukwila International Blvd Fourth Fl	Seattle	WA	98168	206-281-8700	282-9951
Web: www.sabey.com					
San Diego Family Housing LLC 3360 Murray Ridge Rd	San Diego	CA	92123	858-874-8100	
Web: www.lincolnmilitary.com					
Sares-Regis Group 18802 Bardeen Ave	Irvine	CA	92612	949-756-5959	756-5955
Web: www.sares-regis.com					
Saul Centers Inc 7501 Wisconsin Ave Ste 1500E	Bethesda	MD	20814	301-986-6200	986-6079
NYSE: BFS ■ *Web:* www.saulcenters.com					
Saxe Real Estate Management Service 1999 Van Ness Ave	San Francisco	CA	94109	415-474-3171	447-8652
Web: www.saxerealestate.com					
Schatten Properties Management Company Inc 1514 S St	Nashville	TN	37212	615-329-3011	327-2343
TF: 800-892-1315 ■ *Web:* www.schattenproperties.com					
Sea Island Co PO Box 30351	Sea Island	GA	31561	912-638-3611	634-3961
TF: 800-732-4752 ■ *Web:* seaisland.com					
Selig Enterprises Inc 1100 Spring St NW Ste 550	Atlanta	GA	30309	404-876-5511	875-2629
Web: www.seligenterprises.com					
Seligman & Assoc One Town Sq Ste 1913	Southfield	MI	48076	248-862-8000	
Web: www.seligmangroup.com					
Sen Plex Corp 938 Kohou St	Honolulu	HI	96817	808-848-0111	848-0210
Web: www.senplex.com					
Senior Housing Properties Trust 255 Washington St	Newton	MA	02458	617-796-8350	796-8349
NYSE: SNH ■ *TF:* 866-511-5038 ■ *Web:* www.snhreit.com					
Sentinel Real Estate Corp 1251 Ave of the Americas	New York	NY	10020	212-408-5000	603-8253
Web: www.sentinelcorp.com					
Simon Property Group Inc 225 W Washington St	Indianapolis	IN	46204	317-636-1600	263-7658*
NYSE: SPG ■ **Fax:* Cust Svc ■ *Web:* www.simon.com					
SL Green Realty Corp 420 Lexington Ave	New York	NY	10170	212-594-2700	216-1790
NYSE: SLG ■ *Web:* www.slgreen.com					
SonomaWest Holdings Inc 2064 Hwy 116	Sebastopol	CA	95472	707-824-2534	829-4630
Web: sonomawestholdings.com					
SR Weiner & Assoc Inc 1330 Boylston St	Chestnut Hill	MA	02467	617-232-8900	734-4661
Web: www.wsdevelopment.com					
Stanmar Inc 321 Commonwealth Rd Ste 201	Wayland	MA	01778	508-310-9922	310-0479
Web: www.stanmar-inc.com					
Stirling Properties 109 Northpark Blvd Ste 300	Covington	LA	70433	985-898-2022	898-2077
TF: 888-261-2022 ■ *Web:* www.stirlingprop.com					
SUHRCO Management Inc 2010 156th Ave NE Ste 100	Bellevue	WA	98007	425-455-0900	462-1943
Web: suhrcorp.com/					
Sun Communities Inc 27777 Franklin Rd Ste 200	Southfield	MI	48034	248-208-2500	208-2640
NYSE: SUI ■ *Web:* www.suncommunities.com					
Supertel Hospitality Inc 309 N Fifth St PO Box 1448	Norfolk	NE	68701	402-371-2520	
NASDAQ: SPPR ■ *Web:* www.supertelinc.com					
Susquehanna Real Estate 140 E Market St PO Box 2026	York	PA	17401	717-848-5500	771-1430
Web: www.susquehanna-realestate.com					
Tanger Factory Outlet Centers Inc 3200 Northline Ave Ste 360	Greensboro	NC	27408	336-292-3010	852-2096
NYSE: SKT ■ *TF:* 800-720-6728 ■ *Web:* www.tangeroutlet.com					
Targa Real Estate Services Inc 720 S 348th St A2	Federal Way	WA	98003	253-815-0393	815-0191
Web: www.targarealestate.com					
Taubman Centers Inc 200 E Long Lk Rd Ste 300	Bloomfield Hills	MI	48303	248-258-6800	258-7683
NYSE: TCO ■ *TF:* 800-297-6003 ■ *Web:* www.taubman.com					
Thackeray Partners 5207 McKinney Ave Ste 200	Dallas	TX	75205	214-360-7830	
Web: www.thackeraypartners.com					
Topa Management Co 1800 Ave of the Stars Ste 1400	Los Angeles	CA	90067	310-203-9199	229-9788
Web: www.topamanagement.com					
Tower Properties Co 1000 Walnut St Ste 900	Kansas City	MO	64106	816-421-8255	
Web: www.towerproperties.com					
Trammell Crow Co 2100 McKinney Ave Suite 800	Dallas	TX	75201	214-863-4101	863-4493
Web: www.trammellcrow.com					
Transcontinental Realty Investors Inc 1603 Lyndon B Johnson Fwy Ste 800	Dallas	TX	75234	469-522-4200	522-4299
NYSE: TCI ■ *TF:* 800-400-6407 ■ *Web:* www.transconrealty-invest.com					

Phone Fax

Transwestern Commercial Services
1900 W Loop S Ste 1300 .... Houston TX 77027 713-270-7700 270-6285
Web: www.transwestern.net

Tridel Corp 4800 Dufferin St Ste 200 .... Toronto ON M3H5S9 416-661-9394
Web: www.tridel.com

TSI International Group
One Robert Speck Pkwy Ste 960 .... Mississauga ON L4Z3M3 905-602-7463
Web: www.tsi-international.com

Tucson Realty & Trust Co
333 N Wilmont Rd Ste 340 .... Tucson AZ 85711 520-577-7000 918-3031
Web: www.tucsonrealty.com

Underwood Investments 11502 Juniper Ridge Dr .... Austin TX 78759 512-336-1155
Web: underwoodinvestments.com

United Capital Corp Nine Pk Pl .... Great Neck NY 11021 516-466-6464 829-4301
OTC: UCAP ■ *Web:* www.unitedcapitalcorp.net

United Mobile Homes Inc 3499 Rt 9 N Ste 3C .... Freehold NJ 07728 732-577-9997 577-9980
NYSE: UMH ■ *Web:* www.umh.com

Universal Health Realty Income Trust
367 S Gulph Rd .... KingofPrussia PA 19406 610-265-0688
NYSE: UHT ■ *Web:* www.uhrit.com

University City Housing (UCH)
3418 Sansom St .... Philadelphia PA 19104 215-222-2000 222-5449
Web: www.universitycityhousing.com

Urban Retail Properties Co
900 N Michigan Ave Ste 900 .... Chicago IL 60611 312-915-2000
Web: www.urbanretail.com

Urstadt Biddle Properties Inc
321 Railroad Ave .... Greenwich CT 06830 203-863-8200 861-6755
NYSE: UBA ■ *Web:* www.ubproperties.com

USAA Real Estate Co
9830 Colonnade Blvd Ste 600 .... San Antonio TX 78230 800-531-8182 641-8425*
**Fax Area Code:* 210 ■ *TF:* 800-531-8182 ■ *Web:* www.usrealco.com

Vangard Investment Properties
118 N State College Blvd .... Fullerton CA 92831 714-446-0100
Web: www.vanguardproperty.com

Vann Realty Co 10330 Regency Pkwy Dr Ste 204 .... Omaha NE 68114 402-734-4800 734-5248
Web: www.vannrealtyco.com

Ventas Inc 353 N Clark St Ste 3300 .... Chicago IL 60654 877-483-6827
NYSE: VTR ■ *TF:* 877-483-6827 ■ *Web:* www.ventasreit.com

Vestar Development
2425 E Camelback Rd Ste 750 .... Phoenix AZ 85016 602-866-0900 955-2298
Web: www.vestar.com

Viceroy Homes Ltd 414 Croft St E .... Port Hope ON L1A4H1 905-885-0400
Web: www.viceroy.com

Village Green Cos 30833 NW Hwy .... Farmington Hills MI 48334 248-851-9600 851-6161
TF: 800-521-2220 ■ *Web:* www.villagegreen.com

Vornado Realty Trust 888 Seventh Ave .... New York NY 10019 212-894-7000 902-9316
NYSE: VNO ■ *TF:* 800-294-1322 ■ *Web:* www.vno.com

Wal-Mart Realty 2001 SE Tenth St .... Bentonville AR 72716 479-273-4682
Web: www.walmartrealty.com

Walton Street Capital LLC
900 N Michigan Ave Ste 1900 .... Chicago IL 60611 312-915-2800
Web: www.waltonst.com

Warren Properties Inc PO Box 469114 .... Escondido CA 92046 800-831-0804 480-7327*
**Fax Area Code:* 760 ■ *Web:* www.warrenproperties.com

Washington Real Estate Investment Trust (WRIT)
6110 Executive Blvd Ste 800 .... Rockville MD 20852 301-984-9400 984-9610
NYSE: WRE ■ *TF:* 800-565-9748 ■ *Web:* www.writ.com

Weingarten Realty Investors
2600 Citadel Plz Dr Ste 300 .... Houston TX 77008 713-866-6000 866-6049
NYSE: WRI ■ *TF:* 800-688-8865 ■ *Web:* www.weingarten.com

Westfield America Inc
2049 Century Park E .... Century City CA 90067 310-478-4456
Web: www.westfield.com

Westgate Management Co Inc
133 Franklin Corner Rd .... Lawrence Township NJ 08648 609-895-8890 895-0058

White Co 1600 S Brentwood Blvd Ste 770 .... Saint Louis MO 63144 314-961-4480 961-5903
Web: www.white-co.com

Wings Event Center 3600 Van Rick Dr .... Kalamazoo MI 49001 269-345-1125 258-3050*
**Fax Area Code:* 720 ■ *Web:* www.wingsstadium.com

Winthrop Realty Trust 7 Bulfinch Pl Ste 500 .... Boston MA 02114 617-570-4614 570-4746
NYSE: FUR ■ *TF:* 800-622-6757 ■ *Web:* www.winthropreit.com

Woodmont Real Estate Services (WRES)
1050 Ralston Ave .... Belmont CA 94002 650-592-3960 591-4577
Web: www.wres.com

WP Carey & Company LLC
50 Rockefeller Plz Second Fl .... New York NY 10020 212-492-1100 492-8922
NYSE: WPC ■ *TF:* 800-972-2739 ■ *Web:* www.wpcarey.com

Wright Runstad & Co 1201 Third Ave Ste 2700 .... Seattle WA 98101 206-447-9000 223-8791
Web: www.wrightrunstad.com

Zamias Services Inc 300 Market St .... Johnstown PA 15901 814-535-3563 536-5969
Web: www.zamias.com

Zions Securities Corp
Five Triad Ctr Ste 450 .... Salt Lake City UT 84180 801-321-8700 320-4600
Web: www.utpma.com

659 ◦ REALTOR ASSOCIATIONS - STATE

SEE ALSO Real Estate Professionals Associations p. 1807
Listed here are the state branches of the National Association of Realtors.

Phone Fax

Alabama Assn of Realtors
522 Washington Ave PO Box 4070 .... Montgomery AL 36104 334-262-3808 263-9650
TF: 800-446-3808 ■ *Web:* www.alabamarealtors.com

Alaska Assn of Realtors 4205 Minnesota Dr .... Anchorage AK 99503 907-563-7133 561-1779
Web: www.alaskarealtors.com

Arizona Assn of Realtors
255 E Osborne Rd Ste 200 .... Phoenix AZ 85012 602-248-7787 351-2474
TF: 800-426-7274 ■ *Web:* www.aaronline.com

Arkansas Realtors Assn
11224 Executive Ctr Dr .... Little Rock AR 72211 501-225-2020 225-7131
TF: 888-333-2206 ■ *Web:* www.arkansasrealtors.com

Phone Fax

Axiom Xcell Inc 6150 Lusk Blvd Ste 203 .... San Diego CA 92121 858-453-9700
Web: www.axiomxcell.com

Beach Properties of Hilton Head Inc
64 Arrow Rd PO Box 7408 .... Hilton Head Island SC 29928 843-671-5155
Web: www.beach-property.com

California Assn of Realtors
525 S Virgil Ave .... Los Angeles CA 90020 213-739-8200 480-7724
Web: www.car.org

Carolina Designs Realty Inc 1197 Duck Rd .... Kitty Hawk NC 27949 252-261-3934
Web: www.carolinadesigns.com

Colorado Assn of Realtors
309 Inverness Way S .... Englewood CO 80112 303-790-7099 790-7299
TF: 800-944-6550 ■ *Web:* www.coloradorealtors.com

Connecticut Assn of Realtors
111 Founders Plz Ste 1101 .... East Hartford CT 06108 860-290-6601 290-6615
TF: 800-335-4862 ■ *Web:* www.ctrealtor.com

Countryside Asset Management Corp
7490 Clubhouse Rd Ste 201 .... Boulder CO 80301 303-530-0700
Web: www.csamc.com

Delaware Assn of Realtors 134 E Water St .... Dover DE 19901 302-734-4444 734-1341
TF: 800-305-4445 ■ *Web:* www.delawarerealtor.com

Flaherty & Collins Properties Inc
8900 Keystone Crossing Ste 1200 .... Indianapolis IN 46240 317-816-9300
Web: flco.com

Florida Assn of Realtors
7025 Augusta National Dr .... Orlando FL 32822 407-438-1400 438-1411
Web: www.floridarealtors.org

Georgia Assn of Realtors
3200 Presidential Dr .... Atlanta GA 30340 770-451-1831 458-6992
TF: 866-280-0576 ■ *Web:* www.garealtor.com

Goodman Real Estate Inc
2801 Alaskan Way Ste 310 .... Seattle WA 98121 206-448-0259
Web: www.goodmanre.com

Grand Peaks Properties Inc
4582 S Ulster St Pkwy Ste 1200 .... Denver CO 80237 720-889-9200
Web: www.grandpeaks.com

Greater Capital Area Assn of Realtors
8757 Georgia Ave Ste 600 .... Silver Spring MD 20910 301-590-2000
Web: www.gcaar.com

Growth Properties Investment Managers Inc
1329 Bristol Pike Ste 182 .... Bensalem PA 19020 215-546-5980
Web: www.gpim.net

Hawaii Assn of Realtors
1136 12th Ave Ste 220 .... Honolulu HI 96816 808-733-7060 737-4977
TF: 866-693-6767 ■ *Web:* www.hawaiirealtors.com

Idaho Assn of Realtors 10116 W Overland Rd .... Boise ID 83702 208-342-3585 336-7958
TF: 800-621-7553 ■ *Web:* www.idahorealtors.com

Illinois Assn of Realtors 522 S Fifth St .... Springfield IL 62701 217-529-2600 529-3904
Web: www.illinoisrealtor.org

Indiana Assn of Realtors
7301 N Shadeland Ave Ste A .... Indianapolis IN 46250 317-842-0890 842-1076
TF: 800-284-0084 ■ *Web:* www.indianarealtors.com

Intracorp Projects Ltd
25 Centurian Dr Ste 204 .... Markham ON L3R5N8 905-940-6555
Web: intracorp.ca

Iowa Assn of Realtors 1370 NW 114th St Ste 100 .... Clive IA 50325 515-453-1064 453-1070
TF: 800-532-1515 ■ *Web:* www.iowarealtors.com

Jacobson Companies Inc, The 1334 S Fifth Ave .... Yuma AZ 85364 928-782-1801
Web: www.jacobsoncompanies.com

JEM Strapping Systems 116 Shaver St .... Brantford ON N3T5M1 519-754-5432
Web: www.jemline.com

Kansas Assn of Realtors 3644 SW Burlingame Rd .... Topeka KS 66611 785-267-3610 267-1867
TF: 800-366-0069 ■ *Web:* www.kansasrealtor.com

Kentucky Assn of Realtors
161 Prosperous Pl .... Lexington KY 40509 859-263-7377 263-7565
TF: 800-264-2185 ■ *Web:* www.kar.com

Maine Assn of Realtors 19 Community Dr .... Augusta ME 04330 207-622-7501 623-3590
Web: www.mainerealtors.com

Management Group Inc, The
7710 Ne Vancouver Mall Dr Ste A .... Vancouver WA 98662 360-892-4000
Web: www.tmgnw.com

Maryland Assn of Realtors 2594 Riva Rd .... Annapolis MD 21401 410-841-6080 261-8369*
**Fax Area Code:* 301 ■ *TF:* 800-638-6425 ■ *Web:* www.mdrealtor.org

Massachusetts Assn of Realtors
256 Second Ave .... Waltham MA 02451 781-890-3700 890-4919
TF: 800-725-6272 ■ *Web:* www.marealtor.com

Mentor Group Inc, The
1775 E Palm Canyon Dr Ste 110-132 .... Palm Springs CA 92264 760-325-6411
Web: www.mentorgroupinc.com

Michael L. Shular 2682 S Mckenzie St .... Foley AL 36535 251-943-9100
Web: www.shularhospitality.com

Michigan Assn of Realtors
720 N Washington Ave .... Lansing MI 48906 517-372-8890 334-5568
TF: 800-454-7842 ■ *Web:* www.mirealtors.com

Minnesota Assn of Realtors
5750 Lincoln Dr .... Minneapolis MN 55436 952-935-8313 835-3815
TF: 800-862-6097 ■ *Web:* www.mnrealtor.com

Mississippi Assn of Realtors
4274 Lakeland Dr PO Box 321000 .... Jackson MS 39232 601-932-9325 932-0382
TF: 800-747-1103 ■ *Web:* www.msrealtors.org

Missouri Assn of Realtors
2601 Bernadette Pl .... Columbia MO 65203 573-445-8400 445-7865
TF: 800-403-0101 ■ *Web:* www.missourirealtor.org

MLS Property Information Network Inc
904 Hartford Tpke .... Shrewsbury MA 01545 508-845-1011
Web: www.mlspin.com

Montana Assn of Realtors
One S Montana Ave Ste M1 .... Helena MT 59601 406-443-4032 443-4220
TF: 800-477-1864 ■ *Web:* www.montanarealtors.org

Nebraska Realtors Assn 800 S 13th St Ste 200 .... Lincoln NE 68508 402-323-6500 323-6501
TF: 800-777-5231 ■ *Web:* www.nebraskarealtors.com

Nevada Assn of Realtors 760 Margrave Dr Ste 200 .... Reno NV 89502 775-829-5911 829-5915
TF: 800-748-5526 ■ *Web:* www.nvar.org

Phone Fax

New Hampshire Assn of Realtors
115A Airport Rd .... Concord NH 03301 603-225-5549 228-0385
TF: 800-335-4862 ■ *Web:* nhar.org

New Jersey Assn of Realtors 295 Pierson Ave .... Edison NJ 08837 732-494-5616 494-4723
Web: www.njar.com

New York State Assn of Realtors
130 Washington Ave................................ Albany NY 12210 518-463-0300 462-5474
TF: 800-462-7585 ■ *Web:* www.nysar.com

North Carolina Assn of Realtors Inc
4511 Weybridge Ln............................. Greensboro NC 27407 336-294-1415 299-7872
TF: 800-443-9956 ■ *Web:* www.ncrealtors.org

North Dakota Assn of Realtors
318 W Apollo Ave................................ Bismarck ND 58503 701-355-1010 258-7211
TF: 800-279-2361 ■ *Web:* www.ndrealtors.com

Ohio Assn of Realtors 200 E Town St............... Columbus OH 43215 614-228-6675 228-2601
Web: www.ohiorealtors.org

Oklahoma Assn of Realtors
9807 N Broadway .... Oklahoma City OK 73114 405-848-9944 848-9947
TF: 800-375-9944 ■ *Web:* www.oklahomarealtors.com

Oregon Assn of Realtors 2110 Mission St SE .... Salem OR 97308 503-362-3645 362-9615
TF: 800-252-9115 ■ *Web:* oregonrealtors.org

Pennsylvania Assn of Realtors
4501 Chambers Hill Rd .... Harrisburg PA 17111 717-561-1303 561-8796
TF: 800-555-3390 ■ *Web:* www.parealtor.org

Phoenix Housing Network 7050 S G St............... Tacoma WA 98408 253-471-5340
Web: ccsww.convio.net

Rainier Group Investment Advisory LLC
500 108th Ave N E Ste 2000......................... Bellevue WA 98004 425-463-3000
Web: rainiergroup.com

Real Estate Institute of Canada, The
5407 Eglinton Ave W Ste 208........................ Toronto ON M9C5K6 416-695-9000
Web: www.reic.ca

Realtors Assn of New Mexico 2201 Bros Rd .... Santa Fe NM 87505 505-982-2442 983-8809
TF: 800-224-2282 ■ *Web:* www.nmrealtor.com

Rhode Island Assn of Realtors 100 Bignall St .... Warwick RI 02888 401-785-9898 941-5360
TF: 866-438-8345 ■ *Web:* www.riliving.com

RPI Media Inc 265 Racine Dr Ste 201............... Wilmington NC 28403 910-763-2100
Web: www.rpisales.com

Senior Resource Group
500 Stevens Ave Ste 100 .... Solana Beach CA 92075 858-792-9300
Web: www.srgseniorliving.com

Signature Homes Inc 4670 Willow Rd Ste 200........ Pleasanton CA 94588 925-463-1122
Web: www.sigprop.com

SMI properties 5239 zMax Blvd.................... Harrisburg NC 28075 704-455-9499
Web: www.smiproperties.com

South Carolina Assn of Realtors
3780 Fernandina Rd............................. Columbia SC 29210 803-772-5206 798-6650
TF: 800-233-6381 ■ *Web:* www.screaltors.org

South Dakota Assn of Realtors
204 N Euclid Ave .... Pierre SD 57501 605-224-0554 224-8975
TF: 800-227-5877 ■ *Web:* www.sdrealtor.org

staySky Resort Management
7011 Grand National Dr Ste 104...................... Orlando FL 32819 407-992-0430
Web: www.skyresortmanagement.com

Tennessee Assn of Realtors (TAR)
901 19th Ave S.................................. Nashville TN 37212 615-321-1477 321-4905
TF: 877-321-1477 ■ *Web:* www.tarnet.com

Texas Assn of Realtors
1115 San Jacinto Blvd Ste 200........................ Austin TX 78701 512-480-8200 370-2390
TF: 800-873-9155 ■ *Web:* www.texasrealestate.com/

Utah Assn of Realtors
230 W Towne Ridge Pkwy Ste 500 .... Sandy UT 84070 801-676-5200 676-5225
TF: 800-594-8933 ■ *Web:* www.utahrealtors.com

Vermont Assn of Realtors 148 State St............. Montpelier VT 05602 802-229-0513 229-0995
Web: www.vtrealtor.com

Victoria Inn, The 1604 Quintard Ave................. Anniston AL 36202 256-236-0503
Web: www.thevictoria.com

Virginia Assn of Realtors
10231 Telegraph Rd .... Glen Allen VA 23059 804-264-5033 262-0497
TF: 800-755-8271 ■ *Web:* www.varealtor.com

Washington Assn of Realtors
504 14th Ave SE Ste 200 .... Olympia WA 98501 360-943-3100
Web: www.warealtor.org

West Virginia Assn of Realtors
2110 Kanawha Blvd E............................. Charleston WV 25311 304-342-7600 343-5811
TF: 800-445-7600 ■ *Web:* www.wvrealtors.com

Wisconsin Realtors Assn
4801 Forest Run Rd Ste 201........................ Madison WI 53704 608-241-2047 241-2901
TF: 800-279-1972 ■ *Web:* www.wra.org

Wyoming Assn of Realtors 951 Werner Ct Ste 300....... Casper WY 82601 307-237-4085 237-7929
TF: 800-676-4085 ■ *Web:* www.wyorealtors.com

660 RECORDING COMPANIES

Phone Fax

ABKCO Music & Records Inc
85 Fifth Ave Ste 11.............................. New York NY 10003 212-399-0300
Web: www.abkco.com

Alligator Records & Artist Management Inc
PO Box 60234 .... Chicago IL 60660 773-973-7736 973-2088
Web: www.alligator.com

American Gramaphone LLC 9130 Mormon Bridge Rd..... Omaha NE 68152 402-457-4341 457-4332
TF: 800-348-3434 ■ *Web:* store.mannheimsteamroller.com/home.htm

Balboa Records Inc 10900 Washington Blvd .... Culver City CA 90232 310-204-3792 204-0886
Web: www.balboarecords.com

Cambria Music PO Box 374.......................... Lomita CA 90717 310-831-1322 833-7442
Web: www.cambriamus.com

Century Media 2323 W El Segundo Blvd............. Hawthorne CA 90250 323-418-1400 418-0118
Web: www.centurymedia.com

Curb Records 48 Music Sq E .... Nashville TN 37203 615-321-5080
Web: www.curb.com

Dualtone Music Group 3 Mcferrin Ave............... Nashville TN 37206 615-320-0620 320-0692
Web: www.dualtone.com

EMI Music Canada 109 Atlantic Ave .... Toronto ON M6K1X4 416-583-5000
Web: www.universalmusic.ca

Geffen Records 2220 Colorado Ave.............. Santa Monica CA 90404 310-865-4000
Web: www.interscope.com

Hollywood Records Inc 500 S Buena Vista St.......... Burbank CA 91521 818-560-5670 845-4313
Web: www.hollywoodrecords.com

Integrity Music 4050 Lee Vance View .... Colorado Springs CO 80918 719-536-0100
TF: 888-888-4726 ■ *Web:* www.integritymusic.com

Interscope Records 2220 Colorado Ave.......... Santa Monica CA 90404 310-865-1000 865-1405
Web: www.interscope.com

Mack Avenue Records Ii LLC
19900 Harper Ave........................... Harper Woods MI 48225 313-640-8414
Web: www.mackavenue.com

Malaco Music Group Inc 3023 W Northside Dr......... Jackson MS 39213 601-982-4522 982-4528
TF Cust Svc: 800-272-7936 ■ *Web:* www.malaco.com

Mosaic Records 35 Melrose Pl..................... Stamford CT 06902 203-327-7111 323-3526
Web: www.mosaicrecords.com

Narada Productions Inc
4650 N Port Washington Rd........................ Milwaukee WI 53212 414-961-8350 961-8351

Naxos of America Inc 1810 Columbia Ave............. Franklin TN 37064 615-771-9393 771-6747
TF: 877-629-6723 ■ *Web:* www.naxos.com

Nightingale-Conant Corp 6245 W Howard St .... Niles IL 60714 800-557-1660 647-5989*
**Fax Area Code:* 847 ■ *TF Cust Svc:* 800-557-1660 ■ *Web:* www.nightingale.com

Nonesuch Records
1290 Ave of the Americas Ste 23 .... New York NY 10104 212-275-2000
Web: www.nonesuch.com

Psychopathic Record 32575 Folsom Rd....... Farmington Hills MI 48336 248 426 0800
Web: www.psychopathicrecords.com

Rainmaker Recording & Creative
1901 E Franklin St Ste 101........................ Richmond VA 23223 804-771-9300
Web: www.rainmakerstudios.com

RCA Records 550 Madison Ave...................... New York NY 10022 800-745-3000
Web: www.rcarecords.com

Record Plant Inc 1032 N Sycamore Ave .... Hollywood CA 90038 323-993-9300 466-8835
Web: www.recordplant.com

Rhino Records 3400 W Olive Ave...................... Burbank CA 91505 800-546-3670 956-0529*
**Fax Area Code:* 212 ■ *TF:* 800-827-4466 ■ *Web:* www.rhino.com

Righteous Babe Records
341 Delaware Ave PO Box 95 .... Buffalo NY 14202 716-852-8020 852-2741
TF: 800-664-3769 ■ *Web:* www.righteousbabe.com

Silvercup Studios 3402 Starr Ave .... Long Island City NY 11101 718-906-3000
Web: www.silvercupstudios.com

Skaggs Family Records PO Box 2478 .... Hendersonville TN 37077 615-264-8877 264-8899
Web: www.skaggsfamilyrecords.com

Smithsonian Folkways Recordings
600 Maryland Ave SW Ste 200...................... Washington DC 20024 202-633-6450 633-6477
TF: 800-410-9815 ■ *Web:* www.folkways.si.edu

Soar Corp (SOAR) 5200 Constitution Ave NE .... Albuquerque NM 87110 505-268-6110 464-0445*
**Fax Area Code:* 215 ■ *TF:* 866-616-4450

Sony Music Entertainment
550 Madison Ave Rm 2316 .... New York NY 10022 212-833-8000 833-5828*
**Fax:* Sales ■ *Web:* www.sonymusic.com

Sony Music Nashville 1400 18th Ave S .... Nashville TN 37212 615-301-4488
Web: www.sonymusicnashville.com

Sony Wonder 550 Madison Ave .... New York NY 10022 212-833-8100
Web: www.sonywondertechlab.com

SubPop Records 2013 Fourth Ave Third Fl .... Seattle WA 98121 206-441-8441 441-8245
Web: www.subpop.com

Telarc International Corp
23307 Commerce Pk Rd.......................... Cleveland OH 44122 216-464-2313 360-9663
Web: concordmusicgroup.com/labels/telarc/

Victory Records Inc 346 N Justine St 5th Fl............ Chicago IL 60607 312-666-8661 666-8665
Web: www.victoryrecords.com

Walt Disney Records 500 S Buena Vista St............ Burbank CA 91521 818-560-1000
Web: www.disney.go.com/disneyrecords

Walt Disney Studios 500 S Buena Vista St .... Burbank CA 91521 407-939-5277
Web: www.disneyworld.disney.go.com

Warner Bros Records 3300 Warner Blvd .... Burbank CA 91505 818-846-9090
Web: www.warnerbrosrecords.com

Warner Music Group
75 Rockefeller Plz 30th Fl.......................... New York NY 10019 212-275-2000
Web: www.wmg.com

Word Entertainment 25 Music Sq W .... Nashville TN 37203 615-251-0600 726-7868
Web: www.wordentertainment.com

Worldly Voices LLC 2610 Westwood Dr .... Nashville TN 37204 615-321-8802
Web: www.worldlyvoices.com

661 RECORDING MEDIA - MAGNETIC & OPTICAL

SEE ALSO Photographic Equipment & Supplies p. 2927

Phone Fax

Allied Vaughn 7600 Parklawn Ste 300............. Minneapolis MN 55435 952-832-3100 832-3179
TF: 800-323-0281 ■ *Web:* www.alliedvaughn.com

Ampex Corp 500 Broadway..................... Redwood City CA 94063 650-367-2011 367-4669*
**Fax:* Hum Res ■ *TF:* 800-835-5095 ■ *Web:* www.ampex.com

Applied Data Resources Inc
1303 N Glenville Dr .... Richardson TX 75081 972-238-8111

Athana Inc 1624 W 240 St....................... Harbor City CA 90710 310-539-7280 539-6596
TF: 800-421-1591 ■ *Web:* www.athana.com

Cine Magnetics Inc 100 Business Pk Dr Ste 1.......... Armonk NY 10504 914-273-7500 273-7575
TF: 800-431-1102 ■ *Web:* cinemagnetics.com

Cinram International Inc 2255 Markham Rd....... Scarborough ON M1B2W3 416-298-8190 298-0612
Web: cinramgroup.com

Conduant Corp 1501 S Sunset St Ste C............ Longmont CO 80501 303-485-2721
Web: www.conduant.com

Digital Excellence 300 York Ave.................. Saint Paul MN 55101 651-772-5100 771-5629
TF: 800-608-8008 ■ *Web:* www.digx.com

Duplication Factory Inc 4275 Norex Dr .... Chaska MN 55318 952-227-8106
TF: 800-279-2009 ■ *Web:* www.duplicationfactory.com

Phone Fax

eScholar LLC 222 Bloomingdale Rd Ste 107 .... White Plains NY 10605 914-989-2900
Web: www.escholar.com

Farstone Technology Inc
1758-B N Shoreline Blvd .... Mountain View CA 94043 562-373-5370 969-4567*
**Fax Area Code:* 650 ■ *Web:* www.farstone.com

Fujifilm Mfg USA Inc 211 Pucketts Ferry Rd......... Greenwood SC 29649 864-223-2888
Web: fujifilmusa.com/about

Imagine Express 2633 Minnehaha Ave .... Minneapolis MN 55406 612-728-1500
Web: www.digidigi.com

Imation Corp One Imation Pl ....Oakdale MN 55128 651-704-4000 704-7100
NYSE: IMN ■ *TF:* 888-466-3456 ■ *Web:* www.imation.com

LaserCard Corp 1875 N Shoreline Blvd.......... Mountain View CA 94043 650-969-4428 969-3140
Web: www.hidglobal.com

Maxell Corp of America
3 Garret Mountain Plaza 3rd Fl Ste 300 ....Woodland Park NJ 07424 973-653-2400 653-2450
TF: 800-533-2836 ■ *Web:* www.maxell-usa.com

Mediostream Inc 4962 El Cmno Real 201 ....Los Altos CA 94022 650-625-8900 625-9900
Web: www.mediostream.com

Optical Disc Solutions Inc 1767 Sheridan St .... Richmond IN 47374 765-935-7574 894-7281*
**Fax Area Code:* 423 ■ *TF:* 888-987-6334 ■ *Web:* www.odiscs.com

Peripheral Manufacturing Inc 4775 Paris St...........Denver CO 80239 303-371-8651 371-8643
TF: 800-468-6888 ■ *Web:* www.periphman.com

Sony DADC US INC 1800 N Fruitridge Ave .... Terre Haute IN 47804 812-462-8100
Web: www.sonydadc.com

Stanton Magnetics Inc
772 S Military Trl ....Deerfield Beach FL 33442 954-949-9600
Web: www.stantondj.com

TDK Electronics Corp 525 RXR Plz................. Uniondale NY 11556 516-535-2600
Web: www.tdk.com

TDK USA Corp 525 RXR Plaza PO Box 9302 .... Uniondale NY 11556 516-535-2600 294-8318*
**Fax:* Sales ■ *TF General:* 800-285-2783 ■ *Web:* www.tdk.com

Verbatim Americas LLC
1200 W WT Harris Blvd .... Charlotte NC 28262 704-547-6500 547-6609
TF: 800-538-8589 ■ *Web:* www.verbatim.com

Viva Magnetics (Canada) Ltd
1663 Neilson Rd............................. Scarborough ON M1X1T1 416-321-0622
Web: www.vivacan.com

662 RECREATION FACILITY OPERATORS

SEE ALSO Bowling Centers p. 1885

Phone Fax

Clicks Billiards 3100 Monticello Ave Ste 350 .... Dallas TX 75205 214-521-7001 521-1449
Web: clicks.com

Dave & Buster's Inc 2481 Manana Dr.................. Dallas TX 75220 214-357-9588 636-5454*
**Fax Area Code:* 302 ■ *TF:* 800-842-5369 ■ *Web:* www.daveandbusters.com

663 RECYCLABLE MATERIALS RECOVERY

Included here are companies that recycle post-consumer trash, tires, appliances, batteries, etc. as well as industrial recyclers of plastics, paper, wood, glass, solvents, and so on.

Phone Fax

A.J. Catagnus Inc 1299 W James St................Norristown PA 19401 610-277-2727
Web: www.ajcatagnus.com

ACC Recycling Corp 1190 20th St N........... Saint Petersburg FL 33713 727-892-9216 822-4923

Active Recycling Company Inc
2000 W Slauson Ave...........................Los Angeles CA 90047 323-295-7774
Web: www.activelosangeles.com

Advanced Environmental Recycling Technologies Inc
914 N Jefferson St ....Springdale AR 72764 479-756-7400 756-7410
OTC: AERT ■ *Web:* aert.com

All American Recycling Corp 2 Hope St............Jersey City NJ 07307 201-656-3363 792-5693
Web: allamericanrecyclingcorp.com

Ambit Pacific Recycling Inc
16228 S Figueroa St...............................Gardena CA 90248 310-538-3798 327-7114
Web: www.ambitpacific.com

American Paper Recycling Corp
301 W Lake St ....Northlake IL 60164 708-344-6789 344-0262
TF Cust Svc: 800-762-6790 ■ *Web:* aprcorp.com

Apollo Wood Recovery Inc 14253 Whittram Ave........Fontana CA 92335 909-356-2735
Web: www.apollowood.com

Appliance Recycling Centers of America Inc
7400 Excelsior Blvd .... Minneapolis MN 55426 952-930-9000 930-1800
NASDAQ: ARCI ■ *TF:* 800-452-8680 ■ *Web:* www.arcainc.com

Arrow Value Recovery 9101 Burnet Rd Ste 203.......... Austin TX 78758 800-393-7627
TF: 800-393-7627 ■ *Web:* www.intechra.com

Asbury Environmental Services
9119 Birch St...................................Spring Valley CA 91977 619-463-1126
Web: www.asburyenv.com

Balcones Resources Inc 9301 Johnny Morris Rd........ Austin TX 78724 512-472-3355
Web: www.balconesresources.com

Better Management Corp (BMC)
41738 Esterly Dr...............................Columbiana OH 44408 330-482-7070 482-5929
TF: 877-293-4300 ■ *Web:* www.bmcohio.com

Canusa Hershman Recycling Co
45 NE Industrial Rd............................. Branford CT 06405 203-488-0887 483-9943
Web: www.chrecycling.com

Chemtron Corp 35850 Schneider Ct .... Avon OH 44011 440-937-6348
Web: www.chemtron-corp.com

Clean Earth of North Jersey Inc
115 Jacobus Ave...............................South Kearny NJ 07032 973-344-4004 344-8652
TF: 877-445-3478 ■ *Web:* cleanearthinc.com

Continental Paper Grading Company Inc
1623 S Lumber St.................................Chicago IL 60616 312-226-2010 226-2025
Web: www.cpgco.com

Dallas Waste Disposal & Recycling Inc
3303 Pluto St................................... Dallas TX 75212 214-634-1831
Web: www.dallasrecycling.net

Energy Answers Corp 79 N Pearl St ....Albany NY 12207 518-434-1227 436-6343
Web: www.energyanswers.com

Federal International Inc
7935 Clayton Rd.............................. Saint Louis MO 63117 314-721-3377 721-2007
TF: 800-972-7277 ■ *Web:* www.federalinternational.com

Friedman Recycling Co 3640 W Lincoln St............Phoenix AZ 85009 602-269-9324
Web: www.friedmanrecycling.com

Fritz Enterprises Inc 1650 W Jefferson Ave .... Trenton MI 48183 734-362-3200 362-3250
Web: www.fritzinc.com

Geep International
2501 N Great SW Pkwy.........................Grand Prairie TX 75050 972-602-2905
Web: www.geepglobal.com

Giordano s Solid Waste Removal
110 N Mill Rd .... Vineland NJ 08360 856-696-2068
Web: www.giordanosrecycling.com

GreenMan Technologies Inc
Seven Kimball Ln Bldg A ....Lynnfield MA 01940 781-224-2411 224-0114
Web: www.americanpowergroupinc.com

Greentec International Inc 95 Struck Ct............Cambridge ON N1R8L2 519-624-3300
Web: www.greentec.com

Horry County Solid Waste Authority Inc
1886 Hwy 90 .... Conway SC 29526 843-347-1651
Web: www.solidwasteauthority.org

Hvf West LLC 6581 E Drexel Rd........................Tucson AZ 85706 520-750-9454
Web: www.hvfwest.com

International Metals Reclamation Company Inc
One Inmetco Dr.............................. Ellwood City PA 16117 724-758-2800 758-2845
Web: www.inmetco.com

Jupiter Aluminum Corp 4825 Scott St .... Schiller Park IL 60176 847-928-5930 928-0795
TF: 800-392-7265 ■ *Web:* www.jupiteraluminum.com

Marborg Industries 728 E Yanonali St .... Santa Barbara CA 93103 805-963-1852 962-0552
TF: 800-798-1852 ■ *Web:* www.marborg.com

MCF Systems Atlanta Inc
5353 Snapfinger Woods Dr.......................... Decatur GA 30035 770-593-9434
Web: www.mcfsystems.com

Mervis Industries Inc 3295 E Main St ....Danville IL 61834 217-442-5300 477-9245
TF: 800-637-3016 ■ *Web:* www.mervis.com

Metro Recycling Co Inc 2424 Beekman St........... Cincinnati OH 45214 513-251-1800 836-1047*
**Fax Area Code:* 519

Minergy Corp 1512 S Commercial St.................. Neenah WI 54956 920-727-1919 727-1418
Web: www.minergy.com

Newalta Corp 211 11 Ave SW .... Calgary AB T2R0C6 403-806-7000
Web: www.newalta.com

North Shore Recycled Fibers Inc
53 Jefferson Ave.................................. Salem MA 01970 978-744-4330 744-8857
TF: 800-225-2369 ■ *Web:* newarkgroup.com

Pall Corp 2200 Northern Blvd ....East Hills NY 11548 516-484-5400 801-9754
NYSE: PLL ■ *TF:* 800-645-6532 ■ *Web:* www.pall.com

Paper Tigers, The
2201 Waukegan Rd Ste 180 ....Bannockburn IL 60015 847-919-6500 919-6501
TF: 800-621-1774 ■ *Web:* www.papertigers.com

Pioneer Paper Stock 155 Irving Ave N............ Minneapolis MN 55405 612-374-2280 374-5982
TF: 800-821-8512 ■ *Web:* www.pioneerintl.com

Potential Industries Inc 922 E E St............... Wilmington CA 90744 310-549-5901 513-1361
Web: potentialindustries.com

ReCommunity Recycling 809 W Hill St............. Charlotte NC 28208 704-697-2000 375-2949
Web: www.recommunity.com

Recycle Ann Arbor Inc
2420 S Industrial Hwy .... Ann Arbor MI 48104 734-662-6288
Web: www.recycleannarbor.org

Recycling Center of Live Oak Inc, The
700 Houston Ave NW .... Live Oak FL 32064 386-364-5865
Web: www.biggreenball.org

ROUND2 Inc
1340 Airport Commerce Dr Bldg 3 Ste 300 .... Austin TX 78741 512-342-8855
Web: www.round2.net

Royal Waste Services Inc 18740 Hollis Ave ....Hollis NY 11423 718-468-8679
Web: royalwaste.com

Strategic Materials Inc
16365 Pk Ten Pl Ste 200 ....Houston TX 77084 281-647-2700 647-2710
Web: www.strategicmaterials.com

Sun Valley Paper Stock Inc
11166 Pendleton St ....Sun Valley CA 91352 818-875-2613

Texas Recycling Surplus Inc
2835 Congressman Ln............................. Dallas TX 75220 214-357-0262
Web: www.texasrecycling.com

United Plastic Recycling Inc
4290 Alatex Rd .... Montgomery AL 36108 334-288-5002
Web: unitedplasticrecycling.com

Utah Metal Works Inc (UMW)
805 Everett Ave PO Box 1073................... Salt Lake City UT 84116 877-364-5679 364-5676*
**Fax Area Code:* 801 ■ *TF:* 877-221-0099 ■ *Web:* www.umw.com

Vexor Technology Inc 955 W Smith Rd .... Medina OH 44256 330-721-9773
Web: www.vexortechnology.com

WTE Corp Seven Alfred Cir............................ Bedford MA 01730 781-275-6400 275-8612
Web: www.wte.com

664 RECYCLED PLASTICS PRODUCTS

SEE ALSO Flooring - Resilient p. 2292

Phone Fax

Allen Ventures Inc 517 State Farm Rd................ Deerfield WI 53531 608-423-9800 423-9804
TF: 877-423-9800 ■ *Web:* www.allenventures.com

Amazing Recycled Products Inc PO Box 312 ....Denver CO 80201 303-699-7693 699-2102
TF: 800-241-2174 ■ *Web:* www.amazingrecycled.com

American Recycled Plastic Inc
773 N. Union Grove Rd......................... Friendsville TN 37737 865-738-3439 738-3731
TF: 866-674-1525 ■ *Web:* www.itsrecycled.com

Bedford Technology LLC
2424 Armour Rd PO Box 609................ Worthington MN 56187 507-372-5558 372-5726
TF: 800-721-9037 ■ *Web:* plasticboards.com/

Everlast Plastic Lumber 800 Market St............... Auburn PA 17922 570-754-7440
Web: plasticlumber.org

	City	State	Zip	Phone	Fax
GP Harmon Recycling LLC Two Jericho Plz Ste 110 *Web:* www.eharmongp.com	Jericho	NY	11753	516-997-3400	997-3409
J-MacLumber Inc 4154 Faust St. *Web:* www.maclumber.com	Bamberg	SC	29003	803-245-1700	245-1701
Koller Craft Plastic Products 1400 S Old Hwy PO Box 718 *Web:* www.koller-craft.com	Fenton	MO	63026	636-343-9220	343-1034
Parkland Plastics Inc 104 Yoder Dr PO Box 339 *TF:* 800-835-4110 ■ *Web:* www.parklandplastics.com	Middlebury	IN	46540	574-825-4336	
Plastic Lumberyard LLC 220 E Washington St *Web:* www.plasticlumberyard.com	Norristown	PA	19401	610-277-3900	277-3970
Plastic Recycling of Iowa Falls Inc 10252 Hwy 65 *TF:* 800-338-1438 ■ *Web:* www.plasticrecycling.us	Iowa Falls	IA	50126	641-648-5073	648-5074
Plastiques Cascades Re-Plast 1350 Ch Quatre-Saisons *TF:* 800-567-5813 ■ *Web:* www.cascadesreplast.com	Notre-Dame-du-Bon-Conseil	QC	J0C1A0	819-336-2440	336-2442
Polymer Concentrates Inc 179 Woodlawn St PO Box 42 *Web:* www.polymerconcentrates.com	Clinton	MA	01510	978-365-7335	368-0438
Renew Plastics 112 Fourth St PO Box 480 *TF:* 800-666-5207 ■ *Web:* www.renewplastics.com	Luxemburg	WI	54217	920-845-2326	845-2335
Resco Plastics Inc 93783 Newport Ln *TF:* 800-266-5097 ■ *Web:* www.rescoplastics.com	Coos Bay	OR	97420	541-269-5485	269-2572
Witt Industries Inc 4600 Mason-Montgomery Rd. **Fax Area Code: 877* ■ *TF:* 800-543-7417 ■ *Web:* www.witt.com	Mason	OH	45040	800-543-7417	891-8200*

665 REFRACTORIES - CLAY

	City	State	Zip	Phone	Fax
BNZ Materials Inc 6901 S Pierce St Ste 260 *TF:* 800-999-0890 ■ *Web:* www.bnzmaterials.com	Littleton	CO	80128	303-978-1199	978-0308
HarbisonWalker International *ANH Refractories Co* 600 Grant St Ste 50 *Web:* www.hwr.com	Pittsburgh	PA	15219	412-562-6200	562-6209
Magneco/Metrel Inc 223 W I- Rd. *Web:* www.magneco-metrel.com	Addison	IL	60101	630-543-6660	543-1479
Minerals Technologies Inc 405 Lexington Ave. *Web:* mineralstech.com	New York	NY	10174	212-661-9711	
Permatech Inc 911 E Elm St. *Web:* www.permatech.net	Graham	NC	27253	336-578-0701	578-7758
RENO Refractories Inc 601 Reno Dr. *TF:* 800-741-7366 ■ *Web:* www.renorefractories.com	Morris	AL	35116	205-647-0240	647-2115
RENO Refractories Inc Reftech Div 601 Reno Dr **Fax Area Code: 205* ■ *TF General:* 800-741-7366 ■ *Web:* renorefractories.com	Morris	AL	35116	800-741-7366	647-2115*
Resco Products Inc Two Penn Ctr W Ste 430 *TF:* 888-283-5505 ■ *Web:* www.rescoproducts.com	Pittsburgh	PA	15276	412-494-4491	494-4571
Riverside Refractories Inc 201 Truss Ferry Rd *TF:* 800-924-0637 ■ *Web:* www.riversiderefractories.com	Pell City	AL	35128	205-338-3366	338-7456
Shenango Advanced Ceramics LLC 606 McCleary Ave *Web:* rescoproducts.com	New Castle	PA	16101	724-652-6668	
Utah Refractories Corp 2200 North 1200 West *Web:* utah-refractories-corp.com	Lehi	UT	84043	801-768-3591	768-2684
Whitacre Greer Fireproofing Inc 1400 S Mahoning Ave *TF Cust Svc:* 800-947-2837 ■ *Web:* www.wgpaver.com	Alliance	OH	44601	330-823-1610	823-5502

666 REFRACTORIES - NONCLAY

	City	State	Zip	Phone	Fax
Allied Mineral Products Inc 2700 Scioto Pkwy. *Web:* www.alliedmineral.com	Columbus	OH	43221	614-876-0244	876-0981
C-E Minerals Inc 901 E Eigth Ave. *Web:* www.ceminerals.com	King of Prussia	PA	19406	610-265-6880	337-8122
Fedmet Resources Corp PO Box 278. *TF:* 800-609-5711 ■ *Web:* www.fedmet.com	Montreal	QC	H3Z2T2	514-931-5711	931-8378
Inland Refractories Co 38600 Chester Rd PO Box 239 *TF:* 800-321-0767 ■ *Web:* www.refractoriesinstitute.org	Avon	OH	44011	440-934-6600	934-6601
Magnesita Refractories Co 425 S Salem Church Rd **Fax:* Sales ■ *Web:* magnesita.com.br	York	PA	17403	717-792-3611	848-2294*
McDanel Advanced Ceramic Technologies LLC 510 Ninth Ave. *Web:* www.ceramics.com/vesuvius	Beaver Falls	PA	15010	724-843-8300	359-1201
Minco Inc 510 Midway Cir *TF:* 800-525-9753 ■ *Web:* www.mincoitc.com	Midway	TN	37809	423-422-6051	422-4802
Minerals Technologies Inc 405 Lexington Ave. *Web:* mineralstech.com	New York	NY	10174	212-661-9711	
New Castle Refractories Co Inc 915 Industrial St. *TF:* 888-396-3566 ■ *Web:* www.refractoriesinstitute.org	New Castle	PA	16102	724-654-7711	654-6322
Permatech Inc 911 E Elm St *Web:* www.permatech.net	Graham	NC	27253	336-578-0701	578-7758
Plibrico Co 1010 N Hooker St. *Web:* plibrico.com	Chicago	IL	60622	312-337-9000	337-9003
Ransom & Randolph Co 3535 Briarfield Blvd. *TF:* 800-800-7496 ■ *Web:* www.ransom-randolph.com	Maumee	OH	43537	419-865-9497	865-9997
RENO Refractories Inc 601 Reno Dr. *TF:* 800-741-7366 ■ *Web:* www.renorefractories.com	Morris	AL	35116	205-647-0240	647-2115
RENO Refractories Inc Reftech Div 601 Reno Dr **Fax Area Code: 205* ■ *TF General:* 800-741-7366 ■ *Web:* renorefractories.com	Morris	AL	35116	800-741-7366	647-2115*
TYK America Inc 301 BrickyaRd Rd. *TF:* 800-569-9359 ■ *Web:* www.tykamerica.com	Clairton	PA	15025	412-384-4259	384-4242

	City	State	Zip	Phone	Fax
Wahl Refractory Solutions LLC 767 OH-19 *TF:* 800-837-9245 ■ *Web:* www.wahlref.com	Fremont	OH	43420	419-334-2658	334-9445
Worldwide Refractories Inc 6th St.	Tarentum	PA	15084	724-224-8800	224-3353

667 REFRIGERATION EQUIPMENT - MFR

SEE ALSO Air Conditioning & Heating Equipment - Commercial/Industrial p. 1726

	City	State	Zip	Phone	Fax
Adelt Mechanical Ltd 2640 Argentia Rd. *Web:* www.adeltmechanical.com	Mississauga	ON	L5N6C5	905-812-7900	
Advance Energy Technologies Inc One Solar Dr. *TF:* 800-724-0198 ■ *Web:* www.advanceet.com	Clifton Park	NY	12065	518-371-2140	371-0737
American Panel Corp 5800 SE 78th St. *TF:* 800-327-3015 ■ *Web:* www.americanpanel.com	Ocala	FL	34472	352-245-7055	245-0726
Applied Process Cooling Corp 555 Price Ave **Fax Area Code: 707* ■ *TF:* 877-231-6406 ■ *Web:* www.apcco.net	Redwood City	CA	94063	650-595-0665	433-1310*
Arctic Star Refrigeration Mfg Company Inc 3540 W Pioneer Pkwy. *TF:* 800-229-6562 ■ *Web:* www.arcticstar.com	Arlington	TX	76013	817-274-1396	277-4828
Berg Co 2160 Industrial Dr. *Web:* www.bergliquorcontrols.com	Monona	WI	53713	608-221-4281	221-1416
Bessam-Aire Inc 26881 Cannon Rd *Web:* www.bessamaire.com	Cleveland	OH	44146	440-439-1200	
Beverage-Air Corp 3779 Champion Blvd *TF:* 800-845-9800 ■ *Web:* www.beverage-air.com	Winston-Salem	NC	27105	336-245-6400	245-6453
Burch Industries Inc 21381 Charles Craft Ln PO Box 1049. *Web:* www.burchindustries.com	Laurinburg	NC	28352	910-844-3688	844-3689
CIMCO Refrigeration 65 Villiers St. *Web:* www.cimcorefrigeration.com	Toronto	ON	M5A3S1	416-465-7581	
Coldmatic Products International LLC 8500 Keele St *Web:* www.coldmatic.com	Concord	ON	L4K2A6	905-326-7600	
Compu-Aire Inc 8167 Byron Rd. *Web:* www.compu-aire.com	Whittier	CA	90606	562-945-8971	
Contract Manufacturers Inc 729 N Fleishel Ave *Web:* www.contractmanufacturersltd.com	Tyler	TX	75702	903-597-8297	
CrownTonka Inc 15600 37th Ave N Ste 100 *TF:* 800-523-7337 ■ *Web:* www.crowntonka.com	Plymouth	MN	55446	763-541-1410	541-1563
Custom Coolers LLC 5609 Azle Ave *TF:* 800-627-0488 ■ *Web:* www.cccoolers.com	Fort Worth	TX	76114	817-626-3737	626-1213
Delfield Co 980 S Isabella Rd *TF:* 800-733-8821 ■ *Web:* www.delfield.com	Mount Pleasant	MI	48858	989-773-7981	773-3210
Dole Refrigerating Co 1420 Higgs Rd *TF:* 800-251-8990 ■ *Web:* www.doleref.com	Lewisburg	TN	37091	931-359-6211	359-8664
Eliason Corp 9229 Shaver Rd. *TF Cust Svc:* 800-828-3655 ■ *Web:* www.eliasoncorp.com	Portage	MI	49024	269-327-7003	327-7006
Federal Industries Div Standex Corp 215 Federal Ave **Fax Area Code: 608* ■ *TF:* 800-356-4206 ■ *Web:* www.federalind.com	Belleville	WI	53508	800-356-4206	424-3234*
FRL Furniture 460 Grand Blvd *TF:* 800-529-4375 ■ *Web:* www.frlalternatives.com	Westbury	NY	11590	516-333-4400	333-4759
Harris Environmental Systems Inc 11 Connector Rd. *Web:* www.harris-env.com	Andover	MA	01810	978-470-8600	475-7903
Haws Corp 1455 Kleppe Ln. *TF:* 888-640-4297 ■ *Web:* www.hawsco.com	Sparks	NV	89431	775-359-4712	359-7424
Heatcraft Refrigeration Products 2175 W Pk Pl Blvd *TF:* 800-321-1881 ■ *Web:* www.heatcraftrpd.com	Stone Mountain	GA	30087	770-465-5600	465-5990
Hill PHOENIX Inc 1003 Sigman Rd. *TF:* 800-518-6630 ■ *Web:* www.hillphoenix.com	Conyers	GA	30013	770-285-3264	285-3080
Howe Corp 1650 N Elston Ave. *Web:* www.howecorp.com	Chicago	IL	60642	773-235-0200	235-1530
Hussmann Corp 12999 St Charles Rock Rd. *TF:* 800-592-2060 ■ *Web:* www.hussmann.com	Bridgeton	MO	63044	314-291-2000	298-4756
Ice Air LLC 80 Hartford Ave *Web:* www.ice-air.com	Mount Vernon	NY	10553	914-668-4700	
Ice-O-Matic 11100 E 45th Ave. *TF:* 800-423-3367 ■ *Web:* www.iceomatic.com	Denver	CO	80239	303-371-3737	371-6296
IMI Cornelius Inc 101 Broadway St W *TF:* 800-238-3600 ■ *Web:* www.cornelius.com	Osseo	MN	55369	763-488-8200	488-4298
IntelliChoice Energy LLC 2355 W Utopia Rd. *Web:* www.iceghp.com	Phoenix	AZ	85027	623-879-4664	
International Cold Storage Company Inc 215 E 13th St *TF:* 800-835-0001 ■ *Web:* www.icsco.com	Andover	KS	67002	316-733-1385	733-2434
KDIndustries 1525 E Lake Rd *TF:* 800-840-9577 ■ *Web:* www.kold-draft.com	Erie	PA	16511	814-453-6761	455-6336
Kloppenberg & Co 2627 W Oxford Ave. *TF:* 800-346-3246 ■ *Web:* www.kloppenberg.com	Englewood	CO	80110	303-761-1615	789-1741
Kolpak 2915 Tennessee Ave N. *TF:* 800-826-7036 ■ *Web:* www.kolpak.com	Parsons	TN	38363	731-847-5328	847-5387
Kysor Panel Systems 4201 N Beach St. *TF:* 800-633-3426 ■ *Web:* www.kysorpanel.com	Fort Worth	TX	76137	817-281-5121	281-5521
Lancer Corp 6655 Lancer Blvd *TF:* 800-729-1500 ■ *Web:* www.lancercorp.com	San Antonio	TX	78219	210-310-7000	310-7250
Leer LP 206 Leer St *TF Cust Svc:* 800-766-5337 ■ *Web:* www.leerinc.com	New Lisbon	WI	53950	608-562-7100	562-6022
Lytron Inc 55 Dragon Ct *Web:* www.lytron.com	Woburn	MA	01801	781-933-7300	
Manitowoc Ice 2110 S 26th St **Fax:* Sales ■ *TF:* 800-545-5720 ■ *Web:* www.manitowocice.com	Manitowoc	WI	54220	920-682-0161	683-7589*
McCann's Engineering & Manufacturing Co 4570 W Colorado Blvd *TF:* 800-423-2429 ■ *Web:* www.manitowocbeverage.com	Los Angeles	CA	90039	818-637-7200	637-7222
Micro Matic USA Inc 10726 N Second St. **Fax:* Sales ■ *TF:* 866-291-5756 ■ *Web:* www.micro-matic.com	Machesney Park	IL	61115	815-968-7557	968-0363*

Phone | Fax

MicroMetl Corp
3035 N Shadeland Ave Ste 300 .... Indianapolis IN 46226 800-662-4822 524-5499*
*Fax Area Code: 317 ■ TF: 800-662-4822 ■ Web: www.micrometl.com

Morris & Assoc Inc 803 Morris Dr .... Garner NC 27529 919-582-9200 582-9100
Web: www.morris-associates.com

Nance International Inc 2915 Milam St .... Beaumont TX 77701 409-838-6127
Web: nanceinternational.com

Nor-Lake Inc 727 Second St PO Box 248 .... Hudson WI 54016 715-386-2323 386-6149
TF: 800-388-5253 ■ Web: www.norlake.com

Norcold Inc 600 S Kuther Rd .... Sidney OH 45365 937-493-0033 497-3092
TF: 800-543-1219 ■ Web: www.norcold.com

Ontor Ltd 12 Leswyn Rd .... Toronto ON M6A1K3 416-781-5286
Web: www.ontor.com

Perlick Corp 8300 W Good Hope Rd .... Milwaukee WI 53223 414-353-7060 353-7069
TF: 800-558-5592 ■ Web: www.perlick.com

Refplus Inc 2777 Grande Allee .... St-hubert QC J4T2R4 450-641-2665
Web: www.refplus.com

Scotsman Ice Systems
775 Corporate Woods Pkwy .... Vernon Hills IL 60061 847-215-4500 913-9844
TF Cust Svc: 800-726-8762 ■ Web: www.scotsman-ice.com

Semco Manufacturing Co 705 E Business 83 .... Pharr TX 78577 956-787-4203 781-0620
Web: semcoice.com

Silver King Refrigeration Inc
1600 Xenium Ln N .... Minneapolis MN 55441 763-923-2441 553-1209
TF: 800-328-3329 ■ Web: www.silverking.com

Specific Systems Ltd 7655 E 41st St .... Tulsa OK 74145 918-663-9321
Web: specificsystems.com

Suburban Manufacturing Co 676 Broadway St .... Dayton TN 37321 423-775-2131
Web: www.suburbanmanufacturing.com

Tigerflow Systems Inc 4034 Mint Way .... Dallas TX 75237 214-337-8780
Web: www.tigerflow.com

True Manufacturing Co 2001 E Terra Ln .... O'Fallon MO 63366 636-240-2400 272-2408
TF: 800-325-6152 ■ Web: www.truemfg.com

Turbo Refrigerating 1000 W Ormsby Ave .... Louisville KY 40210 502-635-3000 634-0479
TF: 800-853-8648 ■ Web: www.vogtice.com

Victory Refrigeration Inc
110 Woodcrest Rd .... Cherry Hill NJ 08003 856-428-4200 428-7299
TF: 800-523-5008 ■ Web: www.victoryrefrigeration.com

Vintage Air Inc 18865 Goll St .... San Antonio TX 78266 210-654-7171
Web: www.vintageair.com

Vogt Ice 1000 W Ormsby Ave Ste 19 .... Louisville KY 40210 502-635-3000 634-0479
TF: 800-853-8648 ■ Web: www.vogtice.com

WA Brown & Son Inc 209 Long Meadow Dr .... Salisbury NC 28147 704-636-5131 637-0919
TF: 800-438-2316 ■ Web: www.wabrown.com

Weather-Rite LLC 616 N Fifth St .... Minneapolis MN 55401 612-338-1401
Web: www.weather-rite.com

Winvale Group LLC, The
1012 14th St NW Fifth Fl .... Washington DC 20005 202-296-5505
Web: www.winvale.com

Xetex Inc 9405 Holly St NW .... Minneapolis MN 55433 612-724-3101
Web: www.xetexinc.com

668 REFRIGERATION EQUIPMENT - WHOL

SEE ALSO Plumbing, Heating, Air Conditioning Equipment & Supplies - Whol p. 2947

Phone | Fax

Abco Refrigeration Supply Corp
49-70 31st St .... Long Island City NY 11101 718-937-9000 937-9776

Allied Supply Company Inc 1100 E Monument Ave .... Dayton OH 45402 937-224-9833 224-5648
TF: 800-589-5690 ■ Web: www.alliedsupply.com

Alpha Distributors Inc
4700 N Ronald St .... Harwood Heights IL 60706 708-867-5200
Web: www.alphadist.com

American Refrigeration Supplies
2632 E Chambers St .... Phoenix AZ 85040 602-243-2792 243-2893
Web: www.ars-net.com

Automatic Ice & Beverage Inc
1400 Tuscaloosa Ave SW .... Birmingham AL 35211 205-787-9640
Web: aibnow.com

Baker Distributing Co
PO Box 2954 Ste 100 .... Jacksonville FL 32203 800-217-4698 407-8440*
*Fax Area Code: 904 ■ TF: 800-217-4698 ■ Web: www.bakerdist.com

Broich Enterprises Inc 6440 City W Pkwy .... Eden Prairie MN 55344 952-941-2270 941-3066
TF: 800-853-3508 ■ Web: www.arcticairco.com

Cannon Marketing Inc 4684 US Hwy 70 W .... Kinston NC 28504 252-527-3361
Web: www.1cmi.com

Cardinal Ice Equipment Inc
3311 Gilmore Industrial B .... Louisville KY 40213 502-966-4579
Web: iceguys.com

Dennis Supply Co PO Box 3376 .... Sioux City IA 51102 712-255-7637 255-4913
TF: 800-352-4618 ■ Web: www.dennissupply.com

Don Stevens Inc 980 Discovery Rd .... Eagan MN 55121 651-452-0872 452-4189
TF: 800-444-2299 ■ Web: www.donstevens.com

Downriver Refrigeration Supply Co
38170 N Executive Dr N .... Westland MI 48185 734-728-0795
Web: www.downriversupply.com

Ernest F Mariani Company Inc
573 West 2890 South .... Salt Lake City UT 84115 800-453-2927 531-9615*
*Fax Area Code: 801 ■ TF: 800-453-2927 ■ Web: efmco.com

Gustave A Larson Co PO Box 910 .... Pewaukee WI 53072 262-542-0200 542-1400
TF: 800-829-9609 ■ Web: www.galarson.com

Hart & Price Corp PO Box 36368 .... Dallas TX 75235 214-521-9129 350-4143
TF: 800-777-9129 ■ Web: www.hartprice.com

Insco Distributing Inc
12501 Network Blvd .... San Antonio TX 78249 210-690-8400 690-1524
TF: 855-282-4295 ■ Web: www.inscohvac.com

ISI Commercial Refrigeration LP
9136 Viscount Row .... Dallas TX 75247 214-631-7980 631-6813
TF: 800-777-5070 ■ Web: www.isi-texas.com

Luce, Schwab & Kase Inc Nine Gloria Ln .... Fairfield NJ 07007 973-227-4840
Web: www.lskair.com

Minus Forty Technologies Corp
30 Armstrong Ave .... Georgetown ON L7G4R9 905-702-1441
Web: www.minusforty.com

Modern Ice Equipment & Supply Co
5709 Harrison Ave .... Cincinnati OH 45248 513-367-2101 367-5762
TF: 800-543-1581 ■ Web: www.modernice.com

Norm's Refrigeration & Ice Equipment Inc
1175 N Knollwood Cir .... Anaheim CA 92801 714-236-3600
Web: www.normsrefrigeration.com

Preston Refrigeration Company Inc
3200 Fiberglass Rd .... Kansas City KS 66115 913-621-1813 621-6962
Web: www.prestonrefrigeration.com

RE Lewis Refrigeration Inc
803 S Lincoln St PO Box 92 .... Creston IA 50801 641-782-8183 782-8156
TF Cust Svc: 800-264-0767 ■ Web: www.relewisinc.com

Redico Inc 1850 S Lee Ct .... Buford GA 30518 800-242-3920 614-1403*
*Fax Area Code: 770 ■ TF: 800-242-3920 ■ Web: www.redicoinc.com

Refricenter of Miami Inc 7101 NW 43rd St .... Miami FL 33166 305-477-8880 599-9323
Web: www.refricenter.net

Rogers Supply Company Inc PO Box 740 .... Champaign IL 61824 217-356-0166 356-1768
TF: 800-252-0406 ■ Web: www.rogerssupply.com

Schroeder America 5620 Business Park .... San Antonio TX 78218 210-662-8200
Web: schroederamerica.com

Sid Harvey Industries Inc 605 Locust St .... Garden City NY 11530 516-745-9200 222-9027
Web: www.sidharvey.com

Southern Refrigeration Corp
3140 Shenandoah Ave .... Roanoke VA 24017 540-342-3493 343-2163
TF: 800-763-4433 ■ Web: www.southernrefcorp.com

Stafford-Smith Inc 3414 S Burdick St .... Kalamazoo MI 49001 269-343-1240 343-2509
TF: 800-968-2442 ■ Web: www.staffordsmith.com

Supermarket Systems Inc 6419 Bannington Rd .... Charlotte NC 28226 704-542-6000
TF: 800-553-1905 ■ Web: www.supermarketsystems.com

SWH Supply Co 242 E Main St .... Louisville KY 40202 502-589-9287 585-3812
TF: 800-321-3598 ■ Web: www.swhsupply.com

Taylor Freezer Sales Company Inc
2032 Atlantic Ave .... Chesapeake VA 23324 800-768-6945 545-7908*
*Fax Area Code: 757 ■ TF: 800-768-6945 ■ Web: www.taylorfreezer.com

Thermo King of Houston LP 772 McCarty St .... Houston TX 77029 713-671-2700
Web: www.tkofhouston.net

Transport Refrigeration Inc 301 Lawrence Dr .... De Pere WI 54115 920-339-5700 339-5717
TF: 888-502-3569 ■ Web: thermokinggreenbay.com

United Refrigeration Inc
11401 Roosevelt Blvd .... Philadelphia PA 19154 215-698-9100 698-9493*
*Fax: Financial ■ TF General: 888-578-9100 ■ Web: www.uri.com

Western Pacific Distributors Inc
1739 Sabre St .... Hayward CA 94545 510-732-0100 732-0155
Web: www.teamwpd.com

669 RELOCATION CONSULTING SERVICES

Phone | Fax

Cartus Corp 40 Apple Ridge Rd .... Danbury CT 06810 203-205-3400 205-6575
Web: www.cartus.com

Coldwell Banker Gundaker
2458 Old Dorsett Rd Ste 300 .... Maryland Heights MO 63043 314-298-5000
TF: 800-325-1978 ■ Web: www.cbgundaker.com

Crye-Leike Inc 6525 N Quail Hollow Rd .... Memphis TN 38120 866-310-3102 758-5641*
*Fax Area Code: 901 ■ Web: www.crye-leike.com

RE/MAX LLC 5075 S Syracuse St .... Denver CO 80237 800-525-7452 796-3599*
*Fax Area Code: 303 ■ TF: 800-525-7452 ■ Web: www.remax.com

RELO Direct Inc 161 N Clark St Ste 1250 .... Chicago IL 60601 312-384-5900 384-5988
TF: 800-621-7356 ■ Web: www.relodirect.com

Relocation America 25800 NW Hwy Ste 210 .... Southfield MI 48075 877-500-4466 263-0093*
*Fax Area Code: 248 ■ TF: 877-500-4466 ■ Web: www.relocationamerica.com

Runzheimer International Runzheimer Pk .... Rochester WI 53167 262-971-2200 971-2254
TF: 800-558-1702 ■ Web: www.runzheimer.com

SIRVA Inc 700 Oakmont Ln .... Terrace IL 60181 630-570-8900 468-4761
TF: 888-444-4765 ■ Web: www.sirva.com

Windermere Relocation Inc
5424 Sand Point Way NE .... Seattle WA 98105 206-527-3801
TF: 866-740-9589 ■ Web: www.windermere.com

670 REMEDIATION SERVICES

SEE ALSO Consulting Services - Environmental p. 2110; Environmental Organizations p. 1770; Waste Management p. 3293

Remediation services include clean-up, restorative, and corrective work to repair or minimize environmental damage caused by lead, asbestos, mining, petroleum, chemicals, and other pollutants.

Phone | Fax

911 Restoration Enterprises Inc
7721 Densmore Ave .... Van Nuys CA 91406 888-243-6653
TF: 888-243-6653 ■ Web: www.911restoration.com

AAC Contracting Inc 175 Humboldt St .... Rochester NY 14610 585-527-8000
Web: www.aac-contracting.com

Abscope Environmental Inc
7086 Commercial Dr .... Canastota NY 13032 315-697-8437
Web: www.abscope.com

Allstate Power Vac Inc 928 E Hazelwood Ave .... Rahway NJ 07065 732-815-0220 815-9892

Antea Group 5910 Rice Creek Pkwy Ste 100 .... Saint Paul MN 55126 651-639-9449 639-9473
TF: 800-477-7411 ■ Web: www.anteagroup.com

BELFOR (Canada) Inc 3300 Bridgeway St .... Vancouver BC V5K1H9 604-432-1123
Web: www.belfor.com

Bristol Environmental Inc 1123 Beaver St .... Bristol PA 19007 215-788-6040
Web: www.beigroup.com

Brook Environmental & Engineering Corp
11419 Cronridge Dr Ste 10 .... Owings Mills MD 21117 410-356-5073
Web: carrollcountytimes.com

Carylon Corp 2500 W Arthington St .... Chicago IL 60612 312-666-7700 666-5810
TF: 800-621-4342 ■ Web: www.carylon.com

Phone | Fax

Central Insulation Systems Inc
300 Murray Rd . . . Cincinnati OH 45217 513-242-0600
Web: www.centralinsulation.com

Chemical Waste Management Inc
1001 Fannin St Ste 4000 . . . Houston TX 77002 713-512-6200
TF: 800-633-7871 ■ *Web:* www.wm.com

Clean Harbors Inc 42 Longwater Dr PO Box 9149 . . . Norwell MA 02061 781-792-5000
NYSE: CLH ■ *TF:* 800-282-0058 ■ *Web:* www.cleanharbors.com

Clean Venture/Cycle Chem Inc
201 S First St . . . Elizabeth NJ 07206 908-355-5800 355-0562
TF: 800-347-7672 ■ *Web:* www.cyclechem.com

Contaminant Recovery Systems (CONREC)
Nine Rocky Hill Rd . . . Smithfield RI 02917 401-231-3770
Web: www.conrec.net

Crosby & Overton Inc 1610 W 17th St . . . Long Beach CA 90813 562-432-5445 436-7540
TF: 800-827-6729 ■ *Web:* www.crosbyoverton.com

Custom Environmental Services Inc
8041 N I 70 Frontage Rd # 5 . . . Arvada CO 80002 303-423-9949
Web: www.customsvcs.com

Dec-Tam Corp 50 Concord St . . . North Reading MA 01864 978-470-2860
Web: www.dectam.com

Ecology Control Industries Inc
255 Parr Blvd . . . Richmond CA 94801 510-235-1393 235-3709
Web: www.ecologycontrol.com

EMR Inc 2110 Delaware St Ste B . . . Lawrence KS 66046 785-842-9013
Web: www.emr-inc.com

Environmental Enterprises Inc (EEI)
10163 Cincinnati Dayton Rd . . . Cincinnati OH 45241 513-772-2818 782-8950
TF: 800-722-2818 ■ *Web:* www.eeienv.com

Envirovantage Inc 629 Calef Hwy Ste 200 . . . Epping NH 03042 603-679-9682
Web: www.envirovantage.com

Garner Environmental Services Inc
1717 W 13th St . . . Deer Park TX 77536 281-930-1200
Web: www.garner-es.com

Greenleaf Environmental Group Inc
4943 Austin Park Ave . . . Buford GA 30518 678-714-8420
Web: www.greenleafgroup.net

H & s Environmental Inc
160 E Main St Ste 2F . . . Westborough MA 01581 508-366-7442
Web: www.hsenv.com

H Barber & Sons Inc 15 Raytkwich Rd . . . Naugatuck CT 06770 203-729-9000
Web: hbarber.com

MCM Management Corp
35980 Woodward Ave Ste 210 . . . Bloomfield Hills MI 48304 248-932-9600 932-9638
TF: 800-843-7512 ■ *Web:* www.mcmmanagement.com

Metson Marine Inc 2060 Knoll Dr Ste 100 . . . Ventura CA 93003 805-658-2628
Web: www.metsonmarine.com

NACHER Corp, The 111 E Angus Dr . . . Youngsville LA 70592 337-856-9144
Web: nacher.net

Paragon Environmental Construction Inc
5664 Mud Mill Rd . . . Brewerton NY 13029 315-699-0840
Web: paragonec.net

Parc Specialty Contractors 1400 Vinci Ave . . . Sacramento CA 95838 916-992-5405
Web: www.parcspecialty.com

Perma-Fix Environmental Services Inc
8302 Dunwoody Pl Ste 250 . . . Atlanta GA 30350 770-587-9898 587-9937
NASDAQ: PESI ■ *TF:* 800-365-6066 ■ *Web:* www.perma-fix.com

Perma-Fix Northwest Inc 2025 Battelle Blvd . . . Richland WA 99354 509-375-5160

PW Stephens Inc
15201 Pipeline Ln Unit B . . . Huntington Beach CA 92649 714-892-2028 891-9807
TF: 800-750-7733 ■ *Web:* www.pwsei.com

R W Collins Co 7225 W 66th St . . . Chicago IL 60638 708-458-6868
Web: www.rwcollins.com

Remediation Services Inc
2735 S 10th St PO Box 587 . . . Independence KS 67301 620-331-1200
Web: www.rsi-ks.com

S Brewer Enterprises
2151 Jamieson Ave Ste 1607 . . . Alexandria VA 22314 703-567-1284

Safety & Ecology Corp
2800 Solway Rd SEC Business Center . . . Knoxville TN 37931 865-690-0501
Web: www.sec-tn.com

Safety-Kleen Corp
2600 N Central Expwy Ste 400 . . . Richardson TX 75080 800-323-5040 265-2990*
**Fax Area Code:* 972 ■ *TF:* 800-669-5740 ■ *Web:* www.safety-kleen.com

SEACOR Holdings Inc
2200 Eller Dr PO Box 13038 . . . Fort Lauderdale FL 33316 954-523-2200 524-9185
NYSE: CKH ■ *TF:* 800-516-6203 ■ *Web:* www.seacorholdings.com

Sevenson Environmental Services Inc
2749 Lockport Rd . . . Niagara Falls NY 14305 716-284-0431 284-7645
TF: 800-777-3836 ■ *Web:* www.sevenson.com

Sigma Environmental Services Inc
1300 W Canal St . . . Milwaukee WI 53233 414-643-4200 643-4210
Web: www.thesigmagroup.com

Terra Contracting Services LLC
5787 Stadium Dr . . . Kalamazoo MI 49009 269-375-9595
Web: www.terracontracting.net

US Ecology 300 E Mallard Dr Ste 300 . . . Boise ID 83706 208-331-8400 331-7900
NASDAQ: ECOL ■ *TF:* 800-590-5220 ■ *Web:* www.americanecology.com

UXB International Inc
2020 Kraft Dr Ste 2100 . . . Blacksburg VA 24060 540-443-3700 443-3701
TF: 800-422-4892 ■ *Web:* www.uxb.com

Waste Control Specialists LLC
5430 LBJ Fwy Ste 1700 . . . Dallas TX 75240 972-715-9800 448-1419
Web: www.wcstexas.com

Winter Environmental
3350 Green Pointe Pkwy Ste 200 . . . Norcross GA 30092 404-588-3300 946-6494*
**Fax:* Hum Res ■ *Web:* www.winter-environmental.com

WRR Environmental Services 5200 Ryder Rd . . . Eau Claire WI 54701 715-834-9624
TF: 800-727-8760 ■ *Web:* www.wrres.com

Young's Environmental Cleanup Inc
G-5305 N Dort Hwy . . . Flint MI 48505 810-789-7155
Web: www.youngsenvironmental.com

Phone | Fax

671 RESEARCH CENTERS & INSTITUTIONS

SEE ALSO Market Research Firms p. 2716; Public Policy Research Centers p. 2978; Testing Facilities p. 3226

Phone | Fax

3D Biomatrix Inc
1600 Huron Pkwy Bldg 520 Second Fl . . . Ann Arbor MI 48109 734-272-4688
Web: 3dbiomatrix.com

Aaron Diamond AIDS Research Ctr
455 First Ave 7th Fl . . . New York NY 10016 212-448-5000 725-1126
Web: www.adarc.org

ADA Technologies Inc
8100 Shaffer Pkwy Ste 130 . . . Littleton CO 80127 303-792-5615
TF: 800-232-0296 ■ *Web:* www.adatech.com

Adaption Technologies Ventures Ltd
1009 Pruitt Rd . . . Spring TX 77380 281-465-3320
Web: adpt-tech.com

Adherent Technologies Inc
11208 Cochiti SE . . . Albuquerque NM 87123 505-346-1688
Web: www.adherent-tech.com

Adial Pharmaceuticals
1001 Research Park Blvd Ste 100 . . . Charlottesville VA 22911 434-422-9800
Web: www.adialpharma.com

Adlyfe Inc 9430 Key W Ave . . . Rockville MD 20850 703-868-3050
Web: www.adlyfe.com

Advanced Cell Diagnostics Inc
3960 Point Eden Way . . . Hayward CA 94545 510-576-8800
TF: 877-576-3636 ■ *Web:* www.acdbio.com

Advanced Focus 44 E 32nd St Fourth Fl . . . New York NY 10016 212-217-2000
Web: www.advancedfocus.com

Advanced Technology for Large Structural Systems Ctr (ATLSS)
117 ATLSS Dr . . . Bethlehem PA 18015 610-758-3525 758-5902
Web: www.atlss.lehigh.edu

Advantagene Inc 440 Lexington St . . . Auburndale MA 02466 617-916-5445
Web: www.advantagene.com

Advion BioSciences Inc 19 Brown Rd . . . Ithaca NY 14850 607-266-0665 266-0749
TF: 877-523-8466 ■ *Web:* www.advion.com

Aegera Therapeutics Inc 810 ch Du Golf . . . Montreal QC H3E1A8 514-288-5532 288-9280
Web: www.aegera.com

Aerodyne Research Inc 45 Manning Rd . . . Billerica MA 01821 978-663-9500 663-4918
Web: www.aerodyne.com

Aeronautical Systems Ctr (ASC)
5215 Thurlow St Bldg 70, Ste 4B . . . Wright Patterson OH 45433 937-522-3252 656-7088
Web: www.wpafb.af.mil/asc

Aeronix Inc 1775 W Hibiscus Blvd Ste 200 . . . Melbourne FL 32901 321-984-1671
Web: www.aeronix.com

Aerospace Corp, The
2310 E El Segundo Blvd PO Box 92957 . . . Los Angeles CA 90009 310-336-5000 336-7055
Web: www.aerospace.org

Affinium Pharmaceuticals Ltd
200 Front St W Ste 3004 . . . Toronto ON M5V3K2 416-645-6613
Web: pint.com

Air Force Office of Scientific Research (AFOSR)
875 N Randolph St Ste 325 Rm 3112 . . . Arlington VA 22203 703-696-7551 696-9556
Web: www.wpafb.af.mil

Air Force Research Laboratory (AFRL)
AFRL/PA
1864 Fourth St Bldg 15 Rm 225 . . . Wright-Patterson AFB OH 45433 800-222-0336 255-2219*
**Fax Area Code:* 937 ■ *TF:* 800-222-0336 ■ *Web:* www.afsbirsttr.com

Air Resources Laboratory
5830 University Research Ct Rm. 4204 . . . Silver Spring MD 20740 301-713-0684 713-0119
Web: www.arl.noaa.gov

Akebia Therapeutics Inc 245 St 1 Ste 1100 . . . Cambridge MA 02142 617-871-2098 871-2099
Web: www.akebia.com

Alaska Fisheries Science Ctr (AFSC)
National Marine Fisheries Service
7600 Sand Pt Way NE Bldg 4 . . . Seattle WA 98115 206-526-4000 526-4004
Web: www.afsc.noaa.gov

Albany International Research Co
216 Airport Dr . . . Rochester NH 03867 603-330-5850
TF: 888-797-6735 ■ *Web:* www.albint.com

Allied Business Intelligence Inc 249 S St . . . Oyster Bay NY 11771 516-624-2500
Web: www.abiresearch.com

ALLPoints Research Inc
200 W First St Ste 300 . . . Winston Salem NC 27101 336-896-2200
Web: www.allpoints.biz

American Institute for Cancer Research
1759 R St NW . . . Washington DC 20009 202-328-7744 328-7226
TF: 800-843-8114 ■ *Web:* www.aicr.org

American Institutes for Research
1000 Thomas Jefferson St NW . . . Washington DC 20007 202-403-5000 403-5454
TF: 877-334-3499 ■ *Web:* www.air.org

American Type Culture Collection (ATCC)
10801 University Blvd PO Box 1549 . . . Manassas VA 20108 703-365-2700 365-2701
TF Cust Svc: 800-638-6597 ■ *Web:* www.atcc.org

Ames Laboratory 111 TASF Iowa State University . . . Ames IA 50011 515-294-9557 294-3226
Web: www.ameslab.gov

Amplimmune Inc 45 W Watkins Mill Rd . . . Gaithersburg MD 20878 301-309-9800
Web: www.amplimmune.com

Amunix Operating Inc 500 Ellis St . . . Mountain View CA 94043 650-428-1800
Web: www.amunix.com

Anasys Instruments Corp
121 Gray Ave Ste 100 . . . Santa Barbara CA 93101 805-730-3310
Web: www.anasysinstruments.com

Annapolis Micro Systems Inc
190 Admiral Cochrane Dr . . . Annapolis MD 21401 410-841-2514 841-2518
Web: www.annapmicro.com

Applied Physics Laboratory
University of Washington 1013 NE 40th St
PO Box 355640 . . . Seattle WA 98105 206-543-1300 543-6785
Web: www.apl.washington.edu

Phone Fax

Applied Research Laboratory
Pennsylvania State University
N Atherton St PO Box 30 State College PA 16804 814-865-6531 865-3105
Web: www.arl.psu.edu

Aptima Inc 12 Gill St Ste 1400 Woburn MA 01801 781-935-3966 935-4385
TF: 866-461-7298 ■ *Web:* www.aptima.com

Aquarian Capital LLC 5345 Annabel Ln Plano TX 75093 469-361-2177
Web: www.aquariancapital.com

Arbor Research & Trading LLC
1000 Hart Rd Ste 260 Barrington IL 60010 847-304-1550
Web: www.arborresearch.com

Arca Biopharma Inc 8001 Arista Pl Ste 200 Broomfield CO 80021 720-940-2100 208-9261
NASDAQ: ABIO ■ *Web:* www.arcabiopharma.com

Arctic Region Supercomputing Ctr
505 S Chandlar Dr PO Box 756020 Fairbanks AK 99775 907-450-8600 450-8601
Web: www.arsc.edu

Arctic Research Consortium of the US (ARCUS)
3535 College Rd Ste 101 Fairbanks AK 99709 907-474-1600 474-1604
Web: www.arcus.org

Argonne National Laboratory (ANL)
9700 S Cass Ave Argonne IL 60439 630-252-2000 252-3379
Web: www.anl.gov

Armed Forces Radiobiology Research Institute (AFRRI)
8901 Wisconsin Ave Bethesda MD 20889 301-295-1210 295-4967
Web: www.afrri.usuhs.mil

Atlantic Oceanographic & Meteorological Laboratory (AOML)
4301 Rickenbacker Cswy Miami FL 33149 305-361-4300 361-4449
Web: www.aoml.noaa.gov

aTyr Pharma Inc
3545 General Atomics Ct Ste 250 San Diego CA 92121 858-731-8389
Web: www.atyrpharma.com

Autism Research Institute (ARI)
4182 Adams Ave San Diego CA 92116 619-281-7165 563-6840
Web: www.autism.com

Avaxia Biologics Inc 128 Spring St Ste 620 Lexington MA 02421 781-861-0062
Web: www.avaxiabiologics.com

Avcom SMT Inc 213 E Broadway Westerville OH 43081 614-882-8176
Web: www.avcomsmt.com

Aveo Pharmaceuticals Inc 75 Sidney St Cambridge MA 02139 617-299-5000 995-4995
NASDAQ: AVEO ■ *Web:* www.aveooncology.com

Axikin Pharmaceuticals Inc
4940 Carroll Canyon Rd Ste 100 San Diego CA 92121 858-458-1890
Web: www.axikin.com

Azaya Therapeutics Inc
12500 Network Blvd Ste 207 San Antonio TX 78249 210-341-6600
Web: www.azayatherapeutics.com

Baker Institute for Animal Health
Cornell University College of Veterinary Medicine
Hungerford Hill Rd Ithaca NY 14850 607-256-5600 256-5608

Barbara Ann Karmanos Cancer Institute
4100 John R St Detroit MI 48201 800-527-6266
TF: 800-527-6266 ■ *Web:* www.karmanos.org

Barrios Technology Inc
16441 Space Ctr Blvd Ste B-100 Houston TX 77058 281-280-1900 280-1901
Web: www.barrios.com

Battelle Memorial Institute Inc
505 King Ave Columbus OH 43201 614-424-6424 424-5263
TF: 800-201-2011 ■ *Web:* www.battelle.org

BC Systems Inc 200 Belle Mead Rd Setauket NY 11733 631-751-9370
Web: www.bcpowersys.com

Belle W Baruch Institute for Marine & Coastal Sciences
University of S Carolina 609 EWS Bldg Columbia SC 29208 803-777-5288 777-3935
Web: artsandsciences.sc.edu

Beltsville Human Nutrition Research Ctr
USDA/ARS BARC-E Bldg 307-C Rm 117
10300 Baltimore Blvd Beltsville MD 20705 301-504-8157 504-9381
Web: www.ars.usda.gov/main/site_main.htm?modecode=12-35-00-00

Bend Research Inc 64550 Research Rd Bend OR 97701 541-382-4100 382-2713
Web: www.bendresearch.com

Berkeley Sensor & Actuator Ctr (BSAC)
University of California
497 Cory Hall MC Ste 1774 Berkeley CA 94720 510-643-6690 643-6637
TF: 800-549-1002 ■ *Web:* www-bsac.eecs.berkeley.edu

Beta Research Corp 6400 Jericho Tpke Syosset NY 11791 516-935-3800
Web: www.betaresearch.com

BioLegend Inc 11080 Roselle St San Diego CA 92121 858-455-9588
TF: 877-246-5343 ■ *Web:* www.biolegend.com

bioLytical Laboratories Inc
1108 - 13351 Commerce Pkwy Richmond BC V6V2X7 604-204-6784
TF: 866-674-6784 ■ *Web:* www.biolytical.com

BioMarker Pharmaceuticals Inc
5941 Optical Ct San Jose CA 95138 408-257-2000
Web: www.biomarkerinc.com

Biomerix Corp 47757 Fremont Blvd Fremont CA 94538 510-933-3450
TF: 888-308-3620 ■ *Web:* www.biomerix.com

BioResource International Inc
4222 Emperor Blvd Ste 460 Durham NC 27703 919-993-3389
Web: www.briworldwide.com

BioVascular Inc
12230 El Camino Real Ste 100 San Diego CA 92130 858-455-5000
Web: www.biovascularinc.com

BN ImmunoTherapeutics Inc
2425 Garcia Ave Mountain View CA 94043 650-681-4660
Web: www.bavarian-nordic.com

Boyce Thompson Institute for Plant Research Inc
Cornell University Twr Rd Ithaca NY 14853 607-254-1234 254-1242
Web: bti.cornell.edu

BPR Inc 4655 Wilfrid-Hamel Blvd Quebec City QC G1P2J7 418-871-8151 871-9625
Web: bpr.ca

Brain Research Institute
695 Charles Young Dr S Los Angeles CA 90095 310-825-5061 206-5855
Web: www.bri.ucla.edu

BrainCells Inc 3636 Nobel Dr Ste 215 San Diego CA 92122 858-812-7700
Web: www.braincellsinc.com

Brainstorm SMS Services LLC
2402 Sidney St Pittsburgh PA 15203 415-287-0372
Web: www.cs.smashcode.com

Brookhaven National Laboratory (BNL) PO Box 5000 Upton NY 11973 631-344-8000 344-3000
Web: www.bnl.gov

Bureau of Economic Analysis (BEA)
1441 L St NW Washington DC 20005 202-606-9900 606-5311
Web: www.bea.gov

C & C Market Research Inc
1200 S Waldron Rd Ste 138 Fort Smith AR 72903 479-785-5637
Web: www.ccmarketresearch.com

Caelum Research Corp
1700 Research Blvd Ste 250 Rockville MD 20850 301-424-8205 424-8183
Web: www.caelum.com

California Pacific Medical Ctr Research Institute
475 Brannan St Ste 220 San Francisco CA 94107 415-600-1600 600-1753
TF: 855-354-2778 ■ *Web:* www.cpmc.org/professionals/research

Cancer Research Ctr of Hawaii
University of Hawaii 1236 Lauhala St Honolulu HI 96813 808-586-3013 586-3052
Web: www.crch.org

CardioKinetix Inc 925 Hamilton Ave Menlo Park CA 94025 650-364-7016
Web: www.cardiokinetix.com

Carmell Therapeutics Corp
3636 Boulevard of the Allies Pittsburgh PA 15213 412-508-6519
Web: www.carmellrx.com

Carnegie Institution of Washington
1530 P St NW Washington DC 20005 202-387-6400 387-8092
Web: www.carnegiescience.edu

Carson Energy Services Ltd Hwy 361 W Lampman SK S0C1N0 306-487-2281
Web: urs.com

Celator Pharmaceuticals Inc
303B College Rd E Princeton NJ 08540 609-243-0123
Web: celatorpharma.com

Center for Advanced Biotechnology & Medicine
Rutgers The State University of New Jersey
679 Hoes Ln Piscataway NJ 08854 732-235-5310 235-5318
Web: www3.cabm.rutgers.edu

Center for Automation Research
University of Maryland
AV Williams Bldg 115 Rm 4413 College Park MD 20742 301-405-4526 314-9115
TF: 800-868-0094 ■ *Web:* www.cfar.umd.edu

Center for Biofilm Engineering (CBE)
Montana State University PO Box 173980 Bozeman MT 59717 406-994-4770 994-6098
Web: www.biofilm.montana.edu

Center for Biophysical Sciences & Engineering (CBSE)
University of Alabama CBSE 100
1720 2nd Ave S Birmingham AL 35294 205-934-5329 934-0480
Web: www.uab.edu

Center for Crops Utilization Research
Iowa State University 1041 Food Sciences Bldg Ames IA 50011 515-294-0160 294-6261
Web: www.ccur.iastate.edu

Center for Education
Rice University 320 IBC Bldg P. O. Box 1892 Houston TX 77251 713-348-5145 348-4229
Web: www.centerforeducation.rice.edu

Center for Electromechanics
University of Texas at Austin
10100 Burnet Rd Bldg 133 Austin TX 78758 512-471-4496 471-0781
Web: www.utexas.edu/research/cem

Center for Engineering Logistics & Distribution
University of Arkansas Dept of Industrial Engineering
4207 Bell Engineering Ctr Fayetteville AR 72701 479-575-2124 575-8431
Web: www.celdi.ineg.uark.edu

Center for Global Change & Arctic System Research (CGC)
University of Alaska-Fairbanks
930 Koyukuk Dr Rm 306 PO Box 757740 Fairbanks AK 99775 907-474-5818 474-6722
Web: www.cgc.uaf.edu

Center for Global Change Science
Massachusetts Institute of Technology
77 Massachusetts Ave Cambridge MA 02139 617-253-4902 253-0354
Web: cgcs.mit.edu

Center for Grain & Animal Health Research
1515 College Ave Manhattan KS 66502 800-627-0388 776-2789*
**Fax Area Code: 785* ■ *TF:* 800-627-0388 ■
Web: www.ars.usda.gov/main/site_main.htm?modecode=54300000

Center for High Performance Software Research (HiPerSoft)
Rice University 6100 Main St MS-41 Houston TX 77005 713-348-5186 348-3111
Web: www.hipersoft.rice.edu

Center for Information Systems Research (CISR)
Massachusetts Institute of Technology
5 Cambridge Ctr NE25 7th Fl Cambridge MA 02142 617-253-2348 253-4424
Web: cisr.mit.edu

Center for Integrative Toxicology
Michigan State University
165C Food Safety & Toxicology Bldg East Lansing MI 48824 517-353-6469 355-4603
Web: www.cit.msu.edu

Center for International Trade in Forest Products (CINTRAFOR)
University of Washington PO Box 352100 Seattle WA 98195 206-543-8684 685-0790
Web: www.cintrafor.org

Center for Lesbian & Gay Studies (CLAGS)
University of New York 365 Fifth Ave Rm 7115 New York NY 10016 212-817-1955 817-1567
Web: www.clags.org/

Center for Medical Agricultural & Veterinary Entomology (CMAVE)
1700 SW 23rd Dr Gainesville FL 32608 352-374-5901 374-5852
Web: www.ars.usda.gov/saa/cmave

Center for Nanophysics & Advanced Materials
University of Maryland College Park MD 20742 301-405-8285 405-3779
Web: www.csr.umd.edu

Center for Radiophysics & Space Research
Cornell University 314 Space Sciences Bldg Ithaca NY 14853 607-255-1955 255-3433
Web: www.astro.cornell.edu

Center for Research in Mathematics & Science Education
San Diego State University
6475 Alvarado Rd Ste 206 San Diego CA 92120 619-594-5090 594-1581
TF: 800-573-8804 ■ *Web:* www.sci.sdsu.edu

	City	State	Zip	Phone	Fax
Center for Research on the Context of Teaching 520 Galvez Mall CERAS Bldg Fourth Fl *Web:* www.stanford.edu/group/crc	Stanford	CA	94305	650-723-0572	
Center for Space Plasma & Aeronomic Research University of Alabama Huntsville *TF:* 800-824-2255 ■ *Web:* www.uah.edu	Huntsville	AL	35899	256-961-7403	961-7730
Center for Space Research University of Texas 3925 W Braker Ln Ste 200 *Web:* www.csr.utexas.edu	Austin	TX	78759	512-471-5573	471-3570
Center for Sustainable Environmental Technologies Iowa State University 1140 Biorenewables Research Laboratory *Web:* www.cset.iastate.edu	Ames	IA	50011	515-294-7936	294-3091
Center for the Study of Language & Information Stanford University Cordura Hall 210 Panama St *Web:* www-csli.stanford.edu	Stanford	CA	94305	650-725-3286	723-0758
Center for the Study of Teaching & Policy (CTP) University of Washington PO Box 353600 *Web:* www.depts.washington.edu	Seattle	WA	98195	206-221-4114	616-8158
Center on Education & Training for Employment Ohio State University 1900 Kenny Rd *TF:* 800-848-4815 ■ *Web:* cete.osu.edu	Columbus	OH	43210	614-292-6869	292-3742
Center on Human Development & Disability University of Washington 1701 NE Columbia Rd PO Box 357920 *TF:* 800-636-1089 ■ *Web:* www.depts.washington.edu/chdd	Seattle	WA	98195	206-543-2832	543-3561
National Center for Environmental Health 4770 Buford Hwy Bldg 101 *TF:* 800-232-4636 ■ *Web:* www.cdc.gov	Atlanta	GA	30341	404-639-3311	
National Institute for Occupational Safety & Health 200 Independence Ave SW *TF:* 800-356-4674 ■ *Web:* www.cdc.gov/niosh	Washington	DC	20201	404-639-3286	
Centrose LLC 802 Deming Way *Web:* www.centrosepharma.com	Madison	WI	53717	608-836-0207	
Charles River Laboratories Inc 251 Ballardvale St *NYSE: CRL* ■ **Fax Area Code:* 978 ■ *TF:* 800-522-7287 ■ *Web:* www.criver.com	Wilmington	MA	01887	781-222-6000	658-7132*
Charles Stark Draper Laboratory Inc 555 Technology Sq *Web:* www.draper.com	Cambridge	MA	02139	617-258-1000	258-1131
CHI Solutions Inc 801 W Ellsworth Rd Ste 202 *Web:* www.chisolutionsinc.com	Ann Arbor	MI	48108	734-662-6363	
Children's Nutrition Research Ctr USDA/ARS Baylor College of Medicine 1100 Bates St *Web:* www.bcm.edu/cnrc	Houston	TX	77030	713-798-6767	798-7046
Children's Research Institute Children's National Medical Ctr 111 Michigan Ave NW Research Fl 5 *TF:* 888-884-2327 ■ *Web:* www.childrensnational.org	Washington	DC	20010	888-884-2327	
Cibus Global 6455 Nancy Ridge Dr Ste 100 *Web:* www.cibus.com	San Diego	CA	92121	858-450-0008	
Cincinnati Children's Hospital Research Foundation 3333 Burnet Ave *TF:* 800-344-2462 ■ *Web:* www.cincinnatichildrens.org/research	Cincinnati	OH	45229	513-636-4200	636-8453
Clarassance Inc 9700 Great Seneca Hwy *Web:* www.clarassance.com	Rockville	MD	20850	301-452-2899	
Clark Martire & Bartolomeo 375 Sylvan Ave *Web:* www.cmbinc.com	Englewood Cliffs	NJ	07632	201-568-0011	
Cleveland Biolabs Inc 73 High St *NASDAQ: CBLI* ■ *Web:* www.cbiolabs.com	Buffalo	NY	14203	716-849-6810	
Climatronics Corp 140 Wilbur Pl *Web:* www.climatronics.com	Bohemia	NY	11716	631-567-7300	
CNA Corp 4825 Mark Ctr Dr *TF:* 800-344-0007 ■ *Web:* www.cna.org	Alexandria	VA	22311	703-824-2000	824-2949
Coastal & Marine Institute San Diego State University 4165 Spruance Rd *Web:* www.sci.sdsu.edu/cmi	San Diego	CA	92101	619-594-1308	
Cobalt Technologies Inc 500 Clyde Ave *Web:* cobalttech.com/	Mountain View	CA	94043	650-230-0760	
Cogent Research LLC 125 Cambridge Park Dr *Web:* www.axiomresearch.com	Cambridge	MA	02140	617-441-9944	
Cold Spring Harbor Laboratory (CSHL) One Bungtown Rd *Web:* www.cshl.edu	Cold Spring Harbor	NY	11724	516-367-8800	367-8455
Colorado Ctr for Astrodynamics Research (CCAR) University of Colorado ECNT 320 UCB 431 *Web:* ccar.colorado.edu	Boulder	CO	80309	303-492-3105	492-2825
Columbia Environmental Research Ctr (CERC) 4200 New Haven Rd *TF:* 888-283-7626 ■ *Web:* www.cerc.usgs.gov	Columbia	MO	65201	573-875-5399	876-1896
Columbia Institute for Tele-Information (CITI) Columbia University 3022 Broadway Uris Hall Ste 1A *Web:* www8.gsb.columbia.edu/citi	New York	NY	10027	212-854-4222	854-1471
Comcor Environmental Ltd 320 Pinebush Rd Ste 12 *Web:* www.comcor.com	Cambridge	ON	N1T1Z6	519-621-6669	
Computer Emergency Response Team (CERT) SEI Carnegie Mellon University 4500 Fifth Ave *Web:* www.cert.org	Pittsburgh	PA	15213	412-268-7090	268-6989
Computer Science & Artificial Intelligence Laboratory (CSAIL) 32 Vassar St Bldg 32 *Web:* www.csail.mit.edu	Cambridge	MA	02139	617-253-5851	258-8682
Conservation & Production Research Laboratory (CPRL) USDA/ARS PO Box 10 *Web:* www.cprl.ars.usda.gov	Bushland	TX	79012	806-356-5724	356-5750
Coriell Institute for Medical Research 403 Haddon Ave *TF:* 800-752-3805 ■ *Web:* www.coriell.org	Camden	NJ	08103	856-966-7377	
Cornell NanoScale Science & Technology Facility (CNF) Cornell University 250 Duffield Hall *Web:* www.cnf.cornell.edu	Ithaca	NY	14853	607-255-2329	255-8601
Courant Institute of Mathematical Sciences (CIMS) *New York University* 251 Mercer St *Web:* www.cims.nyu.edu	New York	NY	10012	212-998-1212	995-4121
Creare Inc 16 Great Hollow Rd *Web:* www.creare.com	Hanover	NH	03755	603-643-3800	643-4657
CRG Global Inc Three Signal Ave Ste A *Web:* www.crgglobalinc.com	Ormond Beach	FL	32174	386-677-5644	
CureSearch for Children's Cancer 4600 East-West Hwy Ste 600 *TF:* 800-458-6223 ■ *Web:* www.curesearch.org	Bethesda	MD	20814	301-718-0047	
Curriculum Research & Development Group University of Hawaii 1776 University Ave *Web:* manoa.hawaii.edu	Honolulu	HI	96822	808-956-7961	956-9486
Dana-Farber Cancer Institute 44 Binney St **Fax:* PR ■ *TF:* 866-408-3324 ■ *Web:* www.dana-farber.org	Boston	MA	02115	617-632-3000	632-5520*
Data Sciences International 2033 Corporate Dr *Web:* datasci.com/buxco	Wilmington	NC	28405	910-794-6980	
Data Storage Systems Ctr (DSSC) *Carnegie Mellon University ECE Dept* 5000 Forbes Ave *TF:* 800-864-8287 ■ *Web:* www.dssc.ece.cmu.edu	Pittsburgh	PA	15213	412-268-6600	268-3497
DEKA Research & Development Corp 340 Commercial St *Web:* www.dekaresearch.com	Manchester	NH	03101	603-669-5139	
Dell'Oro Group Inc 230 Redwood Shores Pkwy *Web:* www.delloro.com	Redwood City	CA	94065	650-622-9400	
Desert Research Institute 2215 Raggio Pkwy *Web:* www.dri.edu	Reno	NV	89512	775-673-7300	673-7397
Diabetes Research Institute 1450 NW Tenth Ave **Fax Area Code:* 305 ■ *Web:* www.diabetesresearch.org	Miami	FL	33136	954-964-4040	243-4404*
Digital Monitoring Products Inc 2500 N Partnership Blvd *TF:* 800-641-4282 ■ *Web:* www.dmp.com	Springfield	MO	65803	417-831-9362	
Digitec Inc 2731 Van Dorn Rd *TF:* 888-761-3382 ■ *Web:* www.digitecinc.com	Milford	NE	68405	402-761-3382	
Discera Inc 1961 Concourse Dr *Web:* www.discera.com	San Jose	CA	95131	408-432-8600	
DisplayLink Corp 480 S California Ave Ste 304 *Web:* www.displaylink.com	Palo Alto	CA	94306	650-838-0481	
Diversified Laboratories Inc 4150 Lafayette Ctr Dr *Web:* www.diversifiedlaboratories.com	Chantilly	VA	20151	703-222-8700	222-0786
Dryden Flight Research Ctr PO Box 273 *Web:* www.nasa.gov/centers	Edwards	CA	93523	661-276-3311	276-3566
Dycor Technologies Ltd 1851 94 St *TF:* 800-663-9267 ■ *Web:* www.dycor.com	Edmonton	AB	T6N1E6	780-486-0091	486-3535
Earth Sciences & Resources Institute 901 Sumter St Ste 301 *Web:* www.esri.sc.edu	Columbia	SC	29208	803-777-4243	777-2972
Earth System Research Laboratory NOAA/ESRL 325 Broadway *Web:* www.esrl.noaa.gov	Boulder	CO	80305	303-497-6643	497-6951
Eastern Regional Research Ctr (ERRC) 600 E Mermaid Ln *Web:* www.ars.usda.gov/main/site_main.htm?modecode=19350000	Wyndmoor	PA	19038	215-233-6400	233-6559
Edison Biotechnology Institute Ohio University Konneker Research Laboratories The Ridges *TF:* 800-444-2420 ■ *Web:* www.ohio.edu	Athens	OH	45701	740-593-4713	593-4795
Eikos Inc 2 Master Dr *TF:* 888-345-6712 ■ *Web:* www.eikos.com	Franklin	MA	02038	508-528-0300	
EmPower Research LLC 404 E 79th St Ste 16E *Web:* www.empowerresearch.com	New York	NY	10075	646-472-7908	
Enanta Pharmaceuticals Inc 500 Arsenal St *Web:* www.enanta.com	Watertown	MA	02472	617-607-0800	
Endacea Inc Two Davis Dr *Web:* www.endacea.com	Research Triangle Park	NC	27709	919-406-1888	
Energy & Environmental Research Ctr (EERC) University of N Dakota 15 N 23rd St S 9018 *Web:* www.eerc.und.nodak.edu	Grand Forks	ND	58202	701-777-5000	777-5181
Energy Institute Pennsylvania State University Coal Utilization Laboratory Rm C211 *Web:* www.energy.psu.edu	University Park	PA	16802	814-865-3093	863-7432
Engineering Research Ctr for Net Shape Mfg Ohio State University 1971 Neil Ave Rm 339 *Web:* nsmwww.eng.ohio-state.edu	Columbus	OH	43210	614-292-9267	292-7219
Environmental Management Inc 5200 NE Hwy 33 *TF:* 800-510-8510 ■ *Web:* www.emiok.com	Guthrie	OK	73044	405-282-8510	
Environmental Science Assoc 225 Bush St Ste 1700 *Web:* www.esassoc.com	San Francisco	CA	94104	415-896-5900	896-0332
EPIEN Medical Inc 4225 White Bear Pkwy Ste 600 *TF:* 888-884-4675 ■ *Web:* www.epien.com	St Paul	MN	55110	651-653-3380	
Epiphany Biosciences Inc One California St Ste 2800 *Web:* www.epiphanybio.com	San Francisco	CA	94111	415-765-7193	
Epitomics Inc 863 Mitten Rd Ste 103 *TF:* 888-772-2226 ■ *Web:* www.epitomics.com	Burlingame	CA	94010	650-583-6688	
EPRI 3420 Hillview Ave *Web:* www.epri.com	Palo Alto	CA	94304	650-855-2000	

Name / Address	City	State	Zip	Phone	Fax
Eunice Kennedy Shriver Ctr 200 Trapelo Rd *Web:* www.umassmed.edu/shriver	Waltham	MA	02452	781-642-0001	642-0114
Evans Data Corp 340 Soquel Ave *Web:* www.evansdata.com	Santa Cruz	CA	95062	831-425-8451	
Exponent Inc 149 Commonwealth Dr *NASDAQ: EXPO* ■ *TF:* 888-656-3976 ■ *Web:* www.exponent.com	Menlo Park	CA	94025	650-326-9400	326-8072
Expression Pathology Inc 9620 Medical Ctr Dr Ste100 *Web:* www.expressionpathology.com	Rockville	MD	20850	301-977-3654	
Aviation Research Div 800 Independence Ave SW Rm 528A *TF:* 866-835-5322 ■ *Web:* www.faa.gov	Washington	DC	20591	202-267-9251	267-5320
Federal Judicial Ctr 1 Columbus Cir NE *Web:* www.fjc.gov	Washington	DC	20544	202-502-4000	
Fels Institute for Cancer Research & Molecular Biology Temple Univ School of Medicine 3400 N Broad St *Web:* www.temple.edu	Philadelphia	PA	19140	215-707-6356	707-2783
Fermi National Accelerator Laboratory PO Box 500 *Web:* www.fnal.gov	Batavia	IL	60510	630-840-3000	840-4343
Florida Resources & Environmental Analysis Ctr *Florida State University* UCC 2200 FSU *Web:* www.freac.fsu.edu	Tallahassee	FL	32306	850-644-2007	644-7360
Florida Solar Energy Ctr 1679 Clearlake Rd *TF:* 877-777-4778 ■ *Web:* www.fsec.ucf.edu	Cocoa	FL	32922	321-638-1000	638-1010
Focus Forward LLC 950 W Valley Rd Ste 2700 *Web:* www.focusfwd.com	Wayne	PA	19087	215-367-4000	
Focus Pointe 100 E Penn Sq Ste 1200 *Web:* www.phonelab.com	Philadelphia	PA	19107	215-561-5500	
Focus Vision 7 River Park Pl E Ste 110 *Web:* www.decipherinc.com	Fresno	CA	93720	559-436-6940	
Food Research Institute University of Wisconsin Madison 1550 Linden Dr *Web:* fri.wisc.edu	Madison	WI	53706	608-263-7777	263-1114
Fox Chase Cancer Ctr 333 Cottman Ave *TF:* 888-369-2427 ■ *Web:* www.fccc.edu	Philadelphia	PA	19111	215-728-6900	728-2682
Framingham Heart Study 73 Mt Wayte Ave Ste 2 *Web:* www.framinghamheartstudy.org	Framingham	MA	01702	508-935-3418	626-1262
Francis Bitter Magnet Laboratory Massachusetts Institute of Technology 150 Albany St NW 14 *Web:* web.mit.edu/fbml	Cambridge	MA	02139	617-253-5478	253-5405
Fred Hutchinson Cancer Research Ctr 1100 Fairview Ave N PO Box 19024 *Web:* www.fhcrc.org	Seattle	WA	98104	206-667-5000	667-4051
Friends Research Institute Inc 1040 Pk Ave Ste 103 *TF:* 800-822-3677 ■ *Web:* www.friendsresearch.org	Baltimore	MD	21201	410-823-5116	823-5131
Social Research Ctr 1040 Pk Ave Ste 103 *Web:* www.friendsresearch.org	Baltimore	MD	21201	410-837-3977	752-4218
Functional Genetics Inc 708 Quince Orchard Rd	Gaithersburg	MD	20878	240-631-6790	
Galleon Pharmaceuticals Inc 213 Witmer Rd *Web:* www.galleonpharma.com	Horsham	PA	19044	267-803-1970	
Gas Technology Institute (GTI) 1700 S Mt Prospect Rd *Web:* www.gastechnology.org	Des Plaines	IL	60018	847-768-0500	768-0501
Gatorade Sports Science Institute 617 W Main St *TF:* 800-616-4774 ■ *Web:* www.gssiweb.org	Barrington	IL	60010	800-616-4774	
Gem Mobile Treatment Services Inc 2525 Cherry Ave Ste 105 *Web:* www.gem-mobile.com	Signal Hill	CA	90755	562-595-7075	
Gemmus Pharma Inc 409 Illinois St *Web:* www.gemmuspharma.com	San Francisco	CA	94158	415-978-2151	
Genemed Biotechnologies Inc 458 Carlton Ct S San Francisco *TF:* 877-436-3633 ■ *Web:* www.genemed.com	San Fransisco	CA	94080	650-952-0110	
GenePharm Inc 1237 Midas Way *Web:* www.genepharminc.com	Sunnyvale	CA	94085	408-773-0106	
General Atomics 3550 General Atomics Ct PO Box 85608 *TF:* 800-669-6820 ■ *Web:* www.ga.com	San Diego	CA	92121	858-455-3000	455-3621
General Resonance LLC One Resonance Way	Havre De Grace	MD	21078	410-939-2343	
Genocea Biosciences Inc 100 Acorn Park Dr Ste 2C *Web:* www.genocea.com	Cambridge	MA	02140	617-876-8191	
Geophysical Fluid Dynamics Laboratory NOAA/OAR/GFDL 201 Forrestal Rd *Web:* www.gfdl.noaa.gov	Princeton	NJ	08540	609-452-6500	987-5063
Georgia Tech Fusion Research Ctr Boggs Bldg Rm 3-29 *Web:* www.frc.gatech.edu	Atlanta	GA	30332	404-894-3758	894-3733
Georgia Tech Research Institute (GTRI) *Georgia Institute of Technology* 250 14th St NW *Web:* www.gtri.gatech.edu	Atlanta	GA	30318	404-407-7400	894-9875
Gerontology Research Ctr 4940 Eastern Ave 5600 Nathan Shock Dr *Web:* www.grc.nia.nih.gov	Baltimore	MD	21224	410-558-8110	
GFK Arbor LLC 1 W Third St *Web:* valientmarketresearch.com/	Media	PA	19063	610-566-8700	
Giner Inc 89 Rumford Ave *Web:* www.ginerinc.com	Newton	MA	02466	781-529-0500	
Glen Research Corp 22825 Davis Dr *TF:* 800-327-4536 ■ *Web:* www.glenres.com	Sterling	VA	20164	703-437-6191	
Glenn Research Ctr 21000 Brookpark Rd *Web:* www.nasa.gov/centers/glenn/home	Cleveland	OH	44135	216-433-4000	433-8000
Goddard Institute for Space Studies 2880 Broadway *TF:* 888-661-1620 ■ *Web:* www.giss.nasa.gov	New York	NY	10025	212-678-5510	678-5552
Goddard Space Flight Ctr 8800 Greenbelt Rd **Fax:* PR ■ *Web:* www.nasa.gov/centers/goddard	Greenbelt	MD	20771	301-286-2000	286-1707*
Gongos Research Inc 2365 Pontiac Rd *Web:* www.gongos.com	Auburn Hills	MI	48326	248-239-2300	
Grand Forks Human Nutrition Research Ctr USDA/ARS 2420 Second Ave N PO Box 9034 *Web:* www.ars.usda.gov/Main/docs.htm?docid=3898	Grand Forks	ND	58202	701-795-8353	795-8395
Great Lakes Environmental Research Laboratory (GLERL) 4840 S State St *Web:* www.glerl.noaa.gov	Ann Arbor	MI	48108	734-741-2235	741-2055
Gustavson Assoc LLC 5757 Central Ave Ste D *Web:* www.gustavson.com	Boulder	CO	80301	303-443-2209	
H Lee Moffitt Cancer Ctr & Research Institute University of S Florida 12902 Magnolia Dr **Fax Area Code:* 813 ■ *TF:* 800-456-3434 ■ *Web:* www.moffitt.org	Tampa	FL	33612	888-663-3488	745-4064*
Hamner Institutes for Health Sciences, The Six Davis Dr PO Box 12137 *Web:* www.thehamner.org	Research Triangle Park	NC	27709	919-558-1200	558-1400
Harry K Dupree Stuttgart National Aquaculture Research Ctr 2955 Hwy 130 E PO Box 1050 *Web:* www.ars.usda.gov/main/site_main.htm?modecode=62251000	Stuttgart	AR	72160	870-673-4483	673-7710
Harvard-Smithsonian Ctr for Astrophysics 60 Garden St *Web:* www.cfa.harvard.edu	Cambridge	MA	02138	617-495-7100	495-7468
Hatfield Marine Science Ctr 2030 SE Marine Science Dr *Web:* www.hmsc.oregonstate.edu	Newport	OR	97365	541-867-0100	867-0138
Hawaii Insitute of Geophysics & Planetology University of Hawaii 1680 E-W Rd PO Box 602B *Web:* www.higp.hawaii.edu	Honolulu	HI	96822	808-956-8760	956-3188
Hazen Research Inc 4601 Indiana St *Web:* www.hazenusa.com	Golden	CO	80403	303-279-4501	278-1528
HemoShear LLC 501 Locust Ave Ste 301 *Web:* www.hemoshear.com	Charlottesville	VA	22902	434-872-0196	872-0199
High Performance Computing Collaboratory PO Box 9627 *TF:* 800-521-4041 ■ *Web:* www.erc.msstate.edu	Mississippi State	MS	39762	662-325-8278	325-7692
Holifield Radioactive Ion Beam Facility (HRIBF) Oak Ridge National Laboratory Bldg 6000 PO Box 2008 *Web:* www.phy.ornl.gov/hribf	Oak Ridge	TN	37831	865-574-4493	574-1268
Houston Advanced Research Ctr (HARC) 4800 Research Forest Dr *Web:* www.harc.edu	The Woodlands	TX	77381	281-367-1348	363-7914
Howard Hughes Medical Institute 4000 Jones Bridge Rd *Web:* www.hhmi.org	Chevy Chase	MD	20815	301-215-8500	215-8863
Human Resources Research Organization (HumRRO) 66 Canal Ctr Plz Ste 400 *Web:* www.humrro.org	Alexandria	VA	22314	703-549-3611	549-9025
Huntingdon Life Sciences Inc *Princeton Research Centre* Mettlers Rd PO Box 2360 *Web:* www.huntingdon.com	East Millstone	NJ	08875	732-873-2550	873-3992
Hyperion Biotechnology Inc 13302 Langtry St *Web:* hyperionbiotechnology.com	San Antonio	TX	78248	210-493-7452	
Iconoculture Inc 244 First Ave N Ste 200 *Web:* www.iconoculture.com	Minneapolis	MN	55401	612-642-2222	
Idaho National Laboratory (INL) 2525 Fremont Ave PO Box 1625 *TF:* 866-495-7440 ■ *Web:* inlportal.inl.gov	Idaho Falls	ID	83415	866-495-7440	
IFOS Inc 2363 Calle Del Mundo *Web:* www.ifos.com	Santa Clara	CA	95054	408-565-9000	
IIT Research Institute (IITRI) 10 W 35th St **Fax:* Hum Res ■ *Web:* www.iitri.org	Chicago	IL	60616	312-567-4000	567-4838*
Immune Design Corp 1616 Eastlake Ave E Ste 310 *Web:* www.immunedesign.com	Seattle	WA	98102	206-682-0645	
Immunotope Inc The Pennsylvania Biotechnology Ctr 3805 Old Easton Rd *Web:* www.immunotope.com	Doylestown	PA	18902	215-253-4180	
in-sync Consumer Insight Corp 90 Eglinton Ave E Ste 403 *Web:* www.insyncstrategy.com	Toronto	ON	M4P2Y3	416-932-0921	
Indiana Molecular Biology Institute Indiana University 915 E 3rd St *Web:* imbi.bio.indiana.edu	Bloomington	IN	47405	812-855-4183	855-6082
Industrial Partnership for Research in Interfacial & Materials Engineering (IPRIME) University of Minnesota 151 Amundson Hall 421 Washington Ave SE *Web:* www.iprime.umn.edu	Minneapolis	MN	55455	612-626-9509	626-7246
Institute for Astronomy University of Hawaii 2680 Woodlawn Dr *TF:* 800-351-1330 ■ *Web:* www.ifa.hawaii.edu	Honolulu	HI	96822	808-956-8312	988-2790
Institute for Basic Research in Developmental Disabilities 1050 Forest Hill Rd *Web:* opwdd.ny.gov	Staten Island	NY	10314	718-494-0600	494-0833
Institute for Defense Analyses (IDA) 4850 Mark Ctr Dr *Web:* www.ida.org	Alexandria	VA	22311	703-845-2000	845-2588
Institute for Diabetes Obesity & Metabolism University of Pennsylvania 700 Clinical Research Bldg *Web:* med.upenn.edu/idom	Philadelphia	PA	19104	215-898-4365	898-5408
Institute for Molecular Virology (IMV) 413 RM Bock Laboratories 1525 Linden Dr *Web:* virology.wisc.edu	Madison	WI	53706	608-262-4540	262-4570

	City	State	ZIP	Phone	Fax
Institute for Physical Research & Technology (IPRT) *Iowa State University* 2156 Gilman Hall *Web:* www.iprt.iastate.edu	Ames	IA	50011	515-294-3045	294-2361
Institute for Research on Poverty University of Wisconsin Madison 1180 Observatory Dr 3412 William H Sewell Social Sciences Bldg *TF:* 866-301-1753 ■ *Web:* www.irp.wisc.edu	Madison	WI	53706	608-262-6358	265-3119
Institute for Scientific Analysis 390 Fourth St Ste D *Web:* www.scientificanalysis.org	San Francisco	CA	94107	415-777-2352	563-9940
Institute for Simulation & Training (IST) 3100 Technology Pkwy *Web:* www.ist.ucf.edu	Orlando	FL	32826	407-882-1300	658-5059
Institute for Social Behavioral & Economic Research University of California 2201 N Hall *Web:* www.isber.ucsb.edu	Santa Barbara	CA	93106	805-893-2548	893-7995
Institute for Social Research University of Michigan 426 Thompson St *Web:* home.isr.umich.edu	Ann Arbor	MI	48104	734-764-8354	936-9708
Institute for Systems Research University of Maryland 2173 AV Williams Bldg *TF:* 866-675-8967 ■ *Web:* www.isr.umd.edu	College Park	MD	20742	301-405-6615	314-9920
Institute for Telecommunications Sciences 325 Broadway *Web:* www.its.bldrdoc.gov	Boulder	CO	80305	303-497-5216	
Institute of Arctic & Alpine Research (INSTAAR) University of Colorado 1560 30th St PO Box 450 *Web:* instaar.colorado.edu	Boulder	CO	80309	303-492-6387	492-6388
Institute of Behavioral Science University of Colorado 1416 Broadway *Web:* www.colorado.edu/IBS	Boulder	CO	80302	303-492-8147	492-6924
Institute of Ecosystem Studies (IES) 2801 Sharon Tpke PO Box AB *Web:* www.caryinstitute.org	Millbrook	NY	12545	845-677-5343	677-5976
Institute of Education Sciences (IES) US Dept of Education 555 New Jersey Ave NW Rm 600 *Web:* www.ies.ed.gov	Washington	DC	20208	202-219-1385	219-1466
Institute of Gerontology University of Michigan 300 N Ingalls St *TF:* 877-865-2167 ■ *Web:* med.umich.edu	Ann Arbor	MI	48109	734-936-2107	936-2116
Institute of Human Origins (IHO) Arizona State Univ PO Box 874101 *Web:* iho.asu.edu	Tempe	AZ	85287	480-727-6580	727-6570
Institute of Materials Science University of Connecticut 97 N Eagleville Rd *TF:* 800-528-7411 ■ *Web:* www.ims.uconn.edu	Storrs	CT	06269	860-486-4623	486-4745
Intelligent Mechatronic Systems Inc 435 King St N *TF:* 866-818-6637 ■ *Web:* www.intellimec.com	Waterloo	ON	N2J2Z5	519-745-8887	
Intematix Corp 46410 Fremont Blvd *Web:* www.intematix.com	Fremont	CA	94538	510-933-3300	
International Arctic Research Ctr (IARC) 930 Koyukuk Dr PO Box 757340 *Web:* www.iarc.uaf.edu	Fairbanks	AK	99775	907-474-6016	474-5662
International Ctr for Advanced Internet Research (iCAIR) 750 N Lk Shore Dr Ste 600 *Web:* www.icair.org	Chicago	IL	60611	312-503-0735	
International Institute of Tropical Forestry (IITF) Jardin Botanico Sur 1201 Calle Ceiba *Web:* www.fs.fed.us/global/iitf	San Juan	PR	00926	787-766-5335	766-6302
Ionian Technologies Inc 4940 Carroll Canyon Rd Ste 100 *Web:* www.ionian-tech.com	San Diego	CA	92121	858-642-0998	
Issues & Answers Network Inc 5151 Bonney Rd Ste 100 *Web:* www.issans.net	Virginia Beach	VA	23462	757-456-1100	
itherX Pharmaceuticals Inc 10790 Roselle St *Web:* www.itxpharma.com	San Diego	CA	92121	858-824-1100	
ITN Energy Systems Inc 8130 Shaffer Pkwy *Web:* www.itnes.com	Littleton	CO	80127	303-420-1141	
Jackson Laboratory, The 600 Main St *Web:* www.jax.org	Bar Harbor	ME	04609	207-288-6000	288-6076
James Cancer Hospital & Solove Research Institute, The 300 W Tenth Ave Ste 519 *Web:* cancer.osu.edu/	Columbus	OH	43210	614-293-5066	293-3132
Jamie Whitten Delta States Research Ctr Experiment Stn Rd PO Box 225 *Web:* www.ars.usda.gov/main/site_main.htm?modecode=64-02-00-00	Stoneville	MS	38776	662-686-5265	686-5459
Jean Mayer USDA Human Nutrition Research Ctr on Aging 711 Washington St *Web:* hnrca.tufts.edu	Boston	MA	02111	617-556-3000	556-3344
Jet Propulsion Laboratory (JPL) 4800 Oak Grove Dr *Web:* www.jpl.nasa.gov	Pasadena	CA	91109	818-354-4321	
John A Volpe National Transportation Systems Ctr 55 Broadway *Web:* www.volpe.dot.gov	Cambridge	MA	02142	617-494-2000	
John F. Kennedy Space Ctr *TF:* 866-737-5235 ■ *Web:* www.nasa.gov/centers/kennedy	Kennedy Space Center	FL	32899	321-867-5000	
Johns Hopkins University Applied Physics Laboratory 11100 Johns Hopkins Rd *Web:* www.jhuapl.edu	Laurel	MD	20723	240-228-5000	228-1093
Johnson Space Ctr 2101 NASA Pkwy *Web:* www.nasa.gov	Houston	TX	77058	281-483-0123	483-2000
Joint Institute for Laboratory Astrophysics (JILA) University of Colorado 440 UCB *Web:* jila.colorado.edu	Boulder	CO	80309	303-492-7789	492-5235
Joint Institute for Marine & Atmospheric Research University of Hawaii at Manoa 1000 Pope Rd MSB Bldg 312 *Web:* www.soest.hawaii.edu	Honolulu	HI	96822	808-956-8083	956-4104
Joint Institute for Marine Observations (JIMO) Scripps Institution of Oceanography -Univ of California 9500 Gilman Dr *Web:* www.jimo.ucsd.edu	La Jolla	CA	92093	858-534-4100	
Joseph Stokes Jr Research Institute Children's Hospital of Philadelphia 3615 Civic Ctr Blvd *Web:* stokes.chop.edu	Philadelphia	PA	19104	215-590-3800	590-3804
Joslin Diabetes Ctr 1 Joslin Pl *Web:* www.joslin.org	Boston	MA	02215	617-732-2400	732-2542
KemPharm Inc 2656Crosspark Rd Ste 100 *TF:* 877-695-3638 ■ *Web:* www.kempharm.com	Coralville	IA	52241	319-665-2575	665-2577
Kendle International Inc 441 Vine St 1200 Carew Twr *TF:* 800-733-1572 ■ *Web:* www.kendle.com	Cincinnati	OH	45202	513-381-5550	381-5870
Keweenaw Research Ctr Michigan Technological University 1400 Townsend Dr *Web:* www.mtukrc.org	Houghton	MI	49931	906-487-2750	487-2202
Knowledge Systems & Research Inc 120 Madison St 15th Fl *Web:* www.ksrinc.com	Syracuse	NY	13202	315-470-1350	
Kresge Hearing Research Institute (KHRI) University of Michigan Medical School 1150 W Medical Ctr Dr Rm 4605 Med Sci 2 *Web:* www.khri.med.umich.edu	Ann Arbor	MI	48109	734-764-8110	764-0014
Laboratory for Laser Energetics 250 E River Rd *Web:* www.lle.rochester.edu	Rochester	NY	14623	585-275-5101	275-5960
Lamont-Doherty Earth Observatory 61 Rt 9w *Web:* www.ldeo.columbia.edu	Palisades	NY	10964	845-359-2900	359-2931
Langley Research Ctr Eight Lindbergh Wy *Web:* www.nasa.gov/centers/langley	Hampton	VA	23681	757-864-1000	
Lawrence Berkeley National Laboratory *Advanced Light Source* One Cyclotron Rd MS 6-2100 *Web:* www-als.lbl.gov	Berkeley	CA	94720	510-486-7745	486-4773
Lawrence Livermore National Laboratory (LLNL) 7000 E Ave PO Box 808 *Web:* www.llnl.gov	Livermore	CA	94550	925-422-1100	422-1370
LC Sciences LLC 2575 W Bellfort St Ste 270 *Web:* www.lcsciences.com	Houston	TX	77054	713-664-7087	
Learning Research & Development Ctr (LRDC) University of Pittsburgh 3939 O'Hara St *TF:* 800-397-0071 ■ *Web:* www.lrdc.pitt.edu	Pittsburgh	PA	15260	412-624-7020	624-9149
Learning Systems Institute 4600 University Ctr *Web:* www.lsi.fsu.edu	Tallahassee	FL	32306	850-644-2570	644-4952
Lerner Research Institute 9500 Euclid Ave *TF:* 800-223-2273 ■ *Web:* www.lerner.ccf.org	Cleveland	OH	44195	216-444-3900	444-3279
LifeSensors Inc 271 Great Vly Pkwy Ste 100 *Web:* www.lifesensors.com	Malvern	PA	19355	610-644-8845	
Lightwaves 2020 Inc 1323 Great Mall Dr *Web:* www.lightwaves2020.com	Milpitas	CA	95035	408-503-8888	
LIMRA International Inc 300 Day Hill Rd *TF:* 866-540-4505 ■ *Web:* www.limra.com	Windsor	CT	06095	860-688-3358	298-9555
Lincoln Laboratory Massachusetts Institute of Technology 244 Wood St **Fax:* Hum Res ■ *TF:* 800-445-8667 ■ *Web:* www.ll.mit.edu	Lexington	MA	02420	781-981-5500	981-7086*
Lineagen Inc 423 Wakara Way Ste 200 *TF:* 888-888-6736 ■ *Web:* www.lineagen.com	Salt Lake City	UT	84108	801-931-6200	
Lodestar Research Corp 2400 Central Ave Ste P-5 *Web:* www.lodestar.com	Boulder	CO	80301	303-449-9691	449-3865
Los Alamos National Laboratory (LANL) PO Box 1663 *TF:* 877-723-4101 ■ *Web:* www.lanl.gov	Los Alamos	NM	87545	505-667-7000	
Los Angeles Biomedical Research Institute 1124 W Carson St **Fax Area Code:* 310 ■ *TF:* 877-452-2674 ■ *Web:* www.labiomed.org	Torrance	CA	90502	877-452-2674	222-3640*
Lovelace Respiratory Research Institute (LRRI) 2425 Ridgecrest Dr SE *Web:* www.lrri.org	Albuquerque	NM	87108	505-348-9400	348-8541
Lutonix Inc 9409 Science Ctr Dr *Web:* www.lutonix.com	New Hope	MN	55428	763-445-2352	
Mahoney Institute of Neurological Sciences 3535 Market St Mezzanine *Web:* www.med.upenn.edu	Philadelphia	PA	19104	215-662-2560	349-8312
Mailman Research Ctr *McLean Hospital* 115 Mill St *TF:* 800-333-0338 ■ *Web:* mcleanhospital.org/research/mrc	Belmont	MA	02478	617-855-2000	855-3479
Marine Biological Laboratory (MBL) 7 MBL St *TF:* 800-222-1222 ■ *Web:* www.mbl.edu	Woods Hole	MA	02543	508-548-3705	540-6902
Marine Environmental Research Institute (MERI) *MERI Center for Marine Studies* 55 Main St PO Box 1652 *Web:* www.meriresearch.org	Blue Hill	ME	04614	207-374-2135	374-2931
Marine Science Institute University of California *Web:* www.msi.ucsb.edu	Santa Barbara	CA	93106	805-893-4093	893-8062
Marinus Pharmaceuticals Inc 21 Business Park Dr *Web:* www.marinuspharma.com	Branford	CT	06405	203-315-0566	
Market Probe Inc 2655 N Mayfair Rd *TF:* 800-282-1376 ■ *Web:* w3.marketprobe.com	Milwaukee	WI	53226	414-778-6000	
Martec Group Inc, The 105 W Adams St Ste 2125 *TF:* 888-811-5755 ■ *Web:* www.martecgroup.com	Chicago	IL	60603	312-606-9690	
Massa Products Corp 280 Lincoln St *TF:* 800-962-7543 ■ *Web:* www.massa.com	Hingham	MA	02043	781-749-4800	

				Phone	Fax
Massey Cancer Ctr *Virginia Commonwealth University* 401 College St PO Box 980037 *TF:* 877-462-7739 ■ *Web:* www.massey.vcu.edu	Richmond	VA	23298	804-828-0450	828-8453
MAX Technologies Inc 7005 Taschereau Blvd 3rd Fl *Web:* www.maxt.com	Brossard	QC	J4Z1A7	450-443-3332	443-1618
MBI International 3815 Technology Blvd *Web:* www.mbi.org	Lansing	MI	48910	517-337-3181	337-2122
McArdle Laboratory for Cancer Research University of Wisconsin Dept of Oncology 1400 University Ave *Web:* mcardle.oncology.wisc.edu	Madison	WI	53706	608-262-2177	262-2824
McCrone Assoc Inc 850 Pasquinelli Dr *Web:* www.mccroneassociates.com	Westmont	IL	60559	630-887-7100	887-7417
MCEER Red Jacket Quadrangle *Web:* mceer.buffalo.edu	Buffalo	NY	14260	716-645-3391	645-3733
Mechanical Technology Inc 431 New Karner Rd *NASDAQ: MKTY* ■ *TF:* 800-937-5449 ■ *Web:* www.mechtech.com	Albany	NY	12205	518-533-2200	218-2500
Membrane Technology & Research Inc 1360 Willow Rd Ste 103 *Web:* www.mtrinc.com	Menlo Park	CA	94025	650-328-2228	328-6580
Memorial Sloan-Kettering Cancer Ctr 1275 York Ave *TF:* 800-525-2225 ■ *Web:* www.mskcc.org	New York	NY	10065	212-639-2000	
Mersana Therapeutics Inc 840 Memorial Dr *Web:* www.mersana.com	Cambridge	MA	02139	617-498-0020	
Metabolon Inc 3410 Industrial Blvd Ste 103 *Web:* www.lipomics.com	West Sacramento	CA	95691	916-371-7974	669-0475
Metrics Inc 1240 Sugg Pkwy *Web:* www.metricsinc.com	Greenville	NC	27834	252-752-3800	758-8522
Miami Project to Cure Paralysis 1095 NW 14th Terr Lois Pope LIFE Ctr *TF General:* 800-782-6387 ■ *Web:* www.miamiproject.miami.edu	Miami	FL	33136	305-243-6001	243-6017
Michigan Mfg Technology Ctr 47911 Halyard Dr **Fax Area Code:* 734 ■ *TF:* 888-414-6682 ■ *Web:* www.mmtc.org	Plymouth	MI	48170	888-414-6682	451-4201*
Mid-Continent Research for Education & Learning (McREL) 4601 DTC Blvd Ste 500 *Web:* www.mcrel.org	Denver	CO	80237	303-337-0990	337-3005
Midwest Research Institute (MRI) 425 Volker Blvd *Web:* www.mriglobal.org	Kansas City	MO	64110	816-753-7600	753-8420
MIT Media Laboratory Massachusetts Institute of Technology 77 Massachusetts Ave Bldg E15 *Web:* www.media.mit.edu	Cambridge	MA	02139	617-253-5960	258-6264
MITRE Corp 202 Burlington Rd *Web:* www.mitre.org	Bedford	MA	01730	781-271-2000	271-2271
Monell Chemical Senses Ctr 3500 Market St *TF:* 800-732-0999	Philadelphia	PA	19104	267-519-4700	519-4805
Monteith Engineering Research Center *North Carolina State University* 2410 Campus Shore Dr Centennial Campus *Web:* www.ncsu.edu	Raleigh	NC	27606	919-515-2030	515-5055
Mote Marine Laboratory 1600 Ken Thompson Pkwy *Web:* www.mote.org	Sarasota	FL	34236	941-388-4441	388-4312
MSU-DOE Plant Research Laboratory Michigan State University 106 Plant Biology *TF:* 800-875-5090 ■ *Web:* www.prl.msu.edu	East Lansing	MI	48824	517-353-2270	353-9168
NAHB Research Ctr 400 Prince Georges Blvd *TF:* 800-638-8556 ■ *Web:* www.homeinnovation.com	Upper Marlboro	MD	20774	301-249-4000	430-6180
NanoBio Corp 2311 Green Rd Ste A *Web:* www.nanobio.com	Ann Arbor	MI	48105	734-302-4000	
Nanotechnology Research Ctr *Georgia Institute of Technology* 791 Atlantic Dr *TF:* 800-424-9300 ■ *Web:* ien.gatech.edu/nrc-transition-page/	Atlanta	GA	30332	404-894-5100	894-5028
Nathan S Kline Institute for Psychiatric Research 140 Old Orangeburg Rd Bldg 35 *Web:* www.rfmh.org/nki	Orangeburg	NY	10962	845-398-5500	398-5508
National Astronomy & Ionosphere Ctr (NAIC) Cornell University Space Sciences Bldg *Web:* www.naic.edu	Ithaca	NY	14853	607-255-3735	255-8803
National Biodynamics Laboratory (NBDL) *University of New Orleans College of Engineering* 2000 Lakeshore Dr **Fax Area Code:* 504 ■ *TF:* 888-514-4275 ■ *Web:* www.uno.edu	New Orleans	LA	70148	888-514-4275	280-7413*
National Bureau of Economic Research 1050 Massachusetts Ave *TF:* 800-621-8476 ■ *Web:* www.nber.org	Cambridge	MA	02138	617-868-3900	868-2742
National Cancer Institute at Frederick 1050 Boyles St PO Box B *Web:* ncifrederick.cancer.gov	Frederick	MD	21702	301-846-1108	846-1494
National Ctr for Agricultural Utilization Research USDA/ARS 1815 N University St *Web:* www.ars.usda.gov/Main/docs.htm?docid=3153	Peoria	IL	61604	309-685-4011	681-6686
National Ctr for Atmospheric Research (NCAR) 1850 Table Mesa Dr PO Box 3000 **Fax:* PR ■ *Web:* www.ncar.ucar.edu	Boulder	CO	80305	303-497-1000	497-8610*
National Ctr for Computational Toxicology US Environmental Protection Agency 109 TW Alexander Dr *Web:* www.epa.gov	Research Triangle Park	NC	27709	919-541-3850	
National Ctr for Ecological Analysis & Synthesis (NCEAS) University of California Santa Barbara 735 State St Ste 300 *Web:* www.nceas.ucsb.edu	Santa Barbara	CA	93101	805-892-2500	892-2510
National Ctr for Electron Microscopy (NCEM) Lawrence Berkeley National Laboratory MS 72-150 *Web:* foundry.lbl.gov/facilities/ncem	Berkeley	CA	94720	510-486-4000	486-5888
National Ctr for Genetic Resources Preservation (NCGRP) 1111 S Mason St *Web:* www.ars.usda.gov/npa/ftcollins/ncgrp	Fort Collins	CO	80521	970-495-3200	221-1427
National Ctr for Genome Resources 2935 Rodeo Pk Dr E *TF:* 800-450-4854 ■ *Web:* www.ncgr.org	Santa Fe	NM	87505	505-995-4451	995-4432
National Ctr for Mfg Sciences (NCMS) 3025 Boardwalk *TF:* 800-222-6267 ■ *Web:* www.ncms.org	Ann Arbor	MI	48108	734-995-0300	995-1150
National Ctr for Supercomputing Applications University of Illinois Urbana-Champaign 1205 W Clark St Rm 1008 MC-257 *Web:* www.ncsa.illinois.edu	Urbana	IL	61801	217-244-0072	244-8195
National Development & Research Institutes Inc 71 W 23rd St Eighth Fl **Fax Area Code:* 917 ■ *Web:* www.ndri.org	New York	NY	10010	212-845-4400	438-0894*
National Energy Research Scientific Computing Ctr (NERSC) Lawrence Berkeley National Laboratory *TF:* 800-666-3772 ■ *Web:* www.nersc.gov	Berkeley	CA	94720	510-486-5849	486-4300
National Energy Technology Laboratory (NETL) 3610 Collins Ferry Rd *TF:* 800-432-8330 ■ *Web:* www.netl.doe.gov	Morgantown	WV	26505	304-285-4764	285-4919
National Exposure Research Laboratory US Environmental Protection Agency TW Alexander **Fax Area Code:* 919 ■ *Web:* www.epa.gov	Research Triangle Park	NC	27709	202-564-6620	541-0605*
National Hansen's Disease Program (NHDP) 1770 Physicians Pk Dr *TF:* 800-642-2477 ■ *Web:* hrsa.gov	Baton Rouge	LA	70816	225-756-3700	
National Health & Environmental Effects Research Laboratory US Environmental Protection Agency 109 TW Alexander Dr **Fax Area Code:* 919 ■ *Web:* www.epa.gov/nheerl	Research Triangle Park	NC	27709	202-564-6665	541-4324*
National High Magnetic Field Laboratory (NHMFL) 1800 E Paul Dirac Dr *Web:* www.magnet.fsu.edu	Tallahassee	FL	32310	850-644-0311	644-8350
National Homeland Security Research Ctr US Environmental Protection Agency 26 W Martin Luther King Dr *TF:* 888-372-7341 ■ *Web:* www.epa.gov	Cincinnati	OH	45268	513-569-7907	487-2555
National Institute Child Health (CRMC) 6100 Executive Blvd	Rockville	MD	20852	301-496-5593	
National Institute of Standards & Technology (NIST) 100 Bureau Dr Sp 1070 *TF:* 800-877-8339 ■ *Web:* www.nist.gov	Gaithersburg	MD	20899	301-975-6478	926-1630
Boulder Laboratories 325 Broadway MS 104 **Fax Area Code:* 303 ■ *Web:* www.boulder.nist.gov	Boulder	CO	80305	301-975-6478	497-6235*
National Institute on Disability & Rehabilitation Research (NIDRR) Potomac Center Plz 550 12th St SW Rm 5142 *Web:* www.ed.gov/about/offices/list/osers/nidrr	Washington	DC	20202	202-245-6211	245-7323
Clinical Ctr 10 Ctr Dr Bldg 10 *Web:* www.cc.nih.gov	Bethesda	MD	20892	301-496-2563	402-2984
National Cancer Institute Public Inquiries Office 6116 Executive Blvd Rm 3036A *TF:* 800-422-6237 ■ *Web:* www.cancer.gov	Bethesda	MD	20892	301-435-3848	
National Eye Institute 2020 Vision Pl *Web:* www.nei.nih.gov	Bethesda	MD	20892	301-496-5248	402-1065
National Human Genome Research Institute 31 Ctr Dr Bldg 31 Rm 4B09 *Web:* www.genome.gov	Bethesda	MD	20892	301-402-0911	402-2218
National Institute of Arthritis & Musculoskeletal & Skin Diseases 31 Ctr Dr MSC 2350 Bldg 31 Rm 4C02 *Web:* www.niams.nih.gov	Bethesda	MD	20892	301-496-8190	480-2814
National Institute of Dental & Craniofacial Research 31 Ctr Dr *Web:* www.nidcr.nih.gov	Bethesda	MD	20892	301-496-3571	402-2185
National Institute of Environmental Health Sciences PO Box 12233 *Web:* www.niehs.nih.gov	Research Triangle Park	NC	27709	919-541-3201	541-2260
National Institute of General Medical Sciences 45 Ctr Dr MSC 6200 *Web:* www.nigms.nih.gov	Bethesda	MD	20892	301-496-7301	
National Institute of Mental Health 6001 Executive Blvd Rm 8184 MSC 9663 *TF:* 866-615-6464 ■ *Web:* www.nimh.nih.gov	Bethesda	MD	20892	301-443-4513	443-4279
National Institute of Neurological Disorders & Stroke PO Box 5801 *TF:* 800-352-9424 ■ *Web:* www.ninds.nih.gov	Bethesda	MD	20824	301-496-5751	
National Institute of Nursing Research 31 Ctr Dr Bldg 31 Rm 5B10 *Web:* www.ninr.nih.gov	Bethesda	MD	20892	301-496-8230	594-3405
National Institute on Aging 31 Ctr Dr Bldg 31 Rm 5C27 MSC 2292 *Web:* www.nia.nih.gov	Bethesda	MD	20892	301-496-1752	496-1072
National Institute on Alcohol Abuse & Alcoholism 5635 Fishers Ln MSC 9304 *Web:* www.niaaa.nih.gov	Bethesda	MD	20892	301-443-3885	443-7043
National Institute on Deafness & Other Communication Disorders 31 Ctr Dr Bldg 31 Rm 3C35 *TF:* 800-241-1044 ■ *Web:* www.nidcd.nih.gov	Bethesda	MD	20892	301-496-7243	402-0018
National Library of Medicine *Lister Hill National Center for Biomedical Communications* 8600 Rockville Pike Bldg 38A 7th Fl *Web:* www.lhncbc.nlm.nih.gov	Bethesda	MD	20894	301-496-4441	480-3035
National Optical Astronomy Observatories 950 N Cherry Ave *TF:* 888-809-4012 ■ *Web:* www.noao.edu	Tucson	AZ	85719	520-318-8163	318-8360

	City	State	Zip	Phone	Fax
National Radio Astronomy Observatory (NRAO)					
520 Edgemont Rd	Charlottesville	VA	22903	434-296-0211	296-0278
Web: www.nrao.edu					
National Renewable Energy Laboratory (NREL)					
1617 Cole Blvd	Golden	CO	80401	303-275-3000	275-4053
Web: www.nrel.gov					
National Research Ctr for Coal & Energy (NRCCE)					
West Virginia University					
385 Evansdale Dr PO Box 6064	Morgantown	WV	26506	304-293-2867	293-3749
TF: 800-624-8301 ■ *Web:* www.nrcce.wvu.edu					
National Research Ctr on English Learning & Achievement (CELA)					
School of Education University of Albany B9					
1400 Washington Ave	Albany	NY	12222	518-442-5026	442-5933
Web: www.albany.edu					
National Risk Management Research Laboratory					
US Environmental Protection Agency					
26 Martin Luther King Dr	Cincinnati	OH	45268	513-569-7418	569-7680
Web: www.epa.gov/ordntrnt/ord/nrmrl					
National Sedimentation Laboratory PO Box 1157	Oxford	MS	38655	662-232-2924	281-5706
Web: www.ars.usda.gov/main/site_main.htm?modecode=64-08-05-00					
National Severe Storms Laboratory (NSSL)					
120 David L Boren Blvd	Norman	OK	73072	405-325-6907	
Web: www.nssl.noaa.gov					
National Soil Erosion Research Laboratory					
USDA/ARS 275 S Russell St	West Lafayette	IN	47907	765-494-8689	494-5948
Web: www.ars.usda.gov/main/site_main.htm?modecode=36021500					
National Technical Information Service (NTIS)					
5285 Port Royal Rd	Springfield	VA	22161	703-605-6000	605-6900
TF Orders: 800-553-6847 ■ *Web:* www.ntis.gov					
National Toxicology Program (NTP)					
PO Box 12233	Research Triangle Park	NC	27709	919-541-0530	541-3687
Web: ntp.niehs.nih.gov/					
National Undersea Research Ctr for Hawaii & the Western Pacific					
University of Hawaii at Manoa	Honolulu	HI	96822	808-956-6335	956-9772
TF: 888-800-0460 ■ *Web:* www.soest.hawaii.edu/hurl					
National Undersea Research Ctr for the Caribbean					
Perry Institute for Marine Science Caribbean Marine Research Ctr					
100 N US Hwy 1 Ste 202	Jupiter	FL	33477	561-741-0192	741-0193
Web: www.perryinstitute.org					
National Undersea Research Ctr for the Mid-Atlantic Bight					
Institute of Marine & Coastal Sciences					
Rutgers University 71 Dudley Rd	New Brunswick	NJ	08901	732-932-6555	932-8578
TF: 888-776-6537 ■ *Web:* www.marine.rutgers.edu					
National Undersea Research Ctr for the North Atlantic & Great Lakes (NURC)					
University of Connecticut at Avery Pt					
1080 Shennecossett Rd	Groton	CT	06340	860-405-9121	445-2969
Web: nurtec.uconn.edu/					
National Undersea Research Ctr for the Southeastern US & Gulf of Mexico (NURC)					
University of N Carolina at Wilmington					
5600 Marvin K Moss Ln	Wilmington	NC	28409	910-962-2440	962-2444
Web: www.nurp.noaa.gov					
National Wetlands Research Ctr					
700 Cajundome Blvd	Lafayette	LA	70506	337-266-8500	266-8513
Web: www.nwrc.usgs.gov					
National Wildlife Health Ctr					
6006 Schroeder Rd	Madison	WI	53711	608-270-2400	270-2415
TF: 800-232-4636 ■ *Web:* www.nwhc.usgs.gov					
National Wildlife Research Ctr					
4101 LaPorte Ave	Fort Collins	CO	80521	970-266-6000	266-6032
Web: www.aphis.usda.gov					
Nationwide Children's Hospital					
700 Children's Dr	Columbus	OH	43205	614-722-2700	722-2716
Web: www.nationwidechildrens.org					
Natural Hazards Ctr					
University of Colorado CB 482	Boulder	CO	80309	303-492-6818	492-2151
Web: www.colorado.edu/hazards					
Natural Resource Ecology Laboratory					
Colorado State University					
Campus Delivery 1499	Fort Collins	CO	80523	970-491-1982	491-1965
Web: www.nrel.colostate.edu					
Natural Resources Research Institute (NRRI)					
University of Minnesota Duluth					
5013 Miller Trunk Hwy	Duluth	MN	55811	218-720-4294	720-4219
TF: 800-234-0054 ■ *Web:* www.nrri.umn.edu					
Naval Health Research Ctr (NHRC)					
140 Sylvester Rd	San Diego	CA	92106	619-553-8400	553-9389
Web: www.med.navy.mil/sites/nhrc					
Naval Institute for Dental & Biomedical Research (NDRI)					
310-A B St Bldg 1-H	Great Lakes	IL	60088	847-688-1900	
Web: www.dentalmercury.com					
Naval Research Laboratory (NRL)					
4555 Overlook Ave SW Code 1000	Washington	DC	20375	202-767-3403	404-7419
Web: www.nrl.navy.mil					
Naval Submarine Medical Research Laboratory (NSMRL)					
PO Box 900	Groton	CT	06349	703-681-9025	694-4809*
**Fax Area Code:* 860 ■ *Web:* www.med.navy.mil					
Naval Surface Warfare Ctr (NSWC)					
1333 Isaac Hull Ave SE	Washington Navy Yard	DC	20376	202-781-5425	
Web: www.navsea.navy.mil/nswc					
Carderock Div 9500 MacArthur Blvd	West Bethesda	MD	20817	202-781-0000	227-3574*
**Fax Area Code:* 301 ■ *Web:* www.navsea.navy.mil/nswc/carderock					
Dahlgren Div 6149 Welsh Rd Ste 203	Dahlgren	VA	22448	877-845-5656	
TF: 877-845-5656 ■ *Web:* www.navsea.navy.mil					
Naval Undersea Warfare Ctr (NUWC)					
1176 Howell St	Newport	RI	02841	401-832-7742	832-4396
Web: www.navsea.navy.mil/nuwc					
Keyport Div 610 Dowell St	Keyport	WA	98345	360-396-2699	396-2387
Web: www.navsea.navy.mil/nuwc/keyport/default.aspx					
Newport Div 1176 Howell St	Newport	RI	02841	401-832-7742	832-4661
Web: www.navsea.navy.mil/nuwc/default.aspx					
Nebraska Ctr for Materials & Nanoscience					
855 N. 16th Street N201 NANO	Lincoln	NE	68588	402-472-7886	472-2879
Web: www.unl.edu/ncmn					

	City	State	Zip	Phone	Fax
NEC Laboratories America Inc					
Four Independence Way	Princeton	NJ	08540	609-520-1555	951-2481
Web: www.nec-labs.com					
Nereus Pharmaceuticals Inc					
10480 Wateridge Cir	San Diego	CA	92121	858-587-4090	
Web: www.nereuspharm.com					
Neumedicines Inc 133 N Altadena Dr Ste 310	Pasadena	CA	91107	626-844-3800	
Web: www.neumedicines.com					
Neurotech Pharmaceuticals Inc					
900 Highland Corporate Dr	Cumberland	RI	02864	401-333-3880	
Web: www.neurotechusa.com					
Neurotez Inc 991 Hwy 22 Ste 200 A	Bridgewater	NJ	08807	908-998-1340	
Web: neurotez.com					
New England Primate Research Ctr (NEPRC)					
1 Pine Hill Dr PO Box 9102	Southborough	MA	01772	617-432-1000	786-3317*
**Fax Area Code:* 508 ■ *Web:* www.hms.harvard.edu					
NGM Biopharmaceuticals Inc					
630 Gateway Blvd	South San Francisco	CA	94080	650-243-5555	
Web: www.ngmbio.com					
NOAA's Undersea Research Program					
Florida Keys Research Program					
1315 EW Hwy	Silver Spring	MD	20910	301-734-1000	713-1967
Web: nurp.noaa.gov					
Noblis 3150 Fairview Pk Dr S	Falls Church	VA	22042	703-610-2000	
Web: www.noblis.org					
Non-Intrusive Inspection Technology Inc					
23031 Ladbrook Dr	Dulles	VA	20166	703-661-0283	
Web: www.niitek.com					
North American Science Assoc Inc					
6750 Walcs Rd	Northwood	OH	43619	419-666-9455	662-4386
TF: 866-666-9455 ■ *Web:* www.namsa.com					
North Central Agricultural Research Laboratory (NGIRL)					
USDA/ARS 2923 Medary Ave	Brookings	SD	57006	605-693-3241	693-5240
Web: www.ars.usda.gov/main/docs.htm?docid=2357					
Northeast Fisheries Science Ctr					
166 Water St	Woods Hole	MA	02543	508-495-2000	495-2258
Web: www.nefsc.noaa.gov					
Northern Power Systems Inc 29 Pitman Rd	Barre	VT	05641	802-461-2955	
TF: 877-906-6784 ■ *Web:* www.northernpower.com					
Northern Prairie Wildlife Research Ctr					
8711 37th St SE	Jamestown	ND	58401	701-253-5500	253-5553
Web: www.npwrc.usgs.gov					
Northern Research Station					
11 Campus Blvd Ste 200	Newtown Square	PA	19073	610-557-4017	557-4095
Web: www.nrs.fs.fed.us					
Northwest Fisheries Science Ctr					
2725 Montlake Blvd E	Seattle	WA	98112	206-860-3200	860-3217
Web: www.nwfsc.noaa.gov					
Notre Dame Radiation Laboratory					
University of Notre Dame	Notre Dame	IN	46556	574-631-6163	631-8068
Web: www.rad.nd.edu					
Oak Ridge National Laboratory (ORNL)					
PO Box 2008	Oak Ridge	TN	37831	865-576-2900	574-0595*
**Fax:* PR ■ *Web:* www.ornl.gov					
Oceanic Institute 41-202 Kalanianaole Hwy	Waimanalo	HI	96795	808-259-7951	259-5971
Web: www.oceanicinstitute.org					
Office of Naval Research (ONR)					
875 N Randolph St Ste 1425	Arlington	VA	22217	703-696-5031	696-5940
Web: onr.navy.mil					
Office of Population Research					
Princeton University					
Wallace Hall Second Fl	Princeton	NJ	08544	609-258-4870	258-1039
Web: www.opr.princeton.edu					
Ohio State University Police, The					
1680 Madison Ave	Wooster	OH	44691	330-287-0111	202-3579
TF: 800-358-4678 ■ *Web:* www.oardc.ohio-state.edu					
Oklahoma Medical Research Foundation (OMRF)					
825 NE 13th St	Oklahoma City	OK	73104	405-271-6673	271-7510
TF: 800-522-0211 ■ *Web:* www.omrf.org					
Oracle Capital LLC 1985 E River Rd Ste 111	Tucson	AZ	85718	520-319-9958	
Web: www.oraclecapital.com					
Orca Systems Inc 13025 Danielson St Ste 106	Poway	CA	92064	858-679-9115	
Web: www.orcasystems.com					
Oregon National Primate Research Ctr (ONPRC)					
3181 SW Sam Jackson Pk Rd	Portland	OR	97239	503-494-8311	
Web: www.ohsu.edu					
Pacific Disaster Ctr 1305 N Holopono St Ste 2	Kihei	HI	96753	808-891-0525	891-0526
TF: 888-808-6688 ■ *Web:* www.pdc.org					
Pacific Institute for Research & Evaluation					
11720 Beltsville Dr Ste 900	Calverton	MD	20705	301-755-2738	755-2799
Web: www.pire.org					
Pacific International Ctr for High Technology Research (PICHTR)					
1440 Kapiolani Blvd Ste 1225	Honolulu	HI	96814	808-943-9581	943-9582
Web: www.pichtr.org					
Pacific Island Ecosystems Research Ctr (PIERC)					
677 Ala Moana Blvd Ste 615	Honolulu	HI	96813	808-587-7452	587-7451
Web: www.usgs.gov					
Pacific Marine Environmental Laboratory (PMEL)					
7600 Sand Pt Way NE	Seattle	WA	98115	206-526-6239	526-6815
Web: www.pmel.noaa.gov					
Pacific Northwest National Laboratory (PNNL)					
902 Battelle Blvd PO Box 999	Richland	WA	99352	509-375-2121	375-2507*
**Fax:* Mail Rm ■ *TF:* 888-375-7665 ■ *Web:* www.pnl.gov					
Pacific Northwest Research Station					
333 SW First Ave	Portland	OR	97204	503-808-2100	808-2130
Web: www.fs.fed.us/pnw					
Pacific Southwest Research Station					
800 Buchanan St W Annex Bldg	Albany	CA	94710	510-559-6300	559-6440
Web: www.fs.fed.us/psw					
Palo Alto Research Ctr Inc (PARC)					
3333 Coyote Hill Rd	Palo Alto	CA	94304	650-812-4000	812-4970
Web: www.parc.com					
PAREXEL International Corp 195 W St	Waltham	MA	02451	781-487-9900	487-0525
NASDAQ: PRXL ■ *TF:* 800-301-5033 ■ *Web:* www.parexel.com					

Organization	City	State	ZIP	Phone	Fax
Parker Mktg Research LLC 5405 Dupont Cir *Web:* parkerinsights.com	Milford	OH	45150	513-248-8100	
Parks Assoc Inc 5310 Harvest Hill Rd Ste 235 PO Box 162 *TF:* 800-727-5711 ■ *Web:* www.parksassociates.com	Dallas	TX	75230	972-490-1113	
Patrick Ctr for Environmental Research 1900 Benjamin Franklin Pkwy *Web:* www.ansp.org/research/pcer	Philadelphia	PA	19103	215-299-1000	299-1079
Patuxent Wildlife Research Ctr 12100 Beech Forest Rd. *Web:* www.pwrc.usgs.gov	Laurel	MD	20708	301-497-5500	497-5505
Percivia LLC One Hampshire St Fifth Fl *Web:* www.percivia.com	Cambridge	MA	02139	617-301-8800	
Peryam & Kroll Research Corp 6323 N Avondale Ave *TF:* 800-747-5522	Chicago	IL	60631	800-281-3155	
Pfenex Inc 10790 Roselle St. *Web:* www.pfenex.com	San Diego	CA	92121	858-352-4400	
Phantom Laboratory Inc, The 2727 SR- 29 *TF:* 800-525-1190 ■ *Web:* www.phantomlab.com	Greenwich	NY	12834	518-692-1190	692-3329
Pittsburgh Supercomputing Ctr 300 S Craig St *TF:* 800-221-1641 ■ *Web:* www.psc.edu	Pittsburgh	PA	15213	412-268-4960	268-5832
Planet Biotechnology Inc 25571 Clawiter Rd *Web:* www.planetbiotechnology.com	Hayward	CA	94545	510-887-1461	
Plasma Science & Fusion Ctr Massachusetts Institute of Technology 77 Massachusetts Ave NW16 *Web:* www.psfc.mit.edu	Cambridge	MA	02139	617-253-8100	253-0238
Pleora Technologies Inc 340 Terry Fox Dr Suite 300 *TF:* 888-687-6877 ■ *Web:* www.pleora.com	Kanata	ON	K2K3A2	613-270-0625	270-1425
Plexxikon Inc 91 Bolivar Dr *Web:* plexxikon.com	Berkeley	CA	94710	510-647-4000	
Plum Island Animal Disease Ctr 1400 Independence Ave. SW *Web:* www.ars.usda.gov/main/site_main.htm?modecode=19400000	Washington	DC	20250	631-323-3200	323-2507
Polisher Research Institute Abramson Ctr for Jewish Life 1425 Horsham Rd. *Web:* www.pgc.org/pri	North Wales	PA	19454	215-371-1895	371-3015
Population Council One Dag Hammarskjold Plz Ninth Fl. *Web:* www.popcouncil.org	New York	NY	10017	212-339-0500	755-6052
Population Research Ctr University of Chicago 1155 E 60th St. *Web:* popcenter.uchicago.edu	Chicago	IL	60637	773-256-6315	256-6313
Population Research Institute Pennsylvania State University 601 Oswald Tower *Web:* www.pop.psu.edu	University Park	PA	16802	814-865-0486	863-8342
Positron Inc 5101 Buchan St Ste 220 *Web:* www.positronpower.com	Montreal	QC	H4P2R9	514-345-2200	345-2271
PPD Inc 929 N Front St *NASDAQ: PPDI* ■ *Web:* www.ppdi.com	Wilmington	NC	28401	910-251-0081	762-5820
Precision Filters Inc 240 Cherry St *Web:* www.pfinc.com	Ithaca	NY	14850	607-277-3550	
Princeton Plasma Physics Laboratory (PPPL) James Forrestal Campus Princeton University PO Box 451 *TF:* 800-772-2222 ■ *Web:* www.pppl.gov	Princeton	NJ	08543	609-243-2750	243-2751
Public Health Research Institute (PHRI) International Ctr for Public Health 225 Warren St. *Web:* www.phri.org	Newark	NJ	07103	973-854-3100	854-3101
Quantiam Technologies Inc 1651 - 94 St NW *Web:* www.quantiam.com	Edmonton	AB	T6N1E6	780-462-0707	465-6603
Quintessence Biosciences Inc 505 S Rosa Rd *Web:* www.quintbio.com	Madison	WI	53719	608-441-2950	
Quintiles Transnational Corp 4820 Emperor Blvd. *TF:* 866-267-4479 ■ *Web:* www.quintiles.com	Durham	NC	27703	919-998-2000	998-2003
Radiant Research Inc 11500 Northlake Dr Ste 320 *TF:* 866-232-8484 ■ *Web:* www.radiantresearch.com	Cincinnati	OH	45249	513-247-5500	247-5588
Regional Research Institute for Human Services (RRI) Portland State University 1600 SW Fourth Ave Ste 900 *Web:* www.rri.pdx.edu	Portland	OR	97201	503-725-4040	725-2140
Renaissance Computing Institute (RENCI) 100 Europa Dr Ste 540 *Web:* www.renci.org	Chapel Hill	NC	27517	919-445-9640	445-9669
Research Board Inc, The 1325 Ave of the Americas 17th Fl *Web:* www.researchboard.com	New York	NY	10019	212-632-7600	
Research for Better Schools Inc 112 N Broad St *Web:* www.rbs.org	Philadelphia	PA	19102	215-568-6150	568-7260
Research Foundation of City University of New York, The 230 W 41st St Seventh Fl *Web:* www.rfcuny.org	New York	NY	10036	212-417-8300	
Research Institute on Addictions (RIA) 1021 Main St *Web:* buffalo.edu/ria.html	Buffalo	NY	14203	716-887-2566	887-2252
Research Laboratory of Electronics Massachusetts Institute of Technology 77 Massachusetts Ave Rm 36-413 *Web:* www.rle.mit.edu	Cambridge	MA	02139	617-253-2519	253-1301
Research Triangle Institute 3040 Cornwallis Rd PO Box 12194 *TF:* 800-334-8571 ■ *Web:* www.rti.org	Research Triangle Park	NC	27709	919-541-6000	541-5985
Ricerca Biosciences LLC 7528 Auburn Rd PO Box 1000 *TF:* 888-742-3722 ■ *Web:* www.ricerca.com	Concord	OH	44077	440-357-3300	354-6276
Rivel Research Group Inc 830 Post Rd E. *Web:* www.rivel.com	Westport	CT	06880	203-226-0800	
Robotics Institute Carnegie Mellon University 5000 Forbes Ave. *TF:* 800-767-8483 ■ *Web:* www.ri.cmu.edu	Pittsburgh	PA	15213	412-268-3818	268-6436
Rocky Mountain Research Station *US Forest Service* 240 W Prospec *Web:* www.fs.fed.us/rm	Fort Collins	CO	80526	970-498-1100	498-1010
Rodale Institute 611 Siegfriedale Rd. *Web:* www.rodaleinstitute.org	Kutztown	PA	19530	610-683-1400	683-8548
Rose F. Kennedy Ctr *Albert Einstein College of Medicine* 1410 Pelham Pkwy S *Web:* www.einstein.yu.edu	Bronx	NY	10461	718-430-8500	918-7505
Roswell Park Cancer Institute Elm and Carlton St *TF:* 877-275-7724 ■ *Web:* www.roswellpark.org	Buffalo	NY	14263	716-845-2300	845-8335
Roubini Global Economics LLC 95 Morton St Sixth Fl *Web:* roubini.com	New York	NY	10014	212-645-0010	
Roy J Carver Biotechnology Ctr 1206 W Gregory. *TF:* 800-550-3033 ■ *Web:* www.biotech.illinois.edu	Urbana	IL	61801	217-333-1695	244-0466
Russell Sage Foundation 112 E 64th St *Web:* www.russellsage.org	New York	NY	10021	212-750-6000	371-4761
Rutgers Business School (RBS) One Washington Park Rm 526 *Web:* www.business.rutgers.edu/default.aspx?id=645	Newark	NJ	07102	973-353-1821	
Sabrient Systems LLC 115 S La Cumbre Ln Ste 100 *Web:* www.sabrient.com	Santa Barbara	CA	93105	805-730-7777	
Safety Analysis & Forensic Engineering 5665 Hollister Ave Ste 100 *Web:* www.saferesearch.com	Goleta	CA	93117	805-964-0676	964-7669
Salk Institute for Biological Studies PO Box 85800 *TF:* 800-245-9757 ■ *Web:* www.salk.edu	San Diego	CA	92186	858-453-4100	552-8285
San Diego Supercomputer Ctr (SDSC) 9500 Gilman Dr *Web:* www.sdsc.edu	La Jolla	CA	92093	858-534-5000	534-5056
SanBio Inc 231 S Whisman Rd. *Web:* www.san-bio.com	Mountain View	CA	94041	650-625-8965	
Sandelman & Assoc Inc 257 La Paloma Ste 1 *TF:* 888-897-7881 ■ *Web:* www.sandelman.com	San Clemente	CA	92672	949-388-5600	
Sandia National Laboratories - California (SNL) 7011 E Ave PO Box 969 *Web:* www.sandia.gov	Livermore	CA	94551	925-294-3000	
Sandia National Laboratories - New Mexico (SNL) 1515 Eubank SE PO Box 5800 *Web:* www.sandia.gov	Albuquerque	NM	87123	505-845-0011	
Sarnoff Corp 201 Washington Rd PO Box 5300 *Web:* sri.com/engage/products-solutions	Princeton	NJ	08543	609-734-2000	734-2221
Savannah River National Laboratory Savannah River Site *Web:* srnl.doe.gov	Aiken	SC	29808	803-725-2854	725-1660
SC&A Inc 1608 Spring Hill Rd Ste 400 *Web:* www.scainc.com	Vienna	VA	22182	703-893-6600	821-8236
Schiefelbusch Institute for Life Span Studies *Univ of Kansas Robert Dole Human Development Ctr* 1000 Sunnyside Ave Rm 1052 *Web:* www.lsi.ku.edu/lsi	Lawrence	KS	66045	785-864-4295	864-5323
Science Applications International Corp 10260 Campus Pt Dr **Fax Area Code: 858* ■ *Web:* www.saic.com	San Diego	CA	92121	703-676-4300	826-6634*
Scripps Institution of Oceanography (SIO) 8622 Kennel Way *Web:* scripps.ucsd.edu	La Jolla	CA	92037	858-534-3624	
Scripps Research Institute 10550 N Torrey Pines Rd **Fax: Hum Res* ■ *Web:* www.scripps.edu	La Jolla	CA	92037	858-784-1000	784-9004*
SEDL 4700 Mueller Blvd *Web:* www.sedl.org	Austin	TX	78723	512-476-6861	476-2286
SEMATECH 2706 Montopolis Dr *Web:* www.sematech.org	Austin	TX	78741	512-356-3500	
Sensor Technology Systems Inc 2794 Indian Ripple Rd *Web:* www.sts-eo.com	Beavercreek	OH	45440	937-490-2509	
SERVE 5900 Summit Ave Ste 201 *TF:* 800-755-3277 ■ *Web:* www.serve.org	Browns Summit	NC	27214	336-315-7400	315-7457
Shamrock Structures LLC 1440 Davey Rd. *Web:* www.shamrockstructures.com	Woodridge	IL	60517	630-739-3215	
Sharp Laboratories Of America Inc 5750 NW Pacific Rim Blvd *Web:* www.sharplabs.com	Camas	WA	98607	360-817-8400	817-7544
Shiley-Marcos Alzheimer's Disease Research Ctr 8950 Villa La Jolla Dr Ste C129 *Web:* www.adrc.ucsd.edu	La Jolla	CA	92037	858-622-5800	622-1012
Sidney Kimmel Comprehensive Cancer Ctr at Johns Hopkins 401 N Broadway The Harry & Jeanette Weinberg Bldg Ste 1100 *Web:* www.hopkinsmedicine.org	Baltimore	MD	21231	410-955-5222	955-6787
SIS International Research Inc 11 E 22nd St Second Fl *Web:* www.sisinternational.com	New York	NY	10010	212-505-6805	
Siteman Cancer Ctr 4921 Parkview Pl *TF:* 800-600-3606 ■ *Web:* www.siteman.wustl.edu	Saint Louis	MO	63110	314-362-5196	
SIU's Advanced Coal and Energy Research Center Southern Illinois University 504 W Grand. *Web:* acerc.siu.edu	Carbondale	IL	62902	618-536-5521	453-7346

Phone | Fax

Smith-Kettlewell Eye Research Institute
2318 Fillmore St. San Francisco CA 94115 415-345-2000 345-8455
Web: www.ski.org

Smithsonian Environmental Research Ctr
647 Contees Wharf Rd PO Box 28 Edgewater MD 21037 443-482-2200 482-2380
Web: www.serc.si.edu

Smithsonian Tropical Research Institute (STRI)
9100 Panama City PL Washington DC 20521 703-487-3770 786-2557*
**Fax Area Code:* 202 ■ *Web:* www.stri.si.edu

SNBL USA Ltd 6605 Merrill Creek Pkwy Everett WA 98203 425-407-0121
Web: snbl.com

Social & Economic Sciences Research Ctr (SESRC)
Washington State University
Wilson Hall Rm 133 PO Box 644014 Pullman WA 99164 509-335-1511 335-0116
TF: 800-932-5393 ■ *Web:* www.sesrc.wsu.edu

Socratic Technologies Inc
2505 Mariposa St San Francisco CA 94110 415-430-2200
Web: www.sotech.com

Software Engineering Institute (SEI)
4500 Fifth Ave. Pittsburgh PA 15213 412-268-5800 268-6257*
**Fax:* Cust Svc ■ *TF:* 888-201-4479 ■ *Web:* www.sei.cmu.edu

Software Engineering Services Corp
1311 Ft Crook Rd S Bellevue NE 68005 402-292-8660 292-3271
TF: 800-244-1278 ■ *Web:* www.sessolutions.com

Somnus Therapeutics Inc
135 Us Hwy 202/206 Ste 9 Bedminster NJ 07921 908-901-0300
Web: www.softekinfo.com

Southeast Fisheries Science Ctr
75 Virginia Beach Dr. Miami FL 33149 305-361-4200 361-4219
Web: www.sefsc.noaa.gov

Southern California Earthquake Ctr
3651 Trousdale Pkwy Ste 169 Los Angeles CA 90089 213-740-5843 740-0011
Web: www.scec.org

Southern Regional Research Ctr (SRRC)
1100 Robert E Lee Blvd PO Box 19687 New Orleans LA 70179 706-546-3527 286-4419*
**Fax Area Code:* 504 ■ *Web:* www.ars.usda.gov/main/site_main.htm?modecode=64350000

Southern Research Institute
2000 Ninth Ave S Birmingham AL 35205 205-581-2000 581-2726
TF: 800-967-6774 ■ *Web:* www.sri.org

Southern Research Station
USDA Forest Service 200 Weaver Blvd. Asheville NC 28804 828-257-4300 257-4840
Web: www.srs.fs.usda.gov

Southwest National Primate Research Ctr (SNPRC)
Texas Biomedical Research Institute
PO Box 760549 San Antonio TX 78245 210-258-9400
Web: txbiomed.org/primate-research-center

Southwest Research Institute (SwRI)
6220 Culebra Rd. San Antonio TX 78238 210-684-5111 522-3496*
**Fax:* Hum Res ■ *Web:* swri.org/

Space Dynamics Laboratory
1695 N Research Pkwy North Logan UT 84341 435-797-4600 797-4495
TF: 866-487-2365 ■ *Web:* www.sdl.usu.edu

Space Physics Research Laboratory
2455 Hayward St University of Michigan Ann Arbor MI 48109 734-936-7775 763-0437
Web: www.sprl.umich.edu

Space Science & Engineering Ctr
University of Wisconsin 1225 W Dayton St Madison WI 53706 608-262-0544 262-5974
TF: 866-391-1753 ■ *Web:* www.ssec.wisc.edu

Space Telescope Science Institute
3700 San Martin Dr Baltimore MD 21218 410-338-4700 338-4767
Web: www.stsci.edu

SPAWAR (SPAWAR) 53560 Hull St. San Diego CA 92152 619-553-2717
Web: www.public.navy.mil/spawar/Pages/default.aspx

SPINS Inc 1111 Plaza Dr Ste 800 Schaumburg IL 60173 847-908-1200
Web: www.spins.com

SRI International 333 Ravenswood Ave Menlo Park CA 94025 650-859-2000 326-5512
Web: www.sri.com

Stanford Cancer Ctr
875 Lake Blake Wilbur Dr Stanford CA 94305 650-498-6000 724-1433
TF: 800-422-6237 ■ *Web:* cancer.stanford.edu/

Stanford Linear Accelerator Ctr (SLAC)
2575 Sand Hill Rd Menlo Park CA 94025 650-926-3300 926-4999
Web: www.slac.stanford.edu

Stanford Prevention Research Ctr (SPRC)
291 Campus Dr Li Ka Shing Bldg Stanford CA 94305 650-723-6254 725-6906
Web: prevention.stanford.edu

Stanford Synchrotron Radiation Lightsource (SSRL)
2575 Sand Hill Rd MS 69 Menlo Park CA 94025 650-926-2079 926-3600
Web: www-ssrl.slac.stanford.edu

Stevenson Co, The
10002 Shelbyville Rd Ste 201 Louisville KY 40223 502-271-5250
Web: www.stevensoncompany.com

Superclick Networks Inc
10222 Blvd Saint-Michel Montreal QC H1H5H1 514-847-0333

Supercomputing Institute for Digital Simulation & Advanced Computation
University of Minnesota
599 Walter Library 117 Pleasant St SE Minneapolis MN 55455 612-625-1818 624-8861
Web: www.msi.umn.edu

Survey Sampling International LLC
Six Research Dr Shelton CT 06484 203-567-7200
Web: www.surveysampling.com

Synchrotron Radiation Ctr (SRC)
3731 Schneider Dr Stoughton WI 53589 608-877-2000 877-2001
Web: www.src.wisc.edu

Synergy Co of Utah LLC, The
2279 S Resource Blvd Moab UT 84532 800-723-0277
TF: 800-723-0277 ■ *Web:* www.thesynergycompany.com

Syntron Bioresearch Inc 2774 Loker Ave W Carlsbad CA 92010 760-930-2200 930-2212
Web: www.syntron.net

Syracuse Research Corp (SRC)
7502 Round Pond Rd North Syracuse NY 13212 315-452-8000
TF: 800-724-0451 ■ *Web:* www.srcinc.com

Phone | Fax

Technology Service Corp
962 Wayne Ave Ste 800 Silver Spring MD 20910 301-565-2970 565-0673
TF: 800-324-7700 ■ *Web:* tsc.com

Tempra Technology Inc 6140 15th St E Bradenton FL 34203 941-739-8900
Web: www.tempratech.com

TERC 2067 Massachusetts Ave Second Fl Cambridge MA 02140 617-547-0430 349-3535
Web: www.terc.edu

Texas Ctr for Superconductivity
3201 Cullen Blvd Ste 202 Houston TX 77204 713-743-8200 743-8201
Web: www.tcsuh.com

Therapeutics Inc 9025 Balboa Ave Ste 100 San Diego CA 92123 858-571-1800
Web: www.therapeuticsinc.com

Thomas Jefferson National Accelerator Facility
12000 Jefferson Ave Newport News VA 23606 757-269-7100 269-7363
Web: www.jlab.org

TMR Inc 450 Pkwy Broomall PA 19008 610-359-0696
Web: www.tmrinfo.com

Transportation Research Ctr Inc (TRC Inc)
10820 State Rt 347 PO Box B-67 East Liberty OH 43319 937-666-2011 666-5066
TF: 800-837-7872 ■ *Web:* www.trcpg.com

Transportation Technology Ctr Inc
55500 DOT Rd PO Box 11130 Pueblo CO 81001 719-584-0750 584-0711
Web: www.aar.com

Trex Enterprises Corp 10455 Pacific Ctr Ct San Diego CA 92121 858-646-5300 646-5301
TF: 800-626-5885 ■ *Web:* www.trexenterprises.com

TRICOR Systems Inc 1650 Todd Farm Dr Elgin IL 60123 847-742-5542
Web: www.tricor-systems.com

Tris Pharma Inc
2033 Rt 130 Brunswick Business Pk
Ste D Monmouth Junction NJ 08852 732-940-2800 940-2855
Web: www.trispharma.com

Turner-Fairbank Highway Research Ctr
6300 Georgetown Pike McLean VA 22101 800-424-9071 493-3170*
**Fax Area Code:* 202 ■ *Web:* www.fhwa.dot.gov

UAB Comprehensive Cancer Ctr
University of Alabama at Birmingham
1824 Sixth Ave S Birmingham AL 35294 205-934-4011
TF: 800-294-7780 ■ *Web:* www3.ccc.uab.edu

UNC Neuroscience Ctr
University of N Carolina
115 Mason Farm Rd CB 7250 Chapel Hill NC 27599 919-843-8536 966-1050
TF: 800-862-4938 ■ *Web:* www.med.unc.edu/neuroscience

University of Maryland Ctr for Environmental Science (UMCES)
2020 Horn Pt Rd Cambridge MD 21613 410-228-9250 228-3843
TF: 866-842-2520 ■ *Web:* www.umces.edu

University of Michigan Transportation Research Institute (UMTRI)
2901 Baxter Rd Ann Arbor MI 48109 734-764-6504 936-1081
Web: www.umtri.umich.edu

University of Texas Institute for Geophysics (UTIG)
JJ Pickle Research Campus Bldg 196
10100 Burnet Rd (RR2200) Austin TX 78758 512-471-6156 471-8844
Web: www.ig.utexas.edu

US Army Aeromedical Research Laboratory
MCMR-UAC Bldg 6901 Fort Rucker AL 36362 334-255-6920 255-6933
TF: 888-386-7635 ■ *Web:* www.usaarl.army.mil

US Army Armament Research Development & Engineering Ctr (ARDEC)
Technical & Industrial Liaison Officer Picatinny NJ 07806 973-724-9623 724-3044
Web: www.pica.army.mil

US Army Aviation & Missile Research Development & Engineering Ctr (AMRDEC)
5400 Bldg. Redstone Arsenal AL 35898 256-313-5742 876-9142
Web: www.redstone.army.mil/amrdec

US Army Corps of Engineers Institute for Water Resources
Hydrologic Engineering Ctr 609 Second St Davis CA 95616 530-756-1104 756-8250
Web: www.hec.usace.army.mil

US Army Engineer Research & Development Ctr (ERDC)
3909 Halls Ferry Rd Vicksburg MS 39180 601-634-3188 634-2388
TF: 800-522-6937 ■ *Web:* www.erdc.usace.army.mil

US Army Institute of Surgical Research (USAISR)
3698 Chambers Pass Ste B Fort Sam Houston TX 78234 210-539-3219 227-8502
Web: www.usaisr.amedd.army.mil

US Army Medical Research & Materiel Command (USAMRMC)
820 Chandler St Fort Detrick MD 21702 301-619-2471
Web: www.mrmc.smallbusopps.army.mil

US Army Medical Research Institute of Chemical Defense (USAMRICD)
3100 Ricketts Point Rd Aberdeen Proving Ground MD 21010 410-436-3276 436-1960
Web: usamricd.apgea.army.mil

US Army Medical Research Institute of Infectious Diseases (USAMRIID)
Attn: MCMR-UIZ-R 1425 Porter St Frederick MD 21702 301-619-2285
Web: www.usamriid.army.mil

US Army Research Laboratory (ARL)
Attn: AMSRD-ARL-O-PA 2800 Powder Mill Rd Adelphi MD 20783 301-394-2500 394-1174
Web: www.arl.army.mil

US Coast Guard Research & Development Ctr
1082 Shennecossett Rd Groton CT 06340 860-441-2600 441-2792
Web: www.uscg.mil/hq

US Dairy Forage Research Ctr (DFRC)
1925 Linden Dr W Madison WI 53706 608-890-0050
Web: ars.usda.gov

US Horticultural Research Laboratory
2001 S Rock Rd Fort Pierce FL 34945 772-462-5800 462-5986
Web: www.ars.usda.gov/Main/docs.htm?docid=7376

US Salinity Laboratory
USDA/ARS 450 W Big Springs Rd Riverside CA 92507 951-369-4815 369-4818
Web: www.ars.usda.gov/AboutUs/AboutUs.htm?modecode=53-10-20-00

US Vegetable Laboratory
USDA/ARS 2700 Savannah Hwy Charleston SC 29414 843-402-5300
Web: www.ars.usda.gov/main/docs.htm?docid=5953

USC Information Sciences Institute
4676 Admiralty Way Ste 1001 Marina del Rey CA 90292 310-822-1511 823-6714
Web: isi.edu

USGS Forest & Rangeland Ecosystem Science Ctr
777 NW Ninth St Ste 400 Corvallis OR 97330 541-750-1030 750-1069
Web: fresc.usgs.gov

Phone *Fax*

USGS Leetown Science Ctr
11649 Leetown Rd .... Kearneysville WV 25430 304-724-4400 724-4410
Web: www.lsc.usgs.gov

USGS Northern Rocky Mountain Science Ctr (NRMSC)
2327 University Way Ste 2 .... Bozeman MT 59715 406-994-4293 994-6556
Web: www.nrmsc.usgs.gov

USGS Southwest Biological Science Ctr
2255 N Gemini Dr MS-9394 .... Flagstaff AZ 86001 928-556-7094 556-7092
Web: sbsc.wr.usgs.gov

USGS Upper Midwest Environmental Sciences Ctr
2630 Fanta Reed Rd .... La Crosse WI 54603 608-783-6451 783-6066
Web: www.umesc.usgs.gov

USGS Western Fisheries Research Ctr
US Geological Survey 6505 NE 65th St .... Seattle WA 98115 206-526-6282 526-6654
Web: wfrc.usgs.gov

UT-Battelle LLC 1201 Oak Ridge Tpke Ste 100 .... Oak Ridge TN 37830 865-220-5101

Vanderbilt Kennedy Ctr for Research on Human Development
21st Ave S .... Nashville TN 37203 615-322-8240 322-8236
TF: 800-772-1213 ■ *Web:* vkc.mc.vanderbilt.edu/

Vaxin Inc 19 Firstfield Rd Ste 200 .... Gaithersburg MD 20878 240-654-1450
Web: www.vaxin.com

Venture Design Services Inc 1051 SE St .... Anaheim CA 92805 714-765-3740
Web: www.venture.com.sg

Virginia Institute of Marine Science (VIMS)
1208 Greate Rd PO Box 1346 .... Gloucester Point VA 23062 804-684-7000 684-7097
Web: www.vims.edu

Virobay Inc 1360 Willow Rd Ste 100 .... Menlo Park CA 94025 650-833-5700
Web: www.virobayinc.com

Visidyne Inc 111 S Bedford St S Bedford St .... Burlington MA 01803 781-273-2820 272-1068
Web: www.visidyne.com

Wadsworth Ctr
Biggs Laboratory New York Dept of Health
Empire State Plz PO Box 509 .... Albany NY 12201 518-474-2160
Web: www.wadsworth.org

Waisman Ctr
University of Wisconsin 1500 Highland Ave .... Madison WI 53705 608-263-5940 263-0529
TF: 888-428-8476 ■ *Web:* www.waisman.wisc.edu

Walter Reed Army Institute of Research (WRAIR)
MCMR-UWZ 503 Robert Grant Ave .... Silver Spring MD 20910 301-319-9471 319-9227
Web: wrair-www.army.mil

Washington National Primate Research Ctr (WNPRC)
1705 NE Pacific St PO Box 357330 .... Seattle WA 98195 206-543-0440 616-6771
Web: www.wanprc.org

WestEd 730 Harrison St Fifth Fl .... San Francisco CA 94107 415-565-3000 565-3012
TF: 877-493-7833 ■ *Web:* www.wested.org

Western Environmental Technology Laboratories Inc
620 Applegate St .... Philomath OR 97370 541-929-5650
Web: www.wetlabs.com

Western Regional Research Ctr (WRRC)
800 Buchanan St .... Albany CA 94710 510-559-5600 559-5963
Web: www.ars.usda.gov/main/docs.htm?docid=5819

Western Research Institute 365 N Ninth St .... Laramie WY 82072 307-721-2011 721-2345
Web: westernresearch.org

Wisconsin Ctr for Education Research
University of Wisconsin Madison
1025 W Johnson St .... Madison WI 53706 608-263-4200 263-6448
Web: www.wcer.wisc.edu

Wisconsin National Primate Research Ctr
1220 Capitol Ct .... Madison WI 53715 608-263-3500 265-2067
TF: 800-833-7050 ■ *Web:* www.primate.wisc.edu

Wistar Institute 3601 Spruce St .... Philadelphia PA 19104 215-898-3700 898-3715
TF: 800-724-6633 ■ *Web:* wistar.org

WM Keck Ctr for Comparative & Functional Genomics
1201 W Gregory Dr .... Urbana IL 61801 217-244-3930 244-0466
Web: www.biotech.uiuc.edu

WM Keck Observatory 65-1120 Mamalahoa Hwy .... Kamuela HI 96743 808-885-7887 885-4464
Web: www.keckobservatory.org

Woods Hole Oceanographic Institution (WHOI)
86 Water St MS Ste 19 .... Woods Hole MA 02543 508-289-2282 457-2109*
**Fax:* Hum Res ■ *Web:* www.whoi.edu

Xenon Pharmaceuticals Inc 3650 Gilmore Way .... Burnaby BC V5G4W8 604-484-3300 484-3450
Web: www.xenon-pharma.com

Yale Child Study Ctr
Yale University 230 S Frontage Rd .... New Haven CT 06520 203-785-2540 785-7611
Web: www.medicine.yale.edu

Yerkes National Primate Research Ctr
Emory University 954 Gatewood Rd .... Atlanta GA 30322 404-727-7732 727-3108
Web: www.yerkes.emory.edu

672 RESORTS & RESORT COMPANIES

SEE ALSO Casinos p. 1904; Dude Ranches p. 2209; Hotels - Conference Center p. 2525; Hotels & Hotel Companies p. 2530; Spas - Hotel & Resort p. 3176

Alabama

Phone *Fax*

Joe Wheeler Resort Lodge & Convention Ctr
4401 McLean Dr .... Rogersville AL 35652 256-247-5461 247-5471
TF: 800-544-5639 ■ *Web:* www.alapark.com/joewheeler

Perdido Beach Resort
27200 Perdido Beach Blvd .... Orange Beach AL 36561 251-981-9811 981-5670
TF: 800-634-8001 ■ *Web:* www.perdidobeachresort.com

StillWaters Resort 797 Moonbrook Dr .... Dadeville AL 36853 256-825-1353 825-1717
Web: www.stillwatersgolf.com

Alaska

Phone *Fax*

Alyeska Prince Hotel & Resort
1000 Arlberg Ave PO Box 249 .... Girdwood AK 99587 907-754-1111 754-2200
TF: 800-880-3880 ■ *Web:* www.alyeskaresort.com

Pybus Point Lodge PO Box 33497 .... Juneau AK 99803 907-790-4866 790-4866
Web: pybuspoint.com

Alberta

Phone *Fax*

Fairmont Banff Springs PO Box 960 .... Banff AB T1L1J4 403-762-2211 762-5755
TF: 800-441-1414 ■ *Web:* www.fairmont.com

Fairmont Chateau Lake Louise
111 Lk Louise Dr .... Lake Louise AB T0L1E0 403-522-3511 522-3834
TF: 800-441-1414 ■ *Web:* www.fairmont.com

Rimrock Resort Hotel, The
300 Mountain Ave PO Box 1110 .... Banff AB T1L1J2 403-762-3356 762-4132
TF: 888-746-7625 ■ *Web:* www.rimrockresort.com

Waterton Lakes Lodge Resort
101 Clematis Ave PO Box 4 .... Waterton Park AB T0K2M0 403-859-2150 859-2229
TF: 888-985-6343 ■ *Web:* www.watertonlakeslodge.com

Arizona

Phone *Fax*

Arizona Biltmore Resort & Spa
2400 E Missouri .... Phoenix AZ 85016 602-955-6600 381-7600
TF: 800-950-0086 ■ *Web:* www.arizonabiltmore.com

Arizona Golf Resort & Conference Ctr
425 S Power Rd .... Mesa AZ 85206 480-832-3202 981-0151
TF: 800-528-8282 ■ *Web:* www.arizonagolfresort.com

Arizona Grand Resort
8000 S Arizona Grand Pkwy .... Phoenix AZ 85044 602-438-9000 431-6535
TF: 866-267-1321 ■ *Web:* www.arizonagrandresort.com

Boulders Resort & Golden Door Spa
34631 N Tom Darlington Dr PO Box 2090 .... Carefree AZ 85377 480-488-9009 488-4118
TF: 888-579-2631 ■ *Web:* www.theboulders.com

Camelback Inn JW Marriott Resort Golf Club & Spa
5402 E Lincoln Dr .... Scottsdale AZ 85253 480-948-1700 596-7029
TF: 800-242-2635 ■ *Web:* www.marriott.com

Canyon Ranch Tucson 8600 E Rockcliff Rd .... Tucson AZ 85750 520-749-9000 749-1646
TF: 800-742-9000 ■ *Web:* www.canyonranch.com/tucson

Chaparral Suites Resort & Conference Ctr
5001 N Scottsdale Rd .... Scottsdale AZ 85250 480-949-1414 947-2675
TF: 866-534-1797 ■ *Web:* www.chaparralsuites.com

CopperWynd Resort & Club
13225 N Eagle Ridge Dr .... Fountain Hills AZ 85268 480-333-1900 333-1901
TF: 877-707-7760 ■ *Web:* www.copperwynd.com

Doubletree Paradise Valley Resort
5401 N Scottsdale Rd .... Scottsdale AZ 85250 480-947-5400 443-9702
TF: 800-222-8733 ■ *Web:* www3.hilton.com

Enchantment Resort 525 Boynton Canyon Rd .... Sedona AZ 86336 800-826-4180 282-9249*
**Fax Area Code:* 928 ■ *TF:* 800-826-4180 ■ *Web:* www.enchantmentresort.com

Esplendor Resort at Rio Rico
1069 Camino Caralampi .... Rio Rico AZ 85648 520-281-1901 281-7132
TF: 800-288-4746 ■ *Web:* www.esplendor-resort.com

Fairmont Scottsdale Princess
7575 E Princess Dr .... Scottsdale AZ 85255 480-585-4848 585-0086
TF: 800-257-7544 ■ *Web:* www.fairmont.com

FireSky Resort & Spa 4925 N Scottsdale Rd .... Scottsdale AZ 85251 480-945-7666 946-4056
TF: 800-528-7867 ■ *Web:* www.fireskyresort.com

Four Seasons Resort Scottsdale at Troon North
10600 E Crescent Moon Dr .... Scottsdale AZ 85262 480-515-5700 515-5599
TF: 800-332-3442 ■ *Web:* www.fourseasons.com

Francisco Grande Hotel & Golf Resort
26000 Gila Bend Hwy .... Casa Grande AZ 85222 520-836-6444 421-0544
TF General: 800-237-4238 ■ *Web:* www.franciscogrande.com

Gold Canyon Golf Resort
6100 S Kings Ranch Rd .... Gold Canyon AZ 85118 480-982-9090 830-5211
TF: 800-624-6445 ■ *Web:* www.gcgr.com

Hacienda del Sol Guest Ranch Resort
5501 N Hacienda Del Sol Rd .... Tucson AZ 85718 520-299-1501 299-5554
TF: 800-728-6514 ■ *Web:* www.haciendadelsol.com

Harrah's Ak-Chin Casino Resort
15406 Maricopa Rd .... Maricopa AZ 85139 480-802-5000
TF General: 800-427-7247 ■ *Web:* www.totalrewards.com

Hilton Sedona Resort & Spa 90 Ridge Trl Dr .... Sedona AZ 86351 928-284-4040
TF General: 877-273-3762 ■ *Web:* www1.hilton.com

JW Marriott Desert Ridge Resort & Spa
5350 E Marriott Dr .... Phoenix AZ 85054 480-293-5000 293-3600
TF: 800-845-5279 ■ *Web:* www.marriott.com/hotels/travel/phxdr

Lake Powell Resorts & Marinas 100 Lakeshore Dr .... Page AZ 86040 888-896-3829 326-2670*
**Fax Area Code:* 580 ■ *TF:* 800-622-6317 ■ *Web:* www.travelok.com

Legacy Golf Resort 6808 S 32nd St .... Phoenix AZ 85042 602-305-5500 305-5501
TF: 888-828-3673 ■ *Web:* www.shellhospitality.com

Lodge at Ventana Canyon - A Wyndham Luxury Resort
6200 N Clubhouse Ln .... Tucson AZ 85750 520-577-1400 577-4065
TF: 800-828-5701 ■ *Web:* www.thelodgeatventanacanyon.com

Loews Ventana Canyon Resort 7000 N Resort Dr .... Tucson AZ 85750 520-299-2020 299-6832
TF: 800-234-5117 ■ *Web:* www.loewshotels.com

Los Abrigados Resort 160 Portal Ln .... Sedona AZ 86336 928-282-1777 282-2614
TF: 877-374-2582 ■ *Web:* www.diamondresorts.com

Millennium Resort Scottsdale McCormick Ranch
7401 N Scottsdale Rd .... Scottsdale AZ 85253 716-681-2400 991-5572*
**Fax Area Code:* 480 ■ *TF:* 800-243-1332 ■ *Web:* millenniumhotels.com

Omni Tucson National Golf Resort & Spa
2727 W Club Dr .... Tucson AZ 85742 520-297-2271 297-7544
Web: www.tucsonnational.com

Orange Tree Golf & Conference Resort
10601 N 56th St .... Scottsdale AZ 85254 480-948-6100 483-6074
TF: 866-729-7159 ■
Web: shellhospitality.com/en/orange-tree-golf-resort

Phoenician, The 6000 E Camelback Rd .... Scottsdale AZ 85251 480-941-8200 947-4311
TF: 800-888-8234 ■ *Web:* www.thephoenician.com

	City	State	Zip	Phone	Fax
Pointe Hilton at Squaw Peak Resort 7677 N 16th St	Phoenix	AZ	85020	602-997-2626	875-1652*
**Fax Area Code:* 281 ■ *TF:* 800-685-0550 ■ *Web:* www.pointehilton.com					
Pointe Hilton Resort at Tapatio Cliffs 11111 N Seventh St	Phoenix	AZ	85020	602-866-7500	875-1652*
**Fax Area Code:* 281 ■ *TF:* 800-947-9784 ■ *Web:* www.pointehilton.com					
Rancho de los Caballeros 1551 S Vulture Mine Rd	Wickenburg	AZ	85390	928-684-5484	684-2267
TF: 800-684-5030 ■ *Web:* www.ranchodeloscaballeros.com					
Ritz-Carlton Phoenix 2401 E Camelback Rd	Phoenix	AZ	85016	602-468-0700	468-0793
TF: 800-241-3333 ■ *Web:* www.ritzcarlton.com/hotels/phoenix					
Royal Palms Resort & Spa 5200 E Camelback Rd	Phoenix	AZ	85018	602-840-3610	840-6927
TF: 800-672-6011 ■ *Web:* www.royalpalmshotel.com					
Saguaro Lake Ranch 13020 Bush Hwy	Mesa	AZ	85215	480-984-2194	
Web: www.saguarolakeranch.com					
Sanctuary on Camelback Mountain 5700 E McDonald Dr	Paradise Valley	AZ	85253	480-948-2100	948-7314
TF: 800-245-2051 ■ *Web:* www.sanctuaryoncamelback.com					
Scottsdale Camelback Resort 6302 E Camelback Rd	Scottsdale	AZ	85251	480-947-3300	994-0594
TF: 800-891-8585 ■ *Web:* www.scottsdalecamelback.com					
Scottsdale Cottonwoods Resort & Suites 6160 N Scottsdale Rd	Scottsdale	AZ	85253	480-991-1414	951-3350
Scottsdale Plaza Resort 7200 N Scottsdale Rd	Scottsdale	AZ	85253	480-948-5000	998-5971
TF: 800-832-2025 ■ *Web:* www.scottsdaleplaza.com					
Sheraton Wild Horse Pass Resort & Spa 5594 W Wild Horse Pass Blvd	Chandler	AZ	85226	602-225-0100	225-0300
TF: 800-325-3535 ■ *Web:* www.wildhorsepassresort.com					
Tanque Verde Guest Ranch 14301 E Speedway Blvd	Tucson	AZ	85748	520-296-6275	721-9426
TF: 800-234-3833 ■ *Web:* www.tvgr.com					
Westward Look Resort 245 E Ina Rd	Tucson	AZ	85704	520-297-1151	297-9023
TF: 800-722-2500 ■ *Web:* www.westwardlook.com					
Wigwam Golf Resort & Spa 300 E Wigwam Blvd	Litchfield Park	AZ	85340	623-935-3811	935-3737
TF: 800-327-0396 ■ *Web:* wigwamarizona.com					

Arkansas

	City	State	Zip	Phone	Fax
Arlington Resort Hotel & Spa 239 Central Ave	Hot Springs	AR	71901	501-623-7771	623-2243
TF: 800-643-1502 ■ *Web:* www.arlingtonhotel.com					
Best Western Inn of the Ozarks 207 W Van Buren	Eureka Springs	AR	72632	479-253-9768	253-9768
TF: 800-552-3785 ■ *Web:* www.bestwestern.com					
Gaston's White River Resort 1777 River Rd	Lakeview	AR	72642	870-431-5202	431-5216
Web: www.gastons.com					

British Columbia

	City	State	Zip	Phone	Fax
Coast Hotels & Resorts Canada 1090 W Georgia St	Vancouver	BC	V6E3V7	604-682-7982	682-8942
Web: www.coasthotels.com					
Delta Victoria Ocean Pointe Resort & Spa 45 Songhees Rd	Victoria	BC	V9A6T3	250-360-2999	360-5871
TF: 800-667-4677 ■ *Web:* www.deltahotels.com					
Delta Whistler Village Suites 4308 Main St	Whistler	BC	V0N1B4	604-905-3987	938-6335
TF: 888-299-3987 ■ *Web:* www.deltahotels.com					
Fairmont Chateau Whistler 4599 Chateau Blvd	Whistler	BC	V0N1B4	604-938-8000	938-2291
TF: 800-441-1414 ■ *Web:* www.fairmont.com					
Four Seasons Resort Whistler 4591 Blackcomb Way	Whistler	BC	V0N1B4	604-935-3400	935-3455
Web: www.fourseasons.com/whistler					
Harrison Hot Springs Resort & Spa 100 Esplanade Ave	Harrison Hot Springs	BC	V0M1K0	604-796-2244	796-3682
TF: 800-663-2266 ■ *Web:* www.harrisonresort.com					
Hilton Whistler Resort & Spa 4050 Whistler Way	Whistler	BC	V0N1B4	604-932-1982	966-5093
TF: 800-515-4050 ■ *Web:* www.hiltonwhistler.com					
Holiday Inn SunSpree Resort Whistler Village 4295 Blackcomb Way	Whistler	BC	V0N1B4	604-938-0878	938-9943
Web: www.ihg.com					
Holiday Trails Resorts (Western) Inc 53730 Bridal Falls Rd	Rosedale	BC	V0X1X1	604-794-7876	794-3756
TF: 800-663-2265 ■ *Web:* www.holidaytrailsresorts.com					
Intrawest ULC 326 - 375 Water St The Landing	Vancouver	BC	V6B5C6	604-689-8816	682-7842
Web: www.intrawest.com					
Pan Pacific Whistler Mountainside 4320 Sundial Crescent	Whistler	BC	V0N1B4	604-905-2999	905-2995
TF: 888-905-9995 ■ *Web:* www.panpacific.com					
River Rock Casino Resort 8811 River Rd	Richmond	BC	V6X3P8	604-247-8900	207-2641
TF: 866-748-3718 ■ *Web:* www.riverrock.com					
Tantalus Resort Lodge 4200 Whistler Way	Whistler	BC	V0N1B4	604-932-4146	932-2405
TF: 888-633-4046 ■ *Web:* www.tantaluslodge.com					
Whistler Blackcomb Mountain Ski Resort 4545 Blackcomb Way	Whistler	BC	V0N1B4	604-932-3434	938-7527
TF: 800-766-0449 ■ *Web:* www.whistlerblackcomb.com					

California

	City	State	Zip	Phone	Fax
Alisal Guest Ranch & Resort 1054 Alisal Rd	Solvang	CA	93463	805-688-6411	688-2510
TF: 800-425-4725 ■ *Web:* www.alisal.com					
Alpine Meadows Ski Resort 2600 Alpine Meadows Rd	Tahoe City	CA	96145	800-403-0206	583-0963*
**Fax Area Code:* 530 ■ *TF:* 800-403-0206 ■ *Web:* www.skialpine.com					
Bacara Resort & Spa 8301 Hollister Ave	Santa Barbara	CA	93117	805-968-0100	968-1800
TF: 855-968-0100 ■ *Web:* www.bacararesort.com					
Bahia Resort Hotel 998 W Mission Bay Dr	San Diego	CA	92109	858-488-0551	488-7055
TF: 800-576-4229 ■ *Web:* www.bahiahotel.com					
Barona Resort & Casino 1932 Wildcat Canyon Rd	Lakeside	CA	92040	619-443-2300	443-2856
TF: 888-722-7662 ■ *Web:* www.barona.com					
Bear Mountain Golf Course 43101 Gold Mine Dr PO Box 77	Big Bear Lake	CA	92315	909-866-5766	585-6805
Web: www.bigbearmountainresorts.com					
Calistoga Ranch 580 Lommel Rd	Calistoga	CA	94515	707-254-2800	254-2825
TF: 800-942-4220 ■ *Web:* calistogaranch.aubergeresorts.com/					
Carmel Valley Ranch Resort One Old Ranch Rd	Carmel	CA	93923	831-625-9500	624-2858
TF: 866-405-5037 ■ *Web:* www.carmelvalleyranch.com					
Casa Palmero 1518 Cypress Dr	Pebble Beach	CA	93953	831-622-6650	622-6655
TF: 800-654-9300 ■ *Web:* pebblebeach.com					
Catalina Canyon Resort & Spa 888 Country Club Dr PO Box 736	Avalon	CA	90704	310-510-0325	510-0900
Web: www.catalinacanyonresort.com					
Chaminade One Chaminade Ln	Santa Cruz	CA	95065	831-475-5600	476-4798
TF: 800-283-6569 ■ *Web:* www.chaminade.com					
Claremont Resort & Spa 41 Tunnel Rd	Berkeley	CA	94705	510-843-3000	848-6208
TF: 800-551-7266 ■ *Web:* www.claremontresort.com					
Costanoa Coastal Lodge & Camp 2001 Rossi Rd	Pescadero	CA	94060	650-879-1100	879-2275
TF: 877-262-7848 ■ *Web:* www.costanoa.com					
Desert Hot Springs Spa Hotel 10805 Palm Dr	Desert Hot Springs	CA	92240	760-329-6000	329-6915
TF: 800-808-7727 ■ *Web:* www.dhsspa.com					
Desert Springs Marriott Resort & Spa 74855 Country Club Dr	Palm Desert	CA	92260	760-341-2211	341-1872
TF: 888-538-9459 ■ *Web:* www.marriott.com					
Doral Desert Princess Palm Springs Resort 67967 Vista Chino	Cathedral City	CA	92234	760-322-7000	322-6853
TF: 800-433-0431 ■ *Web:* www.desertprincessgolfresort.com					
Double Eagle Resort & Spa 5587 Hwy 158 PO Box 736	June Lake	CA	93529	760-648-7004	648-8225
Web: www.doubleeagle.com					
Dr Wilkinson's Hot Springs Resort 1507 Lincoln Ave	Calistoga	CA	94515	707-942-4102	942-4412
Web: www.drwilkinson.com					
Elkhorn Golf Club 1050 Elkhorn Dr	Stockton	CA	95209	209-474-3900	
Web: www.elkhorngc.com					
Estancia La Jolla Hotel & Spa 9700 N Torrey Pines Rd	La Jolla	CA	92037	858-550-1000	550-1001
TF: 866-437-8262 ■ *Web:* estancialajolla.com					
Fairmont Sonoma Mission Inn & Spa, The PO Box 1447	Sonoma	CA	95476	707-938-9000	938-4250
TF: 866-540-4499 ■ *Web:* www.fairmont.com/sonoma					
Fess Parker's Doubletree Resort (FPDTR) 633 E Cabrillo Blvd	Santa Barbara	CA	93103	805-564-4333	
TF: 800-879-2929 ■ *Web:* www.fessparkersantabarbarahotel.com					
Flamingo Resort Hotel & Conference Ctr 2777 Fourth St	Santa Rosa	CA	95405	707-545-8530	528-1404
TF: 800-848-8300 ■ *Web:* www.flamingohotel.com					
Four Seasons Resort Santa Barbara 1260 Ch Dr	Santa Barbara	CA	93108	805-969-2261	565-8323
TF: 800-819-5053 ■ *Web:* www.fourseasons.com					
Furnace Creek Inn & Ranch Resort Hwy 190 PO Box 187	Death Valley	CA	92328	760-786-2345	786-2514
TF: 800-236-7916 ■ *Web:* www.furnacecreekresort.com					
Grand Pacific Palisades Resort & Hotel 5805 Armada Dr	Carlsbad	CA	92008	760-827-3200	827-3210
TF: 800-725-4723 ■ *Web:* www.grandpacificpalisades.com					
Greenhorn Creek Resort 711 McCauley Ranch Rd	Angels Camp	CA	95222	209-729-8111	736-4728
TF: 888-736-5900 ■ *Web:* www.greenhorncreek.com					
Handlery Hotel & Resort 950 Hotel Cir N	San Diego	CA	92108	619-298-0511	298-9793
TF: 800-676-6567 ■ *Web:* www.handlery.com					
Harrah's Rincon Casino & Resort 777 Harrah's Rincon Way	Valley Center	CA	92082	760-751-3100	751-3200
TF: 800-522-4700 ■ *Web:* www.totalrewards.com					
Hilton San Diego Resort 1775 E Mission Bay Dr	San Diego	CA	92109	619-276-4010	275-8944
TF: 800-445-8667 ■ *Web:* www.hilton.com					
Hotel Del Coronado 1500 Orange Ave	Coronado	CA	92118	619-435-6611	522-8262
TF: 800-468-3533 ■ *Web:* www.hoteldel.com					
Indian Springs Resort & Spa 1712 Lincoln Ave	Calistoga	CA	94515	707-942-4913	942-4919
TF: 800-877-3623 ■ *Web:* www.indianspringscalistoga.com					
Indian Wells Resort Hotel 76-661 Hwy 111	Indian Wells	CA	92210	760-345-6466	772-5083
TF: 800-248-3220 ■ *Web:* www.indianwellsresort.com					
Inn at Rancho Santa Fe 5951 Linea Del Cielo PO Box 869	Rancho Santa Fe	CA	92067	858-756-1131	759-1604
TF: 800-843-4661 ■ *Web:* www.theinnatrsf.com					
Inn at Spanish Bay, The 2700 17-Mile Dr	Pebble Beach	CA	93953	831-647-7500	622-3603
TF: 800-654-9300 ■ *Web:* www.pebblebeach.com					
Knott's Berry Farm Resort 7675 Crescent Ave	Buena Park	CA	90620	714-995-1111	220-5124
TF: 866-752-2444 ■ *Web:* www.knotts.com					
L'Auberge Del Mar 1540 Camino del Mar PO Box 2880	Del Mar	CA	92014	858-259-1515	755-4940
TF: 800-245-9757 ■ *Web:* www.laubergedelmar.com					
La Costa Resort & Spa 2100 Costa del Mar Rd	Carlsbad	CA	92009	760-438-9111	931-7569
TF: 800-854-5000 ■ *Web:* www.lacosta.com					
La Jolla Beach & Tennis Club 2000 Spindrift Dr	La Jolla	CA	92037	858-454-7126	456-3805
TF: 888-828-0948 ■ *Web:* www.ljbtc.com					
La Quinta Resort & Club 49-499 Eisenhower Dr	La Quinta	CA	92253	760-564-4111	564-7625
TF: 800-598-3828 ■ *Web:* www.laquintaresort.com					
Laguna Cliffs Marriott Resort 25135 Pk Lantern	Dana Point	CA	92629	949-661-5000	661-5358
TF: 800-545-7483 ■ *Web:* www.lagunacliffs.com					

	City	State	ZIP	Phone	Fax
Lake Arrowhead Resort & Spa 27984 Hwy 189 — *TF:* 800-800-6792 ■ *Web:* www.lakearrowheadresort.com	Lake Arrowhead	CA	92352	909-336-1511	744-3088
Lakeland Village Beach & Mountain Resort 3535 Lake Tahoe Blvd — *TF:* 888-484-7094 ■ *Web:* lakeland--village.com	South Lake Tahoe	CA	96150	530-544-1685	
Le Parker Meridien Palm Springs 4200 E Palm Canyon Dr — *Web:* www.starwoodhotels.com/lemeridien	Palm Springs	CA	92264	760-770-5000	324-2188
Leisure Sports Inc 7077 Koll Ctr Pkwy Ste 110 — **Fax Area Code:* 949 ■ *TF:* 888-239-0930 ■ *Web:* clubsports.com	Pleasanton	CA	94566	925-600-1966	643-7950*
Lodge at Pebble Beach 1700 17-Mile Dr — *TF:* 800-654-9300 ■ *Web:* www.pebblebeach.com	Pebble Beach	CA	93953	831-624-3811	625-8598
Lodge at Sonoma - A Renaissance Resort & Spa 1325 Broadway — *TF:* 866-263-0758 ■ *Web:* www.marriott.com	Sonoma	CA	95476	707-935-6600	935-6829
Lodge at Torrey Pines Inn 11480 N Torrey Pines Rd — *Web:* www.lodgeattorreypines.com	La Jolla	CA	92037	858-453-4420	550-3908
Loews Coronado Bay Resort 4000 Coronado Bay Rd — *TF:* 800-815-6397 ■ *Web:* www.loewshotels.com/hotels/sandiego	Coronado	CA	92118	619-424-4000	424-4400
Mammoth Mountain Resort One Minaret Rd PO Box 24 — *TF:* 800-626-6684 ■ *Web:* www.mammothmountain.com	Mammoth Lakes	CA	93546	760-934-2571	934-0615
Meadowood Napa Valley 900 Meadowood Ln — *TF:* 800-458-8080 ■ *Web:* www.meadowood.com	Saint Helena	CA	94574	707-963-3646	963-3532
Miramonte Resort & Spa 45000 Indian Wells Ln — *TF:* 800-237-2926 ■ *Web:* www.miramonteresort.com	Indian Wells	CA	92210	760-341-2200	568-0541
Montage Resort & Spa 30801 S Coast Hwy — *TF:* 866-271-6953 ■ *Web:* montagehotels.com/lagunabeach/	Laguna Beach	CA	92651	949-715-6000	715-6070
Morgan Run Resort & Club 5690 Cancha de Golf — *TF Resv:* 800-378-4653 ■ *Web:* www.clubcorp.com	Rancho Santa Fe	CA	92091	858-756-2471	
Morongo Casino Resort & Spa 49500 Seminole Dr — *TF:* 800-252-4499 ■ *Web:* www.morongocasinoresort.com	Cabazon	CA	92230	951-849-3080	755-5735
Mount Shasta Resort 1000 Siskiyou Lk Blvd — *TF:* 800-958-3363 ■ *Web:* www.mountshastaresort.com	Mount Shasta	CA	96067	530-926-3030	926-0333
Northstar-at-Tahoe PO Box 129 — **Fax Area Code:* 530 ■ *TF:* 800-466-6784 ■ *Web:* www.northstarcalifornia.com	Truckee	CA	96160	800-466-6784	562-3812*
Ojai Valley Inn & Spa 905 Country Club Rd — *TF:* 800-422-6524 ■ *Web:* www.ojairesort.com	Ojai	CA	93023	805-640-2068	646-0904
Pacific Palms Conference Resort 1 Industry Hills Pkwy — *TF Cust Svc:* 800-524-4557 ■ *Web:* www.pacificpalmsresort.com	City of Industry	CA	91744	626-810-4455	964-9535
Pala Casino Resort & Spa 35008 Pala-Temecula Rd — *TF:* 877-946-7252 ■ *Web:* www.palacasino.com	Pala	CA	92059	760-510-5100	510-5191
Pala Mesa Resort 2001 Old Hwy 395 — *TF:* 800-722-4700 ■ *Web:* www.palamesa.com	Fallbrook	CA	92028	760-728-5881	723-8292
Palm Mountain Resort & Spa 155 S BelaRdo Rd — *TF:* 800-622-9451 ■ *Web:* www.palmmountainresort.com	Palm Springs	CA	92262	760-325-1301	323-8937
Paradise Point Resort & Spa 1404 W Vacation Rd — *TF:* 800-344-2626 ■ *Web:* www.paradisepoint.com	San Diego	CA	92109	858-274-4630	581-5924
Pechanga Resort & Casino 45000 Pechanga Pkwy — *TF:* 877-711-2946 ■ *Web:* www.pechanga.com	Temecula	CA	92592	951-693-1819	695-7410
Quail Lodge Resort & Golf Club 8205 Valley Greens Dr — *TF:* 866-675-1101 ■ *Web:* www.quaillodge.com	Carmel	CA	93923	831-624-2888	
Rancho Valencia Resort 5921 Valencia Cir PO Box 9126 — *TF:* 800-548-3664 ■ *Web:* www.ranchovalencia.com	Rancho Santa Fe	CA	92067	858-756-1123	756-0165
Renaissance Esmeralda Resort 44-400 Indian Wells Ln — *TF:* 888-236-2427 ■ *Web:* www.marriott.com	Indian Wells	CA	92210	760-773-4444	346-9308
Resort at Squaw Creek 400 Squaw Creek Rd PO Box 3333 — *TF:* 800-327-3353 ■ *Web:* www.squawcreek.com	Olympic Valley	CA	96146	530-583-6300	581-6632
Ritz-Carlton Half Moon Bay One Miramontes Pt Rd — *TF General:* 800-241-3333 ■ *Web:* www.ritzcarlton.com	Half Moon Bay	CA	94019	650-712-7000	712-7015
Ritz-Carlton Laguna Niguel, The One Ritz Carlton Dr — *TF:* 800-542-8680 ■ *Web:* www.ritzcarlton.com/resorts/laguna_niguel	Dana Point	CA	92629	949-240-2000	
Saint Regis Monarch Beach Resort & Spa One Monarch Beach Resort — *TF:* 800-722-1543 ■ *Web:* www.stregismb.com	Dana Point	CA	92629	949-234-3200	234-3201
San Vicente Inn & Golf Course 24157 San Vicente Rd — *TF:* 800-776-1289 ■ *Web:* www.sdcea.net	Ramona	CA	92065	760-789-3788	788-6115
San Ysidro Ranch 900 San Ysidro Ln — *Web:* www.sanysidroranch.com	Santa Barbara	CA	93108	805-565-1700	565-1995
Sea Venture Resort 100 Ocean View Ave — *TF:* 800-443-7778 ■ *Web:* www.seaventure.com	Pismo Beach	CA	93449	805-773-4994	773-0924
Shadow Mountain Resort & Club 45-750 San Luis Rey — *TF:* 800-472-3713 ■ *Web:* www.shadowmountainresort.com	Palm Desert	CA	92260	760-346-6123	346-6518
Silverado Resort & Spa 1600 Atlas Peak Rd — *TF:* 800-532-0500 ■ *Web:* www.silveradoresort.com	Napa	CA	94558	707-257-0200	257-2867
Snow Valley Mountain Resort 35100 State Hwy 18 PO Box 2337 — *TF:* 800-680-7669 ■ *Web:* www.snow-valley.com	Running Springs	CA	92382	909-867-2751	867-7687
Spa Resort, The 100 N Indian Canyon Dr — **Fax Area Code:* 760 ■ *TF:* 800-854-1279 ■ *Web:* www.sparesortcasino.com	Palm Springs	CA	92262	800-854-1279	325-3344*
Squaw Valley USA PO Box 2007 — *TF:* 800-403-0206 ■ *Web:* squawalpine.com	Olympic Valley	CA	96146	530-583-6955	581-7106
Stonepine 150 E Carmel Vly Rd — *Web:* www.stonepineestate.com	Carmel Valley	CA	93924	831-659-2245	659-5160
Sycuan Casino 5485 Casino Way — *Web:* sycuan.com/resort/	El Cajon	CA	92019	619-445-6002	445-6752
Tahoe Seasons Resort 3901 Saddle Rd PO Box 16300 — *TF:* 800-540-4874 ■ *Web:* tahoeseasonsresort.net/	South Lake Tahoe	CA	96151	530-541-6700	541-0653
Temecula Creek Inn 44501 Rainbow Canyon Rd — **Fax Area Code:* 951 ■ *TF:* 877-517-1823 ■ *Web:* www.temeculacreekinn.com	Temecula	CA	92592	855-685-9299	676-8961*
Town & Country Resort Hotel 500 Hotel Cir N — *TF:* 800-772-8527 ■ *Web:* www.towncountry.com	San Diego	CA	92108	619-291-7131	291-3584
Two Bunch Palms Resort & Spa 67425 Two Bunch Palms Trl — *TF:* 800-472-4334 ■ *Web:* www.twobunchpalms.com	Desert Hot Springs	CA	92240	760-329-8791	329-1874
Ventana Inn 48123 Hwy 1 — *TF:* 800-628-6500 ■ *Web:* www.ventanainn.com	Big Sur	CA	93920	831-667-2331	667-0573
Welk Resort San Diego 8860 Lawrence Welk Dr — *TF Resv:* 800-932-9355 ■ *Web:* welkresorts.com	Escondido	CA	92026	760-749-3000	749-9537
Winner's Cir Resort 550 Via de la Valle — *TF:* 800-874-8770 ■ *Web:* www.winnerscircleresort.com	Solana Beach	CA	92075	858-755-6666	481-3706

Colorado

	City	State	ZIP	Phone	Fax
Aspen Meadows Resort 845 Meadows Rd — *TF:* 800-452-4240 ■ *Web:* www.aspenmeadows.com	Aspen	CO	81611	970-925-4240	925-7790
Aspen Skiing Co 117 ABC — *TF:* 855-754-2863 ■ *Web:* www.aspensnowmass.com	Aspen	CO	81611	970-925-1220	925-2647
Beaver Run Resort & Conference Ctr 620 Village Rd — *TF:* 800-525-2253 ■ *Web:* www.beaverrun.com	Breckenridge	CO	80424	970-453-6000	453-2454
Broadmoor, The One Lake Ave — *TF:* 866-837-9520 ■ *Web:* www.broadmoor.com	Colorado Springs	CO	80906	719-577-5775	577-5738
C Lazy U Ranch 3640 Colorado Hwy 125 PO Box 379 — *Web:* www.clazyu.com	Granby	CO	80446	970-887-3344	887-3917
Copper Mountain Resort 209 Ten Mile Cir PO Box 3001 — *TF:* 888-219-2441 ■ *Web:* www.coppercolorado.com	Copper Mountain	CO	80443	970-968-2882	968-3155
Crested Butte Mountain Resort (CBMR) 12 Snowmass Rd PO Box 5700 — *TF:* 800-810-7669 ■ *Web:* www.skicb.com/cbmr	Crested Butte	CO	81224	970-349-2222	349-2250
Destination Hotels & Resorts Inc 10333 E Dry Creek Rd Ste 450 — *TF:* 855-893-1011 ■ *Web:* www.destinationhotels.com	Englewood	CO	80112	303-799-3830	799-6011
Durango Mountain Resort One Skier Pl — *TF:* 800-982-6103 ■ *Web:* www.durangomountainresort.com	Durango	CO	81301	970-247-9000	385-2107
Grand Lodge Crested Butte 12 Snowmass Rd — *TF:* 877-547-5143 ■ *Web:* www.skicb.com/cbmr/grand-lodge.aspx	Crested Butte	CO	81224	970-349-2222	349-4265
Hot Springs Lodge & Pool 415 E Sixth St PO Box 308 — *TF:* 800-537-7946 ■ *Web:* www.hotspringspool.com	Glenwood Springs	CO	81602	970-945-6571	947-2950
Indian Hot Springs 302 Soda Creek Rd PO Box 1990 — *Web:* www.indianhotsprings.com	Idaho Springs	CO	80452	303-989-6666	567-9304
Inverness Hotel & Golf Club 200 Inverness Dr W — *TF:* 800-346-4891 ■ *Web:* www.invernesshotel.com	Englewood	CO	80112	303-799-5800	799-5874
Keystone Resort 21996 Hwy 6 PO Box 38 — *TF:* 877-625-1556 ■ *Web:* www.keystoneresort.com	Keystone	CO	80435	970-496-2316	
Lion Square Lodge & Conference Ctr 660 W Lionshead Pl — *TF:* 800-525-1943 ■ *Web:* www.wyndhamvacationrentals.com	Vail	CO	81657	970-476-2281	476-7423
Manor Vail Lodge 595 E Vail Vly Dr — *TF:* 800-950-8245 ■ *Web:* www.manorvail.com	Vail	CO	81657	970-476-5000	476-4982
Mountain Lodge at Telluride 457 Mtn Village Blvd — *TF:* 866-368-6867 ■ *Web:* www.mountainlodgetelluride.com	Telluride	CO	81435	970-369-5000	369-4317
Omni Interlocken Resort 500 Interlocken Blvd — *TF:* 800-843-6664 ■ *Web:* www.omnihotels.com	Broomfield	CO	80021	303-438-6600	464-3236
Park Hyatt Beaver Creek Resort & Spa 136 E Thomas Pl — *TF Cust Svc:* 800-233-1234 ■ *Web:* www.beavercreek.hyatt.com	Avon	CO	81620	970-949-1234	949-4164
Peaks Resort & Golden Door Spa 136 Country Club Dr — **Fax Area Code:* 970 ■ *TF:* 800-789-2220 ■ *Web:* www.thepeaksresort.com	Telluride	CO	81435	800-789-2220	728-6175*
Ritz-Carlton Bachelor Gulch 0130 Daybreak Ridge — *TF:* 800-241-3333 ■ *Web:* www.ritzcarlton.com	Avon	CO	81620	970-748-6200	343-1070
Saint Regis Resort Aspen 315 E Dean St — **Fax Area Code:* 704 ■ *TF:* 888-627-7198 ■ *Web:* www.stregisaspen.com	Aspen	CO	81611	970-920-3300	825-7723*
Snowmass Club PO Box G-2 — *Web:* www.snowmassclub.com	Snowmass Village	CO	81615	970-923-5600	923-6944
Sonnenalp Resort of Vail 20 Vail Rd — *TF:* 800-654-8312 ■ *Web:* www.sonnenalp.com	Vail	CO	81657	970-476-5656	476-1639
Steamboat Grand Resort Hotel & Conference Ctr 2300 Mt Werner Cir — *TF:* 877-269-2628 ■ *Web:* www.steamboatgrand.com	Steamboat Springs	CO	80487	970-871-5500	871-5501
Steamboat Ski & Resort Corp 2305 Mt Werner Cir — *TF:* 877-237-2628 ■ *Web:* www.steamboat.com	Steamboat Springs	CO	80487	970-879-6111	879-4757
Torian Plum Condo Resort 1855 Ski Time Sq Dr — *TF:* 800-228-2458 ■ *Web:* www.wyndhamvacationrentals.com	Steamboat Springs	CO	80487	970-879-8811	
Vail Cascade Resort & Spa 1300 Westhaven Dr — *TF:* 800-420-2424 ■ *Web:* www.vailcascade.com	Vail	CO	81657	970-476-7111	479-7020
Vail Resorts Management Co 390 Interlocken Crescent Ste 1000 — *NYSE:* MTN ■ *TF:* 800-842-8062 ■ *Web:* www.vailresorts.com	Broomfield	CO	80021	303-404-1800	404-6415

Phone | Fax

Village at Breckenridge Resort
535 S Pk Ave .... Breckenridge CO 80424 970-453-3000
Web: www.breckenridgesports.com

Wyndham Vacation Rentals 14 Sylvan Way .... Parsippany NJ 07054 973-753-6300 870-7813*
**Fax Area Code:* 970 ■ *TF:* 800-467-3529 ■ *Web:* www.wyndhamvacationrentals.com

Connecticut

Phone | Fax

Heritage Hotel 522 Heritage Rd .... Southbury CT 06488 203-264-8200 264-5035
TF: 800-932-3466 ■ *Web:* www.heritagesouthbury.com

Interlaken Inn 74 Interlaken Rd Rt 12 .... Lakeville CT 06039 860-435-9878 435-2980
TF: 800-222-2909 ■ *Web:* www.interlakeninn.com

Mohegan Sun Resort & Casino
One Mohegan Sun Blvd .... Uncasville CT 06382 860-862-8150
TF: 888-226-7711 ■ *Web:* www.mohegansun.com

Saybrook Point Inn & Spa Two Bridge St .... Old Saybrook CT 06475 860-395-2000 388-1504
TF: 800-243-0212 ■ *Web:* www.saybrook.com

Water's Edge Resort & Spa
1525 Boston Post Rd PO Box 688 .... Westbrook CT 06498 860-399-5901 399-8644
TF: 800-222-5901 ■ *Web:* www.watersedgeresortandspa.com

Florida

Phone | Fax

Amelia Island Plantation
39 Beach Lagoon Rd .... Amelia Island FL 32034 904-261-6161
TF: 800-834-4900 ■ *Web:* www.villasofameliaisland.com

Americano Beach Resort
1260 N Atlantic Ave .... Daytona Beach FL 32118 386-255-7431 253-9513
TF: 800-874-1824 ■ *Web:* www.americanobeachresort.com

Bahia Mar Beach Resort & Yachting Ctr
801 Seabreeze Blvd .... Fort Lauderdale FL 33316 954-764-2233 523-5424
TF: 888-802-2442 ■ *Web:* www.bahiamarhotel.com

Banana Bay Resort 4590 Overseas Hwy .... Marathon FL 33050 866-689-4217 743-2670*
**Fax Area Code:* 305 ■ *TF:* 866-689-4217 ■ *Web:* www.bananabay.com

Banyan Resort 323 Whitehead St .... Key West FL 33040 305-296-7786 294-1107
TF: 866-371-9222 ■ *Web:* www.thebanyanresort.com

Bay Hill Golf Club & Lodge
9000 Bay Hill Blvd .... Orlando FL 32819 407-876-2429 876-1035
TF: 888-422-9445 ■ *Web:* www.bayhill.com

Beachcomber Resort Hotel & Villas
1200 S Ocean Blvd .... Pompano Beach FL 33062 954-941-7830 942-7680
TF: 800-231-2423 ■ *Web:* www.beachcomberresort.com

Biltmore Hotel & Conference Ctr of the Americas
1200 Anastasia Ave .... Coral Gables FL 33134 305-445-1926 913-3159
TF Cust Svc: 800-727-1926 ■ *Web:* www.biltmorehotel.com

Bluewater Bay Resort 2000 Bluewater Blvd .... Niceville FL 32578 850-897-3613 897-2424
TF: 800-874-2128 ■ *Web:* www.bwbresort.com

Boca Raton Resort & Club
501 E Camino Real .... Boca Raton FL 33432 561-447-3000 447-5073
TF: 888-543-1224 ■ *Web:* www.bocaresort.com

Breakers, The One S County Rd .... Palm Beach FL 33480 561-655-6611 659-8403
TF: 888-273-2537 ■ *Web:* www.thebreakers.com

Buena Vista Hospitality Group Inc
6750 Forum Dr Ste 316 .... Orlando FL 32821 407-352-7161 352-2413
Web: www.bvhg.com

Buena Vista Palace Hotel & Spa
1900 N Buena Vista Dr .... Lake Buena Vista FL 32830 866-397-6516 827-6034*
**Fax Area Code:* 407 ■ *TF:* 866-397-6516 ■ *Web:* www.buenavistapalace.com

Casa Marina Resort & Beach Club
1500 Reynolds St .... Key West FL 33040 888-303-5717 296-4633*
**Fax Area Code:* 305 ■ *TF:* 888-303-5717 ■ *Web:* www.casamarinaresort.com

Casa Ybel Resort 2255 W Gulf Dr .... Sanibel Island FL 33957 239-472-3145 472-2109
TF: 800-276-4753 ■ *Web:* www.casaybelresort.com

Choice Hotels International Inc
621 S Atlantic Ave .... Ormond Beach FL 32176 386-672-4550
Web: ascendcollection.com

Club Med Sandpiper
4500 SE Pine Vly St .... Port Saint Lucie FL 34952 772-398-5100 398-5103
TF: 888-932-2582 ■ *Web:* clubmed.co.in/

Deauville Beach Resort 6701 Collins Ave .... Miami Beach FL 33141 305-865-8511 861-2367
TF: 800-327-6656 ■ *Web:* www.deauvillebeachresort.com

Disney's All-Star Movies Resort
1901 W Buena Vista Dr .... Lake Buena Vista FL 32830 407-939-7000 939-7111
Web: disneyworld.disney.go.com/resorts/all-star-movies-resort

Disney's All-Star Music Resort
1801 W Buena Vista Dr .... Lake Buena Vista FL 32830 407-939-6000 939-7222
Web: disneyworld.disney.go.com

Disney's All-Star Sports Resort
1701 W Buena Vista Dr .... Lake Buena Vista FL 32830 407-939-5000 939-7333
Web: www.disneyworld.disney.go.com

Disney's Animal Kingdom Lodge
2901 Osceola Pkwy .... Lake Buena Vista FL 32830 407-938-3000 938-4799
TF: 855-878-9582 ■
Web: disneyworld.disney.go.com/resorts/animal-kingdom-lodge

Disney's BoardWalk Resort
2101 N Epcot Resort Blvd .... Lake Buena Vista FL 32830 407-939-5100 939-5150
Web: disneyworld.disney.go.com

Disney's BoardWalk Villas
2101 N Epcot Resort Blvd .... Lake Buena Vista FL 32830 407-939-5100 939-5150
Web: disneyworld.disney.go.com

Disney's Caribbean Beach Resort
900 Cayman Way .... Lake Buena Vista FL 32830 407-934-3400
Web: disneyworld.disney.go.com/resorts/caribbean-beach-resort

Disney's Contemporary Resort
4600 N World Dr .... Lake Buena Vista FL 32830 407-824-1000 824-3539
Web: disneyworld.disney.go.com/resorts/contemporary-resort

Disney's Coronado Springs Resort
1000 W Buena Vista Dr .... Lake Buena Vista FL 32830 407-939-1000 939-1001
Web: www.disneyworld.disney.go.com

Phone | Fax

Disney's Fort Wilderness Resort & Campground
4510 Ft Wilderness Trl .... Lake Buena Vista FL 32830 407-824-2900 824-3508
Web: www.disneyworld.disney.go.com

Disney's Grand Floridian Resort & Spa
4401 Floridian Way .... Lake Buena Vista FL 32830 407-824-3000 824-3186
Web: www.disneyworld.disney.go.com

Disney's Old Key West Resort
1510 N Cove Rd .... Lake Buena Vista FL 32830 407-827-7700 827-7710
Web: disneyworld.disney.go.com/resorts/old-key-west-resort

Disney's Polynesian Resort
1600 Seven Seas Dr .... Lake Buena Vista FL 32830 407-824-2000 824-3174
Web: disneyworld.disney.go.com/resorts/polynesian-resort

Disney's Pop Century Resort
1050 Century Dr .... Lake Buena Vista FL 32830 407-938-4000 938-4040
Web: disneyworld.disney.go.com

Disney's Port Orleans Resort-French Quarter
2201 Orleans Dr .... Lake Buena Vista FL 32830 407-934-5000 934-5353
Web: www.disneyworld.disney.go.com

Disney's Port Orleans Resort-Riverside
1251 Riverside Dr .... Lake Buena Vista FL 32830 407-934-6000 934-5777
Web: disneyworld.disney.go.com/resorts/port-orleans-resort-riverside

Disney's Wilderness Lodge
901 Timberline Dr .... Lake Buena Vista FL 32830 407-824-3200 824-3232
Web: disneyworld.disney.go.com/resorts/wilderness-lodge-resort

Disney's Yacht Club Resort
1700 EPCOT Resorts Blvd .... Lake Buena Vista FL 32830 407-934-7000 934-3850
Web: www.disneyworld.disney.go.com

Don CeSar Beach Resort - A Loews Hotel
3400 Gulf Blvd .... Saint Pete Beach FL 33706 727-360-1881 360-1881*
**Fax:* Sales ■ *TF:* 866-563-9792 ■ *Web:* www.loewshotels.com

Don Shula's Hotel & Golf Club
6842 Main St .... Miami Lakes FL 33014 305-821-1150 820-8087
Web: www.donshulahotel.com

Doral Golf Resort & Spa 4400 NW 87th Ave .... Miami FL 33178 305-592-2000 592-2000
TF: 800-713-6725 ■ *Web:* www.trumphotelcollection.com

DoubleTree Resort by Hilton Hotel Grand Key (DGKR)
3990 S Roosevelt Blvd .... Key West FL 33040 305-293-1818 296-6962
TF: 888-844-0454 ■ *Web:* doubletree3.hilton.com

Eden Roc - A Renaissance Beach Resort & Spa
4525 Collins Ave .... Miami Beach FL 33140 305-531-0000 674-5555
TF: 855-433-3676 ■ *Web:* edenrocmiami.com

Fisher Island Club & Resort
One Fisher Island Dr .... Miami FL 33109 305-535-6000 535-6003
TF Resv: 800-537-3708 ■ *Web:* www.fisherislandclub.com

Fontainebleau Miami Beach
4441 Collins Ave .... Miami Beach FL 33140 305-538-2000 531-2845
TF: 800-548-8886 ■ *Web:* fontainebleau.com

Fort Lauderdale Grande Hotel & Yacht Club
1881 SE 17th St .... Fort Lauderdale FL 33316 954-463-4000 527-6705
TF: 888-554-2131 ■ *Web:* www.fortlauderdalemarinahotel.com

Four Seasons Resort Palm Beach
2800 S Ocean Blvd .... Palm Beach FL 33480 561-582-2800 547-1374
TF: 800-432-2335 ■ *Web:* www.fourseasons.com/palmbeach

Galleon Resort & Marina 617 Front St .... Key West FL 33040 305-296-7711 296-0821
TF: 800-544-3030 ■ *Web:* www.galleonresort.com

Gaylord Palms Resort & Convention Ctr
6000 W Osceola Pkwy .... Kissimmee FL 34746 407-586-0000 586-2199
Web: www.marriott.com

Grand Palms Hotel & Golf Resort
110 Grand Palms Dr .... Pembroke Pines FL 33027 954-431-8800 435-5988
TF: 800-327-9246 ■ *Web:* www.grandpalmsresort.com

Grenelefe Golf & Tennis Resort
3200 State Rd 546 E .... Haines City FL 33844 863-422-7511
Web: www.thelefe.com

Hammock Beach Resort 200 Ocean Crest Dr .... Palm Coast FL 32137 386-246-5500
TF: 866-841-0287 ■ *Web:* www.hammockbeach.com

HARBORSIDE SUITES AT LITTLE HARBOR
611 Destiny Dr .... Ruskin FL 33570 800-327-2773 922-6171*
**Fax Area Code:* 813 ■ *TF:* 800-327-2773 ■ *Web:* www.staylittleharbor.com

Hard Rock Hotel at Universal Orlando Resort
5800 Universal Blvd .... Orlando FL 32819 407-503-2000 503-2010
TF: 888-430-4999 ■ *Web:* www.loewshotels.com

Hawk's Cay Resort & Marina
61 Hawk's Cay Blvd .... Duck Key FL 33050 305-743-7000 743-5215
TF: 888-395-5539 ■ *Web:* www.hawkscay.com

Hilton Longboat Key Beach Resort
4711 Gulf of Mexico Dr .... Longboat Key FL 34228 941-383-2451 383-7979
Web: www1.hilton.com

Hilton Marco Island Beach Resort
560 S Collier Blvd .... Marco Island FL 34145 239-394-5000 394-8410
Web: www1.hilton.com

Hilton Sandestin Beach Golf Resort & Spa
4000 Sandestin Blvd S .... Destin FL 32550 850-267-9500 267-3076
TF: 800-559-1805 ■ *Web:* hiltonsandestinbeach.com/

Holiday Inn Express & Suites Oceanfront
3301 S Atlantic Ave .... Daytona Beach Shores FL 32118 386-767-1711 271-0000
TF: 800-633-8464 ■ *Web:* www.ihg.com

Holiday Inn Resort Lake Buena Vista
13351 SR 535 .... Orlando FL 32821 407-239-4500 239-7713
TF Sales: 866-808-8833 ■ *Web:* www.hiresortlbv.com

Holiday Isle Beach Resort & Marina
84001 Overseas Hwy .... Islamorada FL 33036 305-664-2321 664-2703
TF: 800-327-7070 ■ *Web:* www.holidayisle.com

Innisbrook Resort & Golf Club
36750 US Hwy 19 N .... Palm Harbor FL 34684 727-942-2000 942-5576
TF: 800-492-6899 ■ *Web:* www.innisbrookgolfresort.com

Inverrary Resort 3501 Inverrary Blvd .... Fort Lauderdale FL 33319 954-485-0500 733-0236
TF: 800-241-0363 ■ *Web:* inverrary.com

Janus Hotels & Resorts Inc
2300 Corporate Blvd NW Ste 232 .... Boca Raton FL 33431 561-997-2325 997-5331
TF: 800-327-2110 ■ *Web:* www.janushotels.com

Jupiter Beach Resort Five N A1A .... Jupiter FL 33477 561-746-2511
TF: 877-389-0571 ■ *Web:* www.jupiterbeachresort.com

				Phone	Fax

JW Marriott Orlando Grande Lakes Resort
4040 Central Florida Pkwy .... Orlando FL 32837 407-206-2300 206-2301
TF: 800-576-5750 ■ *Web:* www.grandelakes.com

Key Largo Grande Resort & Beach Club
97000 S Overseas Hwy .... Key Largo FL 33037 305-852-5553 852-8669
Web: www.keylargoresort.com

Key Largo Marriott Bay Resort
103800 Overseas Hwy .... Key Largo FL 33037 305-453-0000 453-0093
TF Resv: 888-731-9056 ■ *Web:* www.marriottkeylargo.com

La Cita Country Club 777 Country Club Dr .... Titusville FL 32780 321-383-2582 267-4209
Web: www.lacitacc.com

La Playa Beach & Golf Resort
9891 Gulf Shore Dr .... Naples FL 34108 239-597-3123 597-6278
TF: 800-237-6883 ■ *Web:* www.laplayaresort.com

Lago Mar Resort & Club
1700 S Ocean Ln .... Fort Lauderdale FL 33316 954-678-3915 524-6627
TF: 855-209-5677 ■ *Web:* www.lagomar.com

Little Palm Island Resort & Spa
28500 Overseas Hwy MM 28.5 .... Little Torch Key FL 33042 305-872-2524 872-4843
TF: 800-343-8567 ■ *Web:* www.littlepalmisland.com

Lodge & Club at Ponte Vedra Beach
607 Ponte Vedra Blvd .... Ponte Vedra Beach FL 32082 888-839-9145 273-0210*
**Fax Area Code:* 904 ■ *TF:* 800-243-4304 ■ *Web:* www.pontevedra.com

Longboat Key Club 220 Sands Point Rd .... Longboat Key FL 34228 941-383-8821
TF: 800-237-8821 ■ *Web:* www.longboatkeyclub.com

Marco Beach Ocean Resort
480 S Collier Blvd .... Marco Island FL 34145 239-393-1400 393-1401
TF: 800-715-8517 ■ *Web:* www.marcoresort.com

Miami Beach Resort & Spa
4833 Collins Ave .... Miami Beach FL 33140 305-532-3600 534-7409
TF: 866-765-9090 ■ *Web:* www.miamibeachresortandspa.com

Mission Inn Resort & Club
10400 County Rd 48 .... Howey in the Hills FL 34737 352-324-3101 324-2636
TF: 800-874-9053 ■ *Web:* www.missioninnresort.com

Naples Bay Resort 1500 Fifth Ave S .... Naples FL 34102 239-530-1199 436-8024
TF: 866-605-1199 ■ *Web:* www.naplesbayresort.com

Naples Beach Hotel & Golf Club
851 Gulf Shore Blvd N .... Naples FL 34102 239-261-2222 261-7380
TF: 800-237-7600 ■ *Web:* www.naplesbeachhotel.com

Nickelodeon Family Suites by Holiday Inn
14500 Continental Gateway .... Orlando FL 32821 407-387-5437 387-1488
TF: 877-642-5111 ■ *Web:* www.nickhotel.com

Ocean Key Resort & Spa 0 Duval St .... Key West FL 33040 305-296-7701 292-7685
TF: 800-328-9815 ■ *Web:* www.oceankey.com

Ocean Manor Resort
4040 Galt Ocean Dr .... Fort Lauderdale FL 33308 954-566-7500 564-3075
TF: 800-955-0444 ■ *Web:* www.oceanmanor.com

Ocean Sands Resort & Spa
1350 N Ocean Blvd .... Pompano Beach FL 33062 954-590-1000 590-1101
TF: 800-721-7033 ■
Web: www.marriott.com/hotels/travel/fllpb-residence-inn-fort-lauderdale-pompano-beach-oceanfront

Omni Orlando Resort at Championsgate
1500 Masters Blvd .... Champions Gate FL 33896 407-390-6664 390-6600
TF: 800-843-6664 ■ *Web:* www.omnihotels.com

Orange Lake Country Club Inc (OLCC)
8505 W Irlo Bronson Memorial Hwy .... Kissimmee FL 34747 407-239-0000 239-5119
TF: 800-877-6522 ■ *Web:* www.orangelake.com

Palms, The 3025 Collins Ave .... Miami Beach FL 33140 305-534-0505 534-0515
TF: 800-550-0505 ■ *Web:* www.thepalmshotel.com

Park Shore Resort 600 Neapolitan Way .... Naples FL 34103 239-263-2222 263-0946
TF: 800-548-2077 ■ *Web:* www.parkshorefl.com

PGA National Resort & Spa
400 Ave of the Champions .... Palm Beach Gardens FL 33418 561-627-2000 625-6204
TF: 866-633-9150 ■ *Web:* www.pgaresort.com

Pier House Resort Caribbean Spa
One Duval St .... Key West FL 33040 305-296-4600 296-7569
TF: 800-723-2791 ■ *Web:* www.pierhouse.com

Plantation Inn & Golf Resort
9301 W Ft Island Trl .... Crystal River FL 34429 352-795-4211 795-1156
TF: 800-632-6262 ■ *Web:* www.plantationoncrystalriver.com

Plaza Resort & Spa 600 N Atlantic Ave .... Daytona Beach FL 32118 386-255-4471 238-7984
TF: 800-429-8662 ■ *Web:* www.plazaresortandspa.com

Ponte Vedra Inn & Club
200 Ponte Vedra Blvd .... Ponte Vedra Beach FL 32082 904-285-1111 285-1111
TF: 800-234-7842 ■ *Web:* www.pontevedra.com

Portofino Bay Hotel at Universal Orlando - A Loews Hotel
5601 Universal Blvd .... Orlando FL 32819 407-503-1000 503-1010
TF: 800-235-6397 ■ *Web:* www.loewshotels.com

Quality Inn & Suites Naples Golf Resort
4100 Golden Gate Pkwy .... Naples FL 34116 239-455-1010 455-4038
TF: 800-277-0017 ■ *Web:* www.naplesgolfresort.com

Radisson Resort Parkway 2900 PkwyBlvd .... Kissimmee FL 34747 407-396-7000 396-6792
TF: 800-333-3333 ■ *Web:* www.radisson.com

Reach Resort 1435 Simonton St .... Key West FL 33040 305-296-5000 296-2830
TF: 888-318-4316 ■ *Web:* www.reachresort.com

Renaissance Orlando Resort at SeaWorld
6677 Sea Harbor Dr .... Orlando FL 32821 407-351-5555 351-9991
TF: 800-327-6677 ■ *Web:* www.marriott.com/default.mi

Renaissance Resort at World Golf Village
500 S Legacy Trl .... Saint Augustine FL 32092 904-940-8000 940-8008
TF: 888-740-7020 ■ *Web:* www.worldgolfrenaissance.com

Renaissance Vinoy Resort & Golf Club
501 Fifth Ave NE .... Saint Petersburg FL 33701 727-894-1000
TF: 800-468-3571 ■ *Web:* www.marriott.com/default.mi

Resort at Singer Island
3800 N Ocean Dr .... Riviera Beach FL 33404 561-340-1700 340-1705
TF: 800-721-7033 ■ *Web:* marriott.com

Ritz-Carlton Amelia Island
4750 Amelia Island Pkwy .... Amelia Island FL 32034 904-277-1100 261-9064
TF: 800-241-3333 ■ *Web:* www.ritzcarlton.com/resorts/amelia_island

Ritz-Carlton Key Biscayne
455 Grand Bay Dr .... Key Biscayne FL 33149 305-365-4500 365-4505
TF: 800-241-3333 ■ *Web:* www.ritzcarlton.com/resorts/key_biscayne

Ritz-Carlton Naples 280 Vanderbilt Beach Rd .... Naples FL 34108 239-598-3300 598-6690
Web: www.ritzcarlton.com/resorts/naples

Ritz-Carlton Naples Golf Resort
2600 Tiburon Dr .... Naples FL 34109 239-593-2000 254-3300
TF Resv: 888-856-2164 ■ *Web:* www.ritzcarlton.com

Ritz-Carlton Orlando Grande Lakes
4012 Central Florida Pkwy .... Orlando FL 32837 407-206-2400 206-2401
TF: 800-576-5760 ■ *Web:* www.ritzcarlton.com

Ritz-Carlton Sarasota 1111 Ritz-Carlton Dr .... Sarasota FL 34236 941-309-2000 309-2100
TF: 800-241-3333 ■ *Web:* www.ritzcarlton.com

Rosen Hotels & Resorts Inc
9840 International Dr .... Orlando FL 32819 407-996-9840 996-0865
TF: 800-204-7234 ■ *Web:* www.rosenhotels.com

Royal Pacific Resort at Universal Orlando - A Loews Hotel
6300 Hollywood Way .... Orlando FL 32819 407-503-3000 503-3010
TF: 800-232-7827 ■ *Web:* www.loewshotels.com

Safety Harbor Resort & Spa
105 N Bayshore Dr .... Safety Harbor FL 34695 727-726-1161 726-4268
TF: 888-237-8772 ■ *Web:* www.safetyharborspa.com

Sandals Resorts International 4950 SW 72nd Ave .... Miami FL 33155 305-284-1300 666-5332*
**Fax:* PR ■ *TF:* 888-726-3257 ■ *Web:* www.sandals.com

Sandestin Golf & Beach Resort
9300 Emerald Coast Pkwy W .... Sandestin FL 32550 850-267-8000
TF: 800-277-0800 ■ *Web:* www.sandestin.com

Sanibel Harbour Marriott Resort & Spa
17260 Harbour Pt Dr .... Fort Myers FL 33908 239-466-4000 466-2266
TF: 800-767-7777 ■ *Web:* www.marriott.com

Sawgrass Marriott Resort & Beach Club
1000 PGA Tour Blvd .... Ponte Vedra Beach FL 32082 904-285-7777 285-0906
TF: 800-228-9290 ■ *Web:* www.marriott.com

Sea Gardens Beach & Tennis Resort
615 N Ocean Blvd .... Pompano Beach FL 33062 954-943-6200 783-0047
Web: www.seagardens.com

Seminole Hard Rock Hotel & Casino Hollywood
1 Seminole Way .... Hollywood FL 33314 954-327-7625
TF: 888-236-4848 ■ *Web:* www.seminolehardrock.com

Sheraton Sand Key Resort
1160 Gulf Blvd .... Clearwater Beach FL 33767 727-595-1611 596-8488
TF: 800-456-7263 ■ *Web:* www.sheratonsandkey.com

South Seas Island Resort 5400 Plantation Rd .... Captiva FL 33924 239-472-5111 472-7541
TF: 866-565-5089 ■ *Web:* www.southseas.com

Standard, The 40 Island Ave .... Miami Beach FL 33139 305-673-1717 673-8181
TF: 800-327-8363 ■ *Web:* standardhotels.com

Sundial Beach & Golf Resort
1451 Middle Gulf Dr .... Sanibel FL 33957 239-472-4151
TF: 866-717-2323 ■ *Web:* www.theinnsofsanibel.com

Sunset Beach Resort 3287 W Gulf Dr .... Sanibel Island FL 33957 239-472-1700
TF: 866-565-5091 ■ *Web:* www.theinnsofsanibel.com

Sunset Key Guest Cottages at Westin Resort
245 Front St .... Key West FL 33040 305-292-5300 292-5395
Web: www.westinsunsetkeycottages.com

Trump International Sonesta Beach Resort
18001 Collins Ave .... Sunny Isles Beach FL 33160 305-692-5600 692-5601
TF: 800-766-3782 ■ *Web:* www.sonesta.com

Vanderbilt Beach Resort 9225 Gulf Shore Dr N .... Naples FL 34108 239-597-3144 597-2199
TF: 800-243-9076 ■ *Web:* www.vanderbiltbeachresort.com

Villas of Grand Cypress Golf Resort
One N Jacaranda .... Orlando FL 32836 407-239-4700 239-7219
TF: 800-835-7377 ■ *Web:* www.grandcypress.com

Walt Disney World Dolphin
1500 Epcot Resorts Blvd .... Lake Buena Vista FL 32830 407-934-4000 934-4884
TF: 888-828-8850 ■ *Web:* www.swandolphin.com

Walt Disney World Resorts
4600 N World Dr .... Lake Buena Vista FL 32830 407-824-1000 827-2096
Web: disneyworld.disney.go.com

Walt Disney World Swan
1200 Epcot Resorts Blvd .... Lake Buena Vista FL 32830 407-934-4000 934-4884
TF: 888-828-8850 ■ *Web:* www.swandolphin.com

West Wind Inn 3345 W Gulf Dr .... Sanibel FL 33957 239-472-1541 472-8134
TF: 800-824-0476 ■ *Web:* www.westwindinn.com

Westin Diplomat Resort & Spa
501 Diplomat Pkwy .... Hallandale FL 33009 954-883-4444
Web: www.diplomatgolf.com

Westin Key West Resort & Marina
245 Front St .... Key West FL 33040 305-294-4000 294-4086
TF: 866-837-4250 ■ *Web:* www.westinkeywestresort.com

Georgia

				Phone	Fax

Barnsley Gardens 597 Barnsley Gardens Rd .... Adairsville GA 30103 770-773-7480 773-1779
TF: 877-773-2447 ■ *Web:* www.barnsleyresort.com

Brasstown Valley Resort 6321 US Hwy 76 .... Young Harris GA 30582 706-379-9900 379-9999
TF: 800-201-3205 ■ *Web:* www.brasstownvalley.com

Callaway Gardens 17800 Hwy 27 .... Pine Mountain GA 31822 706-663-2281 663-5122
TF: 800-225-5292 ■ *Web:* www.callawaygardens.com

Chateau Elan Resort & Conference Ctr
100 Rue Charlemagne .... Braselton GA 30517 678-425-0900 425-6000
TF: 800-233-9463 ■ *Web:* www.chateauelan.com

Forrest Hills Mountain Resort & Conference Ctr
135 Forrest Hills Rd .... Dahlonega GA 30533 706-864-6456 864-0757
TF: 800-654-6313 ■ *Web:* www.foresths.com

Jekyll Island Club Hotel
371 Riverview Dr .... Jekyll Island GA 31527 912-635-2600 635-2818
TF: 800-535-9547 ■ *Web:* www.jekyllclub.com

King & Prince Beach & Golf Resort
201 Arnold Rd .... Saint Simons Island GA 31522 912-638-3631 638-7699
TF: 800-342-0212 ■ *Web:* www.kingandprince.com

Lake Lanier Islands Resort 7000 Holiday Rd .... Buford GA 30518 770-945-8787 271-7381
TF: 800-840-5253 ■ *Web:* www.lakelanierislands.com

Reynolds Plantation 100 Linger Longer Rd .... Greensboro GA 30642 706-467-0600
TF: 800-800-5250 ■ *Web:* www.reynoldsplantation.com

	City	State	ZIP	Phone	Fax
Ritz-Carlton Lodge Reynolds Plantation One Lk Oconee Trl.	Greensboro	GA	30642	706-467-0600	467-7124
TF: 800-826-1945 ■ *Web:* www.ritzcarlton.com					
Sea Palms Golf & Tennis Resort 5445 Frederica Rd	Saint Simons Island	GA	31522	912-638-3351	634-8029
TF: 800-841-6268 ■ *Web:* www.seapalms.com					
Sky Valley Golf Club 568 Sky Vly Way	Sky Valley	GA	30537	706-746-5302	
Web: skyvalleycountryclub.com					
Villas by the Sea Resort 1175 N Beachview Dr	Jekyll Island	GA	31527	912-635-2521	635-2569
TF: 800-841-6262 ■ *Web:* www.villasbythesearesort.com					

Hawaii

	City	State	ZIP	Phone	Fax
Fairmont Kea Lani Maui 4100 Wailea Alanui Dr	Wailea-makena	HI	96753	808-875-4100	875-1200
TF: 800-659-4100 ■ *Web:* www.fairmont.com					
Fairmont Orchid Hawaii One N Kaniku Dr	Kamuela	HI	96743	808-885-2000	885-5778
TF: 800-845-9905 ■ *Web:* www.fairmont.com/orchid					
Four Seasons Resort Hualalai 100 Ka'upulehu Dr	Kailua Kona	HI	96740	808-325-8000	325-8200
TF: 888-340-5662 ■ *Web:* www.fourseasons.com/hualalai					
Four Seasons Resort Maui at Wailea 3900 Wailea Alanui Dr	Wailea	HI	96753	808-874-8000	874-2244
TF: 800-334-6284 ■ *Web:* www.fourseasons.com					
Grand Hyatt Kauai Resort & Spa 1571 Poipu Rd	Koloa	HI	96756	808-742-1234	742-1557
TF: 800-233-1234 ■ *Web:* kauai.hyatt.com					
Grand Wailea Resort & Spa 3850 Wailea Alanui Dr	Wailea	HI	96753	808-875-1234	879-4077
TF: 800-888-6100 ■ *Web:* www.grandwailea.com					
Hanalei Bay Resort & Suites 5380 Honoiki Rd	Princeville	HI	96722	808-826-6522	
TF: 877-344-0688 ■ *Web:* www.hanaleibayresort.com					
Hapuna Beach Prince Hotel 62-100 Kauna'oa Dr	Kamuela	HI	96743	808-880-1111	880-3142
TF: 800-882-6060 ■ *Web:* www.princeresortshawaii.com					
Hawaii Prince Hotel Waikiki, The 100 Holomoana St	Honolulu	HI	96815	888-977-4623	944-4491*
**Fax Area Code:* 808 ■ *TF:* 888-977-4623 ■ *Web:* www.princeresortshawaii.com					
Hilton Hawaiian Village 2005 Kalia Rd	Honolulu	HI	96815	808-949-4321	951-5458
TF: 800-445-8667 ■ *Web:* www.hilton.com					
Hilton Waikoloa Village 425 Waikoloa Beach Dr	Waikoloa	HI	96738	808-886-1234	886-2900
TF: 866-931-1679 ■ *Web:* www.hiltonwaikoloavillage.com					
Hyatt Regency Maui Resort & Spa 200 Nohea Kai Dr	Lahaina	HI	96761	808-661-1234	667-4497
TF: 800-633-7313 ■ *Web:* www.maui.hyatt.com					
Kapalua Villas, The 2000 Village Rd	Lahaina	HI	96761	808-665-5400	669-2702
TF: 800-545-0018 ■ *Web:* www.outrigger.com/hotels-resorts/hawaiian-islands/maui/the-kapalua-villas					
Lodge at Koele One Keomoku Hwy	Lanai City	HI	96763	808-565-4000	
Web: www.lodgeatkoele.com					
Marriott Kaua'i Resort & Beach Club 3610 Rice St Kalapaki Beach	Lihue	HI	96766	808-245-5050	245-5049
TF: 800-220-2925 ■ *Web:* www.marriott.com					
Mauna Kea Beach Hotel 62-100 Maunakea Beach Dr	Island of Hawaii	HI	96743	808-882-7222	882-5700
TF: 866-977-4589 ■ *Web:* www.princeresortshawaii.com					
Mauna Lani Bay Hotel & Bungalows 68-1400 Mauna Lani Dr	Kohala Coast	HI	96743	808-885-6622	881-7000
TF: 800-367-2323 ■ *Web:* www.maunalani.com					
Napili Kai Beach Club 5900 Honoapiilani Rd	Lahaina	HI	96761	808-669-6271	669-5740
TF: 800-367-5030 ■ *Web:* www.napilikai.com					
Outrigger Enterprises Group 2375 Kuhio Ave	Honolulu	HI	96815	808-921-6941	369-9403*
**Fax Area Code:* 303 ■ *TF:* 800-462-6262 ■ *Web:* www.outrigger.com					
Outrigger Hotels & Resorts 2375 Kuhio Ave	Honolulu	HI	96815	808-921-6941	926-4368*
**Fax:* Sales ■ *TF:* 800-688-7444 ■ *Web:* www.outrigger.com					
Outrigger Kanaloa at Kona 78-261 Manukai St	Kailua-Kona	HI	96740	808-322-9625	322-3818
TF: 800-688-7444 ■ *Web:* www.outrigger.com					
Outrigger Reef on the Beach 2169 Kalia Rd	Honolulu	HI	96815	808-923-3111	924-4957
TF: 800-688-7444 ■ *Web:* www.outrigger.com					
Prince Resorts Hawaii 100 Holomoana St	Honolulu	HI	96815	808-956-1111	944-4491
TF: 888-977-4623 ■ *Web:* www.princeresortshawaii.com					
Ritz-Carlton Kapalua 1 Ritz-Carlton Dr Kapalua	Maui	HI	96761	808-669-6200	669-1566
TF Resv: 800-262-8440 ■ *Web:* www.ritzcarlton.com/resorts/kapalua					
Royal Hawaiian 2259 Kalakaua Ave	Honolulu	HI	96815	808-923-7311	931-7098
Web: royal-hawaiian.com					
Royal Lahaina Resort 2780 Kekaa Dr	Lahaina	HI	96761	808-661-3611	661-6150
TF: 800-222-5642 ■ *Web:* www.hawaiianhotels.com					
Sheraton Kauai Resort 2440 Hoonani Rd	Koloa	HI	96756	808-742-1661	742-4041
TF Resv: 800-325-3535 ■ *Web:* sheraton-kauai.com					
Sheraton Maui Resort 2605 Kaanapali Pkwy	Lahaina	HI	96761	808-661-0031	661-0458
TF: 866-716-8109 ■ *Web:* sheraton-maui.com					
Sheraton Waikiki 2255 Kalakaua Ave	Honolulu	HI	96815	808-922-4422	
TF: 800-325-3535 ■ *Web:* sheraton-waikiki.com					
Travaasa Hana 5031 Hana Hwy	Hana	HI	96713	808-248-8211	248-7202
TF: 855-868-7282 ■ *Web:* travaasa.com					
Turtle Bay Resort 57-091 Kamehameha Hwy	Kahuku	HI	96731	808-293-6000	293-9147
TF: 866-475-2567 ■ *Web:* www.turtlebayresort.com					
Wailea Beach Marriott Resort & Spa 3700 Wailea Alanui Dr	Wailea	HI	96753	808-879-1922	778-2049*
**Fax Area Code:* 817 ■ *TF:* 800-845-5279 ■ *Web:* www.marriott.com					

Idaho

	City	State	ZIP	Phone	Fax
Aston Hotel & Resorts Sunvalley 333 S Main St	Ketchum	ID	83340	208-622-6400	
TF: 877-997-6667 ■ *Web:* www.astonhotels.com					
Coeur d'Alene Resort 115 S Second St	Coeur d'Alene	ID	83814	208-765-4000	664-7276
TF: 800-688-5253 ■ *Web:* www.cdaresort.com					
Red Lion Templin's Hotel on the River 414 E First Ave	Post Falls	ID	83854	208-773-1611	773-4192
TF: 800-733-5466 ■ *Web:* www.redlion.com					
Sun Valley Resort 1 Sun Valley Rd	Sun Valley	ID	83353	208-622-4111	
TF: 800-786-8259 ■ *Web:* www.sunvalley.com					

Illinois

	City	State	ZIP	Phone	Fax
Eagle Ridge Inn & Resort 444 Eagle Ridge Dr	Galena	IL	61036	815-777-2444	777-4502
TF: 800-892-2269 ■ *Web:* www.eagleridge.com					
Eaglewood Resort & Spa 1401 Nordic Rd	Itasca	IL	60143	630-773-1400	773-1709
TF: 877-285-6150 ■ *Web:* www.eaglewoodresort.com					
Indian Lakes Resort 250 W Schick Rd	Bloomingdale	IL	60108	630-529-0200	529-9271
TF: 800-334-3417 ■ *Web:* www.indianlakesresort.com					
Pheasant Run Resort & Spa 4051 E Main St	Saint Charles	IL	60174	630-584-6300	584-4693
Web: www.pheasantrun.com					

Indiana

	City	State	ZIP	Phone	Fax
Belterra Casino Resort 777 Belterra Dr	Florence	IN	47020	812-427-7777	427-7823
TF: 888-235-8377 ■ *Web:* www.belterracasino.com					
Brickyard Crossing Golf Resort & Inn 4400 W 16th St	Indianapolis	IN	46222	317-241-2500	
Web: brickyardcrossing.com					
Eagle Pointe Golf Resort 2250 E Pt Rd	Bloomington	IN	47401	812-824-4040	824-6860
Web: www.eaglepointe.com					
Fourwinds Resort & Marina 9301 Fairfax Rd	Bloomington	IN	47401	812-824-2628	824-9816
TF: 800-824-2628 ■ *Web:* www.bestinboating.com					
French Lick Resort 8670 W State Rd 56	French Lick	IN	47432	812-936-9300	936-2100
TF: 888-936-9360 ■ *Web:* www.frenchlick.com					
Potawatomi Inn Pokagan State Pk 6 Ln 100A Lk James	Angola	IN	46703	260-833-1077	833-4087
TF: 877-768-2928 ■ *Web:* www.in.gov/dnr/parklake/inns/potawatomi					

Iowa

	City	State	ZIP	Phone	Fax
Grand Harbor Resort & Waterpark 350 Bell St	Dubuque	IA	52001	563-690-4000	690-0558
TF: 866-690-4006 ■ *Web:* www.grandharborresort.com					

Kansas

	City	State	ZIP	Phone	Fax
Terradyne Resort Hotel & Country Club 1400 Terradyne Dr	Andover	KS	67002	316-733-2582	733-9149
Web: www.terradyne-resort.com					

Kentucky

	City	State	ZIP	Phone	Fax
General Butler State Resort Park 1608 US Hwy 227	Carrollton	KY	41008	502-732-4384	732-4270
TF: 866-462-8853 ■ *Web:* www.parks.ky.gov					
Griffin Gate Marriott Resort 1800 Newtown Pk	Lexington	KY	40511	859-231-5100	255-9944
TF: 800-228-9290 ■ *Web:* www.marriott.com					
Lake Cumberland State Resort Park 5465 State Pk Rd	Jamestown	KY	42629	270-343-3111	343-5510
Web: www.state.ky.us					

Maine

	City	State	ZIP	Phone	Fax
Atlantic Oakes 119 Eden St	Bar Harbor	ME	04609	207-288-5801	288-8402
TF: 800-356-3585 ■ *Web:* www.barharbor.com					
Bar Harbor Inn Oceanfront Resort Newport Dr PO Box 7	Bar Harbor	ME	04609	207-288-3351	288-8454
TF: 800-248-3351 ■ *Web:* www.barharborinn.com					
Bethel Inn & Country Club 21 Broad St PO Box 49	Bethel	ME	04217	207-824-2175	824-2233
TF: 800-654-0125 ■ *Web:* www.bethelinn.com					
Black Point Inn Resort 510 Black Pt Rd	Scarborough	ME	04074	207-883-2500	883-9976
Web: www.blackpointinn.com					
Cliff House Resort & Spa 591 Shore Rd	Cape Neddick	ME	03902	207-361-1000	361-2122
Web: www.cliffhousemaine.com					
Colony Hotel 140 Ocean Ave	Kennebunkport	ME	04046	207-967-3331	967-8738
TF: 800-552-2363 ■ *Web:* www.thecolonyhotel.com					
Inn by the Sea 40 Bowery Beach Rd	Cape Elizabeth	ME	04107	207-799-3134	799-4779
TF: 800-888-4287 ■ *Web:* www.innbythesea.com					
Samoset Resort 220 Warrenton St	Rockport	ME	04856	207-594-2511	594-0722
TF: 800-341-1650 ■ *Web:* www.samosetresort.com					
Sebasco Harbor Resort 29 Keynon Rd	Phippsburg	ME	04562	207-389-1161	389-2004
TF: 800-225-3819 ■ *Web:* www.sebasco.com					
Spruce Point Inn 88 Grandview Ave PO Box 237	Boothbay Harbor	ME	04538	207-633-4152	
Web: www.sprucepointinn.com					
Stage Neck Inn Eight Stage Neck Rd Rt 1A PO Box 70	York Harbor	ME	03911	207-363-3850	363-2221
TF: 800-222-3238 ■ *Web:* www.stageneck.com					
Sugarloaf/USA 5092 Access Rd	Carrabassett Valley	ME	04947	207-237-2000	237-3768
TF: 800-843-5623 ■ *Web:* www.sugarloaf.com					
Sunday River Ski Resort 15 S Ridge Rd PO Box 4500	Newry	ME	04261	207-824-3500	824-5110
TF: 800-543-2754 ■ *Web:* sundayriver.com					

Maryland

	City	State	ZIP	Phone	Fax
Coconut Malorie Resort 200 59th St *TF:* 855-826-6361 ■ *Web:* vacationcondos.com/coconut-malorie-festiva-resort	Ocean City	MD	21842	443-513-0175	
Francis Scott Key Family Resort 12806 Ocean Gateway PO Box 468 *TF:* 800-213-0088 ■ *Web:* www.fskmotel.com	Ocean City	MD	21842	410-213-0088	213-2854
Harbourtowne Golf Resort & Conference Ctr 9784 Martingham Dr *TF:* 800-446-9066 ■ *Web:* www.harbourtowne.com	Saint Michaels	MD	21663	410-745-9066	745-9124
Ritz-Carlton Hotel Co LLC, The 4445 Willard Ave Ste 800 **Fax Area Code:* 801 ■ *TF:* 800-241-3333 ■ *Web:* www.ritzcarlton.com	Chevy Chase	MD	20815	301-547-4700	468-4069*
Ritz-Carlton Huntington Hotel & Spa 4445 Willard Ave Ste 800 **Fax Area Code:* 801 ■ *TF:* 800-241-3333 ■ *Web:* www.ritzcarlton.com	Chevy Chase	MD	20815	301-547-4700	468-4069*
Turf Valley Resort & Conference Ctr 2700 Turf Vly Rd *Web:* www.turfvalley.com	Ellicott City	MD	21042	410-465-1500	465-9282

Massachusetts

	City	State	ZIP	Phone	Fax
Bayside Resort Hotel 225 Massachusetts 28 *TF:* 800-243-1114 ■ *Web:* www.baysideresort.com	West Yarmouth	MA	02673	508-775-5669	775-8862
Blue Water Resort 291 S Shore Dr *TF:* 800-367-9393 ■ *Web:* www.redjacketresorts.com/blue-water-resort.php	South Yarmouth	MA	02664	508-398-2288	
Canyon Ranch Lenox 165 Kemble St *TF Resv:* 800-742-9000 ■ *Web:* www.canyonranch.com	Lenox	MA	01240	413-637-4100	637-0057
Cape Codder Resort & Spa 1225 Iyanough Rd Rt 132 Bearse's Way *TF:* 888-297-2200 ■ *Web:* www.capecodderresort.com	Hyannis	MA	02601	508-771-3000	790-8145
Captain Gosnold Village 230 Gosnold St *Web:* www.captaingosnold.com	Hyannis	MA	02601	508-775-9111	
Chatham Bars Inn 297 Shore Rd *TF:* 800-527-4884 ■ *Web:* www.chathambarsinn.com	Chatham	MA	02633	508-945-0096	945-6785
Cranwell Resort Spa & Golf Club 55 Lee Rd *TF:* 800-272-6935 ■ *Web:* www.cranwell.com	Lenox	MA	01240	413-637-1364	637-4364
New Seabury Resort 20 Red Brook Rd *TF:* 877-687-3228 ■ *Web:* www.newseabury.com	Mashpee	MA	02649	508-539-8200	539-8634
Ocean Edge Resort & Golf Club 2907 Main St *TF:* 800-343-6074 ■ *Web:* www.oceanedge.com	Brewster	MA	02631	508-896-9000	896-9123
Ocean Mist Resort 97 S Shore Dr *TF:* 800-655-1972 ■ *Web:* www.oceanmistcapecod.com	South Yarmouth	MA	02664	508-398-2633	398-2122
Sea Crest Resort & Conference Ctr 350 Quaker Rd *TF:* 800-225-3110 ■ *Web:* www.seacrestbeachhotel.com	North Falmouth	MA	02556	508-540-9400	548-0556

Michigan

	City	State	ZIP	Phone	Fax
Bay Valley Hotel & Resort 2470 Old Bridge Rd *TF:* 888-241-4653 ■ *Web:* www.bayvalley.com	Bay City	MI	48706	989-686-3500	
Boyne Highlands Resort 600 Highlands Dr *TF:* 800-462-6963 ■ *Web:* www.boyne.com	Harbor Springs	MI	49740	231-526-3000	526-3100
Boyne Mountain Resort 11521 Huffman Lake Rd PO Box 91252 *TF:* 800-462-6963 ■ *Web:* www.boyneresorts.com	Boyne Falls	MI	49713	231-549-6060	549-6094
Crystal Mountain Resort 12500 Crystal Mtn Dr *TF:* 800-968-7686 ■ *Web:* www.crystalmountain.com	Thompsonville	MI	49683	231-378-2000	378-2998
Evergreen Resort 7880 Mackinaw Trail **Fax Area Code:* 231 ■ *TF:* 800-634-7302 ■ *Web:* www.mcguiresresort.com	Cadillac	MI	49601	800-634-7302	775-9621*
Garland Resort 4700 N Red Oak Rd *TF:* 877-442-7526 ■ *Web:* www.garlandusa.com	Lewiston	MI	49756	989-786-2211	786-1016
Grand Traverse Resort & Spa 100 Grand Traverse Blvd PO Box 404 *TF:* 800-236-1577 ■ *Web:* www.grandtraverseresort.com	Acme	MI	49610	231-534-6000	
Homestead Resort, The One Wood Ridge Rd *Web:* www.thehomesteadresort.com	Glen Arbor	MI	49636	231-334-5000	334-5246
Indianhead Mountain Resort 500 Indianhead Rd **Fax Area Code:* 906 ■ *TF:* 800-346-3426 ■ *Web:* www.indianheadmtn.com	Wakefield	MI	49968	800-346-3426	229-5920*
Inn at Bay Harbor, The 3600 Village Harbor Dr *TF:* 800-462-6963 ■ *Web:* www.innatbayharbor.com	Bay Harbor	MI	49770	231-439-4000	439-4094
Lakewood Shores Resort 7751 Cedar Lake Rd *TF:* 800-882-2493 ■ *Web:* www.lakewoodshores.com	Oscoda	MI	48750	989-739-2073	739-1351
Marsh Ridge Resort 4815 Old US Hwy 27 S *Web:* www.marshridge.com	Gaylord	MI	49735	989-732-5552	732-2134
Mission Point Resort 6633 Main St *TF:* 800-833-7711 ■ *Web:* www.missionpoint.com	Mackinac Island	MI	49757	800-833-7711	
Otsego Club 696 M-32 E Main St PO Box 556 *TF:* 800-752-5510 ■ *Web:* www.otsegoclub.com	Gaylord	MI	49734	989-732-5181	732-0497
Shanty Creek Resort 5780 Shanty Creek Rd *TF:* 800-678-4111 ■ *Web:* www.shantycreek.com	Bellaire	MI	49615	231-533-8621	533-7020
Treetops Resort 3962 Wilkinson Rd *TF:* 866-348-5249 ■ *Web:* www.treetops.com	Gaylord	MI	49735	989-732-6711	732-8459

Minnesota

	City	State	ZIP	Phone	Fax
Arrowwood Resort & Conference Ctr 2100 Arrowwood Ln NW *TF Resv:* 866-386-5263 ■ *Web:* www.arrowwoodresort.com	Alexandria	MN	56308	320-762-1124	762-0133
Breezy Point Resort 9252 Breezy Pt Dr *TF:* 800-432-3777 ■ *Web:* www.breezypointresort.com	Breezy Point	MN	56472	218-562-7811	562-4510
Caribou Highlands Lodge 371 Ski Hill Rd PO Box 99 *TF:* 800-642-6036 ■ *Web:* www.caribouhighlands.com	Lutsen	MN	55612	218-663-7241	663-7920
Carlson *Radisson Hotels & Resorts* 701 Carlson Pkwy *TF:* 800-333-3333 ■ *Web:* www.carlson.com	Minnetonka	MN	55305	763-212-5000	
Cascade Lodge 3719 W Hwy 61 *TF:* 800-322-9543 ■ *Web:* www.cascadelodgemn.com	Lutsen	MN	55612	218-387-1112	387-1113
Cragun's Conference & Golf Resort 11000 Cragun's Dr **Fax Area Code:* 218 ■ *TF:* 800-272-4867 ■ *Web:* www.craguns.com	Brainerd	MN	56401	800-272-4867	829-9188*
Eagle's Nest Resort 6103 Lavaque Rd *Web:* eaglesnestfishlake.com	Duluth	MN	55803	218-721-4147	
Fair Hills Resort 24270 County Hwy 20 *TF Resv:* 800-323-2849 ■ *Web:* www.fairhillsresort.com	Detroit Lakes	MN	56501	218-847-7638	532-2068
Grand Casino Hinckley 777 Lady Luck Dr **Fax Area Code:* 320 ■ *TF:* 800-472-6321 ■ *Web:* www.grandcasinomn.com	Hinckley	MN	55037	800-472-6321	384-4775*
Grand Casino Mille Lacs 777 Grand Ave PO Box 343 **Fax Area Code:* 320 ■ *TF:* 800-626-5825 ■ *Web:* www.grandcasinomn.com	Onamia	MN	56359	800-626-5825	532-8103*
Grand Portage Lodge & Casino PO Box 233 *TF:* 800-543-1384 ■ *Web:* www.grandportage.com	Grand Portage	MN	55605	218-475-2401	475-2309
Grand View Lodge 23521 Nokomis Ave *TF:* 866-801-2951 ■ *Web:* www.grandviewlodge.com	Nisswa	MN	56468	218-963-2234	963-2269
Izatys Golf Resort 40005 85th Ave *Web:* www.izatys.com	Onamia	MN	56359	320-532-4574	
Lake Breeze Motel Resort 9000 Congdon Blvd *TF:* 800-738-5884 ■ *Web:* www.lakebreeze.com	Duluth	MN	55804	218-525-6808	525-2986
Lutsen Resort 5700 W Hwy 61 PO Box 9 *TF:* 800-258-8736 ■ *Web:* www.lutsenresort.com	Lutsen	MN	55612	218-663-7212	663-0145
Madden's on Gull Lake 11266 Pine Beach Peninsula *TF:* 800-642-5363 ■ *Web:* www.maddens.com	Brainerd	MN	56401	218-829-2811	829-6583
Ruttger's Bay Lake Lodge 25039 Tame Fish Lk Rd PO Box 400 *TF:* 800-450-4545 ■ *Web:* www.ruttgers.com	Deerwood	MN	56444	218-678-2885	678-2864
Superior Shores Resort 1521 Superior Shores Dr *TF:* 800-242-1988 ■ *Web:* www.superiorshores.com	Two Harbors	MN	55616	218-834-5671	834-5677

Mississippi

	City	State	ZIP	Phone	Fax
Beau Rivage Resort & Casino 875 Beach Blvd *TF:* 888-750-7111 ■ *Web:* www.beaurivage.com	Biloxi	MS	39530	228-386-7111	386-7414
Gulf Hills Hotel 13701 Paso Rd *TF:* 866-875-4211 ■ *Web:* www.gulfhillshotel.com	Ocean Springs	MS	39564	228-875-4211	875-4213
IP Casino Resort & Spa 850 Bayview Ave *TF Resv:* 888-946-2847 ■ *Web:* www.ipbiloxi.com	Biloxi	MS	39530	228-436-3000	432-3260
Treasure Bay Casino & Hotel 1980 Beach Blvd *TF General:* 800-747-2839 ■ *Web:* www.treasurebay.com	Biloxi	MS	39531	228-385-6000	385-6082

Missouri

	City	State	ZIP	Phone	Fax
Big Cedar Lodge 612 Devil's Pool Rd *Web:* www.big-cedar.com	Ridgedale	MO	65739	417-335-2777	335-2340
Dogwood Hills Golf Resort 1252 State Hwy KK *TF:* 800-220-6571 ■ *Web:* www.dogwoodhillsresort.com	Osage Beach	MO	65065	573-348-1735	348-0014
Indian Point Resort 71 Dogwood Pk Trl *TF:* 800-888-1891 ■ *Web:* www.indianpoint.com	Branson	MO	65616	417-338-2250	338-3507
Lilleys' Landing Resort 367 River Ln *TF:* 866-545-5397 ■ *Web:* www.lilleyslanding.com	Branson	MO	65616	417-334-6380	334-6311
Lodge of Four Seasons 315 Four Seasons Dr PO Box 215 *TF Resv:* 888-265-5500 ■ *Web:* www.4seasonsresort.com	Lake Ozark	MO	65049	573-365-3000	
Peak Resorts 17409 Hidden Vly Dr *Web:* www.peakresorts.com	Wildwood	MO	63025	636-938-7474	549-0064
Resort at Port Arrowhead, The 3080 Bagnell Dam Blvd PO Box 1930 *TF:* 800-532-3575 ■ *Web:* theresortatportarrowhead.com	Lake Ozark	MO	65049	573-365-2334	365-6887
Tan-Tar-A Resort Golf Club & Spa 494 Tantara Dr PO Box 188TT *TF Resv:* 800-826-8272 ■ *Web:* www.tan-tar-a.com	Osage Beach	MO	65065	573-348-3131	348-3206
Thousand Hills Golf Resort 245 S Wildwood Dr *TF:* 877-262-0430 ■ *Web:* www.thousandhills.com	Branson	MO	65616	417-336-5873	337-5740
Welk Resort Branson 1984 State Hwy 165 *TF:* 800-505-9355 ■ *Web:* welkresorts.com	Branson	MO	65616	417-336-3575	336-3165

Montana

Name / Address	City	State	Zip	Phone	Fax
Big Sky Resort One Lone Mtn Trl PO Box 160001 *TF:* 800-548-4486 ■ *Web:* www.bigskyresort.com	Big Sky	MT	59716	406-995-5000	995-5001
Fairmont Hot Springs Resort 1500 Fairmont Rd *TF:* 800-332-3272 ■ *Web:* www.fairmontmontana.com	Fairmont	MT	59711	406-797-3241	797-3337
Glacier Park Inc PO Box 2025 *Web:* www.glacierparkinc.com	Columbia Falls	MT	59912	406-892-2525	892-1375
Meadow Lake Resort 100 St Andrews Dr *TF:* 800-321-4653 ■ *Web:* www.meadowlake.com	Columbia Falls	MT	59912	406-892-8700	892-8731
Rock Creek Resort 6380 US Hwy 212 *TF:* 800-667-1119 ■ *Web:* www.rockcreekresort.com	Red Lodge	MT	59068	406-446-1111	237-9851
Triple Creek Ranch 5551 W Fork Rd *TF:* 800-654-2943 ■ *Web:* www.triplecreekranch.com	Darby	MT	59829	406-821-4600	821-4666

Nebraska

Name / Address	City	State	Zip	Phone	Fax
Radisson Palm Beach Shores Resort & Vacation Villas 11340 Blondo S Ste 100 *TF:* 800-615-7253 ■ *Web:* www.radisson.com	Omaha	NE	68164	800-615-7253	

Nevada

Name / Address	City	State	Zip	Phone	Fax
Alexis Park Resort 375 E Harmon Ave *TF:* 800-582-2228 ■ *Web:* www.alexispark.com	Las Vegas	NV	89169	702-796-3300	796-4334
Aquarius Casino Resort 1900 S Casino Dr *TF:* 888-662-5825 ■ *Web:* www.aquariuscasinoresort.com	Laughlin	NV	89029	702-298-5111	
Atlantis Casino Resort 3800 S Virginia St *TF:* 800-723-6500 ■ *Web:* www.atlantiscasino.com	Reno	NV	89502	775-825-4700	332-2211
Bellagio Hotel & Casino 3600 Las Vegas Blvd S *TF:* 888-987-7111 ■ *Web:* www.bellagio.com	Las Vegas	NV	89109	702-693-7111	693-8585
Casablanca Resort 950 W Mesquite Blvd *TF:* 800-459-7529 ■ *Web:* www.casablancaresort.com	Mesquite	NV	89027	702-346-7529	346-6888
Club Cal Neva Hotel Casino, The 38 E Second St PO Box 2071 *TF:* 877-777-7303 ■ *Web:* www.clubcalneva.com	Reno	NV	89501	775-323-1046	335-2614
Don Laughlin's Riverside Resort & Casino 1650 Casino Dr *TF:* 800-227-3849 ■ *Web:* www.riversideresort.com	Laughlin	NV	89029	702-298-2535	298-2695
Golden Nugget Hotel 129 E Fremont St *TF:* 800-634-3454 ■ *Web:* www.goldennugget.com	Las Vegas	NV	89101	702-385-7111	385-7111
Golden Nugget Laughlin 2300 S Casino Dr *TF:* 800-950-7700 ■ *Web:* www.goldennugget.com	Laughlin	NV	89029	702-298-7111	298-3023
Grand Sierra Resort & Casino 2500 E Second St *TF:* 800-501-2651 ■ *Web:* www.grandsierraresort.com	Reno	NV	89595	775-789-2000	789-2130
Hard Rock Hotel & Casino 4455 Paradise Rd *TF:* 800-693-7625 ■ *Web:* www.hardrockhotel.com	Las Vegas	NV	89169	702-693-5000	693-5331
John Ascuaga's Nugget Hotel Casino 1100 Nugget Ave **Fax:* Resv ■ *TF:* 800-648-1177 ■ *Web:* www.janugget.com	Sparks	NV	89431	775-356-3300	356-3434*
JW Marriott Resort Las Vegas 221 N Rampart Blvd *TF:* 877-869-8777 ■ *Web:* www.marriott.com	Las Vegas	NV	89144	702-869-7777	869-7339
Las Vegas Sands Corp 3355 Las Vegas Blvd S *NYSE: LVS* ■ *Web:* www.sands.com	Las Vegas	NV	89109	702-414-1000	414-4884
Mandalay Bay Resort & Casino 3950 Las Vegas Blvd S *TF:* 877-632-7800 ■ *Web:* www.mandalaybay.com	Las Vegas	NV	89119	702-632-7777	632-7234
MGM Grand Hotel & Casino 3799 Las Vegas Blvd S *TF:* 877-880-0880 ■ *Web:* www.mgmgrand.com	Las Vegas	NV	89109	702-891-1111	891-3036
Mirage, The 3400 Las Vegas Blvd S *TF:* 800-627-6667 ■ *Web:* www.mirage.com	Las Vegas	NV	89109	702-791-7111	791-7414
Monarch Casino & Resort Inc 3800 S Virginia St *NASDAQ: MCRI* ■ *Web:* www.monarchcasino.com	Reno	NV	89502	775-335-4600	332-9171
Monte Carlo Resort & Casino 3770 Las Vegas Blvd S *TF:* 800-311-8999 ■ *Web:* www.montecarlo.com	Las Vegas	NV	89109	702-730-7777	730-7200
Planet Hollywood Resort & Casino 3667 Las Vegas Blvd S *TF:* 866-919-7472 ■ *Web:* www.planethollywoodresort.com	Las Vegas	NV	89109	702-785-5555	785-5080
Primm Valley Resort & Casino 31900 S Las Vegas Blvd **Fax Area Code:* 702 ■ *TF:* 800-926-4455 ■ *Web:* www.primmvalleyresorts.com	Primm	NV	89019	800-926-4455	679-5424*
Ridge Tahoe 400 Ridge Club Dr PO Box 5790 *TF:* 800-334-1600 ■ *Web:* www.ridgetahoeresort.com	Stateline	NV	89449	775-588-3553	588-1551
Riviera Hotel & Casino 2901 Las Vegas Blvd S **Fax Area Code:* 800 ■ *TF Resv:* 866-275-6030 ■ *Web:* www.rivierahotel.com	Las Vegas	NV	89109	702-734-5110	232-9236*
Treasure Island Hotel & Casino 3300 Las Vegas Blvd S *TF:* 800-288-7206 ■ *Web:* www.treasureisland.com	Las Vegas	NV	89109	702-894-7111	894-7414
Tropicana Resort & Casino 3801 Las Vegas Blvd S *TF Resv:* 800-462-8767 ■ *Web:* www.troplv.com	Las Vegas	NV	89109	702-739-2222	739-3648
Venetian Resort Hotel & Casino 3355 Las Vegas Blvd S *TF:* 866-659-9643 ■ *Web:* www.venetian.com	Las Vegas	NV	89109	702-414-1000	414-1100

New Hampshire

Name / Address	City	State	Zip	Phone	Fax
Cranmore Mountain Resort One Skimobile Rd PO Box 1640 *TF:* 800-786-6754 ■ *Web:* www.cranmore.com	North Conway	NH	03860	603-356-5543	356-8526
Margate on Winnipesaukee, The 76 Lake St *Web:* www.themargate.com	Laconia	NH	03246	603-524-5210	
Mount Washington Hotel & Resort Rt 302 *TF:* 800-314-1752 ■ *Web:* www.brettonwoods.com	Bretton Woods	NH	03575	603-278-1000	278-8828
Waterville Valley Resort One Ski Area Rd PO Box 540 *TF:* 800-468-2553 ■ *Web:* www.waterville.com	Waterville Valley	NH	03215	603-236-8311	236-4344
White Mountain Hotel & Resort 2560 W Side Rd PO Box 1828 *TF:* 800-533-6301 ■ *Web:* www.whitemountainhotel.com	North Conway	NH	03860	603-356-7100	356-7100

New Jersey

Name / Address	City	State	Zip	Phone	Fax
Bally's Atlantic City 1900 Pacific Ave *TF:* 800-772-7777 ■ *Web:* www.ballysac.com	Atlantic City	NJ	08401	609-340-2000	
Caesars Atlantic City Hotel Casino 2100 Pacific Ave *TF:* 800-522-4700 ■ *Web:* www.totalrewards.com	Atlantic City	NJ	08401	609-348-4411	343-2405
Dolce International 28 W Grand Ave *Web:* www.dolce.com	Montvale	NJ	07645	201-307-8700	307-8837
Montreal Inn Beach Dr & Madison Ave *TF:* 800-525-7011 ■ *Web:* montrealbeachresort.com/	Cape May	NJ	08204	609-884-7011	884-4559
Mountain Creek Resort 200 Rt 94 *Web:* mountaincreek.com/	Vernon	NJ	07462	973-827-2000	
Ocean Place Resort & Spa One Ocean Blvd *TF:* 800-411-6493 ■ *Web:* www.oceanplace.com	Long Branch	NJ	07740	732-571-4000	
Resorts Casino Hotel 1133 Boardwalk *TF:* 800-334-6378 ■ *Web:* www.resortsac.com	Atlantic City	NJ	08401	800-334-6378	
Tropicana Entertainment 2831 Boardwalk *OTC: TPCA* ■ **Fax Area Code:* 609 ■ *TF:* 800-843-8767 ■ *Web:* www.tropicana.net	Atlantic City	NJ	08401	800-843-8767	340-4457*
Trump Taj Mahal Casino Resort 1000 Boardwalk & Virginia Ave *TF:* 800-426-2537 ■ *Web:* www.trumptaj.com	Atlantic City	NJ	08401	609-449-1000	

New Mexico

Name / Address	City	State	Zip	Phone	Fax
Angel Fire Resort PO Box 130 **Fax Area Code:* 505 ■ *TF:* 800-633-7463 ■ *Web:* www.angelfireresort.com	Angel Fire	NM	87710	575-377-6401	377-4200*
Inn of the Mountain Gods 287 Carrizo Canyon Rd *TF:* 800-545-9011 ■ *Web:* www.innofthemountaingods.com	Mescalero	NM	88340	800-545-9011	
La Posada de Santa Fe Resort & Spa 330 E Palace Ave **Fax Area Code:* 970 ■ *TF:* 866-280-3810 ■ *Web:* rockresorts.com	Santa Fe	NM	87501	505-986-0000	476-7425*
Lifts West Condominium Resort Hotel PO Box 330 *TF:* 800-221-1859 ■ *Web:* www.redrivernm.com/liftswest	Red River	NM	87558	505-754-2778	754-6617

New York

Name / Address	City	State	Zip	Phone	Fax
Bonnie Castle Resort 31 Holland St *TF:* 800-955-4511 ■ *Web:* www.bonniecastle.com	Alexandria Bay	NY	13607	315-482-4511	482-9600
Canoe Island Lodge 3820 Lakeshore Dr *Web:* www.canoeislandlodge.com	Diamond Point	NY	12824	518-668-5592	668-2012
Doral Arrowwood Conference Resort 975 Anderson Hill Rd **Fax Area Code:* 914 ■ *TF:* 844-211-0512 ■ *Web:* www.arrowwood.com	Rye Brook	NY	10573	844-214-5500	323-5500*
Gurney's Montauk Resort & Seawater Spa 290 Old Montauk Hwy *Web:* www.gurneysinn.com	Montauk	NY	11954	631-668-2345	
High Peaks Resort 2384 Saranac Ave *TF:* 800-755-5598 ■ *Web:* highpeaksresort.com	Lake Placid	NY	12946	518-523-4411	523-1120
Holiday Valley Resort Rt 219 PO Box 370 *TF:* 800-323-0020 ■ *Web:* www.holidayvalley.com	Ellicottville	NY	14731	716-699-2345	699-5204
Mohonk Mountain House 1000 Mtn Rest Rd *TF:* 800-772-6646 ■ *Web:* www.mohonk.com	New Paltz	NY	12561	845-255-1000	256-2161
Montauk Yacht Club Resort & Marina 32 Star Island Rd *TF:* 888-692-8668 ■ *Web:* www.montaukyachtclub.com	Montauk	NY	11954	631-668-3100	668-6181
Otesaga, The 60 Lake St *TF:* 800-348-6222 ■ *Web:* www.otesaga.com	Cooperstown	NY	13326	607-547-9931	547-9675
Peek 'n Peak Resort 1405 Olde Rd PO Box 360 *Web:* www.pknpk.com	Findley Lake	NY	14736	716-355-4141	355-4542
Point, The PO Box 1327 *TF:* 800-255-3530 ■ *Web:* thepointsaranac.com	Saranac Lake	NY	12983	518-891-5674	891-1152
Roaring Brook Ranch & Tennis Resort Rte 9N S *TF:* 800-882-7665 ■ *Web:* www.roaringbrookranch.com	Lake George	NY	12845	518-668-5767	
Rocking Horse Ranch Resort 600 Rt 44-55 *TF:* 800-647-2624 ■ *Web:* www.rockinghorseranch.com	Highland	NY	12528	845-691-2927	691-6434
Sagamore, The 110 Sagamore Rd *TF:* 866-384-1944 ■ *Web:* www.thesagamore.com	Bolton Landing	NY	12814	518-644-9400	743-6036
Starwood Hotels & Resorts Worldwide Inc *Saint Regis Hotels & Resorts* 1111 Westchester Ave *TF:* 888-625-4988 ■ *Web:* www.starwoodhotels.com	White Plains	NY	10604	914-640-8100	640-8310
Villa Roma Resort & Conference Ctr 356 Villa Roma Rd *TF:* 800-533-6767 ■ *Web:* www.villaroma.com	Callicoon	NY	12723	845-887-4880	887-4824
Whiteface Club & Resort 373 Whiteface Inn Ln *TF:* 800-422-6757 ■ *Web:* www.whitefaceclubresort.com	Lake Placid	NY	12946	518-523-2551	523-4278
Woodcliff Hotel & Spa 199 Woodcliff Dr *TF:* 800-365-3065 ■ *Web:* www.woodcliffhotelspa.com	Fairport	NY	14450	585-381-4000	381-2673

North Carolina

Phone *Fax*

Ballantyne Resort Hotel
10000 Ballantyne Commons Pkwy .... Charlotte NC 28277 704-248-4000 248-4005
TF: 866-248-4824 ■ *Web:* www.theballantynehotel.com

Eseeola Lodge, The
175 Linville Ave PO Box 99 .... Linville NC 28646 828-733-4311
TF: 800-742-6717 ■ *Web:* www.eseeola.com

Fontana Village Resort
300 Woods Rd PO Box 68 .... Fontana Dam NC 28733 828-498-2211
TF: 800-849-2258 ■ *Web:* fontanavillage.com

Grove Park Inn Resort & Spa 290 Macon Ave......... Asheville NC 28804 828-252-2711 253-7053
TF: 800-438-5800 ■ *Web:* www.groveparkinn.com

High Hampton Inn & Country Club
1525 Hwy 107 S................................. Cashiers NC 28717 828-743-2450 743-5991
TF: 800-334-2551 ■ *Web:* www.highhamptoninn.com

Holiday Inn SunSpree Resort Wrightsville Beach
1706 N Lumina Ave .... Wrightsville Beach NC 28480 910-256-2231
TF: 888-211-9874 ■ *Web:* www.ihg.com

Hound Ears Lodge & Club 328 Shulls Mill Rd........... Boone NC 28607 828-963-4321 963-8030
Web: www.houndears.com

Maggie Valley Resort & Country Club
1819 Country Club Dr .... Maggie Valley NC 28751 828-926-1616 926-2906
TF: 800-438-3861 ■ *Web:* www.maggievalleyclub.com

Mid Pines Inn & Golf Club
1010 Midland Rd .... Southern Pines NC 28387 910-692-2114 692-5349
TF: 800-747-7272 ■ *Web:* www.pineneedles-midpines.com

Pine Needles Lodge & Golf Club
PO Box 88 .... Southern Pines NC 28388 910-692-7111 692-5349
TF: 800-747-7272 ■ *Web:* www.pineneedles-midpines.com

Pinehurst Resort & Country Club
80 Carolina Vista Dr.............................Pinehurst NC 28374 910-295-6811 295-8466
TF: 800-487-4653 ■ *Web:* www.pinehurst.com

Pinnacle Inn Resort
301 Pinnacle Inn Rd........................ Beech Mountain NC 28604 828-387-2231
TF: 800-405-7888 ■ *Web:* www.pinnacleinn.com

Sanderling Resort & Spa 1461 Duck Rd................ Duck NC 27949 252-261-4111 261-1638
TF: 800-701-4111 ■ *Web:* www.sanderling-resort.com

Waynesville Inn Golf & Country Club, The
176 Country Club Dr ....Waynesville NC 28786 828-456-3551 456-3555
TF: 800-627-6250 ■ *Web:* www.thewaynesvilleinn.com

Wolf Ridge Ski Resort 578 Vly View Cir.............. Mars Hill NC 28754 828-689-4111 689-9819
TF: 800-817-4111 ■ *Web:* www.skiwolfridgenc.com

North Dakota

Phone *Fax*

Prairie Knights Casino & Resort
7932 Hwy 24 .... Fort Yates ND 58538 701-854-7777 854-7786
TF: 800-425-8277 ■ *Web:* www.prairieknights.com

Nova Scotia

Phone *Fax*

Atlantica Hotel & Marina Oak Island
36 Treasure Dr PO Box 6 ....Western Shore NS B0J3M0 902-627-2600 627-2020
TF: 800-565-5075 ■ *Web:* www.atlanticaoakisland.com

Pines Resort, The 103 Shore Rd PO Box 70.............Digby NS B0V1A0 902-245-2511 245-6133
TF: 800-667-4637 ■ *Web:* digbypines.ca

Ohio

Phone *Fax*

Atwood Lake Resort 2650 Lodge Rd ....Sherrodsville OH 44675 330-735-2211
Web: www.atwoodresort.com

Glenmoor Country Club 4191 Glenmoor Rd.............Canton OH 44718 330-966-3600 966-3611
Web: www.glenmoorcc.com

Hueston Woods Lodge & Conference Ctr
5201 Lodge Rd............................ College Corner OH 45003 513-664-3500 523-1522
Web: huestonwoodslodge.com

Quail Hollow Resort
11080 Concord-Hambden Rd......................Painesville OH 44077 440-497-1100 350-3594
Web: www.quailhollowresort.com

Sawmill Creek Resort 400 Sawmill Creek Dr............ Huron OH 44839 419-433-3800 433-7610
TF: 800-729-6455 ■ *Web:* www.sawmillcreekresort.com

Oklahoma

Phone *Fax*

Cherokee Casino & Resort 777 W Cherokee St ....Catoosa OK 74015 800-760-6700
TF: 800-760-6700 ■ *Web:* www.cherokeestarrewards.com

Fin & Feather Resort Inc 445889 Hwy 10-A .... Gore OK 74435 918-487-5148 487-5025
Web: finandfeather.publishpath.com/

Lake Murray Resort Park 3323 Lodge Rd .... Ardmore OK 73401 580-223-6600 326-2670
TF: 800-622-6317 ■ *Web:* www.travelok.com

Quartz Mountain Resort & Conference Ctr
22469 Lodge Rd................................ Lone Wolf OK 73655 580-563-2424 563-2422
TF: 877-999-5567 ■ *Web:* www.quartzmountainresort.com

Ontario

Phone *Fax*

Deerhurst Resort 1235 Deerhurst Dr................ Huntsville ON P1H2E8 705-789-6411 789-2431
TF Sales: 800-461-6522 ■ *Web:* www.deerhurstresort.com

Delta Meadowvale 6750 Mississauga Rd.......... Mississauga ON L5N2L3 905-821-1981 542-4036
TF: 800-422-8238 ■ *Web:* www.deltahotels.com

Fallsview Casino Resort
6380 Fallsview Blvd .... Niagara Falls ON L2G7X5 888-325-5788 371-7952*
**Fax Area Code:* 905 ■ *TF:* 888-325-5788 ■ *Web:* www.fallsviewcasinoresort.com

Phone *Fax*

Pinestone Resort 4252 County Rd Ste 21............Haliburton ON K0M1S0 705-457-1800 457-1783
TF: 800-461-0357 ■ *Web:* www.pinestone-resort.com

Oregon

Phone *Fax*

Black Butte Ranch
12930 Hawks BeaRd Rd PO Box 8000 .... Black Butte Ranch OR 97759 541-595-1252 595-2077
TF: 866-901-2961 ■ *Web:* www.blackbutteranch.com

Gearhart By the Sea 1157 N Marion Ave ....Gearhart OR 97138 503-738-8331 738-0881
TF: 800-547-0115 ■ *Web:* www.gearhartresort.com

Mount Bachelor Village Resort & Conference Ctr
19717 Mt Bachelor Dr .... Bend OR 97702 541-389-5900 388-7401
TF: 800-547-5204 ■ *Web:* www.mtbachelorvillage.com

Resort at the Mountain 68010 E Fairway Ave ....Welches OR 97067 503-622-3101 622-2222
TF: 877-439-6774 ■ *Web:* www.theresort.com

Salishan Lodge & Golf Resort
PO Box 118 ....Gleneden Beach OR 97388 800-452-2300 764-3681*
**Fax Area Code:* 541 ■ *TF:* 800-452-2300 ■ *Web:* www.salishan.com

Seventh Mountain Resort 18575 SW Century Dr .... Bend OR 97702 541-382-8711 382-3517
TF: 800-452-6810 ■ *Web:* www.seventhmountain.com

Sunriver Resort 17600 Ctr Dr PO Box 3609 ....Sunriver OR 97707 541-593-1000
TF: 800-547-3922 ■ *Web:* www.sunriver-resort.com

Timberline Lodge
27500 E Timberline Rd.....................Government Camp OR 97028 503-272-3311
TF: 800-547-1406 ■ *Web:* www.timberlinelodge.com

Village Green Resort & Gardens
725 Row River Rd............................ Cottage Grove OR 97424 541-942-2491 942-2386
TF: 800-343-7666 ■ *Web:* www.villagegreenresortandgardens.com

Pennsylvania

Phone *Fax*

Allenberry Resort
1559 Boiling Springs Rd ....Boiling Springs PA 17007 717-258-3211 960-5280
TF: 800-430-5468 ■ *Web:* www.allenberry.com

Carroll Valley Golf Resort
78 Country Club Trail..........................Carroll Valley PA 17320 717-642-8282 642-6534
TF: 855-784-0330 ■ *Web:* libertymountainresort.com

Cove Haven Pocono Palace
5222 Milford Rd............................East Stroudsburg PA 18302 800-432-9932 226-6982*
**Fax Area Code:* 570 ■ *TF:* 877-822-3333 ■ *Web:* www.covepoconoresorts.com

Felicita Resort 2201 Fishing Creek Vly Rd...........Harrisburg PA 17112 717-599-5301
Web: www.felicitaresort.com

Fernwood Resort 5785 Milford Rd ....East Stroudsburg PA 18302 888-337-6966 588-7112*
**Fax Area Code:* 570 ■ *TF:* 888-337-6966 ■ *Web:* fernwoodresortpoconos.com

Heritage Hills Golf Resort & Conference Ctr
2700 Mt Rose Ave..York PA 17402 717-755-0123 812-9303
TF: 877-782-9752 ■ *Web:* www.heritagehillsresort.com

Hershey Entertainment & Resorts Co
27 W Chocolate Ave ....Hershey PA 17033 800-437-7439 534-3324*
**Fax Area Code:* 717 ■ *TF:* 800-437-7439 ■ *Web:* www.hersheypa.com

Hidden Valley Resort & Conference Ctr
1 Craighead Dr PO Box 4420 .... Hidden Valley PA 15502 814-443-8000 443-8254
TF: 800-452-2223 ■ *Web:* www.hiddenvalleyresort.com

Hotel Hershey, The 100 Hotel Rd ....Hershey PA 17033 717-533-2171 534-8887
TF: 800-437-7439 ■ *Web:* www.thehotelhershey.com

Lancaster Host Resort 2300 Lincoln Hwy E...........Lancaster PA 17602 717-299-5500 295-5104
TF Resv: 800-233-0121 ■ *Web:* www.lancasterhost.com

Liberty Mountain Resort & Conference Ctr
78 Country Club Trl ....Carroll Valley PA 17320 717-642-8282
Web: www.libertymountainresort.com

Mountain Laurel Resort & Spa
Rt 940 PO Box 9.............................. White Haven PA 18661 570-443-8411 443-5518
TF: 888-243-9300 ■ *Web:* www.mountainlaurelresort.com

Nemacolin Woodlands Resort & Spa
1001 Lafayette Dr............................. Farmington PA 15437 724-329-8555 329-6198
TF: 800-422-2736 ■ *Web:* www.nemacolin.com

Pocono Manor Golf Resort & Spa
one Manor Dr Rt 314 ....Pocono Manor PA 18349 570-839-7111 839-3407
TF: 800-233-8150 ■ *Web:* www.poconomanor.com

Seven Springs Mountain Resort
777 Waterwheel Dr............................... Champion PA 15622 814-352-7777
TF: 800-452-2223 ■ *Web:* www.7springs.com

Skytop Lodge One Skytop...........................Skytop PA 18357 570-595-7401 595-9618
TF: 800-345-7759 ■ *Web:* www.skytop.com

Split Rock Resort 100 Moseywood Rd ....Lake Harmony PA 18624 570-722-9111 722-8831
TF: 800-255-7625 ■ *Web:* www.splitrockresort.com

Tamiment Resort & Conference Ctr
Bushkill Falls Rd................................Tamiment PA 18371 570-588-6652 588-9800
Web: worldgolf.com

Willow Valley Resort & Conference Ctr
2400 Willow St Pike ....Lancaster PA 17602 717-464-2711 464-4784
TF: 800-444-1714 ■ *Web:* www.willowvalley.com

Woodlands Inn, The 1073 Hwy 315.............. Wilkes-Barre PA 18702 570-824-9831 824-8865
TF: 844-779-8472 ■ *Web:* ascendcollection.com

Puerto Rico

Phone *Fax*

Caribe Hilton One San Geronimo St.................San Juan PR 00901 787-721-0303 725-8849
Web: www.caribehilton.com

El Conquistador Resort & Golden Door Spa
1000 El Conquistador Ave .... Fajardo PR 00738 787-863-1000 863-6500
TF Resv: 888-543-1282 ■ *Web:* www.elconresort.com

Las Casitas Village & Golden Door Spa
1000 El Conquistador Ave .... Fajardo PR 00738 787-863-1000 863-6831
Web: www.lascasitasvillage.com

Ritz-Carlton San Juan, The
6961 Ave of the Governors Isla Verde..................Carolina PR 00979 787-253-1700 253-1777
TF: 800-241-3333 ■ *Web:* www.ritzcarlton.com/en/properties/sanjuan

Quebec

				Phone	Fax
Fairmont Le Chateau Montebello 392 Notre Dame St *TF:* 800-441-1414 ■ *Web:* www.fairmont.com	Montebello	QC	J0V1L0	819-423-6341	423-1133
Hotel Cheribourg 2603 Ch du Parc *TF:* 877-845-5344 ■ *Web:* www.hotelsvillegia.com	Orford	QC	J1X8C8	819-843-3308	843-2639
Hotel du Lac 121 Rue Cuttle *TF:* 800-567-8341 ■ *Web:* www.clubtremblant.com	Mont-Tremblant	QC	J8E1B9	819-425-2731	425-5617
Manoir du Lac Delage 40 Ave du Lac *TF:* 888-202-3242 ■ *Web:* www.lacdelage.com	Lac Delage	QC	G3C5C4	418-848-2551	848-1352
Westin Resort Tremblant 100 Ch Kandahar *TF:* 800-937-8461 ■ *Web:* www.westintremblant.com	Mont-Tremblant	QC	J8E1E2	819-681-8000	

Rhode Island

				Phone	Fax
Castle Hill Inn & Resort 590 Ocean Dr. *TF:* 888-466-1355 ■ *Web:* www.castlehillinn.com	Newport	RI	02840	401-849-3800	849-3838
Inn on Long Wharf Five Washington St *Web:* extraholidays.com	Newport	RI	02840	401-847-7800	845-0127

South Carolina

				Phone	Fax
Barefoot Resort & Golf 4980 Barefoot Resort Bridge Rd *TF:* 866-638-4818 ■ *Web:* www.barefootgolf.com	North Myrtle Beach	SC	29582	843-390-3200	390-3213
Bay Watch Resort & Conference Ctr 2701 S Ocean Blvd *TF:* 866-270-2172 ■ *Web:* oceanaresorts.com	North Myrtle Beach	SC	29582	843-272-4600	
Beach Colony Resort 5308 N Ocean Blvd. *TF General:* 800-222-2141 ■ *Web:* www.beachcolony.com	Myrtle Beach	SC	29577	843-449-4010	449-2810
Bluewater Resort 2001 S Ocean Blvd. *TF:* 800-845-6994 ■ *Web:* www.bluewaterresort.com	Myrtle Beach	SC	29577	843-626-8345	448-2310
Breakers Resort 3002 N Ocean Blvd. *TF:* 800-952-4507 ■ *Web:* www.breakers.com	Myrtle Beach	SC	29577	843-448-8082	626-5001
Caravelle Resort Hotel & Villas 6900 N Ocean Blvd. *TF:* 800-507-9145 ■ *Web:* www.thecaravelle.com	Myrtle Beach	SC	29572	843-918-8000	918-8199
Caribbean Resort & Villas 3000 N Ocean Blvd. *TF:* 800-552-8509 ■ *Web:* www.caribbeanresort.com	Myrtle Beach	SC	29577	800-552-8509	
Compass Cove Ocean Resort 2311 S Ocean Blvd *TF:* 800-331-0934 ■ *Web:* www.compasscove.com	Myrtle Beach	SC	29577	843-448-8373	448-5444
Coral Beach Resort & Suites 1105 S Ocean Blvd. **Fax Area Code:* 843 ■ *TF:* 800-843-2684 ■ *Web:* www.coralbeachmyrtlebeachresort.com	Myrtle Beach	SC	29577	800-556-1754	626-0156*
Disney's Hilton Head Island Resort 22 Harborside Ln *Web:* www.disneyvacationclub.disney.go.com	Hilton Head Island	SC	29928	843-341-4100	341-4130
Hilton Charleston Harbor Resort & Marina 20 Patriots Pt Rd. *Web:* www.charlestonharborresort.com	Mount Pleasant	SC	29464	843-856-0028	856-8333
Hilton Head Island Beach & Tennis Resort 40 Folly Field Rd *Web:* www.hhibeachandtennis.com	Hilton Head Island	SC	29928	843-842-4402	842-3323
Hilton Myrtle Beach Resort 10000 Beach Club Dr *TF:* 800-445-8667 ■ *Web:* www.hilton.com	Myrtle Beach	SC	29572	843-449-5000	497-0168
Holiday Inn Oceanfront at Surfside Beach 1601 N Ocean Blvd. *TF Resv:* 866-661-5139 ■ *Web:* www.ihg.com	Surfside Beach	SC	29575	843-238-5601	238-4758
Kiawah Island Golf Resort One Sancturay Beach Dr **Fax:* Resv ■ *TF Resv:* 800-654-2924 ■ *Web:* www.kiawahresort.com/golf	Kiawah Island	SC	29455	843-768-2121	768-2736*
Litchfield Beach & Golf Resort 14276 Ocean Hwy. *TF:* 888-766-4633 ■ *Web:* www.litchfieldbeach.com	Pawleys Island	SC	29585	843-237-3000	237-3282
Myrtle Beach Marriott Resort at Grande Dunes 8400 Costa Verde Dr. *Web:* www.marriott.com	Myrtle Beach	SC	29572	843-449-8880	449-8669
Myrtle Beach Resort Vacations 5905 S Kings Hwy PO Box 3936 *TF:* 888-627-3767 ■ *Web:* www.myrtle-beach-resort.com	Myrtle Beach	SC	29578	843-238-1559	238-2424
Mystic Sea Resort 2105 S Ocean Blvd *TF:* 800-443-7050 ■ *Web:* www.mysticsea.com	Myrtle Beach	SC	29577	843-448-8446	626-2024
Ocean Reef Resort 7100 N Ocean Blvd. *TF:* 888-322-6411 ■ *Web:* www.oceanreefmyrtlebeach.com	Myrtle Beach	SC	29572	843-449-4441	497-3041
Palmetto Dunes Resort 4 Queen Folly Rd *TF:* 866-380-1778 ■ *Web:* www.palmettodunes.com	Hilton Head Island	SC	29928	866-380-1778	
Palms Resort 2500 N Ocean Blvd. *TF:* 800-300-1198 ■ *Web:* www.palmsresort.com	Myrtle Beach	SC	29577	843-626-8334	448-1950
Patricia Grand Resort 2710 N Ocean Blvd. *TF:* 800-255-4763 ■ *Web:* www.oceanaresorts.com	Myrtle Beach	SC	29577	843-448-8453	448-3080
Pawleys Plantation 70 Tanglewood Dr. *TF:* 800-367-9959 ■ *Web:* www.pawleysplantation.com	Pawleys Island	SC	29585	843-237-6000	
Player's Club Resort 35 Deallyon Ave *TF:* 800-497-7529 ■ *Web:* spinnakerresorts.com	Hilton Head Island	SC	29928	843-785-3355	785-9185
Reef Resort 2101 S Ocean Blvd *TF Cust Svc:* 800-845-1212 ■ *Web:* www.reefmyrtlebeach.com	Myrtle Beach	SC	29577	843-448-1765	626-9971
Resort at Seabrook Island 3772 Seabrook Island Rd *Web:* www.discoverseabrook.com	Seabrook Island	SC	29455	843-768-2500	768-7524
Sand Dunes Resort Hotel 201 74th Ave N *TF:* 800-726-3783 ■ *Web:* www.sandsresorts.com	Myrtle Beach	SC	29572	843-449-3313	449-5036
Sea Mist Resort 1200 S Ocean Blvd *TF:* 800-793-6507 ■ *Web:* www.myrtlebeachseamist.com	Myrtle Beach	SC	29577	843-448-1551	893-1108
Seacrest Oceanfront Resort on the South Beach 803 S Ocean Blvd. **Fax Area Code:* 843 ■ *TF:* 888-889-8113 ■ *Web:* www.myrtlebeach-resorts.com	Myrtle Beach	SC	29577	888-889-8113	913-5801*
Shore Crest Vacation Villas 4709 S Ocean Blvd *Web:* www.bluegreenrentals.com	North Myrtle Beach	SC	29582	843-361-3600	361-3601
Wild Dunes Resort 5757 Palm Blvd. *TF:* 800-845-8880 ■ *Web:* www.wilddunes.com	Isle of Palms	SC	29451	843-886-6000	886-2916
Wyndham Vacation Resorts King Cotton Villas One King Cotton Rd *TF:* 800-251-8736 ■ *Web:* www.wyndhamvacationresorts.com	Edisto Beach	SC	29438	843-869-2561	869-2384

South Dakota

				Phone	Fax
Spearfish Canyon Resort 10619 Roughlock Falls Rd *TF:* 877-975-6343 ■ *Web:* www.spfcanyon.com	Lead	SD	57754	605-584-3435	584-3990
Spring Creek Resort 28229 Spring Creek Pl. *Web:* www.springcreekventure.com	Pierre	SD	57501	605-224-8336	

Tennessee

				Phone	Fax
Brookside Resort 463 E Pkwy *TF:* 800-251-9597 ■ *Web:* brooksideresort.com	Gatlinburg	TN	37738	865-436-5611	436-0039

Texas

				Phone	Fax
Bahia Mar Resort & Conference Ctr 6300 Padre Blvd **Fax Area Code:* 956 ■ *Web:* pirentals.com	South Padre Island	TX	78597	800-926-6926	761-6287*
Columbia Lakes Resort & Conference Ctr 188 Freeman Blvd. *Web:* www.columbialakesgolf.com	West Columbia	TX	77486	979-345-5151	345-3049
Four Seasons Resort & Club Dallas at Las Colinas 4150 N MacArthur Blvd *TF:* 800-332-3442 ■ *Web:* www.fourseasons.com/dallas	Irving	TX	75038	972-717-0700	717-2550
Hilton Galveston Island Resort 5400 Seawall Blvd *TF:* 800-475-3386 ■ *Web:* www1.hilton.com	Galveston	TX	77551	409-744-5000	740-2209
Houstonian Hotel Club & Spa 111 N Post Oak Ln *TF Resv:* 800-231-2759 ■ *Web:* www.houstonian.com	Houston	TX	77024	713-680-2626	680-2992
Inn of the Hills River Resort 1001 Junction Hwy. *TF:* 800-292-5690 ■ *Web:* www.innofthehills.com	Kerrville	TX	78028	830-895-5000	895-6020
Omni Barton Creek Resort & Spa 8212 Barton Club Dr. *TF:* 800-336-6158 ■ *Web:* www.bartoncreek.com	Austin	TX	78735	512-329-4000	329-4597
Quorum Hotels & Resorts 5429 Lyndon B Johnson Fwy #625. *Web:* www.quorumhotels.com	Dallas	TX	75240	972-458-7265	991-5647
Rancho Viejo Resort & Country Club One Rancho Viejo Dr *TF:* 800-531-7400	Rancho Viejo	TX	78575	956-350-4000	350-5696
Rosewood Hotels & Resorts 500 Crescent Ct Ste 300. *TF:* 888-767-3966 ■ *Web:* www.rosewoodhotels.com	Dallas	TX	75201	214-880-4200	880-4201
San Luis Resort Spa & Conference Ctr 5222 Seawall Blvd *TF Cust Svc:* 800-445-0090 ■ *Web:* www.sanluisresort.com	Galveston Island	TX	77551	409-744-1500	744-8452
Silverleaf Resorts Inc 1221 Riverbend Dr Ste 120. *TF:* 800-613-0310 ■ *Web:* www.silverleafresorts.com	Dallas	TX	75247	214-631-1166	637-0585
South Shore Harbour Resort & Conference Ctr 2500 S Shore Blvd *TF Resv:* 800-442-5005 ■ *Web:* www.sshr.com	League City	TX	77573	281-334-1000	334-1157
Tanglewood Resort Hotel & Conference Ctr 290 Tanglewood Cir *TF:* 800-833-6569 ■ *Web:* www.tanglewoodresort.com	Pottsboro	TX	75076	903-786-2968	786-2128
Tapatio Springs Golf Resort & Conference Ctr One Resort Way *TF:* 800-999-3299 ■ *Web:* www.tapatio.com	Boerne	TX	78006	800-999-3299	

Utah

				Phone	Fax
Alta Lodge PO Box 8040 *TF Cust Svc:* 800-707-2582 ■ *Web:* www.altalodge.com	Alta	UT	84092	801-742-3500	742-3504
Canyons Resort, The 4000 The Canyons Resort Dr *TF:* 888-226-9667 ■ *Web:* www.thecanyons.com	Park City	UT	84098	435-649-5400	649-7374
Deer Valley Resort Lodging PO Box 889. *TF:* 800-558-3337 ■ *Web:* www.deervalley.com	Park City	UT	84060	435-645-6626	645-6538
Homestead Resort 700 N Homestead Dr **Fax Area Code:* 435 ■ *TF:* 888-327-7220 ■ *Web:* www.homesteadresort.com	Midway	UT	84049	888-327-7220	654-5087*
Little America Hotels & Resorts 500 S Main St. *TF:* 800-281-7899 ■ *Web:* www.littleamerica.com	Salt Lake City	UT	84101	801-596-5700	
Park City Mountain Resort (PCMR) 1345 Lowell Ave PO Box 39 *TF:* 800-222-7275 ■ *Web:* www.parkcitymountain.com	Park City	UT	84060	435-649-8111	647-5374
Rustler Lodge 10380 East Hwy 210 PO Box 8030 *TF:* 888-532-2582 ■ *Web:* www.rustlerlodge.com	Alta	UT	84092	801-742-2200	742-3832
Snowbasin Ski Resort 3925 E Snowbasin Rd *TF:* 888-437-5488 ■ *Web:* www.snowbasin.com	Huntsville	UT	84317	801-620-1100	620-1314

Resort	City	State	Zip	Phone	Fax
Snowbird Ski & Summer Resort Hwy 210 PO Box 929000 *TF:* 800-453-3000 ■ *Web:* www.snowbird.com	Snowbird	UT	84092	801-742-2222	947-8227
Solitude Ski Resort 12000 Big Cottonwood Canyon *TF:* 800-748-4754 ■ *Web:* www.skisolitude.com	Brighton	UT	84121	801-534-1400	517-7705
Stein Eriksen Lodge 7700 Stein Way *TF:* 800-453-1302 ■ *Web:* www.steinlodge.com	Park City	UT	84060	435-649-3700	649-5825

Vermont

Resort	City	State	Zip	Phone	Fax
Basin Harbor Club 4800 Basin Harbor Rd *TF:* 800-622-4000 ■ *Web:* www.basinharbor.com	Vergennes	VT	05491	802-475-2311	475-6545
Equinox, The 3567 Main St Rt 7A *TF:* 800-362-4747 ■ *Web:* www.equinoxresort.com	Manchester Village	VT	05254	802-362-4700	362-4861
Hawk Inn & Mountain Resort 75 Billings Rd *TF:* 800-685-4295 ■ *Web:* www.hawkresort.com	Plymouth	VT	05056	802-672-3811	672-5585
Inn at Stratton Mountain 5 Village Lodge Rd *TF:* 800-787-2886 ■ *Web:* www.stratton.com	Stratton Mountain	VT	05155	802-297-2500	297-4300
Jay Peak Resort 830 Jay Peak Rd *TF:* 800-451-4449 ■ *Web:* www.jaypeakresort.com	Jay	VT	05859	802-988-2611	988-4049
Killington Resort & Pico Mountain 228 E Mountain Rd *TF:* 800-621-6867 ■ *Web:* www.killington.com	Killington	VT	05751	802-422-6200	422-6113
Lake Morey Resort One Clubhouse Rd *TF:* 800-423-1211 ■ *Web:* www.lakemoreyresort.com	Fairlee	VT	05045	802-333-4311	333-4553
Smugglers' Notch Resort 4323 Vermont Rt 108 S *TF:* 800-451-8752 ■ *Web:* www.smuggs.com	Jeffersonville	VT	05464	802-644-8851	644-1230
Stowe Mountain Resort 5781 Mountain Rd *TF:* 800-253-4754 ■ *Web:* www.stowe.com	Stowe	VT	05672	802-253-3000	
Stoweflake Mountain Resort & Spa 1746 Mountain Rd PO Box 369 *TF:* 800-253-2232 ■ *Web:* www.stoweflake.com	Stowe	VT	05672	802-253-7355	253-6858
Sugarbush Resort & Inn 1840 Sugarbush Access Rd *TF:* 800-537-8427 ■ *Web:* www.sugarbush.com	Warren	VT	05674	802-583-6300	583-6390
Topnotch at Stowe Resort & Spa 4000 Mountain Rd **Fax Area Code:* 802 ■ *TF:* 800-451-8686 ■ *Web:* www.topnotchresort.com	Stowe	VT	05672	800-451-8686	253-9263*
Trapp Family Lodge 700 Trapp Hill Rd PO Box 1428 *TF:* 800-826-7000 ■ *Web:* www.trappfamily.com	Stowe	VT	05672	802-253-8511	
Woodstock Inn & Resort 14 The Green *TF:* 800-448-7900 ■ *Web:* www.woodstockinn.com	Woodstock	VT	05091	802-457-1100	457-6699

Virginia

Resort	City	State	Zip	Phone	Fax
Alamar Resort Inn 311 16th St *TF:* 800-346-5681 ■ *Web:* www.alamarresortinn.net	Virginia Beach	VA	23451	757-428-7582	
Boar's Head Inn 200 Ednam Dr *TF:* 800-476-1988 ■ *Web:* www.boarsheadinn.com	Charlottesville	VA	22903	434-296-2181	972-6024
Breakers Resort Inn 16th & Oceanfront *TF:* 800-237-7532 ■ *Web:* www.breakersresort.com	Virginia Beach	VA	23451	757-428-1821	422-9602
Cavalier Hotel 4201 Atlantic Ave *TF:* 800-446-8199 ■ *Web:* www.cavalierhotel.com	Virginia Beach	VA	23451	757-425-8555	
Crestline Hotels & Resorts 3950 University Dr Ste 301 *Web:* www.crestlinehotels.com	Fairfax	VA	22030	571-529-6100	529-6095
Great Wolf Lodge Williamsburg 549 E Rochambeau Dr *TF:* 800-551-9653 ■ *Web:* www.greatwolf.com	Williamsburg	VA	23188	757-229-9700	229-9780
Kingsmill Resort & Spa 1010 Kingsmill Rd *TF:* 800-832-5665 ■ *Web:* www.kingsmill.com	Williamsburg	VA	23185	757-253-1703	253-8246
Massanutten Resort 1822 Resort Dr *Web:* www.massresort.com	McGaheysville	VA	22840	540-289-9441	289-6981
OMNI HOMESTEAD RESORT, THE 7696 Sam Snead Hwy *TF:* 800-838-1766 ■ *Web:* www.thehomestead.com	Hot Springs	VA	24445	540-839-1766	
Shenvalee Golf Resort 9660 Fairway Dr PO Box 930 *TF:* 888-339-3181 ■ *Web:* www.shenvalee.com	New Market	VA	22844	540-740-3181	740-8931
Turtle Cay Resort 600 Atlantic Ave *TF:* 888-989-7788 ■ *Web:* www.vacationrentalsvabeach.com	Virginia Beach	VA	23451	757-437-5565	437-9104
Virginia Beach Resort Hotel & Conference Ctr 2800 Shore Dr *TF:* 800-468-2722 ■ *Web:* www.virginiabeachresort.com	Virginia Beach	VA	23451	757-481-9000	496-7429
Virginia Crossings Resort 1000 Virginia Ctr Pkwy *TF:* 888-444-6553 ■ *Web:* www.wyndhamvirginiacrossings.com	Glen Allen	VA	23059	804-727-1400	727-1690
Williamsburg Inn 136 E Francis St *TF:* 800-447-8679 ■ *Web:* www.colonialwilliamsburg.com	Williamsburg	VA	23185	757-229-1000	220-7096

Washington

Resort	City	State	Zip	Phone	Fax
Alderbrook Resort & Spa 7101 E SR-106 *TF:* 800-622-9370 ■ *Web:* www.alderbrookresort.com	Union	WA	98592	360-898-2200	898-4610
Campbell's Resort 104 W Woodin Ave PO Box 278 *TF:* 800-553-8225 ■ *Web:* www.campbellsresort.com	Chelan	WA	98816	509-682-2561	682-2177
Coast Hotels & Resorts USA 2003 Western Ave Ste 500 *Web:* www.coasthotels.com	Seattle	WA	98121	206-826-2700	826-2701
Desert Canyon Golf Resort 1201 Desert Canyon Blvd *TF:* 800-258-4173 ■ *Web:* www.desertcanyon.com	Orondo	WA	98843	509-784-1111	784-2701
Freestone Inn at Wilson Ranch 31 Early Winters Dr *TF:* 800-639-3809 ■ *Web:* www.freestoneinn.com	Mazama	WA	98833	509-996-3906	996-3907
Lake Quinault Lodge 345 S Shore Rd *TF:* 800-562-6672 ■ *Web:* www.olympicnationalparks.com	Quinault	WA	98575	360-288-2900	288-2901
Little Creek Casino Resort 91 W State Rt 108 *TF:* 800-667-7711 ■ *Web:* www.little-creek.com	Shelton	WA	98584	360-427-7711	427-7868
Polynesian Resort, The 615 Ocean Shores Blvd NW *TF:* 800-562-4836 ■ *Web:* www.thepolynesian.com	Ocean Shores	WA	98569	360-289-3361	289-0294
Resort Semiahmoo 9565 Semiahmoo Pkwy *TF:* 855-917-3767 ■ *Web:* www.semiahmoo.com	Blaine	WA	98230	360-318-2000	318-2087
Rosario Resort & Spa 1400 Rosario Rd *TF:* 800-562-8820 ■ *Web:* www.rosarioresort.com	Eastsound	WA	98245	360-376-2222	376-2289
Salish Lodge & Spa 6501 Railroad Ave DE PO Box 1109 *TF:* 800-272-5474 ■ *Web:* www.salishlodge.com	Snoqualmie	WA	98065	425-888-2556	888-9634
Sun Mountain Lodge 604 Patterson Lk Rd PO Box 1000 *TF:* 800-572-0493 ■ *Web:* www.sunmountainlodge.com	Winthrop	WA	98862	509-996-2211	996-3133

West Virginia

Resort	City	State	Zip	Phone	Fax
Canaan Valley Resort & Conference Ctr 230 Main Lodge Rd *TF:* 800-622-4121 ■ *Web:* www.canaanresort.com	Davis	WV	26260	304-866-4121	866-2172
Glade Springs Resort 255 Resort Dr *TF:* 866-562-8054 ■ *Web:* www.gladesprings.com	Daniels	WV	25832	866-562-8054	
Greenbrier, The 300 W Main St *TF:* 800-453-4858 ■ *Web:* www.greenbrier.com	White Sulphur Springs	WV	24986	304-536-1110	536-7854
Lakeview Golf Resort & Spa One Lakeview Dr *TF:* 800-624-8300 ■ *Web:* www.lakeviewresort.com	Morgantown	WV	26508	304-594-1111	
Oglebay Resort & Conference Ctr Rt 88 N Oglebay Pk *TF:* 800-624-6988 ■ *Web:* www.oglebay-resort.com	Wheeling	WV	26003	304-243-4000	243-4070
Pipestem Resort State Park PO Box 150 *Web:* www.pipestemresort.com	Pipestem	WV	25979	304-466-1800	466-2803
Snowshoe Mountain Resort 10 Snowshoe Dr *TF:* 877-441-4386 ■ *Web:* www.snowshoemtn.com	Snowshoe	WV	26209	304-572-1000	572-5407
Stonewall Resort 940 Resort Dr *TF:* 888-278-8150 ■ *Web:* www.stonewallresort.com	Roanoke	WV	26447	304-269-7400	269-8818
Woods Resort & Conference Ctr Mountain Lk Rd PO Box 5 **Fax Area Code:* 304 ■ *TF:* 800-248-2222 ■ *Web:* www.thewoods.com	Hedgesville	WV	25427	800-248-2222	754-8146*

Wisconsin

Resort	City	State	Zip	Phone	Fax
Abbey Resort & Fontana Spa 269 Fontana Blvd *TF:* 800-709-1323 ■ *Web:* www.theabbeyresort.com	Fontana	WI	53125	262-275-9000	
Alpine Resort 7715 Alpine Rd PO Box 200 *Web:* www.alpineresort.com	Egg Harbor	WI	54209	920-868-3000	868-2576
American Club, The 419 Highland Dr *TF:* 800-344-2838 ■ *Web:* www.americanclubresort.com	Kohler	WI	53044	920-457-8000	457-0299
Chanticleer Inn 1458 E Dollar Lk Rd *TF:* 800-752-9193 ■ *Web:* www.chanticleerinn.com	Eagle River	WI	54521	715-479-4486	479-0004
Chula Vista Resort 2501 River Rd *TF:* 800-388-4782 ■ *Web:* www.chulavistaresort.com	Wisconsin Dells	WI	53965	608-254-8366	254-7653
Devil's Head Resort & Convention Ctr S 6330 Bluff Rd *TF:* 800-472-6670 ■ *Web:* www.devilsheadresort.com	Merrimac	WI	53561	608-493-2251	493-2176
Fox Hills Resort & Convention Ctr 250 W Church St *TF:* 800-950-7615 ■ *Web:* www.foxhillsresort.com	Mishicot	WI	54228	920-755-2376	755-2186
Grand Geneva Resort & Spa 7036 Grand Geneva Way *TF:* 800-558-3417 ■ *Web:* www.grandgeneva.com	Lake Geneva	WI	53147	262-248-8811	249-4763
Great Wolf Resorts Inc 525 Junction Rd Ste 6000 S *NASDAQ: WOLF* ■ *Web:* www.greatwolf.com	Madison	WI	53717	608-253-2222	661-4701
Heidel House Resort 643 Illinois Ave *TF:* 800-444-2812 ■ *Web:* www.heidelhouse.com	Green Lake	WI	54941	920-294-3344	294-6128
Holiday Acres Resort 4060 S Shore Dr PO Box 460 *TF:* 800-261-1500 ■ *Web:* www.holidayacres.com	Rhinelander	WI	54501	715-369-1500	369-3665
Lake Lawn Resort 2400 E Geneva St *TF:* 800-338-5253 ■ *Web:* www.lakelawnresort.com	Delavan	WI	53115	262-728-7950	728-2347
Landmark Resort 7643 Hillside Rd *TF:* 800-273-7877 ■ *Web:* www.thelandmarkresort.com	Egg Harbor	WI	54209	920-868-3205	868-2569
Maxwelton Braes Golf Resort 7670 Hwy 57 *Web:* maxweltonbraes.com	Baileys Harbor	WI	54202	920-839-2321	839-2729
Olympia Resort & Spa 1350 Royale Mile Rd *TF:* 800-558-9573 ■ *Web:* www.olympiaresort.com	Oconomowoc	WI	53066	262-369-4999	369-4998
Osthoff Resort, The 101 Osthoff Ave PO Box 151 *TF:* 800-876-3399 ■ *Web:* www.osthoff.com	Elkhart Lake	WI	53020	920-876-3366	876-3228
Tundra Lodge Resort & Waterpark 865 Lombardi Ave *TF:* 877-886-3725 ■ *Web:* www.tundralodge.com	Green Bay	WI	54304	920-405-8700	405-1997

Wyoming

Resort	City	State	Zip	Phone	Fax
Amangani Resort 1535 NE Butte Rd *TF:* 877-734-7333 ■ *Web:* www.amanresorts.com	Jackson	WY	83001	307-734-7333	734-7332
Aramark Parks & Destinations 27655 Hwy 26 & 287 *TF:* 866-278-4245 ■ *Web:* www.togwoteelodge.com	Moran	WY	83013	307-543-2847	543-2391

Phone | Fax

Four Seasons Resort Jackson Hole
7680 Granite Loop Rd PO Box 544 . . . Teton Village WY 83025 307-732-5000 732-5001
TF: 800-914-5110 ■ *Web:* www.fourseasons.com/jacksonhole

Grand Targhee Resort 3300 E Ski Hill Rd . . . Alta WY 83414 307-353-2300 353-8148
TF: 800-827-4433 ■ *Web:* www.grandtarghee.com

Grand Teton Lodge Co
5 Miles N Hwy 89 PO Box 250 . . . Moran WY 83013 307-543-2811 543-3143*
**Fax:* Resv ■ *TF Resv:* 800-628-9988 ■ *Web:* www.gtlc.com

Jackson Hole Mountain Resort
3395 Cody Ln PO Box 290 . . . Teton Village WY 83025 307-733-2292 739-2737
TF: 800-450-0477 ■ *Web:* www.jacksonhole.com

Jackson HoleResort Lodging
3200 W McCollister Dr PO Box 510 . . . Teton Village WY 83025 307-733-3990
TF: 800-443-8613 ■ *Web:* www.jhrl.com

Jackson Lake Lodge PO Box 250 . . . Moran WY 83013 307-543-2811 543-3143
TF: 800-628-9988 ■ *Web:* www.gtlc.com

Rusty Parrot Lodge & Spa PO Box 1657 . . . Jackson WY 83001 307-733-2000 733-5566
TF: 800-458-2004 ■ *Web:* www.rustyparrot.com

Signal Mountain Lodge PO Box 50 . . . Moran WY 83013 307-543-2831 543-2569
Web: www.signalmtnlodge.com

Snow King Resort
400 E Snow King Ave Jackson Hole . . . Jackson WY 83001 307-733-5200 733-4086
TF: 800-522-5464 ■ *Web:* www.snowking.com

Teton Pines Resort & Country Club
3450 N Clubhouse Dr . . . Wilson WY 83014 307-733-1005 733-2860
Web: www.tetonpines.com

673 RESTAURANT COMPANIES

SEE ALSO Food Service p. 2320; Franchises p. 2330; Ice Cream & Dairy Stores p. 2550; Bakeries p. 1847

Phone | Fax

94th Aero Squadron Restaurants
16320 Raymer St . . . Van Nuys CA 91406 818-994-7437
Web: www.94thvannuys.com/94thvannuys

Al Copeland Investments Inc
1001 Harimaw Ct S . . . Metairie LA 70001 504-830-1000 401-0401
TF: 800-401-0401 ■ *Web:* www.alcopeland.com

Aloha Restaurants Inc
204 Main St Ste 960 . . . Newport Beach CA 92661 949-250-0331 673-5085
Web: aloharestaurants.com

Arby's Restaurant Group Inc
1155 Perimeter Ctr W . . . Atlanta GA 30338 678-514-4100
Web: www.arbys.com

Arctic Cir Restaurants Inc PO Box 339 . . . Midvale UT 84047 801-561-3620 561-9646
Web: www.acburger.com

Ark Restaurants Corp 85 Fifth Ave 14th Fl . . . New York NY 10003 212-206-8800 206-8814
NASDAQ: ARKR ■ *Web:* www.arkrestaurants.com

Aurelio's Pizza 18162 Harwood Ave . . . Homewood IL 60430 708-798-8050 798-6692
Web: www.aureliospizza.com

Azteca Mexican Restaurants
15735 Ambaum Blvd SW . . . Seattle WA 98166 206-243-7021 246-0429
Web: www.aztecamex.com

BAB Inc 500 Lk Cook Rd Ste 475 . . . Deerfield IL 60015 800-251-6101 405-8140*
OTC: BABB ■ **Fax Area Code:* 847 ■ *TF:* 800-251-6101 ■ *Web:* www.babcorp.com

Back Yard Burgers Inc 500 Church St Ste 200 . . . Nashville TN 37219 615-620-2300 620-2301
Web: www.backyardburgers.com

Baker's Burgers Inc
1875 Business Ctr Dr . . . San Bernardino CA 92408 909-884-5233 885-4059
Web: www.bakersdrivethru.com

Barbato's Italian Restaurants 3512 Buffalo Rd . . . Erie PA 16510 814-899-3423 899-5293
Web: www.barbatos.com

Battleground Restaurant Group Inc
1337 Winstead Pl . . . Greensboro NC 27408 336-272-9355 272-5568
Web: www.brginc.com

Beef O'Bradys Inc 5660 W Cypress St Ste A . . . Tampa FL 33607 813-226-2333 226-0030
TF: 800-728-8878 ■ *Web:* www.beefobradys.com

Bellacino's Corp 10096 Shaver Rd . . . Portage MI 49024 269-329-0782 329-0930
TF: 877-379-0700 ■ *Web:* bellacinos.com

Bennett's Bar-B-Que Inc 3538 Peoria St Ste 508 . . . Aurora CO 80010 303-792-3088 792-5801
Web: www.bennettsbbq.com

Bennigan's 5151 Beltline Rd Ste 300 . . . Dallas TX 75254 469-248-4419
Web: bennigans.com

Bertucci's Restaurant Corp 155 Otis St . . . Northborough MA 01532 508-351-2500 393-1231
Web: www.bertuccis.com

BF Nashville 1101 Kermit Dr Ste 310 . . . Nashville TN 37217 615-399-9700 399-3373

Biaggi's Ristorante Italiano
1705 Clearwater Ave . . . Bloomington IL 61704 309-664-2148 664-2149
Web: www.biaggis.com

Bice Ristorante 7 E 54th St . . . New York NY 10022 212-688-1999 752-1329
Web: www.bicenewyork.com

Bickford's Family Restauarants Inc
37 Oak St Ext . . . Brockton MA 02301 800-969-5653
TF: 800-969-5653 ■ *Web:* www.bickfordsrestaurants.com

Big Boy Restaurants International LLC
4199 Marcy St . . . Warren MI 48091 586-759-6000
Web: www.bigboy.com

Big Buck Brewery & Steakhouse Inc
550 S Wisconsin Ave . . . Gaylord MI 49735 989-732-5781 732-3990
Web: www.bigbuck.com

Bill Miller Bar-B-Q Inc
430 S Santa Rosa St PO Box 839925 . . . San Antonio TX 78207 210-225-4461 302-1533*
**Fax:* Sales ■ *TF:* 800-339-3111 ■ *Web:* www.billmillerbbq.com

Biscuitville Inc 1414 Yanceyville St . . . Greensboro NC 27405 336-553-3700 553-3701
Web: www.biscuitville.com

BJ's Restaurants Inc
7755 Ctr Ave Ste 300 . . . Huntington Beach CA 92647 714-500-2400 848-8287
NASDAQ: BJRI ■ *Web:* bjsrestaurants.com/

Bob Evans Farms Inc 3776 S High St . . . Columbus OH 43207 800-939-2338 497-4318*
NASDAQ: BOBE ■ **Fax Area Code:* 614 ■ **Fax:* Hum Res ■ *TF:* 800-939-2338 ■ *Web:* www.bobevans.com

Bobby Rubino's Place for Ribs
2501 N Federal Hwy . . . Pompano Beach FL 33064 954-781-7550
Web: www.bobbyrubinos.com

Boddie-Noell Enterprises Inc (BNEINC)
1021 Noell Ln PO Box 1908 . . . Rocky Mount NC 27804 252-937-2000 937-6991
Web: www.bneinc.com

Bojangles' Restaurants Inc
9432 Southern Pine Blvd . . . Charlotte NC 28273 704-335-1804 523-6676
TF: 800-366-9921 ■ *Web:* www.bojangles.com

Bonefish Grill 2202 NW Shore Blvd . . . Tampa FL 33607 813-282-1225
Web: www.bonefishgrill.com

Bongos Cuban Cafe 420 Jefferson Ave . . . Miami Beach FL 33139 305-695-7072 695-7160
Web: www.bongoscubancafe.com

Bono's Pit Bar-B-Q
10645 Phillips Hwy Bldg 200 . . . Jacksonville FL 32256 904-880-8310 880-8373
Web: www.bonosbarbq.com

Boomerang Grille 9200 S Western . . . Oklahoma City OK 73139 405-378-7049
Web: www.boomeranggrille.com

Boston Beanery Restaurants Inc
689 Fairchance Rd . . . Morgantown WV 26508 304-594-0095 594-0081
Web: www.bostonbeanery.com

Boston Market Corp 14103 Denver W Pkwy . . . Golden CO 80401 303-278-9500 216-5339
TF General: 800-877-2870 ■ *Web:* www.bostonmarket.com

Boston Pizza Restaurants LP
1501 LBJ Fwy Ste 450 . . . Dallas TX 75234 972-484-9022 484-7630
TF: 866-277-8721 ■ *Web:* www.bostons.com

BRAVO | BRIO Restaurant Group
777 Goodale Blvd Ste 100 . . . Columbus OH 43212 614-326-7944 326-7943
TF: 888-452-7286 ■ *Web:* www.bestitalianusa.com

Briad Group, The 78 Okner Pkwy . . . Livingston NJ 07039 973-597-6433 597-6422
Web: www.briad.com

Brigantine Restaurants Inc 7889 Ostrow St . . . San Diego CA 92111 858-268-1030 268-5727
Web: www.brigantine.com

Brinker International Inc 6820 LBJ Fwy . . . Dallas TX 75240 972-980-9917 770-9593
NYSE: EAT ■ *TF:* 800-983-4637 ■ *Web:* www.brinker.com

Bristol Bar & Grille Inc
1308 BaRdstown Rd PO Box 4607 . . . Louisville KY 40204 502-456-6762 456-6784
Web: bristolbarandgrille.com

Brock & Company Inc 257 Great Vly Pkwy . . . Malvern PA 19355 610-647-5656 647-0867
TF: 866-468-2783 ■ *Web:* www.brockco.com

Bubba Gump Shrimp Co LLC 2501 Seawall Blvd . . . Galveston TX 77550 409-766-4952
TF: 800-552-6379 ■ *Web:* www.bubbagump.com

Buca di Beppo 1204 Harmon Pl . . . Minneapolis MN 55403 612-288-0138 341-0496
TF: 866-328-2822 ■ *Web:* www.bucadibeppo.com

Buca Inc 1204 Harmon Pl . . . Minneapolis MN 55403 612-288-0138 341-0496
TF: 866-328-2822 ■ *Web:* www.bucadibeppo.com

Buck's Pizza Franchising Corp Inc PO Box 405 . . . Du Bois PA 15801 800-310-8848 371-4214*
**Fax Area Code:* 814 ■ *TF:* 800-310-8848 ■ *Web:* www.buckspizza.com

Buffalo Wild Wings Inc
5500 Wayzata Blvd Ste 1600 . . . Minneapolis MN 55416 952-593-9943 593-9787
NASDAQ: BWLD ■ *Web:* www.buffalowildwings.com

Buffalo's Franchise Concepts Inc
9606 Santa Monica Blvd Ste 105 . . . Beverly Hills CA 90210 310-402-0606
TF: 800-459-4647 ■ *Web:* www.buffaloscafe.com

Burger King Corp 5505 Blue Lagoon Dr . . . Miami FL 33126 305-378-3000
TF: 855-673-3725 ■ *Web:* www.bk.com

Burgerville USA 109 W 17th St . . . Vancouver WA 98660 360-694-1521 694-9114
TF: 888-827-8369 ■ *Web:* www.burgerville.com

Cafe Express LLC 19443 Gulf Fwy . . . Webster TX 77598 281-554-6999 554-5501
Web: www.cafe-express.com

California Cafe Restaurants
Old Town 50 University Ave Ste 260 . . . Los Gatos CA 95030 408-354-8118 354-1400
Web: www.californiacafe.com

California Pizza Kitchen Inc
18601 Airport Way Ste 135 . . . Santa Ana CA 92707 949-252-6125
NASDAQ: CPKI ■ *TF:* 800-919-3227 ■ *Web:* www.cpk.com

Capital Restaurant Concepts Ltd (CRC)
1305 Wisconsin Ave NW . . . Washington DC 20007 202-339-6800 339-6801
Web: www.capitalrestaurants.com

Captain D's LLC
624 Grassmere Park Dr Ste 30 . . . Nashville TN 37211 615-391-5461
TF: 800-314-4819 ■ *Web:* www.captainds.com

Carey Hilliard's Restaurants
11111 Abercom St . . . Savannah GA 31419 912-925-3225 925-1699
Web: careyhilliards.com

Carino's Italian 150 Cascade Mall Dr . . . Burlington WA 98233 360-757-4535
Web: www.carinos.com

Carlson Restaurants 4201 Marsh Ln . . . Carrollton TX 75007 972-662-5400
TF: 800-374-3297 ■ *Web:* www.carlson.com

Carrols Restaurant Group Inc 968 James St . . . Syracuse NY 13203 315-424-0513 425-8874*
NASDAQ: TAST ■ **Fax:* Mktg ■ *Web:* www.carrols.com

Carvers Steak & Chops
11940 Bernardo Plz Dr . . . San Diego CA 92128 858-485-1262
Web: www.carverssteak.com

Cask 'n' Cleaver 8689 Ninth St . . . Rancho Cucamonga CA 91730 909-981-5771 981-9734
TF: 800-995-4452 ■ *Web:* www.caskncleaver.com

Catalina Restaurant Group Inc
2200 Faraday Ave Ste 250 . . . Carlsbad CA 92008 760-804-5750 476-5141
Web: www.catalinarestaurantgroup.com

CEC Entertainment Inc
4441 W Airport Fwy PO Box 152077 . . . Irving TX 75062 972-258-8507 258-5524
NYSE: CEC ■ *TF:* 888-778-7193 ■ *Web:* www.chuckecheese.com

Champps Entertainment Inc
19111 Dallas Pkwy Ste 370 . . . Dallas TX 75287 972-581-1171
TF General: 800-229-2118 ■ *Web:* www.champps.com

Charley's Grilled Subs
2500 Farmers Dr Ste 140 . . . Columbus OH 43235 614-923-4700 923-4701
TF: 800-437-8325 ■ *Web:* www.charleys.com

Chart House Restaurants 1510 W Loop S . . . Houston TX 77027 713-850-1010 386-7707
TF: 800-552-6379 ■ *Web:* www.chart-house.com

Checkers Drive-In Restaurants Inc
4300 W Cypress St Ste 600 . . . Tampa FL 33607 813-283-7000 283-7208
TF: 800-800-8072 ■ *Web:* www.checkers.com

Company	City	State	ZIP	Phone	Fax
Cheddar's Casual Cafe 700 I- 635 Service Rd	Irving	TX	75063	972-409-0300	409-0302
Web: cheddars.com					
Cheesecake Factory Inc					
26901 Malibu Hills Rd	Calabasas Hills	CA	91301	818-871-3000	871-3001
NASDAQ: CAKE ■ *Web:* www.thecheesecakefactory.com					
Chefs International Inc					
62 Broadway	Point Pleasant Beach	NJ	08742	732-295-0350	295-4514
Web: www.lobster.com					
Chelo's Inc 1725 Mendon Rd Ste 209	Cumberland	RI	02864	401-312-6500	312-6501
Web: www.chelos.com					
Chesapeake Bay Seafood House Assoc LLC					
1960 Gallows Rd Ste 200	Vienna	VA	22182	703-827-0320	893-1536
Web: www.chesapeakerestaurants.com					
Chevys Inc 5660 Katella Ave Ste 100	Cypress	CA	90630	858-205-1123	
Web: www.chevys.com					
Chick-fil-A Inc 5200 Buffington Rd	Atlanta	GA	30349	404-765-8000	810-5926*
**Fax Area Code:* 904 ■ **Fax:* Mktg ■ *TF:* 800-232-2677 ■ *Web:* www.chick-fil-a.com					
China Grill Management Inc (CGM) 60 W 53rd St	New York	NY	10019	212-333-7788	
Web: www.chinagrillmgt.com					
Chipotle Mexican Grill Inc 1401 Wynkoop St	Denver	CO	80202	303-595-4000	
NYSE: CMG ■ *Web:* www.chipotle.com					
Chuck's Steak House Inc 20 Segar St	Danbury	CT	06810	203-792-5555	
Web: www.chuckssteakhouse.com					
CiCi Enterprises LP 1080 W Bethel Rd	Coppell	TX	75019	972-745-4200	745-4204
Web: www.cicispizza.com					
City Barbeque Inc 6175 Emerald Pkwy	Dublin	OH	43016	614-583-0999	
Web: citybbq.com					
Clock Restaurants					
902 Clint Moore Rd Ste 126	Boca Raton	FL	33487	561-994-3440	994-3655
Clyde's Restaurant Group 3236 M St NW	Washington	DC	20007	202-333-9180	625-7429
Web: www.clydes.com					
Corporate Chefs Inc 22 Parkridge Rd	Haverhill	MA	01835	978-372-7400	
Web: www.corporatechefs.com					
Cosi Inc 1751 Lk Cook Rd Ste 600	Deerfield	IL	60015	847-597-8800	597-8884
NASDAQ: COSI ■ *TF:* 800-822-2076 ■ *Web:* www.getcosi.com					
Cousins Submarines Inc					
N83 W13400 Leon Rd	Menomonee Falls	WI	53051	262-253-7700	253-7710
TF: 800-238-9736 ■ *Web:* www.cousinssubs.com					
Cozymels Restaurant 2655 Grapevine Mills	Grapevine	TX	76051	972-724-0277	443-2001*
**Fax Area Code:* 214 ■ *Web:* www.cozymels.com					
Cracker Barrel Old Country Store Inc					
PO Box 787	Lebanon	TN	37088	615-444-5533	444-5533
NASDAQ: CBRL ■ *TF:* 800-333-9566 ■ *Web:* www.crackerbarrel.com					
Culver Franchising System Inc					
1240 Water St	Prairie du Sac	WI	53578	608-643-7980	643-7982
Web: www.culvers.com					
D'Angelo Sandwich Shops 600 Providence Hwy	Dedham	MA	02026	781-461-1200	461-1896
TF: 800-727-2446 ■ *Web:* www.dangelos.com					
Darden Restaurants Inc (DRI) 5900 Lk Ellenor Dr	Orlando	FL	32809	407-245-4000	245-5114
NYSE: DRI ■ *Web:* www.darden.com					
Davanni's Inc 1100 Xenium Ln N	Plymouth	MN	55441	952-927-2300	927-2323
Web: www.davannis.com					
DavCo Restaurants Inc 1657 Crofton Blvd	Crofton	MD	21114	410-721-3770	793-0754
TF General: 800-523-1411 ■ *Web:* www.wendavco.com					
Debos Diners Inc					
7625 Hamilton Pk Dr Ste 26	Chattanooga	TN	37421	423-855-4650	
Web: debosdiners.com					
Del Taco Inc					
25521 Commercentre Dr Ste 200	Lake Forest	CA	92630	949-462-9300	462-7444
TF Cust Svc: 800-852-7204 ■ *Web:* www.deltaco.com					
Deli Management Inc 2400 Broadway	Beaumont	TX	77702	409-838-1976	838-1906
Web: jasonsdeli.com					
Deli Partners LLC 1608 Rogers Rd	Fort Worth	TX	76107	817-738-9355	
Denny's Corp 203 E Main St	Spartanburg	SC	29319	864-597-8000	
NASDAQ: DENN ■ *TF Cust Svc:* 800-733-6697 ■ *Web:* www.dennys.com					
Denny's Inc 203 E Main St	Spartanburg	SC	29319	864-597-8000	597-7708*
**Fax:* Mktg ■ *Web:* www.dennys.com					
Dick's Last Resort 2211 N Lambar St	Dallas	TX	75202	214-747-0001	385-1745
Web: www.dickslastresort.com					
Dixie Restaurants Inc					
1215 Rebsamen Pk Rd	Little Rock	AR	72202	501-666-3494	666-8900
Web: www.dixiecafe.com					
Doctor's Assoc Inc 325 Bic Dr	Milford	CT	06461	203-877-4281	783-7293
TF: 800-888-4848 ■ *Web:* www.subway.co.in					
Dolly's Pizza Franchising Inc					
1097 Union Lake Rd	White Lake	MI	48386	248-360-6440	360-7020
TF: 866-336-5597 ■ *Web:* www.dollyspizza.com					
Domino's Pizza Inc					
30 Frank Lloyd Wright Dr	Ann Arbor	MI	48106	734-930-3030	930-3580*
NYSE: DPZ ■ **Fax:* Mail Rm ■ *Web:* dominos.com					
Don's Restaurants 8905 Lake Ave	Cleveland	OH	44102	216-961-6700	961-1966
Web: www.strangcorp.com					
Donatos Pizza 935 Taylor Stn Rd	Columbus	OH	43230	800-366-2867	416-7701*
**Fax Area Code:* 614 ■ *TF:* 800-366-2867 ■ *Web:* www.donatos.com					
DRM Inc 5324 N 134th Ave	Omaha	NE	68164	402-556-4098	573-0171
Web: www.drmarbys.com					
Dutchman Hospitality Group					
4985 Walnut St PO Box 158	Walnut Creek	OH	44687	330-893-2926	893-2637
Web: www.dhgroup.com					
Dynaco Inc 7050 N Fresno St Ste 210	Fresno	CA	93720	559-485-8520	256-5820
Web: brg.co					
Eat'n Park Hospitality Group Inc					
285 E Waterfront Dr PO Box 3000	Homestead	PA	15120	412-461-2000	461-6000
TF: 800-947-4033 ■ *Web:* www.eatnpark.com					
Edo Japan International Inc 32 St SE Ste 4838	Calgary	AB	T2B2S6	403-215-8800	215-8801
TF: 888-336-9888 ■ *Web:* www.edojapan.com					
Eegee's Inc 3360 E Ajo Way	Tucson	AZ	85713	520-294-3333	889-4340
Web: www.eegees.com					
Einstein Noah Restaurant Group Inc					
555 Zang St Ste 300	Lakewood	CO	80228	303-568-8000	
Web: einsteinnoah.com					
El Centro Foods Inc					
6930 1/2 Tujunga Ave	North Hollywood	CA	91605	818-766-4395	

Company	City	State	ZIP	Phone	Fax
El Fenix Corp 11075 Harry Hines Blvd	Dallas	TX	75229	972-241-2171	241-3031
TF: 877-591-1918 ■ *Web:* www.elfenix.com					
El Pollo Loco 3535 Harbor Blvd Ste 100	Costa Mesa	CA	92626	714-599-5000	
TF: 877-375-4968 ■ *Web:* www.elpolloloco.com					
El Torito Restaurants Inc					
5660 Katella Ave Ste 100	Cypress	CA	90630	562-346-1200	
Web: www.eltorito.com					
Elephant Bar Restaurant					
10100 Stockdale Hwy Ste 315	Bakersfield	CA	93311	661-663-3020	
Web: www.elephantbar.com					
Emeril's Homebase 829 St Charles Ave	New Orleans	LA	70130	504-524-4241	558-3937
Web: www.emerils.com					
Erik's Deli Cafe 365 Coral St	Santa Cruz	CA	95060	831-458-1818	458-9797
Web: www.eriksdelicafe.com					
Escape Enterprises Ltd 222 Neilston St	Columbus	OH	43215	614-224-0300	224-6460
Web: www.steakescape.com					
Famous Dave's of America Inc					
12701 Whitewater Dr Ste 200	Minnetonka	MN	55343	952-294-1300	822-9921*
NASDAQ: DAVE ■ **Fax Area Code:* 612 ■ *TF:* 800-929-4040 ■ *Web:* www.famousdaves.com					
Fatburger North America Inc					
301 Arizona Ave Ste 200	Santa Monica	CA	90401	310-319-1850	319-1863
TF: 800-315-3901 ■ *Web:* www.fatburger.com					
Fatz Cafe 4324 Wade Hampton Blvd	Taylors	SC	29687	864-322-1331	322-1332
Web: www.fatz.com					
Fausto's Fried Chicken Inc 905 E Fourth St	Dequincy	LA	70633	337-786-7264	
Faz Restaurants Inc 5121 HopyaRd Rd	Pleasanton	CA	94588	925-460-0444	469-1604
Web: www.fazrestaurants.com					
Figaro's Italian Pizza Inc					
1500 Liberty St SE Ste 160	Salem	OR	97302	503-371-9318	363-5364
TF: 888-344-2767 ■ *Web:* www.figaros.com					
Firehouse Restaurant Group Inc					
3400 Kori Rd Ste 8	Jacksonville	FL	32257	904-886-8300	886-2111
TF: 877-309-7332 ■ *Web:* www.firehousesubs.com					
Flamers Charbroiled Hamburgers					
1515 International Pkwy Ste 2013	Heathrow	FL	32746	407-574-8363	333-8852
TF: 866-749-4889 ■ *Web:* www.flamersgrill.com					
Flanigan's Enterprises Inc					
5059 NE 18th Ave	Fort Lauderdale	FL	33334	954-377-1961	377-1980
NYSE: BDL ■ *Web:* www.flanigans.net					
Folks Southern Kitchen					
1384 Buford Business Blvd Ste 500	Buford	GA	30518	770-904-6595	904-6805
Web: www.folkskitchen.com					
Food Concepts International LP					
2575 S Loop 289	Lubbock	TX	79423	806-785-8686	785-8866
Web: www.abuelos.com					
Fosters Freeze LLC 630 Central Ave	Alameda	CA	94501	510-521-1242	
Web: www.fostersfreeze.com					
Fox's Pizza Den Inc					
4425 Willaim Penn Hwy	Murrysville	PA	15668	724-733-7888	325-5479
TF: 800-899-3697 ■ *Web:* www.foxspizza.com					
Fresh Enterprises Inc					
5900-A Katella Ave Ste 101	Cypress	CA	90630	562-391-2400	
TF: 877-225-2373 ■ *Web:* www.bajafresh.com					
Freshens Frozen Treats 1750 The Exchange	Atlanta	GA	30339	678-627-5400	627-5454
Web: www.freshens.com					
Friendly Ice Cream Corp 1855 Boston Rd	Wilbraham	MA	01095	413-731-4000	543-5844
TF: 800-966-9970 ■ *Web:* www.friendlys.com					
Frisch's Restaurants Inc 2800 Gilbert Ave	Cincinnati	OH	45206	513-961-2660	559-5160
NYSE: FRS ■ *TF:* 800-873-3633 ■ *Web:* www.frischs.com					
Frullati Cafe & Bakery					
9311 E Via de Ventura	Scottsdale	AZ	85258	480-362-4800	362-4812
TF: 866-452-4252 ■ *Web:* www.frullati.com					
Garden Fresh Restaurant Corp					
15822 Bernardo Ctr Dr Ste A	San Diego	CA	92127	858-675-1600	675-1616
TF: 800-874-1600 ■ *Web:* www.souplantation.com					
Garduno's 10031 Coors Blvd NW	Albuquerque	NM	87114	505-890-7000	
Web: www.gardunosrestaurants.com					
Gastronomy Inc 48 W Market St Ste 250	Salt Lake City	UT	84101	801-322-2020	363-5275
Web: marketstreetgrill.com					
Gates Bar-B-Q 4621 Paseo Blvd	Kansas City	MO	64110	816-923-0900	923-3922
TF: 800-662-7427 ■ *Web:* www.gatesbbq.com					
Giorgio Restaurants 222 boul Saint Laurent	Montreal	QC	H2Y2Y3	514-845-4221	844-0071
Web: www.giorgio.ca					
Godfathers Pizza Inc 2808 N 108th St	Omaha	NE	68164	402-391-1452	
Web: godfathers.com					
Gold Star Chili 650 Lunken Pk Dr	Cincinnati	OH	45226	513-231-4541	624-4415
TF: 800-643-0465 ■ *Web:* www.goldstarchili.com					
Golden Corral Corp 5151 Glenwood Ave	Raleigh	NC	27612	919-781-9310	881-4654
Web: goldencorral.com					
Golden Franchising Corp					
1131 Rockingham Ste 250	Richardson	TX	75080	972-831-0911	831-0401
Web: www.goldenchick.com					
Golden Griddle Corp, The					
1500 Matheson Blvd Ste 900	Mississauga	ON	L4W3Z4	905-629-1460	985-8105
Web: www.goldengriddleinc.com					
Good Eats Inc 12200 Stemmons Fwy Ste 100	Dallas	TX	75234	972-241-5500	888-8198
TF: 800-275-1337 ■ *Web:* www.goodeatsgrill.com					
Good Times Restaurants Inc 601 Corporate Cir	Golden	CO	80401	303-384-1400	273-0177
NASDAQ: GTIM ■ *Web:* www.goodtimesburgers.com					
Great Steak & Potato Co					
9311 E Via de Ventura	Scottsdale	AZ	85258	480-362-4800	362-4812
TF: 866-452-4252 ■ *Web:* www.thegreatsteak.com					
Great Wraps! Inc 4 Executive Pk E Ste 315	Atlanta	GA	30329	404-248-9900	248-0180
Web: www.greatwraps.com					
Griff's of America Inc					
1202 Richardson Dr Ste 312	Richardson	TX	75080	972-238-9561	238-9564
Web: griffshamburgers.com					
Grill Concepts Inc					
6300 Canoga Ave Ste 600	Woodland Hills	CA	91367	818-251-7000	999-4745
OTC: GLLC ■ *Web:* www.dailygrill.com					
Grinner's Food Systems Ltd 105 Walker	Truro	NS	B2N4B1	902-893-4141	
Web: www.greco.ca					

Phone *Fax*

Grotto Pizza Inc 20376 Coastal Hwy . . . Rehoboth Beach DE 19971 302-227-3567 227-4566
Web: www.grottopizza.com

Hacienda Mexican Restaurants
1501 N Ironwood Dr . . . South Bend IN 46635 800-541-3227 272-6055*
**Fax Area Code:* 574 ■ *TF:* 800-541-3227 ■ *Web:* www.haciendafiesta.com

Haddad Restaurant Group Inc
3100 Gillham Rd . . . Kansas City MO 64109 816-931-2261 931-9044

Hal Smith Restaurant Group Inc
3101 W Tecumseh Rd . . . Norman OK 73072 405-321-2600
Web: www.ehsrg.com

Happy Chef Systems Inc 51646 US Hwy 169 . . . Mankato MN 56001 507-388-2953

Happy Joe's Inc 2705 Happy Joe Dr . . . Bettendorf IA 52722 563-332-8811 332-5822
Web: www.happyjoes.com

Hard Times Cafe 1404 King St . . . Alexandria VA 22314 703-837-0050 837-0057
Web: www.hardtimes.com

Harman Management Corp 199 First St Ste 212 . . . Los Altos CA 94022 650-941-5681 948-7532

Heidi's Family Restaurant Inc
106 E Adams St Ste 206 . . . Carson City NV 89706 775-884-1415 884-2091
Web: heidisfamilyrestaurants.com

Hero Systems Inc. 7327 SW Barnes Rd Ste 718 . . . Portland OR 97204 503-228-4376 228-8778
Web: www.bigtownhero.com

High Plains Pizza Inc 7 W PkwyBlvd . . . Liberal KS 67901 620-624-5638 624-5411
Web: highplainspizza.com

Hillstone Restaurant Group
147 S Beverly Dr . . . Beverly Hills CA 90212 310-385-7343 385-7119
TF: 800-230-9787 ■ *Web:* www.hillstone.com

Ho-Lee-Chow 2204 Danforth Ave . . . Toronto ON M4C1K3 416-996-3333 778-6818
TF: 800-465-3324 ■ *Web:* www.holeechow.com

Hof's Hut Restaurants Inc
2601 E Willow St . . . Signal Hill CA 90755 562-596-0200 430-0480
Web: www.hofshut.com

Holcomb Bridge at Grimes Bridge
690 Holcomb Bridge Rd . . . Roswell GA 30076 770-594-9117
Web: www.myfriendsplacedeli.com

Holland Inc 109 W 17th St . . . Vancouver WA 98660 360-694-1521 694-9114
Web: www.hollandinc.com

Home Run Inn Inc 1300 Internationale Pkwy . . . Woodridge IL 60517 630-783-9696 783-0069
TF: 800-636-9696 ■ *Web:* www.homeruninnpizza.com

Homestyle Dining LLC 3701 W Plano Pkwy Ste 200 . . . Plano TX 75075 972-244-8900 588-5905
Web: www.ponderosasteakhouses.com

Hot Dog on a Stick 5942 Priestly Dr . . . Carlsbad CA 92008 760-930-0456
TF: 877-639-2361 ■ *Web:* www.hotdogonastick.com

Houlihan's Restaurants Inc
8700 State Line Rd Ste 100 . . . Leawood KS 66206 913-901-2500 901-2673
Web: www.houlihans.com

House of Blues Entertainment Inc
7060 Hollywood Blvd . . . Hollywood CA 90028 323-769-4600 769-4787
TF: 877-632-7600 ■ *Web:* www.houseofblues.com

Huddle House Inc
5901 Peachtree Dunwoody Ste B450 . . . Atlanta GA 30328 770-325-1300
Web: www.huddlehouse.com

Humperdink's Texas LLC PO Box 542465 . . . Dallas TX 75354 214-358-4159
Web: www.humperdinks.com

Humpty's Restaurants International Inc
2505 Macleod Terr S . . . Calgary AB T2G5J4 403-269-4675 266-1973
Web: www.humptys.com

Hungry Howie's Pizza & Subs Inc
30300 Stephenson Hwy Ste 200 . . . Madison Heights MI 48071 248-414-3300 414-3301
Web: www.hungryhowies.com

Hyde Park Restaurant Systems
26300 Chagrin Blvd Ste 1 . . . Beachwood OH 44122 216-464-0688 595-8267
Web: www.hydeparkrestaurants.com

Ignite Restaurant Group Inc
9900 Wpark Dr Ste 300 . . . Houston TX 77063 713-366-7500
Web: igniterestaurants.com

IHOP Corp 450 N Brand Blvd . . . Glendale CA 91203 818-240-6055 637-4730
TF: 800-901-5248 ■ *Web:* www.ihop.com

Il Fornaio America Corp
770 Tamalpais Dr Ste 400 . . . Corte Madera CA 94925 415-945-0500 286-6632*
**Fax Area Code:* 408 ■ *TF:* 888-454-6246 ■ *Web:* www.ilfornaio.com

In-N-Out Burger Inc 4199 Campus Dr Ninth Fl . . . Irvine CA 92612 949-509-6200 509-6389
TF Cust Svc: 800-786-1000 ■ *Web:* www.in-n-out.com

Interfoods of America Inc
9500 S Dadeland Blvd Ste 720 . . . Miami FL 33156 305-670-0746 670-0767

International Dairy Queen Corp
7505 Metro Blvd . . . Minneapolis MN 55439 952-830-0200 830-0270
TF: 866-793-7582 ■ *Web:* www.dairyqueen.com

International Restaurant Management Group Inc (IRMG)
4104 Aurora St . . . Coral Gables FL 33146 305-476-1611 476-9622
Web: www.irmgusa.com

Iron Hill Brewery 2502 W Sixth St . . . Wilmington DE 19805 302-472-2739 652-4115
Web: www.ironhillbrewery.com

Isaac's Deli Inc 354 N Prince St Ste 220 . . . Lancaster PA 17603 717-394-0623 393-0955
Web: www.isaacsdeli.com

Islands Restaurants 5750 Fleet St Ste 120 . . . Carlsbad CA 92008 760-268-1800 918-1500
Web: www.islandsrestaurants.com

J & S Cafeteria Inc PO Box 5748 . . . High Point NC 27262 336-884-0404 884-0815
Web: www.jandscafeteria.com

J A Sutherland Inc 228 MN St . . . Red Bluff CA 96080 530-529-1470 527-1959
Web: www.jasutherland.com

J Alexander's Corp 3401 W End Ave Ste 260 . . . Nashville TN 37203 615-269-1900 269-1999
NASDAQ: JAX ■ *TF:* 888-528-1991 ■ *Web:* www.jalexanders.com

J Gilbert's Wood Fired Steaks
8700 State Line Rd Ste 100 . . . Leawood KS 66206 913-642-8070 901-2673
Web: www.jgilberts.com

Jack in the Box Inc 9330 Balboa Ave . . . San Diego CA 92123 858-571-2121 571-2101
NASDAQ: JACK ■ *TF:* 800-955-5225 ■ *Web:* www.jackinthebox.com

Jack's Family Restaurants Inc
2831 19th St S . . . Homewood AL 35209 205-879-9321 945-8167
TF: 800-422-3893 ■ *Web:* www.eatatjacks.com

Jake's Pizza Enterprises Inc
1931 Rohlwing Rd Ste B . . . Rolling Meadows IL 60008 847-368-1990 368-1995

Phone *Fax*

James Coney Island Inc 1750 Stebbins Dr . . . Houston TX 77043 713-932-1500 932-0061
Web: www.jamesconeyisland.com

Jan Cos 35 Sockanosset Cross Rd . . . Cranston RI 02920 401-946-4000 946-4392
TF: 888-693-6844 ■ *Web:* www.jancompanies.com

Jerry's Famous Deli Inc
12711 Ventura Blvd Ste 400 . . . Studio City CA 91604 818-766-8311 766-8315
Web: www.jerrysfamousdeli.com

Jerry's Systems Inc
15942 Shady Grove Rd . . . Gaithersburg MD 20877 800-990-9176 948-3508*
**Fax Area Code:* 301 ■ *TF:* 800-990-9176 ■ *Web:* www.jerrysusa.com

Jet's America Inc 37501 Mound Rd . . . Sterling Heights MI 48310 586-268-5870 268-6762
Web: www.jetspizza.com

Jim's Restaurants 8520 Crownhill Blvd . . . San Antonio TX 78209 210-828-1493 822-8606
Web: www.jimsrestaurants.com

Jimmy John's Franchise Inc 2212 Fox Dr . . . Champaign IL 61820 217-356-9900 359-2956
TF: 800-546-6904 ■ *Web:* www.jimmyjohns.com

Jocks & Jills & Frankie's Sports Grill
5600 Roswell Rd NE Ste 100-A . . . Atlanta GA 30342 770-209-0920
Web: www.jocks-frankies.com

Joey's Only Seafood Franchising Corp
514-42nd Ave SE . . . Calgary AB T2G1Y6 403-243-4584 243-8989
TF: 800-661-2123 ■ *Web:* www.joeys.ca

John Harvard's Brew House 33 Dunster St . . . Cambridge MA 02138 617-868-3585 868-4341
Web: www.johnharvards.com

JRN Inc 209 W Seventh St . . . Columbia TN 38401 931-381-3000
Web: kfc.com

K-Bob's USA Inc 141 E Palace Ave . . . Santa Fe NM 87501 505-982-3438
Web: k-bobs.com

K-Mac Enterprises Inc PO Box 6538 . . . Fort Smith AR 72906 479-646-2053 646-8748
TF: 800-947-9277 ■ *Web:* www.kmaccorp.com

Kahala Corp 9311 E Via de Ventura . . . Scottsdale AZ 85258 480-362-4800 362-4812
TF: 866-452-4252 ■ *Web:* www.blimpie.com

Kahunaville Island Restaurant & Party Bar
3300 Las Vegas Blvd S . . . Las Vegas NV 89109 702-894-7390
Web: www.kahunaville.com

Keg Steakhouse 10100 Shellbridge Way . . . Richmond BC V6X2W7 604-276-0242 276-2681
Web: www.kegsteakhouse.com

Kellys Roast Beef Inc 605 Broadway Ste 300 . . . Saugus MA 01906 781-233-5700

KFC Corp 1441 Gardiner Ln . . . Louisville KY 40213 818-780-6990
TF: 800-225-5532 ■ *Web:* www.kfc.com

Kimpton Hotel & Restaurant Group LLC
222 Kearny St Ste 200 . . . San Francisco CA 94108 415-397-5572 296-8031
TF: 800-546-7866 ■ *Web:* www.kimptonhotels.com

King Taco Restaurants Inc 3421 E 14th St . . . Los Angeles CA 90023 323-266-3585 266-6565
Web: www.kingtaco.com

King's Seafood Co 3185 Airway Ave . . . Costa Mesa CA 92626 714-432-0400 432-0111
Web: www.kingsseafood.com

Kings Family Restaurants
1820 Lincoln Hwy . . . North Versailles PA 15137 412-823-0324
Web: www.kingsfamily.com

Kobe Japanese Steakhouse Inc
468 W Hwy 436 . . . Altamonte Springs FL 32714 407-862-6099 788-8887
Web: www.kobesteakhouse.com

Kona Grill Inc 7150 E Camelback Rd Ste 220 . . . Scottsdale AZ 85251 480-922-8100 991-6811
NASDAQ: KONA ■ *TF:* 866-328-5662 ■ *Web:* www.konagrill.com

L & L Hawaiian Barbecue
931 University Ave Ste 202 . . . Honolulu HI 96826 808-951-9888 951-0888
Web: www.hawaiianbarbecue.com

La Salsa Fresh Mexican Grill
320 Commerce Ste 100 . . . Irvine CA 92602 949-270-8900
TF: 866-452-7257 ■ *Web:* lasalsa.com

LaBelle Management Inc
405 S Mission Rd . . . Mount Pleasant MI 48858 989-772-2902 773-7521
Web: www.labellemgt.com

Lambert's Cafe Inc 2305 E Malone . . . Sikeston MO 63801 573-471-4261 471-7563
Web: www.throwedrolls.com

Lamppost Pizza Franchise Corp 3002 Dow Ave . . . Tustin CA 92780 714-731-6171
Web: www.lamppost-backstreet.com

Landry's Restaurants Inc 1510 W Loop S . . . Houston TX 77027 713-850-1010 632-4702*
**Fax Area Code:* 281 ■ *TF:* 800-552-6379 ■ *Web:* www.landrysinc.com

LaRosa's Inc 2334 Boudinot Ave . . . Cincinnati OH 45238 513-347-5660
Web: www.larosas.com

Lawry's Restaurants Inc
234 E Colorado Blvd Ste 500 . . . Pasadena CA 91101 626-440-5234
TF: 888-552-9797 ■ *Web:* www.lawrysonline.com

LEDO Pizza System Inc
2001 Tidewater Colony Dr . . . Annapolis MD 21401 410-721-6887 571-8395

Legal Sea Foods Inc 1 Seafood Way . . . Boston MA 02210 617-530-9000 530-9649
TF: 800-477-5342 ■ *Web:* www.legalseafoods.com

Lettuce Entertain You Enterprises Inc
5419 N Sheridan Rd . . . Chicago IL 60640 773-878-7340 878-8468
Web: www.leye.com

Levy Restaurants 980 N Michigan Ave Ste 400 . . . Chicago IL 60611 312-664-8200 280-2739
Web: www.levyrestaurants.com

Libby Hill Seafood Restaurants Inc
4517 W Market St . . . Greensboro NC 27407 336-294-0505 292-6005
Web: www.libbyhill.com

Little Caesars Inc 2211 Woodward Ave . . . Detroit MI 48201 313-983-6409
TF: 800-722-3727 ■ *Web:* www.littlecaesars.com

Lone Star Steakhouse & Saloon Inc
5055 W Pk Blvd Ste 500 . . . Plano TX 75093 972-295-8600
Web: www.lonestarsteakhouse.com

Lone Star Texas Grill 472 Morden Rd Ste 101 . . . Oakville ON L6K3W4 905-845-5852 845-7091
Web: www.lonestartexasgrill.com

Long John Silver's Restaurants Inc
9505 Williamsburg Plaza . . . Louisville KY 40222 502-815-6100
Web: www.ljsilvers.com

LongHorn Steakhouse 1000 Darden Ctr Dr . . . Orlando FL 32837 888-221-0642
Web: www.longhornsteakhouse.com

Luby's Inc 13111 NW Fwy Ste 600 . . . Houston TX 77040 713-329-6800 329-6859
NYSE: LUB ■ *TF:* 800-886-4600 ■ *Web:* www.lubys.com

Lunan Corp 414 N Orleans St Ste 402 . . . Chicago IL 60654 312-645-9898 646-0654
Web: www.arbysrestaurants.com

Company	City	State	Zip	Phone	Fax
Macayo Mexican Restaurants 12637 S 48th St. Web: www.macayo.com	Phoenix	AZ	85044	480-598-5101	
Maggiano's Little Italy 205 Northpark Ctr Ste 205 Web: www.maggianos.com	Dallas	TX	75225	214-360-0707	360-0756
Magic Time Machine 8520 Crownhill Blvd Web: www.magictimemachine.com	San Antonio	TX	78209	210-828-1493	822-8830
Malnati Organization Inc 3685 Woodhead Dr. TF: 800-568-8646 ■ Web: www.loumalnatis.com	Northbrook	IL	60062	847-562-1814	562-1950
Mancha Development Co 2275 Sampson Ave Ste 201	Corona	CA	92879	951-271-4100	
Marie Callender Restaurant & Bakery 27101 Puerta Real Ste 260 TF: 800-776-7437 ■ Web: mariecallenders.com/	Mission Viejo	CA	92691	800-776-7437	
Maui Tacos International Inc 2001 Palmer Ave. Ste 105 TF: 866-388-3758 ■ Web: www.mauitacos.com	Larchmont	NY	10538	866-388-3758	
Maui Wowi Inc 1509 York St Ste 300 Web: www.mauiwowi.com	Denver	CO	80206	303-781-7800	781-2438
Maz Mezcal Inc 316 E 86th St Web: mazmezcal.com	New York	NY	10028	212-472-1599	
McDonald's Corp One McDonald's Plz NYSE: MCD ■ TF: 800-244-6227 ■ Web: www.mcdonalds.com	Oak Brook	IL	60523	630-623-3000	623-5500
McDonald's Restaurants of Canada Ltd One McDonald's Pl Web: www.mcdonalds.ca	Toronto	ON	M3C3L4	416-443-1000	446-3443
Me-N-Ed's-Bullard/West 1731 W Bullard Ste 101 Web: www.meneds.com	Fresno	CA	93711	559-431-7331	
Melting Pot Restaurants Inc 8810 Twin Lakes Blvd TF: 800-783-0867 ■ Web: www.meltingpot.com	Tampa	FL	33614	813-881-0055	889-9361
Mercedes Restaurants Inc 2402 W Nebraska Ave Web: mercedesrestaurants.com	Peoria	IL	61604	309-676-6443	
Meritage Hospitality Group Inc 3310 Eagle Park Dr Ste 205 OTC: MHGU ■ Web: www.meritagehospitality.com	Grand Rapids	MI	49525	616-776-2600	364-2810
Mexican Restaurants Inc 1135 Edgebrook St. OTC: CASA ■ *Fax Area Code: 832 ■ TF: 800-444-2090 ■ Web: www.mexicanrestaurantsinc.com	Houston	TX	77034	713-943-7574	300-5859*
Milio's Sandwiches 901 Deming Way Ste 202 Web: www.milios.com	Madison	WI	53717	608-662-3000	662-3001
Mirabile Investment Corp 1900 Whitten Rd Web: www.mic-memphis.com	Memphis	TN	38133	901-324-0450	
Mitchco International Inc 4801 Sherburn Ln. Web: www.mitchcointernational.com	Louisville	KY	40207	502-896-9653	896-2989
Mo's Restaurants 657 SW Bay Blvd Web: www.moschowder.com	Newport	OR	97365	541-265-7512	265-9323
Monical Pizza Corp 530 N Kinzie Ave TF: 800-929-3227 ■ Web: monicals.com/	Bradley	IL	60915	815-937-1890	937-9828
Morgan's Foods Inc 4829 Galaxy Pkwy Ste S Web: www.morgansfoods.com	Cleveland	OH	44128	216-360-7500	
Mr Gatti's Inc 5912 Balcones Dr. Web: www.mrgattis.com	Austin	TX	78731	512-459-4796	454-4990
Mr Goodcents Franchise Systems Inc 8997 Commerce Dr *Fax Area Code: 913 ■ TF: 800-648-2368 ■ Web: goodcentssubs.com	DeSoto	KS	66018	800-648-2368	583-3500*
Mr Hero Restaurants 7010 Engle Rd Ste 100 TF: 888-860-5082 ■ Web: www.mrhero.com	Middleburg Heights	OH	44130	440-625-3080	625-3081
Mr Jim's Pizza Inc 2521 Pepperwood St TF: 800-583-5960 ■ Web: www.mrjimspizza.net	Dallas	TX	75234	972-267-5467	
Myriad Restaurant Group Inc 249 W Broadway Web: www.myriadrestaurantgroup.com	New York	NY	10013	212-219-9500	219-2380
Nancy's Pizza 7929 W 171st St Web: www.nancyspizza.com	Tinley Park	IL	60477	708-614-6100	
Nathan's Famous Inc One Jericho Plz Second Fl NASDAQ: NATH ■ TF: 800-628-4267 ■ Web: www.nathansfamous.com	Jericho	NY	11753	516-338-8500	338-7220
National Coney Island Inc 27947 Groesback Hwy Web: www.nationalconeyisland.com	Roseville	MI	48066	586-771-7744	771-9578
Nations Foodservice Inc 11090 San Pablo Ave Ste 200 Web: nationsrestaurants.com	El Cerrito	CA	94530	510-237-1952	
New York Fries 1220 Yonge St Ste 400 Web: www.newyorkfries.com	Toronto	ON	M4T1W1	416-963-5005	963-4920
Newport Bay Restaurants 2865 NW Town Ctr Loop. Web: www.newportbay.com	Portland	OR	97006	503-645-2526	620-6149
Nexdine LLC 100 Pleasant St Web: www.nexdine.com	Dracut	MA	01826	978-674-8464	
Ninety-Nine Restaurant & Pubs 160 Olympia Ave. Web: www.99restaurants.com	Woburn	MA	01801	781-933-8999	
Noble Roman's Pizza Inc One Virginia Ave Ste 300 Web: www.nobleromans.com	Indianapolis	IN	46204	317-634-3377	636-3207
Noodles & Co 520 Zang St Web: www.noodles.com	Broomfield	CO	80021	720-214-1900	214-1933
Norsan Group Inc 2445 Meadowbrook Pkwy *Fax Area Code: 770 ■ Web: norsan.net	Duluth	GA	30096	678-242-1654	414-0617*
North Beach Pizza Inc 1462 Grant Ave Web: www.northbeachpizza.com	San Francisco	CA	94133	415-433-2444	433-7217
NPC International Inc 7300 W 129th St TF: 866-299-1148 ■ Web: www.npcinternational.com	Overland Park	KS	66213	913-327-5555	327-5850
O'Charley's Inc 3038 Sidco Dr NASDAQ: CHUX ■ Web: ocharleys.com	Nashville	TN	37204	615-256-8500	782-5043
Office Beer Bar & Grill 728 Thompson Ave Rt 22 W Web: www.office-beerbar.com	Bridgewater	NJ	08805	732-469-0066	469-7041
Old Chicago Restaurants 100 Superior Plaza Way Ste 100 *Fax Area Code: 303 ■ Web: www.oldchicago.com	Superior	CO	80027	720-304-2048	664-4199*
Old Country Buffet Restaurants (OCB) 405 Lancaster Avenue Web: www.oldcountrybuffet.com/	Greer	SC	29650	651-994-8608	365-2356
Old Spaghetti Factory Inc (OSF) 0715 SW Bancroft St Web: www.osf.com	Portland	OR	97239	503-225-0433	226-6214
Olga's Kitchen Inc 1940 Northwood Dr. Web: www.olgas.com	Troy	MI	48084	248-362-0001	362-2013
Olive Garden 1000 Darden Center Dr PO Box 695017 *Fax: Mail Rm ■ Web: www.olivegarden.com	Orlando	FL	32869	407-245-4336	245-5389*
Orange Julius of America 7505 Metro Blvd. *Fax: Mktg ■ TF: 866-793-7582 ■ Web: www.dairyqueen.com	Minneapolis	MN	55439	952-830-0200	*
Original Pancake House Franchising Inc 8601 SW 24th Ave Web: www.originalpancakehouse.com	Portland	OR	97219	503-246-9007	
Outback Steakhouse Inc 2202 NW Shore Blvd 5th Fl Web: www.outback.com	Tampa	FL	33607	813-282-1225	281-2114
PacPizza LLC 220 Porter Dr Ste 100 Web: pacpizza.com	San Ramon	CA	94583	925-838-8567	838-5801
Palm Management Corp 1730 Rhode Island Ave NW Ste 900 TF: 800-388-7256 ■ Web: www.thepalm.com	Washington	DC	20036	202-775-7256	775-8292
Palomino Restaurant Rotisseria Bar 1420 Fifth Ave. Web: www.palomino.com	Seattle	WA	98101	206-623-1300	547-4829
Panchero's Mexican Grill 2475 Coral Ct Ste B TF: 888-639-2378 ■ Web: www.pancheros.com	Coralville	IA	52241	319-545-6565	545-6570
Panda Express 1717 Walnut Grove Ave TF: 800-877-8988 ■ Web: www.pandaexpress.com	Rosemead	CA	91770	626-312-5401	312-9508
Panda Restaurant Group Inc 1683 Walnut Grove Ave TF: 800-877-8988 ■ Web: www.pandarg.com	Rosemead	CA	91770	626-799-9898	372-8288
Papa Gino's Inc 600 Providence Hwy. TF: 800-727-2446 ■ Web: www.papaginos.com	Dedham	MA	02026	781-461-1200	461-1896
Papa Murphy's International Inc 8000 NE Pkwy Dr Ste 350 TF: 800-778-7879 ■ Web: www.papamurphys.com	Vancouver	WA	98662	360-260-7272	260-0500
Pappas Restaurants Inc 13939 NW Fwy TF: 877-277-2748 ■ Web: www.pappas.com	Houston	TX	77040	713-869-0151	869-4932
Pappas Seafood House 13939 NW Fwy TF: 877-277-2748 ■ Web: www.pappas.com	Houston	TX	77040	713-869-0151	869-4932
Pappasito's Cantina 13070 Hwy 290 Web: www.pappasitos.com	Houston	TX	77040	713-462-0246	
Parco Ltd Co 998 Fremont Ave	Dubuque	IA	52003	563-557-1337	
Pasta House Co 1143 Macklind Ave. Web: www.pastahouse.com	Saint Louis	MO	63110	314-535-6644	531-2499
Pasta Pomodoro Inc 851 Cherry Ave Ste 27 Web: www.pastapomodoro.com	San Bruno	CA	94066	415-241-5200	431-8940
Pat O'Brien's International Inc 718 St Peter St TF: 800-597-4823 ■ Web: www.patobriens.com	New Orleans	LA	70116	504-525-4823	582-6918
Patina Group 400 S Hope St 9th Fl. Web: www.patinagroup.com	Los Angeles	CA	90071	213-239-2500	239-2506
Paul Revere's Pizza International Ltd 1570 42nd St NE Web: www.paulreverespizza.com	Cedar Rapids	IA	52402	319-395-9113	395-9115
Pei Wei 7676 E Pinnacle Peak Rd. Web: www.peiwei.com	Scottsdale	AZ	85255	480-888-3000	
Penguin Point Franchise Systems Inc 2691 E US 30 PO Box 975 TF: 800-577-5755 ■ Web: www.penguinpoint.com	Warsaw	IN	46580	574-267-3107	267-3154
Pepe's Inc 1325 W 15th St Web: www.pepes.com	Chicago	IL	60608	312-733-2500	733-2564
Perkins Restaurant & Bakery 6075 Poplar Ave Ste 800 TF: 800-877-7375 ■ Web: www.perkinsrestaurants.com	Memphis	TN	38119	901-766-6400	766-6482
Peter Piper Inc 950 W Behrend Dr Ste 102 TF: 800-899-3425 ■ Web: www.peterpiperpizza.com	Phoenix	AZ	85027	480-609-6400	609-6577
PF Chang's China Bistro Inc 7676 E Pinnacle Peak Rd NASDAQ: PFCB ■ TF: 866-732-4264 ■ Web: www.pfchangs.com	Scottsdale	AZ	85255	480-888-3000	
Piatti Restaurant Co 625 Redwood Hwy. Web: www.piatti.com	Mill Valley	CA	94941	415-380-2525	380-2530
Piccadilly Cafeterias Inc 3332 S Sherwood Forest Blvd *Fax Area Code: 318 ■ TF: 800-552-7422 ■ Web: www.piccadilly.com	Baton Rouge	LA	70816	225-293-4853	445-4740*
Piccadilly Circus Pizza 1007 Okoboji Ave PO Box 188 *Fax Area Code: 712 ■ TF: 800-338-4340 ■ Web: www.pcpizza.com	Milford	IA	51351	800-338-4340	338-2263*
Pitt Grill Inc 928 Shady Ln	Lake Charles	LA	70601	337-479-1320	582-4297
Pizza Boli's 5721 Falls Rd 5725 Falls Rd TF: 800-234-2654 ■ Web: www.pizzabolis.com	Baltimore	MD	21209	410-323-3278	323-7745
Pizza Factory Inc 49430 Rd 426 TF: 800-654-4840 ■ Web: www.pizzafactory.com	Oakhurst	CA	93644	559-683-3377	683-6879
Pizza Inn Inc 3551 Plano Pkwy. NASDAQ: RAVE ■ TF: 800-880-9955 ■ Web: www.pizzainn.com	The Colony	TX	75056	469-384-5000	384-5058
Pizza King Inc 221 Farabee Dr Web: theoriginalpizzaking.com	Lafayette	IN	47905	765-447-2172	447-5491
Pizza Plus Pizza Inc 299 Franklin Dr. TF: 800-675-1220 ■ Web: www.pizzaplusinc.com	Blountville	TN	37617	423-279-9335	279-0551
Pizza Pro Inc 2107 N Second St PO Box 1285 TF: 800-777-7554 ■ Web: www.pizzapro.com	Cabot	AR	72023	501-605-1175	605-1204
Pizza Ranch Inc 204 19th St SE TF: 800-321-3401 ■ Web: www.pizzaranch.com	Orange City	IA	51041	800-321-3401	
Planet Hollywood International Inc 4700 Millenia Blvd Ste 400 Web: www.planethollywoodintl.com	Orlando	FL	32839	407-903-5500	
Popeyes Louisiana Kitchen 5555 Glenridge Connector NE Ste 300 Web: www.popeyes.com	Atlanta	GA	30342	404-459-4450	459-4533
Potbelly Sandwich Works 222 Merchandise Mart Plz Ste 2300 Web: www.potbelly.com	Chicago	IL	60654	312-951-0600	951-0300

	City	State	Zip	Phone	Fax
Pretzelmaker 1346 Oakbrook Dr Ste 170	Norcross	GA	30093	877-639-2361	
TF: 877-639-2361 ■ *Web:* pretzelmaker.com					
Qdoba Restaurant Corp 4865 WaRd Rd Ste 500	Wheat Ridge	CO	80033	720-898-2300	898-2396
Web: www.qdoba.com					
Quality Dining Inc 4220 Edison Lakes Pkwy	Mishawaka	IN	46545	574-271-4600	271-4612
TF: 800-589-3820 ■ *Web:* www.qdi.com					
Quiznos Corp 1275 Grant St Ste 200	Denver	CO	80203	720-359-3300	359-3399
TF: 866-486-2783 ■ *Web:* www.quiznos.com					
Rafferty's Inc 1750 Scottsville Rd Ste 2	Bowling Green	KY	42104	270-781-2857	781-2860
Web: www.raffertys.com					
Rainforest Cafe 1510 W Loop S	Houston	TX	77027	713-850-1010	
Web: www.rainforestcafe.com					
Ram Restaurant & Brewery PO Box 98768 PO Box 99010	Lakewood	WA	98499	253-584-3191	588-9617
Ram's Horn Restaurant 26200 W 12 Mile Rd	Southfield	MI	48034	248-350-3430	
Web: ramshornrestaurants.com					
Red Robin Gourmet Burgers Inc 6312 S Fiddlers Green Cir Ste 200-N	Greenwood Village	CO	80111	303-846-6000	846-6013
NASDAQ: RRGB ■ *TF:* 877-733-6543 ■ *Web:* www.redrobin.com					
Republic Foods Inc 1101 Wootton Pkwy Ste 460	Rockville	MD	20852	301-656-6687	656-3934
Web: www.republicfoods.com					
Restaurant Assoc Inc 132 West 31st Street Ste 601	New York	NY	10001	212-613-5500	
Web: www.restaurantassociates.com					
Restaurant Developers Corp 7010 Engle Rd Ste 100	Cleveland	OH	44130	440-625-3080	
TF: 888-860-5082 ■ *Web:* www.mrhero.com					
Restaurants Unlimited Inc 411 First Ave S Ste 200	Seattle	WA	98104	206-634-0550	
TF: 877-855-6106 ■ *Web:* www.r-u-i.com					
Rib Crib Corp 4535 S Harvard Ave	Tulsa	OK	74135	918-712-7427	728-6945
TF: 800-275-9677 ■ *Web:* www.ribcrib.com					
Riscky's Barbecue 2314 Azle Ave	Fort Worth	TX	76164	817-624-8662	624-3777
Web: www.risckys.com					
Roc Management & Assoc Inc 1601 Keokuk Ave	Spirit Lake	IA	51360	712-336-3933	
Rocky Rococo 105 E Wisconsin Ave	Oconomowoc	WI	53066	262-569-5580	569-5591
TF: 800-888-7625 ■ *Web:* www.rockyrococo.com					
Romano's Macaroni Grill 4535 Belt Line Rd	Addison	TX	75001	972-386-3831	386-9535
Web: www.macaronigrill.com					
Rosati's Pizza 28381 Davis Pkwy Ste 701	Warrenville	IL	60555	630-393-2280	393-2281
Web: rosatispizza.com					
Rosebud Restaurant 1419 W Diversey Pkwy	Chicago	IL	60614	773-325-9700	325-9708
Web: www.rosebudrestaurants.com					
Roy's Restaurants 1300 Dove St Ste 105	Newport Beach	CA	92660	949-222-2223	
Web: www.roysrestaurant.com					
RPM Pizza LLC 15384 Fifth St	Gulfport	MS	39503	228-832-4000	832-1092
Web: www.rpmpizza.com					
Rubio's Restaurants Inc 1902 Wright Pl Ste 300	Carlsbad	CA	92008	760-929-8226	929-8203
TF: 800-354-4199 ■ *Web:* www.rubios.com					
Ruby Tuesday Inc 150 W Church Ave	Maryville	TN	37801	865-379-5700	380-7639*
NYSE: RT ■ **Fax:* Mktg ■ *TF:* 800-325-0755 ■ *Web:* www.rubytuesday.com					
Runza National Inc 5931 S 58th St	Lincoln	NE	68516	402-423-2394	
Web: runza.com					
Russ' Restaurants Inc 390 E Eigth St	Holland	MI	49423	616-396-6571	396-6755
TF: 800-521-1778 ■ *Web:* www.russrestaurants.com					
Rusty's Pizza Parlors Inc 228 W Carillo St Ste F	Santa Barbara	CA	93101	805-963-9127	962-5054
Web: www.rustyspizza.com					
Ruth's Hospitality Group Inc 1030 W Canton Ave Ste 100`	Winter Park	FL	32789	407-333-7440	833-9625
NASDAQ: RUTH ■ *TF Sales:* 800-544-0808 ■ *Web:* www.ruthschris.com					
Sagebrush Steakhouse 129 Fast Ln	Mooresville	NC	28117	704-660-5939	799-6199
TF: 877-704-5939 ■ *Web:* www.sagebrushsteakhouse.com					
Sandella's LLC Nine Brookside Rd	West Redding	CT	06896	203-544-9984	544-9981
Web: www.sandellas.com					
Sasnak Management Corp 1877 N Rock Rd	Wichita	KS	67206	316-683-2611	
Schwartz Bros Restaurants 325 118th Ave SE Ste 106	Bellevue	WA	98005	425-455-3948	451-3573
Web: www.schwartzbros.com					
Select Restaurants Inc 2000 Auburn Dr 1 Chagrin Highlands	Cleveland	OH	44122	216-464-6606	464-8565
Web: www.selectrestaurants.com					
Selrico Services Inc 717 W Ashby Pl	San Antonio	TX	78212	210-737-8220	737-7994
Web: selricoservices.com					
SERVUS 4201 Mannheim Rd Ste A	Jasper	IN	47546	812-482-3212	482-4013
Web: www.brsidal.com					
Shakey's USA 2200 W Valley Blvd	Alhambra	CA	91803	626-576-0616	284-6870
TF: 888-444-6686 ■ *Web:* www.shakeys.com					
Shari's Restaurant & Pies 9400 SW Gemini Dr	Beaverton	OR	97008	503-605-4299	605-4260
TF: 800-433-5334 ■ *Web:* www.sharis.com					
Shoney's Restaurants Inc 1717 Elm Hill Pk Ste B1	Nashville	TN	37210	615-231-2333	
Web: www.shoneys.com					
Shuhei Inc 23360 Chagrin Blvd	Beachwood	OH	44122	216-464-1720	
Web: shuheirestaurant.com					
Silver Diner Inc 12276 Rockville Pk	Rockville	MD	20852	301-770-0333	770-2832
TF: 866-561-0518 ■ *Web:* www.silverdiner.com					
Sizzler Restaurants 25910 Acero Rd Ste 350	Mission Viejo	CA	92691	855-895-9703	
Web: www.sizzler.com					
Sizzling Wok International Inc 2560 Shell Rd	Richmond	BC	V6X0B8	604-207-8871	
Skyline Chili Inc 4180 Thunderbird Ln	Fairfield	OH	45014	513-874-1188	874-3591
TF General: 800-443-4371 ■ *Web:* www.skylinechili.com					
Small Sun Inc 2204 Danforth Ave	Toronto	ON	M4C1K3	416-996-3333	
Web: www.holeechow.com					
Smith & Wollensky Restaurant Group Inc 318 N State St	Chicago	IL	60654	312-670-9900	
Web: www.smithandwollensky.com					
Smith Bros Restaurant Corp 16 N Marengo Ave Ste 609	Pasadena	CA	91101	626-577-2400	577-8330
Web: www.smithbrothersrestaurants.com					
Smitty's Canada Ltd 501 18th Ave SW Ste 600	Calgary	AB	T2S0C7	403-229-3838	229-3899
Web: www.smittys.ca					
Snappy Tomato Pizza Co 6111 A Burgundy Hill Dr	Burlington	KY	41005	859-525-4680	525-4686
TF: 888-463-7627 ■ *Web:* www.snappytomato.com					
Sobik's Subs 620 Crown Oak Ctr Dr Ste 104	Longwood	FL	32750	407-671-2600	671-0260
Web: www.sobiks.com					
Sonic Corp 300 Johnny Bench Dr	Oklahoma City	OK	73104	405-225-5000	
NASDAQ: SONC ■ *TF:* 877-828-7868 ■ *Web:* sonicdrivein.com					
Sonic Drive-in Restaurants 300 Johnny Bench Dr	Oklahoma City	OK	73104	405-225-5000	
TF: 877-828-7868 ■ *Web:* www.sonicdrivein.com					
Sonny Bryan's Smokehouse 12720 Hilcrest Rd Ste 910	Dallas	TX	75230	214-350-1800	350-3738
Web: www.sonnybryans.com					
Sonny's Franchise Co 2605 Maitland Ctr Pkwy Ste C	Maitland	FL	32751	407-660-8888	660-9050
Web: www.sonnysbbq.com					
Souplantation 15822 Bernardo Ctr Dr Ste A	San Diego	CA	92127	858-675-1600	
Web: www.souplantation.com					
Southern Multifoods Inc 101 E Cherokee St	Jacksonville	TX	75766	903-586-1524	
Web: www.smi-tex.com					
Spaghetti Warehouse Inc 1255 W I-20	Arlington	TX	76017	817-557-0321	550-0908*
**Fax Area Code:* 972 ■ *Web:* www.meatballs.com					
Spangles Inc 437 N Hillside St	Wichita	KS	67214	316-685-8817	685-1671
Web: www.spanglesinc.com					
Specialty Restaurants Corp 8191 E Kaiser Blvd	Anaheim	CA	92808	714-279-6100	998-7574
Web: www.specialtyrestaurants.com					
Stanford's Restaurant & Bar 913 Lloyd Ctr Ste 200	Portland	OR	97232	503-335-0811	
Web: www.stanfords.com					
Steak Escape 222 Neilston St	Columbus	OH	43215	614-224-0300	224-6460
Web: www.steakescape.com					
Steak N Shake Co 3810 W Washington Holt Rd	Indianapolis	IN	46241	317-241-0483	
TF: 877-785-6745 ■ *Web:* www.steaknshake.com					
Stockade Cos 113 E Third St	Taylor	TX	78681	512-352-5030	297-2578
Web: www.stockadecompanies.com					
Strang Corp 8905 Lake Ave	Cleveland	OH	44102	216-961-6767	961-1966
Web: www.strangcorp.com					
Strategic Restaurants Inc 3000 Executive Pkwy Ste 515	San Ramon	CA	94583	925-328-3300	328-3333
Web: www.strategicrestaurants.com					
Stuart Anderson's Black Angus 4410 El Camino Real	Los Altos	CA	94022	800-382-3852	
TF: 800-382-3852 ■ *Web:* www.stuartanderson.com					
Stuckey's Corp 8555 16th St Ste 850	Silver Spring	MD	20910	301-585-8222	585-8997
TF: 800-423-6171 ■ *Web:* www.stuckeys.com					
Stuft Pizza Franchise Corp 50855 Washington St Ste 210	La Quinta	CA	92253	760-777-1660	777-1948
Web: www.stuftpizza.com					
Sub Station II Inc PO Box 2260	Sumter	SC	29151	803-773-4711	775-2220
Web: www.substationii.com					
Summerwood Corp 14 Balligomingo Rd	Conshohocken	PA	19428	610-520-1000	
TF: 800-760-0950 ■ *Web:* www.summerwood.biz					
Super Subby's Inc 8924 N Dixie Dr	Dayton	OH	45414	937-898-0996	898-2367
Web: www.subbys.com					
Sushi Doraku 1104 Lincoln Rd	Miami Beach	FL	33139	305-695-8383	695-1441
Web: www.dorakusushi.com					
Sweet Tomatoes 15822 Bernardo Ctr Dr Ste A	San Diego	CA	92127	858-675-1600	
Web: www.souplantation.com					
Tacala LLC 3750 Corporate Woods Dr	Vestavia Hills	AL	35242	205-443-9600	443-9700
TF: 800-822-6235 ■ *Web:* www.tacala.com					
Taco Bell Corp 1 Glen Bell Way	Irvine	CA	92618	949-863-4000	863-2252
Web: www.tacobell.com					
Taco Cabana Inc 8918 Tesoro Dr Ste 200	San Antonio	TX	78217	210-804-0990	804-1970
TF: 800-357-9924 ■ *Web:* www.tacocabana.com					
Taco Mayo 10405 Greenbriar Pl	Oklahoma City	OK	73159	405-691-8226	
Web: www.tacomayo.com/default.html					
Taco Time International Inc 9311 E Via de Venutra	Scottsdale	AZ	85258	480-362-4800	362-4812
TF: 866-452-4252 ■ *Web:* www.tacotime.com					
Tacoma Inc 328 E Church St	Martinsville	VA	24112	276-666-9417	666-9427
TF: 800-352-9417 ■ *Web:* www.gototaco.com					
Tacos Mexico Inc 5120 E Olympic Blvd	Los Angeles	CA	90022	323-266-0482	266-1721
Web: tacosmexico.com					
Tavistock Restaurants LLC 6475 Christie Ave Ste 300	Emeryville	CA	94608	510-594-4262	654-8295
Web: tavistockrestaurants.com					
Ted's Hot Dogs 95 Roger Chaffee Dr	Amherst	NY	14228	716-691-3731	
Web: www.tedshotdogs.com					
Tee Jaye's Country Place Restaurants 1363 Parsons Ave PO Box 06359	Columbus	OH	43206	614-443-9773	443-0613
Web: www.barnyardbuster.com					
Temple Square Hospitality Corp 15 E S Temple St 9th Fl	Salt Lake City	UT	84150	801-531-1000	539-3117
Web: www.templesquare.com					
Texas Roadhouse Inc 6040 Dutchmans Ln Ste 400	Louisville	KY	40205	502-426-9984	426-9924
NASDAQ: TXRH ■ *TF:* 800-839-7623 ■ *Web:* www.texasroadhouse.com					
Thompson Hospitality 505 Huntmar Pk Dr Ste 350	Herndon	VA	20170	703-964-5500	759-1538
TF: 800-842-2737 ■ *Web:* www.thompsonhospitality.com					
Thundercloud Subs 1102 W Sixth St	Austin	TX	78703	512-479-8805	479-8806
Web: www.thundercloud.com					

	Phone	Fax
Tim Hortons Inc 874 Sinclair Rd. Oakville ON L6K2Y1 *NYSE:* THI ■ *TF:* 888-601-1616 ■ *Web:* www.timhortons.com	905-845-6511	845-0265
Toarmina's Pizza 32785 Cherry Hill Rd. Westland MI 48186 *Web:* www.toarminas.com	734-728-0060	
TooJays Original Gourmet Deli 3654 Georgia Ave West Palm Beach FL 33405 *Web:* www.toojays.com	561-659-9011	659-9703
Trader Vic's Inc Nine Anchor Dr Emeryville CA 94608 *Web:* www.tradervics.com	510-653-3400	653-9384
Trail Dust Steak Houses Inc 2300 E Lamar Arlington TX 76006 *Web:* www.traildust.com	817-640-6411	640-2930
Travaglini Enterprises 231 Chestnut St. Meadville PA 16335	814-724-4880	
Tri City Foods Inc 1400 Opus Pl Ste 900 Downers Grove IL 60515 *Web:* www.heartlandfoodcorp.com	630-598-3300	
Tripps Restaurants 1337 Winstead Pl Greensboro NC 27408 *Web:* www.trippsrestaurants.com	336-272-9355	272-5568
TS Restaurants of California & Hawaii 2335 Kalakaua Ave Ste 116 Honolulu HI 96815 *Web:* www.hulapie.com	808-922-2268	
Tubbys Grilled Submarines 31920 Groesbeck Hwy Fraser MI 48026 **Fax Area Code:* 586 ■ *TF:* 800-752-0644 ■ *Web:* www.tubby.com	800-752-0644	293-5088*
Tudor's Biscuit World PO Box 3603 Charleston WV 25336 *Web:* www.tudorsbiscuitworld.com	304-343-4026	
Tumbleweed Inc 2301 River Rd Louisville KY 40206 *Web:* www.tumbleweedrestaurants.com	502-893-0323	893-6676
TWA Restaurant Group Inc 16012 Metcalf Ave Ste 1 Overland Park KS 66085 *Web:* www.twabrands.com	913-239-0266	239-9768
Uno Chicago Grill 100 Charles Pk Rd Boston MA 02132 *TF:* 866-600-8667 ■ *Web:* www.unos.com	617-323-9200	469-3949
Uno Restaurant Corp 100 Charles Pk Rd Boston MA 02132 *TF:* 866-600-8667 ■ *Web:* www.unos.com	617-323-9200	323-6906
V & J Holding Cos Inc 6933 W Brown Deer Rd Milwaukee WI 53223 *Web:* www.vjfoods.com	414-365-9003	365-9467
Valentino's 2601 S 70th St Lincoln NE 68506 **Fax Area Code:* 308 ■ *TF:* 888-240-8257 ■ *Web:* www.valentinos.com	402-434-9350	382-7146*
Villa Enterprises Management Ltd Inc 25 Washington St Morristown NJ 07960 *Web:* www.villapizza.com	973-285-4800	695-0912
Village Inn 400 W 48th Ave Denver CO 80216 **Fax:* Cust Svc ■ *TF:* 800-800-3644 ■ *Web:* www.villageinn.com	303-296-2121	672-2676*
Viva Burrito Co 860 E 16th St Tucson AZ 85719 *Web:* vivaburritoco.com	520-882-8713	
Vocelli Pizza 1005 S Bee St Pittsburgh PA 15220 *Web:* www.vocellipizza.com	412-919-2100	937-9204
Waffle House Inc 5986 Financial Dr Norcross GA 30071 **Fax Area Code:* 555 ■ *TF:* 877-992-3353 ■ *Web:* www.wafflehouse.com	770-729-5700	555-5555*
Wahoo's Fish Taco 2855 Pullman St Santa Ana CA 92705 *Web:* www.wahoos.com	949-222-0670	222-0750
Ward's Food Systems Inc 5133 Lincoln Rd Ext Hattiesburg MS 39402 *Web:* wardsrestaurants.com	601-268-9273	
Weathervane Seafood Restaurant 306 US Rt 1 Kittery ME 03904 *TF:* 800-914-1774 ■ *Web:* www.weathervaneseafoods.com	207-439-0330	439-7754
Wendy's International Inc 1 Dave Thomas Blvd Dublin OH 43017 *Web:* www.wendys.com	614-764-3100	764-3330
Whataburger Restaurants LP 300 Concord Plz PO Box 791990 San Antonio TX 78216 *Web:* www.whataburger.com	210-476-6000	
Willie G's 1605 Post Oak Blvd Houston TX 77056 *Web:* www.williegs.com	713-840-7190	840-7820
Winger's USA Inc 404 East 4500 South Ste A12 Murray UT 84107 *Web:* www.wingers.info	801-261-3700	
Wingstop Restaurants Inc 1101 E Arapaho Rd Ste 150 Richardson TX 75081 *Web:* www.wingstop.com	972-686-6500	686-6502
Wolfgang Puck Worldwide Inc 100 N Crescent Dr Ste 100 Beverly Hills CA 90210 *Web:* www.wolfgangpuck.com	310-432-1640	432-1640
World Wrapps 3023 80th Ave SE Ste 200 Mercer Island WA 98040 **Fax Area Code:* 425 ■ *TF:* 888-233-9727 ■ *Web:* www.worldwrapps.com	206-233-9727	232-5540*
Yamashiro Inc 1999 N Sycamore Ave Hollywood CA 90068 *Web:* yamashirohollywood.com	323-466-5125	
Yard House Restaurant 71 Fortune Dr Irvine CA 92618 *Web:* www.yardhouse.com	949-753-9373	
Yaya's Flame Broiled Chicken 521 S Dort Hwy Flint MI 48503 *Web:* www.yayas.com	810-235-6550	235-5210
Yoshinoya Beef Bowl 991 Knox St Torrance CA 90502 *TF:* 800-576-8017 ■ *Web:* www.yoshinoyaamerica.com	310-527-6060	527-6050
Yum! Brands Inc 1441 Gardiner Ln Louisville KY 40213 *NYSE:* YUM ■ *TF:* 800-225-5532 ■ *Web:* www.yum.com	502-874-8300	874-8323
Zero's Subs 3760 Virginia Beach Blvd Virginia Beach VA 23452 *Web:* zerossubs.com	757-463-9114	
Zyng Inc RPO Atwater PO Box 72108 Montreal QC H3J2Z6 *Web:* www.zyng.com	514-288-8800	939-8808

674 RESTAURANTS (INDIVIDUAL)

SEE ALSO Shopping/Dining/Entertainment Districts p. 1823; Restaurant Companies p. 3069

Individual restaurants are organized by city names within state and province groupings. (Canadian provinces are interfiled among the US states, in alphabetical order.)

	Phone	Fax
Cubs' Ac 1950 S Industrial Hwy Ann Arbor MI 48104 *Web:* www.coloniallanescubsac.com	734-665-4474	
Sodexo Canada Ltd 3350 S Service Rd Burlington ON L7N3M6 *Web:* ca.sodexo.com	905-632-8592	
F Gs Inc 815 W Van Buren St Ste 302 Chicago IL 60607 *Web:* fgs-inc.com	312-421-3060	
Reunion Tower 300 Reunion Blvd E Dallas TX 75207 *Web:* www.reuniontower.com	214-651-1234	
Alumni Center, The 1241 University Dr N Fargo ND 58102 *Web:* www.ndsualumni.com	701-231-6800	
La Fontaine Bleue Inc 7514 S Ritchie Hwy Glen Burnie MD 21061 *Web:* www.lafontainebleu.com	410-760-4115	
Abbington Distinctive Banquets 3s002 Il Route 53 Glen Ellyn IL 60137 *Web:* www.abbingtonbanquets.com	630-942-8600	
Pine Mountain Lake Association 19228 Pine Mtn Dr Groveland CA 95321 *Web:* www.pinemountainlake.com	209-962-8600	
Stonegate Conference & Banquet Centre, The 2401 W Higgins Rd Hoffman Estates IL 60169 *Web:* www.thestonegate.com	847-884-7000	
Valenti Mid-south Management LLC 1775 Moriah Woods Blvd Ste 5 Memphis TN 38117 *Web:* www.valentirestaurants.com	901-684-1215	
Mesquite Championship Rodeo Inc 1818 Rodeo Dr Mesquite TX 75149 *Web:* www.mesquiterodeo.com	972-285-8777	
W Montreal Hotel 901 Victoria Sq Montreal QC H2Z1R1 *Web:* www.wmontrealhotel.com	514-395-3100	
Really Simple LLC 225 W 35th St Ste 1101 New York NY 10001 *Web:* www.reallysimple.com	212-683-4696	
COCO Development LLC 7101 Mercy Rd Ste 300 Omaha NE 68106 *Web:* benaissance.com	402-884-7021	
Palm-Aire Country Club in Pompano Beach 2600 N Palm Aire Dr Pompano Beach FL 33069 *Web:* www.palmairegolf.com	954-975-6225	
Birchwood Manor 111 N Jefferson Rd Whippany NJ 07981 *Web:* birchwoodmanor.com	973-887-1414	

Alabama

	Phone	Fax
Bottega 2240 Highland Ave S Birmingham AL 35205 *Web:* bottegarestaurant.com	205-939-1000	939-1536
Daniel George 2837 Culver Rd Birmingham AL 35223 *Web:* www.birminghammenus.com/danielgeorge	205-871-3266	871-7266
Dreamland BBQ 1427 14th Ave S Birmingham AL 35205 *TF:* 800-752-0544 ■ *Web:* www.dreamlandbbq.com	205-933-2133	933-9770
Highlands Bar & Grill 2011 11th Ave S Birmingham AL 35205 *Web:* www.highlandsbarandgrill.com	205-939-1400	939-1405
Hot & Hot Fish Club 2180 11th Ct S Birmingham AL 35205 *Web:* www.birminghammenus.com	205-933-5474	933-6243
J Alexanders 3320 Galleria Cir Birmingham AL 35244 *NASDAQ:* JAX ■ *Web:* www.jalexanders.com	205-733-9995	733-8461
Jim-n-Nick's 1908 11th Ave S Birmingham AL 35205 *Web:* jimnnicks.com	205-320-1060	637-2977
La Dolce Vita 1851 Montgomery Hwy Birmingham AL 35244 *Web:* ladolcevitahoover.com	205-985-2909	
Little Savannah 3811 Clairmont Ave Birmingham AL 35222 *Web:* www.birminghammenus.com	205-591-1119	
Ming's Cuisine 514 Cahaba Pk Cir Birmingham AL 35242 *Web:* mingsmenu.com	205-991-3803	
Niki's West 233 Finley Ave W Birmingham AL 35204 *Web:* nikiswest.com	205-252-5751	252-8163
Ocean 1218 20th St S Birmingham AL 35205 *Web:* www.oceanbirmingham.com	205-933-0999	933-0998
Sabor Latino Restaurant 112 Green Springs Hwy Birmingham AL 35209 *Web:* www.misaborlatino.webs.com	205-942-9480	942-9428
Shula's Steak House 1000 Riverchase Galleria Birmingham AL 35244 *Web:* www.donshula.com	205-444-5750	987-0454
Sol Y Luna 2811 Seventh Ave S Birmingham AL 35233 *Web:* www.birminghammenus.com	205-322-1186	322-1708
Surin West 1918 11th Ave S Birmingham AL 35205 *Web:* www.surinwest.com	205-324-1928	
Taste of Thailand 3321 Lorna Rd Birmingham AL 35216	205-978-6863	
Cocina Superior 587 Brookwood Village Homewood AL 35209 *Web:* www.thecocinasuperior.com	205-259-1980	259-1987
Nabeel's Cafe 1706 Oxmoor Rd Homewood AL 35209 *Web:* www.nabeels.com	205-879-9292	879-9291
Stix 3250 Galleria Cir Hoover AL 35244 *Web:* www.stixonline.com	205-982-3070	982-3073
Big Spring Cafe 2906 Governors Dr Huntsville AL 35805	256-539-9994	
Cafe 302 2700 Winchester Rd NE Huntsville AL 35811	256-852-3442	
Logan's Roadhouse 4249 Balmoral Dr SW Huntsville AL 35801 *Web:* www.logansroadhouse.com	256-881-0584	881-3296
Rolo's Cafe 975 Airport Rd Huntsville AL 35802	256-883-7656	
Scrugg's Barbeque 7529 Moores Mill Rd Huntsville AL 35811 *Web:* www.scruggsbbq.com	256-859-6800	
Thai Garden Restaurant Inc 800 Wellman Ave NE Huntsville AL 35801 *Web:* www.ilovethaigarden.com/i_love_thai_garden/thai_garden_restaurant.html	256-534-0122	564-7341
Brick Pit 5456 Old Shell Rd Mobile AL 36608 *Web:* www.brickpit.com	251-343-0001	
Cafe 615 615 Dauphin St Mobile AL 36602 *Web:* cafe615mobile.com	251-432-8434	433-9885
Downtowners 107 Dauphin St Mobile AL 36602	251-433-8868	
Saucy-Q Bar B Que 1111 Government St Mobile AL 36604 *Web:* saucyqbbq.com	251-433-7427	433-7428
Dreamland Bar-B-Que Ribs 101 Tallapoosa St Montgomery AL 36104 *Web:* www.dreamlandbbq.com	334-273-7427	273-7857
Island Delight Caribbean Restaurant 323 Airbase Blvd Montgomery AL 36108	334-264-0041	
Ixtapa 6132 Atlanta Hwy Montgomery AL 36117	334-272-5232	
King Buffet 2727 Bell Rd Montgomery AL 36117	334-273-8883	
Lek's Taste of Thailand 5421 Atlanta Hwy Montgomery AL 36109	334-244-8994	

				Phone	Fax
Mings Garden Chinese Restaurant 1741 Eastern Bypass *Web:* www.mingsgardenmontgomery.com	Montgomery	AL	36117	334-277-8188	
Peyton's Place 5344 Atlanta Hwy *Web:* peytonsplacelunch.tripod.com	Montgomery	AL	36109	334-396-3630	
Zoes Kitchen 7218 EastChase Pkwy *Web:* www.zoeskitchen.com	Montgomery	AL	36117	334-270-9115	
Baumhower's of Tuscaloosa 500 Harper Lee Dr *Web:* www.baumhowers.com	Tuscaloosa	AL	35404	205-556-5658	556-5639
Bento 1306 University Blvd Ste D	Tuscaloosa	AL	35401	205-758-7426	
Buffalo Phil's 1149 University Blvd *Web:* buffalophils.com	Tuscaloosa	AL	35401	205-758-3318	758-3310
Cypress Inn, The 501 Rice Mine Rd N *Web:* www.cypressinnrestaurant.com	Tuscaloosa	AL	35406	205-345-6963	345-6997
DePalma's Italian Cafe 2300 University Blvd *Web:* depalmasdowntown.com	Tuscaloosa	AL	35401	205-759-1879	
Dreamland Bar-B-que 5535 15th Ave E *Web:* www.dreamlandbbq.com	Tuscaloosa	AL	35405	205-758-8135	758-5158
Evangeline's 1653 McFarland Blvd *Web:* www.evangelinesrestaurant.com	Tuscaloosa	AL	35406	205-752-0830	
Kozy's Restaurant 3510 Loop Rd *Web:* www.killionrestaurants.com	Tuscaloosa	AL	35404	205-556-4112	633-4034
Los Tarascos 1759 Skyland Blvd.	Tuscaloosa	AL	35405	205-553-8896	
Rama Jama's 1000 Paul Bryant Dr	Tuscaloosa	AL	35401	205-750-0901	
Sol Azteca 1360 Montgomery Hwy Ste 128	Vestavia Hills	AL	35216	205-979-4902	

Alaska

				Phone	Fax
Aladdin's Fine Mediterranean 4240 Old Seward Hwy *Web:* www.aladdinsalaska.com	Anchorage	AK	99503	907-561-2373	563-5117
Bombay Deluxe 555 W Northern Lights Blvd *Web:* www.bombaydeluxe.com	Anchorage	AK	99503	907-277-1200	
Bradley House 11321 Old Seward Hwy *Web:* alaskabradleyhouse.com	Anchorage	AK	99515	907-336-7177	336-7178
Club Paris 417 W Fifth Ave *Web:* www.clubparisrestaurant.com	Anchorage	AK	99501	907-277-6332	277-6544
Crow's Nest 939 W Fifth Ave Hotel Captain Cook	Anchorage	AK	99501	907-343-2217	
Don Jose's 2052 E Northern Lights Blvd *Web:* www.alaskadonjoses.com	Anchorage	AK	99508	907-279-5111	279-2053
Glacier Brew House 737 W Fifth Ave *Web:* www.glacierbrewhouse.com	Anchorage	AK	99501	907-274-2739	277-1033
Gweenie's Old Alaska Restaurant 4333 SpenaRd Rd *Web:* gwenniesrestaurant.com	Anchorage	AK	99517	907-243-2090	
Jen's Restaurant 701 W 36th Ave *Web:* www.jensrestaurant.com	Anchorage	AK	99503	907-561-5367	561-5325
Kincaid Grill 6700 Jewel Lk Rd. *Web:* www.kincaidgrill.com	Anchorage	AK	99502	907-243-0507	243-5110
Kumagoro Restaurant 533 W Fourth Ave.	Anchorage	AK	99501	907-272-9905	
La Cabana 312 E Fourth Ave *Web:* alaskalacabana.com	Anchorage	AK	99501	907-272-0135	
Little Italy 2300 E 88th Ave. *Web:* littleitalyalaska.com	Anchorage	AK	99507	907-344-1515	
Los Arcos 2000 E Dowling St. *Web:* www.losarcosak.com	Anchorage	AK	99507	907-562-0477	
Marx Bros Cafe 627 W Third Ave *Web:* www.marxcafe.com	Anchorage	AK	99501	907-278-2133	258-6279
Peking Wok 4000 W Dimond Blvd *Web:* pekingwokak.com	Anchorage	AK	99502	907-248-1648	
Sacks Cafe 328 G St *Web:* www.sackscafe.com	Anchorage	AK	99501	907-276-3546	
Sea Galley Restaurant 4101 Credit Union Dr *Web:* seagalleyanchorage.com	Anchorage	AK	99503	907-563-3520	563-6382
Simon & Seafort's Saloon & Grill 420 L St *Web:* www.simonandseaforts.com	Anchorage	AK	99501	907-274-3502	274-2487
Snow Goose Restaurant 717 W Third Ave *Web:* www.alaskabeers.com	Anchorage	AK	99501	907-277-7727	277-0606
Sourdough Mining Co 5200 Juneau St. *Web:* www.sourdoughmining.com	Anchorage	AK	99518	907-563-2272	
Southside Bistro 1320 Huffman Pk Dr *Web:* www.southsidebistro.com	Anchorage	AK	99515	907-348-0088	348-0089
Villa Nova Restaurant 5121 Arctic Blvd Ste I *Web:* villanovaalaska.com	Anchorage	AK	99503	907-561-1660	
Alaska Salmon Bake In Alaskaland 2300 Airport Way *TF:* 800-354-7274 ■ *Web:* www.akvisit.com/salmon.html	Fairbanks	AK	99701	907-452-7274	
Cookie Jar 1006 Cadillac Ct *Web:* www.cookiejarfairbanks.com	Fairbanks	AK	99701	907-479-8319	479-8329
Gambardella's Pasta Bella 706 Second Ave *Web:* www.gambardellas.com	Fairbanks	AK	99701	907-457-4992	456-3425
Geraldo's 701 College Rd	Fairbanks	AK	99701	907-452-2299	452-7634
Ivory Jack's 2581 Goldstream Rd *Web:* www.ivoryjacks.alaskansavvy.com	Fairbanks	AK	99709	907-455-6665	455-4254
Lavelle's Bistro 575 First Ave *Web:* www.lavellesbistro.com	Fairbanks	AK	99701	907-450-0555	450-0444
Pump House, The 796 Chena Pump Rd. *Web:* www.pumphouse.com	Fairbanks	AK	99709	907-479-8452	479-8432
Soapy Smith's Pioneer Restaurant 543 Second Ave	Fairbanks	AK	99701	907-451-8380	
Thai House 412 Fifth Ave. *Web:* thaihousefairbanks.com	Fairbanks	AK	99701	907-452-6123	452-6124
Turtle Club 2098 Old Steese Hwy *Web:* www.alaskanturtle.com	Fairbanks	AK	99712	907-457-3883	
Vallata 2190 Goldstream Rd	Fairbanks	AK	99709	907-455-6600	
Zach's Catering 1717 University Ave S	Fairbanks	AK	99709	907-374-6582	
Seven Glaciers Restaurant 1000 Arlberg Ave *Web:* www.alyeska.com	Girdwood	AK	ESORT	907-754-2237	
Best Western Grandma's Feather Bed 9300 Glacier Hwy *TF:* 888-781-5005 ■ *Web:* www.grandmasfeatherbed.com	Juneau	AK	99801	907-789-5005	
Canton House 8585 Old Dairy Rd. *Web:* www.cantonhouse.net	Juneau	AK	99801	907-789-5075	790-2172
El Sombrero 157 S Franklin St. *Web:* elsombrerojuneau.com	Juneau	AK	99801	907-586-6770	586-6772
Glacier Restaurant Lounge 1873 Shell Simmons Dr Ste 220	Juneau	AK	99801	907-789-9538	789-3090
Hangar On The Wharf Two Marine Way Ste 106 *Web:* hangaronthewharf.com	Juneau	AK	99801	907-586-5018	586-8173
Mi Casa 9200 Glacier Hwy	Juneau	AK	99801	907-789-3636	789-1969
Red Dog Saloon 278 S Franklin St *Web:* www.reddogsaloon.com	Juneau	AK	99801	907-463-3658	
Seong's Sushi Bar 740 W Ninth St *Web:* seongssushibar.com	Juneau	AK	99801	907-586-4778	

Alberta

				Phone	Fax
Abruzzo Ristorante 402 Eigth St SW. *Web:* abruzzoristorante.com	Calgary	AB	T2P1Z9	403-237-5660	237-5661
Aida's Mediterranean Bistro 2208 Fourth St SW *Web:* www.aidasbistro.ca	Calgary	AB	T2S1W9	403-541-1189	
Antonio's Garlic Clove 2206 Fourth St SW	Calgary	AB	T2S1W9	403-228-0866	
Bonterra Trattoria 1016 Eigth St SW *Web:* www.bonterra.ca	Calgary	AB	T2R1K2	403-262-8480	
Buddha's Veggie Restaurant 5802 MacLeod Trail SW *Web:* www.buddhasveggie.com	Calgary	AB	T2H0K1	403-252-8830	
Buon Giorno Ristorante Italiano 823 17th Ave SW *Web:* buongiornoristoranteitaliano.ca	Calgary	AB	T2T0A1	403-244-5522	244-5631
Cactus Club Cafe 7010 MacLeod Trl S *Web:* www.cactusclubcafe.com	Calgary	AB	T2H0L3	403-255-1088	255-1049
Caesar's Steak House 512 Fourth Ave SW. *Web:* caesarssteakhouse.com	Calgary	AB	T2P0J6	403-264-1222	264-9933
Carver's Steakhouse 2620 32nd Ave NE	Calgary	AB	T1Y6B8	403-250-6327	
Catch Oyster Bar/Seafood Restaurant 100 Eigth Ave SE *Web:* hyatt.com	Calgary	AB	T2G0K6	403-206-0000	206-0005
Chianti Cafe 1438 17th Ave SW *Web:* www.chianticafe.ca	Calgary	AB	T2T0C8	403-229-1600	
China Rose Restaurant 228 28th St SE *Web:* www.chinarose.ca	Calgary	AB	T2A6J9	403-248-2711	248-6810
Cilantro 338 17th Ave SW *Web:* www.crmr.com/cilantro	Calgary	AB	T2S0A8	403-229-1177	245-5239
Co Do Vietnamese Restaurant 1411 17th Ave SW	Calgary	AB	T2T0C3	403-228-7798	
Coup, The 924 17th Ave SW *Web:* www.thecoup.ca	Calgary	AB	T2T0A2	403-541-1041	
Da Guido Ristorante 2001 Centre St N *Web:* www.daguido.ca	Calgary	AB	T2E2S9	403-276-1365	
Ed's Restaurant 202 17th Ave SE. *Web:* www.edsrestaurant.com	Calgary	AB	T2G1H4	403-262-3500	
Fiore Cantina Italiana 638 17th Ave SW *Web:* www.fiore.ca	Calgary	AB	T2S0B4	403-244-6603	
Hana Sushi 1803 Fourth St SW. *Web:* hanasushi.ca	Calgary	AB	St SW	403-229-1499	
IL Sogno 24 Fourth St NE *Web:* www.ilsogno.org	Calgary	AB	T2E3R7	403-232-8901	232-8816
James Joyce Authentic Irish Pub 114 Eigth Ave SW. *Web:* stthomasac.com	Calgary	AB	T2P1B3	403-262-0708	262-0709
Joey Eau Claire 208 Barclay Parade SW Ste 200 Eau Claire Market *Web:* joeyrestaurants.com/menu/	Calgary	AB	T2P4R4	403-263-6336	
KEG Steakhouse & Bar 7104 MacLeod Trl S. *Web:* www.kegsteakhouse.com	Calgary	AB	T2H0L3	403-253-2534	253-2875
King & I 822 11th Ave SW *Web:* www.kingandi.ca	Calgary	AB	T2R0E5	403-264-7241	264-8490
La Chaumiere Restaurant Ltd 17th Ave SW Ste 139 *Web:* www.lachaumiere.ca	Calgary	AB	T2R0A1	403-228-5690	228-4448
Limerick Traditional Public House 7304 MacLeod Trail SE. *Web:* calgarysbestpubs.com	Calgary	AB	T2H0L9	403-252-9190	252-9174
Marathon Ethiopian Restaurant 130 Tenth St NW. *Web:* marathonethiopian.com	Calgary	AB	T2N1V3	403-283-6796	
Melrose Cafe & Bar 730 17th Ave SW *Web:* www.melrosecalgary.com	Calgary	AB	T2S0B7	403-228-3566	228-5708
Molly Malone's Irish Pub 1153 Kensington Crescent NW. *Web:* mollymalones.ca	Calgary	AB	T2N3P7	403-296-3220	
Moti Mahal 1805 14 St SW. *Web:* www.motimahal.ca	Calgary	AB	T2T3T1	403-228-9990	
Q Haute Cuisine 100 LaCaille Pl SW *Web:* www.qhautecuisine.com	Calgary	AB	T2P5E2	403-262-5554	237-6108
Rajdoot 2424 Fourth St SW. *Web:* www.rajdoot.ca	Calgary	AB	T2S2T4	403-245-0181	455-4017
Redwater Rustic Grille 9223 MacLeod Trl S *Web:* www.redwatergrille.com	Calgary	AB	T2J0P6	403-253-4266	253-9045
River Cafe 25 Prince's Island Pk *Web:* www.river-cafe.com	Calgary	AB	T2P0R1	403-261-7670	261-8795
Rouge 1240 Eigth Ave SE. *Web:* www.rougecalgary.com	Calgary	AB	T2G0M7	403-531-2767	531-2768
Sakana Grill 116 Second Ave SW. *Web:* sakanagrill.ca	Calgary	AB	T2P3J9	403-290-1118	290-1120

				Phone	Fax
Salt & Pepper 6515 Bowness Rd NW *Web:* www.saltnpepper.ca	Calgary	AB	T3B0E8	403-247-4402	
Santorini Greek Taverna 1502 Centre St N *Web:* www.santorinirestaurant.com	Calgary	AB	T2E2R9	403-276-8363	276-8399
Silver Dragon Restaurant 106 Third Ave SE	Calgary	AB	T2G0B6	403-264-5326	
Singapore Sam's 555 11th Ave SW Ste 101 *Web:* www.singaporesams.com	Calgary	AB	T2R1P6	403-234-8088	266-6883
Smuggler's Inn 6920 MacLeod Trl S *Web:* www.smugglers.ca	Calgary	AB	T2H0L3	403-253-5355	259-4787
Thai Sa-On 351 Tenth Ave SW *Web:* www.thai-sa-on.com	Calgary	AB	T2R0A5	403-264-3526	264-3526
Villa Firenze 610 First Ave NE *Web:* villafirenze.ca	Calgary	AB	T2E0B6	403-264-4297	
Vintage Chophouse & Tavern 320 11 Ave SW *Web:* www.vintagechophouse.com	Calgary	AB	T2R0C5	403-262-7262	262-7263
Allegro Italian Kitchen 10011-109 St *Web:* www.allegroitaliankitchen.ca	Edmonton	AB	T5J3S8	780-424-6644	
Ban Thai 15726 100th Ave *Web:* www.banthai.com	Edmonton	AB	T5P0L1	780-444-9345	
Bul-Go-Gi House 8813 92 St NW *Web:* www.edmontonkoreanfood.com	Edmonton	AB	T6C3P9	780-466-2330	
Cafe Mosaics 10844 82nd Ave *Web:* cafemosaics.com	Edmonton	AB	T6E2B3	780-433-9702	
Characters 10257 105th St *Web:* www.characters.ca	Edmonton	AB	T5J1E6	780-421-4100	425-1550
Chiante Cafe & Restaurant 10501 82nd Ave *Web:* chianticafe.ca	Edmonton	AB	ve NW	780-439-9829	439-4071
Creperie, The 10220 103rd St NW *Web:* www.thecreperie.com	Edmonton	AB	T5J4C9	780-420-6656	
Dan Shing 15912 Stony Plain Rd	Edmonton	AB	T5P4A1	780-483-1143	
Furusato 10012 82nd Ave *Web:* furusatojapaneserestaurant.com	Edmonton	AB	T6E1Y9	780-439-1335	
Hardware Grill 9698 Jasper Ave *Web:* www.hardwaregrill.com	Edmonton	AB	T5H3V5	780-423-0969	423-4739
Il Pasticcio Trattoria 11520 100th Ave *Web:* www.ilpasticcio.ca	Edmonton	AB	T5K1V4	780-488-9543	
Julio's Barrio 10450 82nd Ave *Web:* www.juliosbarrio.com	Edmonton	AB	T6E2A2	780-431-0774	
Khazana 10177 107th St *Web:* www.khazana.ab.ca	Edmonton	AB	T5J1J5	780-702-0330	990-0342
Louisiana Purchase Restaurant 10320 111th St NW *Web:* www.louisianapurchase.ca	Edmonton	AB	T5K1M9	780-420-6779	
Normand's 11639 A Jasper Ave *TF:* 866-308-4438 ■ *Web:* www.normands.com	Edmonton	AB	T5K2S7	780-482-2600	
Old Country Inn 9906 72nd Ave *Web:* www.barbandernies.com	Edmonton	AB	T6E0Z3	780-433-3242	
Parkallen 7018 109th St *Web:* www.parkallen.com	Edmonton	AB	T6H3C1	780-436-8080	
Pearl River Restaurant 4728 99th St NW *Web:* www.lusoft.ca/pearlriver	Edmonton	AB	T6E5H5	780-435-2015	431-2758
Red Ox Inn 9420 91st St *Web:* www.theredoxinn.com	Edmonton	AB	T6C1Z5	780-465-5727	
Tasty Tom's Bistro 9965 82nd Ave NW	Edmonton	AB	T6E1Z1	780-437-5761	

Arizona

				Phone	Fax
Haus Murphy's 5739 W Glendale Ave *Web:* www.hausmurphys.com	Downtown Glendale	AZ	85301	623-939-2480	
August Moon Chinese Restaurant 1300 S Milton Rd *Web:* augustmoonflagstaff.com	Flagstaff	AZ	86001	928-774-5280	
Beaver Street Brewery 11 S Beaver St *Web:* www.beaverstreetbrewery.com	Flagstaff	AZ	86001	928-779-0079	
Black Barts Steakhouse Saloon 2760 E Butler Ave *Web:* www.blackbartssteakhouse.com	Flagstaff	AZ	86004	928-779-3142	774-1113
Brandy's 1500 E Cedar Ave Ste 40 *Web:* www.brandysrestaurant.com	Flagstaff	AZ	86004	928-779-2187	
Collins Irish Pub Two N Laroux St *Web:* www.collinsirishpub.com	Flagstaff	AZ	86001	928-214-7363	
Cottage Place 126 W Cottage Ave *Web:* www.cottageplace.com	Flagstaff	AZ	86001	928-774-8431	774-0374
Dara Thai 14 S San Francisco St *Web:* darathaiflagstaff.com	Flagstaff	AZ	86001	928-774-0047	
Dehli Palace Cuisine of India 2700 S Woodlands Village Blvd	Flagstaff	AZ	86001	928-556-0019	
El Capitan Fresh Mexican Grill 1800 S Milton Rd Ste 21 *Web:* www.elcapitanfmg.com	Flagstaff	AZ	86001	928-774-1083	774-0447
Granny's Closet 218 S Milton Rd *Web:* grannysclosetflagstaff.com	Flagstaff	AZ	86001	928-774-8331	
Josephine's 503 N Humphreys St *Web:* www.josephinesrestaurant.com	Flagstaff	AZ	86001	928-779-3400	226-0910
Little Thai Kitchen 1051 S Milton Rd	Flagstaff	AZ	86001	928-226-9422	
Miz Zips Cafe 2924 E Rt 66	Flagstaff	AZ	86004	928-526-0104	
Mountain Oasis 11 E Aspen Ave	Flagstaff	AZ	86001	928-214-9270	214-0020
Sakura Restaurant 1175 W Rt 66 *Web:* www.radisson.com	Flagstaff	AZ	86001	928-773-9118	
Romeo's Euro Cafe 207 N Gilbert Rd Ste 105 *Web:* www.eurocafe.com	Gilbert	AZ	85234	480-962-4224	558-2033
Ajo Al's *Arrowhead* 7458 W Bell Rd *Web:* www.ajoals.com	Glendale	AZ	85308	623-334-9899	
Babbo Italian Eatery 20211 N 67th Ave *Web:* babboitalian.com	Glendale	AZ	85308	623-566-9898	566-5561
Bitz-Ee Mama's 7023 N 58th Ave *Web:* www.bitz-eemamas.com	Glendale	AZ	85301	623-931-0562	
Caramba 5421 W Glendale Ave *Web:* carambamex.com	Glendale	AZ	85301	623-934-8888	487-1934

				Phone	Fax
Kiss the Cook Restaurant 4915 W Glendale Ave *Web:* www.kissthecook.net	Glendale	AZ	85301	623-939-4663	939-2989
La Perla Cafe 5912 W Glendale Ave	Glendale	AZ	85301	623-939-7561	939-0339
Mimi's Cafe 7450 W Bell Rd *Web:* www.mimiscafe.com	Glendale	AZ	85308	623-979-4500	979-4339
Pedro's 4938 W Glendale Ave *Web:* pedrosmexicanfood.com	Glendale	AZ	85301	623-937-0807	551-8069
Ah-So 1919 S Gilbert Rd *Web:* ahsomesa.com	Mesa	AZ	85204	480-497-1114	497-1115
Aloha Kitchen 2950 S Alma School Rd Ste 12 *Web:* alohakitchen.com	Mesa	AZ	85210	480-897-2451	897-7295
Baby Kay's Cajun Kitchen 2051 S Dobson Rd *Web:* www.babykayscajunkitchen.com	Mesa	AZ	85202	480-800-4811	
Bavarian Point Restaurant 4815 E Main St *Web:* www.bavarianpoint.net	Mesa	AZ	85205	480-830-0999	830-0530
Golden Gate 2640 W Baseline Rd	Mesa	AZ	85202	480-897-1335	
Hodori 1116 S Dobson Rd *Web:* hodoriaz.com	Mesa	AZ	85202	480-668-7979	
Landmark Restaurant 809 W Main St *Web:* www.landmarkrestaurant.com	Mesa	AZ	85201	480-962-4652	
On The Border mexican grill & cantina 1710 S Power Rd *Web:* www.ontheborder.com	Mesa	AZ	85206	602-247-7510	
Rosa's Mexican Grill 328 E University Dr *Web:* rosasgrill.com	Mesa	AZ	85201	480-964-5451	
SN Pacific Rim Asian Kitchen 1236 E Baseline Rd *Web:* www.asiaaz.com	Mesa	AZ	85204	480-892-0688	
El Chorro Lodge 5550 E Lincoln Dr *Web:* www.elchorro.com	Paradise Valley	AZ	85253	480-948-5170	
Alexi's Grill 3550 N Central Ave Ste 120 *Web:* www.alexisgrillphx.com	Phoenix	AZ	85012	602-279-0982	
Alice Cooperstown 101 E Jackson St *Web:* www.alicecooperstown.com	Phoenix	AZ	85004	602-253-7337	253-4866
Avanti's 2728 E Thomas Rd *Web:* www.avanti-az.com	Phoenix	AZ	85016	602-956-0900	468-1913
Barrio Cafe 2814 N 16th St *Web:* www.barriocafe.com	Phoenix	AZ	85006	602-636-0240	
Bill Johnson's Big Apple 3757 E Van Buren St *Web:* www.billjohnsons.com	Phoenix	AZ	85008	602-275-2107	
Christopher's Crush 2502 E Camelback Rd *Web:* www.christophersaz.com	Phoenix	AZ	85016	602-522-2344	468-0314
Coup des Tartes 4626 N 16th St *Web:* nicetartes.com	Phoenix	AZ	85016	602-212-1082	212-1138
Desert Jade 3215 E Indian School Rd *Web:* desertjadeaz.com	Phoenix	AZ	85018	602-954-0048	
Different Pointe of View 11111 N Seventh St *Web:* www.pointehilton.com	Phoenix	AZ	85020	602-866-6350	866-6358
Durant's Restaurant 2611 N Central Ave *Web:* www.durantsaz.com	Phoenix	AZ	85004	602-264-5967	264-5112
Giuseppe's Italian Kitchen 2824 E Indian School Rd *Web:* giuseppeson28th.com	Phoenix	AZ	85016	602-381-1237	381-3669
La Pinata 3330 N 19th Ave *Web:* lapinatarestaurantaz.com	Phoenix	AZ	85015	602-279-1763	200-0931
Majerle's Sports Grill 24 N Second St *Web:* www.majerles.com	Phoenix	AZ	85004	602-253-0118	
Melting Pot of Ahwatukee, The 3626 E Ray Rd *Web:* www.meltingpot.com	Phoenix	AZ	85044	480-704-9206	704-2973
Michelina's 3241 E Shea Blvd *Web:* www.michelinasrestaurant.com	Phoenix	AZ	85028	602-996-8977	996-9041
Pizzeria Bianco 623 E Adams St *Web:* www.pizzeriabianco.com	Phoenix	AZ	85004	602-258-8300	
T Cook's 5200 E Camelback Rd *TF:* 800-672-6011 ■ *Web:* royalpalmshotel.com/dining/tcooks-restaurant-phoenix	Phoenix	AZ	85018	602-808-0766	840-6927
Tarbell's 3213 E Camelback *Web:* www.tarbells.com	Phoenix	AZ	85018	602-955-8100	955-8181
That's Italiano 3717 E Indian School Rd	Phoenix	AZ	85018	602-778-9100	
Vincent Guerithault on Camelback 3930 E Camelback Rd *Web:* www.vincentsoncamelback.com	Phoenix	AZ	85018	602-224-0225	956-5400
Arcadia Farms Cafe 7014 E First Ave *Web:* arcadiafarmscafe.com	Scottsdale	AZ	85251	480-941-5665	
Atlas Bistro 2515 N Scottsdale Rd Ste 18 *Web:* www.azeats.com	Scottsdale	AZ	85257	480-990-2433	
Blue Adobe Grille 10885 N Frank Lloyd Wright Blvd *Web:* www.blueadobegrille.com	Scottsdale	AZ	85259	480-314-0550	
Cowboy Ciao Wine Bar & Grill 7133 E Stetson Dr *Web:* www.cowboyciao.com	Scottsdale	AZ	85251	480-946-3111	
Don & Charlie's 7501 E Camelback Rd *Web:* www.donandcharlies.com	Scottsdale	AZ	85251	480-990-0900	
George & Sons 11291 E Via Linda *Web:* www.georgeandsonsasiancuisine.com	Scottsdale	AZ	85259	480-661-6336	
J & G's Steakhouse 6000 E Camelback Rd *Web:* www.spgrestaurantsandbars.com/united-states/arizona/scottsdale/jg-steakhouse	Scottsdale	AZ	85251	480-214-8000	214-8001
Jalapeno Inferno 23587 N Scottsdale *Web:* www.jalapenoinferno.com	Scottsdale	AZ	85255	480-585-6442	
Kazimierz World Wine Bar 7137 E Stetson Dr *Web:* www.kazbar.net	Scottsdale	AZ	85251	480-946-3004	
Kona Grill & Sushi Bar 7014 E Camelback Rd *Web:* konagrill.com	Scottsdale	AZ	85251	480-429-1100	
Los Olivos Mexican Patio 7328 E Second St *Web:* losolivosrestaurants.com	Scottsdale	AZ	85251	480-946-2256	
Palm Court, The 7700 E McCormick Pkwy *Web:* thescottsdaleresort.com	Scottsdale	AZ	85258	480-596-7700	
Pepin restaurant 7363 Scottsdale Mall *Web:* www.pepinrestaurant.com	Scottsdale	AZ	85251	480-990-9026	

Restaurant	City	State	ZIP	Phone	Fax
Rancho Pinot Grill 6208 N Scottsdale Rd *Web:* www.ranchopinot.com	Scottsdale	AZ	85253	480-367-8030	443-0680
Remington's 7200 N Scottsdale Rd *Web:* scottsdaleplaza.com	Scottsdale	AZ	85253	480-951-5101	
Salt Cellar 550 N Hayden Rd *Web:* www.saltcellarrestaurant.com	Scottsdale	AZ	85257	480-947-1963	941-0929
Sassi Ristorante 10455 E Pinnacle Peak Pkwy *Web:* www.sassi.biz	Scottsdale	AZ	85255	480-502-9095	
Sushi on Shea 7000 E Shea Blvd *Web:* sushionshea.com	Scottsdale	AZ	85254	480-483-7799	
Taggia 4925 N Scottsdale Rd *Web:* www.taggiascottsdale.com	Scottsdale	AZ	85251	480-424-6095	425-8966
Veneto Trattoria 6137 N Scottsdale Rd *Web:* www.venetotrattoria.com	Scottsdale	AZ	85250	480-948-9928	
L'Auberge de Sedona 301 L'Auberge Ln *TF:* 855-905-5745 ■ *Web:* www.lauberge.com	Sedona	AZ	86336	928-282-1661	282-2885
Byblos Restaurant 3332 S Mill Ave *Web:* www.amdest.com	Tempe	AZ	85282	480-894-1945	
Caffe Boa 398 S Mill Ave *Web:* www.cafeboa.com	Tempe	AZ	85281	480-968-9112	
Casey Moore's Oyster House 850 S Ash Ave *Web:* caseymoores.com	Tempe	AZ	85281	480-968-9935	968-6193
Cervantes 3318 S Mill Ave *Web:* cervantesrestaurant.com	Tempe	AZ	85282	480-921-9113	
House of Tricks 114 E Seventh St *Web:* www.houseoftricks.com	Tempe	AZ	85281	480-968-1114	968-0080
Monti's La Casa Vieja 100 S Mill Ave *Web:* www.montis.com	Tempe	AZ	85281	480-967-7594	967-8129
Pita Jungle 1250 E Apache Blvd *Web:* pitajungle.com	Tempe	AZ	85281	480-804-0234	
Urban Cafe 1212 E Apache Blvd *Web:* www.theurbancafe.com	Tempe	AZ	85281	480-968-8888	
Wong's Place 1825 E Baseline Rd *Web:* wongsplacetempe.com	Tempe	AZ	85283	480-838-8988	
Z'Tejas 20 W Sixth St *Web:* ztejas.com	Tempe	AZ	85281	480-377-1170	377-1167
Athens on Fourth Avenue 500 N Fourth Ave *Web:* athenson4thave.com	Tucson	AZ	85705	520-624-6886	
Cafe Poca Cosa 110 E Pennington St Ste 100 *Web:* cafepocacosatucson.com	Tucson	AZ	85701	520-622-6400	
Casa Molina 6225 E Speedway *Web:* www.casamolina.com	Tucson	AZ	85712	520-886-5468	
Char Thai 5039 Fifth St	Tucson	AZ	85711	520-795-1715	
Delectables 533 N Fourth Ave *Web:* www.delectables.com	Tucson	AZ	85705	520-884-9289	
El Charro Cafe 311 N Ct Ave *Web:* www.elcharrocafe.com	Tucson	AZ	85701	520-622-1922	
El Corral 2201 E River Rd *Web:* elcorraltucson.com	Tucson	AZ	85718	520-299-6092	
Feast 3719 E Speedway *Web:* www.eatatfeast.com	Tucson	AZ	85712	520-326-9363	326-9245
Gandhi 150 W Ft Lowell Rd *Web:* gandhicuisineofindia.com	Tucson	AZ	85705	520-292-1738	
Gold Room 245 E Ina Rd *Web:* westwardlook.com	Tucson	AZ	85704	520-297-1151	297-9023
Grill at Hacienda del Sol 5501 N Hacienda del Sol Rd *TF:* 800-728-6514 ■ *Web:* www.haciendadelsol.com	Tucson	AZ	85718	520-529-3500	
Janos 3770 E Sunrise Dr *Web:* www.janos.com	Tucson	AZ	85718	520-615-6100	615-3334
Jonathan's Tucson Cork 6320 E Tanque Verde Rd *Web:* www.jonathanscork.com	Tucson	AZ	85715	520-296-1631	296-0765
Kingfisher Bar & Grill 2564 E Grant Rd *Web:* www.kingfishertucson.com	Tucson	AZ	85716	520-323-7739	795-7810
Le Rendez-vous 3844 E Ft Lowell Rd *Web:* www.lerendez-vous.com	Tucson	AZ	85716	520-323-7373	
Mi Nidito Restaurant 1813 S Fourth Ave *Web:* www.minidito.net	Tucson	AZ	85713	520-622-5081	
Michelangelo 420 W Magee Rd *Web:* www.michelangelotucson.com	Tucson	AZ	85704	520-297-5775	
Michelangelo Ristorante 420 W Magee Rd *Web:* www.michelangelotucson.com	Tucson	AZ	85704	520-297-5775	
Pastiche Modern Eatery 3025 N Campbell Ave *Web:* www.pasticheme.com	Tucson	AZ	85719	520-325-3333	
Sushi Ten 4500 E Speedway Blvd *Web:* sushiten.webs.com	Tucson	AZ	85712	520-324-0010	
Thunder Canyon Brewery 7401 N La Cholla Blvd *Web:* thundercanyonbrewery.com	Tucson	AZ	85741	520-797-2652	797-2589
Wildflower 7037 N Oracle Rd *Web:* wildflowertucson.com	Tucson	AZ	85704	520-219-4230	
Yoshimatsu 2660 N Campbell Ave *Web:* www.yoshimatsuaz.com	Tucson	AZ	85719	520-320-1574	

Arkansas

Restaurant	City	State	ZIP	Phone	Fax
Catfish Cove 1615 Phoenix Ave	Fort Smith	AR	72901	479-646-8835	646-8835
Taliano's Restaurant 201 N 14th St *Web:* talianos.net	Fort Smith	AR	72901	479-785-2292	785-2640
Back Porch Grill, The 4810 Central Ave *Web:* www.backporchgrill.com	Hot Springs	AR	71913	501-525-0885	
Cafe 1217 1217 Malvern Ave *Web:* cafe1217.net	Hot Springs	AR	71901	501-318-1094	624-4931
Cajun Boilers 2806 Albert Pike Rd *Web:* cajunboilers.com	Hot Springs	AR	71913	501-767-5695	
Chuck's Southern Bar-B-Que 1118 Airport Rd	Hot Springs	AR	71913	501-760-3223	
Hamilton House Estate Bed & Breakfast 132 Van Lyell Terr *Web:* www.hamiltonhouseestate.com	Hot Springs	AR	71913	501-520-4040	520-4023
King's 3310 Central Ave	Hot Springs	AR	71913	501-318-1888	
McClard's Bar-B-Q 505 Albert Pike Rd *TF:* 866-622-5273 ■ *Web:* www.mcclards.com	Hot Springs	AR	71901	501-623-9665	
Mickey's CMB BBQ 1622 Pk Ave *Web:* www.mickeysbbq.net	Hot Springs National Park	AR	71901	501-624-1247	
1620 SAVOY 1620 Market St *Web:* www.1620savoy.com/	Little Rock	AR	72211	501-221-1620	221-1921
Acadia 3000 Kavanaugh Blvd Ste 202 *Web:* www.acadiahillcrest.com	Little Rock	AR	72205	501-603-9630	603-0477
Anderson's Cajun Wharf 2400 Cantrell Rd *Web:* www.cajunswharf.com	Little Rock	AR	72202	501-375-5351	375-5354
Black Angus 10907 N Rodney Parham Rd *Web:* blackanguscafe.com	Little Rock	AR	72212	501-228-7800	
Brave New Restaurant (BNR) 2300 Cottondale Ln Ste 105 *Web:* www.bravenewrestaurant.com	Little Rock	AR	72202	501-663-2677	
Buffalo Grill 1611 Rebsamen Pk Rd *Web:* www.buffalogrilllr.com	Little Rock	AR	72211	501-296-9535	
Capers 14502 Cantrell Rd *Web:* www.capersrestaurant.com	Little Rock	AR	72223	501-868-7600	868-4294
Dave's Place 210 Ctr St *Web:* www.davesplacerestaurant.com	Little Rock	AR	72201	501-372-3283	
Doe's Eat Place 1023 W Marckham St *Web:* www.doeseatplace.net	Little Rock	AR	72201	501-376-1195	
El Chico 8409 I-30 *Web:* elchico.com	Little Rock	AR	72209	501-562-3762	
Fu Lin Chinese Restaurant 200 N Bowman Rd	Little Rock	AR	72211	501-225-8989	
Graffiti's Italian Restaurant 7811 Cantrell Rd *Web:* littlerockgraffitis.net	Little Rock	AR	72227	501-224-9079	224-9161
Juanita's 614 President Clinton *Web:* www.juanitas.com	Little Rock	AR	72201	501-372-1228	
Loca Luna 3519 Old Cantrell Rd *Web:* www.localuna.com	Little Rock	AR	72202	501-663-4666	664-4176
Markham Street Grill & Pub 11321 W Markham St Ste 6 *Web:* markhamstreetpub.com	Little Rock	AR	72211	501-224-2010	
Shogun Japanese Steak House 2815 Cantrell Rd *Web:* www.shogunlr.com	Little Rock	AR	72202	501-666-7070	
Shorty Small's Great American Restaurant 11100 N Rodney Parham Rd *Web:* www.shortysmalls.com	Little Rock	AR	72212	501-224-3344	
Sonny Williams' Steak Room 500 President Clinton Ave *Web:* www.sonnywilliamssteakroom.com	Little Rock	AR	72201	501-324-2999	324-4888
Trio's 8201 Cantrell Rd *Web:* www.triosrestaurant.com	Little Rock	AR	72227	501-221-3330	221-1002

British Columbia

Restaurant	City	Prov.	Postal Code	Phone	Fax
Afghan Horseman 1833 Anderson St *Web:* afghanhorsemen.com	Vancouver	BC	V6H4E5	604-873-5923	
Athene's 3618 W Broadway *Web:* athenesrestaurant.ca	Vancouver	BC	V6R2B7	604-731-4135	
Banana Leaf 820 W Broadway *Web:* www.bananaleaf-vancouver.com	Vancouver	BC	V5Z1J9	604-731-6333	
Bin 941 Tapas Parlour 941 Davie St *Web:* www.bin941.com	Vancouver	BC	V6Z1B9	604-683-1246	683-1206
Bishop's 2183 W Fourth Ave *Web:* www.bishopsonline.com	Vancouver	BC	V6K1N7	604-738-2025	738-4622
Bistro Pastis 2153 Fourth Ave W *Web:* www.bistropastis.com	Vancouver	BC	V6K1N7	604-731-5020	
Blue Water Cafe 1095 Hamilton St *Web:* www.bluewatercafe.net	Vancouver	BC	V6B5T4	604-688-8078	688-8978
Bridges Restaurant 1696 Duranleau St *Web:* www.bridgesrestaurant.com	Vancouver	BC	V6H3S4	604-687-4400	
C Restaurant 2-1600 Howe St *Web:* www.crestaurant.com	Vancouver	BC	V6Z2L9	604-681-1164	605-8263
Cardero's 1583 Coal Harbour Quay *Web:* www.vancouverdine.com/carderos	Vancouver	BC	V6G3E7	604-669-7666	669-7609
Chambar 562 Beatty St *Web:* www.chambar.com	Vancouver	BC	V6B2L3	604-879-7119	879-7118
CinCin Ristorante 1154 Robson St 2nd Fl *Web:* www.cincin.net	Vancouver	BC	V6E3V5	604-688-7338	688-7339
Cioppino's Mediterranean Grill & Enoteca 1133 Hamilton St *Web:* cioppinosyaletown.com	Vancouver	BC	V6B5P6	604-688-7466	
Diva at the Met 645 Howe St *Web:* www.metropolitan.com/diva	Vancouver	BC	V6C2Y9	604-602-7788	643-7267
Five Sails Restaurant 999 Canada Pl Ste 410 *Web:* www.fivesails.ca	Vancouver	BC	V6C3E1	604-844-2855	682-6321
Glowbal Grill & Satay Bar 1079 Mainland St *Web:* www.glowbalgroup.com	Vancouver	BC	V6B5P9	604-602-0835	602-7523
Go Fish! Ocean Emporium 1505 W First Ave	Vancouver	BC	V6J1E8	604-730-5040	
Gotham Steakhouse & Cocktail Bar 615 Seymour St *Web:* www.gothamsteakhouse.com	Vancouver	BC	V6B3K3	604-605-8282	605-8285
Las Margaritas Restaurante 1999 W Fourth Ave *Web:* www.lasmargaritas.com	Vancouver	BC	V6J1M7	604-734-7117	734-3528
Maurya Indian Cuisine 1643 W Broadway *Web:* www.mauryaindiancuisine.com	Vancouver	BC	V6J1W9	604-742-0622	
Mr Pickwick's 8620 Granville St *Web:* mrpickwicksbc.com	Vancouver	BC	V6P5A1	604-266-2340	
Original Tandoori Kitchen King 7215 Main St *Web:* originaltandoorikitchens.com/	Vancouver	BC	V5X3J3	604-327-8900	

Name / Address	City	State	Zip	Phone	Fax
Ouisi Bistro 3014 Granville St. *Web:* www.ouisibistro.com	Vancouver	BC	V6H3J8	604-732-7550	
Panos Greek Taverna 654 SE Marine Dr. *Web:* panosgreekvancouver.ca	Vancouver	BC	V5X2T4	604-322-8824	
Pink Pearl Chinese Seafood 1132 E Hastings St *Web:* www.pinkpearl.com	Vancouver	BC	V6A1S2	604-253-4316	253-4316
Raincity Grill 1193 Denman St. *Web:* www.raincitygrill.com	Vancouver	BC	V6G2N1	604-685-7337	
Reef Caribbean Restaurants, The 4172 Main St *Web:* www.thereefrestaurant.com	Vancouver	BC	B8W1K9	604-874-5375	
Sawasdee Thai 4250 Main St *Web:* www.sawasdeethairestaurant.com	Vancouver	BC	V5V3P9	604-876-4030	876-4035
Sequoia Grill at the Teahouse 1583 Coal Harbour Quay *Web:* www.vancouverdine.com	Vancouver	BC	V6G3E7	604-687-5684	669-7699
Simply Thai 1211 Hamilton St *Web:* www.simplythairestaurant.com	Vancouver	BC	V6B6L2	604-642-0123	
Stepho's 1124 Davie St.	Vancouver	BC	V6E1N1	604-683-2555	
Sun Sui Wah Seafood Restaurant 3888 Main St *Web:* sunsuiwah.com	Vancouver	BC	V5V3N9	604-872-8822	876-1638
Tojo's *Tojo's Restaurant* 1133 W Broadway *Web:* www.tojos.com	Vancouver	BC	V6H1G1	604-872-8050	872-8060
Yew Restaurant & Bar 791 W Georgia St Second Fl. *Web:* www.fourseasons.com	Vancouver	BC	V6C2T4	604-692-4939	844-6749

California

Name / Address	City	State	Zip	Phone	Fax
Anaheim Marriott 700 W Convention Way *TF:* 800-845-5279 ■ *Web:* www.marriott.com	Anaheim	CA	92802	714-750-8000	750-9100
Anaheim White House 887 S Anaheim Blvd. *Web:* www.anaheimwhitehouse.com	Anaheim	CA	92805	714-772-1381	772-7062
Catal Restaurant & Uva Bar 1580 S Disneyland Dr # 106 *Web:* www.patinagroup.com	Anaheim	CA	92802	714-774-4442	
Catch, The 2100 E Katella Ave Ste 104 *Web:* www.catchanaheim.com	Anaheim	CA	92806	714-935-0101	935-0105
Hibachi Steak House 108 S Fairmont Blvd.	Anaheim	CA	92808	714-998-4110	
JT Schmid's Restaurant & Brewery 2610 E Katella Ave *Web:* www.jtschmidsrestaurants.com	Anaheim	CA	92806	714-634-9200	634-9200
Merhaba 2801 W Ball Rd *Web:* merhabarestaurant.com	Anaheim	CA	92804	714-826-8859	
Naples 1550 S Disneyland Dr # 101 *Web:* www.patinagroup.com	Anaheim	CA	92802	714-776-6200	776-6340
Pepe's 2429 W Ball Rd. *Web:* pepesmexicanfood.com	Anaheim	CA	92804	714-952-9410	
Ralph Brennan's Jazz Kitchen 1590 S Disneyland Dr Downtown Disney *Web:* www.rbjazzkitchen.com	Anaheim	CA	92802	714-776-5200	999-2123
Rosine's 721 S Weir Canyon Rd *Web:* www.rosines.com	Anaheim	CA	92808	714-283-5141	283-0158
Storytellers Cafe 1600 S Disneyland Dr. *Web:* disneyland.disney.go.com/	Anaheim	CA	92802	714-781-3463	
Tortilla Jo's 1510 Disneyland Dr Downtown Disney *Web:* www.patinagroup.com/tortillaJos	Anaheim	CA	92802	714-535-5000	535-5700
Benji's 4001 Rosedale Hwy	Bakersfield	CA	93308	661-328-0400	328-0423
Bill Lee's Bamboo Chopsticks 1203 18th St. *Web:* www.billlees.com	Bakersfield	CA	93301	661-324-9441	324-7811
Bit of Germany 1901 Flower St.	Bakersfield	CA	93305	661-325-8874	872-0854
Buck Owens' Crystal Palace Steakhouse 2800 Buck Owens Blvd. *Web:* www.buckowens.com	Bakersfield	CA	93308	661-328-7560	328-7565
Cafe Med Restaurant 4809 Scottdale Hwy *Web:* www.cafemedrestaurant.com	Bakersfield	CA	93309	661-834-4433	
Chalet Basque 200 Oak St.	Bakersfield	CA	93304	661-327-2915	
Chuy's Mesquite Broiler 2500 New Stine Rd *Web:* bajachuys.com	Bakersfield	CA	93309	661-833-3469	833-3130
Cope's Knotty Pine Cafe 1530 Norris Rd.	Bakersfield	CA	93308	661-399-0120	
Imperial Chinese Restaurant 4525 Ming Ave *Web:* imperialchineseonline.com	Bakersfield	CA	93309	661-836-0288	
Izumo Sushi 4412 Ming Ave	Bakersfield	CA	93309	661-398-0608	
Jake's Tex-Mex Cafe 1710 Oak St *Web:* www.jakestexmex.com	Bakersfield	CA	93301	661-322-6380	322-3731
Mama Tosca's 9000 Ming Ave Ste K2-K3 *Web:* www.mamatoscas.com	Bakersfield	CA	93311	661-831-1242	663-7436
Mossman's Southwest 3610 Wible Rd *Web:* mossmanscatering.com	Bakersfield	CA	93309	661-832-5130	832-4783
Tahoe Joe's 9000 Ming Ave *Web:* www.tahoejoes.com	Bakersfield	CA	93311	661-664-7750	664-7732
Uricchio's Trattoria 1400 17th St. *Web:* uricchios-trattoria.com	Bakersfield	CA	93301	661-326-8870	326-8829
Wool Growers 620 E 19th St. *Web:* woolgrowers.net	Bakersfield	CA	93305	661-327-9584	
Meritage at the Claremont 41 Tunnel Rd *Web:* meritageclaremont.com	Berkeley	CA	94705	510-549-8510	
Belvedere, The 9882 S Santa Monica Blvd *Web:* peninsula.com	Beverly Hills	CA	90212	310-788-2306	788-2319
Lawry's the Prime Rib 100 N La Cienega Blvd. *Web:* www.lawrysonline.com	Beverly Hills	CA	90211	310-652-2827	657-5463
Mastro's Steakhouse 246 N Canon Dr. *Web:* mastrosrestaurants.com	Beverly Hills	CA	90210	310-888-8782	
Matsuhisa Restaurant 129 N La Cienega Blvd *Web:* www.nobumatsuhisa.com	Beverly Hills	CA	90211	310-659-9639	659-0492
Tanzore 50 N La Cienega Blvd. *Web:* tanzore.com	Beverly Hills	CA	90211	310-652-3838	
Anton & Michel PO Box 4917 *Web:* www.carmelsbest.com/antonmichel	Carmel	CA	93921	831-624-2406	625-1542
Bouchee Mission St *Web:* www.andresbouchee.com	Carmel	CA	93923	831-626-7880	
Casanova Fifth St-between Mission & San Carlos PO Box GG *Web:* www.casanovarestaurant.com	Carmel	CA	93921	831-625-0501	625-9799
Flying Fish Grill Mission St *Web:* flyingfishgrill.com	Carmel	CA	93921	831-625-1962	
Grasing's Sixth & Mission Sts *Web:* www.grasings.com	Carmel	CA	93923	831-624-6562	624-7431
Pacific's Edge 120 Highland Dr. *Web:* pacificsedge.com	Carmel	CA	93923	831-622-5445	
Rio Grill 101 the Crossroads *Web:* www.riogrill.com	Carmel	CA	93923	831-625-5436	625-2950
Robata Grill 3658 The Barnyard *Web:* robata-barnyard.com	Carmel	CA	93923	831-624-2643	
Leon's at Desert Princess 28-555 Landau Blvd *Web:* desertprincesscc.com	Cathedral City	CA	92234	760-325-5002	
Aunt Emma's 700 E St. *Web:* www.auntemmaspancakes.com	Chula Vista	CA	91910	619-427-2722	
Meakwan 230 Third Ave *Web:* www.meakwanthaicuisine.com	Chula Vista	CA	91910	619-426-5172	
Carmen & Family Bar-B-Q 41986 Fremont Blvd *Web:* carmenandfamilybbq.com	Fremont	CA	94538	510-657-5464	
China Chili 39116 State St	Fremont	CA	94538	510-791-1688	791-5181
Country Way 5325 Mowry Ave	Fremont	CA	94536	510-797-3188	
El Patio Restaurant 37311 Fremont Blvd *Web:* elpatiooriginaldining.com	Fremont	CA	94536	510-796-1733	
Fremont Market Broiler 43406 Christy St. *Web:* www.marketbroiler.com	Fremont	CA	94538	510-791-8675	791-6172
Ho Chow Restaurant 47966 Warm Springs Blvd *Web:* www.hochow.com	Fremont	CA	94539	510-657-0683	657-9026
Massimo's 5200 Mowry Ave. *Web:* www.massimos.com	Fremont	CA	94538	510-792-2000	792-7041
Norman's Family Restaurant 4949 Stevenson Blvd	Fremont	CA	94538	510-226-7777	
Papillon Restaurant 37296 Mission Blvd. *Web:* www.papillonrestaurant.com	Fremont	CA	94536	510-793-6331	793-2789
Campagnia 1185 E Champlain Dr *Web:* www.campagnia.net	Fresno	CA	93720	559-433-3300	433-3066
Chopsticks 4783 E Olive Ave	Fresno	CA	93702	559-255-0489	
Livingstone's Restaurant & Pub 831 E Fern Ave. *Web:* towerdistrict.org	Fresno	CA	93728	559-485-5198	485-3439
Maxs Bistro 1784 W Bullard Ave *Web:* www.maxsbistro.com	Fresno	CA	93711	559-439-6900	439-7206
Ripe Tomato 5064 N Palm Ave *Web:* tripadvisor.com	Fresno	CA	93704	559-225-1850	
Sequoia Brewing Co 777 E Olive St *Web:* sequoiabrewing.com	Fresno	CA	93728	559-264-5521	
Tokyo Garden 1711 Fulton St *Web:* tokyogardenfresno.com	Fresno	CA	93721	559-268-3596	
Yoshino Restaurant 6226 N Blackstone Ave	Fresno	CA	93710	559-431-2205	
Azteca 12911 Main St *Web:* www.theazteca.com	Garden Grove	CA	92840	714-638-3790	638-3737
California Grill 11999 Harbor Blvd Hyatt Regency Orange County *TF:* 800-233-1234 ■ *Web:* orangecounty.hyatt.com	Garden Grove	CA	92840	714-740-6047	740-0465
Carolina's 12045 Chapman Ave *Web:* carolinasitalianrestaurant.com	Garden Grove	CA	92840	714-971-5551	971-5552
Casa De Soto 8562 Garden Grove Blvd. *Web:* www.casadesoto.com	Garden Grove	CA	92844	714-530-4200	
Furiwa Seafood 13826 Brookhurst St *Web:* furiwa.com	Garden Grove	CA	92843	714-534-3996	534-5327
Pho 79 9941 Hazard Ave. *Web:* pho79.com	Garden Grove	CA	92844	714-531-2490	
Seafood Cove 8547 Westminster Blvd	Garden Grove	CA	92844	714-895-7964	
Tokyo Love 12565 S Harbor Blvd	Garden Grove	CA	92840	714-534-4751	
Barragan's 814 S Central Ave. *Web:* barragansrestaurants.com	Glendale	CA	91204	818-243-1103	243-2637
Carousel Restaurant 304 N Brand Blvd *Web:* www.carouselrestaurant.com	Glendale	CA	91203	818-246-7775	246-6627
Damon's Steak House 317 N Brand Blvd *Web:* www.damonsglendale.com	Glendale	CA	91203	818-507-1510	240-0087
Far Niente Ristorante 204 1/2 N Brand Blvd *Web:* farnienteglendale.com	Glendale	CA	91203	818-242-3835	242-2956
Fresco Ristorante 514 S Brand Blvd. *Web:* www.frescoristorante.com	Glendale	CA	91204	818-247-5541	247-1964
Gennaro's Ristorante 1109 N Brand Blvd *Web:* www.gennarosristorante.com	Glendale	CA	91202	818-243-6231	
La Cabanita 3447 N Verdugo Rd *Web:* cabanitarestaurant.com	Glendale	CA	91208	818-957-2711	
Max's of Manila 313 W Broadway *Web:* www.maxschicken.com	Glendale	CA	91204	818-637-7751	637-2325
Notte Luna 113 N Maryland Ave *Web:* www.notteluna.com	Glendale	CA	91206	818-552-4100	552-3522
Scarantino's 1524 E Colorado St. *Web:* www.scarantinos.com	Glendale	CA	91205	818-247-9777	
Tep Thai 209 W Wilson Ave *Web:* www.tepthai.com	Glendale	CA	91203	818-246-0380	
Two Guys From Italy 405 N Verdugo Rd *Web:* www.glendaletwoguysfromitaly.com	Glendale	CA	91206	818-240-0020	240-0972

Phone Fax

Varouj's Kabobs 1110 S Glendale Ave. . . . Glendale CA 91205 818-243-9870
Baci 18748 Beach Blvd. . . . Huntington Beach CA 92648 714-965-1194 965-4106
Web: www.bacirestaurant.com
Beachfront 301 301 Main St. . . . Huntington Beach CA 92648 714-374-3399 374-1088
Web: www.beachfront301.com
Capone's Cucina
19688 Beach Blvd Ste 10 . . . . Huntington Beach CA 92646 714-593-2888 705-0467
Web: www.caponescucina.com
Hyatt Regency Huntington Beach Resort & Spa
21500 Pacific Coast Hwy . . . . Huntington Beach CA 92648 714-698-1234 845-4990
TF: 800-633-7313 ■ *Web:* huntingtonbeach.hyatt.com
Longboard Restaurant & Pub
217 Main St . . . . Huntington Beach CA 92648 714-960-1896 960-8447
Web: longboardpub.com
Lou's Red Oak BBQ Grill
21501 Brookhurst St. . . . Huntington Beach CA 92646 714-965-5200
Web: www.lousbbq.com
Mario's Restaurant 18603 Main St. . . . Huntington Beach CA 92648 714-842-5811 842-0292
Web: mariosmexicanfoodcantina.com
Matsu Japanese Restaurant
18035 Beach Blvd. . . . Huntington Beach CA 92648 714-848-4404 842-4049
Web: matsusogood.com
Ruby's Diner One Main St. . . . Huntington Beach CA 92648 714-969-7829 969-1630
Web: www.rubys.com
Sea Siam Restaurant
16103 Bolsa Chica St . . . . Huntington Beach CA 92649 714-846-8986
Web: seasiamhb.com
Shades Restaurant
21100 Pacific Coast Hwy . . . . Huntington Beach CA 92640 714-845-8000 845-8424
Web: www.waterfrontresort.com/dining/shades
Spark Woodfire Grill
300 Pacific Coast Hwy Ste 202 . . . . Huntington Beach CA 92648 714-960-0996 960-7332
Web: www.sparkwoodfiregrill.com
West Coast Club
21100 Pacific Coast Hwy
Hilton Waterfront Beach Resort . . . . Huntington Beach CA 92648 714-845-8000 845-8425
TF: 800-548-8690 ■ *Web:* waterfrontresort.com
Zubie's Dry Dock 9059 Adams Ave . . . . Huntington Beach CA 92646 714-963-6362
Web: zubiesdrydock.com
Baja Fresh 320 Commerce Ste 100 . . . . Irvine CA 92602 949-270-8900 270-8901
TF: 877-225-2373 ■ *Web:* www.bajafresh.com
Marine Room, The 2000 Spindrift Dr . . . . La Jolla CA 92037 858-459-7222 551-4673
TF: 866-644-2351 ■ *Web:* www.marineroom.com
Piatti 2182 Avenida de la Playa . . . . La Jolla CA 92037 858-454-1589 454-1799
Web: piatti.com
Roppongi 875 Prospect St Ste 102 . . . . La Jolla CA 92037 858-551-5252
Web: www.roppongiusa.com
Tapenade 7612 Fay Ave . . . . La Jolla CA 92037 858-551-7500 551-9913
Web: www.tapenaderestaurant.com
Napoli Italian Restaurant
24960 Redlands Blvd . . . . Loma Linda CA 92354 909-796-3770 478-7756
Web: napoli-italian.com
555 East 555 E Ocean Blvd . . . . Long Beach CA 90802 562-437-0626
Web: www.555east.com
Alegria Cocina Latina Restaurant
115 Pine Ave. . . . Long Beach CA 90802 562-436-3388 436-9108
Web: www.alegriacocinalatina.com
Attic, The 3441 E Broadway . . . . Long Beach CA 90803 562-433-0153 433-2735
Web: theatticonbroadway.com
Bangkok Thai Cuisine 3426 E Fourth St . . . . Long Beach CA 90814 562-433-0093
Web: bangkokthaicuisinelbc.com
Belmont Brewing Co 25 39th Pl . . . . Long Beach CA 90803 562-433-3891 434-0604
Web: www.belmontbrewing.com
Cafe Piccolo 3222 E Broadway . . . . Long Beach CA 90803 562-438-1316
Web: www.cafepiccolo.com
Caffe La Strada 4716 E Second St . . . . Long Beach CA 90803 562-433-8100
Web: www.lastradalongbeach.com
Christy's On Broadway 3937 E Broadway . . . . Long Beach CA 90803 562-433-1171
Web: christysonbroadway.com
Crab Pot Restaurant & Bar, The
215 N Marina Dr . . . . Long Beach CA 90803 562-430-0272 799-0686
Web: www.crabpotlongbeach.com
George's Greek Cafe 5316 E Second St . . . . Long Beach CA 90803 562-433-1755
Web: georgesgreekcafe.com
Green Field Churrascaria
5305 E Pacific Coast Hwy . . . . Long Beach CA 90804 562-597-0906 597-0916
Web: greenfieldlongbeach.com
Johnny Rebs' Southern Roadhouse
4663 Long Beach Blvd . . . . Long Beach CA 90805 562-423-7327 422-9681
Web: www.johnnyrebs.com
King's Fish House 100 W Broadway . . . . Long Beach CA 90802 562-432-7463 435-6143
Web: www.kingsfishhouse.com
L'Opera 101 Pine Ave . . . . Long Beach CA 90802 562-491-0066 436-1108
Web: www.lopera.com
La Traviata Restaurant 301 N Cedar Ave . . . . Long Beach CA 90802 562-432-8022
Web: www.latraviata301.com
Lucille's Smokehouse Bar-B-Que
7411 Carson St . . . . Long Beach CA 90808 562-938-7427 627-1947
Web: www.lucillesbbq.com
Parker's Lighthouse
435 Shoreline Village Dr . . . . Long Beach CA 90802 562-432-6500 436-3551
Web: www.parkerslighthouse.com
Phil Trani's 3490 Long Beach Blvd . . . . Long Beach CA 90807 562-426-3668 426-1218
Web: philtrani.com
Reef Restaurant, The
880 S Harbor Scenic Dr . . . . Long Beach CA 90802 562-435-8013 432-6823
Web: www.reefrestaurant.com
Roscoe's House of Chicken & Waffles
730 E Broadway . . . . Long Beach CA 90802 562-437-8355
Web: www.roscoeschickenandwaffles.com
Sir Winston's Restaurant & Lounge
1126 Queens Hwy . . . . Long Beach CA 90802 562-435-3511
TF: 877-342-0738 ■ *Web:* www.queenmary.com

Phone Fax

Sky Room 40 S Locust Ave . . . . Long Beach CA 90802 562-983-2703
Web: theskyroom.com
Utopia 445 E First St . . . . Long Beach CA 90802 562-432-6888 432-8687
Web: www.utopiarestaurant.net
Yard House 401 Shoreline Village Dr . . . . Long Beach CA 90802 562-628-0455 435-5544
Web: www.yardhouse.com
Shenandoah at the Arbor
10631 Los Alamitos Blvd . . . . Los Alamitos CA 90720 562-431-1990 431-1910
Web: www.shenandoahatthearbor.com
Angeli Caffe 7274 Melrose Ave . . . . Los Angeles CA 90046 323-936-9086 938-9873
Web: www.angelicaffe.com
Angelini Osteria 7313 Beverly Blvd . . . . Los Angeles CA 90036 323-297-0070 297-0072
Web: www.angeliniosteria.com
AOC Wine Bar & Restaurant
8700 W Third St . . . . Los Angeles CA 90048 310-859-9859
Web: www.aocwinebar.com
Bamboo Restaurant 10835 Venice Blvd . . . . Los Angeles CA 90034 310-287-0668 287-0229
Web: bamboorestaurant.net
Ca'Brea 346 S La Brea Ave . . . . Los Angeles CA 90036 323-938-2863 938-8659
Cafe Pinot 700 W Fifth St . . . . Los Angeles CA 90071 213-239-6500
Web: www.patinagroup.com
Cafe Stella 3932 W Sunset Blvd . . . . Los Angeles CA 90029 323-666-0265 666-0258
Web: www.cafestella.com
Carlitos Gardel 7963 Melrose Ave . . . . Los Angeles CA 90046 323-655-0891 655-1576
Web: www.carlitosgardel.com
Cha Cha Cha 656 N Virgil Ave . . . . Los Angeles CA 90004 323-664-7723 664-7769
Web: www.theoriginalchachacha.com
Chi Dynasty 1813 Hillhurst Ave . . . . Los Angeles CA 90027 323-667-3388 667-3393
Web: www.chidynasty.com
Cicada 617 S Olive St . . . . Los Angeles CA 90014 213-488-9488 488-9546
Web: www.cicadarestaurant.com
Encounter Restaurant 209 World Way . . . . Los Angeles CA 90045 310-215-5156
Web: www.encounterrestaurant.com
Engine Co No 28 644 S Figueroa St . . . . Los Angeles CA 90017 213-624-6996 625-1600
Web: www.engineco.com
Farfalla Trattoria 1978 Hillhurst Ave . . . . Los Angeles CA 90027 323-661-7365 661-5956
Web: trattoriafarfalla.com
Genghis Cohen 740 N Fairfax Ave . . . . Los Angeles CA 90046 323-653-0640 653-0701
Web: www.genghiscohen.com
Gumbo Pot 6333 W Third St . . . . Los Angeles CA 90036 323-933-0358 932-6820
Web: www.thegumbopotla.com
Hamasaku 11043 Santa Monica Blvd . . . . Los Angeles CA 90025 310-479-7636 479-3116
Web: www.hamasakula.com
Harold & Belle's 2920 W Jefferson Blvd . . . . Los Angeles CA 90018 323-735-9023
Web: haroldandbellesrestaurant.com
Hilton Checkers Los Angeles
535 S Grand Ave . . . . Los Angeles CA 90071 213-624-0000
Web: checkerslosangeles.hilton.com/diningcd.php
Hu's Szechwan Restaurant
10450 National Blvd . . . . Los Angeles CA 90034 310-837-0252
Web: www.husrestaurant.com
IL Grano 11359 Santa Monica Blvd . . . . Los Angeles CA 90025 310-477-7886 477-7775
Web: ilgrano.com
India's Oven 7231 Beverly Blvd . . . . Los Angeles CA 90036 323-936-1000 936-1792
Web: www.laindiasoven.com
India's Tandoori 5468 Wilshire Blvd . . . . Los Angeles CA 90036 323-936-2050 936-0187
Web: www.indiastandoori.net
Ivy, The 113 N Robertson Blvd . . . . Los Angeles CA 90048 310-274-8303
Web: theivyrestaurants.com
JAR 8225 Beverly Blvd . . . . Los Angeles CA 90048 323-655-6566 655-6577
Web: www.thejar.com
Jitlada 5233 1/2 W Sunset Blvd . . . . Los Angeles CA 90027 323-667-9809 663-3104
Web: jitladala.com
Kendall's Brasserie & Bar
135 N Grand Ave . . . . Los Angeles CA 90012 213-972-7322 972-7331
Web: www.patinagroup.com/kendallsbrasserie
Kitchen, The 4348 Fountain Ave . . . . Los Angeles CA 90029 323-664-3663
Web: www.thekitchen.la
La Barca 2414 S Vermont Ave . . . . Los Angeles CA 90007 323-735-6567
Little Door 8164 W Third St . . . . Los Angeles CA 90048 323-951-1210 951-0487
Web: www.thelittledoor.com
Locanda Veneta 8638 W Third St . . . . Los Angeles CA 90048 310-274-1893 274-4217
Web: www.locandaveneta.net
Loteria! Grill 6333 W Third St . . . . Los Angeles CA 90036 323-930-2211 930-2282
Web: www.loteriagrill.com
Lucques 8474 Melrose Ave . . . . Los Angeles CA 90069 323-655-6277 655-3925
Web: www.lucques.com
Marino 6001 Melrose Ave . . . . Los Angeles CA 90038 323-466-8812 466-9010
Web: marinorestaurant.net
Mario's Peruvian 5786 Melrose Ave . . . . Los Angeles CA 90038 323-466-4181
Marouch 4905 Santa Monica Blvd . . . . Los Angeles CA 90029 323-662-9325 664-4229
Web: www.marouchrestaurant.com
Moishe's 6333 W Third St . . . . Los Angeles CA 90036 323-936-4998
Web: moishes-la.com
Mori Sushi 11500 W Pico Blvd . . . . Los Angeles CA 90064 310-479-3939
Web: www.morisushi.org
Nick & Stef's Steakhouse 330 S Hope St . . . . Los Angeles CA 90071 213-680-0330 680-0052
Web: www.patinagroup.com
Ocean Seafood 750 N Hill St . . . . Los Angeles CA 90012 213-687-3088 687-8549
Web: www.oceansf.com
Palms Thai 5900 Hollywood Blvd . . . . Los Angeles CA 90028 323-462-5073
Web: palmsthai.com
Papa Cristos 2771 W Pico Blvd . . . . Los Angeles CA 90006 323-737-2970 737-3571
Web: papacristos.com
Patina 141 S Grand Ave . . . . Los Angeles CA 90012 213-972-3331 972-3531
Web: www.patinagroup.com
Shabu Shabu House
127 Japanese Village Plz Mall . . . . Los Angeles CA 90012 213-680-3890
Sunnin 1776 Westwood Blvd . . . . Los Angeles CA 90024 310-475-3358
Web: www.sunnin.com
Tam O'Shanter Inn 2980 Los Feliz Blvd . . . . Los Angeles CA 90039 323-664-0228 664-4915
Web: www.lawrysonline.com

Name / Address	City	State	Zip	Phone	Fax
Taylor's Steak House 3361 W Eigth St	Los Angeles	CA	90005	213-382-8449	382-2372
Web: www.taylorssteakhouse.com					
Traxx Restaurant 800 N Alameda St	Los Angeles	CA	90012	213-625-1999	625-2999
Web: www.traxxrestaurant.com					
Tuk Tuk Thai 8875 W Pico Blvd	Los Angeles	CA	90035	310-860-1872	492-0003
Web: delivery.com					
Vermont 1714 N Vermont Ave	Los Angeles	CA	90027	323-661-6163	
Web: rockwell-la.com					
Water Grill 544 S Grand Ave	Los Angeles	CA	90071	213-891-0900	629-1891
Web: www.watergrill.com					
Appetez 825 W Roseburg Ave	Modesto	CA	95350	209-577-5099	577-5598
Web: www.appetez.com					
Dewz 1505 J St	Modesto	CA	95354	209-549-1101	
El Rosal 3430 Tully Rd	Modesto	CA	95350	209-523-7871	
Fruit Yard, The 7948 Yosemite Blvd	Modesto	CA	95357	209-577-3093	577-0600
Web: www.thefruityard.com					
Fuzio Universal Pasta 1020 Tenth St Ste 100	Modesto	CA	95354	209-557-9711	557-9717
Web: www.fuzio.com					
Galletto Ristorante 1101 J St	Modesto	CA	95354	209-523-4500	
Web: www.galletto.biz					
Marcella Restaurant 3507 Tully Rd	Modesto	CA	95356	209-577-3777	
Web: marcellasmexicanrestaurant.com					
MikiSushi 180 Leveland Ln	Modesto	CA	95350	209-524-3555	
Minnie's 107 McHenry Ave	Modesto	CA	95354	209-524-4621	524-6043
Web: minniesmodesto.com					
Noah's Hof Brau 1311 J St	Modesto	CA	95354	209-527-1090	527-8039
P Wexford's Pub 3313 McHenry Ave	Modesto	CA	95350	209-576-7939	576-7934
Papachino's 1212 J St	Modesto	CA	95354	209-578-5225	
Web: mypapachinos.com					
Strings Italian Cafe 2601 Oakdale Rd	Modesto	CA	95355	209-578-9777	578-5266
Web: stringscafe.com					
Tasty Thai 1401 Coffee Rd	Modesto	CA	95355	209-571-8424	571-8164
Web: tastythaimodesto.com					
Torii Japanese Restaurant					
2401 E Orangeburg Ave Ste 590	Modesto	CA	95355	209-529-8697	
Web: toriis.com					
Velvet Grill & Creamery 2204 McHenry Ave	Modesto	CA	95350	209-544-9029	
Web: www.velvetgrill.net					
Verona's Cucina Italiana 1700 McHenry Ave	Modesto	CA	95350	209-549-8876	
Abalonetti Seafood Trattoria					
57 Fisherman's Wharf Ste 1	Monterey	CA	93940	831-373-1851	373-2058
TF: 877-643-4972 ■ *Web:* www.restauranteur.com/abalonetti					
Bullwacker's 653 Cannery Row	Monterey	CA	93940	831-373-1353	373-0196
Cafe Fina 47 Fisherman's Wharf Ste 1	Monterey	CA	93940	831-372-5200	372-5209
TF: 800-843-3462 ■ *Web:* www.cafefina.com					
Domenico's on the Wharf					
50 Fisherman's Wharf # 1	Monterey	CA	93940	831-372-3655	372-2073
Web: www.domenicosmonterey.com					
Duck Club, The 400 Cannery Row	Monterey	CA	93940	831-646-1706	646-5425
Web: www.montereyplazahotel.com					
Epsilon Greek Restaurant 422 Tyler St	Monterey	CA	93940	831-655-8108	655-1791
Web: epsilonrestaurant.com					
Montrio 414 Calle Principal	Monterey	CA	93940	831-648-8880	648-8241
Web: www.montrio.com					
Old Fishermans Grotto 39 Fishermans Wharf	Monterey	CA	93940	831-375-4604	375-0391
Web: www.oldfishermansgrotto.com					
Sardine Factory, The 701 Wave St	Monterey	CA	93940	831-373-3775	373-4241
Web: www.sardinefactory.com					
Tarpy's Roadhouse 2999 Monterey-Salinas Hwy	Monterey	CA	93940	831-647-1444	
Web: www.tarpys.com					
Whaling Station Prime Steaks & Seafood					
763 Wave St	Monterey	CA	93940	831-373-3778	373-2460
Web: www.whalingstation.net					
Naya Restaurant 1057 Second Ave	New York	NY	10022	212-319-7777	
Web: www.nayarestaurants.com					
Banana Blossom Thai 4228 Pk Blvd	Oakland	CA	94602	510-336-0990	
Web: www.bananablossomthai.com					
Battambang 850 Broadway	Oakland	CA	94607	510-839-8815	
Web: themenupage.com					
Bay Wolf Restaurant 3853 Piedmont Ave	Oakland	CA	94611	510-655-6004	
Web: www.baywolf.com					
Dopo/Adesso 4293 Piedmont Ave	Oakland	CA	94611	510-652-3676	597-0265
Web: www.dopoadesso.com/dopo					
El Huarache Azteca 3842 International Blvd	Oakland	CA	94601	510-533-2395	
Web: elhuaracheazteca.net					
Everett & Jones Barbeque 126 Broadway	Oakland	CA	94607	510-663-2350	663-8856
Web: www.eandjbbq.com					
Holy Land 677 Rand Ave	Oakland	CA	94610	510-272-0535	
Web: holylandrestaurant.com					
Le Cheval Restaurant 1007 Clay St	Oakland	CA	94607	510-763-8495	763-7610
Web: www.lecheval.com					
Legendary Palace 708 Franklin St	Oakland	CA	94607	510-663-9188	
Mama's Royal Cafe 4012 Broadway	Oakland	CA	94611	510-547-7600	
Web: mamasroyalcafeoakland.com					
Marica Seafood Restaurant 5301 College Ave	Oakland	CA	94618	510-985-8388	
Web: maricafood.wordpress.com					
Mezze					
Mezze Restaurant & Bar 3407 Lakeshore Ave	Oakland	CA	94610	510-663-2500	
Web: www.mezze.com					
Oliveto Cafe & Restaurant 5655 College Ave	Oakland	CA	94618	510-547-5356	
Web: www.oliveto.com					
Pho84 354 17th St	Oakland	CA	94612	510-832-1338	
Web: pho84.com					
Quinn's Lighthouse 1951 Embarcadero Cove	Oakland	CA	94606	510-536-2050	535-1285
Web: www.quinnslighthouse.com					
Restaurant Peony 388 Ninth St Ste 288	Oakland	CA	94607	510-286-8866	
Web: restaurantpeony.com					
Scott's Seafood Grill & Bar					
Jack London Square Two Broadway	Oakland	CA	94607	510-444-3456	302-0995
Web: www.scottsjls.com					
Soi Four Bangkok Eatery 5421 College Ave	Oakland	CA	94618	510-655-0889	
Web: soifour.com					

Name / Address	City	State	Zip	Phone	Fax
Spettro 3355 Lakeshore Ave	Oakland	CA	94610	510-451-7738	
Web: themenupage.com					
Uzen Japanese Cuisine 5415 College Ave	Oakland	CA	94618	510-654-7753	
PlumpJack Cafe					
1920 Squaw Vly Rd PO Box 2407	Olympic Valley	CA	96146	530-583-1576	583-1734*
**Fax:* Hotel ■ *Web:* www.plumpjack.com					
Big Daddy O's Beach BBQ 2333 Roosevelt Blvd	Oxnard	CA	93035	805-984-0014	
BJ's Restaurant & Brewhouse 461 Esplanade Dr	Oxnard	CA	93030	805-485-1124	485-2246
Web: www.bjsrestaurants.com					
Cabo Seafood Grill & Cantina					
1041 S Oxnard Blvd	Oxnard	CA	93030	805-487-6933	487-6954
Web: www.caboseafoodgrill.com					
El Ranchero 131 W Second St	Oxnard	CA	93030	805-486-5665	
Kampai Japanese Restaurant 2367 N Oxnard Blvd	Oxnard	CA	93036	805-983-3333	
Korean Barbeque Swan 2061 N Oxnard Blvd	Oxnard	CA	93036	805-278-9611	
Pilar's Cafe 746 S 'A' St	Oxnard	CA	93030	805-487-1444	
Pirates Grub & Grog 450 S Victoria Ave	Oxnard	CA	93030	805-984-0046	382-6623
Web: www.piratesgrubngrog.net					
Plaza Grill 600 E Esplanade Dr	Oxnard	CA	93036	805-278-5070	
Favaloro's 545 Lighthouse Ave	Pacific Grove	CA	93950	831-373-8523	
Web: favalorosbignightbistro.com					
Passionfish 701 Lighthouse Ave	Pacific Grove	CA	93950	831-655-3311	655-3454
Web: www.passionfish.net					
Vito's Italian Restaurant					
1180 Forest Ave Ste A	Pacific Grove	CA	93950	831-375-3070	
Web: www.vitospacificgrove.com					
Pearl Dragon 15229 W Sunset Blvd	Pacific Palisades	CA	90272	310-459-9790	
Web: www.thepearldragon.com					
Al Dente Pasta 491 N Palm Canyon Dr	Palm Springs	CA	92262	760-325-1160	325-2199
Web: www.aldente-palmsprings.com					
Chop House 262 S Palm Canyon Dr	Palm Springs	CA	92262	760-320-4500	320-6940
Web: chophousepalmsprings.com					
El Mirasol Regional Cuisines of Mexico					
140 E Palm Canyon Dr	Palm Springs	CA	92264	760-323-0721	
Web: elmirasolrestaurants.com					
Europa Restaurant 1620 S Indian Trl	Palm Springs	CA	92264	760-327-2314	322-3794
TF: 800-245-2314 ■ *Web:* www.villaroyale.com					
Fisherman's Market & Grill					
235 S Indian Canyon Dr	Palm Springs	CA	92262	760-327-1766	
Web: www.fishermans.com					
Johanne's 196 S Indian Canyon Dr	Palm Springs	CA	92262	760-778-0017	778-1447
Web: www.johannesrestaurants.com					
John Henry's Cafe					
1785 E Tahquitz Canyon Way	Palm Springs	CA	92262	760-327-7667	
Web: johnhenryscafe.com/					
Kaiser Grille 205 S Palm Canyon Dr	Palm Springs	CA	92262	760-323-1003	323-5522
Web: www.restaurantsofpalmsprings.com					
Las Casuelas Terraza					
222 S Palm Canyon Dr	Palm Springs	CA	92262	760-325-2794	327-4174
Web: lascasuelas.com					
Le Vallauris 385 W Tahquitz Canyon Way	Palm Springs	CA	92262	760-325-5059	
Web: www.palmsprings.com					
Melvyn's 200 W Ramon Rd	Palm Springs	CA	92264	760-325-2323	325-0710
Web: www.inglesideinn.com					
Norma's 4200 E Palm Canyon Dr	Palm Springs	CA	92264	760-770-5000	342-2188
Web: www.starwoodhotels.com/lemeridien					
Sammy G's 265 S Palm Canyon Dr	Palm Springs	CA	92262	760-320-8041	
Web: sammygsrestaurant.com					
Spencer's Restaurant 701 W Barista Rd	Palm Springs	CA	92262	760-327-3446	327-5125
Web: www.spencersrestaurant.com					
Thai Smile 651 N Palm Canyon Dr	Palm Springs	CA	92262	760-320-5503	320-5584
Web: thaismilepalmsprings.com					
Arroyo Chop House 536 S Arroyo Pkwy	Pasadena	CA	91105	626-577-7463	577-1089
Web: www.arroyochophouse.com					
Parkway Grill 510 S Arroyo Pkwy	Pasadena	CA	91105	626-795-1001	796-6221
Web: www.theparkwaygrill.com					
Akina Teppan & Sushi 195 E Alessandro Blvd	Riverside	CA	92508	951-789-0443	
Chen Ling Palace 9856 Magnolia Ave	Riverside	CA	92503	951-351-8511	351-8162
Web: chenlingpalace.com					
Ciao Bella 1630 Spruce St	Riverside	CA	92507	951-781-8840	781-1970
Web: www.ciaobellariverside.com					
City Cuisine 2586 Main St	Riverside	CA	92501	951-682-9566	682-8649
Duane's 3649 Mission Inn Ave	Riverside	CA	92501	951-784-0300	683-1342
TF: 800-843-7755 ■ *Web:* www.missioninn.com					
Kountry Folks 3653 La Sierra Ave	Riverside	CA	92505	951-354-0437	354-7728
Web: www.kountry.com					
Mario's Place 3646 Mission Inn Ave	Riverside	CA	92501	951-684-7755	
Web: www.mariosplace.com					
Sevilla Riverside 3252 Mission Inn Ave	Riverside	CA	92507	951-778-0611	530-0083
Web: www.cafesevilla.com					
33rd Street Bistro 3301 Folsom Blvd	Sacramento	CA	95816	916-455-2233	457-2189
Web: www.33rdstreetbistro.com					
Aioli Bodega Espanola 1800 L St	Sacramento	CA	95811	916-447-9440	
Web: aiolibodega.com					
Alamar Restaurant & Marina					
5999 Garden Hwy	Sacramento	CA	95837	916-922-0200	
Biba 2801 Capitol Ave	Sacramento	CA	95816	916-455-2422	455-0542
Web: www.biba-restaurant.com					
Caballo Blanco Restaurante					
5604 Franklin Blvd	Sacramento	CA	95824	916-428-6706	
Casablanca 3516 Fair Oaks Blvd	Sacramento	CA	95864	916-979-1160	
El Novillero 4216 Franklin Blvd	Sacramento	CA	95820	916-456-4287	456-4149
Web: www.elnov.com					
Enotria Cafe & Wine Bar					
1431 Del Paso Blvd	Sacramento	CA	95815	916-922-6792	
Web: enotria.com					
Ernesto's Mexican Food 1901 16th St	Sacramento	CA	95814	916-441-5850	441-2154
Web: www.ernestosmexicanfood.com					
Esquire Grill 1213 K St	Sacramento	CA	95814	916-448-8900	
Web: www.paragarys.com					
Firehouse, The 1112 Second St	Sacramento	CA	95814	916-442-4772	442-6617
Web: www.firehouseoldsac.com					

Name / Address	City	State	ZIP	Phone	Fax
Gonuls J Street Cafe 3839 J St. Web: jstreetcafe.com	Sacramento	CA	95816	916-457-1155	
House of Chang 1589 W El Camino Ave	Sacramento	CA	95833	916-925-2138	
Il Fornaio 400 Capitol Mall Web: www.ilfornaio.com	Sacramento	CA	95814	916-446-4100	
JR's Texas Bar-B-Que 180 Otto Cir Web: www.jrtexasbbq.com	Sacramento	CA	95822	916-424-3520	424-9915
Kamon 2210 16th St. Web: jensaisushi.com	Sacramento	CA	95818	916-443-8888	
Kaveri Madras Cuisine 1148 Fulton Ave Web: kaverimadrascuisine.com	Sacramento	CA	95825	916-481-9970	
Kitchen Restaurant, The 2225 Hurley Way Web: thekitchenrestaurant.com	Sacramento	CA	95825	916-568-7171	
Lemon Grass 601 Munroe St Web: www.starginger.com	Sacramento	CA	95825	916-486-4891	486-1627
Lucca Restaurant & Bar 1615 J St. Web: www.luccarestaurant.com	Sacramento	CA	95814	916-669-5300	669-2848
MacQue's 8101 Elder Creek Rd. Web: www.macques.com	Sacramento	CA	95824	916-381-4119	
Marrakech 1833 Fulton Ave. Web: www.marrakechrestaurant.com	Sacramento	CA	95825	916-486-1944	
Nishiki Sushi 1501 16th St. Web: nishikisushi.com	Sacramento	CA	95814	916-446-3629	
Piatti Ristorante & Bar Sacramento 571 Pavilions Ln. Web: www.piatti.com	Sacramento	CA	95825	916-649-8885	649-8907
Rio City Cafe 1110 Front St Web: www.riocitycafe.com	Sacramento	CA	95814	916-442-8226	
Riverside Clubhouse 2633 Riverside Blvd Web: www.riversideclubhouse.com	Sacramento	CA	95818	916-448-9988	
Tapa the World 2115 J St. Web: www.tapatheworld.com	Sacramento	CA	95816	916-442-4353	442-4348
Texas West Bar-B-Que 1600 Fulton Ave Web: www.texaswestbbq.com	Sacramento	CA	95825	916-483-7427	483-8636
Tower Cafe 1518 Broadway. Web: www.towercafe.com	Sacramento	CA	95818	916-441-0222	
Waterboy, The 2000 Capitol Ave Web: www.waterboyrestaurant.com	Sacramento	CA	95811	916-498-9891	498-9893
Zinfandel Grille 2384 Fair Oaks Blvd. Web: zinfandelgrille.com	Sacramento	CA	95825	916-485-7100	484-7728
Alfredo's Pizza & Pasta 251 W Baseline St Web: alfredospizzaandpasta.com	San Bernardino	CA	92410	909-885-0218	
Addison The Grand Del Mar 5200 Grand Del Mar Way Web: www.addisondelmar.com	San Diego	CA	92130	858-314-1900	314-2001
Albie's Beef Inn 1201 Hotel Cir S Web: albiesbeefinn.com	San Diego	CA	92108	619-291-1103	
Anthony's Fish Grotto 1360 N Harbor Dr Web: www.gofishanthonys.com	San Diego	CA	92101	619-232-5103	425-8370
Ashoka the Great 9474 Black Mountain Rd. Web: ashokasd.com	San Diego	CA	92126	858-695-9749	695-9279
Bandar 845 Fourth Ave Web: www.bandarrestaurant.com	San Diego	CA	92101	619-238-0101	
Bernard'O Restaurant 12457 Rancho BernaRdo Rd. Web: bernardorestaurant.wordpress.com	San Diego	CA	92128	858-487-7171	487-7185
Berta's 3928 Twiggs St Web: www.bertasinoldtown.com	San Diego	CA	92110	619-295-2343	
Bertrand at Mister A's 2550 Fifth Ave 12th Fl Web: www.bertrandatmisteras.com	San Diego	CA	92103	619-239-1377	239-1379
Blue Point Coastal Cuisine 565 Fifth Ave Web: cohnrestaurants.com	San Diego	CA	92101	619-233-6623	
Buon Appetito 1609 India St Web: www.sandiegouniontribune.com/	San Diego	CA	92101	619-238-9880	
Cafe Japengo 8960 University Ctr Ln. Web: www.cafejapengo.com	San Diego	CA	92122	858-450-3355	552-6104
Cafe on Park 3831 Pk Blvd. Web: cafeonpark.com	San Diego	CA	92103	619-293-7275	
Cafe Zucchero 1731 India St Web: www.cafezucchero.com	San Diego	CA	92101	619-531-1731	531-7053
Candelas 416 Third Ave Web: www.candelas-sd.com	San Diego	CA	92101	619-702-4455	
Celadon 3671 Fifth Ave. Web: celadoncanteen.com	San Diego	CA	92103	619-297-8424	
Cohn Restaurant Group 2225 Hancock St Ste 120 Web: www.cohnrestaurants.com	San Diego	CA	92110	619-236-1299	236-1300
Corvette Diner 2965 Historic Decatur Rd. Web: cohnrestaurants.com	San Diego	CA	92103	619-542-1476	
De Medici 815 Fifth Ave. Web: demedicisandiego.com	San Diego	CA	92101	619-702-7228	
Dobson's 956 Broadway Cir Web: www.dobsonsrestaurant.com	San Diego	CA	92101	619-231-6771	
Edgewater Grill 861 W Harbor Dr Web: www.edgewatergrill.com	San Diego	CA	92101	619-232-7581	
Emerald Chinese Seafood Restaurant 3709 Convoy St Web: www.emeraldrestaurant.com	San Diego	CA	92111	858-565-6888	
Field, The 544 Fifth Ave Web: www.thefield.com	San Diego	CA	92101	619-232-9840	232-9842
Georgia's Greek Cuisine 3550 Rosecrans St. Web: www.georgiasgreekcuisine.com	San Diego	CA	92110	619-523-1007	523-2455
Greek Palace 8878 Clairmont Mesa Blvd. Web: www.greekpalace.com	San Diego	CA	92123	858-573-0155	573-9645
Greystone the Steakhouse 658 Fifth Ave Web: www.greystonesteakhouse.com	San Diego	CA	92101	619-232-0225	233-3606
Hob-Nob Hill 2271 First Ave. Web: hobnobhill.com	San Diego	CA	92101	619-239-8176	
Humphreys Restaurant 2241 Shelter Island Dr TF: 800-377-1177 ■ Web: www.humphreysbythebay.com	San Diego	CA	92106	619-224-3411	224-9438
Indigo Grill 1536 India St Web: www.cohnrestaurants.com	San Diego	CA	92101	619-234-6802	234-6868
Jack & Giulio's 2391 San Diego Ave Web: jackandgiulios.com	San Diego	CA	92110	619-294-2074	
JSix Restaurant 616 J St Web: www.jsixrestaurant.com	San Diego	CA	92101	619-531-8744	393-0131
La Gran Tapa 611 B St. Web: www.lagrantapa.com	San Diego	CA	92101	619-234-8272	
Lou & Mickey's 224 Fifth Ave. Web: www.louandmickeys.com	San Diego	CA	92101	619-237-4900	233-4977
Old Trieste 2335 Morena Blvd Web: www.oldtriesterestaurant.com	San Diego	CA	92110	619-276-1841	
Osteria Panevino 722 Fifth Ave Web: www.osteriapanevino.com	San Diego	CA	92101	619-595-7959	
Pampas Bar & Grill 8690 Aero Dr. Web: www.pampasrestaurant.com	San Diego	CA	92123	858-278-5971	
Panda Inn 506 Horton Plz Web: pandainn.com	San Diego	CA	92101	619-233-7800	
Park House Eatery 4574 Pk Blvd. Web: www.parkhouseeatery.com	San Diego	CA	92116	619-295-7275	
Phil's BBQ 3750 Sports Arena Blvd Web: www.philsbbq.net	San Diego	CA	92110	619-226-6333	
Princess Pub & Grille 1665 India St. Web: www.princesspub.com	San Diego	CA	92101	619-702-3021	
Rama 327 Fourth Ave Web: www.ramarestaurant.com	San Diego	CA	92101	619-501-8424	546-5304
Rancho Bernardo Inn 17550 Bernardo Oaks Dr Web: www.ranchobernardoinn.com	San Diego	CA	92128	858-675-8500	675-8501
Rei do Gado 939 Fourth Ave Web: www.reidogado.net	San Diego	CA	92101	619-702-8464	
Saigon on Fifth 3900 Fifth Ave Ste 120 Web: saigononfifth.menutoeat.com	San Diego	CA	92103	619-220-8828	
Star of the Sea 1360 N Harbor Dr Web: www.staroftheseа.com	San Diego	CA	92101	619-232-7408	232-2128
Sushi Ota 4529 Mission Bay Dr. Web: sushiota.com	San Diego	CA	92109	858-270-5670	
Taka Restaurant 555 Fifth Ave. Web: www.takasushi.com	San Diego	CA	92101	619-338-0555	
Tapas Picasso 3923 Fourth Ave Web: tapas-picasso.com	San Diego	CA	92103	619-294-3061	
Terra 7091 El Cajon Blvd Web: www.terrasd.com	San Diego	CA	92115	619-293-7088	293-7193
Tom Ham's Lighthouse 2150 Harbor Island Dr Web: www.tomhamslighthouse.com	San Diego	CA	92101	619-291-9110	
Westgate Hotel, The 1055 Second Ave TF: 800-522-1564 ■ Web: westgatehotel.com	San Diego	CA	92101	619-238-1818	557-3737
WineSellar & Brasserie 9550 Waples St Ste 115 Web: www.winesellar.com	San Diego	CA	92121	858-450-9557	
Absinthe Brasserie & Bar 398 Hayes St Web: www.absinthe.com	San Francisco	CA	94102	415-551-1590	255-2385
Acquerello 1722 Sacramento St. Web: www.acquerello.com	San Francisco	CA	94109	415-567-5432	567-6432
Albona Ristorante Istriano 545 Francisco St. Web: albonarestaurant.com	San Francisco	CA	94133	415-441-1040	
Alfred's Steakhouse 659 Merchant St Web: www.alfredssteakhouse.com	San Francisco	CA	94111	415-781-7058	397-1928
Ana Mandara 891 Beach St. Web: www.anamandara.com	San Francisco	CA	94109	415-771-6800	
Anzu 222 Mason St Hotel Nikko Web: www.hotelnikkosf.com	San Francisco	CA	94102	415-394-1100	394-1102
asiaSF 201 Ninth St. Web: www.asiasf.com	San Francisco	CA	94103	415-255-2742	
Aziza 5800 Geary Blvd Web: www.aziza-sf.com	San Francisco	CA	94121	415-752-2222	
Betelnut 2030 Union St. Web: www.betelnutrestaurant.com	San Francisco	CA	94123	415-929-8855	929-8894
Big Four Restaurant 1075 California St. Web: big4restaurant.com	San Francisco	CA	94108	415-771-1140	345-2891
Bistro Aix 3340 Steiner St. Web: www.bistroaix.com	San Francisco	CA	94123	415-202-0100	202-0153
Bix Restaurant 56 Gold St Web: www.bixrestaurant.com	San Francisco	CA	94133	415-433-6300	433-4574
Blue Mermaid Chowder House & Bar 471 Jefferson St Web: www.bluemermaidsf.com	San Francisco	CA	94109	415-771-2222	447-4014
Blue Plate, The 3218 Mission St. Web: www.blueplatesf.com	San Francisco	CA	94110	415-282-6777	282-8053
Boulevard One Mission St Web: www.boulevardrestaurant.com	San Francisco	CA	94105	415-543-6084	495-2936
Campton Place Restaurant 340 Stockton St Web: www.camptonplacesf.com	San Francisco	CA	94108	415-955-5555	955-5559
Chaya Brasserie 132 The Embarcadero Web: www.thechaya.com	San Francisco	CA	94105	415-777-8688	247-9952
Chenery Park 683 Chenery St Web: www.chenerypark.com	San Francisco	CA	94131	415-337-8537	337-0390
Chez Papa Bistrot 1401 18th St.	San Francisco	CA	94107	415-824-8205	
Chez Spencer 82 14th St Web: www.chezspencer.net	San Francisco	CA	94103	415-864-2191	864-2199
Crustacean 1475 Polk St Third Fl Web: houseofan.com	San Francisco	CA	94109	415-776-2722	
Delfina 3621 18th St Web: www.delfinasf.com	San Francisco	CA	94110	415-552-4055	552-4095
Ebisu 1283 Ninth Ave Web: www.ebisusushi.com	San Francisco	CA	94122	415-566-1770	
Farallon 450 Post St Web: www.farallonrestaurant.com	San Francisco	CA	94102	415-956-6969	834-1234

	City	State	ZIP	Phone	Fax
Fior D'Italia 2237 Mason St *Web:* www.fior.com	San Francisco	CA	94133	415-986-1886	
Foreign Cinema 2534 Mission St *Web:* www.foreigncinema.com	San Francisco	CA	94110	415-648-7600	648-7669
Frascati 1901 Hyde St *Web:* www.frascatisf.com	San Francisco	CA	94109	415-928-1406	928-1983
Fringale 570 Fourth St *Web:* www.fringalesf.com	San Francisco	CA	94107	415-543-0573	
Garcon Restaurant 1101 Valencia St *Web:* www.garconsf.com	San Francisco	CA	94110	415-401-8959	401-8960
Garibaldis 347 Presidio Ave *Web:* www.hurleyhafen.com	San Francisco	CA	94115	415-563-8841	563-3731
Grand Cafe 501 Geary St *Web:* monaco-sf.com/san-francisco-restaurant/index.html	San Francisco	CA	94102	415-292-0101	
Greens Fort Mason Ctr Bldg A *Web:* www.greensrestaurant.com	San Francisco	CA	94123	415-771-6222	
Harris' Restaurant 2100 Van Ness Ave *Web:* www.harrisrestaurant.com	San Francisco	CA	94109	415-673-1888	673-8817
Hog Island Oyster Co One Ferry Bldg # 11A *Web:* hogislandoysters.com	San Francisco	CA	94111	415-391-7117	391-7118
House 1230 Grant Ave *Web:* www.thehse.com	San Francisco	CA	94133	415-986-8612	
House of Prime Rib 1906 Van Ness Ave *Web:* houseofprimerib.net	San Francisco	CA	94109	415-885-4605	
Hyde Street Seafood House 1509 Hyde St *Web:* hydestseafoodhouse.com	San Francisco	CA	94109	415-931-3474	
Incanto 1550 Church St *Web:* www.incanto.biz	San Francisco	CA	94131	415-641-4500	641-4546
Indian Oven 233 Fillmore St *Web:* www.indianovensf.com	San Francisco	CA	94117	415-626-1628	
Isa 3324 Steiner St *Web:* www.isarestaurant.com	San Francisco	CA	94123	415-567-9588	
Jardiniere 300 Grove St *Web:* www.jardiniere.com	San Francisco	CA	94102	415-861-5555	861-5580
Kabuto Sushi 5121 Geary Blvd *Web:* www.kabutosushi.com	San Francisco	CA	94118	415-752-5652	
Kokkari Estiatorio 200 Jackson St *Web:* www.kokkari.com	San Francisco	CA	94111	415-981-0983	982-0983
Kyo-ya Two New Montgomery St *Web:* www.sfpalace.com	San Francisco	CA	94105	415-512-1111	537-6299
La Folie 2316 Polk St *Web:* www.lafolie.com	San Francisco	CA	94109	415-776-5577	776-3431
Little Nepal 925 Cortland Ave *Web:* www.littlenepalsf.com	San Francisco	CA	94110	415-643-3881	643-8088
Manora's Thai Cuisine 1600 Folsom St *Web:* www.manorathai.com	San Francisco	CA	94103	415-861-6224	861-1731
Masa's Restaurant 648 Bush St *Web:* www.masasrestaurant.com	San Francisco	CA	94108	415-989-7154	989-3141
Maykadeh 470 Green St *Web:* www.maykadehrestaurant.com	San Francisco	CA	94133	415-362-8286	
Millennium 580 Geary St *Web:* www.millenniumrestaurant.com	San Francisco	CA	94102	415-345-3900	345-3941
One Market One Market St *Web:* www.onemarket.com	San Francisco	CA	94105	415-777-5577	
Ozumo 161 Steuart St *Web:* www.ozumosanfrancisco.com	San Francisco	CA	94105	415-882-1333	882-1794
Piperade 1015 Battery St *Web:* www.piperade.com	San Francisco	CA	94111	415-391-2555	391-1159
Postrio 545 Post St *Web:* prescotthotel.com/	San Francisco	CA	94102	415-776-7825	
Puccini & Pinetti 129 Ellis St *Web:* pucciniandpinetti.com	San Francisco	CA	94102	415-392-5500	
Quince 470 Pacific Ave Cross Streets Sansome & Montgomery *Web:* www.quincerestaurant.com	San Francisco	CA	94133	415-775-8500	775-8501
Restaurant Gary Danko 800 N Pt St *Web:* www.garydanko.com	San Francisco	CA	94109	415-749-2060	
Ristorante Bacco 737 Diamond St *Web:* baccosf.com	San Francisco	CA	94114	415-282-4969	
Roy's 575 Mission St *Web:* www.roysrestaurant.com	San Francisco	CA	94105	415-777-0277	777-0377
Scala's Bistro 432 Powell St *Web:* www.scalasbistro.com	San Francisco	CA	94102	415-395-8555	395-8549
Schroeder's Cafe 240 Front St *Web:* www.schroederssf.com	San Francisco	CA	94111	415-421-4778	421-2217
Seven Hills 1550 Hyde St *Web:* sevenhillssf.com	San Francisco	CA	94109	415-775-1550	
Silks 222 Sansome St *TF:* 800-526-6566 ■ *Web:* www.mandarinoriental.com	San Francisco	CA	94104	415-986-2020	
Slanted Door One Ferry Bldg Ste 3 *Web:* www.slanteddoor.com	San Francisco	CA	94111	415-861-8032	
Sociale 3665 Sacramento St *Web:* caffesociale.com	San Francisco	CA	94118	415-921-3200	
South Park Cafe 108 S Pk St *Web:* www.southparkcafe.com	San Francisco	CA	94107	415-495-7275	
Straits Restaurant 845 Market St Fourth Fl *Web:* www.straitsrestaurants.com	San Francisco	CA	94103	415-668-1783	538-8496
Town Hall 342 Howard St *Web:* www.townhallsf.com	San Francisco	CA	94105	415-908-3900	908-3700
Trattoria Contadina 1800 Mason St **Fax Area Code:* 418 ■ *Web:* www.trattoriacontadina.com	San Francisco	CA	94133	415-982-5728	982-5746*
Tsunami Sushi & Sake Bar 1306 Fulton St *Web:* dajanigroup.net	San Francisco	CA	94117	415-567-7664	
Venticello 1257 Taylor St *Web:* www.venticello.com	San Francisco	CA	94108	415-922-2545	776-6583
Yank Sing 49 Stevenson St *Web:* www.yanksing.com	San Francisco	CA	94105	415-541-4949	541-0308
Zuni Cafe & Grill 1658 Market St *Web:* www.zunicafe.com	San Francisco	CA	94102	415-552-2522	
71 Sainte Peter 71 N San Pedro St *Web:* www.71saintpeter.com	San Jose	CA	95110	408-971-8523	938-3440
Amber India 377 Santana Row Ste 1140 *Web:* www.amber-india.com	San Jose	CA	95128	408-248-5400	248-5401
Aqui Cal-Mex Grill 1145 Lincoln Ave *Web:* aquicalmex.com	San Jose	CA	95125	408-995-0381	995-0385
Arcadia 100 W San Carlos St *Web:* michaelmina.net	San Jose	CA	95113	408-278-4555	278-4556
Bella Mia Restaurant & Bar 58 S First St	San Jose	CA	95113	408-280-1993	280-5624
Blowfish 355 Santana Row Ste 1010 *Web:* www.blowfishsushi.com	San Jose	CA	95128	408-345-3848	
ChaatCafe.com 834 Blossom Hill Rd *Web:* www.chaatcafes.com	San Jose	CA	95123	408-225-2233	516-9059
Cheesecake Factory South San Jose 925 Blossom Hill Rd *Web:* www.thecheesecakefactory.com	San Jose	CA	95123	408-225-6948	225-6957
Emile's 545 S Second St *Web:* www.emilesrestaurant.com	San Jose	CA	95112	408-289-1960	998-1245
Gecko Grill 855 N 13th St	San Jose	CA	95112	408-971-1826	
Grill on, The Alley, The 172 S Market St *Web:* www.thegrill.com	San Jose	CA	95113	408-294-2244	294-2255
Henry's Hi-life 301 W St John St *Web:* henryshilife.com	San Jose	CA	95110	408-295-5414	295-5431
House of Siam 151 S Second St *Web:* houseofsiamsanjose.com	San Jose	CA	95113	408-295-3397	
Korean Palace 2297A Stevens Creek Blvd	San Jose	CA	95128	408-947-8600	
Krung Thai 642 S Winchester Blvd *Web:* www.originalkrungthai.com	San Jose	CA	95128	408-260-8224	
La Foret 21747 Bertram Rd *Web:* www.laforetrestaurant.com	San Jose	CA	95120	408-997-3458	
La Pastaia 233 W Santa Clara St *Web:* www.lapastaia.com	San Jose	CA	95113	408-286-1000	
Le Papillon 410 Saratoga Ave *Web:* www.lepapillon.com	San Jose	CA	95129	408-296-3730	247-7812
Menara 41 E Gish Rd *Web:* menara41.com	San Jose	CA	95112	408-453-1983	
Original Joe's 301 S First St *Web:* www.originaljoes.com	San Jose	CA	95113	408-292-7030	
Paolo's Restaurant 333 W San Carlos St Ste 150 *Web:* www.paolosrestaurant.com	San Jose	CA	95110	408-294-2558	
Picasso's 62 W Santa Clara St *Web:* www.picassostapas.com	San Jose	CA	95113	408-298-4400	
Rosy's Fish City 2882 Story Rd *Web:* rosysfishcity.com	San Jose	CA	95127	408-272-2088	
Straits Cafe 333 Santana Row Ste 1100 *Web:* www.straitsrestaurants.com	San Jose	CA	95128	408-246-6320	246-6397
Sushi Factory Japanese Restaurant 4632 Meridian Ave *Web:* www.sushifactorysj.com	San Jose	CA	95124	408-723-2598	723-2579
Teske's Germania 255 N First St *Web:* www.teskes-germania.com	San Jose	CA	95113	408-292-0291	292-0347
Tomisushi 4336 Moorpark Ave *Web:* www.tomisushi.us	San Jose	CA	95129	408-257-4722	
50 Forks 3601 W Sunflower Ave *Web:* new.artinstitutes.edu	Santa Ana	CA	92704	714-338-1325	
Antonello Ristorante 3800 S Plz Dr *Web:* www.antonello.com	Santa Ana	CA	92704	714-751-7153	751-8650
Colima 130 N Fairview St *Web:* colimamexicanandseafood.com	Santa Ana	CA	92703	714-836-1254	543-6169
Darya Restaurant 3800 S Plaza Dr *Web:* daryasouthcoastplaza.com/	Santa Ana	CA	92704	714-557-6600	
El Gallo Giro 1442 S Bristol St *Web:* gallogiro.com	Santa Ana	CA	92704	714-549-2011	
Favori 3502 W First St *Web:* www.favorirestaurant.com	Santa Ana	CA	92703	714-531-6838	
Gypsy Den 125 N Broadway Ave *Web:* www.gypsyden.com	Santa Ana	CA	92701	714-835-8840	
Hacienda, The 1725 College Ave *Web:* tivoliterrace.com/wedding-packages/	Santa Ana	CA	92706	714-558-1304	
Memphis 201 N Broadway *Web:* memphiscafe.com	Santa Ana	CA	92701	714-564-1064	
Olde Ship, The 1120 W 17th St *Web:* www.theoldeship.com	Santa Ana	CA	92706	714-550-6700	550-6702
Polly's 2660 N Main St *Web:* www.pollypies.com	Santa Ana	CA	92705	714-547-9681	547-5302
Royal Khyber 1621 W Sunflower Ave *Web:* www.royalkhyber.com	Santa Ana	CA	92704	714-436-1010	436-9188
Spoons California Grill 2601 Hotel Terr *Web:* www.spoonsoc.com	Santa Ana	CA	92705	714-556-0700	957-8997
Tangata 2002 N Main St *Web:* www.patinagroup.com	Santa Ana	CA	92706	714-550-0906	667-3471
Taqueria De Anda 1029 E Fourth St *Web:* taqueriadeanda.com	Santa Ana	CA	92701	714-558-0856	
Yellow Basket Restaurant 2860 S Main St *Web:* www.yellowbasket.com	Santa Ana	CA	92707	714-545-8219	
Border Grill *Santa Monica* 1445 Fourth St *Web:* www.bordergrill.com	Santa Monica	CA	90401	310-451-1655	394-2049
Chinois on Main 2709 Main St *TF:* 888-646-3387 ■ *Web:* www.wolfgangpuck.com	Santa Monica	CA	90405	310-392-9025	396-5102
Ivy at the Shore 1535 Ocean Ave *Web:* theivyrestaurant.com	Santa Monica	CA	90401	310-393-3113	
JiRaffe Restaurant 502 Santa Monica Blvd *Web:* www.jirafferestaurant.com	Santa Monica	CA	90401	310-917-6671	917-6677
Josie 2424 Pico Blvd *Web:* www.josierestaurant.com	Santa Monica	CA	90405	310-581-9888	581-4202
Melisse 1104 Wilshire Blvd *Web:* www.melisse.com	Santa Monica	CA	90401	310-395-0881	395-3810

Name / Address	City	State	ZIP	Phone	Fax
Valentino Santa Monica 3115 Pico Blvd.	Santa Monica	CA	90405	310-829-4313	315-2791
Web: valentinosantamonica.com					
Delius Restaurant 2951 Cherry Ave	Signal Hill	CA	90755	562-426-0694	426-0694
Web: www.deliusrestaurant.com					
Thai Nakorn 11951 Beach Blvd.	Stanton	CA	90680	714-799-2031	
Web: thainakornrestaurant.com					
Angelina's 1563 E Fremont St	Stockton	CA	95205	209-948-6609	948-2477
Web: www.angelinas.com					
Bangkok Restaurant 3255 W Hammer Ln Ste 18	Stockton	CA	95209	209-476-8616	
Basil's 2324 Grand Canal Blvd.	Stockton	CA	95207	209-478-6290	
Breadfruit Tree 8095 Rio Blanco Rd	Stockton	CA	95219	209-952-7361	
Web: www.breadfruittree.com					
Bud's Seafood Grill 314 Lincoln Ctr	Stockton	CA	95207	209-956-0270	
Web: www.budsseafood.com					
Chitiva's Salsa & Sports Bar & Grille 445 W Weber Ave	Stockton	CA	95203	209-941-8605	
Web: www.chitiva.net					
Cocoro Bistro & Sushi Bar 2105 Pacific Ave	Stockton	CA	95204	209-941-6053	
Web: cocorobistro.com					
Dave Wong's 2828 W March Ln	Stockton	CA	95219	209-951-4152	951-5106
Web: davewongsrestaurant.com					
El Rancho Steak House 1457 E Mariposa Rd	Stockton	CA	95205	209-467-1529	467-1525
Garlic Bros 6629 Embarcadero Dr.	Stockton	CA	95219	209-474-6585	
Web: garlicbrothersonline.com					
House of Shaw 227 Dorris Pl	Stockton	CA	95204	209-948-4300	
Mi Ranchito Cafe 425 S Ctr St.	Stockton	CA	95203	209-946-9257	939-0227
Miguel's 7555 Pacific Ave.	Stockton	CA	95207	209-951-1931	
Web: miguelsmexicanrestaurantstockton.com					
Papapavlo's Bistro & Bar 501 N Lincoln Ctr.	Stockton	CA	95207	209-477-6133	477-6132
Web: www.papapavlos.com					
Sho Mi 419 Lincoln Ctr.	Stockton	CA	95207	209-951-3525	951-3628
Web: shomirestaurant.com					
Stockton Joe's 236 Lincoln Ctr	Stockton	CA	95207	209-951-2980	
Web: modesto.backpage.com					
Yasso Yani Restaurant 326 E Main St	Stockton	CA	95202	209-464-3108	
Sushi Nozawa 11288 Ventura Blvd Ste C	Studio City	CA	91604	818-508-7017	
Web: sushinozawa.com					
Ca'del Sole 4100 Cahuenga Blvd	Toluka Lake	CA	91602	818-985-4669	
Web: www.cadelsole.com					
Rockenwagner *3 Square Cafe + Bakery* 1121 Abbot Kinney Blvd.	Venice	CA	90291	310-399-6504	399-6518
Web: www.rockenwagner.com					
House of Blues 8430 W Sunset Blvd	West Hollywood	CA	90069	323-848-5100	
Web: www.houseofblues.com					
Vivoli Cafe & Trattoria of West Hollywood 7994 Sunset Blvd	West Hollywood	CA	90046	323-656-5050	656-0419
Web: www.vivolicafe.com					
Eduardo's Border Grill 1830 Westwood Blvd	West Los Angeles	CA	90025	310-475-2410	
Web: www.eduardosbordergrill.com					
Wood Ranch Barbecue & Grill Inc 2835 Townsgate Rd Ste 200	Westlake Village	CA	91361	805-719-9000	
Web: www.woodranch.com					
Bistro Jeanty 6510 Washington St.	Yountville	CA	94599	707-944-0103	944-0370
Web: www.bistrojeanty.com					

Colorado

Name / Address	City	State	ZIP	Phone	Fax
Cache Cache Bistro 205 S Mill St	Aspen	CO	81611	970-925-3835	544-8248
Web: www.cachecache.com					
Campo de Fiori 205 S Mill St.	Aspen	CO	81611	970-920-7717	920-3098
Web: www.campodefiori.net					
Hickory House Ribs *Aspen* 730 W Main St	Aspen	CO	81611	970-925-2313	
Web: www.hickoryhouseribs.com					
Matsuhisa 303 E Main St.	Aspen	CO	81611	970-544-6628	544-6630
Web: matsuhisaaspen.com					
Pinons 105 S Mill St	Aspen	CO	81611	970-920-2021	
Web: www.pinons.net					
Syzygy 308 E Hawkins Ave	Aspen	CO	81611	970-925-3700	
Web: www.syzygyrestaurant.com					
Takah Sushi 320 S Mill St.	Aspen	CO	81611	970-925-8588	925-4255
Web: www.takahsushi.com					
Dozens 2180 S Havana St	Aurora	CO	80014	303-337-6627	
Web: www.dozensrestaurant.com					
East Cafe Chinese Restaurant 15140 E Mississippi Ave	Aurora	CO	80012	303-369-6103	
El Alamo 1708 S Chambers Rd	Aurora	CO	80017	303-614-9806	
Web: elalamogrande.comcastbiz.net					
Helga's German Restaurant 14197 E Exposition Ave	Aurora	CO	80012	303-344-5488	344-5101
Web: www.helgasdeli.com					
La Cueva 9742 E Colfax Ave.	Aurora	CO	80010	303-367-1422	367-4071
Web: www.lacueva.net					
Royal Hilltop 18581 E Hampden Ave Ste 134	Aurora	CO	80013	303-690-7738	
Web: www.royalhilltop.com					
Sam's No 3 2580 S Havana St	Aurora	CO	80014	303-751-0347	
Web: www.samsno3.com					
Senor Ric's 13200 E Mississippi Ave	Aurora	CO	80012	303-750-9000	750-9006
Web: www.senorrics.net					
Summit Steakhouse, The 2700 S Havana St	Aurora	CO	80014	303-751-2112	
Web: www.thesummitsteakhouse.com					
Boulder ChopHouse & Tavern 921 Walnut St	Boulder	CO	80302	303-443-1188	443-4876
Web: www.boulderchophouse.com					
Boulder Cork 3295 30th St.	Boulder	CO	80301	303-443-9505	443-0193
Web: www.bouldercork.com					
Buff Restaurant 2600 Canyon Blvd	Boulder	CO	80302	303-442-9150	
Web: www.buffrestaurant.com					
Carelli's of Boulder 645 30th St	Boulder	CO	80303	303-938-9300	938-4077
Web: www.carellis.com					
Casa Alvarez 3161 Walnut St	Boulder	CO	80301	303-546-0630	
Web: www.casaalvarezcolorado.com					
Chautauqua Dining Hall 900 Baseline Rd	Boulder	CO	80302	303-440-3776	440-0926
Web: www.chautauqua.com					
Chez Thuy 2655 28th St.	Boulder	CO	80301	303-442-1700	
Web: www.chezthuy.com					
Falafel King Restaurant 1314 Pearl St	Boulder	CO	80302	303-449-9321	443-8965
Web: falafelkingboulder.com					
Flagstaff House 1138 Flagstaff Rd	Boulder	CO	80302	303-442-4640	442-8924
Web: www.flagstaffhouse.com					
Greenbriar Inn, The 8735 N Foothills Hwy.	Boulder	CO	80302	303-440-7979	449-2054
TF: 800-253-1474 ■ *Web:* www.greenbriarinn.com					
Illegal Pete's 1447 Pearl St	Boulder	CO	80302	303-440-3955	
Web: illegalpetes.com					
Japango 1136 Pearl St	Boulder	CO	80302	303-938-0330	938-0101
Web: www.boulderjapango.com					
Jax Fish House 928 Pearl St.	Boulder	CO	80302	303-444-1811	
Web: jaxfishhouse.com/boulder/					
L'Atelier 1739 Pearl St	Boulder	CO	80302	303-442-7233	
Web: www.latelierboulder.com					
Lucile's 2124 14th St.	Boulder	CO	80302	303-442-4743	939-9848
Web: www.luciles.com					
Pasta Jays 1001 Pearl St	Boulder	CO	80302	303-444-5800	
Web: www.pastajays.com					
Ras Kassa's Ethiopian Restaurant 2111 30th St.	Boulder	CO	80301	303-447-2919	
Web: www.raskassas.com					
Spruce 2115 13th St	Boulder	CO	80302	303-442-4880	
Sushi Tora 2014 Tenth St.	Boulder	CO	80302	303-444-2280	
Web: sushitoraboulder.com					
Sushi Zanmai 1221 Spruce St.	Boulder	CO	80302	303-440-0733	440-6676
Web: www.sushizanmai.com					
Taj Restaurant 2630 Baseline Rd	Boulder	CO	80305	303-494-5216	
Web: tajcolorado.com					
Thyme on the Creek 1345 28th St	Boulder	CO	80302	303-998-3835	443-1480
TF: 866-866-8086 ■ *Web:* www.millenniumhotels.com					
Walnut Brewery 1123 Walnut St	Boulder	CO	80302	303-447-1345	447-0067
Web: www.walnutbrewery.com					
Walnut Cafe 3073 Walnut St.	Boulder	CO	80301	303-447-2315	
Web: www.walnutcafe.com					
Zolo Grill 2525 Arapahoe Ave.	Boulder	CO	80302	303-449-0444	
Web: www.zologrill.com					
Amanda's Fonda 3625 W Colorado Ave	Colorado Springs	CO	80904	719-227-1975	578-0285
Web: amandasfonda.com					
Bamboo Court 4935 Centennial Blvd	Colorado Springs	CO	80919	719-599-7383	599-7098
Web: bamboocourtcoloradosprings.com					
Blue Star, The 1645 S Tejon St.	Colorado Springs	CO	80905	719-632-1086	
Web: www.thebluestar.net					
China Town 326 S Nevada Ave	Colorado Springs	CO	80903	719-632-5151	
Web: chinatown-restaurant.com					
Edelweiss 34 E Ramona Ave.	Colorado Springs	CO	80905	719-633-2220	471-8413
Web: www.restauranteur.com					
Flying W Ranch Inc 3330 Chuckwagon Rd.	Colorado Springs	CO	80919	719-598-4000	598-4600
TF: 800-232-3599 ■ *Web:* www.flyingw.com					
Fratelli 124 N Nevada Ave.	Colorado Springs	CO	80903	719-575-9571	
Web: www.fratelliristorante.com					
Jake & Telly's 2616 W Colorado Ave	Colorado Springs	CO	80904	719-633-0406	473-1153
Web: www.jakeandtellys.com					
Jun Japanese Restaurant 1760 Dublin Blvd	Colorado Springs	CO	80918	719-531-9368	
Web: www.coloradojijo.com					
La Carreta 35 N Iowa Ave	Colorado Springs	CO	80909	719-477-1157	
MacKenzie's Chop House Restaurant 128 S Tejon St	Colorado Springs	CO	80903	719-635-3536	635-1225
Web: www.mackenzieschophouse.com					
Marigold Cafe 4605 Centennial Blvd.	Colorado Springs	CO	80919	719-599-4776	
Web: marigoldcoloradosprings.com					
Mason Jar, The 2925 W Colorado Ave.	Colorado Springs	CO	80904	719-632-4820	632-0392
Web: www.masonjarcolorado.com					
Penrose Room One Lake Ave	Colorado Springs	CO	80906	719-634-7711	
Web: www.broadmoor.com					
Pepper Tree, The 888 W Moreno Ave	Colorado Springs	CO	80905	719-471-4888	471-0997
Web: www.peppertreecs.com					
Phantom Canyon Brewing Co Two E Pikes Peak Ave	Colorado Springs	CO	80903	719-635-2800	635-9930
Web: www.phantomcanyon.com					
Uwes German Restaurant 31 Iowa Ave	Colorado Springs	CO	80909	719-475-1611	
Web: bestgermanrestaurant.com					
1515 On Market 1515 Market St	Denver	CO	80202	303-571-0011	
Web: www.1515restaurant.com					
Barolo Grill 3030 E Sixth Ave	Denver	CO	80206	303-393-1040	333-9240
Web: www.barologrilldenver.com					
Bella Vista Mexican Restaurant 127 E 20th Ave	Denver	CO	80205	303-297-9020	297-8866
Bistro Vendome 1420 Larimer St.	Denver	CO	80202	303-825-3232	825-3240
Web: www.bistrovendome.com					
Broker Restaurant, The 821 17th St	Denver	CO	80202	303-292-5065	292-2652
Web: www.thebrokerrestaurant.com					
Cafe Brazil 4408 Lowell Blvd	Denver	CO	80211	303-480-1877	
Web: www.cafebrazildenver.com					
Carmine's on Penn 92 S Pennsylvania	Denver	CO	80209	303-777-6443	777-4129
Web: www.carminesonpenn.net					
Celtic Tavern, The 1801 Blake St	Denver	CO	80202	303-308-1795	308-1576
Web: www.theceltictavern.com					
Corkhouse, The 4900 E Colfax Ave.	Denver	CO	80220	303-355-4488	355-1336
Web: corkhousebroker.com					
Damascus 2276 S Colorado Blvd.	Denver	CO	80222	303-757-3515	
El Taco de Mexico 714 Santa Fe Dr	Denver	CO	80204	303-623-3926	
Web: eltacodemexicodenver.com					
Fado Irish Pub 1735 19th St Ste 150	Denver	CO	80202	303-297-0066	297-0055
Web: www.fadoirishpub.com					

Restaurant	City	State	ZIP	Phone	Fax
Hapa Sushi Grill & Sake Bar 2780 E Second Ave *Web:* www.hapasushi.com	Denver	CO	80206	303-322-9554	355-3449
India's 7400 E Hampden Ave Ste F *Web:* www.indiasrestaurant.com	Denver	CO	80231	303-755-4284	752-9814
Le Central 112 E Eigth Ave *Web:* www.lecentral.com	Denver	CO	80203	303-863-8094	863-0219
Little India 330 E Sixth Ave *Web:* www.littleindiadenver.com	Denver	CO	80203	303-871-9777	871-1907
Luca d'Italia 711 Grant St *Web:* www.lucadenver.com	Denver	CO	80203	303-832-6600	823-3532
New Saigon 630 S Federal Blvd *Web:* newsaigon.com	Denver	CO	80219	303-936-4954	
Panzano 909 17th St *Web:* www.panzano-denver.com	Denver	CO	80202	303-296-3525	
Parisi 4401 Tennyson St *Web:* www.parisidenver.com	Denver	CO	80212	303-561-0234	480-5514
Potager 1109 Ogden St *Web:* www.potagerrestaurant.com	Denver	CO	80218	303-832-5788	
Solera 5410 E Colfax Ave *Web:* www.solerarestaurant.com	Denver	CO	80220	303-388-8429	
Sullivan's Steakhouse 1745 Wazee St *Web:* sullivanssteakhouse.com	Denver	CO	80202	303-295-2664	
Sushi Den 1487 S Pearl St *Web:* www.sushiden.net	Denver	CO	80210	303-777-0826	
Tamayo 1400 Larimer St *Web:* www.richardsandoval.com	Denver	CO	80202	720-946-1433	946-1434
Venice Ristorante & Wine Bar 1700 Wynkoop St *Web:* www.veniceristorante.com	Denver	CO	80202	303-534-2222	893-0560
Wynkoop Brewing Co 1634 18th St *Web:* www.wynkoop.com	Denver	CO	80202	303-297-2700	297-2958
Zengo 1610 Little Raven St *Web:* www.richardsandoval.com	Denver	CO	80202	720-904-0965	904-0966
6512 Restaurant 6512 durango *Web:* www.6512restaurant.com	Durango	CO	81301	970-247-9083	
Carver Brewing Co 1022 Main Ave *Web:* www.carverbrewing.com	Durango	CO	81301	970-259-2545	
Christina's Grill & Bar 21382 Hwy 160 W *Web:* www.christinasgrill.com	Durango	CO	81303	970-382-3844	382-3865
Cyprus Cafe 725 E Second Ave *Web:* www.cypruscafe.com	Durango	CO	81301	970-385-6884	
East by Southwest 160 E College Dr *Web:* www.eastbysouthwest.com	Durango	CO	81301	970-247-5533	
Francisco's Restaurante y Cantina 619 Main Ave *Web:* franciscosdurango.com	Durango	CO	81301	970-247-4098	247-2008
Ken & Sue's 636 Main Ave *Web:* www.kenandsues.com	Durango	CO	81301	970-385-1810	385-1801
Lady Falconburgh's Barley Exchange 640 Main Ave	Durango	CO	81301	970-382-9664	382-9625
Mahogany Grille 699 Main Ave *Web:* www.mahoganygrille.com	Durango	CO	81301	970-247-4433	259-2208
Bisetti's Italian Restaurant 120 S College Ave *Web:* www.bisettis.com	Fort Collins	CO	80524	970-493-0086	493-1701
Enzio's Italian Kitchen 126 W Mountain Ave *Web:* www.enzios.com	Fort Collins	CO	80524	970-484-8466	484-8490
Jay's Bistro 135 W Oak St *Web:* www.jaysbistro.net	Fort Collins	CO	80524	970-482-1876	482-1897
Moot House 2626 S College Ave *Web:* www.themoothouse.com	Fort Collins	CO	80525	970-226-2121	
Nimo's Sushi Bar & Japanese 921 E Harmony Rd Ste 104 *Web:* www.nimossushi.com	Fort Collins	CO	80525	970-221-1040	
Rainbow Restaurant 212 W Laurel St *Web:* rainbowfortcollins.com	Fort Collins	CO	80521	970-221-2664	
Suehiro 223 Linden St *Web:* suehirofc.com	Fort Collins	CO	80524	970-482-3734	
Young's Cafe 3307 S College Rd *Web:* www.youngscafe.com	Fort Collins	CO	80525	970-223-8000	223-4923
Sam Taylor's Barbeque 435 S Cherry St *Web:* samtaylorsbbq.com	Glendale	CO	80246	303-388-9300	388-2276
240 Union 240 Union Blvd *Web:* www.240union.com	Lakewood	CO	80228	303-989-3562	989-3565
Casa Bonita 6715 W Colfax Ave *Web:* www.casabonitadenver.com	Lakewood	CO	80214	303-232-5115	232-7801
Briarhurst Manor 404 Manitou Ave *TF:* 877-685-1448 ■ *Web:* www.briarhurst.com	Manitou Springs	CO	80829	719-685-1864	685-9638
Krabloonik 4250 Divide Rd PO Box 5517 *Web:* www.krabloonik.com	Snowmass Village	CO	81615	970-923-3953	923-0246

Connecticut

Restaurant	City	State	ZIP	Phone	Fax
Bloodroot 85 Ferris St *Web:* www.bloodroot.com	Bridgeport	CT	06605	203-576-9168	
Captain's Cove Seaport 1 Bostwick Ave *Web:* www.captainscoveseaport.com	Bridgeport	CT	06605	203-335-7104	335-6793
Field Restaurant & Bar, The 3001 Fairfield Ave *Web:* www.fieldrestaurant.com	Bridgeport	CT	06605	203-333-0043	
Joseph's Steakhouse 360 Fairfield Ave *Web:* www.josephssteakhouse.com	Bridgeport	CT	06604	203-337-9944	337-9996
Ralph 'N Rich's 815 Main St *Web:* ralphnrichsct.com	Bridgeport	CT	06604	203-366-3597	
Tony's Huntington Inn 437 Huntington Tpke *Web:* www.thpizza.com	Bridgeport	CT	06610	203-374-5541	
Vazzy's Brick Oven Restaurant 513 Broadbridge Rd *Web:* www.vazzysrest.com	Bridgeport	CT	06610	203-371-8046	371-4293
Barcelona Restaurant & Wine Bar 4180 Black Rock Tpke *Web:* www.barcelonawinebar.com	Fairfield	CT	06824	203-255-0800	255-0225
Shiki Hana 222 Post Rd *Web:* shikihanafairfield.com	Fairfield	CT	06824	203-259-5950	259-5428
Asiana Cafe 130 E Putnam Ave *Web:* www.asianacafe.com	Greenwich	CT	06830	203-622-6833	861-2680
Elm Street Oyster House 11 W Elm St *Web:* www.elmstreetoysterhouse.com	Greenwich	CT	06830	203-629-5795	629-8515
L'Escale 500 Steamboat Rd *Web:* www.lescalerestaurant.com	Greenwich	CT	06830	203-661-4600	661-4601
Meli-Melo 362 Greenwich Ave *Web:* melimelogreenwich.com	Greenwich	CT	06830	203-629-6153	
Morello Bistro 253 Greenwich Ave *Web:* www.morellobistro.com	Greenwich	CT	06830	203-661-3443	661-3588
Penang Grill 55 Lewis St	Greenwich	CT	06830	203-861-1988	861-0003
Polpo 554 Old Post Rd *Web:* www.polporestaurant.com	Greenwich	CT	06830	203-629-1999	629-1718
Tengda Asian Bistro 21 Field Pt Rd *Web:* tengdaasian.com	Greenwich	CT	06830	203-625-5338	
Thomas Henkelmann Restaurant 420 Field Pt Rd *Web:* www.homesteadinn.com	Greenwich	CT	06830	203-869-7500	869-7502
Carbone's Ristorante 588 Franklin Ave *Web:* www.carbonesct.com	Hartford	CT	06114	860-296-9646	296-2785
City Steam Brewery Cafe 942 Main St *Web:* www.citysteambrewerycafe.com	Hartford	CT	06103	860-525-1600	244-2255
Costa del Sol 901 Wethersfield Ave *Web:* www.costadelsolrestaurant.net	Hartford	CT	06114	860-296-1714	296-9250
Coyote Flaco 635 New Britain Ave *Web:* www.mycoyoteflaco.com	Hartford	CT	06106	860-953-1299	953-1954
Ficara's 577 Franklin Ave *Web:* www.ficarasrestaurant.com	Hartford	CT	06114	860-296-3238	296-3238
First & Last Tavern 939 Maple Ave *Web:* www.firstandlasttavern.com	Hartford	CT	06114	860-956-6000	956-9783
Hot Tomato's One Union Pl *Web:* www.hottomatos.net	Hartford	CT	06103	860-249-5100	524-8120
Koji 17 Asylum St	Hartford	CT	06103	860-247-5654	677-5359
Max Downtown 185 Asylum St *Web:* www.maxrestaurantgroup.com	Hartford	CT	06103	860-522-2530	246-5279
New Park 1615 Pk St	Hartford	CT	06106	860-232-1565	
Oporto 2074 Park St *Web:* www.oportohartford.com	Hartford	CT	06106	860-233-3184	951-7770
Peppercorn's Grill 357 Main St *Web:* www.peppercornsgrill.com	Hartford	CT	06106	860-547-1714	724-7612
Trumbull Kitchen 150 Trumbull St *Web:* maxrestaurantgroup.com	Hartford	CT	06103	860-493-7412	493-7416
Vito's by the Park 26 Trumbull St *Web:* www.vitosct.com	Hartford	CT	06103	860-244-2200	244-2210
VIVO Seasonal Trattoria 200 Columbus Blvd *Web:* vivohartford.com	Hartford	CT	06103	860-760-2333	
Cavey's 45 E Ctr St *Web:* www.caveysrestaurant.com	Manchester	CT	06040	860-643-2751	
Adriana's 771 Grand Ave *Web:* adrianasnewhaven.com	New Haven	CT	06511	203-865-6474	865-4846
Akasaka 1450 Whalley Ave	New Haven	CT	06515	203-387-4898	397-3069
Archie Moore's Bar & Restaurant 188 1/2 Willow St *Web:* www.archiemoores.com	New Haven	CT	06511	203-773-9870	773-9799
Bentara 76 Orange St *Web:* www.bentara.com	New Haven	CT	06510	203-562-2511	562-0892
Brazi's Italian Restaurant 201 Food Terminal Plz *Web:* brazis.com	New Haven	CT	06511	203-498-2488	498-1652
Carmen Anthony Steakhouse 660 State St *Web:* www.carmenanthony.com	New Haven	CT	06511	203-773-1444	772-4853
Carmine's Tuscan Grill Ristorante 1500 Whalley Ave *Web:* www.carminestuscangrill.com	New Haven	CT	06515	203-389-2805	
Christopher Martin's 860 State St *Web:* www.christophermartins.com	New Haven	CT	06511	203-776-8835	777-8875
Claire's Corner Copia 1000 Chapel St *Web:* www.clairescornercopia.com	New Haven	CT	06510	203-562-3888	
Consiglio's 165 Wooster St *Web:* www.consiglios.com	New Haven	CT	06511	203-865-4489	
Fireside Restaurant 810 Woodward Ave *Web:* firesidebarandgrillct.com	New Haven	CT	06512	203-466-1919	466-1589
Mamoun's Falafel Restaurant 85 Howe St *Web:* www.mamouns.com	New Haven	CT	06511	203-562-8444	562-1474
Miya 68 Howe St *Web:* www.miyassushi.com	New Haven	CT	06511	203-777-9760	
Sage American Bar & Grill 100 S Water St *Web:* www.sageamerican.com	New Haven	CT	06519	203-787-3466	777-8274
Tre Scalini 100 Wooster St *Web:* www.trescalinirestaurant.com	New Haven	CT	06510	203-777-3373	787-5360
Union League Cafe 1032 Chapel St *Web:* unionleaguecafe.com	New Haven	CT	06510	203-562-4299	562-6712
Zaroka 148 York St *Web:* www.zaroka.com	New Haven	CT	06511	203-776-8644	776-0051
Zinc 964 Chapel St *Web:* www.zincfood.com	New Haven	CT	06510	203-624-0507	624-9156
Sabatiello Gourmet Pizza 1072 E Putnam Ave *Web:* www.pizzashops.info/connecticut//riverside/sabatiellogourmetpizza	Riverside	CT	06878	203-344-9339	
La Scogliera Restaurant 474 River Rd *Web:* www.lascoglierarestaurant.com	Shelton	CT	06484	203-922-1179	922-1176
Bobby Valentine's Sports Gallery Cafe 225 Main St *Web:* www.bobbyv.com	Stamford	CT	06901	203-348-0010	359-9395
Brasitas 954 E Main St *Web:* www.brasitas.com	Stamford	CT	06902	203-323-3176	353-8102
Columbus Park Trattoria 205 Main St *Web:* www.columbusparktrattoria.com	Stamford	CT	06901	203-967-9191	967-4724

Restaurant	City	State	Zip	Phone	Fax
Crab Shell 46 Southfield Ave *Web:* www.crabshell.com	Stamford	CT	06902	203-967-7229	967-7233
Eclisse Restaurant 700 Canal St	Stamford	CT	06902	203-325-3773	327-2308
Hugo's Restaurant 161 Stillwater Ave	Stamford	CT	06902	203-323-5577	
Kotobuki 457 Summer St *Web:* www.kotobukijapaneserestaurant.com	Stamford	CT	06901	203-359-4747	357-7522
Ole Mole 1030 High Ridge Rd *Web:* olemolestamford.com	Stamford	CT	06905	203-461-9962	329-7438
Arugula 953 Farmington Ave *Web:* arugula-bistro.com	West Hartford	CT	06107	860-561-4888	
Chengdu 179 Pk Rd *Web:* chengduwesthartford.com	West Hartford	CT	06119	860-232-6455	232-3002
Grant's 977 Farmington Ave *Web:* billygrant.com	West Hartford	CT	06107	860-236-1930	
Max's Oyster Bar 964 Farmington Ave *Web:* www.maxrestaurantgroup.com	West Hartford	CT	06107	860-236-6299	233-6969
Murasaki 23 LaSalle Rd *Web:* murasakijapaneserestaurant.com	West Hartford	CT	06107	860-236-7622	
Pond House Cafe 1555 Asylum Ave *Web:* www.pondhousecafe.com	West Hartford	CT	06117	860-231-8823	231-8731
Restaurant Bricco 78 LaSalle Rd *Web:* www.billygrant.com	West Hartford	CT	06107	860-233-0220	233-7503

Delaware

Restaurant	City	State	Zip	Phone	Fax
Rusty Rudder Restaurant 113 Dickinson St *Web:* rustyrudderdewey.com	Dewey Beach	DE	19971	302-227-3888	226-2402
Starboard Restaurant 2009 Hwy 1 *Web:* www.thestarboard.com	Dewey Beach	DE	19971	302-227-4600	227-4601
Two Seas Restaurant 1300 Delaware 1 *Web:* dinehere.us	Dewey Beach	DE	19971	302-227-2610	
Roma Italian Restaurant Three President Dr *Web:* www.romadover.com	Dover	DE	19901	302-678-1041	
US 13 Grill & Catering 1115 S Governors Ave	Dover	DE	19904	302-730-3551	
Where Pigs Fly 617 E Loockerman St *Web:* wherepigsflyrestaurant.com	Dover	DE	19901	302-678-0586	735-7675
Sambo's Tavern 283 Front St	Leipsic	DE	19901	302-674-9724	
Big Fish Grill 20298 Coastal Hwy *Web:* www.bigfishgrill.com	Rehoboth Beach	DE	19971	302-227-3474	227-1705
Blue Moon Restaurant 35 Baltimore Ave *Web:* www.bluemoonrehoboth.com	Rehoboth Beach	DE	19971	302-227-6515	227-3702
Dos Locos 208 Rehoboth Ave *Web:* www.doslocos.com	Rehoboth Beach	DE	19971	302-227-3353	227-2213
Jake's Seafood House Restaurant 29 Baltimore Ave *Web:* www.jakesseafoodhouse.com	Rehoboth Beach	DE	19971	302-227-6237	226-5137
Ristorante Zebra 32 Lake Ave *Web:* ristorantezebra.us	Rehoboth Beach	DE	19971	302-226-1160	226-4985
Victoria's Restaurant Two Olive Ave Boardwalk Plz Hotel *Web:* www.boardwalkplaza.com/restaurant.htm	Rehoboth Beach	DE	19971	302-227-0615	
Blue Parrott Bar & Grille 1934 W Sixth St *Web:* www.blueparrotgrille.com	Wilmington	DE	19805	302-655-8990	655-9488
Bonhouse 4713 Kirkwood Hwy	Wilmington	DE	19808	302-633-1218	
Bull's Eye Saloon & Restaurant 3734 Kirkwood Hwy *Web:* www.bullseyesaloon.com	Wilmington	DE	19808	302-633-6557	
Corner Bistro 3604 Silverside Rd *Web:* www.mybistro.com	Wilmington	DE	19810	302-477-1778	
Deep Blue Bar & Grill 111 W 11th St *Web:* www.deepbluebarandgrill.com	Wilmington	DE	19801	302-777-2040	777-1012
Eclipse Bistro 1020 N Union St *Web:* www.platinumdininggroup.com	Wilmington	DE	19805	302-658-1588	661-1080
Green Room at the Hotel duPont 11th & Market St *TF:* 800-441-9019 ■ *Web:* www.hoteldupont.com	Wilmington	DE	19801	302-594-3100	594-3108
Harry's Savoy Grill 2020 Naamans Rd *Web:* harryshospitalitygroup.com/harrys-savoy-grill	Wilmington	DE	19810	302-475-3000	475-9990
Harry's Seafood Grill 101 S Market St *Web:* harryshospitalitygroup.com/harrys-seafood-grill	Wilmington	DE	19801	302-777-1500	777-2406
LaTolteca 2209 Concord Pk *Web:* authenticmex.com	Wilmington	DE	19803	302-778-4646	
Luigi Vitrone's Pastabilities 415 N Lincoln St *Web:* www.ljv-pastabilities.com	Wilmington	DE	19805	302-656-9822	
Madeline's Italian Restaurant 531 N DuPont St *Web:* www.madelinesitalianrestaurant.com	Wilmington	DE	19805	302-656-4505	
Mexican Post 3100 Naamans Rd *Web:* www.mexicanpost.com	Wilmington	DE	19810	302-478-3939	478-5599
Mikimoto's 1212 N Washington St *Web:* www.mikimotos.com	Wilmington	DE	19801	302-656-8638	656-7423
Moro 1307 N Scott St *Web:* www.mororestaurant.net	Wilmington	DE	19806	302-777-1800	777-2350
Mrs Robino's Restaurant 520 N Union St *Web:* www.mrsrobinos.com	Wilmington	DE	19801	302-652-9223	658-8124
Piccolina Toscana 1412 N DuPont St *Web:* www.piccolinatoscana.com	Wilmington	DE	19806	302-654-8001	654-8250
Stanley's Tavern 2038 Foulk Rd *Web:* www.stanleystavern.com	Wilmington	DE	19810	302-475-1887	475-0904
Union City Grille 805 N Union St *Web:* www.unioncitygrille.com	Wilmington	DE	19805	302-654-9780	654-0238
Valle Cucina Italiana 4752 Limestone Rd *Web:* www.vallecucina.com	Wilmington	DE	19808	302-998-9999	
Walter's Steak House & Saloon 802 N Union St *Web:* walters-steakhouse.com	Wilmington	DE	19805	302-652-6780	

District of Columbia

Restaurant	City	State	Zip	Phone	Fax
Marriott International Inc 10400 Fernwood Road *NASDAQ: MAR* ■ **Fax Area Code: 336* ■ **Fax:* Mail Rm ■ *TF:* 800-450-4442 ■ *Web:* www.marriott.com	Bethesda	MD	20817	301-380-3000	665-6522*
15 Ria 1515 Rhode Island Ave NW *Web:* www.15ria.com	Washington	DC	20005	202-742-0015	332-8436
1789 Restaurant 1226 36th St NW *Web:* www.1789restaurant.com	Washington	DC	20007	202-965-1789	337-1541
701 Restaurant 701 Pennsylvania Ave NW *Web:* www.701restaurant.com	Washington	DC	20004	202-393-0701	393-0242
Al Tiramisu 2014 P St NW *Web:* www.altiramisu.com	Washington	DC	20036	202-467-4466	467-4468
Ardeo 3311 Connecticut Ave NW *Web:* www.ardeobardeo.com	Washington	DC	20008	202-244-6550	
Bistro Bis 15 E St NW *Web:* www.bistrobis.com	Washington	DC	20001	202-661-2700	661-2747
Bombay Club 815 Connecticut Ave NW *Web:* www.bombayclubdc.com	Washington	DC	20006	202-659-3727	659-5012
Cactus Cantina 3300 Wisconsin Ave NW *Web:* www.cactuscantina.com	Washington	DC	20016	202-686-7222	362-5649
Cafe Atlantico 405 Eigth St NW *Web:* www.cafeatlantico.com	Washington	DC	20004	202-393-0812	393-0555
Cashion's Eat Place 1819 Columbia Rd NW *Web:* www.cashionseatplace.com	Washington	DC	20009	202-797-1819	797-0048
Ceiba 701 14th St NW *Web:* www.ceibarestaurant.com	Washington	DC	20005	202-393-3983	393-1863
Charlie Palmer Steak 101 Constitution Ave NW *TF:* 877-632-7800	Washington	DC	20001	202-547-8100	
City Lights of China 1731 Connecticut Ave NW *Web:* www.citylightsofchina.com	Washington	DC	20009	202-265-6688	265-1369
Coeur de Lion 926 Massachusetts Ave NW *Web:* www.henleypark.com	Washington	DC	20001	202-414-0500	414-0513
Corduroy 1122 Ninth St NW *Web:* corduroydc.com	Washington	DC	20001	202-589-0699	
DC Coast 1401 K St NW *Web:* www.dccoast.com	Washington	DC	20005	202-216-5988	371-2221
Equinox 818 Connecticut Ave NW *Web:* www.equinoxrestaurant.com	Washington	DC	20006	202-331-8118	331-0809
Filomena Ristorante 1063 Wisconsin Ave NW	Washington	DC	20007	202-338-8800	338-8806
Heritage India 1337 Connecticut Ave NW *Web:* heritageindiausa.com	Washington	DC	20036	202-331-1114	
I Ricchi 1220 19th St NW *Web:* www.iricchi.net	Washington	DC	20036	202-835-0459	872-1220
Indique 3512 Connecticut Ave NW *Web:* www.indique.com	Washington	DC	20008	202-244-6600	244-6603
Jaleo 480 Seventh St NW *Web:* www.jaleo.com	Washington	DC	20004	202-628-7949	628-7952
Johnny's Half Shell 400 N Capitol St NW *Web:* www.johnnyshalfshell.net	Washington	DC	20001	202-737-0400	737-3026
Jyoti 2433 18th St NW *Web:* jyotidc.com	Washington	DC	20009	202-518-5892	518-5892
Kaz Sushi Bistro 1915 I St NW *Web:* www.kazsushibistro.com	Washington	DC	20006	202-530-5500	530-5501
Komi 1509 17th St NW *Web:* www.komirestaurant.com	Washington	DC	20036	202-332-9200	330-5909
Little Fountain Cafe 2339 18th St NW *Web:* www.littlefountaincafe.com	Washington	DC	20009	202-462-8100	
Loews Madison Hotel 1177 15th St NW *Web:* loewshotels.com	Washington	DC	20005	202-862-1600	
Makoto 4822 MacArthur Blvd NW *Web:* makotorestaurantdc.com	Washington	DC	20007	202-298-6866	625-6602
Marcel's 2401 Pennsylvania Ave NW *Web:* www.marcelsdc.com	Washington	DC	20037	202-296-1166	296-6466
Marrakesh 617 New York Ave NW	Washington	DC	20001	202-393-9393	737-3737
Montmarte 327 Seventh St SE *Web:* montmartredc.com	Washington	DC	20003	202-544-1244	544-4038
New Heights Restaurant 2317 Calvert St NW *Web:* www.newheightsrestaurant.com	Washington	DC	20008	202-234-4110	
Nora 2132 Florida Ave NW *Web:* www.noras.com	Washington	DC	20008	202-462-5143	234-6232
Obelisk 2029 P St NW	Washington	DC	20036	202-872-1180	
Oceanaire Seafood Room 1201 F St NW *Web:* www.theoceanaire.com	Washington	DC	20004	202-347-2277	347-9858
Old Ebbitt Grill 675 15th St NW *Web:* www.ebbitt.com	Washington	DC	20005	202-347-4800	347-6136
Palena 3529 Connecticut Ave NW	Washington	DC	20008	202-537-9250	
Peacock Cafe 3251 Prospect St NW *Web:* www.peacockcafe.com	Washington	DC	20007	202-625-2740	625-1402
Prime Rib, The 2020 K St NW *Web:* www.theprimerib.com	Washington	DC	20006	202-466-8811	466-2010
Rice 1608 14th St NW *Web:* www.ricerestaurant.com	Washington	DC	20009	202-234-2400	234-2737
Sakana 2026 P St NW	Washington	DC	20036	202-887-0900	
Sea Catch 1054 31st St NW *Web:* www.seacatchrestaurant.com	Washington	DC	20007	202-337-8855	337-7159
Sushi Ko Glover Park 2309 Wisconsin Ave NW *Web:* sushikorestaurants.com	Washington	DC	20007	202-333-7594	
Sushi Taro 1503 17th St NW *Web:* www.sushitaro.com	Washington	DC	20036	202-462-8999	328-3756
Tabard Inn 1739 N St NW *Web:* www.tabardinn.com	Washington	DC	20036	202-331-8528	785-6173
Taberna Del Alabardero 1776 I St NW *Web:* www.alabardero.com	Washington	DC	20006	202-429-2200	775-3713
Tosca 1112 F St NW *Web:* www.toscadc.com	Washington	DC	20004	202-367-1990	367-1999

				Phone	Fax
Vidalia 1990 M St NW *Web:* www.vidaliadc.com	Washington	DC	20036	202-659-1990	223-8572
Zaytinya 701 Ninth St NW *Web:* www.zaytinya.com	Washington	DC	20001	202-638-0800	638-6969

Florida

				Phone	Fax
Sandbar Seafood & Spirits 100 Spring Ave. *Web:* sandbar.groupersandwich.com	Anna Maria	FL	34216	941-778-0444	778-3997
Chef Allen's 19088 NE 29th Ave *Web:* www.chefallens.com	Aventura	FL	33180	305-935-2900	
Addison, The Two E Camino Real *Web:* www.theaddison.com	Boca Raton	FL	33432	561-372-0568	372-0570
Kathy's Gazebo Cafe 4199 N Federal Hwy *Web:* www.kathysgazebo.com	Boca Raton	FL	33431	561-395-6033	395-6335
Ke-e Grill 17940 N Military Trl. *Web:* wix.com	Boca Raton	FL	33496	561-995-5044	995-5024
Le Vieux Paris 170 W Camino Real	Boca Raton	FL	33432	561-368-7910	
Max's Grille 404 Plz Real *Web:* www.maxsgrille.com	Boca Raton	FL	33432	561-368-0080	
New York Prime 2350 Executive Ctr Dr NW *Web:* www.newyorkprime.com	Boca Raton	FL	33431	561-998-3881	998-5761
Uncle Tai's 5250 Town Ctr Cir. *Web:* uncletais.com	Boca Raton	FL	33486	561-368-8806	
Caffe Vialetto 4019 Le Jeune Rd *Web:* www.cafevialetto.com	Coral Gables	FL	33134	305-446-5659	446-3532
Christy's 3101 Ponce de Leon Blvd. *Web:* www.christysrestaurant.com	Coral Gables	FL	33134	305-446-1400	446-3257
Francesco 325 Alcazar Ave. *Web:* www.francesco.com.pe	Coral Gables	FL	33134	305-446-1600	
Maroosh 223 Valencia Ave *Web:* www.maroosh.com	Coral Gables	FL	33134	305-476-9800	476-3999
Ortanique Restaurant 278 Miracle Mile. *Web:* ortaniquerestaurants.com	Coral Gables	FL	33134	305-446-7710	446-9895
Pascal's on Ponce 2611 Ponce de Leon Blvd. *Web:* www.pascalmiami.com	Coral Gables	FL	33134	305-444-2024	444-9798
Runyon's 9810 W Sample Rd *Web:* www.runyonsofcoralsprings.com	Coral Springs	FL	33065	954-752-2333	752-2401
Shorty's Bar-B-Q 5989 S University Dr *Web:* www.shortys.com	Davie	FL	33328	954-680-9900	
Angell & Phelps Chocolate Factory 154 S Beach St. *Web:* angellandphelps.com	Daytona Beach	FL	32114	386-252-6531	
Anna's Trattoria 304 Seabreeze Blvd	Daytona Beach	FL	32118	386-239-9624	
Caribbean Jack's 721 Ballough Rd. *Web:* www.caribbeanjacks.com	Daytona Beach	FL	32114	386-523-3000	252-7362
Cellar, The 220 Magnolia Ave. *Web:* www.thecellarrestaurant.com	Daytona Beach	FL	32114	386-258-0011	
Gene's Steak House 3674 W International Speedway Blvd	Daytona Beach	FL	32124	386-255-2059	
Ocean Deck 127 S Ocean Ave. *Web:* www.oceandeck.com	Daytona Beach	FL	32118	386-253-5224	253-7226
Oyster Pub 555 Seabreeze Blvd. *Web:* www.oysterpub.com	Daytona Beach	FL	32118	386-255-6348	258-7489
Pasha 919 W International Speedway Blvd *Web:* pashacafedaytona.com	Daytona Beach	FL	32114	386-257-7753	
Porto-Fino Restaurant 3124 S Atlantic Ave. *Web:* portofinodaytona.com	Daytona Beach	FL	32118	386-767-9484	
Top of Daytona Restaurant 2625 S Atlantic Ave. *Web:* topofdaytona.com	Daytona Beach	FL	32118	386-767-5791	
Baja Cafe Dos 1310 S Federal Hwy *Web:* www.bajacafedeerfield.com	Deerfield Beach	FL	33441	954-596-1305	
Tamarind Asian Grill & Sushi Bar 949 S Federal Hwy *Web:* www.tamarindgrill.com	Deerfield Beach	FL	33441	954-428-8009	
32 East 32 E Atlantic Ave *Web:* www.32east.com	Delray Beach	FL	33444	561-276-7868	276-7894
Fifth Avenue Grill 821 SE Fifth Ave Federal Hwy.	Delray Beach	FL	33483	561-265-0122	
3030 Ocean 3030 Holiday Dr *Web:* www.3030ocean.com	Fort Lauderdale	FL	33316	954-765-3030	
Ambry 3016 E Commercial Blvd. *Web:* ambryrestaurant.net	Fort Lauderdale	FL	33308	954-771-7342	
Bistro 17 1617 SE 17th St. *Web:* marriott.com	Fort Lauderdale	FL	33316	954-626-1748	626-1717
Bistro Mezzaluna 1821 SE Tenth Ave *Web:* www.bistromezzaluna.com	Fort Lauderdale	FL	33316	954-522-9191	
Cafe Martorano 3343 E Oakland Pk Blvd *Web:* www.cafemartorano.com	Fort Lauderdale	FL	33308	954-561-2554	630-2082
Cafe Seville 2768 E Oakland Pk Blvd *Web:* www.cafeseville.com	Fort Lauderdale	FL	33306	954-565-1148	
Cafe Vico 1125 N Federal Hwy *Web:* www.cafevicorestaurant.com	Fort Lauderdale	FL	33304	954-565-9681	565-6978
Casa D'Angelo 1201 N Federal Hwy. *Web:* casa-d-angelo.com	Fort Lauderdale	FL	33304	954-564-1234	564-1235
Casablanca Cafe 3049 Alhambra St. *Web:* www.casablancacafeonline.com	Fort Lauderdale	FL	33304	954-764-3500	764-3815
Eduardo de San Angel 2822 E Commercial Blvd *Web:* www.eduardodesanangel.com	Fort Lauderdale	FL	33308	954-772-4731	772-0794
Greek Islands Taverna 3300 N Ocean Blvd. *Web:* www.greekislandstaverna.com	Fort Lauderdale	FL	33308	954-565-5505	565-4675
Hi-Life Cafe 3000 N Federal Hwy *Web:* www.hilifecafe.com	Fort Lauderdale	FL	33306	954-563-1395	
Johnny V 625 E Las Olas Blvd *Web:* www.johnnyvlasolas.com	Fort Lauderdale	FL	33301	954-761-7920	761-3495
Las Vegas 2807 E Oakland Pk Blvd *Web:* www.lasvegascubancuisine.com	Fort Lauderdale	FL	33306	954-564-1370	
Mango's 904 E Las Olas Blvd *Web:* www.mangosonlasolas.com	Fort Lauderdale	FL	33301	954-523-5001	523-5355
Nick's 3496 N Ocean Blvd *Web:* nicksitalianonline.com	Fort Lauderdale	FL	33308	954-563-6441	
Rainbow Palace 2787 E Oakland Pk Blvd *Web:* www.rainbowpalace.com	Fort Lauderdale	FL	33306	954-565-5652	565-4175
Sage 2378 N Federal Hwy. *Web:* www.sagecafe.net	Fort Lauderdale	FL	33305	954-565-2299	565-3309
Sea Watch Restaurant 6002 N Ocean Blvd. *Web:* www.seawatchontheocean.com	Fort Lauderdale	FL	33308	954-781-2200	783-0282
Sunfish Grill 2775 E Oakland Park Blvd *Web:* sunfishgrill.com	Fort Lauderdale	FL	33306	954-561-2004	
Sushi Rock Cafe 1515 E Las Olas Blvd	Fort Lauderdale	FL	33301	954-462-5541	
Thai on the Beach 901 N Ft Lauderdale Beach Blvd.	Fort Lauderdale	FL	33304	954-565-0015	
Timpano Italian Chophouse 450 E Las Olas Blvd *Web:* timpanochophouse.net	Fort Lauderdale	FL	33301	954-462-9119	462-9109
Tokyo Sushi 1499 SE 17th St *Web:* iluvtokyosushi.net	Fort Lauderdale	FL	33316	954-767-9922	
Tom Jenkins' Bar-B-Q 1236 S Federal Hwy *Web:* www.tomjenkins.net	Fort Lauderdale	FL	33316	954-522-5046	
Amelia's 235 S Main St Ste 107 *Web:* www.ameliasgainesville.com	Gainesville	FL	32601	352-373-1919	374-8565
David's Barbecue 5121 NW 39th Ave *Web:* davidsbbq.com	Gainesville	FL	32606	352-373-2002	372-8492
Emiliano's Cafe Seven SE First Ave. *Web:* www.emilianoscafe.com	Gainesville	FL	32601	352-375-7381	
La Fiesta Mexican Restaurant 908 NW 69th Terrace	Gainesville	FL	32605	352-332-0878	332-0878
Leonardo's 706 706 W University Ave. *Web:* www.leonardosgainesville.com	Gainesville	FL	32601	352-378-2001	
Mildred's Big City Food 3445 W University Ave *Web:* www.mildredsbigcityfood.com	Gainesville	FL	32607	352-371-1711	371-3290
Miya Sushi 3222 SW 35th Blvd. *Web:* miyasushi.net	Gainesville	FL	32608	352-335-3030	335-2288
Northwest Grille 5115 NW 39th Ave	Gainesville	FL	32606	352-376-0500	
Sushi Matsuri 3418 SW Archer Rd. *Web:* www.matsuritime.com	Gainesville	FL	32608	352-335-1875	
Tim's Thai 501 NW 23rd Ave Ste A *Web:* www.timsthairestaurant.com	Gainesville	FL	32609	352-372-5424	372-5424
Tangelo's Grille 3121 Beach Blvd S. *Web:* www.tangelosgrille.com	Gulfport	FL	33707	727-894-1695	821-7027
Molina's Ranch Restaurant 4090 E Eigth Ave. *Web:* www.molinasranchrestaurant.com	Hialeah	FL	33013	305-693-4440	693-9255
Dave & Buster's 3000 Oakwood Blvd. **Fax Area Code:* 214 ■ *TF:* 844-515-5157 ■ *Web:* www.daveandbusters.com	Hollywood	FL	33020	954-923-5505	904-2370*
Taverna Opa 800 N Ocean Dr *Web:* www.tavernaopa.com	Hollywood	FL	33019	954-922-2256	922-2258
Islamorada Fish Co 81532 Overseas Hwy PO Box 283 **Fax Area Code:* 305 ■ *TF:* 800-258-2559 ■ *Web:* www.ifcstonecrab.com	Islamorada	FL	33036	800-258-2559	664-5071*
BB's Restaurant & Bar 1019 Hendricks Ave *Web:* www.bbsrestaurant.com	Jacksonville	FL	32207	904-306-0100	306-0118
Biscotti's Restaurant 3556 St Johns Ave. *Web:* www.biscottis.net	Jacksonville	FL	32205	904-387-2060	387-0051
JJ's Bistro de Paris 7643 Gate Pkwy Ste 105. *Web:* www.jjbistro.com	Jacksonville	FL	32256	904-996-7557	996-7577
Marker 32 14549 Beach Blvd *Web:* www.marker32.com	Jacksonville	FL	32250	904-223-1534	223-7763
Matthew's 2107 Hendricks Ave *Web:* www.matthewsrestaurant.com	Jacksonville	FL	32207	904-396-9922	396-5222
Pastiche 4260 Herschel St *Web:* patioatpastiche.com	Jacksonville	FL	32210	904-387-6213	
Wine Cellar 1314 Prudential Dr *Web:* www.winecellarjax.com	Jacksonville	FL	32207	904-398-8989	
Dwight's Bistro 1527 Penman Rd *Web:* www.dwightsbistro.com	Jacksonville Beach	FL	32250	904-241-4496	
Eleven South 216 11th Ave S *Web:* www.elevensouth.com	Jacksonville Beach	FL	32250	904-241-1112	241-1109
A & B Lobster House 700 Front St. *Web:* www.aandblobsterhouse.com	Key West	FL	33040	305-294-5880	294-6871
Ambrosia 1401 Simonton St *Web:* keywestambrosia.com	Key West	FL	33040	305-293-0304	
Bagatelle 115 Duval St. *Web:* www.bagatellekeywest.com	Key West	FL	33040	305-296-6609	294-7304
Blue Heaven 729 Thomas St. **Fax Area Code:* 910 ■ *TF:* 800-986-0958 ■ *Web:* www.blueheavenkw.homestead.com	Key West	FL	33040	305-296-8666	299-0850*
BO's Fish Wagon 801 Caroline St. *Web:* bosfishwagon.com	Key West	FL	33040	305-294-9272	
Cafe Marquesa 600 Fleming St *Web:* www.marquesa.com	Key West	FL	33040	305-292-1244	
Cafe Sole 1029 Southard St *Web:* cafesole.com	Key West	FL	33040	305-294-0230	296-8286
Camille's 1202 Simonton St *Web:* www.camilleskeywest.com	Key West	FL	33040	305-296-4811	294-8983
Duffy's Steak & Lobster House 1007 Simonton St. *Web:* duffyskeywest.com	Key West	FL	33040	305-296-4900	
Grand Cafe Key West 314 Duval St. *Web:* www.grandcafekeywest.com	Key West	FL	33040	305-292-4740	

Name / Address	City	State	Zip	Phone	Fax
Hard Rock Cafe Key West 313 Duval St.	Key West	FL	33040	305-293-0230	
Web: www.hardrock.com					
Hog's Breath Saloon Key West 400 Front St Ste C	Key West	FL	33040	305-296-4222	292-8472
Web: www.hogsbreath.com					
Jimmy Buffet's Margaritaville 500 Duval St	Key West	FL	33040	305-292-1435	294-9147
Web: www.margaritaville.com					
Kelly's Caribbean Bar Grill & Brewery 301 Whitehead St	Key West	FL	33040	305-293-8484	296-0047
Web: www.kellyskeywest.com					
Latitudes Beach Cafe 245 Front St	Key West	FL	33040	305-292-5394	292-5395
Web: westinsunsetkeycottages.com					
Louie's Backyard 700 Waddell Ave	Key West	FL	33040	305-294-1061	294-0002
Web: www.louiesbackyard.com					
Mangia Mangia 900 Southard St	Key West	FL	33040	305-294-2469	
Web: www.mangia-mangia.com					
Mangoes 700 Duval St	Key West	FL	33040	305-292-4606	
Web: www.mangoskeywest.com					
Michael's 532 Margaret St	Key West	FL	33040	305-295-1300	295-1378
Web: www.michaelskeywest.com					
Mo's 1116 White St.	Key West	FL	33040	305-296-8955	
Pisces 1007 Simonton St.	Key West	FL	33040	305-294-7100	
Web: www.pisceskeywest.com					
Square One 1075 Duval St Ste C12	Key West	FL	33040	305-296-4300	
Web: squareonekeywest.com					
Turtle Kraals Restaurant & Bar 231 Margaret St	Key West	FL	33040	305-294-2640	
Web: www.turtlekraals.com					
Artist Point 901 Timberline Dr	Lake Buena Vista	FL	32830	407-824-3200	
Web: disneyworld.disney.go.com					
bluezoo 1500 Epcot Resorts Blvd PO Box 22653	Lake Buena Vista	FL	32830	407-934-1111	934-4882
Web: www.swandolphin.com/bluezoo					
Disney 4401 Grand Floridian Way Disney's Grand Floridian Resort	Lake Buena Vista	FL	32830	407-934-7639	824-3186
Web: disneyworld.disney.go.com/					
House of Blues Orlando 1490 E Lk Buena Vista Dr	Lake Buena Vista	FL	32830	407-934-2583	934-1100
Web: www.houseofblues.com					
Blue Moon Fish Co 4405 W Tradewinds Ave	Lauderdale-by-the-Sea	FL	33308	954-267-9888	267-9006
Web: www.bluemoonfishco.com					
Rosey Baby 4587 N University Dr	Lauderhill	FL	33351	954-749-5627	749-5733
Web: www.roseybaby.com					
Cap's Place Island Restaurant 2765 NE 28th Ct	Lighthouse Point	FL	33064	954-941-0418	941-2346
Web: www.capsplace.com					
Le Bistro 4626 N Federal Hwy	Lighthouse Point	FL	33064	954-946-9240	
Web: www.lebistrorestaurant.com					
Chart House 201 Gulf of Mexico Dr	Longboat Key	FL	34228	941-383-5593	383-5879
Web: www.chart-house.com					
Euphemia Haye 5540 Gulf of Mexico Dr	Longboat Key	FL	34228	941-383-3633	387-8336
Web: www.euphemiahaye.com					
Harry's Continental Kitchens 525 St Judes Dr	Longboat Key	FL	34228	941-383-0777	383-2029
Web: www.harryskitchen.com					
Pattigeorge's 4120 Gulf of Mexico Dr.	Longboat Key	FL	34228	941-383-5111	
Web: www.pattigeorges.com					
Azul 500 Brickell Key Dr	Miami	FL	33131	305-913-8358	913-3825
Web: www.mandarinoriental.com					
Bali Cafe 109 NE Second Ave	Miami	FL	33132	305-358-5751	
Bizcaya Grill 3300 SW 27th Ave.	Miami	FL	33133	305-644-4675	
Web: ritzcarlton.com					
Cancun Grill 15406 NW 77th Ct	Miami	FL	33016	305-826-8571	826-7994
Web: cancungrillmiamilakes.com					
Captain's Tavern Restaurant Inc 9625 S Dixie Hwy	Miami	FL	33156	305-666-5979	665-9753
Web: www.captainstavernmiami.com					
Casa Juancho 2436 SW Eigth St	Miami	FL	33135	305-642-2452	642-2524
Web: www.casajuancho.com					
Garcia's 398 NW N River Dr	Miami	FL	33128	305-375-0765	375-0167
Web: garciasmiami.com					
Graziano's 9227 SW 40th St.	Miami	FL	33165	305-225-0008	221-1949
Web: grazianosgroup.com					
La Loggia 68 W Flagler St	Miami	FL	33130	305-373-4800	373-7350
Web: laloggia.org					
Lan Pan Asian Cafe 8332 S Dixie Hwy	Miami	FL	33143	305-661-8141	
Web: lanpanasian.com					
Lombardi's 401 Biscayne Blvd	Miami	FL	33132	888-286-3792	381-9366*
**Fax Area Code:* 305 ■ *TF:* 888-286-3792 ■ *Web:* www.lombardifamilyconcepts.com					
Melting Pot of Miami, The 11520 Sunset Dr	Miami	FL	33173	305-279-8816	598-8931
Web: www.meltingpot.com					
Perricone's Marketplace & Cafe 15 SE Tenth St	Miami	FL	33131	305-374-9449	371-6647
Web: www.perricones.com					
Romeo's Cafe 2257 SW 22nd St Coral Way	Miami	FL	33145	305-859-2228	859-8566
Web: romeoscafe.com					
Tony Chan's Water Club 1717 N Bayshore Dr.	Miami	FL	33132	305-374-8888	
Web: www.tonychans.com					
Tropical Chinese Restaurant 7991 SW 40th St	Miami	FL	33155	305-262-7576	262-1552
Web: www.tropicalchinesemiami.com					
Tutto Pasta 1751 SW Third Ave	Miami	FL	33129	305-857-0709	
Web: www.tuttopasta.com					
Versailles 3555 SW Eigth St.	Miami	FL	33135	305-444-0240	444-0774
Web: versaillesrestaurant.com					
A Fish Called Avalon 700 Ocean Dr.	Miami Beach	FL	33139	305-532-1727	913-6818
Web: www.afishcalledavalon.com					
Cafe Prima Pasta 414 71st St	Miami Beach	FL	33141	305-867-0106	
Web: www.primapasta.com					
Escopazzo 1311 Washington Ave	Miami Beach	FL	33139	305-674-9450	532-8770
Forge, The 432 41st St	Miami Beach	FL	33140	305-538-8533	538-7733
Web: www.theforge.com					
Grillfish 1444 Collins Ave	Miami Beach	FL	33139	305-538-9908	538-2203
Web: www.grillfish.com					
Hosteria Romana 429 Espanola Way.	Miami Beach	FL	33139	305-532-4299	673-2570
Web: www.hosteriaromana.com					
Icebox Cafe 1855 Purdy Ave.	Miami Beach	FL	33139	305-538-8448	538-6405
Web: www.iceboxcafe.com					
Joe's Stone Crab 11 Washington Ave	Miami Beach	FL	33139	305-673-0365	673-0295
Web: www.joesstonecrab.com					
Macaluso's 1747 Alton Rd.	Miami Beach	FL	33139	305-604-1811	
Web: macalusosmiami.com					
Nemo 100 Collins Ave 2nd Fl	Miami Beach	FL	33139	305-532-4550	
Web: www.mylesrestaurantgroup.com					
News Cafe 800 Ocean Dr.	Miami Beach	FL	33139	305-538-6397	538-7817
Web: www.newscafe.com					
Nikki Beach One Ocean Dr S Beach	Miami Beach	FL	33139	305-538-1111	779-5895
Web: www.nikkibeachmiami.com					
Pelican Cafe 826 Ocean Dr	Miami Beach	FL	33139	305-673-3373	673-3255
Web: www.pelicanhotel.com					
Prime 112 112 Ocean Dr.	Miami Beach	FL	33139	305-532-8112	674-7317
Web: www.mylesrestaurantgroup.com					
Spris 721 Lincoln Rd	Miami Beach	FL	33139	305-673-2020	532-1706
Web: www.spris.cc					
SushiSamba 600 Lincoln Rd	Miami Beach	FL	33139	305-673-5337	673-5451
Web: www.sushisamba.com					
Tap Tap 819 Fifth St	Miami Beach	FL	33139	305-672-2898	
Web: www.taptaprestaurant.com					
Toni's Sushi Bar 1208 Washington Ave	Miami Beach	FL	33139	305-673-9368	
Web: www.tonisushi.com					
Yuca 501 Lincoln Rd	Miami Beach	FL	33139	305-532-9822	673-8276
Web: www.yuca.com					
Beverly Hills Cafe 7321 Miami Lakes Dr.	Miami Lakes	FL	33014	305-558-8201	
Web: www.thebeverlyhillscafe.com					
El Novillo Restaurant 15450 New Barn Rd	Miami Lakes	FL	33014	305-819-2755	819-7570
Web: www.elnovillorestaurant.com					
Shula's Steak 2 15255 Bull Run Rd	Miami Lakes	FL	33014	305-820-8047	820-8039
Web: www.donshula.com					
Bistro 821 821 Fifth Ave S.	Naples	FL	34102	239-261-5821	261-1972
Web: www.bistro821.com					
Campiello 1177 Third St S	Naples	FL	34102	239-435-1166	
Web: www.campiello.damico.com					
Chop's City Grill 837 Fifth Ave S	Naples	FL	34102	239-262-4677	430-2227
Web: www.chopscitygrill.com					
Dock at Crayton Cove 845 12th Ave S	Naples	FL	34102	239-263-9940	
Web: www.dockcraytoncove.com					
Jasmine 7231 Radio Rd.	Naples	FL	34104	239-352-5528	352-5285
Web: jasminechinesefood.com					
M Waterfront Grille 4300 Gulf Shore Blvd N.	Naples	FL	34103	239-263-4421	263-3509
Web: www.mwaterfrontgrille.com					
Pazzo! 853 Fifth Ave S	Naples	FL	34102	239-434-8494	430-2227
Web: gr8food.net					
Ristorante Ciao 835 Fourth Ave S.	Naples	FL	34102	239-263-3889	263-3658
Web: www.ristoranteciao.com					
Watermark Grille 11280 Tamiami Trl N.	Naples	FL	34110	239-596-1400	596-1402
Web: www.watermarkgrille.com					
Yabba Island Grill 711 Fifth Ave S.	Naples	FL	34102	239-262-5787	262-7767
Web: www.yabbaislandgrill.com					
Emeril's Miami Beach 829 St Charles Ave.	New Orleans	LA	33139	504-524-4241	695-4551*
**Fax Area Code:* 305 ■ *Web:* www.emerils.com					
Ayothaya Thai Cuisine 7555 W Sand Lake	Orlando	FL	32819	407-345-0040	345-0495
Web: www.ayothayathaicuisineoforlando.com					
Bahama Breeze 8849 International Dr	Orlando	FL	32819	407-248-2499	248-2494
TF: 877-500-9715 ■ *Web:* www.bahamabreeze.com					
Boheme, The 325 S Orange Ave.	Orlando	FL	32801	407-313-9000	313-9001
TF: 866-663-0024 ■ *Web:* www.grandbohemianhotel.com/theboheme					
Cafe Tu Tu Tango 8625 International Dr	Orlando	FL	32819	407-248-2222	352-3696
Web: www.cafetututango.com					
Capital Grille Offices, The 1000 Darden Ctr Dr	Orlando	FL	32837	202-737-6200	637-8821
Web: www.thecapitalgrille.com					
Cariera's Cucina Italiana 7600 Dr Phillips Blvd Ste 12	Orlando	FL	32819	407-351-1187	351-1565
Web: www.carierasorlando.com					
Cedar's 7732 W Sand Lk Rd	Orlando	FL	32819	407-351-6000	355-0607
Web: www.cedarsoforlando.com					
Charley's Steak House 8255 International Dr.	Orlando	FL	32819	407-363-0228	354-4617
Web: www.talkofthetownrestaurants.com					
Chatham's Place Restaurant 7575 Doctor Philips Blvd	Orlando	FL	32819	407-345-2992	345-0307
Web: www.chathamsplace.com					
Cheesecake Factory 4200 Conroy Rd.	Orlando	FL	32839	407-226-0333	226-9020
Web: www.thecheesecakefactory.com					
Christini's 7600 Dr Phillips Blvd	Orlando	FL	32819	407-345-8770	345-8700
Web: www.christinis.com					
Ciao Italia 6149 Westwood Blvd.	Orlando	FL	32821	407-354-0770	370-0124
Web: www.ciaoitaliaonline.com					
Emeril's Orlando 6000 Universal Blvd Ste 702	Orlando	FL	32819	407-224-2424	224-2525
Web: www.emerils.com					
Emeril's Tchoup Chop 6300 Hollywood Way	Orlando	FL	32819	407-503-2467	503-3344
Web: www.emerils.com					
Hemisphere 9300 Airport Blvd.	Orlando	FL	32827	407-825-1234	825-1270
Web: www.hyatt.com					
Hue Restaurant 629 E Central Blvd	Orlando	FL	32801	407-849-1800	
Web: socothorntonpark.com/					
Julie's Waterfront 4201 S Orange Ave	Orlando	FL	32806	407-240-2557	857-5850
K Restaurant & Wine Bar 1710 Edgewater Dr.	Orlando	FL	32804	407-872-2332	
Web: krestaurant.net					
Le Coq Au Vin 4800 S Orange Ave	Orlando	FL	32806	407-851-6980	
Web: www.lecoqauvinrestaurant.com					
Linda's La Cantina 4721 E Colonial Dr	Orlando	FL	32803	407-894-4491	894-6415
Web: www.lindaslacantina.com					

				Phone	Fax
Little Saigon 1106 E Colonial Dr *Web:* littlesaigonrestaurant.com	Orlando	FL	32803	407-423-8539	
Ming Court 9188 International Dr *Web:* www.ming-court.com	Orlando	FL	32819	407-351-9988	
MoonFish 7525 W Sand Lk Rd *Web:* www.talkofthetownrestaurants.com	Orlando	FL	32819	407-363-7262	345-0097
Palm 5800 Universal Blvd Hard Rock Hotel *TF:* 866-333-7256 ■ *Web:* www.thepalm.com	Orlando	FL	32819	407-503-7256	503-2383
Seasons 52 7700 Sand Lk Rd *Web:* www.seasons52.com	Orlando	FL	32819	407-354-5212	345-1109
Sushi House of Orlando 8204 Crystal Clear Ln Ste 1300 *Web:* www.sushihouseint.com	Orlando	FL	32809	407-610-5921	
Vito's Chop House 8633 International Dr *Web:* www.talkofthetownrestaurants.com	Orlando	FL	32819	407-354-2467	226-0914
Cafe Cellini 2505 S Ocean Blvd *Web:* cafecellini.com	Palm Beach	FL	33480	561-588-1871	582-0335
Cafe L'Europe 331 S County Rd *Web:* www.cafeleurope.com	Palm Beach	FL	33480	561-655-4020	659-6619
Chez Jean-Pierre Bistro 132 N County Rd *Web:* chezjean-pierre.com	Palm Beach	FL	33480	561-833-1171	835-0482
Echo 230A Sunrise Ave *Web:* www.echopalmbeach.com	Palm Beach	FL	33480	561-802-4222	
Trevini 150 Worth Ave *Web:* www.treviniristorante.com	Palm Beach	FL	33480	561-833-3883	835-9115
Cafe Chardonnay 4533 PGA Blvd *Web:* www.cafechardonnay.com	Palm Beach Gardens	FL	33418	561-627-2662	627-3413
Ironwood Grille 400 Ave of the Champions *Web:* www.pgaresort.com	Palm Beach Gardens	FL	33418	561-627-4852	
River House, The 2373 PGA Blvd *Web:* www.riverhouserestaurant.com	Palm Beach Gardens	FL	33410	561-694-1188	694-1204
Capriccio 2424 N University Dr *Web:* www.capriccios.net	Pembroke Pines	FL	33024	954-432-7001	432-7560
Angus, The 1101 Scenic Hwy *Web:* www.anguspensacola.com	Pensacola	FL	32503	850-432-0539	433-9060
Horizen 3103 E Strong St *Web:* horizenpensacola.com	Pensacola	FL	32503	850-432-7899	436-7599
Jackson's Steakhouse 400 S Palafox St *Web:* greatsouthernrestaurants.com/	Pensacola	FL	32502	850-469-9898	
Los Rancheros 7250 Plantation Rd *Web:* larumbamexicanrestaurant.com	Pensacola	FL	32504	850-476-1623	
McGuire's Irish Pub 600 E Gregory St *Web:* www.mcguiresirishpub.com	Pensacola	FL	32502	850-433-6789	
Melting Pot of Pensacola, The 418 Gregory St Ste 500 *TF:* 800-783-0867 ■ *Web:* www.meltingpot.com	Pensacola	FL	32501	850-438-4030	433-7664
Petrella's Italian Cafe 2174 W Nine Mile Rd *Web:* www.petrellasitaliancafe.com	Pensacola	FL	32534	850-471-9444	
Tokyo Japanese Steakhouse 312 E Nine Mile Rd *Web:* gotokyopensacola.com	Pensacola	FL	32514	850-479-9111	479-5881
Yamato Oriental Cuisine 131 N New Warrington Rd *Web:* www.yamatodining.com	Pensacola	FL	32506	850-453-3461	456-5967
India House 1711 N University Dr *Web:* www.indiahouserestaurant.com	Plantation	FL	33322	954-565-5701	
Cafe Maxx 2601 E Atlantic Blvd *Web:* www.cafemaxx.com	Pompano Beach	FL	33062	954-782-0606	782-0648
Booth's Bowery 3657 S Nova Rd *Web:* www.boothsbowery.com	Port Orange	FL	32129	386-761-9464	761-7518
Acapulco Mexican Restaurant 12 Avenida Menendez *Web:* www.acapulcorestaurants.com	Saint Augustine	FL	32084	904-808-9933	808-9937
Barnacle Bill's 14 Castillo Dr *Web:* www.barnaclebillsonline.com	Saint Augustine	FL	32084	904-824-3663	
Beachcomber Restaurant Two A St	Saint Augustine	FL	32080	904-471-3744	
Cap's 4325 Myrtle St *Web:* www.capsonthewater.com	Saint Augustine	FL	32084	904-824-8794	829-0709
Conch House Restaurant 57 Comares Ave Conch House Marina Resort *TF:* 800-940-6256 ■ *Web:* conch-house.com	Saint Augustine	FL	32080	904-829-8646	
Cortesse's Bistro 1910 US 1	Saint Augustine	FL	32086	904-825-6775	
Creekside Dinery 160 Nix Boat Yard Rd *Web:* creeksidedinery.com	Saint Augustine	FL	32084	904-829-6113	
Kingfish Grill 252 Yacht Club Dr *Web:* www.kingfishgrill.com	Saint Augustine	FL	32084	904-824-2111	819-6765
Kings Head British Pub 6460 US Hwy 1 N *Web:* kingsheadbritishpub.com	Saint Augustine	FL	32095	904-823-9787	823-1466
Le Pavillon 45 San Marco Ave *Web:* www.lepav.com	Saint Augustine	FL	32084	904-824-6202	824-1024
Manatee Cafe 525 SR 16 Ste 106 Westgate Plz *Web:* www.manateecafe.com	Saint Augustine	FL	32084	904-826-0210	826-4080
Mikato Japanese Steak House 1092 S Ponce de Leon Blvd *Web:* mymikato.com	Saint Augustine	FL	32084	904-824-7064	
O'Steen's Restaurant 205 Anastasia Blvd *Web:* osteensrestaurant.com	Saint Augustine	FL	32080	904-829-6974	
Oasis Deck & Restaurant 4000 A1A Ocean Trace Rd *Web:* www.worldfamousoasis.com	Saint Augustine	FL	32080	904-471-3424	
Raintree 102 San Marco Ave *Web:* www.raintreerestaurant.com	Saint Augustine	FL	32084	904-824-7211	
Reef, The 4100 Coastal Hwy *Web:* www.thereefstaugustine.com	Saint Augustine	FL	32084	904-824-8008	

				Phone	Fax
Salt Water Cowboy's 299 Dondanville Rd *Web:* www.saltwatercowboys.com	Saint Augustine	FL	32084	904-471-2332	471-8997
Santa Maria Restaurant 135 Avenida Menendez	Saint Augustine	FL	32084	904-829-6578	824-9214
South Beach Grill 45 Cubbedge Rd *Web:* www.southbeachgrill.net	Saint Augustine	FL	32080	904-471-8700	
9 Bangkok Restaurant 571 Central Ave *Web:* 9bangkok.info	Saint Petersburg	FL	33701	727-894-5990	826-6164
Athenian Garden 6940 22nd Ave N *Web:* www.atheniangardens.com	Saint Petersburg	FL	33710	727-345-7040	345-0765
Chattaway 358 22nd Ave S *Web:* thechattaway.com	Saint Petersburg	FL	33705	727-823-1594	
Marchand's Bar & Grill 501 Fifth Ave NE Renaissance Vinoy Resort *Web:* www.marriott.com	Saint Petersburg	FL	33701	727-824-8072	824-5044
Melting Pot ST Petersburg, The 2221 Fourth St N *Web:* www.meltingpot.com	Saint Petersburg	FL	33704	727-895-6358	894-7383
Red Mesa Restaurant 4912 Fourth St N *Web:* www.redmesarestaurant.com	Saint Petersburg	FL	33703	727-527-8728	
Siam Garden Thai Restaurant 3125 MLK St N *Web:* www.siamgardenthai1.com	Saint Petersburg	FL	33704	727-822-0613	898-2933
Ted Peter's Famous Smoked Fish 1350 Pasadena Ave S *Web:* tedpetersfish.com	Saint Petersburg	FL	33707	727-381-7931	
Tokyo Bay Japanese Restaurant & Sushi 5901 Sun Blvd *Web:* www.tokyobayrestaurant.com	Saint Petersburg	FL	33715	727-867-0770	
Cafe Amici 1371 Main St *Web:* www.cafeamicisrq.com	Sarasota	FL	34236	941-951-6896	951-6897
Cafe Baci 4001 S Tamiami Trl *Web:* www.cafebacisarasota.com	Sarasota	FL	34231	941-921-4848	923-8643
Captain Brian's Seafood Market & Restaurant 8421 N Tamiami Trl *Web:* www.captainbriansseafood.com	Sarasota	FL	34243	941-313-7682	355-1973
Chutney's Etc 1944 Hillview St *Web:* www.chutneysetc.com	Sarasota	FL	34239	941-954-4444	
Columbia 411 St Armands Cir *Web:* www.columbiarestaurant.com	Sarasota	FL	34236	941-388-3987	388-3321
Demetrio's 4410 S Tamiami Trail *Web:* www.demetriospizzeria.com	Sarasota	FL	34231	941-922-1585	
Mediterraneo 1970 Main St *Web:* mediterraneorest.com	Sarasota	FL	34236	941-365-4122	954-0106
Michael's on East 1212 E Ave S *Web:* bestfood.com	Sarasota	FL	34239	941-366-0007	953-3463
Morel Restaurant 3809 S Tuttle Ave *Web:* www.morelrestaurant.com	Sarasota	FL	34239	941-927-8716	922-3390
Old Salty Dog 1601 Ken Thompson Pkwy *Web:* www.theoldsaltydog.com	Sarasota	FL	34236	941-388-4311	388-3902
Phillippi Creek Village Restaurant & Oyster Bar 5353 S Tamiami Trl *Web:* www.creekseafood.com	Sarasota	FL	34231	941-925-4444	923-2861
Saga Japanese Steak House 8383 S Tamiami Trl *Web:* sagasteakhouse.com	Sarasota	FL	34238	941-924-2800	
Selva Grill 1345 Main St *Web:* www.selvagrill.com	Sarasota	FL	34236	941-362-4427	362-2867
Ophelia's on the Bay 9105 Midnight Pass Rd *Web:* www.opheliasonthebay.net	Siesta Key	FL	34242	941-349-2212	349-3328
Songkran Thai Restaurant 2309 S Ridgewood Ave *Web:* songkran-thai-restaurant.com	South Daytona	FL	32119	386-760-0300	
Two Chefs 8287 S Dixie Hwy *Web:* twochefsrestaurant.com	South Miami	FL	33143	305-663-2100	663-0220
Andrew's 228 228 S Adams St *Web:* www.andrewsdowntown.com	Tallahassee	FL	32301	850-222-3444	222-2433
Bahn Thai Restaurant 1319 S Monroe St	Tallahassee	FL	32301	850-224-4765	
Cabo's Island Grill & Bar 1221 Apalachee Pkwy *Web:* www.cabosgrill.com	Tallahassee	FL	32301	850-878-7707	878-7835
Clusters & Hops 707 N Monroe St *Web:* www.winencheese.com	Tallahassee	FL	32303	850-222-2669	222-0469
Cypress, The 320 E Tennessee St *Web:* www.cypressrestaurant.com	Tallahassee	FL	32301	850-513-1100	513-0020
Georgio's 3425 Thomasville Rd *Web:* georgiostallahassee.com	Tallahassee	FL	32309	850-893-4161	
Julie's Place 2901 N Monroe St *Web:* www.juliesplace.net	Tallahassee	FL	32303	850-386-7181	422-3619
Kitcho 1415 Timberlane Rd Ste 121 *Web:* www.kitchorestaurant.com	Tallahassee	FL	32312	850-893-7686	
Los Compadres 2102 W Pensacola St *Web:* bestmexicanfoodtallahassee.com	Tallahassee	FL	32304	850-576-8946	
Marie Livingston's Steakhouse & Saloon 2705 Apalachee Pkwy *Web:* marielivingstonsteakhouse.com	Tallahassee	FL	32301	850-562-2525	
Mom & Dad's 4175 Apalachee Pkwy *Web:* momanddadstlh.com	Tallahassee	FL	32311	850-877-4518	
Samrat 2529 Apalachee Pkwy *Web:* samratindianrestaurantfl.com	Tallahassee	FL	32301	850-942-1993	942-8091
Z Bardhi 3596 Kinhega Dr *Web:* www.zbardhis.com	Tallahassee	FL	32312	850-894-9919	
Armani's Restaurant 2900 Bayport Dr *Web:* www.hyatt.com	Tampa	FL	33607	813-207-6800	207-6709
Bern's Steak House 1208 S Howard Ave *Web:* www.bernssteakhouse.com	Tampa	FL	33606	813-251-2421	251-5001
Byblos Cafe 2832 S MacDill Ave *Web:* www.bybloscafe.com	Tampa	FL	33629	813-805-7977	837-0951

				Phone	Fax
Caffe Paridiso 4205 S MacDill Ave	Tampa	FL	33611	813-835-6622	835-9773
Capdevila at Lateresita 3248 W Columbus Dr *Web:* www.lateresitarestaurant.com	Tampa	FL	33607	813-879-9704	871-2321
Columbia Restaurant 2025 E Seventh Ave *Web:* www.columbiarestaurant.com	Tampa	FL	33605	813-248-3000	247-5881
Haven Restaurant 2208 W Morrison Ave *Web:* www.sideberns.com	Tampa	FL	33606	813-258-2233	
Jackson's Bistro 601 S Harbor Island Blvd *Web:* www.jacksonsbistro.com	Tampa	FL	33602	813-277-0112	277-0114
Jimbo's Pit BBQ 4103 W Kennedy Blvd *Web:* www.jimbosbarbq.com	Tampa	FL	33609	813-289-9724	289-1006
Kojak's House of Ribs 2808 W Gandy Blvd *Web:* kojaksbbq.net	Tampa	FL	33611	813-837-3774	
Mangroves Bar & Grille 208 S Howard Ave *Web:* www.mangroves-restaurants.com	Tampa	FL	33606	813-258-3302	
Melting Pot of Tampa, The 13164 N Dale Mabry Hwy *TF:* 800-783-0867 ■ *Web:* www.meltingpot.com	Tampa	FL	33618	813-962-6936	963-0125
Mise En Place 442 W Kennedy Blvd *Web:* miseonline.com	Tampa	FL	33606	813-254-5373	254-3392
Rusty Pelican 2425 N Rocky Pt Dr *Web:* www.therustypelican.com	Tampa	FL	33607	813-281-1943	289-3782
Sawatdee Thai Cuisine 10938 N 56th St *Web:* sawatdeethaioftampa.com	Tampa	FL	33617	813-985-2071	
Six Tables 4267 Henderson Blvd *Web:* www.sixtablestampa.com	Tampa	FL	33629	813-207-0527	
Taj Indian Cuisine 2734 E Fowler Ave *Web:* tajtampaindiancuisine.com	Tampa	FL	33612	813-971-8483	
Thai Terrace 2055 N Dale Mabry Hwy *Web:* thaiterrace.net	Tampa	FL	33607	813-877-8955	980-0444
Bimini Twist 8480 Okeechobee Blvd *Web:* mybiminitwist.com	West Palm Beach	FL	33411	561-784-2660	784-2660
Cabana 533 Clematis St *Web:* www.cabanarestaurant.com	West Palm Beach	FL	33401	561-833-4773	514-0655
City Cellar Wine Bar & Grill 700 S Rosemary Ave *Web:* bigtimerestaurants.com	West Palm Beach	FL	33401	561-366-0071	366-8541
La Sirena 6316 S Dixie Hwy *Web:* www.lasirenaonline.com	West Palm Beach	FL	33405	561-585-3128	
Maison Carlos 3010 S Dixie Hwy *Web:* www.maisoncarlos.com	West Palm Beach	FL	33405	561-659-6524	
Okeechobee Steakhouse 2854 Okeechobee Blvd *Web:* www.okeesteakhouse.com	West Palm Beach	FL	33409	561-683-5151	684-7402
Raindancer Steak House 2300 Palm Beach Lakes Blvd *Web:* www.raindancersteakhouse.com	West Palm Beach	FL	33409	561-684-2810	
Rhythm Cafe 3800 S Dixie Hwy *Web:* www.rhythmcafe.cc	West Palm Beach	FL	33405	561-833-3406	
Stresa 2710 Okeechobee Blvd	West Palm Beach	FL	33409	561-615-0200	615-0200
Boondocks Restaurant 3948 S Peninsula Dr *Web:* boondocks-restaurant.com	Wilbur by the Sea	FL	32127	386-760-9001	
Old Florida Seafood House 1414 NE 26th St *Web:* www.oldflaseafood.com	Wilton Manors	FL	33305	954-566-1044	566-1048

Georgia

				Phone	Fax
Di Paolo Cucina 8560 Holcomb Bridge Rd *Web:* www.dipaolorestaurant.com	Alpharetta	GA	30022	770-587-1051	
10 Degrees South 4183 Roswell Rd NE *Web:* www.10degreessouth.com	Atlanta	GA	30342	404-705-8870	
5 Seasons Brewing Co 5600 Roswell Rd Ste 21 *Web:* www.5seasonsbrewing.com	Atlanta	GA	30342	404-255-5911	255-5966
Agave 242 Blvd SE *Web:* www.agaverestaurant.com	Atlanta	GA	30312	404-588-0006	588-0909
Anis Cafe & Bistro 2974 Grandview Ave *Web:* www.anisbistro.com	Atlanta	GA	30305	404-233-9889	233-4894
Annie's Thai Castle 3195 Roswell Rd NE *Web:* www.anniesthaifood.com	Atlanta	GA	30305	404-264-9546	
Antica Posta 519 E Paces Ferry Rd *Web:* www.anticaposta.com	Atlanta	GA	30305	404-262-7112	262-7335
Aria Restaurant 490 E Paces Ferry Rd NE *Web:* www.aria-atl.com	Atlanta	GA	30305	404-233-7673	262-5208
Atlanta Fish Market 265 Pharr Rd NE *Web:* www.buckheadrestaurants.com	Atlanta	GA	30305	404-240-1833	601-1315
Atlanta Grill 181 Peachtree St NE *Web:* www.ritzcarlton.com/en/Properties/Atlanta/Dining/AtlantaGrill/Default.htm	Atlanta	GA	30303	404-659-0400	688-0400
Atmosphere 1620 Piedmont Ave *Web:* www.atmospherebistro.com	Atlanta	GA	30324	678-702-1620	
Babette's Cafe 573 N Highland Ave *Web:* www.babettescafe.com	Atlanta	GA	30307	404-523-9121	
Bacchanalia 1198 Howell Mill Rd *Web:* starprovisions.com	Atlanta	GA	30318	404-365-0410	365-8020
Bangkok Thai 1492-A Piedmont Ave *Web:* www.bangkokatl.com	Atlanta	GA	30324	404-874-2514	
Baraonda 710 Peachtree St *Web:* www.baraondaatlanta.com	Atlanta	GA	30308	404-879-9962	
Basil's Restaurant & Tapas Bar 2985 Grandview Ave NE *Web:* www.basils.net	Atlanta	GA	30305	404-233-9755	
Beautiful Restaurant, The 2260 Cascade Rd SW *Web:* www.beautifulrestaurant-atlanta.com	Atlanta	GA	30311	404-752-5931	758-4767
Benihana 229 Peachtree St NE *Web:* www.benihana.com	Atlanta	GA	30303	404-522-9629	
Blue Ridge Grill 1261 W Paces Ferry Rd *Web:* www.blueridgegrill.com	Atlanta	GA	30327	404-233-5030	233-5023
BluePointe 3344 Peachtree Rd *Web:* www.buckheadrestaurants.com	Atlanta	GA	30326	404-237-9070	237-2387
Bone's Restaurant 3130 Piedmont Rd NE *Web:* www.bonesrestaurant.com	Atlanta	GA	30305	404-237-2663	233-5704
Buckhead Diner 3073 Piedmont Rd NE *Web:* www.buckheadrestaurants.com	Atlanta	GA	30305	404-262-3336	262-3593
Cafe Sunflower 2140 Peachtree Rd *Web:* www.cafesunflower.com	Atlanta	GA	30309	404-352-8859	
Cafe, The 3434 Peachtree Rd NE Ritz-Carlton Buckhead *TF:* 800-241-3333 ■ *Web:* www.ritzcarlton.com	Atlanta	GA	30326	404-237-2700	239-0078
Canoe 4199 Paces Ferry Rd NW *Web:* www.canoeatl.com	Atlanta	GA	30339	770-432-2663	
Capital Grille, The 255 E Paces Ferry Rd *Web:* www.thecapitalgrille.com	Atlanta	GA	30305	404-262-1162	262-1163
China Cooks 215 Northwood Dr	Atlanta	GA	30342	404-252-6611	
Chops/Lobster Bar 70 W Paces Ferry Rd NW *Web:* www.buckheadrestaurants.com	Atlanta	GA	30305	404-262-2675	240-6645
Eclipse di Luna 764 Miami Cir *Web:* www.eclipsediluna.com	Atlanta	GA	30324	404-846-0449	869-7418
Fat Matt's Rib Shack 1811 Piedmont Ave *Web:* www.fatmattsribshack.com	Atlanta	GA	30324	404-607-1622	
Figo Pasta/Osteria del Figo 1170 Collier Rd NW # B *Web:* www.figopasta.com	Atlanta	GA	30318	404-351-9667	351-9677
Floataway Cafe 1123 Zonolite Rd Ste 15 *Web:* www.starprovisions.com	Atlanta	GA	30306	404-892-1414	892-8833
Flying Biscuit Cafe 1655 McLendon Ave *Web:* www.flyingbiscuit.com	Atlanta	GA	30307	404-687-8888	687-8838
Fritti 309 N Highland Ave *Web:* www.frittirestaurant.com	Atlanta	GA	30307	404-880-9559	880-0462
Georgia Grille 2290 Peachtree Rd *Web:* www.thereynoldsgroupinc.com	Atlanta	GA	30309	404-352-3517	
Goldfish 4400 Ashford Dunwoody Rd *Web:* h2sr.com	Atlanta	GA	30346	770-671-0100	671-1887
Grand China Restaurant 2975 Peachtree Rd NE *Web:* www.grandchinaatl.com	Atlanta	GA	30305	404-231-8690	231-5415
Hal's on Old Ivy 30 Old Ivy Rd *Web:* www.hals.net	Atlanta	GA	30342	404-261-0025	814-1248
Harry & Sons 820 N Highland Ave *Web:* www.harryandsonsrestaurant.com	Atlanta	GA	30306	404-873-2009	
Haven 1441 Dresden Dr NE Ste 100 *Web:* www.havenrestaurant.com	Atlanta	GA	30319	404-969-0700	969-0701
Horseradish Grill 4320 Powers Ferry Rd *Web:* www.horseradishgrill.com	Atlanta	GA	30342	404-255-7277	847-0603
Hsu's Gourmet Chinese Restaurant 192 Peachtree Ctr Ave *Web:* www.hsus.com	Atlanta	GA	30303	404-659-2788	577-3456
Kyma 3085 Piedmont Rd *Web:* www.buckheadrestaurants.com	Atlanta	GA	30305	404-262-0702	841-9924
La Grotta 2637 Peachtree Rd *Web:* www.la-grotta.com	Atlanta	GA	30305	404-231-1368	231-1274
La Tavola Trattoria 992 Virginia Ave *Web:* www.latavolatrattoria.com	Atlanta	GA	30306	404-873-5430	
Le Mridien Atlanta Perimeterrestaurant 111 Perimeter Ctr W *Web:* www.lemeridienatlantaperimeter.com	Atlanta	GA	30346	770-396-6800	
Malaya 857 Collier Rd *Web:* malayaatlanta.com	Atlanta	GA	30318	404-609-9991	
Mali Restaurant 961 Amsterdam Ave NE *Web:* www.malirestaurant.com	Atlanta	GA	30306	404-874-1411	874-5112
McKendrick's Steak House 4505 Ashford Dunwoody Rd *Web:* www.mckendricks.com	Atlanta	GA	30346	770-512-8888	379-1470
Mu Lan 824 Juniper St NE *Web:* mulanatlanta.net	Atlanta	GA	30308	404-877-5797	877-5798
Nakato 1776 Cheshire Bridge Rd NE *Web:* www.nakatorestaurant.com	Atlanta	GA	30324	404-873-6582	874-7897
Nan Thai 1350 Spring St NW *Web:* www.nanfinedining.com	Atlanta	GA	30309	404-870-9933	870-9955
Nava 3060 Peachtree Rd *Web:* www.buckheadrestaurants.com	Atlanta	GA	30305	404-240-1984	240-1381
Nikolai's Roof 255 Courtland St *Web:* www.nikolaisroof.com	Atlanta	GA	30303	404-221-6362	
Nino's 1931 Chesire Bridge Rd *Web:* www.ninosatlanta.com	Atlanta	GA	30324	404-874-6505	874-3596
Nuevo Laredo 1495 Chattahoochee Ave *Web:* www.nuevolaredocantina.com	Atlanta	GA	30318	404-352-9009	352-9202
Pacific Rim Bistro 303 Peachtree Ctr Ave *Web:* www.pacificrimbistro.com	Atlanta	GA	30308	404-893-0018	893-0020
Park 75 75 14th St *Web:* fourseasons.com	Atlanta	GA	30309	404-253-3840	253-3935
Paul's Restaurant 10 King Cir *Web:* greatfoodinc.com	Atlanta	GA	30305	404-231-4113	
Pricci 500 Pharr Rd *Web:* www.buckheadrestaurants.com	Atlanta	GA	30305	404-237-2941	261-0058
Prime 3393 Peachtree Rd *Web:* h2sr.com	Atlanta	GA	30326	404-812-0555	812-0225
Rathbun's 112 Krog St Ste R *Web:* www.kevinrathbun.com	Atlanta	GA	30307	404-524-8280	524-8580
Ray's in the City 240 Peachtree St NW *Web:* www.raysrestaurants.com	Atlanta	GA	30303	404-524-9224	524-9229
Ritz-Carlton Dining Room 3434 Peachtree Rd *Web:* ritzcarlton.com	Atlanta	GA	30326	404-237-2700	239-0078
Sotto Sotto Cucina Italiana 313 N Highland Ave *Web:* www.sottosottorestaurant.com	Atlanta	GA	30307	404-523-6678	880-0462
South City Kitchen 1144 Crescent Ave *Web:* fifthgroup.com	Atlanta	GA	30309	404-873-7358	873-0317
Surin of Thailand 810 N Highland Ave NE *Web:* www.surinofthailand.com	Atlanta	GA	30306	404-892-7789	892-8344
Tamarind Seed 1197 Peachtree St NW Ste 110 *Web:* www.tamarindseed.com	Atlanta	GA	30361	404-873-4888	873-4886

Name / Address	City	State	Zip	Phone	Fax
Thai Chili 2169 Briarcliff Rd NE *Web:* www.thaichilicuisine.com	Atlanta	GA	30329	404-315-6750	315-9367
Tierra Restaurant 1425 Piedmont Ave NE *Web:* tierrarestaurant.com	Atlanta	GA	30309	404-874-5951	
Top Spice 3007 N Druid Hills Rd *Web:* www.topspiceatlanta.com	Atlanta	GA	30329	404-728-0588	
Veni-Vidi-Vici 41 Fourteenth St *Web:* www.buckheadrestaurants.com	Atlanta	GA	30309	404-875-8424	875-6533
Wisteria 471 N Highland Ave *Web:* www.wisteria-atlanta.com	Atlanta	GA	30307	404-525-3363	525-3313
Woodfire Grill 1782 Cheshire Bridge Rd *Web:* www.woodfiregrill.com	Atlanta	GA	30324	404-347-9055	347-9566
yahoo finance 3011 Paces Mill Rd SE *Web:* www.ovivinings.com	Atlanta	GA	30339	770-438-2282	438-0653
Beamie's 865 Reynolds St	Augusta	GA	30901	706-724-6593	724-7466
California Dreaming 3241 Washington Rd *Web:* www.centraarchy.com	Augusta	GA	30907	706-860-6206	860-4699
Calvert's Restaurant 475 Highland Ave *Web:* www.calvertsrestaurant.com	Augusta	GA	30909	706-738-4514	312-2121
Formosa's 3830 Washington Rd	Augusta	GA	30907	706-855-8998	855-9742
French Market Grille 425 Highland Ave *Web:* www.thefrenchmarketgrille.com	Augusta	GA	30909	706-737-4865	733-0275
La Maison on Telfair 404 Telfair St *Web:* www.lamaisontelfair.com	Augusta	GA	30901	706-722-4805	722-1753
Rhinehart's Oyster Bar 3051 Washington Rd *Web:* rhineharts.com	Augusta	GA	30907	706-860-2337	
Sconyer's Bar-B-Que 2250 Sconyers Way *Web:* sconyersbar-b-que.com	Augusta	GA	30906	706-790-5411	790-1505
T's Restaurant 3416 Mike Pagett Hwy *Web:* www.tsrestaurant.com	Augusta	GA	30906	706-798-4145	793-8474
Villa Europa 3044 Deans Bridge Rd *Web:* www.villaeuropa.com	Augusta	GA	30906	706-798-6211	798-0066
Harmony Vegetarian Chinese Restaurant 4897 Buford Hwy Ste 109 *Web:* www.harmonyvegetarian.com	Chamblee	GA	30341	770-457-7288	
Country's Barbecue 2016 12th Ave *TF General:* 800-285-4267 ■ *Web:* www.countrysbarbecue.com	Columbus	GA	31901	706-327-7702	324-5859
Don Chuco's 5770 Milgen Rd	Columbus	GA	31907	706-561-3040	
Los Amigos Mexican Restaurant 5935 Veterans Pkwy	Columbus	GA	31909	706-322-1993	
Macon Road Barbecue 2703 Avalon Rd	Columbus	GA	31907	706-563-0542	
Mikata Japanese Steakhouse 5300 Sidney Simons Blvd *Web:* www.mikatasteakhouse.com	Columbus	GA	31904	706-327-5100	
Shangri La Chinese Gourmet 4248 Buena Vista Rd *Web:* www.shangrilacolumbus.c	Columbus	GA	31907	706-568-7554	
Dawson's Kitchen 3360 Brookdale Ave *Web:* www.dawsonskitchen.com	Macon	GA	31204	478-742-9852	
Downtown Grill 562 Mulberry St Ln *Web:* www.macondowntowngrill.com	Macon	GA	31201	478-742-5999	742-9708
Marco 4581 Forsyth Rd *Web:* www.marcomacon.com	Macon	GA	31210	478-405-5660	405-5668
Natalia's 201 N Macon St *Web:* natalias.net	Macon	GA	31210	478-741-1380	743-9388
Saleem Fish Supreme 2198 Pio Nono Ave	Macon	GA	31206	478-788-8600	
Aqua Blue 1564 Holcomb Bridge Rd *Web:* www.aquablueatl.com	Roswell	GA	30076	770-643-8886	643-8851
17 Hundred 90 Restaurant 307 E President St *Web:* www.17hundred90.com	Savannah	GA	31401	912-236-7122	236-7123
45 Bistro 123 E Broughton St *Web:* www.marshallhouse.com	Savannah	GA	31401	912-234-3111	233-9672
Alligator Soul 114 Barnard St *Web:* alligatorsoul.com	Savannah	GA	31401	912-232-7899	232-7898
Belford's Savannah 315 W St Julian St *Web:* www.belfordssavannah.com	Savannah	GA	31401	912-233-2626	
Cotton Exchange Tavern 201 E River St	Savannah	GA	31401	912-232-7088	
Elizabeth on 37th 105 E 37th St *Web:* www.elizabethon37th.net	Savannah	GA	31401	912-236-5547	
Garibaldi Cafe 315 W Congress St *Web:* garibaldisavannah.com	Savannah	GA	31401	912-232-7118	232-7957
Lady & Sons, The 102 W Congress St *Web:* www.ladyandsons.com	Savannah	GA	31401	912-233-2600	233-8283
Olde Pink House 23 Abercorn St *Web:* plantersinnsavannah.com	Savannah	GA	31401	912-232-4286	231-1934
Pirates' House 20 E Broad St *Web:* www.thepirateshouse.com	Savannah	GA	31401	912-233-5757	234-1212
River House Seafood Restaurant 125 W River St **Fax:* Orders ■ *Web:* www.riverhouseseafood.com	Savannah	GA	31401	912-234-1900	341-0277*
Sapphire Grill 110 W Congress St *Web:* www.sapphiregrill.com	Savannah	GA	31401	912-443-9962	443-9964
Savannah ePASS 7000 LaRoche Ave *Web:* savannahmenu.com	Savannah	GA	31406	912-352-8221	
Shell House Restaurant, The Eight Gateway Blvd *Web:* shellhouseseafoodsavannah.com/	Savannah	GA	31419	912-927-3280	920-4814
Six Pence Pub 245 Bull St *Web:* www.sixpencepub.com	Savannah	GA	31401	912-233-3151	233-4576
Toucan Cafe 531 Stephenson Ave *Web:* www.toucancafe.com	Savannah	GA	31406	912-352-2233	352-2258
Tubby's Tank House 2909 River Dr *Web:* www.savannahmenu.com	Savannah	GA	31404	912-354-9040	354-1374
Uncle Bubba's Oyster House 104 Bryan Woods Rd *Web:* www.unclebubbas.com	Savannah	GA	31410	912-897-6101	897-6811
Wilkes Dining Room 107 W Jones St *Web:* mrswilkes.com	Savannah	GA	31401	912-232-5997	

Hawaii

Name / Address	City	State	Zip	Phone	Fax
3660 on the Rise 3660 Waialae Ave *Web:* www.3660.com	Honolulu	HI	96816	808-737-1177	735-6105
Alan Wong's 1857 S King St *Web:* www.alanwongs.com	Honolulu	HI	96826	808-949-2526	951-9520
Auntie Pasto's Restuarant 1099 S Beretania St *Web:* www.auntiepastos.com	Honolulu	HI	96814	808-523-8855	523-8857
Bali Steak & Seafood 2005 Kalia Rd *Web:* www.hiltonhawaiianvillage.com/dining/bali-steak-and-seafood	Honolulu	HI	96815	808-949-4321	947-7926
Chef Mavro 1969 S King St *Web:* www.chefmavro.com	Honolulu	HI	96826	808-944-4714	944-3903
Chuck's Steak House 2335 Kalakaua Ave *Web:* www.chuckshawaii.com	Honolulu	HI	96815	808-923-1228	733-7503
El Burrito 550 Piikoi St	Honolulu	HI	96814	808-596-8225	
Genki Sushi Hawaii 677 Ala Moana Blvd Ste 612 *Web:* www.genkisushiusa.com	Honolulu	HI	96813	808-523-3315	523-3316
Gyotaku 1824 King St *Web:* www.gyotakuhawaii.com	Honolulu	HI	96826	808-949-4584	486-3106
Hard Rock Cafe International Inc 1837 Kapiolani Blvd *Web:* www.hardrock.com	Honolulu	HI	96826	808-955-7383	949-6040
Hee Hing 449 Kapahulu Ave *Web:* www.heehinghawaii.com	Honolulu	HI	96815	808-735-5544	732-6026
Hiroshi Eurasian Tapas 500 Ala Moana Blvd *Web:* www.hiroshihawaii.com	Honolulu	HI	96813	808-533-4476	536-0667
Hoku's 5000 Kahala Ave *Web:* www.kahalaresort.com	Honolulu	HI	96816	808-739-8888	739-8800
Hy's Steak House 2440 Kuhio Ave *Web:* hyswaikiki.com/	Honolulu	HI	96815	808-922-5555	926-5089
Keo's 2028 Kuhio Ave *Web:* www.keosthaicuisine.com	Honolulu	HI	96815	808-951-9355	953-2325
Kincaid's Fish Chop & Steak House 1050 Ala Moana Blvd *Web:* www.kincaids.com	Honolulu	HI	96814	808-591-2005	591-2501
Longhi's *Ala Moana Shopping Ctr* 1450 Ala Moana Blvd Ste 3001 *Web:* www.longhis.com	Honolulu	HI	96814	808-947-9899	944-3733
Mariposa 1450 Ala Moana Blvd *Web:* neimanmarcus.com	Honolulu	HI	96814	808-951-3420	
Michel's 2895 Kalakaua Ave Colony Surf Hotel *Web:* www.michelshawaii.com	Honolulu	HI	96815	808-923-6552	926-6063
Ruth's Chris Steak House 500 Ala Moana Blvd Restaurant Row *Web:* www.ruthschris.com	Honolulu	HI	96813	808-599-3860	533-0786
Ryan's Grill at Ward Centre 1200 Ala Moana Blvd *Web:* www.ryansgrill.com	Honolulu	HI	96814	808-591-9132	591-0034
Sansei Seafood Restaurant & Sushi Bar *Waikiki Beach Marriot Resort & Spa* 2552 Kalakauna Ave *Web:* www.sanseihawaii.com	Honolulu	HI	96815	808-931-6286	924-0667
Shorebird Beach Broiler 2169 Kalia Rd Outrigger Reef Hotel *Web:* www.shorebirdwaikiki.com	Honolulu	HI	96815	808-922-2887	926-5372
Side Street Inn 1225 Hopaka St *Web:* www.sidestreetinn.com	Honolulu	HI	96814	808-591-0253	732-7333
Sorabol *Sorabol Korean Restaurant* 805 Keeaumoku St *Web:* www.sorabolhawaii.com	Honolulu	HI	96814	808-947-3113	947-6861
Stage Restaurant 1250 Kapiolani Blvd Second Fl *Web:* www.stagerestauranthawaii.com	Honolulu	HI	96814	808-237-5429	956-1255
Tanaka of Tokyo East 131 Kaiulani Ave Third Fl *Web:* www.tanakaoftokyo.com	Honolulu	HI	96815	808-922-4233	922-6948
Duke's Huntington Beach 130 Kai Malina Pkwy **Fax Area Code:* 714 ■ *Web:* www.hulapie.com	Lahaina	HI	96761	808-667-4800	374-6546*

Idaho

Name / Address	City	State	Zip	Phone	Fax
Angell's Bar & Grill 999 W Main St 1 Capital Ctr *Web:* www.angellsbarandgrill.com	Boise	ID	83702	208-342-4900	342-3971
Barbacoa Grill 276 W Bobwhite Ct *Web:* www.barbacoa-boise.com	Boise	ID	83706	208-338-5000	338-5004
Bitter Creek Ale House 246 N Eigth St *Web:* bcrfl.com	Boise	ID	83702	208-429-6340	
Cottonwood Grille 913 W River St *Web:* www.cottonwoodgrille.com	Boise	ID	83702	208-333-9800	333-1450
Fujiyama 283 N Milwaukee St *Web:* www.fujiyamaboise.com	Boise	ID	83704	208-672-8227	672-8247
Mai Thai 750 W Idaho St *Web:* www.maithaigroup.com	Boise	ID	83702	208-344-8424	344-2445
Shige Japanese Cuisine 100 N Eigth St Ste 215	Boise	ID	83702	208-338-8423	
Smoky Mountain Pizzeria Grill 408 E 41st St *Web:* www.smokymountainpizza.com	Boise	ID	83714	208-433-9596	433-9588
Bamboo Garden 1200 Yellowstone Ave *Web:* orderbamboogarden.com	Pocatello	ID	83201	208-238-2331	
Buddy's Italian Restaurant 626 E Lewis St	Pocatello	ID	83201	208-233-1172	
Mama Inez 390 Yellowstone Ave *Web:* mamainezid.com	Pocatello	ID	83201	208-234-7674	234-2707
Mandarin House 675 Yellowstone Ave Ste D *Web:* www.mandarinhouse.takeout1.com	Pocatello	ID	83201	208-233-6088	233-6089

Illinois

Phone Fax

Bacaro 113 N Walnut St . . . Champaign IL 61820 217-398-6982
Web: www.bacarowinelounge.com
Empire Chinese Restaurant 410 E Green St . . . Champaign IL 61820 217-328-0832
Web: cu-empire.com
Fiesta Cafe 216 S First St . . . Champaign IL 61820 217-352-5902
Web: www.fiestacafe.com
Kamakura 715 S Neil St . . . Champaign IL 61820 217-351-9898
Web: www.kamakurajapaneserestaurant.com
Li'l Porgy's Bar-B-Q
1917 W Springfield Ave . . . Champaign IL 61821 217-398-8575
Web: www.lilporgysbbq.com
Radio Maria 119 N Walnut St . . . Champaign IL 61820 217-398-7729
Web: radiomariarestaurant.com
Ryan's Family Steak House
1004 W Anthony Dr . . . Champaign IL 61821 217-352-7403 352-8344
Web: www.ryans.com
Taffie's 301 S Mattis Ave . . . Champaign IL 61821 217-359-4201
Web: taffiesrestaurant.com
A Tavola 2148 W Chicago Ave . . . Chicago IL 60622 773-276-7567
Web: atavolachi.com/
Adobo Grill Chicago 1610 N Wells St . . . Chicago IL 60614 312-266-7999 266-9299
Web: www.adobogrill.com
Alinea 1723 N Halsted St . . . Chicago IL 60614 312-867-0110
Web: website.alinearestaurant.com
Aria 200 N Columbus Dr . . . Chicago IL 60601 312-444-9494 856-1032
TF: 888-495-1829 ■ *Web:* www.ariachicago.com
Arun's 4156 N Kedzie Ave . . . Chicago IL 60618 773-539-1909 539-2125
Web: www.arunsthai.com
Atwood Cafe One W Washington St . . . Chicago IL 60602 312-368-1900 357-2875
Web: atwoodrestaurant.com/
Avec Restaurant 615 W Randolph St . . . Chicago IL 60661 312-377-2002 377-2008
Web: www.avecrestaurant.com
BIN 36 339 N Dearborn St . . . Chicago IL 60654 312-755-9463
Web: www.bin36.com
Bistrot Margot 1437 N Wells St . . . Chicago IL 60610 312-587-3660 587-3668
Web: www.bistrotmargot.com
Blackbird 619 W Randolph St . . . Chicago IL 60606 312-715-0708 715-0774
Web: www.blackbirdrestaurant.com
Bongo Room 1470 N Milwaukee Ave . . . Chicago IL 60622 773-489-0690
Web: www.thebongoroom.com
Buona Terra 2535 N California Ave . . . Chicago IL 60647 773-289-3800
Web: www.buona-terra.com
Cafe Absinthe 1954 W N Ave . . . Chicago IL 60622 773-278-4488 278-5291
Web: cafe-absinthe.com
Chicago Chop House 60 W Ontario St . . . Chicago IL 60654 312-787-7100 787-3219
Web: www.chicagochophouse.com
Coco Pazzo 300 W Hubbard St . . . Chicago IL 60654 312-836-0900 836-0257
Web: www.cocopazzochicago.com
Everest 440 S LaSalle St 40th Fl . . . Chicago IL 60605 312-663-8920
Web: www.everestrestaurant.com
Fat Willy's 2416 W Schubert Ave . . . Chicago IL 60647 773-782-1800 782-1818
Web: www.fatwillys.com
Francesca's on Taylor 1400 W Taylor St . . . Chicago IL 60607 312-829-2828 829-2831
Web: www.francescarestaurants.com
Frontera Grill 445 N Clark St . . . Chicago IL 60654 312-661-1434 661-1830
Web: www.rickbayless.com
Geja's Cafe 340 W Armitage Ave . . . Chicago IL 60614 773-281-9101 281-0849
Web: www.gejascafe.com
Gene & Georgetti 500 N Franklin St . . . Chicago IL 60654 312-527-3718 527-2039
Web: www.geneandgeorgetti.com
Gibsons Steakhouse 1028 N Rush St . . . Chicago IL 60611 312-266-8999 266-3327
Web: www.gibsonssteakhouse.com
Green Zebra 1460 W Chicago Ave . . . Chicago IL 60642 312-243-7100 226-3360
Web: www.greenzebrachicago.com
Indian Garden 247 E Ontario St Second Fl . . . Chicago IL 60611 312-280-4910 280-4934
Web: www.indiangardenchicago.com
Japonais Chicago 600 W Chicago Ave . . . Chicago IL 60610 312-822-9600 822-9623
Web: japonaismorimoto.com/
Jin Ju 5203 N Clark St . . . Chicago IL 60640 773-334-6377
Web: jinjurestaurant.com
Joe's Seafood Prime Steak & Stone Crab
60 E Grand Ave . . . Chicago IL 60611 312-379-5637 494-9787
Web: www.leye.com
Kiki's Bistro 900 N Franklin St . . . Chicago IL 60610 312-335-5454
Web: www.kikisbistro.com
L2O Restaurant 2300 N Lincoln Pk W . . . Chicago IL 60614 773-868-0002 868-0001
Web: www.l2orestaurant.com
La Petite Folie 1504 E 55th St . . . Chicago IL 60615 773-493-1394 493-1450
Web: www.lapetitefolie.com
Le Colonial 937 N Rush St . . . Chicago IL 60611 312-255-0088 255-1108
Web: www.lecolonialchicago.com
Les Nomades 222 E Ontario St . . . Chicago IL 60611 312-649-9010 649-0608
Web: www.lesnomades.net
Merlo on Maple 16 W Maple St . . . Chicago IL 60610 312-335-8200 335-8205
Web: www.merlochicago.com
Mike Ditka's Restaurant 100 E Chestnut St . . . Chicago IL 60611 312-587-8989 587-8980
Web: www.ditkasrestaurants.com
Mirai Sushi 2020 W Div St . . . Chicago IL 60622 773-862-8500 862-8510
Web: www.miraisushi.com
MK Restaurant 868 N Franklin St . . . Chicago IL 60610 312-482-9179 482-9171
Web: www.mkchicago.com
Mon Ami Gabi 2300 N Lincoln Pk W . . . Chicago IL 60614 773-348-8886 472-9077
Web: www.monamigabi.com
Nacional 27 325 W Huron St . . . Chicago IL 60654 312-664-2727 649-0256
Web: www.leye.com
Naha 500 N Clark St . . . Chicago IL 60654 312-321-6242
Web: www.naha-chicago.com

Phone Fax

Nick's Fishmarket Grill & Bar
222 W Merchandise Mart Plaza #135 . . . Chicago IL 60654 312-621-0200
Web: www.nicksfishmarketchicago.com
NoMI 800 N Michigan Ave . . . Chicago IL 60611 312-335-1234 239-4000
Web: parkchicago.hyatt.com
North Pond 2610 N Cannon Dr . . . Chicago IL 60614 773-477-5845
Web: www.northpondrestaurant.com
Petterino's 150 N Dearborn St . . . Chicago IL 60601 312-422-0150
Web: www.petterinos.com
Public Chicago 1301 N State Pkwy . . . Chicago IL 60610 312-787-3700
Web: www.publichotels.com
Quartino 626 N State St . . . Chicago IL 60610 312-698-5000
Web: www.quartinochicago.com
Rise Sushi & Sake Lounge
3401 N Southport Ave . . . Chicago IL 60657 773-525-3535 525-3522
Web: www.risesushi.com
Rockwell's Neighborhood Grill
4632 N Rockwell St . . . Chicago IL 60625 773-509-1871
Web: www.rockwellsgrill.com
Sai Cafe 2010 N Sheffield Ave . . . Chicago IL 60614 773-472-8080 472-0699
Web: www.saicafe.com
Salpicon 1252 N Wells St . . . Chicago IL 60610 312-988-7811 988-7715
Web: www.salpicon.com
Shanghai Terrace 108 E Superior St Fourth Fl . . . Chicago IL 60611 312-573-6744 573-6697
Web: chicago.peninsula.com
Shaw's Crab House Chicago 21 E Hubbard St . . . Chicago IL 60611 312-527-2722 527-4740
Web: www.shawscrabhouse.com
South Water Kitchen 225 N Wabash Ave . . . Chicago IL 60601 312-236-9300 960-8538
Web: www.southwaterkitchen.com
Spiaggia 980 N Michigan Ave . . . Chicago IL 60611 312-280-2750 943-8560
Web: www.spiaggiarestaurant.com
Trattoria No 10 10 N Dearborn St . . . Chicago IL 60602 312-984-1718 984-1525
Web: www.trattoriaten.com
Tre Kronor 3258 W Foster Ave . . . Chicago IL 60625 773-267-9888
Web: trekronorrestaurant.com
Tru 676 N St Clair St . . . Chicago IL 60611 312-202-0001 202-0003
Web: www.trurestaurant.com
University Club of Chicago 76 E Monroe St . . . Chicago IL 60603 312-726-2840 726-0620
Web: www.ucco.com
Vivere 71 W Monroe St . . . Chicago IL 60603 312-332-4040 332-2656
Web: www.italianvillage-chicago.com
Yoshi's Cafe 3257 N Halsted St . . . Chicago IL 60657 773-248-6160
Web: www.yoshiscafe.com
Captain Merry Guesthouse & Fine Dining
399 Sinsinawa Ave . . . East Dubuque IL 61025 815-747-3644
TF: 866-351-9586 ■ *Web:* www.privatestay.com
Agatucci's 2607 N University St . . . Peoria IL 61604 309-688-8200
Web: agatuccis.com
Fairview Farms 5911 Heuermann Rd . . . Peoria IL 61607 309-697-4111
Web: www.fairview-farm.com
Fish House, The 4919 N University St . . . Peoria IL 61614 309-691-9358
Web: fishhousepeoria.com
Flat Top Grill 5201 W War Memorial Dr . . . Peoria IL 61615 309-693-9966 693-9846
Web: www.flattopgrill.com
Jim's Downtown Steakhouse 110 SW Jefferson St . . . Peoria IL 61602 309-673-5300 673-9335
Web: www.jimssteakhouse.net
Sushigawa 2601 W Lake Ave . . . Peoria IL 61615 309-679-9300
Abreo 515 E State St . . . Rockford IL 61104 815-968-9463 968-9792
Web: www.abreorockford.com
Capri 313 E State St . . . Rockford IL 61104 815-965-6341
Web: caprirockford.com
Cliffbreakers River Restaurant
700 W Riverside Blvd . . . Rockford IL 61103 815-282-3033 282-6505
Web: www.cliffbreakers.com
Garrett's Cafe 1631 N Bell School Rd . . . Rockford IL 61107 815-484-9473 397-7593
Web: www.garrettsrestaurantbar.com
Giovanni's Restaurant & Convention Ctr
610 N Bell School Rd . . . Rockford IL 61107 815-398-6411 398-6416
TF: 800-383-7829 ■ *Web:* www.giodine.com
Great Wall Restaurant 4228 E State St . . . Rockford IL 61108 815-226-0982
Web: www.greatwall.lk
Hoffman House 7550 E State St . . . Rockford IL 61108 815-397-5800 397-0175
Web: www.hoffmanhouserockford.com
Imperial Palace 3415 E State St . . . Rockford IL 61108 815-516-5240 316-0721
Web: imperialpalacerockford.com
JMK Nippon 2551 N Perryville Rd . . . Rockford IL 61107 815-877-0505 877-0681
Web: jmkrockford.com
Maria's Italian Restaurant
828 Cunningham St . . . Rockford IL 61102 815-968-6781
Octane Interlounge 124 N Main St . . . Rockford IL 61101 815-965-4012
Web: www.octane.net
Olympic Tavern 2327 N Main St . . . Rockford IL 61103 815-962-8758 962-8760
Web: www.theolympictavern.com
Rathskeller, The 1132 Auburn St . . . Rockford IL 61103 815-963-2922
Web: www.derrathskeller.net
Augie's Front Burner 109 S Fifth St . . . Springfield IL 62701 217-544-6979 544-7088
Web: www.augiesfrontburner.com
Chesapeake Seafood House
3045 Clear Lk Ave . . . Springfield IL 62702 217-522-5220 522-5993
Web: www.chesapeakeseafoodhouse.com
Fritz's Wagon Wheel Restaurant
2709 S MacArthur Blvd . . . Springfield IL 62704 217-546-9888 726-5357
Indigo 3013 Lindbergh Blvd . . . Springfield IL 62704 217-726-3487 726-4563
Web: www.indigocuisine.com
Lime Street Cafe 951 S Durkin Dr . . . Springfield IL 62704 217-793-1905 793-7860
Maldaner's 222 S Sixth St . . . Springfield IL 62701 217-522-4313 522-1720
Web: www.maldaners.com
Courier Cafe 111 N Race St . . . Urbana IL 61801 217-328-1811 328-1880
Web: www.couriersilvercreek.com
Kennedy's at Stone Creek
2560 Stone Creek Blvd . . . Urbana IL 61802 217-384-8111
Web: www.kennedysatstonecreek.com

				Phone	Fax
Milo's Restaurant 2870 S Philo Rd *Web:* www.milosurbana.com	Urbana	IL	61802	217-344-8946	344-8922
Timpone's 710 S Goodwin Ave *Web:* www.timpones-urbana.com	Urbana	IL	61801	217-344-7619	344-7648

Indiana

				Phone	Fax
Buffa Louie's 114 S Indiana Ave *Web:* www.buffalouies.com	Bloomington	IN	47408	812-333-3030	334-3945
Chapman's Restaurant 4506 E Third St *Web:* www.chapmansrestaurant.com	Bloomington	IN	47401	812-337-9999	
Crazy Horse 214 W Kirkwood Ave *Web:* www.crazyhorseindiana.com	Bloomington	IN	47404	812-336-8877	336-8011
Dragon Chinese Restaurant 3261 W Third St	Bloomington	IN	47404	812-332-6610	
Esan Thai 221 E Kirkwood Ave Ste D *Web:* esanthairest.com/	Bloomington	IN	47408	812-333-8424	
Fairfax Inn 8660 S Fairfax Rd *Web:* www.thefairfaxinn.com	Bloomington	IN	47401	812-824-8552	824-2634
Grazie Italian Eatery 106 W Sixth St *Web:* www.grazieitalianeatery.com	Bloomington	IN	47401	812-323-0303	
Irish Lion 212 W Kirkwood Ave *Web:* www.irishlion.com	Bloomington	IN	47404	812-336-9076	
Laughing Planet Cafe 322 E Kirkwood Ave *Web:* thelaughingplanetcafe.com	Bloomington	IN	47408	812-323-2233	323-1336
Le Petit Cafe 308 W Sixth St *Web:* lpc1977.com	Bloomington	IN	47404	812-334-9747	
Malibu Grill 106 N Walnut St *Web:* www.malibugrill.net	Bloomington	IN	47404	812-332-4334	333-2282
Michael's Uptown Cafe 102 E Kirkwood Ave *Web:* www.the-uptown.com	Bloomington	IN	47408	812-339-0900	331-6025
Nick's English Hut 423 E Kirkwood Ave *Web:* www.nicksenglishhut.com	Bloomington	IN	47408	812-332-4040	339-0282
Restaurant Tallent 208 N Walnut *Web:* www.restauranttallent.com	Bloomington	IN	47404	812-330-9801	
Scholars Inn Gourmet Cafe 717 N College Ave *TF:* 800-765-3466 ■ *Web:* www.scholarsinn.com	Bloomington	IN	47404	812-332-1892	
Trojan Horse 100 E Kirkwood Ave *Web:* www.thetrojanhorse.com	Bloomington	IN	47408	812-332-1101	330-7092
Upland Brewing Co 350 W 11th St *Web:* www.uplandbeer.com	Bloomington	IN	47404	812-336-2337	330-7421
Yogi's Grill & Bar 519 E Tenth St *Web:* www.yogis.com	Bloomington	IN	47408	812-323-9644	323-8898
Angelo's 305 Main St *Web:* angelosevansville.com	Evansville	IN	47708	812-428-6666	428-6699
Canton Inn Restaurant 947 N Pk Dr *Web:* www.cantoninnrestaurant.com	Evansville	IN	47710	812-428-6611	
Chopstick House 5412 E Indiana St *Web:* www.chopstickhouserestaurant.net	Evansville	IN	47715	812-473-5551	
Hacienda Mexican Restaurant 711 N First Ave *Web:* www.haciendafiesta.com	Evansville	IN	47710	812-423-6355	
Lorenzo's Bread Bistro 972 S Hebron Ave *Web:* lorenzosbistro.net	Evansville	IN	47714	812-475-9477	475-9478
Moe's Southwest Grill 6401 E Lloyd Expy Ste 5 *Web:* www.moes.com	Evansville	IN	47715	812-491-6637	491-6617
Raffi's 1100 N BurkehaRdt Rd	Evansville	IN	47715	812-479-9166	491-0318
Raffis Italian Cuisine 1100 N Burkhart Rd	Evansville	IN	47715	812-479-9166	491-0318
Western Rib-Eye & Ribs 1401 N Boeke Rd *Web:* www.westernribeye.com	Evansville	IN	47711	812-476-5405	473-4850
Wolf's Bar-B-Q Restaurant 6600 N First Ave *Web:* www.wolfsbarbq.com	Evansville	IN	47710	812-424-8891	424-8905
Baan Thai 4634 Coldwater Rd *Web:* baanthaiin.com	Fort Wayne	IN	46825	260-471-2929	471-2020
Bandido's Inc 6060 E State Blvd *Web:* www.bandidos.com	Fort Wayne	IN	46815	260-493-0607	493-0806
Casa Ristoranti 7539 W Jefferson Blvd *Web:* www.casarestaurants.net	Fort Wayne	IN	46825	260-399-2455	745-5503
Club Soda 235 E Superior St *Web:* www.clubsodafortwayne.com	Fort Wayne	IN	46802	260-426-3442	426-4214
Cork'N Cleaver 221 E Washington Ctr Rd *Web:* corkncleaveronline.com	Fort Wayne	IN	46825	260-484-7772	
Don Hall's Old Gas House 305 E Superior St *Web:* www.donhalls.com	Fort Wayne	IN	46802	260-426-3411	424-2903
Double Dragon 117 W Wayne St	Fort Wayne	IN	46802	260-422-6426	
Eddie Merlot's 1502 Illinois Rd S *Web:* www.eddiemerlots.com	Fort Wayne	IN	46804	260-459-2222	459-8896
Flanagan's Restaurant & Pub 6525 Covington Rd *Web:* www.eatatflanagans.com	Fort Wayne	IN	46804	260-432-6666	432-6799
Mi Pueblo IV 2419 W Jefferson Blvd *Fax Area Code: 408	Fort Wayne	IN	46802	260-432-6462	263-7780*
Rib Room 1235 E State Blvd *Web:* www.theribroom.com	Fort Wayne	IN	46805	260-483-9767	
Taj Mahal 6410 W Jefferson Blvd *Web:* tajmahalindianrestaurant.net	Fort Wayne	IN	46804	260-432-8993	432-8486
Takaoka of Japan 305 E Superior St *Web:* donhalls.com	Fort Wayne	IN	46802	260-424-3183	
Amalfi 1351 W 86th St *Web:* www.amalfiristoranteitaliano.com	Indianapolis	IN	46260	317-253-4034	
Circle City Bar & Grille 350 W Maryland St *Web:* indymarriott.com	Indianapolis	IN	46225	317-405-6100	822-1002
Dunaway's 351 SE St *Web:* www.dunaways.com	Indianapolis	IN	46204	317-638-7663	638-7677
Fujiyama Japanese Steakhouse 5149 Victory Dr *Web:* www.fujiyama-indy.com	Indianapolis	IN	46203	317-787-7900	
Greek Islands Restaurant 906 S Meridian St *Web:* www.greekislandsrestaurant.com	Indianapolis	IN	46225	317-636-0700	636-2347
Hard Rock Cafe Indianapolis 49 S Meridian St *Web:* www.hardrock.com	Indianapolis	IN	46204	317-636-2550	636-2551
Hollyhock Hill 8110 N College Ave *Web:* www.hollyhockhill.com	Indianapolis	IN	46240	317-251-2294	251-2295
Iaria's Italian Restaurant 317 S College Ave *Web:* www.iariasrestaurant.com	Indianapolis	IN	46202	317-638-7706	687-9232
Iron Skillet Restaurant, The 2489 W 30th St *Web:* www.ironskillet.net	Indianapolis	IN	46222	317-923-6353	923-5209
Kona Jack's Fish Market & Sushi Bar 9419 N Meridian St *Web:* jacksarebetter.net	Indianapolis	IN	46260	317-843-1609	571-6987
Mama Carolla's Old Italian Restaurant 1031 E 54th St *Web:* www.mamacarollas.com	Indianapolis	IN	46220	317-259-9412	
Marker, The 2544 Executive Dr *Fax Area Code:* 317 ■ *Web:* wyndham.com	Indianapolis	IN	46241	877-999-3223	381-6170*
Melting Pot of Indianapolis, The 5650 E 86th St Ste A *TF:* 800-783-0867 ■ *Web:* www.meltingpot.com	Indianapolis	IN	46250	317-841-3601	841-1207
Mikado Japanese Restaurant 148 S Illinois St *Web:* indymikado.com/	Indianapolis	IN	46225	317-972-4180	972-4191
Oakley's Bistro 1464 W 86th St *Web:* www.oakleysbistro.com	Indianapolis	IN	46260	317-824-1231	824-0938
Oceanaire Seafood Room, The 30 S Meridian St Ste 100 *Web:* www.theoceanaire.com	Indianapolis	IN	46204	317-955-2277	955-2278
Oh Yumm! Bistro 5615 N Illinois St *Web:* www.ohyummbistro.com	Indianapolis	IN	46208	317-251-5656	255-1840
Plump's Last Shot 6416 Cornell Ave *Web:* plumpslastshot.com	Indianapolis	IN	46220	317-257-5867	
R Bistro 888 Massachusetts Ave *Web:* www.rbistro.com	Indianapolis	IN	46204	317-423-0312	
Rathskeller Restaurant 401 E Michigan St *Web:* www.rathskeller.com	Indianapolis	IN	46204	317-636-0396	630-4652
Rick's Cafe Boatyard 4050 Dandy Trl *Web:* www.rickscafeboatyard.com	Indianapolis	IN	46254	317-290-9300	291-1043
Saint Elmo Steak House 127 S Illinois St *Web:* www.stelmos.com	Indianapolis	IN	46225	317-635-0636	687-9162
Sakura 7201 N Keystone Ave *Web:* www.indysakura.com	Indianapolis	IN	46240	317-259-4171	253-7846
Starwood Hotels & Resorts Worldwide Inc. 123 S Illinois St *Web:* lemeridienindianapolis.com//go/restaurant.html	Indianapolis	IN	46225	317-737-1600	685-2519
Hana Yori 3601 Grape Rd *Web:* www.hanayori.com	Mishawaka	IN	46545	574-258-5817	258-6045
Main Street Grille 112 N Main St *Web:* www.mainstgrille.com	Mishawaka	IN	46544	574-254-4995	
Carriage House 24460 Adams Rd *Web:* www.carriagehousedining.com	South Bend	IN	46628	574-272-9220	272-6179
Frankie's Barbecue 1621 W Washington St *Web:* frankiesbbq.net	South Bend	IN	46628	574-287-8993	
LaSalle Grill 115 W Colfax Ave *TF:* 800-382-9323 ■ *Web:* www.lasallegrill.com	South Bend	IN	46601	574-288-1155	288-2012
Matuba 2930 McKinley Ave	South Bend	IN	46615	574-251-0674	251-0675
Parisi's Italian Ristorante 1412 S Bend Ave *Web:* www.parisisrestaurant.com	South Bend	IN	46617	574-232-4244	232-4257
Rocco's 537 N St Louis Blvd *Web:* roccosoriginalpizza.com	South Bend	IN	46617	574-233-2464	288-0168
Simeri's Old Town Tap 1505 W Indiana Ave *Web:* simerisoldtowntap.webs.com	South Bend	IN	46613	574-289-1361	
Tippecanoe Place 620 W Washington St *Web:* www.tippe.com	South Bend	IN	46601	574-234-9077	
Volcano Restaurant 3700 Lincoln Way W *Web:* volcanosb.com	South Bend	IN	46628	574-287-5775	

Iowa

				Phone	Fax
Biaggi's Ristorante 320 Collins Rd NE *Web:* biaggis.com	Cedar Rapids	IA	52402	319-393-6593	393-6594
El Rancho 2747 16th Ave SW *Web:* www.elranchomexican.com	Cedar Rapids	IA	52404	319-298-8844	286-0048
Irish Democrat Pub 3207 First Ave SE *Web:* www.irishdemocrat.net	Cedar Rapids	IA	52402	319-364-9896	368-8020
Olive Tree Restaurant 2201 16th Ave SW	Cedar Rapids	IA	52404	319-364-0781	
Texas Roadhouse 2605 Edgewood Rd SW *Web:* www.texasroadhouse.com	Cedar Rapids	IA	52404	319-396-3300	396-1500
Third Base Sports Bar & Brewery 500 Blairs Ferry Rd NE *Web:* www.3rdbasebrewery.com	Cedar Rapids	IA	52402	319-378-9090	378-9154
Vito's 4100 River Ridge Dr NE *Web:* www.vitoson42nd.com	Cedar Rapids	IA	52402	319-393-8727	393-3981
Zio Johno's Spaghetti House 2925 Williams Blvd SW *Web:* www.ziojohnosonline.com	Cedar Rapids	IA	52404	319-396-1700	
Cosi Cucina 1975 NW 86th St *Web:* www.cosicucina.com	Clive	IA	50325	515-278-8148	
Taste of Italy 8421 University Blvd *Web:* atasteofitalyia.com	Clive	IA	50325	515-221-0743	309-3156

				Phone	Fax
Barattas 2320 S Union St *Web:* barattas.com	Des Moines	IA	50315	515-243-4516	243-5324
China Chef Restaurant 5010 SW Ninth St	Des Moines	IA	50315	515-256-8005	256-1848
Chuck's Restaurant 3610 Sixth Ave *Web:* www.chucksdesmoines.com	Des Moines	IA	50313	515-244-4104	
Court Avenue Brewing Co 309 Ct Ave *Web:* www.courtavebrew.com	Des Moines	IA	50309	515-282-2739	282-3789
Gino's Restaurant & Lounge 2809 Sixth Ave.	Des Moines	IA	50313	515-282-4029	
Iowa Beef Steakhouse 1201 E Euclid Ave *Web:* www.iowabeefsteakhouse.com	Des Moines	IA	50316	515-262-1138	
Latin King 2200 Hubbell Ave. *Web:* www.tursislatinking.com	Des Moines	IA	50317	515-266-4466	264-1096
Raccoon River Brewing Co 200 Tenth St.	Des Moines	IA	50309	515-362-5222	243-4317
Thai Flavors 1254 E 14th St *Web:* www.thaiflavorsiowa.com	Des Moines	IA	50316	515-262-4658	
Bridge Restaurant 31 Locust St *Web:* www.bridgerest.com	Dubuque	IA	52001	563-557-7280	
Champps Americana 3100 Dodge St Best Western Midway *Web:* www.champpsdubuque.com	Dubuque	IA	52003	563-690-2040	
Mario's Italian Restaurant 1298 Main St *Web:* mariosofdubuque.com	Dubuque	IA	52001	563-556-9424	
Pepper Sprout 378 Main St *Web:* www.peppersprout.com	Dubuque	IA	52001	563-556-2167	583-6428
Yen Ching 926 Main St *Web:* yenchingdbq.com	Dubuque	IA	52001	563-556-2574	556-2574
Trostel's Greenbrier Restaurant 5010 Merle Hay Rd. *Web:* greenbriartrostels.com	Johnston	IA	50131	515-253-0124	
Biaggi's 5990 University Ave. *Web:* www.biaggis.com	West Des Moines	IA	50266	515-221-9900	221-9901
Rock Bottom Restaurant & Brewery 4508 University Ave *Web:* rockbottom.com	West Des Moines	IA	50266	515-267-8900	267-1400
Waterfront Seafood Market 2900 University Ave *Web:* www.waterfrontseafoodmarket.com	West Des Moines	IA	50266	515-223-5106	224-9665

Kansas

				Phone	Fax
Arthur Bryant Barbecue 1702 Village W Pkwy *Web:* arthurbryantsbbq.com	Kansas City	KS	66111	913-788-7500	788-2333
Gates Bar-B-Que 1026 State Ave *Web:* www.gatesbbq.com	Kansas City	KS	66102	913-621-1134	
Oklahoma Joe's BBQ & Catering 3002 W 47th Ave *Web:* www.oklahomajoesbbq.com	Kansas City	KS	66103	913-722-3366	722-6644
Rosedale Barbeque 600 SW Blvd. *Web:* rosedalebarbeque.com	Kansas City	KS	66103	913-262-0343	
Vietnam Cafe 2200 W 39th St *Web:* thevietnamcafe.com	Kansas City	KS	66103	913-262-8552	
Cheeseburger in Paradise 10562 US Hwy 98W *Web:* www.cheeseburgerinparadise.com	Miramar Beach	FL	32550	850-837-0197	837-0866
Ruchi 11168 Antioch Rd. *Web:* www.ruchicuisine.com	Overland Park	KS	66210	913-661-9088	338-3662
Blind Tiger Brewery & Restaurant 417 SW 37th St *Web:* www.blindtiger.com	Topeka	KS	66611	785-267-2739	267-7527
Boss Hawg's 2833 SW 29th St *Web:* www.bosshawgsbbq.com	Topeka	KS	66614	785-273-7300	273-0077
Casa 3320 SW Topeka Blvd	Topeka	KS	66611	785-266-4503	266-4539
New City Cafe 4005 SW Gage Ctr Dr	Topeka	KS	66604	785-271-8646	271-8636
Paisano's 4043 SW Tenth St. *Web:* www.paisanoskansas.com	Topeka	KS	66604	785-273-0100	
Pepe & Chela's 1001 SW Tyler St *Web:* www.pepeandchelas.com	Topeka	KS	66612	785-357-8332	
Bamboo Stix 2243 N Tyler Rd Ste 101 *Web:* www.bamboostix.com	Wichita	KS	67205	316-722-8886	462-0888
Cafe Bel Ami 229 E William St Ste 101 *Web:* www.cafebelami.biz	Wichita	KS	67202	316-267-3433	267-3070
Felipe's 2241 N Woodlawn *Web:* www.felipeswichita.com	Wichita	KS	67220	316-652-0027	
Great Wall 410 N Hillside Ave *Web:* greatwallwichita.com	Wichita	KS	67214	316-688-0881	612-4825
Harvest Kitchen & Bar 400 W Waterman *Web:* harvestkitchenandbar.com	Wichita	KS	67202	316-613-6300	293-1200
La Chinita 1451 N Broadway St. *Web:* mexicancateringwichitaks.com	Wichita	KS	67214	316-267-1552	267-7097
Larkspur Restaurant & Grill 904 E Douglas St *Web:* www.larkspuronline.com	Wichita	KS	67202	316-262-5275	262-1292
NuWay Burgers 3441 E Harry *Web:* www.nuwayburgers.com	Wichita	KS	67218	316-684-6132	
Sal's Japanese Steakhouse 6829 E Kellogg Dr.	Wichita	KS	67207	316-682-8880	

Kentucky

				Phone	Fax
Casa Fiesta 801 Louisville Rd *Web:* links2frankfort.com	Frankfort	KY	40601	502-226-5010	
China Buffet 1300 US Hwy 127 S.	Frankfort	KY	40601	502-226-3400	226-3800
China Wok 111 E Wood Shopping Ctr. *Web:* www.chinawokky.com	Frankfort	KY	40601	502-695-9388	
Jim's Seafood 950 Wilkinson Blvd. *Web:* jimseafood.com	Frankfort	KY	40601	502-223-7448	227-7419
La Fiesta Grande 314 Versailles Rd	Frankfort	KY	40601	502-695-8378	695-8378
A La Lucie 159 N Limestone St *Web:* www.alalucie.com	Lexington	KY	40507	859-252-5277	225-5027
Billy's Hickory Pit Bar B-Q 101 Cochran Rd *Web:* www.billysbarbq.com	Lexington	KY	40502	859-269-9593	266-7865
Cheapside Bar & Grill 131 Cheapside St *Web:* www.cheapsidebarandgrill.com	Lexington	KY	40507	859-254-0046	233-2146
Dudley's 259 Westshort St. *Web:* www.dudleysonshort.com	Lexington	KY	40507	859-252-1010	253-9383
Durango's 2121 Richmond Rd	Lexington	KY	40502	859-268-0723	
Gratz Park Inn 120 W Second St *TF:* 800-752-4166 ■ *Web:* www.gratzparkinn.com	Lexington	KY	40507	859-231-1777	233-7593
Malone's *Bluegrass Hospitality Group* 3347 Tates Creek Rd *Web:* www.bluegrasshospitality.com	Lexington	KY	40502	859-335-6500	335-1815
Mansion at Griffin Gate 1800 Newtown Pk *Web:* www.mansionatgriffingate.com	Lexington	KY	40511	859-231-5100	288-6216
Merrick Inn, The 1074 Merrick Dr. *Web:* themerrickinn.com	Lexington	KY	40502	859-269-5417	
Natasha's Bistro & Bar 112 Esplanade *Web:* www.beetnik.com	Lexington	KY	40507	859-259-2754	
Portofino 249 E Main St *Web:* www.portofinolexington.com	Lexington	KY	40507	859-253-9300	258-2488
211 Clover Lane 211 Clover Ln *Web:* 211clover.com	Louisville	KY	40207	502-896-9570	
610 Magnolia 610 Magnolia Ave *Web:* www.610magnolia.com	Louisville	KY	40208	502-636-0783	636-0787
Against the Grain Brewery 401 E Main St Louisville Slugger Field *Web:* www.atgbrewery.com	Louisville	KY	40202	502-515-0174	
August Moon 2269 Lexington Rd *Web:* www.augustmoonbistro.com	Louisville	KY	40206	502-456-6569	456-4669
Bazo's Fresh Mexican Grill 4014 Dutchmans Ln *Web:* bazosgrill.com	Louisville	KY	40207	502-899-9600	
Buck's Restaurant 425 W Ormsby Ave *Web:* www.bucksrestaurantandbar.com	Louisville	KY	40203	502-637-5284	
De La Torre's 1606 BaRdstown Rd. *Web:* www.delatorres.com	Louisville	KY	40205	502-456-4955	
El Mundo 2345 Frankfort Ave. *Web:* www.502elmundo.com	Louisville	KY	40206	502-899-9930	
Equus 122 Sears Ave *Web:* www.equusrestaurant.com	Louisville	KY	40207	502-897-9721	897-0535
Lilly's Bistro 1147 BaRdstown Rd. *Web:* www.lillyslapeche.com	Louisville	KY	40204	502-451-0447	
Lynn's Paradise Cafe 984 Barret Ave *Web:* www.lynnsparadisecafe.com	Louisville	KY	40204	502-583-3447	583-0211
Pat's Steak House 2437 Brownsboro Rd. *Web:* www.patssteakhouselouisville.com	Louisville	KY	40206	502-893-2062	893-2062
Porcini 2730 Frankfort Ave *Web:* www.porcinilouisville.com	Louisville	KY	40206	502-894-8686	899-1798
Shah's Mongolian Grill 9148 Taylorsville Rd *Web:* www.shahsmongoliangrill.com	Louisville	KY	40299	502-493-0234	
Uptown Cafe 1624 BaRdstown Rd *Web:* www.uptownlouisville.com	Louisville	KY	40205	502-458-4212	458-4252
Vincenzo's 150 S Fifth St *Web:* www.vincenzositalianrestaurant.com	Louisville	KY	40202	502-580-1350	580-1355
Yang Kee Noodle Club 7900 Shelbyville Rd *Web:* www.yangkeenoodle.com	Louisville	KY	40222	502-426-0800	426-9080

Louisiana

				Phone	Fax
Boutin's 8322 Bluebonnet Blvd	Baton Rouge	LA	70810	225-819-9862	
Chimes Restaurant & Tap Room 3357 Highland Rd. *Web:* www.thechimes.com	Baton Rouge	LA	70802	225-383-1754	387-5413
Copelands of New Orleans 4957 Essen Ln *Web:* www.copelandsofneworleans.com	Baton Rouge	LA	70809	225-769-1800	769-1812
Gino's 4542 Bennington Ave *Web:* www.ginosrestaurant.com	Baton Rouge	LA	70808	225-927-7156	
India's Restaurant 5230 Essen Ln	Baton Rouge	LA	70809	225-769-0600	
Juban's 3739 Perkins Rd. *Web:* www.jubans.com	Baton Rouge	LA	70808	225-346-8422	387-2601
Mansur's 5720 Corporate Blvd Ste A *Web:* www.mansursontheboulevard.com	Baton Rouge	LA	70808	225-923-3366	
Mike Anderson's Seafood Restaurant 1031 W Lee Dr	Baton Rouge	LA	70809	225-766-7823	
Ninfa's Restaurant 4738 Constitution Ave *Web:* ninfaslouisiana.com	Baton Rouge	LA	70808	225-924-0377	924-5620
Thai Kitchen 4335 Perkins Rd *Web:* www.thaikitchenla.com	Baton Rouge	LA	70808	225-346-1230	346-5113
L'Italiano 701 Barksdale Blvd *Web:* litalianorestaurant.webs.com	Bossier City	LA	71111	318-747-7777	
Ralph & Kacoo's 1700 Old Minden Rd Ste 141 *Web:* ralphandkacoos.com	Bossier City	LA	71111	318-747-6660	747-9816
Antoni's Italian Cafe 1118 Coolidge Blvd Ste A.	Lafayette	LA	70503	337-232-8384	232-4311
Bailey's Seafood & Grill 5520-A Johnston St *Web:* www.baileyscss.com	Lafayette	LA	70503	337-988-6464	988-6494
Cafe Vermilionville 1304 W Pinhook Rd. *Web:* www.cafev.com	Lafayette	LA	70503	337-237-0100	233-5599
Charley G's Seafood Grill 3809 Ambassador Caffery Pkwy *Web:* www.charleygs.com	Lafayette	LA	70503	337-981-0108	981-5899
Don's Seafood & Steakhouse 301 E Vermilion St *Web:* www.donsdowntown.com	Lafayette	LA	70501	337-235-3551	235-6707
Picante Mexican Restaurant 3235 NW Evangeline Thwy *Web:* www.picantesrestaurant.com	Lafayette	LA	70507	337-896-1200	896-1202

Name	City	State	Zip	Phone	Fax
Prejean's Restaurant 3480 NE Evangeline Trwy *Web:* www.prejeans.com	Lafayette	LA	70507	337-896-3247	896-3278
Carreta's Grill 2320 Veterans Memorial Blvd *Web:* carretasgrill.com	Metairie	LA	70002	504-837-6696	
Casa Garcia 8814 Veterans Memorial Blvd *Web:* casa-garcia.com	Metairie	LA	70003	504-464-0354	
Deanie's Seafood 1713 Lake Ave *Web:* www.deanies.com	Metairie	LA	70005	504-834-1225	837-2166
Drago's 3232 N Arnoult Rd *Web:* www.dragosrestaurant.com	Metairie	LA	70002	504-888-9254	888-9255
Fausto's Bistro 530 Veterans Memorial Blvd *Web:* www.faustosbistro.com	Metairie	LA	70005	504-833-7121	833-7632
Impastato's 3400 16th St *Web:* www.impastatos.com	Metairie	LA	70002	504-455-1545	833-1816
Peppermill Restaurant 3524 Severn Ave *Web:* www.riccobonos.com	Metairie	LA	70002	504-455-2266	
Siamese Thai Cuisine 6601 Veterans Memorial Blvd Ste 29-30 *Web:* www.siamesecuisine.com	Metairie	LA	70003	504-454-8752	
Sun Ray Grill 619 Pink St *Web:* www.sunraygrill.com	Metairie	LA	70005	504-837-0055	835-2555
Vega Tapas Cafe 2051 Metairie Rd *Web:* www.vegatapascafe.com	Metairie	LA	70005	504-836-2007	
Acme Oyster House 724 Iberville St **Fax Area Code:* 504 ■ *Web:* www.acmeoyster.com	New Orleans	LA	70130	225-906-2372	524-1595*
Antoine's 713 St Louis St *Web:* www.antoines.com	New Orleans	LA	70130	504-581-4422	
Arnaud's 813 Bienville St *TF:* 866-230-8895 ■ *Web:* www.arnaudsrestaurant.com	New Orleans	LA	70112	504-523-5433	355-5730
August 301 Tchoupitoulas St *Web:* www.rest-august.com	New Orleans	LA	70130	504-299-9777	299-1199
Bayona 430 Rue Dauphine *Web:* www.bayona.com	New Orleans	LA	70112	504-525-4455	522-0589
Bon Ton Cafe 401 Magazine St *Web:* www.thebontoncafe.com	New Orleans	LA	70130	504-524-3386	
Bourbon House Seafood & Oyster Bar 144 Bourbon St *Web:* www.bourbonhouse.com	New Orleans	LA	70130	504-522-0111	522-0333
Brigtsen's 723 Dante St *Web:* www.brigtsens.com	New Orleans	LA	70118	504-861-7610	866-7397
Broussard's Restaurant 819 Rue Conti *Web:* www.broussards.com	New Orleans	LA	70112	504-581-3866	581-3873
Byblos 3218 Magazine St *Web:* www.byblosrestaurants.com	New Orleans	LA	70115	504-894-1233	894-1239
Cafe Degas 3127 Esplanade Ave *Web:* www.cafedegas.com	New Orleans	LA	70119	504-945-5635	943-5255
Cafe Giovanni 117 Rue Decatur St *Web:* www.cafegiovanni.com	New Orleans	LA	70118	504-529-2154	529-3352
Ciro's Cote Sud 7918 Maple St *Web:* www.cotesudrestaurant.com	New Orleans	LA	70118	504-866-9551	
Clancy's 6100 Annunciation St *Web:* clancysneworleans.com	New Orleans	LA	70118	504-895-1111	
Dick & Jenny's 4501 Tchoupitoulas St *Web:* www.dickandjennys.com	New Orleans	LA	70115	504-894-9880	
Elizabeth's 601 Gallier St *Web:* elizabethsrestaurantnola.com	New Orleans	LA	70117	504-944-9272	
Emeril's 800 Tchoupitoulas St *Web:* www.emerils.com	New Orleans	LA	70130	504-528-9393	558-3925
Emeril's Delmonico 1300 St Charles Ave *Web:* www.emerils.com	New Orleans	LA	70130	504-525-4937	595-2206
Galatoire's 209 Bourbon St *Web:* www.galatoires.com	New Orleans	LA	70130	504-525-2021	525-5900
GW Fins 808 Bienville St *Web:* www.gwfins.com	New Orleans	LA	70112	504-581-3467	565-5459
Herbsaint Bar & Restaurant 701 St Charles Ave *Web:* herbsaint.com	New Orleans	LA	70130	504-524-4114	522-1679
Horinoya 920 Poydras St	New Orleans	LA	70112	504-561-8914	561-8919
Irene's Cuisine 539 St Phillip St	New Orleans	LA	70116	504-529-8811	527-5273
Jacques-Imo's Cafe 8324 Oak St *Web:* jacques-imos.com	New Orleans	LA	70118	504-861-0886	314-1585
K-Paul's Louisiana Kitchen 416 Chartres St *Web:* www.kpauls.com	New Orleans	LA	70130	504-596-2530	596-2540
Kyoto 4920 Prytania St *Web:* kyotonola.com	New Orleans	LA	70115	504-891-3644	891-3694
La Crepe Nanou 1410 Robert St *Web:* www.lacrepenanou.com	New Orleans	LA	70115	504-899-2670	
Le Meritage at the Maison Dupuy 1001 Rue Toulouse *Web:* www.maisondupuy.com	New Orleans	LA	70112	504-522-8800	525-5334
Liborio's 321 Magazine St *Web:* www.liboriocuban.com	New Orleans	LA	70130	504-581-9680	
Lilette 3637 Magazine St *Web:* www.liletterestaurant.com	New Orleans	LA	70115	504-895-1636	895-3622
Louisiana Bistro 337 Dauphine St *Web:* louisianabistro.net	New Orleans	LA	70112	504-525-3335	
Martinique Bistro 5908 Magazine St *Web:* www.martiniquebistro.com	New Orleans	LA	70115	504-891-8495	
Mat & Naddie's Restaurant 937 Leonidas St *Web:* www.matandnaddies.com	New Orleans	LA	70118	504-861-9600	
Mr B's Bistro 201 Royal St *Web:* www.mrbsbistro.com	New Orleans	LA	70130	504-523-2078	521-8304
Muriel's 801 Chartres St *Web:* www.muriels.com	New Orleans	LA	70116	504-568-1885	568-9795
NewOrleans Restaurants 300 Bourbon St *Web:* neworleansrestaurants.com/desire/	New Orleans	LA	70130	504-779-5188	
Ninja 8433 Oak St *Web:* ninjasushineworleans.com	New Orleans	LA	70118	504-866-1119	
NOLA 534 St Louis St *Web:* www.emerils.com	New Orleans	LA	70130	504-522-6652	524-6178
Orleans Grapevine Wine Bar & Bistro 718 - 720 Orleans Ave *Web:* www.orleansgrapevine.com	New Orleans	LA	70116	504-523-1930	523-1245
Palace Cafe 605 Canal St *Web:* www.palacecafe.com	New Orleans	LA	70130	504-523-1661	
Pelican Club 312 Exchange Alley *Web:* www.pelicanclub.com	New Orleans	LA	70130	504-523-1504	522-2331
Port of Call 838 Esplanade Ave *Web:* portofcallnola.com	New Orleans	LA	70116	504-523-0120	529-7678
Red Fish Grill 115 Bourbon St *Web:* www.redfishgrill.com	New Orleans	LA	70130	504-598-1200	598-1211
RioMar 800 S Peters St *Web:* www.riomarseafood.com	New Orleans	LA	70130	504-525-3474	
Sake Cafe 2830 Magazine St *Web:* sakecafeuptown.us	New Orleans	LA	70115	504-894-0033	894-1546
Sara's 724 Dublin St *Web:* hugedomains.com/domain_profile.cfm?d=sarasrestaurant&e=com	New Orleans	LA	70118	504-861-0565	
Stella! 1032 Chartres St *Web:* www.restaurantstella.com	New Orleans	LA	70116	504-587-0091	587-0092
Upperline 1413 Upperline St *Web:* www.upperline.com	New Orleans	LA	70115	504-891-9822	
Bella Fresca Restaurant 6307 Line Ave *Web:* www.bellafresca.com	Shreveport	LA	71106	318-865-6307	
Chianti Restaurant 6535 Line Ave *Web:* chiantirestaurant.net	Shreveport	LA	71106	318-868-8866	865-7119
Copeland's of New Orleans 1665 E Industrial Loop *Web:* www.copelandsofneworleans.com	Shreveport	LA	71106	318-797-0143	797-7135
Ernest's Orleans Restaurant & Cocktail Lounge 1601 Spring St S *Web:* www.ernestsorleans.com	Shreveport	LA	71101	318-226-1325	425-0900
Mabry House 1540 Irving Pl	Shreveport	LA	71101	318-227-1121	227-1121
Ming Garden 1250 Shreveport Barksdale Hwy *Web:* chineserestaurantshreveport.com	Shreveport	LA	71105	318-861-2741	865-7222
Monjunis 1315 Louisiana Ave *Web:* www.monjunis.com	Shreveport	LA	71101	318-227-0847	227-9499
Superior Bar & Grill 6123 Line Ave *Web:* superiorgrill.com	Shreveport	LA	71106	318-869-3243	868-7688
Trejo's 9122 Mansfield Rd *Web:* trejosmexicanrestaurant.com	Shreveport	LA	71118	318-687-6192	687-8187
Village Grille 1313 Louisiana Ave	Shreveport	LA	71101	318-424-2874	

Maine

Name	City	State	Zip	Phone	Fax
Margaritas 390 Western Ave *Web:* www.margs.com	Augusta	ME	04330	207-622-7874	622-7908
Red Barn 455 Riverside Dr *Web:* theredbarnmaine.com	Augusta	ME	04330	207-623-9485	
Riverfront Barbeque & Grill 300 Water St *Web:* riverfrontbbq.com	Augusta	ME	04330	207-622-8899	
Bugaboo Creek Steak House 24 Bangor Mall Blvd *Web:* bugaboocreek.com	Bangor	ME	04401	207-945-5515	945-5445
Captain Nick's 1165 Union St *Web:* captainnicksmaine.com	Bangor	ME	04401	207-942-6444	
China Light 571 Broadway *Web:* chinalightbangor.com	Bangor	ME	04401	207-947-6759	
Geaghan's Restaurant & Pub 570 Main St *Web:* www.geaghanspub.com	Bangor	ME	04401	207-945-3730	941-6758
Oriental Jade Bangor Mall Blvd *Web:* www.orientaljade.com	Bangor	ME	04401	207-947-6969	942-7170
Panda Garden 123 Franklin St *Web:* bangorpanda.com	Bangor	ME	04401	207-942-2704	942-2704
Thistle's 175 Exchange St *Web:* www.thistlesrestaurant.com	Bangor	ME	04401	207-945-5480	990-3836
Cafe Blue Fish 122 Cottage St *Web:* www.cafebluefishbarharbor.com	Bar Harbor	ME	04609	207-288-3696	
Geddy's Pub 19 Main St PO Box 955 *Web:* www.geddys.com	Bar Harbor	ME	04609	207-288-5077	288-9927
Havana 318 Main St *Web:* havanamaine.com	Bar Harbor	ME	04609	207-288-2822	
Mama DiMatteo's 34 Kennebec Pl *Web:* www.mamadimatteos.com	Bar Harbor	ME	04609	207-288-3666	
Michelle's 194 Main St *Web:* www.ivymanor.com	Bar Harbor	ME	04609	207-288-0038	
Poor Boy's Gourmet 300 Main St *Web:* www.poorboysgourmet.com	Bar Harbor	ME	04609	207-288-4148	
Rosalie's 46 Cottage St *Web:* rosaliespizza.com	Bar Harbor	ME	04609	207-288-5666	
Route 66 21 Cottage St *Web:* barharborroute66.com	Bar Harbor	ME	04609	207-288-3708	
Rupununi Bar & Grill 119 Main St *Web:* www.rupununi.com	Bar Harbor	ME	04609	207-288-2886	
West Street Cafe 76 W St *Web:* www.weststreetcafe.com	Bar Harbor	ME	04609	207-288-5242	
Ground Round 215 Whitten Rd PO Box 426 *Web:* sparetimerec.com	Hallowell	ME	04347	207-623-0022	621-2860
Hattie's Chowder House 103 Water St *Web:* www.hattieschowderhouse.com	Hallowell	ME	04347	207-621-4114	621-2622
Bar Harbor Lobster Bakes 10 State Hwy 3 PO Box 177 *Web:* www.barharborlobsterbakes.com	Hulls Cove	ME	04644	207-288-4055	288-5767
Back Bay Grill 65 Portland St *Web:* www.backbaygrill.com	Portland	ME	04101	207-772-8833	
Benkay Two India St *Web:* sushimanme.info	Portland	ME	04101	207-773-5555	
Bintliff's American Cafe 98 Portland St *Web:* www.bintliffscafe.com	Portland	ME	04101	207-774-0005	774-2505
Blue Spoon 89 Congress St *Web:* bluespoonme.com	Portland	ME	04101	207-773-1116	773-1119

Name	City	State	Zip	Phone	Fax
Cinque Terre 10 Dana St. *Web:* www.vignolamaine.com	Portland	ME	04101	207-772-1330	
DiMillo's on the Water 25 Long Wharf *Web:* www.dimillos.com	Portland	ME	04101	207-772-2216	772-1081
Duckfat 43 Middle St *Web:* www.duckfat.com	Portland	ME	04101	207-774-8080	774-0262
Fore Street 288 Fore St. *Web:* forestreet.biz	Portland	ME	04101	207-775-2717	
Gilbert's Chowder House 92 Commercial St *Web:* gilbertschowderhouse.com	Portland	ME	04101	207-871-5636	
Katahdin Restaurant 27 Forest Ave *Web:* www.katahdinrestaurant.com	Portland	ME	04101	207-774-1740	774-1740
Maria's 337 Cumberland Ave *Web:* mariasrestaurant.com	Portland	ME	04101	207-772-9232	
Pepperclub 78 Middle St. *Web:* pepperclubrestaurant.com	Portland	ME	04101	207-772-0531	
Portland Lobster Co 180 Commercial St *Web:* www.portlandlobstercompany.com	Portland	ME	04112	207-775-2112	
Ri Ra Irish Pub & Restaurant 72 Commercial St. *Web:* www.rira.com	Portland	ME	04101	207-761-4446	761-4447
Ribollita 41 Middle St. *Web:* ribollitamaine.com	Portland	ME	04101	207-774-2972	
Sapporo Restaurant 230 Commercial St *Web:* www.sappororestaurant.com	Portland	ME	04101	207-772-1233	871-9275
Walter's Cafe Two Portland Sq. *Web:* www.waltersportland.com	Portland	ME	04101	207-871-9258	871-1018
Joe's Boathouse One Spring Pt Dr. *Web.* www.joesboathouse.com	South Portland	ME	04106	207-741-2780	347-5718

Manitoba

Name	City	Prov	Postal Code	Phone	Fax
529 Wellington 529 Wellington Crescent *Web:* wowhospitality.ca	Winnipeg	MB	R3M0B9	204-487-8325	
Amici 326 Broadway *Web:* www.amiciwpg.com	Winnipeg	MB	R3C0S5	204-943-4997	943-0369
Bailey's 185 Lombard Ave. *Web:* www.baileysprimedining.com	Winnipeg	MB	R3B0W4	204-944-1180	944-0449
Bella Vista 53 Maryland St.	Winnipeg	MB	R3G1C3	204-775-4485	
Bombolini 326 Broadway *Web:* amiciwpg.com	Winnipeg	MB	R3C0S5	204-943-5066	943-0369
Cafe Carlo 243 Lilac St. *Web:* www.cafecarlo.com	Winnipeg	MB	R3M2S2	204-477-5544	477-1652
East India Co 349 York Ave. *Web:* www.eastindiaco.com	Winnipeg	MB	R3C3S9	204-947-3097	947-5019
Elephant & Castle/Delta Winnipeg Hotel 350 St Mary Ave. *Web:* www.elephantcastle.com	Winnipeg	MB	R3C3J2	204-942-5555	947-0275
Fusion Grill 550 Academy Rd *Web:* fusiongrill.mb.ca	Winnipeg	MB	R3N0E3	204-489-6963	
Gasthaus Gutenberger 2583 Portage Ave *Web:* www.gasthausgutenberger.com	Winnipeg	MB	R3J0P5	204-888-3133	
Hy's Steakhouse & Cocktail Bar One Lombard Pl Main Fl Richardson Bldg *Web:* www.hyssteakhouse.com	Winnipeg	MB	R3B0X3	204-942-1000	
Ichiban 189 Carlton St. *Web:* www.ichiban.ca	Winnipeg	MB	R3C3H7	204-925-7400	957-1697
King's Head Pub 120 King St. *Web:* www.kingshead.ca	Winnipeg	MB	R3B1M3	204-957-7710	
Maxime 1131 St Mary's Rd **Fax Area Code: 207* ■ *Web:* maximesrestaurant.ca	Winnipeg	MB	R2M3T9	204-257-1521	257-1521*
Mei Ji Sushi 454 River Ave *Web:* www.meijisushi.ca	Winnipeg	MB	R3L0C6	204-284-3996	
Mitchell Block, The 173 McDermot Ave *Web:* www.trevisirestaurant.com	Winnipeg	MB	R3B0S1	204-949-9032	943-7540
Mona Lisa 1697 Corydon Ave. *Web:* www.monalisarestaurant.ca/	Winnipeg	MB	R3N0J9	204-488-3684	489-1679
Mondragon 91 Albert St. *Web:* www.mondragon.ca	Winnipeg	MB	R3B1G5	204-946-5241	956-1505
Pembina Village Restaurant 333 Pembina Hwy. *Web:* www.pembinavillagerestaurant.com	Winnipeg	MB	R3L2E4	204-477-5439	
Resto Gare 630 Des Meurons St. *Web:* www.restogare.com	Winnipeg	MB	R2H2P9	204-237-7072	837-3624
Toad in the Hole 112 Osborne St *Web:* toadinthehole.ca	Winnipeg	MB	R3L1Y5	204-284-7201	474-1490
Tropikis 878 Ellice Ave	Winnipeg	MB	R3G0C6	204-788-4733	
White Tower 3670 Roblin Blvd *Web:* weebly.com	Winnipeg	MB	R3R0E1	204-896-0406	837-3873

Maryland

Name	City	State	Zip	Phone	Fax
Adam's Ribs East 921C Chesapeake Ave. *Web:* www.adamsribseast.com	Annapolis	MD	21403	410-267-0064	
Cafe Normandie 185 Main St. *Web:* www.cafenormandie.com	Annapolis	MD	21401	410-263-3382	263-8824
Cantler's Riverside Inn 458 Forest Beach Rd. *Web:* www.cantlers.com	Annapolis	MD	21409	410-757-1311	757-6784
Castlebay Irish Pub 193-A Main St	Annapolis	MD	21401	410-626-0165	
Famous Dave's Barbeque 181 Jennifer Rd *Web:* www.famousdaves.com	Annapolis	MD	21401	410-224-2207	224-2088
Federal House Bar & Grille 22 Market Space *Web:* federalhouserestaurant.com	Annapolis	MD	21401	410-268-2576	280-0195
Galway Bay Irish Pub 63 Maryland Ave *Web:* www.galwaybayannapolis.com	Annapolis	MD	21401	410-263-8333	263-8989
Harry Browne's 66 State Cir *Web:* www.harrybrownes.com	Annapolis	MD	21401	410-263-4332	263-8049
Jalapenos 85 Forest Dr. *Web:* jalapenosonline.com	Annapolis	MD	21401	410-266-7580	266-7582
Joss Cafe & Sushi Bar 195 Main St *Web:* josssushi.com	Annapolis	MD	21401	410-263-4688	263-4764
Lebanese Taverna 2478 Solomons Island Rd Annapolis Harbour Ctr *Web:* www.lebanesetaverna.com	Annapolis	MD	21401	410-897-1111	897-9099
Les Folies 2552 Riva Rd *Web:* www.lesfoliesbrasserie.com	Annapolis	MD	21401	410-573-0970	573-9131
Lewnes' Steakhouse 401 Fourth St *Web:* www.lewnessteakhouse.com	Annapolis	MD	21403	410-263-1617	
Main Ingredient 914 Bay Ridge Rd *Web:* www.themainingredient.com	Annapolis	MD	21403	410-626-0388	626-0204
Mangia 81 Main St *Web:* mangiasannapolis.com	Annapolis	MD	21401	410-268-1350	
Melting Pot of Annapolis, The 2348 Solomons Island Rd *TF:* 800-783-0867 ■ *Web:* www.meltingpot.com	Annapolis	MD	21401	410-266-8004	266-8431
O'Brien's Oyster Bar & Restaurant 113 Main St *Web:* www.obriensoysterbar.com	Annapolis	MD	21401	410-268-6288	267-7767
O'Leary's Seafood Restaurant 310 Third St. *Web:* www.olearysseafood.com	Annapolis	MD	21403	410-263-0884	
Osteria 177 177 Main St. *Web:* www.osteria177.com	Annapolis	MD	21401	410-267-7700	
Paul's Homewood Cafe 919 W St. *Web:* pauls.publishpath.com/	Annapolis	MD	21401	410-267-7891	
Piccola Roma 200 Main St. *Web:* piccolaromaannapolis.com	Annapolis	MD	21401	410-268-7898	
Red Hot & Blue Restaurants Inc 200 Old Mill Bottom Rd S. *Web:* www.redhotandblue.com	Annapolis	MD	21401	410-626-7427	757-5095
Reynolds Tavern Seven Church Cir *Web:* www.reynoldstavern.org	Annapolis	MD	21401	410-295-9555	295-9559
Sam's on the Waterfront 2020 Chesapeake Harbour Dr E *Web:* www.samsonthewaterfront.com	Annapolis	MD	21403	410-263-3600	263-3654
Abacrombie Inn 58 W Biddle St	Baltimore	MD	21201	410-244-7227	
Akbar 823 N Charles St *Web:* www.akbar-restaurant.com	Baltimore	MD	21201	410-539-0944	
Aldo's 306 S High St *Web:* www.aldositaly.com	Baltimore	MD	21202	410-727-0700	625-3700
Ambassador Dining Room 3811 Canterbury Rd *Web:* www1.nyc.gov	Baltimore	MD	21218	410-366-1484	
Amicci's of Little Italy 231 S High St *Web:* www.amiccis.com	Baltimore	MD	21202	410-528-1096	685-6259
B - A Bolton Hill Bistro 1501 Bolton St. *Web:* www.b-bistro.com	Baltimore	MD	21217	410-383-8600	383-1017
Birches 641 S Montford Ave *Web:* www.birchesrestaurant.com	Baltimore	MD	21224	410-732-3000	
Black Olive 814 S Bond St *Web:* www.theblackolive.com	Baltimore	MD	21231	410-276-7141	276-7143
Brewers Art 1106 N Charles St. *Web:* www.thebrewersart.com	Baltimore	MD	21201	410-547-6925	547-7417
Brightons Orangerie 550 Light St. *Web:* sonesta.com	Baltimore	MD	21202	410-347-9750	659-5925
Carlyle, The 500 W University Pkwy *Web:* www.morgan-properties.com/thecarlyle	Baltimore	MD	21210	410-467-9890	
Charleston 1000 Lancaster St *Web:* www.charlestonrestaurant.com	Baltimore	MD	21202	410-332-7373	332-8425
Da Mimmo Italian Cuisine 217 S High St. *Web:* www.damimmo.com	Baltimore	MD	21202	410-727-6876	727-1927
Dalesio's of Little Italy 829 Eastern Ave *Web:* www.dalesios.com	Baltimore	MD	21202	410-539-1965	
Dukem 1100 Maryland Ave **Fax Area Code: 202* ■ *Web:* www.dukemrestaurant.com	Baltimore	MD	21201	410-385-0318	667-2488*
Faidley's Seafood 203 N Paca St *Web:* www.faidleyscrabcakes.com	Baltimore	MD	21201	410-727-4898	
Gertrude's 10 Art Museum Dr. *Web:* gertrudesbaltimore.com	Baltimore	MD	21218	410-889-3399	889-9689
Helmand, The 806 N Charles St. *Web:* www.helmand.com	Baltimore	MD	21201	410-752-0311	752-0511
Henninger's Tavern 1812 Bank St *Web:* www.henningerstavern.com	Baltimore	MD	21231	410-342-2172	
Hull Street Blues 1222 Hull St. *Web:* www.hullstreetblues.com	Baltimore	MD	21230	410-727-7476	576-2343
Ikaros 4901 Eastern Ave. *Web:* www.ikarosrestaurant.com	Baltimore	MD	21224	410-633-3750	633-7881
Kali's Court 1606 Thames St. *Web:* www.kaliscourt.com	Baltimore	MD	21231	410-276-4700	276-2420
Kali's Mezze 1606 Thames St. *Web:* www.kalismezze.com	Baltimore	MD	21231	410-563-7600	276-2420
La Scala of Little Italy 1012 Eastern Ave *Web:* www.lascaladining.com	Baltimore	MD	21202	410-783-9209	783-5949
La Tavola 248 Albemarle St *Web:* www.la-tavola.com	Baltimore	MD	21202	410-685-1859	685-1891
Little Havana 1325 Key Hwy. *Web:* www.littlehavanas.com	Baltimore	MD	21230	410-837-9903	332-0775
Louisiana Restaurant 1708 Aliceanna St. *Web:* www.louisianasrestaurant.com	Baltimore	MD	21231	410-327-2610	
Mama's on the Half Shell 2901 O'Donnell St *Web:* www.mamasonthehalfshell.com	Baltimore	MD	21224	410-276-3160	327-7140
Matsuri Restaurant 1105 S Charles St. *Web:* www.matsuri-restaurant.com/	Baltimore	MD	21230	410-752-8561	752-9919
Nacho Mama's 2907 O'Donnell St *Web:* www.nachomamascanton.com	Baltimore	MD	21224	410-675-0898	
Peter's Inn 504 S Ann St. *Web:* www.petersinn.com	Baltimore	MD	21231	410-675-7313	
Petit Louis Bistro 4800 Roland Ave. *Web:* www.petitlouis.com	Baltimore	MD	21210	410-366-9393	366-9019
Red Maple 930 N Charles St *Web:* www.930redmaple.com	Baltimore	MD	21201	410-385-0520	

Name / Address	City	State	Zip	Phone	Fax
Rocco's Capriccio 846 Fawn St *Web:* roccosinlittleitaly.com	Baltimore	MD	21202	410-685-2710	
Sabatino's 901 Fawn St *Web:* www.sabatinos.com	Baltimore	MD	21202	410-727-9414	837-6540
Samos 600 Oldham St *Web:* www.samosrestaurant.com	Baltimore	MD	21224	410-675-5292	
Sascha's 527 N Charles St *Web:* www.saschas.com	Baltimore	MD	21201	410-539-8880	
Sotto Sopra 405 N Charles St *Web:* sottosoprainc.com	Baltimore	MD	21201	410-625-0534	625-2642
Sushi-San Thai Jai Dee 2748 Lighthouse Pt *Web:* sushisanbaltimore.com	Baltimore	MD	21224	410-534-8888	534-8665
Suzie's Soba 1009 W 36th St	Baltimore	MD	21211	410-243-0051	
Tapas Teatro 1711 N Charles St *Web:* www.tapasteatro.com	Baltimore	MD	21201	410-332-0110	
Thai Arroy 1019 Light St *Web:* www.thaiarroy.com	Baltimore	MD	21230	410-385-8587	
Thai Landing 1207 N Charles St *Web:* www.thailandingmd.com	Baltimore	MD	21201	410-727-1234	
Tio Pepe 10 E Franklin St *Web:* tiopepebaltimore.com	Baltimore	MD	21202	410-539-4675	
Viccino 1317 N Charles St *Web:* www.viccino.com	Baltimore	MD	21201	410-347-0349	783-1938
La Hacienda Restaurant 11033 Nicholas Ln *Web:* www.oclahacienda.com	Berlin	MD	21811	410-208-1383	
Marlin Moon Grille 1183 Beach Blvd *Web:* www.marlinmoongrille.com	Jax Beach	FL	32250	904-372-4438	
Angler Restaurant 312 Talbot St *Web:* angleroc.net	Ocean City	MD	21842	410-289-7424	
BJ's On the Water 115 75th St *Web:* www.bjsonthewater.com	Ocean City	MD	21842	410-524-7575	524-7624
Bonfire, The 7009 Coastal Hwy *Web:* www.thebonfirerestaurant.com	Ocean City	MD	21842	410-524-7171	524-4228
Buxy's Salty Dog 2707 Philadelphia Ave *Web:* buxys.com	Ocean City	MD	21842	410-289-0973	289-0038
Captain's Galley 12817 Harbor Rd *Web:* captainsgalley2.com	Ocean City	MD	21842	410-213-2525	213-0702
Coral Reef Restaurant 1701 Atlantic Ave *Web:* ocmdhotels.com	Ocean City	MD	21842	410-289-2612	289-3381
Fager's Island Restaurant 201 60th St *Web:* www.fagers.com	Ocean City	MD	21842	410-524-5500	723-2055
Hall's Restaurant 60th St Bayside *Web:* www.halls-oc.com	Ocean City	MD	21842	410-524-5008	524-5377
Harrison's Harbor Watch Restaurant 806 S Boardwalk *Web:* www.harborwatchrestaurant.com	Ocean City	MD	21842	410-289-5121	
JR's Place for Ribs 131st St & Coastal *TF:* 800-879-7742 ■ *Web:* www.jrsribs.com	Ocean City	MD	21842	410-250-3100	
Jules 11805 Coastal Hwy *Web:* ocjules.com	Ocean City	MD	21842	410-524-3396	
Macky's Bayside Bar & Grill 54th St on the Bay *Web:* www.mackys.com	Ocean City	MD	21842	410-723-5565	
Marina Deck 306 Dorchester St *Web:* www.marinadeckrestaurant.com	Ocean City	MD	21842	410-289-4411	
Nick's Original House of Ribs 145th St & Coastal Hwy *Web:* www.nickshouseofribs.com	Ocean City	MD	21842	410-250-1984	
Ocean City Maryland Hotels 6600 Coastal Hwy *Web:* www.ocmdhotels.com	Ocean City	MD	21842	410-524-5252	
Ocean Club Night Club 10100 Coastal Hwy *Web:* oceancity.com	Ocean City	MD	21842	410-703-1970	
Phillips Crab House 2004 N Philadelphia Ave *Web:* www.phillipsseafood.com	Ocean City	MD	21842	410-289-6821	289-4258
Tequila Mockingbird 130th St Montego Bay Shopping Ctr *Web:* www.octequila.com	Ocean City	MD	21842	410-250-4424	
Crab Alley 9703 Golf Course Rd *Web:* craballeyoc.com	West Ocean City	MD	21842	410-213-7800	213-1048

Massachusetts

Name / Address	City	State	Zip	Phone	Fax
Outermost Inn 81 Lighthouse Rd *Web:* www.outermostinn.com	Aquinnah	MA	02535	508-645-3511	645-3514
29 Newbury 29 Newbury St *Web:* www.29newbury.com	Boston	MA	02116	617-536-0290	
75 Chestnut 75 Chestnut St *Web:* www.75chestnut.com	Boston	MA	02108	617-227-2175	227-3675
Abe & Louie's 793 Boylston St *Web:* www.abeandlouies.com	Boston	MA	02116	617-536-6300	437-6291
Addis Red Sea 544 Tremont St *Web:* www.addisredsea.com	Boston	MA	02116	617-426-8727	695-3677
Antico Forno 93 Salem St *Web:* www.anticofornoboston.com	Boston	MA	02113	617-723-6733	
Aquitaine 569 Tremont St *Web:* www.aquitaineboston.com	Boston	MA	02118	617-424-8577	424-0249
Assaggio 29 Prince St *Web:* www.assaggioboston.com	Boston	MA	02113	617-227-7380	742-3512
Atlantic Fish Co 761 Boylston St *Web:* www.backbayrestaurantgroup.com	Boston	MA	02116	617-267-4000	
B & G Oysters 550 Tremont St *Web:* www.bandgoysters.com	Boston	MA	02116	617-423-0550	
Bangkok Blue 651 Boylston St *Web:* www.bkkblueboston.com	Boston	MA	02116	617-266-1010	266-9747
Bin 26 Enoteca 26 Charles St *Web:* www.bin26.com	Boston	MA	02114	617-723-5939	
Blu Four Avery St Fourth Fl *Web:* www.blurestaurant.com	Boston	MA	02111	617-375-8550	375-8201
Bristol, The 200 Boylston St *TF:* 800-819-5053 ■ *Web:* www.fourseasons.com	Boston	MA	02116	617-338-4400	423-0154
Brown Sugar Cafe 1033 Commonwealth Ave *Web:* www.brownsugarcafe.com	Boston	MA	02215	617-787-4242	783-1365
Butcher Shop, The 552 Tremont St *Web:* www.thebutchershopboston.com	Boston	MA	02118	617-423-4800	
Cantina Italiana 346 Hanover St *Web:* www.cantinaitaliana.com	Boston	MA	02113	617-723-4577	723-6357
Capital Grille 900 Boylston St **Fax Area Code:* 617 ■ *TF:* 866-518-9113 ■ *Web:* www.thecapitalgrille.com	Boston	MA	02115	866-518-9113	262-9449*
Carmen 33 N Sq *Web:* www.carmenboston.com	Boston	MA	02113	617-742-6421	
Casa Romero 30 Gloucester St *Web:* www.casaromero.com	Boston	MA	02115	617-536-4341	536-6191
Clio 370A Commonwealth Ave *Web:* www.cliorestaurant.com	Boston	MA	02215	617-536-7200	
Davide 326 Commercial St *Web:* www.daviderestaurant.com	Boston	MA	02109	617-227-5745	
East Ocean City 27 Beach St *Web:* www.eastoceancity.com	Boston	MA	02111	617-542-2504	
Franklin Cafe 278 Shawmut Ave *Web:* www.franklincafe.com	Boston	MA	02118	617-350-0010	
Ginza 16 Hudson St	Boston	MA	02111	617-338-2261	426-3563
Grill 23 & Bar 161 Berkeley St *Web:* www.grill23.com	Boston	MA	02116	617-542-2255	542-5114
Grotto 37 Bowdoin St *Web:* www.grottorestaurant.com	Boston	MA	02114	617-227-3434	
Hamersley's Bistro 553 Tremont St	Boston	MA	02116	617-423-2700	
India Quality 484 Commonwealth Ave *Web:* www.indiaquality.com	Boston	MA	02215	617-267-4499	267-4477
KO Prime 90 Tremont St *TF:* 866-906-9090 ■ *Web:* www.ninezero.com	Boston	MA	02108	617-772-0202	772-5810
L'Espalier 774-Bayleston St *Web:* www.lespalier.com	Boston	MA	02199	617-262-3023	375-9297
Lala Rokh 97 Mt Vernon St *Web:* www.lalarokh.com	Boston	MA	02108	617-720-5511	
Legal Sea Foods 26 Pk Plz *Web:* www.legalseafoods.com	Boston	MA	02116	617-426-4444	338-7629
Les Zygomates 129 S St *Web:* winebar129.com/	Boston	MA	02111	617-542-5108	482-8806
Lucca 226 Hanover St *Web:* www.luccaboston.com	Boston	MA	02113	617-742-9200	723-2081
Mamma Maria's Three N Sq *Web:* www.mammamaria.com	Boston	MA	02113	617-523-0077	523-4348
Meritage 70 Rowes Wharf *Web:* www.meritagetherestaurant.com	Boston	MA	02110	617-439-3995	
Metropolis Cafe 584 Tremont St *Web:* www.metropolisboston.com	Boston	MA	02118	617-247-2931	247-2495
Mistral 223 Columbus Ave *Web:* www.mistralbistro.com	Boston	MA	02116	617-867-9300	351-2601
Montien 63 Stuart St *Web:* www.montien-boston.com	Boston	MA	02116	617-338-5600	338-5348
No 9 PARK Nine Pk St *Web:* www.no9park.com	Boston	MA	02108	617-742-9991	742-9993
O Ya Nine E St Pl *Web:* www.oyarestaurantboston.com	Boston	MA	02111	617-654-9900	654-9909
Oak Room 138 St James Ave *Web:* oaklongbarkitchen.com	Boston	MA	02116	617-585-7222	
Oishii Boston 1166 Washington St *Web:* www.oishiiboston.com	Boston	MA	02118	617-482-8868	482-8869
Peach Farm Four Tyler St *Web:* peachfarmboston.com	Boston	MA	02111	617-482-1116	
Prezza 24 Fleet St *Web:* www.prezza.com	Boston	MA	02113	617-227-1577	227-1587
Ruby Room 155 Portland St *Web:* www.rubyroomboston.com	Boston	MA	02114	617-557-9950	557-0005
Sakurabana 57 Broad St *Web:* sakurabanaboston.com	Boston	MA	02109	617-542-4311	542-2320
Sonsie 327 Newbury St *Web:* www.sonsieboston.com	Boston	MA	02115	617-351-2500	
Strega 379 Hanover St *Web:* www.stregaristorante.com	Boston	MA	02113	617-523-8481	
Tapeo 266 Newbury St *Web:* www.tapeo.com	Boston	MA	02116	617-267-4799	267-1602
Taranta 210 Hanover St *Web:* www.tarantarist.com	Boston	MA	02113	617-720-0052	507-0492
Teatro 177 Tremont St *Web:* teatroboston.com	Boston	MA	02111	617-778-6841	778-6844
Terramia Ristorante 98 Salem St *Web:* www.terramiaristorante.com	Boston	MA	02113	617-523-3112	
Tresca 233 Hanover St *Web:* www.trescanorthend.com	Boston	MA	02113	617-742-8240	742-8246
Troquet 140 Boylston St *Web:* www.troquetboston.com	Boston	MA	02116	617-695-9463	
Union Bar & Grille 1357 Washington St *Web:* www.unionrestaurant.com	Boston	MA	02118	617-423-0555	423-6055
Via Matta 79 Pk Plz *Web:* www.viamattarestaurant.com	Boston	MA	02116	617-422-0008	422-0014
Wagamama Quincy Market Bldg *Web:* www.wagamama.us	Boston	MA	02109	617-742-9242	742-9241
Bramble Inn 2019 Main St *Web:* www.brambleinn.com	Brewster	MA	02631	508-896-7644	896-9332
Chillingsworth 2449 Main St *Web:* www.chillingsworth.com	Brewster	MA	02631	508-896-3640	
Fireplace 1634 Beacon St *Web:* www.fireplacerest.com	Brookline	MA	02446	617-975-1900	975-1600
East Coast Grill & Raw Bar 1271 Cambridge St *Web:* www.eastcoastgrill.net	Cambridge	MA	02139	617-491-6568	868-4278
Elephant Walk 2067 Massachusetts Ave *Web:* www.elephantwalk.com	Cambridge	MA	02140	617-492-6900	

				Phone	Fax
Harvest 44 Brattle St	Cambridge	MA	02138	617-868-2255	
Web: www.harvestcambridge.com					
Helmand Restaurant 143 First St	Cambridge	MA	02142	617-492-4646	
Web: www.helmandrestaurant.com					
Oleana Restaurant 134 Hampshire St	Cambridge	MA	02139	617-661-0505	661-3336
Web: www.oleanarestaurant.com					
Red Pheasant 905 Main St	Dennis	MA	02638	508-385-2133	
Web: www.redpheasantinn.com					
Nauset Beach Club 222 Main St	East Orleans	MA	02643	508-255-8547	
Web: www.nausetbeachclub.com					
Atria 137 Main St PO Box 561	Edgartown	MA	02539	508-627-5850	627-9389
Web: www.atriamv.com					
Water Street 131 N Water St	Edgartown	MA	02539	508-627-7000	627-8417
TF: 800-225-6005 ■ *Web:* www.harbor-view.com					
La Cucina Sul Mare 237 Main St	Falmouth	MA	02540	508-548-5600	
Web: www.lacucinasulmare.com					
Buca's Tuscan Roadhouse Four Depot Rd	Harwich	MA	02645	508-432-6900	
Web: www.bucasroadhouse.com					
L'Alouette 787 Massachusetts 28	Harwich Port	MA	02646	508-430-0405	
Web: www.lalouettebistro.com					
Delaney House Three County Club Rd Rt 5 Smith's Ferry	Holyoke	MA	01040	413-532-1800	533-7137
Web: logcabin-delaney.com					
Brazilian Grill 680 Main St	Hyannis	MA	02601	508-771-0109	771-1070
Web: www.braziliangrill-capecod.com					
Cooke's Seafood 1120 Rt 132	Hyannis	MA	02601	508-775-0450	
Web: www.cookesseafood.com					
Fazio's Trattoria 294 Main St	Hyannis	MA	02601	508-775-9400	
Web: www.fazio.net					
Misaki Sushi 379 W Main St	Hyannis	MA	02601	508-771-3771	771-4431
Web: www.misakisushi.com					
Naked Oyster Bistro & Raw Bar 410 Main St	Hyannis	MA	02601	508-778-6500	
Web: www.nakedoyster.com					
Paddock, The 20 Scudder Ave	Hyannis	MA	02601	508-775-7677	771-9517
Web: www.paddockcapecod.com					
Sam Diego's 950 Iyanough Rd Rt 132	Hyannis	MA	02601	508-771-8816	771-0174
Web: www.samdiegos.com					
Tiki Port 714 Iyanough Rd	Hyannis	MA	02601	508-771-5220	771-2775
Web: www.tikiport.com					
Company of the Cauldron Five India St	Nantucket	MA	02554	508-228-4016	
Web: www.companyofthecauldron.com					
Le Languedoc Bistro 24 Broad St	Nantucket	MA	02554	508-228-2552	228-4682
Web: www.lelanguedoc.com					
Straight Wharf Six Harbor Sq	Nantucket	MA	02554	508-228-4499	
Web: straightwharfrestaurant.com					
Topper's 120 Wauwinet Rd	Nantucket	MA	02584	508-228-8768	
Web: wauwinet.com					
Lumiere 1293 Washington St	Newton	MA	02465	617-244-9199	796-9178
Web: www.lumiererestaurant.com					
Abba 89 Old Colony Way	Orleans	MA	02653	508-255-8144	
Web: www.abbarestaurant.com					
Academy Ocean Grille Two Academy Pl	Orleans	MA	02653	508-240-1585	
Web: www.academyoceangrille.com					
Captain Linnell House 137 Skaket Beach Rd	Orleans	MA	02653	508-255-3400	255-5377
Web: www.linnell.com					
Front Street 230 Commercial St	Provincetown	MA	02657	508-487-9715	487-7748
Web: www.frontstreetrestaurant.com					
Mews Restaurant & Cafe 429 Commercial St	Provincetown	MA	02657	508-487-1500	487-3700
Web: mews.com					
Red Inn 15 Commercial St	Provincetown	MA	02657	508-487-7334	487-5115
TF: 866-473-3466 ■ *Web:* www.theredinn.com					
Ross' Grill 237 Commercial St Second Fl PO Box 304	Provincetown	MA	02657	508-487-8878	
Web: www.rossgrille.com					
Dali Restaurant 415 Washington St	Somerville	MA	02143	617-661-3254	661-2813
Web: www.dalirestaurant.com					
Riverway Lobster House 1338 Massachusetts 28	South Yarmouth	MA	02664	508-398-2172	
Web: www.riverwaylobsterhouserestaurant.com					
A Touch of Garlic Restaurant 427 White St	Springfield	MA	01108	413-739-0236	
Web: atouchofgarlicrestaurant.com					
Big Mamou 63 Liberty St	Springfield	MA	01103	413-732-1011	
Web: www.chefwaynes-bigmamou.com					
Cafe Lebanon 1390 Main St	Springfield	MA	01103	413-737-7373	737-5773
Web: www.cafelebanon.com					
Casa De Nana 995 Boston Rd	Springfield	MA	01119	413-783-1549	
Web: www.casadenana.com					
Lido's 555 Worthington St	Springfield	MA	01105	413-736-0887	
Web: www.lidosrestaurant.com					
Max's Tavern 1000 W Columbus Blvd	Springfield	MA	01105	413-746-6299	
Web: maxtavern.com					
Pho Saigon 398 Dickinson St	Springfield	MA	01108	413-781-4488	
Web: phosaigonspringfield.com					
Salvatore's 1333 Boston Rd	Springfield	MA	01119	413-782-9968	796-7601
Web: www.salvatoresrestaurant.net					
Student Prince Cafe, The 8 Fort St	Springfield	MA	01103	413-734-7475	739-7303
Web: www.studentprince.com					
Theodore's Booze Blues & BBQ 201 Worthington St	Springfield	MA	01103	413-736-6000	
Web: theodoresbbq.com					
Typical Sicilian 497 Belmont Ave	Springfield	MA	01108	413-739-7100	
Web: www.typicalsicilian.com					
Il Capriccio 888 Main St	Waltham	MA	02453	781-894-2234	
Web: www.bostonchefs.com					
Blue Ginger 583 Washington St	Wellesley	MA	02482	781-283-5790	283-5772
Web: www.ming.com					
Bistro 5 5 Playstead Rd	West Medford	MA	02155	781-395-7464	395-0130
Web: www.bistro5.com					
Debbie Wong 878 Memorial Ave	West Springfield	MA	01089	413-781-1711	
Web: debbiewongrestaurant.com					
111 Chop House 111 Shrewsbury St	Worcester	MA	01604	508-799-4111	791-7224
Web: www.111chophouse.com					
Boynton Family Restaurant 117 Highland St	Worcester	MA	01609	508-756-8458	
Web: boyntonrestaurant.com					
Dalat Restaurant 425 Pk Ave	Worcester	MA	01610	508-753-6036	
Dino's 13 Lord St	Worcester	MA	01604	508-753-9978	753-5646
Web: www.dineatdinos.com					
El Basha 424 Belmont St	Worcester	MA	01604	508-797-0884	
Web: www.elbasharestaurant.com					
Flying Rhino Cafe 278 Shrewsbury St	Worcester	MA	01604	508-757-1450	754-8102
Web: flyingrhinocafe.com					
Leo's Ristorante 11 Leo Turo Wy	Worcester	MA	01604	508-753-9490	797-5123
Web: www.leosristorante.net					
Maxwell Silverman's Toolhouse Lincoln Sq	Worcester	MA	01608	508-755-1200	753-8217
Web: www.maxwellmaxine.com					
Nancy Chang 372 Chandler St	Worcester	MA	01602	508-752-8899	798-6688
Web: www.nancychang.com					
O'Connor's Restaurant & Bar 1160 W Boylston St	Worcester	MA	01606	508-853-0789	853-2879
Web: www.oconnorsrestaurant.com					
Sahara Restaurant 143 Highland St	Worcester	MA	01609	508-798-2181	798-9164
Web: eatsahara.com					
Sole Proprietor, The 118 Highland St	Worcester	MA	01609	508-798-3474	753-4889
Web: www.thesole.com					
Viva Bene 144 Commercial St	Worcester	MA	01608	508-799-9999	753-0434
Web: www.viva-bene.com					
Webster House Restaurant One Webster St	Worcester	MA	01603	508-757-7208	
Web: websterhouseweb.com					
Colonial House Inn 277 Main St Rt 6A	Yarmouth Port	MA	02675	508-362-4348	362-8034
TF: 800-999-3416 ■ *Web:* www.colonialhousecapecod.com/dine.html					
Inaho 157 Rt 6A	Yarmouth Port	MA	02675	508-362-5522	
Web: www.inahocapecod.com					

Michigan

				Phone	Fax
Amadeus 122 E Washington St	Ann Arbor	MI	48104	734-665-8767	
Web: www.amadeusrestaurant.com					
Arbor Brewing Co 114 E Washington St	Ann Arbor	MI	48104	734-213-1393	213-2835
Web: www.arborbrewing.com					
Argiero's 300 Detroit St	Ann Arbor	MI	48104	734-665-0444	665-2653
Web: argieros.net					
Blue Nile Ethiopian Restaurant - Ann Arbor, The 221 E Washington St	Ann Arbor	MI	48104	734-998-4746	
Web: www.bluenilemi.com					
Chia Shiang 2016 Packard St	Ann Arbor	MI	48104	734-741-0778	
Chop House Ann Arbor, The 322 S Main St	Ann Arbor	MI	48104	734-669-9977	669-7177
Web: thechophouseannarbor.com					
Earle, The 121 W Washington St	Ann Arbor	MI	48104	734-994-0211	994-3466
Web: www.theearle.com					
Gandy Dancer 401 Depot St	Ann Arbor	MI	48104	734-769-0592	769-0415
TF: 800-552-6379 ■ *Web:* www.muer.com					
Grizzly Peak Brewing Co 120 W Washington St	Ann Arbor	MI	48104	734-741-7325	
Web: www.grizzlypeak.net					
Knight's Steak House 2324 Dexter Ave	Ann Arbor	MI	48103	734-665-8644	665-7948
Web: www.knightsrestaurants.com					
Mediteranno Restaurant 2900 S State St	Ann Arbor	MI	48108	734-332-9700	
Web: mediterrano.com					
Metzger's German Restaurant 305 N Zeeb Rd	Ann Arbor	MI	48103	734-668-8987	668-9028
Web: www.metzgers.net					
Miki Japanese Restaurant 106 S First St	Ann Arbor	MI	48104	734-665-8226	
Prickly Pear Southwest Cafe 328 S Main St	Ann Arbor	MI	48104	734-930-0047	930-1561
Web: pricklypearcafe.com					
Raja Rani 400 S Div St	Ann Arbor	MI	48104	734-995-1545	995-5999
Web: rajaraniannarbor.com					
Sabor Latino 211 N Main St	Ann Arbor	MI	48104	734-214-7775	
Web: annarborsabor.com					
Shalimar 307 S Main St	Ann Arbor	MI	48104	734-663-1500	929-9129
Web: www.shalimarrestaurant.com					
Tuptim 4896 Washtenaw Ave	Ann Arbor	MI	48108	734-528-5588	528-2569
Web: www.tuptim.com					
Vinology 110 S Main St	Ann Arbor	MI	48104	734-222-9841	
Web: vinologya2.com					
West End Grill, The 120 W Liberty Ave	Ann Arbor	MI	48104	734-747-6260	
Web: westendgrillannarbor.com					
Zingerman's Roadhouse 2501 Jackson Rd	Ann Arbor	MI	48103	734-663-3663	
Web: www.zingermansroadhouse.com					
Andiamo 400 Renaissance Ctr Ste A403	Detroit	MI	48243	313-567-6700	567-6701
Web: www.andiamoitalia.com					
Armando's Mexican Restaurant 4242 W Vernor Hwy	Detroit	MI	48209	313-554-0666	554-0667
Web: www.mexicantown.com					
Atlas Global Bistro 3111 Woodward Ave	Detroit	MI	48201	313-831-2241	831-4023
Web: www.atlasglobalbistro.com					
Atwater Brewing Co 237 Joseph Campau Ave	Detroit	MI	48207	313-877-9205	877-9206
Web: atwaterbeer.com					
Cuisine 670 Lothrop Rd	Detroit	MI	48202	313-872-5110	
Web: www.cuisinerestaurant.com					
DaEdoardo Foxtown Grille 2203 Woodward Ave	Detroit	MI	48201	313-471-3500	471-3499
Web: www.daedoardo.com					
El Zocalo Mexican Restaurant 3400 Bagley St	Detroit	MI	48216	313-841-3700	
Web: elzocalodetroit.net					
Giovanni's Ristorante 330 S Oakwood Blvd	Detroit	MI	48217	313-841-0122	841-3947
Web: www.giovannisristorante.com					
Hockeytown Cafe 2301 Woodward Ave	Detroit	MI	48201	313-471-3400	471-3466
Web: hockeytowncafe.com					
Iridescence 2901 Grand River Ave	Detroit	MI	48201	313-237-6732	961-0966
Web: www.motorcitycasino.com					
Louisiana Creole Gumbo Restaurant 2051 Gratiot Ave	Detroit	MI	48207	313-567-1200	
Web: www.detroitgumbo.com					

Phone Fax

Mario's 4222 Second Ave Detroit MI 48201 313-832-1616 832-1460
Web: www.mariosdetroit.com
Opus One 565 E Larned St Detroit MI 48226 313-961-7766 961-9243
Web: www.opus-one.com
Pegasus Taverna 558 Monroe St Detroit MI 48226 313-964-6800 964-0869
Web: pegasusdetroit.com
Roma Cafe 3401 Riopelle St Detroit MI 48207 313-831-5940 831-2253
Web: www.romacafe.com
Small Plates 1521 Broadway St Detroit MI 48226 313-963-0702 963-0702
Web: www.smallplates.com
Taqueria Mi Pueblo Mexican Restaurant
7278 Dix St Detroit MI 48209 313-841-3315
Web: www.mipueblorestaurant.com
Union Street 4145 Woodward Ave Detroit MI 48201 313-831-3965 831-2553
Web: www.unionstreetdetroit.com
Vincente's Cuban Cuisine 1250 Library St Detroit MI 48226 313-962-8800 962-0898
Web: www.vicente.us
Whitney, The 4421 Woodward Ave Detroit MI 48201 313-832-5700 832-2159
Web: www.thewhitney.com
Xochimilco Restaurant 3409 Bagley St Detroit MI 48216 313-843-0179
Beggar's Banquet 218 Abbott Rd East Lansing MI 48823 517-351-4540 351-3585
Web: www.beggarsbanquet.com
English Inn, The 677 S Michigan Rd Eaton Rapids MI 48827 517-663-2500 663-2643
TF: 800-858-0598 ■ *Web:* www.englishinn.com
Blue Nile 545 W Nine-Mile Rd Ferndale MI 48220 248-547-6699 547-3165
Web: www.bluenilemi.com
Badawest Restaurant 4018 Corruna Rd Flint MI 48532 810-232-2479 232-3326
Churchill's Food & Spirits 340 S Saginaw St Flint MI 48502 810-238-3800
Web: churchillsflint.com
Golden Moon 4527 Miller Rd Flint MI 48507 810-733-7030
Web: goldenmoonflint.com
Latina Restaurant & Pizzeria 1370 W Bristol Rd Flint MI 48507 810-767-8491
Web: latinarestaurant.com
Redwood Steakhouse 5304 Gateway Ctr Dr Flint MI 48507 810-233-8000 233-8833
Web: theredwoodlodge.com
Roma Pizzeria Flint G5227 N Saginaw St Flint MI 48505 810-787-1061 787-6788
Web: www.romaspizza.com
Salvatore Scallopini Restaurant 3227 Miller Rd Flint MI 48503 810-732-1070 732-1538
Web: www.salvatorescallopini.com
Beltline Bar 16 28th St SE Grand Rapids MI 49548 616-245-0494 245-3955
Web: beltlinebar.com
Bistro Bella Vita 44 Grandville Ave SW Grand Rapids MI 49503 616-222-4600 222-4601
Web: www.bistrobellavita.com
Bombay Cuisine 1420 Lake Dr Grand Rapids MI 49506 616-456-7055
Brann's Steakhouse & Grille
401 Leonard St NW Grand Rapids MI 49504 616-454-9368 454-7702
Web: www.branns.com
Charley's Crab Restaurant
63 Market St SW Grand Rapids MI 49503 616-459-2500 459-8142
Web: www.muer.com
China Chef 4335 Lake Michigan Dr NW Grand Rapids MI 49534 616-791-4488
Web: chinachef49534.com
DoubleTree by Hilton Grand Rapids Airport Hotel
4747 28th St SE Grand Rapids MI 49512 616-957-0100 977-5632
Web: www.hiltongrandrapids.com
Maggie's Kitchen 636 Bridge St NW Grand Rapids MI 49504 616-458-8583
Mikado 3971 28th St SE Grand Rapids MI 49512 616-285-7666 977-0509
Web: mikadogr.com
Noto's Old World Italian
6600 28th St SE Grand Rapids MI 49546 616-493-6686 493-6682
Web: www.notosoldworld.com
One Trick Pony 136 E Fulton St Grand Rapids MI 49503 616-235-7669
Web: www.onetrick.biz
San Chez 38 Fulton St W Grand Rapids MI 49503 616-774-8272 774-9954
Web: www.sanchezbistro.com
Seoul Garden Restaurant 3321 28th St Grand Rapids MI 49512 616-956-1522 956-1801
Starbucks Corporation 187 Monroe Ave NW Grand Rapids MI 49503 616-774-2000 776-6489
Web: starbucks.com
Tillman's 1245 Monroe Ave NW Grand Rapids MI 49505 616-451-9266 451-2227
Web: tillmansrestaurant.com
Tre Cugini 122 Monroe Ctr NW Grand Rapids MI 49503 616-235-9339 235-9449
Web: trecugini.com
XO Asian Cuisine 58 Monroe Ctr Grand Rapids MI 49503 616-235-6969 235-2801
Web: www.xoasiancuisine.com/
Z's Bar & Restaurant 168 Louis Campau Grand Rapids MI 49503 616-454-3141
Web: www.zsbar.com
Tokyo Grill & Sushi Restaurant
4478 Breton Rd SE Kentwood MI 49508 616-455-3433 455-0385
Web: tokyogrillsushi.com
Christie's Bistro 925 S Creyts Rd Lansing MI 48917 517-323-4190 323-2180
Web: www.ihg.com
Clara's 637 E Michigan Ave Lansing MI 48912 517-372-7120 372-0157
Web: www.claras.com
Deluca's Restaurant 2006 W Willow St Lansing MI 48917 517-487-6087 487-3633
Web: www.delucaspizza.com
Emil's 2012 E Michigan Ave Lansing MI 48912 517-482-4430 482-9390
House of Ing 4113 S Cedar St Lansing MI 48910 517-393-4848 393-6868
Web: www.houseofing.com
Knight Cap, The 320 E Michigan Ave Lansing MI 48933 517-484-7676
Web: www.theknightcap.com
La Senorita 2706 Lk Lansing Rd Lansing MI 48912 517-485-0166 485-8350
Web: www.lasenorita.com
Piazzano's Restaurant 1825 N Grand River Ave Lansing MI 48906 517-484-0150
Web: www.piazzanos.com
Apple Jade
300 N Clippert St Lansing Charter Township MI 48912 517-332-1111
Gracie's Place 151 S Putnam St Williamston MI 48895 517-655-1100
Web: www.graciesplacewilliamston.com
Bangkok View 1233 28th St SW Wyoming MI 49509 616-531-8070

Minnesota

Phone Fax

Lindey's Prime Steak House
3600 N Snelling Ave Arden Hills MN 55112 651-633-9813
TF: 866-491-0538 ■ *Web:* www.theplaceforsteak.com
Timber Lodge Steakhouse
7989 Southtown Dr Bloomington MN 55431 952-881-5509 949-1205*
**Fax Area Code:* 970 ■ *Web:* www.timberlodgesteakhouse.com
Angie's Cantina 11 E Buchanan St Duluth MN 55802 218-727-6117 727-8235
TF: 800-706-7672 ■ *Web:* www.grandmasrestaurants.com/littleangies
Beijing Restaurant 1219 E Superior St Duluth MN 55802 218-724-2578
Web: beijingrestaurant.org
Bellisio's Italian Restaurant & Wine Bar
405 Lake Ave S Duluth MN 55802 218-727-4921
Web: www.grandmasrestaurants.com
Chinese Dragon 108 E Superior St Duluth MN 55802 218-723-4036
Fitger's Brewery Complex 600 E Superior St Duluth MN 55802 218-722-8826 722-8826
TF: 888-348-4377 ■ *Web:* www.fitgers.com
Grandma's Saloon & Grill 522 Lake Ave S Duluth MN 55802 218-727-4192 723-1986
TF: 800-706-7672 ■ *Web:* www.grandmasrestaurants.com/gmas_cp.htm
Grandma's Sports Garden Bar & Grill
425 Lake Ave S Duluth MN 55802 218-722-4724 720-3804
Web: www.grandmasrestaurants.com/sportsgarden/family.htm
Jade Fountain 305 N Central Ave Duluth MN 55807 218-624-4212
Web: jadefountainduluth.com
Lake Avenue Cafe 394 S Lake Ave Ste 107A Duluth MN 55802 218-722-2355
Web: www.lakeavenuecafe.com
New Scenic Cafe 5461 N Shore Dr Duluth MN 55804 218-525-6274 525-0737
Web: www.sceniccafe.com
Old Chicago 327 Lake Ave S Duluth MN 55802 218-720-2966 720-2930
Web: www.oldchicago.com
Porter's 200 W First St Duluth MN 55802 218-727-6746 722-0233
Web: hiduluth.com
Sir Benedict's Tavern 805 E Superior St Duluth MN 55802 218-728-1192 728-9878
Web: www.sirbens.com
Sneakers Sports Bar & Grill 207 W Superior St Duluth MN 55802 218-727-7494
4 Bells Restaurant 1610 Harmon Pl Minneapolis MN 55403 612-904-1163
Web: www.joes-garage.com
Alma 528 University Ave SE Minneapolis MN 55414 612-379-4909
Web: www.restaurantalma.com
Black Forest Inn 1 E 26th St Minneapolis MN 55404 612-872-0812 872-0423
Web: www.blackforestinnmpls.com
Brit's Pub & Eating Establishment
1110 Nicollet Mall Minneapolis MN 55403 612-332-3908 332-8032
Web: www.britspub.com
Broders Southside Pasta Bar
5000 Penn Ave S Minneapolis MN 55419 612-925-9202
Web: www.broders.com
Cafe Barbette 1600 W Lake St Minneapolis MN 55408 612-827-5710 822-6305
Web: www.barbette.com
Cafe Lurcat 1624 Harmon Pl Minneapolis MN 55403 612-486-5500
Web: www.cafelurcat.com
Cafe Twenty-Eight 2724 W 43rd St Minneapolis MN 55410 612-926-2800 926-2804
Cave Vin 5555 Xerxes Ave S Minneapolis MN 55410 612-922-0100
Web: cave-vin.net
Christo's 2632 Nicollet Ave Minneapolis MN 55408 612-871-2111 871-8129
Web: www.christos.com
Dakota Jazz Club & Restaurant
1010 Nicollet Ave Minneapolis MN 55403 612-332-1010 332-7070
Web: www.dakotacooks.com
Erte Restaurant 323 13th Ave NE Minneapolis MN 55413 612-623-4211
Web: www.ertedining.com
Famous Dave's Bar-B-Que
3001 Hennepin Ave Minneapolis MN 55408 612-822-9900
Web: www.famousdaves.com
Gardens of Salonica 19 NE Fifth St Minneapolis MN 55413 612-378-0611
Web: gardensofsalonica.com
La Belle Vie 510 Groveland Ave Minneapolis MN 55403 612-874-6440
Web: www.labellevie.us
Local, The 931 Nicollet Mall Minneapolis MN 55402 612-904-1000 904-1005
Web: www.the-local.com
Lucia's 1432 W 31st St Minneapolis MN 55408 612-825-1572 824-4553
Web: www.lucias.com
Mandarin Kitchen 8766 Lyndale Ave S Minneapolis MN 55420 952-884-5356
Manny's Steak House 825 Marquette Ave Minneapolis MN 55403 612-339-9900 341-2373
Web: www.mannyssteakhouse.com
Melting Pot, The 80 S Ninth St Minneapolis MN 55402 612-338-9900 312-2855
Web: www.meltingpot.com
Mission American Kitchen 77 S Seventh St Minneapolis MN 55402 612-339-1000 339-8700
Web: www.missionamerican.com
Modern Cafe 337 13th Ave NE Minneapolis MN 55413 612-378-9882
Web: moderncafeminneapolis.com
Murray's 26 S Sixth St Minneapolis MN 55402 612-339-0909
Web: www.murraysrestaurant.com
Nami 251 N First Ave Ste 100 Minneapolis MN 55401 612-333-1999
Web: namiminneapolis.com
Nicollet Island Inn 95 Merriam St Minneapolis MN 55401 612-331-1800 331-6528
Web: www.nicolletislandinn.com
Prima 5325 Lyndale Ave S Minneapolis MN 55419 612-827-7376 827-7534
Web: primampls.com
Quang 2719 Nicollet Ave Minneapolis MN 55408 612-870-4739 879-4739
Web: www.quangrestaurant.com
Rainbow Chinese 2739 Nicollet Ave S Minneapolis MN 55408 612-870-7084 872-6204
Web: www.rainbowrestaurant.com
Rock Bottom Brewery 800 LaSalle Plz Minneapolis MN 55402 612-332-2739 332-1508
Web: rockbottom.com
Salsa a la Salsa 1420 Nicollet Ave Minneapolis MN 55403 612-813-1970 813-1972
Web: www.salsaalasalsa.com
Sapor Cafe & Bar 428 Washington Ave N Minneapolis MN 55401 612-375-1971
Web: www.saporcafe.com

Restaurant	City	State	ZIP	Phone	Fax
Sawatdee 607 Washington Ave S *Web:* www.sawatdee.com	Minneapolis	MN	55415	612-338-6451	338-6498
Zelo 831 Nicollet Mall *Web:* zelomn.com	Minneapolis	MN	55402	612-333-7000	333-7707
Speak Easy 1001 30th Ave S *Web:* speakeasyrestaurant.com	Moorhead	MN	56560	218-233-1326	233-6012
Khan's Mongolian Barbecue 500 E 78th St *Web:* www.khansmongolianbarbecue.com	Richfield	MN	55423	612-861-7991	
Canadian Honker 1203 Second St SW *Web:* canadianhonker.com	Rochester	MN	55902	507-282-6572	
Fiesta Cafe Bar 1645 N Broadway *Web:* fiestacafeandbar.com	Rochester	MN	55906	507-288-1116	
Jenpachi Japanese Steak House 3160 Wellner NE *Web:* jenpachisteakhouse.com	Rochester	MN	55906	507-292-1688	
Redwood Room 300 First Ave NW	Rochester	MN	55901	507-281-2978	
Roscoe's Root Beer & Ribs 603 Fourth St SE *Web:* roscoesbbq.com	Rochester	MN	55904	507-285-0501	
Sky Dragon Buffet 34 17th Ave NW	Rochester	MN	55901	507-281-1813	
Victoria's Seven First Ave NW *Web:* www.victoriasmn.com	Rochester	MN	55902	507-280-6232	280-6288
128 Cafe 128 Cleveland Ave N *Web:* the128cafe.com	Saint Paul	MN	55104	651-645-4128	
Beirut Restaurant 1385 Robert St S *Web:* www.beirutrestaurantanddeli.com	Saint Paul	MN	55118	651-457-4886	
El Burrito Mercado 175 Cesar Chavez St Ste 2 *Web:* www.elburritomercado.com	Saint Paul	MN	55107	651-227-2192	227-2411
Everest on Grand 1278 Grand Ave *Web:* www.everestongrand.com	Saint Paul	MN	55105	651-696-1666	
Forepaugh's 276 S Exchange St *Web:* www.forepaughs.com	Saint Paul	MN	55102	651-224-5606	
Fuji-Ya 465 N Wabasha St *Web:* www.fujiyasushi.com	Saint Paul	MN	55102	651-310-0111	
Green Mill Restaurant & Bar 1342 Grand Ave *Web:* www.greenmill.com	Saint Paul	MN	55105	651-203-3100	203-3101
Heartland 289 E Fifth St *Web:* www.heartlandrestaurant.com	Saint Paul	MN	55101	651-699-3536	
Lexington, The 1096 Grand Ave *Web:* www.snapagency.com	Saint Paul	MN	55105	651-222-5878	
Luci Ancora 2060 Randolph Ave *Web:* luciancora.com	Saint Paul	MN	55105	651-698-6889	698-6696
Mai Village 394 University Ave *Web:* maivillage.net	Saint Paul	MN	55103	651-290-2585	
Mancini's Char House 531 Seventh St W *Web:* www.mancinis.com	Saint Paul	MN	55102	651-224-7345	224-9367
Moscow on the Hill 371 Selby Ave *Web:* www.moscowonthehill.com	Saint Paul	MN	55102	651-291-1236	
Muffuletta Cafe 2260 Como Ave *Web:* www.muffuletta.com	Saint Paul	MN	55108	651-644-9116	644-5329
Pad Thai Restaurant 1681 Grand Ave *Web:* padthaiongrand.com	Saint Paul	MN	55105	651-690-1393	
Pazzaluna 360 St Peter St *Web:* pazzaluna.com	Saint Paul	MN	55102	651-223-7000	227-1296
Peking Garden 1488 University Ave *Web:* www.pekinggardenmn.com	Saint Paul	MN	55104	651-644-0888	644-1738
Saji-Ya 695 Grand Ave *Web:* www.sajiya.com	Saint Paul	MN	55105	651-292-0444	225-4881
Sakura Japanese Restaurant 350 St Peter St *Web:* www.sakurastpaul.com	Saint Paul	MN	55102	651-224-0185	225-9350
St Paul Grill, The 350 Market St *Web:* www.stpaulgrill.com	Saint Paul	MN	55102	651-224-7455	
Tavern on Grand 656 Grand Ave *Web:* www.tavernongrand.com	Saint Paul	MN	55105	651-228-9030	229-0090
Trattoria da Vinci 400 Sibley St *Web:* www.trattoriadavinci.com	Saint Paul	MN	55101	651-222-4050	224-4545
Wild Onion 788 Grand Ave *Web:* www.wild-onion.net	Saint Paul	MN	55105	651-291-2525	

Mississippi

Restaurant	City	State	ZIP	Phone	Fax
Jazzeppi's 195 B Porter Ave	Biloxi	MS	39530	228-374-9660	374-9692
Mary Mahoney's 110 Rue Magnolia *Web:* www.marymahoneys.com	Biloxi	MS	39530	228-374-0163	432-1387
Mr Greek 1670 H Pass Rd *Web:* mrgreekbiloxi.com	Biloxi	MS	39531	228-432-7888	432-8379
Blow Fly Inn 1201 Washington Ave *Web:* blow-fly-inn.com	Gulfport	MS	39507	228-896-9812	
El Mexicano Inn 1215 30th Ave	Gulfport	MS	39501	228-863-3691	
Lil Ray's 500A Courthouse Rd *Web:* lilraysrestaurant.com	Gulfport	MS	39507	228-896-9601	
South China 548 Courthouse Rd	Gulfport	MS	39507	228-896-9832	
Bianchis Pizzeria 128 E Front St *Web:* www.bianchispizzeria.com	Hattiesburg	MS	39401	601-450-1263	
Cuco's Mexican Cafe 6104 Hwy 49 S *Web:* cucos-mexican-restaurant-hattiesburg.com	Hattiesburg	MS	39401	601-545-8241	
Donanelle's Bar & Grill 4321 U S Hwy 49 *Web:* www.donanelles.com	Hattiesburg	MS	39401	601-545-3860	
Front Porch Barbecue & Seafood 205 Thornhill Dr	Hattiesburg	MS	39401	601-264-3536	
La Fiesta Brava 6168 Hwy 49 N	Hattiesburg	MS	39401	601-584-9484	
Leatha's Bar-B-Que Inn 6374 US Hwy 98	Hattiesburg	MS	39402	601-271-6003	
Purple Parrot Cafe 3810 Hardy St *Web:* www.nsrg.com	Hattiesburg	MS	39402	601-264-0657	264-0681
Rayner's Seafood House 7343 Hwy 49	Hattiesburg	MS	39401	601-268-2639	
Walnut Cir Grill 115 Walnut St *Web:* www.walnutcirclegrill.com	Hattiesburg	MS	39401	601-544-2202	
Bonsai Japanese Steak House 1925 Lakeland Dr *Web:* facebook.com	Jackson	MS	39216	601-981-0606	
Bravo I-55 N Exit 100 *Web:* www.bravobuzz.com	Jackson	MS	39211	601-982-8111	362-2990
Elite Restaurant 141 E Capitol St	Jackson	MS	39201	601-352-5606	
Hal & Mal's 200 S Commerce St *Web:* www.halandmals.com	Jackson	MS	39204	601-948-0888	
Keifer's 710 Poplar Blvd	Jackson	MS	39202	601-355-6825	355-0380
La Cazuela Mexican Grill 1401 E Ftification St *Web:* lacazuela.com	Jackson	MS	39202	601-353-3014	
Que Sera Sera 2801 N State St *Web:* queserams.com	Jackson	MS	39216	601-981-2520	981-2522
Sakura Bana 4800 I-55 N LeFleur's Gallery	Jackson	MS	39211	601-982-3035	982-3075
Thai House Restaurant 1405 Old Sq Rd	Jackson	MS	39211	601-982-9991	
Cancun Mexican Restaurant 201 N Gloster St *Web:* cancunmexicantupelo.com	Tupelo	MS	38804	662-842-9557	
China Capital 530 N Gloster St	Tupelo	MS	38804	662-841-0484	
Harvey's 424 S Gloster St *TF:* 888-222-9550 ■ *Web:* www.eatwithus.com	Tupelo	MS	38801	662-842-6763	327-1672
Las Margaritas 123 S Industrial Rd	Tupelo	MS	38801	662-844-7399	
Tellini's 504 S Gloster St *Web:* www.tellinis.com	Tupelo	MS	38801	662-620-9955	
Vanelli's 1302 N Gloster St *Web:* vanellis.com	Tupelo	MS	38804	662-844-4410	
Woody's 619 N Gloster St *Web:* woodyssteak.com	Tupelo	MS	38804	662-840-0460	

Missouri

Restaurant	City	State	ZIP	Phone	Fax
Baldknobbers Restaurant 2845 W 76 Country Blvd *Web:* www.baldknobbers.com	Branson	MO	65616	417-334-7202	339-3505
Branson Cafe 120 W Main St *Web:* downtownbransoncafe.com	Branson	MO	65616	417-334-3021	
BT Bones 2280 Shepherd Hill Expy	Branson	MO	65616	417-335-2002	335-2109
Buckingham's Restaurant & Oasis 2820 W Hwy 76 *Web:* clarionhotelbranson.com	Branson	MO	65616	417-337-7777	337-5335
Casa Fuentes 1107 W Hwy 76 *Web:* www.casafuentes.com	Branson	MO	65616	417-339-3888	
Charlie's Steak-Ribs-Ale 3009 W State Hwy 76	Branson	MO	65616	417-334-6090	336-4038
Chateau Grille 415 N State Hwy 265 *TF:* 888-333-5253 ■ *Web:* www.chateauonthelake.com	Branson	MO	65616	417-334-1161	339-5566
Farmhouse Restaurant 119 W Main St *Web:* farmhouserestaurantbranson.com	Branson	MO	65616	417-334-9701	
Landry's Seafood House 2900 W Missouri Hwy 76 *Web:* www.landrysseafood.com	Branson	MO	65616	417-339-1010	339-3801
Plaza View 245 N Wildwood Dr *Web:* bransongrandplaza.com	Branson	MO	65616	417-335-2798	
Rocky's Italian Restaurant 120 N Sycamore St	Branson	MO	65616	417-335-4765	
Whipper Snapper's 2421 W Hwy 76 *Web:* www.bransonsbestrestaurant.com	Branson	MO	65616	417-334-3282	
Spiro's 1054 N Woods Mill Rd *Web:* www.spiros-restaurant.com	Chesterfield	MO	63017	314-878-4449	878-1090
Cardwell's 8100 Maryland Ave *Web:* www.cardwellsinclayton.com	Clayton	MO	63105	314-726-5055	
63 Diner, The 5801 Hwy 763 N *Web:* www.63dinercolumbia.com	Columbia	MO	65202	573-815-0017	
Addison's An American Grill 709 Cherry St *Web:* www.addisonsgrill.com/	Columbia	MO	65201	573-256-1995	256-2836
Bangkok Gardens 811 Cherry St *Web:* bangkokgardens.com	Columbia	MO	65201	573-874-3284	
CJ's in Tiger Country 704 E Broadway *Web:* www.cjsintigercountry.com	Columbia	MO	65201	573-442-7777	
Ernie's Cafe 1005 E Walnut St *Web:* erniescolumbia.com	Columbia	MO	65201	573-874-7804	
Flat Branch Pub & Brewing Co 115 S Fifth St *Web:* www.flatbranch.com	Columbia	MO	65201	573-499-0400	
Formosa Restaurant 913 E Broadway Ste A *Web:* www.formosatogo.com	Columbia	MO	65201	573-449-3339	
Italian Village Pizza 711 Vandiver Dr Ste B *Web:* theitalianvillagepizza.com	Columbia	MO	65202	573-442-8821	442-3571
Jack's Gourmet Restaurant 1903 Business Loop 70 E *Web:* www.jacksgourmetrestaurant.com	Columbia	MO	65201	573-449-3927	442-9881
Jimmy's Family Steak House 3101 S Providence Rd	Columbia	MO	65203	573-443-1796	
Murry's 3107 Green Meadows Way *Web:* murrysrestaurant.net	Columbia	MO	65203	573-442-4969	
Wine Cellar & Bistro 505 Cherry St *Web:* www.winecellarbistro.com	Columbia	MO	65201	573-442-7281	441-8318
54th Street Grill 18700 E 38th Terr *Web:* www.54thstreetgrill.com	Independence	MO	64057	816-795-7077	
El Maguey 3738 S Noland Rd	Independence	MO	64055	816-252-6868	
Englewood Cafe 10904 E Winner Rd	Independence	MO	64052	816-461-9588	
Rheinland Restaurant 208 N Main St *Web:* www.rheinlandrestaurant.com	Independence	MO	64050	816-461-5383	
V's Italiano Ristorante 10819 E US Hwy 40 *Web:* www.vsrestaurant.com	Independence	MO	64055	816-353-1241	353-0004
Zio's Italian Kitchen 3901 S Bolger Dr *Web:* www.zios.com	Independence	MO	64055	816-350-1011	350-1211
Alexandro's 2125 Missouri Blvd *Web:* alexandrosandtgs.com	Jefferson City	MO	65109	573-634-7740	
Cajun Catfish House 6819 Hwy 50 W *Web:* cajuncatfishhouse.com	Jefferson City	MO	65109	573-893-4665	
Capitol Plaza Hotel 415 W McCarty St *TF:* 800-338-8088 ■ *Web:* capitolplazajeffersoncity.com	Jefferson City	MO	65101	573-635-1234	635-4565

Name / Address	City	State	Zip	Phone	Fax
Das Stein Haus 1436 Southridge Dr *Web:* www.dasseinhaus.com	Jefferson City	MO	65109	573-634-3869	
Hunan Restaurant 1416 Missouri Blvd *Web:* hunan-restaurant.com	Jefferson City	MO	65109	573-634-5253	
Madison's Cafe 216 Madison St *Web:* www.madisonscafe.com	Jefferson City	MO	65101	573-634-2988	634-3740
Yen Ching Restaurant 2208 Missouri Blvd	Jefferson City	MO	65109	573-635-5225	
Arthur Bryant's Barbeque 1727 Brooklyn Ave *Web:* arthurbryantsbbq.com	Kansas City	MO	64127	816-231-1123	
Blue Bird Bistro 1700 Summit St *Web:* bluebirdbistro.com	Kansas City	MO	64108	816-221-7559	221-7901
Bluestem 900 Westport Rd *Web:* kansascitymenus.com/goodbye.html	Kansas City	MO	64111	816-561-1101	561-5726
Bo Ling's 4800 Main St *Web:* www.bolings.com	Kansas City	MO	64112	816-753-1718	753-8819
Cafe Al Dente 412D Delaware *Web:* cafealdentekc.com	Kansas City	MO	64105	816-472-9444	
Californos 4124 Pennsylvania Ave *Web:* www.californos.com	Kansas City	MO	64111	816-531-7878	531-1894
Cascone's 3737 N Oak Trafficway *Web:* www.cascones.com	Kansas City	MO	64116	816-454-7977	
Cupini's Fresh Pasta & Panini 1809 Westport Rd *Web:* www.cupinis.com	Kansas City	MO	64111	816-753-7662	753-7564
EBT Restaurant 1310 Carondelet Dr *Web:* www.ebtrestaurant.com	Kansas City	MO	64114	816-942-8870	941-8532
Europa! 323 E 55th St *Web:* cafeeuropakc.com	Kansas City	MO	64113	816-523-1212	
Fiorella's Jack Stack Barbecue 13441 Holmes Rd *Web:* www.jackstackbbq.com	Kansas City	MO	64145	816-942-9141	941-8762
Garozzo's 526 Harrison St *Web:* www.garozzos.com	Kansas City	MO	64106	816-221-2455	221-7174
Grand Street Cafe 4740 Grand Ave *Web:* www.grandstreetcafe.com	Kansas City	MO	64112	816-561-8000	
Grinders 417 E 18th St *Web:* grinderspizza.com	Kansas City	MO	64108	816-472-5454	
Houston's 4640 Wornall Rd *Web:* hillstone.com	Kansas City	MO	64112	816-561-8542	561-0423
Jasper's 1201 W 103rd St *Web:* www.jasperskc.com	Kansas City	MO	64114	816-941-6600	941-4121
Jess & Jim's Steakhouse 517 E 135th St *Web:* www.jessandjims.com	Kansas City	MO	64145	816-941-9499	942-6348
KatoSushi 6340 NW Barry Rd *Web:* www.katosushi.com	Kansas City	MO	64154	816-584-8883	
La Bodega 703 SW Blvd *Web:* labodegakc.com	Kansas City	MO	64108	816-472-8272	
Le Fou Frog 400 E Fifth St *Web:* www.lefoufrog.com	Kansas City	MO	64106	816-474-6060	
Lidia's Kansas City 101 W 22nd St *Web:* www.lidias-kc.com	Kansas City	MO	64108	816-221-3722	842-1960
Majestic Steakhouse 931 Broadway *Web:* www.majestickc.com	Kansas City	MO	64105	816-221-1888	
Malay Cafe 6003 NW Barry Rd *Web:* friendsofmalaysia.org	Kansas City	MO	64154	816-741-3616	
New Peking 540 Westport Rd *Web:* newpekingkansas.com	Kansas City	MO	64111	816-531-6969	531-9188
Osteria Il Centro 5101 Main St *Web:* osteriailcentro.com	Kansas City	MO	64111	816-561-2369	
Peach Tree 6800 Eastwood TFWY *Web:* www.peachtreerestaurants.com	Kansas City	MO	64129	816-923-0099	923-3844
Pierpont's at Union Station 30 W Pershing Rd Union Station *Web:* www.herefordhouse.com	Kansas City	MO	64108	816-221-5111	
PotPie 904 Westport Rd *Web:* www.kcpotpie.com	Kansas City	MO	64111	816-561-2702	
Red Snapper 8430 Ward Pkwy *Web:* www.kcredsnapper.com	Kansas City	MO	64114	816-333-8899	333-8893
Smokin' Guns BBQ 1218 Swift Ave *Web:* www.smokingunsbbq.com	Kansas City	MO	64116	816-221-2535	221-2606
Streetcar Named Desire 2450 Grand Ave *Web:* streetcar.bizhosting.com	Kansas City	MO	64108	816-472-5959	
Thai Place 4130 Pennsylvania Ave *Web:* www.kcthaiplace.com	Kansas City	MO	64111	816-753-8424	753-5595
Thomas Restaurant 1815 W 39th St *Web:* www.thomaskc.com	Kansas City	MO	64111	816-561-3663	
Blue Owl Restaurant, The 6116 Second St *Web:* www.theblueowl.com	Kimmswick	MO	63053	636-464-3128	464-8108
Chappell's Restaurant & Sports Museum 323 Armour Rd *Web:* chappellsrestaurant.com	North Kansas City	MO	64116	816-421-0002	472-7141
Al's Restaurant 1200 N First St *Web:* www.alsrestaurant.net	Saint Louis	MO	63102	314-421-6399	421-0357
Bandana's Bar-B-Q 11750 Gravois Rd *Web:* www.bandanasbbq.com	Saint Louis	MO	63127	314-849-1162	729-1126
Bar Italian Ristorante-Caffe 13 Maryland Plz *Web:* www.baritaliastl.com	Saint Louis	MO	63108	314-361-7010	361-6131
Broadway Oyster Bar 736 S Broadway *Web:* www.broadwayoysterbar.com	Saint Louis	MO	63102	314-621-8811	621-1995
Carmine's Steak House 20 S Fourth St *Web:* www.lombardosrestaurants.com	Saint Louis	MO	63102	314-241-1631	
Clark Street Grill 811 Spruce St *Web:* www.clarkstreetgrill.com	Saint Louis	MO	63102	314-552-5850	
Cunetto House of Pasta 5453 Magnolia Ave *Web:* www.cunetto.com	Saint Louis	MO	63139	314-781-1135	781-5674
Giuseppe's 4141 S Grand Blvd *Web:* www.giuseppesongrand.com	Saint Louis	MO	63118	314-832-3779	832-7598
Harry's Restaurant & Bar 2144 Market St *Web:* www.harrysrestaurantandbar.com	Saint Louis	MO	63103	314-421-6969	241-2755
House of India 8501 Delmar Blvd *Web:* www.hoistl.com	Saint Louis	MO	63124	314-567-6850	567-5282
I Love Mr Sushi 9443 Olive Blvd *Web:* mrsushistl.com	Saint Louis	MO	63132	314-432-8898	
Kemoll's 211 N Broadway *Web:* www.kemolls.com	Saint Louis	MO	63102	314-421-0555	436-9692
Kreis' Restaurant 535 S Lindbergh Blvd *Web:* www.kreisrestaurant.com	Saint Louis	MO	63131	314-993-0735	993-3020
Lorenzo's Trattoria 1933 Edwards St *Web:* www.lorenzostrattoria.com	Saint Louis	MO	63110	314-773-2223	773-0689
LoRusso's Cucina 3121 Watson Rd *Web:* www.lorussos.com	Saint Louis	MO	63139	314-647-6222	647-2821
Mike Shannon's 620 Market St *Web:* www.shannonsteak.com	Saint Louis	MO	63101	314-421-1540	241-5642
Modesto 5257 Shaw Ave *Web:* www.saucecafe.com/modesto	Saint Louis	MO	63110	314-772-8272	
Nobu's 8643 Olive Blvd *Web:* www.nobusushistl.com	Saint Louis	MO	63132	314-997-2303	
Pho Grand 3195 S Grand Blvd *Web:* www.phogrand.com	Saint Louis	MO	63118	314-664-7435	
Sam's Steakhouse 10205 Gravois Rd *Web:* www.samssteakhouse.com	Saint Louis	MO	63123	314-849-3033	
Sidney Street Cafe 2000 Sidney St *Web:* www.sidneystreetcafe.com	Saint Louis	MO	63104	314-771-5777	771-7016
Soulard's Restaurant 1731 S Seventh St *Web:* www.soulards.com	Saint Louis	MO	63104	314-241-7956	241-7956
SqWire's 1415 S 18th St *Web:* www.sqwires.com	Saint Louis	MO	63104	314-865-3522	865-3524
Tenderloin Room 232 N KingsHwy Blvd *Web:* www.tenderloinroom.com	Saint Louis	MO	63108	314-361-0900	
Top of the Riverfront 200 S Fourth St 28th Fl *Web:* www.millenniumhotels.com	Saint Louis	MO	63102	314-241-3191	
Trattoria Marcella 3600 Watson Rd *Web:* trattoriamarcella.com	Saint Louis	MO	63109	314-352-7706	352-0848
Tucker's Place *Historic Soulard* 2117 S 12th St *Web:* www.tuckersplacestl.com	Saint Louis	MO	63104	314-772-5977	
Vin de Set Rooftop Bar & Bistro 2017 Chouteau Ave *Web:* www.1111-m.com	Saint Louis	MO	63103	314-241-8989	621-5550
Yemanja Brasil 2900 Missouri Ave Pestalozzi St *Web:* www.yemanjabrasil.com	Saint Louis	MO	63118	314-771-7457	771-0296
Zia's 5256 Wilson Ave *Web:* www.zias.com	Saint Louis	MO	63110	314-776-0020	776-5778
Dominic's 5101 Wilson Ave *Web:* www.dominicsrestaurant.com	South Saint Louis	MO	63110	314-771-1632	771-1695
Bangkok City 1129 E Walnut St *Web:* wordpress.com	Springfield	MO	65806	417-799-1221	
Buckingham's BBQ 2002 S Campbell Ave *Web:* buckinghambbq.com	Springfield	MO	65807	417-886-9979	
Cielito Lindo Mexicano 2953 S National Ave	Springfield	MO	65804	417-886-3320	
Gem of India 211 W Battlefield St *Web:* gemofindia.net	Springfield	MO	65807	417-881-9558	
Gilardi's 820 E Walnut St *Web:* gilardisonwalnut.com	Springfield	MO	65806	417-862-6400	
Hemingway's Blue Water Cafe 1935 S Campbell *Web:* restaurants.basspro.com	Springfield	MO	65898	417-891-5100	887-5204
Lucy's Chinese Food 3330 S Campbell *Web:* www.lucyschinesefood.com	Springfield	MO	65807	417-882-5383	
Nonna's Italian American Cafe 306 S Ave *Web:* nonnascafe.com	Springfield	MO	65806	417-831-1222	
Pappy's Place 943 N Main Ave	Springfield	MO	65802	417-866-8744	
Shanghai Inn 1937 N Glenstone Ave	Springfield	MO	65803	417-865-5111	
Springfield Brewing Co 305 S Market Ave *Web:* www.springfieldbrewingco.com	Springfield	MO	65806	417-832-8277	

Montana

Name / Address	City	State	Zip	Phone	Fax
Bistro Enzo 1502 Rehberg Ln *Web:* bistroenzobillings.com	Billings	MT	59102	406-651-0999	
Don Luis 15 N 26th St *Web:* donluismt.com	Billings	MT	59101	406-256-3355	256-3359
Guadalajara Family Mexican 17 N 29th St	Billings	MT	59101	406-259-8930	259-8950
Jake's 2701 First Ave N *Web:* jakesbillings.com	Billings	MT	59101	406-259-9375	259-1142
Juliano's 2912 Seventh Ave N *Web:* wordpress.com	Billings	MT	59101	406-248-6400	
Montana Brewing Co 113 N 28th St *Web:* www.montanabrewingcompany.com	Billings	MT	59101	406-252-9200	259-3329
Rex, The 2401 Montana Ave	Billings	MT	59101	406-245-7477	
3-D International 1825 Smelter Ave *Web:* 3dinternationalrest.com	Black Eagle	MT	59414	406-453-6561	
Borrie's 1800 Smelter Ave	Black Eagle	MT	59414	406-761-0300	761-2021
Cattlemen's Cut Supper Club 369 Vaughn Frontage Rd S *Web:* cattlemenscut.com	Great Falls	MT	59404	406-452-0702	
Dante's Creative Cuisine 1325 Eigth Ave N	Great Falls	MT	59401	406-453-9599	453-9599
El Comedor 1120 25th St S	Great Falls	MT	59405	406-761-5500	761-5502
Maple Garden 5401 Ninth Ave S	Great Falls	MT	59405	406-727-0310	
Prime Cut Restaurant 3219 Tenth Ave S	Great Falls	MT	59405	406-727-2141	
Bert & Ernie's Saloon 361 N Last Chance Gulch *Web:* www.bertanderniesofhelena.com	Helena	MT	59601	406-443-5680	443-7857
Brewhouse Brew Pub & Grill 939 1/2 Getchell St *Web:* atthebrewhouse.com	Helena	MT	59601	406-457-9390	457-9296

				Phone	Fax
Jade Garden Helena 3128 N Montana Ave	Helena	MT	59602	406-443-8899	443-8390
Web: jadegardenhelena.com					
Jorgenson's 1720 11th Ave	Helena	MT	59601	406-442-6380	
Web: www.jorgensons.com					
Mediterranean Grill 42 S Pk Ave	Helena	MT	59601	406-495-1212	
Web: www.mediterraneangrillhelena.com					
Miller's Crossing 52 S Pk Ave	Helena	MT	59601	406-442-3290	
Web: www.millerscrossing.biz					
Montana Club 24 W Sixth Ave	Helena	MT	59601	406-442-5980	442-0276
Web: www.mtclub.org					
On Broadway 106 Broadway	Helena	MT	59601	406-443-1929	
Web: onbroadwayinhelena.com					
Windbag Saloon & Grill 19 S Last Chance Gulch	Helena	MT	59601	406-443-9669	
Marysville House 153 Main St	Marysville	MT	59640	406-443-6677	

Nebraska

				Phone	Fax
Billy's 1301 H St	Lincoln	NE	68508	402-474-0084	474-3391
Web: www.billysrestaurant.com					
Doozy's 101 N 14th St Ste 3	Lincoln	NE	68508	402-438-1616	
Web: www.downtowndoozys.com					
El Toro 2600 S 48th St	Lincoln	NE	68506	402-488-3939	488-7746
Web: facebook.com					
Green Gateau 330 S Tenth St	Lincoln	NE	68508	402-477-0330	477-0782
Web: www.greengateau.com					
La Paz					
La PazMexican Restaurant 321 N Cotner Blvd	Lincoln	NE	68505	402-466-9111	466-9244
Web: www.getintolapaz.com					
Lazlo's Brewery & Grill 210 N Seventh St	Lincoln	NE	68508	402-434-5636	434-3291
Web: lazlosbreweryandgrill.com					
Mazatlan 211 N 70th St	Lincoln	NE	68505	402-464-7201	464-7527
Misty's Steakhouse & Brewery 200 N 11th St	Lincoln	NE	68508	402-476-7766	476-7796
Web: www.mistyslincoln.com					
Oven, The 201 N Eigth St	Lincoln	NE	68508	402-475-6118	475-1281
Web: www.theoven-lincoln.com					
Parthenon 56th & Hwy 2	Lincoln	NE	68516	402-423-2222	423-2228
Web: www.theparthenon.net					
Sher-E-Punjab 1601 Q St	Lincoln	NE	68508	402-477-3090	
Web: sherepunjablincoln.com					
Steak House, The 3441 Adams St	Lincoln	NE	68504	402-466-2472	466-4897
Web: thesteakhouse.drupalgardens.com					
Tandoor 3530 Village Dr	Lincoln	NE	68516	402-423-2007	
Web: www.tandoorindiancuisinelincoln.com					
Tico's 317 S 17th St	Lincoln	NE	68508	402-475-1048	475-3291
Web: www.ticosoflincoln.com					
Ahmad's Persian 1006 Howard St	Omaha	NE	68102	402-341-9616	
Anthony's 7220 F St	Omaha	NE	68127	402-331-7575	331-1497
Web: www.anthonyssteakhouse.com					
Bangkok Cuisine 1905 Farnam St	Omaha	NE	68102	402-346-5874	
Bohemian Cafe 1406 S 13th St	Omaha	NE	68108	402-342-9838	
Web: www.bohemiancafe.net					
Brother Sebastian's Steak House					
1350 S 119th St	Omaha	NE	68144	402-330-0300	330-4814
Web: www.brothersebastians.com					
Caniglia's Venice Inn 6920 Pacific St	Omaha	NE	68106	402-556-3111	
Web: canigliasveniceinn.com					
Cascio's Steak House 1620 S Tenth St	Omaha	NE	68108	402-345-8313	
Web: www.casciossteakhouse.com					
Charlie's on the Lake 4150 S 144th St	Omaha	NE	68137	402-894-9411	894-9415
Web: www.charliesonthelake.net					
Fleming's Prime Steakhouse & Wine Bar					
140 Regency Pkwy	Omaha	NE	68114	402-393-0811	393-0958
Web: www.flemingssteakhouse.com					
Gorat's Steakhouse 4917 Ctr St	Omaha	NE	68106	402-551-3733	
Web: www.goratsomaha.com					
Greek Islands 3821 Ctr St	Omaha	NE	68105	402-346-1528	345-7428
Web: greekislandsomaha.com					
HIRO 88 Restaurants 3655 N 129th St	Omaha	NE	68164	402-933-0091	
Web: www.hiro88.com					
Jack & Mary's Restaurant 655 N 114th St	Omaha	NE	68154	402-496-2090	
Web: www.jackandmarysrestaurant.com					
Jaipur, The 10922 Elm St	Omaha	NE	68144	402-392-7331	
Web: www.jaipurbrewhouse.com					
Jazz A Louisiana Kitchen 1421 Farnam St	Omaha	NE	68102	402-342-3662	934-1258
Web: www.jazzkitchens.com					
Jim & Jennie's Greek Village 3026 N 90th St	Omaha	NE	68134	402-571-2857	
Web: jimandjennies.com					
Johnny's Cafe 4702 S 27th St	Omaha	NE	68107	402-731-4774	731-6698
Web: www.johnnyscafe.com					
Lo Sole Mio 3001 S 32nd Ave	Omaha	NE	68105	402-345-5656	345-5859
Web: www.losolemio.com					
M's Pub 422 S 11th St	Omaha	NE	68102	402-342-2550	342-3035
Web: www.mspubomaha.com					
McFoster's Natural Kind Cafe 302 S 38th St	Omaha	NE	68131	402-345-7477	
Web: mcfosters.com					
Mediterranean Bistro 1712 N 120th St	Omaha	NE	68154	402-493-3080	
Web: www.medbistro.com					
Piccolo Pete's 2202 S 20th St	Omaha	NE	68108	402-342-9038	
Web: www.piccolopetesrestaurant.net					
Upstream Brewing Co 514 S 11th St	Omaha	NE	68102	402-344-0200	344-0451
Web: www.upstreambrewing.com					

Nevada

				Phone	Fax
Adele's 1112 N Carson St	Carson City	NV	89701	775-882-3353	882-0437
Web: www.adelesrestaurantandlounge.com					
China East 1810 Hwy 50 E	Carson City	NV	89701	775-885-6996	
Garibaldi's 307 N Carson St	Carson City	NV	89701	775-884-4574	246-4529
Web: garibaldisristoranteitaliano.com					

				Phone	Fax
Glen Eagles 3700 N Carson St	Carson City	NV	89706	775-884-4414	
Web: www.gleneaglesrestaurant.com					
Grandma Hattie's 2811 S Carson St	Carson City	NV	89701	775-882-4900	
Heidi's 1020 N Carson St	Carson City	NV	89701	775-882-0486	884-2091
Web: heidisfamilyrestaurants.com					
Ming's 2330 S Carson St	Carson City	NV	89701	775-887-8878	887-0570
Web: officialmobilesite.com					
Panda Kitchen 1986 Hwy 50 E	Carson City	NV	89701	775-882-8128	882-3236
Web: pandakitchencarsoncity.com					
Playa Azul 415 E William St	Carson City	NV	89701	775-883-2244	
Red's Old 395 Grill 1055 S Carson St	Carson City	NV	89701	775-887-0395	887-5640
Web: reds395.com					
Taqueria Uruaban 4601 Goni Rd	Carson City	NV	89706	775-883-7609	
Thurman's Ranch House 2943 Hwy 50 E	Carson City	NV	89701	775-883-1773	
Web: thurmansranchhouse.com					
Tito's 444 E William St	Carson City	NV	89701	775-885-0309	
America 3790 Las Vegas Blvd S	Las Vegas	NV	89109	702-740-6451	
Web: www.arkvegas.com					
Andre's 401 S Sixth St	Las Vegas	NV	89101	702-385-5016	385-1742
Web: andrelv.com					
Archi's Thai Kitchen 6360 W Flamingo Rd	Las Vegas	NV	89103	702-880-5550	870-5551
Web: archithai.com					
Aureole 3950 Las Vegas Blvd S	Las Vegas	NV	89119	702-632-7401	
Web: www.charliepalmer.com					
Bartolotta Ristorante diMare					
3131 Las Vegas Blvd S	Las Vegas	NV	89109	702-770-9966	
Web: www.wynnlasvegas.com					
Border Grill Las Vegas					
3950 Las Vegas Blvd S					
Mandalay Bay Resort & Casino	Las Vegas	NV	89119	702-632-7403	632-6945
Web: www.bordergrill.com					
Bouchon 3355 Las Vegas Blvd S	Las Vegas	NV	89109	702-414-6200	
Web: bouchonbistro.com					
Buzio's 3700 W Flamingo Rd	Las Vegas	NV	89103	702-777-7697	
Web: riolasvegas.com					
Caesar's Palace					
3570 Las Vegas Blvd S Caesar's Palace	Las Vegas	NV	89109	702-731-7110	866-1700
TF: 800-634-6001 ■ *Web:* www.caesars.com					
Canaletto 3355 Las Vegas Blvd S	Las Vegas	NV	89109	702-414-1000	414-1100
TF: 866-659-9643 ■ *Web:* www.venetian.com					
Chicago Joe's 820 S Fourth St	Las Vegas	NV	89101	702-382-5637	
Web: www.chicagojoesrestaurant.com					
Craftsteak 3799 Las Vegas Blvd S	Las Vegas	NV	89109	702-891-7318	891-5899
Web: craftrestaurantsinc.com					
Delmonico Steakhouse					
3355 Las Vegas Blvd S					
Venetian Resort Hotel & Casino	Las Vegas	NV	89109	702-414-3737	414-3838
Web: www.emerils.com					
Eiffel Tower Restaurant					
3655 Las Vegas Blvd S	Las Vegas	NV	89109	702-948-6937	942-0004
Web: www.eiffeltowerrestaurant.com					
Emeril's New Orleans Fish House					
3799 Las Vegas Blvd S MGM Grand Hotel	Las Vegas	NV	89109	702-891-7374	891-7338
Web: www.emerils.com/restaurant/4/emerils-new-orleans-fish-house					
Ferraro's 4480 Paradise Rd	Las Vegas	NV	89169	702-364-5300	
Web: www.ferraroslasvegas.com					
Fiamma Trattoria 3799 Las Vegas Blvd S	Las Vegas	NV	89109	702-891-7600	
Web: mgmgrand.com					
Gandhi India's Cuisine 4080 Paradise Rd	Las Vegas	NV	89109	702-734-0094	734-3445
Web: www.gandhicuisine.com					
Grotto Ristorante 129 E Fremont St	Las Vegas	NV	89101	702-385-7111	
Web: www.goldennugget.com					
Hugo's Cellar 202 Fremont St	Las Vegas	NV	89101	404-659-0400	
Web: www.hugoscellar.com					
Le Cirque 3600 Las Vegas Blvd S	Las Vegas	NV	89109	702-693-7111	693-8585
TF: 888-987-6667 ■ *Web:* www.bellagio.com					
Lillie's Asian Cuisine 129 E Fremont St	Las Vegas	NV	89101	702-385-7111	
TF: 800-634-3454 ■ *Web:* www.goldennugget.com/dining/lillies.asp					
Lotus of Siam 953 E Sahara Ave	Las Vegas	NV	89104	702-735-3033	735-3033
Web: saipinchutima.com					
McCormick & Schmick's 335 Hughes Ctr Dr	Las Vegas	NV	89109	702-836-9000	836-9500
Web: www.mccormickandschmicks.com					
Michael Mina 3600 Las Vegas Blvd S	Las Vegas	NV	89109	702-693-7223	693-8512
Web: michaelmina.net/restaurants/locations/mmlv.php					
N9ne Steakhouse 4321 W Flamingo Rd	Las Vegas	NV	89103	702-933-9900	942-8072
Web: www.palms.com					
Nob Hill					
3799 Las Vegas Blvd S MGM Grand Hotel	Las Vegas	NV	89109	702-891-1111	891-3036
TF Resv: 800-929-1111 ■ *Web:* www.mgmgrand.com					
Olives 3600 Las Vegas Blvd S	Las Vegas	NV	89109	702-693-8181	
Web: cheftoddenglish.com					
Onda Ristorante 3400 Las Vegas Blvd S	Las Vegas	NV	89109	702-791-7111	
Web: www.mirage.com					
Osaka 4205 W Sahara Ave	Las Vegas	NV	89102	702-876-4988	876-0259
Web: lasvegas-sushi.com					
Osteria Del Circo 3600 Las Vegas Blvd S	Las Vegas	NV	89109	888-987-6667	693-8585*
**Fax Area Code:* 702 ■ *TF:* 866-259-7111 ■ *Web:* www.bellagio.com/restaurants/circo.aspx					
Pamplemousse 400 E Sahara Ave	Las Vegas	NV	89104	702-733-2066	733-9139
Web: www.pamplemousserestaurant.com					
PF Chang's China Bistro					
3667 Las Vegas Blvd S	Las Vegas	NV	89109	702-836-0955	
Web: www.pfchangs.com					
Pinot Brasserie 3355 Las Vegas Blvd S	Las Vegas	NV	89109	702-414-8888	414-3885
Web: www.patinagroup.com/pinotbrasserie					
Second Street Grill 200 E Fremont St	Las Vegas	NV	89101	702-385-3232	
Web: fremontcasino.com					
Spago 3500 Las Vegas Blvd S Ste G1	Las Vegas	NV	89109	702-369-6300	369-0361
TF: 800-241-3333 ■ *Web:* www.wolfgangpuck.com					
Steak House 2880 Las Vegas Blvd S	Las Vegas	NV	89109	702-794-3767	
Web: circuscircus.com					
Sterling Brunch 3645 Las Vegas Blvd S	Las Vegas	NV	89109	702-967-7999	
Web: ballyslasvegas.com					

Restaurant	City	State	Zip	Phone	Fax
STRIPSTEAK 3950 Las Vegas Blvd S *Web:* www.mandalaybay.com	Las Vegas	NV	89119	702-632-7200	
Sushi Roku 3500 Las Vegas Blvd S *Web:* www.innovativedining.com	Las Vegas	NV	89109	702-733-7373	
SW Steakhouse 3131 Las Vegas Blvd S *TF:* 888-320-7198 ■ *Web:* wynnlasvegas.com	Las Vegas	NV	89109	702-770-9966	770-1570
Thai Spice 4433 W Flamingo Rd *Web:* thaispicelv.com	Las Vegas	NV	89103	702-362-5308	
Trattoria Del Lupo 3950 Las Vegas Blvd S *TF:* 800-275-8273 ■ *Web:* www.wolfgangpuck.com/restaurants/fine-dining/3860	Las Vegas	NV	89119	702-740-5522	740-5533
Verandah 3960 Las Vegas Blvd S *Web:* www.fourseasons.com	Las Vegas	NV	89119	702-632-5000	632-5195
Willy & Jose's Mexican Cantina 5111 Boulder Hwy *Web:* samstownlv.com	Las Vegas	NV	89122	702-456-7777	
Wolfgang Puck's Bar & Grill 3799 Las Vegas Blvd S *Web:* www.wolfgangpuck.com	Las Vegas	NV	89109	702-891-3000	891-3263
Zeffirino Ristorante 3377 Las Vegas Blvd S *Web:* www.zeffirinolasvegas.com	Las Vegas	NV	89109	702-414-3500	
Atlantis Seafood Steakhouse 3800 S Virginia St Atlantis Casino Resort **Fax Area Code: 775* ■ *TF:* 800-723-6500 ■ *Web:* www.atlantiscasino.com	Reno	NV	89502	800-723-6500	827-1518*
Bavarian World 595 Valley Rd *Web:* bavarianworldreno.com	Reno	NV	89512	775-323-7646	
Beaujolais Bistro 753 Riverside Dr *Web:* www.beaujolaisbistro.com	Reno	NV	89503	775-323-2227	
Black Bear Diner 2323 S Virginia St *Web:* www.blackbeardiner.com	Reno	NV	89502	775-827-5570	
Bricks 1695 S Virginia St *Web:* bricksrestaurant.com	Reno	NV	89502	775-786-2277	
Cafe de Thai 7499 Longly Ln *Web:* cafedethaireno.net	Reno	NV	89511	775-829-8424	
China East Restaurant 1086 S Virginia St Ste A	Reno	NV	89502	775-348-7020	348-1956
Flowing Tide Pub 10580 N McCarran Blvd *Web:* www.flowingtidepub.com	Reno	NV	89503	775-747-7707	
Golden Flower 205 W Fifth St *Web:* goldenflowerreno.com	Reno	NV	89503	775-323-1628	
Johnny's 4245 W Fourth St *Web:* johnnysristorante.com	Reno	NV	89523	775-747-4511	
La Strada 345 N Virginia St *Web:* eldoradoreno.com	Reno	NV	89501	775-348-9297	
Louis' Basque Corner 301 E Fourth St *Web:* louisbasquecorner.com	Reno	NV	89512	775-323-7203	
Paisan's 4826 Longley Ln *Web:* paisanscatering.com	Reno	NV	89502	775-826-9444	856-9593
Palais de Jade 960 W Moana Ln *Web:* www.palaisdejadereno.com	Reno	NV	89509	775-827-5233	
Pho 777 Vietnamese Restaurant 102 E Second St	Reno	NV	89501	775-323-7777	
Pneumatic Diner 501 W First St	Reno	NV	89503	775-786-8888	
Romanza 2707 S Virginia St Peppermill Hotel Casino *Web:* www.peppermillreno.com	Reno	NV	89502	775-826-2121	
Sushi Club 294 E Moana Ln	Reno	NV	89502	775-828-7311	828-5426
Sushi Pier 1290 E Plumb Ln *Web:* mysushipier.com	Reno	NV	89502	775-825-6776	
Washoe Steakhouse 4201 W Fourth St *Web:* www.washoesteakhouse.com	Reno	NV	89523	775-786-1323	

New Hampshire

Restaurant	City	State	Zip	Phone	Fax
Bedford Village Inn Two Olde Bedford Way *Web:* www.bedfordvillageinn.com	Bedford	NH	03110	603-472-2001	472-2379
Angelina's Ristorante Italiano 11 Depot St *Web:* www.angelinasrestaurant.com	Concord	NH	03301	603-228-3313	228-3775
Barley House 132 N Main St *Web:* thebarleyhouse.com	Concord	NH	03301	603-228-6363	228-6565
Cheers 17 Depot St *Web:* www.cheersnh.com	Concord	NH	03301	603-228-0180	226-3459
Common Man, The 25 Water St *Web:* www.thecman.com	Concord	NH	03301	603-228-3463	224-5722
Corner View Restaurant 80 1/2 S St	Concord	NH	03301	603-229-4554	229-0932
Hermanos Cocina Mexicana 11 Hills Ave *Web:* www.hermanosmexican.com	Concord	NH	03301	603-224-5669	
Margarita's One Bicentennial Sq *Web:* www.margs.com	Concord	NH	03301	603-224-2821	224-3023
Moritomo 32 Ft Eddy Rd *Web:* moritomonh.com	Concord	NH	03301	603-224-8363	224-8038
Red Blazer, The 72 Manchester St *Web:* www.theredblazer.com	Concord	NH	03301	603-224-4101	224-7118
Siam Orchid 12 N Main St *Web:* www.siamorchid.net	Concord	NH	03301	603-228-1529	
Szechuan Garden Restaurant 108 Fisherville Rd	Concord	NH	03303	603-226-2650	
Tea Garden Restaurant 184 N Main St *Web:* teagarden-nh.com	Concord	NH	03301	603-228-4420	224-9820
Belmont Hall & Restaurant 718 Grove St *Web:* belmonthall.net	Manchester	NH	03103	603-625-8540	
Cactus Jacks Southwest Grill 782 S Willow St *Web:* go2cjs.com	Manchester	NH	03103	603-627-8600	434-3200
Chateau Restaurant 201 Hanover St *Web:* chateaunh.com	Manchester	NH	03104	603-627-2677	
Derryfield Restaurant, The 625 Mammoth Rd *Web:* www.thederryfield.com	Manchester	NH	03104	603-623-2880	623-6850
Don Quijote 362 Union St	Manchester	NH	03103	603-622-2246	
Fratello's Ristorante Italiano 155 Dow St *Web:* www.fratellos.com	Manchester	NH	03101	603-624-2022	629-9465
Gaucho's Churrascaria 62 Lowell St *Web:* www.gauchosbraziliansteakhouse.com	Manchester	NH	03101	603-669-9460	
Lakorn Thai Restaurant 470 S Main St *Web:* lakornthainh.com	Manchester	NH	03102	603-626-4545	
Piccola Italia 815 Elm St *Web:* www.piccolaitalianh.com	Manchester	NH	03101	603-606-5100	
Shorty's 1050 Bicentennial Dr *Web:* shortysmex.com	Manchester	NH	03104	603-625-1730	625-1770
Szechuan House 245 Maple St *Web:* szechuanhousenh.com	Manchester	NH	03103	603-669-8811	
Thousand Crane 1000 Elm St *Web:* thousandcranenh.com	Manchester	NH	03101	603-634-0000	
Yard, The 1211 S Mammoth Rd *Web:* www.theyardrestaurant.com	Manchester	NH	03109	603-623-3545	625-8420
Puritan Backroom Restaurant 245 Hooksett Rd *Web:* www.puritanbackroom.com	North Manchester	NH	03104	603-669-6890	623-3788

New Jersey

Restaurant	City	State	Zip	Phone	Fax
Angelo's Fairmount Tavern 2300 Fairmount Ave *Web:* www.angelosfairmounttavern.com	Atlantic City	NJ	08401	609-344-2439	348-1043
Atlantic City Bar & Grill 1219 Pacific Ave *Web:* www.acbarandgrill.com	Atlantic City	NJ	08401	609-348-8080	
Bobby Flay Steak One Borgata Way *Web:* www.bobbyflaysteak.com	Atlantic City	NJ	08401	609-317-1000	
Cuba Libre 2801 Pacific Ave *Web:* www.cubalibrerestaurant.com	Atlantic City	NJ	08401	609-348-6700	348-6704
Dock's Oyster House 2405 Atlantic Ave *Web:* www.docksoysterhouse.com	Atlantic City	NJ	08401	609-345-0092	345-7893
Girasole Ristorante & Lounge 3108 Pacific Ave *Web:* www.girasoleac.com	Atlantic City	NJ	08401	609-345-5554	
Knife & Fork Inn, The 3600 Atlantic Ave *Web:* www.knifeandforkinn.com	Atlantic City	NJ	08401	609-344-1133	344-3533
Los Amigos 1926 Atlantic Ave *Web:* www.losamigosrest.com	Atlantic City	NJ	08401	609-344-2293	344-2373
Mia Restaurant 2100 Pacific Ave *Web:* www.miaac.com	Atlantic City	NJ	08401	609-441-2345	
Sea Blue 1 Borgata Way *TF Cust Svc:* 877-786-9900 ■ *Web:* www.theborgata.com	Atlantic City	NJ	08401	609-317-1000	317-1039
Sal Deforte's 1400 PkwyAve Serenity Plz *Web:* www.saldefortesristorante.com	Ewing	NJ	08628	609-406-0123	
Rams Head Inn 9 W White Horse Pike *Web:* ramsheadinn.com	Galloway	NJ	08205	609-652-1700	
Baja 104 14th St	Hoboken	NJ	07030	201-653-0610	
Amelia's Bistro 187 Warren St *Web:* ameliasbistro.com	Jersey City	NJ	07302	201-332-2200	
Amiya 160 Green St Harborside Financial Ctr Plz 5 *Web:* www.amiyarestaurant.com	Jersey City	NJ	07311	201-433-8000	433-8866
Casa Dante 737 Newark Ave *Web:* www.casadante.com	Jersey City	NJ	07306	201-795-2750	795-1225
Confucius Asian Bistro 558 Washington Blvd *Web:* confucius558.com	Jersey City	NJ	07310	201-386-8898	386-8896
Iron Monkey 97 Greene St *Web:* ironmonkey.com	Jersey City	NJ	07302	201-435-5756	433-0762
Komegashi 103 Montgomery St *Web:* www.komegashi.com	Jersey City	NJ	07302	201-433-4567	333-8946
Laico's 67 Terhune Ave *Web:* www.laicosjc.com	Jersey City	NJ	07305	201-434-4115	434-4116
Liberty House 76 Audrey Zapp Dr *Web:* www.libertyhouserestaurant.com	Jersey City	NJ	07305	201-395-0300	
Light Horse Tavern 199 Washington St *Web:* www.lighthorsetavern.com	Jersey City	NJ	07302	201-946-2028	946-2029
Madame Claude Cafe 364 1/2 Fourth St *Web:* www.madameclaudecafe.com	Jersey City	NJ	07302	201-876-8800	
Marco & Pepe 289 Grove St *Web:* www.marcoandpepe.com	Jersey City	NJ	07302	201-860-9688	
Marker's Restaurant 153 Plaza II Harborside Financial Ctr *Web:* www.markersrestaurant.com	Jersey City	NJ	07311	201-433-6275	433-0399
Merchant, The 279 Grove St *Web:* www.themerchantnj.com	Jersey City	NJ	07302	201-200-0202	200-9945
Puccini's 1064 Westside Ave *Web:* www.puccinisrestaurant.com	Jersey City	NJ	07306	201-432-4111	432-9026
Rita & Joe's 142 Broadway *Web:* www.rita-joes.com	Jersey City	NJ	07306	201-451-3606	
Acacia 2637 Lawrenceville Rd *Web:* www.acacianj.com	Lawrenceville	NJ	08648	609-895-9885	
Steve & Cookies By the Bay 9700 Amherst Ave *Web:* www.steveandcookies.com	Margate	NJ	08402	609-823-1163	
Adega Grill 130 Ferry St *Web:* www.adegagrill.com	Newark	NJ	07105	973-589-8830	
Campino Restaurant 70 Jabez St	Newark	NJ	07105	973-589-4004	
Casa Vasca 141 Elm St *Web:* casavascarestaurant.com	Newark	NJ	07105	973-465-1350	465-7335
Don Pepe Restaurant & Catering 844 McCarter Hwy *Web:* www.donpeperestaurant.com	Newark	NJ	07102	973-623-4662	623-5402
Fernandes Steak House 158 Fleming Ave *Web:* www.fernandessteakhouse.com	Newark	NJ	07105	973-589-4344	589-6312
Fornos of Spain 47 Ferry St *Web:* www.fornosrestaurant.com	Newark	NJ	07105	973-589-4767	589-1482
Iberia Peninsula Restaurant 67 Ferry St *Web:* www.iberiarestaurants.com	Newark	NJ	07105	973-344-5611	344-2067

	City	State	Zip	Phone	Fax
Maize					
Maize Restaurant 50 Pk Pl	Newark	NJ	07102	973-733-2202	639-1600
Web: www.maizerestaurant.com					
Spain Restaurant 419 Market St	Newark	NJ	07105	973-344-0994	344-2669
Web: www.spainrestaurant.com					
Spanish Tavern 103 McWhorter St.	Newark	NJ	07105	973-589-4959	589-4148
Web: www.spanishtavern.com					
Tony da Caneca 72 Elm Rd	Newark	NJ	07105	973-589-6882	589-0036
Web: www.tonydacaneca.com					
Albasha 1076 Main St.	Paterson	NJ	07503	973-345-3700	
Web: www.albashanj.com					
Bonfire 999 Market St	Paterson	NJ	07513	973-278-2400	278-1380
Web: www.bonfirerestaurant.com					
Brownstone House 351 W Broadway	Paterson	NJ	07522	973-595-8582	595-1141
Web: www.thebrownstone.com					
D'Classico 58-60 Ellison St	Paterson	NJ	07505	973-569-4300	
E & V Restaurant 320 Chamberlain Ave.	Paterson	NJ	07502	973-942-4664	942-0060
Web: www.evrestaurant.com					
Hacienda Restaurant 102 McLean Blvd.	Paterson	NJ	07514	973-345-1255	
Web: haciendanj.com					
Kikiriki 215 Market St	Paterson	NJ	07505	973-225-0336	
Web: kikirikirestaurant.com					
King Wok 712 Main St.	Paterson	NJ	07503	973-881-8818	
Patsy's 72 Seventh Ave	Paterson	NJ	07524	973-742-9596	
Seven Bros Grill 846 Market St	Paterson	NJ	07513	973-684-2579	
Tierras Colombians Restaurant 395 21st Ave	Paterson	NJ	07513	973-684-4066	
Blue Point Grill 258 Nassau St.	Princeton	NJ	08542	609-921-1211	
Web: bluepointgrill.com					
Crab Trap Two Broadway	Somers Point	NJ	08244	609-927-7377	927-5979
Web: www.thecrabtrap.com					
Amici Milano Restaurant 600 Chesnut Ave.	Trenton	NJ	08611	609-396-6300	396-3926
Web: www.amicimilano.com					
Blue Danube Elm & Adeline Sts	Trenton	NJ	08611	609-393-6133	393-1596
Web: www.bluedanuberestaurant.net					
Yoshi Sono Japanese Restaurant					
643 Eagle Rock Ave	West Orange	NJ	07052	973-325-2005	325-2571
Web: www.yoshi-sono.com					

New Mexico

	City	State	Zip	Phone	Fax
66 Diner 1405 Central Ave NE	Albuquerque	NM	87106	505-247-1421	
Web: www.66diner.com					
Antiquity 112 Romero St NW	Albuquerque	NM	87104	505-247-3545	
Web: antiquityrestaurant.com					
Artichoke Cafe 424 Central SE	Albuquerque	NM	87102	505-243-0200	243-3365
Web: www.artichokecafe.com					
Chama River Brewing Co					
4939 Pan American Fwy	Albuquerque	NM	87109	505-342-1800	342-2018
Web: www.chamariverbrewery.com					
County Line 9600 Tramway Blvd NE	Albuquerque	NM	87122	505-856-7477	856-7479
Web: www.countyline.com					
El Pinto 10500 Fourth St NW	Albuquerque	NM	87114	505-898-1771	890-0498
Web: www.elpinto.com					
Forque Kitchen and Bar					
330 Tijeras Ave NW					
Hyatt Regency Albuquerque	Albuquerque	NM	87102	505-842-1234	
Gold Street Caffe 218 Gold Ave SW	Albuquerque	NM	87102	505-765-1633	
Web: goldstreetcaffe.com					
High Finance Restaurant 40 Tramway Rd NE.	Albuquerque	NM	87122	505-243-9742	247-8501
Web: sandiapeakrestaurants.com					
India Kitchen 6910 Montgomery Blvd NE	Albuquerque	NM	87109	505-884-2333	
Web: www.indiakitchenabq.com					
Monte Vista Fire Station					
3201 Central Ave NE.	Albuquerque	NM	87106	505-255-2424	255-2521
Web: montevistafirestation.com					
Mr Powdrell's Barbeque House					
11301 Central Ave NE.	Albuquerque	NM	87123	505-298-6766	298-0025
Web: mrpowdrellsbbq.com					
Pelican's Restaurant					
9800 Montgomery Blvd NE.	Albuquerque	NM	87111	505-298-7678	293-9953
Web: pelicansabq.com					
Ragin' Shrimp 3624 Central Ave SE	Albuquerque	NM	87108	505-254-1544	
Web: www.raginshrimp.com					
Ranchers Club of New Mexico					
1901 University Blvd NE.	Albuquerque	NM	87102	505-889-8071	
Web: www.theranchersclubofnm.com					
Sadie's 6230 Fourth St NW	Albuquerque	NM	87107	505-345-5339	
Web: www.sadiessalsa.com					
Samurai Grill & Sushi Bar					
9500 Montgomery Blvd NE.	Albuquerque	NM	87111	505-275-6601	275-4146
Web: www.abqsamurai.com					
Sandiago's Mexican Grill at the Tram					
40 Tramway Rd NE	Albuquerque	NM	87122	505-856-6692	856-6692
Web: www.sandiapeakrestaurants.com					
Scalo Northern Italian Grill					
3500 Central Ave SE.	Albuquerque	NM	87106	505-255-8781	265-7850
Web: www.scalonobhill.com					
Seasons Rotisserie & Grill					
2031 Mountain Rd NW	Albuquerque	NM	87104	505-766-5100	766-5252
Web: www.seasonsabq.com					
Yanni's Mediterranean Bar & Grill					
3109 Central Ave NE.	Albuquerque	NM	87106	505-268-9250	
Web: yannisandopabar.com					
Zinc Wine Bar & Bistro					
3009 Central Ave NE.	Albuquerque	NM	87106	505-254-9462	
Web: zincabq.com					
Chilito's 2405 S Valley Dr	Las Cruces	NM	88005	575-526-4184	532-1104
Web: chilitos.net					
Farley's 3499 Foothills Rd.	Las Cruces	NM	88011	575-522-0466	
Web: www.farleyspub.com					
Los Compas Cafe 603 S Nevarez St	Las Cruces	NM	88001	575-523-1778	527-5590
Mesilla Valley Kitchen 2001 E Lohman.	Las Cruces	NM	88001	575-523-9311	
Web: www.mesillavalleykitchen.com					
Meson de Mesilla 1891 Avenida de Mesilla	Las Cruces	NM	88005	575-652-4953	
Web: www.mesondemesilla.com					
Mix Express 1001 E University Ave Ste D-3	Las Cruces	NM	88001	575-532-1382	532-2046
Nellie's Cafe 1226 W Hadley Ave.	Las Cruces	NM	88005	575-524-9982	
Roberto's 908 E Amador Ave	Las Cruces	NM	88001	575-523-1851	
Si Senor Restaurant 1551 E Amador Ave.	Las Cruces	NM	88001	575-527-0817	527-0412
Web: www.sisenor.com					
Spanish Kitchen 2960 N Main St	Las Cruces	NM	88001	575-526-4275	
Teriyaki Chicken House 805 El Paseo Rd	Las Cruces	NM	88001	575-541-1696	
Web: teriyakichickenhouse.com					
Cattle Baron Restaurants Inc					
901 S Main St Ste A	Roswell	NM	88203	575-622-3311	623-8801
Web: www.cattlebaron.com					
Annapurna Chai House 1620 St Michaels	Santa Fe	NM	87505	505-988-9688	988-9914
Web: www.chaishoppe.com					
Bull Ring of Santa Fe, The					
150 Washington Ave.	Santa Fe	NM	87501	505-983-3328	982-8254
Web: santafebullring.com					
Chow's Contemporary Chinese Food					
720 St Michaels Dr.	Santa Fe	NM	87505	505-471-7120	
Web: www.mychows.com					
Coyote Cafe 132 W Water St	Santa Fe	NM	87501	505-983-1615	
Web: www.coyotecafe.com					
El Farol 808 Canyon Rd	Santa Fe	NM	87501	505-983-9912	
Web: www.elfarolsf.com					
Fuego 330 E Palace Ave.	Santa Fe	NM	87501	505-986-0000	
TF Sales: 855-811-0050 ■ *Web:* www.laposadadesantafe.com					
Geronimo 724 Canyon Rd.	Santa Fe	NM	87501	505-982-1500	
Web: www.geronimorestaurant.com					
IL Vicino 321 W San Francisco St	Santa Fe	NM	87501	505-986-8700	820-0524
Web: www.ilvicino.com					
Kohnami 313 S Guadalupe St	Santa Fe	NM	87501	505-984-2002	
Web: kohnamirestaurant.com					
Maria's New Mexican Kitchen					
555 W Cordova Rd	Santa Fe	NM	87505	505-983-7929	
Web: www.marias-santafe.com					
Mariscos La Playa 537 W Cordova Rd	Santa Fe	NM	87505	505-982-2790	
Mu Du Noodles 1494 Cerrillos Rd.	Santa Fe	NM	87505	505-983-1411	
Web: www.mudunoodles.com					
Old House 309 W San Francisco St	Santa Fe	NM	87501	505-988-4455	995-4543
TF: 800-955-4455 ■ *Web:* www.eldoradohotel.com					
Rio Chama Steakhouse 414 Old Santa Fe Trl	Santa Fe	NM	87501	505-955-0765	955-8579
Web: www.riochamasteakhouse.com					
Santacafe 231 Washington Ave	Santa Fe	NM	87501	505-984-1788	
Web: www.santacafe.com					
Shed, The 113 1/2 E Palace Ave	Santa Fe	NM	87501	505-982-9030	982-0902
Web: www.sfshed.com					
Tecolote Cafe 1203 Cerrillos Rd	Santa Fe	NM	87505	505-988-1362	
Web: tecolotecafe.com					
Tomasita's Restaurant & Bar					
500 S Guadalupe St	Santa Fe	NM	87501	505-983-5721	983-0780
Web: www.tomasitas.com					
Tortilla Flats 3139 Cerrillos Rd	Santa Fe	NM	87507	505-471-8685	
Web: tortillaflats.net					

New York

	City	State	Zip	Phone	Fax
Cafe Capriccio 49 Grand St.	Albany	NY	12207	518-465-0439	465-6822
Web: www.cafecapriccio.com					
Caffe Italia Ristorante 662 Central Ave	Albany	NY	12206	518-459-8029	482-9433
CH Evans Brewing Company at the Albany Pump Station					
19 Quackenbush Sq	Albany	NY	12207	518-447-9000	465-1410
Web: www.evansale.com					
Desmond Albany Hotel, The					
660 Albany-Shaker Rd	Albany	NY	12211	518-869-8100	869-7659
TF: 800-448-3500 ■ *Web:* www.desmondhotelsalbany.com					
El Loco Mexican Cafe 465 Madison Ave.	Albany	NY	12210	518-436-1855	
Web: ellocomexicancafe.com					
El Mariachi 144 Washington Ave.	Albany	NY	12210	518-465-2568	
Web: elmariachisrestaurant.com					
Jack's Oyster House 42 State St.	Albany	NY	12207	518-465-8854	434-2134
Web: www.jacksoysterhouse.com					
My Linh 272 Delaware Ave	Albany	NY	12209	518-465-8899	465-8898
Web: www.mylinhrestaurant.com					
Provence 1475 Western Ave Stuyvesant Plz	Albany	NY	12203	518-689-7777	689-7780
Web: www.milano-restaurant.com/provence					
Scotch & Sirloin 3999 Maple Rd.	Amherst	NY	14226	716-837-4900	
Web: scotchnsirloinrestaurant.net					
Erawan Thai Cuisine 42-31 Bell Blvd	Bayside	NY	11361	718-428-2112	428-2098
Web: www.erawanthaibayside.com					
Elia 8611 Third Ave.	Brooklyn	NY	11209	718-748-9891	
Web: www.eliarestaurant.com/elia					
Frankies 457 Court Street Spuntino					
457 Ct St	Brooklyn	NY	11231	718-403-0033	403-9260
Web: frankiesspuntino.com/					
Grocery, The 288 Smith St.	Brooklyn	NY	11231	718-596-3335	
Web: www.thegroceryrestaurant.com					
ICI Restaurant 246 DeKalb Ave.	Brooklyn	NY	11205	718-789-2778	
Web: www.icirestaurant.com					
Kai 20 Jay St Ste 530	Brooklyn	NY	11201	718-250-4000	246-1325
TF: 888-832-7832 ■ *Web:* www.itoen.com					
Peter Luger Steak House 178 Broadway	Brooklyn	NY	11211	718-387-7400	387-3523
Web: www.peterluger.com					
Saul 200 Eastern Pkwy	Brooklyn	NY	11238	718-935-9842	
Web: www.saulrestaurant.com					
Acropolis Family Restaurant 708 Elmwood Ave	Buffalo	NY	14222	716-886-2977	
Web: www.acropolisopa.com					
Bijou Grille, The 643 Main St	Buffalo	NY	14203	716-847-1512	852-3041
Web: www.bijougrille.com					

Restaurant	City	State	ZIP	Phone	Fax
Bing's 1952 Kensington Ave	Buffalo	NY	14215	716-839-5788	
Web: bingsrestaurant.biz					
Blackthorn Restaurant & Pub 2134 Seneca St	Buffalo	NY	14210	716-825-9327	
Web: blackthornrestaurant.com					
Duff's 3651 Sheridan Dr	Buffalo	NY	14226	716-834-6234	831-5513
Web: duffswings.com					
Fat Bob's Smokehouse 41 Virginia Pl	Buffalo	NY	14202	716-887-2971	332-1201
Web: www.fatbobs.com					
Frank & Teressa's Anchor Bar & Restaurant 651 Delaware Ave	Buffalo	NY	14202	716-883-1134	
Web: www.anchorbar.com					
Gigi's Restaurant 257 E Ferry St	Buffalo	NY	14208	716-883-1438	
Hutch's 1375 Delaware Ave	Buffalo	NY	14209	716-885-0074	
Web: www.hutchsrestaurant.com					
Ilio DiPaolo's 3785 S Pk Ave	Buffalo	NY	14219	716-825-3675	825-1054
Web: www.iliodipaolos.com					
Left Bank 511 Rhode Island St	Buffalo	NY	14213	716-882-3509	
Web: www.leftbankrestaurant.com					
Marco's 1085 Niagara St	Buffalo	NY	14213	716-882-5539	
Web: marcosbuffalo.com					
Mother's 33 Virginia Pl	Buffalo	NY	14202	716-882-2989	
Oliver's 2095 Delaware Ave	Buffalo	NY	14216	716-877-9662	877-8291
Web: www.oliverscuisine.com					
Pearl Street Grill & Brewery 76 Pearl St	Buffalo	NY	14202	716-856-2337	849-0839
Web: buffalobrewerydistrict.com/pearl					
Rue Franklin 341 Franklin St	Buffalo	NY	14202	716-852-4416	
Web: www.ruefranklin.com					
Santasiero's 1329 Niagara St	Buffalo	NY	14213	716-886-9197	884-9338
Hunan Village Restaurant 1402A N Loop 336 W	Conroe	NY	77304	936-539-6811	
Web: www.hunanvillageconroe.com					
Salvatore's Italian Gardens 6461 Transit Rd	Depew	NY	14043	716-683-7990	
TF: 877-456-4097 ■ *Web:* www.salvatores.net					
Tavern 104 Limestone Pl	Fayetteville	NY	13066	315-637-8321	
Web: pascalerestaurant.com					
Alain Ducasse at the Essex House 60 W 55th St	New York	NY	10019	646-943-7373	943-7330
Web: www.alain-ducasse.com					
Annisa 13 Barrow St	New York	NY	10014	212-741-6699	
Web: www.annisarestaurant.com					
Aquagrill Inc 210 Spring St	New York	NY	10012	212-274-0505	274-0587
Web: www.aquagrill.com					
Aquavit 65 E 55th St	New York	NY	10022	212-307-7311	
Web: www.aquavit.org					
Babbo 110 Waverly Pl	New York	NY	10011	212-777-0303	
Web: www.babbonyc.com					
Balthazar 80 Spring St	New York	NY	10012	212-965-1414	
Web: www.balthazarny.com					
Bar Americain 152 W 52nd St	New York	NY	10019	212-265-9700	
Web: www.baramericain.com					
Barbuto 775 Washington St	New York	NY	10014	212-924-9700	924-9300
Web: www.barbutonyc.com					
BLT Prime 111 E 22nd St	New York	NY	10010	212-995-8500	
Web: www.e2hospitality.com/blt-prime-new-york					
Blue Fin 1567 Broadway	New York	NY	10036	212-918-1400	918-1300
Web: bluefinnyc.com					
Blue Hill 75 Washington Pl	New York	NY	10011	212-539-1776	539-0959
Web: bluehillfarm.com					
Blue Ribbon 97 Sullivan St	New York	NY	10012	212-274-0404	274-1318
Web: www.blueribbonrestaurants.com					
Blue Water Grill 31 Union Sq W	New York	NY	10003	212-675-9500	675-1899
Web: bluewatergrillnyc.com					
Bouley 163 Duane St	New York	NY	10013	212-964-2525	
Web: www.davidbouley.com					
Cafe Boulud 20 E 76th St	New York	NY	10021	212-772-2600	772-7755
Web: www.danielnyc.com					
Cafe Centro 200 Pk Ave	New York	NY	10166	212-818-1222	949-8266
Web: patinagroup.com					
Casa Mono 52 Irving Pl	New York	NY	10003	212-253-2773	253-5318
Web: casamononyc.com					
Caviar Russe 538 Madison Ave Second Fl	New York	NY	10022	212-980-5908	871-1842
Web: www.caviarrusse.com					
Chanterelle 2 Harrison St	New York	NY	10013	212-966-6143	
Web: www.chanterellenyc.com					
Churrascaria Plataforma 316 W 49th St	New York	NY	10019	212-245-0505	974-8250
Web: www.churrascariaplataforma.com					
Craft 43 E 19th St	New York	NY	10003	212-780-0880	
Web: www.craftrestaurantsinc.com					
Daniel 60 E 65th St	New York	NY	10065	212-288-0033	
Web: www.danielnyc.com					
Dawat 210 E 58th St	New York	NY	10022	212-355-7555	
Web: dawatny.com					
db Bistro Moderne 55 W 44th St	New York	NY	10036	212-391-2400	391-1188
Web: www.danielnyc.com					
Del Frisco's Double Eagle Steak House 1221 Ave of the Americas	New York	NY	10020	212-575-5129	
Web: www.delfriscos.com					
Del Posto 85 Tenth Ave	New York	NY	10011	212-497-8090	
Web: www.delposto.com					
Devi Eight E 18th St	New York	NY	10003	212-691-1300	691-1695
Web: www.devinyc.com					
Elle 300 W 57th St 24th Fl	New York	NY	10019	212-903-5000	
Web: elle.com					
Erminia 250 E 83rd St	New York	NY	10028	212-879-4284	
Web: erminiarestaurant.com					
Estiatorio Milos 125 W 55th St	New York	NY	10019	212-245-7400	245-4828
Web: www.milos.ca					
Felidia 243 E 58th St	New York	NY	10022	212-758-1479	
Web: www.felidia-nyc.com					
Four Seasons 99 E 52nd St	New York	NY	10022	212-754-9494	754-1077
Web: www.fourseasonsrestaurant.com					
Gordon Ramsay at the London 151 W 54th St	New York	NY	10019	212-468-8888	
Web: www.thelondonnyc.com					
Gotham Bar & Grill 12 E 12th St	New York	NY	10003	212-620-4020	
Web: www.gothambarandgrill.com					
Gramercy Tavern 42 E 20th St	New York	NY	10003	212-477-0777	
Web: www.gramercytavern.com					
Hangawi 12 E 32nd St	New York	NY	10016	212-213-0077	689-0780
Web: www.hangawirestaurant.com					
Harrison, The 355 Greenwich St	New York	NY	10013	212-274-9310	274-9376
Web: www.theharrison.com/harrison.php					
IL Mulino 86 W Third St	New York	NY	10012	212-673-3783	673-9875
Web: www.ilmulino.com					
IL Palazzo 151 Mulberry St	New York	NY	10013	212-343-7000	343-1508
Web: littleitalynyc.com					
Jean Georges One Central Pk W	New York	NY	10023	212-299-3900	
Web: www.jean-georges.com					
Jewel Bako 239 E Fifth St	New York	NY	10003	212-979-1012	
Web: www.degustationnyc.com					
Joe Allen 326 W 46th St	New York	NY	10036	212-581-6464	265-3383
Web: www.joeallenrestaurant.com					
JoJo 160 E 64th St	New York	NY	10021	212-223-5656	755-9038
Web: jojorestaurantnyc.com					
Kuruma Zushi Seven E 47th St Second Fl	New York	NY	10017	212-317-2802	317-2803
Web: kurumazushi.com					
L'Absinthe Restaurant 227 E 67th St	New York	NY	10065	212-794-4950	794-1589
Web: www.labsinthe.com					
La Grenouille Three E 52nd St	New York	NY	10022	212-752-1495	593-4964
Web: www.la-grenouille.com					
Le Perigord 405 E 52nd St	New York	NY	10022	212-755-6244	
Web: www.leperigord.com					
Lupa Osteria Romana 170 Thompson St	New York	NY	10012	212-982-5089	982-5490
Web: www.luparestaurant.com					
Maloney & Porcelli 37 E 50th St	New York	NY	10022	212-750-2233	750-2252
Web: www.maloneyandporcelli.com					
MAS (Farmhouse) 39 Downing St	New York	NY	10014	212-255-1790	255-0279
Web: masfarmhouse.com					
Masa 10 Columbus Cir Time Warner Ctr Fourth Fl	New York	NY	10019	212-823-9800	
Web: www.masanyc.com					
Megu 62 Thomas St	New York	NY	10013	212-964-7777	
Mercer Kitchen 99 Prince St	New York	NY	10012	212-966-5454	965-3855
Web: www.jean-georges.com					
Michael Jordan's Steak House 23 Vanderbilt Ave	New York	NY	10017	212-655-2300	
Web: michaeljordansnyc.com					
Michael's New York 24 W 55th St	New York	NY	10019	212-767-0555	581-6778
Web: www.michaelsnewyork.com					
NIOS Restaurant & Wine Bar 130 W 46th St	New York	NY	10036	212-485-2999	485-2789
Web: www.niosrestaurant.com					
Nobu 105 Hudson St	New York	NY	10013	212-219-0500	219-1441
Web: www.noburestaurants.com					
Oceana 120 W 49th St	New York	NY	10020	212-759-5941	759-6076
Web: www.oceanarestaurant.com					
Old Homestead Steakhouse 56 Ninth Ave	New York	NY	10011	212-242-9040	727-1637
Web: www.theoldhomesteadsteakhouse.com					
One if by Land Two if by Sea 17 Barrow St	New York	NY	10014	212-255-8649	304-2900*
**Fax Area Code:* 646 ■ *Web:* www.oneifbyland.com					
Ouest 2315 Broadway	New York	NY	10024	212-580-8700	580-1360
Web: www.ouestny.com					
Palm Restaurant 837 Second Ave	New York	NY	10017	212-687-2953	983-4584
TF: 866-333-7256 ■ *Web:* www.thepalm.com					
Pampano 209 E 49th St	New York	NY	10017	212-751-4545	
Web: www.richardsandoval.com					
Pearl Oyster Bar 18 Cornelia St	New York	NY	10014	212-691-8211	
Web: www.pearloysterbar.com					
Peasant 194 Elizabeth St	New York	NY	10012	212-965-9511	965-8741
Web: www.peasantnyc.com					
Per Se 10 Columbus Cir Fourth Fl	New York	NY	10019	212-823-9335	
Web: www.perseny.com					
Periyali 35 W 20th St	New York	NY	10011	212-463-7890	924-9403
Web: www.periyali.com					
Picholine 35 W 64th St	New York	NY	10023	212-724-8585	875-8979
Web: www.picholinenyc.com					
Po 31 Cornelia St	New York	NY	10014	212-645-2189	367-9448
Web: www.porestaurant.com					
Poke 343 E 85th St	New York	NY	10028	212-249-0569	
Web: www.pokesushinyc.com					
Post House, The 28 E 63rd St	New York	NY	10021	212-935-2888	
Web: www.theposthouse.com					
Prime Grill, The 25 W 56th St	New York	NY	10019	212-692-9292	697-3652
Web: www.theprimegrill.primehospitalityny.com					
Ramen-Ya 181 W Fourth St	New York	NY	10014	212-989-5440	
Web: www.ramen-ya.net					
Remi 145 W 53rd St	New York	NY	10019	212-581-4242	262-2507
Web: remi-nyc.com					
Rothmann's Steakhouse & Grill Three E 54th St	New York	NY	10022	212-319-5500	319-5540
Web: www.rothmanns54.com					
Scalini Fedeli 165 Duane St	New York	NY	10013	212-528-0400	587-8773
Web: www.scalinifedeli.com					
Sea Grill Restaurant 19 W 49th St	New York	NY	10020	212-332-7610	332-7677
Web: www.patinagroup.com					
Shun Lee Palace 155 E 55th St	New York	NY	10022	212-371-8844	752-1936
Web: www.shunleepalace.com					
Sparks Steak House 210 E 46th St	New York	NY	10017	212-687-4855	557-7409
Web: www.sparkssteakhouse.com					
Spice Market 403 W 13th St	New York	NY	10014	212-675-2322	675-4365
Web: www.jean-georges.com					
Strip House 13 E 12th St	New York	NY	10003	212-328-0000	
Web: striphouse.com					
Sugiyama 251 W 55th St	New York	NY	10019	212-956-0670	956-0671
Web: www.sugiyama-nyc.com					
Sushi of Gari 402 E 78th St	New York	NY	10075	212-517-5340	
Web: sushiofgari.com					

				Phone	Fax
Sushi Seki 1143 First Ave *Web:* sushiseki.com	New York	NY	10065	212-371-0238	
Sushi Yasuda 204 E 43rd St *Web:* www.sushiyasuda.com	New York	NY	10017	212-972-1001	972-1717
Sushi Zen 108 W 44th St *Web:* www.sushizen-ny.com	New York	NY	10036	212-302-0707	944-7710
Tamarind 43 E 22nd St # 42 *Web:* tamarind22.com	New York	NY	10010	212-674-7400	674-4449
Thalia 828 Eigth Ave *Web:* www.restaurantthalia.com	New York	NY	10019	212-399-4444	399-3268
Tocqueville One E 15th St *Web:* www.tocquevillerestaurant.com	New York	NY	10003	212-647-1515	647-7148
Tomoe Sushi 172 Thompson St *Web:* tomoesushi.com	New York	NY	10012	212-777-9346	
Trattoria dell'Arte 900 Seventh Ave *Web:* www.trattoriadellarte.com	New York	NY	10106	212-245-9800	
Triomphe 49 W 44th St *Web:* www.iroquoisny.com	New York	NY	10036	212-453-4233	827-0464
Union Square Cafe 21 E 16th St *Web:* unionsquarecafe.com	New York	NY	10003	212-243-4020	627-2673
Veritas 43 E 20th St *Web:* www.veritas-nyc.com	New York	NY	10003	212-353-3700	
Wallse 344 W 11th St *Web:* kg-ny.com	New York	NY	10014	212-352-2300	
Wolfgang's Steakhouse Four Pk Ave *Web:* www.wolfgangssteakhouse.net	New York	NY	10016	212-889-3369	889-6845
Butcher Block 15 Booth Dr *Web:* www.butcherblockrestaurant.com	Plattsburgh	NY	12901	518-563-0920	566-1201
Agatina's 2967 Buffalo Rd *Web:* www.agatinas.com	Rochester	NY	14624	585 426 0510	
Aladdin's Natural Eatery 646 Monroe Ave *Web:* myaladdins.com/monroe.html	Rochester	NY	14607	585-442-5000	
Bacco's 263 Pk Ave *Web:* baccosristorante.com	Rochester	NY	14607	585-442-5090	
Bathtub Billy's 630 Ridge Rd W *Web:* www.bathtubbillys.com	Rochester	NY	14615	585-865-6510	865-6323
Benucci's 3349 Monroe Ave *Web:* www.benuccis.com	Rochester	NY	14618	585-264-1300	264-1926
Bernard's Grove 187 Long Pond Rd *Web:* www.bernardsgrove.com	Rochester	NY	14612	585-227-6405	723-5915
Brook House 920 Elmridge Ctr Dr	Rochester	NY	14626	585-723-9988	
California Rollin' 274 N Goodman St *Web:* californiarollin.com	Rochester	NY	14607	585-271-8990	
Edibles Restaurant & Bar 704 University Ave *Web:* www.ediblesrochester.com	Rochester	NY	14607	585-271-4910	
Elmwood Inn, The 1256 Mt Hope Ave *Web:* elmwoodinn.net	Rochester	NY	14620	585-271-5195	
Hogan's Hideaway 197 Pk Ave *Web:* www.hoganshideaway.com	Rochester	NY	14607	585-442-4293	461-4965
Lucano 1815 E Ave *Web:* www.ristorantelucano.com	Rochester	NY	14610	585-244-3460	
Mamasan 2800 Monroe Ave *Web:* www.mamasans.com	Rochester	NY	14618	585-461-3290	
Mario's Via Abruzzi 2740 Monroe Ave *Web:* www.mariosit.com	Rochester	NY	14618	585-271-1111	
Phillips European Restaurant 26 Corporate Woods *Web:* www.phillipseuropean.com	Rochester	NY	14623	585-272-9910	272-1778
Remington's Restaurant 425 Merchants Rd	Rochester	NY	14609	585-482-4434	
Salena's Mexican Restaurant 302 N Goodman St At the Vlg Gate *Web:* www.salenas.com	Rochester	NY	14607	585-256-5980	
Angelina's Ristorante 399 Ellis St *Web:* angelinasristorante.com	Staten Island	NY	10307	718-227-2900	227-3329
1060 at the Genesee Grande 1060 E Genesee St *Web:* 1060restaurant.com	Syracuse	NY	13210	315-476-9000	
Alto Cinco 526 Westcott St *Web:* www.altocinco.net	Syracuse	NY	13210	315-422-6399	
Angotti's 725 Burnet Ave	Syracuse	NY	13203	315-472-8403	
Blue Tusk 165 Walton St *Web:* www.bluetusk.com	Syracuse	NY	13202	315-472-1934	
Casa Di Copani 3414 Burnet Ave *Web:* casadicopani.com	Syracuse	NY	13206	315-463-1031	
Delmonico's Italian Steakhouse Syracuse 2950 Erie Blvd E *Web:* www.delmonicositaliansteakhouse.com	Syracuse	NY	13224	315-445-1111	445-0257
Joey's Restaurant 6594 Thompson Rd *Web:* joeysitalianrestaurant.com	Syracuse	NY	13206	315-432-0315	
King David's 129 Marshall St *Web:* www.kingdavids.com	Syracuse	NY	13210	315-471-5000	
Luigi's 1524 Valley Dr	Syracuse	NY	13207	315-492-9997	
Mission, The 304 E Onondaga St *Web:* themissionrestaurant.com	Syracuse	NY	13202	315-475-7344	475-7340
Phoebe's 900 E Genesee St *Web:* www.phoebessyracuse.com	Syracuse	NY	13210	315-475-5154	
Riley's 312 Pk St	Syracuse	NY	13203	315-471-7111	
Syracuse Suds Factory 320 S Clinton St *Web:* s502965190.onlinehome.us/	Syracuse	NY	13202	315-471-2253	
Thai Flavor 2863 Erie Blvd E *Web:* syracusethaiflavor.com	Syracuse	NY	13224	315-251-1366	
Tokyo-Seoul 3180 Erie Blvd E *Web:* tokyoseoulsyracuse.com	Syracuse	NY	13214	315-449-2688	
Scharf's Schiller Park Restaurant 2683 Clinton St *Web:* www.scharfsrest.com	West Seneca	NY	14224	716-895-7249	
Sripraphai 64-13 39th Ave *Web:* sripraphairestaurant.com	Woodside	NY	11377	718-899-9599	
Caridad & Louie's Restaurant 187 S Broadway	Yonkers	NY	10701	914-375-9777	
La Lanterna 23 Grey Oaks Ave *Web:* www.lalanterna.com	Yonkers	NY	10710	914-476-3060	375-3008
Rory Dolan's 890 McLean Ave *Web:* www.rorydolans.com	Yonkers	NY	10704	914-776-2946	776-6538
Tombolino Restaurant 356 Kimball Ave *Web:* www.tombolinoristorante.com	Yonkers	NY	10704	914-237-1266	237-1254
Zuppa 59 Main St *Web:* www.zupparestaurant.com	Yonkers	NY	10701	914-376-6500	376-4900

North Carolina

				Phone	Fax
Charlotte Street Grill & Pub 157 Charlotte St *Web:* charlottestreetpub.com/	Asheville	NC	28801	828-252-2948	
Doc Chey's Noodle House 37 Biltmore Ave *Web:* www.doccheys.com	Asheville	NC	28801	828-252-8220	
Laughing Seed Cafe 40 Wall St *Web:* laughingseed.jackofthewood.com	Asheville	NC	28801	828-252-3445	
Market Place, The 20 Wall St *Web:* www.marketplace-restaurant.com	Asheville	NC	28801	828-252-4162	253-3120
Moose Cafe 570 BrevaRd Rd *Web:* eatatthemoosecafe.com	Asheville	NC	28806	828-255-0920	255-0042
Omni Grove Park Inn, The 290 Macon Ave	Asheville	NC	28804	828-252-2711	252-7053
Ristorante da Vincenzo 10 N Market St	Asheville	NC	28801	828-254-4698	
Salsa Six Patton Ave *Web:* salsasnc.com	Asheville	NC	28801	828-252-9805	252-9805
Savoy Restaurant & Martini Bar 641 Merrimon Ave *Web:* www.savoyasheville.com	Asheville	NC	28804	828-253-1077	252-6776
Sunset Terrace 290 Macon Ave **Fax Area Code: 805* ■ *Web:* www.groveparkinn.com	Asheville	NC	28804	828-252-2711	497-4825*
Tupelo Honey Cafe 12 College St *Web:* www.tupelohoneycafe.com	Asheville	NC	28801	828-255-4863	255-4864
Yoshida Japanese Steak House Four Regent Pk Blvd	Asheville	NC	28806	828-252-5903	258-3514
Zambra! 85 W Walnut St *Web:* www.zambratapas.com	Asheville	NC	28801	828-232-1060	
Ruth's Chris Steakhouse 2010 Renaissance Pk Pl *Web:* www.ruthschris.com	Cary	NC	27513	919-677-0033	677-8633
Aria Tuscan Grill 100 N Tryon St *Web:* www.sonomarestaurants.net	Charlotte	NC	28202	704-376-8880	344-2563
Baoding 4722 Sharon Rd Ste F *Web:* baodingsouthpark.com	Charlotte	NC	28210	704-552-8899	552-8828
Barrington's 7822 Fairview Rd *Web:* www.barringtonsrestaurant.com	Charlotte	NC	28226	704-364-5755	
Big Ben British Pub & Restaurant 2000 S Blvd *Web:* www.bigbenpub.com	Charlotte	NC	28203	704-817-9697	
Bill Spoon's Barbecue 5524 S Blvd *Web:* spoonsbarbecue.com	Charlotte	NC	28217	704-525-8865	
Blue Restaurant & Bar 206 N College St *Web:* www.bluecharlotte.com	Charlotte	NC	28202	704-927-2583	927-0555
Bonterra Dining & Wine Room 1829 Cleveland Ave *Web:* www.bonterradining.com	Charlotte	NC	28203	704-333-9463	372-9463
Cajun Queen 1800 E Seventh St *Web:* www.cajunqueen.net	Charlotte	NC	28204	704-377-9017	
Carpe Diem 1535 Elizabeth Ave *Web:* www.carpediemrestaurant.com	Charlotte	NC	28204	704-377-7976	377-7975
Greek Isles 200 E Bland St *Web:* www.greekislesrestaurant.com	Charlotte	NC	28203	704-444-9000	373-2883
Ilios Noche 11508 Providence Rd *Web:* www.xeniahospitality.com	Charlotte	NC	28277	704-814-9882	
Mama Ricotta's 601 S Kings Dr *Web:* www.mamaricottasrestaurant.com	Charlotte	NC	28204	704-343-0148	377-7461
McNinch House 511 N Church St *Web:* www.mcninchhouserestaurant.com	Charlotte	NC	28202	704-332-6159	376-0212
Melting Pot of Charlotte, The 901 S Kings Dr Ste 140B *TF:* 800-783-0867 ■ *Web:* www.meltingpot.com	Charlotte	NC	28204	704-334-4400	334-0535
Mert's Heart & Soul 214 N College St *Web:* www.uptown2go.com	Charlotte	NC	28202	704-342-4222	342-4499
Mickey & Mooch The other Joint 8128 Providence Rd Ste 1200 *Web:* www.mickeyandmooch.com	Charlotte	NC	28277	704-752-8080	
Mimosa Grill 327 S Tryon St *Web:* www.harpersgroup.com	Charlotte	NC	28202	704-343-0700	343-9002
Miro Spanish Grille 12239 N Community House Rd *Web:* www.mirospanishgrille.com	Charlotte	NC	28277	704-540-7374	540-7388
Musashi 10110 Johnston Rd *Web:* www.musashi-nc.com	Charlotte	NC	28210	704-543-5181	
New South Kitchen & Bar 8140 Providence Rd Ste 300 *Web:* www.newsouthkitchen.com	Charlotte	NC	28277	704-541-9990	541-1163
Nikko 1300 S Blvd *Web:* www.nikkosushibar.net	Charlotte	NC	28203	704-370-0100	370-0123
Old Hickory House Restaurant 6538 N Tryon St	Charlotte	NC	28213	704-596-8014	596-0922
Senor Tequila 6414 Rea Rd *Web:* senortequilacantinagrill.com	Charlotte	NC	28277	704-543-0706	
Thai Orchid 4223 Providence Rd *Web:* thaiorchidrestaurantcharlotte.com	Charlotte	NC	28211	704-364-1134	
Toscana 6401 Morrison Blvd *Web:* conterestaurantgroup.com	Charlotte	NC	28211	704-367-1808	367-0854
Upstream *Harper's Restaurant Group* 6902 Phillips Pl Ct *Web:* www.harpersgroup.com/upstream.asp	Charlotte	NC	28210	704-556-7730	552-2793
Villa Antonio 4707 S Blvd *Web:* www.villaantonio.com	Charlotte	NC	28217	704-523-1594	523-5697

Phone | Fax

Volare Ristorante Italiano
1523 Elizabeth Ave ... Charlotte NC 28204 704-370-0208
Web: www.volareristoranteitaliano.com

Zebra 4521 Sharon Rd ... Charlotte NC 28211 704-442-9525 442-9546
Web: www.zebrarestaurant.net

Bennett Pointe Grill & Bar
4625 Hillsborough Rd ... Durham NC 27705 919-382-9431
Web: www.bpgrill.com

Blue Corn Cafe 716 Ninth St ... Durham NC 27705 919-286-9600 416-0862
Web: bluecorncafedurham.com

Bullock's Bar-B-Que 3330 Quebec Dr. ... Durham NC 27705 919-383-3211 383-6202
Web: www.bullocksbbq.com

Cafe Parizade 2200 W Main St ... Durham NC 27705 919-286-9712 416-9706
Web: www.parizadedurham.com

El Rodeo 3404 Westgate Dr ... Durham NC 27707 919-402-9190
Web: elrodeodurhamnc.com

Fairview Restaurant 3001 Cameron Blvd. ... Durham NC 27705 919-493-6699 681-3514
Web: washingtondukeinn.com

Fishmonger's 806 W Main St ... Durham NC 27701 919-682-0128
Web: www.fishmongers.net

Four Square 2701 Chapel Hill Rd ... Durham NC 27707 919-401-9877 401-9878
Web: www.foursquarerestaurant.com

Hog Heaven Bar-B-Q 2419 Guess Rd. ... Durham NC 27705 919-286-7447
Web: www.hogheavenbarbecue.com

Jamaica Jamaica 4857 NC Hwy 55 ... Durham NC 27713 919-544-1532

Kurama Seafood & Steakhouse
3644 Chapel Hill Blvd. ... Durham NC 27707 919-489-2669 489-4400
Web: www.kuramadurham.com

Nana's 2514 University Dr ... Durham NC 27707 919-493-8545 403-8487
Web: www.nanasdurham.com

Neo-Asia Restaurant 4015 University Dr ... Durham NC 27707 919-489-2828 489-9898
Web: www.neo-china.com

Original Q Shack, The 2510 University Dr ... Durham NC 27707 919-402-4227
Web: theqshackoriginal.com

Satisfaction Restaurant 905 W Main St Ste 37 ... Durham NC 27701 919-682-7397 682-6642
Web: www.satisfactionrestaurant.com

Shiki Sushi 207 N Carolina 54 ... Durham NC 27713 919-484-4108
Web: shikinc.com

Spice & Curry 2105 E Hwy 54 ... Durham NC 27713 919-544-7555

Torero's 800 W Main St. ... Durham NC 27701 919-682-4197 682-2662
Web: torerosmexicanrestaurants.com

Vin Rouge Bistro
GHG Restaurant Group 2010 Hillsborough Rd. ... Durham NC 27705 919-416-0466
Web: www.vinrougerestaurant.com

Acropolis Restaurant 416 N Eugene St ... Greensboro NC 27401 336-273-3306 675-0913*
**Fax Area Code: 410*

Anton's 1628 Battleground Ave ... Greensboro NC 27408 336-273-1386 273-1225

Asahi 4520 W Market St. ... Greensboro NC 27407 336-855-8883

Bangkok Cafe 1203 S Holden Rd. ... Greensboro NC 27407 336-855-9370

Boba House 332 S Tate St. ... Greensboro NC 27403 336-379-7444
Web: www.bobahouse.com

Cafe Pasta 305 State St ... Greensboro NC 27408 336-272-1308 272-1352
Web: www.cafepasta.com

Cooper's Ale House 5340 W Market St. ... Greensboro NC 27409 336-294-0575
Web: www.coopersalehouse.com

Darryl's Wood Fired Grill 3300 High Pt Rd ... Greensboro NC 27407 336-294-1781 294-2242
Web: darryls.com

George K's Catering & Banquet Hall
2108 Cedar Fork Dr ... Greensboro NC 27407 336-854-0008

Green Valley Grill 622 Green Vly Rd ... Greensboro NC 27408 336-854-2015 544-9000
Web: www.greenvalleygrill.com

Leblon 106 S Holden Rd ... Greensboro NC 27407 336-294-2605
Web: leblonsteakhouse.com

Liberty Oak Restaurant & Bar
100 W Washington St Ste D ... Greensboro NC 27401 336-273-7057 273-7111
Web: www.libertyoakrestaurant.com

Marisol 5834 High Pt Rd ... Greensboro NC 27407 336-852-3303 852-0347
Web: www.themarisol.com

Melting Pot of Greensboro, The
2924 Battleground Ave ... Greensboro NC 27408 336-545-6233 545-6448
Web: www.meltingpot.com

Monterrey 3724 Battleground Ave ... Greensboro NC 27410 336-282-5588
Web: monterrey29.com

Sapporo Fantasy Japanese Steak
2939 C Battleground Ave ... Greensboro NC 27408 336-282-5345 282-5379

Southern Lights 2415 Lawndale Dr ... Greensboro NC 27408 336-379-9414
Web: southernlightsbistro.com

Stamey's Barbecue 2206 High Pt Rd ... Greensboro NC 27403 336-299-9888 294-2599
Web: www.stameys.com

Taste of Thai 1500 Mill St ... Greensboro NC 27408 336-273-1318
Web: www.tasteofthaigreensboro.com

Undercurrent, The 327 Battleground Ave. ... Greensboro NC 27401 336-370-1266
Web: www.undercurrentrestaurant.com

Village Tavern 1903 Westridge Rd. ... Greensboro NC 27410 336-282-3063
Web: www.villagetavern.com

Villarosa Italian Restaurant & Grill
6010 Landmark Ctr Blvd. ... Greensboro NC 27407 336-294-8688
Web: villarosa.us

518 West 518 W Jones St ... Raleigh NC 27603 919-829-2518 829-0248
Web: www.518west.com

Angus Barn 9401 Glenwood Ave. ... Raleigh NC 27617 919-781-2444 783-5568
TF: 800-277-2270 ■ *Web:* www.angusbarn.com

Bella Monica 3121 EdwaRds Mill Rd Ste 103 ... Raleigh NC 27612 919-881-9778
Web: www.bellamonica.com

Bloomsbury Bistro
509 W Whitaker Mill Rd Ste 101 ... Raleigh NC 27608 919-834-9011 834-9096
Web: www.bloomsburybistro.com

Caffe Luna 136 E Hargett St ... Raleigh NC 27601 919-832-6090 832-0176
Web: www.cafeluna.com

Clyde Cooper's BBQ 109 E Davie St ... Raleigh NC 27601 919-832-7614
Web: clydecoopersbbq.com

Irregardless Cafe 901 W Morgan St. ... Raleigh NC 27603 919-833-8898
Web: irregardless.com

Kanki Japanese House of Steaks
4500 Old Wake Forest Rd ... Raleigh NC 27609 919-782-9708 876-7699
Web: www.kanki.com

Melting Pot of Raleigh, The
3100 Wake Forest Rd ... Raleigh NC 27609 919-878-0477 878-0815
Web: www.meltingpot.com

Neo-Asia / Neo-China (Weekend Lunch Dim Sum)
6602 Glenwood Ave ... Raleigh NC 27612 919-783-8383 783-8353
Web: www.neo-china.com

Nina's 8801 Lead Mine Rd ... Raleigh NC 27615 919-845-1122
Web: ninasrestaurant.com

Rey's 1130 Buck Jones Rd ... Raleigh NC 27606 919-380-0122 380-0411
Web: www.reysrestaurant.com

Saint-Jacques 6112 Falls of the Neuse Rd ... Raleigh NC 27609 919-862-2770 862-2771
Web: saintjacquesfrenchcuisine.com

Second Empire 330 Hillsborough St ... Raleigh NC 27603 919-829-3663
Web: www.second-empire.com

ShabaShabu 3080 Wake Forest Rd. ... Raleigh NC 27609 919-501-7755 501-7479
Web: shabashabu.net

Sushi Blues 301 Glenwood Ave. ... Raleigh NC 27603 919-664-8061 664-8070
Web: www.sushibluescafe.com

Waraji 5910 Duraleigh Rd ... Raleigh NC 27612 919-783-1883
Web: www.warajijapaneserestaurant.com

Zely & Ritz 301 Glenwood Ave. ... Raleigh NC 27603 919-828-0018 828-2937
Web: www.zelyandritz.com

Texas Steakhouse 711 Sutters Creek Blvd ... Rocky Mount NC 27804 252-443-3888
Web: www.texassteakhouse.com

1703 Restaurant 1703 Robin Hood Rd ... Winston-Salem NC 27104 336-725-5767 725-5768
Web: www.localedge.com

A Noble Grille 380 Knollwood St. ... Winston-Salem NC 27103 336-777-8477
Web: www.noblesgrille.com

Cha-Da Thai 420-J Jonestown Rd. ... Winston-Salem NC 27104 336-659-8466 659-8458
Web: chadathai-nc.com

Hill's Lexington Barbecue
4005 Patterson Ave. ... Winston-Salem NC 27105 336-767-2184
Web: ncbbqsociety.com

ISE Sushi & Japanese Restaurant
121 Stark St ... Winston-Salem NC 27103 336-774-0433 774-0451
Web: winstonsalemsushi.com

Midtown Cafe & Dessertery
151 S Stratford Rd ... Winston-Salem NC 27104 336-724-9800 724-9830
Web: www.midtowncafews.com

MJM Reynolda Laundromat
2802 Reynolda Rd ... Winston-Salem NC 27106 336-724-4242

Newtown Bistro & Bar
420 Jonestown Rd Ste U. ... Winston-Salem NC 27104 336-659-8062 659-9835

Old Fourth Street Filling Station, The
871 W Fourth St ... Winston-Salem NC 27101 336-724-7600
Web: www.theoldfourthstreetfillingstation.com

Paul's Fine Italian Dining
3443-B Robinhood Rd ... Winston-Salem NC 27106 336-768-2645
Web: paulsfineitaliandining.com

Ryan's 719 Coliseum Dr. ... Winston-Salem NC 27106 336-724-6132 724-5761
Web: www.ryansrestaurant.com

Sampan Chinese Restaurant
985 Peters Creek Pkwy ... Winston-Salem NC 27103 336-777-8266

Sweet Potatoes 529 N Trade St. ... Winston-Salem NC 27101 336-727-4844 727-4808
Web: www.sweetpotatoes-arestaurant.com

Szechuan Palace 3040 Healy Dr. ... Winston-Salem NC 27103 336-768-7123

North Dakota

Phone | Fax

40 Steak & Seafood 1401 Interchange Ave ... Bismarck ND 58501 701-255-4040 258-7229

Bistro An American Cafe 1103 E Front Ave ... Bismarck ND 58504 701-224-8800 224-0398
Web: www.bistro1100.com

China Garden 1929 N Washington St ... Bismarck ND 58501 701-224-0698

Famous Dave's 401 E Bismarck Expy ... Bismarck ND 58504 701-530-9800 223-2485
Web: www.famousdaves.com

Grand China 658 Kirkwood Mall ... Bismarck ND 58504 701-222-1518 222-1519
Web: www.grandchinabismarck.com

Hong Kong Chinese Restaurant
1055 E Interstate Ave ... Bismarck ND 58503 701-223-2130

Little Cottage Cafe 2513 E Main Ave ... Bismarck ND 58501 701-223-4949

Peacock Alley 422 E Main St ... Bismarck ND 58501 701-255-7917 255-7231
Web: www.peacock-alley.com

Space Aliens Grill & Bar 1304 E Century Ave ... Bismarck ND 58503 701-223-6220 223-2252
Web: www.spacealiens.com

Walrus, The 1136 N 3rd St ... Bismarck ND 58501 701-250-0020
Web: www.thewalrus.com

Wood House Restaurant 1825 N 13th St ... Bismarck ND 58501 701-255-3654

Bison Turf 1211 N University Dr ... Fargo ND 58102 701-235-9118
Web: thebisonturfnd.com

Cafe Aladdin 530 Sixth Ave N. ... Fargo ND 58102 701-298-0880
Web: cafealaddinfargo.com

Granite City Food & Brewery Ltd (GCFB)
1636 42nd St SW ... Fargo ND 58103 701-293-3000 492-0724
Web: www.gcfb.com

Juano's 402 Broadway ... Fargo ND 58102 701-232-3123
Web: juanosrestaurant.com

Mexican Village 814 Main Ave ... Fargo ND 58103 701-293-0120
Web: www.mexicanvillage.com/

Nine Dragons Restaurant 4525 17th Ave S ... Fargo ND 58104 701-232-2411
Web: www.9dragonsrestaurant.com

Seasons at Rose Creek 1500 Rose Creek Pkwy E ... Fargo ND 58104 701-235-5000 235-3010
Web: www.seasonsatrosecreek.com

Shang Hai 3051 25th St SW ... Fargo ND 58103 701-280-5818 232-9433
Web: fargoshanghai.com

Timberlodge Steakhouse 1111 38th St SW ... Fargo ND 58103 701-282-8987
Web: www.timberlodgesteakhouse.com

Restaurant	City	State	Zip	Phone	Fax
Eagle's Crest Grill 5301 S Columbia Rd *Web:* eaglescrestgrill.com	Grand Forks	ND	58201	701-787-3491	787-3494
Italian Moon 810 S Washington St *Web:* www.italianmoon.com	Grand Forks	ND	58201	701-772-7277	
Red Pepper 1011 University Ave *Web:* www.redpepper.com	Grand Forks	ND	58203	701-775-9671	746-7268
Sanders 1907 22 S Third St	Grand Forks	ND	58201	701-746-8970	

Nova Scotia

Restaurant	City	State	Zip	Phone	Fax
Baan Thai Restaurant 5234 Blowers St Second Fl *Web:* www.baanthai.ca	Halifax	NS	B3J1J7	902-446-4301	
Chives Canadian Bistro 1537 Barrington St *Web:* www.chives.ca	Halifax	NS	B3J1Z4	902-420-9626	422-7238
Cousin's Restaurant 3545 Robie St *Web:* www.cousinsrestaurant.webs.com	Halifax	NS	B3K4S7	902-455-8931	
Da Maurizio *Fine Dining* 1496 Lower Water St *Web:* www.damaurizio.ca	Halifax	NS	B3J1R9	902-423-0859	
Dharma Sushi 1576 Argyle St *Web:* www.dharmasushi.com	Halifax	NS	B3J2B3	902-425-7785	425-7250
Economy Shoe Shop Cafe & Bar 1663 Argyle St Ste 1661 *Web:* www.economyshoeshop.ca	Halifax	NS	B3J2B5	902-423-8845	423-5880
Fid 1569 Dresden Row *Web:* fidresto.ca	Halifax	NS	B3J2K4	902-422-9162	422-0018
Five Fishermen Restaurant & Grill, The 1740 Argyle St *Web:* www.fivefishermen.com	Halifax	NS	B3J2B6	902-422-4421	
Hamachi House 5190 Morris St *Web:* www.hamachirestaurants.com	Halifax	NS	B3J1B3	902-425-7711	444-4068
McKelvie's 1680 Lower Water St *Web:* www.mckelvies.com	Halifax	NS	B3J2Y3	902-421-6161	425-8949
Mexico Lindo 3635 Dutch Village Rd *Web:* www.mexicolindo.ca	Halifax	NS	B3N2S4	902-445-0996	
Murphy's Cable Wharf 1751 Lower Water St PO Box 2378 *Web:* www.mtcw.ca	Halifax	NS	B3J3E4	902-420-1015	423-7942
Wooden Monkey 1707 Grafton St *Web:* www.thewoodenmonkey.ca	Halifax	NS	B3J2C6	902-444-3844	444-3693
Your Father's Moustache 5686 Spring Garden Rd *Web:* www.yourfathersmoustache.ca	Halifax	NS	B3J1H5	902-423-6766	422-0054

Ohio

Restaurant	City	State	Zip	Phone	Fax
Bill Hwang's Restaurant 879 Canton Rd *Web:* billhwangsrestaurant.com	Akron	OH	44312	330-784-7167	
Bricco One W Exchange St *Web:* www.briccoakron.com	Akron	OH	44308	330-475-1600	475-1604
Dontino's La Vita Gardens 555 E Cuyahoga Falls Ave *Web:* www.dontinos.com	Akron	OH	44310	330-928-9530	
Duffy's Restaurant 231 Darrow Rd *Web:* duffysrestaurantandgrill.com	Akron	OH	44305	330-784-5043	
El Rincon 1485 S Arlington St	Akron	OH	44306	330-785-3724	785-2816
Gasoline Alley 870 N Cleveland Massillon Rd *Web:* gasolinealleyinbath.com	Akron	OH	44333	330-666-2670	
House of Hunan 12 E Exchange St Ste 1 *Web:* thehouseofhunan.com	Akron	OH	44308	330-253-1888	
Hyde Park Grille 4073 Medina Rd *Web:* www.hydeparkrestaurants.com	Akron	OH	44333	330-670-6303	670-6174
Ido Bar & Grill 1537 S Main St *Web:* www.idobar.com	Akron	OH	44301	330-773-1724	
Ken Stewart's Grille 1970 W Market St *Web:* kenstewarts.com	Akron	OH	44313	330-867-2555	
Lanning's 826 N Cleveland-Massillon Rd *Web:* www.lannings-restaurant.com	Akron	OH	44333	330-666-1159	
Larry's Main Entrance 1964 W Market St	Akron	OH	44313	330-864-8162	
New Era Restaurant 10 Massillon Rd	Akron	OH	44312	330-784-0087	
Otani Japanese Seafood & Steakhouse 1684 Merriman Rd	Akron	OH	44313	330-836-1500	
Papa Joe's 1561 Akron Peninsula Rd *Web:* papajoes.com	Akron	OH	44313	330-923-7999	923-8009
Platinum Dragon 814 1/2 W Market St	Akron	OH	44303	330-434-8108	434-1908
Vaccaro's Trattoria 1000 Ghent Rd *Web:* www.vactrat.com	Akron	OH	44333	330-666-6158	666-4558
Antone's Italian Cafe 4837 Mahoning Ave *Web:* chadanthonys.com	Austintown	OH	44515	330-793-0707	793-2857
Asuka Japanese Cuisine 7381 Market St *Web:* asukajapanese.com	Boardman	OH	44512	330-629-8088	629-6880
Ambar 350 Ludlow Ave *Web:* www.ambarindia.com	Cincinnati	OH	45220	513-281-7000	281-7001
Amol India 354 Ludlow Ave *Web:* amolindiacincinnati.com	Cincinnati	OH	45220	513-961-3600	961-3665
Andy's Mediterranean Grille 906 Nassau St *Web:* www.andyskabob.com	Cincinnati	OH	45206	513-281-9791	751-0416
Bacall's Cafe 6118 Hamilton Ave *Web:* www.bacallscafe.com	Cincinnati	OH	45224	513-541-8804	
Barresi's 4111 Webster Ave *Web:* www.barresis.com	Cincinnati	OH	45236	513-793-2540	
BBQ Revue 4725 Madison Rd	Cincinnati	OH	45227	513-871-3500	
Big Art's BBQ 2796 Struble Rd *Web:* bigartsbbq.com	Cincinnati	OH	45251	513-825-4811	
Brown Dog Cafe 5893 Pfeiffer Rd *Web:* www.browndogcafe.com	Cincinnati	OH	45242	513-794-1610	794-1613
Celestial Restaurant 1071 Celestial St *Web:* www.thecelestial.com	Cincinnati	OH	45202	513-241-4455	241-4855
China Gourmet 3340 Erie Ave *Web:* thechinagourmet.com	Cincinnati	OH	45208	513-871-6612	
El Coyote 7404 State Rd Off 5 Mile Rd *Web:* www.elcoyotecincy.com	Cincinnati	OH	45230	513-232-5757	232-3094
El Rancho Grande 7860 Montgomery Rd *Web:* www.elranchogrande.info	Cincinnati	OH	45236	513-791-5215	
Hibachi Master 8160 Beechmont Ave *Web:* hibachimaster.com	Cincinnati	OH	45255	513-474-9888	
Jeff Ruby's Steakhouse 700 Walnut St *Web:* www.jeffruby.com	Cincinnati	OH	45202	513-321-8080	
Mt Adams Fish House 940 Pavilion St *Web:* www.mtadamsfishhouse.com	Cincinnati	OH	45202	513-421-3250	421-1446
Nectar Restaurant 1000 Delta Ave *Web:* www.tastenectar.com/	Cincinnati	OH	45208	513-929-0525	
Nicholson's Tavern & Pub 625 Walnut St *Web:* www.tavernrestaurantgroup.com	Cincinnati	OH	45202	513-564-9111	
Nicola's 1420 Sycamore St *Web:* nicolasotr.com	Cincinnati	OH	45202	513-721-6200	721-1777
Palace, The 601 Vine St *TF:* 800-942-9000 ■ *Web:* www.palacecincinnati.com	Cincinnati	OH	45202	513-381-6006	651-0256
Primavista 810 Matson Pl *Web:* www.pvista.com	Cincinnati	OH	45204	513-251-6467	251-4669
Restaurant at the Phoenix 812 Race St *Web:* www.thephx.com/restaurant	Cincinnati	OH	45202	513-721-8901	721-1475
Shanghai Mama's 216 E Sixth St *Web:* www.shanghaimamas.com	Cincinnati	OH	45202	513-241-7777	
Teak Thai Cuisine 1049-51 St Gregory St *Web:* www.teakthaicuisine.com	Cincinnati	OH	45202	513-665-9800	665-9861
Trio 7565 Kenwood Rd *Web:* www.triobistro.com	Cincinnati	OH	45236	513-984-1905	984-3873
Blue Point Grille 700 W St Clair Ave *Web:* hrcleveland.com	Cleveland	OH	44113	216-875-7827	902-8175
Bo Loong Restaurant 3922 St Clair Ave	Cleveland	OH	44114	216-391-3113	391-8407
China Jade 2190 Brookpark Rd *Web:* chinajadechineserestaurant.com	Cleveland	OH	44134	216-749-4720	
Don's Lighthouse Grille 8905 Lake Ave *Web:* www.donslighthouse.com	Cleveland	OH	44102	216-961-6700	961-1966
Fahrenheit 2417 Professor Ave *Web:* chefroccowhalen.com/fahrenheit-cleveland/	Cleveland	OH	44113	216-781-8858	781-8867
Fat Cats 2061 W Tenth St *Web:* coolplacestoeat.com	Cleveland	OH	44113	216-579-0200	
Fire 13220 Shaker Sq *Web:* www.firefoodanddrink.com	Cleveland	OH	44120	216-921-3473	921-1957
Flying Fig 2523 Market St *Web:* www.theflyingfig.com	Cleveland	OH	44113	216-241-4243	241-0255
Frank Sterles Slovenian Restaurant 1401 E 55th St *Web:* www.sterlescountryhouse.com	Cleveland	OH	44103	216-881-4181	
Gene's Place 3730 Rocky River Dr	Cleveland	OH	44111	216-252-1741	252-1742
Ginza Sushi House 1105 Carnegie Ave	Cleveland	OH	44115	216-589-8503	
Gusto 12022 Mayfield Rd *Web:* www.gustolittleitaly.com	Cleveland	OH	44106	216-791-9900	791-9903
Harp, The 4408 Detroit Ave *Web:* www.the-harp.com	Cleveland	OH	44113	216-939-0200	939-0068
Hyde Park Steakhouse 123 Prospect Ave W *Web:* www.hydeparkrestaurants.com	Cleveland	OH	44115	216-344-2444	344-2726
Johnny's Bar on Fulton 3164 Fulton Rd *Web:* johnnyscleveland.com	Cleveland	OH	44109	216-281-0055	
Johnny's Downtown 1406 W Sixth St *Web:* www.johnnyscleveland.com	Cleveland	OH	44113	216-623-0055	623-1248
Lemon Grass Thai Cuisine 2179 Lee Rd *Web:* www.bestlemongrass.com	Cleveland	OH	44118	216-321-0210	321-2180
Light Bistro 2801 Bridge Ave *Web:* www.lightbistro.com	Cleveland	OH	44113	216-771-7130	771-8130
Lolita 900 Literary Rd *Web:* lolitarestaurant.com	Cleveland	OH	44113	216-771-5652	
Momocho Mod Mex 1835 Fulton Rd *Web:* www.momocho.com	Cleveland	OH	44113	216-694-2122	
Mortons the Steakhouse 1600 W Second St *Web:* www.mortons.com	Cleveland	OH	44113	216-621-6200	621-7745
Parallax 2179 W 11th St *Web:* www.parallaxtremont.com	Cleveland	OH	44113	216-583-9999	583-0720
Sans Souci 24 Public Sq *Web:* www.sanssoucicleveland.com	Cleveland	OH	44113	216-902-4095	696-0432
Sun Luck Garden 1901 S Taylor Rd *Web:* sunluckgarden.com	Cleveland	OH	44118	216-397-7676	
Sushi Rock 1276 W Sixth St *Web:* www.sushirockohio.com	Cleveland	OH	44113	216-623-1212	
Tommy's Restaurant 1824 Coventry Rd *Web:* www.tommyscoventry.com	Cleveland	OH	44118	216-321-7757	321-8377
Villa Y Zapata 8505 Madison Ave	Cleveland	OH	44102	216-961-4369	
XO Prime Steaks 500 W St Claire Ave *Web:* xoprimesteaks.com	Cleveland	OH	44113	216-861-1919	861-0374
Cafe Tandoor 2096 S Taylor Rd *Web:* cafetandoorcleveland.com	Cleveland Heights	OH	44118	216-371-8500	371-8560
Mad Greek 2466 Fairmount Blvd *Web:* www.madgreekcleveland.com	Cleveland Heights	OH	44106	216-421-3333	421-8821
Aladdin's Eatery 2931 N High St *Web:* www.aladdinseatery.com	Columbus	OH	43202	614-262-2414	262-2450
Alana's Food & Wine 2333 N High St *Web:* www.alanas.com	Columbus	OH	43202	614-294-6783	
Anna's Greek Cuisine 7370 Sawmill Rd *Web:* annasgreekfood.com	Columbus	OH	43235	614-799-2207	
Barcelona 263 E Whittier St *Web:* www.barcelonacolumbus.com	Columbus	OH	43206	614-443-3699	444-0539
Barley's Smokehouse & Brewpub 1130 Dublin Rd *Web:* www.smokehousebrewing.com	Columbus	OH	43215	614-485-0227	
Basi Italia 811 Highland St *Web:* basi-italia.com	Columbus	OH	43215	614-294-7383	
Brio Tuscan Grille 3993 Easton Stn St *Web:* www.brioitalian.com	Columbus	OH	43219	614-416-4745	416-4747

				Phone	Fax
Cafe Istanbul 3983 Worth Ave	Columbus	OH	43219	614-473-9144	473-9133
Web: www.cafeistanbul.com					
Cameron Mitchell Restaurants 515 Pk St	Columbus	OH	43215	614-291-3663	
Web: www.cameronmitchell.com					
Columbus Fish Market 1245 Olentangy River Rd	Columbus	OH	43212	614-291-3474	291-7258
Web: mitchellsfishmarket.com					
Due Amici 67 E Gay St	Columbus	OH	43215	614-224-9373	227-0015
Web: www.due-amici.com					
El Vaquero 2195 Riverside Dr	Columbus	OH	43221	614-486-4547	486-4050
Web: vaquerorestaurant.com					
G Michael's Bistro 595 S Third St	Columbus	OH	43215	614-464-0575	
Web: gmichaelsbistroandbar.com					
Haiku Poetic Food & Art 800 N High St	Columbus	OH	43215	614-294-8168	294-3868
Web: haikucolumbus.com					
Handke's Cuisine 520 S Front St	Columbus	OH	43215	614-621-2500	621-2626
Web: www.chefhandke.com					
Hunan House 2350 E Dublin Granville Rd	Columbus	OH	43229	614-895-3330	
Web: www.hunancolumbus.com					
Hyde Park Prime Steakhouse 569 N High St	Columbus	OH	43215	614-224-2204	
Web: hydeparkrestaurants.com					
J Alexander's 7550 Vantage Dr	Columbus	OH	43235	614-847-1166	847-1332
Web: www.jalexanders.com					
Japanese Steak House 479 N High St	Columbus	OH	43215	614-228-3030	
Web: japanesesteakhousecolumbusoh.com					
L'Antibes 772 N High St Ste 106	Columbus	OH	43215	614-291-1666	
Web: www.lantibes.com					
Latitude 41 50 N Third St	Columbus	OH	43215	614-233-7541	
Web: www.latitude41restaurant.com					
Lemongrass 641 N High St	Columbus	OH	43215	614-224-1414	221-2535
Web: www.lemongrassfusion.com					
Lindey's 169 E Beck St	Columbus	OH	43206	614-228-4343	228-8920
Web: www.lindeys.com					
M at Miranova 2 Miranova PL Ste 100	Columbus	OH	43215	614-629-0000	221-5020
TF: 877-491-1267 ■ *Web:* www.matmiranova.com					
Martini Italian Bistro 445 N High St	Columbus	OH	43215	614-224-8259	224-8780
Web: www.martinimodernitalian.com					
Mitchell's Fish Market 1245 Olentangy River Rd	Columbus	OH	43212	614-410-3474	
Web: www.mitchellsfishmarket.com					
Mitchell's Ocean Club 4002 Easton Stn	Columbus	OH	43219	614-416-2582	416-2800
Web: www.mitchellsoceanclub.com					
Mitchell's Steakhouse 45 N Third St	Columbus	OH	43215	614-621-2333	621-2898
Web: www.mitchellssteakhouse.com					
Refectory Resturant & Bistro 1092 Bethel Rd	Columbus	OH	43220	614-451-9774	451-4434
Web: www.therefectoryrestaurant.com					
Rigsby's Kitchen 698 N High St	Columbus	OH	43215	614-461-7888	228-5639
Web: www.rigsbyskitchen.com					
Rossi Bar & Kitchen 895 N High St	Columbus	OH	43215	614-299-2810	
Web: rossibarandkitchen.com					
Schmidt's Sausage Haus 240 E Kossuth St	Columbus	OH	43206	614-444-6808	445-3072
Web: www.schmidthaus.com					
Shoku 1312 Grandview Ave	Columbus	OH	43212	614-485-9490	
Web: shokugrandview.com					
Thai Taste 1178 Kenny Centre Mall	Columbus	OH	43220	614-451-7605	
Trattoria Roma 1447 Grandview Ave	Columbus	OH	43212	614-488-2104	488-4452
Web: www.trattoria-roma.com					
Windward Passage 4739 Reed Rd	Columbus	OH	43220	614-451-2497	
Akashi Sushi Bar 2020 Harshman Rd	Dayton	OH	45424	937-233-8005	233-8845
Web: akashidayton.com					
Amber Rose 1400 Valley St	Dayton	OH	45404	937-228-2511	222-0479
Web: www.theamberrose.com					
Barnsider 5202 N Main St	Dayton	OH	45415	937-277-1332	277-0567
Web: barnsider-restaurant.com					
Citilites 109 N Main St Ste 305	Dayton	OH	45402	937-222-0623	222-1504
Web: victoriatheatre.com					
Dublin Pub 300 Wayne Ave	Dayton	OH	45410	937-224-7822	224-0355
Web: www.dubpub.com					
Elsa's 3618 Linden Ave	Dayton	OH	45410	937-252-9635	
Web: elsas.net					
Franco's Ristorante Italiano 824 E Fifth St	Dayton	OH	45402	937-222-0204	222-1380
Web: www.francos-italiano.com					
I-Zu Japanese Restaurant & Grocery 5252 N Dixie Dr	Dayton	OH	45414	937-277-9596	
Jay's Seafood Restaurant *Woods Construction Co Inc, The* 225 E Sixth St	Dayton	OH	45402	937-222-2892	222-7547
Web: www.jays.com					
Mamma DiSalvo's Italian Ristorante 1375 E Stroop Rd	Dayton	OH	45429	937-299-5831	299-1752
Web: www.mammadisalvo.com					
North China 6090 Far Hills Ave	Dayton	OH	45459	937-433-6837	
Web: northchinadayton.com					
Pine Club, The 1926 Brown St	Dayton	OH	45409	937-228-7463	228-5371
Web: www.thepineclub.com					
Thai9 11 Brown St	Dayton	OH	45402	937-222-3227	222-3235
Web: www.thai9restaurant.com					
La Petite France 3177 Glendale-Milford Rd	Evendale	OH	45241	513-733-8383	733-0038
Web: www.lapetitefrance.biz					
Max & Erma's 3750 W Market St	Fairlawn	OH	44333	330-666-1002	666-3001
Web: maxandermas.com					
Otani 1625 Golden Gate Plz	Mayfield Heights	OH	44124	440-442-7098	442-7138
Web: www.otanicleveland.com					
Montgomery Inn 9440 Montgomery Rd	Montgomery	OH	45242	513-791-3482	992-8678*
**Fax Area Code:* 914 ■ *Web:* www.montgomeryinn.com					
356th Fighter Group 4919 Mt Pleasant Rd	North Canton	OH	44720	330-494-3500	494-5509
Phnom Penh 27080 Lorain Ave	North Olmsted	OH	44070	216-201-9141	
Web: ohiorestaurant.com					
Cousino's Steak House 1842 Woodville Rd	Oregon	OH	43616	419-693-0862	
Saffron Patch 20600 Chagrin Blvd Twr E Bldg	Shaker Heights	OH	44122	216-295-0400	295-1320
Web: www.thesaffronpatch.com					
Avenue Bistro Restaurant 6710 W Central Ave	Toledo	OH	43617	419-841-5944	842-1435
Web: centralavenuebistro.com					
Beirut 4082 Monroe St	Toledo	OH	43606	419-473-0885	473-8947
Web: beirutrestaurant.com					
Dolly & Joe's 1045 S Reynolds St	Toledo	OH	43615	419-385-2441	
Dorr Street Cafe 5243 Dorr St	Toledo	OH	43615	419-531-4446	
Web: dorrstreetcafe.com					
Eddie Lee's 4700 Nantucket Dr	Toledo	OH	43623	419-882-0616	
El Camino Real 2500 W Sylvania Ave	Toledo	OH	43613	419-472-0700	
Web: elcaminorealtoledo.com					
Fritz & Alfredo's 3025 N Summit St	Toledo	OH	43611	419-729-9775	
Web: toledostripletreat.com					
Georgio's Cafe International 426 N Superior St	Toledo	OH	43604	419-242-2424	242-2155
Web: www.georgiostoledo.com					
Mancy's 953 Phillips Ave	Toledo	OH	43612	419-476-4154	
Web: www.mancys.com					
Mango Tree 217 S Reynolds Rd	Toledo	OH	43615	419-536-2883	
Web: mangotreedining.com					
Manos Greek Restaurant & Bar 1701 Adams St	Toledo	OH	43604	419-244-4479	
Web: www.manosgreekrestaurant.com					
Real Seafood Co 22 Main St	Toledo	OH	43605	419-697-4400	
Web: mainstreetventuresinc.com					
Rockwell's 27 Broadway	Toledo	OH	43604	419-243-1302	243-9256
Web: oh-rockwells.com					
Rose Thai 5333 Monroe St	Toledo	OH	43623	419-841-8467	
Shorty's Bar-B-Cue 5111 Monroe St	Toledo	OH	43623	419-841-9505	843-2158
Web: www.mancys.com					
Tony Packo's 1902 Front St	Toledo	OH	43605	419-691-1953	
TF: 866-472-2567 ■ *Web:* www.tonypacko.com					
Ventura's 7742 W Bancroft St	Toledo	OH	43617	419-841-7523	
Web: toledostripletreat.com					
China Dynasty 1689 W Ln Ave	Upper Arlington	OH	43221	614-486-7126	486-4131
Web: www.chinadynasty-cmh.com					
Kikyo 3706 Riverside Dr	Upper Arlington	OH	43221	614-457-5277	
Web: www.thekikyo.com					
Golden Dawn 1245 Logan Ave	Youngstown	OH	44505	330-746-0393	
Golden Hunan Restaurant 3111 Belmont Ave	Youngstown	OH	44505	330-759-7197	
Main Moon 1760 Belmont Ave	Youngstown	OH	44504	330-743-1638	
Nicolinni's 1912 S Raccoon Rd	Youngstown	OH	44515	330-799-9999	
Web: www.nicolinnis.com					
Station Square Restaurant 4250 Belmont Ave	Youngstown	OH	44505	330-759-8802	
Web: thestationsquare.com					
Upstairs Restaurant, The 4500 Mahoning Ave	Youngstown	OH	44515	330-793-5577	259-0658
Web: theupstairsrestaurant.com					
Youngstown Crab Co 3917 Belmont Ave	Youngstown	OH	44505	330-759-5480	759-7811
Web: www.youngstowncrabco.com					

Oklahoma

				Phone	Fax
Pelicans 291 N Air Depot Blvd	Midwest City	OK	73110	405-732-4392	
Web: pelicansok.com					
Ajanta 12215 N Pennsylvania Ave	Oklahoma City	OK	73120	405-752-5283	
Web: www.ajantaokc.com					
Alvarado's Mexican Restaurant 11641 S Western Ave	Oklahoma City	OK	73170	405-692-2007	
Web: www.alvaradosmexican.com					
Bricktown Brewery One N Oklahoma Ave	Oklahoma City	OK	73104	405-232-2739	601-8961
Web: www.bricktownbrewery.com					
Charleston's 5907 NW Expy St	Oklahoma City	OK	73132	405-721-0060	
Web: charlestons.ehsrg.com					
Coach House 6437 Avondale Dr	Oklahoma City	OK	73116	405-842-1000	843-9777
Web: www.thecoachhouseokc.com					
Deep Fork Grill 5418 N Western Ave	Oklahoma City	OK	73118	405-848-7678	840-0624
Web: www.deepforkgrill.com					
Dot Wo 3101 N Portland Ave	Oklahoma City	OK	73112	405-942-1376	
Web: www.dot-wo.com					
Earl's Rib Palace 6816 N Western Ave	Oklahoma City	OK	73116	405-843-9922	
Web: www.earlsribpalace.com					
Haunted House 7101 Miramar Blvd	Oklahoma City	OK	73111	405-478-1417	
Web: hauntedhouserestaurant.com					
Metro Wine Bar & Bistro 6418 N Western Ave	Oklahoma City	OK	73116	405-840-9463	
Web: www.metrowinebar.com					
Mickey Mantle's Steakhouse Seven Mickey Mantle Dr	Oklahoma City	OK	73104	405-272-0777	232-7111
Web: mickeymantlesteakhouse.com					
Musashi's Japanese Steakhouse 4315 N Western	Oklahoma City	OK	73118	405-602-5623	602-5574
Web: www.musashis.com					
Papa Dio's 10712 N May Ave	Oklahoma City	OK	73120	405-755-2255	
Web: papadiosokc.com					
Pearl's Oyster Bar 5641 N Classen Blvd	Oklahoma City	OK	73118	405-848-8008	840-0382
Web: funfresh.publishpath.com/					
Redrock Canyon Grill 9221 Lk Hefner Pkwy	Oklahoma City	OK	73120	405-749-1995	
Web: redrockcanyongrill.com					
Royal Bavaria Brewery 3401 S Sooner Rd	Oklahoma City	OK	73165	405-799-7666	
Web: www.royal-bavaria.com					
Sushi Neko 4318 N Western	Oklahoma City	OK	73118	405-528-8862	521-9877
Web: www.sushineko.com					
Ted's Cafe Escondido 2836 NW 68th St	Oklahoma City	OK	73116	405-848-8337	840-5865
Web: tedscafe.com					
Tokyo Japanese Restaurant 7516 N Western Ave	Oklahoma City	OK	73116	405-848-6733	
Web: www.tokyookc.com					
Trapper's Fishcamp & Grill 4300 W Reno St	Oklahoma City	OK	73107	405-943-9111	
Web: funfresh.publishpath.com/					

Name / Address	City	State	Zip	Phone	Fax
Albert G's Bar-BQ 2748 S Harvard Ave *Web:* www.albertgs.com	Tulsa	OK	74114	918-747-4799	
Binh-Le 5903 E 31st St	Tulsa	OK	74135	918-835-7722	
Bodean Seafood Restaurant 3376 E 51st St *Web:* www.bodean.net	Tulsa	OK	74135	918-749-1407	747-9352
Brookside by Day 3313 S Peoria Ave *Web:* brooksidebyday.com	Tulsa	OK	74105	918-745-9989	
Chalkboard, The 1324 S Main St *Web:* chalkboardtulsa.com/	Tulsa	OK	74119	918-582-1964	382-6013
Chimi's 1304 E 15th St *Web:* chimismexican.com	Tulsa	OK	74120	918-587-4411	587-0402
French Hen 7143 S Yale Ave *Web:* frenchhentulsa.net	Tulsa	OK	74136	918-492-2596	
Fuji 8226 E 71st St *Web:* www.fujisushibar.com	Tulsa	OK	74133	918-250-1821	459-5012
In the Raw Sushi 3321 S Peoria *Web:* www.intherawsushi.com	Tulsa	OK	74105	918-744-1300	744-1311
Kilkenny's Irish Pub & Eatery 1413 E 15th St *Web:* www.tulsairishpub.com	Tulsa	OK	74120	918-582-8282	582-3931
Mahogany Prime Steak House 6823 S Yale Ave *Web:* www.mahogany.ehsrg.com	Tulsa	OK	74136	918-494-4043	494-0209
McGill's 1560 E 21st St *Web:* dinemcgills.com	Tulsa	OK	74114	918-742-8080	
New Hong Kong Restaurant 2623 E 11th St	Tulsa	OK	74104	918-585-5328	
Polo Grill 2038 Utica Sq *Web:* www.pologrill.com	Tulsa	OK	74114	918-744-4280	749-7082
Spudder, The 6536 E 50th St *Web:* www.thespudder.com	Tulsa	OK	74145	918-665-1416	477-7719
Taste of China 11360 E 31st St	Tulsa	OK	74146	918-664-2252	
United States Beef Corp 4923 E 49th St *Web:* www.usbeefcorp.com	Tulsa	OK	74135	918-665-0740	610-2200
White Lion Pub 6927 S Canton Ave *Web:* kelv.net	Tulsa	OK	74136	918-491-6533	
Zio's 7111 S Mingo Rd *Web:* zios.com	Tulsa	OK	74133	918-250-5999	252-1287

Ontario

Name / Address	City	State	Zip	Phone	Fax
Mandarin Eight Clipper Crt *Web:* www.mandarinrestaurant.com	Brampton	ON	L6W4T9	905-451-4100	456-3411
Grappa 690 The Queensway *Web:* www.grapparestaurant.ca	Etobicoke	ON	M8Y1K8	416-535-3337	
Capone's 1701 Woodroffe Ave *Web:* www.capones.com	Nepean	ON	K2G1W2	613-226-6947	226-7080
Beckta Dining & Wine 226 Nepean St *Web:* www.beckta.com	Ottawa	ON	K2P0B8	613-238-7063	231-7474
Black Tomato 11 George St *Web:* www.theblacktomato.com	Ottawa	ON	K1N8W5	613-789-8123	
Blue Cactus Bar & Grill Two ByWard Market *Web:* www.bluecactusbarandgrill.com	Ottawa	ON	K1N7A1	613-241-7061	241-4504
Cafe Spiga 271 Dalhousie St *Web:* www.cafespiga.com	Ottawa	ON	K1N7E5	613-241-4381	
Coriander 282 Kent St *Web:* corianderthai.com	Ottawa	ON	K2P2A4	613-233-2828	
D'Arcy McGee's Irish Pub 44 Sparks St *Web:* www.primepubs.com	Ottawa	ON	K1P5A8	613-230-4433	230-3849
Giovanni's 362 Preston St *Web:* www.giovannis-restaurant.com	Ottawa	ON	K1S4M7	613-234-3156	
Golden Palace 2195 Carling Ave *Web:* goldenpalacerestaurant.ca	Ottawa	ON	K2B7E8	613-820-8444	
Green Door 198 Main St *Web:* www.greendoor.ca	Ottawa	ON	K1S1C6	613-234-9597	
Haveli Restaurant 39 Clarence St *Web:* www.haveli.com	Ottawa	ON	K1N1G9	613-241-1700	
Heart & Crown 67 Clarence St *Web:* www.heartandcrown.ca	Ottawa	ON	K1N5P5	613-562-0674	562-3278
Indian Biriyani House 1589 Bank St *Web:* indianbiriyanihouse.ca	Ottawa	ON	K1H7Z3	613-260-3893	
Island Jerk 1800 Bank St	Ottawa	ON	K1V0W3	613-737-5163	
Juniper 245 Richmond Rd	Ottawa	ON	K1Z6W7	613-728-0220	728-3993
Luxe Bistro 47 York St *Web:* www.luxebistro.com	Ottawa	ON	K1N5S7	613-241-8805	241-8886
Mamma Grazzi's Kitchen 25 George St *Web:* www.mammagrazzis.com	Ottawa	ON	K1N8W5	613-241-8656	241-5738
Manx, The 370 Elgin St *Web:* manxpub.com	Ottawa	ON	K2P1N1	613-231-2070	
Mezzanotte Cafe 50 Murray St Byward Market *Web:* www.mezzanotte-bistro.com	Ottawa	ON	K1N9M5	613-562-3978	
Murray Street Kitchen 110 Murray St *Web:* www.murraystreet.ca	Ottawa	ON	K1N5M6	613-562-7244	562-9770
New Mee Fung 350 Booth St *Web:* newmeefung.com	Ottawa	ON	K1R7K1	613-567-8228	
Nokham Thai 747 Richmond Rd *Web:* nokhamthai.ca	Ottawa	ON	K2A3Z9	613-724-6135	724-6620
Pancho Villa 361 Elgin St	Ottawa	ON	K2P1M7	613-234-8872	234-7786
Pub Italia 434 1/2 Preston St *Web:* www.pubitalia.ca	Ottawa	ON	K1S4N4	613-232-2326	
Sante Restaurant 45 Rideau St Second Fl *Web:* www.santerestaurant.com	Ottawa	ON	K1N5W8	613-241-7113	
Shanghai Restaurant 651 Somerset St W	Ottawa	ON	K1R5K3	613-233-4001	
Suisha Garden Japanese Restaurant 208 Slater St *Web:* japaninottawa.com	Ottawa	ON	K1P5H8	613-236-9602	
Sweet Basil 1585 Bank St *Web:* sweetbasilottawa.com	Ottawa	ON	K1H7Z3	613-731-8424	
Tosca Ristorante 144 O'Connor St *Web:* www.tosca-ristorante.ca	Ottawa	ON	K2P2G7	613-565-3933	
Vietnam Palace Restaurant 819 Somerset St W	Ottawa	ON	K1R6R5	613-238-6758	
Vineyards Wine Bar Bistro 54 York St *Web:* www.vineyards.ca	Ottawa	ON	K1N5T1	613-241-4270	241-5538
Vittoria Trattoria 35 William St *Web:* www.vittoriatrattoria.com	Ottawa	ON	K1N6Z9	613-789-8959	730-5239
Yangtze Dining Lounge 700 Somerset W *Web:* www.yangtze.ca	Ottawa	ON	K1R6P3	613-236-0555	
Acqua Fine Foods 671 The Queensway *Web:* www.acqua.ca	Toronto	ON	M8Y1K8	416-368-7171	368-6171
Adega 33 Elm St *Web:* www.adegarestaurante.ca	Toronto	ON	M5G1H1	416-977-4338	977-9339
Bangkok Garden 18 Elm St *Web:* www.bangkokgarden.ca	Toronto	ON	M5G1G7	416-977-6748	977-8280
Barberian's Steak House Seven Elm St *Web:* www.barberians.com	Toronto	ON	M5G1H1	416-597-0335	597-1407
Biagio 155 King St E *Web:* biagioristorante.ca	Toronto	ON	M5C1G9	416-366-4040	366-4765
Big Daddy's 212 King St W *Web:* www.bigdaddys.ca	Toronto	ON	M5H1K5	416-599-5200	599-8582
Bodega Restaurant 30 Baldwin St *Web:* www.bodegarestaurant.com	Toronto	ON	M5T1L3	416-977-1287	408-1941
Cafe 668 885 Dundas St W *Web:* www.cafe668.com	Toronto	ON	M6J1V9	416-703-0668	
Celestin 623 Mt Pleasant Rd *Web:* celestinrestaurant.ca	Toronto	ON	M4S2M9	416-544-9035	
Chiado 864 College St *Web:* www.chiadorestaurant.com	Toronto	ON	M6H1A3	416-538-1910	588-8383
Coppi 3363 Yonge St *Web:* www.coppiristorante.com	Toronto	ON	M4N2M6	416-484-4464	
Courtyard Cafe 18 St Thomas St *TF Cust Svc:* 877-999-2767 ■ *Web:* www.windsorarmshotel.com	Toronto	ON	M5S3E7	416-921-2921	921-9121
Dhaba 309 King St W *Web:* www.dhaba.ca	Toronto	ON	M5V1J5	416-740-6622	740-4519
EDO Sushi 484 Eglinton Ave W *Web:* edorestaurants.com	Toronto	ON	M5N1A5	416-322-3033	322-2272
Edo-ko 431 Spadina Rd *Web:* edorestaurants.com	Toronto	ON	M5P2W3	416-482-8973	
El Sol 1448 Danforth Ave *Web:* elsol.ca	Toronto	ON	M4J1N4	416-405-8074	
Far Niente 187 Bay St PO Box 517 *Web:* www.farnienterestaurant.com	Toronto	ON	M5L1G5	416-214-9922	214-1895
Fifth inc, The 225 Richmond St W *Web:* www.thefifth.com	Toronto	ON	M5V1W2	416-979-3000	979-9877
George 111 Queen St E *Web:* www.georgeonqueen.com	Toronto	ON	M5C1S2	416-863-6006	368-6093
Golden Thai 105 Church St *Web:* www.goldenthai.ca	Toronto	ON	M5C2G3	416-868-6668	
Harbour Sixty Steakhouse 60 Harbour St *Web:* www.harboursixty.com	Toronto	ON	M5J1B7	416-777-2111	777-2110
Hemispheres Restaurant & Bistro 108 Chestnut St *Web:* www.metropolitan.com	Toronto	ON	M5G1R3	416-599-8000	977-9513
Il Gatto Nero 720 College St	Toronto	ON	M6G1C2	416-536-3132	
Joso's 202 Davenport Rd *Web:* josos.com	Toronto	ON	M5R1J2	416-925-1903	925-6567
La Fenice 319 King St W *Web:* www.lafenice.ca	Toronto	ON	M5V1J5	416-585-2377	
Lai Wah Heen 108 Chestnut St *Web:* laiwahheen.com	Toronto	ON	M5G1R3	416-977-9899	977-8027
Le Papillon on Front 69 Front St E *Web:* papillononfront.com	Toronto	ON	M5E1B5	416-367-0303	
Le Saint Tropez 315 King St W *TF:* 888-627-2357 ■ *Web:* www.marcels.com	Toronto	ON	M5V1J5	416-591-8600	591-7689
Morton's of Chicago Four Ave Rd *Web:* www.mortons.com	Toronto	ON	M5R2E8	416-925-0648	925-7593
New Generation Sushi 493 Bloor St W *Web:* newgenerationsushi.com	Toronto	ON	M5S1Y2	416-963-8861	
North 44 Degrees 2537 Yonge St *Web:* north44.mcewangroup.ca	Toronto	ON	M4P2H9	416-487-4897	
Opus 37 Prince Arthur Ave *Web:* www.opusrestaurant.com	Toronto	ON	M5R1B2	416-921-3105	921-9353
ORO Restaurant 45 Elm St *Web:* www.ororestaurant.com	Toronto	ON	M5G1H1	416-597-0155	597-2819
Panagaea Restaurant 1221 Bay St *Web:* www.pangaearestaurant.com	Toronto	ON	M5R3P5	416-920-2323	
REDS Wine Tavern 77 Adelaide St W *Web:* www.redswinetavern.com	Toronto	ON	M5H1P9	416-862-7337	
Ristorante SOTTO SOTTO 116A Ave Rd *Web:* www.sottosotto.ca	Toronto	ON	M5R2H4	416-962-0011	962-2509
Rodney's Oyster House 469 King St W *Web:* www.rodneysoysterhouse.com	Toronto	ON	M5V1K4	416-363-8105	363-6638
Rol San 323 Spadina Ave	Toronto	ON	M5T2E9	416-977-1128	
Rosewater Supper Club 19 Toronto St *Web:* www.libertygroup.com	Toronto	ON	M5C2R1	416-214-5888	214-2412
Sassafraz 100 Cumberland St *Web:* www.sassafraz.ca	Toronto	ON	M5R1A6	416-964-2222	964-2402
Scaramouche Restaurant One Benvenuto Pl *Web:* www.scaramoucherestaurant.com	Toronto	ON	M4V2L1	416-961-8011	961-1922
Segovia Five St Nicholas St *Web:* www.segoviarestaurant.ca	Toronto	ON	M4Y1W5	416-960-1010	
Signatures 220 Bloor St W	Toronto	ON	M5S1T8	416-324-5885	
Southern Accent 595 Markham St *Web:* www.southernaccent.com	Toronto	ON	M6G2L7	416-536-3211	536-3548
Splendido's 88 Harbord St *Web:* splendido.ca	Toronto	ON	M5S1G6	416-929-7788	929-3501
Spuntini 116 Ave Rd *Web:* www.spuntini.ca	Toronto	ON	M5R2H4	416-962-1110	934-0179
Trattoria Nervosa 75 Yorkville Ave *Web:* www.eatnervosa.com	Toronto	ON	M5R1B8	416-961-4642	967-4642
Young Thailand 936 King St W *Web:* www.youngthailand.com	Toronto	ON	M5V1P5	416-366-8424	
Zucca Trattoria 2150 Yonge St *Web:* www.zuccatrattoria.com	Toronto	ON	M4S2A7	416-488-5774	

Oregon

Restaurant	City	State	ZIP	Phone	Fax
Skippers Seafood & Chowder House 2987 Santiam Hwy SE *Web:* www.skippersseafoodandchowder.com	Albany	OR	97322	541-926-8623	
Ambrosia Restaurant 174 E Broadway *Web:* www.ambrosiarestaurant.com	Eugene	OR	97401	541-342-4141	345-6965
Anatolia's 992 Willamette St *Web:* poppisanatolia.com	Eugene	OR	97401	541-343-9661	
Beppe & Gianni's Tratorria 1646 E 19th Ave *Web:* beppeandgiannis.net	Eugene	OR	97403	541-683-6661	485-9698
Cafe Soriah 384 W 13th Ave *Web:* www.soriah.com	Eugene	OR	97401	541-342-4410	
Chao Pra Ya Thai Cuisine 580 Adams St	Eugene	OR	97402	541-344-1706	344-1181
Chapala 136 Oakway Rd *Web:* chapalamex.com	Eugene	OR	97401	541-434-6113	434-6267
Fisherman's Market 830 W Seventh Ave *Web:* eugenefishmarket.com	Eugene	OR	97402	541-484-2722	
Lotus Garden 810 Charnelton St *Web:* lotusgardenveg.com	Eugene	OR	97401	541-344-1928	
Marche 296 E Fifth Ave *Web:* www.marcherestaurant.com	Eugene	OR	97401	541-342-3612	342-3611
McGrath's Fish House 1036 Vly River Way *Web:* www.mcgrathsfishhouse.com	Eugene	OR	97401	541-342-6404	342-6079
Morning Glory Cafe 450 Willamette St *Web:* morninggloryeugene.com	Eugene	OR	97401	541-687-0709	
Oregon Electric Station 27 E Fifth Ave *Web:* oesrestaurant.com	Eugene	OR	97401	541-485-4444	484-6149
Ring of Fire 1099 Chambers St *Web:* www.ringoffirerestaurant.com	Eugene	OR	97402	541-344-6475	684-0732
Sixth Street Grill 55 W Sixth Ave *Web:* www.sixthstreetgrill.com	Eugene	OR	97401	541-485-2961	485-3080
Steelhead Brewery & Cafe 199 E Fifth Ave *Web:* www.steelheadbrewery.com	Eugene	OR	97401	541-686-2739	342-5338
Sushi Station 199 E Fifth Ave	Eugene	OR	97401	541-484-1334	
Vintage, The 837 Lincoln St *Web:* thevintageeugene.com	Eugene	OR	97401	541-349-9181	
3 Doors Down Cafe 1429 SE 37th St *Web:* www.3doorsdowncafe.com	Portland	OR	97214	503-236-6886	235-9221
Amalfi's 4703 NE Fremont St *Web:* www.amalfisrestaurant.com	Portland	OR	97213	503-284-6747	
Andina 1314 NW Glisan *Web:* www.andinarestaurant.com	Portland	OR	97209	503-228-9535	228-0788
Basta's Trattoria 410 NW 21st Ave *Web:* www.bastastrattoria.com	Portland	OR	97209	503-274-1572	
Berlin Inn 3131 SE 12th Ave *Web:* www.berlininn.com	Portland	OR	97202	503-236-6761	238-4068
Bluehour 250 NW 13th Ave *Web:* www.bluehouronline.com	Portland	OR	97209	503-226-3394	
Bombay Cricket Club Restaurant 1925 SE Hawthorne Blvd *Web:* www.bombaycricketclubrestaurant.com	Portland	OR	97214	503-231-0740	
Cafe Castagna 1752 SE Hawthorne Blvd *Web:* www.castagnarestaurant.com	Portland	OR	97214	503-231-9959	
Cafe du Berry 6439 SW MacAdam Ave *Web:* cafeduberry.ypguides.net	Portland	OR	97239	503-244-5551	
Caffe Mingo 807 NW 21st Ave *Web:* barmingonw.com	Portland	OR	97209	503-226-4646	
Campbell's Bar-B-Q 8701 SE Powell Blvd *Web:* www.campbellsbbq.com	Portland	OR	97266	503-777-9795	
Canton Grill 2610 SE 82nd Ave *Web:* canton-grill.com	Portland	OR	97266	503-774-1135	
Castagna 1752 SE Hawthorne Blvd *Web:* www.castagnarestaurant.com	Portland	OR	97214	503-231-7373	231-7474
Cha! Cha! Cha! 1208 NW Glisan St *Web:* chachachapdx.com	Portland	OR	97209	503-221-2111	
Clay's Smokehouse Grill 2932 SE Div St *Web:* clayssmokehouse.ypguides.net	Portland	OR	97202	503-235-4755	
Giorgio's 1131 NW Hoyt St *Web:* www.giorgiospdx.com	Portland	OR	97209	503-221-1888	
Heathman Restaurant 1001 SW Broadway *Web:* www.heathmanrestaurantandbar.com	Portland	OR	97205	503-790-7752	790-7105
Higgins Restaurant & Bar 1239 SW Broadway *Web:* higginsportland.com	Portland	OR	97205	503-222-9070	222-1244
Iron Horse 6034 SE Milwaukie Ave *Web:* www.portlandironhorse.com	Portland	OR	97202	503-232-1826	236-3988
Jake's Famous Crawfish 401 SW 12th Ave SW Stark *TF:* 800-552-6379 ■ *Web:* www.mccormickandschmicks.com	Portland	OR	97205	503-226-1419	220-1856
Jake's Grill 611 SW Tenth Ave *TF:* 800-552-6379 ■ *Web:* www.mccormickandschmicks.com	Portland	OR	97205	503-220-1850	226-8365
Kell's 112 SW Second Ave *Web:* www.kellsirish.com	Portland	OR	97204	503-227-4057	593-1227
Koji Osakaya 606 SW Broadway *Web:* www.koji.com	Portland	OR	97205	503-294-1169	294-1169
London Grill 309 SW Broadway *Web:* www.coasthotels.com	Portland	OR	97205	503-228-2000	471-3924
McCormick & Schmick's Harborside 0309 SW Montgomery *Fax Area Code: 614 ■ *TF Resv:* 888-262-4386 ■ *Web:* www.mccormickandschmicks.com	Portland	OR	97201	503-220-1865	476-3663*
Mint Restaurant & Bar 816 N Russell St *Web:* www.mintand820.com	Portland	OR	97227	503-284-5518	
Mio Sushi 2271 NW Johnson St *Web:* www.miosushi.com	Portland	OR	97210	503-221-1469	827-4932
Mother's Bistro & Bar 212 SW Stark St *Web:* www.mothersbistro.com	Portland	OR	97204	503-464-1122	525-5877
Noble Rot 1111 E Burnside Fourth Fl *Web:* www.noblerotpdx.com	Portland	OR	97214	503-233-1999	
Oba! 555 NW 12th Ave *Web:* www.obarestaurant.com	Portland	OR	97209	503-228-6161	228-2673
OM Seafood Restaurant 7632 SE Powell Blvd *Web:* omseafood.com	Portland	OR	97206	503-788-3128	471-2101
Paley's Place 1204 NW 21st Ave *Web:* www.paleysplace.net	Portland	OR	97209	503-243-2403	223-8041
Pambiche 2811 NE Glisan St *Web:* www.pambiche.com	Portland	OR	97232	503-233-0511	233-0495
Piazza Italia 1129 NW Johnson St *Web:* www.piazzaportland.com	Portland	OR	97209	503-478-0619	227-5199
Portland City Grill 111 SW Fifth Ave Unico US Bank Twr 30th Fl *Web:* www.portlandcitygrill.com	Portland	OR	97204	503-450-0030	
Red Star Tavern & Roast House 503 SW Alder St *Web:* www.redstartavern.com	Portland	OR	97204	503-222-0005	417-3334
Ringside SteakHouse, The 2165 W Burnside St *Web:* www.ringsidesteakhouse.com	Portland	OR	97210	503-223-1513	223-6908
Saucebox 214 SW Broadway *Web:* www.saucebox.com	Portland	OR	97205	503-241-3393	
Sin Ju 1022 NW Johnson St *Web:* www.sinjurestaurant.com	Portland	OR	97209	503-223-6535	
Slide Inn, The 2348 SE Ankeny *Web:* www.slideinnpdx.com	Portland	OR	97214	503-236-4997	
Southpark Seafood Grill & Wine Bar 901 SW Salmon St *Web:* southparkseafood.com	Portland	OR	97205	503-326-1300	326-1301
Stickers Asian Cafe 6808 SE Milwaukie Ave *Web:* www.stickersasiancafe.com	Portland	OR	97202	503-239-8739	
Veritable Quandary 1220 SW First Ave *Web:* veritablequandary.com	Portland	OR	97204	503-227-7342	
Adam's Rib 1210 State St *Web:* adams-rib-smoke-house.com	Salem	OR	97301	503-362-2194	362-2196
Almost Home Restaurant & Steakhouse 3310 Market St NE	Salem	OR	97301	503-378-0100	
Casa Baez 1292 Lancaster Dr NE	Salem	OR	97301	503-371-3867	
Flight Deck Restaurant & Lounge 2680 Aerial Way *Web:* www.flightdeckrestaurant.com	Salem	OR	97302	503-581-5721	
India Palace 377 Ct St	Salem	OR	97301	503-371-4808	
La Margarita Co 545 Ferry St SE *Web:* lamargaritasalem.com	Salem	OR	97301	503-362-8861	
Los Arcos Mexican Grill 4120 Commercial St SE	Salem	OR	97302	503-581-2740	
Los Baez 2920 Commercial St SE	Salem	OR	97302	503-363-3109	581-0701
Lucky Fortune 1401 Lancaster Dr NE *Web:* salemluckyfortune.com	Salem	OR	97301	503-399-9189	581-7810
Lum-Yuen 3190 Portland Rd NE *Web:* lumyuensalem.com	Salem	OR	97303	503-581-2912	581-2903
Macedonia 189 Liberty St NE *Web:* reedoperahouse.com	Salem	OR	97301	503-316-9997	316-9997
Marco Polo Global Restaurant 300 Liberty St SE	Salem	OR	97301	503-364-4833	364-4833

Pennsylvania

Restaurant	City	State	ZIP	Phone	Fax
Altland House Center Sq Rt 30 PO Box 448 *Web:* www.altlandhouse.com	Abbottstown	PA	17301	717-259-9535	259-9956
Aladdin 651 Union Blvd *Web:* aladdinlv.com	Allentown	PA	18109	610-437-4023	
Bay Leaf 935 W Hamilton St *Web:* www.allentownbayleaf.com	Allentown	PA	18101	610-433-4211	433-2652
Oasis Restaurant 2355 Schoenersville Rd	Allentown	PA	18109	610-264-1955	
Ritz Barbecue 302 17th St	Allentown	PA	18104	610-432-0952	
Robata of Tokyo 39 S Ninth St *Web:* www.icloud.com	Allentown	PA	18102	610-821-6900	
Sunset Grille 6751 Ruppsville Rd *Web:* www.sunset-grille.com	Allentown	PA	18106	610-395-9622	
Youell's Oyster House 2249 Walnut St *Web:* youellsoysterhouse.com	Allentown	PA	18104	610-439-1203	
Cashtown Inn Restaurant 1325 Old Rt 30 *TF:* 800-367-1797 ■ *Web:* cashtowninn.com	Cashtown	PA	17310	717-334-9722	334-4679
Bertrand's 18 N Pk Row *Web:* bertrandsbistro.com	Erie	PA	16501	814-871-6477	464-9029
Calamari's Squid Row 1317 State St *Web:* www.calamaris-squidrow.com	Erie	PA	16501	814-459-4276	455-5635
Colao's Ristorante 2826 Plum St *Web:* colaos.com	Erie	PA	16508	814-866-9621	
Colony Pub & Grille 2670 W Eigth St *Web:* colonypub.com	Erie	PA	16505	814-838-2162	838-9804
El Canelo 2709 W 12th St *Web:* elcanelo.net	Erie	PA	16505	814-835-2290	836-0334
Hibachi Japanese Steak House 3000 W 12th St *Web:* www.hibachijapan.com	Erie	PA	16505	814-838-2495	
Hoss's Steak & Sea House 3302 W 26th St	Erie	PA	16506	814-838-6718	
Joe Roots Grill 2826 W Eigth St	Erie	PA	16505	814-836-7668	
Panos Restaurant 1504 W 38th St	Erie	PA	16508	814-866-0517	
Petra 3602 W Lake Rd *TF:* 866-906-2931 ■ *Web:* www.petrarestaurant.com	Erie	PA	16505	814-838-7197	833-9543
Pufferbelly 414 French St *Web:* thepufferbelly.com	Erie	PA	16507	814-454-1557	455-6138
Ricardo's 2112 E Lake Rd *Web:* ricardos-erie.com	Erie	PA	16511	814-455-4947	461-9177
Smokey Bones BBQ 2074 Interchange Rd *Web:* www.smokeybones.com	Erie	PA	16565	814-868-3388	
Sullivan's Pub & Eatery 301 French St	Erie	PA	16507	814-452-3446	
Syd's Place 2992 W Lake Rd	Erie	PA	16505	814-838-3089	
Avenue Restaurant, The 21 Steinwehr Ave *Web:* www.avenuerestaurant.net	Gettysburg	PA	17325	717-334-3235	334-5209
Blue & Gray Bar & Grill Two Baltimore St	Gettysburg	PA	17325	717-334-1999	
Blue Parrot Bistro 35 Chambersburg St *Web:* blueparrotbistro.com	Gettysburg	PA	17325	717-337-3739	338-9345
Dobbin House Inc 89 Steinwehr Ave *Web:* www.dobbinhouse.com/map.htm	Gettysburg	PA	17325	717-334-2100	334-6905

Name / Address	City	State	ZIP	Phone	Fax
Dunlap's 90 Buford Ave *Web:* www.dunlapsrestaurant.com	Gettysburg	PA	17325	717-334-4816	334-2053
Ernie's Texas Lunch 58 Chambersburg St	Gettysburg	PA	17325	717-334-1970	
Farnsworth House Inn 401 Baltimore St *Web:* www.farnsworthhouseinn.com	Gettysburg	PA	17325	717-334-8838	334-5862
General Pickett's Buffet 571 Steinwehr Ave *Web:* generalpickettsbuffets.com	Gettysburg	PA	17325	717-334-7580	334-3701
Gettysburg Hotel One Lincoln Sq Best Western Gettysburg Hotel *Web:* www.hotelgettysburg.com	Gettysburg	PA	17325	717-337-2000	337-2075
Herr Tavern & Public House 900 Chambersburg Rd *TF:* 800-362-9849 ■ *Web:* www.innatherrridge.com	Gettysburg	PA	17325	717-334-4332	334-3332
La Bella Italia 402 York St *Web:* labellaitalia.org	Gettysburg	PA	17325	717-334-1978	334-0781
Mamma Ventura 13 Chambersburg St *Web:* mammaventuras.com	Gettysburg	PA	17325	717-334-5548	334-7231
O'Rorke's Eatery & Spirits 44 Steinwehr Ave *Web:* ororkes.com	Gettysburg	PA	17325	717-334-2333	
Ping's Cafe 34 Baltimore St *Web:* www.pingscafe.com	Gettysburg	PA	17325	717-334-2234	
Aangan Classic Indian & Napalese Cuisine 3500 Walnut St *Web:* www.aanganonline.com	Harrisburg	PA	17109	717-909-7777	909-7979
Appalachian Brewing Co 50 N Cameron St *Web:* www.abcbrew.com	Harrisburg	PA	17101	717-221-1080	221-1083
Fuji Do Restaurant 1701 Paxton St	Harrisburg	PA	17104	717-232-1437	
Gabriella 3907 Jonestown Rd *Web:* gabriellaristorante.com	Harrisburg	PA	17109	717-540-0040	
Isaac's 421 Friendship Rd *Web:* www.isaacsdeli.com	Harrisburg	PA	17111	717-920-5757	920-3955
McGrath's Pub & Restaurant 202 Locust St *Web:* mcgrathspub.net	Harrisburg	PA	17101	717-232-9914	
Miyako 227 N Second St	Harrisburg	PA	17101	717-234-3250	
Molly Brannigans 31 N Second St *Web:* www.mollybrannigans.com	Harrisburg	PA	17101	717-260-9242	260-9244
Passage to India 520 Race St *Web:* www.passagetoindiaharrisburgpa.com	Harrisburg	PA	17104	717-233-1202	
Stocks on Second 211 N Second St *Web:* www.stocksonsecond.com	Harrisburg	PA	17101	717-233-6699	
Ted's Bar & Grill 6197 Allentown Blvd *Web:* tedsbarandgrill.com	Harrisburg	PA	17112	717-652-3832	
Vietnamese Garden 304 Reily St	Harrisburg	PA	17102	717-238-9310	
Wharf, The 6852 Derry St *Web:* www.thewharfbarandgrill.com	Harrisburg	PA	17111	717-564-9920	
Carr's Restaurant 50 W Grant St *Web:* www.carrsrestaurant.com	Lancaster	PA	17603	717-299-7090	
El Serrano 2151 Columbia Ave *Web:* www.elserrano.com	Lancaster	PA	17603	717-397-6191	
Gibraltar 931 Harrisburg Ave *Web:* www.kearesrestaurants.com	Lancaster	PA	17603	717-397-2790	397-3622
La Fleur 2285 Lincoln Hwy E Continental Inn *Web:* www.continentalinn.com/lafleur.asp	Lancaster	PA	17602	717-299-0421	
Lancaster Brewing Co 302 N Plum St *Web:* www.lancasterbrewing.com	Lancaster	PA	17602	717-391-6258	391-6015
Loft Restaurant, The 201 W Orange St *Web:* www.theloftlancaster.com	Lancaster	PA	17603	717-299-0661	299-2010
Lombardo's 216 Harrisburg Ave *Web:* www.lombardosrestaurant.com	Lancaster	PA	17603	717-394-3749	394-7179
Pressroom Restaurant 26-28 W King St *Web:* www.pressroomrestaurant.com	Lancaster	PA	17603	717-399-5400	399-5463
Symposium 125 S Centerville Rd *Web:* www.symposiumcafe.com	Lancaster	PA	17603	717-391-7656	391-0749
Tony Wang's 2217 Lincoln Hwy E	Lancaster	PA	17602	717-399-1915	399-8475
Log Cabin 11 Lehoy Forest Dr *Web:* www.logcabinrestaurant.com	Leola	PA	17540	717-625-2142	626-1181
Nana's Pasta House 1223 Springbrook Ave *Web:* www.nanaspastahouse.com	Moosic	PA	18507	570-457-9612	
New Amber Indian Restaurant 3505 Birney Ave *Web:* www.newamberindian.com	Moosic	PA	18507	570-344-7100	
Hickory Bridge Farm 96 Hickory Bridge Rd *Web:* www.hickorybridgefarm.com	Orrtanna	PA	17353	717-642-5261	624-6419
Alma de Cuba 1623 Walnut St *Web:* www.almadecubarestaurant.com	Philadelphia	PA	19103	215-988-1799	988-0807
Barclay Prime 237 S 18th St *Web:* www.barclayprime.com	Philadelphia	PA	19103	215-732-7560	732-7560
Bistro Romano 120 Lombard St *Web:* www.bistroromano.com	Philadelphia	PA	19147	215-925-8880	925-9888
Buddakan 325 Chestnut St *Web:* www.buddakan.com	Philadelphia	PA	19106	215-574-9440	574-8994
Chloe 232 Arch St *Web:* www.chloebyob.com	Philadelphia	PA	19106	215-629-2337	
Continental, The 138 Market St *Web:* www.continentalmartinibar.com	Philadelphia	PA	19106	215-923-6069	923-2955
Cuba Libre Restaurant 10 S Second St *Web:* www.cubalibrerestaurant.com	Philadelphia	PA	19106	215-627-0666	627-6193
Cucina Forte 768 S Eigth St *Web:* cucinaforte.com	Philadelphia	PA	19147	215-238-0778	
Dahlak Restaurant inc 4708 Baltimore Ave *Web:* www.dahlakrestaurant.com	Philadelphia	PA	19143	215-726-6464	
El Vez 121 S 13th St *Web:* www.elvezrestaurant.com	Philadelphia	PA	19107	215-928-9800	928-9889
Fork 306 Market St *Web:* www.forkrestaurant.com	Philadelphia	PA	19106	215-625-9425	
Friday Saturday Sunday 261 S 21st St *Web:* www.frisatsun.com	Philadelphia	PA	19103	215-546-4232	
Hikaru 607 S Second St *Web:* hikaruphilly.com	Philadelphia	PA	19147	215-627-7110	
Il Cantuccio 701 N Third St	Philadelphia	PA	19123	215-627-6573	627-6573
Karma 114 Chestnut St *Web:* karmaphilly.com	Philadelphia	PA	19106	215-925-1444	
L'Angolo Ristorante 1415 Porter St *Web:* www.salentorestaurant.com	Philadelphia	PA	19145	215-389-4252	
La Famiglia Eight S Front St *Web:* www.lafamiglia.com	Philadelphia	PA	19106	215-922-2803	922-7495
Lacroix at the Rittenhouse 210 W Rittenhouse Sq *Web:* www.rittenhousehotel.com	Philadelphia	PA	19103	215-790-2533	546-9858
Macaroni's 9315 Old Bustleton Ave *Web:* macaronis.net	Philadelphia	PA	19115	215-464-3040	
Matyson 37 S 19th St *Web:* www.matyson.com	Philadelphia	PA	19103	215-564-2925	
Meritage Philadelphia 500 S 20th St *Web:* www.meritagephiladelphia.com	Philadelphia	PA	19103	215-985-1922	985-0455
Morimoto 723 Chestnut St *Web:* www.morimotorestaurant.com	Philadelphia	PA	19106	215-413-9070	413-9075
Morning Glory Diner 735 S Tenth St *Web:* www.themorninggloryciner.com	Philadelphia	PA	19147	215-413-3999	
Panorama 14 N Front St *Web:* panoramaristorante.com	Philadelphia	PA	19106	215-922-7800	922-7642
Pod Restaurant 3636 Sansom St *Web:* www.podrestaurant.com	Philadelphia	PA	19104	215-387-1803	387-1809
Radicchio 402 Wood St *Web:* www.radicchio-cafe.com	Philadelphia	PA	19106	215-627-6850	627-6801
Rose Tattoo Cafe 1847 Callowhill St *Web:* www.rosetattoocafe.com	Philadelphia	PA	19130	215-569-8939	947-9786
Saloon 750 S Seventh St *Web:* www.saloonrestaurant.net	Philadelphia	PA	19147	215-627-1811	
Sansom Street Oyster House 1516 Sansom St *Web:* www.oysterhousephilly.com	Philadelphia	PA	19102	215-567-7683	
Scannicchio 2500 S Broad St *Web:* www.scannicchio.com	Philadelphia	PA	19145	215-468-3900	468-3900
Shiao Lan Kung 930 Race St	Philadelphia	PA	19107	215-928-0282	
Smith & Wollensky 210 W Rittenhouse Sq **Fax Area Code:* 857 ■ *Web:* www.smithandwollensky.com	Philadelphia	PA	19103	215-545-1700	239-9219*
Standard Tap 901 N 2nd St *Web:* news.standardtap.com.s86406.gridserver.com	Philadelphia	PA	19123	215-238-0630	
Sweet Lucy's Smokehouse 7500 State Rd *Web:* www.sweetlucys.com	Philadelphia	PA	19136	215-333-9663	331-3185
Tai Lake Restaurant 134 N Tenth St *Web:* www.tailakeseafoodrest.com	Philadelphia	PA	19107	215-922-0698	922-0347
Tequilas 1602 Locust St *Web:* tequilasphilly.com	Philadelphia	PA	19103	215-546-0181	546-9953
Umbria 7131 Germantown Ave *Web:* www.umbria-byo.com	Philadelphia	PA	19119	215-242-6470	
Valanni Restaurant & Lounge 1229 Spruce St *Web:* www.valanni.com	Philadelphia	PA	19107	215-790-9494	790-9642
Vetri 1312 Spruce St *Web:* www.vetrifamily.com	Philadelphia	PA	19107	215-732-3478	732-3487
Vientiane Cafe 4728 Baltimore Ave	Philadelphia	PA	19143	215-726-1095	
Vietnam Restaurant 221 N 11th St *Web:* www.eatatvietnam.com	Philadelphia	PA	19107	215-592-1163	
White Dog Cafe 3420 Sansom St *Web:* www.whitedog.com	Philadelphia	PA	19104	215-386-9224	
Ali Baba 404 S Craig St *Web:* www.alibabapittsburgh.com	Pittsburgh	PA	15213	412-682-2829	
Amel's Restaurant 435 McNeilly Rd *Web:* www.amelsrestaurantpgh.com	Pittsburgh	PA	15226	412-563-3466	
Cafe du Jour 1107 E Carson St	Pittsburgh	PA	15203	412-488-9695	
Carlton Restaurant 500 Grant St 1 Mellon Bank Ctr *Web:* www.thecarltonrestaurant.com	Pittsburgh	PA	15219	412-391-4152	281-1704
Casbah 229 S Highland Dr *Web:* www.bigburrito.com	Pittsburgh	PA	15206	412-661-5656	
Christos Mediterranean Grille 130 Sixth St *Web:* christosmediterraneangrille.com	Pittsburgh	PA	15222	412-261-6442	
Church Brew Works 3525 Liberty Ave *Web:* www.churchbrew.com	Pittsburgh	PA	15201	412-688-8200	688-8201
Del's 4428 Liberty Ave *Web:* www.delsrest.com	Pittsburgh	PA	15224	412-683-1448	683-3863
Eleven 1150 Smallman St *Web:* www.bigburrito.com	Pittsburgh	PA	15222	412-201-5656	201-5655
Grand Concourse 100 W Stn Sq Dr *Web:* www.muer.com	Pittsburgh	PA	15219	412-261-1717	261-6041
India Garden 328 Atwood St *Web:* www.indiagarden.net	Pittsburgh	PA	15213	412-682-3000	682-3130
Kaya 2000 Smallman St *Web:* www.bigburrito.com	Pittsburgh	PA	15222	412-261-6565	261-1526
Kiku 225 W Stn Sq Dr *Web:* kikupittsburgh.net	Pittsburgh	PA	15219	412-765-3200	765-3202
Lidia's Italy 1400 Smallman St *Web:* www.lidias-pittsburgh.com	Pittsburgh	PA	15222	412-552-0150	
Mallorca 2228 E Carson St *Web:* mallorcarestaurantpgh.com	Pittsburgh	PA	15203	412-488-1818	488-1320
Max's Allegheny Tavern 537 Suismon St *Web:* www.maxsalleghenytavern.com	Pittsburgh	PA	15212	412-231-1899	231-5099
Meat & Potatoes 649 Penn Ave *Web:* meatandpotatoespgh.com	Pittsburgh	PA	15222	412-325-7007	
Mullaney's Harp & Fiddle 2329 Penn Ave *Web:* www.harpandfiddle.com	Pittsburgh	PA	15222	412-642-6622	
Nakama Japanese Steakhouse 1611 E Carson St *Web:* www.eatatnakama.com	Pittsburgh	PA	15203	412-381-6000	381-6643
Original Fish Market 1001 Liberty Ave *Web:* www.originalfishmarket.com	Pittsburgh	PA	15222	412-227-3657	227-3658
Penn Brewery, The 800 Vinial St *Web:* www.pennbrew.com	Pittsburgh	PA	15212	412-237-9400	

Name	City	State	Zip	Phone	Fax
Pittsburgh Steak Co 1924 E Carson St	Pittsburgh	PA	15203	412-381-5505	488-6628
Web: www.pghsteak.com					
Pleasure Bar & Restaurant 4729 Liberty Ave.	Pittsburgh	PA	15224	412-682-9603	
Web: pleasurebarpittsburgh.com					
Primanti Bros 46 18th St	Pittsburgh	PA	15222	412-263-2142	
Web: primantibros.com					
Sesame Inn 715 Washington Rd.	Pittsburgh	PA	15228	412-341-2555	341-6887
Web: sesameinn.com					
Soba 5847 Ellsworth Ave	Pittsburgh	PA	15232	412-362-5656	
Web: www.bigburrito.com					
Spice Island Tea House 253 Atwood St	Pittsburgh	PA	15213	412-687-8821	
Web: spiceislandteahouse.com					
Sushi Kim 1241 Penn Ave	Pittsburgh	PA	15222	412-281-9956	281-9957
Tessaro's 4601 Liberty Ave	Pittsburgh	PA	15224	412-682-6809	
Web: tessaros.com					
Thai Place Restaurant 5528 Walnut St	Pittsburgh	PA	15232	412-687-8586	
Web: www.thaiplacepgh.com					
Tram's Kitchen 4050 Penn Ave	Pittsburgh	PA	15224	412-682-2688	
Umi 5849 Ellsworth Ave.	Pittsburgh	PA	15232	412-362-6198	
Web: bigburrito.com					
Wilson's Bar-B-Q 700 N Taylor Ave	Pittsburgh	PA	15212	412-322-7427	
Susanna Foo 555 E Lancaster Ave	Radnor	PA	19087	610-688-8808	688-8055
Web: www.susannafoo.com					
Cooper's Seafood House 701 N Washington Ave.	Scranton	PA	18509	570-346-6883	
Web: www.coopers-seafood.com					
Foliage 122 N Main Ave	Scranton	PA	18504	570-347-1071	
Kelly's Pub & Eatery 1802 Cedar Ave.	Scranton	PA	18505	570-346-9758	
Web: kpehotwings.com					
La Trattoria 522 Moosic St	Scranton	PA	18505	570-961-1504	
Web: thelatrattoria.com					
Russell's 1918 Ash St	Scranton	PA	18510	570-961-8949	
Stirna's 120 W Market St	Scranton	PA	18508	570-343-5742	
Web: stirnas.com					
Hunan Springs 4939 Hamilton Blvd	Wescosville	PA	18106	610-366-8338	366-7184
Web: hunansprings.com					

Quebec

Name	City	State	Postal Code	Phone	Fax
3 Amigos 1657 Ste Catherine W	Montreal	QC	H3H1L9	514-939-3329	939-4194
Web: www.3amigosrestaurant.com					
Ariel Restaurant 2072 Drummond St	Montreal	QC	H3G1W9	514-282-9790	
Web: lasouris.ca/#!ariel-to-la-souris/c5zr					
Beijing 92 Rue de la Gauchetiere O	Montreal	QC	H2Z1C1	514-861-2003	
Web: www.restaurantbeijing.net					
Bombay Mahal 1001 Rue Jean-Talon Ouest	Montreal	QC	H3N1T2	514-273-3331	
Web: www.restaurantbombaymahal.ca					
Buffet Maharaja 1481 Rene Levesque Blvd W	Montreal	QC	H3G1T8	514-934-0655	934-0695
Web: www.buffetmaharaja.com					
Carlos & Pepe's 1420 Peel St	Montreal	QC	H3A1S8	514-288-3090	
Web: carlospepes.com					
Chez la Mere Michel 1209 Rue Guy	Montreal	QC	H3H2L3	514-934-0473	
Web: www.chezlameremichel.ca					
Coco Rico 3907 St-Laurent Blvd	Montreal	QC	H2W1X9	514-849-5554	286-0967
Europea 1227 de la Montagne	Montreal	QC	H3G1Z2	514-397-9161	398-9718
Web: www.europea.ca					
Ferreira Cafe 1446 Peel St	Montreal	QC	H3A1S8	514-848-0988	848-9375
Web: www.ferreiracafe.com					
Frite Alors! 1562 Laurier St E	Montreal	QC	H2J1H9	514-524-6336	
Web: www.fritealors.com					
Globe Bar-Restaurant 3455 St Laurent Blvd	Montreal	QC	H2X2T6	514-284-3823	284-3531
Hwang-Kum 5908 Sherbrooke St W	Montreal	QC	H4A1X7	514-487-1712	
L'Entrecote St-Jean 2022 Peel St	Montreal	QC	H3A2W5	514-281-6492	274-6411
Web: www.lentrecotestjean.com					
L'Estaminet 1340 Fleury E	Montreal	QC	H2C1R3	514-389-0596	
Web: www.lestaminet.ca					
L'Express 3927 St Denis St	Montreal	QC	H2W2M4	514-845-5333	843-7576
Web: restaurantlexpress.ca					
La Buona Forchetta 2407 Mont-Royal E	Montreal	QC	H2H1L2	514-521-6766	
Web: buonaforchettasd.com					
La Chronique 104 Ave Laurier Ouest	Montreal	QC	H2T2N7	514-271-3095	
Web: www.lachronique.qc.ca					
La Colombe 554 Duluth E	Montreal	QC	H2L1A9	514-849-8844	879-6686
Web: lacolomberestaurant.com					
La Mer 1840 Ren,L,vesque Est	Montreal	QC	H2K4P1	514-522-3003	522-0467
Web: lamer.ca					
Laloux 250 Pine Ave E	Montreal	QC	H2W1P3	514-287-9127	281-0682
Web: www.laloux.com					
Le Mas Des Oliviers Restaurant 1216 Rue Bishop	Montreal	QC	H3G2E3	514-861-6733	
Web: www.lemasdesoliviers.ca					
Le Nil Bleu 3706 St-Denis	Montreal	QC	H2X3L7	514-285-4628	
Les Chenets 2075 Rue Bishop	Montreal	QC	H3G2G2	514-844-1842	
Maestro SVP 3615 St Laurent Blvd	Montreal	QC	H2X1V5	514-842-6447	
Web: www.maestrosvp.com					
Milos 5357 du Parc Ave	Montreal	QC	H2V4G9	514-272-3522	
Web: www.milos.ca					
Moishes Steakhouse 3961 St Laurent Blvd	Montreal	QC	H2W1Y4	514-845-3509	845-9504
Web: www.moishes.ca					
Molivos 2310 Guy	Montreal	QC	H3H2M2	514-846-8818	846-1263
Web: molivos.ca					
Oishii Sushi 277 Bernard Ouest	Montreal	QC	H2V1T5	514-271-8863	
Web: www.oishii.ca					
Pho Bang New York 1001 St-Laurent Blvd.	Montreal	QC	H2Z1J4	514-954-2032	
Restaurant Gandhi 230 Rue St Paul Oeust	Montreal	QC	H2Y1Z9	514-845-5866	
Web: www.restaurantgandhi.com					
Restaurant Jano Grillades 3883 St-Laurent Blvd	Montreal	QC	H2W1X9	514-849-0646	849-3628
Restaurant Mysore 4216 St Laurent	Montreal	QC	H2W1Z3	514-844-4733	
Web: restaurant-mysore.com					
Ristorante DaVinci 1180 Bishop St	Montreal	QC	H3G2M5	514-874-2001	
Web: www.davinci.ca					
Rotisserie Italienne 1933 Sainte-Catherine St W	Montreal	QC	H3H1M4	514-935-4436	
Web: wordpress.com					
Toque 900 Pl Jean-Paul Riopelle	Montreal	QC	H2Z2B2	514-499-2084	499-0292
Web: www.restaurant-toque.com					
Upstairs Jazz Bar & Grill 1254 MacKay St.	Montreal	QC	H3G2H4	514-931-6808	931-5213
Web: www.upstairsjazz.com					
YOY Sushi Bar 4526 St Denis St W	Montreal	QC	H2J2L3	514-844-9884	
Web: montrealyoysushi.com					
LOEWS HOTELS 667 Madison Ave	New York	QC	10065	615-340-2000	657-5817*
**Fax Area Code:* 418 ■ *Web:* www.loewshotels.com					
Chez Leveque 1030 Laurier Ave W	Outremont	QC	H2V2K8	514-279-7355	279-1737
Web: www.chezleveque.ca					
Au Petit Coin Breton 1029 Rue Saint-Jean	Quebec	QC	G1R1R6	418-694-0758	
Web: aupetitcoinbreton.com					
Auberge du Tresor 20 Rue Sainte-Anne	Quebec	QC	G1R3X2	418-694-1876	694-0563
Web: www.aubergedutresor.com					
Aux Anciens Canadiens 34 rue Saint-Louis Casier postal 175 succursale Haute-Ville	Quebec	QC	G1R4P3	418-692-1627	692-5419
Web: www.auxancienscanadiens.qc.ca					
Cochon Dingue Le 46 Champlain Blvd	Quebec	QC	G1R2A4	418-692-2013	
Web: www.cochondingue.com					
Cosmos Cafe 575 Grande Allee E	Quebec	QC	G1R2K4	418-640-0606	640-0520
Web: lecosmos.com					
Entrecote Saint Jean 1080 St Jean St	Quebec	QC	G1R1S4	418-694-0234	694-2172
Web: www.entrecotesaintjean.com					
L'Echaude 73 Rue Sault-au-Matelot St	Quebec	QC	G1K3Y9	418-692-1299	692-1133
Web: www.echaude.com					
La Cremaillere 73 rue Sainte-Anne	Quebec	QC	G1R3X4	418-692-2216	692-5202
Web: www.cremaillere.qc.ca					
La Grolla 815 Cote d'Abraham	Quebec	QC	G1R1A4	418-529-8107	
Web: www.restaurantlagrolla.com					
Laurie Raphael 117 Dalhousie St.	Quebec	QC	G1K9C8	418-692-4555	692-4175
TF: 877-876-4555 ■ *Web:* www.laurieraphael.com					
Le Beffroi Steakhouse 775 Honore-Mercier Ave.	Quebec	QC	G1R5M9	418-380-2638	
Le Patriarche 17 St Stanislas St	Quebec	QC	G1R4G7	418-692-5488	692-0370
Web: www.lepatriarche.com					
Le Saint-Amour 48 rue Sainte-Ursule	Quebec	QC	G1R4E2	418-694-0667	694-0967
Web: www.saint-amour.com					
Pub Saint-Alexandre 1087 St Jean St	Quebec	QC	G1R1S3	418-694-0015	694-0178
Web: www.pubstalexandre.com					
Restaurant Aviatic Club 450 de la Gare-du-Palais	Quebec	QC	G1K3X2	418-522-3555	522-6404
Restaurant L'Initiale 54 St-Pierre St	Quebec	QC	G1K4A1	418-694-1818	694-2387
Web: restaurantinitiale.com					
Apsara 71 Rue D'Auteuil	Quebec City	QC	G1R4C3	418-694-0232	
Web: restaurantapsara.com					
Charbon Steakhouse 450 Gare du Palais	Quebec City	QC	G1K3X2	418-522-0133	522-6404
Web: charbonsteakhouse.com					
Ciccio Cafe 875 Claire-Fontaine	Quebec City	QC	G1R3A8	418-525-6161	
Le Lapin Saute 52 ru du Petit-Champlain	Quebec City	QC	G1K4H4	418-692-5325	692-2195
Web: www.lapinsaute.com					
Mistral Gagnant 160 St-Paul	Quebec City	QC	G1K3W1	418-692-4260	
Web: mistralgagnant.ca					
Pub St Patrick 1200 St-Jean St	Quebec City	QC	G1R1S8	418-694-0618	694-2120
Restaurant Chez Rabelais 2 Rue Du Petit-Champlain	Quebec City	QC	G1K4H5	418-522-3240	
Marie-Clarisse 12 du Petit-Champlain St.	Vieux Qu,bec	QC	G1K4H5	418-692-5085	
Pub St-Paul 124 St Paul St E	Vieux-Montreal	QC	H2Y1G6	514-874-0485	
Web: www.pubstpaul.com					
D'Orsay Restaurant Pub 65 Rue de Buade	Vieux-Quebec	QC	G1R4A2	418-694-1582	694-1587
Web: www.dorsayrestaurant.com					
Le Continental 26 rue St-Louis	Vieux-Qu,bec	QC	G1R3Y9	418-694-9995	694-2109
Web: www.restaurantlecontinental.com					

Rhode Island

Name	City	State	Zip	Phone	Fax
Basta 2195 Broad St	Cranston	RI	02905	401-461-2300	
Web: bastaonbroad.com					
22 Bowen's 22 Bowen's Wharf	Newport	RI	02840	401-841-8884	841-8883
Web: www.22bowens.com					
Black Pearl, The Bannister's Wharf	Newport	RI	02840	401-846-5264	846-0360
Web: www.blackpearlnewport.com					
Brick Alley Pub & Restaurant 140 Thames St	Newport	RI	02840	401-849-6334	848-5640
Web: www.brickalley.com					
Cafe Zelda 528 Lower Thames St	Newport	RI	02840	401-849-4002	846-4578
Web: www.cafezelda.com					
Christie's of Newport 14 Perry Mill Wharf	Newport	RI	02840	401-847-5400	
Web: www.41north.com					
Clarke Cooke House One Bannister's Wharf	Newport	RI	02840	401-846-4500	849-8750
Web: www.bannistersnewport.com					
Mamma Luisa 673 Thames St	Newport	RI	02840	401-848-5257	849-8415
Web: www.mammaluisa.com					
Mooring, The Sayer's Wharf	Newport	RI	02840	401-846-2260	846-8950
Web: www.mooringrestaurant.com					
Red Parrot, The 348 Thames St PO Box 340	Newport	RI	02840	401-847-3800	845-2530
Web: www.redparrotrestaurant.com					
Restaurant Bouchard 505 Thames St	Newport	RI	02840	401-846-0123	841-8565
Web: www.restaurantbouchard.com					
Salvation Cafe 140 Broadway	Newport	RI	02840	401-847-2620	
Web: www.salvationcafe.com					
Sardella's Restaurant 30 Memorial Blvd W	Newport	RI	02840	401-849-6312	848-0190
Web: www.sardellas.com					
Scales & Shells Restaurant & Raw Bar 527 Thames St	Newport	RI	02840	401-846-3474	848-7706
Web: www.scalesandshells.com					
Spiced Pear 117 Memorial Blvd	Newport	RI	02840	401-847-2244	847-3620
Web: thechanler.com					

Name / Address	City	State	Zip	Phone	Fax
Thai Cuisine at Thames 517 Thames St *Web:* thaicuisinemenu.com	Newport	RI	02840	401-841-8822	845-8338
White Horse Tavern 26 Marlborough St *Web:* www.whitehorsenewport.com	Newport	RI	02840	401-849-3600	
Al Forno Restaurant 577 S Main St *Web:* alforno.com	Providence	RI	02903	401-273-9760	
Andreas 268 Thayer St *Web:* andreasri.com	Providence	RI	02906	401-331-7879	331-7300
Blue Grotto 210 Atwells Ave *Web:* www.bluegrottorestaurant.com	Providence	RI	02903	401-272-9030	272-4818
Camilles Restaurant 71 Bradford St *Web:* www.camillesonthehill.com	Providence	RI	02903	401-751-4812	
Cassarino's Restaurant 177 Atwells Ave *Web:* www.cassarinosri.com	Providence	RI	02903	401-751-3333	
CAV Restaurant 14 Imperial Pl *Web:* www.cavrestaurant.com	Providence	RI	02903	401-751-9164	274-9107
Chez Pascal 960 Hope St *Web:* www.chez-pascal.com	Providence	RI	02906	401-421-4422	
Chilangos 447 Manton Ave	Providence	RI	02909	401-383-4877	
Classic Cafe 865 Westminster St *Web:* classiccaferi.com	Providence	RI	02903	401-273-0707	
Don Jose Tequila's 351 Atwells Ave *Web:* www.donjoseteq.com	Providence	RI	02903	401-454-8951	
Haruki East 172 Wayland Ave *Web:* harukisushi.com	Providence	RI	02906	401-223-0332	490-3243
Hemenway's Seafood Grille 121 S Main St Providence Washington Plaza *Web:* www.hemenwaysrestaurant.com	Providence	RI	02903	401-351-8570	351-8594
Julian's 318 Broadway *Web:* www.juliansprovidence.com	Providence	RI	02909	401-861-1770	831-3706
Lot 401 44 Hospital St	Providence	RI	02903	401-490-3980	
Mandarin Garden 555 Chalkstone Ave	Providence	RI	02908	401-751-0144	
Mill's Tavern 101 N Main St *Web:* www.millstavernrestaurant.com	Providence	RI	02903	401-272-3331	272-4453
New Rivers Restaurant Seven Steeple St *Web:* www.newriversrestaurant.com	Providence	RI	02903	401-751-0350	
Nick's on Broadway 500 Broadway *Web:* nicksonbroadway.com	Providence	RI	02909	401-421-0286	
Not Just Snacks 833 Hope St *Web:* letseat.at	Providence	RI	02906	401-831-1150	
OPA Restaurant 230 Atwells Ave *Web:* opaprovidence.com	Providence	RI	02903	401-351-8282	
Pakarang 303 S Main St *Web:* www.pakarangrestaurant.com	Providence	RI	02903	401-453-3660	453-3661
Pane E Vino 365 Atwells Ave *Web:* www.panevino.net	Providence	RI	02903	401-223-2230	223-4322
Parkside Rotisserie & Bar 76 S Main St *Web:* www.parksideprovidence.com	Providence	RI	02903	401-331-0003	
Pot Au Feu 44 Custom House St *Web:* potaufeuri.com	Providence	RI	02903	401-273-8953	273-8963
Providence Oyster Bar 283 Atwells Ave *Web:* www.providenceoysterbar.com	Providence	RI	02903	401-272-8866	
Sawaddee Thai Restaurant 93 Hope St *Web:* www.sawaddeerestaurant.com	Providence	RI	02906	401-831-1122	831-1121
Taste of India 230 Wickenden St *Web:* www.tasteofindiari.com	Providence	RI	02903	401-421-4355	751-1432
Ten Prime Steak & Sushi 55 Pine St *Web:* www.tenprimesteakandsushi.com	Providence	RI	02903	401-453-2333	
Tokyo Restaurant 388 Wickenden St	Providence	RI	02903	401-331-5330	
Waterman Grille, The Four Richmond Sq *Web:* www.watermangrille.com	Providence	RI	02906	401-521-9229	521-9351
Wes' Rib House 38 Dike St *Web:* www.wesribhouse.com	Providence	RI	02909	401-421-9090	
XO Cafe 125 N Main St *Web:* www.xocafe.com	Providence	RI	02903	401-273-9090	

South Carolina

Name / Address	City	State	Zip	Phone	Fax
Mi Tierra Mexican Restaurant 27 Mellichamp Dr Ste 101 *Web:* www.mitierrabluffton.com	Bluffton	SC	29910	843-757-7200	
39 Rue De Jean 39 John St *Web:* www.holycityhospitality.com	Charleston	SC	29403	843-722-8881	722-8835
82 Queen 82 Queen St *TF:* 800-849-0082 ■ *Web:* www.82queen.com	Charleston	SC	29401	843-723-7591	577-7463
AW Shuck's 35 S Market St *Web:* awshucks.menu	Charleston	SC	29401	843-723-1151	
Basil *Basil Thai Restaurant* 460 King St *Web:* www.eatatbasil.com	Charleston	SC	29403	843-724-3490	
Blossom Restaurant 171 E Bay St *Web:* magnolias-blossom-cypress.com	Charleston	SC	29401	843-722-9200	
Bubba Gump Shrimp Co 99 S Market St *Web:* www.bubbagump.com	Charleston	SC	29401	843-723-5665	723-5220
Charleston Crab House 145 Wappoo Creek Dr *Web:* www.charlestoncrabhouse.com	Charleston	SC	29412	843-795-1963	762-4866
Charleston Grill 224 King St *Web:* www.charlestongrill.com	Charleston	SC	29401	843-577-4522	
Circa 1886 149 Wentworth St *Web:* www.circa1886.com	Charleston	SC	29401	843-853-7828	720-5292
Cru Cafe 18 Pinckney St *Web:* www.crucafe.com	Charleston	SC	29401	843-534-2434	534-2439
Cypress Lowcountry Grille 167 E Bay St *Web:* www.magnolias-blossom-cypress.com/cypresshome.asp?catid=20427	Charleston	SC	29401	843-727-0111	
FIG restaurant 232 Meeting St *Web:* www.eatatfig.com	Charleston	SC	29401	843-805-5900	805-5996
Fish 442 King St *Web:* www.fishrestaurantcharleston.com	Charleston	SC	29403	843-722-3474	937-0406
Fulton Five Five Fulton St *Web:* www.fultonfive.com	Charleston	SC	29401	843-853-5555	853-6212
Grill 225 225 E Bay St *TF:* 877-440-2250 ■ *Web:* www.marketpavilion.com/grill225.cfm	Charleston	SC	29401	843-266-4222	723-4320
Hank's Seafood Restaurant 10 Hayne St *Web:* www.hanksseafoodrestaurant.com	Charleston	SC	29401	843-723-3474	
Harbor View Restaurant 301 Savannah Hwy *Fax Area Code: 843 ■ *Web:* ihg.com	Charleston	SC	29407	843-556-7100	556-6176*
High Cotton Maverick Bar & Grill 199 E Bay St *Web:* www.mavericksouthernkitchens.com	Charleston	SC	29401	843-724-3815	724-3816
Hominy Grill 207 Rutledge Ave *Web:* www.hominygrill.com	Charleston	SC	29403	843-937-0930	937-0931
Il Cortile Del Re 193 King St *Web:* ilcortiledelre.com	Charleston	SC	29401	843-853-1888	
Jestine's Kitchen 251 Meeting St *Web:* jestineskitchen.com	Charleston	SC	29401	843-722-7224	722-1133
McCrady's Two Unity Alley *Web:* www.mccradysrestaurant.com	Charleston	SC	29401	843-577-0025	577-3681
Middleton Place 4300 Ashley River Rd *TF:* 800-782-3608 ■ *Web:* www.middletonplace.org	Charleston	SC	29414	843-556-6020	766-4460
Peninsula Grill 112 N Market St *Web:* www.peninsulagrill.com	Charleston	SC	29401	843-723-0700	577-2125
Poogan's Porch 72 Queen St *Web:* www.poogansporch.com	Charleston	SC	29401	843-577-2337	577-2493
Slightly North of Broad 192 E Bay St *Web:* www.mavericksouthernkitchens.com	Charleston	SC	29401	843-723-3424	724-3811
Sticky Fingers 235 Meeting St *TF:* 800-784-2597 ■ *Web:* www.stickyfingers.com	Charleston	SC	29401	843-853-7427	853-0132
Tristan 7671 Northwoods Blvd *Web:* tristanevents.com	Charleston	SC	29406	843-534-2155	254-2156
Trotters Restaurant 2008 Savannah Hwy *Web:* www.thetownandcountryinn.com	Charleston	SC	29401	843-571-1000	766-9444
Wasabi 61 State St	Charleston	SC	29401	843-577-5222	
Baan Sawan 2135 Devine St *Web:* baansawan.blogspot.com	Columbia	SC	29205	803-252-8992	
Blue Marlin 1200 Lincoln St *Web:* www.bluemarlincolumbia.com	Columbia	SC	29201	803-799-3838	799-5606
Delhi Palace 542 St Andrew Rd	Columbia	SC	29210	803-750-7760	750-7765
Eric's San Jose 6118 Garners Ferry Rd *Web:* ericssanjose.com	Columbia	SC	29209	803-783-6650	
Gervais & Vine 620-A Gervais St *Web:* www.gervine.com	Columbia	SC	29201	803-799-8463	
Hampton Street Vineyard 1201 Hampton St *Web:* www.hamptonstreetvineyard.com	Columbia	SC	29202	803-252-0850	931-0193
Melting Pot of Columbia, The 1410 Colonial Life Blvd *TF:* 800-783-0867 ■ *Web:* www.meltingpot.com	Columbia	SC	29210	803-731-8500	731-8569
Motor Supply Company Bistro 920 Gervais St *Web:* www.motorsupplycobistro.com	Columbia	SC	29201	803-256-6687	
Mr Friendly's New Southern Cafe 2001 Greene St *Web:* www.mrfriendlys.com	Columbia	SC	29205	803-254-7828	254-8219
Palmetto Pig 530 Devine St *Web:* palmettopig.com	Columbia	SC	29201	803-733-2556	733-5860
Saluda's 751 Saluda Ave *Web:* www.saludas.com	Columbia	SC	29205	803-799-9500	
Villa Tronco 1213 Blanding St *Web:* www.villatronco.com	Columbia	SC	29201	803-256-7677	256-4336
Yamato Steak House of Japan 360 Columbian Dr *Web:* www.yamatoinc.com	Columbia	SC	29212	803-407-0033	
Yesterday's Resturant & Tavern 2030 Devine St 5 Pts *Web:* www.yesterdayssc.com	Columbia	SC	29205	803-799-0196	256-0860
Zorba's 6169 St Andrews Rd	Columbia	SC	29212	803-772-4617	772-0342
Addy's Dutch Cafe & Restaurant 17 E Coffee St *Web:* addys.net	Greenville	SC	29601	864-232-2339	
Augusta Grill 1818 Augusta Rd *Web:* www.augustagrill.com	Greenville	SC	29605	864-242-0316	232-0151
Blue Ridge Brewing Co 217 N Main St *Web:* www.blueridgebrewing.com	Greenville	SC	29601	864-232-4677	232-4680
Chicora Alley 608B S Main St *Web:* www.chicoraalley.com	Greenville	SC	29601	864-232-4100	
Chophouse '47 36 Beacon Dr *Web:* www.centraarchy.com/chophouse47.php	Greenville	SC	29615	864-286-8700	286-8733
Henry's Smokehouse 240 Wade Hampton Blvd *Web:* www.henryssmokehouse.com	Greenville	SC	29607	864-232-7774	232-7237
Irashiai Sushi Pub & Japanese Restaurant 115 Pelham Rd *Web:* www.irashiai.com	Greenville	SC	29615	864-271-0900	
Joy of Tokyo 15 Pelham Rd Ste 110 *Web:* joyoftokyo.tv	Greenville	SC	29615	864-232-2888	
Larkin's on the River 318 S Main St *Web:* www.larkinsontheriver.com	Greenville	SC	29601	864-467-9777	467-3028
Saskatoon 477 Haywood Rd *Web:* saskatoonrestaurant.com	Greenville	SC	29607	864-297-7244	
Soby's 207 S Main St *Web:* www.sobys.com	Greenville	SC	29601	864-232-7007	232-5282
Trattoria Giorgio 121 S Main St *Web:* trattoriagiorgio.net	Greenville	SC	29601	864-271-9166	
Alexander's Seafood Restaurant & Wine Bar 76 Queens Folly Rd *Web:* www.alexandersrestaurant.com	Hilton Head Island	SC	29928	843-785-4999	785-2117
Aunt Chilada's Easy Street Cafe 69 Pope Ave *Web:* auntchiladashhi.com	Hilton Head Island	SC	29928	843-785-7700	842-9936
Charlie's L'Etoile Verte Eight New Orleans Rd *Web:* www.charliesgreenstar.com	Hilton Head Island	SC	29928	843-785-9277	
CQ's Restaurant 140-A Lighthouse Rd Harbour Town *Web:* www.cqsrestaurant.com	Hilton Head Island	SC	29928	843-671-2779	671-6787

				Phone	Fax
Crane's Tavern & Steakhouse 26 New Orleans Rd *Web:* cranestavern.com	Hilton Head Island	SC	29928	843-341-2333	341-3089
Crazy Crab 104 William Hilton Pkwy *Web:* www.thecrazycrab.com	Hilton Head Island	SC	29926	843-681-5021	681-8233
Fiesta Fresh Mexican Grill 51 New Orleans Rd Ste 4 *Web:* fiestafreshmexicangrill.com	Hilton Head Island	SC	29928	843-785-4788	
Hudson's Seafood House on the Docks One Hudsons Rd *Web:* www.hudsonsonthedocks.com	Hilton Head Island	SC	29926	843-681-2772	681-2774
Kingfisher Seafood & Steak House 18 Harborside Ln Shelter Cove Harbour *Web:* www.kingfisherseafood.com	Hilton Head Island	SC	29928	843-785-4442	785-6792
Mangiamo 2000 Main St *Web:* www.hhipizza.com	Hilton Head Island	SC	29926	843-682-2444	682-3355
Market Street Cafe One N Forest Beach Blvd *Web:* www.marketstreetcafe.com	Hilton Head Island	SC	29928	843-686-4976	
Marley's Island Grille 35 Office Pk Rd *Web:* marleyshhi.com	Hilton Head Island	SC	29928	843-686-5800	686-4765
Michael Anthony's Cucina Italiana 37 New Orleans Rd Ste L *Web:* www.michael-anthonys.com	Hilton Head Island	SC	29928	843-785-6272	671-3513
Old Fort Pub 65 Skull Creek Dr *Web:* oldfortpub.com	Hilton Head Island	SC	29926	843-681-2386	681-9287
Old Oyster Factory 101 Marshland Rd *Web:* www.oldoysterfactory.com	Hilton Head Island	SC	29926	843-681-6040	
Red Fish Eight Archer Rd *Web:* www.redfishofhiltonhead.com	Hilton Head Island	SC	29928	843-686-3388	
Sage Room 81 Pope Ave *Web:* www.thesageroom.com	Hilton Head Island	SC	29928	843-785-5352	785-5354
Salty Dog Cafe, The 232 S Sea Pines Dr *TF:* 877-725-8936 ■ *Web:* www.saltydog.com	Hilton Head Island	SC	29928	843-671-5199	671-6498
Santa Fe Cafe 807 William Hilton Pkwy *Web:* santafecafehiltonhead.com	Hilton Head Island	SC	29928	843-785-3838	785-2496
Signe's Bakery & Cafe 93 Arrow Rd *TF:* 866-807-4463 ■ *Web:* www.signesbakery.com	Hilton Head Island	SC	29928	843-785-9118	785-6144
Smokehouse, The 34 Palmetto Bay Rd *Web:* www.smokehousehhi.com	Hilton Head Island	SC	29928	843-842-4227	
Steamer Seafood Co One N Forest Beach Dr Ste 28 Calligny Plz *Web:* www.steamerseafood.com	Hilton Head Island	SC	29928	843-785-2070	
Boathouse, The 101 Palm Blvd *Web:* www.boathouserestaurants.com	Isle of Palms	SC	29451	843-886-8000	
Bovine's 3979 Hwy 17 Business *Web:* www.bovinesrestaurant.com	Murrells Inlet	SC	29576	843-651-2888	651-0211
Bangkok House 318 N Kings Hwy	Myrtle Beach	SC	29577	843-626-5384	
Captain George's 1401 29th Ave *Web:* www.captaingeorges.com	Myrtle Beach	SC	29577	843-916-2278	443-9097
El Cerro Grande 108 S Kings Hwy	Myrtle Beach	SC	29577	843-946-9562	448-4431
Fiesta Del Burroloco 960 Jason Blvd *Web:* www.centraarchy.com	Myrtle Beach	SC	29577	843-626-1756	626-1860
Flamingo Grille 7050 N Kings Hwy *Web:* flamingogrill.com	Myrtle Beach	SC	29572	843-449-5388	449-4551
Giant Crab 9597 N Kings Hwy *Web:* www.giantcrab.com	Myrtle Beach	SC	29572	843-449-1097	449-3575
Miyabi 9732 N Kings Hwy *Web:* miyabimyrtlebeach.com	Myrtle Beach	SC	29572	843-449-9294	692-2274
Original Benjamin's, The 9593 N Kings Hwy *Web:* www.originalbenjamins.com	Myrtle Beach	SC	29572	843-449-0821	
Sea Captain's House 3002 N Ocean Blvd *Web:* www.seacaptains.com	Myrtle Beach	SC	29577	843-448-8082	
Senor Frogs 1304 Celebrity Cir Bldg R-8 *Web:* www.senorfrogs.com	Myrtle Beach	SC	29577	843-444-5506	
Sugami 4813 N Kings Hwy *Web:* sugamimyrtlebeach.com	Myrtle Beach	SC	29577	843-692-7709	
Thoroughbreds 9706 N Kings Hwy *Web:* www.thoroughbredsrestaurant.com	Myrtle Beach	SC	29572	843-497-2636	497-6474
Crabby Mike's Calabash Seafood 290 Hwy 17 N *Web:* www.crabbymikes.com	Surfside Beach	SC	29575	843-238-3524	238-3526

South Dakota

				Phone	Fax
Cattleman's Club Steakhouse & Lounge 29608 SD Hwy 34 *Web:* cattlemansclubsteakhouse.com	Pierre	SD	57501	605-224-9774	
Jake's Good Time Place 620 S Cleveland *Web:* dexknows.com	Pierre	SD	57501	605-945-0485	
La Minestra 106 E Dakota Ave *Web:* www.laminestra.com	Pierre	SD	57501	605-224-8090	
Longbranch Restaurant & Lounge 351 S Pierre St	Pierre	SD	57501	605-224-6166	945-2240
Mad Mary's Steakhouse & Saloon 110 E Dakota Ave	Pierre	SD	57501	605-224-6469	
Outpost Lodge 28229 Cow Creek Rd *Web:* www.theoutpostlodge.com	Pierre	SD	57501	605-264-5450	264-5369
Botticelli Italian Restaurant 523 Main St *Web:* botticelliristorante.net	Rapid City	SD	57701	605-348-0089	
Colonial House 2501 Mt Rushmore Rd *Web:* www.colonialhousernb.com	Rapid City	SD	57701	605-342-4640	341-0445
Firehouse Brewing Co 610 Main St *Web:* firehousebrewing.com	Rapid City	SD	57701	605-348-1915	
Golden Phoenix 2421 W Main St	Rapid City	SD	57702	605-348-4195	
Hong Kong Buffet 927 E N St *Web:* cocopalaces.com	Rapid City	SD	57701	605-716-4664	
Hunan 1720 Mt Rushmore Rd *Web:* bhhunan.com	Rapid City	SD	57701	605-341-3888	399-3203
Mongolian Grill 1415 N Lacrosse St Ste 1 *Web:* www.mongoliangrill.ca	Rapid City	SD	57701	605-388-3187	
Saigon 221 E N St *Web:* saigonrestaurantrc.com	Rapid City	SD	57701	605-348-8523	
Casa Del Rey 901 W Russell St *Web:* www.casadelrey.com	Sioux Falls	SD	57104	605-338-6078	
Cherry Creek Grill 3104 E 26th St *Web:* cherrycreek-grill.com	Sioux Falls	SD	57103	605-336-2333	
Dynasty 5326 W 26th St *Web:* www.dynastysf.com	Sioux Falls	SD	57106	605-361-7788	
Falls Landing 200 E Eigth St *Web:* falls-landing.com	Sioux Falls	SD	57103	605-336-2290	
Incas 3312 S Holly Ave *Web:* incasiouxfalls.com	Sioux Falls	SD	57105	605-367-1992	367-1993
Minerva's 301 S Phillips Ave *Web:* www.minervas.net	Sioux Falls	SD	57104	605-334-0386	334-9585
Sanaa's 401 E Eigth St *Web:* sanaacooks.com	Sioux Falls	SD	57103	605-275-2516	
Spezia Restaurant 4801 S Louise Ave *Web:* bigthreerestaurants.com	Sioux Falls	SD	57106	605-334-7491	
Sushi Masa 423 S Phillips Ave	Sioux Falls	SD	57104	605-977-6968	
Touch of Europe 337 S Phillips Ave *Web:* www.touchofeurope.net	Sioux Falls	SD	57104	605-336-3066	

Tennessee

				Phone	Fax
Corky's 100 Franklin Rd *Web:* corkysbbq.com	Brentwood	TN	37027	615-373-1020	371-1638
212 Market Restaurant 212 Market St *Web:* www.212market.com	Chattanooga	TN	37402	423-265-1212	267-6757
Acropolis, The 2213 Hamilton Pl Blvd *Web:* www.acropolisgrill.com	Chattanooga	TN	37421	423-899-5341	899-6587
Amigo Mexican Restaurant 3805 Ringgold Rd *Web:* amigorestaurantonline.com	Chattanooga	TN	37412	423-624-4345	
Broad Street Grille at the Chattanoogan 1201 Broad St *Web:* www.chattanooganhotel.com	Chattanooga	TN	37402	423-424-3700	756-3404
China Moon 5600 Brainerd Rd *Web:* chinamoontn.com	Chattanooga	TN	37411	423-893-8088	855-5288
Chop House, The 2011 Gunbarrel Rd *Web:* www.thechophouse.com	Chattanooga	TN	37421	423-892-1222	
India Mahal 5970 Brainerd Rd	Chattanooga	TN	37421	423-510-9651	
Kanpai of Tokyo 2200 Hamilton Pl Blvd *Web:* www.kanpaioftokyo.com	Chattanooga	TN	37421	423-855-8204	855-9687
Mount Vernon Restaurant 3535 Broad St	Chattanooga	TN	37409	423-266-6591	
Na Go Ya 4921 Brainerd Rd *Web:* chattanooganagoya.com	Chattanooga	TN	37411	423-899-9252	
Porker's BBQ 1251 Market St *Web:* porkersbbq.com	Chattanooga	TN	37402	423-267-2726	
Saint John's Restaurant 1278 Market St *Web:* www.stjohnsrestaurant.com	Chattanooga	TN	37402	423-266-4400	267-3004
Sekisui of Chattanooga 1120 Houston St *Web:* www.sekisuichattanooga.com	Chattanooga	TN	37402	423-267-4600	
Southern Star 1300 Broad St *Web:* www.southernstarrestaurant.com	Chattanooga	TN	37402	423-267-8899	
Sushi Nabe of Chattanooga 110 River St *Web:* www.sushinabechattanooga.com	Chattanooga	TN	37405	423-634-0171	
Terra Nostra 105 Frazier Ave *Web:* www.terranostratapas.com	Chattanooga	TN	37405	423-634-0238	
Jims Place Grille 3660 S Houston Levee *Web:* jimsplacegrille.com	Collierville	TN	38017	901-861-5000	
Alta Cucina 1200 N Roan St *Web:* altacucinajc.com/	Johnson City	TN	37601	423-928-2092	
Bello Vita 2927 N Roan St Bldg 2	Johnson City	TN	37601	423-282-8600	
Cafe One 11 111 Broyles St Sunset Shopping Ctr Ste 1 *Web:* www.cafeone11jc.com	Johnson City	TN	37601	423-283-4633	283-0550
Cafe Pacific 1033 W Oakland Ave *Web:* www.cafepacificjtn.com	Johnson City	TN	37604	423-610-0117	610-0880
Dixie Barbecue Co 3301 N Roan St *Web:* dixiebarbeque.net	Johnson City	TN	37601	423-283-7447	
Firehouse Restaurant 627 W Walnut St *Web:* www.thefirehouse.com	Johnson City	TN	37604	423-929-7377	929-2080
Harbor House Seafood 2510 N Roan St *Web:* www.harborhousejc.com	Johnson City	TN	37601	423-282-5122	
Horseshoe Restaurant & Lounge 908 W Market St	Johnson City	TN	37604	423-928-8992	
Misaki Seafood & Steak House of Japan 3104 Bristol Hwy	Johnson City	TN	37601	423-282-5451	
Moto Japanese Restaurant 2607 N Roan St	Johnson City	TN	37601	423-282-6686	282-0132
Peerless Steak House 2531 N Roan St *Web:* www.peerlesseatout.com	Johnson City	TN	37601	423-282-2351	283-0439
Red Pig Bar-B-Q 2201 Ferguson Rd	Johnson City	TN	37604	423-282-6585	282-6309
Bayou Bay Seafood House 7117 Chapman Hwy *Web:* bayoubayseafoodhouseknoxville.com	Knoxville	TN	37920	865-573-7936	
Bistro by the Tracks 215 Brookview Centre Way Ste 109 *Web:* www.bistrobythetracks.com	Knoxville	TN	37919	865-558-9500	
Buddy's Bar-B-Q 4401 Chapman Hwy *Web:* buddysbarbq.com	Knoxville	TN	37920	865-579-1747	579-3315

	City	State	Zip	Phone	Fax
Calhoun's 10020 Kingston Pk *Web:* calhouns.com	Knoxville	TN	37922	865-673-3444	
Chesapeake's 500 Henley St *Web:* www.coppercellar.com	Knoxville	TN	37902	865-673-3433	673-3435
Copper Cellar 1807 Cumberland Ave PO Box 50370 *Web:* www.coppercellar.com	Knoxville	TN	37950	865-673-3400	522-8526
Downtown Grill & Brewery 424 S Gay St *Web:* www.downtownbrewery.com	Knoxville	TN	37902	865-633-8111	633-8954
King Tut's Grill 4132 Martin Mill Pk	Knoxville	TN	37920	865-573-6021	
Litton's Market & Restaurant & Bakery 2803 Essary Dr *Web:* www.littonsdirecttoyou.com/home.aspx	Knoxville	TN	37918	865-688-0429	
Misaki Japanese Steak House 8207 Kingston Pk	Knoxville	TN	37919	865-691-3121	691-3218
Nama Sushi Bar 506 S Gay St **Fax Area Code:* 615 ■ *Web:* www.namasushibar.com	Knoxville	TN	37902	865-633-8539	739-5819*
Naples Italian Restaurant 5500 Kingston Pk *Web:* naplesitalianrestaurant.net	Knoxville	TN	37919	865-584-5033	584-9415
Orangery, The 5412 Kingston Pk *Web:* www.orangeryknoxville.com	Knoxville	TN	37919	865-588-2964	
Pelanchos Mexican Grill 1516 Downtown W Blvd *Web:* www.pelanchos.com	Knoxville	TN	37919	865-694-9060	
Savelli's 3055 Sutherland Ave *Web:* savellisknoxville.com	Knoxville	TN	37919	865-521-9085	
Sitar Indian Cuisine 6004 Kingston Pk *Web:* sitarknoxville.com	Knoxville	TN	37919	865-588-1828	588-1830
Tomato Head 12 Market Sq *Web:* thetomatohead.com	Knoxville	TN	37902	865-637-4067	637-4019
Wasabi Japanese Steak House 226 Lovell Rd *Web:* www.wasabi-steakhouse.com	Knoxville	TN	37934	865-675-0201	
Ye Olde Steak House 6838 Chapman Hwy *Web:* www.yeoldesteakhouse.com	Knoxville	TN	37920	865-577-9328	
Automatic Slim's 83 S Second St *Web:* www.automaticslimsmemphis.com	Memphis	TN	38103	901-525-7948	526-6642
Bar-B-Q Shop, The 1782 Madison Ave *Web:* dancingpigs.com	Memphis	TN	38104	901-272-1277	272-9085
BB King's Blues Club 143 Beale St *Web:* www.bbkingclubs.com	Memphis	TN	38103	901-524-5464	524-5454
Bhan Thai 1324 Peabody Ave *Web:* www.bhanthairestaurant.com	Memphis	TN	38104	901-272-1538	272-2487
Boscos Squared 827 S Main *Web:* www.boscosbeer.com	Memphis	TN	38106	901-278-0087	278-3040
Buckley's 5355 Poplar Ave *Web:* www.buckleysgrill.com	Memphis	TN	38119	901-683-4538	
Cafe 1912 243 S Cooper at Peabody *Web:* cafe1912.com	Memphis	TN	38104	901-722-2700	
Cafe Society 212 N Evergreen St *Web:* cafesocietymemphis.com	Memphis	TN	38112	901-722-2177	722-2186
Celtic Crossing Irish Pub & Restaurant 903 S Cooper St *Web:* www.celticcrossingmemphis.com	Memphis	TN	38104	901-274-5151	274-5159
Central BBQ 2249 Central Ave *Web:* cbqmemphis.com	Memphis	TN	38104	901-272-9377	728-5850
Cupboard, The 1400 Union Ave *Web:* www.thecupboardrestaurant.com	Memphis	TN	38104	901-276-8015	728-5518
Erling Jensen Restaurant 1044 S Yates Rd *Web:* www.ejensen.com	Memphis	TN	38119	901-763-3700	763-3800
Folk's Folly Prime Steak House 551 S Mendenhall Rd *Web:* www.folksfolly.com	Memphis	TN	38117	901-762-8200	328-2287
Frank Grisanti's 1022 S Shady Grove Rd *Web:* frankgrisanti.com	Memphis	TN	38120	901-761-9462	761-2245
Golden India 2097 Madison Ave	Memphis	TN	38104	901-728-5111	
Grill83 83 Madison Ave *Web:* www.eighty3memphis.com	Memphis	TN	38103	901-333-1224	333-1210
Grove Grill 4550 Poplar Ave *Web:* www.thegrovegrill.com	Memphis	TN	38117	901-818-9951	
Happy Mexican Restaurant & Cantina 6080 Primacy Pkwy *Web:* www.happymexican.com	Memphis	TN	38119	901-683-0000	
Huey's 1927 Madison Ave *Web:* www.hueyburger.com	Memphis	TN	38104	901-726-4372	278-9073
Jim Neely's Interstate Barbeque 2265 S Third St *Web:* www.interstatebarbecue.com	Memphis	TN	38109	901-775-2304	775-3149
King's Palace Cafe 162 Beale St *Web:* kingspalacecafe.com	Memphis	TN	38103	901-521-1851	
Mollie's La Casita Restaurant 2006 Madison Ave *Web:* www.mollyslacasita.com	Memphis	TN	38104	901-726-1873	726-1876
Owen Brennan's Restaurant 6150 Poplar Ave *Web:* www.brennansmemphis.com	Memphis	TN	38119	901-761-0990	761-9177
Saigon Le 51 N Cleveland St	Memphis	TN	38104	901-276-5326	
Sekisui 25 S Belvedere Blvd **Fax Area Code:* 956 ■ *Web:* www.sekisuiusa.com	Memphis	TN	38104	901-725-0005	380-8256*
Sekisui Japanese Restaurant 4724 Poplar Ave Ste 16 *Web:* www.sekisuiusa.com	Memphis	TN	38117	901-767-7770	747-2118
Silky O'Sullivan's 183 Beale St *Web:* www.silkyosullivans.com	Memphis	TN	38103	901-522-9596	522-8462
Texas de Brazil 150 Peabody Pl Ste 103 *Web:* www.texasdebrazil.com	Memphis	TN	38103	901-526-7600	526-7615
Amerigo Nashville 1920 W End Ave *Web:* www.amerigo.net	Nashville	TN	37203	615-320-1740	320-0644
Anatolia 48 White Bridge Rd *Web:* www.anatolia-restaurant.com	Nashville	TN	37205	615-356-1556	356-1551
Antonios' of Nashville 7097 Old HaRding Rd *Web:* antoniosofnashville.com	Nashville	TN	37221	615-646-9166	
Blackstone Restaurant & Brewery 1918 W End Ave *Web:* blackstone-pub.com/	Nashville	TN	37203	615-327-9969	327-4131
Bound'ry 911 20th Ave S *Web:* boundrynashville.com	Nashville	TN	37212	615-321-3043	321-0984
Cock of the Walk 2624 Music Vly Dr *Web:* www.cockofthewalkrestaurant.com	Nashville	TN	37214	615-889-1930	889-0047
Copper Kettle Cafe 4004 Granny White Pk *Web:* copperkettlenashville.com	Nashville	TN	37204	615-383-7242	383-7949
Goten Japanese Steak & Sushi Bar 1719 W End Ave Ste 101W	Nashville	TN	37203	615-321-4537	321-3105
Hog Heaven 115 27th Ave N *Web:* www.hogheavenbbq.com	Nashville	TN	37203	615-329-1234	
Jack's Bar-B-Que 334 W Trinity Ln *Web:* www.jacksbarbque.com	Nashville	TN	37207	615-228-4600	228-4700
Jim 'N Nick's 7004 Charlotte Pk *Web:* jimnnicks.com	Nashville	TN	37209	615-352-5777	
Jimmy Kelly's 217 Louise Ave *Web:* www.jimmykellys.com	Nashville	TN	37203	615-329-4349	320-7882
Kalamata's 3764 Hillsboro Pike *Web:* www.eatatkalamatas.com	Nashville	TN	37215	615-383-8700	
Ken's 1108 Murfreesboro Pk *Web:* www.kensushi.com	Nashville	TN	37217	615-321-2444	
Kien Giang 5845 Charlotte Pk	Nashville	TN	37209	615-353-1250	
Kobe Steaks Nashville 210 25th Ave N Ste 100 *Web:* www.kobesteaks.net	Nashville	TN	37203	615-327-9081	327-9083
Korea House 6410 Charlotte Pk Ste 108	Nashville	TN	37209	615-352-2790	
Mad Platter, The 1239 Sixth Ave N *Web:* www.madplatternashville.com	Nashville	TN	37208	615-242-2563	
Margot Cafe & Bar 1017 Woodland St *Web:* margotcafe.com	Nashville	TN	37206	615-227-4668	
Midtown Cafe 102 19th Ave S *Web:* www.midtowncafe.com	Nashville	TN	37203	615-320-7176	320-0920
Palm, The 140 Fifth Ave S *Web:* www.thepalm.com	Nashville	TN	37203	615-742-7256	742-9028
Park Cafe 4403 Murphy Rd *Web:* parkcafenashville.com	Nashville	TN	37209	615-383-4409	383-4829
Rotier's 2413 Elliston Pl *Web:* rotiersrestaurant.com	Nashville	TN	37203	615-327-9892	
Ru San's 505 12th Ave S *Web:* rusansjapanese.com	Nashville	TN	37203	615-252-8787	
Siam Cafe 316 McCall St	Nashville	TN	37211	615-834-3181	
Sonobana Japanese Restaurant & Grocery 40 White Bridge Rd *Web:* www.sonobananashville.com	Nashville	TN	37205	615-356-6600	
South Street Restaurant 907 20th Ave S *Web:* pansouth.net/southstreet	Nashville	TN	37212	615-320-5555	
Sperry's 5109 Harding Pike *Web:* www.sperrys.com	Nashville	TN	37205	615-353-0809	353-0814
Sunset Grill 2001 Belcourt Ave *Web:* www.sunsetgrill.com	Nashville	TN	37212	615-386-3663	
Tin Angel 3201 W End Ave *Web:* tinangel.net	Nashville	TN	37203	615-298-3444	
Yellow Porch, The 734 Thompson Ln *Web:* www.theyellowporch.com	Nashville	TN	37204	615-386-0260	

Texas

	City	State	Zip	Phone	Fax
Abilene Seafood Tavern 1882 S Clack St *Web:* abileneseafoodtavern.com	Abilene	TX	79605	325-695-1770	
Alfredo's Mexican Food 2849 S 14th St	Abilene	TX	79605	325-698-0104	
Catfish Corner 780 S Treadaway Blvd	Abilene	TX	79602	325-672-3620	
Cotton Patch Cafe 3302 S Clack St *Web:* www.cottonpatch.com	Abilene	TX	79606	325-691-0509	
Cypress Street Station 158 Cypress St *Web:* www.cypress-street.com	Abilene	TX	79601	325-676-3463	676-0715
Eckos Restaurant 2410 Adam Ave	Abilene	TX	79602	325-672-3792	
Joe Allen's Pit Bar-B-Que 301 S 11th St	Abilene	TX	79602	325-672-6082	672-3015*
Little Panda 1035 N Judge Ely Blvd *Web:* www.littlepandaonline.com	Abilene	TX	79601	325-670-9393	670-9392
Lytle Land & Cattle Co 1150 E S 11th St PO Box 3877 *Web:* www.lytlelandandcattle.com	Abilene	TX	79602	325-677-1925	677-0951
Towne Crier Steak House 818 US Hwy 80 E *Web:* www.townecriersteakhouse.com	Abilene	TX	79601	325-673-4551	673-0065
Abuelo's Mexican Food Embassy 3501 W 45th Ave *Web:* www.abuelos.com	Amarillo	TX	79109	806-354-8294	
Amarillo Club 600 S Tyler St *Web:* amarilloclub.net	Amarillo	TX	79101	806-373-4361	372-2606
Big Texan Steak Ranch 7701 I-40 E **Fax Area Code:* 651 ■ *TF Cust Svc:* 800-657-7177 ■ *Web:* www.bigtexan.com	Amarillo	TX	79118	806-372-6000	604-8499*
BL Bistro 2203 S Austin St *Web:* www.blbistro.com	Amarillo	TX	79109	806-355-7838	373-8481
Buns Over Texas 6045 SW 34th *Web:* bunsovertexas.com	Amarillo	TX	79109	806-358-6808	
Coyote Bluff Cafe 2417 S Grand St *Web:* coyotebluffcafe.com	Amarillo	TX	79103	806-373-4640	
Doug's Hickory Pit Bar B Que 3313 S Georgia St	Amarillo	TX	79109	806-352-8471	
Golden Light Cafe 2908 W Sixth Ave *Web:* www.goldenlightcafe.com	Amarillo	TX	79106	806-374-9237	
Hoffbrau Steaks 7203-G IH- I-40 W *Web:* www.hoffbrausteaks.com	Amarillo	TX	79106	806-358-6595	354-8411
Hummer's Sports Cafe 2600 Paramount Blvd	Amarillo	TX	79109	806-353-0723	353-4249
Jorge's Taco Garcia Mexican Cafe 1100 S Ross St *Web:* www.tacosgarcia.com	Amarillo	TX	79102	806-371-0411	371-0538

Restaurant	City	State	Zip	Phone	Fax
Kabuki Japanese Steakhouse 8130 I 40 W *Web:* kabukiromanza.com	Amarillo	TX	79106	806-358-7799	
Macaroni Joe's 1619 S Kentucky St Ste 1500-D *Web:* www.macaronijoes.com	Amarillo	TX	79102	806-358-8990	322-1325
My Thai 2029 Coulter Dr *Web:* www.mythaiamarillo.com	Amarillo	TX	79106	806-355-9541	
Pacific Rim 2061 Paramount *Web:* www.pacificrimam.com	Amarillo	TX	79109	806-353-9179	358-7888
Ruby Tequila's 2001 S Georgia *Web:* www.rubytequilas.com	Amarillo	TX	79109	806-358-7829	
Arlington Steak House 1724 W Div St *Web:* thearlingtonsteakhouse.com	Arlington	TX	76012	817-275-7881	275-7881
Bigotes 1821 E Abram St	Arlington	TX	76010	817-274-1350	
Cacharel Restaurant & Grand Ballroom 2221 E Lamar Blvd *Web:* www.cacharel.net	Arlington	TX	76006	817-640-9981	633-5737
La Isla 611 W Pk Row	Arlington	TX	76010	817-460-1180	
Mariano's Mexican Cuisine 2614 Majesty Dr *Web:* laharanch.com	Arlington	TX	76011	817-640-5118	
Nagoya Japanese Restaurant 1155 W Arbrook Blvd *Web:* www.txnagoya.com	Arlington	TX	76015	817-466-3688	466-3684
Pappadeaux Seafood Kitchen 1304 E Copeland Rd *Web:* www.pappadeaux.com	Arlington	TX	76011	817-543-0545	543-0548
Piccolo Mondo 829 E Lamar Blvd *Web:* www.piccolomondo.com	Arlington	TX	76011	817-265-9174	226-3474
Spring Creek Barbeque 2340 W I- 20 Ste 100 *TF:* 888-467-0505 ■ *Web:* www.springcreekbarbeque.com	Arlington	TX	76017	817-467-0505	493-5216
Tandoor Indian Restaurant 1200 N Fielder Rd Ste 532 *Web:* www.tandoorrestaurant.net	Arlington	TX	76012	817-261-6604	548-9026
Alborz Persian Cuisine 3300 W Anderson Ln Ste 303 *Web:* www.alborzpersiancuisine.com	Austin	TX	78757	512-420-2222	
Asti Trattoria 408C E 43rd St *Web:* www.astiaustin.com	Austin	TX	78751	512-451-1218	
Austin Land & Cattle Co 1205 N Lamar Blvd *Web:* alcsteaks.com	Austin	TX	78703	512-472-1813	472-1815
Casa de Luz 1701 Toomey Rd *Web:* www.casadeluz.org	Austin	TX	78704	512-476-2535	476-0198
Chez Nous 510 Neches St *Web:* cheznousaustin.com	Austin	TX	78701	512-473-2413	236-8468
Chez Zee American Bistro 5406 Balcones Dr *Web:* www.chez-zee.com	Austin	TX	78731	512-454-2666	454-0034
Clay Pit 1601 Guadalupe St *Web:* www.claypit.com	Austin	TX	78701	512-322-5131	322-9514
Curra's Grill 614 E Oltorf St *Web:* www.currasgrill.com	Austin	TX	78704	512-444-0012	
Cypress Grill 4404 W William Cannon Ste L *Web:* www.cypressgrill.net	Austin	TX	78749	512-358-7474	358-7472
Din Ho's Chinese BBQ 8557 Research Blvd *Web:* www.dinhochinesebbq.com	Austin	TX	78758	512-832-8788	
Dog & Duck Pub, The 406 W 17th St *Web:* www.dogandduckpub.com	Austin	TX	78701	512-479-0598	
Driskill Grill 604 Brazos St *Web:* www.driskillgrill.com	Austin	TX	78701	512-391-7162	391-7059
Eastside Cafe 2113 Manor Rd *Web:* www.eastsidecafeaustin.com	Austin	TX	78722	512-476-5858	477-5847
El Sol Y La Luna 600 E Sixth St *Web:* elsolylalunaaustin.com	Austin	TX	78701	512-444-7770	444-4554
Fado's Irish Pub 214 W Fourth St *Web:* www.fadoirishpub.com	Austin	TX	78701	512-457-0172	457-0519
Fonda San Miguel 2330 W N Loop Blvd *Web:* www.fondasanmiguel.com	Austin	TX	78756	512-459-4121	459-5792
Four Seasons Hotel Austin 98 San Jacinto Blvd *Web:* fourseasons.com	Austin	TX	78701	512-478-4500	478-3117
Green Pastures 811 W Live Oak St *Web:* www.greenpasturesrestaurant.com	Austin	TX	78704	512-444-4747	444-3912
Habana 2728 S Congress Ave *Web:* www.habanaaustin.com	Austin	TX	78704	512-443-4252	
Hudson's on the Bend 3509 Ranch Rd 620 N *TF:* 800-996-7655 ■ *Web:* www.hudsonsonthebend.com	Austin	TX	78734	512-266-1369	266-1399
Hula Hut 3825 Lk Austin Blvd *Web:* www.hulahut.com	Austin	TX	78703	512-476-4852	477-1604
Hyde Park Bar & Grill 4206 Duval St *Web:* www.hpbng.com	Austin	TX	78751	512-458-3168	458-6722
III Forks 111 Lavaca St *Web:* www.3forks.com	Austin	TX	78701	512-474-1776	
Jeffrey's Restaurant 1204 W Lynn St *Web:* www.jeffreysofaustin.com	Austin	TX	78703	512-477-5584	474-7279
Kim Phung 7601 N Lamar Blvd Ste I *Web:* kplamar.com	Austin	TX	78752	512-451-2464	451-8083
La Traviata 314 Congress Ave *Web:* latraviata.net	Austin	TX	78701	512-479-8131	479-8545
Madam Mam's 2514 Guadalupe St *Web:* madammam.com	Austin	TX	78705	512-472-8306	236-3040
Magnolia Cafe 2304 Lk Austin Blvd *Web:* www.themagnoliacafe.com	Austin	TX	78703	512-478-8645	494-1722
Mikado Ryotei 9033 Research Blvd *Web:* www.mikadoryotei.com	Austin	TX	78758	512-833-8188	
Moonshine Patio Bar & Grill 303 Red River St *Web:* www.moonshinegrill.com	Austin	TX	78701	512-236-9599	236-8816
Musashino Sushi Dokoro 3407 Greystone Dr *Web:* www.musashinosushi.com	Austin	TX	78731	512-795-8593	343-7613
Oasis, The 6550 Comanche Trl *Web:* www.oasis-austin.com	Austin	TX	78732	512-266-2442	266-9296
Rocco's Grill 900 Ranch Rd 620 S Ste A106 *Web:* www.roccosgrill.com	Austin	TX	78734	512-263-8204	263-5332
Satay 3202 W Anderson Ln *Web:* www.satayusa.com	Austin	TX	78757	512-467-6731	467-9640

Restaurant	City	State	Zip	Phone	Fax
Shoreline Grill 98 San Jacinto Blvd *Web:* www.shorelinegrill.com	Austin	TX	78701	512-477-3300	477-6392
Star of India 2900 W Anderson Ln Ste 12D *Web:* www.starofindiaaustin.com	Austin	TX	78757	512-452-8199	
Sunflower 8557 Research Blvd	Austin	TX	78758	512-339-7860	
Sushi Japon 6801 N IH-35 *Web:* www.sushijaponaustin.com	Austin	TX	78752	512-323-6663	323-6789
Sushi Zushi 1611 W Fifth St *Web:* www.sushizushi.com	Austin	TX	78703	512-474-7000	
Threadgill's 6416 N Lamar Blvd *Web:* www.threadgills.com	Austin	TX	78752	512-451-5440	451-5033
Uchi 801 S Lamar Blvd *Web:* www.uchiaustin.com	Austin	TX	78704	512-916-4808	916-4806
Umi Sushi Bar & Grill 5510 S IH-35 Ste 400 *Web:* umiaustin.com	Austin	TX	78745	512-383-8681	383-8802
Veggie Heaven 1914 Guadalupe St *Web:* veggieheavenaustin.com	Austin	TX	78705	512-457-1013	
Vespaio 1610 S Congress Ave *Web:* austinvespaio.com	Austin	TX	78704	512-441-6100	441-7746
Wink Restaurant 1014 N Lamar Blvd *Web:* www.winkrestaurant.com	Austin	TX	78703	512-482-8868	482-9477
Z Tejas Grill 9400-A Arboreum Blvd *Web:* www.ztejas.com	Austin	TX	78759	512-346-3506	346-6328
Antonio's Mexican Village 840 Paredes Rd	Brownsville	TX	78521	956-542-6504	542-1125
Blue Mermaid Cafe 119 Billy Mitchell Blvd	Brownsville	TX	78521	956-544-2157	
Cobbleheads Bar & Grill 3154 Central Blvd *Web:* www.cobbleheads.com	Brownsville	TX	78520	956-546-6224	546-6772
Los Camperos 2500 N Expy *Web:* camperosgrillandbar.com	Brownsville	TX	78526	956-546-8172	541-7315
Lotus Inn 905 N Expy *Web:* lotuscafe.us	Brownsville	TX	78520	956-542-5715	541-6973
Oyster Bar I 157 E Levee St	Brownsville	TX	78520	956-542-9786	
Sylvia's Restaurant 1843 Southmost Rd	Brownsville	TX	78521	956-542-9220	
Vermillion, The 115 Paredes Line Rd *Web:* www.thevermillion.com	Brownsville	TX	78521	956-542-9893	
El Rinconcitos 4025 Prescott St	Corpus Christi	TX	78416	361-851-8020	
Executive Surf Club 309 N Water St *Web:* www.executivesurfclub.com	Corpus Christi	TX	78401	361-884-7873	882-2865
Kiko's 5514 Everhart Rd *Web:* kikosmexicanfood.com	Corpus Christi	TX	78411	361-991-1211	
Little Manila Lumpia House 2124 Waldron Rd	Corpus Christi	TX	78418	361-937-5651	
Peoples 9738 Up River Rd *Web:* www.peoplesrestaurant.com	Corpus Christi	TX	78410	361-241-8087	241-8089
Pier 99 2822 N Shoreline Blvd *Web:* pier99restaurant.com	Corpus Christi	TX	78402	361-887-0764	887-8840
Republic of Texas Bar & Grill 900 N Shoreline Blvd *Web:* omnihotels.com	Corpus Christi	TX	78401	361-887-1600	886-3530
Snoopy's Pier 13313 S Padre Island Dr *Web:* snoopyspier.com	Corpus Christi	TX	78418	361-949-8815	949-9778
Torch Restaurant 4425 S Alameda St	Corpus Christi	TX	78412	361-992-7491	
Water Street Market 309 N Water St *Web:* www.waterstmarketcc.com	Corpus Christi	TX	78401	361-882-8683	
Abacus *Kent Rathbun* 4511 McKinney Ave *Web:* www.kentrathbun.com/abacus	Dallas	TX	75205	214-559-3111	559-3113
Al Biernat's 4217 Oak Lawn Ave *Web:* www.albiernats.com	Dallas	TX	75219	214-219-2201	219-2093
Amore 6931 Snider Plz *Web:* amoreitalianrestaurant.com	Dallas	TX	75205	214-739-0502	
Anderson's BBQ House 5410 Harry Hines Blvd *Web:* www.mikeandersonsbbq.com	Dallas	TX	75235	214-630-0735	630-1686
Asian Mint 11617 N Central Expy Ste 135 *Web:* www.asianmint.com	Dallas	TX	75243	214-363-6655	363-6686
Avila's 4714 Maple Ave *Web:* avilasrestaurant.com	Dallas	TX	75219	214-520-2700	
AW Shucks restaurant 3601 Greenville Ave *Web:* www.awshucksdallas.com	Dallas	TX	75206	214-821-9449	821-4581
Bob's Steak & Chop House 4300 Lemmon Ave *Web:* www.bobs-steakandchop.com	Dallas	TX	75219	214-528-9446	526-8159
Cafe Izmir 3711 Greenville Ave *Web:* www.cafeizmir.com	Dallas	TX	75206	214-826-7788	827-4359
Cafe Madrid 4501 Travis St *Web:* www.cafemadrid-dallas.com	Dallas	TX	75205	214-528-1731	522-8752
Celebration Restaurant & Catering 4503 W Lovers Ln PO Box 7330 *Web:* www.celebrationrestaurant.com	Dallas	TX	75209	214-351-5681	904-1716
City Cafe 5757 W Lovers Ln *Web:* www.thecitycafedallas.com	Dallas	TX	75209	214-351-2233	351-1936
Cosmic Cafe 2912 Oak Lawn *Web:* www.cosmiccafedallas.com	Dallas	TX	75219	214-521-6157	521-9195
Deep Sushi 2624 Elm St *Web:* www.deepsushi.com	Dallas	TX	75226	214-651-1177	
Del Frisco's of dallas 5251 Spring Vly Rd *Web:* www.delfriscos.com	Dallas	TX	75254	972-490-9000	934-0867
Fadi's Mediterranean Grill 3001 Knox St *Web:* www.fadiscuisine.com	Dallas	TX	75205	214-528-1800	528-1807
Fearing's 2121 McKinney Ave *Web:* www.fearingsrestaurant.com	Dallas	TX	75201	214-922-4848	
French Room 1321 Commerce St *Web:* www.hoteladolphus.com	Dallas	TX	75202	214-742-8200	651-3575
Fuji Steakhouse & Sushi Bar 12817 Preston Rd *Web:* www.fujidallas.com	Dallas	TX	75230	972-661-5662	661-1751
Genghis Grill 4901 LBJ Fwy Ste 150 *Web:* www.genghisgrill.com	Dallas	TX	75244	214-774-4240	
Grape, The 2808 Greenville Ave *Web:* www.thegraperestaurant.com	Dallas	TX	75206	214-828-1981	
Green Papaya 3211 Oak Lawn Ave Ste B *Web:* www.greenpapayadallas.com	Dallas	TX	75219	214-521-4811	521-4685

Name / Address	City	State	ZIP	Phone	Fax
Hibiscus 2927 N Henderson *Web:* www.hibiscusdallas.com	Dallas	TX	75206	214-827-2927	827-2929
III Forks Steakhouse 17776 Dallas Pkwy *Web:* 3forks.com/	Dallas	TX	75287	972-267-1776	267-1799
India Palace Restaurant 12817 Preston Rd Ste 105 *Web:* www.indiapalacedallas.com	Dallas	TX	75230	972-392-0190	392-3188
Jade Garden 4800 Bryan St	Dallas	TX	75204	214-821-0675	821-0675
Javier's Gourmet Mexicano 4912 Cole Ave *Web:* www.javiers.net	Dallas	TX	75205	214-521-4211	521-5239
La Duni Latin Cafe 4264 Oak Lawn Ave *Web:* www.laduni.com	Dallas	TX	75219	214-520-7300	520-7390
La Madeleine de Corps Inc 12201 Merit Dr Ste 900 *Web:* www.lamadeleine.com	Dallas	TX	75251	214-696-6962	692-8496
Lavendou 19009 Preston Rd Ste 200 *Web:* www.lavendou.com	Dallas	TX	75252	972-248-1911	248-1660
May Dragon 4848 Beltline Rd *Web:* www.maydragon.com	Dallas	TX	75254	972-392-9998	490-5023
Mercury Grill, The 11909 Preston Rd Ste 1418 *Web:* www.mcrowd.com	Dallas	TX	75230	972-960-7774	960-7988
MI PIACI 8411 Preston Rd Ste 132 *Web:* www.ilsole-dallas.com	Dallas	TX	75225	972-934-8424	
Nick & Sam's Grill 3008 Maple Ave *Web:* www.nick-sams.com	Dallas	TX	75201	214-871-7444	871-7663
Old Warsaw, The 2610 Maple Ave *Web:* www.oldwarsaw.com	Dallas	TX	75201	214-528-0032	
Palm The Restaurant 701 Ross Ave *Web:* www.thepalm.com	Dallas	TX	75202	214-698-0470	
Place At Perry's 2680 Cedar Springs Rd *Web:* www.placeatperrys.com	Dallas	TX	75201	214-871-9991	871-0302
Primo's 3309 McKinney Ave *Web:* www.primosdallas.com	Dallas	TX	75204	214-220-0510	220-2786
Pyramid Grill 1717 N Akard St *Web:* www.pyramidrestaurant.com	Dallas	TX	75201	214-720-5249	720-5282
Rosewood Hotels and Resorts LLC 2821 Turtle Creek Blvd *Web:* www.rosewoodhotels.com	Dallas	TX	75219	214-559-2100	528-4187
Royal Thai 5500 Greenville Ave *Web:* royalthaitexas.com	Dallas	TX	75206	214-691-3555	691-6718
S & D Oyster Co 2701 McKinney Ave *Web:* sdoyster.com	Dallas	TX	75204	214-880-0111	
Saint Martin's Wine Bistro 3020 Greenville Ave *Web:* www.stmartinswinebistro.com	Dallas	TX	75206	214-826-0940	826-1229
Sammy's Barbeque 2126 Leonard St *Web:* sammystexasbbq.com	Dallas	TX	75201	214-880-9064	
Sevy's Grill 8201 Preston Rd Ste 100 *Web:* www.sevys.com	Dallas	TX	75225	214-265-7389	265-8949
Simply Fondue 2108 Greenville Ave **Fax Area Code:* 800 ■ *Web:* www.simplyfondue.com	Dallas	TX	75206	214-827-8878	378-9016*
Steel Restaurant & Lounge 3102 Oaklawn Ave *Web:* www.steeldallas.com	Dallas	TX	75219	214-219-9908	219-9929
Suze 4345 W NW Hwy *Web:* www.suzedallas.com	Dallas	TX	75220	214-350-6135	350-6178
Tei Tei Robata Bar 2906 N Henderson St *Web:* www.teiteirobata.com	Dallas	TX	75206	214-828-2400	
Teppo Yakitori & Sushi Bar 2014 Greenville Ave	Dallas	TX	75206	214-826-8989	
YO Ranch Steakhouse 702 Ross Ave *Web:* www.yoranchsteakhouse.com	Dallas	TX	75202	214-744-3287	
Ziziki's Restaurant & Bar 4514 Travis St Ste 122 *Web:* www.zizikis.com	Dallas	TX	75205	214-521-2233	521-2722
Salt Lick 18300 FM 1826 *Web:* www.saltlickbbq.com	Driftwood	TX	78619	512-858-4959	858-2038
Bella Napoli 6331 N Mesa St *Web:* www.bellanapoliristorante.com	El Paso	TX	79912	915-584-3321	584-3466
Cafe Central 109 N Oregon St *Web:* www.cafecentral.com	El Paso	TX	79901	915-545-2233	545-2884
Cappetto's 2711 N Stanton St *Web:* www.nuovocappetto.com	El Paso	TX	79902	915-532-0700	
Clock Family Restaurant 8409 Dyer St	El Paso	TX	79904	915-751-6367	
Dona Lupe Cafe 2919 Pershing Dr *Web:* donalupecafe.com	El Paso	TX	79903	915-566-9833	
Edge of Texas Steakhouse 8690 Edge of Texas *Web:* theedgeoftexassteakhouse.com	El Paso	TX	79934	915-822-3343	
Forti's Mexican Elder 321 Chelsea St *Web:* fortisrestaurant.com	El Paso	TX	79905	915-772-0066	772-0067
Japanese Kitchen 4024 N Mesa St	El Paso	TX	79902	915-533-4267	542-1015
Julio's Cafe Corona 8050 Gateway Blvd E *Web:* julioscafecorona.com	El Paso	TX	79907	915-591-7676	592-1294
L & J Cafe 3622 E Missouri St *Web:* landjcafe.com	El Paso	TX	79903	915-566-8418	566-4070
Mediterranean Cuisine 4111 N Mesa St	El Paso	TX	79902	915-542-1012	
Michelinos 3615 Rutherglen St	El Paso	TX	79925	915-592-1700	
Pelican's Steak & Seafood 130 Shadow Mtn Rd *Web:* pelicanselpaso.com	El Paso	TX	79912	915-581-1392	
Pho Tre Bien 6946 Gateway E *Web:* www.photrebien.com	El Paso	TX	79915	915-598-0166	
Senor Fish 9530 Viscount Blvd Ste 1A	El Paso	TX	79925	915-598-3630	
State Line 1222 Sunland Pk Dr *Web:* www.countyline.com	El Paso	TX	79922	915-581-3371	833-4843
Trattoria Bella Sera 9449 Montana Ave *Web:* trattoriabellasera.com	El Paso	TX	79925	915-598-7948	
Cattleman's Steakhouse 3450 S Fabens Carlsbad Rd *Web:* www.cattlemanssteakhouse.com	Fabens	TX	79838	915-544-3200	
Blue Mesa Grill 1600 S University Dr *Web:* www.bluemesagrill.com	Fort Worth	TX	76107	817-332-6372	332-6398
Bonnell's 4259 Bryant Irvin Rd *Web:* bonnellstexas.com	Fort Worth	TX	76109	817-738-5489	738-4953
Byblos Byblos Lebanese Restaurant 1406 N Main St *Web:* www.byblostx.com	Fort Worth	TX	76106	817-625-9667	625-8319
Cafe Modern 3200 Darnell St *Web:* www.themodern.org	Fort Worth	TX	76107	817-738-9215	735-1161
Celaborelle Phoenician Buffet 2257 Hemphill St	Fort Worth	TX	76110	817-922-8118	
Dixie House Cafe 6200 E Lancaster Ave *Web:* www.dixiehousecafe.com	Fort Worth	TX	76112	817-451-6180	
Edelweiss German Restaurant 3801 SW Blvd A *Web:* www.edelweissgermanrestaurant.com	Fort Worth	TX	76116	817-738-5934	738-6946
Fort Worth Chop House 301 Main St *Web:* www.fortworthchophouse.com	Fort Worth	TX	76102	817-336-4129	332-6773
H3 Ranch 105 E Exchange Ave Stockyards Hotel *Web:* www.h3ranch.com	Fort Worth	TX	76164	817-624-1246	624-2571
Joe T Garcia's 2201 N Commerce St *Web:* www.joets.com	Fort Worth	TX	76164	817-626-4356	626-0581
Keg, The 5760 SW Loop 820 *Web:* www.kegsteakhouse.com	Fort Worth	TX	76132	817-731-3534	
La Familia Restaurant 841 Foch St *Web:* www.lafamilia-fw.com	Fort Worth	TX	76107	817-870-2002	
Lanny's Alta Cocina Mexicana 3405 W Seventh St *Web:* www.lannyskitchen.com	Fort Worth	TX	76107	817-850-9996	
Lonesome Dove Western Bistro 2406 N Main St *Web:* www.lonesomedovebistro.com	Fort Worth	TX	76164	817-740-8810	740-8632
Los Molcajetes 4320 Western Ctr Blvd *Web:* www.losmolcajetes.com	Fort Worth	TX	76137	817-306-9000	306-9033
Lucille's Stateside Bistro 4700 Camp Bowie Blvd *Web:* lucillesstatesidebistro.com	Fort Worth	TX	76107	817-738-4761	
Maharaja Restaurant 6308 Hulen Bend Blvd *Web:* maharajadfw.com	Fort Worth	TX	76132	817-263-7156	
MiCocina 509 Main St *Web:* micocinarestaurants.com	Fort Worth	TX	76102	817-877-3600	332-4182
Piranha 335 W Third St *Web:* www.piranhakillersushi.com	Fort Worth	TX	76102	817-348-0200	
Railhead Smokehouse 2900 Montgomery St *Web:* railheadsmokehouse.com	Fort Worth	TX	76107	817-738-9808	732-4059
Reata 310 Houston St *Web:* www.reata.net	Fort Worth	TX	76102	817-336-1009	336-0267
Saint Emilion 3617 W Seventh St *Web:* www.saint-emilionrestaurant.com	Fort Worth	TX	76107	817-737-2781	
Silver Fox Steakhouse 1651 S University Dr *Web:* www.silverfoxcafe.com	Fort Worth	TX	76107	817-332-9060	332-9073
Spiral Diner 1314 W Magnolia *Web:* www.spiraldiner.com	Fort Worth	TX	76104	817-332-8834	332-8834
Tres Jose's 4004 White Settlement Rd *Web:* tresjosestexmex.com	Fort Worth	TX	76107	817-763-0456	
West Side Cafe 7950 Camp Bowie W	Fort Worth	TX	76116	817-560-1996	
China Star 2425 W Walnut St Ste 222 *Web:* garlandchinastar.com	Garland	TX	75042	972-487-8311	
Crazy Catfish 1410 W Buckingham Rd	Garland	TX	75042	972-487-2100	
Ernesto's 1202 NW Hwy	Garland	TX	75041	972-681-8112	
Fish City Grill 445 Coneflower Dr *Web:* www.fishcitygrill.com	Garland	TX	75040	972-675-1600	
Golden Wok Buffet 1311 Plz Dr	Garland	TX	75041	972-686-8691	
Lucky China Buffet 1102 NW Hwy	Garland	TX	75041	972-270-3430	270-8839
Luna de Noche 7602 N Jupiter Rd **Fax Area Code:* 972 ■ *Web:* www.lunadenochetexmex.com	Garland	TX	75044	469-246-8271	414-2654*
On the Border Cafe 1350 NW Hwy *Web:* ontheborder.com	Garland	TX	75041	972-865-7988	
Soulman's Barbeque 3410 Broadway Blvd *Web:* soulmans.com	Garland	TX	75043	972-271-6885	
Uncle Wing Chinese Restaurant 107 N First St	Garland	TX	75040	972-272-2775	
Yen China Cafe 1225 Belt Line Rd *Web:* garlandyenchinacafe.com	Garland	TX	75040	972-495-9779	495-4929
Grey Moss Inn 19010 Scenic Loop Rd *Web:* www.grey-moss-inn.com	Helotes	TX	78023	210-695-8301	695-3237
Arcodoro 5000 Westheimer Rd Ste 120 *Web:* www.arcodoro.com	Houston	TX	77056	713-621-6888	621-6886
Arcodoro & Pomodoro 5000 Westheimer Ste 100 *Web:* www.arcodoro.com	Houston	TX	77056	713-621-6888	621-6886
Armandos 2630 Westheimer Rd *Web:* www.armandosrestaurant.com	Houston	TX	77098	713-520-1738	520-5748
Ashiana Indian Restaurant 12610 Briar Forest Rd *Web:* ashianarestaurant.net	Houston	TX	77077	281-679-5555	493-0981
Babin's Seafood House 17485 Tomball Pkwy *Web:* www.babinsseafood.com	Houston	TX	77064	281-477-9300	477-9322
Backstreet Cafe 1103 S Shepherd Dr *Web:* www.backstreetcafe.net	Houston	TX	77019	713-521-2239	520-5724
Baker's Ribs 2223 S Voss Rd *Web:* www.bakersribs.com	Houston	TX	77057	713-977-8725	977-9705
Benjy's 2424 Dunstan Rd Ste 125 *Web:* www.benjys.com	Houston	TX	77005	713-522-7602	522-7655
Bocados Restaurant 1312 W Alabama St *Web:* www.bocadoshouston.com	Houston	TX	77006	713-523-5230	
Bonnie's Beef & Seafood Co 6867 Gulf Fwy *Web:* www.bonniesbeefandseafood.com	Houston	TX	77087	713-641-2397	641-4235
Brennan's of Houston 3300 Smith St *Web:* www.brennanshouston.com	Houston	TX	77006	713-522-9711	
Brenner's Steakhouse 10911 Katy Fwy *Web:* www.brennerssteakhouse.com	Houston	TX	77079	713-465-2901	465-6205
Cafe Rabelais 2442 Times Blvd *Web:* www.caferabelais.com	Houston	TX	77005	713-520-8841	524-0071
Carmelo's 14795 Memorial Dr *Web:* www.carmelosrestaurant.com	Houston	TX	77079	281-531-0696	531-0249

Restaurant	City	State	Zip	Phone	Fax
Charivari 2521 Bagby St *Web:* www.charivarirest.com	Houston	TX	77006	713-521-7231	521-4697
Churrasco's 2055 Westheimer Rd *Web:* www.cordua.com	Houston	TX	77098	713-527-8300	527-0847
Da Marco 1520 Westheimer Rd *Web:* www.damarcohouston.com	Houston	TX	77006	713-807-8857	807-8301
Damian's Cucina Italiana 3011 Smith St *Web:* www.damians.com	Houston	TX	77006	713-522-0439	522-4408
El Tiempo Cantina 3130 Richmond Ave *Web:* www.eltiempocantina.com	Houston	TX	77098	713-807-1600	807-1616
Empire Turkish Grill 12448 Memorial Dr *Web:* www.empiretrgrill.com	Houston	TX	77024	713-827-7475	463-7719
Fadi's Mediterranean Cuisine 8383 Westheimer Rd *Web:* www.fadiscuisine.com	Houston	TX	77063	713-532-0666	532-0677
Farrago 318 Gray St *Web:* farragohouston.com	Houston	TX	77002	713-523-6404	523-6405
Fogo de Chao 8250 Westheimer Rd *Web:* www.fogodechao.com	Houston	TX	77063	713-978-6500	978-6501
Frenchie's 1041 NASA Pkwy *Web:* frenchiesvillacapri.com	Houston	TX	77058	281-486-7144	486-3952
Fung's Kitchen 7320 SW Fwy Ste 115 *Web:* eatatfungs.com	Houston	TX	77074	713-779-2288	271-2288
Goode Co Texas Barbecue 5109 Kirby Dr *Web:* www.goodecompany.com	Houston	TX	77098	713-522-2530	522-3873
Goode Company Seafood 2621 Westpark Dr *Web:* goodecompany.com	Houston	TX	77098	713-523-7154	523-0774
Hugo's 1600 Westheimer Rd *Web:* www.hugosrestaurant.net	Houston	TX	77006	713-524-7744	524-7719
Hunan Village 3311 S Shepherd Dr *Web:* houstonhunanvillage.com	Houston	TX	77098	713-528-4651	
Ibiza Food & Wine Bar 2450 Louisiana St *Web:* www.ibizafoodandwinebar.com	Houston	TX	77006	713-524-0004	524-5687
Indika 516 Westheimer Rd *Web:* www.indikausa.com	Houston	TX	77006	713-524-2170	984-1755
Jasmine Asian Cuisine 9938 Bellaire Blvd Ste D *Web:* jasmineasianrestaurant.com	Houston	TX	77036	713-272-8188	272-8187
Kam's 4500 Montrose Blvd *TF:* 800-510-3663 ■ *Web:* kamscuisine.com	Houston	TX	77006	713-529-5057	529-5486
Kiran's Restaurant & Bar 4100 Westheimer Rd *Web:* www.kiranshouston.com	Houston	TX	77027	713-960-8472	993-0739
Kubo's Sushi Bar & Grill 2414 University Blvd 200 *Web:* www.kubos-sushi.com	Houston	TX	77005	713-528-7878	528-9150
La Griglia 2002 W Gray St *Web:* www.lagrigliarestaurant.com	Houston	TX	77019	713-526-4700	526-9249
Lynn's Steakhouse 955 Dairy Ashford *Web:* www.lynnssteakhouse.com	Houston	TX	77079	281-870-0807	870-0888
Madras Pavilion 3910 Kirby Dr *Web:* madraspavilion.us	Houston	TX	77098	713-521-2617	
Maggiano's Little Italy Restaurant 2019 Post Oak Blvd *Web:* www.maggianos.com	Houston	TX	77056	713-961-2700	961-4550
Mark's American Cuisine 1658 Westheimer Rd *Web:* www.marks1658.com	Houston	TX	77006	713-523-3800	523-9292
Masraff's 1753 S Post Oak Ln *Web:* www.masraffs.com	Houston	TX	77056	713-355-1975	355-1965
Massa's 1160 Smith St *Web:* www.massas.com	Houston	TX	77002	713-650-0837	650-0165
Mockingbird Bistro 1985 Welch St *Web:* www.mockingbirdbistro.com	Houston	TX	77019	713-533-0200	533-0215
Morton's The Steakhouse 5000 Westheimer Rd *TF:* 800-552-6379 ■ *Web:* www.mortons.com	Houston	TX	77056	713-629-1946	629-4348
Nino's Vincent's Grappino di Nino 2817 W Dallas St *Web:* www.ninos-vincents.com	Houston	TX	77019	713-522-5120	528-1008
Noe Restaurant & Bar 4 Riverway *TF:* 800-809-6664 ■ *Web:* noerestaurant.com	Houston	TX	77056	713-871-8177	871-0719
Osaka Japanese Restaurant 515 Westheimer Rd	Houston	TX	77006	713-533-9098	
Piatto Ristorante 4925 W Alabama St *Web:* www.piattoristorante.com	Houston	TX	77056	713-871-9722	871-9190
Prego 2520 Amherst St *Web:* www.prego-houston.com	Houston	TX	77005	713-529-2420	526-3181
Rainbow Lodge 2011 Ella Blvd *Web:* www.rainbow-lodge.com	Houston	TX	77008	713-861-8666	861-8405
Reef 2600 Travis St *Web:* www.reefhouston.com	Houston	TX	77006	713-526-8282	526-8266
Rio Ranch 9999 Westheimer Rd *Web:* www.rioranch.com	Houston	TX	77042	713-952-5000	952-2263
Sabor! 5712 Bellaire Blvd	Houston	TX	77081	713-667-6001	
Saltgrass Steak House 520 Meyerland Plz Mall *Web:* www.saltgrass.com	Houston	TX	77096	713-665-2226	877-3176
Shiva 2514 Times Blvd *Web:* www.shivarestaurant.com	Houston	TX	77005	713-523-4753	523-4754
Spanish Flower 4701 N Main St *Web:* spanish-flowers.com	Houston	TX	77009	713-869-1706	869-1734
Spindletop 1200 Louisiana St *Web:* hyatt.com	Houston	TX	77002	713-375-4775	
Taste of Texas Restaurant 10505 Katy Fwy *Web:* www.tasteoftexas.com	Houston	TX	77024	713-932-6901	461-6177
Tony Mandola's Gulf Coast Kitchen 1212 Waugh Dr *Web:* www.tonymandolas.com	Houston	TX	77019	713-528-3474	528-4438
Tony's 3755 Richmond Ave *Web:* www.tonyshouston.com	Houston	TX	77046	713-622-6778	
Vieng Thai 6929 Long Pt St	Houston	TX	77055	713-688-9910	
Bruno's 9462 N MacArthur Blvd *Web:* brunosristorante.com	Irving	TX	75063	972-556-2465	
Cool River Cafe 1045 Hidden Ridge *Web:* www.coolrivercafe.com	Irving	TX	75038	972-871-8881	871-8882
Danal's Mexican Restaurant 508 N O'Connor Rd *Web:* danals-restaurant.com	Irving	TX	75061	972-254-2666	259-7483
Empress of China 2648 N Belt Line Rd *Web:* www.eocrestaurant.com	Irving	TX	75062	972-252-7677	258-6776
Hanasho Japanese Restaurant 2938 N Belt Line Rd *Web:* www.hanashojapaneserestaurant.com	Irving	TX	75062	972-258-0250	
I Fratelli 7701 N MacArthur Blvd *Web:* www.ifratelli.net	Irving	TX	75063	972-501-9700	501-9704
Italian Cafe 387 Las Colinas Blvd E *Web:* italianitaliancafe.com	Irving	TX	75039	972-401-0000	401-9193
Jinbeh 301 E Las Colinas Blvd *Web:* www.jinbeh.com	Irving	TX	75039	972-869-4011	869-4311
Pasand Indian Cuisine 2600 N Belt Line Rd *Web:* www.pasandrestaurant.com	Irving	TX	75062	972-594-0693	594-8935
Pei Wei Asian Diner 7600 N MacArthur Blvd *Web:* peiwei.com	Irving	TX	75063	972-373-8000	373-8133
Piman Asian Bistro 4835 N O'Connor Rd *Web:* www.pimanasian.com	Irving	TX	75062	972-650-0001	
Sonny Bryan's Smoke House 4030 N MacArthur Blvd Ste 222 **Fax Area Code: 214* ■ *Web:* www.sonnybryans.com	Irving	TX	75038	972-650-9564	596-1081*
Texadelphia 7601 N MacArthur Blvd *Web:* www.texadelphia.com	Irving	TX	75063	972-432-0725	373-8810
Trevi's 221 Las Colinas Blvd E *Web:* omnihotels.com	Irving	TX	75039	972-869-5550	556-0800
Via Real Restaurant 4020 N MacArthur Blvd *Web:* www.viareal.com	Irving	TX	75038	972-650-9001	541-0215
50 Yard Line Steakhouse 2549 Loop 289 S *Web:* 50-yardline.com	Lubbock	TX	79423	806-745-3991	
Bless Your Heart 3701 19th St *Web:* byhlubbock.com	Lubbock	TX	79410	806-791-2211	791-5330
Cagle Steaks 118 N Inler Ave *Web:* www.caglesteaks.com	Lubbock	TX	79416	806-795-3879	797-3967
Choochai Thai Cuisine 2330 19th St	Lubbock	TX	79401	806-747-1767	
Fortune Cookie 7006 University Ave Ste 6 *Web:* lubbockfortunecookie.com	Lubbock	TX	79413	806-745-2205	745-0126
Gardski's 2009 Broadway *Web:* gardskisloft.com	Lubbock	TX	79401	806-744-2391	744-0181
Jake's Sports Cafe 5025 50th St *Web:* www.jakes-sportscafe.com	Lubbock	TX	79414	806-687-5253	
Jazz Restaurant 3703C 19th St *Web:* www.jazzkitchen.com	Lubbock	TX	79410	806-799-2124	799-7870
Joe's Crab Shack 5802 W Loop S 289 *Web:* www.joescrabshack.com	Lubbock	TX	79424	806-797-8600	
Orlando's 2402 Ave Q *Web:* www.orlandos.com	Lubbock	TX	79411	806-747-5998	747-3501
Rudy's Country Store & Bar BQ 4930 S Loop 289 *Web:* www.rudysbbq.com	Lubbock	TX	79414	806-797-1777	
Texas Cafe & Bar 3604 50th St	Lubbock	TX	79413	806-792-8544	
Thai Thai 5018 50th St	Lubbock	TX	79414	806-791-0024	
Bavarian Grill 221 W Parker Rd *Web:* www.bavariangrill.com	Plano	TX	75023	972-881-0705	422-0664
Big Easy New Orleans Style Sandwiches 1915 N Central Expy Ste 200 *Web:* www.bigeasyplano.com	Plano	TX	75075	972-424-5261	
Blue Goose Cantina 4757 W Pk Blvd *Web:* www.bluegoosecantina.com	Plano	TX	75093	972-596-8882	596-8722
Cathy's Wok 3948 Legacy Dr Ste 103 *Web:* www.cathyswok.com	Plano	TX	75023	972-491-7267	491-2621
Chettinaad Palace 2205 N Central Expy *Web:* www.chettinaadpalace.com	Plano	TX	75075	469-229-9100	229-9101
Covino's 3265 Independence Pkwy *Web:* covinos.com	Plano	TX	75075	972-519-0345	778-2363
Fishmonger's Seafood 1901 N Central Expy *Web:* www.fishmongersplano.com	Plano	TX	75075	972-423-3699	
Greek Isles Grille & Taverna 3309 N Central Expy Ste 370 *Web:* greekislesgrille.com	Plano	TX	75023	972-423-7778	
Jade Palace 820 W Spring Creek Pkwy Ste 214 *Web:* www.jadepalacechinese.com	Plano	TX	75023	972-424-5578	424-9689
Japon Steak House & Sushi Bar 4021 Preston Rd *Web:* www.japonsteakhouseandsushi.com	Plano	TX	75093	972-781-2818	608-0083
Jorg's Cafe Vienna 1037 E 15th St *Web:* cafevienna.us	Plano	TX	75074	972-509-5966	
Kosta's Cafe 4621 W Pk Blvd Ste 100 *Web:* www.kostascafe.com	Plano	TX	75093	972-596-8424	
Love & War In Texas 601 E Plano Pkwy *Web:* www.loveandwarintexas.com	Plano	TX	75074	972-422-6201	633-1225
Mango's Thai Cuisine 4701 W Pk Blvd Ste 104 *Web:* www.mangoplano.com	Plano	TX	75093	972-599-0289	599-7013
Ojeda's 2001 Coit Rd Ste 102 *Web:* ojedasrestaurant.com	Plano	TX	75075	972-599-1300	
Osaka Sushi 5012 W Pk Blvd *Web:* osaka-plano.com	Plano	TX	75093	972-931-8898	
Paesano's 508 E 14th St *Web:* www.paesanosrestaurant.net	Plano	TX	75074	972-578-2727	
Patrizio's Restaurant 1900 Preston Rd *Web:* patrizios.net	Plano	TX	75093	972-964-2200	596-1743
Picasso's Italian Ristorante 3948 Legacy Dr *Web:* www.picassosrestaurant.us	Plano	TX	75023	972-618-4143	
Posados Cafe 3421 N Central Expy *Web:* posados.com	Plano	TX	75023	972-509-4999	509-4949
Rockfish Seafood Grill 4701 W Pk Blvd Ste 105 *Web:* rockfish.com	Plano	TX	75093	972-599-2190	964-6898
Steve Fields Steak & Lobster Lounge 5013 W Pk Blvd *Web:* www.stevefieldsrestaurant.com	Plano	TX	75093	972-596-7100	599-3950
Taste of the Islands 909 W Spring Creek Pkwy *Web:* tasteoftheislands.net	Plano	TX	75023	972-517-5900	
Vincent's 2432 Preston Rd	Plano	TX	75093	972-612-6208	

				Phone	Fax
Piranha Killer Sushi 7100 Blvd 26 Ste 208 *Web:* www.piranhakillersushi.com	Richland Hills	TX	76180	682-626-5953	626-5954
Alamo Cafe 10060 W IH-10 *Web:* www.alamocafe.com	San Antonio	TX	78230	210-691-8827	691-0056
Anaqua Grill 555 S Alamo St **Fax Area Code:* 817 ■ *TF:* 800-845-5279	San Antonio	TX	78205	210-229-1000	778-2049*
Biga on the Banks 203 S St Mary's St *Web:* www.biga.com	San Antonio	TX	78205	210-225-0722	225-1052
Bistro Vatel 218 E Olmos Dr *Web:* www.bistrovatel.com	San Antonio	TX	78212	210-828-3141	828-5177
Boardwalk Bistro 4011 Broadway *Web:* www.boardwalkbistro.net	San Antonio	TX	78209	210-824-0100	824-0100
Bohanan's Prime Steaks & Seafood 219 E Houston St Second Fl *Web:* www.bohanans.com	San Antonio	TX	78205	210-472-2600	472-2276
Boudro's On the Riverwalk 421 E Commerce St *Web:* www.boudros.com	San Antonio	TX	78205	210-224-8484	225-2839
Cappy's 5011 Broadway St *Web:* www.cappysrestaurant.com	San Antonio	TX	78209	210-828-9669	828-3041
Chris Madrid's 1900 Blanco Rd *Web:* chrismadrids.com	San Antonio	TX	78212	210-735-3552	
Cove, The 606 W Cypress St *Web:* thecove.us	San Antonio	TX	78212	210-227-2683	
Crumpets 3920 Harry Wurzbach St *Web:* www.crumpetsa.com	San Antonio	TX	78209	210-821-5600	821-5624
Demo's 2501 N St Mary's St *Web:* www.demosgreekfood.com	San Antonio	TX	78212	210-732-7777	731-9002
El Mirador 722 S St Mary St *Web:* www.elmiradorsatx.com	San Antonio	TX	78205	210-225-9444	271-3236
Fig Tree 515 Villita St *Web:* www.figtreerestaurant.com	San Antonio	TX	78205	210-224-1976	271-9180
Formosa Garden 1011 NE Loop 410 *Web:* www.formosagarden.com	San Antonio	TX	78209	210-828-9988	826-2566
Golden Wok 8822 Wurzbach Rd *Web:* www.golden-wok.com	San Antonio	TX	78240	210-615-8282	615-8284
Hard Rock Cafe 111 W Crocket St *TF:* 888-519-6683 ■ *Web:* www.hardrock.com	San Antonio	TX	78205	210-224-7625	224-7693
India Oven 1031 Patricia *Web:* www.indiaoven.biz	San Antonio	TX	78213	210-366-1030	
Kirby's Steakhouse 123 N Loop 1604 E *Web:* www.kirbyssteakhouse.com	San Antonio	TX	78232	210-404-2221	404-2225
La Fogata 2427 Vance Jackson Rd *Web:* www.lafogata.com	San Antonio	TX	78213	210-340-1337	349-6467
Little Rhein Steakhouse 231 S Alamo St *Web:* www.littlerheinsteakhouse.com	San Antonio	TX	78205	210-225-2111	271-9180
Melting Pot of San Antonio, The 14855 Blanco Rd Ste 110 *TF:* 800-783-0867 ■ *Web:* www.meltingpot.com	San Antonio	TX	78216	210-479-6358	479-8106
Old San Francisco Steak House 10223 Sahara Dr *Web:* www.theoldsanfrancisco.com	San Antonio	TX	78216	210-342-2321	340-3135
Piatti Ristorante & Bar San Antonio 255 E Basse Rd Ste 500 *Web:* www.piatti.com	San Antonio	TX	78209	210-832-0300	832-0303
Picante Grill 3810 Broadway *Web:* picantegrill.com	San Antonio	TX	78209	210-822-3797	
Rio Rio Cantina 421 E Commerce St *Web:* www.rioriocantina.com	San Antonio	TX	78205	210-226-8462	226-8443
Silo 1133 Austin Hwy *Web:* www.siloelevatedcuisine.com	San Antonio	TX	78209	210-824-8686	805-8452
Texas Land & Cattle Steak House 9911 W IH- 10 *TF:* 855-685-1622 ■ *Web:* www.txlc.com	San Antonio	TX	78230	210-699-8744	699-8292
Tamolly's 5940 Summerhill Rd *Web:* www.tamollys.com	Texarkana	TX	75503	903-792-0732	

Utah

				Phone	Fax
Athenian 252 East 2500 South	Ogden	UT	84401	801-621-4911	395-2456
Bistro 258 258 25th St *Web:* bistro258.net	Ogden	UT	84404	801-394-1595	
Eastern Winds 3740 Washington Blvd *Web:* easternwindsrestaurant.com	Ogden	UT	84403	801-627-2739	627-2739
El Matador 2564 Ogden Ave *Web:* elmatadorogden.com	Ogden	UT	84401	801-393-3151	
Golden Dynasty 3433 Washington Blvd	Ogden	UT	84401	801-621-6789	
Javiers 703 Washington Blvd *Web:* javiersmexicanfood.com	Ogden	UT	84404	801-393-4747	
Jeremiah's 1307 West 1200 South *Web:* jeremiahsutah.com	Ogden	UT	84404	801-394-3273	627-6579
Prairie Schooner Restaurant 445 Pk Blvd *Web:* www.prairieschoonerrestaurant.com	Ogden	UT	84401	801-392-2712	393-1626
Rooster's 253 25th St *Web:* roostersbrewingco.com	Ogden	UT	84401	801-627-6171	
Ruby River Steak House 4286 Riverdale Rd *Web:* www.rubyriver.com	Ogden	UT	84405	801-622-2320	
Timber Mine 1701 Pk Blvd *Web:* www.timbermine.com	Ogden	UT	84401	801-393-2155	
Tona 210 25th St *Web:* www.tonarestaurant.com	Ogden	UT	84401	801-622-8662	
Union Grill 2501 Wall Ave *Web:* www.uniongrillogden.com	Ogden	UT	84401	801-621-2830	621-7946
Windy's Sukiyaki 3809 Riverdale Rd *Web:* www.windyssukiyaki.com	Ogden	UT	84405	801-621-4505	
Brick Oven 111 East 800 North *Web:* www.brickovenrestaurants.com	Provo	UT	84606	801-374-8800	
Demae Japanese Restaurant 82 W Ctr St *Web:* demae-japanese.com	Provo	UT	84601	801-374-0306	373-3308
Happy Sumo at the Riverwoods 4801 N University Ave *Web:* www.happysumosushi.com	Provo	UT	84604	801-225-9100	
OZZ - Event & Fun Ctr 490 N Freedom Blvd *Web:* hugedomains.com/domain_profile.cfm?d=ozzfun&e=com	Provo	UT	84601	801-818-9000	
Ruby River Steakhouse 1454 S University Ave *Web:* www.rubyriver.com	Provo	UT	84601	801-371-0648	
Saigon Cafe 440 West 300 South *Web:* saigoncafeprovo.biz	Provo	UT	84601	801-812-1173	
Sam Hawk 660 N Freedom Blvd	Provo	UT	84601	801-377-7766	
Thai Ruby 744 East 820 North *Web:* thairubyfood.com	Provo	UT	84606	801-375-6840	
Tucanos Brazilian Grill 4801 N University Ave Unit 790 *Web:* www.tucanos.com	Provo	UT	84604	801-224-4774	
Aristo's 224 South 1300 East *Web:* aristosslc.com	Salt Lake City	UT	84102	801-581-0888	
Bambara Restaurant 202 S Main St *Web:* www.bambara-slc.com	Salt Lake City	UT	84101	801-363-5454	363-5888
Benihana of Tokyo 165 SW Temple *Web:* www.benihana.com	Salt Lake City	UT	84101	801-322-2421	575-6415
Blue Iguana 165 SW Temple *Web:* www.blueiguanarestaurant.net	Salt Lake City	UT	84101	801-533-8900	
Bombay House 2731 Parleys Way *Web:* www.bombayhouse.com	Salt Lake City	UT	84109	801-581-0222	
Cafe Rio 3025 East 3300 South *Web:* www.caferio.com	Salt Lake City	UT	84109	801-463-7250	
Cafe Trang 200 South 307 West *Web:* www.cafetrangrestaurant.com	Salt Lake City	UT	84101	801-539-1638	328-1066
Caffe Molise 55 West 100 South *Web:* www.caffemolise.com	Salt Lake City	UT	84101	801-364-8833	
Christopher's Seafood & Steak House 134 W Pierpont Ave *Web:* christophersutah.com	Salt Lake City	UT	84101	801-519-8515	
Citris Grill 2991 East 3300 South *Web:* www.citrisgrill.com	Salt Lake City	UT	84109	801-466-1202	
Desert Edge Brewery 273 Trolley Sq *Web:* www.desertedgebrewery.com	Salt Lake City	UT	84102	801-521-8917	
Em's 271 N Ctr St *Web:* www.emsrestaurant.com	Salt Lake City	UT	84103	801-596-0566	
Fresco Italian Cafe 1513 S 1500 E *Web:* www.frescoitaliancafe.com	Salt Lake City	UT	84105	801-486-1300	487-5379
Hong Kong Tea House 565 W 200 S *Web:* www.hongkongteahouse.com	Salt Lake City	UT	84101	801-531-7010	531-7033
Koyo Restaurant 2275 East 33rd South *Web:* www.koyoslc.com	Salt Lake City	UT	84109	801-466-7111	
Lamb's Grill Cafe 169 S Main St *Web:* www.lambsgrill.com	Salt Lake City	UT	84111	801-364-7166	355-1644
Log Haven 6451 East Milcreek Canyon *Web:* www.log-haven.com	Salt Lake City	UT	84109	801-272-8255	
Market Street Broiler 260 South 1300 East *Web:* marketstreetgrill.com	Salt Lake City	UT	84102	801-583-8808	
Market Street Oyster Bar 54 W Market St *Web:* marketstreetgrill.com	Salt Lake City	UT	84101	801-531-6044	531-0730
Mazza 1515 S 1500 E *Web:* www.mazzacafe.com	Salt Lake City	UT	84105	801-484-9259	484-4277
New Yorker 60 W Market St *Web:* newyorkerslc.com	Salt Lake City	UT	84101	801-363-0166	
Oasis Cafe 151 South 500 East *Web:* www.oasiscafeslc.com	Salt Lake City	UT	84102	801-322-0404	
Paris Bistro 1500 South 1500 East *Web:* www.theparis.net	Salt Lake City	UT	84105	801-486-5585	
Red Iguana 736 W N Temple St *Web:* www.rediguana.com	Salt Lake City	UT	84116	801-322-1489	322-4834
Red Rock Brewing Co 254 South 200 West *Web:* www.redrockbrewing.com	Salt Lake City	UT	84101	801-521-7446	
Rio Grande Cafe 270 S Rio Grande St	Salt Lake City	UT	84101	801-364-3302	
Rodizio Grill 600 South 700 East *Web:* www.rodiziogrill.com	Salt Lake City	UT	84102	801-220-0500	
Rumbi Island Grill 358 South 700 East *Web:* rumbi.com	Salt Lake City	UT	84102	801-530-1000	
Sage's Cafe 234 W 900 S *Web:* www.sagescafe.com	Salt Lake City	UT	84101	801-322-3790	
Sampan 675 East 2100 South *Web:* www.esampan.com	Salt Lake City	UT	84106	801-467-3663	466-4120
Shogun 321 S Main St *Web:* shogunslc.com	Salt Lake City	UT	84111	801-364-7142	
Spencer's for Steaks & Chops 255 SW Temple St *Web:* www.spencersforsteaksandchops.com	Salt Lake City	UT	84101	801-238-4748	
Squatter's Pub Brewery 147 West Broadway *Web:* www.squatters.com	Salt Lake City	UT	84101	801-363-2739	
Thai Siam 1435 S State St *Web:* www.thaisiam.net	Salt Lake City	UT	84115	801-474-3322	
Tuscany 2832 East 6200 South *Web:* www.tuscanyslc.com	Salt Lake City	UT	84121	801-277-9919	
La Caille at Quail Run 9565 Wasatch Blvd *Web:* www.lacaille.com	Sandy	UT	84092	801-942-1751	944-8990
Temari 458 E 40th St *Web:* www.mytemari.com	South Ogden	UT	84403	801-399-9536	

Vermont

				Phone	Fax
Bove's of Vermont 68 Pearl St *Web:* www.boves.com	Burlington	VT	05403	802-864-6651	
Daily Planet 15 Ctr St *Web:* www.dailyplanet15.com	Burlington	VT	05401	802-862-9647	

	City	State	ZIP	Phone	Fax
Halvorson's Upstreet Cafe 16 Church St	Burlington	VT	05401	802-658-0278	
Web: halvorsonsupstreetcafe.com					
India House Restaurant 207 Colchester Ave	Burlington	VT	05401	802-862-7800	
L'Amante 126 College St	Burlington	VT	05401	802-863-5200	
Web: www.lamante.com					
Leunig's Bistro 115 Church St	Burlington	VT	05401	802-863-3759	658-6332
Web: www.leunigsbistro.com					
New World Tortilla 696 Pine St	Burlington	VT	05401	802-865-1058	
Web: www.newworldtortilla.com					
Pauline's 1834 Shelburne Rd	Burlington	VT	05403	802-862-1081	862-6842
Web: www.paulinescafe.com					
Ri Ra 123 Church St	Burlington	VT	05401	802-860-9401	
Web: www.rira.com					
Single Pebble 133 Bank St	Burlington	VT	05401	802-865-5200	
Web: www.asinglepebble.com					
Sweetwaters 120 Church St	Burlington	VT	05401	802-864-9800	864-4913
Web: www.sweetwatersvt.com					
Trattoria Delia 152 St Paul St	Burlington	VT	05401	802-864-5253	
Web: www.trattoriadelia.com					
Chef's Table 118 Main St	Montpelier	VT	05602	802-229-9202	
Web: neci.edu					
China Star Chinese Restaurant 15 Main St	Montpelier	VT	05602	802-223-0808	
House of Tang 114 River St	Montpelier	VT	05602	802-223-6020	223-3388
Web: houseoftang.com					
J Morgan's Steakhouse 100 State St	Montpelier	VT	05602	802-223-5222	
Web: www.capitolplaza.com					
Julio's Restaurant 54 State St	Montpelier	VT	05602	802-229-9348	
Web: www.julioscantina.com					
Main Street Grill & Bar 118 Main St	Montpelier	VT	05602	802-223-3188	223-9285
Web: www.neci.edu					
McGillicuddy's Irish Pub 14 Langdon St	Montpelier	VT	05862	802-223-2721	
Web: mcgillicuddysvt.com					
Sarducci's Three Main St	Montpelier	VT	05602	802-223-0229	
Web: www.sarduccis.com					
Trader Duke's 1117 Williston Rd	South Burlington	VT	05403	802-660-7523	660-7516
TF: 800-445-8667 ■ Web: www.hilton.com					
Peking Duck House 79 W Canal St	Winooski	VT	05404	802-655-7474	
Web: www.pekingduckhousevt.com					

Virginia

	City	State	ZIP	Phone	Fax
219 Restaurant 219 King St	Alexandria	VA	22314	703-549-1141	549-0035
Web: www.219restaurant.com					
A La Lucia 315 Madison St	Alexandria	VA	22314	703-836-5123	548-9463
Web: www.alalucia.com					
Afghan Restaurant 2700 Jefferson Davis Hwy	Alexandria	VA	22301	703-548-0022	548-0673
Web: afghanrestaurantva.com					
Akasaka Japanese Restaurant 514-C S Van Dorn St	Alexandria	VA	22304	703-751-3133	764-0956*
*Fax Area Code: 905 ■ Web: akasakasushi.com					
Atlantis Restaurant 3648 King St	Alexandria	VA	22302	703-671-0250	
Web: alexandriaitalianfood.com					
Bombay Curry Co 3110 Mt Vernon Ave The Calvert Bldg	Alexandria	VA	22305	703-836-6363	
Web: www.bombaycurrycompany.com					
Chart House Restaurant 1 Cameron St	Alexandria	VA	22314	703-684-5080	684-7364
Web: www.chart-house.com					
Evening Star Cafe 2000 Mt Vernon Ave	Alexandria	VA	22301	703-549-5051	549-8520
Web: www.eveningstarcafe.net					
Finn & Porter 5000 Seminary Rd	Alexandria	VA	22311	703-379-2346	845-7662
Web: www.finnandporter.com					
Fish Market 105 King St	Alexandria	VA	22314	703-836-5676	684-9424
Web: www.fishmarketva.com					
Geranio Ristorante 722 King St	Alexandria	VA	22314	703-548-0088	548-0091
Web: www.geranio.net					
Grille at Morrison House, The 116 S Alfred St	Alexandria	VA	22314	703-838-8000	519-7709
Web: www.thegrillealexandria.com					
Hee Been 6231 Little River Tpke	Alexandria	VA	22312	703-941-3737	941-2721
Web: www.heebeen.com					
House of Dynasty 7550 Telegraph Rd	Alexandria	VA	22315	703-922-5210	922-5211
Web: www.houseofdynasty.com					
IL Porto Ristorante 121 King St	Alexandria	VA	22314	703-836-8833	836-8835
Web: www.ilportoristorante.com					
Indigo Landing Restaurant One Marina Dr	Alexandria	VA	22314	703-548-0001	548-2296
Web: indigolanding.com					
La Bergerie 218 N Lee St	Alexandria	VA	22314	703-683-1007	519-6114
Web: www.labergerie.com					
Landini Bros 115 King St	Alexandria	VA	22314	703-836-8404	549-3596
Web: www.landinibrothers.com					
Le Refuge Restaurant 127 N Washington St	Alexandria	VA	22314	703-548-4661	
Web: www.lerefugealexandria.com					
Morrison House 116 S Alfred St	Alexandria	VA	22314	703-838-8000	684-6283
TF: 866-834-6628 ■ Web: www.morrisonhouse.com					
Murphy's Grand Irish Pub 713 King St	Alexandria	VA	22314	703-548-1717	739-4583
Web: www.murphyspub.com					
Restaurant Eve 110 S Pitt St	Alexandria	VA	22314	703-706-0450	706-0968
Web: www.restauranteve.com					
Rocklands 25 S Quaker Ln	Alexandria	VA	22314	703-778-8000	778-8007
Web: www.rocklands.com					
RT's 3804 Mt Vernon Ave	Alexandria	VA	22305	703-684-6010	548-0417
Web: www.rtsrestaurant.net					
Satay Sarinah 512A S Van Dorn St	Alexandria	VA	22304	703-370-4313	370-9672
Web: www.sataysarinah.com					
Savio's 516 S Van Dorn St	Alexandria	VA	22304	703-212-9651	212-9652
Web: www.saviosrestaurant.com					
Shooter McGees 5239 Duke St	Alexandria	VA	22304	703-751-9266	
Web: www.shootermcgees.com					
Southside 815 815 S Washington St	Alexandria	VA	22314	703-836-6222	549-6985
Web: www.southside815.com					

	City	State	ZIP	Phone	Fax
Taqueria el Poblano 2400B Mt Vernon Ave	Alexandria	VA	22301	703-548-8226	
Web: www.taqueriapoblano.com					
Taverna Cretekou 818 King St	Alexandria	VA	22314	703-548-8688	683-2739
Web: www.tavernacretekou.com					
Tempo Restaurant 4231 Duke St	Alexandria	VA	22304	703-370-7900	370-7902
Web: www.temporestaurant.com					
Thai Lemon Grass Restaurant 506 S Van Dorn St	Alexandria	VA	22304	703-751-4627	
Union Street Public House 121 S Union St	Alexandria	VA	22314	703-548-1785	548-0705
Web: www.unionstreetpublichouse.com					
Vermilion 1120 King St	Alexandria	VA	22314	703-684-9669	684-9614
Web: www.vermilionrestaurant.com					
Warehouse Bar & Grill 214 King St	Alexandria	VA	22314	703-683-6868	683-6928
Web: www.warehousebarandgrill.com					
Yamazato 6303 Little River Tpke	Alexandria	VA	22312	703-914-8877	914-8833
Web: www.yamazato.net					
Athena Pallas 556 22nd St S	Arlington	VA	22202	703-521-3870	521-3877
Web: www.athenapallas.com					
Bangkok 54 2919 Columbia Pk	Arlington	VA	22204	703-521-4070	521-4069
Web: www.bangkok54restaurant.com					
Bangkok Bistro 715 N Glebe Rd	Arlington	VA	22203	703-243-9669	243-9668
Web: www.bangkokbistrodc.com					
Cafe Asia 1550 Wilson Blvd	Arlington	VA	22209	703-741-0870	741-7666
Web: www.cafeasia.com					
Caribbean Grill 5183 Lee Hwy	Arlington	VA	22207	703-241-8947	
Carlyle 4000 Campbell Ave	Arlington	VA	22206	703-931-0777	931-9420
Web: www.greatamericanrestaurants.com					
Clarendon Grill 1101 N Highland St	Arlington	VA	22201	703-524-7455	524-9598
Web: www.cgrill.com					
Crystal Thai 4819 First St N	Arlington	VA	22203	703-522-1311	522-1331
Web: www.crystalthai.com					
El Paso Cafe 4235 N Pershing Dr	Arlington	VA	22203	703-243-9811	243-0064
Web: elpasocafeva.com					
El Pollo Rico 932 N Kennmore St	Arlington	VA	22201	703-522-3220	522-3282
Web: elpolloricorestaurant.com					
Freddie's Beach Bar & Restaurant 555 23rd St S	Arlington	VA	22202	703-685-0555	685-0877
Web: freddiesbeachbar.com					
Guajillo 1727 Wilson Blvd	Arlington	VA	22201	703-807-0840	
Web: www.guajillogrill.com					
Hunan Gate 4233 N Fairfax Dr	Arlington	VA	22203	703-243-5678	
Web: hunangate.com					
Johnny Rockets 1100 S Hayes St	Arlington	VA	22202	703-415-3510	415-3510
TF: 888-856-4669 ■ Web: johnnyrockets.com					
La Cote d'Or Cafe 6876 Lee Hwy	Arlington	VA	22213	703-538-3033	573-0409
Web: www.lacotedorcafe.com					
Laylalina Restaurant 5216 Wilson Blvd	Arlington	VA	22205	703-525-1170	
Web: layalinarestaurant.com					
Melting Pot of Arlington, The 1110 N Glebe Rd	Arlington	VA	22201	703-243-4490	243-4547
Web: www.meltingpot.com					
Mexicali Blues 2933 Wilson Blvd	Arlington	VA	22201	703-812-9352	
Web: www.mexicali-blues.com					
Minh's 2500 Wilson Blvd	Arlington	VA	22201	703-525-2828	525-2829
Web: minhdcrestaurant.com					
Portabellos 2109 N Pollard St	Arlington	VA	22207	703-528-1557	
Web: portabellos.net					
Ray's the Steaks 2300 Wilson Blvd	Arlington	VA	22201	703-841-7297	
Web: raysthesteaks.com					
Rhodeside Grill 1836 Wilson Blvd	Arlington	VA	22201	703-243-0145	243-8454
Web: www.rhodesidegrill.com					
Ristorante Murali 1201 S Joyce St	Arlington	VA	22202	703-415-0411	415-0410
Web: www.muraliva.com					
SoBe Seafood Co 3100 Clarendon Blvd	Arlington	VA	22201	703-527-1283	832-8840
Taqueria Poblano 2503 N Harrison St	Arlington	VA	22207	703-237-8250	237-9502
Web: www.taqueriapoblano.com					
THAI 4029 Campbell Ave	Arlington	VA	22206	703-931-3203	
Web: www.thaiinshirlington.com					
Thaiphoon 1301 S Joy St	Arlington	VA	22202	703-413-8200	413-8868
Web: www.thaiphoon.com					
Tutto Bene 501 N Randolph St	Arlington	VA	22203	703-522-1005	527-0863
Village Bistro, The 1723 Wilson Blvd	Arlington	VA	22209	703-522-0284	522-7797
Web: frenchitalianarlingtonva.com/					
Court House Cafe 350 S Battlefield Blvd	Chesapeake	VA	23322	757-482-7077	
Web: gbcourthousecafe.com					
Daikichi Sushi Japanese Bistro 1400 N Battlefield Blvd	Chesapeake	VA	23320	757-549-0200	549-0200
Web: www.welovesushi.net					
El Loro 801 Volvo Pkwy	Chesapeake	VA	23320	757-436-3415	
Web: www.elloromexican.com					
Great Bridge BBQ 800 Battlefield Blvd S Ste 112	Chesapeake	VA	23322	757-546-2270	
Web: greatbridgebbq.com					
Jade Garden Restaurant 1200 Battlefield Blvd N Ste 119	Chesapeake	VA	23320	757-436-1010	
Web: gojadegarden.com					
Kyoto Japanese Steak House & Sushi Bar 1412 Greenbrier Pkwy	Chesapeake	VA	23320	757-420-0950	
Web: kyotochesapeakeva.com					
Nagoya Sushi 109 Gainsborough Sq	Chesapeake	VA	23320	757-549-7977	549-3458
Pirate's Cove 109 Gainsborough Sq	Chesapeake	VA	23320	757-549-7272	
Web: piratescoveva.com					
Rancho Grande 1320 S Military Hwy	Chesapeake	VA	23320	757-366-5128	
Web: ranchogrande12.com					
Smokey Bones BBQ & Grill 1405 Greenbrier Pkwy	Chesapeake	VA	23320	757-361-6843	361-6849
Web: www.smokeybones.com					
Tida Thai Cuisine 1937 S Military Hwy	Chesapeake	VA	23320	757-422-1027	
Web: tidathai.com					
Hana Tokyo Seafood & Steak House 1275 Post Rd	Fairfield	CT	06824	203-256-0800	
Web: www.hanatokyo.com					

Name / Address	City	State	Zip	Phone	Fax
Awful Arthur's Seafood Co 6078 Mechanicsville Tpke *Web:* www.awfularthurs.com	Mechanicsville	VA	23111	804-559-4370	
Kabuto Inc 13158 Midlothian Tpke *Web:* kabutorichmond.com	Midlothian	VA	23113	804-379-7979	
Alfresco 11710 Jefferson Ave *Web:* www.alfrescoitalianrestaurant.com	Newport News	VA	23606	757-873-0644	873-2355
Chung Oak 15320 A & B Warwick Blvd	Newport News	VA	23608	757-874-3505	
Das Waldcafe 12529 Warwick Blvd	Newport News	VA	23606	757-930-1781	
Japan Samurai 12233 Jefferson Ave *Web:* japansamurainn.com	Newport News	VA	23602	757-249-4400	
Port Arthur 11137 Warwick Blvd *Web:* www.portarthurva.com	Newport News	VA	23601	757-599-6474	
RJ's Restaurant & Sports Pub 12743 Jefferson Ave	Newport News	VA	23602	757-874-4246	
Schlesinger's Chop House 1106 William Styron Sq S *Web:* www.schlesingerssteaks.com	Newport News	VA	23606	757-599-4700	599-4707
So Ya Japenese Restaurant 12715 Warwick Blvd Ste J	Newport News	VA	23606	757-930-0156	
456 Fish 456 Granby St *Web:* www.456fish.com	Norfolk	VA	23507	757-625-4444	626-3692
Banque, The 1849 E Little Creek Rd *Web:* thebanque.com	Norfolk	VA	23518	757-480-3600	
Bodega 442 Granby St *Web:* www.bodegaongranby.com	Norfolk	VA	23510	757-622-8527	
Empire Little Bar & Bistro, The 257 Granby St	Norfolk	VA	23510	757-626-3100	626-3124
Fellini's 3910 Colley Ave *Web:* fellinisva.com	Norfolk	VA	23508	757-625-3000	625-0717
Franco's 6200 N Military Hwy	Norfolk	VA	23518	757-853-0177	
Freemason Abbey 209 W Freemason St *Web:* www.freemasonabbey.com	Norfolk	VA	23510	757-622-3966	622-3592
Havana's 255 Granby St	Norfolk	VA	23510	757-627-5800	
Luna Maya 2010 Colley Ave and 21st St *Web:* www.lunamayarestaurant.com	Norfolk	VA	23517	757-622-6986	
Max & Erma's Restaurant 1500 N Military Hwy *Web:* www.maxandermas.com	Norfolk	VA	23502	757-625-7771	
Omar's Carriage House 313 W Bute St *Web:* omarscarriagehouse.com	Norfolk	VA	23510	757-622-4990	622-8122
Rajput Indian Cuisine 742 W 21st St *Web:* www.rajputonline.com	Norfolk	VA	23517	757-625-4634	
Regino's 3816 E Little Creek Rd *Web:* reginosrestaurantofnorfolk.com	Norfolk	VA	23518	757-588-4300	
Sai Gai Japanese Steakhouse 7521 Granby St	Norfolk	VA	23505	757-423-1000	
San Antonio Sams 1501 Colley Ave *Web:* www.sanantoniosams.com	Norfolk	VA	23517	757-623-0233	623-5977
Todd Jurich's Bistro 150 W Main St Ste 100 *Web:* www.toddjurichsbistro.com	Norfolk	VA	23510	757-622-3210	962-7638
Uptown Buffet 1050 N Military Hwy	Norfolk	VA	23502	757-893-9293	
Voila! 509 Botetourt St *Web:* voilacuisine.com	Norfolk	VA	23510	757-640-0343	
Acacia mid-town 2601 W Cary St *Web:* www.acaciarestaurant.com	Richmond	VA	23220	804-562-0138	562-0248
Bella Italia 6407 Iron Bridge Rd *Web:* work-telephone-manners.com/	Richmond	VA	23234	804-743-1116	
Capital Ale House 623 E Main St *Web:* www.capitalalehouse.com	Richmond	VA	23219	804-780-2537	
Helen's 2527 W Main St *Web:* helensrva.com	Richmond	VA	23220	804-358-4370	
India K'Raja 9051 W Broad St *Web:* www.indiakraja.com	Richmond	VA	23294	804-965-6345	
Lemaire 101 W Franklin St *Web:* www.lemairerestaurant.com	Richmond	VA	23220	804-649-4629	
Mamma 'Zu 501 S Pine St	Richmond	VA	23220	804-788-4205	
Melting Pot of Richmond, The 9704 Gayton Rd *Web:* www.meltingpot.com	Richmond	VA	23233	804-741-3120	741-2781
Millie's 2603 E Main St *Web:* www.milliesdiner.com	Richmond	VA	23223	804-643-5512	648-4321
Old Original Bookbinder's 2306 E Cary St *Web:* bookbindersrichmond.com	Richmond	VA	23223	804-643-6900	
Palani Drive 401 Libbie Ave *Web:* www.palanidrive.com	Richmond	VA	23226	804-285-3200	
Sam Miller's Restaurant 1210 E Cary St *Web:* www.sammillers.com	Richmond	VA	23219	804-644-5465	
Sine Irish Pub & Restaurant 1327 E Cary St *Web:* www.sineirishpub.com/cms_richmond	Richmond	VA	23219	804-649-7767	649-0661
Skilligalee 5416 Glenside Dr	Richmond	VA	23228	804-672-6200	755-1312
Sticky Rice 2232 W Main St *Web:* www.ilovestickyrice.com	Richmond	VA	23220	804-358-7870	
Tobacco Company Restaurant 1201 E Cary St *Web:* www.thetobaccocompany.com	Richmond	VA	23219	804-782-9555	788-8913
Zeus Gallery Cafe 201 N Belmont Ave	Richmond	VA	23221	804-359-3219	
419 West 3865 Electric Rd *Web:* 419-west.com	Roanoke	VA	24018	540-776-0419	
Alexander's 105 S Jefferson St *Web:* alexandersva.com	Roanoke	VA	24011	540-982-6983	
Carlos Brazilian International Cuisine 4167 Electric Rd SW *Web:* carlosbrazilian.com	Roanoke	VA	24018	540-776-1117	
Coach & Four Restaurant 5206 Williamson Rd *Web:* www.coachandfour.com	Roanoke	VA	24012	540-362-4220	
El Toreo 3790 Peter's Creek Rd Ext SW *Web:* eltoreoroanoke.com	Roanoke	VA	24018	540-342-7060	
Frankie Rowland's Steakhouse 104 Jefferson St *Web:* frankierowlandssteakhouse.com	Roanoke	VA	24011	540-527-2333	
Kabuki Japanese Steak House 3503 Franklin Rd SW *Web:* kabukiva.com	Roanoke	VA	24014	540-981-0222	
Kobe Japanese Steak House 3214 Electric Rd *Web:* www.kobesteakhouse.com	Roanoke	VA	24018	540-776-0008	
Metro! 14 Campbell Ave SE *Web:* www.metroroanoke.com	Roanoke	VA	24011	540-345-6645	345-6647
Ragazzi's 3843 Electric Rd *Web:* www.ragazzis.com	Roanoke	VA	24018	540-989-9022	
Szechuan 5207 Bernard Dr *Web:* szechuan1.net	Roanoke	VA	24018	540-989-7947	
Woo Lae Oak 8240 Leesburg Pk *Web:* www.woolaeoak.com	Vienna	VA	22182	703-827-7300	827-7302
22nd St Raw Bar & Grill, The 202 22nd St *Web:* rawbarandgrille.com	Virginia Beach	VA	23451	757-491-2222	
Aberdeen Barn 5805 Northampton Blvd *Web:* www.aberdeenbarn.com	Virginia Beach	VA	23455	757-464-1580	
Aldo's Ristorante 1860 Laskin Rd *Web:* aldosvb.com	Virginia Beach	VA	23454	757-491-1111	
Boulevard Pizzeria & Italian Eatery 2935 Virginia Beach Blvd *Web:* boulevard-pizzeria.com	Virginia Beach	VA	23452	757-463-1311	
Captain George's Seafood 1956 Laskin Rd *Web:* www.captaingeorges.com	Virginia Beach	VA	23454	757-428-3494	
Ensenada 2824 Virginia Beach Blvd	Virginia Beach	VA	23452	757-631-1090	
Hot Tuna Bar & Grill 2817 Shore Dr *Web:* hottunavb.com	Virginia Beach	VA	23451	757-481-2888	
Il Giardino 910 Atlantic Ave *Web:* www.ilgiardino.com	Virginia Beach	VA	23451	757-422-6464	422-1175
Kin's Wok 4001 Virginia Beach Blvd Ste 118 *Web:* kinswokvb.com	Virginia Beach	VA	23452	757-340-6898	
Lynnhaven Fish House 2350 Starfish Rd *Web:* www.lynnhavenfishhouse.net	Virginia Beach	VA	23451	757-481-0003	481-3474
Melting Pot of Virginia Beach, The 1564 Laskin Rd *Web:* www.meltingpot.com	Virginia Beach	VA	23451	757-425-3463	
Mi Casita 3600 Bonney Rd *Web:* micasitamexican.com	Virginia Beach	VA	23452	757-463-3819	
Mo Mo Sushi 1385 Fordham Dr	Virginia Beach	VA	23464	757-366-3188	
Nara Sushi 1115 Independence Blvd Ste 104 *Web:* www.narasushi.com	Virginia Beach	VA	23455	757-456-5111	490-0109
North Beach Bar & Grill 3107 Atlantic Ave *Web:* hamptoninnvirginiabeachoceanfront.com	Virginia Beach	VA	23451	757-491-1800	
One Fish - Two Fish 2109 W Great Neck Rd *Web:* www.onefish-twofish.com	Virginia Beach	VA	23451	757-496-4350	
Plaza Azteca 4292 Holland Rd *Web:* plazaazteca.com	Virginia Beach	VA	23452	757-431-8135	
Reginella's 4000 Virginia Beach Blvd *Web:* reginellas.com	Virginia Beach	VA	23452	757-498-9770	
Steinhilbers Thalia 653 Thalia Rd *Web:* www.steinys.com	Virginia Beach	VA	23452	757-340-1156	340-8134
Tautog's 205 23rd St *Web:* www.tautogs.com	Virginia Beach	VA	23451	757-422-0081	
Waterman's Grill 415 Atlantic Ave *Web:* www.watermans.com	Virginia Beach	VA	23451	757-428-3644	
Zia Marie 4497 Lookout Rd	Virginia Beach	VA	23455	757-460-0715	
Blue Talon Bistro 420 Prince George St *Web:* www.bluetalonbistro.com	Williamsburg	VA	23185	757-476-2583	
Captain George's Seafood Restaurant 5363 Richmond Rd *Web:* www.captaingeorges.com	Williamsburg	VA	23188	757-565-2323	
Fat Canary 410 W Duke of Gloucester St *Web:* fatcanarywilliamsburg.com	Williamsburg	VA	23185	757-229-3333	
Jefferson Restaurant 1453 Richmond Rd	Williamsburg	VA	23185	757-229-2296	
La Tolteca 3048 Richmond Rd	Williamsburg	VA	23185	757-253-2939	
Le Yaca 1430 High St *Web:* leyacawilliamsburg.com	Williamsburg	VA	23185	757-220-3616	
Nawab Indian Cuisine 204 Monticello Ave Monticello Shopping Ctr *Web:* www.nawabonline.com	Williamsburg	VA	23185	757-565-3200	
Old Chickahominy House 1211 Jamestown Rd *Web:* oldchickahominy.com	Williamsburg	VA	23185	757-229-4689	
Peking 120 Waller Mill Rd *Web:* peking-va.com	Williamsburg	VA	23185	757-229-2288	
Sal's 1242 Richmond Rd *Web:* www.salsbyvictor.com	Williamsburg	VA	23185	757-220-2641	
Seafare of Williamsburg 1632 Richmond Rd *Web:* superstarrealty.visualshows.com	Williamsburg	VA	23185	757-229-0099	
Second Street Restaurant & Tavern 140 Second St *Web:* www.secondst.com	Williamsburg	VA	23185	757-220-2286	
Trellis Restaurant 403 W Duke of Gloucester St *Web:* www.thetrellis.com	Williamsburg	VA	23185	757-229-8610	
Williamsburg Hospitality House 415 Richmond Rd Williamsburg Hospitality House *Web:* letspartyvirginia.com	Williamsburg	VA	23185	757-229-4020	
Yorkshire Steak & Seafood Restaurant 700 York St *Web:* www.theyorkshirerestaurant.com	Williamsburg	VA	23185	757-229-9790	

Washington

Name / Address	City	State	Zip	Phone	Fax
Longhorn BBQ 635 C St SW *Web:* www.thelonghornbbq.com	Auburn	WA	98001	253-804-9600	804-5493

Restaurant	City	State	ZIP	Phone	Fax
Budd Bay Cafe 525 Columbia St NW *Web:* www.buddbaycafe.com	Olympia	WA	98501	360-357-6963	
Casa Mia 716 Plum St *Web:* www.casamiarestaurants.com	Olympia	WA	98501	360-352-0440	
El Sarape 4043 Martin Way E *Web:* www.elsarape.net	Olympia	WA	98506	360-459-5525	
Emperor's Palace 400 Cooper Pt Rd SW *Web:* www.eprestaurant.com	Olympia	WA	98502	360-352-0777	754-2188
Fishbowl Brew Pub & Cafe 515 Jefferson St SE *Web:* fishtalebrewpub.com	Olympia	WA	98501	360-943-3650	943-6983
Gardner's Seafood & Pasta 111 Thurston Ave NW *Web:* gardnersrestaurant.com	Olympia	WA	98501	360-786-8466	
Koibito 1707 Harrison Ave NW *Web:* koibitosushi.com	Olympia	WA	98502	360-352-4751	
Lemon Grass Restaurant 212 Fourth Ave W	Olympia	WA	98501	360-705-1832	
Mekong 125 Columbia St NW	Olympia	WA	98501	360-352-9620	
Mercato 111 Market St NW *Web:* www.mercatoristorante.com	Olympia	WA	98501	360-528-3663	
Oyster House 320 Fourth Ave W *Web:* www.oysterhouse.com	Olympia	WA	98501	360-753-7000	
Ramblin Jack's 520 Fourth Ave E *Web:* www.ramblinjacks.com	Olympia	WA	98501	360-754-8909	
Saigon Rendez-vous 117 Fifth Ave SW *Web:* saigonrendezvous.com	Olympia	WA	98501	360-352-1989	
Trinacria Ristorante 113 Capitol Way N	Olympia	WA	98501	360-352-8892	
Urban Onion 116 Legion Way SE *Web:* theurbanonion.com	Olympia	WA	98501	360-943-9242	
13 Coins 125 Boren Ave N *Web:* www.13coins.com	Seattle	WA	98109	206-682-2513	
611 Supreme 611 E Pine St *Web:* 611supreme.com	Seattle	WA	98122	206-328-0292	
Agua Verde Cafe 1303 NE Boat St *Web:* www.aguaverde.com	Seattle	WA	98105	206-545-8570	
Al Boccalino One Yesler Way *Web:* seattleslittleitaly.com	Seattle	WA	98104	206-622-7688	622-1798
Andaluca 407 Olive Way *Web:* www.andaluca.com	Seattle	WA	98101	206-382-6999	382-6997
Anthony's Pier 66 2201 Alaskan Way *Web:* www.anthonys.com	Seattle	WA	98121	206-448-6688	728-2500
Assaggio Ristorante 2010 Fourth Ave *Web:* www.assaggioseattle.com	Seattle	WA	98121	206-441-1399	
BluWater Bistro 102 Lakeside Ave *Web:* www.bluwaterbistro.com	Seattle	WA	98122	206-328-2233	447-6977
Brad's Swingside Cafe 4212 Fremont Ave N *Web:* swingsidecafe.com	Seattle	WA	98103	206-633-4057	
Brasserie Margaux 401 Lenora St *Web:* www.margauxseattle.com	Seattle	WA	98121	206-219-2224	
Brooklyn Seafood Steak & Oyster House 1212 Second Ave *Web:* thebrooklyn.com	Seattle	WA	98101	206-224-7000	224-7088
Cactus 4220 E Madison *Web:* www.cactusrestaurants.com	Seattle	WA	98112	206-324-4140	
Cafe Flora 2901 E Madison St *Web:* www.cafeflora.com	Seattle	WA	98112	206-325-9100	
Cafe Lago 2305 24th Ave E *Web:* www.cafelago.com	Seattle	WA	98112	206-329-8005	
Campagne 1600 Post Alley *Web:* cafecampagne.com	Seattle	WA	98101	206-728-2800	443-3804
Canlis Restaurant 2576 Aurora Ave N *Web:* www.canlis.com	Seattle	WA	98109	206-283-3313	283-1766
Chandler's Crabhouse 901 Fairview Ave N *Web:* chandlerscrabhouse.com	Seattle	WA	98109	206-223-2722	223-9380
Chinook's at Salmon Bay 1900 W Nickerson St Ste 103 *Web:* anthonys.com	Seattle	WA	98119	206-283-4665	283-3705
Chiso Restaurant 3520 Fremont Ave N *Web:* www.chisoseattle.com	Seattle	WA	98103	206-632-3430	
Chutneys 605 15th Ave E *Web:* chutneysgrille.com	Seattle	WA	98112	206-726-1000	
Cutters Bayhouse 2001 Western Ave *Web:* www.cuttersbayhouse.com	Seattle	WA	98121	206-448-4884	727-2194
Dahlia Lounge 2001 Fourth Ave *Web:* www.tomdouglas.com	Seattle	WA	98121	206-682-4142	467-0568
Daniel's Broiler 809 Fairview Pl N **Fax Area Code: 206* ■ *Web:* www.schwartzbros.com	Seattle	WA	98109	425-990-6310	748-7765*
El Gaucho-Aqua 2801 Alaskan Way Pier 70 *Web:* elgaucho.com	Seattle	WA	98121	206-956-9171	956-8090
Elliott's Oyster House 1201 Alaskan Way Pier 56 *Web:* www.elliottsoysterhouse.com	Seattle	WA	98101	206-623-4340	224-0154
Etta's Seafood 2020 Western Ave *Web:* www.tomdouglas.com	Seattle	WA	98121	206-443-6000	443-0648
Eva Restaurant 2227 N 56th St *Web:* evarestaurant.com	Seattle	WA	98103	206-633-3538	
Flying Fish 300 Westlake Ave N *Web:* www.flyingfishseattle.com	Seattle	WA	98109	206-728-8595	728-1551
Georgian, The 411 University St *Web:* fairmont.com	Seattle	WA	98101	206-621-7889	
Harvest Vine 2701 E Madison St *Web:* www.harvestvine.com	Seattle	WA	98112	206-320-9771	
Icon Grill 1933 Fifth Ave *Web:* www.icongrill.net	Seattle	WA	98101	206-441-6330	441-7037
Il Bistro 93-A Pike St *Web:* www.ilbistro.net	Seattle	WA	98101	206-682-3049	223-0234
Il Terrazzo Carmine 411 First Ave S *Web:* www.ilterrazzocarmine.com	Seattle	WA	98104	206-467-7797	
India Bistro 2301 NW Market St *Web:* www.seattleindiabistro.com	Seattle	WA	98107	206-783-5080	297-9069
Ivar's Acres of Clams 1001 Alaskan Way Pier 54 *Web:* www.ivars.com	Seattle	WA	98104	206-624-6852	624-4895
JaK's Grill 3701 NE 45th St *Web:* www.jaksgrill.com	Seattle	WA	98105	206-985-8545	
Kabul Afghan Cuisine 2301 N 45th St *Web:* www.kabulrestaurant.com	Seattle	WA	98103	206-545-9000	
Kingfish Cafe 602 19th Ave E *Web:* thekingfishcafe.com	Seattle	WA	98112	206-320-8757	
La Medusa 4857 Rainier Ave S *Web:* www.lamedusarestaurant.com	Seattle	WA	98118	206-723-2192	
La Rustica 4100 Beach Dr SW *Web:* www.larusticarestaurant.com	Seattle	WA	98116	206-932-3020	
La Vita E Bella 2411 Second Ave *Web:* www.lavitaebella.us	Seattle	WA	98121	206-441-5322	
Le Gourmand 425 NW Market St *Web:* www.legourmandrestaurant.com	Seattle	WA	98107	206-784-3463	
Le Pichet 1933 First Ave *Web:* lepichetseattle.com	Seattle	WA	98101	206-256-1499	
Lola 2000 Fourth Ave *Web:* www.tomdouglas.com	Seattle	WA	98121	206-441-1430	441-5224
Maneki 304 Sixth Ave S *Web:* manekirestaurant.com	Seattle	WA	98104	206-622-2631	
Matt's in the Market 94 Pike St Ste 32 *Web:* www.mattsinthemarket.com	Seattle	WA	98101	206-467-7909	
McCormick's Fish House & Bar 722 Fourth Ave *Web:* www.mccormickandschmicks.com	Seattle	WA	98104	206-682-3900	667-0081
Metropolitan Grill 820 Second Ave *Web:* www.themetropolitangrill.com	Seattle	WA	98104	206-624-3287	389-0042
Nell's 6804 E Green Lk Way N *Web:* www.nellsrestaurant.com	Seattle	WA	98115	206-524-4044	
Ototo Sushi Seven Boston St *Web:* www.ototosushi.com	Seattle	WA	98109	206-691-3838	691-3839
Pabla Indian Cuisine 1516 Second Ave *Web:* pablaindiacuisine.com	Seattle	WA	98101	206-623-2868	
Palace Kitchen 2030 Fifth Ave *Web:* www.tomdouglas.com	Seattle	WA	98121	206-448-2001	
Palisade 2601 W Marina Pl *Web:* www.palisaderestaurant.com	Seattle	WA	98199	206-285-1000	285-7087
Palomino 1420 Fifth Ave *Web:* www.palomino.com	Seattle	WA	98101	206-623-1300	467-1386
Paseo 4225 Fremont Ave N *Web:* paseoseattle.com	Seattle	WA	98103	206-545-7440	
Phoenecia at Alki 2716 Alki Ave SW *Web:* phoeneciawestseattle.com	Seattle	WA	98116	206-935-6550	
Pink Door, The 1919 Post Alley *Web:* www.thepinkdoor.net	Seattle	WA	98101	206-443-3241	443-3341
Place Pigalle 81 Pike St *Web:* www.placepigalle-seattle.com	Seattle	WA	98101	206-624-1756	
Ponti Seafood Grill 3014 Third Ave N *Web:* www.pontiseafoodgrill.com	Seattle	WA	98109	206-284-3000	284-4768
Queen City Grill 2201 First Ave *Web:* www.queencitygrill.com	Seattle	WA	98121	206-443-0975	973-5345
Ray's Boathouse 6049 Seaview Ave NW *Web:* www.rays.com	Seattle	WA	98107	206-789-3770	781-1960
Restaurant Zoe 1318 E Union St *Web:* www.restaurantzoe.com	Seattle	WA	98122	206-256-2060	
Rock Salt Steak House 1232 Westlake Ave N *Web:* www.rocksaltlakeunion.com	Seattle	WA	98109	206-284-1047	298-1379
Rover's 2808 E Madison St *Web:* www.thechefinthehat.com	Seattle	WA	98112	206-325-7442	
Salty's on Alki Beach 1936 Harbor Ave SW *Web:* www.saltys.com	Seattle	WA	98126	206-937-1600	937-1430
Serafina 2043 Eastlake Ave E *Web:* www.serafinaseattle.com	Seattle	WA	98102	206-323-0807	325-2766
Shiro's Sushi Restaurant 2401 Second Ave *Web:* www.shiros.com	Seattle	WA	98121	206-443-9844	443-9974
SkyCity Restaurant 400 Broad St *Web:* www.spaceneedle.com	Seattle	WA	98109	206-905-2100	
Sorrento Hotel 900 Madison St *Web:* www.hotelsorrento.com	Seattle	WA	98104	206-622-6400	343-6159
Sunfish 2800 Alki Ave SW	Seattle	WA	98116	206-938-4112	
Szmania's 3321 W McGraw St *Web:* www.szmanias.com	Seattle	WA	98199	206-284-7305	
Tango 1100 Pike St *Web:* tangorestaurant.com	Seattle	WA	98101	206-583-0382	
Ten Mercer 10 Mercer St *Web:* www.tenmercer.com	Seattle	WA	98109	206-691-3723	
Thai Heaven 352 Roy St *Web:* thaiheavenseattle.com	Seattle	WA	98109	206-285-1596	
Tilth Restaurant 1411 N 45th St *Web:* mariahinesrestaurants.com	Seattle	WA	98103	206-633-0801	633-0801
Tulio Ristorante 1100 Fifth Ave *Web:* www.tulio.com	Seattle	WA	98101	206-624-5500	
Volterra 5411 Ballard Ave NW *Web:* www.volterrarestaurant.com	Seattle	WA	98107	206-789-5100	
Wild Ginger Asian Restaurant 1401 Third Ave *Web:* www.wildginger.net	Seattle	WA	98101	206-623-4450	623-8265
Azar's 2501 N Monroe St *Web:* azarsrestaurant.com	Spokane	WA	99205	509-326-7171	
Cathay Inn 3714 N Div St *Web:* www.cathayinn.com	Spokane	WA	99207	509-326-2226	323-4810
China Dragon 27 E Queen Ave *Web:* chinadragonspokane.com	Spokane	WA	99207	509-483-5209	
Clinkerdagger 621 W Mallon Ave *Web:* www.clinkerdagger.com	Spokane	WA	99201	509-328-5965	
Downriver Grill 3315 W NW Blvd *Web:* www.downrivergrillspokane.com	Spokane	WA	99205	509-323-1600	326-3642
Elk Public House 1931 W Pacific Ave *Web:* wedonthaveone.com	Spokane	WA	99204	509-363-1973	
Linnie Thai Cuisine 1301 W Third Ave	Spokane	WA	99201	509-835-5800	
Luna 5620 S Perry St *Web:* www.lunaspokane.com	Spokane	WA	99223	509-448-2383	448-9765
Mamma Mia's 420 W Francis Ave *Web:* mammamiaspokane.com	Spokane	WA	99205	509-467-7786	467-7761

	City	State	ZIP	Phone	Fax
Ming Wah 1618 W Third Ave	Spokane	WA	99201	509-455-9474	
Mizuna 214 N Howard St	Spokane	WA	99201	509-747-2004	
Web: www.mizuna.com					
Mustard Seed 4750 N Div	Spokane	WA	99207	509-483-1500	
Web: www.mustardseedweb.com					
O'Doherty's Irish Grill 525 W Spokane Falls Blvd	Spokane	WA	99201	509-747-0322	
Web: odohertyspub.com					
Rancho Chico 2023 W NW Blvd	Spokane	WA	99205	509-327-2723	
Web: ranchochico.biz					
Spencer's 322 N Spokane Falls Ct	Spokane	WA	99220	509-744-2372	744-2396
Web: www.spencersforsteaksandchops.com					
Tomato Street North 6220 N Div	Spokane	WA	99208	509-484-4500	
Web: www.tomatostreet.com					
Twigs Bistro & Bar 808 W Main Ave Third Fl Riverpark Sq	Spokane	WA	99201	509-232-3376	755-0779
Web: www.twigsbistro.com					
Anthony's at Point Defiance 5910 N Waterfront Dr	Tacoma	WA	98407	253-752-9700	752-1929
Web: www.anthonys.com					
El Gaucho 2119 Pacific Ave	Tacoma	WA	98402	253-272-1510	
Web: www.elgaucho.com					
Europa Bistro 2515 N Proctor St	Tacoma	WA	98406	253-761-5660	
Web: www.europabistro.net					
Galanga 1129 Broadway	Tacoma	WA	98402	253-272-3393	
Web: www.galangathai.com					
Harmon Brewing Co 1938 Pacific Ave	Tacoma	WA	98402	253-383-2739	
Web: harmonbrewingco.com					
Indochine Asian Dining Lounge 1924 Pacific Ave	Tacoma	WA	98402	253-272-8200	
Web: www.indochinedowntown.com					
Johnny's Dock 1900 E D St	Tacoma	WA	98421	253-627-3186	
Web: www.johnnysdock.com					
Kabuki Japanese Restaurant 2919 S 38th St Ste B	Tacoma	WA	98409	253-474-1650	
Web: japanesefoodtacoma.com					
Le-Le 1012 S Martin Luther King Jr Way	Tacoma	WA	98405	253-572-9491	
Web: lelerestaurant.com					
Lobster Shop South 4015 Ruston Way	Tacoma	WA	98402	253-759-2165	752-9640
Web: wp.lobstershop.com					
Marzano 516 Garfield St S	Tacoma	WA	98444	253-537-4191	
Web: www.dinemarzano.com					
Moctezuma's 4102 S 56th St	Tacoma	WA	98409	253-474-5593	
Web: www.moctezumas.com					
North China Garden 2303 Sixth Ave	Tacoma	WA	98403	253-572-5106	
Web: northchinagardentacoma.com					
Sakura Japanese Steakhouse 3630 S Cedar St	Tacoma	WA	98409	253-475-1300	
Southern Kitchen 1716 Sixth Ave	Tacoma	WA	98405	253-627-4282	
Web: southernkitchen-tacoma.com					
Stanley & Seafort's 115 E 34th St	Tacoma	WA	98404	253-473-7300	
Web: www.stanleyandseaforts.com					
Sushi Tama 3919 Sixth Ave	Tacoma	WA	98406	253-761-1014	
Tacos Guaymas 2630 S 38th St	Tacoma	WA	98409	253-471-2224	
Web: www.tacosguaymas.com					
Falls Terrace 106 Deschutes Way SW	Tumwater	WA	98501	360-943-7830	
Web: www.fallsterrace.com					
Beaches Restaurant & Bar 1919 SE Columbia River Dr	Vancouver	WA	98661	360-699-1592	699-0724
Web: www.beachesrestaurantandbar.com					
Cactus Ya Ya 15704 SE Mill Plain Blvd	Vancouver	WA	98684	360-944-9292	
Canton Chinese Buffet 1118 NE 78th St	Vancouver	WA	98665	360-576-8699	
Carol's Corner Cafe 7800 NE St Johns Blvd	Vancouver	WA	98665	360-573-6357	
Dragon King 1401 NE 78th St	Vancouver	WA	98665	360-574-6684	
Web: dragonking78.com					
Hudson's Bar & Grill 7805 NW Greenwood Dr	Vancouver	WA	98662	360-816-6100	
Web: www.hudsonsbarandgrill.com					
Jerusalem Restaurant & Cafe 106 E Evergreen Blvd	Vancouver	WA	98660	360-906-0306	
Web: thejerusalemcafe.com					
Little Italy's Trattoria 901 Washington St	Vancouver	WA	98660	360-737-2363	
Web: www.littleitalystrattoria.com					
McMenamins on the Columbia 1801 S Access Rd	Vancouver	WA	98661	360-699-1521	
Web: mcmenamins.com					
Namaste Indian Cuisine 6300 NE 117th Ave	Vancouver	WA	98662	360-891-5857	891-5906
Web: www.namasteindiancuisine.com					
Patrick's Hawaiian Cafe 316 SE 123rd Ave	Vancouver	WA	98683	360-885-0881	
Web: www.hawaiiancafe.com					
Thai Little Home 3214 E Fourth Plain Blvd	Vancouver	WA	98661	360-693-4061	
Web: thailittletogo.com					
Tiger's Garden 312 W Eigth St	Vancouver	WA	98660	360-693-9585	
Web: tigersgardenrestaurant.com					
Who-Song & Larry's 111 SE Columbia Way	Vancouver	WA	98661	360-695-1198	
Web: www.eltorito.com					
Herbfarm, The 14590 NE 145th St	Woodinville	WA	98072	425-485-5300	424-2925
Web: www.theherbfarm.com					

West Virginia

	City	State	ZIP	Phone	Fax
Fifth Quarter 201 Clendenin St	Charleston	WV	25301	304-345-3933	
Web: fifthquarterofcharleston.com					
Joe Fazio's 1008 Bullitt St	Charleston	WV	25301	304-344-3071	
Web: fazios.net					
Laury's 350 MacCorkle Ave SE	Charleston	WV	25314	304-343-0055	343-0078
Web: www.laurysrestaurant.com					
Leonoro's Spaghetti House 1507 Washington St E	Charleston	WV	25311	304-343-1851	
Web: leonorosspaghettihouse.com					
Rio Grande 160 Ct St Ste 7	Charleston	WV	25301	304-344-8616	
Sitar of India 702 Lee St E	Charleston	WV	25311	304-346-3745	720-6260
Web: sitarofindia.org					
Tidewater Grill 1060 Charleston Town Ctr	Charleston	WV	25389	304-345-2620	345-5624
TF: 888-456-3463 ■ *Web:* mainstreetventuresinc.com					
Whitewater Grille 200 Lee St E	Charleston	WV	25301	304-353-3636	353-3722
TF: 800-845-5279					
Cafe Bacchus 76 High St	Morgantown	WV	26505	304-296-9234	
Web: cafebacchus.net					
Casa D'Amici 485 High St	Morgantown	WV	26507	304-292-4400	
Web: www.casadamici.com					
Glasshouse Grille 709 Beechurst Ave	Morgantown	WV	26505	304-296-8460	
Web: www.theglasshousegrille.com					
Great Chinese Buffet 5000 Greenbag Rd	Morgantown	WV	26505	304-296-4050	
Maxwell's One Wall St	Morgantown	WV	26505	304-292-0982	
Oliverio's Ristorante on the Wharf 52 Clay St	Morgantown	WV	26505	304-296-2565	296-2564
Web: www.oliverios.sites.morgantowns.com					
Peking House 1125 Van Voorhis Rd	Morgantown	WV	26505	304-598-3333	
Web: pekinghousewv.com					
Puglioni's 1137 Van Voorhis Rd	Morgantown	WV	26505	304-599-7521	
Web: pugspasta.com					
Voyagers Restaurant 110 Hartfield Rd	Morgantown	WV	26505	304-777-4120	
Web: www.alibabaexpress.com					
Abbeys 145 Zane St	Wheeling	WV	26003	304-233-0729	
Bella Via One Burkham Ct	Wheeling	WV	26003	304-242-8181	242-8182
Web: bellavialic.com					
Coleman's Fish Market 2226 Centre Market	Wheeling	WV	26003	304-232-8510	
Figaretti's 1035 Mt de Chantel Rd	Wheeling	WV	26003	304-243-5625	
Web: figarettisrestaurant.com					
Generations Restaurant & Pub 338 National Rd	Wheeling	WV	26003	304-232-7917	233-0385
Web: www.generationswhg.com					
Golden Chopsticks 329 N York St	Wheeling	WV	26003	304-232-2888	
Panda Chinese Kitchen 1133 Market St	Wheeling	WV	26003	304-232-7572	
River City Ale Works 1400 Main St	Wheeling	WV	26003	304-233-4555	
Web: rivercitybanquets.com					

Wisconsin

	City	State	ZIP	Phone	Fax
Brett Favre's Steakhouse 1004 Brett Favre Pass	Green Bay	WI	54304	920-499-6874	405-6896
Web: foodspot.com/clients					
China Palace 213 N Washington St	Green Bay	WI	54301	920-433-0688	
Web: chinapalacegreenbay.com					
Grazies Italian Grill 2851 S Oneida St	Green Bay	WI	54304	920-499-6365	499-7983
Web: www.graziesitaliangrill.com					
Hinterland Brewery & Restaurant 313 Dousman St	Green Bay	WI	54303	920-438-8050	438-8053
Web: www.hinterlandbeer.com					
Kavarna 143 N Broadway	Green Bay	WI	54303	920-430-3200	
Web: www.kavarna.com					
Krolls West 1990 S Ridge Rd	Green Bay	WI	54304	920-497-1111	497-0237
Web: www.krollswest.com					
Legends Brewhouse & Eatery 2840 Shawano Ave	Green Bay	WI	54313	920-662-1111	
Web: legendseatery.com					
Little Tokyo 121B N Broadway	Green Bay	WI	54303	920-433-9323	433-9523
Web: thegreenbaysushi.com					
Los Banditos 1258 Main St	Green Bay	WI	54302	920-432-9462	
Web: foodspot.com/clients/wi/greenbay/losbanditos/default.aspx?accid=13619					
Luigi's Italian Bistro 2733 Mantiwoc Rd	Green Bay	WI	54311	920-468-4900	
Web: luigisitalianbistro.com					
Mackinaws Grill & Spirits 2925 Voyager Dr	Green Bay	WI	54311	920-406-8000	406-8840
Web: www.mackinaws.com					
Rock Garden 1951 Bond St	Green Bay	WI	54303	920-497-4701	499-5242
Web: comfortsuitesgb.com					
Titletown Brewing Co 200 Dousman St	Green Bay	WI	54303	920-437-2337	437-2739
Web: www.titletownbrewing.com					
Wellington, The 1060 Hansen Rd	Green Bay	WI	54304	920-499-2000	
Web: wellingtonsteakhouse.com					
Admiralty Room 666 Wisconsin Ave	Madison	WI	53703	608-256-9071	
TF: 800-922-5512 ■ *Web:* isthmus.com/					
Avenue Bar, The 1128 E Washington Ave	Madison	WI	53703	608-257-6877	
Web: avenuebarmadison.com					
Babe's Grill & Bar 5614 Schroeder Rd	Madison	WI	53711	608-274-7300	274-3201
Web: www.babesmadison.com					
Bandung Indonesian Restaurant 600 Williamson St	Madison	WI	53703	608-255-6910	
Web: www.bandungrestaurant.com					
Blue Moon Bar & Grill 2535 University Ave	Madison	WI	53705	608-233-0441	
Web: www.bluemoonbar.com					
Capitol Chophouse Nine E Wilson St	Madison	WI	53703	608-255-0165	
Web: chophouse411.com/chophouse_location_cch.asp					
Eldorado Grill 744 Williamson St	Madison	WI	53703	608-280-9378	
Web: eldoradogrillmadison.com					
Eno Vino Wine Bar & Bistro 601 Junction Rd	Madison	WI	53717	608-664-9565	664-9563
Web: www.eno-vino.com					
Essen Haus 514 E Wilson St	Madison	WI	53703	608-255-4674	258-8632
TF: 800-448-0158 ■ *Web:* www.essen-haus.com					
Food Fight inc 117 MLK Jr Blvd	Madison	WI	53703	608-467-3130	
Web: www.foodfightinc.com					
Husnu's 547 State St	Madison	WI	53703	608-256-0900	
Web: www.husnus.com					
Imperial Garden 4214 E Washington Ave	Madison	WI	53704	608-249-0466	
Web: imperialgardenmadison.com					
Johnny Delmonico's 130 S Pinckney St	Madison	WI	53703	608-257-8325	257-8324
Web: www.foodfightinc.com					
Jolly Bob's 1210 Williamson St	Madison	WI	53703	608-251-3902	
Web: jollybobs.com					
L'Etoile One S Pinckney St	Madison	WI	53703	608-251-0500	251-7577
Web: www.letoile-restaurant.com					
La Hacienda 515 S Pk St	Madison	WI	53715	608-255-8227	

Restaurant	City	State	ZIP	Phone	Fax
Lao Laan-Xang 1146 Williamson St *Web:* llx-restaurant.com	Madison	WI	53703	608-280-0104	
Laredo's 694 S Whitney Way *Web:* laredosrestaurante.com	Madison	WI	53711	608-278-0585	
Lombardino's 2500 University Ave *Web:* www.lombardinos.com	Madison	WI	53705	608-238-1922	218-9810
Mariner's Inn, The 5339 Lighthouse Bay Dr *Web:* marinersmadison.com	Madison	WI	53704	608-246-3120	
Nau-Ti-Gal 5360 Westport Rd *Web:* nautigal.com	Madison	WI	53704	608-246-3130	
Otto's Restaurant & Bar 6405 Mineral Pt Rd *Web:* www.ottosrestaurant.com	Madison	WI	53705	608-274-4044	274-1358
Pedro's Mexican Restaurante 3555 E Washington Ave *Web:* www.pedrosmexicanrestaurant.com	Madison	WI	53704	608-241-8110	241-8248
Porta Bella 425 N Frances St *Web:* www.portabellarestaurant.biz	Madison	WI	53703	608-256-3186	256-1210
Sa Bai Thong 2840 University Ave. *Web:* www.sabaithong.com	Madison	WI	53705	608-238-3100	
Smoky's Club 3005 University Ave *Web:* www.smokysclub.com	Madison	WI	53705	608-233-2120	
State Street Brats 603 State St *Web:* www.statestreetbrats.com	Madison	WI	53703	608-255-5544	
Taj Indian Restaurant 1256 S Pk St *Web:* www.tajmadison.com	Madison	WI	53715	608-268-0772	268-0774
Tornado Club Steak House 116 S Hamilton St *Web:* tornadosteakhouse.com	Madison	WI	53703	608-256-3570	
Wasabi Japanese Restaurant 449 State St. *Web:* wasabi-madison.com	Madison	WI	53703	608-255-5020	
Captain Bill's Seafood Co 2701 Century Harbor Rd *Web:* www.capbills.com	Middleton	WI	53562	608-831-7327	831-0634
Alioto's 3041 N Mayfair Rd *Web:* www.foodspot.com	Milwaukee	WI	53222	414-476-6900	476-6902
Apollo Cafe 1310 E Brady St *Web:* apollocafe.com	Milwaukee	WI	53202	414-272-2233	272-2344
Bacchus Restaurant 925 E Wells St *Web:* www.bacchusmke.com	Milwaukee	WI	53202	414-765-1166	765-1161
Beans & Barley 1901 E N Ave *Web:* www.beansandbarley.com	Milwaukee	WI	53202	414-278-7878	278-6013
Botanas 816 S Fifth St *Web:* www.botanasrestaurant.com	Milwaukee	WI	53204	414-672-3755	672-2771
Caterina's Ristorante 9104 W Oklahoma Ave *Web:* www.caterinasristorante.com	Milwaukee	WI	53227	414-541-4200	541-4221
Cempazuchi 1205 E Brady St *Web:* www.cempazuchi.com	Milwaukee	WI	53202	414-291-5233	291-5254
Coast 931 E Wisconsin Ave *Web:* www.coastrestaurant.com	Milwaukee	WI	53202	414-727-5555	727-0777
Coquette Cafe 316 N Milwaukee St *Web:* www.coquettecafe.com	Milwaukee	WI	53202	414-291-2655	
County Clare 1234 N Astor St *Web:* www.countyclare-inn.com	Milwaukee	WI	53202	414-272-5273	290-6300
Crawdaddy's 6414 W Greenfield Ave *TF:* 800-727-9477 ■ *Web:* foodspot.com/search/destination.aspx?fs=19985&st=1	Milwaukee	WI	53214	414-778-2228	
Eddie Martini's 8612 W Watertown Plank Rd *Web:* www.foodspot.com	Milwaukee	WI	53226	414-771-6680	771-5034
Elsa's on the Park 833 N Jefferson St *Web:* www.elsas.com	Milwaukee	WI	53202	414-765-0615	
Emperor of China Restaurant 1010 E Brady St *Web:* www.emperorofchinarestaurant.com	Milwaukee	WI	53202	414-271-8889	
Filippo's 6915 W Lincoln Ave	Milwaukee	WI	53219	414-321-4040	
Historic Turner Restaurant 1034 N Fourth St *Web:* www.foodspot.com	Milwaukee	WI	53203	414-276-4844	276-0442
Izumi's 2150 N Prospect Ave *Web:* www.izumis.com	Milwaukee	WI	53202	414-271-5258	
Jackson Grill 3736 W Mitchell St *Web:* www.jacksongrill.com	Milwaukee	WI	53215	414-384-7384	
Karl Ratzsch's Old World Restaurant 320 E Mason St *Web:* www.karlratzsch.com	Milwaukee	WI	53202	414-276-2720	276-3534
Kegels German Inn 5901 W National Ave *Web:* kegelsinn.com	Milwaukee	WI	53214	414-257-9999	774-4517
King & I, The 830 N Old World Third St *Web:* www.kingandirestaurant.com	Milwaukee	WI	53203	414-276-4181	276-4387
La Fuente 625 S Fifth St *Web:* www.ilovelafuente.com	Milwaukee	WI	53204	414-271-8595	271-8594
Mader's German Restaurant 1041 N Old World Third St *Web:* www.madersrestaurant.com	Milwaukee	WI	53203	414-271-3377	271-7914
Maharaja 1550 N Farwell Ave	Milwaukee	WI	53202	414-276-2250	
Milwaukee Chop House 633 N Fifth St *Web:* chophouse411.com/chophouse_location_mch.asp	Milwaukee	WI	53203	414-226-2467	
Mimma's Cafe 1307 E Brady St *Web:* www.mimmas.com	Milwaukee	WI	53202	414-271-7337	272-4543
Old Town 522 W Lincoln Ave	Milwaukee	WI	53207	414-672-0206	
Osteria del Mondo 1028 E Juneau Ave *Web:* www.getbianchini.com	Milwaukee	WI	53202	414-291-3770	291-0840
Packing House 900 E Layton Ave. *TF:* 800-727-9477 ■ *Web:* www.foodspot.com/clients/wi/milwaukee	Milwaukee	WI	53207	414-483-5054	483-3481
Palms 221 N Broadway	Milwaukee	WI	53202	414-298-3000	
River Lane Inn 4313 W River Ln *Web:* theriverlaneinn.com	Milwaukee	WI	53223	414-354-1995	
Safe House 779 N Front St *Web:* safe-house.com	Milwaukee	WI	53202	414-271-2007	271-2676
Sanford Restaurant 1547 N Jackson St *Web:* www.sanfordrestaurant.com	Milwaukee	WI	53202	414-276-9608	278-8509
Saraphino's 3074 E Layton Ave St Francis	Milwaukee	WI	53235	414-744-0303	
Saz's 5539 W State St *Web:* www.sazs.com	Milwaukee	WI	53208	414-453-2410	256-8778
Shahrazad 2847 N Oakland Ave *Web:* www.shahrazadrestaurant.com	Milwaukee	WI	53211	414-964-5475	964-5471
Singha Thai 2237 S 108th St *Web:* www.singhathaimilwaukee.com	Milwaukee	WI	53227	414-541-1234	
Speed Queen BBQ 1130 W Walnut St *Web:* www.foodspot.com	Milwaukee	WI	53205	414-265-2900	265-7001
Swig 217 N Broad Way St *Web:* www.swigmilwaukee.com	Milwaukee	WI	53202	414-431-7944	
Tess 2499 N Bartlett Ave *Web:* tess2499.com	Milwaukee	WI	53211	414-964-8377	964-7790
Third Ward Caffe 225 E St Paul Ave *Web:* foodspot.com/clients/wi/milwaukee/thirdwardcaffe/	Milwaukee	WI	53202	414-224-0895	
Three Bros 2414 S St Clair St **Fax Area Code:* 301	Milwaukee	WI	53207	414-481-7530	595-8888*
Trocadero 1758 N Water St. *Web:* www.trocaderogastrobar.com	Milwaukee	WI	53202	414-272-0205	
Water Street Brewery 1101 N Water St *Web:* www.waterstreetbrewery.com	Milwaukee	WI	53202	414-272-1195	272-0406
Hammond Steakhouse 1402 N Fifth St *Web:* hammondliquor.com	Superior	WI	54880	715-392-3269	392-8374
Lan-Chi's Restaurant 1320 Belknap St	Superior	WI	54880	715-394-4496	395-2431
IL MITO Trattoria e Enoteca 6913 W N Ave *Web:* www.ilmito.com	Wauwatosa	WI	53213	414-443-1414	

Wyoming

Restaurant	City	State	ZIP	Phone	Fax
Dorn's Fireside 1745 Cy Ave *Web:* dornsfireside.com	Casper	WY	82604	307-235-6831	235-6304
Goose Egg Inn 10580 Goose Egg Rd	Casper	WY	82604	307-473-8838	
JS Chinese 116 W Second St	Casper	WY	82601	307-577-0618	
La Costa 1600 E Second St *Web:* webs.com	Casper	WY	82601	307-235-6599	
Poor Boys Steakhouse 739 N Ctr St *Web:* poorboyssteakhouse.com	Casper	WY	82601	307-237-8325	
Sanford's Grub & Pub 241 Ctr St *Web:* thegrubandpub.com	Casper	WY	82601	307-234-4555	
Silver Fox Restaurant & Lounge 3422 S Energy Ln *Web:* www.silverfoxcasper.com	Casper	WY	82604	307-235-3000	
Avanti 4620 Grandview Ave *Web:* avanticheyenne.com	Cheyenne	WY	82009	307-634-3432	
Casa de Trujillo 122 W Sixth St	Cheyenne	WY	82007	307-635-1227	
Good Friends 507 E Lincolnway	Cheyenne	WY	82001	307-778-7088	
Guadalajara 1745 Dell Range Blvd	Cheyenne	WY	82009	307-432-6803	
Korean House 3219 Snyder Ave	Cheyenne	WY	82001	307-638-7938	
Little Bear Inn 1700 Little Bear Rd *Web:* littlebearinn.com	Cheyenne	WY	82009	307-634-3684	
Renzios Greek Food 1400 Dell Range Blvd *Web:* renziosgreekfood.com	Cheyenne	WY	82007	307-637-5411	
T-Joe's Steakhouse & Saloon 12700 I-80 Service Rd *Web:* www.tjoessteakhouse.com	Cheyenne	WY	82009	307-634-8750	
Twin Dragons 1809 Carey Ave	Cheyenne	WY	82001	307-637-6622	
Bar-T-5 Covered Wagon Cook Out & Wild West Show 812 Cache Creek Dr *TF:* 800-772-5386 ■ *Web:* www.bart5.com	Jackson	WY	83001	307-733-5386	739-9183
Blue Lion Restaurant 160 N Millward St *Web:* www.bluelionrestaurant.com	Jackson	WY	83001	307-733-3912	733-3915
BonAppeThai 245 W Pearl St *Web:* bonappethai.com	Jackson	WY	83001	307-734-0245	
Bubba's 100 Flat Creek Dr *Web:* www.bubbasjh.com	Jackson	WY	83001	307-733-2288	
Bunnery Bakery & Restaurant, The 130 N Cache Dr *Web:* bunnery.com/restaurant2.php?	Jackson	WY	83001	307-733-5474	
Calico Restaurant & Bar Teton Village Rd *Web:* www.calicorestaurant.com	Jackson	WY	83014	307-733-2460	
Chinatown 850 W Broadway	Jackson	WY	83001	307-733-8856	
Gun Barrel Steak & Game House 862 W Broadway *Web:* www.gunbarrel.com	Jackson	WY	83002	307-733-3287	733-6090
Nikai Sushi 225 N Cache St PO Box 14250 *Web:* www.nikaisushi.com	Jackson	WY	83001	307-734-6490	734-6488
Ocean City 340 W Broadway *Web:* oceancitychinabistro.com	Jackson	WY	83001	307-734-9768	734-0454
Snake River Brewing Co 265 S Millward St *Web:* www.snakeriverbrewing.com	Jackson	WY	83001	307-739-2337	739-2296
Snake River Grill 84 E Broadway *Web:* www.snakerivergrill.com	Jackson	WY	83001	307-733-0557	733-5767
Sweetwater Restaurant 85 King St PO Box 3271 *Web:* sweetwaterjackson.com	Jackson	WY	83001	307-733-3553	
Thai Me Up 75 E Pearl St *Web:* www.thaijh.com	Jackson	WY	83001	307-733-0005	
Mangy Moose PO Box 590 *Web:* mangymoose.com	Teton Village	WY	83025	307-733-4913	

675 RETIREMENT COMMUNITIES

SEE ALSO Long-Term Care Facilities p. 2676

Listed here are senior communities where the majority of residents live independently but where nursing care and/or other personal care is available on-site. The listings in this category are organized alphabetically by state names.

Community	City	State	ZIP	Phone	Fax
Ability Center of Greater Toledo Inc 5605 Monroe St *Web:* www.abilitycenter.org	Sylvania	OH	43560	419-885-5733	
Arbutus Park Retirement Community 207 Ottawa St *Web:* arbutusparkmanor.com	Johnstown	PA	15904	814-266-8621	

Name / Address	City	State	Zip	Phone	Fax
Beauvais Manor On The Park 3625 Magnolia Ave	Saint Louis	MO	63110	314-771-2990	
Web: www.beauvaismanor.com					
Birchwood Plaza 1426 W Birchwood	Chicago	IL	60626	773-274-4405	
Web: www.birchwoodplaza.com					
Bishop Spencer Place Redevelopment Corp 4301 Madison Ave	Kansas City	MO	64111	816-931-4277	
Web: www.bishopspencerplace.org					
Corn Heritage Village 106 W Adams St Apt 1	Corn	OK	73024	580-343-2295	
Web: cornheritage.org					
Cornwall Manor One Boyd St	Cornwall	PA	17016	717-273-2647	
Web: www.cornwallmanor.org					
Covenant Woods 7090 Covenant Woods Dr	Mechanicsville	VA	23111	804-569-8000	
Web: www.covenantwoods.com					
CSSS d'Antoine-Labelle 515 boul Dr Albiny-Paquette	Mont-laurier	QC	J9L1K8	819-623-6127	
Web: www.csssal.org					
Damar Services Inc 6067 Decatur Blvd	Indianapolis	IN	46241	317-856-5201	
Web: www.damar.org					
Eastside Retirement Association 10901 17th Cir NE	Redmond	WA	98052	425-556-8100	
Web: www.emeraldheights.com					
Elm Terrace Gardens 660 N Broad St	Lansdale	PA	19446	215-361-5600	
Web: www.elmterracegardens.org					
General Baptist Nursing Home US Hwy 62 W	Campbell	MO	63933	573-246-2155	
Web: generalbaptisthealthcare.com					
Greencroft Retirement Communities Inc 1721 Greencroft Blvd	Goshen	IN	46527	574-537-4000	
Web: www.greencroft.org					
H&H Total Care Services Inc 8382 156 St	Surrey	BC	V3S3R7	604-597-7931	
Web: www.hhtotalcare.com					
Hillcrest Convalescent Hospital Inc 3401 Cedar Ave	Long Beach	CA	90807	562-426-4461	
Web: www.hillcrestcare.com					
Kingsway Arms Retirement Residences Inc Ste 209 5409 Eglinton Ave W	Etobicoke	ON	M9C5K6	647-288-2942	
Web: retirementliving.kingswayarms.com					
Lifespace Communities Inc 100 E Grand Ave Ste 200	Des Moines	IA	50309	515-288-5805	
Web: www.lifespacecommunities.com					
Mennonite Friendship Communities 600 W Blanchard Rd	South Hutchinson	KS	67505	620-663-7175	
Web: www.mennofriend.com					
Michigan Masonic Home 1200 Wright Ave	Alma	MI	48801	989-463-3141	
Web: masonicpathways.com					
Montereau Inc 6800 S Granite Ave	Tulsa	OK	74136	918-495-1500	
Web: www.montereau.net					
Moravian Manor 300 W Lemon St	Lititz	PA	17543	717-626-0214	
Web: www.moravianmanor.org					
Moravian Village of Bethlehem 526 Wood St	Bethlehem	PA	18018	610-625-4885	
Web: www.moravianvillage.com					
Mother of Good Counsel Home 6825 Natural Bridge Rd	St. Louis	MO	63121	314-383-4765	
Web: mogch.org					
New Jersey Firemen's Home 565 Lathrop Ave	Boonton	NJ	07005	973-334-0024	
Web: www.njfh.org					
Pennswood Village 1382 Newtown-Langhorne Rd	Newtown	PA	18940	215-968-9110	
Web: pennswood.org					
People Inc 1219 N Forest Rd	Williamsville	NY	14231	716-634-8132	
Web: www.people-inc.org					
Peppermint Ridge Inc 825 Magnolia Ave	Corona	CA	92879	951-273-7320	
Web: peppermintridge.org					
Peter Becker Community 800 Maple Ave	Harleysville	PA	19438	215-256-9501	
Web: peterbeckercommunity.com					
Quarryville Presbyterian Retirement Community 625 Robert Fulton Hwy	Quarryville	PA	17566	717-786-7321	
Web: www.quarryville.com					
Sarasota-Manatee Jewish Housing Council Inc 1951 N Honore Ave	Sarasota	FL	34235	941-377-0781	
Web: www.kobernickanchin.org					
Galleria Woods 3850 Galleria Woods Dr	Birmingham	AL	35244	205-985-7537	987-2146
Web: brookdale.com/					
Atria Campana del Rio 1550 E River Rd	Tucson	AZ	85718	520-299-1941	529-2572
Web: www.atriaseniorliving.com					
Atria Chandler Villas 101 S Yucca St	Chandler	AZ	85224	480-899-7650	899-4485
Web: www.atriaseniorliving.com					
Beatitudes Campus of Care 1610 W Glendale Ave	Phoenix	AZ	85021	602-995-2611	995-4854
Web: beatitudescampus.org					
Forum at Desert Harbor, The 13840 N Desert Harbor Dr	Peoria	AZ	85381	623-972-0995	796-8385*
**Fax Area Code:* 617 ■ *Web:* theforumatdesertharbor.com					
Forum at Tucson 2500 N Rosemont Blvd	Tucson	AZ	85712	520-325-4800	319-4076
Web: theforumattucson.com					
Friendship Village of Tempe 2645 E Southern Ave	Tempe	AZ	85282	480-831-5000	413-0285
TF: 800-824-1112 ■ *Web:* www.friendshipvillageaz.com					
Glencroft 8611 N 67th Ave	Glendale	AZ	85302	623-939-9475	
Web: www.glencroft.com					
La Posada at Park Centre 350 E Morningside Rd	Green Valley	AZ	85614	520-648-8131	648-8397
Web: www.laposadagv.com					
Terraces at Phoenix, The 7550 N 16th St	Phoenix	AZ	85020	602-906-4024	371-9181
TF: 800-836-4281 ■ *Web:* www.theterracesphoenix.com					
Butterfield Trail Village 1923 E Joyce Blvd	Fayetteville	AR	72703	479-442-7220	442-2019
Web: www.butterfieldtrailvillage.com					
Atherton Baptist Homes 214 S Atlantic Blvd	Alhambra	CA	91801	626-289-4178	
Web: www.abh.org					
Atria Rancho Park 801 Cypress Way	San Dimas	CA	91773	626-339-5426	
Web: atriaranchopark.com					
Bixby Knolls Towers 3737 Atlantic Ave	Long Beach	CA	90807	562-426-6123	426-2571
Web: www.bixbyknollstowers.org					
Carmel Valley Manor 8545 Carmel Vly Rd	Carmel	CA	93923	831-624-1281	622-4543
TF: 800-544-5546 ■ *Web:* www.cvmanor.com					
Casa Dorinda 300 Hot Springs Rd	Montecito	CA	93108	805-969-8011	969-8686
Web: casadorinda.org					
Castle Hill Retirement Village 3575 N Moorpark Rd	Thousand Oaks	CA	91360	805-492-2471	
Channing House 850 Webster St	Palo Alto	CA	94301	650-327-0950	
Web: www.channinghouse.org					
Covenant Village of Turlock 2125 N Olive Ave	Turlock	CA	95382	209-216-5610	565-3809*
**Fax Area Code:* 617 ■ *TF:* 800-485-7844 ■ *Web:* www.covenantvillageofturlock.org					
Eskaton Inc 5105 Manzanita Ave	Carmichael	CA	95608	916-334-0810	338-1248
Web: www.eskaton.org					
Eskaton Village 3939 Walnut Ave	Carmichael	CA	95608	916-974-2000	974-2022
TF: 800-300-3929 ■ *Web:* www.eskaton.org					
Freedom Village 23442 El Toro Rd	Lake Forest	CA	92630	949-472-4700	
TF: 800-584-8084 ■ *Web:* www.freedomvillage.org					
Grand Lake Gardens 401 Santa Clara Ave	Oakland	CA	94610	800-416-6091	893-0114*
**Fax Area Code:* 510 ■ *TF:* 800-416-6091 ■ *Web:* www.grandlakegardens.com					
Hillcrest Homes 2705 Mtn View Dr	La Verne	CA	91750	909-392-4375	596-5538
Web: www.livingathillcrest.org					
Lake Park Retirement Residences 1850 Alice St	Oakland	CA	94612	510-835-5511	273-0529
Web: www.lakeparkretirement.org					
Los Gatos Meadows 110 Wood Rd	Los Gatos	CA	95030	408-354-0211	354-4193
Web: jtm-esc.org/lgm/index					
Morningside of Fullerton 800 Morningside Dr	Fullerton	CA	92835	714-256-8000	
TF: 800-803-7597 ■ *Web:* www.morningsideoffullerton.com					
Mount Miguel Covenant Village 325 Kempton St	Spring Valley	CA	91977	619-479-4790	565-3809*
**Fax Area Code:* 617 ■ *TF:* 877-407-4790 ■ *Web:* www.mountmiguelcovenantvillage.org					
O'Connor Woods 3400 Wagner Heights Rd	Stockton	CA	95209	209-956-3400	
TF: 800-957-3308 ■ *Web:* www.oconnorwoods.org					
Park Lane, The 200 Glenwood Cir	Monterey	CA	93940	831-250-6159	
Web: www.theparklanemonterey.com					
Peninsula Regent, The One Baldwin Ave	San Mateo	CA	94401	650-579-5500	579-0446
Web: www.peninsularegent.com					
Piedmont Gardens 110 41st St	Oakland	CA	94611	510-596-2600	
Web: www.piedmontgardens.com					
Plymouth Village 900 Salem Dr	Redlands	CA	92373	909-793-9195	798-5504
TF: 800-391-4552 ■ *Web:* www.plymouthvillage.org					
Quaker Gardens 12151 Dale St	Stanton	CA	90680	714-530-9100	530-0945*
**Fax:* Mktg ■ *Web:* www.quakergardens.com					
Regents Point 19191 Harvard Ave	Irvine	CA	92612	949-988-0849	247-3871*
**Fax Area Code:* 818 ■ *TF General:* 800-347-3735 ■ *Web:* www.thebegroup.org					
Remington Club 16925 Hierba Dr	San Diego	CA	92128	858-673-6300	673-6318
Web: theremingtonclub.com					
Rosewood Retirement Community 1301 New Stine Rd	Bakersfield	CA	93309	661-834-0620	834-0280
TF: 800-984-4216 ■ *Web:* www.rosewoodretirement.org					
Samarkand, The 2550 Treasure Dr	Santa Barbara	CA	93105	805-687-0701	687-3386
Web: thesamarkand.org					
San Joaquin Gardens 5555 N Fresno St	Fresno	CA	93710	559-439-4770	439-2457
Web: theterracesatsanjoaquin.com					
Sequoias Portola Valley, The *Northern California Presbyterian Homes & Services* 501 Portola Rd	Portola Valley	CA	94028	650-851-1501	851-5007
Web: www.ncphs.org					
Sequoias San Francisco 1400 Geary Blvd	San Francisco	CA	94109	415-922-9700	567-2576
Web: www.ncphs.org					
Smith Ranch Homes 400 Deer Vly Rd Ste L	San Rafael	CA	94903	415-491-4918	491-0254
TF: 800-772-6264 ■ *Web:* www.smithranchhomes.com					
Solheim Lutheran Home (SLH) 2236 Merton Ave	Los Angeles	CA	90041	323-257-7518	255-3544
TF: 888-257-7518 ■ *Web:* www.solheimlutheran.org					
Spring Lake Village 5555 Montgomery Dr	Santa Rosa	CA	95409	707-538-8400	
Web: jtm-esc.org					
Tamalpais, The 501 Via Casitas	Greenbrae	CA	94904	415-461-2300	461-0241
Web: www.ncphs.org					
Terraces at Los Altos, The 2478 W El Camino Real	Mountain View	CA	94040	650-917-9661	
Web: www.theterracesatlosaltos.com					
Terraces of Los Gatos 800 Blossom Hill Rd	Los Gatos	CA	95032	408-356-1006	356-9647
Web: www.theterracesoflosgatos.com					
Valle Verde 900 Calle de los Amigos	Santa Barbara	CA	93105	805-883-4000	687-5540
TF: 800-750-5089 ■ *Web:* www.valleverde.org					
Villa Gardens 842 E Villa St	Pasadena	CA	91101	626-463-5329	568-9606
TF: 800-958-4552 ■ *Web:* www.villagardens.org					
Villa Marin 100 Thorndale Dr	San Rafael	CA	94903	415-492-2408	
Web: www.villa-marin.com					
Villa Valencia 24552 Paseo de Valencia	Laguna Hills	CA	92653	949-581-6111	837-1082
Web: www.villavalenciaretirement.com					
Village, The 2200 W Acacia Ave	Hemet	CA	92545	951-658-3369	658-4295
TF: 800-257-7888 ■ *Web:* thevillageriversidecounty.com/					
Vista del Monte 3775 Modoc Rd	Santa Barbara	CA	93105	805-687-0793	687-6350
TF: 800-736-1333 ■ *Web:* www.vistadelmonte.org					
White Sands of La Jolla 516 Burchett St	Glendale	CA	92037	818-247-0420	247-3871
TF: 800-347-3735 ■ *Web:* www.thebegroup.org					
Englewood Meridian 3455 S Corona St	Englewood	CO	80113	888-221-7317	221-2289*
**Fax Area Code:* 615 ■ *TF:* 855-444-7658 ■ *Web:* brookdaleliving.com/					
Heritage Club 2020 S Monroe St	Denver	CO	80210	303-756-0025	
TF: 888-221-7317 ■ *Web:* brookdale.com/heritage-club-denver.aspx					
Parkplace 111 Emerson St	Denver	CO	80218	303-744-0400	
Web: brookdale.com/parkplace-.aspx					
Villa Pueblo Towers 2501 E 104th Ave	Thornton	CO	80233	303-255-4100	844-2025
TF: 888-808-8828 ■ *Web:* centuraseniors.org					
Arbors of Hop Brook 403 W Ctr St	Manchester	CT	06040	860-647-9343	434-5790
TF: 866-689-0846 ■ *Web:* www.arborsct.com					
Covenant Village of Cromwell & Pilgrim Manor 52 Missionary Rd	Cromwell	CT	06416	860-635-2690	632-2407
Web: www.covenantvillageofcromwell.org					
Duncaster 40 Loeffler Rd	Bloomfield	CT	06002	860-380-5006	242-8004
Web: www.duncaster.org					

	City	State	ZIP	Phone	Fax
Elim Park Place 140 Cook Hill Rd	Cheshire	CT	06410	203-272-3547	250-6282
TF: 800-994-1776 ■ *Web:* www.elimpark.org					
Essex Meadows 30 Bokum Rd	Essex	CT	06426	860-767-7201	767-0014
TF: 800-767-7201 ■ *Web:* www.essexmeadows.com					
Evergreen Woods 88 Notch Hill Rd	North Branford	CT	06471	203-488-8000	488-9429
TF General: 866-413-6378 ■ *Web:* evergreenwoods.com					
Pomperaug Woods 80 Heritage Rd	Southbury	CT	06488	203-262-6555	264-2155
TF: 866-817-8935 ■ *Web:* www.pomperaugwoods.com					
Watermark at 3030 Park, The 3030 Pk Ave	Bridgeport	CT	06604	203-502-7593	374-2871
Web: www.watermarkcommunities.com/3030park					
Whitney Ctr 200 Leeder Hill Dr	Hamden	CT	06517	203-848-2641	
TF: 800-237-3847 ■ *Web:* www.whitneycenter.com					
Cokesbury Village 726 Loveville Rd	Hockessin	DE	19707	302-235-6000	239-2650
Web: actsretirement.org					
Methodist Country House 4830 Kennett Pk	Wilmington	DE	19807	302-654-5101	426-8108
Web: www.actsretirement.org					
Methodist Manor House 1001 Middleford Rd	Seaford	DE	19973	302-629-4593	
TF: 800-775-4593 ■ *Web:* www.actsretirement.org					
Stonegates 4031 Kennett Pk	Greenville	DE	19807	302-658-6200	658-1510
Web: www.stonegates.com					
Ingleside Rock Creek 3050 Military Rd NW	Washington	DC	20015	202-363-8310	363-0950
Web: www.ircdc.org					
Knollwood 6200 Oregon Ave NW	Washington	DC	20015	202-541-0400	364-2856
TF: 800-541-4255 ■ *Web:* www.armydistaff.org					
Abbey Delray 2000 Lowson Blvd	Delray Beach	FL	33445	561-454-2000	
TF: 888-791-9363 ■					
Web: lifespacecommunities.com/senior-living-delray-beach/ad/					
Atria Meridian Assisted Living Community					
3061 Donnelly Dr	Lantana	FL	33462	561-902-1085	
Web: www.atriaseniorliving.com					
Bay Village 8400 Vamo Rd	Sarasota	FL	34231	941-966-5611	966-4040
Web: www.bayvillage.org					
Covenant Village of Florida					
9215 W Broward Blvd	Plantation	FL	33324	954-472-2860	472-5934
Web: www.covenantretirement.org					
East Ridge Retirement Village					
19301 SW 87th Ave	Miami	FL	33157	800-856-8097	
TF: 800-856-8097 ■ *Web:* www.eastridgeatcutlerbay.com					
Edgewater Pointe Estates					
23315 Blue Water Cir	Boca Raton	FL	33433	561-391-6305	
TF General: 888-339-2287 ■ *Web:* www.actsretirement.org					
Fleet Landing Retirement Community					
1 Fleet Landing Blvd	Atlantic Beach	FL	32233	904-246-9900	246-9900
TF General: 877-591-6547 ■ *Web:* www.fleetlanding.com					
Florida Presbyterian Homes 16 Lk Hunter Dr	Lakeland	FL	33803	863-688-5521	682-4644
TF: 866-294-3352 ■ *Web:* www.fphi.org					
Gulf Coast Village					
1333 Santa Barbara Blvd	Cape Coral	FL	33991	239-772-1333	772-0242*
**Fax:* Mktg ■ *Web:* www.gulfcoastvillage.com					
Harbour's Edge 401 E Linton Blvd	Delray Beach	FL	33483	561-272-7979	
TF: 888-417-9281 ■					
Web: lifespacecommunities.com/senior-living-delray-beach/he/					
Indian River Estates					
2250 Indian Creek Blvd W	Vero Beach	FL	32966	772-562-7400	778-7747
TF Mktg: 800-544-0277 ■ *Web:* www.actsretirement.org					
Lake Seminole Square 8333 Seminole Blvd	Seminole	FL	33772	727-391-0500	392-9497
TF: 866-785-9025 ■ *Web:* brookdale.com/lake-seminole-square.aspx					
Mayflower Retirement Community					
1620 Mayflower Ct	Winter Park	FL	32792	407-672-1620	671-6336
TF: 800-228-6518 ■ *Web:* www.themayflower.com					
Mease Manor Retirement Living 700 Mease Plz	Dunedin	FL	34698	727-738-3000	
Web: www.measemanor.com					
Moorings Park 120 Moorings Pk Dr	Naples	FL	34105	239-643-9111	262-7040
TF: 866-802-4302 ■ *Web:* www.mooringspark.org					
Palace Renaissance & Royale 11355 SW 84th St	Miami	FL	33173	305-270-7000	
Web: www.thepalace.org					
Park Summit of Coral Springs					
8500 Royal Palm Blvd	Coral Springs	FL	33065	954-752-9500	755-9559
Web: parksummit.com					
Plymouth Harbor 700 John Ringling Blvd	Sarasota	FL	34236	941-365-2600	957-1812
Web: www.plymouthharbor.org					
Saint Andrews Estates 6152 Verde Trail N	Boca Raton	FL	33433	561-487-4728	883-3823
TF Mktg: 866-897-3490 ■ *Web:* www.actsretirement.org					
Saint Mark Village 2655 Nebraska Ave	Palm Harbor	FL	34684	727-785-2580	
Web: www.stmarkvillage.com					
Shell Point Village 15101 Shell Pt Blvd	Fort Myers	FL	33908	239-466-1131	454-2220
TF Mktg: 800-780-1131 ■ *Web:* www.shellpoint.org					
Stratford Court 45 Katherine Blvd	Palm Harbor	FL	34684	727-787-1500	787-1506
TF: 888-434-4648 ■ *Web:* www.sunriseseniorliving.com					
Village on the Green 500 Village Pl	Longwood	FL	32779	407-682-0230	682-3893*
**Fax:* Mktg ■ *TF Mktg:* 888-541-3443 ■					
Web: lifespacecommunities.com/senior-living-orlando/					
Waterford, The 601 Universe Blvd	Juno Beach	FL	33408	561-627-3800	
TF: 888-335-1678 ■					
Web: lifespacecommunities.com/senior-living-juno-beach/					
Westminster Bradenton Manor					
1700 21st Ave W	Bradenton	FL	34205	941-748-4161	
TF: 866-846-8046 ■ *Web:* www.westminsterretirement.com					
Westminster Oaks 4449 Meandering Way	Tallahassee	FL	32308	850-878-1136	942-4924
TF: 866-937-6257 ■ *Web:* www.westminsterretirement.com					
Westminster Towers 80 W Lucerne Cir	Orlando	FL	32801	407-841-1310	849-0900
TF: 800-416-2612 ■ *Web:* www.westminsterretirement.com					
Clairmont Place 2100 Clairmont Lake	Decatur	GA	30033	404-633-8875	633-9417
Web: clairmontplace.com					
Arcadia Retirement Residence					
1434 Punahou St	Honolulu	HI	96822	808-941-0941	949-4965
Web: www.arcadia-hi.org					
Admiral at the Lake 929 W Foster Ste 7	Chicago	IL	60660	773-433-1800	
Web: admiral.kendal.org					
Church Creek 1250 W Central Rd	Arlington Heights	IL	60005	847-506-3200	506-2598
Web: www.sunriseseniorliving.com					
Clark-Lindsey Village 101 W Windsor Rd	Urbana	IL	61802	217-344-2144	344-9147
TF: 800-998-2581 ■ *Web:* www.clark-lindsey.com					
Covenant Retirement Communities Inc					
5700 Old OrchaRd Rd Ste 100	Skokie	IL	60077	773-878-2294	
Web: www.covenantretirement.org					
Friendship Manor 1209 21st Ave	Rock Island	IL	61201	309-786-9667	786-5611
TF: 888-382-1222 ■ *Web:* www.friendshipmanor.org					
Hallmark, The 2960 N Lk Shore Dr	Chicago	IL	60657	773-880-2960	880-2966
Web: brookdale.com/					
Holmstad, The 700 W Fabyan Pkwy	Batavia	IL	60510	630-879-4100	879-1153
Web: www.covenantretirement.org					
Oak Crest DeKalb Area Retirement Ctr					
2944 Greenwood Acres Dr	DeKalb	IL	60115	815-756-8461	756-6515
Web: www.oakcrestdekalb.org					
Providence Life Services					
18601 N Creek Dr	Tinley Park	IL	60477	708-342-8100	342-8000
TF: 800-509-2800 ■ *Web:* www.providencelifeservices.com					
Senior Lifestyle Corp					
111 E Wacker Dr Ste 2200	Chicago	IL	60601	312-673-4333	673-4440
Web: www.seniorlifestyle.com					
Vi 71 S Wacker Dr	Chicago	IL	60606	312-803-8800	803-8801
TF: 800-421-1442 ■ *Web:* www.viliving.com					
Westminster Place 3200 Grant St	Evanston	IL	60201	847-570-3422	492-2850
TF: 800-896-9095 ■ *Web:* www.presbyterianhomes.org					
Four Seasons Retirement Ctr 1901 Taylor Rd	Columbus	IN	47203	812-372-8481	378-6184
Web: www.fourseasonsretirement.com					
Greenwood Village South 295 Village Ln	Greenwood	IN	46143	317-881-2591	881-1299
Web: www.greenwoodvillagesouth.com					
Hoosier Village 5300 W 96th St	Indianapolis	IN	46268	317-873-3349	873-8224
Web: www.hoosiervillage.com					
Lutheran Life Villages					
6701 S Anthony Blvd	Fort Wayne	IN	46816	260-447-1591	447-7369
Web: www.lutheranlifevillages.org					
Marquette 8140 Township Line Rd	Indianapolis	IN	46260	317-875-9700	875-7504
Web: www.retirement-living.org					
Meadowood Retirement Community					
2455 Tamarack Trl	Bloomington	IN	47408	812-336-7060	333-8917
Web: www.meadowoodretirement.com					
Towne House, The 2209 St Joe Ctr Rd	Fort Wayne	IN	46825	260-483-3116	969-8072
Web: www.townehouse.org					
Wesley Manor 1555 N Main St	Frankfort	IN	46041	765-659-1811	654-5596
Web: www.wesleymanor.org					
Westminster Village 1120 E Davis Dr	Terre Haute	IN	47802	812-232-7533	232-3304
Web: www.westminstervillagein.com					
Friendship Village 600 Pk Ln	Waterloo	IA	50702	319-291-8100	291-8324
Web: www.friendshipvillageiowa.com					
Meth-Wick Community 1224 13th St NW	Cedar Rapids	IA	52405	319-365-9171	363-5312
Web: www.methwick.org					
Western Home Communities 420 E 11th St	Cedar Falls	IA	50613	319-277-2141	268-8338
Web: www.westernhomecommunities.org					
Aldersgate Village 7220 SW Asbury Dr	Topeka	KS	66614	785-478-9440	478-9104
Web: www.aldersgatevillage.org					
Brewster Place 1205 SW 29th St	Topeka	KS	66611	785-274-3350	267-9355
Web: brewsterliving.org/					
Delmar Gardens of Lenexa Inc 9701 Monrovia St	Lenexa	KS	66215	913-492-1130	492-0586
Web: www.delmargardens.com					
Kansas Christian Home 1035 SE Third St	Newton	KS	67114	316-283-6600	283-6375
Web: kschristianhome.org					
Larksfield Place 7373 E 29th St N	Wichita	KS	67226	316-858-3910	636-5790
TF: 866-232-8484 ■ *Web:* www.larksfieldplace.org					
Wesley Towers 700 Monterey Pl	Hutchinson	KS	67502	620-663-9175	663-2961
TF: 888-663-9175 ■ *Web:* www.wesleytowers.com					
Forum at Brookside 200 Brookside Dr	Louisville	KY	40243	502-245-3048	244-6327*
**Fax:* Mktg ■ *Web:* theforumatbrookside.com					
Treyton Oak Towers 211 W Oak St	Louisville	KY	40203	502-589-3211	589-7263
Web: www.treytonoaktowers.com					
Seniorsplus Eight Falcon Rd PO Box 659	Lewiston	ME	04243	207-795-4010	795-4009
TF: 800-427-1241 ■ *Web:* www.seniorsplus.org					
Asbury Methodist Village					
201 Russell Ave	Gaithersburg	MD	20877	301-216-4100	
TF: 800-327-2879 ■ *Web:* www.asburymethodistvillage.org					
Bedford Court 3701 International Dr	Silver Spring	MD	20906	301-598-2900	598-8588
Web: www.sunriseseniorliving.com					
Broadmead 13801 York Rd	Cockeysville	MD	21030	410-527-1900	527-0259
Web: www.broadmead.org					
Carroll Lutheran Village 300 St Luke Cir	Westminster	MD	21158	410-848-0090	848-8133
TF: 877-848-0095 ■ *Web:* www.carrolllutheranvillage.org					
Charlestown Retirement Community (CCI)					
715 Maiden Choice Ln	Catonsville	MD	21228	410-242-2880	737-8854
TF: 800-917-8649 ■					
Web: ericksonliving.com/catonsville/catonsville-senior-living.asp					
Collington Episcopal Community					
10450 Lottsford Rd	Mitchellville	MD	20721	301-925-9610	925-7357
Web: collington.kendal.org					
Edenwald 800 Southerly Rd	Baltimore	MD	21286	410-339-6000	583-8786
Web: www.edenwald.org					
Fairhaven 7200 Third Ave	Sykesville	MD	21784	410-795-8801	970-2035
TF: 877-696-6775 ■ *Web:* www.fairhavenccrc.org					
Ginger Cove 4000 River Crescent Dr	Annapolis	MD	21401	410-266-7300	266-6144
TF: 800-299-2683 ■ *Web:* www.gingercove.com					
Glen Meadows 11630 Glen Arm Rd	Glen Arm	MD	21057	800-630-4689	
TF: 800-630-4689 ■ *Web:* www.glenmeadows.org					
Heron Point of Chestertown					
501 E Campus Ave	Chestertown	MD	21620	410-778-7300	810-2915
TF: 800-327-9138 ■ *Web:* www.actsretirement.org					
Homewood at Williamsport					
16505 Virginia Ave	Williamsport	MD	21795	301-582-1750	582-1819
Web: www.homewood.com					
Roland Park Place 830 W 40th St	Baltimore	MD	21211	410-243-5700	243-4929
Web: www.rolandparkplace.org					
Brookhaven at Lexington 1010 Waltham St	Lexington	MA	02421	781-863-9660	863-9944*
**Fax:* Admin ■ *Web:* www.aboutbrookhaven.org					
Carleton-Willard Village (CWV)					
100 Old Billerica Rd	Bedford	MA	01730	781-275-8700	275-5787
Web: www.cwvillage.org					

Name / Address	City	State	Zip	Phone	Fax
Epoch Senior Living 51 Sawyer Rd Ste 500	Waltham	MA	02453	781-891-0777	891-0774
TF: 877-376-2475 ■ *Web:* www.epochsl.com					
Fox Hill Village 10 Longwood Dr	Westwood	MA	02090	781-329-4433	461-2464
Web: foxhillvillage.com					
Loomis Communities 246 N Main St	South Hadley	MA	01075	413-532-5325	532-8676
TF: 800-865-7655 ■ *Web:* www.loomiscommunities.org					
New Pond Village 180 Main St	Walpole	MA	02081	508-660-1555	668-8893
Web: www.norwoodma.brightviewseniorliving.com					
Willows, The 1 Lyman St	Westborough	MA	01581	508-366-4730	898-3982
TF: 800-464-8060 ■ *Web:* www.salmonfamily.com					
Friendship Village Kalamazoo					
1400 N Drake Rd	Kalamazoo	MI	49006	269-381-0560	
TF: 800-613-3984 ■ *Web:* www.friendshipvillagemi.com					
Glacier Hills 1200 Earhart Rd	Ann Arbor	MI	48105	734-769-6410	769-3092
Web: www.glacierhills.org					
Porter Hills 3600 E Fulton St	Grand Rapids	MI	49546	616-949-4971	954-1795
Web: www.porterhills.org					
Vista Grande Villa 2251 Springport Rd	Jackson	MI	49202	517-787-0222	787-6909
TF: 800-889-8499 ■ *Web:* www.vistagrandevilla.com					
Covenant Village of Golden Valley					
5800 St Croix Ave	Minneapolis	MN	55422	763-546-6125	565-3809*
**Fax Area Code:* 617 ■ *TF:* 877-224-5051 ■ *Web:* www.covenantvillageofgoldenvalley.org					
Armed Forces Retirement Home - Gulfport					
1800 Beach Dr	Gulfport	MS	39507	800-422-9988	541-7519*
**Fax Area Code:* 202 ■ *TF:* 800-422-9988 ■ *Web:* www.afrh.gov					
Methodist Senior Services 300 Airline Rd	Columbus	MS	39702	662-327-6716	482-5567*
**Fax Area Code:* 601 ■ *Web:* www.mss.org/					
Friendship Village of South County					
12503 Village Cir Dr	Saint Louis	MO	63127	314-842-6840	525-7500
Web: www.friendshipvillagestl.com					
John Knox Village 400 NW Murray Rd	Lee's Summit	MO	64081	816-251-8000	246-4739
TF: 800-892-5669 ■ *Web:* www.johnknoxvillage.org					
Kingswood Senior Living Community					
10000 Wornall Rd	Kansas City	MO	64114	816-942-0994	942-2455*
**Fax:* Sales ■ *TF Sales:* 888-942-2715 ■ *Web:* www.kingswoodathome.org					
Parkside Meadows Retirement Community					
2150 W Randolph St	Saint Charles	MO	63301	636-946-4966	
Web: stcharlesretirement.com/					
Village North Retirement Community					
11160 Village N Dr	Saint Louis	MO	63136	314-355-8010	
Web: villagenorthretirement.org					
Eastmont Towers 6315 'O' St	Lincoln	NE	68510	402-486-2281	486-2331
Web: www.eastmonttowers.com					
Northfield Villa & Residency					
Villa & Vista, The 2550 21st St	Gering	NE	69341	308-436-3101	436-3493
Web: www.northfieldretirement.net					
Skyline Retirement Community					
7300 Graceland Dr # 120B	Omaha	NE	68134	402-572-5750	
Web: skylinerc.com					
Havenwood-Heritage Heights Havenwood Campus					
33 Christian Ave	Concord	NH	03301	603-224-5363	229-1188
TF: 800-457-6833 ■ *Web:* www.hhhinfo.com					
Kendal at Hanover 80 Lyme Rd	Hanover	NH	03755	603-643-8900	643-7099
Web: kah.kendal.org					
RiverMead Retirement Community					
150 RiverMead Rd	Peterborough	NH	03458	603-924-0062	924-6507
TF: 800-200-5433 ■ *Web:* rivermead.org					
Cadbury Retirement Community 2150 Rt 38	Cherry Hill	NJ	08002	856-667-4550	667-3653
TF: 800-422-3287 ■ *Web:* www.cadbury.org					
Crestwood Manor 50 Lacey Rd	Whiting	NJ	08759	732-849-4900	
TF General: 877-467-1652 ■ *Web:* www.crestwoodmanoronline.org					
Evergreens, The 309 Bridgeboro Rd	Moorestown	NJ	08057	856-439-2000	*
**Fax:* Mktg ■ *TF:* 877-673-8234 ■ *Web:* www.evergreens.org					
Franciscan Oaks 19 Pocono Rd	Denville	NJ	07834	973-586-6000	586-6030
TF: 800-237-3330 ■ *Web:* www.franciscanoaks.com					
Harrogate 400 Locust St	Lakewood	NJ	08701	732-905-7070	905-4059
TF: 888-551-5531 ■ *Web:* harrogatelifecare.org/					
Medford Leas One Medford Leas Way	Medford	NJ	08055	609-654-3000	654-7894
TF: 800-331-4302 ■ *Web:* www.medfordleas.org					
La Vida Llena 10501 Lagrima de Oro NE	Albuquerque	NM	87111	505-293-4001	291-3199
TF: 800-922-1344 ■ *Web:* www.lavidallena.com					
Montebello on Academy, The					
10500 Academy Rd NE	Albuquerque	NM	87111	505-294-9944	294-1808
Web: themontebelloseniorliving.com					
Andrus on Hudson 185 Old Broadway	Hastings-on-Hudson	NY	10706	914-478-3700	478-3541
Web: andrusonhudson.org					
Fountains at Millbrook, The 79 Flint Rd	Millbrook	NY	12545	845-605-4457	
Web: www.watermarkcommunities.com					
Kendal at Ithaca 2230 N Triphammer Rd	Ithaca	NY	14850	607-266-5300	266-5353
TF: 800-253-6325 ■ *Web:* www.kai.kendal.org					
Arbor Acres 1240 Arbor Rd	Winston-Salem	NC	27104	336-724-7921	721-0271
TF: 866-658-2724 ■ *Web:* www.arboracres.org					
Bermuda Village 142 Bermuda Village Dr	Advance	NC	27006	800-843-5433	940-2140*
**Fax Area Code:* 336 ■ **Fax:* Mktg ■ *TF Mktg:* 800-843-5433 ■ *Web:* www.bermudavillage.net					
Carol Woods Retirement Community					
750 Weaver Dairy Rd	Chapel Hill	NC	27514	919-968-4511	918-3349
TF: 800-518-9333 ■ *Web:* carolwoods.org					
Carolina Meadows 100 Carolina Meadows	Chapel Hill	NC	27517	919-942-4014	929-7808
TF: 800-458-6756 ■ *Web:* www.carolinameadows.org					
Carolina Village					
600 Carolina Village Rd	Hendersonville	NC	28792	828-692-6275	692-7876
Web: www.carolinavillage.com					
Covenant Village 1351 Robinwood Rd	Gastonia	NC	28054	704-867-2319	861-8893
Deerfield Episcopal Retirement Community					
1617 Hendersonville Rd	Asheville	NC	28803	828-274-1531	274-0238
TF: 800-284-1531 ■ *Web:* www.deerfieldwnc.org					
Forest at Duke 2701 Pickett Rd	Durham	NC	27705	919-490-8000	490-0887
TF: 800-474-0258 ■ *Web:* www.forestduke.org					
Pines at Davidson 400 Avinger Ln	Davidson	NC	28036	704-896-1100	896-1119
Web: www.thepinesatdavidson.org					
Sharon Towers 5100 Sharon Rd	Charlotte	NC	28210	704-553-1670	553-1877
Web: www.sharontowers.org					

Name / Address	City	State	Zip	Phone	Fax
Springmoor Life Care Retirement Community					
1500 Sawmill Rd	Raleigh	NC	27615	919-848-7000	848-7392
Web: www.springmoor.org					
Breckenridge Village 36851 Ridge Rd	Willoughby	OH	44094	440-942-4342	
Web: www.oprs.org					
First Community Village 1800 Riverside Dr	Columbus	OH	43212	614-324-4455	
TF: 877-364-2570 ■ *Web:* www.nationalchurchresidences.org					
Friendship Village of columbus					
5800 Forest Hills Blvd	Columbus	OH	43231	614-890-8282	890-2661
Web: www.friendshipvillageoh.com					
Hilltop Village 25900 Euclid Ave	Euclid	OH	44132	216-261-8383	261-6816
Web: www.hilltopvillage.com					
Kendal at Oberlin 600 Kendal Dr	Oberlin	OH	44074	800-548-9469	775-9880*
**Fax Area Code:* 440 ■ *TF Mktg:* 800-548-9469 ■ *Web:* www.kao.kendal.org					
Laurel Lake Retirement Community					
200 Laurel Lk Dr	Hudson	OH	44236	866-650-2100	655-1738*
**Fax Area Code:* 330 ■ *TF:* 866-650-2100 ■ *Web:* laurellake.org/					
Maple Knoll Communities Inc					
11100 Springfield Pk	Cincinnati	OH	45246	513-782-2400	782-4324
TF: 800-272-3900 ■ *Web:* www.mapleknoll.org					
Methodist ElderCare Services 5155 N High St	Columbus	OH	43214	614-396-4990	436-6012
TF: 855-636-2225 ■ *Web:* www.wesleyridge.com/wesleyglen_home.aspx					
Otterbein Retirement Living Communities					
580 N SR 741	Lebanon	OH	45036	513-933-5400	932-1054
TF: 888-513-9131 ■ *Web:* www.otterbein.org					
Renaissance, The 26376 John Rd	Olmsted Township	OH	44138	440-235-7100	235-7115
Rockynol Retirement Community 1150 W Market St	Akron	OH	44313	330-867-2150	
Web: www.oprs.org					
Twin Towers 5343 Hamilton Ave	Cincinnati	OH	45224	513-853-2000	853-2703
Web: lec.org					
Westlake Village 28550 Westlake Village Dr	Westlake	OH	44145	855-308-2432	
Westminster-Thurber Community 717 Neil Ave	Columbus	OH	43215	614-228-8888	228-8898
Web: www.westminsterthurber.org					
Epworth Villa 14901 N Pennsylvania Ave	Oklahoma City	OK	73134	405-752-1200	755-4813
TF: 800-579-8776 ■ *Web:* www.epworthvilla.com					
Golden Oaks Village 5801 N Oakwood Rd	Enid	OK	73703	580-249-2600	
TF: 800-259-0914 ■ *Web:* www.goldenoaks.com					
Spanish Cove 11 Palm Ave	Yukon	OK	73099	800-965-2683	
TF: 800-965-2683 ■ *Web:* www.spanishcove.com					
Capital Manor 1955 Dallas Hwy NW	Salem	OR	97304	503-362-4101	371-9021
TF: 800-637-0327 ■ *Web:* www.capitalmanor.com					
Friendsview Retirement Community					
1301 E Fulton St	Newberg	OR	97132	503-538-3144	538-6371
TF: 866-307-4371 ■ *Web:* friendsview.org					
Mennonite Village 5353 Columbus St SE	Albany	OR	97322	541-928-7232	917-1399
Web: www.mennonitevillage.org					
Rogue Valley Manor 1200 Mira Mar Ave	Medford	OR	97504	541-857-7214	857-7599
TF: 800-848-7868 ■ *Web:* www.retirement.org/rvm					
Willamette View 12705 SE River Rd	Portland	OR	97222	503-654-6581	652-6260
TF: 800-446-0670 ■ *Web:* www.willametteview.org					
Beaumont at Bryn Mawr 601 N Ithan Ave	Bryn Mawr	PA	19010	610-526-7000	525-0293
Web: www.beaumontretirement.com					
Bethany Village 325 Wesley Dr	Mechanicsburg	PA	17055	717-766-0279	766-0870
Web: www.bethanyvillage.org					
Brittany Pointe Estates					
1001 S Valley Forge Rd	Lansdale	PA	19446	215-855-4109	
TF: 800-504-2287 ■ *Web:* www.actsretirement.org					
Cross Keys Village					
2990 Carlisle Pk PO Box 128	New Oxford	PA	17350	717-624-5350	624-5252
TF Mktg: 888-624-8242 ■ *Web:* www.crosskeysvillage.org					
Foulkeways at Gwynedd 1120 Meetinghouse Rd	Gwynedd	PA	19436	215-643-2200	646-2917
Web: www.foulkeways.org					
Foxdale Village 500 E Marylyn Ave	State College	PA	16801	814-272-2117	238-2920
TF: 800-253-4951 ■ *Web:* www.foxdalevillage.org					
Friendship Village of South Hills					
1290 Boyce Rd	Upper Saint Clair	PA	15241	724-941-3100	941-6331
Web: lifespacecommunities.com/senior-living-pittsburgh/					
Granite Farms Estates 1343 W Baltimore Pike	Media	PA	19063	610-358-3440	
TF: 888-499-2287 ■ *Web:* www.actsretirement.org					
Kendal at Longwood & Crosslands					
PO Box 100	Kennett Square	PA	19348	610-388-1441	388-5503
TF: 800-216-1920 ■ *Web:* kcc.kendal.org					
Lebanon Valley Brethren Home 1200 Grubb Rd	Palmyra	PA	17078	717-838-5406	838-3826
Web: www.lvbh.org					
Lima Estates 411 N Middletown Rd	Media	PA	19063	610-565-7020	
TF: 888-398-2287 ■ *Web:* www.actsretirement.org					
Lutheran Community at Telford					
12 Lutheran Home Dr	Telford	PA	18969	215-723-9819	723-3623
TF: 877-343-7518 ■ *Web:* www.lctelford.org					
Martins Run 100 Halcyon Dr	Media	PA	19063	610-353-7660	355-1339
TF: 877-824-3935 ■ *Web:* www.martinsrun.org					
Meadowood 3205 Skippack Pike PO Box 670	Worcester	PA	19490	610-584-1000	584-3645
Web: www.meadowood.net					
Menno Village 2075 Scotland Ave	Chambersburg	PA	17201	717-262-2373	263-6988
Web: www.mennohaven.org					
Moravian Hall Square 175 W N St	Nazareth	PA	18064	610-746-1000	746-1023
Web: www.moravian.com					
Normandy Farms Estates Morris Rd Rt 202	Blue Bell	PA	19422	215-616-8500	
Web: www.normandyfarm.com					
Passavant Retirement Community					
401 S Main St	Zelienople	PA	16063	724-452-5400	452-3684
TF: 888-498-7753 ■ *Web:* www.lutheranseniorlife.org					
Philadelphia Protestant Home					
6500 Tabor Rd	Philadelphia	PA	19111	215-697-8000	697-8137
Web: www.pphfamily.org					
Pine Run Community 777 Ferry Rd	Doylestown	PA	18901	215-345-9000	340-5128
TF: 888-992-8992 ■ *Web:* www.pinerun.org					
Quadrangle, The 3300 Darby Rd	Haverford	PA	19041	610-642-3000	642-5743
Web: www.sunriseseniorliving.com					
Riddle Village 1048 W Baltimore Pk	Media	PA	19063	610-891-3700	891-3671
Web: www.riddlevillage.com					

	City	State	Zip	Phone	Fax
Rydal Park 1515 The Fairway *Web:* www.rydalpark.org	Rydal	PA	19046	215-885-6800	885-4560
Sherwood Oaks 100 Norman Dr *TF:* 800-642-2217 ■ *Web:* www.sherwood-oaks.com	Cranberry Township	PA	16066	724-776-8100	776-8468
Simpson House 2101 Belmont Ave *Web:* www.simpsonhouse.org	Philadelphia	PA	19131	215-878-3600	878-6701
Spring House Estates 728 Norristown Rd *TF:* 888-365-2287 ■ *Web:* www.actsretirement.org	Lower Gwynedd	PA	19002	215-628-8110	628-9701
Watermark at Logan Square Two Franklin Town Blvd *Web:* www.watermarkcommunities.com/logansquare	Philadelphia	PA	19103	215-240-8915	
Waverly Heights 1400 Waverly Rd *Web:* www.waverlyheightsltd.org	Gladwyne	PA	19035	610-645-8600	645-8611
White Horse Village 535 Gradyville Rd *Web:* www.whitehorsevillage.org	Newtown Square	PA	19073	610-558-5000	558-5001
Willow Valley Lakes Manor 300 Willow Vly Lakes Dr *TF:* 800-770-5445 ■ *Web:* www.willowvalleyretirement.com	Willow Street	PA	17584	717-464-0800	464-2560
Bethea Baptist Retirement Community 157 Home Ave *Web:* bethearetirement.com	Darlington	SC	29532	843-393-2867	393-2458
Presbyterian Homes of SC 2817 Ashland Rd *TF:* 888-842-4855 ■ *Web:* preshomesc.org	Columbia	SC	29210	803-772-5885	772-5872
White Oak Manor Inc 130 E Main St PO Box 3347 *TF:* 800-826-6762 ■ *Web:* www.whiteoakmanor.com	Spartanburg	SC	29304	864-582-7503	573-9107
Brookdale Senior Living Inc 111 Westwood Pl Ste 400 *TF:* 866-785-9025 ■ *Web:* brookdale.com/	Brentwood	TN	37027	615-221-2250	221-2289
Army Residence Community 7400 Crestway *TF:* 800-725-0083 ■ *Web:* www.armyresidence.com	San Antonio	TX	78239	210-646-5316	646-5313
Bayou Manor 4141 S Braeswood Blvd *Web:* houstonretirement.org	Houston	TX	77025	713-666-2651	660-4800
Capital Senior Living Corp 14160 Dallas Pkwy Ste 300 *NYSE: CSU* ■ *Web:* www.capitalsenior.com	Dallas	TX	75254	972-770-5600	770-5666
Forum at Lincoln Heights 311 W Nottingham Pl *Web:* theforumatlincolnheights.com	San Antonio	TX	78209	210-824-2314	824-6556
Forum at Park Lane 7831 Pk Ln *Web:* theforumatparklane.com	Dallas	TX	75225	214-369-9902	373-1836
Grace Presbyterian Village 550 E Ann Arbor Ave *Web:* www.gracepresbyterianvillage.org	Dallas	TX	75216	214-376-1701	376-4350
John Knox Village of the Rio Grande Valley 1300 S Border Ave *Web:* johnknoxvillagergv.com	Weslaco	TX	78596	956-968-4575	968-4570
Manor Park Inc 2208 N Loop 250 W *TF:* 800-523-9898 ■ *Web:* www.manorparkinc.org	Midland	TX	79707	432-689-9898	694-2551
Rolling Meadows 3006 McNiel Ave *Web:* www.rmeadows.com	Wichita Falls	TX	76309	940-691-7511	696-5154
Temple Meridian 4312 S 31st St *TF:* 855-444-7658 ■ *Web:* brookdaleliving.com/	Temple	TX	76502	254-771-2350	
Westminster Manor 4100 Jackson Ave *Web:* westminsteraustintx.org	Austin	TX	78731	512-454-4643	371-7308
Brandermill Woods 14311 Brandermill Woods Trl *Web:* www.brandermillwoods.com	Midlothian	VA	23112	804-744-1173	744-4894
Colonnades, The 2600 Barracks Rd *Web:* www.sunriseseniorliving.com	Charlottesville	VA	22901	434-963-4198	963-4108
Culpeper Baptist Retirement Community 12425 Village Loop *TF:* 800-894-2411 ■ *Web:* culpeperretirement.org	Culpeper	VA	22701	540-825-2411	825-5123
Fairfax, The 9140 Belvoir Woods Pkwy *Web:* sunriseseniorliving.com	Fort Belvoir	VA	22060	703-799-1200	781-2448
Goodwin House 4800 Fillmore Ave *Web:* www.goodwinhouse.org	Alexandria	VA	22311	703-578-1000	824-1353
Goodwin House Bailey's Crossroads 3440 S Jefferson St *Web:* www.goodwinhouse.org	Falls Church	VA	22041	703-820-1488	578-7519
Hermitage, The 1600 Westwood Ave *Web:* www.hermitage-vumh.com/	Richmond	VA	23227	804-474-1800	358-0854
Jefferson, The 900 N Taylor St *Web:* www.sunriseseniorliving.com	Arlington	VA	22203	703-516-9455	516-9459
Lakewood Manor 1900 Lauderdale Dr *TF:* 866-521-9100 ■ *Web:* www.lakewoodmanor.org	Richmond	VA	23238	804-740-2900	740-3774
Shenandoah Valley Westminster-Canterbury 300 Westminster-Canterbury Dr *TF:* 800-492-9463 ■ *Web:* www.svwc.org	Winchester	VA	22603	540-665-5914	
Virginian, The 9229 Arlington Blvd *Web:* www.thevirginian.org	Fairfax	VA	22031	703-385-0555	
Washington House 5100 Fillmore Ave *Web:* www.watermarkcommunities.com/washingtonhouse	Alexandria	VA	22311	703-291-0188	
Westminster-Canterbury of Lynchburg 501 VES Rd *TF:* 800-962-3520 ■ *Web:* www.wclynchburg.org	Lynchburg	VA	24503	434-386-3500	386-3535
Westminster-Canterbury on Chesapeake Bay 3100 Shore Dr *TF:* 800-349-1722 ■ *Web:* www.wcbay.com	Virginia Beach	VA	23451	757-496-1100	496-1122
Westminster-Canterbury Richmond 1600 Westbrook Ave *TF:* 800-445-9904 ■ *Web:* www.wcrichmond.org	Richmond	VA	23227	804-264-6000	264-4579
Williamsburg Landing 5700 Williamsburg Landing Dr *TF:* 800-554-5517 ■ *Web:* www.williamsburglanding.com	Williamsburg	VA	23185	757-565-6505	565-6537
Bayview Retirement Community 11 W Aloha St *Web:* www.bayviewcommunity.org	Seattle	WA	98119	206-284-7330	284-9640
Hearthstone at Green Lake, The 6720 E Green Lk Way N *Web:* www.hearthstone.org	Seattle	WA	98103	206-525-9666	
Judson Park 23600 Marine View Dr S *TF:* 800-401-4113 ■ *Web:* www.judsonpark.com	Des Moines	WA	98198	206-824-4000	878-6404
Panorama City 1751 Cir Ln SE *TF:* 800-999-9807 ■ *Web:* www.panoramacity.org	Lacey	WA	98503	360-456-0111	438-5901
Park Shore 1630 43rd Ave E *Web:* www.parkshore.org	Seattle	WA	98112	206-329-0770	329-0227
Rockwood Retirement Community 2903 E 25th Ave *TF:* 800-727-6650 ■ *Web:* www.rockwoodretirement.org	Spokane	WA	99223	509-536-6650	536-6662
Wesley Homes 815 S 216th St *TF:* 866-937-5390 ■ *Web:* wesleyhomes.org	Des Moines	WA	98198	206-824-5000	870-1209
Milwaukee Catholic Home 2330 & 2462 N Prospect Ave *Web:* www.milwaukeecatholichome.org	Milwaukee	WI	53211	414-224-9700	224-1666
Oakwood Village West 5565 Tancho Dr *Web:* www.oakwoodvillage.net	Madison	WI	53705	608-230-4000	230-3286
Saint John's On the Lake 1840 N Prospect Ave *Web:* www.saintjohnsmilw.org	Milwaukee	WI	53202	414-831-7300	831-6760
Village at Manor Park, The (VMP) 3023 S 84th St *Web:* www.vmpcares.com	Milwaukee	WI	53227	414-607-4100	607-4504

676 RETREATS - SPIRITUAL

The facilities listed here offer basic amenities and services such as bed linens, food preparation, maid service, etc. Although physical activity may play a role in the programs offered, the focus is on the spiritual.

	City	State	Zip	Phone	Fax
Ashram, The PO Box 8009 *Web:* www.theashram.com	Calabasas	CA	91372	818-222-6900	222-7393
Benedict Inn Retreat & Conference Ctr 1402 Southern Ave *Web:* benedictine.com	Beech Grove	IN	46107	317-788-7581	782-3142
Bethany Retreat House 2202 Lituanica Ave *Web:* www.bethanyretreathouse.org	East Chicago	IN	46312	219-398-5047	398-9329
Bishop's Ranch 5297 Westside Rd *Web:* www.bishopsranch.org	Healdsburg	CA	95448	707-433-2440	433-3431
Bridge-Between Retreat Ctr, The 4471 Flaherty Ln *Web:* www.bridge-between.com	Denmark	WI	54208	920-864-7230	864-7044
Campion Renewal Ctr 319 Concord Rd *Web:* www.campioncenter.org	Weston	MA	02493	781-419-1337	894-5864
Catholic Diocese of Buffalo 6892 Lake Shore Rd PO Box 816 *Web:* www.buffalodiocese.org	Derby	NY	14047	716-947-4708	
Chopra Ctr at La Costa Resort & Spa 2013 Costa del Mar Rd *TF:* 888-424-6772 ■ *Web:* www.chopra.com	Carlsbad	CA	92009	760-494-1600	494-1608
Christ the King Retreat Ctr 621 First Ave S *Web:* www.kingshouse.com	Buffalo	MN	55313	763-682-1394	682-3453
Conception Abbey PO Box 501 *Web:* www.conceptionabbey.org	Conception	MO	64433	660-944-3100	944-2811
Elat Chayyim 116 Johnson Rd **Fax Area Code:* 860 ■ *TF:* 800-398-2630 ■ *Web:* isabellafreedman.org	Falls Village	CT	06031	800-398-2630	824-7228*
Enders Island PO Box 399 *Web:* www.endersisland.com	Mystic	CT	06355	860-536-0565	572-7655
Esalen Institute 55000 Hwy 1 *Web:* www.esalen.org	Big Sur	CA	93920	831-667-3000	667-2724
Expanding Light 14618 Tyler Foote Rd *TF:* 800-346-5350 ■ *Web:* www.expandinglight.org	Nevada City	CA	95959	530-478-7518	478-7519
Franciscan Spirituality Ctr 920 Market St *Web:* www.franciscanspiritualitycenter.org	La Crosse	WI	54601	608-791-5295	
Genesis Spiritual Life Ctr 53 Mill St *Web:* www.genesiscenter.us	Westfield	MA	01085	413-562-3627	572-1060
Harbin Hot Springs 18424 Harbin Springs Rd PO Box 782 *TF:* 800-622-2477 ■ *Web:* www.harbin.org	Middletown	CA	95461	707-987-2477	987-0616
Hollyhock PO Box 127 *TF:* 800-933-6339 ■ *Web:* www.hollyhock.ca	Mansons Landing	BC	V0P1K0	250-935-6576	935-6424
Holy Cross Monastery 1615 Rt 9W *Web:* www.holycrossmonastery.com	West Park	NY	12493	845-384-6660	384-6031
Jesuit Ctr for Spiritual Growth 501 N Church Rd *Web:* jesuitcenter.org	Wernersville	PA	19565	610-670-3642	670-3650
Jesuit Retreat House 300 Manresa Way *Web:* www.elretiro.org	Los Altos	CA	94022	650-917-4000	
Jesuit Spiritual Ctr 5361 S Milford Rd *Web:* www.jesuitspiritualcenter.com	Milford	OH	45150	513-248-3500	248-3503
Kalani Oceanside Retreat 12-6860 Kapoho Kalapana Rd *TF:* 800-800-6886 ■ *Web:* www.kalani.com	Pahoa	HI	96778	808-965-7828	965-0527
Kirkridge Retreat & Study Ctr 2495 Fox Gap Rd *TF:* 800-231-2222 ■ *Web:* www.kirkridge.org	Bangor	PA	18013	610-588-1793	588-8510
Kordes Retreat Ctr 841 E 14th St *Web:* www.thedome.org	Ferdinand	IN	47532	812-367-2777	367-2313
Laurelville Mennonite Church Ctr 941 Laurelville Ln *TF:* 800-839-1021 ■ *Web:* www.laurelville.org	Mount Pleasant	PA	15666	724-423-2056	423-2096
Linwood Spiritual Ctr 50 Linwood Rd *Web:* www.linwoodspiritualctr.org	Rhinebeck	NY	12572	845-876-4178	876-1920
Louhelen Baha'i School 3208 S State Rd *TF:* 800-894-9716 ■ *Web:* louhelen.org	Davison	MI	48423	810-653-5033	653-7181
Loyola House 5420 Hwy 6 N *Web:* www.loyolahouse.com	Guelph	ON	N1H6J2	519-824-1250	767-0994
Loyola Retreat House 161 James St *Web:* www.loyola.org	Morristown	NJ	07960	973-539-0740	898-9839
Manna House of Prayer 323 E Fifth St *Web:* www.mannahouse.org	Concordia	KS	66901	785-243-4428	243-4321
Marguerite Centre 700 Mackay St *Web:* www.margueritecentre.com	Pembroke	ON	K8A1G6	613-732-9925	

Phone Fax

Marie Joseph Spiritual Ctr 10 Evans Rd ... Biddeford ME 04005 207-284-5671 286-1371
Web: www.mariejosephspiritual.org

Marycrest Assisted Living 2850 Columbine Rd ... Denver CO 80221 303-433-0282
Web: www.marycrest.org

Mercy Ctr 2300 Adeline Dr ... Burlingame CA 94010 650-340-7474 340-1299
Web: www.mercy-center.org

Mercy Ctr at Madison 167 Neck Rd PO Box 191 ... Madison CT 06443 203-245-0401 245-8718
Web: www.mercybythesea.org

Mercy Ctr for Healing the Whole Person
520 W Buena Ventura ... Colorado Springs CO 80907 719-633-2302 633-1031
Web: www.mercycenter.com

Monastery of Saint Gertrude
465 Keuterville Rd ... Cottonwood ID 83522 208-962-3224 962-7212
Web: www.stgertrudes.org

Montserrat Jesuit Retreat House
600 N Shady Shores Dr PO Box 1390 ... Lake Dallas TX 75065 940-321-6020 321-6040
Web: www.montserratretreat.org

Mount Calvary Retreat House
PO Box 1296 ... Santa Barbara CA 93102 805-962-9855
Web: www.mount-calvary.org

Mount Carmel Ctr 4600 W Davis St ... Dallas TX 75211 214-331-6224
Web: www.mountcarmelcenter.org

Omega Institute for Holistic Studies
150 Lake Dr ... Rhinebeck NY 12572 845-266-4444 266-3769
TF: 800-944-1001 ■ *Web:* www.eomega.org

Omega Retreat & Spirituality Ctr
216 W Highland ... Boerne TX 78006 830-816-8504
Web: www.boernebenedictines.com

Our Lady of Fatima Retreat House
5353 E 56th St ... Indianapolis IN 46226 317-545-7681 545-0095
TF: 800-480-2520 ■ *Web:* www.archindy.org

Pecos Benedictine Monastery
Our Lady of Guadalupe Abbey PO Box 1080 ... Pecos NM 87552 505-757-6415
Web: www.pecosmonastery.org

Pendle Hill 338 Plush Mill Rd ... Wallingford PA 19086 610-566-4507 566-3679
TF: 800-742-3150 ■ *Web:* www.pendlehill.org

Priory Spirituality Ctr 500 College St NE ... Lacey WA 98516 360-438-2595 438-9236
Web: www.stplacid.org

Pumpkin Hollow Farm 1184 Rt 11 ... Craryville NY 12521 518-325-3583 325-5633
TF: 877-325-3583 ■ *Web:* www.pumpkinhollow.org

Quaker Hill Conference Ctr
10 Quaker Hill Dr ... Richmond IN 47374 765-962-5741
Web: www.qhcc.org/facilities.shtml

Redemptorist Retreat Ctr
1800 N Timber Trail Ln ... Oconomowoc WI 53066 262-567-6900 567-0134
Web: redemptoristretreat.org/

Rowe Camp & Conference Ctr
22 Kings Hwy Rd PO Box 273 ... Rowe MA 01367 413-339-4954 339-5728
Web: www.rowecenter.org

Saint Andrew's Abbey 31001 N Valyermo Rd ... Valyermo CA 93563 661-944-2178 944-1076
Web: www.valyermo.com

Saint Anthony Retreat Ctr 300 E Fourth St ... Marathon WI 54448 715-443-2236 443-2235
Web: www.sarcenter.com

Saint Francis Retreat Ctr
549 Mission VineyaRd Rd ... San Juan Bautista CA 95045 831-623-4234 623-9046
Web: www.stfrancisretreat.com

Saint Meinrad Archabbey 200 Hill Dr ... Saint Meinrad IN 47577 812-357-6585 357-6325
TF: 800-682-0988 ■ *Web:* www.saintmeinrad.edu

San Damiano Retreat Ctr
710 Highland Dr PO Box 767 ... Danville CA 94526 925-837-9141 837-0522
Web: www.sandamiano.org

Satchidananda Ashram Yogaville (SAYVA)
108 Yogaville Way ... Buckingham VA 23921 434-969-3121 969-1303*
**Fax Area Code:* 804 ■ *TF Resv:* 800-858-9642 ■ *Web:* yogaville.org

Serra Retreat Ctr 3401 Serra Rd ... Malibu CA 90265 310-456-6631 456-9417
Web: www.serraretreat.com

Shalom Prayer Ctr 840 S Main St ... Mount Angel OR 97362 503-845-6773
Web: www.benedictine-srs.org

Shambhala Mountain Ctr
151 Shambhala Wy ... Red Feather Lakes CO 80545 970-881-2184 881-2909
TF: 888-788-7221 ■ *Web:* www.shambhalamountain.org

Siena Ctr 5635 Erie St ... Racine WI 53402 262-639-4100 639-9702
Web: racinedominicans.org

Song of the Morning Yoga Retreat Ctr
9607 Sturgeon Vly Rd ... Vanderbilt MI 49795 989-983-4107
Web: www.songofthemorning.org

Sophia Spirituality Ctr 751 S Eigth St ... Atchison KS 66002 913-360-6173
Web: www.mountosb.org

Spiritual Life Ctr 7100 E 45th St N ... Wichita KS 67226 316-744-0167 744-8072
TF: 800-348-2440 ■ *Web:* catholicdioceseofwichita.org

Tabor Retreat Ctr 60 Anchor Ave ... Oceanside NY 11572 516-536-3004
Web: www.taborretreatcenter.org

Vivekananda Retreat Ridgely
101 Leggett Rd ... Stone Ridge NY 12484 845-687-4574 687-4578
Web: www.ridgely.org

Wainwright House 260 Stuyvesant Ave ... Rye NY 10580 914-967-6080 967-6114
Web: www.wainwright.org

Wisdom House Retreat & Conference Ctr
229 E Litchfield Rd ... Litchfield CT 06759 860-567-3163 567-3166
Web: www.wisdomhouse.org

WomanWell 1784 La Crosse Ave ... Saint Paul MN 55119 651-739-7953 739-7475

677 ROLLING MILL MACHINERY

SEE ALSO Metalworking Machinery p. 2757

Phone Fax

Abbey International Ltd 11140 Ave Rd ... Perrysburg OH 43552 419-874-4301 874-8200
Web: www.abbeyintl.com

Ampco-Pittsburgh Corp
600 Grant St Ste 4600 ... Pittsburgh PA 15219 412-456-4400 456-4404
NYSE: AP ■ *Web:* www.ampcopittsburgh.com

Bonell Manufacturing Co 13521 S Halsted St ... Riverdale IL 60827 708-849-1770 849-3434
Web: www.bonellmfg.com

Bradbury Company Inc 1200 E Cole ... Moundridge KS 67107 620-345-6394 345-6381
TF: 800-397-6394 ■ *Web:* bradburygroup.com

Fairfield Machine Company Inc
1143 Lower Elkton Rd PO Box 27 ... Columbiana OH 44408 330-482-3388 482-5052
Web: www.fairfieldmachine.com

Formtek Metal Forming Inc
4899 Commerce Pkwy ... Cleveland OH 44128 216-292-4460 831-7948
TF: 800-631-0520 ■ *Web:* www.formtekinc.com

Magnum Integrated Technologies Inc
200 First Gulf Blvd ... Brampton ON L6W4T5 905-595-1998 455-0422
TF: 800-830-0642 ■ *Web:* www.mit-world.com

T Sendzimir Inc 269 Brookside Rd ... Waterbury CT 06708 203-756-4617 756-4610
Web: www.sendzimir.com

WHEMCO Inc 5 Hot Metal St ... Pittsburgh PA 15203 412-390-2700 539-0645*
**Fax Area Code:* 724 ■ *TF:* 800-800-7686 ■ *Web:* www.whemco.com

678 ROYALTY TRUSTS

Phone Fax

ARC Resources Ltd 308 Fourth Ave SW Ste 1200 ... Calgary AB T2P0H7 403-503-8600
TSE: ARX ■ *TF:* 888-272-4900 ■ *Web:* www.arcresources.com

Great Northern Iron Ore Properties
332 Minnesota St Rm W1290 ... Saint Paul MN 55101 651-224-2385 224-2387
NYSE: GNI ■ *TF:* 800-468-9716 ■ *Web:* www.gniop.com

Harvest Energy Trust
330 Fifth Ave SW Ste 2100 ... Calgary AB T2P0L4 403-265-1178 266-3490
TF: 866-666-1178 ■ *Web:* www.harvestenergy.ca

Hugoton Royalty Trust
901 Main St 17th Fl PO Box 830650 ... Dallas TX 75283 214-209-2400 289-2431
NYSE: HGT

Marine Petroleum Trust
901 Main St Bank of America Plz 17th Fl ... Dallas TX 75202 214-209-2400
NASDAQ: MARPS ■ *Web:* www.marps-marine.com

North European Oil Royalty Trust
43 W Front St Ste 19A ... Red Bank NJ 07701 732-741-4008 741-3140
NYSE: NRT ■ *TF:* 800-368-5948 ■ *Web:* www.neort.com

Pengrowth Energy Trust
222 Third Ave SW Ste 2100 ... Calgary AB T2P0B4 403-233-0224 265-6251
NYSE: PGH ■ *TF:* 800-223-4122 ■ *Web:* www.pengrowth.com

Penn West Energy Trust
425 First St SW Ste 2200 ... Calgary AB T2P3L8 403-777-2500 777-2699
TF: 866-693-2707 ■ *Web:* www.pennwest.com

TAQA North Ltd 308-4th Ave ... Calgary AB T2P0H7 403-724-5000 724-5001
Web: taqaglobal.com

Texas Pacific Land Trust
1700 Pacific Ave Ste 2770 ... Dallas TX 75201 214-969-5530 871-7139
NYSE: TPL ■ *TF:* 877-231-7500 ■ *Web:* www.tpltrust.com

679 RUBBER GOODS

Phone Fax

Aero Tec Labs Inc 45 Spear Rd Industrial Pk ... Ramsey NJ 07446 201-825-1400 825-1962
TF: 800-526-5330 ■ *Web:* www.atlinc.com

Alliance Rubber Co 210 Carpenter Dam Rd ... Hot Springs AR 71901 800-626-5940 262-3948*
**Fax Area Code:* 501 ■ *TF:* 800-626-5940 ■ *Web:* www.rubberband.com

Biltrite Corp 51 Sawyer Rd ... Waltham MA 02454 781-647-1700 647-4205
TF: 800-877-8775 ■ *Web:* www.biltrite.com

BRP Manufacturing Co 637 N Jackson St ... Lima OH 45801 419-228-4441 222-5010
TF: 800-858-0482 ■ *Web:* www.brpmfg.com

Dawson Mfg Co 1042 N Crystal Ave ... Benton Harbor MI 49022 269-925-0100 925-0997
Web: www.dawsonmfg.com

Durable Products Inc PO Box 826 ... Crossville TN 38557 931-484-3502 456-7682
TF: 800-373-3502 ■ *Web:* www.durableproductsinc.com

Dynatect Mfg 2300 S Calhoun Rd ... New Berlin WI 53151 262-786-1500 786-3280
Web: www.gortite.com

EAM World 5502 NW 37th Ave ... Miami FL 33142 305-871-4050 637-8632
Web: www.theraft.com

Flexsys America LP 260 Springside Dr ... Akron OH 44333 330-666-4111
TF: 800-455-5622 ■ *Web:* www.eastman.com

Griswold Corp One River St PO Box 638 ... Moosup CT 06354 860-564-3321 564-9103
TF: 800-472-8788 ■ *Web:* www.griswoldcorp.com

Hutchinson Aerospace & Industry Inc
82 S St ... Hopkinton MA 01748 508-417-7000 417-7224*
**Fax:* Sales ■ *TF:* 800-227-7962 ■ *Web:* www.barrycontrols.com

Interstate Foam & Supply Inc PO Box 338 ... Conover NC 28613 828-459-9700 459-0300
Web: interstatefoamandsupply.com

Itran Precision Rubber
375 Metuchen Rd ... South Plainfield NJ 07080 908-754-8100 757-1820
Web: www.itranrubber.com

Jet Rubber Company Inc 4457 Tallmadge Rd ... Rootstown OH 44272 330-325-1821 325-2876
Web: www.jetrubber.com

Kent Elastomer Products Inc 1500 St Claire Ave ... Kent OH 44240 330-673-1011 673-1351
TF Cust Svc: 800-331-4762 ■ *Web:* www.kentelastomer.com

Koneta Inc 1400 Lunar Dr ... Wapakoneta OH 45895 419-739-4200 739-4247
TF: 800-331-0775 ■ *Web:* knrubber.com

Ludlow Composites Corp 2100 Commerce Dr ... Fremont OH 43420 800-628-5463 332-7776*
**Fax Area Code:* 419 ■ *TF:* 800-628-5463 ■ *Web:* www.ludlow-comp.com

Mitchell Rubber Products Inc
10220 San Sevaine Way ... Mira Loma CA 91752 800-453-7526 681-1479*
**Fax Area Code:* 951 ■ *TF:* 800-453-7526 ■ *Web:* www.mitchellrubber.com

Mosites Rubber Company Inc PO Box 2115 ... Fort Worth TX 76113 817-335-3451 870-1564
Web: www.mositesrubber.com

MSM Industries Inc 802 Swan Dr ... Smyrna TN 37167 615-355-4355 355-6874
TF: 800-648-6648 ■ *Web:* www.msmind.com

Musson Rubber Company Inc 1320 E Archwood Ave ... Akron OH 44306 330-773-7651 773-3254
TF Cust Svc: 800-321-2381 ■ *Web:* www.mussonrubber.com

				Phone	Fax
National Rubber Technologies Corp 35 Cawthra Ave. Toronto	ON	M6N5B3		416-657-1111	656-1231
TF: 800-387-8501 ■ *Web:* www.knrubber.com					
Patch Rubber Co PO Box H Roanoke Rapids	NC	27870		252-536-2574	536-4108
Web: www.patchrubber.com					
Pawling Corp 32 Nelson Hill Rd PO Box 200 Wassaic	NY	12592		800-431-3456	373-9300*
**Fax Area Code:* 845 ■ *TF:* 800-431-3456 ■ *Web:* www.pawling.com					
Philpott Rubber Co 1010 Industrial Pkwy Brunswick	OH	44212		330-225-3344	225-1999
Web: www.philpottrubber.com					
Plasticoid Co 249 W High St Elkton	MD	21921		410-398-2800	398-2803
Web: www.plasticoid.com					
Proco Products Inc PO Box 590 Stockton	CA	95201		209-943-6088	943-0242
TF: 800-344-3246 ■ *Web:* www.procoproducts.com					
R & K Industrial Products Co 1945 Seventh St Richmond	CA	94801		510-234-7212	234-1923
TF: 800-842-7655 ■ *Web:* www.rkwheels.com					
Regupol America 33 Keystone Dr Lebanon	PA	17042		800-537-8737	675-2199*
**Fax Area Code:* 717 ■ *TF:* 800-537-8737 ■ *Web:* www.regupol.com					
Rubber Industries Inc 200 Cavanaugh Dr Shakopee	MN	55379		952-445-1320	445-7934
Web: www.rubberindustries.com					
Seismic Energy Products LP (SEP) 518 Progress Way Athens	TX	75751		903-675-8571	677-4980
Web: www.sepbearings.com					
Shercon Inc 6262 Katella Ave Cypress	CA	90630		714-548-3999	
TF: 888-227-5847 ■ *Web:* www.caplugs.com					
SMR Technologies Inc 93 Nettie Fenwick Rd Fenwick	WV	26202		304-846-6636	846-2024
TF: 800-767-6899 ■ *Web:* www.smrtech.com					
Star-Glo Industries LLC Two Carlton Ave East Rutherford	NJ	07073		201-939-6162	939-4054
Web: www.starglo.com					
Swarco Industries Inc PO Box 89 Columbia	TN	38402		931-388-5900	388-4039
Web: www.swarco.com					
Teknor Apex Co 505 Central Ave Pawtucket	RI	02861		401-725-8000	725-8095
TF: 800-556-3864 ■ *Web:* www.teknorapex.com					
Vulcan Corp 30 Garfield Pl Ste 1040 Cincinnati	OH	45202		513-621-2850	241-8199
TF Sales: 800-447-1146 ■ *Web:* www.vulcorp.com					

680 RUBBER GOODS - MECHANICAL

Mechanical rubber goods are rubber components used in machinery, such as o-rings, sprockets, sleeves, roller covers, etc.

			Phone	Fax
Acme Machell 2000 Airport Rd Waukesha	WI	53188	262-521-2870	521-2894
AGC Inc 106 Evansville Ave Meriden	CT	06451	203-639-7125	235-6543
Web: www.agcincorporated.com				
AirBoss of America Corp 16441 Yonge St Newmarket	ON	L3X2G8	905-751-1188	751-1101
TSE: BOS ■ *Web:* www.airbossofamerica.com				
American National Rubber Co Main & High St Ceredo	WV	25507	304-453-1311	453-2347*
**Fax:* Sales ■ *TF Cust Svc:* 800-624-3410 ■ *Web:* www.anr-co.com				
American Roller Co 1440 13th Ave Union Grove	WI	53182	262-878-8665	878-1932
Web: www.americanroller.com				
Ames Corp 19 Ames Blvd Hamburg	NJ	07419	973-827-9101	827-8893
Web: www.theamescorp.com				
Armada Rubber Mfg Co 24586 Armada Ridge Rd PO Box 579 Armada	MI	48005	586-784-9135	784-5023
TF: 800-842-8311 ■ *Web:* www.armadarubber.com				
Ashtabula Rubber Co 2751 W Ave Ashtabula	OH	44004	440-992-2195	992-7829
Web: www.ashtabularubber.com				
Atlantic India Rubber Co 1437 Kentucky Rt 1428 Hagerhill	KY	41222	800-476-6638	789-9098*
**Fax Area Code:* 606 ■ *TF:* 800-476-6638 ■ *Web:* www.atlanticindia.com				
BRC Rubber Group Inc PO Box 227 Churubusco	IN	46723	260-693-2171	693-6511
Web: www.brcrp.com				
Buckhorn Rubber Products Inc 5151 Industrial Dr Hannibal	MO	63401	573-221-8933	221-7144
Web: www.buckhornrubber.com				
Central Rubber & Plastics 17416 County Rd 34 Goshen	IN	46528	574-534-6411	
Web: www.centralrubbercompany.com				
Colonial Diversified Polymer Products LLC 2055 Forrest St Ext PO Box 930 Dyersburg	TN	38025	731-287-3636	287-3691
Web: www.colonialdpp.com				
Connor Corp 10633 Coldwater Rd Ste 200 Fort Wayne	IN	46845	260-424-1601	
Web: www.connorcorp.com				
Da/Pro Rubber Inc 601 N Poplar Ave Broken Arrow	OK	74012	918-258-9386	258-3286
Web: www.daprorubber.com				
Derby Cellular Products Inc 150 Roosevelt Dr Derby	CT	06418	203-735-4661	
Fabreeka International Inc 1023 Tpke St Stoughton	MA	02072	781-341-3655	341-3983
TF Cust Svc: 800-322-7352 ■ *Web:* www.fabreeka.com				
Finzer Roller Co 129 Rawls Rd Des Plaines	IL	60018	847-390-6200	390-6201
TF: 888-486-1900 ■ *Web:* www.finzerroller.com				
Flexan Corp 6626 W Dakin St Chicago	IL	60634	773-685-6446	685-6630
Web: www.flexan.com				
Flexible Products Co 2600 Auburn Ct Auburn Hills	MI	48326	248-852-5500	852-8620
Web: www.flexible-products.com				
Grand River Rubber & Plastics Co 2029 Aetna Rd Ashtabula	OH	44004	440-998-2900	
Web: www.grrp.com				
Griffith Rubber Mills 2625 NW Industrial St Portland	OR	97210	503-226-6971	226-6976
TF: 800-321-9677 ■ *Web:* griffithrubber.com				
Hiawatha Rubber Co 1700 67th Ave N Minneapolis	MN	55430	763-566-0900	566-9537
Web: www.hiawatharubber.com				
Holz Rubber Company Inc 1129 S Sacramento St Lodi	CA	95240	209-368-7171	368-3246
TF: 800-285-1600 ■ *Web:* www.holzrubber.com				
IER Fujikura Inc 8271 Bavaria Rd Macedonia	OH	44056	330-425-7125	425-7596
Web: www.ierfujikura.com				
Jamak Fabrication Inc 1401 N Bowie Dr Weatherford	TX	76086	817-594-8771	594-8324
TF: 800-543-4747 ■ *Web:* www.jamak.com				
Jasper Rubber Products Inc 1010 First Ave Jasper	IN	47546	812-482-3242	482-0816
TF: 800-457-7457 ■ *Web:* www.jasperrubber.com				
Johnson Bros Rubber Inc 42 W Buckeye St West Salem	OH	44287	419-853-4122	853-4062
Web: www.johnsonbrosrubbercompany.com				
Jonal Laboratories Inc PO Box 743 Meriden	CT	06450	203-634-4444	634-4448
Web: www.jonal.com				
Karman Rubber Co 2331 Copley Rd Akron	OH	44320	330-864-2161	864-2124
Web: www.karman.com				
Kirkhill Manufacturing Co 12023 Woodruff Ave Downey	CA	90241	562-803-1117	803-3117
Web: www.rubbersales.com				
Kirkhill-TA Co 300 E Cypress St Brea	CA	92821	714-529-4901	529-6775
Web: www.esterline.com				
Lauren Mfg 2228 Reiser Ave SE New Philadelphia	OH	44663	330-339-3373	339-1515
TF: 855-989-9090 ■ *Web:* www.lauren.com				
Lavelle Industries Inc 665 McHenry St Burlington	WI	53105	262-763-2434	763-5607
TF: 800-528-3553 ■ *Web:* www.lavelle.com				
Longwood Elastomers Inc 706 Green Valley Rd Ste 212 Greensboro	NC	27408	336-272-3710	272-3710
Web: www.longwoodindustries.com				
Lord Corp 111 Lord Dr Cary	NC	27511	919-468-5979	
TF: 877-275-5673 ■ *Web:* www.lord.com				
Mantaline Corp 4754 E High St Mantua	OH	44255	330-274-2264	274-8850
Web: www.mantaline.com				
MGI Coutier 603 W Seventh St Cadillac	MI	49601	231-775-6571	775-8731
Web: mgicoutier.com				
Minor Rubber Company Inc 49 Ackerman St Bloomfield	NJ	07003	973-338-6800	893-1399
TF: 800-433-6886 ■ *Web:* www.minorrubber.com				
MOCAP Inc 409 Parkway Dr Park Hills	MO	63601	314-543-4000	543-4111
TF: 800-633-6775 ■ *Web:* www.mocap.com				
Molded Rubber & Plastic Corp 13161 W Glendale Ave Butler	WI	53007	262-781-7122	781-5353
Web: www.mrpcorp.com				
Neff-Perkins Co 16080 Industrial Pkwy Middlefield	OH	44062	440-632-1658	632-1206
Web: www.neffp.com				
OMNI Products Inc 3911 Dayton St Mchenry	IL	60050	815-344-3100	
Web: www.omnirail.com				
Pamarco 171 E Marquardt Dr Wheeling	IL	60090	847-459-6000	459-6277
TF Sales: 800-323-7735 ■ *Web:* www.pamarcoglobal.com				
Polymeric Technology Inc 1900 Marina Blvd San Leandro	CA	94577	510-895-6001	
Web: ww.poly-tek.com				
Polyneer Inc 259-D Samuel Barnet Blvd New Bedford	MA	02745	508-998-5225	
Web: www.polyneer.com				
Precision Assoc Inc 3800 N Washington Ave Minneapolis	MN	55412	612-333-7464	342-2417
TF: 800-394-6590 ■ *Web:* www.precisionassoc.com				
Precix Inc 744 Bellville Ave New Bedford	MA	02745	508-998-4000	998-4100
Web: www.precixinc.com				
Prince Rubber & Plastics Company Inc 137 Arthur St Buffalo	NY	14207	716-877-7400	877-0743
Web: www.princerp.com				
Quality Synthetic Rubber Inc 1700 Highland Rd Twinsburg	OH	44087	330-425-8472	425-7976
Web: www.qsr-inc.com				
Reiss Manufacturing Inc 75 Mt Vernon Rd Englishtown	NJ	07726	732-446-6100	446-1394
Web: www.reissbuilt.com				
RotaDyne Corp 8140 S Cass Ave Darien	IL	60561	630-769-9700	769-9255
Web: www.rotadyne.com				
RPP Corp 12 Ballard Way Lawrence	MA	01843	978-689-2800	
Web: www.rppcorp.com				
Sperry & Rice Mfg Company LLC 9146 US Hwy 52 Brookville	IN	47012	765-647-4141	647-3302
TF: 800-541-9277 ■ *Web:* www.sperryrice.com				
Thermodyn Corp 3550 Silica Rd Sylvania	OH	43560	419-841-7782	841-3139
TF: 800-654-6518 ■ *Web:* www.thermodyn.com				
Triangle Rubber Company Inc PO Box 95 Goshen	IN	46527	574-533-3118	534-0416
Web: www.trianglerubberco.com				
Trostel Ltd 901 Maxwell St Lake Geneva	WI	53147	262-248-4481	248-6406
Web: www.trostel.com				
Universal Polymer & Rubber Ltd 15730 Madison Rd Middlefield	OH	44062	440-632-1691	632-5761
TF: 800-782-2375 ■ *Web:* www.universalpolymer.com				
Vail Rubber Works Inc 521 Langley Ave Saint Joseph	MI	49085	269-983-1595	983-0155
Web: www.vailrubber.com				
Vernay Laboratories Inc 120 E S College St Yellow Springs	OH	45387	937-767-7261	767-7913*
**Fax:* Sales ■ *Web:* www.vernay.com				
Wabtec Rubber Products 269 Donohue Rd Greensburg	PA	15601	724-838-1317	832-5630
Web: www.wabtec.com				
West American Rubber Co LLC 1337 Braden Ct Orange	CA	92868	714-532-3355	532-2238
Web: www.warco.com				
YUSA Corp 151 Jamison Rd SW Washington Court House	OH	43160	740-335-0335	335-0330
Web: yusa-oh.com				

681 SAFETY EQUIPMENT - MFR

SEE ALSO Medical Supplies - Mfr p. 2733; Personal Protective Equipment & Clothing p. 2914

			Phone	Fax
ACR Electronics Inc 5757 Anglers Ave Fort Lauderdale	FL	33312	954-981-3333	983-5087
TF: 800-432-0227 ■ *Web:* www.acrartex.com				
Adams Elevator Equipment Co 6310 W Howard St Niles	IL	60714	847-581-2900	581-2949
TF: 800-929-9247 ■ *Web:* www.adamselevator.com				
Aerial Machine & Tool Corp 4298 Jeb Stuart Hwy PO Box 222 Vesta	VA	24177	276-952-2006	952-2231
Web: www.aerialmachineandtool.com				
Air Cruisers Co 1747 New Jersey 34 Wall Township	NJ	07727	732-681-3527	681-9163
Web: zodiacaerospace.com/en/zodiac-aero-evacuation-systems-air-cruisers				
ALP Industries Inc 1229 W Lincoln Hwy Coatesville	PA	19320	610-384-1300	384-7300
TF: 800-220-2571 ■ *Web:* www.alpind.com				
Amerex Corp 7595 Gadsden Hwy PO Box 81 Trussville	AL	35173	205-655-3271	655-3279
Web: www.amerex-fire.com				
AmSafe Inc 1043 N 47th Ave Phoenix	AZ	85043	602-850-2850	850-2812
Web: www.amsafe.com				

	City	State	ZIP	Phone	Fax
Ancra International LLC 4880 W Rosecrans Ave *TF:* 800-973-5092 ■ *Web:* www.ancra-llc.com	Hawthorne	CA	90250	310-973-5000	973-1138
Autoliv Inc 3350 Airport Rd *NYSE: ALV* ■ *Web:* www.autoliv.com	Ogden	UT	84405	801-625-8200	629-9111
Bradley Corp W 142 N 9101 Fountain Blvd *TF:* 800-272-3539 ■ *Web:* www.bradleycorp.com	Menomonee Falls	WI	53051	262-251-6000	251-5817
Buckeye Fire Equipment Co 110 Kings Rd PO Box 428 *Web:* www.buckeyef.com	Kings Mountain	NC	28086	704-739-7415	739-7418
Carsonite Composites LLC 19845 US Hwy 76 *TF:* 800-648-7916 ■ *Web:* www.carsonite.com	Newberry	SC	29108	803-321-1185	276-8940
Central Research Laboratories 3965 Pepin Ave *Web:* www.centres.com	Red Wing	MN	55066	651-388-3565	388-1232
CSE Corp 600 Seco Rd *TF:* 800-245-2224 ■ *Web:* www.csecorporation.com	Monroeville	PA	15146	412-856-9200	856-9203
Delta Scientific Corp 40355 Delta Ln *Web:* www.deltascientific.com	Palmdale	CA	93551	661-575-1100	575-1109
Encon Safety Products Co 6825 W Sam Houston Pkwy N PO Box 3826 *TF:* 800-283-6266 ■ *Web:* www.enconsafety.com	Houston	TX	77041	713-466-1449	466-1703
Energy Absorption Systems Inc 35 E Wacker Dr Ste 1100 *Web:* www.energyabsorption.com	Chicago	IL	60601	312-467-6750	467-1356
Gemtor Inc One Johnson Ave *TF:* 800-405-9048 ■ *Web:* www.gemtor.com	Matawan	NJ	07747	732-583-6200	290-9391
Hawkins Traffic Safety Supply 1255 E Shore Hwy **Fax Area Code:* 510 ■ *TF:* 800-772-3995 ■ *Web:* hawkinstraffic.com	Berkeley	CA	94710	800-236-0112	525-2861*
Herbert S Hiller Corp 401 Commerce Pt *TF:* 800-833-5211 ■ *Web:* www.hillercompanies.com	New Orleans	LA	70123	504-736-0008	736-0030
Key Safety Systems Inc 7000 Nineteen Mile Rd *OTC: BDTTZ* ■ *Web:* www.keysafetyinc.com	Sterling Heights	MI	48314	586-726-3800	726-4150
Mercedes Textiles Ltd 5838 Cypihot St *Web:* www.mercedestextiles.com	Ville Saint Laurent	QC	H4S1Y5	514-335-4337	335-9633
Monaco Enterprises Inc 14820 E Sprague Ave PO Box 14129 *Web:* www.monaco.com	Spokane	WA	99216	509-926-6277	924-4980
North American Fire Hose 910 E Noble Way *Web:* www.northamericanfirehose.com	Santa Maria	CA	93454	805-922-7076	922-0086
Ocenco Inc 10225 82nd Ave *TF:* 800-932-2293 ■ *Web:* www.ocenco.com	Pleasant Prairie	WI	53158	262-947-9000	947-9020
Peck & Hale LLC 180 Div Ave *Web:* www.peckhale.com	West Sayville	NY	11796	631-589-2510	589-2925
Peerless Chain Co 1416 E Sanborn St **Fax Area Code:* 800 ■ *TF:* 800-533-8056 ■ *Web:* www.peerlesschain.com	Winona	MN	55987	507-457-9100	356-1149*
Peerless Industrial Group PO Box 949 **Fax Area Code:* 503 ■ *TF:* 800-547-6806 ■ *Web:* www.peerlesschain.com	Clackamas	OR	97015	800-873-1916	656-4836*
Plastic Safety Systems Inc 2444 Baldwin Rd **Fax Area Code:* 216 ■ *TF:* 800-662-6338 ■ *Web:* www.plasticsafety.com	Cleveland	OH	44104	800-662-6338	231-2702*
Potter-Roemer 17451 Hurley St *TF:* 800-366-3473 ■ *Web:* www.potterroemer.com	City of Industry	CA	91744	626-855-4890	937-4777
Reflexite North America 315 S St *TF:* 800-654-7570 ■ *Web:* www.orafol.com	New Britain	CT	06051	860-223-9297	832-9267
Rite-Hite Corp 8900 N Arbon Dr *TF:* 800-456-0600 ■ *Web:* www.ritehite.com	Milwaukee	WI	53224	414-355-2600	355-9248
Rostra Precision Controls Inc 2519 Dana Dr *TF Cust Svc:* 800-782-3379 ■ *Web:* www.rostra.com	Laurinburg	NC	28352	910-276-4853	276-1354
Safety Components International Inc 40 Emery St *Web:* www.safetycomponents.com	Greenville	SC	29605	864-240-2692	
Simulaids 16 Simulaids Dr PO Box 1289 *Web:* www.simulaids.com	Saugerties	NY	12477	845-679-2475	679-8996
Takata Inc 2500 Takata Dr *Web:* www.takata.com	Auburn Hills	MI	48326	248-373-8040	377-2897
Tread Corp 176 Eastpark Dr *Web:* www.treadcorp.com	Roanoke	VA	24019	540-982-6881	344-7536

682 SAFETY EQUIPMENT - WHOL

	City	State	ZIP	Phone	Fax
Allstar Fire Equipment Inc 12328 Lower Azusa Rd *TF:* 800-425-5787 ■ *Web:* www.allstarfire.com	Arcadia	CA	91006	626-652-0900	652-0920
Arbill PO Box 820542 *TF:* 800-523-5367 ■ *Web:* www.arbill.com	Philadelphia	PA	19154	800-523-5367	426-5808
Brooks Equipment Company Inc 10926 David Taylor Dr Ste 300 *TF:* 800-826-3473 ■ *Web:* www.brooksequipment.com	Charlotte	NC	28269	800-826-3473	433-9265
Broward Fire Equipment & Service Inc 101 SW Sixth St *TF:* 800-866-3473 ■ *Web:* www.browardfire.com	Fort Lauderdale	FL	33301	954-467-6625	467-6640
Calolympic Glove & Safety Company Inc 1720 Delilah St *TF:* 800-421-6630 ■ *Web:* www.caloly-safety.com	Corona	CA	92879	951-340-2229	340-3337
Choctaw-Kaul Distribution Co 3540 Vinewood Ave *Web:* www.choctawkaul.com	Detroit	MI	48208	313-894-9494	894-7977
Continental Safety Equipment 2935 Waters Rd Ste 140 *TF:* 800-844-7003 ■ *Web:* www.csesafety.com	Eagan	MN	55121	651-454-7233	454-3217
Dunn Safety Products Inc 37 S Sangamon St *Web:* www.dunnsafety.com	Chicago	IL	60607	312-666-5800	666-5090
Empire Safety & Supply Inc 10624 Industrial Ave **Fax Area Code:* 888 ■ *TF:* 800-995-1341 ■ *Web:* www.empiresafety.com	Roseville	CA	95678	916-781-3003	882-9060*
Fire Fighters Equipment Co 3053 Rt 10 E *Web:* www.ffecnj.com	Denville	NJ	07834	973-366-4466	
Fire Protection Service Inc 8050 Harrisburg Blvd *Web:* www.fps-usa.com	Houston	TX	77012	713-924-9600	923-6272
International Fire Equipment Corp 500 Telser Rd *Web:* www.intlfire.com	Lake Zurich	IL	60047	847-438-2343	438-1869
La Grand Industrial Supply Co 2620 SW First Ave *Web:* lagrandindustrial.net	Portland	OR	97201	503-224-5800	
LaFrance Equipment Corp 516 Erie St *TF:* 800-873-8808 ■ *Web:* www.lafrance-equipment.com	Elmira	NY	14904	607-733-5511	733-0482
LN Curtis & Sons 1800 Peralta St *TF:* 800-443-3556 ■ *Web:* www.lncurtis.com	Oakland	CA	94607	510-839-5111	839-5325
Mid-Continent Safety 8225 E 35th St N *TF General:* 800-776-0956 ■ *Web:* www.midsafe.com/store/index.cfm	Wichita	KS	67226	316-522-0900	
Minnesota Conway 575 Minnehaha Ave W St *TF:* 800-223-2587 ■ *Web:* www.summitfire.com	Saint Paul	MN	55103	651-251-1880	251-1879
Nardini Fire Equipment Company Inc 405 County Rd E W *TF:* 888-627-3464 ■ *Web:* www.nardinifire.com	Saint Paul	MN	55126	651-483-6631	483-6945
Orr Safety Corp 11601 Interchange Dr *TF:* 800-726-6789 ■ *Web:* www.orrsafety.com	Louisville	KY	40229	502-774-5791	776-8030
PK Safety Supply 2005 Clement Ave Bldg 9 *TF:* 800-829-9580 ■ *Web:* www.pksafety.com	Alameda	CA	94501	510-337-8880	337-8890
Reliable Fire Equipment Co 12845 S Cicero Ave *Web:* www.reliablefire.com	Alsip	IL	60803	708-597-4600	389-1150
Saf-T-Gard International Inc 205 Huehl Rd *TF:* 800-548-4273 ■ *Web:* www.saftgard.com	Northbrook	IL	60062	847-291-1600	291-1610
Safety Products Inc 3517 Craftsman Blvd **Fax Area Code:* 800 ■ *TF:* 800-248-6860 ■ *Web:* www.spisafety.com	Lakeland	FL	33803	863-665-3601	330-0395*
Safety Supply South Inc 100 Centrum Dr **Fax Area Code:* 803 ■ *TF Cust Svc:* 800-522-8344 ■ *Web:* www.safetysupplysouth.com	Irmo	SC	29063	800-522-8344	732-3696*
Safeware Inc 3200 HubbaRd Rd *TF Cust Svc:* 800-331-6707 ■ *Web:* www.safewareinc.com	Landover	MD	20785	301-683-1234	683-1200
Sanderson Safety Supply Co 1101 SE Third Ave *Web:* www.sandersonsafety.com	Portland	OR	97214	503-238-5700	238-6443
Stauffer Glove & Safety PO Box 45 *Web:* my.stauffersafety.com	Red Hill	PA	18076	215-679-4446	679-5053
Sun Devil Fire Equipment Inc 2929 W Clarendon Ave **Fax Area Code:* 602 ■ *TF:* 800-536-3845 ■ *Web:* www.sundevilfire.com	Phoenix	AZ	85017	623-245-0636	495-9291*
United Fire Equipment Co 335 N Fourth Ave *TF:* 800-362-0150 ■ *Web:* unitedfire.net	Tucson	AZ	85705	520-622-3639	882-3991
Wayest Safety Inc 3750 N I-44 Service Rd *TF:* 800-256-1003 ■ *Web:* northernsafety.com/wayest	Oklahoma City	OK	73112	405-942-7101	942-5289
Wenaas AGS Inc 12211 Parc Crest Dr Bldg Ste 100 *TF:* 888-576-2668 ■ *Web:* www.wenaasusa.com	Stafford	TX	77477	281-931-4300	931-4328

683 SALT

SEE ALSO Spices, Seasonings, Herbs p. 2311

Companies listed here produce salt that may be used for a variety of purposes, including as a food ingredient or for deicing, water conditioning, or other chemical or industrial applications.

	City	State	ZIP	Phone	Fax
Cargill Inc North America 15407 McGinty Rd *Web:* cargill.com	Wayzata	MN	55391	952-742-7575	
Cargill Salt Inc PO Box 5621 *TF:* 888-385-7258 ■ *Web:* www.cargill.com	Minneapolis	MN	55440	888-385-7258	
Compass Minerals International 9900 W 109th St Ste 100 *NYSE: CMP* ■ *TF Cust Svc:* 866-755-1743 ■ *Web:* www.compassminerals.com	Overland Park	KS	66210	913-344-9200	
Morton Salt Inc 123 N Wacker Dr **Fax:* Cust Svc ■ *TF:* 800-725-8847 ■ *Web:* www.mortonsalt.com	Chicago	IL	60606	312-807-2000	807-2899*
North American Salt Co 9900 W 109th St Ste 100 *Web:* www.nasalt.com	Overland Park	KS	66210	913-344-9100	
United Salt Corp 4800 San Felipe St *TF:* 800-554-8658 ■ *Web:* www.unitedsalt.com	Houston	TX	77056	713-877-2600	877-2609

684 SATELLITE COMMUNICATIONS SERVICES

SEE ALSO Cable & Other Pay Television Services p. 1897; Internet Service Providers (ISPs) p. 2589; Telecommunications Services p. 3208

	City	State	ZIP	Phone	Fax
American International Radio Inc 3601 E Algonquin Rd Ste 800 *Web:* www.airadio.com	Rolling Meadows	IL	60008	847-818-9999	
ARINC Inc 2551 Riva Rd *TF:* 866-321-6060 ■ *Web:* www.arinc.com	Annapolis	MD	21401	410-266-4000	573-3300
Broken Arrow Communications Inc 8316 Corona Loop NE *Web:* www.bacom-inc.com	Albuquerque	NM	87113	505-877-2100	877-2101
Bytemobile Inc 2860 De La Cruz Blvd Second Fl *Web:* www.citrix.com	Santa Clara	CA	95050	408-327-7700	327-7701
Cableworks Communications Inc 3112 Main St Unit #3 *Web:* www.cableworkscommunications.com	Salisbury	NB	E4J2L6	506-372-9542	
CapRock Communications Inc 4400 S Sam Houston Pkwy E *Web:* www.harriscaprock.com	Houston	TX	77048	832-668-2300	668-2388
Fleet Management Solutions Inc 3426 Empresa Dr Ste 100 *Web:* www.fmsgps.com	San Luis Obispo	CA	93401	805-787-0508	

	City	State	Zip	Phone	Fax
Force10 Networks Inc 1415 N McDowell Blvd. *TF:* 866-600-5100 ■ *Web:* www.force10networks.com	Petaluma	CA	94954	707-665-4400	792-4938
Globalstar LP 3200 Zanker Rd Bldg 260 *TF:* 877-728-7466 ■ *Web:* www.globalstar.com	San Jose	CA	95134	408-933-4000	933-4100
Ground Control Systems Inc 3100 El Camino Real *Web:* www.groundcontrol.com	Atascadero	CA	93422	805-783-4600	
Intelsat Ltd 3400 International Dr NW *Web:* www.intelsat.com	Washington	DC	20008	703-559-6800	559-7898
International Satellite Services Inc 1004 Collier Ctr Way Ste 205 *Web:* www.internationalsatelliteservices.com	Naples	FL	34110	239-598-2241	
ISYS Technologies Inc 801 W Mineral Ave Ste 105 *Web:* www.isystechnologies.com	Littleton	CO	80120	303-290-8922	
Lightriver Technologies Inc 2150 John Glenn Dre Ste 200 **Fax Area Code:* 925 ■ *TF:* 888-544-4825 ■ *Web:* www.lightriver.com	Concord	CA	94520	941-552-9410	299-9521*
Linkus Enterprises Inc 5595 W San Madele Ave *Web:* linkuscorp.com	Fresno	CA	93722	559-256-6600	
MDU Communications International Inc 60 D Commerce Way *OTC:* MDTV ■ *TF:* 866-286-9638 ■ *Web:* mymdu.com	Totowa	NJ	07512	973-237-9499	237-9243
Microspace Communications Corp 3100 Highwoods Blvd Ste 120 *Web:* www.microspace.com	Raleigh	NC	27604	919-850-4500	850-4518
MTN/ATC Teleports 3044 N Commerce Pkwy *TF:* 877-464-4686 ■ *Web:* www.mtnsat.com	Miramar	FL	33025	954-538-4000	431-4077
Northstar Broadband LLC 3660 E Covington Ave Ste C *Web:* www.northstarbroadband.net	Post Falls	ID	83854	208-262-9394	
ORBCOMM 22265 Pacific Blvd Ste 200 *TF Cust Svc:* 877-538-7764 ■ *Web:* www.orbcomm.com	Dulles	VA	20166	703-433-6300	
Outerlink Corp 187 Ballardvale St Ste A260 *TF:* 877-688-3770 ■ *Web:* www.outerlink.com	Wilmington	MA	01887	978-284-6070	268-5444
Quantum Dimension Inc 15061 Springdale St Ste 202 *Web:* www.qdimension.com	Huntington Beach	CA	92649	714-893-6004	
SES World Skies Four Research Way **Fax:* Mktg ■ *Web:* www.ses.com	Princeton	NJ	08540	609-987-4000	987-4517*
SpaceNet Inc 1750 Old Meadow Rd **Fax Area Code:* 800 ■ *Web:* www.spacenet.com	McLean	VA	22102	703-848-1000	325-9202*
SS8 Networks Inc 750 Tasman Dr *Web:* www.ss8.com	Milpitas	CA	95035	408-944-0250	428-3732
Star West Satellite Inc 580 Pronghorn Dr *Web:* www.starwestsatellite.net	Bozeman	MT	59718	406-522-8402	
Stratos Global Corp 6550 Rock Spring Dr Ste 650 *TF:* 800-563-2255 ■ *Web:* www.stratosglobal.com	Bethesda	MD	20817	301-214-8800	214-8801
Telesat 1601 Telesat Ct *Web:* www.telesat.com	Ottawa	ON	K1B5P4	613-748-0123	748-8712
United Launch Alliance LLC Galileo Operations Ctr 9501 E Panorama Cir *Web:* www.ulalaunch.com	Centennial	CO	80112	720-922-7100	
ViaSat Inc 6155 El Camino Real *NASDAQ:* VSAT ■ *TF:* 877-363-7396 ■ *Web:* www.viasat.com	Carlsbad	CA	92009	760-476-2200	929-3941

685 SAW BLADES & HANDSAWS

SEE ALSO Tools - Hand & Edge p. 3242

	City	State	Zip	Phone	Fax
Blount Outdoor Products Group 4909 SE International Way *Web:* blount.com	Portland	OR	97222	503-653-8881	653-4402
California Saw & Knife Works 721 Brannan St *TF:* 888-729-6533 ■ *Web:* www.calsaw.com	San Francisco	CA	94103	415-861-0644	861-0406
Carlton Co 3901 SE Naef Rd *Web:* carltonproducts.com	Milwaukie	OR	97267	503-659-8911	659-8616
Contour Saws Inc 1217 E Thacker St *TF:* 800-458-9034 ■ *Web:* contoursawsinc.com	Des Plaines	IL	60016	847-824-1146	803-9467
Diamond Saw Works Inc 12290 Olean Rd *TF:* 800-828-1180 ■ *Web:* www.diamondsaw.com	Chaffee	NY	14030	716-496-7417	496-8969
Disston Precision Inc 6795 State Rd *TF Cust Svc:* 800-238-1007 ■ *Web:* www.disstonprecision.com	Philadelphia	PA	19135	215-338-1200	338-7060
Great Neck Saw Manufacturing Inc 165 E Second St *TF Cust Svc:* 800-457-0600 ■ *Web:* www.greatnecksaw.com	Mineola	NY	11501	516-746-5352	746-5358
ICS Blount Inc 4909 SE International Way **Fax Area Code:* 503 ■ *TF:* 800-321-1240 ■ *Web:* www.icsbestway.com	Portland	OR	97222	800-321-1240	653-4201*
LS Starrett Co 121 Crescent St *NYSE:* SCX ■ *TF:* 800-482-8710 ■ *Web:* www.starrett.com	Athol	MA	01331	978-249-3551	249-8495
Marvel Mfg Company Inc 3501 Marvel Dr *TF:* 800-472-9464 ■ *Web:* www.marvelsaws.com	Oshkosh	WI	54902	920-236-7200	236-7209
MK Diamond Products Inc 1315 Storm Pkwy *TF:* 800-421-5830 ■ *Web:* www.mkdiamond.com	Torrance	CA	90501	310-539-5221	539-5158
MK Morse Co 1101 11th St SE *TF:* 800-733-3377 ■ *Web:* www.mkmorse.com	Canton	OH	44707	330-453-8187	453-1111
Simonds International 135 Intervale Rd *TF:* 800-343-1616 ■ *Web:* www.simondsint.com	Fitchburg	MA	01420	800-343-1616	541-6224

686 SAWMILLS & PLANING MILLS

	City	State	Zip	Phone	Fax
Anderson-Tully Co 775 Ridgelake Blvd Ste 1050 *Web:* www.andersontully.com	Memphis	TN	38120	901-576-1400	
Anthony Forest Products Co 309 N Washington Ave *TF:* 800-221-2326 ■ *Web:* www.anthonyforest.com	El Dorado	AR	71730	870-862-3414	863-4296
Anthony Timberlands Inc 111 S Plum St PO Box 137 *Web:* www.anthonytimberlands.com	Bearden	AR	71720	870-687-3611	687-2283
Balfour Lumber Company Inc 800 W Clay St *Web:* balfourlumber.com	Thomasville	GA	31792	229-226-6086	
Barrette-Chapais Ltee CP 248 Km 346 Rt 113 *Web:* www.barrette-chapais.qc.ca	Chapais	QC	G0W1H0	418-745-2545	
Bayway Lumber & Home Center (inc) 400 Ashton Ave *Web:* www.baywaylumber.com	Linden	NJ	07036	908-486-4480	
Beadles Lumber Company Inc 900 Sixth St NE PO Box 3457 *TF:* 800-763-2400 ■ *Web:* www.beadleslumber.com	Moultrie	GA	31776	229-985-6996	890-6050
Beasley Forest Products Inc 712 Uvalda Hwy *Web:* www.beasleyforestproducts.com	Hazlehurst	GA	31539	912-375-5174	
Bennett Lumber Products Inc 3759 Hwy 6 PO Box 130 *Web:* www.bennett-lumber.com	Princeton	ID	83857	208-875-1121	875-0191
Bradford Forest Inc 18385 Rt 287 *Web:* www.bradfordforest.com	Tioga	PA	16946	814-368-3701	368-3720
Buse Timber & Sales Inc 3812 28th Pl NE *TF:* 800-305-2577 ■ *Web:* www.busetimber.com	Everett	WA	98201	425-258-2577	259-6956
Buskirk Lumber Co 319 Oak St *TF:* 800-860-9663 ■ *Web:* www.buskirklumber.com	Freeport	MI	49325	616-765-5103	765-3380
Canadian Forest Products Ltd 5162 Northwood Pulp Mill Rd PO Box 9000 **Fax:* Acctg ■ *Web:* www.canfor.com	Prince George	BC	V2L4W2	250-962-3500	962-3473*
Carl Diebold Lumber Co 725 Nw Dunbar Ave *Web:* dieboldlumber.com	Troutdale	OR	97060	503-669-8226	
Carrier Lumber Ltd 4722 Continental Way *Web:* www.carrierlumber.bc.ca	Prince George	BC	V2N5S5	250-563-9271	
Catawissa Wood & Components Inc 1015 W Valley Ave *Web:* www.catlmbr.com	Elysburg	PA	17824	570-644-1928	486-2800
Cersosimo Lumber Co Inc 1103 Vernon St **Fax Area Code:* 413 ■ *TF:* 800-326-5647 ■ *Web:* www.cersosimolumber.com	Brattleboro	VT	05301	802-254-4508	477-6585*
Claude Howard Lumber Company Inc 600 Pk Ave *Web:* sbcontract.com	Statesboro	GA	30458	912-764-5407	764-6279
Coastal Timbers Inc 1310 Jane St PO Box 10537 *Web:* www.coastaltimbers.com	New Iberia	LA	70563	337-369-3017	365-0003
Collins Cos 1618 SW First Ave Ste 500 **Fax Area Code:* 503 ■ *TF:* 800-329-1219 ■ *Web:* www.collinsco.com	Portland	OR	97201	800-329-1219	227-5349*
Collum's Lumber Products LLC 1723 Barnwell Hwy PO Box 535 *Web:* www.collumlumber.com	Allendale	SC	29810	803-584-3451	584-2783
Columbia Vista Corp PO Box 489 *Web:* www.columbiavistacorp.com	Vancouver	WA	98666	360-892-0770	944-8229
Conner Industries Inc 3800 Sandshell Dr Ste 235 *Web:* www.connerindustries.com	Fort Worth	TX	76137	817-847-0361	
Crone Lumber Company Inc 501 N Park Ave *Web:* www.cronelbr.com	Martinsville	IN	46151	765-342-2259	
Cronland Lumber Co PO Box 574 *Web:* www.cronlandlumber.com	Lincolnton	NC	28093	704-736-2691	735-8493
Crownover Lumber Company Inc 501 Fairview Ave *Web:* www.crownoverlumber.com	Mc Arthur	OH	45651	740-596-5229	
Cumberland Lumber & Manufacturing Co 202 Red Rd	McMinnville	TN	37110	931-473-9542	473-6259
Cut - to - Size Technology Inc 345 S Fairbank St *Web:* www.cuttosizetech.com	Addison	IL	60101	630-543-8328	
David R Webb Company Inc 206 S Holland St PO Box 8 *Web:* www.davidrwebb.com	Edinburgh	IN	46124	812-526-2601	526-5842
Deltic Timber Corp PO Box 7200 *NYSE:* DEL ■ *Web:* www.deltic.com	El Dorado	AR	71731	870-881-9400	881-6454
DLH Nordisk Inc 2307 W Cone Boulvard Ste 200 *Web:* www.dlh-usa.com	Greensboro	NC	27408	336-852-8341	
Domtar Corp 395 de Maisonneuve W *NYSE:* UFS ■ *TF:* 877-848-4466 ■ *Web:* www.domtar.com	Montreal	QC	H3A1L6	514-848-5555	
DR Johnson Lumber Co 1991 Pruner Rd PO Box 66 *Web:* www.drjlumber.com	Riddle	OR	97469	541-874-2231	874-3337
Dur-A-Flex Inc 95 Goodwin St *Web:* www.dur-a-flex.com	East Hartford	CT	06108	860-528-9838	
Dwight G Lewis Lumber Company Inc 1895 Pennsylvania 87	Hillsgrove	PA	18619	570-924-3507	
ECO Building Products Inc 909 W Vista Way	Vista	CA	92083	909-519-5470	
Fitzgerald Lumber & Log Company Inc 403 E 29th St PO Box 188 *Web:* www.fitzgeraldlumber.com	Buena Vista	VA	24416	540-261-3430	
Fitzpatrick & Weller Inc 12 Mill St PO Box 490 *Web:* www.fitzweller.com	Ellicottville	NY	14731	716-699-2393	699-2893
Forest Products Manufacturing Co 51 E 30th St PO Box 606 *Web:* forestp.com	Jasper	IN	47547	812-482-5625	482-9148
Frank Lumber Company Inc PO Box 79 *Web:* franklumberco.com	Mill City	OR	97360	503-897-2371	
Freeman Brothers Inc 2401 S Arkansas Ave	Russellville	AR	72802	479-968-4986	967-9989
Fulghum Industries 317 S Main St **Fax:* Sales ■ *TF:* 800-841-5980 ■ *Web:* www.fulghum.com	Wadley	GA	30477	478-252-5223	252-0454*
Gram Lumber Co 985 NW Second St *Web:* rsgfp.com	Kalama	WA	98625	360-673-5231	673-5558
Greenpak Development Inc 3001 Gateman Dr *Web:* www.greenpak.com	Parkersburg	WV	26101	304-420-1028	

	City	State	Zip	Phone	Fax
Griffin Lumber Co 1603 Drayton Rd *Web:* www.griffithlumber.net	Cordele	GA	31015	229-273-3113	273-4909
Groupe Savoie Inc 251, Rt 180 *Web:* www.groupesavoie.com	St-quentin	NB	E8A2K9	506-235-2228	235-3200
Hampton Affiliates 9600 SW Barnes Rd Ste 200 *TF:* 888-310-1464 ■ *Web:* www.hamptonaffiliates.com	Portland	OR	97225	503-297-7691	
Hardwoods of Michigan Inc 430 Div St *TF:* 800-327-2812 ■ *Web:* www.hmilumber.com	Clinton	MI	49236	517-456-7431	456-4931
Hartzell Hardwoods 1025 S Roosevelt Ave *Web:* www.hartzellhardwoods.com	Piqua	OH	45356	937-773-7054	773-6160
Hedstrom Lumber Company Inc 1504 Gunflint Trl *Web:* www.hedstromlumber.com	Grand Marais	MN	55604	218-387-2995	387-2204
Hoge Lumber Co 701 S Main St PO Box 159 *Web:* www.hoge.com	New Knoxville	OH	45871	419-753-2263	753-2963
Hughes Hardwood International Inc 500 Hwy 13 S *Web:* www.hugheshardwood.com	Collinwood	TN	38450	931-724-6258	724-6259
Hunt Forest Products 401 E Reynolds Dr PO Box 1263 *TF:* 800-390-8589 ■ *Web:* www.huntforpro.com	Ruston	LA	71273	318-255-2245	255-4048
Impact Guns 2710 South 1900 West *TF:* 888-505-3086 ■ *Web:* www.impactguns.com	Ogden	UT	84401	801-393-2474	
Independence Lumber Inc 407 Lumber Ln *Web:* www.indlbr.com	Independence	VA	24348	276-773-3744	773-3723
Indiana Dimension Inc 1621 W Market St *Web:* indianadimension.com	Logansport	IN	46947	574-739-2319	
Indiana Hardwood Specialists Inc 4341 N US Hwy 231 *Web:* indianahardwoodspec.com	Spencer	IN	47460	812-829-4866	829 4860
Industrial Timber & Lumber Corp (ITL) 23925 Commerce Pk Rd *TF:* 800-829-9663 ■ *Web:* www.itlcorp.com	Beachwood	OH	44122	216-831-3140	831-4734
Interfor Pacific Inc 2211 Rimland Dr Ste 220 *Web:* www.interfor.com	Bellingham	WA	98226	360-788-2299	
Jerry G Williams & Sons Inc 524 Brogden Rd PO Box 2430	Smithfield	NC	27577	919-934-4115	
JW Jones Lumber Company Inc 1443 Northside Rd *Web:* mackeysferrysawmill.com	Elizabeth City	NC	27909	252-771-2497	771-8252
Kasco-Sharptech Corp 1569 Tower Grove Ave *Web:* www.kascosharptech.com	St. Louis	MO	63110	314-771-1550	
Kitchens Bros Manufacturing Co 601 Carpenter St PO Box 217	Utica	MS	39175	601-885-6001	885-8501
Komo Machine Inc One Gusmer Dr *Web:* www.komo.com	Lakewood	NJ	08701	732-719-6222	
Kretz Lumber Company Inc W11143 County Hwy G *Web:* www.kretzlumber.com	Antigo	WI	54409	715-623-5410	
Langdale Forest Products Co 1202 Madison Hwy *Web:* www.langdaleforest.com	Valdosta	GA	31603	229-333-2500	333-2533
Lewisohn Sales Company Inc 4001 Dell Ave *Web:* www.lewisohn.com	North Bergen	NJ	07047	201-864-0300	
Lon Musolf Distributing Inc 985 E Berwood Ave *Web:* www.lonmusolf.com	Vadnais Heights	MN	55110	651-484-3020	
Louisiana-Pacific Corp 414 Union St Ste 2000 *NYSE:* LPX ■ *TF:* 888-820-0325 ■ *Web:* www.lpcorp.com	Nashville	TN	37219	615-986-5600	986-5666
Maibec Inc 1984, 5e Rue Ste 202 *Web:* www.maibec.com	L,vis	QC	G6W5M6	418-659-3323	
Manke Lumber Company Inc 1717 Marine View Dr *TF:* 800-426-8488 ■ *Web:* www.mankelumber.com	Tacoma	WA	98422	253-572-6252	383-2489
Matson Lumber Company Inc 132 Main St *Web:* www.matsonlumber.com	Brookville	PA	15825	814-849-5334	849-3811
MC Dixon Lumber Company Inc 605 W Washington St *Web:* dixonlumber.com	Eufaula	AL	36027	334-687-8204	687-8208
Menominee Tribal Enterprises PO Box 10 *Web:* www.mtewood.com	Neopit	WI	54150	715-756-2311	799-4323
Merritt Bros Lumber Co Inc 5400 E Hwy 54 *Web:* www.merrittbros.com	Athol	ID	83801	208-683-3321	683-3328
Mid South Lumber Inc 1115 C St *Web:* www.mid-southlumber.com	Meridian	MS	39301	601-483-4389	
Midwest Hardwood Corp 9540 83rd Ave N *Web:* www.midwesthardwood.com	Maple Grove	MN	55369	763-425-8700	391-6740
Mill & Timber Products Ltd 12770- 116th Ave *Web:* www.millandtimber.com	Surrey	BC	V3V7H9	604-580-2781	
Moose River Lumber Co Inc 25 Talpey Rd *Web:* www.mooseriverlumber.com	Moose River	ME	04945	207-668-4193	668-5381
Morgan Lumber Company Inc 628 Jeb Stuart Hwy *Web:* www.morganlumber.com	Red Oak	VA	23964	434-735-8151	
Nicholson Manufacturing Ltd 9896 Galaran Rd *Web:* www.debarking.com	Sidney	BC	V8L3S6	250-656-3131	
North American Forest Products Inc PO Box 600 *Web:* www.nafpinc.com	Edwardsburg	MI	49112	269-663-8500	663-2073
Ochoco Lumber Co 200 SE Combs Flat Rd PO Box 668 *Web:* www.ochocolumber.com	Prineville	OR	97754	541-447-6296	382-6131
Ohio Valley Veneer Inc 165 No Name Rd	Piketon	OH	45661	740-289-4979	
Oregon Canadian Forest Products Inc 31950 Comml St NW PO Box 279 *Web:* www.ocfp.com	North Plains	OR	97133	503-647-5011	647-0910
Pacific Fibre Products Inc 20 Fibre Way *Web:* www.pacfibre.com	Longview	WA	98632	360-577-7112	
Parton Lumber Company Inc 251 Parton Rd *TF:* 800-624-1501 ■ *Web:* www.partonlumber.com	Rutherfordton	NC	28139	828-287-4257	287-3308
Pike Lumber Company Inc PO Box 247 *TF:* 800-356-4554 ■ *Web:* www.pikelumber.com	Akron	IN	46910	574-893-4511	893-7400

	City	State	Zip	Phone	Fax
Pleasant River Lumber Co 432 Milo Rd *Web:* www.pleasantriverlumber.com	Dover Foxcroft	ME	04426	207-564-8520	
Plum Creek Timber Company Inc 601 Union St Ste 3100 *NYSE:* PCL ■ *TF:* 800-858-5347 ■ *Web:* www.plumcreek.com	Seattle	WA	98101	206-467-3600	467-3795
Plummer Forest Products Inc 810 N Henry St Ste 420B *Web:* www.plummerforest.com	Post Falls	ID	83854	208-457-1060	
Potlatch Corp 601 W First Ave Ste 1600 *NASDAQ:* PCH ■ *Web:* www.potlatchcorp.com	Spokane	WA	99201	509-835-1500	835-1555
Potlatch Corp Wood Products Div 805 Mill Rd PO Box 1388 **Fax Area Code:* 208 ■ *Web:* www.potlatchcorp.com	Lewiston	ID	83501	509-835-1500	799-1918*
Pyramid Mountain Lumber Inc 379 Boy Scout Rd PO Box 549 *Web:* www.pyramidlumber.com	Seeley Lake	MT	59868	406-677-2201	677-2509
Riephoff Sawmill Inc 763 Rt 524 *Web:* www.riephoffsawmill.com	Allentown	NJ	08501	609-259-7265	
Robbins Inc 4777 Eastern Ave *TF:* 800-543-1913 ■ *Web:* www.robbinsfloor.com	Cincinnati	OH	45226	513-871-8988	871-7998
Robbins Lumber Co 53 Ghent Rd PO Box 9 *Web:* www.rlco.com	Searsmont	ME	04973	207-342-5221	342-5201
Rogers Lumber Company Inc 937 Hwy 7 N *Web:* rogerspallet.com	Camden	AR	71701	870-574-0231	574-1206
Rosboro Lumber Co 2509 Main St *Web:* www.rosboro.com	Springfield	OR	97477	541-746-8411	726-8919
Roseburg Forest Products Co PO Box 1088 *TF:* 800-245-1115 ■ *Web:* www.roseburg.com	Roseburg	OR	97470	541-679-3311	
RSG Forest Products Inc 985 NW Second St *Web:* www.rsgfp.com	Kalama	WA	98625	360-673-2825	673-5558
Rushmore Forest Products 23848 Hwy 385 PO Box 619 *TF:* 866-466-5254 ■ *Web:* neimanenterprises.com	Hill City	SD	57745	605-574-2512	574-4154
Rutland Plywood Corp One Ripley Rd *Web:* www.rutply.com	Rutland	VT	05701	802-747-4000	
Scotch Gulf Lumber 1850 Conception St Rd *TF:* 800-496-3307 ■ *Web:* www.gulflumber.com	Mobile	AL	36610	251-457-6872	452-7110
Scotch Lumber Co 119 W Main St PO Box 38 *TF:* 800-936-4424 ■ *Web:* scotchplywood.com	Fulton	AL	36446	334-636-4424	636-7107
Scott Industries Inc 1573 Hwy 136 W PO Box 7 *TF:* 800-951-9276 ■ *Web:* www.scott-mfg.com	Henderson	KY	42419	270-831-2037	831-2039
Seattle Snohomish Mill Co Inc 9525 Airport Way *Web:* www.sea-sno.com	Snohomish	WA	98296	360-568-2171	
Seneca Sawmill Co 90201 Hwy 99 *Web:* www.senecasawmill.com	Eugene	OR	97440	541-689-1011	
Sierra Forest Products 9000 Rd 234 *Web:* www.sierrafp.com	Terra Bella	CA	93270	559-535-4893	
Sierra Pacific Industries 19794 Riverside Ave *Web:* spi-ind.com	Anderson	CA	96007	530-378-8000	378-8109
Simpson Timber Co 917 E 11th St *Web:* www.simpson.com	Tacoma	WA	98421	253-779-6400	680-6855
Sims Bark Company Inc 1765 Spring Vly Rd *Web:* www.simsbark.com	Tuscumbia	AL	35674	256-381-8323	
Smith Flooring Inc 1501 W Hwy 60 PO Box 99 *Web:* www.smithflooring.com	Mountain View	MO	65548	417-934-2291	934-2295
South Coast Lumber Co 885 Railroad Ave PO Box 670 *Web:* www.socomi.com	Brookings	OR	97415	541-469-2136	469-3487
Stella-Jones Inc 3100 de la Cote-Vertu Blvd Ste 300 *Web:* www.stella-jones.com	St-laurent	QC	H4R2J8	514-934-8666	934-5327
Stimson Lumber Co 520 SW Yamhill St Ste 700 *TF:* 800-445-9758 ■ *Web:* www.stimsonlumber.com	Portland	OR	97204	503-222-1676	222-2682
Sun Mountain Lumber 181 Greenhouse Rd *Web:* www.sunmtnlumber.com	Deer Lodge	MT	59722	406-846-1600	
Swaner Hardwood Co Inc 5 W Magnolia Blvd PO Box 4200 *TF:* 800-368-1108 ■ *Web:* www.swanerhardwood.com	Burbank	CA	91503	818-953-5350	846-3662
Teal-Jones Group, The 17897 Triggs Rd *Web:* www.tealjones.com	Surrey	BC	V4N4M8	604-587-8700	
Tembec Inc 800 Boul Rene Levesque O Bureau 1050 *TSE:* TMB ■ *Web:* www.tembec.com	Montreal	QC	H3B1X9	514-871-0137	397-0896
Terminal Forest Products Ltd 12180 Mitchell Rd *Web:* www.terminalforest.com	Richmond	BC	V6V1M8	604-717-1200	
TR Miller Mill Company Inc 215 Deer St PO Box 708 *TF:* 800-633-6740 ■ *Web:* www.trmillermill.com	Brewton	AL	36427	251-867-4331	867-6882
Tucker Lumber Cos LLC 601 N Pearl St *Web:* www.cmtuckerlumber.com	Pageland	SC	29728	843-672-6135	672-5393
United Lumber & Remanufacturing LLC 980 Ford Rd *Web:* www.unitedlumber.net	Muscle Shoals	AL	35661	256-381-4151	
United Treating & Distribution LLC 338 E Washington Dr *Web:* unitedtreating.com	Muscle Shoals	AL	35661	256-248-0944	
Universal Forest Products Inc (UFPI) 2801 E Beltline Ave NE *NASDAQ:* UFPI ■ *TF:* 800-598-9663 ■ *Web:* www.ufpi.com	Grand Rapids	MI	49525	616-364-6161	361-7534
USNR 1981 Schurman Way PO Box 310 *TF:* 800-289-8767 ■ *Web:* www.coemfg.com	Woodland	WA	98674	360-225-8267	225-8017
West Coast Engineering Group Ltd 7984 River Rd *Web:* www.wceng.com	Delta	BC	V4G1E3	604-946-1256	946-1203
West Fraser Timber Company Ltd (WFT) 501-858 Beatty St Ste 501 *NYSE:* WFT ■ *Web:* www.westfraser.com	Vancouver	BC	V6B1C1	604-895-2700	681-6061
Westervelt Company Inc, The PO Box 48999 *Web:* www.westervelt.com	Tuscaloosa	AL	35404	205-562-5000	562-5012

Phone | Fax

Weyerhaeuser Co 33663 Weyerhaeuser Way S ...... Federal Way WA 98003 253-924-2345 924-2685
NYSE: WY ■ *TF:* 800-525-5440 ■ *Web:* www.weyerhaeuser.com

687 SCALES & BALANCES

SEE ALSO Laboratory Apparatus & Furniture p. 2619

Phone | Fax

Advance Scale of MD LLC
2400 Egg Harbor Rd .... Lindenwold NJ 08021 856-627-0700
Web: advancescale.com

Avery Weigh-Tronix Inc 1000 Armstrong Dr .... Fairmont MN 56031 507-238-4461 238-8258*
**Fax:* Mktg ■ *TF:* 800-458-7062 ■ *Web:* www.averyweigh-tronix.com

BRK Brands Inc 3901 Liberty St Rd .... Aurora IL 60504 630-851-7330 851-7452
TF: 800-323-9005 ■ *Web:* www.firstalert.com

Cardinal Detecto Scale Manufacturing Co
203 E Daugherty St .... Webb City MO 64870 417-673-4631 673-5001
TF: 800-441-4237 ■ *Web:* www.cardet.com

Compuweigh Corp 50 Middle Quarter Rd .... Woodbury CT 06798 203-262-9400
Web: www.compuweigh.com

Detecto Scale Co
203 E Daugherty St PO Box 151 .... Webb City MO 64870 417-673-4631 673-4631
TF: 800-641-2008 ■ *Web:* www.detecto.com

Emery Winslow Scale Co 73 Cogwheel Ln .... Seymour CT 06483 203-881-9333 881-9477
TF: 800-891-3952 ■ *Web:* www.emerywinslow.com

Fairbanks Scales Inc 821 Locust St .... Kansas City MO 64106 816-471-0231 471-0241
TF: 800-451-4107 ■ *Web:* www.fairbanks.com

Industrial Data Systems Inc
3822 E La Palma Ave .... Anaheim CA 92807 714-921-9212 399-0286
TF: 800-854-3311 ■ *Web:* www.industrialdata.com

Intercomp Co 3839 County Rd 116 .... Medina MN 55340 763-476-2531 476-2613
TF: 800-328-3336 ■ *Web:* www.intercompcompany.com

Jarden Consumer Solutions
2381 Executive Ctr Dr .... Boca Raton FL 33431 561-912-4100
TF: 800-777-5452 ■ *Web:* www.jardencs.com

Johnson Scale Company Inc 36 Stiles Ln .... Pine Brook NJ 07058 800-572-2531 882-8068*
**Fax Area Code:* 973 ■ *TF:* 800-572-2531 ■ *Web:* www.johnsonscale.net

LSI Robway Pty Ltd 9633 Zaka Rd .... Houston TX 77064 281-664-1330
Web: www.loadsystems.com

Measurement Specialties Inc 1000 Lucas Way ...... Hampton VA 23666 757-766-1500 766-4297
NASDAQ: MEAS ■ *TF:* 800-745-8008 ■ *Web:* www.meas-spec.com

Medela Inc 1101 Corporate Dr .... Mchenry IL 60050 815-363-1166
Web: www.medela.us

Merrick Industries Inc 10 Arthur Dr .... Lynn Haven FL 32444 850-265-3611 265-9768*
**Fax:* Hum Res ■ *Web:* www.merrick-inc.com

Ohaus Corp 19-A Chapin Rd PO Box 2033 .... Pine Brook NJ 07058 973-377-9000 944-7177
TF: 800-672-7722 ■ *Web:* asiapacific.ohaus.com

Premier Tech Industrial Equipment Group
One Premier Ave .... Rivere-du-Loup QC G5R6C1 418-867-8884 862-6642
Web: www.ptchronos.com

Schenck Trebel Corp 535 Acorn St .... Deer Park NY 11729 631-242-4010 242-5077
TF: 800-873-2357 ■ *Web:* www.schenck-usa.com

Setra Systems Inc 159 Swanson Rd .... Boxborough MA 01719 978-263-1400 264-0292
TF: 800-257-3872 ■ *Web:* www.setra.com

Tanita Corp of America Inc
2625 S Clearbrook Dr .... Arlington Heights IL 60005 847-640-9241 640-9261
Web: www.tanita.com

TCI Scales Inc PO Box 1648 .... Snohomish WA 98291 425-353-4384 609-1021
TF: 800-522-2206 ■ *Web:* www.tciscales.com

Thayer Scale Corp 91 Schoosett St .... Pembroke MA 02359 781-826-8101 826-0072*
**Fax:* Cust Svc ■ *TF:* 800-225-0450 ■ *Web:* www.thayerscale.com

Wisconsin Electrical Mfg Company Inc (WEM)
2501 S Moorland Rd PO Box 510767 .... New Berlin WI 53151 262-782-2340 782-2653
Web: www.wemautomation.com

Yamato Corp 1775 S Murray Blvd .... Colorado Springs CO 80916 719-591-1500 591-1045
TF: 800-538-1762 ■ *Web:* www.yamatocorp.com

688 SCHOOL BOARDS (PUBLIC)

Phone | Fax

A.C. White Transfer & Storage Co Inc
1775 Founders Pkwy .... Alpharetta GA 30009 770-325-9100 325-9175
Web: acwhitemoving.com

Abbeville County School District 60
400 Greenville St .... Abbeville SC 29620 864-366-5427
Web: www.acsd.k12.sc.us

Abbotsford Virtual School 33952 Pine St .... Abbotsford BC V2S2P3 604-859-9803
Web: avs.sd34.bc.ca

Aberdeen School District 5 216 N G St .... Aberdeen WA 98520 360-538-2000
Web: www.asd5.org

Abrams Hebrew Academy 31 W College Ave .... Yardley PA 19067 215-493-1800
Web: abramsonline.org

Academy of Notre Dame De Namur
560 Sproul Rd .... Villanova PA 19085 610-687-0650
Web: www.ndapa.org

Acalanes Union High School Dist
1212 Pleasant Hill Rd .... Lafayette CA 94549 925-280-3900 932-2336
Web: www.acalanes.k12.ca.us

Adair County Board of Education
1204 Greensburg St .... Columbia KY 42728 270-384-2476
Web: adair.k12.ky.us

Adams County School District 50
6933 Raleigh St .... Westminster CO 80030 303-428-3511
Web: www.adams50.org

Airport Community Schools 11270 Grafton Rd .... Carleton MI 48117 734-654-2414 654-3424

Aiton Elementary School 533 48th Pl Ne .... Washington DC 20019 202-671-6060
Web: www.zillow.com

Akron Public Schools 70 N Broadway Ave .... Akron OH 44308 330-761-1661 761-3225
Web: www.akronschools.com

Al Huda Islamic School 12227 Hawthorne Way .... Hawthorne CA 90250 310-973-0500
Web: www.ichla.org

Phone | Fax

Alamance-Burlington School District
1712 Vaughn Rd .... Burlington NC 27217 336-570-6060 570-6218
TF: 888-764-7001 ■ *Web:* www.abss.k12.nc.us

Alameda Bible Church Home of Victory Christian School
220 El Pueblo Rd Nw .... Albuquerque NM 87114 505-898-2311
Web: www.alamedabiblechurch.com

Albany County School 1948 E Grand Ave .... Laramie WY 82070 307-721-4400
Web: www.acsd1.org

Albuquerque Public Schools (APS)
6400 Uptown Blvd NE .... Albuquerque NM 87110 505-880-3700 889-4883*
**Fax:* Hum Res ■ *TF:* 866-563-9297 ■ *Web:* www.aps.edu

Alden Hebron High School 9604 Illinois St .... Hebron IL 60034 815-648-2442
Web: www.alden-hebron.org

Alexander Smith Academy Inc
10255 Richmond Ave Ste 100 .... Houston TX 77042 713-266-0920
Web: www.alexandersmith.com

Alisal Union Elementary School District
1205 E Market St .... Salinas CA 93905 831-753-5700 753-5709
TF: 800-782-7463 ■ *Web:* www.alisal.org

Allegheny Valley School District
300 PEARL Ave .... Cheswick PA 15024 724-274-5300 274-8040
Web: avsdweb.org

Allen Village School 706 W 42nd St .... Kansas City MO 64111 816-561-2602
Web: www.allenvillageschool.com

Allentown School District (ASD) 31 S Penn St ...... Allentown PA 18105 484-765-4000 765-4140
TF: 877-262-1492 ■ *Web:* www.allentownsd.org

Alpena Public Schools (Inc) 2373 Gordon Rd .... Alpena MI 49707 989-358-5040 358-5041
Web: www.alpenaschools.com

Alta Loma School District 9390 Baseline Rd .... Alta Loma CA 91701 909-484-5151 484-5195
Web: www.alsd.k12.ca.us

Amador County Unified School District
217 Rex Ave .... Jackson CA 95642 209-223-1750
Web: www.amadorcoe.org

Amarillo Independent School District (AISD)
7200 I- 40 W .... Amarillo TX 79106 806-326-1000 354-4378*
**Fax:* Hum Res ■ *Web:* amaisd.org

American Quality Schools Corp
910 W. Van Buren St .... Chicago IL 60607 312-226-3355
Web: www.aqs.org

Ames Community School District 415 Stanton Ave .... Ames IA 50014 515-268-6600 268-6633
TF: 800-262-3867 ■ *Web:* www.ames.k12.ia.us

Anaheim City School District - Capital Facilities Corp
1001 SE St .... Anaheim CA 92805 714-517-7500
Web: www.acsd.k12.ca.us

Anaheim Union High School District (AUHSB)
501 N Crescent Way .... Anaheim CA 92801 714-999-3511 520-9752*
**Fax:* Admin ■ *Web:* www.auhsd.us

Anchor Bay School District
5201 County Line Rd Ste 100 .... Casco Township MI 48064 586-725-2861 725-0290
TF: 800-285-4460 ■ *Web:* www.anchorbay.misd.net

Anchorage School District 3580 E Tudor Rd .... Anchorage AK 99507 907-742-4000 742-4176
Web: www.asdk12.org

Anoka-Hennepin Independent School District 11
2727 N Ferry St .... Anoka MN 55303 763-506-1000 506-1003
TF: 800-729-6164 ■ *Web:* www.anoka.k12.mn.us

Anthony Wayne Board of Education
PO Box 2487 .... Whitehouse OH 43571 419-877-5377
Web: www.anthonywayneschools.org

Apollo-Ridge School District
PO Box 219 .... Spring Church PA 15686 724-478-6000
Web: www.apolloridge.com

Apple Valley Unified School District (AVUSD)
12555 Navajo Rd .... Apple Valley CA 92308 760-247-8001
Web: www.avusd.org

Appling County Board of Education
249 Blackshear Hwy .... Baxley GA 31513 912-367-8600
TF: 866-632-9992 ■ *Web:* www.appling.k12.ga.us

Archway Programs Inc PO Box 668 .... Atco NJ 08004 856-767-5757
Web: www.archwayprograms.org

Arlington Central School District
144 Todd Hill Rd .... LaGrangeville NY 12540 845-486-4460 486-4457
TF: 800-225-2527 ■ *Web:* www.arlingtonschools.org

Arlington School District 315 N French Ave .... Arlington WA 98223 360-618-6200 618-6221
TF: 888-535-0747 ■ *Web:* www.asd.wednet.edu

Armbrae Academy 1400 Oxford St .... Halifax NS B3H3Y8 902-423-7920
Web: www.armbrae.ns.ca

Armijo High School 824 Washington St .... Fairfield CA 94533 707-422-7500
Web: www.fsusd.org

Armstrong School District 410 Main St .... Ford City PA 16226 724-763-5200 763-7295
TF: 888-573-5733 ■ *Web:* www.asd.k12.pa.us

Ashbury College 362 Mariposa Ave .... Rockcliffe ON K1M0T3 613-749-5954
Web: www.ashbury.on.ca

Asheville Catholic School 12 Culvern St .... Asheville NC 28804 828-252-7896
Web: www.ashevillecatholic.org

Ashland Independent School District
PO Box 3000 .... Ashland KY 41105 606-327-2706 327-2705
TF: 800-752-6200 ■ *Web:* www.ashland.kyschools.us

Ashley Hall School 172 Rutledge Ave .... Charleston SC 29403 843-722-4088
Web: ashleyhall.org

Ashtabula Area City School District
2630 W 13th St .... Ashtabula OH 44004 440-992-1200 992-1209
Web: www.aacs.net

Ashwaubenon School District
1055 Griffiths Ln .... Green Bay WI 54304 920-492-2900 492-2911
Web: www.ashwaubenon.k12.wi.us

Athens City School District
25 S Plains Rd .... The Plains OH 45780 740-797-4544
Web: www.athenscity.k12.oh.us

Atkinson County School System
98 Roberts Ave E .... Pearson GA 31642 912-422-7373 422-7369
TF: 800-639-0850 ■ *Web:* www.atkinson.k12.ga.us

Atlanta Public Schools 130 Trinity Ave SW .... Atlanta GA 30303 404-802-3500 802-1803
Web: www.atlanta.k12.ga.us

Name / Address	City	State	Zip	Phone	Fax
Au Authum Ki Inc 665 E Morelos St Ste 101 *Web:* www.authumki.com	Chandler	AZ	85225	480-497-1997	377-1143
Auburn City School District PO Box 3270 *TF:* 866-277-9644 ■ *Web:* www.auburnschools.org	Auburn	AL	36831	334-887-2100	887-2107
Auburn Union School District 255 Epperle Ln *Web:* www.auburn.k12.ca.us	Auburn	CA	95603	530-885-7242	885-5170
Austin Elementary School 1900 Duncan St *Web:* www.pampaisd.net	Pampa	TX	79065	806-669-4760	
Austin Jewish Academy 7300 Hart Ln *Web:* www.austinjewishacademy.org	Austin	TX	78731	512-735-8350	
Ave Intervision LLC 1840 W State St *TF:* 800-448-9126 ■ *Web:* www.amvonet.com	Alliance	OH	44601	800-448-9126	
Avondale House 3611 Cummins St *Web:* www.avondalehouse.org	Houston	TX	77027	713-993-9544	
Avonworth School District 258 Josephs Ln *Web:* www.avonworth.k12.pa.us	Pittsburgh	PA	15237	412-369-8738	369-8746
Axis Construction Corp 125 Laser Ct *Web:* www.theaxisgroup.com	Hauppauge	NY	11788	631-243-5970	243-5973
Bakersfield City School District 1300 Baker St *Web:* www.bcsd.com	Bakersfield	CA	93305	661-631-4600	326-1485
Balboa City Schools 525 Hawthorn St *Web:* www.balboaschool.com	San Diego	CA	92101	619-243-1170	
Baltimore City Public Schools 200 E N Ave **Fax Area Code:* 410 ■ *Web:* www.baltimorecityschools.org	Baltimore	MD	21202	443-984-2000	545-0897*
Baltimore Polytechnic Institute 1400 W Cold Spring Ln *Web:* www.bpi.edu	Baltimore	MD	21209	410-396-7026	
Bank of Highland Park Financial Corp 1835 First St PO Box 546 *TF:* 877-651-7800 ■ *Web:* www.firstbankhp.com	Highland Park	IL	60035	847-432-7800	433-2156
Banks County Board of Education PO Box 248 *Web:* www.banks.k12.ga.us	Homer	GA	30547	706-677-2224	
Barbers Hill Isd (BHISD) 9600 Eagle Dr PO Box 1108 *Web:* www.bhisd.net	Mont Belvieu	TX	77580	281-576-2221	
Barnard & Sons Construction LLC 3054 Simpson Hwy 13 PO Box 517 *Web:* www.barnardandsons.com	Mendenhall	MS	39114	601-847-2420	847-0110
Barney Trucking Inc 235 State Rt 24 **Fax Area Code:* 435 ■ *TF:* 800-524-7930 ■ *Web:* www.barneytrucking.com	Salina	UT	84654	800-524-7930	529-7314*
Barstow School, The 11511 State Line Rd *Web:* www.barstowschool.org	Kansas City	MO	64114	816-942-3255	
Bartlett High School 701 W Schick Rd *Web:* www.u-46.org	Bartlett	IL	60103	630-372-4700	
Bastrop Isd 906 Farm St *Web:* www.bisdtx.org	Bastrop	TX	78602	512-308-9253	
Battle River Regional Div 5402 48a Ave *Web:* www.brsd.ab.ca	Camrose	AB	T4V0L3	780-672-6131	
Baugo Community School Indiana 29125 County Rd 22 W *Web:* www.baugo.com	Elkhart	IN	46517	574-293-8583	
Bay City Public Schools 910 N Walnut St *Web:* www.bcschools.net	Bay City	MI	48706	989-686-9700	686-7626
Bayview Glen Public School 42 Limcombe Dr *Web:* www.yrdsb.ca	Markham	ON	L3T2V5	905-889-2448	
Beam Construction Company Inc 601 E Main St *Web:* www.beamconstruction.com	Cherryville	NC	28021	704-435-3206	435-8412
Beantree Learning 43629 Greenway Corporate Dr *Web:* beantreelearning.com	Ashburn	VA	20147	571-223-3110	
Bear Branch Elementary School 8909 Fm 1488 Rd *Web:* www.magnoliaisd.org	Magnolia	TX	77354	281-356-4771	
Beaufort County Board of Education 321 Smaw Rd *Web:* www.beaufort.k12.nc.us	Washington	NC	27889	252-946-6593	
Beaumont School 3301 N Park Blvd *Web:* www.beaumontschool.org	Cleveland Heights	OH	44118	216-321-2954	
Beavercreek Board of Education 3040 Kemp Rd *Web:* www.beavercreek.k12.oh.us	Dayton	OH	45431	937-426-1522	429-7517
Bedford Public Schools 1623 W Sterns Rd *TF:* 866-261-9184 ■ *Web:* www.bedford.k12.mi.us	Temperance	MI	48182	734-850-6000	850-6099
Beemac Trucking 2747 Litionville Rd *TF:* 800-282-8781 ■ *Web:* beemactrucking.com	Ambridge	PA	15003	724-266-8781	266-5638
Belle Chasse Academy Inc 100 Fifth St *Web:* www.bellechasseacademy.com	Belle Chasse	LA	70037	504-433-5850	
Bellefonte Area School District 318 N Allegheny St *TF:* 866-632-9992 ■ *Web:* www.basd.net	Bellefonte	PA	16823	814-355-4814	
Belton School District 110 W Walnut St *Web:* www.beltonschools.org	Belton	MO	64012	816-348-1000	348-1068
Bemidji Ind School District 31 3300 Gillett Dr NW *Web:* www.bemidji.k12.mn.us	Bemidji	MN	56601	218-333-3110	
Berea City School District 390 Fair St *Web:* www.berea.k12.oh.us	Berea	OH	44017	216-898-8300	898-8551
Bernards Township Board of Education 101 Peachtree Rd *Web:* www.bernardsboe.com	Basking Ridge	NJ	07920	908-204-2600	
Berrien Resa 711 Saint Joseph Ave *Web:* www.berrienresa.org	Berrien Springs	MI	49103	269-471-7725	
Beth Ramacher Development Ctr 710 N Hughes Ave *Web:* www.fcoe.org	Fresno	CA	93728	559-497-3955	
Bettendorf Community School District 3311 18th St *Web:* www.bettendorf.k12.ia.us	Bettendorf	IA	52722	563-359-3681	359-3685
Beverly Hills Unified School District 255 S Lasky Dr *TF:* 800-334-5847 ■ *Web:* www.bhusd.org	Beverly Hills	CA	90212	310-551-5100	277-6137
Bexley City School District 348 S Cassingham Rd *TF:* 800-282-1780 ■ *Web:* www.bexleyschools.org	Columbus	OH	43209	614-231-7611	
Bialik Hebrew Day School 2760 Bathurst St *Web:* bialik.ca	Toronto	ON	M6B3A1	416-783-3346	
Big Country Elementary School 2250 Pue Rd *Web:* www.swisd.net	San Antonio	TX	78245	210-645-7560	
Big Spring Independent School District 708 E 11th Pl *TF:* 866-632-9992 ■ *Web:* bigspringisd.net	Big Spring	TX	79720	432-264-3600	264-3646
Biltmore Construction Company Inc 1055 Ponce De Leon Blvd *Web:* www.biltmoreconstruction.com	Belleair	FL	33756	727-585-2084	585-2088
Binghamton City School District (BCSD) 164 Hawley St PO Box 2126 *Web:* binghamtonschools.org	Binghamton	NY	13902	607-762-8100	
Birmingham Board of Education (BCS) 2015 Pk Pl N *Web:* www.bhamcityschools.org	Birmingham	AL	35203	205-231-4600	
Bishop George Ahr High School One Tingley Ln *Web:* www.bgahs.org	Edison	NJ	08820	732-549-1108	
Bishop Kelly Foundation Inc 7009 W Franklin Rd *Web:* www.bk.org	Boise	ID	83709	208-375-6010	
Bishop Loughlin Memorial High School 357 Clermont Ave *Web:* blmhs.org	Brooklyn	NY	11238	718-857-2700	
Bishop Miege High School 5041 Reinhardt Dr *Web:* www.bishopmiege.com	Roeland Park	KS	66205	913-262-2700	
Bishop O'Dowd High School 9500 Stearns Ave *Web:* www.bishopodowd.org	OAKLAND	CA	94605	510-577-9100	
Bishop Whelan Elementary School 244 rue de la Presentation *Web:* bishopwhelan.lbpsb.qc.ca	Dorval	QC	H9S3L6	514-634-0550	
Black Horse Pike Regional School District 580 Erial Rd *Web:* www.bhprsd.org	Blackwood	NJ	08012	856-227-4105	227-6835
Blackburn Elementary School 2401 Concord St *Web:* www.catawbaschools.net	Forney	TX	75126	972-564-7008	
Blackfoot School District 55 270 E Bridge St *Web:* www.d55.k12.id.us	Blackfoot	ID	83221	208-785-8800	785-8809
Blacksburg High 201 W Ramseur Dr *Web:* www.mcps.org	Blacksburg	SC	29702	864-839-6371	
Blast Intermediate Unit 17 2400 Reach Rd *Web:* www.iu17.org	Williamsport	PA	17701	570-323-8561	
Blount County Schools 204 Second Ave E *Web:* www.blountboe.net	Oneonta	AL	35121	205-625-4102	
Blue Mountain School District Inc PO Box 188 *Web:* www.bmsd.org	Orwigsburg	PA	17961	570-366-0515	
Blythe Park Elementary School 735 Leesley Rd *Web:* www.district96.org	Riverside	IL	60546	708-447-2168	
Boarder to Boarder Trucking Inc PO Box 328 *TF:* 800-678-8789 ■ *Web:* www.btbtrucking.com	Edinburg	TX	78541	956-316-4444	316-4445
Boces Lower Hudson Regional Information Ctr 44 Executive Blvd *Web:* www.lhric.org	Elmsford	NY	10523	914-592-4203	
Bodwell High School 955 Harbourside Dr *Web:* www.bodwell.edu	North Vancouver	BC	V7P3S4	604-924-5056	
Boise City Independent School District 8169 W Victory Rd *Web:* www.sd01.k12.id.us	Boise	ID	83709	208-854-4000	854-4003
Bookman Road Elementary School 1245 Bookman Rd *Web:* www.richland2.org	Elgin	SC	29045	803-699-1724	
Borger High School 600 W First St *Web:* www.borgerisd.net	Borger	TX	79007	806-273-1029	
Borough-bogota Board-education One Henry C Luthin Pl *Web:* bogotaboe.com	Bogota	NJ	07603	201-441-4800	
Borton Lc 200 E First Ave *Web:* borton.biz	Hutchinson	KS	67501	620-669-8211	
Boulder Country Day School 4820 Nautilus Court N *Web:* bouldercountryday.org	Boulder	CO	80301	303-527-4931	
Bowling Green City Schools (BGCS) 137 Clough St *Web:* www.bgcs.k12.oh.us	Bowling Green	OH	43402	419-352-3576	352-1701
Bowling Green Independent School District 1211 Ctr St *Web:* b-g.k12.ky.us	Bowling Green	KY	42101	270-746-2200	
Bozeman School District 7 PO Box 520 *Web:* www.bsd7.org	Bozeman	MT	59771	406-522-6000	
Bradford Area School District Inc PO Box 375 *Web:* www.bradfordareaschools.org	Bradford	PA	16701	814-362-3841	
Brandon School Division 813 26th St *Web:* www.bsd.ca	Brandon	MB	R7B2B6	204-729-3955	
Breckinridge County School District 86 Airport Rd *TF:* 800-325-1713 ■ *Web:* breckinridgecountyky.com	Hardinsburg	KY	40143	270-756-2186	
Brecksville Broadview Hts Csd 6638 Mill Rd *Web:* www.bbhcsd.org	Brecksville	OH	44141	440-740-4000	740-4004
Brentwood Christian School Association of Parents, Teachers & Friends 11908 N Lamar Blvd *Web:* www.russianbibleschool.com	Austin	TX	78753	512-835-5983	

Name / Address	City	State	Zip	Phone	Fax
Brentwood High School Pto 5304 Murray Ln *Web:* www.ptobhs.org	Brentwood	TN	37027	615-472-4220	
Brentwood School 100 S Barrington Pl *Web:* www.bwscampus.com	Los Angeles	CA	90049	310-476-9633	476-4087
Bridges Public Charter School 1250 Taylor St Nw Ste A *Web:* bridgespcs.org	Washington	DC	20011	202-545-0515	
Bristol-Warren Regional School District 151 State St *Web:* www.bw.k12.ri.us	Bristol	RI	02809	401-253-4000	
Bronx Charter School for Excellence 1960 Benedict Ave *Web:* bronxexcellence.org	Bronx	NY	10462	718-828-7301	
Brookhaven School District PO Box 540 *Web:* www.brookhaven.k12.ms.us	Brookhaven	MS	39602	601-833-6661	833-4154
Brookline College 2445 W Dunlap Ave Ste 100 *Web:* brooklinecollege.edu	Phoenix	AZ	85021	602-242-6265	
Brooklyn Ascend Charter School 205 Rockaway Pkwy *Web:* www.ascendlearning.org	Brooklyn	NY	11212	718-240-9162	
Brooks Elementary School 3225 Sangamon Dr *Web:* www.dist428.org	Dekalb	IL	60115	815-754-9936	
Brookwood Middle School 1020 Hunters Ridge Dr *Web:* www.tcss.net	Genoa City	WI	53128	262-279-1053	
Broward County Public Schools 600 SE Third Ave *Web:* www.browardschools.com	Fort Lauderdale	FL	33301	754-321-0000	321-2701
Browne Academy 5917 Telegraph Rd *Web:* www.browneacademy.org	Alexandria	VA	22310	703-960-3000	
Browning School Inc 52 E 62nd St *Web:* www.browning.edu	New York	NY	10065	212-838-6280	355-5602
Brownsville Area School Dist Five Falcon Dr *Web:* www.basd.org	Brownsville	PA	15417	724-785-2021	785-4333
Brownsville Independent School District 1900 E Price Rd *Web:* www.bisd.us	Brownsville	TX	78521	956-548-8000	548-8019
Brunswick City School District 3643 Ctr Rd *Web:* www.bcsoh.org	Brunswick	OH	44212	330-225-7731	273-0507
Brunswick County Board of Education 35 Referendum Dr *TF:* 800-662-7030 ■ *Web:* www.bcswan.net	Bolivia	NC	28422	910-253-2900	253-2983
Bucher Elementary School 450 Candlewyck Rd *Web:* www.mtwp.net	Lancaster	PA	17601	717-569-4291	
Buckingham Browne & Nichols School 46 Belmont St *Web:* www.bbns.org	Watertown	MA	02472	617-547-6100	
Buckley School, The 3900 Stansbury Ave *Web:* www.buckley.org	Sherman Oaks	CA	91423	818-783-1610	461-6714
Buffalo City School District 712 City Hall *Web:* buffaloschools.org	Buffalo	NY	14202	716-816-3500	851-3535
Bullis Charter School 102 W Portola Ave *Web:* www.bullischarterschool.com	Los Altos	CA	94022	650-947-4939	
Bulloch County Board of Education 150 Williams Rd Ste A *Web:* www.bulloch.k12.ga.us	Statesboro	GA	30458	912-212-8500	764-8436
Bullock Creek Public Schools 1420 S Badour Rd *TF:* 877-706-2508 ■ *Web:* www.bcreek.k12.mi.us	Midland	MI	48640	989-631-9022	631-2882
Burke County Public Schools 789 Burke Veterans Pkwy *Web:* www.burke.k12.ga.us	Waynesboro	GA	30830	706-554-5101	554-8051
Burnet Middle School 8401 Hathaway Dr *Web:* www.austinisd.org	Austin	TX	78757	512-414-3225	
Burnham Wood Charter School 7310 Bishop Flores Dr *Web:* burnhamwood.org	El Paso	TX	79912	915-584-9499	
Bush School, The 3400 E Harrison St *Web:* bush.edu	Seattle	WA	98112	206-322-7978	
Butler Area School District 110 Campus Ln *TF:* 888-800-5583	Butler	PA	16001	724-287-8720	
Butler County Board of Education 215 Administrative Dr *Web:* www.butlerco.k12.al.us	Greenville	AL	36037	334-382-2665	
Butts County Board of Education 181 N Mulberry St *Web:* www.butts.k12.ga.us	Jackson	GA	30233	770-504-2300	504-2305
Cabarrus County School District 4401 Old Airport Rd *Web:* cabarrus.k12.nc.us	Concord	NC	28025	704-786-6191	786-6141
Cabrillo Unified School District 498 Kelly Ave *Web:* www.cabrillo.k12.ca.us	Half Moon Bay	CA	94019	650-712-7100	726-0279
Cache County School District 2063 N 1200 E *TF:* 888-837-6437 ■ *Web:* www.ccsdut.org	North Logan	UT	84341	435-752-3925	753-2168
Caddo Mills Isd 100 Fox Ln *Web:* www.caddomillsisd.org	Caddo Mills	TX	75135	903-527-6056	
Caddo Parish School Board 1961 Midway Ave PO Box 32000 **Fax:* Hum Res ■ *Web:* caddo.k12.la.us	Shreveport	LA	71130	318-603-6300	603-6559*
Cadillac Area Public Schools 421 S Mitchell St *Web:* vikingnet.org	Cadillac	MI	49601	231-876-5000	
Calhoun City of Schools Superintendents Offic 380 Barrett Rd *Web:* www.calhounschools.org	Calhoun	GA	30701	706-629-2900	
Calhoun County Board of Education PO Box 2084 *Web:* www.calhoun.k12.al.us	Anniston	AL	36202	256-741-7400	237-5332
Calhoun School Inc, The 160 W 74th St *Web:* www.calhoun.org	New York	NY	10023	212-497-6500	
Caliche Jr Sr. High School 26324 County Rd 65 *Web:* www.re1valleyschools.org	Iliff	CO	80736	970-522-8200	
Calvary Christian School Sys. 2331 E Little Creek Rd *Web:* www.ccss-va.org	Norfolk	VA	23518	757-583-9730	
Calvary Church of Pacific 701 Palisades Dr *Web:* calvarychristian.org	Pacific Palisades	CA	90272	310-454-6537	
Camden Central School District 51 Third St *Web:* www.camdenschools.org	Camden	NY	13316	315-245-2500	
Campbell Christian Schools 1075 E Campbell Ave *Web:* www.campbellchristian.org	Campbell	CA	95008	408-370-4900	
Campbell County Board of Education 101 Orchard Ln *TF:* 800-942-3767 ■ *Web:* campbell.k12.ky.us	Alexandria	KY	41001	859-635-2173	448-2428
Campbell County Dept of Education PO Box 843 *Web:* www.campbell.k12.tn.us	Jacksboro	TN	37757	423-562-8377	566-7562
Campbell Union High School District 3235 Union Ave *Web:* www.cuhsd.org	San Jose	CA	95124	408-371-0960	
Campbell Union School District 155 N Third St *Web:* www.campbellusd.org	Campbell	CA	95008	408-364-4200	
Camphill Special School Inc 1784 Fairview Rd *Web:* camphillspecialschool.org	Glenmoore	PA	19343	610-469-9236	
Canandaigua City School District 143 N Pearl St *Web:* www.canandaiguaschools.org	Canandaigua	NY	14424	585-396-3700	
Canby School District 1130 S Ivy St *TF:* 800-475-7785 ■ *Web:* www.canby.k12.or.us	Canby	OR	97013	503-266-7861	266-0022
Canton Public School District 403 Lincoln St *Web:* www.cantonschools.net	Canton	MS	39046	601-859-4110	
Capital High School 1500 Greenbrier St *Web:* www.capitalhigh.org	Charleston	WV	25311	304-348-6500	
Cardinal Hayes High School 650 grand concourse *Web:* www.cabrinihs.com	Bronx	NY	10451	718-292-6100	
Cardinal O'hara High School 39 Ohara Rd *Web:* www.cardinalohara.com	Tonawanda	NY	14150	716-695-2600	
Carl Sandburg Jr High School 2600 Martin Ln *Web:* www.ccsd15.net	Rolling Meadows	IL	60008	847-963-7800	
Carlbrook School LLC, The 3046 Carlbrook Rd *Web:* www.carlbrook.org	South Boston	VA	24592	434-476-2406	
Carlinville Primary School 18456 Shipman Rd *Web:* www.carlinvilleschools.net	Carlinville	IL	62626	217-854-9823	
Carlthorp School 438 San Vicente Blvd *Web:* carlthorp.org	Santa Monica	CA	90402	310-451-1332	
Carlynton School District 435 Kings Hwy *Web:* www.carlynton.k12.pa.us	Carnegie	PA	15106	412-429-8400	
Carroll County Board of Ed 125 N Court St Ste 101 *Web:* www.carrollk12.org	Westminster	MD	21157	410-751-3000	
Cartersville School Board PO Box 3310 *Web:* www.cartersville.k12.ga.us	Cartersville	GA	30120	770-382-3666	
Cary Academy 1500 N Harrison Ave *Web:* www.caryacademy.org	Cary	NC	27513	919-677-3873	
Casa Di Mir Montessori School 90 E Latimer Ave *Web:* www.casadimir.org	Campbell	CA	95008	408-370-3073	
Case Raymond Elementary School 8565 Shasta Lily Dr *Web:* egusd.net	Elk Grove	CA	95624	916-681-8820	
Castilleja School Foundation 1310 Bryant St *Web:* www.castilleja.org	Palo Alto	CA	94301	650-328-3160	
Castle High School 3344 State Rt 261 *Web:* www.warrickschools.com	Newburgh	IN	47630	812-853-3331	
Catalina High School 3645 E Pima St *Web:* www.catalinahighschoolfoundation.org	Tucson	AZ	85716	520-232-8400	
Cataract Elementary School 6070 State Hwy 27 *Web:* www.sparta.org	Sparta	WI	54656	608-366-3453	
Cathedral High School 1253 Bishops Rd *Web:* www.cathedralhighschool.com	Los Angeles	CA	90012	323-225-2438	
Catholic High School 4552 Princess Anne Rd *Web:* catholichigh.org	Virginia Beach	VA	23462	757-467-2881	
Cedar Riverside Community School 1610 S Sixth St Ste 100 *Web:* www.crcs-school.org	Minneapolis	MN	55454	612-339-5767	
Centennial Independent School District No 12 4757 N Rd	Circle Pines	MN	55014	763-792-5000	
Centennial School District 18135 SE Brooklyn *Web:* www.centennial.k12.or.us	Portland	OR	97236	503-760-7990	762-3689
Center Independent School Dist 404 Mosby St *Web:* www.centerisd.org	Center	TX	75935	936-598-5642	
Centinela Elementary School 1123 Marlborough Ave *Web:* inglewood.k12.ca.us	Inglewood	CA	90302	310-680-5440	
Central Montcalm Public School 1480 S Sheridan Rd *Web:* www.central-montcalm.org	Stanton	MI	48888	989-831-5243	
Central Union High School District 351 W Ross Ave *Web:* www.cuhsd.net	El Centro	CA	92243	760-336-4500	353-3606
Centronia 1420 Columbia Rd Nw Fl 1 *Web:* www.centronia.org	Washington	DC	20009	202-332-4200	

Name / Address	City	State	Zip	Phone	Fax
Century Junior High School 10801 W 159th St. *Web:* www.orland135.org	Orland Park	IL	60467	708-873-6400	
Champion Construction Corp 941 Forest Ave *Web:* www.championcc.homestead.com	Staten Island	NY	10310	718-818-8202	818-8238
Chapa Elementary School 5670 N Doffing Rd. *Web:* lajoyaisd.com	Mission	TX	78574	956-580-6150	
Chaparral Elementary School 451 Chaparral Dr *Web:* chpes.capousd.ca.schoolloop.com	Claremont	CA	91711	909-624-9146	
Chaparral High School 1600 N Cuyamaca St. *Web:* chaparral.guhsd.net	El Cajon	CA	92020	619-956-4600	
Chariho Regional School District 455 Switch Rd *Web:* www.chariho.k12.ri.us	Wood River Junction	RI	02894	401-364-7575	415-6076
Charleston County School District (CCSD) 75 Calhoun St. *TF:* 800-255-7688 ■ *Web:* www.ccsdschools.com	Charleston	SC	29401	843-937-6300	937-6300
Charleston School of Law LLC, The 81 Mary St *Web:* www.charlestonlaw.edu	Charleston	SC	29403	843-329-1000	
Charlevoix Public Schools 104 E St Marys Dr *Web:* www.rayder.net	Charlevoix	MI	49720	231-547-3200	547-0556
Charlotte Latin Schools Inc 9502 Providence Rd *Web:* www.charlottelatin.org	Charlotte	NC	28277	704-846-1100	
Charlotte-Mecklenburg Schools 701 E ML King Jr Blvd *TF:* 800-244-6224 ■ *Web:* www.cms.k12.nc.us	Charlotte	NC	28202	980-343-3000	343-5661
Chatham Central School District 50 Woodbridge Ave *Web:* www.chathamcentralschools.com	Chatham	NY	12037	518-392-2400	
Cherokee County Board of Education 221 W Main PO Box 769 *Web:* www.cherokee.k12.ga.us	Canton	GA	30169	770-479-1871	
Cherokee County School District 1 141 Twin Lk Rd PO Box 460 *Web:* www.cherokee1.k12.sc.us	Gaffney	SC	29342	864-206-2201	
Chester County School District 109 Hinton St. *Web:* www.chester.k12.sc.us	Chester	SC	29706	803-385-6122	
Cheverus High School 267 Ocean Ave *Web:* www.cheverus.org	Portland	ME	04103	207-774-6238	
Chicago Board of Education 125 S Clark St. *Web:* www.cps.edu/about_cps/Pages/AboutCPS.aspx	Chicago	IL	60603	773-553-1600	553-3543
Chico Unified School District 1163 E Seventh St *Web:* chicousd.org	Chico	CA	95928	530-891-3000	891-3220
Chignecto-central Regional 60 Lorne St *Web:* www.ccrsb.ca	Truro	NS	B2N3K3	902-897-8923	
Childventures Early Learning Academy Inc Burlington Campus 2180 Itabashi Way *Web:* www.childventures.ca	Burlington	ON	L7M5A5	905-637-8481	
Chino Hills High School 16150 Pomona Rincon Rd *Web:* chino.k12.ca.us	Chino Hills	CA	91709	909-606-7540	
Chisum High School 3250 S Church St. *Web:* www.chisumisd.org	Paris	TX	75462	903-737-2824	
Christ The King School Mothers Club Inc 4100 Colgate Ave *Web:* www.cks.org	Dallas	TX	75225	214-365-1234	
Christian County Public Schools 200 Glass Ave PO Box 609 *TF:* 800-274-7374 ■ *Web:* www.christian.kyschools.us	Hopkinsville	KY	42240	270-887-7000	887-1316
Churchill County School District 545 E Richards St *TF:* 800-232-6382 ■ *Web:* www.churchill.k12.nv.us	Fallon	NV	89406	775-423-5184	423-2959
Circleville City School District 388 Clark Dr *TF:* 800-418-6423 ■ *Web:* www.circlevillecityschools.org	Circleville	OH	43113	740-474-4340	474-6600
Citrus County School District 1007 W Main St *Web:* www.citrus.k12.fl.us	Inverness	FL	34450	352-726-1931	
Clarendon Hall School 1140 S Dukes St *Web:* clarendonhall.com	Summerton	SC	29148	803-485-3550	
Clark County School District (CCSD) 5100 W Sahara Ave. *TF:* 866-799-8997 ■ *Web:* www.ccsd.net	Las Vegas	NV	89146	702-799-5000	799-5125
Cleveland Municipal School District (CMSD) 1380 E Sixth St. **Fax:* Hum Res ■ *Web:* www.clevelandmetroschools.org	Cleveland	OH	44114	216-838-0000	361-2018*
Clinton Public School District PO Box 300 *Web:* www.clintonpublicschools.com	Clinton	MS	39060	601-924-7533	
Clio Area School District 430 N Mill St. *TF:* 866-984-3962 ■ *Web:* www.clioschools.org	Clio	MI	48420	810-591-0500	
Clovis Unified School District 1450 Herndon Ave *TF:* 800-498-9055 ■ *Web:* www.cusd.com	Clovis	CA	93611	559-327-9000	327-9109
Clyde's Transfer Inc 8015 Industrial Pk Rd *TF:* 800-342-8758 ■ *Web:* clydestransfer.com	Mechanicsville	VA	23116	804-746-1135	746-8898
Coachella Valley Unified School District PO Box 847 *Web:* www.coachella.k12.ca.us	Thermal	CA	92274	760-399-5137	
Cobleskill-Richmondville Central School District 155 Washington Ave. *Web:* www.crcs.k12.ny.us	Cobleskill	NY	12043	518-234-4032	
Cogun Inc 11369 Market St PO Box 704 **Fax Area Code:* 330	North Lima	OH	44452	800-258-5540	549-5328*
Coil Construction Inc 209 E Broadway *Web:* www.coilconstruction.com	Columbia	MO	65203	573-874-1444	443-3039
Coldwater Community Schools 401 Sauk River Dr. *Web:* www.coldwaterschools.org	Coldwater	MI	49036	517-279-5910	279-7651
Coleman Isd 2400 S Concho St *Web:* www.coleman.netxv.net	Coleman	TX	76834	325-625-4369	
Colfax Elementary School 24825 Ben Taylor Rd *Web:* www.colfax.k12.ca.us	Colfax	CA	95713	530-346-2202	
College Jean De Brebeuf 3200 Ch De La Cote-sainte-catherine *Web:* www.brebeuf.qc.ca	Montreal	QC	H3T1C1	514-342-1320	
College Notre Dame, Quebec 3791 chemin Queen Mary *Web:* www.collegenotre-dame.qc.ca	Montreal	QC	H3V1A8	514-739-3371	
College Regina Assumpta 1750 Rue Sauriol E *Web:* www.reginaassumpta.qc.ca	Montreal	QC	H2C1X4	514-382-4121	
Collier County School Board 5775 Osceola Trl *Web:* www.collier.k12.fl.us	Naples	FL	34109	239-377-0001	377-0336
Colorado Academy 3800 S Pierce St *Web:* www.coloradoacademy.org	Denver	CO	80235	303-986-1501	
Colorado Springs School District #11 1115 N El Paso St. *TF:* 800-273-8255 ■ *Web:* d11.org	Colorado Springs	CO	80903	719-520-2000	577-4546
Colts Neck High School 59 Five Points Rd. *Web:* www.frhsd.com	Colts Neck	NJ	07722	732-761-0190	
Columbus City Schools 270 E State St. *Web:* www.columbus.k12.oh.us	Columbus	OH	43215	614-365-5000	365-5652
Columbus County Schools PO Box 729 *Web:* www.columbus.k12.nc.us	Whiteville	NC	28472	910-642-5168	640-1010
Columbus Humanities Arts & Technology Academy 1333 Morse Rd *Web:* columbushumanitiesata.org	Columbus	OH	43229	614-261-1200	
Colusa County Office of Education 146 Seventh St *Web:* www.colusacountyclerk.com	Colusa	CA	95932	530-458-0350	
Community High School District 99 6301 Springside Ave. *Web:* csd99.org	Downers Grove	IL	60516	630-795-7100	
Community Unit School District 200 130 W Pk Ave *Web:* www.cusd200.org	Wheaton	IL	60189	630-682-2000	682-2227
Conestoga Valley School District 2110 Horseshoe Rd *TF:* 800-732-0025 ■ *Web:* www.cvsd.k12.pa.us	Lancaster	PA	17601	717-397-2421	397-0442
Conneaut School District 219 W School Dr *Web:* www.conneautsd.org	Linesville	PA	16424	814-683-5900	
Conseil Des Ecoles Publique De L'est De L'ontario 2445 St Laurent Blvd *Web:* www.cepeo.on.ca	Ottawa	ON	K1G6C3	613-742-8960	
Continental Development Corp 2041 Rosecrans Ave Ste 200 PO Box 916 *Web:* www.continentaldevelopment.com	El Segundo	CA	90245	310-640-1520	414-9279
Cooper High School 3639 Sayles Blvd *Web:* abileneisd.org	Abilene	TX	79605	325-691-1000	
Copperas Cove Independent School District 703 W Ave D. *TF:* 866-632-9992 ■ *Web:* www.ccisd.com	Copperas Cove	TX	76522	254-547-1227	
Coquihalla Middle School 2975 Clapperton Ave *Web:* www.sd58.bc.ca	Merritt	BC	V1K1A3	250-378-6104	
Cordova High School 1800 Berryhill Rd *Web:* www.cadetsofcordova.org	Cordova	TN	38016	901-416-4540	
Cornelia Connelly School of The Holy Child 2323 W Broadway *Web:* www.connellyhs.org	Anaheim	CA	92804	714-776-1717	
Cornwall Lebanon School District 105 E Evergreen Rd *Web:* www.clsd.k12.pa.us	Lebanon	PA	17042	717-272-2031	274-2786
Corona-Norco Unified School District 2820 Clark Ave *Web:* www.cnusd.k12.ca.us	Norco	CA	92860	951-736-5000	
Corunna Public School District 124 N Shiawassee St *TF:* 866-632-9992 ■ *Web:* www.corunna.k12.mi.us	Corunna	MI	48817	989-743-6338	743-4474
Council Rock School District 30 N Chancellor St *Web:* www.crsd.org	Newtown	PA	18940	215-944-1000	
Counterpane Montessori Inc 839 Hwy 314 *Web:* www.counterpane.org	Fayetteville	GA	30214	770-461-2304	
Crane Country Day School 1795 San Leandro Ln *Web:* www.craneschool.org	Santa Barbara	CA	93108	805-969-7732	
Craven County School (CCS) 3600 Trent Rd *Web:* www.craven.k12.nc.us	New Bern	NC	28562	252-514-6300	514-6351
Crawford Ausable School District 1135 N Old 27 *Web:* www.casdk12.net	Grayling	MI	49738	989-344-3500	
Crawford Central School District 11280 Mercer Pk *Web:* www.craw.org	Meadville	PA	16335	814-724-3960	
Crawford County School District 190 E Crusselle St PO Box 8 *Web:* www.crawfordcounty.schoolinsites.com	Roberta	GA	31078	478-836-3131	836-3114
Creative Contractors Inc 620 Drew St. *Web:* www.creativecontractors.com	Clearwater	FL	33755	727-461-5522	447-4808
Crespi Carmelite High School Inc 5031 Alonzo Ave. *Web:* www.crespi.org	Encino	CA	91316	818-345-1672	
Crete-monee School District No 201-u 1500 S Sangamon St *Web:* www.cm201u.org	Crete	IL	60417	708-367-8300	
Crisp County Board of Education PO Box 729 *Web:* www.crispschools.org	Cordele	GA	31015	229-276-3400	276-3406
Cristo Rey Jesuit High School 1852 W 22nd Pl *Web:* www.cristorey.net	Chicago	IL	60608	773-890-6889	

Phone | Fax

Crossroads School For Arts & Sciences
1714 21st St — Santa Monica CA 90404 310-829-7391 828-5636
Web: www.xrds.org

CSLI Inc 188 Nelson St — Vancouver NT V6B6J8 604-683-2754
Web: www.csli.com

Cuba Rushford Central School 5476 Rt 305 — Cuba NY 14727 585-968-2650 968-2651
Web: www.crcs.wnyric.org

Cullman City School 301 First St Ne Ste 100 — Cullman AL 35055 256-734-2233
Web: www.cullmancats.net

Cullman County Board of Education
PO Box 1590 — Cullman AL 35056 256-734-2933
Web: www.ccboe.org

Culver City Unified School District (CCUSD)
4034 Irving Pl — Culver City CA 90232 310-842-4220 842-4205
TF: 855-446-2673 ■ *Web:* www.ccusd.org

Cunningham-Limp Co
39300 W 12 Mile Rd Ste 200 — Farmington Hills MI 48331 248-489-2300 489-2310
Web: www.cunninghamlimp.com

Curie Metropolitan High School
4959 S Archer Ave — Chicago IL 60632 773-535-2100
Web: curiehs.org

Currituck County Board of Education
2958 Caratoke Hwy — Currituck NC 27929 252-232-2223 232-3655
Web: www.currituck.k12.nc.us

Cushman School - Elementary School
592 Ne 60th St — Miami FL 33137 305-757-1966
Web: www.cushmanschool.org

Cypress-Fairbanks Independent School District
PO Box 692003 — Houston TX 77269 281-897-4000
Web: www.cfisd.net

D & T Trucking Inc
3686 140th St E PO Box 510 — Rosemount MN 55068 651-480-7961
TF: 800-624-8130 ■ *Web:* bayandbay.com/index.php

Dakota Hills Middle School
4183 Braddock Trl Ste 1 — Saint Paul MN 55123 651-683-6800
Web: rschooltoday.com

Dallas Ctr - Grimes Community School District
1414 Walnut St Ste 200 — Dallas Center IA 50063 515-992-3866
Web: dcgschools.com/

Dallas Independent School District
3700 Ross Ave — Dallas TX 75204 972-925-3700 925-4201
TF: 866-796-3682 ■ *Web:* www.dallasisd.org

Dallastown Area School District
700 New School Ln — Dallastown PA 17313 717-244-4021
Web: www.dallastown.net

Dalton Public Schools
300 W Waugh St PO Box 1408 — Dalton GA 30722 706-876-4000 226-4583
Web: www.daltonpublicschools.com

Dalton Schools Inc 108 E 89th St — New York NY 10128 212-423-5200
Web: www.dalton.org

Dassel-Cokato Public Schools PO Box 1700 — Cokato MN 55321 320-286-4100
Web: www.dc.k12.mn.us

Davie County Schools 220 Cherry St — Mocksville NC 27028 336-751-5921 751-9013
Web: www.davie.k12.nc.us

Davis Elementary School 1050 Arlington Dr — Costa Mesa CA 92626 714-424-7930
Web: davis.nmusd.us

Dawson County Board of Education, The
517 Allen St — Dawsonville GA 30534 706-265-3246 265-1226
TF: 866-632-9992 ■ *Web:* www.dawsoncountyschools.org

Dayton City Schools 115 S Ludlow St — Dayton OH 45402 937-542-3000 542-3188
Web: www.dps.k12.oh.us

De Soto Public School District 73
610 Vineland School Rd — De Soto MO 63020 636-586-1000
Web: www.desoto.k12.mo.us

Decatur Isd Education Foundation Inc
501 E Collins St — Decatur TX 76234 940-393-7100
Web: www.decaturisd.us

Decatur Public Schools 110 Cedar St — Decatur MI 49045 269-423-6800
Web: raiderpride.org

Delano Union School District 1405 12th Ave — Delano CA 93215 661-721-5000 725-2446
Web: www.duesd.org

Delaware City School District
248 N Washington St — Delaware OH 43015 740-833-1100 833-1149
Web: www.dcs.k12.oh.us

Delaware Company Christian School
462 Malin Rd — Newtown Square PA 19073 610-353-6522
Web: www.dccs.org

Delaware County Intermediate Unit
200 Yale Ave — Morton PA 19070 610-938-9000 938-9887
TF: 800-441-3215 ■ *Web:* www.dciu.org

Dennis Chavez Es-203-Ichs Cluster Elementary School
7500 Barstow St Ne — Albuquerque NM 87109 505-821-1810
Web: www.dcchavez.com

Dennis-Yarmouth Regional School District
296 Stn Ave — South Yarmouth MA 02664 508-398-7600 398-7622
Web: www.dy-regional.k12.ma.us

Denver Public Schools 900 Grant St — Denver CO 80203 720-423-3200 423-3413
TF: 866-726-0033 ■ *Web:* dpsk12.org

Des Moines Independent School District
901 Walnut St — Des Moines IA 50309 515-242-7911 242-7579
TF: 800-452-1111 ■ *Web:* www.dmschools.org

Desert Sands Charter High School
3030 E Palmdale Blvd Ste G — Palmdale CA 93550 661-272-0044
Web: www.dschs.org

Desoto Parish School District
201 Crosby St — Mansfield LA 71052 318-872-2836 872-1324
TF: 888-741-0205 ■ *Web:* desotopsb.com

Destinta Theatres 215 Quassaick Ave — New Windsor NY 12553 845-569-8181 473-8808*
**Fax Area Code:* 973 ■ *Web:* www.destinta.com

Detroit Community High School 12675 Burt Rd — Detroit MI 48228 313-537-3570
Web: www.detcomschools.org

Detroit Public Schools 3031 W Grand Blvd — Detroit MI 48202 313-873-7927 873-4564
TF: 800-656-4673 ■ *Web:* www.detroitk12.org

Diamond Bar High School
21400 Pathfinder Rd — Diamond Bar CA 91765 909-594-1405
Web: dbhs.wvusd.k12.ca.us

Dickenson County School District
PO Box 1127 — Clintwood VA 24228 276-926-4643 926-6374
TF: 866-632-9992 ■ *Web:* www.dickenson.k12.va.us

Dillard Academy Charter School
504 W Elm St — Goldsboro NC 27530 919-581-0166
Web: www.dillardacademy.org

Dinwiddie County Public School
14016 Boydton Plank Rd PO Box 7 — Dinwiddie VA 23841 804-469-4190 469-4197
Web: www.dinwiddie.k12.va.us

District of Columbia Public Schools (DCPS)
1200 First St NE — Washington DC 20002 202-442-5885 442-5026
Web: www.dcps.dc.gov

Division Scolaire Franco-Manitobaine No 49
1263 Dawson Rd — Lorette MB R0A0Y0 204-878-9399
Web: www.dsfm.mb.ca

Donegal School District 1051 Koser Rd — Mount Joy PA 17552 717-653-1447
Web: www.donegal.k12.pa.us

Douglas County Board of Education
9030 Hwy 5 PO Box 1077 — Douglasville GA 30134 770-651-2000
Web: www.douglas.k12.ga.us

Downey High School 11040 Brookshire Ave — Downey CA 90241 562-869-7301
Web: www.dusd.net

Duarte Unified School District
1620 Huntington Dr — Duarte CA 91010 626-599-5000 599-5069
TF: 888-225-7377 ■ *Web:* www.duarte.k12.ca.us

Dublin Unified School District
7471 Larkdale Ave — Dublin CA 94568 925-828-2551 829-6532
Web: www.dublin.k12.ca.us

Dufour Petroleum LP 1374 US 11 — Petal MS 39465 601-583-9991

Durham Academy Inc 3130 Pickett Rd — Durham NC 27705 919-489-9118
TF: 888-904-9149 ■ *Web:* www.da.org

Duval County School System
1701 Prudential Dr — Jacksonville FL 32207 904-390-2000 390-2586
Web: www.duvalschools.org

Eagleville Elementary School
S101w34511 County Rd Lo — Eagle WI 53119 262-363-6258
Web: www.methacton.org

Earle Baum Center of The Blind
4539 Occidental Rd — Santa Rosa CA 95401 707-523-3222
Web: www.earlebaum.org

Earlimart School District PO Box 11970 — Earlimart CA 93219 661-849-3386
Web: www.earlimart.org

Early County School District
11927 Columbia St — Blakely GA 39823 229-723-4337
Web: www.early.k12.ga.us

East Bernard Isd 723 College St — East Bernard TX 77435 979-335-7519
Web: www.ebisd.org

East Cleveland Board of Education
14305 Shaw Ave — Cleveland OH 44112 216-268-6600
Web: www.east-cleveland.k12.oh.us

East Maine School District 63 (EMSD)
10150 Dee Rd — Des Plaines IL 60016 847-299-1900 299-9963
TF: 866-752-6850 ■ *Web:* www.emsd63.org

East Penn School District 800 Pine St — Emmaus PA 18049 610-966-8300
Web: new.eastpennsd.org/

East Ramapo Central School District
105 S Madison Ave — Spring Valley NY 10977 845-577-6000 577-6038
Web: www.eram.k12.ny.us

East Side Union High School District
830 N Capitol Ave — San Jose CA 95133 408-347-5000 347-5045
Web: www.esuhsd.org

East Valley School District 361
12325 E Grace Ave — Spokane WA 99216 509-924-1830 927-9500
Web: www.evsd.org

Eastconn 376 Hartford Tpke — Hampton CT 06247 860-455-0707
Web: www.eastconn.org

Eastern Lancaster County School District
669 E Main St PO Box 609 — New Holland PA 17557 717-354-1500 354-1512
TF: 877-935-5655 ■ *Web:* www.elanco.k12.pa.us

Eastern Nc School for The Deaf
1311 Us Hwy 301 N — Wilson NC 27893 252-237-2450
Web: encsd.net

Easton Area School District Inc
1801 Bushkill Dr — Easton PA 18040 610-250-2400
Web: www.eastonsd.org

Eastside Union School District
45006 30th St E — Lancaster CA 93535 661-952-1200 952-1220
TF: 877-263-7995 ■ *Web:* www.eastside.k12.ca.us

Ecampusalberta 1301 16 Ave Nw — Calgary AB T2M0L4 403-284-8777
Web: www.ecampusalberta.ca

Ecole De La Cle-des-champs
3858 Rue Principale — Dunham QC J0E1M0 450-295-2722
Web: cle-des-champs.csvdc.qc.ca

Edcouch-Elsa Independent School District
PO Box 127 — Edcouch TX 78538 956-262-6000 262-6032
Web: www.eeisd.org

Edison School Elementary School
246 S Fair Ave — Elmhurst IL 60126 630-834-4272
Web: elmhurst205.org

EdisonLearning Inc 900 S Gay St Ste 1000 — Knoxville TN 37902 865-329-3600
Web: www.edisonlearning.com

Edwardsburg Public Schools
69410 Section St — Edwardsburg MI 49112 269-663-1031
Web: www.edwardsburgpublicschools.org

Edwardsville Community School District 7
708 St Louis St — Edwardsville IL 62025 618-656-1182 692-7423
Web: www.ecusd7.org

El Campo Independent School District
700 W Norris St — El Campo TX 77437 979-543-6771
Web: www.ecisd.org

Phone | Fax

El Centro Elementary School District
1256 Broadway St. . . . El Centro CA 92243 760-352-5712
Web: www.ecesd.com

El Monte City School District
3540 Lexington Ave . . . El Monte CA 91731 626-453-3700
Web: web.emcsd.org

El Monte Union High School District
3537 Johnson Ave . . . El Monte CA 91731 626-444-9005 448-8419
Web: www.emuhsd.k12.ca.us

El Paso Independent School District
6531 Boeing Dr . . . El Paso TX 79925 915-779-3781 779-4280*
**Fax:* Hum Res ■ *Web:* episd.org

Elbert County Board of Education
50 Laurel Dr . . . Elberton GA 30635 706-213-4000
Web: www.elbert.k12.ga.us

Elim Christian School
13020 S Central Ave. . . . Palos Heights IL 60463 708-389-0555
Web: www.elimcs.org

Elisabeth Morrow School, The
435 Lydecker St . . . Englewood NJ 07631 201-568-5566
Web: elisabethmorrow.org

Ellington Elementary School 3001 Lindell Ave . . . Quincy IL 62301 217-222-5697
Web: www.qps.org

Elmont Union Free School District
135 Elmont Rd . . . Elmont NY 11003 516-326-5500 326-5574
Web: www.elmontschools.org

Elmore County Public School System
100 H H Robison Dr PO Box 817 . . . Wetumpka AL 36092 334-567-1200
Web: www.elmoreco.com

Elzinga & Volkers 86 E Sixth St. . . . Holland MI 49423 616-392-2383 392-3752
TF General: 800-632-7734 ■ *Web:* www.elzinga-volkers.com

Emanuel County Board of Education
PO Box 130 . . . Swainsboro GA 30401 478-237-6674 237-3404
Web: www.emanuel.k12.ga.us

Emek Hebrew Academy 15365 Magnolia Blvd. . . . Sherman Oaks CA 91403 818-380-9950
Web: www.emek.org

Encinitas Union School District Educational Facilities Corp
101 S Rancho Santa Fe Rd . . . Encinitas CA 92024 760-944-4300
Web: www.eusd.k12.ca.us

Engineering Design Technologies (EDT)
1705 Entp Way SE Ste 200 . . . Marietta GA 30067 770-988-0400 988-0300
Web: www.edtinc.net

Ennis Independent School District
303 W Knox PO Box 1420 . . . Ennis TX 75120 972-872-7000 875-8667
Web: www.ennis.k12.tx.us

Ericson Elementary School 4774 E Yale Ave. . . . Fresno CA 93703 559-253-6450
Web: fresnounified.org

Erie 2-Chautauqua Cattaraugus Boces (ECCB)
8685 Erie Rd . . . Angola NY 14006 716-549-4454
TF: 800-228-1184 ■ *Web:* www.e2ccb.org

Etiwanda School District (ESD) 6061 E Ave. . . . Etiwanda CA 91739 909-899-2451 899-1235
TF: 800-300-1506 ■ *Web:* www.etiwanda.k12.ca.us

Eugene School District 4J 200 N Monroe St. . . . Eugene OR 97402 541-687-3123 687-3691
Web: www.4j.lane.edu

Eureka Union School District
5455 Eureka Rd . . . Granite Bay CA 95746 916-791-4939 791-5527
Web: www.eureka-usd.k12.ca.us

Evanston/Skokie School District 65
1500 Mcdaniel Ave. . . . Evanston IL 60201 847-859-8000 859-8707
Web: www.district65.net

Evergreen Public Schools
13501 NE 28th St PO Box 8910 . . . Vancouver WA 98668 360-604-4000 892-5307
Web: evergreenps.org

Evesham Township Board of Education
25 S Maple Ave. . . . Marlton NJ 08053 856-983-1800
Web: www.evesham.k12.nj.us

Exploris 401 Hillsborough St. . . . Raleigh NC 27603 919-715-3690
Web: www.exploris.org

Fairhill School & Diagnostic 16150 Preston Rd. . . . Dallas TX 75248 972-233-1026
Web: fairhill.org

Fairview Elementary School 300 Salem Dr . . . Plymouth WI 53073 920-892-2621
Web: www.plymouth.k12.wi.us

Fannin County Board of Education
2290 E First St . . . Blue Ridge GA 30513 706-632-3771 632-7583
TF: 800-308-2145 ■ *Web:* www.fannin.k12.ga.us

Far Horizons Montessori 264 N Main St . . . Orange CA 92868 714-997-8333
Web: www.farhorizonsmontessori.org

Farwest Freight Systems Inc 4504 E Vly Hwy E. . . . Sumner WA 98390 253-826-4565

Fayette County Board of Education
210 Stonewall Ave . . . Fayetteville GA 30214 770-460-3535 460-8191
TF: 800-550-5131 ■ *Web:* www.fcboe.org

Fayette County Public Schools
701 E Main St. . . . Lexington KY 40502 859-381-4100 381-4271*
**Fax:* Hum Res ■ *Web:* fcps.net

Ferndale School District 502
6041 Vista Dr PO Box 698 . . . Ferndale WA 98248 360-383-9200 383-9201
Web: www.ferndale.wednet.edu

Ferry Transportation Inc Five Thames Ave. . . . Laurel MS 39440 601-425-5542
Web: www.ferrytrans.com

First Farmers & Merchants National Bank
816 S Garden St PO Box 1148 . . . Columbia TN 38401 931-388-3145 380-8359
OTC: FIME ■ *TF:* 800-882-8378 ■ *Web:* www.myfirstfarmers.com

Flint Community Schools 923 E Kearsley St . . . Flint MI 48503 810-760-1000
Web: www.flintschools.org

Floresville Independent School District
908 Tenth St . . . Floresville TX 78114 830-393-5300
Web: floresvilleathletics.us

Floyd Blinsky Trucking Inc 210 Keys Rd. . . . Yakima WA 98901 509-457-3484 457-0832
TF: 800-537-9599 ■ *Web:* www.blinsky.com

Floyd County Board of Education
600 Riverside Pkwy NE . . . Rome GA 30161 706-234-1031 236-1824
Web: www.floydboe.net

Phone | Fax

Foley High School 621 Penn St. . . . Foley MN 56329 320-968-7246
Web: www.bcbe.org

Forest Hills Local School 7550 Forest Rd . . . Cincinnati OH 45255 513-231-3600
Web: www.foresthills.edu

Forest Lake Area School District
6100 210th St N . . . Forest Lake MN 55025 651-982-8100 982-8137
TF: 866-632-9992 ■ *Web:* www.forestlake.k12.mn.us

Forney Independent School District (Inc)
600 S Bois D ARC St . . . Forney TX 75126 972-564-4055
Web: www.forneyisd.net

Forsyth County Board of Education
1120 Dahlonega Hwy . . . Cumming GA 30040 770-887-2461 781-6632
Web: www.forsyth.k12.ga.us

Fort Bragg Unified School District
312 S Lincoln St. . . . Fort Bragg CA 95437 707-961-2850
TF: 800-734-7793 ■ *Web:* www.fbusd.us

Fort Mill School District 4
120 E Elliott St . . . Fort Mill SC 29715 803-548-2527 547-4696
Web: www.fort-mill.k12.sc.us

Fort Wayne Community Schools (FWCS)
1200 S Clinton St. . . . Fort Wayne IN 46802 260-467-2009 467-1186
Web: www.fwcs.k12.in.us

Fort Worth Independent School District
100 N University Dr . . . Fort Worth TX 76107 817-871-2000 814-2935
Web: fwisd.org

Fox Chapel Area School District
611 Field Club Rd. . . . Pittsburgh PA 15238 412-967-2453 967-0697
Web: www.fcasd.edu

Franklin Local School District
PO Box 428 . . . Duncan Falls OH 43734 740-674-5203
TF: 800-846-4976 ■ *Web:* www.franklin-local.k12.oh.us

Franklin Special School District
507 New Hwy 96 W . . . Franklin TN 37064 615-794-6624 790-4716
Web: www.fssd.org

Franklin-Pierce Schools 315 129th St S . . . Tacoma WA 98444 253-298-3000
Web: fpschools.org

Fredericksburg City Public Schools
817 Princess Anne St . . . Fredericksburg VA 22401 540-372-1130 372-1111
TF: 800-846-4464 ■ *Web:* www.cityschools.com

Free The Children 233 Carlton St . . . Toronto ON M5A2L2 416-925-5894
Web: www.freethechildren.com

Freedom Middle School 3016 Ridgeland Ave . . . Berwyn IL 60402 708-795-5800
Web: www.bsd100.org

Fremont Public Schools 220 W Pine St. . . . Fremont MI 49412 231-924-2350 924-5264
TF: 800-822-9433 ■ *Web:* www.fremont.net

Fremont Unified School District PO Box 5008 . . . Fremont CA 94537 510-657-2350 770-9851
TF: 800-544-5248 ■ *Web:* www.fremont.k12.ca.us

Fresno Unified School District 2309 Tulare St . . . Fresno CA 93721 559-457-3000 457-3528*
**Fax:* Hum Res ■ *Web:* www.fresno.k12.ca.us

Friends School of Wilmington Inc
350 Peiffer Ave . . . Wilmington NC 28409 910-792-1811
Web: www.fsow.org

Friendship House PO Box 3778 . . . Scranton PA 18505 570-342-8305 344-1178
Web: www.friendshiphousepa.org

Frontier Central School District
5120 Orchard Ave. . . . Hamburg NY 14075 716-926-1710

Fulton School District 58 Two Hornet Dr. . . . Fulton MO 65251 573-590-8000
Web: www.fulton58.org

Futures High School
26440 La Alameda Ste 6026. . . . Mission Viejo CA 92691 949-348-0608
Web: www.halstromacademy.org

Gainesville City Schools 508 Oak St. . . . Gainesville GA 30501 770-536-5275 287-2019
TF: 800-533-0682 ■ *Web:* www.gcssk12.net

Galveston Independent School District (GISD)
3904 Ave PO Box 660. . . . Galveston TX 77550 409-766-5100 762-8391
TF: 877-262-1492 ■ *Web:* www.gisd.org

Garden Grove Unified School District
10331 Stanford Ave . . . Garden Grove CA 92840 714-663-6000 663-6100
Web: www.ggusd.us

Garfield Elementary School 1514 S Ninth Ave . . . Maywood IL 60153 708-450-2009
Web: www.maywood89.org

Garland Independent School District (GISD)
501 S Jupiter PO Box 469026 . . . Garland TX 75046 972-494-8201 485-4936
TF: 800-252-5555 ■ *Web:* www.garlandisd.net

Gaston County School
943 Osceola St PO Box 1397 . . . Gastonia NC 28054 704-866-6117
Web: www.gaston.k12.nc.us

Gateway Unified School Disrict
4411 Mtn Lakes Blvd . . . Redding CA 96003 530-245-7900
Web: www.gateway-schools.org

Genesee Intermediate School District
2413 W Maple Ave . . . Flint MI 48507 810-591-4400
Web: www.geneseeisd.org

Geneseo Community Unit School District 228
209 S College Ave . . . Geneseo IL 61254 309-945-0450 945-0445
Web: www.dist228.org

Geneva County Board of Education PO Box 250. . . . Geneva AL 36340 334-684-5690
Web: www.genevacountyschools.com

Giddings Independent Schl Dst
2337 N Main St . . . Giddings TX 78942 979-542-2854 542-9264
Web: giddingsisd.net

Gilmer Junior High 111 Bruce St. . . . Gilmer TX 75645 903-843-3808
Web: www.gilmerisd.org

Gilroy Unified School District
7810 Arroyo Cir . . . Gilroy CA 95020 408-847-2700 842-1158
Web: www.gusd.k12.ca.us

Gladstone School District 115
17789 Webster Rd . . . Gladstone OR 97027 503-655-2777 655-5201
TF: 800-328-0272 ■ *Web:* www.gladstone.k12.or.us

Glen Ellyn School District 41
793 N Main St . . . Glen Ellyn IL 60137 630-790-6400 790-1867
Web: www.d41.dupage.k12.il.us

				Phone	Fax
Glen Grove Elementary School 3900 Glenview Rd *Web:* www.glenview34.org	Glenview	IL	60025	847-998-5030	
Glens Falls City School District 15 Quade St *Web:* www.gfsd.org	Glens Falls	NY	12801	518-792-1212	
Goleta Union School District 401 N Fairview Ave *Web:* www.goleta.k12.ca.us	Goleta	CA	93117	805-681-1200	
Goliad Independent School District PO Box 830 *TF:* 800-750-9911 ■ *Web:* www.goliadisd.org	Goliad	TX	77963	361-645-3259	
Gordon County Board of Education 205 Warrior Path PO Box 12001 *Web:* www.gcbe.org	Calhoun	GA	30703	706-629-7366	625-5671
Gordon Sevig Trucking Co (GSTC) 400 Hwy 151 E *Web:* www.gstcinc.com	Walford	IA	52351	319-846-5500	846-5541
Goshen County School District 1 626 W 25th Ave *Web:* www.goshen.k12.wy.us	Torrington	WY	82240	307-532-2171	532-7085
Grand Rapids Public Schools (GRPS) 1331 Franklin St SE PO Box 117 *Web:* www.grps.k12.mi.us	Grand Rapids	MI	49506	616-819-2000	819-2104
Grandview Heights City School District 1587 W Third Ave *Web:* www.grandviewschools.org	Columbus	OH	43212	614-481-3600	
Granite Falls School District 307 N Alder Ave *TF:* 888-651-8931 ■ *Web:* www.gfalls.wednet.edu	Granite Falls	WA	98252	360-691-7717	691-4459
Grant Career Center 718 W Plane St *Web:* www.grantcareer.com	Bethel	OH	45106	513-734-6222	
Granville Central School District 58 Quaker St *Web:* www.granvillecsd.org	Granville	NY	12832	518-642-1051	642-4544
Grapeland Elementary School 210 Third St *Web:* www.grapelandisd.net	Grapeland	TX	75844	936-687-2317	
Gratiot-Isabella Regional Education Service District 1131 E Ctr St PO Box 310 *Web:* giresd.net	Ithaca	MI	48847	989-875-5101	875-2858
Gray Transportation Inc 2459 GT Dr *TF:* 800-234-3930 ■ *Web:* www.graytran.com	Waterloo	IA	50703	319-234-3930	234-8841
Greenfield Union School District 1624 Fairview Rd *Web:* www.gfusd.k12.ca.us	Bakersfield	CA	93307	661-837-6000	832-2873
Greenwood School District 50 1855 Calhoun Rd PO Box 248 *TF:* 888-260-9430 ■ *Web:* www.gwd50.org	Greenwood	SC	29648	864-941-5400	941-5427
Grosse Ile Township Schools 23276 E River Rd *Web:* www.gischools.org	Grosse Ile	MI	48138	734-362-2555	
Guidance Charter School, The 1125 E Palmdale Blvd # B *Web:* www.thegcs.org	Palmdale	CA	93550	661-272-1701	
Guilford County Schools 617 W Market St *TF:* 866-286-7337 ■ *Web:* www.gcsnc.com	Greensboro	NC	27401	336-370-8100	370-8398
Gulf Coast Bank & Trust Co 200 St Charles Ave *TF:* 800-223-2060 ■ *Web:* www.gulfbank.com	New Orleans	LA	70130	504-561-6100	581-3583
Gulf County School District 150 Middle School Rd *Web:* www.gulf.k12.fl.us	Port Saint Joe	FL	32456	850-229-8256	229-6089
Guy Shavender Trucking Inc PO Box 206 *TF:* 800-682-2447 ■ *Web:* www.shavender.com	Pantego	NC	27860	252-943-3379	943-6434
Habersham County Board of Education 132 W Stanford Mill Rd PO Box 70 *Web:* www.habershamschools.com	Clarkesville	GA	30523	706-754-2118	754-1549
Hale County Board of Education 1115 Powers St *Web:* www.halek12.org	Greensboro	AL	36744	334-624-8836	
Halifax County Public Schools 1030 Mary Bethune St PO Box 1849 *TF:* 800-253-2687 ■ *Web:* www.halifax.k12.va.us	Halifax	VA	24558	434-476-2171	476-1858
Hall County Schools 711 Green St NW Ste 100 *TF:* 800-505-4732 ■ *Web:* www.hallco.org	Gainesville	GA	30501	770-534-1080	535-7404
Hamblen County Board of Education 210 E Morris Blvd *Web:* www.hcboe.net	Morristown	TN	37813	423-586-7700	586-7747
Hamburg Area School District (HASD) 701 Windsor St *Web:* www.hasdhawks.org	Hamburg	PA	19526	610-562-2241	562-2634
Hamilton City School District (HCSD) 533 Dayton St PO Box 627 *Web:* www.hamiltoncityschools.com	Hamilton	OH	45012	513-887-5000	887-5014
Hamilton County Dept of Education 3074 Hickory Vly Rd **Fax:* Hum Res ■ *Web:* www.hcde.org	Chattanooga	TN	37421	423-209-8400	209-8539*
Hamilton County Educational Service Ctr (HCESC) 11083 Hamilton Ave *TF:* 800-964-8211 ■ *Web:* www.hcesc.org	Cincinnati	OH	45231	513-674-4200	742-8339
Hanning Construction Inc 815 Swan St *Web:* www.hannigconstruction.com	Terre Haute	IN	47807	812-235-6218	235-1218
Hardee County School District PO Box 1678 *Web:* www.hardee.k12.fl.us	Wauchula	FL	33873	863-773-9058	
Harlandale Isd 102 Genevieve Dr *Web:* www.harlandale.net	San Antonio	TX	78214	210-989-4322	
Harlem Children's Zone Inc 35 E 125th St *Web:* www.hcz.org	New York	NY	10035	212-360-3255	289-0661
Harlingen High School 1201 Marshall St *Web:* hcisd.org	Harlingen	TX	78550	956-427-3600	
Harnett County Board of Education 1008 11th Street PO Box 1029 *TF:* 800-942-3767 ■ *Web:* www.harnett.k12.nc.us	Lillington	NC	27546	910-893-8151	893-8839
Harrisburg School District Inc 1601 State St *Web:* www.hbgsd.k12.pa.us	Harrisburg	PA	17103	717-703-4000	
Harrow District High School 45 Wellington *Web:* www.gecdsb.on.ca	Harrow	ON	N0R1G0	519-738-2234	
Hart County Board of Education PO Box 696 *Web:* www.hart.k12.ga.us	Hartwell	GA	30643	706-376-5141	376-7046
Hartford Public Schools 960 Main St **Fax:* Hum Res ■ *Web:* www.hartfordschools.org	Hartford	CT	06103	860-695-8000	722-8454*
Haslett Public School 5593 Franklin St *Web:* www.haslett.k12.mi.us	Haslett	MI	48840	517-339-8242	
Hatboro-Horsham School District 229 Meetinghouse Rd *TF:* 866-771-3170 ■ *Web:* www.hatboro-horsham.org	Horsham	PA	19044	215-672-5660	420-5262
Hauppauge School District (HSP) 495 Hoffman Ln PO Box 6006 *Web:* www.hauppauge.k12.ny.us	Hauppauge	NY	11788	631-761-8208	
Hawaii Dept of Education Honolulu District Office 4967 Kilauea Ave *TF:* 800-437-8641 ■ *Web:* www.hawaiipublicschools.org	Honolulu	HI	96816	808-733-4950	733-4953
Hays Consolidated I S D 21003 I- 35 *Web:* www.hayscisd.net	Kyle	TX	78640	512-268-2141	268-2147
Hayward Unified School District (HUSD) 24411 Amador St PO Box 5000 *Web:* www.husd.k12.ca.us	Hayward	CA	94540	510-784-2600	784-2641
Hebrew Academy of The Five Towns & Rockaway Inc 389 Central Ave *Web:* www.haftr.org	Lawrence	NY	11559	516-569-3370	
Hemlock Public Schools District PO Box 260 *Web:* www.hemlock.k12.mi.us	Hemlock	MI	48626	989-642-5282	
Henderson Isd 200 N High St *Web:* www.hendersonisd.org	Henderson	TX	75652	903-657-8511	
Henry Carlson Co 1205 W Russell St PO Box 84010 *Web:* henrycarlson.com	Sioux Falls	SD	57104	605-336-2410	332-1314
Hereford Independent School District 601 N 25 Mile Ave *Web:* www.herefordisd.net	Hereford	TX	79045	806-363-7600	363-7699
Hertford County School District PO Box 158 *Web:* www.hertford.k12.nc.us	Winton	NC	27986	252-358-1761	
Highland Central School District 320 Pancake Hollow Rd *Web:* www.highland-k12.org	Highland	NY	12528	845-691-1000	
Highland Falls-Ft Montgomery School District PO Box 287 *Web:* www.hffmcsd.org	Highland Falls	NY	10928	845-446-9575	
Hillsboro City Schools 39 Willetsville Pk *Web:* www.hillsboro.k12.oh.us	Hillsboro	OH	45133	937-393-3475	
Hillsboro Community Unit School District 3 1311 Vandalia Rd *Web:* www.hillsboroschools.net	Hillsboro	IL	62049	217-532-2942	532-3137
Hillsboro School District 3083 NE 49th Pl *Web:* www.hsd.k12.or.us	Hillsboro	OR	97124	503-844-1500	844-1540
Hillsborough County Public Schools 901 E Kennedy Blvd *TF:* 800-962-2873 ■ *Web:* www.sdhc.k12.fl.us	Tampa	FL	33602	813-272-4000	272-4073
Hillsborough Township Board of Education 379 S Branch Rd *TF:* 800-272-1325 ■ *Web:* www.htps.us	Hillsborough	NJ	08844	908-431-6600	369-8286
Hilltop Elementary School 2615 W Lincoln Rd *Web:* www.d15.org	Mchenry	IL	60051	815-385-4421	
Hinds County School District 13192 Hwy 18 *Web:* www.hinds.k12.ms.us	Raymond	MS	39154	601-857-5222	857-8548
Hingham School District 220 Central St *Web:* www.hingham-ma.com	Hingham	MA	02043	781-741-1500	
Hoffmeier Inc 3210 N Lewis Ave *Web:* www.hoffmeier.com	Tulsa	OK	74110	918-428-5823	430-0820
Holiday Express Corp 721 S 28th St *TF:* 800-831-5078 ■ *Web:* www.holidayxpress.net	Estherville	IA	51334	712-362-5812	362-3019
Holland Patent Central School District 9601 Main St *Web:* www.hpschools.org	Holland Patent	NY	13354	315-865-7200	
Holland Public Schools 156 W 11th St *Web:* www.hollandpublicschools.org	Holland	MI	49423	616-494-2000	392-8225
Holmes District School Board (HDSB) 701 E Pennsylvania Ave *Web:* www.hdsb.org	Bonifay	FL	32425	850-547-9341	547-3568
Homer Central School District PO Box 500 *Web:* www.homercentral.org	Homer	NY	13077	607-749-7241	
Hopkins County Board-Education 320 S Seminary St *Web:* hopkins.k12.ky.us	Madisonville	KY	42431	270-825-6000	825-6072
Houston Independent School District 228 McCarty St *TF:* 800-446-2821 ■ *Web:* www.houstonisd.org	Houston	TX	77029	713-556-6000	556-6006
Hueneme Elementary School Dist 205 N Ventura Rd *TF:* 866-431-2478 ■ *Web:* www.huensd.k12.ca.us	Port Hueneme	CA	93041	805-488-3588	488-1779
Humble Independent School District PO Box 2000 *Web:* www.humble.k12.tx.us	Humble	TX	77347	281-641-1000	641-1050
Huntington Union Free School District 3 PO Box 1500 *Web:* www.hufsd.edu	Huntington	NY	11743	631-673-2185	
Huntsville Board of Education 200 White St **Fax:* Hum Res ■ *TF:* 877-517-0020 ■ *Web:* www.huntsvillecityschools.org	Huntsville	AL	35801	256-428-6800	428-6838*
Hyde Park Central School District (Inc) PO Box 2033 *Web:* www.hpcsd.org	Hyde Park	NY	12538	845-229-4000	
Idaho Falls School District 91 Education Foundation Inc 690 John Adams Pkwy *TF:* 888-993-7120 ■ *Web:* www.d91.k12.id.us	Idaho Falls	ID	83401	208-525-7500	525-7596

				Phone	Fax
Ilex Construction & Woodworking 131 N Washington St Ste 400 *TF:* 866-551-4539 ■ *Web:* www.ilexconstruction.com	Easton	MD	21601	410-820-4393	820-4394
Iman Academy 10929 Almeda Genoa Rd *Web:* www.imanacademy.org	Houston	TX	77034	713-910-3626	
Imperial High School 517 W Barioni Blvd *Web:* imperialhighschool.org	Imperial	CA	92251	760-355-3220	
Imperial Valley Rop 687 W State St *Web:* www.ivrop.org	El Centro	CA	92243	760-482-2600	
Indianapolis Public Schools 120 E Walnut St *Web:* myips.org	Indianapolis	IN	46204	317-226-4000	
Ingleside High School 2807 Mustang Dr *Web:* www.inglesideisd.org	Ingleside	TX	78362	361-776-2712	
J.M. Bozeman Enterprises Inc 166 Seltzer Ln *TF General:* 800-472-1836 ■ *Web:* jmbozeman.com	Malvern	AR	72104	501-844-4060	844-4133
Jackson County Intermediate School District (JCISD) 6700 Browns Lk Rd *Web:* jacksoncisd.schoolwires.com/site/default.aspx?pageid=1	Jackson	MI	49201	517-768-5200	
Jackson County School District 6 300 Ash St *TF:* 800-978-3040 ■ *Web:* www.district6.org	Central Point	OR	97502	541-494-6200	664-1637
Jackson County School District 9 PO Box 548 *Web:* www.eaglepnt.k12.or.us	Eagle Point	OR	97524	541-830-1200	
Jackson County School System 1660 Winder Hwy *TF:* 800-760-3727 ■ *Web:* www.jackson.k12.ga.us	Jefferson	GA	30549	706-367-5151	367-9457
Jackson Public Schools 662 S President St *Web:* www.jackson.k12.ms.us	Jackson	MS	39201	601-960-8700	960-8713
Jacksonville Independent School District PO Box 631 *TF:* 866-914-5202 ■ *Web:* www.jisd.org	Jacksonville	TX	75766	903-586-6511	586-3133
Jacksonville School District 117 516 Jordan St *Web:* jsd117.org	Jacksonville	IL	62650	217-243-9411	243-6844
Jaffrey-Rindge School District 81 Fitzgerald Dr Unit 2 *Web:* sau47.org	Jaffrey	NH	03452	603-532-8100	
James Jordan Middle School 20040 Parthenia St *Web:* www.jamesjordanms.com	Northridge	CA	91324	818-882-2496	
Jamesville-Dewitt Central School Dist (Inc) 6845 Edinger Dr PO Box 606 *Web:* www.jamesvilledewitt.org	Fayetteville	NY	13066	315-445-8300	445-8477
Jefferson Area Local School District 906 W Main St *Web:* www.west-jefferson.k12.oh.us	West Jefferson	OH	43162	614-879-7654	
Jefferson Davis Parish Parish Schools 203 E Plaquemine St PO Box 640 *Web:* www.webserver.jeffersondavis.org	Jennings	LA	70546	337-824-1834	
Jefferson Schools 2400 N Dixie Hwy *Web:* www.jeffersonschools.org	Monroe	MI	48162	734-289-5550	
Jenison Public Schools (JPS) 8375 20th Ave *Web:* www.jpsonline.org	Jenison	MI	49428	616-457-1402	457-8090
Jennings County Schools 34 W Main St *TF:* 866-346-3724 ■ *Web:* www.jenningscounty-in.gov	North Vernon	IN	47265	812-346-4483	
Joan of Arc Academy 2221 Elmira Dr *Web:* joanofarcacademy.com	Ottawa	ON	K2C1H3	613-728-6364	
John Carroll School, The 703 Churchville Rd *Web:* www.johncarroll.org	Bel Air	MD	21014	410-879-2480	
John Cooper School One John Cooper Dr *Web:* www.johncooper.org	The Woodlands	TX	77381	281-367-0900	
John Hersey High School 1900 E Thomas St *Web:* jhhs.d214.org	Arlington Heights	IL	60004	847-718-4800	
Johnston Community School District PO Box 10 *Web:* www.johnston.k12.ia.us	Johnston	IA	50131	515-278-0470	278-5884
Joliet Public School District 86 420 N Raynor Ave *Web:* www.joliet86.org	Joliet	IL	60435	815-740-3196	
Jubilee Christian Center 105 Nortech Pkwy *Web:* jubilee.org	San Jose	CA	95134	408-262-0900	
Julian Charter School Inc 1704 Cape Horn *TF:* 866-853-0003 ■ *Web:* www.juliancharterschool.org	Julian	CA	92036	760-765-3847	
Junipero Serra High School 31422 Camino Capistrano *Web:* serra.capousd.ca.schoolloop.com	San Juan Capistrano	CA	92675	949-489-7216	
K12 Inc 2300 Corporate Pk Dr *NYSE: LRN* ■ *TF:* 866-512-2273 ■ *Web:* www.k12.com	Herndon	VA	20171	703-483-7000	483-7330
Kansas City Missouri School District 1211 McGee St *Web:* www.kcpublicschools.org	Kansas City	MO	64106	816-418-7000	418-7766
Katherine Delmar Burke School 195 32nd Ave *Web:* www.kdbs.org	San Francisco	CA	94121	415-751-0177	
Kaweah High School 21215 Ave 300 *Web:* www.kaweah.org	Exeter	CA	93221	559-592-9467	
KBT Inc 3885 W Michigan St **Fax Area Code:* 937	Sidney	OH	45365	800-860-9455	497-1870*
Kelseyville Unified School District 4410 Konocti Rd *Web:* www.kusd.lake.k12.ca.us	Kelseyville	CA	95451	707-279-1511	
Kentwood Public Schools 5820 Eastern Ave SE *Web:* www.kentwoodps.org	Grand Rapids	MI	49508	616-455-4400	455-4476
Keppel Union School District PO Box 186 *Web:* www.keppel.k12.ca.us	Pearblossom	CA	93553	661-944-2155	944-2933
Kern County High School District 5801 Sundale Ave *Web:* www.khsd.k12.ca.us	Bakersfield	CA	93309	661-827-3100	827-3300

				Phone	Fax
Kershaw County School District 2029 W DeKalb St *Web:* www.kershaw.k12.sc.us	Camden	SC	29020	803-432-8416	425-8918
Keystone School District 451 Huston Ave *Web:* www.keyknox.com	Knox	PA	16232	814-797-5921	
King City Union Elementary School District 800 Broadway St *Web:* www.kcusd.org	King City	CA	93930	831-385-1144	
King's Academy Inc, The 8401 Belvedere Rd *Web:* www.tka.net	West Palm Beach	FL	33411	561-686-4244	
Kingsway College School 4600 Dundas St W *Web:* www.kcs.on.ca	Etobicoke	ON	M9A1A5	416-234-5073	
Kirkwood School District R-7 Inc 11289 Manchester Rd *Web:* www.kirkwoodschools.org	Kirkwood	MO	63122	314-213-6100	984-0002
Klein Independent School District 7200 Spring Cypress Rd *Web:* www.kleinisd.net	Spring	TX	77379	832-249-4000	
La Citadelle International Academy of Arts & Science 15 Mallow Rd *Web:* www.lacitadelleacademy.com	North York	ON	M3B1G2	416-385-9685	
La Mesa-Spring Valley School District 4750 Date Ave *Web:* www.lmsvsd.k12.ca.us	La Mesa	CA	91941	619-668-5700	
La Tercera Elementary School 1600 Albin Way *Web:* laterceraschool.org	Petaluma	CA	94954	707-765-4303	
Lab School of Washington, The 4759 Reservoir Rd Nw *Web:* www.labschool.org	Washington	DC	20007	202-965-6600	
Lafayette Parish School System 113 Chaplin Dr *Web:* www.lpssonline.com	Lafayette	LA	70508	337-521-7000	
Laingsburg Community School District 205 S Woodhull Rd *Web:* www.laingsburg.k12.mi.us	Laingsburg	MI	48848	517-651-2705	651-9075
Lake Superior Ind Sch Dist 381 1640 2 Hwy *TF:* 888-878-0136 ■ *Web:* www.isd381.k12.mn.us	Two Harbors	MN	55616	218-834-8201	834-8239
Lake Travis Independent School District 3322 Ranch Rd 620 S *Web:* www.laketravis.txed.net	Austin	TX	78738	512-533-6000	533-6001
Lake Washington School District 414 16250 NE 74th St PO Box 97039 *Web:* www.lwsd.org	Redmond	WA	98073	425-936-1200	936-1213
Lake Worth Independent School District (LWISD) 6805 Telephone Rd *Web:* www.lwisd.org	Lake Worth	TX	76135	817-306-4200	237-2583
Lakeside Lutheran High School 231 Woodland Beach Rd *Web:* www.llhs.org	Lake Mills	WI	53551	920-648-2321	
Lamesa Independent School District PO Box 261 *TF:* 888-286-6700 ■ *Web:* www.lamesaisd.net	Lamesa	TX	79331	806-872-5461	872-6220
Lamphere Schools 31201 Dorchester Ave *Web:* www.lamphere.k12.mi.us	Madison Heights	MI	48071	248-589-1990	589-2618
Lancaster City School District 345 E Mulberry St *TF:* 888-647-4729 ■ *Web:* www.lancaster.k12.oh.us	Lancaster	OH	43130	740-687-7300	
Lanier County Board of Education 247 S Hway 221 *Web:* www.lanier.k12.ga.us	Lakeland	GA	31635	229-482-3966	482-3020
Las Cruces Public Schools 505 S Main St Ste 249 **Fax: Hum Res* ■ *TF:* 888-222-1498 ■ *Web:* www.lcps.k12.nm.us	Las Cruces	NM	88001	575-527-5800	527-6658*
Laurel Highlands School District (LHSD) 304 Bailey Ave *Web:* www.lhsd.org	Uniontown	PA	15401	724-437-2821	437-8929
Laurens County Board of Education 467 Firetower Rd *Web:* www.lcboe.net	Dublin	GA	31021	478-272-4767	277-2619
Lawrence Public Schools 110 McDonald Dr *TF:* 800-772-1213 ■ *Web:* www.usd497.org	Lawrence	KS	66044	785-832-5000	832-5016
Leadership Public Schools 344 Thomas L Berkley Way *Web:* www.leadps.org	Oakland	CA	94612	510-830-3780	225-2575
Lebanon City School District 700 Holbrook Ave *Web:* www.lebanon.k12.oh.us	Lebanon	OH	45036	513-934-5770	
Leflore County School District 1901 Hwy 82 W *Web:* www.leflorecountyschools.org	Greenwood	MS	38930	662-453-8566	
Lemont High School 800 Porter St *Web:* lhs210.net	Lemont	IL	60439	630-257-6211	
Lenoir County Public School (LCPS) 2017 W Vernon Ave PO Box 729 *TF:* 888-684-8404 ■ *Web:* www.lenoir.k12.nc.us	Kinston	NC	28504	252-527-1109	527-6884
Leon County Schools (LCS) 2757 W Pensacola St	Tallahassee	FL	32304	850-487-7306	*
Lewis S. Mills High School 24 Lyon Rd *TF:* 800-673-2411 ■ *Web:* www.region10ct.org	Burlington	CT	06013	860-673-0423	673-9128
Lexington City Board of Education 1010 Fair St *Web:* www.lexcs.org	Lexington	NC	27292	336-242-1527	
Lexington School District 4 607 E Fifth St *Web:* www.lexington4.net	Swansea	SC	29160	803-568-1000	568-1020
Liberal High School 205 N Paine *Web:* www.liberal.k12.mo.us	Liberal	MO	64762	417-843-2125	
Liberty Independent School District 1600 Grand Ave *Web:* www.libertyisd.net	Liberty	TX	77575	936-336-7215	

Phone / Fax

Liberty-Eylau Independent School District
2901 Leopard Dr. Texarkana TX 75501 903-832-1535 838-9444
Web: www.leisd.net

Libertyville School District 70
1381 W Lake St Libertyville IL 60048 847-362-8393
Web: www.d70.k12.il.us

Light of Christ Rcssd 16
9301 19th Ave. North Battleford SK S9A3N5 306-445-6158
Web: www.loccsd.ca

Limestone County School District
300 S Jefferson St Athens AL 35611 256-232-5353 233-6461
Web: www.lcsk12.org

Lincoln Public Schools PO Box 82889 Lincoln NE 68510 402-436-1000 436-1620*
*Fax: Hum Res ■ *Web:* www.lps.org

Lincoln Unified School District
2010 W Swain Rd Stockton CA 95207 209-953-8700
Web: www.lusd.net

Lincoln-Way Central High School
1801 E Lincoln Hwy New Lenox IL 60451 815-462-2100
Web: www.lw210.org

Linden Kildare 205 Kildare Rd Linden TX 75563 903-756-7071
Web: www.lkcisd.net

Little Cypress-Mauriceville Cisd Inc
6586 FM 1130 Orange TX 77632 409-883-2232
Web: www.lcmcisd.org

Little Friends Inc 140 N Wright St. Naperville IL 60540 630-355-6533
Web: littlefriendsinc.org

Little Rock School District
810 W Markham St. Little Rock AR 72201 501-447-1000 447-1162*
*Fax: Hum Res ■ *Web:* www.lrsd.org

Locust Valley Central School District
22 Horse Hollow Rd Locust Valley NY 11560 516-277-5000
Web: www.lvcsd.k12.ny.us

Lompoc Unified School District 1301 N A St. Lompoc CA 93436 805-742-3300 735-8452
Web: www.lusd.org

London City School District 380 Elm St London OH 43140 740-852-5700
Web: www.london.k12.oh.us

Long County Board of Education PO Box 428 Ludowici GA 31316 912-545-2367 545-2380
Web: www.longcountyps.com

Long Valley Charter School 436 Susan Dr 965 Doyle CA 96109 530-827-2395
Web: www.longvalleycs.org

Longview School District 2715 Lilac St Longview WA 98632 360-575-7000 575-7231
TF: 800-533-7881 ■ *Web:* www.longview.k12.wa.us

Los Alamitos Unified School District
10293 Bloomfield St. Los Alamitos CA 90720 562-799-4700 799-4711
Web: www.losal.org

Los Altos School District 201 Covington Rd Los Altos CA 94024 650-947-1150 947-0118
Web: www.lasdschools.org

Los Angeles Unified School District (LAUSD)
333 S Beaudry Ave Los Angeles CA 90017 213-241-1000
TF: 877-772-6273

Los Banos California 645 Seventh St Los Banos CA 93635 209-827-7034
Web: www.losbanos.org

Los Gatos Union Elementary School District
17010 Roberts Rd. Los Gatos CA 95032 408-335-2000
Web: www.lgusd.org

Louis Riel School Division 900 St Mary's Rd. Winnipeg MB R2M3R3 204-257-7827
Web: www.lrsd.net

Louisville Municipal School District
112 S Columbus Ave PO Box 909 Louisville MS 39339 662-773-3411 773-4013
Web: www.louisville.k12.ms.us

Loyola Academy 1100 Laramie Wilmette IL 60091 847-256-1100
Web: www.goramblers.org

Lubbock-Cooper Independent School District
16302 Loop 493 Lubbock TX 79423 806-863-2282
Web: www.lcisd.net

Luling Independent School District
212 E Bowie St Luling TX 78648 830-875-3191
Web: www.luling.txed.net

Lyons Elementary School District 103
4100 Joliet Ave. Lyons IL 60534 708-783-4100
Web: www.sd103.com

Macomb Community Unit School District 185
323 W Washington St. Macomb IL 61455 309-833-4161
Web: www.medfd.org

Madera Unified School District 1902 HowaRd Rd. Madera CA 93637 559-675-4500 675-1186
TF: 800-322-6384 ■ *Web:* www.madera.k12.ca.us

Madison Local Board of Educuation
1379 Grace St. Mansfield OH 44905 419-589-2600
Web: www.madison-richland.k12.oh.us

Madison Metropolitan School District
545 W Dayton St. Madison WI 53703 608-663-1879 204-0346*
*Fax: Hum Res ■ *Web:* www.madison.k12.wi.us

Mahanoy Area School District
One Golden Bear Dr Mahanoy City PA 17948 570-773-3443
Web: www.mabears.net

Maine Endwell Central School
712 Farm to Market Rd. Endwell NY 13760 607-754-1400 754-1650
Web: www.me.stier.org

Malvern Prep School 418 S Warren Ave. Malvern PA 19355 484-595-1100
Web: malvernprep.org

Malverne Union Free School District 12
301 Wicks Ln Malverne NY 11565 516-887-6400
Web: www.malverne.k12.ny.us

Mandell School, The 795 Columbus Ave. New York NY 10025 212-222-2925
Web: www.mandellschool.org

Manteno High School 443 N Maple St. Manteno IL 60950 815-928-7100
Web: www.manteno5.org

Manteo High School 829 Wingina St Manteo NC 27954 252-473-5841
Web: daretolearn.org

Maple Valley School District
11090 Nashville Hwy Vermontville MI 49096 517-852-9699
Web: www.mvs.k12.mi.us

Marana Unified School District 6
11279 W Grier Rd Ste 127 Marana AZ 85653 520-682-4757 616-4515
Web: www.maranausd.org

Mardel Inc 7727 SW 44th St. Oklahoma City OK 73179 405-745-1300 745-1337
Web: www.mardel.com

Marin Academy 1600 Mission Ave San Rafael CA 94901 415-453-4550
Web: www.ma.org

Marine Military Academy Air Wing Inc
320 Iwo Jima Blvd Harlingen TX 78550 956-423-6006
Web: www.mma-tx.org

Marinette School District 2139 Pierce Ave. Marinette WI 54143 715-735-1406
Web: www.marinette.k12.wi.us

Marion County Board of Education Inc
200 Gaston Ave. Fairmont WV 26554 304-367-2100
Web: www.marionboe.com

Marion Ctr Area School District
PO Box 156 Marion Center PA 15759 724-397-5551
Web: www.mcasd.net

Mark Young Construction Inc 7200 Miller Pl Frederick CO 80504 303-776-1449 776-1729
Web: www.markyoungconstruction.com

Marshall Independent School District (Inc)
1305 E Pinecrest Dr Marshall TX 75670 903-927-8701 935-0203
Web: www.marshallisd.com

Marshall Middle School 401 S Saratoga St. Marshall MN 56258 507-537-6938
Web: swmn.org

Martin County West High School
16 W Fifth St. Sherburn MN 56171 507-764-4661
Web: martin.k12.mn.us

Martinez Unified School District
921 Susana St Martinez CA 94553 925-335-5800 335-5960
Web: www.martinezusd.net

Massillon City School District
207 Oak Ave SE Massillon OH 44646 330-830-3900
Web: massillonschools.org

Masters Academy of Central Florida Inc, The
1500 Lukas Ln Oviedo FL 32765 407-971-2221
Web: www.mastersacademy.com

Mbc Computer Service Inc 11112 Downs Rd Pineville NC 28134 704-525-7590
Web: www.mbcservice.com

McCrory Construction Company LLC
1280 Assembly St PO Box 145 Columbia SC 29201 803-799-8100 254-9800
Web: www.mccroryconstruction.com

McIntosh County Board of Education
200 Pine St. Darien GA 31305 912-437-6645
Web: www.mcintosh.k12.ga.us

Mclean School of Maryland Inc, The
8224 Lochinver Ln Potomac MD 20854 301-299-8277
Web: www.mcleanschool.org

McLeod Express LLC 5002 Cundiff Ct. Decatur IL 62526 800-709-3936 875-7914*
*Fax Area Code: 217 ■ *TF General:* 800-709-3936 ■ *Web:* www.mcleodtrucking.com

Mead School District 2323 E Farwell Rd Mead WA 99021 509-465-6000 465-6020
Web: www.mead354.org

Meadowridge School 12224 240 St Maple Ridge BC V4R1N1 604-467-4444
Web: www.meadowridge.bc.ca

Mechanicsburg Area School District (Inc)
100 E Elmwood Ave Second Fl Mechanicsburg PA 17055 717-691-4500 691-3438
Web: www.mbgsd.org

Mecosta-Osceola Intermediate School District
15760 190th Ave. Big Rapids MI 49307 231-796-3543
TF: 877-211-5253 ■ *Web:* www.moisd.org

Medford Township Board of Education
128 Rt 70 Ste 1 Medford NJ 08055 609-654-6416 654-7436
Web: www.medford.k12.nj.us

Melvindale-Northern Allen Park Public Schools
18530 Prospect St Melvindale MI 48122 313-389-3300 389-3312
Web: www.melnap.k12.mi.us

Memphis City Board of Education
2597 Avery Ave. Memphis TN 38112 901-416-5300 416-5578
Web: www.mcsk12.net

Mentor Public Schools 6451 Center St Mentor OH 44060 440-255-4444
Web: www.mentorschools.net

Meramec Valley R-3 School District
126 N Payne St. Pacific MO 63069 636-271-1400 271-1406
TF: 866-632-9992 ■ *Web:* www.mvr3.k12.mo.us

Merion Mercy Academy
511 Montgomery Ave Merion Station PA 19066 610-664-6655
Web: www.merion-mercy.com

Meriwether County Schools
2100 Gaston St PO Box 70 Greenville GA 30222 706-672-4297
Web: www.meriwether.k12.ga.us

Mesa Grande School Elementary School
9172 Third Ave Hesperia CA 92345 760-244-3709
Web: mesagrande-husd-ca.schoolloop.com

Metairie Park Country Day School Alumni Association Inc, The
300 Park Rd Metairie LA 70005 504-837-5204
Web: mpcds.com

Metropolitan Construction Services LLC (MCS)
2803 Butterfield Rd Ste 100 Oak Brook IL 60523 630-691-7200 691-7234
Web: www.metroconstructionllc.com

Metropolitan Nashville Public Schools (MNPS)
2601 Bransford Ave Nashville TN 37204 615-259-8531 214-8890
TF: 800-848-0298 ■ *Web:* www.mnps.org

Miami-Dade County Public Schools (M-DCPS)
1450 NE Second Ave Miami FL 33132 305-995-1000
Web: www.dadeschools.net

Michener Institute for Applied
222 Saint Patrick St Toronto ON M5T1V4 416-596-3101
Web: www.michener.ca

Mid-central Educational Cooperative Office
612 Main Ave Platte SD 57369 605-337-2636
Web: midcentral-coop.org

Phone | Fax

Mid-East Career & Technology Centers
400 RichaRds Rd . . . Zanesville OH 43701 740-454-0101 454-0731
Web: www.mid-east.k12.oh.us

Middlebury Community Schools
57853 Northridge Dr. . . . Middlebury IN 46540 574-825-9425 825-9426
TF: 866-632-9992 ■ *Web:* www.mcsin-k12.org

Middlesex County Educational Service Commission
1660 Stelton Rd . . . Piscataway NJ 08854 732-777-9848
Web: www.mresc.k12.nj.us

Middlesex County Vocational & Technical High Schools
PO Box 1070 . . . East Brunswick NJ 08816 732-257-3300
Web: www.mcvts.net

Middleton Cross Plains Area School District
7106 S Ave . . . Middleton WI 53562 608-829-9000
Web: www.mcpasd.k12.wi.us

Middletown Area School District (Inc)
55 W Water St Ste 2 . . . Middletown PA 17057 717-948-3300 948-3329
Web: www.raiderweb.org

Middletown City School 1515 Girard Ave . . . Middletown OH 45044 513-423-0781 420-4579
Web: middletowncityschools.com

Midland High School 1301 Eastlawn Dr . . . Midland MI 48642 989-923-5181
Web: www.midlandisd.net

Midwestern Intermediate Unit Iv
453 Maple St . . . Grove City PA 16127 724-458-6700 458-5083
TF: 800-942-8035 ■ *Web:* www.miu4.k12.pa.us

Mifflin County School District
201 Eigth St . . . Lewistown PA 17044 717-248-0148
Web: www.mcsdk12.org

Miken Builders Inc 32782 Cedar Dr Unit 1 . . . Millville DE 19967 302-537-4444 537-4525
TF: 800-888-7501 ■ *Web:* www.mikenbuilders.com

Mildred High School 5475 S Us Hwy 287 . . . Corsicana TX 75109 903-872-6505
Web: www.mildredisd.org

Milford Exempted Village School District
1039 St Rt 28 . . . Milford OH 45150 513-831-9690 831-3208
Web: www.milfordschools.org

Milken Community High School
15800 Zeldins Way . . . Los Angeles CA 90049 310-440-3500
Web: www.milkenschool.org

Millburn Township New Jersey Board Education
434 Millburn Ave . . . Millburn NJ 07041 973-376-3600
Web: www.millburn.org

Miller Jordan Middle School
700 N Mccullough St . . . San Benito TX 78586 956-361-6666
Web: mjms.sbcisd.net

Millet Learning Ctr 3660 Southfield Dr . . . Saginaw MI 48601 989-777-2520
Web: www.sisd.cc

Milwaukee Public Schools 5225 W Vliet St . . . Milwaukee WI 53208 414-475-8393 475-8722*
**Fax:* Hum Res ■ *Web:* mpsportal.milwaukee.k12.wi.us

Minisink Valley Central Sd PO Box 217 . . . Slate Hill NY 10973 845-355-5100
Web: www.minisink.com

Minneapolis Public Schools
3345 Chicago Ave. . . . Minneapolis MN 55407 612-668-0000 668-0525
TF: 800-543-7709 ■ *Web:* www.mpls.k12.mn.us

Minnehaha Academy 3100 W River Pkwy . . . Minneapolis MN 55406 612-729-8321
Web: www.minnehahaacademy.net

Minnetonka Public School Service Ctr
5621 County Rd 101 . . . Minnetonka MN 55345 952-401-5000 401-5093
Web: www.minnetonka.k12.mn.us

Minnewaska Area High School
25122 State Hwy 28 . . . Glenwood MN 56334 320-239-4820
Web: www.minnewaska.k12.mn.us

Minot Public School District 1
215 Second St SE . . . Minot ND 58701 701-857-4400 857-4432
Web: minot.k12.nd.us

Minuteman Regional High School
758 Marrett Rd . . . Lexington MA 02421 781-861-6500
Web: www.minuteman.org

Missouri School Boards Association
2100 I-70 Dr SW . . . Columbia MO 65203 573-445-9920
Web: www.msbanet.org

Mitchell Elementary School 14429 Condon Ave . . . Lawndale CA 90260 310-676-6140
Web: www.lawndale.k12.ca.us

Mobile County Public Schools
1 Magnum Pass PO Box 180069 . . . Mobile AL 36618 251-221-4000 221-4545*
**Fax:* Hum Res ■ *TF:* 800-605-1033 ■ *Web:* www.mcpss.com

Modesto City Schools 426 Locust St . . . Modesto CA 95351 209-576-4011 576-4846*
**Fax:* Hum Res ■ *TF:* 800-942-3767 ■ *Web:* monet.k12.ca.us

Mohawk Council of Akwesasne
Stn Main Po Box 579 . . . Cornwall ON K6H5T3 613-575-2250
Web: www.akwesasne.ca

Monache High School 960 N Newcomb St . . . Porterville CA 93257 559-782-7178
Web: mhs.portervilleschools.org

Monroe County Intermediate School District
1101 S Raisinville Rd . . . Monroe MI 48161 734-242-5799
Web: www.misd.k12.mi.us

Monrovia Unified School District
325 E Huntington Dr . . . Monrovia CA 91016 626-471-2000
Web: www.monroviaschools.net

Monte Vista High School Keynoters
3131 Stone Vly Rd . . . Danville CA 94526 925-552-5530
Web: www.mvkeynoters.org

Montebello Unified School District (MUSD)
123 S Montebello Blvd . . . Montebello CA 90640 323-887-7900
Web: www.montebello.k12.ca.us

Montgomery Public Schools
307 S Decatur St PO Box 1991 . . . Montgomery AL 36104 334-223-6700 269-3076
Web: www.mps.k12.al.us

Monticello Central School District
237 Forestburgh Rd . . . Monticello NY 12701 845-794-7700
TF: 866-805-0990 ■ *Web:* www.monticelloschools.net

Montini Catholic High School 19w070 16th St . . . Lombard IL 60148 630-627-6930
Web: montini.org

Montrose County School District Re-1j Inc
PO Box 10000 . . . Montrose CO 81402 970-249-7726 249-7173
Web: www.mcsd.org

Mooresville Graded School District
305 N Main St . . . Mooresville NC 28115 704-658-2530 663-3005
TF: 800-222-1222 ■ *Web:* www.mgsd.k12.nc.us

Morgan County Schools 1325 Pt Mallard Pkwy . . . Decatur AL 35601 256-353-6442 309-2141
Web: www.morgank12.org

Moriah School of Engelwood
53 S Woodland St . . . Englewood NJ 07631 201-567-0208
Web: www.moriahschool.org

Morris School District 31 Hazel St . . . Morristown NJ 07960 973-292-2300
Web: www.morrisschooldistrict.org

Morris-Union Jointure Commission
340 Central Ave . . . New Providence NJ 07974 908-464-7625
Web: www.mujc.org

Morton High School 500 Champion Dr . . . Morton TX 79346 806-266-5523
Web: mhs.morton709.org

Mountain Empire Unified School District
3291 Buckman Springs Rd . . . Pine Valley CA 91962 619-473-9022 473-9728
Web: www.meusd.k12.ca.us

Mountain Mission School 1760 Edgewater Dr . . . Grundy VA 24614 276-935-2954
Web: www.mountainmissionschool.org

Mountain View School District (MVSD)
3320 Gilman Rd . . . El Monte CA 91732 626-652-4000 652-4052
Web: www.mtviewschools.com

Mt Pleasant Central School District
825 Westlake Dr . . . Thornwood NY 10594 914-769-5500 769-3733
Web: www.mtplcsd.org

Mt Street Michael High School 4300 Murdock Ave . . . Bronx NY 10466 718-515-6400
Web: mtstmichael.org

Mt. Lebanon School District 7 Horsman Dr . . . Pittsburgh PA 15228 412-344-2000 344-2047
TF: 800-587-3257 ■ *Web:* www.mtlsd.org

Mukwonago Area School District
385 County Rd NNE . . . Mukwonago WI 53149 262-363-6300 363-6272
Web: www.masd.k12.wi.us

Murray Co 1807 Pk 270 Dr Ste 460 . . . Saint Louis MO 63146 314-576-2818 434-5780
TF: 888-323-5560 ■ *Web:* www.murray-company.com

N e Florida Educational Consortium
3841 Reid St . . . Palatka FL 32177 386-329-3800
Web: nefec.org

Nashoba Regional School District Inc
50 Mechanic St . . . Bolton MA 01740 978-779-0539
Web: www.nrsd.net

Nassau County School District
1201 Atlantic Ave . . . Fernandina Beach FL 32034 904-491-9900
Web: www.edline.net/pages/nassau_county_school_district

National Children's Ctr Inc
6200 Second St NW . . . Washington DC 20011 202-722-2300
TF: 866-632-9992 ■ *Web:* www.nccinc.org

National Outdoor Leadership School
284 Lincoln St . . . Lander WY 82520 307-332-5300 332-1220
TF: 800-710-6657 ■ *Web:* www.nols.edu

National School District 1500 N Ave . . . National City CA 91950 619-336-7500 336-7521
Web: www.nsd.us

Nationwide Magazine & Book Distributors Inc
3000 E Grauwyler Rd PO Box 170427 . . . Irving TX 75017 972-438-7852 721-0613
TF General: 800-777-9068 ■ *Web:* www.nationwidemagazine.com

Nebraska City Middle School
909 First Corso . . . Nebraska City NE 68410 402-873-5591
Web: nebraskacity.ne.schoolwebpages.com

Netcong Elementary School 26 College Rd . . . Netcong NJ 07857 973-347-0020
Web: www.netcongschool.org

Netivot Hatorah 18 Atkinson Ave . . . Thornhill ON L4J8C8 905-771-1234
Web: www.netivot.com

New Brighton Area School District
3225 43rd St . . . New Brighton PA 15066 724-843-1795 843-6144
TF: 866-950-1040 ■ *Web:* www.nbasd.org

New Haven Unified School District
34200 Alvarado Niles Rd . . . Union City CA 94587 510-471-1100
Web: www.nhusd.k12.ca.us

New Hope 459 W King St . . . York PA 17401 717-845-4046
Web: challengeacademy.net

New Lenox School District 122 (NLSD)
102 S Cedar Rd . . . New Lenox IL 60451 815-485-2169
Web: www.nlsd122.org

New Trier Township High School District 203
Seven Happ Rd . . . Northfield IL 60093 847-446-7000 784-7500
Web: www.newtrier.k12.il.us

New York City Dept of Education 65 Ct St . . . Brooklyn NY 11201 718-935-4000
Web: schools.nyc.gov

Newberg School District 29 Jt 714 E Sixth St . . . Newberg OR 97132 503-554-5000 538-4374
Web: www.newberg.k12.or.us

Newton-Conover City Sch Dist 605 N Ashe Ave . . . Newton NC 28658 828-464-3191
Web: www.nccs.k12.nc.us

Niagara Fresh Fruit Co 5796 Wilson Burt Rd . . . Burt NY 14028 716-778-7631 778-8768
Web: niagarafreshfruit.com

Niles Community School 111 Spruce St . . . Niles MI 49120 269-683-0732
TF: 877-622-2321 ■ *Web:* nilesschools.schoolwires.net

Niskayuna Central School District (NCSD)
1239 Van Antwerp Rd . . . Schenectady NY 12309 518-377-4666 377-4074
TF: 866-893-6337 ■ *Web:* www.niskyschools.org

Noble & Greenough School 10 Campus Dr . . . Dedham MA 02026 781-326-3700
Web: www.teachingcompany.com

Nokomis Regional High School 266 Williams Rd . . . Newport ME 04953 207-368-4354
Web: rsu19.org

Nordonia Hills School District
9370 Olde 8 Rd . . . Northfield OH 44067 330-467-0580
Web: www.nordoniaschools.org

Norfolk Academy 1585 Wesleyan Dr . . . Norfolk VA 23502 757-461-6236
Web: www.norfolkacademy.org

Norfolk Collegiate School 7336 Granby St . . . Norfolk VA 23505 757-480-2885
Web: www.norfolkcollegiate.org

Name / Address	City	State	Zip	Phone	Fax
Norfolk Public Schools 800 E City Hall Ave *TF:* 800-846-4464 ■ *Web:* www.nps.k12.va.us	Norfolk	VA	23510	757-628-3843	628-3820
Norman Howard School 275 Pinnacle Rd *Web:* www.normanhoward.org	Rochester	NY	14623	585-334-8010	
Normandy School District 3855 Lcas Hunt Rd Ste 100 *Web:* www.normandy.k12.mo.us	Saint Louis	MO	63121	314-493-0400	493-0414
North Boone Middle School 17641 Poplar Grove Rd *Web:* nbcusd.org	Poplar Grove	IL	61065	815-765-9274	
North Elementary School 300 W Seventh St *Web:* www.esc14.net	Breckenridge	TX	76424	254-559-6511	
North Hunterdon-Voorhees Regional High School District 1445 SR- 31 *Web:* www.nhvweb.net	Annandale	NJ	08801	908-735-2846	735-6914
North Love Christian School 5301 E Riverside Blvd *Web:* northlove.org	Rockford	IL	61114	815-877-6021	
North Mason School District Inc 71 E Campus Dr *Web:* www.nmsd.wednet.edu	Belfair	WA	98528	360-277-2300	
North Monterey County Unified School District 8142 Moss Landing Rd *Web:* www.nmcusd.org	Moss Landing	CA	95039	831-633-3343	633-2937
North Ridgeville City School District 5490 Mills Creek Ln *TF:* 877-644-6457 ■ *Web:* www.nrcs.k12.oh.us	North Ridgeville	OH	44039	440-327-4444	
North Rose-Wolcott Central School District 11631 Salter Colvin Rd *TF:* 855-707-2267 ■ *Web:* www.nrwcs.org	Wolcott	NY	14590	315-594-3141	594-2352
North Sanpete School District Inc 390 East 700 South *Web:* www.nsh.nsanpete.k12.ut.us	Mount Pleasant	UT	84647	435-462-2452	462-3112
North Santiam School District 29 J 1155 N Third Ave *Web:* nsantiam.orvsd.org	Stayton	OR	97383	503-769-6924	769-3578
North Schuylkill School District 15 Academy Ln *Web:* www.northschuylkill.net	Ashland	PA	17921	570-874-0466	874-3334
North Shore School District 112 (NSSD) 1936 Green Bay Rd *Web:* www.nssd112.org	Highland Park	IL	60035	224-765-3000	
Northampton County School District 701 N Church St PO Box 158 *Web:* www.northampton.k12.nc.us	Jackson	NC	27845	252-534-1371	534-4631
Northeast Wyoming Board of Cooperative Educational Services Boces 410 N Miller Ave *Web:* www.newboces.com	Gillette	WY	82716	307-682-0231	
Northern Burlington County School District 160 Mansfield Rd E *Web:* www.nburlington.com	Columbus	NJ	08022	609-298-3900	
Northern Local School District 8700 Sheridan Dr *Web:* www.nlsd.k12.oh.us	Thornville	OH	43076	740-743-1303	743-3301
Northview Public School 4451 Hunsberger NE *TF:* 866-632-9992 ■ *Web:* www.nvps.net	Grand Rapids	MI	49525	616-363-4857	361-3494
Northwest Local School District (NWLSD) 3240 Banning Rd *TF:* 800-374-2806 ■ *Web:* www.nwlsd.org	Cincinnati	OH	45239	513-923-1000	923-3644
Northwest R-1 School District 2843 Community Ln *Web:* www.nwr1.k12.mo.us	High Ridge	MO	63049	636-677-3473	677-5480
Northwestern Lehigh Sch Dist 6493 Rt 309 *Web:* www.nwlehighsd.org	New Tripoli	PA	18066	610-298-8661	
Norwin School District 281 Mcmahon Dr *Web:* www.norwinsd.org	Irwin	PA	15642	724-861-3000	863-9467
Nye County School District Inc (NCSD) PO Box 113 *TF:* 800-796-6273 ■ *Web:* nyecounty.schoolinsites.com	Tonopah	NV	89049	775-482-6258	482-8573
O H Anderson Elementary School 666 Warner Ave S *Web:* www.mahtomedi.k12.mn.us	Saint Paul	MN	55115	651-407-2300	
Oak Creek-Franklin Joint School District 7630 S Tenth St	Oak Creek	WI	53154	414-768-5880	
Oak Meadows Elementary School 28600 Poinsettia St *Web:* omes.buckeyeusd.org	Murrieta	CA	92563	951-246-4210	
Oakland Elementary School 2415 Brockton Ave *Web:* www.royaloakschools.com	Royal Oak	MI	48067	248-542-4406	
Oakland Schools Inc 2111 Pontiac Lk Rd *Web:* www.oakland.k12.mi.us	Waterford	MI	48328	248-209-2000	209-2206
Oakland Unified School District 1025 Second Ave *TF:* 888-604-4636 ■ *Web:* www.ousd.k12.ca.us	Oakland	CA	94606	510-879-8582	
Oceanside Union Free School District 11 145 Merle Ave *Web:* oceansideschools.org	Oceanside	NY	11572	516-678-1200	
Oconee County School District PO Box 146 *Web:* www.oconee.k12.ga.us	Watkinsville	GA	30677	706-769-5130	769-3500
Ohio Council of Community Schools 3131 Executive Pkwy Ste 306 *Web:* ohioschools.org	Toledo	OH	43606	419-720-5200	
Ohio County Board of Education 315 E Union St *Web:* ohio.k12.ky.us	Hartford	KY	42347	270-298-3249	
Oklahoma City Public Schools 2500 NE 30th St *Web:* www.okcps.org	Oklahoma City	OK	73111	405-587-0000	
Olympia School District 1113 Legion Way SE *TF:* 855-846-8376 ■ *Web:* www.osd.wednet.edu	Olympia	WA	98501	360-596-6100	596-6111
Omaha Public Schools 3215 Cuming St *Web:* www.ops.org	Omaha	NE	68131	402-557-2222	
Oneida City School District Inc 565 Sayles St *Web:* www.oneidacsd.org	Oneida	NY	13421	315-363-2550	363-6728
Ontario Christian High School 931 W Philadelphia St *Web:* www.couleurcafe.com	Ontario	CA	91762	909-984-1756	
Orange County Public Schools 445 W Amelia St **Fax:* Hum Res ■ *TF:* 800-378-9264 ■ *Web:* www.ocps.net	Orlando	FL	32801	407-317-3200	317-3392*
Orangeburg Consolidated School District 5 578 Ellis Ave *Web:* www.ocsd5schools.org	Orangeburg	SC	29115	803-534-5454	533-7953
Oregon City School District 62 PO Box 2110 *Web:* www.orecity.k12.or.us	Oregon City	OR	97045	503-785-8000	
Orleans Parish School Board 3520 General DeGaulle Dr *Web:* www.nops.k12.la.us	New Orleans	LA	70114	504-304-3520	
Oroville Union High School District 2211 Washington Ave *Web:* ouhsd.org	Oroville	CA	95966	530-538-2300	
Osprey Central School 408053 Grey Rd 4 *Web:* www.bwdsb.on.ca	Maxwell	ON	N0C1J0	519-922-2341	
Ossining Union Free School District 190 Croton Ave *TF:* 877-769-7447 ■ *Web:* www.ossiningufsd.org	Ossining	NY	10562	914-941-7700	941-7291
Oswego Community Unit School District 308 4175 SR- 71 *Web:* www.oswego308.org	Oswego	IL	60543	630-554-3447	554-2168
Our Lady Queen of Peace Catholic School 1600 Hwy 2004 *Web:* www.olqpschool.org	Richwood	TX	77531	979-265-3909	
Owatonna Senior High School 333 E School St *Web:* www.owatonna.k12.mn.us	Owatonna	MN	55060	507-444-8800	
Owosso Public Schools 645 Alger St PO Box 340 *Web:* www.owosso.k12.mi.us	Owosso	MI	48867	989-723-8131	723-7777
Oxford Academy & Central School 50 S Washington Ave PO Box 192 *Web:* www.oxac.org	Oxford	NY	13830	607-843-2025	843-3241
Pacific Bldg Group 9752 Aspen Creek Ct Ste 150 *Web:* www.pacificbuildinggroup.com	San Diego	CA	92126	858-552-0600	552-0604
Pacific Ridge School 6269 El Fuerte St *Web:* www.pacificridge.org	Carlsbad	CA	92009	760-448-9820	
Paideia School Inc, The 1509 Ponce De Leon Ave NE *Web:* www.paideiaschool.org	Atlanta	GA	30307	404-377-3491	377-0032
Palisades Charter High School 15777 Bowdoin St *Web:* www.palihigh.org	Pacific Palisades	CA	90272	310-230-6623	
Palm Beach County School District, The 3300 Forest Hill Blvd **Fax:* Hum Res ■ *TF:* 866-930-8402 ■ *Web:* www.palmbeach.k12.fl.us	West Palm Beach	FL	33406	561-434-8000	434-8899*
Palmerton Area School District 680 Fourth St *TF:* 800-732-0999 ■ *Web:* www.palmerton.k12.pa.us	Palmerton	PA	18071	610-826-7101	826-4958
Palmyra Area School District 1125 Pk Dr *Web:* pasd.us	Palmyra	PA	17078	717-838-3144	
Paradise Valley Unified School District 15002 N 32nd St *Web:* www.pvschools.net	Phoenix	AZ	85032	602-449-2000	
Paramount 1027 E Main St Ste A *Web:* www.jennifer4homes.com	Alhambra	CA	91801	626-458-0939	
Park County District No 6 919 Cody Ave *Web:* park6.org	Cody	WY	82414	307-587-4253	
Park Tudor School 7200 N College Ave *Web:* www.parktudor.org	Indianapolis	IN	46240	317-415-2700	
Parkland School District 1210 Springhouse Rd *TF:* 866-632-9992 ■ *Web:* www.parklandsd.org	Allentown	PA	18104	610-351-5503	351-5509
Parsons Elem. School 899 Hollywood St *Web:* nbtschools.org	North Brunswick	NJ	08902	732-289-3400	
Paul Risk Assoc Inc 11 W State St *Web:* www.paulrisk.com	Quarryville	PA	17566	717-786-7308	786-2848
Pawling Central School District 515 Rt 22 *Web:* www.pawlingschools.org	Pawling	NY	12564	845-855-4600	
Peace Wapiti Public School Division No 76 8611 108 St *Web:* www.pwsd76.ab.ca	Grande Prairie	AB	T8V4C5	780-532-8133	
Peach County School District Inc 523 Vineville St *TF:* 866-632-9992 ■ *Web:* www.peachschools.org	Fort Valley	GA	31030	478-825-5933	825-9970
Pearl City High School 100 S Summit St *Web:* www.pearlcityhs.org	Pearl City	IL	61062	815-443-2715	
Pembroke Hill School 400 W 51st St *Web:* www.pembrokehill.org	Kansas City	MO	64112	816-936-1200	
Peninsula High School 300 Piedmont Ave *Web:* www.phs.psd401.net	San Bruno	CA	94066	650-558-2499	
Penn Hills School District 260 Aster St *Web:* www.phsd.k12.pa.us	Pittsburgh	PA	15235	412-793-7000	793-6402
Penn. Manor Senior High School 100 E Cottage Ave *Web:* www.pennmanor.net	Millersville	PA	17551	717-872-9520	
Pennridge School District 1200 N Fifth St *Web:* pennridge.org	Perkasie	PA	18944	215-257-5011	
Penns Grove-Carneys Point Regional Board of Education 100 Iona Ave *TF:* 877-652-7624 ■ *Web:* pgcpschools.org	Penns Grove	NJ	08069	856-299-4250	299-5226

Name / Address	City	State	ZIP	Phone	Fax
Perris Union High School District 155 E Fourth St *Web:* www.puhsd.org	Perris	CA	92570	951-943-6369	
Person Centered Services Inc 240 N Union St *Web:* www.pcs4dd.com	Stockton	CA	95205	209-466-2448	
Person County Public Schools 304 S Morgan St *TF:* 866-724-6650 ■ *Web:* www.person.k12.nc.us	Roxboro	NC	27573	336-599-2191	
Petaluma City Schools (PCS) 200 Douglas St *Web:* www.petalumacityschools.org	Petaluma	CA	94952	707-778-4813	
Phase North 6601 Xylon Ave N *Web:* www.district287.org	Minneapolis	MN	55428	763-533-3821	
Phillipsburg Board of Education 445 Marshall St *Web:* www.pburgsd.net	Phillipsburg	NJ	08865	908-454-3400	
Phoenix Elementary School District 1817 N Seventh St **Fax:* Hum Res ■ *Web:* www.phxelem.k12.az.us	Phoenix	AZ	85006	602-257-3755	257-6077*
Phoenix Union High School District (PUHSD) 4502 N Central Ave *Web:* www.phxhs.k12.az.us	Phoenix	AZ	85012	602-764-1100	
Pickaway-Ross County Joint Vocational School District 895 Crouse Chapel Rd *Web:* pickawayross.com	Chillicothe	OH	45601	740-642-1200	
Pickens County School District (PCSD) 1348 Griffin Mill Rd *Web:* www.pickens.k12.sc.us	Easley	SC	29640	864-397-1000	855-8159
Pickerington Local School District 777 Long Rd *Web:* www.pickerington.k12.oh.us	Pickerington	OH	43147	614-833-2110	833-2143
Pima County School Superintendent 130 W Congress St Fourth Fl **Fax:* Hum Res ■ *Web:* www.schools.pima.gov	Tucson	AZ	85701	520-740-8451	623-9308*
Pinckney Community Schools 2130 E MI 36 *Web:* www.pinckneyschools.org	Pinckney	MI	48169	810-225-3900	
Pine Grove Area School Dist 103 School St *Web:* www.pgasd.com	Pine Grove	PA	17963	570-345-2731	
Pine Road Elementary School 3737 Pine Rd *Web:* www.lmtsd.org	Huntingdon Valley	PA	19006	215-938-0290	
Pinelands Regional School District PO Box 248 *TF:* 866-850-0511 ■ *Web:* www.prsdnj.org	Tuckerton	NJ	08087	609-296-3106	
Pinewood Preparatory School 1114 Orangeburg Rd *Web:* pinewoodprep.com	Summerville	SC	29483	843-873-1643	
Pittsburgh Public Schools (PPS) 341 S Bellefield Ave *Web:* www.pps.k12.pa.us	Pittsburgh	PA	15213	412-622-7920	
Pittsylvania County School Board 39 Bank St SE PO Box 232 *TF:* 888-440-6520 ■ *Web:* www.pcs.k12.va.us	Chatham	VA	24531	434-432-2761	432-9560
Placentia-Yorba Linda Unified School District (PYLUSD) 1301 E Orangethorpe Ave *Web:* www.pylusd.org	Placentia	CA	92870	714-996-2550	
Placer Union High School District PO Box 5048 *Web:* www.puhsd.k12.ca.us	Auburn	CA	95604	530-886-4400	886-4439
Plain Local School District 901 44th St NW *Web:* www.plainlocal.org	Canton	OH	44709	330-492-3500	493-5542
Plainfield Central School District 75 Canterbury Rd *Web:* www.plainfieldschools.org	Plainfield	CT	06374	860-564-6437	
Plainfield Community Consolidated School District 202 15732 S Howard St *Web:* psd202.org	Plainfield	IL	60544	815-577-4000	436-7824
Plainwell Community School District 600 School Dr *Web:* www.plainwellschools.org	Plainwell	MI	49080	269-685-5823	685-1108
Plaquemines Parish School Board 557 F Edward Hebert Blvd *TF:* 877-453-2721 ■ *Web:* www.ppsb.org	Belle Chasse	LA	70037	504-595-6400	392-4973
Pleasant Valley Sch District 600 Temple Ave *Web:* www.pvsd.k12.ca.us	Camarillo	CA	93010	805-482-2763	987-5511
Pleasantville Union Free School District 60 Romer Ave *Web:* www.pleasantvilleschools.com	Pleasantville	NY	10570	914-741-1400	741-1499
Pope John Paul Ii High School Office 1901 Jaguar Dr *Web:* pjp.org	Slidell	LA	70461	985-649-0914	
Portage Community School District 904 De Witt St *Web:* www.portage.k12.wi.us	Portage	WI	53901	608-742-4867	
Portland Public Schools 501 N Dixon St *TF:* 800-766-8206 ■ *Web:* www.pps.k12.or.us	Portland	OR	97227	503-916-2000	916-3110
Portola School 300 Amador Ave *Web:* sbpsd.k12.ca.us	San Bruno	CA	94066	650-624-3175	
Positive Education Program Inc 3100 Euclid Ave *Web:* www.pepcleve.org	Cleveland	OH	44115	216-361-4400	361-8600
Poudre School District 2407 LaPorte Ave *Web:* psdschools.org	Fort Collins	CO	80521	970-482-7420	490-3514
Powhatan County School District 2320 Skaggs Rd *Web:* www.powhatan.k12.va.us	Powhatan	VA	23139	804-598-5700	
Prairie Lakes Area Education Agency 1235 Fifth Ave S *Web:* www.plaea.org	Fort Dodge	IA	50501	515-574-5500	
Prairie View Sr. High School 13731 Ks Hwy 152 *Web:* www.pv362.org	Lacygne	KS	66040	913-757-4447	
Preble-Shawnee School District 124 Bloomfield St	Camden	OH	45311	937-452-1283	
Prestwood Elementary School 343 E Macarthur St *Web:* prestwoodschool.org	Sonoma	CA	95476	707-935-6030	
Prince Edward County School District 35 Eagle Dr *Web:* www.pecps.k12.va.us	Farmville	VA	23901	434-315-2100	
Princeton Regional School District 25 Valley Rd Administration Bldg *TF:* 877-652-2873 ■ *Web:* www.prs.k12.nj.us	Princeton	NJ	08540	609-806-4200	
Prior Lake-Savage Area Public School District 719 4540 Tower St SE *TF:* 855-346-1650 ■ *Web:* www.priorlake-savage.k12.mn.us	Prior Lake	MN	55372	952-226-0000	226-0049
Proteus Inc 1830 N Dinuba Blvd *Web:* www.proteusinc.org	Visalia	CA	93291	559-733-5423	
Provision Ministry Group PO Box 19700 *TF:* 800-233-3880 ■ *Web:* www.provision.org	Irvine	CA	92623	800-233-3880	
Provo School District 280 West 940 North *Web:* www.provo.edu	Provo	UT	84604	801-374-4800	374-4808
Puget Sound Educational Service District 800 Oakesdale Ave SW *TF:* 800-664-4549 ■ *Web:* www.psesd.org	Renton	WA	98057	425-917-7600	
Pulaski County School District (PCPS) 202 N Washington Ave *Web:* www.pcva.us	Pulaski	VA	24301	540-994-2550	994-2552
Pullman School District 267 240 SE Dexter St *Web:* www.psd267.org	Pullman	WA	99163	509-332-3581	334-0375
Putnam Valley School District Inc 146 Peekskill Hollow Rd *TF:* 800-666-5327 ■ *Web:* www.pvcsd.org	Putnam Valley	NY	10579	845-528-8143	528-8386
Quaker Valley School District 203 Graham St *Web:* www.qvsd.org	Sewickley	PA	15143	412-749-3600	
Queensbury Union Free School 429 Aviation Rd *Web:* www.queensburyschool.org	Queensbury	NY	12804	518-824-5699	
Rabun County School District 963 Tiger Connector *TF:* 866-632-9992 ■ *Web:* www.rabun.k12.ga.us	Tiger	GA	30576	706-212-4350	782-6224
Radnor Township School Authority 135 S Wayne Ave Ste 1 *Web:* www.rtsd.org	Wayne	PA	19087	610-688-8100	
Ralston Middle School 8202 Lakeview St *Web:* ralstonschools.org	Omaha	NE	68127	402-331-4701	
Ramsey Board of Education 266 E Main St *Web:* www.ramsey.k12.nj.us	Ramsey	NJ	07446	201-785-2300	934-6623
RE Crawford Construction Inc 6771 Professional Pkwy W Ste 100 *Web:* www.recrawford.com	Sarasota	FL	34240	941-907-0010	
Red Clay Consolidated School District 1502 Spruce Ave *Web:* www.redclay.k12.de.us	Wilmington	DE	19808	302-552-3700	
Red Lion Christian Academy 1390 Red Lion Rd *Web:* www.redlionca.org	Bear	DE	19701	302-834-2526	
Red River Valley School Division 233 Main St N *Web:* www.rrvsd.ca	Morris	MB	R0G1K0	204-746-2317	
Redmond School District 145 SE Salmon Ave *Web:* www.redmond.k12.or.us	Redmond	OR	97756	541-923-5437	923-5142
Redwood City School District (RCSD) 750 Bradford St *Web:* www.rcsd.k12.ca.us/site/default.aspx?pageid=1	Redwood City	CA	94063	650-423-2200	423-2294
Redwood Day School Parents & Guardians Association 3245 Sheffield Ave *Web:* www.rdschool.org	Oakland	CA	94602	510-534-0800	
Regis School 7330 Westview Dr *Web:* www.theregisschool.org	Houston	TX	77055	713-682-8383	
Retail Construction Services Inc (RCS) 11343 39th St N *Web:* www.retailconstruction.com	Lake Elmo	MN	55042	651-704-9000	704-9100
Reynolds School District 7 Inc 1204 NE 201st Ave *Web:* www.reynolds.k12.or.us	Fairview	OR	97024	503-661-7200	667-6932
Richland County School District One 1616 Richland St **Fax:* Hum Res ■ *Web:* www.richlandone.org	Columbia	SC	29201	803-231-7000	231-7417*
Richmond City Public Schools 301 N Ninth St *Web:* web.richmond.k12.va.us	Richmond	VA	23219	804-780-7700	780-4122
Richmond County School System 864 Broad St *Web:* www.rcboe.org/home.asp	Augusta	GA	30901	706-826-1000	
Ripon Elementary School 509 W Main St *Web:* riponusd.net	Ripon	CA	95366	209-599-4225	
River East Transcona School Division 589 Roch St *Web:* www.retsd.mb.ca	Winnipeg	MB	R2K2P7	204-667-7130	
River School 4880 Macarthur Blvd Nw *Web:* riverschool.net	Washington	DC	20007	202-337-3554	
River View Local School District 26496 SR- 60 *Web:* www.river-view.k12.oh.us	Warsaw	OH	43844	740-824-3521	
Riverdale Country School 5250 Fieldston Rd *Web:* www.riverdale.edu	Bronx	NY	10471	718-549-8810	519-2795
Riverside Unified School District (RUSD) 3380 14th St PO Box 2800 *Web:* www.rusdlink.org	Riverside	CA	92501	951-788-7135	
Riverton Elementary School 209 N Seventh St *Web:* www.rivertonschools.org	Riverton	IL	62561	217-629-6001	
Riverview Intermediate Unit Number 6 Administrative Offices 270 Mayfield Rd *Web:* www.riu6.org	Clarion	PA	16214	814-226-7103	
Robbinsdale Area Schools 4148 Winnetka Ave N *Web:* www.rdale.org	New Hope	MN	55427	763-504-8000	

				Phone	Fax
Robert e Webber Institute for Worship Studies, The 151 Kingsley Ave *Web:* iws.edu	Orange Park	FL	32073	904-264-2172	
Robert Frost Middle School 2206 W 167th St *Web:* gpa.me	Markham	IL	60428	708-210-9929	
Robstown High School 609 Hwy 44 *Web:* www.robstownisd.org	Robstown	TX	78380	361-387-5999	
Rochester City School District 131 W Broad St *Web:* www.rcsdk12.org	Rochester	NY	14614	585-262-8100	262-5151
Rocklin Academy, The 6532 Turnstone Way *Web:* www.rocklinacademy.com	Rocklin	CA	95765	916-632-6580	
Roman Catholic Diocese of Fresno 1550 N Fresno St *Web:* www.dioceseoffresno.org	Fresno	CA	93703	559-488-7400	
Rome City School District 508 E Second St *Web:* www.rcs.rome.ga.us	Rome	GA	30161	706-236-5050	802-4311
Romeo Community School District 316 N Main St *TF:* 888-427-6818 ■ *Web:* www.romeo.k12.mi.us	Romeo	MI	48065	586-752-0200	752-0228
Ronald C Wornick Jewish Day School 800 Foster City Blvd *Web:* www.wornickjds.org	Foster City	CA	94404	650-378-2600	
Ronald Reagan Middle School 620 Division St *Web:* dixonschools.org	Dixon	IL	61021	815-284-7729	
Roncalli High Sch. Sisters 2000 Mirro Dr. *Web:* roncallijets.net	Manitowoc	WI	54220	920-682-8801	
Rose Tree Media School District 308 N Olive St *Web:* www.rtmsd.org	Media	PA	19063	610-627-6000	
Rosetta Stone Ltd 1919 N Lynn St 7th Fl *NYSE: RST* ■ **Fax Area Code:* 540 ■ *TF:* 800-788-0822 ■ *Web:* www.rosettastone.com	Arlington	VA	22209	800-788-0822	432-0953*
Roseville Joint Union High School District Fin Corp 1750 Cirby Way *Web:* www.rjuhsd.k12.ca.us	Roseville	CA	95661	916-786-2051	786-2681
Ross Valley School District 110 Shaw Dr *TF:* 800-322-6384 ■ *Web:* www.rossvalleyschools.org	San Anselmo	CA	94960	415-454-2162	
Round Rock ISD 1311 Round Rock Ave *Web:* www.roundrockisd.org	Round Rock	TX	78681	512-464-6000	
Rush-Henrietta Central School District 2034 Lehigh Stn Rd *Web:* www.rhnet.org	Henrietta	NY	14467	585-359-5000	359-5045
Rusk High School 203 E Seventh St *Web:* www.ruskisd.net	Rusk	TX	75785	903-683-5401	
Sachem Central School District At Holbrook 245 Union Ave *Web:* www.sachem.edu	Holbrook	NY	11741	631-471-1300	
Sacramento City Unified School District 5735 47th Ave *Web:* www.scusd.edu	Sacramento	CA	95824	916-643-7400	643-9440
Safford Unified School District 1 734 W 11th St *Web:* www.saffordusd.k12.az.us	Safford	AZ	85546	928-348-7000	
Saint Jude The Apostle School 32036 Lindero Canyon Rd *Web:* saintjude.net	Westlake Village	CA	91361	818-889-9483	
Saint Louis Public Schools 801 N 11th St **Fax:* Hum Res ■ *Web:* www.slps.org	Saint Louis	MO	63101	314-231-3720	345-2650*
Saint Patrick School 9040 Hutchins St *Web:* stpatrickwhitelake.org	White Lake	MI	48386	248-698-3240	
Salem-Keizer Public Schools 2450 Lancaster Dr NE **Fax:* Hum Res ■ *TF:* 877-293-1090 ■ *Web:* www.salkeiz.k12.or.us	Salem	OR	97305	503-399-3000	375-7802*
Salesian High School 2851 Salesian Ave *Web:* www.inn-sys.com	Richmond	CA	94804	510-234-4433	
Salin Bank 8455 Keystone Xing *TF:* 800-320-7536 ■ *Web:* www.salin.com	Indianapolis	IN	46240	317-452-8000	532-2263
Saline Area Schools 7265 Saline Ann Arbor Rd *Web:* www.salineschools.org	Saline	MI	48176	734-429-8000	429-8010
Salt Lake School District 440 East 100 South *Web:* slcschools.org	Salt Lake City	UT	84111	801-578-8599	578-8689
Sampson County Schools 437 Rowan Rd PO Box 439 *Web:* www.sampson.k12.nc.us	Clinton	NC	28329	910-592-1401	590-2445
San Antonio Independent School District (SAISD) 141 Lavaca St **Fax:* Hum Res ■ *TF:* 800-943-6422 ■ *Web:* www.saisd.net	San Antonio	TX	78210	210-554-2200	299-5600*
San Diego Jewish Academy 11860 Carmel Creek Rd *Web:* www.sdja.com	San Diego	CA	92130	858-704-3700	704-3750
San Diego Unified School District 4100 Normal St *Web:* www.sandi.net	San Diego	CA	92103	619-725-8000	725-8001
San Francisco Unified School District 555 Franklin St *Web:* www.sfusd.edu	San Francisco	CA	94102	415-241-6000	241-6429
San Jacinto Valley Academy Inc 480 N San Jacinto Ave *Web:* www.sjva.net	San Jacinto	CA	92583	951-654-6113	
San Jose Unified School District 855 Lenzen Ave **Fax:* Hum Res ■ *TF:* 800-433-3243 ■ *Web:* www.sjusd.org	San Jose	CA	95126	408-535-6000	535-2377*
San Leandro Adult School 2255 Bancroft Ave *Web:* www.sanleandroadultschool.org	San Leandro	CA	94577	510-618-4420	
San Lorenzo Unified School District (SLZUSD) 15510 Usher St *Web:* www.slzusd.org	San Lorenzo	CA	94580	510-317-4600	
San Luis Obispo High School 1499 San Luis Dr *Web:* www.slcusd.org	San Luis Obispo	CA	93401	805-596-4040	
San Miguel Joint Un School Dst. 1601 L St *Web:* www.sanmiguelschools.org	San Miguel	CA	93451	805-467-3216	
San Ysidro School District 4350 Otay Mesa Rd *Web:* www.sysd.k12.ca.us	San Ysidro	CA	92173	619-428-4476	428-1505
Santa Barbara Unified School District 720 Santa Barbara St *Web:* www.sbunified.org	Santa Barbara	CA	93101	805-963-4338	
Santa Fe Independent School District PO Box 370 *Web:* www.sfisd.org	Santa Fe	TX	77510	409-925-3526	
Santa Fe Preparatory School 1101 Camino De Cruz Blanca *Web:* www.sfprep.org	Santa Fe	NM	87505	505-982-1829	
Santa Margarita Catholic High School 22062 antonio pkwy *Web:* www.eaglesfootball.com	Rancho Santa Margarita	CA	92688	949-766-6000	
Santa Maria-Bonita School Dist 708 S Miller St *Web:* www.smbsd.org	Santa Maria	CA	93454	805-928-1783	
Santee School District 9625 Cuyamaca St *Web:* www.santeesd.net	Santee	CA	92071	619-258-2300	
Saucon Valley School District 2097 Polk Vly Rd *TF:* 866-632-9992 ■ *Web:* svpanthers.org	Hellertown	PA	18055	610-838-7026	
Sauder School of Business 2389 Health Sciences Mall *Web:* www.sauder.ubc.ca	Vancouver	BC	V6T1Z2	604-822-8399	
Saugus High School 21900 Centurion Way *Web:* www.hartdistrict.org	Santa Clarita	CA	91350	661-297-3900	
Scarsdale Union Free School District 2 Brewster Rd *TF:* 888-837-6437 ■ *Web:* www.scarsdaleschools.k12.ny.us	Scarsdale	NY	10583	914-721-2410	
Schalmont Central School District Four Sabre Dr *Web:* www.schalmont.org	Schenectady	NY	12306	518-355-9200	355-9203
School Board of Highlands County Florida PO Box 9300 *TF:* 877-357-7456 ■ *Web:* www.highlands.k12.fl.us	Sebring	FL	33871	863-471-5555	386-6179
School District of Cheltenham Township 2000 Ashbourne Rd *Web:* www.cheltenham.org	Elkins Park	PA	19027	215-886-9500	884-6929
School District of Hartford 675 E Rossman St *Web:* www.hartfordjt1.k12.wi.us	Hartford	WI	53027	262-673-3155	673-3548
School District of Philadelphia 440 N Broad St *Web:* www.phila.k12.pa.us	Philadelphia	PA	19130	215-400-4000	
School District of The Chathams 58 Meyersville Rd *TF:* 800-225-5425 ■ *Web:* www.chatham-nj.org	Chatham	NJ	07928	973-457-2500	701-0146
School Nurse Supply Co 1690 Wright Blvd *Web:* www.schoolnursesupplyinc.com	Schaumburg	IL	60193	847-352-9364	
Schools Wstrn Area Career & Techlgy Center; Main Ofc 688 Western Ave *Web:* www.wactc.net	Canonsburg	PA	15317	724-746-2890	
Schuylkill Haven Area School Authority 120 Haven St *Web:* www.haven.k12.pa.us	Schuylkill Haven	PA	17972	570-385-6705	
Schuylkill Valley School District 929 Lakeshore Dr *TF:* 888-883-8237 ■ *Web:* www.schuylkillvalley.org	Leesport	PA	19533	610-926-1706	926-3960
Scotch Plains-Fanwood Board of Education 2280 Evergreen Ave *Web:* www.spfk12.org	Scotch Plains	NJ	07076	908-889-5331	889-9332
Scotts Valley Unified School District Inc 4444 Scotts Vly Dr Ste 5b *Web:* www.svusd.santacruz.k12.ca.us	Scotts Valley	CA	95066	831-438-2312	
Scranton School District 425 N Washington Ave *Web:* scrsd.org	Scranton	PA	18503	570-348-3402	348-3563
Seaman Unified School District 345 901 NW Lyman Rd *Web:* www.usd345.com	Topeka	KS	66608	785-575-8600	575-8620
Seattle Public Schools PO Box 34165 *Web:* www.seattleschools.org	Seattle	WA	98124	206-252-0000	
Security Bancshares Co 735 11th St E PO Box 218 *Web:* www.security-banks.com	Glencoe	MN	55336	320-864-3171	864-5133
Seguin Independent School District 1221 E Kingsbury St *TF:* 866-632-9992 ■ *Web:* www.seguin.k12.tx.us	Seguin	TX	78155	830-372-5771	379-0392
Seneca Falls School District 98 Clinton St *Web:* www.sfcs.k12.ny.us	Seneca Falls	NY	13148	315-568-5818	
Seton Home Study School 1350 Progress Dr *Web:* www.setonhome.org	Front Royal	VA	22630	540-636-9990	
Seven Arrows Elementary School Inc 15240 La Cruz Dr *Web:* www.sevenarrows.com	Pacific Palisades	CA	90272	310-230-0257	
Shamrock High School 100 S Illinois St *Web:* www.region16.net	Shamrock	TX	79079	806-256-2126	
Shelton City School District 382 Long Hill Ave *Web:* www.sheltonpublicschools.org	Shelton	CT	06484	203-924-1023	924-6851
Shepherd Valley Waldorf School 6500 Dry Creek Pkwy *Web:* shepherdvalley.org	Niwot	CO	80503	303-652-0130	
Shikellamy School District 200 Island Blvd *Web:* www.shikbraves.org	Sunbury	PA	17801	570-286-3720	
Siast Administrative Offices 119 Fourth Ave S *Web:* www.siast.sk.ca	Saskatoon	SK	S7K5X2	306-933-7331	

Phone Fax

Sidney Transportation Services
777 W Russell Rd PO Box 748 . . . Sidney OH 45365 937-498-2323 492-4025
TF: 800-743-6391 ■ *Web:* www.sidneytransportationservices.com

Silver Springs-Martin Luther School
512 W Township Line Rd . . . Plymouth Meeting PA 19462 610-825-4440
Web: www.silver-springs.org

Sioux Falls School District
201 E 38th St . . . Sioux Falls SD 57105 605-367-7900 367-4637*
**Fax:* Hum Res ■ *Web:* www.sf.k12.sd.us

Siuslaw School District 97j 2111 Oak St . . . Florence OR 97439 541-997-2651
Web: www.greatschools.org

Slaton Independent School District
140 E Panhandle St . . . Slaton TX 79364 806-828-6591
Web: www.slatonisd.net

Sneed Elementary School 9855 Pagewood Ln . . . Houston TX 77042 713-789-6979
Web: sneed.aliefisd.net

Snodgrass & Son's Construction Company Inc
2700 S George Washington Bldg . . . Wichita KS 67210 316-687-3110 687-5853
Web: snodgrassconstruction.com

Socrates Academy 3909 Weddington Rd . . . Matthews NC 28105 704-321-1711
Web: socratesacademy.us

Solanco School District 121 S Hess St . . . Quarryville PA 17566 717-786-8401 786-8245
Web: www.solanco.k12.pa.us

Solex Academy Inc 350 E Dundee Rd Ste 200 . . . Wheeling IL 60090 847-229-9595
Web: www.solex.edu

Sonoma Valley Unified School District (SVUSD)
17850 Railroad Ave. . . . Sonoma CA 95476 707-935-6000
Web: www.svusdca.org

Sonoran Science Academy 5741 E Ironwood St . . . Tucson AZ 85708 520-300-5699
Web: www.sonoranschools.org

Souderton Area School District
760 Lower Rd . . . Souderton PA 18964 215-723-6061 723-8897
Web: www.soudertonsd.org

Soundview Preparatory School
370 Underhill Ave. . . . Yorktown Heights NY 10598 914-962-2780
Web: www.soundviewprep.org

South Bay Union School District
601 Elm Ave . . . Imperial Beach CA 91932 619-628-1600 628-1608
Web: www.sbusd.org

South Haven Public Schools Inc
554 Green St. . . . South Haven MI 49090 269-637-0520
Web: www.shps.org

South Kitsap School District
1962 Hoover Ave SE. . . . Port Orchard WA 98366 360-874-7000 874-7068
Web: www.skitsap.wednet.edu

South Orangetown School District (Inc), The
160 Van Wyck Rd . . . Blauvelt NY 10913 845-680-1000
Web: socsd.org

South Plains Academy 4008 Ave R. . . . Lubbock TX 79412 806-744-0330
Web: stdsapi.com

South San Antonio Independent School District
5622 Ray Ellison Dr . . . San Antonio TX 78242 210-977-7000
Web: www.southsanisd.net

South San Francisco Unified School District
398 B St . . . South San Francisco CA 94080 650-877-8700
Web: ssfusd.org

South Summit School District
375 East 300 South . . . Kamas UT 84036 435-783-4301
Web: www.ssummit.k12.ut.us

South Whidbey School Dist 206 PO Box 346 . . . Langley WA 98260 360-221-6100 221-3835
Web: www.sw.wednet.edu

Southern Lehigh School District
5775 Main St . . . Center Valley PA 18034 610-282-3121 282-0193
Web: www.slsd.org

Southern Regional High School District Board of Education
105 Cedar Bridge Rd . . . Manahawkin NJ 08050 609-597-9481 978-0298
TF: 866-850-0511 ■ *Web:* www.srsd.net

Southern Tioga School District 241 Main St . . . Blossburg PA 16912 570-638-2183
Web: www.southerntioga.org

Southgate Community School District
13305 Reeck Rd . . . Southgate MI 48195 734-246-4600 283-6791
TF: 888-263-5897 ■ *Web:* www.southgateschools.com

Southview Special Educatn Schl
11660 Eddie And Park Rd. . . . Sappington MO 63126 314-989-8900
Web: www.ssdmo.org

Southwest Local School District
230 S Elm St. . . . Harrison OH 45030 513-367-4139
Web: www.southwestschools.org

Southwestern Central School District
600 Hunt Rd . . . Jamestown NY 14701 716-664-1881
Web: www.swcs.wnyric.org

Southwick Tolland Regional SD
86 Powder Mill Rd . . . Southwick MA 01077 413-569-5391
Web: www.stgrsd.org

Spackenkill Union Free School Districts (Inc)
15 Croft Rd . . . Poughkeepsie NY 12603 845-463-7800
Web: www.spackenkillschools.org

Sparta Area Schools 465 S Union St . . . Sparta MI 49345 616-887-8253
Web: www.spartaschools.org

Speech & Language Development
8699 Holder St . . . Buena Park CA 90620 714-821-3620
Web: www.sldc.net

Splendora Independent School District
23419 FM 2090 Rd. . . . Splendora TX 77372 281-689-3128 689-7509
TF: 866-861-2010 ■ *Web:* www.splendoraisd.org

Spring-Ford Area School District
857 S Lewis Rd. . . . Royersford PA 19468 610-705-6000 705-6245
Web: www.spring-ford.net

Springfield Public School District #186
1900 W Monroe St . . . Springfield IL 62704 217-525-3000 525-3005
TF: 877-632-7753 ■ *Web:* www.sps186.org

Phone Fax

Springfield Public Schools
1359 E St Louis St . . . Springfield MO 65802 417-523-0000 523-0196*
**Fax:* Mail Rm ■ *Web:* www.springfieldpublicschoolsmo.org

St Ann's Catholic School
365 N Cool Spring St . . . Fayetteville NC 28301 910-483-3902
Web: stanncatholicschool.org

St Basil Academy High School
711 Fox Chase Rd . . . Jenkintown PA 19046 215-885-3771
Web: stbasilacademy.org

St Cecilia Catholic School 1311 Sycamore Ave. . . . Tustin CA 92780 714-544-1533
Web: www.saintceciliaschool.org

St Charles Inc 151 S 84th St. . . . Milwaukee WI 53214 414-476-3710
Web: www.stcharlesinc.org

St Edwards High School 13500 Detroit Ave . . . Lakewood OH 44107 216-221-3776
Web: www.sehs.net

St Francis De Sales High School
2323 W Bancroft St. . . . Toledo OH 43607 419-531-1618
Web: www.sfstoledo.org

St Francis High School
1885 Miramonte Ave. . . . Mountain View CA 94040 650-968-1213
Web: www.sfhs.com

St Francis Xavier High School 15 School St. . . . Sumter SC 29150 803-773-0210
Web: www.sfxhs.com

St Henry District High School
3755 Scheben Dr . . . Erlanger KY 41018 859-525-0255
Web: shdhs.org

St Ignatius College Prep 1076 W Roosevelt Rd . . . Chicago IL 60608 312-421-5900
Web: www.siprep.org

St James Academy 3100 Monkton Rd . . . Monkton MD 21111 410-771-4816
Web: www.saintjamesacademy.org

St James Episcopal School
602 S Carancahua St . . . Corpus Christi TX 78401 361-883-0835
Web: www.sjes.org

St John Neumann Regional Catholic School
791 Tom Smith Rd Sw . . . Lilburn GA 30047 770-381-0557
Web: www.sjnrcs.org

St John The Apostle School
7421 Glenview Dr . . . Richland Hills TX 76180 817-284-2228
Web: stjs.org

St Johns Unified District
450 S 13th St W . . . Saint Johns AZ 85936 928-337-2255
Web: www.sjusd.net

St Lukes Episcopal Day School
8833 Goodwood Blvd . . . Baton Rouge LA 70806 225-926-5343
Web: www.stlukesbr.org

St Mary's Dominican High School Corp
7701 Walmsley Ave . . . New Orleans LA 70125 504-865-9401
Web: www.stmarysdominican.org

St Matthew Catholic School 11525 Elm Ln. . . . Charlotte NC 28277 704-544-2070
Web: www.charlottediocese.org

St Olivier School 325 Beckwell Ave . . . Radville SK S0C2G0 306-869-3221
Web: www.holyfamilyrcssd.ca

St Paul Education Regional Division No 1
4901-47 St . . . St Paul AB T0A3A3 780-645-3323
Web: www.stpauleducation.ab.ca

St Paul High School
9635 Greenleaf Ave. . . . Santa Fe Springs CA 90670 562-698-6246
Web: stpaulhs.org

St Stephen's Catholic School 16701 S St . . . Omaha NE 68135 402-896-0754
Web: www.stephen.org

St. Anastasia School 8631 Stanmoor Dr. . . . Los Angeles CA 90045 310-645-8816
Web: www.st-anastasia.org

St. Clair County Regional Educational Service Agency
499 Range Rd . . . Marysville MI 48040 810-364-8990
Web: www.sccresa.org

St. John Vianney High School 540 Line Rd. . . . Holmdel NJ 07733 732-739-0800
Web: www.sjvhs.com

St. Margaret's School 1080 Lucas Ave. . . . Victoria BC V8X3P7 250-479-7171
Web: www.stmarg.ca

St. Mary's Home for Children
420 Fruit Hill Ave . . . North Providence RI 02911 401-353-3900
Web: www.smhfc.org

St. Sebastian's School 815 Broad Ave . . . Belle Vernon PA 15012 724-929-5143
Web: www.stsebs.org

Steinhauer Elementary School
25 N Fellowship Rd . . . Maple Shade NJ 08052 856-779-7323
Web: www.mapleshade.org

Stephen Mack Middle School
11810 Old River Rd . . . Rockton IL 61072 815-624-2611
Web: rockton140.org

Stephenville Independent School District
2655 W Overhill Dr. . . . Stephenville TX 76401 254-968-4141
Web: www.sville.us

Stockton Unified School District
701 N Madison St. . . . Stockton CA 95202 209-933-7000 933-7031
Web: stocktonusd.net

Stoughton Area School District 320 N St . . . Stoughton WI 53589 608-877-5000
Web: www.stoughton.k12.wi.us

Stow-Munroe Falls City School District
4350 Allen Rd. . . . Stow OH 44224 330-689-5445
Web: smfschools.org

Study (the) 3233 The Blvd. . . . Westmount QC H3Y1S4 514-935-9352
Web: www.thestudy.qc.ca

Sturgis Public Schools 107 W W St. . . . Sturgis MI 49091 269-659-1500
Web: www.sturgisps.org

Sugar Creek Board of Education
3757 Upper Bellbrook Road . . . Bellbrook OH 45305 937-848-6251
Web: www.sugarcreek.k12.oh.us

Summit Construction Company Inc
1107 Burdsal Pkwy PO Box 88126 . . . Indianapolis IN 46208 317-634-6112 264-2529
Web: www.summitconst.com

Sumner School District 1202 Wood Ave . . . Sumner WA 98390 253-891-6000 891-6098
TF: 866-548-3847 ■ *Web:* www.sumner.wednet.edu

Phone | Fax

Sunrise School Division 536 Park Ave . . . Beausejour MB R0E0C0 204-268-4832
Web: www.sunrisesd.ca

Sunset Ridge School District 29
525 Sunset Ridge Rd . . . Northfield IL 60093 847-881-9400 446-6388
TF: 888-331-2195 ■ *Web:* www.sunsetridge29.net

Surry County School
209 N Crutchfield St PO Box 364 . . . Dobson NC 27017 336-386-8211 386-4279
Web: www.surry.k12.nc.us

Swan Valley School Dist 8380 Ohern Rd . . . Saginaw MI 48609 989-921-3701
Web: swanvalleyschools.com

Sweet Home Central School District
1901 Sweet Home Rd . . . Amherst NY 14228 716-250-1400
Web: sweethomeschools.org

Sweet Home School District 55
1920 Long St . . . Sweet Home OR 97386 541-367-7126
Web: www.sweethome.k12.or.us

Sweetwater County School District 2
320 Monroe Ave . . . Green River WY 82935 307-872-5500
Web: www.sw2.k12.wy.us

Syracuse City School District, The
725 Harrison St . . . Syracuse NY 13210 315-435-4499 435-4023
Web: www.syracusecityschools.com

Tahoe Truckee Unified School District (TTUSD)
11603 Donner Pass Rd . . . Truckee CA 96161 530-582-2500 582-7606
Web: www.ttusd.org

Talbot County Public Schools PO Box 1029 . . . Easton MD 21601 410-822-0330 820-4260
Web: www.tcps.k12.md.us

Tattnall County School
146 W Brazell St PO Box 157 . . . Reidsville GA 30453 912-557-4726 557-3036
Web: www.tattnallschools.org

Taylor Independent School District
602 W 12th St . . . Taylor TX 76574 512-352-6361 365-3800
Web: www.taylorisd.org

Team Hardinger Transportation/Warehousing
1314 W 18th St . . . Erie PA 16502 814-453-6587 453-4919
Web: www.team-h.com

Telfair County School District
212 W Huckabee St PO Box 240 . . . McRae GA 31055 229-868-5661 868-5549
Web: www.telfairschools.org

Temecula Valley Unified School District School Facilities Corp
31350 Rancho Vista Rd . . . Temecula CA 92592 951-676-2661 695-7121
Web: www.tvusd.k12.ca.us

Tempe Elementary Schools 3205 S Rural Rd . . . Tempe AZ 85282 480-730-7100
Web: www.tempeschools.org

Templeton Unified School District
960 Old County Rd . . . Templeton CA 93465 805-434-5800 434-5879
TF: 800-316-6142 ■ *Web:* tusd.ca.schoolloop.com

Tennyson High School 27035 Whitman St . . . Hayward CA 94544 510-293-8591
Web: ths-haywardusd-ca.schoolloop.com

Tforce Energy Services
6143 S Willow Ste 320 . . . Greenwood Village CO 80111 877-234-1444 770-6461*
*Fax Area Code: 303 ■ *TF:* 877-234-1444 ■ *Web:* www.tforceenergy.com

TheAcademy.com
Contact Information 10223 McAllister
Ste 206 . . . San Antonio TX 78216 210-530-2700
Web: www.theacademy.com

Thornapple Kellogg Schools
10051 Green Lk Rd . . . Middleville MI 49333 269-795-3313 795-5492
Web: www.tkschools.org

Thornton Fractional South High School
18500 Burnham Ave . . . Lansing IL 60438 708-585-2000
Web: www.tfd215.org

Thunderbird School of Global Management
One Global Pl . . . Glendale AZ 85306 602-978-7000 978-9663
TF: 800-848-9084 ■ *Web:* www.thunderbird.edu

Thurman G Smith Elementary School
3600 Falcon Rd . . . Springdale AR 72762 479-750-8846
Web: springdaleschools.org

Tipton County Schools 1580 Hwy 51 S . . . Covington TN 38019 901-476-7148 476-4870
Web: www.tipton-county.com

Tomball Independent School District
221 W Main St . . . Tomball TX 77375 281-357-3100 357-3128
TF: 877-382-4357 ■ *Web:* www.tomballisd.net

Topeka Public Schools 624 SW 24th St . . . Topeka KS 66611 785-295-3000 575-6162*
*Fax: Hum Res ■ *Web:* www.topekapublicschools.net

Toppenish School District 202 306 Bolin Dr . . . Toppenish WA 98948 509-865-4455 865-2067
TF: 888-730-1101 ■ *Web:* www.toppenish.wednet.edu

Torrance Unified School District
2335 Plz Del AMO . . . Torrance CA 90501 310-972-6500
Web: www.tusd.org

Trenton Public School System
108 N Clinton Ave . . . Trenton NJ 08609 609-656-4900 989-2682
Web: www.trenton.k12.nj.us

Tri-Valley Local School District PO Box 125 . . . Dresden OH 43821 740-754-1442 754-6400
Web: www.tri-valley.k12.oh.us

Trinity Academy Inc 12345 E 21st St N . . . Wichita KS 67206 316-634-0909
Web: www.trinityacademy.org

Trinity Area School District 231 Pk Ave . . . Washington PA 15301 724-223-2000
Web: www.trinitypride.k12.pa.us

Trinity Elementary School
4410 Murfreesboro Rd . . . Franklin TN 37067 615-472-4850
Web: www.wcs.edu

Triway Local School District 3205 Shreve Rd . . . Wooster OH 44691 330-264-9491 262-3955
Web: www.triway.k12.oh.us

Tuckahoe Union Free School District
65 Siwanoy Blvd . . . Eastchester NY 10709 914-337-6600
Web: tuckahoeschools.org

Tucson Unified School District No 1
1010 E Tenth St . . . Tucson AZ 85719 520-225-6070 798-8767
Web: www.tusd1.org

Tulare Joint Union High School District
426 N Blackstone Ave . . . Tulare CA 93274 559-688-2021 687-7317
TF: 800-942-3767 ■ *Web:* www.tulare.k12.ca.us

Tulsa Public Schools 3027 S New Haven Ave . . . Tulsa OK 74114 918-746-6800 746-6144*
*Fax: Hum Res ■ *TF:* 866-632-9992 ■ *Web:* tulsaschools.org

Tupelo Public School District 72 S Green St . . . Tupelo MS 38804 662-841-8850 841-8887
Web: www.tupeloschools.com

Turner County Board of Education
423 N Cleveland St . . . Ashburn GA 31714 229-567-3338 567-3285
Web: www.turner.k12.ga.us

Tuscarora Intermediate Unit 11
2527 US 522 S Hwy . . . McVeytown PA 17051 717-899-7143 542-2569*
*Fax Area Code: 824 ■ *Web:* www.tiu11.org

Twin Falls School District 411
201 Main Ave W . . . Twin Falls ID 83301 208-733-6900 733-6987
TF: 800-726-0003 ■ *Web:* www.tfsd.k12.id.us

Twin Rivers Unified School District
3222 Winona Way . . . North Highlands CA 95660 916-566-1628 566-3586
TF: 888-674-6854 ■ *Web:* www.twinriversusd.org

Unified School District 428
201 S Patton Rd . . . Great Bend KS 67530 620-793-1500
Web: www.usd428.net

Unified School District of Antigo
120 S Dorr St . . . Antigo WI 54409 715-627-4355 623-3279
TF: 800-795-3272 ■ *Web:* www.antigo.k12.wi.us

Union County Public Schools
510 S Mart St . . . Morganfield KY 42437 270-389-1694 389-9806
Web: www.union.kyschools.us

Unity Elementary School
6846 Unity School Rd . . . Brookport IL 62910 618-564-2582
Web: unity.massac.org

Unlimited Construction Services Inc
1696 Haleukana St . . . Lihue HI 96766 808 241 1400 245 6611
Web: www.unlimitedhawaii.com

Upland Unified School District
390 N Euclid Ave . . . Upland CA 91786 909-985-1864 949-7863
Web: www.upland.k12.ca.us

Upper Dauphin Area School District (UDASD)
5668 State Rt 209 . . . Lykens PA 17048 717-362-8134 362-3050
TF: 866-632-9992 ■ *Web:* www.udasd.org

Upper Freehold Regional Board of Education (Inc)
27 High St . . . Allentown NJ 08501 609-259-7292
Web: www.ufrsd.net

Upper Merion Area School District
435 Crossfield Rd . . . King of Prussia PA 19406 610-205-6400 205-6433
Web: www.umasd.org

Upper Perkiomen School District
2229 E Buck Rd Ste 2 . . . Pennsburg PA 18073 215-679-7961
Web: www.upsd.org

US Special Delivery Inc 821 E Blvd . . . Kingsford MI 49802 906-774-1931 774-2032
TF: 800-821-6389 ■ *Web:* usspecial.com

Utica Community Schools (UCS)
11303 Greendale Dr . . . Sterling Heights MI 48312 586-797-1000 797-1001
TF: 800-877-8339 ■ *Web:* www.uticak12.org

Uvalde Consolidated Independent School District
PO Box 1909 . . . Uvalde TX 78802 830-278-6655 591-4927
Web: www.ucisd.net

Vail Mountain School 3000 Booth Falls Rd . . . Vail CO 81657 970-476-3850
Web: www.vmts.org

Val Verde Unified School District
975 Morgan St . . . Perris CA 92571 951-940-6100
Web: www.valverde.edu

Valley Ctr-Pauma Unified School District
28751 Cole Grade Rd . . . Valley Center CA 92082 760-749-0464 749-1208
Web: www.vcpusd.net

Van Buren Public Schools (VBPS)
555 W Columbia Ave . . . Belleville MI 48111 734-697-9123 697-6385
Web: www.vanburenschools.net

Vancouver Talmud Torah Association
998 26th Ave W . . . Vancouver BC V5Z2G1 604-736-7307
Web: www.talmudtorah.com

Varnett School - East, The 804 Maxey Rd . . . Houston TX 77013 713-637-6574
Web: www.varnett.org

Vernon Parish School Board 201 Belview Rd . . . Leesville LA 71446 337-239-3401 392-2517
TF: 800-621-1742 ■ *Web:* www.vpsb.k12.la.us

Vernon Township Board of Education (Inc)
PO Box 99 . . . Vernon NJ 07462 973-764-2900
Web: www.vtsd.com

Vestal Central School District 201 Main St . . . Vestal NY 13850 607-757-2241 757-2227
Web: vestal.stier.org

Vestavia Hills Board of Education
1204 Montgomery Hwy . . . Birmingham AL 35216 205-402-5100
Web: www.vestavia.k12.al.us

Victor Elementary School District (VESD)
15579 Eigth St . . . Victorville CA 92392 760-245-1691 245-6245
Web: www.vesd.net

Volmar Construction Inc 4400 Second Ave . . . Brooklyn NY 11232 718-832-2444 499-4045
Web: www.volmar.com

W. N. Morehouse Truck Line Inc
4010 Dahlman Ave . . . Omaha NE 68107 402-733-2200 733-6316
TF: 800-228-9378 ■ *Web:* www.morehousetruckline.com

Wahluke School District 73
411 E Saddle Mt Dr . . . Mattawa WA 99349 509-932-4565
Web: www.wsd73.wednet.edu

Wake Christian Academy Inc
5500 Wake Academy Dr . . . Raleigh NC 27603 919-772-6264
Web: www.wakechristianacademy.com

Wake County Public School System
3600 Wake Forest Rd . . . Raleigh NC 27609 919-850-1600
Web: www.wcpss.net

Wakefield School District 60 Farm St . . . Wakefield MA 01880 781-246-6400
Web: wakefieldpublicschools.org/

Walbon & Company Inc
4230 Pine Bend Trial Ste A . . . Rosemount MN 55068 651-437-2011 437-2087
Web: www.walbon.com

	City	State	Zip	Phone	Fax
Walker County Board of Education 1710 Alabama Ave PO Box 311 *TF:* 866-276-7735 ■ *Web:* www.walkercountyschools.com	Jasper	AL	35501	205-387-0555	221-5636
Wall Timber Products Inc 1825 Effingham Hwy *Web:* www.walltimber.com	Sylvania	GA	30467	912-863-5108	863-7478
Wallingford-Swarthmore School District 200 S Providence Rd *Web:* www.wssd.org	Wallingford	PA	19086	610-892-3470	
Wallkill Central School District (WCSD) 19 Main St PO Box 310 *Web:* www.wallkillcsd.k12.ny.us/education/district/district.php?sectionid=7785	Wallkill	NY	12589	845-895-7100	895-3630
Washington Company School District PO Box 716 *Web:* www.washington.k12.ga.us	Sandersville	GA	31082	478-552-3981	
Washington County Board of Education 802 Washington St *Web:* www.washingtonco.k12.nc.us	Plymouth	NC	27962	252-793-5171	793-5062
Washington International School 3100 Macomb St NW *Web:* www.wis.edu	Washington	DC	20008	202-243-1815	
Washington School District Inc 201 Allison Ave *TF:* 855-846-8376 ■ *Web:* www.washington.k12.pa.us	Washington	PA	15301	724-223-5085	223-5046
Washoe County School District 425 E Ninth St **Fax Area Code:* 814 ■ *Web:* www.washoe.k12.nv.us	Reno	NV	89512	775-348-0200	689-3962*
Watauga County Schools PO Box 1790 *Web:* www.watauga.k12.nc.us	Boone	NC	28607	828-264-7190	264-7196
Waterloo Community Unit School Dst 5 219 Pk St *Web:* www.wcusd5.net	Waterloo	IL	62298	618-939-3453	939-4578
Watertown-Mayer Public Schools 1001 Hwy 25 NW *Web:* www.wm.k12.mn.us	Watertown	MN	55388	952-955-0480	955-0251
Waxahachie Independent School District 411 N Gibson St *Web:* www.wisd.org	Waxahachie	TX	75165	972-923-4631	923-4759
Wayne Highlands School District 474 Grove St *Web:* www.waynehighlands.org	Honesdale	PA	18431	570-253-4661	253-9409
Weimar Junior High School 101 N W St *Web:* www.weimarisd.org	Weimar	TX	78962	979-725-9515	
Wellsboro Area School District 227 Nichols *Web:* www.wellsborosd.k12.pa.us	Wellsboro	PA	16901	570-724-4424	
West Clermont Local School District 4350 Aicholtz Rd Ste 220 *Web:* www.westcler.k12.oh.us	Cincinnati	OH	45245	513-943-5000	752-6158
West Fargo School District 6 207 Main Ave W *Web:* www.west-fargo.k12.nd.us	West Fargo	ND	58078	701-356-2000	356-2009
West Genesee Central School District 300 Sanderson Dr *Web:* www.westgenesee.org	Camillus	NY	13031	315-487-4562	487-2999
West Irondequoit Central School District 321 List Ave *Web:* www.westirondequoit.org	Rochester	NY	14617	585-342-5500	
West Millbrook Middle School Booster Club 8115 Strickland Rd *Web:* wmms.net	Raleigh	NC	27615	919-870-4050	
West Oaklane Charter School 7115 Stenton Ave *Web:* wolcs.org	Philadelphia	PA	19138	215-927-7995	
West Valley School District 208 8902 Zier Rd *Web:* www.wvsd208.org	Yakima	WA	98908	509-972-6000	
Western Placer Unified School District Finanacing Corp 600 Sixth St *Web:* www.wpusd.k12.ca.us	Lincoln	CA	95648	916-645-6350	
Western Suffolk Boces (suffolk 3) 507 Deer Park Rd *Web:* www.monroebup.org	Dix Hills	NY	11746	631-549-4900	
Westfield Board of Education Inc 302 Elm St *TF:* 800-355-2583 ■ *Web:* www.westfieldnjk12.org	Westfield	NJ	07090	908-789-4401	
Westminster School District 14121 Cedarwood St *TF:* 800-678-9133 ■ *Web:* www.wsd.k12.ca.us	Westminster	CA	92683	714-894-7311	899-2781
Wharton Independent School District 2100 N Fulton St *TF:* 800-818-3453 ■ *Web:* www.whartonisd.net	Wharton	TX	77488	979-532-3612	532-6228
Wheaton Academy 900 Prince Crossing Rd *Web:* wheatonacademy.org	West Chicago	IL	60185	630-293-4179	
Whitcomb School 350 W Mauna Loa Ave *Web:* mie.marlborough.schoolfusion.us	Glendora	CA	91740	626-852-4550	
Whittier City School District 7211 Whittier Ave *Web:* www.whittiercity.k12.ca.us	Whittier	CA	90602	562-789-3000	907-9425
Wicomico County Board of Education PO Box 1538 *Web:* www.wcboe.org	Salisbury	MD	21802	410-677-4400	677-4444
William B Meyer Inc 255 Long Beach Blvd *TF:* 800-727-5985 ■ *Web:* www.williambmeyer.com	Stratford	CT	06615	203-375-5801	375-9820
Williams Valley School District 10400 US 209	Tower City	PA	17980	717-647-2181	
Williamsburg-James City County Educational Foundation Inc PO Box 8783 *Web:* wjccschools.org/web/	Williamsburg	VA	23187	757-253-6777	
Williamsport Area School District 201 W Third St *TF:* 888-448-4642 ■ *Web:* www.wasd.org	Williamsport	PA	17701	570-327-5500	327-8122
Williamston Community Schools Inc 418 Highland St *Web:* www.gowcs.net	Williamston	MI	48895	517-655-4361	
Willoughby Eastlake City Schools 37047 Ridge Rd *Web:* www.weschools.org	Willoughby	OH	44094	440-946-5000	946-4671
Wills Point Independent School Distric 338 W N Commerce St *Web:* www.wpisd.com	Wills Point	TX	75169	903-873-3161	873-2462
Winchester-Thurston School 555 Morewood Ave *Web:* winchesterthurston.org	Pittsburgh	PA	15213	412-578-7500	578-7504
Windsor High School 6208 Us Hwy 61/67 *Web:* windsor.k12.mo.us	Imperial	MO	63052	636-464-4408	
Winnebago Community Unit District 323 304 E Mcnair Rd *Web:* www.winnebagoschools.org	Winnebago	IL	61088	815-335-2456	
Winston-Salem/Forsyth County Schools (WS/FCS) 1605 Miller St *Web:* www.wsfcs.k12.nc.us	Winston-Salem	NC	27103	336-727-2816	661-6572
Winton Woods City Schools 1215 W Kemper Rd *Web:* www.wintonwoods.org	Cincinnati	OH	45240	513-619-2300	619-2300
Woodland School District 50 1105 N Hunt Club Rd *Web:* www.dist50.net	Gurnee	IL	60031	847-596-5600	680-8266
Woodstock Community Unit School District 200 227 W Judd St *Web:* www.woodstockschools.org	Woodstock	IL	60098	815-338-8200	338-2005
Woodward Academy 1662 Rugby Ave *Web:* www.woodward.edu	College Park	GA	30337	404-765-4000	
Wooster City Board of Education 144 N Market St *Web:* www.woostercityschools.org	Wooster	OH	44691	330-264-0869	262-3407
Worcester Public Schools 20 Irving St *Web:* www.worcesterschools.org	Worcester	MA	01609	508-799-3115	799-3119
Wyoming Valley West School District 450 N Maple Ave *Web:* www.wvwspartans.org	Kingston	PA	18704	570-288-6551	288-1564
Wythe County Public Schools Foundation for Excellence Inc 1570 W Reservoir St *Web:* wytheexcellence.org	Wytheville	VA	24382	276-228-5411	
Xaverian Brothers High School Inc 800 clapboardtree st *Web:* www.xbhs.com	Westwood	MA	02090	781-326-6392	
Xavier High School Corporation of Middletown 181 Randolph Rd *Web:* xavierhighschool.org	Middletown	CT	06457	860-346-7735	
Yale Public Schools 315 E Chicago Ave *Web:* www.yale.k12.ok.us	Yale	OK	74085	918-387-2434	387-2503
Yancey County Schools Foundation Inc, The PO Box 190 *Web:* www.yanceync.net	Burnsville	NC	28714	828-682-6101	682-7110
Yeshivat Noam 70 W Century Rd *Web:* www.yeshivatnoam.org	Paramus	NJ	07652	201-261-1919	
York Catholic High School 601 E Springettsbury Ave *Web:* yorkcatholic.org	York	PA	17403	717-846-8871	
Zachary Community School Board 3755 Church St *Web:* zacharyschools.org	Zachary	LA	70791	225-658-4969	
Zanesville City School Board 160 N Fourth St *TF:* 866-280-7377 ■ *Web:* www.zanesville.k12.oh.us	Zanesville	OH	43701	740-454-9751	
Zumbrota-mazeppa Senior High School 705 Mill St *Web:* www.zmschools.us	Zumbrota	MN	55992	507-732-7395	

689 SCRAP METAL

SEE ALSO Recyclable Materials Recovery p. 3046

	City	State	Zip	Phone	Fax
A Tenenbaum Company Inc 4500 W Bethany Rd *Web:* www.trg.net	North Little Rock	AR	72117	501-945-0881	945-3865
Advantage Metals Recycling LLC 3005 Manchester Trfy *TF:* 866-527-4733 ■ *Web:* www.advantagerecycling.com	Kansas City	MO	64129	816-861-2700	861-7670
Alco Iron & Metal Co 2140 Davis St *Web:* www.alcometals.com	San Leandro	CA	94577	510-562-1107	562-1354
Allan Industries PO Box 999 *Web:* allanrecyclers.com	Wilkes-Barre	PA	18703	570-826-0123	829-4099
Alter Trading Corp 700 Office Pkwy *TF:* 888-337-2727 ■ *Web:* www.altertrading.com	Saint Louis	MO	63141	314-872-2400	872-2420
Amcep Metals 4484 E Tennessee St *Web:* amcepmetals.com	Tucson	AZ	85714	520-748-1900	748-2752
AMG Resources Corp 2 Robinson Plaza # 350 *TF:* 800-633-3606 ■ *Web:* www.amgresources.com	Pittsburgh	PA	15205	412-777-7300	331-0972
Azcon Corp 820 W Jackson Blvd Ste 425 *Web:* azcon.net	Chicago	IL	60607	312-559-3100	559-1543
Baker Iron & Metal Company Inc 740 Rock Castle Ave *Web:* www.bakeriron.com	Lexington	KY	40505	859-255-5676	252-3590
Borg Compressed Steel Corp 1032 N Lewis Ave *Web:* yaffeco.net	Tulsa	OK	74110	918-587-2511	587-2520
Calbag Metals Co 2495 NW Nicolai St *TF:* 800-398-3441 ■ *Web:* www.calbag.com	Portland	OR	97210	503-226-3441	228-0184
City Carton Company Inc Three E Benton St *TF:* 800-369-6112 ■ *Web:* www.citycarton.com	Iowa City	IA	52240	319-351-2848	351-3818
Cleveland Corp 42810 N Green Bay Rd *TF:* 800-281-3464 ■ *Web:* www.clevelandcorp.com	Zion	IL	60099	847-872-7200	872-0827
Cohen Bros Inc 1723 Woodlawn Ave *TF:* 800-878-3697 ■ *Web:* www.cohenusa.com	Middletown	OH	45044	513-422-3696	422-9018
Connell LP One International Pl 31st Fl *Web:* www.connell-lp.com	Boston	MA	02110	617-391-5577	737-1617

	Phone	Fax
Cycle Systems Inc 2580 Broadway SW .... Roanoke VA 24014	540-981-1211	
David J Joseph Co (DJJ) 300 Pike St .... Cincinnati OH 45202 *Web:* www.djj.com	513-419-6200	419-6222
Davis Industries Inc 9920 Richmond Hwy .... Lorton VA 22079	703-550-7402	
Dimco Steel Inc 3901 S Lamar St .... Dallas TX 75215 *TF:* 877-428-8336 ■ *Web:* www.dimcosteel.com	214-428-8336	428-1929
ELG Metals Inc 369 River Rd .... McKeesport PA 15132 *Web:* www.elg.de	412-672-9200	672-0824
FPT Pontiac Div 500 Collier Rd .... Pontiac MI 48340 *Web:* www.fptscrap.com	248-335-8141	335-8714
Franklin Iron & Metal Corp 1939 E First St .... Dayton OH 45403 *Web:* franklinironandmetal.liveonatt.com	937-253-8184	
Gachman Metals & Recycling Company Inc 2600 Shamrock Ave .... Fort Worth TX 76107 *TF:* 800-749-0423 ■ *Web:* www.gachman.com	817-334-0211	877-1528
Gershow Recycling Corp 71 Peconic Ave PO Box 526 .... Medford NY 11763 *Web:* www.gershow.com	631-289-6188	289-6368
Grossman Iron & Steel Five N Market St .... Saint Louis MO 63102 *TF:* 800-969-9423 ■ *Web:* www.grossmaniron.com	314-231-9423	231-6983
Iron & Metals Inc 5555 Franklin St .... Denver CO 80216 *TF:* 800-776-7910 ■ *Web:* www.ironandmetals.com	303-292-5555	292-0513
Joe Krentzman & Son Inc 3175 Back Maitland Rd .... Lewistown PA 17044 *Web:* www.krentzman.net	717-543-4000	
Keywell LLC 11900 S Cottage Grove Ave .... Chicago IL 60628 *Web:* www.keywell.com	773-660-2060	660-2064
Langley Recycling 503 SE Branner St .... Topeka KS 66607 *Web:* www.langleyrecycling.com	785-234-2691	354-8019
Lionetti Assoc 450 S Front St .... Elizabeth NJ 07202 *TF:* 800-734-0910 ■ *Web:* www.lorcopetroleum.com	908-820-8800	820-8412
Louis Padnos Iron & Metal Co PO Box 1979 .... Holland MI 49422 *TF:* 800-442-3509 ■ *Web:* www.padnos.com	616-396-6521	396-7789
M Lipsitz & Co Inc 100 Elm St .... Waco TX 76704 *Web:* www.mlipsitzco.com	254-756-6661	752-0175
Mayer Pollock Steel Corp Industrial Hwy .... Pottstown PA 19464 *TF General:* 855-773-2848 ■ *Web:* www.mayerpollock.com	610-323-5500	323-5506
Mervis Industries Inc 3295 E Main St .... Danville IL 61834 *TF:* 800-637-3016 ■ *Web:* www.mervis.com	217-442-5300	477-9245
Metal Exchange Corp 111 W Port Plaza Ste 350 .... Saint Louis MO 63146 *Web:* www.metalexchangecorp.com	314-434-3500	434-2196
Metalico Annaco Inc 943 Hazel St .... Akron OH 44305 *TF:* 800-966-1499 ■ *Web:* www.metalico.com	330-376-1400	376-9696
Metalsco Inc 1828 Craig Rd .... Saint Louis MO 63146 *Web:* www.metalsco.com	314-997-5200	997-5921
Metro Metals Northwest 5611 NE Columbia Blvd .... Portland OR 97218 *TF:* 800-610-5680 ■ *Web:* www.metrometalsnw.com	503-287-8861	287-5569
Mid State Trading Co 2525 Trenton Ave .... Williamsport PA 17701	570-326-9431	326-5028
Midland Iron & Steel Corp 3301 Fourth Ave .... Moline IL 61265 *Web:* midlanddavis.com	309-764-6723	764-6729
Miller Compressing Co 1640 W Bruce St .... Milwaukee WI 53204	414-671-5980	671-7191
Minkin Chandler Corp 15400 Oakwood Dr .... Romulus MI 48174 *Web:* minkinchandler.weebly.com	734-229-9200	
Newell Recycling of San Antonio 726 Probandt .... San Antonio TX 78204 *Web:* newellrecyclingsa.com	210-227-3141	227-8948
Northern Metal Recycling LLC 2800 Pacific St N .... Minneapolis MN 55411 *Web:* www.northernmetalrecycling.com	612-529-9221	529-2548
OmniSource Corp 7575 W Jefferson Blvd .... Fort Wayne IN 46804 *TF:* 800-666-4789 ■ *Web:* www.omnisource.com	260-422-5541	423-8500
Pascap Company Inc 4250 Boston Rd .... Bronx NY 10475 *Web:* pascapco.com	718-325-7200	325-7595
Progress Rail Services 1600 Progress Dr PO Box 1037 .... Albertville AL 35950 *TF:* 800-476-8769 ■ *Web:* www.progressrail.com	256-505-6600	593-1249
PSC 5151 San Felipe Ste 1100 .... Houston TX 77056 **Fax Area Code:* 713 ■ *TF:* 800-726-1300 ■ *Web:* www.pscnow.com	800-726-1300	985-5318*
River Metals Recycling 2045 River Rd .... Louisville KY 40206 *Web:* www.rmrecycling.com	502-585-5331	587-8699
River Recycling Industries Inc 4195 Bradley Rd .... Cleveland OH 44109 *Web:* riverrecyclingind.com	216-459-2100	749-8107
Riverside Scrap Iron 2993 Sixth St .... Riverside CA 92507 *Web:* www.riversidemetalrecycling.com	951-686-2129	686-8933
Rocky Mountain Recycling (RMR) 6510 Brighton Blvd .... Commerce City CO 80022 *Web:* www.rmrscrap.com	303-288-6868	288-0250
SA Recycling LLC 2411 N Glassell St .... Orange CA 92865 *TF:* 800-468-7272 ■ *Web:* www.sarecycling.com	714-632-2000	630-5836
Sadoff & Rudoy Industries LLP 240 W Arndt St .... Fond du Lac WI 54936 *TF General:* 877-972-3633 ■ *Web:* www.sadoff.com	920-921-2070	921-1283
SD Richman Sons Inc 2435 Wheatsheaf Ln .... Philadelphia PA 19137 *TF:* 800-648-3576 ■ *Web:* www.sdrichmansons.com	215-535-5100	288-1043
Simon Metals LLC 2202 E River St .... Tacoma WA 98421 *TF:* 800-562-8464 ■ *Web:* www.simonmetals.com	253-272-9364	
Sims Bros Inc 1011 S Prospect St PO Box 1170 .... Marion OH 43301 *TF:* 800-536-7465 ■ *Web:* www.simsbros.com	740-387-9041	
SLC Recycling Industries Inc 8701 E 8 Mile Rd .... Warren MI 48089 *Web:* fptscrap.com	586-759-6600	759-6518
Soave Enterprises LLC 3400 E Lafayette St .... Detroit MI 48207 *Web:* www.soave.com	313-567-7000	567-0966
Sol Tick & Co 1180 N 22nd St PO Box 1605 .... Decatur IL 62521 *Web:* www.mervis.com	217-429-4148	429-7565
Sugar Creek Scrap Inc 1201 W National Ave .... West Terre Haute IN 47885 *TF:* 800-466-7462 ■ *Web:* www.sugarcreekscrap.com	812-533-2147	533-2140
Tennessee Valley Recycling LLC 821 W College St .... Pulaski TN 38478 *Web:* tvrllc.com	931-363-3593	363-8065
Thalheimer Bros Inc 5550 Whitaker Ave .... Philadelphia PA 19124 *Web:* www.thalheimerbrothers.com	215-537-5200	533-3993
Thermo Fluids Inc 4301 W Jefferson St .... Phoenix AZ 85043 *TF:* 800-350-7565 ■ *Web:* www.thermofluids.com	602-272-2400	
Tri-State Iron & Metal Co 1725 E Ninth St .... Texarkana AR 71854 **Fax Area Code:* 800 ■ *TF:* 800-773-8409 ■ *Web:* www.tsimco.com	870-773-8409	772-3086*
Tube City IMS Corp (TMS) 12 Monongahela Ave .... Glassport PA 15045 *NYSE: TMS* ■ *TF:* 800-860-2442 ■ *Web:* www.tubecityims.com	412-678-6141	675-8295
Universal Steel Co, The 6600 Grant Ave .... Cleveland OH 44105 *Web:* univsteel.com	216-883-4972	
Upstate Shredding LLC 1 Recycle Dr Tioga Industrial Pk .... Owego NY 13827 *TF:* 800-245-3133 ■ *Web:* www.upstateshredding.com	607-687-7777	687-7746
Weiner Iron & Metal Corp PO Box 359 .... Pottsville PA 17901	570-622-6543	622-3175
Western Scrap Processing Co 3315 Drennan Industrial Loop S .... Colorado Springs CO 80910 *Web:* www.westernscrap.com	719-390-7986	390-3852
Yaffe Cos Inc, The 1200 S G St .... Muskogee OK 74403 *TF:* 800-759-2333 ■ *Web:* yaffeco.net	918-687-7543	

690 SCREEN PRINTING

	Phone	Fax
A Plus Designs Inc & Outfitters Plus Outlet Store 56988 635th St .... Atlantic IA 50022 *Web:* www.aplusdesignsinc.com	712-243-4379	
Action Screen Print Inc 30w260 Butterfield Rd Unit 203 .... Warrenville IL 60555 *Web:* actionscreen.com	630-393-1990	
Aim Screen Printing Supply LLC 2731 Willow Ridge Dr .... Naperville IL 60564 *Web:* aimsupply.net	630-357-4293	
Allied Advertising Agency Inc 3700 Blanco Rd .... San Antonio TX 78212 *Web:* www.alliedad.com	210-732-7874	
Ares Sportswear Ltd 3704 Lacon Rd .... Hilliard OH 43026 *Web:* www.areswear.com	614-767-1950	
Art Brands LLC 225 Business Ctr Dr .... Blacklick OH 43004 *Web:* www.artbrands.com	614-755-4278	
Artco (US) Inc One Staery Pl .... Rexburg ID 83441 *Web:* www.stylartstore.com	208-359-1000	
Chimes Inc, The 4815 Seton Dr .... Baltimore MD 21215 *Web:* www.chimes.org	410-358-6400	
Designer Decal Inc 1120 E First Ave .... Spokane WA 99202 *TF:* 800-622-6333 ■ *Web:* www.designerdecal.com	509-535-0267	535-1476
Empire Screen Printing Inc N5206 Marco Rd PO Box 218 .... Onalaska WI 54650 *Web:* www.empirescreen.com	608-783-3301	783-3306
Excel Screen Printing & Embroidery Inc 10507 Delta Pkwy .... Schiller Park IL 60176 *Web:* www.excelscreenprinting.com	847-801-5200	
F&E Sportswear Corp 1230 Newell Pkwy .... Montgomery AL 36110 *Web:* fandesportswear.us	334-244-6477	
Faux Pas Prints Inc 620 Papworth Ave .... Metairie LA 70005 *Web:* www.fauxpasprints.com	504-834-8342	
Fisher Printing Inc 8640 S Oketo Ave .... Bridgeview IL 60455 *Web:* fisherprinting.com	708-598-1500	
Flow-Eze Co 3209 Auburn St .... Rockford IL 61101 *TF:* 800-435-4873 ■ *Web:* www.flow-eze.com	815-965-1062	965-1329
Garment Graphics LLC 220 W Ft Lowell Rd .... Tucson AZ 85705 *Web:* www.garmentgraphics.net	520-544-0529	
GFX International Inc 333 Barron Blvd .... Grayslake IL 60030 *Web:* www.gfxi.com	847-543-4600	
Gill Studios Inc 10800 Lackman Rd .... Lenexa KS 66219 *Web:* www.gill-line.com	913-888-4422	
Gillespie Graphics 27676 SW Pkwy Ave .... Wilsonville OR 97070 *Web:* www.gillespie-graphics.com	503-682-1122	
Graphic Trends Inc 7301 Adams St .... Paramount CA 90723 *Web:* www.graphictrends.net	562-531-2339	
Gwin's Commercial Printing & Engraving 957 Spring Hill Ave .... Mobile AL 36604 *Web:* gwins.cc	251-438-2226	
Haapanen Brothers Inc 1400 Saint Paul Ave .... Gurnee IL 60031 *Web:* hb-graphics.net	847-662-1542	
Hanson Sign & Screen Process Corp 82 Carter St .... Falconer NY 14733 *Web:* www.hansonsign.com	716-484-8564	
Image Sport Inc 1115 SE Westbrooke Dr .... Waukee IA 50263 *Web:* www.imagesport.com	515-987-7699	
Ink Enterprises 400 Casey Dr .... Maumelle AR 72113 *Web:* inkenterprises.com	501-851-6916	
Innerworkings Inc 600 W Chicago Ave Ste 850 .... Chicago IL 60610 *NASDAQ: INWK* ■ *Web:* www.inwk.com	312-642-3700	642-3704
J.N. White Designs Digital Inc 129 N Ctr St PO Box 219 .... Perry NY 14530 *Web:* www.jnwhitedesigns.com	585-237-5191	
Kapta Inc 2220 1re Av .... Notre-dame-des-pins QC G0M1K0 *Web:* kapta.ca	418-774-5688	
Kay Automotive Graphics 57 Kay Industrial Dr .... Lake Orion MI 48359 *TF:* 800-443-0190 ■ *Web:* www.kayautomotive.com	248-377-4999	377-2097
Kerusso Activewear Inc 402 Hwy 62 Spur .... Berryville AR 72616 *Web:* www.kerusso.com	870-423-6242	
Killeen Dynamic Designs Inc 2100 E Stan Schlueter Loop Ste F .... Killeen TX 76542 *Web:* www.dynamicdesignsinc.com	254-628-8272	
Law Elder Law 2275 Church Rd .... Aurora IL 60502 *Web:* lawelderlaw.com	630-585-5200	

				Phone	Fax

Litho Technical Services Inc
1600 W 92nd St — Bloomington MN 55431 952-888-7945
Web: lithotechusa.com

M & M Designs Inc
1981 Quality Blvd PO Box 1049 — Huntsville TX 77320 800-627-0656 295-9286*
**Fax Area Code:* 936 ■ *TF:* 800-627-0656 ■ *Web:* www.m-mdesigns.com

Mastro Graphic Arts Inc 67 Deep Rock Rd — Rochester NY 14624 585-436-7570
Web: www.mastrographics.com

Mitographers Inc, The 4720 N Fourth Ave — Sioux Falls SD 57104 605-336-1818
Web: mito.com

Modagrafics Inc 5300 Newport Dr — Rolling Meadows IL 60008 847-392-3980
Web: www.modagrafics.com

Motson Graphics Inc 1717 Bethlehem Pk — Flourtown PA 19031 215-233-0500 233-5014
TF: 800-972-1986 ■ *Web:* www.motson.com

New Life Industries Inc
140 Chappells Dairy Rd — Somerset KY 42503 606-679-3616
Web: www.newlifeshopper.com

NSO Press Inc 1921 E 68th Ave — Denver CO 80229 303-227-1400
Web: www.nsopress.com

Offset Impressions Inc 122 Mtn View Rd — Reading PA 19607 610-378-1851
Web: www.offsetimpress.com

Oscar Printing Co 57 Columbia Sq — San Francisco CA 94103 415-626-8818
Web: opportunitymart.com

Otis Graphics Inc 290 Grant Ave — Lyndhurst NJ 07071 201-438-7120
Web: www.otisgraphics.com

Petra Manufacturing Co 6600 W Armitage Ave — Chicago IL 60707 773-622-1475
Web: www.petramanufacturing.com

Primary Color Inc 9239 Premier Row — Dallas TX 75247 214-630-8800
Web: www.primarycolorinc.com

Ram Graphics Inc 2408 S Pk Ave — Alexandria IN 46001 800-531-4656 551-6846
TF: 800-531-4656 ■ *Web:* www.ramgraphics.com

Screen Graphics of Florida Inc
1801 N Andrews Ave — Pompano Beach FL 33069 800-346-4420
TF: 800-346-4420 ■ *Web:* www.screen-graphics.com

Screen Industry Art Inc
214 Industrial Park Dr — Soddy Daisy TN 37379 423-332-6190
Web: businessdirectory.lebanondemocrat.com

Screen Machine Inc 3855 Wabash Ave — San Diego CA 92104 619-281-3355 281-2033
Web: scrnmach.com

Select Design Ltd 208 Flynn Ave Ste 1a — Burlington VT 05401 802-864-9075
Web: www.selectdesign.com

Selecto-Flash Inc 18 Central Ave — West Orange NJ 07052 973-677-3500
Web: www.selectoflash.com

Sensical Inc Decals 31115 Aurora Rd — Solon OH 44139 216-641-1141
Web: sensical.com

Serigraph Inc 3801 E Decorah Rd — West Bend WI 53095 262-335-7200 335-7699
Web: www.serigraph.com

Service Graphics LLC 8350 Allison Ave — Indianapolis IN 46268 317-471-8246
Web: www.mysgi.com

Signcraft Screenprint Inc 100 A J Harle Dr — Galena IL 61036 815-777-3030
Web: www.signcraftinc.com

Silkworm Inc 102 S Sezmore Dr — Murphysboro IL 62966 618-687-4077
Web: www.silkwormink.com

Starline Printing Inc
7111 Pan American W Svc Ne — Albuquerque NM 87109 505-345-8900
Web: www.starlineprinting.com

Sun Line Products 1454 E Summitry Cir — Katy TX 77449 281-398-6655
Web: www.sunlineproducts.com

Superior Imaging Group Inc 22710 72nd Ave South — Kent WA 98032 253-872-7200
Web: www.superiorimaging.com

Technigraph Corp 850 W Third St — Winona MN 55987 507-454-3830 454-6470
Web: www.technigraph.net

Technigraphics 3212 S Cravens Rd — Fort Worth TX 76119 817-457-8412
Web: www.craftmarkid.com

Thomas Graphics Inc 9501 N IH 35 — Austin TX 78753 512-719-3535
Web: www.thomasgraphicsinc.com

Top Promotions Inc 8831 S Greenview Dr — Middleton WI 53562 608-836-9111
Web: www.toppromotions.com

Trau & Loevner Inc 5817 Centre Ave — Pittsburgh PA 15206 412-361-7700 361-8221
Web: www.trau-loevner.com

Triple Crown Products Inc 814 Ela Ave — Waterford WI 53185 262-534-7878
Web: www.tcpcaps.com

Trust-franklin Press Inc 41 Terminal Way — Pittsburgh PA 15219 412-481-6442
Web: www.trust-franklinpress.com

Vincent Printing Company Inc
1512 Sholar Ave — Chattanooga TN 37406 800-251-7262
TF: 800-251-7262 ■ *Web:* www.vincentprinting.com

William Frick & Co 2600 Commerce Dr — Libertyville IL 60048 847-918-3700
Web: fricknet.com

Windy City Silkscreening 2715 S Archer Ave — Chicago IL 60608 312-842-0030
Web: windycitysilkscreening.net

691 SCREENING - WOVEN WIRE

				Phone	Fax

ACS Industries Inc 191 Social St — Woonsocket RI 02895 401-769-4700 333-6088
TF: 866-783-4838 ■ *Web:* www.acsindustries.com

Belleville Wire Cloth Inc 18 Rutgers Ave — Cedar Grove NJ 07009 973-239-0074 239-3985
TF: 800-631-0490 ■ *Web:* www.bwire.com

Buffalo Wire Works Co 1165 Clinton St — Buffalo NY 14206 716-826-4666 826-8271
TF: 800-828-7028 ■ *Web:* www.buffalowire.com

Cleveland Wire Cloth & Manufacturing Co
3573 E 78th St — Cleveland OH 44105 216-341-1832 341-1876
TF: 800-321-3234 ■ *Web:* www.wirecloth.com

Edward J Darby & Son Inc
2200 N Eigth St PO Box 50049 — Philadelphia PA 19133 215-236-2203 236-2203
TF: 800-875-6374 ■ *Web:* www.darbywiremesh.com

Gerard Daniel Worldwide 34 Barnhart Dr — Hanover PA 17331 717-637-5901 633-7095
TF: 800-232-3332 ■ *Web:* www.gerarddaniel.com

Halliburton Screen Co
3000 N Sam Houston Pkwy E — Houston TX 77032 281-871-4000
NYSE: HAL ■ *Web:* www.halliburton.com

Hanover Wire Cloth 500 E Middle St — Hanover PA 17331 717-637-3795 637-4766
Web: www.newyorkwireind.com

Jelliff Corp 354 Pequot Ave — Southport CT 06890 203-259-1615 255-7908
TF: 800-243-0052 ■ *Web:* www.jelliff.com

King Wire Partitions Inc
6044 N Figueroa St — Los Angeles CA 90042 323-256-4848 256-1950
Web: www.kingwireusa.com

Metal Textiles 970 New Durham Rd — Edison NJ 08818 732-287-0800 287-8546*
**Fax:* Sales ■ *Web:* www.metexcorp.com

National Wire Fabric 701 Arkansas St — Star City AR 71667 870-628-4201 628-3700

TWP Inc 2831 Tenth St — Berkeley CA 94710 510-548-4434 548-3073
TF: 800-227-1570 ■ *Web:* www.twpinc.com

United Capital Corp Nine Pk Pl — Great Neck NY 11021 516-466-6464 829-4301
OTC: UCAP ■ *Web:* www.unitedcapitalcorp.net

Universal Wire Cloth Co 16 N Steel Rd — Morrisville PA 19067 215-736-8981 736-8994
TF: 800-523-0575 ■ *Web:* www.universalwirecloth.com

Wayne Wire Cloth Products Inc
200 E Dresden St — Kalkaska MI 49646 231-258-9187 258-5504
Web: www.waynewire.com

Western Wire Group 4025 NW Express Ave — Portland OR 97210 503-222-1644 222-6843
Web: www.thewesterngroup.com

Wire Cloth Filter Manufacturing Co
611 St Charles Rd — Maywood IL 60153 708-410-1800 410-1807
Web: wireclothfilter.net

692 SEATING - VEHICULAR

				Phone	Fax

Advanced Components Technologies Inc
91 - 16th St S — Northwood IA 50459 641-324-2231 324-1231

American Metal Fab Inc
55515 Franklin Dr — Three Rivers MI 49093 269-279-5108 279-5356
Web: www.americanmetalfab.com

Beloates Aircraft Trim Inc
4408 N Haltom Rd — Haltom City TX 76117 817-485-5013 485-5014
Web: beloates-aircraft-trim-inc.sbcontract.com

Bridgewater Interiors LLC 4617 W Fort St — Detroit MI 48209 313-842-3300 842-3452
Web: bridgewater-interiors.com

Custom Aircraft Interiors 3701 Industry Ave — Lakewood CA 90712 562-426-5098 490-0213
Web: www.customaircraftinteriors.com

Freedman Seating Co 4545 W Augusta Blvd — Chicago IL 60651 773-524-2440 252-7450
TF: 800-443-4540 ■ *Web:* www.freedmanseating.com

Gill Industries Inc
5271 Plainfield Ave NE — Grand Rapids MI 49525 616-559-2700 559-8850
Web: www.gill-industries.com

HO Bostrom Company Inc 818 Progress Ave — Waukesha WI 53186 262-542-0222 542-3784
TF: 800-332-5415 ■ *Web:* www.hobostrom.com

Johnson Controls Inc Automotive Systems Group
49200 Halyard Dr — Plymouth MI 48170 734-254-5000 254-5843*
**Fax:* Hum Res ■ *Web:* www.johnsoncontrols.com

Kustom Fit/Hi-Tech Seating
8990 Atlantic Ave — South Gate CA 90280 323-564-4481 564-5754
Web: www.kustomfit.com

Milsco Mfg Co 9009 N 51st St — Milwaukee WI 53223 414-354-0500 354-0508
TF: 800-255-0337 ■ *Web:* www.milsco.com

Sears Manufacturing Co
1718 S Concord St PO Box 3667 — Davenport IA 52808 563-383-2800 383-2810
TF Cust Svc: 800-553-3013 ■ *Web:* www.searsseating.com

Seats Inc 1515 Industrial St — Reedsburg WI 53959 608-524-8261
TF: 800-443-0615 ■ *Web:* www.seatsinc.com

693 SECURITIES BROKERS & DEALERS

SEE ALSO Commodity Contracts Brokers & Dealers p. 2010; Electronic Communications Networks (ECNs) p. 2232; Investment Advice & Management p. 2590; Mutual Funds p. 2807

				Phone	Fax

1&1 Internet Inc 701 Lee Rd Ste 300 — Chesterbrook PA 19087 877-461-2631 560-1501*
**Fax Area Code:* 610 ■ *TF:* 877-461-2631 ■ *Web:* www.1and1.com

195 Lumber Company Killeen Ltd
3032 S Ft Hood St — Killeen TX 76542 254-634-2188
Web: www.195lumberco.com

1st Discount Brokerage Inc
8927 Hypoluxo Rd Ste A-5 — Lake Worth FL 33467 561-515-3200 515-3201
TF: 888-642-2811 ■ *Web:* www.1db.com

360 Trading Networks Inc
521 Fifth Ave 38th Fl — New York NY 10175 212-776-2900
Web: www.360t.com

AB Watley Direct Inc 50 Broad St Ste 1614 — New York NY 10004 646-753-9301
TF: 877-993-4886 ■
Web: www.dittotrade.com/index.php?option=com_content&view=article&id=255

ABG Sundal Collier Inc
535 Madison Ave 17th Fl — New York NY 10022 212-605-3800
Web: www.abgsc.com

Access Financial Resources Inc
3621 NW 63rd Ste A1 — Oklahoma City OK 73116 405-848-9826
Web: afradvice.com

Access Securities Inc 30 Buxton Farm Rd — Stamford CT 06905 203-322-3377
TF: 800-331-6171 ■ *Web:* www.accesssecurities.com

Acculease Construction Equipment Inc
63 Clifton St — Farmingdale NY 11735 631-577-0101
Web: www.acculease.com

achoo! ALLERGY & AIR Products Inc
3411 Pierce Dr Ste 100 — Atlanta GA 30341 770-455-9999
Web: www.achooallergy.com

				Phone	Fax
Actinver Securities Inc 5075 Wheimer Rd Galleria Financial Tower Ste 650	Houston	TX	77056	713-885-9843	
Web: www.actinversecurities.com					
Adventures Unlimited Press One Adventure Pl	Kempton	IL	60946	815-253-6390	
Web: www.adventuresunlimitedpress.com					
Akar Capital Management 8551 W Sunrise Blvd Ste 102A	Plantation	FL	33322	954-476-7011	
Web: akarcapital.com					
Alamo Capital Financial Services 201 N Civic Dr Ste 145	Walnut Creek	CA	94596	925-472-5700	
Web: www.alamocapital.com					
Albert Fried & Company LLC 45 Broadway 24th Fl	New York	NY	10006	212-542-8266	
Web: www.albertfried.com					
Alchem Chemical Co 5360 Tulane Dr	Atlanta	GA	30336	404-696-9202	
Web: www.alchemchemical.com					
All-Phase Electric Supply Co 4216 Legacy Pkwy Ste D	Lansing	MI	48911	517-394-1461	
Web: all-phaselansing.com					
Allen & Co Inc 1401 South Florida Avenue	Lakeland	FL	33803	863-688-9000	
TF: 800-950-2526					
Allen & Company of Florida Inc 1401 S Florida Ave	Lakeland	FL	33803	863-688-9000	
Web: alleninvestments.com					
Allen C Ewing & Co 50 N Laura St Ste 3625	Jacksonville	FL	32202	904-354-5573	
Web: www.allenewing.com					
Alliance Advisory & Securities Inc 3390 Auto Mall Dr	Westlake Village	CA	91362	805-371-8020	
Web: www.allianceadvisory.com					
Alpine Investors LP Three Embarcadero Ctr Ste 2330	San Francisco	CA	94111	415-392-9100	
Web: www.alpine-investors.com					
Alpine Securities Corp 39 Exchange Pl	Salt Lake City	UT	84111	801-355-5588	
Web: www.alpine-securities.com					
AmeriFile Inc 1940 W Oak Cir	Marietta	GA	30062	770-420-1978	
Web: www.amerifile.net					
Ameriprise Brokerage 70400 Ameriprise Financial Ctr	Minneapolis	MN	55474	800-535-2001	624-2259
TF: 800-535-2001 ■ *Web:* www.ameriprise.com					
Anachemia Canada Inc 255 Rue Norman	Lachine	QC	H8R1A3	514-489-5711	
Web: www.anachemia.com					
Andrew Garrett Inc 140 E 45th St 11th Fl	New York	NY	10017	212-682-8833	
Web: www.andrewgarrett.com					
Antaeus Capital Inc 1100 Glendon Ave PH Ste 9	Los Angeles	CA	90024	310-443-9000	443-9005
Web: www.antaeuscap.com					
Ardour Capital Investments LLC The Empire State Bldg 350 Fifth Ave Ste 3018	New York City	NY	10118	212-375-2950	
Web: www.ardourcapital.com					
Aronson + Johnson + Ortiz LP 230 S Broad St 20th Fl	Philadelphia	PA	19102	215-546-7500	546-7506
Web: www.ajopartners.com					
Arque Capital Ltd 7501 E McCormick Pkwy Ste 111 N Ct	Scottsdale	AZ	85258	602-971-9000	
Web: www.arquecapital.com					
Artspace.com Markets Inc 915 Broadway Ste 602	New York	NY	10010	212-675-5804	
Web: www.artspace.com					
Atlantic Forest Products LLC 240 W Dickman St	Baltimore	MD	21230	410-752-8092	
Web: www.atlanticforest.com					
Atlas Advisors LLC 140 E 45th St 23rd Fl	New York	NY	10017	212-471-4100	
Web: www.atlasadvisors.com					
Auerbach Grayson & Company LLC 25 W 45th St	New York	NY	10036	212-557-4444	
Web: agco.com					
Ausdal Financial Partners 220 N Main St Ste 400	Davenport	IA	52801	563-326-2064	
Web: www.ausdal.com					
Avalon Ventures 1134 Kline St	La Jolla	CA	92037	858-348-2180	
Web: www.avalon-ventures.com					
Avisen Securities Inc 3620 American River Dr Ste 145	Sacramento	CA	95864	916-480-2747	
TF: 800-230-7704 ■ *Web:* www.avisensecurities.com					
AVM LP 777 Yamato Rd	Boca Raton	FL	33431	561-544-4600	
Web: www.avmlp.com					
B Riley & Company LLC 11100 Santa Monica Blvd Ste 800	Los Angeles	CA	90025	310-966-1444	
Web: www.brileyco.com					
Baird Patrick & Company Inc 305 Plz Ten	Jersey City	NJ	07311	201-680-7300	680-7301
TF: 800-221-7747 ■ *Web:* www.bairdpatrick.com					
Banca IMI Securities Corp One William St	New York	NY	10004	212-326-1100	
Web: www.bancaimi.com					
Barclays Capital Inc 200 Pk Ave	New York	NY	10166	212-412-4000	412-7300*
**Fax:* Hum Res ■ *TF:* 888-227-2275 ■ *Web:* www.barcap.com					
BaxterBoo 7025 S Fulton St Ste 150	Centennial	CO	80112	888-887-0063	
TF: 888-887-0063 ■ *Web:* www.baxterboo.com					
Bayview Capital Group LLC 214 Minnetonka Ave S	Wayzata	MN	55391	952-345-2000	
Web: www.bayviewcap.com					
BBS Securities Inc 4100 Yonge St Ste 507	Toronto	ON	M2P2B5	416-235-0200	
Web: www.bbssecurities.com					
Bear Forest Products Inc 4685 Brookhollow Cir	Riverside	CA	92509	951-727-1767	
Web: www.bearfp.com					
Bell Supply Inc 7221 Rt 130	Pennsauken	NJ	08110	856-663-3900	665-2196
TF: 888-834-2371 ■ *Web:* www.bellsupplyinc.com					
Bernard L Madoff Investment Securities Co 885 Third Ave 18th Fl	New York	NY	10022	212-230-2424	
TF: 800-334-1343 ■ *Web:* www.madofftrustee.com					
Berry-Shino Securities Inc 15100 N 78th Way Ste 100	Scottsdale	AZ	85260	480-315-3660	
Web: www.berry-shino.com					
Berthel Fisher & Co 701 Tama St Bldg B PO Box 609	Marion	IA	52302	319-447-5700	447-4250
TF: 800-356-5234 ■ *Web:* www.berthel.com					
BHK Securities LLC 2200 Lakeshore Dr Ste 250	Birmingham	AL	35209	205-322-2025	
TF: 888-529-2610 ■ *Web:* www.bhkllc.com					
Bia Digital Partners Lp 15120 Enterprise Ct	Chantilly	VA	20151	703-227-9600	
Web: www.biadigitalpartners.com					
Big Ceramic Store LLC 543 Vista Blvd	Sparks	NV	89434	775-351-2888	
Web: www.bigceramicstore.com					
Black Canyon Capital LLC 2000 Ave of the Stars 11th Fl	Los Angeles	CA	90067	310-272-1800	
Web: www.blackcanyoncapital.com					
Blackstone Group 345 Pk Ave 6th Fl	New York	NY	10154	212-583-5000	583-5749
Web: www.blackstone.com					
Blowfish Direct LLC 11130 Holder St	Cypress	CA	90630	877-725-6934	
TF: 877-725-6934 ■ *Web:* www.blowfishshoes.com					
Blue 9 Capital 145 Hudson St Ste 401	New York	NY	10013	212-798-0400	
Web: www.blue9capital.com					
Blue Fire Capital LLC 311 S Wacker Dr Ste 2000	Chicago	IL	60606	312-242-0500	
Web: www.bluefirecap.com					
Bluelinx Holdings Inc 4300 Wildwood Pkwy	Atlanta	GA	30339	770-953-7000	
Web: www.bluelinxco.com					
BluePointe Capital Management LLC 400 S El Camino Real Ste 760	San Mateo	CA	94402	650-293-4545	
Web: www.bluepointecapital.com					
BNP Paribas 787 Seventh Ave	New York	NY	10019	212-841-3000	841-2146
Web: www.bnpparibas.com					
Bobcat of St. Louis 401 W Outer Rd	Valley Park	MO	63088	636-225-2900	
Web: www.bobcatstl.com					
BOS Innovations Ltd 888 E Belvidere Rd Ste 218	Grayslake	IL	60030	847-665-1080	
Web: www.blacklight.com					
Boston Partners 909 Third Ave 32nd Fl	New York	NY	10022	212-908-9500	908-9672
Web: www.robecoinvest.com					
Bourbon & Boots Inc 419 Main St	North Little Rock	AR	72114	855-623-3562	
TF: 855-623-3562 ■ *Web:* www.bourbonandboots.com					
Brant Securities Ltd Ste 300-220 Bay St	Toronto	ON	M5J2W4	416-596-4545	
Web: www.brantsec.com					
Bridgepoint Merchant Banking 816 P St Ste 200	Lincoln	NE	68508	402-817-7900	
Web: bridgepointmb.com					
Brighton Securities Corp 1703 Monroe Ave Ste 1	Rochester	NY	14618	585-473-3590	
Web: www.brightonsecurities.com					
Brill Securities Inc 152 W 57th St 16th Fl	New York	NY	10019	212-957-5700	
TF: 800-933-0800 ■ *Web:* www.brillsec.com					
Broadband Capital Management LLC 712 Fifth Ave 22nd Fl	New York	NY	10019	212-759-2020	
Web: www.broadbandcapital.com					
Bruml Capital Corp 1801 E Ninth St Ste 1620	Cleveland	OH	44114	216-771-6660	
Web: www.brumlcapital.com					
BTIG LLC 600 Montgomery St Sixth Fl	San Francisco	CA	94111	415-248-2200	
Web: wwwca01.btig.com					
Bull Wealth Management Group Inc 4100 Yonge St Ste 612	Toronto	ON	M2P2B5	416-223-2053	
TF: 866-623-2053 ■ *Web:* www.bullwealth.com					
Burch & Company Inc 4151 N Mulberry Dr Ste 235	Kansas City	MO	64116	816-842-4660	
Web: www.burchco.com					
Burgess Steel LLC 200 W Forest Ave	Englewood	NJ	07631	201-871-3500	
Web: www.burgesssteel.com					
Burgundy Asset Management Ltd Bay Wellington Tower Brookfield Pl 181 Bay St Ste 4510	Toronto	ON	M5J2T3	416-869-3222	
Web: www.burgundyasset.com					
Burt Martin Arnold Securities Inc 608 Silver Spur Rd Ste 100	Rolling Hills Estates	CA	90274	310-544-3545	
Web: www.bmasecurities.com					
Butler Capital Investments LLC 222 Court Sq Second Fl Ste 3	Charlottesville	VA	22902	434-295-5888	
Web: www.butlercap.com					
BUYandHOLD.com Securities Corp *c/o Freedom Investments, Inc* 375 Raritan Ctr Pkwy Ste D	Edison	NJ	08837	800-646-8212	934-3095*
**Fax Area Code:* 732 ■ *TF:* 800-646-8212 ■ *Web:* www.buyandhold.com					
Cabinets To Go LLC 6901 Crestwood Blvd	Birmingham	AL	35210	205-623-2209	
Web: www.cabinetstogo.com					
Cabrera Capital Markets LLC 10 S La Salle St Ste 1050	Chicago	IL	60603	312-236-8888	236-8936
Web: www.cabreracapital.com					
Cal-Sierra Pipe LLC 3033 S 99 Hwy W Frontage Rd	Stockton	CA	95215	209-466-0988	
Web: www.calsierrapipe.com					
Caldwell Securities Ltd 150 King St W Ste 1710	Toronto	ON	M5H1J9	416-862-7755	
TF: 800-387-0859 ■ *Web:* www.caldwellsecurities.com					
Calton & Assoc Inc 14497 N Dale Mabry Hwy	Tampa	FL	33618	813-264-0440	962-8695
TF: 800-942-0262 ■ *Web:* calton.com					
Camfour Inc 65 Wfield Industrial Park Rd	Westfield	MA	01085	413-564-2300	
Cantor Fitzgerald LP 499 Pk Ave	New York	NY	10022	212-938-5000	
Web: www.cantor.com					
Capital Lumber Company Inc 5110 N 40th St Ste 242	Phoenix	AZ	85018	602-381-0709	
Web: www.capital-lumber.com					
Capitol Securities Management Inc 100 Concourse Blvd Glen Allen	Richmond	VA	23059	804-612-9700	
Web: www.capitolsecurities.com					

Phone Fax

Capstone Investments Research Div
12760 High Bluff Dr Ste 120 San Diego CA 92130 858-875-4500
Web: www.capstoneinvestments.com

Carlyle Capital Markets Inc
14755 Preston Rd Ste510 Dallas TX 75254 972-404-8686
Web: www.carlylecapitalmarkets.com

Cedar Hill Associates LLC
120 S LaSalle St Ste 1750 Chicago IL 60603 312-445-2900
Web: www.cedhill.com

Centaurus Financial
2300 E Katella Ave Ste 200 Anaheim CA 92806 714-456-1790
Web: centaurusfinancial.com

Centurion Counsel Inc 1282 Pacific Oaks Pl Escondido CA 92029 760-471-8536
Web: www.centurioncounsel.com

Ceros Financial Services Inc
1445 Research Blvd Ste 530 Rockville MD 20850 866-842-3356
TF: 866-842-3356 ■ *Web:* www.cerosfs.com

Cetera Financial Group Inc
200 N Sepulveda Blvd Ste 1200 El Segundo CA 90245 866-489-3100
TF: 866-489-3100 ■ *Web:* www.cetera.com

Charles Schwab & Co Inc 211 Main St San Francisco CA 94105 415-667-1009
TF Cust Svc: 800-648-5300 ■ *Web:* www.schwab.com

Charter Brokerage LLC 383 Main Ave Ste 506 Norwalk CT 06851 203-840-7500
Web: charterbrokerage.net

Chase Plastic Services Inc
6467 Waldon Ctr Dr Clarkston MI 48346 248-620-2120
TF: 800-232-4273 ■ *Web:* www.chaseplastics.com

Chatsworth Securities LLC
95 East Putnam Ave Greenwich CT 06830 203-629-2612 629-2375
Web: www.chatsworthgroup.com

Cheevers & Company Inc
440 S LaSalle St Ste 710 Chicago IL 60605 312-224-7922
Web: www.cheeversco.com

Chopper Trading LLC
141 W Jackson Blvd Ste 2201A Chicago IL 60604 312-628-3500
Web: www.choppertrading.com

Cinco Energy Land Services
9235 Katy Fwy Ste 400 Houston TX 77024 713-463-6009
Web: cincoland.com

City Securities Corp
30 S Meridian St Ste 600 Indianapolis IN 46204 317-634-4400 955-2509
TF: 800-800-2489 ■ *Web:* www.citysecurities.com

CJS Securities Inc
Westchester Financial Ctr 50 Main St
Ste 325 White Plains NY 10606 914-287-7600
Web: www.cjssecurities.com

CL King & Associates Inc Nine Elk St Albany NY 12207 518-431-3500
Web: clking.com

Clark Food Service Equipment
2209 Old Philadelphia Pk Lancaster PA 17602 717-392-7363
Web: www.clarkfoodserviceequipment.biz

CLS Investments LLC 4020 S 147th St Omaha NE 68137 402-493-3313
Web: www.clsinvest.com

CME Group Index Services LLC PO Box 300 Princeton NJ 08543 609-520-7249
Web: www.djindexes.com

CNBS Inc 7200 W 132nd St Ste 240 Overland Park KS 66213 800-222-0978
TF: 800-222-0978 ■ *Web:* www.cnbsnet.com

Cobblestone Capital Advisors LLC
140 Allens Creek Rd Rochester NY 14618 585-473-3333
Web: cobblestonecap.com

Colorado West Investments Inc
1731 E Niagara Rd Montrose CO 81401 970-249-9882
Web: cowestinvest.com

Columbia West Capital LLC
14624 N Scottsdale Rd Ste 124 Scottsdale AZ 85254 480-664-3949
Web: www.columbiawestcap.com

Community Banc Investments Inc
26 E Main St New Concord OH 43762 740-826-7601
Web: www.cbibankstocks.com

Compass Point Research & Trading LLC
3000 K St NW Ste 340 Washington DC 20007 202-540-7300
Web: www.compasspointllc.com

Conceptual Financial Planning Inc
3962 N Richmond St Ste B Appleton WI 54913 920-731-9500
Web: www.viainsurance.com

Concord International Investments Group LP
725 Fifth Ave 15th Fl New York NY 10022 212-759-2375
Web: www.concordus.com

Construction Book Express Inc
401 S Wright Rd Janesville WI 53546 608-743-8031
Web: www.constructionbook.com

Continental Stock Transfer & Trust Company Inc
17 Battery Pl New York NY 10004 212-509-4000
Web: www.continentalstock.com

Convergex Holdings LLC 1633 Broadway 48th Fl New York NY 10019 212-468-7713
Web: www.convergex.com

Corinthian Partners LLC 10 E 53rd St 28th Fl New York NY 10022 212-287-1500
TF: 800-899-8950 ■ *Web:* www.corinthianpartners.com

CP Capital Securities Inc
1428 Brickell Ave Ste 600 Miami FL 33131 305-702-5500
Web: www.cpcapital.com

Credit Suisse 11 Madison Ave New York NY 10010 212-325-2000 325-6665
TF: 800-222-8977 ■ *Web:* www.credit-suisse.com

Crest Industries Inc
231 Larkin Williams Industrial Ct Fenton MO 63026 636-349-4800
Web: www.crestmidwest.com

Cronin & Company Inc
800 Nicollet Mall Ste 2520 Minneapolis MN 55402 612-339-8561
Web: www.cronincoinc.com

Crowell Weedon & Co
One Wilshire Blvd 26th Fl Los Angeles CA 90017 213-620-1850 244-9388
TF: 800-227-0319 ■ *Web:* www.crowellweedon.com

Currenex Inc
1230 Ave of the Americas 18th Fl New York NY 10020 212-340-1780
Web: www.currenex.com

Cutler Group LP
101 Montgomery St Ste 700 San Francisco CA 94104 415-645-6745
Web: www.cutlergrouplp.com

Cypress Asset Management Inc
4545 Post Oak Pl Dr Ste 205 Houston TX 77027 713-512-2100
Web: cypressasset.com

DA Davidson & Company Inc
Eight Third St N Great Falls MT 59401 406-727-4200 791-7380
TF: 800-332-5915 ■ *Web:* www.davidsoncompanies.com/indv

Daewoo Securities (america) Inc
600 Lexington Ave Ste 301 New York NY 10022 212-407-1000
Web: www.bestez.com

Daiwa Capital Markets America Inc
Financial Sq 32 Old Slip New York NY 10005 212-612-7000
Web: www.us.daiwacm.com

DAK Group Ltd, The 195 Rt 17 S Rochelle Park NJ 07662 201-712-9555
Web: www.dakgroup.com

Davenport & Co LLC
901 E Cary St One James Center Ste 1100 Richmond VA 23219 804-780-2000 780-2026
TF: 800-846-6666 ■ *Web:* www.davenportllc.com

Davidge Data Systems Corp
20 Exchange Pl 39th Fl New York NY 10005 212-269-0901
Web: www.davidge.com

Davidson Cos Eight Third St N PO Box 5015 Great Falls MT 59401 406-727-4200
Web: www.davidsoncompanies.com

Davidson's Inc 6100 Wilkinson Dr Prescott AZ 86301 928 776 8055
Web: www.galleryofguns.com

Decision Software Inc 116 John St New York NY 10038 212-385-1662
Web: www.dsoftware.com

Deep Liquidity Inc
6101 W Courtyard Dr Bldg 1 Ste 110 Austin TX 78730 512-372-8001
Web: www.deepliquidity.com

DeMatteo Monness LLC 780 Third Ave 45th Fl New York NY 10017 212-833-9900
Web: www.dmllc.com

Demeter Advisory Group LLC
220 Halleck St Ste 110 San Francisco CA 94129 415-632-4400
Web: www.demetergroup.net

DH Capital LLC 1540 Broadway Ste 1610 New York NY 10036 212-774-3720
Web: www.dhcapital.com

DiscountMugs.com 12610 NW 115th Ave Medley FL 33178 800-569-1980
TF: 800-569-1980 ■ *Web:* www.discountmugs.com

DM Kelly & Co 3900 Ingersoll Ave Ste 300 Des Moines IA 50312 515-221-1133
Web: www.dmkc.com

Domestic Securities Inc 160 Summit Ave Montvale NJ 07645 201-505-9855
TF: 877-690-2274 ■ *Web:* mojo.myfoxphilly.com

Dot Com Holdings of Buffalo Inc
1460 Military Rd Buffalo NY 14217 877-636-3673
Web: www.dotcomholdingsofbuffalo.com

Dougherty & Company LLC
90 S Seventh St Ste 4300 Minneapolis MN 55402 612-376-4000 338-7732
TF: 800-328-4000 ■ *Web:* www.doughertymarkets.com

Douglas P Bates 144 Genesee St Auburn NY 13021 315-253-2782

Dowling & Yahnke Inc 12340 El Camino Real San Diego CA 92130 858-509-9500
Web: dywealth.com

Dresner Partners 20 N Clark St Ste 3550 Chicago IL 60602 312-726-3600
Web: www.dresnerpartners.com

Dreyfus Corp 200 Pk Ave New York NY 10166 212-495-1784 922-6880
Web: public.dreyfus.com

DRW Trading Group 540 W Madison St Ste 2500 Chicago IL 60661 312-542-1000
Web: www.drw.com

Duncan-Williams Inc 6750 Poplar Ave Ste 300 Memphis TN 38138 901-260-6800 260-6994
Web: www.duncanwilliams.com

Duquesne Capital Mgt LLC 40 W 57th St Fl 25 New York NY 10019 212-397-8596

E*Trade Financial Corp
1271 Ave of the Americas 14th Fl New York NY 10020 800-387-2331
NASDAQ: ETFC ■ *TF:* 800-387-2331 ■ *Web:* about.etrade.com

E1 Asset Management Inc 44 Wall St 9th Fl New York NY 10005 212-425-2670
Web: e1am.com

eBX LLC 65 Franklin St Ste 201 Boston MA 02110 617-350-1600
TF: 800-958-4813 ■ *Web:* www.levelats.com

ECMD Inc Two Grandview St North Wilkesboro NC 28659 336-667-5976
TF: 888-222-3961 ■ *Web:* www.ecmd.com

EdgePoint Capital Advisors LLC
3700 Park E Dr Ste 160 Beachwood OH 44122 216-831-2430
Web: www.edgepoint.com

Edward Jones 12555 Manchester Rd Saint Louis MO 63131 314-515-2000 515-3269
Web: www.edwardjones.com

EFG Capital International Corp
701 Brickell Ave Ninth Fl Miami FL 33131 305-482-8000
Web: www.efgcapital.com

EKRiley Investments LLC
1420 Fifth Ave Ste 3300 Seattle WA 98101 206-832-1520
Web: www.ekriley.com

Ellie Fashion Group Inc
1447 Second St Third Fl Santa Monica CA 90401 888-926-9615
TF: 888-926-9615 ■ *Web:* www.ellie.com

Ema Brokerage LLC 1300 Rt 73 Ste 306 Mount Laurel NJ 08054 856-216-0211 216-8242
Web: emabrokerage.com

Emergent Financial Group Inc
3600 American Blvd W Ste 670 Bloomington MN 55431 952-829-1212
Web: www.emergentfinancial.com

Emerson Equity LLC 155 Bovet Rd Ste 725 San Mateo CA 94402 650-312-0200
Web: www.emersonequity.com

Endeavour Capital Inc
920 S W Sixth Ave Ste 1400 Portland OR 97204 503-223-2721
Web: www.endeavourcapital.com

Energy Spectrum Advisors Inc
5956 Sherry Ln Ste 900 Dallas TX 75225 214-987-6100
Web: www.energyspectrumadvisors.com

				Phone	Fax
Energynet.com Inc 7201 I-40 W Ste 319 *Web:* www.energynet.com	Amarillo	TX	79106	806-351-2953	354-2835
Envestnet Inc 35 E Wacker Dr Ste 2400 *Web:* www.envestnet.com	Chicago	IL	60601	312-827-2800	
Equinox Securities Inc 760 S Rochester Ave Ste E *Web:* www.equinoxsecurities.net	Ontario	CA	91761	909-218-8950	
Equitec Group LLC 111 W Jackson Blvd Fl 20 *Web:* www.eqtc.com	Chicago	IL	60604	312-692-5000	
Essex National Securities Inc 550 Gateway Dr Ste 210 *TF:* 855-444-3674 ■ *Web:* www.ensinet.com	Napa	CA	94558	707-258-5000	
Euro Pacific Canada Inc 130 King St W Ste 2820 *Web:* www.europac.ca	Toronto	ON	M5X1A9	416-649-4273	
Evans Investment Advisors LLC 6713 Perkins Rd	Baton Rouge	LA	70808	225-761-7870	
Everest Group Inc, The 9912 Carver Rd Ste 100 *Web:* www.everestrealestate.com	Cincinnati	OH	45242	513-769-2500	
Exane Inc 640 Fifth Ave 15th Fl *Web:* www.exane.com	New York	NY	10019	212-634-4990	
ExRx.net LLC 4236 Bell St *Web:* www.exrx.net	Kansas City	MO	64111	913-481-9335	
Fairbridge Capital Markets Inc City Tower Plz Carr 165 Km 12 Ste 48 *Web:* www.fairbridgecap.com	Guaynabo	PR	00968	787-622-3473	
Fairmount Partners LP 100 Four Falls Corporate Ctr Ste 660 *Web:* fairmountpartners.com	West Conshohocken	PA	19428	610-260-6200	
Fastener Supply Co 13410 S Ridge Dr PO Box 7369 *TF:* 800-888-9519 ■ *Web:* www.fastenersupply.com	Charlotte	NC	28241	704-596-7634	598-0116
Fidus Partners LLC 227 W Trade St Ste 1910 *Web:* www.fiduspartners.com	Charlotte	NC	28202	704-334-2222	334-2202
Fieldpoint Private Bank & Trust 100 Field Pt Rd *TF:* 877-438-4338 ■ *Web:* www.fieldpointprivate.com	Greenwich	CT	06830	203-413-9300	
Fieldstone Partners 1800 Bering Dr Ste 430 *Web:* fieldstone.com	Houston	TX	77057	713-850-0080	
FIMAC Solutions LLC Denver Technological Ctr 5299 DTC Blvd Ste 950 *Web:* www.fimacsolutions.com	Greenwood Village	CO	80111	303-320-1900	
Financial America Securities Inc 1325 Carnegie Ave *Web:* www.fasinv.com	Cleveland	OH	44115	216-781-5060	
Financial Service Corp 2300 Windy Ridge Pkwy Ste 1100 *TF:* 800-547-2382 ■ *Web:* www.fscorp.com	Atlanta	GA	30339	770-916-6500	
Financial West Investment Group Inc 4510 E Thousand Oaks Blvd *Web:* www.fwg.com	Westlake Village	CA	91362	805-497-9222	
Fincantieri Marine Systems North America Inc 800-C Principal Ct *TF:* 877-436-7643 ■ *Web:* www.fincantierimarinesystems.com	Chesapeake	VA	23320	757-548-6000	
Fintegra LLC 6120 Earle Brown Dr Ste 550 *Web:* www.fintegra.com	Minneapolis	MN	55430	763-585-0503	
First Dallas Securities 2905 Maple Ave *Web:* www.firstdallas.com	Dallas	TX	75201	214-954-1177	954-1281
First Heartland Capital Inc 1839 Lk St Louis Blvd	Lake St Louis	MO	63367	636-625-0900	
First London Securities Corp 2603 Fairmount St *Web:* www.firstlondon.com	Dallas	TX	75201	214-220-0699	
First Manhattan Co 399 Park Ave *Web:* www.firstmanhattan.com	New York	NY	10022	212-756-3300	
First New York Securities LLC 90 Pk Ave Fl 5 *Web:* www.firstny.com	New York	NY	10016	212-848-0600	888-3174
First Options of Chicago Inc 70 W Madison St Ste 2100 *Web:* www.pfitrading.com	Chicago	IL	60602	312-933-5884	
First Southwest Co 325 N St Paul St Ste 800 *TF:* 800-678-3792 ■ *Web:* firstsw.com	Dallas	TX	75201	214-953-4000	953-4050
First Tryon Securities LLC 1355 Greenwood Cliff Ste 401 *Web:* www.firsttryon.com	Charlotte	NC	28204	704-372-6118	
FirstEnergy Capital Corp 311-6th Ave SW Ste 1100 *Web:* www.firstenergy.com	Calgary	AB	T2P3H2	403-262-0600	
Fisc Investment Services Corp 1849 Clairmont Rd *TF:* 800-241-3203 ■ *Web:* www.palmeragency.com	Decatur	GA	30033	404-321-1212	
Fisgard Capital Corp 3378 Douglas St *Web:* www.fisgard.com	Victoria	BC	V8Z3L3	250-382-9255	
Flagship Investment Group Inc 3939 W Ridge Rd Ste A-103 *Web:* raymondjames.com	Erie	PA	16506	814-835-1150	
Fogel International Inc 5110 N 32nd St Ste 206 *Web:* www.fogelinternational.com	Phoenix	AZ	85018	602-508-0728	
Force Capital Management LLC 767 Fifth Ave 8th Fl *Web:* www.bakercapital.com	New York	NY	10153	212-451-9150	
Fordham Financial Management Inc 14 Wall St *Web:* www.fordhamfinancial.com	New York	NY	10005	212-732-8500	
FOREXcom 44 Wall St Seventh Fl *Web:* www.forex.com	New York	NY	10005	908-731-0750	
Forshaw Industries Inc 650 State St *Web:* www.forshaw.com	Charlotte	NC	28208	704-372-6790	
Franklin Templeton Investments 3344 Quality Dr **Fax Area Code:* 916 ■ **Fax:* Cust Svc ■ *TF:* 800-632-2350 ■ *Web:* www.franklintempleton.com	Rancho Cordova	CA	95670	650-312-2000	463-1125*
Freedom Investments Inc 375 Raritan Ctr Pkwy *TF:* 800-944-4033 ■ *Web:* www.freedominvestments.com	Edison	NJ	08837	800-944-4033	830-1855
Fremont Realty Capital 199 Fremont St Ste 2200 *Web:* www.fremontrealtycapital.com	San Francisco	CA	94105	415-284-8665	
Friedman Billings Ramsey Group Inc 1001 19th St N *TF:* 800-846-5050 ■ *Web:* www.fbr.com	Arlington	VA	22209	703-312-9500	312-9501
Frost Securities Inc 2727 N Harwood St Ste 1000 *Web:* www.frostsecurities.com	Dallas	TX	75201	214-515-4400	515-4455
FSB Warner Financial 1001 Peoples Sq *Web:* fsbfs.com	Waterloo	IA	50702	319-235-6561	
Full Access Brokerage 1240 Charnelton St *Web:* fullaccess.org	Eugene	OR	97401	541-284-5070	
Galileo Global Advisors LLC 10 Rockefeller Plz Ste 1001 *Web:* www.galileoadvisors.com	New York	NY	10020	212-332-6055	
Gar Wood Securities LLC 440 S LaSalle St Ste 2201 *Web:* www.garwoodsecurities.net	Chicago	IL	60605	312-566-0740	
Garban Capital Markets LLC 1100 Plaza Five *Web:* www.icap.com	Jersey City	NJ	07311	207-000-5000	
Gardner Rich & Co 401 S Financial Pl	Chicago	IL	60605	312-922-3333	922-2144
GBS Financial Corp 558 B St Ste 200 *Web:* www.gbsfinancial.com	Santa Rosa	CA	95401	707-568-2400	
GE Richards Graphic Supplies Company Inc 928 Links Ave *TF:* 800-233-0410 ■ *Web:* www.gerichards.com	Landisville	PA	17538	717-898-3151	
Geary Pacific Corp 1908 N Enterprise St *TF:* 800-444-3279 ■ *Web:* www.gearypacific.com	Orange	CA	92865	714-279-2950	
Geneos Wealth Management Inc 9055 E Mineral Cir Ste 200 *Web:* www.geneoswealth.com	Centennial	CO	80112	303-785-8470	
General Parts LLC 11311 Hampshire Ave S *Web:* generalparts.com	Bloomington	MN	55438	952-944-5800	
George K Baum & Co 4801 Main St Ste 500 Ste 500 *TF:* 800-821-7195 ■ *Web:* www.gkbaum.com	Kansas City	MO	64112	816-474-1100	283-5180
Georgeson Securities Corp 480 Washington Blvd 27th Fl *TF:* 800-428-0717 ■ *Web:* www.georgesonsecurities.com	Jersey City	NJ	07310	800-428-0717	
Gifts On Time LLC 80 Front St Ste 21 *Web:* www.giftsontime.com	Scituate	MA	02066	781-545-0799	
Gilford Securities Inc 777 Third Ave *TF:* 800-445-3673 ■ *Web:* www.gilfordsecurities.com	New York	NY	10017	212-888-6400	826-9738
Gleacher & Co Inc 1290 Ave of the Americas *Web:* www.gleacher.com	New York	NY	10104	212-273-7100	
Glendale Securities Inc 15233 Ventura Blvd Ste 712 *Web:* www.glendalesecurities.com	Sherman Oaks	CA	91403	818-907-1505	
Glickenhaus & Co 546 Fifth Ave Seventh Fl	New York	NY	10036	212-938-2100	983-8436
Global Arena Capital Corp 708 Third Ave 11th Fl *Web:* www.globalarenacapital.com	New York	NY	10017	212-508-4700	
Global Maxfin Investments Inc 100 Mural St Ste 201 *Web:* www.globalmaxfin.ca	Richmond Hill	ON	L4B1J3	416-741-1544	
Global Security Management Agency Inc 1781 Vineyard Dr *Web:* gsmasecurity.com	Antioch	CA	94509	925-262-4181	
Global Strategic Investments LLC 701 Brickell Ave Ste 1420 *Web:* www.gscorporation.com	Miami	FL	33131	305-373-3326	
GMP Securities LLC 331 Madison Ave *Web:* www.gmpsecuritiesllc.com	New York	NY	10017	212-692-5100	
GMS Group LLC, The Five N Regent St Ste 513 *Web:* www.gmsgroup.com	Livingston	NJ	07039	973-535-5000	
Grace Financial Group LLC 83 Jobs Ln *TF:* 866-817-6047 ■ *Web:* www.gracefg.com	Southampton	NY	11968	631-287-4633	
Great Pacific Fixed Income Securities Inc 151 Kalmus Dr Ste H-8 *TF:* 800-284-4804 ■ *Web:* www.greatpac.com	Costa Mesa	CA	92626	714-619-3000	619-3018
GreenChem Industries LLC 222 Clematis St Ste 207 *Web:* www.greenchemindustries.com	West Palm Beach	FL	33401	561-659-2236	
Greenland (America) Inc 1905 Woodstock Rd Ste 2200 *Web:* www.greenlandamerica.com	Roswell	GA	30075	770-435-1100	
Greenling Inc 3913 Todd Ln Ste 618 *Web:* www.greenling.com	Austin	TX	78744	512-440-8449	
Greenspun Corp Inc, The 901 N Green Vly Pkwy Ste 210	Henderson	NV	89074	702-259-4023	
Gridley & Company LLC 10 E 53rd St 24th Fl *Web:* www.gridleyco.com	New York	NY	10022	212-400-9720	
Group One Trading LP 440 S La Salle Ste 3232 *Web:* www.group1.com	Chicago	IL	60605	312-922-2620	
GVC Capital LLC 5350 S Roslyn St Ste 400 *Web:* www.gvccap.com	Greenwood Village	CO	80111	303-694-0862	694-6287
GWN Securities Inc 11440 N Jog Rd *Web:* www.gwnsecurities.com	Palm Beach Gardens	FL	33418	561-472-2700	
Hampton Securities Ltd 141 Adelaide St W Ste 1800 *Web:* www.hamptonsecurities.com	Toronto	ON	M5H3L5	416-862-7800	
Hanover Partners Inc 425 California St Ste 1700 *Web:* www.hanoverpartners.com	San Francisco	CA	94104	415-788-8680	

Name / Address	City	State	Zip	Phone	Fax
Hansen-Mueller Co 12231 Emmet St Ste 1	Omaha	NE	68164	402-491-3385	
Web: www.hansenmueller.com					
Harch Capital Management LLC 751 Park of Commerce Dr Ste 118	Boca Raton	FL	33487	561-226-6199	
Web: www.harchcapital.com					
Harpeth Capital LLC 3100 W End Ave Ste 710	Nashville	TN	37203	615-296-9840	
Web: www.harpethcapital.com					
Harris Financial Services Inc 940 Spokane Ave	Whitefish	MT	59937	406-862-4400	
Web: harrisfsi.com					
Hazlett Burt & Watson Inc 1300 Chapline St	Wheeling	WV	26003	304-233-3312	
Web: www.hazlettburt.com					
HC Wainwright & Co Inc 430 Park Ave 4th Fl	New York	NY	10022	212-356-0500	
Web: www.hcwainwright.com					
Heartland Investment Associates Inc 2202 Heritage Green Dr	Hiawatha	IA	52233	319-393-8913	
Web: www.heartlandinv.com					
Hencorp Inc 777 Brickell Ave Ste 1010	Miami	FL	33131	305-373-9000	
Web: www.hencorp.com					
Henley & Company LLC 1290 RXR Plz	Uniondale	NY	11556	516-794-5520	
Web: www.henleyandcompany.com					
Henry H Armstrong Associates Inc One Gateway Ctr 420 Ft Duquesne Blvd Ste 1825	Pittsburgh	PA	15222	412-471-1551	
Web: www.henryarmstrong.com					
Hilco Industrial LLC 31555 W Fourteen Mile Rd Ste 207	Farmington Hills	MI	48334	248-254-9999	
Web: www.hilcoind.com					
Hilco Merchant Resources LLC Five Revere Dr Ste 206	Northbrook	IL	60062	847-509-1100	
Web: www.hilcomerchantresources.com					
Hirzel Capital Management LLC 3963 Maple Ave Ste 170	Dallas	TX	75129	214-999-0014	
Web: www.hirzelcapital.com					
Hogan-Knotts Financial Group, The 298 Broad St	Red Bank	NJ	07701	732-842-7400	
Web: hkfg.biz					
Horan Associates Inc 4990 E Galbraith Rd	Cincinnati	OH	45236	513-745-0707	
Web: www.horanassoc.com					
Houlihan Capital LLC 500 W Madison St Ste 2600	Chicago	IL	60661	312-450-8600	
Web: www.houlihan.com					
Houston Asset Management Inc 1800 W Loop S	Houston	TX	77027	713-629-1534	
Web: www.houstonassetmgmt.com					
HoustonStreet Inc One New Hampshire Ave Ste 207	Portsmouth	NH	03801	603-766-8716	
Web: www.houstonstreet.com					
Howe Barnes Hoefer & Arnett Inc 222 S Riverside Plz Seventh Fl	Chicago	IL	60606	312-655-3000	
Web: www.howebarnes.com					
Huntleigh Securities Corp 7800 Forsyth Blvd Fifth Fl	Saint Louis	MO	63105	314-236-2400	236-2401
TF: 800-727-5405 ■ *Web:* www.hntlgh.com					
Hurlen Corp 9841 Bell Ranch Dr	Santa Fe Springs	CA	90670	562-941-5330	
Web: kenigaero.com/					
Hutchinson Shockey Erley & Co 222 W Adams St Ste 1700	Chicago	IL	60606	312-443-1550	
Web: www.hsemuni.com					
Icor Technology Inc 935 Ages Dr	Ottawa	ON	K1G6L3	613-745-3600	
Web: icortechnology.com					
IDI Distributors Inc 8303 Audubon Rd	Chanhassen	MN	55317	952-279-6400	
TF: 888-843-1318 ■ *Web:* idi-insulation.com					
IEX Group Inc Seven World Trade Ctr 30th Fl	New York	NY	10007	646-568-2320	
Web: iextrading.com					
IKON Global Markets Inc 88 Pine St Wall St Plz Fifth Fl	New York	NY	10005	212-482-8408	
Web: www.ikongm.com					
Illinois Fair Plan Association 130 East Randolph Ste 1050	Chicago	IL	60601	312-861-0385	861-0485
TF: 800-972-4480 ■ *Web:* www.illinoisfairplan.com					
Impulse Technologies Ltd 920 Gana Crt	Mississauga	ON	L5S1Z4	905-564-9266	
Web: impulsetechnologies.com					
Incapital LLC 200 S Wacker Dr Ste 3700	Chicago	IL	60606	312-379-3700	
Web: www.incapital.com					
Index Funds Advisors Inc 19200 Von Karman Ave Ste 150	Irvine	CA	92612	949-502-0050	
Web: ifa.com					
IndexIQ Inc 800 Westchester Ave Ste N-611	Rye Brook	NY	10573	888-934-0777	
Web: www.indexiq.com					
Industrial Source Inc 1574 W Sixth Ave	Eugene	OR	97402	541-344-1438	
Web: www.industrialsource.com					
Industrial Tube & Steel Corp 4658 Crystal Pkwy	Kent	OH	44240	330-474-5530	
TF: 800-662-9567 ■ *Web:* www.industrialtube.com					
Infinity Insurance Solutions LLC 10707 Barkley St	Leawood	KS	66211	913-338-3200	
Web: www.infinityins.com					
ING Financial Markets Llc 1325 Ave of the Americas	New York	NY	10019	646-424-6000	424-6060
Web: ing.com					
Insight Capital Investments 4101 Gateway Dr	Colleyville	TX	76034	817-545-1959	399-9225
Web: www.onealinvestments.com					
Interwest Capital Corp 8910 University Ctr Ln The Aventine Bldg Ste 580	San Diego	CA	92122	858-622-4900	
Web: www.interwestcapital.com					
Investec Ernst & Co One Battery Pk Plz Second Fl	New York	NY	10004	212-898-6200	895-3555
Web: www.investec.com					
Investment Professionals Inc 16414 San Pedro Ave Ste 150	San Antonio	TX	78232	210-308-8800	308-8707
Web: www.invpro.com					
Investors Security Company Inc 127 E Washington St Ste 101	Suffolk	VA	23434	757-539-2396	
Web: investorssecurity.com					
Investrade Discount Securities 950 N Milwaukee Ave Ste 102	Glenview	IL	60025	847-375-6080	367-8466*
**Fax Area Code:* 877 ■ **Fax:* Cust Svc ■ *TF Cust Svc:* 800-498-7120 ■ *Web:* www.investrade.com					
Ironwood Capital Ltd 45 Nod Rd	Avon	CT	06001	860-409-2100	
Web: www.ironwoodcap.com					
Isaak Bond Investments Inc 3900 S Wadsworth Blvd Ste 590	Lakewood	CO	80202	303-623-7500	623-4252
TF: 800-279-4426 ■ *Web:* www.isaakbond.com					
ITG Derivatives LLC 601 S LaSalle Ste 300	Chicago	IL	60605	312-334-8000	
Web: www.redskysecurities.com					
ITG Inc One Liberty Plz 165 Broadway	New York	NY	10006	212-588-4000	444-6292
TF: 800-215-4484 ■ *Web:* www.itginc.com					
Janney Montgomery Scott LLC 1801 Market St	Philadelphia	PA	19103	215-665-6000	665-6197*
**Fax:* Sales ■ *TF:* 800-526-6397 ■ *Web:* www.janney.com					
Javelin Capital Markets LLC 443 Park Ave S 10th Fl	New York	NY	10016	212-779-2300	
TF: 877-528-9244 ■ *Web:* www.thejavelin.com					
Jaypee International Inc 30 S Wacker Dr Ste 1700	Chicago	IL	60606	312-655-7606	
Web: www.jaypeeusa.com					
JD Ford & Company LLC 650 S Cherry St Ste 1200	Denver	CO	80246	303-333-3673	
TF: 888-999-9495 ■ *Web:* www.jdford.com					
Jefferies Group Inc 520 Madison Ave 10th Fl	New York	NY	10022	212-284-2300	
NYSE: JEF ■ *Web:* www.jefferies.com					
JJB Hilliard WL Lyons Inc 500 W Jefferson St	Louisville	KY	40202	502-588-8400	585-8901*
**Fax:* Hum Res ■ *TF:* 800-444-1854 ■ *Web:* www.hilliard.com					
Jobast Holdings Inc 377 Oak St Ste 402	Garden City	NY	11530	516-997-4490	
Johnston Lemon & Company Inc 1101 Vermont Ave NW Ste 800	Washington	DC	20005	202-842-5500	842-7185
Web: www.johnstonlemon.com					
JonesTrading Institutional Services LLC 32133 Lindero Canyon Rd Ste 208	Westlake Village	CA	91361	818-991-5500	
Web: www.jonestrading.com					
Juniper Advisory LLC 191 N Wacker Dr Ste 900	Chicago	IL	60606	312-506-3000	230-5713*
**Fax Area Code:* 322 ■ *Web:* www.juniperadvisory.com					
Kane Reid Securities Group Inc 13024 Ballantyne Corporate Pl Ste 500	Charlotte	NC	28277	877-495-5464	
TF: 877-495-5464 ■ *Web:* www.tradeking.com					
Katalyst Surgical LLC 754 Goddard Ave	Chesterfield	MO	63005	888-452-8259	
TF: 888-452-8259 ■ *Web:* www.katalystsurgical.com					
Kaufman Bros LP 800 Third Ave 30th Fl	New York	NY	10022	212-292-8100	
Web: www.kbro.com					
Keefe Bruyette & Woods Inc 787 Seventh Ave The Equitable Bldg Fourth Fl	New York	NY	10019	212-887-7777	
Web: www.kbw.com					
Kelso & Company Inc 320 Pk Ave 24th Fl	New York	NY	10022	212-751-3939	223-2379
Web: www.kelso.com					
Kidd & Company LLC 1455 E Putnam Ave	Old Greenwich	CT	06870	203-661-0070	
Web: www.kiddcompany.com					
KippsDeSanto & Co 8000 Towers Crescent Dr Ste 1200	Tysons Corner	VA	22182	703-442-1400	
Web: www.kippsdesanto.com					
Knight Capital Group Inc 545 Washington Blvd	Jersey City	NJ	07310	201-222-9400	557-6853
NYSE: KCG ■ *TF:* 800-544-7508 ■ *Web:* www.kcg.com					
Kohlberg Capital Corp 295 Madison Ave Sixth Fl	New York	NY	10017	212-455-8300	983-7654
Web: www.kohlbergcapital.com					
Kovack Securities Inc 6451 N Federal Hwy # 1201	Fort Lauderdale	FL	33308	954-782-4771	943-7331
TF: 800-711-4078 ■ *Web:* www.kovacksecurities.com					
L B L Group 4281 Katella Ave Ste 221	Los Alamitos	CA	90720	714-236-8270	
TF: 800-451-8037 ■ *Web:* www.lblgroup.com					
LaBranche & Company Inc 33 Whitehall St Eighth Fl	New York	NY	10004	212-425-1144	
Web: labfs.com					
Ladenburg Thalmann Financial Services Inc 4400 Biscayne Blvd 12th Fl	Miami	FL	33137	212-409-2000	572-4199*
NYSE: LTS ■ **Fax Area Code:* 305 ■ *TF:* 800-523-8425 ■ *Web:* www.ladenburg.com					
Lake Shore Securities Lp 401 S La Salle St Ste 1000	Chicago	IL	60605	312-663-1307	
Web: www.lakeshoresecurities.com					
Lasalle St Securities LLC 940 N Industrial Dr	Elmhurst	IL	60126	630-600-0500	
Web: lasallest.com					
Lasting Legacy Ltd 812 Busse Hwy	Park Ridge	IL	60068	847-685-8402	
Web: raymondjames.com					
Laux & Co 672 W Liberty St	Medina	OH	44256	330-721-0100	
Web: www.lauxco.com					
Lazard 30 Rockefeller Plz	New York	NY	10112	212-632-2685	
NYSE: LAZ ■ *TF:* 877-266-8601 ■ *Web:* www.lazard.com					
Leader Capital Corp 919 N East 19th Ave Ste 200	Portland	OR	97232	503-294-1010	
Web: www.leadercapital.com					
Leaders LLC Two Portland Fish Pier Ste 301	Portland	ME	04101	888-583-7770	
TF: 888-583-7770 ■ *Web:* www.leaders-llc.com					
Lebenthal Wealth Advisors 230 Park Ave Fl 32	New York	NY	10169	212-425-6006	867-1787
TF: 877-425-6006 ■ *Web:* www.lebenthal.com					
Leede Financial Markets Inc Ste 2300 First Alberta Pl 777 Eighth Ave SW	Calgary	AB	T2P3R5	403-531-6800	
Web: www.leedefinancial.com					
Legg Mason Inc (LMI) 100 International Dr	Baltimore	MD	21202	410-539-0000	454-3101*
NYSE: LM ■ **Fax:* Hum Res ■ *TF:* 800-822-5544 ■ *Web:* www.leggmason.com					
Leigh Baldwin & Company LLC One Hopper St	Utica	NY	13501	315-734-1410	
TF: 800-659-8044 ■ *Web:* www.leighbaldwin.com					

Phone | Fax

Lenox Group LLC, The
3384 Peachtree Rd N E Ste 300 ... Atlanta GA 30326 404-419-1660
Web: www.lenoxgroupllc.com

Lepercq de Neuflize & Co
156 W 56th St 12th Fl ... New York NY 10019 212-698-0700 262-0155
Web: www.lepercq.com

Lexington Investment Mortgage Company LLC
2365 Harrodsburg Rd Ste B375 ... Lexington KY 40504 859-224-7073
Web: www.lexinvest.com

Liberty Group LLC 3923 Grand Ave ... Oakland CA 94610 510-658-1880
Web: www.libertygroupllc.com

Liebherr-Canada Ltd 1015 Sutton Dr ... Burlington ON L7L5Z8 905-319-9222
Web: www.liebherr.ca

Lime Brokerage LLC 625 Broadway 12th Fl ... New York NY 10012 212-824-5000
Web: www.limebrokerage.com

Lincolnshire Management Inc
780 Third Ave 40th Fl ... New York NY 10017 212-319-3633 755-5457
Web: www.lincolnshiremgmt.com

Livingston Technologies
45 Horse Hill Rd Ste 105B ... Cedar Knolls NJ 07927 973-322-5671

Loop Capital Markets LLC
111 W Jackson Blvd Ste 1901 ... Chicago IL 60604 312-913-4900 913-4928
TF: 888-294-8898 ■ *Web:* www.loopcap.com

Louisiana Chemical Equipment Company LLC
7911 Wrenwood Ste A ... Baton Rouge LA 70896 225-923-3602
Web: www.lcec.com

LPL Financial Services 75 State St 24th Fl ... Boston MA 02109 800-877-7210
TF: 800-877-7210 ■ *Web:* www.joinlpl.com

LTVtrade LLC 501 Madison Ave Ste 501 ... New York NY 10022 212-616-4600
Web: www.ltvtrade.com

Lyons Equipment Company Inc
5445 Nys Rt 353 ... Little Valley NY 14755 716-938-9175
Web: www.lyonstimbertalk.com

M Ramsey King Securities Inc
93 Tomlin Cir ... Burr Ridge IL 60527 630-789-0607
Web: mramseyking.com

Maguire Investments Inc
1862 S Broadway Ste 100 ... Santa Maria CA 93454 805-922-6901
Web: www.maguire-investments.com

Mailender Inc 9500 Glades Dr ... Hamilton OH 45011 513-942-5453
TF: 800-998-5453 ■ *Web:* www.mailender.com

Manhattan Beach Trading Inc
1926 E Maple Ave ... El Segundo CA 90245 310-647-4281
Web: www.mbtrading.com

Marco Polo Securities Inc
30 Vesey St 14th Fl ... New York NY 10007 212-220-2700
Web: mpsecurities.com

Marquette Partners LP 801 W Adams Ste 500 ... Chicago IL 60607 312-224-2400
Web: www.marquettepartners.com

Memorial Investments Corp
110 The American Rd ... Morris Plains NJ 07950 973-538-2808

Mercator Asset Management LP
5200 Town Ctr Cir Boca Ctr Ste 550 ... Boca Raton FL 33486 561-361-1079
Web: www.mercatorasset.com

Mercury Marine Ltd 8698 Escarpment Way ... Milton ON L9T0M1 905-636-4700

Mercy Home Care & Medical Supplies Inc
2001 McDonald Ave ... Brooklyn NY 11223 718-376-3131
Web: www.mercymedsupplies.com

Meridian Capital LLC 2025 First Ave Ste 1170 ... Seattle WA 98121 206-623-4000 623-8221
Web: www.meridianllc.com

Meridian Equity Partners Inc
Five Hanover Sq 21st Fl ... New York NY 10004 212-500-6650
Web: meptraders.com

Merrion Group LLC 210 Elmer St ... Westfield NJ 07090 908-654-0033
Web: www.merriongroup.net

Mesa Products Inc 4445 S 74th E Ave ... Tulsa OK 74145 918-627-3188
Web: www.mesaproducts.com

Mesirow Financial Inc 350 N Clark St ... Chicago IL 60610 312-595-6000 595-4246*
**Fax: Hum Res* ■ *TF:* 888-681-0082 ■ *Web:* www.mesirowfinancial.com

Millennium Management LLC
666 Fifth Ave Eighth Fl ... New York NY 10103 212-841-4100
Web: www.mlp.com

MISA Metal Processing of Tennessee Inc
104 Western Dr ... Portland TN 37148 615-325-5454
Web: www.misa.com

Mizuho Securities USA 1251 Sixth Ave ... New York NY 10020 212-282-3000 209-9427
TF Sales: 866-216-1851 ■ *Web:* www.mizuhosecurities.com

MKM Partners LLC
300 First Stamford Pl E Fourth Fl ... Stamford CT 06902 203-861-9060
Web: www.mkmpartners.com

MLV & Co 1301 Ave of the Americas 43rd Fl ... New York NY 10019 212-542-5880
Web: www.mlvco.com

Moag & Company LLC 323 W Camden St Ste 400 ... Baltimore MD 21201 410-230-0105
Web: www.moagandcompany.com

Money Concepts International Inc
11440 N Jog Rd ... Palm Beach Gardens FL 33418 561-472-2000
Web: www.moneyconcepts.com

Montgomery Investment Management Inc
6550 Rock Spring Dr Ste 600A ... Bethesda MD 20817 301-897-9783
Web: www.miminvest.com

Morgan Stanley 1585 Broadway ... New York NY 10036 212-761-4000
NYSE: MS ■ *TF General:* 800-223-2440 ■ *Web:* www.morganstanley.com

Morgan Stanley Investment Management
1221 Ave of the Americas 5th Fl ... New York NY 10020 212-296-6600 452-0390*
**Fax Area Code:* 646 ■ *TF General:* 800-223-2440 ■ *Web:* www.morganstanley.com/im

MS Howells & Co 20555 N Pima Rd Ste 100 ... Scottsdale AZ 85255 480-563-2000
Web: www.mshowells.com

Municipal Capital Markets Group Inc
4851 Lyndon B Johnson Fwy Ste 200 ... Dallas TX 75244 972-386-0200
Web: www.municapital.com

Murfie Inc Seven N Pinckney St Ste 300 ... Madison WI 53703 608-515-8180
Web: www.murfie.com

Muzinich & Company Inc 450 Park Ave Ste 1804 ... New York NY 10022 212-888-3413
Web: www.muzinich.com

NASDAQ OMX Commodities Clearing Co
311 S Wacker Dr Ste 1750 ... Chicago IL 60606 312-568-5900

National Alliance Capital Markets
515 Congress Ave Ste 2410 ... Austin TX 78701 512-609-1700
Web: www.natalliance.com

National Commerce Bank Services Inc
80 Monroe Ave Ste 250 ... Memphis TN 38103 800-264-2609
TF: 800-264-2609 ■ *Web:* www.ncbs.com

National Securities Corp
410 Park Ave 14th Fl ... New York NY 10022 212-417-8000
TF: 800-742-7730 ■ *Web:* www.nationalsecurities.com

Natixis Securities Americas LLC
1251 Ave of the Americas ... New York NY 10020 212-891-6100
Web: www.blr.natixis.com

Needham & Co Inc 445 Pk Ave 3rd Fl ... New York NY 10022 212-371-8300 751-1450
TF: 800-903-3268 ■ *Web:* www.needhamco.com

Neidiger Tucker Bruner Inc
9540 S Maroon Cir Ste 250 ... Englewood CO 80112 303-825-1825
Web: www.ntbinc.com

New Century Capital Partners Inc
1510 11th St Ste 1100 ... Santa Monica CA 90401 310-451-9073
Web: www.newcenturycap.com

New England Capital Partners Inc
One Gateway Ctr Ste 405 ... Newton MA 02458 617-964-7300 964-7301
Web: www.necapitalpartners.com

Newbridge Securities Corp
1451 W Cypress Creek Rd ... Fort Lauderdale FL 33309 954-334-3450
Web: www.newbridgefinancial.com

Newport CH International LLC
1100 W Town & Country Rd Ste 1388 ... Orange CA 92868 714-572-8881
Web: www.newportchintl.com

Newport Group Securities Inc
300 International Pkwy Ste 270 ... Heathrow FL 32746 407-333-2905
Web: felc.com

NexBank Securities Inc 13455 Noel Rd 22nd Fl ... Dallas TX 75240 972-308-6700
Web: nexbank.com

NEXT Financial Holdings Inc
2500 Wilcrest Dr Ste 620 ... Houston TX 77042 713-789-7122
Web: www.nextfinancialholdings.com

Nollenberger Capital Partners Inc
101 California St Ste 3100 ... San Francisco CA 94111 415-402-6000
Web: www.nollenbergercapital.com

Nomura Securities International Inc
2 World Financial Ctr Bldg B ... New York NY 10281 212-667-9300 667-1058
Web: www.nomura.com

Northeast Capital & Advisory Inc
Seven Airport Pk Blvd Second Fl ... Latham NY 12110 518-426-0100 786-0105
Web: www.northeastcapital.net

Northern Industrial Sales Ltd
3526 Opie Cres ... Prince George BC V2N2P9 250-562-4435
TF: 800-668-3317 ■ *Web:* www.northernindustrialsales.ca

Northern Trust Securities
50 S La Salle St 12th Fl ... Chicago IL 60603 312-630-6000
Web: www.northerntrust.com

Northstar Financial Services Group LLC
17605 Wright St ... Omaha NE 68130 402-895-1600
Web: nstar-financial.com

Northwest Bank & Trust Co
100 E Kimberly Rd ... Davenport IA 52806 563-388-2511
Web: www.northwestbank.com

Novasel & Schwarte Investments Inc
3170 Hwy 50 Ste 10 ... South Lake Tahoe CA 96150 530-577-5050

NSK Canada Inc 5585 Mcadam Rd ... Mississauga ON L4Z1N4 905-890-0740 890-0434
Web: nskamericas.com

Nunami Services LLC 410 17th St Ste 570 ... Denver CO 80202 303-914-2819
Web: www.stockborrow.net

Nuveen Investments Inc 333 W Wacker Dr ... Chicago IL 60606 312-917-7700
TF: 800-257-8787 ■ *Web:* www.nuveen.com

NYLIFE Securities Inc 51 Madison Ave Rm 251 ... New York NY 10010 800-695-4785
TF: 800-695-4785 ■ *Web:* www.newyorklife.com

Oberweis Securities Inc
3333 Warrenville Rd Ste 500 ... Lisle IL 60532 630-577-2300 245-0467
TF: 800-323-6166 ■ *Web:* www.oberweis.net

Octagon Capital Corp
181 University Ave Ste 400 ... Toronto ON M5H3M7 416-368-3322
TF: 888-478-8888 ■ *Web:* www.octagoncap.com

Odeon Capital Group LLC
750 Lexington Ave 27th Fl ... New York NY 10022 212-257-6970
Web: www.odeoncap.com

Office Products Recycling Assoc Inc
100 W 18th Ave ... North Kansas City MO 64116 816-584-1000
Web: www.oprausa.com

Open E Cry LLC 9482 Wedgewood Blvd Ste 150 ... Powell OH 43065 614-792-2690

Orizon Investment Counsel LLC
16924 Frances St Ste 200 ... Omaha NE 68130 402-330-7008
Web: hsmcorizon.com

Oscar Gruss & Son Inc 55 E 59th st 15th Fl ... New York NY 10022 212-419-4000 317-5907
Web: www.oscargruss.com

Pacific Crest Securities Inc
111 SW Fifth Ave 42nd Fl ... Portland OR 97204 503-248-0721
TF: 800-314-9837 ■ *Web:* www.pacific-crest.com

Packaging Material Direct Inc
30405 Solon Rd Ste 9 ... Solon OH 44139 440-914-0530
Web: www.packagingsuppliesbymail.com

Paint Applicator Corp of America
Seven Harbor Park Dr ... Port Washington NY 11050 516-284-3000
Web: www.pacoa.com

Palladium Equity Partners LLC
1270 Ave of the Americas ... New York NY 10020 212-218-5150 218-5155
Web: www.palladiumequity.com

Company / Address	City	State	Zip	Phone	Fax
Pangaea Partners Ltd 1210 N Wfield Rd *Web:* www.pangaeapartners.com	Madison	WI	53717	608-347-0192	
PAR Capital Management Inc One International Pl Ste 2401 *Web:* www.parcapital.com	Boston	MA	02110	617-526-8990	
ParaCap Group LLC 6150 Parkland Blvd Ste 250 Mayfield Heights *Web:* www.paracapgroup.com	Cleveland	OH	44124	440-869-2100	
Parchman Vaughan & Co LLC Symphony Ctr Ste 120 1040 Park Ave *Web:* www.parchmanvaughan.com	Baltimore	MD	21201	410-244-8971	
Park Hill Group LLC 345 Park Ave 15th Fl *Web:* www.parkhillgroup.com	New York	NY	10154	212-583-5799	
Parnassus Investments One Market St Steuart Tower Ste 1600 *Web:* www.parnassus.com	San Francisco	CA	94105	415-778-0200	
Patriot Flooring Supply Inc 110 Commerce Way *TF:* 866-444-4433 ■ *Web:* www.patriothardwoodfloors.com	Woburn	MA	01801	866-444-4433	
Paulson Investment Company Inc 811 SW Naito Pkwy Ste 200 *Web:* www.paulsoninvestment.com	Portland	OR	97204	503-243-6000	243-6018
PDI Financial Group 601 N Lynndale Dr *TF:* 800-234-7341 ■ *Web:* www.pdifinancial.com	Appleton	WI	54914	920-739-2303	739-2205
Pennsylvania Trust Co Five Radnor Corp Ctr Ste 450 *TF:* 800-975-4316 ■ *Web:* penntrust.com	Radnor	PA	19087	610-975-4300	975-4324
Penso Capital Markets LLC 68 Carman Ave *Web:* penso.com	Cedarhurst	NY	11516	516-791-3800	
People's Securities Inc 850 Main St **Fax:* Cust Svc ■ *TF:* 800-772-4400 ■ *Web:* psi.peoples.com	Bridgeport	CT	06601	203-338-0800	338-3087*
Perimeter Financial Corp Two Queen St E Ste 1800 *Web:* www.pfin.ca	Toronto	ON	M5C3G7	416-703-7800	
PERMAC Securities Inc 285 Grand Ave Bldg No 3 *Web:* www.victorsecurities.com	Englewood	NJ	07631	646-820-8732	
Phillips & Company Securities Inc 1300 Sw Fifth Ave Ste 2100 *Web:* www.phillipsandco.com	Portland	OR	97201	503-224-0858	
Pico Quantitative Trading LLC 120 Wall St 16th Fl *Web:* www.picotrading.com	New York	NY	10005	646-701-6120	
Pikes Peak Financial Consultants 1544 Shane Cir	Colorado Springs	CO	80907	719-266-8890	
Piper Jaffray Cos 800 Nicollet Mall Ste 800 *NYSE: PJC* ■ **Fax:* PR ■ *TF:* 800-333-6000 ■ *Web:* www.piperjaffray.com	Minneapolis	MN	55402	612-303-6000	303-1309*
Planesmart! Aviation LLC Addison Airport 15841 Addison Rd *TF:* 888-228-4283 ■ *Web:* www.planesmart.com	Addison	TX	75001	972-380-8004	
Pointe Capital LLC 501 E Kennedy Blvd Ste 1400 *Web:* www.jhscapital.com	Tampa	FL	33602	813-202-7960	
PolySource LLC 1003 Industrial Dr *Web:* www.polysource.net	Pleasant Hill	MO	64080	816-540-5300	
Precision IBC Inc 8054 Mcgowin Dr *TF:* 800-544-7069 ■ *Web:* www.precisionibc.com	Fairhope	AL	36532	251-990-6789	
PRICE Futures Group Inc, The 141 W Jackson Blvd Ste 1340A *Web:* www.pricegroup.com	Chicago	IL	60604	312-264-4300	
Prime Capital Services Inc 11 Raymond Ave *Web:* www.primefs.com	Poughkeepsie	NY	12603	845-485-3338	
Professional Sales & Service LC 3545 West 1500 South *Web:* pro-sales.com	Salt Lake City	UT	84104	801-977-3961	
Quality Oil Inc 55 N 400 E *Web:* www.qualityoil.com	Valparaiso	IN	46383	219-462-2951	
Questar Capital Corp 5701 Golden Hills Dr **Fax Area Code:* 763 ■ *TF:* 888-446-5872 ■ *Web:* www.questarcapital.com	Minneapolis	MN	55416	888-446-5872	765-5996*
R Seelaus & Company Inc 25 Deforest Ave Ste 304 *TF:* 800-922-0584 ■ *Web:* www.rseelaus.com	Summit	NJ	07901	800-922-0584	
Radius Partners LLC 21 Charles St Ste 410 *Web:* www.radiuspartnersllc.com	Westport	CT	06880	203-557-3845	
Raymond James Financial Inc 880 Carillon Pkwy *NYSE: RJF* ■ **Fax:* Cust Svc ■ *TF:* 800-248-8863 ■ *Web:* www.raymondjames.com	Saint Petersburg	FL	33716	727-567-1000	573-8622*
RBC Capital Markets 1 Liberty Plaza **Fax:* Hum Res ■ *TF:* 800-387-1122 ■ *Web:* www.rbccm.com	New York	NY	10006	212-428-6200	428-6200*
RBC Dain Rauscher Inc 60 S Sixth St Dain Rauscher Plz *Web:* www.rbcwm-usa.com	Minneapolis	MN	55402	612-371-7270	
RCI Capital Group Inc 1030 W Georgia St Ste 1300 *Web:* www.rcicapitalgroup.com	Vancouver	BC	V6E2Y3	604-689-0881	
Reams Asset Management Company LLC 227 Washington St *Web:* www.reamsasset.com	Columbus	IN	47202	812-372-6606	
Redwood Capital Group LLC 885 Third Ave 25th Fl *Web:* www.redcapgroup.com	New York	NY	10022	212-508-7100	
Regal Discount Securities Inc 950 Milwaukee Ave Ste 102 *Web:* www.eregal.com	Glenview	IL	60025	847-375-6024	
Renaissance Technologies Corp 800 Third Ave *Web:* www.rentec.com	New York	NY	10022	212-486-6780	
Residex LLC 248 Cox St *Web:* www.residex.com	Roselle	NJ	07203	908-272-4383	
Reva Capital Markets LLC 45 Broadway Eighth Fl *Web:* www.revacap.com	New York	NY	10025	212-464-7363	
Rice Financial Products Co 17 State St 40th Fl *Web:* www.ricefinancialproducts.com	New York	NY	10004	212-908-9200	908-9299
RM Burritt Motors Inc 340 Rt 104 E *Web:* www.burrittmotors.com	Oswego	NY	13126	315-343-8948	
Robert W Baird & Company Inc PO Box 672 *TF:* 800-792-2473 ■ *Web:* www.rwbaird.com	Milwaukee	WI	53201	414-765-3500	765-3600
Roberts Mitani LLC 145 W 57th St 21st Fl *Web:* www.robertsmitani.com	New York	NY	10019	212-582-9800	
Rockwell Automation Canada Inc 135 Dundas St *Web:* ca.rockwellautomation.com	Cambridge	ON	N1R5N9	519-623-1810	740-9871
Roehl & Yi Investment Advisors LLC 450 Country Club Rd Ste 160 *Web:* roehl-yi.com	Eugene	OR	97401	541-683-2085	
Roger a Soape Inc 450 Gears Rd Ste 780 *Web:* www.rasoape.com	Houston	TX	77067	281-440-6347	
Roosevelt & Cross Inc One Exchange Plz 55 Broadway 22nd Fl *TF:* 800-348-3426 ■ *Web:* www.roosevelt-cross.com	New York	NY	10006	212-344-2500	
Ross Sinclaire & Associates LLC 700 Walnut St Ste 600 *Web:* www.rsanet.com	Cincinnati	OH	45202	513-381-3939	
Royal Alliance Assoc Inc One World Financial Ctr 14th Fl *TF:* 800-821-5100 ■ *Web:* www.royalalliance.com	New York	NY	10281	800-821-5100	
Royal Securities Co 4095 Chicago Dr SW Ste 120 *TF:* 800 421 3518 ■ *Web:* investwithjw.com	Grandville	MI	49418	616-538-2550	538-3360
Rutberg & Company LLC 351 California St Ste 1100 *Web:* www.rutbergco.com	San Francisco	CA	94104	415-371-1186	371-1187
SagePoint Financial Inc 2800 N Central Ave Ste 2100 *TF:* 800-552-3319 ■ *Web:* www.sagepointfinancial.com	Phoenix	AZ	85004	800-552-3319	
Salman Partners Inc 1095 W Pender St 17th Fl *Web:* www.salmanpartners.com	Vancouver	BC	V6E2M6	604-685-2450	
Samuel A Ramirez & Co Inc 61 Broadway Ste 2924 **Fax Area Code:* 212 ■ *TF:* 800-888-4086 ■ *Web:* www.ramirezco.com	New York	NY	10006	800-888-4086	248-0528*
Sandler O'Neill + Partners LP 1251 Avenue of the Americas 6th Fl *TF:* 800-635-6851 ■ *Web:* www.sandleroneill.com	New York	NY	10020	212-466-7800	466-7888
Sands Brothers Asset Management 15 Valley Dr *Web:* www.sandsbros.com	Greenwich	CT	06831	203-661-7500	
Schroder Investment Management North America Inc (SIMNA) 875 Third Ave 22nd Fl **Fax Area Code:* 212 ■ *TF:* 800-730-2932 ■ *Web:* www.schroders.com/us	New York	NY	10022	800-730-2932	632-2954*
Schroder US Holdings Inc 875 Third Ave. *Web:* www.millbrookllc.com	New York	NY	10022	212-542-3600	
Schwabe & Assoc Inc 8525 SW 92nd St Ste B6	Miami	FL	33156	305-270-1990	
Scotia Capital Markets One Liberty Plz *TF:* 877-294-3435 ■ *Web:* www.gbm.scotiabank.com	New York	NY	10006	212-225-5000	225-5090
Scotttrade 8205 E Regal Ct *Web:* www.scottrade.com	Tulsa	OK	74133	918-369-4333	
Seasongood & Mayer LLC 414 Walnut St Ste 300 *Web:* www.rbccm.com	Cincinnati	OH	45202	513-621-0580	
SecondMarket Inc 636 Ave of the Americas *Web:* www.SecondMarket.com	New York	NY	10011	212-463-0200	
Securities Center Inc, The 245 E St *Web:* www.securitiescenter.com	Chula Vista	CA	91910	619-426-3550	
Securities Service Network Inc 9729 Cogdill Rd Ste 301 *TF:* 866-843-4635 ■ *Web:* www.ssnetwork.com	Knoxville	TN	37932	866-843-4635	
Seer Capital Management LP 489 Fifth Ave 17th Fl *Web:* seercap.com	New York	NY	10017	212-850-9000	
Seidel & Shaw LLC 40 Exchange Pl *Web:* www.seidelshaw.com	New York	NY	10005	212-269-9008	
Sentinel Brokers Company Inc 20 Broadway Ste 1	Massapequa	NY	11758	516-541-9100	
SFE Investment Counsel Inc 801 S Figueroa St Ste 2100 *Web:* www.sfeic.com	Los Angeles	CA	90017	213-612-0220	
Shank Wealth Management LLC 2627 Chestnut Ridge Dr Ste 110 *Web:* shankwm.com	Kingwood	TX	77339	281-359-3133	
Shay Financial Services Inc 1000 Brickell Ave Ste 500 *Web:* www.shay.com	Miami	FL	33131	305-379-6656	
Shorcan Brokers Ltd 20 Adelaide St E Ste 1000 *Web:* www.shorcan.com	Toronto	ON	M5C2T6	416-360-2500	
Shore Morgan Young 300 W Wilson Bridge Rd *Web:* shoremorganyoung.com	Worthington	OH	43085	614-888-2117	
Siebert Brandford Shank & Co LLC 100 Wall St 18th Fl *TF:* 800-334-6800 ■ *Web:* www.sbsco.com	New York	NY	10005	646-775-4850	576-9680
Sigma Financial Corp 300 Parkland Plz *Web:* www.sigmafinancial.com	Ann Arbor	MI	48103	734-663-1611	
SII Investments Inc 5555 W Grande Market Dr *Web:* www.siionline.com	Appleton	WI	54913	920-996-2600	
Silver Legacy Capital Corp 407 N Virginia St *TF:* 800-687-8733 ■ *Web:* www.silverlegacycasino.com	Reno	NV	89501	800-687-8733	
Silverwood Partners LLC Silverwood Farm Pl 32 Pleasant St *Web:* www.silverwoodpartners.com	Sherborn	MA	01770	508-651-2194	
SMITH HAYES Financial Services Corp 1225 L St Ste 200 *Web:* www.smithhayes.com	Lincoln	NE	68508	402-476-3000	

Phone Fax

South Street Securities LLC
825 Third Ave 35th Fl. . . . . New York NY 10022 212-824-0738
Web: www.southstreetsecurities.com

Spartan Securities Group Ltd
15500 Roosevelt Blvd Ste 303 . . . . Clearwater FL 33760 727-502-0508
Web: www.spartansecurities.com

Spence Asset Management Inc
2455 E Missouri Ave Ste C. . . . . Las Cruces NM 88001 575-556-8500
Web: spenceassetmanagement.com

Spencer Clarke LLC 410 Park Ave Ste 1500 . . . . New York NY 10022 212-446-6100
Web: www.spencerclarke.com

SSI Investment Management Inc
9440 Santa Monica Blvd Eighth Fl . . . . Beverly Hills CA 90210 310-595-2000
Web: www.ssi-invest.com

Standard Investment Chartered Inc
2801 Bristol St Ste 100. . . . . Costa Mesa CA 92626 714-444-4300
Web: www.standardinvestment.com

Starshak Winzenburg & Co
55 W Monroe St Ste 2530 . . . . Chicago IL 60603 312-444-9367 444-9519
Web: www.swandco.com

Stephens Inc 111 Ctr St. . . . . Little Rock AR 72201 501-377-2000 377-2470*
**Fax:* Mail Rm ■ *TF:* 800-643-9691 ■ *Web:* www.stephens.com

Stern Brothers & Co
8000 Maryland Ave Ste 800 . . . . St. Louis MO 63105 314-743-4005
Web: www.sternbrothers.com

Sterne Agee & Leach Inc
800 Shades Creek Pkwy Ste 700 . . . . Birmingham AL 35209 205-949-3500 949-3607
TF: 800-240-1438 ■ *Web:* www.sterneagee.com

Stifel Financial Corp 501 N Broadway . . . . Saint Louis MO 63102 800-679-5446 342-2051*
NYSE: SF ■ **Fax Area Code:* 314 ■ *TF:* 800-679-5446 ■ *Web:* www.stifel.com

Stifel Nicolaus & Co Inc 501 N Broadway . . . . Saint Louis MO 63102 314-342-2000 342-2151
TF: 800-679-5446 ■ *Web:* www.stifel.com

Stock USA Investments Inc 1717 Rt 6. . . . . Carmel NY 10512 845-225-5132
Web: www.speedtrader.com

Stonegate Securities Inc
5950 Sherry Ln Ste 410 . . . . Dallas TX 75225 214-987-4121
Web: www.stonegateinc.com

Stonehenge Partners Inc
191 W Nationwide Blvd Ste 600 . . . . Columbus OH 43215 614-246-2500
Web: www.stonehengepartners.com

StormHarbour Securities LP
140 E 45th St Two Grand Central Tower
33rd Fl . . . . New York NY 10017 212-905-2500
Web: www.stormharbour.com

Success Trade Securities Inc
1900 L St N W Ste 525. . . . . Washington DC 20036 202-466-6890
Web: www.successtrade.com

Summer Street Capital Partners LLC
70 W Chippewa St Ste 500. . . . . Buffalo NY 14202 716-566-2900
Web: www.summerstreetcapital.com

Sunbelt Securities Inc
5065 Westheimer Ste 600. . . . . Houston TX 77056 713-965-9510
Web: www.sunbeltsecurities.com

SunTrust Robinson Humphrey Capital Markets
3333 Peachtree Rd NE . . . . Atlanta GA 30326 404-926-5000
TF: 800-634-7928 ■ *Web:* www.suntrustrh.com

SURFACExchange LLC 37 Brookside Dr . . . . Greenwich CT 06830 203-987-6900
Web: www.surfacexchange.com

Susquehanna International Group LLP
401 City Ave Ste 220 . . . . Bala Cynwyd PA 19004 610-617-2600
Web: www.sig.com

Sutter Securities Inc
220 Montgomery St Ste 1700. . . . . San Francisco CA 94104 415-352-6300
Web: www.suttersecurities.com

SWS Financial Services Inc
1201 Elm St Ste 3500. . . . . Dallas TX 75270 214-859-1800
Web: swst.com

Symphony Asset Management Inc
555 California St. . . . . San Francisco CA 94104 415-676-4000 676-2480
Web: www.symphonyasset.com

Symphony Capital LLC 880 Third Ave 12th Fl . . . . New York NY 10022 212-632-5400 632-5401
Web: www.symphonycapital.com

Synergy Advisors LLC 840 Apollo St Ste 213 . . . . El Segundo CA 90245 310-414-3200
Web: www.synergyadvisorsllc.com

Tano Capital LLC
One Franklin Pkwy Bldg 970 Second Fl . . . . San Mateo CA 94403 650-212-0330
Web: www.tanocapital.com

Tejas Inc 8226 Bee Caves Rd . . . . Austin TX 78746 512-306-8222 306-1348
TF: 800-846-6803 ■ *Web:* www.tejassec.com

Thornhill Securities Inc
336 S Congress Ave Ste 200 . . . . Austin TX 78704 512-472-7171 478-2616
Web: www.thornhillsecurities.com

TimeCapital Securities Corp
One Roosevelt Ave . . . . Port Jefferson Station NY 11776 631-331-1400
Web: www.timecapital.com

Tocco Financial Services Inc
6236 E Pima Ste 190 . . . . Tucson AZ 85712 520-881-1149
Web: toccofinancial.com

Toll Cross Securities Inc
Ste 200 1 Toronto St. . . . . Toronto ON M5C2V6 416-365-1960
Web: www.tollcross.ca

Topeka Capital Markets Inc
40 Wall St Ste 1702 . . . . New York NY 10005 212-709-5701
Web: www.topekacapitalmarkets.com

TradeHelm Inc 5727 S Lewis Ave Ste 300. . . . . Tulsa OK 74105 918-561-6900
Web: www.tradehelm.com

Tradelink Securities LLC
71 S Wacker Dr Ste 1900 . . . . Chicago IL 60606 312-264-2000
Web: www.tradelinkllc.com

Trader's Library LLC
6310 Stevens Forest Rd Ste 200. . . . . Columbia MD 21046 410-964-0026
Web: www.traderslibrary.com

TradeStation Group Inc
8050 SW Tenth St Ste 2000 . . . . Plantation FL 33324 954-652-7000 652-7300
TF: 800-871-3577 ■ *Web:* www.tradestation.com

TradeStation Securities Inc
8050 SW Tenth St Ste 2000 . . . . Plantation FL 33324 954-652-7000 652-7898
TF: 800-808-9336 ■ *Web:* www.tradestation.com

Trading Direct
160 Broadway E Bldg Seventh Fl . . . . New York NY 10038 212-766-0230 766-0914
TF: 800-925-8566 ■ *Web:* www.tradingdirect.com

TradingMarkets.com Inc
15260 Ventura Blvd Ste 2200. . . . . Sherman Oaks CA 91403 213-955-5858
Web: www.tradingmarkets.com

Tradition Asiel Securities Inc
75 Park Pl Fourth Fl . . . . New York NY 10007 212-791-4500
Web: www.tradition-na.com

TranscriptionGear Inc 7280 Auburn Rd . . . . Concord OH 44077 440-392-9882
Web: www.transcriptiongear.com

Trefethen Advisors LLC
6710 E Camelback Rd Ste 200 . . . . Scottsdale AZ 85251 480-922-9966
Web: www.trefethenadvisors.com

Tricor Pacific Capital Inc
200 Burrard St Ste 200. . . . . Vancouver BC V6C3L6 604-688-7669
Web: www.tricorpacific.com

Triton Capital Partners Ltd
566 W Lake St Ste 235. . . . . Chicago IL 60661 312-575-0190
Web: www.tritoncap.com

Trubee Collins & Company Inc
1350 One M & T Plz. . . . . Buffalo NY 14203 716-849-1401
Web: www.trubeecollins.com

trueEX Group LLC 162 Fifth Ave Ninth Fl. . . . . New York NY 10010 646 786 8520
Web: www.trueex.com

Trumaker Inc 701 Sutter St Fl 5. . . . . San Francisco CA 94109 855-623-3878
TF: 855-623-3878 ■ *Web:* www.trumaker.com

TVC Capital LLC
11260 El Camino Real Ste 220. . . . . San Diego CA 92130 858-704-3261
Web: www.tvccapital.com

Twenty-First Securities Corp 780 Third Ave . . . . New York NY 10017 212-418-6000
Web: www.twenty-first.com

Two Sigma Investments LLC
100 Ave of the Americas 16th Fl. . . . . New York NY 10013 212-625-5700
Web: www.twosigma.com

UBS Financial Services Inc
1285 Ave of the Americas. . . . . New York NY 10019 212-713-2000
TF: 800-221-3260 ■ *Web:* financialservicesinc.ubs.com

UBS Warburg LLC 677 Washington Blvd. . . . . Stamford CT 06901 203-719-3000
TF: 800-221-3260 ■ *Web:* www.ubs.com

Ulivi Wealth 369 S Glassell St . . . . Orange CA 92866 714-771-6000
Web: www.ulivi.com

Union Securities Ltd
700 W Georgia St Ste 900 . . . . Vancouver BC V7Y1H4 604-687-2201
Web: www.union-securities.com

Vanguard Brokerage Services PO Box 2600 . . . . Valley Forge PA 19482 610-669-1000 669-6366
TF: 800-992-8327 ■ *Web:* investor.vanguard.com

Veris Wealth Partners LLC
90 Broad St 24th Fl. . . . . New York NY 10004 212-349-4172
Web: www.veriswp.com

Veronis Suhler Stevenson (VSS)
55 E 52nd St 33rd Fl. . . . . New York NY 10055 212-935-4990 381-8168
Web: www.vss.com

vFinance Inc 1200 N Federal Hwy Ste 400 . . . . Boca Raton FL 33432 561-981-1000 283-0480
Web: www.vfinance.com

ViewTrade Securities Inc
525 Washington Blvd 24th Fl . . . . Jersey City NJ 07310 201-215-9850
Web: www.viewtrade.com

Vining Sparks IBG LP 775 Ridge Lk Blvd . . . . Memphis TN 38120 901-766-3000
Web: www.viningsparks.com

Virtual Brokers 4100 Yonge St Ste 506. . . . . Toronto ON M2P2B5 416-288-8028
Web: www.virtualbrokers.com

Wachtel & Company Inc
1101 14th St NW Eigth Fl Ste 800 . . . . Washington DC 20005 202-898-1144
Web: www.wachtelco.com

Wallace Financial Group Inc 4390 Earney Rd . . . . Woodstock GA 30188 770-751-7411
Web: lpl.com

WallachBeth Capital LLC 100 Wall St Ste 6600 . . . . New York NY 10005 646-237-8585
Web: www.wallachbeth.com

Warbros Venture Partners PO Box 1033. . . . . Westerly RI 02891 401-596-8960
Web: www.warbros.com

Wayne Hummer Investments LLC
222 S Riverside Pz 28th Fl . . . . Chicago IL 60606 866-943-4732
TF: 800-621-4477 ■ *Web:* www.wintrustwealth.com

Wesbild Holdings Ltd
666 Burrard St Park Pl Ste 2650. . . . . Vancouver BC V6C2X8 604-694-8800
Web: www.wesbild.com

Western International Securities Inc
70 S Lake Ave Ste 700 . . . . Pasadena CA 91101 888-793-7717
TF: 888-793-7717 ■ *Web:* www.wisdirect.com

WestPark Capital Inc
1900 Ave of the Stars Ste 310. . . . . Los Angeles CA 90067 310-843-9300
Web: www.wpcapital.com

William Blair & Company LLC 222 W Adams St. . . . . Chicago IL 60606 312-236-1600 236-1875
TF: 800-621-0687 ■ *Web:* www.williamblair.com

Wilson-Davis & Company Inc
236 South Main . . . . Salt Lake City UT 84101 801-532-1313
Web: www.wdco.com

Winetasting Network, The 578 Gateway Dr . . . . Napa CA 94558 800-435-2225
TF: 800-435-2225 ■ *Web:* www.winetasting.com

Wm Sword & Co Inc 90 Nassau St. . . . . Princeton NJ 08542 609-924-6710
Web: swordrowe.com/

Wolfe & Hurst Bond Brokers Inc
30 Montgomery St Ste 1040. . . . . Jersey City NJ 07302 201-938-0400
Web: www.wolfehurstbbi.com

Phone Fax

Wolverton Securities Ltd
777 Dunsmuir St 17th Fl ... Vancouver BC V7Y1J5 604-622-1000
Web: www.wolverton.ca

World Equity Group
1650 N Arlington Heights Rd
Ste 100 ... Arlington Heights IL 60004 847-342-1700
Web: www.worldequitygroup.com

WR Hambrecht & Co
909 Montgomery St 3rd Fl ... San Francisco CA 94133 415-551-8600 551-8686
TF Cust Svc: 855-753-6484 ■ *Web:* www.wrhambrecht.com

Wunderlich Securities Inc
6000 Poplar Ave Ste 150 ... Memphis TN 38119 901-251-1330
Web: www.wunderlichsecurities.com

Wyser-Pratte Management Company Inc
504 Guard Hill Rd ... Bedford NY 10506 914-234-4930
Web: www.wyser-pratte.com

Xpert Financial Inc 1825 S Grant St Ste 400 ... San Mateo CA 94402 650-212-1535
Web: www.xpertfinancial.com

Yellow Point Equity Partners LP
1285 W Pender St Ste 1000 ... Vancouver BC V6E4B1 604-659-1898
Web: www.ypoint.ca

Ziegler Capital Markets Investment Services
200 S Wacker ... Chicago IL 60606 414-978-6400 334-3433*
**Fax Area Code:* 262 ■ **Fax:* Hum Res ■ *Web:* ziegler.com

694 SECURITIES & COMMODITIES EXCHANGES

Phone Fax

Able Global Partners LLC
641 Lexington Ave 15th Fl ... New York NY 10022 212-581-7011
Web: www.ableglobalps.com

Accelon Capital 2470 El Camino Real Ste 210 ... Palo Alto CA 94306 650-213-8353
Web: www.acceloncapital.com

Advanced Equities Financial Corp
311 S Wacker Dr Ste 1650 ... Chicago IL 60606 312-377-5300
Web: www.advancedequities.com

Alinian Capital Group LLC
3343 W Commercial Blvd Ste 103 ... Fort Lauderdale FL 33309 954-495-2040
Web: www.alinian.com

Arcady Bay Partners LLC 40417 Aldie Springs Dr ... Aldie VA 20105 703-359-4773
Web: www.arcadybay.com

AtlasBanc Holdings Corp
301 S Missouri Ave ... Clearwater FL 33756 727-446-6660
Web: www.atlasbanc.com

Axial Inc 45 E 20th St 12th Fl ... New York NY 10003 800-860-4519
TF: 800-860-4519 ■ *Web:* www.axial.net

Bats Trading Inc 8050 Marshall Dr Ste 120 ... Lenexa KS 66214 913-815-7000
Web: www.batstrading.com

BizXchange Inc 3600 136th Pl SE Ste 270 ... Bellevue WA 98006 425-998-5055
Web: www.bizx.com

Border Gold Corp 15234 N Bluff Rd ... White Rock BC V4B3E6 604-535-3287
Web: www.bordergold.com

Bulltick Capital Markets Holdings LLC
701 Brickell Ave Ste 2550 ... Miami FL 33131 305-533-1541
Web: www.bulltick.com

Cape Securities Inc 2005 Pennsylvania Ave ... Mcdonough GA 30253 678-583-1120
Web: www.capesecurities.com

Capital Growth Planning Inc
405 E Lexington Ave Ste 201 ... El Cajon CA 92020 619-440-7023
Web: www.capplan.com

Capital Guardian Holding LLC
1355 Greenwood Cliff Ste 250 ... Charlotte NC 28204 704-705-1860
Web: www.capitalguardianllc.com

CBOE Stock Exchange LLC 400 S LaSalle St ... Chicago IL 60605 312-786-7449
Web: www.cbsx.com

Cedar Ventures LLC 2870 Peachtree Rd Ste 493 ... Atlanta GA 30305 404-239-8416
Web: cedarventures.com

Ceia USA Ltd 9155 Dutton Dr ... Twinsburg OH 44087 330-405-3190
Web: www.ceia-usa.com

Chapin Davis Investments
Two Village Sq Ste 200 ... Baltimore MD 21210 410-435-3200
Web: www.chapindavis.com

Chicago Board Options Exchange (CBOE)
400 S La Salle St ... Chicago IL 60605 312-786-5600 786-8818
TF: 800-678-4667 ■ *Web:* www.cboe.com

Chicago Stock Exchange 440 S LaSalle St ... Chicago IL 60605 312-663-2222 663-2721
Web: chx.com

CME Group Inc 20 S Wacker Dr ... Chicago IL 60606 312-930-1000 466-4410
NASDAQ: CME ■ *TF:* 866-716-7274 ■ *Web:* www.cmegroup.com

CNSX Markets Inc 220 Bay St Ninth Fl ... Toronto ON M5J2W4 416-572-2000
Web: www.cnsx.ca

Coker & Palmer Inc 1667 Lelia Dr ... Jackson MS 39216 601-354-0860
Web: www.cokerpalmer.com

Convergent Wealth Advisors LLC
12505 Park Potomac Ave Ste 400 ... Potomac MD 20854 301-770-6300
Web: www.convergentwealth.com

Culver Capital Group Inc
1600 Sunflower Ave Ste 120 ... Costa Mesa CA 92626 714-380-3000
Web: www.culvercapital.com

DN Partners LLC 180 N LaSalle St Ste 2630 ... Chicago IL 60601 312-332-7960
Web: www.dnpartners.com

England & Company LLC
888 17th St NW Ste 304 ... Washington DC 20006 202-386-6500
Web: www.englandco.com

Eris Exchange LLC 311 S Wacker Dr Ste 950 ... Chicago IL 60606 212-561-5472
Web: www.erisfutures.com

Farmington Capital Partners PO Box 1461 ... Hartford CT 06144 860-284-1096
Web: www.farmingtoncapital.com

FMA Advisory Inc 1631 N Front St ... Harrisburg PA 17102 717-232-8850
Web: fma-advisory.com

Phone Fax

G2 Investment Group LLC
142 W 57th St 12th Fl ... New York NY 10019 212-887-1150
Web: www.g2investmentgroup.com

Geneva Trading USA LLC
980 N Michigan Ave Ste 1710 ... Chicago IL 60611 312-587-7000
Web: www.geneva-trading.com

Granite Tower Capital 324 Traders Blvd E ... Mississauga ON L4Z1W7 905-366-2551
Web: www.granitetowercapital.com

Ice Futures One N End Ave 13th Fl ... New York NY 10282 212-748-4000
Web: www.theice.com

Impetus Capital LLC 145 W 57th St 16 Fl ... New York NY 10019 212-258-2782
Web: www.impetuscapital.com

IPC Securities Corp
2680 Skymark Ave Ste 700 ... Mississauga ON L4W5L6 905-212-9788
Web: www.ipcsecurities.com

JDB Capital Partners LLC
20645 N Pima Rd Ste 110 ... Scottsdale AZ 85255 480-502-9200
Web: www.jdbcapital.com

Jitney Trade Inc 360 St-Jacques St W 16th Fl ... Montreal QC H2Y1P5 514-985-8080
Web: www.jitneytrade.com

Kansas City Board of Trade
4800 Main St Ste 303 ... Kansas City MO 64112 816-753-7500 753-3944
Web: www.cmegroup.com

KeyImpact Sales & Systems Inc
1701 Crossroads Dr ... Odenton MD 21113 410-381-1239
Web: www.kisales.com

Lazear Capital Partners Ltd
401 N Front St Ste 350 ... Columbus OH 43215 614-221-1616
Web: www.lazearcapital.com

Linch Capital LLC
3384 Peachtree Rd NW Ste 575 ... Atlanta GA 30326 404-334-7047
Web: www.linchcapital.com

Lucent Capital Inc
9454 Wilshire Blvd Ste 525 ... Beverly Hills CA 90212 310-876-8454
Web: www.lucentcapital.com

M3 Capital Partners 150 S Wacker Dr 31st Fl ... Chicago IL 60606 312-499-8500
Web: www.mcp-llc.com

MAM Global Financial Services
16161 Ventura Blvd PO Box 631 ... Encino CA 91436 818-784-8752
Web: www.mamgfs.com

Manulife Securities Inc
500-1235 N Service Rd W ... Oakville ON L6M2W2 905-469-2100
Web: www.manulifesecurities.ca

Market Street Consulting Group Inc
6965 El Camino Real Ste 105599 ... Carlsbad CA 92009 760-518-2310 621-5904*
**Fax Area Code:* 888 ■ *Web:* www.marketstreetfs.com

MAS Capital Inc 2715 Coney Island Ave ... Brooklyn NY 11235 866-553-7493
TF: 866-553-7493 ■ *Web:* www.mascapital.com

MBF Clearing Corp
One N End Ave World Financial Ctr Ste 1201 ... New York NY 10282 212-845-5000
Web: www.mbfcc.com

Milestone Partners LLC
6047 Tyvola Glen Cir ... Charlotte NC 28217 704-414-6532
Web: www.milestonex.com

Minneapolis Grain Exchange
400 S Fourth St 130 Grain Exchange Bldg ... Minneapolis MN 55415 612-321-7101 339-1155
TF: 800-827-4746 ■ *Web:* www.mgex.com

Montreal Exchange
800 Victoria Sq Third Fl PO Box 61 ... Montreal QC H4Z1A9 514-871-2424 871-3565
TF: 800-361-5353 ■ *Web:* www.m-x.ca

MSB Fairway Capital Partners
1800 St James Pl Ste 450 ... Houston TX 77056 713-622-9961
Web: www.msbfairway.com

Nasdaq Stock Market Inc 165 Broadway ... New York NY 10006 212-401-8700
Web: www.nasdaq.com

National Stock Exchange (NSX)
440 S LaSalle St Ste 2600 ... Chicago IL 60605 201-499-3700 939-7239*
**Fax Area Code:* 312 ■ *TF:* 800-843-3924 ■ *Web:* www.nsx.com

Nations Financial Group Inc
4000 River Ridge Dr NE PO Box 908 ... Cedar Rapids IA 52406 319-393-9541
Web: www.nationsfg.com

NMS Capital Group LLC
433 N Camden Dr Fourth Fl ... Beverly Hills CA 90210 800-716-2080
TF: 800-716-2080 ■ *Web:* nmscapital.com

NYSE Arce 115 Samsone St ... San Francisco CA 94104 877-729-7291
TF: 877-729-7291 ■ *Web:* www.nyse.com

NYSE Euronext 11 Wall St ... New York NY 10005 212-656-3000 656-2126
NYSE: NYX ■ *TF:* 866-873-7422 ■ *Web:* www.nyse.com

Oliver Capital Partners Inc
102 3016 Fifth Ave NE ... Calgary AB T2A6K4 403-313-4645
Web: www.olcapa.com

Partnership Capital Growth Advisors
One Embarcadero Ctr Ste 3810 ... San Francisco CA 94111 415-705-8008
Web: www.pcg-advisors.com

Pavilion Financial Corp
1001 Corydon Ave Ste 300 ... Winnipeg MB R3M0B6 204-954-5101
Web: www.pavilioncorp.com

Pelion Financial Group Inc
369 Lexington Ave Ste 311 ... New York NY 10017 917-639-5450
Web: www.peliongroup.com

ProFutures Inc 11719 Bee Cave Rd Ste 200 ... Austin TX 78738 512-263-3800
Web: www.profutures.com

RainMaker Securities LLC
500 N Michigan Ave Ste 600 ... Chicago IL 60611 312-254-5048
Web: www.rainmakersecurities.com

Raymond James (USA) Ltd
2200 - 925 W Georgia St ... Vancouver BC V6C3L2 877-570-7558
TF: 877-570-7558 ■ *Web:* www.rjlu.com

Sprott Global Resource Investments Ltd
1910 Palomar Point Way Ste 200 ... Carlsbad CA 92008 800-477-7853
Web: www.sprottglobal.com

				Phone	Fax
Stone Key Group LLC Two Sound View Dr Second Fl *Web:* www.stonekey.com	Greenwich	CT	06830	203-930-3700	
TerraPass Inc 527 Howard St Fourth Fl *Web:* www.terrapass.com	San Francisco	CA	94105	415-692-3411	
Tigress Financial Partners LLC 500 Fifth Ave 15th Fl *Web:* www.tigressfp.com	New York	NY	10036	212-430-8700	
Timucuan Asset Management Inc 200 W Forsyth St Ste 1600 *Web:* www.timucuan.com	Jacksonville	FL	32202	904-356-1739	
Toronto Stock Exchange 130 King St W *TF:* 888-873-8392 ■ *Web:* www.tmx.com	Toronto	ON	M5X1J2	416-947-4670	947-4662
Trade Exchange of America 23200 Coolidge Hwy *Web:* www.tradefirst.com	Oak Park	MI	48237	248-544-1350	
Unified Financial Services Inc 2353 Alexandria Dr *Web:* www.unified.com	Lexington	KY	40504	859-422-0347	
VectorGlobal WMG Inc 801 Brickell Ave Ste 2500 (PH1) *Web:* www.vectorglobalwmg.com	Miami	FL	33131	305-350-3350	
Wall Street Financial Group Inc 255 Woodcliff Dr *Web:* www.wsfg.com	Fairport	NY	14450	585-267-8000	
Williams Financial Group Inc 2711 N Haskell Ave Cityplace Tower Ste 2900 *Web:* www.williams-financial.com	Dallas	TX	75204	972-661-8700	
Wilmington Capital Securities LLC 600 Old Country Rd Ste 200 *Web:* wilmingtoncap.com	Garden City	NY	11530	516-750-6200	
World Currency USA Inc 16 W Main St *TF:* 888-593-7927 ■ *Web:* www.worldcurrencyusa.com	Marlton	NJ	08053	888-593-7927	

695 SECURITY PRODUCTS & SERVICES

SEE ALSO Fire Protection Systems p. 2289; Audio & Video Equipment p. 1825; Signals & Sirens - Electric p. 3173

				Phone	Fax
3M 639 N Rosemead Blvd *Web:* www.cogentsystems.com	Pasadena	CA	91107	626-325-9600	
ADS Security LP 3001 Armory Dr Ste 100 *Web:* www.adsalarms.com	Nashville	TN	37204	800-448-8652	
ADT Security Services Inc 14200 E Exposition Ave **Fax Area Code:* 877 ■ **Fax:* Hum Res ■ *TF:* 800-238-2455 ■ *Web:* www.adt.com	Aurora	CO	80012	800-238-2455	238-3307*
Advantor Systems Corp 12612 Challenger Pkwy Ste 300 **Fax:* Sales ■ *TF:* 800-238-2686 ■ *Web:* www.advantor.com	Orlando	FL	32809	407-859-3350	857-1635*
AFA Protective Systems Inc 155 Michael Dr *OTC:* AFAP ■ *Web:* afap.com	Syosset	NY	11791	516-496-2322	496-2848
Akal Security Inc Seven Infinity Loop *TF:* 888-325-2527 ■ *Web:* www.akalsecurity.com	Espanola	NM	87532	505-692-6600	753-8689
Alken Inc 40 Hercules Dr *TF:* 800-357-4777 ■ *Web:* www.polhemus.com	Colchester	VT	05446	802-655-3159	
Allied Fire & Security Inc 425 W Second Ave **Fax:* Acctg ■ *TF Acctg:* 888-333-2632 ■ *Web:* www.alliedfireandsecurity.com	Spokane	WA	99201	509-321-8778	321-8767*
Alphacorp Inc 2211 West 2300 South *Web:* www.alphacorpsecurity.com	West Valley	UT	84119	801-977-8608	
AMAG Technology Inc 20701 Manhattan Pl *TF:* 800-889-9138 ■ *Web:* www.amag.com	Torrance	CA	90501	310-518-2380	834-0685
American Locker Group Inc 815 S Main St *OTC:* ALGI ■ *TF:* 800-828-9118 ■ *Web:* www.americanlocker.com	Grapevine	TX	76051	817-329-1600	421-8618
American Locker Security Systems Inc 608 Allen St *TF Sales:* 800-828-9118 ■ *Web:* www.americanlocker.com	Jamestown	NY	14701	716-664-9600	664-2949
American Science & Engineering Inc 829 Middlesex Tpke *NASDAQ:* ASEI ■ *TF:* 800-225-1608 ■ *Web:* www.as-e.com	Billerica	MA	01821	978-262-8700	262-8804
American Security Products Inc 11925 Pacific Ave *TF:* 800-421-6142 ■ *Web:* www.amsecusa.com	Fontana	CA	92337	951-685-9680	685-9685
APi Systems Group Inc 10575 Vista Park Rd *TF General:* 877-828-1200 ■ *Web:* www.apisystemsgroup.com	Dallas	TX	75238	214-291-1200	291-1340
Apollo Security Inc 2150 Boston Providence Hwy *Web:* apollointernational.com/	Walpole	MA	02081	508-660-1197	
Argyle Security Inc 12903 Delivery Dr *Web:* isisecurity.com/	San Antonio	TX	78247	210-495-5245	828-7300
Ascent Capital Group Inc 5251 DTC Pkwy Ste 1000 *Web:* www.ascentcapitalgroupinc.com	Greenwood Village	CO	80111	303-628-5600	
Astrophysics Inc 21481 Ferrero Pkwy *Web:* www.astrophysicsinc.com	City Of Industry	CA	91789	909-598-5488	
Authentix Inc 4355 Excel Pkwy Ste 100 *TF:* 866-434-1402 ■ *Web:* www.authentix.com	Addison	TX	75001	469-737-4400	737-4409
B & G Security International 6631 Hwy 42 *Web:* www.bgsecurity.com	Rex	GA	30273	770-507-6409	
Baltimore Alarm & Security 5314 Reistertown Rd *Web:* www.baltoalarm.com	Baltimore	MD	21215	410-358-8600	
BI Inc 6400 Lookout Rd *TF:* 800-241-2911 ■ *Web:* www.bi.com	Boulder	CO	80301	303-218-1000	218-1250
Black Hat Inc 1932 First Ave Ste 204 *TF:* 866-203-8081 ■ *Web:* www.blackhat.com	Seattle	WA	98101	206-443-5489	
Bosch Security Systems 130 Perinton Pkwy *TF:* 800-289-0096 ■ *Web:* us.boschsecurity.com	Fairport	NY	14450	585-223-4060	223-9180
Brivo Systems LLC 4350 E W Hwy Ste 201 *TF Tech Supp:* 866-692-7486 ■ *Web:* www.brivo.com	Bethesda	MD	20814	301-664-5242	664-5264
BSM Wireless Inc 75 International Blvd Ste 100 *TF:* 866-768-4771 ■ *Web:* www.bsmwireless.com	Toronto	ON	M9W6L9	416-675-1201	

				Phone	Fax
Carter Bros LLC 100 Hartsfield Ctr Pkwy Ste 140 **Fax Area Code:* 404 ■ *TF:* 888-818-0152 ■ *Web:* carterbrothers.com	Atlanta	GA	30354	888-818-0152	767-2568*
Central Signaling 2033 Hamilton Rd *TF:* 800-554-1104 ■ *Web:* www.censignal.com	Columbus	GA	31904	706-322-3756	596-8552
CFP Group Inc, The 1401 Chain Bridge Rd Ste 300 *Web:* www.thecfpgroup.com	Mclean	VA	22101	703-752-0570	
Checkpoint Systems Inc 101 Wolf Dr *NYSE:* CKP ■ *TF:* 800-257-5540 ■ *Web:* www.checkpointsystems.com	Thorofare	NJ	08086	856-848-1800	848-0937
CompuDyne Corp 2530 Riva Rd Ste 201 *Web:* www.compudyne.com	Annapolis	MD	21401	410-224-4415	
Corby Industries Inc 1501 E Pennsylvania St *TF Sales:* 800-652-6729 ■ *Web:* www.corby.com	Allentown	PA	18109	610-433-1412	435-1963
DEI Holdings Inc One Viper Way *OTC:* DEIX ■ *TF:* 800-876-0800 ■ *Web:* deiholdings.com	Vista	CA	92081	760-598-6200	598-6400
Detector Electronics Corp 6901 W 110th St *Web:* det-tronics.com/	Minneapolis	MN	55438	952-941-5665	
Detex Corp 302 Detex Dr *TF:* 800-729-3839 ■ *Web:* www.detex.com	New Braunfels	TX	78130	830-629-2900	620-6711
deView Electronics USA Inc 708 Vly Ridge Cir Ste 1 *TF:* 877-433-8439 ■ *Web:* www.deviewelectronics.com	Lewisville	TX	75057	214-222-3332	
Diebold Inc 5995 Mayfair Rd *NYSE:* DBD ■ *TF:* 800-999-3600 ■ *Web:* www.diebold.com	North Canton	OH	44720	330-490-4000	
Digital Security Controls (DSC) 3301 Langstaff Rd *Web:* www.dsc.com	Concord	ON	L4K4L2	905-760-3000	760-3004
Doyle Security Systems Inc 792 Calkins Rd *TF:* 800-836-9538 ■ *Web:* godoyle.com	Rochester	NY	14623	585-244-3400	271-8273
eDist 97 McKee Dr **Fax Area Code:* 800 ■ *TF:* 800-800-6624 ■ *Web:* www.edist.com	Mahwah	NJ	07430	201-512-1400	391-5078*
ELK Products Inc 3266 Us 70 W *TF:* 800-797-9355 ■ *Web:* www.elkproducts.com	Connelly Springs	NC	28612	828-397-4200	
EZ Electric Inc 1250 Birchwood Dr *Web:* www.ez-electric.com	Sunnyvale	CA	94089	408-734-4282	734-0798
Federal APD Inc (FAPD) 28100 Cabot Dr Ste 200 *TF:* 877-992-7749 ■ *Web:* 3m.com/	Novi	MI	48377	248-374-9600	
Felts Lock & Alarm Company Inc 4000 E Indiana St *Web:* www.feltsonline.com	Evansville	IN	47715	812-473-4000	
Fiber SenSys LLC 2925 NW Aloclek Dr Ste 130 *TF:* 800-641-8150 ■ *Web:* www.fibersensys.com	Hillsboro	OR	97124	503-692-4430	
FireKing Security Group 101 Security Pkwy *TF:* 800-457-2424 ■ *Web:* www.fireking.com	New Albany	IN	47150	812-948-8400	
First Action Security Security Team Inc 18702 Crestwood Dr *TF Cust Svc:* 800-372-7447 ■ *Web:* www.firstactionteam.com	Hagerstown	MD	21742	301-797-2124	797-2189
Fortress Technology Inc 51 Grand Marshall Dr *TF:* 888-220-8737 ■ *Web:* www.fortresstechnology.com	Toronto	ON	M1B5N6	416-754-2898	
Frontier Systems Integrator LLC 2751 Prosperity Ave *Web:* www.frontier-si.com	Fairfax	VA	22031	703-289-9930	
Gateway Group One Inc 604-608 Market St *Web:* www.gatewaygroupone.com	Newark	NJ	07105	973-465-8006	
GE Analytical Instruments Inc 6060 Spine Rd *TF:* 800-255-6964 ■ *Web:* www.geinstruments.com	Boulder	CO	80301	303-444-2009	
Gentex Corp 600 N Centennial St *NASDAQ:* GNTX ■ *Web:* www.gentex.com	Zeeland	MI	49464	616-772-1800	772-7348
George Risk Industries Inc 802 S Elm St *OTC:* RSKIA ■ *TF Sales:* 800-523-1227 ■ *Web:* www.grisk.com	Kimball	NE	69145	308-235-4645	235-2609
Guardian Alarm 20800 Southfield Rd *TF:* 800-782-9688 ■ *Web:* www.guardianalarm.com	Southfield	MI	48075	248-423-1000	423-3009
Hanchett Entry Systems Inc (HES) 22630 N 17th Ave *TF:* 800-626-7590 ■ *Web:* www.hesinnovations.com	Phoenix	AZ	85027	623-582-4626	582-4641
HandyTrac Systems LLC 510 Staghorn Ct *TF:* 800-665-9994 ■ *Web:* www.handytrac.com	Alpharetta	GA	30004	678-990-2305	
Hikvision USA Inc 908 Canada Ct *Web:* hikvision.com	City Of Industry	CA	91748	909-895-0400	
Honeywell Automation & Control Solutions 11 W Spring St *Web:* www.honeywell.com	Freeport	IL	61032	815-235-5500	
Honeywell Security Group Two Corporate Ctr Dr Ste 100 *TF:* 800-467-5875 ■ *Web:* www.security.honeywell.com	Melville	NY	11747	516-577-2000	
IDenticard Systems Inc 40 Citation Ln *TF:* 800-233-0298 ■ *Web:* www.identicard.com	Lititz	PA	17543	717-569-5797	569-2390
Infinova Corp 51 Stouts Ln *Web:* www.infinova.com	Monmouth Junction	NJ	08852	732-355-9100	
Integrated Biometrics Inc 121 Broadcast Dr *TF:* 888-840-8034 ■ *Web:* www.integratedbiometrics.com	Spartanburg	SC	29303	864-990-3711	
Interface Security Systems LLC 6340 International Pkwy Ste 100 *TF:* 866-593-3480	Plano	TX	75093	972-996-2800	996-2801
International Electronics Inc 427 Tpke St *TF:* 800-343-9502 ■ *Web:* linearcorp.com/iei_access_solutions.php	Canton	MA	02021	781-821-5566	821-4443
ISS International Inc Aspen Corporate Park 1480 Us Hwy 9 N Ste 202 *Web:* www.isscctv.com	Woodbridge	NJ	07095	732-855-1111	
Johnson Controls Fire & Security Solutions 4100 Gardian St Ste 200 *TF:* 800-229-4076 ■ *Web:* www.johnsoncontrols.com/security	Simi Valley	CA	93063	805-522-5555	582-7888
KWJ Engineering Inc 8430 Central Ave Ste C *TF:* 800-472-6626 ■ *Web:* www.kwjengineering.com	Newark	CA	94560	510-794-4296	574-8341
Loomis Fargo & Co 2500 Citywest Blvd Ste 900 *TF:* 866-383-5069 ■ *Web:* www.loomis.us	Houston	TX	77042	713-435-6700	
Lumenera Corp Seven Capella Ct *Web:* www.lumenera.com	Ottawa	ON	K2E8A7	613-736-4077	

Phone Fax

Mace Security International Inc
240 Gibraltar Rd Ste 220 ... Horsham PA 19044 267-317-4009
OTC: MACE ■ *Web:* corp.mace.com
Matrix Systems Inc 1041 Byers Rd ... Miamisburg OH 45342 937-438-9033 438-0900
TF: 800-562-8749 ■ *Web:* www.matrixsys.com
MDI Security Systems Inc
12500 Network Dr Ste 303 ... San Antonio TX 78249 210-477-5400 477-5401
TF: 866-435-7634 ■ *Web:* www.mdisecure.com
MMF Industries 1111 S Wheeling Rd ... Wheeling IL 60090 800-323-8181
TF: 800-323-8181 ■ *Web:* www.mmfind.com
Monitronics International Inc
2350 Valley View Ln Ste 100 ... Dallas TX 75234 972-243-7443 243-1064
TF Cust Svc: 800-290-0709 ■ *Web:* www.monitronics.com
MorphoTrust USA Inc 296 Concord Rd ... Billerica MA 01821 978-215-2400
TF: 888-245-1114 ■ *Web:* www.morphotrust.com
MSA Security Nine Murray St Second Fl ... New York NY 10007 212-509-1336
Web: www.msasecurity.net
NAPCO Security Systems Inc
333 Bayview Ave ... Amityville NY 11701 631-842-9400 842-9137
NASDAQ: NSSC ■ *TF:* 800-645-9445 ■ *Web:* www.napcosecurity.com
National Fingerprint Inc 6999 Dolan Rd ... Glouster OH 45732 740-767-3853
TF: 888-823-7873 ■ *Web:* www.nationalfingerprint.com
New England Security Inc 10 Industrial Dr ... Westerly RI 02891 401-596-0660
TF: 800-556-7395 ■ *Web:* newenglandsecurityinc.com
Norment Security Group Inc
3224 Mobile Hwy ... Montgomery AL 36108 800-466-3007 286-6421*
**Fax Area Code:* 334 ■ *TF:* 800-466-3007 ■ *Web:* cornerstonedetention.com/
Nortek Security & Control LLC
1950 Camino Vida Roble Ste 150 ... Carlsbad CA 92008 760 438 7000 931-1340
TF Cust Svc: 800-421-1587 ■ *Web:* www.linearcorp.com
OpenEye Inc 23221 E Knox Ave ... Liberty Lake WA 99019 509-232-5261
Web: www.openeye.net
Optex Inc 13661 Benson Ave Bldg C ... Chino CA 91710 909-993-5770 628-5560
TF: 800-966-7839 ■ *Web:* www.optexamerica.com
OSI Systems Inc 12525 Chadron Ave ... Hawthorne CA 90250 310-978-0516 644-1727
NASDAQ: OSIS ■ *Web:* www.osi-systems.com
Owlstone Nanotech Inc 761 Main Ave ... Norwalk CT 06851 203-908-4848
Web: www.owlstonenanotech.com
Paragon Systems Inc
13655 Dulles Technology Dr Ste 100 ... Herndon VA 20171 703-263-7176
Web: www.parasys.com
Parking Products Inc 2517 Wyandotte Rd ... Willow Grove PA 19090 215-657-7500 657-4321
Web: www.parkingproducts.com
PCSC Corp 3541 Challenger St ... Torrance CA 90503 310-303-3600
Web: www.pcscsecurity.com
Per Mar Security 1910 E Kimberly Rd ... Davenport IA 52807 563-359-3200 359-6700
TF: 800-473-7627 ■ *Web:* www.permarsecurity.com
PerkinElmer Inc 940 Winter St ... Waltham MA 02451 203-925-4602 944-4904
NYSE: PKI ■ *Web:* www.perkinelmer.com
protection One Alarm Monitoring
1035 N Third St Ste 101 ... Lawrence KS 66044 877-776-1911
TF: 800-438-4357 ■ *Web:* www.protection1.com
Public Safety Equipment Inc
10986 N Warson Rd ... St Louis MO 63114 314-426-2700
Web: code3pse.com/
PV Labs Inc 1074 Cooke Blvd Ste 400A ... Burlington ON L7T4A8 905-667-7202
TF: 888-667-7202 ■ *Web:* www.pv-labs.com
Qualys Inc 1600 Bridge Pkwy ... Redwood Shores CA 94065 650-801-6100 801-6101
TF: 866-801-6161 ■ *Web:* www.qualys.com
Radiance Technologies Inc 350 Wynn Dr ... Huntsville AL 35805 256-704-3400 704-3412
Web: www.radiancetech.com
Revo America Inc 700 Freeport Pkwy Ste 100 ... Coppell TX 75019 469-464-2800
Web: www.revoamerica.com
Ronco Consulting Corp
6710 Oxon Hill Rd Ste 200 ... Oxon Hill MD 20745 240-493-3910
Web: www.roncoconsulting.com
RS2 Technologies LLC 400 Fisher St Ste G ... Munster IN 46321 219-836-9002
Web: www.rs2tech.com
Safeguards Technology LLC 75 Atlantic St ... Hackensack NJ 07601 201-488-1022
Web: www.safeguards.com
SAFLOK 31750 Sherman Ave ... Madison Heights MI 48071 248-837-3700 583-3228
TF: 800-999-6213 ■ *Web:* www.saflok.com
Seco-Larm USA Inc 16842 Millikan Ave ... Irvine CA 92606 949-261-2999 261-7326
TF: 800-662-0800 ■ *Web:* www.seco-larm.com
SecureUSA Inc 4250 Keith Bridge Rd Ste 160 ... Cumming GA 30041 770-205-0789
Web: www.secureusa.net
Securitas Security Services USA Inc
2 Campus Dr ... Parsippany NJ 07054 973-267-5300 832-0871*
**Fax Area Code:* 323 ■ *TF:* 800-555-0906 ■ *Web:* www.securitas.com
Security Corp 22325 Roethel Dr ... Novi MI 48375 877-374-5700 374-5750*
**Fax Area Code:* 248 ■ *TF:* 877-374-5700 ■ *Web:* www.securitycorp.com
Security Defense Systems Corp 160 Pk Ave ... Nutley NJ 07110 800-325-6339 235-0132*
**Fax Area Code:* 973 ■ *TF:* 800-325-6339 ■ *Web:* www.securitydefense.com
Security Signal Devices Inc 1740 N Lemon St ... Anaheim CA 92801 800-888-0444
TF: 800-888-0444 ■ *Web:* www.ssdsystems.com
Sensormatic Electronics Corp
6600 Congress Ave ... Boca Raton FL 33487 561-912-6000 912-6097
TF: 800-327-1765 ■ *Web:* www.sensormatic.com
Sentry Group 900 Linden Ave ... Rochester NY 14625 585-381-4900 381-2940*
**Fax:* Cust Svc ■ *TF Cust Svc:* 800-828-1438 ■ *Web:* www.sentrysafe.com
Sentry Technology Corp 1881 Lakeland Ave ... Ronkonkoma NY 11779 800-645-4224 739-2124*
OTC: SKVY ■ **Fax Area Code:* 631 ■ *TF:* 800-645-4224 ■ *Web:* www.sentrytechnology.com
Sielox LLC 170 E Ninth Ave ... Runnemede NJ 08078 856-939-9300
Web: www.sielox.com
SIRCHIE Finger Print Laboratories Inc
100 Hunter Pl ... Youngsville NC 27596 919-554-2244 554-2266
TF: 800-356-7311 ■ *Web:* www.sirchie.com
Sizemore Inc 2116 Walton Way ... Augusta GA 30904 706-736-1456
TF: 800-445-1748 ■ *Web:* www.sizemoreinc.com
Slomin's Inc 125 Lauman Ln ... Hicksville NY 11801 516-932-7000
TF: 800-252-7663 ■ *Web:* www.slomins.com
Sofradir EC Inc 373 Rt 46W ... Fairfield NJ 07004 973-882-0211 882-0997
TF: 800-759-9577 ■ *Web:* www.electrophysics.com

Phone Fax

Southern Folger Detention Equipment Co
4634 S Presa St ... San Antonio TX 78223 210-533-1231 533-2211
TF: 888-745-0530 ■ *Web:* www.southernfolger.com
Teletrac Inc 7391 Lincoln Way ... Garden Grove CA 92841 714-897-0877 379-6378
TF: 800-500-6009 ■ *Web:* www.teletrac.com
Texas Industrial Security
101 Summit Ave Ste 404 ... Fort Worth TX 76102 817-335-3046 335-3048
Web: www.txsecurity.com
TrakLok Corp 11020 Solway School Rd Ste 105 ... Knoxville TN 37931 865-927-4911
Web: www.traklok.com
Tyco Fire & Security 6600 Congress Ave ... Boca Raton FL 33487 561-912-6000
Web: www.tyco.com
Tyco International Ltd Nine Roszel Rd ... Princeton NJ 08540 609-720-4200 720-4208
NYSE: TYC ■ *TF:* 800-685-4509 ■ *Web:* www.tyco.com
Unisec Inc 2555 Nicholson St ... San Leandro CA 94577 800-982-4587 352-6707*
**Fax Area Code:* 510 ■ *TF:* 800-982-4587 ■ *Web:* www.ultrabarrier.com
Universal Security Instruments Inc
11407 Cronhill Dr ... Owings Mills MD 21117 410-363-3000 363-2218
TSE: UUU ■ *TF:* 800-390-4321 ■ *Web:* www.universalsecurity.com
VASCO Data Security International Inc
1901 S Meyers Rd Ste 210 ... Oakbrook Terrace IL 60181 630-932-8844 932-8852
NASDAQ: VDSI ■ *Web:* www.vasco.com
Vector Security Inc 2000 Ericsson Dr ... Warrendale PA 15086 800-832-8575 741-2299*
**Fax Area Code:* 724 ■ *TF:* 800-832-8575 ■ *Web:* www.vectorsecurity.com
Verint Video Solutions 330 South Service Rd ... Melville NY 11747 800-483-7468 483-9790*
**Fax Area Code:* 301 ■ *TF:* 800-638-5969 ■ *Web:* www.verint.com
Videolarm Inc 2525 Park Central Blvd ... Decatur GA 30035 770-987-7550
Web: www.videolarm.com
Winner International LLC 32 W State St ... Sharon PA 16146 724-981-1152 981-1034
TF: 800-258-2321 ■ *Web:* www.winner-intl.com

696 SECURITY & PROTECTIVE SERVICES

SEE ALSO Investigative Services p. 2590

Phone Fax

2GIG Technologies Inc
2961 West Maple Loop Dr Ste 300 ... Lehi UT 84043 801-221-9162
Web: www.2gig.com
5 Alarm Fire & Safety Equipment LLC
350 Austin Cir ... Delafield WI 53018 262-646-5911
TF: 800-615-6789 ■ *Web:* www.5alarm.com
A & R Security Service Inc
2552 W 135th St ... Blue Island IL 60406 708-389-3830 389-7734
Web: www.universalpro.com
A b s Advanced Business Solutions
600 S John Redditt Dr ... Lufkin TX 75904 936-639-4744
A Better Solution Inc 4303 Cedar Lk Cv ... Conley GA 30288 770-252-1500
Web: www.abs-consulting.com
A10 Networks Inc Three W Plumeria Dr ... San Jose CA 95134 408-325-8668
TF: 888-210-6363 ■ *Web:* www.a10networks.com
AAA Alarm Systems Ltd 180 Nature Park Way ... Winnipeg MB R3P0X7 204-949-0078
Web: www.aaaalarms.ca
ABC Security Service Inc 1840 Embarcadero ... Oakland CA 94606 510-436-0666
ABM Industries Inc 8020 W Doe Ste C ... Visalia SC 93291 559-651-1612 579-9578*
**Fax Area Code:* 864 ■ *Web:* www.abm.com
Accurate Controls 326 Blackburn St ... Ripon WI 54971 920-748-6603
Web: www.accuratecontrols.com
Accuvant Inc 1125 17th St Ste 1700 ... Denver CO 80202 303-298-0600 298-0868
TF: 800-574-0896 ■ *Web:* www.accuvant.com
Action Security Inc 243 E Fifth Ave ... Anchorage AK 99501 907-279-7050
Web: actionsecurity.com
Admiral Security Services Inc
5550 W Touhy Ave Ste 101 ... Skokie IL 60077 847-588-0888
Web: www.admiralsecuritychicago.com
Advanced Alarm Systems Inc
101 Lindsey St Ste 12 ... Fall River MA 02720 508-675-1937
Web: www.advancedalarmsystems.com
Advent Security Corp 101 Roesch Ave ... Oreland PA 19075 215-576-7111
Web: www.adventsecurity.com
Aiphone Corp 1700 130th Ave NE ... Bellevue WA 98005 425-455-0510
Web: www.aiphone.com
Alarm Security Group LLC
12301 Kiln Court Ste A ... Beltsville MD 20705 301-937-8880
Web: www.asgsecurity.com
All American Private Security Inc
421 S Glendora Ave Ste A ... West Covina CA 91790 626-962-9620
Web: www.allamericansecurity.com
All Phase Security Inc
2959 Promenade St Ste 200 ... West Sacramento CA 95691 916-375-6640
Web: www.allphasesecurity.com
Allegiance Security Group LLC
2900 Arendell St Ste 18 ... Morehead City NC 28557 252-247-1138
TF: 866-747-2748 ■ *Web:* www.allegiancesecurityteam.com
Alliance Home Health Care Inc
5930 Hohman Ave Ste 102 ... Hammond IN 46320 219-852-5101
Web: alliancehomehealthcare.net
AlliedBarton Security Services
150 S Warner Rd ... King of Prussia PA 19406 484-654-3800 239-1107
TF: 866-703-7666 ■ *Web:* www.alliedbarton.com
Alrod Enterprises Inc 119 N Sycamore St ... Petersburg VA 23803 804-732-3972
Web: www.alrodenterprises.com
Am-Gard Security Inc 600 Main St ... Pittsburgh PA 15215 412-781-5800
Web: www.am-gard.com
American Services Inc 1300 Rutherford Rd ... Greenville SC 29609 864-292-7450
TF: 877-292-7450 ■ *Web:* www.american-services-inc.com
Ameriguard Security Services Inc
5470 W Spruce Ave Ste 102 ... Fresno CA 93722 559-271-5984
Web: ameriguard.publishpath.com/
Amherst Alarm Inc 435 Lawrence Bell Dr ... Amherst NY 14221 716-632-4600
Web: www.amherstalarm.com

Phone | Fax

Anderson Security Agency Ltd
2555 W Morningside Dr ... Phoenix AZ 85023 602-331-7000
Web: www.andersonsecurity.com
Andy Frain Services Inc 761 Shoreline Dr ... Aurora IL 60504 630-820-3820
TF: 877-707-4771 ■ *Web:* www.andyfrain.com
Apex3 Security 8750 W Bryn Mawr Ave ... Chicago IL 60631 773-867-9204
Web: levysecurity.com
APG Security Inc 116 N Broadway ... South Amboy NJ 08879 732-553-1537
Web: www.apgsecurity.com
Api Security Services & Investigations Inc
867 High St Ste D ... Worthington OH 43085 614-310-1980
Web: apisecurity.us
APL Access & Security Inc
115 S William Dillard Dr ... Gilbert AZ 85233 480-497-9471
TF: 866-873-2288 ■ *Web:* www.aplsecurity.com
Arkansas Automatic Sprinklers Inc 185 Arena Rd ... Cabot AR 72023 501-843-9392
Web: www.arautosprinklers.com
Arrow Security Patrols 60 Knickerbocker Ave ... Bohemia NY 11716 631-675-2430
Web: www.arrowsecurity.net
Asia Pacific Center for Security
2058 Maluhia Rd ... Honolulu HI 96815 808-971-8900
Web: www.apcss.org
ASP Inc 460 Brant St Ste 212 ... Burlington ON L7R4B6 905-333-4242 481-1966*
*Fax Area Code: 416 ■ *TF:* 877-552-5535 ■ *Web:* www.security-asp.com
ASSI Security Inc 1370 Reynolds Ave Ste 201 ... Irvine CA 92614 949-955-0244
Web: www.assisecurity.com
ASSIST Aviation Solutions LLC
117 Perimeter Rd ... Nashua NH 03063 603-505-4668
Web: www.assist-us.com
Atcc 757 Barbershop Rd ... Edinburg VA 22824 540-984-8443
Avante Security Inc 1959 Leslie St ... Toronto ON M3B2M3 416-923-6984
Web: www.avantesecurity.com
AWP Inc 826 Overholt Rd ... Kent OH 44240 800-343-2650
Web: www.awptrafficsafety.com
B b C Security & Communication Inc
401 Mclean Ave ... Yonkers NY 10705 914-969-4000
Web: bbcsecurity.com
Barnes Alarm Systems Inc
3201 Flagler Ave Ste 503 ... Key West FL 33040 305-294-6753
Web: barnesalarmsystems.com
Bms Integrated Services Inc
1277 Georgia St E ... Vancouver BC V6A2A9 604-676-0136
Web: bmscom.com
Bonafide Security Solutions
3605 N 126th St ... Brookfield WI 53005 262-790-9400
Web: www.bonafidesafe.com
Bot Home Automation Inc 1523 26th St ... Santa Monica CA 90404 310-929-7085
Web: www.ring.com
Boyd & Assoc Inc 6319 Colfax Ave ... North Hollywood CA 91606 818-752-1888
Web: www.boydsecurity.com
Brink's Inc 555 Dividend Dr Ste 100 ... Coppell TX 75019 469-549-6000
TF: 800-274-6575 ■ *Web:* www.brinksinc.com
Brokers International Financial Services LLC
102 Se 13th St ... Panora IA 50216 641-755-4635
Web: www.brokersifs.com
Business Protection Specialists Inc
250 Gorham St Ste 4 ... Canandaigua NY 14424 585-394-5112
Web: www.securingpeople.com
By Taylor Made Irrigation 750 Barsby St ... Vista CA 92084 760-945-0118
C & d Security Management Inc
306 Delaware Dr ... Colorado Springs CO 80909 719-597-0750
Web: www.canddsecurity.com
Cansec Systems Ltd 3105 Unity Dr Unit 9 ... Mississauga ON L5L4L2 905-820-2404
Web: www.cansec.com
Cass 1810 Water Pl SE Ste 180 ... Atlanta GA 30339 770-916-0060
Web: www.cassecurity.com
Castlegarde Inc 4911 S W Shore Blvd ... Tampa FL 33611 813-872-4844
Web: www.castlegarde.com
Caveon LLC 6905 South 1300 East Ste 468 ... Midvale UT 84047 801-208-0103
Web: www.caveon.com
Cbm 2614 Hickory St ... Santa Ana CA 92707 714-424-9250
Web: www.cbme.net
CelAccess Systems Inc 13619 Inwood Rd Ste 360 ... Dallas TX 75244 972-231-1999
Web: www.celaccess.com
Central Defense Security
50 Vantage Way Ste 251 ... Nashville TN 37228 615-256-0300
Web: www.centdef.com
Checkview Corp 8180 upland cir ... Chanhassen MN 55317 952-227-5853
Web: www.checkview.com
Cincinnatus Consulting LLC
1721 Spruce St ... Philadelphia PA 19103 267-872-0313
Web: www.cincinnatus-consulting.com
CNB Technology USA Inc
2310 E Artesia Blvd ... Long Beach CA 90805 562-728-8500
Web: www.cnbusa.com
Command Security Corp
388 Westchester Ave Ste 1J/H ... Port Chester NY 10573 914-937-2969 939-2808
TF: 877-331-8056 ■ *Web:* www.commandsecurity.com
Control Microsystems Inc 48 Steacie Dr ... Kanata ON K2K2A9 613-591-1943
Web: www2.schneider-electric.com
Convergint Technologies LLC
1651 Wilkening Rd ... Schaumburg IL 60173 847-229-0222
Web: www.convergint.com
Cook Security Group Inc
5841 SE International Way ... Milwaukie OR 97222 503-786-5173
Web: www.cooksecuritygroup.com
Counterforce Inc
2740 Matheson Blvd E Unit 2A ... Mississauga ON L4W4X3 905-282-6200
Web: www.counterforce.com
Creative Security Company Inc
150 S Autumn St Ste B ... San Jose CA 95110 408-295-2600
Web: www.creativesecurity.com
Crimetek Security Services
3448 N Golden State Blvd ... Turlock CA 95382 209-668-6208
Web: www.crimetek.com
CTC International Group Inc
330 Clematis St Ste 220 ... West Palm Beach FL 33401 561-655-3111
Web: ctcintl.com
Custom Communications Inc
1661 Greenview Dr SW ... Rochester MN 55902 507-288-5522
Web: www.custom-alarm.com
Denco Security System LLC
4605 Clear Creek Pkwy ... Northport AL 35475 205-333-9931
Dial Security Inc 760 W Ventura Blvd ... Camarillo CA 93010 805-389-6700
Web: www.dialcomm.com
Diamond Group 13101 Preston Rd Ste 212 ... Dallas TX 75240 972-788-1111 788-0077
Web: www.thediamondgroup.ws
DIGIOP Inc
3850 Priority Way S Dr Ste 200 ... Indianapolis IN 46240 317-489-0413
Web: www.digiop.com
Digital Watchdog Inc 5436 W Crenshaw St ... Tampa FL 33634 813-888-9555
Web: digital-watchdog.com
Dk Security 5160 falcon view ave se ... Grand rapids MI 49512 616-656-0123
Web: www.dksecurity.com
DSA Detection LLC 120 Water St Ste 211 ... North Andover MA 01845 978-975-3200
Web: www.dsadetection.com
DSX Access Systems Inc 10731 Rockwall Rd ... Dallas TX 75238 214-553-6140 553-6147
TF: 888-419-8353 ■ *Web:* www.dsxinc.com
Dynamic Security Inc 1102 Woodward Ave ... Muscle Shoals AL 35661 256-383-5798
Web: www.dynamic.cc
E P S 8845 Basil Western Rd ... Canal Winchester OH 43110 614-834-9126
Web: www.epsohio.com
East Coast Security Services Inc 68 Stiles Rd ... Salem NH 03079 603-898-6823
TF: 800-639-2086 ■ *Web:* www.ecss.com
ECSI International Inc
790 Bloomfield Ave Bldg C-1 ... Clifton NJ 07012 973-574-8555
Web: www.ecsiinternational.com
Electroworld Security Systems 867 E 26th St ... Brooklyn NY 11210 718-338-5831
eLine Technology
1070 W 124th Ave Ste B-100 ... Westminster CO 80234 303-938-1133
Web: www.elinetechnology.com
Elite Investigations Ltd 538 W 29th St ... New York NY 10001 212-629-3131
Web: www.eliteinvestigation.com
EMERgency24 Inc 4179 W Irving Park Rd ... Chicago IL 60641 773-777-0707
Web: www.emergency24.com
eV Microelectronics Inc 373 Saxonburg Blvd ... Saxonburg PA 16056 724-352-5288
Web: www.evmicroelectronics.com
Excelsior Defense Inc
2232 Central Ave ... Saint Petersburg FL 33712 727-527-9600
Web: www.excelsiordefense.com
Execushield Inc 4104 24th St ... San Francisco CA 94114 415-508-0825
Web: www.execushield.com
Executive Technologies Corp
8731 Northpark Blvd Ste B ... Charleston SC 29406 843-824-5906
Web: www.executivetechcorp.com
FE Moran Security Solutions
201 W University Ave ... Champaign IL 61820 217-403-6444
Web: www.femoranalarm.com
Federal Protection Inc
2500 N Airport Commerce Ave ... Springfield MO 65803 417-869-9192
TF: 800-299-5400
Fidelco Guide Dog Foundation Inc
103 Vision Way ... Bloomfield CT 06002 860-243-5200
Web: fidelco.org
Finotex USA Corp 6942 NW 50th St ... Miami FL 33166 305-470-2400
Web: www.finotex.com
First Alarm Security & Patrol Inc
1111 Estates Dr ... Aptos CA 95003 831-476-1111
TF: 800-684-1111 ■ *Web:* www.firstalarm.com
FJC Security Services Inc
275 Jericho Tpke ... Floral Park NY 11001 516-328-6000
TF: 888-832-6352 ■ *Web:* www.fjcsecurity.com
Fluent Home Ltd 7319 104 St NW ... Edmonton AB T6E4B9 855-238-4826
TF: 855-238-4826 ■ *Web:* myfluenthome.com
Galaxy Integrated Technologies
100 Leo M Birmingham Pkwy ... Brighton MA 02135 617-202-6388
Web: www.galaxyintegrated.com
Garda World Security Corp 1390 Barre St ... Montreal QC H3C1N4 514-281-2811 281-2811
TSE: GW ■ *TF:* 800-859-1599 ■ *Web:* www.gardaglobal.com
General Security Services Corp
9110 Meadowview Rd ... Minneapolis MN 55425 952-858-5000
Web: www.gssc.net
Geutebruck Security Inc
750 Miller Dr Ste A-5 ... Leesburg VA 20175 703-378-4856
Web: geutebrueck.com
GHS Interactive Security Inc
2081 Arena Blvd Ste 260 ... Sacramento CA 95834 855-208-2447
TF: 855-208-2447 ■ *Web:* ghssecurity.com
Gillmore Security Systems Inc
26165 Broadway Ave ... Cleveland OH 44146 440-232-1000
TF: 800-899-8995 ■ *Web:* www.gillmoresecurity.com
Global Security Assoc LLC
825 E Gate Blvd Ste 301 ... Garden City NY 11530 516-414-0487
Web: www.globaleliteinc.com
Golden Glow Investigative & Protective Services
147 Belmont Blvd ... Elmont NY 11003 516-437-7486
Web: goldenglowsecurity.com
Greater Alarm Company Inc 17992 Cowan ... Irvine CA 92614 949-474-0555
Web: www.interfacesys.com
Grupo Golan Company Inc 18619 Long Lk Dr ... Boca Raton FL 33496 561-483-9972
Guard Systems Inc
1190 Monterey Pass Rd ... Monterey Park CA 91754 323-881-6711 261-7841
TF: 800-606-6711 ■ *Web:* www.guardsystemsinc.com
Guardian Alarm 20800 Southfield Rd ... Southfield MI 48075 248-423-1000 423-3009
TF: 800-782-9688 ■ *Web:* www.guardianalarm.com

				Phone	Fax
Guardian Protection Services Inc 174 Thorn Hill Rd	Warrendale	PA	15086	855-779-2001	741-3541*
*Fax Area Code: 724 ■ TF Cust Svc: 877-314-7092 ■ Web: www.guardianprotection.com					
guardNOW Inc 16209 Victory Blvd Ste 302	Van Nuys	CA	91406	877-482-7366	
TF: 877-482-7366 ■ Web: www.guardnow.com					
Guardsmark Inc 10 Rockefeller Plz 12th Fl	New York	NY	10020	212-765-8226	
TF: 800-238-5878 ■ Web: www.guardsmark.com					
Habitec Security Inc 2926 S Republic Blvd	Toledo	OH	43615	419-537-6768	
TF: 888-422-4832 ■ Web: www.habitecsecurity.com					
Hannon Security Services Inc 9036 Grand Ave S	Minneapolis	MN	55420	952-881-5865	
TF: 800-328-3877 ■ Web: www.hannonsecurity.com					
Hepaco Inc 2711 Burch Dr PO Box 26308	Charlotte	NC	28269	704-598-9782	598-7823
TF: 800-888-7689 ■ Web: www.hepaco.com					
Honor Guard Security Inc 1965 Bernice Rd Ste 1 NW 1045	Lansing	IL	60438	708-418-3059	
Web: www.hgsecurity.biz					
Houston Harris Div Patrol Inc 6420 Richmond Ave	Houston	TX	77057	713-975-9922	
TF: 877-975-9922 ■ Web: www.hhdpi.com					
Huffmaster Crisis Management 1300 Combermere Dr	Troy	MI	48083	248-588-1600	
Web: huffmaster.com					
Hy-Safe Technology Inc 960 Commerce Dr	Union Grove	WI	53182	262-752-2400	
Web: www.hysafe.com					
IBI Armored Services Inc 37-06 61st St	Woodside	NY	11377	718-458-4000	458-5371
Web: www.ibiarmored.com					
Id Experts Corp 10300 SW Greenburg Rd Ste 570	Portland	OR	97008	503-726-4500	
Web: www.idexpertscorp.com					
Imaging Locators Inc 3751 S Seneca	Pahrump	NV	89048	775-751-6931	
Web: www.imaginglocators.com					
Information Network Assoc Inc 5235 N Front St	Harrisburg	PA	17110	717-599-5505	
TF: 800-443-0824 ■ Web: www.ina-inc.com					
Innovative Industrial Solutions Inc 2830 Skyline Dr	Russellville	AR	72802	479-968-4266	
TF: 888-684-8249 ■ Web: www.i-i-s.net					
Intec Video Systems Inc 23301 Vista Grande Dr	Laguna Hills	CA	92653	949-859-3800	
TF: 800-468-3254 ■ Web: www.intecvideo.com					
Ionit Technologies Inc 601 Academy Dr	Northbrook	IL	60062	847-205-9651	
Web: www.ionitusa.com					
IPC International Corp 2111 Waukegan Rd	Bannockburn	IL	60015	847-444-2000	444-2001
Ipss Inc 150 Isabella St	Ottawa	ON	K1S1V7	613-232-2228	231-4888
Web: ipss.ca					
Isr 264 Main St	Sugar Grove	IL	60554	630-466-7800	
Web: www.isr-usa.com					
Itech Digital LLC 4287 W 96th St	Indianapolis	IN	46268	317-704-0440	
Web: itechdigital.com					
J & J Security Services Corp 2922 Howland Blvd Ste 2	Deltona	FL	32725	386-789-5555	
Web: www.jandjsecurity.com					
JBM Patrol & Protection Corp 3110 Kingsley Way	Madison	WI	53713	608-222-5156	
Web: jbmpatrol.com					
JMG Security Systems Inc 17150 Newhope St Ste 109	Fountain Valley	CA	92708	714-545-8882	
TF: 800-900-4564 ■ Web: www.jmgsecurity.com					
Kent Security Services Inc 14600 Biscayne Blvd	North Miami Beach	FL	33181	305-919-9400	
TF: 800-273-5368 ■ Web: www.kentsecurity.com					
King Security Services Inc 1458 Howard St	San Francisco	CA	94103	415-556-5464	
Web: www.kingsecurity.com					
Knight Security Systems LLC 10105 Technology Blvd W Ste 100	Dallas	TX	75220	214-350-1632	
Web: www.knightsecurity.com					
L3 Stratis 941 mercantile dr	Hanover	MD	21076	410-694-4900	
Web: l-3nss.com					
Lantz Security Systems Inc 43440 Sahuayo St	Lancaster	CA	93535	661-949-3565	
Web: www.lantzsecurity.com					
Law Enforcement Assoc Corp (LEA) 120 Penmarc Dr Ste 125	Raleigh	NC	27616	919-872-6210	872-6431
OTC: LAWEQ ■ TF: 800-354-9669 ■ Web: www.leacorp.com					
Logitech WiLife 132 East 13065 South Ste 200	Draper	UT	84020	801-316-4700	
Web: online.wilife.com					
Loomis Armored US Inc 2500 Citywest Blvd Ste 900	Houston	TX	77042	713-435-6700	
TF: 866-383-5069 ■ Web: www.loomis.us					
Madison Security Group Inc 31 Kirk St	Lowell	MA	01852	978-459-5911	
Web: www.madisonsg.com					
Maloney Security Inc 1055 Laurel St	San Carlos	CA	94070	650-593-0163	593-1101
Web: www.maloneysecurityinc.com					
MaxBotix Inc 7594 S Long Lk Bay Rd	Brainerd	MN	56401	218-454-0766	
Web: www.maxbotix.com					
McRoberts Protective Agency Inc 87 Nassau St	New York	NY	10038	212-425-6500	
Web: www.mcroberts1876.com					
Merchants Building Maintenance LLC 786 Monterey Pass Rd	Monterey Park	CA	91754	323-881-6700	
Web: www.mbmonline.com					
Mijac Alarm 9339 Charles Smith Ave Ste 100	Rancho Cucamonga	CA	91730	909-982-7612	481-0124
TF: 800-982-7612 ■ Web: www.mijacalarm.com					
Mircom Technologies Ltd 25 Interchange Way	Vaughan	ON	L4K5W3	905-660-4655	660-4113
TF: 888-660-4655 ■ Web: www.mircom.com					
Monument Security Inc 5844 Price Ave	Sacramento	CA	95652	916-564-4234	
Web: monumentsecurity.com					
Murray Guard Inc 58 Murray Guard Dr	Jackson	TN	38305	731-668-3400	664-1343
TF: 800-238-3830 ■ Web: www.murrayguard.com					
MVM Inc 44620 Guilford Dr	Ashburn	VA	20147	571-223-4500	223-4474
Web: www.mvminc.com					

				Phone	Fax
My Alarm Center LLC 3803 W Chester Pike Ste 100	Newtown Square	PA	19073	866-484-4800	
TF: 866-484-4800 ■ Web: www.myalarmcenter.com					
Nabco Inc 1001 Corporate Dr Ste 205	Canonsburg	PA	15317	724-746-9617	
Web: www.nabcoinc.com					
National Monitoring Center 26800 Aliso Viejo Pkwy Ste 250	Aliso Viejo	CA	92656	800-662-1711	
Web: www.nmccentral.com					
Network Multi-Family Security Corp 4221 W John Carpenter Fwy	Irving	TX	75063	972-490-9902	
TF: 800-541-3138 ■ Web: protection1.com/business/multifamily-security-systems/					
Nevis Networks Inc 295 Bernardo Ave	Mountain View	CA	94043	650-254-2500	
Web: www.nevisnetworks.com					
New York Merchants Protective Company Inc 75 W Merrick Rd	Freeport	NY	11520	516-561-5210	
TF: 888-696-7911 ■ Web: www.nympc.com					
Next Level Security Systems Inc 6353 Corte Del Abeto Ste 102	Carlsbad	CA	92011	760-444-1410	
Web: www.nlss.com					
Northwest Protective Service Inc 801 S Fidalgo 2nd Fl	Seattle	WA	98108	206-448-4040	448-2461
TF: 866-877-1965 ■ Web: www.nwprotective.com					
Northwestern Ohio Security Systems Inc 121 E High St	Lima	OH	45801	614-527-7037	
TF: 800-833-6416 ■ Web: www.nwoss.com					
Nuclear Security Services Corp 701 Willowbrook Centre Pkwy	Willowbrook	IL	60527	630-920-1488	
Web: www.g4s.us					
O'Gara Group Inc, The 7870 E Kemper Rd Ste 460	Cincinnati	OH	45249	513-338-0660	
Web: www.ogaragroup.com					
Okaloosa - Walton Security & Surveillancellc 593 Hubbard St	Defuniak Springs	FL	32435	850-892-4550	
Web: okaloosa-waltonsecurityandsurveillance.com					
Olympic Security Services Inc 631 Strander Blvd Ste A	Tukwila	WA	98188	206-575-8531	
Web: www.olympiksecurity.com					
Omega Security Service Inc 103 Yost Blvd Ste 100A	Pittsburgh	PA	15221	412-349-0850	
Web: www.omega-security.com					
OpSec Security Inc 1857 Colonial Village Ln	Lancaster	PA	17601	717-293-4110	
Web: www.aotgroup.com					
Optellios Inc 11 Penns Trl Ste 300	Newtown	PA	18940	267-364-5298	
Web: www.optellios.com					
OSI Security Devices Inc 1580 Jayken Way	Chula Vista	CA	91911	619-628-1000	
TF: 800-711-6814 ■ Web: www.omnilock.com					
Pacific Security Integrations Inc 99-1285 Halawa Vly Rd	Aiea	HI	96701	808-484-4000	
Web: pacsecinc.com					
Pasek Corp Nine W Third St	South Boston	MA	02127	617-269-7110	
TF: 800-628-2822 ■ Web: www.pasek.com					
Pass Security LLC 340 Office Court Ste B	Fairview Heights	IL	62208	618-394-1144	
Web: www.passsecurity.com					
Patrol One 630 S Grand Ave Ste 101	Santa Ana	CA	92705	714-541-0999	
Web: www.patrol-one.com					
Perey Turnstiles Inc 308 Bishop Ave	Bridgeport	CT	06610	203-333-9400	
Web: www.turnstile.com					
Perimeter Security Solutions Inc 1900 Fannin St	Vernon	TX	76384	940-552-2942	
Web: www.perimetersecuritysolutions.com					
Photo-scan of Los Angeles 743 Cochran St Ste C	Simi Valley	CA	93065	805-581-4448	
Web: www.pslasecurity.com					
Pierce County Security Inc 2002 99th St E	Tacoma	WA	98445	253-535-4433	
TF: 800-773-4432 ■ Web: www.pcswa.com					
Pivot Point Security 1245 Whitehorse Mercerville Rd	Trenton	NJ	08619	609-581-4600	
Web: pivotpointsecurity.com					
Point 2 Point Global Security Inc 14346 Jarrettsville Pike Ste 200	Phoenix	MD	21131	410-638-8788	
Web: www.p2pgsi.net					
Pontis Research Inc 4195 E Thousand Oaks Blvd Ste 105	Westlake Village	CA	91362	805-777-7424	
Web: www.pontisresearch.com					
Port Security International LLC 40 Calhoun St Ste 230	Charleston	SC	29401	843-723-9255	
Web: www.secureports.com					
Post Alarm Systems Inc 47 E Saint Joseph St	Arcadia	CA	91006	626-446-7159	
Web: www.postalarm.com					
Premier Electronics Inc 465 Rockaway Ave	Valley Stream	NY	11581	516-837-3160	
Prestige Alarm & Specialty Products Inc 7640 Commerce Ln P.O. Box 9	Trussville	AL	35173	205-661-4822	
Web: www.prestigealarm.com					
Prestige Security 5855 Green Vly Cir	Culver City	CA	90230	310-670-5999	
Web: www.prestigesecurity.com					
Pro Security Group 301B S Robinson Dr	Robinson	TX	76706	254-753-7766	
Web: prosecuritygroup.com					
Prodco International Inc 4529 de Castille	Montreal	QC	H1H1Y3	514-324-9796	
Web: www.prodcotech.com					
Protran Technology LLC 52 Paterson Ave	Newton	NJ	07860	973-250-4176	
Web: www.protrantechnology.com					
Pyro-Comm Systems Inc 15531 Container Ln	Huntington Beach	CA	92649	714-902-8000	
Web: www.pyrocomm.com					
R & d Professional Services LLC 3000 Keller Springs Rd Ste 200	Carrollton	TX	75006	214-483-5342	
Web: www.rndconsult.com					

				Phone	Fax
Rancho Santa Fe Protective Services Inc 1991 Vlg Pk Way Ste 100 *Web:* www.rsfsecurity.com	Encinitas	CA	92024	760-942-0688	
Ranger American Calle Marginal Lodi 605 Ave 65 Infanteria Villa Capri Rio Piedras *Web:* www.rangeramerican.com	San Juan	PR	00924	787-999-6060	
Rapid Focus Security LLC 253 Summer St Ste 303 *TF:* 855-793-1337 ■ *Web:* www.pwnieexpress.com	Boston	MA	02210	855-793-1337	
Rapid Response Monitoring Services Inc 400 W Division St. *TF:* 800-558-7767 ■ *Web:* www.rrms.com	Syracuse	NY	13204	800-558-7767	
Razberi Technologies Inc 1628 Valwood Pkwy Ste 148 *Web:* www.razberi.net	Carrollton	TX	75006	469-828-3380	
Rebellion Photonics Inc 7547 South Fwy *Web:* rebellionphotonics.com	Houston	TX	77021	713-218-0101	
RECON Dynamics LLC 2300 Carillon Point *TF:* 877-480-3551 ■ *Web:* www.recondynamics.com	Kirkland	WA	98033	877-480-3551	
Redrock Security & Cabling Inc 6 Morgan Ste 150 *Web:* www.itredrock.com	Irvine	CA	92618	949-900-3460	
Redwire LLC 1136 Thomasville Rd *Web:* redwireus.com	Tallahassee	FL	32303	850-219-9473	
Reliance Protectron Security Services 4209-99 St Ste 102 *Web:* www.voxcom.com	Edmonton	AB	T6E5V7	780-462-1657	
RIEtech Global LLC 3700 Singer Blvd NE Ste A *Web:* www.sagebrushtech.com	Albuquerque	NM	87109	505-299-6623	
RLE Technologies Inc 104 Racquette Dr *Web:* rletech.com	Fort Collins	CO	80524	970 484 6510	
Rochester Armored Car Company Inc 3937 Leavenworth St *Web:* www.rochesterarmoredcar.com	Omaha	NE	68105	402-558-9323	
Rodbat Security Services 8125 Somerset Blvd *Web:* www.rmiintl.com	Paramount	CA	90723	562-806-9098	
Safe Home Security Inc 55 Sebethe Dr *Web:* www.safehomesecurityinc.com	Cromwell	CT	06416	860-262-4000	
Safe Security 3550 Nw Byron St Ste A *Web:* safesecurity.us	Silverdale	WA	98383	360-698-9800	
Safeguard Security & Communications Inc 8454 N 90th St *TF:* 800-426-6060 ■ *Web:* safeguardsecurity.com/	Scottsdale	AZ	85258	480-609-6200	
Safety Service Systems Inc 4036 N Nashville Ave *Web:* www.safetyservicesystems.com	Chicago	IL	60634	773-282-4900	
Scarsdale Security Systems Inc 132 Montgomery Ave *Web:* scarsdalesecurity.com/index.html	Scarsdale	NY	10583	914-722-2200	
SDI Chicago 33 West Monroe Ste 400 *TF:* 888-968-7734 ■ *Web:* www.sdisolutions.com	Chicago	IL	60603	312-580-7500	580-7600
Secom International 9610 Bellanca Ave *Web:* www.secomintl.com	Los Angeles	CA	90045	310-641-1290	
Secure Mentem Inc 1910 Towne Centre Blvd Ste 250 *Web:* www.securementem.com	Annapolis	MD	21401	443-603-0200	
Securenet Alarm Systems Inc 10501 W Hampton Lakes St *Web:* www.securenetalarms.com	Maize	KS	67101	316-945-5630	
Securiguard Inc 6858 Old Dominion Dr Ste 307 *Web:* www.securiguardinc.com	Mclean	VA	22101	703-821-6777	
Security & Access Systems 3811 Rutledge Rd Ne *Web:* www.securityandaccess.com	Albuquerque	NM	87109	505-823-1561	
Security & Data Technologies Inc 101 Pheasant Run	Newtown	PA	18940	215-579-7000	579-7080
Security Equipment Inc 13505 C St *Web:* www.sei-security.com	Omaha	NE	68144	402-333-3233	
Security Horizon Inc 5350 Tomah Dr Ste 3200 *Web:* www.securityhorizon.com	Colorado Springs	CO	80918	719-488-4500	
Security Information Systems Inc 6314 Kingspointe Pkwy Ste 3 *Web:* www.securitysoftware.com	Orlando	FL	32819	407-345-1550	
Security Instrument Corp of Delaware 309 W Newport Pk *Web:* www.securityinstrument.com	Wilmington	DE	19804	302-633-5621	
Security Management Systems Inc 225 Community Dr Ste 150 *Web:* www.securitymgt.com	Great Neck	NY	11021	516-450-3120	
Security Resource Group Inc 300-1914 Hamilton St *Web:* www.securityresourcegroup.com	Regina	SK	S4P3N6	306-522-0135	
Seico Security Systems 132 Court St *Web:* seicosecurity.com	Pekin	IL	61554	309-347-3200	
Select Engineered Systems 7991 W 26th Ave *TF:* 800-342-5737 ■ *Web:* www.selectses.com	Hialeah	FL	33016	305-823-5410	
Senstar Corp 119 John Cavanaugh Dr *Web:* senstar.com	Carp	ON	K0A1L0	613-839-5572	
Sentinel Offender Services LLC 220 Technology Dr Ste 200 *Web:* www.sentrak.com	Irvine	CA	92618	949-453-1550	
Sentry 360 Security Inc 1280 Iroquois Ave Ste 102 *Web:* sentry360.com	Naperville	IL	60563	630-355-3440	
Sentry Alarm Systems of America Inc Eight Thomas Owens Way *Web:* sentryalarm.com	Monterey	CA	93940	831-375-2727	
Sentry Security LLC 339 Egidi Dr *TF:* 888-272-7080 ■ *Web:* www.sentrysecurity.com	Wheeling	IL	60090	847-353-7200	

				Phone	Fax
Sentry Watch Inc 1705 Holbrook St *Web:* www.sentrywatch.com	Greensboro	NC	27403	336-292-6468	
SFI Electronics Inc 400A Clanton Rd *Web:* www.sfi-electronics.com	Charlotte	NC	28217	704-522-0800	
SFRi LLC 242 California St *Web:* www.sfrillc.com	San Francisco	CA	94111	415-394-3900	
SIC Biometrics Inc 172 Harwood Blvd *Web:* www.sic.ca	Dorion	QC	J7V1Y2	450-424-2772	
Silver Shield Security Inc 2107 N First St Ste 100 *Web:* hugedomains.com/domain_profile.cfm?d=silvershieldsecurity&e=com	San Jose	CA	95131	408-435-1111	
Smith Monitoring Inc 550 E 15th St *Web:* www.smithmonitoring.com	Plano	TX	75074	469-250-8866	
Smith Protective Services Inc 8918 John W Carpenter Fwy *Web:* www.smithprotective.com	Dallas	TX	75247	214-631-4444	631-4241
SNUPI Technologies Inc 4512 University Way NE *Web:* www.wallyhome.com	Seattle	WA	98105	206-673-2707	
Sonavation Inc 3970 RCA Blvd Ste 7003 *Web:* sonavation.com	Palm Beach Gardens	FL	33410	561-209-1201	
St Moritz Security Services Inc 4600 Clairton Blvd *TF:* 800-218-9156 ■ *Web:* www.smssi.com	Pittsburgh	PA	15236	412-885-3144	
Staff Pro Inc 15272 Newsboy Cir *Web:* www.staffpro.com	Huntington Beach	CA	92649	714-230-7200	
Starr Security Services 601 W 51st St *Web:* starrsecurityservices.com	New York	NY	10019	212-767-1110	
Stealth Monitoring Inc 15182 Marsh Lane *TF:* 855-783-2584 ■ *Web:* www.stealthmonitoring.com	Dallas	TX	75001	214-341-0123	
Strongauth Inc 10846 Via San Marino *Web:* www.strongauth.com	Cupertino	CA	95014	408-331-2000	
Summit Security Services Inc 390 Rexcorp Plz W Tower - Lobby Level *TF:* 800-615-5888 ■ *Web:* www.summitsecurity.com	Uniondale	NY	11556	516-240-2400	
Superior Alarm Systems 9001 Canoga Ave *Web:* www.sassecurity.com	Canoga Park	CA	91304	818-700-7100	
Supreme Security Systems Inc 1565 Union Ave *Web:* www.supremesecurity.com	Union	NJ	07083	908-810-8822	
Systemes De Securite Paradox Ltee 780 Industrial Blvd *Web:* www.paradox.ca	St-eustache	QC	J7R5V3	450-491-7444	
Tenable Protective Services Inc 2423 Payne Ave *Web:* www.anchor-security.com	Cleveland	OH	44114	216-361-0002	
Texas Dept of Public Safety 1001 E Coke Rd	Winnsboro	TX	75494	903-342-0982	
Titan Protection & Consulting Inc 9350 Metcalf Ave Ste 210 *Web:* www.tpcsecurity.com	Overland Park	KS	66212	913-441-0911	
Top Guard Inc 131 Kings Way Ste 100 *Web:* www.topguardinc.com	Hampton	VA	23669	757-722-3961	
Totevision 1319 Dexter Ave N Ste 20 *Web:* www.totevision.com	Seattle	WA	98109	206-623-6000	
Triad Security Systems 971 Lehigh Ave *Web:* www.triadsecurity.com	Union	NJ	07083	908-964-5252	
Trident Security Service 4968 Dorchester Rd *Web:* www.tsecurityservices.com	Charleston	SC	29418	843-767-3855	
Triple s Alarm Company Inc 2820 Cantrell Rd *Web:* www.triplesalarm.com	Little Rock	AR	72202	501-664-4599	
Twin City Security Inc 519 Coon Rapids Blvd *Web:* www.twincitysecurity.com	Minneapolis	MN	55433	763-784-4160	
Tyco International Ltd Nine Roszel Rd *NYSE: TYC* ■ *TF:* 800-685-4509 ■ *Web:* www.tyco.com	Princeton	NJ	08540	609-720-4200	720-4208
UCIT Online Security 6441 Northam Dr *TF:* 866-756-7847 ■ *Web:* www.ucitonline.com	Mississauga	ON	L4V1J2	905-405-9898	
United Security Inc 4295 Arthur Kill Rd *Web:* www.usisecurity.com	Staten Island	NY	10309	718-967-6820	
Universal Protection Service 27134 Malibu Cove Colony Dr *Web:* universalpro.com	Malibu	CA	90265	310-589-5728	
Universal Services of America Inc 1551 N Tustin Ave Ste 650 *TF:* 866-877-1965 ■ *Web:* www.universalpro.com	Santa Ana	CA	92705	714-619-9700	619-9701
US Protection Service LLC 5785 Emporium Sq *Web:* www.uspsvc.com	Columbus	OH	43231	614-794-4950	
US Security Assoc Inc 200 Mansell Ct Fifth Fl *TF:* 800-730-9599 ■ *Web:* www.ussecurityassociates.com	Roswell	GA	30076	770-625-1500	625-1509
US Security Inc 4544 NW 10th St *TF:* 877-917-5566 ■ *Web:* www.ussecurity.com	Oklahoma City	OK	73127	405-947-3377	
Vanguard Products Group Inc 720 Brooker Creek Blvd Ste 223 *Web:* vanguardprotexglobal.com/	Oldsmar	FL	34677	813-855-9639	
Verant Identification Systems Inc 2496 Ridge Rd W Ste 203 *TF:* 866-257-4351 ■ *Web:* www.verantid.com	Rochester	NY	14626	585-214-2451	
Vescom Corp 705 Main Rd N *TF:* 800-841-1769 ■ *Web:* www.vescomcorp.com	Hampden	ME	04444	207-945-5051	
Vinson Guard Service Inc 955 Howard Ave *TF:* 800-441-7899 ■ *Web:* www.vinsonguard.com	New Orleans	LA	70113	504-529-2260	
Voice Security Systems Inc 24591 Seth Cir *Web:* www.voice-security.com	Dana Point	CA	92629	949-493-4030	
Vss Security Services 1717 W Northern Ave Ste 200 *Web:* www.vss-security-services.com	Phoenix	AZ	85021	602-861-9900	
Weiser Security Services Inc 3939 Tulane Ave *Web:* www.weisersecurity.com	New Orleans	LA	70119	504-949-7558	

Phone Fax

Whelan Security Co 1699 S Hanley Rd Ste 350 St Louis MO 63144 314-644-3227
TF: 888-494-3526 ■ *Web:* www.whelansecurity.com

Xator Corp 543 Harbor Blvd Ste 501 Destin FL 32541 850-460-2860
Web: www.xatorcorp.com

Yale Assoc Inc 1150 Portion Rd Ste 1 Holtsville NY 11742 631-320-3088
Web: www.yaleassociates.com

Zinus Inc 30799 Wiegman Rd Hayward CA 94544 925-417-2100
Web: zinus.com

Zvetco Biometrics LLC 6820 Hanging Moss Rd Orlando FL 32807 407-681-0111
Web: www.zvetcobiometrics.com

697 SEED COMPANIES

SEE ALSO Farm Supplies p. 2285

Seed production and development companies (horticultural and agricultural).

Phone Fax

AgriGold Hybrids 5381 Akin Rd Saint Francisville IL 62460 618-943-5776
TF: 800-262-7333 ■ *Web:* www.agrigold.com

Albert Lea Seed House 1414 W Main St Albert Lea MN 56007 507-373-3161 373-7032
TF: 800-352-5247 ■ *Web:* www.alseed.com

Ampac Seed Co 32727 Hwy 99 E Tangent OR 97389 541-928-1651 928-2430
TF: 800-547-3230 ■ *Web:* www.ampacseed.com

Applewood Seed Co 5380 Vivian St Arvada CO 80002 303-431-7333 467-7886
Web: www.applewoodseed.com

Barenbrug USA Inc 33477 Hwy 99 E PO Box 239 Tangent OR 97389 541-926-5801 926-9435*
**Fax:* Sales ■ *Web:* www.barenbrug.com

Foremostco Inc 8457 NW 66th St Miami FL 33166 305-592-8986 426-1362*
**Fax Area Code:* 800 ■ *TF:* 800-421-8986 ■ *Web:* www.foremostco.com

Gries Seed Farms Inc 2348 N Fifth St Fremont OH 43420 419-332-5571 233-3350*
**Fax Area Code:* 402 ■ *Web:* seedtoday.com

Harris Moran Seed Co PO Box 4938 Modesto CA 95352 800-320-4672 527-5312*
**Fax Area Code:* 209 ■ *TF:* 800-808-7333 ■ *Web:* www.harrismoran.com

Johnny's Selected Seeds 955 Benton Ave Winslow ME 04901 207-861-3900 861-8363
TF: 877-564-6697 ■ *Web:* www.johnnyseeds.com

JW Jung Seed Co 335 S High St Randolph WI 53956 800-297-3123 692-5864
TF: 800-297-3123 ■ *Web:* www.jungseed.com

Keithly-Williams Seeds Inc
420 Palm Ave PO Box 177 Holtville CA 92250 760-356-5533 356-2409
TF: 800-533-3465 ■ *Web:* www.keithlywilliams.com

Latham Seed Co 131 180th St Alexander IA 50420 641-692-3258 692-3250
TF: 877-465-2842 ■ *Web:* www.lathamseeds.com

Lebanon Seaboard Corp 1600 E Cumberland St Lebanon PA 17042 717-273-1685 273-9466
TF: 800-233-0628 ■ *Web:* www.lebsea.com

Nunhems USA Inc 1200 Anderson Corner Rd Parma ID 83660 208-674-4000 674-4090*
**Fax:* Cust Svc ■ *TF Cust Svc:* 800-733-9505 ■
Web: www.nunhemsusa.com/www/NunhemsInternet.nsf/id/US_EN_Home

Park Seed Co One Parkton Ave Greenwood SC 29647 800-845-3369 941-4502*
**Fax Area Code:* 864 ■ *TF Orders:* 800-845-3369 ■ *Web:* www.parkseed.com

Pennington Seed Inc 1280 AtlantaHwy Madison GA 30650 706-342-1234 342-8071
TF: 800-285-7333 ■ *Web:* www.penningtonseed.com

Red River Commodities Inc 501 42nd St N Fargo ND 58102 701-282-2600 282-5325
TF: 800-437-5539 ■ *Web:* www.redriv.com

Renee's Garden Seeds Inc 7389 W Zayante Rd Felton CA 95018 831-335-7228 335-7227
TF: 888-880-7228 ■ *Web:* www.reneesgarden.com

Sakata Seed America Inc
18095 Serene Dr PO Box 880 Morgan Hill CA 95037 408-778-7758 778-7768
Web: www.sakata.com

Sand Seed Service Inc 4765 Hwy 143 Marcus IA 51035 712-376-4135 376-4140
TF: 800-352-2228 ■ *Web:* www.sandsofiowa.com

Schlessman Seed Co 11513 US Rt 250 Milan OH 44846 419-499-2572 499-2574
TF: 888-534-7333 ■ *Web:* www.schlessman-seed.com

Seedway LLC 1734 Railroad Pl Hall NY 14463 585-526-6391 526-6832
TF: 800-836-3710 ■ *Web:* www.seedway.com

Sharp Bros Seed Co 1005 S Sycamore Healy KS 67850 620-398-2231 398-2220
TF: 800-462-8483 ■ *Web:* www.sharpseed.com

Stock Seed Farms 28008 Mill Rd Murdock NE 68407 402-867-3771 867-2442
TF: 800-759-1520 ■ *Web:* www.stockseed.com

Stratton Seed Co 1530 Hwy 79 S Stuttgart AR 72160 870-673-4433 673-4290
TF: 800-264-4433 ■ *Web:* www.strattonseed.com

W Atlee Burpee Co 300 Pk Ave Warminster PA 18974 215-674-4900 674-4170
TF Cust Svc: 800-333-5808 ■ *Web:* www.burpee.com

Weeks Seed Company Inc 1050 Moye Blvd Greenville NC 27834 252-757-1234 757-0978
TF: 800-322-1234 ■ *Web:* www.weeksseeds.com

Wetsel Inc 961 N Liberty St Harrisonburg VA 22802 540-434-6753
TF Cust Svc: 800-572-4018 ■ *Web:* bfgsupply.com/

698 SEMICONDUCTOR MANUFACTURING SYSTEMS & EQUIPMENT

Phone Fax

Adcotron EMS Inc 12 Ch St Marine Industrial Pk Boston MA 02210 617-598-3000 598-3001
Web: www.adcotron.com

Advanced Energy Industries Inc
1625 Sharp Pt Dr Fort Collins CO 80525 970-221-4670 221-5583
NASDAQ: AEIS ■ *TF:* 800-446-9167 ■ *Web:* www.advanced-energy.com

Aehr Test Systems 400 Kato Terr Fremont CA 94539 510-623-9400 623-9450
NASDAQ: AEHR ■ *TF:* 800-962-4284 ■ *Web:* www.aehr.com

Akrion Systems LLC
6330 Hedgewood Dr Ste 150 Allentown PA 18106 610-391-9200 391-1982*
**Fax:* Sales ■ *Web:* www.akrionsystems.com

Amistar Automation Inc 1269 Linda Vista San Marcos CA 92078 760-471-1700 471-9065
Web: www.amistarautomation.com

Amtech Systems Inc 131 S Clark Dr Tempe AZ 85281 480-967-5146 968-3763
NASDAQ: ASYS ■ *Web:* www.amtechsystems.com

Applied Materials Inc
3050 Bowers Ave PO Box 58039 Santa Clara CA 95054 408-727-5555 748-9943
NASDAQ: AMAT ■ *TF:* 877-356-9175 ■ *Web:* www.appliedmaterials.com

Applied Materials/Semitool
655 W Reserve Dr Kalispell MT 59901 406-752-2107 752-5522
TF: 877-356-9175 ■ *Web:* www.appliedmaterials.com

Phone Fax

ASM America Inc 3440 E University Dr Phoenix AZ 85034 602-470-5700 437-1403
Web: www.asm.com

ASML US Inc 8555 S River Pkwy Tempe AZ 85284 480-383-4422 383-3995
TF: 800-227-6462 ■ *Web:* www.asml.com

Axcelis Technologies Inc 108 Cherry Hill Dr Beverly MA 01915 978-787-4000 787-4200
NASDAQ: ACLS ■ *Web:* www.axcelis.com

Brooks Automation Inc 15 Elizabeth Dr Chelmsford MA 01824 978-262-2400 262-2500
NASDAQ: BRKS ■ *TF:* 800-698-6149 ■ *Web:* www.brooks.com

BTU International Inc 23 Esquire Rd North Billerica MA 01862 978-667-4111 667-9068
NASDAQ: BTUI ■ *TF:* 800-998-0666 ■ *Web:* www.btu.com

Conceptronic Inc 1860 Smithtown Ave Ronkonkoma NY 11779 631-981-7081 981-7095
Web: www.conceptronic.com

Contact Systems Inc 50 Miry Brook Rd Danbury CT 06810 203-743-3837
Web: www.contactsystems.com

CVD Equipment Corp 1860 Smithtown Ave Ronkonkoma NY 11779 631-981-7081 981-7095
NASDAQ: CVV ■ *Web:* www.cvdequipment.com

Cymer Inc 17075 Thornmint Ct San Diego CA 92127 858-385-7300 385-7100
NASDAQ: CYMI ■ *Web:* www.cymer.com

Data I/O Corp 6464 185th Ave NE Ste 101 Redmond WA 98052 425-881-6444 881-6444
NASDAQ: DAIO ■ *TF:* 800-426-1045 ■ *Web:* dataio.com

Ebara Technologies Inc 51 Main Ave Sacramento CA 95838 916-920-5451 925-6654
TF: 800-535-5376 ■ *Web:* www.ebaratech.com

EG Systems LLC 30974 Santana St Hayward CA 94544 408-528-3000 528-3562
Web: www.electroglas.com

EMCORE Corp 10420 Research Rd SE Albuquerque NM 87123 505-332-5000 332-5038
NASDAQ: EMKR ■ *Web:* www.emcore.com

Engent Inc 3140 Northwoods Pkwy Ste 300A Norcross GA 30071 678-990-3320 990-3324
TF: 888-768-4357 ■ *Web:* www.engentaat.com

Entegris Inc 129 Concord Rd Bldg 2 Billerica MA 01021 970-436-6500 436-6735
NASDAQ: ENTG ■ *TF:* 877-695-7654 ■ *Web:* www.entegris.com

FormFactor Inc 7005 SouthFront Rd Livermore CA 94551 925-290-4000 290-4010
NASDAQ: FORM ■ *Web:* www.formfactor.com

Fortrend Corp 687 N Pastoria Ave Sunnyvale CA 94085 408-734-9311 734-4299
TF: 888-937-3637 ■ *Web:* www.fortrend.com

FSI International Inc 3455 Lyman Blvd Chaska MN 55318 952-448-5440 448-2825
NASDAQ: FSII ■ *Web:* www.tel.com

Gem City Engineering & Mfg Co, The 401 Leo St Dayton OH 45404 937-223-5544 226-1908
Web: www.gemcity.com

Gem Services USA Inc 2880 Lakeside Dr Santa Clara CA 95054 408-566-8866 566-8858
Web: www.gemservices.com

Global Communication Semiconductors Inc
23155 Kashiwa Ct Torrance CA 90505 310-530-7274 517-8200
Web: www.gcsincorp.com

Hittite Microwave Corp 20 Alpha Rd Chelmsford MA 01824 978-250-3343 250-3373
NASDAQ: ADI ■ *Web:* www.hittite.com

I.B.I.S. Inc 30 Technology Pkwy S Ste 400 Norcross GA 30092 770-368-4000 368-1186
TF: 888-477-7989 ■ *Web:* www.ibisinc.com

Imtec Acculine Inc 49036 Milmont Dr Fremont CA 94538 510-770-1800 770-1400
Web: www.imtecacculine.com

KDF Electronic & Vacuum Services Inc
10 Volvo Dr Rockleigh NJ 07647 201-784-5005 784-0202
TF: 877-533-3343 ■ *Web:* www.kdf.com

KLA-Tencor Corp One Technology Dr Milpitas CA 95035 408-875-3000 875-4144
NASDAQ: KLAC ■ *TF:* 800-600-2829 ■ *Web:* www.kla-tencor.com

Kokusai Semiconductor Equipment Corp
2460 N First St Ste 290 San Jose CA 95131 408-456-2750 456-2760
TF: 800-800-5321 ■ *Web:* www.ksec.com

Kulicke & Soffa Industries Inc (K&S)
1005 Virginia Dr Fort Washington PA 19034 215-784-6000 784-6001
NASDAQ: KLIC ■ *Web:* www.kns.com

Lam Research Corp 4650 Cushing Pkwy Fremont CA 94538 510-572-0200 572-1093*
NASDAQ: LRCX ■ **Fax:* Cust Svc ■ *TF:* 800-526-7678 ■ *Web:* lamresearch.com

Lansdale Semiconductor Inc 5245 S 39th St Phoenix AZ 85040 602-438-0123 438-0138
Web: www.lansdale.com

Loranger International Corp 817 Fourth Ave Warren PA 16365 814-723-2250 723-5391
Web: www.loranger.com

Mattson Technology Inc 47131 Bayside Pkwy Fremont CA 94538 510-657-5900 492-5911
NASDAQ: MTSN ■ *TF:* 800-315-6607 ■ *Web:* www.mattson.com

MaxLinear Inc
2051 Palomar Airport Rd Ste 100 Carlsbad CA 92011 760-692-0711 444-8598
NYSE: MXL ■ *TF:* 888-505-4369 ■ *Web:* www.maxlinear.com

MCT Worldwide LLC 121 S Eigth St Ste 960 Minneapolis MN 55402 612-436-3240 436-3242
Web: www.mct.com

N J R Corp 125 Nicholson Ln San Jose CA 95134 408-321-0200 232-6060
TF: 800-800-5441 ■ *Web:* www.njr.com

Neutronix-Quintel (NXQ) 685 Jarvis Dr # A Morgan Hill CA 95037 408-776-5190 776-1039
Web: www.neutronixinc.com

Rudolph Technologies Inc
One Rudolph Rd PO Box 1000 Flanders NJ 07836 973-691-1300 691-4863
NASDAQ: RTEC ■ *TF:* 877-467-8365 ■ *Web:* www.rudolphtech.com

Semi-Kinetics Inc 20191 Windrow Dr Ste A Lake Forest CA 92630 949-830-7364 830-7385
Web: www.semi-kinetics.com

Sensitron Semiconductor 221 W Industry Ct Deer Park NY 11729 631-586-7600 586-6053
Web: www.sensitron.com

Shin-Etsu Microsi Inc 10028 S 51st St Phoenix AZ 85044 480-893-8898 893-8637
Web: www.microsi.com

Small Precision Tools Inc 1330 Clegg St Petaluma CA 94954 707-765-4545 778-2271
Web: www.smallprecisiontools.com

Solid State Equipment Corp 185 Gibraltar Rd Horsham PA 19044 215-328-0700 328-9410
Web: www.ssecusa.com

Spintrac Systems Inc 690 Aldo Ave Santa Clara CA 95054 408-980-1155 980-1267
Web: www.spintrac.com

Spire Corp 1 Patriots Pk Bedford MA 01730 781-275-6000 275-7470
OTC: SPIR ■ *TF:* 800-510-4815 ■ *Web:* www.spirecorp.com

Tegal Corp 2201 S McDowell Blvd Petaluma CA 94954 707-763-5600 765-9311
TF: 800-828-3425 ■ *Web:* www.collabrx.com

Tek-Vac Industries Inc 176 Express Dr S Brentwood NY 11717 631-436-5100 436-5154
Web: www.tekvac.com

Tokyo Electron America Inc 2400 Grove Blvd Austin TX 78741 512-424-1000 424-1001
TF: 800-828-6596 ■ *Web:* tel.com

Trio-Tech International 14731 Califa St Van Nuys CA 91411 818-787-7000 787-9130
NYSE: TRT ■ *Web:* www.triotech.com

Phone Fax

Ultra Clean Holdings Inc 26462 Corporate Ave .... Hayward CA 94545 510-576-4400 576-4401
NASDAQ: UCTT ■ *Web:* www.uct.com
Ultratech Inc 3050 Zanker Rd .... San Jose CA 95134 408-321-8835 577-3378
NASDAQ: UTEK ■ *TF:* 800-222-1213 ■ *Web:* www.ultratech.com
United Memories Inc
4815 List Dr Ste 109 .... Colorado Springs CO 80919 719-594-4238
Web: www.unitedmemories.com
Universal Instruments Corp (UIC)
33 Broome Corporate Pk .... Conklin NY 13748 607-779-7522 779-4466
TF: 800-842-9732 ■ *Web:* uic.com
Varian Semiconductor Equipment Assoc Inc
35 Dory Rd .... Gloucester MA 01930 978-282-2000 283-6376
TF: 800-344-1111 ■ *Web:* www.vsea.com
Veeco Instruments Inc One Terminal Dr .... Plainview NY 11803 516-677-0200 714-1200
NASDAQ: VECO ■ *TF:* 888-248-3326 ■ *Web:* www.veeco.com

699 SEMICONDUCTORS & RELATED DEVICES

SEE ALSO Electronic Components & Accessories - Mfr p. 2232; Printed Circuit Boards p. 2963

Phone Fax

8x8 Inc 810 W Maude Ave .... Sunnyvale CA 94085 408-727-1885 980-0432
NASDAQ: EGHT ■ *TF:* 888-898-8733 ■ *Web:* www.8x8.com
Actel Corp 2061 Stierlin Ct .... Mountain View CA 94043 650-318-4200 318-4600
TF: 800-262-1060 ■ *Web:* www.microsemi.com
Advanced Micro Devices Inc (AMD)
One AMD Pl PO Box 3453 .... Sunnyvale CA 94088 408-749-4000
NYSE: AMD ■ *TF:* 800-538-8450 ■ *Web:* www.amd.com
Advanced Photonix Inc 2925 Boardwalk .... Ann Arbor MI 48104 734-864-5600 998-3474
NYSE: API ■ *Web:* www.advancedphotonix.com
Advantage Electronic Product Development
34 Garden Ctr .... Broomfield CO 80020 303-410-0292
Web: www.advantage-dev.com
Aeroflex Inc 35 S Service Rd PO Box 6022 .... Plainview NY 11803 516-694-6700 694-0658
TSE: ARX ■ *TF:* 800-843-1553 ■ *Web:* www.aeroflex.com
AKM Semiconductor Inc
1731 Technology Dr Ste 500 .... San Jose CA 95110 408-436-8580
Web: www.akm.com
Allegro Microsystems Inc 115 NE Cutoff .... Worcester MA 01606 508-853-5000 853-2431
Web: www.allegromicro.com
Alliance Semiconductor Corp
10755 Scripps Poway Pkwy Ste 302 .... San Diego CA 92131 408-855-4900 855-4999
OTC: ALSC ■ *Web:* www.alsc.com
Altera Corp 101 Innovation Dr .... San Jose CA 95134 408-544-7000 544-6403*
NASDAQ: ALTR ■ **Fax:* Cust Svc ■ *TF Cust Svc:* 800-767-3753 ■ *Web:* www.altera.com
Amalfi Semiconductor Inc
475 Alberto Way Ste 200 .... Los Gatos CA 95032 408-399-5360
Ambarella Inc 2975 San Ysidro Way .... Santa Clara CA 95054 408-734-8888
Web: www.ambarella.com
American Arium 14811 Myford Rd .... Tustin CA 92780 714-731-1661 731-6344
TF: 877-508-3970 ■ *Web:* www.arium.com
Amkor Technology Inc 1900 S Price Rd .... Chandler AZ 85248 480-821-5000
NASDAQ: AMKR ■ *Web:* www.amkor.com
ANADIGICS Inc 141 Mt Bethel Rd .... Warren NJ 07059 908-668-5000 668-5068
NASDAQ: ANAD ■ *Web:* www.anadigics.com
Analog Devices Inc Three Technology Way .... Norwood MA 02062 781-329-4700 461-3113
NASDAQ: ADI ■ *TF:* 800-262-5643 ■ *Web:* www.analog.com
Analogix Semiconductor Inc
3211 Scott Blvd Ste 103 .... Santa Clara CA 95054 408-988-8848
Web: www.analogix.com
Apogee Technology Inc 129 Morgan Dr .... Norwood MA 02062 781-551-9450 769-9107
OTC: ATCS ■ *Web:* www.apogeebio.com
Applied Micro Circuits Corp
215 Moffett Pk Dr .... Sunnyvale CA 94089 408-542-8600 542-8601
NASDAQ: AMCC ■ *Web:* www.apm.com
ARM Inc 141 Caspian Ct .... Sunnyvale CA 94089 408-734-5600 734-5050
Web: www.arm.com
Arsenal Capital Partners
100 Park Ave 31st Fl .... New York NY 10017 212-771-1717
Web: www.arsenalcapital.com
Ascent Solar Technologies Inc
12300 Grant St .... Thornton CO 80241 720-872-5000
Web: www.ascentsolar.com/
Atmel Corp 2325 Orchard Pkwy .... San Jose CA 95131 408-441-0311 436-4200
NASDAQ: ATML ■ *Web:* www.atmel.com
AuthenTec Inc 100 Rialto Pl # 100 .... Melbourne FL 32901 321-308-1300 308-1430
Avanex Corp 40919 Encyclopedia Cir .... Fremont CA 94538 510-897-4188
Web: www.avanex.com
Aware Inc 40 Middlesex Tpke .... Bedford MA 01730 781-276-4000 276-4001
NASDAQ: AWRE ■ *Web:* www.aware.com
Axsun Technologies Inc One Fortune Dr .... Billerica MA 01821 978-262-0049 262-0035
TF: 866-462-9786 ■ *Web:* www.axsun.com
AXT Inc 4281 Technology Dr .... Fremont CA 94538 510-438-4700 353-0668
NASDAQ: AXTI ■ *Web:* www.axt.com
B & B Electronics Manufacturing Co
PO Box 1040 .... Ottawa IL 61350 815-433-5100 433-5109
TF: 800-346-3119 ■ *Web:* www.bb-elec.com
BI Technologies Corp 4200 Bonita Pl .... Fullerton CA 92835 714-447-2300 447-2745
Web: www.bitechnologies.com
BKM Technology Partners LLC
3620 E Campbell Ave Ste A-2 .... Phoenix AZ 85018 480-922-4933
Web: www.bkmtechnologypartners.com
Brion Technologies Inc 4211 Burton Dr .... Santa Clara CA 95054 408-653-1500
Web: www.brion.com
Broadcom Corp 5300 California Ave .... Irvine CA 92617 949-926-5000 926-5203
NASDAQ: BRCM ■ *TF:* 877-577-2726 ■ *Web:* www.broadcom.com
Busch Semiconductor Vacuum Group LLC
18430 Sutter Blvd .... Morgan Hill CA 95037 408-782-0800
Web: www.buschsvg.com
Calxeda Inc 7000 N Mopac Expy Ste 250 .... Austin TX 78731 512-961-3680

Phone Fax

Cavium Inc 2315 Nfirst St .... San Jose CA 95131 408-943-7100
Web: investor.caviumnetworks.com
Celis Semiconductor Corp
4775 Centennial Blvd .... Colorado Springs CO 80919 719-260-9133
CEVA Inc 1943 Landings Dr .... San Jose CA 94043 650-417-7900
TF: 800-894-0972 ■ *Web:* www.ceva-dsp.com
Cirrus Logic Inc 2901 Via Fortuna .... Austin TX 78746 512-851-4000 851-4977
NASDAQ: CRUS ■ *TF:* 800-888-5016 ■ *Web:* www.cirrus.com
Clare Inc 78 Cherry Hill Dr .... Beverly MA 01915 978-524-6700 524-4700
Web: www.ixysic.com
Clearspeed Technology Inc 3031 Tisch Way .... San Jose CA 95128 408-557-2067
Web: www.clearspeed.com
Conexant Systems Inc 1901 Main St Ste 300 .... Irvine CA 92614 949-483-4600 370-8990*
**Fax Area Code:* 781 ■ *TF:* 888-855-4562 ■ *Web:* www.conexant.com
Cooper Crouse-Hinds MTL Inc
4300 Fortune Pl Ste A .... West Melbourne FL 32904 321-725-8000
Web: www.atlanticscientific.com
Cree Inc 4600 Silicon Dr .... Durham NC 27703 919-313-5300 313-5451*
NASDAQ: CREE ■ **Fax:* Sales ■ *TF:* 800-533-2583 ■ *Web:* www.cree.com
Crossfield Technology LLC
9390 Research Blvd Bldg 200 .... Austin TX 78759 512-795-0220
Web: www.crossfieldtech.com
Cypress Semiconductor Corp 198 Champion Ct ...... San Jose CA 95134 408-943-2600 943-4730*
NASDAQ: CY ■ **Fax:* Mktg ■ *TF:* 800-541-4736 ■ *Web:* www.cypress.com
Dakota Systems Inc 1057 Broadway Rd Rt 113 .... Dracut MA 01826 978-275-0600 275-0606
Web: www.dakotasystems.com
Dallas Semiconductor Corp
4401 S Beltwood Pkwy .... Dallas TX 75244 972-371-3726 371-3715*
**Fax:* Cust Svc ■ *Web:* www.maximintegrated.com
Deca Technologies Inc 7855 S River Pkwy Ste 111 .... Tempe AZ 85284 480-345-9895
Web: www.decatechnologies.com
Dialight Corp 1501 SR 34 .... Farmingdale NJ 07727 732-919-3119 751-5778
Web: www.dialight.com
Diodes Inc 15660 N Dallas Pkwy Ste 850 .... Dallas TX 75248 972-385-2810 446-4850*
NASDAQ: DIOD ■ **Fax Area Code:* 805 ■ *Web:* www.diodes.com
Dornerworks Ltd
3445 Lk Eastbrook Blvd SE .... Grand Rapids MI 49546 616-245-8369
Web: www.dornerworks.com
DSP Group Inc 2580 N First St Ste 460 .... San Jose CA 95131 408-986-4300 986-4323
NASDAQ: DSPG ■ *Web:* www.dspg.com
E/g Electro-graph Inc
2365 Camino Vida Roble .... Carlsbad CA 92011 760-438-9090 438-3923
TF: 800-782-6659 ■ *Web:* plansee.com/en
EMCORE Corp 10420 Research Rd SE .... Albuquerque NM 87123 505-332-5000 332-5038
NASDAQ: EMKR ■ *Web:* www.emcore.com
Energy Xtreme LLC 2215 Westlake Dr .... Austin TX 78746 512-617-7902
Web: www.energyxtreme.net
Enphase Energy Inc 1420 N Mcdowell Blvd .... Petaluma CA 94954 707-763-4784
TF: 877-797-4743 ■ *Web:* investor.enphase.com
Epson Electronics America Inc
150 River Oaks Pkwy .... San Jose CA 95134 408-922-0200 922-0238
TF: 800-228-3964 ■ *Web:* www.eea.epson.com
Equator Technologies Inc 520 Pike St Ste 900 .... Seattle WA 98101 206-267-4500 812-1285
ESS Technology Inc 48401 Fremont Blvd .... Fremont CA 94538 510-492-1088 492-1098
Web: www.esstech.com
Exar Corp 48720 Kato Rd .... Fremont CA 94538 510-668-7000 668-7011
NYSE: EXAR ■ *Web:* www.exar.com
Fairchild Imaging Inc 1801 McCarthy Blvd .... Milpitas CA 95035 408-433-2500 435-7352
TF: 800-325-6975 ■ *Web:* www.fairchildimaging.com
Fairchild Semiconductor Corp
82 Running Hill Rd .... South Portland ME 04106 207-775-8100 761-6139
NASDAQ: FCS ■ *TF:* 800-341-0392 ■ *Web:* www.fairchildsemi.com
Freescale Semiconductor Inc
6501 William Cannon Dr W .... Austin TX 78735 512-895-2000 895-2652
TF Tech Supp: 800-521-6274 ■ *Web:* www.freescale.com
GCT Semiconductor Inc 2121 Ringwood Ave .... San Jose CA 95131 408-434-6040 434-6050
Web: www.gctsemi.com
Gel-Pak LLC 31398 Huntwood Ave .... Hayward CA 94544 510-576-2220 576-2282
TF: 888-621-4147 ■ *Web:* www.gelpak.com
Gennum Corp 4281 Harvestar Rd .... Burlington ON L7L5M4 905-632-2996 632-2055
Web: www.gennum.com
GHO Ventures LLC 92 Nassau St 2nd Fl .... Princeton NJ 08542 732-458-3681
Web: www.ghoventures.com
GigOptix Inc 130 Baytech Dr .... San Jose CA 95134 408-522-3100
Web: ir.gigoptix.com
Global Equipment Services Corp
2372-East Qume Dr .... San Jose CA 95131 408-441-0682
Web: www.geservs.com
Global Solar Energy Inc 8500 S Rita Rd .... Tucson AZ 85747 520-546-6313 546-6318
TF: 866-999-8422 ■ *Web:* www.globalsolar.com
Grinding & Dicing Services Inc
925 Berryessa Rd .... San Jose CA 95133 408-451-2000
Web: www.wafergrind.com
GSI Technology Inc 2360 Owen St .... Santa Clara CA 95054 408-980-8388 980-8377
NASDAQ: GSIT ■ *Web:* www.gsitechnology.com
GT Advanced Technologies Inc
243 DANIEL WEBSTER Hwy .... Merrimack NH 03054 603-883-5200
Web: www.gtat.com
HEI Inc 1495 Steiger Lk Ln .... Victoria MN 55386 952-443-2500 443-2668
TF: 866-720-2397 ■ *Web:* www.heii.com
Hitachi Canada Ltd
5450 Explore Dr Suite 501 .... Mississauga ON L4W5N1 905-629-9300 290-0141
TF: 866-797-4332 ■ *Web:* www.hitachi.ca
Hitachi High Technologies America Inc
10 N Martingale Rd Ste 500 .... Schaumburg IL 60173 847-273-4141 273-4407
Web: www.hitachi-hta.com
Holt Integrated Circuits Inc
23351 Madero .... Mission Viejo CA 92691 949-859-8800 859-9643
Web: www.holtic.com
Hynix Semiconductor America Inc
3101 N First St .... San Jose CA 95134 408-232-8000 232-8103
Web: www.hynix.com

Company	City	State	ZIP	Phone	Fax
Hysitron Inc 9625 W 76th St *Web:* www.hysitron.com	Minneapolis	MN	55344	952-835-6366	
Hytel Group Inc 290 Industrial Dr *Web:* www.hytel.com	Hampshire	IL	60140	847-683-9800	683-7940
I-O Corp 14852 S Heritage Crest Way 1-A *Web:* www.iocorp.com	Bluffdale	UT	84065	801-973-6767	974-5683
i2a Technologies Inc 3399 W Warren Ave *Web:* www.ipac.com	Fremont	CA	94538	510-770-0322	
Ikanos Communications 47669 Fremont Blvd *NASDAQ: IKAN* ■ *Web:* www.ikanos.com	Fremont	CA	94538	510-979-0400	979-0500
Impinj Inc 701 N 34th St Ste 300 *TF:* 866-467-4650 ■ *Web:* www.impinj.com	Seattle	WA	98103	206-517-5300	517-5262
Inabata America Corp 1270 Ave of the Americas Ste 602 *Web:* us.inabata.com	New York	NY	10020	212-586-7764	245-2876
Integrated Device Technology Inc 6024 Silver Creek Vly Rd *NASDAQ: IDTI* ■ *TF:* 800-345-7015 ■ *Web:* www.idt.com	San Jose	CA	95138	408-284-8200	284-2775
Integrated Silicon Solution Inc (ISSI) 1940 Zanker Rd *NASDAQ: ISSI* ■ *TF:* 800-379-4774 ■ *Web:* www.issi.com	San Jose	CA	95112	408-969-6600	969-7800
Intel Corp 2200 Mission College Blvd *NASDAQ: INTC* ■ *TF Cust Svc:* 800-628-8686 ■ *Web:* www.intel.in	Santa Clara	CA	95052	408-765-8080	
InterDigital Communications Corp 781 Third Ave *Web:* www.interdigital.com	King of Prussia	PA	19406	610-878-7800	878-7842
Intermolecular Inc 3011 N First St *TF:* 877-251-1860 ■ *Web:* www.intermolecular.com	San Jose	CA	95134	408-582-5700	
International Rectifier Corp 101 N Sepulveda Blvd *Web:* www.irf.com	El Segundo	CA	90245	310-322-3331	
Intersil Corp 1001 Murphy Ranch Rd *NASDAQ: ISIL* ■ *TF:* 888-468-3774 ■ *Web:* www.intersil.com	Milpitas	CA	95035	408-432-8888	434-5351
Invensense Inc 1197 Borregas Ave *NYSE: INVN* ■ *Web:* www.invensense.com	Sunnyvale	CA	94089	408-988-7339	988-8104
IQE Inc 119 Technology Dr *Web:* www.iqep.com	Bethlehem	PA	18015	610-861-6930	861-5273
Irvine Sensors Corp 3001 Redhill Ave B3-108vv *Web:* www.irvine-sensors.com	Costa Mesa	CA	92626	714-444-8700	
iWatt Inc 675 Campbell Technology Pkwy Ste 150 *Web:* www.iwatt.com	Campbell	CA	95008	408-374-4200	
IXYS Corp 3540 Bassett St *NASDAQ: IXYS* ■ *Web:* www.ixys.com	Santa Clara	CA	95054	408-982-0700	748-9788
Jazz Semiconductor Inc 4321 Jamboree Rd *Web:* www.jazzsemi.com	Newport Beach	CA	92660	949-435-8000	435-8757
JDS Uniphase Inc 61 Bill Leathem Dr *Web:* www.jdsu.com	Ottawa	ON	K2J0P7	613-843-3000	
Johnstech International Corp 1210 New Brighton Blvd *Web:* www.johnstech.com	Minneapolis	MN	55413	612-378-2020	378-2030
Judson Technologies LLC 221 Commerce Dr *Web:* www.judsontechnologies.com	Montgomeryville	PA	18936	215-368-6900	362-6107
Kilopass Technology Inc 3333 Octavius Dr Ste 101 *Web:* www.kilopass.com	Santa Clara	CA	95054	408-980-8808	980-8856
Kleer Corp 19925 Stevens Creek Blvd Ste 111 *Web:* www.kleer.com	Cupertino	CA	95014	408-973-7255	
Kopin Corp 125 N Dr *NASDAQ: KOPN* ■ *Web:* www.kopin.com	Westborough	MA	01581	508-870-5959	822-1381
Kyocera America Inc 8611 Balboa Ave *TF:* 888-955-0800 ■ *Web:* global.kyocera.com	San Diego	CA	92123	858-576-2600	569-9412
Kyocera Solar Inc 7812 E Acoma Dr Ste 2 *TF:* 800-544-6466 ■ *Web:* www.kyocerasolar.com	Scottsdale	AZ	85260	480-948-8003	483-6431
Laser Diode Inc Four Olsen Ave *Web:* www.laserdiode.com	Edison	NJ	08820	732-549-9001	906-1559
Lattice Semiconductor Corp 5555 NE Moore Ct *NASDAQ: LSCC* ■ *TF:* 800-528-8423 ■ *Web:* www.latticesemi.com	Hillsboro	OR	97124	503-268-8000	268-8347
Lightel Technologies Inc 2210 Lind Ave SW Ste 100 *Web:* www.lighteltech.com	Renton	WA	98057	425-277-8000	
Lilliputian Systems Inc 36 Jonspin Rd *Web:* www.lilliputiansystems.com	Wilmington	MA	01887	978-203-1700	
Linear Technology Corp 1630 McCarthy Blvd *NASDAQ: LLTC* ■ *TF:* 888-500-6973 ■ *Web:* www.linear.com	Milpitas	CA	95035	408-432-1900	434-0507
Lite Access Technologies Inc 2180-21331 Gordon Way *Web:* www.liteaccess.com	Richmond	BC	V6W1J9	604-247-4704	
Logic Devices Inc 1375 Geneva Dr *OTC: LOGC* ■ *TF:* 800-233-2518 ■ *Web:* www.logicdevices.com	Sunnyvale	CA	94089	408-542-5400	542-0080
LSI Computer Systems Inc 1235 Walt Whitman Rd *Web:* www.lsicsi.com	Melville	NY	11747	631-271-0400	271-0405
LSI Logic Corp 1320 Ridder Park Dr *NASDAQ: LSI* ■ *TF:* 800-372-2447 ■ *Web:* www.lsi.com	San Jose	CA	95131	408-433-8000	433-7715
M Cubed Technologies Inc 921 Main St *Web:* www.mmmt.com	Monroe	CT	06468	203-452-2333	452-2335
M/A-COM Technology Solutions Inc 100 Chelmsford St *TF:* 800-366-2266 ■ *Web:* macom.com/	Lowell	MA	01851	978-656-2500	
Macronix America Inc 680 N McCarthy Blvd *Web:* www.macronix.com	Milpitas	CA	95035	408-262-8887	262-8810
Magnum Semiconductor Inc 591 Yosemite Dr *Web:* www.magnumsemi.com	Milpitas	CA	95035	408-934-3700	
Marvell Technology Group Ltd 5488 Marvell Ln *NASDAQ: MRVL* ■ *Web:* www.marvell.com	Santa Clara	CA	95054	408-222-2500	988-8279
Maxim Integrated 6440 Oak Canyon Ste 100 *Web:* www.maximintegrated.com	Irvine	CA	92618	714-508-8800	
Maxim Integrated Products Inc 120 San Gabriel Dr *NASDAQ: MXIM* ■ *TF:* 888-629-4642 ■ *Web:* www.maximintegrated.com	Sunnyvale	CA	94086	408-737-7600	737-7194
Medtronic Microelectronics Ctr (MMC) 710 Medtronic Pkwy *TF:* 800-633-8766 ■ *Web:* www.medtronic.com	Minneapolis	MN	55432	763-514-4000	
Memsic Inc One Tech Dr Ste 325 *Web:* www.memsic.com	Andover	MA	01810	978-738-0900	
Micrel Inc 2180 Fortune Dr *NASDAQ: MCRL* ■ *TF:* 800-538-8450 ■ *Web:* www.micrel.com	San Jose	CA	95131	408-944-0800	474-1000
Microchip Technology Inc 2355 West Chandler Blvd *NASDAQ: MCHP* ■ **Fax Area Code:* 602 ■ *TF:* 877-860-3951 ■ *Web:* www.microchip.com	Chandler	AZ	85224	480-792-7200	687-4646*
MicroLink Devices Inc 6457 W Howard St *Web:* www.mldevices.com	Niles	IL	60714	847-588-3001	
Micropac Industries Inc 905 E Walnut St *OTC: MPAD* ■ *Web:* www.micropac.com	Garland	TX	75040	972-272-3571	487-6918
Microsemi Corp 2381 Morse Ave *NASDAQ: MSCC* ■ *TF:* 800-713-4113 ■ *Web:* www.microsemi.com	Irvine	CA	92614	949-221-7100	756-0308
Mindspeed Technologies Inc 4000 MacArthur Blvd *NASDAQ: MSPD* ■ *Web:* macom.com	Newport Beach	CA	92660	949-579-3000	
Mini-Circuits Laboratories Inc 13 Neptune Ave *TF:* 800-654-7949 ■ *Web:* www.minicircuits.com	Brooklyn	NY	11235	718-934-4500	332-4661
MIPS Technologies Inc 955 E Arques Ave *NASDAQ: MIPS* ■ **Fax Area Code:* 650 ■ *Web:* www.imgtec.com	Sunnyvale	CA	94085	408-530-5000	530-5150*
Monolithic Power Systems Inc (MPS) 6409 Guadalupe Mines Rd *NASDAQ: MPWR* ■ *Web:* www.monolithicpower.com	San Jose	CA	95120	408-826-0600	826-0601
Moschip Semiconductor Technology USA 3335 Kifer Rd *Web:* www.moschip.com	Santa Clara	CA	95051	408-737-7141	737-7708
MoSys Inc 3301 Olcott St *TF:* 877-360-6690 ■ *Web:* www.mosys.com	Santa Clara	CA	95054	408-418-7500	
N&K Technology Inc 80 Las Colinas Ln *Web:* www.nandk.com	San Jose	CA	95119	408-513-3800	
National Semiconductor Corp 2900 Semiconductor Dr *Web:* www.ti.com	Santa Clara	CA	95051	408-721-5000	739-9803
NEC Electronics America Inc 2801 Scott Blvd *TF Tech Supp:* 800-366-9782 ■ *Web:* www.am.renesas.com	Santa Clara	CA	95050	408-588-6000	588-6130
NeoPhotonics Corp 2911 Zanker Rd *Web:* www.neophotonics.com	San Jose	CA	95134	408-232-9200	351-8899
Netlist Inc 51 Discovery Ste 150 *Web:* www.netlist.com	Irvine	CA	92618	949-435-0025	
Neurosky Inc 125 S Market St Ste 900 *Web:* www.neurosky.com	San Jose	CA	95113	408-600-0129	
Nikon Precision Inc 1399 Shoreway Rd *Web:* www.nikon.com	Belmont	CA	94002	650-508-4674	
Nitronex Corp 2305 Presidential Dr *Web:* www.nitronex.com	Durham	NC	27703	919-807-9100	
NVE Corp 11409 Vly View Rd *NASDAQ: NVEC* ■ *TF:* 800-467-7141 ■ *Web:* www.nve.com	Eden Prairie	MN	55344	952-829-9217	996-1600
O2Micro International Ltd 3118 Patrick Henry Dr *NASDAQ: OIIM* ■ *Web:* www.o2micro.com	Santa Clara	CA	95054	408-987-5920	987-5929
Oclaro Inc 46429 Landing Pkwy *NASDAQ: OCLR* ■ *Web:* oclaro.com	Fremont	CA	94538	510-580-8828	
OEM Group Inc 2120 W Guadalupe Rd *Web:* www.oemgroupinc.com	Gilbert	AZ	85233	480-558-9200	
OmniVision Technologies Inc 4275 Burton Dr *NASDAQ: OVTI* ■ *Web:* www.ovt.com	Santa Clara	CA	95054	408-542-3000	542-3001
ON Semiconductor Corp 5005 E McDowell Rd *NASDAQ: ON* ■ *TF:* 800-282-9855 ■ *Web:* www.onsemi.com	Phoenix	AZ	85008	602-244-6600	
Optek Technology Inc 1645 Wallace Dr *TF:* 800-341-4747 ■ *Web:* www.optekinc.com	Carrollton	TX	75006	972-323-2200	323-2396
OSI Systems Inc 12525 Chadron Ave *NASDAQ: OSIS* ■ *Web:* www.osi-systems.com	Hawthorne	CA	90250	310-978-0516	644-1727
Peregrine Semiconductor Corp 9380 Carroll Pk Dr *Web:* www.psemi.com	San Diego	CA	92121	858-731-9400	731-9499
Pericom Semiconductor Corp 3545 N First St *NASDAQ: PSEM* ■ *TF:* 800-435-2336 ■ *Web:* www.pericom.com	San Jose	CA	95134	408-435-0800	435-1100
PerkinElmer Inc 940 Winter St *NYSE: PKI* ■ *Web:* www.perkinelmer.com	Waltham	MA	02451	203-925-4602	944-4904
Photronics Inc 15 Secor Rd *NASDAQ: PLAB* ■ **Fax:* Hum Res ■ *Web:* www.photronics.com	Brookfield	CT	06804	203-775-9000	740-5630*
Pixelworks Inc 224 Airport Pkwy Ste 400 *NASDAQ: PXLW* ■ *Web:* www.pixelworks.com	San Jose	CA	95110	408-200-9200	200-9201
Plascore Inc 615 N Fairview St *TF:* 800-630-9257 ■ *Web:* www.plascore.com	Zeeland	MI	49464	616-772-1220	772-1289
PLX Technology Inc 870 W Maude Ave *NASDAQ: PLXT* ■ *TF:* 800-759-3735 ■ *Web:* www.plxtech.com	Sunnyvale	CA	94085	408-774-9060	774-2169
PMC-Sierra Inc 1380 Bordeaux Dr *NASDAQ: PMCS* ■ *TF:* 866-268-7116 ■ *Web:* pmcs.com	Sunnyvale	CA	94089	408-239-8000	492-1157
Point Source Power Inc 132 Tharp Dr *Web:* www.pointsourcepower.com	Moraga	CA	94556	925-708-7845	
Power Integrations 5245 Hellyer Ave *NASDAQ: POWI* ■ *Web:* www.powerint.com	San Jose	CA	95138	408-414-9200	414-9201
Powerex Inc 173 Pavilion Ln *TF:* 800-451-1415 ■ *Web:* www.pwrx.com	Youngwood	PA	15697	724-925-7272	925-4393
Powerfilm Inc 2337 230th St *TF:* 888-354-7773 ■ *Web:* www.powerfilmsolar.com	Ames	IA	50014	515-292-7606	
QLogic Corp 26650 Aliso Viejo Pkwy *NASDAQ: QLGC* ■ *TF:* 800-662-4471 ■ *Web:* www.qlogic.com	Aliso Viejo	CA	92656	949-389-6000	389-6114
QuickLogic Corp 1277 Orleans Dr *NASDAQ: QUIK* ■ *Web:* www.quicklogic.com	Sunnyvale	CA	94089	408-990-4000	990-4040
Rambus Inc 1050 Enterprise Way Ste 700 *NASDAQ: RMBS* ■ *Web:* www.rambus.com	Sunnyvale	CA	94089	408-462-8000	462-8001

Phone *Fax*

Ramtron International Corp
1850 Ramtron Dr .... Colorado Springs CO 80921 719-481-7000 481-9294
NASDAQ: RMTR ■ *TF:* 800-541-4736 ■ *Web:* www.cypress.com

Rayotek Scientific Inc
11499 Sorrento Vly Rd .... San Diego CA 92121 858-558-3671
Web: www.rayotek.com

Raytek Inc 1201 Shaffer Rd Bldg 2 .... Santa Cruz CA 95061 831-458-3900 425-4561
TF: 800-227-8074 ■ *Web:* www.raytek.com

Raytheon RF Components (RRFC) 870 Winter St...... Waltham MA 02451 781-522-3000
Web: www.raytheon.com

RF Micro Devices Inc 7628 Thorndike Rd........... Greensboro NC 27409 336-664-1233 931-7454
NASDAQ: RFMD ■ *TF:* 800-937-5449 ■ *Web:* www.rfmd.com

Samsung Semiconductors Inc 3655 N First St........ San Jose CA 95134 408-544-4000 544-4980
TF General: 800-726-7864 ■ *Web:* www.usa.samsungsemi.com

Seiko Instruments USA Inc
21221 S Western Ave Ste 250...................... Torrance CA 90501 310-517-7700 517-7709
TF Sales: 800-688-0817 ■ *Web:* www.seikoinstruments.com

Semiconductor Process Equipment Corp
27963 Franklin Pkwy .... Valencia CA 91355 661-257-0934
Web: www.team-spec.com

Semifab Inc 150 Great Oaks Blvd.................... San Jose CA 95119 408-414-5928
Web: www.semifab.com

Semikron Inc 11 Executive Dr .... Hudson NH 03051 603-883-8102
Web: semikron.com/

Semtech Corp 200 Flynn Rd .... Camarillo CA 93012 805-498-2111 498-3804
NASDAQ: SMTC ■ *Web:* www.semtech.com

Senspex Inc 9798 Coors Blvd Nw Bldg B........... Albuquerque NM 87114 505-891-0034
Web: www.senspex.com

Sharp Microelectronics of the Americas
5700 NW Pacific Rim Blvd .... Camas WA 98607 360-834-2500 834-8903
Web: www.sharpsma.com

Sheldahl Inc 1150 Sheldahl Rd .... Northfield MN 55057 507-663-8000 663-8545
TF: 800-927-3580 ■ *Web:* www.sheldahl.com

Shin-Etsu Handotai America Inc PO Box 8965...... Vancouver WA 98668 360-883-7053 883-7074
Web: www.sehamerica.com

Showa Denko America
420 Lexington Ave Ste 2850........................ New York NY 10170 212-370-0033 370-4566
Web: www.showadenko.us

Sigma Designs Inc 1778 Mcarthy Blvd .... Milpitas CA 95035 408-262-9003 957-9740
NASDAQ: SIGM ■ *Web:* www.sigmadesigns.com

Silicon Image Inc 1060 E Arques Ave .... Sunnyvale CA 94085 408-616-4000 830-9530
TF: 800-633-8284 ■ *Web:* www.siliconimage.com

Silicon Laboratories Inc 400 W Cesar Chavez........... Austin TX 78701 512-416-8500 416-9669
NASDAQ: SLAB ■ *TF:* 877-444-3032 ■ *Web:* www.silabs.com

Siliconix Inc 2201 Laurelwood Rd .... Santa Clara CA 95054 408-988-8000 567-8950
Web: www.vishay.com

Siltronic Corp 7200 NW Front Ave................... Portland OR 97210 503-243-2020 564-3219*
**Fax Area Code:* 898 ■ **Fax:* Sales ■ *TF:* 800-922-5371 ■ *Web:* www.siltronic.com

SkyFuel Inc 18300 W Hwy 72......................... Arvada CO 80007 303-330-0276
Web: www.skyfuel.com

Skyworks Solutions Inc 20 Sylvan Rd................ Woburn MA 01801 781-376-3000 376-3300
NASDAQ: SWKS ■ *Web:* www.skyworksinc.com

Solar Solutions & Distribution LLC
2500 W Fifth Ave .... Denver CO 80204 303-948-6300
TF: 855-765-3478 ■ *Web:* www.soldist.com

Solatube International Inc 2210 Oak Ridge Way .... Vista CA 92081 760-477-1120
TF: 888-765-2882 ■ *Web:* www.solatube.com

Solid State Devices Inc
14701 Firestone Blvd .... La Mirada CA 90638 562-404-4474
Web: www.ssdi-power.com

Solitron Devices Inc
3301 Electronics Way...................... West Palm Beach FL 33407 561-848-4311 863-5946*
OTC: SODI ■ **Fax:* Mktg ■ *Web:* www.solitrondevices.com

Spectrolab Inc 12500 Gladstone Ave .... Sylmar CA 91342 818-365-4611 361-5102
TF: 800-936-4888 ■ *Web:* www.spectrolab.com

SRS Labs Inc 2909 Daimler St.................... Santa Ana CA 92705 949-442-1070 852-1099
NASDAQ: SRSL ■ *TF General:* 800-243-2733 ■ *Web:* dts.com

STMicroelectronics NV
Pmb #192 134 Vintage Park Blvd Ste A .... Houston TX 77070 281-469-2035 469-2194
TF: 888-356-1766 ■ *Web:* www.st.com

Stretch Inc 1322 Orleans Dr...................... Sunnyvale CA 94089 408-543-2700 747-5736
TF: 800-468-6853 ■ *Web:* www.stretchinc.com

Sumitomo Electric Industries Ltd
2355 Zanker Rd .... San Jose CA 95131 408-232-9500 428-9111
Web: www.us.eudyna.com

SunEdison Semiconductor Ltd
501 Pearl Dr.......................... Saint Peters MO 63376 636-474-5000 474-5158*
NASDAQ: SEMI ■ **Fax:* Sales ■ *Web:* sunedisonsemi.com/

SunPower Corp 77 Rio Robles........................ San Jose CA 95134 408-240-5500
NASDAQ: SPWR ■ *TF:* 800-786-7693

Symetrix Corp
5055 Mark Dabling Blvd.................... Colorado Springs CO 80918 719-594-6145 598-3437
Web: www.symetrixcorp.com

Taiwan Semiconductor Mfg Company Ltd (TSMC)
2585 Junction Ave .... San Jose CA 95134 408-382-8000 382-8008
NYSE: TSM ■ *TF:* 877-248-4237 ■ *Web:* www.tsmc.com

Teledyne DALSA Inc 888 East Arques Ave............ Sunnyvale CA 94085 408-736-6000
Web: www.rad-icon.com

Teledyne Electronics & Communications
1049 Camino Dos Rios...................... Thousand Oaks CA 91360 805-373-4545
Web: www.tet.com

Tellurex Corp 1462 International Dr............... Traverse City MI 49686 231-947-0110 947-5821
TF: 877-774-7468 ■ *Web:* www.tellurex.com

Tensilica Inc 3255 Scott Blvd Ste 6............ Santa Clara CA 95054 408-986-8000 986-8919
Web: ip.cadence.com/

Tessera Technologies Inc 3099 Orchard Dr .... San Jose CA 95134 408-894-0700 894-0768
NASDAQ: TSRA ■ *Web:* www.tessera.com

Texas Advanced Optoelectronic Solutions Inc (TAOS)
1001 Klein Rd Ste 300 .... Plano TX 75074 469-298-4200 298-5991
Web: www.taosinc.com

Texas Instruments Inc 12500 TI Blvd.................. Dallas TX 75243 972-995-3773 927-6377
NASDAQ: TXN ■ *TF Cust Svc:* 800-336-5236 ■ *Web:* www.ti.com

Phone *Fax*

Tezzaron Semiconductor Corp
1415 Bond St Ste 111.......................... Naperville IL 60563 630-505-0404 505-9292
Web: www.tachyonsemi.com

Thorlabs Quantum Electronics Inc
10335 Guilford Rd .... Jessup MD 20794 240-456-7100 456-7200
TF: 877-226-8342 ■ *Web:* www.covega.com

Time Domain Corp
4955 Corporate Dr
Ste 101 Cummings Research Park .... Huntsville AL 35805 256-922-9229
Web: www.timedomain.com

Toppan Photomasks Inc
131 Old Settlers Blvd .... Round Rock TX 78664 512-310-6500 310-6544
Web: www.photomask.com

Toshiba America Electronic Components Inc
19900 MacArthur Blvd Ste 400.......................... Irvine CA 92612 949-623-2900 462-2200*
**Fax:* Hum Res ■ *TF:* 800-879-4963 ■ *Web:* www.toshiba.com/taec

Tosoh SMD Inc 3600 Gantz Rd.................... Grove City OH 43123 614-875-7912 875-0031
Web: www.tosohsmd.com

TranSwitch Corp Three Enterprise Dr .... Shelton CT 06484 203-929-8810
Web: www.websolutions.com/

Trident Microsystems Inc 1170 Kifer Rd............ Sunnyvale CA 94086 408-962-5000
Web: www.tridentmicro.com

TriQuint Semiconductor Inc
2300 NE Brookwood Pkwy .... Hillsboro OR 97124 503-615-9000 615-8900
NASDAQ: TQNT ■ *TF:* 855-367-8768 ■ *Web:* www.triquint.com

Tru-Si Technologies 657 N Pastoria Ave............ Sunnyvale CA 94085 408-720-3333
Web: www.trusi.com

Tvia Inc 4800 Great America Pkwy Ste 405 .... Santa Clara CA 95054 408-327-8033 612-2805*
**Fax Area Code:* 972 ■ *Web:* www.tvia.com

United Microelectronics Corp
488 De Guigne Dr.......................... Sunnyvale CA 94085 408-523-7800 733-8090
NYSE: UMC ■ *TF:* 800-990-1135 ■ *Web:* www.umc.com

Universal Display Corp 375 Phillips Blvd .... Ewing NJ 08618 609-671-0980 671-0995
NASDAQ: OLED ■ *Web:* www.udcoled.com

Variosystems Inc 901 S Kimball Ave .... Southlake TX 76092 817-416-7535
Web: www.variosystems.com

Veritec Inc 2445 Winnetka Ave N................ Golden Valley MN 55427 763-253-2670
TF: 866-546-1011 ■ *Web:* www.veritecinc.com

VIA Technologies Inc 940 Mission Ct................ Fremont CA 94539 510-683-3300 687-4654
TF: 888-524-9382 ■ *Web:* www.via.com.tw/en

Vishay Intertechnology Inc 63 Lancaster Ave.......... Malvern PA 19355 610-644-1300 296-0657
NYSE: VSH ■ *TF:* 800-567-6098 ■ *Web:* www.vishay.com

Vishay Precision Group Inc 63 Lancaster Ave.......... Malvern PA 19355 610-644-1300 321-5301*
NYSE: VPG ■ **Fax Area Code:* 484 ■ *Web:* www.vishay.com

Vitesse Semiconductor Corp 741 Calle Plano .... Camarillo CA 93012 805-388-3700 987-5896
TF: 800-642-1687 ■ *Web:* www.vitesse.com

Vlsip Technologies Inc
750 Presidential Dr.......................... Richardson TX 75081 972-437-5506 644-1286
Web: www.vlsip.com

Volterra Semiconductor Corp
47467 Fremont Blvd.......................... Fremont CA 94538 510-743-1200 743-1600
NASDAQ: VLTR ■ *Web:* www.maximintegrated.com

Wabash Technologies
1375 Swan St PO Box 829...................... Huntington IN 46750 260-355-4100 355-4265*
**Fax:* Sales ■ *TF:* 800-487-6865 ■ *Web:* www.wabashtech.com

Wafertech LLC 5509 NW Parker St .... Camas WA 98607 360-817-3000 817-3590
Web: www.wafertech.com

Wallco Inc 53 E Jackson St # 55.................. Wilkes Barre PA 18701 570-823-6181 829-5952
TF: 800-392-5526 ■ *Web:* www.wallcoinc.com

West Coast Quartz Corp (WCQ)
1000 Corporate Way PO Box 14066.................. Fremont CA 94539 510-249-2160 651-4617
Web: www.westcoastquartz.com

Winbond Electronics Corp America
2727 N First St.......................... San Jose CA 95134 408-943-6666 474-1600
Web: www.winbond.com

Winslow Automation Inc 905 Montague Expy.......... Milpitas CA 95035 408-262-9004 956-0199
Web: www.winslowautomation.com

X-fab Texas Inc 2301 N University Ave .... Lubbock TX 79415 806-747-4400 747-3111
Web: www.xfab.com

Xilinx Inc 2100 Logic Dr.......................... San Jose CA 95124 408-559-7778 559-7114
NASDAQ: XLNX ■ *TF:* 800-594-5469 ■ *Web:* www.xilinx.com

ZiLOG Inc 1590 Buckeye Dr.......................... Milpitas CA 95035 408-513-1500 365-8535
Web: www.zilog.com

Zoran Corp 1390 Kifer Rd .... Sunnyvale CA 94086 408-523-6500 523-6501
NASDAQ: ZRAN

700 SHEET METAL WORK

SEE ALSO Plumbing, Heating, Air Conditioning Contractors p. 2098; Roofing, Siding, Sheet Metal Contractors p. 2103

Phone *Fax*

A p Machine & Tool Inc 1301 Elm St .... Terre Haute IN 47807 812-232-4939
Web: apmachineandtool.com

A-1 Tool Corp 1425 Armitage Ave................ Melrose Park IL 60160 708-345-5000
Web: www.a1toolco.com

A2mg Inc 8601 E Us Hwy 40.................... Kansas City MO 64129 816-874-4500
Web: www.a2mg.com

Abalon Precision Mfg Corp 1040 Home St............... Bronx NY 10459 718-589-5682 589-0300
TF: 800-888-2225 ■ *Web:* www.abalonmfg.com

Abrams Airborne Manufacturing Inc
3735 N Romero Rd.......................... Tucson AZ 85705 520-887-1727 293-8807
Web: www.abrams.com

AC Horn & Co 1269 Majesty Dr...................... Dallas TX 75247 214-630-3311
Web: www.achornco.com

Accede Mold & Tool Company Inc
1125 Lexington Ave .... Rochester NY 14606 585-254-6490
Web: www.accedemold.com

Accu-Fab Inc 801 Beacon Lk Dr .... Raleigh NC 27610 919-212-6400
Web: www.accufabnc.com

Accuduct Manufacturing Inc 316 Ellingson Rd......... Algona WA 98001 253-939-7741
Web: www.accuduct.com

Company	City	State	ZIP	Phone	Fax
Ace Irrigation & Manufacturing Co 4740 E 39th St *Web:* www.acenebraska.com	Kearney	NE	68847	308-237-5173	
Aero Trades Manufacturing Corp 65 Jericho Tpke *Web:* www.aerotrades.com	Mineola	NY	11501	516-746-3360	746-3417
Aerospace Fabrications of Georgia Inc 305 Butler Industrial Dr *Web:* www.afog.com	Dallas	GA	30132	770-505-8801	
Ag Machining & Industries Inc 4607 S Windermere St *Web:* www.agmachining.com	Englewood	CO	80110	303-783-0081	
AHR Metals Inc 20 Division St *Web:* www.ahrmetals.com	Bessemer	AL	35020	205-428-8888	
Air Comfort Corp 2550 Braga Dr *TF:* 800-466-3779 ■ *Web:* www.aircomfort.com	Broadview	IL	60155	708-345-1900	345-2730
Air Conditioning Products Co 30350 Ecorse Rd *Web:* www.acpshutters.com	Romulus	MI	48174	734-326-0050	326-9632
Air Vent Inc 4117 Pinnacle Pnt Dr Ste 400 **Fax Area Code:* 214 ■ *TF:* 800-247-8368 ■ *Web:* www.airvent.com	Dallas	TX	75211	800-247-8368	630-7413*
Aircom Mfg Inc 6205 E 30th St *TF:* 800-925-2426 ■ *Web:* www.aircommfg.com	Indianapolis	IN	46219	317-545-5383	542-7365
Airecon Manufacturing Corp 5271 Brotherton Ct *Web:* www.airecon.com	Cincinnati	OH	45227	513-561-5522	
Airolite Company LLC PO Box 410 *Web:* www.airolite.com	Schofield	WI	54476	715-841-8757	841-8773
Airtronics Metal Products Inc 1991 Senter Rd *Web:* www.airtronics.com	San Jose	CA	95112	408-977-7800	977-7810
All Metals Fabricating Inc 200 Allentown Pkwy *Web:* www.k-flex.us	Allen	TX	75002	972-747-1230	
Allendale Machinery Systems Inc 16 Park Way *Web:* hfoallendale.com	Upper Saddle River	NJ	07458	201-327-5215	
Allied Tool & Die Company LLC 3807 S Seventh St *Web:* www.alliedtool.com	Phoenix	AZ	85040	602-276-2439	
Aluminum Line Products Co 24460 Sperry Cir *TF:* 800-321-3154 ■ *Web:* www.aluminumline.com	Westlake	OH	44145	440-835-8880	835-8879
American Aircraft Products Inc 15411 S Broadway *Web:* www.americanaircraft.com	Gardena	CA	90248	310-532-7434	
American Fabricators Inc 570 Metroplex Dr *Web:* www.americanfabricators.com	Nashville	TN	37211	615-834-8700	
American Warming & Ventilating Inc 7301 International Dr *Web:* www.american-warming.com	Holland	OH	43528	419-865-5000	865-1375
Amtex Precision Fabrication 3920 Bahler Ave *Web:* www.amtexprecision.com	Manvel	TX	77578	281-489-7042	489-1992
Amuneal Manufacturing Corp 4737 Darrah St *Web:* www.amuneal.com	Philadelphia	PA	19124	215-535-3000	
APX Enclosures Inc 200 Oregon St *Web:* www.apx-enclosures.com	Mercersburg	PA	17236	717-328-9399	
Arizona Precision Sheet Metal 2140 W Pinnacle Peak Rd *TF:* 800-443-7039 ■ *Web:* www.apsm-jit.com	Phoenix	AZ	85027	623-516-3700	516-3701
Arrow United Industries 450 Riverside Dr PO Box 69 *Web:* www.arrowunited.com	Wyalusing	PA	18853	570-746-1888	746-9286
ASC Profiles Inc 2110 Enterprise Blvd *TF Cust Svc:* 800-360-2477 ■ *Web:* www.ascprofiles.com	West Sacramento	CA	95691	916-372-0933	372-7606
Assembled Products 300 Hastings Dr *Web:* www.aproducts.com	Buffalo Grove	IL	60089	847-215-1948	
Associated Materials Inc 3773 State Rd *TF:* 800-257-4335 ■ *Web:* www.associatedmaterials.com	Cuyahoga Falls	OH	44223	330-929-1811	922-2296
Atlantic Air Enterprises Inc 856 Elston St *Web:* www.atlanticairent.com	Rahway	NJ	07065	732-381-4000	
Atlantic Ventilating & Equipment Co 25 Sebethe Dr	Cromwell	CT	06416	860-635-1300	632-7412
Atlas Mfg 2950 Weeks Ave SE *Web:* www.atlasmfg.com	Minneapolis	MN	55414	612-331-2566	331-1295
ATS Systems Inc 30222 Esperanza *TF:* 800-321-1833 ■ *Web:* www.ats-s.com	Rancho Santa Margarita	CA	92688	949-888-1744	
Automated Quality Technologies Inc 563 Shoreview Park Rd *TF:* 800-250-9297 ■ *Web:* www.lionprecision.com	St Paul	MN	55126	651-484-6544	
AW Mercer Inc 104 Industrial Dr PO Box 508 *Web:* www.awmercer.com	Boyertown	PA	19512	610-367-8460	367-7491
Baldwin Metals Company Inc 1901 W Commerce St Ste A *Web:* baldwinmetals.com	Dallas	TX	75208	214-747-6722	
Ballew's Aluminum Products Inc Two Shelter Dr *Web:* www.ballews.com	Greer	SC	29650	864-272-4453	
Bandy Inc 201 S International Rd *Web:* www.bandyco.com	Garland	TX	75042	972-272-5455	
Basmat Inc 1531 240th St *Web:* www.mcstarlite.com	Harbor City	CA	90710	310-325-2063	325-9682
Bauer Manufacturing Inc 100 N Fm 3083 Rd *Web:* www.bauer-conroe.com	Conroe	TX	77303	936-539-5030	
Berger Bldg Products Inc 805 Pennsylvania Blvd *TF Cust Svc:* 800-523-8852 ■ *Web:* www.bergerbp.com	Feasterville	PA	19053	215-355-1200	355-7738
Bert R Huncilman & Son 115 Security Pkwy	New Albany	IN	47150	812-945-3544	
Best Cutting Die Co 8080 Mccormick Blvd *Web:* www.bestcuttingdie.com	Skokie	IL	60076	847-675-5522	
BHW Sheet Metal Co 113 Johnson St *Web:* bhwsm.com	Jonesboro	GA	30236	770-471-9303	478-7923

Company	City	State	ZIP	Phone	Fax
Blazing Technologies Inc 4631A Morgantown Rd *Web:* www.blazingtech.net	Mohnton	PA	19540	484-722-4800	
Branch Manufacturing Co 6420 Pine St *Web:* www.branchmfg.com	North Branch	MN	55056	651-674-4441	674-4442
Burgess Speciality Fabrication Inc 8222 Fawndale Ln *Web:* www.burgessfab.com	Houston	TX	77040	713-462-0293	
California Precision Products Inc 6790 Flanders Dr *Web:* www.cal-precision.com	San Diego	CA	92121	858-638-7300	
Captive-aire Systems Inc 4641 Paragon Pk Rd *TF:* 800-334-9256 ■ *Web:* www.captiveaire.com	Raleigh	NC	27616	919-882-2410	882-5204
CEEMCO Inc 3330 E Kemper Rd *Web:* www.ceemco.com	Cincinnati	OH	45241	513-563-8822	
Center Industries Corp 2505 S Custer *Web:* www.centerindustries.com	Wichita	KS	67217	316-942-8255	
Chantland-MHS 502 Seventh St N *Web:* www.chantland.com	Dakota City	IA	50529	515-332-4045	
Chapco Inc 10 Denlar Dr *Web:* www.chapcoinc.com	Chester	CT	06412	860-526-9535	
Chapman Engineering Corp 2321 Cape Cod Way *Web:* www.chapmanengineering.com	Santa Ana	CA	92703	714-542-1942	
Chirch Global Mfg LLC 1150 Ridgeview Dr *Web:* www.chirchmfg.com	Mchenry	IL	60050	815-385-5600	
Christensen Industries 2990 S Main St *Web:* www.christensenindustries.com	Salt Lake City	UT	84115	801-466-3334	466-1441
Ci Metal Fabrication 6205 St Louis St *Web:* www.cimetalfab.com/	Meridian	MS	39307	601-483-6281	693-6529
CID Performance Tooling Inc Six Willey Rd *Web:* www.cidtools.com	Saco	ME	04072	207-206-3319	
Cincinnati Ventilating Company Inc 7410 Industrial Rd *Web:* www.cvc-fab.com	Florence	KY	41042	859-371-1320	
Clark Specialty Co Inc 323 West Morris St *Web:* www.clarkspecialty.com	Bath	NY	14810	607-776-3193	776-3190
Cody Company Inc 4200 N I-45 *Web:* www.codycompany.com	Ennis	TX	75119	972-875-5884	875-0308
Coltwell Industries Inc 55 Winans Ave *Web:* www.coltwell.com	Cranford	NJ	07016	908-276-7600	
Computer Components Corp 2751 S Hampton Rd *Web:* compcomp.com	Philadelphia	PA	19154	215-676-7600	464-7876
Connell LP One International Pl 31st Fl *Web:* www.connell-lp.com	Boston	MA	02110	617-391-5577	737-1617
Consolidated Systems Inc 650 Rosewood Dr **Fax Area Code:* 803 ■ *TF:* 800-654-1912 ■ *Web:* www.csisteel.com	Columbia	SC	29202	800-654-1912	771-7920*
Contech Construction Products Inc 9025 Centre Pt Dr Ste 400 *TF:* 800-338-1122 ■ *Web:* www.conteches.com	West Chester	OH	45069	513-645-7000	645-7993
Continuous Metal Technology 439 W Main St *Web:* www.powdered-metal.com	Ridgway	PA	15853	814-772-9274	
Corchran Inc 1340 State St S *Web:* www.corchran.com	Waseca	MN	56093	507-835-3910	835-1382
Cortec Precision Sheet Metal Inc 2231 Will Wool Dr *Web:* www.cortecprecision.com	San Jose	CA	95112	408-278-8540	
Craftech Metal Forming Inc 24100 Water Ave Ste B *Web:* www.craftechmetal.com	Perris	CA	92570	951-940-6444	
Craftsman Custom Metals LLC 3838 N River Rd *Web:* www.ccm.com	Schiller Park	IL	60176	847-655-0040	
Crown Products Company Inc 6390 Phillips Hwy *TF:* 800-683-7144 ■ *Web:* www.crownproductsco.com	Jacksonville	FL	32216	904-737-7144	737-3533
Custom Metalcraft Inc 2332 E Division PO Box 10587 *Web:* www.custom-metalcraft.com	Springfield	MO	65808	417-862-0707	
CWR Mfg Corp 7000 Fly Rd *Web:* www.cwronline.com	Syracuse	NY	13057	315-437-1032	437-1493
Dalsin Industries Inc 9111 Grand Ave S *Web:* www.dalsinind.com	Bloomington	MN	55420	952-881-2260	
Danco Metal Products Inc 760 Moore Rd *Web:* www.dancometal.com	Avon Lake	OH	44012	440-871-2300	
Daria Metal Fabricators 1507 W Park Ave *Web:* www.dariametalfabricators.com	Perkasie	PA	18944	215-453-2110	
Data Transformation Corp One Penn Plz Ste 4515 *Web:* www.dtcss.com	New York	NY	10119	212-563-7565	
Data-matique 2110 Sherwin St *Web:* www.data-matique.com	Garland	TX	75041	972-272-3446	
Datagenic Tool & Die Inc 4280 Motor Ave	Culver City	CA	90232	310-253-9918	
Datamation Systems Inc 125 Louis St *Web:* www.pc-security.com	South Hackensack	NJ	07606	201-329-7200	
Dauntless Molds 806 N Grand Ave *Web:* www.dauntlessmolds.com	Covina	CA	91724	626-966-4494	
Daviess County Metal Sales Inc 9929 E US Hwy 50 *TF:* 800-279-4299 ■ *Web:* www.dcmetal.com	Cannelburg	IN	47519	812-486-4299	295-4344
Davis Tool & Die Company Inc 888 Bolger Ct *Web:* www.davistool.com	Fenton	MO	63026	636-343-0828	
Dawson Metal Company Inc 825 Allen St *Web:* www.dawsonmetal.com	Jamestown	NY	14701	716-664-3815	664-3485
Defabco Inc 3765 E Livingston Ave *Web:* www.defabco.com	Columbus	OH	43227	614-231-2700	
Detronic Industries Inc 35800 Beattie Dr *Web:* www.detronic.com	Sterling Heights	MI	48312	586-977-5660	939-5340
Domaille Engineering LLC 7100 Dresser Dr Ne *Web:* www.domailleengineering.com	Rochester	MN	55906	507-281-0275	
Du-Mont Co 7800 N Pioneer Ct *Web:* www.du-mont.com	Peoria	IL	61615	309-692-7240	693-2937

Company / Address	City	State	ZIP	Phone	Fax
Duggan Manufacturing LLC 50150 Ryan Rd Ste 15 *Web:* www.dugganmfg.com	Shelby Township	MI	48317	586-254-7400	
Dura-Bilt Products Inc PO Box 188 *Web:* www.durabilt.com	Wellsburg	NY	14894	570-596-2000	596-3296
Durand Forms Inc 6200 Equitable Rd *Fax Area Code: 989 ■ *TF:* 800-545-6342 ■ *Web:* www.durandforms.com	Kansas City	MO	64120	800-545-6342	288-2128*
Duratrack Inc 950 Morse Ave *Web:* www.duratrack.com	Elk Grove Village	IL	60007	847-806-0202	
Duwest Tool & Die Inc 8400 Madison Ave *Web:* duwesttool.com	Cleveland	OH	44102	216-631-1060	
Dynamic Tool Company Inc 1421 Vanderbilt Dr *Web:* www.dynamictool.com	El Paso	TX	79935	915-598-2330	
Eagle Cornice Co Inc 89 Pettaconsett Ave *Web:* www.eaglecornice.com	Cranston	RI	02920	401-781-5978	781-6570
EDAK Inc 630 Distribution Dr *Web:* www.edak.com	Melbourne	FL	32904	321-674-6804	
Edco & Arrowhead Products Inc 8700 Excelsior Blvd *TF:* 800-333-2580 ■ *Web:* www.edcoproducts.com	Hopkins	MN	55343	952-945-2680	938-4950
EDM Zap Parts Inc 1108 Front St Ste 2 *Web:* www.edmzap.com	Lisle	IL	60532	630-852-1699	
El Dorado Molds Inc 2691 Mercantile Dr Ste 104 *Web:* www.eldoradomolds.com	Rancho Cordova	CA	95742	916-635-4558	
Electro-Space Fabricators Inc 300 W High St *Web:* www.esfinc.com	Topton	PA	19562	610-682-7181	682-2133
Electromet Corp 879 Commonwealth Ave *Web:* www.electromet.com	Hagerstown	MD	21740	301-797-5900	
Elimetal Inc 1515 Boul Pitfield *Web:* elimetal.com	St Laurent	QC	H4S1G3	514-956-7400	956-8110
Elixir Industries Inc 24800 Chrisanta Dr Ste 210 *TF:* 800-421-1942 ■ *Web:* www.elixirind.com	Mission Viejo	CA	92691	949-860-5000	860-5011
Endicott Precision Inc 1328 Campville Rd *Web:* www.endicottprecision.com	Endicott	NY	13760	607-754-7076	
Engravers Metal Fabricators 124 Imperial St *Web:* www.emfinc.net	Merritt Island	FL	32952	321-453-3670	
Enprotech Corp 4259 E 49th St *Web:* www.enprotech.com	Cleveland	OH	44125	216-206-0081	
Enprotech Mechanical Services Inc 2200 Olds Ave *Web:* www.enpromech.com	Lansing	MI	48915	517-372-0950	
Epic Metals Corp 11 Talbot Ave *TF:* 877-696-3742 ■ *Web:* www.epicmetals.com	Rankin	PA	15104	412-351-3913	351-3913
Evansville Sheet Metal Works Inc 1901 W Maryland St *Web:* www.esmw.com	Evansville	IN	47712	812-423-7871	
EVS Metal Inc One Kenner Ct *Web:* www.evsmetal.com	Riverdale	NJ	07457	973-839-4432	
Exact Inc 5285 Ramona Blvd	Jacksonville	FL	32205	904-783-6640	
Experi-Metal Inc 6385 Wall St *Web:* www.experi-metal.com	Sterling Heights	MI	48312	586-977-7800	977-6981
Eze Lap Diamond Products 3572 Arrowhead Dr *Web:* www.eze-lap.com	Carson City	NV	89706	775-888-9500	
Fabrication Concepts Corp 1800 E St Andrew Pl *Web:* www.fabcon.com	Santa Ana	CA	92705	714-881-2000	881-2001
Fabrico Inc 10 Old Webster Rd	Oxford	MA	01540	508-987-5900	
Falstrom Co 147 Falstrom Ct *Web:* www.falstromcompany.com	Passaic	NJ	07055	973-777-0013	777-6396
Flat Rock Metal Inc (FRM) 26601 W Huron River Dr PO Box 1090 *Web:* www.frm.com	Flat Rock	MI	48134	734-782-4454	782-5640
Flexbar Machine Corp 250 Gibbs Rd *TF:* 800-879-7575 ■ *Web:* www.flexbar.com	Islandia	NY	11749	631-582-8440	
Floturn Inc 4236 Thunderbird Ln *Web:* www.floturn.com	Fairfield	OH	45014	513-860-8040	860-8044
Frank M Booth Inc 222 Third St *Web:* www.frankbooth.com	Marysville	CA	95901	530-742-7134	742-8109
Fred Christen & Sons Co 714 George St *Web:* toledochamber.com	Toledo	OH	43608	419-243-4161	243-1292
Frost Roofing Inc Two Broadway St *Web:* www.frost-roofing.com	Wapakoneta	OH	45895	419-739-2701	
FS Tool Corp 71 Hobbs Gate *TF:* 800-387-9723 ■ *Web:* www.fstoolcorp.com	Markham	ON	L3R9T9	905-475-1999	
G&G Steel Inc PO Box 179 *Web:* www.ggsteel.com	Russellville	AL	35653	256-332-6652	332-0143
Gasbarre Products Inc 590 Division St *Web:* www.gasbarre.com	Dubois	PA	15801	814-371-3015	
Gauthier Industries Inc 3105 22nd St NW *Web:* www.gauthind.com	Rochester	MN	55901	507-289-0731	
Gentek Bldg Products Inc 11 Craigwood Rd *TF:* 800-548-4542 ■ *Web:* www.gentekinc.com	Avenel	NJ	07001	732-381-0900	
Gerome Mfg Co Inc 80 Laurel View Dr PO Box 1089 *Web:* www.geromemfg.com	Smithfield	PA	15478	724-438-8544	437-5608
Gerref Industries 206 N York St *Web:* www.gerref.com	Belding	MI	48809	616-794-3110	
Gilbert Mechanical Contractors Inc 4451 W 76th St *Web:* www.gilbertmech.com	Edina	MN	55435	952-835-3810	835-4765
Girtz Industries Inc 5262 N E Shafer Dr *Web:* www.girtz.com	Monticello	IN	47960	574-278-7510	
Global Power Equipment Group Inc 400 E Las Colinas Blvd Ste 400 *NASDAQ: GLPW* ■ *Web:* www.globalpower.com	Irving	TX	75039	214-574-2700	853-4744
Goldberg Bros Inc 8000 E 40th Ave *Web:* www.goldbergbrothers.com	Denver	CO	80207	303-321-1099	388-0749
Gomez & Associates Company LLC 3216 Industry Dr Ste C *Web:* www.cryogenics.net	North Charleston	SC	29418	843-552-4552	
Gordons Specialties Inc 720 W Wintergreen Rd *Web:* www.gsihighway.com	Hutchins	TX	75141	972-225-1660	
Grayd-A Metal Fabricators 13233 Florence Ave *Web:* www.grayd-a.com	Santa Fe Springs	CA	90670	562-944-8951	944-2326
Greene Metal Products Inc 24500 Capital Blvd	Clinton Township	MI	48036	586-465-6800	465-0136
Group Manufacturing Services Inc 1928 Hartog Dr *Web:* www.groupmanufacturing.com	San Jose	CA	95131	408-436-1040	
H & H Industrial Corp 7612 Rt 130 *TF:* 800-982-0341 ■ *Web:* www.hhindustrial.com	Pennsauken	NJ	08110	856-663-4444	663-4446
H & S Manufacturing Co 2913 Singleton St *Web:* www.hsmfg.com	Rowlett	TX	75088	972-475-4747	
Hagerty Steel & Aluminum Co 601 N Main *Web:* www.hagertysteel.com	East Peoria	IL	61611	309-699-7251	
Hamilton Form Company Ltd 7009 Midway Rd *Web:* www.hamiltonform.com	Fort Worth	TX	76118	817-590-2111	595-1110
Handy Industries LLC 600 W Second Ave PO Box 223 *Web:* www.handyindustries.com	Sully	IA	50251	641-752-5446	
Harrington Mold 1906 S Quaker Ridge Pl *Web:* www.harringtonmold.com	Ontario	CA	91761	909-923-2627	
HASCO America Inc 270 Rutledge Rd Unit B *TF:* 800-387-9609 ■ *Web:* www.hasco.com	Fletcher	NC	28732	828-650-2600	
Hawkeye Industries Inc 1126 N Eason Blvd *Web:* hawkeye.ws	Tupelo	MS	38804	662-842-3333	
Herold Precision Metals LLC 1370 Hammond Rd White Bear Township *Web:* www.heroldprecision.com	Saint Paul	MN	55110	651-490-5550	
Herr Industrial Inc 610 E Oregon Rd *Web:* www.herrindustrial.com	Lititz	PA	17543	717-569-6619	
Hi-Tech Fabrication Inc Leesville Industrial Park 8900 Midway W Rd *Web:* www.htfi.com	Raleigh	NC	27617	919-781-2552	
HiMEC Mechanical 1400 Seventh St NW *Web:* www.himec.com	Rochester	MN	55901	507-281-4000	281-5206
HM White Inc 12855 Burt Rd *Web:* paintfinishingsystems.com	Detroit	MI	48223	313-531-8477	531-0522
HS Die & Engineering Inc 0-215 Lk Michigan Dr NW *Web:* www.hsdie.com	Grand Rapids	MI	49534	616-453-5451	
Humanetics II Ltd 1700 Columbian Club Dr *Web:* www.humanetics.com	Carrollton	TX	75006	972-416-1304	416-4163
Hutchinson Manufacturing Inc 720 Hwy 7 W *Web:* www.hutchmfg.com	Hutchinson	MN	55350	320-587-4653	
Hydraulic Technology Inc 3833 Cincinnati Ave *Web:* www.hydraulictechnology.com	Rocklin	CA	95765	916-645-3317	
IMCO Inc 858 N Lenola Rd *Web:* imco-inc.net	Moorestown	NJ	08057	856-235-7540	727-1637
IMM Inc 758 Isenhauer Rd *Web:* www.imm.net	Grayling	MI	49738	989-344-7662	
In-place Machining Company Inc 3811 N Holton St *Web:* inplace.com	Milwaukee	WI	53212	414-562-2000	
Industrial Air Inc 428 Edwardia Dr PO Box 8769 *Web:* www.industrialairinc.com	Greensboro	NC	27409	336-292-1030	855-7763
Industrial Louvers Inc 511 Seventh St S *TF:* 800-328-3421 ■ *Web:* www.industriallouvers.com	Delano	MN	55328	763-972-2981	972-2911
Industrial Revolution Inc 9225 151st Ave NE *Web:* www.industrialrev.com	Redmond	WA	98052	425-883-6600	
Irving Tool & Mfg Company Inc 2249 Wall St *Web:* irvingtool.com	Garland	TX	75041	972-926-4000	926-4099
J & E Metal Fabricators One Coan Pl *Web:* www.metalfab.com	Metuchen	NJ	08840	732-548-9650	
J & K Contracting 8903 Pioneer Rd *Web:* www.jandkcontracting.com	Neenah	WI	54956	920-836-9539	
Jaquith Industries Inc 600 E Brighton Ave *Web:* www.jaquith.com	Syracuse	NY	13210	315-478-5700	478-5707
Jensen Bridge & Supply Co 400 Stoney Creek Dr *Web:* www.jensenbridge.com	Sandusky	MI	48471	810-648-3000	648-3549
JET Equipment & Tools Ltd 49 Schooner St *TF:* 800-472-7685 ■ *Web:* www.jetgroupbrands.com/brands/view/index.php?lang=eng	Coquitlam	BC	V3K0B3	604-523-8665	
John W McDougall Company Inc (JWMCD) 3731 Amy Lynn Dr *Web:* www.jwmcd.com	Nashville	TN	37218	615-321-3900	329-9069
Jones Metal Products Inc 3201 Third Ave *TF:* 800-967-1750 ■ *Web:* www.jonesmetalproducts.com	Mankato	MN	56001	507-625-4436	625-2994
Jor-Mac Company Inc 155 E Main St *Web:* www.jor-mac.com	Lomira	WI	53048	920-269-8500	
Juniper Industries Inc 72-15 Metropolitan Ave PO Box 148 *Web:* www.juniperind.com	Middle Village	NY	11379	718-326-2546	326-3786
K y Diamond Ltd 2645 Rue Diab *Web:* kydiamond.ca	St Laurent	QC	H4S1E7	514-333-5606	339-5493
Kees Inc 400 Industrial Dr *Web:* www.kees.com	Elkhart Lake	WI	53020	920-876-3391	
Kingsbury Corp 15 Business Center Dr *Web:* www.optimation.us	Swanzey	NH	03446	603-352-5212	
Kirk Williams Company Inc 2734 Home Rd *Web:* www.kirkwilliamsco.com	Grove City	OH	43123	614-875-9023	875-9214
Klauer Manufacturing Co 1185 Roosevelt Ext PO Box 59 *Web:* www.klauer.com	Dubuque	IA	52004	563-582-7201	582-2022
Krueger Sheet Metal Co 731 N Superior St *Web:* kruegersheetmetal.com	Spokane	WA	99202	509-489-0221	489-6539

Company	City	State	ZIP	Phone	Fax
KSM Industries Inc N 115 W 19025 Edison Dr *Web:* www.ksmindustries.com	Germantown	WI	53022	262-251-9510	251-4865
Kuest Corp PO Box 33007 *Web:* www.kuestcorp.com	San Antonio	TX	78265	210-655-1220	655-1220
Laciny Bros Inc 6622 Vernon Ave *Web:* www.lacinybros.com	Saint Louis	MO	63130	314-862-8330	
Landmark Manufacturing Corp 28100 Quick Ave *Web:* www.landmarkfab.com	Gallatin	MO	64640	660-663-2185	663-2417
LB Foster Co 415 Holiday Dr *NASDAQ: FSTR* ■ **Fax Area Code:* 412 ■ **Fax:* Sales ■ *TF:* 800-255-4500 ■ *Web:* www.lbfoster.com	Pittsburgh	PA	15220	800-255-4500	928-7891*
Leader Industries Inc 2509 Cruzen St *Web:* www.leaderindustries.com	Nashville	TN	37211	615-256-3500	
Lewis Corp 15136 W Hunziker Rd *Web:* www.lcorp.com	Pocatello	ID	83202	208-238-1202	
Lifetime Nut Covers Inc 720 320th St *Web:* lifetimenutcovers.com	Britt	IA	50423	641-565-3566	
Limco Airepair Inc 5304 S Lawton Ave *Web:* www.limcoairepair.com	Tulsa	OK	74107	918-445-4300	445-2210
Link-Burns Mfg Company Inc 253 American Way *Web:* linkburns.com	Voorhees	NJ	08043	856-429-6844	429-3734
Lippincott Marine 327 14th Ave S *Web:* www.lippincottmarine.com	St Petersburg	FL	33701	727-821-5949	
Livers Bronze Co 4621 E 75th Terr *Web:* www.liversbronze.com	Kansas City	MO	64132	816-300-2828	300-0864
Lyco Manufacturing Inc 115 Commercial Dr *Web:* www.lycomfg.com	Columbus	WI	53925	920-623-4152	
Lynx Enterprises 724 E Grant Line Rd Ste B *Web:* www.lynxent.com	Tracy	CA	95304	209-833-3400	
M K Specialty Metal Fabricators 725 W Wintergreen Rd *Web:* www.mkspecialty.com	Hutchins	TX	75141	972-225-6562	
M&M Manufacturing Co 4001 Mark IV Pkwy *Web:* www.mmmfg.com	Fort Worth	TX	76106	817-336-2311	
M2 Global Inc 5714 Epsilon *Web:* www.m2global.com	San Antonio	TX	78249	210-561-4800	561-4852
Mac Cal Company Inc 1737 Junction Ave *Web:* www.maccal.com	San Jose	CA	95112	408-441-1435	
Maddox Metal Works Inc 4116 Bronze Way *Web:* www.maddoxmetalworks.com	Dallas	TX	75237	214-333-2311	337-8169
Magic Metals Inc 3401 Bay St *Web:* www.magicmetals.com	Union Gap	WA	98903	509-453-1690	
Magnus-hitech Industries Inc 1605 Lake St *Web:* www.magnushitech.com	Melbourne	FL	32901	321-724-9731	
Majestic Industries Inc 15378 Hallmark Ct *Web:* www.majesticind.net	Macomb	MI	48042	586-786-9100	
Majestic Metals Inc 7770 Washington St *Web:* majesticmetals.com	Denver	CO	80229	303-288-6855	
Malmberg Engineering Inc 550 Commerce Way *Web:* www.malmbergeng.com	Livermore	CA	94551	925-606-6500	
Mantz Automation Inc 1630 Innovation Way *Web:* www.mantzautomation.com	Hartford	WI	53027	262-673-7560	
Mapes Panels LLC 2929 Cornhusker Hwy PO Box 80069 *TF:* 800-228-2391 ■ *Web:* mapes.com	Lincoln	NE	68504	800-228-2391	737-6756
Matcor Metal Fabrication Inc 1021 W Birchwood St *Web:* www.matcor-matsu.com/	Morton	IL	61550	309-266-7176	263-1866
Mayco Industries LLC 18 W Oxmoor Rd *TF:* 800-749-6061 ■ *Web:* www.maycoindustries.com	Birmingham	AL	35209	205-942-4242	945-8704
Mayville Products Corp 403 Degner Ave *TF:* 800-230-0136 ■ *Web:* optimastantron.com/en/optima-stantron/	Mayville	WI	53050	920-387-3000	387-7196
McCorvey Sheet Metal Works LP 8610 Wallisville Rd *TF:* 800-580-7545 ■ *Web:* www.mccorvey.com	Houston	TX	77029	713-672-7545	672-0509
McFarlane Inc 3473 N Washington St *Web:* mcfarlane-e3.com	Grand Forks	ND	58203	701-772-9511	
McGill Airflow Corp 900 Pinder Ave **Fax Area Code:* 614 ■ *Web:* www.mcgillairflow.com	Grinnell	IA	50112	641-236-1580	829-1291*
McHone Metal Fabricators Inc 10300 County Rd 304 *Web:* www.kwikbilt.com	Terrell	TX	75160	972-524-7775	524-2777
Mech-Tronics Corp 1635 N 25th Ave *Web:* www.mech-tronics.com	Melrose Park	IL	60160	708-344-9823	344-0067
Melanson Company Inc, The 353 W St *Web:* www.melanson.com	Keene	NH	03431	603-352-4232	
Menches Tool & Die Inc 30995 San Benito St *TF:* 877-592-2328 ■ *Web:* www.menches.com	Hayward	CA	94544	510-476-1160	
Mercury Aircraft Inc 17 Wheeler Ave *Web:* www.mercurycorp.com	Hammondsport	NY	14840	607-569-4231	569-4306
Metal Standard Corp 286 Hedcor St *Web:* www.metalstd.com	Holland	MI	49423	616-396-4890	
Metal Trades Inc PO Box 129 *Web:* www.metaltrades.com	Hollywood	SC	29449	843-889-6441	
Metal-Fab Inc 3025 May St *TF:* 800-835-2830 ■ *Web:* www.mtlfab.com	Wichita	KS	67213	316-943-2351	943-2717
Metalcraft Technologies Inc 526 N Aviation Way *Web:* www.metalcraft.net	Cedar City	UT	84720	435-586-3871	586-0289
Metaltech Inc 206 Prospect Ave *Web:* www.metaltechinc.net	Saint Louis	MO	63122	314-965-4550	965-4234
Metalworks Inc 902 E Fourth St *Web:* metalworks1.com	Ludington	MI	49431	231-845-5136	845-1043
Metcam Inc 305 Tidwell Cir *Web:* www.metcam.com	Alpharetta	GA	30004	770-475-9633	442-3425
Mid-Continent Engineering Inc 405 35th Ave NE *Web:* www.mid-continent.com	Minneapolis	MN	55418	612-781-0260	782-1320
Middle Atlantic Products Inc 300 Fairfield Rd *Web:* www.middleatlantic.com	Fairfield	NJ	07004	973-839-1011	
Milbank Mfg Company Inc 4801 Deramus Ave *Web:* www.milbankmfg.com	Kansas City	MO	64120	816-483-5314	483-6357
Miller-Leaman 800 Orange Ave *Web:* www.millerleaman.com	Daytona Beach	FL	32114	386-248-0500	
Missouri Metals LLC 9970 Page Boulvard *Web:* www.missourimetals.com	St. Louis	MO	63132	314-222-7100	
Mitchell Metal Products Inc 19250 Hwy 12 E PO Box 789 *TF:* 800-258-6137 ■ *Web:* www.mitchellmetal.net	Kosciusko	MS	39090	662-289-7110	289-7112
Models & Tools 51400 Bellestri Ct *Web:* www.modelsandtools.com	Shelby Township	MI	48315	586-580-6900	
Modern Tool Inc 1200 Northdale Blvd *Web:* www.moderntoolinc.com	Coon Rapids	MN	55448	763-754-7337	754-7557
Morse Industries Inc 25811 74th Ave S *TF:* 800-325-7513 ■ *Web:* www.morseindustries.com	Kent	WA	98032	800-325-7513	
Multi-metal & Manufacturing Company Inc 1500 E Interstate 30 *Web:* www.multi-metal.com	Rockwall	TX	75087	972-771-1376	
Murray Sheet Metal Co Inc 3112 Seventh St *TF:* 800-464-8801 ■ *Web:* www.murraysheetmetal.com	Parkersburg	WV	26104	304-422-5431	428-4623
Myrmidon Corp 10555 W Little York Rd *Web:* myrmcorp.com	Houston	TX	77041	713-880-0044	880-4720
N-fab Inc 14925 Stuebner Airline Rd Ste 207 *Web:* www.n-fab.com	Houston	TX	77069	281-880-6322	
Napco Ply Gem Inc 5020 Weston Pkwy Ste 400 *TF:* 800-786-2726 ■ *Web:* napco.plygem.com	Cary	MO	27153	888-975-9436	842-3991
National Fabtronix Inc 28800 Hesperian Blvd *Web:* www.natfab.com	Hayward	CA	94545	510-785-3135	785-1253
National Metal Fabricators 2395 Greenleaf Ave *TF:* 800-323-8849 ■ *Web:* www.nmfrings.com	Elk Grove Village	IL	60007	847-439-5321	439-4774
New Age Metal Fabricating Company Inc 26 Daniel Rd *Web:* www.namf.com	Fairfield	NJ	07004	973-227-9107	
Newjac Inc 415 S Grant St *Web:* www.newjac.com	Lebanon	IN	46052	765-483-2190	
Noll Manufacturing Co 1320 Performance Dr	Stockton	CA	95206	209-234-1600	234-5925
Northern Manufacturing Company Inc 132 N Railroad St *Web:* www.northernmfg.com	Oak Harbor	OH	43449	419-898-2821	
Northwest Precision Fabricators Inc 1765 Red Soils Ct Ste 100 *Web:* www.nwprecision.com	Oregon City	OR	97045	503-557-1951	
Nsa Industries LLC 210 Pierce Rd PO Box 54 *Web:* www.nsaindustries.com	St. Johnsbury	VT	05819	802-748-5007	748-0067
Nu-Way Industries Inc 555 Howard Ave *TF:* 888-488-5631 ■ *Web:* www.nuwayindustries.com	Des Plaines	IL	60018	847-298-7710	635-8650
OMAX Corp 21409 72nd Ave S *TF:* 800-838-0343 ■ *Web:* www.omax.com	Kent	WA	98032	253-872-2300	
Panavise Products Inc 7540 Colbert Dr *TF:* 800-759-7535 ■ *Web:* www.panavise.com	Reno	NV	89511	775-850-2900	
Paramount Precision Products Inc 15255 W Eleven Mile Rd	Oak Park	MI	48237	248-543-2100	
Passaic Metal Products Co Five Central Ave Ste 1 *Web:* www.pampco.com	Clifton	NJ	07011	973-546-9000	
Pegasus Manufacturing Inc 422 Timber Ridge Rd *Web:* www.pegasusmfg.com	Middletown	CT	06457	860-635-8811	
Petersen Aluminum Corp 1005 Tonne Rd **Fax Area Code:* 800 ■ *TF:* 800-323-1960 ■ *Web:* www.pac-clad.com	Elk Grove Village	IL	60007	847-228-7150	722-7150*
PKM Steel Service Inc 228 E Ave A *Web:* www.pkmsteel.com	Salina	KS	67401	785-827-3638	
Platt & Labonia Co 70 Stoddard Ave *TF:* 800-505-9099 ■ *Web:* www.plattlabonia.com	North Haven	CT	06473	203-239-5681	234-7978
Poly Tech Diamond Co Four E St PO Box 6 *Web:* www.polytechdiamond.com	North Attleboro	MA	02760	508-695-3561	
Precise Industries Inc 610 Neptune Ave *Web:* www.preciseind.com	Brea	CA	92821	714-482-2333	
Precision Kidd Steel Company Inc One Quality Way *Web:* www.precisionkidd.com	Aliquippa	PA	15001	724-378-7670	
Precorp Inc 2024 N Chappel Dr *Web:* www.precorp.net	Spanish Fork	UT	84660	801-798-5425	
Pro Fabrication Inc 201 First St *Web:* www.pro-fabrication.com	Madison Lake	MN	56063	507-243-3441	
Protocase Inc 46 Wabana Court Harbourside Industrial Park *Web:* www.protocase.com	Sydney	NS	B1P0B9	902-567-3335	
PTMW Inc 5040 NW US Hwy 24 *Web:* www.ptmw.com	Topeka	KS	66618	785-232-7792	
Puritan Manufacturing Inc 1302 Grace St *Web:* www.purmfg.com	Omaha	NE	68110	402-341-3753	
QPM Aerospace Inc 14341 Fryelands Blvd *Web:* www.qpm2000.com	Monroe	WA	98272	360-794-9925	
Qual-fab Inc 34250 Mills Rd *Web:* www.qual-fab.net	Avon	OH	44011	440-327-5000	
Quality Industries Inc 130 Jones Blvd *Web:* www.qualityind.com	La Vergne	TN	37086	615-793-3000	
Quality Metal Fabricators Inc 2610 E Fifth Ave *Web:* www.qmf.com	Tampa	FL	33605	813-831-7320	
Quality Metal Products Inc Orange Rd PO Box 273 *Web:* www.qualmet.com	Dallas	PA	18612	570-333-4248	333-4967
Quality Tool Inc 1220 Energy Park Dr *Web:* www.qualitytool.com	Saint Paul	MN	55108	651-646-7433	
Rain Trade Corp 19 Skokie Vly Rd *Web:* www.guttersupply.com	Lake Bluff	IL	60044	847-283-0006	

Phone | Fax

Recovered Energy Inc 3411 Hawthorne Rd .... Pocatello ID 83201 208-637-0645
Web: www.recoveredenergy.com

RF Knox Company Inc 4865 Martin Ct SE .... Smyrna GA 30082 770-434-7401 433-1783
Web: www.rfknox.com

RG Smith Co 1249 Dueber Ave SW .... Canton OH 44706 330-456-3415 456-9638
Web: www.rgscontractors.com

Roll Forming Corp (RFC)
1070 Brooks Industrial Rd .... Shelbyville KY 40065 502-633-4435
Web: www.rfcorp.com

Rollex Corp 800 Chasa Ave .... Elk Grove Village IL 60007 847-437-3000 437-7561
TF Cust Svc: 800-251-3300 ■ *Web:* www.rollex.com

RuMar Manufacturing Corp 925 S St .... Mayville WI 53050 920-387-2104 387-2367
Web: www.rumar.com

Ruskin Manufacturing Co
3900 Doctor Greaves Rd .... Grandview MO 64030 816-761-7476 765-8955
Web: www.ruskin.com

S & S X-Ray Products Inc 10625 Telge Rd .... Houston TX 77095 281-815-1300
Web: www.ss-technology.com

Saferack Manufactoring 219 Safety Ave .... Andrews SC 29510 843-264-8096
Web: www.saferack.com

Saint Regis Culvert Inc 202 Morrell St .... Charlotte MI 48813 517-543-3430 543-2313
TF: 800-527-4604 ■ *Web:* www.stregisculvert.com

Schadegg Mechanical Inc
225 Bridgepoint Dr S .... St. Paul MN 55075 651-292-9933
Web: www.schadegg-mech.com

Serra Corp 3590 Snell Ave .... San Jose CA 95133 510-651-7333 657-5860
Web: www.serracorp.com

Seyer Industries Inc 66 Patmos Ct .... St. Peters MO 63376 636-928-1190
Web: www.seyerind.com

Sheet Metal Engineers Inc 383 Tower Rd .... Augusta GA 30907 706-863-6575

Ship & Shore Environmental Inc
2474 N Palm Dr .... Signal Hill CA 90755 562-997-0233
Web: www.shipandshore.com

Simpson Dura-Vent Inc 877 Cotting Ct .... Vacaville CA 95688 707-446-1786 446-4740
TF: 800-835-4429 ■ *Web:* www.duravent.com

SMT Inc 7300 ACC Blvd .... Raleigh NC 27617 919-782-4804 781-1498
Web: www.smtcoinc.com

Soldream Inc 203 Hartford Tpke .... Tolland CT 06084 860-871-6883
Web: www.soldream.com

Southbridge Sheet Metal Works Inc
441 Main St .... Sturbridge MA 01566 508-347-7800 347-9118
Web: ssmwusa.com

Southwark Metal Mfg Company Inc
2800 Red Lion Rd .... Philadelphia PA 19114 215-735-3401 735-0411
TF: 800-523-1052 ■ *Web:* southwarkmetal.com

Spartan Carbide 34110 Riviera .... Fraser MI 48026 586-285-9786
Web: www.spartancarbide.com

Special Products & Manufacturing Inc
2625 Discovery Blvd .... Rockwall TX 75032 972-771-8851 771-8563
Web: www.spmfg.com

Specialty Engineering Inc 1766 Hwy 36 E .... Maplewood MN 55109 651-777-8311 777-2707
Web: www.specialtyeng.com

Specialty Fabrications Inc
2674 Westhills Ct .... Simi Valley CA 93065 805-579-9730
Web: www.specfabinc.com

Spencer Fabrications Inc 29511 County Rd 561 .... Tavares FL 32778 352-343-0014
Web: www.spenfab.com

Spray Enclosure Technologies Inc
1427 N Linden Ave .... Rialto CA 92376 909-419-7011
Web: www.spraytech.com

STANDARD Iron & Wire Works Inc
524 Pine St .... Monticello MN 55362 763-295-8700
Web: www.std-iron.com

Standard Metal Products 1541 W 132nd St .... Gardena CA 90249 310-532-9861
Web: www.sheet-metal.com

Standley Batch Systems Inc
505 Aquamsi St .... Cape Girardeau MO 63702 573-334-2831
Web: www.standleybatch.com

Star Precision LLC 7300 Miller Dr .... Longmont CO 80504 303-926-0559
Web: www.starprecision.com

Streimer Sheet Metal Works Inc
740 N Knott St .... Portland OR 97227 503-288-9393 288-3327
TF: 888-288-3828 ■ *Web:* www.streimer.com

Structures Unlimited Inc 88 Pine St .... Manchester NH 03103 603-645-6539 625-0798
TF: 800-225-3895 ■ *Web:* www.structuresunlimitedinc.com

Superior Air Handling Corp
200 East 700 South .... Clearfield UT 84015 801-776-1997
Web: www.sahco.com

Sureway Tool & Engineering
2959 Hart Ct .... Franklin Park IL 60131 847-451-1784
Web: www.surewaytool.com

Swift Atlanta 3605 Swiftwater Park Dr .... Suwanee GA 30024 770-945-1084
Web: www.swiftatlanta.com

T & C Industries Inc PO Box 629 .... Darien WI 53114 262-882-1227
Web: www.royal-basket.com

Tarus Products Inc
38100 Commerce Dr .... Sterling Heights MI 48312 586-977-1400
Web: www.tarus.com

Taylor Dynamometer Inc
3602 W Wheelhouse Rd .... Milwaukee WI 53208 414-755-0040
Web: www.taylordyno.com

Technifab Products Inc
10339 N Industrial Park Dr .... Brazil IN 47834 812-442-0520
Web: www.technifab.com

Tella Tool & Mfg 1015 N Ridge Ave .... Lombard IL 60148 630-495-0545 495-3056
Web: www.tellatool.com

Tenere Inc 700 Kelly Ave .... Dresser WI 54009 715-247-4242
Web: www.tenere.com

TF System The Vertical ICF Inc
3030c Holmgren Way .... Green Bay WI 54304 920-983-9960
Web: tfsystem.com

TH Martin Inc 8500 Brookpark Rd .... Cleveland OH 44129 216-741-2020
Web: www.thmartin.net

Thybar Corp 913 S Kay Ave .... Addison IL 60101 630-543-5300 543-5309
TF: 800-666-2872 ■ *Web:* www.thybar.com

Titan Air Inc 13901 16th St .... Osseo WI 54758 715-597-2050
Web: www.titan-air.com

Tobar Industries 912 Olinder Ct .... San Jose CA 95122 408-494-3530
Web: www.tobar-ind.com

Top Tool Co 3100 84th Ln Ne .... Blaine MN 55449 763-786-0030
Web: www.toptool.com

Trend Technologies LLC 4626 Eucalypus Ave .... Chino CA 91710 909-597-7861 597-2284
Web: www.trendtechnologies.com

Tru-Fab Technology Inc 34820 Lakeland Blvd .... Eastlake OH 44095 440-954-9760
Web: www.trufab.com

Unist 4134 36th St SE .... Grand Rapids MI 49512 616-949-0853
Web: www.unist.com

United McGill Corp One Mission Pk .... Groveport OH 43125 614-829-1200 829-1291
Web: www.unitedmcgill.com

United Tool & Stamping Company of North Carolina Inc
2817 Enterprise Ave .... Fayetteville NC 28306 910-323-8588
TF: 800-883-6087 ■ *Web:* www.uts-nc.com

Unruh Fire Inc 100 Industrial Dr .... Sedgwick KS 67135 316-772-5400
Web: www.unruhfire.com

USAch Technologies Inc 1524 Davis Rd .... Elgin IL 60123 847-888-0148
Web: www.usach.com

V M Systems 3125 Hill Ave .... Toledo OH 43607 419-535-1044
Web: www.vmsystemsinc.com

Valley Joist 3019 Gault Ave N .... Fort Payne AL 35967 256-845-2330 845-2597
TF: 800-263-0324 ■ *Web:* www.valleyjoist.com

Valley Tool & Die Inc
10020 York Theta Dr .... North Royalton OH 44133 440-237-0160
Web: www.valcocleve.com

Vander Bend Manufacturing LLC
2701 Orchard Pkwy .... San Jose CA 95134 408-245-5150
Web: www.vander-bend.com

Vaughn Mfg Company Inc 757 Douglas Ave .... Nashville TN 37207 615-262-5775
Web: www.vaughnmfg.com

Vector Industries Inc
1520 - 80th St SW Bldg B .... Everett WA 98203 425-347-6696
Web: www.vectorindustries.com

Vent Products Company Inc
1901 S Kilbourn Ave .... Chicago IL 60623 773-521-1900 521-5613

Vent-A-Hood Ltd 1000 N Greenville Ave .... Richardson TX 75081 972-235-5201 231-0663
Web: www.ventahood.com

Versatile Fabrication 2708 Ninth St .... Muskegon MI 49444 231-739-7115
Web: versatilefab.com

Virtual Solutions LLC
21644 N Ninth Ave Ste 201 .... Phoenix AZ 85027 623-580-0775
Web: www.vsols.com

Voisard Mfg Inc 60 Scott St .... Shiloh OH 44878 419-896-3191 896-2127
Web: www.voisard.com

Votaw Precision Technologies Inc
13153 Lakeland Rd .... Santa Fe Springs CA 90670 562-944-0661
Web: www.votaw.com

Western Bay Sheet Metal Inc
2311 Marconi Ct .... San Diego CA 92154 619-233-1753
Web: www.westernbay.net

Western Industries Inc Watertown Metal Products Div
1141 S Tenth St .... Watertown WI 53094 920-261-0660 261-3832
Web: www.westernind.com

Wiley Metal Fabricating Inc 4589 N Wabash Rd .... Marion IN 46952 765-671-7865
Web: www.wileymetal.com

Wilson Manufacturing Co
4725 Green Park Rd .... Saint Louis MO 63123 314-416-8900
Web: www.wilsonmfg.com

Wilson Tool International Inc
12912 Farnham Ave .... White Bear Lake MN 55110 651-286-6001
TF: 800-328-9646 ■ *Web:* www.wilsontool.com

Wisco Products Inc 109 Commercial St .... Dayton OH 45402 937-228-2101 228-2407
TF: 800-367-6570 ■ *Web:* www.wiscoproducts.com

Wise Alloys LLC 4805 Second St .... Muscle Shoals AL 35661 256-386-6000 386-6980
TF Sales: 855-287-1922 ■ *Web:* www.wisealloys.com

Wolfe Engineering Inc 3040 N First St .... San Jose CA 95134 408-232-2600
Web: www.e-wolfe.com

Woodings Industrial Corp 218 Clay Ave .... Mars PA 16046 724-625-3131
Web: www.woodingsindustrial.com

Wyoming Machine Inc 30680 Forest Blvd .... Stacy MN 55079 651-462-4156
Web: www.wyomingmachine.com

York Metal Fabricators Inc
27 Ne 26th St .... Oklahoma City OK 73105 405-528-7495
Web: www.yorkmetal.com

701 SHIP BUILDING & REPAIRING

Phone | Fax

Al Larson Boat Shop Inc 1046 S Seaside Ave .... San Pedro CA 90731 310-514-4100 831-4912
Web: larsonboat.com

Allied Marine & Industrial Inc
118 W St .... Port Colborne ON L3K4C9 905-834-8275
Web: www.allmind.com

Allied Shipyard Inc 310 Ledet Ln .... Larose LA 70373 985-693-3323 693-3687

Allison Marine Contractors Inc 9828 Hwy 182 E .... Amelia LA 70340 985-631-2000
Web: www.allisonmarine.net

Austal USA LLC One Dunlap Dr .... Mobile AL 36602 251-434-8000
Web: www.austal.com

Bath Iron Works Corp 700 Washington St .... Bath ME 04530 207-443-3311 442-1567
Web: gdbiw.com

Bay Diesel Corp 3736 Cook Blvd .... Chesapeake VA 23323 757-485-0075
Web: www.baydiesel.com

Bay Ship & Yacht Co 2900 Main St Ste 2100 .... Alameda CA 94501 510-337-9122 337-0154
Web: www.bay-ship.com

Bay Shipbuilding Co 605 N Third Ave .... Sturgeon Bay WI 54235 920-743-5524
Web: bayshipbuildingcompany.com

Company	City	State	ZIP	Phone	Fax
Boland Marine & Mfg Company Inc 1000 Tchoupitoulas St *Web:* www.bolandmarine.com	New Orleans	LA	70130	504-581-5800	581-5814
Bollinger Algiers Inc 434 Powder St *Web:* www.bollingershipyards.com	New Orleans	LA	70114	504-362-7960	361-1679
Bollinger Gretna 4640 Peters Rd *Web:* bollingershipyards.com	Harvey	LA	70058	504-367-8080	
Bollinger Shipyards Inc 8365 Louisiana 308 *Web:* www.bollingershipyards.com	Lockport	LA	70374	985-532-2554	532-7225
C & G Boat Works Inc 401 Cochran Bridge Causeway Hwy 98 *Web:* www.cgboatworks.com	Mobile	AL	36603	251-694-1300	
Cascade General Inc 5555 N Ch Ave *Fax: Hum Res ■ *TF:* 855-844-6799 ■ *Web:* www.vigorindustrial.com	Portland	OR	97217	503-247-1777	247-6050*
Colonna's Shipyard Inc 400 E Indian River Rd *TF:* 800-265-6627 ■ *Web:* www.colonnaship.com	Norfolk	VA	23523	757-545-2414	543-2480
Conrad Industries Inc 1501 Front St *Web:* www.conradindustries.com	Morgan City	LA	70380	985-384-3060	385-4090
Continental Maritime of San Diego Inc 1995 Bay Front St *TF:* 877-631-0020 ■ *Web:* www.continentalmaritime.com	San Diego	CA	92113	619-234-8851	696-7358
Dakota Creek Industries Inc 820 Fourth St PO Box 218 *Web:* www.dakotacreek.com	Anacortes	WA	98221	360-293-9575	293-6432
Davis Boat Works Inc 99 Jefferson Ave *Web:* www.davisboat.com	Newport News	VA	23607	757-247-0101	
Derecktor Shipyards Inc 311 E Boston Post Rd *Web:* www.derecktor.com	Mamaroneck	NY	10543	914-698-5020	
Detyens Shipyards Inc 1670 Drydock Ave Bldg 236 Ste 200 *Web:* www.detyens.com	North Charleston	SC	29405	843-308-8000	308-8059
Earl Industries LLC 2 Harper Ave *TF:* 800-433-7300 ■ *Web:* www.nasscoearl.com	Portsmouth	VA	23707	757-215-2500	215-2504
Elevating Boats LLC 201 Dean Ct *TF:* 800-843-2895 ■ *Web:* www.ebi-inc.com	Houma	LA	70363	985-868-9655	868-9656
Elliott Bay Design Group LLC 5305 Shilshole Ave NW Ste 100 *Web:* www.ebdg.com	Seattle	WA	98107	206-782-3082	
Essex Boat Works Inc Ferry St PO Box 37 *TF:* 866-378-3748 ■ *Web:* essexboatworks.com	Essex	CT	06426	860-767-8276	767-1729
Fraser Shipyards Inc One Clough Ave *Web:* www.frasershipyards.com	Superior	WI	54880	715-394-7787	394-2807
General Dynamics Electric Boat Corp (GDEB) 75 Eastern Pt Rd *Fax: Hum Res ■ *Web:* gdeb.com	Groton	CT	06340	860-433-3000	433-1400*
General Dynamics NASSCO 2798 E Harbor Dr *Web:* www.nassco.com	San Diego	CA	92113	619-544-3400	544-3541
General Ship Repair Corp, The 1449 Key Hwy *Web:* www.generalshiprepair.com	Baltimore	MD	21230	410-752-7620	
Gladding-Hearn Shipbuilding One Riverside Ave PO Box 300 *Web:* www.gladding-hearn.com	Somerset	MA	02726	508-676-8596	672-1873
Goltens New York Corp 160 Van Brunt St *Web:* www.goltens.com	Brooklyn	NY	11231	718-855-7200	802-1147
Greenbrier Co One Centerpointe Dr Ste 200 *NYSE:* GBX ■ *TF:* 800-343-7188 ■ *Web:* www.gbrx.com	Lake Oswego	OR	97035	503-684-7000	684-7553
Gulf Copper & Mfg Corp 7200 Hwy 87 *Web:* www.gulfcopper.com	Port Arthur	TX	77642	409-989-0300	985-6349
Gulf Craft LLC 320 Boro Ln *Web:* www.gulfcraft.com	Franklin	LA	70538	337-828-2580	828-2586
Hodgdon Yachts Inc 14 School St PO Box 505 *Web:* www.hodgdonyachts.com	East Boothbay	ME	04544	207-633-4194	
Horizon Shipbuilding Inc 13980 Shell Belt Rd *Web:* www.horizonshipbuilding.com	Bayou La Batre	AL	36509	251-824-1660	
Huntington Ingalls Industries 4101 Washington Ave *NYSE:* HII ■ *Web:* www.huntingtoningalls.com	Newport News	VA	23607	757-380-2000	
Huntington Ingalls Shipbuilding Inc 1000 Access Rd *Web:* ingalls.huntingtoningalls.com	Pascagoula	MS	39567	228-935-1122	
Indmar Products Company Inc 5400 Old Millington Rd *Web:* www.indmar.com	Millington	TN	38053	901-353-9930	
International Submarine Engineering Ltd 1734 Broadway St *Web:* www.ise.bc.ca	Port Coquitlam	BC	V3C2M8	604-942-5223	942-7577
Irving Shipbuilding Inc 3099 Barrington St *Web:* www.irvingshipbuilding.com	Halifax	NS	B3K5M7	902-423-9271	
J. M. Martinac Shipbuilding Corp 401 E 15th St *Web:* www.martinacship.com	Tacoma	WA	98421	253-572-4005	627-2816
Jupiter Marine International Holdings 1103 12th AveEast *Web:* www.jupitermarine.com	Palmetto	FL	34221	941-729-5000	
Kvichak Marine Industries 469 NW Bowdoin Pl *Web:* www.kvichak.com	Seattle	WA	98107	206-545-8485	545-3504
Lake Union Drydock Co 1515 Fairview Ave E *Web:* ludd.com	Seattle	WA	98102	206-323-6400	
Leevac Shipyards Inc 111 Bunge St *TF:* 800-244-3262 ■ *Web:* leevac.com	Jennings	LA	70546	337-824-2210	824-2970
Lyon Shipyard Inc PO Box 2180 *Web:* www.lyonshipyard.com	Norfolk	VA	23501	757-622-4661	625-7137
Malibu Boats LLC 5075 Kimberly Way *Web:* www.malibuboats.com	Loudon	TN	37774	209-383-7469	
Malin International Ship Repair & Drydock Inc 320 77th St Pier 41 *Web:* www.malinshiprepair.com	Galveston	TX	77554	409-740-3314	
MARCO Global 4259 22nd Ave W *TF:* 866-966-2726 ■ *Web:* www.marcoglobal.com	Seattle	WA	98199	206-285-3200	282-8520
Marine Hydraulics International Inc (MHI) 543 E Indian River Rd *Web:* www.mhi-shiprepair.com	Norfolk	VA	23523	757-545-6400	545-8169
Marine Systems Inc 116 Capital Blvd *Web:* www.kirbycorp.com	Houma	LA	70360	985-223-7100	
Marinette Marine Corp 1600 Ely St *Fax: Cust Svc ■ *Web:* marinettemarine.com	Marinette	WI	54143	715-735-9341	735-3516*
Marisco Ltd 91-607 Malakole Rd *Web:* www.marisco.net	Kapolei	HI	96707	808-682-1333	
Metro Machine Corp PO Box 1860 PO Box 1860 *Fax: Hum Res ■ *Web:* www.memach.com	Norfolk	VA	23501	757-543-6801	494-0430*
Mitsubishi Heavy Industries America Inc 630 Fifth Ave Ste 2650 *Web:* www.mitsubishitoday.com	New York	NY	10111	212-969-9000	262-2113
Mship Co 401 W A St Ste 2125 *Web:* www.mshipco.com	San Diego	CA	92101	619-232-8937	
Newport Shipyard One Washington St *Web:* www.newportshipyard.com	Newport	RI	02840	401-846-6000	846-6001
Nichols Bros Boat Builders Inc 5400 Cameron Rd *Web:* www.nicholsboats.com	Freeland	WA	98249	360-331-5500	331-7484
North River Boats Inc 1750 Green Siding Rd *Web:* www.northriverboats.com	Roseburg	OR	97471	541-673-2438	
Northrop Grumman Newport News 13560 Jefferson Ave *Fax: Hum Res ■ *TF:* 888-493-7386 ■ *Web:* www.newport-news.org	Newport News	VA	23603	757-886-7777	886-7920*
Ocean Shipholdings Inc 16211 Pk Ten Pl *Web:* www.oceanshipholdings.com	Houston	TX	77084	281-579-3700	579-0671
Orange Shipbuilding Co Inc 710 Market St *Web:* www.conradindustries.com	Orange	TX	77631	409-883-6666	
Pacific Fisherman Inc 5351 24th Ave NW *TF:* 877-644-6148 ■ *Web:* pacificfishermen.com	Seattle	WA	98107	206-784-2562	784-1986
Pacific Shipyards International LLC 41 Sand Island Access Rd PO Box 31328 *Web:* www.pacificshipyards.com	Honolulu	HI	96819	808-848-6211	848-6279
Pacord Inc 240 W 30th St *Web:* I-3mps.com	National City	CA	91950	619-336-2200	
Pocock Racing Shells 615 80Th St Sw *Web:* www.pocock.com	Everett	WA	98203	425-438-9048	
Robishaw Engineering Inc 10106 Mathewson Ln *TF:* 800-877-1706 ■ *Web:* www.flexifloat.com	Houston	TX	77043	713-468-1706	468-5822
Ship Supply of Florida Inc 15065 NW Seventh Ave *Web:* www.ship-supply.com	Miami	FL	33168	305-681-7447	
Southwest Shipyard L P 18310 Market St *Web:* www.swslp.com	Channelview	TX	77530	281-860-3200	860-3215
Stabbert Mantime Management 2629 Nw 54th St Ste 201 *Web:* www.stabbertmaritime.com	Seattle	WA	98107	206-547-6161	
Swiftships Inc 1105 Levee Rd *Web:* www.swiftships.com	Morgan City	LA	70380	985-384-1700	380-2559
Tecnico Corp 831 Industrial Ave *TF General:* 800-786-2207 ■ *Web:* www.tecnicocorp.com	Chesapeake	VA	23324	757-545-4013	545-4925
Trinity Marine Products Inc 2525 N Stemmons Fwy *TF:* 877-876-5463 ■ *Web:* www.trin.net	Dallas	TX	75207	214-589-8446	
United States Marine Inc 10011 Lorraine Rd *Web:* www.usmi.com	Gulfport	MS	39503	228-679-1005	
Victoria Shipyards Company Ltd 825 Admirals Rd *Web:* www.vicship.com	Victoria	BC	V9A2P1	250-380-1602	
VT Halter Marine Inc 900 Bayou Casotte Pkwy *Web:* www.vthaltermarine.com	Pascagoula	MS	39581	228-696-6888	696-6899

702 SHUTTERS - WINDOW (ALL TYPES)

Company	City	State	ZIP	Phone	Fax
All Broward Hurricane & Aeicor Metal Products 472 W McNab Rd	Fort Lauderdale	FL	33309	954-974-3300	247-3491
Atlantic Premium Shutters 29797 Beck Rd *TF:* 866-288-2726 ■ *Web:* thetapcogroup.com/brands/atlantic	Wixom	MI	48393	248-668-6408	
Champion Window Mfg Inc 12121 Champion Way *TF:* 877-424-2674 ■ *Web:* www.championwindow.com	Cincinnati	OH	45241	513-346-4600	346-4614
Commonwealth Laminating & Coating Inc 345 Beaver Creek Dr *TF General:* 888-321-5111 ■ *Web:* www.suntekfilms.com	Martinsville	VA	24112	276-632-4991	632-0173
Perfect Shutters Inc 12213 Rte 173 *TF:* 800-548-3336 ■ *Web:* www.shuttersinc.com	Hebron	IL	60034	815-648-2401	648-4510
Roll Shutter Systems Inc 21633 N 14th Ave *TF:* 800-551-7655 ■ *Web:* www.rollshuttersystemsusa.com	Phoenix	AZ	85027	623-869-7057	581-3116
Roll-A-Way Inc 1661 Glenlake Ave *Fax Area Code:* 630 ■ *TF:* 866-749-5424 ■ *Web:* www.roll-a-way.com	Itasca	IL	60143	866-749-5424	980-6364*
Rolling Shield Inc 2500 NW 74th Ave *Fax Area Code:* 305 ■ *TF:* 800-474-9404 ■ *Web:* www.rollingshield.com	Miami	FL	33122	800-474-9404	436-5523*
Shutter Mill Inc 8517 S Perkins Rd *TF:* 800-416-6455 ■ *Web:* www.kirtz.com	Stillwater	OK	74074	405-377-6455	377-1010
Sunburst Shutters 6480 W Flamingo Rd Ste D *TF:* 877-786-2877 ■ *Web:* www.sunburstshutters.com	Las Vegas	NV	89103	702-367-1600	367-8525
Tapco Group 29797 Beck Rd *TF:* 800-367-8741 ■ *Web:* www.tapcogroup.com	Wixom	MI	48393	248-668-6400	668-6466
Vantage Products Corp 960 Almon Rd *TF:* 800-481-3303 ■ *Web:* www.vantageproducts.com	Covington	GA	30014	770-788-0136	788-0361

703 SIGNALS & SIRENS - ELECTRIC

Company	City	State	ZIP	Phone	Fax
ADDCO LLC 240 Arlington Ave E *TF:* 800-616-4408 ■ *Web:* www.addco.com	Saint Paul	MN	55117	651-488-8600	558-3600

Phone *Fax*

ECCO 833 W Diamond St ... Boise ID 83705 208-395-8000 688-3226*
Fax Area Code: 800 ■ *TF:* 800-635-5900 ■ *Web:* www.eccolink.com

Econolite Control Products Inc
3360 E La Palma Av ... Anaheim CA 92806 714-630-3700 630-6349
TF: 800-225-6480 ■ *Web:* www.econolite.com

Federal Signal Corp Emergency Products Div
2645 Federal Signal Dr ... University Park IL 60466 708-534-3400 534-9050
Web: www.fedsig.com

Harrington Signal Co 2519 Fourth Ave ... Moline IL 61265 309-762-0731 762-8215
Web: www.harringtonsignal.com

Rothenbuhler Engineering
524 Rhodes Rd PO Box 708 ... Sedro Woolley WA 98284 360-856-0836 856-2183
Web: www.rothenbuhlereng.com

Safetran Traffic Systems Inc
1485 Garden of the Gods Rd ... Colorado Springs CO 80907 719-599-5600 599-3853
Web: www.safetran-traffic.com

Western Cullen Hayes Inc 2700 W 36th Pl ... Chicago IL 60632 773-254-9600 254-1110
Web: wch.com

Whelen Engineering Company Inc
51 Winthrop Rd & Rt 145 ... Chester CT 06412 860-526-9504 526-4078
Web: www.whelen.com

WL Jenkins Co 1445 Whipple Ave SW ... Canton OH 44710 330-477-3407 477-8404
Web: www.wljenkinsco.com

704 SIGNS

SEE ALSO Displays - Exhibit & Trade Show p. 2202; Displays - Point-of-Purchase p. 2203; Signals & Sirens - Electric p. 3173

Phone *Fax*

Ace Sign Systems Inc 3621 W Royerton Rd ... Muncie IN 47304 765-288-1000 288-1010
Web: www.acesign.com

Ad Art Co 3260 E 26th St ... Los Angeles CA 90058 323-981-8941 980-0515
TF: 800-266-7522 ■ *Web:* www.adartco.com

Ad Display Sign Systems Inc 27255 Katy Fwy ... Katy TX 77494 281-392-2828 392-7446
Web: addisplaysigns.com

Adamsahern Sign Solutions Inc
30 Arbor St Ste 27 ... Hartford CT 06106 860-523-8835
Web: www.adamsahern.com

Advance Corp Braille-Tac Div
8200 97th St S ... Cottage Grove MN 55016 651-771-9297 771-2121
TF: 800-328-9451 ■ *Web:* www.advancecorp.com

Advantage Sign Supply Inc
3939 N Greenbrooke SE ... Grand Rapids MI 49512 616-554-3300
Web: advantagesgs.com/

Allen Industries Inc 6434 Burnt Poplar Rd ... Greensboro NC 27409 336-668-2791 668-7875
TF: 800-967-2553 ■ *Web:* www.allenindustries.com

Always a Good Sign
407 Bloomfield Dr Ste 3 ... West Berlin NJ 08091 856-753-7800
Web: alwaysagoodsign.com

American Porcelain Enamel Co
203 W Church St ... Crandall TX 75114 972-427-6654

Anza Inc 312 Ninth Ave SE Ste B ... Watertown SD 57201 605-886-3889
Web: www.anza.com

APCO Graphics Inc 388 Grant St SE ... Atlanta GA 30312 404-688-9000
TF: 877-988-2726 ■ *Web:* www.apcosigns.com

Apex Digital Imaging Inc
16057 Tampa Palms Blvd W ... Tampa FL 33647 813-973-3034
TF: 866-973-3034 ■ *Web:* www.apexdigitalimaging.com

Art Guild Inc 300 Wolf Dr ... West Deptford NJ 08086 856-853-7500
Web: www.artguildinc.com

Artcraft Signs Co 1717 S Acoma St ... Denver CO 80223 303-777-7771 778-7175
Web: www.artcraftsign.com

ASC Signal Corp 1120 Jupiter Rd Ste 102 ... Plano TX 75074 214-291-7654
Web: www.ascsignal.com

ASL Services 3700 Commerce Blvd Ste 216 ... Kissimmee FL 34741 407-518-7900
Web: www.aslservices.com

Atlantic Sign Media Inc 151 McArthur Ln ... Burlington NC 27217 336-584-1375 584-3848
Web: atlanticsignmedia.com

Banana Banner Signs 3148 Duke St ... Alexandria VA 22314 703-823-5933
Web: bananabanner.com

Beyond Digital Imaging 36 Apple Creek Blvd ... Markham ON L3R4Y4 905-415-1888 415-1583
TF: 888-689-1888 ■ *Web:* www.bdimaging.com

Brady Corp 6555 W Good Hope Rd ... Milwaukee WI 53223 414-358-6600 292-2289*
NYSE: BRC ■ *Fax Area Code:* 800 ■ *Fax:* Cust Svc ■ *TF Cust Svc:* 800-541-1686 ■ *Web:* www.bradycorp.com

Budget 1 Hour Signs Inc
2535 E Indian School Rd ... Phoenix AZ 85016 602-955-4686
Web: budgetsignsaz.com

Caasco Signs 2719 Texas Ave ... Texas City TX 77590 281-332-1502 332-1503
Web: creativesigntc.com

California Neon Products Inc
4530 Mission Gorge Pl ... San Diego CA 92120 619-283-2191 283-9503
TF: 800-822-6366 ■ *Web:* www.cnpsigns.com

Carousel Signs & Designs Inc
2312 Commerce Ctr Dr Ste B ... Rockville VA 23146 804-620-3200
Web: www.carouselsigns.com

Century Graphics & Metals Inc
550 S N Lake Blvd Ste 1000 ... Altamonte Springs FL 32701 800-327-5664 262-8291*
Fax Area Code: 407 ■ *TF:* 800-327-5664 ■ *Web:* www.centurygraphics.com

Club Colors Inc 420 E State Pkwy ... Schaumburg IL 60173 847-490-3636
Web: www.clubcolors.com

Coast 2 Coast Sign Surveys Inc
7704 Basswood Dr ... Chattanooga TN 37416 423-296-9000
Web: www.c2csurveys.com

Colorado Time Systems 1551 E 11th St ... Loveland CO 80537 970-667-1000 667-5876
TF: 800-279-0111 ■ *Web:* www.colotime.com

Couch & Philippi Inc 10680 Fern Ave PO Box A ... Stanton CA 90680 714-527-2261 827-2077
TF Orders: 800-854-3360 ■ *Web:* www.couchandphilippi.com

Cummings Signs Inc 15 Century Blvd Ste 200 ... Nashville TN 37214 800-489-7446
TF: 800-489-7446 ■ *Web:* cummingsbrandnew.com

Phone *Fax*

Di Highway Sign & Structure Corp
40 Greenman Ave ... New York Mills NY 13417 315-736-8312
Web: www.dihighway.com

DiAZiT Company Inc
941 US 1 Hwy PO Box 276 ... Youngsville NC 27596 919-556-5188 556-3757
TF Cust Svc: 800-334-6641 ■ *Web:* www.diazit.com

Douglas Corp 9650 Valley View Rd ... Eden Prairie MN 55344 952-941-2944 942-3125
Web: www.douglascorp.com

Doyle Signs Inc 232 W IH- Rd ... Addison IL 60101 630-543-9490 543-9493
Web: www.doylesigns.com

Dualite Sales & Service Inc
1 Dualite Ln ... Williamsburg OH 45176 513-724-7100 724-7100
TF: 800-543-7271 ■ *Web:* www.dualite.com

Dynasign Corp 44040 Fremont Blvd ... Fremont CA 94538 510-405-5988
Web: www.dynasign.net

Eastern Metal/USA-SIGN 1430 Sullivan St ... Elmira NY 14901 607-734-2295 734-8783
TF Sales: 800-872-7446 ■ *Web:* www.usa-sign.com

Everbrite Inc 4949 S 110th St PO Box 20020 ... Greenfield WI 53220 414-529-3500 529-7191
TF: 800-558-3888 ■ *Web:* www.everbrite.com

Fairmont Sign Company Inc 3750 E Outer Dr ... Detroit MI 48234 313-368-4000
Web: www.fairmontsign.com

FASTSIGNS International Inc
2542 Highlander Way ... Carrollton TX 75006 972-447-0777 248-8201
TF: 800-827-7446 ■ *Web:* www.fastsigns.com

Federal Heath Sign Co 4602 N Ave ... Oceanside CA 92056 760-941-0715 941-0719
Web: www.federalheath.com

FLOORgraphics Inc
200 American Metro Blvd ... Hamilton Township NJ 08619 609-528-9200

Formetco Inc 2963 Pleasant Hill Rd ... Duluth GA 30096 770-476-7000
TF: 800-367-6382 ■ *Web:* www.formetco.com

Forms & Surfaces Inc 30 Pine St ... Pittsburgh PA 15223 412-781-9003
Web: www.forms-surfaces.com

GableSigns Inc 7440 Ft Smallwood Rd ... Baltimore MD 21226 410-255-6400 437-5336
TF: 800-854-0568 ■ *Web:* www.gablesigns.com

Gemini Inc 103 Mensing Way ... Cannon Falls MN 55009 507-263-3957 263-4887
TF: 800-538-8377 ■ *Web:* www.signletters.com

George Patton Assoc Inc 55 Broadcommon Rd ... Bristol RI 02809 401-247-0333
TF: 800-572-2194 ■ *Web:* www.displays2go.com

Gopher Sign Co 1310 Randolph Ave ... Saint Paul MN 55105 651-698-5095 699-3727
TF: 800-383-3156 ■ *Web:* www.gophersign.com

Gordon Sign 2930 W Ninth Ave ... Denver CO 80204 303-629-6121 629-1024
Web: www.gordonsign.com

Grandwell Industries Inc
121 Quantum St ... Holly Springs NC 27540 919-557-1221 552-9830
TF Cust Svc: 800-338-6554 ■ *Web:* www.grandwell.com

Graphic Specialties Inc
3110 Washington Ave N ... Minneapolis MN 55411 612-522-5287
TF: 800-486-4605 ■ *Web:* www.signsbygsi.com

Gulf Coast Signs of Sarasota Inc
1713 Northgate Blvd ... Sarasota FL 34234 941-355-8841
Web: www.gulfcoastsigns.com

Hackley Architectural Signage Inc
1999 Alpine Way ... Hayward CA 94545 510-940-2608
Web: www.hackley.net

Hall Signs Inc 4495 W Vernal Pk ... Bloomington IN 47404 800-284-7446 332-9816*
Fax Area Code: 812 ■ *TF:* 800-284-7446 ■ *Web:* www.hallsigns.com

Hallmark Nameplate Inc 1717 E Lincoln Ave ... Mount Dora FL 32757 352-383-8142 383-8146
TF: 800-874-9063 ■ *Web:* www.hallmarknameplate.com

Hawkins Traffic Safety Supply
1255 E Shore Hwy ... Berkeley CA 94710 800-236-0112 525-2861*
Fax Area Code: 510 ■ *TF:* 800-772-3995 ■ *Web:* hawkinstraffic.com

Highland Containers 100 Ragsdale Rd ... Jamestown NC 27282 336-887-5400
Web: www.stronghaven.com

Hy-Ko Products Co 60 Meadow Ln ... Northfield OH 44067 330-467-7446 467-7442
TF: 800-292-0550 ■ *Web:* www.hy-ko.com

Icon Identity Solutions
1418 Elmhurst Rd ... Elk Grove Village IL 60007 888-724-0380 364-1517*
Fax Area Code: 847 ■ *TF:* 888-724-0380 ■ *Web:* www.iconid.com

iHighcom Inc 325 W Main St Third Fl ... Lexington KY 40507 859-514-3839
Web: www.ihigh.com

Image National Inc 16265 Star Rd ... Nampa ID 83687 208-345-4020 336-9886
Web: www.imagenational.com

Insignia Systems Inc 8799 Brooklyn Blvd ... Minneapolis MN 55445 763-392-6200 392-6222
NASDAQ: ISIG ■ *TF:* 800-874-4648 ■ *Web:* www.insigniasystems.com

International Display Systems Inc
5008 Veterans Memorial Hwy ... Holbrook NY 11741 631-218-1802 218-1801
Web: www.idsmenus.com

International Patterns Inc 50 Inez Dr ... Bay Shore NY 11706 631-952-2000
TF: 800-471-6368 ■ *Web:* www.internationalpatterns.com

Interstate Highway Sign Corp
7415 Lindsey Rd ... Little Rock AR 72206 501-490-4242 490-1090
Web: www.interstatesigns.com

Kessler Sign Co 5804 Poe Ave ... Dayton OH 45414 937-898-0633
Web: www.kesslersignco.com

Kieffer & Company Inc 3322 Washington Ave ... Sheboygan WI 53081 800-458-4394 451-3360*
Fax Area Code: 920 ■ *TF:* 800-458-4394 ■ *Web:* www.kieffersigns.com

King Signs & Graphics 3858 Jackson River Rd ... Monterey VA 24465 540-468-2932

LaFrance Corp
One LaFrance Way PO Box 5002 ... Concordville PA 19331 610-361-4300 361-4301
Web: www.lafrancecorp.com

Lake Shore Industries Inc (LSI)
1817 Poplar St PO BOX 3427 ... Erie PA 16508 800-458-0463 453-4293*
Fax Area Code: 814 ■ *TF:* 800-458-0463 ■ *Web:* www.lsisigns.com

Lauretano Sign Group 1 Tremco Dr ... Terryville CT 06786 860-582-0233 583-0949
Web: www.lauretano.com

LNI Custom Manufacturing Inc
12536 Chadron Ave ... Hawthorne CA 90250 310-978-2000
TF: 800-338-3387 ■ *Web:* www.lnisigns.com

LSI Industries Inc 10000 Alliance Rd ... Cincinnati OH 45242 513-793-3200 984-1335
NASDAQ: LYTS ■ *Web:* www.lsi-industries.com

Lynn Sign Eight Gleason St ... Andover MA 01810 978-470-1194

M-R Sign Company Inc 1706 First Ave N ... Fergus Falls MN 56537 218-736-5681 736-4070
TF: 800-231-5564 ■ *Web:* www.mrsigncompany.com

Phone Fax

Magnetsigns Adv Inc 4225 38th St .... Camrose AB T4V3Z3 780-672-8720 672-8716
TF: 800-219-8977 ■ *Web:* www.magnetsigns.com

MC Sign Company Inc 8959 Tyler Blvd .... Mentor OH 44060 440-953-2280
Web: www.mcsign.com

McLoone 75 Sumner St .... La Crosse WI 54603 608-784-1260 782-3711
TF: 800-624-6641 ■ *Web:* www.mcloone.com

National Sign Corp 1255 Westlake Ave N .... Seattle WA 98109 206-282-0700 285-3091
Web: www.nationalsigncorp.com

National Stock Sign Co 1040 El Dorado Ave .... Santa Cruz CA 95062 831-476-2020 476-1734
TF: 800-462-7726 ■ *Web:* nationalstocksign.com

NW Sign Industries Inc 360 Crider Ave .... Moorestown NJ 08057 856-802-1677
Web: www.nwsignindustries.com

O'Ryan Group Inc 4010 Pilot Ste 108 .... Memphis TN 38118 901-794-4610 794-3206
TF: 800-253-0750 ■ *Web:* www.oryangroup.com

Pannier Graphics 345 Oak Rd .... Gibsonia PA 15044 724-265-4900 265-4300
TF: 800-544-8428 ■ *Web:* www.panniergraphics.com

Pattison Sign Group 555 Ellesmere Rd .... Scarborough ON M1R4E8 416-759-1111 759-9560*
**Fax Area Code:* 855 ■ *TF:* 800-268-6536 ■ *Web:* www.pattisonsign.com

Philadelphia Sign Co 707 W Spring Garden St .... Palmyra NJ 08065 856-829-1460 829-8549
Web: www.philadelphiasign.com

Poblocki Sign Company LLC 922 S 70th St .... West Allis WI 53214 414-453-4010 453-3070
TF: 800-776-7064 ■ *Web:* www.poblocki.com

Precision Solar Controls Inc 2985 Market St .... Garland TX 75041 972-278-0553 271-9583
TF: 800-686-7414 ■ *Web:* www.precisionsolarcontrols.com

Prismaflex Inc 1645 Queens Way E .... Mississauga ON L4X3A3 905-279-9793 279-1330
TF: 888-454-2244 ■ *Web:* www.prismaflex.com

Progressive Promotions Inc 145 Cedar Ln .... Englewood NJ 07631 201-945-0500
Web: progressivepromotions.com

Protection Services Inc 635 Lucknow Rd .... Harrisburg PA 17110 717-236-9307 236-1281
TF: 866-489-1234 ■ *Web:* www.protectionservices.com

Quality Manufacturing Inc
969 Labore Industrial Ct .... Saint Paul MN 55110 651-483-5473 483-1101
TF: 800-243-5473 ■ *Web:* www.qualitymanufacturing.com

Quiel Bros Sign Co 272 S 'I' St .... San Bernardino CA 92410 909-885-4476 888-2239
Web: www.quielsigns.com

Recognition Specialties Inc
1710 Harbeck Rd .... Grants Pass OR 97527 541-476-3166
Web: nicebadge.com

SA-SO Co 525 N Great SW Pkwy .... Arlington TX 76011 972-641-4911 660-3684
Web: www.sa-so.com

Safeway Sign Co 9875 Yucca Rd .... Adelanto CA 92301 760-246-7070 246-5512
TF: 800-637-7233 ■ *Web:* www.safewaysign.com

Scioto Sign Company Inc 6047 US Rt 68 N .... Kenton OH 43326 419-673-1261 675-3298
TF: 800-572-4686 ■ *Web:* www.sciotosigns.com

Scott Sign Systems Inc
7525 Pennsylvania Ave Ste 101 .... Sarasota FL 34243 941-355-5171 351-1787
TF: 800-237-9447 ■ *Web:* www.scottsigns.com

SFC Graphics 110 E Woodruff Ave .... Toledo OH 43604 419-255-1283
TF: 800-537-1130 ■ *Web:* www.sfcgraphics.com

Sign Builders Inc
4800 Jefferson Ave PO Box 28380 .... Birmingham AL 35228 800-222-7330 923-2124*
**Fax Area Code:* 205 ■ *TF:* 800-222-7330 ■ *Web:* www.signbuilders.com

Sign Designs Inc 204 Campus Way .... Modesto CA 95350 209-524-4484 521-0272
TF: 800-421-7446 ■ *Web:* www.signdesigns.com

Sign Resource Inc 6135 District Blvd .... Maywood CA 90270 323-771-2098
Web: www.signresource.net

Sign-A-Rama 2121 Vista Pkwy .... West Palm Beach FL 33411 561-640-5570 640-5580
TF All: 800-776-8105 ■ *Web:* www.signarama.com

Signs by Tomorrow USA Inc
8681 Robert Fulton Dr .... Columbia MD 21046 410-312-3600 312-3520
TF: 800-765-7446 ■ *Web:* www.signsbytomorrow.com

Signs First Corp 720 Wildwood Trace .... Winchester TN 37398 931-636-4031
TF: 800-598-5845 ■ *Web:* www.signsfirst.com

Signs Now 5368 Dixie Hwy Ste 1 .... Waterford MI 48329 248-596-8600 596-8601
TF: 800-356-3373 ■ *Web:* www.signsnow.com

Signtech Electrical Adv Inc
4444 Federal Blvd .... San Diego CA 92102 619-527-6100 275-6115*
**Fax Area Code:* 866 ■ *TF:* 877-885-1135 ■ *Web:* www.signtech.com

Signtex Imaging LP 1225 Alma St Ste C .... Tomball TX 77375 281-351-2776 351-0170
Web: www.signtex.com

Signtronix 1445 W Sepulveda Blvd .... Torrance CA 90501 800-729-4853 539-3554*
**Fax Area Code:* 310 ■ **Fax:* Sales ■ *TF:* 800-729-4853 ■ *Web:* www.signtronix.com

Spectrum Corp 10048 Easthaven Blvd .... Houston TX 77075 713-944-6200 944-1290
TF: 800-392-5050 ■ *Web:* www.specorp.com

Spotlight Promotions Inc
2000 Van Ness Ave Ste 101 .... San Francisco CA 94109 415-202-7100
Web: www.spotlightsf.com

Stouse Inc 300 New Century Pkwy .... New Century KS 66031 913-764-5757
Web: www.stouse.com

STOUT 6425 W Florissant Ave .... Saint Louis MO 63136 314-385-4600
Web: www.stoutsign.com

Tool Sport & Sign Co 1060 S Lapeer Rd .... Oxford MI 48371 248-969-5850
Web: toolsportandsign.com

Tube Art Group (TAG) 11715 SE Fifth St .... Bellevue WA 98005 206-223-1122 223-1123
TF: 800-562-2854 ■ *Web:* www.tubeart.com

Turnroth Sign Company Inc
1207 E Rock Falls Rd .... Rock Falls IL 61071 815-625-1155 625-1158

U s Nameplate Company Inc Hwy 30 W .... Mount Vernon IA 52314 319-895-8804
Web: www.usnameplate.com

Vomar Products Inc 7800 Deering Ave .... Canoga Park CA 91304 818-610-5115 610-5123
Web: www.vomarproducts.com

Vomela Specialty Co 274 E Fillmore Ave .... Saint Paul MN 55107 651-228-2200 228-2295
TF: 800-645-1012 ■ *Web:* www.vomela.com

Walter Haas & Sons Inc 123 W 23rd St .... Hialeah FL 33010 305-883-2257 883-0598
TF: 800-552-3845 ■ *Web:* www.haasprint.com

Werner Tool & Mfg Co Inc
12301 E McNichols Rd .... Detroit MI 48205 313-526-6020 526-6070
TF: 800-362-8491 ■ *Web:* www.trivision.com

White Way Sign 451 Kingston Ct .... Mount Prospect IL 60056 847-391-0200 391-0099
Web: www.whiteway.com

Phone Fax

World Wide Concessions Inc
440 Benigno Blvd Ste E .... Bellmawr NJ 08031 856-933-9900
Web: www.wwconcessions.com

Worldwide Sign Systems 446 N Cecil St .... Bonduel WI 54107 800-874-3334
TF: 800-874-3334 ■ *Web:* www.wwsign.com

Young Electric Sign Co
2401 Foothill Dr .... Salt Lake City UT 84109 801-464-4600 483-0998
TF: 888-959-3726 ■ *Web:* www.yesco.com

Zumar Industries Inc
9719 Santa Fe Springs Rd .... Santa Fe Springs CA 90670 562-941-4633 941-4643
TF: 800-654-7446 ■ *Web:* www.zumar.com

705 SILVERWARE

SEE ALSO Cutlery p. 2183; Metal Stampings p. 2746

Phone Fax

Empire Silver Company Inc
6520 New Utrecht Ave .... Brooklyn NY 11219 718-232-3389 232-0680

Great American Products Inc
1661 S Seguin Ave .... New Braunfels TX 78130 830-620-4400 620-8430
TF: 800-341-4436 ■ *Web:* www.gap1.com

Metallics Inc W7274 County Hwy Z PO Box 99 .... Onalaska WI 54650 608-781-5200 781-2254
Web: www.metallics.net

Old Newbury Crafters 36 Main St Ste 2 .... Amesbury MA 01913 800-343-1388 388-8430*
**Fax Area Code:* 978 ■ *TF:* 800-343-1388 ■ *Web:* www.silvercrafters.com

Olde Country Reproductions Inc 722 W Market St .... York PA 17405 717-848-1859 845-7129
TF Cust Svc: 800-358-3997 ■ *Web:* www.pewtarex.com

Pfaltzgraff Co PO Box 21769 .... York PA 17402 800-999-2811 717-2481*
**Fax:* Cust Svc ■ *TF:* 800-999-2811 ■ *Web:* www.pfaltzgraff.com

Salisbury Inc 29085 Airpark Dr .... Easton MD 21601 410-770-4901
TF: 855-255-5309 ■ *Web:* salisburyinc.net/

Towle Silversmiths PO Box 21379 .... York PA 17402 800-264-0758
Web: www.lifetimesterling.com

Tropar Manufacturing Inc
Five Vreeland Rd .... Florham Park NJ 07932 973-822-2400 822-2891
Web: www.airflyte.com

Utica Cutlery Co 820 Noyes St PO Box 10527 .... Utica NY 13503 315-733-4663 733-6602
Web: www.uticacutlery.com

Woodbury Pewterers Inc 860 Main St S .... Woodbury CT 06798 800-648-2014 263-2657*
**Fax Area Code:* 203 ■ *TF:* 800-648-2014 ■ *Web:* www.woodburypewter.com

706 SIMULATION & TRAINING SYSTEMS

Phone Fax

Bemco Inc 2255 Union Pl .... Simi Valley CA 93065 805-583-4970 583-5033
Web: www.bemcoinc.com

CACI MTL Systems Inc 2685 Hibiscus Way .... Beavercreek OH 45431 937-426-3111
Web: www.caci.com

CAE Inc 8585 Cote de Liesse .... Saint Laurent QC H4T1G6 514-341-6780 341-7699
NYSE: CAE ■ *TF:* 866-999-6223 ■ *Web:* www.cae.com

Cubic Corp 9333 Balboa Ave PO Box 85587 .... San Diego CA 92186 858-277-6780 505-1523
NYSE: CUB ■ *TF:* 800-937-5449 ■ *Web:* www.cubic.com

Cubic Defense Systems 9333 Balboa Ave .... San Diego CA 92123 858-277-6780 505-1524
TF: 800-937-5449 ■ *Web:* www.cubic.com

Doron Precision Systems Inc
150 Corporate Dr PO Box 400 .... Binghamton NY 13904 607-772-1610 772-6760
Web: www.doronprecision.com

DRS C3 Systems LLC 400 Professional Dr .... Gaithersburg MD 20879 301-921-8100 921-8010
TF: 800-694-5005 ■ *Web:* www.drs.com

Energy Concepts Inc 404 Washington Blvd .... Mundelein IL 60060 847-837-8191 837-8171
TF: 800-621-1247 ■ *Web:* www.eci-info.com

Environmental Tectonics Corp
125 James Way .... SouthHampton PA 18966 215-355-9100 357-4000
OTC: ETCC ■ *Web:* www.etcusa.com

Evans & Sutherland Computer Corp
770 Komas Dr .... Salt Lake City UT 84108 801-588-1000 588-4500*
OTC: ESCC ■ **Fax:* Hum Res ■ *TF Sales:* 800-327-5707 ■ *Web:* www.es.com

Faac Inc 1229 Oak Valley Dr .... Ann Arbor MI 48108 734-761-5836 761-5368
TF: 877-322-2387 ■ *Web:* www.faac.com

Frasca International Inc 906 E Airport Rd .... Urbana IL 61802 217-344-9200 344-9207
Web: www.frasca.com

Malwin Electronics Corp 52 E 22nd St .... Paterson NJ 07514 973-881-1500 881-1686
Web: www.malwin.com

Meggitt Training Systems Inc 296 Brogdon Rd .... Suwanee GA 30024 678-288-1090 288-1515
TF: 800-813-9046 ■ *Web:* www.meggitttrainingsystems.com

Nida Corp 300 S John Rodes Blvd .... Melbourne FL 32904 321-727-2265 727-2655
TF: 800-327-6432 ■ *Web:* www.nida.com

Ternion Corp 2223 Drake Ave .... Huntsville AL 35805 256-881-9933 881-9957
Web: www.ternion.com

707 SMART CARDS

Phone Fax

CardLogix 16 Hughes Ste 100 .... Irvine CA 92618 949-380-1312 380-1428
TF: 866-392-8326 ■ *Web:* www.cardlogix.com

Clever Devices Ltd 300 Crossways Pk Dr .... Woodbury NY 11797 516-433-6100
TF: 800-872-6129 ■ *Web:* www.cleverdevices.com

Credit Card Systems Inc 180 Shepard Ave .... Wheeling IL 60090 847-459-8320
TF: 800-747-1269 ■ *Web:* www.ccsplastech.com

DataCard Corp 11111 Bren Rd W .... Minnetonka MN 55343 952-933-1223 933-7971
TF: 800-328-8623 ■ *Web:* www.datacard.com

MDI Security Systems Inc
12500 Network Dr Ste 303 .... San Antonio TX 78249 210-477-5400 477-5401
TF: 866-435-7634 ■ *Web:* www.mdisecure.com

Perfect Plastic Printing Corp
311 Kautz Rd Ste 4 .... Saint Charles IL 60174 630-584-1600 584-0648
Web: www.perfectplastic.com

				Phone	Fax
Smart Card Integrators Inc (SCI) 2424 N Ontario St ... *Web:* www.sci-s.com	Burbank	CA	91504	818-847-1022	847-1454

708 SNOWMOBILES

SEE ALSO Sporting Goods p. 3182

				Phone	Fax
Arctic Cat Inc 601 Brooks Ave S ... *NASDAQ: ACAT* ■ *TF:* 877-228-2687 ■ *Web:* www.arcticcat.com	Thief River Falls	MN	56701	218-681-8558	681-9859
Polaris Industries Inc 2100 Hwy 55 ... *NYSE: PII* ■ *Web:* www.polaris.com	Medina	MN	55340	763-542-0500	542-0599
Yamaha Motor Corp USA 6555 Katella Ave ... *TF Cust Svc:* 800-656-7695 ■ *Web:* www.yamaha-motor.com	Cypress	CA	90630	800-656-7695	

SOFTWARE

SEE Computer Software p. 2040

709 SPAS - HEALTH & FITNESS

SEE ALSO Health & Fitness Centers p. 2451; Spas - Hotel & Resort p. 3176; Weight Loss Centers & Services p. 3296

Facilities listed here provide multi-day programs designed to increase health and well-being. Types of programs offered include (but are not limited to) relaxation, smoking cessation, weight loss, and physical fitness.

				Phone	Fax
Amerispa 90 Stanstead St ... *Web:* www.amerispa.ca	Bromont	QC	J2L1K6	450-534-2717	534-0599
Birdwing Spa 21398 575th Ave ... *Web:* www.birdwingspa.com	Litchfield	MN	55355	320-693-6064	693-7026
Black Hills Health & Education Ctr PO Box 19 ... *Web:* bhhec.org/	Hermosa	SD	57744	605-255-4101	255-4687
Body/Mind Restoration Retreats 56 Lieb Rd ... *Web:* www.bodymindretreats.com	Spencer	NY	14883	607-277-7779	277-7801
Cal-a-Vie Spa 29402 Spa Havens Way ... *TF:* 866-772-4283 ■ *Web:* www.cal-a-vie.com	Vista	CA	92084	760-945-2055	630-0074
Calistoga Spa Hot Springs 1006 Washington St ... *TF:* 866-822-5772 ■ *Web:* www.calistogaspa.com	Calistoga	CA	94515	707-942-6269	942-4214
Cooper Wellness Program 12230 Preston Rd ... *TF:* 800-444-5192 ■ *Web:* cooperaerobics.com	Dallas	TX	75230	972-386-4777	386-0039
Cornelia Day Resort 663 Fifth Ave Eighth Fl ... *TF:* 866-663-1700 ■ *Web:* www.cornelia.com	New York	NY	10022	212-871-3050	
Deerfield Spa 650 Resica Falls Rd ... *TF:* 800-852-4494 ■ *Web:* www.deerfieldspa.com	East Stroudsburg	PA	18302	570-223-0160	
Dr Wilkinson's Hot Springs Resort 1507 Lincoln Ave ... *Web:* www.drwilkinson.com	Calistoga	CA	94515	707-942-4102	942-4412
Duke Diet & Fitness Ctr (DFC) 501 Douglas St ... *TF:* 800-235-3853 ■ *Web:* dukemedicine.org/treatments/treatments/weight-loss-and-wellness	Durham	NC	27705	919-688-3079	684-6176
Golden Door PO Box 463077 ... *TF:* 866-420-6414 ■ *Web:* www.goldendoor.com	Escondido	CA	92046	760-744-5777	471-2393
Grand Wailea Resort & Spa 3850 Wailea Alanui Dr ... *TF:* 800-888-6100 ■ *Web:* www.grandwailea.com	Wailea	HI	96753	808-875-1234	879-4077
Green Mountain at Fox Run 262 Fox Ln PO Box 358 ... *TF:* 800-448-8106 ■ *Web:* www.fitwoman.com	Ludlow	VT	05149	802-228-8885	228-8887
Green Valley Spa & Resort 1871 W Canyon View Dr ... *TF:* 800-237-1068 ■ *Web:* www.greenvalleyspa.com	Saint George	UT	84770	800-237-1068	
Heartland Spa 1237 E 1600 N Rd ... **Fax Area Code:* 815 ■ *TF:* 800-545-4853 ■ *Web:* www.heartlandspa.com	Gilman	IL	60938	800-545-4853	683-2144*
Hills Health Ranch 4871 Caribou Hwy 97 PO Box 26 ... *TF:* 800-668-2233 ■ *Web:* www.spabc.com	108 Mile Ranch	BC	V0K2Z0	250-791-5225	791-6384
Hilton Head Health Institute 14 Valencia Rd ... *TF:* 800-292-2440 ■ *Web:* www.hhhealth.com	Hilton Head Island	SC	29928	843-785-7292	686-5659
Himalayan Institute Ctr for Health & Healing 952 Bethany Tpke ... *Web:* www.himalayaninstitute.org	Honesdale	PA	18431	570-253-5551	253-9078
Hippocrates Health Institute Life-Change Ctr 1443 Palmdale Ct ... *TF:* 800-842-2125 ■ *Web:* www.hippocratesinst.org	West Palm Beach	FL	33411	561-471-8876	471-9464
Kerr House 17777 Beaver St PO Box 363 ... *Web:* www.thekerrhouse.com	Grand Rapids	OH	43522	419-832-1733	832-4303
Kohala Spa 69-425 Waikoloa Beach Dr ... *Web:* www.kohalaspa.com	Waikoloa	HI	96738	808-886-2828	886-2953
Kripalu Ctr for Yoga & Health 57 Interlaken Rd ... *TF:* 800-741-7353 ■ *Web:* www.kripalu.org	Stockbridge	MA	01262	413-448-3400	448-3384
Lodge & Spa at Cordillera 2205 Cordillera Way ... *TF:* 800-877-3529 ■ *Web:* www.cordilleralodge.com	Edwards	CO	81632	970-926-2200	926-2486
Miraval AZ Resort & Spa 5000 E Via Estancia Miraval ... **Fax Area Code:* 520 ■ *TF:* 800-232-3969 ■ *Web:* www.miravalresorts.com	Tucson	AZ	85739	800-232-3969	825-5163*
New Age Health Spa PO Box 658 ... *TF:* 800-682-4348 ■ *Web:* www.newagehealthspa.com	Neversink	NY	12765	845-985-7600	985-2467
Northern Pines on Crescent Lake Bed & Breakfast Plus 31 Big Pine Rd ... *Web:* people.maine.com	Raymond	ME	04071	207-655-7624	935-7574
Oaks at Ojai 122 E Ojai Ave ... *TF:* 800-753-6257 ■ *Web:* www.oaksspa.com	Ojai	CA	93023	805-646-5573	640-1504
Ocean Waters Spa 600 N Atlantic Ave ... *TF:* 844-284-2685 ■ *Web:* plazaresortandspa.com	Daytona Beach	FL	32118	386-267-1660	
Ojo Caliente Mineral Springs Resort 50 Los Banos Dr PO Box 68 ... *TF:* 800-222-9162 ■ *Web:* www.ojospa.com	Ojo Caliente	NM	87549	505-583-2233	583-2045
Optimum Health Institute 6970 Central Ave ... *TF:* 800-993-4325 ■ *Web:* www.optimumhealth.org	Lemon Grove	CA	91945	619-464-3346	589-4098
Pritikin Longevity Ctr & Spa 8755 NW 36th St ... **Fax:* Resv ■ *TF:* 800-327-4914 ■ *Web:* www.pritikin.com	Doral	FL	33178	305-935-7131	935-7371*
Raj, The 1734 Jasmine Ave ... *TF:* 800-248-9050 ■ *Web:* www.theraj.com	Fairfield	IA	52556	641-472-9580	472-2496
Sagestone Spa & Salon *Red Mountain Resort* 1275 East Red Mtn Cir ... *TF:* 877-246-4453 ■ *Web:* www.redmountainresort.com	Ivins	UT	84738	435-673-4905	
Spa at Coeur d'Alene 115 S Second St ... *TF:* 800-684-0514 ■ *Web:* cdaresort.com/discover/spa	Coeur d'Alene	ID	83814	208-765-4000	676-7298
Spa at Grand Lake 1667 Exeter Rd Rt 207 ... *Web:* spasofamerica.com	Lebanon	CT	06249	860-642-4306	
Spa at Peninsula Beverly Hills 9882 S Santa Monica Blvd ... *TF:* 800-462-7899 ■ *Web:* www.peninsula.com/beverly_hills/en	Beverly Hills	CA	90212	310-551-2888	788-2319
Spa at The Setai 2001 Collins Ave ... **Fax Area Code:* 305 ■ *Web:* www.thesetaihotel.com	Miami Beach	FL	33139	888-625-7500	520-6600*
Spa Radiance 3011 Fillmore St ... *Web:* www.sparadiance.com	San Francisco	CA	94123	415-346-6281	346-6170
Structure House 3017 Pickett Rd ... *TF:* 800-553-0052 ■ *Web:* structurehouse.crchealth.com	Durham	NC	27705	919-493-4205	490-0191
Tennessee Fitness Spa 299 Natural Bridge Pk Rd ... *TF:* 800-235-8365 ■ *Web:* www.tfspa.com	Waynesboro	TN	38485	931-722-5589	722-9113
Tracie Martyn Salon 59 Fifth Ave Ste 1 ... *TF:* 866-862-7896 ■ *Web:* www.traciemartyn.com	New York	NY	10003	212-206-9333	206-8399
Two Bunch Palms Resort & Spa 67425 Two Bunch Palms Trl ... *TF:* 800-472-4334 ■ *Web:* www.twobunchpalms.com	Desert Hot Springs	CA	92240	760-329-8791	329-1874
Uchee Pines Lifestyle Ctr 30 Uchee Pines Rd PO Box 75 ... *TF:* 877-824-3374 ■ *Web:* ucheepines.org	Seale	AL	36875	334-855-4764	855-9014
Vail Cascade Resort & Spa 1300 Westhaven Dr ... *TF:* 800-420-2424 ■ *Web:* www.vailcascade.com	Vail	CO	81657	970-476-7111	479-7020
Wiesbaden Hot Springs 625 5th St PO Box 349 ... *Web:* www.wiesbadenhotsprings.com	Ouray	CO	81427	970-325-4347	325-4358

710 SPAS - HOTEL & RESORT

SEE ALSO Spas - Health & Fitness p. 3176

				Phone	Fax
100 Fountain Spa at the Pillar & Post Inn 48 John St PO Box 48 ... *TF:* 888-669-5566 ■ *Web:* www.vintage-hotels.com	Niagara-on-the-Lake	ON	L0S1J0	905-468-2123	468-3551
74 State LLC 74 State St ... *Web:* www.74state.com	Albany	NY	12207	518-434-7410	
Abbey Resort & Fontana Spa 269 Fontana Blvd ... *TF:* 800-709-1323 ■ *Web:* www.theabbeyresort.com	Fontana	WI	53125	262-275-9000	
Abhasa Waikiki Spa at the Royal Hawaiian Hotel 2259 Kalakaua Ave ... *Web:* www.abhasa.com	Honolulu	HI	96815	808-922-8200	922-3557
Accent Inns Ltd 3233 Maple St ... *Web:* www.accentinns.com	Victoria	BC	V8X4Y9	250-475-7500	
AdVantis Hospitality Alliance LLC 615 N Highland Ste 2A ... *Web:* www.vistarez.com	Murfreesboro	TN	37130	615-904-6133	
Alamo City Riverwalk Plaza Hotel 100 Villita St ... *Web:* www.riverwalkplaza.com	San Antonio	TX	78205	210-225-1234	
Aliante Gaming LLC 7300 Aliante Pkwy ... *Web:* www.aliantegaming.com	North Las Vegas	NV	89084	702-692-7777	
Allegria Spa at the Park Hyatt Beaver Creek 100 E Thomas Pl ... *Web:* www.allegriaspa.com	Avon	CO	81620	970-748-7500	748-7501
Aloft Broomfield Denver 8300 Arista Pl ... *Web:* www.aloftbroomfielddenver.com	Broomfield	CO	80021	303-635-2000	
Aloft Chicago O'hare 9700 Balmoral Ave ... *Web:* www.aloftchicagoohare.com	Rosemont	IL	60018	847-671-4444	
Alpine Lodge 434 Indian Creek Cir ... *Web:* www.alpinelodgeresort.com	Branson	MO	65616	417-338-2514	
AM Resorts LLC Seven Campus Blvd ... *Web:* www.amresorts.com	Newtown Square	PA	19073	610-359-8130	
Amadeus Spa at the Marriott Napa Valley 3425 Solano Ave ... *Web:* marriott.com/hotels/travel/sfonp-napa-valley-marriott-hotel-and-spa	Napa	CA	94558	707-254-3330	
Amoray Dive Resort Inc 104250 Overseas Hwy ... *Web:* www.amoray.com	Key Largo	FL	33037	305-451-3595	
Anara Spa at the Hyatt Regency Kauai 1571 Poipu Rd ... *Web:* www.anaraspa.com	Koloa	HI	96756	808-742-1234	240-6599
Ancient Cedars Spa at the Wickaninnish Inn 500 Osprey Ln PO Box 250 ... *TF:* 800-333-4604 ■ *Web:* www.wickinn.com	Tofino	BC	V0R2Z0	250-725-3113	725-3110
Andre Balazs Properties 23 E Fourth St Fl 5 ... *Web:* www.andrebalazsproperties.com	New York	NY	10002	212-226-5656	
Antoine du Chez 2700 E Second Ave ... *Web:* www.antoineduchez.com	Denver	CO	80206	303-320-6012	996-1061
Aquae Sulis Spa at the JW Marriott Resort Las Vegas 221 N Rampart Blvd ... *TF:* 877-869-8777 ■ *Web:* www.marriott.com	Las Vegas	NV	89144	702-869-7807	869-7772
Aquaterra Spa at the Surf & Sand Resort 1555 S Coast Hwy ... *Web:* www.surfandsandresort.com	Laguna Beach	CA	92651	949-376-2772	376-2773
Aria Spa & Club at the Vail Cascade Resort 1300 Westhaven Dr ... *TF:* 888-824-5772 ■ *Web:* vailcascade.com/colorado-mountain-spa.php	Vail	CO	81657	970-479-5942	476-7405

				Phone	Fax
Arizona Biltmore Resort & Spa 2400 E Missouri *TF:* 800-950-0086 ■ *Web:* www.arizonabiltmore.com	Phoenix	AZ	85016	602-955-6600	381-7600
Arlington Residence Court Hotel 1200 N Courthouse Rd *Web:* www.arlingtoncourthotel.com	Arlington	VA	22201	703-524-4000	
Au Naturel Wellness & Medical Spa at the Brookstreet Hotel 525 Legget Dr *TF:* 888-826-2220 ■ *Web:* www.brookstreethotel.com	Ottawa	ON	K2K2W2	613-271-1800	
Auberge De La Fontaine b & b Inn 1301 Rue Rachel E *Web:* www.aubergedelafontaine.com	Montreal	QC	H2J2K1	514-597-0166	
Baccarat New York LLC 20 W 53rd St *Web:* www.baccarathotels.com	New York	NY	10019	212-790-8800	
Bartell Hotels 4875 N Harbor Dr *Web:* www.bartellhotels.com	San Diego	CA	92106	619-224-1556	
Bathhouse at Calistoga Ranch 580 Lommel Rd *Web:* calistogaranch.aubergeresorts.com/	Calistoga	CA	94515	707-254-2820	254-2825
Battery Wharf Hotel & Spa, The Three Battery Wharf *Web:* www.batterywharfhotelboston.com	Boston	MA	02109	617-994-9000	
Beekman Arms-delamater Inn Inc 6387 Mill St *Web:* www.beekmandelamaterinn.com	Rhinebeck	NY	12572	845-876-7077	
Belamar Hotel, The 3501 Sepulveda Blvd *Web:* www.thebelamar.com	Manhattan Beach	CA	90266	310-750-0300	
Best Western Tuscan Inn 425 N Point St *Web:* www.tuscaninn.com	San Francisco	CA	94133	415-561-1100	
Bittersweet Ski Resort Snowline 600 River Rd *Web:* www.skibittersweet.com	Otsego	MI	49078	269-694-2032	
Blue Haven Resort 1851 Lk Shore Dr *Web:* www.branson.com	Branson	MO	65616	417-334-3917	
Bluestar Resort & Golf LLC 8800 N Gainey Ctr Dr Ste 350 *Web:* www.bluestargolf.com	Scottsdale	AZ	85258	480-348-6519	
Boutique Spa at the Ritz-Carlton Georgetown 3100 S St NW *TF:* 800-241-3333 ■ *Web:* www.ritzcarlton.com	Washington	DC	20007	202-912-4175	912-4199
Boxer Hotel, The 107 Merrimac St *Web:* www.theboxerboston.com	Boston	MA	02114	617-624-0202	
Brampton (City of) Two Wellington St W *Web:* www.brampton.ca	Brampton	ON	L6Y4R2	905-874-2600	
Canyon Ranch SpaClub at the Venetian 3355 Las Vegas Blvd S Ste 1159 *TF:* 877-220-2688 ■ *Web:* canyonranch.com/visit	Las Vegas	NV	89109	702-414-3606	414-3801
Cape Codder Resort & Spa 1225 Iyanough Rd Rt 132 Bearse's Way *TF:* 888-297-2200 ■ *Web:* www.capecodderresort.com	Hyannis	MA	02601	508-771-3000	790-8145
Capella Hotels & Resorts 3384 Peachtree Rd Ste 375 *Web:* www.capellahotels.com	Atlanta	GA	30326	404-649-7030	
Carefree Resort & Conference Ctr 37220 Mule Train Rd *TF:* 888-692-4343 ■ *Web:* www.carefree-resort.com	Carefree	AZ	85377	888-692-4343	
Carneros Inn, The 4048 Sonoma Hwy *TF:* 888-400-9000 ■ *Web:* www.thecarnerosinn.com	Napa	CA	94559	707-299-4900	299-4950
Casa Marina Hotel & Restaurant 691 First St N *Web:* www.casamarinahotel.com	Jacksonville Beach	FL	32250	904-270-0025	
Centre for Well-Being at the Phoenician 6000 E Camelback Rd **Fax Area Code:* 480 ■ *TF:* 800-843-2392 ■ *Web:* www.thephoenician.com	Scottsdale	AZ	85251	800-843-2392	423-2582*
Century City Fitness Club & Spa 10220 Constellation Blvd *Web:* www.equinox.com	Century City	CA	90067	310-286-2900	286-0208
CEPA Le Baluchon Inc 3550 chemin des Trembles *Web:* www.baluchon.com	Saint-paulin	QC	J0K3G0	819-268-2555	
Chateau Elan Spa at the Chateau Elan Atlanta 100 Rue Charlemagne *TF:* 800-233-9463 ■ *Web:* www.chateauelan.com	Braselton	GA	30517	678-425-0900	
Chateau Resort & Conference Center, The 300 Camelback Rd *Web:* chateauresort.com	Tannersville	PA	18372	570-629-5900	
Chateau Rouge 1505 S Broadway Ave *Web:* www.chateaurouge.com	Red Lodge	MT	59068	406-446-1601	
Cheeca Lodge & Spa 81801 Overseas Hwy Mile Marker 82 *TF:* 800-327-2888 ■ *Web:* www.cheeca.com	Islamorada	FL	33036	305-664-4651	
Cliff Spa at Snowbird Hwy 210 PO Box 929000 *TF:* 800-453-3000 ■ *Web:* www.snowbird.com	Snowbird	UT	84092	801-933-2225	
Columbia Room Inc 1108 E Marina Way *Web:* www.hoodriverinn.com	Hood River	OR	97031	541-386-2200	
Condado Vanderbilt Hotel Towers 1055 Ashford Ave *Web:* www.condadovanderbilt.com	San Juan	PR	00907	787-721-5500	
CopperWynd Resort and Club 13225 N Eagle Ridge Dr *TF:* 877-707-7760 ■ *Web:* www.copperwynd.com	Fountain Hills	AZ	85268	480-333-1831	
Coral Kay Resort 2300 Caravelle Cir *Web:* www.staycoralcay.com	Kissimmee	FL	34746	407-787-0718	
Cranwell Resort Spa & Golf Club 55 Lee Rd *TF:* 800-272-6935 ■ *Web:* www.cranwell.com	Lenox	MA	01240	413-637-1364	637-4364
Cupertino Inn 10889 N De Anza Blvd *Web:* m.cupertinoinn.com	Cupertino	CA	95014	408-996-7700	
Deer Lodge Hotels Ltd 106 Circle Dr *Web:* www.travelodge.ca	Saskatoon	SK	S7L4L6	306-242-8881	
Delta Montreal Hotel 475 President Kennedy Ave *Web:* www.deltamontreal.com	Montreal	QC	H3A1J7	514-286-1986	
Disney's Grand Floridian Spa 4401 Floridian Wy **Fax:* Cust Svc ■ *TF:* 800-169-0730 ■ *Web:* disneyworld.disney.go.com	Lake Buena Vista	FL	32830	407-824-2332	824-3186*
Dmi 235 W Jefferson Ave *Web:* www.dmihotels.com	Naperville	IL	60540	630-428-1000	
Econo Lodge 2934 Polynesian Isle Blvd *Web:* www.econolodge.com	Kissimmee	FL	34746	407-787-4100	
Edward Thomas Companies, The 9950 Santa Monica Blvd *Web:* www.edwardthomasco.com	Beverly Hills	CA	90212	310-859-9366	
El Caribe Resort 2125 S Atlantic Ave *Web:* elcaribe.com	Daytona Beach	FL	32118	386-252-1558	
Elite Island Resorts Inc 1065 SW 30th Ave *Web:* www.eliteislandresorts.com	Deerfield Beach	FL	33442	954-481-8787	
Elizabeth Arden Red Door Spa at Mystic Marriott Hotel & Spa 625 N Rd *TF:* 866-449-7390 ■ *Web:* www.marriott.com	Groton	CT	06340	860-446-2500	446-2696
Elizabeth Arden Red Door Spa at the Seaview Marriott Resort & Spa 400 E Fairway Ln *Web:* www.reddoorspas.com	Galloway	NJ	08205	609-404-4100	404-4110
Embassy San Diego - Downtown #66378 601 Pacific Hwy *Web:* sandiegobay.embassysuites.com	San Diego	CA	92101	619-233-9922	
Embassy Suites Tysons Corner Hotel 8517 Leesburg Pk *Web:* embassysuites1.hilton.com	Vienna	VA	22182	703-883-0707	
Emerson Resort & Spa 5340 Rt 28 *TF:* 877-688-2828 ■ *Web:* www.emersonresort.com	Mount Tremper	NY	12457	845-688-7900	688-2829
Estancia La Jolla Hotel & Spa 9700 N Torrey Pines Rd *TF:* 866-437-8262 ■ *Web:* estancialajolla.com	La Jolla	CA	92037	858-550-1000	550-1001
EZ8 Motels Inc 2484 Hotel Cir Pl *Web:* www.ez8motels.com	San Diego	CA	92108	619-291-8252	
Felicita Resort 2201 Fishing Creek Vly Rd *Web:* www.felicitaresort.com	Harrisburg	PA	17112	717-599-5301	
Festival Inn, The 1144 Ontario St *Web:* www.festivalinnstratford.com	Stratford	ON	N5A6Z3	519-273-1150	
Ford Hotel Supply Company Inc 2204 N Broadway *Web:* www.fordstl.com	Saint Louis	MO	63102	314-231-8400	
Four Seasons Spa at the Four Seasons Hotel Las Vegas 3960 Las Vegas Blvd S *TF:* 800-332-3442 ■ *Web:* www.fourseasons.com/lasvegas	Las Vegas	NV	89119	702-632-5302	632-5450
Four Seasons Spa at the Four Seasons Hotel Los Angeles at Beverly Hills 300 S Doheny Dr *TF:* 800-819-5053 ■ *Web:* www.fourseasons.com/losangeles	Los Angeles	CA	90048	310-786-2229	860-8966
Four Seasons Spa at the Four Seasons Resort Jackson Hole 7680 Granite Loop Rd PO Box 544 *TF:* 800-819-5053 ■ *Web:* www.fourseasons.com/jacksonhole	Teton Village	WY	83025	307-732-5120	732-5121
Four Seasons Spa at the Four Seasons Resort Maui 3900 Wailea Alanui Dr *TF:* 800-334-6284 ■ *Web:* www.fourseasons.com/maui	Wailea	HI	96753	808-874-2925	874-2269
Four Seasons Spa at the Four Seasons Resort Santa Barbara 1260 Ch Dr *TF General:* 800-819-5053 ■ *Web:* www.fourseasons.com/santabarbara	Santa Barbara	CA	93108	805-565-8250	565-8451
Fox Harb'r Resort & Spa 1337 Fox Harbour Rd *TF:* 866-257-1801 ■ *Web:* www.foxharbr.com	Wallace	NS	B0K1Y0	902-257-1801	257-1852
Galvestonian Condominium Association 1401 E Beach Dr *Web:* www.galvestonian.com	Galveston	TX	77550	409-765-6161	
Garden Spa at MacArthur Place 29 E MacArthur St *TF:* 800-722-1866 ■ *Web:* www.macarthurplace.com	Sonoma	CA	95476	707-933-3193	933-9833
Gaylord Texan Resort & Convention Center 1501 Gaylord Trl *Web:* www.gaylordtexan.com	Grapevine	TX	76051	817-778-2000	
General Hotels Corp 2501 S High School Rd *Web:* genhotels.com	Indianapolis	IN	46241	317-243-1000	
Glacial Waters Spa at Grand View Lodge 23521 Nokomis Ave *TF:* 866-801-2951 ■ *Web:* www.grandviewlodge.com	Nisswa	MN	56468	218-963-2234	963-8791
Global Sports Consultants LLC 196 Route 202 N *Web:* www.jetsetsports.com	Far Hills	NJ	07931	908-766-1001	
Gold Key Resorts Phr Career Center 313 Laskin Rd Ste 103 *Web:* goldkeyphr.com	Virginia Beach	VA	23451	757-213-4344	
Grand Hotel & Conference Center Peoria 4400 N Brandywine Dr *Web:* www.grandhotelpeoria.com	Peoria	IL	61614	309-686-8000	
Grand Hotel Marriott Resort Golf Club & Spa One Grand Blvd PO Box 639 *TF:* 800-544-9933 ■ *Web:* www.marriott.com	Point Clear	AL	36564	251-928-9201	928-1149
Grand Lodge of The Order of The Sons of Hermann in the State of Texas 515 S Saint Marys St *Web:* www.texashermannsons.org	San Antonio	TX	78205	210-892-0254	
Grand Toronto Venture LP Four Ave Rd *Web:* www.parktoronto.hyatt.com	Toronto	ON	M5R2E8	416-925-1234	
Greek Peak Ski Resort 2000 State Rt 392 *Web:* greekpeakmtnresort.com	Cortland	NY	13045	607-835-6111	
Green Valley Ranch Resort Casino & Spa 2300 Paseo Verde Pkwy *TF Resv:* 866-782-9487 ■ *Web:* greenvalleyranch.sclv.com	Henderson	NV	89052	702-617-7777	
Greenbrier, The 300 W Main St *TF:* 800-453-4858 ■ *Web:* www.greenbrier.com	White Sulphur Springs	WV	24986	304-536-1110	536-7854
Groupe Germain Inc 1200 des-Soeurs-du-Bon-Pasteur Ste 500 *Web:* www.groupegermain.com	Quebec	QC	G1S0B1	418-687-1123	
Groupe Riotel Hospitality Inc 250 Ave du Phare Est *Web:* www.riotel.com	Matane	QC	G4W3N4	418-566-2651	

Phone *Fax*

Grouse Mountain Resorts Ltd
6400 Nancy Greene Way.................... North Vancouver BC V7R4K9 604-984-0661
Web: www.grousemountain.com

Grove Park Inn Resort & Spa 290 Macon Ave......... Asheville NC 28804 828-252-2711 253-7053
TF: 800-438-5800 ■ *Web:* www.groveparkinn.com

Guildford Ventures Ltd 15269 104th Ave............... Surrey BC V3R1N5 604-582-9288
Web: www.sheratonguildford.com

Haddon Hall Hotel 1500 Collins Ave.............. Miami Beach FL 33139 305-531-1251
Web: haddonhallmiamibeach.com

Hard Rock Hotel Palm Springs
150 S Indian Canyon Dr....................... Palm Springs CA 92262 760-325-9676
Web: www.hrhpalmsprings.com

Hibiscus Spa at the Myrtle Beach Marriott Resort at Grande Dunes
8400 Costa Verde Dr.......................... Myrtle Beach SC 29572 843-692-3730 449-8669
Web: www.csspagroup.com

Hilton Akron Fairlawn 3180 W Market St.............Fairlawn OH 44333 330-867-5024
Web: www.akronhilton.com

Hilton Mystic Hotel 20 Coogan Blvd.................. Mystic CT 06355 860-572-0731
Web: www.hiltonmystic.com

Hilton Pasadena Hotel 168 S Los Robles Ave .... Pasadena CA 91101 626-577-1000
Web: www.daytonahilton.com

Hilton Short Hills 41 JFK Pkwy .... Short Hills NJ 07078 973-379-0100 379-6870
TF: 800-445-8667 ■ *Web:* www.hiltonshorthills.com

Hilton Suites Toronto/Markham Conference Centre & Spa
8500 Warden Ave .... Markham ON L6G1A5 905-470-8500 477-8611
TF: 800-445-8667 ■ *Web:* www3.hilton.com

Hilton Tampa Airport Westshore, The
2225 N Lois Ave.................................. Tampa FL 33607 813-877-6688
Web: www.hiltontampawestshore.com

Holly Shores Best Holiday 491 Route 9............ Cape May NJ 08204 609-886-1234
Web: www.hollyshores.com

Home2 Suites by Hilton
4035 Sycamore Dairy Rd .... Fayetteville NC 28303 910-223-1170
Web: home2suites1.hilton.com

Homestead Resort 700 N Homestead Dr .... Midway UT 84049 888-327-7220 654-5087*
**Fax Area Code:* 435 ■ *TF:* 888-327-7220 ■ *Web:* www.homesteadresort.com

Horizon Hotels Ltd 99 Corvett Way Ste 302........... Eatontown NJ 07724 732-935-9553
Web: www.horizonhotels.com

Hotel 373 Fifth Avenue 373 Fifth Ave................ New York NY 10016 212-213-3388
Web: www.hotel373.com

Hotel Elegante Event & Conference Center
2886 South Cir Dr .... Colorado Springs CO 80906 719-576-5900
Web: www.hotelelegante.com

Hotel Mortagne 1228 Rue Nobel .... Boucherville QC J4B5H1 450-655-9966
Web: www.hotelmortagne.com

Hotel Nelligan 110 Rue Saint-paul O .... Montreal QC H2Y1Z3 514-788-2040
Web: hotelnelligan.com

Hotel Sorella 800 sorella ct .... Houston TX 77024 713-973-1600
Web: www.valenciagroup.com

Hotel Valencia Riverwalk
150 E Houston St .... San Antonio TX 78205 210-227-9700
Web: www.hotelvalencia-riverwalk.com

Hotels at Home Inc 208 Passaic Ave.................. Fairfield NJ 07004 973-882-8437
Web: www.hotelsathome.com

Hualalai Resort Corp
At Historic Ka'upulehu Post Office Box 1119
.... Kailua-kona HI 96745 808-325-8455
Web: www.hualalairesort.com

Hualalai Sports Club & Spa at the Four Seasons Resort Hualalai
100 Kaupulehu Dr............................ Kaupulehu-Kona HI 96740 808-325-8440 325-8451
Web: www.fourseasons.com/hualalai

Hutton Hotel, The 1808 W End Ave.................. Nashville TN 37203 615-340-9333
Web: www.huttonhotel.com

Hyatt Boston Harbor 101 Harborside Dr............... Boston MA 02128 617-568-1234
Web: www.bostonharbor.hyatt.com

Hyatt Deerfield 1750 Lk Cook Rd.................... Deerfield IL 60015 847-945-3400
Web: www.hyattdeerfield.com

Hyatt Regency Scottsdale Resort at Gainey Ranch
7500 E Doubletree Ranch Rd .... Scottsdale AZ 85258 480-483-5558 483-5544
TF: 800-233-1234 ■ *Web:* scottsdale.hyatt.com

Hyatt Rosemont 6350 N River Rd.................. Rosemont IL 60018 847-518-1234
Web: rosemont.hyatt.com

Il Fornello Management Ltd 112 Isabella St .... Toronto ON M4Y1P1 416-920-9410
Web: www.ilfornello.com

Imc Resort Services LLC
Two Corpus Christie Pl..................... Hilton Head Island SC 29928 843-785-4775
Web: www.imcresortservices.com

Indian Springs Resort & Spa
1712 Lincoln Ave .... Calistoga CA 94515 707-942-4913 942-4919
TF: 800-877-3623 ■ *Web:* www.indianspringscalistoga.com

Jefferson Hotel Washington Dc, The
1200 16th St Nw............................... Washington DC 20036 202-448-2300
Web: www.jeffersondc.com

Jiminy Peak Mountain Resort LLC 37 Corey Rd ...... Hancock MA 01237 413-738-5500
Web: www.jiminypeak.com

Jurlique Spa 4925 N Scottsdale Rd .... Scottsdale AZ 85251 480-424-6072
TF: 800-528-7867 ■ *Web:* www.fireskyresort.com

JW Starr Pass Resort & Spa
3800 W Starr Pass Blvd .... Tucson AZ 85745 520-792-3500 778-2049*
**Fax Area Code:* 817 ■ *TF:* 800-845-5279 ■ *Web:* www.marriott.com

Kea Lani Spa at the Fairmont Kea Lani Maui
4100 Wailea Alanui Dr .... Maui HI 96753 808-875-2229 875-1200
TF: 800-659-4100 ■ *Web:* www.fairmont.com

Kelco Management & Development Inc
1020 Oriental Gardens Rd...................... Jacksonville FL 32207 904-858-9919
Web: www.kelcohotels.com

Kohler Waters Spa 501 Highlands Dr .... Kohler WI 53044 920-457-7777 208-4934
TF: 866-928-3777 ■ *Web:* www.americanclubresort.com

L.A. Hotel Downtown, The
333 S Figueroa St............................ Los Angeles CA 90071 213-617-1133
Web: www.thelahotel.com

Phone *Fax*

Labovitz Enterprises
227 W First St 880 Missabe Bldg..................... Duluth MN 55802 218-727-7765
Web: www.labovitzenterprises.com

Lafayette Park Hotel 3287 Mt Diablo Blvd .... Lafayette CA 94549 925-283-3700 284-1621
TF: 877-283-8787 ■ *Web:* www.lafayetteparkhotel.com

Lake Austin Spa Resort 1705 S Quinlan Pk Rd .... Austin TX 78732 512-372-7380 266-1572
TF: 800-847-5637 ■ *Web:* www.lakeaustin.com

Lake Natoma Ltd 702 Gold Lk Dr.................... Folsom CA 95630 916-932-2769
Web: www.lakenatomainn.com

Lansdowne Resort 44050 Woodridge Pkwy .... Leesburg VA 20176 703-729-4036 729-4096
TF: 877-509-8400 ■ *Web:* www.lansdowneresort.com

Larry Blumberg & Associates Inc
2733 Ross Clark Cir .... Dothan AL 36301 334-793-6855
Web: lbaproperties.com

Lexington New York City, The
511 Lexington Ave 48th St .... New York NY 10017 212-755-4400
Web: www.lexingtonhotelnyc.com

Lido Beach Resort 700 Ben Franklin Dr............... Sarasota FL 34236 941-388-2161
Web: www.lidobeachresort.com

Living Spa at El Monte Sagrado
317 Kit Carson Rd .... Taos NM 87571 575-758-3502 737-2985
TF: 888-213-4419 ■ *Web:* www.elmontesagrado.com

Lodgco Management LLC
5225 E Pickard Rd .... Mount Pleasant MI 48858 989-773-2400
Web: lodgco.net

Lodging Dynamics Hospitality Group LLC
5314 North River Run Dr Ste 310........................ Provo UT 84604 801-919-3440
Web: www.lodgingdynamics.com

Los Willows Inn & Spa
530 Stewart Canyon Rd .... Fallbrook CA 92028 760-731-9400 728-3622
Web: www.loswillows.com

Luxe City Center Hotel
1020 S Figueroa St............................ Los Angeles CA 90015 213-748-1291
Web: www.luxecitycenter.com

Magnuson Hotels PO Box 1434 .... Spokane WA 99210 509-747-8713
Web: www.magnusonhotels.com

Manga Hotels Inc 3279 Caroga Dr .... Mississauga ON L4V1A3 905-672-4821
Web: www.mangahotels.com

Marcus Whitman Hotel & Conference Center LLC
Six W Rose St.................................. Walla Walla WA 99362 509-525-2200
Web: www.marcuswhitmanhotel.com

Marina del Rey Hotel 13534 Bali Way .... Marina Del Rey CA 90292 310-301-1000
Web: www.marinadelreyhotel.com

Massage Ctr at Mohonk Mountain House
1000 Mtn Rest Rd................................ New Paltz NY 12561 845-255-1000 256-2737
TF: 800-772-6646 ■ *Web:* www.mohonk.com

Mauna Lani Spa at Mauna Lani Resort
68-1365 Pauoa Rd .... Kohala Coast HI 96743 808-881-7922 885-4440
Web: www.maunalani.com

MHG of Pensacola, Florida LLC
481 Creighton Rd................................. Pensacola FL 32504 850-484-7022
Web: www.mckibbon.com

Mii Amo at Enchantment Resort
525 Boynton Canyon Rd............................ Sedona AZ 86336 928-203-8500 282-9249
TF: 888-749-2137 ■ *Web:* www.miiamo.com

MileNorth Chicago Hotel 166 E Superior St .... Chicago IL 60611 312-787-6000
Web: www.milenorthhotel.com

Milestone Hospitality Management LLC
717 Light St .... Baltimore MD 21230 561-981-8828
Web: www.milestonehotels.com

Mirbeau Inn & Spa 851 W Genesee St .... Skaneateles NY 13152 315-685-5006 685-5150
TF: 877-647-2328 ■ *Web:* www.mirbeau.com

Mirror Lake Inn Resort & Spa
77 Mirror Lk Dr................................ Lake Placid NY 12946 518-523-2544 523-2871
Web: www.mirrorlakeinn.com

MODERN Honolulu, The 1775 Ala Moana Blvd......... Honolulu HI 96815 808-943-5800
Web: www.themodernhonolulu.com

Mokara Hotel & Spa 212 W Crockett St .... San Antonio TX 78205 210-396-5800 226-0389
TF: 866-605-1212 ■ *Web:* www.mokarahotels.com

Montecito Inn Inc
1295 Coast Village Rd .... Santa Barbara CA 93108 805-969-7854
Web: www.montecitoinn.com

Moonstone Hotel Properties Inc
2905 Burton Dr.................................. Cambria CA 93428 805-927-4200
Web: www.moonstonehotels.com

Morrissey Hospitality Companies Inc
345 St Peter St Ste 2000......................... Saint Paul MN 55102 651-221-0815
Web: www.morrisseyhospitality.com

Motif Seattle 1415 Fifth Ave .... Seattle WA 98101 206-971-8000
Web: www.motifseattle.com

Mountain Laurel Spa at Stonewall Resort
940 Resort Dr .... Roanoke WV 26447 304-269-8881 269-4358
TF: 888-278-8150 ■ *Web:* www.stonewallresort.com

Music Road Hotel LLC
303 Henderson Chapel Rd .... Pigeon Forge TN 37863 865-429-7700
Web: www.musicroadhotel.com

Na Ho'ola Spa at Hyatt Regency Waikiki Resort
2424 Kalakaua Ave .... Honolulu HI 96815 808-923-1234 926-3415
TF: 800-233-1234 ■ *Web:* www.waikiki.hyatt.com

New Suncadia LLC 3600 Suncadia Trl .... Cle Elum WA 98922 509-649-6400
Web: www.suncadiaresort.com

Northern Rockies Lodge
Mile 462 Alaska Hwy .... Muncho Lake BC V0C1Z0 250-776-3481
Web: www.northern-rockies-lodge.com

Oak Hotels Inc 2424 State Route 52........... Hopewell Junction NY 12533 845-223-3603
Web: www.oakhotels.com

Oakwood Inn Resort Golf & Spa
Grand Bend Reservations .... Grand Bend ON N0M1T0 519-238-2324
Web: oakwoodresort.ca

Ocean Drive Clevelander Inc
1020 Ocean Dr .... Miami Beach FL 33139 305-534-2700
Web: www.clevelander.com

Name / Address	City	State	Zip	Phone	Fax
Ocean House Hotel Partners LLC One Bluff Ave *Web:* www.oceanhouseri.com	Watch Hill	RI	02891	401-584-7000	
Ohio House Motel 600 N La Salle Dr *Web:* www.ohiohousemotel.com	Chicago	IL	60654	312-943-6000	
Omni Interlocken Resort 500 Interlocken Blvd *TF:* 800-843-6664 ■ *Web:* www.omnihotels.com	Broomfield	CO	80021	303-438-6600	464-3236
Omni Rancho Las Palmas Resort & Spa 41000 Bob Hope Dr *TF:* 866-423-1195 ■ *Web:* www.rancholaspalmas.com/spa	Rancho Mirage	CA	92270	760-568-2727	568-5845
Osprey Valley Resorts 18821 Main St *Web:* www.ospreyvalleygolf.com	Alton	ON	L7K1R1	519-927-9034	
P Saa 5142 State St *Web:* skipa.com	White Haven	PA	18661	570-443-0963	
Pacific Hospitality Group LLC 2532 Dupont Dr *Web:* www.pacifichospitality.com	Irvine	CA	92612	949-861-4700	
Pala Casino Resort & Spa 35008 Pala-Temecula Rd *TF:* 877-946-7252 ■ *Web:* www.palacasino.com	Pala	CA	92059	760-510-5100	510-5191
Palm Garden Hotel 495 N Ventu Park Rd *Web:* www.palmgardenhotel.com	Thousand Oaks	CA	91320	805-716-4100	
Peaks Resort & Golden Door Spa 136 Country Club Dr **Fax Area Code:* 970 ■ *TF:* 800-789-2220 ■ *Web:* www.thepeaksresort.com	Telluride	CO	81435	800-789-2220	728-6175*
Pineapple Hospitality Co 155 108th Ave NE Ste 350 *Web:* www.staypineapple.com	Bellevue	WA	98004	425-455-5825	
Portofino Spa at Portofino Island Resort 10 Portofino Dr *TF:* 866-849-0223 ■ *Web:* www.portofinoisland.com	Pensacola	FL	32561	850-916-5000	
Post Ranch Inn Hwy 1 PO Box 219 *Web:* www.postranchinn.com	Big Sur	CA	93920	831-667-2200	
Promise Hotels Inc 2201 N 77th E Ave *Web:* www.promisehotels.com	Tulsa	OK	74115	918-858-2779	
Rainbow Courts Motel & Apartments 915 E Cameron Ave *Web:* www.rainbowcourts.com	Rockdale	TX	76567	512-446-2361	
Raindance Spa at the Lodge at Sonoma Renaissance Resort 1325 Broadway *TF:* 866-263-0758 ■ *Web:* www.marriott.com	Sonoma	CA	95476	707-935-6600	931-2137
Raleigh, The 1775 Collins Ave *Web:* www.raleighhotel.com	Miami Beach	FL	33139	305-534-6300	
Ramada Hotel & Suites Lethbridge 2375 Mayor Magrath Dr S Hwy 4 and Mayor Magrath Dr *Web:* www.ramadalethbridge.ca	Lethbridge	AB	T1K7M1	403-380-5050	
Ramada Mall of America 2300 E American Blvd *Web:* www.ramadamoa.com	Bloomington	MN	55425	952-548-3609	
Red Lion Honalae, The 2270 Hotel Cir N *Web:* www.hanaleihotel.com	San Diego	CA	92108	619-297-1101	
Renoir Hotel 45 McAllister St *Web:* www.renoirhotel.com	San Francisco	CA	94102	415-626-5200	
Residence Inn Mystic 40 Whitehall Ave *Web:* www.lakesregion.org	Mystic	CT	06355	860-536-5150	
Resort At Pelican Hill 22701 pelican hill rd s *Web:* www.irvineco.com	Newport Beach	CA	92657	949-467-6800	
Resort at Squaw Creek 400 Squaw Creek Rd PO Box 3333 *TF:* 800-327-3353 ■ *Web:* www.squawcreek.com	Olympic Valley	CA	96146	530-583-6300	581-6632
Revere Hotel Boston Common 200 Stuart St *Web:* www.reverehotel.com	Boston	MA	02116	617-482-1800	
Revive Spa at the JW Marriott Desert Ridge Resort Phoenix 5350 E Marriott Dr *TF:* 800-845-5279 ■ *Web:* www.marriott.com	Phoenix	AZ	85054	480-293-3700	
Ritz-Carlton Hotel Company, The 1111 Ritz-Carlton Dr **Fax Area Code:* 801 ■ *TF:* 800-241-3333 ■ *Web:* www.ritzcarlton.com	Sarasota	FL	34236	866-922-6882	468-4069*
Ritz-Carlton Tysons Corner, The 1700 Tysons Blvd *TF:* 800-241-3333 ■ *Web:* www.ritzcarlton.com	McLean	VA	22102	703-506-4300	506-2694
Safety Harbor Resort & Spa 105 N Bayshore Dr *TF:* 888-237-8772 ■ *Web:* www.safetyharborspa.com	Safety Harbor	FL	34695	727-726-1161	726-4268
Saint Regis Aspen 315 E Dean St *TF General:* 888-627-7198 ■ *Web:* www.stregisaspen.com	Aspen	CO	81611	970-920-3300	
Sanctuary Beach Resort Monterey Bay 3295 Dunes Rd *Web:* www.thesanctuarybeachresort.com	Marina	CA	93933	831-883-9478	
Sea Spa at Loews Coronado Bay Resort 4000 Loews Coronado Bay Rd *TF:* 800-815-6397 ■ *Web:* www.loewshotels.com	Coronado	CA	92118	619-424-4000	424-4000
Seasons Restaurant at Highland Lake Inn 86 Lilly Pad Ln *Web:* hlinn.com	Flat Rock	NC	28731	828-696-9094	
Secret Garden Spa at the Prince of Wales Hotel Six Picton St PO Box 46 *TF:* 888-669-5566 ■ *Web:* www.vintage-hotels.com	Niagara-on-the-Lake	ON	L0S1J0	905-468-3246	468-5521
Senator Inn & Spa of Augusta 284 Western Ave *TF:* 877-772-2224 ■ *Web:* www.senatorinn.com	Augusta	ME	04330	207-622-8800	622-8803
ShaNah Spa at the Bishop's Lodge 1297 Bishop *Web:* www.bishopslodge.com/shanahspa	Santa Fe	NM	87506	505-983-6377	
Shell Island Ocean Front Suites 2700 N Lumina Ave *Web:* www.shellisland.com	Wrightsville Beach	NC	28480	910-256-8696	
Sheraton Agoura Hills Hotel 30100 Agoura Rd *Web:* www.sheratonagourahills.com	Agoura Hills	CA	91301	818-707-1220	
Sheraton Denver Tech Center Hotel 7007 S Clinton St *Web:* www.sheraton.com	Greenwood Village	CO	80112	303-799-6200	
Sheraton Fishermans Wharf (San Francisco, CA) 2500 Mason St *Web:* www.sheratonatthewharf.com	San Francisco	CA	94133	415-362-5500	
Sheraton Gunter Hotel 205 E Houston St *Web:* www.gunterhotel.com	San Antonio	TX	78205	210-227-3241	
Sheraton North Houston Hotel At George Bush Intercontinental 15700 JFK Blvd *Web:* www.sheratonnorthhouston.com	Houston	TX	77032	281-442-5100	
Sheraton Phoenix Downtown Hotel 340 N Third St *Web:* www.sheratonphoenixdowntown.com	Phoenix	AZ	85004	602-262-2500	
Sheraton Raleigh Hotel 421 S Salisbury St *Web:* www.sheratonraleigh.com	Raleigh	NC	27601	919-834-9900	
Sheraton Safari Hotel & Suites 12205 S Apopka Vineland Rd *Web:* www.sheratonlakebuenavistaresort.com	Orlando	FL	32836	407-239-0444	
Sheraton Washington North Hotel 4095 Powder Mill Rd *Web:* www.sheratoncollegeparknorth.com	Beltsville	MD	20705	301-937-4422	
Shui Spa at Crowne Pointe Historic Inn 82 Bradford St *Web:* www.crownepointe.com	Provincetown	MA	02657	508-487-6767	487-5554
Sixty Hotels 54 Thompson St *Web:* sixtyhotels.com	New York	NY	10012	212-431-0400	
SLS Hotel South Beach 1701 Collins Ave *Web:* slshotels.com	Miami Beach	FL	33139	305-674-1701	
Sofitel Philadelphia Hotel 120 S 17th St *Web:* www.sofitel.com	Philadelphia	PA	19103	215-569-8300	
Soho House Beach House LLC 4385 collins ave *Web:* www.sohobeachhouse.com	Miami Beach	FL	33140	786-507-7900	
Solage Calistoga 755 Silverado Trl *Web:* www.solagecalistoga.com	Calistoga	CA	94515	707-266-7531	
Sole East LLC 90 Second House Rd *Web:* www.soleeast.com	Montauk	NY	11954	631-668-2105	
Spa & Fitness Club at the Four Seasons Hotel Washington 2800 Pennsylvania Ave NW *TF:* 800-819-5053 ■ *Web:* www.fourseasons.com/washington	Washington	DC	20007	202-944-2022	944-2072
Spa at Big Cedar Lodge 612 Devil's Pool Rd *TF:* 800-225-6343 ■ *Web:* big-cedar.com/	Ridgedale	MO	65739	417-339-5201	779-5363
Spa at Eagle Crest Resort 1522 Cline Falls Hwy PO Box 1215 *TF:* 800-682-4786 ■ *Web:* www.eagle-crest.com	Redmond	OR	97756	541-923-9647	504-1420
Spa at Kingsmill Resort 1010 Kingsmill Rd *Web:* www.kingsmill.com	Williamsburg	VA	23185	757-253-8230	258-1629
Spa at Le Merigot JW Marriott Beach Hotel Santa Monica 1740 Ocean Ave *TF:* 888-236-2427 ■ *Web:* www.marriott.com	Santa Monica	CA	90401	310-395-9700	395-9200
Spa at Pebble Beach 1518 Cypress Dr *TF:* 800-654-9300 ■ *Web:* www.pebblebeach.com	Pebble Beach	CA	93953	831-649-7615	
Spa at Pinehurst Resort 80 Carolina Vista Dr PO Box 4000 *TF:* 800-487-4653 ■ *Web:* www.pinehurst.com	Pinehurst	NC	28374	910-235-8320	235-8306
Spa at the Beverly Wilshire, The 9500 Wilshire Blvd *TF:* 800-545-4000 ■ *Web:* www.fourseasons.com	Beverly Hills	CA	90212	310-385-7023	
Spa at the Bodega Bay Lodge 103 Coast Hwy 1 *TF:* 888-875-2250 ■ *Web:* www.bodegabaylodge.com	Bodega Bay	CA	94923	707-875-3525	875-2428
Spa at the Breakers One S County Rd *TF:* 888-273-2537 ■ *Web:* www.thebreakers.com	Palm Beach	FL	33480	561-653-6656	653-6675
Spa at the Broadmoor One Lake Ave *TF:* 800-634-7711 ■ *Web:* www.broadmoor.com	Colorado Springs	CO	80906	719-634-7711	577-5766
Spa at the Buena Vista Palace Resort in the Walt Disney World Resort 1900 Buena Vista Dr PO Box 22206 *TF:* 866-397-6516 ■ *Web:* www.buenavistapalace.com/services_and_activities/spa.cfm	Lake Buena Vista	FL	32830	407-827-3200	827-3136
Spa at the Camelback Inn JW Marriott Resort Golf Club & Spa 5402 E Lincoln Dr *TF:* 800-922-2635 ■ *Web:* www.camelbackspa.com	Scottsdale	AZ	85253	480-596-7040	596-7000
Spa at the Chattanooga 1201 S Broad St *TF:* 800-619-0018 ■ *Web:* www.chattanooganhotel.com	Chattanooga	TN	37402	423-424-3779	756-3404
Spa at the Diplomat Country Club 501 Diplomat Pkwy *Web:* www.diplomatresort.com	Hallandale	FL	33009	954-883-4900	
Spa at the Equinox Resort 3567 Main St Rt 7-A **Fax Area Code:* 802 ■ *TF:* 800-362-4747 ■ *Web:* www.equinoxresort.com	Manchester Village	VT	05254	800-362-4747	362-4861*
Spa at the Fairmont Inn Sonoma Mission Inn 100 Boyes Blvd *TF:* 877-289-7354 ■ *Web:* www.fairmont.com	Sonoma	CA	95476	707-938-9000	938-8012
Spa at the Hotel Hershey 100 Hotel Rd *TF:* 877-772-9988 ■ *Web:* www.chocolatespa.com	Hershey	PA	17033	717-520-5888	520-5880
Spa at the JW Marriott Desert Springs Resort Palm Desert 74855 Country Club Dr **Fax Area Code:* 817 ■ *TF:* 800-845-5279 ■ *Web:* www.marriott.com	Palm Desert	CA	92260	760-341-2211	778-2049*
Spa at the Marriott Harbor Beach Resort 3030 Holiday Dr *Web:* www.marriott.com	Fort Lauderdale	FL	33316	954-765-3032	766-6101
Spa at the Norwich Inn 607 W Thames St *TF:* 800-275-4772 ■ *Web:* www.thespaatnorwichinn.com	Norwich	CT	06360	860-886-2401	886-9299
Spa at the Orlando World Ctr Marriott Resort & Convention Ctr 8701 World Ctr Dr *Web:* www.marriott.com	Orlando	FL	32821	407-238-8705	238-8777
Spa at the PGA National Resort 450 Ave of the Champions *TF:* 800-633-9150 ■ *Web:* www.pgaresort.com	Palm Beach Gardens	FL	33418	561-627-3111	627-6056
Spa at the Ponte Vedra Inn & Club 200 Ponte Vedra Blvd *TF:* 800-234-7842 ■ *Web:* www.pvspa.com	Ponte Vedra Beach	FL	32082	904-273-7700	273-7706

				Phone	Fax
Spa at the Ritz-Carlton Amelia Island 4750 Amelia Island Pkwy *TF:* 800-241-3333 ■ *Web:* www.ritzcarlton.com	Amelia Island	FL	32034	904-277-1087	277-1071
Spa at the Ritz-Carlton Bachelor Gulch 0130 Daybreak Ridge *TF:* 800-241-3333 ■ *Web:* www.ritzcarlton.com	Avon	CO	81620	970-748-6200	343-1126
Spa at the Ritz-Carlton Half Moon Bay One Miramontes Pt Rd *TF:* 800-241-3333 ■ *Web:* www.ritzcarlton.com	Half Moon Bay	CA	94019	650-712-7040	712-7070
Spa at the Ritz-Carlton New Orleans 921 Canal St *TF:* 800-241-3333 ■ *Web:* www.ritzcarlton.com	New Orleans	LA	70112	504-670-2929	670-2930
Spa at the Saddlebrook Resort 5700 Saddlebrook Way *TF:* 800-729-8383	Wesley Chapel	FL	33543	813-907-4419	
Spa at the Sagamore 110 Sagamore Rd *TF:* 866-384-1944 ■ *Web:* www.thesagamore.com	Bolton Landing	NY	12814	518-743-6081	
Spa at the Sanderling Resort 1461 Duck Rd *TF:* 855-412-7866 ■ *Web:* www.sanderling-resort.com	Duck	NC	27949	252-261-7744	261-1352
Spa at the Vail Marriott Mountain Resort 715 W Lionshead Cir *TF:* 800-648-0720 ■ *Web:* www.marriott.com	Vail	CO	81657	970-479-5004	
Spa at the Villagio Inn 6481 Washington St *TF:* 800-351-1133 ■ *Web:* www.villagio.com	Yountville	CA	94599	707-948-5050	948-5054
Spa at White Oaks Conference Resort 253 Taylor Rd *TF:* 800-263-5766 ■ *Web:* www.whiteoaksresort.com	Niagara-on-the-Lake	ON	L0S1J0	905-641-2599	
Spa Esmeralda at the Renaissance Esmeralda Resort 44400 Indian Wells Ln **Fax Area Code:* 817 ■ *TF:* 800-845-5279 ■ *Web:* www.marriott.com	Indian Wells	CA	92210	760-836-1265	778-2049*
Spa Gaucin at the Saint Regis Monarch Beach One Monarch Beach Resort *TF:* 800-722-1543 ■ *Web:* www.spagaucin.com	Dana Point	CA	92629	949-234-3367	234-3365
Spa Grande at the Grand Wailea Resort Maui 3850 Wailea Alanui Dr *TF:* 800-772-1933 ■ *Web:* www.grandwailea.com/spa	Wailea	HI	96753	808-875-1234	874-2424
Spa La Quinta at La Quinta Resort 49499 Eisenhower Dr *TF:* 877-527-7721 ■ *Web:* www.laquintaresort.com	La Quinta	CA	92253	760-777-4800	564-5723
Spa Moana at the Hyatt Regency Maui Resort & Spa 200 Nohea Kai Dr *TF:* 800-233-1234 ■ *Web:* www.maui.hyatt.com	Lahaina	HI	96761	808-667-4725	667-4503
Spa Shiki at the Lodge of Four Seasons 315 Horseshoe Bend Pkwy *TF:* 800-843-5253 ■ *Web:* spashiki.com	Lake Ozark	MO	65049	573-365-8108	365-8101
Spa Suites at Kahala Hotel & Resort 5000 Kahala Ave *TF:* 800-367-2525 ■ *Web:* www.kahalaresort.com	Honolulu	HI	96816	808-739-8938	739-8939
Spa Terre at LaPlaya Beach & Golf Resort 9891 Gulf Shore Dr *Web:* www.laplayaresort.com	Naples	FL	34108	239-597-3123	597-6278
Spa Terre at Paradise Point Resort 1404 Vacation Rd *TF:* 800-344-2626 ■ *Web:* www.paradisepoint.com	San Diego	CA	92109	858-581-5998	490-6688
Spa Terre at the Hotel Viking One Bellevue Ave *TF:* 800-556-7126 ■ *Web:* www.hotelviking.com	Newport	RI	02840	401-847-3300	
Spa Terre at the Inn & Spa at Loretto 211 Old Santa Fe Trl *TF:* 800-727-5531 ■ *Web:* www.innatloretto.com	Santa Fe	NM	87501	505-984-7997	
Spa Toccare at Borgata Hotel Casino 1 Borgata Way *TF:* 877-448-5833 ■ *Web:* www.theborgata.com	Atlantic City	NJ	08401	609-317-7555	317-1039
Spa Torrey Pines at the Lodge at Torrey Pines 11480 N Torrey Pines Rd *TF:* 800-656-0087 ■ *Web:* www.spatorreypines.com	La Jolla	CA	92037	858-453-4420	777-6698
SpaHalekulani at the Halekulani Hotel 2199 Kalia Rd *TF:* 800-367-2343 ■ *Web:* www.halekulani.com	Honolulu	HI	96815	808-931-5322	931-5337
Spire Hospitality LLC 111 S Pfingsten Rd Ste 425 *Web:* www.spirehotels.com	Deerfield	IL	60015	847-498-6650	
Sportsmen's Lodge Hotel 12825 Ventura Blvd *Web:* www.slhotel.com	Studio City	CA	91604	818-769-4700	
Springmaid Beach Resort 3200 S Ocean Blvd *TF:* 866-764-8501 ■ *Web:* springmaidbeach.com	Myrtle Beach	SC	29577	866-764-8501	
Staybridge Suites Hotel 6095 Emerald Pkwy *Web:* www.staybridge.com	Dublin	OH	43016	614-734-9882	
Stillwater Spa at the Hyatt Regency Newport One Goat Island *TF:* 800-233-1234 ■ *Web:* www.newport.hyatt.com	Newport	RI	02840	401-851-3225	851-3201
Studio 6 P O Box 809092 *Web:* www.staystudio6.com	Dallas	TX	75380	614-601-4060	
Sundestin Beach Resort 1040 Hwy 98 E *Web:* sundestinresort.com	Destin	FL	32541	850-837-7093	
Sunstone Hotel Properties Inc 903 Calle Amanecer Ste 100 *Web:* www.sunstonehotels.com	San Clemente	CA	92673	949-369-4000	
Sunway Hotel Group Inc 8500 College Blvd *Web:* www.sunwayhotel.com	Overland Park	KS	66210	913-345-2111	
Taboo Resort Golf & Spa 1209 Muskoka Beach Rd **Fax Area Code:* 705 ■ *TF:* 800-461-0236	Gravenhurst	ON	P1P1R1	800-461-0236	687-7474*
Tampa Marriott Waterside Hotel & Marina 700 S Florida Ave *TF:* 888-268-1616 ■ *Web:* www.marriott.com	Tampa	FL	33602	813-204-6300	204-6342
Ten Thousand Waves Japanese Health Spa 3451 Hyde Pk Rd *Web:* www.tenthousandwaves.com	Santa Fe	NM	87501	505-982-9304	
Tillicum Village & Tours Inc 1101 Alaskan Way Pier 55 *Web:* www.tillicumvillage.com	Seattle	WA	98101	206-623-1445	
TMI Hospitality Inc 4850 32nd Ave South *Web:* www.tharaldson.com	Fargo	ND	58104	701-235-1060	
Toll House Hotel 140 S Santa Cruz Ave *Web:* www.tollhousehotel.com	Los Gatos	CA	95030	408-395-7070	
Treasure Island Resort & Casino 5734 Sturgeon Lk Rd *Web:* www.ticasino.com	Welch	MN	55089	651-385-2786	
Trump Soho New York 246 Spring St *Web:* www.trumpsohohotel.com	New York	NY	10013	212-842-5500	
Tulalip Resort Casino 10200 Quil Ceda Blvd *TF:* 888-272-1111 ■ *Web:* www.tulalipresortcasino.com	Tulalip	WA	98271	888-272-1111	
Turtle Cove Spa at Mountain Harbor Resort 181 Club House Dr *Web:* www.turtlecovespa.com	Mount Ida	AR	71957	870-867-1220	867-4678
Urgo Hotels LP 6710A Rockledge Dr Ste 420 *Web:* www.urgohotels.com	Bethesda	MD	20817	301-657-2130	
Vail Mountain Lodge & Spa, The 352 E Meadow Dr *TF:* 888-794-0410 ■ *Web:* www.vailmountainlodge.com	Vail	CO	81657	970-476-0700	477-3225
Verandah Club, The 2201 Stemmons Fwy *Web:* www.verandahclub.com	Dallas	TX	75207	214-761-7878	
W Fort Lauderdale Hotel & Residences 401 N Ft Lauderdale Beach Blvd *Web:* www.wfortlauderdalehotel.com	Fort Lauderdale	FL	33304	954-414-8200	
Well Spa at Miramonte Resort 45000 Indian Wells Ln *TF:* 866-843-9355 ■ *Web:* www.miramonteresort.com	Indian Wells	CA	92210	760-837-1652	837-2330
Westglow Resort & Spa 224 Westglow Cir *TF:* 800-562-0807 ■ *Web:* www.westglowresortandspa.com	Blowing Rock	NC	28605	828-295-4463	295-5115
Westin Harbour Castle One Harbour Sq *Web:* www.westinharbourcastletoronto.com	Toronto	ON	M5J1A6	416-869-1600	
Westin Imagine Orlando, The 9501 Universal Blvd *Web:* www.westinimagineorlando.com	Orlando	FL	32819	407-233-2200	
Westin Kierland Resort & Spa 6902 E Greenway Pkwy *TF:* 800-354-5892 ■ *Web:* www.kierlandresort.com	Scottsdale	AZ	85254	480-624-1000	624-1001
Westin Maui Resort & Spa, The 2365 Kaanapali Pkwy *TF:* 866-716-8112 ■ *Web:* www.westinmaui.com	Lahaina	HI	96761	808-667-2525	661-5764
Westin Mission Hills Resort 71333 Dinah Shore Dr *Web:* www.westinmissionhills.com	Rancho Mirage	CA	92270	760-328-5955	
Westin Resort & Spa 4090 Whistler Way *TF:* 888-627-8979 ■ *Web:* www.westinwhistler.com	Whistler	BC	V0N1B4	604-905-5000	
Willow Stream Spa at Fairmont Scottsdale Princess 7575 E Princess Dr *TF:* 800-908-9540 ■ *Web:* www.fairmont.com	Scottsdale	AZ	85255	480-585-2732	585-0086
Willow Stream Spa at the Fairmont Banff Springs 405 Spray Ave *TF:* 800-404-1772 ■ *Web:* www.fairmont.com	Banff	AB	T1L1J4	403-762-1772	762-1766
Willow Stream Spa at the Fairmont Empress 633 Humboldt St *TF:* 866-854-7444 ■ *Web:* www.fairmont.com	Victoria	BC	V8W1A6	250-995-4650	995-4651
Wingate by Wyndham Calgary Hotel 400 Midpark Way SE *Web:* www.wingatebywyndhamcalgary.com	Calgary	AB	T2X3S4	403-514-0099	
Wintergreen Resort Rt 664 PO Box 706 *TF:* 800-266-2444 ■ *Web:* www.wintergreenresort.com	Wintergreen	VA	22958	855-699-1858	

711 SPEAKERS BUREAUS

				Phone	Fax
3 Arts Entertainment Inc 9460 Wilshire Blvd *Web:* 3arts.com	Beverly Hills	CA	90212	310-888-3200	
Abrams Artists Agency 9200 Sunset Blvd 11th Fl *Web:* www.abramsartists.com	Los Angeles	CA	90069	310-859-0625	
Add Rob Litho LLC 11 W Passaic St *Web:* www.addroblitho.com	Rochelle Park	NJ	07662	201-556-0700	
AEI Speakers Bureau 214 Lincoln St Ste 113 *TF:* 800-447-7325 ■ *Web:* aeispeakers.com	Allston	MA	02134	617-782-3111	782-3444
Agency For the Performing Arts Inc 405 S Beverly Dr *Web:* www.apa-agency.com	Beverly Hills	CA	90212	310-888-4200	
Ambassador Speakers Bureau PO Box 50358 *Web:* www.ambassadorspeakers.com	Nashville	TN	37205	615-370-4700	661-4344
Anderson Daymon Worldwide LLC 1301 Fourth Ave NW Ste 100 *Web:* www.adww.com	Issaquah	WA	98027	425-507-3100	
Atlantic Speakers Bureau 980 Rt 730 *Web:* www.atlanticspeakersbureau.com	Scotch Ridge	NB	E3L5L2	506-465-0990	
Atlas Performing Arts Center 1333 H St Ne *Web:* atlasarts.org	Washington	DC	20002	202-399-7993	
Barber & Assoc 1308 Sumac Dr PO Box 11669 *Web:* www.barberusa.com	Knoxville	TN	37939	865-546-0000	
Bronx Defenders, The 860 Courtlandt Ave *Web:* www.bronxdefenders.org	Bronx	NY	10451	718-838-7878	
Brooks International Speakers Bureau 763 Santa Fe Dr *Web:* www.brooksinternational.com	Denver	CO	80204	303-825-8700	825-8701
Capitol City Speakers Bureau 1620 S Fifth St *TF:* 800-397-3183 ■ *Web:* www.capcityspeakers.com	Springfield	IL	62703	217-544-8552	544-1496
Debt Marketplace Inc, The 10440 Pioneer Blvd Ste 2 *Web:* debtmarketplace.com	Santa Fe Springs	CA	90670	562-903-7220	

	City	State	Zip	Phone	Fax
Eclipse Advertising Inc 2255 N Ontario St Ste 230	Burbank	CA	91504	818-238-9388	
Web: www.eclipseadvertising.com					
Elk Valley Rancheria 2332 Howland Hill Rd	Crescent City	CA	95531	707-464-4680	
Web: www.elk-valley.com					
Everingham & Kerr Inc 1300 Route 73 Ste 103	Mount Laurel	NJ	08054	856-546-6655	
Web: www.everkerr.com					
Executive Speakers Bureau 8567 Cordes Cir	Germantown	TN	38139	901-754-9404	756-4237
TF: 800-754-9404 ■ *Web:* www.executivespeakers.com					
Florexpo LLC 1960 Kellogg Ave	Carlsbad	CA	92008	760-930-3567	
Web: www.florexpo.com					
Glyphic Technologies Inc 1001 Ave Of The Amrcas	New York	NY	10018	212-625-9170	
Web: www.glytec.com					
Greater Talent Network Inc 437 Fifth Ave Seventh Fl	New York	NY	10016	212-645-4200	627-1471
TF: 800-326-4211 ■ *Web:* www.greatertalent.com					
H2f Comedy Productions 102 E Magnolia Blvd	Burbank	CA	91502	818-845-9721	
Web: www.flapperscomedy.com					
Harry Walker Agency Inc (HWA) 355 Lexington Ave 21st Fl	New York	NY	10017	646-227-4900	227-4901
Web: www.harrywalker.com					
Infinedi LLC 7912 E 31st Ct Ste 300	Tulsa	OK	74145	918-249-4450	
Web: www.infinedi.net					
International Speakers Bureau Inc 2128 Boll St	Dallas	TX	75204	214-744-3885	744-3888
Web: business-bankruptcies.com					
J Reynolds & Company Inc 369 Sansom Blvd	Saginaw	TX	76179	817-306-9596	
Web: www.jreynoldsroofing.com					
Janas Consulting 201 S Lk Ave Ste 302	Pasadena	CA	91101	626-432-7000	
Web: www.janascorp.com					
Joanne Rile Artists Management Inc 93 York Rd Ste 222	Jenkintown	PA	19046	215-885-6400	
Web: www.rilearts.com					
Justifacts Credential Verification Inc 5250 Logan Ferry Rd	Murrysville	PA	15668	412-798-4790	
Web: www.justifacts.com					
Keppler Speakers Bureau 3030 Clarendon Blvd Seventh Fl	Arlington	VA	22201	703-516-4000	516-4819
Web: www.kepplerspeakers.com					
Key Speakers Bureau Inc 3500 E Coast Hwy Ste 6	Corona del Mar	CA	92625	949-675-7856	675-1478
TF: 800-675-1175 ■ *Web:* www.keyspeakers.com					
Laser Rite Technologies Inc 1744 Independence Blvd	Sarasota	FL	34234	941-955-2737	
Web: www.laserrite.com					
Leading Authorities Inc 1990 M St Ste 800	Washington	DC	20036	202-783-0300	783-0301
TF: 800-773-2537 ■ *Web:* www.leadingauthorities.com					
Lytmos Group Inc 400 SW Longview Blvd Ste 290	Lee's Summit	MO	64081	816-347-9449	
Web: www.lytmos.com					
MediVista Media LLC 1100 Spring St Ste 750	Atlanta	GA	30309	404-817-7767	
Web: www.everwell.com					
National Speakers Bureau 1177 W Bdwy Ste 300	Vancouver	BC	V6H1G3	604-734-3663	734-8906
TF: 800-661-4110 ■ *Web:* www.nsb.com					
National Speakers Bureau Inc 14047 W Petronalla Dr Ste 102	Libertyville	IL	60048	847-295-1122	367-5499
TF: 800-323-9442 ■ *Web:* www.nationalspeakers.com					
Orlando Shakespeare Theater Inc 812 E Rollins St Ste 100	Orlando	FL	32803	407-447-1700	
Web: www.orlandoshakes.org					
Powerzone Volleyball Inc Three Luger Rd	Denville	NJ	07834	973-983-8208	
Web: www.powerzonevb.com					
Publicitas North America 330 Seventh Ave Fl 5	New York	NY	10001	212-330-0720	
Web: www.publicitas.com					
Santa Barbara Speakers Bureau LLC (SBSB) PO Box 30768	Santa Barbara	CA	93130	805-682-7474	
Web: www.sbsb.net					
Semple Brown Design PC 1160 Santa Fe Dr	Denver	CO	80204	303-571-4137	
Web: www.sbdesign-pc.com					
Six Degrees LLC 8040 E Gelding Dr	Scottsdale	AZ	85260	480-627-9850	
Web: www.six-degrees.com					
Solix Inc 30 Lanidex Plz W PO Box 685	Parsippany	NJ	07054	973-581-6700	
Web: www.solixinc.com					
Speak Inc Speakers Bureau 10680 Treena St Ste 230	San Diego	CA	92131	858-228-3771	228-3989
Web: www.speakinc.com					
Speakers Guild Inc 35 Discovery Hill Rd	East Sandwich	MA	02537	508-888-6702	
Web: businessfinder.masslive.com					
Speakers Unlimited PO Box 27225	Columbus	OH	43227	614-864-3703	864-3876
TF: 888-333-6676 ■ *Web:* www.speakersunlimited.com					
Speakers.com 130 Lubrano Dr Ste 110	Annapolis	MD	21401	410-897-1970	897-1971
Web: www.speakers.com					
Steven Barclay Agency 12 Western Ave	Petaluma	CA	94952	707-773-0654	778-1868
TF: 888-965-7323 ■ *Web:* www.barclayagency.com					
Venture Opportunities Inc 13140 Coit Rd Ste 211	Dallas	TX	75240	972-783-1662	
Web: www.bizdealmaker.com					
Walters International Speakers Bureau 18825 Hicrest Rd	Glendora	CA	91741	626-335-8069	
Washington Speakers Bureau 1663 Prince St	Alexandria	VA	22314	703-684-0555	684-9378
Web: www.washingtonspeakers.com					
WME | IMG SPEAKERS 304 Pk Ave S	New York	NY	10010	212-774-6735	
Web: www.imgspeakers.com					
World Class Speakers & Entertainers 5200 Kanan Rd Ste 210	Agoura Hills	CA	91301	818-991-5400	991-2226
Web: www.wcspeakers.com					

712 SPEED CHANGERS, INDUSTRIAL HIGH SPEED DRIVES, GEARS

SEE ALSO Controls & Relays - Electrical p. 2151; Aircraft Parts & Auxiliary Equipment p. 1733; Machine Shops p. 2680; Motors (Electric) & Generators p. 2776; Automotive Parts & Supplies - Mfr p. 1839; Power Transmission Equipment - Mechanical p. 2956

	City	State	Zip	Phone	Fax
Amarillo Gear Co 2401 W Sundown Ln	Amarillo	TX	79118	806-622-1273	622-3258
Web: www.amarillogear.com					
Auburn Gear Inc 400 E Auburn Dr	Auburn	IN	46706	260-925-3200	925-4725
Web: www.auburngear.com					
Avion Technologies Inc 1203 Lorimar Dr	Mississauga	ON	L5S1M9	905-670-1570	670-1568
Web: www.avion-tech.com					
Bison Gear & Engineering Corp 3850 Ohio Ave	Saint Charles	IL	60174	630-377-4327	377-6777
TF: 800-282-4766 ■ *Web:* www.bisongear.com					
BMT Aerospace USA Inc 18559 Malyn Blvd	Fraser	MI	48026	586-285-7700	
Web: www.bmtaerospace.com					
Bonfiglioli USA 3541 Hargrave Ct	Hebron	KY	41048	859-334-3333	
Web: www.bonfigliolíusa.com					
Charles Bond Co 11 Green St PO Box 105	Christiana	PA	17509	610-593-5171	593-5378
Web: www.bondgear.com					
Chicago Gear-DO James Corp 2823 W Fulton St	Chicago	IL	60612	773-638-0508	638-7161
Web: www.oc-gear.com					
Cleveland Gear Co 3249 E 80th St	Cleveland	OH	44104	216-641-9000	641-2731
TF: 800-423-3169 ■ *Web:* www.clevelandgear.com					
Columbia Gear Corp 530 County Rd 50	Avon	MN	56310	320-356-7301	356-2131
TF: 800-323-9838 ■ *Web:* www.columbiagear.com					
Cone Drive Operations Inc - A Textron Co 240 E 12th St	Traverse City	MI	49685	231-946-8410	907-2663*
**Fax Area Code:* 888 ■ *TF Sales:* 888-994-2663 ■ *Web:* www.conedrive.com					
Cotta Transmission Company LLC 1301 Prince Hall Dr	Beloit	WI	53511	608-368-5600	368-5605
Web: www.cotta.com					
Curtis Machine Company Inc 2500 E Trl St	Dodge City	KS	67801	620-227-7164	
Web: www.curtismachine.com					
Dalton Gear Co 212 Colfax Ave N	Minneapolis	MN	55405	612-374-2150	374-2467
TF: 800-328-7485 ■ *Web:* www.daltongear.com					
Designatronics Inc 2101 Jericho Tpke	New Hyde Park	NY	11040	516-328-3300	326-8827
TF Orders: 800-345-1144 ■ *Web:* www.sdp-si.com					
Electro Sales Inc 100 Fellsway W	Somerville	MA	02145	617-666-0500	628-2800
Emerson Industrial Automation 12005 Technology Dr	Eden Prairie	MN	55344	952-995-8000	
Web: www.emerson.com					
Fairchild Industrial Products Co 3920 Westpoint Blvd	Winston-Salem	NC	27103	336-659-3400	659-9323*
**Fax:* Sales ■ *TF:* 800-334-8422 ■ *Web:* www.fairchildproducts.com					
Fairfield Mfg Company Inc 2309 Concord Rd	Lafayette	IN	47909	765-772-4000	772-4001
Web: www.oerlikon.com					
Gear Motions Inc 1750 Milton Ave	Syracuse	NY	13209	315-488-0100	488-0196
Web: www.gearmotions.com					
Geartronics Industries Inc 100 Chelmsford Rd	North Billerica	MA	01862	978-663-6566	667-3130
Web: www.geartronics.com					
Hankscraft Inc 300 Wengel Dr	Reedsburg	WI	53959	608-524-4341	524-4342
Web: www.hankscraft.com					
HECO Inc 2350 Del Monte St	West Sacramento	CA	95691	916-372-5411	
Web: www.hecogear.com					
Horsburgh & Scott Co 5114 Hamilton Ave	Cleveland	OH	44114	216-431-3900	432-5850
Web: www.horsburgh-scott.com					
Hub City Inc 2914 Industrial Ave	Aberdeen	SD	57401	605-225-0360	225-0567
TF: 800-482-2489 ■ *Web:* www.hubcityinc.com					
Imperial Electric Co 1503 Exeter Rd	Akron	OH	44306	330-734-3600	734-3601
Web: www.imperialelectric.com					
Industrial Motion Control LLC 1444 S Wolf Rd	Wheeling	IL	60090	847-459-5200	459-3064
Web: www.camcoindex.com					
Koellmann Gear Corp Eight Industrial Park	Waldwick	NJ	07463	201-447-0200	
Web: www.koellmann.com					
Kurz Electric Solutions Inc 1325 McMahon Dr	Neenah	WI	54956	920-886-8200	886-8201
TF: 800-776-3629 ■ *Web:* www.kurz.com					
L & H Industrial 913 L J Ct	Gillette	WY	82718	307-682-7238	686-1646
Web: www.lnh.net					
Leedy Manufacturing Co 210 Hall St SW	Grand Rapids	MI	49507	616-245-0517	245-3888
Web: www.leedymfg.com					
Leeson Electric Corp 2100 Washington St	Grafton	WI	53024	262-377-8810	
Web: www.leeson.com					
Lenze 630 Douglas St	Uxbridge	MA	01569	508-278-9100	
TF: 800-217-9100 ■ *Web:* lenzeamericas.com					
Martin Sprocket & Gear Inc 3100 Sprocket Dr PO Box 91588	Arlington	TX	76015	817-258-3000	258-3333
Web: www.martinsprocket.com					
Milwaukee Gear Co 5150 N Port Washington Rd	Milwaukee	WI	53217	414-962-3532	962-2774
Web: www.milwaukeegear.com					
Nixon Gear Inc 1750 Milton Ave	Syracuse	NY	13209	315-488-0100	488-0196
Web: gearmotions.com/about-gear-motions/nixon-gear-oliver-gear/					
Nuttall Gear LLC 2221 Niagra Falls Blvd	Niagara Falls	NY	14304	716-298-4100	298-4101
TF: 800-724-6710 ■ *Web:* www.nuttallgear.com					
Oliver Gear Inc 1120 Niagara St	Buffalo	NY	14213	716-885-1080	885-1145
Web: www.gearmotions.com					
Overton Chicago Gear Inc 530 Westgate Dr	Addison	IL	60101	630-543-9570	543-7440
Web: www.ocgear.com/					
Peerless-Winsmith Inc 172 Eaton St	Springville	NY	14141	716-592-9310	592-9362
Web: www.winsmith.com					
Perfection Gear Inc Nine N Bear Creek Rd	Asheville	NC	28806	828-253-0000	253-2649
Web: www.perfectiongear.com					
Piller Inc 45 Turner Rd	Middletown	NY	10941	800-597-6937	692-0295*
**Fax Area Code:* 845 ■ *TF:* 800-597-6937 ■ *Web:* www.piller.com					

	City	State	Zip	Phone	Fax
Precision Technology USA Inc 225 Glade View Dr *Web:* www.pt-usa.net	Roanoke	VA	24012	540-857-9871	
Regal-Beloit Corp 200 State St *NYSE:* RBC ■ *TF:* 800-672-6495 ■ *Web:* www.regalbeloit.com	Beloit	WI	53511	608-364-8800	364-8818
Regal-Beloit Corp Durst Div PO Box 298 *TF:* 800-356-0775 ■ *Web:* www.durstdrives.com	Beloit	WI	53512	608-365-2563	365-2182
Richmond Gear PO Box 238 *TF Sales:* 800-934-2727 ■ *Web:* www.richmondgear.com	Liberty	SC	29657	864-843-9231	843-1276
Rush Gears Inc 550 Virginia Dr **Fax Area Code:* 800 ■ *TF:* 800-523-2576 ■ *Web:* www.rushgear.com	Fort Washington	PA	19034	215-542-9000	635-6273*
Schafer Gear Works Inc 4701 Nimtz Pkwy *Web:* schaferindustries.com/schafer-gear-works/about-schafer-gear-works	South Bend	IN	46628	574-234-4116	234-4115
SEW-Eurodrive Inc 1295 Old Spartanburg Hwy *Web:* www.seweurodrive.com	Lyman	SC	29365	864-439-7537	439-0566
Standard Machine Ltd 868-60th St E *Web:* www.standardmachine.ca	Saskatoon	SK	S7K8G8	306-931-3343	
Sterling Electric Inc 7997 Allison Ave *TF Cust Svc:* 800-654-6220 ■ *Web:* www.sterlingelectric.com	Indianapolis	IN	46268	317-872-0471	872-0907
Sumitomo Machinery Corp of America 4200 Holland Blvd *TF:* 800-762-9256 ■ *Web:* www.sumitomodrive.com	Chesapeake	VA	23323	757-485-3355	485-7490
Superior Gearbox Co 803 W Hwy 32 *TF:* 800-346-5745 ■ *Web:* www.superiorgearbox.com	Stockton	MO	65785	417-276-5191	276-3492
TECO-Westinghouse Motor Co 5100 N IH-35 *TF:* 800-451-8798 ■ *Web:* www.tecowestinghouse.com	Round Rock	TX	78681	512-255-4141	244-5512
Textron Fluid & Power Inc 40 Westminster St *Web:* www.textron.com	Providence	RI	02903	401-421-2800	621-5045

713 SPORTING GOODS

SEE ALSO Cord & Twine p. 2167; Exercise & Fitness Equipment p. 2280; Firearms & Ammunition (Non-Military) p. 2289; All-Terrain Vehicles p. 1740; Gym & Playground Equipment p. 2443; Handbags, Totes, Backpacks p. 2444; Motor Vehicles - Commercial & Special Purpose p. 2773; Personal Protective Equipment & Clothing p. 2914; Snowmobiles p. 3176; Swimming Pools p. 3202; Tarps, Tents, Covers p. 3204; Bicycles & Bicycle Parts & Accessories p. 1868; Boats - Recreational p. 1874

	City	State	Zip	Phone	Fax
40-Up Tackle Co 16 Union Ave PO Box 442 *Web:* www.40uptackleco.com	Westfield	MA	01086	413-562-0385	
Abel Automatics Inc 165 Aviador St *TF:* 866-511-7444 ■ *Web:* www.abelreels.com	Camarillo	CA	93010	805-484-8789	482-0701
Acushnet Co 333 Bridge St **Fax:* Hum Res ■ *TF:* 800-225-8500 ■ *Web:* www.acushnetcompany.com	Fairhaven	MA	02719	508-979-2000	979-3927*
AcuSport Corp 1 Hunter Pl **Fax:* Sales ■ *TF:* 800-543-3150 ■ *Web:* www.acusport.com	Bellefontaine	OH	43311	937-593-7010	592-5625*
Adams Golf 2801 E Plano Pkwy *TF:* 800-709-6142 ■ *Web:* www.adamsgolf.com	Plano	TX	75074	972-673-9000	398-8818
Adams USA Inc 610 S Jefferson Ave **Fax Area Code:* 931 ■ *TF:* 800-251-6857 ■ *Web:* www.adamsusa.com	Cookeville	TN	38501	800-251-6857	526-8357*
Air Chair Inc 2175 N Kiowa Blvd Ste 101 *Web:* www.airchair.com	Lake Havasu City	AZ	86403	928-505-2226	505-2229
Aldila Inc 14145 Danielson St Ste B *OTC:* ALDA ■ *TF:* 800-854-2786 ■ *Web:* www.aldila.com	Poway	CA	92064	858-513-1801	513-1870
Alpine Archery 3101 N S Hwy PO Box 319 *Web:* www.alpinearchery.com	Lewiston	ID	83501	208-746-4717	746-1635
American Classic Sales 1142 South 2475 West	Salt Lake City	UT	84104	801-977-3935	
American Sports 74 Albe Dr Ste 1 *TF:* 866-207-3179 ■ *Web:* www.americansports.com	Newark	DE	19702	302-369-9480	250-4024
AMF Bowling Worldwide Inc 7313 Bell Creek Rd *TF:* 800-342-5263 ■ *Web:* www.amf.com	Mechanicsville	VA	23111	800-342-5263	
Aqua-Leisure Industries Inc PO Box 239 **Fax Area Code:* 508 ■ *TF:* 866-807-3998 ■ *Web:* www.aqualeisure.com	Avon	MA	02322	866-807-3998	587-5318*
Aqualung America Inc 2340 Cousteau Ct *TF:* 800-446-2671 ■ *Web:* www.aqualung.com	Vista	CA	92083	760-597-5000	597-4900
Arrow Surfboards 1115 Thompson Ave Ste 7 *Web:* www.arrowsurfshop.com	Santa Cruz	CA	95062	831-462-2791	
Atomic USA 2030 Lincoln Ave **Fax Area Code:* 801 ■ *TF:* 800-258-5020 ■ *Web:* www.atomic.com	Ogden	UT	84401	800-258-5020	334-4503*
Austin Surfboards 513 19th St *Web:* www.austinsurfboards.com	Virginia Beach	VA	23451	757-428-7873	
Bankshot Sports Organization 842 B Rockville Pike *TF:* 800-933-0140 ■ *Web:* www.bankshot.com	Rockville	MD	20852	301-309-0260	309-0263
BAUER 100 Domain Dr *Web:* www.bauer.com	Exeter	NH	03833	603-430-2111	430-3010
Bauer Premium Fly Reels 585 Clover Ln Ste 1 *TF:* 888-484-4165 ■ *Web:* www.bauerflyreel.com	Ashland	OR	97520	541-488-8246	488-8244
Bell Sports Corp 6225 N St Hwy 161 Ste 300 *TF:* 866-525-2357 ■ *Web:* bellsports.com	Irving	TX	75038	469-417-6600	492-1639
Big Rock Sports LLC 173 Hankison Dr *TF:* 800-334-2661 ■ *Web:* www.bigrocksports.com	Newport	NC	28570	252-808-3500	726-8352
Biscayne Rod Manufacturing Inc 425 E Ninth St *TF:* 866-969-0808 ■ *Web:* www.biscaynerod.com	Hialeah	FL	33010	305-884-0808	884-3017
Bison Inc 603 L St **Fax Area Code:* 800 ■ *TF:* 800-247-7668 ■ *Web:* www.bisoninc.com	Lincoln	NE	68508	402-474-3353	638-0698*
Bombardier Recreational Products (BRP) 565 de la Montagne *Web:* www.brp.com	Valcourt	QC	J0E2L0	450-532-2211	532-5133
Bravo Sports Corp 12801 Carmenita Rd *TF Cust Svc:* 800-234-9737 ■ *Web:* www.bravosportscorp.com	Santa Fe Springs	CA	90670	562-484-5100	484-5183
Bridgestone Golf Inc 15320 Industrial Pk Blvd NE *TF:* 800-358-6319 ■ *Web:* www.bridgestonegolf.com	Covington	GA	30014	770-787-7400	786-6416
Brine Inc 32125 Hollingsworth Ave **Fax Area Code:* 586 ■ **Fax:* Cust Svc ■ *TF:* 800-968-7845 ■ *Web:* www.brine.com	Warren	MI	48092	800-968-7845	446-1162*
Brunswick Corp One N Field Ct *NYSE:* BC ■ *Web:* www.brunswick.com	Lake Forest	IL	60045	847-735-4700	735-4765
Bullet Weights Inc 182 S Apollo Dr *Web:* www.bulletweights.com	Alda	NE	68810	308-382-7436	382-2906
Callaway Golf Co 2180 Rutherford Rd *NYSE:* ELY ■ *TF:* 800-588-9836 ■ *Web:* www.callawaygolf.com	Carlsbad	CA	92008	760-931-1771	931-8013
Carstens Industries Inc 733 W Main St *Web:* www.carstensindustries.com	Melrose	MN	56352	320-256-3919	256-4052
Cascade Designs Inc 4000 First Ave S *TF Cust Svc:* 800-531-9531 ■ *Web:* www.cascadedesigns.com	Seattle	WA	98134	206-505-9500	505-9525
Catalyst 109 N Orlando Ave	Cocoa Beach	FL	32931	321-783-1530	799-1643
Century Sports Inc 1995 Rutgers University Blvd *TF Sales:* 800-526-7548 ■ *Web:* www.centurysportsinc.com	Lakewood	NJ	08701	732-905-4422	901-7766
Century Tool & Mfg 90 McMillen Rd **Fax Area Code:* 847 ■ *TF:* 800-635-3831 ■ *Web:* www.centurycamping.com	Antioch	IL	60002	800-635-3831	395-3305*
Champion Shuffleboard Ltd 7216 Burns St *TF:* 800-826-7856 ■ *Web:* www.championshuffleboard.com	Richland Hills	TX	76118	817-284-3499	595-1506
Cleveland Golf Co 5601 Skylab Rd **Fax Area Code:* 714 ■ *TF Cust Svc:* 800-999-6263 ■ *Web:* www.clevelandgolf.com	Huntington Beach	CA	92647	800-999-6263	889-5890*
Cobra Mfg Co Inc 7909 E 148th St S *TF:* 800-352-6272 ■ *Web:* www.cobraarchery.com	Bixby	OK	74008	918-366-7484	
Coleman Co 1100 Stearns Dr **Fax Area Code:* 415 ■ *TF:* 800 328 3208 ■ *Web:* www.coleman.com/	Sauk Rapids	MN	56379	320-252-1642	453-8585*
Coleman Company Inc 3600 N Hydraulic *TF Cust Svc:* 800-835-3278 ■ *Web:* www.coleman.com	Wichita	KS	67219	316-832-2653	832-3060
Columbia Industries Inc PO Box 746 *TF:* 800-531-5920 ■ *Web:* www.columbia300.com	Hopkinsville	KY	42240	270-881-1300	
Confluence Watersports Co 575 Mauldin Rd Ste 200 *TF:* 800-595-2925 ■ *Web:* confluenceoutdoor.com/	Greenville	SC	29607	800-595-2925	
Connelly Skis Inc 20621 52nd Ave W *Web:* www.connellyskis.com	Lynnwood	WA	98036	425-775-5416	778-9590
Cortland Line Company Inc 3736 Kellogg Rd *Web:* www.cortlandline.com	Cortland	NY	13045	607-756-2851	753-8835
Coverstar LLC 1795 West 200 North *TF:* 800-617-7283 ■ *Web:* www.coverstar.com	Lindon	UT	84042	801-373-4777	373-5095
Creative Playthings Ltd 33 Loring Dr *Web:* www.creativeplaythings.com	Framingham	MA	01702	508-620-0900	872-3120
Current Designs PO Box 247 *Web:* www.cdkayak.com	Winona	MN	55987	507-454-5430	454-5448
Daisy Outdoor Products 400 W Stribling Dr *TF:* 800-643-3458 ■ *Web:* www.daisy.com	Rogers	AR	72756	479-636-1200	636-1601
Daiwa Corp 12851 Midway Pl *TF:* 800-736-4653 ■ *Web:* www.daiwa.com	Cerritos	CA	90703	562-802-9589	546-0066
Douglas Industries Co 3441 S 11th Ave *TF:* 800-553-8907 ■ *Web:* www.douglas-sports.com	Eldridge	IA	52748	563-285-4162	285-4163
Dover Saddlery Inc 525 Great Rd PO Box 1100 *NASDAQ:* DOVR ■ *TF:* 800-406-8204 ■ *Web:* www.doversaddlery.com	Littleton	MA	01460	978-952-8062	952-8063
Dynastar 1413 Crt Dr *TF:* 888-243-6722 ■ *Web:* www.dynastar.com	Park City	UT	84098	435-252-3300	
Eagle One Golf Products Inc 1340 N Jefferson St *TF:* 800-448-4409 ■ *Web:* www.eagleonegolf.com	Anaheim	CA	92807	714-983-0050	
Eastaboga Tackle Mfg Co Inc 261 Mudd St *Web:* www.eastabogatackle.com	Eastaboga	AL	36260	256-831-9682	835-2524
Easton Tru-Flite LLC 2709 S Freeman Rd *Web:* eastonarchery.com	Monticello	IN	47960	574-583-5131	
Easy Rider Canoe & Kayak Co PO Box 88108 *Web:* www.easyriderkayaks.com	Seattle	WA	98138	425-228-3633	277-8778
Ebonite International Inc PO Box 746 *TF:* 800-326-6483 ■ *Web:* www.ebonite.com	Hopkinsville	KY	42241	270-881-1200	881-1201
Eddyline Kayaks 11977 Westar Ln *Web:* www.eddyline.com	Burlington	WA	98233	360-757-2300	757-2302
Eppinger Manufacturing Co 6340 Schaefer Rd *TF:* 888-771-8277 ■ *Web:* www.eppinger.net	Dearborn	MI	48126	313-582-3205	582-0110
Escalade Inc 817 Maxwell Ave *NASDAQ:* ESCA ■ *TF Cust Svc:* 800-426-1421 ■ *Web:* www.escaladesports.com	Evansville	IN	47711	812-467-1200	467-1300
Facility Merchandising Inc 5959 Topanga Canyon Blvd Ste 125 *Web:* www.facilitymerchandising.com	Woodland Hills	CA	91367	818-703-6690	703-6576
Folbot Inc 4209 Pace St *TF:* 800-533-5099 ■ *Web:* www.folbot.com	Charleston	SC	29405	843-744-3483	744-7783
Franklin Sports Inc 17 Campanelli Pkwy PO Box 508 *TF:* 800-225-8649 ■ *Web:* www.franklinsports.com	Stoughton	MA	02072	781-344-1111	341-0333
G & H Decoys Inc PO Box 1208 *TF Orders:* 800-443-3269 ■ *Web:* www.ghdecoys.com	Henryetta	OK	74437	918-652-3314	652-3400
Game Country Inc 2403 Commerce Ln *Web:* www.gamecountry.biz	Albany	GA	31707	229-883-4706	883-4766
Gamma Sports 200 Waterfront Dr *TF:* 800-333-0337 ■ *Web:* www.gammasports.com	Pittsburgh	PA	15222	412-323-0335	323-0317
Gared Sports Inc 707 N Second St Ste 220 *TF:* 800-325-2682 ■ *Web:* www.garedsports.com	Saint Louis	MO	63102	314-421-0044	421-6014
Gexco 3460 Vine St *Web:* gexcoenterprises.com	Norco	CA	92860	951-735-4951	
Gill Athletics Inc 2808 Gemini Ct *TF Cust Svc:* 800-637-3090 ■ *Web:* www.gillathletics.com	Champaign	IL	61822	217-367-8438	367-8440
Goal Sporting Goods Inc 37 Industrial Pk Rd PO Box 236 **Fax Area Code:* 860 ■ *TF:* 800-334-4625 ■ *Web:* www.goalsports.com	Essex	CT	06426	800-334-4625	767-9121*
Goals & Poles 7575 Jefferson Hwy *TF:* 800-275-0317 ■ *Web:* www.goalsandpoles.com	Baton Rouge	LA	70806	225-923-0622	926-0934
Goalsetter Systems Inc 1041 Cordova Ave **Fax Area Code:* 641 ■ *TF:* 800-362-4625 ■ *Web:* www.goalsetter.com	Lynnville	IA	50153	800-362-4625	594-3343*

	City	State	Zip	Phone	Fax
Golf Instruments Co					
3210 Production Ave Unit A	Oceanside	CA	92058	760-722-1129	967-7268
Web: www.golfinstruments.com					
Golfsmith International Inc 11000 N IH-35	Austin	TX	78753	512-821-4050	837-1245
TF Sales: 800-396-0099 ■ *Web:* www.golfsmith.com					
GolfWorks, The 4820 Jacksontown Rd PO Box 3008	Newark	OH	43055	740-328-4193	323-0311
TF: 800-848-8358 ■ *Web:* www.golfworks.com					
Green Grass Golf Corp 282 Newbridge Rd	Hicksville	NY	11801	516-935-6722	935-7064
Web: www.greengrassgolf.com					
Grundmann's Athletic Co 3018 Galleria Dr	Metairie	LA	70001	504-833-6602	833-6899
Web: www.grundmanns.com					
Harlick & Company Inc 893 American St	San Carlos	CA	94070	650-593-2093	593-9704
Web: www.harlick.com					
HEAD USA Inc One Selleck St	Norwalk	CT	06855	203-855-8666	866-9573
TF: 800-874-3235 ■ *Web:* www.head.com					
HEAD/Penn Racquet Sports 306 S 45th Ave	Phoenix	AZ	85043	800-289-7366	329-7366*
**Fax Area Code:* 888 ■ **Fax:* Cust Svc ■ *TF:* 800-289-7366 ■ *Web:* www.pennracquet.com					
Hillerich & Bradsby Company Inc					
800 W Main St	Louisville	KY	40202	502-585-5226	585-1179
TF: 800-282-2287 ■ *Web:* www.slugger.com					
Hireko Trading Company Inc					
16185 Stephens St	City of Industry	CA	91745	800-367-8912	367-8912*
**Fax Area Code:* 888 ■ *TF:* 800-367-8912 ■ *Web:* www.hirekogolf.com					
Hobie Cat Co 4925 Oceanside Blvd	Oceanside	CA	92056	760-758-9100	758-1841
TF: 800-462-4349 ■ *Web:* www.hobiecat.com					
Hoyt 543 N Neil Armstrong Rd	Salt Lake City	UT	84116	801-363-2990	537-1470
Web: hoyt.com					
Hunter Company Inc 3300 W 71st Ave	Westminster	CO	80030	303-427-4626	
TF: 800-676-4868 ■ *Web:* www.huntercompany.com					
Hunter's Specialties Inc					
6000 Huntington Ct NE	Cedar Rapids	IA	52402	319-395-0321	395-0326
TF: 800-530-7149 ■ *Web:* www.hunterspec.com					
International Billiards Inc					
2311 Washington Ave	Houston	TX	77007	713-869-3237	869-8420
Web: www.intlbilliards.com					
Intex Recreation Corp					
1665 Hughes Way PO Box 1440	Long Beach	CA	90801	310-847-6981	
TF Cust Svc: 800-234-6839 ■ *Web:* www.intexcorp.com					
J & B Importers Inc 11925 SW 128th St	Miami	FL	33186	305-238-1866	235-8056
Web: jbi.bike/web/					
Jayhawk Bowling Supply Inc					
355 N Iowa St PO Box 685	Lawrence	KS	66044	785-842-3237	842-9667
TF: 800-255-6436 ■ *Web:* www.jayhawkbowling.com					
Jerry's Sport Ctr Inc					
100 Capital Rd	Jenkins Township	PA	18640	800-234-2612	388-8452
TF: 800-234-2612 ■ *Web:* www.jerryssportscenter.com					
Johnson Outdoors Inc 555 Main St	Racine	WI	53403	262-631-6600	631-6601
NASDAQ: JOUT ■ *TF:* 800-468-9716 ■ *Web:* www.johnsonoutdoors.com					
Jugs Sports 11885 SW Herman Rd	Tualatin	OR	97062	800-547-6843	691-1100*
**Fax Area Code:* 503 ■ *TF:* 800-547-6843 ■ *Web:* www.jugssports.com					
K2 Sports 4201 Sixth Ave S	Seattle	WA	98108	206-805-4800	*
**Fax:* Cust Svc ■ *TF:* 800-426-1617 ■ *Web:* www.k2sports.com					
Kawasaki Motors Corp USA PO Box 25252	Santa Ana	CA	92799	949-770-0400	460-5600
Web: www.kawasaki.com					
Kent Sporting Goods Company Inc					
433 Pk Ave S	New London	OH	44851	419-929-7021	929-1769
Web: www.kentwatersports.com					
KL Industries Inc 1790 Sun Dolphin Dr	Muskegon	MI	49444	231-733-2725	739-4502
TF: 800-733-2727 ■ *Web:* www.klindustries.com					
Kolpin Powersports 205 N Depot St PO Box 107	Fox Lake	WI	53933	920-928-3118	928-3687*
**Fax:* Cust Svc ■ *TF:* 877-956-5746 ■ *Web:* www.kolpinpowersports.com					
Kwik Goal Ltd 140 Pacific Dr	Quakertown	PA	18951	215-536-2200	778-8869*
**Fax Area Code:* 800 ■ *TF:* 800-531-4252 ■ *Web:* www.kwikgoal.com					
Lakes Mall LLC, The 5600 Harvey St	Muskegon	MI	49444	231-798-7104	798-7129
Web: www.thelakesmall.com					
Lamartek Inc 175 NW Washington St	Lake City	FL	32055	386-752-1087	755-0613
TF Orders: 800-495-1046 ■ *Web:* www.diverite.com					
Lamiglas Inc 1400 Atlantic Ave	Woodland	WA	98674	360-225-9436	225-5050
Web: www.lamiglas.com					
Laughing Loon 344 GaRdiner Rd	Jefferson	ME	04348	207-549-3531	
Web: www.laughingloon.com					
Lifetime Products Inc					
Freeport Ctr Bldg D-11 PO Box 160010	Clearfield	UT	84016	801-776-1532	
TF: 800-242-3865 ■ *Web:* www.lifetime.com					
Linden Surfboards 1027 S Cleveland St	Oceanside	CA	92054	760-722-8956	722-8972
Web: www.lindensurfboards.com					
Lobster Sports Inc 7340 Fulton Ave	North Hollywood	CA	91605	818-764-6000	764-6061
TF: 800-210-5992 ■ *Web:* www.lobstersports.com					
Local Motion Inc 870 Kawaiahao St	Honolulu	HI	96813	808-523-7873	521-6413
Web: www.localmotionhawaii.com					
Louisville Golf Club Co					
2320 Watterson Trail	Louisville	KY	40299	502-491-5490	491-6189
TF: 800-456-1631 ■ *Web:* www.louisvillegolf.com					
MacNeill Engineering Company Inc					
140 Locke Dr PO Box 735	Marlborough	MA	01752	508-481-8830	303-4923
TF: 800-652-4267 ■ *Web:* www.champspikes.com					
Manns Bait Co 1111 State Docks Rd	Eufaula	AL	36027	800-841-8435	687-4352*
**Fax Area Code:* 334 ■ *TF:* 800-841-8435 ■ *Web:* www.mannsbait.com					
Maravia Corp of Idaho 602 E 45th St	Boise	ID	83714	208-322-4949	322-5016
TF: 800-223-7238 ■ *Web:* www.maravia.com					
Marble Arms (MA) 420 Industrial Pk Dr	Gladstone	MI	49837	906-428-3710	428-3711
Web: www.marblearms.com					
Mares America Corp One Selleck St	Norwalk	CT	06855	203-855-0631	866-9573
TF: 800-874-3236 ■ *Web:* www.mares.com					
Martin Archery Inc 3134 Heritage Rd	Walla Walla	WA	99362	509-529-2554	529-2186
TF: 800-541-8902 ■ *Web:* www.martinarchery.com					
Master Industries Inc 14420 Myford Rd	Irvine	CA	92606	714-918-4650	660-1678*
**Fax Area Code:* 949 ■ *Web:* www.masterindustries.com					
Master Pitching Machine					
4200 NE Birmingham Rd	Kansas City	MO	64117	816-452-0228	452-7581
Web: www.masterpitch.com					
Mitsven Surfboards 1157 Cushman Ave	San Diego	CA	92110	619-299-7873	
Web: mitsvensurfboards.com					
Mizuno USA 4925 Avalon Ridge Pkwy	Norcross	GA	30071	770-441-5553	448-3234
TF: 800-966-1211 ■ *Web:* www.mizunousa.com					
Moultrie Feeders 150 Industrial Rd	Alabaster	AL	35007	205-664-6700	664-6706
TF: 800-653-3334 ■ *Web:* www.moultriefeeders.com					
Murrey International Inc					
14150 S Figueroa St	Los Angeles	CA	90061	310-532-6091	217-0504
TF: 800-421-1022 ■ *Web:* murreybowling.com					
National Billiard Manufacturing Co					
3315 Eugenia Ave	Covington	KY	41015	859-431-4129	431-4179
TF: 800-543-0880 ■ *Web:* www.nationalbilliard.com					
Nicklaus Design					
11780 US Hwy 1 Ste 500	North Palm Beach	FL	33408	561-227-0300	227-0548
Web: www.nicklaus.com					
North Face, The 14450 Doolittle Dr	San Leandro	CA	94577	877-992-0111	
TF: 855-500-8639 ■ *Web:* www.thenorthface.com					
NuStep Inc 5111 Venture Dr Ste 1	Ann Arbor	MI	48108	734-769-3939	
Web: www.nustep.com					
O'Brien International 14615 NE 91st St	Redmond	WA	98052	425-202-2100	202-2199
TF: 800-662-7436 ■ *Web:* www.obrien.com					
O'Neill Wetsuits USA					
1071 41st Ave PO Box 6300	Santa Cruz	CA	95063	831-475-7500	475-0544
Web: www.oneill.com					
Ocean Kayak 125 Gilman Falls Ave Bldg B	Old Town	ME	04468	800-852-9257	827-3647*
**Fax Area Code:* 207 ■ *TF:* 800-852-9257 ■ *Web:* www.oceankayak.com					
Ocean Management Systems Inc PO Box 146	Montgomery	NY	12549	216-667-5411	
Web: www.omsdive.com					
Oceanic USA 2002 Davis St	San Leandro	CA	94577	510-562-0500	569-5404
TF: 800-435-3483 ■ *Web:* www.oceanicworldwide.com					
Old Town Canoe Co					
125 Gilman Falls Ave Bldg B PO Box 548	Old Town	ME	04468	207-827-5513	827-3647
TF: 800-343-1555 ■ *Web:* www.oldtowncanoe.com					
Orvis International Travel					
178 Conservation Way	Sunderland	VT	05250	802-362-8790	362-8795
TF: 800-547-4322 ■ *Web:* www.orvis.com					
Parker Compound Bows Inc PO Box 105	Mint Spring	VA	24463	540-337-5426	332-2715*
**Fax Area Code:* 800 ■ *Web:* www.parkerbows.com					
Penn Fishing Tackle Manufacturing Co					
3028 W Hunting Pk Ave	Philadelphia	PA	19132	215-229-9415	223-3017
Web: pennfishing.com/					
Pentair Ltd 1351 Rt 55	Lagrangeville	NY	12540	845-463-7200	463-7291
TF: 888-711-7487 ■ *Web:* www.paragonaquatics.com					
PIC Skate 22 Village Dr	Riverside	RI	02915	401-490-9334	438-5419
TF: 800-882-3448 ■ *Web:* www.picskate.com					
Ping Inc 2201 W Desert Cove Ave PO Box 82000	Phoenix	AZ	85071	800-474-6434	687-5046*
**Fax Area Code:* 602 ■ **Fax:* Cust Svc ■ *TF:* 800-474-6434 ■ *Web:* www.ping.com					
Poolmaster Inc 770 Del Paso Rd	Sacramento	CA	95834	916-567-9800	567-9880
TF: 800-854-1492 ■ *Web:* www.poolmaster.com					
Powell Skate One Corp					
30 S La Patera Ln	Santa Barbara	CA	93117	805-964-1330	964-0511
TF: 800-288-7528 ■ *Web:* www.skateone.com					
Precision Shooting Equipment Inc					
2727 N Fairview Ave	Tucson	AZ	85705	520-884-9065	884-1479
TF: 800-477-7789 ■ *Web:* www.pse-archery.com					
Prince Global Sports LLC One Advantage Ct	Bordentown	NJ	08505	609-291-5800	291-5900
TF All: 800-283-6647 ■ *Web:* www.princetennis.com					
Reebok-CCM Hockey Inc 3400 Raymond Lasnir	Montreal	QC	H4R3L3	514-461-8000	232-9226*
**Fax Area Code:* 800 ■ *Web:* www.thehockeycompany.com					
Resilite Sports Products PO Box 764	Sunbury	PA	17801	570-473-3529	473-8988
TF: 800-843-6287 ■ *Web:* www.resilite.com					
Riedell Shoes Inc 122 Cannon River Ave	Red Wing	MN	55066	651-388-8251	385-5500
TF: 800-698-6893 ■ *Web:* www.riedellskates.com					
RL Winston Rod Co					
500 S Main St PO Box 411	Twin Bridges	MT	59754	406-684-5674	684-5533
Web: www.web.winstonrods.com					
Roller Derby Skate Corp PO Box 930	Litchfield	IL	62056	217-324-3961	324-2213
Web: www.rollerderby.com					
Rome Specialty Company Inc Rosco Div					
501 W Embargo St	Rome	NY	13440	315-337-8200	339-2523
TF: 800-794-8357 ■ *Web:* www.roscoinc.com					
Ross Reels 11 Ponderosa Ct	Montrose	CO	81401	970-249-0606	
TF: 866-587-6747 ■ *Web:* www.rossreels.com					
RSR Group Inc 4405 Metric Dr	Winter Park	FL	32792	407-677-1000	677-4489
TF: 800-541-4867 ■ *Web:* www.rsrgroup.com					
Sampo Inc 119 Remsen Rd	Barneveld	NY	13304	315-896-2606	896-6575
Web: www.sampoinc.com					
Saunders Archery Co					
1874 14th Ave PO Box 1707	Columbus	NE	68601	402-564-7176	564-3260
TF Cust Svc: 800-228-1408 ■ *Web:* www.sausa.com					
Scott Fly Rod Co 2355 Air Pk Way	Montrose	CO	81401	800-728-7208	249-4172*
**Fax Area Code:* 970 ■ *TF:* 800-728-7208 ■ *Web:* www.scottflyrod.com					
Scott USA Inc PO Box 2030	Sun Valley	ID	83353	208-622-1000	622-1005
TF: 800-292-5874 ■ *Web:* www.scott-sports.com					
Sea Eagle Boats Inc					
19 N Columbia St Ste 1	Port Jefferson	NY	11777	631-473-7308	473-7398
TF: 800-748-8066 ■ *Web:* www.seaeagle.com					
Seeker Rod Co 1340 W Cowles St	Long Beach	CA	90813	562-491-0076	435-7599
Web: seekerrods.com					
Shakespeare Fishing Tackle Co 7 Science Ct	Columbia	SC	29203	803-754-7000	
TF Cust Svc: 800-466-5643 ■ *Web:* www.shakespeare-fishing.com					
Sheldons' Inc 626 Ctr St	Antigo	WI	54409	715-623-2382	623-3001
Web: www.mepps.com					
Shimano American Corp 1 Holland Dr	Irvine	CA	92618	949-951-5003	768-0920
Web: www.shimano.com					
Simms Fishing Products Corp 101 Evergreen Dr	Bozeman	MT	59715	406-585-3557	585-3562
TF: 800-217-4667 ■ *Web:* www.simmsfishing.com					
Spalding PO Box 90015	Bowling Green	KY	42103	855-253-4533	729-4800*
**Fax Area Code:* 877 ■ *TF:* 855-253-4533 ■ *Web:* www.spalding.com					
Sport Supply Group Inc 1901 Diplomat Dr	Dallas	TX	75234	972-484-9484	243-0149
TF: 800-527-7510 ■ *Web:* www.sportsupplygroup.com					
Sportco Sporting Goods Inc					
2580 E Sunset Rd	Las Vegas	NV	89120	702-739-9750	739-9021
Web: sportcolv.com					

	City	State	ZIP	Phone	Fax
Sportline Inc Four Executive Plz. *Web:* www.sportline.com	Yonkers	NY	10701	914-964-5200	
Standard Golf Co 6620 Nordic Dr *Web:* www.standardgolfcompany.com	Cedar Falls	IA	50613	319-266-2638	266-9627
Stewart Surfboards 2102 S El Camino Real *Web:* www.stewartsurfboards.com	San Clemente	CA	92672	949-492-1085	492-2344
Storm Products Inc 165 South 800 West *TF:* 800-369-4402 ■ *Web:* www.stormbowling.com	Brigham City	UT	84302	435-723-0403	734-0338
Summit Treestands LLC 715 Summit Dr *Web:* www.summitstands.com	Decatur	AL	35601	256-353-0634	353-9818
Talon 1552 Down River Dr PO Box 907 *Web:* www.talon-graphite.com	Woodland	WA	98674	360-225-8247	225-7737
TaylorMade - Adidas Golf 5545 Fermi Ct *TF Cust Svc:* 800-555-1212 ■ *Web:* www.taylormadegolf.com	Carlsbad	CA	92008	760-918-6000	918-6014
Tecnica USA 19 Technology Dr. *TF:* 800-258-3897 ■ *Web:* tecnicausa.com	West Lebanon	NH	03784	603-298-8032	298-5790
Toobs Inc 347 Quintana Rd *TF:* 800-795-8662 ■ *Web:* www.toobs.com	Morro Bay	CA	93442	800-795-8662	
True Temper Sports 8275 Tournament Dr Ste 200 *TF:* 800-355-8783 ■ *Web:* www.truetemper.com	Memphis	TN	38125	901-746-2000	746-2160
Underwater Kinetics (UK) 13400 Danielson St *TF:* 800-852-7483 ■ *Web:* www.uwkinetics.com	Poway	CA	92064	858-513-9100	513-3602
Victoria Skimboards 2955 Laguna Canyon Rd Ste 1 *Web:* ocean.victoriaskimboards.com	Laguna Beach	CA	92651	949-494-0059	494-5485
Weed USA Inc 5780 Harrow Glen Ct *TF:* 800-933-3758 ■ *Web:* www.weedusa.com	Galena	OH	43021	740-548-3881	548-3882
West Coast Trends 17811 Jamestown Ln *TF:* 800-736-4568 ■ *Web:* www.clubglove.com	Huntington Beach	CA	92647	714-843-9288	843-9020
Wiley Waterski and Wakeboard Pro Shop 1417 S Trenton *TF:* 800-962-0785 ■ *Web:* www.wileyski.com	Seattle	WA	98108	206-762-1300	762-7339
Wilson Sporting Goods Co 8750 W Bryn Mawr Ave *TF:* 800-874-5930 ■ *Web:* www.wilson.com	Chicago	IL	60631	773-714-6400	714-4565
Wittek Golf Supply Co Inc 3865 N Commercial Ave *TF:* 800-869-1800 ■ *Web:* www.wittekgolf.com	Northbrook	IL	60062	847-943-2399	412-9591
Worldwide Golf Shops Inc 1430 S Village Way *TF:* 888-216-5252 ■ *Web:* www.worldwidegolfshops.com	Santa Ana	CA	92705	714-543-8284	
Worth Co, The 214 Sherman Ave PO Box 88 *TF:* 800-944-1899 ■ *Web:* www.worthco.com	Stevens Point	WI	54481	715-344-6081	344-3021
Wright & McGill Co 4245 E 46th Ave **Fax Area Code:* 303 ■ *Web:* www.wright-mcgill.com	Denver	CO	80216	720-941-8700	321-4750*
Yakima Bait Company Inc PO Box 310 *TF:* 800-527-2711 ■ *Web:* www.yakimabait.com	Granger	WA	98932	509-854-1311	854-2263
Yamaha Motor Corp USA 6555 Katella Ave *TF Cust Svc:* 800-656-7695 ■ *Web:* www.yamaha-motor.com	Cypress	CA	90630	800-656-7695	
Yonex Corp 20140 S Western Ave *TF:* 800-449-6639 ■ *Web:* www.yonex.com	Torrance	CA	90501	310-793-3800	793-3899

714 SPORTING GOODS STORES

	City	State	ZIP	Phone	Fax
2nd Swing Inc 13031 Ridgedale Dr *Web:* www.2ndswing.com	Minnetonka	MN	55305	952-546-1906	546-1908
2nd Wind Exercise Equipment Inc 7585 Equitable Dr *Web:* www.2ndwindexercise.com	Eden Prairie	MN	55344	952-544-5249	544-5053
3balls.com 319 Manley St Ste 1 *Web:* www.3balls.com	West Bridgewater	MA	02379	888-289-0300	
5 Star Equine Products Inc 4589 Hwy 71 S *Web:* www.5starequineproducts.com	Hatfield	AR	71945	870-389-6328	
A T R Sales Inc 41 Talbot Rd *Web:* www.atrsales.com	Northborough	MA	01532	508-393-8529	
Academy Sports & Outdoors 1800 N Mason Rd *TF:* 888-922-2336 ■ *Web:* www.academy.com	Katy	TX	77449	281-646-5200	646-5204
Action Water Sports 4155 32nd Ave *Web:* www.actionwater.com	Hudsonville	MI	49426	616-896-3100	
Advanced Cable Ties Inc 245 Suffolk Ln *Web:* www.actfs.com	Gardner	MA	01440	978-630-3900	
Adventure 16 Inc 4620 Alvarado Canyon Rd **Fax:* Hum Res ■ *TF:* 800-854-2672 ■ *Web:* www.adventure16.com	San Diego	CA	92120	619-283-2362	283-7956*
Aero Tech Designs Cycling Apparel 1132 Fourth Ave *Web:* www.aerotechdesigns.com	Coraopolis	PA	15108	412-262-3255	
AFP International LLC 1730 Berkeley St *Web:* www.afproducts.com	Santa Monica	CA	90404	310-559-9949	
Alabama Outdoors Inc 3054 Independence Dr *TF:* 800-870-0011 ■ *Web:* www.alabamaoutdoors.com	Birmingham	AL	35209	205-870-1919	870-5505
Alaska Mining & Diving Supply Inc 3222 Commercial Dr *Web:* akmining.com	Anchorage	AK	99501	907-277-1741	
Allstar Fasteners Inc 1550 Arthur Ave *Web:* www.allstarfasteners.com	Elk Grove Village	IL	60007	847-640-7827	
Alpina Sports Corp 93 Etna Rd *Web:* www.alpinasports.com	Lebanon	NH	03766	603-448-3101	448-1586
Alpine Accessories Ski, Snowboard, Paddle Board Shop 9219 S State Rt 31 *Web:* www.alpineaccessories.com	Lake In The Hills	IL	60156	847-854-4754	
Altrec.com Inc 725 SW Umatilla Ave *TF:* 800-369-3949 ■ *Web:* www.altrec.com	Redmond	OR	97756	541-316-2400	
Ambush Boarding Co 2555 Cobb Pl Ln Nw *Web:* www.ambushboardco.com	Kennesaw	GA	30144	770-420-9111	
American Outfitters Ltd 3700 Sunset Ave *Web:* www.americanoutfitters.com	Waukegan	IL	60087	847-623-3959	
Ammo Alley LLC 11562 County Rd 395 *Web:* www.wholesalehunter.com	Hartsburg	MO	65039	573-634-6196	
Anaconda Sports Inc 85 Katrine Ln *Web:* www.anacondasports.com	Lake Katrine	NY	12449	845-336-4024	
Andy & Bax Sporting Goods & Gi Surplus 324 Se Grand Ave *Web:* www.andyandbax.com	Portland	OR	97214	503-234-7538	
Apple Saddlery 1875 Innes Rd *TF:* 800-867-8225 ■ *Web:* www.applesaddlery.com	Ottawa	ON	K1B4C6	613-744-4040	
Arco Ideas & Design Inc 212 N Tennessee St *Web:* www.arcoideas.com	Cartersville	GA	30120	770-386-2799	
ASLU LLC 12087 Landon Dr *Web:* www.activerideshop.com	Mira Loma	CA	91752	951-934-4200	
Aspen Ski & Board Co 1170 E Powell Rd *Web:* aspenskiandboard.com	Lewis Center	OH	43035	614-848-6600	
Associated Electrics Inc 26021 Commercentre Dr *Web:* www.teamassociated.com	Lake Forest	CA	92630	949-544-7500	
Athletic Supply Co 16101 NE 87th St *TF:* 800-732-9259 ■ *Web:* www.kimmelathletic.com	Redmond	WA	98052	425-882-1456	497-4727
Athletic Training Equipment Company Inc 655 Spice Island Dr *Web:* www.atecsports.com	Sparks	NV	89431	775-352-2800	
Atlantic Firearms LLC 10337 Bunting Rd *Web:* www.atlanticfirearms.com	Bishopville	MD	21813	410-352-5183	
Atomic Aquatics Inc 16742 Burke Ln *Web:* atomicaquatics.com	Huntington Beach	CA	92647	714-375-1433	
Austad's Golf 2801 E 10th St *TF Cust Svc:* 800-444-1234 ■ *Web:* www.austads.com	Sioux Falls	SD	57103	316-838-5557	
Backcountry Gear LLC 1855 W Second Ave *Web:* www.backcountrygear.com	Eugene	OR	97402	541-485-4007	
Backwoods 3300 N IH35 Ste 149 *Web:* www.backwoods.com	Austin	TX	78705	512-583-1700	370-3636
Backwoods Guns & Wildlife Taxidermy Inc 3322 Us Rt 60 *Web:* backwoodsgunstore.com	Huntington	WV	25705	304-521-6888	
Barnes Bullets Inc 38 N Frontage Rd *Web:* www.barnesbullets.com	Mona	UT	84645	435-856-1000	
Barts Water Sports 7581 E 800 N *Web:* www.bartswatersports.com	North Webster	IN	46555	574-834-7666	
Baseball Express Inc 5750 NW Pkwy Ste 100 *TF:* 800-937-4824 ■ *Web:* www.baseballexpress.com	San Antonio	TX	78249	210-348-7000	525-9339
Basilius Inc 4338 S Ave *Web:* www.basilius.com	Toledo	OH	43615	419-536-5810	
Bass Pro Shops Outdoor World 1935 S Campbell Ave *Web:* www.basspro.com	Springfield	MO	65807	417-887-7334	885-0072
Beads Galore International Inc 3320 S Priest Dr Ste 3 *Web:* www.beadsgalore.com	Tempe	AZ	85282	480-921-3949	
Bell Lifestyle Products Inc 3164 Pepper Mill Ct *Web:* www.belllifestyleproducts.com	Mississauga	ON	L5L4X4	905-820-7000	
Bent Gate Mountaineering 1313 Washington Ave *Web:* www.bentgate.com	Golden	CO	80401	303-271-9382	
Berg's Ski & Snowboard Shop 367 W 13th Ave *Web:* www.bergsskishop.com	Eugene	OR	97401	541-683-1300	
Berts Bikes & Sports 4050 Southwestern Blvd *Web:* www.bertsbikes.com	Orchard Park	NY	14127	716-646-0028	
Beval Saddlery Ltd 50 Pine St *Web:* www.beval.com	New Canaan	CT	06840	203-966-7828	
Bicycle Garage of Indy Inc 4340 E 82nd St *Web:* bgifitness.com	Indianapolis	IN	46250	317-842-4140	
Bicycle Warehouse 4670 Santa Fe St *Web:* www.bicyclewarehouse.com	San Diego	CA	92109	858-273-7300	
Big 5 Sporting Goods Corp 2525 E El Segundo Blvd *NASDAQ:* BGFV ■ *TF:* 800-898-2994 ■ *Web:* big5sportinggoods.com	El Segundo	CA	90245	310-536-0611	297-7580
Bike Gallery Portland Inc 5329 NE Sandy Blvd *Web:* bikegallery.com	Portland	OR	97213	503-281-9800	
Bike Line Corp 700 Lawrence Dr *Web:* www.bikeline.com	West Chester	PA	19380	610-429-4370	429-4295
Bike USA Inc 2811 Brodhead Rd *Web:* www.bikeusainc.com	Bethlehem	PA	18020	610-868-7652	
Bilenky Cycle Works Inc 5319 N Second St *Web:* www.bilenky.com	Philadelphia	PA	19120	215-329-4744	
Birdie Golf Balls Golf Equipment 208 Margate Ct *Web:* www.birdiegolfballstore.com	Margate	FL	33063	954-973-2741	
Bit of Britain Inc 141 Union School Rd *Web:* www.bitofbritain.com	Oxford	PA	19363	610-998-0400	
Black Box Inc 2777 Loker Ave W Unit A *Web:* www.blackboxdist.com	Carlsbad	CA	92010	760-804-3300	
Black Hills Shooters Supply Inc 2875 Creek Dr *Web:* www.bhshooters.com	Rapid City	SD	57703	605-348-4477	
Blade-Tech Industries Inc 5530 184th St East *TF:* 877-331-5793 ■ *Web:* www.blade-tech.com	Puyallup	WA	98375	253-655-8059	
Blue Quill Angler Inc 1532 Bergen Pkwy *Web:* www.bluequillangler.com	Evergreen	CO	80439	303-674-4700	
Blue Ribbon Products Fishng Tackl Dlr 1701 W Academy St *Web:* www.bettstackle.net	Fuquay Varina	NC	27526	919-552-2226	
Blue Sky Cycling Inc 2530 Randolph St *Web:* www.blueskycycling.com	Huntington Park	CA	90255	323-585-3934	

Company / Address	City	State	ZIP	Phone	Fax
Blue Sky Sports Center of Euless LLC 7801 Main St *Web:* www.blueskysportscenter.com	The Colony	TX	75056	469-384-3400	
Bob Reeves Brass Mouthpieces 25574 Rye Canyon Rd Ste D *Web:* www.bobreeves.com	Valencia	CA	91355	661-775-8820	
Bob Ward & Sons Inc 3015 Paxson St *TF:* 800-800-5083 ■ *Web:* www.bobwards.com	Missoula	MT	59801	406-728-3220	728-5230
Body Bar Inc 1942 Broadway St Ste 314 *Web:* www.bodybars.com	Boulder	CO	80302	303-938-6865	
Boulder Running Co 2775 Pearl St Ste 103 *Web:* www.boulderrunningcompany.com	Boulder	CO	80302	303-786-9255	
Boyne Country Sports 1200 Bay View Rd *TF:* 800-462-6963 ■ *Web:* www.boyne.com	Petoskey	MI	49770	231-439-4906	439-4960
Brainsport The Running Store 704 Broadway Ave *Web:* www.brainsport.ca	Saskatoon	SK	S7N1B4	306-244-0955	
Brighton Feed & Saddlery 370 N Main St *Web:* www.brightonsaddlery.com	Brighton	CO	80601	303-659-0721	
Brooklyn Gallery of Coins & Stamps Inc 8725 4th Ave *Web:* brooklyngallery.com	Brooklyn	NY	11209	718-745-5701	745-2775
Buchbinder Tunick & Company LLP One Penn Plz Ste 5335 *Web:* www.buchbinder.com	New York	NY	10119	212-695-5003	
Burghardt Sporting Goods 14660 W Capitol Dr *Web:* www.burghardtsportinggoods.com	Brookfield	WI	53005	262-790-1170	
Busy Body Home Fitness 9990 Empire St **Fax Area Code:* 949 ■ *TF:* 800-466-3348 ■ *Web:* www.busybody.com	San Diego	CA	92126	800-466-3348	258-5744*
C W I Inc 650 Three Springs Raod *Web:* www.campingworld.com	Bowling Green	KY	42104	888-626-7576	
C Walters Intercoastal Corp Inc 20081 Ellipse *Web:* www.destinationwater.com	Foothill Ranch	CA	92610	949-448-9940	
Cabela's Inc One Cabela Dr *NYSE:* CAB ■ **Fax:* Mktg ■ *TF:* 800-237-8888 ■ *Web:* www.cabelas.com	Sidney	NE	69160	308-254-5505	254-6102*
Cabela's Outdoor Adventures Inc 610 Glover Rd Ste A *TF:* 800-346-8747 ■ *Web:* www.cabelasoutdooradventures.com	Sidney	NE	69162	800-346-8747	
Cambria Bicycle Outfitter 2885 Santa Rosa Ave *Web:* www.cambriabike.com	Santa Rosa	CA	95407	707-579-5400	
Campmor Inc 400 Corporate Dr PO Box 680 *Web:* campmor.com	Mahwah	NJ	07430	201-335-9064	
Cannon Sports Inc 11614 Pendleton Steet *Web:* www.cannonsports.com	Sun Valley	CA	91352	818-683-1000	
CAP Barbell Inc 10820 Westpark *Web:* www.capbarbell.com	Houston	TX	77042	713-977-3090	
Capt Harrys Fishing Supply Company Inc 8501 Nw Seventh Ave *Web:* www.captharry.com	Miami	FL	33150	305-756-3474	
Carl's Golfland Inc 1976 S Telegraph Rd *Web:* www.carlsgolfland.com	Bloomfield Hills	MI	48302	248-335-8095	
Cascade Bicycle Club 7400 Sand Point Way Ne Ste 101s *Web:* www.cascade.org	Seattle	WA	98115	206-522-3222	
Centaur Products Inc 6855 Antrim Ave *Web:* www.centaurproducts.com	Burnaby	BC	V5J4M5	604-430-3088	
Century Martial Art Supply Inc 1000 Century Blvd *TF Sales:* 800-626-2787 ■ *Web:* www.centurymartialarts.com	Oklahoma City	OK	73110	405-732-2226	737-8954
Century Tool & Gage Co 200 S Alloy Dr *Web:* www.centurytool.com	Fenton	MI	48430	810-629-0784	
Champions for Life Sports Center 453 Grant Ave Rd *Web:* championsforlife.org	Auburn	NY	13021	315-252-9305	
Champs Sports 311 Manatee Ave W **Fax Area Code:* 941 ■ **Fax:* Mktg ■ *TF:* 800-991-6813 ■ *Web:* www.champssports.com	Bradenton	FL	34205	800-991-6813	741-7582*
Channel Islands Surfboards Inc 36 Anacapa St *Web:* www.almerrick.com	Santa Barbara	CA	93101	805-966-7213	
Chicagoland Bicycle Federation Nine W Hubbard St Ste 402 *Web:* www.activetrans.org	Chicago	IL	60654	312-427-3325	
Chick's 18011 S Dupont Hwy *Web:* chicksaddlery.com	Harrington	DE	19952	302-398-4630	
Christy Sports LLC 875 Parfet St *Web:* www.christysports.com	Lakewood	CO	80215	303-237-6321	233-5946
CIC Photonics Inc 9000 Washington St *Web:* www.cicp.com	Albuquerque	NM	87113	505-343-9500	
City Bikes 8401 Connecticut Ave Ste 111 *Web:* www.citybikes.com	Chevy Chase	MD	20815	301-652-1777	
Clear Water Outdoor LLC 744 W Main St *Web:* www.clearwateroutdoor.com	Lake Geneva	WI	53147	262-348-2420	
CMC Rescue Inc 41 Aero Camino *Web:* www.cmcrescue.com	Goleta	CA	93117	805-562-9120	
CMMG Inc 620 County Rd 118 *Web:* www.cmmginc.com	Fayette	MO	65248	660-248-2293	
Coghlan's Ltd 121 Irene St *Web:* www.coghlans.com	Winnipeg	MB	R3T4C7	204-284-9550	
Cole Sport Inc 1615 Park Ave *Web:* www.colesport.com	Park City	UT	84060	435-649-4800	
Colonial Country Club Inc 3735 Country Club Cir *Web:* www.colonialfw.com	Fort Worth	TX	76109	817-927-4200	
Colorado Ski Country USA Inc 1444 Wazee S Ste 320 *Web:* www.coloradoski.com	Denver	CO	80202	303-837-0793	
Concept Molds Inc 12273 N Us 131 *Web:* www.conceptmolds.com	Schoolcraft	MI	49087	269-679-2100	679-2157
Condor Outdoor Products 5268 Rivergrade Rd *Web:* www.condoroutdoor.com	Irwindale	CA	91706	626-358-3270	
Coontail Corner 5466 Park St *Web:* coontailsports.com	Boulder Junction	WI	54512	715-385-2582	
Cosfibel Inc 60 E 42nd St Ste 2301 *Web:* www.cosfibelgroup.com	New York	NY	10165	212-867-4133	
Cox Sales Co 2035 Cook Dr *Web:* www.glue4you.com	Salem	VA	24153	540-345-2636	
Crown Enterprises Inc 145 Hutton Ranch Rd *Web:* www.sportsmanskihaus.com	Kalispell	MT	59901	406-755-6484	758-7425
Cycle-safe Inc 5211 Cascade Rd Se Ste 210 *Web:* cyclesafe.com	Grand Rapids	MI	49546	616-954-9977	
D & R Sports Ctr Inc 8178 W Main St *TF:* 800-992-1520 ■ *Web:* www.dandrsports.com	Kalamazoo	MI	49009	269-372-2277	372-9072
D&S Pump & Supply Co 3784 Danbury Rd *Web:* www.dspumpco.com	Brewster	NY	10509	845-279-3784	
Daddies Board Shop LLC 7126 NE Sandy Blvd *Web:* www.daddiesboardshop.com	Portland	OR	97213	503-281-5123	
Dallas Athletic Club Po Box 570649 *Web:* www.123access.net	Dallas	TX	75357	972-279-6517	
Dan Bailey Fly Shop 209 W Park St *Web:* www.dan-bailey.com	Livingston	MT	59047	406-222-1673	
Dan's Competition Inc One Competition Way *Web:* www.danscomp.com	Mount Vernon	IN	47620	812-838-2691	
Darien Sport Shop Inc, The 1127 Post Rd *Web:* dariensport.com	Darien	CT	06820	203-655-2575	
Dart World Inc 140 Linwood St *Web:* www.dartworld.com	Lynn	MA	01905	781-581-6035	
Dave'S Pawn Shop 1576 N Main St *Web:* davespawnshop.com	Crossville	TN	38555	931-484-8947	
Del-Ton Inc 330 Aviation Pkwy *Web:* www.del-ton.com	Elizabethtown	NC	28337	910-645-2172	
Delta Mold Inc 9415 Stockport Pl *Web:* www.deltamold.com	Charlotte	NC	28273	704-588-6600	
Dharma Trading Co 1604 Fourth St *Web:* dharmatrading.com	San Rafael	CA	94901	415-456-1211	
DHM Adhesives Inc 509 S Wall St Ste A *Web:* www.dhmadhesives.com	Calhoun	GA	30701	706-629-7960	
Diamond Supply Co 451 N Fairfax Ave *Web:* www.diamondsupplyco.com	Los Angeles	CA	90036	323-966-5970	
Diamond Tour 203 E Lincoln Hwy *Web:* www.diamondtour.com	Dekalb	IL	60115	815-787-2649	
Direct Sports Inc 1720 Curve Rd *Web:* directsports.com	Pearisburg	VA	24134	800-456-0072	
Dive N' Surf Inc 504 N Broadway *Web:* www.divensurf.com	Redondo Beach	CA	90277	310-372-8423	
Dixie Gun Works Inc 1412 W Reelfoot Ave PO Box 130 *TF Orders:* 800-238-6785 ■ *Web:* www.dixiegun.com	Union City	TN	38281	731-885-0700	885-0440
Dollamur LP 1734 E El Paso St *Web:* www.dollamur.com	Fort Worth	TX	76102	817-534-3344	
Dolphin Swim School Inc 1530 El Camino Ave *Web:* www.dolphinscuba.com	Sacramento	CA	95815	916-929-8188	
Doms Outdoor Outfitters 1870 First St *Web:* www.domsoutdoor.com	Livermore	CA	94550	925-447-9629	
Double J Saddlery Inc 2243 US Hwy 77A S *Web:* www.doublejsaddlery.com	Yoakum	TX	77995	361-293-6364	
Dowdle Sports Inc 4415 Donelson Dr *Web:* www.dowdlesports.com	Eads	TN	38028	901-466-7706	
Downtown Athletic Store Inc 1180 Seminole Trail Ste 210 *TF:* 800-348-2649 ■ *Web:* www.downtownathletic.com	Charlottesville	VA	22901	434-975-3696	975-2845
Duke's Source for Sports 3876 Bloor St W *Web:* dukes.sourceforsports.com	Etobicoke	ON	M9B1L3	416-233-2011	
Duluth Pack 365 Canal Park Dr *Web:* www.duluthpack.com	Duluth	MN	55802	218-722-1707	
Dynamic Pro Shop 4330 Thousand Oaks Dr *Web:* dynamicjudo.com	San Antonio	TX	78217	210-650-5560	
Dynamic Tool & Design Inc W133 N5180 Campbell Dr *Web:* www.dyntool.com	Menomonee Falls	WI	53051	262-783-6340	
Eagle Grips Inc 460 Randy Rd *Web:* eaglegrips.com	Carol Stream	IL	60188	630-260-0400	
Eagle Quest Golf Centers Inc 1001 United Blvd *Web:* www.eaglequestgolf.com	Coquitlam	BC	V3K4S8	604-523-6400	
Earth Sports LLC 746 W Algonquin Rd *Web:* www.erehwon.com	Arlington Heights	IL	60005	847-439-1400	
Eastern Mountain Sports 1 Vose Farm Rd *TF:* 888-463-6367 ■ *Web:* www.ems.com	Peterborough	NH	03458	603-924-7231	924-4320
Eastern Skateboard Supply Inc 6612 Amsterdam Way *Web:* www.easternskatesupply.com	Wilmington	NC	28405	910-791-8240	
Easy Picker Golf Products Inc 415 Leonard Blvd N *Web:* www.easypicker.com	Lehigh Acres	FL	33971	239-368-6600	
Efinger Sporting Goods Company Inc 513 W Union Ave *Web:* www.efingersports.com	Bound Brook	NJ	08805	732-356-0604	356-0604
Electra Bicycle Company LLC 3270 Corporate View Ste A *Web:* www.electrabike.com	Vista	CA	92081	760-607-2453	
Entest Inc 2015 Midway Rd Ste 114 *Web:* www.entest.net	Carrollton	TX	75006	972-980-9876	960-7044
Equinox Ltd 1307 Park Ave *Web:* www.equinoxltd.com	Williamsport	PA	17701	570-322-5900	
Eternal Board Shop 45 E Freeport Blvd *Web:* www.eternalsnow.com	Sparks	NV	89431	775-358-1002	

Company / Address	City	State	ZIP	Phone	Fax
Evaporated Coatings Inc 2365 Maryland Rd *Web:* www.evaporatedcoatings.com	Willow Grove	PA	19090	215-659-3080	
Excel Sports Boulder 2045 32nd St *Web:* www.excelsports.com	Boulder	CO	80301	303-444-6737	
Exerplay Inc 12001 State Hwy 14 N *Web:* www.exerplay.com	Cedar Crest	NM	87008	505-281-0151	
Exkate 26212 Dimension Dr Ste 160 *Web:* exkate.com	Lake Forest	CA	92630	949-951-9500	
Eyeline Golf 2990 W 29th St Unit 7 *Web:* www.eyelinegolf.com	Greeley	CO	80631	970-353-0393	
Fairway Golf Inc 5040 Convoy St Ste A *Web:* www.fairwaygolfusa.com	San Diego	CA	92111	858-268-1702	
Fanzz 2657 South 1030 West *TF:* 888-326-9946 ■ *Web:* www.fanzz.com	Salt Lake City	UT	84119	801-325-2700	
Farwest Sports Inc 4602 20th St E *Web:* sportco.com	Fife	WA	98424	253-922-2581	
Fibar Group LLC, The 80 Business Park Dr Suit 300 *Web:* www.fibar.com	Armonk	NY	10504	914-273-8770	
Fin-feather-fur Outfitters 652 Us Hwy 250 E *Web:* finfeatherfuroutfitters.com	Ashland	OH	44805	419-281-2557	
Finlandia Sauna Products Inc 14010 Sw 72nd Ave Ste B *Web:* www.finlandiasauna.com	Portland	OR	97224	503-684-8289	
First to The Finish Inc 1325 N Broad St *Web:* www.firsttothefinish.com	Carlinville	IL	62626	217-854-8305	
Fishtech 5802 W Dempster St *Web:* www.fishtechmg.com	Morton Grove	IL	60053	847-966-5900	
Fitness Club Warehouse Inc 2210 S Sepulveda Blvd *Web:* www.fitnessblowout.com	Los Angeles	CA	90064	310-235-2040	
Fitness Zone 3439 Colonnade Pkwy Se 800 *TF:* 800-875-9145 ■ *Web:* www.fitnesszone.com	Birmingham	AL	35243	800-875-9145	
Flite Hockey Inc 3400 Ridgeway Dr Unit 2 *Web:* www.flitehockey.com	Mississauga	ON	L5L0A2	905-828-6030	
Florida Custom Mold Inc 1806 Gunn Hwy *Web:* www.fla-mold.com	Odessa	FL	33556	813-343-5080	
Flow Sports Inc 1021 Calle Recodo *Web:* www.flow.com	San Clemente	CA	92673	949-361-5260	
Fluid Industrial Associates Inc Seven Sixth Rd Ste 2414 *Web:* fiainc.com	Woburn	MA	01801	781-938-8900	
Fly Fishing Shop E 67296 Hwy 26 *Web:* www.flyfishingevents.com	Welches	OR	97067	503-622-4607	
Foreman Tool & Mold Corp 3850 Swenson Ave *Web:* www.foremantool.com	Saint Charles	IL	60174	630-377-6389	
Forzani Group Ltd 824 41st Ave NE *Web:* www.fglsports.com	Calgary	AB	T2E3R3	403-717-1400	
Fourteen Company Ltd 18271 W McDurmott St Ste F *Web:* www.fourteengolf.com	Irvine	CA	92614	949-852-8811	
Fox Creek Leather Inc 2029 Elk Creek Pkwy *Web:* www.foxcreekleather.com	Independence	VA	24348	276-773-3131	
Fram Trak Industries Inc 205 Hallock Ave Ste B *Web:* www.framtrak.com	Middlesex	NJ	08846	732-424-8400	
Free Flite Inc 2949 Canton Rd Ste 1000 *Web:* www.freeflite.com	Marietta	GA	30066	770-422-5237	
Freebord Manufacturing Inc 455 Irwin St Unit 104 *Web:* www.freebord.com	San Francisco	CA	94107	415-285-2673	
French Creek Outfitters Inc 270 Schuylkill Rd *Web:* www.frenchcreekoutfitters.com	Phoenixville	PA	19460	610-933-7200	
Gander Mountain Co 180 Fifth St E Ste 1300 *Web:* gandermountain.com	Saint Paul	MN	55101	651-325-4300	
Garber C s & Sons Inc 7928 Boyertown Pk *Web:* www.csgarber.com	Boyertown	PA	19512	610-689-9500	
Gazelle Sports 3930 28th St Se *Web:* www.gazellesports.com	Grand Rapids	MI	49512	616-940-9888	
Gem Manufacturing Company Inc 78 Brookside Rd *Web:* www.gemmfg.com	Waterbury	CT	06708	203-574-1466	
Genesis Bicycles 126 Bushkill St *Web:* genesisbicycles.com	Easton	PA	18042	610-253-1140	
Gerry Cosby & Company Inc 11 Pennsylvania Plz *TF:* 877-563-6464 ■ *Web:* www.cosbysports.com	New York	NY	10001	212-563-6464	967-0876
Getboards.com 40905 Big Bear Blvd *Web:* www.getboards.com	Big Bear Lake	CA	92315	909-878-3155	
Girl Skateboard Company Inc, The 22500 S Vermont Ave *Web:* www.girlskateboards.com	Torrance	CA	90502	310-783-1900	
Gita Sporting Goods Ltd 12500 Steele Creek Rd *Web:* www.gitabike.com	Charlotte	NC	28273	704-588-7555	
Gold Tip LLC 368 S Gold Tip Dr *Web:* www.goldtip.com	Orem	UT	84058	801-229-1666	
Golf & Ski Warehouse Inc 290 Plainfield Rd *Web:* www.golfskiwarehouse.com	West Lebanon	NH	03784	603-298-8282	
Golf Etc of America Inc 2201 Commercial Ln *TF:* 800-806-8633 ■ *Web:* www.golfetc.com	Granbury	TX	76048	817-579-5263	579-1162
Golf Shack Inc 1631 N Bell School Rd *TF:* 888-446-5390 ■ *Web:* www.golfshack.com	Rockford	IL	61107	815-397-3709	397-7593
Golf Shoe Centers of America 9899 N Kings Hwy *Web:* www.golfshoesonly.com	Myrtle Beach	SC	29572	843-497-0507	
Golfballs.com Inc 126 Arnould Blvd *Web:* www.golfballs.com	Lafayette	LA	70506	337-210-4653	
Golfer's Warehouse Inc 75 Brainard Rd *Web:* www.golferswarehouse.com	Hartford	CT	06114	860-522-6829	
Golfsmith International Inc 11000 N IH-35 *TF Sales:* 800-396-0099 ■ *Web:* www.golfsmith.com	Austin	TX	78753	512-821-4050	837-1245
Good Sports Outdoor Outfitters 12730 W Interstate 10 Ste 300 *Web:* www.goodsports.com	San Antonio	TX	78230	210-694-0881	
Graf & Sons Whlse. Dept Inc 4050 S Clark St *Web:* www.grafs.com	Mexico	MO	65265	573-581-2266	
Great Skate Hockey Supl Co 3395 Sheridan Dr *Web:* www.greatskate.com	Buffalo	NY	14226	716-838-5100	
Green Top Sporting Goods Corp PO Box 1015 *Web:* www.greentophuntfish.com	Glen Allen	VA	23060	804-550-2188	550-2693
Gregg's Greenlake Cycle 7007 Woodlawn Ave NE *Web:* www.greggscycles.com	Seattle	WA	98115	206-523-1822	523-5330
Guildcraft Inc 100 Fire Tower Dr *Web:* www.guildcraftinc.com	Tonawanda	NY	14150	800-345-5563	
Gulf States Distributors Inc 6000 E Shirley Ln *Web:* www.gulfstatesdist.com	Montgomery	AL	36117	334-271-2010	
Gun Lake Band Health & Human Services 1743 142nd Ave Ste 6 *Web:* www.mbpi.org	Dorr	MI	49323	616-681-0360	
Gunsite Academy Inc 2900 W Gunsite Rd *Web:* www.gunsite.com	Paulden	AZ	86334	928-636-4565	
Gym Source 40 E 52nd St *TF:* 800-496-3499 ■ *Web:* www.gymsource.com	New York	NY	10022	212-688-4222	750-2886
H E Anderson Company Inc 2100 Anderson Dr *Web:* www.heanderson.com	Muskogee	OK	74403	918-687-4426	
Haddrell's Point Tackle & Supply 47 Windermere Blvd *Web:* www.haddrellspoint.com	Charleston	SC	29407	843-573-3474	
Half Hitch Tackle Company Inc 2206 Thomas Dr *Web:* www.halfhitch.com	Panama City	FL	32408	850-234-2621	
Half Moon Outfitters 15 E Broughton St *Web:* www.recarts.com	Savannah	GA	31401	912-201-9393	
Hansen Surfboards 1105 S Coast Hwy 101 *Web:* www.hansensurf.com	Encinitas	CA	92024	760-753-6595	
Hawaiian Island Creations Inc 348 Hahani St *Web:* www.hicsurf.com	Kailua	HI	96734	808-266-6730	
Heerema Co 200 Sixth Ave *Web:* www.heeremacompany.com	Hawthorne	NJ	07506	973-423-0505	
Hibbett Sporting Goods Inc 451 Industrial Ln *Web:* www.hibbett.com	Birmingham	AL	35211	205-942-4292	912-7290
His Tackle Box Inc 40 Chestnut Ave *Web:* www.histacklebox.com	South San Francisco	CA	94080	650-588-1200	
Hoigaards Inc 5425 Excelsior Blvd *TF:* 800-266-8157 ■ *Web:* www.hoigaards.com	Minneapolis	MN	55416	952-929-1351	929-2669
Holabird Sports LLC 9220 Pulaski Hwy *Web:* www.holabirdsports.com	Middle River	MD	21220	410-687-6400	
Holiday Diver Inc 180 Gulf Stream Way *Web:* www.diversdirect.com	Dania Beach	FL	33004	954-926-4420	
Hometown Sportswear Inc 3692 Us Rt 60 E *Web:* hometownsportswear.com	Barboursville	WV	25504	304-736-4021	
Hopkins Sporting Goods Inc 5485 NW Beaver Dr *Web:* www.hopkinssportinggoods.com	Johnston	IA	50131	515-270-0132	
Hot Melt Technologies Inc 1723 W Hamlin Rd *Web:* www.hotmelt-tech.com	Rochester Hills	MI	48309	248-853-2011	
Hunter Banks Company Inc 29 Montford Ave *Web:* hunterbanks.com	Asheville	NC	28801	828-252-3005	
Hunter'S Friend LLC 340 Low Gap Frk *Web:* huntersfriend.com	Oil Springs	KY	41238	606-297-1011	
Ice Box Sports Center 21902 Telegraph Rd *Web:* www.norianproperties.com	Brownstown Twp	MI	48183	734-676-5500	
In The Swim Inc 320 Industrial Dr **Fax Area Code:* 800 ■ *TF:* 800-288-7946 ■ *Web:* www.intheswim.com	West Chicago	IL	60185	630-876-0040	766-5329*
Industrial Ride Shop 3111 W Chandler Blvd Ste 2198 *Web:* www.industrialrideshop.com	Chandler	AZ	85226	480-812-8881	
Inside Edge Ski & Bike Shop 643 Glen St *Web:* www.reliableracing.com	Queensbury	NY	12804	518-793-5677	
Ironmind Enterprises Inc 11992 Charles Dr *Web:* www.ironmind.com	Grass Valley	CA	95945	530-272-3579	
Island Surf 1009 Orange Ave *Web:* www.islandsurf.com	Coronado	CA	92118	619-435-1527	
Isometric Tool & Design Inc 330 Wisconsin Dr *Web:* www.isotool.com	New Richmond	WI	54017	715-246-7005	
J & G Sales Inc 440 Miller Vly Rd *Web:* jgsales.com	Prescott	AZ	86301	928-445-9650	
J. & M. Golf Inc 319 Industrial Dr *Web:* jandmgolf.com	Griffith	IN	46319	219-922-1787	
Jan's Mountain Outfitters 1600 Pk Ave PO Box 280 *TF:* 800-745-1020 ■ *Web:* www.jans.com	Park City	UT	84060	435-649-4949	649-7511
Jax Outdoor Gear 1200 N College Ave *Web:* jaxmercantile.com	Fort Collins	CO	80524	970-221-0544	
Jay's Sporting Goods Inc 8800 S Clare Ave *Web:* www.jayssportinggoods.com	Clare	MI	48617	989-386-3475	386-3496
Jumping Brook Country Club 210 Jumping Brook Rd *Web:* www.jumpingbrookcc.com	Neptune	NJ	07753	732-922-3653	
Karla Colletto Swimwear Inc 319d Mill St Ne *Web:* www.karlacolletto.com	Vienna	VA	22180	703-281-3262	

Phone | Fax

Keep Me in Stitches 14833 N Dale Mabry Hwy .... Tampa FL 33618 813-908-3889
Web: www.kmisinc.com
Killer Dana Surf Shop 24621 Del Prado ....Dana Point CA 92629 949-489-8380
Web: www.killerdana.com
Kirkham's Outdoor Products
3125 S State St.............................. Salt Lake City UT 84115 801-486-4161
Web: www.kirkhams.com
Kittery Trading Post 301 US 1 .... Kittery ME 03904 603-334-1157 439-8001*
**Fax Area Code:* 207 ■ *TF:* 888-587-6246 ■ *Web:* www.kitterytradingpost.com
Kitty Hawk Kites Inc
306 W Lk Dr Unit K........................... Kill Devil Hills NC 27948 252-441-4127
Web: www.kittyhawk.com
Kona Sports Center 103 E Rio Grande Ave .... Wildwood NJ 08260 609-522-7899
Web: konasports.com
Korney Board Aids Sporting 312 Harrison Ave ....Roxton TX 75477 903-346-3269
Web: www.kbacoach.com
Kreinik Manufacturing Company Inc
1708 Gihon Rd..................................Parkersburg WV 26101 304-422-8900
Web: www.kreinik.com
Kwik Industries Inc 4725 Nall Rd .... Dallas TX 75244 972-458-9761 458-0948
Web: kwikind.com
Lacrosse Unlimited Inc 59 Gilpin Ave .... Hauppauge NY 11788 631-582-2500
Web: www.lacrosseunlimited.com
Lancaster Archery Supply Inc
2195a Old Phila Pk.....................................Lancaster PA 17602 717-394-7229
Web: www.lancasterarchery.com
Laux Sporting Goods Inc 25 Pineview Dr ....Amherst NY 14228 716-691-3367 691-4393
Web: www.lauxsportinggoods.com
Lee's Cyclery 202 W Laurel St ....Fort Collins CO 80521 970-482-6006
Web: www.leescyclery.com
Leisure Pro 42 W 18th St ....New York NY 10011 212-645-1234
Web: www.leisurepro.com
Lombardi Sports Inc 1600 Jackson St .... San Francisco CA 94109 415-771-0600 771-0600
Web: www.lombardisports.com
Lone Mountain Sports Mountain Vlg .... Big Sky MT 59716 406-995-4471
Web: www.lonemountainsports.net
Look Cycle Usa 6300 San Ignacio Ave Ste G .... San Jose CA 95119 408-363-1406
Web: www.lookcycle.com
Love to Swim & Tumble School
15502 Huebner Rd Ste 111.......................San Antonio TX 78248 210-492-2606
Web: www.love-to-swim.com
Lumberjack Building Centers
3470 Pointe Tremble Rd............................Algonac MI 48001 810-794-4921
Web: www.lumber-jack.com
Macks Prairie Wings 2335 Hwy 63 N.................Stuttgart AR 72160 870-673-6960
Web: www.mackspw.com
Mad Dogg Athletics Inc 2111 Narcissus Ct............. Venice CA 90291 310-823-7008
Web: www.spinning.com
Magnum Research Inc
7110 University Ave NE .... Minneapolis MN 55432 763-574-1868
Web: www.magnumresearch.com
Mancom Manufacturing Inc 1335 Osprey Dr......... Ancaster ON L9G4V5 905-304-6141
Web: www.mancomsystems.com
Marin Mountain Bikes Inc
265 Bel Marin Keys Blvd ....Novato CA 94949 415-382-6000
Web: www.marinbikes.com
Marks Outdoor Sports Inc
1400 Montgomery Hwy Ste B........................Vestavia AL 35216 205-822-2010
Web: marksoutdoors.com
Markwort Sporting Goods Co
1101 Research Blvd .... St. Louis MO 63132 314-652-8935
Web: markwort.com
Marman Industries Inc 1701 Earhart................ La Verne CA 91750 909-392-2136
Web: marman.com
Martin Kilpatrick Table Tennis
4482 Technology Dr NW..................................Wilson NC 27896 252-291-8202
Web: www.butterflyonline.com
Mass Movement Inc 65 Green St Ste 1................Foxboro MA 02035 508-543-2073
Web: www.massmovement.com
Mathews Inc 919 River Rd............................ Sparta WI 54656 608-269-2728
Web: www.mathewsinc.com
MC Sports 3070 Shaffer Ave SE...................Grand Rapids MI 49512 616-942-2600 942-2786
TF: 800-626-1762 ■ *Web:* www.mcsports.com
McCormick's Enterprises Inc
216 W Campus Dr Ste 101.................. Arlington Heights IL 60004 847-398-8680
Web: www.mccormicksnet.com
Medallion Athletic Products Inc
150 River Park Rd..................................Mooresville NC 28117 704-660-3000
Web: www.medallionathletics.com
Mel Cotton's Sales & Rentals Inc
1266 W San Carlos St .... San Jose CA 95126 408-287-5994 298-3536
Web: www.melcottons.com
Midwest Gun & Supply Inc 16 E Peoria.................Paola KS 66071 913-557-4867
Web: midwestgunandsupply.com
Midwest Mountaineering Inc
309 Cedar Ave S............................... Minneapolis MN 55454 612-339-3433
Web: www.midwestmtn.com
Midwest Sports Supply Inc
11613 Reading Rd .... Cincinnati OH 45241 513-956-4900
Web: www.midwestsports.com
Minco Tool & Mold Co 5690 Webster St...................Dayton OH 45414 937-890-7905
Web: www.mincogroup.com
Mission Bicycles Inc 766 Valencia St .... San Francisco CA 94110 415-683-6166
Web: missionbicycle.com
Modell's Sporting Goods
498 Seventh Ave 20th Fl.............................New York NY 10018 800-275-6633
TF: 888-645-8667 ■ *Web:* www.modells.com
MOL (America) Inc
700 E Butterfield Rd Ste 150....................... Lombard IL 60148 630-812-3700
Web: www.molpower.com
Mold Craft Inc 200 Stillwater Rd PO Box 458 .... Willernie MN 55090 651-426-3216
Web: www.mold-craft.com

Phone | Fax

Moldex 823 Bessemer St...........................Meadville PA 16335 814-337-3190
Web: www.moldexcorp.com
Mollusk Surf Shop LLC 4500 Irving St .... San Francisco CA 94122 415-564-6300
Web: mollusksurfshop.com
Monogram Center 437 Amboy Ave.............. Perth Amboy NJ 08861 732-442-1800
Web: www.njtees.com
Motion Fitness LLC 1400 W Northwest Hwy........... Palatine IL 60067 847-963-8969
Web: www.motionfitness.com
Motrec Inc 200 rue Des PME St.................. Sherbrooke QC J1C0R2 819-846-2010
Web: www.motrec.com
Mountain Equipment Co-operative
149 W Fourth Ave..............................Vancouver BC V5Y4A6 604-707-3300
Web: www.mec.ca
Mountain Tools Inc 225 Crossroads Blvd..............Carmel CA 93923 831-620-0911
Web: www.mtntools.com
Mud Hole Custom Tackle Inc 400 Kane Ct ....Oviedo FL 32765 407-447-7637
Web: www.mudhole.com
Mueller Recreational Products Inc
4825 S 16th St .... Lincoln NE 68512 402-423-8888
Web: www.muellers.com
Mystic Valley Wheel Works Inc 480 Trapelo Rd ....Belmont MA 02478 617-489-3577
Web: www.wheelworks.com
Nagel Gun & Sports Shop
6201 San Pedro Ave...........................San Antonio TX 78216 210-342-5420
Web: nagelsguns.net
National Sports Center Foundation, The
1700 105th Ave Ne........................... Minneapolis MN 55449 763-785-5600
Web: www.nscsports.org
Nerel Corp Dba Wheat Ridge Cyclery
7085 W 38th Ave .... Wheat Ridge CO 80033 303-424-3221
New York Golf Center 131 W 35th St ....New York NY 10001 212-564-2255
Web: www.nygolfcenter.com
Nicros Inc 845 Phalen Blvd....................... Saint Paul MN 55106 651-778-1975
Web: www.nicros.com
Nill Bros Sports 2814 S 44th St ....Kansas City KS 66106 913-384-4242 384-0107
Web: www.nillbros.com
NLC Products Inc
3801 Woodland Heights Rd Ste 100................Little Rock AR 72212 501-227-9050
Web: www.huntsmart.com
No Fault Sports Products 2101 Briarglen Dr ....Houston TX 77027 713-683-7101
Web: nofaultsports.com
North Carolina Railroad Co
2809 Highwoods Blvd Ste 100....................... Raleigh NC 27604 919-954-7601
Web: www.ncrr.com
North Shore Country Club 1340 Glenview Rd .... Glenview IL 60025 847-729-1200
Web: www.north-shorecc.org
Northern Wholesale Supply Inc
6800 Otter Lk Rd.................................Lino Lakes MN 55038 651-429-1515
Web: www.northernwholesale.com
Northland Fishing Tackle LLC
1001 Naylor Dr Se .... Bemidji MN 56601 218-751-6723
Web: www.northlandtackle.com
Northwest Outlet 1814 Belknap St .... Superior WI 54880 715-392-1122
Web: www.northwestoutlet.com
Notubes 202 Daniel Zenker Dr...................... Big Flats NY 14814 607-562-2877
Web: www.notubes.com
Nova Fitness Equipment 4511 S 119th Cir ....Omaha NE 68137 402-343-0552
Web: www.novafitnessequipment.com
NRC Sports Inc 603 Pleasant St ....Paxton MA 01612 800-243-5033 852-8206*
**Fax Area Code:* 508 ■ *TF:* 800-243-5033 ■ *Web:* www.nrcsports.com
Okuma Fishing Tackle Corp 2310 E Locust Ct .... Ontario CA 91761 909-923-2828
Web: www.okumafishing.com
Old Harbor Outfit 480 Barnum Ave.................Bridgeport CT 06608 203-540-5150
Web: www.oldharboroutfitters.com
Olympia Sports Five Bradley Dr..................Westbrook ME 04092 207-854-2794 854-4168
Web: www.olympiasports.net
Onion River Sports Inc 20 Langdon St..............Montpelier VT 05602 802-229-9409
Web: www.onionriver.com
Otis Technology 6987 Laura St PO Box 582.......... Lyons Falls NY 13368 315-348-4300
Web: www.otisgun.com
Out-fit 25 W Easy St Ste 306 .... Simi Valley CA 93065 805-584-1500
Web: www.out-fit.net
Outcast Sporting Gear 2021 E Wilson Ln............ Meridian ID 83642 208-955-0476
Web: aireindustrial.net
Outdoor Sports Center 80 Danbury Rd................ Wilton CT 06897 203-762-8797
Web: www.outdoorsports.com
Outdoor Ventures 10579 S Main St................. Hayward WI 54843 715-634-4447
TF: 866-710-2846 ■ *Web:* www.outdoorventureshayward.com
Palco Marketing Inc 8555 Revere Ln N .... Maple Grove MN 55369 763-559-5539
Web: www.palcosports.com
Palos Sports Inc 11711 S Austin Ave.................... Alsip IL 60803 708-396-2555
Web: www.palossports.com
Pape's Archery Inc 250 Terry Blvd ....Louisville KY 40229 502-955-8118
Web: www.papesinc.com
Paragon Sporting Goods Corp
867 Broadway 18th St..............................New York NY 10003 212-255-8889 929-1831
TF: 800-961-3030 ■ *Web:* www.paragonsports.com
Pedigree Ski Shop Inc
355 Mamaroneck Ave........................... White Plains NY 10605 914-948-2995 948-1599
Web: www.pedigreeskishop.com
Perani's Hockey World 1600 Cochran Rd .... Pittsburgh PA 15220 412-343-5857
Web: hockeyworld.com
Perform Better Inc 11 Amflex Dr .... Cranston RI 02921 401-942-9363
Web: www.everythingtrackandfield.com
Performance Inc One Performance Way........... Chapel Hill NC 27514 800-727-2453 942-5431*
**Fax Area Code:* 919 ■ *TF Cust Svc:* 800-727-2453 ■ *Web:* www.performancebike.com
Peter Glenn Ski & Sports
2901 W Oakland Pk Blvd.....................Fort Lauderdale FL 33311 954-484-3606 739-5724
TF: 800-818-0946 ■ *Web:* www.peterglenn.com
Planet Bike 2402 Vondron Rd .... Madison WI 53718 608-256-8510
Web: www.planetbike.com

Company / Address	City	State	Zip	Phone	Fax
Playnation of Wnc 542 Hendersonville Rd *Web:* playnationofwnc.com	Asheville	NC	28803	828-776-2731	
Playspace Designs Inc 6321 S Heughs Canyon Dr *Web:* www.playspacedesigns.com	Salt Lake City	UT	84121	801-274-0212	
Playwell Group, The 4743 Iberia Ave Ste C *Web:* www.playwellgroup.com	Dallas	TX	75207	800-726-1816	
Playworks Inc 12824 141 St Nw *Web:* www.playworks.ca	Edmonton	AB	T5L4N8	780-453-6903	
Power Gripps Usa Inc 41 Pomola Ave *Web:* www.versagripps.com	Sorrento	ME	04677	207-422-2051	
Pro Hockey Life Sporting Goods Inc 4440 Autoroute 440 *Web:* www.prohockeylife.com	Laval	QC	H7T2P7	450-681-8440	
Pro Performance Sports LLC 2081 Faraday Ave *TF:* 877-225-7275 ■ *Web:* www.sklz.com	Carlsbad	CA	92008	877-225-7275	
Proactive Sports Inc 1200 SE Second Ave *Web:* proactivesports.com	Canby	OR	97013	503-263-8583	
Proline Distributors Inc 1191 S Rogers Cir *Web:* www.prolinedist.com	Boca Raton	FL	33487	561-241-7000	
Protek Cargo 1568 Airport Blvd *Web:* www.protekcargo.com	Napa	CA	94558	707-562-3578	
Pummills Sporting Goods Inc 2400 W 16th St *Web:* www.pummillsports.com	Sedalia	MO	65301	660-826-0150	
Quarq Technology Inc 3100 First Ave *Web:* www.quarq.com	Spearfish	SD	57783	605-642-2226	
R K Sport Inc 26900 Jefferson Ave *Web:* www.stretchformingcorp.com	Murrieta	CA	92562	951-894-7883	
Randall Scott Cycle Company LLC 2897 Mapleton Ave Ste 100 *Web:* www.rscycle.com	Boulder	CO	80301	720-214-0714	
RD Rogers Co, The 515 N Garfield Cir *Web:* www.pushpedalpull.com	Sioux Falls	SD	57104	605-334-7740	
Recreational Equipment Inc (REI) 6750 S 228th St *TF Orders:* 800-426-4840 ■ *Web:* www.rei.com	Kent	WA	98032	253-395-3780	891-2523
Redden Marine Supply Inc 1411 Roeder Ave *Web:* www.reddenmarine.com	Bellingham	WA	98225	360-733-0250	
Reeds Family Outdoor Outfitters 522 Minnesota Ave NW *Web:* www.reedssports.com	Walker	MN	56484	800-346-0019	
Retail Concepts Inc 10560 Bissonnet St Ste 100 *Web:* www.retailconcepts.cc	Stafford	TX	77099	281-340-5000	
Rhino Gun Safes 607 Garber St *Web:* www.rhinosafe.com	Caldwell	ID	83605	208-454-5545	
Rich n Ton Calls Inc 2315 Hwy 63 N *Web:* www.rntcalls.com	Stuttgart	AR	72160	870-673-4274	
Richardson Bike Mart Inc 1451 W Campbell Rd *Web:* bikemart.com	Richardson	TX	75080	972-644-1466	
Risse Racing Technology Inc 1240 Redwood Blvd *Web:* www.risseracing.com	Redding	CA	96003	530-246-8700	
RJR Fashion Fabrics 2203 Dominguez Way *Web:* www.rjrfabrics.com	Torrance	CA	90501	310-222-8782	
Robart Manufacturing Co 625 N 12th St *Web:* www.robart.com	Saint Charles	IL	60174	630-584-7616	
Ron Jon Surf Shop 3850 S Banana River Blvd *TF:* 888-757-8737 ■ *Web:* www.ronjonsurfshop.com	Cocoa Beach	FL	32931	321-799-8888	799-8805
Royal Oaks Country Club Club House 7915 Greenville Ave *Web:* roccdallas.com	Dallas	TX	75231	214-691-6091	
Royer Corp 805 East St *Web:* www.royercorp.com	Madison	IN	47250	812-265-3133	
Rubenstein & Ziff Inc 1055 American Blvd E *Web:* www.quiltworksonline.com	Minneapolis	MN	55420	952-854-1460	
Ruby Hill Golf Shop 3404 W Ruby Hill Dr *Web:* rubyhill.com	Pleasanton	CA	94566	925-417-5850	
Rudolph Brothers 6550 Oley Speaks Way *Web:* www.rudolphbros.com	Canal Winchester	OH	43110	614-833-0707	
Runner's Edge Inc, The 3195 N Federal Hwy *Web:* runnersedgeboca.com	Boca Raton	FL	33431	561-361-1950	
Runners Forum of Carmel Inc 620 Station Dr *Web:* www.runnersforum.com	Carmel	IN	46032	317-844-1558	
Rusted Moon Outfitters Inc 6410 Cornell Ave *Web:* www.rustedmoonoutfitters.com	Indianapolis	IN	46220	317-253-4453	
San Juan Golf & Country Club Golf Shop 806 Golf Course Rd *Web:* sanjuangolfandcountryclub.com	Friday Harbor	WA	98250	360-378-2254	
Scottsdale Gun Club 14860 N Northsight Blvd *Web:* www.scottsdalegunclub.com	Scottsdale	AZ	85260	480-348-1111	
Scouts Canada 1345 Baseline Rd *Web:* www.scouts.ca	Ottawa	ON	K2C0A7	613-225-2770	
Scuba Com Inc 1752 Langley Ave *Web:* www.scuba.com	Irvine	CA	92614	949-221-9300	
Seattle Golf Club Pro Shop LLC 210 Nw 145th St *Web:* www.seattlegolfclub.com	Shoreline	WA	98177	206-363-8811	
SeeMore Putter Co, The 277 Mallory Sta Ste 119 *Web:* www.seemore.com	Franklin	TN	37067	615-435-8015	
Shatz Norman C Company Inc 3570 St Rd *Web:* www.shatzusa.com	Bensalem	PA	19020	215-245-5511	
Shuert Industries Inc 6600 Dobry Rd *Web:* www.shuert.com	Sterling Heights	MI	48314	586-254-4590	
Sierra Bullets LLC 1400 W Henry St *Web:* www.sierrabullets.com	Sedalia	MO	65301	660-827-6300	
SKI Pro 1924 W Eigth St *Web:* www.skipro.com	Mesa	AZ	85201	480-962-6910	
Ski Stop 197 S Service Rd *Web:* www.sunandski.com	Plainview	NY	11803	516-249-7980	249-5636
Skiershop PO Box 1542 *Web:* www.skiershop.com	Stowe	VT	05672	802-253-9400	
Slocum Adhesives Corp 2500 Carroll Ave *Web:* www.slocumadhesives.com	Lynchburg	VA	24501	434-847-5671	
Soccer 4 All 1306 Fm 1092 Rd Ste 101 *Web:* www.soccer4all.com	Missouri City	TX	77459	281-499-6665	499-7411
Sonoma Outfitters 145 Third St *Web:* www.sonomaoutfitters.com	Santa Rosa	CA	95401	707-528-1920	
South Hills Country Club Golf Shop 2655 S Citrus St *Web:* www.southhillscountryclub.org	West Covina	CA	91791	626-339-1231	
Spokes Etc Inc 1545 N Quaker Ln *Web:* www.spokesetc.com	Alexandria	VA	22302	703-820-2200	
Sport Chalet Inc One Sport Chalet Dr *NASDAQ: SPCHB* ■ *TF:* 888-801-9162 ■ *Web:* www.sportchalet.com	La Canada	CA	91011	818-949-5300	
Sporting Goods Intelligence Inc 442 Featherbed Ln *Web:* www.sginews.com	Glen Mills	PA	19342	610-459-4040	
Sports Authority Inc, The 1050 W Hampden Ave *Web:* sportsauthority.com	Englewood	CO	80110	303-200-5050	
Sports Excellence Corporation Inc 915 rue Philippe-Paradis *Web:* www.sec.ca	Quebec	QC	G1N4E3	418-687-0133	
Sports Imports Inc Po Box 21040 *Web:* www.sportsimports.com	Columbus	OH	43221	614-771-0246	
Sports One Inc 9640 SW Sunshine Court Ste 400 *Web:* www.etzelagency.com	Portland	OR	97005	503-721-7477	
Sports Promotion Network PO Box 200548 **Fax Area Code: 866* ■ *TF:* 800-460-9989 ■ *Web:* www.gotospn.com	Arlington	TX	76006	800-460-9989	300-5333*
Sports Warehouse Inc 181 Suburban Rd *Web:* www.tennis-warehouse.com	San Luis Obispo	CA	93401	805-781-6464	
Sportsman's Warehouse 7035 High Tech Dr *Web:* www.sportsmanswarehouse.com	Midvale	UT	84047	801-566-6681	
Spot-hogg Archery Products 125 Smith St *Web:* spot-hogg.com	Harrisburg	OR	97446	541-995-3702	
Spyder Ii 65 Pier Ave *Web:* www.spydersurf.com	Hermosa Beach	CA	90254	310-374-2494	
St Bernard Sports 5570 W Lovers Ln Ste 388 *Web:* www.stbernardsports.com	Dallas	TX	75209	214-357-9700	357-0107
Starline Inc 1300 W Henry St *Web:* starlinebrass.com	Sedalia	MO	65301	660-827-6640	
STI International Inc 114 Halmar Cove *Web:* stiguns.com	Georgetown	TX	78628	512-819-0656	
Stic-adhesive Products Company Inc 3950 Medford St *Web:* www.sticadhesive.com	Los Angeles	CA	90063	323-268-2956	
Stoneybrook West Golf Club LLC 15501 Towne Commons Blvd *Web:* www.stoneybrookgolf.com	Winter Garden	FL	34787	407-877-8533	
Stretch Boards 983 Tower Pl *Web:* www.stretchboards.com	Santa Cruz	CA	95062	831-479-7309	
Summit Canyon Mountaineering 732 Grand Ave *Web:* summitcanyon.com	Glenwood Springs	CO	81601	970-945-6994	
Summit Hut 5045 E Speedway Blvd *Web:* www.summithut.com	Tucson	AZ	85712	520-325-1554	795-7350
Sun & Ski Sports 4001 Greenbriar St Ste 100 *Web:* www.sunandski.com	Stafford	TX	77477	281-340-5000	340-5020
Sun & Snow Sports Inc 2471 W Stadium Blvd *Web:* www.sunandsnow.com	Ann Arbor	MI	48103	734-663-9515	
Sundance Beach 59 S La Patera Ln *Web:* www.sundancebeach.com	Goleta	CA	93117	805-966-2474	
Super Runners Shop Inc 355 New York Ave *Web:* www.superrunnersshop.com	Huntington	NY	11743	631-549-3006	
Surf Associates Inc 1701 N Federal Hwy *Web:* www.bcsurf.com	Fort Lauderdale	FL	33305	954-563-1366	
Surf Technicians LLC 2685 Mattison Ln *Web:* www.surftech.com	Santa Cruz	CA	95062	831-479-4944	
Switlik Parachute Company Inc 1325 E State St *Web:* www.switlik.com	Trenton	NJ	08609	609-587-3300	
Syndrome Distribution Inc 1410 Vantage Ct *Web:* www.syndromedist.com	Vista	CA	92081	760-560-0440	
Tabata U.S.A. Inc 2380 Mira Mar Ave *Web:* www.tusa.com	Long Beach	CA	90815	562-498-3708	
Tack Room Too Inc 201 Lee St Sw *Web:* www.tackroomtoo.com	Tumwater	WA	98501	360-357-4268	
Tahoe Mountain Sports 11200 Donner Pass Rd Ste 5e *TF:* 866-891-9177 ■ *Web:* www.tahoemountainsports.com	Truckee	CA	96161	866-891-9177	
Tam O'shanter Country Club 5051 Orchard Lk Rd *Web:* www.blendedlearningworkshop.com	West Bloomfield	MI	48323	248-855-1900	
Tennis Express 11022 Westheimer Rd *Web:* www.tennisexpress.com	Houston	TX	77042	713-781-4848	781-1237
Tennis Pro Shop 19101 Peninsula Club Dr *Web:* www.thepeninsulaclub.com	Cornelius	NC	28031	704-896-7676	
Texford Battery Co 2002 Milby St *Web:* www.texford.com	Houston	TX	77003	713-222-0125	
Tie Fast Vest Tools 847 W Fifth St *Web:* tie-fast.com	Chico	CA	95928	530-345-4261	
Toledo Physical Education Supply Inc 5101 Advantage Dr *Web:* www.tpesonline.com	Toledo	OH	43612	419-726-8122	
Toledo Ticket Co 3963 Catawba St *Web:* www.toledoticket.com	Toledo	OH	43612	419-476-5424	

				Phone	Fax
Total Hockey Inc 5833 Suemandy Rd *Web:* www.totalhockey.net	Saint Peters	MO	63376	636-397-6370	
Traditions Performance Firearms 1375 Boston Post Rd *Web:* www.traditionsfirearms.com	Old Saybrook	CT	06475	860-388-4656	
Treads Bicycle Outfitters 16701 E Iliff Ave *Web:* www.treads.com	Aurora	CO	80013	303-750-1671	
Trek Bicycle Superstore 4240 Kearny Mesa Rd Ste 108 *Web:* www.trekbicyclesuperstore.com	San Diego	CA	92111	858-974-8735	
Trek Bikes of Ventura 4060 E Main St *Web:* www.trekbikesofventura.com	Ventura	CA	93003	805-644-8735	
Tri-State Pumps Inc 1162 Chastain Rd *Web:* www.tsppumps.com	Liberty	SC	29657	864-843-8100	
Triathlete Sports 186 Exchange St *Web:* www.triathletesports.com	Bangor	ME	04401	207-990-2013	
Trijicon Inc 49385 Shafer Ave PO Box 930059 *Web:* www.trijicon.com	Wixom	MI	48393	248-960-7700	
TriSports.com 4495 S Coach Dr *TF:* 888-293-3934 ■ *Web:* www.trisports.com	Tucson	AZ	85714	888-293-3934	
Tum Yeto Inc 2001 Commercial St *Web:* www.tumyeto.com	San Diego	CA	92113	619-232-7523	
Turbo 2 n 1 Grip 46460 Continental Dr *Web:* www.turbogrips.com	Chesterfield	MI	48047	586-598-3948	
Turner's Outdoorsman 11738 Sanmarino St Ste A *Web:* www.turners.com	Rancho Cucamonga	CA	91730	909-923-3009	923-3022
U.S. Kids Golf LLC 3040 Northwoods Pkwy *Web:* www.uskidsgolf.com	Norcross	GA	30071	770-441-3077	
Val Surf Inc 4810 Whitsett Ave *TF:* 888-825-7873 ■ *Web:* www.valsurf.com	Valley Village	CA	91607	818-769-6977	769-4318
Van Cliburn Foundation Inc 2525 Ridgmar Blvd Ste 307 *Web:* www.cliburn.org	Fort Worth	TX	76116	817-738-6536	738-6534
Vance Outdoors Inc 3723 Cleveland Ave *Web:* www.vancesshooterssupplies.com	Columbus	OH	43224	614-471-7000	
Viking Ski Shop Inc 3422 W Fullerton Ave *Web:* vikingskishop.com	Chicago	IL	60647	773-276-1222	
Volquartsen Custom Ltd 24276 240th St *Web:* volquartsen.com	Carroll	IA	51401	712-792-4238	
Wapsi Fly Co 27 County Rd 458 *Web:* www.wapsifly.com	Mountain Home	AR	72653	870-425-9500	
Warehouse Skateboards Inc 1638 Military Cutoff Rd Ste 101 *Web:* www.warehouseskateboards.com	Wilmington	NC	28403	910-509-9599	
Warrior Custom Golf Inc 15 Mason Ste A *TF:* 800-600-5113 ■ *Web:* www.warriorcustomgolf.com	Irvine	CA	92618	949-699-2499	
Wave Loch Inc 210 Westbourne St *Web:* www.waveloch.com	La Jolla	CA	92037	858-454-1777	
Western Power Sports Inc 601 E Gowen Rd *TF:* 800-999-3388 ■ *Web:* www.wps-inc.com	Boise	ID	83716	208-376-8400	375-8901
Wheel & Sprocket 6940 N Santa Monica Blvd *Web:* www.wheelsprocket.com	Milwaukee	WI	53217	414-247-8100	
Wheel & Sprocket Inc 5722 S 108th St *TF:* 866-892-6059 ■ *Web:* wheelandsprocket.com	Hales Corners	WI	53130	414-529-6600	247-8105
Wilmette Bicycle & Sport Shop 605 Green Bay Rd *Web:* www.wilmettesportshop.com	Wilmette	IL	60091	847-251-1404	
Worldwide Golf Company 560 E 2100 S *Web:* www.worldwidegolfshops.com	Salt Lake City	UT	84106	801-487-8233	466-5713
WrestlingGearCom Ltd 655 W Grand Ave Ste 140 *Web:* www.wrestlinggear.com	Elmhurst	IL	60126	630-832-0500	
Xs Sight Systems Inc 2401 Ludelle St *Web:* www.xssights.com	Fort Worth	TX	76105	817-536-0136	
Zimmer Enterprises Inc 911 Senate Dr *Web:* www.pbj-sport.com	Dayton	OH	45459	937-428-1057	

715 SPORTS COMMISSIONS & REGULATORY AGENCIES - STATE

				Phone	Fax
Arizona Racing Dept 1110 W Washington St Ste 260 *Web:* racing.az.gov/	Phoenix	AZ	85007	602-364-1700	364-1703
Arkansas Racing Commission 1515 W Seventh St Rm 505 *Web:* www.dfa.arkansas.gov	Little Rock	AR	72203	501-682-1467	682-5273
California Athletic Commission 1430 Howe Ave *Web:* www.dca.ca.gov	Sacramento	CA	95825	916-263-2195	263-2197
California Horse Racing Board 1010 Hurley Way Rm 300 *Web:* www.chrb.ca.gov	Sacramento	CA	95825	916-263-6000	263-6042
Delaware Harness Racing Commission 2320 S Dupont Hwy *Web:* dda.delaware.gov	Dover	DE	19901	302-698-4599	697-6287
Delaware Thoroughbred Racing Commission 2320 S DuPont Hwy *Web:* dda.delaware.gov	Dover	DE	19901	302-698-4599	
Energy and Environment Cabinet 500 Mero St Ste 5 *Web:* www.eec.ky.gov	Frankfort	KY	40601	502-564-3350	564-3969
Idaho Racing Commission 700 S Stratford Dr *Web:* isp.idaho.gov	Meridian	ID	83642	208-884-7080	884-7098
Illinois Racing Board 100 W Randolph St Ste 5-700 **Fax Area Code:* 866 ■ *Web:* www2.illinois.gov	Chicago	IL	60601	312-814-2600	323-0273*
Indiana Horse Racing Commission 150 W Market St Ste 530 *Web:* www.in.gov	Indianapolis	IN	46204	317-233-3119	233-4470
Kentucky Horse Racing Authority 4063 Iron Works Pkwy Bldg B *Web:* khrc.ky.gov	Lexington	KY	40511	859-246-2040	246-2039
Louisiana Racing Commission 320 N Carrollton Ave Ste 2-B *Web:* horseracing.louisiana.gov	New Orleans	LA	70119	504-483-4000	483-4898
Maryland Racing Commission 500 N Calvert St Rm 201 *Web:* www.dllr.state.md.us	Baltimore	MD	21202	410-230-6320	
Maryland State Athletic Commission 500 N Calvert St Rm 304 *Web:* www.dllr.state.md.us/license/occprof/athlet.html	Baltimore	MD	21202	410-230-6223	333-6314
Massachusetts State Boxing Commission 1 Ashburton Pl Rm 1301 *Web:* www.mass.gov/mbc	Boston	MA	02108	617-727-3200	727-5732
Massachusetts State Racing Commission 1 Ashurton Pl 11th Fl *Web:* www.mass.gov	Boston	MA	02108	617-727-2581	
Michigan Racing Commissioners Office 525 W Allegan St PO Box 30773 *Web:* www.michigan.gov	Lansing	MI	48909	517-335-1420	241-3018
Nebraska State Racing Commission 5903 Walker Ave *Web:* nebraskaracingcommission.com/	Lincoln	NE	68507	402-471-4155	
Nevada State Athletic Commission 555 E Washington Ave Ste 3300 *Web:* www.boxing.nv.gov	Las Vegas	NV	89101	702-486-2575	486-2577
New Jersey Racing Commission 140 E Front St *Web:* www.njpublicsafety.org	Trenton	NJ	08625	609-292-0613	599-1785
New Jersey State Athletic Control Board 25 Market Street 1st Fl W Wing *Web:* www.state.nj.us/lps/sacb	Trenton	NJ	08625	609-292-0317	292-3756
New Mexico Racing Commission 4900 Alameda NE *Web:* www.nmrc.state.nm.us	Albuquerque	NM	87113	505-222-0700	222-0713
New York Athletic Commission 123 William St 20th Fl *TF:* 866-269-3769 ■ *Web:* www.dos.ny.gov	New York	NY	10038	212-417-5700	417-4987
North Dakota Racing Commission 500 N Ninth St *Web:* www.ndracingcommission.com	Bismarck	ND	58501	701-328-4290	
Ohio Racing Commission 77 S High St 18th Fl *Web:* www.racing.ohio.gov	Columbus	OH	43215	614-466-2757	466-1900
Pennsylvania State Athletic Commission 2601 N Third St *Web:* dos.state.pa.us/portal/server.pt/community/state_athletic_commission/12431	Harrisburg	PA	17110	717-787-5720	783-0824
South Dakota Gaming Commission 221 W Capitol Ave Ste 101 *Web:* sd.gov	Pierre	SD	57501	605-773-6050	773-6053
Texas Racing Commission 8505 Cross Pk Dr Ste 110 *Web:* txrc.state.tx.us	Austin	TX	78754	512-833-6699	833-6907
Utah Sports Commission 201 S Main St Ste 2002 *Web:* www.utahsportscommission.com	Salt Lake City	UT	84111	801-328-2372	328-2389
Washington Horse Racing Commission 6326 Martin Way Ste 209 *Web:* www.whrc.wa.gov	Olympia	WA	98516	360-459-6462	459-6461
West Virginia Racing Commission 900 Pennsylvania Ave Ste 533 *Web:* www.racing.wv.gov	Charleston	WV	25302	304-558-2150	558-6319

SPORTS FACILITIES

SEE Racing & Racetracks p. 2997; Stadiums & Arenas p. 3192; Motor Speedways p. 2772

716 SPORTS TEAMS - BASEBALL

SEE ALSO Sports Organizations p. 1785

				Phone	Fax
Major League Baseball (Office of the Commissioner) 245 Pk Ave 31st Fl **Fax:* PR ■ *TF Cust Svc:* 866-800-1275 ■ *Web:* mlb.mlb.com	New York	NY	10167	212-931-7800	949-5654*
3D Lacrosse LLC 1301 S Jason St Unit K *Web:* www.3dlacrosse.com	Denver	CO	80223	303-346-2888	
Alabama Sports Festival 2530 E South Blvd *Web:* www.alagames.net	Montgomery	AL	36116	334-280-0065	
Arizona Diamondbacks 401 E Jefferson St *Web:* arizona.diamondbacks.mlb.com	Phoenix	AZ	85004	602-462-6500	462-6600
Atlanta Braves PO Box 4064 *TF:* 800-326-4000 ■ *Web:* atlanta.braves.mlb.com	Atlanta	GA	30302	404-522-7630	614-1329
Boston Red Sox Fenway Pk 4 Yawkey Way *Web:* boston.redsox.mlb.com	Boston	MA	02215	617-226-6000	236-6797
Camden Riversharks 401 N Delware Ave *Web:* riversharks.com	Camden	NJ	08102	856-963-2600	
Catholic Memorial High School 235 Baker St *Web:* www.catholicmemorial.org	West Roxbury	MA	02132	617-469-8000	
Chicago Cubs 1060 W Addison St Ste 1 **Fax:* PR ■ *Web:* chicago.cubs.mlb.com	Chicago	IL	60613	773-404-2827	404-4129*
Chicago White Sox US Cellular Field 333 W 35th St *Web:* chicago.whitesox.mlb.com	Chicago	IL	60616	312-674-1000	
Cincinnati Reds 100 Joe Nuxhall Way *TF:* 877-647-7337 ■ *Web:* cincinnati.reds.mlb.com	Cincinnati	OH	45202	513-381-7337	765-7342
Cleveland Indians 2401 Ontario St **Fax:* Cust Svc ■ *Web:* cleveland.indians.mlb.com	Cleveland	OH	44115	216-420-4487	420-4799*
Colorado Rockies Coors Field 2001 Blake St **Fax:* PR ■ *Web:* colorado.rockies.mlb.com	Denver	CO	80205	303-292-0200	312-2115*
Detroit Tigers Comerica Pk 2100 Woodward Ave **Fax:* PR ■ *TF:* 866-800-1275 ■ *Web:* detroit.tigers.mlb.com	Detroit	MI	48201	313-962-4000	471-2138*

Phone *Fax*

Edmonton Eskimo Football Club, The
11000 Stadium Rd .... Edmonton AB T5H4E2 780-448-1525
Web: www.esks.com

Houston Astros
Minute Maid Pk 501 Crawford St .... Houston TX 77002 713-259-8000 799-9562
TF: 800-771-2303 ■ *Web:* houston.astros.mlb.com

Kansas City Royals
Kauffman Stadium 1 Royal Way .... Kansas City MO 64129 816-921-8000 921-5775
TF Sales: 800-676-9257 ■ *Web:* kansascity.royals.mlb.com

Lancaster Barnstormers & Keystone Baseball
650 N Prince St .... Lancaster PA 17603 717-509-1340
Web: www.lancasterbarnstormers.com

Los Angeles Angels of Anaheim
Angel Stadium 2000 Gene Autry Way .... Anaheim CA 92806 714-940-2000 940-2205*
**Fax:* PR ■ *Web:* losangeles.angels.mlb.com

Los Angeles Dodgers
Dodger Stadium 1000 Elysian Pk Ave .... Los Angeles CA 90012 323-224-1500 224-1269*
**Fax:* PR ■ *Web:* losangeles.dodgers.mlb.com

Milwaukee Brewers Miller Pk 1 Brewers Way .... Milwaukee WI 53214 414-902-4452 902-4588
TF: 877-722-6458 ■ *Web:* milwaukee.brewers.mlb.com

Minnesota Twins
Metrodome 34 Kirby Puckett Pl .... Minneapolis MN 55415 612-375-1366
TF: 800-338-9467 ■ *Web:* minnesota.twins.mlb.com

New Britain Rock Cats
230 John Karbonic Way S Main St New Britain Stadium
.... New Britain CT 06051 860-224-8383
Web: newbritain.rockcats.milb.com

New York Jets LLC One Jets Dr .... Florham Park NJ 07932 973-549-4800
Web: www.newyorkjets.com

New York Mets
Shea Stadium 123-01 Roosevelt Ave .... Flushing NY 11368 718-507-6387 507-6395
TF: 888-652-7467 ■ *Web:* newyork.mets.mlb.com

New York Yankees
Yankee Stadium 161st St & River Ave .... Bronx NY 10451 718-293-4300 293-8431
Web: newyork.yankees.mlb.com

Norfolk Tides Baseball
150 Park Ave Harbor Park .... Norfolk VA 23510 757-622-2222
Web: norfolk.tides.milb.com

Oakland Athletics
7000 Coliseum Way McAfhee Stadium .... Oakland CA 94621 510-638-4900 568-3770
Web: oakland.athletics.mlb.com

Philadelphia Phillies
Citizens Bank Pk 1 Citizens Bank Pk Way .... Philadelphia PA 19148 215-463-1000
Web: philadelphia.phillies.mlb.com

Pinnacle Sports LLC 313 Medina Rd .... Medina OH 44256 330-239-0616
Web: www.pinnaclesports.org

Pittsburgh Pirates
115 Federal St PO Box 7000 .... Pittsburgh PA 15212 412-321-2827
TF: 800-289-2827 ■ *Web:* pittsburgh.pirates.mlb.com

Real Salt Lake 9256 South State .... Sandy UT 84070 801-727-2700
Web: www.realsaltlake.com

Richard Childress Racing Enterprises Inc
425 Industrial Dr .... Welcome NC 27374 336-731-3334
Web: www.rcrracing.com

Rochester Yacht Club 5555 Saint Paul Blvd .... Rochester NY 14617 585-342-5511
Web: www.rochesteryc.com

Roush Fenway Racing LLC 4600 Roush Pl NW .... Concord NC 28027 704-720-4600
Web: www.roushracing.com

San Diego Padres Petco Pk 100 Park Blvd .... San Diego CA 92101 619-795-5000 795-5035
Web: sandiego.padres.mlb.com

San Francisco Giants
AT & T Pk 24 Willie Mays Plaza
24 Willie Mays Plz .... San Francisco CA 94107 415-972-2000
Web: sanfrancisco.giants.mlb.com

Seattle Mariners
Safeco Field 1250 First Ave S .... Seattle WA 98134 206-346-4000 346-4050
TF: 800-255-7932 ■ *Web:* seattle.mariners.mlb.com

Sport Systems Unlimited Corp 685 Rupert St .... Waterloo ON N2V1N7 519-747-1856
Web: www.sportsystemscorp.com

St. Paul Saints Baseball Club Inc
1771 Energy Park Dr .... Saint Paul MN 55108 651-644-6659
Web: www.saintsbaseball.com

Texas Rangers
Rangers Ballpark in Arlington
1000 Ballpark Way .... Arlington TX 76011 817-273-5222 273-5190
TF: 866-800-1275 ■ *Web:* texas.rangers.mlb.com

Toledo Mud Hens Baseball Club Inc
406 Washington St .... Toledo OH 43604 419-725-4367
Web: www.mudhens.com

Toronto Blue Jays One Blue Jays Way Ste 3200 .... Toronto ON M5V1J1 416-341-1000 341-1250*
**Fax:* PR ■ *TF:* 888-654-6529 ■ *Web:* toronto.bluejays.mlb.com

Winston-Salem Dash 926 Brookstown Ave .... Winston-salem NC 27101 336-714-2287
Web: winstonsalem.dash.milb.com

717 SPORTS TEAMS - BASKETBALL

SEE ALSO Sports Organizations p. 1785

717-1 National Basketball Association (NBA)

Phone *Fax*

National Basketball Association (NBA)
645 Fifth Ave .... New York NY 10022 212-407-8000 832-3861
Web: www.nba.com

Atlanta Hawks
Centennial Tower 101 Marietta St NW Ste 1900 .... Atlanta GA 30303 404-827-3800 827-3880
Web: www.nba.com/hawks

Boston Celtics 226 Cswy St Fourth Fl .... Boston MA 02114 617-854-8000 367-4286
Web: www.nba.com

Charlotte Bobcats 333 E Trade St .... Charlotte NC 28202 704-688-8600 688-8732
Web: www.nba.com/bobcats

Chicago Bulls 1901 W Madison St .... Chicago IL 60612 312-455-4000
Web: www.nba.com

Cleveland Cavaliers
Quicken Loans Arena 1 Ctr Ct .... Cleveland OH 44115 216-420-2000 420-2298*
**Fax:* PR ■ *TF:* 800-332-2287 ■ *Web:* www.nba.com

Dallas Mavericks 2909 Taylor St .... Dallas TX 75226 214-747-6287 658-7121
Web: www.nba.com

Denver Nuggets 1000 Chopper Cir .... Denver CO 80204 303-405-1100 405-1315
Web: www.nba.com

Detroit Pistons
Palace at Auburn Hills
5 Championship Dr .... Auburn Hills MI 48326 248-377-0100 377-4262
Web: www.nba.com

Golden State Warriors 1011 Broadway .... Oakland CA 94607 510-986-2200 827-3880*
**Fax Area Code:* 404 ■ *TF:* 866-648-4668 ■ *Web:* www.nba.com

Houston Rockets 1510 Polk St .... Houston TX 77002 713-758-7200 758-7396*
**Fax:* Hum Res ■ *TF:* 866-648-4668 ■ *Web:* www.nba.com/rockets

Indiana Pacers
Conseco Fieldhouse
125 S Pennsylvania St .... Indianapolis IN 46204 317-917-2500 917-2599
Web: www.nba.com/pacers

Los Angeles Clippers
Staples Ctr 1111 S Figueroa St Ste 1100 .... Los Angeles CA 90015 213-742-7100 742-7550
TF: 855-895-0872 ■ *Web:* www.nba.com/clippers

Los Angeles Lakers 555 N Nash St .... El Segundo CA 90245 310-426-6000 426-6105
TF: 866-648-4668 ■ *Web:* www.nba.com/lakers

Memphis Grizzlies FedExForum 191 Beale St .... Memphis TN 38103 901-205-1234 205-1235
Web: www.nba.com/grizzlies

Miami Heat
American Airlines Arena 601 Biscayne Blvd .... Miami FL 33132 786-777-1000 777-1615
Web: www.nba.com

Milwaukee Bucks
Bradley Ctr 1001 N Fourth St .... Milwaukee WI 53203 414-227-0500 227-0543
Web: www.nba.com

Minnesota Timberwolves
Target Ctr 600 First Ave N .... Minneapolis MN 55403 612-673-1600 673-1699
TF: 855-895-0872 ■ *Web:* www.nba.com

New Jersey Nets
Nets Champion Ctr
390 Murray Hill Pkwy .... East Rutherford NJ 07073 201-935-8888
TF: 800-346-6387 ■ *Web:* www.nba.com

New Orleans Hornets 1250 Poydras St Fl 19 .... New Orleans LA 70113 504-593-4700
Web: www.nba.com

New York Knicks
Madison Sq Garden 2 Pennsylvania Plz
14th Fl .... New York NY 10121 212-465-6471 465-6498*
**Fax:* PR ■ *Web:* www.nba.com/knicks

Orlando Magic 8701 Maitland Summit Blvd .... Orlando FL 32810 407-916-2400 916-2953
Web: www.nba.com

Philadelphia 76ers 3601 S Broad St .... Philadelphia PA 19148 215-339-7600 339-7615
Web: www.nba.com

Phoenix Suns
US Airways Ctr 201 E Jefferson St .... Phoenix AZ 85004 602-379-7900 379-7990
TF: 866-648-4668 ■ *Web:* www.nba.com/suns

Sacramento Kings ARCO Arena 1 Sports Pkwy .... Sacramento CA 95834 916-928-0000 928-0727
TF: 866-746-7622 ■ *Web:* www.nba.com/kings

San Antonio Spurs One AT & T Ctr .... San Antonio TX 78219 210-444-5000 444-5003
Web: www.nba.com/spurs

Seattle SuperSonics 1201 Third Ave Ste 1000 .... Seattle WA 98101 206-281-5800 281-5839
TF: 800-743-7021 ■ *Web:* www.nba.com

Utah Jazz
301 W S Temple St
Energy Solutions Arena .... Salt Lake City UT 84101 801-325-2500 325-2578*
**Fax:* PR ■ *Web:* www.nba.com

Washington Wizards Verizon Ctr 601 F St NW .... Washington DC 20004 202-661-5000
Web: www.nba.com

717-2 Women's National Basketball Association (WNBA)

Phone *Fax*

Women's National Basketball Assn (WNBA)
645 Fifth Ave .... New York NY 10022 212-688-9622 750-9622
Web: www.wnba.com

Chicago Sky 20 W Kinzie St Ste 1000 .... Chicago IL 60610 312-828-9550
Web: www.wnba.com

Connecticut Sun 1 Mohegan Sun Blvd .... Uncasville CT 06382 860-862-4000 862-4010
TF: 877-329-9622 ■ *Web:* www.wnba.com

Detroit Shock
5 Championship Dr
Palace at Auburn Hills .... Auburn Hills MI 48326 248-377-0100 377-3260
Web: www.wnba.com/shock

Houston Comets 1730 Jefferson St .... Houston TX 77003 713-739-7442 739-7709*
**Fax:* Hum Res ■ *Web:* www.wnba.com

Indiana Fever
Conseco Fieldhouse
125 S Pennsylvania St .... Indianapolis IN 46204 317-917-2500 917-2899
TF: 877-275-9007 ■ *Web:* www.wnba.com/fever

Los Angeles Sparks
865 S Figueroa St Ste 104 .... Los Angeles CA 90017 213-929-1300 929-1325
TF: 888-694-3278 ■ *Web:* www.wnba.com

Minnesota Lynx 600 First Ave N Target Ctr .... Minneapolis MN 55403 612-673-1600 673-8407
Web: www.wnba.com/lynx

New York Liberty
Madison Sq Garden 2 Pennsylvania Plz .... New York NY 10121 212-564-9622 465-6250
Web: www.wnba.com/liberty

Phoenix Mercury
US Airways Ctr 201 E Jefferson St .... Phoenix AZ 85004 602-514-8333 514-8303
Web: www.wnba.com/mercury

Sacramento Monarchs
ARCO Arena 1 Sports Pkwy .... Sacramento CA 95834 916-928-6900 928-8109
TF: 877-329-9622 ■ *Web:* www.wnba.com/monarchs

				Phone	Fax
San Antonio Silver Stars One AT & T Ctr .... San Antonio *Web:* wnba.com/stars/	TX	78219		210-444-5090	444-5003
Seattle Storm 351 Elliott Ave W Ste 500 .... Seattle *TF:* 877-329-9622 ■ *Web:* www.wnba.com	WA	98119		206-281-5800	281-5839
Washington Mystics 627 N Glebe Rd Ste 850 .... Arlington *TF:* 877-329-9622 ■ *Web:* www.wnba.com	VA	22203		202-266-2200	266-2220

718 SPORTS TEAMS - FOOTBALL

SEE ALSO Sports Organizations p. 1785

718-1 Arena Football League (AFL)

			Phone	Fax
Arena Football League (AFL) 640 N LaSalle St Ste 557 .... Chicago *Web:* www.arenafootball.com	IL	60654	312-465-2200	496-3055
Arizona Rattlers 14287 N 87th St Ste 120 .... Scottsdale *Web:* www.azrattlers.com	AZ	85260	602-514-8383	

718-2 Canadian Football League (CFL)

			Phone	Fax
Canadian Football League 50 Wellington St E Third Fl .... Toronto *Web:* www.cfl.ca	ON	M5E1C8	416-322-9650	322-9651
BC Lions 10605 135th St .... Surrey *Web:* www.bclions.com	BC	V3T4C8	604-930-5466	583-7882
Calgary Stampeders 1817 Crowchild Trail NW McMahon Stadium .... Calgary *Web:* www.stampeders.com	AB	T2M4R6	403-289-0205	262-4332
Montreal Alouettes 1260 University St Ste 100 .... Montreal *Web:* www.montrealalouettes.com	QC	H3B3B9	514-871-2266	871-2277
Saskatchewan Roughriders 1910 Piffles Taylor Way PO Box 1966 .... Regina *TF:* 888-474-3377 ■ *Web:* www.riderville.com	SK	S4P3E1	306-569-2323	566-4280
Toronto Argonauts One Blue Jays Way Ste 3300 .... Toronto *Web:* www.argonauts.ca	ON	M5V1J3	416-341-2700	
Winnipeg Blue Bombers 1465 Maroons Rd .... Winnipeg *Web:* www.bluebombers.com	MB	R3G0L6	204-784-2583	783-5222

718-3 National Football League (NFL)

			Phone	Fax
Arizona Cardinals 8701 S Hardy Dr .... Tempe *TF:* 800-999-1402 ■ *Web:* www.azcardinals.com	AZ	85284	602-379-0101	379-1819
Atlanta Falcons 4400 Falcon Pkwy .... Flowery Branch *Web:* www.atlantafalcons.com	GA	30542	770-965-3115	965-3185
Baltimore Ravens 1101 Russell St .... Baltimore *Web:* www.baltimoreravens.com	MD	21230	410-261-7283	
Buffalo Bills Ralph Wilson Stadium 1 Bills Dr .... Orchard Park *TF:* 877-228-4257 ■ *Web:* www.buffalobills.com	NY	14127	716-648-1800	
Carolina Panthers Bank of America Stadium 800 S Mint St .... Charlotte *TF:* 888-297-8673 ■ *Web:* www.panthers.com	NC	28202	704-358-7000	358-7618
Chicago Bears 1000 Football Dr .... Lake Forest *Web:* www.chicagobears.com	IL	60045	847-295-6600	295-8986
Cincinnati Bengals One Paul Brown Stadium .... Cincinnati *TF:* 866-621-8383 ■ *Web:* www.bengals.com	OH	45202	513-621-3550	621-3570
Cleveland Browns 76 Lou Groza Blvd .... Berea *Web:* www.clevelandbrowns.com	OH	44017	440-891-5000	891-5009
Dallas Cowboys One Cowboys Pkwy .... Irving *Web:* www.dallascowboys.com	TX	75063	972-556-9900	556-9304
Denver Broncos 13655 Broncos Pkwy .... Englewood *Web:* www.denverbroncos.com	CO	80112	303-649-9000	649-9354
Detroit Lions 222 Republic Dr .... Allen Park *TF:* 800-745-3000 ■ *Web:* www.detroitlions.com	MI	48101	313-216-4000	216-4056
Green Bay Packers 1265 Lombardi Ave PO Box 10628 .... Green Bay *Web:* www.packers.com	WI	54304	920-569-7500	569-7301
Houston Texans Two NRG Park .... Houston *Web:* www.houstontexans.com	TX	77054	832-667-2002	667-2100
Indianapolis Colts 7001 W 56th St .... Indianapolis *TF:* 800-805-2658 ■ *Web:* www.colts.com	IN	46254	317-297-2658	297-8971
Kansas City Chiefs Arrowhead Stadium 1 Arrowhead Dr .... Kansas City *TF:* 800-332-6048 ■ *Web:* www.kcchiefs.com	MO	64129	816-920-9300	920-4315
Miami Dolphins 7500 SW 30th St .... Davie **Fax Area Code:* 954 ■ **Fax:* PR ■ *Web:* www.miamidolphins.com	FL	33314	305-943-8000	452-7055*
Minnesota Vikings 9520 Viking Dr .... Eden Prairie *TF:* 877-722-6458 ■ *Web:* www.vikings.com	MN	55344	952-828-6500	828-6540
New Orleans Saints 5800 Airline Dr .... Metairie *Web:* www.neworleanssaints.com	LA	70003	504-733-0255	731-1782
New York Giants 1925 Giants Dr .... East Rutherford *Web:* www.giants.com	NJ	07073	201-935-8111	
Oakland Raiders 1220 Harbor Bay Pkwy .... Alameda *TF:* 800-724-3377 ■ *Web:* www.raiders.com	CA	94502	510-864-5000	864-5134
Philadelphia Eagles NovaCare Complex 1 NovaCare Way .... Philadelphia *Web:* www.philadelphiaeagles.com	PA	19145	215-463-2500	339-5464
Pittsburgh Steelers 3400 S Water St .... Pittsburgh *Web:* www.steelers.com	PA	15203	412-432-7800	432-7878
San Diego Chargers 4020 Murphy Canyon Rd .... San Diego *TF:* 877-242-7437 ■ *Web:* www.chargers.com	CA	92123	858-874-4500	292-2760
San Francisco 49ers 4949 Centennial Blvd .... Santa Clara *Web:* www.49ers.com	CA	95054	408-562-4949	727-4937
Seattle Seahawks 12 Seahawks Way .... Renton *TF:* 888-635-4295 ■ *Web:* www.seahawks.com	WA	98056	888-635-4295	
Tampa Bay Buccaneers One Buccaneer Pl .... Tampa *Web:* www.buccaneers.com	FL	33607	813-870-2700	
Tennessee Titans 460 Great Cir Rd .... Nashville *TF:* 800-334-4628 ■ *Web:* www.titansonline.com	TN	37228	615-565-4000	565-4006
Washington Redskins 21300 Redskin Pk Dr .... Ashburn *Web:* www.redskins.com	VA	20147	703-726-7000	726-7086

719 SPORTS TEAMS - HOCKEY

SEE ALSO Sports Organizations p. 1785

			Phone	Fax
National Hockey League (NHL) 1185 Ave of the Americas .... New York *Web:* www.nhl.com	NY	10036	212-789-2000	789-2020
Anaheim Ducks 2695 E Katella Ave .... Anaheim **Fax Area Code:* 714 ■ *TF:* 877-945-3946 ■ *Web:* ducks.nhl.com	CA	92806	877-945-3946	940-2953*
Boston Bruins 100 Legends Way .... Boston *Web:* bruins.nhl.com	MA	02114	617-624-1900	523-7184
Buffalo Sabres HSBC Arena 1 Seymour H Knox III Plz .... Buffalo *TF:* 888-467-2273 ■ *Web:* sabres.nhl.com	NY	14203	716-855-4100	855-4115
Calgary Flames Pengrowth Saddledome 555 Saddledome Rise SE .... Calgary **Fax:* PR ■ *Web:* flames.nhl.com	AB	T2G2W1	403-777-2177	777-2195*
Carolina Hurricanes RBC Ctr 1400 Edwards Mill Rd .... Raleigh *TF:* 800-521-7521 ■ *Web:* hurricanes.nhl.com	NC	27607	919-467-7825	462-7030
Chicago Blackhawks 1901 W Madison St .... Chicago **Fax:* PR ■ *Web:* blackhawks.nhl.com	IL	60612	312-455-7000	455-7041*
Colorado Avalanche Pepsi Ctr 1000 Chopper Cir .... Denver *Web:* avalanche.nhl.com	CO	80204	303-405-1100	
Columbus Blue Jackets Nationwide Arena 200 W Nationwide Blvd Ste Level .... Columbus *Web:* bluejackets.nhl.com	OH	43215	614-246-4625	246-4007
Dallas Stars 2601 Ave of the Stars .... Frisco *Web:* stars.nhl.com	TX	75034	214-387-5500	387-5599
Detroit Red Wings Joe Louis Arena 600 Civic Ctr Dr .... Detroit **Fax:* PR ■ *Web:* redwings.nhl.com	MI	48226	313-396-7444	567-0296*
Edmonton Oilers 11230 110th St .... Edmonton *TF:* 866-414-4625 ■ *Web:* oilers.nhl.com	AB	T5G3H7	780-414-4000	409-5890
Florida Panthers BankAtlantic Ctr 1 Panther Pkwy .... Sunrise **Fax:* Sales ■ *Web:* panthers.nhl.com	FL	33323	954-835-7000	835-7200*
Los Angeles Kings Staples Ctr 1111 S Figueroa St .... Los Angeles *TF:* 888-546-4752 ■ *Web:* kings.nhl.com	CA	90015	213-742-7100	
Minnesota Wild 317 Washington St .... Saint Paul *TF:* 866-242-5006 ■ *Web:* wild.nhl.com	MN	55102	651-602-6000	222-1055
Montreal Canadiens Bell Centre 1260 de la Gauchetiere St W .... Montreal **Fax:* PR ■ *TF:* 800-363-8162 ■ *Web:* canadiens.nhl.com	QC	H3B5E8	514-989-2841	925-2144*
Nashville Predators 501 Broadway .... Nashville *Web:* predators.nhl.com	TN	37203	615-770-2355	770-2341
New York Islanders 1535 Old Country Rd .... Plainview *TF:* 800-843-5678 ■ *Web:* islanders.nhl.com	NY	11803	516-501-6700	501-6729
New York Rangers Two Pennsylvania Plz .... New York *Web:* rangers.nhl.com	NY	10121	212-465-6553	465-6494
Ottawa Senators 1000 Palladium Dr Scotia Bank Pl .... Kanata *TF:* 800-444-7367 ■ *Web:* senators.nhl.com	ON	K2V1A5	613-599-0100	
Philadelphia Flyers Wachovia Ctr 3601 S Broad St .... Philadelphia *Web:* flyers.nhl.com	PA	19148	215-465-4500	389-9476
Phoenix Coyotes 6751 N Sunset Blvd Ste 200 .... Glendale *TF:* 877-448-4483 ■ *Web:* coyotes.nhl.com	AZ	85305	623-772-3200	772-3201
Pittsburgh Penguins 1001 Fifth Avenue .... Pittsburgh *TF:* 800-642-7367 ■ *Web:* penguins.nhl.com	PA	15219	412-642-1300	642-1859
San Jose Sharks HP Pavilion at San Jose 525 W Santa Clara St .... San Jose *TF:* 800-755-5050 ■ *Web:* sharks.nhl.com	CA	95113	408-287-7070	999-5797
Tampa Bay Lightning St Pete Times Forum 401 Channelside Dr .... Tampa *TF:* 800-745-3000 ■ *Web:* lightning.nhl.com	FL	33602	813-301-6500	301-1482
Toronto Maple Leafs Air Canada Ctr 40 Bay St Ste 400 .... Toronto *Web:* mapleleafs.nhl.com	ON	M5J2X2	416-815-5700	359-9205
Vancouver Canucks 800 Griffiths Way .... Vancouver *TF:* 877-788-3937 ■ *Web:* canucks.nhl.com	BC	V6B6G1	604-899-7400	899-7401
Washington Capitals 627 N Glebe Rd Ste 850 .... Arlington *Web:* capitals.nhl.com	VA	22203	202-266-2200	

720 SPORTS TEAMS - SOCCER

SEE ALSO Sports Organizations p. 1785

			Phone	Fax
Major League Soccer (MLS) 420 Fifth Ave Seventh Fl .... New York *Web:* www.mlssoccer.com	NY	10018	212-450-1200	
Big League Dreams USA LLC 16333 Fairfield Ranch Rd .... Chino Hills *Web:* www.bigleaguedreams.com	CA	91709	909-287-6900	
Bobcats Basketball LLC 333 E Trade St .... Charlotte *Web:* www.timewarnercablearena.com	NC	28202	704-688-9000	
Brooklyn Cyclones 1904 Surf Ave MCU Park .... Brooklyn *Web:* www.brooklyncyclones.com	NY	11224	718-449-8497	

Phone *Fax*

Chicago Fire 7000 S Harlem Ave .... Bridgeview IL 60455 708-594-7200 496-6050
TF: 888-657-3473 ■ *Web:* www.chicago-fire.com

Club Deportivo Chivas USA
Home Depot Ctr 18400 Avalon Blvd Ste 500 .... Carson CA 90746 310-630-4550 630-4551
TF Sales: 877-244-8271 ■ *Web:* www.cdchivasusa.com

Colorado Rapids 6000 Victory Way .... Commerce City CO 80022 303-727-3500 727-3536
Web: www.coloradorapids.com

Colorado Storm Soccer Assoc
7002 S Revere Pkwy Ste 60 .... Centennial CO 80112 303-799-0151
Web: www.shippertmedical.com

DC United 2400 E Capitol St SE .... Washington DC 20003 202-587-5000 587-5400
Web: www.dcunited.com

FC Dallas 9200 World Cup Way Ste 202 .... Frisco TX 75034 214-705-6700 705-6799
Web: fcdallasstadium.com

FMC Ice Sports 100 Schoosett St Bldg 3 .... Pembroke MA 02359 781-826-3085
Web: www.fmcicesports.com

Front Row Motorsports 2670 Peachtree Rd .... Statesville NC 28625 704-873-6445
Web: teamfrm.com

Global Sports & Entertainment Inc
300 N Continental Blvd Ste 140 .... El Segundo CA 90245 310-414-2690
Web: www.globalsports-ent.com

Houston Astros Inc 501 Crawford St Ste 400 .... Houston TX 77002 713-259-8000
Web: www.mlb.com

Houston Dynamo 1415 Louisiana St Ste 3400 .... Houston TX 77002 713-276-7500 276-7580
Web: www.houstondynamo.com

Los Angeles Galaxy
Home Depot Ctr 18400 Avalon Blvd Ste 200 .... Carson CA 90746 310-630-2200 630-2250
TF: 877-342-5299 ■ *Web:* www.lagalaxy.com

Manchester Monarchs 555 Elm St .... Manchester NH 03101 603-626-7825
Web: www.manchestermonarchs.com

Milwaukee Wave LLC 510 W Kilbourn Ave .... Milwaukee WI 53203 414-224-9283 224-9290
TF: 800-745-3000 ■ *Web:* www.milwaukeewave.com

Monumental Sports & Entertainment LLC
601 F St NW .... Washington DC 20004 202-628-3200
Web: www.monumentalsports.com

MVP Sports Spot 3701 32nd St SE .... Grand Rapids MI 49512 616-464-1000
Web: www.soccerspot.net

Natick Junior Redmen 15 W St .... Natick MA 01760 508-653-9900
Web: www.natickpolice.com

New England Revolution
Gillette Stadium 1 Patriot Pl .... Foxboro MA 02035 877-438-7387 384-9128*
**Fax Area Code:* 508 ■ *TF:* 877-438-7387 ■ *Web:* www.revolutionsoccer.net

New York Red Bulls 600 Cape May St Eighth Fl .... Harrison NJ 07029 877-727-6223
TF: 877-727-6223 ■ *Web:* www.newyorkredbulls.com

Ontario Minor Hockey Association Inc
3-25 Brodie Dr .... Richmond Hill ON L4B3K7 905-780-6642
Web: www.omha.net

Reading Royals Hockey Club
645 Penn St Third Fl .... Reading PA 19601 610-898-7825
Web: www.royalshockey.com

Richmond Kickers Soccer Club Inc
2001 Maywill St Ste 203 .... Richmond VA 23230 804-644-5425
Web: www.richmondkickers.com

Suwanee Sports Academy 3640 Burnette Rd .... Suwanee GA 30024 770-614-6686
Web: ssasports.com

Swix Sport USA Inc 600 Research Dr .... Wilmington MA 01887 978-657-4820
Web: www.swixsport.com

Trail Blazers Inc 1 N Center Ct St Ste 200 .... Portland OR 97227 503-234-9291
Web: www.trailblazers.org

Wolfpack Sports Marketing PO Box 37100 .... Raleigh NC 27627 919-831-9653
Web: www.gopack.com

721 SPRINGS - HEAVY-GAUGE

Phone *Fax*

Automatic Spring Products Corp
803 Taylor Ave .... Grand Haven MI 49417 616-842-7800 842-4380
Web: www.automaticspring.com

Barnes Group Inc 123 Main St .... Bristol CT 06011 860-583-7070 589-3507
NYSE: B ■ *TF:* 800-877-8803 ■ *Web:* barnesgroupinc.com

General Wire Spring Co
1101 Thompson Ave .... McKees Rocks PA 15136 412-771-6300 771-6317
TF: 800-245-6200 ■ *Web:* www.generalwirespring.com

Pa-Ted Spring Company Inc
137 Vincent P Kelly Rd .... Bristol CT 06010 860-582-6368 583-1044
Web: patedspring.com

Perfection Spring & Stamping Corp
1449 E Algonquin Rd .... Mount Prospect IL 60056 847-437-3900 437-1322
Web: www.pss-corp.com

Rockford Spring Co 3801 S Central Ave .... Rockford IL 61102 815-968-3000 968-3100
Web: www.rockfordspring.com

Service Spring Corp 4370 Moline Martin Rd .... Millbury OH 43447 419-838-6081 838-6071
TF: 800-752-8522 ■ *Web:* www.sscorp.com

Southern Spring & Stamping Inc 401 Sub Stn Rd .... Venice FL 34285 941-488-2276 485-9156
TF: 800-450-5882 ■ *Web:* www.southernspring.com

Stanley Spring & Stamping Corp
5050 W Foster Ave .... Chicago IL 60630 773-777-2600 777-3894
Web: www.stanleyspring.com

722 SPRINGS - LIGHT-GAUGE

Phone *Fax*

American Coil Spring Co 1041 E Keating Ave .... Muskegon MI 49442 231-726-4021
Web: americancoil.com

Atlantic Spring PO Box 650 .... Flemington NJ 08822 908-788-5800 788-0511
TF: 877-231-6474 ■ *Web:* www.mw-ind.com

Century Spring Corp 222 E 16th St .... Los Angeles CA 90015 213-749-1466 749-3802
TF: 800-237-5225 ■ *Web:* www.centuryspring.com

Connecticut Spring & Stamping Corp
48 Spring Ln .... Farmington CT 06034 860-677-1341 677-7199*
**Fax:* Cust Svc ■ *Web:* ctspring.com

Dudek & Bock Spring Mfg Co
5100 W Roosevelt Rd .... Chicago IL 60644 773-379-4100 379-4108
Web: www.dudek-bock.com

Economy Spring & Stamping Co
29 DePaolo Dr PO Box 651 .... Southington CT 06489 860-621-7358 621-7882
TF: 800-237-5225 ■ *Web:* www.mw-ind.com

Exacto Spring Corp 1201 Hickory St .... Grafton WI 53024 262-377-3970 377-3854
Web: www.exacto.com

Fennell Spring LLC 295 Hemlock St .... Horseheads NY 14845 607-739-3541 739-7601

General Wire Spring Co
1101 Thompson Ave .... McKees Rocks PA 15136 412-771-6300 771-6317
TF: 800-245-6200 ■ *Web:* www.generalwirespring.com

Hickory Springs Mfg Co 235 Second Ave NW .... Hickory NC 28601 800-438-5341
TF: 800-438-5341 ■ *Web:* www.hickorysprings.com

John Evans' Sons Inc
One Spring Ave PO Box 885 .... Lansdale PA 19446 215-368-7700 368-9019
Web: www.springcompany.com

Lee Spring Company Inc 140 58th St Ste 3C .... Brooklyn NY 11220 718-236-2222 236-3919
TF: 800-110-2500 ■ *Web:* www.leespring.com

Leggett & Platt Inc
Number 1 Leggett Rd PO Box 757 .... Carthage MO 64836 417-358-8131 358-6996
NYSE: LEG ■ *TF:* 800-888-4569 ■ *Web:* www.leggett.com

Maryland Precision Spring Co 8900 Kelso Dr .... Baltimore MD 21221 410-391-7400 687-9223
Web: www.mw-ind.com

Mastercoil Spring 4010 Albany .... McHenry IL 60050 815-344-0051 344-0071
Web: www.mastercoil.com

Michigan Spring & Stamping LLC
2700 Wickham Dr .... Muskegon MI 49441 231-755-1691 755-3449
Web: www.msands.com/

Micromatic Spring & Stamping Company Inc
45 N Church St .... Addison IL 60101 847-671-6600 671-3452
Web: www.micromaticspring.com

Mid-West Spring & Stamping Co
1404 Joliet Rd Unit C .... Romeoville IL 60446 630-739-3800 643-9781*
**Fax Area Code:* 888 ■ *TF:* 800-619-0909 ■ *Web:* www.mwspring.com

Monticello Spring Corp
3137 Freeman Rd PO Box 705 .... Monticello IN 47960 574-583-8090 583-9299
Web: www.monticellospring.com

Newcomb Spring Corp 235 Spring St .... Southington CT 06489 860-621-0111 621-7048
TF: 888-579-3051 ■ *Web:* www.newcombspring.com

O & G Spring & Wire Forms Specialty Co
4500 W Div St .... Chicago IL 60651 773-772-9331 772-6578
Web: www.ogspring.com

Pa-Ted Spring Company Inc
137 Vincent P Kelly Rd .... Bristol CT 06010 860-582-6368 583-1044
Web: patedspring.com

Perfection Spring & Stamping Corp
1449 E Algonquin Rd .... Mount Prospect IL 60056 847-437-3900 437-1322
Web: www.pss-corp.com

Peterson Spring 21200 Telegraph Rd .... Southfield MI 48033 248-799-5400 357-3176
Web: www.pspring.com

Plymouth Spring Company Inc 281 Lake Ave .... Bristol CT 06010 860-584-0594 584-0943
Web: www.plymouthspring.com

Precision Coil Spring Co 10107 Rose Ave .... El Monte CA 91731 626-444-0561 444-3712
Web: www.pcspring.com

QS/Togo Inc 355 Jay St .... Coldwater MI 49036 517-278-2391 279-4680
Web: www.qsti.com

R & L Spring Co 1097 Geneva Pkwy .... Lake Geneva WI 53147 262-249-7854 249-7866
Web: www.rlspring.com

Rockford Spring Co 3801 S Central Ave .... Rockford IL 61102 815-968-3000 968-3100
Web: www.rockfordspring.com

Rowley Spring & Stamping Corp
210 Redstone Hill Rd .... Bristol CT 06010 860-582-8175 589-8718
Web: www.rowleyspring.com

Southern Spring & Stamping Inc 401 Sub Stn Rd .... Venice FL 34285 941-488-2276 485-9156
TF: 800-450-5882 ■ *Web:* www.southernspring.com

Spring Dynamics Inc 7378 Research Dr .... Almont MI 48003 810-798-2622 798-2902
TF: 888-274-8432 ■ *Web:* www.springdynamics.com

Spring Engineers Inc 9740 Tanner Rd .... Houston TX 77041 713-690-9488 690-1199
TF: 800-899-9488 ■ *Web:* springhouston.com

Stanley Spring & Stamping Corp
5050 W Foster Ave .... Chicago IL 60630 773-777-2600 777-3894
Web: www.stanleyspring.com

Twist Inc 47 S Limestone St .... Jamestown OH 45335 937-675-9581 675-6781
Web: www.twistinc.com

Walker Corp 1555 Vintage Ave .... Ontario CA 91761 909-390-4300 390-4301
Web: www.walkercorp.com

Winamac Coil Spring Inc 512 N Smith St .... Kewanna IN 46939 574-653-2186 653-2645
Web: www.winamaccoilspring.com

Wire Products Company Inc
14601 Industrial Pkwy .... Cleveland OH 44135 216-267-0777 267-7972
Web: www.wire-products.com

Yost Superior Co PO Box 1487 .... Springfield OH 45501 937-323-7591 323-5180
Web: www.yostsuperior.com

723 STADIUMS & ARENAS

SEE ALSO Convention Centers p. 2153; Performing Arts Facilities p. 2900

Phone *Fax*

500 Festival Inc
500 Festival Bldg 21 Virginia Ave
Ste 500 .... Indianapolis IN 46204 317-927-3378
Web: www.500festival.com

Air Canada Centre 40 Bay St .... Toronto ON M5J2X2 416-815-5500
Web: www.theaircanadacentre.com

Alamodome 100 Montana St .... San Antonio TX 78203 210-207-3663 207-3646
TF: 800-884-3663 ■ *Web:* www.alamodome.com

Albert Lea City Arena 701 Lk Chapeau Dr .... Albert Lea MN 56007 507-377-4374
Web: cityofalbertlea.org

				Phone	Fax
Alerus Ctr 1200 42nd St S *Web:* www.aleruscenter.com	Grand Forks	ND	58201	701-792-1200	746-6511
Allen County War Memorial Coliseum 4000 Parnell Ave. *TF:* 800-745-3000 ■ *Web:* www.memorialcoliseum.com	Fort Wayne	IN	46805	260-482-9502	484-1637
Allstate Arena 6920 Mannheim Rd *Web:* rosemont.com/allstate/	Rosemont	IL	60018	847-635-6601	635-6606
Aloha Stadium 99-500 Salt Lk Blvd *Web:* www.alohastadium.hawaii.gov	Honolulu	HI	96818	808-483-2500	483-2823
American Airlines Arena 601 Biscayne Blvd. **Fax:* Hum Res ■ *Web:* www.aaarena.com	Miami	FL	33132	786-777-1000	777-1230*
American Airlines Ctr 2500 Victory Ave. *TF:* 800-745-3000 ■ *Web:* www.americanairlinescenter.com	Dallas	TX	75219	214-222-3687	665-4850
Angel Stadium 2000 Gene Autry Way. *TF:* 866-800-1275 ■ *Web:* losangeles.angels.mlb.com	Anaheim	CA	92806	714-940-2000	940-2244
Arrowhead Stadium One Arrowhead Dr **Fax:* PR ■ *Web:* www.kcchiefs.com/arrowhead	Kansas City	MO	64129	816-920-9300	923-4719*
Arts Midwest 2908 Hennepin Ave Ste 200 *Web:* www.artsmidwest.org	Minneapolis	MN	55408	612-341-0755	
AT & T Park 24 Willie Mays Plaza	San Francisco	CA	94107	415-972-1800	
AT&T Ctr One AT&T Ctr Pkwy *TF Resv:* 800-745-3000 ■ *Web:* www.attcenter.com	San Antonio	TX	78219	210-444-5000	444-5100
Bank of America Stadium 800 S Mint St *Web:* www.panthers.com	Charlotte	NC	28202	704-358-7000	358-7615
Bankers Life Fieldhouse 125 S Pennsylvania St *Web:* www.bankerslifefieldhouse.com	Indianapolis	IN	46204	317-917-2500	917-2599
Bay Area Renaissance Festival at Mosi 11315 N 46th St *Web:* bayarearenfest.com	Tampa	FL	33617	813-983-0111	
Big Night Entertainment Group One Boylston Pl *Web:* www.bneg.com	Boston	MA	02116	617-338-4343	
Big Sandy Superstore Arena One Civic Ctr Plz *Web:* www.bigsandyarena.com	Huntington	WV	25701	304-696-5990	696-4463
Billy Bob's Texas 2520 Rodeo Plz *Web:* billybobstexas.com	Fort Worth	TX	76164	817-624-7117	
BMO Harris Bradley Center 1001 N Fourth St *Web:* www.bmoharrisbradleycenter.com	Milwaukee	WI	53203	414-227-0400	
Bon Secours Wellness Arena 650 N Academy St *Web:* bonsecoursarena.com	Greenville	SC	29601	864-241-3800	250-4939
Bridgestone Arena 501 Broadway *Web:* www.bridgestonearena.com	Nashville	TN	37203	615-770-2000	
British Columbia Place Stadium 777 Pacific Blvd *Web:* www.bcplacestadium.com	Vancouver	BC	V6B4Y8	604-669-2300	661-3412
Broome County Veterans Memorial Arena 1 Stuart St. *Web:* broomearenaforum.com	Binghamton	NY	13901	607-778-1528	
Busch Stadium 700 Clark St *Web:* stlouis.cardinals.mlb.com	Saint Louis	MO	63102	314-345-9600	345-9523
Camp Randall Stadium 1440 Monroe St *Web:* www.uwbadgers.com	Madison	WI	53711	608-262-1866	
Canal Park Stadium 300 S Main St. *TF:* 855-977-8225 ■ *Web:* www.milb.com	Akron	OH	44308	330-253-5151	
Chase Field 401 E Jefferson St *Web:* azchasefield.com	Phoenix	AZ	85004	602-462-6500	462-6600
Cincinnati Gardens 2250 Seymour Ave *Web:* www.cincygardens.com	Cincinnati	OH	45212	513-631-7793	351-5898
Clark County Event Center at The Fairgrounds 17402 Ne Delfel Rd. *Web:* www.clarkcofair.com	Ridgefield	WA	98642	360-397-6180	
Cleveland Indians Team Shops 2401 Ontario St *TF:* 800-388-7423	Cleveland	OH	44115	216-420-4444	420-4799
Columbus Civic Ctr 400 Fourth St *TF:* 800-745-3000 ■ *Web:* www.columbusciviccenter.org	Columbus	GA	31901	706-653-4482	653-4481
Coors Field 2001 Blake St. *Web:* colorado.rockies.mlb.com	Denver	CO	80205	303-292-0200	312-2115
Cowtown Coliseum 121 E Exchange Ave *Web:* stockyardsrodeo.com	Fort Worth	TX	76164	817-625-1025	625-1148
David S Palmer Arena 100 W Main St *Web:* www.palmerarena.com	Danville	IL	61832	217-431-2424	431-6444
DCU Ctr 50 Foster St. *Web:* www.dcucenter.com	Worcester	MA	01608	508-755-6800	929-0111
Denver Coliseum 4600 Humboldt St *Web:* www.denvercoliseum.com	Denver	CO	80216	720-865-2475	865-2467
Dodger Stadium 1000 Elysian Pk Ave *Web:* dodgers.com	Los Angeles	CA	90012	323-224-1500	224-1269
Dunkin' Donuts Ctr 1 LaSalle Sq. *Web:* www.dunkindonutscenter.com	Providence	RI	02903	401-331-0700	751-6792
Ed Smith Stadium 2700 12th St *Web:* baltimore.orioles.mlb.com	Sarasota	FL	34237	941-954-4101	365-1587
Endeavor Hall 6008 Center St *Web:* cityofclayton.org	Clayton	CA	94517	925-673-7300	
Energy Solutions Arena 301 West South Temple **Fax:* PR ■ *Web:* www.energysolutionsarena.com	Salt Lake City	UT	84101	801-325-2000	325-2578*
Eyebeam Atelier 540 W 21st St. *Web:* www.eyebeam.org	New York	NY	10011	212-937-6580	
Family Arena 2002 Arena Pkwy *Web:* www.familyarena.com	Saint Charles	MO	63303	636-896-4242	896-4205
FARGODOME 1800 N University Dr. *TF:* 855-694-6367 ■ *Web:* www.fargodome.com	Fargo	ND	58102	701-241-9100	237-0987
FedEx Field 1600 FedEx Way *Web:* www.redskins.com	Landover	MD	20785	301-276-6000	276-6001
FedEx Forum 191 Beale St *Web:* www.nba.com/grizzlies	Memphis	TN	38103	901-205-1234	205-1235
Fenway Park Four Yawkey Way *TF:* 877-733-7699 ■ *Web:* boston.redsox.mlb.com	Boston	MA	02215	617-226-6000	226-6682
Fiesta San Antonio Commission Inc, The 2611 Broadway St. *Web:* www.fiesta-sa.org	San Antonio	TX	78215	210-227-5191	
First Niagara Ctr One Seymour Knox III Plz *TF:* 888-223-6000 ■ *Web:* www.firstniagaracenter.com	Buffalo	NY	14203	716-855-4100	855-4122
Florida Repertory Theatre Inc 2267 First St. *Web:* www.floridarep.org	Fort Myers	FL	33901	239-332-4665	
Ford Field 2000 Brush St Ste 200 *Web:* www.detroitlions.com	Detroit	MI	48226	313-262-2000	262-2808
Frank Erwin Ctr 1701 Red River PO Box 2929 *Web:* www.uterwincenter.com	Austin	TX	78701	512-471-7744	471-9652
Freeman Coliseum 3201 E Houston St *Web:* www.freemancoliseum.com	San Antonio	TX	78219	210-226-1177	226-5081
Georgia Dome 1 Georgia Dome Dr NW *TF:* 888-333-4406 ■ *Web:* www.gadome.com	Atlanta	GA	30313	404-223-9200	223-8011
Gila River Arena 9400 W Maryland Ave *Web:* www.jobingarena.com	Glendale	AZ	85305	623-772-3200	772-3201
Gillette Stadium One Patriots Pl *Web:* www.gillettestadium.com	Foxboro	MA	02035	508-543-8200	543-0285
Globe Life Park In Arlington 1000 Ballpark Way *Web:* Www.texas.rangers.mlb.com	Arlington	TX	76011	817-273-5222	
Golden Spike Event Ctr 1000 North 1200 West *Web:* www.goldenspikeeventcenter.com	Ogden	UT	84404	801-399-8798	392-1995
Greater Austin Performing Arts Center Inc 701 W Riverside Dr. *Web:* thelongcenter.org	Austin	TX	78704	512-457-5100	
Greensboro Coliseum Complex 1921 W Lee St *Web:* www.greensborocoliseum.com	Greensboro	NC	27403	336-373-7400	373-2170
Hampton Coliseum 1000 Coliseum Dr PO Box 7309 *Web:* www.hamptoncoliseum.org	Hampton	VA	23666	757-838-5650	838-2595
Harvey Wheeler Community Ctr 1276 Main St. *Web:* www.concordnet.org	Concord	MA	01742	978-318-3020	
Hawthorne Direct Inc 300 N 16th St *Web:* www.hawthornedirect.com	Fairfield	IA	52556	641-472-3800	
Heinz Field 100 Art Rooney Ave *Web:* www.steelers.com	Pittsburgh	PA	15212	412-697-7181	697-7701
Hersheypark Arena & Stadium 550 W Hersheypark Dr *Web:* www.giantcenter.com	Hershey	PA	17033	717-534-3911	534-8996
Hippodrome State Theatre 25 SE Second Pl *Web:* thehipp.org	Gainesville	FL	32601	352-373-5968	
Honda Ctr 2695 E Katella Ave *TF:* 877-945-3946 ■ *Web:* www.hondacenter.com	Anaheim	CA	92806	714-704-2400	704-2443
Houston Arts Alliance 3201 Allen Pkwy Ste 250 *Web:* www.houstonartsalliance.com	Houston	TX	77019	713-527-9330	
HP Pavilion at San Jose 525 W Santa Clara St *TF:* 800-745-3000 ■ *Web:* www.sapcenteratsanjose.com	San Jose	CA	95113	408-287-7070	999-5797
Hubert H Humphrey Metrodome 900 S Fifth St *Web:* msfa.com/	Minneapolis	MN	55415	612-332-0386	332-8334
i Wireless Ctr 1201 River Dr *TF:* 800-745-3000 ■ *Web:* www.iwirelesscenter.com	Moline	IL	61265	309-764-2001	764-2192
Independence Stadium 3301 Pershing Blvd *Web:* independencebowl.org/	Shreveport	LA	71109	318-673-7789	
Iowa State Fair (state House) Po Box 57130 *Web:* www.iowastatefair.org	Des Moines	IA	50317	515-262-3111	
Jacksonville Municipal Stadium 1 EverBank Field Dr **Fax:* Mktg ■ *TF:* 877-452-4784 ■ *Web:* www.jaguars.com	Jacksonville	FL	32202	904-633-6000	633-6055*
Jacksonville Veterans Memorial Arena 300 A Philip Randolph Blvd *Web:* www.jaxevents.com	Jacksonville	FL	32202	904-630-3900	854-0601
James J. Eagan Civic Center One James J Eagan Dr *Web:* www.florissantmo.com	Florissant	MO	63033	314-921-4466	
Jcd Sports Group Inc 1300 Nw 17th Ave Ste 272 *Web:* www.jcdsportsgroup.com	Delray Beach	FL	33445	561-265-0255	
Jeld-Wen Field 1844 SW Morrison St *Web:* www.jeld-wenfield.com	Portland	OR	97205	503-553-5400	553-5405
JHE Production Group Inc 6427 Saddle Creek Ct. *Web:* www.gojhe.com	Harrisburg	NC	28075	704-455-8888	
Kansas Coliseum 1279 E 85th St N *Web:* www.kansascoliseum.com	Park City	KS	67147	316-440-0888	
Kauffman Stadium One Royal Way *TF:* 800-676-9257 ■ *Web:* kansascity.royals.mlb.com	Kansas City	MO	64129	816-921-8000	921-5775
Kemper Arena & American Royal Centers 1701 American Royal Ct *TF:* 800-634-3942 ■ *Web:* www.visitkc.com	Kansas City	MO	64102	816-221-5242	513-4211
Kentucky Fair & Expo Ctr 937 Phillips Ln. *Web:* www.kyfairexpo.org	Louisville	KY	40209	502-367-5000	367-5139
Key Arena 305 Harrison St *Web:* www.seattlecenter.com	Seattle	WA	98109	206-684-7202	684-7343
LA STAGE Alliance 4200 Chevy Chase Dr *Web:* www.lastagealliance.com	Los Angeles	CA	90039	213-614-0556	
Ladd-Peebles Stadium 1621 Virginia St *Web:* www.laddpeeblesstadium.com	Mobile	AL	36604	251-208-2500	208-2514
Lambeau Field Atrium 1265 Lombardi Ave *Web:* www.packers.com	Green Bay	WI	54304	920-569-7500	569-7301
Laredo Energy Arena 6700 Arena Blvd *Web:* www.learena.com	Laredo	TX	78041	956-791-9192	523-7777
LC Walker Arena & Conference Ctr 955 Fourth St *Web:* www.lcwalkerarena.com	Muskegon	MI	49440	231-724-5225	
Long Beach Arena 300 E Ocean Blvd. *Web:* longbeachcc.com	Long Beach	CA	90802	562-436-3636	436-9491

Name / Address	City	State	Zip	Phone	Fax
Los Angeles Memorial Coliseum & Sports Arena 3939 S Figueroa St *Web:* www.lacoliseum.com	Los Angeles	CA	90037	213-747-7111	746-9346
LP Field One Titans Way *Web:* www.titansonline.com	Nashville	TN	37213	615-565-4300	565-4444
Lubbock Municipal Auditorium/Coliseum 1625 13th St *TF:* 800-735-2989 ■ *Web:* www.mylubbock.us/departmental-websites/departments/civic-center/home	Lubbock	TX	79415	806-775-2242	775-3240
Lucas Oil Stadium 500 S Capitol Ave *Web:* www.icclos.com	Indianapolis	IN	46225	317-262-8600	262-5700
M&T Bank Stadium 1101 Russell St *Web:* www.baltimoreravens.com	Baltimore	MD	21230	410-261-7283	
Macon Centreplex Coliseum 200 Coliseum Dr *TF:* 877-532-6144 ■ *Web:* www.maconcentreplex.com	Macon	GA	31217	478-751-9152	751-9154
Martin Luther King Jr Arena 301 W Oglethorpe Ave *Web:* www.savannahga.gov	Savannah	GA	31401	912-651-6550	651-6552
Meeting House, The 5885 Robert Oliver Pl *Web:* www.themeetinghouse.org	Columbia	MD	21045	410-730-4090	
Mellon Arena 1001 Fifth Ave *Web:* www.consolenergycenter.com	Pittsburgh	PA	15219	412-642-1800	642-1925
Mercedes-Benz Superdome 1500 Girod St PO Box 52439	New Orleans	LA	70112	504-587-3663	587-3848
MetraPark Arena 308 Sixth Ave N *TF:* 800-366-8538 ■ *Web:* www.metrapark.com	Billings	MT	59101	406-256-2400	254-7991
MGM Grand Garden Arena 3799 Las Vegas Blvd S *TF:* 800-646-9143 ■ *Web:* www.mgmgrand.com	Las Vegas	NV	89109	702-891-1111	891-3036
Michigan Stadium 1201 S Main St University of Michigan *TF:* 866-296-6849 ■ *Web:* www.mgoblue.com	Ann Arbor	MI	48104	734-647-2583	764-3221
Minute Maid Park 501 Crawford St *TF:* 877-927-8767 ■ *Web:* houston.astros.mlb.com	Houston	TX	77002	713-259-8000	259-8981
Mississippi Veterans Memorial Stadium 2531 N State St *Web:* www.ms-veteransstadium.com	Jackson	MS	39216	601-354-6021	354-6019
Mullins Ctr 200 Commonwealth Ave University of Massachusetts *Web:* www.mullinscenter.com	Amherst	MA	01003	413-545-3001	545-3005
Municipal Auditorium Arena 301 W 13th St *TF:* 800-821-7060 ■ *Web:* visitkc.com/convention-center/index.aspx	Kansas City	MO	64105	816-513-5000	513-5001
Musicians On Call Inc 39 W 32nd St Ste 1103 *Web:* www.musiciansoncall.org	New York	NY	10001	212-741-2709	
Nassau Veterans Memorial Coliseum 1255 Hempstead Tpke *TF:* 800-745-3000 ■ *Web:* www.nassaucoliseum.com	Uniondale	NY	11553	516-794-9300	794-9389
Nationwide Arena 200 W Nationwide Blvd *TF:* 800-645-2657 ■ *Web:* www.nationwidearena.com	Columbus	OH	43215	614-246-2000	246-4300
Norfolk Scope Arena 201 E Brambleton Ave *TF:* 800-745-3000 ■ *Web:* www.sevenvenues.com	Norfolk	VA	23510	757-664-6464	664-6990
North Charleston Coliseum & Convention Ctr 5001 Coliseum Dr *Web:* www.northcharlestoncoliseumpac.com	North Charleston	SC	29418	843-529-5050	529-5010
Northwest Washington Fair Association 1775 Front St *Web:* www.nwwafair.com	Lynden	WA	98264	360-354-4111	
Oakland Arena & McAfee Coliseum 7000 Coliseum Way *Web:* www.coliseum.com	Oakland	CA	94621	510-569-2121	569-4246
Ohio Stadium 411 Woody Hayes Dr *Web:* www.ohiostatebuckeyes.com	Columbus	OH	43210	614-292-7572	292-0506
Olympic Ctr Arena 2634 Main St *TF:* 800-462-6236 ■ *Web:* www.orda.org	Lake Placid	NY	12946	518-523-1655	523-9275
Oriole Park at Camden Yards 333 Camden St *TF:* 888-848-2473 ■ *Web:* baltimore.orioles.mlb.com/	Baltimore	MD	21201	410-547-6100	
Palace of Auburn Hills Six Championship Dr **Fax:* PR ■ *Web:* www.palacenet.com	Auburn Hills	MI	48326	248-377-0100	377-3260*
Paul Brown Stadium 1 Paul Brown Stadium *TF:* 866-621-8383 ■ *Web:* www.bengals.com/stadium/index.html	Cincinnati	OH	45202	513-621-3550	621-3570
Perani Arena & Event Ctr 3501 Lapeer Rd *Web:* www.peraniarena.com	Flint	MI	48503	810-744-0580	744-2906
Petco Park 100 Pk Blvd *TF:* 866-800-1275 ■ *Web:* sandiego.padres.mlb.com	San Diego	CA	92101	619-795-5000	
Philips Arena One Philips Dr *Web:* www.philipsarena.com	Atlanta	GA	30303	404-878-3000	878-3055
PNC Arena 1400 EdwaRds Mill Rd *TF:* 800-745-3000 ■ *Web:* www.thepncarena.com	Raleigh	NC	27607	919-861-2300	861-2310
PNC Park 115 Federal St *TF:* 866-800-1275 ■ *Web:* www.pittsburgh.pirates.mlb.com/pit/ballpark	Pittsburgh	PA	15212	412-321-2827	
Power Balance Pavilion One Sports Pkwy *Web:* www.sleeptrainarena.com	Sacramento	CA	95834	916-928-0000	928-0727
Pratt Fine Arts Center 1902 S Main St *Web:* www.pratt.org	Seattle	WA	98144	206-328-2200	
Qualcomm Stadium 9449 Friars Rd *TF:* 800-400-7115 ■ *Web:* www.sandiego.gov/qualcomm	San Diego	CA	92108	619-641-3100	283-0460
Quicken Loans Arena One Ctr Ct *TF:* 888-894-9424 ■ *Web:* www.theqarena.com	Cleveland	OH	44115	216-420-2000	420-2298
Qwest Arena 233 S Capitol Blvd *TF:* 888-330-8497 ■ *Web:* www.centurylinkarenaboise.com	Boise	ID	83702	208-424-2200	424-2222
Rabobank Arena Theater & Convention Ctr 1001 Truxtun Ave *Web:* rabobankarena.com	Bakersfield	CA	93301	661-852-7300	861-9904
Ralph Wilson Stadium One Bills Dr *Web:* www.buffalobills.com	Orchard Park	NY	14127	716-648-1800	649-6446
Ravinia Festival Association 418 Sheridan Rd *Web:* www.ravinia.org	Highland Park	IL	60035	847-266-5000	
Raymond James Stadium 4201 N Dale Mabry Hwy *Web:* www.tampasportsauthority.com	Tampa	FL	33607	813-350-6500	673-4308
Reliant Park One Reliant Pk *Web:* www.reliantpark.com	Houston	TX	77054	832-667-1400	
Reno Rodeo Association 1350 N Wells Ave *Web:* www.ci.reno.nv.us	Reno	NV	89512	775-329-3877	
Richmond Coliseum 601 E Leigh St *TF:* 800-228-9290 ■ *Web:* www.richmondcoliseum.net	Richmond	VA	23219	804-780-4970	780-4606
Roanoke Civic Ctr 710 Williamson Rd *TF:* 877-482-8496 ■ *Web:* roanokecivicenter.com	Roanoke	VA	24016	540-853-2241	853-2748
Robert F Kennedy Stadium 2400 E Capitol St SE *Web:* eventsdc.com/venues/rfkstadium/contactinfo.aspx	Washington	DC	20003	202-608-1100	547-7460
Rockford MetroCentre 300 Elm St *TF:* 800-745-3000 ■ *Web:* thebmoharrisbankcenter.com	Rockford	IL	61101	815-968-5600	968-5451
Roger Dean Stadium 4751 Main St *TF:* 800-926-7678 ■ *Web:* www.rogerdeanstadium.com	Jupiter	FL	33458	561-775-1818	691-6886
Rogers Arena 800 Griffiths Way *Web:* rogersarena.com	Vancouver	BC	V6B6G1	604-899-7400	899-7401
Rogers Centre 1 Blue Jays Way Ste 3000 *Web:* www.rogerscentre.com	Toronto	ON	M5V1J1	416-341-3034	341-3110
Rose Bowl 1001 Rose Bowl Dr *Web:* www.rosebowlstadium.com	Pasadena	CA	91103	626-577-3100	405-0992
Royal Farms Arena 201 W Baltimore St *Web:* www.1stmarinerarena.com	Baltimore	MD	21201	410-347-2020	347-2042
Rupp Arena 430 W Vine St *Web:* www.rupparena.com	Lexington	KY	40507	859-233-4567	253-2718
Safeco Field 1250 First Ave S *Web:* seattle.mariners.mlb.com	Seattle	WA	98134	206-346-4000	346-4050
San Jose Municipal Stadium 588 E Alma Ave *Web:* www.milb.com	San Jose	CA	95112	408-297-1435	297-1453
Scottrade Ctr 1401 Clark Ave *Web:* www.scottradecenter.com	Saint Louis	MO	63103	314-622-5400	622-5410
Scottsdale Stadium 7408 E Osborn Rd *TF:* 877-229-5042 ■ *Web:* www.scottsdaleaz.gov/stadium	Scottsdale	AZ	85251	480-312-2856	312-7729
Seattle Ctr 305 Harrison St *Web:* www.seattlecenter.com	Seattle	WA	98109	206-684-7200	684-7342
Seattle Theatre Group 911 Pine St *Web:* www.stgpresents.org	Seattle	WA	98101	206-467-5510	
Selland Arena 700 M St *Web:* www.fresnoconventioncenter.com	Fresno	CA	93721	559-445-8100	445-8110
Show Me Ctr 1333 N Sprigg St *Web:* www.showmecenter.biz	Cape Girardeau	MO	63701	573-651-2297	651-5054
Sioux Falls Arena 1201 NW Ave *TF:* 800-338-3177 ■ *Web:* www.sfarena.com	Sioux Falls	SD	57104	605-367-7288	338-1463
Sky Sox Stadium 4385 Tutt Blvd Security Service Field *TF:* 866-698-4253 ■ *Web:* www.milb.com	Colorado Springs	CO	80922	719-597-1449	597-2491
Soccer City LLC 5770 Springdale Rd *Web:* indoorsoccercity.com	Cincinnati	OH	45247	513-741-8480	
Soldier Field 1410 S Museum Campus Dr *TF:* 800-322-5868 ■ *Web:* www.soldierfield.net	Chicago	IL	60605	312-235-7000	235-7030
Sovereign Bank Arena 81 Hamilton Ave *Web:* www.sunnationalbankcenter.com	Trenton	NJ	08611	609-656-3200	656-3201
Sports Authority Field at Mile High 1701 Bryant St *Web:* www.sportsauthorityfieldatmilehigh.com	Denver	CO	80204	720-258-3000	258-3050
St Pete Times Forum 401 Channelside Dr *Web:* www.tampabaytimesforum.com	Tampa	FL	33602	813-301-6500	301-1481
Staples Ctr 1111 S Figueroa St *Web:* www.staplescenter.com	Los Angeles	CA	90015	213-742-7100	742-7296
State Fair & Exposition 1001 Beulah Ave *Web:* www.coloradostatefair.com	Pueblo	CO	81004	719-404-2018	
Studio Theatre 1501 14th St NW *Web:* www.studiotheatre.org	Washington	DC	20005	202-232-7267	
Sullivan Arena 1600 Gambell St *Web:* www.sullivanarena.com	Anchorage	AK	99501	907-279-0618	274-0676
Sun Devil Stadium 500 E Veterans Way Arizona State University *TF:* 888-786-3857 ■ *Web:* www.thesundevils.com/viewarticle.dbml?atclid=208254937	Tempe	AZ	85281	480-965-3482	965-1261
Sun Life Stadium 347 Don Shula Dr *Web:* www.sunlifestadium.com	Miami Gardens	FL	33056	305-943-8000	
Taco Bell Arena 1910 University Dr *Web:* www.tacobellarena.com	Boise	ID	83725	208-426-1900	426-1998
Tacoma Dome Arena & Exhibition Hall 2727 E 'D' St **Fax:* Mktg ■ *Web:* www.tacomadome.org	Tacoma	WA	98421	253-272-3663	593-7620*
Target Ctr Arena 600 First Ave N *Web:* www.targetcenter.com	Minneapolis	MN	55403	612-673-1300	673-1387
Texas Stadium 1 Cowboys Pkwy *Web:* www.dallascowboys.com	Irving	TX	75063	972-785-4800	785-4744
Thomas & Mack Ctr/Sam Boyd Stadium 4505 S Maryland Pkwy PO Box 450003 *Web:* thomasandmack.com	Las Vegas	NV	89154	702-895-3761	
Times Union Ctr 51 S Pearl St *TF:* 866-308-3394 ■ *Web:* www.timesunioncenter-albany.com	Albany	NY	12207	518-487-2000	487-2020
Toyota Ctr 1510 Polk St *TF:* 866-446-8849 ■ *Web:* www.houstontoyotacenter.com	Houston	TX	77002	713-758-7200	758-7315
Tropicana Field One Tropicana Dr *TF:* 888-326-7297	Saint Petersburg	FL	33705	727-825-3137	825-3204
United Ctr 1901 W Madison St *Web:* www.unitedcenter.com	Chicago	IL	60612	312-455-4500	455-4511
University of Phoenix Stadium One Cardinals Dr *Web:* www.azcardinalsstadium.com	Glendale	AZ	85305	623-433-7100	
US Airways Ctr 201 E Jefferson St *Web:* www.usairwayscenter.com	Phoenix	AZ	85004	602-379-2000	379-2093
US Cellular Ctr 370 First Ave E *TF:* 800-745-3000 ■ *Web:* www.uscellularcenter.com	Cedar Rapids	IA	52401	319-398-5211	362-2102
US Cellular Field 333 W 35th St **Fax:* Hum Res ■ *Web:* chicago.whitesox.mlb.com/cws/ballpark/index.jsp	Chicago	IL	60616	312-674-1000	674-5104*

Name / Address	City	State	ZIP	Phone	Fax
US Olympic Training Ctr 1750 E Boulder St	Colorado Springs	CO	80909	719-866-4618	325-8995
TF: 800-775-8762 ■ *Web:* www.teamusa.org					
Valley View Casino Ctr 3500 Sports Arena Blvd	San Diego	CA	92110	619-224-4171	224-3010
TF: 800-745-3000 ■ *Web:* www.valleyviewcasinocenter.com					
Van Andel Arena 130 Fulton St W	Grand Rapids	MI	49503	616-742-6600	742-6197
Web: www.vanandelarena.com					
Verizon Arena One Verizon Arena Way	North Little Rock	AR	72114	501-340-5660	
TF: 800-745-3000 ■ *Web:* www.verizonarena.com					
Verizon Ctr 601 F St NW	Washington	DC	20004	202-628-3200	
Web: verizoncenter.monumentalnetwork.com					
Verizon Wireless Arena 555 Elm St	Manchester	NH	03101	603-644-5000	644-1575
Web: www.verizonwirelessarena.com					
Webster Bank Arena 600 Main St Second St	Bridgeport	CT	06604	203-345-2300	335-1719
TF: 800-745-3000 ■ *Web:* www.websterbankarena.com					
Will Rogers Memorial Ctr 3401 W Lancaster Ave	Fort Worth	TX	76107	817-392-7469	392-8170
Web: fortworthtexas.gov					
Winnipeg Centennial Folk Festival Inc, The 211 Bannatyne Ave Ste 203	Winnipeg	MB	R3B3P2	204-231-0096	
Web: www.winnipegfolkfestival.ca					
Winnipeg Goldeyes Baseball Club Inc One Portage Ave E	Winnipeg	MB	R3B3N3	204-982-2273	
Web: www.goldeyes.com					
Winston-Salem Entertainment-Sports Complex 2825 University Pkwy	Winston-Salem	NC	27105	336-758-2410	727-2922
Web: www.ljvm.com					
Wrigley Field 1060 W Addison St	Chicago	IL	60613	773-404-2827	404-4129
TF: 866-800-1275 ■ *Web:* chicago.cubs.mlb.com					
Yankee Stadium 161st St & River Ave	Bronx	NY	10451	718-293-4300	293-8431
Web: newyork.yankees.mlb.com					
Zed Ink Inc 228 Main St Ste 17	Venice	CA	90291	310-460-2424	
Web: zedink.com					

724 STAFFING SERVICES

SEE ALSO Employment Offices - Government p. 2250; Employment Services - On-line p. 2251; Executive Recruiting Firms p. 2279; Modeling Agencies p. 2765; Professional Employer Organizations (PEOs) p. 2975; Talent Agencies p. 3203

Name / Address	City	State	ZIP	Phone	Fax
ABM Industries Inc 8020 W Doe Ste C	Visalia	SC	93291	559-651-1612	579-9578*
**Fax Area Code:* 864 ■ *Web:* www.abm.com					
Accountants International 2535 Townsgate Rd Ste 107	Westlake Village	CA	91361	805-496-6888	496-2700
Web: accountantsinternational.com					
Accounting Principals 10151 Deerwood Park Blvd Ste 400	Jacksonville	FL	32256	800-981-3849	360-2394*
**Fax Area Code:* 904 ■ *TF:* 800-981-3849 ■ *Web:* www.accountingprincipals.com					
Ace Personnel (AP) 5909 Woodson Rd	Mission	KS	66202	913-384-1100	378-1912
Web: www.acepersonnel.com					
Acentron Technologies Inc PO Box 78378	Charlotte	NC	28271	704-335-0030	675-1061*
**Fax Area Code:* 864 ■ *Web:* www.acentron.com					
Adecco Inc 175 Broad Hollow Rd	Melville	NY	11747	631-844-7650	844-7614*
**Fax:* Mktg ■ *TF General:* 800-978-3729 ■ *Web:* www.adeccousa.com					
Advantage Resourcing 220 Norwood Pk S	Norwood	MA	02062	781-251-8000	676-7172*
**Fax Area Code:* 325 ■ *TF:* 800-343-4314 ■ *Web:* www.advantageresourcing.com					
Aerotek Inc 7301 Pkwy Dr	Hanover	MD	21076	410-694-5100	
TF: 800-237-6835 ■ *Web:* www.aerotek.com					
Allegis Group Inc 7301 Pkwy Dr	Hanover	MD	21076	410-579-3000	540-7556
TF: 800-927-8090 ■ *Web:* www.allegisgroup.com					
Allied Health Group LLC 145 Technology Pkwy NW	Norcross	GA	30092	800-741-4674	245-7142*
**Fax Area Code:* 678 ■ *TF:* 800-741-4674 ■ *Web:* www.alliedhealth.com					
ALTRES Inc 967 Kapiolani Blvd	Honolulu	HI	96814	808-591-4940	591-4914
TF: 888-425-8737 ■ *Web:* www.altres.com					
American Healthcare Services LLC 1000 John R Ste 250	Troy	MI	48083	248-588-9700	774-0780*
**Fax Area Code:* 540 ■ *TF:* 866-227-9998 ■ *Web:* www.americanhealthcareservices.com					
AMN Healthcare Services Inc 12400 High Bluff Dr Ste 100	San Diego	CA	92130	866-871-8519	282-1211*
NYSE: AHS ■ **Fax Area Code:* 800 ■ *TF:* 866-871-8519 ■ *Web:* www.amnhealthcare.com					
APEX Systems Inc 4400 Cox Rd Ste 100	Glen Allen	VA	23060	804-254-2600	254-7290
TF: 800-452-7391 ■ *Web:* www.apexsystemsinc.com					
AppleOne Employment Services Inc 327 W Broadway	Glendale	CA	91204	310-750-3400	265-5514*
**Fax Area Code:* 818 ■ *TF:* 800-872-2677 ■ *Web:* www.appleone.com					
Aquent LLC 711 Boylston St	Boston	MA	02116	617-535-5000	429-6244*
**Fax Area Code:* 208 ■ *TF:* 855-767-6333 ■ *Web:* www.aquent.com					
ARC Industries Inc 2879 Johnstown Rd	Columbus	OH	43219	800-734-7007	342-5680*
**Fax Area Code:* 614 ■ *TF:* 800-734-7007 ■ *Web:* www.arcind.com					
Area Temps Inc 1228 Euclid Ave	Cleveland	OH	44115	440-646-1333	
TF: 866-995-5627 ■ *Web:* www.areatemps.com					
Artech Information Systems LLC 240 Cedar Knolls Rd Ste 100	Cedar Knolls	NJ	07927	973-998-2500	998-2599
TF: 800-950-9496 ■ *Web:* www.artechinfo.com					
Attorney Resource 3300 Oak Lawn Ave Ste 510	Dallas	TX	75201	214-922-8050	871-3041
Web: www.attorneyresource.com					
Baldwin & Gilman LLC 4760 Red Bank Rd Ste 216	Cincinnati	OH	45227	513-272-2400	
Web: baldwingilman.com					
BarkerGilmore LLC 1387 Fairport Rd Ste 845	Fairport	NY	14450	585-598-6555	
Web: www.barkergilmore.com					
Bartech Group 17199 N Laurel Pk Dr Ste 224	Livonia	MI	48152	734-953-5050	
TF: 800-828-4410 ■ *Web:* www.bartechgroup.com					
Bay Area Anesthesia Inc PO Box 1547	Ukiah	CA	95482	707-462-9420	
Web: www.fastgas.com					
Bergaila & Assoc Inc 1155 Dairy Ashford Rd Ste 600	Houston	TX	77079	281-496-0803	496-4705
Web: www.bergaila.com					
Bolton Group 2860 Carradale Dr	Roseville	CA	95661	916-783-4486	
Web: www.boltongrp.com					
Bowdoin Group Inc, The 40 William St	Wellesley	MA	02481	781-239-9933	
Web: www.bowdoingroup.com					
C & A Industries Inc 13609 California St	Omaha	NE	68154	402-891-0009	891-9461
TF: 800-574-9829 ■ *Web:* www.ca-industries.com					
Calian Technology Ltd 340 Legget Dr Ste 101	Ottawa	ON	K2K1Y6	613-599-8600	599-8650
TSE: CTY ■ *TF:* 877-225-4264 ■ *Web:* www.calian.com					
CareerStaff Unlimited Inc 6363 N State Hwy 161 Ste 525	Irving	TX	75038	888-993-4599	
TF: 888-993-4599 ■ *Web:* www.therapistsunlimited.com					
CDI Corp 1717 Arch St 35th Fl	Philadelphia	PA	19103	215-569-2200	561-1750
NYSE: CDI ■ *Web:* www.cdicorp.com					
Cejka Search Inc Four Cityplace Dr Ste 300	Saint Louis	MO	63141	314-726-1603	726-0026
TF: 800-678-7858 ■ *Web:* www.cejkasearch.com					
Command Ctr Inc 3901 N Schreiber Wy	Coeur D Alene	ID	83815	208-773-7450	773-7467
OTC: CCNI ■ *TF:* 866-464-5844 ■ *Web:* www.commandonline.com					
CompHealth Inc 6440 S Millrock Dr Ste 175 Ste 175	Salt Lake City	UT	84121	801-930-3000	
TF: 800-453-3030 ■ *Web:* www.chghealthcare.com					
Compunnel Software Group Inc 103 Morgan Ln Suite 102	Plainsboro	NJ	08536	800-696-8128	
TF: 800-696-8128 ■ *Web:* www.compunnel.com					
Computer Consulting Assoc International (CCAII) 200 Pequot Ave	Southport	CT	06890	203-255-8966	
Web: www.ccaii.com					
Computer Enterprises Inc (CEI) 1000 Omega Dr Ste 1150	Pittsburgh	PA	15205	412 341 3541	341-0519
Web: www.ceiamerica.com					
Compuware Corp Professional Services Div 7760 France Ave S Ste 430	Bloomington	MN	55435	612-851-2200	851-2300
TF: 800-288-8974 ■ *Web:* www.compuware.com					
Consultnet LLC 10813 S River Front Pkwy Ste 150	South Jordan	UT	84095	801-208-3700	208-3643
TF: 888-215-9675 ■ *Web:* consultnet.com					
Continuum Legal 1651 Old Meadow Rd Ste 600	McLean	VA	22102	703-734-7474	734-8839
Web: www.continuumlegal.com					
CORESTAFF Services 1775 St James Pl Ste 150& 200	Houston	TX	77056	713-438-1400	558-8011*
**Fax:* Mktg ■ *Web:* www.corestaff.com					
CPC Logistics Inc 14528 S Outer 40 Rd Ste 210	Chesterfield	MO	63017	314-542-2266	542-0666
TF: 800-274-3746 ■ *Web:* www.callcpc.com					
Cross Country Healthcare Inc 6551 Pk of Commerce Blvd	Boca Raton	FL	33487	561-998-2232	998-8533
NASDAQ: CCRN ■ *TF:* 800-347-2264 ■ *Web:* www.crosscountryhealthcare.com					
CyberStaff America Ltd 253 W 35th St Ste 2600	New York`	NY	10001	212-244-2300	
Web: www.cyberstaff.com					
Davis Cos 325 Donald J Lynch Blvd	Marlborough	MA	01752	508-481-9500	481-8519
TF: 800-482-9494 ■ *Web:* www.daviscos.com					
Debbie's Staffing Services Inc 4431 Cherry St Ste 50	Winston Salem	NC	27105	336-744-2393	776-1661
Web: www.debbiesstaffing.com					
Design Group Staffing Inc 10012 Jasper Ave	Edmonton	AB	T5J1R2	780-428-1505	428-7095
Web: dg.ca					
DLH Holdings Corp 1776 Peachtree St NW Ste 300S	Atlanta	GA	30309	770-554-3545	
NASDAQ: DLHC ■ *TF:* 866-352-5304 ■ *Web:* www.dlhcorp.com					
Duran Human Capital Partners Inc 300 Orchard City Dr Ste 142	Campbell	CA	95008	408-540-0070	540-0073
TF: 800-287-9682 ■ *Web:* www.duranhcp.com					
Durham Cos Inc 6300 Transit Rd	Depew	NY	14043	716-684-3333	681-7408
TF: 800-633-7724 ■ *Web:* www.durhamstaffing.com					
Durham Exchange Club Industries Inc 1717 E Lawson St	Durham	NC	27703	919-596-1341	596-6380
Web: www.deci.org					
Eagle Professional Resources Inc 67 Yonge St Ste 200	Toronto	ON	M5E1J8	416-861-0636	861-8401
TF: 800-281-2339 ■ *Web:* www.eagleonline.com					
Energy Services Group International Inc (ESG) 3601 La Grange Pkwy	Toano	VA	23168	757-741-4040	741-4045
Web: www.esgi.net					
Ensearch Management Consultants 905 E Cotati Ave	Cotati	CA	94931	888-667-5627	795-6200*
**Fax Area Code:* 707 ■ *TF:* 888-667-5627 ■ *Web:* www.ensearch.com					
Entegee Inc 70 BlanchaRd Rd Ste 102	Burlington	MA	01803	781-221-5800	221-4544
TF: 800-230-7232 ■ *Web:* www.entegee.com					
Execupharm Inc 500 N Gulph Rd Ste 120	King Of Prussia	PA	19406	610-272-8771	272-8056
Web: www.execupharm.com					
Express Employment Professionals 8516 NW Expy	Oklahoma City	OK	73162	405-840-5000	717-5665
TF: 800-222-4057 ■ *Web:* www.expresspros.com					
G&A Partners 4801 Woodway Dr Ste 210W	Houston	TX	77056	713-784-1181	784-2705
TF: 800-253-8562 ■ *Web:* www.gnapartners.com					
General Employment Enterprises Inc one Tower Ln Ste 2200	Oakbrook Terrace	IL	60181	630-954-0400	954-0447
NYSE: JOB ■ *Web:* www.generalemployment.com					
Gibson Arnold & Assoc 5433 Westheimer Rd Ste 1016	Houston	TX	77056	713-572-3000	572-4664
TF: 800-879-2007 ■ *Web:* www.gibsonarnold.com					
Godshall & Godshall Personnel Po Box 1984	Greenville	SC	29602	864-242-3491	
Web: www.sccareersearch.com					
Hawkins Assoc Inc 909 NE Loop 410 Ste 104	San Antonio	TX	78209	210-349-9911	349-3393
Web: www.hawkinspersonnel.com					
Headway Corporate Resources Inc 421 Fayetteville St Ste 1020	Raleigh	NC	27601	919-376-4929	672-6599*
**Fax Area Code:* 212 ■ *Web:* www.headwaycorp.com					
Helbling & Associates Inc 9000 Brooktree Rd Ste 150	Wexford	PA	15090	724-935-7500	
Web: www.helblingsearch.com					

Name / Address	City	State	Zip	Phone	Fax
Hire Image LLC Six Alcazar Ave *Web:* www.hireimage.com	Johnston	RI	02919	401-490-2202	
Integrity Staffing Solutions Inc 750 Shipyard Dr Ste 300 *TF:* 888-458-8367 ■ *Web:* www.integritystaffing.com	Wilmington	DE	19801	302-661-8776	661-8779
Interim HealthCare Inc 1601 Sawgrass Corporate Pkwy *TF:* 800-338-7786 ■ *Web:* www.interimhealthcare.com	Sunrise	FL	33323	954-858-6000	858-2720
IPC Technologies Inc 7200 Glen Forest Dr Ste 100 *Web:* www.ipctech.com	Richmond	VA	23226	804-622-7288	
Jean Simpson Personnel Services Inc 1318 Shreveport Barksdale *Web:* www.jeansimpson.com	Shreveport	LA	71105	318-869-3494	868-0790
Joule Inc 1245 US Rt 1 S *TF:* 800-341-0341 ■ *Web:* www.jouleinc.com	Edison	NJ	08837	732-548-5444	494-6346
Judge Group Inc 300 Conshohocken State Rd Ste 300 *TF:* 888-228-7162 ■ *Web:* www.judge.com	West Conshohocken	PA	19428	610-667-7700	667-1058
Justin Bradley 1725 I St Nw Ste 300 *Web:* www.justinbradley.com	Washington	DC	20006	202-457-8400	
Kelly Law Registry Inc 999 W Big Beaver Rd *Web:* www.kellyservices.us	Troy	MI	48084	248-362-4444	244-4483
Kelly Services Inc 999 W Big Beaver Rd *NASDAQ: KELYA* ■ **Fax:* Mail Rm ■ *Web:* www.kellyservices.com	Troy	MI	48084	248-362-4444	244-5292*
Kforce Inc 1001 E Palm Ave *NASDAQ: KFRC* ■ *TF:* 888-663-3626 ■ *Web:* www.kforce.com	Tampa	FL	33605	813-552-5000	552-1482
Kimco Staffing Services Inc 17872 Cowan Ave *TF:* 800-649-5627 ■ *Web:* kimco.com	Irvine	CA	92614	949-752-6996	752-7298
Labor Finders International Inc 11426 N Jog Rd *TF:* 800-864-7749 ■ *Web:* www.laborfinders.com	Palm Beach Gardens	FL	33418	561-627-6507	627-6556
Lakeshore Staffing Inc 1 N Franklin St *TF:* 877-685-2432 ■ *Web:* www.livinglakeshore.com	Chicago	IL	60606	312-251-7575	
LJ Gonzer Assoc Inc 14 Commerce Dr Ste 305 *TF:* 866-692-4538 ■ *Web:* www.gonzer.com	Cranford	NJ	07016	908-709-9494	709-9077
Lucas Assoc Inc 3384 Peachtree Rd Ste 900 *TF:* 800-515-0819 ■ *Web:* www.lucasgroup.com	Atlanta	GA	30326	800-466-4489	
Lumen Legal 1025 N Campbell Rd *TF:* 877-933-1330 ■ *Web:* www.lumenlegal.com	Royal Oak	MI	48067	248-597-0400	597-0410
Magnum Staffing Services Inc 2900 Smith St Ste 250 *Web:* www.magnumstaffing.com	Houston	TX	77006	713-658-0068	523-3621
Major Legal Services 1301 E Ninth St Ste 1414 *Web:* majorlegalservices.com	Cleveland	OH	44114	216-579-9782	579-1662
ManpowerGroup 100 Manpower Pl *NYSE: MAN* ■ *Web:* www.manpower.us	Milwaukee	WI	53212	414-961-1000	906-7822
Marketstar Corp 2475 Washington Blvd *TF:* 800-877-8259 ■ *Web:* www.marketstar.com	Ogden	UT	84401	801-393-1155	393-4115
Medical Staffing Assoc Inc 6731 Whittier Ave 3rd Fl **Fax Area Code:* 703 ■ *TF:* 800-235-5105 ■ *Web:* www.medstaffer.com	McLean	VA	22101	800-235-5105	893-7358*
Medical Staffing Network Holdings Inc 901 Yamato Rd Ste 110 **Fax Area Code:* 561 ■ *TF:* 800-676-8326 ■ *Web:* www.msnhealth.com	Boca Raton	FL	33431	800-676-8326	322-1200*
Medvantx Inc 5626 Oberlin Dr Ste 110 *TF:* 866-744-0621 ■ *Web:* www.medvantx.com	San Diego	CA	92121	858-625-2990	625-2999
Midcom Corp 1275 N Manassero St Ste 200 *TF:* 800-737-1632 ■ *Web:* www.midcom.com	Anaheim	CA	92807	714-630-1999	459-7061
Minute Men Staffing Services 3740 Carnegie Ave *TF:* 877-873-8856 ■ *Web:* www.minutemeninc.com	Cleveland	OH	44115	216-426-9675	426-2246
Motion Recruitment Partners 131 Clarendon St 3rd Fl *Web:* www.motionrecruitment.com	Boston	MA	02116	617-585-6500	536-9154
National Engineering Service Corp 72 Mirona Rd **Fax Area Code:* 800 ■ *TF:* 800-562-3463 ■ *Web:* www.nesc.com	Portsmouth	NH	03801	603-431-9740	637-2562*
Nextgen Information Services Inc 906 Olive St Ste 1100 *Web:* www.nextgen-is.com	Saint Louis	MO	63101	314-588-1212	588-1211
North Highland Co, The 3333 Piedmont Rd NE Ste 1000 *Web:* www.northhighland.com	Atlanta	GA	30305	404-233-1015	233-4930
Nursefinders Inc 524 E Lamar Blvd Ste 300 *TF:* 800-445-0459 ■ *Web:* www.nursefinders.com	Arlington	TX	76011	817-460-1181	462-9146
On Assignment Inc 26745 Malibu Hills Rd *NYSE: ASGN* ■ *TF:* 800-426-9196 ■ *Web:* www.assignment.net	Calabasas	CA	91301	818-878-7900	
Orion International Consulting Group Inc 912 Capital of Texas Hwy S Ste 220 *TF:* 800-336-7466 ■ *Web:* www.orioninternational.com	Austin	TX	78746	512-327-7111	327-4286
Oxford Global Resources Inc 100 Cummings Ctr Ste 206L *TF:* 800-426-9196 ■ *Web:* www.oxfordcorp.com	Beverly	MA	01915	978-236-1182	236-1077
Peak Technical Services Inc 583 Epsilon Dr *TF:* 888-888-7325 ■ *Web:* www.peaktechnical.com	Pittsburgh	PA	15238	412-696-1080	696-1083
Pinnacle Staffing Inc 127 Tanner Rd PO Box 17589 *Web:* pinnaclestaffing.com	Greenville	SC	29606	864-297-4212	987-7351
Plus Group Inc, The (TPG) 7425 Janes Ave Ste 201 *Web:* www.theplusgroup.com	Woodridge	IL	60517	630-515-0500	515-0510
Premier Staffing Services of New York Inc one N Broadway Ste 801 *Web:* www.thepremiergroup.com	White Plains	NY	10601	914-428-2233	428-5547
Prime Staffing Inc 3806 N Cicero Ave *Web:* www.primestaffing.com	Chicago	IL	60641	773-685-9399	685-9565
Principal Technical Services Inc 9960 Research Dr Ste 200 **Fax Area Code:* 949 ■ *TF:* 888-787-3711 ■ *Web:* www.ptsstaffing.com	Irvine	CA	92618	888-787-3711	268-4040*
Pro Staff Personnel Services 2999 W County Rd 42 Ste 220 *Web:* www.prostaff.com	Burnsville	MN	55306	952-892-3240	
Productive Data Solutions Inc (PDSINC) 6160 S Syracuse Way Ste B160 *TF:* 800-404-7165 ■ *Web:* ww1.productivedatasolutions.com	Greenwood Village	CO	80111	303-220-7165	
Professional Placement Inc 4040 E Camelback Ste 235 *Web:* www.proplacement.com	Phoenix	AZ	85018	602-955-0870	955-0604
Professional Staffing Group 155 Federal St *Web:* www.psgstaffing.com	Boston	MA	02110	617-250-1000	250-1099
Profiles International Inc 5205 Lk Shore Dr *TF:* 866-751-1644 ■ *Web:* www.profilesinternational.com	Waco	TX	76710	254-751-1644	776-5405
PRWT Services Inc 1835 Market St Eighth Fl *Web:* www.prwt.com	Philadelphia	PA	19103	215-569-8810	569-9893
Raymond International 410 High St *Web:* www.globalrecruiter.com	Santa Cruz	CA	95060	831-429-1234	
RCM Technologies Inc 2500 McClellan Ave Ste 350 *NASDAQ: RCMT* ■ *TF:* 800-322-2885 ■ *Web:* www.rcmt.com	Pennsauken	NJ	08109	856-356-4500	356-4600
Remedy Temp Inc 3820 State St *TF:* 800-688-6162 ■ *Web:* www.remedystaff.com	Santa Barbara	CA	93105	805-882-2200	898-7111
Research Pharmaceutical Services Inc 520 Virginia Dr *TF General:* 866-777-1151 ■ *Web:* www.rpsweb.com	Fort Washington	PA	19034	215-540-0700	540-0770
Resources Global Professionals 17101 Armstrong Ave *NASDAQ: RECN* ■ *TF:* 800-900-1131 ■ *Web:* www.resourcesglobal.com	Irvine	CA	92614	714-430-6400	433-6100
Right at Home Inc 6464 Crt St Ste 150 *TF:* 877-697-7537 ■ *Web:* www.rightathome.net	Omaha	NE	68106	402-697-7537	697-0289
Robert Half International Inc 2884 Sand Hill Rd Ste 200 *NYSE: RHI* ■ *Web:* www.roberthalf.com	Menlo Park	CA	94025	650-234-6000	
Robert Half International Inc Accountemps Div 2884 Sand Hill Rd Ste 200 **Fax Area Code:* 650 ■ **Fax:* Mktg ■ *Web:* www.roberthalf.com	Menlo Park	CA	94025	855-396-4598	234-6915*
Robert Half International Inc Affiliates Div 2884 Sand Hill Rd Ste 200 **Fax Area Code:* 650 ■ *Web:* www.roberthalf.com	Menlo Park	CA	94025	844-266-2182	234-6930*
Robert Half International Inc OfficeTeam Div 2884 Sand Hill Rd Ste 200 **Fax:* Mktg ■ *Web:* www.roberthalf.com	Menlo Park	CA	94025	650-234-6000	234-6998*
Roth Staffing Cos LP 333 City Blvd W Ste 100 *Web:* www.rothstaffing.com	Orange	CA	92868	714-939-8600	939-8688
Sacramento Employment & Training Agency 925 Del Paso Blvd *Web:* www.seta.net	Sacramento	CA	95815	916-263-3800	263-3825
Salem Group, The Two TransAm Plz Dr Ste 170 *Web:* www.saleminc.com	Oakbrook Terrace	IL	60181	630-932-7000	932-7010
SEEK Careers/Staffing Inc PO Box 148 *TF:* 800-870-7181 ■ *Web:* www.seekcareers.com	Grafton	WI	53024	262-377-8888	375-6677
Select Staffing 3820 State St *TF:* 800-688-6162 ■ *Web:* www.selectstaffing.com	Santa Barbara	CA	93105	805-882-2200	898-7111
Show Pros Entertainment Services Inc PO Box 12599 *Web:* www.showprostaff.com	Charlotte	NC	28220	704-525-3784	525-3785
Sigma Systems Inc 201 Boston Post Rd Ste 201 *TF:* 888-867-4462 ■ *Web:* www.sigmainc.com	Marlborough	MA	01752	508-925-3200	357-6301
Silicon Valley Staffing 2200 Powell St Ste 510 *TF:* 877-660-6000 ■ *Web:* www.svsjobs.com	Emeryville	CA	94608	510-923-9898	923-9313
Softworld Inc 281 Winter St Ste 301 *TF:* 877-899-1166 ■ *Web:* www.softworldinc.com	Waltham	MA	02451	781-466-8882	466-8885
SOS Staffing Services Inc 2650 S Decker Lk Blvd Ste 500 *Web:* elwoodstaffing.com/redirect.html	Salt Lake City	UT	84119	801-484-4400	483-4283
Sourcing Interests Group (SIG) 221 N Hogan St #389 *Web:* www.sig.org	Jacksonville	FL	32202	904-310-9560	
Southwest Medical Assoc Inc 638 E Market St PO Box 2168 **Fax Area Code:* 361 ■ *TF:* 800-929-4854 ■ *Web:* www.swmed.com	Rockport	TX	78382	800-929-4854	729-8854*
Special Counsel Inc 10201 Centurion Pkwy N Ste 400 *TF:* 800-737-3436 ■ *Web:* www.specialcounsel.com	Jacksonville	FL	32256	904-737-3436	360-2307
Sterling Computer Corp 600 Stevens Port Dr Ste 200 *TF:* 877-242-4074 ■ *Web:* www.sterlingcomputers.com	Dakota Dunes	SD	57049	605-242-4000	242-4001
Stivers Staffing Services Inc 200 W Monroe St Ste 1300 **Fax:* Hum Res ■ *Web:* www.stivers.com	Chicago	IL	60606	312-558-3550	558-1934*
Superior Technical Resources Inc 250 International Dr *TF:* 800-568-8310 ■ *Web:* superiorgroup.com	Williamsville	NY	14221	716-929-1400	633-2026
Surgical Staff Inc 120 St Matthews Ave *TF:* 800-339-9599 ■ *Web:* surgicalstaffinc.net	San Mateo	CA	94401	650-558-3999	558-3949
TAJ Technologies Inc 1168 Northland Dr *TF:* 877-825-2801 ■ *Web:* www.tajtech.com	Mendota Heights	MN	55120	651-688-2801	688-8321
Team Health Inc 265 Brookview Ctr Way Ste 400 *TF:* 800-342-2898 ■ *Web:* www.teamhealth.com	Knoxville	TN	37919	865-693-1000	539-8030
TEKsystems Inc 7437 Race Rd *TF:* 888-519-0776 ■ *Web:* www.teksystems.com	Hanover	MD	21076	410-540-7700	540-7556
Temporary Solutions Inc 10550 Linden Lk Plz Ste 200 *TF:* 888-222-0457 ■ *Web:* www.eeihr.com	Manassas	VA	20109	703-361-2220	368-3594
Thinkpath Inc 9080 Springboro Pk Ste 300 *Web:* www.thinkpath.com	Miamisburg	OH	45342	937-291-8374	

Phone Fax

Thompson Technologies Inc
114 Townpark Dr Ste 100 Kennesaw GA 30144 770-794-8380 794-8381
TF: 888-794-7947 ■ *Web:* www.thompsontechnologies.com

Transforce Inc 6551 Loisdale Ct Ste 801 Springfield VA 22150 703-838-5580 838-5585
TF: 800-308-6989 ■ *Web:* www.transforce.com

True Blue Inc PO Box 2910 Tacoma WA 98401 253-383-9101 733-0399*
NYSE: TBI ■ **Fax Area Code:* 877 ■ *TF:* 800-610-8920 ■ *Web:* www.trueblue.com

TSR Inc 400 Oser Ave Ste 150 Hauppauge NY 11788 631-231-0333 435-1428
NASDAQ: TSRI ■ *Web:* www.tsrconsulting.com

UltraStaff 1818 Memorial Dr Ste 200 Houston TX 77007 713-522-7100 522-0744
TF: 800-522-7707 ■ *Web:* www.ultrastaff.com

US Legal Support Inc
363 N Sam Houston Pkwy E Ste 900 Houston TX 77060 713-653-7100 653-7171
TF: 800-567-8757 ■ *Web:* www.uslegalsupport.com

Vaco 5410 Maryland Way Ste 460 Brentwood TN 37027 615-324-8226 324-8245
Web: www.vaco.com

VMC Consulting Corp 11611 Willows Rd NE Redmond WA 98052 425-558-7700 558-7703
TF: 877-393-8622 ■ *Web:* www.vmc.com

Volt Services Group
1065 Ave of the Americas 20th Fl New York NY 10018 212-704-2400
NYSE: VISI ■ *Web:* volt.com

White Glove Placement Inc 85 Bartlett St Brooklyn NY 11206 718-387-8181 387-8359
TF: 866-387-8100 ■ *Web:* whiteglovecare.com

Winston Resources Inc 122 E 42nd St Ste 320 New York NY 10168 212-557-5000 682-1056
TF: 800-494-6786 ■ *Web:* www.winstonresources.com

Wolff r L & Associates 2138 Richmond Ave Houston TX 77098 713-523-2655
Web: rlwolff.com

Workstream Inc 2200 Lucien Way Ste 201 Maitland FL 32751 407-475-5500 475-5517

York Solutions LLC
One Westbrook Corporate Ctr Ste 910 Westchester IL 60154 708-531-8362 531-8361
TF: 877-700-9675 ■ *Web:* www.yorksolutions.net

725 STAGE EQUIPMENT & SERVICES

Phone Fax

Angstrom Lighting 837 N Cahuenga Blvd Hollywood CA 90038 323-462-4246 462-8190
Web: www.angstromlighting.com

Apollo Design Technology Inc
4130 Fourier Dr Fort Wayne IN 46818 260-497-9191 497-9192
TF: 800-288-4626 ■ *Web:* www.internetapollo.com

ARTEC Consultants Inc 77 Water St 5th Fl New York NY 10005 212-242-0120 645-8635
Web: www.artecconsultants.com

BlueScreen LLC
137 N Larchmont Blvd Ste 508 Los Angeles CA 90004 323-467-7572
Web: www.bluescreen.com

Chapman/Leonard Studio Equipment Inc
12950 Raymer St North Hollywood CA 91605 818-764-6726 764-6730
TF: 888-883-6559 ■ *Web:* www.chapman-leonard.com

Creative Stage Lighting Company Inc
149 Rt 28 N PO Box 567 North Creek NY 12853 518-251-3302 251-2908
Web: www.creativestagelighting.com

Dreamworld Backdrops
6450 Lusk Blvd Ste E-106 San Diego CA 92121 800-737-9869
TF: 800-737-9869 ■ *Web:* www.dreamworldbackdrops.com

Fisher Dachs Assoc 22 W 19th St Sixth Fl New York NY 10011 212-691-3020 633-1644
Web: www.fda-online.com

Grosh Scenic Rentals 4114 Sunset Blvd Los Angeles CA 90029 877-363-7998 664-7526*
**Fax Area Code:* 323 ■ *TF:* 877-363-7998 ■ *Web:* www.grosh.com

High End Systems Inc 2105 Gracy Farms Ln Austin TX 78758 512-836-2242 837-5290
TF: 800-890-8989 ■ *Web:* www.highend.com

Holzmueller Productions Corp
1000 25th St San Francisco CA 94107 415-826-8383 826-2608
Web: www.holzmueller.com

Janson Industries 1200 Garfield Ave SW Canton OH 44706 330-455-7029 455-5919
TF: 800-548-8982 ■ *Web:* www.jansonindustries.com

Lycian Stage Lighting
1144 Kings Hwy PO Box D Sugar Loaf NY 10981 845-469-2285 469-5355
Web: www.lycian.com

Musson Theatrical Inc 890 Walsh Ave Santa Clara CA 95050 408-986-0210 986-9552
TF: 800-843-2837 ■ *Web:* www.musson.com

Production Resource Group LLC
539 Temple Hill Rd New Windsor NY 12553 845-567-5700 567-5800
Web: www.prg.com

Rosco Laboratories Inc 52 Harbor View Ave Stamford CT 06902 203-708-8900 708-8919
TF: 800-767-2669 ■ *Web:* www.rosco.com

Schuler & Shook 750 N Orleans St Ste 400 Chicago IL 60654 312-944-8230 944-8297
Web: www.schulershook.com

Screen Works 2201 W Fulton St Chicago IL 60612 312-243-8265 243-8290
TF Cust Svc: 800-294-8111 ■ *Web:* www.thescreenworks.com

Secoa Inc 8650 109th Ave N Champlin MN 55316 763-506-8800 506-8844
TF: 800-328-5519 ■ *Web:* www.secoa.com

Syracuse Scenery & Stage Lighting Company Inc
101 Monarch Dr Liverpool NY 13088 315-453-8096 453-7897
TF: 800-453-7775 ■ *Web:* www.syracusescenery.com

Triangle Scenery Drapery & Lighting Co
1215 Bates Ave Los Angeles CA 90029 323-662-8129 662-8120
Web: www.tridrape.com

726 STEEL - MFR

Phone Fax

A Finkl & Sons Co 2011 N Southport Ave Chicago IL 60614 773-975-2510 348-5347
TF: 800-343-2562 ■ *Web:* www.finkl.com

Action Sales & Metal Company Inc
1625 E Pacific Coast Hwy Wilmington CA 90744 310-549-5666
Web: actionsalesmetal.com

Air-Cure Inc 8501 Evergreen Blvd Minneapolis MN 55433 763-717-0707
Web: www.aircure.com

AK Steel Corp 9227 Centre Pt Dr West Chester OH 45069 513-425-5000 601-4332*
NYSE: AKS ■ **Fax Area Code:* 312 ■ *TF:* 800-331-5050 ■ *Web:* www.aksteel.com

Aleris International Inc
25825 Science Pk Dr Ste 400 Beachwood OH 44122 216-910-3400 910-3650
TF: 866-266-2586 ■ *Web:* www.aleris.com

Allegheny Technologies Inc
1000 Six PPG Pl Pittsburgh PA 15222 412-394-2800 394-3034*
NYSE: ATI ■ **Fax:* Hum Res ■ *TF Sales:* 800-258-3586 ■ *Web:* www.atimetals.com

American Tank & Fabricating Co (AT&F)
12314 Elmwood Ave Cleveland OH 44111 216-252-1500 251-4963
TF: 800-544-5316 ■ *Web:* www.atfco.com

ATI Allegheny Ludlum Corp 100 River Rd Brackenridge PA 15014 724-224-1000
TF Sales: 800-258-3586 ■ *Web:* www.atimetals.com

Block Steel Corp 6101 Oakton St Ste 2 Skokie IL 60077 847-966-3000 966-5906
Web: www.blocksteel.com

Borgeson Universal Company Inc
91 Technology Park Dr Torrington CT 06790 860-482-8283
Web: borgeson.com

Bushwick Metals LLC 560 N Washington Ave Bridgeport CT 06604 203-576-1800
Web: bushwickmetals.thomaswebs.net

Cadillac Casting Inc 1500 Fourth Ave Cadillac MI 49601 231-779-9600
Web: cadillaccasting.com

Calstrip Steel Corp 7140 Bandini Blvd Los Angeles CA 90040 323-726-1345 722-8269
Web: calstripsteel.com

Canam Group Inc
11505 First Ave Bureau 500 Saint-Georges QC G5Y7H5 418-228-8031
TSE: CAM ■ *TF:* 877-499-6049 ■ *Web:* groupecanam.com/en/

Carpenter Specialty Alloys Operations
101 W Bern St Reading PA 19601 610-208-2000 208-3716
TF: 800-654-6543 ■ *Web:* www.cartech.com/sao_products

Carpenter Technology Corp PO Box 14662 Reading PA 19612 610-208-2000 208-3716
NYSE: CRS ■ *TF:* 800-654-6543 ■ *Web:* www.cartech.com

Cascade Steel Rolling Mills Inc (CSRM)
3200 N Hwy 99 W PO Box 687 McMinnville OR 97128 503-472-4181 434-5739
TF: 800-283-2776 ■ *Web:* www.cascadesteel.com

Central Illinois Steel Co
21050 Rt 4 PO Box 78 Carlinville IL 62626 217-854-3251 854-4771

Charleston Steel & Metal Co
2700 Spruill Ave PO Box 814 North Charleston SC 29405 843-722-7278
Web: www.charlestonsteelandmetal.com

Charter Mfg Company Inc 1212 W Glen Oaks Ln Mequon WI 53092 262-243-4700 243-4767
Web: www.chartermfg.com

Chicago Heights Steel Acquisition Corp
211 E Main St Chicago Heights IL 60411 708-756-5648 756-5628
TF: 800-424-4487 ■ *Web:* chs.com

Claret Medical Inc
1745 Copperhill Pkwy Ste 1 Santa Rosa CA 95403 707-528-9300
Web: www.claretmedical.com

Colibri Technologies Inc 293 Lesmill Rd North York ON M3B2V1 416-483-0100
Web: colibritech.com

Commercial Metals Co (CMC)
6565 N MacArthur Blvd Ste 800 Irving TX 75039 214-689-4300 689-4300
NYSE: CMC ■ *Web:* www.cmc.com

Corey Steel Co 2800 S 61st Ct Cicero IL 60804 708-735-8000 735-8100
TF: 800-323-2750 ■ *Web:* www.coreysteel.com

Creform Corp PO Box 830 Greer SC 29652 864-989-1700 877-3863
TF: 800-839-8823 ■ *Web:* www.creform.com

Crucible Materials Corp 575 State Fair Blvd Syracuse NY 13209 315-487-4111 470-9358*
**Fax:* Sales ■ *TF:* 800-365-1180 ■ *Web:* www.crucible.com

Delphinus Medical Technologies LLC
46701 Commerce Ctr Dr Plymouth MI 48170 734-233-3088
Web: www.delphinusmt.com

Dunkirk Specialty Steel Corp 830 Brigham Rd Dunkirk NY 14048 716-366-1000 366-0478
Web: www.dunkirkspecialtysteel.com

E&h Steel Corp 3635 Alabama 134 Midland City AL 36350 334-983-6405 983-6173
Web: www.ehsteel.com

Electralloy Corp 175 Main St Oil City PA 16301 814-678-4100 678-4100
TF: 800-458-7273 ■ *Web:* www.electralloy.com

Ellwood Engineered Castings Co
7158 Hubbard Masury Rd Hubbard OH 44425 330-534-8668
Web: ellwoodengineeredcastings.com

F & D Head Co 3040 E Peden Rd Fort Worth TX 76179 817-236-8773 236-1061
Web: www.fwfdhead.com

Feroleto Steel Company Inc
300 Scofield Ave Bridgeport CT 06605 203-366-3263 366-8058
TF: 800-243-2839 ■ *Web:* www.feroletosteel.com

Gerdau Ameristeel 2300 Oklahoma 97 Sand Springs OK 74063 918-245-1335 245-9343

Gerdau AmeriSteel Corp
4221 W Boy Scout Blvd Ste 600 Tampa FL 33607 813-286-8383
TF Sales: 800-876-7833 ■ *Web:* www.gerdau.com

Gibraltar Industries Inc 3556 Lakeshore Rd Buffalo NY 14219 716-826-6500 826-1589*
NASDAQ: ROCK ■ **Fax:* Sales ■ *TF:* 800-247-8368 ■ *Web:* www.gibraltar1.com

GO Carlson Inc
350 Marshallton Thorndale Rd Downingtown PA 19335 610-384-2800 383-3429
TF: 800-338-5622 ■ *Web:* www.electralloy.com

Greer Steel Co 624 Blvd Dover OH 44622 330-343-8811 343-1700
TF Sales: 800-388-2868 ■ *Web:* www.greersteel.com

Guided Delivery Systems Inc
2355 Calle de Luna Santa Clara CA 95054 408-727-1105
Web: www.gdsmed.com

Gulf Coast Machine & Supply Company Inc
6817 Industrial Rd Beaumont TX 77705 409-842-1311 842-4621
TF: 800-231-3032 ■ *Web:* www.gulfco.com

Harris Steel Co 1223 S 55th Ct Cicero IL 60804 708-656-5500 656-0151
Web: www.harrissteelco.com

Heidtman Steel Products Inc 2401 Front St Toledo OH 43605 419-691-4646 698-1150
Web: www.heidtman.com

Huron Valley Steel Corp
1650 W Jefferson Ste 100 Trenton MI 48183 734-479-3500 479-3413
Web: www.hvsc.net

Image Diagnostics Inc 310 Authority Dr Fitchburg MA 01420 978-829-0009
Web: www.imagediagnostics.com

Intsel Steel Distributors LP
11310 W Little York Houston TX 77041 713-937-9500 937-1091
TF: 800-762-3316 ■ *Web:* www.intselsteel.com

				Phone	Fax
Jersey Shore Steel Co 70 Maryland Ave PO Box 5055 *TF:* 800-833-0277 ■ *Web:* www.jssteel.com	Jersey Shore	PA	17740	570-753-3000	753-3782
JFE Steel Corp 350 Pk Ave 27th Fl *Web:* www.jfe-steel.co.jp	New York	NY	10022	212-310-9320	308-9292
Kardium Inc 12851 Rowan Pl Ste 100 *Web:* www.kardium.com	Richmond	BC	V6V2K5	604-248-8891	
Kentucky Electric Steel LLC 2704 S Big Run Rd W *TF:* 800-333-3012 ■ *Web:* www.kentuckyelectricsteel.com	Ashland	KY	41102	606-929-1200	929-1219
Keystone Steel & Wire Co 7000 S Adams St **Fax Area Code:* 309 ■ *TF:* 800-447-6444 ■ *Web:* www.redbrand.com	Peoria	IL	61641	800-447-6444	697-7487*
Kobe Steel USA Inc 535 Madison Ave 5th Fl *Web:* www.kobelco.co.jp	New York	NY	10022	212-751-9400	355-5564
LBIW Inc 2020 W 14th St	Long Beach	CA	90813	562-432-5451	
LOKRING Technology LLC 38376 Apollo Pkwy *Web:* www.lokring.com	Willoughby	OH	44094	440-942-0880	
Lynchburg Steel & Specialty Co 275 Francis Ave *Web:* lynchburgsteel.com	Monroe	VA	24574	434-929-0951	929-2613
Metalex Corp 1530 Artaius Pkwy PO Box 399 *TF:* 800-323-0792 ■ *Web:* www.metlx.com	Libertyville	IL	60048	847-362-8300	362-7939
Mevion Medical Systems Inc 300 Foster Sreet *Web:* www.stillriversystems.com	Littleton	MA	01460	978-540-1500	
Mill Steel Co 5116 36th St SE **Fax Area Code:* 616 ■ *TF:* 800-247-6455 ■ *Web:* www.millsteel.com	Grand Rapids	MI	49512	800-247-6455	977-9411*
Millerbernd Manufacturing Co PO Box 98 *Web:* www.millerberndmfg.com	Winsted	MN	55395	320-485-2111	485-4420
Mobisante Inc 8201 164th Ave NE Ste 200 *Web:* www.mobisante.com	Redmond	WA	98052	425-605-0600	
Moore Erection LP 19921 Fm 2252 *Web:* melpsteel.com	San Antonio	TX	78266	210-648-7461	648-1340
Niagara Corp 667 Madison Ave *TF:* 877-289-2277 ■ *Web:* www.niagaralasalle.com	New York	NY	10021	212-317-1000	317-1001
Nisshin USA LLC 1701 Golf Rd Continental Tower 3 Ste 1004 *Web:* www.nisshin-steel.co.jp	Rolling Meadows	IL	60008	847-290-5100	290-0826
Nucor Corp 1915 Rexford Rd *NYSE: NUE* ■ *TF:* 800-294-1322 ■ *Web:* www.nucor.com	Charlotte	NC	28211	704-366-7000	362-4208
Nucor Corp Cold Finish Div 2800 N Governor Williams Hwy **Fax Area Code:* 843 ■ **Fax:* Sales ■ *TF:* 800-333-0590 ■ *Web:* www.nucor.com	Darlington	SC	29540	704-366-7000	395-8759*
Nucor Corp Steel Div 1455 Hagan Ave **Fax:* Sales ■ *TF:* 800-424-9300 ■ *Web:* www.nucorsteel.com	Huger	SC	29450	843-336-6000	336-6108*
Nucor-Yamato Steel Co 5929 E State Hwy 18 *TF:* 800-289-6977 ■ *Web:* www.nucoryamato.com	Blytheville	AR	72315	870-762-5500	762-1130
Reference Metals Company Inc 1000 Old Pond Rd *Web:* cbmm.com.br	Bridgeville	PA	15017	412-221-7008	
Regional Fabricators Inc 1905 Diver Dr *Web:* www.regionalfab.com	New Iberia	LA	70560	337-367-3488	
ROHN Products LLC One Fairholm Ave *Web:* www.rohnnet.com	Peoria	IL	61603	309-566-3000	
Sandmeyer Steel Co One Sandmeyer Ln *TF:* 800-523-3663 ■ *Web:* www.sandmeyersteel.com	Philadelphia	PA	19116	215-464-7100	677-1430
Schnitzer Steel Industries Inc 3200 NW Yeon Ave *NASDAQ: SCHN* ■ *TF:* 800-562-9876 ■ *Web:* www.schnitzersteel.com	Portland	OR	97210	503-224-9900	323-2804
Scion Steel Inc 21555 Mullin Ave *TF:* 800-288-2127 ■ *Web:* www.scionsteel.com	Warren	MI	48089	586-755-4000	757-5210
Shasta Inc 300 Steel St *Web:* shastainc.com	Aliquippa	PA	15001	724-378-8280	
Standard Steel LLC 500 N Walnut St *Web:* www.standardsteel.com	Burnham	PA	17009	717-248-4911	248-8050
Steel Dynamics Inc 7575 W Jefferson Blvd Ste 200 *NASDAQ: STLD* ■ *TF:* 866-740-8700 ■ *Web:* www.steeldynamics.com	Fort Wayne	IN	46804	260-969-3500	969-3590
Steel of West Virginia Inc 17th St & Second Ave *TF:* 800-624-3492 ■ *Web:* www.swvainc.com	Huntington	WV	25703	304-696-8200	529-1479
Tempel Steel Co 5500 N Wolcott Ave **Fax:* Cust Svc ■ *Web:* www.tempel.com	Chicago	IL	60640	773-250-8000	250-8910*
Tenaris 530-8th Ave SW Ste 400 *Web:* www.tenaris.com	Calgary	AB	T2P3S8	403-767-0100	767-0299
Thompson Steel Co 120 Royall St *Web:* www.thompsonsteelco.com	Canton	MA	02021	781-828-8800	
Tube Products Corp 14420 Ewing Ave S	Burnsville	MN	55306	952-894-2817	
TWB Co 1600 Nadeau Rd *Web:* www.twbcompany.com	Monroe	MI	48162	734-289-6400	289-6555
Ulbrich Stainless Steels & Special Metals Inc (USSM) 57 Dodge Ave **Fax:* Sales ■ *TF:* 800-243-1676 ■ *Web:* www.ulbrich.com	North Haven	CT	06473	203-239-4481	239-7479*
Union Electric Steel Corp 726 Bell Ave *Web:* www.uniones.com	Carnegie	PA	15106	412-429-7655	276-1711
United Performance Metals 3475 Symmes Rd *TF:* 888-282-3292 ■ *Web:* www.fergusonmetals.com	Hamilton	OH	45015	513-860-6500	874-6857
US Steel Corp 600 Grant St *NYSE: X* ■ **Fax:* Hum Res ■ *Web:* www.ussteel.com	Pittsburgh	PA	15219	412-433-6791	433-6779*
USS-POSCO Industries 900 Loveridge Rd *TF:* 800-877-7672 ■ *Web:* www.ussposco.com	Pittsburg	CA	94565	925-439-6000	439-6722
Western Steel Inc Attn Fred Campbell 3360 Davey Allison Blvd *Web:* westernsteelinc.com	Hueytown	AL	35023	205-744-2230	
Worthington Specialty Processing 4905 S Meridian Rd *Web:* worthingtonindustries.com	Jackson	MI	49201	517-789-0200	
Worthington Steel Co 1127 Dearborn Dr **Fax:* Sales ■ *TF:* 800-944-3733 ■ *Web:* worthingtonindustries.com	Columbus	OH	43085	614-438-3210	840-4681*

727 STONE (CUT) & STONE PRODUCTS

				Phone	Fax
Adam Ross Cut Stone Co 1003 Broadway *Web:* www.adamrosscutstone.com	Albany	NY	12204	518-463-6674	463-0710
Akdo Intertrade Inc 1435 State St *TF:* 800-811-2536 ■ *Web:* www.akdo.com	Bridgeport	CT	06605	203-336-5199	
American Slate Co 1900 Olympic Blvd Ste 200 *Web:* www.americanslate.com	Walnut Creek	CA	94596	925-977-4880	
Austin Countertops 11108 Bluff Bend Dr *Web:* www.austincountertops.com	Austin	TX	78753	512-835-5100	339-1796
AZ Countertops Inc 1445 S Hudson Ave *TF:* 800-266-3524 ■ *Web:* azcountertopsinc.com	Ontario	CA	91762	909-983-5386	983-5495
Benson Stone Co 1100 11th St *Web:* www.bensonstone.com	Rockford	IL	61104	815-227-2000	227-2001
Biesanz Stone Co Inc 4600 Goodview Rd *TF:* 800-247-8322 ■ *Web:* www.biesanzstone.com	Winona	MN	55987	507-454-4336	454-8140
Briar Hill Stone Co, The 12470 State Rt 520 PO Box 457 *Web:* www.briarhillstone.com	Glenmont	OH	44628	330-377-5100	377-5110
Bristol Memorial Works Inc 797 King St *TF:* 888-987-7821	Bristol	CT	06010	860-583-1654	
Bybee Stone Company Inc 6293 N Matthews Dr *TF:* 800-457-4530 ■ *Web:* www.bybeestone.com	Ellettsville	IN	47429	812-876-2215	876-6329
C & H Stone Company Inc 4000 S Rockport Rd *Web:* chstoneinc.com	Bloomington	IN	47403	812-336-2560	331-7292
Cold Spring Granite Inc 17482 Granite W Rd *TF:* 800-328-5040 ■ *Web:* www.coldspringusa.com	Cold Spring	MN	56320	320-685-3621	685-8490
Coldspring 17482 Granite W Rd *TF:* 800-328-5040 ■ *Web:* www.coldspringusa.com	Cold Spring	MN	56320	800-328-5040	473-4881
Columbus Marble Works Corp 2415 Hwy 45 N PO Box 791 *TF Cust Svc:* 800-647-1055 ■ *Web:* www.columbusmarbleworks.net	Columbus	MS	39703	662-328-1477	328-5002
Continental Cast Stone Manufacturing Inc 22001 W 83rd St **Fax Area Code:* 913 ■ *TF:* 800-989-7866 ■ *Web:* www.continentalcaststone.com	Shawnee	KS	66227	800-989-7866	422-7272*
Dakota Granite Co 48391 150th St PO Box 1351 *TF:* 800-843-3333 ■ *Web:* dakotagranite.com	Milbank	SD	57252	605-432-5580	432-6155
Dakota Marble Inc 902 W 19th St *TF:* 800-697-7241 ■ *Web:* www.dakotamarble.com	Yankton	SD	57078	605-665-7241	665-7241
Daprato Rigali Inc 6030 N NW Hwy *Web:* www.dapratorigali.com	Chicago	IL	60631	773-763-5511	763-5522
Dutch Quality Stone Inc 18012 Dover Rd *Web:* www.dutchqualitystone.com	Mount Eaton	OH	44659	330-359-7866	
Environmental Materials LLC 6300 E Stapleton Dr S *Web:* www.estoneworks.com	Denver	CO	80216	303-309-3040	
Finger Lakes Stone Company Inc 33 Quarry Rd *Web:* www.fingerlakesstone.net	Ithaca	NY	14850	607-273-4646	273-4692
Glenrock International Inc 985 E Linden Ave *TF:* 800-453-6762 ■ *Web:* glenrock.com	Linden	NJ	07036	908-862-3433	862-0430
Hilltop Slate Three County Rt 21 PO Box 201 *Web:* www.hilltopslate.com	Middle Granville	NY	12849	518-642-2270	642-1220
Intercontinental Marble Corp 8228 NW 56th St *Web:* www.intercontinentalmarble.com	Miami	FL	33166	305-591-2207	
Keystone Retaining Wall Systems Inc 4444 W 78th St *TF:* 800-642-3887 ■ *Web:* www.keystonewalls.com	Minneapolis	MN	55435	952-897-1040	
Kollmann Monumental Works Inc 1915 W Div St *TF:* 800-659-8010 ■ *Web:* www.kollmann.com	Saint Cloud	MN	56301	320-251-8010	251-8019
Kotecki Rock of Ages Memorials 3636 Pearl Rd *Web:* www.koteckifamilymemorials.com	Cleveland	OH	44109	216-749-2880	749-7221
Little Falls Granite Works 10802 Hwy 10 PO Box 240 *TF:* 800-862-2417 ■ *Web:* lfgranite.com	Little Falls	MN	56345	320-632-9277	632-3342
Mankato-Kasota Stone Inc 818 N Willow St *Web:* www.mankato-kasota-stone.com	Mankato	MN	56001	507-625-2746	
Maryland Materials Inc 233 Stevenson Rd *Web:* www.marylandmaterials.com	North East	MD	21901	410-287-8177	
Milwaukee Marble & Granite Co 4535 W Mitchell St *TF:* 877-645-6272 ■ *Web:* www.milwaukeemarble.com	Milwaukee	WI	53214	414-645-0305	645-2620
Monumental Sales Inc 537 22nd Ave N PO Box 667 *TF:* 800-442-1660 ■ *Web:* www.sunburstmemorials.com	Saint Cloud	MN	56302	320-251-6585	251-6547
North Carolina Granite Corp 151 Granite Quarry Trl PO Box 151 *TF:* 800-227-6242 ■ *Web:* www.ncgranite.com	Mount Airy	NC	27030	336-786-5141	719-2623
Northfield Block Co One Hunt Ct *TF:* 800-358-3003 ■ *Web:* northfieldblock.com	Mundelein	IL	60060	847-949-3600	816-9072
Northwestern Marble & Granite Co 7705 Bush Lake Rd Ste A *Web:* www.northwesternmarble.com	Edina	MN	55439	952-941-8601	941-0994
Polycor Inc 139 St-Pierre St *Web:* www.polycor.com	Quebec City	QC	G1K8B9	418-692-4695	
RJ Marshall Co 26776 W 12-Mile Rd **Fax Area Code:* 800 ■ *TF Cust Svc:* 888-514-8600 ■ *Web:* www.rjmarshallco.com	Southfield	MI	48034	248-353-4100	338-7900*
Rock of Ages Corp 560 Graniteville Rd *TF:* 800-421-0166 ■ *Web:* www.rockofages.com	Graniteville	VT	05654	802-476-3119	
Solidia Technologies Inc 11 Colonial Dr *Web:* www.solidiatech.com	Piscataway	NJ	08854	908-315-5901	

Phone Fax

Starrett Tru-Stone Technologies Div
1101 Prosper Dr PO Box 430 .... Waite Park MN 56387 320-251-7171 259-5073
TF: 800-959-0517 ■ *Web:* www.starrett.com

StonePeak Ceramics Inc 314 W Superior Ste 201 ...... Chicago IL 60610 312-506-2800
Web: www.stonepeakceramics.com

Tri-State Cut Stone & Brick Co
10333 Van's Dr .... Frankfort IL 60423 815-469-7550 464-5096
Web: www.stone-brick.com

Vermont Structural Slate Company Inc
Three Prospect St PO Box 98 .... Fair Haven VT 05743 802-265-4933 265-3865
TF: 800-343-1900 ■ *Web:* www.vermontstructuralslate.com

Vetter Stone Co (VSC) 23894 Third Ave .... Mankato MN 56001 507-345-4568 345-4777
TF: 800-878-2850 ■ *Web:* www.vetterstone.com

WE Neal Slate Co 2840 Hwy 25 .... Watertown MN 55388 952-955-3340 955-3341
Web: www.nealslate.com

Winona Monument Company Inc 174 W Third St ...... Winona MN 55987 507-452-4672
Web: winonamonument.net

WS Hampshire Inc 365 Keyes Ave .... Hampshire IL 60140 847-683-4400 683-4407
TF: 800-541-0251 ■ *Web:* www.wshampshire.com

728 STUDENT ASSISTANCE PROGRAMS

Phone Fax

Alabama Commission on Higher Education
100 N Union St PO Box 302000 .... Montgomery AL 36104 334-242-1998 242-0268
Web: ache.alabama.gov

Alabama Prepaid Affordable College Tuition (PACT) Program
100 N Union St Ste 660 .... Montgomery AL 36130 334-242-7514
TF: 800-252-7228 ■ *Web:* www.treasury.state.al.us

Alaska Commission on Postsecondary Education
PO Box 110510 .... Juneau AK 99811 907-465-2962 465-5316
TF: 800-441-2962 ■ *Web:* acpe.alaska.gov

Arkansas Financial Aid Office
114 Silas Hunt Hall .... Fayetteville AR 72701 479-575-3806 575-7790
TF: 800-547-8839 ■ *Web:* finaid.uark.edu

California Student Aid Commission
PO Box 419027 .... Rancho Cordova CA 95741 916-526-8999 526-8002
TF: 888-224-7268 ■ *Web:* www.csac.ca.gov

Colorado CollegeInvest 1560 Broadway Ste 1700 .... Denver CO 80202 303-376-8800 296-4811
TF: 800-448-2424 ■ *Web:* collegeinvest.org

Council for Opportunity in Education
1025 Vermont Ave NW Ste 900 .... Washington DC 20005 202-347-7430 347-0786
TF: 800-633-7313 ■ *Web:* www.coenet.us

DC Tuition Assistance Grant Program
810 First St NE .... Washington DC 20001 202-727-2824 727-2834
TF: 877-485-6751 ■ *Web:* www.osse.dc.gov

Dollars for Scholars
Scholarship America 1 Scholarship Way .... Saint Peter MN 56082 507-931-1682 931-9168
TF: 800-248-8080 ■ *Web:* www.scholarshipamerica.org

EdVest PO Box 55244 .... Boston MA 02205 888-338-3789 266-2647*
**Fax Area Code:* 608 ■ *TF:* 888-338-3789 ■ *Web:* mobile.edvest.com/materials.shtml

FastWeb Inc 444 N Michigan Ave Ste 3000 .... Chicago IL 60611 444-536-1212 467-0638*
**Fax Area Code:* 312 ■ *TF:* 800-829-1040 ■ *Web:* www.fastweb.com

FinAid Page LLC PO Box 2056 .... Cranberry Township PA 16066 724-538-4500 538-4502
TF: 800-433-3243 ■ *Web:* www.finaid.org

Florida Prepaid College Board
PO Box 6567 .... Tallahassee FL 32314 800-552-4723 309-1766*
**Fax Area Code:* 850 ■ **Fax:* Cust Svc ■ *Web:* www.myfloridaprepaid.com

Florida Student Financial Assistance Office
1940 N Monroe St Ste 70 .... Tallahassee FL 32303 850-410-5200 488-3612
TF: 888-827-2004 ■ *Web:* www.floridastudentfinancialaid.org

Georgia Student Finance Commission
2082 E Exchange Pl Ste 200 .... Tucker GA 30084 770-724-9000 724-9089
TF: 800-505-4732 ■ *Web:* www.gsfc.org

Harry S Truman Scholarship Foundation
712 Jackson Pl NW .... Washington DC 20006 202-395-4831 395-6995
Web: www.truman.gov

Hawaii Postsecondary Education Commission
2444 Dole St Bachman Hall Rm 209 .... Honolulu HI 96822 808-956-8213 956-5156
TF: 877-531-2333 ■ *Web:* hawaii.edu

Idaho Scholarship Office
650 W State St Rm 307 PO Box 83720 .... Boise ID 83720 208-334-2270 334-2632
Web: www.boardofed.idaho.gov

Illinois Student Assistance Commission
1755 Lake Cook Rd .... Deerfield IL 60015 847-948-8500 831-8549*
**Fax:* Cust Svc ■ *TF:* 800-899-4722 ■ *Web:* collegeillinois.org/

Indiana Students Assistance Commission
150 W Market St Ste 500 .... Indianapolis IN 46204 317-232-2350 232-3260
TF: 888-528-4719 ■ *Web:* www.in.gov

Iowa College Student Aid Commission
603 E 12th St Fl 5th .... Des Moines IA 50319 515-725-3400 725-3401
TF: 800-383-4222 ■ *Web:* www.iowacollegeaid.gov

Kansas Board of Regents, The
1000 SW Jackson St Ste 520 .... Topeka KS 66612 785-296-3421 296-0983
Web: www.kansasregents.org

Kentucky Higher Education Assistance Authority (KHEAA)
100 Airport Rd .... Frankfort KY 40602 800-928-8926
TF: 800-928-8926 ■ *Web:* www.kheaa.com

Louisiana Office of Student Financial Assistance (LOSFA)
602 N Fifth St PO Box 91202 .... Baton Rouge LA 70802 225-219-1012 208-1496
TF: 800-259-5626 ■ *Web:* www.osfa.la.gov

Maine Finance Authority of Maine (FAME)
5 Community Dr PO Box 949 .... Augusta ME 04332 207-623-3263 623-0095
TF: 800-228-3734 ■ *Web:* www.famemaine.com

Maryland Student Financial Assistance Office
839 Bestgate Rd Ste 400 .... Annapolis MD 21401 410-260-4565 260-3200
TF: 800-974-0203 ■ *Web:* www.mhec.state.md.us

Michigan Education Trust (MET) PO Box 30198 .... Lansing MI 48909 517-335-4767 373-6967
TF General: 800-638-4543 ■ *Web:* www.setwithmet.com

Michigan Student Financial Services Bureau
Austin Bldg 430 W Allegan .... Lansing MI 48922 888-447-2687 335-6792*
**Fax Area Code:* 517 ■ *TF General:* 800-642-5626 ■ *Web:* www.michigan.gov/mistudentaid

Minnesota Office of Higher Education
1450 Energy Pk Dr Ste 350 .... Saint Paul MN 55108 651-642-0567 642-0675
TF: 800-657-3866 ■ *Web:* www.ohe.state.mn.us

Mississippi Student Financial Aid Office
3825 Ridgewood Rd .... Jackson MS 39211 601-432-6997 432-6527
TF: 800-327-2980 ■ *Web:* www.ihl.state.ms.us/financialaid

Montana Higher Education Board of Regents
2500 Broadway St PO Box 203201 .... Helena MT 59620 406-444-6570 444-1469
TF: 877-501-1722 ■ *Web:* www.mus.edu

Morris K Udall Foundation 130 S Scott Ave .... Tucson AZ 85709 520-901-8500 670-5530
Web: www.udall.gov

National Merit Scholarship Corp
1560 Sherman Ave Ste 200 .... Evanston IL 60201 847-866-5100 866-5113
Web: www.nationalmerit.org

Nebraska Coordinating Commission for Postsecondary Educatio
140 N Eigth St Ste 300 PO Box 95005 .... Lincoln NE 68509 402-471-2847 471-2886
Web: www.ccpe.state.ne.us

New Hampshire Postsecondary Education Commission
64 South Street Ste 300 .... Concord NH 03301 603-271-2555 271-2696
TF: 800-735-2964 ■ *Web:* www.nh.gov

New Jersey Higher Education Student Assistance Authority
4 Quakerbridge Plaza PO Box 540 .... Trenton NJ 08625 609-584-4480 588-7389
TF: 800-792-8670 ■ *Web:* www.hesaa.org

New Mexico Financial Aid & Student Services Unit
2048 Galisteo St .... Santa Fe NM 87505 505-476-8400 476-8453
TF: 800-279-9777 ■ *Web:* www.hed.state.nm.us

New York Higher Education Services Corp
99 Washington Ave .... Albany NY 12255 518-473-1574 473-3749
TF: 888-697-4372 ■ *Web:* www.hesc.ny.gov

North Carolina State Education Assistance Authority (NCSEAA)
PO Box 14103 .... Research Triangle Park NC 27709 919-549-8614 549-8481
TF: 800-700-1775 ■ *Web:* www.ncseaa.edu

North Dakota Student Financial Assistance Program
600 E Blvd Ave 10th Fl Dept 215 .... Bismarck ND 58505 701-328-2960 328-2961
Web: www.ndus.nodak.edu

Ohio Tuition Trust Authority
580 S High St Ste 208 .... Columbus OH 43215 614-752-9400
TF Cust Svc: 800-233-6734 ■ *Web:* www.collegeadvantage.com

Oklahoma State Regents for Higher Education
655 Research Pkwy Ste 200 .... Oklahoma City OK 73104 405-225-9100 225-9235
Web: www.okhighered.org

Oregon Student Assistance Commission
1500 Valley River Dr Ste 100 .... Eugene OR 97401 541-687-7400
Web: oregonstudentaid.gov

Pennsylvania Higher Education Assistance Agency
1200 N Seventh St .... Harrisburg PA 17102 800-233-0557 720-3901*
**Fax Area Code:* 717 ■ *TF:* 800-233-0557 ■ *Web:* www.pheaa.org

Scholarship America
One Scholarship Way PO Box 297 .... Saint Peter MN 56082 507-931-1682 931-9168
TF: 800-537-4180 ■ *Web:* www.scholarshipamerica.org

South Carolina Higher Education Tuition Grants Commission
115 Atrium Wy Ste 102 .... Columbia SC 29203 803-896-1120 896-1126
TF: 877-382-4357 ■ *Web:* www.sctuitiongrants.com

Tennessee Student Assistance Corp
404 James Robertson Pkwy Ste 1510 .... Nashville TN 37243 615-741-1346 741-6101
Web: www.state.tn.us/tsac

Tennessee Treasurer
Tennessee State Capitol
1st Fl 600 Charlotte Ave .... Nashville TN 37243 615-741-2956
Web: www.treasury.state.tn.us

Texas Higher Education Coordinating Board
1200 E Anderson Ln .... Austin TX 78752 512-427-6101 427-6169
Web: www.thecb.state.tx.us

Thurgood Marshall Scholarship Fund
80 Maiden Ln Ste 2204 .... New York NY 10038 212-573-8888 573-8497
TF: 866-632-9992 ■ *Web:* www.thurgoodmarshallfund.net

Utah Higher Education Assistance Authority
PO Box 145112 .... Salt Lake City UT 84114 801-321-7294 366-8431
TF: 877-336-7378 ■ *Web:* www.uheaa.org

Vermont Student Assistance Corp (VSAC)
PO Box 2000 .... Winooski VT 05404 802-655-9602 654-3765
TF: 800-642-3177 ■ *Web:* www.vsac.org

Virginia College Savings Plan
9001 Arboretum Pkwy PO Box 607 .... Richmond VA 23236 804-786-0719
TF: 888-567-0540 ■ *Web:* www.virginia529.com

Virginia State Council of Higher Education
101 N 14th St 9th Fl .... Richmond VA 23219 804-225-2600 225-2604
Web: www.schev.edu

Washington Higher Education Coordinating Board
917 Lakeridge Way PO Box 43430 .... Olympia WA 98504 360-753-7800 753-7808
Web: www.wsac.wa.gov

West Virginia Higher Education Policy Commission
1018 Kanawha Blvd E Ste 700 .... Charleston WV 25301 304-558-2101
TF: 888-825-5707 ■ *Web:* wvhepc.com

Wisconsin Higher Educational Aids Board (HEAB)
131 W Wilson S PO Box 7885 .... Madison WI 53707 608-267-2206 267-2808
Web: www.heab.state.wi.us

Wyoming Community College Commission
2300 Capitol Ave Fl 5 Ste B .... Cheyenne WY 82002 307-777-7763 777-6567
Web: communitycolleges.wy.edu

729 SUBSTANCE ABUSE TREATMENT CENTERS

SEE ALSO General Hospitals - Canada p. 2490; General Hospitals - US p. 2492; Psychiatric Hospitals p. 2519; Self-Help Organizations p. 1784

Phone Fax

AdCare Hospital of Worcester
107 Lincoln St .... Worcester MA 01605 508-799-9000 753-3733
TF: 800-252-6465 ■ *Web:* www.adcare.com

Aletheia House 201 Finley Ave W .... Birmingham AL 35204 205-324-6502
Web: specialkindofcaring.org

Phone | Fax

Anchor Hospital 5454 Yorktowne Dr, Atlanta GA 30349 770-991-6044 991-3843
Web: www.anchorhospital.com

Anthony Louis Ctr 115 Forestview Ln, Plymouth MN 55441 763-542-9212 542-9248
Web: www.anthonylouiscenter.com

Apex Behavioral Health Western Wayne PLLC
1547 S Wayne Rd, Westland MI 48186 734-729-3133
Web: www.apexbehavioralhealth.com

Applewood Centers Inc 2525 E 22nd St, Cleveland OH 44115 216-696-5800
Web: www.applewoodcenters.org

APT Foundation One Long Wharf Dr Ste 321, New Haven CT 06511 203-781-4600
Web: aptfoundation.org

AREBA Casriel Inc (ACI) 500 W 57th St, New York NY 10019 212-293-3000 293-3020
TF: 800-724-4444 ■ *Web:* www.acirehab.org

Arizona Foundation for the Handicapped
3146 E Windsor Ave, Phoenix AZ 85008 602-956-0400
Web: www.azafh.com

Arms Acres 75 Seminary Hill Rd, Carmel NY 10512 845-225-3400
TF: 800-989-2676 ■ *Web:* www.armsacres.com

Baker Places Inc
1000 Brannan St Ste 401, San Francisco CA 94103 415-864-4655
Web: www.bakerplaces.org

Baltimore Behavioral Health (BBH)
1101 W Pratt St, Baltimore MD 21223 410-962-7180 962-7194
TF: 800-789-2647 ■ *Web:* baltimorecity.md.networkofcare.org

Betty Ford Ctr 39000 Bob Hope Dr, Rancho Mirage CA 92270 760-773-4100 773-4126
TF: 800-854-9211 ■ *Web:* www.bettyfordcenter.org

Blue Hills Hospital 500 Vine St, Hartford CT 06112 860-293-6400 293-6470
Web: www.ct.gov

Bradford Health Services
2101 Magnolia Ave S Ste 518, Birmingham AL 35205 205-251-7753 251-7760
TF: 800-217-2849 ■ *Web:* www.bradfordhealth.com

Brighton Hospital 12851 E Grand River Ave, Brighton MI 48116 810-227-1211 227-1869
TF Cust Svc: 800-523-8198 ■ *Web:* www.brightonhospital.org

CenterPointe Inc 2633 P St, Lincoln NE 68503 402-475-8717
Web: www.centerpointe.org

Central Street Health Ctr 26 Central St, Somerville MA 02143 617-591-6033 591-6452
TF: 800-909-2677 ■ *Web:* www.challiance.org

Child Guidance Resource Centers
2000 Old W Chester Pk, Havertown PA 19083 484-454-8700
Web: www.cgrc.org

Circle Family Care 3919 N Albany Ave, Chicago IL 60618 773-478-4747
Web: www.circlefamilycare.org

Clear Brook Lodge 890 Bethel Hill Rd, Shickshinny PA 18655 570-864-3116

Clear Brook Manor 1100 E Northampton St, Laurel Run PA 18706 800-582-6241 823-1582*
**Fax Area Code:* 570 ■ *TF:* 800-582-6241 ■ *Web:* clearbrookinc.com

Coleman Professional Services 24 7 Emergency C
3920 Lovers Ln, Ravenna OH 44266 330-296-3555
Web: www.colemanservices.org

Columbia Community Mental Health
58646 McNulty Way, Saint Helens OR 97051 503-397-5211
Web: www.ccmh1.com

COMHAR Inc 100 W Lehigh Ave, Philadelphia PA 19133 215-203-3000
Web: comhar.org

Community Partnership of The Ozarks Inc
330 N Jefferson Ave Ste A, Springfield MO 65806 417-888-2020
Web: www.commpartnership.org

Conifer Park 79 Glenridge Rd, Schenectady NY 12302 518-399-6446 952-8228
TF: 800-989-6446 ■ *Web:* www.coniferpark.com

Copper Country Mental Healths Services
901 Memorial Rd, Houghton MI 49931 906-482-9400
Web: cccmh.org

Cornerstone Medical Arts Ctr Hospital
159-05 Union Tpke, Fresh Meadows NY 11366 718-906-6700 906-6840
TF: 800-233-9999 ■ *Web:* www.cornerstoneny.com

Daymark Recovery Services Inc Stanly Center
1000 N First St Ste 1, Albemarle NC 28001 704-983-2117
Web: www.daymarkrecovery.org

Dayton Rehabilitation Institute
One Elizabeth Pl, Dayton OH 45417 937-424-8200
Web: reliantdayton.com

Detroit Central City Community Mental Health Inc
10 Peterboro St, Detroit MI 48201 313-831-3160
Web: www.dcccmh.org

Eagleville Hospital 100 Eagleville Rd, Eagleville PA 19408 610-539-6000 539-6249
TF General: 800-255-2019 ■ *Web:* www.eaglevillehospital.org

El Rincon Community Clinic 3809 W Grand Ave, Chicago IL 60651 773-276-0200
Web: elrinconclinic.org

Fairbanks Hospital 8102 Clearvista Pkwy, Indianapolis IN 46256 317-849-8222 849-8222
TF: 800-225-4673 ■ *Web:* fairbankscd.org

Family Behavioral Resources Inc
400 Oakbrook Dr Oakbrook Commons Ste 2300
PO Box 879, Greensburg PA 15601 724-850-8118
Web: www.familybehavioralresources.com

Family Guidance Center of Warren County Inc
492 Route 57 W, Washington NJ 07882 908-689-1000
Web: www.familyguidancecenterofwc.info

Fellowship Hall Inc 5140 Dunstan Rd, Greensboro NC 27405 336-621-3381 621-7513
TF: 800-659-3381 ■ *Web:* www.fellowshiphall.com

Florida Ctr for Addictions & Dual Disorders
100 W College Dr, Avon Park FL 33825 863-452-3858 452-3863
Web: tchsonline.org/

Fountain House Inc 425 W 47th St, New York NY 10036 212-582-0340
Web: www.fountainhouse.org

Friary of Lakeview Ctr, The
4400 Hickory Shores Blvd, Gulf Breeze FL 32563 850-932-9375 934-1281
TF: 800-332-2271 ■ *Web:* www.thefriary.org

Gateway Foundation Inc 1080 E Pk St, Carbondale IL 62901 877-505-4673
TF: 877-505-4673 ■ *Web:* www.recovergateway.org

Gaudenzia 106 W Main St, Norristown PA 19401 610-239-9600 239-9195
Web: www.gaudenzia.org

Glenbeigh Health Source 2863 SR 45, Rock Creek OH 44084 440-563-3400 563-9619
TF: 800-234-1001 ■ *Web:* www.glenbeigh.com

Grand Lake Mental Health Center Inc
114 W Delaware, Nowata OK 74048 918-273-1841
Web: www.glmhc.net

Greenleaf Ctr 2209 Pineview Dr, Valdosta GA 31602 229-671-6700 242-1252
TF: 800-247-2747 ■ *Web:* www.greenleafcounseling.net

Griffin Memorial Hospital 900 E Main St, Norman OK 73071 405-321-4880
TF General: 800-955-3468 ■ *Web:* ok.gov

Gulf Coast Mental Health Center
1600 Broad Ave, Gulfport MS 39501 228-863-1132
Web: www.gcmhc.com

Hamm Memorial Psychiatric Clnc
408 Saint Peter St Ste 429, Saint Paul MN 55102 651-224-0614
Web: www.hammclinic.org

Hampton Behavioral Health Center
650 Rancocas Rd, Westampton NJ 08060 800-603-6767
TF: 800-603-6767 ■ *Web:* hamptonhospital.com

Harmony Foundation Inc
1600 Fish Hatchery Rd, Estes Park CO 80517 970-586-4491
Web: www.harmonyfoundationinc.com

Hathaway-Sycamores Child & Family Services
210 S DeLacey Ave Ste 110, Pasadena CA 91105 626-395-7100
Web: www.hathaway-sycamores.org

Hazelden Chicago 867 N Dearborn St, Chicago IL 60610 312-943-3534 943-3530
TF: 800-257-7810 ■ *Web:* www.hazelden.org

Hazelden Ctr for Youth & Families (HCYF)
11505 36th Ave N, Plymouth MN 55441 763-509-3800 559-0149
TF: 800-257-7810 ■ *Web:* www.hazelden.org

Hazelden Foundation
15251 Pleasant Vly Rd, Center City MN 55012 651-213-4200 213-4411
TF: 800-257-7810 ■ *Web:* www.hazelden.org

Hazelden New York 322 Eigth Ave 12th Fl, New York NY 10001 212-420-9520 420-9664
TF: 800-257-7800 ■ *Web:* www.hazelden.org

Hazelden Springbrook 1901 Esther St, Newberg OR 97132 503-554-4300 537-7007
TF: 866-866-4662 ■ *Web:* www.hazelden.org

HealthSource Saginaw 3340 Hospital Rd, Saginaw MI 48603 989-790-7700 790-9297
TF: 800-662-6848 ■ *Web:* www.healthsourcesaginaw.org

Highland Ridge Hospital 7309 South 180 West, Midvale UT 84047 801-569-2153 567-9006
Web: www.highlandridgehospital.com

Horizon Human Services Inc
210 E Cottonwood Ln, Casa Grande AZ 85122 520-836-1688
Web: www.horizonhumanservices.org

Impact Drug & Alcohol Treatment Ctr
1680 N Fair Oaks Ave PO Box 93607, Pasadena CA 91103 626-798-0884 798-6970
TF: 866-734-4200 ■ *Web:* www.impacthouse.com

Indian Creek Foundation 420 Cowpath Rd, Souderton PA 18964 267-203-1500
Web: www.indiancreekindustries.com

Judson Center Inc 4410 W 13 Mile Rd, Royal Oak MI 48073 248-549-4339
Web: www.judsoncenter.org

Julian F Keith Alcohol & Drug Abuse Treatment Ctr
201 Tabernacle Rd, Black Mountain NC 28711 828-257-6200 257-6300

Keystone Ctr 2001 Providence Ave, Chester PA 19013 610-876-9000 876-5441
TF: 800-558-9600 ■ *Web:* www.keystonecenter.net

La Hacienda Treatment Ctr 145 La Hacienda Way, Hunt TX 78024 830-238-4222 238-3120
TF: 800-749-6160 ■ *Web:* www.lahacienda.com

Lester A. Drenk Behavioral Health Center, The
1289 Route 38 W Ste 203, Hainesport NJ 08036 609-267-5656
Web: www.drenk.org

Lifetime Recovery 10290 Southton Rd, San Antonio TX 78223 210-633-0201
Web: www.lifetimerecoverytx.org

Livengrin Foundation 4833 Hulmeville Rd, Bensalem PA 19020 215-638-5200 638-2603
TF: 800-245-4746 ■ *Web:* www.livengrin.org

Malvern Institute 940 W King Rd, Malvern PA 19355 610-647-0330 647-2572
TF: 888-643-3869 ■ *Web:* www.malverninstitute.com

Mental Health Center of North Iowa
235 S Eisenhower Ave, Mason City IA 50401 641-424-2075
Web: www.mhconi.org

Miami Valley Family Care Center
922 W Riverview Ave, Dayton OH 45402 937-223-7217
Web: www.cssmv.org

Missouri Home Therapy
9191 W Florissant Ave Ste 200, Saint Louis MO 63136 314-524-3958
Web: www.missourihometherapy.com

Mohave Mental Health Clinic Inc
3505 Western Ave, Kingman AZ 86409 928-757-8111
Web: www.mmhc-inc.org

Momentum For Mental Health 438 N White Rd, San Jose CA 95127 408-254-6828
Web: www.momentumformentalhealth.org

Monadnock Family Services 64 Main St Ste 201, Keene NH 03431 603-357-4400
Web: www.mfs.org

Mount Regis Ctr 405 Kimball Ave, Salem VA 24153 877-217-3447 389-6539*
**Fax Area Code:* 540 ■ *TF:* 877-217-3447 ■ *Web:* www.mtregis.com

Mountain Manor Treatment Ctr
9701 Keysville Rd, Emmitsburg MD 21727 301-447-2361
TF: 800-537-3422 ■ *Web:* www.mountainmanor.org

New Directions Inc 30800 Chagrin Blvd, Cleveland OH 44124 216-591-0324 591-1243
TF: 800-750-6709 ■ *Web:* www.newdirect.org

Nicasa 31979 N Fish Lk Rd, Round Lake IL 60073 847-546-6450
Web: www.nicasa.org

Nordoff-robbins Music Therapy Clinic
26 Washington Pl, New York NY 10003 212-998-5151
Web: steinhardt.nyu.edu

North Oklahoma County Mental Health Center
4436 NW 50th St, Oklahoma City OK 73112 405-858-2700
Web: www.northcare.com

Northeast Guidance Center 2900 Conner Bldg A, Detroit MI 48215 313-308-1400
Web: www.neguidance.org

Nulton Diagnostic & Treatment Center PC
214 College Park, Johnstown PA 15904 814-262-0025
Web: www.nulton.com

Oaklawn Psychiatric Center Inc
330 Lakeview Dr, Goshen IN 46527 574-533-1234
Web: www.oaklawn.org

Phone Fax

Oesterlen-services for Youth Inc
1918 Mechanicsburg Rd. Springfield OH 45503 937-399-6101
Web: oesterlen.org

OnTrack Inc 221 W Main St Medford OR 97501 541-772-1777
Web: www.ontrackrecovery.org

Oriana House Inc 885 E Buchtel Ave Akron OH 44305 330-535-8116
Web: www.orianahouse.org

Osceola Mental Health Inc 206 Park Pl Blvd Kissimmee FL 34741 407-846-0023
Web: www.ppbh.org

Ozark Guidance Center Inc 2400 S 48th St Springdale AR 72762 479-750-2020
Web: www.ozarkguidance.org

Palmetto Lowcountry Behavioral Health LLC
2777 Speissegger Dr North Charleston SC 29405 843-747-5830
Web: palmettobehavioralhealth.com

Park Center Inc 909 E State Blvd Fort Wayne IN 46805 260-481-2700
Web: www.parkcenter.org

Peak Wellness Center 1263 N 15th St Laramie WY 82072 307-745-8915
Web: www.peakwellnesscenter.org

Perception Programs Inc 54 N St Willimantic CT 06226 860-450-7122
Web: perceptionprograms.org

Phoenix House Foundation Inc (PHF)
164 W 74th St 4th Fl New York NY 10023 888-671-9392 595-6365*
**Fax Area Code:* 212 ■ *TF:* 800-378-4435 ■ *Web:* www.phoenixhouse.org

Prestera Center for Mental Health Services Inc
3375 Us Route 60 Huntington WV 25705 304-525-7851
Web: www.prestera.org

Progress Unlimited Inc
11431 Cronhill Dr Ste C Owings Mills MD 21117 410-363-8550
Web: www.progressunlimited.org

Prototypes 1000 N Alameda St Ste 390 Los Angeles CA 90012 213-542-3838
Web: www.prototypes.org

Providence Behavioral Health Hospital
1233 Main St Holyoke MA 01040 413-536-5111 786-3059
TF: 800-274-7724 ■ *Web:* www.mercycares.com

Reconnect Mental Health Services
2150 Islington Ave Etobicoke ON M9P3V4 416-248-2050
Web: www.reconnect.on.ca

Ridgeview Institute Inc 3995 S Cobb Dr Smyrna GA 30080 770-434-4567
Web: www.ridgeviewinstitute.con

Rimrock Foundation 1231 N 29th St Billings MT 59101 406-248-3175 248-3821
TF: 800-227-3953 ■ *Web:* www.rimrock.org

Riverside General Hospital (RGH)
Houston Recovery Ctr 4514 Lyons Ave Houston TX 77020 713-331-2501
Web: riversidegeneralhospital.org

Rivervalley Behavioral Health Hospital
1000 Industrial Dr. Owensboro KY 42301 270-689-6800 689-6799
TF: 800-755-8477 ■ *Web:* www.rvbh.com

Riverwood Center 1485 M 139 Benton Harbor MI 49022 269-925-0585
Web: riverwoodcenter.org

Rutland Mental Health Services Inc
78 S Main St Rutland VT 05701 802-775-2381
Web: www.rmhsccn.org

Safety Council of The Ozarks
1111 S Glenstone Ave Ste 1-103 Springfield MO 65804 417-869-2121
Web: nscozarks.org

Samaritan Village 138-02 Queens Blvd Briarwood NY 11435 718-206-2000 206-2399
TF: 800-532-4357 ■ *Web:* samaritanvillage.org

Schick Shadel Hospital 12101 Ambaum Blvd SW Seattle WA 98146 800-500-6395 431-9142*
**Fax Area Code:* 206 ■ *TF:* 800-500-6395 ■ *Web:* schickshadel.com

Senior World 719 N Kumpf Blvd Peoria IL 61601 309-495-4530
Web: ipmr.org

Serenity Lane 616 E 16th Ave Eugene OR 97401 541-687-1110 687-9041
TF: 800-543-9905 ■ *Web:* www.serenitylane.org

Sierra Tucson Inc 39580 S Lago Del Oro Pkwy Tucson AZ 85739 520-624-4000 818-5869
TF: 800-842-4487 ■ *Web:* sierratucson.crchealth.com

Spectrum Programs Inc 11031 NE Sixth Ave Miami FL 33161 305-757-0602 757-2387

Spencer Recovery Centers Inc
1316 S Coast Hwy Laguna Beach CA 92651 800-334-0394 376-6862*
**Fax Area Code:* 949 ■ *TF:* 800-334-0394 ■ *Web:* www.spencerrecovery.com

Substance Abuse Foundation
3125 E Seventh St Long Beach CA 90804 562-987-5722 438-6891
TF: 888-476-2743 ■ *Web:* www.safinc.org

Talbott Recovery Campus 5448 Yorktowne Dr Atlanta GA 30349 770-994-0185 994-2024
TF: 800-445-4232 ■ *Web:* www.talbottcampus.com

Turning Point Hospital
3015 Veterans Pkwy PO Box 1177 Moultrie GA 31776 229-985-4815 890-1614
TF: 800-342-1075 ■ *Web:* www.turningpointcare.com

Turning Point of Tampa 6227 Sheldon Rd Tampa FL 33615 813-882-3003 885-6974
TF: 800-397-3006 ■ *Web:* rehabisforquitters.com

Twin Town Treatment Ctr
1706 University Ave Saint Paul MN 55104 651-645-3661 645-0959
Web: meridianprograms.com

Upper Bay Counseling & Support Services Inc
200 Booth St Elkton MD 21921 410-996-5104
Web: www.upperbay.org

Valley Forge Medical Ctr & Hospital
1033 W Germantown Pk Norristown PA 19403 610-539-8500 539-0910
TF: 888-539-8500 ■ *Web:* www.vfmc.net

Villa of Hope 3300 Dewey Ave Rochester NY 14616 585-865-1550 865-5219
Web: www.villaofhope.org

Village South Inc 3050 Biscayne Blvd 9th Fl Miami FL 33137 305-573-3784 576-1348
TF: 800-443-3784 ■ *Web:* www.villagesouth.com

Wake County Alcoholism Treatment Ctr
3000 Falstaff Rd Raleigh NC 27610 919-250-1500
Web: www.wakegov.com

Walter B Jones Alcohol & Drug Abuse Treatment Ctr
2577 W Fifth St Greenville NC 27834 252-830-3426 830-8585
TF: 800-422-1884 ■ *Web:* ncdhhs.gov

Warwick Manor Behavioral Health
3680 Warwick Rd East New Market MD 21631 410-943-8108
Web: www.warwickmanor.org

Willingway Hospital 311 Jones Mill Rd Statesboro GA 30458 912-764-6236 764-7063
TF: 800-242-9455 ■ *Web:* www.willingway.com

Wilmington Treatment Ctr 2520 Troy Dr Wilmington NC 28401 910-762-2727 762-7923
TF: 877-762-3750 ■ *Web:* wilmingtontreatmentcenter.crchealth.com

Youth Home Inc 20400 Colonel Glenn Rd Little Rock AR 72210 501-821-5500
Web: www.youthhome.org

730 SURVEYING, MAPPING, RELATED SERVICES

SEE ALSO Engineering & Design p. 2256

Phone Fax

AD Potts & Assoc Inc
11524 Jefferson Ave Newport News VA 23601 757-595-4610

Aerotech Mapping Inc 2580 Montessouri St Las Vegas NV 89117 702-228-6277
Web: www.atmlv.com

Allen & Major Associates Inc 100 Commerce Way Woburn MA 01888 781-935-6889
Web: www.allenmajor.com

Atzl Scatassa & Zigler Land Surveyors & Engineers PC
234 N Main St New City NY 10956 845-634-4694

Austin Exploration Inc 10333 Westoffice Dr Houston TX 77042 713-780-7141 780-3118
Web: austinex.com

B H Suhr & Company Inc 840 Custer Evanston IL 60202 847-864-6315
Web: bhsuhr.com

Bock & Clark Corp 3550 W Market St Ste 200 Akron OH 44333 330-665-4821
Web: www.bockandclark.com

Bowman Consulting Group
14020 Thunderbolt Pl # 300 Chantilly VA 20151 703-464-1000 481-8410
Web: www.bowmanconsulting.com

Brill J Michael & Associates
5053 Ritter Rd Ste 200 Mechanicsburg PA 17055 717-691-0200
Web: www.jmichaelbrill.com

Chastain Homer L & Associates LLP
Five N Country Club Rd Decatur IL 62521 217-422-8544
Web: hlcllp.com

Coast Surveying Inc 15031 Pkwy Loop Ste B Tustin CA 92780 714-918-6266
Web: coastsurvey.com

Cochrane Technologies Inc PO Box 81276 Lafayette LA 70598 337-837-3334 837-7134
TF: 800-346-3745 ■ *Web:* www.cochranetech.com

Cooper Aerial Survey Co 1692 W Grant Rd Tucson AZ 85745 520-884-7580
Web: cooperaerial.com

Core Design Inc 14711 NE 29th Pl Ste 101 Bellevue WA 98007 425-885-7877
Web: www.coredesigninc.com

D W Smith Associates LLC
149 Yellowbrook Rd Ste 101 Farmingdale NJ 07727 732-363-5850
Web: www.dwsmith.com

Day & Zimmermann Group Inc
1818 Market St Philadelphia PA 19130 215-299-8000
TF: 877-319-0270 ■ *Web:* www.dayzim.com

Doyle & Wachtstetter Inc 131 Commerce St Clute TX 77531 979-265-3622
Web: www.dw-surveyor.com

Fugro Chance Inc 6100 Hillcroft St Ste 300 Houston TX 77081 713-346-3700 346-3671
Web: www.fugrochance.com

Fugro Pelagos Inc 3574 Ruffin Rd San Diego CA 92123 858-292-8922 292-5308
Web: www.fugro-pelagos.com

Gabriel E Senor PC 90 N Central Ave Hartsdale NY 10530 914-422-0070

Geodetic Designs 2300 N Grand River Ave Lansing MI 48906 517-908-0008
Web: geodeticdesigns.com

Geokinetics Management Inc
1500 Citywest Blvd Ste 800 Houston TX 77042 713-850-7600
Web: www.geokinetics.com

Geophysics GPR International Inc
2545 Delorimier Longueuil QC J4K3P7 450-679-2400
Web: www.geophysicsgpr.com

GeoStrata Resources Inc 9727 Horton Rd SW Calgary AB T2V2X5 403-319-0922
Web: www.geostrata.ca

Geotech Ltd 245 Industrial Pkwy N Aurora ON L4G4C4 905-841-5004
Web: www.geotech.ca

Ghiotto & Assoc Inc 2426 Phillips Hwy Jacksonville FL 32207 904-886-0071
Web: www.ghiotto.com

Greene & Bradford Inc
3501 Constitution Dr Springfield IL 62711 217-793-8844
Web: greeneandbradford.com

Ground Penetrating Radar Systems Inc
7540 New West Rd Ste E1 Toledo OH 43617 419-843-9804
Web: www.gp-radar.com

GX Technology Corp 2105 CityWest Blvd Ste 900 Houston TX 77042 713-789-7250
Web: www.iongeo.com

Gymo, Architecture, Engineering & Land Surveying PC
220 Sterling St Watertown NY 13601 315-788-3900
Web: www.gymopc.com

H2 Engineering Surveying LLC 8880 N Hess St Hayden ID 83835 208-772-6600
Web: h2survey.com

HadenStanziale PA 2200 W Main St Ste 560 Durham NC 27705 919-286-7440
Web: www.hadenstanziale.com

Hagedorn Inc 1924 Broadway St Ste B Vancouver WA 98663 360-696-4428

Hanover Design Services PA
1123 Floral Pkwy Wilmington NC 28403 910-343-8002

Hillwig-Goodrow Inc 31407 Outer Hwy 10 Redland CA 92373 909-794-2673
Web: hillwig-goodrow.com

HMA Land Services Ltd
7710 - Fifth St SE Ste 100 Calgary AB T2H2L9 403-692-0850
Web: www.hmaland.com

HRG Pllc 416 W Third St Owensboro KY 42301 270-683-7558
Web: hrgpllc.com

Huitt-Zollars Inc 1717 McKinney Ave Ste 1400 Dallas TX 75202 214-871-3311 871-0757
TF: 866-667-6572 ■ *Web:* www.huitt-zollars.com

Ingersoll Watson & Mcmachen Inc
1133 E Milham Rd Portage MI 49002 269-344-6165
Web: iwmeng.com

Inland Aerial Surveys Inc
7117 Arlington Ave Ste A Riverside CA 92503 951-687-4252
Web: inlandaerial.com

Company	City	State	Zip	Phone	Fax
Intermap Technologies Inc 8310 S Vly Hwy Ste 400 *Web:* www.intermap.com	Englewood	CO	80112	303-708-0955	
Joseph A. Schudt & Associates Inc 19350 S Harlem Ave *Web:* www.jaseng.com	Frankfort	IL	60423	708-720-1000	
JSD Professional Services Inc 161 Horizon Dr Ste 101 *Web:* www.jsdinc.com	Verona	WI	53593	608-848-5060	
KCI Technologies Inc 936 Ridgebrook Rd *TF:* 800-572-7496 ■ *Web:* kci.com	Sparks	MD	21152	410-316-7800	316-7817
Keystone Aerial Surveys Inc 9800 Ashton Rd *Web:* www.keystoneaerialsurveys.com	Philadelphia	PA	19114	215-677-3119	
Lamp, Rynearson & Associates Inc 14710 W Dodge Rd Ste 100 *Web:* www.lra-inc.com	Omaha	NE	68154	402-496-2498	
Landiscor 7310 N 16th St Ste 275 *TF:* 866-221-8578 ■ *Web:* www.landiscor.com	Phoenix	AZ	85020	602-248-8989	266-8116
Landpoint Surveys Inc 611 El Dorado Rd *Web:* www.landpoint.net	Magnolia	AR	71753	870-234-6384	
Lewis Yockey & Brown Inc 505 N Main St *Web:* www.lybinc.com	Bloomington	IL	61701	309-829-2552	
Loureiro Engineering Associates 100 Northwest Dr *Web:* www.loureiro.com	Plainville	CT	06062	860-747-6181	
MacDonald Dettwiler & Assoc Ltd 13800 Commerce Pkwy *TSE: MDA* ■ *Web:* www.mdacorporation.com	Richmond	BC	V6V2J3	604-278-3411	231-2768
Mackie Consultants LLC 9575 W Higgins Rd Ste 500 *Web:* www.mackieconsult.com	Rosemont	IL	60018	847-696-1400	
Northeast Civil Solutions Inc 381 Payne Rd *Web:* www.northeastcivilsolutions.com	Scarborough	ME	04074	207-883-1000	883-1001
NuTech Energy Alliance Ltd 7702 FM 1960 E Ste 300 *Web:* www.nutechenergy.com	Houston	TX	77346	281-812-4030	
Poepping Stone Bach & Assoc Inc Engr 100 S 54th St *Web:* psba.com	Quincy	IL	62305	217-223-4605	
Print-O-Stat Inc 1011 W Market St *TF:* 800-711-8014 ■ *Web:* www.printostat.com	York	PA	17404	717-854-7821	846-4084
Quantapoint Inc 275 Curry Hollow Rd *Web:* www.quantapoint.com	Pittsburgh	PA	15236	412-653-0100	653-2940
Quantec Geoscience Ltd 146 Sparks Ave *Web:* www.quantecgeoscience.com	Toronto	ON	M2H2S4	416-306-1941	
R e Warner & Associates Inc 25777 Detroit Rd Ste 200 *Web:* www.rewarner.com	Westlake	OH	44145	440-835-9400	
R&M Consultants Inc 9101 Vanguard Dr *Web:* www.rmconsult.com	Anchorage	AK	99507	907-522-1707	
Ramsey Land Surveying LLC 8718 SW Pkwy	Austin	TX	78735	512-301-9398	
Raudenbush Engineering Inc 29 S Union St *Web:* raudeng.com	Middletown	PA	17057	717-944-0883	
Rice Assoc Inc 10625 Gaskins Way *Web:* ricesurveys.com	Manassas	VA	20109	703-968-3200	
Rouse-sirine Associates Ltd 333 Office Sq Ln Ste 100 *Web:* www.rouse-sirine.com	Virginia Beach	VA	23462	757-490-2308	
Sidwell Co Inc 675 Sidwell Ct *TF:* 877-743-9355 ■ *Web:* www.sidwellco.com	Saint Charles	IL	60174	630-549-1000	549-1111
Surdex Corp 520 Spirit of St Louis Blvd *Web:* www.surdex.com	Chesterfield	MO	63005	636-368-4400	
Surveying Services Inc 41 Heritage Sq	Jackson	TN	38305	731-664-0807	
T3 Global Strategies Inc 10 Emerson Ln Ste 808	Bridgeville	PA	15017	412-221-2003	
Teletrac Inc 7391 Lincoln Way *TF:* 800-500-6009 ■ *Web:* www.teletrac.com	Garden Grove	CA	92841	714-897-0877	379-6378
Terra Remote Sensing Inc 1962 Mills Rd *Web:* www.terraremote.com	Sidney	BC	V8L5Y3	250-656-0931	
Tim Miller Assoc Inc 10 N St *Web:* timmillerassociates.com	Cold Spring	NY	10516	845-265-4400	
Wade-Trim Group Inc 500 Griswold Ave Ste 2500 *TF:* 800-482-2864 ■ *Web:* www.wadetrim.com	Detroit	MI	48226	313-961-3650	961-0898
XNR Productions Inc 931 E Main St Ste 24 *Web:* xnrproductions.com	Madison	WI	53703	608-663-4600	

731 SWIMMING POOLS

Company	City	State	Zip	Phone	Fax
Anthony & Sylvan Pools Corp 3739 Easton Rd Rt 611 *TF:* 800-366-7958 ■ *Web:* www.anthonysylvan.com	Doylestown	PA	18901	215-489-5600	489-5610
Delair Group LLC 8600 River Rd *TF:* 800-235-0185 ■ *Web:* jerith.com/delgard/	Delair	NJ	08110	800-235-0185	
Fox Pool Corp 3490 BoaRd Rd *TF:* 800-723-1011 ■ *Web:* www.foxpool.com	York	PA	17406	717-764-8581	764-4293
Gary Pools Inc 438 Sandau Rd *Web:* www.garypools.com	San Antonio	TX	78216	210-341-5153	341-5154
Hoffinger Industries Inc 315 Sebastian St	West Helena	AR	72390	870-572-3466	572-9711
Hornerxpress Inc 5755 Powerline Rd *TF:* 800-432-6966 ■ *Web:* www.hornerxpress.com	Fort Lauderdale	FL	33309	954-772-6966	772-6970
Imperial Pools Inc 33 Wade Rd *TF:* 800-444-9977 ■ *Web:* www.imperialpoolsb2b.com	Latham	NY	12110	518-786-1200	786-0954
Mission Pools of Escondido 755 W Grand Ave *Web:* www.missionpools.com	Escondido	CA	92025	760-743-2605	743-0384
Morgan Bldg Systems Inc 2800 McCree Rd *TF:* 800-935-0321 ■ *Web:* www.morganusa.com	Garland	TX	75041	972-864-7300	864-7307
Radiant Pools Div Trojan Leisure Products LLC 440 N Pearl St *TF:* 866-697-5870 ■ *Web:* www.radiantpools.com	Albany	NY	12207	518-434-4161	432-6554
Viking Pools Inc 121 Crawford Rd PO Box 96 *TF:* 800-854-7665 ■ *Web:* www.vikingpools.net	Williams	CA	95987	530-473-5319	473-5393
Vogue Pool Products 7050 St Patrick St *TF:* 800-363-3232 ■ *Web:* www.piscinesvogue.com	LaSalle	QC	H8N1V2	514-363-3232	363-1772

732 SWITCHGEAR & SWITCHBOARD APPARATUS

SEE ALSO Transformers - Power, Distribution, Specialty p. 3248; Wiring Devices - Current-Carrying p. 3298

Company	City	State	Zip	Phone	Fax
Acorn Technology 23103 Miles Rd *Web:* www.acorntechnology.com	Cleveland	OH	44128	216-663-1244	
Actelis Networks Inc 6150 Stevenson Blvd *Web:* www.actelis.com	Fremont	CA	94538	510-545-1045	
Atkinson Industries Inc 1801 E 27th St Terr *Web:* www.azz.com	Pittsburg	KS	66762	620-231-6900	231-7154
AudioCodes Inc 27 World'S Fair Dr *Web:* audiocodes.com	Somerset	NJ	08873	732-469-0880	
AZZ Inc 3100 W Seventh St Ste 500 *Web:* www.azz.com	Fort Worth	TX	76107	817-810-0095	336-5354
Bel Fuse Inc 206 Van Vorst St *NASDAQ: BELFA* ■ *TF:* 800-235-3873 ■ *Web:* www.belfuse.com	Jersey City	NJ	07302	201-432-0463	432-9542
Cleaveland Price Inc 14000 Rt 993 *Web:* www.cleavelandprice.com	Trafford	PA	15085	724-864-4177	
Cole Instrument Corp 2650 S Croddy Way **Fax:* Sales ■ *Web:* www.cole-switches.com	Santa Ana	CA	92704	714-556-3100	241-9061*
Components Corp of America 5950 Berkshire Ln # 1550 *Web:* www.components-corp-amer.com	Dallas	TX	75225	214-969-0166	969-5905
Comus International Inc 454 Allwood Rd *Web:* www.comus-intl.com	Clifton	NJ	07012	973-777-6900	
Custom Control Solutions Inc 8500 Fowler Ave *Web:* www.ccsinc-florida.com	Pensacola	FL	32534	850-473-8704	
CW Industries 130 James Way *Web:* www.cwind.com	SouthHampton	PA	18966	215-355-7080	355-1088
Delta Systems Inc 1734 Frost Rd *Web:* phoenixtechnologyit.com/	Streetsboro	OH	44241	330-626-2811	
Electroswitch Corp 180 King Ave *Web:* www.electroswitch.com	Weymouth	MA	02188	781-335-5200	335-4253
FIC Corp 12216 Parklawn Dr *Web:* www.ficcorp.com	Rockville	MD	20852	301-881-8124	
Grayhill Inc 561 W Hillgrove Ave *Web:* www.grayhill.com	La Grange	IL	60525	708-354-1040	354-2820
Guardian Electric Mfg Company Inc 1425 Lake Ave *TF:* 800-762-0369 ■ *Web:* www.guardian-electric.com	Woodstock	IL	60098	815-334-3600	337-0377
HVB AE Power Systems Inc 7250 Mcginnis Ferry Rd *TF:* 866-362-0798 ■ *Web:* hvbi.hitachi.us	Suwanee	GA	30024	770-495-1755	
Indak Manufacturing Corp 1915 Techny Rd *Web:* www.indak.com	Northbrook	IL	60062	847-272-0343	272-0697
Indicon Corp 6417 Center Dr Ste 110 *Web:* www.indicon.com	Sterling Heights	MI	48312	586-274-0505	
Inertia Engineering 6665 Hardaway Rd *Web:* www.inertiaworks.com	Stockton	CA	95215	209-931-1670	
Instruments Inc 7263 Engineer Rd Ste G *Web:* www.instrumentsinc.com	San Diego	CA	92111	858-571-1111	571-0188
ITW Switches 2550 Mill Brook Dr *TF:* 800-544-3354 ■ *Web:* www.itwswitches.com	Buffalo Grove	IL	60089	847-876-9400	876-9440
JMS North America Corp 22320 Foothill Blvd Ste 350 *Web:* www.jmsna.net	Hayward	CA	94541	510-888-9090	
Kasa Industrial Controls Inc 418 E Ave B *TF:* 800-755-5272 ■ *Web:* www.kasacontrols.com	Salina	KS	67401	785-825-7181	825-1663
Keystone Electrical Manufacturing Co 2511 Bell Ave *Web:* www.keystoneemc.com	Des Moines	IA	50321	515-283-2567	283-0418
Kraus & Naimer 760 New Brunswick Rd *Web:* www.krausnaimer.com	Somerset	NJ	08873	732-560-1240	560-8823
LayerZero Power Systems Inc 1500 Danner Dr *Web:* www.layerzero.com	Aurora	OH	44202	440-399-9000	
Littelfuse Inc 8755 W Higgins Rd Ste 500 *NASDAQ: LFUS* ■ *TF Sales:* 800-227-0029 ■ *Web:* www.littelfuse.com	Chicago	IL	60631	773-628-1000	
Logic Technologies Inc 117 Bellamy Pl *Web:* logictechnologies.com	Stockbridge	GA	30281	770-389-4964	
Lumitex Inc 8443 Dow Cir *TF:* 800-969-5483 ■ *Web:* www.lumitex.com	Strongsville	OH	44136	440-243-8401	243-8402
Mac Products Inc 60 Pennsylvania Ave PO Box 469 *Web:* www.macproducts.net	Kearny	NJ	07032	973-344-0700	344-5368
Marathon Special Products 13300 Van Camp Rd PO Box 468 *Web:* www.marathonsp.com	Bowling Green	OH	43402	419-352-8441	352-0875
MCC Control Systems LP 859 Cotting Ct Ste G *Web:* www.mcccontrolsystems.com	Vacaville	CA	95688	707-449-0341	
Mechanical Products Co 1112 N Garfield St *Web:* www.mechprod.com	Lombard	IL	60148	630-953-4100	
Mersen Inc 374 Merrimac St *Web:* www.mersen.com	Newburyport	MA	01950	978-462-6662	462-7934
Mitsubishi Electric Power Products Inc Thorn Hill Industrial Park 530 Keystone Dr *Web:* www.meppi.com	Warrendale	PA	15086	724-772-2555	
Multitech Industries Inc 350 Village Dr *Web:* www.multitechind.com	Carol Stream	IL	60188	630-784-9200	784-9225

Company	City	State	Zip	Phone	Fax
Norberg-ies 4237 S 74th E Ave *TF:* 800-739-9145 ■ *Web:* www.nema7.com	Tulsa	OK	74145	918-665-6888	
Otto Engineering Inc 2 E Main St *TF:* 888-234-6886 ■ *Web:* www.ottoexcellence.com	Carpentersville	IL	60110	847-428-7171	428-1956
Pacs Industries Inc 61 Steamboat Rd *Web:* www.pacsindustries.com	Great Neck	NY	11024	516-829-9060	829-9557
Powell Industries Inc 8550 Mosely Dr *NASDAQ: POWL* ■ *TF:* 800-480-7273 ■ *Web:* www.powellind.com	Houston	TX	77075	713-944-6900	947-4453
Power Distribution Inc 4200 Oakleys Ct *TF:* 800-225-4838 ■ *Web:* smithspower.com/brands/pdi/	Richmond	VA	23223	804-737-9880	
Powercon Corp PO Box 477 *TF:* 800-638-5055 ■ *Web:* www.powerconcorp.com	Severn	MD	21144	410-551-6500	551-8451
Professional Power Products Inc 448 W Madison St *Web:* www.professionalpowerproducts.com	Darien	WI	53114	262-882-9000	882-9010
PSI Control Solutions Inc 5808 Long Creek Park Dr *Web:* psicontrolsolutions.com	Charlotte	NC	28269	704-596-5617	
Reliance Controls Corp 2001 Young Ct *TF:* 800-634-6155 ■ *Web:* www.reliancecontrols.com	Racine	WI	53404	262-634-6155	634-6436
Revere Control Systems Inc 2240 Rocky Ridge Rd *TF:* 800-536-2525 ■ *Web:* www.reverecontrol.com	Birmingham	AL	35216	205-824-0004	824-0439
Romac Supply Company Inc 7400 Bandini Blvd *Web:* www.romacsupply.com	Commerce	CA	90040	323-721-5810	
Russelectric Inc 99 Industrial Pk Rd *TF:* 800-225-5250 ■ *Web:* www.russelectric.com	Hingham	MA	02043	781-749-6000	749-8077
S & C Electric Co 6601 N Ridge Blvd *TF:* 800-621-5546 ■ *Web:* www.sandc.com	Chicago	IL	60626	773-338-1000	338-3657
Satin American Corp 40 Oliver Terr **Fax Area Code:* 203 ■ *TF:* 877-356-5050 ■ *Web:* www.satinamerican.com	Shelton	CT	06484	877-356-5050	929-9684*
Sigma-Netics Inc Two N Corporate Dr *Web:* www.sigmanetics.com	Riverdale	NJ	07457	973-227-6372	
Signature Group Holdings Inc 15303 Ventura Blvd Ste 1600 *Web:* www.signaturegroupholdings.com	Sherman Oaks	CA	91403	805-409-4340	
Southwest Electric Co PO Box 82639 *Web:* www.swelectric.com	Oklahoma City	OK	73148	405-869-1100	869-1105
SPD Electrical Systems 13500 Roosevelt Blvd *Web:* l-3com.com	Philadelphia	PA	19116	215-677-4900	
Superior Electric 28 Spring Ln Ste 3 *TF:* 800-390-6405 ■ *Web:* www.danaherspecialtyproducts.com	Farmington	CT	06032	860-507-2025	507-2050
Tapeswitch Corp 100 Schmitt Blvd *TF:* 800-234-8273 ■ *Web:* www.tapeswitch.com	Farmingdale	NY	11735	631-630-0442	630-0454
Taqua LLC 740 E Campbell Rd Second Fl *Web:* www.taqua.com	Richardson	TX	75081	972-692-1800	437-2762
TopWorx Inc 3300 Fern Vly Rd *Web:* www2.emersonprocess.com	Louisville	KY	40213	502-969-8000	969-5911
Turner Electric LLC 131 Enterprise Dr *Web:* www.turnerswitch.com	Edwardsville	IL	62025	618-797-5000	
Uniforce Technologies Inc 1805 E Fifth St	North Little Rock	AR	72114	501-945-3283	

733 TABLE & KITCHEN SUPPLIES - CHINA & EARTHENWARE

SEE ALSO

Company	City	State	Zip	Phone	Fax
Bradshaw International Inc 9409 Buffalo Ave *Web:* www.bradshawintl.com	Rancho Cucamonga	CA	91730	909-476-3884	476-3616
Hall China Co One Anna Ave PO Box 989 **Fax Area Code:* 800 ■ *Web:* www.hallchina.com	East Liverpool	OH	43920	330-385-2900	837-4950*
Heritage Mint Ltd PO Box 13750 *TF:* 888-860-6245 ■ *Web:* www.heritagemint.com	Scottsdale	AZ	85267	480-860-1300	860-8174
Homer Laughlin China Co 672 Fiesta Dr *TF:* 800-452-4462 ■ *Web:* hlcdinnerware.com	Newell	WV	26050	304-387-1300	387-0593
Lenox Corp PO Box 2006 *TF:* 800-223-4311 ■ *Web:* www.lenox.com	Bristol	PA	19007	800-223-4311	
Lipper International Inc 235 Washington St *TF:* 800-243-3129 ■ *Web:* www.lipperinternational.com	Wallingford	CT	06492	203-269-8588	284-8637
Luna Garcia 201 San Juan Ave *Web:* www.lunagarcia.com	Venice	CA	90291	310-396-8026	
Original Hartstone Pottery, The 1719 Dearborn St *TF:* 800-339-4278 ■ *Web:* www.hartstonepottery.com	Zanesville	OH	43701	740-452-9000	452-5369
Pfaltzgraff Co PO Box 21769 **Fax:* Cust Svc ■ *TF:* 800-999-2811 ■ *Web:* www.pfaltzgraff.com	York	PA	17402	800-999-2811	717-2481*
True West 8549 PR 2414 PO Box 441 *Web:* www.truewesthome.com	Royse City	TX	75189	972-636-7922	635-2059
Waterford Wedgwood USA Inc 1330 Campus Pkwy *Web:* wedgwood.com/	Wall	NJ	07753	732-938-5800	

734 TALENT AGENCIES

SEE ALSO Literary Agents p. 2671; Modeling Agencies p. 2765

Company	City	State	Zip	Phone	Fax
Buddy Lee Attractions Inc 38 Music Sq E Ste 300 *Web:* www.buddyleeattractions.com	Nashville	TN	37203	615-244-4336	726-0429
CAA Sports 2000 Ave of the Stars *Web:* sports.caa.com	Los Angeles	CA	90067	424-288-2000	288-2900
CESD Talent Agency Inc 10635 Santa Monica Blvd Ste 130 *Web:* www.cesdtalent.com	Los Angeles	CA	90025	310-475-2111	474-5307
CM Artists New York 127 W 96th St Ste 13 B *Web:* www.cmartists.com	New York	NY	10025	212-864-1005	864-1066
Columbia Artists Management LLC 1790 Broadway *Web:* www.cami.com	New York	NY	10019	212-841-9500	841-9744
Creative Artists Agency Inc (CAA) 2000 Ave of the Stars *Web:* www.caa.com	Los Angeles	CA	90067	424-288-2000	288-2900
Don Buchwald & Assoc 6500 Wilshire Blvd Ste 2200 *Web:* www.buchwald.com	Los Angeles	CA	90048	323-655-7400	655-7470
Endeavor Agency 9601 Wilshire Blvd 3rd Fl *Web:* www.wmeentertainment.com	Beverly Hills	CA	90210	310-385-1362	285-9010
Gersh Agency 9465 Wilshire Blvd *Web:* www.gershcomedy.com	Beverly Hills	CA	90212	310-274-6611	
Gersh Agency, The (TGA) 41 Madison Ave 33rd Fl *Web:* www.gershcomedy.com	New York	NY	10010	212-997-1818	
Gorfaine/Schwartz Agency 4111 W Alameda Ave Ste 509 *Web:* www.gsamusic.com	Burbank	CA	91505	818-260-8500	260-8522
Great North Artists Management 350 Dupont St *Web:* tamac.ca	Toronto	ON	M5R1V9	416-925-2051	925-3904
Hartig Hilepo Agency Ltd 54 W 21st St Ste 610 *Web:* hartighilepo.com	New York	NY	10010	212-929-1772	929-1266
HS International 9871 Irvine Ctr Dr *Web:* www.hsi.net	Irvine	CA	92618	949-753-9153	753-9253
IMG Artists 152 W 57th St Ste 5 *Web:* www.imgartists.com	New York	NY	10019	212-994-3500	994-3550
IMG Inc 1360 E Ninth St *Web:* img.com	Cleveland	OH	44114	216-522-1200	522-1145
Innovative Artists 1505 Tenth St *Web:* www.innovativeartists.com	Santa Monica	CA	90401	310-656-0400	656-0456
Kraft-Engel Management 15233 Ventura Blvd Ste 200 *Web:* www.kraft-engel.com	Sherman Oaks	CA	91403	818-380-1918	380-2609
Media Talent Group 9200 Sunset Blvd Ste 550	West Hollywood	CA	90069	310-275-7900	275-7910
Monterey International 200 W Superior St Ste 202 *Web:* www.montereyinternational.net	Chicago	IL	60654	312-640-7500	640-7515
Monterey Peninsula Artists/Paradigm 404 W Franklin St *Web:* www.paradigmagency.com	Monterey	CA	93940	831-375-4889	375-2623
Nettwerk 1650 W Second Ave *Web:* www.nettwerk.com	Vancouver	BC	V6J4R3	604-654-2929	654-1993
One Entertainment 12 W 57th St Ste 1	New York	NY	10019	212-974-3900	
Original Artists 9465 Wilshire Blvd Ste 870	Beverly Hills	CA	90212	310-275-6765	
Paradigm Talent & Literary Agency 360 N Crescent Dr N Bldg *Web:* paradigmagency.com	Beverly Hills	CA	90210	310-288-8000	288-2000
Parseghian Planco LLC 322 Eigth Ave Ste 601	New York	NY	10001	212-777-7786	
Peter Strain & Assoc 5455 Wilshire Blvd Ste 1812 *Web:* natacharoi.com	Los Angeles	CA	90036	323-525-3391	525-0881
Randsman Artist Management 250 W 57th St Ste 2401 *Web:* www.randsman.com	New York	NY	10107	212-290-2281	290-2284
Rogers & Cowan Pacific Design Ctr 8687 Melrose Ave 7th Fl *Web:* www.rogersandcowan.com	Los Angeles	CA	90069	310-854-8100	854-8106
Rosebud Agency PO Box 170429 *Web:* www.rosebudus.com	San Francisco	CA	94117	415-386-3456	386-0599
Sfx Live Nation 5335 Wisconsin Ave NW *Web:* prnewswire.co.uk	Washington	DC	20015	202-686-2000	
Shapiro/West & Assoc 141 El Camino Dr Ste 205	Beverly Hills	CA	90212	310-278-8896	278-7238
Stone Manners Agency 9911 W Pico Blvd Ste 1400	Los Angeles	CA	90035	323-655-1313	389-1577
TalentWorks 3500 W Olive Ave Ste 1400 *Web:* www.talentworks.us	Burbank	CA	91505	818-972-4300	955-6411
United Talent Agency Inc (UTA) 9336 Civic Ctr Dr Ste 500 *Web:* www.unitedtalent.com	Beverly Hills	CA	90210	310-273-6700	247-1111
William Morris Agency 1325 Ave of the Americas *Web:* www.wma.com	New York	NY	10019	212-586-5100	246-3583

TAPE - ADHESIVE

SEE Medical Supplies - Mfr p. 2733

735 TAPE - CELLOPHANE, GUMMED, MASKING, PRESSURE SENSITIVE

SEE ALSO Medical Supplies - Mfr p. 2733

Company	City	State	Zip	Phone	Fax
3M Canada Co 300 Tartan Dr **Fax Area Code:* 800 ■ *TF:* 888-364-3577 ■ *Web:* 3m.com/intl/ca/	London	ON	N5V4M9	888-364-3577	479-4453*
Adchem Corp 1852 County Rd 58 *Web:* www.adchem.com	Riverhead	NY	11901	631-727-6000	727-6010
Adhesive Applications Inc 41 O'Neill St *TF General:* 800-356-3572 ■ *Web:* www.stik-2.com	EastHampton	MA	01027	413-527-7120	527-7249
American Biltrite Inc 57 River St *OTC: ABLT* ■ *Web:* www.ambilt.com	Wellesley Hills	MA	02481	781-237-6655	237-6880
American Biltrite Inc Tape Products Div (ABI) 105 Whittendale Dr **Fax Area Code:* 888 ■ *Web:* www.abitape.com	Moorestown	NJ	08057	856-778-0700	224-6325*
Avery Dennison Specialty Tapes Div 250 Chester St Bldg 5 **Fax Area Code:* 440 ■ *TF:* 866-462-8379 ■ *Web:* www.averydennison.com	Painesville	OH	44077	626-304-2000	358-3341*

	City	State	Zip	Phone	Fax
Bemis Company Inc One Neenah Ctr Fourth Fl PO Box 669	Neenah	WI	54957	920-727-4100	
NYSE: BMS ■ *Web:* www.bemis.com					
Brady Coated Products 6555 W Good Hope Rd	Milwaukee	WI	53223	414-358-6600	541-1686*
**Fax Area Code:* 800 ■ *TF:* 800-662-1191 ■ *Web:* www.coatedproducts.com					
Brite-Line LLC 10660 E 51st Ave	Denver	CO	80239	888-201-6448	208-0758
TF: 888-201-6448 ■ *Web:* www.brite-line.com					
Decker Tape Products Inc Six Stewart Pl	Fairfield	NJ	07004	973-227-5350	808-9418
TF: 800-227-5252 ■ *Web:* www.deckertape.com					
DeWAL Industries Inc 15 Ray Trainor Dr	Narragansett	RI	02882	401-789-9736	783-6780
TF: 800-366-8356 ■ *Web:* www.dewal.com					
Eternabond 75 E Div St	Mundelein	IL	60060	847-837-9400	837-9449
TF: 888-336-2663 ■ *Web:* www.eternabond.com					
FiberMark Inc 161 Wellington Rd	Brattleboro	VT	05301	802-257-0365	257-5907*
**Fax:* Sales ■ *Web:* www.fibermark.com					
Gaska-Tape Inc 1810 W Lusher Ave	Elkhart	IN	46517	574-294-5431	293-4504
TF: 800-423-1571 ■ *Web:* www.gaska.com					
Harris Industries Inc 5181 Argosy Ave	Huntington Beach	CA	92649	714-898-8048	898-7108
TF: 800-222-6866 ■ *Web:* www.harrisind.com					
Hawkeye International Ltd 5760 VT Rt 100	North Hyde Park	VT	05665	802-635-7500	635-7900
Web: www.hawkeyeintl.com/home.htm					
Holland Mfg Co Inc 15 Main St PO Box 404	Succasunna	NJ	07876	973-584-8141	584-6845
TF: 800-345-0492 ■ *Web:* www.hollandmfg.com					
JHL Industries 10012 Nevada Ave	Chatsworth	CA	91311	818-882-2233	882-4350
TF: 800-255-6636 ■ *Web:* www.jhlindustries.com					
Kruse Adhesive Tape Inc 1610 E McFadden Ave	Santa Ana	CA	92705	714-640-2130	640-2134
TF: 800-992-7702 ■ *Web:* www.krusetape.com					
M & C Specialties Co 90 James Way	SouthHampton	PA	18966	215-322-1600	322-1620
TF Cust Svc: 800-441-6996 ■ *Web:* www.mcspecialties.com					
Neptco Inc 30 Hamlet St	Pawtucket	RI	02861	401-722-5500	722-6378
TF: 800-354-5445 ■ *Web:* www.neptco.com					
Plymouth Rubber Company Inc 275 Tpke St Ste 310	Canton	MA	02021	781-828-0220	828-6041
Web: www.plymouthrubber.com					
Presto Tape Inc 1626 Bridgewater Rd	Bensalem	PA	19020	215-245-8555	245-8554
TF: 800-331-1373 ■ *Web:* www.prestotape.com					
Pro Tapes & Specialties PO Box 53026	Newark	NJ	07101	732-346-0900	729-7440
TF: 800-345-0234 ■ *Web:* www.protapes.com					
Shurtape Technologies LLC 1712 Eigth St Dr SE	Hickory	NC	28602	828-322-2700	335-7651*
**Fax Area Code:* 800 ■ *TF:* 888-442-8273 ■ *Web:* www.shurtape.com					
STA Overlaminations 100 S Puente St	Brea	CA	92821	714-255-7888	990-6851
TF: 800-235-8273 ■ *Web:* www.sekisui-ta.com					
TapeSouth Inc 10302 Deerwood Pk Ste 125	Jacksonville	FL	32256	904-642-1800	642-7006
Web: www.tapesouth.com					
Tesa Tape Inc 5825 Carnegie Blvd	Charlotte	NC	28209	704-554-0707	852-8831*
**Fax Area Code:* 800 ■ **Fax:* Cust Svc ■ *TF:* 800-426-2181 ■ *Web:* www.tesatape.com					
Thomas Tape Co 1713 Sheridan Ave	Springfield	OH	45505	937-325-6414	325-2850
Web: www.thomastape.com					
Tommy Tape 378 Four Rod Rd	Berlin	CT	06037	860-378-0111	378-0113
TF: 888-866-8273 ■ *Web:* www.tommytape.com					
Venture Tape Corp 30 Commerce Rd	Rockland	MA	02370	781-331-5900	871-0065
TF: 800-343-1076 ■ *Web:* venturetape.com					
VIBAC Canada Inc 12250 Industrial Blvd	Montreal	QC	H1B5M5	514-640-0250	640-1577
TF: 800-557-0192 ■ *Web:* www.vibacgroup.com					
WTP Inc PO Box 937	Coloma	MI	49038	269-468-3399	468-3391
TF: 800-521-0731 ■ *Web:* www.wtp-inc.com					

736 TARPS, TENTS, COVERS

SEE ALSO Bags - Textile p. 1847; Sporting Goods p. 3182

	City	State	Zip	Phone	Fax
Aero Industries Inc 4243 W Bradbury Ave	Indianapolis	IN	46241	317-244-2433	244-1311
TF Sales: 800-535-9545 ■ *Web:* www.aeroindustries.com					
American Pavilion 1706 Warrington Ave	Danville	IL	61832	217-443-0800	443-9619
Web: www.americanpavilion.com					
Anchor Industries Inc 1100 Burch Dr	Evansville	IN	47725	812-867-2421	867-1429
TF: 800-544-4445 ■ *Web:* www.anchorinc.com					
Canvas Products Co 274 S Waterman St	Detroit	MI	48209	877-293-1669	
TF: 877-293-1669 ■ *Web:* www.canvaspc.com					
Canvas Specialty 7344 E Bandini Blvd	Los Angeles	CA	90040	323-722-1156	724-3848
Web: www.can-spec.com					
Carefree of Colorado 2145 W Sixth Ave	Broomfield	CO	80020	303-469-3324	469-4742
TF: 800-621-2617 ■ *Web:* www.carefreeofcolorado.com					
Clamshell Structures Inc 1101 Maulhardt Ave	Oxnard	CA	93030	805-988-1340	988-2266
TF: 800-360-8853 ■ *Web:* www.clamshell.com					
Commonwealth Canvas Inc Five Perkins Way	Newburyport	MA	01950	978-499-3900	499-3933
TF: 877-922-6827 ■ *Web:* www.commonwealthcanvas.com					
CR Daniels Inc 3451 Ellicott Ctr Dr	Ellicott City	MD	21043	410-461-2100	461-2987
TF: 800-933-2638 ■ *Web:* www.crdaniels.com					
DC Humphrys Inc 5744 Woodland Ave	Philadelphia	PA	19143	215-724-8181	724-8706
TF Sales: 800-645-2059 ■ *Web:* dc-humphrys-co-inc.sbcontract.com					
Diamond Brand Canvas Products 145 Cane Creek Industrial Pk Rd Ste 1	Fletcher	NC	28732	828-684-9848	687-0965
TF Sales: 800-459-6262 ■ *Web:* www.diamondbrand.com					
Eide Industries Inc 16215 Piuma Ave	Cerritos	CA	90703	562-402-8335	924-2233
TF: 800-422-6827 ■ *Web:* www.eideindustries.com					
Estex Mfg Co Inc 402 E Broad St PO Box 368	Fairburn	GA	30213	800-749-1224	964-7534*
**Fax Area Code:* 770 ■ *TF:* 800-749-1224 ■ *Web:* www.estexmfg.com					
Fisher Canvas Products Inc 415 St Mary St	Burlington	NJ	08016	800-892-6688	239-2728*
**Fax Area Code:* 609 ■ *TF:* 800-892-6688 ■ *Web:* www.fishercanvas.com					
Harry Miller Co Inc 850 Albany St	Boston	MA	02119	617-427-2300	442-1152
Web: www.harrymiller.com					
John Johnson Co 274 S Waterman St	Detroit	MI	48209	313-496-0600	496-0252
TF: 800-991-1394 ■ *Web:* www.johnjohnsonco.com					
Johnson Outdoors Inc 555 Main St	Racine	WI	53403	262-631-6600	631-6601
NASDAQ: JOUT ■ *TF:* 800-468-9716 ■ *Web:* www.johnsonoutdoors.com					
Loop-Loc Ltd 390 Motor Pkwy	Hauppauge	NY	11788	631-582-2626	582-2636
TF: 800-562-5667 ■ *Web:* www.looploc.com					
Mauritzon Inc 3939 W Belden Ave	Chicago	IL	60647	773-235-6000	235-1479
TF: 800-621-4352 ■ *Web:* www.mauritzononline.com					
Midwest Canvas Corp 4635 W Lake St	Chicago	IL	60644	773-287-4400	854-2017
TF General: 800-433-4701 ■ *Web:* www.midwestcanvas.com					
North Sails Group LLC 125 Old Gate Ln	Milford	CT	06460	203-877-7621	874-6059
TF: 866-427-4747 ■ *Web:* www.na.northsails.com					
Rainier Industries Ltd 18375 Olympic Ave S	Tukwila	WA	98188	425-251-1800	251-5065
TF: 800-869-7162 ■ *Web:* www.rainier.com					
Robertson Manufacturing Inc 112 Woodland Ave	West Grove	PA	19390	610-869-9600	869-6365
TF: 800-260-5423					
Shur-Co Inc 2309 Shur-Lok St PO Box 713	Yankton	SD	57078	605-665-6000	665-0501
TF: 800-474-8756 ■ *Web:* www.shurco.com					
Steele Canvas Basket Corp 201 William St PO Box 6267 IMCN	Chelsea	MA	02150	617-889-0202	889-0524
TF: 800-541-8929 ■ *Web:* steelecanvas.com					
Trimaco LLC 2300 Gateway Centre Blvd Ste 200	Morrisville	NC	27560	919-674-3460	674-3461
TF: 800-325-7356 ■ *Web:* www.trimaco.com					
Troy Sunshade Co 607 Riffle Ave	Greenville	OH	45331	937-548-2466	548-6102
TF: 800-833-8769 ■ *Web:* bagsbytroy.com					
Universal Fabric Structures Inc 2200 Kumry Rd	Quakertown	PA	18951	215-529-9921	529-9936
TF: 800-634-8368 ■ *Web:* www.ufsinc.com					
Webb Manufacturing Co 1241 Carpenter St	Philadelphia	PA	19147	215-336-5570	336-4422
Web: www.webbmfg.com					

737 TAX PREPARATION SERVICES

	City	State	Zip	Phone	Fax
1-2-3 Payroll & HR Services Inc PO Box 96	Holtsville	NY	11742	631-654-1811	
Web: www.1-2-3payroll.com					
Abdo Eick & Meyers LLP 5201 Eden Ave	Edina	MN	55436	952-835-9090	
Web: www.aemcpas.com					
AccessPoint LLC 42400 Grand River Ave Ste 200	Novi	MI	48375	248-353-1400	
Web: www.accesspointhr.com					
Accume Partners LLC 341 New Albany Rd	Moorestown	NJ	08057	856-914-9500	
Web: www.accumepartners.com					
Active Professionals Inc 9647b Folsom Blvd	Sacramento	CA	95827	916-361-0931	
Web: activeprofessionalconferences.com					
Acumen Fiscal Agent LLC 4542 E Inverness Ave Ste 210	Mesa	AZ	85206	480-497-0343	
Web: www.acumenfiscalagent.com					
Adamy Valuation Advisors 161 Ottawa Ave NW Ste 408	Grand Rapids	MI	49503	616-284-3700	
Web: www.adamyvaluation.com					
Advantage One Tax Consulting Inc 20610 Quarterpath Trace Cir	Sterling	VA	20165	703-584-5533	
Web: www.aotax.com					
Advantec Inc 4890 W Kennedy Blvd Ste 500	Tampa	FL	33609	813-289-9442	
Web: www.advantec-hr.com					
AFJ Consulting Group 5455 Wilshire Blvd Ste 2020	Los Angeles	CA	90036	323-782-9391	
Web: www.afjconsulting.com					
Alliance Benefit Group Financial Services Corp 201 E Clark St PO Box 1206	Albert Lea	MN	56007	507-377-2919	
Web: www.abgfs.com					
AmCheck Inc 5030 E Sunrise Dr	Phoenix	AZ	85044	480-763-5900	
Web: www.amcheck.com					
APA Services 4150 International Plz Tower I Ste 510	Fort Worth	TX	76109	877-425-5023	
TF: 877-425-5023 ■ *Web:* www.apaservices.net					
Arthur Consulting Group Inc 31355 Oak Crest Dr Ste 200	Westlake Village	CA	91361	818-735-4800	
Web: www.arthurconsulting.com					
Audit Technology Group 1850 W Winchester Rd	Libertyville	IL	60048	847-281-8703	
Web: www.atgaudits.com					
Audits & Systems Inc C/O 464 Central Rd	Northfield	IL	60093	847-446-5244	
Avitus Group P.O. Box 81590	Billings	MT	59108	800-454-2446	
TF: 800-454-2446 ■ *Web:* www.avitusgroup.com					
Barry W James & Associates LLP 721 E Texas Ave	Baytown	TX	77520	281-420-1040	
Web: www.bwjames.com					
Bayerkohler & Graff Ltd 11132 Zealand Ave N	Champlin	MN	55316	763-427-2542	
Web: bayergraff.com					
BCRS Assoc LLC 77 Water St	New York	NY	10005	212-440-0800	
Web: bcrsllc.com					
BDB Payroll Inc 768 Bedford Ave	Brooklyn	NY	11205	718-522-2000	
TF: 800-729-7687 ■ *Web:* www.bdbpayroll.com					
Bederson LLP 405 Northfield Ave	West Orange	NJ	07052	973-736-3333	
Web: www.bederson.com					
Benefit Administrative Services International Corp 9246 Portage Industrial Dr	Portage	MI	49024	269-327-1922	
Web: www.basiconline.com					
BGBC Partners LLP 300 N Meridian St Ste 1100	Indianapolis	IN	46204	317-633-4700	
Web: www.bgbc.co					
Bradley & Associates 201 S Capitol Ave Ste 910	Indianapolis	IN	46225	317-237-5500	
Web: www.bradleycpa.com					
Building Block Computer 3209 Terminal Dr Ste 100	Saint Paul	MN	55121	651-687-9435	
Web: www.bbcusa.com					
Cannon & Co 5605 Murray Ave	Memphis	TN	38119	901-761-1710	
Web: www.cannoncpa.com					
Canyon Tax & Bookkeeping Service 22342 Avenida Empresa Ste 280	Rancho Santa Margarita	CA	92688	949-888-2829	
Web: canyontax.com					

Name / Address	City	State	ZIP	Phone	Fax
CAPS LLC 10600 Virginia Ave *Web:* www.capspayroll.com	Culver City	CA	90232	310-280-0755	
CASA Payroll Service LLC 3120 Fire Rd *Web:* www.casapayroll.com	Egg Harbor Township	NJ	08234	609-383-0677	383-0907
CeFO Inc 88 Inverness Cir E Ste L107 *Web:* www.cefo.net	Englewood	CO	80112	720-506-4105	
Central Tax Inc 534 Notre-Dame St Ste 240 *Web:* www.centraletaxes.com	Repentigny	QC	J6A2T8	450-585-8293	
CF & Company LLP 8750 N Central Expy Ste 300 *Web:* www.cfllp.com	Dallas	TX	75231	972-387-4300	
Christopher Smith Leonard Bristow Stanell & Wells PA Suntrust Bank Bldg 1001 Third Ave W Ste 700 *Web:* www.cslcpa.com	Bradenton	FL	34205	941-748-1040	
City of Bay Village Ohio 350 Dover Ctr Rd *Web:* www.cityofbayvillage.com	Bay Village	OH	44140	440-899-3412	
Clairmount Group Plc 18424 Mack Ave *Web:* clairmount.com	Grosse Pointe Farms	MI	48236	313-642-1102	
COBRA Solutions Inc 4500 S Lakeshore Dr *Web:* www.cobra-solutions.com	Tempe	AZ	85282	480-831-6078	
Cohen & Co 1350 Euclid Ave Ste 800 *Web:* www.cohencpa.com	Cleveland	OH	44115	216-579-1040	
Collabrus Inc 111 Sutter St Ste 900 *Web:* www.collabrus.com	San Francisco	CA	94104	415-288-1826	
Connolly Consulting Associates Inc 50 Danbury Rd *Web:* www.connollyhealthcare.com	Wilton	CT	06897	203-529-2000	
Cordano Severson & Assoc Ltd 2321 Plainfield Rd *Web:* csatax.com	Crest Hill	IL	60403	815-744-1900	
Corporate Payroll Services Inc 1000 Miller Ct W *Web:* www.corpay.com	Norcross	GA	30071	770-446-7289	
Cort Software Inc 855 S W Yates Dr Ste 201 *Web:* www.nuviewinc.com	Bend	OR	97702	541-617-5100	
Crowe Horwath International 488 Madison Ave Ste 202 *Web:* www.crowehorwath.net	New York	NY	10022	212-808-2000	
Cytak Inc 444 de Haro Ste 210 *Web:* www.cytak.com	San Francisco	CA	94107	415-738-1650	
Daddy Don'S Tax Service 8235 Santa Monica Blvd Ste 210 *Web:* daddydon.com	West Hollywood	CA	90046	323-656-7532	
Davidson & Company LLP 1200 - 609 Granville St Pacific Centre *Web:* www.davidson-co.com	Vancouver	BC	V7Y1G6	604-687-0947	
DAWSON & ASSOCIATES 3250 Mary St Ste 401 *Web:* www.flacpa.com	Coconut Grove	FL	33133	305-443-1500	
Defense Finance & Accounting Service 8899 E 56th St *TF:* 888-332-7411 ■ *Web:* www.dfas.mil	Indianapolis	IN	46249	888-332-7411	
Diverse Staffing Inc 1800 E Lambert Rd Ste 100 *Web:* www.dss-staffing.com	Brea	CA	92821	714-482-0499	
DuCharme McMillen & Assoc Inc 6610 Mutual Dr *Web:* www.dmainc.com	Fort Wayne	IN	46825	260-484-8631	482-8152
Ease Entertainment Services LLC 8383 Wilshire Blvd Ste 100 *Web:* www.easeentertainment.com	Beverly Hills	CA	90211	310-469-7300	
Eastridge Workforce Solutions 2375 Northside Dr Ste 360 *TF:* 877-862-2632 ■ *Web:* www.eastridge.com	San Diego	CA	92108	877-337-5422	
EBS Associates Inc 14020 SE Johnson Rd Ste 101 *Web:* www.teachmequickbooks.com	Portland	OR	97267	503-885-0776	
Employer Flexible 7850 N Sam Houston Parkway W Ste 100 *TF:* 866-501-4942 ■ *Web:* www.employerflexible.com	Houston	TX	77064	866-501-4942	
Employer Solutions Group Inc 4844 North 300 West Ste 100 *Web:* www.esghr.com	Provo	UT	84604	801-223-7007	
EP Canada Film Services Inc 130 Bloor St W Ste 500 *Web:* epcanada.com	Toronto	ON	M5S1N5	416-923-9255	
Etonien LLC 222 N Sepulveda Blvd Ste 1507 *Web:* www.etonien.com	El Segundo	CA	90245	310-321-5800	
Exactax Inc 2301 W Lincoln Ave Ste 100 *Web:* www.exactax.com	Anaheim	CA	92801	714-284-4802	
Exerve Inc 2909 Langford Rd Ste 400B *Web:* www.exerve.com	Norcross	GA	30071	770-447-1566	
Farm Business Consultants Inc 150 3015 Fifth Ave Ne *Web:* www.fbc.ca	Calgary	AB	T2A6T8	403-735-6105	
Feldman Financial Advisors Inc 1001 Connecticut Ave NW Ste 840 *Web:* www.feldmanfinancial.com	Washington	DC	20036	202-467-6862	
Fesnak & Associates LLP 1777 Sentry Pkwy W Ste 300 *TF:* 800-274-3978 ■ *Web:* www.fesnak.com	Blue Bell	PA	19422	267-419-2200	
Fgmk LLC 2801 Lakeside Dr Third Fl *Web:* www.fgmk.net	Bannockburn	IL	60015	847-374-0400	
Fiducial 1370 Ave of the Americas 31st Fl *TF:* 866-343-8242 ■ *Web:* www.fiducial.com	New York	NY	10019	212-207-4700	308-2613
Fiducial Franchising 10100 Old Columbia Rd Third Fl *TF:* 800-323-9000 ■ *Web:* www.fiducial.com	Columbia	MD	21046	410-290-8296	910-5903
Financial Intelligence LLC 1451 Grant Rd Ste 200 *Web:* www.financial-intelligence.com	Mountain View	CA	94040	650-264-2252	
First Choice Software LLC PO Box 1657 *Web:* www.fcs-software.com	West Chester	PA	19380	610-436-6825	
Fortune Industries Inc 6402 Corporate Dr *Web:* www.ffi.net	Indianapolis	IN	46278	317-532-1374	
G&J Seiberlich & Company LLP 3264 Villa Ln *Web:* www.gjscollp.com	Napa	CA	94558	707-224-7948	
Global Tax Network US LLC 750 Boone Ave N Ste 102 *Web:* www.gtn.com	Minneapolis	MN	55427	763-746-4556	
Goff Backa Alfera & Company LLC 3325 Saw Mill Run Blvd *Web:* www.gbaco.com	Pittsburgh	PA	15227	412-885-5045	
H & R Block Tax Services Inc 4400 Main St **Fax Area Code:* 816 ■ *TF:* 800-472-5625 ■ *Web:* www.hrblock.com	Kansas City	MO	64111	800-472-5625	753-5346*
Harding & Carbone Inc 3903 Bellaire Blvd *Web:* www.hctax.com	Houston	TX	77025	713-664-1215	
Harrison Accountancy Corp 2850 Mesa Verde Dr E Ste 101	Costa Mesa	CA	92626	714-966-0644	
HK Payroll Services 2345 JFK Rd *Web:* www.hkpayroll.com	Dubuque	IA	52004	563-556-0123	
HUMACare Inc 9501 Union Cemetery Rd *Web:* humacare.net	Loveland	OH	45140	513-605-3522	
Industry Consulting Group Inc 2777 N Stemmons Fwy Ste 940 *Web:* www.icgtax.com	Dallas	TX	75207	972-991-0391	
Infiniti HR LLC 3905 National Dr Ste 400 *Web:* www.infinitihr.com	Burtonsville	MD	20866	301-841-6380	
Innovative Employee Solutions Inc 9665 Granite Ridge Dr Ste 420 *Web:* www.innovativeemployeesolutions.com	San Diego	CA	92123	858-715-5100	
Inova Payroll Inc 176 Thompson Ln Ste 204 *TF:* 888-244-6106 ■ *Web:* www.inovapayroll.com	Nashville	TN	37211	615-921-0600	
Jackson Hewitt Inc Three Sylvan Way Ste 301 *OTC:* JHTXQ ■ *TF:* 800-234-1040 ■ *Web:* www.jacksonhewitt.com	Parsippany	NJ	07054	800-234-1040	
JD Clark & Co 2225 Washington Blvd Ste 300 *Web:* www.jdclark.com	Ogden	UT	84401	801-737-4000	
JG Tax Group 1430 S Federal Hwy *TF:* 866-477-5291 ■ *Web:* www.jgtaxgroup.com	Deerfield Beach	FL	33441	866-477-5291	
John L Henss Ltd 8980 Hickman Rd Ste 102	Clive	IA	50325	515-254-9959	
Johnson & Sheldon PC 500 S Taylor Plz II Ste 200 *Web:* www.amacpas.com	Amarillo	TX	79105	806-371-7661	
Kafafian Group Inc, The 2001 Rt 46 Ste 310 *Web:* www.kafafiangroup.com	Parsippany	NJ	07054	973-299-0300	299-1002
Karuna Advisors LLP 1550 El Camino Real Ste 250 *Web:* www.karunaadvisors.com	Menlo Park	CA	94025	650-328-2758	
Katz Cassidy An Accountancy Corp Olympic *Web:* www.katzcassidy.com	Los Angeles	CA	90064	310-477-6300	
KMJ Corbin & Company LLP 555 Anton Blvd Ste 1000 *Web:* www.corbincocpa.com	Costa Mesa	CA	92626	714-380-6565	
Knight James E & Associates Pc 14825 Saint Marys Ln *TF:* 800-896-4500 ■ *Web:* www.ktjcpas.com	Houston	TX	77079	281-493-5080	
Lauka & Assoc 3511 Se Milwaukie Ave *Web:* laukaweb.com	Portland	OR	97202	503-233-2177	
Liberty Tax Service Inc 1716 Corporate Landing Pkwy *TF Cust Svc:* 800-790-3863 ■ *Web:* www.libertytax.com	Virginia Beach	VA	23454	757-493-8855	493-0169
LINK Staffing Services Inc 1800 Bering Dr Ste 800 *Web:* www.linkstaffing.com	Houston	TX	77057	713-784-4400	
Lippa Assoc Inc 3633 Camino Del Rio S 207	San Diego	CA	92108	619-283-2581	
Maahs & Vanlahr PC 3911 Old Lee Hwy Ste 43E *Web:* maahsandvanlahrcpa.com	Fairfax	VA	22030	703-691-8632	
MaloneBailey LLP 9801 Westheimer Rd Ste 1100 *Web:* www.malonebailey.com	Houston	TX	77042	713-343-4286	
Martini Iosue & Akpovi CPAs 16830 Ventura Blvd Ste 415 *Web:* www.miacpas.com	Encino	CA	91436	818-789-1179	
Maxwell Locke & Ritter LLP 401 Congress Ave Ste 1100 *Web:* www.mlrpc.com	Austin	TX	78701	512-370-3200	
Meadows Urquhart Acree & Cook LLP 1802 Bayberry Court Ste 102 *Web:* www.muacllp.com	Richmond	VA	23226	804-249-5786	
Medical Practice Partners 29 Naek Rd *Web:* www.healthwisema.com	Vernon Rockville	CT	06066	860-872-2289	
Mengel Metzger Barr & Company LLP 100 Chestnut St Ste 1200 *Web:* www.mengelmetzgerbarr.com	Rochester	NY	14604	585-423-1860	
Michael West & Assoc 5356 Clayton Rd Ste 216 *Web:* westfinancial.net	Concord	CA	94521	925-676-7437	
Mid-Atlantic Diamond Ventures 1801 Liacouras Walk 503 Alter Hall *Web:* www.fox.temple.edu	Philadelphia	PA	19122	215-204-3082	
Moody Famiglietti & Andronico LLP One Highwood Dr *Web:* mfa-cpa.com	Tewksbury	MA	01876	978-557-5300	
Morgan Jacoby Thurn Boyle & Assoc PA 700 20th St *Web:* www.mjtbcpa.com	Vero Beach	FL	32960	772-562-4158	
Morrissey Family Businesses Inc 5919 Spring Creek Rd *Web:* www.morrisseyfamily.com	Rockford	IL	61114	815-282-4600	
MTS Consulting LLC 7444 Long Ave *Web:* www.mtsconsulting.com	Skokie	IL	60077	847-675-6666	

	City	State	Zip	Phone	Fax
Multistate Tax Commission 444 N Capitol St Nw Ste 425	Washington	DC	20001	202-624-8699	
Web: www.mtc.gov					
National Tax Search LLC 303 E Wacker Dr Ste 900	Chicago	IL	60601	312-233-6440	
Web: www.nationaltaxsearch.com					
Nextaff LLC 11225 College Blvd Ste 250	Overland Park	KS	66210	913-562-5620	
Web: www.nextaff.com					
Ogden Cos Inc 606 Green Meadow N	Colleyville	TX	76034	817-656-8570	
Opportune LLP 711 Louisiana St Ste 3100	Houston	TX	77002	713-490-5050	
Web: www.opportune.com					
Payce Inc 1220B E Joppa Rd Ste 324	Towson	MD	21286	443-279-9000	
Web: www.paycepayroll.com					
Paycom 7501 W Memorial Rd	Oklahoma City	OK	73142	800-580-4505	
TF: 800-580-4505 ■ *Web:* www.paycomonline.com					
Payroll Solutions Plus 180 Amt Tech Dr.	Rocky Mount	VA	24151	540-484-0361	
Web: www.payrollsolutionsplus.com					
Payworks Inc 1565 Willson Pl	Winnipeg	MB	R3T4H1	866-788-3500	779-0538*
**Fax Area Code:* 204 ■ *TF:* 866-788-3500 ■ *Web:* www.payworks.ca					
Perry-Smith & Company LLP 400 Capital Mall Ste 1200	Sacramento	CA	95814	916-441-1000	
Web: www.perry-smith.com					
Phyphar Inc 29 Walter Hammond Pl Ste 1	Waldwick	NJ	07463	201-444-4648	
Web: www.phyphar.com					
PKF Pacific Hawaii LLP 1132 Bishop St.	Honolulu	HI	96813	808-536-0066	
Web: www.pkfpacifichawaii.com					
Premier Tax & Financial Services 121 W 27th St Ste 1003A	New York	NY	10001	212-807-8201	
Web: premiertaxandfinancial.com					
Premium Transportation Staffing Inc 190 Highland Dr	Medina	OH	44256	330-722-7974	
Web: www.premiumtransportation.com					
PrO Unlimited Inc 301 Yamato Rd Ste3199	Boca Raton	FL	33431	800-291-1099	
TF: 800-291-1099 ■ *Web:* www.prounlimited.com					
Professional Employer Plans Inc 1911 US Hwy 301 N Ste 450	Tampa	FL	33619	813-246-5657	
Web: www.peplans.com					
Pursuit of Excellence Inc 10440 N Central Expy Ste 1250	Dallas	TX	75231	214-452-7881	
Web: www.pursuitofexcellenceinc.com					
Quantum Management Services Ltd 2000 McGill College Ave Ste 1800	Montreal	QC	H3A3H3	514-842-5555	849-8846
Web: www.quantum.ca					
Questco LLC 100 Commercial Cir Building B	Conroe	TX	77304	936-756-1980	
Web: questco.net					
Quigley Tax Service SC 5822 W Fond Du Lac Ave Second Fl	Milwaukee	WI	53218	414-461-1800	
Web: quigleytaxserv.com					
Relevante Inc 1235 Westlakes Dr Ste 280	Berwyn	PA	19312	484-403-4100	
Web: www.relevante.com					
Resourcing Edge Inc 1309 Ridge Rd Ste 200	Rockwall	TX	75087	214-771-4411	
Web: www.resourcingedge.com					
Revenew International LLC 9 Greenway PlZ Ste 1950	Houston	TX	77046	281-276-4500	
Web: www.revenew.net					
Richter LLP 1981 McGill College 11th Fl	Montreal	QC	H3A0G6	514-934-3400	
Web: www.richter.ca					
Rockoff Harlan & Rasof Ltd 3818 Oakton St.	Skokie	IL	60076	847-675-7777	
Web: www.rhrcpa.com					
Rose Financial Services LLC Two Research Pl Ste 300	Rockville	MD	20850	301-527-1130	
Web: www.rosefinancial.com					
Rubino & McGeehin Consulting Group Inc 6903 Rockledge Dr Ste 1200	Bethesda	MD	20817	301-564-3636	
Web: www.rubino.com					
Rylander Clay & Opitz LLP 3200 Riverfront Dr Ste 200	Fort Worth	TX	76107	817-332-2301	338-4608
Web: www.rylander-cpa.com					
Safstrom & Company PS 1411 Fourth Ave Ste 1120	Seattle	WA	98101	206-622-6456	
Web: safstrom.com					
SALT Group, The 1845 Sidney Baker St	Kerrville	TX	78028	830-257-1290	
Web: thesaltgroup.com					
Sam S Sloven CPA Inc 3025 S Parker Rd Ste 733	Aurora	CO	80014	303-750-0050	
Schechter Dokken Kanter CPA'S 100 Washington Ave S Ste 1600	Minneapolis	MN	55401	612-332-5500	
Web: www.sdkcpa.com					
Shwiff Levy & Polo LLP 433 California St Ste 1000	San Francisco	CA	94104	415-291-8600	
Web: www.slpconsults.com					
Sidney Tax Service Inc 115 Second St Ne	Sidney	MT	59270	406-433-3131	
Silver Creek Financial ServicesInc 175 Hwy 82	Lostine	OR	97857	541-569-2272	
Web: silvercreekteam.com					
Silver Freedman Taff & Tiernan LLP 3299 K St NW Ste 100	Washington	DC	20007	202-295-4500	
Web: www.sftlaw.com					
Silver Lerner Schwartz Fertel 8707 Skokie Blvd Ste 400	Skokie	IL	60077	847-676-2000	
Web: www.slsf.com					
Skoda Minotti 6685 Beta Dr	Cleveland	OH	44143	440-449-6800	
Web: www.skodaminotti.com					
StaffingSolutions Inc 1390 S Eufaula Ave	Eufaula	AL	36027	334-687-7460	
Web: www.staffingsolutions.com					
Sterlings Bookkeeping & Tax Services 5418 Saint Charles Ave	Dallas	TX	75223	214-330-4682	
Web: www.sterlingstax.com					
Strategic Compliance Solutions LLC 18 Mallard Point Rd	Essex	CT	06426	860-767-3006	
Web: www.strategiccompliancesolutions.com					
Swan Employer Services Inc 1306 East 74th Ave Ste 200	Anchorage	AK	99518	907-344-7926	
Web: www.swanhr.com					
Sweeney Conrad PS 2606 116th Ave NE 200	Bellevue	WA	98004	425-629-1990	
Web: sweeneyconrad.com					
Talagy Inc 245 Riverside Ave Ste 250	Jacksonville	FL	32202	904-224-1400	224-1410
Tax Savvy 401 S Birmingham St	Wylie	TX	75098	972-442-5226	
Web: www.taxsavvy.biz					
Tax Smart Accounting Services 19616 E Benwood St	Covina	CA	91724	626-974-5152	
Web: www.taxsmartaccounting.com					
TGG Accounting 10188 Telesis Ct Ste 130	San Diego	CA	92121	760-697-1033	
Web: www.tgg-accounting.com					
Thurman Campbell Group PLC 324 Franklin St	Clarksville	TN	37040	931-552-7474	
Web: www.tccpas.com					
Traphagen Financial Group 234 Kinderkamack Rd	Oradell	NJ	07649	201-262-1040	
Web: www.traphagen-financial.com					
Trapp Online LLC 7360 E. Acoma Dr Ste 2	Scottsdale	AZ	85260	602-443-9145	
Web: www.trapponline.com					
TravisWolff Independent Advisors & Accountants 15950 N Dallas Pkwy Ste 600	Dallas	TX	75248	972-661-1843	
Web: www.traviswolff.com					
Utilisave LLC 129 W 27th St 11th Fl	New York	NY	10001	718-382-4500	
Web: www.utilisave.com					
Valuation Advisory Group Inc, The 445 Pharr Rd NE	Atlanta	GA	30305	404-841-0992	
Web: www.valuationadvisory.com					
Verified Audit Circulation Inc 900 Larkspur Landing Cir	Larkspur	CA	94939	415-461-6006	
TF: 800-775-3332 ■ *Web:* www.verifiedaudit.com					
Vic's Accounting 897 Henderson Hwy	Winnipeg	MB	R2K2L8	204-668-3441	
Web: allyear.ca					
Victory Education Partners Inc 22 W 19th St Ninth Fl	New York	NY	10011	212-265-1742	
Web: victoryep.com					
Walthall Drake & Wallace LLP 6300 Rockside Rd	Cleveland	OH	44131	216-573-2330	
Web: www.walthall.com					
Wayne Long & Co 1502 Mill Rock Way Ste 200	Bakersfield	CA	93311	661-664-0909	
Web: welcpa.com					
Wilhelm Monroe Gallagher 256 N Washington St	Falls Church	VA	22046	703-241-5403	
Web: www.lowtaxsolutions.com					
Windes & McClaughry Accountancy Corp Landmark Sq 111 W Ocean Blvd 22nd Fl	Long Beach	CA	90802	562-435-1191	
Web: www.windes.com					
WISS & Company LLP 354 Eisenhower Pkwy	Livingston	NJ	07039	973-994-9400	
Web: www.wiss.com					
Wm Stukey & Associates LLC 1705 W Northwest Hwy Ste 220	Grapevine	TX	76051	817-481-3265	
Web: www.midcitiescpa.com					
Wolfe & Co 99 High St	Boston	MA	02110	617-439-9700	
Web: www.wolfandco.com					
Xpitax LLC 10 Forbes Rd W	Braintree	MA	02184	781-303-0136	
Web: www.xpitax.com					
Zimmermans Acctg & Tax Service Inc 804 Carpenter Ave	Iron Mountain	MI	49801	906-774-4529	

738 TELECOMMUNICATIONS EQUIPMENT & SYSTEMS

SEE ALSO Modems p. 2012; Radio & Television Broadcasting & Communications Equipment p. 3026

	City	State	Zip	Phone	Fax
ABB Flexible Automation Inc 12040 Regency Pkwy	Cary	NC	27518	919-856-2360	807-5022
Web: www.abb.com					
ADTRAN Inc 901 Explorer Blvd	Huntsville	AL	35806	256-963-8000	963-8004
NASDAQ: ADTN ■ *TF:* 800-923-8726 ■ *Web:* www.adtran.com					
AirNet Communications Corp 3950 Dow Rd Ste C	Melbourne	FL	32934	321-984-1990	676-9914
Web: www.aircom.com					
Airspan Networks Inc 777 Yamato Rd Ste 105	Boca Raton	FL	33431	561-893-8670	893-8671
OTC: AIRO ■ *Web:* www.airspan.com					
AltiGen Communications Inc 410 E Plumeria Dr	San Jose	CA	95134	408-597-9000	597-9020
OTC: ATGN ■ *TF:* 888-258-4436 ■ *Web:* www.altigen.com					
Amtelco 4800 Curtin Dr	McFarland	WI	53558	608-838-4194	838-8367
TF: 800-356-9148 ■ *Web:* www.amtelco.com					
AOC Technologies Inc 6690 Amador Plz Rd Ste 110	Dublin	CA	94568	925-875-0808	
Web: www.aoctech.com					
Argon ST Inc 12701 Fair Lakes Cir Ste 800	Fairfax	VA	22033	703-322-0881	322-0885
Web: www.argonst.com					
AT & T Inc 175 E Houston St PO Box 2933	San Antonio	TX	78299	210-821-4105	
NYSE: AT&T ■ *TF:* 800-351-7221 ■ *Web:* www.att.com					
Atris Inc 1151 S Trooper Rd Ste E	Norristown	PA	19403	800-724-3384	
TF: 800-724-3384 ■ *Web:* www.atris.biz					
Audiovox Corp 180 Marcus Blvd	Hauppauge	NY	11788	631-231-7750	
NASDAQ: VOXX ■ *TF:* 800-645-4994 ■ *Web:* www.voxxintl.com					
Aurora Networks Inc 5400 Betsy Ross Dr	Santa Clara	CA	95054	408-235-7000	
Web: www.aurora.com					
Axesstel Inc 6815 Flanders Dr Ste 210	San Diego	CA	92121	858-625-2100	625-2110
OTC: AXST ■ *Web:* www.axesstel.com					
Bo-Sherrel Company Inc 3340 Tree Swallow Pl	Fremont	CA	94555	510-792-0354	797-2038
Call One Inc 400 Imperial Blvd PO Box 9002	Cape Canaveral	FL	32920	321-783-2400	799-9222
TF: 800-749-3160 ■ *Web:* www.calloneonline.com					
Ceragon Networks Inc 10 Forest Ave	Paramus	NJ	07652	201-845-6955	845-5665
NASDAQ: CRNT ■ *TF Tech Supp:* 877-342-3247 ■ *Web:* www.ceragon.com					
Charles Industries Ltd 5600 Apollo Dr	Rolling Meadows	IL	60008	847-806-6300	806-6231
TF: 800-458-4747 ■ *Web:* www.charlesindustries.com					

Company	City	State	Zip	Phone	Fax
CiDRA Corp 50 Barnes Pk N *TF:* 877-243-7277 ■ *Web:* www.cidra.com	Wallingford	CT	06492	203-265-0035	294-4211
CIENA Corp 1201 Winterson Rd. *NASDAQ: CIEN* ■ *TF:* 800-921-1144 ■ *Web:* www.ciena.com	Linthicum	MD	21090	410-694-5700	694-5750
ClearOne Communications Inc 5225 Wiley Post Way *TF:* 800-945-7730 ■ *Web:* www.clearone.com	Salt Lake City	UT	84116	801-975-7200	977-0087
CoAdna Photonics Inc 733 Palomar Ave *Web:* www.coadna.com	Sunnyvale	CA	94085	408-736-1100	
COM DEV International Ltd 155 Sheldon Dr *TSE: CDV* ■ *Web:* www.comdev.ca	Cambridge	ON	N1R7H6	519-622-2300	622-1691
Comarco Inc 25541 Commerce Ctr Dr *OTC: CMRO* ■ *TF:* 800-792-0250 ■ *Web:* www.comarco.com	Lake Forest	CA	92630	949-599-7400	599-1415
Comarco Wireless Technologies Inc 25541 Commerce Ctr Dr. *TF Cust Svc:* 800-792-0250 ■ *Web:* www.comarco.com	Lake Forest	CA	92630	949-599-7400	599-1415
Communication Technologies Inc 14151 Newbrook Dr Ste 400 *TF:* 888-266-8358 ■ *Web:* www.comtechnologies.com	Chantilly	VA	20151	703-961-9080	961-1330
Communications Systems Inc 10900 Red Cir Dr *NASDAQ: JCS* ■ *Web:* www.commsystems.com	Minnetonka	MN	55343	952-996-1674	
Communications Test Design Inc 1339 Enterprise Dr *TF:* 800-223-3910 ■ *Web:* www.ctdi.com	West Chester	PA	19380	610-436-5203	
Compunetix Inc 2420 Mosside Blvd *TF:* 800-879-4266 ■ *Web:* www.compunetix.com	Monroeville	PA	15146	412-373-8110	373-2720
Comverse Network Systems Inc 200 Quannapowitt Pkwy *Web:* www.comverse.com	Wakefield	MA	01880	781 246 9000	224 8135
Consolidated Communications Holdings Inc 121 S 17th St *NASDAQ: CNSL* ■ *Web:* consolidated.com	Mattoon	IL	61938	217-235-3311	235-3311
Cyber Digital Inc 400 Oser Ave Ste 1650 *OTC: CYBD* ■ *Web:* www.cyberdigitalinc.com	Hauppauge	NY	11788	631-231-1200	231-1446
Digital Voice Corp 1201 S Beltline Rd Ste 150 *TF Cust Svc:* 800-777-8329 ■ *Web:* www.digitalvoicecorp.com	Coppell	TX	75019	469-635-6500	635-6500
DynaMetric Inc 717 S Myrtle Ave *TF:* 800-525-6925 ■ *Web:* www.dynametric.com	Monrovia	CA	91016	626-358-2559	359-5701
Dynamic Concepts Inc (DCI) 1730 17th St NE *Web:* www.dcihq.com	Washington	DC	20002	202-944-8787	526-7233
Ecessa Corp 2800 Campus Dr Ste 140 *TF:* 800-669-6242 ■ *Web:* www.ecessa.com	Plymouth	MN	55441	763-694-9949	551-0664
ECI Telecom Ltd 5100 NW 33rd Ave Ste 150 *Web:* www.ecitele.com	Fort Lauderdale	FL	33309	954-772-3070	351-4404
Electro Standards Laboratories Inc 36 Western Industrial Dr *TF:* 877-943-1164 ■ *Web:* www.electrostandards.com	Cranston	RI	02921	401-943-1164	
Electronic Tele-Communications Inc 1915 MacArthur Rd *OTC: ETCIA* ■ *TF:* 888-746-4382 ■ *Web:* www.etcia.com	Waukesha	WI	53188	262-542-5600	542-1524
Ericsson Inc 6300 Legacy Dr *Web:* www.ericsson.com	Plano	TX	75024	972-583-0000	
Ever Win International Corp 17579 Railroad St *Web:* www.everwin.com	City Of Industry	CA	91748	626-810-8218	
FleetBoss Global Positioning Solutions Inc 241 O'Brien Rd *TF:* 877-265-9559 ■ *Web:* www.fleetboss.com	Fern Park	FL	32730	407-265-9559	265-0365
Fujitsu America Inc 1250 E Arques Ave *TF:* 800-538-8460 ■ *Web:* www.fujitsu.com	Sunnyvale	CA	94085	408-746-6200	746-6260
GAI-Tronics Corp 400 E Wyomissing Ave *TF:* 800-492-1212 ■ *Web:* www.gai-tronics.com	Mohnton	PA	19540	610-777-1374	775-6540
General DataComm Inc 6 Rubber Ave *Web:* www.gdc.com	Naugatuck	CT	06770	203-729-0271	723-2883
Genesys Telecommunications Laboratories Inc 2001 Junipero Serra Blvd *TF:* 888-436-3797 ■ *Web:* genesys.com	Daly City	CA	94014	650-466-1100	466-1260
GN US Inc 77 NE Blvd. *TF:* 800-327-2230 ■ *Web:* www.jabra.com	Nashua	NH	03062	603-598-1100	598-1122
Harris Corp 1025 W NASA Blvd *NYSE: HRS* ■ *TF:* 800-442-7747 ■ *Web:* www.harris.com	Melbourne	FL	32919	321-727-9100	
Honeywell International Inc 101 Columbia Rd PO Box M6/LM *NYSE: HON* ■ *TF:* 877-841-2840 ■ *Web:* www.honeywell.com	Morristown	NJ	07962	480-353-3020	
Hughes Network Systems LLC 11717 Exploration Ln *TF:* 888-748-6288 ■ *Web:* www.hughes.com	Germantown	MD	20876	301-428-5500	428-1868
I Wireless 4135 NW Urbandale Dr *TF Cust Svc:* 888-550-4497 ■ *Web:* www.iwireless.com	Urbandale	IA	50322	515-258-7000	258-7100
iDirect Technologies Inc 13865 Sunrise Valley Dr Ste 100 *TF:* 888-362-5475 ■ *Web:* www.idirect.net	Herndon	VA	20171	703-648-8118	648-8014
Infinera Corp 140 Caspian Ct. *NASDAQ: INFN* ■ *TF:* 877-742-3427 ■ *Web:* www.infinera.com	Sunnyvale	CA	94089	408-572-5200	572-5454
InnoMedia Inc 128 Baytech Dr *TF:* 888-251-6250 ■ *Web:* www.innomedia.com	San Jose	CA	95134	408-432-5400	941-8152
ISCO International LLC 1450 Arthur Ave Ste A *TF:* 888-948-4726 ■ *Web:* www.iscointl.com	Elk Grove Village	IL	60007	224-222-1666	222-1691
ITUS Corp 900 Walt Whitman Rd *OTC: COPY* ■ *Web:* ctipatents.com/	Melville	NY	11747	631-549-5900	549-5974
JTech Communications Inc 6413 Congress Ave Ste 150 **Fax Area Code:* 561 ■ *TF:* 800-321-6221 ■ *Web:* www.jtech.com	Boca Raton	FL	33487	800-321-6221	995-2260*
Kaiam Corp 39655 Eureka Dr *Web:* www.kaiamcorp.com	Newark	CA	94560	510-344-2231	
L-3 Communications Corp 600 Third Ave 34-35 Fl. *NYSE: LLL* ■ *TF:* 800-351-8483 ■ *Web:* www.l-3com.com	New York	NY	10016	212-697-1111	490-0731
Lantronix Inc 167 Technology Dr *NASDAQ: LTRX* ■ *TF Orders:* 800-526-8766 ■ *Web:* www.lantronix.com	Irvine	CA	92618	949-453-3990	450-7249
LCC International Inc 7900 Westpark Dr Ste A300 *Web:* www.lcc.com	McLean	VA	22102	703-873-2000	873-2100
Mercury Systems Inc 267 Lowell Road Suite 101 *NASDAQ: MRCY* ■ *Web:* rf.mrcy.com	Hudson	NH	03051	603-546-4100	
Metro-Tel Corp 11640 Arbor St Ste 100 *TF:* 888-998-8300 ■ *Web:* www.metrotelcorp.com	Omaha	NE	68144	402-498-2964	493-5100
Microlog Corp 401 Professional Dr Ste 125 *Web:* www.mlog.com	Gaithersburg	MD	20879	301-540-5500	330-2450
Microphase Corp 587 Connecticut Ave. *Web:* www.microphase.com	Norwalk	CT	06854	203-866-8000	866-6727
Microsemi-RFIS 1000 Avenida Acaso. *Web:* www.microsemi.com	Camarillo	CA	93012	805-388-1345	484-2191
Mitel Networks Corp 350 Legget Dr PO Box 13089 *TF:* 800-722-1301 ■ *Web:* www.mitel.com	Kanata	ON	K2K2W7	613-592-2122	592-4724
Molex Premise Networks 2222 Wellington Ct. *TF:* 866-733-6659 ■ *Web:* www.molexpn.com	Lisle	IL	60532	630-969-4550	969-1352
Motorola Inc IDEN Group 8000 W Sunrise Blvd *Web:* motorola-mobility-en-in.custhelp.com	Plantation	FL	33322	800-102-2344	
Movius Interactive 11360 Lakefield Dr. *TF Tech Supp:* 800-688-4001 ■ *Web:* www.moviuscorp.com	Duluth	GA	30097	770-283-1000	
NDS Americas 3500 Highland Ave *TF:* 866-398-8749 ■ *Web:* www.cisco.com	Costa Mesa	CA	92626	714-434-2100	434-2474
NEC America Inc 6555 N State Hwy 161 *TF Cust Svc:* 866-632-3226 ■ *Web:* www.necam.com	Irving	TX	75039	214-262-2000	262-2114
Network Equipment Technologies Inc 6900 Paseo Padre Pkwy *NASDAQ: NWK*	Fremont	CA	94555	510-713-7300	574-4000
NextIO Inc 8303 N MoPac Expy	Austin	TX	78759	512-439-5350	439-5391
NICE Systems Inc 301 Rt 17 N 10th Fl. *TF:* 800-994-4498 ■ *Web:* www.nice.com	Rutherford	NJ	07070	201-964-2600	964-2610
Nokia Inc 200 S Mathilda Ave *NYSE: NOK* ■ **Fax Area Code:* 914 ■ *Web:* www.nokia.com	Sunnyvale	CA	94086	408-530-7600	368-0501*
Norsat International Inc 110-4020 Viking Way *TSE: NII* ■ *TF:* 800-644-4562 ■ *Web:* www.norsat.com	Richmond	BC	V6V2N2	604-821-2800	821-2801
Numerex Corp 1600 Parkwood Cir Fifth Fl. *NASDAQ: NMRX* ■ *TF:* 800-665-5686 ■ *Web:* www.numerex.com	Atlanta	GA	30339	770-693-5950	693-5951
Oplink Communications Inc 46335 Landing Pkwy *NASDAQ: OPLK* ■ *Web:* www.oplink.com	Fremont	CA	94538	510-933-7200	933-7300
Optelian Inc 1700 Enterprise Way SE Ste 101 *Web:* www.optelian.com	Marietta	GA	30067	770-690-9575	
Optoplex Corp 3374-3390 Gateway Blvd *Web:* www.optoplex.com	Fremont	CA	94538	510-490-9930	
Orion Systems Inc 602 Masons Mill Business Pk *Web:* www.orionsystemsinc.net	Huntingdon Valley	PA	19006	215-659-1207	659-4234
OSRAM Sylvania Inc 100 Endicott St *Web:* www.sylvania.com	Danvers	MA	01923	978-777-1900	750-2152
PBE Group, The 1459 Wittens Mill Rd *Web:* www.pyottboone.com	Tazewell	VA	24630	276-988-5505	988-6820
Pics Telecom International Corp 1920 Lyell Ave *TF:* 800-521-7427 ■ *Web:* www.picstelecom.com	Rochester	NY	14606	585-295-2000	295-2020
Plantronics Inc 345 Encinal St *NYSE: PLT* ■ *TF:* 800-544-4660 ■ *Web:* www.plantronics.com	Santa Cruz	CA	95060	831-426-5858	426-6098
Polycom Inc 4750 Willow Rd **Fax:* Hum Res ■ *TF:* 800-765-9266 ■ *Web:* www.polycom.com	Pleasanton	CA	94588	800-765-9266	*
Protel Inc 4150 Kidron Rd. *TF:* 800-925-8882 ■ *Web:* www.protelinc.com	Lakeland	FL	33811	863-644-5558	646-5855
Proxim Wireless Corp 1561 Buckeye Dr. *OTC: PRXM* ■ *TF:* 800-229-1630 ■ *Web:* www.proxim.com	Milpitas	CA	95035	408-383-7600	383-7680
Pulse Communications Inc 2900 Towerview Rd **Fax:* Cust Svc ■ *TF Cust Svc:* 800-381-1997 ■ *Web:* www.pulse.com	Herndon	VA	20171	703-471-2900	471-2951*
Qualcomm Inc 5775 Morehouse Dr. *NASDAQ: QCOM* ■ *Web:* www.qualcomm.com	San Diego	CA	92121	858-587-1121	658-2100
Quintron Systems Inc 2105 S Blosser Rd. *Web:* www.quintron.com	Santa Maria	CA	93458	805-928-4343	928-9914
RAD Data Communications Ltd 900 Corporate Dr. *TF:* 800-444-7234 ■ *Web:* www.rad.com	Mahwah	NJ	07430	201-529-1100	529-1157
Redcom Laboratories Inc One Redcom Ctr *Web:* www.redcom.com	Victor	NY	14564	585-924-7550	924-6572
RFL Electronics Inc 353 Powerville Rd *Web:* www.rflelect.com	Boonton	NJ	07005	973-334-3100	334-3863
SAJE Technology LLC 765 Dixon Ct *Web:* www.saje-tech.com	Hoffman Estates	IL	60192	847-756-7603	496-4515
Samsung Telecommunications America LLP 1301 E Lookout Dr *TF:* 800-726-7864 ■ *Web:* www.samsung.com	Richardson	TX	75082	972-761-7000	761-7001
Sanyo Fisher Co 21605 Plummer St *Web:* us.sanyo.com	Chatsworth	CA	91311	818-998-7322	
Siemens Canada Ltd 1550 Appleby Line *Web:* www.siemens.com	Burlington	ON	L7L6X7	905-319-3600	319-7170
SmarTrunk Systems Inc 867 Bowsprit Rd *Web:* www.smartrunk.com	Chula Vista	CA	91914	619-426-3781	426-3788
Sonetronics Inc PO Box L *Web:* www.sonetronics.com	West Belmar	NJ	07719	732-681-5016	681-5216
SPL Integrated Solutions 6301 Benjamin Rd Ste 101 *TF:* 800-292-4125 ■ *Web:* www.avispl.com	Tampa	FL	33634	813-884-7168	882-9508
Star Dynamics Corp 100 Outwater Ln *Web:* www.stardynamic.com	Garfield	NJ	07026	973-340-3883	340-1530
STM Wireless Inc Two Faraday *Web:* emcsatcom.com/	Irvine	CA	92618	949-273-6800	
Superior Essex Communications LP 6120 Powers Ferry Rd Ste 150 *TF:* 800-551-8948 ■ *Web:* www.superioressex.com	Atlanta	GA	30339	770-657-6000	657-6652
Suttle 1001 E Hwy 212 *TF:* 800-852-8662 ■ *Web:* www.suttleonline.com	Hector	MN	55342	320-848-6711	848-6218

Phone Fax

Symetrics Industries Inc 1615 W NASA Blvd .... Melbourne FL 32901 321-254-1500 259-4122
Web: www.symetrics.com

Symmetricom Inc 2300 Orchard Pkwy .... San Jose CA 95131 408-433-0910 428-7998
NASDAQ: SYMM ■ *TF:* 888-367-7966 ■ *Web:* microsemi.com/index.php

Syntellect Inc
16610 N Black Canyon Hwy Ste 100 .... Phoenix AZ 85053 800-788-9733 789-2899*
**Fax Area Code:* 602 ■ *TF:* 800-788-9733 ■ *Web:* www.syntellect.com

System Engineering International Inc (SEI)
5115 Pegasus Ct Ste Q .... Frederick MD 21704 301-694-9601 694-9608
TF: 800-765-4734 ■ *Web:* www.seipower.com

TAG Solutions LLC 12 Elmwood Rd .... Albany NY 12204 518-292-6500 292-6510
TF: 800-724-0023 ■ *Web:* www.tagsolutions.com

Taylored Systems Inc
14701 Cumberland Rd Ste 100 .... Noblesville IN 46060 317-776-4000 776-4004
Web: www.taylored.com

Technical Communications Corp 100 Domino Dr ..... Concord MA 01742 978-287-5100 371-1280
NASDAQ: TCCO ■ *TF:* 800-952-4082 ■ *Web:* www.tccsecure.com

Tekelec 5200 Paramount Pkwy .... Morrisville NC 27560 919-460-5500 460-0877
NASDAQ: TKLC ■ *TF:* 800-633-0738 ■
Web: oracle.com/us/corporate/acquisitions/tekelec/index.html

Tel Electronics Inc
313 S 740 E St Suite 1 .... American Fork UT 84003 801-756-9606 756-9135
TF: 800-564-9424 ■ *Web:* www.tel-electronics.com

Telco Systems Inc 15 Berkshire Rd .... Mansfield MA 02048 781-255-2120 255-2122
TF: 800-227-0937 ■ *Web:* www.telco.com

Telect Inc 23321 E Knox Ave .... Liberty Lake WA 99019 509-926-6000 926-8915
TF Cust Svc: 800-551-4567 ■ *Web:* www.telect.com

Telemobile Inc 19840 Hamilton Ave .... Torrance CA 90502 310-538-5100 532-8526
Web: www.telemobile.com

Tellabs Inc 1415 W Diehl Rd .... Naperville IL 60563 630-798-8800 798-2000
NASDAQ: TLAB ■ *Web:* www.tellabs.com

Teo Technologies Inc 11609 49th Pl W .... Mukilteo WA 98275 425-349-1000 349-1010
TF: 800-524-0024 ■ *Web:* www.tonecommander.com

Tollgrade Communications Inc
3120 Unionville Rd Ste 400 .... Cranberry Township PA 16066 412-820-1400 820-1530
TF Cust Svc: 800-878-3399 ■ *Web:* www.tollgrade.com

Toshiba America Inc
1251 Ave of the Americas Ste 4100 .... New York NY 10020 212-596-0600 593-3875
TF: 800-457-7777 ■ *Web:* www.toshiba.com

Tricomm Services Corp
1247 N Church St Ste 8 .... Moorestown NJ 08057 856-914-9001 914-9065
TF: 800-872-2401 ■ *Web:* www.tricommcorp.com

TSI Global Cos 700 Fountain Lakes Blvd .... Saint Charles MO 63301 636-949-8889 925-2111
TF: 800-875-5605 ■ *Web:* www.tsi-global.com

Tyco Telecommunications 60 Columbia Rd .... Morristown NJ 07960 973-656-8000
Web: www.tycotelecom.com

Uniden America Corp 4700 Amon Carter Blvd .... Fort Worth TX 76155 817-858-3300 858-3300*
**Fax:* Hum Res ■ *TF Cust Svc:* 800-297-1023 ■ *Web:* www.uniden.com

UTStarcom Inc 1732 North First St Ste 220 .... San Jose CA 95112 408-453-4557 996-7273*
NASDAQ: UTSI ■ **Fax Area Code:* 510 ■ *TF:* 877-547-6340 ■ *Web:* www.utstar.com

Valcom Inc 5614 Hollins Rd .... Roanoke VA 24019 540-563-2000 362-9800
TF: 800-825-2661 ■ *Web:* www.valcom.com

Vbrick Systems Inc 12 Beaumont Rd .... Wallingford CT 06492 203-265-0044 265-6750
TF: 866-827-4251 ■ *Web:* www.vbrick.com

VCON Inc 578 Main St .... Hackensack NJ 07601 201-883-1220
Web: www.clearone.com

Vela Research LP 5540 Rio Vista Dr .... Clearwater FL 33760 727-507-5300 507-5312
Web: www.vela.com

Veramark Technologies Inc
1565 Jefferson Rd .... Rochester NY 14623 585-381-6000 383-6800
Web: www.veramark.com

VTech Communications Inc
9590 SW Gemini Dr Ste 120 .... Beaverton OR 97008 503-596-1200 644-9887
TF: 800-595-9511 ■ *Web:* www.vtech.com

Westell Technologies Inc 750 N Commons Dr .... Aurora IL 60504 630-898-2500 375-4931*
NASDAQ: WSTL ■ **Fax:* Sales ■ *TF:* 800-323-6883 ■ *Web:* www.westell.com

Wireless Telecom Group Inc 25 Eastmans Rd ...... Parsippany NJ 07054 973-386-9696 386-9191
NYSE: WTT ■ *Web:* www.wirelesstelecomgroup.com

XETA Technologies Inc 1814 W Tacoma St .... Broken Arrow OK 74012 918-664-8200 664-6876

Zhone Technologies Inc 7001 Oakport St .... Oakland CA 94621 510-777-7000 777-7001
NASDAQ: ZHNE ■ *TF:* 877-946-6320 ■ *Web:* www.zhone.com

739 TELECOMMUNICATIONS SERVICES

Phone Fax

4g Wireless Inc 8871 Research Dr .... Irvine CA 92618 949-748-6100
Web: www.4gwireless.com

Access America 673 Emory Vly Rd .... Oak Ridge TN 37830 865-482-2140 482-2306
TF: 800-860-2140 ■ *Web:* www.accessam.com

Access Point Inc 1100 Crescent Green .... Cary NC 27518 919-851-4838
TF: 877-419-4274 ■ *Web:* www.accesspointinc.com

Accessory Export LLC 4105 Indus Way .... Riverside CA 92503 951-687-1140
Web: www.empirecase.com

Acision 6404 International Pkwy Ste 2048 .... Plano TX 75093 972-246-5400
Web: www.acision.com

Acotel Interactive Inc 80 Pine St 29th Fl .... New York NY 10005 212-400-1212
Web: www.flycell.com

ACT Conferencing
1526 Cole Blvd Bldg 3 Ste 300 .... Lakewood CO 80401 303-233-3500 238-0096
TF: 800-433-2900 ■ *Web:* www.actconferencing.com

Advanced 2000 Systems Inc 718 Circle Dr E .... Saskatoon SK S7K3T7 306-955-2355
Web: www.airsource.net

Advanced Telecom Services Inc
996 Old Eagle School Rd Ste 1105 .... Wayne PA 19087 610-688-6000
Web: www.atsmobile.com

AirIQ Inc 1815 Ironstone Manor Unit 10 .... Pickering ON L1W3W9 905-831-6444
Web: airiq.com

Airvoice Wireless LLC
2425 Franklin Rd .... Bloomfield Hills MI 48302 888-944-2355
TF: 888-944-2355 ■ *Web:* www.airvoicewireless.com

Alaska Communications Systems Group Inc
600 Telephone Ave .... Anchorage AK 99503 907-563-8000 297-3100
NASDAQ: ALSK ■ *TF:* 800-808-8083 ■ *Web:* www.alaskacommunications.com

Allstream Corp 200 Wellington St W .... Toronto ON M5V3G2 416-345-2000 363-0962
TF Cust Svc: 888-288-2273 ■ *Web:* www.allstream.com

AmeriCom Inc PO Box 2146 .... Sandy UT 84091 801-571-2446 257-6643*
**Fax Area Code:* 775 ■ *TF:* 800-820-6296 ■ *Web:* www.americom.com

Aperto Networks Inc 598 Gibraltar Dr .... Milpitas CA 95035 408-719-9977 719-9970
Web: www.apertonet.com

AT & T Inc 175 E Houston St PO Box 2933 .... San Antonio TX 78299 210-821-4105
NYSE: AT&T ■ *TF:* 800-351-7221 ■ *Web:* www.att.com

Auragan LLC PO Box 1501 .... New Canaan CT 06840 866-644-2872
TF: 866-644-2872 ■ *Web:* www.advection.net

Bell Aliant Regional Communications
7 S Maritime Centre 1505 Barrington St .... Halifax NS B3J3K5 800-267-1110
TSE: BA ■ *TF:* 800-555-1212 ■ *Web:* www.bellaliant.net

Bell Canada
1050 Beaver Hall Hill Bureau 3700 .... Montreal QC H2Z1S4 800-667-0123
TF: 800-667-0123 ■ *Web:* www.bell.ca

Birch Communications Inc
2300 Main St 6th Fl .... Kansas City MO 64108 816-300-3000
TF: 866-424-5100 ■ *Web:* www.birch.com

Bledsoe Telephone Co-op Corp (BTC)
338 Cumberland Ave PO Box 609 .... Pikeville TN 37367 423-447-2121 447-2498
TF: 888-382-1222 ■ *Web:* www.bledsoe.net

Bluegrass Cellular Inc
2902 Ring Rd PO Box 5012 .... Elizabethtown KY 42702 270-769-0339
TF: 800-928-2355 ■ *Web:* www.bluegrasscellular.com

Blumerich Communications Service
6403 W Pierson Rd .... Flushing MI 48433 810-659-5000
Web: www.blumerich.com

Brazoria Telephone Co 314 W Texas St .... Brazoria TX 77422 979-798-2121 798-3005
Web: www.btel.com

Broadview Networks Holdings Inc
800 Westchester Ave Ste N-501 .... Rye Brook NY 10573 914-922-7000 922-7001
TF: 800-260-8766 ■ *Web:* www.broadviewnet.com

Bruce Telecom 3145 Hwy 21 N R R#3 .... Tiverton ON N0G2T0 519-368-2000
Web: www.brucetelecom.com

Cap Rock Telephone Co-op Inc PO Box 300 .... Spur TX 79370 806-271-3336 271-3601
Web: www.caprock-spur.com

Cavalier Telephone LLC 2134 W Laburnum Ave ...... Richmond VA 23227 800-442-2410 422-4200*
**Fax Area Code:* 804 ■ *TF:* 800-683-3944 ■ *Web:* www.cavtel.com

Cellhire USA LLC 3520 W Miller Rd Ste 100 .... Garland TX 75041 214-355-5200
Web: www.cellhire.com

Cellular Communications Inc
3301 13th Ave S Ste 109 .... Fargo ND 58103 701-241-4394
Web: www.cellcominc.com

Century Interactive LLC
8750 N Central Expy Ste 720 .... Dallas TX 75231 214-446-7867
TF: 877-921-7992 ■ *Web:* www.centuryinteractive.com

Cesium Telecom Inc 5798 Ferrier .... Montreal QC H4P1M7 514-798-8686
Web: www.cesiumonline.com

Cincinnati Bell Inc 221 E Fourth St .... Cincinnati OH 45202 513-397-9900 241-1264
NYSE: CBB ■ *TF:* 800-387-3638 ■ *Web:* www.cincinnatibell.com

Circa Enterprises Inc 206-5 Richard Way SW .... Calgary AB T3E7M8 403-258-2011
Web: www.circaent.com

Citizens Telephone Co-op PO Box 137 .... Floyd VA 24091 540-745-2111 745-3791
TF: 800-941-0426 ■ *Web:* www.citizens.coop

Co-op Communications Inc 210 Clay Ave .... Lyndhurst NJ 07071 800-833-2700 531-0150*
**Fax Area Code:* 201 ■ *TF:* 800-833-2700 ■ *Web:* www.cooperativenet.com

Commenco Inc 4901 Bristol Ave .... Kansas City MO 64129 816-753-2166
Web: www.commenco.com

Commonwealth Telephone Co
1 Newbury Street Suite 103 .... Peabody MA 01960 978-536-9500
TF: 800-439-7170 ■ *Web:* www.commonwealthtel.com

Communication Services Inc 2151 E Broadway Rd ...... Tempe AZ 85282 480-905-8689 905-8818
Web: www.com-serv.com

Comporium Communications 332 E Main St .... Rock Hill SC 29730 888-403-2667 326-5708*
**Fax Area Code:* 803 ■ *TF:* 866-922-5922 ■ *Web:* www.comporium.com

Computer Consulting Operations Specialists Inc
600 Corporate Pointe .... Culver City CA 90230 310-568-5000 417-7991
Web: www.ccops.com

Conference Plus Inc 1051 E Woodfield Rd .... Schaumburg IL 60173 847-619-6100
Web: conferenceplus.com

Convergent Media Systems Corp
190 Bluegrass Vly Pkwy 1 Convergent Ctr .... Alpharetta GA 30005 770-369-9000 369-9100
Web: www.convergent.com

Corporate Telephone Services 184 W Second St .... Boston MA 02127 617-625-1200 625-1201
TF: 800-274-1211 ■ *Web:* corptelserv.com

CPA2Biz Inc 100 Broadway Sixth Fl .... New York NY 10005 646-233-5000 233-5090
TF: 888-777-7077 ■ *Web:* www.cpa2biz.com

Criticom Inc 4211 Forbes Blvd .... Lanham MD 20706 301-306-0600
TF: 800-449-3384 ■ *Web:* www.ultra-3eti.com

Cypress Communications Inc
3565 Piedmont Rd NE .... Atlanta GA 30305 404-869-2500 869-2525
TF: 844-276-2386 ■ *Web:* www.broadvox.com

D2 Technologie 2119 Boul Marcel-laurin .... Saint-laurent QC H4R1K4 514-904-5888
Web: d2technologie.com

Dakota Central Telecommunications Co-op
630 Fifth St N .... Carrington ND 58421 701-652-3184 674-8121
TF: 800-771-0974 ■ *Web:* www.daktel.com

Deltacom Inc 7037 Old Madison Pike .... Huntsville AL 35806 800-239-3000
TF: 800-239-3000 ■ *Web:* www.deltacom.com

deltathree Inc 75 Broad St .... New York NY 10004 212-500-4850 500-4888
PINK: DDDC ■ *TF:* 888-335-8230 ■ *Web:* deltathree.com

Develcon Inc 401 Magnetic Dr Units 15-17 .... Toronto ON M3J3H9 416-385-1390
Web: www.develcon.com

Digerati Technologies Inc
3463 Magic Dr Ste 355 .... San Antonio TX 78229 210-614-7240 614-7264
OTC: DTGI ■ *TF:* 855-202-5683 ■ *Web:* www.digerati-inc.com

Eastex Telephone Co-op Inc PO Box 150 .... Henderson TX 75653 903-854-1000 854-1203
TF: 800-232-7839 ■ *Web:* www.eastex.com

Company	City	State	Zip	Phone	Fax
EATELCORP Inc 913 S Burnside Ave *TF:* 800-621-4211 ■ *Web:* eatel.com	Gonzales	LA	70737	225-621-4300	
Electronique Mercier Ltee 162 Rue Fraser *Web:* www.emercier.com	Riviere-du-loup	QC	G5R1C8	418-862-7269	
Empire Telephone Corp 34 Main St PO Box 349 *TF:* 800-338-3300 ■ *Web:* www.empiretelephone.com	Prattsburgh	NY	14873	607-522-3712	
Etex Telephone Co-op Inc 1013 Hwy 155 N. *TF:* 877-482-3839 ■ *Web:* www.etex.net	Gilmer	TX	75644	903-797-2711	797-6666
Excel Telecommunications 433 Las Colinas Blvd Ste 400. *TF:* 877-668-0808 ■ *Web:* www.excel.com	Irving	TX	75039	972-910-1900	
FairPoint Communications Inc 521 E Morehead St Ste 250 *NASDAQ: FRP* ■ *TF:* 866-740-2764 ■ *Web:* www.fairpoint.com	Charlotte	NC	28202	704-344-8150	
Farmers Telecommunications Co-op (FTC) 144 McCurdy Ave N PO Box 217 *TF:* 866-638-2144 ■ *Web:* www.farmerstel.com	Rainsville	AL	35986	256-638-2144	638-4830
Farmers Telephone Co-op Inc 1101 E Main St. *TF:* 888-218-5050 ■ *Web:* www.ftc-i.net	Kingstree	SC	29556	843-382-2333	382-2333
Faxaway 417 Second Ave W *TF:* 800-906-4329 ■ *Web:* www.faxaway.com	Seattle	WA	98119	206-301-7000	301-7500
FaxBack Inc 7007 SW Cardinal Ln Ste 105 *TF:* 800-329-2225 ■ *Web:* www.faxback.com	Portland	OR	97224	503-597-5350	597-5399
FiberTower Corp 185 Berry St Ste 4800 *OTC: FTWRQ* ■ *Web:* www.fibertower.com	San Francisco	CA	94107	415-659-3500	
Fido Solutions Inc 800 De La Gauchetiere St W Ste 4000 *Web:* www.fido.ca	Montreal	QC	H5A1K3	514-933-3436	
Filer Mutual Telephone Co PO Box 89 *Web:* www.filertel.com	Filer	ID	83328	208-326-4331	326-3190
Frontier Communications Corp Three High Ridge Pk. *NASDAQ: FTR* ■ *TF:* 800-877-4390 ■ *Web:* www.frontier.com	Stamford	CT	06905	203-614-5600	614-4602
Fusion Telecommunications International Inc 420 Lexington Ave Ste 1718. *OTC: FSNN* ■ *TF:* 888-301-1721 ■ *Web:* fusionconnect.com/	New York	NY	10170	212-201-2400	972-7884
General Communication Inc 2550 Denali St Ste 1000. *NASDAQ: GNCMA* ■ *TF:* 800-770-7886 ■ *Web:* www.gci.com	Anchorage	AK	99503	907-265-5600	868-5676
GetWireless LLC 10901 Red Cir Dr. *Web:* www.getwirelessllc.com	Minnetonka	MN	55343	952-890-6669	
Global Domains International Inc 701 Palomar Airport Rd Ste 300. *Web:* www.worldsite.ws	Carlsbad	CA	92009	760-602-3000	602-3099
Golden State Cellular 17400 High School Rd *TF:* 800-453-8255 ■ *Web:* www.goldenstatecellular.com	Jamestown	CA	95327	209-984-8700	
Golden West Telecommunications 415 Crown St PO Box 411 *TF:* 866-279-2161 ■ *Web:* www.goldenwest.com	Wall	SD	57790	605-279-2161	279-2727
GPShopper LLC 584 Broadway Ste 904 *Web:* www.gpshopper.com	New York	NY	10012	212-488-2222	
Granite Telecommunications LLC 100 Newport Ave Ext. *TF:* 866-847-1500 ■ *Web:* www.granitenet.com	Quincy	MA	02171	617-933-5500	328-0312
Graphnet Inc 40 Fultron St 28th Fl. *TF:* 800-327-1800 ■ *Web:* www.graphnet.com	New York	NY	10038	212-994-1100	994-1199
GTT Communications Inc 7900 Tysons One Pl Ste 1450. *NYSE: GTT* ■ *TF:* 866-250-3887 ■ *Web:* www.gtt.net	McLean	VA	22102	703-442-5500	
GTX Corp 117 W Ninth St Ste 1214 *Web:* www.gtxcorp.com	Los Angeles	CA	90015	213-489-3019	
Guadalupe Valley Telephone Co-op (GVTC) 36101 FM 3159 *TF:* 800-367-4882 ■ *Web:* www.gvtc.com	New Braunfels	TX	78132	830-885-4411	885-2400
Guidance Solutions Inc 4134 Del Rey Ave *Web:* www.guidance.com	Marina del Rey	CA	90292	310-754-4000	754-4010
Hargray Communications 856 William Hilton Pkwy PO Box 5986 *TF:* 800-726-1266 ■ *Web:* www.hargray.com	Hilton Head Island	SC	29938	843-341-1501	
Harrisonville Telephone Co 213 S Main St PO Box 149. *TF:* 888-482-8353 ■ *Web:* htc.net	Waterloo	IL	62298	618-939-6112	939-4826
Hayneville Telephone Company Inc PO Box 175 *Web:* www.htcnet.net	Hayneville	AL	36040	334-548-2101	548-2051
Hop-on Inc 2222 Michelson Dr Ste 222 *Web:* hop-on.com	Irvine	CA	92612	949-756-9008	
Horry Telephone Co-op Inc (HTC) 3480 Hwy 701 N PO Box 1820. *TF:* 800-824-6779 ■ *Web:* www.htcinc.net	Conway	SC	29528	843-365-2151	365-0855
iBasis Inc 20 Second Ave *Web:* www.ibasis.com	Burlington	MA	01803	781-505-7500	505-7300
IDT Corp 520 Broad St *NYSE: IDT* ■ *Web:* www.idt.net	Newark	NJ	07102	973-438-1000	438-1453
Ingenicomm Inc 14120 Parke Long Court Ste 210 *Web:* www.ingenicomm.net	Chantilly	VA	20151	703-665-4333	
Integra Telecom Inc 1201 NE Lloyd Blvd Ste 500. *TF General:* 866-468-3472 ■ *Web:* www.integratelecom.com	Portland	OR	97232	503-453-8000	453-8221
Inter-Community Telephone Co (ICTC) PO Box 8 *TF:* 800-350-9137 ■ *Web:* www.ictc.com	Nome	ND	58062	701-924-8815	924-8808
InterCall 8420 W Bryn Mawr Ste 1100 *TF:* 800-374-2441 ■ *Web:* www.intercall.com	Chicago	IL	60631	773-399-1600	399-1588
Interop Technologies LLC 13500 Powers Centre *Web:* www.interoptechnologies.com	Fort Myers	FL	33912	239-425-3000	
Intrado Inc 1601 Dry Creek Dr *TF:* 877-262-3775 ■ *Web:* www.intrado.com	Longmont	CO	80503	720-494-5800	494-6600
Iridium Satellite LLC 6701 Democracy Blvd *TF:* 866-947-4348 ■ *Web:* www.iridium.com	Bethesda	MD	20817	301-571-6200	571-6250
IVCi LLC 601 Old Willets Path *TF:* 800-224-7083 ■ *Web:* www.ivci.com	Hauppauge	NY	11788	631-273-5800	273-7277
J2 Global Communications Inc 6922 Hollywood Blvd Eighth Fl *TF Sales:* 888-718-2000 ■ *Web:* www.j2global.com	Los Angeles	CA	90028	323-860-9200	
Japan Telecom America Inc 100 Wall St Ste 1803 *Web:* www.jt-america.com	New York	NY	10005	212-422-4650	
Kaplan Telephone Company Inc (KTC) 220 N Cushing Ave. *TF:* 866-643-7171 ■ *Web:* www.ktconline.net	Kaplan	LA	70548	337-643-7171	643-6000
KDDI America Inc 825 Third Ave Third Fl *Web:* kddia.com	New York	NY	10022	212-295-1200	295-1080
Kennebec Telephone Company Inc 220 S Main St. *TF:* 888-868-3390 ■ *Web:* www.kennebectelephone.com	Kennebec	SD	57544	605-869-2220	869-2221
Kentec Communications Inc 915 W Main St *Web:* kci.net	Sterling	CO	80751	970-522-8107	
Lambeau Telecom 1807 N Ctr St *TF Cust Svc:* 800-444-4014 ■ *Web:* bcntele.com	Beaver Dam	WI	53916	920-887-3148	
Liberty Global Inc 12300 Liberty Blvd. *NASDAQ: LBTYA* ■ *Web:* www.libertyglobal.com	Englewood	CO	80112	303-220-6600	220-6601
LICT Corp 401 Theodore Fremd Ave. *TF:* 800-690-6903 ■ *Web:* www.lictcorp.com	Rye	NY	10580	914-921-8821	921-6410
Lightower Fiber Networks 80 Central St. *TF:* 888-583-4237 ■ *Web:* www.lightower.com	Boxborough	MA	01719	978-264-6000	
Linkedin Corp 2029 Stierlin Ct. *Web:* www.linkedin.com	Mountain View	CA	94043	650-687-3600	687-0505
Matanuska Telephone Assn Inc 1740 S Chugach St. *Web:* www.mta-telco.com	Palmer	AK	99645	907-745-3211	761-2481
Mckay Brothers LLC 2355 broadway. *Web:* www.mckay-brothers.com	Oakland	CA	94612	510-891-1731	
Mercury Wireless LLC 2825 se california ave. *TF:* 800-354-4915 ■ *Web:* www.mercurywireless.com	Topeka	KS	66605	800-354-4915	
Meru Networks Inc 894 Ross Dr *Web:* www.merunetworks.com	Sunnyvale	CA	94089	408-215-5300	
Microserve 276 Fifth Ave Ste 1011 *Web:* www.mserve.com	New York	NY	10001	212-683-2811	
Midcontinent Communications PO Box 5010 *TF:* 800-888-1300 ■ *Web:* www.midcocomm.com	Sioux Falls	SD	57117	605-274-9810	
Modern Wireless Inc 1163 N Patt St *Web:* www.modernwirelessusa.com	Anaheim	CA	92801	714-535-6399	
Molalla Communications Co 211 Robbins St PO Box 360. *TF:* 800-332-2344 ■ *Web:* www.molalla.net	Molalla	OR	97038	503-829-1100	829-7781
Multiband Corp 9449 Science Ctr Dr. *NASDAQ: MBND* ■ *Web:* www.multibandusa.com	New Hope	MN	55428	763-504-3000	504-3060
National Field Service Corp (NFS) 162 Orange Ave *Web:* nfsco.com	Suffern	NY	10901	845-368-1600	368-1989
NativeX LLC 1900 Medical Arts Ave S. *Web:* nativex.com	Sartell	MN	56377	320-257-7500	
Net Access Corp Nine Wing Dr *TF:* 800-638-6336 ■ *Web:* www.nac.net	Cedar Knolls	NJ	07927	973-590-5000	590-5080
Net Talk.Com Inc 1080 NW 163rd Dr. *Web:* www.nettalk.com	Miami	FL	33169	305-621-1200	
Net2Phone Inc 520 Broad St. *TF:* 800-386-6438 ■ *Web:* www.net2phone.com	Newark	NJ	07102	973-438-3111	412-2829
Netwolves Corp 4710 Eisenhower Blvd Ste E-8 *Web:* www.netwolves.com	Tampa	FL	33634	813-579-3200	882-0209
Network Communications International Corp (NCIC) PO Box 551 *TF:* 800-382-2887 ■ *Web:* www.ncic.com	Longview	TX	75601	903-757-4455	247-2057
Network Services LLC 2065 Kensington Ave *Web:* www.ns-wny.com	Amherst	NY	14226	716-839-5309	839-5301
New Global Telecom Inc 143 Union Blvd Ste 400 *Web:* www.ngt.com	Lakewood	CO	80228	303-278-0700	278-0728
New Ulm Telecom Inc 27 N Minnesota St. *OTC: NULM* ■ *TF:* 888-873-6853 ■ *Web:* www.newulmtel.net	New Ulm	MN	56073	507-354-4111	354-1982
Nexius Inc 825 Market St Ste 250. *Web:* www.nexius.com	Allen	TX	75013	703-650-7777	
NII Holdings Inc 1875 Explorer St Ste 1000 *NASDAQ: NIHD* ■ *Web:* www.nii.com	Reston	VA	20190	703-390-5100	390-5149
North Central Telephone Co-op Corp PO Box 70 *TF:* 888-882-1693 ■ *Web:* www.nctc.com	Lafayette	TN	37083	615-666-2151	666-6772
North State Communications 111 N Main St *Web:* www.northstate.net	High Point	NC	27261	336-886-3600	887-7418
NTELOS Holdings Corp 1154 Shenandoah Village Dr PO Box 1990 *NASDAQ: NTLS* ■ *TF:* 877-468-3567 ■ *Web:* www.ntelos.com	Waynesboro	VA	22980	540-946-3500	
NTT DoCoMo USA Inc 757 Third Ave 16th Fl. **Fax Area Code:* 212 ■ *TF:* 888-362-6661 ■ *Web:* www.docomo-usa.com	New York	NY	10017	888-362-6661	994-7219*
01 Communications Inc 1515 K St Ste 100 **Fax Area Code:* 916 ■ *TF:* 888-444-1111 ■ *Web:* www.o1.com	Sacramento	CA	95814	888-444-1111	933-6958*
Oakes Motor Sports 1210 S Seventh St *Web:* drtel.net	Oakes	ND	58474	701-742-2936	
Omnitracs LLC 10290 Campus Point Dr *TF:* 800-647-3325 ■ *Web:* www.omnitracs.com	San Diego	CA	92121	800-647-3325	
Oncologix Tech Inc 206 Crown St SW	Grand Rapids	MI	49548	616-977-9933	
One Communications Corp 100 Chestnut St *Web:* www.onecommunications.com	Rochester	NY	14604	877-355-1501	
Otelco Inc 505 Third Ave E *NASDAQ: OTT* ■ *TF:* 800-344-7483 ■ *Web:* www.otelco.net	Oneonta	AL	35121	205-625-3574	625-3523
OTZ Telephone Co-op Inc PO Box 324 *TF:* 800-478-3111 ■ *Web:* otz.net	Kotzebue	AK	99752	907-442-3114	

Company	City	State	ZIP	Phone	Fax
Ovation Wireless Management Inc 19315 W Catawba Ave Ste 220 *Web:* www.ovationwm.com	Cornelius	NC	28031	704-714-2111	
P & R Communications Service Inc 700 E First St *Web:* www.pandrcommunications.com	Dayton	OH	45402	937-512-8100	
Panhandle Telecommunication Systems Inc (PTSI) 2222 NW Hwy *TF:* 800-562-2556 ■ *Web:* www.ptci.net	Guymon	OK	73942	580-338-2556	
Penasco Valley Telecommunications (PVT) 4011 W Main St **Fax Area Code:* 575 ■ *TF:* 800-505-4844 ■ *Web:* www.pvt.com	Artesia	NM	88210	800-505-4844	746-4142*
Pioneer Long Distance Inc PO Box 539 *TF:* 888-782-2667 ■ *Web:* www.pldi.net	Kingfisher	OK	73750	888-782-2667	
Pioneer Telephone Assn Inc PO Box 707 *TF:* 800-308-7536 ■ *Web:* www.pioncomm.net	Ulysses	KS	67880	620-356-3211	356-3242
Pioneer Telephone Co-op Inc 108 E Roberts Ave PO Box 539 **Fax:* Mktg ■ *Web:* www.ptci.com	Kingfisher	OK	73750	405-375-0411	699-3053*
Pratt Communications 2913 Tech Ctr *TF General:* 800-980-2323 ■ *Web:* www.prattcommunications.com	Santa Ana	CA	92705	714-540-6840	
Primus Telecommunications (PTGi) 7901 Jones Ranch Dr Ste 900 *NYSE: PTGI* ■ *TF:* 866-385-3360 ■ *Web:* www.ptgi.com	McLean	VA	22102	703-902-2800	902-2814
PRTC Inc (PRTC) PO Box 249 *Web:* www.prtcnet.com	Laurens	SC	29360	864-682-3131	682-8888
PWR LLC 6402 Deere Rd Ste 3 *TF:* 800-342-0878 ■ *Web:* www.pwrllc.com	Syracuse	NY	13206	315-701-0210	701-0217
Qualicom Systems Inc 2100 Electronics Ln *Web:* www.lightningradio.net	Fort Myers	FL	33912	239-481-8700	
Questar InfoComm Inc 180 East 100 South PO Box 45433 *TF:* 800-729-6790 ■ *Web:* www.questarpipeline.com	Salt Lake City	UT	84145	801-324-5856	
QuickPlay Media Inc 190 Liberty St Second Fl *Web:* www.quickplay.com	Toronto	ON	M6K3L5	416-916-7529	
Redknee Solutions Inc 2560 Matheson Blvd E Ste 500 *Web:* www.redknee.com	Mississauga	ON	L4W4Y9	905-625-2622	
Reiko Wireless 1218 flushing ave *Web:* www.reikowireless.com	Brooklyn	NY	11237	212-213-1102	
Reserve Telephone Company Inc PO Box T *TF:* 888-611-6111 ■ *Web:* www.rtconline.com	Reserve	LA	70084	985-536-1111	536-4815
RFIP Inc 100 W Wilshire Blvd Ste C4 *Web:* rfip.com	Oklahoma City	OK	73116	405-286-0928	
Rnk Inc 333 Elm St Ste 310 *TF:* 877-323-2486	Dedham	MA	02026	781-613-6000	297-2091
Rogers Communications Inc 333 Bloor St E 10th Fl *TSE: RCI.B* ■ *Web:* www.rogers.com	Toronto	ON	M4W1G9	416-935-7777	935-3599
Rogers Wireless Communications Inc 333 Bloor St. E, 4th Fl *TF:* 800-575-9090 ■ *Web:* www.rogers.com	Toronto	ON	M4W1G9	888-764-3771	
Rural Telephone Service Company Inc PO Box 158 *TF:* 877-625-7872 ■ *Web:* www.nex-tech.com	Lenora	KS	67645	785-567-4281	567-4401
Russell Cellular Inc 5624 S Hwy FF *Web:* www.russellcellular.com	Battlefield	MO	65619	417-886-7542	
S & p Communications 6712 Randolph Blvd *Web:* www.spcomm.com	Live Oak	TX	78233	210-656-5073	
Sage Telecom Inc 3300 E Renner Rd Ste 350 Bldg 2 *TF:* 877-742-5622 ■ *Web:* www.sagetelecom.net	Richardson	TX	75082	214-495-4700	495-4895
Sandhill TelephoneCo-op Inc PO Box 519 *Web:* www.shtc.net	Jefferson	SC	29718	843-658-3434	658-7700
Securus Technologies Inc 14651 Dallas Pkwy *TF:* 800-844-6591 ■ *Web:* www.securustech.net	Dallas	TX	75254	972-277-0300	277-0301
Shawnee Telephone Co PO Box 69 *TF:* 800-461-3956 ■ *Web:* myshawnee.net	Equality	IL	62934	618-276-4211	
Shenandoah Telecommunications Co 500 Shentel Way *NASDAQ: SHEN* ■ *TF:* 800-743-6835 ■ *Web:* www.shentel.com	Edinburg	VA	22824	540-984-5224	984-3438
SignalPoint Communications Corp 433 Hackensack Ave Continental Plz 6th Fl *TF:* 877-928-3292 ■ *Web:* www.signalpointcommunications.com	Hackensack	NJ	07601	201-968-9797	968-1886
Skyline Telephone Membership Corp PO Box 759 *TF:* 877-475-9546 ■ *Web:* www.skyline.org	West Jefferson	NC	28694	336-877-3111	
SkyTel Corp PO Box 2469 **Fax Area Code:* 601 ■ **Fax:* Hum Res ■ *TF Cust Svc:* 800-759-8737 ■ *Web:* www.skytel.com	Jackson	MS	39225	800-759-8737	460-8736*
Smart City Networks 5795 W Badura Ave Ste 110 *TF:* 888-446-6911 ■ *Web:* www.smartcity.com	Las Vegas	NV	89118	702-943-6000	943-6001
Smithville Communications Inc 1600 W Temperance St *Web:* www.smithville.com/	Ellettsville	IN	47429	812-876-2211	339-3313
SnapOne Inc 3490 Route 1 Bldg 16 *Web:* www.snapone.com	Princeton	NJ	08540	609-720-1900	
Solarus 440 E Grand Ave *TF:* 800-421-9282 ■ *Web:* www.solarus.net	Wisconsin Rapids	WI	54494	715-421-8111	421-6081
SoundBite Communications Inc 22 Crosby Dr *NASDAQ: SDBT* ■ **Fax Area Code:* 650 ■ *TF:* 888-436-3797 ■ *Web:* genesys.com/soundbite	Bedford	MA	01730	877-768-6324	466-1260*
South Central Rural Telephone Co-op Corp Inc PO Box 159 *TF:* 877-678-2111 ■ *Web:* www.scrtc.com	Glasgow	KY	42142	270-678-2111	528-2361
Southern Communications Services Inc 5555 Glenridge Connector Ste 500 **Fax Area Code:* 678 ■ *TF:* 800-818-5462 ■ *Web:* www.southernlinc.com	Atlanta	GA	30342	800-818-5462	443-1533*
Spanlink Communications Inc 605 Hwy 169 N Ste 900 *TF Sales:* 800-303-1239 ■ *Web:* www.spanlink.com	Minneapolis	MN	55441	763-971-2000	971-2300
Spotwave Wireless Inc 500 Van Buren St Box 550 *Web:* www.spotwave.com	Kemptville	ON	K0G1J0	613-591-1662	
Startec Global Communications Corp 11300 Rockville Pike Ste 900 **Fax Area Code:* 877 ■ *TF:* 800-827-3374 ■ *Web:* www.startec.com	Rockville	MD	20852	301-610-4300	329-2882*
T-Mobile USA Inc 12920 SE 38th St *TF:* 800-318-9270 ■ *Web:* www.t-mobile.com	Bellevue	WA	98006	425-383-4000	378-4040
Tango Networks Inc 3801 Parkwood Blvd *Web:* www.tango-networks.com	Frisco	TX	75034	469-229-6000	
TDS Telecommunications Corp 525 Junction Rd *TF:* 866-571-6662 ■ *Web:* www.tdstelecom.com	Madison	WI	53717	608-664-4000	830-5569
TelAlaska Inc 201 E 56th St *TF:* 888-570-1792 ■ *Web:* www.telalaska.com	Anchorage	AK	99518	907-563-2003	565-5539
Telecom Management Inc 39 Darling Ave *Web:* www.pioneertelephone.com	South Portland	ME	04106	207-774-9500	
Telefonica USA Inc 1111 Brickell Ave 10th Fl *Web:* www.us.telefonica.com	Miami	FL	33131	305-925-5300	373-1685
Telephone Service Co 2 Willipie St *TF:* 800-743-5707 ■ *Web:* www.telserco.com	Wapakoneta	OH	45895	419-739-2200	739-2299
Telephone Systems International Inc (TSI) 4400 Marsh Landing Blvd Ste 3 *Web:* www.tsiglobe.com	Ponte Vedra Beach	FL	32082	904-686-1470	686-1709
Teligent Inc 210 Brookwood Rd **Fax Area Code:* 888 ■ *TF:* 888-411-1175 ■ *Web:* www.teligent.com	Atmore	AL	36502	251-368-8600	841-1957*
Thumb Cellular Ltd. Partnership 82 S Main St *Web:* www.thumbcellular.com	Pigeon	MI	48755	989-453-4333	
Time Warner Telecom Inc 10475 Pk Meadow Dr *NASDAQ: TWTC* ■ *Web:* www.twtelecom.com	Littleton	CO	80124	303-566-1000	566-1011
TNS Inc 11480 Commerce Pk Dr Ste 600 *NYSE: TNS* ■ *TF:* 800-240-2824 ■ *Web:* www.tnsi.com	Reston	VA	20191	703-453-8300	453-8599
Total Telcom Inc 540 1632 Dickson Ave *TF:* 877 860 3762 ■ *Web:* www.totaltelcom.com	Kelowna	BC	V1Y7T2	877-860-3762	
Tower Ventures LLC 4091 Viscount Ave *Web:* www.towerventures.com	Memphis	TN	38118	901-794-9494	
TracFone Wireless Inc 9700 NW 112th Ave. *TF:* 800-876-5753 ■ *Web:* www.tracfone.com	Miami	FL	33178	305-640-2000	640-2070
Trans National Communications International Inc (TNCI) 2 Charlesgate W Ste 500 *TF:* 800-800-8400 ■ *Web:* www.tncii.com	Boston	MA	02215	617-369-1000	369-1111
Twin Lakes Telephone Co-op 200 Telephone Ln *TF Cust Svc:* 800-644-8582 ■ *Web:* www.twlakes.net	Gainesboro	TN	38562	931-268-2151	268-2734
United Telecomp LLC 225 US Hwy 46 Ste 9 *Web:* www.utc.net	Totowa	NJ	07512	973-639-6700	
United Utilities Inc 5450 A St *TF:* 800-478-2020 ■ *Web:* www.unicom-alaska.com	Anchorage	AK	99509	907-561-1674	273-5322
Unitel Inc PO Box 165 *TF:* 888-760-1048 ■ *Web:* www.unitelme.com	Unity	ME	04988	207-948-3900	948-3021
Universal Service Administrative Co (USAC) 2000 L St NW Ste 200 *TF:* 888-641-8722 ■ *Web:* www.usac.org	Washington	DC	20036	202-776-0200	776-0080
Universal Service Administrative Company Schools & Libraries Div 2000 L St NW Ste 200 *TF:* 888-203-8100 ■ *Web:* www.usac.org	Washington	DC	20036	888-203-8100	276-8736
Upper Peninsula Telephone Co PO Box 86 *TF:* 800-950-8506 ■ *Web:* www2.michbbs.com	Carney	MI	49812	906-639-2111	639-9935
US Cellular Corp (USCC) 8410 W Bryn Mawr Ave Ste 700 *NYSE: USM* ■ *TF:* 888-944-9400 ■ *Web:* www.uscellular.com	Chicago	IL	60631	773-399-8900	399-8936
USA Datanet Corp 109 S Warren St Ste 602 *TF:* 800-566-8655 ■ *Web:* www.usadatanet.com	Syracuse	NY	13202	800-566-8655	
USA Mobility Inc 6677 Richmond Hwy *TF:* 800-231-2556 ■ *Web:* www.usamobility.com	Alexandria	VA	22306	703-660-6677	660-6994
Valley Telephone Co-op Inc 752 E Maley St *TF:* 800-421-5711 ■ *Web:* www.vtc.net	Willcox	AZ	85643	520-384-2231	384-2831
VeriSign Inc 350 Ellis St *NASDAQ: VRSN* ■ *TF Sales:* 866-893-6565 ■ *Web:* www.verisign.com	Mountain View	CA	94043	650-426-3100	961-7300
Verizon Business 1 Verizon Way *TF Cust Svc:* 877-297-7816 ■ *Web:* www.verizonenterprise.com	Basking Ridge	NJ	07920	908-559-2000	
Verizon Communications Inc 140 W St *NYSE: VZ* ■ *Web:* www.verizon.com	New York	NY	10007	212-395-1000	
Verizon Wireless 180 Washington Valley Rd **Fax:* Hum Res ■ *TF:* 800-922-0204 ■ *Web:* www.verizonwireless.com	Bedminster	NJ	07921	908-306-7000	306-6927*
Virgin Mobile USA Inc 10 Independence Blvd *TF:* 888-322-1122 ■ *Web:* www.virginmobileusa.com	Warren	NJ	07059	908-607-4000	607-4822
Voicecom 5900 Windward Pkwy Ste 500 *TF:* 888-468-3554 ■ *Web:* intelliverse.com/	Alpharetta	GA	30005	888-468-3554	
Vonage Holdings Corp 23 Main St *NYSE: VG* ■ *TF:* 877-862-2562 ■ *Web:* www.vonage.com	Holmdel	NJ	07733	732-528-2600	834-0189
Wabash Telephone Co-op Inc PO Box 299 *TF:* 800-228-9824 ■ *Web:* www.wabashtelephone.coop	Louisville	IL	62858	618-665-3311	665-4188
Warwick Valley Telephone Co 47 Main St PO Box 592 *NASDAQ: WWVY* ■ *TF Cust Svc:* 800-952-7642 ■ *Web:* www.wvtc.com	Warwick	NY	10990	845-986-8080	986-6699
Wavedivision Holdings LLC 401 Kirkland Prk Pl Ste 500 *TF:* 866-928-3123 ■ *Web:* www.wavebroadband.com	Kirkland	WA	98033	425-576-8200	576-8221
Webtech Wireless Inc Ste 215 4299 Canada Way *Web:* www.webtechwireless.com	Burnaby	BC	V5G1H3	604-434-7337	
West Central Wireless 3389 Knickerbocker Rd. *Web:* www.wcc.net	San Angelo	TX	76904	325-223-6680	
West River Co-op Telephone Co (WRCTC) 801 Coleman Ave PO Box 39 *Web:* www.sdplains.com	Bison	SD	57620	605-244-5213	244-7288
West River Telecommunications Co-op PO Box 467 *TF:* 800-748-7220 ■ *Web:* www.westriv.com	Hazen	ND	58545	701-748-2211	748-6800
West Texas Rural TelephoneCo-op Inc PO Box 1737 *Web:* www.wtrt.net	Hereford	TX	79045	806-364-3331	276-5219
Windstream Corp 4001 Rodney Parham Rd *Web:* www.windstream.com	Little Rock	AR	72212	501-748-7000	
Wireless Mike's 301 S 21st St *Web:* wirelessmikes.com	Mattoon	IL	61938	217-258-8771	

				Phone	Fax
WQN Inc 14911 Quorum Dr Ste 140	Dallas	TX	75254	866-661-6176	980-8996*
OTC: WQNI ■ **Fax Area Code:* 972 ■ *TF:* 866-661-6176 ■ *Web:* www.wqn.com					
XO Communications Inc 13865 Sunrise Vly Dr	Herndon	VA	20171	703-547-2000	547-2881
TF: 866-349-0134 ■ *Web:* www.xo.com					
Yak Communications Corp 48 Yonge St Ste 1200	Toronto	ON	M5E1G6	877-925-4925	216-9923*
**Fax Area Code:* 866 ■ *TF:* 877-925-4925 ■ *Web:* www.yak.ca					
York Telecom Corp 81 Corbett Way	Eatontown	NJ	07724	732-413-6000	413-6060
TF: 866-836-8463 ■ *Web:* www.yorktel.com					

740 TELEMARKETING & OTHER TELE-SERVICES

Both inbound and outbound telephone marketing as well as other tele-services are included here.

				Phone	Fax
Aegis Communications Group Inc					
8201 Ridgepoint Dr	Irving	TX	75063	972-830-1800	830-1801
TF: 877-892-3447 ■ *Web:* www.aegisglobal.com					
Alta Resources 120 N Commercial St	Neenah	WI	54956	877-464-2582	727-9954*
**Fax Area Code:* 920 ■ *TF:* 877-464-2582 ■ *Web:* www.altaresources.com					
America's Call Center Inc					
7901 Baymeadows Way Ste 14	Jacksonville	FL	32256	904-224-2000	
Web: www.webcallusa.com					
American Home Base 428 Childers St	Pensacola	FL	32534	850-857-0860	484-8661
TF General: 800-549-0595 ■ *Web:* www.amhomebase.com					
Ameridial Inc 4535 Strausser St NW	North Canton	OH	44720	800-445-7128	497-5500*
**Fax Area Code:* 330 ■ *TF:* 800-445-7128 ■ *Web:* www.ameridial.com					
Aria Communications Corp					
717 W Saint Germain St	St. Cloud	MN	56301	800-955-9924	
TF: 800-955-9924 ■ *Web:* www.ariacallsandcards.com					
Bluestem Brands Inc					
6509 Flying Cloud Dr	Eden Prairie	MN	55344	952-656-3700	656-4112
Web: bluestembrands.silkroad.com					
Calling Solutions By Phone Power Inc					
2200 McCullough Ave	San Antonio	TX	78212	210-822-7400	
TF Cust Svc: 800-683-5500 ■ *Web:* www.callingsolutions.com					
Connection, The 11351 Rupp Dr	Burnsville	MN	55337	952-948-5488	948-5498
TF Sales: 800-883-5777 ■ *Web:* www.the-connection.com					
Convergys Corp 201 E Fourth St	Cincinnati	OH	45202	513-723-7000	
NYSE: CVG ■ *TF:* 888-284-9900 ■ *Web:* www.convergys.com					
Dale Corp 28091 Dequindre	Madison Heights	MI	48071	248-542-2400	542-6007
Web: www.dalecorporation.com					
DialAmerica Marketing Inc 960 MacArthur Blvd	Mahwah	NJ	07495	201-327-0200	327-4066
Web: www.dialamerica.com					
EBSCO TeleServices					
4150 Belden Village Ave NW Ste 401	Canton	OH	44718	330-492-5105	492-5202
TF: 800-456-5105 ■ *Web:* www.call-ets.com					
Evolve IP LLC 989 Old Eagle School Rd Ste 815	Wayne	PA	19087	610-964-8000	
Web: www.evolveip.net					
Gage 10000 Hwy 55	Minneapolis	MN	55441	763-595-3800	595-3871
Web: www.gage.com					
Harte-Hanks Response Management					
2800 Wells Branch Pkwy	Austin	TX	78728	512-434-1100	
TF: 800-456-9748 ■ *Web:* hartehanks.com/					
Holden Marketing Support Services					
5000 Lima St	Denver	CO	80239	720-374-3700	
InfoCision Management Corp 325 Springside Dr	Akron	OH	44333	330-668-1400	668-1401
TF: 800-210-6269 ■ *Web:* www.infocision.com					
InService America Inc 129 Vista Centre Dr	Forest	VA	24551	434-316-7400	
Web: www.inserviceamerica.com					
Integretel Inc 5883 Rue Ferrari	San Jose	CA	95138	408-362-4000	
TF: 888-302-2750					
Intelemark LLC 2120 E Rose Garden Ln Ste D2	Phoenix	AZ	85024	602-943-7111	
Web: www.intelemark.com					
iSky 1700 Pennsylvania Ave NW Ste 560	Washington	DC	20006	855-475-4759	
TF: 855-475-4759 ■ *Web:* www.isky.com					
Julie Inc 3275 Executive Dr	Joliet	IL	60431	815-741-5000	
Web: www.illinois1call.com					
Kipany Productions Ltd 32 E 39th St	New York	NY	10016	212-883-8300	
Web: www.kipany.com					
Lester Inc 19 Business Pk Dr	Branford	CT	06405	203-488-5265	483-0408
TF: 800-999-5265 ■ *Web:* www.lesterusa.com					
Lexicon Marketing Corp					
6380 Wilshire Blvd	Los Angeles	CA	90048	323-782-7400	
TF: 800-650-4444 ■ *Web:* www.lexiconmarketing.com					
Mars Stout Inc 4500 Majestic Dr	Missoula	MT	59808	406-721-6280	
Web: www.marsstout.com					
Meyer Assoc Inc 14 Seventh Ave N	Saint Cloud	MN	56303	320-259-4000	259-4044
TF: 800-676-9233					
Miratel Solutions Inc 2501 Steeles Ave W	North York	ON	M3J2P1	416-650-7850	
Web: www.miratelinc.com					
My Receptionist					
800 Wisconsin St PO Box 109	Eau Claire	WI	54703	800-686-0162	615-4921
TF: 800-686-0162 ■ *Web:* www.myreceptionist.com					
Nordia Inc 5200 Blvd de l'Ormiere	Quebec City	QC	G1P4B2	418-864-7359	
Web: www.nordia.ca					
ProCom Inc 28838 US Hwy 69 PO Box 27	Lamoni	IA	50140	641-784-8841	784-4100
TF: 800-433-9893 ■ *Web:* www.procom-inc.com					
Quez Media Marketing 1138 Prospect Ave E	Cleveland	OH	44115	216-910-0202	
Web: www.quezmedia.com					
Research First Consulting Inc					
4066 Somerset Rdg	Birmingham	AL	35242	205-995-8866	
Web: www.researchfirst.com					
Results Telemarketing Inc					
499 E Sheridan St Ste 400	Dania Beach	FL	33004	954-921-2400	923-8070
Web: www.resultstel.com					
SITEL Corp					
2 American Ctr 3102 W End Ave Ste 1000	Nashville	TN	37203	615-301-7100	
TF: 866-957-4835 ■ *Web:* www.sitel.com					
Telax Voice Solutions 365 Evans Ave	Etobicoke	ON	M8Z1K2	416-207-1795	
Web: www.telax.com					
Tele Business USA 1945 Techny Rd Ste 3	Northbrook	IL	60062	877-315-8353	480-6055*
**Fax Area Code:* 847 ■ *TF:* 877-315-8353 ■ *Web:* www.tbiz.com					
Teleperformance USA					
1991 South 4650 West	Salt Lake City	UT	84104	801-257-5800	257-6246
Web: www.teleperformance.com					
Telerx 723 Dresher Rd	Horsham	PA	19044	267-942-3300	347-6010*
**Fax Area Code:* 215 ■ *TF:* 800-283-5379 ■ *Web:* www.telerx.com					
TeleServices Direct					
5305 Lakeview Pkwy S Dr	Indianapolis	IN	46268	317-216-2240	216-2248
TF: 888-646-6626 ■ *Web:* www.teleservicesdirect.com					
TeleTech Holdings Inc 9197 S Peoria St	Englewood	CO	80112	303-397-8100	397-8695
NASDAQ: TTEC ■ *TF General:* 800-835-3832 ■ *Web:* www.teletech.com					
Telexpertise Inc					
7790 E Arapahoe Rd Ste 240	Centennial	CO	80112	720-200-0590	
Web: www.telexpertise.com					
Thumbs-Up Telemarketing Inc					
13545 Barrett Pkwy Dr Ste 101	Ballwin	MO	63021	314-821-8111	
Web: thumbsupinc.com					
Torcom 25 Kessel Ct Ste 107	Madison	WI	53711	608-276-0709	
Web: torco.com					
TRG Holdings LLC 1700 Pennsylvania Ave NW	Washington	DC	20006	202-289-9898	
Web: www.ibexglobal.com					
TTC Marketing Solutions 3945 N Neenah	Chicago	IL	60634	800-530-7189	
TF: 800-530-7189 ■ *Web:* www.ttcmarketingsolutions.com					
Turn-Key Solutions Inc					
4920 W Thunderbird Ave Ste C-120	Glendale	AZ	85306	602-863-0269	
Web: www.tksnation.com					
USA 800 Inc 9808 E 66th Terr PO Box 16795	Kansas City	MO	64133	816-358-1303	358-8845
TF: 800-821-7539 ■ *Web:* www.usa800.com					
VOX Data 1155 Metcalfe St 18th Fl	Montreal	QC	H3B2V6	514-871-1920	
Web: www.voxdata.com					
West Corp 11808 Miracle Hills Dr	Omaha	NE	68154	800-232-0900	573-1030*
**Fax Area Code:* 402 ■ *TF Sales:* 800-232-0900 ■ *Web:* www.west.com					
Working Solutions 1820 Preston Pk Blvd Ste 2000	Plano	TX	75093	972-964-4800	964-4802
TF: 866-857-4800 ■ *Web:* www.workingsolutions.com					
Young America Corp 10 S 5th St 7th Fl	Minneapolis	MN	55402	800-533-4529	
TF: 800-533-4529 ■ *Web:* www.yaengage.com					

TELEVISION - CABLE

SEE Television Networks - Cable p. 3212; Cable & Other Pay Television Services p. 1897

741 TELEVISION COMPANIES

				Phone	Fax
A. Smith & Company Productions Inc					
9911 W Pico Blvd Ste 250	Los Angeles	CA	90035	310-432-4800	
Web: www.asmithco.com					
Acme Communications Inc					
2101 E Fourth St Ste 202	Santa Ana	CA	92705	714-245-9499	245-9494
PINK: ACME ■ *Web:* www.acmecommunications.com					
Allbritton Communications Co					
1000 Wilson Blvd Ste 2700	Arlington	VA	22209	703-647-8700	
Web: allbritton.com/					
Ask Associates Inc 1505 Kasold Dr	Lawrence	KS	66047	785-841-8194	
Web: www.askusa.com					
California Oregon Broadcasting Inc					
125 S Fir St	Medford	OR	97501	541-779-5555	779-5564
Web: www.kobi5.com					
Capitol Broadcasting Co Inc					
2619 Western Blvd	Raleigh	NC	27606	919-890-6000	890-6095
TF: 800-234-4857 ■ *Web:* capitolbroadcasting.com					
CBS Television Stations Group 51 W 52nd St	New York	NY	10019	212-975-4321	975-3154
Web: www.cbs.com					
Christian Television Network Inc (CTN)					
6922 142nd Ave N	Largo	FL	33771	727-535-5622	531-2497
TF: 800-716-7729 ■ *Web:* www.ctnonline.com					
Communications Corp of America					
700 St John St Ste 300	Lafayette	LA	70501	337-237-1142	
Web: comcorpusa.com					
Community Educational Television					
10902 S Wilcrest Dr	Houston	TX	77099	281-561-5828	561-9793
Web: myedutv.org					
CW Network LLC, The 3300 Olive Ave	Burbank	CA	91505	818-977-2500	954-7667
Web: www.cwtv.com					
Diversified Business Communications					
121 Free St	Portland	ME	04101	207-842-5500	842-5503
Web: divcom.com					
Elevation Ltd 1027 33rd St Nw Ste 260	Washington	DC	20007	202-380-3230	
Web: www.elevation-us.com					
Emmis Communications Corp					
40 Monument Cir 1 Emmis Plz Ste 700	Indianapolis	IN	46204	317-266-0100	631-3750
NASDAQ: EMMS ■ *Web:* www.emmis.com					
Entravision Communications Corp					
2425 Olympic Blvd Ste 6000 W	Santa Monica	CA	90404	310-447-3870	447-3899
NYSE: EVC ■ *Web:* www.entravision.com					
EW Scripps Co 312 Walnut St Ste 2800	Cincinnati	OH	45202	513-977-3000	977-3800*
NYSE: SSP ■ **Fax:* Hum Res ■ *TF:* 800-888-3000 ■ *Web:* www.scripps.com					
Fisher Communications Inc					
140 Fourth Ave N Ste 500	Seattle	WA	98109	206-404-7000	404-6037
NASDAQ: FSCI ■ *Web:* www.sbgi.net					
Flinn Broadcasting 6080 Mt Moriah Rd Ext	Memphis	TN	38115	901-375-9324	375-0041
Web: www.flinn.com					
Fort Group Inc					
100 Challenger Rd Eighth Fl	Ridgefield Park	NJ	07660	201-445-0202	
Web: www.fortgroupinc.com					
Forum Communications Co 101 Fifth St N	Fargo	ND	58102	701-451-5629	241-5406
TF: 800-747-7311 ■ *Web:* www.forumcomm.com					
Fox Television Stations Inc					
1999 S Bundy Dr	Los Angeles	CA	90025	310-584-2000	584-2012
Web: www.myfoxla.com					

				Phone	Fax
Freedom Communications Inc 17666 Fitch *TF:* 866-262-7678 ■ *Web:* www.freedom.com	Irvine	CA	92614	949-253-2300	474-7675
Gannett Company Inc 7950 Jones Branch Dr *NYSE: GCI* ■ *Web:* www.gannett.com	McLean	VA	22107	703-854-6000	
Granite Broadcasting Corp 767 Third Ave 34th Fl *Web:* www.granitetv.com	New York	NY	10017	212-826-2530	826-2858
Gray Television Inc 4370 Peachtree Rd NE *NYSE: GTN* ■ *Web:* www.gray.tv	Atlanta	GA	30319	404-504-9828	
Hearst-Argyle Television Inc 300 W 57th St 39th Fl *Web:* www.hearsttelevision.com	New York	NY	10019	212-887-6800	887-6855
Kota 518 St Joseph St	Rapid City	SD	57701	605-342-2000	342-7305
LeSea Broadcasting Corp 61300 S Ironwood Rd *TF:* 800-365-3732 ■ *Web:* www.lesea.com	South Bend	IN	46614	574-291-8200	291-9043
Lieberman Productions 455 Ninth St *Web:* www.lieberman.com	San Francisco	CA	94103	415-955-0855	
McGraw-Hill Cos Inc Broadcasting Group 1221 Ave of the Americas *Web:* www.mcgraw-hill.com	New York	NY	10020	800-338-3987	
Media General Broadcast Group 111 N Fourth St *TF:* 800-937-5449 ■ *Web:* www.mediageneral.com	Richmond	VA	23219	804-649-6000	
Meredith Corp 1716 Locust St *NYSE: MDP* ■ *Web:* www.meredith.com	Des Moines	IA	50309	515-284-3000	284-3806
Metrovision Production Group LLC 508 W 24th St *Web:* www.metrovision-nyc.com	New York	NY	10011	212-989-1515	
Morgan Murphy Broadcasting Group 7025 Raymond Rd *Web:* www.channel3000.com	Madison	WI	53719	608-271-4321	271-6111
Morris Multimedia Inc 27 Abercorn St *Web:* www.morrismultimedia.com	Savannah	GA	31401	912-233-1281	232-4639
Omnivision Entertainment Inc The Film Ctr 630 Ninth Ave Ste 1012 *Web:* www.mydamnchannel.com	New York	NY	10036	212-582-2199	
On Event Services LLC 6550 McDonough Dr *Web:* www.oneventservices.com	Norcross	GA	30093	770-457-0966	
Pappas Telecasting Cos 823 W Center Ave	Visalia	CA	93291	559-733-7800	733-7878
Post-Newsweek Stations Inc 550 W Lafayette Blvd *Web:* ghco.com/phoenix.zhtml?c=62487&p=irol-landing	Detroit	MI	48226	313-223-2260	
Quincy Newspapers Inc 130 S Fifth St *TF:* 800-373-9444 ■ *Web:* www.whig.com	Quincy	IL	62301	217-223-5100	223-9757
Raycom Media Inc 201 Monroe St RSA Tower 20th Fl *Web:* www.raycommedia.com	Montgomery	AL	36104	334-206-1400	206-1555
Red River Broadcasting Co LLC 2001 London Rd *Web:* www.fox21online.com	Duluth	MN	55812	218-722-2861	728-8932
Roadtrip Productions Ltd 1626 Placentia Ave *Web:* roadtripnation.com	Costa Mesa	CA	92626	949-764-9121	
Saga Communications Inc 73 Kercheval Ave *NYSE: SGA* ■ *TF:* 800-777-3674 ■ *Web:* sagacom.com	Grosse Pointe Farms	MI	48236	313-886-7070	886-7150
Sarkes Tarzian Inc 205 N College Ave Ste 800	Bloomington	IN	47404	812-332-7251	331-4575
Sinclair Broadcast Group Inc 10706 Beaver Dam Rd *NASDAQ: SBGI* ■ *Web:* www.sbgi.net	Hunt Valley	MD	21030	410-568-1500	568-1533
Smart MultiMedia Inc 2311 Canal St Ste 208 *Web:* www.smartgeometrics.com	Houston	TX	77003	713-574-6690	
Tribune Co 435 N Michigan Ave Ste 1800 *Web:* www.tribune.com	Chicago	IL	60611	312-222-9100	
Univision Television Group Inc 5999 Ctr Dr *TF:* 800-594-5387 ■ *Web:* www.univision.com	Los Angeles	CA	90045	310-846-2800	
Verite Inc 608 West 9320 South *Web:* www.verite.com	Sandy	UT	84070	801-553-1101	
Visual Data Media Services Inc 610 N Hollywood Way *Web:* www.visualdatainc.com	Burbank	CA	91505	818-558-3363	
Weigel Broadcasting 26 N Halstead St *Web:* metvnetwork.com	Chicago	IL	60661	312-705-2600	705-2656
Wicks Group of Cos LLC 405 Pk Ave Ste 702 *Web:* www.wicksgroup.com	New York	NY	10022	212-838-2100	223-2109
WMFE 11510 E Colonial Dr *Web:* www.wmfe.org	Orlando	FL	32817	407-273-2300	
WYOMedia Inc 1856 Skyview Dr	Casper	WY	82601	307-577-5923	577-5928
Xanadoo Co 225 City Ave Ste 100	Bala Cynwyd	PA	19004	610-934-7000	
ZGS Communications 2000 N 14th St Ste 400 *Web:* www.zgsgroup.com	Arlington	VA	22201	703-528-5656	526-0879

742 TELEVISION NETWORKS - BROADCAST

				Phone	Fax
ABC Inc 77 W 66th St *Web:* www.abc.go.com	New York	NY	10023	212-456-7777	456-2795
CBS Broadcasting Inc 51 W 52nd St *Web:* www.cbs.com	New York	NY	10019	212-975-4321	
CBS Corp 51 W 52nd St *NYSE: CBS* ■ *Web:* www.cbscorporation.com	New York	NY	10019	212-975-4321	975-4516
Fox Broadcasting Co 10201 W Pico Blvd *Web:* www.fox.com	Los Angeles	CA	90035	310-369-1350	
Nstreams Technologies Inc 1914 Junction Ave *Web:* www.nstreams.com	San Jose	CA	95131	408-734-8889	734-8886
Public Broadcasting Service (PBS) 2100 Crystal Dr *Web:* www.pbs.org	Arlington	VA	22202	703-739-5000	739-0775
Univision Communications Inc 1999 Ave of the Stars Ste 3050 *Web:* www.univision.com	Los Angeles	CA	90067	310-348-3672	556-7615

743 TELEVISION NETWORKS - CABLE

				Phone	Fax
A&E Television Networks LLC 235 E 45th St *Web:* www.aenetworks.com	New York	NY	10017	212-210-1400	210-1308
Accent Health 60 E 42nd St Ste 1543 **Fax Area Code:* 813 ■ *TF:* 800-235-4930 ■ *Web:* www.accenthealth.com	New York	NY	10165	800-235-4930	349-7299*
AMC Networks Inc 11 Penn Plaza 2nd Fl *NASDAQ: AMCX* ■ **Fax Area Code:* 516 ■ *Web:* www.amcnetworks.com	New York	NY	10001	212-324-8500	803-3003*
Artv 1400 Rene-Levesque Blvd E Bureau A-53-1 *Web:* www.artv.ca	Montreal	QC	H2L2M2	514-597-3636	
Asian Television Network (ATN) 330 Cochrane Dr *Web:* www.asiantelevision.com	Markham	ON	L3R8E4	905-948-8199	948-8108
Astral Television Networks 181 Bay St Ste 100 PO Box 787 *Web:* www.bellmedia.ca	Toronto	ON	M5J2T3	416-956-2010	956-2018
Auto Ch 332 W Broadway Ste 1604 *Web:* www.theautochannel.com	Louisville	KY	40202	502-992-0200	992-0201
BBC America 1120 Ave of the Americas Fifth Fl *Web:* www.bbcamerica.com	New York	NY	10036	212-705-9300	705-9338
BET Networks & BET Interactive LLC 1235 W St NE *Web:* www.bet.com	Washington	DC	20018	202-608-2000	608-2599
Bloomberg Television 731 Lexington Ave *Web:* www.bloomberg.com/tv	New York	NY	10022	212-318-2000	
Book Television 299 Queen St W *Web:* www.booktelevision.com	Toronto	AB	M5V2Z5	416-384-8000	591-5117
Business News Network (BNN) 299 Queen St W *TF:* 855-326-6266 ■ *Web:* www.bnn.ca	Toronto	ON	M5V2Z5	416-384-6600	
C-SPAN Extra 400 N Capitol St NW Ste 650 *Web:* www.c-span.org	Washington	DC	20001	202-737-3220	737-3323
C-SPAN3 400 N Capitol St NW Ste 650 *Web:* www.c-span.org	Washington	DC	20001	202-737-3220	
Cable Public Affairs Ch (CPAC) PO Box 81099 **Fax Area Code:* 613 ■ *TF:* 877-287-2722 ■ *Web:* www.cpac.ca	Ottawa	ON	K1P1B1	877-287-2722	567-2749*
Cable Satellite Public Affairs Network (C-SPAN) 400 N Capitol St NW Ste 650 *Web:* www.c-span.org	Washington	DC	20001	202-737-3220	737-3323
Cartoon Network Inc, The 1015 Techwood Drive *Web:* www.cartoonnetwork.com	Atlanta	GA	30318	404-878-0694	885-0620
Christian Broadcasting Network (CBN) 977 Centerville Tpke CBN Ctr *TF:* 800-759-0700 ■ *Web:* www.cbn.com	Virginia Beach	VA	23463	757-226-7000	226-2017
Cinemax 1100 Ave of the Americas *Web:* www.cinemax.com	New York	NY	10036	212-512-1000	
Classic Arts Showcase PO Box 828 *Web:* www.classicartsshowcase.org	Burbank	CA	91503	323-878-0283	878-0329
CNBC Inc 900 Sylvan Ave *Web:* www.cnbc.com	Englewood Cliffs	NJ	07632	201-735-2622	
Comedy Central 1775 Broadway *Web:* cc.com/	New York	NY	10019	212-767-8600	767-8592
Country Music Television (CMT) 330 Commerce St *Web:* www.cmt.com	Nashville	TN	37201	615-335-8400	335-8614
CRN Digital Talk Radio 10487 Sunland Blvd *TF:* 800-336-2225 ■ *Web:* www.crntalk.com	Sunland	CA	91040	818-352-7152	352-3229
Cross TV 370 W Camino Gardens Blvd Ste 300 *Web:* www.crosstv.com	Boca Raton	FL	33432	561-367-7454	
Crown Media Holdings Inc 12700 Ventura Blvd Ste 200 *NASDAQ: CRWN* ■ *TF:* 800-479-7328 ■ *Web:* www.hallmarkchannel.com	Studio City	CA	91604	818-755-2400	755-2461
CTV Edmonton 18520 Stony Plain Rd NW	Edmonton	AB	T5S1A8	780-483-3311	
Daystar Television Network 3901 Hwy 121 PO Box 610546 *TF:* 800-329-0029 ■ *Web:* daystar.com	Bedford	TX	76021	817-571-1229	571-7458
Deep Dish TV 339 Lafayette St Third Fl *Web:* www.deepdishtv.org	New York	NY	10012	212-473-8933	
Discovery Ch LLC One Discovery Pl *Web:* discovery.com/	Silver Spring	MD	20910	240-662-2000	
Discovery Comm Latin America 6505 Blue Lagoon Dr Ste 190 *Web:* corporate.discovery.com	Miami	FL	33126	786-273-4700	
Discovery Communications Inc One Discovery Pl *NASDAQ: DISCA* ■ *TF:* 877-324-5850 ■ *Web:* corporate.discovery.com	Silver Spring	MD	20910	240-662-2000	
Discovery Life Cannel 1 Discovery Pl *Web:* discoveryfitandhealth.com/	Silver Spring	MD	20910	240-662-2000	
Documentary Ch 1207 16th Ave S *Web:* www.pivot.tv	Nashville	TN	37212	615-322-9333	
E! Entertainment Television 5750 Wilshire Blvd **Fax Area Code:* 213 ■ *Web:* www.eonline.com	Los Angeles	CA	90036	323-954-2400	954-2621*
ESPN 545 Middle St *Web:* www.espn.go.com	Bristol	CT	06010	877-710-3776	
ESPN Classic Canada 9 Ch Nine Ct *Web:* www.tsn.ca	Scarborough	ON	M1S4B5	416-384-7624	
ESPN Classic Inc ESPN Plaza *Web:* espn.go.com	Bristol	CT	06010	877-710-3776	
ESPN Deportes Two Alhambra Plz Ninth Fl *TF:* 800-337-6783 ■ *Web:* espndeportes.com	Coral Gables	FL	33134	305-567-3797	
Eternal Word Television Network (EWTN) 5817 Old Leeds Rd *Web:* www.ewtn.com	Irondale	AL	35210	205-271-2900	
EVINE Live Inc 6740 Shady Oak Rd **Fax:* Hum Res ■ *TF:* 800-676-5523 ■ *Web:* www.evine.com	Eden Prairie	MN	55344	800-676-5523	*

	City	State	Zip	Phone	Fax
Fashion Television Ch					
Bell Media Inc 299 Queen St W	Toronto	ON	M5V2Z5	416-332-5000	384-0080
Web: www.fashiontelevision.com					
FOX News Ch 1211 Ave of the Americas	New York	NY	10036	212-301-3000	301-8274*
**Fax:* News Rm ■ *Web:* www.foxnews.com					
FOX Sports Net 10201 W Pico Blvd	Los Angeles	CA	90035	310-369-6000	
Web: www.msn.foxsports.com					
Free Speech TV (FSTV) PO Box 44099	Denver	CO	80201	303-542-4813	
Web: www.freespeech.org					
God's Learning Ch (GLC) PO Box 61000	Midland	TX	79711	432-563-0420	563-1736
TF: 800-707-0420 ■ *Web:* www.glc.us.com					
Hallmark Ch 12700 Ventura Blvd Ste 200	Studio City	CA	91604	818-755-2400	755-2564
TF: 888-390-7474 ■ *Web:* www.hallmarkchannel.com					
Hispanic Information & Telecommunications Network Inc					
63 Flushing Ave Unit 281	Brooklyn	NY	11205	212-966-5660	966-5725
Web: www.hitn.org					
History Ch					
A&E Television Networks LLC					
235 E 45th St 8th Fl	New York	NY	10017	212-210-1400	210-1308
TF: 866-582-5613 ■ *Web:* www.history.com					
Idea Ch 2002 Filmore Ave Ste 1	Erie	PA	16506	814-833-7107	833-7415
Web: www.ideachannel.com					
iN DEMAND 345 Hudson St 17th Fl	New York	NY	10014	646-638-8200	486-0855
Web: www.indemand.com					
Ion Media Networks					
601 Clearwater Pk Rd	West Palm Beach	FL	33401	561-659-4122	597-5903*
**Fax Area Code:* 646 ■ **Fax:* PR ■ *TF:* 800-987-9936 ■ *Web:* www.ionmedianetworks.com					
Les Chaines Tele Astral					
1800 Ave McGill College Bureau 1000	Montreal	QC	H3A3J6	514-938-3320	939-3151
Web: www.bellmedia.ca					
Liberty Ch 1971 University Blvd	Lynchburg	VA	24506	434-582-2000	
TF: 800-332-1883 ■ *Web:* www.liberty.edu					
MSG Network Two Pennsylvania Plz	New York	NY	10121	212-465-6741	465-6024
Web: www.msg.com					
MTV Networks 1515 Broadway	New York	NY	10036	212-846-6000	422-6630*
**Fax Area Code:* 201 ■ *Web:* www.mtv.com					
MTV Networks On Campus Inc (MTVU)					
1540 Broadway 33rd Fl	New York	NY	10036	877-800-4483	
Web: www.mtvu.com					
NASA TV 300 E St SW	Washington	DC	20546	202-358-0000	358-4338
TF: 877-546-1574 ■ *Web:* www.nasa.gov					
National Geographic Ch (NGC) 1145 17th St NW	Washington	DC	20036	202-912-6500	912-6603
Web: channel.nationalgeographic.com					
New England Cable News (NECN) 160 Wells Ave	Newton	MA	02459	617-630-5000	630-5055
Web: www.necn.com					
New England Sports Network (NESN)					
480 Arsenal St Bldg 1	Watertown	MA	02472	617-536-9233	536-7814
Web: www.nesn.com					
NFL Network 345 Park Avenue	New York	NY	10154	212-450-2000	681-7599
TF: 800-724-3377 ■ *Web:* www.nfl.com/nflnetwork					
Nickelodeon 1515 Broadway 38th Fl	New York	NY	10036	212-258-7500	258-7705
Web: www.nick.com					
nuvoTV 700 N Central Ave Ste 600	Glendale	CA	91203	323-256-8900	
Web: www.mynuvotv.com					
Oasis TV Inc 2029 Century Pk E Ste 1400	Los Angeles	CA	90067	310-553-4300	
Web: watchotv.com					
Outdoor Ch 43445 Business Pk Dr Ste 103	Temecula	CA	92590	951-699-6991	699-6313
NASDAQ: OUTD ■ *TF:* 800-770-5750 ■ *Web:* www.outdoorchannel.com					
Ovation The Arts Network					
2850 Ocean Pk Blvd Ste 225	Santa Monica	CA	90405	310-430-7575	
Web: www.ovationtv.com					
Pet Network 105 Gordon Baker Rd Eighth Fl	Toronto	ON	M2H3P8	416-756-2404	756-5526
Web: www.thepetnetwork.tv					
QVC Inc 1200 Wilson Dr	West Chester	PA	19380	484-701-1000	701-1138*
**Fax:* Cust Svc ■ *TF:* 800-367-9444 ■ *Web:* www.qvc.com					
Resort Sports Network					
Outside Television 33 Riverside Ave 4th Fl	Westport	CT	06880	203-221-9240	
TF: 888-795-9488 ■ *Web:* www.outsidetelevision.com					
SCOLA 21557 270th St	McClelland	IA	51548	712-566-2202	566-2502
Web: www.scola.org					
Score, The 500 King St W 4th Fl	Toronto	ON	M5V1L9	416-479-8812	361-2045
Web: thescore.com					
Scripps Networks LLC 9721 Sherrill Blvd	Knoxville	TN	37932	865-694-2700	531-8933
Web: www.diynetwork.com					
Shopping Ch, The					
Credit Card Dept 59 Ambassador Dr	Mississauga	ON	L5T2P9	905-362-2020	202-0877*
**Fax Area Code:* 877 ■ *TF:* 888-202-0888 ■ *Web:* www.theshoppingchannel.com					
Showtime Networks Inc 1633 Broadway 15th Fl	New York	NY	10019	212-708-1600	708-1217
Web: www.sho.com					
SoapNet LLC 500 S Buena Vista St	Burbank	CA	91521	818-560-1000	
Web: abc.go.com/shows					
Starz Encore Group LLC 8900 Liberty Cir	Englewood	CO	80112	720-852-7700	852-7710
Web: www.starz.com					
Starz LLC 8900 Liberty Cir	Englewood	CO	80112	720-852-7700	852-7710
Web: www.starz.com					
Stornoway Communications					
105 Gordon Baker Rd 8th Fl	Toronto	ON	M2H3P8	416-756-2404	756-5526
Web: www.stornoway.com					
Sundance Ch 1633 Broadway Eighth Fl	New York	NY	10019	212-708-1500	654-4724
Web: sundance.tv/					
TBS Superstation Inc 1050 Techwood Dr NW	Atlanta	GA	30318	404-827-1700	
Web: www.tbs.com					
TCT Ministries Inc 11717 N Rt 37 PO Box 1010	Marion	IL	62959	618-997-4700	993-9778
TF: 800-232-9855 ■ *Web:* www.tct.tv					
Telelatino Network Inc (TLN) 5125 Steeles Ave W	Toronto	ON	M9L1R5	416-744-8200	744-0966
TF: 800-551-8401 ■ *Web:* www.tlntv.com					
Teletoon Canada Inc					
181 Bay St Ste 100 Brookfield Pl	Toronto	ON	M5J2T3	416-956-2060	956-2070
Web: www.teletoon.com					
Tennis Ch 2850 Ocean Pk Blvd Ste 150	Santa Monica	CA	90405	310-314-9400	314-9433
Web: www.tennischannel.com					
TFC USA 150 Shoreline Dr	Redwood City	CA	94065	650-508-6000	
TF: 800-345-2465 ■ *Web:* www.abs-cbnglobal.com					
Total Living Network (TLN) 2880 Vision Ct	Aurora	IL	60506	630-801-3838	801-3839
Web: www.tln.com					
Travel Ch LLC 5425 Wisconsin Ave Ste 500	Chevy Chase	MD	20815	301-244-7500	
Web: www.travelchannel.com					
Trinity Broadcasting Network (TBN) PO Box A	Santa Ana	CA	92711	714-832-2950	
TF: 888-731-1000 ■ *Web:* www.tbn.org					
Turner Broadcasting System Inc (TBS)					
One CNN Ctr	Atlanta	GA	30303	404-827-1700	
Web: www.turner.com					
Turner Classic Movies (TCM) 1050 Techwood Dr NW	Atlanta	GA	30318	404-827-1700	
Web: www.tcm.turner.com					
TV Asahi America Inc 875 Third Ave 3rd Fl	New York	NY	10022	212-644-6300	644-0003
Web: www.tv-asahi.net					
TV One 1010 Wayne Ave 10th Fl	Silver Spring	MD	20910	301-755-0400	429-3202
Web: tvone.tv					
USA Network 30 Rockefeller Plaza 21st Fl	New York	NY	10112	212-664-4444	664-6365
Web: www.usanetwork.com					
VH1 Classic 1515 Broadway 21st Fl	New York	NY	10036	212-258-6000	654-4743
Web: www.vh1.com					
Video Hits One (VH1) 1515 Broadway 20th Fl	New York	NY	10036	212-846-6000	422-6630*
**Fax Area Code:* 201 ■ **Fax:* Hum Res ■ *Web:* www.vh1.com					
W Network 25 Dockside Dr Unit 18	Toronto	ON	M5A0B5	416-479-6784	
Web: www.wnetwork.com					
Weather Ch Inc, The					
300 I N Pkwy Po Box 724554	Atlanta	GA	30339	770-226-0000	226-2632
TF: 866-843-0392 ■ *Web:* www.weather.com					
Weather Network, The 2655 Bristol Cir	Oakville	ON	L6H7W1	905-829-1159	829-5800
Web: www.theweathernetwork.com					
WGN America 2501 W Bradley Pl	Chicago	IL	60618	773-528-2311	
Web: www.wgnamerica.com					
Worship Network PO Box 428	Safety Harbor	FL	34695	800-728-8723	
TF: 800-728-8723 ■ *Web:* www.worship.net					

744 TELEVISION STATIONS

SEE ALSO Internet Broadcasting p. 2588

ABC	American Broadcasting Co	**PBS**	Public Broadcasting Service
CBC	Canadian Broadcasting Corp	**QS**	Television Quatre Saisons
CBS	Columbia Broadcasting System	**SRC**	Societe Radio-Canada
CTV	Canadian Television Network	**TBN**	Trinity Broadcasting Network
Fox	Fox Broadcasting Co	**Tele**	Telemundo Communications Group
GTN	Global Television Network	**TVA**	Groupe TVA
Ind	Independent	**Uni**	Univision Television Network
NBC	National Broadcasting Co	**UPN**	United Paramount Network
PAX	Paxson Communications Corp	**WB**	Warner Bros Television

	City	State	Zip	Phone	Fax
CBET-TV Ch 9 (CBC) 825 Riverside Dr W	Windsor	ON	N9A5K9	519-255-3411	
Web: cbc.ca/news/canada/windsor/					
CFCM-TV Ch 4 (TVA) 1000 Myrand Ave	Sainte-Foy	QC	G1V2W3	418-688-9330	688-0413
Web: tva.canoe.ca					
Channel 45 WHFT TV 3324 Pembroke Rd	Hollywood	FL	33021	954-962-1700	
Web: tbn.org					
CKVR-TV Ch 3 (Ind) 299 Queen St W	Toronto	ON	M5V2Z5	416-384-5000	
TF: 866-690-6179 ■ *Web:* www.ctv.ca					
EW Scripps Co, The 1866 E Chisholm	Nampa	ID	83687	208-336-0500	381-6682
Web: jrn.com/kivitv					
Global TV 121 Bloor St E	Toronto	ON	M4W3M5	416-967-1174	
TF: 877-345-9195 ■ *Web:* www.globaltv.com					
Iowa Public Television 6450 Corporate Dr	Johnston	IA	50131	515-242-3100	725-9836
TF: 800-532-1290 ■ *Web:* www.iptv.org					
KAAL-TV Ch 6 (ABC) 1701 Tenth Pl NE	Austin	MN	55912	507-437-6666	433-9560
Web: www.kaaltv.com					
KABC-TV Ch 7 (ABC) 500 Cir Seven Dr	Glendale	CA	91201	818-863-7777	863-7080
Web: www.abclocal.go.com					
KAFT-TV Ch 13 (PBS) 350 S Donaghey Ave	Conway	AR	72034	501-682-2386	682-4122
TF: 800-662-2386 ■ *Web:* www.aetn.org					
KAIL-TV Ch 7 1590 Alluvial Ave	Clovis	CA	93611	559-299-9753	299-1523
Web: www.kail.tv					
KARE-TV Ch 11 (NBC) 8811 State Hwy 55	Golden Valley	MN	55427	763-546-1111	546-8606
TF: 888-966-4532 ■ *Web:* www.kare11.com					
KAZT-TV Ch 7 (Ind) 3211 Tower Rd	Prescott	AZ	86305	928-778-6770	
Web: aztv.com					
KBHE-TV Ch 9 (PBS)					
555 N Dakota St PO Box 5000	Vermillion	SD	57069	800-333-0789	677-5010*
**Fax Area Code:* 605 ■ *TF:* 800-333-0789 ■ *Web:* www.sdpb.org					
KBYU-TV Ch 11 (PBS)					
2000 Ironton Blvd Brigham Young University	Provo	UT	84606	801-422-8450	422-8478
TF: 800-298-5298 ■ *Web:* www.kbyutv.org					
KCAL-TV Ch 9 (Ind) 4200 Radford Ave	Studio City	CA	91604	818-655-2000	
Web: losangeles.cbslocal.com					
KCBA-TV Ch 35 (Fox) 1550 Moffett St	Salinas	CA	93905	831-422-3500	422-9365
Web: www.kionrightnow.com					
KCBS-TV Ch 2 (CBS) 4200 Radford Ave	Studio City	CA	91604	818-655-2000	
Web: losangeles.cbslocal.com					
KCTV-TV Ch 5 (CBS) 4500 Shawnee Mission Pkwy	Fairway	KS	66205	913-677-5555	677-7243
Web: www.kctv5.com					
KCWC-TV Ch 4 (PBS) 2660 Peck Ave	Riverton	WY	82501	307-856-6944	856-3893
Web: wyomingpbs.org/					
KCWY-TV Ch 13 (NBC)					
141 Progress Cir PO Box 1450	Mills	WY	82644	307-577-0013	577-5251
TF: 800-955-5739 ■ *Web:* kcwy13.com					
KDTX-TV Ch 58 (TBN) 2823 W Irving Blvd	Irving	TX	75061	972-313-1333	790-5853
Web: www.tbn.org					
KESQ-TV Ch 3 (ABC) 42650 Melanie Pl	Palm Desert	CA	92211	760-568-6830	343-7480
TF: 888-776-8538 ■ *Web:* www.kesq.com					
KETG-TV Ch 9 (PBS) 350 S Donaghey Ave	Conway	AR	72034	501-682-2386	682-4122
TF: 800-662-2386 ■ *Web:* www.aetn.org					

				Phone	Fax
KETS-TV Ch 2 (PBS) 350 S Donaghey Ave. *TF:* 800-662-2386 ■ *Web:* www.aetn.org	Conway	AR	72034	501-682-2386	682-4122
KFBB-TV 3200 Old Havre Hwy PO Box 1139 *TF:* 800-854-7720 ■ *Web:* www.kfbb.com	Black Eagle	MT	59414	406-453-4377	
KFPX-TV Ch 39 (I) 4570 114th St *Web:* www.ionmedia.tv	Urbandale	IA	50322	515-331-3939	331-1312
KGBT-TV Ch 4 (CBS) 9201 W Expy 83 *Web:* www.valleycentral.com	Harlingen	TX	78552	956-366-4444	366-4494
KICU-TV Ch 36 (Ind) 2102 Commerce Dr *Web:* www.ktvu.com	San Jose	CA	95131	408-953-3636	
KIMT-TV Ch 3 (CBS) 112 N Pennsylvania Ave *TF:* 800-323-4883 ■ *Web:* www.kimt.com	Mason City	IA	50401	641-423-2540	423-9309
KION-TV Ch 46 (CBS) 1550 Moffett St *Web:* www.kionrightnow.com	Salinas	CA	93905	831-422-3500	422-9365
KIVI-TV Ch 6 (ABC) 1866 E Chisholm Dr *Web:* jrn.com/kivitv	Nampa	ID	83687	208-336-0500	381-6682
KMAX-TV Ch 31 (CBS) 2713 Kovr Dr *TF:* 800-374-8813 ■ *Web:* sacramento.cbslocal.com	West Sacramento	CA	95605	916-374-1313	374-1304
KMBH-TV Ch 60 (PBS) 1701 Tennessee St	Harlingen	TX	78550	956-421-4111	
KMIR-TV Ch 6 (NBC) 72920 Parkview Dr **Fax:* Sales ■ *Web:* kmir.com/	Palm Desert	CA	92260	760-568-3636	568-1176*
KMIZ-TV Ch 17 (ABC) 501 Business Loop 70 E *TF:* 800-345-4109 ■ *Web:* www.abc17news.com	Columbia	MO	65201	573-449-0917	875-7078
KMOS-TV Ch 6 (PBS) University of Central Missouri **Fax Area Code:* 660 ■ *TF:* 800-753-3436 ■ *Web:* www.kmos.org	Warrensburg	MO	64093	800-753-3436	543-8863*
KMSP-TV Ch 9 (Fox) 11358 Viking Dr *Web:* www.myfoxtwincities.com	Eden Prairie	MN	55344	952-944-9999	942-0455
KMTR-TV Ch 16 (NBC) 3825 International Ct *Web:* www.kmtr.com	Springfield	OR	97477	541-746-1600	747-0866
KNTV-TV Ch 11 (NBC) 2450 N First St *Web:* www.nbcbayarea.com	San Jose	CA	95131	408-432-6221	
KNVO-TV Ch 48 (Uni) 801 N Jackson Rd *Web:* knvotv48.com	McAllen	TX	78501	956-687-4848	687-7784
KNWA-TV Ch 51 (NBC) 609 W Dickson St Third Flr *Web:* www.nwahomepage.com	Fayetteville	AR	72701	479-571-5100	571-8914
KOAA-TV Ch 5/30 (NBC) 2200 Seventh Ave *Web:* www.koaa.com	Pueblo	CO	81003	719-544-5781	295-6677
KOMU-TV Ch 8 (NBC) 5550 Hwy 63 S *TF:* 800-286-3932 ■ *Web:* www.komu.com	Columbia	MO	65201	573-884-6397	
KPDX-TV Ch 49 (MNT) 14975 NW Greenbrier Pkwy *TF:* 866-906-1249 ■ *Web:* www.kptv.com	Beaverton	OR	97006	503-906-1249	548-6920
KPLC-TV Ch 7 (NBC) 320 Div St *Web:* www.kplctv.com	Lake Charles	LA	70601	337-439-9071	437-7600
KPLO-TV Ch 6 (CBS) 501 S Phillips Ave *TF:* 800-888-5356 ■ *Web:* www.keloland.com	Sioux Falls	SD	57104	605-336-1100	336-0202
KPTV-TV Ch 12 (Fox) 14975 NW Greenbrier Pkwy *TF:* 866-906-1249 ■ *Web:* www.kptv.com	Beaverton	OR	97006	503-906-1249	548-6920
KPXD-TV Ch 68 (I) 600 Six Flags Dr Ste 652	Arlington	TX	76011	817-633-6843	633-3176
KPXE-TV Ch 50 (I) 4220 Shawnee Mission Pkwy Ste 110 B *TF:* 800-646-7296 ■ *Web:* www.ionmedianetworks.com	Fairway	KS	66205	913-722-0798	722-1217
KQED Inc 1585 Schallenberger Rd *Web:* www.kqed.org	San Jose	CA	95131	415-864-2000	
KRCG-TV Ch 13 (CBS) 10188 Old Hwy 54 N *Web:* www.connectmidmissouri.com	New Bloomfield	MO	65063	573-896-5144	896-5193
KRGV-TV Ch 5 (ABC) 900 E Expy PO Box 5 *Web:* www.krgv.com	Weslaco	TX	78596	956-968-5555	973-5016
KSBW-TV Ch 8 (NBC) 238 John St *Web:* www.ksbw.com	Salinas	CA	93901	831-758-8888	424-3750
KSMO-TV Ch 62 (MNT) 4500 Shawnee Mission Pkwy *Web:* www.kctv5.com	Fairway	KS	66205	913-677-5555	621-4703
KSMQ-TV Ch 15 (PBS) 2000 Eigth Ave NW *TF:* 800-658-2539 ■ *Web:* www.ksmq.org	Austin	MN	55912	507-433-0678	433-0670
KSPX-TV Ch 29 (I) 3352 Mather Field Rd **Fax Area Code:* 646 ■ *TF:* 800-987-9936 ■ *Web:* www.ionmedia.tv	Rancho Cordova	CA	95670	916-368-2929	597-5903*
KSTW-TV Ch 11 (CW) 1000 Dexter Ave N Ste 205 *TF:* 866-313-5789 ■ *Web:* cwseattle.cbslocal.com	Seattle	WA	98109	206-441-1111	861-8915
KTBN-TV Ch 40 (TBN) 2442 Michelle Dr *TF:* 888-731-1000 ■ *Web:* www.tbn.org	Tustin	CA	92780	714-832-2950	
KTEH-TV Ch 54 (PBS) 1585 Schallenberger Rd *Web:* www.kqed.org	San Jose	CA	95131	415-864-2000	
KTNL-TV Ch 13 (CBS/I) 520 Lake St *Web:* www.cbssoutheastak.com	Sitka	AK	99835	907-747-5749	747-8440
KTSC-TV Ch 8 (PBS) 2200 Bonforte Blvd *Web:* www.rmpbs.org	Pueblo	CO	81001	719-543-8800	549-2208
KTSD-TV Ch 10 (PBS) 555 N Dakota St PO Box 5000 **Fax Area Code:* 605 ■ *TF:* 800-333-0789 ■ *Web:* www.sdpb.org	Vermillion	SD	57069	800-333-0789	677-5010*
KTSF-TV Ch 26 (Ind) 100 Valley Dr *TF:* 800-772-1213 ■ *Web:* www.ktsf.com	Brisbane	CA	94005	415-468-2626	467-7559
KTVU-TV Ch 2 (Fox) Two Jack London Sq *Web:* www.ktvu.com	Oakland	CA	94607	510-834-1212	272-9957
KUSD-TV Ch 2 (PBS) 555 N Dakota St PO Box 5000 **Fax Area Code:* 605 ■ *TF:* 800-333-0789 ■ *Web:* www.sdpb.org	Vermillion	SD	57069	800-333-0789	677-5010*
KUSM-TV Ch 9 (PBS) Visual Communications Bldg Rm 183 *TF:* 800-426-8243 ■ *Web:* www.montanapbs.org	Bozeman	MT	59717	406-994-3437	994-6545
KVEA-TV Ch 52 (Tele) 3000 W Alameda Ave *Web:* www.telemundo52.com	Burbank	CA	91523	202-237-2280	
KVVU-TV Ch 5 (Fox) 25 TV 5 Dr *Web:* www.fox5vegas.com	Henderson	NV	89014	702-435-5555	451-4220
KWKB-TV Ch 20 (CW) 1547 Baker Ave *Web:* kwkb.com	West Branch	IA	52358	319-643-5952	
KWPX-TV Ch 33 (I) 8112-C 304th Ave SE PO Box 426 *TF:* 888-467-2988 ■ *Web:* www.ionmedianetworks.com	Preston	WA	98050	425-222-6010	222-6032
KWWL-TV Ch 7 (NBC) 500 E Fourth St *TF:* 800-947-7746 ■ *Web:* www.kwwl.com	Waterloo	IA	50703	319-291-1200	291-1255
KWYB-TV Ch 18 (ABC) 3825 Harrison Ave *Web:* www.abcfoxmontana.com	Butte	MT	59701	406-782-7185	723-9269
KXLF-TV Ch 4 (CBS) 1003 S Montana St *Web:* www.kxlf.com	Butte	MT	59701	406-496-8400	782-8906
Liberman Broadcasting, INC 1845 Empire Ave *TF:* 866-576-5353 ■ *Web:* www.lbimedia.com	Burbank	CA	91504	818-729-5300	
Maryland Public Television 11767 Owings Mills Blvd *Web:* www.mpt.org	Owings Mills	MD	21117	410-581-4097	581-4338
UNC-TV Ch 4 (PBS) 10 TW Alexander Dr PO Box 14900 *TF:* 800-906-5050 ■ *Web:* www.unctv.org	Research Triangle Park	NC	27709	919-549-7000	549-7201
WADL-TV Ch 38 (Fox) 35000 Adell Dr *Web:* www.wadldetroit.com	Clinton Township	MI	48035	586-790-3838	790-3841
WAND-TV Ch 17 (ABC) 904 S Side Dr *Web:* www.wandtv.com	Decatur	IL	62521	217-424-2500	424-2583
WAOE-TV Ch 59 (MNT) 2907 Springfield Rd *Web:* www.my59.tv	East Peoria	IL	61611	309-674-5900	674-5959
WAVY-TV Ch 10 (NBC) 300 Wavy St *Web:* www.wavy.com	Portsmouth	VA	23704	757-393-1010	397-8279
WBBZ-TV Ch 67 (Ind) 4545 Transit Rd Ste 750 *Web:* www.wbbz.tv	Williamsville	NY	14221	716-630-9229	630-9233
WBIN TV 11 A St *Web:* www.wbintv.com	Derry	NH	03038	603-845-1000	434-8627
WBND-TV Ch 57 (Ind) 53550 Generations Dr *Web:* www.abc57.com	South Bend	IN	46635	574-344-5500	344-5094
WBNX-TV Ch 55 (CW) 2690 State Rd *TF:* 800-282-0515 ■ *Web:* www.wbnx.com	Cuyahoga Falls	OH	44223	330-922-5500	929-2410
WBOC-TV Ch 16 (CBS) 1729 N Salisbury Blvd *Web:* www.wboc.com	Salisbury	MD	21801	410-749-1111	742-5190
WBRE-TV Ch 28 (NBC) 62 S Franklin St *TF:* 800-367-9222 ■ *Web:* www.pahomepage.com	Wilkes-Barre	PA	18701	570-823-2828	829-0440
WCAU-TV Ch 10 (NBC) 10 Monument Rd *Web:* www.nbcphiladelphia.com	Bala Cynwyd	PA	19004	610-668-5510	668-3700
WCAX-TV Ch 3 (CBS) 30 Joy Dr *TF:* 855-669-9657 ■ *Web:* www.wcax.com	South Burlington	VT	05403	802-658-6300	652-6399
WCBB-TV Ch 10 (PBS) 1450 Lisbon St *TF:* 800-884-1717 ■ *Web:* www.mpbn.net	Lewiston	ME	04240	207-783-9101	783-5193
WCBD-TV Ch 2 (NBC) 210 W Coleman Blvd *Web:* www.counton2.com	Mount Pleasant	SC	29464	843-884-2222	881-3410
WCBI-TV Ch 4 (CBS) 201 Fifth St S *Web:* www.wcbi.com	Columbus	MS	39701	662-327-4444	328-5222
WCIA-TV Ch 3 (CBS) PO Box 20 *TF:* 800-676-3382 ■ *Web:* www.illinoishomepage.net	Champaign	IL	61824	217-356-8333	402-9750
WCLF-TV Ch 22 (Ind) PO Box 6922 *Web:* www.ctnonline.com	Clearwater	FL	33758	727-535-5622	531-2497
WCTX-TV Ch 59 (MNT) Eight Elm St	New Haven	CT	06510	203-782-5900	
WCVB-TV Ch 5 (ABC) Five TV Pl *Web:* www.wcvb.com	Needham	MA	02494	781-449-0400	433-4510
WCYB-TV Ch 5 (NBC) 101 Lee St *Web:* www.wcyb.com	Bristol	VA	24201	276-645-1555	
WDAM-TV Ch 7 (NBC) PO Box 16269 *TF:* 800-844-9326 ■ *Web:* www.wdam.com	Hattiesburg	MS	39404	601-544-4730	584-9302
WDSC-TV 1200 W International Speedway Blvd *TF:* 866-273-5825 ■ *Web:* www.wdsctv.org	Daytona Beach	FL	32114	386-506-4415	506-4427
WEAO-TV Ch 49 (PBS) 1750 Campus Ctr Dr *TF:* 800-544-4549 ■ *Web:* westernreservepublicmedia.org	Kent	OH	44240	330-677-4549	678-0688
WEAR-TV Ch 3 (ABC) 4990 Mobile Hwy **Fax Area Code:* 410 ■ *TF:* 877-903-7867 ■ *Web:* www.weartv.com	Pensacola	FL	32506	850-456-3333	568-1691*
WECT-TV Ch 6 (NBC) 322 Shipyard Blvd *Web:* www.wect.com	Wilmington	NC	28412	910-791-8070	791-9535
WEEK-TV Ch 25 (NBC) 2907 Springfield Rd *Web:* www.cinewsnow.com	East Peoria	IL	61611	309-698-2525	698-9335
WEHT-TV Ch 25 (ABC) 800 Marywood Dr *TF:* 800-879-8542 ■ *Web:* www.tristatehomepage.com	Henderson	KY	42420	270-826-6281	826-9301
WELF-TV Ch 23 (TBN) 384 S Campus Rd *Web:* www.tbn.org	Lookout Mountain	GA	30750	706-820-1663	820-1735
WENH-TV Ch 11 (PBS) 268 Mast Rd *Web:* www.nhptv.org	Durham	NH	03824	603-868-1100	868-7552
WESH-TV Ch 2 (NBC) 1021 N Wymore Rd *Web:* www.wesh.com	Winter Park	FL	32789	407-645-2222	539-7948
WETA-TV Ch 26 (PBS) 2775 S Quincy St *Web:* www.weta.org	Arlington	VA	22206	703-998-2600	998-3401
WEYI-TV Ch 25 (NBC) 2225 W WillaRd Rd *Web:* www.minbcnews.com	Clio	MI	48420	810-687-1000	687-4925
WFFF-TV Ch 44 (Fox) 298 Mountain View Dr *TF:* 888-344-7233 ■ *Web:* www.mychamplainvalley.com	Colchester	VT	05446	802-660-9333	660-8673
WFMY-TV Ch 2 (CBS) 1615 Phillips Ave *Web:* wfmynews2.com/	Greensboro	NC	27405	336-379-9369	273-9433
WFMZ-TV Ch 69 (Ind) 300 E Rock Rd *Web:* www.wfmz.com	Allentown	PA	18103	610-478-6500	791-9994
WFSB-TV Ch 3 (CBS) 333 Capital Blvd *Web:* www.wfsb.com	Rocky Hill	CT	06067	860-728-3333	728-0263
WFTC-TV Ch 29 (MNT) 11358 Viking Dr *Web:* www.my29tv.com	Eden Prairie	MN	55344	952-944-9999	942-0455
WFXT-TV Ch 25 (Fox) 25 Fox Dr *Web:* www.myfoxboston.com	Dedham	MA	02026	781-467-2525	467-7213
WGAL-TV Ch 8 (NBC) 1300 Columbia Ave *Web:* www.wgal.com	Lancaster	PA	17604	717-393-5851	295-7457
WGBH-TV Ch 2 (PBS) 1 Guest St *TF:* 800-492-1111 ■ *Web:* www.wgbh.org	Brighton	MA	02135	617-300-2000	300-1026
WGGS-TV Ch 16 (Ind) 3409 Rutherford Rd Ext *TF General:* 800-849-3683 ■ *Web:* www.wggs16.com	Taylors	SC	29687	864-244-1616	292-8481

Station / Address	City	State	ZIP	Phone	Fax
WGHP-TV Ch 8 (Fox) 2005 Francis St *TF:* 800-808-6397 ■ *Web:* myfox8.com	High Point	NC	27263	336-841-8888	841-5169
WGPX-TV Ch 16 (I) 1114 N Ohenry Blvd	Greensboro	NC	27405	336-272-9227	272-9298
WHKY-TV Ch 14 (Ind) PO Box 1059 *Web:* www.whky.com	Hickory	NC	28603	828-322-1290	322-8256
WHLT-TV Ch 22 (CBS) 5912 Hwy 49 Cloverleaf Mall Ste A *TF:* 866-328-1987 ■ *Web:* www.whlt.com	Hattiesburg	MS	39401	601-545-2077	545-3589
WHMB-TV Ch 40 (Ind) 10511 Greenfield Ave *Web:* www.whmbtv.com	Noblesville	IN	46060	317-773-5050	776-4051
WHOI-TV Ch 19 (ABC) 2907 Springfield Rd *Web:* www.cinewsnow.com	East Peoria	IL	61611	309-698-2525	
WICD-TV Ch 15 (ABC) 250 S Country Fair Dr *Web:* www.newschannel20.com/	Champaign	IL	61821	217-351-8500	
WILL-TV Ch 12 (PBS) 300 N Goodwin Ave *Web:* www.will.illinois.edu	Urbana	IL	61801	217-333-7300	333-7151
WITV-TV Ch 7 (PBS) 1101 Geroge Rogers Blvd *Web:* www.scetv.org	Columbia	SC	29201	803-737-3200	737-3476
WJAR-TV Ch 10 (NBC) 23 Kenney Dr *Web:* www.turnto10.com	Cranston	RI	02920	401-455-9100	455-9140
WJBK-TV Ch 2 (Fox) PO Box 2000 *Web:* www.myfoxdetroit.com	Southfield	MI	48037	248-557-2000	
WJLA-TV Ch 7 (ABC) 1100 Wilson Blvd *Web:* www.wjla.com	Arlington	VA	22209	703-236-9552	236-2331
WJWJ-TV Ch 16 (PBS) PO Box 1165 *Web:* www.scetv.org	Beaufort	SC	29901	843-524-0808	
WJYS-TV Ch 62 (Ind) 18600 Oak Pk Ave *Web:* www.wjys.tv	Tinley Park	IL	60477	708-633-0001	
WKAR-TV Ch 23 (PBS) MSU 283 Communications Arts Bldg *Web:* wkar.org/tv	East Lansing	MI	48824	517-884-4700	
WKBD-TV Ch 50 (CW) 26905 W 11-Mile Rd *Web:* cwdetroit.cbslocal.com	Southfield	MI	48034	248-355-7000	355-7000
WKMJ-TV Ch 68 (PBS) 600 Cooper Dr *TF:* 800-432-0951 ■ *Web:* www.ket.org	Lexington	KY	40502	859-258-7000	258-7399
WKNO-TV Ch 10 (PBS) 7151 Cherry Farms Rd *TF:* 877-717-7822 ■ *Web:* www.wkno.org	Cordova	TN	38016	901-729-8765	729-8176
WKPC-TV Ch 15 (PBS) 600 Cooper Dr *TF:* 800-432-0951 ■ *Web:* www.ket.org	Lexington	KY	40502	859-258-7000	258-7399
WKPT-TV Ch 19 (ABC) 222 Commerce St *TF:* 877-768-5048 ■ *Web:* www.abc19.tv	Kingsport	TN	37660	423-246-9578	246-1863
WLAE-TV Ch 32 (PBS) 3330 N Cswy Blvd Ste 345 *Web:* www.wlae.com	Metairie	LA	70002	504-866-7411	840-9838
WLGA-TV Ch 66 (CW) 1501 13th Ave *Web:* www.wlgatv.com	Columbus	GA	31901	706-257-6703	
WLIW-TV Ch 21 (PBS) 825 Eighth Ave *Web:* www.wliw.org	New York	NY	10019	516-367-2100	
WLNY-TV Ch 55 (Ind) 270 S Service Rd Ste 55 *Web:* newyork.cbslocal.com	Melville	NY	11747	631-777-8855	
WLOX-TV Ch 13 (ABC) 208 Debuys Rd **Fax:* News Rm ■ *Web:* www.wlox.com	Biloxi	MS	39531	228-896-1313	896-2596*
WMDT-TV Ch 47 (ABC) 202 Downtown Plz *Web:* www.wmdt.com	Salisbury	MD	21801	410-742-4747	742-5767
WMGM NBC40.Net 1601 New Rd	Linwood	NJ	08221	609-927-4440	927-7014
WMHT-TV Ch 17 (PBS) Four Global View *Web:* www.wmht.org	Troy	NY	12180	518-880-3400	880-3409
WMTW-TV Ch 8 (ABC) 99 Danville Corner Rd *TF:* 800-248-6397 ■ *Web:* www.wmtw.com	Auburn	ME	04210	207-782-1800	783-7371
WMUR-TV Ch 9 (ABC) 100 S Commercial St *Web:* www.wmur.com	Manchester	NH	03101	603-669-9999	641-9005
WMYD-TV Ch 20 (MNT) 2777 Franklin Rd Ste 1220 *TF:* 800-825-0770 ■ *Web:* wxyz.com/tv20detroit/	Southfield	MI	48034	248-355-2020	
WNEM-TV Ch 5 (CBS) 107 N Franklin St *TF:* 800-522-9636 ■ *Web:* www.wnem.com	Saginaw	MI	48607	989-755-8191	758-2110
WNEP-TV Ch 16 (ABC) 16 Montage Mtn Rd **Fax:* News Rm ■ *TF:* 800-982-4374 ■ *Web:* www.wnep.com	Moosic	PA	18507	570-346-7474	341-1344*
WNET PO Box 5776 *Web:* www.njtvonline.org	Englewood	NJ	07631	609-777-0031	
WNJU-TV Ch 47 (Tele) 2200 Fletcher Ave 6th Fl *Web:* www.telemundo47.com	Fort Lee	NJ	07024	877-478-3536	
WNOL-TV Ch 38 (CW) One Galeria Blvd Ste 850 *Web:* wgno.com	Metairie	LA	70001	504-525-3838	569-0908
WOFL-TV Ch 35 (Fox) 35 Skyline Dr *Web:* www.myfoxorlando.com	Lake Mary	FL	32746	407-644-3535	741-5189
WOI-TV Ch 5 (ABC) 3903 Westown Pkwy **Fax:* Sales ■ *TF:* 800-858-5555 ■ *Web:* weareiowa.com/home/	West Des Moines	IA	50266	515-457-9645	457-1034*
WOUC-TV Ch 44 (PBS) 35 S College St *Web:* www.woub.org	Athens	OH	45701	740-593-1771	593-0240
WOWK-TV Ch 13 (CBS) 555 Fifth Ave *TF:* 800-333-7636 ■ *Web:* www.wowktv.com	Huntington	WV	25701	304-525-1313	523-0545
WPBF-TV Ch 25 (ABC) 3970 RCA Blvd Ste 7007 *Web:* www.wpbf.com	Palm Beach Gardens	FL	33410	561-694-2525	624-1089
WPLG-TV Ch 10 (ABC) 3401 W Hallandale Beach Blvd **Fax Area Code:* 305 ■ **Fax:* News Rm ■ *Web:* www.local10.com	Pembroke Park	FL	33023	954-364-2500	375-2480*
WPMT-TV Ch 43 (Fox) 2005 S Queen St *TF:* 866-976-8747 ■ *Web:* www.fox43.com	York	PA	17403	717-843-0043	814-5530
WPNE-TV Ch 38 (PBS) 821 University Ave *Web:* www.wpt.org	Madison	WI	53706	608-263-2121	
Wpri TV 25 Catamore Blvd	East Providence	RI	02914	401-438-7200	228-1774
WPTZ-TV Ch 5 (NBC) Five Television Dr *Web:* www.wptz.com	Plattsburgh	NY	12901	518-561-5555	561-1201
WPXD-TV Ch 31 (I) 3975 Varsity Dr *TF:* 888-467-2988 ■ *Web:* www.ionmedianetworks.com	Ann Arbor	MI	48108	734-973-7900	973-7906
WPXL-TV Ch 49 (I) 3900 Veterans Blvd Ste 202	Metairie	LA	70002	504-887-9795	887-1518
WPXT-TV Ch 12 (CW) Four Ledgeview Dr *Web:* ourmaine.com	Westbrook	ME	04092	207-774-0051	774-6849
WPXW-TV Ch 66 (I) 6199 Old Arrington Ln	Fairfax Station	VA	22039	703-503-7966	503-1225
WQCW-TV Ch 30 (CW) 800 Gallia St	Portsmouth	OH	45662	740-353-3391	
WRBW-TV Ch 65 (MNT) 35 Skyline Dr *Web:* www.my65orlando.com	Lake Mary	FL	32746	407-644-3535	741-5189
WRGB-TV Ch 6 (CBS) 1400 Balltown Rd *Web:* www.cbs6albany.com	Schenectady	NY	12309	518-346-6666	
WSAZ-TV Ch 3 (NBC) PO Box 2115 *Web:* www.wsaz.com	Huntington	WV	25721	304-697-4780	690-3066
WSBT-TV Ch 22 (CBS) 1301 E Douglas Rd *TF:* 877-634-7181 ■ *Web:* www.wsbt.com	Mishawaka	IN	46545	574-232-6397	289-0622
WSCV-TV Ch 51 (NBC) 15000 SW 27th St *Web:* www.telemundo51.com	Miramar	FL	33027	954-622-7710	622-7700
WSET-TV Ch 13 (ABC) 2320 Langhorne Rd *TF:* 800-639-7847 ■ *Web:* www.wset.com	Lynchburg	VA	24501	434-528-1313	847-0458
WSKY-TV Ch 4 (Ind) 920 Corporate Ln *Web:* www.sky4tv.com	Chesapeake	VA	23320	757-382-0004	382-0365
WSRE-TV Ch 23 (PBS) 1000 College Blvd *Web:* www.wsre.org	Pensacola	FL	32504	850-484-1200	484-1255
WSYR-TV Ch 9 (ABC) 5904 Bridge St *Web:* localsyr.com:80/	East Syracuse	NY	13057	315-446-9999	251-1567
WTAT-TV Ch 24 (Fox) 4301 Arco Ln *Web:* www.foxcharleston.com	North Charleston	SC	29418	843-744-2424	554-9649
WTGL-TV Ch 45 (Ind) 31 Skyline Dr *Web:* www.tv45.org	Lake Mary	FL	32746	407-215-6745	215-6789
WTIU-TV Ch 30 (PBS) 1229 E Seventh St *TF:* 800-662-3311 ■ *Web:* www.wtiu.indiana.edu	Bloomington	IN	47405	812-855-5900	855-0729
WTJP-TV Ch 60 (TBN) 313 Rosedale Ave *Web:* www.tbn.org	Gadsden	AL	35901	256-546-8860	543-8623
WTLH-TV Ch 49 (Fox) 950 Commerce Blvd *Web:* www.myfoxtallahassee.com	Midway	FL	32343	850-576-4990	576-0200
WTLJ-TV Ch 54 (Ind) 10290 48th Ave	Allendale	MI	49401	616-895-4154	
WTNH-TV Ch 8 (ABC) Eight Elm St **Fax:* Mktg ■ *Web:* www.wtnh.com	New Haven	CT	06510	203-784-8888	789-2010*
WTVA-TV Ch 9 (NBC) PO Box 350 *Web:* www.wtva.com	Tupelo	MS	38802	662-842-7620	
WTVJ-TV Ch 6 (NBC) 15000 SW 27th St *Web:* www.nbcmiami.com	Miramar	FL	33027	954-622-6000	622-6107
WTXL-TV Ch 27 (ABC) 1620 Commerce Blvd *Web:* www.wtxl.com	Midway	FL	32343	850-893-3127	668-0423
WUGA-TV Ch 32 (PBS) 120 Hooper St *Web:* www.uga.edu	Athens	GA	30602	706-542-3000	
WUNI-TV Ch 27 (Uni) 33 Fourth Ave *Web:* www.wunitv.com	Needham	MA	02494	781-433-2727	433-2750
WUNL-TV Ch 26 (PBS) 10 TW Alexander Dr PO Box 14900 *Web:* www.unctv.org	Research Triangle Park	NC	27709	919-549-7000	
WVIT-TV Ch 30 (NBC) 1422 New Britain Ave *TF:* 800-523-9848 ■ *Web:* www.nbcconnecticut.com	West Hartford	CT	06110	860-521-3030	521-3110
WVNY-TV Ch 22 (ABC) 298 Mountain View Dr *Web:* www.mychamplainvalley.com	Colchester	VT	05446	802-660-9333	660-8673
WWJ-TV Ch 62 (CBS) 26905 W 11-Mile Rd *Web:* detroit.cbslocal.com	Southfield	MI	48034	248-355-7000	
WWMT-TV Ch 3 (CBS) 590 W Maple St **Fax Area Code:* 269 ■ *TF:* 800-875-3333 ■ *Web:* www.wwmt.com	Kalamazoo	MI	49008	800-875-3333	388-8322*
WWOR-TV Ch 9 (MNT) 9 Broadcast Plaza *Web:* www.my9nj.com	Secaucus	NJ	07096	201-330-7846	330-3777
WXPX-TV Ch 66 (I) 14444 66th St N *Web:* www.ionmedia.tv	Clearwater	FL	33764	727-479-1053	479-1055
WXXV-TV Ch 25 (Fox) 14351 Hwy 49 N *Web:* www.wxxv25.com	Gulfport	MS	39503	228-832-2525	832-4442
WXYZ-TV Ch 7 (ABC) 20777 W 10-Mile Rd *TF:* 800-825-0770 ■ *Web:* www.wxyz.com	Southfield	MI	48037	248-827-7777	827-9444
WYES-TV Ch 12 (PBS) 111 Veterans Blvd Ste 250 *Web:* www.wyes.org	Metairie	LA	70005	504-486-5511	840-9954
WYOU-TV Ch 22 (CBS) 62 S Franklin St *TF:* 855-241-5144 ■ *Web:* www.pahomepage.com	Wilkes-Barre	PA	18701	570-961-2222	829-0440
WYPX-TV Ch 55 (I) One Charles Blvd *Web:* www.ionmedianetworks.com	Guilderland	NY	12084	518-464-0143	464-0633
WYZZ-TV Ch 43 (Fox) 2714 E Lincoln St *Web:* www.centralillinoisproud.com	Bloomington	IL	61701	309-661-4343	663-6943

744-1 Abilene, TX

Station / Address	City	State	ZIP	Phone	Fax
KRBC-TV Ch 9 (NBC) 4510 S 14th St *Web:* www.bigcountryhomepage.com	Abilene	TX	79605	325-692-4242	692-8265
KTAB-TV Ch 32 (CBS) 4510 S 14th St *Web:* www.bigcountryhomepage.com	Abilene	TX	79605	325-695-2777	695-9922
KTXS-TV Ch 12 (ABC) 4420 N Clack St **Fax:* News Rm ■ *Web:* www.ktxs.com	Abilene	TX	79601	325-677-2281	672-5307*

744-2 Albany, NY

Station / Address	City	State	ZIP	Phone	Fax
WNYT-TV Ch 13 (NBC) 715 N Pearl St *TF:* 800-999-9698 ■ *Web:* www.wnyt.com	Albany	NY	12204	518-436-4791	434-0659
WTEN-TV Ch 10 (ABC) 341 Northern Blvd **Fax:* News Rm ■ *TF:* 800-888-9836 ■ *Web:* www.news10.com	Albany	NY	12204	518-436-4822	426-4792*

744-3 Albuquerque/Santa Fe, NM

Station / Address	City	State	ZIP	Phone	Fax
KASY-TV Ch 50 (MNT) 8341 Washington St NE	Albuquerque	NM	87113	505-797-1919	

Station	City	State	ZIP	Phone	Fax
KLUZ-TV Ch 41 (Uni) 2725 F Broadbent Pkwy NE *Web:* www.kluz.tv	Albuquerque	NM	87107	505-342-4141	341-9264
KNAT-TV Ch 23 (TBN) 1510 Coors Blvd NW *Web:* www.tbn.org	Albuquerque	NM	87121	505-836-6585	831-8725
KNME-TV Ch 5 (PBS) 1130 University Blvd NE University of New Mexico *TF:* 800-328-5663 ■ *Web:* www.newmexicopbs.org	Albuquerque	NM	87102	505-277-2121	277-2191
KOAT-TV Ch 7 (ABC) 3801 Carlisle Blvd NE *TF:* 877-871-0165 ■ *Web:* www.koat.com	Albuquerque	NM	87107	505-884-7777	884-6354
KOB-TV Ch 4 (NBC) Four Broadcast Plz SW *Web:* www.kob.com	Albuquerque	NM	87104	505-243-4411	764-2522
KRQE-TV Ch 13 (CBS) 13 Broadcast Plz SW *TF:* 800-283-4227 ■ *Web:* www.krqe.com	Albuquerque	NM	87104	505-243-2285	842-8483

744-4 Amarillo, TX

Station	City	State	ZIP	Phone	Fax
KACV-TV Ch 2 (PBS) PO Box 447 *Web:* www.kacvtv.org	Amarillo	TX	79178	806-371-5222	371-5258
KAMR-TV Ch 4 (NBC) 1015 S Fillmore St *Web:* myhighplains.com	Amarillo	TX	79101	806-383-3321	220-0941
KCIT-TV Ch 14 (Fox) 1015 S Fillmore St *Web:* www.myhighplains.com	Amarillo	TX	79101	806-374-1414	322-0123
KFDA-TV Ch 10 (CBS) 7900 Broadway *Web:* www.newschannel10.com	Amarillo	TX	79105	806-383-1010	381-9859

744-5 Anchorage, AK

Station	City	State	ZIP	Phone	Fax
KAKM-TV Ch 7 (PBS) 3877 University Dr *Web:* www.alaskapublic.org	Anchorage	AK	99508	907-550-8400	550-8401
KTBY-TV Ch 4 (Fox) 2700 E Tudor Rd *TF:* 877-304-1313 ■ *Web:* www.youralaskalink.com	Anchorage	AK	99507	907-561-1313	561-1377
KTUU-TV Ch 2 (NBC) 701 E Tudor Rd Ste 220 *Web:* www.ktuu.com	Anchorage	AK	99503	907-762-9202	563-3318
KTVA-TV Ch 11 (CBS) 1001 Northway Dr St 202 *Web:* www.ktva.com	Anchorage	AK	99508	907-274-1111	334-9427
KYUR-TV Ch 13 (ABC) 2700 E Tudor Rd *TF:* 877-304-1313 ■ *Web:* www.youralaskalink.com	Anchorage	AK	99507	907-561-1313	561-8934

744-6 Asheville, NC/Greenville, SC/Spartanburg, SC

Station	City	State	ZIP	Phone	Fax
WLOS-TV Ch 13 (ABC) 110 Technology Dr **Fax Area Code:* 410 ■ *TF:* 800-209-2293 ■ *Web:* www.wlos.com	Asheville	NC	28803	828-684-1340	568-1691*
WMYA-TV Ch 40 (MNT) 33 Villa Rd *TF:* 800-288-2413 ■ *Web:* www.my40.tv	Greenville	SC	29615	828-684-1340	
WRET-TV Ch 49 (PBS) PO Box 4069 *Web:* www.scetv.org	Spartanburg	SC	29305	864-503-9371	503-3615
WSPA-TV Ch 7 (CBS) 250 International Dr *TF:* 800-207-6397 ■ *Web:* www.wspa.com	Spartanburg	SC	29303	864-576-7777	587-4480
WYFF-TV Ch 4 (NBC) 505 Rutherford St *TF:* 800-453-9933 ■ *Web:* www.wyff4.com	Greenville	SC	29609	864-242-4404	240-5305

744-7 Atlanta, GA

Station	City	State	ZIP	Phone	Fax
WAGA-TV Ch 5 (Fox) 1551 Briarcliff Rd NE **Fax:* News Rm ■ *Web:* www.myfoxatlanta.com	Atlanta	GA	30306	404-875-5555	898-0169*
WATL-TV Ch 36 (MNT) One Monroe Pl *Web:* 11alive.com	Atlanta	GA	30324	404-892-1611	885-7639
WGCL-TV Ch 46 (CBS) 425 14th St NW *Web:* cbs46.com/	Atlanta	GA	30318	404-327-3194	327-3004
WPBA-TV Ch 30 (PBS) 740 Bismark Rd NE *Web:* www.pba.org	Atlanta	GA	30324	678-686-0321	686-0356
WSB-TV Ch 2 (ABC) 1601 W Peachtree St NE *Web:* www.wsbtv.com	Atlanta	GA	30309	404-897-7000	897-7370
WUPA-TV Ch 69 (CW) 2700 NE Expy Bldg A *Web:* cwatlanta.cbslocal.com	Atlanta	GA	30345	404-325-6929	633-4567
WXIA-TV Ch 11 (NBC) One Monroe Pl **Fax:* News Rm ■ *Web:* www.11alive.com	Atlanta	GA	30324	404-892-1611	881-0675*

744-8 Augusta, GA

Station	City	State	ZIP	Phone	Fax
WAGT-TV Ch 26 (NBC) 1336 Augusta W Pkwy *Web:* www.nbc26.tv	Augusta	GA	30909	706-826-0026	
WFXG-TV Ch 54 (Fox) 3933 Washington Rd *Web:* www.wfxg.com	Augusta	GA	30907	706-650-5400	650-8411
WRDW-TV Ch 12 (CBS) PO Box 1212 *TF:* 866-591-2502 ■ *Web:* www.wrdw.com	Augusta	GA	30903	803-278-1212	279-8316

744-9 Austin, TX

Station	City	State	ZIP	Phone	Fax
FOX 7 Austin 119 E Tenth St *Web:* www.myfoxaustin.com	Austin	TX	78701	512-476-7777	495-7060
KEYE-TV Ch 42 (CBS) 10700 Metric Blvd *TF:* 800-621-3362 ■ *Web:* www.keyetv.com	Austin	TX	78758	512-835-0042	490-2111
KLRU-TV Ch 18 (PBS) 2504-B Whitis Ave *Web:* www.klru.org	Austin	TX	78712	512-471-4811	475-9090
KNVA-TV Ch 54 (CW) 908 W ML King Jr Blvd *Web:* www.thecwaustin.com	Austin	TX	78701	512-478-5400	476-1520
KVUE-TV Ch 24 (ABC) 3201 Steck Ave **Fax:* News Rm ■ *Web:* www.kvue.com	Austin	TX	78757	512-459-6521	533-2233*
KXAN News 908 W Martin Luther King Jr Bl *Web:* www.kxan.com	Austin	TX	78701	512-476-3636	469-0630

744-10 Bakersfield, CA

Station	City	State	ZIP	Phone	Fax
KERO-TV Ch 23 (ABC) 321 21st St **Fax:* News Rm ■ *Web:* www.turnto23.com	Bakersfield	CA	93301	661-637-2323	323-5538*
KGET-TV Ch 17 (NBC) 2120 L St *Web:* www.kerngoldenempire.com	Bakersfield	CA	93301	661-283-1700	
KUVI-TV Ch 45 (MNT) 5801 Truxtun Ave	Bakersfield	CA	93309	661-324-0045	

744-11 Baltimore, MD

Station	City	State	ZIP	Phone	Fax
WBAL-TV Ch 11 (NBC) 3800 Hooper Ave *TF:* 800-622-4121 ■ *Web:* www.wbaltv.com	Baltimore	MD	21211	410-467-3000	338-6460
WBFF-TV Ch 45 (Fox) 2000 W 41st St *Web:* www.foxbaltimore.com	Baltimore	MD	21211	410-467-4545	467-5090
WJZ-TV Ch 13 (CBS) 3725 Malden Ave *Web:* baltimore.cbslocal.com	Baltimore	MD	21211	410-466-0013	578-7502

744-12 Bangor, ME

Station	City	State	ZIP	Phone	Fax
WABI-TV Ch 5 (CBS) 35 Hildreth St *Web:* wabi.tv	Bangor	ME	04401	207-947-8321	941-9378
WLBZ-TV Ch 2 (NBC) 329 Mt Hope Ave *TF:* 800-244-6306 ■ *Web:* www.wlbz2.com	Bangor	ME	04401	207-942-4821	942-2109
WMEB-TV Ch 12 (PBS) 63 Texas Ave *Web:* www.mpbn.net	Bangor	ME	04401	207-941-1010	942-2857
WVII-TV Ch 7 (ABC) 371 Target Industrial Cir *TF General:* 888-820-8458 ■ *Web:* www.foxbangor.com	Bangor	ME	04401	207-945-6457	

744-13 Baton Rouge, LA

Station	City	State	ZIP	Phone	Fax
BRProud 10000 Perkins Rd *Web:* www.fox44.com	Baton Rouge	LA	70810	225-766-3233	768-9293
KLPB-TV Ch 24 (PBS) 7733 Perkins Rd *TF:* 800-272-8161 ■ *Web:* www.lpb.org	Baton Rouge	LA	70810	225-767-5660	767-4421
KLTS-TV Ch 24 (PBS) 7733 Perkins Rd *Web:* www.lpb.org	Baton Rouge	LA	70810	225-767-5660	767-4299
NBC 33 TV 10000 Perkins Rd *Web:* www.nbc33tv.com	Baton Rouge	LA	70810	225-766-3233	768-9293
WAFB-TV Ch 9 (CBS) 844 Government St *TF:* 888-677-2900 ■ *Web:* www.wafb.com	Baton Rouge	LA	70802	225-215-4700	
WBRZ-TV Ch 2 (ABC) 1650 Highland Rd **Fax:* News Rm ■ *Web:* theadvocate.com	Baton Rouge	LA	70802	225-387-2222	336-2347*
WLPB-TV Ch 27 (PBS) 7733 Perkins Rd **Fax:* News Rm ■ *TF:* 800-272-8161 ■ *Web:* www.lpb.org	Baton Rouge	LA	70810	225-767-5660	767-4421*
WVLA 10000 Perkins Rd *Web:* nbc33tv.com	Baton Rouge	LA	70810	225-766-3233	

744-14 Billings, MT

Station	City	State	ZIP	Phone	Fax
KSVI-TV Ch 6 (ABC) 445 S 24th St W *Web:* www.yourbigsky.com	Billings	MT	59102	406-652-4743	652-6963
KTVQ-TV Ch 2 (CBS) 3203 Third Ave N *TF:* 800-908-4490 ■ *Web:* www.ktvq.com	Billings	MT	59101	406-252-5611	252-9938
KULR-TV Ch 8 (NBC) 2045 Overland Ave *Web:* www.kulr8.com	Billings	MT	59102	406-656-8000	652-8207

744-15 Birmingham, AL

Station	City	State	ZIP	Phone	Fax
WABM-TV Ch 68 (MNT) 651 Beacon Pkwy W Ste 105 *Web:* www.wabm68.com	Birmingham	AL	35209	205-403-3340	
WBIQ-TV Ch 10 (PBS) 2112 11th Ave S Ste 400 *TF:* 800-239-5233 ■ *Web:* www.aptv.org	Birmingham	AL	35205	205-328-8756	251-2192
WBRC-TV Ch 6 (Fox) 1720 Vly View Dr *Web:* www.myfoxal.com	Birmingham	AL	35209	205-322-6666	583-4356
WCFT-TV Ch 33 (ABC) 800 Concourse Pkwy Ste 200 **Fax:* News Rm ■ *TF:* 800-819-0121 ■ *Web:* www.abc3340.com	Birmingham	AL	35244	205-403-3340	982-3942*
WEIQ-TV Ch 42 (PBS) 2112 11th Ave S Ste 400 *TF:* 800-239-5233 ■ *Web:* www.aptv.org	Birmingham	AL	35205	205-328-8756	251-2192
WHIQ-TV Ch 24 (PBS) 2112 11th Ave S Ste 400 *TF:* 800-239-5233 ■ *Web:* www.aptv.org	Birmingham	AL	35205	205-328-8756	251-2192
WTTO-TV Ch 21 (CW) 651 Beacon Pkwy W Ste 105 *Web:* www.wtto21.com/birmingham_al	Birmingham	AL	35209	205-943-2168	290-2114
WVTM-TV Ch 13 (NBC) 1732 Valley View Dr *TF:* 844-248-7698 ■ *Web:* www.alabamas13.com	Birmingham	AL	35209	205-933-1313	558-7389

744-16 Bismarck, ND

Station	City	State	Zip	Phone	Fax
KBMY-TV Ch 17 (ABC) 1811 N 15th St *Web:* wday.com/	Bismarck	ND	58501	701-223-1700	
KFYR-TV Ch 5 (NBC) 200 N Fourth St *Web:* www.kfyrtv.com	Bismarck	ND	58501	701-255-5757	255-8220
KNDX-TV Ch 26 (Fox) 3130 E Broadway Ave	Bismarck	ND	58501	701-355-0026	
KXMB-TV Ch 12 (CBS) 1811 N 15th St *Web:* www.kxnet.com	Bismarck	ND	58501	701-223-9197	355-9140

744-17 Boise, ID

Station	City	State	Zip	Phone	Fax
KTVB-TV Ch 7 (NBC) 5407 Fairview **Fax Area Code:* 313 ■ *TF:* 800-537-8939 ■ *Web:* www.ktvb.com	Boise	ID	83706	208-375-7277	223-4650*

744-18 Boston, MA

Station	City	State	Zip	Phone	Fax
WHDH-TV Ch 7 (NBC) 7 Bulfinch Pl *Web:* whdh.com	Boston	MA	02114	617-725-0777	723-6117

744-19 Brownsville, TX

Station	City	State	Zip	Phone	Fax
KVEO-TV Ch 23 (NBC) 394 N Expy *Web:* www.kveo.com	Brownsville	TX	78521	956-544-2323	544-4636

744-20 Buffalo, NY

Station	City	State	Zip	Phone	Fax
WGRZ-TV Ch 2 (NBC) 259 Delaware Ave *Web:* www.wgrz.com	Buffalo	NY	14202	716-849-2200	849-7602
WIVB-TV Ch 4 (CBS) 2077 Elmwood Ave **Fax:* News Rm ■ *TF:* 800-794-3687 ■ *Web:* www.wivb.com	Buffalo	NY	14207	716-874-4410	874-8173*
WKBW-TV Ch 7 (ABC) 7 Broadcast Plaza **Fax:* News Rm ■ *TF:* 888-373-7888 ■ *Web:* www.wkbw.com	Buffalo	NY	14202	716-845-6100	840-7820*
WNED-TV Ch 17 (PBS) 140 Lower Terr Horizons Plz *Web:* www.wned.org	Buffalo	NY	14202	716-845-7000	845-7036
WNYO-TV Ch 49 (MNT) 699 Hertel Ave Ste 100 *Web:* www.mytvbuffalo.com	Buffalo	NY	14207	716-447-3200	875-4919
WUTV-TV Ch 29 (Fox) 699 Hertel Ave Ste 100 *Web:* www.wutv29.com	Buffalo	NY	14207	716-447-3200	875-4919

744-21 Calgary, AB

Station	City	State	Zip	Phone	Fax
CBC 1724 Westmount Blvd NW *Web:* www.cbc.ca	Calgary	AB	T2N3G7	403-521-6000	521-6079
CFCN-TV Ch 3 (CTV) 80 Patina Rise SW *Web:* calgary.ctvnews.ca	Calgary	AB	T3H2W4	403-240-5600	240-5689

744-22 Casper, WY

Station	City	State	Zip	Phone	Fax
KGWC-TV Ch 14 (CBS) 1856 Skyview Dr	Casper	WY	82601	307-234-1111	234-4005
KTWO-TV Ch 2 (ABC) 1896 Skyview Dr *Web:* www.k2tv.com	Casper	WY	82601	307-237-3711	234-9866
Wyo Media Inc 1856 Skyview Dr	Casper	WY	82601	307-577-5923	577-5928

744-23 Cedar Rapids, IA

Station	City	State	Zip	Phone	Fax
KCRG-TV Ch 9 (ABC) 501 Second Ave SE *TF:* 800-332-5443 ■ *Web:* www.kcrg.com	Cedar Rapids	IA	52401	319-398-8422	398-8378
KFXA-TV Ch 28 (Fox) 600 Old Marion Rd NE **Fax Area Code:* 319 ■ *TF:* 800-222-5426 ■ *Web:* www.fox28iowa.com	Cedar Rapids	IA	52402	800-222-5426	395-7028*
KGAN-TV Ch 2 (CBS) 600 Old Marion Rd NE *TF:* 800-642-6140 ■ *Web:* www.cbs2iowa.com	Cedar Rapids	IA	52402	319-395-9060	395-0987
KPXR-TV Ch 48 (I) 1957 Blairs Ferry Rd NE *Web:* www.iontelevision.com	Cedar Rapids	IA	52402	319-378-1260	378-0076

744-24 Charleston, SC

Station	City	State	Zip	Phone	Fax
WCIV-TV Ch 4 (ABC) PO Box 22165 **Fax:* News Rm ■ *Web:* www.abcnews4.com	Charleston	SC	29413	843-881-4444	849-2519*
WCSC-TV Ch 5 (CBS) 2126 Charlie Hall Blvd *Web:* www.live5news.com	Charleston	SC	29414	843-577-6397	402-5744

744-25 Charleston, WV

Station	City	State	Zip	Phone	Fax
WCHS-TV Ch 8 (ABC) 1301 Piedmont Rd *TF:* 888-696-9247 ■ *Web:* www.wchstv.com	Charleston	WV	25301	304-346-5358	346-4765
WVAH-TV Ch 11 (Fox) 1301 Piedmont Rd *Web:* www.wvah.com	Charleston	WV	25301	304-346-5358	346-4765

744-26 Charlotte, NC

Station	City	State	Zip	Phone	Fax
WAXN-TV Ch 64 (ABC) 1901 N Tryon St *TF:* 888-664-6835 ■ *Web:* www.wsoctv.com	Charlotte	NC	28206	704-335-4786	
WBTV-TV Ch 3 (CBS) One Julian Price Pl *Web:* www.wbtv.com	Charlotte	NC	28208	704-374-3500	374-3671
WCCB-TV Ch 18 (Fox) One Television Pl *Web:* wccbcharlotte.com	Charlotte	NC	28205	704-372-1800	
WCNC-TV Ch 36 (NBC) 1001 Wood Ridge Ctr Dr *Web:* www.wcnc.com	Charlotte	NC	28217	704-329-3636	357-4975
WJZY-TV Ch 46 (CW) 3501 Performance Rd **Fax Area Code:* 254 ■ *TF:* 888-369-4762 ■ *Web:* www.myfoxcarolinas.com	Charlotte	NC	28214	704-398-0046	297-5386*
WMYT-TV Ch 12 (MNT) 3501 Performance Rd *Web:* www.wmyt12.com	Charlotte	NC	28214	704-398-0046	393-8407
WSOC-TV Ch 9 (ABC) 1901 N Tryon St *TF:* 800-247-6299 ■ *Web:* www.wsoctv.com	Charlotte	NC	28206	704-338-9999	335-4736
WTVI-TV Ch 42 (PBS) 3242 Commonwealth Ave *Web:* www.wtvi.org	Charlotte	NC	28205	704-372-2442	335-1358

744-27 Chattanooga, TN

Station	City	State	Zip	Phone	Fax
WDEF-TV Ch 12 (CBS) 3300 Broad St *Web:* www.wdef.com	Chattanooga	TN	37408	423-785-1200	785-1271
WDSI-TV Ch 61 (Fox) 1101 E Main St *Web:* www.myfoxchattanooga.com	Chattanooga	TN	37408	423-265-0061	
WRCB-TV Ch 3 (NBC) 900 Whitehall Rd **Fax:* News Rm ■ *Web:* www.wrcbtv.com	Chattanooga	TN	37405	423-267-5412	756-3148*
WTCI-TV Ch 45 (PBS) 7540 Bonnie Shire Dr *Web:* www.wtcitv.org	Chattanooga	TN	37416	423-702-7800	702-7823
WTVC-TV Ch 9 (ABC) 4279 Benton Dr *Web:* www.newschannel9.com	Chattanooga	TN	37406	423-756-5500	757-7400

744-28 Cheyenne, WY

Station	City	State	Zip	Phone	Fax
KGWN-TV Ch 5 (CBS) 2923 E Lincolnway *Web:* www.kgwn.tv	Cheyenne	WY	82001	307-634-7755	638-0182

744-29 Chicago, IL

Station	City	State	Zip	Phone	Fax
WCIU-TV Ch 26 (Ind) 26 N Halsted St *Web:* www.wciu.com	Chicago	IL	60661	312-705-2600	660-8323
WCPX-TV Ch 38 (I) 333 S Desplaines St Ste 101 *TF:* 800-531-5000 ■ *Web:* www.ionmedianetworks.com	Chicago	IL	60661	312-376-8520	575-8735
WFLD-TV Ch 32 (Fox) 205 N Michigan Ave Ground Fl *Web:* www.myfoxchicago.com	Chicago	IL	60601	312-565-5532	819-1332
WGN-TV Ch 9 (CW) 2501 W Bradley Pl *Web:* www.wgntv.com	Chicago	IL	60618	773-528-2311	
WMAQ-TV Ch 5 (NBC) 454 N Columbus Dr NBC Twr *Web:* www.nbcchicago.com	Chicago	IL	60611	312-836-5555	527-5925
WPWR-TV Ch 50 (Fox) 205 N Michigan Ave *Web:* www.my50chicago.com	Chicago	IL	60601	312-565-5532	819-1332
WTTW-TV Ch 11 (PBS) 5400 N St Louis Ave *Web:* www.wttw.com	Chicago	IL	60625	773-583-5000	583-3046
WYCC-TV Ch 20 (PBS) 6258 S Union Ave *Web:* www.wycc.org	Chicago	IL	60621	773-224-3300	783-2906

744-30 Cincinnati, OH

Station	City	State	Zip	Phone	Fax
WCET-TV Ch 48 (PBS) 1223 Central Pkwy *Web:* www.cetconnect.org	Cincinnati	OH	45214	513-381-4033	381-7520
WCPO-TV Ch 9 (ABC) 1720 Gilbert Ave *Web:* www.wcpo.com	Cincinnati	OH	45202	513-721-9900	721-7717
WKRC-TV Ch 12 (CBS) 1906 Highland Ave *TF:* 877-889-5610 ■ *Web:* www.local12.com	Cincinnati	OH	45219	513-763-5500	421-3820
WLWT-TV Ch 5 (NBC) 1700 Young St *Web:* www.wlwt.com	Cincinnati	OH	45202	513-412-5000	
WSTR-TV Ch 64 (MNT) 5177 Fishwick Dr *Web:* www.star64.tv	Cincinnati	OH	45216	513-641-4400	242-2633
WXIX-TV Ch 19 (Fox) 635 W Seventh St 19 Broadcast Plz *Web:* fox19.com/	Cincinnati	OH	45203	513-421-1919	421-3022

744-31 Cleveland/Akron, OH

Station	City	State	Zip	Phone	Fax
ideastream 1375 Euclid Ave *Web:* www.wviz.org	Cleveland	OH	44115	216-916-6100	

Station	City	State	ZIP	Phone	Fax
WDLI-TV Ch 17 (TBN) PO Box A *TF:* 888-731-1000 ■ *Web:* www.tbn.org	Santa Ana	CA	92711	714-832-2950	
WEWS-TV Ch 5 (ABC) 3001 Euclid Ave *Web:* www.newsnet5.com	Cleveland	OH	44115	216-431-5555	431-3666
WJW-TV Ch 8 (Fox) 5800 S Marginal Rd *Web:* fox8.com	Cleveland	OH	44103	216-431-8888	391-9559
WKYC-TV Ch 3 (NBC) 1333 Lakeside Ave E *TF:* 877-790-7370 ■ *Web:* www.wkyc.com	Cleveland	OH	44114	216-344-3333	344-3314
WOIO-TV Ch 19 (CBS) 1717 E 12th St *TF:* 877-929-1943 ■ *Web:* www.19actionnews.com	Cleveland	OH	44114	216-771-1943	515-7152

744-32 Colorado Springs, CO

Station	City	State	ZIP	Phone	Fax
KKTV-TV Ch 11 (CBS) 3100 N Nevada Ave *Web:* www.kktv.com	Colorado Springs	CO	80907	719-634-2844	634-3741
KXRM-TV Ch 21 (Fox) 560 Wooten Rd *Web:* www.fox21news.com	Colorado Springs	CO	80915	719-596-2100	591-4180

744-33 Columbia, SC

Station	City	State	ZIP	Phone	Fax
ABC Columbia 5807 Shakespeare Rd *Web:* abccolumbia.com	Columbia	SC	29223	803-754-7525	754-6147
WACH-TV Ch 57 (Fox) 1400 Pickens St Ste 6 *Web:* www.wach.com	Columbia	SC	29201	803-252-5757	212-7270
WHMC-TV Ch 23 (PBS) 1101 George Rogers Blvd *Web:* www.scetv.org	Columbia	SC	29201	803-737-3200	737-3417
WIS-TV Ch 10 (NBC) 1111 Bull St *Web:* www.wistv.com	Columbia	SC	29201	803-799-1010	758-1155
WLTX-TV Ch 19 (CBS) 6027 Garner's Ferry Rd *Web:* www.wltx.com	Columbia	SC	29209	803-776-3600	695-3714
WRLK-TV Ch 35 (PBS) 1101 George Rogers Blvd *TF:* 800-922-5437 ■ *Web:* www.scetv.org	Columbia	SC	29201	803-737-3200	

744-34 Columbus, GA

Station	City	State	ZIP	Phone	Fax
WLTZ-TV Ch 38 (NBC) 6140 Buena Vista Rd *Web:* www.wltz.com	Columbus	GA	31907	706-561-3838	563-8467
WRBL-TV Ch 3 (CBS) 1350 13th Ave *Web:* www.wrbl.com	Columbus	GA	31901	706-323-3333	323-0841
WTVM-TV Ch 9 (ABC) 1909 Wynnton Rd *Web:* www.wtvm.com	Columbus	GA	31906	706-494-5400	322-7527

744-35 Columbus, OH

Station	City	State	ZIP	Phone	Fax
WBNS-TV Ch 10 (CBS) 770 Twin Rivers Dr **Fax:* News Rm ■ *Web:* www.10tv.com	Columbus	OH	43215	614-460-3700	460-2891*
WCMH-TV Ch 4 (NBC) 3165 Olentangy River Rd *Web:* www.nbc4i.com	Columbus	OH	43202	614-263-4444	263-0166
WOSU-TV Ch 34 (PBS) 2400 Olentangy River Rd *Web:* wosu.org/2012/television/	Columbus	OH	43210	614-292-9678	292-7625
WSYX-TV Ch 6 (ABC) 1261 Dublin Rd **Fax:* News Rm ■ *Web:* www.abc6onyourside.com	Columbus	OH	43215	614-481-6666	481-6624*
WTTE-TV Ch 28 (Fox) 1261 Dublin Rd *Web:* www.myfox28columbus.com	Columbus	OH	43215	614-481-6666	481-6624

744-36 Corpus Christi, TX

Station	City	State	ZIP	Phone	Fax
KDF-TV Ch 47 (Fox) 409 S Staples St *Web:* www.kristv.com	Corpus Christi	TX	78401	361-886-6100	886-6116
KEDT-TV Ch 16 (PBS) 4455 S Padre Island Dr Ste 38 *TF:* 800-307-5338 ■ *Web:* www.kedt.org	Corpus Christi	TX	78411	361-855-2213	855-3877
KIII-TV Ch 3 (ABC) 5002 S Padre Island Dr *TF:* 800-882-9539 ■ *Web:* www.kiiitv.com	Corpus Christi	TX	78411	361-986-8300	986-8440
KRIS-TV Ch 6 (NBC) 301 Artesian St *Web:* www.kristv.com	Corpus Christi	TX	78401	361-886-6100	886-6175
KZTV-TV Ch 10 (CBS) 301 Artesian St **Fax:* News Rm ■ *Web:* www.kztv10.com	Corpus Christi	TX	78401	361-883-7070	884-8111*

744-37 Dallas/Fort Worth, TX

Station	City	State	ZIP	Phone	Fax
KDFW FOX 4 400 N Griffin St *Web:* www.myfoxdfw.com	Dallas	TX	75202	214-720-4444	720-3263
KERA-TV Ch 13 (PBS) 3000 Harry Hines Blvd *Web:* www.kera.org	Dallas	TX	75201	214-871-1390	754-6035
KTVT-TV Ch 11 (CBS) 5233 Bridge St *Web:* dfw.cbslocal.com	Fort Worth	TX	76103	817-451-1111	496-7739
KXAS-TV Ch 5 (NBC) 3900 Barnett St *Web:* www.nbcdfw.com	Fort Worth	TX	76103	817-429-5555	654-6325
KXTX-TV Ch 39 (Tele) 4805 Amon Carter Blvd *TF:* 877-266-8365 ■ *Web:* www.telemundodallas.com	Fort Worth	TX	76155	877-266-8365	
WFAA-TV Ch 8 (ABC) 606 Young St Communications Ctr *Web:* www.wfaa.com	Dallas	TX	75202	214-748-9631	977-6585

744-38 Dayton, OH

Station	City	State	ZIP	Phone	Fax
WDTN-TV Ch 2 (NBC) 4595 S Dixie Ave *Web:* www.wdtn.com	Dayton	OH	45439	937-293-2101	296-7147
WHIO-TV Ch 7 (CBS) 1414 Wilmington Ave *Web:* whio.com//	Dayton	OH	45420	937-259-2111	259-2005
WPTD-TV Ch 16 (PBS) 110 S Jefferson St *TF:* 800-247-1614 ■ *Web:* www.thinktv.org	Dayton	OH	45402	937-220-1600	220-1642

744-39 Denver, CO

Station	City	State	ZIP	Phone	Fax
KCEC-TV Ch 50 (Uni) 777 Grant St Fifth Fl *Web:* www.entravision.com	Denver	CO	80203	303-832-0050	832-3410
KCNC-TV Ch 4 (CBS) 1044 Lincoln St *Web:* denver.cbslocal.com	Denver	CO	80203	303-861-4444	830-6380
KDVR-TV Ch 31 (Fox) 100 E Speer Blvd *TF:* 888-397-3742 ■ *Web:* kdvr.com	Denver	CO	80203	303-595-3131	
KMGH-TV Ch 7 (ABC) 123 E Speer Blvd *Web:* www.thedenverchannel.com	Denver	CO	80203	303-832-7777	832-0119
KRMA-TV Ch 6 (PBS) 1089 Bannock St *TF:* 800-274-6666 ■ *Web:* www.rmpbs.org	Denver	CO	80204	303-892-6666	620-5600
KUSA-TV Ch 9 (NBC) 500 Speer Blvd *Web:* www.9news.com	Denver	CO	80203	303-871-9999	698-4700
KWGN-TV Ch 2 (CW) 100 E Speer Blvd *Web:* kwgn.com	Denver	CO	80203	303-595-3131	566-2931

744-40 Des Moines, IA

Station	City	State	ZIP	Phone	Fax
KCCI-TV Ch 8 (CBS) 888 Ninth St *Web:* www.kcci.com	Des Moines	IA	50309	515-247-8888	244-0202
KDSM-TV Ch 17 (Fox) 4023 Fleur Dr *Web:* www.kdsm17.com	Des Moines	IA	50321	515-287-1717	287-0064
WHO-TV Ch 13 (NBC) 1801 Grand Ave **Fax:* News Rm ■ *TF:* 800-777-8398 ■ *Web:* www.whotv.com	Des Moines	IA	50309	515-242-3500	242-3796*

744-41 Detroit, MI

Station	City	State	ZIP	Phone	Fax
WDIV-TV Ch 4 (NBC) 550 W Lafayette Blvd *Web:* www.clickondetroit.com	Detroit	MI	48226	313-222-0500	222-0592

744-42 Duluth, MN

Station	City	State	ZIP	Phone	Fax
KDLH-TV Ch 3 (CBS) 246 S Lake Ave *Web:* www.northlandsnewscenter.com	Duluth	MN	55802	218-720-9600	720-9660
KQDS-TV Ch 21 (Fox) 2001 London Rd *Web:* www.fox21online.com	Duluth	MN	55812	218-722-2861	728-1557
WDIO-TV Ch 10 (ABC) 10 Observation Rd *TF:* 800-477-1013 ■ *Web:* www.wdio.com	Duluth	MN	55811	218-727-6864	727-4415
WDSE-TV Ch 8 (PBS) 632 Niagara Ct *TF:* 888-563-9373 ■ *Web:* www.wdse.org	Duluth	MN	55811	218-788-2831	

744-43 Edmonton, AB

Station	City	State	ZIP	Phone	Fax
CFRN-TV Ch 3 (CTV) 18520 Stony Plain Rd *Web:* edmonton.ctvnews.ca	Edmonton	AB	T5S1A8	780-483-3311	489-5883

744-44 El Paso, TX

Station	City	State	ZIP	Phone	Fax
ElPaso Proud 801 N Oregon St *Web:* www.ktsm.com	El Paso	TX	79902	915-532-5421	496-4590
KCOS-TV Ch 13 (PBS) 9050 Viscount Blvd Ste A-440 *Web:* www.kcostv.org	El Paso	TX	79925	915-590-1313	594-5394
KFOX-TV Ch 14 (Fox) 6004 N Mesa St *Web:* www.kfoxtv.com	El Paso	TX	79912	915-833-8585	833-8717
KINT-TV Ch 26 (Uni) 5426 N Mesa St *Web:* www.kint.com	El Paso	TX	79912	915-581-1126	
KTDO-TV Ch 48 (Tele) 10033 Carnegie Ave	El Paso	TX	79925	915-591-9595	591-9896
KVIA-TV Ch 7 (ABC) 4140 Rio Bravo St **Fax:* News Rm ■ *TF:* 800-433-7300 ■ *Web:* www.kvia.com	El Paso	TX	79902	915-496-7777	532-0505*

744-45 Erie, PA

Station	City	State	ZIP	Phone	Fax
WFXP-TV Ch 66 (Fox) 8455 Peach St *Web:* www.yourerie.com	Erie	PA	16509	814-864-2400	
WICU-TV Ch 12 (NBC) 3514 State St *Web:* www.erietvnews.com	Erie	PA	16508	814-454-5201	454-3753
WJET-TV Ch 24 (ABC) 8455 Peach St *Web:* yourerie.com	Erie	PA	16509	814-864-2400	868-3041
WQLN-TV Ch 54 (PBS) 8425 Peach St *TF:* 800-727-8854 ■ *Web:* www.wqln.org	Erie	PA	16509	814-864-3001	864-4077
WSEE-TV Ch 35 (CBS) 3514 State St *TF:* 888-346-8982 ■ *Web:* www.erietvnews.com	Erie	PA	16508	814-454-5201	

744-46 Eugene, OR

Station	Address	City	State	Zip	Phone	Fax
KEZI-TV Ch 9 (ABC) PO Box 7009 *Web:* www.kezi.com		Eugene	OR	97408	541-485-5611	686-8004
KVAL-TV Ch 13 (CBS) 4575 Blanton Rd PO Box 1313 *Web:* www.kval.com		Eugene	OR	97405	541-342-4961	342-2635

744-47 Evansville, IN

Station	City	State	Zip	Phone	Fax
WEVV-TV Ch 44 (CBS) 44 Main St *Web:* www.wevv.com	Evansville	IN	47708	812-464-4444	465-4559
WFIE-TV Ch 14 (NBC) 1115 Mt Auburn Rd *TF:* 800-832-0014 ■ *Web:* www.14news.com	Evansville	IN	47720	812-426-1414	425-2482
WNIN-TV Ch 9 (PBS) 405 Carpenter St *TF:* 855-888-9646 ■ *Web:* www.wnin.org	Evansville	IN	47708	812-423-2973	428-7548

744-48 Fairbanks, AK

Station	City	State	Zip	Phone	Fax
KATN-TV Ch 2 (ABC) 516 2nd Ave Ste 400 *Web:* www.youralaskalink.com	Fairbanks	AK	99701	907-452-2125	456-8225
KFXF-TV Ch 7 (Fox) 3650 Bradock St Ste 2 *Web:* www.tvtv.com	Fairbanks	AK	99701	907-452-3697	456-3428
KTVF-TV Ch 11 (NBC) 3650 Braddock St. *TF:* 855-255-5975 ■ *Web:* www.webcenter11.com	Fairbanks	AK	99701	907-458-1800	458-1820
KUAC-TV Ch 9 (PBS) University of Alaska PO Box 755620 *TF:* 800-727-6543 ■ *Web:* kuac.org	Fairbanks	AK	99775	907-474-7491	474-5064

744-49 Fargo/Grand Forks, ND

Station	City	State	Zip	Phone	Fax
KBME-TV Ch 3 (PBS) 207 N Fifth St *TF:* 800-359-6900 ■ *Web:* www.prairiepublic.org	Fargo	ND	58102	701-241-6900	239-7650
KFME-TV Ch 13 (PBS) 207 N Fifth St *TF:* 800-359-6900 ■ *Web:* www.prairiepublic.org	Fargo	ND	58102	701-241-6900	239-7650
KGFE-TV Ch 2 (PBS) 207 N Fifth St *TF:* 800-359-6900 ■ *Web:* www.prairiepublic.org	Fargo	ND	58102	701-241-6900	239-7650
KVLY-TV Ch 11 (NBC) 1350 21st Ave S *TF:* 800-450-5844 ■ *Web:* www.valleynewslive.com	Fargo	ND	58103	701-237-5211	232-0493
KXJB-TV Ch 4 (CBS) 1350 21st Ave S *TF:* 877-571-0774 ■ *Web:* www.valleynewslive.com	Fargo	ND	58103	701-237-5211	232-0493
WDAY-TV Ch 6 (ABC) 301 S Eigth St *Web:* www.inforum.com	Fargo	ND	58103	701-237-6500	241-5358
WDAZ-TV Ch 8 (ABC) 2220 S Washington St. *TF:* 877-382-4357 ■ *Web:* www.wdaz.com	Grand Forks	ND	58201	701-775-2511	241-5217

744-50 Flint, MI

Station	City	State	Zip	Phone	Fax
WJRT-TV Ch 12 (ABC) 2302 Lapeer Rd **Fax:* News Rm ■ *Web:* www.abclocal.go.com	Flint	MI	48503	810-233-3130	257-2812*
WSMH-TV Ch 66 (Fox) 3463 W Pierson Rd Ste G *Web:* www.wsmh.com	Flint	MI	48504	810-785-8866	785-8963

744-51 Fort Smith, AR

Station	City	State	Zip	Phone	Fax
KFSM-TV Ch 5 (CBS) 318 N 13th St *Web:* 5newsonline.com	Fort Smith	AR	72902	479-783-3131	783-3295
KHBS-TV Ch 40 (ABC) 2415 N Albert Pike *TF General:* 855-253-7122 ■ *Web:* www.4029tv.com	Fort Smith	AR	72904	479-783-4040	785-5375

744-52 Fort Wayne, IN

Station	City	State	Zip	Phone	Fax
WANE-TV Ch 15 (CBS) 2915 W State Blvd. *Web:* www.wane.com	Fort Wayne	IN	46808	260-424-1515	
WFWA-TV Ch 39 (PBS) 2501 E Coliseum Blvd *TF:* 888-484-8839 ■ *Web:* www.wfwa.org	Fort Wayne	IN	46805	260-484-8839	482-3632
WPTA-TV Ch 21 (ABC) 3401 Butler Rd *Web:* www.indianasnewscenter.com	Fort Wayne	IN	46808	260-483-0584	483-2568

744-53 Fresno, CA

Station	City	State	Zip	Phone	Fax
KFSN-TV Ch 30 (ABC) 1777 G St. *Web:* abc30.com/	Fresno	CA	93706	559-442-1170	266-5024
KFTV-TV Ch 21 (Uni) 601 W Univision Plaza **Fax Area Code:* 604 ■ *TF:* 866-783-2645 ■ *Web:* univisionfresno.univision.com	Fresno	CA	93650	212-455-5200	251-7898*
KGPE-TV Ch 47 (CBS) 4880 N First St. *Web:* www.yourcentralvalley.com	Fresno	CA	93726	559-222-2411	
KMPH-TV Ch 26 (Fox) 5111 E McKinley Ave. *TF:* 800-101-2045 ■ *Web:* www.kmph.com	Fresno	CA	93727	559-453-8850	255-9626
KNXT-TV Ch 49 (Ind) 1550 N Fresno St. *Web:* www.knxt.tv	Fresno	CA	93703	559-488-7440	488-7444
KSEE-TV Ch 24 (NBC) 5035 E McKinley Ave *Web:* www.yourcentralvalley.com	Fresno	CA	93727	559-745-5733	
Valley PBS 1544 Van Ness Ave *Web:* www.kvpt.org	Fresno	CA	93721	559-266-1800	650-1880

744-54 Grand Rapids, MI

Station	City	State	Zip	Phone	Fax
WGVU-TV Ch 35 (PBS) 301 W Fulton St *TF:* 800-442-2771 ■ *Web:* www.wgvu.org	Grand Rapids	MI	49504	616-331-6666	331-6625
WOOD-TV Ch 8 (NBC) 120 College Ave SE *Web:* www.woodtv.com	Grand Rapids	MI	49503	616-456-8888	456-5755
WOTV-TV Ch 4 (ABC) 120 College Ave *Web:* www.wotv4women.com	Grand Rapids	MI	49503	616-456-8888	456-9169
WXMI-TV Ch 17 (Fox) 3117 Plz Dr NE *Web:* www.fox17online.com	Grand Rapids	MI	49525	616-364-8722	364-8506
WZPX-TV Ch 43 (I) 2610 Horizon Dr SE Ste E *TF:* 800-987-9936 ■ *Web:* www.ionmedianetworks.com	Grand Rapids	MI	49546	616-222-4343	493-2677
WZZM-TV Ch 13 (ABC) 645 3-Mile Rd NW *Web:* www.wzzm13.com	Grand Rapids	MI	49544	616-785-1313	785-1301

744-55 Great Falls, MT

Station	City	State	Zip	Phone	Fax
KRTV-TV Ch 3 (CBS) PO Box 2989 *Web:* www.krtv.com	Great Falls	MT	59403	406-791-5400	791-5479

744-56 Green Bay, WI

Station	City	State	Zip	Phone	Fax
NBC 26 1391 N Rd *Web:* jrn.com/nbc26	Green Bay	WI	54313	920-494-2626	490-2500
WBAY-TV Ch 2 (ABC) 115 S Jefferson St. *TF:* 800-261-9229 ■ *Web:* www.wbay.com	Green Bay	WI	54301	920-432-3331	432-1190
WCWF-TV Ch 14 (CW) 787 Lombardi Ave. *Web:* www.cw14online.com	Green Bay	WI	54304	920-494-8711	494-8782
WFRV-TV Ch 5 (CBS) 1181 E Mason St PO Box 19055 *Web:* www.wearegreenbay.com	Green Bay	WI	54301	920-437-5411	437-4576
WLUK-TV Ch 11 (Fox) 787 Lombardi Ave *TF:* 800-242-8067 ■ *Web:* www.fox11online.com	Green Bay	WI	54304	920-494-8711	494-8782

744-57 Harrisburg, PA

Station	City	State	Zip	Phone	Fax
WHP-TV Ch 21 (CBS) 3300 N Sixth St. *Web:* www.local21news.com	Harrisburg	PA	17110	717-238-2100	238-4903
WHTM-TV Ch 27 (ABC) 3235 Hoffman St *Web:* www.abc27.com	Harrisburg	PA	17110	717-236-2727	236-1263

744-58 Hartford, CT

Station	City	State	Zip	Phone	Fax
WTIC-TV Ch 61 (Fox) 285 Broad St. *Web:* foxct.com	Hartford	CT	06115	860-527-6161	293-0178
WUVN-TV Ch 18 (Uni) One Constitution Plz Seventh Fl *Web:* www.wuvntv.com	Hartford	CT	06103	860-278-1818	278-1811

744-59 Helena, MT

Station	City	State	Zip	Phone	Fax
KTVH 100 W Lyndale Ave Ste A *Web:* www.beartoothnbc.com	Helena	MT	59601	406-457-1212	442-5106

744-60 Honolulu, HI

Station	City	State	Zip	Phone	Fax
KBFD-TV Ch 32 (Ind) 1188 Bishop St Ste PH 1 *Web:* www.kbfd.com	Honolulu	HI	96813	808-521-8066	521-5233
KHET-TV Ch 11 (PBS) 2350 Dole St. *Web:* www.pbshawaii.org	Honolulu	HI	96822	808-973-1000	973-1090
KHNL-TV Ch 8 (NBC) 420 Waiakamilo Rd Ste 205 *Web:* www.hawaiinewsnow.com	Honolulu	HI	96817	808-847-3246	845-3616
KHON-TV Ch 2 (Fox) 88 Piikoi St. *TF:* 877-926-8300 ■ *Web:* www.khon2.com	Honolulu	HI	96814	808-591-4278	593-2418
KIKU-TV Ch 20 (Ind) 737 Bishop St Mauka Twr Ste 1430 *Web:* www.kikutv.com	Honolulu	HI	96813	808-847-2021	841-3326
KITV-TV Ch 4 (ABC) 801 S King St *Web:* www.kitv.com	Honolulu	HI	96813	808-535-0240	536-8993
KPXO-TV Ch 66 (I) 875 Waimanu St Ste 630 *TF:* 800-987-9936 ■ *Web:* ionmedia.tv	Honolulu	HI	96813	808-591-1275	591-1409
KWHE-TV Ch 14 (Ind) 1188 Bishop St Ste 502 *TF:* 800-218-1414 ■ *Web:* www.kwhe.com	Honolulu	HI	96813	808-538-1414	526-0326

744-61 Houston, TX

Station	City	State	Zip	Phone	Fax
KETH-TV Ch 14 (TBN) 10902 S Wilcrest Dr *Web:* myedutv.org	Houston	TX	77099	281-561-5828	561-9793

Station	City	State	Zip	Phone	Fax
KHOU-TV Ch 11 (CBS) 1945 Allen Pkwy *Web:* www.khou.com	Houston	TX	77019	713-526-1111	520-7763
KPRC-TV Ch 2 (NBC) 8181 SW Fwy *Web:* www.click2houston.com	Houston	TX	77074	713-222-2222	771-4930
KPXB-TV Ch 49 (I) 256 N Sam Houston Pkwy E Ste 49	Houston	TX	77060	281-820-4900	
KRIV-TV Ch 26 (Fox) 4261 SW Fwy **Fax:* News Rm ■ *Web:* www.myfoxhouston.com	Houston	TX	77027	713-479-2600	479-2859*
KTBU-TV Ch 55 (Ind) 7007 NW 77th Ave *NASDAQ: SBSA* ■ **Fax Area Code:* 866 ■ *Web:* www.spanishbroadcasting.com	Miami	FL	33166	305-441-6901	269-1521*
KTMD-TV Ch 47 (Tele) 1235 N Loop W Ste 125 *Web:* www.telemundohouston.com	Houston	TX	77008	713-974-4848	
KTRK-TV Ch 13 (ABC) 3310 Bissonnet St *Web:* abc13.com/	Houston	TX	77005	713-666-0713	
KTXH-TV Ch 20 (MNT) 4261 SW Fwy *Web:* www.my20houston.com	Houston	TX	77027	713-479-2801	479-2859
KUHT-TV Ch 8 (PBS) 4343 Elgin St *Web:* houstonpublicmedia.org/	Houston	TX	77204	713-748-8888	743-8867
KXLN-TV Ch 45 (Uni) 5100 SW Fwy *Web:* houston.univision.com	Houston	TX	77056	713-662-4545	965-2604

744-62 Huntsville, AL

Station	City	State	Zip	Phone	Fax
WAAY-TV Ch 31 (ABC) 1000 Monte Sano Blvd SE **Fax:* News Rm ■ *TF:* 888-407-4747 ■ *Web:* www.waaytv.com	Huntsville	AL	35801	256-533-3131	728-7118*
WAFF-TV Ch 48 (NBC) 1414 Memorial PkwyNW *Web:* www.waff.com	Huntsville	AL	35801	256-533-4848	534-4101
WHDF-TV Ch 15 (CW) 200 Andrew Jackson Way *Web:* www.lbgtv.com	Huntsville	AL	35801	256-536-1550	
WHNT-TV Ch 19 (CBS) PO Box 19 *TF:* 800-533-8819 ■ *Web:* www.whnt.com	Huntsville	AL	35804	256-533-1919	536-9468
WZDX-TV CH 54 (Fox) 1309 N Memorial Pkwy *Web:* www.fox54.com	Huntsville	AL	35801	256-533-5454	203-8320

744-63 Indianapolis, IN

Station	City	State	Zip	Phone	Fax
WFYI-TV Ch 20 (PBS) 1630 N Meridian St *Web:* www.wfyi.org	Indianapolis	IN	46202	317-636-2020	283-6645
WISH-TV Ch 8 (CBS) 1950 N Meridian St *Web:* www.wishtv.com	Indianapolis	IN	46202	317-923-8888	931-2242
WRTV-TV Ch 6 (ABC) 1330 N Meridian St **Fax:* News Rm ■ *TF:* 877-667-4265 ■ *Web:* www.theindychannel.com	Indianapolis	IN	46202	317-635-9788	269-1445*
WTHR-TV Ch 13 (NBC) 1000 N Meridian St *Web:* www.wthr.com	Indianapolis	IN	46204	317-636-1313	636-3717
WTTV-TV Ch 4 (CW) 6910 Network Pl **Fax:* News Rm ■ *Web:* fox59.com	Indianapolis	IN	46278	317-632-5900	687-6556*
WXIN-TV Ch 59 (Fox) 6910 Network Pl *Web:* www.fox59.com	Indianapolis	IN	46278	317-632-5900	715-6251

744-64 Jackson, MS

Station	City	State	Zip	Phone	Fax
WAPT-TV Ch 16 (ABC) 7616 Ch 16 Way *Web:* www.wapt.com	Jackson	MS	39209	601-922-1607	
WJTV-TV Ch 12 (CBS) 1820 TV Rd *Web:* www.wjtv.com	Jackson	MS	39204	601-372-6311	372-8798
WLBT-TV Ch 3 (NBC) 715 S Jefferson St *Web:* www.msnewsnow.com	Jackson	MS	39201	601-948-3333	355-7830

744-65 Jacksonville, FL

Station	City	State	Zip	Phone	Fax
WCWJ-TV Ch 17 (CW) 9117 Hogan Rd *Web:* www.yourjax.com	Jacksonville	FL	32216	904-641-1700	642-7201
WJCT-TV Ch 7 (PBS) 100 Festival Pk Ave *Web:* www.wjct.org	Jacksonville	FL	32202	904-353-7770	
WJXT-TV Ch 4 (Ind) Four Broadcast Pl **Fax:* News Rm ■ *Web:* www.news4jax.com	Jacksonville	FL	32207	904-399-4000	393-9822*
WJXX-TV Ch 25 (ABC) 1070 E Adams St **Fax:* News Rm ■ *Web:* www.firstcoastnews.com	Jacksonville	FL	32202	904-354-1212	633-8899*
WTLV-TV Ch 12 (NBC) 1070 E Adams St **Fax:* News Rm ■ *Web:* www.firstcoastnews.com	Jacksonville	FL	32202	904-354-1212	633-8899*

744-66 Jefferson City, MO

Station	City	State	Zip	Phone	Fax
KNLJ-TV Ch 25 (Ind) 311 W Dunklin *Web:* www.knlj.tv	Jefferson City	MO	65101	573-896-5105	896-0251

744-67 Johnson City, TN

Station	City	State	Zip	Phone	Fax
WJHL-TV Ch 11 (CBS) 338 E Main St **Fax Area Code:* 804 ■ *TF:* 800-861-5255 ■ *Web:* www.wjhl.com	Johnson City	TN	37601	423-926-2151	887-7062*

744-68 Juneau, AK

Station	City	State	Zip	Phone	Fax
KATH-TV Ch 5 (NBC) 1107 W Eigth St *Web:* www.kath.tv	Juneau	AK	99801	907-586-8384	586-8394
KJUD-TV Ch 8 (ABC) 2700 E Tudor Rd *TF:* 877-304-1313 ■ *Web:* www.youralaskalink.com	Anchorage	AK	99507	907-561-1313	561-1377
KTOO-TV Ch 3 (PBS) 360 Egan Dr *Web:* www.ktoo.org	Juneau	AK	99801	907-586-1670	

744-69 Kansas City, KS & MO

Station	City	State	Zip	Phone	Fax
KCPT-TV Ch 19 (PBS) 125 E 31st St *Web:* www.kcpt.org	Kansas City	MO	64108	816-756-3580	931-2500
KCWE-TV Ch 29 (CW) 6455 Winchester Ave **Fax:* Sales ■ *Web:* www.kmbc.com/kcwe/index.html	Kansas City	MO	64133	816-221-2900	421-4163*
KMBC-TV Ch 9 (ABC) 6455 Winchester Ave *Web:* www.kmbc.com	Kansas City	MO	64133	816-221-9999	421-4163
KMCI-TV Ch 38 (Ind) 4720 Oak St *Web:* www.kshb.com	Kansas City	MO	64112	816-753-4141	932-4145
KSHB-TV Ch 41 (NBC) 4720 Oak St *TF:* 800-222-1222 ■ *Web:* www.kshb.com	Kansas City	MO	64112	816-753-4141	932-4145
WDAF-TV Ch 4 (Fox) 3030 Summit *Web:* www.fox4kc.com	Kansas City	MO	64108	816-753-4567	

744-70 Knoxville, TN

Station	City	State	Zip	Phone	Fax
Rev Rocket, LLC 9000 Executive Pk Dr Bldg D Ste 300 *Web:* foxville43.revrocket.us/	Knoxville	TN	37923	865-693-4343	691-6904
WATE-TV Ch 6 (ABC) 1306 Broadway *Web:* www.wate.com	Knoxville	TN	37917	865-637-6666	525-4091
WBIR-TV Ch 10 (NBC) 1513 Hutchinson Ave *Web:* www.wbir.com	Knoxville	TN	37917	865-637-1010	637-6380
WBXX-TV Ch 20 (CW) 10427 Cogdill Rd Ste 100 *Web:* www.lbgtv.com	Knoxville	TN	37932	865-777-9220	777-9221
WKOP-TV Ch 17 (PBS) 1611 E Magnolia Ave *Web:* www.etptv.org	Knoxville	TN	37917	865-595-0220	595-0300
WVLT-TV Ch 8 (CBS) 6450 Papermill Dr *Web:* www.local8now.com	Knoxville	TN	37919	865-450-8888	450-8869

744-71 Lafayette, LA

Station	City	State	Zip	Phone	Fax
KADN Fox15 1500 Eraste Landry Rd *Web:* www.kadn.com	Lafayette	LA	70506	337-237-1500	237-2237
KATC-TV Ch 3 (ABC) 1103 Eraste Landry Rd *Web:* www.katc.com	Lafayette	LA	70506	337-235-3333	
KLFY-TV Ch 10 (CBS) 1808 Eraste Landry Rd PO Box 90665 **Fax:* Sales ■ *Web:* www.klfy.com	Lafayette	LA	70509	337-981-4823	984-8323*

744-72 Lansing, MI

Station	City	State	Zip	Phone	Fax
WILX-TV Ch 10 (NBC) 500 American Rd *TF:* 866-653-4261 ■ *Web:* www.wilx.com	Lansing	MI	48911	517-393-0110	393-8555
WLAJ-TV Ch 3 (ABC) 5815 S Pennsylvania Ave *Web:* www.wlns.com	Lansing	MI	48911	517-394-5300	
WLNS-TV Ch 6 (CBS) 2820 E Saginaw St *Web:* www.wlns.com	Lansing	MI	48912	517-372-8282	374-7610
WSYM-TV Ch 47 (Fox) 600 W St Joseph St Ste 47 *Web:* jrn.com/fox47news	Lansing	MI	48933	517-484-7747	484-3144

744-73 Las Vegas, NV

Station	City	State	Zip	Phone	Fax
KINC-TV Ch 15 (Uni) 500 Pilot Rd Ste D *Web:* www.entravision.com	Las Vegas	NV	89119	702-434-0015	434-0527
KLAS-TV Ch 8 (CBS) 3228 Ch 8 Dr **Fax:* News Rm ■ *Web:* www.8newsnow.com	Las Vegas	NV	89109	702-792-8888	792-2977*
KLVX-TV Ch 10 (PBS) 3050 E Flamingo *Web:* www.vegaspbs.org	Las Vegas	NV	89121	702-799-1010	799-5586
KTNV-TV Ch 13 (ABC) 3355 S Valley View Blvd *TF:* 800-877-1620 ■ *Web:* jrn.com/ktnv	Las Vegas	NV	89102	702-876-1313	876-2237
Sinclair Broadcast Group, Inc 10706 Beaver Dam Rd *Web:* www.sbgi.net	Cockeysville	MD	21030	702-382-2121	952-4683

744-74 Lexington, KY

Station	City	State	Zip	Phone	Fax
WDKY-TV Ch 56 (Fox) 836 Euclid Ave Ste 201 *Web:* www.foxlexington.com	Lexington	KY	40502	859-269-5656	293-1578
WKYT-TV Ch 27 (CBS) 2851 Winchester Rd **Fax:* News Rm ■ *Web:* www.wkyt.com	Lexington	KY	40509	859-299-0411	293-1578*
WTVQ-TV Ch 36 (ABC) 6940 Man O War Blvd *Web:* www.wtvq.com	Lexington	KY	40509	859-294-3636	293-5002

744-75 Lincoln, NE

Station	City	State	Zip	Phone	Fax
KLKN-TV Ch 8 (ABC) 3240 S Tenth St *Web:* www.klkntv.com	Lincoln	NE	68502	402-434-8000	436-2236
KOLN-TV Ch 10 (CBS) 840 N 40th *TF:* 800-475-1011 ■ *Web:* www.1011now.com	Lincoln	NE	68503	402-467-4321	467-9210
NET Radio 1800 N 33rd St *TF:* 800-868-1868 ■ *Web:* www.netnebraska.org	Lincoln	NE	68503	800-868-1868	

744-76 Little Rock, AR

Station	City	State	Zip	Phone	Fax
KATV-TV Ch 7 (ABC) 401 S Main St *Web:* www.katv.com	Little Rock	AR	72201	501-324-7777	
KTHV-TV Ch 11 (CBS) 720 S Izard St *TF:* 800-621-3362 ■ *Web:* www.thv11.com	Little Rock	AR	72201	501-376-1111	376-1645

744-77 Los Angeles, CA

Station	City	State	Zip	Phone	Fax
KCET-TV Ch 28 (PBS) 4401 Sunset Blvd *Web:* www.kcet.org	Los Angeles	CA	90027	323-666-6500	
KJLA-TV Ch 57 (Ind) 2323 Corinth Ave *TF:* 800-588-5788 ■ *Web:* www.kjla.com	Los Angeles	CA	90064	310-943-5288	943-5299
KLCS-TV Ch 58 (PBS) 1061 W Temple St *Web:* www.klcs.org	Los Angeles	CA	90012	213-241-4000	481-1019
KSCI-TV Ch 18 (Ind) 1990 S Bundy Dr Ste 850 *Web:* www.la18.tv	Los Angeles	CA	90025	310-478-1818	479-8118
KTLA-TV Ch 5 (CW) 5800 W Sunset Blvd *Web:* ktla.com	Los Angeles	CA	90028	323-460-5500	460-5333
KTTV FOX 11 1999 S Bundy Dr *Web:* www.myfoxla.com	Los Angeles	CA	90025	310-584-2000	
KTTV-TV Ch 11 (Fox) 1999 S Bundy Dr *Web:* www.myfoxla.com	Los Angeles	CA	90025	310-584-2000	584-2024

744-78 Louisville, KY

Station	City	State	Zip	Phone	Fax
WAVE-TV Ch 3 (NBC) 725 S Floyd St PO Box 32970 *TF:* 800-223-2579 ■ *Web:* www.wave3.com	Louisville	KY	40203	502-585-2201	561-4115
WDRB-TV Ch 41 (Fox) 624 W Muhammad Ali Blvd *Web:* www.wdrb.com	Louisville	KY	40203	502-584-6441	589-5559
WHAS-TV Ch 11 (ABC) 520 W Chestnut *Web:* www.whas11.com	Louisville	KY	40202	502-582-7711	582-7279
WLKY-TV Ch 32 (CBS) 1918 Mellwood Ave *Web:* www.wlky.com	Louisville	KY	40206	502-893-3671	896-0725

744-79 Lubbock, TX

Station	City	State	Zip	Phone	Fax
KAMC-TV Ch 28 (ABC) 7403 S University Ave *Web:* everythinglubbock.com	Lubbock	TX	79423	806-745-2345	748-2250
KCBD-TV Ch 11 (NBC) 5600 Ave A *Web:* www.kcbd.com	Lubbock	TX	79404	806-744-1414	749-1111
KLBK-TV Ch 13 (CBS) 7403 S University Ave *Web:* everythinglubbock.com	Lubbock	TX	79423	806-745-2345	748-2250
KTTZ-TV Ch 5 (PBS) 17th & Indiana Ave PO Box 42161 *Web:* www.kttz.org	Lubbock	TX	79409	806-742-2209	742-1274

744-80 Macon, GA

Station	City	State	Zip	Phone	Fax
WGNM-TV Ch 64 (Ind) 178 Steven Dr *Web:* www.wgnm.com	Macon	GA	31210	478-474-8400	474-4777
WMAZ-TV Ch 13 (CBS) 1314 Gray Hwy *Web:* www.13wmaz.com	Macon	GA	31211	478-752-1313	752-1331
WMGT-TV Ch 41 (NBC) 301 Poplar St *Web:* 41nbc.com	Macon	GA	31201	478-745-4141	742-2626

744-81 Madison, WI

Station	City	State	Zip	Phone	Fax
NBC15 615 Forward Dr *TF:* 800-894-4222 ■ *Web:* nbc15.com	Madison	WI	53711	608-274-1515	271-5194
WHA-TV Ch 21 (PBS) 821 University Ave *Web:* www.wpt.org	Madison	WI	53706	608-263-2121	
WISC-TV Ch 3000 (CBS) 7025 Raymond Rd *Web:* www.channel3000.com	Madison	WI	53719	608-271-4321	271-0800
WKOW-TV Ch 27 (ABC) 5727 Tokay Blvd *Web:* www.wkow.com	Madison	WI	53719	608-274-1234	274-9514
WMSN-TV Ch 47 (Fox) 7847 Big Sky Dr *Web:* www.fox47.com	Madison	WI	53719	608-833-0047	274-9569

744-82 Memphis, TN

Station	City	State	Zip	Phone	Fax
WHBQ-TV Ch 13 (Fox) 485 S Highland St *Web:* www.myfoxmemphis.com	Memphis	TN	38111	901-320-1313	320-1366
WMC-TV Ch 5 (NBC) 1960 Union Ave *Web:* wmcactionnews5.com/	Memphis	TN	38104	901-726-0555	278-7633
WPTY-TV Ch 24 (ABC) 2701 Union Ave Ext *Web:* www.localmemphis.com	Memphis	TN	38112	901-323-2430	452-1820
WREG-TV Ch 3 (CBS) 803 Ch Three Dr *Web:* www.wreg.com	Memphis	TN	38103	901-543-2333	543-2167

744-83 Miami/Fort Lauderdale, FL

Station	City	State	Zip	Phone	Fax
WBFS-TV Ch 33 (MNT) 8900 NW 18th Terr *Web:* miami.cbslocal.com	Miami	FL	33172	305-591-4444	477-3040
WFOR-TV Ch 4 (CBS) 8900 NW 18th Terr *Web:* miami.cbslocal.com	Miami	FL	33172	305-591-4444	477-3040
WLRN-TV Ch 17 (PBS) 172 NE 15th St *Web:* www.wlrn.org	Miami	FL	33132	305-995-1717	995-2299
WPBT-TV Ch 2 (PBS) 14901 NE 20th Ave **Fax:* News Rm ■ *TF:* 800-222-9728 ■ *Web:* www.wpbt2.org	Miami	FL	33181	305-949-8321	944-4211*
WSFL-TV Ch 39 (CW) 200 E Las Olas Blvd 11th Fl *Web:* www.southflorida.com	Fort Lauderdale	FL	33301	954-627-7349	355-2000
WSVN-TV Ch 7 (Fox) 1401 79th St Cswy *Web:* www.wsvn.com	Miami	FL	33141	305-751-6692	

744-84 Milwaukee, WI

Station	City	State	Zip	Phone	Fax
WCGV-TV Ch 24 (MNT) 4041 N 35th St *Web:* www.my24milwaukee.com	Milwaukee	WI	53216	414-442-7050	874-1899
WDJT-TV Ch 58 (CBS) 809 S 60th St *Web:* www.cbs58.com	Milwaukee	WI	53214	414-777-5800	777-5802
WISN-TV Ch 12 (ABC) 759 N 19th St *Web:* www.wisn.com	Milwaukee	WI	53233	414-342-8812	342-7505
WITI-TV Ch 6 (Fox) 9001 N Green Bay Rd **Fax:* News Rm ■ *Web:* www.fox6now.com	Milwaukee	WI	53209	414-355-6666	586-2141*
WMVS-TV Ch 10 1036 N Eigth St *Web:* www.mptv.org	Milwaukee	WI	53233	414-271-1036	297-8549
WPXE-TV Ch 55 (I) 6161 N Flint Rd Ste F *Web:* www.ionmedia.tv	Milwaukee	WI	53209	414-247-0117	247-1302
WTMJ-TV Ch 4 (NBC) 720 E Capitol Dr *Web:* jrn.com/tmj4	Milwaukee	WI	53212	414-332-9611	967-5378
WVCY-TV Ch 30 (Ind) 3434 W Kilbourn Ave *TF:* 800-729-9829 ■ *Web:* www.vcyamerica.org	Milwaukee	WI	53208	414-935-3000	935-3015
WVTV-TV Ch 18 (CW) 4041 N 35th St *Web:* www.cw18milwaukee.com	Milwaukee	WI	53216	414-442-7050	203-2300

744-85 Minneapolis/Saint Paul, MN

Station	City	State	Zip	Phone	Fax
KSTP-TV Ch 5 (ABC) 3415 University Ave W *Web:* www.kstp.com	Saint Paul	MN	55114	651-646-5555	642-4409
KTCA-TV Ch 2 (PBS) 172 E Fourth St *Web:* www.tpt.org	Saint Paul	MN	55101	651-222-1717	229-1282
KTCI-TV Ch 17 (PBS) 172 E Fourth St *Web:* www.tpt.org	Saint Paul	MN	55101	651-222-1717	229-1282
WCCO-TV Ch 4 (CBS) 90 S 11th St *Web:* minnesota.cbslocal.com	Minneapolis	MN	55403	612-339-4444	330-2767
WUCW-TV Ch 23 (CW) 1640 Como Ave *Web:* thecw23.com	Saint Paul	MN	55108	651-646-2300	646-1220

744-86 Mobile, AL

Station	City	State	Zip	Phone	Fax
WALA-TV Ch 10 (Fox) 1501 Satchel Paige Dr *Web:* www.fox10tv.com	Mobile	AL	36606	251-434-1010	434-1073
WKRG-TV Ch 5 (CBS) 555 Broadcast Dr *Web:* www.wkrg.com	Mobile	AL	36606	251-479-5555	473-8130
WMPV-TV Ch 21 (TBN) 1668 W I-65 Service Rd S *Web:* www.tbn.org	Mobile	AL	36693	251-661-2101	661-7121
WPMI-TV Ch 15 (NBC) 661 Azalea Rd *Web:* www.local15tv.com	Mobile	AL	36609	251-602-1500	602-1550

744-87 Monterey, CA

Station	City	State	Zip	Phone	Fax
Entavision Communication Corp 67 Garden Ct *Web:* www.ksmstv.com	Monterey	CA	93940	831-373-6767	373-6700

744-88 Montgomery, AL

Station	City	State	Zip	Phone	Fax
WAIQ-TV Ch 26 (PBS) 1255 Madison Ave **Fax Area Code:* 334 ■ *TF:* 800-239-5239 ■ *Web:* www.aptv.org	Montgomery	AL	36107	205-328-8756	264-7045*
WAKA-TV Ch 8 (CBS) 3020 Eastern Blvd *TF:* 800-467-0401 ■ *Web:* www.waka.com	Montgomery	AL	36116	334-271-8888	244-7859
WCOV-TV Ch 20 (Fox) One W Cov Ave *Web:* www.wcov.com	Montgomery	AL	36111	334-288-7020	288-5414

Station	City	State	ZIP	Phone	Fax
WNCF-TV Ch 32 (ABC) 3251 Harrison Rd *TF:* 800-467-0424 ■ *Web:* www.alabamanews.net	Montgomery	AL	36109	334-270-2834	272-6444
WSFA-TV Ch 12 (NBC) 12 E Delano Ave **Fax:* News Rm ■ *Web:* www.wsfa.com	Montgomery	AL	36105	334-288-1212	613-8303*

744-89 Montreal, QC

Station	City	State	ZIP	Phone	Fax
CBMT-TV Ch 6 (CBC) 1400 Rene-Levesque Blvd E Rm B 62-1 *Web:* cbc.ca/news/canada/montreal/	Montreal	QC	H2L2M2	514-597-6000	597-6354
CFCF-TV Ch 12 (CTV) 1205 Papineau Ave *Web:* montreal.ctvnews.ca	Montreal	QC	H2K4R2	514-273-6311	273-1973

744-91 Myrtle Beach, SC

Station	City	State	ZIP	Phone	Fax
WBTW-TV Ch 13 (CBS) 101 McDonald Ct *Web:* www.wbtw.com	Myrtle Beach	SC	29588	843-293-1301	293-7701
WFXB-TV Ch 43 (Fox) 3364 Huger St *Web:* www.wfxb.com	Myrtle Beach	SC	29577	843-828-4300	828-4343

744-92 Naples/Fort Myers, FL

Station	City	State	ZIP	Phone	Fax
WBBH-TV Ch 20 (NBC) 3719 Central Ave PO Box 7578 *Web:* www.nbc-2.com	Fort Myers	FL	33901	239-939-2020	936-7771
WFTX-TV Ch 4 (Fox) 621 SW Pine Island Rd *Web:* jrn.com/fox4now	Cape Coral	FL	33991	239-574-3636	574-2025
WGCU-TV Ch 30 (PBS) 10501 FGCU Blvd *TF General:* 888-824-0030 ■ *Web:* www.wgcu.org	Fort Myers	FL	33965	239-590-2300	590-2310
WINK-TV Ch 11 (CBS) 2824 Palm Beach Blvd *Web:* www.winknews.com	Fort Myers	FL	33916	239-334-1111	332-0767
WZVN-TV Ch 26 (ABC) 3719 Central Ave *TF:* 888-232-8635 ■ *Web:* www.abc-7.com	Fort Myers	FL	33901	239-939-2020	936-7771

744-93 Nashville, TN

Station	City	State	ZIP	Phone	Fax
WKRN-TV Ch 2 (ABC) 441 Murfreesboro Rd *TF:* 800-222-5555 ■ *Web:* www.wkrn.com	Nashville	TN	37210	615-369-7222	369-7329
WNPT-TV Ch 8 (PBS) 161 Rains Ave *Web:* www.wnpt.org	Nashville	TN	37203	615-259-9325	248-6120
WSMV-TV Ch 4 (NBC) 5700 Knob Rd *Web:* www.wsmv.com	Nashville	TN	37209	615-353-4444	353-2343
WTVF-TV Ch 5 (CBS) 474 James Robertson Pkwy **Fax:* News Rm ■ *Web:* jrn.com/newschannel5	Nashville	TN	37219	615-244-5000	244-9883*
WUXP-TV Ch 30 (MNT) 631 Mainstream Dr PO Box 17 *Web:* www.mytv30web.com	Nashville	TN	37228	615-259-5617	259-3962
WZTV-TV Ch 17 (Fox) 631 Mainstream Dr PO Box 17 *Web:* www.fox17.com	Nashville	TN	37228	615-259-5617	259-5684

744-94 New Orleans, LA

Station	City	State	ZIP	Phone	Fax
WDSU-TV Ch 6 (NBC) 846 Howard Ave *TF:* 888-925-4127 ■ *Web:* www.wdsu.com	New Orleans	LA	70113	504-679-0600	679-0752
WHNO-TV Ch 20 (Ind) 839 St Charles Ave *Web:* www.whno.com	New Orleans	LA	70130	504-681-0120	681-0180
WUPL-TV Ch 54 (MNT) 1024 N Rampart St *Web:* www.upltv.com	New Orleans	LA	70116	504-529-4444	529-6472
WVUE-TV Ch 8 (Fox) 1025 S Jefferson Davis Pkwy *Web:* www.fox8live.com	New Orleans	LA	70125	504-486-6161	483-1543
WWL-TV Ch 4 (CBS) 1024 N Rampart St *Web:* www.wwltv.com	New Orleans	LA	70116	504-529-4444	529-6472

744-95 New York, NY

Station	City	State	ZIP	Phone	Fax
PIX 11 220 E 42nd St *Web:* wpix.com	New York	NY	10017	212-949-1100	
WABC-TV Ch 7 (ABC) Seven Lincoln Sq *Web:* www.abclocal.go.com	New York	NY	10023	917-260-7000	
WCBS-TV Ch 2 (CBS) 51 W 52th St *Web:* newyork.cbslocal.com	New York	NY	10019	212-975-4321	975-9387
WNBC-TV Ch 4 (NBC) 30 Rockefeller Plz *Web:* www.nbcnewyork.com	New York	NY	10112	212-664-4444	
WNET-TV Ch 13 (PBS) 450 W 33rd St *Web:* www.thirteen.org	New York	NY	10001	212-560-1313	560-1314
WNYW-TV Ch 5 (Fox) 205 E 67th St *Web:* www.myfoxny.com	New York	NY	10065	212-452-5800	249-1182
WPXN-TV Ch 31 (I) 810 Seventh Ave 30th Fl *TF:* 800-987-9936 ■ *Web:* www.ionmedianetworks.com	New York	NY	10019	212-603-8419	664-5918
WTBY-TV Ch 54 (TBN) 111 E 15th St *Web:* www.tbn.org	New York	NY	10003	819-770-2333	770-2338

744-96 Norfolk/Virginia Beach, VA

Station	City	State	ZIP	Phone	Fax
WHRO-TV Ch 15 (PBS) 5200 Hampton Blvd *Web:* www.whro.org	Norfolk	VA	23508	757-889-9400	489-0007
WTKR-TV Ch 3 (CBS) 720 Boush St *TF:* 866-347-2423 ■ *Web:* www.wtkr.com	Norfolk	VA	23510	757-446-1000	622-1807
WTVZ-TV Ch 33 (MNT) 900 Granby St *Web:* www.mytvz.com	Norfolk	VA	23510	757-622-3333	623-1541
WVEC-TV Ch 13 (ABC) 613 Woodis Ave *Web:* www.wvec.com	Norfolk	VA	23510	757-625-1313	628-5855

744-97 Oklahoma City, OK

Station	City	State	ZIP	Phone	Fax
KETA-TV Ch 13 (PBS) PO Box 14190 *Web:* www.oeta.tv/	Oklahoma City	OK	73113	405-848-8501	841-9216
KFOR-TV Ch 4 (NBC) 444 E Britton Rd *Web:* www.kfor.com	Oklahoma City	OK	73114	405-424-4444	478-6337
KOCB-TV Ch 34 (CW) 1228 E Wilshire Blvd *Web:* www.cwokc.com	Oklahoma City	OK	73111	405-843-2525	478-4343
KOCO-TV Ch 5 (ABC) 1300 E Britton Rd *Web:* www.koco.com	Oklahoma City	OK	73131	405-478-3000	478-6675
KOKH-TV Ch 25 (Fox) 1228 E Wilshire Blvd *Web:* www.okcfox.com	Oklahoma City	OK	73111	405-843-2525	478-4343
KOPX-TV Ch 62 (I) 13424 Railway Dr *Web:* ionmedia.tv	Oklahoma City	OK	73114	405-478-9562	751-6867
KWTV-TV Ch 9 (CBS) 7401 N Kelley Ave *TF:* 888-550-5988 ■ *Web:* www.news9.com	Oklahoma City	OK	73111	405-843-6641	841-9989

744-98 Omaha, NE

Station	City	State	ZIP	Phone	Fax
KETV-TV Ch 7 (ABC) 2665 Douglas St *TF:* 800-279-5388 ■ *Web:* www.ketv.com	Omaha	NE	68131	402-345-7777	522-7740
KMTV Action 3 News 10714 Mockingbird Dr **Fax Area Code:* 414 ■ *TF:* 800-800-6619 ■ *Web:* jrn.com/kmtv	Omaha	NE	68127	402-592-3333	967-5378*
KPTM 42.2 FM 4625 Farnam St *Web:* www.fox42kptm.com	Omaha	NE	68132	402-554-4282	554-4279
KXVO-TV Ch 15 (CW) 4625 Farnam St *Web:* www.kxvo.com	Omaha	NE	68132	402-554-1500	554-4290
WOWT-TV Ch 6 (NBC) 3501 Farnam St *TF:* 866-434-8587 ■ *Web:* www.wowt.com	Omaha	NE	68131	402-346-6666	233-7887

744-99 Orlando, FL

Station	City	State	ZIP	Phone	Fax
ION Media Networks Inc 7091 Grand National Dr Ste 100 *Web:* www.ionmedia.tv	Orlando	FL	32819	407-370-5600	363-1759
WFTV-TV Ch 9 (ABC) 490 E S St *Web:* www.wftv.com	Orlando	FL	32801	407-841-9000	481-2891
WKMG-TV Ch 6 (CBS) 4466 N John Young Pkwy *TF:* 800-435-7352 ■ *Web:* www.clickorlando.com	Orlando	FL	32804	407-521-1200	521-1204

744-100 Ottawa, ON

Station	City	State	ZIP	Phone	Fax
CJOH-TV Ch 13 (CTV) 87 George St *Web:* ottawa.ctvnews.ca	Ottawa	ON	K1N9H7	613-224-1313	

744-101 Peoria, IL

Station	City	State	ZIP	Phone	Fax
WMBD-TV Ch 31 (CBS) 3131 N University St *Web:* www.centralillinoisproud.com	Peoria	IL	61604	309-688-3131	686-8650
WTVP-TV Ch 47 (PBS) 101 State St *TF:* 800-837-4747 ■ *Web:* www.wtvp.org	Peoria	IL	61602	309-677-4747	677-4730

744-102 Philadelphia, PA

Station	City	State	ZIP	Phone	Fax
KYW-TV Ch 3 (CBS) 1555 Hamilton St *Web:* philadelphia.cbslocal.com	Philadelphia	PA	19130	215-977-5333	238-4545
WHYY-TV Ch 12 (PBS) 150 N Sixth St *Web:* www.whyy.org	Philadelphia	PA	19106	215-351-1200	351-3352
WPHL-TV Ch 17 (MNT) 5001 Wynnefield Ave *Web:* phl17.com	Philadelphia	PA	19131	215-878-1700	
WPPX-TV Ch 61 (I) 3901 B Main St Ste 301 *Web:* www.ionmedia.tv	Philadelphia	PA	19127	215-482-4770	482-4777
WPSG-TV Ch 57 (CW) 1555 Hamilton St	Philadelphia	PA	19130	215-977-5700	977-5658
WPVI-TV Ch 6 (ABC) 4100 City Line Ave *Web:* www.abclocal.go.com	Philadelphia	PA	19131	215-878-9700	581-4530
WTXF-TV Ch 29 (Fox) 330 Market St **Fax:* News Rm ■ *Web:* www.myfoxphilly.com	Philadelphia	PA	19106	215-925-2929	982-5494*

744-103 Phoenix, AZ

Station	City	State	Zip	Phone	Fax
KASW-TV Ch 61 (CW) 5555 N Seventh Ave	Phoenix	AZ	85013	480-661-6161	207-3277
KNXV-TV Ch 15 (ABC) 515 N 44th St *TF:* 800-222-4357 ■ *Web:* www.abc15.com	Phoenix	AZ	85008	602-273-1500	685-3000
KPAZ-TV Ch 21 (TBN) 3551 E McDowell Rd *Web:* www.tbn.org	Phoenix	AZ	85008	602-273-1477	267-9427
KPHO-TV Ch 5 (CBS) 4016 N Black Canyon Hwy *Web:* www.kpho.com	Phoenix	AZ	85017	602-264-1000	
KPNX-TV Ch 12 (NBC) 1101 N Central Ave *Web:* www.azcentral.com/12news	Phoenix	AZ	85004	602-257-1212	257-6619
KSAZ-TV Ch 10 (Fox) 511 W Adams St *TF:* 888-369-4762 ■ *Web:* fox10phoenix.com/	Phoenix	AZ	85003	602-257-1234	262-0177
KTVK-TV Ch 3 (Ind) 5555 N Seventh Ave. *Web:* www.azfamily.com	Phoenix	AZ	85013	602-207-3333	207-3477
KTVW-TV Ch 33 (Uni) 6006 S 30th St *Web:* univisionarizona.univision.com	Phoenix	AZ	85042	602-243-3333	
KUTP-TV Ch 45 (MNT) 511 W Adams *Web:* www.my45.com	Phoenix	AZ	85003	602-257-1234	262-0177

744-104 Pittsburgh, PA

Station	City	State	Zip	Phone	Fax
WPGH-TV Ch 53 (Fox) 750 Ivory Ave **Fax:* News Rm ■ *Web:* www.wpgh53.com/pittsburgh_pa	Pittsburgh	PA	15214	412-931-5300	931-8135*
WPMY-TV Ch 22 (MNT) 750 Ivory Ave *Web:* www.mypittsburghtv.com	Pittsburgh	PA	15214	412-931-5300	931-4284
WPXI-TV Ch 11 (NBC) 4145 Evergreen Rd. *TF:* 866-347-4434 ■ *Web:* www.wpxi.com	Pittsburgh	PA	15214	412-237-1100	237-1286
WQED-TV Ch 13 (PBS) 4802 Fifth Ave. *TF:* 800-876-1316 ■ *Web:* www.wqed.org	Pittsburgh	PA	15213	412-622-1370	622-6413
WTAE-TV Ch 4 (ABC) 400 Ardmore Blvd **Fax:* News Rm ■ *Web:* www.wtae.com	Pittsburgh	PA	15221	412-242-4300	244-4628*

744-105 Pocatello, ID

Station	City	State	Zip	Phone	Fax
KIFI-TV Ch 8 (ABC) 1915 N Yellowstone Hwy *Web:* www.localnews8.com	Idaho Falls	ID	83401	208-525-8888	522-1930
KISU-TV Ch 10 (PBS) Idaho State University CB 8111 921 S Eighth Ave *TF:* 800-543-6868 ■ *Web:* www.idahoptv.org	Pocatello	ID	83209	208-282-2857	282-2848
KPVI-TV Ch 6 (NBC) 902 E Sherman St *TF:* 800-829-3676 ■ *Web:* www.kpvi.com	Pocatello	ID	83201	208-232-6666	233-6678

744-106 Portland, ME

Station	City	State	Zip	Phone	Fax
WCSH-TV Ch 6 (NBC) One Congress Sq *TF:* 800-464-1213 ■ *Web:* www.wcsh6.com	Portland	ME	04101	207-828-6666	828-6620
WGME-TV Ch 13 (CBS) 81 Northport Dr *Web:* www.wgme.com	Portland	ME	04103	207-797-1313	878-3505

744-107 Portland, OR

Station	City	State	Zip	Phone	Fax
KATU-TV Ch 2 (ABC) 2153 NE Sandy Blvd. *Web:* www.katu.com	Portland	OR	97232	503-231-4222	231-4263
KGW-TV Ch 8 (NBC) 1501 SW Jefferson St *TF:* 800-669-9777 ■ *Web:* www.kgw.com	Portland	OR	97201	503-226-5000	
KOIN-TV Ch 6 (CBS) 222 SW Columbia St. *Web:* www.koin.com	Portland	OR	97201	503-464-0600	464-0717

744-108 Providence, RI

Station	City	State	Zip	Phone	Fax
WLNE-TV Ch 6 (ABC) 10 Orms St *Web:* www.abc6.com	Providence	RI	02904	401-453-8000	331-4431
WSBE-TV Ch 36 (PBS) 50 Pk Ln *TF:* 866-438-0220 ■ *Web:* www.ripbs.org	Providence	RI	02907	401-222-3636	222-3407

744-109 Raleigh/Durham, NC

Station	City	State	Zip	Phone	Fax
WNCN-TV Ch 17 (NBC) 1205 Front St *Web:* www.wncn.com	Raleigh	NC	27609	919-836-1717	836-1747
WRAL-TV Ch 5 (CBS) 2619 Western Blvd *TF:* 800-245-9725 ■ *Web:* www.wral.com	Raleigh	NC	27606	919-821-8555	821-8541
WRAZ-TV Ch 50 (Fox) 512 S Mangum St *TF:* 877-369-5050 ■ *Web:* www.fox50.com	Durham	NC	27701	919-595-5050	595-5028
WTVD-TV Ch 11 (ABC) 411 Liberty St *TF:* 855-324-8477 ■ *Web:* www.abclocal.go.com	Durham	NC	27701	919-683-1111	687-4373

744-111 Rapid City, SD

Station	City	State	Zip	Phone	Fax
KEVN-TV Ch 7 (Fox) 2001 Skyline Dr PO Box 677 **Fax Area Code:* 202 ■ *Web:* www.blackhillsfox.com	Rapid City	SD	57709	605-394-7777	747-7791*
KNBN-TV Ch 27 (NBC) 2424 S Plz Dr *Web:* www.newscenter1.tv	Rapid City	SD	57702	605-355-0024	355-9274
KOTA-TV Ch 3 (ABC) 518 St Joseph St *TF:* 866-558-4554 ■ *Web:* www.kotatv.com	Rapid City	SD	57701	605-342-2000	342-7305

744-112 Reno/Carson City, NV

Station	City	State	Zip	Phone	Fax
KNPB-TV Ch 5 (PBS) 1670 N Virginia St *Web:* www.knpb.org	Reno	NV	89503	775-784-4555	784-1438
KOLO-TV Ch 8 (ABC) 4850 Ampere Dr **Fax:* News Rm ■ *Web:* www.kolotv.com	Reno	NV	89502	775-858-8888	858-8855*
KRXI-TV Ch 11 (Fox) 4920 Brookside Ct *Web:* www.foxreno.com	Reno	NV	89502	775-856-1100	856-2116
KTVN-TV Ch 2 (CBS) 4925 Energy Way *Web:* www.ktvn.com	Reno	NV	89502	775-858-2222	861-4298

744-113 Richmond, VA

Station	City	State	Zip	Phone	Fax
WCVE-TV Ch 23 (PBS) 23 Sesame St *TF:* 800-476-8440 ■ *Web:* ideastations.org	Richmond	VA	23235	804-320-1301	320-8729
WRIC-TV Ch 8 (ABC) 301 Arboretum Pl. *Web:* www.wric.com	Richmond	VA	23236	804-330-8888	330-8881
WRLH-TV Ch 35 (Fox) 1925 Westmoreland St. *Web:* www.foxrichmond.com	Richmond	VA	23230	804-358-3535	358-1495
WTVR-TV Ch 6 (CBS) 3301 W Broad St. **Fax:* Sales ■ *Web:* www.wtvr.com	Richmond	VA	23230	804-254-3600	342-3418*
WUPV-TV Ch 65 (CW) 5710 Midlothian Tpke *Web:* www.cwrichmond.tv	Richmond	VA	23225	804-230-1212	342-5746
WWBT-TV Ch 12 (NBC) 5710 Midlothian Tpke *Web:* www.nbc12.com	Richmond	VA	23225	804-230-1212	230-2793

744-114 Roanoke, VA

Station	City	State	Zip	Phone	Fax
WFXR-TV Ch 27 (Fox) 2618 Colonial Ave SW *Web:* www.fox2127.com	Roanoke	VA	24015	540-344-2127	345-1912
WSLS-TV Ch 10 (NBC) PO Box 10 *TF:* 800-800-9757 ■ *Web:* www.wsls.com	Roanoke	VA	24022	540-981-9110	343-2059

744-115 Rochester, MN

Station	City	State	Zip	Phone	Fax
KTTC-TV Ch 10 (NBC) 6301 Bandel Rd NW *TF:* 800-288-1656 ■ *Web:* www.kttc.com	Rochester	MN	55901	507-288-4444	288-6324
KXLT-TV Ch 47 (Fox) 6301 Bandel Rd NW *TF:* 800-452-4368 ■ *Web:* www.myfox47.com	Rochester	MN	55901	507-252-4747	252-5050

744-116 Rochester, NY

Station	City	State	Zip	Phone	Fax
WHAM-TV Ch 13 (ABC) 4225 W Henrietta Rd *Web:* www.13wham.com	Rochester	NY	14623	585-334-8700	334-8719
WHEC-TV Ch 10 (NBC) 191 E Ave *Web:* www.whec.com	Rochester	NY	14604	585-546-5670	546-5688
WROC-TV Ch 8 (CBS) 201 Humboldt St. **Fax:* News Rm ■ *Web:* www.rochesterhomepage.net	Rochester	NY	14610	585-288-8400	288-1505*
WUHF-TV Ch 31 (Fox) 201 Humbolt St *Web:* rochesterhomepage.net	Rochester	NY	14610	585-232-3700	288-1505
WXXI-TV Ch 21 (PBS) PO Box 30021 *Web:* interactive.wxxi.org	Rochester	NY	14603	585-325-7500	258-0335

744-117 Rockford, IL

Station	City	State	Zip	Phone	Fax
WIFR-TV Ch 23 (CBS) 2523 N Meridian Rd *Web:* www.wifr.com	Rockford	IL	61101	815-987-5300	965-0981
WREX-TV Ch 13 (NBC) 10322 Auburn Rd **Fax:* News Rm ■ *Web:* www.wrex.com	Rockford	IL	61103	815-335-2213	335-2055*
WTVO-TV Ch 17 (ABC) 1917 N Meridian Rd *Web:* www.mystateline.com	Rockford	IL	61101	815-963-5413	963-6113

744-118 Sacramento, CA

Station	City	State	Zip	Phone	Fax
KCRA-TV Ch 3 (NBC) Three Television Cir *Web:* www.kcra.com	Sacramento	CA	95814	916-446-3333	554-4688
KQCA-TV Ch 58 (MNT) Three Television Cir *Web:* www.kcra.com	Sacramento	CA	95814	916-446-3333	554-4658
KTXL-TV Ch 40 (Fox) 4655 Fruitridge Rd *Web:* www.fox40.com	Sacramento	CA	95820	916-454-4422	739-0559
KVIE-TV Ch 6 (PBS) 2030 W El Camino Ave *TF:* 800-347-5843 ■ *Web:* www.kvie.org	Sacramento	CA	95833	916-929-5843	929-7215

Phone *Fax*

News10 400 Broadway — Sacramento CA 95818 — 916-441-2345 447-6107
TF: 866-397-9884 ■ *Web:* www.news10.net

744-119 Saint Louis, MO

Phone *Fax*

KDNL-TV Ch 30 (ABC) 1215 Cole St — Saint Louis MO 63106 — 314-436-3030
Web: www.abcstlouis.com

KETC-TV Ch 9 (PBS) 3655 Olive St — Saint Louis MO 63108 — 314-512-9000 512-9005
TF: 855-482-5382 ■ *Web:* ninenet.org

KMOV-TV Ch 4 (CBS) 1 Memorial Dr — Saint Louis MO 63102 — 314-621-4444 621-4775
Web: www.kmov.com

KSDK-TV Ch 5 (NBC) 1000 Market St — Saint Louis MO 63101 — 314-421-5055 444-5164*
**Fax:* News Rm ■ *Web:* www.ksdk.com

744-120 Salt Lake City, UT

Phone *Fax*

Good 4 Utah 2175 W 1700 S — Salt Lake City UT 84104 — 801-975-4444 924-8099
Web: www.4utah.com

KJZZ-TV Ch 14 (Ind)
301 West South Temple — Salt Lake City UT 84101 — 801-537-1414
Web: www.kjzz.com

KPNZ-TV Ch 24 (Ind) 1845 Empire Ave — Burbank CA 91504 — 818-729-5300
Web: www.lbimedia.com

KSL-TV Ch 5 (NBC) PO Box 1160 — Salt Lake City UT 84110 — 801-575-5555 575-5560
TF: 800-862-9098 ■ *Web:* www.ksl.com

KSTU-TV Ch 13 (Fox)
5020 Amelia Earhart Dr — Salt Lake City UT 84116 — 801-536-1313
Web: fox13now.com

KUED-TV Ch 7 (PBS)
101 Wasatch Dr Rm 215 — Salt Lake City UT 84112 — 801-581-7777 585-5096
TF: 800-477-5833 ■ *Web:* www.kued.org

KUPX-TV Ch 16 (I) 466C Lawndale Dr — Salt Lake City UT 84115 — 801-474-0016 463-9667
TF: 888-467-2988 ■ *Web:* www.ionmedia.tv

KUTV-TV Ch 2 (CBS)
299 S Main St Ste 150 — Salt Lake City UT 84111 — 801-839-1234 839-1235*
**Fax:* News Rm ■ *TF:* 866-438-0220 ■ *Web:* www.kutv.com

744-121 San Antonio, TX

Phone *Fax*

KABB-TV Ch 29 (Fox) 4335 NW Loop 410 — San Antonio TX 78229 — 210-366-1129 377-4758
TF: 800-987-6038 ■ *Web:* www.foxsanantonio.com

KENS-TV Ch 5 (CBS)
5400 Fredericksburg Rd — San Antonio TX 78229 — 210-366-5000
Web: www.kens5.com

KLRN-TV Ch 9 (PBS) 501 Broadway St — San Antonio TX 78215 — 210-270-9000 270-9078
TF: 800-627-8193 ■ *Web:* www.klrn.org

KMYS-TV Ch 35 (MNT) 4335 NW Loop 410 — San Antonio TX 78229 — 210-366-1129 377-4758*
**Fax:* News Rm ■ *TF:* 800-987-6038 ■ *Web:* www.kmys.tv

KSAT-TV Ch 12 (ABC) 1408 N St Mary's St — San Antonio TX 78215 — 210-351-1200 351-1310*
**Fax:* News Rm ■ *Web:* www.ksat.com

KVDA-TV Ch 60 (Tele) 6234 San Pedro Ave — San Antonio TX 78216 — 210-340-8860

WOAI-TV Ch 4 (NBC) 1031 Navarro St — San Antonio TX 78205 — 210-736-9700 224-9898
Web: www.woai.com

744-122 San Diego, CA

Phone *Fax*

KFMB-TV Ch 8 (CBS) 7677 Engineer Rd — San Diego CA 92111 — 858-571-8888 560-0627
Web: www.cbs8.com

KGTV-TV Ch 10 (ABC) 4600 Airway — San Diego CA 92102 — 619-237-1010 527-0369
Web: www.10news.com

KNSD-TV Ch 39 (NBC) 225 Broadway — San Diego CA 92101 — 619-231-3939 578-0202
Web: www.nbcsandiego.com

KPBS-TV Ch 15 (PBS) 5200 Campanile Dr — San Diego CA 92182 — 619-594-1515 594-3812
TF: 888-399-5727 ■ *Web:* www.kpbs.org

KSWB-TV Ch 5 (Fox) 7191 Engineer Rd — San Diego CA 92111 — 858-492-9269 268-0401*
**Fax:* News Rm ■ *Web:* www.fox5sandiego.com

KUSI-TV Ch 51 (Ind) 4575 Viewridge Ave — San Diego CA 92123 — 858-571-5151 576-9317
Web: www.kusi.com

XETV-TV Ch 6 (CW) 8253 Ronson Rd — San Diego CA 92111 — 858-279-6666 279-0061
TF: 866-700-6397 ■ *Web:* www.sandiego6.com

744-123 San Francisco, CA

Phone *Fax*

KBHK-TV Ch 44 (CW)
855 Battery St Fourth Fl — San Francisco CA 94111 — 415-765-8144
Web: cwsanfrancisco.cbslocal.com

KGO-TV Ch 7 (ABC) 900 Front St — San Francisco CA 94111 — 415-954-7777 956-6402
Web: www.abclocal.go.com

KQED-TV Ch 9 (PBS) 2601 Mariposa St — San Francisco CA 94110 — 415-864-2000 553-2254
TF: 866-573-3123 ■ *Web:* www.kqed.org

KTNC-TV Ch 42 (Ind)
1700 Montgomery St Ste 400 — San Francisco CA 94111 — 415-398-4242 352-1800
Web: www.ktnc.com

744-124 San Juan, PR

Phone *Fax*

WKAQ-TV Ch 2 (Tele) PO Box 366222 — San Juan PR 00936 — 787-758-2222
Web: www.telemundopr.com

744-125 Savannah, GA

Phone *Fax*

WJCL-TV Ch 22 (ABC)
1375 Chatham Pkwy Third Fl — Savannah GA 31405 — 912-925-0022 921-2235
Web: www.wjcl.com

WSAV-TV Ch 3 (NBC) 1430 E Victory Dr — Savannah GA 31404 — 912-651-0300 651-0304
Web: www.wsav.com

WTOC-TV Ch 11 (CBS)
11 the News Pl PO Box 8086 — Savannah GA 31412 — 912-234-1111 232-4945*
**Fax:* News Rm ■ *Web:* www.wtoc.com

744-126 Seattle/Tacoma, WA

Phone *Fax*

KBTC-TV Ch 28 (PBS) 2320 S 19th St — Tacoma WA 98405 — 253-680-7700 680-7725
TF: 888-596-5282 ■ *Web:* www.kbtc.org

KCPQ-TV Ch 13 (Fox) 1813 Westlake Ave N — Seattle WA 98109 — 206-674-1313
Web: q13fox.com

KCTS-TV Ch 9 (PBS) 401 Mercer St — Seattle WA 98109 — 206-728-6463 443-6691
TF: 800-443-9991 ■ *Web:* kcts9.org

KING 5 Television 333 Dexter Ave N — Seattle WA 98109 — 206-448-5555 448-4525
TF: 800-456-3975 ■ *Web:* www.king5.com

KIRO-TV Ch 7 (CBS) 2807 Third Ave — Seattle WA 98121 — 206-728-7777
Web: www.kirotv.com

KOMO-TV Ch 4 (ABC) 140 Fourth Ave N — Seattle WA 98109 — 206-404-4000 404-4422
Web: www.komonews.com

KONG-TV Ch 16 (Ind) 333 Dexter Ave N — Seattle WA 98109 — 206-448-5555 448-4525
Web: www.king5.com

744-128 Shreveport, LA

Phone *Fax*

KMSS-TV Ch 33 (Fox) 3519 Jewella Ave — Shreveport LA 71109 — 318-631-5677 631-4195
Web: www.kmsstv.com

KSLA-TV Ch 12 (CBS) 1812 Fairfield Ave — Shreveport LA 71101 — 318-222-1212 677-6703
Web: www.ksla.com

KTAL-TV Ch 6 (NBC) 3150 N Market St — Shreveport LA 71107 — 318-629-6000 334-0288*
**Fax Area Code:* 903 ■ *TF:* 800-259-4929 ■ *Web:* www.arklatexhomepage.com

KTBS-TV Ch 3 (ABC) 312 E Kings Hwy — Shreveport LA 71104 — 318-861-5800 219-4601
TF: 866-543-3296 ■ *Web:* www.ktbs.com

744-129 Sioux Falls, SD

Phone *Fax*

KDLT-TV Ch 46 (NBC) 3600 S Westport Ave — Sioux Falls SD 57106 — 605-361-5555 361-3982
TF: 800-727-5358 ■ *Web:* kdlt.com

KELO-TV Ch 11 (CBS) 501 S Phillips Ave — Sioux Falls SD 57104 — 605-336-1100 336-0202*
**Fax:* News Rm ■ *TF:* 800-888-5356 ■ *Web:* www.keloland.com

KSFY-TV Ch 13 (ABC)
300 N Dakota Ave Ste 100 — Sioux Falls SD 57104 — 605-336-1300 336-2067
Web: www.ksfy.com

KTTW-TV Ch 7 (Fox) 2817 W 11th St — Sioux Falls SD 57104 — 605-338-0017 338-7173
TF: 800-369-4762 ■ *Web:* www.kttw.com

744-130 South Bend, IN

Phone *Fax*

WNDU-TV Ch 16 (NBC) PO Box 1616 — South Bend IN 46634 — 574-284-3000 284-3009
Web: www.wndu.com

WNIT-TV Ch 34.1 (PBS)
300 W Jefferson Blvd PO Box 7034 — South Bend IN 46601 — 574-675-9648 289-3441
TF: 877-411-3662 ■ *Web:* www.wnit.org

WSJV-TV Ch 28 (Fox) PO Box 28 — South Bend IN 46624 — 574-679-9758 294-1267
TF: 800-435-3803 ■ *Web:* www.fox28.com

744-131 Spokane, WA

Phone *Fax*

KAYU-TV Ch 28 (Fox) 4600 S Regal St — Spokane WA 99223 — 509-448-2828 448-0926
Web: www.myfoxspokane.com

KHQ-TV Ch 6 (NBC) 1201 W Sprague Ave — Spokane WA 99201 — 509-448-6000 448-4644
Web: www.khq.com

KREM-TV Ch 2 (CBS) 4103 S Regal St — Spokane WA 99223 — 509-448-2000 425-1307*
**Fax Area Code:* 870 ■ *TF:* 888-404-3922 ■ *Web:* www.krem.com

KSKN-TV Ch 22 (CW) 4103 S Regal St — Spokane WA 99223 — 509-448-2000 425-1307*
**Fax Area Code:* 870 ■ *TF:* 888-404-3922 ■ *Web:* www.krem.com

KSPS Public TV 3911 S Regal St — Spokane WA 99223 — 509-443-7800
TF: 800-735-2377 ■ *Web:* www.ksps.org

KXLY-TV Ch 4 (ABC) 500 W Boone Ave — Spokane WA 99201 — 509-324-4000 327-3932
Web: www.kxly.com

744-132 Springfield, IL

Phone *Fax*

WICS-TV Ch 20 (ABC) 2680 E Cook St — Springfield IL 62703 — 217-753-5620 753-5681*
**Fax:* News Rm ■ *TF:* 800-263-9720 ■ *Web:* www.wics.com

WRSP-TV Ch 55 (Fox)
3003 Old Rochester Rd — Springfield IL 62703 — 217-523-8855 523-4410
Web: foxillinois.com

744-133 Springfield, MA

Station	City	State	Zip	Phone	Fax
WESTERN MASS NEWS 1300 Liberty St **Fax Area Code:* 816 ■ *TF:* 877-872-2756 ■ *Web:* www.wggb.com	Springfield	MA	01104	413-733-4040	471-7338*
WGBY-TV Ch 57 (PBS) 44 Hampden St *Web:* www.wgby.org	Springfield	MA	01103	413-781-2801	731-5093
WWLP-TV Ch 22 (NBC) PO Box 2210 *Web:* www.wwlp.com	Springfield	MA	01102	413-377-2200	377-2261

744-134 Springfield, MO

Station	City	State	Zip	Phone	Fax
KOLR-TV Ch 10 (CBS) 2650 E Div St *Web:* ozarksfirst.com	Springfield	MO	65803	417-862-1010	831-4209
KOZK-TV Ch 21 (PBS) 901 S National Ave *TF:* 866-684-5695 ■ *Web:* www.optv.org	Springfield	MO	65897	417-836-3500	836-3569
KSPR-TV Ch 33 (ABC) 1359 St Louis St *TF:* 888-435-1464 ■ *Web:* www.kspr.com	Springfield	MO	65802	417-831-1333	831-9358
KYTV-TV Ch 3 (NBC) PO Box 3500 *TF:* 888-435-1464 ■ *Web:* www.ky3.com	Springfield	MO	65808	417-268-3000	268-3364

744-135 Syracuse, NY

Station	City	State	Zip	Phone	Fax
WCNY-TV Ch 24 (PBS) 506 Old Liverpool Rd PO Box 2400 *TF:* 800-638-5163 ■ *Web:* www.wcny.org	Syracuse	NY	13220	315-453-2424	451-8824
WNYS-TV Ch 43 (MNT) 1000 James St *Web:* www.my43.tv	Syracuse	NY	13203	315-472-6800	471-8889
WSYT-TV Ch 68 (Fox) 1000 James St *Web:* www.foxsyracuse.com	Syracuse	NY	13203	315-472-6800	471-8889

744-136 Tallahassee, FL

Station	City	State	Zip	Phone	Fax
WCTV-TV Ch 6 (CBS) 1801 Halstead Blvd *TF:* 888-297-9461 ■ *Web:* www.wctv.tv	Tallahassee	FL	32309	850-893-6666	668-3851
WFSU-TV Ch 11 (PBS) 1600 Red Barber Plz *TF:* 800-322-9378 ■ *Web:* www.wfsu.org	Tallahassee	FL	32310	850-487-3170	487-3093
WTWC-TV Ch 40 (NBC) 8440 Deerlake Rd S *Web:* www.wtwc40.com	Tallahassee	FL	32312	850-893-4140	893-6974

744-137 Tampa/Saint Petersburg, FL

Station	City	State	Zip	Phone	Fax
WEDU-TV Ch 3 (PBS) 1300 N Blvd *Web:* www.wedu.org	Tampa	FL	33607	813-254-9338	253-0826
WFLA-TV Ch 8 (NBC) PO Box 1410 *TF:* 800-338-0808 ■ *Web:* www.wfla.com	Tampa	FL	33601	813-228-8888	225-2770
WFTS-TV Ch 28 (ABC) 4045 N Himes Ave *TF:* 877-833-2828 ■ *Web:* www.abcactionnews.com	Tampa	FL	33607	813-354-2828	870-2828
WMOR-TV Ch 32 (Ind) 7201 E Hillsborough Ave *Web:* www.mor-tv.com	Tampa	FL	33610	813-626-3232	626-1961
WTOG-TV Ch 44 (CW) 365 105th Terr NE *Web:* cwtampa.cbslocal.com	Saint Petersburg	FL	33716	727-576-4444	
WTSP-TV Ch 10 (CBS) 11450 Gandy Blvd N *TF:* 877-762-7824 ■ *Web:* www.wtsp.com	Saint Petersburg	FL	33702	727-577-1010	576-6924
WTTA-TV Ch 38 (MNT) 7622 Bald Cypress Pl *Web:* www.great38.com	Tampa	FL	33614	813-886-9882	225-2770
WTVT-TV Ch 13 (Fox) 3213 W Kennedy Blvd *Web:* www.myfoxtampabay.com	Tampa	FL	33609	813-876-1313	871-3135
WUSF-TV Ch 16 (PBS) 4202 E Fowler Ave *TF:* 800-654-3703 ■ *Web:* www.wusftv.usf.edu	Tampa	FL	33620	813-974-4000	974-4806

744-138 Toledo, OH

Station	City	State	Zip	Phone	Fax
WGTE-TV Ch 30 (PBS) PO Box 30 *Web:* www.wgte.org	Toledo	OH	43614	419-380-4600	380-4710
WLMB-TV Ch 40 (Ind) 825 Capital Commons Dr *Web:* www.wlmb.com	Toledo	OH	43615	419-720-9562	720-9563
WNWO-TV Ch 24 (NBC) 300 S Byrne Rd *Web:* nbc24.com	Toledo	OH	43615	419-535-0024	535-8936
WTOL-TV Ch 11 (CBS) 730 N Summit St *Web:* www.toledonewsnow.com	Toledo	OH	43604	419-248-1111	244-7104
WTVG-TV Ch 13 (ABC) 4247 Dorr St *Web:* www.13abc.com	Toledo	OH	43607	419-531-1313	534-3898

744-139 Topeka, KS

Station	City	State	Zip	Phone	Fax
KSNT-TV Ch 27 (NBC) 6835 NW Hwy 24 *TF:* 800-222-8477 ■ *Web:* www.kansasfirstnews.com	Topeka	KS	66618	785-582-4000	
KTWU-TV Ch 11 (PBS) 1700 College *TF:* 800-866-5898 ■ *Web:* www.ktwu.org	Topeka	KS	66621	785-670-1111	670-1112
WIBW-TV Ch 13 (CBS) 631 SW Commerce Pl *Web:* www.wibw.com	Topeka	KS	66615	785-272-6397	272-1363

744-140 Toronto, ON

Station	City	State	Zip	Phone	Fax
CICA-TV Ch 19 (Ind) 2180 Yonge St Stn Q PO Box 200 *TF:* 800-613-0513 ■ *Web:* tvo.org/	Toronto	ON	M4T2T1	416-484-2600	484-4234
CITY-TV Ch 57 (Ind) 33 Dundas St E *Web:* www.citytv.com/toronto	Toronto	ON	M5B1B8	416-764-3003	

744-141 Tucson, AZ

Station	City	State	Zip	Phone	Fax
KGUN-TV Ch 9 (ABC) 7280 E Rosewood St *Web:* jrn.com/kgun9	Tucson	AZ	85710	520-722-5486	733-7050
KOLD-TV Ch 13 (CBS) 7831 N Business Pk Dr *Web:* www.tucsonnewsnow.com	Tucson	AZ	85743	520-744-1313	744-5235
KUAT-TV Ch 6 (PBS) University of Arizona Modern Languages Bldg 1423 E University Blvd *Web:* stations.fcc.gov/station-profile/kuat-tv	Tucson	AZ	85721	520-621-5828	621-9664
KVOA-TV Ch 4 (NBC) 209 W Elm PO Box 5188 *Web:* www.kvoa.com	Tucson	AZ	85703	520-792-2270	620-1309

744-142 Tulsa, OK

Station	City	State	Zip	Phone	Fax
KJRH-TV Ch 2 (NBC) 3701 S Peoria Ave *Web:* www.kjrh.com	Tulsa	OK	74105	918-743-2222	748-1436
KOKI-TV Ch 23 (Fox) 2625 S Memorial Dr *Web:* www.fox23.com	Tulsa	OK	74129	918-491-0023	491-6650
KOTV-TV Ch 6 (CBS) PO Box 6 *TF:* 888-434-8248 ■ *Web:* www.newson6.com	Tulsa	OK	74101	918-732-6000	732-6185
KTUL-TV Ch 8 (ABC) PO Box 8 *Web:* www.ktul.com	Tulsa	OK	74101	918-445-8888	445-9316
KWHB-TV Ch 47 (Ind) 8835 S Memorial Dr *Web:* www.kwhb.com	Tulsa	OK	74133	918-254-4701	254-5614

744-143 Vancouver, BC

Station	City	State	Zip	Phone	Fax
CIVT-TV Ch 9 (CTV) 750 Burrard St Ste 300 *Web:* bc.ctvnews.ca	Vancouver	BC	V6Z1X5	604-608-2868	608-2698

744-144 Washington, DC

Station	City	State	Zip	Phone	Fax
WDCW-TV 2121 Wisconsin Ave NW Ste 350 *Web:* www.dc50tv.com	Washington	DC	20007	202-965-5050	
WHUT-TV Ch 32 (PBS) 2222 Fourth St NW *Web:* www.whut.org	Washington	DC	20059	202-806-3200	806-3300
WRC-TV Ch 4 (NBC) 4001 Nebraska Ave NW *Web:* www.nbcwashington.com	Washington	DC	20016	202-885-4000	885-4104
WTTG FOX 5 & myfoxdc 5151 Wisconsin Ave NW *Web:* www.myfoxdc.com	Washington	DC	20016	202-244-5151	895-3340
WTTG-TV Ch 5 (Fox) 5151 Wisconsin Ave NW **Fax:* News Rm ■ *TF:* 866-756-3587 ■ *Web:* www.myfoxdc.com	Washington	DC	20016	202-244-5151	*
WUSA-TV Ch 9 (CBS) 4100 Wisconsin Ave NW *Web:* www.wusa9.com	Washington	DC	20016	202-895-5999	

744-145 West Palm Beach, FL

Station	City	State	Zip	Phone	Fax
WFGC-TV Ch 61 (Ind) 1900 S Congress Ave Ste A *Web:* www.wfgctelevision.com	West Palm Beach	FL	33406	561-642-3361	967-5961
WFLX-TV Ch 29 (Fox) 4119 W Blue Heron Blvd *Web:* www.wflx.com	West Palm Beach	FL	33404	561-845-2929	863-1238
WPTV-TV Ch 5 (NBC) 1100 Banyan Blvd **Fax:* News Rm ■ *Web:* www.wptv.com	West Palm Beach	FL	33401	561-655-5455	653-5719*
WTVX-TV Ch 34 (CW) 1700 Palm Beach Lakes Blvd *Web:* cw34.com	West Palm Beach	FL	33401	561-681-3434	
WXEL-TV Ch 42 (PBS) PO Box 6607 *TF:* 800-915-9935 ■ *Web:* www.wxel.org	West Palm Beach	FL	33405	561-737-8000	369-3067

744-146 Wheeling, WV

Station	City	State	Zip	Phone	Fax
WTRF-TV Ch 7 (CBS) 96 16th St **Fax:* News Rm ■ *Web:* www.wtrf.com	Wheeling	WV	26003	304-232-7777	233-5822*

744-147 Wichita, KS

Station	City	State	Zip	Phone	Fax
KAKE-TV Ch 10 (ABC) 1500 NW St *Web:* www.kake.com	Wichita	KS	67203	316-943-4221	943-5374
KPTS-TV Ch 8 (PBS) 320 W 21 St *TF:* 800-794-8498 ■ *Web:* www.kpts.org	Wichita	KS	67203	316-838-3090	838-8586

	City	State	Zip	Phone	Fax
KSAS-TV Ch 24 (Fox) 316 NW St. *Web:* www.foxkansas.com	Wichita	KS	67203	316-942-2424	942-8927
KSCW-TV Ch 33 (CW) 2815 E 37th St N *Web:* kwch.com/kscw-crew/-/22425548/-/cxwku6/-/index.html	Wichita	KS	67219	316-838-1212	
KSNW-TV 833 N Main St *TF:* 800-325-0778 ■ *Web:* www.ksn.com	Wichita	KS	67203	316-265-3333	292-1195
KWCH-TV Ch 12 (CBS) 2815 E 37th St N *TF:* 877-257-6921 ■ *Web:* www.kwch.com	Wichita	KS	67219	316-838-1212	978-3950

744-148 Winnipeg, MB

	City	State	Zip	Phone	Fax
CTV-TV Ch 5 (CTV) 345 Graham Ave Ste 400 *Fax:* News Rm ■ *TF:* 800-461-1542 ■ *Web:* winnipeg.ctvnews.ca	Winnipeg	MB	R3C5S6	204-788-3300	788-3399*

744-149 Winston-Salem, NC

	City	State	Zip	Phone	Fax
WMYV-TV Ch 48 (MNT) 3500 Myer Lee Dr *Web:* www.my48.tv	Winston-Salem	NC	27101	336-760-0706	723-8217
WXII-TV Ch 12 (NBC) 700 Coliseum Dr *Web:* www.wxii12.com	Winston-Salem	NC	27106	336-721-9944	721-0856
WXLV-TV Ch 45 (ABC) 3500 Myer Lee Dr *Web:* www.abc45.com	Winston-Salem	NC	27101	336-722-4545	723-8217

744-150 Youngstown, OH

	City	State	Zip	Phone	Fax
WFMJ-TV Ch 21 (NBC) 101 W Boardman St *TF:* 800-488-9365 ■ *Web:* www.wfmj.com	Youngstown	OH	44503	330-744-8611	742-2472
WKBN-TV Ch 27 (CBS) 3930 Sunset Blvd *Web:* www.wkbn.com/default.aspx	Youngstown	OH	44512	330-782-1144	782-3504
WKBN/WYFX 3930 Sunset Blvd *Web:* www.wkbn.com	Youngstown	OH	44512	330-782-1144	782-3504
WYFX-TV Ch 62 (Fox) 3930 Sunset Blvd. *Web:* www.wkbn.com	Youngstown	OH	44512	330-782-1144	782-3504

744-151

Phone Fax

745 TELEVISION SYNDICATORS

Television syndicators are companies that produce programming in-house and market and distribute the programs to networks on a national or regional basis.

	City	State	Zip	Phone	Fax
A Taste of New York Inc 10 Roberta Ln. *Web:* www.tasteofny.com	Syosset	NY	11791	516-677-0239	
ABC NewsOne 47 W 66th St Third Fl *Web:* www.abcnewsone.tv	New York	NY	10023	212-456-4110	
American Public Television (APT) 55 Summer St 4th Fl. *Web:* aptonline.org/aptweb.nsf/home?readform	Boston	MA	02110	617-338-4455	338-5369
Babe Winkelman Productions PO Box 407 *Fax Area Code:* 218 ■ *TF:* 800-333-0471 ■ *Web:* www.winkelman.com	Brainerd	MN	56401	800-333-0471	822-7436*
bieMEDIA LLC 511 Broadway *Web:* biemedia.com	Denver	CO	80203	303-825-2275	
CBS Newspath 524 W 57th St. *Web:* www.cbsnewspath.com	New York	NY	10019	212-975-6121	541-8630
CBS Television Distribution 2450 Colorado Ave Ste 500E *Web:* www.cbstvd.com	Santa Monica	CA	90404	310-264-3300	264-3301
Disney ABC Domestic Television 500 S Buena Vista St *Web:* www.disneyabc.tv	Burbank	CA	91521	818-560-9300	560-5296
Five Star Productions 42 N Swinton Ave *Web:* www.swoolleyentertainment.com	Delray Beach	FL	33444	561-279-7827	
Guthy-Renker Television Network 3340 Ocean Pk Blvd *TF:* 800-778-1011 ■ *Web:* www.guthy-renker.com	Santa Monica	CA	90405	310-581-6250	581-3232
Hearst Entertainment & Syndication Group 300 W 57th St. *Web:* hearst.com/entertainment	New York	NY	10019	212-969-7553	
Independent Television Service (ITVS) 651 Brannan St Ste 410 *TF:* 800-621-6196 ■ *Web:* www.itvs.org	San Francisco	CA	94107	415-356-8383	356-8391
Information Television Network 6650 Pk of Commerce Blvd *TF:* 800-463-6488 ■ *Web:* www.itvisus.com	Boca Raton	FL	33487	561-997-5433	997-5208
Initiative Corp 5700 Wilshire Blvd Ste 400 *Web:* www.im-na.com	Los Angeles	CA	90036	323-370-8000	
Ivanhoe Broadcast News 2745 W Fairbanks Ave *Web:* www.ivanhoe.com	Winter Park	FL	32789	407-740-0789	740-5320
K Rcr Tv News Channel 7 Tv 755 Auditorium Dr *Web:* www.krcrtv.com	Redding	CA	96001	530-243-7777	
National Educational Telecommunications Assn (NETA) 939 S Stadium Rd. *TF:* 866-270-5141 ■ *Web:* www.netaonline.org	Columbia	SC	29201	803-799-5517	771-4831
RCTV International 4380 NW 128th St *Web:* www.rctvintl.com	Opa-locka	FL	33054	305-688-7475	685-5697
Thomson Reuters Three Times Sq. *Web:* www.thomsonreuters.com	New York	NY	10036	646-223-4000	
Warner Bros Domestic Television Distribution 4000 Warner Blvd *Web:* warnerbros.com	Burbank	CA	91522	818-954-6000	
WPT Enterprises Inc (WPTE) 5700 Wilshire Blvd Ste 350 *Fax Area Code:* 323 ■ *Web:* www.worldpokertour.com	Los Angeles	CA	90036	949-225-2600	330-9901*

746 TESTING FACILITIES

	City	State	Zip	Phone	Fax
2b Technologies Inc 2100 Central Ave Ste 105 *Web:* www.twobtech.com	Boulder	CO	80301	303-273-0559	
A & e Testing 1514 Rochester St. *Web:* www.shawndra.com	Lima	NY	14485	585-624-4500	
A&L Great Lakes Laboratories Inc 3505 Conestoga Dr. *Web:* www.algreatlakes.com	Fort Wayne	IN	46808	260-483-4759	
ABC Research Laboratories 3437 SW 24th Ave *Web:* www.abcr.com	Gainesville	FL	32607	352-372-0436	
Accuratus Lab Services 104 Gold St. *Web:* www.microtestlabs.com	Agawam	MA	01001	413-786-1680	
Accusource Inc 1240 E Ontario Ave Ste 102-140 *Web:* www.accusource-online.com	Corona	CA	92881	951-734-8882	
Accutest Laboratories 2235 Rt 130 Bldg B *TF:* 800-329-0204 ■ *Web:* www.accutest.com	Dayton	NJ	08810	732-329-0200	329-3499
Achaogen Inc 7000 Shoreline Ct Ste 371 *Web:* www.achaogen.com	South San Francisco	CA	94080	650-266-1120	
Acme Analytical Laboratories Ltd 1020 Cordova St E *Web:* www.acmelab.com	Vancouver	BC	V6A4A3	604-253-3158	
Actimis Pharmaceuticals Inc 10835 Rd To The Cure Ste 200 *Web:* www.actimis.com	San Diego	CA	92121	858-458-1890	
Activation Laboratories Ltd 1336 Sandhill Dr *Web:* www.actlabs.com	Ancaster	ON	L9G4V5	905-648-9611	
Adamson Analytical Laboratories Inc 200 Crouse Dr *Web:* www.adamsonlab.com	Corona	CA	92879	951-549-9657	549-9659
ADPEN Laboratories Inc 11757 Central Pkwy *Web:* www.adpen.com	Jacksonville	FL	32224	904-645-9169	
AEDC Public Affairs 100 Kindell Dr Ste B-213 *Fax:* Hum Res ■ *Web:* www.arnold.af.mil	Arnold AFB	TN	37389	931-454-5655	454-6720*
Aegis Sciences Corp 515 Great Cir Rd *Web:* www.aegislabs.com	Nashville	TN	37228	615-255-2400	
Aerotech Laboratories Inc 1501 W Knudsen Dr *Web:* www.emlab.com	Phoenix	AZ	85027	623-780-4800	
AgaMatrix Inc 7C Raymond Ave *Web:* www.agamatrix.com	Salem	NH	03079	603-328-6000	
Aircraft X-Ray Labs Inc 5216 Pacific Blvd *Web:* www.aircraftxray.com	Huntington Park	CA	90255	323-587-4141	588-6410
Akron Rubber Development Laboratory Inc 2887 Gilchrist Rd *Web:* www.ardl.com	Akron	OH	44305	330-794-6600	
Akros Pharma Inc 302 Carnegie Ctr Ste 300 *Web:* www.akrospharma.com	Princeton	NJ	08540	609-919-9570	
Alere Toxicology Services Inc 1111 Newton St *Web:* www.aleretoxicology.com	Gretna	LA	70053	504-361-8989	
ALine Inc 2206 E Gladwick St *TF:* 877-707-8575 ■ *Web:* www.alineinc.com	Rancho Dominguez	CA	90220	877-707-8575	
All Metals Processing of Orange County Inc 8401 Standustrial St. *Web:* www.allmetalsprocessing.com	Stanton	CA	90680	714-828-8238	828-4552
All-Tronics Medical Systems Inc 3289 E 55th St *Web:* www.all-tronics.net	Cleveland	OH	44127	216-429-3000	
Allegro Ophthalmics LLC 31473 Rancho Viejo Rd Ste 204 *Web:* www.allegroeye.com	San Juan Capistrano	CA	92675	949-940-8130	
Alliance Source Testing LLC 214 Central Cir SW *Web:* www.stacktest.com	Decatur	AL	35603	256-351-0121	
Altran Solutions USA 2525 Rt 130 S. *TF:* 855-425-8726 ■ *Web:* www.altran-na.com	Cranbury	NJ	08512	609-409-9790	409-8622
Alturas Analytics Inc 1324 Alturas Dr *Web:* www.alturasanalytics.com	Moscow	ID	83843	208-883-3400	
ALZA Corp 700 Eubanks Dr *Web:* jnj.com	Vacaville	CA	95688	707-453-6400	
American Standards Testing Bureau Inc PO Box 583	New York	NY	10274	212-943-3160	
Amplicon Express Inc 2345 Ne Hopkins Ct *Web:* ampliconexpress.com	Pullman	WA	99163	509-332-8080	
Ana-Lab Corp PO Box 9000 *Web:* www.ana-lab.com	Kilgore	TX	75663	903-984-0551	984-5914
Anabolic Laboratories Inc W251s3879 Rickert Dr *Web:* www.anaboliclabs.com	Waukesha	WI	53189	262-544-2020	
Analysts Inc 22750 Hawthorne Blvd Ste 220 *Fax Area Code:* 310 ■ *TF:* 800-336-3637 ■ *Web:* www.analystsinc.com	Torrance	CA	90505	800-336-3637	320-0970*
Analytica Group-environmental Laboratories 4307 Arctic Blvd *Web:* www.analyticagroup.com	Anchorage	AK	99503	907-258-6634	
Analytics Corp 10329 Stony Run Ln *Web:* analyticscorp.com	Ashland	VA	23005	804-365-3000	

	City	State	Zip	Phone	Fax
Animal & Plant Health Inspection Service (APHIS) *National Veterinary Services Laboratories* 2300 Dayton Ave *Web:* www.aphis.usda.gov	Ames	IA	50010	515-663-7200	
Anrad Corp 4950 Levy St *Web:* www.anrad.com	St Laurent	QC	H4R2P1	514-856-6920	
Apotex Fermentation Inc 50 Scurfield Blvd *Web:* www.apoferm.com	Winnipeg	MB	R3Y1G4	204-989-6830	
Aqua Test Inc 28620 Maple Vly Hwy Se *Web:* aquatestinc.com	Maple Valley	WA	98038	425-432-9360	
Arcadia Biosciences Inc 202 Cousteau Pl Ste 200 *Web:* www.arcadiabio.com	Davis	CA	95618	530-756-7077	
Astro Pak Corp 270 E Baker St Ste 100 **Fax Area Code:* 714 ■ *TF:* 866-492-7876 ■ *Web:* www.astropak.com	Costa Mesa	CA	92626	866-492-7876	434-1376*
Atlantic Pharmaceuticals Inc one Glenlake Pkwy Ste 700 *Web:* www.atlanticpharma.com	Atlanta	GA	30328	678-638-6170	
Atlas Testing Laboratories Inc 9820 Sixth St *Web:* www.atlastesting.com	Rancho Cucamonga	CA	91730	909-373-4130	
Auxogyn Inc 1490 O'Brien Dr Ste A *Web:* www.auxogyn.com	Menlo Park	CA	94025	650-641-2429	
Ballantine Laboratories Inc 312 Old Allerton Rd *Web:* www.ballantinelabs.com	Annandale	NJ	08801	908-713-7742	713-7743
Benaroya Research Institute 1201 Ninth Ave *Web:* www.benaroyaresearch.org	Seattle	WA	98101	206-583-6400	
Benchmark International 2710 W Fifth Ave *Web:* www.benchmark-intl.com/	Eugene	OR	97402	541-484-9212	344-2735
Bio-Research Products Inc 323 W Cherry St *TF:* 800-326-3511 ■ *Web:* www.bio-researchprod.com	North Liberty	IA	52317	319-626-6707	
BioFlorida 525 Okeechobee Blvd Ste 1500 *Web:* www.biofIorida.com	West Palm Beach	FL	33401	561-653-3839	
BIOPAC Systems Inc 42 Aero Camino *TF:* 877-524-6722 ■ *Web:* www.biopac.com	Goleta	CA	93117	805-685-0066	
BIOQUELL Inc 702 Electronic Dr Ste 200 *Web:* www.bioquell.com	Horsham	PA	19044	215-682-0225	
Biosan Laboratories Inc 1950 Tobsal Ct *Web:* www.biosan.com	Warren	MI	48091	586-755-8970	
BioStratum Inc 4825 Creekstone Dr Ste 200 *Web:* www.biostratum.com	Durham	NC	27703	919-572-6515	
Biotech Clinical Laboratories Inc 25775 Meadowbrook *Web:* biotechclinical.com	Novi	MI	48375	248-912-1700	
Biothera Inc 3388 Mike Collins Dr *Web:* www.biotherapharma.com	Eagan	MN	55121	651-675-0300	
bioTheranostics Inc 9640 Towne Centre Dr Ste 200 *Web:* www.biotheranostics.com	San Diego	CA	92121	858-587-5870	
BioWa Inc 9420 Athena Cir *Web:* kyowa-kirin.com/biowa/	La Jolla	CA	92037	858-952-7200	
Blend Therapeutics Inc 134 Coolidge Ave *Web:* www.blendtx.com	Watertown	MA	02472	617-923-4100	
Boca Biolistics LLC 4851 W Hillsboro Blvd Ste A7 *Web:* bocabio.com	Coconut Creek	FL	33073	954-573-1200	
Bosch Automotive Proving Grounds 32104 State Rd 2 *Web:* www.bosch.us	New Carlisle	IN	46552	574-654-4000	654-8755
Brook Environmental & Engineering Corp 11419 Cronridge Dr Ste 10 *Web:* carrollcountytimes.com	Owings Mills	MD	21117	410-356-5073	
Brooks Rand Labs LLC 3958 Sixth Ave NW Ste 4 *Web:* www.brooksrand.com	Seattle	WA	98107	206-632-6206	
Brunswick Laboratories LLC 200 Turnpike Rd *Web:* www.brunswicklabs.com	Southborough	MA	01772	508-281-6660	
Caldwell Manufacturing Inc 2605 Manitou Rd *Web:* www.caldwellmfgco.com	Rochester	NY	14624	585-352-3790	
Camin Cargo Control Inc 230 Marion Ave **Fax:* Hum Res ■ *TF:* 800-756-8798 ■ *Web:* www.camincargo.com	Linden	NJ	07036	908-862-1899	523-0616*
Canadian Environmental & Metallurgical Inc 6927 Antrim Ave *Web:* www.cemi.bc.ca	Burnaby	BC	V5J4M5	604-264-5536	
Cancer Care Ontario 620 University Ave *Web:* www.cancercare.on.ca	Toronto	ON	M5G2L7	416-971-9800	
CanWest DHI 660 Speedvale Ave W *Web:* www.canwestdhi.com	Guelph	ON	N1K1E5	519-824-2320	
CardioNexus Corp 710 N Post Oak Rd Ste 103 *Web:* www.cardionexus.com	Houston	TX	77024	281-769-4201	
Cardiovascular Research Foundation 111 E 59th St *Web:* www.crf.org	New York	NY	10022	646-434-4500	
Carlson Testing Inc 8430 SW Hunziker *Web:* www.carlsontesting.com	Tigard	OR	97223	503-684-3460	
Carrot Medical LLC 22122 20th Ave SE Ste H-166 *Web:* carrotmedical.com	Bothell	WA	98021	425-318-8089	
Catalyst Biosciences Inc 260 Littlefield Ave *Web:* www.catbio.com	South San Francisco	CA	94080	650-871-0761	
CD Diagnostics Inc 650 Naamans Rd Ste 100 *Web:* cddiagnostics.com	Claymont	DE	19703	302-367-7770	
Celsis International 600 W Chicago Ave Ste 625 *TF:* 800-222-8260 ■ *Web:* www.celsis.com	Chicago	IL	60654	312-476-1282	476-1201
Chardon Laboratories Inc 7300 Tussing Rd *Web:* chardonlabs.com	Reynoldsburg	OH	43068	614-860-1000	
Chemir Analytical Services Inc 2672 Metro Blvd *Web:* www.chemir.com	Maryland Heights	MO	63043	314-291-6620	
Cherney Microbiological Services Ltd 1110 S Huron Rd *Web:* cherneymicro.com	Green Bay	WI	54311	920-406-8300	
Christian Alliance for Humanitarian Aid Inc 4401 Rice Dyer Rd *Web:* christian-alliance.org	Pearland	TX	77581	281-412-2285	
Coherex Medical Inc 3598 West 1820 South *Web:* www.coherex.com	Salt Lake City	UT	84104	801-433-9900	
Columbia Analytical Services Inc 1317 S 13th Ave *Web:* www.caslab.com	Kelso	WA	98626	360-577-7222	425-9096
Compact Membrane Systems Inc 335 Water St *Web:* www.compactmembrane.com	Wilmington	DE	19804	302-999-7996	
Con-Test Analytical Laboratory 39 Spruce St 2 *Web:* www.contestlabs.com	East Longmeadow	MA	01028	413-525-2332	
Construction Testing & Engineering Inc 1441 Montiel Road Ste 115 **Fax Area Code:* 209 ■ *TF:* 800-576-2271 ■ *Web:* www.cte-inc.net	Escondido	CA	92026	760-746-4955	839-2895*
Copernicus Group Inc, The One Triangle Dr Ste 100 *Web:* www.cgirb.com	Durham	NC	27713	919-465-4310	
Craft Technologies Inc 4344 Frank Price Church Rd *Web:* www.crafttechnologies.com	Wilson	NC	27893	252-206-7071	
Criterion Laboratories Inc 3370 Progress Dr Ste J *Web:* www.criterionlabs.com	Bensalem	PA	19020	215-244-1300	
Cryogenic Experts Inc 531 Sandy Cir *Web:* www.cexi.com	Oxnard	CA	93036	805-981-4500	
CSP Assoc Inc 55 Cambridge Pkwy Riverfront 2 *Web:* www.cspassociates.com	Cambridge	MA	02142	617-225-2828	
CTLGroup 5400 Old OrchaRd Rd *TF:* 800-522-2285 ■ *Web:* www.ctlgroup.com	Skokie	IL	60077	847-965-7500	965-6541
Curtis & Tompkins Ltd 2323 Fifth St *Web:* curtisandtompkins.com	Berkeley	CA	94710	510-486-0900	
Cyl-tec Inc 950 Industrial Dr *Web:* cyl-tec.com	Aurora	IL	60506	630-844-8800	
D L s Electronic Systems Inc 1250 Peterson Dr *Web:* www.dlsemc.com	Wheeling	IL	60090	847-537-6400	
D-Tech Optoelectronics Inc USA 18007 Cortney Ct *Web:* www.dtechopto.com	City Of Industry	CA	91748	626-956-1100	
Dairyland Laboratories Inc 217 E Main St *Web:* www.dairylandlabs.com	Arcadia	WI	54612	608-323-2123	
DALSA Corp 605 McMurray Rd *Web:* www.dalsa.com.	Waterloo	ON	N2V2E9	519-886-6000	
Daniel B Stephens & Assoc Inc 6020 Academy Ne Ste 100 *Web:* www.dbstephens.com	Albuquerque	NM	87109	505-822-9400	
Davinci Biosciences LLC 1239 victoria st *Web:* www.dvbiologics.com	Costa mesa	CA	92627	949-515-2828	
Dayton T Brown Inc 1175 Church St *TF:* 800-232-6300 ■ *Web:* www.daytontbrown.com	Bohemia	NY	11716	631-589-6300	589-0046
DDL Inc 10200 Vly View Rd Ste 101 *Web:* www.testedandproven.com	Eden Prairie	MN	55344	952-941-9226	
Delsen Testing Laboratories Inc 1024 Grand Central Ave *Web:* delsen.com	Glendale	CA	91201	818-247-4106	
DHL Analytical 2300 Double Creek Dr *Web:* www.dhlanalytical.com	Round Rock	TX	78664	512-388-8222	
Diw Group Inc Dba Specialized Engineering 4845 International Blvd	Frederick	MD	21703	301-607-4180	
Dominion Diagnostics LLC 211 Circuit Dr *Web:* dominiondiagnostics.com	North Kingstown	RI	02852	401-667-0800	
DRG International Inc 841 Mountain Ave *Web:* www.drg-international.com	Springfield	NJ	07081	973-564-7555	
Dugway Proving Ground 5124 Kister Ave *Web:* www.dugway.army.mil	Dugway	UT	84022	435-831-2178	
Dyna Flex Ltd 10403 International Plz Dr *Web:* www.dynaflex.com	Saint Ann	MO	63074	314-426-4020	
E Pi Bio Analytical 9095 W Harristown Blvd *Web:* www.eplbas.com	Niantic	IL	62551	217-963-2143	
Eastern Analytical Inc 25 chenell dr *Web:* www.eailabs.com	Concord	NH	03301	603-228-0525	
Eccs Nationwide Mobile Laboratories 2525 Advance Rd *Web:* www.eccsmobilelab.com	Madison	WI	53718	608-221-8700	
Edward S Babcock & Sons Inc 6100 Quail Vly Ct *Web:* www.babcocklabs.com	Riverside	CA	92507	951-653-3351	
Element Materials Technology 5405 E Schaaf Rd *Web:* www.element.com	Cleveland	OH	44131	216-524-1450	524-1459
Elliott Laboratories Inc 41039 Boyce Rd *Web:* www.nts-cs.com	Fremont	CA	94538	510-578-3500	
Ellis & Associates Inc 7064 Davis Creek Rd *Web:* www.ellisassoc.com	Jacksonville	FL	32256	904-880-0960	
Embryotech Laboratories Inc 140 Hale St *TF:* 800-673-7500 ■ *Web:* www.embryotech.com	Haverhill	MA	01830	978-373-7300	
Empirical Testing Corp 4628 Northpark Dr *Web:* www.empiricaltesting.com	Colorado Springs	CO	80918	719-264-9937	
ENCO Laboratories Inc 10775 Central Port Dr *Web:* encolabs.com	Orlando	FL	32824	407-826-5314	

Name / Address	City	State	Zip	Phone	Fax
eNeura Therapeutics LLC 240 N Wolfe Rd *Web:* www.eneura.com	Sunnyvale	CA	94085	408-245-6400	
Engineering Dynamics Inc 3925 S Kalamath St *Web:* www.engdynamics.com	Englewood	CO	80110	303-761-4367	
Enthalpy Analytical Inc 800-1 Capitola Dr *Web:* www.enthalpy.com	Durham	NC	27713	919-850-4392	
EnviroLogix Inc 500 Riverside Industrial Pkwy *TF:* 866-408-4597 ■ *Web:* www.envirologix.com	Portland	ME	04103	207-797-0300	
Environ Laboratories LLC 9725 Girard Ave S *Web:* environlab.com	Minneapolis	MN	55431	952-888-7795	
Environmental Enterprises Inc (EEI) 10163 Cincinnati Dayton Rd *TF:* 800-722-2818 ■ *Web:* www.eeienv.com	Cincinnati	OH	45241	513-772-2818	782-8950
Ettl Engineers & Consultants Inc 1717 E Erwin St *Web:* www.ettlinc.com	Tyler	TX	75702	903-595-4421	
Evans Analytical Group 810 Kifer Rd *Web:* www.eag.com	Sunnyvale	CA	94086	408-530-3500	530-3501
Evena Medical Inc 339 S San Antonio Rd Ste 1C *Web:* www.evenamed.com	Los Altos	CA	94022	650-209-0398	
Everist Genomics Inc 709 W Ellsworth Rd *TF:* 855-383-7478 ■ *Web:* www.everisthealth.com	Ann Arbor	MI	48108	855-383-7478	
Excalibre Engineering 9201 Irvine Blvd *Web:* www.excaliburengineering.com	Irvine	CA	92618	949-454-6603	
Falcon Genomics Inc 2661 Clearview Rd Ste 1 *Web:* www.falcongenomics.com	Allison Park	PA	15101	412-486-1108	
Fenway Community Health Center Inc 1340 Boylston St *Web:* www.fenwayhealth.org	Boston	MA	02215	617-859-1256	
Forensic Fluids Laboratories Inc 225 Parsons St *TF:* 866-492-2517 ■ *Web:* www.forensicfluids.com	Kalamazoo	MI	49007	269-492-7700	
Forensic It 57 E Southcrest Cir *Web:* www.forensicit.us	Edwardsville	IL	62025	314-241-5103	
Froehling & Robertson Inc 3015 Dumbarton Rd *Web:* www.fandr.com	Richmond	VA	23228	804-264-2701	264-1202
Frontage Laboratories LLC 700 Pennsylvania Dr *Web:* www.frontagelab.com	Exton	PA	19341	610-232-0100	
Fruit Growers Laboratory Inc 853 Corporation St *Web:* www.fglinc.com	Santa Paula	CA	93060	805-392-2000	
G & R Labs 2996 scott blvd *Web:* www.grlabs.com	Santa Clara	CA	95054	408-986-0377	
Galbraith Laboratories Inc 2323 Sycamore Dr *Web:* www.galbraith.com	Knoxville	TN	37921	865-546-1335	
Galson Laboratories Inc 6601 Kirkville Rd *Web:* www.galsonlabs.com	East Syracuse	NY	13057	315-432-5227	
Gamma Medica Inc 12 Manor Pkwy Unit 3 *Web:* www.gammamedica.com	Salem	NH	03079	603-952-4441	
GE Healthcare Bio-Sciences Corp 800 Centennial Ave *Web:* www.gelifesciences.com	Piscataway	NJ	08855	732-457-8000	
GenePOC Inc 360 Rue Franquet Porte 3 Technology Park *Web:* www.genepoc-diagnostics.com	Quebec	QC	G1P4N3	418-650-3535	
Geneva Laboratories Inc 1001 Proctor Dr *Web:* www.genevalabs.com	Elkhorn	WI	53121	262-723-5669	
Genmab Inc 902 Carnegie Ctr Ste 301 *Web:* www.genmab.com	Princeton	NJ	08540	609-430-2481	
Glidewell Laboratories Inc 4141 MacArthur Blvd *TF:* 800-854-7256 ■ *Web:* www.glidewelldental.com	Newport Beach	CA	92660	800-854-7256	
Global ID Group 504 N Fourth St *Web:* www.global-id-group.com	Fairfield	IA	52556	641-472-9979	
Global X-Ray & Testing Corp PO Box 1536 *Web:* www.globalxray.com	Morgan City	LA	70381	985-631-2426	
Glytec LLC 665 N Academy St *Web:* www.glytecsystems.com	Greenville	SC	29601	864-370-3297	
Groupe PARIMA Inc 4450 Cousens Rue *Web:* groupeparima.com	Montreal	QC	H4S1X6	514-338-3780	
GVI Medical Devices Corp 1470 Enterprise Pkwy *Web:* www.gvimd.com	Twinsburg	OH	44087	330-963-4083	
H.P. White Laboratory Inc 3114 Scarboro Rd *Web:* www.hpwhite.com	Street	MD	21154	410-838-6550	
H2m Labs Inc 575 Broadhollow Rd *Web:* www.h2mlabs.com	Melville	NY	11747	631-694-3040	
Hawk Mountain Lab Inc 201 W Clay Ave *Web:* hawkmtnlabs.com	Hazle Township	PA	18202	570-455-6011	
Health-Chem Diagnostics LLC 3341 SW 15th St *Web:* www.healthchemdiagnostics.com	Pompano Beach	FL	33069	954-979-3845	
Healthsense Inc 1191 Northland Dr Ste 100 *Web:* www.healthsense.com	Mendota Heights	MN	55120	952-400-7300	
Heron Systems Inc 20945 Great Mills Rd Ste 201 *Web:* www.heronsystems.com	Lexington Park	MD	20653	301-866-0330	
HNP Pharmaceuticals 381 Van Ness Ave Ste 1507 *Web:* www.hnppharmaceuticals.com	Torrance	CA	90501	310-783-7450	
Hoffman Engineering Corp PO Box 4430 *Web:* www.hoffmanengineering.com	Stamford	CT	06907	203-425-8900	425-8910
HORIBA ABX Diagnostics Inc 34 Bunsen Dr *Web:* eurofex.horiba.com	Irvine	CA	92618	949-453-0500	
Huffman Laboratories Inc 4630 Indiana St *Web:* www.huffmanlabs.com	Golden	CO	80403	303-278-4455	
Huron Technologies International Inc 550 Parkside Dr Unit B6 *Web:* www.huron-technologies.com	Waterloo	ON	N2L5V4	519-886-9013	
Hydro-Photon Inc 262 Ellsworth Rd *Web:* www.steripen.com	Blue Hill	ME	04614	207-374-5800	
Hydro-stat Inc 1111 Sw First Way *Web:* www.hydrostat.com	Deerfield Beach	FL	33441	954-428-7677	
Hydrox Laboratories Inc 825 Tollgate Rd Ste B *Web:* www.hydroxlabs.com	Elgin	IL	60123	847-468-9400	
HyGreen Inc 3630 SW 47th Ave Ste 100 *TF:* 877-574-9473 ■ *Web:* www.hygreeninc.com	Gainesville	FL	32608	877-574-9473	
iHealth Lab Inc 719 N Shoreline Blvd *TF:* 855-816-7705 ■ *Web:* www.ihealthlabs.com	Mountain View	CA	94043	855-816-7705	
Ikonisys Inc Five Science Park *Web:* www.ikonisys.com	New Haven	CT	06511	203-776-0791	
Immuno Concepts NA Ltd 9825 Goethe Rd Ste 350 *TF:* 800-251-5115 ■ *Web:* www.immunoconcepts.com	Sacramento	CA	95827	916-363-2649	
Indyne Inc 11800 Sunrise Vly Dr Ste 250 *Web:* www.indyneinc.com	Reston	VA	20191	703-903-6900	903-4997
InformationWEEK Labs 600 Community Dr *Web:* www.informationweek.com	Manhasset	NY	11030	516-562-5000	562-5036
Infoworld Test Ctr 501 Second St Ste 120 *Web:* www.infoworld.com	San Francisco	CA	94107	415-243-0500	978-3120
Inovatia Laboratories LLC 120 E Davis St *Web:* inovatia.com	Fayette	MO	65248	660-248-1911	
Insight Service 20338 Progress Dr *Web:* www.testoil.com	Strongsville	OH	44149	216-251-2510	
Integrated BioTherapeutics Inc 21 Firstfield Rd Ste 100 *Web:* www.integratedbiotherapeutics.com	Gaithersburg	MD	20878	240-454-8934	
InterCorr International Inc 14503 Bammel N Houston Ste 300 *Web:* www.intercorr.com	Houston	TX	77014	281-444-2282	
International Down & Feather Testing Laboratory 1455 S 1100 E *Web:* www.idfl.com	Salt Lake City	UT	84105	801-467-7611	467-7711
Intertek Automotive Research 5404 Bandera Rd *Web:* intertek.com/petroleum	San Antonio	TX	78238	210-684-2310	684-6074
Introtek International LP 150 Executive Dr *Web:* www.introtek.com	Edgewood	NY	11717	631-242-5425	
Iris Diagnostics Inc 9172 Eton Ave *Web:* www.irisdiagnostics.com	Chatsworth	CA	91311	818-527-7000	
iScreen Vision Inc 110 Timber Creek Dr Ste 2 *Web:* www.iscreenvision.com	Cordova	TN	38018	901-201-6132	
Isotech Laboratories Inc 1308 Parkland Ct *Web:* www.isotechlabs.com	Champaign	IL	61821	217-398-3490	
ITEL Laboratories Inc 6745 Philips Industrial Blvd *Web:* www.itelinc.com	Jacksonville	FL	32256	904-363-0196	
IVDiagnostics Inc 880 Eastport Centre Dr *Web:* www.ivdiagnostics.com	Valparaiso	IN	46383	219-840-0007	
JM Test Systems Inc 7323 Tom Dr *TF:* 800-353-3411 ■ *Web:* www.jmtest.com	Baton Rouge	LA	70806	225-925-2029	
Kar Laboratories Inc 4425 Manchester Rd *Web:* karlabs.com	Kalamazoo	MI	49001	269-381-9666	
Kett Engineering Corp 15500 Erwin St Ste 1029 *TF:* 877-372-6799 ■ *Web:* www.ketteng.com	Van Nuys	CA	91411	818-908-5388	908-5323
Keweenaw Research Ctr Michigan Technological University 1400 Townsend Dr *Web:* www.mtukrc.org	Houghton	MI	49931	906-487-2750	487-2202
Koehler Instrument Company Inc 1595 Sycamore Ave *Web:* www.koehlerinstrument.com	Bohemia	NY	11716	631-589-3800	
L&g Engineering Laboratory LLC 2100 W Expressway 83 *Web:* www.lgengineers.com	Mercedes	TX	78570	956-565-9813	
Labstat International ULC 262 Manitou Dr *Web:* www.labstat.com	Kitchener	ON	N2C1L3	519-748-5409	
Laclede Inc 2103 E University Dr *Web:* www.laclede.com	Rancho Dominguez	CA	90220	310-605-4280	
Lambda Technologies 3929 Virginia Ave *Web:* www.lambdatechs.com	Cincinnati	OH	45227	513-561-0883	
Lancaster Laboratories Inc 2425 New Holland Pk PO Box 12425 *Web:* www.lancasterlabs.com	Lancaster	PA	17605	717-656-2300	656-2681
LaserGen Inc 8052 El Rio St *Web:* www.lasergen.com	Houston	TX	77054	713-747-3380	
Laucks Testing Laboratories Inc 940 S Harney St *Web:* pacelabs.com	Seattle	WA	98108	206-767-5060	767-5063
Ledoux & Company Inc 359 Alfred Ave *Web:* www.ledoux.com	Teaneck	NJ	07666	201-837-7160	837-1235
Leica Microsystems Inc 1700 Leider Ln *Web:* support.leica-microsystems.com	Buffalo Grove	IL	60089	847-405-0123	
M&P Lab Inc, The 2210 Technology Dr *Web:* www.mandplabs.com	Schenectady	NY	12301	518-382-0082	
MagiQ Technologies Inc 11 Ward St *Web:* www.magiqtech.com	Somerville	MA	02143	617-661-8300	
Magna Chek Inc 32701 Edward Ave *TF:* 800-582-8947 ■ *Web:* www.magnachek.com	Madison Heights	MI	48071	248-597-0089	597-0440
Magnetic Inspection Laboratory Inc 1401 Greenleaf Ave *Web:* www.milinc.com	Elk Grove Village	IL	60007	847-437-4488	437-4538
Matech Advanced Materials Inc 31304 Via Colinas Ste 102 *Web:* www.matech.us	Westlake Village	CA	91362	818-991-8500	

Company	City	State	Zip	Phone	Fax
Materials Engineer & Testing 125 Valley Ct *Web:* www.meandt.com	Oak Ridge	TN	37830	865-482-7762	
Maxwell Sensors Inc 10020 Pioneer Blvd Ste 103 *Web:* www.maxwellsensors.com	Santa Fe Springs	CA	90670	562-801-2088	
Mayer Laboratories Inc 1950 Addison St Ste 101 *TF:* 800-426-3633 ■ *Web:* www.mayerlabs.com	Berkeley	CA	94704	510-229-5300	
Mccloy Engineering LLC 3701 Port Union Rd *Web:* www.accutektesting.com	Fairfield	OH	45014	513-984-4112	
Medpace Medical Device Inc 3787 95th Ave NE Ste 100 *Web:* www.medpace.com	Minneapolis	MN	55014	612-234-8500	
Metcut Research Inc 3980 Rosslyn Dr *TF:* 800-966-2888 ■ *Web:* www.metcut.com	Cincinnati	OH	45209	513-271-5100	271-9511
Michelson Laboratories Inc 6280 Chalet Dr *Web:* michelsonlab.com	Commerce	CA	90040	562-928-0553	
Micro Precision Calibration Inc 22835 Industrial Pl *Web:* www.microprecision.com	Grass Valley	CA	95949	530-268-1860	
Micro-Clean Inc 177 N Commerce Way *Web:* www.microcln.com	Bethlehem	PA	18017	610-867-5302	
Microbac Laboratories Inc 101 Bellevue Rd Ste 301 *Web:* microbac.com	Pittsburgh	PA	15229	412-459-1060	
Microbial Insights Inc 2340 Stock Creek Blvd *Web:* www.microbe.com	Rockford	TN	37853	865-573-8188	
MicroFluidic Systems 1252 Quarry Ln Ste B	Pleasanton	CA	94566	510-354-0400	
Micronics Inc 8463 154th Ave NE Bldg G *Web:* micronics.net	Redmond	WA	98052	425-895-9197	
Midwest Institute For Clinical Research Inc 8803 N Meridian St *Web:* micr.com	Indianapolis	IN	46260	317-705-7050	
Midwest Laboratories Inc 13611 B St *Web:* www.midwestlabs.com	Omaha	NE	68144	402-334-7770	
Miltenyi Biotec Inc 2303 Lindbergh St *Web:* www.miltenyibiotec.com	Auburn	CA	95602	530-888-8871	
Mineral Labs Inc 309 Pkwy Dr *Web:* minerallabs.com	Salyersville	KY	41465	606-349-6145	
Mira Vista Diagnostics LLC 4444 Decatur Blvd Ste 300 *Web:* www.miravistalabs.com	Indianapolis	IN	46241	317-856-2681	
Modern Industries Inc 613 W 11th St *Web:* modernind.com	Erie	PA	16501	814-455-8061	453-4382
Morphotek Inc 210 Welsh Pool Rd *Web:* www.morphotek.com	Exton	PA	19341	610-423-6100	
Mountain Research LLC 825 25th St *Web:* www.mountainresearch.com	Altoona	PA	16601	814-949-2034	
MSE Technology Applications Inc 200 Technology Way *Web:* www.mse-ta.com	Butte	MT	59701	406-494-7100	494-7230
Nanolab Technologies Inc 1708 McCarthy Blvd *Web:* www.nanolabtechnologies.com	Milpitas	CA	95035	408-433-3320	
Nanotechnology Research & Education Ctr University of S Florida College of Engineering 4202 E Fowler Ave ENB 118 *Web:* www.nrec.usf.edu	Tampa	FL	33620	813-974-3780	974-3610
National Air & Radiation Environmental Laboratory (NAREL) US Environmental Protection Agency 540 S Morris Ave *Web:* www.epa.gov/narel	Montgomery	AL	36115	334-270-3400	270-3454
National Technical Systems Inc 24007 Ventura Blvd Ste 200 *NASDAQ: NTSC* ■ *TF:* 800-879-9225 ■ *Web:* www.nts.com	Calabasas	CA	91302	818-591-0776	591-0899
National X-Ray Corp 595 Old Norcross Rd *Web:* www.nationalx-ray.com	Lawrenceville	GA	30045	770-682-3090	
NDS Surgical Imaging LLC 5750 Hellyer Ave *Web:* www.ndssi.com	San Jose	CA	95138	408-776-0085	
Neotropix Inc 351 Phoenixville Pk *Web:* www.neotropix.com	Malvern	PA	19355	610-296-8660	
Neuisys LLC 1500 Pinecroft Rd Ste 212 *TF:* 877-299-9052 ■ *Web:* www.neuisys.com	Greensboro	NC	27407	877-299-9052	
Neuronetrix Inc 1044 E Chestnut St *Web:* www.neuronetrix.com	Louisville	KY	40204	502-561-9040	
NeuroVigil Inc 7606 Fay Ave *Web:* www.neurovigil.com	La Jolla	CA	92037	858-454-5134	
Newport Partners LLC 3760 Tanglewood Ln *Web:* newportpartnersllc.com	Davidsonville	MD	21035	301-889-0017	
Next Breath LLC 1450 S Rolling Rd *Web:* www.nextbreath.net	Baltimore	MD	21227	410-455-5904	
Nikkiso Cryo Inc 4661 Eaker St *Web:* nikkisocryo.com	North Las Vegas	NV	89081	702-643-4900	
Norchem Drug Testing Laboratory 1760 E Route 66 *Web:* www.norchemlab.com	Flagstaff	AZ	86004	928-526-1011	
Northwest Aerospace Technologies Inc 2210 Hewitt Ave Ste 300	Everett	WA	98201	425-257-2044	
Northwest Labs of Seattle 241 S Holden St *Web:* www.nwlabs1896.com	Seattle	WA	98108	206-763-6252	763-3949
Norwich Clinical Research Associates Ltd 74 E Main St *Web:* www.ncra.com	Norwich	NY	13815	607-334-5850	
Norwich Pharma Services 6826 State Hwy 12 *Web:* www.norwichpharma.com	Norwich	NY	13815	607-335-3000	
Nova Biologicals Inc 1775 N Loop 336 Ste 4 *Web:* www.novatx.com	Conroe	TX	77301	936-756-5333	
NOVX Systems Inc 9133 Leslie St Ste 110 *Web:* www.novxsystems.com	Richmond Hill	ON	L4B4N1	905-474-5051	
Nsl Analytical 4450 Cranwood Pkwy *Web:* www.nslanalytical.com	Cleveland	OH	44128	216-447-1550	
NSTL Inc 670 Sentry Pkwy *Web:* www.nstl.com	Blue Bell	PA	19422	610-832-8400	
NU Laboratories Inc 312 Old Allerton Rd *Web:* www.nulabs.com	Annandale	NJ	08801	908-713-9300	713-9001
Octapharma Plasma Inc 10644 Westlake Dr *Web:* octapharmaplasma.com	Charlotte	NC	28273	704-654-4600	
Ok Kosher Certification 391 Troy Ave *Web:* www.ok.org	Brooklyn	NY	11213	718-756-7500	
Oncoscope Inc 324 Blackwell St Ste 1120 *Web:* www.oncoscope.com	Durham	NC	27701	919-251-8030	
Online Labs Inc 5870 W Jefferson Blvd Ste A *Web:* www.onlinelabs.com	Los Angeles	CA	90016	310-815-8855	
OSDI Inc 100 Acorn Park Dr *Web:* www.oncogene.com	Cambridge	MA	02140	617-492-3900	
Parabase Genomics Inc 100 Morrissey Blvd University of Massachusetts Venture Development Ctr Wheatley Hall Third Fl *Web:* www.parabasegenomics.com	Boston	MA	02125	857-288-0838	
Passport Systems Inc 70 Treble Cove Rd First Fl *Web:* www.passportsystems.com	Billerica	MA	01862	978-263-9900	
PCAS-Nanosyn LLC 3331 - B Industrial Dr *Web:* www.pcas-nanosyn.com	Santa Rosa	CA	95403	707-526-4526	
Penniman & Browne Inc 6252 Falls Rd PO Box 65309 *Web:* www.fandr.com	Baltimore	MD	21209	410-825-4131	321-7384
Perritt Laboratories Inc 145 S Main St *Web:* www.childsafepackagingroup.com	Hightstown	NJ	08520	609-443-4848	
Phenova Inc 6390 Joyce Dr Ste 100 *Web:* www.phenova.com	Golden	CO	80403	303-940-0033	
Phoenix Environmental Laboratories Inc 587 Middle Tpke E *Web:* www.phoenixlabs.com	Manchester	CT	06040	860-645-3513	
Pikes Peak Test Labs Inc 4750 Edison Ave *Web:* www.pptli.com	Colorado Springs	CO	80915	719-596-0802	
Pipette Calibration Services Inc 81 Deborah Rd *Web:* www.pipettecal.com	Newton	MA	02459	617-964-0039	
PMRS Inc 202 Precision Rd *Web:* www.pmrsinc.com	Horsham	PA	19044	267-960-3300	
PPD Development Inc 929 N Front St *Web:* www.ppdi.com	Wilmington	NC	28401	910-251-0081	762-5820
PreventionGenetics LLC 3700 Downwind Dr *Web:* www.preventiongenetics.com	Marshfield	WI	54449	715-387-0484	
Product Evaluation Systems Inc 637 Donohoe Rd *Web:* www.productevaluationsystems.com	Latrobe	PA	15650	724-834-8848	
Provista Diagnostics Inc 17301 N Perimeter Dr *Web:* www.provistadx.com	Scottsdale	AZ	85255	602-224-5500	
PTS Laboratories 8100 Secura Way *Web:* www.ptslabs.com	Santa Fe Springs	CA	90670	562-907-3607	
Quadrants Scientific Inc 10840 Thornmint Rd Ste 110 *Web:* www.quadscience.com	San Diego	CA	92127	858-618-4708	
Qualtech Laboratories Inc 104 Green Grove Rd *Web:* www.qualtechlabsinc.com	Ocean	NJ	07712	732-918-0207	
Qualtest Inc 5325 Old Winter Garden Rd *Web:* www.qualtest.com	Orlando	FL	32811	407-293-5844	
Quanta Laboratories 3199 De La Cruz Blvd *Web:* www.quantalabs.com	Santa Clara	CA	95054	408-988-0770	
Quantum Laboratories Inc 28221 Beck Rd Ste A-11 *Web:* www.quantumlaboratories.com	Wixom	MI	48393	248-348-8378	
Radiometrics Midwest Corp 12 E Devonwood Ave *Web:* www.radiomet.com	Romeoville	IL	60446	815-293-0772	293-0820
Redwood Toxicology Laboratory Inc 3650 W Wind Blvd *Web:* www.redwoodtoxicology.com	Santa Rosa	CA	95403	707-577-7959	
Resuscitation International LLC 17797 N Perimeter Dr Ste 105 *Web:* resusintl.com	Scottsdale	AZ	85255	480-240-9495	
Retlif Inc Testing Laboratories 795 Marconi Ave *Web:* www.retlif.com	Ronkonkoma	NY	11779	631-737-1500	737-1497
RMC Research Corp 1000 Market St Bldg 2 *Web:* www.rmcresearchcorporation.com	Portsmouth	NH	03801	603-422-8888	
Robin Hood Foundation 826 Broadway Ninth Fl *Web:* www.robinhood.org	New York	NY	10003	212-227-6601	
Rothe Development Inc 4614 Sinclair Rd *Web:* www.rothe.com	San Antonio	TX	78222	210-648-3131	648-4091
Schneider Laboratories Inc 2512 W Cary St *Web:* slabinc.com	Richmond	VA	23220	804-353-6778	
SDK Laboratories 1000 Corey Rd *Web:* www.sdklabs.com	Hutchinson	KS	67501	620-665-5661	
Selerity Technologies Inc 1950 South 900 West Ste S3 *Web:* www.selerity.com	Salt Lake City	UT	84104	801-978-2295	
Sentinel Integrity Solutions Inc 6606 Miller Rd 2 *Web:* sentinelintegrity.com	Houston	TX	77049	281-457-2225	
Sentry Health Monitors 4032 Blackburn Ln *Web:* www.lifeclinic.com	Burtonsville	MD	20866	301-476-9888	
SGS Canada Inc 6490 Vipond Dr *TF General:* 877-887-4163 ■ *Web:* www.sgs.ca	Mississauga	ON	L5T1W8	905-364-3757	364-0344
SGS US Testing Company Inc 291 Fairfield Ave *Web:* www.sgsgroup.us.com	Fairfield	NJ	07004	973-575-5252	575-7175

	City	State	ZIP	Phone	Fax
Sherry Laboratories Inc 9301 Innovation Dr Ste 103 PO Box 569 *Web:* www.sherrylabs.com	Daleville	IN	47334	765-378-4101	
Sigma Test Labs 1480 W 178th St *Web:* www.sigmatestlabs.com	Gardena	CA	90248	310-324-9427	532-6216
Simco Electronics 1178 Bordeaux Dr *TF:* 866-299-6029 ■ *Web:* www.simco.com	Sunnyvale	CA	94089	408-734-9750	734-9754
Sky Cylinder Testing 2220 Lexington Rd *Web:* www.skycylinder.com	Evansville	IN	47720	812-423-1759	
Smithers Group Inc, The 425 W Market St *Web:* smithers.com	Akron	OH	44303	330-762-7441	
Sonoscan Inc 2149 Pratt Blvd *Web:* www.sonoscan.com	Elk Grove Village	IL	60007	847-437-6400	437-1550
Sound-Eklin Inc 6359 Paseo Del Lago *Web:* www.soundeklin.com	Carlsbad	CA	92011	760-918-9626	
Southern Petroleum Lab Inc 8850 Interchange Dr **Fax Area Code:* 225 ■ *TF:* 877-775-5227 ■ *Web:* www.spl-inc.com	Houston	TX	77054	713-660-0901	219-3309*
Spectrum Analytical Inc 830 Silver St *TF:* 800-789-9115 ■ *Web:* www.spectrum-analytical.com	Agawam	MA	01001	413-789-9018	789-4076
Speedie & Assoc Inc 3331 E Wood St *TF:* 800-628-6221 ■ *Web:* www.speedie.net	Phoenix	AZ	85040	602-997-6391	943-5508
SRS Medical Systems Inc 76 Treble Cove Rd Bldg 3 *Web:* www.srsmedical.com	North Billerica	MA	01862	978-663-2800	
St Louis Testing Laboratories 2810 Clark Ave *Web:* www.labinc.com	Saint Louis	MO	63103	314-531-8080	531-8085
Standard Laboratories Inc 147 11th Ave Ste 100 *Web:* standardlabs.com	South Charleston	WV	25303	304-744-6800	
Stimwave Technologies Inc 420 Lincoln Rd Ste 365 *Web:* stimwave.com	Miami Beach	FL	33139	786-565-3342	
Summers Laboratories Inc 103 Gp Clement Dr *Web:* www.sumlab.com	Collegeville	PA	19426	610-454-1471	
Sun Ten Laboratories Inc 9250 Jeronimo Rd *Web:* www.sunten.com	Irvine	CA	92618	949-587-0509	
Syagen Technology Inc 1411 Warner Ave *TF:* 877-258-8250 ■ *Web:* www.syagen.com	Tustin	CA	92780	714-258-4400	
Synergy Environmental Lab Inc 1990 Prospect Ct *Web:* synergy-lab.net	Appleton	WI	54914	920-830-2455	
TecMed Inc 1603 Capitol Ave Ste 209 *Web:* tecmed.com	Cheyenne	WY	82001	307-509-9653	
Tension Member Technology 5721 Research Dr *Web:* www.tmtlabs.com	Huntington Beach	CA	92649	714-898-5641	
Terra Tek Inc 5599 San Felipe 17th Fl *Web:* www.slb.com	Houston	TX	77056	713-375-3535	
Test Devices Inc 571 Main St *Web:* www.testdevices.com	Hudson	MA	01749	978-562-6017	
TestAmerica Laboratories Inc 4625 E Cotton Ctr Blvd Ste 189 *TF:* 866-785-5227 ■ *Web:* www.testamericainc.com	Phoenix	AZ	85040	602-437-3340	454-9303
Testcountry 6310 Nancy Ridge Dr Ste 103 *Web:* www.testcountry.com	San Diego	CA	92121	858-784-6904	
Therapeutic Monitoring Services LLC 134 LaSalle St Ste 4 *Web:* www.tmsbioscience.com	New Orleans	LA	70112	504-208-9696	
Thornton Laboratories Testing & Inspection Services 1145 E Cass St *Web:* www.thorntonlab.com	Tampa	FL	33602	813-223-9702	223-9332
Thought Technology Ltd 2180 Belgrave Ave *Web:* www.thoughttechnology.com	Montreal	QC	H4A2L8	514-489-8251	
Tourney Consulting Group LLC 3401 Midlink Dr *Web:* tourneyconsulting.com	Kalamazoo	MI	49048	269-384-9980	
Toxikon Corp 15 Wiggins Ave *TF:* 800-458-4141 ■ *Web:* www.toxikon.com	Bedford	MA	01730	781-275-3330	271-1138
Transportation Research Ctr Inc (TRC Inc) 10820 State Rt 347 PO Box B-67 *TF:* 800-837-7872 ■ *Web:* www.trcpg.com	East Liberty	OH	43319	937-666-2011	666-5066
Transportation Technology Ctr Inc 55500 DOT Rd PO Box 11130 *Web:* www.aar.com	Pueblo	CO	81001	719-584-0750	584-0711
TransTech Pharma Inc 4170 Mendenhall Oaks Pkwy *Web:* www.asynt.com	High Point	NC	27265	336-841-0300	
TriLink BioTechnologies Inc 9955 Mesa Rim Rd *TF:* 800-863-6801 ■ *Web:* www.trilinkbiotech.com	San Diego	CA	92121	858-546-0004	
Triumf 4004 Wesbrook Mall *Web:* www.triumf.ca	Vancouver	BC	V6T2A3	604-222-1047	
Truesdail Laboratories Inc 14201 Franklin Ave *Web:* www.truesdail.com	Tustin	CA	92780	714-730-6239	730-6462
Tulsa Welding School Inc 2545 E 11th St *Web:* www.weldingschool.com	Tulsa	OK	74104	918-587-6789	
Twin City Testing 662 Cromwell Ave *TF:* 888-645-8378 ■ *Web:* www.element.com	Saint Paul	MN	55114	651-645-3601	659-7348
Twining Laboratories of Southern California Inc 3310 Airport Way *Web:* twininginc.com/	Long Beach	CA	90806	562-426-3355	426-6424
Tyzx Inc 3715 Haven Ave Ste 110 *Web:* www.tyzx.com	Menlo Park	CA	94025	650-282-4500	
UL CCS 47173 Benicia St *Web:* www.ccsemc.com	Fremont	CA	94538	510-771-1000	
UL LLC 10 Water St *TF:* 800-903-5660 ■ *Web:* www.ul.com	Enfield	CT	06082	860-749-8371	749-8234
US Army Yuma Proving Ground 301 C St *Web:* www.yuma.army.mil	Yuma	AZ	85365	928-328-2163	328-6249
V t e C Laboratories Inc 212 Manida St *Web:* www.vteclabs.com	Bronx	NY	10474	718-542-8248	
Valley Lea Laboratories 4609 Grape Rd Ste D-4 	Mishawaka	IN	46545	574-272-8484	272-8485
Verichem Laboratories Inc 90 Narragansett Ave *TF:* 800-552-5859 ■ *Web:* www.verichemlabs.com	Providence	RI	02907	401-461-0180	
VeroScience LLC 1334 Main Rd *Web:* www.veroscience.com	Tiverton	RI	02878	401-816-0525	
VHG Labs Inc 276 Abby Rd *Web:* www.vhglabs.com	Manchester	NH	03103	603-622-7660	
Vibranalysis Inc 220 Plz Western Auto *Web:* www.vibranalysispr.com	Trujillo Alto	PR	00976	787-283-7500	
Vibrant Corp 8330A Washington Pl NE *Web:* www.vibrantndt.com	Albuquerque	NM	87113	505-314-1488	
ViOptix Inc 47224 Mission Falls Ct *Web:* www.vioptix.com	Fremont	CA	94539	510-226-5860	
Vista Analytical Laboratory Inc 1104 Windfield Way *Web:* vista-analytical.com	El Dorado Hills	CA	95762	916-673-1520	673-0106
VJ Technologies Inc 89 Carlough Rd *TF:* 800-858-9729 ■ *Web:* www.vjt.com	Bohemia	NY	11716	631-589-8800	
Wadsworth Ctr *Biggs Laboratory New York Dept of Health* Empire State Plz PO Box 509 *Web:* www.wadsworth.org	Albany	NY	12201	518-474-2160	
Wallops Flight Facility Office of Public Affairs *Web:* www.nasa.gov	Wallops Island	VA	23337	757-824-1579	824-1971
Water Spigot Inc, The 5806 E Hwy 22 *Web:* thewaterspigot.com	Panama City	FL	32404	850-871-1900	
WaveTec Vision Systems Inc 66 Argonaut Ste 170 *Web:* www.wavetecvision.com	Aliso Viejo	CA	92656	949-273-5970	
Weecycle Environmental Consulting Inc 5375 Western Ave Ste B *Web:* www.www.weecycle-env.com	Boulder	CO	80301	303-413-0452	
Westmoreland Mechanical Testing & Research Inc PO Box 388 *Web:* www.wmtr.com	Youngstown	PA	15696	724-537-3131	537-3151
WIL Research Laboratories Inc 1407 George Rd *Web:* www.wilresearch.com	Ashland	OH	44805	419-289-8700	289-3650
WinMed Inc Dundee Park Bldg 17 Door 6 *Web:* www.winmed-inc.com	Andover	MA	01810	978-590-4246	
Wirebenders, The 2075 Lincoln Ave Ste A *Web:* www.thewirebenders.com	San Jose	CA	95125	408-265-5576	
X-Ray Industries Inc 1961 Thunderbird *Web:* www.xritesting.com	Troy	MI	48084	248-362-2242	
XBiotech USA Inc 8201 E Riverside Dr Bldg 4 Ste 100 *Web:* www.xbiotech.com	Austin	TX	78744	512-386-2900	
Zyomyx Inc 6519 Dumbarton Cir	Fremont	CA	94555	510-265-8000	

747 TEXTILE MACHINERY

	City	State	ZIP	Phone	Fax
AB Carter Inc 4801 York Hwy *Web:* www.abcarter.com	Gastonia	NC	28052	704-865-1201	
Advanced Innovative Technologies LLC 530 Wilbanks Dr *Web:* www.aitequipment.com	Ball Ground	GA	30107	770-479-1900	479-4179
Andritz Kusters Inc 201 Zima Pk Dr *Web:* www.andritz.com	Spartanburg	SC	29301	864-587-4848	576-2306
Belmont Textile Machinery Co 1212 W Catawba St PO Box 568 *Web:* www.btmc.com	Mount Holly	NC	28120	704-827-5836	827-8551
Bowman Hollis Manufacturing Inc 2925 Old Steele Creek Rd *TF:* 888-269-2358 ■ *Web:* www.bowmanhollis.com	Charlotte	NC	28208	704-374-1500	333-5520
Cobble Tufting Machines 1731 Kimberly Pk Dr *Web:* www.cobbleusa.com	Dalton	GA	30720	706-278-1857	
Custom Industries Inc 215 Aloe Rd *Web:* www.customindustries.com	Greensboro	NC	27409	336-299-2885	294-2472
Eastman Machine Co 779 Washington St *TF:* 800-872-5571 ■ *Web:* www.eastmancuts.com	Buffalo	NY	14203	716-856-2200	856-1140
Entec Composite Machines Inc 300 West 2975 South *Web:* www.entec.com	Salt Lake City	UT	84115	801-486-8721	484-4363
Gaston County Dyeing Machine Co PO Box 308 *Web:* www.gaston-county.com	Stanley	NC	28164	704-822-5000	822-0753
Gerber Technology Inc 24 Industrial Pk Rd W *TF:* 800-826-3243 ■ *Web:* www.gerbertechnology.com	Tolland	CT	06084	860-871-8082	
GTP Inc 1801 Rutherford Rd *Web:* www.globaltextilepartner.com	Greenville	SC	29609	864-288-5475	
Handy Kenlin Group, The 29 E Hintz Rd *Web:* www.handykenlin.com	Wheeling	IL	60090	847-459-0900	459-0902
HH Arnold Co Inc 529 Liberty St *TF:* 866-868-9603 ■ *Web:* www.hharnold.com	Rockland	MA	02370	781-878-0346	878-7944
Hix Corp 1201 E 27th Terr *TF:* 800-835-0606 ■ *Web:* www.hixcorp.com	Pittsburg	KS	66762	620-231-8568	231-1598
Ioline Corp 14140 NE 200th St *TF:* 800-598-0029 ■ *Web:* www.ioline.com	Woodinville	WA	98072	425-398-8282	398-8383
Lawson-Hemphill Inc 1658 G A R Hwy Ste 6 *Web:* www.lawsonhemphill.com	Swansea	MA	02777	508-679-5364	679-5396
Lummus Corp 225 Bourne Blvd PO Box 929 *TF:* 800-458-6687 ■ *Web:* www.lummus.com	Savannah	GA	31408	912-447-9000	447-9250
Mayer Industries Inc 3777 Industrial Blvd *Web:* mayerind.com	Orangeburg	SC	29118	803-536-3500	536-2545
MB Industries Inc 9205 Rosman Hwy *Web:* www.m-bindustries.com	Rosman	NC	28772	828-862-4201	862-4297

Phone | Fax

McCoy-Ellison Inc 1101 Curtis St PO Box 967 Monroe NC 28111 704-289-5413 283-0480
TF: 800-811-5348 ■ *Web:* www.mccoymachinery.com

Morrison Berkshire Inc 865 S Church St North Adams MA 01247 413-663-6501
Web: www.morrisonberkshire.com

Petty Machine Company Inc 2403 Forbes Rd Gastonia NC 28056 704-864-3254 861-1937

Rando Machine Corp 1071 Rt 31 PO Box 614 Macedon NY 14502 315-986-2761 986-7943
Web: www.randomachine.com

Standex International Corp Mullen Testers Div
939 Chicopee St Chicopee MA 01013 413-536-1311 536-1367
Web: www.mullentesters.com

Stork Prints America Inc 3201 Rotary Dr Charlotte NC 28269 704-598-7171
Web: www.spgprints.com

Thermopatch Corp 2204 Erie Blvd E Syracuse NY 13224 315-446-8110 445-8046
TF: 800-252-6555 ■ *Web:* www.thermopatch.biz/us/en

Tompkins Bros Company Inc 623 Oneida St Syracuse NY 13202 315-422-8763 422-8762
Web: www.tompkinsusa.com

TrimMaster 4860 N Fifth St Hwy Temple PA 19560 610-921-0203 929-8833
TF: 800-356-4237 ■ *Web:* www.trimmaster.com

Tubular Textile Machinery
113 Woodside Dr PO Box 2097 Lexington NC 27292 336-956-6444 956-1795
TF: 800-531-3715 ■ *Web:* www.navisglobal.com

Tuftco Corp 2318 S Holtzclaw Ave Chattanooga TN 37408 423-698-8601 698-0842
TF: 800-288-3826 ■ *Web:* www.tuftco.com

Tuftco Finishing Systems Inc
100 W Industrial Blvd Dalton GA 30720 706-277-1110 277-4334
TF: 800-288-3826 ■ *Web:* www.tuftco.com

Wardwell Braiding Machine Co
1211 High St Central Falls RI 02863 401-724-8800 723-2690
Web: www.wardwell.com

West Point Industries
2021 Stateline Rd PO Box 589 West Point GA 31833 706-643-2101 643-2100
Web: www.westpoint.com

Whirlaway Corp 720 Shiloh Ave Wellington OH 44090 440-647-4711 647-9384
Web: www.whirlawaycorporation.com

748 TEXTILE MILLS

748-1 Broadwoven Fabric Mills

Phone | Fax

Alice Mfg Company Inc 208 E First Ave Easley SC 29640 864-859-6323 859-6328
Web: www.alicemfgco.com

American Cotton Growers Textile Div (ACG)
PO Box 2827 PO Box 430 Lubbock TX 79408 806-763-8011 762-7400
TF: 800-333-8011 ■ *Web:* pcca.com/services/denim/

American Fiber & Finishing Inc PO Box 2488 Albemarle NC 28001 704-983-6102 983-1850
Web: www.affinc.com

American Silk Mills Corp 75 Stark St Plains PA 18705 570-822-7147 829-7044
Web: www.americansilk.com

Central Textiles Inc 237 Mill Ave Central SC 29630 864-639-2491 639-4513
Web: ctextiles.com

Circa 1801 One Jacquard Dr Connelly Springs NC 28612 828-397-7003

Cone Denim LLC 804 Green Valley Rd Ste 300 Greensboro NC 27408 336-379-6220 379-6287
TF: 800-763-0123 ■ *Web:* conedenim.com

Copland Fabrics Inc 1714 Carolina Mill Rd Burlington NC 27217 336-226-0272 226-6452
Web: www.coplandfabrics.com

Covington Industries Inc
470 Seventh Ave Ste 900 New York NY 10018 212-689-2200
Web: covingtonfabric.com

Culp Inc 1823 Eastchester Dr High Point NC 27265 336-889-5161
NYSE: CFI ■ *Web:* www.culpinc.com

DeRoyal Textiles 141 E York St PO Box 400 Camden SC 29020 803-432-2403 424-5112
TF: 800-845-1062 ■ *Web:* www.deroyal.com

Dicey Fabrics Inc 430 Neisler St Shelby NC 28152 704-487-6324

Faribault Woolen MillCo 1500 NW Second Ave Faribault MN 55021 507-412-5510
Web: faribaultmill.com

Fortune Fabrics Inc
Wyoming Weavers 315 Simpson St Swoyersville PA 18704 570-288-3667 283-2124
Web: www.wyomingweavers.com

Garnet Hill Inc 231 Main St Franconia NH 03580 603-823-5545 842-9696*
**Fax Area Code:* 888 ■ *TF:* 800-870-3513 ■ *Web:* www.garnethill.com

Glen Raven Inc 232 Glen Raven Rd Glen Raven NC 27217 336-227-6211 226-8133
TF: 800-675-0032 ■ *Web:* www.glenraven.com

Greenwood Mills Inc 300 Morgan Ave Greenwood SC 29646 864-227-2121
Web: www.greenwoodmills.com

Hamrick Mills Inc 515 W Buford St PO Box 48 Gaffney SC 29341 864-489-4731
TF: 800-600-4305 ■ *Web:* www.hamrickmills.com

Henry Glass & Co 49 W 37th St New York NY 10018 917-229-1080 532-3525*
**Fax Area Code:* 212 ■ *TF:* 800-294-9495 ■ *Web:* www.henryglassfabrics.com

Inman Mills 300 Pk Rd PO Box 207 Inman SC 29349 864-472-2121 472-0261
Web: www.inmanmills.com

JB Martin Co 645 Fifth Ave Ste 400 New York NY 10022 212-421-2020 421-1460
TF: 800-223-0525 ■ *Web:* www.jbmartin.com

Juniata Fabrics Inc 1301 Broadway Altoona PA 16601 814-944-9381 944-1938

Keystone Weaving Mills Inc
1349 Cumberland St Lebanon PA 17042 717-272-4665 272-4840

KM Fabrics Inc 2 Waco St Greenville SC 29611 864-295-2550 295-3356
TF: 800-873-7326

Kuraray America Inc
2625 Bay Area Blvd Ste 600 Houston TX 77058 800-423-9762
TF: 800-423-9762 ■ *Web:* www.kuraray.us.com

Lantal Textiles Inc
1300 Langenthal Dr PO Box 965 Rural Hall NC 27045 336-969-9551
TF: 800-334-3309 ■ *Web:* www.lantal.com

Milliken & Co 920 Milliken Rd Spartanburg SC 29303 864-503-2020 503-2100*
**Fax:* Hum Res ■ *Web:* www.milliken.com

Mount Vernon Mills Inc
503 S Main St PO Box 100 Mauldin SC 29662 864-688-7100 688-7215
TF: 800-845-8857 ■ *Web:* www.mvmills.com

Phone | Fax

Polymer Group Inc 9335 Harris Corners Pkwy Charlotte NC 28269 704-697-5100 697-5116
Web: www.polymergroupinc.com

Precision Fabrics Group Inc
301 N Elm St Ste 600 Greensboro NC 27401 336-510-8000 510-8004
TF: 800-284-8001 ■ *Web:* www.precisionfabrics.com

Raxon Fabrics 261 Fifth Ave New York NY 10016 212-532-6816 481-9361
Web: www.raxon.com

Scalamandre Silks Inc 350 Wireless Blvd Hauppauge NY 11788 631-467-8800 467-9448
TF: 800-932-4361 ■ *Web:* scalamandre.com

Stonecutter Mills Corp 230 Spindale St Spindale NC 28160 828-286-2341 287-7280
OTC: STCMA ■ *Web:* www.stonecuttermills.com

Trelleborg Coated Systems US Inc
790 Reeves St Spartanburg SC 29301 800-344-0714 595-2273*
**Fax Area Code:* 864 ■ *TF:* 800-344-0714 ■ *Web:* www.trelleborg.com

Tweave LLC 138 Barrows St PO Box AV Norton MA 02766 508-285-6701 285-2904
Web: www.gehring-tricot.com

Valdese Weavers LLC 1000 Perkins Rd SE Valdese NC 28690 828-874-2181 874-3920
Web: www.valdeseweavers.com

Vectorply Corp 3500 Lakewood Dr Phenix City AL 36867 334-291-7704 291-7743
TF: 800-577-4521 ■ *Web:* www.vectorply.com

Warm Co 5529 186th Pl SW Lynnwood WA 98037 425-248-2424 248-2422
TF: 800-234-9276 ■ *Web:* www.warmcompany.com

WestPoint Home Inc 28 E 28th St Ste 2 New York NY 10016 212-930-2000
Web: martex.com

748-2 Coated Fabric

Phone | Fax

Adell Plastics Inc 4530 Annapolis Rd Baltimore MD 21227 410-789-7780 789-2804
TF: 800-638-5218 ■ *Web:* www.adellplas.com

Alpha Assoc Inc 145 Lehigh Ave Lakewood NJ 08701 732-634-5700 634-1430
TF: 800-631-5399 ■ *Web:* www.alphainc.com

Archer Rubber Co 213 Central St Milford MA 01757 508-473-1870 478-7078
TF: 800-804-2074 ■ *Web:* www.archerrubber.com

Beckmann Converting Inc 14 Pk Dr Amsterdam NY 12010 518-842-0073 842-0282
Web: www.beckmannconverting.com

Bondcote Corp PO Box 729 Pulaski VA 24301 540-980-2640 980-5636
TF: 800-368-2160 ■ *Web:* www.bondcote.com

Bradford Industries Inc 1857 Middlesex St Lowell MA 01851 978-459-4100 459-2597
Web: www.bradfordind.com

Brookwood Laminating 275 Putnam Rd Wauregan CT 06387 860-774-5001 774-5002
Web: www.brookwoodcos.com

Cellusuede Products Inc 500 N Madison St Rockford IL 61107 815-964-8619 964-7949
Web: www.cellusuede.com

Cooley Group 50 Esten Ave Pawtucket RI 02860 401-724-9000
TF Cust Svc: 800-992-0072 ■ *Web:* www.cooleygroup.com

Dazian Inc 18 Central Blvd South Hackensack NJ 07606 877-232-9426 549-1055*
**Fax Area Code:* 201 ■ *TF:* 877-232-9426 ■ *Web:* www.dazian.com

Deccofelt Corp 555 S Vermont Ave Glendora CA 91740 626-963-8511 963-4981
TF Cust Svc: 800-543-3226 ■ *Web:* www.deccofelt.com

Der-Tex Corp One Lehner Rd Saco ME 04072 800-669-0364 669-9026*
**Fax Area Code:* 207 ■ *TF:* 800-669-0364 ■ *Web:* www.dertexcorp.com

Duracote Corp 350 N Diamond St Ravenna OH 44266 330-296-3487 296-5102
TF: 800-321-2252 ■ *Web:* www.duracote.com

Emtex Inc 42 Cherry Hill Dr # B Danvers MA 01923 978-907-4500 907-4555
Web: www.emtexinc.com

Flexfirm Products Inc
2300 N Chico Ave South El Monte CA 91733 626-448-7627 579-5116
Web: www.flexfirmproducts.com

Haartz Corp 87 HaywaRd Rd Acton MA 01720 978-264-2600 264-2601
Web: www.haartz.com

Herculite Products Inc
105 E Sinking Springs Ln Emigsville PA 17318 717-764-1192 764-5211*
**Fax:* Acctg ■ *TF Cust Svc:* 800-772-0036 ■ *Web:* www.herculite.com

ICG/Holliston
905 Holliston Mills Rd PO Box 478 Church Hill TN 37642 423-357-6141 325-0351*
**Fax Area Code:* 800 ■ *TF:* 800-251-0451 ■ *Web:* www.holliston.com

Middlesex Research Mfg Company Inc
27 Apsley St Hudson MA 01749 978-562-3697 562-7446
TF: 800-424-5188 ■ *Web:* www.middlesexresearch.com

OMNOVA Solutions Inc 175 Ghent Rd Fairlawn OH 44333 330-869-4200 869-4288
NYSE: OMN ■ *Web:* www.omnova.com

Polyguard Products Inc PO Box 755 Ennis TX 75120 972-875-8421 875-9425
Web: www.polyguardproducts.com

Reflexite Corp 120 Darling Dr Avon CT 06001 860-676-7100 676-7199
TF: 800-654-7570 ■ *Web:* www.orafol.com

Seaman Corp 1000 Venture Blvd Wooster OH 44691 330-262-1111 263-6950
TF: 800-927-8578 ■ *Web:* www.seamancorp.com

Swift Textile Metalizing LLC
23 Britton Dr PO Box 66 Bloomfield CT 06002 860-243-1122 243-0848
Web: www.swift-textile.com

Taconic 136 Coonbrook Rd PO Box 69 Petersburg NY 12138 518-658-3202 658-3204
TF: 800-833-1805 ■ *Web:* www.4taconic.com

Twitchell Corp 4031 Ross Clark Cir Dothan AL 36303 334-792-0002
TF General: 800-633-7550 ■ *Web:* www.twitchellcorp.com

Uniroyal Engineered Products LLC
1800 Second St Ste 970 Sarasota FL 34236 941-906-8580
Web: www.naugahyde.com

WL Gore & Assoc Inc 551 Papermill Rd Newark DE 19711 302-738-4880 738-7710
Web: www.gore.com

748-3 Industrial Fabrics

Phone | Fax

Albany International Corp
1373 Broadway PO Box 1907 Albany NY 12204 518-445-2200 249-4514*
NYSE: AIN ■ **Fax Area Code:* 830 ■ *TF:* 888-797-6735 ■ *Web:* www.albint.com

Amatex Corp 1032 Stambridge St Norristown PA 19404 610-277-6100 277-6106
TF: 800-441-9680 ■ *Web:* www.amatex.com

Company	City	State	ZIP	Phone	Fax
AMETEK Inc Chemical Products Div 455 Corporate Blvd. *TF Orders:* 800-441-7777 ■ *Web:* www.ametekfpp.com	Newark	DE	19702	302-456-4400	456-4444
AstenJohnson 4399 Corporate Rd. *TF:* 800-529-7990 ■ *Web:* www.astenjohnson.com	Charleston	SC	29405	843-747-7800	202-6278
Belton Industries Inc 1205 Hanby Rd PO Box 127 *TF:* 800-845-8753 ■ *Web:* www.beltonindustries.com	Belton	SC	29627	864-338-5711	338-5594
BGF Industries Inc 3802 Robert Porcher Way **Fax Area Code:* 336 ■ *TF:* 800-476-4845 ■ *Web:* www.bgf.com	Greensboro	NC	27410	800-476-4845	545-0233*
Carthage Mills 4243 Hunt Rd *TF Sales:* 800-543-4430 ■ *Web:* www.carthagemills.com	Cincinnati	OH	45242	513-794-1600	794-3434
Clear Edge Technical Fabrics 7160 Northland Cir N *TF:* 800-328-3036 ■ *Web:* www.ifcfabrics.com	Minneapolis	MN	55428	763-535-3220	535-6040
Fablok Mills Inc 140 Spring St *Web:* www.fablokmills.com	Murray Hill	NJ	07974	908-464-1950	464-6520
FH Bonn Co 4300 Gateway Blvd. *TF:* 800-323-0143 ■ *Web:* www.fhbonn.com	Springfield	OH	45502	937-323-7024	323-0388
Firestone Fibers & Textiles Co 100 Firestone Ln PO Box 1369 *TF:* 800-441-1336 ■ *Web:* www.firestonefibers.com	Kings Mountain	NC	28086	704-734-2132	734-2104
HFI LLC 2421 McGaw Rd *Web:* hfi-inc.com	Obetz	OH	43207	614-491-0700	491-1899
Mutual Industries Inc 707 W Grange St. *TF:* 800-523-0888 ■ *Web:* www.mutualindustries.com	Philadelphia	PA	19120	215-927-6000	927-3388
Newtex Industries Inc 8050 Victor Mendon Rd *TF:* 800-836-1001 ■ *Web:* www.newtex.com	Victor	NY	14564	585-924-9135	924-4645
Sefar Printing Solutions Inc 111 Calumet St *TF:* 800-995-0531 ■ *Web:* www.sefar.com	Depew	NY	14043	716-683-4050	685-9469
Stern & Stern Industries Inc 188 Thacher St PO Box 556 *Web:* www.sternandstern.com	Hornell	NY	14843	212-972-4040	818-9230
TenCate Geosynthetics North America 365 S Holland Dr *TF:* 888-795-0808 ■ *Web:* www.tencate.com	Pendergrass	GA	30567	706-693-2226	693-4400
TenCate Protective Fabrics USA 6501 Mall Blvd *TF:* 800-241-8630 ■ *Web:* www.tencate.com	Union City	GA	30291	800-241-8630	
Tex-Tech Industries Inc 1 City Ctr 11th Fl. *TF:* 800-441-7089 ■ *Web:* www.textechindustries.com	Portland	ME	04101	207-933-4404	
Ultrafabrics LLC 303 S Broadway *TF:* 888-361-9216 ■ *Web:* www.ultrafabricsllc.com	Tarrytown	NY	10591	914-460-1730	631-3572
Weavexx 51 Flex Way *Web:* www.weavexx.com	Youngsville	NC	27596	919-556-7235	556-2432
Wendell Fabrics Corp 108 E Church St PO Box 128 *Web:* www.wendellfabrics.com	Blacksburg	SC	29702	864-839-6341	839-2911

748-4 Knitting Mills

Company	City	State	ZIP	Phone	Fax
Alamac American Knits LLC 1885 Alamac Rd PO Box 1347 *Web:* www.alamacusa.com	Lumberton	NC	28358	910-739-2811	618-2292
Apex Mills Corp 168 Doughty Blvd *TF:* 800-989-2739 ■ *Web:* www.apexmills.com	Inwood	NY	11096	516-239-4400	239-4951
Asheboro Elastics Corp 150 N Pk St *Web:* www.aecnarrowfabrics.com	Asheboro	NC	27203	336-629-2626	629-3782
Cellunet Mfg Co 1006 Jacksonville Rd	Burlington Township	NJ	08016	609-386-3361	
Clover Knits Inc 1075 Jackson Heights	Clover	SC	29710	803-222-3021	222-4105
Contempora Fabrics Inc 351 Contempora Dr *Web:* www.contemporafabrics.com	Lumberton	NC	28358	910-738-7131	738-9575
Darlington Fabrics Corp 36 Beach St *Web:* www.darlingtonfabrics.com	Westerly	RI	02891	401-315-6279	348-6049
Draper Knitting Co 28 Draper Ln. *TF:* 800-808-7707 ■ *Web:* www.draperknitting.com	Canton	MA	02021	781-828-0029	828-3034
Elastic Fabrics of America 3112 Pleasant Garden Rd *Web:* www.elasticfabrics.com	Greensboro	NC	27406	336-275-9401	378-2631
Fab Industries Corp 98 Cutter Mill Rd Ste 412-N *Web:* fab-industries.com	Great Neck	NY	11021	516-498-3200	498-3200
Gehring Textiles Inc 1225 Franklin Ave Ste 300 *Web:* www.gehring-tricot.com	Garden City	NY	11530	516-747-4555	747-8885
Hornwood Inc 766 Hailey's Ferry Rd *Web:* www.hornwoodinc.com	Lilesville	NC	28091	704-848-4121	848-4555
Klauber Bros Inc 980 Ave of the Americas Second Fl *Web:* www.klauberlace.com	New York	NY	10018	212-686-2531	481-7194
Lace For Less Inc 1500 Main Ave Ste 3 *TF:* 800-533-5223 ■ *Web:* www.parislace.com	Clifton	NJ	07011	973-478-2955	478-8746
Minnesota Knitting Mills 1450 Mendota Heights Rd *Web:* www.mnknit.com	Saint Paul	MN	55120	651-452-2240	452-8915
MoCaro Industries Inc 2201 Mocaro Dr. *Web:* www.mocaro.com	Statesville	NC	28677	704-878-6645	873-6139
Monterey Mills Inc 1725 E Delavan Dr. *TF:* 800-255-9665 ■ *Web:* www.montereymills.com	Janesville	WI	53546	608-754-2866	754-3750
Russ-Knits Inc Hwy 211 E PO Box 130 *Web:* www.russknits.com	Candor	NC	27229	910-974-4114	974-4023
Westchester Lace & Textiles Inc 3901 Liberty Ave. *Web:* www.westchesterlace.com	North Bergen	NJ	07047	201-864-2150	864-2116

748-5 Narrow Fabric Mills

Company	City	State	ZIP	Phone	Fax
Advance Fiber Technologies Corp 344 Lodi St	Hackensack	NJ	07601	201-488-2700	489-5656
American Cord & Webbing Co 88 Century Dr. *Web:* www.acw1.com	Woonsocket	RI	02895	401-762-5500	762-5514
Avery Dennison 950 German St *TF:* 800-444-4947 ■ *Web:* www.rbis.averydennison.com	Lenoir	NC	28645	828-758-2338	
Bally Ribbon Mills 23 N Seventh St. *Web:* www.ballyribbon.com	Bally	PA	19503	610-845-2211	845-8013
Carolina Narrow Fabric Co 1100 N Patterson Ave *Web:* www.carolinanarrowfabric.com	Winston-Salem	NC	27101	336-631-3000	631-3060
Conrad-Jarvis Corp 217 Conant St **Fax:* Orders ■ *Web:* conrad-jarvis.com	Pawtucket	RI	02904	401-722-8700	726-8860*
ELC Industries LLC 1439 Dave Lyle Blvd Ste 16-C *Web:* ricebraid.com	Rock Hill	SC	29730	803-980-7600	980-7676
Fulflex Inc 32 Justin Holden Dr **Fax:* Cust Svc ■ *TF:* 800-283-2500 ■ *Web:* www.fulflex.com	Brattleboro	VT	05301	802-257-5256	257-5602*
Hickory Brands Inc (HBI) 429 27th St NW *TF:* 800-438-5777 ■ *Web:* www.hickorybrands.com	Hickory	NC	28601	800-438-5777	422-3279
Hope Global Engineered Textile Solutions 50 Martin St *TF General:* 800-854-7139 ■ *Web:* www.hopeglobal.com	Cumberland	RI	02864	401-333-8990	334-6442
JRM Industries Inc One Mattimore St *TF:* 800-533-2697 ■ *Web:* www.jrm.com	Passaic	NJ	07055	973-779-9340	779-8017
Julius Koch USA Inc 387 Church St *TF Sales:* 800-522-3652 ■ *Web:* www.jkusa.com	New Bedford	MA	02745	508-995-9565	995-8434
Murdock Webbing Co 27 Foundry St *TF:* 800-375-2052 ■ *Web:* www.murdockwebbing.com	Central Falls	RI	02863	401-724-3000	
Name Maker Inc 4450 Commerce Cir PO Box 43821 *TF:* 800-241-2890 ■ *Web:* www.namemaker.com	Atlanta	GA	30336	404-691-2237	691-7711
Narricot Industries LP 928 Jaymore Rd Ste C150 *Web:* www.narricot.com	SoutHampton	PA	18966	215-322-3900	322-3905
Narrow Fabric Industries Corp 701 Reading Ave. *TF:* 877-523-6373 ■ *Web:* readingeagle.com	Reading	PA	19611	610-376-2891	
NFA Corp 850 Boylston St Ste 428	Chestnut Hill	MA	02467	617-232-6060	
Rhode Island Textile Co 211 Columbus Ave *TF:* 800-556-6488 ■ *Web:* www.ritextile.com	Pawtucket	RI	02861	401-722-3700	726-2840
Ross Matthews Mills Inc 657 Quarry St *TF:* 800-753-7677	Fall River	MA	02723	508-677-0601	
Sequins International Inc 60-01 31st Ave. *Web:* www.sequinsdirect.com	Woodside	NY	11377	718-204-0002	204-0999
Shelby Elastics Inc 639 N Post Rd PO Box 2405 *TF:* 800-562-4507 ■ *Web:* www.shelbyelastics.com	Shelby	NC	28150	704-487-4301	481-9348
South Carolina Elastic Co 201 S Carolina Elastic Rd *Web:* www.ritextile.com	Landrum	SC	29356	864-457-3388	
Southern Weaving Co 1005 W Bramlett Rd *TF:* 800-849-8962 ■ *Web:* www.southernweaving.com	Greenville	SC	29611	864-233-1635	240-9302
State Narrow Fabrics Inc 12-12 43rd Ave. *Web:* www.statenarrow.com	Long Island City	NY	11101	718-392-8787	392-9421
Sturges Mfg Company Inc 2030 Sunset Ave PO Box 59 *Web:* www.sturgesstraps.com	Utica	NY	13502	315-732-6159	732-2314
Tape Craft Corp 200 Tape Craft Dr **Fax Area Code:* 256 ■ *TF Cust Svc:* 800-521-1783 ■ *Web:* www.tapecraft.com	Oxford	AL	36203	800-521-1783	236-6718*
Trimtex Company Inc 400 Pk Ave. *Web:* www.trimtex.com	Williamsport	PA	17701	570-326-9135	326-4250
Wayne Mills Co Inc 130 W Berkley St. *TF:* 800-220-8053 ■ *Web:* www.waynemills.com	Philadelphia	PA	19144	215-842-2134	438-8599

748-6 Nonwoven Fabrics

Company	City	State	ZIP	Phone	Fax
Acme Felt Works Co 6500 Stanford Ave	Los Angeles	CA	90001	323-752-3778	752-7164
Aetna Felt Corp 2401 W Emaus Ave *TF:* 800-526-4451 ■ *Web:* www.aetnafelt.com	Allentown	PA	18103	610-791-0900	791-5791
Airtex Consumer Products a Div of Federal Foam Technologies 150 Industrial Pk Blvd **Fax Area Code:* 320 ■ *TF:* 800-851-8887 ■ *Web:* www.airtex.com	Cokato	MN	55321	800-851-8887	286-2428*
American Felt & Filter Co 361 Walsh Ave *Web:* www.affco.com	New Windsor	NY	12553	845-561-3560	563-4422
Berwick Offray LLC 2015 W Front St **Fax Area Code:* 267 ■ *TF General:* 800-327-0350 ■ *Web:* www.berwickindustries.com	Berwick	PA	18603	570-752-5934	256-7200*
Cerex Advanced Fabrics Inc 610 Chemstrand Rd *TF:* 800-572-3739 ■ *Web:* www.cerex.com	Cantonment	FL	32533	850-968-0100	937-3342
Clark-Cutler-McDermott Co (CCMcD) 5 Fisher St *TF:* 800-922-3019 ■ *Web:* www.ccmcd.com	Franklin	MA	02038	508-528-1200	528-1406
Fiber Bond Corp 110 Menke Rd *Web:* www.fiberbond.net	Michigan City	IN	46360	219-879-4541	874-7502
Fisher Textiles Inc 139 Business Pk Dr *TF:* 800-554-8886 ■ *Web:* www.fishertextiles.com	Indian Trail	NC	28079	704-821-8870	821-8880
Foss Mfg Co LLC 11 Merrill Industrial Dr PO Box 5000 *TF:* 800-343-3277 ■ *Web:* www.fossmfg.com	Hampton	NH	03842	603-929-6000	929-6010
Hobbs Bonded Fibers Inc 200 Commerce Dr. *TF:* 800-433-3357 ■ *Web:* www.hobbsbondedfibers.com	Waco	TX	76710	254-741-0040	772-7238
National Nonwovens PO Box 150 *TF:* 800-333-3469 ■ *Web:* www.nationalnonwovens.com	EastHampton	MA	01027	413-527-3445	527-9570
Orr Felt Co 750 S Main St *Web:* www.orrfelt.com	Piqua	OH	45356	937-773-0551	778-9670

				Phone	Fax
Sellars 6565 N 60th St. *TF:* 800-237-8454 ■ *Web:* sellarscompany.com	Milwaukee	WI	53223	414-353-5650	353-5707
Texollini Inc 2575 E El Presidio St. *Web:* www.texollini.com	Long Beach	CA	90810	310-537-3400	537-3500
Tietex International 3010 N Blackstock Rd. *TF:* 800-843-8390 ■ *Web:* www.tietex.com	Spartanburg	SC	29301	864-574-0500	574-9490
Trenton Mills LLC 400 Factory St PO Box 107. *Web:* www.trentonmills.com	Trenton	TN	38382	731-855-1323	855-9000

748-7 Textile Dyeing & Finishing

				Phone	Fax
Advanced Textile Composites 700 E Parker St *Web:* www.advtextile.com	Scranton	PA	18509	570-207-7000	207-7070
Albert Screen Print Inc 3704 Summit Rd. *TF:* 800-759-2774 ■ *Web:* www.albertinc.com	Norton	OH	44203	330-753-7559	753-1612
Aurora Textile Finishing Co 911 N Lake St PO Box 70 *TF:* 800-864-0303 ■ *Web:* www.auroratextile.com	Aurora	IL	60507	630-892-7651	892-3215
Bradford Printing & Finishing LLC 460 Bradford Rd	Bradford	RI	02808	401-377-2231	377-2234
Buckeye Fabric Finishing Co 1260 E Main St PO Box 216. *Web:* www.buckeyefabric.com	Coshocton	OH	43812	740-622-3251	622-9317
Carlisle Finishing 3863 Carlisle Chester Hwy *Web:* www.itg-global.com/companies/carlisle_finishing.html	Carlisle	SC	29031	864-466-4100	427-4501
Como Textile Prints Inc 193 E Railway Ave	Paterson	NJ	07503	973-279-2950	881-8450
Coral Dyeing & Finishing Corp 555 E 31st St.	Paterson	NJ	07513	973-278-0272	278-9490
Cosmo 12 Kent Way Ste 201 PO Box 737 *Web:* www.cosmofabric.net	Byfield	MA	01922	978-462-7311	465-6223
Cranston Print Works Co 1381 Cranston St *TF:* 800-876-2756 ■ *Web:* www.cranstonvillage.com	Cranston	RI	02920	401-943-4800	275-9333
Deep River Dyeing & Finishing Company Inc 225 Poplar St PO Box 217 *Web:* deepriverdyeing.com	Randleman	NC	27317	336-498-4181	498-7252
Duro Textiles LLC 110 Chace St. *Web:* www.duroindustries.com	Fall River	MA	02724	508-675-0101	677-6791
GJ Littlewood & Son Inc 4045 Main St. *Web:* www.littlewooddyers.com	Philadelphia	PA	19127	215-483-3970	483-6129
Hanes Dye & Finish Inc 600 NW Blvd *Web:* www.hanesfinishing.com	Winston-Salem	NC	27101	336-725-1391	777-3895
Harodite Industries Inc 66 S St. *Web:* www.harodite.com	Taunton	MA	02780	508-824-6961	880-0696
Holt Sublimation Printing & Products 2208 Air Pk Dr	Burlington	NC	27215	336-222-3600	229-7580
Huffman Finishing Co 4919 Hickory Blvd *Web:* duzlo.com/huffmanfinishingco9525739dz	Granite Falls	NC	28630	828-396-1741	
Kenyon Industries Inc 36 Sherman Ave *Web:* www.brookwoodcos.com	Kenyon	RI	02836	401-364-3400	364-6130
Microfibres Inc 1 Moshassuck St. *Web:* www.microfibres.com	Pawtucket	RI	02904	401-725-4883	722-8520
Parthenon Prints Inc PO Box 2505 *Web:* www.parthenonprints.com	Panama City	FL	32402	850-769-8321	769-5374
Royal Carolina Corp 7305 Old Friendly Rd *Web:* www.royalcarolina.com	Greensboro	NC	27410	336-292-8845	294-2396
Westex Inc 122 W 22nd St. *TF:* 866-493-7839 ■ *Web:* www.westex.com	Oak Brook	IL	60523	773-523-7000	523-0965
William J Dixon Company Inc 756 Springdale Dr. *Web:* www.wjdixon.com	Exton	PA	19341	610-524-1131	524-7964
Wolfe Dye & Bleach Works Inc 25 Ridge Rd *Web:* www.wolfedyeandbleachworks.com	Shoemakersville	PA	19555	610-562-7639	
Yates Bleachery Co 503 Flintstone Rd *Web:* www.yatesbleachery.info	Flintstone	GA	30725	706-820-1531	820-9459

748-8 Textile Fiber Processing Mills

				Phone	Fax
Buffalo Industries Inc 99 S Spokane St. *TF:* 800-683-0052 ■ *Web:* www.buffaloindustries.com	Seattle	WA	98134	206-682-9900	682-9907
Claremont Flock LLC 107 Scott Dr. *Web:* www.claremontflock.com	Leominster	MA	01453	978-534-6191	534-7352
Fabritech Inc 5740 Salmen St. *TF:* 888-733-5009 ■ *Web:* www.fabritechonline.com	New Orleans	LA	70123	504-733-5009	
Fiber Conversion Inc 15 E Elm St. *Web:* fiberconversion.net	Broadalbin	NY	12025	518-883-3431	883-8748
JE Herndon Company Inc 1020 J E Herndon Access Rd *TF:* 800-277-0500 ■ *Web:* jeherndon.com	Kings Mountain	NC	28086	704-739-4711	734-0621
Leigh Fibers Inc 1101 Syphrit Rd *Web:* www.leighfibers.com	Wellford	SC	29385	864-439-4111	439-4116
Norman W Paschall Co Inc 1 Paschall Rd *TF:* 800-849-1820 ■ *Web:* www.paschall.com	Peachtree City	GA	30269	770-487-7945	487-0840
Oklahoma Waste & Wiping Rag Company Inc 2013 SE 18th St	Oklahoma City	OK	73129	405-670-3100	670-3993
Royal Processing Co 5710 Old Concord Rd *Web:* steinfibers.com	Charlotte	NC	28213	704-599-2804	599-2805
RSM Co 811 Pressley Rd PO Box 31605 *Web:* www.rsmcompany.com	Charlotte	NC	28231	704-525-6851	525-8368
Spectro Coating Corp 101 Scott Dr *Web:* www.spectrocoating.com	Leominster	MA	01453	978-534-1800	534-4155

748-9 Yarn & Thread Mills

				Phone	Fax
Carolina Mills Inc 618 Newton Rd *Web:* www.carolinamills.com	Maiden	NC	28650	828-428-9911	
Chargeurs Wool USA 178 Wool Rd.	Jamestown	SC	29453	843-257-2212	257-4579
Charles Craft Inc 21381 Charles Craft Ln Laurinburg-Maxton Airport. *TF:* 800-277-1009 ■ *Web:* www.commonthread.us	Laurinburg	NC	28352	910-844-3521	844-3045
Chesterfield Yarn Mills Inc PO Box 427. *Web:* www.chesterfieldwraps.com	Pageland	SC	29728	843-672-7211	672-7210
Clover Yarns Inc 1030 Tanyard Branch Trl	Clover	VA	24534	434-454-7151	454-6725
Coats & Clark Inc 3430 Toringdon Way Ste 301 *Web:* coatsandclark.com	Charlotte	NC	28277	704-329-5800	329-5820
Coats North America 3430 Toringdon Way Ste 301 *TF:* 800-631-0965 ■ *Web:* www.coats.com	Charlotte	NC	28277	704-329-5800	329-5279
Crescent Woolen Mills Co 1016 School St. *Web:* crescentwoolenmills.com	Two Rivers	WI	54241	920-793-3331	793-3818
Dillon Yarn Inc 1019 Titan Rd *Web:* dillonyarn.com	Dillon	SC	29536	843-774-7353	774-0338
DMC Corp 10 Basin Dr Ste 130 *Web:* www.dmc-usa.com	Kearny	NJ	07032	973-589-0606	589-8931
Eddington Thread Manufacturing Co PO Box 446 *TF:* 800-220-8901 ■ *Web:* www.edthread.com	Bensalem	PA	19020	215-639-8900	639 8900
Glen Raven Inc 232 Glen Raven Rd *TF:* 800-675-0032 ■ *Web:* www.glenraven.com	Glen Raven	NC	27217	336-227-6211	226-8133
Hickory Yarns Inc 1025 Tenth St NE *Web:* www.hickoryyarns.com	Hickory	NC	28601	828-322-1550	322-1627
Interstock Premium Cabinets LLC 915 Pennsylvania Blvd *Web:* www.interstockcabinets.com	Feasterville	PA	19053	267-288-1200	288-1206
Kent Wool 671 Runnymede Rd *Web:* www.kentwool.com	Pickens	SC	29671	864-878-6367	878-2723
Liberty Throwing Company Inc 214 Pringle St PO Box 1387 *Web:* www.libertythrowing.com	Kingston	PA	18704	570-287-1114	283-3531
Lion Brand Yarn Co 135 Kero Rd **Fax Area Code:* 201 ■ *TF:* 800-795-5466 ■ *Web:* www.lionbrand.com	Carlstadt	NJ	07072	212-243-8995	804-3918*
Meridian Specialty Yarns Inc 312 Colombo St SW *Web:* www.msyg.com	Valdese	NC	28690	828-874-2151	874-3780
Parkdale Mills Inc 531 Cotton Blossom Cir *TF:* 800-331-1843 ■ *Web:* www.parkdalemills.com	Gastonia	NC	28054	704-874-5000	874-5175
Pharr Yarns LLC 100 Main St PO Box 1939 *Web:* www.pharryarns.com	McAdenville	NC	28101	704-824-3551	824-0072
Regal Mfg Co Inc 990 Third Ave SE.	Hickory	NC	28602	828-328-5381	
RL Stowe Mills Inc 100 N Main St.	Belmont	NC	28012	704-825-5314	825-6608
Sapona Mfg Company Inc 2478 Cedar Falls Rd *Web:* www.saponamfg.com	Cedar Falls	NC	27230	336-625-2727	626-0876
Supreme Corp 325 Spence Rd *TF:* 888-604-6975 ■ *Web:* supremecorporation.com/	Conover	NC	28613	828-322-6975	322-7881
Swift Spinning Inc 16 Corporate Ridge Pkwy PO Box 8767 *TF:* 800-849-1252 ■ *Web:* www.swiftspinning.com	Columbus	GA	31907	706-323-6303	
Tuscarora Yarns Inc 8760 E Franklin St *TF:* 800-849-6527 ■ *Web:* www.tuscarorayarns.com	Mount Pleasant	NC	28124	704-436-6527	436-9461
Ultrafab Inc 1050 Hook Rd. *Web:* www.ultrafab.com	Farmington	NY	14425	585-924-2186	924-7680
Unifi Inc 7201 W Friendly Ave *NYSE: UFI* ■ *Web:* www.unifi.com	Greensboro	NC	27410	336-294-4410	316-5422
Universal Fibers Inc PO Box 8930 *Web:* www.universalfibers.com	Bristol	VA	24203	276-669-1161	669-3304

749 TEXTILE PRODUCTS - HOUSEHOLD

				Phone	Fax
1888 Mills LLC 1520 Kensington Rd Ste 115 **Fax Area Code:* 630 ■ *TF:* 800-346-3660 ■ *Web:* www.1888mills.com	Oak Brook	IL	60523	800-346-3660	586-9303*
Ado Corp 851 Simuel Rd **Fax Area Code:* 864 ■ *TF Cust Svc:* 800-845-0918 ■ *Web:* www.ado-usa.com	Spartanburg	SC	29301	800-845-0918	574-5835*
American Textile Co 10 N Linden St *TF Cust Svc:* 800-289-2826 ■ *Web:* www.americantextile.com	Duquesne	PA	15110	412-948-1020	948-1002
Arden Cos 30400 Telegraph Rd Ste 200 *Web:* www.ardencompanies.com	Bingham Farms	MI	48025	248-415-8500	415-8520
Ascot Enterprises Inc 503 S Main St. *Web:* www.ascotent.com	Nappanee	IN	46550	574-773-7751	773-2894
Bardwil Industries Inc 1071 Ave of the Americas 4th Fl *Web:* bardwilhome.com	New York	NY	10018	212-944-1870	869-3599
Biddeford Blankets 300 Terr Dr **Fax Area Code:* 847 ■ *TF:* 800-789-6441 ■ *Web:* biddefordblankets.com	Mundelein	IL	60060	800-789-6441	566-6431*
Biederlack of America 11501 Bedford Rd NE.	Cumberland	MD	21502	301-759-3633	759-3837
Brentwood Originals Inc 20639 S Fordyce Ave. *Web:* www.brentwoodoriginals.com	Carson	CA	90810	310-637-6804	639-9710
Carole Fabrics Inc PO Box 1436. *TF:* 800-241-0920 ■ *Web:* carolefabrics.com	Augusta	GA	30903	706-863-4742	
CHF Industries Inc One Pk Ave Ninth Fl *TF Cust Svc:* 800-243-7090 ■ *Web:* www.chfindustries.com	New York	NY	10016	212-951-7800	
Cotton Goods Manufacturing Co 259 N California Ave. *Web:* www.cottongoodsmfg.com	Chicago	IL	60612	773-265-0088	265-0096
Creative Bath Products 250 Creative Dr *Web:* www.creativebath.com	Central Islip	NY	11722	631-582-8000	582-2020

	City	State	ZIP	Phone	Fax
Crown Crafts Inc 916 S Burnside *NASDAQ: CRWS* ■ *TF:* 800-433-9560 ■ *Web:* www.crowncrafts.com	Gonzales	LA	70737	225-647-9100	647-8331
Custom Drapery Blinds & Shutters 3402 E T C Jester *TF:* 800-929-9211 ■ *Web:* www.cdbas.com	Houston	TX	77018	713-225-9211	227-0808
Echota Fabrics Inc 1394 US 41 N *Web:* www.echotafabrics.com	Calhoun	GA	30701	706-629-9750	629-5229
Franco Mfg Company Inc 555 Prospect St *Web:* franco-mfg.com/	Metuchen	NJ	08840	732-494-0500	494-8270
Haleyville Drapery Manufacturing Co 1050 Hill Ave	Haleyville	AL	35565	205-486-9257	
Hollander Home Fashions Corp 6501 Congress Avenue Suite 300 *TF:* 800-233-7666 ■ *Web:* www.hollander.com	Boca Raton	FL	33487	561-997-6900	997-8738
Kaslen Textiles 6099 Triangle Dr *TF:* 800-777-5789 ■ *Web:* www.kaslentextiles.com	Commerce	CA	90040	323-588-7700	838-0346
Kay Dee Designs Inc 177 Skunk Hill Rd *TF:* 800-537-3433 ■ *Web:* www.kaydeedesigns.com	Hope Valley	RI	02832	401-539-2405	539-2210
Kellwood Co 600 Kellwood Pkwy *Web:* www.kellwood.com	Chesterfield	MO	63017	314-576-3100	576-3434
Lafayette Venetian Blind Inc 3000 Klondike Rd. P.O. Box 2838 **Fax Area Code:* 765 ■ *TF:* 800-342-5523 ■ *Web:* www.lafvb.com	West Lafayette	IN	47996	800-342-5523	423-2402*
Louis Hornick & Co Inc 117 E 38th St *Web:* www.louishornick.com	New York	NY	10016	212-679-2448	779-7098
Louisville Bedding Co 10400 Bunsen Way *TF:* 800-626-2594 ■ *Web:* www.loubed.com	Louisville	KY	40299	502-491-3370	495-5346
Manual Woodworkers & Weavers Inc 3737 HowaRd Gap Rd *TF:* 800-542-3139 ■ *Web:* www.manualww.com	Hendersonville	NC	28792	828-692-7333	696-2961
Marietta Drapery & Window Coverings Company Inc 22 Trammel St PO Box 569 **Fax:* Mktg ■ *TF Mktg:* 800-762-4774 ■ *Web:* www.mariettadrapery.com	Marietta	GA	30064	770-428-3335	423-3398*
Miller Industries Inc 7 Canal St	Lisbon Falls	ME	04252	207-353-4371	353-5900
Newport Layton Home Fashions Inc 8515 N Columbia Blvd *Web:* www.newportlayton.com	Portland	OR	97203	503-283-4864	283-4895
Pacific Coast Feather Co 1964 Fourth Ave S *TF:* 888-297-1778 ■ *Web:* www.pacificcoast.com	Seattle	WA	98134	206-624-1057	
Paramount Industrial Cos Inc 1112 Kingwood Ave *Web:* www.paramountsleep.com	Norfolk	VA	23502	757-855-3321	855-2029
Pendleton Woolen Mills Inc 220 NW Broadway *TF:* 800-760-4844 ■ *Web:* www.pendleton-usa.com	Portland	OR	97209	503-226-4801	535-5502
Perfect Fit Industries Inc 230 Fifth Ave	New York	NY	10010	212-679-6656	
Phoenix Down Corp 85 US 46 *Web:* www.phoenixdown.com	Totowa	NJ	07512	973-812-8100	812-9077
Riegel Consumer Products 51 Riegel Rd PO Box E *TF:* 800-845-3251 ■ *Web:* www.riegellinen.com	Johnston	SC	29832	803-275-2541	275-2219
S Lichtenberg & Co Inc 295 Fifth Ave Rm 918 *TF Cust Svc:* 800-682-1959 ■ *Web:* www.lichtenberg.com	New York	NY	10016	212-689-4510	
Samson Manufacturing Co 231 E 13th St	Waynesboro	GA	30830	706-554-2129	
Saturday Knight Ltd 2100 Section Rd *Web:* skltd.com	Cincinnati	OH	45237	513-641-1400	242-2805
Standard Textile Company Inc Decorative Products One Knollcrest Dr *TF General:* 800-999-0400 ■ *Web:* www.standardtextile.com	Cincinnati	OH	45237	513-761-9255	761-0467
Surefit Inc 6575 Snowdrift Rd Ste 101 **Fax Area Code:* 610 ■ *Web:* www.surefit.net	Allentown	PA	18106	888-796-0500	336-8995*
Tuway American Group Inc, The 2820 W Maple Rd Ste 101 *Web:* www.tuwaymops.com	Troy	MI	48084	248-649-8790	649-3666
United Feather & Down Inc 414 E Golf Rd *TF:* 800-932-3696 ■ *Web:* www.ufandd.com	Des Plaines	IL	60016	847-296-6610	296-6616
Wesco Fabrics Inc 4001 Forest St *TF:* 800-950-9372 ■ *Web:* www.wescofabrics.com	Denver	CO	80216	303-388-4101	388-3908

750 THEATERS - BROADWAY

SEE ALSO Performing Arts Facilities p. 2900; Theater Companies p. 2913; Theaters - Resident p. 3235

	City	State	ZIP	Phone	Fax
Al Hirschfeld Theatre 302 W 45th St *TF:* 800-432-7780 ■ *Web:* www.telecharge.com	New York	NY	10036	212-239-6262	
Ambassador Theaters 219 W 49th St *Web:* ambassadortheater.com	New York	NY	10019	212-239-6200	
American Airlines Theatre 227 W 42nd St *Web:* www.roundabouttheatre.org	New York	NY	10036	212-719-1300	869-8817
August Wilson 245 W 52nd St **Fax Area Code:* 415 ■ *TF:* 800-432-7250 ■ *Web:* www.telecharge.com	New York	NY	10019	212-239-6200	520-3420*
Biltmore Theatre 261 W 47th St *Web:* www.manhattantheatreclub.com	New York	NY	10036	212-399-3000	399-4329
Booth Theatre 222 W 45th St **Fax Area Code:* 415 ■ *TF:* 800-432-7780 ■ *Web:* www.telecharge.com	New York	NY	10036	212-239-6200	520-3420*
Broadhurst Theatre 235 W 44th St **Fax Area Code:* 415 ■ *TF:* 800-447-7400 ■ *Web:* telecharge.com/go.aspx?md=102&pid=7793	New York	NY	10036	212-239-6200	520-3420*
Circle in the Square Theatre 1633 Broadway **Fax Area Code:* 415 ■ *TF:* 800-432-7250 ■ *Web:* www.telecharge.com	New York	NY	10019	212-239-6200	520-3420*
Helen Hayes Theatre 240 W 44th St **Fax Area Code:* 415 ■ *TF:* 800-447-7400 ■ *Web:* telecharge.com/go.aspx?md=102&pid=8417	New York	NY	10036	212-239-6200	520-3420*
Imperial Theatre 249 W 45th St **Fax Area Code:* 415 ■ *TF:* 800-447-7400 ■ *Web:* www.telecharge.com	New York	NY	10036	212-239-6200	520-3420*
Jacobs Theatre 242 W 45th St **Fax Area Code:* 415 ■ *TF:* 800-447-7400 ■ *Web:* www.telecharge.com	New York	NY	10036	212-239-6200	520-3420*
Longacre Theatre 220 W 48th St **Fax Area Code:* 415 ■ *TF:* 800-447-7400 ■ *Web:* www.telecharge.com	New York	NY	10036	212-239-6200	520-3420*
Lyceum Theatre 149 W 45th St *TF:* 800-432-7780 ■ *Web:* www.telecharge.com	New York	NY	10036	212-239-6200	
Minskoff Theatre 200 W 45th St *TF:* 800-714-8452 ■ *Web:* minskofftheatre.com	New York	NY	10036	212-869-0550	
Richard Rodgers Theatre 226 W 46th St *TF:* 866-755-3075 ■ *Web:* richardrodgerstheatre.com	New York	NY	10036	212-221-1211	
Roundabout Theatre Co 231 W 39th St Ste 1200 *Web:* www.roundabouttheatre.org	New York	NY	10018	212-719-9393	869-8817
Shubert Theatre 225 W 44th St **Fax Area Code:* 415 ■ *TF:* 800-432-7250 ■ *Web:* www.telecharge.com	New York	NY	10036	212-239-6200	520-3420*
Studio 54 Theatre 254 W 54th St *Web:* www.roundabouttheatre.org	New York	NY	10019	212-719-1300	956-9254

751 THEATERS - MOTION PICTURE

	City	State	ZIP	Phone	Fax
AMC Entertainment Inc 920 Main St *TF:* 877-341-6397 ■ *Web:* www.amctheatres.com	Kansas City	MO	64105	816-221-4000	
AMC Star Theatres 25333 W 12-Mile Rd *TF:* 888-262-4386 ■ *Web:* www.amctheatres.com	Southfield	MI	48034	248-368-1802	
AMC Theatres 920 Main St *TF:* 877-341-6397 ■ *Web:* www.amctheatres.com	Kansas City	MO	64105	816-221-4000	
Artisan Cinema & Sound LLC 9171 E Bell Rd Ste 100 *Web:* www.iintegrations.net	Scottsdale	AZ	85260	480-538-1071	
Brenden Theatres 531 Davis St *TF:* 877-638-3456 ■ *Web:* www.brendentheatres.com	Vacaville	CA	95688	707-469-0190	
Carmike Cinemas Inc 1301 First Ave *NASDAQ: CKEC* ■ *Web:* www.carmike.com	Columbus	GA	31901	706-576-3400	576-3880
Celebration! Cinema 2121 Celebration Ave **Fax Area Code:* 301 ■ *Web:* www.celebrationcinema.com	Grand Rapids	MI	49525	616-530-7469	469-3001*
Chakeres Theatres Inc 200 N Murray St *Web:* www.chakerestheatres.com	Springfield	OH	45503	937-323-6447	
Cinemark USA Inc 3900 Dallas Pkwy Ste 500 *TF:* 800-246-3627 ■ *Web:* www.cinemark.com	Plano	TX	75093	972-665-1000	665-1004
Cineplex Entertainment LP 1303 Yonge St *TF:* 800-333-0061 ■ *Web:* www.cineplex.com	Toronto	ON	M4T2Y9	416-323-6600	323-7228
Classic Cinemas 603 Rogers St *Web:* www.classiccinemas.com	Downers Grove	IL	60515	630-968-1600	968-1626
Clearview Cinema Group Inc 200 Pk Ave Ste 3 *Web:* www.bowtiecinemas.com	Florham Park	NJ	07932	908-918-2000	
Cobb Theatres LLC 2000-B Southbridge Pkwy Ste 100 *Web:* www.cobbtheatres.com	Birmingham	AL	35209	205-802-7766	
Coming Attractions Theatres 1644 Ashland St Unit 5 *Web:* www.catheatres.com	Ashland	OR	97520	541-488-1021	
Community Theater 100 S St *Web:* www.mayoarts.org	Morristown	NJ	07960	973-455-1607	
Crest Theater 1013 K St *Web:* www.thecrest.com	Sacramento	CA	95814	916-442-5189	
De Anza Land & Leisure Corp 1615 Cordova St	Los Angeles	CA	90007	323-734-9951	734-2531
Decurion Corp, The 120 N Robertson Blvd *Web:* www.decurion.com	Los Angeles	CA	90048	310-657-8420	
Dickinson Theaters Inc 6801 W 107th St *Web:* www.dtmovies.com	Overland Park	KS	66211	913-432-2334	
Eastern Federal Corp 901 E Blvd *Web:* easternfederal.com	Charlotte	NC	28203	704-377-3495	
Fairfield Theater 70 Sanford St *Web:* fairfieldtheatre.org	Fairfield	CT	06824	203-319-1404	
Harkins Theatres 7511 E Mcdonald Dr *Web:* www.harkinstheatres.com	Scottsdale	AZ	85250	480-627-7777	
Hollywood Blvd a Cinema Bar & Eatery 1001 75th St Ste 153 *Web:* www.atriptothemovies.com	Woodridge	IL	60517	630-427-1880	
Hollywood Theater Holdings Inc 919 SW Taylor St Ste 800 *Web:* www.regmovies.com	Portland	OR	97205	503-221-7090	796-0229
IMAX Corp 2525 Speakman Dr *NYSE: IMAX* ■ *Web:* www.imax.com	Mississauga	ON	L5K1B1	905-403-6500	403-6450
Kerasotes ShowPlace Theatres LLC 224 N Des Plaines Ave *TF:* 877-293-2000 ■ *Web:* showplaceicon.com	Chicago	IL	60661	312-756-3360	
Landmark Theaters 2222 S Barrington Ave *TF Cust Svc:* 888-724-6362 ■ *Web:* www.landmarktheatres.com	Los Angeles	CA	90064	310-473-6701	312-2364
Magnolia Pictures LLC 49 W 27th St Seventh Fl *Web:* www.magpictures.com	New York	NY	10001	212-924-6701	
Malco Theatres Inc 5851 Ridgeway Ctr Pkwy *Web:* www.malco.com	Memphis	TN	38120	901-761-3480	681-2044
Marcus Corp 100 E Wisconsin Ave *NYSE: MCS* ■ *TF:* 800-461-9330 ■ *Web:* www.marcuscorp.com	Milwaukee	WI	53202	414-905-1000	
Marcus Theatres Corp 100 E Wisconsin Ave Ste 19 *TF Cust Svc:* 800-274-0099 ■ *Web:* marcustheatres.com/	Milwaukee	WI	53202	414-905-1000	920-2250
Metropolitan Theaters Corp 8727 W Third St *Web:* www.metrotheatres.com	Los Angeles	CA	90048	310-858-2800	858-2860
National Amusements Inc 846 University Ave *Web:* www.showcasecinemas.com	Norwood	MA	02062	781-461-1600	326-1306
New Federal Theatre 292 Henry St *Web:* www.newfederaltheatre.org	New York	NY	10002	212-353-1176	
Pacific Theatres Corp 120 N Robertson Blvd *Web:* www.pacifictheatres.com	Los Angeles	CA	90048	310-657-8420	
Reading International Inc 500 Citadel Dr Ste 300 *NASDAQ: RDI* ■ *Web:* www.readingrdi.com	Commerce	CA	90040	213-235-2240	235-2229
Regal Entertainment Group 7132 Regal Ln *NYSE: RGC* ■ *TF Cust Svc:* 877-835-5734 ■ *Web:* www.regmovies.com	Knoxville	TN	37918	865-922-1123	922-3188
Regency Theatres Inc 1440 Eastman Ave *Web:* www.regencymovies.com	Ventura	CA	93003	805-658-6544	

Phone Fax

Southern Theatres LLC
305 Baronne St Ste 900 New Orleans LA 70112 504-297-1133
Web: www.thegrandtheatre.com

Starplex Operating LP 12750 Merit Dr Ste 800 Dallas TX 75251 214-692-6494
Web: www.starplexcinemas.com

United Entertainment Corp
3601 18th St S Ste 104 Saint Cloud MN 56301 320-203-1003
Web: www.uecmovies.com

Virginia Air & Space Center
600 Settlers Landing Rd Hampton VA 23669 757-727-0900
Web: www.vasc.org

Vittum Theater 1012 N Noble St Chicago IL 60642 773-342-4141
Web: www.vittumtheater.org

Wometco Enterprises Inc
3195 Ponce De Leon Blvd Coral Gables FL 33134 305-529-1400 529-1466
Web: miamiseaprison.com

752 THEATERS - RESIDENT

SEE ALSO Performing Arts Facilities p. 2900; Theater Companies p. 2913; Theaters - Broadway p. 3234

All of the theaters listed here are members of the League of Resident Theatres (LORT). In order to become a member of LORT, each theater must be incorporated as a non-profit, IRS-approved organization; must rehearse each self-produced production for a minimum of three weeks; must have a playing season of 12 weeks or more; and must operate under a LORT-Equity contract.

Phone Fax

5th Avenue Theatre Association
1308 Fifth Ave. Seattle WA 98101 206-625-1900
Web: www.5thavenuetheatre.org

A Contemporary Theatre (ACT)
700 Union St Kreielsheimer Pl Seattle WA 98101 206-292-7660 292-7670
TF: 888-584-4849 ■ *Web:* www.acttheatre.org

Actors Theatre of Louisville
316 W Main St Louisville KY 40202 502-584-1205 561-3300
TF: 800-428-5849 ■ *Web:* www.actorstheatre.org

Alabama Shakespeare Festival
One Festival Dr Montgomery AL 36117 334-271-5300 271-5348
TF: 800-841-4273 ■ *Web:* www.asf.net

Alley Theatre 615 Texas Ave. Houston TX 77002 713-220-5700 222-6542
Web: www.alleytheatre.org

Alliance Theatre Co
1280 Peachtree St NE Woodruff Arts Ctr. Atlanta GA 30309 404-733-4650 733-4625
Web: www.alliancetheatre.org

American Repertory Theatre (ART)
64 Brattle St Cambridge MA 02138 617-495-2668 495-1705
Web: www.americanrepertorytheater.org

Arden Theatre Co 40 N Second St. Philadelphia PA 19106 215-922-8900 922-7011
Web: www.ardentheatre.org

Arena Stage 1101 Sixth St SW Washington DC 20024 202-554-9066 488-4056
Web: www.arenastage.org

Arkansas Repertory Theatre
601 Main St PO Box 110 Little Rock AR 72201 501-378-0445 378-0012
Web: www.therep.org

Asolo Repertory Theatre 5555 N Tamiami Tr. Sarasota FL 34243 941-351-9010 351-5796
TF: 800-361-8388 ■ *Web:* www.asolorep.org

Barter Theatre 127 W Main St. Abingdon VA 24210 276-628-3991 619-3335
Web: www.bartertheatre.com

Bb Riverboats Inc 101 Riverboat Row Newport KY 41071 859-261-8500
Web: www.bbriverboats.com

Berkeley Repertory Theatre 2025 Addison St Berkeley CA 94704 510-647-2949 647-2975
Web: www.berkeleyrep.org

Berkshire Theatre Festival 83 E Main St Stockbridge MA 01262 413-298-5576 298-3368
Web: www.berkshiretheatregroup.org

Capital Repertory Theatre 432 State St Schenectady NY 12305 518-462-4531 881-1823
Web: www.capitalrep.org

Center Stage 700 N Calvert St Baltimore MD 21202 410-986-4000 539-3912
Web: www.centerstage.org

City Theatre Co 1300 Bingham St Pittsburgh PA 15203 412-431-4400 431-5535
Web: www.citytheatrecompany.org

Clarence Brown Theatre
University of Tennessee 206 McClung Tower Knoxville TN 37996 865-974-5161 974-4867
Web: www.clarencebrowntheatre.com

Comedy Works Inc 1226 15th St. Denver CO 80202 303-595-3637
Web: www.comedyworks.com

Court Theatre 5535 S Ellis Ave Chicago IL 60637 773-702-7005 834-1897
Web: www.courttheatre.org

Dallas Theater Ctr 3636 Turtle Creek Blvd Dallas TX 75219 214-526-8210 521-7666
Web: www.dallastheatercenter.org

Delaware Theatre Co 200 Water St Wilmington DE 19801 302-594-1104 594-1107
Web: www.delawaretheatre.org

Fringe Theatre Adventures Society
10330 84 Ave Nw Edmonton AB T6E2G9 780-448-9000
Web: www.fringetheatre.ca

Geffen Playhouse 10886 Le Conte Ave Los Angeles CA 90024 310-208-5454 208-8383
Web: www.geffenplayhouse.com

Genesee Theatre 221 N Genesee St Waukegan IL 60085 847-782-2366
Web: www.geneseetheatre.com

George Street Playhouse
Nine Livingston Ave New Brunswick NJ 08901 732-246-7717 247-9151
Web: www.georgestreetplayhouse.org

Geva Theatre Ctr 75 Woodbury Blvd Rochester NY 14607 585-232-1366 232-4031
Web: www.gevatheatre.org

Goodman Theatre 170 N Dearborn St Chicago IL 60601 312-443-3811 443-3821
Web: www.goodmantheatre.org

Goodspeed Musicals PO Box A East Haddam CT 06423 860-873-8664 873-2329
TF: 800-262-8721 ■ *Web:* www.goodspeed.org

Great Lakes Theater Festival
1501 Euclid Ave Ste 300 Cleveland OH 44115 216-241-5490 241-6315
Web: www.greatlakestheater.org

Guthrie Theater 818 S Second St Minneapolis MN 55415 612-377-2224 225-6004
TF Resv: 877-447-8243 ■ *Web:* www.guthrietheater.org

Phone Fax

Hartford Stage Co 50 Church St Hartford CT 06103 860-527-5151 247-8243
Web: www.hartfordstage.org

Huntington Theatre Co
264 Huntington Ave Boston University Theatre Boston MA 02115 617-266-7900 353-8300
Web: www.huntingtontheatre.org

Kansas City Repertory Theatre
4949 Cherry St Kansas City MO 64110 816-235-2727 235-5508
Web: www.kcrep.org

La Jolla Playhouse PO Box 12039 La Jolla CA 92039 858-550-1070 550-1075
Web: www.lajollaplayhouse.com

Laguna Playhouse, The
606 Laguna Canyon Rd PO Box 1747 Laguna Beach CA 92651 949-497-2787 497-6948
Web: www.lagunaplayhouse.com

Lincoln Ctr Theater 150 W 65th St New York NY 10023 800-432-7250 873-0761*
**Fax Area Code:* 212 ■ *Web:* www.lct.org

Maltz Jupiter Theatre 1001 E Indiantown Rd Jupiter FL 33477 561-743-2666 743-0107
TF: 800-445-1666 ■ *Web:* www.jupitertheatre.org

Manhattan Theatre Club Inc
311 W 43rd St Eighth Fl New York NY 10036 212-399-3000 399-4329
Web: www.manhattantheatreclub.com

Massey Theatre 735 Eighth Ave New Westminster BC V3M2R2 604-517-5900
Web: vcn.bc.ca

McCarter Theatre 91 University Pl Princeton NJ 08540 609-258-6500 497-0369
Web: www.mccarter.org

Merrimack Repertory Theatre 132 Warren St Lowell MA 01852 978-654-7550 654-7575
Web: www.mrt.org

Milwaukee Repertory Theater 108 E Wells St. Milwaukee WI 53202 414-224-1761 224-9097
Web: www.milwaukeerep.com

New Repertory Theatre 200 Dexter Ave Watertown MA 02472 617-923-7060
Web: www.newrep.org

Northlight Theatre 9501 Skokie Blvd Skokie IL 60077 847-673-6300 679-1879
TF: 800-356-9377 ■ *Web:* www.northlight.org

Old Globe Theatre 1363 Old Globe Way San Diego CA 92101 619-231-1941 231-5879
Web: www.oldglobe.org

One Yellow Rabbit Performance Theatre
225 8 Ave Se. Calgary AB T2G0K8 403-264-3224
Web: oyr.org

Opera Atelier 157 King St E Toronto ON M5C1G9 416-703-3767
Web: www.operaatelier.com

Oregon Shakespeare Festival 15 S Pioneer St. Ashland OR 97520 541-482-2111
Web: www.orshakes.org

Pasadena Playhouse, The 39 S El Molino Ave Pasadena CA 91101 626-356-7529 204-7399
TF: 800-733-2767 ■ *Web:* www.pasadenaplayhouse.org

People's Light & Theatre Co 39 Conestoga Rd Malvern PA 19355 610-647-1900 640-9521
TF: 800-732-0999 ■ *Web:* www.peopleslight.org

Philadelphia Theatre Co
230 S Broad St 10th Fl Philadelphia PA 19107 215-985-1400 985-5800
Web: www.philadelphiatheatrecompany.org

Pittsburgh Public Theater 621 Penn Ave Pittsburgh PA 15222 412-316-8200 316-8219
TF: 800-732-0999 ■ *Web:* www.ppt.org

PlayMakers Repertory Co
150 Country Club Rd Chapel Hill NC 27599 919-962-7529 904-8396*
**Fax Area Code:* 866 ■ *Web:* www.playmakersrep.org

Portland Ctr Stage (PCS) 128 NW Eleventh Ave Portland OR 97209 503-445-3700 445-3701
Web: www.pcs.org

Portland Stage Co PO Box 1458 Portland ME 04104 207-774-1043 774-0576
Web: www.portlandstage.org

Prince Music Theater 1412 Chestnut St Philadelphia PA 19102 267-239-2941
Web: www.princetheater.org

Repertory Theatre of Saint Louis
130 Edgar Rd PO Box 191730 Saint Louis MO 63119 314-968-7340 968-9638
Web: www.repstl.org

River Center-performing Arts Po Box 2425 Columbus GA 31902 706-256-3607
Web: rivercenter.org

Roundabout Theatre Co 231 W 39th St Ste 1200 New York NY 10018 212-719-9393 869-8817
Web: www.roundabouttheatre.org

San Jose Repertory Theatre
101 Paseo de San Antonio San Jose CA 95113 408-367-7255 367-7236

Seattle Repertory Theatre (SRT)
155 Mercer St PO Box 900923 Seattle WA 98109 206-443-2210 443-2379
TF: 877-900-9285 ■ *Web:* www.seattlerep.org

Shakespeare & Company Inc 70 Kemble St. Lenox MA 01240 413-637-1199
Web: www.shakespeare.org

Shakespeare Theatre 516 Eigth St SE. Washington DC 20003 202-547-3230 547-0226
TF: 877-487-8849 ■ *Web:* www.shakespearetheatre.org

South Coast Repertory 655 Town Ctr Dr Costa Mesa CA 92626 714-708-5500 708-5576
Web: www.scr.org

Spotlight on Kids 20 S Main St Ste 22 Janesville WI 53545 608-758-1451
Web: www.janesvillepac.org

Stagestruck 121 W Chestnut St. Goldsboro NC 27530 919-736-4530
Web: stagestruck.org

Syracuse Stage 820 E Genesee St Syracuse NY 13210 315-443-4008 443-9846
Web: www.syracusestage.org

TADA 15 W 28th St Third Fl New York NY 10001 212-252-1619
Web: www.tadatheater.com

Theatre For A New Audience
154 Christopher St Ste 3D New York NY 10014 212-229-2819 229-2911
TF: 866-811-4111 ■ *Web:* www.tfana.org

TheatreWorks 1100 Hamilton Ct. Palo Alto CA 94301 650-463-1950 463-1963
Web: www.theatreworks.org

Trinity Repertory Co 201 Washington St. Providence RI 02903 401-521-1100 751-5577
Web: www.trinityrep.com

Victory Gardens Theater 2257 N Lincoln Ave Chicago IL 60614 773-549-5788
Web: victorygardens.org

Wilma Theater 265 S Broad St. Philadelphia PA 19107 215-893-9456 893-0895
TF: 800-732-0999 ■ *Web:* www.wilmatheater.org

Winnipeg Fringe Festival 174 Market Ave Winnipeg MB R3B0P8 204-956-1340
Web: www.winnipegfringe.com

Yale Repertory Theatre
1120 Chapel St PO Box 1257 New Haven CT 06505 203-432-1234 432-6423
TF: 800-973-2837 ■ *Web:* www.yalerep.org

753 TICKET BROKERS

Company	City	State	ZIP	Phone	Fax
All American Ticket Service 2616 Philadelphia Pike Ste E *Fax Area Code: 302 ■ TF: 800-669-0571 ■ Web: www.allamericantickets.com	Claymont	DE	19703	800-669-0571	798-6552*
Americana Tickets NY 1535 Broadway TF: 800-833-3121 ■ Web: www.americanatickets.com	New York	NY	10036	212-581-6660	262-9627
Broadway.com 729 Seventh Ave TF: 800-762-3929 ■ Web: broadway.com	New York	NY	10019	212-541-8457	541-4892
Casual Apparel Inc 139 S Main St	Sparta	TN	38583	931-836-3004	
Front Row USA Entertainment 900 N Federal Hwy Ste 200 TF: 800-277-8499 ■ Web: www.frontrowusa.com	Hallandale	FL	33009	305-940-8499	
Global Entertainment Ticketing 6751 N Sunset Blvd Ste 200 Web: www.gettix.net	Glendale	AZ	85305	480-423-3546	
Great Seats Inc 7338 Baltimore Ave Ste 108A TF: 800-664-5056 ■ Web: www.greatseats.com	College Park	MD	20740	301-985-6250	985-6254
Select-A-Ticket Inc 25 Rt 23 S TF: 800-735-3288 ■ Web: www.selectaticket.com	Riverdale	NJ	07457	973-839-6100	839-0870
Theatre Development Fund 1501 Broadway 21st Fl TF: 888-424-4685 ■ Web: www.tdf.org	New York	NY	10036	212-221-0885	768-1563
Ticket Heaven Inc 440 Knoll St Ste 144	Wheaton	IL	60187	630-260-0626	260-4831
Ticket Source Inc 5516 E Mockingbird Ln Ste 100 TF: 800-557-6872 ■ Web: www.ticketsource.com	Dallas	TX	75206	214-821-9011	821-9060
Tickets.com Inc 555 Anton Blvd 11th Fl TF: 800-352-0212 ■ Web: www.tickets.com	Costa Mesa	CA	92626	714-327-5400	327-5410
TicketWeb Inc PO Box 77250 TF Cust Svc: 866-777-8932 ■ Web: www.ticketweb.com	San Francisco	CA	94103	866-777-8932	
Western States Ticket Service 143 W McDowell Rd TF: 800-326-0331 ■ Web: www.wstickets.com	Phoenix	AZ	85003	602-254-3300	254-3387

754 TILE - CERAMIC (WALL & FLOOR)

Company	City	State	ZIP	Phone	Fax
American Marazzi Tile Inc 359 Clay Rd TF: 800-289-8453 ■ Web: marazziusa.com/	Sunnyvale	TX	75182	972-232-3801	226-5629
Ann Sacks Tile & Stone Inc 8120 NE 33rd Dr TF: 800-278-8453 ■ Web: www.annsacks.com	Portland	OR	97211	503-281-7751	287-8807
Armstrong World Industries Inc 2500 Columbia Ave NYSE: AWI ■ *Fax: Hum Res ■ TF Cust Svc: 800-233-3823 ■ Web: www.armstrong.com	Lancaster	PA	17603	717-397-0611	396-6133*
B & W Tile Mfg Company Inc 14600 S Western Ave Web: www.bwtile.com	Gardena	CA	90249	310-538-9579	538-2190
Crossville Porcelain Stone/USA PO Box 1168 TF: 800-221-9093 ■ Web: www.crossvilleinc.com	Crossville	TN	38557	931-484-2110	484-2110
Curran Group Inc 286 Memorial Ct Web: www.currangroup.com	Crystal Lake	IL	60014	815-455-5100	455-7894
Dal-Tile International Inc 7834 Hawn Fwy TF: 800-933-8453 ■ Web: www.daltile.com	Dallas	TX	75217	214-398-1411	309-4553
Deutsche Steinzeug America Inc (DSA) 367 Curie Dr Web: www.deutsche-steinzeug.de	Alpharetta	GA	30005	770-442-5500	442-5502
Ege Seramik America Inc 5600 Oakbrook Pkwy Ste 280 Web: www.egeseramik-usa.com	Norcross	GA	30093	678-291-0888	291-0832
Endicott Tile LLC 57120 707 Rd Web: www.endicott.com	Endicott	NE	68350	402-729-3315	729-5804
Epro Tile Inc 10890 E CR 6 TF: 866-818-3776 ■ Web: www.eprotile.com	Bloomville	OH	44818	866-818-3776	343-8453
Florida Tile Industries Inc 998 Governors Ln Ste 300 TF Cust Svc: 800-352-8453 ■ Web: www.floridatile.com	Lexington	KY	40513	859-219-5200	
Florim USA Inc 300 International Blvd TF: 877-356-7461 ■ Web: www.florimusa.com	Clarksville	TN	37040	931-645-5100	647-5974
Interceramic USA 2333 S Jupiter Rd Web: www.interceramicusa.com	Garland	TX	75041	214-503-5500	503-5555
Interstyle Ceramics & Glass Ltd 3625 Brighton Ave TF: 800-667-1566 ■ Web: www.interstyle.ca	Burnaby	BC	V5A3H5	604-421-7229	421-7544
Ironrock Capital Inc 1201 Millerton St SE TF: 800-325-3945 ■ Web: www.ironrock.com	Canton	OH	44707	330-484-4887	484-3584
Jefferson Ceramic Tile Company Inc 405 S Main St TF: 888-739-8399 ■ Web: www.jctc.com	Jefferson	WI	53549	920-674-5725	674-3677
ME Tile 447 Atlas Dr TF: 888-348-8453 ■ Web: www.metile.com	Nashville	TN	37211	888-348-8453	
Meredith Collection 1201 Millerton St SE TF: 888-325-3945 ■ Web: www.meredithtile.com	Canton	OH	44707	330-484-1656	484-9380
Metropolitan Ceramics 1201 Millerton St SE TF: 800-325-3945 ■ Web: www.metroceramics.com	Canton	OH	44707	800-325-3945	
Nudo Products Inc 1500 Taylor Ave TF: 800-826-4132 ■ Web: www.nudo.com	Springfield	IL	62703	217-528-5636	528-8722
Summitville Tiles Inc 15364 Ohio 644 Web: www.summitville.com	Summitville	OH	43962	330-223-1511	223-1414
Wood Pro Inc 421 Washington St PO Box 363 TF: 800-786-5577 ■ Web: www.woodproinc.com	Auburn	MA	01501	508-832-3291	832-9847

755 TIMBER TRACTS

Company	City	State	ZIP	Phone	Fax
American Lumber Distributors & Brokers Inc 2405 Republic Blvd Web: www.americanlumber1.com	Birmingham	AL	35201	205-791-0155	
Authentic Pine Floors Inc 4042 Hwy 42 Web: www.authenticpinefloors.com	Locust Grove	GA	30248	770-957-6038	
Boething Treeland Farms Inc 23475 Long Valley Rd Web: boethingtreeland.com	Woodland Hills	CA	91367	818-883-1222	712-6979
Boise Cascade LLC 1111 W Jefferson St Ste 300 Web: www.bc.com	Boise	ID	83702	208-384-6161	384-7189
Bulbman 3101 Orange Grove Ave Web: www.bulbman.com	North Highlands	CA	95660	916-920-3234	
Cherry Lake Tree Farm 7836 Cherry Lk Rd Web: www.cherrylake.com	Groveland	FL	34736	352-429-2171	
Crescent Resources Inc 227 W Trade St Ste 1000 Web: crescentcommunities.com/	Charlotte	NC	28202	980-321-6000	
Deltic Timber Corp PO Box 7200 NYSE: DEL ■ Web: www.deltic.com	El Dorado	AR	71731	870-881-9400	881-6454
Dutchman Tree Farms 9689 W Walker Rd Web: www.dutchmantreefarms.com	Manton	MI	49663	231-839-7901	
Federal Wage & Labor Institute 7001 W 43rd St Web: www.fwlli.com	Houston	TX	77092	713-690-5676	
Gillies & Prittie Inc 151 Pleasant Hill Rd Web: www.gilliesandprittie.com	Scarborough	ME	04074	207-883-7815	
Haida Corp PO Box 89 TF: 800-478-3721 ■ Web: haidacorporation.com	Hydaburg	AK	99922	907-285-3721	
Holiday Tree Farms Inc 800 NW Cornell Ave TF: 800-289-3684 ■ Web: www.holidaytreefarm.com	Corvallis	OR	97330	541-753-3236	757-8028
Industrial Timber & Lumber Corp (ITL) 23925 Commerce Pk Rd TF: 800-829-9663 ■ Web: www.itlcorp.com	Beachwood	OH	44122	216-831-3140	831-4734
JM Huber Corp 499 Thornall St 8th Fl *Fax: Hum Res ■ TF: 877-418-0038 ■ Web: www.huber.com	Edison	NJ	08837	732-549-8600	549-2239*
Keim Lumber Company Inc 4465 State Rt 557 PO Box 40 Web: www.keimlumber.com	Charm	OH	44617	330-893-2251	
Kohltech International Ltd 583 MacElmon Rd Web: www.kohltech.com	Debert	NS	B0M1G0	902-662-3100	
Koopman Lumber Company Inc 665 Church St Web: www.koopmanlumber.com	Whitinsville	MA	01588	508-234-4545	
Lester Group, The 101 E Commonwealth Blvd Web: www.lestergroup.com	Martinsville	VA	24115	276-632-2195	632-2117
McShan Lumber Company Inc PO Box 27 TF: 800-882-3712 ■ Web: www.mcshanlumber.com	McShan	AL	35471	205-375-6277	375-2773
Mendocino Redwood Company LLC 850 Kunzler Ranch Rd Web: www.mrc.com	Ukiah	CA	95482	707-463-5110	
Moonworks 1137 Park E Dr TF: 800-975-6666 ■ Web: www.moonworkshome.com	Woonsocket	RI	02895	800-975-6666	
Moulures M Warnet Mouldings Inc 100 Rue Marius-Warnet Web: www.mwarnet.com	Blainville	QC	J7C5P9	450-437-1209	437-3679
Olympic Resource Management 19950 Seventh Ave NE Ste 200 NASDAQ: POPE ■ Web: www.orminc.com	Poulsbo	WA	98370	360-697-6626	697-1156
Pike Lumber Company Inc PO Box 247 TF: 800-356-4554 ■ Web: www.pikelumber.com	Akron	IN	46910	574-893-4511	893-7400
Pioneer Millworks 1180 Commercial Dr Web: www.pioneermillworks.com	Farmington	NY	14425	585-924-9970	
Plum Creek Timber Company Inc 601 Union St Ste 3100 NYSE: PCL ■ TF: 800-858-5347 ■ Web: www.plumcreek.com	Seattle	WA	98101	206-467-3600	467-3795
Ring's End Inc 181 W Ave Web: www.ringsend.com	Darien	CT	06820	203-655-2525	
Rossi Building Materials Inc 835 Stewart St Web: www.rossi-ace.com	Fort Bragg	CA	95437	707-964-4086	
Roy O Martin 2189 Memorial Dr PO Box 1110 Web: www.royomartin.com	Alexandria	LA	71301	318-448-0405	473-2624
Shell Lumber & Hardware Co 2733 SW 27th Ave Web: www.shelllumber.com	Miami	FL	33133	305-856-6401	
Sierra Pacific Industries 19794 Riverside Ave Web: spi-ind.com	Anderson	CA	96007	530-378-8000	378-8109
Starker Forests Inc 7240 SW Philomath Blvd Web: www.starkerforests.com	Corvallis	OR	97333	541-929-2477	929-2178
Westervelt Company Inc, The PO Box 48999 Web: www.westervelt.com	Tuscaloosa	AL	35404	205-562-5000	562-5012
Weyerhaeuser Co 33663 Weyerhaeuser Way S NYSE: WY ■ TF: 800-525-5440 ■ Web: www.weyerhaeuser.com	Federal Way	WA	98003	253-924-2345	924-2685
Yule Tree Farms LLC PO Box 429 TF: 888-970-8733 ■ Web: www.yuletreefarm.com	Aurora	OR	97002	503-651-2114	651-2665

756 TIMESHARE COMPANIES

SEE ALSO Hotels & Hotel Companies p. 2530

Company	City	State	ZIP	Phone	Fax
Bluegreen Corp 4960 Conference Way N Ste 100 NYSE: BXG ■ TF: 800-456-2582 ■ Web: bluegreenvacations.com/	Boca Raton	FL	33431	561-912-8000	912-8100

				Phone	Fax
Central Florida Investments Inc 5601 Windhover Dr . . . TF: 800-218-4363 ■ Web: www.westgateresorts.com	Orlando	FL	32819	407-351-3351	352-8935
Club Intrawest 375 Water St Ste 326 . . . *Fax Area Code: 604 ■ TF: 800-649-9243 ■ Web: www.clubintrawest.com	Vancouver	BC	V6B5C6	800-649-9243	682-7842*
Diamond Resorts International 3745 Las Vegas Blvd S . . . Web: www.diamondresorts.com	Las Vegas	NV	89109	702-261-1000	
Disney Vacation Club 1390 Celebration Blvd . . . TF: 800-500-3990 ■ Web: www.disneyvacationclub.disney.go.com	Celebration	FL	34747	407-566-3100	
Festiva Resorts One Vance Gap Rd . . . *Fax: Financial ■ TF Resv: 866-933-7848 ■ Web: festiva.com/	Asheville	NC	28805	828-254-3378	254-2285*
Four Seasons Hotels & Resorts 1165 Leslie St . . . TF: 800-332-3442 ■ Web: www.fourseasons.com	Toronto	ON	M3C2K8	416-449-1750	441-4374
Hilton Grand Vacations Company LLC 6355 Metro W Blvd Ste 180 . . . TF: 800-230-7068 ■ Web: www.hiltongrandvacations.com	Orlando	FL	32835	407-722-3100	521-3112
Hyatt Vacation Ownership Inc 140 Fountain Pkwy N Ste 570 . . . TF: 800-926-4447 ■ Web: www.hyatt.com	Saint Petersburg	FL	33716	727-803-9400	803-9401
Interval International Inc 6262 Sunset Dr PO Box 431920 . . . TF: 800-828-8200 ■ Web: www.intervalworld.com	Miami	FL	33143	305-666-1861	667-2072
Island One Resorts 8680 Commodity Cir . . . Web: www.diamondresorts.com/rentals/florida-resorts	Orlando	FL	32819	407-859-8900	206-2535
Marriott Vacation Club International 6649 Westwood Blvd Ste 500 . . . TF: 800-307-7312 ■ Web: www.marriottvacationclub.com	Orlando	FL	32821	407-206-6000	
One Napili Way 5355 Lower Honoapiilani Hwy . . . TF Cust Svc: 800-841-6284 ■ Web: www.onenapiliway.com	Lahaina	HI	96761	808-669-2007	669-5103
Resort Condominiums International (RCI) 9998 N Michigan Rd . . . *Fax: Cust Svc ■ TF: 800-338-7777 ■ Web: www.rci.com	Carmel	IN	46032	317-805-8000	805-9677*
Royal Aloha Vacation Club 1505 Dillingham Blvd Ste 212 . . . TF: 800-367-5212 ■ Web: www.ravc.com	Honolulu	HI	96817	808-847-8050	841-5467
Shell Vacations Club 40 Skokie Blvd Ste 350 . . . Web: www.shellvacationsclub.com	Northbrook	IL	60062	847-564-4600	564-0703
Silverleaf Resorts Inc 1221 Riverbend Dr Ste 120 . . . TF: 800-613-0310 ■ Web: www.silverleafresorts.com	Dallas	TX	75247	214-631-1166	637-0585
Starwood Vacation Ownership Inc *Sheraton Vistana Resort* 8800 Vistana Ctr Dr . . . TF Resv: 800-847-8262 ■ Web: www.starwoodvacationnetwork.com	Orlando	FL	32821	407-239-3100	903-4300
Sunchaser Vacation Villas 5129 Riverview Gate Rd . . . TF Resv: 877-451-1250 ■ Web: www.sunchaservillas.ca	Fairmont Hot Springs	BC	V0B1L1	250-345-4545	345-6166
Tempus Resorts International 7380 Sand Lake Rd Ste 600 . . . TF: 877-747-4747 ■ Web: www.tempusresorts.com	Orlando	FL	32819	407-226-1000	
Vacation Internationale 1417 116th Ave NE . . . TF: 800-444-6633 ■ Web: www.vacationinternationale.com	Bellevue	WA	98004	425-454-8429	456-0536
WorldMark the Club 9805 Willows Rd NE . . . TF: 800-722-3487 ■ Web: www.worldmarktheclub.com	Redmond	WA	98052	425-498-1950	498-1968

757 TIRES - MFR

				Phone	Fax
Albert Tire LLC 39 Phoenix Dr . . . Web: www.alberttire.com	West Deptford	NJ	08086	856-663-0574	
All Business Machines Inc 2555 Third St Ste 100 . . . TF: 888-880-7801 ■ Web: www.allbusinessmachines.com	Sacramento	CA	95818	888-880-7801	
Bridgestone Americas Holding Inc 535 Marriott Dr . . . TF Cust Svc: 877-201-2373 ■ Web: www.bridgestone-firestone.com	Nashville	TN	37214	615-937-1000	937-3621
Callaghan Tire 1511 38th Ave E . . . Web: www.callaghantire.com	Bradenton	FL	34208	941-746-6188	
Carlisle Tire & Wheel Mfg 23 Windham Blvd . . . TF Sales: 800-827-1001 ■ Web: www.carlisletransportationproducts.com	Aiken	SC	29805	803-643-2919	643-2919
Coker Tire Co 1317 Chestnut St . . . Web: www.cokertire.com	Chattanooga	TN	37402	423-265-6368	
Continental Tire North America Inc 1800 Continental Blvd . . . *Fax: Mktg ■ TF: 877-235-0102 ■ Web: www.conti-online.com	Charlotte	NC	28273	704-583-3900	583-8947*
Cooper Tire & Rubber Co 701 Lima Ave . . . NYSE: CTB ■ TF: 800-854-6288 ■ Web: www.coopertire.com	Findlay	OH	45840	419-423-1321	424-4108
Dunlop Tires PO Box 1109 . . . TF: 800-845-8378 ■ Web: www.dunlopmotorcycle.com	Buffalo	NY	14240	800-845-8378	
Goodyear Tire & Rubber Co 200 Innovation Way . . . NASDAQ: GT ■ *Fax: Cust Svc ■ TF Cust Svc: 800-321-2136 ■ Web: www.goodyear.com	Akron	OH	44316	330-796-2121	796-2222*
Hankook Tire America Corp 1450 Valley Rd . . . TF: 800-426-8252 ■ Web: www.hankooktireusa.com	Wayne	NJ	07470	973-633-9000	633-0028
Hercules Tire & Rubber Co 16380 E US Rt 224 - 200 . . . TF: 800-677-9535 ■ Web: www.herculestire.com	Findlay	OH	45840	419-425-6400	425-6404
Hercules Tire Sales Inc 10130 E 51st St . . . Web: www.herculestiresales.com	Tulsa	OK	74146	918-627-7353	
K&M Tire Inc 965 Spencerville Rd PO Box 279 . . . TF: 877-879-5407 ■ Web: www.kmtire.com	Delphos	OH	45833	419-695-1061	
Kal Tire Ltd 1540 Kalamalka Lk Rd PO Box 1240 . . . Web: www.kaltire.com	Vernon	BC	V1T6N6	250-542-2366	
La Cie Canada Tire Inc 21500 Transcanadienne . . . Web: www.cdatire.com	Baie-D'Urfe	QC	H9X4B7	514-457-0155	457-1158
Lyna Manufacturing Inc 1125 15th St W . . . Web: tirelyna.com	North Vancouver	BC	V7P1M7	604-990-0988	
Martin Wheel Company Inc 342 W Ave . . . TF: 800-462-7846 ■ Web: www.martinwheelco.com	Tallmadge	OH	44278	330-633-3278	633-3303
Michelin North America Inc 1 PkwyS PO Box 19001 . . . *Fax: Cust Svc ■ TF Cust Svc: 800-847-3435 ■ Web: www.michelin.com	Greenville	SC	29602	864-458-5000	458-6359*
Mickey Thompson Tires 4600 Prosper Dr . . . TF: 800-222-9092 ■ Web: www.mickeythompsontires.com	Stow	OH	44224	330-928-9092	928-0503
Millennium Industrial Tires LLC 433 Lane Dr . . . Web: www.millenniumtire.com	Florence	AL	35630	256-764-2900	
Mitchell Industrial Tire Co 2915 Eigth Ave PO Box 71839 . . . *Fax: Sales ■ TF: 800-251-7226 ■ Web: www.mitco.com	Chattanooga	TN	37407	423-698-4442	697-7143*
OTR Wheel Engineering Inc Six Riverside Industrial Park PO Box 1853 . . . Web: www.otrwheel.com	Rome	GA	30162	706-235-9781	
Pete's Road Service Inc 2230 E Orangethorpe Ave . . . Web: www.petesrs.com	Fullerton	CA	92831	714-446-1207	
Purcell Tire & Rubber Co 301 N Hall St . . . *Fax: Hum Res ■ TF: 888-878-2355 ■ Web: www.purcelltire.com	Potosi	MO	63664	573-438-2131	438-2151*
Robbins LLC 3415 Thompson St . . . *Fax Area Code: 800 ■ TF: 800-633-3312 ■ Web: www.robbinsllc.com	Muscle Shoals	AL	35661	256-383-5441	821-7918*
SolidBoss Worldwide Inc 200 Veterans Blvd . . . TF: 888-258-7252 ■ Web: www.solidboss.com	South Haven	MI	49090	269-637-6356	637-6356
Specialty Tires of America Inc 1600 Washington St . . . TF: 800-622-7327 ■ Web: www.stausaonline.com	Indiana	PA	15701	724-349-9010	349-8192
Superior Tire & Rubber Corp 1818 Pennsylvania Ave W PO Box 308 . . . TF Cust Svc: 800-209-1456 ■ Web: www.superiortire.com	Warren	PA	16365	814-723-2370	726-0740
Tech International 200 E Coshocton St . . . TF: 800-336-8324 ■ Web: www.techtirerepairs.com	Johnstown	OH	43031	740-967-9015	967-1039
Titan Tire Co 2345 E Market St . . . TF: 800-872-2327 ■ Web: www.titan-intl.com	Des Moines	IA	50317	515-265-9200	265-9301
Toyo Tire USA Corp 6261 Katella Ave Ste 2B . . . *Fax Area Code: 714 ■ *Fax: Mktg ■ TF: 800-678-3250 ■ Web: toyotires.com	Cypress	CA	90630	800-678-3250	229-6184*
Turbo Wholesale Tires Inc 5793 Martin Rd . . . Web: turbotiresonline.com	Irwindale	CA	91706	626-856-1400	
Valley Tire Company Inc 1002 Arentzen Blvd . . . Web: www.valleytireco.com	Charleroi	PA	15022	724-417-9564	
Yokohama Tire Corp 601 S Acacia Ave . . . TF: 800-423-4544 ■ Web: www.yokohamatire.com	Fullerton	CA	92831	714-870-3800	

758 TIRES & TUBES - WHOL

				Phone	Fax
4 Wheel Parts 8227-100 Ave . . . Web: www.national4wd.com	Fort St. John	BC	V1J1W7	250-787-2566	
A & E Tire Inc 3855 E 52nd Ave . . . Web: www.aetire.com	Denver	CO	80216	303-308-6900	
Allied Oil & Supply Inc 2209 S 24th St . . . TF: 800-333-3717 ■ Web: www.alliedoil.com	Omaha	NE	68108	402-344-4343	344-4360
American Tire Depot 1123 W Commonwealth Ave . . . *Fax Area Code: 562 ■ TF: 855-333-2823 ■ Web: www.phillipstire.com	Fullerton	CA	92833	714-525-2306	677-3956*
Aperia Technologies Inc 1616 Rollins Rd . . . Web: www.aperiatech.com	Burlingame	CA	94010	415-494-9624	
Ball Tire & Gas Inc 620 S Ripley Blvd . . . Web: balltire.net	Alpena	MI	49707	989-354-4186	356-2080
Bauer Built Inc PO Box 248 . . . TF: 800-268-5114 ■ Web: www.bauerbuilt.com	Durand	WI	54736	715-672-4295	672-4675
Ben Tire Distributors Ltd 203 E Madison St PO Box 158 . . . *Fax Area Code: 217 ■ TF: 800-252-8961 ■ Web: www.bentire.com	Toledo	IL	62468	800-252-8961	849-3019*
Best-One Tire & Service LLC 101 N Polk St . . . Web: www.bestonetire.com	Monroe	IN	46772	260-692-6171	
BFGoodrich Tires Inc One Pkwy S . . . TF: 877-788-8899 ■ Web: www.bfgoodrichtires.com	Greenville	SC	29602	877-788-8899	
Bridgestone Canada Inc 5770 Hurontario St Ste 400 . . . Web: www.bridgestone-firestone.ca	Mississauga	ON	L5R3G5	905-890-1990	890-1991
Brookside Equipment 7707 Mosley Rd . . . Web: www.brooksideusa.com	Houston	TX	77017	713-943-7100	943-9102
Clark Tire & Auto Supply Co Inc 220 S Ctr St . . . TF: 800-968-3092 ■ Web: www.clarktire.com	Hickory	NC	28602	828-322-2303	324-2906
Community Imports Inc 8340 W 159th St . . . Web: www.communityhonda.com	Orland Park	IL	60462	708-364-2600	
CRM Co 15800 S Avalon Blvd . . . Web: www.crmrubber.com	Rancho Dominguez	CA	90220	310-538-2222	
Cross-Midwest Tire Co 401 S 42nd St . . . Web: www.crossmidwest.com	Kansas City	KS	66106	913-321-3003	
Dapper Tire Company Inc 4025 Lockridge St . . . TF: 800-266-7172 ■ Web: www.dappertire.com	San Diego	CA	92102	619-266-1397	266-2384
De Ronde Tire Supply Inc 95 Rapin Pl . . . TF: 800-227-4647 ■ Web: www.etrucktire.com	Buffalo	NY	14211	716-897-6690	893-5716
Dealer Tire LLC 3711 Chester Ave . . . Web: www.dealertire.com	Cleveland	OH	44114	216-432-0088	
East Bay Tire Co 2200 Huntington Dr Unit C . . . TF: 800-831-8473 ■ Web: eastbaytire.com	Fairfield	CA	94533	707-437-4700	437-4800
Eddie's Tire Service Inc 3077 Valley Rd . . . Web: eddiestire.net	Berkeley Springs	WV	25411	304-258-1368	258-1777
Eurotire Inc 200 S Biscayne Blvd 55th Fl . . . Web: www.eurotire.net	Miami	FL	33131	305-900-2850	
Free Service Tire Co Inc PO Box 6187 . . . TF: 855-646-1423 ■ Web: www.freeservicetire.com	Johnson City	TN	37602	423-979-2250	979-2262
Friend Tire Co 11 Industrial Dr . . . *Fax Area Code: 417 ■ TF: 800-950-8473 ■ Web: www.friendtire.com	Monett	MO	65708	800-950-8473	235-3062*
Goodyear Canada Inc 450 Kipling . . . Web: www.goodyear.ca	Toronto	ON	M8Z5E1	416-201-4300	
Grismer Tire Co PO Box 337 . . . Web: www.grismertire.com	Dayton	OH	45401	937-643-2526	224-3800

Name / Address	City	State	ZIP	Phone	Fax
K&W Tire Company Inc 735 N Prince St Web: www.kwtire.com	Lancaster	PA	17603	717-397-3596	
Kauffman Tire Inc 2832 Anvil Block Rd Web: www.kauffmantire.com	Ellenwood	GA	30294	404-762-4944	
Ken Jones Tire Inc 73 Chandler St TF: 800-225-9513 ■ Web: www.kenjones.com	Worcester	MA	01609	508-755-5255	755-4397
Kenda USA 7095 Americana Pkwy TF: 866-536-3287 ■ Web: www.kendatire.com	Reynoldsburg	OH	43068	614-866-9803	866-9805
Kumho Tire USA Inc 10299 Sixth St TF: 800-445-8646 ■ Web: www.kumhotireusa.com	Rancho Cucamonga	CA	91730	909-428-3999	
Lakin General Corp 2044 N Dominick St Web: www.lakincorp.com	Chicago	IL	60614	773-871-6675	
Lakin Tire West Inc 15305 Spring Ave TF: 800-488-2752 ■ Web: www.lakintire.com	Santa Fe Springs	CA	90670	562-802-2752	802-7584
Michelin North America (Canada) Inc 3020 Jacques-Bureau Ave Web: www.michelin.ca	Laval	QC	H7P6G2	450-978-4700	
Michelin North America Inc 1 PkwyS PO Box 19001 *Fax: Cust Svc ■ TF Cust Svc: 800-847-3435 ■ Web: www.michelin.com	Greenville	SC	29602	864-458-5000	458-6359*
Net Driven 280 Eureka St TF: 800-647-6133 ■ Web: gatewaytire.net	Batesville	MS	38606	662-563-1143	
OK Tire Stores Inc 19082 21st Ave Web: www.oktire.com	Surrey	BC	V3S3M3	604-542-7999	542-7990
Parrish Tire Company Inc 5130 Indiana Ave TF: 800-849-8473 ■ Web: www.parrishtire.com	Winston-Salem	NC	27106	336-767-0202	744-2716
Pete's Tire Barns Inc 275 E Main St Web: www.petestire.com	Orange	MA	01364	978-544-8811	
Petro Amigos Supply Inc 777 N Eldridge Pkwy Ste 400 Web: www.petro-amigos.com	Houston	TX	77079	281-497-0858	
Piedmont Truck Tires Inc PO Box 18228 TF: 800-274-8473 ■ Web: www.piedmonttrucktires.com	Greensboro	NC	27419	336-668-0091	
Pomps Tire Service Inc 1123 Cedar St TF: 800-236-8911 ■ Web: www.pompstire.com	Green Bay	WI	54301	920-435-8301	435-1546
Reliable Tire Co 805 N Blackhorse Pk *Fax Area Code: 856 ■ TF All: 800-342-3426 ■ Web: www.reliabletire.com	Blackwood	NJ	08012	800-342-3426	232-6583*
Snyder Tire 401 Cadiz Rd TF: 800-967-8473 ■ Web: www.snydertire.com	Steubenville	OH	43953	740-264-5543	
Solideal USA Inc 306 Forsyth Hall Dr	Charlotte	NC	28273	704-374-9700	
South Dade Automotive Inc 2875 NW 77th Ave Web: www.sdatire.com	Doral	FL	33122	305-718-6664	718-3989
Southeastern Wholesale Tire Co 4721 Trademark Dr TF General: 800-849-9215 ■ Web: www.southeasterntireonline.com	Raleigh	NC	27610	919-832-3900	861-4357
Southern Tire Mart LLC 529 Industrial Park Web: www.stmtires.com	Columbia	MS	39429	601-424-3200	
Steepleton Tire Co 777 S Lauderdale St Web: steepletontire.com	Memphis	TN	38126	901-774-6440	774-6445
T BC Corp 4770 Hickory Hill Rd Web: www.tbcprivatebrands.com	Memphis	TN	38141	866-822-4968	
Ted Wiens Tire & Auto Centers 1701 Las Vegas Blvd S Web: www.tedwiens.com	Las Vegas	NV	89104	702-732-2382	
Terry's Tire Town Inc 2360 W Main St PO Box 2405	Alliance	OH	44601	800-235-2921	
Tire Centers LLC 310 Inglesby Pkwy TF: 800-603-2430 ■ Web: www.tirecenters.com	Duncan	SC	29334	864-329-2700	329-2900
Tire Rack 7101 Vorden Pkwy TF: 888-541-1777 ■ Web: www.tirerack.com	South Bend	IN	46628	574-287-2345	236-7707
Tire Warehouse Inc 7500 NW 35 Terr TF: 877-235-0102 ■ Web: www.tiregroup.com	Miami	FL	33122	305-696-0096	696-5926
Tire Wholesalers Co Inc 1783 E 14-Mile Rd TF: 800-577-3353 ■ Web: twitire.com	Troy	MI	48083	248-589-9910	589-9919
Tire's Warehouse Inc 240 Teller St TF: 800-655-8851 ■ Web: tireswarehouse.net	Corona	CA	92879	951-808-0111	808-9062
Tire-Rama Inc 1401 Industrial Ave PO Box 23509 TF: 800-828-1642 ■ Web: www.tirerama.com	Billings	MT	59104	406-245-4006	245-0257
TO Haas Tire Co Inc 2400 'O' St PO Box 81067 TF: 866-393-5204 ■ Web: www.tohaastire.com	Lincoln	NE	68510	402-261-2854	474-0336
Tyres International Inc 4637 Allen Rd Web: www.tyres1.com	Stow	OH	44224	330-374-1000	
WD Tire Warehouse Inc 3805 E Livingston Ave Web: www.wdtire.com	Columbus	OH	43227	614-461-8944	461-0136
Wheels Etc 17521 Mesa St *Fax Area Code: 760 ■ TF: 800-758-4737 ■ Web: www.wheels-etc.com	Hesperia	CA	92345	909-350-8200	949-1000*

759 TOBACCO & TOBACCO PRODUCTS

Name / Address	City	State	ZIP	Phone	Fax
Abel Reel, The 165 Aviador St TF: 866-511-7444 ■ Web: www.abelreels.com	Camarillo	CA	93010	805-484-8789	482-0701
Albert H Notini & Sons Inc 225 Aiken St TF: 800-366-8464 ■ Web: www.ahnotini.com	Lowell	MA	01854	978-459-7151	458-7692
Alliance One International Inc 8001 Aerial Ctr Pkwy PO Box 2009 NYSE: AOI ■ TF: 800-937-5449 ■ Web: www.aointl.com	Morrisville	NC	27560	919-379-4300	379-4346
AMCON Distributing Co 7405 Irvington Rd NYSE: DIT ■ TF: 888-201-5997 ■ Web: www.amcon.com	Omaha	NE	68122	402-331-3727	331-4834
Burklund Distributors Inc 2500 N Main St Ste 3 TF: 800-322-2876 ■ Web: www.burklund.com	East Peoria	IL	61611	309-694-1900	694-6788
Caldwell Wholesale Company Inc 9630 Saint Vincent Ave Web: caldwell-wholesale.com	Shreveport	LA	71106	318-869-3101	
Carolina Group 2405 Westwood Ave Ste 101 *Fax Area Code: 336	Richmond	VA	23230	804-349-4796	335-7414*
Cigar.com Inc 1911 Spillman Dr *Fax Area Code: 877 ■ TF: 800-357-9800 ■ Web: www.cigar.com	Bethlehem	PA	18015	800-357-9800	464-2872*
Commonwealth Altadis Inc 5900 N Andrews Ave Ste 1000 TF Orders: 800-446-5797 ■ Web: www.altadisusa.com	Fort Lauderdale	FL	33309	954-772-9000	938-7811
Core-Mark International 395 Oyster Pt Blvd Ste 415 TF: 800-622-1713 ■ Web: www.coremark.com	South San Francisco	CA	94080	650-589-9445	
Domestic Tobacco Co 830 N Prince St	Lancaster	PA	17603	717-393-0613	397-2381
Eby-Brown Co 280 W Shuman Blvd Ste 280 TF: 800-553-8249 ■ Web: www.eby-brown.com	Naperville	IL	60563	630-778-2800	778-2830
Finck Cigar Co 414 Vera Cruz St TF Orders: 800-221-0638 ■ Web: www.finckcigarcompany.com	San Antonio	TX	78207	210-226-4191	226-2825
Flue-Cured Tobacco Co-op 1304 Annapolis Dr Web: www.ustobaccofarmer.com	Raleigh	NC	27608	919-821-4560	821-4564
Hail & Cotton Inc 2500 S Main St Web: www.hailcotton.com	Springfield	TN	37172	615-384-9576	
Holts Cigar Co 1522 Walnut St TF: 800-523-1641 ■ Web: www.holts.com	Philadelphia	PA	19102	215-732-8500	732-4988
J Polep Distribution Services Inc 705 Meadow St TF: 800-447-6537 ■ Web: www.jpolep.com	Chicopee	MA	01013	413-592-4141	592-5870
JC Newman Cigar Co 2701 16th St TF Orders: 800-477-1884 ■ Web: www.cigarfamily.com	Tampa	FL	33605	813-248-2124	247-2135
Keilson-Dayton Co 107 Commerce Pk Dr TF: 800-759-3174 ■ Web: keilsondayton.com	Dayton	OH	45404	937-236-1070	236-2124
Klafter's Inc 216 N Beaver St *Fax Area Code: 724 ■ TF: 800-922-1233 ■ Web: www.klafters.com/	New Castle	PA	16101	800-922-1233	658-8633*
Macon Cigar & Tobacco Company Inc 575 12th St Web: www.mctweb.com	Macon	GA	31201	478-743-2236	744-0903
Mathew Zechman Company Inc 152 Resar Ct	Elyria	OH	44035	440-366-2442	
Modern Distributors Inc 817 W Columbia St Web: teammodern.com	Somerset	KY	42501	606-679-1178	
National Cigar Corp 407 N Main St PO Box 97 *Fax Area Code: 765 ■ TF: 800-321-0247 ■ Web: www.broadleafcigars.com	Frankfort	IN	46041	800-321-0247	654-6932*
National Tobacco Company LP 5201 Interchange Way TF Cust Svc: 800-579-0975 ■ Web: zigzag.com	Louisville	KY	40229	502-778-4421	
Oliva Tobacco Co 3104 N Armenia Ave Web: olivatobacco.com	Tampa	FL	33607	813-248-4921	
Philip Morris USA 2325 Bells Rd TF: 800-343-0975 ■ Web: www.philipmorrisusa.com	Richmond	VA	23234	804-274-2000	
Queen City Wholesale Inc 1001 E 8th PO Box 1083 Web: queencitywholesale.com	Sioux Falls	SD	57103	605-336-3215	
Reynolds American Inc PO Box 2990 NYSE: RAI ■ Web: www.reynoldsamerican.com	Winston-Salem	NC	27102	336-741-7693	741-0881
RJ Reynolds Tobacco Co 401 N Main St Web: www.rjrt.com	Winston-Salem	NC	27102	336-741-5000	741-2998
Sledd Co 100 E Cove Ext TF General: 800-333-0374 ■ Web: www.sleddco.com	Wheeling	WV	26003	304-243-1820	243-1209
Star Scientific Inc 4470 Cox Rd Ste 110 NASDAQ: RCPI ■ Web: rockcreekpharmaceuticals.com/	Glen Allen	VA	23060	804-527-1970	
Swisher International Inc 459 E 16th St Web: www.swisher.com	Jacksonville	FL	32206	904-353-4311	
Tobacco Superstores Inc 3550 Commerce Rd Web: tobaccosuper.com	Forrest City	AR	72335	870-633-0099	
Universal Leaf Tobacco Co Inc 1501 N Hamilton St PO Box 25099 *Fax: Hum Res ■ Web: www.universalcorp.com	Richmond	VA	23260	804-359-9311	254-3584*

760 TOOL & DIE SHOPS

Name / Address	City	State	ZIP	Phone	Fax
A & M Tool & Die Company Inc 64 Mill St TF: 800-848-4628 ■ Web: www.am-tool.com	Southbridge	MA	01550	508-764-3241	765-1377
A Finkl & Sons Co 2011 N Southport Ave TF: 800-343-2562 ■ Web: www.finkl.com	Chicago	IL	60614	773-975-2510	348-5347
ABA-PGT Inc 10 Gear Dr PO Box 8270 TF: 877-840-2172 ■ Web: www.abapgt.com	Manchester	CT	06040	860-649-4591	643-7619
Able Wire Edm Inc 440 Atlas St Web: www.ableedm.com	Brea	CA	92821	714-255-1967	
Abrasive-Form Inc 454 Scott Dr Web: www.abrasive-form.com	Bloomingdale	IL	60108	630-893-7800	893-6313
Advance Industrial Machine LLP W6335 Design Dr Web: www.aim-msm.com	Greenville	WI	54942	920-757-6786	
Aegis Sales & Engineering Inc 5411 Industrial Rd Web: www.aegisparts.com	Fort Wayne	IN	46825	260-483-4160	
Aerostar Aerospace Manufacturing Inc 20825 N 25th Pl Web: www.aerostaraerospace.com	Phoenix	AZ	85050	602-861-1145	
Ahaus Tool & Engineering Inc PO Box 280 Web: www.ahaus.com	Richmond	IN	47375	765-962-3571	962-3426
Akron Special Machinery Inc 2740 Cory Ave Web: www.polinggroup.com	Akron	OH	44314	330-753-1077	
Alco Industries Inc 820 Adams Ave Ste 130 Web: www.alcoind.com	Norristown	PA	19403	610-666-0930	666-0752
Alcona Tool & Machine Inc PO Box 340 Web: www.alconatool.com	Lincoln	MI	48742	989-736-8151	736-6717
Alden Tool Company Inc 199 New Pk Dr Web: www.aldentool.com	Berlin	CT	06037	860-828-3556	828-8872
Alliance Carolina Tool & Mold Corp 125 Glenn Bridge Rd Web: www.alliance-carolina.com	Arden	NC	28704	828-684-7831	
Alliance Precision Plastics 1220 Lee Rd Web: www.allianceppc.com	Rochester	NY	14606	585-426-5310	426-5081
Allied Pacific 2951 E La Palma Ave Web: www.allied-pacific.com	Anaheim	CA	92806	714-630-8145	

Company / Address	City	State	ZIP	Phone	Fax
Allways Precision Inc 14001 Van Dyke Rd *Web:* allwaysprecision.com	Plainfield	IL	60544	815-577-1600	
Alpha Precision Machining Inc 19652 70th Ave South *Web:* www.alphapre.com	Kent	WA	98032	253-395-7381	
Alt's Tool & Machine Inc 10926 Woodside Ave N *Web:* www.altstool.com	Santee	CA	92071	619-562-6653	
Altest Corp 898 Faulstich Ct *Web:* www.altestcorp.com	San Jose	CA	95112	408-436-9900	
American Tool & Mold Inc 1700 Sunshine Dr *Web:* www.a-t-m.com	Clearwater	FL	33765	727-447-7377	447-0125
Ams Production Machining Inc 800 Andico Rd *Web:* www.amsmachining.com	Plainfield	IN	46168	317-838-9273	
Anchor Tool & Die Co 12200 Brookpark Rd *Web:* www.anchor-mfg.com	Cleveland	OH	44130	216-362-1850	265-7833
Apex Tool Works Inc 3200 Tollview Dr *Web:* www.apextool.com	Rolling Meadows	IL	60008	847-394-5810	394-2739
Arlington Machine & Tool Co 90 New Dutch Ln *Web:* www.arlingtonmachine.com	Fairfield	NJ	07004	973-276-1377	
Armin Industries 1500 N La Fox St *Web:* www.armin-ind.com	South Elgin	IL	60177	847-742-1864	742-0253
Armstrong Mold Corp 6910 Manlius Ctr Rd *Web:* www.armstrongmold.com	East Syracuse	NY	13057	315-437-1517	437-9198
Arobotech Systems Inc 1524 E Avis Dr *Web:* www.arobotech.com	Madison Heights	MI	48071	248-588-9080	
Astro Tool & Machine Company Inc 810 Martin St *Web:* www.astrotoolco.com	Rahway	NJ	07065	732-382-2450	382-6394
Ateliers Lesage Inc (les) 1330 Rue Soucy *Web:* atelierslesage.com	Saint-hubert	QC	J4T1A3	450-445-5088	
Atlas Machining & Welding Inc 777 Smith Ln *Web:* www.atlasmw.com	Northampton	PA	18067	610-262-1374	
Atlas Tool Inc 29880 Groesbeck Hwy *Web:* www.atlastool.com	Roseville	MI	48066	586-778-3570	778-3931
Atscott Manufacturing Company Inc 1150 Holstein Dr NE *Web:* www.atscott.com	Pine City	MN	55063	320-629-2501	
Attodyne Inc One Westside Dr Unit 6 *Web:* www.attodynelasers.com	Toronto	ON	M9C1B2	416-840-9096	
Austro Mold Inc 3 Rutter St *TF:* 800-637-7774 ■ *Web:* www.austromold.com	Rochester	NY	14606	585-458-1410	458-0963
Autodie LLC 44 Coldbrook St NW *Web:* www.autodie.com	Grand Rapids	MI	49503	616-454-9361	356-1429
Aztalan Engineering Inc 100 S Industrial Dr *Web:* www.aztalan.com	Lake Mills	WI	53551	920-648-3411	
Baum Machine Inc N253 Stoney Brook Rd *Web:* www.baummachine.com	Appleton	WI	54915	920-738-6613	
Bent River Machine Inc 951 Rio Torcido *Web:* www.bent-river.com	Clarkdale	AZ	86324	928-634-7568	
Bilco Tool Corp 30076 Dequindre Rd *Web:* www.bilcotool.com	Warren	MI	48092	586-574-9300	574-9340
Birdsall Tool & Gage Co 24735 Crestview Ct *Web:* www.birdsalltool.com	Farmington Hills	MI	48335	248-474-5150	474-5600
Bowden Manufacturing Corp 4590 Beidler Rd *Web:* bowdenmfg.com	Willoughby	OH	44094	440-946-1770	
Brinkman Tool & Die Inc 325 Kiser St *Web:* www.brinkmantool.com	Dayton	OH	45404	937-222-1161	222-2079
Buckeye Machine Fabricators Inc 610 E Lima St *Web:* www.buckeyemachine.com	Forest	OH	45843	419-273-2521	
Busch Precision Inc 8200 N Faulkner Rd *Web:* www.buschprecision.com	Milwaukee	WI	53224	414-362-7300	
Byran Company Inc, The 18092 Redondo Cir *Web:* mail.byranco.com	Huntington Beach	CA	92648	714-841-9808	
C & H Machine Inc 943 S Andreasen Dr *Web:* www.c-hmachine.com	Escondido	CA	92029	760-746-6459	
C&A Tool Engineering Inc 4100 N US 33 PO Box 94 *Web:* www.catool.com	Churubusco	IN	46723	260-693-2167	693-3633
C.B.S. Boring & Machine Company Inc 33750 Riviera Dr *Web:* www.cbsboring.com	Fraser	MI	48026	586-294-7540	
CA Spalding Co 1011 Cedar Ave *Web:* www.caspalding.com	Croydon	PA	19021	267-550-9000	550-9008
Caco-Pacific Corp 813 N Cummings Rd *Web:* www.cacopacific.com	Covina	CA	91724	626-331-3361	966-4219
Calmax Technology Inc 526 Laurelwood Rd *Web:* www.calmaxtechnology.com	Santa Clara	CA	95054	408-748-8660	
Canadian Tool & Die Ltd 1331 Chevrier Blvd *Web:* www.canadiantool.com	Winnipeg	MB	R3T1Y4	204-453-6833	
Carlson Tool & Manufacturing Corp W57 N14386 Doerr Way PO Box 85 *TF:* 800-532-2252 ■ *Web:* www.carlsontool.com	Cedarburg	WI	53012	262-377-2020	377-1751
Carr Lane Mfg 4200 Carr Ln Ct *Web:* www.carrlane.com	Saint Louis	MO	63119	314-647-6200	647-5736
Cbw Automation 3939 automation way *Web:* www.cbwautomation.com	Fort collins	CO	80525	970-229-9500	
Chicago Cutting Die Co 3555 Woodhead Dr *TF:* 800-747-3437 ■ *Web:* www.chicagocuttingdie.com	Northbrook	IL	60062	847-509-5800	509-0355
Chicago Mold Engineering Co 615 Stetson Ave *Web:* www.chicagomold.com	Saint Charles	IL	60174	630-584-1311	584-8695
Church Metal Spinning Co 5050 N 124th St *Web:* www.churchmetal.com	Milwaukee	WI	53225	414-461-6460	
Claret Canada Inc 1400 Rue Joliot-curie *Web:* claretnet.com	Boucherville	QC	J4B7L9	450-449-5774	
Classic Turning Inc 3000 E S St *Web:* www.classicturning.com	Jackson	MI	49201	517-764-1335	
Cleveland Punch & Die Co 666 Pratt St PO Box 769 *TF:* 888-451-4342 ■ *Web:* www.clevelandpunch.com	Ravenna	OH	44266	888-451-4342	451-6877
Clifty Engineering & Tool Company Inc 2949 Clifty Dr *Web:* www.cliftyengineering.com	Madison	IN	47250	812-273-3272	273-3272
CNC Machine Products Inc 1709 W 20th St *Web:* www.cncmp.com	Joplin	MO	64804	417-782-2627	
Coast Composites Inc 1395 S Lyon St *Web:* www.coastcomposites.com	Santa Ana	CA	92705	949-455-0665	455-0061
Coastal Casting Service Inc 2903 Gano St *Web:* www.circleeranch.com	Houston	TX	77009	713-223-4439	
Cockburn Enterprises Inc PO Box 2369 *Web:* www.ckbent.com	Muscle Shoals	AL	35662	256-381-3620	381-9146
Cole Tool & Die Co 241 Ashland Rd *Web:* www.coletool.com	Mansfield	OH	44905	419-522-1272	522-5506
Colonial Machine Co 1041 Mogadore Rd *Web:* www.colonial-machine.com	Kent	OH	44240	330-673-5859	673-5859
Comet Die & Engraving Co 909 Larch Ave *Web:* www.cometdie.com	Elmhurst	IL	60126	630-833-5600	833-2644
Composidie Inc 1295 Rt 380 *Web:* www.composidie.com	Apollo	PA	15613	724-727-3466	727-3788
Custom Mold Engineering Inc 9780 S Franklin Dr *TF:* 800-448-2005 ■ *Web:* www.custommold.com	Franklin	WI	53132	414-421-5444	421-5444
D & D Manufacturing Inc 500 Territorial Dr **Fax Area Code:* 630 ■ *TF:* 888-300-6869 ■ *Web:* www.ddmfg.com	Bolingbrook	IL	60440	888-300-6869	759-0043*
D-M-E Co 29111 Stephenson Hwy *TF:* 800-626-6653 ■ *Web:* www.dme.net	Madison Heights	MI	48071	248-398-6000	544-5705
Danly IEM 6779 Engle Rd Ste A-F **Fax Area Code:* 440 ■ *TF:* 877-534-8986 ■ *Web:* www.danly.com	Cleveland	OH	44130	877-534-8986	239-7605*
Dayton Progress Corp 500 Progress Rd *Web:* www.daytonprogress.com	Dayton	OH	45449	937-859-5111	859-5353
Decatur Mold Tool & Engineering Inc 3330 N State Rd 7 PO Box 387 *Web:* www.decaturmold.com	North Vernon	IN	47265	812-346-5188	346-7357
Del-Tech Manufacturing Inc 9703 Penn Rd *Web:* www.deltech.ca	Prince George	BC	V2N5T6	250-564-3585	
Delaware Machinery & Tool 700 S Mulberry St *Web:* www.delawaredynamics.com	Muncie	IN	47302	765-284-3335	289-7185
Deluxe Stitcher Company Inc 3747 acorn ln *Web:* www.deluxebostitch.com	Franklin Park	IL	60131	773-777-6500	
Delva Tool & Machine Corp 1603 Industrial Hwy *Web:* www.delvatool.com	Cinnaminson	NJ	08077	856-786-8700	786-8708
Demmer Corp 1600 N Larch St Ste 1 *Web:* www.demmercorp.com	Lansing	MI	48906	517-321-3600	321-7449
Detroit Tool & Engineering Co 1107 Springfield Rd *Web:* www.detroittool.com	Lebanon	MO	65536	417-720-8108	532-8367
Diamond Die & Mold Co 35401 Groesbeck Hwy *Web:* www.diamond-die.com	Clinton Township	MI	48035	586-791-0700	791-5419
Diamond Tool & Die Inc 508 29th Ave *TF:* 800-227-1084 ■ *Web:* www.dtdjobshop.com	Oakland	CA	94601	510-534-7050	534-0454
Die Services International 45000 Van Born Rd PO Box 339 *Web:* www.dieservicesinternational.com	Belleville	MI	48111	734-699-3400	699-4081
Diemasters Manufacturing Inc 2100 Touhy Ave *Web:* www.thediemasters.com	Elk Grove Village	IL	60007	847-640-9900	640-9900
Dominion Technologies Inc 15736 Sturgeon St *Web:* www.dominiontec.com	Roseville	MI	48066	586-773-3303	773-2730
Domino Machine Inc 4040 98 St NW *Web:* www.dominomachine.com	Edmonton	AB	T6L3E3	780-462-1354	
Du Hadaway Tool & Die Shop Inc 801 Dawson Dr *Web:* duhadawaytool.com	Newark	DE	19713	302-366-0113	
Durre Brothers Welding & Machine Shop Inc 405 S Chestnut St *Web:* www.durrebros.com	Minonk	IL	61760	309-432-2512	
Eagle Rock Technologies Inc One Eagle Rock Dr *Web:* www.eaglerockonline.com	Bath	PA	18014	610-759-5200	
EF Precision Design Inc 2301 Computer Rd *Web:* www.efgroup.com	Willow Grove	PA	19090	215-784-0861	
Ehrhardt Tool & Machine Co 25 Central Industrial Dr *TF:* 877-386-7856 ■ *Web:* www.ehrhardttool.com	Granite City	IL	62040	314-436-6900	436-6905
Electro-Magnetic Products Inc 355 Crider Ave *Web:* www.empmags.com	Moorestown	NJ	08057	856-235-3011	722-0566
Elizabeth Carbide Die Company Inc 601 Linden St *Web:* www.eliz.com	McKeesport	PA	15132	412-751-3000	754-0755
Estee Mold & Die Inc 1467 Stanley Ave *Web:* www.esteemold.com	Dayton	OH	45404	937-224-7853	228-0257
Esterline & Sons Mfg 6508 Old Clifton Rd *Web:* esterlineandsons.com	Springfield	OH	45502	937-265-5278	
Euclid Industries Inc 1655 Tech Dr *Web:* www.euclidindustries.com	Bay City	MI	48706	989-686-8920	
Ewart-Ohlson Machine Company Inc, The 1435 Main St *Web:* www.ewart-ohlson.com	Cuyahoga Falls	OH	44221	330-928-2171	
Excel Machinery Ltd 12100 I-40 E *Web:* www.excelmach.com	Amarillo	TX	79120	806-335-1553	
Excel Tool Inc 2020 First Ave *Web:* www.exceleti.com	Seymour	IN	47274	812-522-6880	522-6524

Company / Address	City	State	ZIP	Phone	Fax
Falmouth Scientific Inc 1400 Route 28A	Cataumet	MA	02534	508-564-7640	
Web: www.falmouth.com					
Ferriot Inc 1000 Arlington Cir.	Akron	OH	44306	330-786-3000	786-3001
Web: ferriot.com					
First Tool Corp 612 Linden Ave	Dayton	OH	45403	937-254-6197	254-0625
Web: www.firsttoolcorp.com					
Fischer Tool & Die Corp					
7155 Industrial Dr.	Temperance	MI	48182	734-847-4788	847-5027
Web: www.fischertool.com					
Fisher Products LLC 1320 W 22nd Pl	Tulsa	OK	74107	918-582-2204	
Web: www.fisherproductsllc.com					
Formex Metal Industries Inc					
N2b-221 Riverbend Dr	Kitchener	ON	N2B2E8	519-745-2260	
Web: www.formex.on.ca					
Fort Wayne Wire Die Inc 2424 American Way	Fort Wayne	IN	46809	260-747-1681	747-4269
Web: www.fwwd.com					
Frizzelle & Parsons Die Sinking Co					
6602 John Deere Rd	Moline	IL	61265	309-796-1030	796-2935
Web: www.frizzelle-parsons.com					
Futuramic Tool & Engineering Co					
24680 Gibson Dr	Warren	MI	48089	586-758-2200	758-0641
Web: www.futuramic.com					
Future Products Tool Corp 885 Rochester Rd S	Clawson	MI	48017	248-588-1060	588-7303
Web: www.future-products.com					
General Carbide Corp 1151 Garden St	Greensburg	PA	15601	724-836-3000	836-6274
TF: 800-245-2465 ■ *Web:* www.generalcarbide.com					
General Tool Co 101 Landy Ln.	Cincinnati	OH	45215	513-733-5500	733-5604
TF: 800-314-9817 ■ *Web:* www.gentool.com					
Global Concepts Enterprise Inc					
785 Waverly Ct	Holland	MI	49423	616-355-7657	355-7662
Web: www.globalconcepts.com					
GlobalDie 1130 Minot Ave PO Box 1120	Auburn	ME	04211	207-514-7252	514-7202
TF: 888-271-4735 ■ *Web:* www.globaldie.com					
Greenville Tool & Die Co					
1215 S Lafayette St.	Greenville	MI	48838	616-754-5693	754-5500
Web: www.gtd.com					
Gremada Industries Inc 825 28th St SW Ste E	Fargo	ND	58103	701-356-0814	
Web: www.gremada.com					
Grinding Products Company Inc					
11084 E 9 Mile Rd	Warren	MI	48089	586-757-2118	
Web: grindingproducts.net					
Guill Tool & Engineering Company Inc					
10 Pike St	West Warwick	RI	02893	401-828-7600	823-5310
Web: guill.com/					
Hahn Manufacturing Co 5332 Hamilton Ave	Cleveland	OH	44114	216-391-9300	
Web: www.hahnmfg.com					
Hampton Machine Shop Inc 900 39th St	Newport News	VA	23607	757-380-8500	
Web: www.hampmach.com					
Harig Manufacturing Corp 5757 W Howard St	Niles	IL	60714	847-647-9500	647-8351
Web: www.harigmfg.com					
Hercules Machine Tool & Die Co					
13920 E Ten-Mile Rd	Warren	MI	48089	586-778-4120	778-0070
Web: www.hmtd.com					
Hill Engineering Inc 373 Randy Rd	Carol Stream	IL	60188	630-834-4430	834-4755
TF: 800-631-0520 ■ *Web:* www.hillengr.com					
Holdren Brothers Inc 301 Runkle	West Liberty	OH	43357	937-465-7050	
Web: www.holdrenbrothers.com					
Houston Dynamic Service Inc 8150 Lawndale	Houston	TX	77012	713-928-6200	
Web: www.houstondynamic.com					
Howmet TMP Corp 3960 S Marginal Rd	Cleveland	OH	44114	216-361-5229	391-4842
Web: www.alcoa.com/howmet					
Hudson Tool & Die Co					
Hudson Technologies 1327 N US 1	Ormond Beach	FL	32174	386-672-2000	676-6212*
**Fax:* Sales ■ *Web:* www.hudson-technologies.com					
Hydro Carbide 4439 State Rte 982	Latrobe	PA	15650	724-539-9701	539-8140
TF: 800-245-2476 ■ *Web:* www.hydrocarbide.com					
Hygrade Precision Technologies Inc					
329 Cooke St	Plainville	CT	06062	860-747-5773	747-3179
TF: 800-457-1666 ■ *Web:* www.hygrade.com					
Incoe Corp 1740 E Maple Rd.	Troy	MI	48083	248-616-0220	616-0225
Web: www.incoe.com					
Indian Creek Fabricators					
1350 Commerce Pk Dr	Tipp City	OH	45371	937-667-5818	667-4093
TF: 877-769-5880 ■ *Web:* www.indiancreekfab.com					
Ivanhoe Tool & Die Company Inc					
590 Thompson Rd	Thompson	CT	06277	860-923-9541	923-2497
Web: www.ivanhoetool.com					
Ivarson Inc 3100 W Green Tree Rd	Milwaukee	WI	53209	414-351-0700	
Web: ivarsoninc.com					
J & J Machine Inc 12655 Industrial Blvd.	Elk River	MN	55330	763-421-0114	
Web: www.jandjmachine.com					
J & M Machine Products Inc 1821 Manor Dr	Muskegon	MI	49441	231-755-1622	
Web: www.jmmachine.com					
Jaco Engineering 879 S East St.	Anaheim	CA	92805	714-991-1680	
Web: www.jacoengineering.com					
Jade Corp 3063 Philmont Ave	Huntingdon Valley	PA	19006	215-947-3333	947-6838
Web: www.jadecorp.com					
Jasco Tools Inc					
1390 Mt Read Blvd PO Box 60497	Rochester	NY	14606	585-254-7000	254-2655
TF: 800-724-5497 ■ *Web:* www.jascotools.com					
Jennings International Corp					
Three Blue Heron Dr	Collegeville	PA	19426	610-831-1600	272-1737
Web: www.jenningsinternational.com					
Jo-Ad Industries Inc					
31465 Stephenson Hwy	Madison Heights	MI	48071	248-588-4810	588-3448
Web: www.jo-ad.com					
Jones Metal Products Co 200 N Ctr St	West Lafayette	OH	43845	740-545-6381	545-9690
TF: 888-868-6535 ■ *Web:* www.jmpforming.com					
Kalow Technologies Inc					
238 Innovation Dr	North Clarendon	VT	05759	802-775-4633	
Web: www.kalowtech.com					
Kalt Manufacturing Co, The					
36700 Sugar Ridge Rd	North Ridgeville	OH	44039	440-327-2102	
Web: www.kaltmfg.com					
Kapp Surgical Instrument Inc					
4919 Warrensville Ctr Rd Ste 1	Cleveland	OH	44128	216-587-4400	
Web: xlconnect.com					
Kell-Strom Tool Co 214 Church St	Wethersfield	CT	06109	860-529-6851	257-9694
Web: www.kell-strom.com					
Kenmode Tool & Engineering Co					
820 W Algonquin Rd	Algonquin	IL	60102	847-658-5041	658-9150
Web: kenmode.com					
Kennedy Tool & Die Inc 325 W Main St.	Birdsboro	PA	19508	610-582-8735	582-3150
Web: www.ktdmold.com					
Lane Punch Corp 281 Ln Pkwy	Salisbury	NC	28146	704-633-3900	227-6725*
**Fax Area Code:* 800 ■ *Web:* www.lanepunch.com					
Lansing Tool & Engineering Inc					
1313 S Waverly Rd	Lansing	MI	48917	517-372-2550	
Web: www.lansingtool.com					
Leader Engineering Fabrication Inc					
695 Independence Dr	Napoleon	OH	43545	419-592-0008	
Web: www.leaderengineeringfabrication.com					
Leech Tool & Die Works Inc					
13144 Dickson Rd	Meadville	PA	16335	814-336-2141	337-0354
Web: www.leechind.com					
Lenhardt Tool & Die Co 3100 E Broadway	Alton	IL	62002	618-462-1075	462-6306
Web: www.lenhardttool.com					
Lou-Rich Machine Tool Inc 505 W Front St	Albert Lea	MN	56007	507-377-8910	373-7110
TF: 800-893-3235 ■ *Web:* www.lou-rich.com					
Mack Engineering Corp 3215 E 26th St	Minneapolis	MN	55406	612-721-2471	
Web: www.mackengineering.com					
Macro Engineering & Technology Inc					
199 Traders Blvd E	Mississauga	ON	L4Z2E5	905-507-9000	
Web: www.macroeng.com					
Mahuta Tool Corp N118W19137 Bunsen Dr	Germantown	WI	53022	262-502-4100	
Web: www.mahutatool.com					
Manda Machine Co 2683 Myrtle Springs Ave.	Dallas	TX	75220	214-352-5946	
Web: www.mandamachine.com					
Master Machine & Tool Company Inc					
5857 Jefferson Ave	Newport News	VA	23605	757-245-6653	
Web: www.master-machine.com					
Master Precision Machining Inc					
2199 Ronald St	Santa Clara	CA	95050	408-727-0185	
Web: master-precision.com					
Mate Precision Tooling Inc 1295 Lund Blvd.	Anoka	MN	55303	763-421-0230	421-0285
TF: 800-328-4492 ■ *Web:* www.matept.com					
May Tool & Mold Company Inc					
2922 Wheeling Ave.	Kansas City	MO	64129	816-923-6262	923-6277
Web: www.mayinc.com					
McAfee Tool & Die Inc 1717 Boettler Rd	Uniontown	OH	44685	330-896-9555	896-9549
Web: www.mcafeetool.com					
Meta Manufacturing Corp 8901 Blue Ash Rd	Cincinnati	OH	45242	513-793-6382	
Web: metamfg.com					
Metal Technologies of Murfreesboro Inc					
314 W Broad St	Murfreesboro	NC	27855	252-398-4041	
Web: www.metaltechnc.com					
Metro Mold & Design Inc 20600 County Rd 81	Rogers	MN	55374	763-428-8310	
Web: www.metromold.com					
Microcast Technologies Corp (MTC)					
1611 W Elizabeth Ave	Linden	NJ	07036	908-523-9503	523-0910
Web: www.mtcnj.com					
Mid-State Machine Products Inc 83 Verti Dr	Winslow	ME	04901	207-873-6136	872-2017
TF: 800-341-4672 ■ *Web:* hnprecision.com/					
Midwest Tool & Engineering Co 112 Webster St	Dayton	OH	45402	937-224-0756	224-0757
Web: www.themidwesttool.com					
Milwaukee Bearing & Machining Inc					
W134N5235 Campbell Dr.	Menomonee Falls	WI	53051	262-783-1100	
Web: www.milwaukeebearing.com					
Moeller Mfg Company Inc Punch & Die Div					
43938 Plymouth Oaks Blvd	Plymouth	MI	48170	734-416-0000	416-2200
TF: 800-521-7613 ■ *Web:* www.moellerpunch.com					
Mold Base Industries Inc 7501 Derry St	Harrisburg	PA	17111	800-241-6656	564-2250*
**Fax Area Code:* 717 ■ *TF:* 800-241-6656 ■ *Web:* www.moldbase.com					
Mold Masters International Inc					
7500 Clover Ave	Mentor	OH	44060	440-953-0220	953-1016
Web: www.moldmastersintl.com					
Mold-A-Matic Corp 147 River St	Oneonta	NY	13820	607-433-2121	432-7861
TF: 866-886-2626 ■ *Web:* www.mamco-molding.com					
Motor-Services Hugo Stamp Inc					
3190 SW Fourth Ave.	Fort Lauderdale	FL	33315	954-763-3660	
Web: www.mshs.com					
MS Willett Inc 220 Cockeysville Rd	Cockeysville	MD	21030	410-771-0460	771-6972
Web: www.mswillett.com					
National Tool & Mfg Company Inc					
100 N 12th St	Kenilworth	NJ	07033	908-276-1600	
Nexxa Industries Ltd 1-4380 76 Ave Se	Calgary	AB	T2C2J2	403-720-1996	
Web: www.nexxaindustries.com					
NGInstruments Inc 4643 N State Rd 15	Warsaw	IN	46582	574-268-2112	
Web: www.nginstruments.com					
Nitek Laser Inc 305 Rt du Port	Nicolet	QC	J3T1R7	819-293-4887	
Web: www.niteklaser.qc.ca					
Nolte Precise Manufacturing Inc					
6850 Colerain Ave	Cincinnati	OH	45239	513-923-3100	
Web: www.nolteprecise.com					
Nor-arc Steel Fabricators 331567 Hwy 11	Earlton	ON	P0J1E0	705-563-2656	
Web: www.norarc.com					
Northland Machine Inc 35234 US Hwy 2	Grand Rapids	MN	55744	218-328-6479	
Web: www.northlandmachine.com					
Northwestern Tools Inc 3130 Valleywood Dr	Dayton	OH	45429	937-298-9994	298-3715
TF: 800-236-3956 ■ *Web:* www.northwesterntools.com					
Nypromold Inc 144 Pleasant St	Clinton	MA	01510	978-365-4547	365-4548
Web: www.nypromold.com					
O Keller Tool Engineering Co					
12701 Inkster Rd	Livonia	MI	48150	734-425-4504	

				Phone	Fax
Oakdale Precision Inc 7022 Sixth St N *Web:* www.oakdaleprecision.com	Saint Paul	MN	55128	651-730-7700	
Oberg Industries Inc 2301 Silverville Rd PO Box 368 *TF:* 866-487-2365 ■ *Web:* www.oberg.com	Freeport	PA	16229	724-295-2121	295-2588
Ohlinger Industries Inc 1211 W Melinda Ln *Web:* www.ohlingerind.com	Phoenix	AZ	85027	602-285-0911	
OKL Can Line Inc 11235 Sebring Dr *Web:* www.oklcan.com	Cincinnati	OH	45240	513-825-1655	
Ontario Die Co of America 2735 20th St *TF:* 800-763-8272 ■ *Web:* www.ontariodie.com	Port Huron	MI	48060	810-987-5060	987-3688
Ort Tool & Die Corp 6555 S Dixie Hwy **Fax Area Code:* 734 ■ *Web:* www.orttool.com	Erie	MI	48133	419-242-9553	848-4308*
Owens Precision Inc 5966 Morgan Mill Rd *Web:* www.owensprecision.com	Carson City	NV	89701	775-883-4690	
Panoramic Corp 4321 Goshen Rd *TF:* 800-654-2027 ■ *Web:* www.pancorp.com	Fort Wayne	IN	46818	800-654-2027	
Paragon Die & Engineering Co 5225 33rd St SE *Web:* www.paragondie.com	Grand Rapids	MI	49512	616-949-2220	949-2536
Paslin Co 25303 Ryan Rd *TF:* 877-972-7546 ■ *Web:* www.paslin.com	Warren	MI	48091	586-758-0200	758-6602
PCS Co 34488 Doreka Dr *TF:* 800-521-0546 ■ *Web:* www.pcs-company.com	Fraser	MI	48026	586-294-7780	294-7799
Peddinghaus Corp 300 N Washington Ave *TF:* 800-786-2448 ■ *Web:* www.peddinghaus.com	Bradley	IL	60915	815-937-3800	937-4003
Penn State Tool & Die Corp 260 Westec Dr *Web:* www.pennstatetool.com	Mount Pleasant	PA	15666	724-613-5500	864-5300
Penn United Technology Inc 799 N Pike Rd *TF:* 866-572-7537 ■ *Web:* www.pennunited.com	Cabot	PA	16023	724-352-1507	352-4970
Pennsylvania Tool & Gages Inc PO Box 534 *TF:* 877-827-8285 ■ *Web:* www.patool.com	Meadville	PA	16335	814-336-3136	333-9131
Permac Industries Inc 14401 Ewing Ave S *Web:* www.permacindustries.com	Burnsville	MN	55306	952-894-7231	
PHB Inc 7900 W Ridge Rd *Web:* www.phbcorp.com	Fairview	PA	16415	814-474-5511	474-3091
Phinney Tool & Die Co PO Box 270 *Web:* www.phinneytool.com	Medina	NY	14103	585-798-3000	798-5612
PhotoMachining Inc Four Industrial Dr Unit number 4 *Web:* www.photomachining.com	Pelham	NH	03076	603-882-9944	
Piedmont Precision Machine Company Inc 150 Airside Dr *Web:* www.ppmmach.com	Danville	VA	24540	434-793-0677	
Pioneer Manufacturing Inc 740 Beechcroft Rd *Web:* www.pioneerleveler.com	Spring Hill	TN	37174	931-486-2296	
Plasidyne Engineering & Manufacturing Inc 3230 E 59th St *Web:* www.plasidyne.com	Long Beach	CA	90805	562-531-0510	531-1377
Porter Precision Products Inc 2734 Banning Rd *TF:* 800-543-7041 ■ *Web:* www.porterpunch.com	Cincinnati	OH	45239	513-923-3777	923-1111
Power Brake Dies Inc 263 W 154th St *Web:* www.powerbrakedies.com	South Holland	IL	60473	708-339-5951	339-7737
Precision Component Industries 5325 Southway St SW *Web:* www.precision-component.com	Canton	OH	44706	330-477-6287	477-1052
Precision Fasteners Tooling Inc 11530 Western Ave *Web:* www.precisionfastenertooling.com	Stanton	CA	90680	714-898-8558	891-4988
Precision Tool Die & Machine Co Inc 6901 Preston Hwy *Web:* www.nth-works.com	Louisville	KY	40219	877-511-9695	
Prikos & Becker Tool Co 8109 N Lawndale Ave *Web:* prikosandbecker.com	Skokie	IL	60076	847-675-3910	675-3913
Producto Machine Co 800 Union Ave *TF Cust Svc:* 800-722-2606 ■ *Web:* ibizprofile.com	Bridgeport	CT	06607	203-367-8675	367-0418
Progress Pump & Machine Services Inc 918 Kennedy Ave *Web:* www.progresspump.com	Schererville	IN	46375	219-322-3700	
Prospect Mold Inc 1100 Main St *Web:* www.prospectmold.com	Cuyahoga Falls	OH	44221	330-929-3311	920-1338
Proto-1 Manufacturing LLC 10 Tower Rd *Web:* www.proto1mfg.com	Winneconne	WI	54986	920-582-4491	
Quality Metalcraft Inc 33355 Glendale St *Web:* www.qualitymetalcraft.com	Livonia	MI	48150	734-261-6700	261-5180
Rand Machine Products Inc PO Box 72 *Web:* www.randmachine.com	Falconer	NY	14733	716-708-4583	665-3374
Raymath Company Inc 2323 W State Rt 55 *Web:* raymath.com	Troy	OH	45373	937-335-1860	
Reber Machine & Tool Company Inc 1112 S Liberty *Web:* rebermachine.com	Muncie	IN	47302	765-288-0297	
Reddog Industries Inc 2012 E 33rd St *Web:* www.reddog-erie.com	Erie	PA	16510	814-898-4321	899-5671
Reed City Tool & Die Inc 603 E Church St *Web:* www.reedcitytool.com	Reed City	MI	49677	231-832-7500	832-5270
Reliance Tool & Manufacturing Co 900 N State St Ste 101 *Web:* www.reliancetool.com	Elgin	IL	60123	847-695-1234	695-0931
Remmele Engineering Inc 10 Old Hwy 8 SW *TF General:* 800-733-6198 ■ *Web:* rtiintl.com/	New Brighton	MN	55112	651-635-4100	635-4168
Reuther Mold & Mfg Co 1225 Munroe Falls Ave *Web:* www.reuthermold.com	Cuyahoga Falls	OH	44221	330-923-5266	923-9930
Reynolds Manufacturing Co 501 38th St *Web:* www.reynoldsmfg.com	Rock Island	IL	61201	309-788-7443	788-7715
Richardson Manufacturing Co 2209 Old Jacksonville Rd *Web:* www.rmc-bigcnc.com	Springfield	IL	62704	217-546-2249	546-9433
Rocheleau Tool & Die Company Inc 117 Industrial Rd *Web:* www.rocheleautool.com	Fitchburg	MA	01420	978-345-1723	345-5972
Rome Tool & Die Company Inc 113 Hemlock St *TF:* 800-241-3369 ■ *Web:* stemco.com/	Rome	GA	30161	706-234-6743	234-1242
RotoMetrics Group 800 Howerton Ln *TF:* 800-325-3851 ■ *Web:* www.rotometrics.com	Eureka	MO	63025	636-587-3600	587-3701
Ryan Manufacturing Inc 6606 Machmueller St *Web:* ryanmfg.com	Schofield	WI	54476	715-359-2565	
SB Whistler & Sons Inc PO Box 270 *TF:* 800-828-1010 ■ *Web:* www.sbwhistler.com	Medina	NY	14103	585-318-4630	798-5612
Schaffer Specialty Welding Inc 109 Industrial Ave *Web:* www.schafferwelding.com	Milltown	WI	54858	715-825-2424	
Schoitz Engineering Inc 4901 Sergeant Rd Hwy 63 S *Web:* www.schoitz.com	Waterloo	IA	50704	319-234-6615	234-0368
Schroeder & Bogardus Die Company Inc 1130 Red Gum St *Web:* www.schroederinc.com	Anaheim	CA	92806	714-630-2270	630-1739
Scribner Associates Inc 150 E Connecticut Ave *Web:* www.scribner.com	Southern Pines	NC	28387	910-695-8884	
Sea-Lect Plastic Corp 3420 Smith Ave *Web:* sealectplastics.com	Everett	WA	98201	425-339-0288	
Serapid Inc 34100 Mound Rd *Web:* www.serapid.com	Sterling Heights	MI	48310	586-274-0774	
Sidney Tool & Die Inc 1950 Campbell Rd *Web:* www.sidneytool.com	Sidney	OH	45365	937-492-6121	498-9601
Sirois Tool Company Inc 169 White Oak Dr *Web:* www.siroistool.com	Berlin	CT	06037	860-828-5327	
Specialized Products Ltd 200 Summer St *Web:* www.specializedproductsltd.com	Clintonville	WI	54929	715-823-3727	
Specialty Design & Mfg Co PO Box 4039 *TF:* 800-720-0867 ■ *Web:* www.specialtydesign.com	Reading	PA	19606	610-779-1357	370-0269
SPX Corp OTC Div 655 Eisenhower Dr **Fax:* Hum Res ■ *TF:* 800-533-6127 ■ *Web:* www.otctools.com	Owatonna	MN	55060	507-455-7000	455-7300*
Stanfordville Machine & Manufacturing Inc 22 Locust Way *Web:* www.stanfordville.com	Stanfordville	NY	12581	845-868-2266	
Stanley Machining & Tool Corp 425 Maple Ave *Web:* www.stanleymachining.com	Carpentersville	IL	60110	847-426-4560	
Stephens Machine Inc 1600 E Dodge St *Web:* www.stephensdynamics.com	Kokomo	IN	46902	765-459-4017	
Sterling Process Engineering & Services Inc 333 McCormick Blvd *Web:* www.sterlingpe.com	Columbus	OH	43213	614-868-5151	
Sulzer Machine & Manufacturing Inc 2475 Spring Brook Rd *Web:* www.sulzermachine.com	Mosinee	WI	54455	715-443-2569	
SUNBELT Machine Works Corp 13411 Redfish Ln *Web:* sunbeltmachine.com	Stafford	TX	77477	281-499-0051	
Superior Die Set Corp 900 W Drexel Ave **Fax Area Code:* 800 ■ *TF:* 800-558-6040 ■ *Web:* www.supdie.com	Oak Creek	WI	53154	414-764-4900	657-0855*
Superior Die Tool & Machine Co 2301 Fairwood Ave *TF:* 800-292-2181 ■ *Web:* www.superior-dietool.com	Columbus	OH	43207	614-444-2181	444-8712
Superior Jig Inc 1540 N Orangethorpe Way *Web:* www.sji.net	Anaheim	CA	92801	714-525-4777	525-8798
Swan Engineering & Machine Co 2611 State St *Web:* swanengr.com	Bettendorf	IA	52722	563-355-2671	355-5380
Swihart Industries Inc 5111 Webster St *Web:* www.swihartindustries.com	Dayton	OH	45414	937-277-4796	
Swissline Precision Mfg. Inc 23-A Ashton Pkwy *Web:* www.swisslineprecision.com	Cumberland	RI	02864	401-333-8888	
Sylhan LLC 210 Rodeo Dr *Web:* www.sylhan.com	Edgewood	NY	11717	631-243-6600	
Texas Shapes Inc 6470 Rupley Cir *Web:* skyhawkgroup.com	Houston	TX	77087	713-641-1000	
TOG Manufacturing Company Inc 1454 S State St *Web:* www.togmanufacturing.com	North Adams	MA	01247	413-664-6711	
Tom Smith Industries 500 Smith Dr	Clayton	OH	45315	937-832-1555	832-1577
Toolcraft Products Inc 1265 Mc Cook Ave *Web:* www.toolcraftproducts.com	Dayton	OH	45404	937-223-8271	223-1408
Tools & Production Co 4924 N Encinita Ave *Web:* www.toolsandproduction.com	Temple City	CA	91780	626-286-0213	286-3398
Triangle Tool Corp 8609 W Port Ave *Web:* ttool.net	Milwaukee	WI	53224	414-357-7117	357-7610
Tru-Cut Inc 1145 Allied Dr *Web:* www.trucut.com	Sebring	OH	44672	330-938-9806	938-9342
Uniloy Milacron Inc 5550 S Occidental Rd Ste B *Web:* www.uniloymilacron.com	Tecumseh	MI	49286	517-424-8756	423-5671
Unipunch Products Inc 311 Fifth St NW *TF:* 800-828-7061 ■ *Web:* www.unipunch.com	Clear Lake	WI	54005	800-828-7061	453-3994
United Standard Industries Inc 2062 Lehigh Ave *Web:* www.unitedstandard.com	Glenview	IL	60025	847-724-0350	
V&L Tool Inc 2021 MacArthur Rd *Web:* www.vltool.com	Waukesha	WI	53188	262-547-1226	
VRC Inc 696 W Bagley Rd *Web:* www.vrcmfg.com	Berea	OH	44017	440-243-6666	
W Machine Works Inc 13814 Del Sur St *Web:* www.wmwcnc.com	San Fernando	CA	91340	818-890-8049	
Walker Tool & Die Inc 2411 Walker Ave NW *TF:* 877-925-5378 ■ *Web:* www.walkertool.com	Grand Rapids	MI	49544	616-453-5471	453-3765

	City	State	Zip	Phone	Fax
Waterflood Service & Sales Ltd 1314 Third St Box 1490 *Web:* www.waterflood.com	Estevan	SK	S4A2L7	306-634-7212	
Weldangrind Ltd 10323 174 St NW *Web:* www.weldangrind.ca	Edmonton	AB	T5S1H1	780-484-3030	
Wesco Machine Products Inc S84W18569 Enterprise Dr *Web:* wescomachine.com	Muskego	WI	53150	262-679-4799	
Westland Corp 1735 S Maize Rd *TF:* 800-247-1144 ■ *Web:* reilоyusa.com	Wichita	KS	67209	316-721-1144	721-1495
Windsor Beach Technologies Inc 7321 Klier Dr *Web:* www.windsorbeach.com	Fairview	PA	16415	814-474-4900	
Wirtz Mfg Company Inc 1105 24th St PO Box 5006 *Web:* www.wirtzusa.com	Port Huron	MI	48061	810-987-7600	987-8135
Wyatt Precision Machine Inc 3301 E 59th St *Web:* www.wyattprecisionmachine.com	Long Beach	CA	90805	562-634-0524	
X-L Engineering Corp 6150 W Mulford St *Web:* www.xleng.com	Niles	IL	60714	847-965-3030	
Yarema Die & Engineering Co Inc 300 Minnesota Rd *TF:* 800-937-9311 ■ *Web:* www.yarema.com	Troy	MI	48083	248-585-2830	616-1422

761 TOOLS - HAND & EDGE

SEE ALSO Lawn & Garden Equipment p. 2639; Metalworking Devices & Accessories p. 2756; Saw Blades & Handsaws p. 3132

	City	State	Zip	Phone	Fax
Adjustable Clamp Co 404 N Armour St *Web:* www.adjustableclamp.com	Chicago	IL	60642	312-666-0640	666-2723
Allway Tools Inc 1255 Seabury Ave *TF:* 800-422-5592 ■ *Web:* www.allwaytools.com	Bronx	NY	10462	718-792-3636	823-9640
Ames Taping Tools Inc 3350 Breckinridge Blvd Ste 100 **Fax Area Code:* 770 ■ *TF:* 800-408-2801 ■ *Web:* www.amestools.com	Duluth	GA	30096	800-303-1827	243-2658*
Ames True Temper Inc 465 Railroad Ave *TF:* 800-393-1846 ■ *Web:* www.ames.com	Camp Hill	PA	17011	800-393-1846	
Arrow Fastener Co Inc 271 Mayhill St *TF:* 800-776-2228 ■ *Web:* www.arrowfastener.com	Saddle Brook	NJ	07663	201-843-6900	843-3911
BARCO Industries Inc 1020 MacArthur Rd **Fax Area Code:* 610 ■ *TF Cust Svc:* 800-234-8665 ■ *Web:* www.barcotools.com	Reading	PA	19605	800-234-8665	374-6320*
Bondhus Corp 1400 E Broadway St PO Box 660 *TF Cust Svc:* 800-328-8310 ■ *Web:* www.bondhus.com	Monticello	MN	55362	763-295-2162	295-4440
Cal-Van Tools 4300 Waterleaf Ct **Fax Area Code:* 336 ■ *TF:* 800-537-1077 ■ *Web:* www.cal-vantools.com	Greensboro	NC	27410	800-537-1077	299-4003*
Channellock Inc 1306 S Main St *TF Cust Svc:* 800-724-3018 ■ *Web:* www.channellock.com	Meadville	PA	16335	800-724-3018	962-2583
Charles GG Schmidt & Company Inc 301 W Grand Ave *TF:* 800-724-6438 ■ *Web:* www.cggschmidt.com	Montvale	NJ	07645	201-391-5300	391-3565
Consolidated Devices Inc (CDI) 19220 San Jose Ave *TF:* 800-525-6319 ■ *Web:* www.cditorque.com	City of Industry	CA	91748	626-965-0668	810-2759
Cooper Industries 600 Travis St Ste 5400 *NYSE:* ETN ■ *TF:* 866-853-4293 ■ *Web:* www.cooperindustries.com	Houston	TX	77002	713-209-8400	209-8995
Cornwell Quality Tools 667 Seville Rd *TF:* 800-321-8356 ■ *Web:* www.cornwelltools.com	Wadsworth	OH	44281	330-336-3506	336-3337
CS Osborne & Company Inc 125 Jersey St *Web:* www.csosborne.com	Harrison	NJ	07029	973-483-3232	484-3621
CTA Manufacturing Corp 263 Veterans Blvd *Web:* www.ctatools.com	Carlstadt	NJ	07072	201-896-1000	896-1378
Danaher Corp 2200 Pennsylvania Ave NW Ste 800 *NYSE:* DHR ■ *TF:* 800-833-9200 ■ *Web:* www.danaher.com	Washington	DC	20037	202-828-0850	828-0860
Daniels Manufacturing Corp 526 Thorpe Rd *Web:* www.dmctools.com	Orlando	FL	32859	407-855-6161	855-6884
Dasco Pro Inc 340 Blackhawk Pk Ave *TF:* 800-327-2690 ■ *Web:* dascopro.com	Rockford	IL	61104	815-962-3727	
Duo-Fast Corp 2400 Galvin Dr *TF Cust Svc:* 888-386-3278 ■ *Web:* www.itwindfast.com	Elgin	IL	60123	847-783-5500	783-5500
Empire Level Manufacturing Corp 929 Empire Dr PO Box 800 **Fax Area Code:* 262 ■ *TF:* 800-558-0722 ■ *Web:* www.empirelevel.com	Mukwonago	WI	53149	800-558-0722	368-2127*
Emporium Specialties Company Inc 10 Foster St *Web:* www.empspec.com	Austin	PA	16720	814-647-8661	647-5536
Enderes Tool Co 1103 Hershey St **Fax Area Code:* 952 ■ *TF:* 800-874-7776 ■ *Web:* www.enderes.com	Albert Lea	MN	56007	800-874-7776	891-1202*
Estwing Manufacturing Co 2647 Eigth St *Web:* www.estwing.com	Rockford	IL	61109	815-397-9558	397-8665
Everhard Products Inc 1016 Ninth St SW *Web:* www.everhard.com	Canton	OH	44707	330-453-7786	
Fiskars Brands Inc 2537 Daniels St *TF:* 866-348-5661 ■ *Web:* www2.fiskars.com	Madison	WI	53718	866-348-5661	
Fletcher-Terry Company Inc 65 Spring Ln *TF Cust Svc:* 800-843-3826 ■ *Web:* www.fletcherviscom.com	Farmington	CT	06032	860-677-7331	676-8858
General Machine Products Company Inc 3111 Old Lincoln Hwy *TF Tech Supp:* 800-345-6009 ■ *Web:* www.gmptools.com	Trevose	PA	19053	215-357-5500	357-6216
General Tools Mfg Company LLC 80 White St *TF:* 800-697-8665 ■ *Web:* www.generaltools.com	New York	NY	10013	212-431-6100	431-6499
Grobet File Company of America Inc 750 Washington Ave *TF:* 800-847-4188 ■ *Web:* www.grobetusa.com	Carlstadt	NJ	07072	201-939-6700	939-5067
Hastings Fiber Glass Products Inc 770 Cook Rd PO Box 218 *Web:* www.hfgp.com	Hastings	MI	49058	269-945-9541	945-4623
Hexacon Electric Co 161 W Clay Ave *TF:* 888-765-3371 ■ *Web:* www.hexaconelectric.com	Roselle Park	NJ	07204	908-245-6200	245-6176
Huther Bros Inc 1290 University Ave *Web:* hutherbros.com	Rochester	NY	14607	585-473-9462	
Hyde Tools Co 54 Eastford Rd *TF:* 800-872-4933 ■ *Web:* www.hydetools.com	Southbridge	MA	01550	508-764-4344	765-5250
Johnson Level & Tool Mfg Company Inc 6333 W Donges Bay Rd *Web:* www.johnsonlevel.com	Mequon	WI	53092	262-242-1161	242-0189
Jonard Industries Corp 134 Marbledale Rd *Web:* www.jonard.com	Tuckahoe	NY	10707	914-793-0700	793-4527
Ken-Tool Co 768 E N St **Fax Area Code:* 800 ■ *Web:* www.kentool.com	Akron	OH	44305	330-535-7177	872-4929*
Klein Tools Inc 450 Bond St *TF Cust Svc:* 800-553-4676 ■ *Web:* www.kleintools.com	Lincolnshire	IL	60069	800-553-4676	
Leatherman Tool Group Inc 12106 NE Ainsworth Cir *TF:* 800-847-8665 ■ *Web:* www.leatherman.com	Portland	OR	97220	503-253-7826	253-7830
Lisle Corp 813 E Main St *Web:* www.lislecorp.com	Clarinda	IA	51632	712-542-5101	542-6591
LS Starrett Co 121 Crescent St *NYSE:* SCX ■ *TF:* 800-482-8710 ■ *Web:* www.starrett.com	Athol	MA	01331	978-249-3551	249-8495
Mac Tools Inc 505 N Cleveland Ave *TF:* 800-622-8665 ■ *Web:* www.mactools.com	Westerville	OH	43082	614-755-7000	622-3295
Malco Products Inc 14080 State Hwy 55 NW PO Box 400 *TF:* 800-328-3530 ■ *Web:* www.malcoproducts.com	Annandale	MN	55302	320-274-8246	274-2269
Marshalltown Co 104 S Eigth Ave *TF:* 800-888-0127 ■ *Web:* www.marshalltown.com	Marshalltown	IA	50158	641-753-5999	753-6341
Matco Tools 4403 Allen Rd *TF:* 800-368-6651 ■ *Web:* www.matcotools.com	Stow	OH	44224	330-926-5332	926-5320
Mayhew Steel Products Inc 199 Industrial Blvd *TF:* 800-872-0037 ■ *Web:* www.mayhew.com	Turners Falls	MA	01376	413-863-4860	863-8464
MIBRO Group 111 Sinnott Rd *TF:* 866-941-9006 ■ *Web:* www.mibro.com	Toronto	ON	M1L4S6	416-285-9000	285-9500
Newell Rubbermaid Inc Irwin Tools Div 8935 Northpointe Executive Dr *TF:* 800-866-5740 ■ *Web:* www.irwin.com	Huntersville	NC	28078	704-987-4555	987-4506
QEP Co Inc 1001 Broken Sound Pkwy NW Ste A *OTC:* QEPC ■ *TF Sales:* 800-777-8665 ■ *Web:* www.qep.com	Boca Raton	FL	33487	561-994-5550	241-2830
Red Devil Inc 1437 S Boulder **Fax Area Code:* 918 ■ *TF:* 800-423-3845 ■ *Web:* www.reddevil.com	Tulsa	OK	74119	800-423-3845	585-8120*
Reed Manufacturing Co 1425 W Eigth St *TF:* 800-456-1697 ■ *Web:* www.reedmfgco.com	Erie	PA	16502	814-452-3691	455-1697
Relton Corp 317 Rolyn Dr PO Box 60019 **Fax Area Code:* 626 ■ *TF Cust Svc:* 800-423-1505 ■ *Web:* www.relton.com	Arcadia	CA	91066	323-681-2551	446-9671*
Ridge Tool Co 400 Clark St *Web:* www.ridgid.com	Elyria	OH	44035	440-323-5581	323-5204
Ripley Co 46 Nooks Hill Rd *TF:* 800-528-8665 ■ *Web:* www.ripley-tools.com	Cromwell	CT	06416	860-635-2200	635-3631
Seymour Mfg Co Inc PO Box 248 *TF:* 800-815-7253 ■ *Web:* www.seymourmfg.com	Seymour	IN	47274	812-522-2900	522-6109
Snap-on Inc 2801 80th St *NYSE:* SNA ■ *TF:* 877-762-7664 ■ *Web:* www.snapon.com	Kenosha	WI	53143	262-656-5200	656-5577
Stabila Inc 332 Industrial Dr P.O. Box 402 **Fax Area Code:* 847 ■ *TF:* 800-869-7460 ■ *Web:* www.stabila.com	South Elgin	IL	60177	800-869-7460	488-0051*
Stanley Supply & Services Inc 335 Willow St **Fax Area Code:* 800 ■ *TF Cust Svc:* 888-887-9473 ■ *Web:* www.stanleysupplyservices.com	North Andover	MA	01845	978-682-2000	743-8141*
Stanley Tools Inc 480 Myrtle St **Fax Area Code:* 800 ■ *TF Cust Svc:* 800-262-2161 ■ *Web:* www.stanleytools.com	New Britain	CT	06053	860-225-5111	643-3756*
Stride Tool Inc Imperial Div 30333 Emerald Vly Pkwy **Fax Area Code:* 800 ■ *TF:* 888-467-8665 ■ *Web:* imperial-tools.com/	Glenwillow	OH	44139	440-247-4600	527-6383*
Superior Tool Co 100 Hayes Dr Unit C *TF Cust Svc:* 800-533-3244 ■ *Web:* www.superiortool.com	Cleveland	OH	44131	216-398-8600	398-8691
Tamco Inc 1466 Delberts Dr *TF:* 800-826-2672 ■ *Web:* www.tamcotools.com	Monongahela	PA	15063	724-258-6622	258-6692
Triumph Twist Drill Co Inc 1 SW 7th St *TF:* 800-942-1501 ■ *Web:* triumphtwistdrill.com	Chisholm	MN	55719	218-263-3891	263-3887
Ullman Devices Corp 664 Danbury Rd *TF:* 800-784-7796 ■ *Web:* www.users.ntplx.net/~ullman	Ridgefield	CT	06877	203-438-6577	431-9064
Vaughan & Bushnell Manufacturing Co 11414 Maple Ave PO Box 390 *TF:* 800-435-6000 ■ *Web:* vaughanmfg.com	Hebron	IL	60034	815-648-2446	648-4300
Wall Lenk Corp 1950 Dr Martin Luther King Jr *TF Cust Svc:* 888-527-4186 ■ *Web:* www.wlenk.com	Kinston	NC	28501	252-527-4186	527-4189
Walter Meier Mfg Inc 427 New Sanford Rd *Web:* www.wiltontools.com	La Vergne	TN	37086	888-804-7129	605-2101
Warner Manufacturing Co 13435 Industrial Pk Blvd *TF:* 800-444-0606 ■ *Web:* www.warnertool.com	Minneapolis	MN	55441	763-559-4740	559-1364
Wheeler-Rex Inc 3744 Jefferson Rd PO Box 688 *TF:* 800-321-7950 ■ *Web:* www.wheelerrex.com	Ashtabula	OH	44005	440-998-2788	992-2925
Zephyr Mfg Company Inc 201 Hindry Av *TF:* 800-624-3944 ■ *Web:* www.zephyrtool.com	Inglewood	CA	90301	310-410-4907	

TOOLS - MACHINE

SEE Machine Tools - Metal Cutting Types p. 2684; Machine Tools - Metal Forming Types p. 2685

762 TOOLS - POWER

SEE ALSO Lawn & Garden Equipment p. 2639; Metalworking Devices & Accessories p. 2756

	City	State	Zip	Phone	Fax
Alpine Power Systems Inc 24355 Capitol *TF:* 877-769-3762 ■ *Web:* www.alpinepowersystems.com	Redford	MI	48239	313-531-6600	531-2950

Phone | Fax

American Pneumatic Tool Inc
9949 Tabor Pl . . . . . Santa Fe Springs CA 90670 562-204-1555 204-1773
TF: 800-532-7402 ■ *Web:* www.apt-tools.com

Atlas Copco Tools & Assembly Systems
2998 Dutton Rd . . . . . Auburn Hills MI 48326 248-373-3000 373-3001
TF: 800-859-3746 ■ *Web:* atlascopco.com/us/tools/us

Blackstone Industries Inc 16 Stoney Hill Rd . . . . . Bethel CT 06801 203-792-8622 796-7861
Web: www.blackstoneind.com

Blount Inc Oregon Cutting Systems Div
4909 SE International Way . . . . . Portland OR 97222 503-653-8881 653-4201
TF: 800-223-5168 ■ *Web:* www.oregonproducts.com

Chicago Pneumatic Tool Co 1800 Overview Dr . . . . . Rock Hill SC 29730 803-817-7000 228-9096*
**Fax Area Code:* 800 ■ **Fax:* Hum Res ■ *TF:* 800-624-4735 ■ *Web:* www.cp.com

Cooper Industries 600 Travis St Ste 5400 . . . . . Houston TX 77002 713-209-8400 209-8995
NYSE: ETN ■ *TF:* 866-853-4293 ■ *Web:* www.cooperindustries.com

Dremel Inc 4915 21st St . . . . . Racine WI 53406 262-554-1390 554-7654
TF: 800-437-3635 ■ *Web:* www.dremel.com

Dynabrade Inc 8989 Sheridan Dr . . . . . Clarence NY 14031 716-631-0100 631-2073
TF Cust Svc: 800-828-7333 ■ *Web:* www.dynabrade.com

Enerpac P.O. Box 3241 . . . . . Milwaukee WI 53201 262-293-1600 781-1049*
**Fax:* Cust Svc ■ *TF Cust Svc:* 800-433-2766 ■ *Web:* www.enerpac.com

Florida Pneumatic Manufacturing Corp
851 Jupiter Pk Ln . . . . . Jupiter FL 33458 561-744-9500 575-9134
TF: 800-327-9403 ■ *Web:* www.florida-pneumatic.com

Greenlee Textron Inc 4455 Boeing Dr . . . . . Rockford IL 61109 800-435-0786 451-2632
TF: 800-435-0786 ■ *Web:* www.greenlee.com

Hilti Inc 5400 S 122nd E Ave . . . . . Tulsa OK 74146 918-252-6000 879-7000*
**Fax Area Code:* 800 ■ *TF Cust Svc:* 800-879-8000 ■ *Web:* www.us.hilti.com

Hougen Manufacturing Inc 3001 Hougen Dr . . . . . Swartz Creek MI 48473 810-635-7111 635-8277
TF Orders: 800-426-7818 ■ *Web:* www.hougen.com

Makita USA Inc 14930 Northam St Ste C . . . . . La Mirada CA 90638 714-522-8088 522-8133
TF: 800-462-5482 ■ *Web:* www.makitausa.com

Master Appliance Corp 2420 18th St . . . . . Racine WI 53403 262-633-7791 633-9745
TF: 800-558-9413 ■ *Web:* www.masterappliance.com

Milwaukee Electric Tool Corp
13135 W Lisbon Rd . . . . . Brookfield WI 53005 262-781-3600 638-9582*
**Fax Area Code:* 800 ■ **Fax:* Orders ■ *TF:* 800-729-3878 ■ *Web:* www.milwaukeetool.com

P & F Industries Inc 445 Broadhollow Rd . . . . . Melville NY 11747 631-694-9800 694-9804
NASDAQ: PFIN ■ *TF:* 800-327-9403 ■ *Web:* www.pfina.com

Paslode 888 Forest Edge Dr . . . . . Vernon Hills IL 60061 847-634-1900 634-6602
TF Cust Svc: 800-682-3428 ■ *Web:* www.paslode.com

Pioneer Tool & Forge Inc 101 Sixth St . . . . . New Kensington PA 15068 724-337-4700 337-4707
TF: 800-359-6408 ■ *Web:* www.breakersteel.com

Pneutek 17 Friars Dr . . . . . Hudson NH 03051 603-883-1660 882-9165
TF: 800-431-8665 ■ *Web:* www.pneutek.com

Powernail Co 1300 Rose Rd . . . . . Lake Zurich IL 60047 847-634-3000 634-4943
TF: 800-323-1653 ■ *Web:* www.powernail.com

Ridge Tool Co 400 Clark St . . . . . Elyria OH 44035 440-323-5581 323-5204
Web: www.ridgid.com

Robert Bosch Tool Corp
1800 W Central Rd . . . . . Mount Prospect IL 60056 224-232-2000 232-3169
TF: 877-267-2499 ■ *Web:* www.boschtools.com

Ryobi Technologies Inc
1428 Pearman Dairy Rd . . . . . Anderson SC 29625 800-525-2579 261-9435*
**Fax Area Code:* 864 ■ *TF:* 800-525-2579 ■ *Web:* www.ryobitools.com

SENCO Products Inc 4270 Ivy Pt Blvd . . . . . Cincinnati OH 45245 800-543-4596 388-3100*
**Fax Area Code:* 513 ■ *TF Tech Supp:* 800-543-4596 ■ *Web:* www.sencobrands.com

Shopsmith Inc 6530 Poe Ave . . . . . Dayton OH 45414 937-898-6070 722-3965*
OTC: SSMH ■ **Fax Area Code:* 800 ■ *TF Cust Svc:* 800-543-7586 ■ *Web:* www.shopsmith.com

Sioux Tools Inc 250 Snap-on Dr . . . . . Murphy NC 28906 828-835-9765 835-9685
TF Orders: 800-722-7290 ■ *Web:* www.siouxtools.com

Speedgrip Chuck Inc 2000 E Industrial Pkwy . . . . . Elkhart IN 46516 574-294-1506 294-2465
Web: www.speedgrip.com

Stanley Assembly Technologies Div
5335 Avion Pk Dr . . . . . Cleveland OH 44143 440-461-5500 461-2710
TF: 877-787-7830 ■ *Web:* www.stanleyengineeredfastening.com

Stihl Inc 536 Viking Dr . . . . . Virginia Beach VA 23452 757-486-9100 340-0377*
**Fax Area Code:* 303 ■ *TF Cust Svc:* 800-467-8445 ■ *Web:* www.stihlusa.com

Suhner Manufacturing Inc 43 Anderson Rd . . . . . Rome GA 30161 706-235-8046 235-8045
Web: www.suhner.com

Thomas C Wilson Inc 21-11 44th Ave . . . . . Long Island City NY 11101 718-729-3360 361-2872
TF: 800-230-2636 ■ *Web:* www.tcwilson.com

763 TOUR OPERATORS

SEE ALSO Bus Services - Charter p. 1890; Travel Agencies p. 3253

Phone | Fax

Academy Bus LLC 111 Paterson Ave . . . . . Hoboken NJ 07030 201-420-7000 420-8087
TF: 800-442-7272 ■ *Web:* www.academybus.com

Acadia National Park Tours 53 Main St . . . . . Bar Harbor ME 04609 207-288-0300
Web: www.nationalparktours.com

Adventure Alaska Tours Inc PO Box 64 . . . . . Hope AK 99605 907-782-3730 782-3725
TF: 800-365-7057 ■ *Web:* www.adventurealaskatours.com

Adventure Connection PO Box 475 . . . . . Coloma CA 95613 530-626-7385 626-9268
TF: 800-556-6060 ■ *Web:* www.raftcalifornia.com

Adventure Ctr Inc 1311 63rd St Ste 200 . . . . . Emeryville CA 94608 510-654-1879

Adventure Life South America
1655 S Third St W Ste 1 . . . . . Missoula MT 59801 406-541-2677 541-2676
TF: 800-344-6118 ■ *Web:* www.adventure-life.com

Adventures Out West 1680 S 21st St . . . . . Colorado Springs CO 80904 800-755-0935
TF: 800-755-0935 ■ *Web:* www.advoutwest.com

Africa Adventure Co, The
5353 N Federal Hwy Ste 300 . . . . . Fort Lauderdale FL 33308 954-491-8877 491-9060
TF: 800-882-9453 ■ *Web:* www.africa-adventure.com

African Travel Inc 330 N Brand Blvd . . . . . Glendale CA 91205 818-507-7893 507-5802
TF: 800-421-8907 ■ *Web:* www.africantravelinc.com

Agape Tours & Charter 2730 Commerce St . . . . . Wichita Falls TX 76301 940-767-4935 692-8477
Web: www.agapetoursinc.com

Agentours Inc 126 W Portal Ave . . . . . San Francisco CA 94127 415-661-5200
Web: agentours.com

Phone | Fax

AHI International Corp 6400 Shafer Ct . . . . . Rosemont IL 60018 800-323-7373 318-5000*
**Fax Area Code:* 847 ■ *TF:* 800-323-7373 ■ *Web:* www.ahitravel.com

Alaska Heritage Tours Inc
509 W Fourth Ave Ste 405 . . . . . Anchorage AK 99501 907-777-2805
Web: www.alaskaheritagetours.com

All Aboard Travel PO Box 90074 . . . . . Chattanooga TN 37412 423-499-9977
Web: www.allaboardchatt.com

Alpha Omega Tours & Charters
419 N Jefferson St PO Box 97 . . . . . Medical Lake WA 99022 509-299-5595 299-5545
Web: www.alphaomegatoursandcharters.com

Alpine Adventure Trails Tours Inc
7495 Lower Thomaston Rd . . . . . Macon GA 31220 888-478-4004 477-4117*
**Fax Area Code:* 478 ■ *TF:* 888-478-4004 ■ *Web:* www.swisshiking.com

AmaWaterways 26010 Mureau Rd . . . . . Calabasas CA 91302 800-626-0126
TF: 800-626-0126

Ambassadors Group Inc 110 S Ferrall St . . . . . Spokane WA 99202 509-534-6200
NASDAQ: EPAX ■ *TF:* 800-652-8683 ■ *Web:* www.ambassadorsgroup.com

American Trails West (ATW) 92 Middle Neck Rd . . . . . Great Neck NY 11021 516-487-2800 487-2855
TF: 800-645-6260 ■ *Web:* www.atwteentours.com

AmericanTours International LLC (ATI)
6053 W Century Blvd . . . . . Los Angeles CA 90045 310-641-9953 216-5807
TF: 800-800-8942 ■ *Web:* www.americantours.com

Anderson Coach & Travel One Anderson Plz . . . . . Greenville PA 16125 724-588-8310 588-0257
TF: 800-345-3435 ■ *Web:* www.goanderson.com

ATS Tours 300 Continental Blvd Ste 350 . . . . . El Segundo CA 90245 888-410-5770 643-0032*
**Fax Area Code:* 310 ■ *TF:* 888-410-5770 ■ *Web:* travel2-us.com

Backroads 801 Cedar St . . . . . Berkeley CA 94710 510-527-1555 527-1444
TF: 800-462-2848 ■ *Web:* www.backroads.com

Badger Coaches Inc 5501 Femrite Dr . . . . . Madison WI 53718 608-255-1511 258-3484
TF: 800-442-8259 ■ *Web:* www.badgerbus.com

Banff Adventures Unlimited
211 Bear St Bison Courtyard . . . . . Banff AB T1L1A8 403-762-4554 760-3196
TF: 800-644-8888 ■ *Web:* www.banffadventures.com

Beamers Hells Canyon Tours & Excursions
PO Box 1243 . . . . . Lewiston ID 83501 509-758-4800 758-3643
TF: 800-522-6966 ■ *Web:* www.hellscanyontours.com

Bestway Tours & Safaris 8678 Greenall Ave . . . . . Burnaby BC V5J3M6 604-264-7378 264-7774
TF: 800-663-0844 ■ *Web:* www.bestway.com

Big Five Tours & Expeditions 1551 SE Palm Ct . . . . . Stuart FL 34994 772-287-7995 287-5990
TF: 800-244-3483 ■ *Web:* www.bigfive.com

Blue Grass Tours Inc 817 Enterprise Dr . . . . . Lexington KY 40510 859-233-2152 255-4748
TF: 800-755-6956 ■ *Web:* www.bluegrasstours.com

Bonaventure Tours 8 Boudreau Ln . . . . . Haute-Aboujagane NB E4P5N1 506-532-3674 532-6487
TF: 800-561-1213 ■ *Web:* www.aboutbonaventuretours.com

Borderland Tours 2550 W Calle Padilla . . . . . Tucson AZ 85745 520-882-7650 792-9205
TF: 800-525-7753 ■ *Web:* www.borderland-tours.com

Boston Duck Tours Ltd Four Copley Pl Ste 310 . . . . . Boston MA 02116 617-450-0065
TF: 800-226-7442 ■ *Web:* www.bostonducktours.com

Breakaway Tours 3300 Bloor St Ste 1800 . . . . . Toronto ON M8X2X2 416-915-9880 915-9881
TF: 800-465-4257 ■ *Web:* www.breakawaytours.com

Brendan Vacations 21625 Prairie St . . . . . Chatsworth CA 91311 800-687-1002
TF: 800-421-8446 ■ *Web:* www.brendanvacations.com

Brewster Rocky Mountain Adventures PO Box 370 . . . . . Banff AB T1L1A5 403-762-5454 673-2100
TF: 800-691-5085 ■ *Web:* www.brewsteradventures.com

Brewster Travel Canada
100 Gopher St PO Box 1140 . . . . . Banff AB T1L1J3 403-762-6700 762-6750
TF: 866-606-6700 ■ *Web:* www.brewster.ca

Burke International Tours Inc PO Box 890 . . . . . Newton NC 28658 828-465-3900 465-3912
TF: 800-476-3900 ■ *Web:* www.burkechristiantours.com

California Parlor Car Tours
500 Sutter St Ste 401 . . . . . San Francisco CA 94102 415-474-7500 673-1539
TF: 800-227-4250 ■ *Web:* www.calpartours.com

Centennial Travelers 311 S College Ave . . . . . Fort Collins CO 80524 970-484-4988
TF: 800-223-0675 ■ *Web:* www.centennialtravel.com

Chicago Supernatural Tours PO Box 557544 . . . . . Chicago IL 60655 708-499-0300
Web: www.ghosttours.com

Churchill Nature Tours PO Box 429 . . . . . Erickson MB R0J0P0 204-636-2968 636-2557
TF: 877-636-2968 ■ *Web:* www.churchillnaturetours.com

City Tours Maine P.O. Box 167 . . . . . Nobleboro ME 04555 207-563-2288 563-3335
TF: 800-537-5378 ■ *Web:* citytoursmaine.com

Classic Student Tours 75 Rhoads Ctr Dr . . . . . Dayton OH 45458 937-439-0032 439-0041
TF: 800-860-0246 ■ *Web:* classicstudenttours.com

Club Europa 802 W Oregon St . . . . . Urbana IL 61801 217-344-5863 344-4072
TF: 800-331-1882 ■ *Web:* www.clubeuropatravel.com

Coach Tours Ltd 475 Federal Rd . . . . . Brookfield CT 06804 203-740-1118 775-6851
TF: 800-822-6224 ■ *Web:* www.coachtour.com

Complete Travel Services 3841 Nostrand Ave . . . . . Brooklyn NY 11235 718-934-9400 891-8681

Contemporary Tours
1400 Old Country Rd Ste 100 . . . . . Westbury NY 11590 516-484-5032
TF: 800-627-8873 ■ *Web:* www.contemporarytours.com

Contiki Holidays 801 E Katella Ave 3rd Fl . . . . . Anaheim CA 92805 714-935-0808
TF: 800-944-5708 ■ *Web:* www.contiki.com

Convexx 6865 S Ea Ste 101 . . . . . Las Vegas NV 89119 702-450-7662
Web: www.convexx.com

Cook Inlet Region Inc 2525 C St Ste 500 . . . . . Anchorage AK 99503 907-274-8638
Web: www.ciri.com

Cultural Experiences Abroad (CEA)
2999 N 44th St Ste 200 . . . . . Phoenix AZ 85018 480-557-7900 557-7926
TF: 800-266-4441 ■ *Web:* www.ceastudyabroad.com

CYR Bus Tours 153 Gilman Falls Ave . . . . . Old Town ME 04468 207-827-2335 827-6763
TF: 800-244-2335 ■ *Web:* www.cyrbustours.com/#tours

D & m Tours Inc 117 E Seventh St . . . . . Paterson NJ 07524 973-569-1320
Web: www.dmtours.com

Dash Tours 1024 Winnipeg St . . . . . Regina SK S4R8P8 306-352-2222 757-4126
TF: 800-265-0000 ■ *Web:* dashtours.com

Delta Tour & Travel Services Inc
3360 Flair Dr Ste 102 . . . . . El Monte CA 91731 626-300-0033
Web: deltatours.com

Dipert Travel & Transportation Ltd
PO Box 580 . . . . . Arlington TX 76004 800-433-5335 543-3728*
**Fax Area Code:* 817 ■ *TF:* 800-433-5335 ■ *Web:* www.dandipert.com

				Phone	Fax
Earthwatch Institute 114 Western Ave *TF:* 800-776-0188 ■ *Web:* www.earthwatch.org	Boston	MA	02134	978-461-0081	461-2332
Eco Park Resort at Mt. St. Helens Inc 14000 Spirit Lk Hwy PO Box 350 *Web:* www.ecoparkresort.com/tours.htm	Toutle	WA	98649	360-274-7007	
Educational Tours 1123 Sterling Rd **Fax Area Code:* 352 ■ *TF:* 800-343-9003 ■ *Web:* www.edtours-us.com	Inverness	FL	34450	800-343-9003	344-0067*
Educational Travel Consultants (ETC) PO Box 1580 *TF:* 800-247-7969 ■ *Web:* www.educationaltravelconsultants.com	Hendersonville	NC	28793	828-693-0412	692-1591
Educational Travel Tours Inc PO Box 9028 *Web:* www.educationaltraveltours.com	Trenton	NJ	08650	609-587-1550	587-1550
EF Tours One Education St **Fax Area Code:* 617 ■ *TF:* 800-872-8439 ■ *Web:* www.eftours.com	Cambridge	MA	02141	877-205-9909	619-1901*
Especially 4-U Tours & Travel 17 Spur Cir Ste 149 *Web:* www.especially4utours.com	Scottsdale	AZ	85251	480-985-4200	218-5135
Esplanade Tours 160 Commonwealth Ave Ste U-1A *TF:* 800-628-4893 ■ *Web:* esplanadetravel.com	Boston	MA	02116	617-266-7465	262-9829
Explorica Inc 145 Tremont St *TF:* 888-310-7120 ■ *Web:* www.explorica.com	Boston	MA	02111	888-310-7120	310-7088
Fantastic Tours & Travel 6143 Jericho Tpke *TF:* 800-552-6262 ■ *Web:* www.fantastictours.com	Commack	NY	11725	631-462-6262	462-2311
Festive Holidays Inc 5501 New Jersey Ave *TF:* 800-257-8920 ■ *Web:* www.festiveholidays.com	Wildwood Crest	NJ	08260	609-522-6316	729-8606
Flathead Lake Lodge & Ranch 150 Flathead Lodge Rd *Web:* flatheadlakelodge.com	Bigfork	MT	59911	406-837-4391	
Friendly Excursions Inc PO Box 69 *TF:* 800-775-5018 ■ *Web:* www.friendlyexcursions.net	Sunland	CA	91041	818-353-7726	353-3903
Frontiers International Travel PO Box 959 *TF:* 800-245-1950 ■ *Web:* www.frontierstravel.com	Wexford	PA	15090	724-935-1577	935-5388
Gadabout Vacations 1801 E Tahquitz Canyon Way Ste 100 *TF:* 800-952-5068 ■ *Web:* www.gadaboutvacations.com	Palm Springs	CA	92262	760-325-5556	325-5127
General Tours 53 Summer St **Fax Area Code:* 603 ■ *TF:* 800-221-2216 ■ *Web:* alexanderroberts.com	Keene	NH	03431	800-221-2216	357-4548*
Gerber Tours Inc 1400 Old Country Rd Ste 100 *TF:* 800-645-9145 ■ *Web:* www.gerbertours.com	Westbury	NY	11590	516-826-5000	826-5044
Global Educational Tours 7216 Madison Ave Ste U *TF:* 888-508-6877 ■ *Web:* www.globaledtours.com	Indianapolis	IN	46227	317-787-2787	787-2765
Globus 5301 S Federal Cir *TF:* 866-755-8581 ■ *Web:* www.globusjourneys.com	Littleton	CO	80123	303-703-7000	795-0962
Go Next 8000 W 78th St Ste 345 *TF:* 800-842-9023 ■ *Web:* www.gonext.com	Minneapolis	MN	55439	952-918-8950	918-8975
Go West Adventures Inc PO Box 882319 *Web:* www.gowestadventures.com	Los Angeles	CA	90009	310-216-2522	216-2638
Go...With Jo! Tours & Travel Inc 910 Dixieland Rd *TF:* 800-999-1446 ■ *Web:* www.gowithjo.com	Harlingen	TX	78552	956-423-1446	421-5787
Good Time Tours 455 Corday St *TF:* 800-446-0886 ■ *Web:* www.goodtimetours.com	Pensacola	FL	32503	850-476-0046	476-7637
Good Times Travel Inc 17132 Magnolia St *TF:* 888-488-2287 ■ *Web:* www.goodtimestravel.com	Fountain Valley	CA	92708	714-848-1255	848-2855
Grand European Tours 6000 Meadows Rd Ste 520 *TF:* 877-622-9109 ■ *Web:* www.getours.com	Lake Oswego	OR	97035	503-718-2262	718-5198
Gray Line Worldwide 1835 Gaylord St *Web:* www.grayline.com	Denver	CO	80206	303-394-6920	394-6950
Green Tortoise Adventure Travel & Hostels 494 Broadway *TF:* 800-867-8647 ■ *Web:* www.greentortoise.com	San Francisco	CA	94133	415-834-1000	956-4900
Greene Coach Charters & Tours Inc 126 Bohannon Ave	Greeneville	TN	37745	423-638-8271	638-5541
Group Voyagers Inc 5301 S Federal Cir *Web:* www.groupvoyagers.com	Littleton	CO	80123	303-703-7000	
Gutsy Women Travel LLC 801 E Katella Ave *TF:* 866-464-8879 ■ *Web:* www.gutsywomentravel.com	Anaheim	CA	92806	866-464-8879	
Hagey Coach & Tours Nrt 210 Schoolhouse Rd *Web:* hagey.com	Souderton	PA	18964	215-723-4381	
Hampton Golf Inc 10401 Deerwood Park Blvd Ste No. 2130 *Web:* www.hamptongolfclubs.com	Jacksonville	FL	32256	904-564-9129	
Harbor Cruises LLC One Long Wharf *Web:* www.bostonharborcruises.com	Boston	MA	02110	617-227-4321	
Hesselgrave International PO Box 30768 *TF:* 800-457-5522 ■ *Web:* www.hesselgravetours.com	Bellingham	WA	98228	360-734-3570	734-3588
Historic Tours of America Inc 201 Front St Ste 224 *TF General:* 800-844-7601 ■ *Web:* www.historictours.com	Key West	FL	33040	305-296-3609	292-8902
Hole in One International 6195 Ridgeview Ct Ste A *Web:* www.holeinoneinternational.com	Reno	NV	89519	775-828-4653	
Holiday River Expeditions 544 East 3900 South *TF:* 800-624-6323 ■ *Web:* www.bikeraft.com	Salt Lake City	UT	84107	801-266-2087	266-1448
Holiday Tours Inc 10367 Randleman Rd *Web:* www.holidaytoursinc.com	Randleman	NC	27317	336-498-9000	498-2204
Isram World of Travel Inc 233 Pk Ave S 10th Fl *TF:* 800-223-7460 ■ *Web:* www.isram.com	New York	NY	10003	212-661-1193	370-1477
Jade Travel Group 139 Keefer St Ste 202 *Web:* www2.jadetours.com	Vancouver	BC	V6A1X3	604-689-5885	
JALPAK International Hawaii Inc 2270 Kalakaua Ave Ste 1600	Honolulu	HI	96815	808-926-4500	923-4635
Jasmine's China Adventure Tours 6044 Laguna Villa Way	Elk Grove	CA	95758	916-683-1790	
Julian Tours 1721 Crestwood Dr Ste 110 *TF:* 800-541-7936 ■ *Web:* www.juliantours.com	Alexandria	VA	22302	703-379-2300	379-5030
Katmai Coastal Bear Tours PO Box 1503 *TF:* 800-532-8338 ■ *Web:* www.katmaibears.com	Homer	AK	99603	907-235-8337	
Ker & Downey Inc 6703 Hwy Blvd *TF:* 800-423-4236 ■ *Web:* www.kerdowney.com	Katy	TX	77494	281-371-2500	371-2514
Kincaid Coach Lines Inc 9207 Woodend Rd *TF:* 800-998-1901 ■ *Web:* www.kincaidcoach.com	Kansas City	KS	66111	913-441-6200	441-0068
Knight Inlet Grizzly Bear Adventure Tours 8841 Driftwood Rd *Web:* www.grizzlytours.com	Black Creek	BC	V9J1A8	250-337-1953	337-1914
Lakefront Lines Inc 13315 Brookpark Rd *Web:* www.lakefrontlines.com	Brook Park	OH	44142	216-267-8810	
Landmark Tours 1304 University Ave NE Ste 201 *TF:* 888-231-8735 ■ *Web:* landmark-tours.com	Minneapolis	MN	55413	651-490-5408	490-1454
Lemhi Ventures Inc 315 East Lk St Ste 304 *Web:* www.lemhiventures.com	Wayzata	MN	55391	952-908-9680	
Lindblad Expeditions 96 Morton St Ninth Fl *TF:* 800-397-3348 ■ *Web:* www.expeditions.com	New York	NY	10014	212-765-7740	265-3770
Macy's Travel 700 Nicollet Mall *TF:* 800-316-6166 ■ *Web:* www.travel.carlsonwagonlit.com	Minneapolis	MN	55402	800-316-6166	
Maupintour Inc 2690 Weston Rd Ste 200 *TF:* 800-255-4266 ■ *Web:* www.maupintour.com	Weston	FL	33331	954-653-3820	888-9082
Mayflower Tours Inc 1225 Warren Ave PO Box 490 *TF:* 800-323-7604 ■ *Web:* www.mayflowertours.com	Downers Grove	IL	60515	630-435-8500	960-3575
McKinzie Tours Inc 12900 Metcalf Ste 100 *Web:* travelsunrise.com	Overland Park	KS	66213	913-681-2202	681-2685
Micato Safaris 15 W 26th St 11th Fl *TF:* 800-642-2861 ■ *Web:* www.micato.com	New York	NY	10010	212-545-7111	545-8297
Mid-American Coaches Inc 4530 Hwy 47 **Fax Area Code:* 636 ■ *TF:* 866-944-8687 ■ *Web:* www.mid-americancoaches.com	Washington	MO	63090	866-944-8687	660-1505*
Midnight Sun Adventure Travel 1027 Pandora Ave *TF:* 800-255-5057 ■ *Web:* www.midnightsuntravel.com	Victoria	BC	V8V3P6	250-480-9409	483-7422
MLT Inc 700 Central Ave *Web:* www.mltvacations.com	Atlanta	GA	30354	404-559-2270	
Monograms 5301 S Federal Cir **Fax Area Code:* 303 ■ *TF:* 866-270-9841 ■ *Web:* monograms.com	Littleton	CO	80123	866-270-9841	795-0962*
Montana River Outfitters 923 Tenth Ave N *TF:* 800-800-8218 ■ *Web:* www.montanariveroutfitters.com	Great Falls	MT	59401	406-761-1677	452-3833
Moose Travel Network 192 Spadina Ave Unit 408 *Web:* www.moosenetwork.com	Toronto	ON	M5T2C2	604-297-0255	297-0228
Mountain Travel Sobek 1266 66th St Ste 4 *TF:* 888-831-7526 ■ *Web:* www.mtsobek.com	Emeryville	CA	94608	510-594-6000	594-6001
Musiker Discovery Programs Inc 1326 Old Northern Blvd *Web:* www.summerdiscovery.com	Roslyn	NY	11576	516-621-3939	625-3438
National Events Inc 9672 South 700 East Ste 200 *Web:* www.nationaleventservices.com	Sandy	UT	84070	801-495-9118	
Natural Habitat Adventures PO Box 3065 *TF:* 800-543-8917 ■ *Web:* www.nathab.com	Boulder	CO	80307	303-449-3711	449-3712
Networld Inc 300 Lanidex Plz Ste 1 *Web:* www.networldinc.com	Parsippany	NJ	07054	973-884-7474	
Off the Beaten Path Seven E Beall St *TF:* 800-445-2995 ■ *Web:* www.offthebeatenpath.com	Bozeman	MT	59715	406-586-1311	587-4147
Olivia Cruises & Resorts 434 Brannan St *TF:* 800-631-6277 ■ *Web:* www.olivia.com	San Francisco	CA	94107	415-962-5700	962-5710
On Tour 201 Cortsen Rd	Pleasant Hill	CA	94523	925-930-9135	
Onondaga Coach Corp PO Box 277 *TF:* 800-451-1570 ■ *Web:* www.onondagacoach.com	Auburn	NY	13021	315-255-2216	255-0925
Orange Belt Stages PO Box 949 *TF:* 800-266-7433 ■ *Web:* www.orangebelt.com	Visalia	CA	93292	559-733-4408	733-0538
Overseas Adventure Travel 347 Congress St **Fax Area Code:* 617 ■ *TF:* 800-221-0814 ■ *Web:* www.oattravel.com	Boston	MA	02210	800-221-0814	876-0455*
Panorama Balloon Tours 2683 Via De La Valle 625G *TF:* 800-455-3592 ■ *Web:* www.gohotair.com	Del Mar	CA	92014	800-455-3592	
Perillo Tours 577 Chestnut Ridge Rd *TF:* 800-431-1515 ■ *Web:* www.perillotours.com	Woodcliff Lake	NJ	07677	201-307-1234	307-1808
Pilgrim Tours & Travel Inc 3071 Main St PO Box 268 *TF:* 800-322-0788 ■ *Web:* www.pilgrimtours.com	Morgantown	PA	19543	610-286-0788	286-6262
Pink Jeep Tours Las Vegas Inc 3629 W Hacienda Ave *Web:* www.pinkjeeptours.com	Las Vegas	NV	89118	702-895-6777	
Pioneer Golf Inc 609 Castle Ridge Rd. Ste 335 *Web:* www.pioneergolf.com	Austin	TX	78746	512-327-2680	327-8120
Pitmar Tours 7549 140th St Ste 9 *TF:* 877-596-9670 ■ *Web:* www.pitmartours.com	Surrey	BC	V3W5J9	604-596-9670	596-3444
Polynesian Adventure Tours Inc 2880 Kilihau St **Fax:* Resv ■ *TF:* 800-622-3011 ■ *Web:* www.polyadhawaiitours.com	Honolulu	HI	96819	808-833-3000	833-3473*
Premier Alaska Tours Inc 1900 Premier Ct *Web:* www.premieralaskatours.com	Anchorage	AK	99502	907-279-0001	
Premier Tours 21 S 12th St Ninth Fl *TF:* 800-545-1910 ■ *Web:* www.premiertours.com	Philadelphia	PA	19107	800-545-1910	
Presley Tours Inc 16 Presley Pk Dr PO Box 58 *TF:* 800-621-6100 ■ *Web:* www.presleytours.com	Makanda	IL	62958	618-549-0704	549-0404
Rail Europe Group 44 S Broadway **Fax Area Code:* 914 ■ **Fax:* Sales ■ *Web:* www.raileurope.co.in	White Plains	NY	10601	800-622-8600	682-2821*
REI Adventures PO Box 1938 *TF:* 800-622-2236 ■ *Web:* www.rei.com/adventures	Sumner	WA	98390	253-437-1100	395-8160
Richmond Tours 1828 Hylan Blvd *TF:* 800-766-3868	Staten Island	NY	10305	718-979-3111	979-7143
Rivers Oceans & Mountains Adventures Inc (ROAM) 2485 Hwy 3A *TF:* 888-639-1114 ■ *Web:* www.iroamtheworld.com	Nelson	BC	V1L6K7	888-639-1114	639-1114
Roberts Hawaii Inc 680 Iwilei Rd Ste 700 *TF:* 800-831-5541 ■ *Web:* www.robertshawaii.com	Honolulu	HI	96817	808-523-7750	522-7872

Phone Fax

Royal Coach Tours 630 Stockton Ave San Jose CA 95126 408-279-4801 286-1410
TF: 800-927-6925 ■ *Web:* www.royal-coach.com

Royal Tours Inc 109 Irving St PO Box 372 Franklin VA 23851 757-569-7616
Web: www.gowithgaynelle.com

RSVP Vacations 2535 25th Ave S Minneapolis MN 55406 310-432-2300 729-2809*
**Fax Area Code:* 612 ■ *TF:* 800-328-7787 ■ *Web:* www.rsvpvacations.com

Scenic Airlines Inc
3900 Paradise Rd Ste 223 Las Vegas NV 89169 702-638-3300 639-3275
TF: 866-235-9422 ■ *Web:* www.scenic.com

Short Hills Tours
46 Chatham Rd PO Box 310 Short Hills NJ 07078 973-467-2113 467-3353
TF: 800-348-6871 ■ *Web:* www.shorthillstours.com

Silver Fox Tours & Motorcoaches
Three Silver Fox Dr Millbury MA 01527 508-865-6000 865-4660
TF: 800-342-5998 ■ *Web:* www.silverfoxcoach.com

Silverado Stages Inc 241 Prado Rd San Luis Obispo CA 93401 805-545-8400 545-8404
TF: 888-383-8109 ■ *Web:* www.silveradostages.com

South of the Border Tours 7937 E Coronado Rd Tucson AZ 85750 520-760-4000 760-3999

Sports Leisure Vacations
9812 Old Winery Pl Sacramento CA 95827 916-361-2051 361-7995
TF: 800-951-5556 ■ *Web:* www.sportsleisure.com

Sports Travel Inc 60 Main St PO Box 50 Hatfield MA 01038 413-247-7678 247-5700
TF: 800-662-4424 ■ *Web:* www.sportstravelandtours.com

Storm Chasing Adventure Tours
1627 W Main St Ste 105 Bozeman MT 59715 970-367-5395
Web: www.stormchasing.com

Straight A Tours & Travel
6881 Kingspointe Pkwy Ste 18 Orlando FL 32819 407-896-1242 896-1151
TF: 800-237-5440 ■ *Web:* straightatours.com

Student Tours Inc 60 W Ave Vineyard Haven MA 02568 508-693-5078 693-8627
TF: 800-331-7093 ■ *Web:* www.studenttoursinc.com

Student Travel Services Inc
1413 Madison Pk Dr Glen Burnie MD 21061 800-648-4849 787-9580*
**Fax Area Code:* 410 ■ *TF:* 800-648-4849 ■ *Web:* www.ststravel.com

Sunny Land Tours Inc
21 Old Kings Rd N Ste B-212 Palm Coast FL 32137 386-449-0059 449-0060
TF: 800-783-7839 ■ *Web:* www.sunnylandtours.com

Super Holiday Tours 116 Gatlin Ave Orlando FL 32806 800-327-2116 851-0071*
**Fax Area Code:* 407 ■ *TF:* 800-327-2116 ■ *Web:* www.superholiday.com

Tag-A-Long Expeditions 452 N Main St Moab UT 84532 435-259-8946 259-8990
TF: 800-453-3292 ■ *Web:* www.tagalong.com

Talbot Tours Inc 1952 Camden Ave San Jose CA 95124 408-879-0101 879-0183
Web: www.talbottours.com

Tauck World Discovery 10 Norden Pl Norwalk CT 06855 203-899-6500 899-6612*
**Fax:* Hum Res ■ *TF:* 800-468-2825 ■ *Web:* www.tauck.com

Team America Inc 33 W 46th St Frnt 3 New York NY 10036 212-221-5938
Web: www.teamamericany.com

Tempest Tours Inc 711 E Lamar Blvd Arlington TX 76011 817-274-9313
Web: www.tempesttours.com

Timberwolf Tours Ltd 51404 RR 264 Ste 34 Spruce Grove AB T7Y1E4 780-470-4966 339-3960*
**Fax Area Code:* 866 ■ *TF:* 888-467-9697 ■ *Web:* www.timberwolftours.com

Toto Tours Ltd 1326 W Albion Ave Chicago IL 60626 773-274-8686 274-8695
TF: 800-565-1241 ■ *Web:* www.tototours.com

Tour East Holidays (Canada) Inc
15 Kern Rd North York ON M3B1S9 416-929-8017
Web: www.toureast.com

TOUR GCX Partners Inc 450 Park Ave New York NY 10016 212-685-2200
Web: www.tourgcx.com

Touram Limited Partnership
1440 St Catherine St W Ste 800 Montreal QC H3G1R8 514-876-0700
Web: vacations.aircanada.com

Travcoa 100 N Sepulveda Blvd Ste 1700 El Segundo CA 90245 310-649-7104 649-7106
TF: 800-992-2003 ■ *Web:* www.travcoa.com

Tri-State Travel 4349 Industrial Pk Dr Galena IL 61036 815-777-0820 777-8128
TF: 800-779-4869 ■ *Web:* www.tristatetravel.com

Uncharted Outposts Inc Nine Village Ln Santa Fe NM 87505 505-795-7710
Web: www.tusk.org

Upstate Tours & Travel
207 Geyser Rd Saratoga Springs NY 12866 518-584-5252 584-1092
TF: 800-237-5252 ■ *Web:* www.upstatetours.com

USA Student Travel
5080 Robert J Mathews Pkwy El Dorado Hills CA 95762 916-939-6805 939-6806
TF: 800-448-4444 ■ *Web:* www.usastudenttravel.com

V I P Meetings & Conventions
1515 Palisades Dr Ste I Pacific Plsds CA 90272 310-459-4691
Web: vipmeetings.com

VBT Bicycling & Walking Vacations
614 Monkton Rd Bristol VT 05443 802-453-4811
TF: 800-245-3868 ■ *Web:* www.vbt.com

VentureOut 575 Pierce St Ste 604 San Francisco CA 94117 415-626-5678 626-5679
TF: 888-431-6789 ■ *Web:* www.venture-out.com

VIP Tour & Charter Bus Co 129-137 Fox St Portland ME 04101 207-772-4457 772-7020
TF General: 800-231-2222 ■ *Web:* www.vipchartercoaches.com

Vip Tours of California Inc
9830 Bellanca Ave Los Angeles CA 90045 310-641-8114
Web: www.viptoursofcalifornia.com

Visit America Inc 330 Seventh Ave 20th Fl New York NY 10001 212-683-8082 683-8501
Web: www.visitamerica.com

Wade Tours Inc 797 Burdeck St Schenectady NY 12306 518-355-4500 355-4942
TF: 800-955-9233 ■ *Web:* www.wadetours.com

Walking Adventures International
14612 NE Fourth Plain Rd Ste A Vancouver WA 98682 800-779-0353 260-1131*
**Fax Area Code:* 360 ■ *TF:* 800-779-0353 ■ *Web:* www.walkingadventures.com

West Coast Connection 1725 Main St Ste 215 Weston FL 33326 954-888-9780 888-9781
TF: 800-767-0227 ■ *Web:* www.westcoastconnection.com

White Mountain Adventures
131 Eagle Crescent PO Box 4259 Banff AB T1L1A6 403-760-4403 760-4409
TF: 800-408-0005 ■ *Web:* www.whitemountainadventures.com

White Star Tours 26 E Lancaster Ave Reading PA 19607 610-775-5000 775-7155
TF: 800-437-2323 ■ *Web:* www.whitestartours.com

Wilderness Travel 1102 Ninth St Berkeley CA 94710 510-558-2488 558-2489
TF: 800-368-2794 ■ *Web:* www.wildernesstravel.com

Phone Fax

Wildland Adventures Inc
3516 Ne 155th St Lake Forest Park WA 98155 206-365-0686
Web: wildland.com

Wings Tours Inc
11350 McCormick Rd Ste 703 Hunt Valley MD 21031 410-771-0925 771-0928
TF: 800-869-4647

WorldPass Travel Group LLC
5080 Robert J Matthews Pkwy El Dorado Hills CA 95762 916-939-6805 939-6806
TF: 800-949-0650 ■ *Web:* www.goworldpass.com

WorldStrides 218 W Water St Ste 400 Charlottesville VA 22902 800-999-7676 982-8690*
**Fax Area Code:* 434 ■ *TF General:* 800-999-7676 ■ *Web:* dn.educationaltravel.com

764 TOY STORES

Phone Fax

A2Z Science & Nature Store 57 King St NorthHampton MA 01060 413-586-1611 584-7253
TF: 877-261-6171 ■ *Web:* www.a-two-z.com

Alabama Card Systems Inc
500 Gene Reed Dr Ste 102 Birmingham AL 35215 205-833-1116 833-1160
TF: 800-985-7507 ■ *Web:* alabamacard.com

Artists Club, The 13118 Ne Fourth St Vancouver WA 98684 360-260-8900
Web: www.knitpicks.com

Bennett Mineral Co PO Box 28 Walkerton VA 23177 804-769-0546
Web: www.bennettmineral.com

Build-A-Bear Workshop Inc
1954 Innerbelt Business Ctr Dr Saint Louis MO 63114 314-423-8000 423-8188
NYSE: BBW ■ *TF:* 888-560-2327 ■ *Web:* www.buildabear.com

Creative Kid Stuff 3939 E 46th St Minneapolis MN 55406 612-929-2431 876-3981
TF: 800-353-0710 ■ *Web:* www.creativekidstuff.com

CRT Custom Products Inc
7532 Hickory Hills Ct Whites Creek TN 37189 615-876-5490
Web: www.crtcustomproducts.com

Daron Worldwide Trading Inc
24 Stewart Pl Unit 4 Fairfield NJ 07004 973-882-0035
Web: www.daronwwt.com

Digital Engineering Systems Corp
2450 Scott Blvd Ste 300 Santa Clara CA 95050 408-970-8551
Web: www.digi-eng.com

Discount School Supplies
Two Lower Ragsdale Rd Ste 125 Monterey CA 93940 800-919-5238 919-5235
TF: 800-919-5238 ■ *Web:* www.discountschoolsupply.com

FAO Schwarz 767 Fifth Ave 58th St New York NY 10153 212-644-9400
TF: 800-426-8697 ■ *Web:* www.fao.com

Fat Brain Toys LLC 1405 N 205th St Ste 120 Elkhorn NE 68022 402-779-3181
Web: www.fatbraintoys.com

Fibre Craft Materials Corp 6400 W Howard St Niles IL 60714 847-929-5600
Web: www.fibrecraft.com

Funagain Games of Ashland 1662 Ashland St Ashland OR 97520 541-482-1939
Web: funagain.com

Galt Toys 900 N Michigan Ave Chicago IL 60611 312-440-9550
Web: www.galtbaby.com

Game Informer 724 N First St Fl 3 Minneapolis MN 55401 612-486-6100
Web: www.gameinformer.com

Glitterex Corp Seven Commerce Dr Cranford NJ 07016 908-272-9121
Web: glitterex.com

Globalstor Data Corp
9960 Congoga Ave Unit D9 Chatsworth CA 91311 818-701-7771
Web: www.globalstor.com

Golden Gaming Inc 6595 S Jones Blvd Las Vegas NV 89118 702-893-7777
Web: www.goldengamingInc.com

Great Lakes Dart Manufacturing Inc
S84 W19093 Enterprise Dr Muskego WI 53150 262-679-8730
Web: www.gldproducts.com

Happy Hen Toys Ltd
1510 Old Deerfield Rd Ste 115 Highland Park IL 60035 847-831-3630
Web: www.happyhentoys.com

Hobbytown USA 1233 Libra Dr Lincoln NE 68512 402-434-5050
Web: www.hobbytown.com

Horizon Dart Supply 2415 S 50th St Kansas City KS 66106 913-236-9111
Web: www.horizondarts.com

Hosung NY Inc 300 Kingsland Ave Brooklyn NY 11222 718-389-8233
Web: www.hosungny.com

Jeson Enterprises Inc 504 NE Fifth Ave Camas WA 98607 360-834-7728
Web: www.craftwarehouse.com

Learning Express Inc 29 Buena Vista St Devens MA 01434 978-889-1000 889-1010
TF: 800-924-2296 ■ *Web:* www.learningexpress.com

M B Klein Inc 243 Cockeysville Rd Ste A Cockeysville MD 21030 410-229-9995
Web: www.modeltrainstuff.com

Magic Beans LLC 312 Harvard St Brookline MA 02446 617-264-2326
Web: www.mbeans.com

Make It Better LLC 1150 Wilmette Ave Ste J Wilmette IL 60091 847-256-4642
Web: www.makeitbetter.net

Mary Maxim Ltd 75 Scott Ave Paris ON N3L3G5 888-442-2266
TF: 888-442-2266 ■ *Web:* www.marymaxim.ca

MGA Entertainment Inc
16300 Roscoe Blvd Ste 150 Van Nuys CA 91406 818-894-2525 894-8094
TF: 800-222-4685 ■ *Web:* www.mgae.com

Mobile Id Solutions Inc
1574 N Batavia St Ste 1 Orange CA 92867 714-922-1134
Web: www.mobileidsolutions.com

Mountain Boy Sledworks Inc 1070 Greene St Silverton CO 81433 970-387-5077
Web: www.mountainboysleds.com

NetWire Inc 165 Nantasket Beach Ave Hull MA 02045 781-925-1700
Web: www.netwire.com

Next Level Games Inc
208 Robson St Fourth Fl Vancouver BC V6B6A1 604-484-6111
Web: www.nextlevelgames.com

Northstar Ceramic Trading LLC
14500 East Beltwood Pkwy Dallas TX 75244 972-392-3800 392-3808
Web: www.northstarceramics.com

Phone | Fax

Outset Media Corp 106-4226 Commerce Cir Victoria BC V8Z6N6 250-592-7374 592-7522
Web: www.outsetmedia.com

Perfect Game Softball LLC
1203 Rockford Rd Sw Ste A Cedar Rapids IA 52404 319-298-2923
Web: perfectgame.org

Plaster Fun Time 400 Highland Ave Ste 9 Salem MA 01970 978-745-7788
Web: www.plasterfuntime.com

Pun's Toy Shop 839 1/2 Lancaster Ave Bryn Mawr PA 19010 610-525-9789 527-5514
Web: punstoys.com

Reel Games Inc 1501 NE 13th Ave Fort Lauderdale FL 33304 954-563-8253
Web: www.reelgamesinc.com

Thinkfun Inc 1321 Cameron St Alexandria VA 22314 703-549-4999
Web: www.thinkfun.com

Thinkway Toys Inc 8885 Woodbine Ave Markham ON L3R5G1 905-470-8883
Web: www.thinkwaytoys.com

Toys 'R' Us (Canada) Ltd 2777 Langstaff Rd Concord ON L4K4M5 905-660-2000
Web: www.toysrus.ca

Trainworld Associates LLC 751 Mcdonald Ave Brooklyn NY 11218 718-436-7072
Web: www.trainworld.com

Village Toy Shop 2100 Patriot Blvd Glenview IL 60026 847-832-6908
Web: www.kohlchildrensmuseum.org

Workshop Inc, The 339 Broadway Menands NY 12204 518-465-5201
Web: www.ncporg.org

765 TOYS, GAMES, HOBBIES

SEE ALSO Games & Entertainment Software p. 2044; Baby Products p. 1846; Bicycles & Bicycle Parts & Accessories p. 1868

Phone | Fax

Airmate Co Inc 16280 County Rd D Bryan OH 43506 419-636-3184 636-4210
TF: 800-544-3614 ■ *Web:* www.airmatecompany.com

American Girl Inc 8400 Fairway Pl Middleton WI 53562 608-836-4848 836-1999
TF Orders: 800-845-0005 ■ *Web:* www.americangirl.com

American Plastic Toys Inc 799 Ladd Rd Walled Lake MI 48390 248-624-4881 624-4918
TF: 800-521-7080 ■ *Web:* www.americanplastictoys.com

Atlas Model Railroad Company Inc
378 Florence Ave Hillside NJ 07205 908-687-0880 687-8857
TF Orders: 800-872-2521 ■ *Web:* www.atlasrr.com

Bachmann Industries Inc 1400 E Erie Ave Philadelphia PA 19124 215-533-1600 744-4699
TF Cust Svc: 800-356-3910 ■ *Web:* www.bachmanntrains.com

Ball Bounce & Sport Inc/Hedstrom Plastics
One Hedstrom Dr Ashland OH 44805 419-289-9310 281-3371
TF: 800-765-9665 ■ *Web:* www.hedstrom.com

Bravo Sports Corp
12801 Carmenita Rd Santa Fe Springs CA 90670 562-484-5100 484-5183
TF Cust Svc: 800-234-9737 ■ *Web:* www.bravosportscorp.com

Buffalo Games Inc 220 James E Casey Dr Buffalo NY 14206 855-895-4290 827-8163*
**Fax Area Code:* 716 ■ *TF:* 855-895-4290 ■ *Web:* www.buffalogames.com

Cardinal Industries Inc
21-01 51st Ave Long Island City NY 11101 718-784-3000 482-7877
TF: 800-524-8697 ■ *Web:* www.cardinalgames.com

Cepia LLC 121 Hunter Ave Ste 103 Saint Louis MO 63124 314-725-4900 725-4919
TF: 800-225-9319 ■ *Web:* www.cepiallc.com

Commonwealth Toy & Novelty Co
45 W 25th St 7th Fl New York NY 10010 212-242-4070 645-4279
Web: commonwealthtoy.com

Creativity for Kids 9450 Allen Dr Cleveland OH 44125 216-643-4660 643-4663
TF: 800-311-8684 ■ *Web:* www.fabercastell.com

Dentt Inc 10450 S State St Sandy UT 84070 801-561-3821
Web: hammondtoy.com

Douglas Cuddle Toys Company Inc
69 Krif Rd PO Box D Keene NH 03431 603-352-3414 352-1248
TF: 800-992-9002 ■ *Web:* www.douglascuddletoy.com

Effanbee Doll Co 459 Hurley Ave Hurley NY 12443 845-339-8246 339-8326
TF: 888-362-3655 ■ *Web:* www.effanbeedoll.com

Electronic Arts Inc (EA)
209 Redwood Shores Pkwy Redwood City CA 94065 650-628-1500 628-1414
NASDAQ: EA ■ *Web:* www.ea.com

Estes-Cox Corp 1295 H St Penrose CO 81240 719-372-6565 372-3419
TF: 800-525-7561 ■ *Web:* www.estesrockets.com

Fisher-Price Inc 636 Girard Ave East Aurora NY 14052 716-687-3000 687-3476
TF: 800-432-5437 ■ *Web:* www.fisher-price.com

Five Below Inc 1818 Market St Ste 2000 Philadelphia PA 19103 215-546-7909 546-8099
Web: www.fivebelow.com

Gayla Industries Inc PO Box 920800 Houston TX 77292 905-857-5207 682-1357*
**Fax Area Code:* 713 ■ *TF:* 800-231-7508 ■ *Web:* www.gaylainc.com

Goffa International Corp 930 Flushing Ave Brooklyn NY 11206 718-361-8883 361-0506
Web: www.goffausa.com

Great Planes Model Distributors
PO Box 9021 Champaign IL 61826 217-398-3630 398-1104
TF: 800-637-7660 ■ *Web:* www.gpmd.com

Guidecraft USA 55508 Hwy 19 W PO Box U Winthrop MN 55396 507-647-5030 647-3254
TF: 800-524-3555 ■ *Web:* www.guidecraft.com

Gund Inc 1 Runyons Ln Edison NJ 08817 732-248-1500 248-1968
TF Cust Svc: 800-448-4863 ■ *Web:* www.gund.com

Hasbro Inc 1027 Newport Ave Pawtucket RI 02861 401-431-8697 431-8082*
NASDAQ: HAS ■ **Fax:* Cust Svc ■ *TF:* 800-242-7276 ■ *Web:* www.hasbro.com

Hasbro Inc Playskool Div 1027 Newport Ave Pawtucket RI 02861 401-431-8697 727-5544
TF: 800-242-7276 ■ *Web:* www.hasbro.com

Imperial Toy LLC 16641 Roscoe Pl North Hills CA 91343 818-536-6500 536-6501
Web: www.imperialtoy.com

International Playthings Inc
75D Lackawanna Ave Parsippany NJ 07054 973-316-2500 316-5883
TF: 800-631-1272 ■ *Web:* www.intplay.com

JAKKS Pacific Inc 21749 Baker Pkwy Walnut CA 91789 909-594-7771
NASDAQ: JAKK ■ *TF:* 877-875-2557 ■ *Web:* www.jakks.com

K'NEX Industries Inc
2990 Bergey Rd PO Box 700 Hatfield PA 19440 215-997-7722
Web: www.brio.net

Phone | Fax

LeapFrog Enterprises Inc
6401 Hollis St Ste 100 Emeryville CA 94608 510-420-5000 420-5001
NYSE: LF ■ *TF:* 800-701-5327 ■ *Web:* leapfrog.com

Learning Resources 380 N Fairway Dr Vernon Hills IL 60061 847-573-8400 573-8425
TF: 800-222-3909 ■ *Web:* www.learningresources.com

LEGO Systems Inc 555 Taylor Rd Enfield CT 06082 860-763-6731
TF: 877-518-5346 ■ *Web:* www.lego.com

Lionel .com LLC 26750 23 Mile Rd Chesterfield MI 48051 586-949-4100 949-6757*
**Fax:* Hum Res ■ *TF:* 800-454-6635 ■ *Web:* www.lionel.com

Little Tikes Co, The 2180 Barlow Rd Hudson OH 44236 800-321-0183
TF Cust Svc: 800-321-0183 ■ *Web:* www.littletikes.com

Losi 4710 E Guasti Rd Ontario CA 91761 909-390-9595 390-5356
TF: 888-899-5674 ■ *Web:* www.losi.com

Mag-Nif Inc 8820 E Ave Mentor OH 44060 800-869-5463 974-0449*
**Fax Area Code:* 440 ■ *TF:* 800-869-5463 ■ *Web:* www.magnif.com

Maple City Rubber Co 55 Newton St PO Box 587 Norwalk OH 44857 419-668-8261 668-1275
TF: 800-841-9434 ■ *Web:* www.maplecityrubber.com

Mattel Inc 333 Continental Blvd El Segundo CA 90245 310-252-2000
NASDAQ: MAT ■ *TF:* 800-524-8697 ■ *Web:* www.mattel.com

Midwest Products Company Inc 400 S Indiana St Hobart IN 46342 219-942-1134 947-2347*
**Fax:* Sales ■ *TF Orders:* 800-348-3497 ■ *Web:* www.midwestproducts.com

Model Rectifier Corp 80 Newfield Ave Edison NJ 08837 732-225-2100 225-0091
Web: www.modelrec.com

Nintendo of America Inc 4820 150th Ave NE Redmond WA 98052 425-882-2040 882-3585
TF Cust Svc: 800-255-3700 ■ *Web:* www.nintendo.com

Ohio Art Co 1 Toy St Bryan OH 43506 419-636-3141
OTC: OART ■ *TF:* 800-800-3141 ■ *Web:* www.world-of-toys.com

Original Appalachian Artworks Inc
1721 Hwy 75 S PO Box 714 Cleveland GA 30528 706-865-2171 865-5862
Web: www.cabbagepatchkids.com

Patch Products Inc 1400 E Inman Pkwy Beloit WI 53511 608-362-6896 362-8178
TF: 800-524-4263 ■ *Web:* www.patchproducts.com

Paul K Guillow Inc
40 New Salem St PO Box 229 Wakefield MA 01880 781-245-5255 245-4738
Web: www.guillow.com

Pepperball Technologies Inc
6540 Lusk Blvd Ste C137 San Diego CA 92121 858-638-0236 638-0781
TF: 877-887-3773 ■ *Web:* www.pepperball.com

Pioneer National Latex Co 5000 E 29th St N Wichita KS 67220 316-685-2266 329-3864*
**Fax Area Code:* 800 ■ *TF:* 800-386-4438 ■ *Web:* www.pioneernational.com

Plaid Enterprises Inc 3225 Westech Dr Norcross GA 30092 678-291-8100 291-8368*
**Fax:* Mktg ■ *TF:* 800-842-4197 ■ *Web:* www.plaidonline.com

Playmobil USA Inc 26 Commerce Dr Cranbury NJ 08512 609-409-1263 395-3015
Web: www.playmobil.com

Poof-Slinky Inc
4280 S Haggerty Rd PO Box 701394 Canton MI 48188 734-454-9552 454-9540
TF: 800-829-9502 ■ *Web:* www.poof-slinky.com

Pressman Toy Corp 121 New England Ave Piscataway NJ 08854 732-562-1590 562-8407
TF Cust Svc: 800-800-0298 ■ *Web:* www.pressmantoy.com

Radio Flyer Inc 6515 W Grand Ave Chicago IL 60707 773-637-7100 637-8874
TF: 800-621-7613 ■ *Web:* www.radioflyer.com

SEGA of America Inc
350 Rhode Island Street Suite 400 San Francisco CA 94103 415-701-6000 701-6001
Web: www.sega.com

SIG Mfg Company Inc 401 S Front St Montezuma IA 50171 641-623-5154 623-3922
TF Sales: 800-247-5008 ■ *Web:* www.sigmfg.com

Sony Computer Entertainment America Inc
919 E Hillsdale Blvd Foster City CA 94404 650-655-8000 655-8001
Web: playstation.com/en-us/home/

Spin Master Ltd 450 Front St W Toronto ON M5V1B6 416-364-6002 364-5097
TF: 800-622-8339 ■ *Web:* www.spinmaster.com

Steiff North America 24 Albion Rd Ste 220 Lincoln RI 02865 401-312-0080
TF: 888-978-3433 ■ *Web:* www.steiffusa.com

Swibco Inc 4810 Venture Rd Lisle IL 60532 630-968-8900 367-7943*
**Fax Area Code:* 800 ■ *TF:* 877-794-2261 ■ *Web:* www.swibco.com

Tara Toy Corp 40 Adams Ave Hauppauge NY 11788 631-273-8697 273-8583
TF: 800-899-8272 ■ *Web:* www.taratoy.com

Testor Corp 440 Blackhawk Pk Ave Rockford IL 61104 815-962-6654 962-7401
TF: 800-837-8677 ■ *Web:* www.testors.com

TOMY International Inc
1111 W 22nd St Ste 320 Oak Brook IL 60523 800-704-8697 573-7575*
**Fax Area Code:* 630 ■ *TF:* 800-704-8697 ■ *Web:* tomy.com

Tonner Doll Co 301 Wall St PO Box 4410 Kingston NY 12402 845-339-9537 339-1259
TF: 800-794-2107 ■ *Web:* www.tonnerdoll.com

Troxel Co Hwy 57 Moscow TN 38057 901-877-6875 877-6942
Web: www.troxel.com

Uncle Milton Industries Inc
29209 Canwood St Ste 120 Agoura CA 91301 818-707-0800 707-0878
TF General: 800-869-7555 ■ *Web:* www.unclemilton.com

Universal Mfg Co Inc 5030 Mackey S Overland Park KS 66203 913-815-6230 815-6240
TF: 800-524-5860 ■ *Web:* www.umcprint.com

University Games Corp 2030 Harrison St San Francisco CA 94110 415-503-1600 503-0085
TF: 800-347-4818 ■ *Web:* www.ugames.com

Upper Deck Co LLC 5909 Sea Otter Pl Carlsbad CA 92010 800-873-7332 929-3512*
**Fax Area Code:* 760 ■ *TF Cust Svc:* 800-873-7332 ■ *Web:* www.upperdeck.com

Vermont Teddy Bear Company Inc
6655 Shelburne Rd Shelburne VT 05482 802-985-3001 985-1304
TF: 800-988-8277 ■ *Web:* vermontteddybear.com

VTech Electronics North America LLC
1155 W Dundee St Ste 130 Arlington Heights IL 60004 847-400-3600 400-3601
TF: 800-521-2010 ■ *Web:* www.vtechkids.com

Wham-O Inc 6301 Owensmouth Ave Ste 700 Woodland Hills CA 91367 888-942-6650
TF: 888-942-6650 ■ *Web:* www.wham-o.com

Wiffle Ball Inc 275 Bridgeport Ave PO Box 193 Shelton CT 06484 203-924-4643 924-9433
Web: www.wiffle.com

William K Walthers Inc 5601 W Florist Ave Milwaukee WI 53218 414-527-0770 527-4423
TF: 800-877-7171 ■ *Web:* www.walthers.com

Wizards of the Coast Inc
1600 Lind Ave SW Ste 400 Renton WA 98057 425-226-6500 204-5818
TF: 800-324-6496 ■ *Web:* company.wizards.com

TRAILERS - TRUCK

SEE Truck Trailers p. 3259

766 TRAILERS (TOWING) & TRAILER HITCHES

Phone Fax

Blessey Marine Services Inc
1515 River Oaks Rd E . . . Harahan LA 70123 504-734-1156 734-1195
Web: www.blessey.com

Bright Co-op Inc 803 W Seale St . . . Nacogdoches TX 75964 936-564-8378 564-3281
TF: 800-562-0730 ■ *Web:* www.brightcoop.com

Cequent Towing Products 47774 Anchor Ct W . . . Plymouth MI 48170 800-521-0510 656-3009*
**Fax Area Code:* 734 ■ *TF:* 800-521-0510 ■ *Web:* www.draw-tite.com

Cequent Trailer Products 1050 Indianhead Dr . . . Mosinee WI 54455 715-693-1700 693-1799
TF: 800-604-9466 ■ *Web:* www.fultonperformance.com

CM Trailers Inc 200 County Rd PO Box 680 . . . Madill OK 73446 580-795-5536 795-7263
TF: 888-268-7577 ■ *Web:* www.cmtrailers.com

Com-Fab Inc 4657 Price HilliaRds Rd . . . Plain City OH 43064 740-857-1107 857-1757
TF: 866-522-1794 ■ *Web:* www.comfab-inc.com

Creek Hill Welding 13 W Eby Rd . . . Leola PA 17540 717-556-8452
Web: www.creekhillwelding.com

Dethmers Manufacturing Co (DEMCO)
4010 320th St PO Box 189 . . . Boyden IA 51234 712-725-2311 725-2380
TF: 800-543-3626 ■ *Web:* www.demco-products.com

EZ Loader Boat Trailers Inc
717 N Hamilton St . . . Spokane WA 99202 509-489-0181 489-5729
TF: 800-398-5623 ■ *Web:* www.ezloader.com

Gardner Cryogenics 2136 City Line Rd . . . Bethlehem PA 18017 610-264-4523 266-3752
Web: www.gardnercryo.com

Gooseneck Trailer Mfg Co
4400 E Hwy 21 PO Box 832 . . . Bryan TX 77808 979-778-0034 778-0615
TF Cust Svc: 800-688-5490 ■ *Web:* www.gooseneck.net

Hawkeye Leisure Trailers Ltd 1419 11th St N . . . Humboldt IA 50548 515-332-1802 332-1833
Web: www.yachtclubtrailers.com

Karavan Trailers Inc
100 Karavan Dr PO Box 27 . . . Fox Lake WI 53933 920-928-6200 928-6201
Web: www.karavantrailers.com

Load Rite Trailers Inc
265 Lincoln Hwy . . . Fairless Hills PA 19030 215-949-0500 949-1385
TF: 800-562-3783 ■ *Web:* www.loadrite.com

Mac-Lander Inc 509 E Maple . . . Milton IA 52570 641-656-4271 656-4225
Web: www.mac-lander.com

Midwest Industries Inc 122 E State Hwy 175 . . . Ida Grove IA 51445 712-364-3365 364-3361
TF: 800-859-3028 ■ *Web:* www.shorelandr.com

Rigid Hitch Inc 3301 W Burnsville Pkwy . . . Burnsville MN 55337 952-895-5001 895-9150
TF Cust Svc: 800-624-7630 ■ *Web:* www.rigidhitch.com

Sundowner Trailers Inc 9805 S State Hwy 48 . . . Coleman OK 73432 580-937-4255 937-4440
TF: 800-654-3879 ■ *Web:* www.sundownertrailer.com

Take 3 Trailers Inc 1808 Hwy 105 . . . Brenham TX 77833 979-337-9568
TF: 800-428-2533 ■ *Web:* www.take3trailers.com

TriMas Corp
39400 Woodward Ave Ste 130 . . . Bloomfield Hills MI 48304 248-631-5450 631-5455
Web: www.trimascorp.com

Unique Functional Products Corp
135 Sunshine Ln . . . San Marcos CA 92069 760-744-1610 744-4709
TF: 800-854-1905 ■ *Web:* www.ufpnet.com

767 TRAINING & CERTIFICATION PROGRAMS - COMPUTER & INTERNET

Phone Fax

AAIM Employers' Association LLC
1600 S Brentwood Ste 400 . . . St. Louis MO 63144 314-968-3600
Web: www.aaimea.org

Agencia International Inc
110 W 40th St Ste 603 . . . New York NY 10018 212-391-1306
Web: www.agencianyc.com

Altima Technologies Inc
Lisle Executive Ctr 3030 Warrenville Rd
Ste 300 . . . Lisle IL 60532 630-281-6464
Web: www.altimatech.com

Animation Mentor 1400 65th St Ste 250 . . . Emeryville CA 94608 877-326-4628
TF: 877-326-4628 ■ *Web:* www.animationmentor.com

ASPE Inc 114 Edinburgh S Dr Ste 200 . . . Cary NC 27511 877-800-5221
TF: 877-800-5221 ■ *Web:* www.aspeinc.com

Bilingual Education Institute
6060 Richmond Ave Ste 180 . . . Houston TX 77057 713-789-4555
Web: www.bei.edu

Career Step LLC 4692 North 300 West Ste 150 . . . Provo UT 84604 801-489-9393
Web: www.careerstep.com

Computer Workshop Inc, The
5131 Post Rd Ste 102 . . . Dublin OH 43017 614-798-9505
Web: www.tcworkshop.com

Computers 4 Kids 945 Second St Se . . . Charlottesville VA 22902 434-817-1121
Web: www.computers4kids.us

Compuworks Ltd One Fenn St Ste 1 . . . Pittsfield MA 01201 413-499-0607
Web: www.bill-dixon.com

Coyne College Inc 330 N Green St . . . Chicago IL 60607 773-577-8100
Web: www.coynecollege.edu

DSI Inc PO Box 162652 . . . Austin TX 78716 512-389-5127 327-6838
Web: www.dsiinc.com

ECO Canada 308 - 11th Ave SE Ste 200 . . . Calgary AB T2G0Y2 403-233-0748
Web: www.eco.ca

Gainshare Inc 3110 N Central Ave Ste 160 . . . Phoenix AZ 85012 602-266-8500
Web: www.interfacett.com

Global Knowledge Training LLC
9000 Regency Pkwy Ste 500 . . . Cary NC 27518 919-461-8600 461-8646
TF: 800-268-7737 ■ *Web:* www.globalknowledge.com

Phone Fax

Hands on Technology Transfer Inc
One Village Sq Ste 8 . . . Chelmsford MA 01824 978-250-4299
Web: traininghott.com

Health & Safety Institute Inc 1450 Westec Dr . . . Eugene OR 97402 800-447-3177
TF: 800-447-3177 ■ *Web:* www.hsi.com

IHRDC 535 Boylston St 12th Fl . . . Boston MA 02116 617-536-0202
Web: www.honeoyestorage.com

It4ce Inc 1200 Aerowood Dr . . . Mississauga ON L4W2S7 905-206-9947
Web: it4ce.com

Learning Tree International Inc
1831 Michael Faraday Dr . . . Reston VA 20190 703-709-9119
OTC: LTRE ■ *TF Cust Svc:* 800-843-8733 ■ *Web:* www.learningtree.com

Metex Inc 789 Don Mills Rd Ste 218 . . . North York ON M3C1T5 416-203-8388
Web: www.metex.com

Milwaukee Rescue Mission 830 n 19th st . . . Milwaukee WI 53233 414-344-2211
Web: www.milmission.org

Minact Inc 5220 Keele St . . . Jackson MS 39206 601-362-1631 362-5771
Web: www.minact.com

MindLeaders.com Inc 5500 Glendon Ct Ste 200 . . . Dublin OH 43016 614-781-7300 781-6510
TF: 800-223-3732 ■ *Web:* www.mindleaders.com

My Service Depot 8774 Cotter St . . . Lewis Center OH 43035 614-985-1278
Web: www.myservicedepot.com

Natural Healing College 446 E Vine St . . . Stockton CA 95202 209-390-8076
Web: naturalhealingcollege.com

Nevada Area Vocational School
900 W Ashland St . . . Nevada MO 64772 417-448-2090
Web: www.nevada.k12.mo.us

New Horizons Computer Learning Centers Inc
1900 S State College Blvd Ste 450 . . . Anaheim CA 92806 714-940-8000
TF: 888-236-3625 ■ *Web:* www.newhorizons.com

New Horizons Worldwide Inc
1 W Elm St Ste 125 . . . Conshohocken PA 19428 888-236-3625
Web: www.newhorizons.com

Next Level Purchasing
1315 Coraopolis Heights Rd Ste 2002 . . . Moon Township PA 15108 412-294-1990
Web: www.nextlevelpurchasing.com

Online Marketing Institute
2088 Union St Ste 3 . . . San Francisco CA 94123 415-450-9524
Web: www.onlinemarketinginstitute.org

Optimum Talent Inc 25 York St Ste 1802 . . . Toronto ON M5J2V5 416-364-2605
Web: www.optimumtalent.com

PAR Springer-Miller Systems Inc
782 Mountain Rd . . . Stowe VT 05672 802-253-7377
Web: www.springermiller.com

Parker University 2540 Walnut Hill Ln . . . Dallas TX 75229 972-438-6932
Web: www.parkerproproducts.com

PowerScore Inc 57 Hasell St . . . Charleston SC 29401 800-545-1750
TF: 800-545-1750 ■ *Web:* www.powerscore.com

Preferred Solutions Inc
21800 Haggerty Rd Ste 315 . . . Northville MI 48167 248-679-0130
Web: www.prefsol.com

Productivity Point International Inc
2950 Gateway Ctr Blvd . . . Morrisville NC 27560 919-379-5611

Prospero Learning Solutions Inc
1075 Bay St Ste 500 . . . Toronto ON M5S2B1 416-360-0606
Web: www.prosperolearning.com

Reading-muhlenberg Area Vocational-technical Schoo
2615 Warren Rd . . . Reading PA 19604 610-921-7300
Web: www.rmctc.org

Region 4 Education Service Center
7145 W Tidwell Rd . . . Houston TX 77092 713-462-7708
Web: www.esc4.net

Rockford Career College 1130 s alpine rd . . . Rockford IL 61108 815-965-8616
Web: www.rbcsuccess.com

Software Answers Inc
6770 W Snowville Rd Ste 200 . . . Brecksville OH 44141 440-526-0095
Web: software-answers.com

Total Seminars LLC 12929 Gulf Fwy Ste 105 . . . Houston TX 77034 281-922-4166
Web: totalsem.com

Trivac Ltd 3050 Regent Blvd Ste 310 . . . Irving TX 75063 469-484-5400
Web: www.trivac.com

UAW Labor Employment & Training Corp
790 E Willow St . . . Long Beach CA 90806 562-989-7700
Web: www.letc.com

768 TRAINING PROGRAMS - CORPORATE

Phone Fax

AchieveGlobal Inc
8875 Hidden River Pkwy Ste 400 . . . Tampa FL 33637 813-631-5500 631-5796
Web: www.achieveglobal.com

ActionCOACH 5781 S Ft Apache Rd . . . Las Vegas NV 89148 702-795-3188 795-3183
TF: 888-483-2828 ■ *Web:* www.actioncoach.com

Acumen Learning LLC 226 N Orem Blvd . . . Orem UT 84057 801-224-5444
Web: acumenlearning.com

Baker Communications Inc 10101 SW Fwy #630 . . . Houston TX 77074 713-627-7700 587-2051
Web: www.bakercommunications.com

Briljent LLC 7615 W Jefferson Blvd . . . Fort Wayne IN 46804 260-434-0990
Web: www.briljent.com

Center for Creative Leadership
One Leadership Pl PO Box 26300 . . . Greensboro NC 27438 336-545-2810 282-3284
Web: www.ccl.org

Christy Capital Management Inc 2939 Mcmanus Rd . . . Macon GA 31220 478-314-2160
Web: www.christycapital.com

ClickSafety.com Inc
2185 N California Blvd Ste 425 . . . Walnut Creek CA 94596 800-971-1080
TF: 800-971-1080 ■ *Web:* www.clicksafety.com

Creative Training Techniques International Inc
14530 Martin Dr . . . Eden Prairie MN 55344 952-829-1954 829-0260
TF: 800-383-9210 ■ *Web:* www.bobpikegroup.com

				Phone	Fax
Crestcom International Ltd 6900 E Belleview Ave	Greenwood Village	CO	80111	303-267-8200	
Web: www.crestcomleadership.com					
Dale Carnegie & Assoc Inc 290 Motor Pkwy	Hauppauge	NY	11788	800-231-5800	644-5532*
**Fax Area Code:* 212 ■ *TF:* 800-231-5800 ■ *Web:* www.dalecarnegie.com					
Don Hutson Organization 516 Tennessee St Ste 219	Memphis	TN	38103	901-767-0000	767-5959
TF: 800-647-9166 ■ *Web:* www.donhutson.com					
Elite Business Services PO Box 9630	Rancho Santa Fe	CA	92067	800-204-3548	756-4781*
**Fax Area Code:* 858 ■ *TF:* 800-204-3548 ■ *Web:* www.eliteworldwidestore.com					
Envision Group Consulting Inc 103 N Durham Ln Ste 200	Round Lake	IL	60073	847-270-7893	
Web: www.envisiongroupconsulting.com					
Executive Enterprises Institute 12 Skyline Dr	Hawthorne	NY	10532	914-517-1122	
TF: 877-334-4273 ■ *Web:* www.eeiconferences.com					
Forum Corp 265 Franklin St 4th Fl	Boston	MA	02110	617-523-7300	371-3300
TF: 800-367-8611 ■ *Web:* www.forum.com					
Franklin Covey Co 2200 West PkwyBlvd	Salt Lake City	UT	84119	801-817-1776	817-6085
NYSE: FC ■ *TF:* 800-827-1776 ■ *Web:* www.franklincovey.com					
Fred Pryor Seminars 9757 Metcalf Ave	Overland Park	KS	66212	800-780-8476	967-8842*
**Fax Area Code:* 913 ■ *TF:* 800-780-8476 ■ *Web:* www.pryor.com					
Frontline Group of Texas LLC 15021 Katy Fwy Ste 575	Houston	TX	77094	281-453-6000	453-8000
TF: 800-285-5512 ■ *Web:* www.frontline-group.com					
Greenlining Institute, The 1918 University Ave Ste 2	Berkeley	CA	94704	510-926-4000	
Web: greenlining.org					
HealthStream Inc 209 Tenth Ave S Ste 450	Nashville	TN	37203	615-301-3100	301-3200
NASDAQ: HSTM ■ *TF:* 800-933-9293 ■ *Web:* www.healthstream.com					
Hinda Incentives Inc 2440 W 34th St	Chicago	IL	60608	773-890-5900	890-4606
TF: 800-621-4112 ■ *Web:* www.hinda.com					
Insight Information 214 King St W Ste 300	Toronto	ON	M5H3S6	416-777-2020	777-1292*
**Fax Area Code:* 866 ■ *TF:* 888-777-1707 ■ *Web:* www.insightinfo.com					
Inspirica Ltd 850 Seventh Ave Ste 403	New York	NY	10019	212-245-3888	
Web: www.inspirica.com					
Invitechange LLC 110 Third Ave N Ste 102	Edmonds	WA	98020	425-778-3505	
Web: www.invitechange.com					
ITC Learning Corp 1616 Anderson Rd Ste 109	McLean	VA	22102	800-638-3757	852-7174*
**Fax Area Code:* 703 ■ *TF:* 800-638-3757 ■ *Web:* www.itclearning.com					
Jones Knowledge Group Inc 9697 E Mineral Ave	Centennial	CO	80112	303-792-3111	799-0966
TF: 800-350-6914 ■ *Web:* www.jonesknowledge.com					
Leadership Management Inc 4567 Lk Shore Dr	Waco	TX	76710	254-776-2060	772-9588
TF: 800-568-1241 ■ *Web:* www.lmi-world.com					
Levinson Institute Inc 28 Main St Ste 100	Jaffrey	NH	03452	603-532-4700	532-4750
TF: 800-290-5735 ■ *Web:* levinsonandco.com					
Mandel Communications Inc 820 Bay Ave Ste 113	Capitola	CA	95010	831-475-8202	
Web: www.mandel.com					
National Businesswomen's Leadership Assn PO Box 419107	Kansas City	MO	64141	913-432-7755	432-0824
TF: 800-258-7246 ■ *Web:* www.nationalseminarstraining.com					
National Seminars Training 6901 W 63rd St 3rd Fl	Overland Park	KS	66202	913-432-7755	432-0824
TF: 800-258-7246 ■ *Web:* www.nationalseminarstraining.com					
Netlan Technology Center Inc 39 W 37th St Fl 11	New York	NY	10018	212-730-5900	
Web: www.netlan.com					
Nexient Learning Canada Inc 1809 Barrington St Ste 900	Halifax	NS	B3J3K8	902-429-4357	
Web: www.globalknowledge.ca					
NTL Institute 1901 S Bell St Ste 300	Arlington	VA	22202	703-548-1500	
Web: www.ntl.org					
Pacific Institute 1709 Harbor Ave SW	Seattle	WA	98126	206-628-4800	587-6007
TF: 800-426-3660 ■ *Web:* www.thepacificinstituteretail.com					
Patch Plus Consulting Inc Three Raleigh Cir Ste B	Medford	NJ	08055	609-792-6204	
Web: www.patchplusconsulting.com					
Pm Resource Group LLC 10800 Alpharetta Hwy Ste 208-642	Roswell	GA	30076	404-247-6968	
Web: www.pmresourcegroup.com					
Priority Management Systems Inc 11160 Silversmith Pl	Richmond	BC	V7A5E4	604-214-7772	214-7773
Web: www.prioritymanagement.com					
Productivity Inc Four Armstrong Rd Third Fl	Shelton	CT	06484	203-225-0451	225-0771
TF: 800-966-5423 ■ *Web:* www.productivityinc.com					
Rockhurst University Continuing Education Ctr Inc PO Box 419107	Kansas City	MO	64141	913-432-7755	432-0824
TF: 800-258-7246 ■ *Web:* www.nationalseminarstraining.com					
Safety Sam Inc 2626 S Roosevelt St Ste 2	Tempe	AZ	85282	866-478-6980	
TF: 866-478-6980 ■ *Web:* www.safetyservicescompany.com					
Sandler Sales Institute 10411 Stevenson Rd	Stevenson	MD	21153	410-653-1993	358-7858
TF: 800-669-3537 ■ *Web:* www.sandler.com					
Situation Management Systems Inc 98 Spit Brook Rd Ste 201	Nashua	NH	03062	603-897-1200	
Web: situationmanagementsystems.com					
SkillSoft PLC 107 NE Blvd	Nashua	NH	03062	603-324-3000	
TF: 877-545-5763 ■ *Web:* www.skillsoft.com					
SmartPros Ltd 12 Skyline Dr	Hawthorne	NY	10532	914-345-2620	345-2603
NASDAQ: SPRO ■ *Web:* sp.smartpros.com					
Speakeasy Inc 3438 Peachtree Rd Ste 1000 Phipps Twr	Atlanta	GA	30326	404-541-4800	541-4848
Web: www.speakeasyinc.com					
Team Business LLC 1410 Belt St	Baltimore	MD	21230	410-837-1414	
Web: www.teambusiness.com					
Telemedia Inc 750 W Lk Cook Rd Rd Ste 250	Buffalo Grove	IL	60089	847-808-4000	
Web: www.tpctraining.com					
Teleos Leadership Inst LLC 7837 Old York Rd	Elkins Park	PA	19027	267-620-9999	
Web: teleosleaders.com					
Toastmasters International 23182 Arroyo Vista	Rancho Santa Margarita	CA	92688	949-858-8255	858-1207
TF: 877-738-8118 ■ *Web:* www.toastmasters.org					
US Learning Inc 516 Tennessee St Ste 219	Memphis	TN	38103	901-767-5700	767-5959
TF: 800-647-9166 ■ *Web:* www.uslearning.com					
Veriforce LLC 19221 I-45 S Ste 200	Shenandoah	TX	77385	800-426-1604	
TF: 800-426-1604 ■ *Web:* www.veriforce.com					
Voice Pro Inc 2055 Lee Rd Ste 101	Cleveland	OH	44118	216-932-8040	
Web: www.voiceproinc.com					
Wilson Learning Corp 8000 W 78th St Ste 200	Edina	MN	55439	952-944-2880	828-8835
TF: 800-328-7937 ■ *Web:* www.wilsonlearning.com					
Xcelerate Media Inc 61 W Bridge St	Dublin	OH	43017	614-336-9722	
Web: www.xceleratemedia.com					

769 TRAINING PROGRAMS (MISC)

SEE ALSO Children's Learning Centers p. 1948; Training & Certification Programs - Computer & Internet p. 3247; Training Programs - Corporate p. 3247

				Phone	Fax
Academy for Guided Imagery Inc 10780 Santa Monica Blvd Ste 290	Los Angeles	CA	90025	800-726-2070	727-2070
TF: 800-726-2070 ■ *Web:* www.acadgi.com					
American College of Orgonomy 4419 Rt 27	Princeton	NJ	08545	732-821-1144	821-0174
Web: www.orgonomy.org					
Audio-Digest Foundation 1577 E Chevy Chase Dr	Glendale	CA	91206	818-240-7500	240-7379
TF: 800-423-2308 ■ *Web:* www.audio-digest.org					
Canter & Assoc LLC 12975 Coral Tree Pl	Los Angeles	CA	90066	310-578-4700	301-7512
TF Cust Svc: 800-669-9011 ■ *Web:* www.canter.net					
Ed Necco & Assoc 178 Private Dr	South Point	OH	45680	513-771-9600	894-1132*
**Fax Area Code:* 740 ■ *TF:* 866-996-3226 ■ *Web:* www.necco.org					
Executive Protection Institute 16 Penn Plz Ste 1570	New York	NY	10001	212-268-4555	563-4783
Web: www.personalprotection.com					
Global University 1211 S Glenstone Ave	Springfield	MO	65804	417-862-9533	865-7167
TF: 800-443-1083 ■ *Web:* www.globaluniversity.edu					
Megatech Corp 525 Woburn St	Tewksbury	MA	01876	978-937-9600	453-9936
Web: www.megatechcorp.com					
Mission Essential Personnel LLC 4343 Easton Commons Ste 100	Columbus	OH	43219	614-416-2345	416-2346
TF: 888-542-3447 ■ *Web:* www.missionessential.com					
Outward Bound 910 Jackson St	Golden	CO	80401	207-510-7533	510-7535
TF: 866-467-7651 ■ *Web:* www.outwardbound.org					
Penland School of Crafts 67 Doras Trl PO Box 37	Penland	NC	28765	828-765-2359	765-7389
Web: www.penland.org					
Sailboats Inc 250 Marina Dr	Superior	WI	54880	715-392-7131	395-6968
TF: 800-826-7010 ■ *Web:* www.sailboats-inc.com					
Smith & Wesson Academy 299 Page Blvd	Springfield	MA	01104	413-846-6461	736-0776
Web: www.smith-wesson.com					
Yamaha Music Education System 6600 Orangethorpe Ave	Buena Park	CA	90620	714-522-9011	
Web: usa.yamaha.com					

770 TRANSFORMERS - POWER, DISTRIBUTION, SPECIALTY

				Phone	Fax
3 Sixty Manufacturing 6288 San Ignacio Ave Ste E	San Jose	CA	95119	408-365-0360	
Web: www.3-sixtymfg.com					
Active Power Inc 2128 W Breaker Ln	Austin	TX	78758	512-836-6464	836-4511
NASDAQ: ACPW ■ *TF:* 800-625-1731 ■ *Web:* www.activepower.com					
Adcomm Inc 89 Leuning St Ste 9	South Hackensack	NJ	07606	201-342-6349	
Web: adcomminc.com					
Advanced Conversion Technology Inc 2001 Fulling Mill Rd	Middletown	PA	17057	717-939-2300	
Web: www.actpower.com					
AFP Transformers Inc 206 Talmedge Rd	Edison	NJ	08817	732-248-0305	248-0542
TF: 800-843-1215 ■ *Web:* www.afp-transformers.com					
Airex Corp 15 Lilac Ln	Somersworth	NH	03878	603-841-2040	
Web: www.airex.com					
Algonquin Power 2845 Bristol Cir	Oakville	ON	L6H7H7	905-465-4500	
Web: www.algonquinpower.com					
ATCO Power Ltd 400 919-11 Ave SW	Calgary	AB	T2R1P3	403-209-6900	
Web: www.atcopower.com					
Bodine Co 236 S Mt Pleasant Rd	Collierville	TN	38027	901-853-7211	853-5009
TF: 800-223-5728 ■ *Web:* www.bodine.com					
Cam Tran Company Ltd 203 Purdy Rd	Colborne	ON	K0K1S0	905-355-3224	
Web: www.camtran.com					
Central Moloney Inc 2400 W Sixth Ave	Pine Bluff	AR	71601	870-534-5332	536-4002
Web: www.centralmoloneyinc.com					
CG Power Systems USA Inc One Pauwels Dr	Washington	MO	63090	636-239-9300	
Web: cgglobal.com					
Controlled Power Co 1955 Stephenson Hwy Ste G	Troy	MI	48083	248-528-3700	528-0411
TF: 800-521-4792 ■ *Web:* www.controlledpwr.com					
Cooper Power Systems Inc 2300 Badger Dr	Waukesha	WI	53187	262-896-2400	896-2313
Web: www.cooperindustries.com					
Core Power Services Inc 37428 Centralmont Pl	Fremont	CA	94536	510-796-6682	
Web: www.cpspower.com					
Datatronic Distribution Inc 28151 Hwy 74	Romoland	CA	92585	951-928-7700	
Web: www.datatronics.com					
Daykin Electric Corp 7792 BoaRdwalk Rd	Brighton	MI	48116	734-261-3310	261-3352
Web: warnerpower.com/daykin-electric/					
DC Group Inc 1977 W River Rd N	Minneapolis	MN	55411	800-838-7927	529-9518*
**Fax Area Code:* 612 ■ *TF:* 800-838-7927 ■ *Web:* www.dc-group.com					
Delta Star Inc 270 Industrial Rd	San Carlos	CA	94070	800-892-8673	593-0658*
**Fax Area Code:* 650 ■ *TF:* 800-892-8673 ■ *Web:* www.deltastar.com					

	Phone	Fax

Delta Transformers Inc
1311-A rue Ampere . . . Boucherville QC J4B5Z5 450-449-9774
Web: www.delta.xfo.com

Dynapower Corp 85 Meadowland Dr . . . South Burlington VT 05403 802-860-7200
Web: www.dynapower.com

Electric Research & Mfg Co-op Inc
PO Box 1228 . . . Dyersburg TN 38025 731-285-9121 287-4101
TF: 800-238-5587 ■ *Web:* www.ermco-eci.com

Energy Transformation Systems Inc
43353 Osgood Rd Ste B . . . Fremont CA 94539 510-656-2012
Web: www.etslan.com

Ensign Corp 201 Ensign Rd . . . Bellevue IA 52031 563-872-3900 872-4575
Web: www.ensigncorp.com

Federal Pacific PO Box 8200 . . . Bristol VA 24203 276-669-4084 669-1869
Web: www.federalpacific.com

Grand Transformers Inc 1500 Marion Ave . . . Grand Haven MI 49417 616-842-5430
Web: www.gtipower.com

Hitran Corp 362 SR- 31 . . . Flemington NJ 08822 908-782-5525 782-9733
Web: www.hitrancorp.com

Howard Industries Inc 3225 Pendorff Rd . . . Laurel MS 39440 601-425-3151 649-8090
Web: www.howard-ind.com

Hunterdon Transformer Co 75 Industrial Dr . . . Alpha NJ 08865 908-454-2400 454-6266
Web: www.hunterdontransformer.com

Ideal Power Inc Ste 600 5004 Bee Creek Rd . . . Spicewood TX 78669 512-264-1542
Web: www.idealpower.com

Jefferson Electric Inc 9650 S Franklin Dr . . . Franklin WI 53132 414-209-1620
Web: www.jeffersonelectric.com

Johnson Electric Coil Co 821 Watson St . . . Antigo WI 54409 715-627-4367 623-2812
TF: 800-826-9741 ■ *Web:* www.johnsoncoil.com

Lamination Specialties Corp
235 N Artesian Ave . . . Chicago IL 60612 312-243-2181 243-2873
Web: www.laminationspecialties.com

Legend Power Systems Inc 8561 Commerce Ct . . . Burnaby BC V5A4N5 604-420-1500 420-1533
TF: 866-772-8797 ■ *Web:* legendpower.com

Maruson Technology Corp
18557 Gale Ave . . . City Of Industry CA 91748 626-912-8388 912-8680
TF: 888-627-8766 ■ *Web:* marusonusa.com

Mesta Electronics Inc
11020 Parker Dr . . . North Huntingdon PA 15642 412-754-3000 754-3016
TF: 800-535-6798 ■ *Web:* www.mesta.com

MGM Transformer Co 5701 Smithway St . . . Commerce CA 90040 323-726-0888 726-8224
TF: 800-423-4366 ■ *Web:* www.mgmtransformer.com

Micrometals Inc 5615 E La Palma Ave . . . Anaheim CA 92807 714-970-9400
Web: www.micrometals.com

Mirus International Inc 31 Sun Pac Blvd . . . Brampton ON L6S5P6 905-494-1120
Web: www.mirusinternational.com

Moloney Electric Inc 35 Leading Rd . . . Toronto ON M9V4B7 416-534-9226
Web: www.moloney-electric.com

Morlan & Associates Inc 6625 McVey Blvd . . . Columbus OH 43235 614-889-6152
Web: www.flex-core.com

MTE Corp PO Box 9013 . . . Menomonee Falls WI 53051 262-253-8200 253-8222
TF: 800-455-4683 ■ *Web:* www.mtecorp.com

Myers Power Products Inc
2950 E Philadelphia St . . . Ontario CA 91761 909-923-1800
Web: www.myerspowerproducts.com

Neeltran Inc 71 Pickett District Rd . . . New Milford CT 06776 860-350-5964 350-5024
Web: www.neeltran.com

Niagara Transformer Corp 1747 Dale Rd . . . Buffalo NY 14225 716-896-6500 896-8871
TF: 800-817-5652 ■ *Web:* www.niagaratransformer.com

Norlake Mfg Co 39301 Taylor Pkwy . . . Elyria OH 44035 440-353-3200 353-3232
Web: www.norlakemfg.com

North American Substation Services LLC
190 N Westmonte Dr . . . Altamonte Springs FL 32716 407-788-3717
Web: www.northamericansubstationservices.com

Nova Power Solutions
23020 Eaglewood Ct Ste 100 . . . Sterling VA 20166 800-999-6682
Web: www.novapower.com

Olsun Electrics Corp 10901 Commercial St . . . Richmond IL 60071 800-336-5786 678-4909*
*Fax Area Code: 815 ■ *TF:* 800-336-5786 ■ *Web:* www.olsun.com

Pauwels Canada Inc 101 Rockman St . . . Winnipeg MB R3T0L7 204-452-7446
Web: www.cgglobal.com

Philips Advance Light Elctro
10275 W Higgins Rd . . . Rosemont IL 60018 847-390-5000 423-1882*
*Fax Area Code: 888 ■ *TF:* 800-322-2086 ■ *Web:* www.usa.lighting.philips.com

Power Partners Inc 200 Newton Bridge Rd . . . Athens GA 30607 706-548-3121
Web: abb.com/

Powersmiths International Corp 10 Devon Rd . . . Brampton ON L6T5B5 905-791-1493
Web: www.powersmiths.com

Powertronix Inc 1120 Chess Dr . . . Foster City CA 94404 650-345-6800
Web: www.powertronix.com

PWR LLC 6402 Deere Rd Ste 3 . . . Syracuse NY 13206 315-701-0210 701-0217
TF: 800-342-0878 ■ *Web:* www.pwrllc.com

Quality Transformer & Electronics
963 Ames Ave . . . Milpitas CA 95035 408-263-8444 263-8448
Web: www.qte.com

Raf Technologies Inc 200 Lexington Ave . . . Deland FL 32724 386-736-1698 736-7338
TF: 888-876-6424 ■ *Web:* www.raftech.com

Rantec Power Systems Inc
1173 Los Olivos Ave . . . Los Osos CA 93402 805-596-6000
Web: www.rantec.com

RE Uptegraff Manufacturing Co
120 Uptegraff Dr PO Box 182 . . . Scottdale PA 15683 724-887-7700 887-4748
Web: www.uptegraff.com

Saunders Electronics 192 Gannett Dr . . . South Portland ME 04106 207-228-1888
Web: saunderselectronics.com

Shallbetter Inc 3110 Progress Dr . . . Oshkosh WI 54901 920-232-8888
Web: www.shallbetter.com

Shape LLC 2105 Corporate Dr . . . Addison IL 60101 630-620-8394 620-0784
TF: 800-367-5811 ■ *Web:* www.shapellc.com

Southern States LLC 30 Georgia Ave . . . Hampton GA 30228 770-946-4562
Web: www.southernstatesllc.com

Sparta Capital Ltd 303-6707 Elbow Drive SW . . . Calgary AB T2V0E5 306-491-6323
Web: www.spartacapital.com

T & R Electric Supply Company Inc
308 SW Third St . . . Colman SD 57017 605-534-3555 534-3861
TF: 800-843-7994 ■ *Web:* www.t-r.com

T. A. Pelsue Co 2500 S Tejon St . . . Englewood CO 80110 303-936-7432
Web: www.pelsue.com

Unique Lighting Systems Inc
1240 Simpson Way . . . Escondido CA 92029 800-955-4831 740-0977*
*Fax Area Code: 760 ■ *TF:* 800-955-4831 ■ *Web:* www.uniquelighting.com

VanTran Industries Inc 7711 Imperial Dr . . . Waco TX 76712 254-772-9740 772-0016
TF: 800-433-3346 ■ *Web:* www.vantran.com

Victor Products USA
322 Commerce Pk Dr . . . Cranberry Township PA 16066 724-776-4900 776-3855
Web: www.victorproductsusa.com

Virginia Transformer Corp 220 Glade View Dr . . . Roanoke VA 24012 540-345-9892 342-7694
TF: 800-882-3944 ■ *Web:* www.vatransformer.com

Warner Power LLC 40 Depot St . . . Warner NH 03278 603-456-3111 456-3754
Web: www.warnerpower.com

Waukesha Electric Systems Inc
400 S Prairie Ave . . . Waukesha WI 53186 262-547-0121 521-0198
Web: www.spxtransformersolutions.com

WEG Electric Corp 6655 Sugarloaf Pkwy . . . Duluth GA 30097 678-249-2000
Web: www.weg.net

Winkle Electric Company Inc., The
1900 Hubbard Rd . . . Youngstown OH 44501 330-744-5303
Web: www.winkle.com

771 TRANSLATION SERVICES

SEE ALSO Language Schools p. 2620

	Phone	Fax

A William Roberts Jr & Assoc Inc
234 Seven Farms Dr Ste 210 . . . Charleston SC 29492 843-722-8414
Web: scheduledepo.com

ABLE Innovations LLC
1100 Lakeway Dr Ste 200 . . . Bellingham WA 98229 360-714-1390
Web: www.ableinnovations.com

Agnew Multilingual
741 Lakefield Rd Ste C . . . Westlake Village CA 91361 805-494-3999
Web: www.agnew.com

Arch Language Network Inc
1885 University Ave W Ste 75 . . . Saint Paul MN 55104 651-789-7897
Web: www.archlanguage.com

Argo Translation Inc 2420 Ravine Way Ste 200 . . . Glenview IL 60025 847-901-4075
Web: www.argotrans.com

Asist Translation Services
4891 Sawmill Rd Ste 200 . . . Columbus OH 43235 614-451-6744
Web: m.asisttranslations.com

Back to Basics Learning Dynamics Inc
Six Stone Hill Rd . . . Wilmington DE 19803 302-594-0754
Web: backtobasicslearning.com

Birnbaum Interpreting Services
8555 16th St Ste 400 . . . Silver Spring MD 20910 301-587-8885
Web: www.bisworld.com

Boston Language Institute Inc
648 Beacon St Kenmore Sq . . . Boston MA 02215 617-262-3500 262-3595
TF: 877-998-3500 ■ *Web:* www.bostonlanguage.com

Bridge-world Language Center Inc, The
110 Second St S Ste 213 . . . Waite Park MN 56387 320-259-9239
Web: www.bridgelanguage.com

CanTalk (Canada) Inc 400-136 Market Ave . . . Winnipeg MB R3B0P4 204-982-1245
Web: www.cantalk.com

Cosmopolitan Translation Bureau Inc
53 W Jackson Blvd Ste 1260 . . . Chicago IL 60604 312-726-2610
TF: 866-370-1439 ■ *Web:* www.cosmopolitantranslation.net

Cyracom International Inc 5780 N Swan Rd . . . Tucson AZ 85718 520-745-9447
Web: cyracom.com

Deaf Hearing Communication Centre Inc
630 Fairview Rd Ste 100 . . . Swarthmore PA 19081 610-604-0450
Web: www.dhcc.org

Excelsys 3230 N Braeswood Blvd . . . Houston TX 77025 713-662-0172
Web: excelsys.org

Fluent Language Solutions Inc
8801 JM Keynes Dr Ste 400 . . . Charlotte NC 28262 704-532-7446
Web: www.fluentls.com

Ganser German Translations 602 Fairway Rd . . . Belton MO 64012 816-331-1863
Web: www.transimpex.com

Geo Group Six Odana Ct Ste 205 . . . Madison WI 53719 608-230-1000
Web: www.thegeogroup.com

Imani Lee Translations Services; Ili International Services; Ili Business s
11297 Senda Luna Llena Bldg B . . . San Diego CA 92130 858-523-9733
Web: www.imanilee.com

Independent Living Resource Center Inc, The
423 W Victoria St . . . Santa Barbara CA 93101 805-963-1350
Web: www.ilrc-trico.org

Interpreters Unlimited Inc
11199 Sorrento Vly Rd Ste 203 . . . San Diego CA 92121 800-726-9891
TF: 800-726-9891 ■ *Web:* www.interpretersunlimited.com

JLS Language Corp 135 Willow Rd . . . Menlo Park CA 94025 650-321-9832
Web: www.jls.com

Kane Transport Inc
40925 403rd Ave PO Box 126 . . . Sauk Centre MN 56378 320-352-2762 352-6141
TF: 800-892-8557 ■ *Web:* www.kanetransport.com

Language Line Services
One Lower Ragsdale Dr Bldg 2 . . . Monterey CA 93940 800-752-6096
TF: 800-752-6096 ■ *Web:* www.languageline.com

Language Services Associates Inc
455 Business Ctr Dr - Ste 100 . . . Horsham PA 19044 800-305-9673
TF: 800-305-9673 ■ *Web:* www.lsaweb.com

Legal Interpreting Services Inc
26 Court St Ste 1005 . . . Brooklyn NY 11242 718-237-8919
Web: www.lis-translations.com

				Phone	Fax
Lingualinx Language Solutions Inc 122 Remsen St Web: lingualinx.com	Cohoes	NY	12047	518-388-9000	
Linguistics Systems Inc 201 Broadway *Fax Area Code: 617 ■ TF: 877-654-5006 ■ Web: www.linguist.com	Cambridge	MA	02139	877-654-5006	864-5186*
Lionbridge Technologies Inc 1050 Winter St Ste 2300 NASDAQ: LIOX ■ Web: lionbridge.com	Waltham	MA	02451	781-434-6000	434-6034
Master Translating Services Inc 10651 N Kendall Dr Ste 220 Web: www.mastertranslating.com	Miami	FL	33176	305-279-2484	279-4016
Masterword Services, International Inc 303 Stafford St Ste 204 Web: www.masterword.com	Houston	TX	77079	281-589-0810	
Merritt Interpreting Services 3626 N Hall St Ste 504 Web: www.mis-interpreting.com	Dallas	TX	75219	214-969-5585	
Mill Neck Manor School for The Deaf 40 Frost Mill Rd Web: millneck.org	Mill Neck	NY	11765	516-922-3818	
MotionPoint Corp Lyons Technology Ctr 4661 Johnson Rd Ste 14 Web: www.motionpoint.com	Coconut Creek	FL	33073	954-421-0890	
One Planet Corp 850 Ridge Ave Web: www.one-planet.net	Pittsburgh	PA	15212	412-323-1050	
Opies Transport Inc 21 Hwy FF PO Box 89 Web: www.opiestransport.com	Eldon	MO	65026	573-392-6525	392-2284
Pals International 900 Wilshire Dr Ste 105 Web: www.palsintl.com	Troy	MI	48084	248-362-2060	
Professional Translating Services Inc Douglas Rd Web: www.protranslating.com	Coral Gables	FL	33134	305-371-7887	381-9824
Schreiber Translations Inc 51 Monroe St Ste 101 Web: www.schreibernet.com	Rockville	MD	20850	301-424-7737	
SimulTrans LLC 455 N Whisman Rd Ste 400 Web: www.simultrans.com	Mountain View	CA	94043	650-605-1300	605-1301
Spanish-American Translating 330 Eagle Ave Web: arleneboas.com	West Hempstead	NY	11552	516-481-3339	
Syntes Language Group 7465 E Peakview Ave Web: www.syntes.com	Centennial	CO	80111	303-779-1288	
TransPerfect Translations Inc Three Pk Ave 39th Fl Web: www.transperfect.com	New York	NY	10016	212-689-5555	689-1059
Verbatim Solutions LLC 5200 South Highland Dr Ste 201 Web: www.verbatimsolutions.com	Salt Lake City	UT	84117	801-273-5700	
Versacom Inc 1501 Ave McGill College Sixth Fl Web: www.versacom.ca	Montreal	QC	H3A3M8	514-397-1950	
Vocalink Language Services 405 W First St Unit A Web: www.vocalink.net	Dayton	OH	45402	937-223-1415	

772 TRANSPLANT CENTERS - BLOOD STEM CELL

				Phone	Fax
Arthur G James Cancer Hospital & Richard J Solove Research Institute *Bone Marrow Transplant Program* 300 W Tenth Ave Ste 519 *Fax Area Code: 614 ■ TF: 800-293-5066 ■ Web: cancer.osu.edu/	Columbus	OH	43210	800-293-5066	293-4044*
Beth Israel Deaconess Medical Ctr Hematologic Malignancies/Bone Marrow Transplantation Program 330 Brookline Ave TF: 800-439-0183 ■ Web: www.bidmc.org	Boston	MA	02215	617-667-9920	667-9922
Blood & Marrow Transplant Group of Georgia (BMTGA) 5670 Peachtree Dunwoody Rd Ste 1000 Web: www.bmtga.com	Atlanta	GA	30342	404-255-1930	255-1939
Blood Donor Ctr at Presbyterian/St Luke's Medical Ctr 1719 E 19th Ave TF: 800-231-2222 ■ Web: www.pslmc.com	Denver	CO	80218	303-839-6000	
Cedars-Sinai Medical Ctr Blood & Marrow Transplant Program 8700 Beverly Blvd AC1060 TF: 800-265-4186 ■ Web: www.cedars-sinai.edu	Los Angeles	CA	90048	310-423-1160	423-2320
Children's Healthcare of Atlanta at Egleston AFLAC Cancer Ctr & Blood Disorders Service 1405 Clifton Rd NE Web: www.choa.org/OurServices/Transplant/BMT	Atlanta	GA	30322	404-785-1200	785-6288
Children's Hospital & Research Ctr at Oakland Blood & Marrow Transplantation Program 747 52nd St TF: 888-433-9042 ■ Web: www.childrenshospitaloakland.org/t_healthcare.cfm?id=253	Oakland	CA	94609	510-428-3000	601-3916
Children's Hospital Bone Marrow Transplant Program LSU Health Science Ctr 200 Henry Clay Ave Web: www.chnola.org	New Orleans	LA	70118	504-896-9740	896-9758
Children's Hospital of New York-Presbyterian *Pediatric Blood & Marrow Transplantation Program* 3959 Broadway 11 Central TF: 866-463-2778 ■ Web: nyp.org/kids	New York	NY	10032	212-305-5593	305-8428
Children's Hospital of Orange County Blood & Donor Services 505 S Main St TF: 800-228-5234 ■ Web: www.choc.org	Orange	CA	92868	714-532-8339	532-8830
Children's Hospital of Philadelphia Stem Cell Transplant Program 3405 Civic Ctr Blvd *Fax Area Code: 215 ■ Web: www.chop.edu	Philadelphia	PA	19104	800-879-2467	590-4744*
Children's Hospital of Wisconsin Bone Marrow Transplant Clinic (CHW) 9000 W Wisconsin Ave PO Box 1997 TF: 877-266-8989 ■ Web: www.chw.org	Milwaukee	WI	53226	414-266-2000	266-2426
Children's Medical Ctr of Dallas Ctr for Cancer & Blood Disorders (CMC) 1935 Medical District Dr TF: 800-222-1222 ■ Web: www.childrens.com	Dallas	TX	75235	214-456-7000	456-6133
Children's National Medical Ctr Hematology/Oncology Dept 111 Michigan Ave NW Web: www.childrensnational.org.	Washington	DC	20010	888-884-2327	
Cincinnati Children's Hospital Medical Ctr Blood & Marrow Transplantation Program 3333 Burnet Ave Web: www.cincinnatichildrens.org	Cincinnati	OH	45229	513-636-4200	
City of Hope National Medical Ctr Hematology & Hematopoietic Cell Transplantation Div 1500 E Duarte Rd TF: 800-535-7119 ■ Web: cityofhope.org	Duarte	CA	91010	626-256-4673	301-8888
Cleveland Clinic Bone Marrow Transplantation Program 9500 Euclid Ave TF: 800-223-2273 ■ Web: my.clevelandclinic.org	Cleveland	OH	44195	216-444-0261	445-7444
Cook Children's Medical Ctr Bone Marrow Transplant Unit 801 Seventh Ave Web: cookchildrens.org	Fort Worth	TX	76104	682-885-4000	885-7190
Dana-Farber Cancer Institute Stem Cell/Bone Marrow Transplant Program 44 Binney St Dana Bldg 1B Rm 30 TF: 866-408-3324 ■ Web: www.dana-farber.org	Boston	MA	02115	617-632-3591	632-4139
Duke Clinical Research & Treatment Ctr *Bone Marrow & Stem Cell Transplant Program* 2400 Pratt St Ste 7028 Web: dukemedicine.org/	Durham	NC	27710	919-668-1002	668-1091
Fairfax PET Imaging Ctr 8503 Arlington Blvd Ste 120 Low Level TF: 800-358-8831 ■ Web: www.inova.org	Fairfax	VA	22031	703-698-4441	
Fairview University Medical Ctr *Blood & Marrow Transplant Clinic* 420 Delaware St SE Web: www.uofmmedicalcenter.org	Minneapolis	MN	55455	612-273-2800	626-2664
Fox Chase Cancer Ctr Bone Marrow Transplant Program 333 Cottman Ave TF: 888-369-2427 ■ Web: www.fccc.edu	Philadelphia	PA	19111	888-369-2427	
Franciscan Alliance, Inc St Francis Hospital 1600 Albany St TF: 800-361-0016 ■ Web: www.franciscanalliance.org/hospitals/indianapolis/services/cancer/cancer-centers-clinics/blood-marrow-transplant/pages/default.aspx	Beech Grove	IN	46107	317-528-5500	
Froedtert Hospital Bone Marrow Transplant Program 9200 W Wisconsin Ave TF: 800-272-3666 ■ Web: www.froedtert.com	Milwaukee	WI	53226	414-805-3666	
H Lee Moffitt Cancer Ctr & Research Institute Blood & Marrow Transplantation Program 12902 Magnolia Dr TF: 888-663-3488 ■ Web: www.moffitt.org	Tampa	FL	33612	888-663-3488	
Hackensack University Medical Ctr Bone Marrow Transplantation Div 30 Prospect Ave	Hackensack	NJ	07601	201-996-2000	
Hahnemann University Hospital 230 N Broad St *Fax: Admitting ■ Web: www.hahnemannhospital.com	Philadelphia	PA	19102	215-762-7000	762-3272*
Bone Marrow Transplant Program 230 N Broad St MS 451 Web: www.hahnemannhospital.com	Philadelphia	PA	19102	215-762-7000	762-8109
Helen DeVos Children's Hospital Pediatric Hematology/Oncology Program 100 Michigan NE TF: 866-989-7999 ■ Web: www.helendevoschildrens.org	Grand Rapids	MI	49503	616-391-9000	391-9430
Henry Ford Hospital Bone Marrow Transplant Program 2799 W Grand Blvd Web: www.henryford.com	Detroit	MI	48202	800-436-7936	
Indiana University Cancer Ctr Bone Marrow & Stem Cell Transplant Team 550 N University Blvd TF: 888-600-4822 ■ Web: cancer.iu.edu	Indianapolis	IN	46202	317-948-6997	
James Graham Brown Cancer Ctr 529 S Jackson St TF: 866-530-5516 ■ Web: www.browncancercenter.org	Louisville	KY	40202	502-562-4369	
Jewish Hospital Blood & Marrow Transplant Program 4777 E Galbraith Rd Web: e-mercy.com/jewish-hospital.aspx	Cincinnati	OH	45236	513-686-3000	686-5483
Karmanos Cancer Institute Bone Marrow/Stem Cell Transplant Program 4100 John R Rm 1308-A *Fax Area Code: 313 ■ TF: 800-527-6266 ■ Web: www.karmanos.org	Detroit	MI	48201	800-527-6266	576-8422*
Lombardi Comprehensive Cancer Ctr at Georgetown University Bone Marrow Transplantation Program 3800 Reservoir Rd NW Web: lombardi.georgetown.edu	Washington	DC	20057	202-444-0275	
Medical City Hospital Transplant Ctr 7777 Forest Ln Bldg A 12 S TF: 800-348-4318 ■ Web: www.medicalcityhospital.com	Dallas	TX	75230	972-566-7000	566-3897
Blood & Marrow Transplant Program 86 Jonathan Lucas St Web: www.muschealth.com	Charleston	SC	29425	843-792-9300	
Memorial Sloan-Kettering Cancer Ctr Bone Marrow Transplant Service 1275 York Ave TF: 800-525-2225 ■ Web: www.mskcc.org	New York	NY	10065	212-639-6009	
Miami Children's Hospital Bone Marrow Transplant Program 3100 SW 62nd Ave Web: www.mch.com	Miami	FL	33155	305-666-6511	663-8511
Mount Sinai Hospital Bone Marrow Transplant Program 19 E 98th St Ste 4B TF: 866-682-9380 ■ Web: www.mountsinai.org	New York	NY	10029	212-241-6021	410-0978
New York Presbyterian Hospital Stem Cell Transplantation Program 525 E 68th St Ste J-130 Web: www.weillcornell.org	New York	NY	10021	212-746-2119	746-6678
North Shore-Long Island Jewish Health System *Bone Marrow & Blood Cell Transplant Program* 300 Community Dr TF: 888-321-3627 ■ Web: www.northshorelij.com	Manhasset	NY	11030	516-562-8973	734-8836
Northwestern Memorial Hospital 251 E Huron St Web: www.nmh.org	Chicago	IL	60611	312-926-2000	
Oregon Health & Science University *Bone Marrow Transplant Program (OHSU)* 3181 SW Sam Jackson Pk Rd TF: 800-799-7233 ■ Web: www.ohsu.edu	Portland	OR	97239	503-494-1617	494-7086

				Phone	Fax
OU Medical Ctr					
Bone Marrow Transplant Program					
One S Bryant Seventh Fl	Oklahoma City	OK	73104	405-271-8042	
Web: www.oumedicine.com					
Penn State Milton S Hershey Medical Ctr Bone Marrow Transplantation Program					
500 University Dr	Hershey	PA	17033	717-531-1657	531-1656
Web: www.pennstatehershey.org					
Roswell Park Cancer Institute Blood & Marrow Transplantation Program					
Elm & Carlton Sts	Buffalo	NY	14263	716-845-3516	845-8564
TF: 800-685-6825 ■ *Web:* www.roswellpark.org					
Saint Jude Children's Research Hospital Stem Cell Transplantation Div					
262 Danny Thomas Pl	Memphis	TN	38105	901-595-3300	
TF: 800-822-6344 ■ *Web:* www.stjude.org					
Saint Louis University Cancer Ctr Hematology & Oncology Div					
3655 Vista Ave	Saint Louis	MO	63110	314-977-4440	773-1167
TF: 866-977-4440 ■ *Web:* www.slu.edu/x24691.xml					
Scripps Green Hospital Blood & Marrow Transplant Ctr					
10666 N Torrey Pines Rd	La Jolla	CA	92037	858-554-8597	
Web: scripps.org					
Seattle Cancer Care Alliance					
825 Eastlake Ave E PO Box 19023	Seattle	WA	98109	206-288-1024	288-1025
TF: 800-804-8824 ■ *Web:* www.seattlecca.org					
Shands Hospital at the University of Florida Blood & Bone Marrow Transplant Program					
1600 SW Archer Rd PO Box 100403	Gainesville	FL	32610	352-733-0972	
TF: 800-749-7424 ■ *Web:* bethematch.org					
Sidney Kimmel Comprehensive Cancer Ctr at Johns Hopkins Bone Marrow Transplant Program					
401 N Broadway Ste 1100	Baltimore	MD	21231	410-955-5000	502-1153
Web: www.hopkinsmedicine.org					
St Francis Healthcare System of Hawaii					
2226 Liliha St Ste 227	Honolulu	HI	96817	808-547-8030	547-6979
Web: www.stfrancishawaii.org					
Stanford University School of Medicine Blood & Marrow Transplant Program					
300 Pasteur Dr Rm H-3249 MC 5623	Stanford	CA	94305	650-723-0822	725-8950
TF: 888-275-5724 ■ *Web:* bmt.stanford.edu					
Stem Cell Transplantation Ctr					
601 Elmwood Ave	Rochester	NY	14642	585-275-1941	275-5590
Web: www.urmc.rochester.edu					
Texas Children's Hospital Stem Cell & Bone Marrow Transplant Program					
6621 Fannin St MC3-3320	Houston	TX	77030	832-824-5800	
Web: texaschildrens.org					
Texas Transplant Institute					
7700 Floyd Curl Dr	San Antonio	TX	78229	210-575-3817	575-4113
TF: 800-298-7824 ■					
Web: sahealth.com/locations/texas-transplant-institute/					
Thomas Jefferson University Hospital Blood & Marrow Transplant Unit					
125 S Ninth St 2nd Fl	Philadelphia	PA	19107	215-955-6000	955-0412
Web: www.jefferson.edu					
Trustees of the University of Pennsylvania					
Bone Marrow & Stem Cell Transplant Program					
3400 Spruce St	Philadelphia	PA	19104	215-662-4533	615-0071
TF: 800-417-9391 ■ *Web:* www.penncancer.org					
Tufts-New England Medical Ctr					
Bone Marrow Transplant Program					
800 Washington St PO Box 542	Boston	MA	02111	617-636-5000	636-2520
Web: www.tuftsmedicalcenter.org					
UMass Memorial Medical Ctr					
Bone Marrow Transplant Program					
55 Lake Ave N	Worcester	MA	01655	508-334-1000	334-7983
Web: umassmemorialhealthcare.org/umass-memorial-medical-center/					
University Hospitals of Cleveland Blood & Marrow Transplant Program					
11100 Euclid Ave	Cleveland	OH	44106	216-844-1000	
Web: www.uhhospitals.org					
University Medical Ctr Blood & Marrow Transplantation Program					
1501 N Campbell Ave PO Box 24-5176	Tucson	AZ	85724	520-694-0111	694-5009
TF: 800-524-5928 ■ *Web:* www.uahealth.com					
University Medical Ctr Bone Marrow & Blood Stem Cell Transplant Program (UMC)					
602 Indiana Ave	Lubbock	TX	79415	806-775-8200	775-9981
Web: www.umchealthsystem.com					
University of Arkansas for Medical Sciences					
Bone Marrow Transplantation Ctr					
4301 W Markham Ave Slot 816	Little Rock	AR	72205	501-686-8250	526-2273
Web: www.uams.edu					
University of California San Diego Medical Ctr Blood & Marrow Transplantation Program					
3855 Health Sciences Dr	La Jolla	CA	92093	858-657-7000	
Web: www.cancer.ucsd.edu					
University of Chicago Medical Ctr Stem Cell Transplant Program					
5841 S Maryland Ave	Chicago	IL	60637	773-702-1000	
Web: www.uchospitals.edu					
University of Illinois Medical Ctr Stem Cell Transplant Unit					
1740 W Taylor St	Chicago	IL	60612	312-996-3900	996-7049
TF: 866-600-2273 ■ *Web:* hospital.uillinois.edu					
University of Kansas Medical Ctr					
Bone Marrow/Hematopoietic Stem Cell Transplant Program					
3901 Rainbow Blvd	Kansas City	KS	66160	913-588-5000	
Web: kumc.edu					
University of Maryland Greenebaum Cancer Ctr					
22 S Greene St Ste N9E17	Baltimore	MD	21201	410-328-7904	328-3018
TF: 800-888-8823 ■ *Web:* www.umm.edu/cancer/canc_stem.html					
University of Miami Hospital & Clinics (UMHC)					
Sylvester Comprehensive Cancer Ctr					
1475 NW 12th Ave	Miami	FL	33136	305-243-1000	243-1129
TF: 800-545-2292 ■ *Web:* www.sylvester.org					
University of Michigan Cancer Ctr Adult Blood and Marrow Transplantation Clinic					
1540 E Hospital Dr 9th Fl	Ann Arbor	MI	48109	734-232-8838	
Web: www.cancer.med.umich.edu					
University of Mississippi Medical Ctr Bone Marrow Transplant Program (UMMC)					
2500 N State St	Jackson	MS	39216	601-354-6655	984-6289
Web: www.umc.edu					
University of Nebraska Medical Ctr Bone Marrow & Stem Cell Transplantation Program (Adults)					
987400 Nebraska Medical Ctr	Omaha	NE	68198	402-559-2000	
TF: 800-922-0000 ■ *Web:* www.nebraskamed.com					
Horizon 110 N Main St	Greenville	PA	16125	724-588-2100	
TF: 888-447-1122 ■ *Web:* www.upmc.com					
Stem Cell Transplantation Program					
5150 Centre Ave	Pittsburgh	PA	15232	412-235-1052	623-1177
Web: www.upmccancercenter.com					
Hematopoietic Cell Transplant Program					
2201 Inwood Rd Second Fl	Dallas	TX	75390	214-645-4673	645-6926
TF: 866-645-6455 ■ *Web:* www.utsouthwestern.edu					
Blood & Marrow Transplant Program					
50 N Medical Dr	Salt Lake City	UT	84132	801-581-2121	585-5825
TF General: 800-824-2073 ■ *Web:* www.healthcare.utah.edu/hospital					
VA Puget Sound Health Care System - Seattle Div					
1660 S Columbian Way	Seattle	WA	98108	206-762-1010	
TF: 800-329-8387 ■ *Web:* www.va.gov					
Vanderbilt University Medical Ctr Stem Cell Transplant Program					
1301 22nd Ave S Ste B902	Nashville	TN	37232	615-591-9890	936-1812
Web: www.vanderbilthealth.com					
VCU Massey Cancer Center					
Bone Marrow Transplant Program					
401 College St PO Box 980037	Richmond	VA	23298	804-828-4360	
Web: www.massey.vcu.edu					
Wake Forest University Baptist Medical Ctr Comprehensive Cancer Ctr					
Medical Ctr Blvd	Winston-Salem	NC	27157	336-716-2011	716-5687
Web: www.wakehealth.edu					
Westchester Medical Ctr Advanced Imaging					
Bone Marrow & Hematopoietic Stem Cell Transplant program					
19 Bradhurst Ave Ste 2100	Hawthorne	NY	10532	914-493-1448	493-2428
Web: www.westchestermedicalcenter.com					
Western Pennsylvania Hospital Hematology/Oncology Patient Care Unit					
4800 Friendship Ave Ste 2303 NT	Pittsburgh	PA	15224	412-578-5000	578-4391
Web: ahn.org					
Winship Cancer Institute of Emory University					
1365 Clifton Rd NE	Atlanta	GA	30322	404-778-1900	843-5615*
**Fax Area Code:* 678 ■ *TF:* 888-946-7447 ■ *Web:* www.winshipcancer.emory.edu					
Yale-New Haven Hospital Blood Stem Cell Transplant Unit					
20 York St 8 W Pavilion	New Haven	CT	06510	203-688-3430	
Web: www.ynhh.org					

773 TRANSPORTATION EQUIPMENT & SUPPLIES - WHOL

				Phone	Fax
A & K Railroad Materials Inc					
1505 S Redwood Rd	Salt Lake City	UT	84104	801-974-5484	972-2041*
**Fax:* Sales ■ *TF Sales:* 800-453-8812 ■ *Web:* www.akrailroad.com					
A d i Services 25 Lights Addition Dr	Martinsburg	WV	25404	304-263-7722	
Web: www.adiservices.com					
AAR Aircraft Turbine Ctr					
1100 N Wood Dale Rd 1 AAR Pl	Wood Dale	IL	60191	630-227-2000	227-2329
TF General: 800-422-2213 ■ *Web:* www.aarcorp.com					
AAR Corp 1100 N Wood Dale Rd 1 AAR Pl	Wood Dale	IL	60191	630-227-2000	227-2019
NYSE: AIR ■ *TF:* 800-422-2213 ■ *Web:* www.aarcorp.com					
AAR Defense Systems & Logistics					
1100 N Wood Dale Rd 1 AAR Pl	Wood Dale	IL	60191	630-227-2000	
Web: aarcorp.com/parts/inventory-management-programs/defense-programs/					
AAR Distribution					
1100 N Wood Dale Rd 1 AAR Pl	Wood Dale	IL	60191	630-227-2000	
TF: 800-422-2213 ■ *Web:* www.aarcorp.com					
Aero Hardware & Parts Company Inc					
130 Business Pk Dr	Armonk	NY	10504	914-273-8550	273-8612
Web: www.aerohardwareparts.com					
Aero Products Component Services Inc					
551 N 40th St	Show Low	AZ	85901	928-537-1000	
Web: www.aeroproducts.com					
Aero Recip (Canada) Ltd 540 Marjorie St	Winnipeg	MB	R3H0S9	204-788-4765	786-2775
Web: www.aerorecip.com					
Aerodirect Inc 860 Chaddick Dr Bldg A	Wheeling	IL	60090	847-325-4971	
Web: www.aerodirect.com					
Aeronautical Systems Inc					
43671 Trade Ctr Pl Ste 100	Sterling	VA	20166	703-996-8090	
Web: www.aeronautical.com					
AeroSolutions Group Inc					
10681 Frank Marshall Ln	Manassas	VA	20110	703-257-7008	
Web: www.aerosolutions.com					
AerSale Inc 121 Alhambra Plz Ste 1700	Coral Gables	FL	33134	305-764-3200	
Web: www.aersale.com					
Africair Inc 13551 SW 132nd Ave # 1	Miami	FL	33186	305-255-6973	255-4064
Web: www.africair.com					
Agility 480 Production Ave	Madison	AL	35758	256-772-7743	
Web: www.agilitylogistics.com					
Aim Mro Holdings Inc					
8500 Glendale Milford Rd	Camp Dennison	OH	45111	513-831-2938	831-3859
Web: www.aimmro.com					
AIRCO Group 1853 S Eisenhower Ct	Wichita	KS	67209	316-945-0445	945-8014
TF: 800-835-2243 ■ *Web:* www.airco-ict.com					
AirLiance Materials LLC 450 Medinah Rd	Roselle	IL	60172	847-233-5800	233-5900
TF General: 877-233-5800 ■ *Web:* www.airliance.com					
Airline Spares America Inc (ASA)					
1022 E Newport Ctr Dr	Deerfield Beach	FL	33442	954-429-8600	429-8388
Web: www.asaspares.com					
Airparts Company Inc 2310 NW 55th Ct	Fort Lauderdale	FL	33309	954-739-3575	739-9514
TF: 800-392-4999 ■ *Web:* www.airpartsco.com					
Alamo Aircraft Ltd					
2538 SW 36th St PO Box 37343	San Antonio	TX	78237	210-434-5577	434-1030
Web: alamoaircraft.com					
All-system Aerospace Int'l Inc 75 Beacon Dr	Holbrook	NY	11741	631-582-9200	582-9353
Web: allsystem.com					
Allied International Corp					
Seven Hill St	Bedford Hills	NY	10507	914-241-6900	241-6985
Web: www.alliedinter.com					
ALSTOM Signaling Inc 1025 John St	West Henrietta	NY	14586	585-783-2000	
Web: www.alstomsignalingsolutions.com					
American General Supplies Inc					
7840 Airpark Rd	Gaithersburg	MD	20879	301-590-9200	590-3069
Web: www.agsusa.com					

Company	Address	City	State	Zip	Phone	Fax
Amex International Inc	1615 L St Nw Ste 340	Washington	DC	20036	202-429-0222	
	Web: www.amexdc.com					
Amsted Rail Company Inc	311 S Wacker Dr Ste 5300	Chicago	IL	60606	312-922-4501	
	Web: www.amstedrail.com					
Andantex USA Inc	1705 Valley Rd	Wanamassa	NJ	07712	732-493-2812	
	Web: www.andantex.com					
Argo International Corp	160 Chubb Ave	Lyndhurst	NJ	07071	201-561-7010	463-9561*
	*Fax Area Code: 315 ■ *TF:* 877-274-6468 ■ *Web:* www.argointl.com					
Arrow Trading Inc	5290 NW 20th Terr Hngr 57-101	Fort Lauderdale	FL	33309	954-771-9366	771-8966
	Web: www.arrowtrading.com					
ASC Industries Inc	1227 Corporate Dr W	Arlington	TX	76006	817-640-1300	649-2685
	Web: www.ascintl.com					
Atlantic Power Inc	20 Empire State Blvd	Castleton	NY	12033	518-479-7071	
	Web: www.atlanticpowerinc.com					
Atlantic Track & Turnout Co	270 N Broad St	Bloomfield	NJ	07003	973-748-5885	748-4520
	TF: 800-631-1274 ■ *Web:* www.atlantictrack.com					
Aviall Inc	2750 Regent Blvd Dallas Fort Worth Airport	Dallas	TX	75261	972-586-1985	586-1361
	Web: www.aviall.com					
Aviojet Corp	76 Brookside Dr	Upper Saddle River	NJ	07458	201-825-3111	825-6950
	Web: www.aviojet.com					
BBB Tank Services Inc	9225 Leopard St	Corpus Christi	TX	78409	361-241-1001	
	Web: www.bbbtankservices.com					
Bearing Belt & Chain Inc	729 E Buckeye	Phoenix	AZ	85034	602-252-6541	
	Web: bbcarizona.com					
Beier Radio Inc	1150 N Causeway Blvd	Mandeville	LA	70471	504-341-0123	
	Web: www.beierradio.com					
Bell Fork Lift Inc	34660 Centaur Dr	Clinton Township	MI	48035	586-415-5200	
	Web: www.bellforklift.com					
Birmingham Rail & Locomotive Company Inc	PO Box 530157	Birmingham	AL	35253	205-424-7245	424-7436
	TF: 800-241-2260 ■ *Web:* www.bhamrail.com					
Burke Handling Systems	431 Hwy 49 S	Jackson	MS	39218	601-939-6600	
	Web: www.burkehandling.com					
Burkle North America Inc	12802 Vly View St Ste 1213	Garden Grove	CA	92845	714-379-5090	
	Web: burkleusa.com					
Cardinal Carryor Inc	1055 Grade Ln	Louisville	KY	40213	502-363-6641	
	Web: www.cardinalcarryor.com					
Cargo Equipment Corp	640 Church Rd	Elgin	IL	60123	847-741-7272	
	Web: www.cargoequipmentcorp.com					
Centurion Investments Inc	18377 Edison Ave	Chesterfield	MO	63005	636-532-2674	
	Web: www.avmats.com					
Chand LLC	157 Hwy 654	Mathews	LA	70375	985-532-2512	532-3262
	Web: www.chand.com					
Christensen Shipyards Ltd	4400 Se Columbia Way	Vancouver	WA	98661	360-695-3238	
	Web: www.christensenyachts.com					
Core Inc	6590 W Rogers Cir Stes 1 & 2	Boca Raton	FL	33487	561-241-4580	
	Web: www.core-aerospace.com					
Corland Co	327 Isis Ave	Inglewood	CA	90301	310-670-3720	
	Web: www.coreland.com					
Corporate Jet Support Inc	One Graphic Pl	Moonachie	NJ	07074	201-807-0784	
	Web: www.corpjetsupport.com					
Cosgrove Aircraft Service Inc	70 Oser Ave	Hauppauge	NY	11788	631-231-6111	
	Web: www.cosgroveaircraft.com					
Cromer Material Handling Inc	4701 Oakport St	Oakland	CA	94601	510-534-6566	
	Web: www.cromer.com					
Crown Xpress Transport	9931 Via De La Amistad	San Diego	CA	92154	619-671-9611	
	Web: www.crownxt.com					
DAC International Inc	6702 McNeil Dr	Austin	TX	78729	512-331-5323	331-4516
	TF: 800-527-2531 ■ *Web:* www.dacint.com					
Davanac Inc	1936 St. Regis	Dorval	QC	H9P1H6	514-421-0177	421-0188
	Web: www.davanac.com					
Defender Industries Inc	42 Great Neck Rd	Waterford	CT	06385	860-701-3400	701-3424
	TF: 800-628-8225 ■ *Web:* www.defender.com					
Derco Aerospace Inc	8000 W Tower Ave	Milwaukee	WI	53223	414-355-3066	
	Web: www.dercoaerospace.com					
Dodson Aviation Inc	2110 Montana Rd	Ottawa	KS	66067	785-242-4000	
	Web: www.dodson.com					
Donovan Marine Inc	6316 Humphreys St	Harahan	LA	70123	504-488-5731	486-3258
	TF: 800-347-4464 ■ *Web:* www.donovanmarine.com					
Dreyfus-Cortney & Lowery Bros Rigging	4400 N Galvez St	New Orleans	LA	70117	504-944-3366	947-8557
	TF: 800-228-7660 ■ *Web:* www.dcl-usa.com					
Dutch Valley Supply Company Inc (DVS)	970 Progress Ctr Ave	Lawrenceville	GA	30043	770-513-0612	513-0716
	Web: www.dutchvalley.com					
E-Z-GO Division of Textron Inc	1451 Marvin Griffin Rd	Augusta	GA	30906	706-798-4311	771-4609
	TF: 800-241-5855 ■ *Web:* ezgo.com					
East Air Corp	337 Second St	Hackensack	NJ	07601	201-487-6060	487-5938
	Web: www.eastair.com					
Edmo Distributors Inc	12830 E Mirabeau Pkwy	Spokane Valley	WA	99216	509-535-8280	535-8266
	TF: 800-235-3300 ■ *Web:* www.edmo.com					
Ellett Industries Ltd	1575 Kingsway Ave	Port Coquitlam	BC	V3C1S2	604-941-8211	
	Web: www.ellett.ca					
ERS Industries Inc	1005 Indian Church Rd	West Seneca	NY	14224	716-675-2040	675-0300
	TF: 800-993-6446 ■ *Web:* www.ersindustries.com					
Expert Industries Inc	848 E 43rd St	Brooklyn	NY	11210	718-434-6060	
	Web: www.rubiconhx.com					
Farrell e d Company Inc	1225 E Second St	Jamestown	NY	14701	716-488-1759	
	Web: www.edfarrell.com					
Fatair Inc	17033 Evergreen Pl	City of Industry	CA	91745	626-839-7513	839-7523
Fieldtech Avionics & Instruments Inc	3N Meacham Field	Fort Worth	TX	76164	817-625-2719	
	Web: www.ftav.com					
First Aviation Services Inc	15 Riverside Ave	Westport	CT	06880	203-291-3300	291-3330
	Web: www.firstaviation.com					
Fisheries Supply Co	1900 N Northlake Way	Seattle	WA	98103	206-632-4462	634-4600
	TF: 800-426-6930 ■ *Web:* www.fisheriessupply.com					
FleetPro Ocean Inc	4770 Biscayne Blvd Penthouse A	Miami	FL	33137	305-573-6355	
	Web: www.fleetpro-psm.com					
Flight Director Inc	100 Michael Angelo Way	Austin	TX	78728	512-834-2000	833-6097
	Web: flightdirector.com					
Fokker Services Inc	5169 Southridge Pkwy Ste 100	Atlanta	GA	30349	770-991-4373	
	Web: www.twincitytesting.com					
Formsprag Clutch Inc	23601 Hoover Rd	Warren	MI	48089	586-758-5000	
	Web: www.formsprag.com					
Freundlich Supply Co Inc	2200 Arthur Kill Rd	Staten Island	NY	10309	718-356-1500	356-3661
	TF: 800-221-0260 ■ *Web:* www.fresupco.com					
Furuno USA Inc	4400 NW Pacific Rim Blvd	Camas	WA	98607	360-834-9300	
	Web: www.furuno.com					
General Aviation Services LLC	1155 E Ensell Rd	Lake Zurich	IL	60047	847-726-5000	726-7668
	TF: 800-586-5336 ■ *Web:* www.genav.com					
Georgetown Rail Equipment Co	111 Cooperative Way Ste 100	Georgetown	TX	78626	512-869-1542	
	Web: www.georgetownrail.com					
Global Parts Support Inc	2799 SW 32nd Ave	Hollywood	FL	33023	954-989-5988	
	Web: www.globalpartssupport.com					
Gulf Marine & Industrial Supplies Inc	5501 Jefferson Hwy	New Orleans	LA	70123	504-525-6252	525-4761
	Web: www.gulfmarine.net					
Handling Systems Inc	2659 E Magnolia St	Phoenix	AZ	85034	602-275-2228	
	Web: www.handlingsystems.com					
Heli-Mart Inc	3184 Airway Ave Ste E	Costa Mesa	CA	92626	714-755-2999	755-2995
	TF: 800-826-6899 ■ *Web:* www.helimart.com					
Helicopter Support Inc (HSI)	124 Quarry Rd	Trumbull	CT	06611	203-416-4000	416-4291
	TF: 800-795-6051 ■ *Web:* www.hsius.com					
Heubel Material Handling Inc	6311 NE Equitable Rd	Kansas City	MO	64120	816-231-7780	
	Web: www.heubel.com					
Holloway Houston Inc	5833 Armour Dr	Houston	TX	77020	713-674-5631	
	Web: www.hhilifting.com					
Hy-Tek Material Handling Inc	2222 Rickenbacker Pkwy W	Columbus	OH	43217	614-497-2500	
	Web: www.hy-tek.net					
IHI Inc	280 Pk Ave W Bldg 30th Fl	New York	NY	10017	212-599-8100	599-8111
	Web: ihiincus.com					
Industry-Railway Suppliers Inc	811 Golf Ln	Bensenville	IL	60106	630-766-5708	766-0017
	TF: 800-728-0029 ■ *Web:* www.industryrailway.com					
Integrated Procurement Technologies Inc	320 Storke Rd Ste 100	Goleta	CA	93117	805-682-0842	
	Web: www.iptsb.com					
Intermountain Air LLC	301 N 2370 W	Salt Lake City	UT	84116	801-322-1645	
	TF: 800-433-9617 ■ *Web:* keystoneaviation.com					
Jerry's Marine Service	100 SW 16th St	Fort Lauderdale	FL	33315	954-525-0311	525-0361*
	*Fax: Sales ■ *TF:* 800-432-2231 ■ *Web:* jms.qwik-order.com/					
Jet International Company LLC	1811 Elmdale Ave	Glenview	IL	60026	847-657-8666	657-9197
	Web: www.jetinternational.com					
JJ MacKay Canada Ltd	1342 Abercrombie Rd	New Glasgow	NS	B2H5C6	902-752-5124	
	Web: www.mackaymeters.com					
JMA Railroad Supply Co	381 S Main Pl	Carol Stream	IL	60188	630-653-9224	522-1150*
	*Fax Area Code: 812 ■ *TF:* 800-874-0643 ■ *Web:* www.jmarail.com					
Kalmar RT Center LLC	103 Guadalupe Dr	Cibolo	TX	78108	210-599-6541	
	Web: www.kalmarrt.com					
Kampi Components Co Inc	88 Canal Rd	Fairless Hills	PA	19030	215-736-2000	736-9000
	Web: www.kampi.com					
KAPCO/VALTEC	3120 Enterprise St	Brea	CA	92821	714-223-5400	996-3490
	Web: www.kapcousa.com					
Kellogg Marine Supply Inc	Five Enterprise Dr	Old Lyme	CT	06371	860-434-6002	628-1304*
	*Fax Area Code: 800 ■ *TF:* 800-243-9303 ■ *Web:* www.kelloggmarine.com					
Kelsan Technologies Corp	1140 W 15th St	North Vancouver	BC	V7P1M9	604-984-6100	
	Web: www.kelsan.com					
KP McNamara Company Inc	3972 Hamilton Ave	Cleveland	OH	44114	216-361-8955	
	Web: www.kpmcnamara.com					
Lagrange Products Inc	607 S Wayne St	Fremont	IN	46737	260-495-3025	
	Web: www.lagrangeproducts.com					
Lat-Lon LLC	2300 S Jason St	Denver	CO	80223	303-937-7406	
	Web: www.lat-lon.com					
Lewis Marine Supply Co Inc	220 SW 32nd St	Fort Lauderdale	FL	33315	954-523-4371	542-2900*
	*Fax Area Code: 800 ■ *Fax: Sales ■ *Web:* www.lewismarine.com					
Madison Components LLC	Two Marin Way Unit 3	Stratham	NH	03885	603-758-1780	
	Web: www.madisoncomponentsllc.com					
Magno International Lp	11014 Nw 33rd St Ste 100	Doral	FL	33172	305-392-4726	
	Web: www.magnointl.com					
Marine Depot	14271 Corporate Dr	Garden Grove	CA	92843	714-554-8748	
	Web: www.petstore.com					
Mark C Pope Associates	2215 Birmingham Dr	Albany	GA	31705	229-435-2473	
	Web: www.markcpope.com					
Markey Machinery Company Inc	7266 Eigth Ave S	Seattle	WA	98108	206-622-4697	
	Web: www.markeymachinery.com					
Material Handling Products Corp	6601 Joy Rd	East Syracuse	NY	13057	315-437-2891	
	Web: www.mhpcorp.com					

				Phone	Fax
Mecanex USA Inc 119 White Oak Dr *Web:* www.mecanexusa.com	Berlin	CT	06037	860-828-6531	
Mediterranean Shipping Company (USA) Inc 420 Fifth Ave 37th St Eighth Fl *Web:* www.msc.us	New York	NY	10018	212-764-4800	
Meridian Aerospace Group Ltd 3796 Vest Mill Rd *Web:* airunion.us	Winston-Salem	NC	27106	336-748-0292	
Mitchell Aircraft 1160 Alexander Ct *Web:* www.mitchellair.com	Cary	IL	60013	847-516-3773	
MJLF & Associates 300 First Stamford Place *Web:* www.mjlf.com	Stamford	CT	06902	203-326-2800	
Modern Track Machinery 1415 Davis Rd *Web:* www.geismar-mtm.com	Elgin	IL	60123	847-697-7510	
Muncie Power Products Inc 201 E Jackson St *Web:* www.munciepower.com	Muncie	IN	47305	765-284-7721	
Norlift of Oregon Inc 7373 Se Milwaukie Expy *Web:* www.norliftor.com	Portland	OR	97222	503-659-5438	
NTE Aviation Ltd 1800 Waters Ridge Dr Ste 400 *Web:* www.nteaviation.com	Lewisville	TX	75057	972-353-3933	353-3923
O'halloran International Inc PO Box 1804 *TF:* 800-800-6503 ■ *Web:* www.ohallorans.com	Des Moines	IA	50305	515-967-3300	967-0206
Omni Jet Trading Ctr 9415 Jet Ln Ste 3 *Web:* www.omnijet.com	Easton	MD	21601	410-820-7300	820-5082
Orkal Industries LLC 333 Westbury Ave *Web:* www.orkal.com	Carle Place	NY	11514	516-333-2121	
Ottosen Propeller & Accessories Inc 105 S 28th St *Web:* www.hartzellprop.com	Phoenix	AZ	85034	602-275-8514	
Pacific Meridian Group 222 Juana Ave *Web:* pacificfarms.com	San Leandro	CA	94577	510-618-1600	
Parker-Hannifin Corp 1160 Ctr Rd *TF:* 800-272-5464 ■ *Web:* parker.com	Avon	OH	44011	440-937-6211	937-5409
PartsBase Inc 905 Clint Moore Rd *TF Cust Svc:* 888-322-6896 ■ *Web:* www.partsbase.com	Boca Raton	FL	33487	561-953-0700	953-0793
Paxton Co 1111 Ingleside Rd *TF:* 800-234-7290 ■ *Web:* www.paxtonco.com	Norfolk	VA	23502	757-853-6781	853-7709
Polywest Ltd 3240 Idylwyld Dr N *Web:* www.polywest.ca	Saskatoon	SK	S7L5Y7	306-956-7788	
Rail Exchange Inc 1150 State St *Web:* railexchangeinc.com	Chicago Heights	IL	60411	708-757-3317	
Railhead Corp 12549 S Laramie Ave *Web:* www.railheadcorp.com	Alsip	IL	60803	773-779-2400	
Rails Co 101 Newark Way *TF:* 800-217-2457 ■ *Web:* www.railsco.com	Maplewood	NJ	07040	973-763-4320	763-2585
Railtech Ltd 325 Lee Ave *Web:* www.railtech.ca	Montreal	QC	H9X3S3	514-457-4760	457-7111
Relli Technology Inc 1200 S Rogers Cir *Web:* www.relli.com	Boca Raton	FL	33487	561-886-0200	886-0201
Ringfeder Power Transmission USA Corp 165 Carver Ave *Web:* www.ringfeder.com	Westwood	NJ	07675	201-666-3320	
RS Braswell Company Inc 485 S Cannon Blvd *Web:* www.rsbraswell.com	Kannapolis	NC	28082	704-933-2269	
S-Line Cargo Control & Safety Products 11414 Mathis *TF:* 800-687-9900 ■ *Web:* www.s-line.com	Dallas	TX	75234	800-687-9900	
Sabine Universal Products Inc PO Box 295 *Web:* supus.com	Port Arthur	TX	77641	409-985-2448	982-0420
Satair USA Inc 3993 Trade Port Blvd Ste 100 *Web:* www.satair.com	Atlanta	GA	30354	404-675-6333	675-6311
SEA BOX Inc One SEA BOX Dr *Web:* www.seabox.com	Cinnaminson	NJ	08077	856-303-1101	
Sea-Dog Corp 3402 Smith Ave *Web:* www.sea-dog.com	Everett	WA	98201	425-259-0194	
Shea Concrete Products Inc 87 Haverhill Rd *Web:* www.sheaconcrete.com	Amesbury	MA	01913	978-388-1509	
Simtech Inc 66A Floydville Rd *Web:* www.simtech-inc.com	East Granby	CT	06026	860-653-2408	
Sooner Lift Inc 3401 S Purdue St *Web:* www.soonerlift.com	Oklahoma City	OK	73179	405-682-1400	
Spencer Industries Inc 19308 68th Ave S **Fax:* Sales ■ *TF:* 800-367-5646 ■ *Web:* web.applied.com	Kent	WA	98032	253-796-1100	796-1101*
Standard Equipment Company Inc 75 Beauregard St *Web:* www.standardequipmentco.com	Mobile	AL	36602	251-432-1705	
Steiner Shipyard Inc 8640 Hemley St PO Box 742 *Web:* www.steinershipyard.com	Bayou La Batre	AL	36509	251-824-4143	824-4178
Sunbelt Industrial Trucks 1617 Terre Colony Ct *Web:* www.sunbelt-industrial.com	Dallas	TX	75212	214-819-4150	819-4166
Superior Tank Company Inc 9500 Lucas Ranch Rd *Web:* superiortank.com	Rancho Cucamonga	CA	91730	909-912-0580	
Talgo Inc 505 Fifth Ave S Ste 170 *Web:* www.talgoamerica.com	Seattle	WA	98104	206-254-7051	
Tank Connection LLC 3609 N 16th St *Web:* www.tankconnection.com	Parsons	KS	67357	620-423-3010	
Tanks-A-Lot Ltd 1810 Yellowhead Trail N.E. *Web:* www.tanks-a-lot.com	Edmonton	AB	T6S1B4	780-472-8265	478-5699
TBS Shipping Services Inc 612 E Grassy Sprain Rd *Web:* www.tbsship.com	Yonkers	NY	10710	914-961-1000	
Tex-air Parts Inc 3724 N Commerce St *Web:* www.texair.com	Fort Worth	TX	76106	817-624-9882	
Tom's Aircraft Maintenance Inc 2641 E Spring St *Web:* www.tomsaircraft.com	Long Beach	CA	90806	562-426-5331	
Tornado Alley Turbo 300 Airport Rd *Web:* www.taturbo.com	Ada	OK	74820	580-332-3510	
TPS Aviation Inc 1515 Crocker Ave *Web:* tpsaviation.com	Hayward	CA	94544	510-475-1010	475-8817
Tranergy Inc 726 Foster Ave *Web:* tranergy.com	Bensenville	IL	60106	630-238-9338	
Transmarine Navigation Corp 301 E Ocean Blvd Ste 590 *Web:* www.transmarine.com	Long Beach	CA	90802	562-951-8260	
Tri-Lift Inc 180 Main St Annex *Web:* www.triliftinc.com	New Haven	CT	06512	203-467-1686	
Trupar America Inc 160 Wilson Rd *Web:* www.trupar.com	Bentleyville	PA	15314	724-239-2220	
Turbo Resources International Inc 5780 W Oakland St *Web:* www.turboresources.com	Chandler	AZ	85226	480-961-3600	961-1775
Unical Aviation Inc 680 S LemonAve *Web:* www.unical.com	City of Industry	CA	91789	909-348-1700	
Unirex Inc 9310 E 37th St N *Web:* www.unirexinc.com	Wichita	KS	67226	316-636-1228	636-5482
United Aerospace Corp 9800 Premier Pkwy *Web:* unitedaerospace.com	Miramar	FL	33025	954-364-0085	364-0089
Unity Railway Supply Company Inc 805 Golf Ln *Web:* www.unityrailway.com	Bensenville	IL	60106	630-595-4560	
Valley Power Systems Inc 425 S Hacienda Blvd *TF:* 800-924-4265 ■ *Web:* www.valleypowersystems.com	City of Industry	CA	91745	626-333-1243	369-7096
Van Bortel Aircraft Inc 4912 S Collins *TF:* 800-759-4295 ■ *Web:* www.vanbortel.com	Arlington	TX	76018	817-468-7788	468-7886
Varga Enterprises Inc 2350 S Airport Blvd *Web:* www.vargaair.com	Chandler	AZ	85286	480-963-6936	
Washington Chain & Supply Inc 2901 Utah Ave S PO Box 3645 *TF:* 800-851-3429 ■ *Web:* www.wachain.com	Seattle	WA	98124	206-623-8500	621-9834
West Marine Inc 500 Westridge Dr *NASDAQ: WMAR* ■ *TF:* 800-262-8464 ■ *Web:* www.westmarine.com	Watsonville	CA	95076	831-728-2700	728-4360
Western Branch Diesel Inc 3504 Shipwright St *Web:* www.westernbranchdiesel.com	Portsmouth	VA	23703	757-673-7000	673-7190
Yingling Aircraft Inc 2010 Airport Rd *TF:* 800-835-0083 ■ *Web:* www.yinglingaviation.com	Wichita	KS	67209	316-943-3246	943-2484
ZAP 501 Fourth St *OTC: ZAAP* ■ *TF Orders:* 800-251-4555 ■ *Web:* www.zapworld.com	Santa Rosa	CA	95401	707-525-8658	525-8692

774 TRAVEL AGENCIES

SEE ALSO Tour Operators p. 3243; Travel Agency Networks p. 3255

				Phone	Fax
ABC Global Services 6400 Shafer Ct Ste 310 *TF:* 800-722-5179 ■ *Web:* www.abccst.com	Rosemont	IL	60018	800-722-5179	
Adelman Travel Group 6980 N Port Washington Rd *TF Cust Svc:* 800-248-5562 ■ *Web:* www.adelmantravel.com	Milwaukee	WI	53217	414-352-7600	352-3900
ADTRAV Travel Management 4555 S Lake Pkwy *TF:* 800-476-2952 ■ *Web:* www.adtrav.com	Birmingham	AL	35244	205-444-4800	444-4808
AESU Travel Inc 3922 Hickory Ave *TF:* 800-638-7640 ■ *Web:* www.aesu.com	Baltimore	MD	21211	410-366-5494	366-6999
Alamo Travel Group Inc 8930 Wurzbach Rd Ste 100 *TF:* 800-692-5266 ■ *Web:* www.alamotravel.com	San Antonio	TX	78240	210-593-0084	614-2448
Alaska Tour & Travel 9170 Jewel Lk Rd Ste 202 PO Box 221011 *TF:* 800-208-0200 ■ *Web:* www.alaskatravel.com	Anchorage	AK	99502	907-245-0200	245-0400
Alaska Travel Adventures Inc 9085 Glacier Hwy Ste 301 *TF:* 800-323-5757 ■ *Web:* www.alaskarv.com	Juneau	AK	99801	907-789-0052	789-1749
All Aboard Cruise Ctr PO Box 540685 *Web:* www.cruisingfun.com	Grand Prairie	TX	75054	972-262-4638	
All Aboard Cruises Inc 11114 SW 127th Ct **Fax Area Code:* 786 ■ *TF:* 800-883-8657 ■ *Web:* www.allaboardcruises.com	Miami	FL	33186	305-385-8657	419-4873*
All Cruise Travel 1723 Hamilton Ave *TF:* 800-227-8473 ■ *Web:* www.allcruise.com	San Jose	CA	95125	408-295-1200	295-2254
All-Inclusive Vacations Inc 1595 Iris St *TF:* 866-980-6483 ■ *Web:* www.all-inclusivevacations.com	Lakewood	CO	80215	303-980-6483	233-1597
American Express Travel Service Co 200 Vesey St American Express Tower C *Web:* travel.americanexpress.com	New York	NY	10285	212-640-5574	640-0404
Apple Vacations Inc 101 NW Pt Blvd **Fax Area Code:* 847 ■ *TF:* 800-517-2000 ■ *Web:* www.applevacations.com	Elk Grove Village	IL	60007	800-517-2000	640-1950*
Austin Travel 6801 Jericho Tpke Ste 100 *TF:* 800-645-7466 ■ *Web:* www.austintravel.com	Syosset	NY	11791	516-465-1000	
Avanti Destinations Inc 1629 SW Salmon St **Fax Area Code:* 800 ■ *TF:* 800-422-5053 ■ *Web:* www.avantidestinations.com	Portland	OR	97205	503-295-1100	422-9505*
Balboa Travel Management Inc 5414 Oberlin Dr Ste 300 *TF:* 800-359-8773 ■ *Web:* www.balboa.com	San Diego	CA	92121	858-678-3300	678-3399
Best Travel Inc 8600 W Bryn Mawr Ave *TF:* 800-840-4822 ■ *Web:* www.besttravel.com	Chicago	IL	60631	773-380-0150	380-7028
Bon Voyage Travel 1640 E River Rd Ste 115 *TF:* 800-439-7963 ■ *Web:* www.bvtravel.com	Tucson	AZ	85718	520-797-1110	797-2408
Brownell World Travel 216 Summit Blvd Ste 220 *TF:* 800-999-3960 ■ *Web:* www.brownelltravel.com	Birmingham	AL	35243	205-802-6222	414-7167
Burkhalter Travel Agency 6501 Mineral Pt Rd *TF:* 800-556-9286 ■ *Web:* www.burkhaltertravel.com	Madison	WI	53705	608-833-5200	
Carefree Vacations Inc 9710 Scranton Rd Ste 300 *TF:* 800-266-3476 ■ *Web:* www.carefreevacations.com	San Diego	CA	92121	858-459-4074	450-0628
Cass Tours 2621 Green River Rd Ste 105-222 *TF:* 800-593-6510 ■ *Web:* www.casstours.com	Corona	CA	92882	951-371-3511	
Casto Travel Inc 2560 N First St Ste 150 *TF:* 800-832-3445 ■ *Web:* www.casto.com	San Jose	CA	95131	408-984-7000	984-7007

				Phone	Fax
City Escape Holidays 13470 Washington Blvd Ste 101	Marina del Rey	CA	90292	800-222-0022	827-5575*
*Fax Area Code: 310 ■ TF: 800-222-0022 ■ Web: www.cityescapeholidays.com					
Classic Custom Vacations 5893 Rue Ferrari	San Jose	CA	95138	800-635-1333	292-9138*
*Fax Area Code: 408 ■ TF: 800-635-1333 ■ Web: www.classicvacations.com					
Clipper Navigation Inc 2701 Alaskan Way Pier 69	Seattle	WA	98121	206-443-2560	443-2583
TF: 800-888-2535 ■ Web: www.clippervacations.com					
Conlin Travel Inc 3270 Washtenaw Ave	Ann Arbor	MI	48104	734-677-0900	677-0901
TF: 800-426-6546 ■ Web: www.conlintravel.com					
Corporate Travel Management Group 450 E 22nd St	Lombard	IL	60148	630-691-8000	
TF: 866-545-6789 ■ Web: www.corptrav.com					
Covington International Travel 4401 Dominion Blvd	Glen Allen	VA	23060	804-747-7077	273-0009
TF: 800-922-9238 ■ Web: www.covingtontravel.com					
Crown Travel & Cruises 240 Newton Rd Ste 106	Raleigh	NC	27615	919-870-1986	870-1666
TF: 800-869-7447 ■ Web: www.crowncruise.com					
Cruise Brokers 2803 W Busch Blvd Ste 100	Tampa	FL	33618	813-288-9597	932-9650
TF: 800-409-1919 ■ Web: www.cruisebrokers.com					
Cruise Concepts 1329 Eniswood Pkwy	Palm Harbor	FL	34683	727-784-7245	
TF: 800-752-7963 ■ Web: www.cruiseconcepts.com					
Cruise Connection LLC 7932 N Oak Ste 210	Kansas City	MO	64118	816-420-8688	420-8667
TF: 800-572-0004 ■ Web: www.cruiseconnectionllc.com					
Cruise Connections Inc 3411 Healy Dr Ste D	Winston-Salem	NC	27103	800-248-7447	701-1156*
*Fax Area Code: 215 ■ TF: 800-248-7447 ■ Web: cruisedriveflystay.com					
Cruise People Inc 10191 W Sample Rd Ste 215	Coral Springs	FL	33065	954-753-0069	340-1968
TF: 800-642-2469 ■ Web: www.cruisepeople.com					
Cruise People Ltd 1252 Lawrence Ave E Ste 210	Don Mills	ON	M3A1C3	416-444-2410	
TF: 800-268-6523 ■ Web: www.thecruisepeople.ca					
Cruise Shop, The 700 Pasquinelli Dr Ste C	Westmont	IL	60559	630-325-7447	321-1669
TF: 800-622-6456 ■ Web: vikingtvl.com					
Cruise Specialists Inc 221 First Ave W Ste 210	Seattle	WA	98119	206-285-5600	
Web: cruisespecialists.com					
Cruise Vacation Ctr 2042 Central Pk Ave	Yonkers	NY	10710	800-803-7245	337-8672*
*Fax Area Code: 914 ■ TF: 800-803-7245 ■ Web: www.cruisevacationcenter.com					
Cruise Web Inc 8100 Corporate Dr Ste 300	Landover	MD	20785	240-487-0155	487-0154
TF: 800-377-9383 ■ Web: www.cruiseweb.com					
CruiseOne Inc 1201 W Cypress Creek Rd Ste 100	Fort Lauderdale	FL	33309	800-278-4731	
TF: 800-278-4731 ■ Web: www.cruiseone.com					
Cruises Cruises 6604 Antoine Dr	Houston	TX	77091	713-681-9866	957-2076
TF: 800-245-9806 ■ Web: www.cruisescruises.net					
Cruises Inc 1201 W Cypress Creek Rd Ste 100	Fort Lauderdale	FL	33309	888-282-1249	
TF Cust Svc: 888-282-1249 ■ Web: www.cruisesinc.com					
CTS Corporate Travel Solutions 5900 Rowland Rd	Minnetonka	MN	55343	952-746-3500	746-3582
Web: www.ctsinc.com					
Direct Travel 95 New Jersey 17	Paramus	NJ	07652	201-847-9000	847-2170
TF: 800-831-1366 ■ Web: www.dt.com					
E Tour & Travel 3626 Quadrangle Blvd Ste 400	Orlando	FL	32817	407-515-2400	658-1768
TF Sales: 800-339-5120 ■ Web: www.etourandtravel.com					
Elegant Voyages 1802 Keesling Ct	San Jose	CA	95125	408-239-0300	239-0304
TF: 800-555-3534 ■ Web: www.elegantvoyages.com					
Euro Lloyd Travel Inc 1640 Hempstead Tpke	East Meadow	NY	11554	516-228-4970	228-8258
TF: 800-334-2724 ■ Web: www.lcc-eurolloyd.com					
Friendly Cruises 3081 S Sycamore Village Dr	Superstition Mountain	AZ	85118	480-358-1496	
TF: 888-842-1786 ■ Web: www.friendlycruises.com					
Gant Travel Management 304 W Kirkwood Ave Ste 1	Bloomington	IN	47404	800-742-4198	332-6263*
*Fax Area Code: 812 ■ TF Cust Svc: 800-742-4198 ■ Web: www.ganttravel.com					
Gil Tours Travel Inc 1511 Walnut St Ste 200	Philadelphia	PA	19102	215-568-6655	568-0696
TF: 800-223-3855 ■ Web: www.giltravel.com					
Giselle's Travel Inc 1300 Ethan Way Ste 100	Sacramento	CA	95825	916-922-5500	679-3090
TF: 800-782-5545 ■ Web: www.globaltrav.com					
Global Travel 900 W Jefferson St	Boise	ID	83702	208-387-1000	338-6042
TF: 800-584-8888 ■ Web: www.globaltrav.com					
GOGO WorldWide Vacations 69 Spring St	Ramsey	NJ	07446	800-254-3477	934-3764*
*Fax Area Code: 201 ■ TF: 800-254-3477 ■ Web: www.gogowwv.com					
Golden Sports Tours 301 W Parker Rd Ste 206	Plano	TX	75023	800-966-8258	578-0786*
*Fax Area Code: 972 ■ TF: 800-966-8258 ■ Web: www.goldensports.com					
Gwin's Travel Planners Inc 212 N Kirkwood Rd	Saint Louis	MO	63122	314-822-1957	835-1107
TF: 800-433-9211 ■ Web: www.gwins.com					
HRG North America 16 E 34th St Third Fl	New York	NY	10016	212-404-8800	481-2933
Web: www.hrgworldwide.com					
Islands in the Sun Cruises & Tours Inc 121 Bayview	Grasonville	MD	21638	410-827-3812	782-2371*
*Fax Area Code: 443 ■ TF: 800-278-7786 ■ Web: www.crus-sun.com					
Japan Travel Bureau USA Inc 156 W 56th St Third Fl	New York	NY	10019	212-698-4900	586-9686
TF: 800-235-3523 ■ Web: www.jtbusa.com					
JourneyCorp 350 Madison Ave 15th Fl	New York	NY	10017	212-753-5511	
Web: www.journeycorp.com					
Kintetsu International 1290 Ave Ste 900	New York	NY	10104	212-259-9600	259-9625
Web: www.kintetsu.com					
Lawyers' Travel Service 71 Fifth Ave	New York	NY	10003	800-431-1112	
TF General: 800-431-1112 ■ Web: www.lawyerstravel.com					
Liberty Travel Inc 69 Spring St	Ramsey	NJ	07446	201-934-3500	
TF: 888-271-1584 ■ Web: www.libertytravel.com					
Lorraine Travel Bureau Inc 377 Alhambra Cir	Coral Gables	FL	33134	305-446-4433	441-9444*
*Fax: Sales ■ TF: 800-666-8911 ■ Web: www.lorrainetravel.com					

				Phone	Fax
Mark Travel Corp 8907 N Port Washington Rd	Milwaukee	WI	53217	414-228-7472	351-1207
Web: www.marktravel.com					
Marvel Aero International Inc 21 Rancho Cir	Lake Forest	CA	92630	949-829-8264	
Maupin Travel Inc 2501 Blue Ridge Rd	Raleigh	NC	27607	919-821-2146	829-0232
TF: 800-786-2738 ■ Web: www.maupintravel.com					
MC & A Inc 615 Piikoi St Ste 1000	Honolulu	HI	96814	808-589-5500	589-5501
TF General: 877-589-5589 ■ Web: www.mcahawaii.com					
Merit Travel Group Inc 111 Peter St Ste 200	Toronto	ON	M5V2H1	416-364-3775	
TF: 800-268-5940 ■ Web: www.merit.ca					
Miller Travel Services Inc 4380 W 12th St	Erie	PA	16505	814-833-8888	838-0082
TF: 800-989-8747 ■ Web: www.millertravel.com					
Montrose Travel 2355 Honolulu Ave	Montrose	CA	91020	800-766-4687	
TF: 800-766-4687 ■ Web: www.montrosetravel.com					
More Hawaii for Less Inc 1200 Quail St Ste 290	Newport Beach	CA	92660	949-724-5050	724-5046
TF: 800-967-6687 ■ Web: www.hawaii4less.com					
National Discount Cruise Co 1401 N Cedar Crest Blvd Ste 56	Allentown	PA	18104	610-439-4883	439-8086
TF: 800-788-8108 ■ Web: www.nationaldiscountcruise.com					
Northstar Cruises 80 Bloomfield Ave Ste 102	Caldwell	NJ	07006	800-249-9360	228-5014*
*Fax Area Code: 973 ■ TF: 800-249-9360 ■ Web: www.northstarcruises.com					
Ocean One Cruise Outlet 3264 Marilynn St	Lancaster	CA	93536	661-949-2873	949-3311
TF: 888-353-1922 ■ Web: oceanonetravelcenter.agentstudio.com					
Omega World Travel Inc 3102 Omega Office Pk Dr	Fairfax	VA	22031	703-359-0200	359-8880
TF: 800-756-6342 ■ Web: omegatravel.com/					
Orvis International Travel 178 Conservation Way	Sunderland	VT	05250	802-362-8790	362-8795
TF: 800-547-4322 ■ Web: www.orvis.com					
Outdoor Connection Inc 424 Neosho	Burlington	KS	66839	620-364-5500	364-5563
Web: www.outdoor-connection.com					
Paradise Island Vacations 1000 S Pine Island Rd Ste 800	Plantation	FL	33324	954-809-2000	
TF Resv: 888-877-7525 ■ Web: www.atlantis.com					
Pleasant Holidays LLC 2404 Townsgate Rd	Westlake Village	CA	91361	818-991-3390	
TF: 800-742-9244 ■ Web: www.pleasantholidays.com					
Premier Golf 4355 River Green Pkwy	Duluth	GA	30096	770-291-4202	291-5157
TF: 866-260-4409 ■ Web: www.premiergolf.com					
Prestige Travel & Cruises Inc 6175 Spring Mountain Rd	Las Vegas	NV	89146	702-251-5552	367-1067
TF: 800-758-5693 ■ Web: www.prestigecruises.com					
Professional Travel Inc 25000 Great Northern Corporate Ctr Ste 170	Cleveland	OH	44070	440-734-8800	734-4528
TF: 800-247-0060 ■ Web: www.protrav.com					
Protravel International Inc 515 Madison Ave 10th Fl	New York	NY	10022	212-755-4550	593-4907
TF: 800-227-1059 ■ Web: www.protravelinc.com					
Regal Travel 615 Piikoi St Ste 104	Honolulu	HI	96814	808-566-7620	566-7676
TF: 800-799-0865 ■ Web: www.regaltravel.com					
Rich Worldwide Travel Inc 500 Mamaroneck Ave	Harrison	NY	10528	914-835-7600	835-1666
TF: 800-431-1130					
Rocky Mountain Escape PO Box 5029	Hinton	AB	T7V1X3	780-865-0124	
Web: www.ecolodge.com					
Roeder Travel Ltd 9805 York Rd	Cockeysville	MD	21030	410-667-6090	
TF: 800-379-9887 ■ Web: www.roedertravel.com					
Seaside Golf Vacations 218 Main St	North Myrtle Beach	SC	29582	877-732-6999	
TF: 877-732-6999 ■ Web: www.seasidegolf.com					
SGH Golf Inc 9403 Kenwood Rd Ste C110	Cincinnati	OH	45242	513-984-0414	984-9648
TF: 800-284-8884 ■ Web: www.sghgolf.com					
Sita World Travel Inc 16250 Ventura Blvd	Encino	CA	91436	818-990-9530	
TF: 800-421-5643 ■ Web: www.sitatours.com					
Sports Empire PO Box 6169	Lakewood	CA	90714	562-920-2350	920-1828
TF: 800-255-5258 ■ Web: www.sports-empire.com					
Star Travel Services Inc 1025 Acuff Rd Fourth Fl	Bloomington	IN	47404	812-336-6811	331-6670
TF: 800-542-1687 ■ Web: www.startravelservices.com					
Sterling Cruises & Travel 8700 W Flagler St Ste 105	Miami	FL	33174	305-592-2522	592-7442
TF: 800-435-7967 ■ Web: www.cruisewin.com					
Stevens Travel Management Inc 119 W 40th St 14th Fl	New York	NY	10018	212-696-4300	679-5072
TF: 800-275-7400 ■ Web: www.stevenstravel.com					
Studentcity.com Inc 8 Essex Ctr Dr	Peabody	MA	01960	888-777-4642	573-2069*
*Fax Area Code: 978 ■ TF: 888-777-4642 ■ Web: www.studentcity.com					
Sun Islands Hawaii Inc 2299 Kuhio Ave First Fl	Honolulu	HI	96830	808-926-3888	922-6951
Web: www.sunislandshawaii.com					
SunQuest Vacations 77-6435 Kuakini Hwy	Kailua-Kona	HI	96740	808-329-6438	329-5480
TF: 800-367-5168 ■ Web: www.sunquest-hawaii.com					
Sunsational Cruises 2470 E Glen Canyon Rd	Green Valley	AZ	85614	480-491-6248	445-6812*
*Fax Area Code: 520 ■ TF: 800-239-6252 ■ Web: www.sunsationalcruises.com					
Tenenbaum's Vacation Stores Inc 300 Market St	Kingston	PA	18704	570-288-8747	283-0918
TF: 800-545-7099 ■ Web: www.tenenbaums.com					
TNT Vacations Two Charlesgate W	Boston	MA	02215	617-262-9200	
Web: www.funjet.com					
Tower Travel Management 53 Ogden Ave Ste 2520	Clarendon Hills	IL	60514	800-542-9700	954-3040*
*Fax Area Code: 630 ■ TF: 800-542-9700 ■ Web: www.towertravel.com					
Tramex Travel Inc 4505 Spicewood Springs Rd Ste 200	Austin	TX	78759	512-343-2201	343-0022
TF: 800-527-3039 ■ Web: www.tramex.com					
Transat AT Inc 300 Leo-Pariseau St Ste 600	Montreal	QC	H2X4C2	514-987-1616	987-8035
TSE: TRZ.B ■ TF: 800-387-0825 ■ Web: www.transat.com					
Travel & Transport Inc 2120 S 72nd St	Omaha	NE	68124	402-399-4500	398-9950*
*Fax: Hum Res ■ TF: 800-228-2545 ■ Web: www.travelandtransport.com					

Phone | Fax

Travel Authority Inc
702 N Shore Dr Ste 300 .... Jeffersonville IN 47130 812-206-5100 206-5265
TF: 888-501-7010 ■ *Web:* www.thetravelauthority.com

Travel Destinations Management Group Inc
110 Painters Mill Rd .... Owings Mills MD 21117 410-363-3111 363-1816
TF: 800-635-7307 ■ *Web:* www.traveldest.com

Travel Focus
First Class International 8111 LBJ Fwy Ste 900 .... Dallas tx 75251 214-915-9000 915-9009*
**Fax Area Code:* 972 ■ *TF:* 800-222-9968 ■ *Web:* www.travelfocus.com

Travel Holdings Inc
220 E Central Pkwy Ste 4000 .... Altamonte Springs FL 32701 407-667-8700
Web: www.travelholdings.com

Travel Impressions Ltd 465 Smith St .... Farmingdale NY 11735 631-845-8000 845-8095
TF: 800-284-0044 ■ *Web:* www.travimp.com

Travel Inc 4355 River Green Pkwy .... Duluth GA 30096 770-291-4100 291-5232*
**Fax:* Hum Res ■ *Web:* www.travelinc.com

Travel Team Inc 2495 Main St .... Buffalo NY 14214 716-862-7600 862-7650
TF: 800-245-8326 ■ *Web:* profile.thetravelteam.com

Travelennium Inc 556 Colonial Rd .... Memphis TN 38117 901-767-0761 766-0126
TF: 800-844-4924 ■ *Web:* www.travelennium.com

Traveline Travel Agencies Inc
4074 Erie St .... Willoughby OH 44094 440-602-8090 946-3613
TF: 888-700-8747 ■ *Web:* www.traveline.com

Travelmore 212 W Colfax Ave .... South Bend IN 46601 574-232-3061 251-3027
Web: www.travelleaders.com

Travelong Inc 225 W 35th St Ste 1501 .... New York NY 10001 212-736-2166 736-6161
TF: 800-537-6043 ■ *Web:* www.travelong.com

TravelStore Inc 11601 Wilshire Blvd .... Los Angeles CA 90025 310-575-5540 575-5541
TF: 800-850-3224 ■ *Web:* www.travelstore.com

Tzell Travel Group 119 W 40th St 14th Fl .... New York NY 10018 212-944-2121 944-7100
Web: www.tzell.com

Ultramar Travel Management International
14 E 47th St Fifth Fl .... New York NY 10017 888-856-2929 856-0129*
**Fax Area Code:* 212 ■ *TF:* 888-856-2929 ■ *Web:* www.ultramartravel.com

Valerie Wilson Travel Inc 475 Pk Ave S .... New York NY 10016 212-532-3400 779-7073
TF: 800-776-1116 ■ *Web:* www.valeriewilsontravel.com

Virtuoso 505 Main St Ste 5 .... Fort Worth TX 76102 817-870-0300 588-8240*
**Fax Area Code:* 212 ■ *TF:* 800-401-4274 ■ *Web:* www.virtuoso.com

World Travel Bureau Inc 618 N Main St .... Santa Ana CA 92701 714-835-8111 835-8124
TF: 800-899-3370 ■ *Web:* www.wtbtvl.com

World Travel Holdings (WTH)
100 Fordham Rd Bldg C Bldg C .... Wilmington MA 01887 617-424-7990 424-1943
TF: 877-958-7447 ■ *Web:* www.worldtravelholdings.com

World Travel Inc 1724 W Schuylkill Rd .... Douglassville PA 19518 610-327-9000 327-8222
TF: 800-341-2014 ■ *Web:* www.worldtravelinc.com

Worldwide Holidays Inc
7800 Red Rd Ste 112 .... South Miami FL 33143 305-665-0841 661-1457
TF: 800-327-9854 ■ *Web:* www.galapagoscruises.net

Worldwide Travel & Cruise Assoc Inc
150 S University Dr Ste E .... Plantation FL 33324 954-452-8800 446-9008
TF: 800-881-8484 ■ *Web:* www.cruiseco.com

Wright Travel Inc 2505 21st Ave S Fifth Fl .... Nashville TN 37212 615-783-1111 783-1100
TF: 800-577-0888 ■ *Web:* www.wrighttravel.net

775 TRAVEL AGENCY NETWORKS

SEE ALSO Travel Agencies p. 3253

A travel agency network is a consortium of travel agencies in which a host agency provides technology, marketing, distribution, customer support, and other services to the network member agencies in exchange for a percentage of the member agencies' profits.

Phone | Fax

Abbey Travel Ltd 522 N Washington St .... Naperville IL 60563 630-420-0400
Web: www.wehrlitravel.com

Affordabletours.com 11150 Cash Rd Ste 110 .... Stafford TX 77477 281-269-2600 269-2690
Web: www.affordabletours.com

Air Apparent Inc 5432 W 104th St .... Los Angeles CA 90045 310-649-0064
Web: www.air-apparent.com

Airtreks Inc Seven Spring St .... San Francisco CA 94104 415-977-7100
Web: www.airtreks.com

Alice Travel Luxury Cruises & Tour
277 Fairfield Rd Ste 218 .... Fairfield NJ 07004 973-439-1700
Web: www.alicetravel.com

All Direct Travel Services Inc
19000 Macarthur Blvd Ste 625 .... Irvine CA 92612 949-474-8100
Web: www.alldirecttravel.com

Allied T Pro Inc 500 Seventh Ave .... New York NY 10036 212-596-1000 313-9800
Web: www.alliedtpro.com

Altour International Inc
1270 Ave of the Americas 15th Fl Ste 2911 .... New York NY 10020 212-897-5000
Web: www.altour.com

American Express Company Inc
World Financial Ctr 200 Vesey St .... New York NY 10285 212-640-2000 640-0404
NYSE: AXP ■ *TF:* 800-528-4800 ■ *Web:* www.americanexpress.com

Arizona Sports & Tourism Authority
One Cardinals Dr .... Glendale AZ 85305 623-433-7500
Web: www.az-sta.com

ARTA Travel 5700 W Plano Pkwy Ste 1400 .... Plano TX 75093 972-422-4000 422-2331
Web: www.artatravel.com

Baskow & Associates 2948 E Russell Rd .... Las Vegas NV 89120 702-733-7818
Web: www.baskow.com

BCD Travel USA LLC Six Concourse Parkway .... Atlanta GA 30328 678-441-5200 815-6555*
**Fax Area Code:* 404 ■ *Web:* www.bcdtravel.us

Berkeleys Northside Travel Inc
1824 Euclid Ave .... Berkeley CA 94709 510-843-1000
Web: www.berkeley4travel.com

Caldwell Travel Inc 5341 Virginia Way .... Brentwood TN 37027 615-327-2720
Web: www.travelcaldwell.com

Canadian Institute of Chartered Business Valuators
277 Wellington St W Ste 710 .... Toronto ON M5V3H2 416-977-1117
Web: www.cicbv.ca

Phone | Fax

Carlson Wagonlit Travel Inc
701 Carlson Pkwy .... Minnetonka MN 55305 800-213-7295 212-2409*
**Fax Area Code:* 763 ■ *TF:* 800-213-7295 ■ *Web:* www.carlsonwagonlit.com

Cascadia Motivation Inc
4646 Riverside Dr Ste 14 .... Red Deer AB T4N6Y5 403-340-8687 342-5644
Web: www.cascadiamotivation.com

Chamber Discoveries Inc
1300 E Shaw Ave Ste 127 .... Fresno CA 93710 559-244-6600
Web: www.chamberdiscoveries.com

Classic Travel Inc 4767 Okemos Rd .... Okemos MI 48864 517-349-6200
Web: www.classictravelusa.com

ClosingCorp Inc 6165 Greenwich Dr Ste 300 .... San Diego CA 92122 858-551-1500
Web: www.closing.com

Club Cruise 1509 Grass Vly Hwy .... Auburn CA 95603 530-889-2582
Web: clubcruise.com

Colpitts World Travel 875 Providence Hwy .... Dedham MA 02026 781-326-7800
Web: www.colpittswt.com

Corniche Group Inc, The
8721 W Sunset Blvd Ste 200 .... West Hollywood CA 90069 310-854-6000
Web: www.corniche.com

Corporate Incentive Travel Inc
685 S Washington St .... Alexandria VA 22314 703-683-0123
Web: www.corporateincentivetravel.net

Corporate Travel Service
23420 Ford Rd Ste 1 .... Dearborn Heights MI 48127 313-565-8888
Web: ctscentral.net

CP Franchising LLC 3300 University Dr .... Coral Springs FL 33065 954-344-8060 755-5898
TF: 800-683-0206 ■ *Web:* www.cruiseplanners.com

Cruise & Travel Store
5435 Scotts Vly Dr .... Scotts Valley CA 95066 831-438-8844

Cruise Brothers, The 950 Wellington Ave .... Cranston RI 02910 401-780-0903
Web: www.cruisebrothers.com

Cruise Deals.com
11111 Carmel Commons Blvd Ste 210 .... Charlotte NC 28226 704-542-6414
Web: www.cruisedeals.com

Cruisecheapcom
220 Congress Park Dr Ste 140 .... Delray Beach FL 33445 561-243-2100
Web: www.cruisecheap.com

CruiseOne Inc
1201 W Cypress Creek Rd Ste 100 .... Fort Lauderdale FL 33309 800-278-4731
TF: 800-278-4731 ■ *Web:* www.cruiseone.com

Cultural Tourism DC 1250 H St Nw Ste 1000 .... Washington DC 20005 202-661-7581
Web: www.culturaltourismdc.org

D&F Travel Inc 338 Central Ave Ste 320 .... Dunkirk NY 14048 800-832-3516
Web: www.dfbuses.com

Destinations Unlimited Inc
5020 Council St Ne .... Cedar Rapids IA 52402 319-393-1359
Web: www.duagency.com

Discovery World Travel Inc
1045 Pennsylvania Ave .... Sheboygan WI 53081 920-459-2963
Web: www.tldiscovery.com

Do All Travel Company Inc 4620 18th Ave .... Brooklyn NY 11204 718-972-6000
Web: www.doalltravel.com

Dude Girl LLC 11854 Kitzbuhel Rd .... Truckee CA 96161 530-550-3247
Web: www.dudegirl.com

Ecuatours Travel Agency Inc
154 Giralda Ave .... Coral Gables FL 33134 305-446-3999
Web: www.ecuatours.com

Elkhorn Bus Service Inc 511 S Lincoln St .... Elkhorn WI 53121 262-723-4309
Web: www.jonestravel.com

Empire Travel Services 2080 We Ste 129 .... Guilderland NY 12084 518-869-0738
Web: www.empiretravel.com

En Route Travel Service
1545 Bethel Rd Ste 200 .... Columbus OH 43220 614-457-7200
Web: www.enroute-travel.com

Ensemble Travel 256 W 38th St 11th Fl .... New York NY 10018 212-545-7460 546-8081*
**Fax Area Code:* 714 ■ *TF:* 800-576-2378 ■ *Web:* www.ensembletravel.com

Executive Travel Consultants Ltd
345 118th Ave Se Ste 200 .... Bellevue WA 98005 425-453-8200
Web: www.etctravel.com

Executive Travel Inc 1212 O St .... Lincoln NE 68508 402-435-8888
Web: www.executivetravel.com

Expedition Trips.com 6553 California Ave Sw .... Seattle WA 98136 206-547-0700
Web: www.expeditiontrips.com

Flathead Travel Service 500 Main St .... Kalispell MT 59901 406-752-8700
Web: www.flatheadtravel.com

Forest Travel Agency
2440 Ne Miami Gardens Dr Ste 107 .... Miami FL 33180 305-932-5560
Web: www.fnbromney.com

Fredericton Tourism 11 Carleton St .... Fredericton NB E3B4Y7 506-460-2041
Web: www.fredericton.ca

Fredson Travel Inc 11077 Biscayne Blvd Ste 401 .... Miami FL 33161 305-577-8422
Web: www.fredsontravel.com

Frosch International Travel Inc
1 Greenway Plz Ste 800 .... Houston TX 77046 800-866-1623
Web: www.froschtravel.com

Future Media Concepts Inc
299 Broadway Ste 1510 .... New York NY 10007 212-233-3500
Web: www.fmctraining.com

Gateway Travel Service Inc
28470 W 13 Mile Rd Ste 200 .... Farmington Hills MI 48334 248-432-8600
Web: www.gatewaytrvl.com

Georgia Hardy Tours 20 Eglinton Ave East .... Toronto ON M4R1K8 416-483-7533
Web: www.ghardytours.com

Global Enterprises Inc
7951 Shoal Creek Ste 200 .... Austin TX 78757 512-451-8280

Global Travel International
2600 Lk Lucien Dr Ste 201 .... Maitland FL 32751 407-660-7800 875-0711
TF: 800-715-4440 ■ *Web:* www.globaltravel.com

Globe Vacation Inc 13527 Roosevelt Ave Ste 2 .... Flushing NY 11354 718-539-3385
Web: wkka.com

Goway Travel Ltd 3284 Yonge St Ste 300 .... Toronto ON M4N3M7 416-322-1034
Web: www.goway.com

Name / Address	City	State	ZIP	Phone	Fax
Great GetAways Inc 313 Cambridge St *Web:* www.ggatravel.com	Boston	MA	02114	617-720-6100	
Great Southern Travel 3424 S National *Web:* www.greatsoutherntravel.com	Springfield	MO	65807	417-888-4488	
GTI Corporate Travel 111 Township Line Rd *Web:* gtitravel.com	Jenkintown	PA	19046	215-379-6800	
Gulliver's Travel Service Inc 2800 S Hulen Ste 110 *Web:* www.gullivers.com	Fort Worth	TX	76109	817-924-7766	
Handa Travel Services Ltd 2269 Riverside Dr Billings Bridge Plz *Web:* www.handatravelservices.com	Ottawa	ON	K1H8K2	613-731-1111	
Happy Time Tours & Travel 1475 Walsh St W *Web:* www.httours.com	Thunder Bay	ON	P7E4X6	807-473-5955	
Hari World Travel Inc 3400 Peachtree Rd Ne Ste 815 *Web:* www.ymdesign.com	Atlanta	GA	30326	404-233-5005	
Hispano Unidos Multiservice Inc 6051 Arlington Blvd *Web:* www.tm.org	Falls Church	VA	22044	703-534-9800	
HMJ Inc 212 W Colfax Ave *Web:* www.travelmore.com	South Bend	IN	46601	574-232-3061	
Holiday Travel of America 6405 El Camino Real *Web:* www.htoa.com	Carlsbad	CA	92009	760-431-8600	
Hume Travel Corp 1525 Robson St Ste 510 *Web:* www.hume-travel.com	Vancouver	BC	V6G1C3	604-682-7581	
Hunter Travel Managers 4637 Chabot Dr Ste 111 *Web:* www.hunterworldtravel.com	Pleasanton	CA	94588	925-463-0560	
Inn at Wall Street Ltd, The Nine S William St *Web:* www.thewallstreetinn.com	New York	NY	10004	212-747-1500	
Interval Servicing International Co 3363 W Commercial Blvd Ste 202 *Web:* www.intervalservicing.com	Ft Lauderdale	FL	33309	954-485-4998	484-6343
Kahala Travel 3838 Camino Del Rio N Ste 300 *Web:* www.kahalatravel.com	San Diego	CA	92108	619-282-8300	
Luxe Travel Management Inc 16450 Bake Pkwy Ste 100 *Web:* www.luxetm.com	Irvine	CA	92618	949-336-1000	
Luxury Link LLC 5200 W Century Blvd Ste 410 *Web:* www.luxurylink.com	Los Angeles	CA	90045	310-215-8060	
Mansour Travel Company Inc 345 N Maple Dr Ste 210 *Web:* www.mansourtravel.com	Beverly Hills	CA	90210	310-276-2768	
Market Square Travel LLC 13756 83rd Way N *Web:* www.tvlleaders.com	Maple Grove	MN	55369	763-231-8870	
MAST Vacation Partners Inc 635 Butterfield Rd Ste 150 *TF:* 888-778-4722 ■ *Web:* www.mvptravel.com	Oakbrook Terrace	IL	60181	630-889-9817	889-9832
Meridican Incentive Consultants 16 Esna Park Dr Ste 103 *Web:* www.meridican.com	Markham	ON	L3R5X1	905-477-7700	
Metro Travel & Tours 9298 Central Ave Ne Ste 222 *Web:* metrotravel.biz	Minneapolis	MN	55434	763-784-0560	
Morris Murdock LLC 515 South 700 East Ste 1B *Web:* www.morrismurdock.com	Salt Lake City	UT	84102	801-483-6441	
Music Celebrations International 1440 S Priest Dr Ste 102 *Web:* www.musiccelebrations.com	Tempe	AZ	85281	480-894-3330	
National Travel Systems LP 4314 S Loop 289 Ste 300 *Web:* www.nationaltravelsystems.com	Lubbock	TX	79413	806-794-3336	
New Wave Travel 1075 Bay St *Web:* www.newwavetravel.net	Toronto	ON	M5S2B1	416-928-3113	
Newser LLC 222 N Columbus Dr Unit D *Web:* www.newser.com	Chicago	IL	60601	312-284-2300	
Nexion 6225 N State Hwy 161 Ste 450 *TF:* 800-949-6410 ■ *Web:* www.nexion.com	Irving	TX	75038	408-280-6410	271-2039
Ohio Travel Association 130 E Chestnut St Ste 301 *Web:* www.ohiotravel.org	Columbus	OH	43215	614-572-1931	
Ohio Travel Bag Manufacturing Co 6481 Davis Industrial Pkwy *Web:* www.ohiotravelbag.com	Solon	OH	44139	440-498-1955	
Pan American Travel Services 320 East 900 South *Web:* www.panam-tours.com	Salt Lake City	UT	84111	801-364-4300	
Panda Travel 1017 Kapahulu Ave Fl 2 *Web:* www.pandaonline.com	Honolulu	HI	96816	808-734-1961	
Paratransit Services Inc 4810 Auto Ctr Way Ste Z *Web:* www.paratransit.net	Bremerton	WA	98312	360-377-7176	
Peak Travel Group Inc 1723 Hamilton Ave *Web:* www.rainbowtraveler.com	San Jose	CA	95125	408-286-2633	
Premiere Travel Services Inc 7900 Westpark Dr Ste A60 *Web:* www.premieretravel.com	Mclean	VA	22102	703-893-2288	
RADIUS 7700 Wisconsin Ave Ste 400 *TF:* 800-989-3059 ■ *Web:* www.radiustravel.com	Bethesda	MD	20814	301-718-9500	718-4290
Raptim Humanitarian Travel 6420 Inducon Dr W Ste A *TF:* 800-272-7846 ■ *Web:* www.raptim.org	Sanborn	NY	14132	716-754-9232	754-2881
Raritan Center Travel II 110 Fieldcrest Ave Ste 1 *Web:* www.sairealestate.com	Edison	NJ	08837	732-417-1600	
Red Label Vacations Inc 5450 Explorer Dr Ste 100 *Web:* www.redtag.ca	Mississauga	ON	L4W5N1	905-283-6020	
Results Travel 701 Carlson Pkwy *TF:* 800-456-4000 ■ *Web:* www.carlson.com	Minnetonka	MN	55305	763-212-5000	
Rick Steves' Europe Through The Back Door 130 Fourth Ave N *Web:* www.ricksteves.com	Edmonds	WA	98020	425-771-8303	
Ritz Tours & Travel Inc 233 El Camino Real *Web:* www.ritztours.com	Millbrae	CA	94030	650-259-9983	
Riverside Travel Group Inc 12790 SE Stark St Ste 201 *Web:* www.riversidetravel.com	Portland	OR	97233	503-255-2950	
Royal Travel & Tours Inc 122 N First St Ste C *Web:* www.royal-travel.com	Dekalb	IL	60115	815-758-8172	
S Di Travel & Incentives 152 W Huron St Ste 200 *Web:* www.sditravel.com	Chicago	IL	60654	312-587-8200	
S&L Travel Partners Inc 210 Aspen Airport Business Ctr Ste AA *Web:* www.ski.com	Aspen	CO	81611	970-925-9500	
Sabre Travel Network 3150 Sabre Dr *Web:* www.sabretravelnetwork.com/home	Southlake	TX	76092	682-605-1000	
Signal Travel & Tours Inc 219 E Main St *Web:* www.signaltravel.com	Niles	MI	49120	269-684-2880	
Simlab.net 579 Pompton Ave *Web:* www.simlab.net	Cedar Grove	NJ	07009	973-571-0055	
Strong Travel Services Inc 8214 Westche Ste 670 *Web:* www.strongtravel.com	Dallas	TX	75225	214-361-0027	
Sunwing Travel Group Inc 27 Fasken Dr *Web:* www.sunwing.ca	Toronto	ON	M9W1K6	416-620-4955	
Tangerine Travel Ltd 16017 Juanita Woodinville Way Ne Ste 201 *Web:* www.tangerinetravel.com	Bothell	WA	98011	425-822-2333	
Texas Travel Industry Association 3345 Bee Cave Rd Ste 102A *Web:* www.ttia.org	West Lake Hills	TX	78746	512-328-8842	
There & Back Again Travel 35 E Broad St *Web:* www.thereandbackagain.com	Savannah	GA	31401	912-920-8222	
Thor Travel Services Inc 12202 Airport Way Ste 150 *Web:* www.thortravelservices.com	Broomfield	CO	80021	303-439-4100	
Top of the World Travel 5105 - 48 St *Web:* www.topoftheworldtravel.com	Yellowknife	NT	X1A1N5	867-766-6000	
Tour Edge Golf Manufacturing Inc 1301 Pierson Dr *Web:* www.touredge.com	Batavia	IL	60510	630-584-4777	
Tourbillon International LLC 11 W 25th St Eighth Fl	New York	NY	10010	212-627-7732	
Tourism Richmond Inc South Tower 5811 Cooney Rd Ste 205 *Web:* www.tourismrichmond.com	Richmond	BC	V6X3M1	604-821-5474	
Trading Places International Inc 23807 Aliso Creek Rd Ste 100 *Web:* www.tradingplaces.com	Laguna Niguel	CA	92677	949-448-5150	
Travel & Cruise 4331 Wyoming Blvd Ne *Web:* www.rgtravel.com	Albuquerque	NM	87111	505-299-7766	
Travel Berkley Springs 127 Fairfax St *Web:* www.berkeleysprings.com	Berkeley Springs	WV	25411	304-258-9147	
Travel Etc Inc Five The Pines Ct Ste F *Web:* www.gototraveletc.com	Saint Louis	MO	63141	314-469-6003	
Travel Management Partners Inc 7208 Falls of Neuse Rd Ste 220 *Web:* www.tmptravel.com	Raleigh	NC	27615	919-782-3810	
Travel One Inc 8009 34th Ave S 15th Fl *Web:* www.traveloneinc.com	Minneapolis	MN	55425	952-854-2551	
Travel Oriented Inc 15490 S Western Ave *Web:* traveloriented.com	Gardena	CA	90249	310-329-2800	
Travel Society Inc 600 S Cherry St Ste 100 *Web:* www.travelsociety.com	Denver	CO	80246	303-321-0900	321-0025
Travel Turf Inc 7540 Windsor Dr Ste 202 *Web:* www.wcv.com	Allentown	PA	18195	610-391-9094	
Travel Wizard LLC 4380 Redwood Hwy Ste 6 *Web:* www.travelwizard.com	San Rafael	CA	94903	415-446-5252	
Travel-On Ltd 9000 Virginia Manor Rd Ste 201 *Web:* www.tvlon.com	Beltsville	MD	20705	240-387-4000	
Travelex International Inc 2061 N Barrington Rd *TF:* 800-882-0499 ■ *Web:* travelexinternational.com	Hoffman Estates	IL	60169	847-882-0400	882-1212
Travelmart Inc, The 28011 Clemens Rd *Web:* ww.thetravelmart.com	Westlake	OH	44145	440-835-8220	
Travelsavers Inc 71 Audrey Ave *Web:* www.travelsavers.com	Oyster Bay	NY	11771	516-624-0500	624-6024
TRAVELVIDEOSTORE.com Inc 5420 Boran Dr *Web:* www.travelvideostore.com	Tampa	FL	33610	813-630-9778	
UNIGLOBE Travel USA LLC 18662 MacArthur Blvd Ste 100 *TF:* 877-438-4338 ■ *Web:* www.uniglobetravelusa.com	Irvine	CA	92612	949-623-9000	
Vacation.com Inc 1650 King St Ste 450 **Fax Area Code:* 703 ■ *TF:* 800-843-0733 ■ *Web:* www.vacation.com	Alexandria	VA	22314	800-843-0733	548-6815*
Vacations To Go Inc 5851 San Felipe St Ste 500 *Web:* www.vacationstogo.com	Houston	TX	77057	713-974-2121	
Van Zile Travel Services 3540 Winton Pl Ste 2 *Web:* www.vanzile.com	Rochester	NY	14623	585-244-1100	
Venuequest LLC 695 Arboreal Ct *Web:* www.venuequest.com	Alpharetta	GA	30022	678-909-4089	
Virtuoso 505 Main St Ste 5 **Fax Area Code:* 212 ■ *TF:* 800-401-4274 ■ *Web:* www.virtuoso.com	Fort Worth	TX	76102	817-870-0300	588-8240*

Phone Fax

Wcities.com Inc 512 Second St Second Fl .... San Francisco CA 94107 415-495-8090
Web: www.wcities.com

West University Travel 3622 University Blvd .... Houston TX 77005 713-665-4767
Web: www.westutravel.com

Western Assn of Travel Agencies (WESTA)
5933 NE Win Sivers Dr Ste 202 .... Portland OR 97220 503-251-8170

Westwood Partners LLC 51 W 52nd St 12th Fl .... New York NY 10019 212-672-3350 757-4640
Web: www.westwood-partners.com

Whaley Childrens Center
1201 N Grand Traverse St.............................. Flint MI 48503 810-234-3603
Web: www.whaleychildren.org

Wilcox Travel Sandals
One W Pack Sq Ste 1700 .... Asheville NC 28801 828-210-8197
Web: www.wilcoxtravel.com

World Travel Service Inc 10201 Parkside Dr .... Knoxville TN 37922 865-777-1600
Web: www.worldtrav.com

World Travel Services LLC
7645 E 63rd St Ste 101............................... Tulsa OK 74133 918-743-8856
Web: www.worldtraveltoday.com

World Ventures Tours & Travel Inc
6601 Kingston Pike Sequoyah Pl .... Knoxville TN 37919 865-588-7426
Web: www.wvtt.com

WorldClass Travel Network
7831 Southtown Ctr Ste A .... Bloomington MN 55431 952-835-8636 835-2340
TF: 800-234-3576 ■ Web: www.worldclassnetwork.net

WorldTEK Event & Travel Management
One Audubon Ste 400........................... New Haven CT 06511 203-772-0470 865-2034
TF: 800-233-5989 ■ Web: www.worldtek.com

Worldview Travel Management Co
101 W Fourth St Ste 400 .... Santa Ana CA 92701 714-540-7400
Web: www.worldviewtravel.com

Wyndham Jade LLC 202 E Main Ave................. Rockford IA 50468 641-756-3385
Web: www.wynjade.com

Your Travel Agent Corporate
321 N Pine St................................. Spartanburg SC 29302 864-583-3054
Web: www.ytavacations.com

TRAVEL INFORMATION - CITY

SEE Convention & Visitors Bureaus p. 2157

776 TRAVEL SERVICES - ONLINE

SEE ALSO Hotel Reservations Services p. 2524

Phone Fax

Away.com Inc 1001 G St NW..................... Washington DC 20001 202-654-8000 654-8081
Web: www.away.com

BedandBreakfast.com 700 Brazos St Ste B-700........ Austin TX 78701 512-322-2700 320-0883
TF Sales: 800-462-2632 ■ Web: www.bedandbreakfast.com

Cruises.com 100 Fordham Rd Bldg C.............. Wilmington MA 01887 800-288-6006 437-6199*
*Fax Area Code: 617 ■ TF: 800-288-6006 ■ Web: www.cruises.com

Hidden America PO Box 4262..................... River Edge NJ 07661 201-487-1190
Web: www.hiddenamerica.com

Hospitality Enterprises 4220 Howard Ave......... New Orleans LA 70125 504-529-4567
Web: www.bigeasy.com

Hotwire.com 655 Montgomery St Ste 600 .... San Francisco CA 94111 415-343-8400 343-8401
TF Cust Svc: 866-468-9473 ■ Web: www.hotwire.com

Kayak.com 7 Market Street Ste 300.................. Stamford CT 06902 203-899-3100 899-3125
Web: www.kayak.co.in

LastMinuteTravel.com Inc
220 E Central Pkwy Ste 4000 .... Altamonte Springs FL 32701 407-667-8700 667-8850
TF: 800-442-0568 ■ Web: www.lastminutetravel.com

Lonely Planet Online 150 Linden St.................. Oakland CA 94607 510-250-6400 893-8572
TF: 800-275-8555 ■ Web: www.lonelyplanet.com

National Recreation Reservation Service (NRRS)
PO Box 140 .... Ballston Spa NY 12020 518-885-3639
TF: 877-444-6777 ■ Web: www.recreation.gov

Priceline.com LLC 800 Connecticut Ave .... Norwalk CT 06854 800-774-2354 299-8955*
NASDAQ: PCLN ■ *Fax Area Code: 203 ■ *Fax: Mktg ■ TF: 800-774-2354 ■ Web: www.priceline.com

ReserveAmerica Holdings Inc
2480 Meadowvale Blvd Ste 120.................. Mississauga ON L5N8M6 877-444-6777 286-0371*
*Fax Area Code: 905 ■ TF: 877-444-6777 ■ Web: www.reserveamerica.com

Travelzoo Inc 590 Madison Ave 37th Fl............... New York NY 10022 212-484-4900 521-4230
NASDAQ: TZOO ■ Web: www.travelzoo.com

TripAdvisor LLC 464 Hillside Ave Ste 304............. Needham MA 02494 781-444-1113 444-1146
Web: www.tripadvisor.com

Vacation.com Inc 1650 King St Ste 450 .... Alexandria VA 22314 800-843-0733 548-6815*
*Fax Area Code: 703 ■ TF: 800-843-0733 ■ Web: www.vacation.com

Yahoo! Travel 701 First Ave....................... Sunnyvale CA 94089 408-349-5080 349-7821
Web: travel.yahoo.com

777 TRAVEL & TOURISM INFORMATION - CANADIAN

Phone Fax

Canadian Tourism Commission
1055 Dunsmuir St PO Box 49230................... Vancouver BC V7X1L2 604-638-8300
Web: en-corporate.canada.travel

Nova Scotia Dept of Tourism & Culture
1800 Argyle St PO Box 456 .... Halifax NS B3J2R5 902-425-5781 424-2668
TF: 800-565-0000 ■ Web: www.novascotia.com

NWT Tourism PO Box 610.......................... Yellowknife NT X1A2N5 867-873-7200 873-4059
TF: 800-661-0788 ■ Web: www.spectacularnwt.com

Ontario Tourism Marketing Partnership Corp
10 Dundas St E Ste 900 .... Toronto ON M7A2A1 905-282-1721
TF: 800-668-2746 ■ Web: www.ontariotravel.net

Prince Edward Island Tourism
PO Box 2000 .... Charlottetown PE C1A7N8 902-368-4000 368-4438
TF: 800-463-4734 ■ Web: www.gov.pe.ca

Tourism New Brunswick PO Box 12345........... Campbellton NB E3N3T6 800-561-0123 789-2044*
*Fax Area Code: 506 ■ TF: 800-561-0123 ■ Web: www.tourismnewbrunswick.ca

Tourism Saskatchewan 1621 Albert St .... Regina SK S4P2S5 306-787-9600 787-6293
TF: 877-237-2273 ■ Web: tourismsaskatchewan.com/

Tourism Yukon PO Box 2703..................... Whitehorse YT Y1A2C6 800-661-0494 393-7005*
*Fax Area Code: 867 ■ TF: 800-661-0494 ■ Web: www.travelyukon.com

Travel Manitoba 155 Carlton St Seventh Fl............ Winnipeg MB R3C3H8 204-927-7800 927-7828
TF: 800-665-0040 ■ Web: www.travelmanitoba.com

778 TRAVEL & TOURISM INFORMATION - FOREIGN TRAVEL

SEE ALSO Embassies & Consulates - Foreign, in the US p. 2245

Phone Fax

A P F Travel Inc 1721 Garvey Ave Fl 2 .... Alhambra CA 91803 626-282-9988
Web: www.apftravel.com

Action Travel Center Inc 5900 Harper Rd .... Solon OH 44139 440-248-4949
Web: www.actiontvl.com

Air Land & Sea Travel Wedding Crdn
66 N Atlantic Ave Ste 102....................... Cocoa Beach FL 32931 321-783-4900
Web: www.als-travel.com

All World Travel Inc 314 Gilmer St .... Sulphur Springs TX 75482 903-885-0896
Web: www.allworldtravel.com

Anguilla Tourist Marketing Office
246 Central Ave .... White Plains NY 10606 914-287-2400
TF: 800-553-4939 ■ Web: ivisitanguilla.com

Antigua & Barbuda Dept of Tourism & Trade
305 E 47th St 6th Fl .... New York NY 10017 212-541-4117 541-4789
TF: 888-268-4227 ■ Web: www.antigua-barbuda.org

Aruba Tourism Authority
1750 Powder Springs St Ste 190 .... Marietta GA 30064 404-892-7822
TF: 800-862-7822 ■ Web: www.aruba.com

Atlas Travel International Inc
One Maple St Ste 3................................ Milford MA 01757 508-478-8626
Web: www.atlastravel.com

Austrian Tourist Office PO Box 1142................ New York NY 10108 212-944-6880 730-4568
Web: www.austria.info/us

Bahamas Tourism Office
1200 S Pine Island Rd Ste 750..................... Plantation FL 33324 954-236-9292 236-9282
TF: 800-327-7678 ■ Web: www.bahamas.com

Baker Travel Inc 23832 Rockfield Blvd .... Lake Forest CA 92630 949-458-1818
Web: www.bakertravel.com

Belgian Tourist Office
220 E 42nd St Ste 3402 .... New York NY 10017 212-758-8130 355-7675
Web: www.visitbelgium.com

Bermuda Dept of Tourism
675 Third Ave 20th Fl.............................. New York NY 10017 212-818-9800 983-5289
TF: 800-223-6106 ■ Web: www.gotobermuda.com

Bike Friday Travel Systems 3364 W 11th Ave.......... Eugene OR 97402 541-687-0487
Web: bikefriday.com

Blue Ribbon Travel-american
3601 W 76th St Ste 190 .... Minneapolis MN 55435 952-835-2724
Web: www.blueribbontravel.com

Bonaire Government Tourist Office
80 Broad St Ste 3202 32nd Fl....................... New York NY 10004 212-956-5912 956-5913
TF: 800-328-2288 ■ Web: www.infobonaire.com

Byrne's Northpoint Travel
1213 Sheridan Rd.......................... Winthrop Harbor IL 60096 847-872-9223
Web: judicialsystems.com

Caa Niagara 155 Main St E.......................... Grimsby ON L3M1P2 905-945-5555
Web: www.caaniagara.ca

Canyon Creek Travel Inc
333 W Campbell Rd Ste 440..................... Richardson TX 75080 972-238-1998
Web: www.canyoncreektravel.com

Caribbean Tourism Organization
80 Broad St 32nd Fl .... New York NY 10004 212-635-9530 635-9511
Web: www.onecaribbean.org

Cayman Islands Dept of Tourism
350 Fifth Ave...................................... New York NY 10118 212-889-9009 889-9125
TF: 800-235-5888 ■ Web: www.caymanislands.ky

Centro De Servicios & Viajes Inc
30 Colonel Robert Magaw Pl Frnt 1 .... New York NY 10033 212-927-6060
Web: centrodeservicios.org

China National Tourist Office
370 Lexington Ave Ste 912......................... New York NY 10017 212-760-8218 760-8809
Web: www.cnto.org

China Travel Service Chicago Inc
2145b S China Pl .... Chicago IL 60616 312-328-0688
Web: www.nexusholidays.com

Croatian National Tourist Office
350 Fifth Ave Ste 4003 .... New York NY 10118 212-279-8672 279-8683
TF: 800-829-4416 ■ Web: www.croatia.hr

Cyprus Tourism Organization 13 E 40th St........... New York NY 10016 212-683-5280 683-5282
Web: www.visitcyprus.com

Dominican Republic Tourist Board
136 E 57th St Ste 805............................. New York NY 10022 212-588-1012
Web: www.dominicanrepublic.com

Duncan Hill Travel Ltd 2700 Beverly St .... Duncan BC V9L5C7 250-748-0391
Web: www.duncanhilltravel.ca

Egyptian Tourist Authority
45 Rockefeller Plaza Ste 2305....................... New York NY 10011 212-332-2570
Web: www.egypt.travel

Europ Assistance USA Services Inc
4330 East-West Hwy Ste 1000 .... Bethesda MD 20814 240-330-1000
Web: www.europassistance-usa.com

Fiji Visitors Bureau
5777 W Century Blvd Ste 220...................... Los Angeles CA 90045 310-568-1616 670-2318
Web: www.fiji.travel

Flightdeck 2321 W March Ln Ste A.................. Stockton CA 95207 209-952-6616
Web: segaletravel.com

French Government Tourist Office
9454 Wilshire Blvd Ste 210 .... Beverly Hills CA 90212 310-271-6665 276-2835
Web: us.rendezvousenfrance.com#xtor=al-999

Phone | Fax

German National Tourist Office
122 E 42nd St Ste 2000 .... New York NY 10168 212-661-7176 687-4138
Web: www.germany.travel/en

Go Travel 205 Parnell St .... Merritt Island FL 32953 321-453-1702
Web: gotravel.com

Go West Tours Inc
790 Eddy St at Van Ness .... San Francisco CA 94109 415-837-0154
Web: www.gowesttours.com

Golden Anchor Travel 1909 Southwood St .... Sarasota FL 34231 941-922-4070
Web: www.goldenanchortravel.com

Greek National Tourism Organization
305 E 47th St .... New York NY 10017 212-421-5777 826-6940
Web: www.visitgreece.gr

Guided Tours of Trois-Rivieres
1457 Rue Notre Dame .... Trois-Rivieres QC G9A4X4 819-375-1122 375-0022
TF: 800-313-1123 ■ *Web:* www.tourismetroisrivieres.com

Hong Kong Tourism Board
5670 Wilshire Blvd Ste 1230 .... Los Angeles CA 90036 323-938-4582 208-1869*
**Fax Area Code:* 310 ■ *TF:* 800-282-4582 ■ *Web:* www.discoverhongkong.com

India Tourist Office
1270 Ave of the Americas Ste 303 .... New York NY 10020 212-586-4901 582-3274
TF General: 800-425-1414 ■ *Web:* www.incredibleindia.org

Irish Tourist Board 345 Pk Ave 17th Fl .... New York NY 10154 212-418-0800 371-9052
TF: 800-223-6470 ■ *Web:* www.tourismireland.com

Israel Government Tourist Office
800 Second Ave 16th Fl .... New York NY 10017 212-499-5660 658-6543*
**Fax Area Code:* 323 ■ *TF:* 877-248-8687 ■ *Web:* www.goisrael.com

Italian Government Tourist Board
500 N Michigan Ave Ste 2240 .... Chicago IL 60611 312-644-0996 644-3019
Web: www.italiantourism.com

Jamaica Tourist Board
5201 Blue Lagoon Dr Ste 670 .... Miami FL 33126 305-665-0557 666-7239
TF: 800-233-4582 ■ *Web:* www.visitjamaica.com

Japan National Tourist Organization
515 S Figueroa St Ste 1470 .... Los Angeles CA 90071 213-623-1952 623-6301
Web: www.japantravelinfo.com

Jordan Tourism Board (JTB)
1307 Dolley Madison Blvd Ste 2A .... McLean VA 22101 703-243-7404 243-7406
TF: 877-733-5673 ■ *Web:* www.visitjordan.com

Jornee 312 Se 17th St Fl 3 .... Fort Lauderdale FL 33316 954-563-6272
Web: www.jornee.com

Kenya Tourism Board
6442 City W Pkwy 6442 City W Pkwy .... Minneapolis MN 55344 310-649-7718 914-6946*
**Fax Area Code:* 952 ■ *TF:* 800-223-6486 ■ *Web:* www.magicalkenya.com

Korea National Tourism Organization
Two Executive Dr Ste 750 .... Fort Lee NJ 07024 201-585-0909 585-9041
TF: 800-868-7567 ■ *Web:* english.visitkorea.or.kr

Maritime Travel Inc
202-2000 Barrington St Cogswell Tower .... Halifax NS B3J3K1 902-420-1554
Web: www.maritimetravel.ca

Martinique Promotion Bureau
444 Madison Ave 16th Fl .... New York NY 10022 800-391-4909
TF: 800-391-4909 ■ *Web:* www.martinique.org

Mexico Tourism Board (CSTM)
225 N Michigan Ave Ste 1800 .... Chicago IL 60601 800-446-3942 228-0515*
**Fax Area Code:* 312 ■ *TF General:* 800-446-3942 ■ *Web:* www.visitmexico.com

Ministry of Tourism of Dominican Republic
848 Brickell Ave .... Miami FL 33131 305-358-2899
Web: godominicanrepublic.com

Monaco Government Tourist Office
565 Fifth Ave 23rd Fl .... New York NY 10017 212-286-3330 286-9890
TF: 800-753-9696 ■ *Web:* www.visitmonaco.com

Morley Companies Inc One Morley Plz .... Saginaw MI 48603 989-791-2550
Web: www.morleynet.com

Netherlands Board of Tourism & Conventions
215 Park Ave S .... New York NY 10003 212-370-7360 370-9507
Web: www.holland.com

New Zealand Tourism Board
501 Santa Monica Blvd Ste 300 .... Santa Monica CA 90401 310-395-7480 395-5453
Web: www.newzealand.com/travel

Norwegian Tourist Board
655 Third Ave 18th Fl .... New York NY 10017 212-885-9700 885-9710
Web: www.visitnorway.com

Nova Tours & Travel Inc 504 Vine St .... Liverpool NY 13088 315-451-0260
Web: www.novatours.com

Philippine Dept of Tourism
556 Fifth Ave First Fl Mezzanine .... New York NY 10036 212-575-7915 302-6759
Web: www.tourism.gov.ph

Plaza Travel 16545 Ventura Blvd Ste 17 .... Encino CA 91436 818-990-4053
Web: www.plazatravel.com

Polish National Tourist Office
Five Marine View Plz Ste 208 .... Hoboken NJ 07030 201-420-9910 584-9153
Web: www.poland.travel

Puerto Rico Tourism Co
Paseo La Princesa .... Old San Juan PR 00902 787-721-2400 722-1093
TF: 800-866-7827 ■ *Web:* topuertorico.org

Rail Europe Inc 44 S Broadway 11th Fl .... White Plains NY 10601 914-682-2999
Web: www.raileurope.com

Romanian National Tourist Office
355 Lexington Ave 19th Fl .... New York NY 10017 212-545-8484
Web: www.romaniatourism.com

Roseborough Travel Agency Inc
140 E Indiana Ave .... Deland FL 32724 386-734-7245
Web: roseboroughtravel.com

Russian National Tourist Office
224 W 30th St Ste 701 .... New York NY 10001 646-473-2233 473-2205
TF: 877-221-7120 ■ *Web:* www.russia-travel.com

Saint Lucia Tourist Board
800 Second Ave Ninth Fl .... New York NY 10017 212-867-2950 867-2795
TF: 800-456-3984 ■ *Web:* stlucianow.com/?src=orgredirection

Saint Vincent & the Grenadines Tourist Information Office
801 Second Ave 21st Fl .... New York NY 10017 212-687-4981
TF: 800-729-1726 ■ *Web:* www.visitsvg.com

Phone | Fax

SaveOnResorts.com 6727 Flanders Dr Ste 220 .... San Diego CA 92121 858-625-0630
Web: www.saveonresorts.com

Scandinavian Tourist Boards 655 Third Ave .... New York NY 10017 212-885-9700
Web: www.goscandinavia.com

Skyland Escapes.ca 445 Sixth Ave W .... Vancouver BC V5Y1L3 604-685-6008
Web: www.escapes.ca

Swedish Travel & Tourism Council
Grand Central Stn PO Box 4649 .... New York NY 10163 212-885-9700 885-9710
Web: www.visitsweden.com

Switzerland Tourism 608 Fifth Ave Ste 202 .... New York NY 10020 212-757-5944 262-6116
TF: 800-794-7795 ■ *Web:* www.myswitzerland.com

Tahiti Tourism
300 Continental Blvd Ste 160 .... El Segundo CA 90245 310-414-8484 414-8490
Web: www.tahiti-tourisme.com

Taiwan Visitors Assn One E 42nd St Ste 9 .... New York NY 10017 212-867-1632 867-1635
Web: www.taiwan.net.tw

Tourism Australia 6100 Ctr Dr Ste 1150 .... Los Angeles CA 90045 310-695-3200 695-3201
Web: www.australia.com

Tourism Authority of Thailand
611 N Larchmont Blvd First Fl .... Los Angeles CA 90004 323-461-9814 461-9834
Web: www.tourismthailand.org

Tourism Malaysia (MTPB) 120 E 56th St 15th Fl .... New York NY 10022 212-754-1113 754-1116
Web: www.tourismmalaysiausa.com

Tourism Medicine Hat
Eight Gehring Rd Se .... Medicine Hat AB T1B4W1 403-527-6422
Web: www.tourismmedicinehat.com

Tourism Saskatoon 202 Fourth Ave N .... Saskatoon SK S7K0K1 306-242-1206
Web: www.tourismsaskatoon.com

Tourist Office of Spain
845 N Michigan Ave Ste 915-E .... Chicago IL 60611 312-642-1992 642-9817
Web: www.spain.info

Travel Network Corp, The 1920 Ave Rd .... Toronto ON M5M4A1 416-789-3271
Web: www.thetravelnetwork.com

Turks & Caicos Islands Tourism Office
60 E 42nd St Ste 2817 .... New York NY 10165 646-375-8830 375-8835
TF: 800-241-0824 ■ *Web:* www.turksandcaicostourism.com

VEGAS.com LLC 2370 Corporate Cir Third Fl .... Henderson NV 89074 702-992-7990
Web: www.vegas.com

Vip Cruises & Travel 22 Cleveland Ter .... West Orange NJ 07052 973-731-8282
Web: www.myvipcruises.com

Visit Florida
2540 W Executive Ctr Cir Ste 200 .... Tallahassee FL 32301 850-488-5607
Web: www.visitflorida.org

Voyages Groupe Ideal Inc 5415 Pare St Ste 1 .... Montreal QC H4P1P7 514-342-9554
Web: www.groupeideal.ca

Voyages Michel Barrette 100 Rue Saint-joseph .... Alma QC G8B7A6 418-668-3078
Web: voyagesmichelbarrette.com

Welcome Aboard Travel Ltd 107 S State St .... Dover DE 19901 302-678-9480
Web: welcomeaboard.net

Williamsburg Travel Management Companies
570 W Crossville Rd Ste 102 .... Roswell GA 30075 770-650-5515
Web: willtrav.com

779 TREE SERVICES

SEE ALSO Landscape Design & Related Services p. 2620

Phone | Fax

ABC Professional Tree Services Inc
201 Flint Ridge Rd .... Webster TX 77598 281-280-1100
Web: www.abctree.com

Acres Enterprises Inc 610 W Liberty St .... Wauconda IL 60084 847-526-4554
Web: www.acresgroup.com

Akehurst Landscaping Service Inc
712 Philadelphia Rd .... Joppa MD 21085 410-538-4018
Web: www.akehurst.com

Alaska Snow Removal 2134 E 88th Ave .... Anchorage AK 99507 907-349-5000
Web: www.akplow.com

Arbor Masters Tree & Landscape Inc
8250 Cole Pkwy .... Shawnee KS 66227 913-441-8888
Web: www.arbormasters.com

Arbor Tree Surgery Inc
802 Paso Robles St .... Paso Robles CA 93446 805-239-1239
Web: www.arbortree.com

Asplundh Tree Expert Co
708 Blair Mill Rd .... Willow Grove PA 19090 215-784-4200 784-4493
TF: 800-248-8733 ■ *Web:* www.asplundh.com

Atlas Environmental Services Inc
9032 Olive Dr .... Spring Valley CA 91977 619-463-1707
Web: www.atlastree.com

BCI Inc 848 Marshall Phelps Rd .... Windsor CT 06095 860-688-8024
Web: www.thebutlerco.com

BIO Landscape & Maintenance Inc
10892 Shadow Wood Dr .... Houston TX 77043 713-462-8552
Web: www.biolandscape.com

Blue Ridge Landscape & Design Inc
172-12 Imboden Dr .... Winchester VA 22603 540-869-0000
Web: www.blueridgelandscape.com

Breezy Hill Nursery Inc 7530 288th Ave .... Salem WI 53168 262-537-2111
Web: www.breezyhillnursery.com

CableTest Systems Inc 400 Alden Rd .... Markham ON L3R4C1 905-475-2607
Web: www.cabletest.com

Care of Trees Inc 2371 Foster Ave .... Wheeling IL 60090 847-394-4220 394-3376
Web: www.thecareoftrees.com

CoCal Landscape Services Inc 12570 E 39th Ave .... Denver CO 80239 303-399-7877
Web: www.cocal.com

Cti Property Services 5916 Triangle Dr .... Raleigh NC 27617 919-787-3789
Web: www.ctipropertyservices.com

Davey Tree Expert Co 1500 N Mantua St .... Kent OH 44240 330-673-9511 673-7089*
**Fax:* Hum Res ■ *TF:* 800-445-8733 ■ *Web:* www.davey.com

David J. Frank Landscape Contracting Inc
N120 W21350 Freistadt Rd .... Germantown WI 53022 262-255-4888
Web: www.davidjfrank.com

Phone Fax

Dejana Industries Inc
30 Sagamore Hill Dr Port Washington NY 11050 516-944-3100
Web: www.dejanaindustries.com

Del Conte's Landscaping Inc 41900 Boscell Rd Fremont CA 94538 510-353-6030
Web: www.visionrecycling.com

Down To Earth Landscaping Inc
705 Wright-Debow Rd Jackson NJ 08527 732-833-7702
Web: www.downtoearthlandscaping.com

Embark Tree & Landscape Services
2700 Palo Pinto Houston TX 77080 713-462-3261
Web: www.embarkservices.com

FA Bartlett Tree Expert Co 1290 E Main St Stamford CT 06902 203-323-1131 353-0808
TF: 877-227-8538 ■ *Web:* www.bartlett.com

Gachina Landscape Management Inc
1130 O'Brien Dr Menlo Park CA 94025 650-853-0400
Web: www.gachina.com

Gardeners' Guild Inc 2780 Goodrick Ave Richmond CA 94801 510-439-3700
Web: www.gardenersguild.com

Grover Landscape Services Inc
6224 Stoddard Rd Modesto CA 95356 209-545-4401
Web: www.groverlandscapeservices.com

Hou-scape Inc 17725 Telge Rd Cypress TX 77429 281-579-6741
Web: www.hou-scape.com

Lewis Tree Service Inc
300 Lucius Gordon Dr West Henrietta NY 14586 585-436-3208 235-5864
TF: 800-333-1593 ■ *Web:* www.lewistree.com

MainScapes Inc 20400 New Hampshire Ave Brinklow MD 20862 301-260-0190
Web: www.mainscapes.com

Maldonado Nursery & Landscaping Inc
16348 Nacogdoches Rd San Antonio TX 78247 210-599-1219
Web: mnlsa.com

Metco Landscape Inc 2200 Rifle St Aurora CO 80011 303-421-3100
Web: www.metcolandscape.com

Nature's Trees Inc 550 Bedford Rd Bedford Hills NY 10507 914-241-4999
Web: www.savatree.com

Nelson Tree Service Inc
3300 Office Pk Dr Ste 205 Dayton OH 45439 937-294-1313 294-8673
TF: 800-522-4311 ■ *Web:* www.nelsontree.com

Paramount Landscape & Maintenance Inc
402 W Orion St Tempe AZ 85283 480-668-6109
Web: www.paramountlandscape.com

Pattillo Grounds Management
5830 E Ponce De Leon Ave Stone Mountain GA 30083 770-938-6366
Web: www.metsprogram.com

Peabody Landscape Construction Inc
2253 Dublin Rd Columbus OH 43228 614-488-2877
Web: www.peabodylandscape.com

Rainbow Treecare Inc 11571 K-Tel Dr Minnetonka MN 55343 952-922-3810
Web: www.rainbowtreecare.com

Realty Landscaping Corp 2585 Second St Pk Newtown PA 18940 215-598-7334
Web: www.realtylandscaping.com

Shade Tree Service Company Inc 520 S Hwy Dr Fenton MO 63026 636-343-1212 343-5660
Web: www.stsco.net

Terry Hughes Tree Service Inc
15802 Fairview Rd Gretna NE 68028 402-558-8198
Web: www.hughestree.com

Three C's Landscaping Inc 32124 Utica Rd Fraser MI 48026 586-415-4850
Web: www.threecslandscaping.com

Treepeople Inc 12601 Mulholland Dr Beverly Hills CA 90210 818-753-4600
Web: treepeople.com

Trees Inc 650 N Sam Houston Pkwy E Ste 209 Houston TX 77060 281-447-1327 260-0728
TF: 866-865-9617 ■ *Web:* www.treesinc.com

Twin Oaks Landscaping Inc 997 Harvey Rd Oswego IL 60543 630-554-3399
Web: www.twinoakslandscaping.com

United Lawnscape Inc 62170 Van Dyke Rd Washington MI 48094 586-752-5000
Web: www.unitedlawnscape.com

Van Zelst Inc 39400 N Hwy 41 Wadsworth IL 60083 847-623-3580
Web: www.vanzelst.com

West Tree Service Inc 6300 Forbing Rd Little Rock AR 72209 501-568-5111 562-9378
TF: 800-779-2967 ■ *Web:* www.westtree.com

Wolf Tree Experts Inc 3310 Greenway Dr Knoxville TN 37918 865-687-3400
Web: www.wolftreeinc.com

780 TROPHIES, PLAQUES, AWARDS

Phone Fax

Architectural Bronze Aluminum Corp
655 Deerfield Rd Ste 100 Deerfield IL 60015 800-339-6581 266-7301*
**Fax Area Code:* 847 ■ *TF:* 800-339-6581 ■ *Web:* www.architecturalbronze.com

Au Sable Woodworking Co 6677 Frederic St Frederic MI 49733 989-348-7086
Web: www.ausablewood.com

Award Products Inc 4830 N Front St Philadelphia PA 19120 215-324-0414
Web: directory.hawaiitribune-herald.com

Bruce Fox Inc 1909 McDonald Ln New Albany IN 47150 812-945-3511 945-0275
TF: 877-336-9601 ■ *Web:* www.brucefox.com

Champion Awards Inc 3649 Winplace Rd Memphis TN 38118 901-365-4830
Web: www.gochampion.net

Classic Medallics Inc 520 S Fulton Ave Mount Vernon NY 10550 914-530-6259 530-6258
TF: 800-221-1348 ■ *Web:* www.classic-medallics.com

Crown Trophy 529 N State Rd Briarcliff NY 10510 914-941-0020 941-3039
Web: www.crowntrophy.com

F & H Ribbon Co Inc 3010 S Pipeline Rd Euless TX 76040 800-877-5775 344-3010
TF: 800-877-5775 ■ *Web:* www.fhribbon.com

Jostens Inc 3601 Minnesota Ave Ste 400 Minneapolis MN 55435 952-830-3300 830-3293*
**Fax:* Hum Res ■ *TF:* 800-235-4774 ■ *Web:* www.jostens.com

Metallic Arts Inc 914 N Lake Rd Spokane WA 99212 509-489-7173 483-1759
TF: 800-541-3200 ■ *Web:* www.metallicarts.com

Plastic Dress-Up Co 11077 Rush St South El Monte CA 91733 626-442-7711 442-1814
Web: www.pdu.com

Regalia Manufacturing Co 2018 Fourth Ave Rock Island IL 61201 309-788-7471 788-0788
TF: 800-798-7471 ■ *Web:* www.regaliamfg.com

RS Owens & Co 5535 N Lynch Ave Chicago IL 60630 773-282-6000
TF: 800-282-6200 ■ *Web:* www.rsowens.com

Trophyland USA Inc 7001 W 20th Ave Hialeah FL 33014 800-327-5820 823-4836*
**Fax Area Code:* 305 ■ *TF:* 800-327-5820 ■ *Web:* www.trophyland.com

US Bronze Sign Co 811 Second Ave New Hyde Park NY 11040 516-352-5155 352-1761
TF: 800-872-5155 ■ *Web:* www.usbronze.com

Wilson Trophy Co 1724 Frienza Ave Sacramento CA 95815 916-927-9733 927-9955
TF: 800-635-5005 ■ *Web:* www.wilsontrophy.com

TRUCK BODIES

SEE Motor Vehicles - Commercial & Special Purpose p. 2773

781 TRUCK RENTAL & LEASING

Phone Fax

Barco Rent a Truck
717 South 5600 West Salt Lake City UT 84104 801-532-7777
Web: www.barcorentatruck.com

Brody Transportation Co Inc
621 S Bentalou St Baltimore MD 21223 410-947-7000 947-5858

Carco National Lease Inc 2905 N 32nd St Fort Smith AR 72904 479-441-3200 441-3212
TF: 800-643-2596 ■ *Web:* carcotrans.com

DeCarolis Truck Rental Inc 333 Colfax St Rochester NY 14606 585-254-1169 458-4072
TF: 800-666-1169 ■ *Web:* www.decarolis.com

Idealease Inc 430 N Rand Rd North Barrington IL 60010 847-304-6000 304-0076
TF: 800-435-3273 ■ *Web:* www.idealease.com

Interstate NationaLease 2700 Palmyra Rd Albany GA 31707 229-883-7250
Web: interstatenationalease.com

Kris Way Truck Leasing Inc
43 Hemco Rd Ste 1 South Portland ME 04106 207-799-8593 799-8657
Web: www.kris-way.com

Lily Transportation Corp 145 Rosemary St Needham MA 02494 781-449-8811 449-7128
Web: www.lily.com

Mendon Truck Leasing & Rental
8215 Foster Ave Brooklyn NY 11236 718-209-9886
Web: www.mendonleasing.com

MHC Kenworth 1524 N Corrington Ave Kansas City MO 64120 816-483-7035 483-4391
TF: 888-259-4826 ■ *Web:* www.mhctruck.com

National Truck Leasing System
450 S Summit Ave Oakbrook IL 60181 630-953-8878 953-0040
TF: 800-729-6857 ■ *Web:* nationalease.com

PACCAR Leasing Corp 777 106th Ave NE Bellevue WA 98004 425-468-7877 468-8211
TF: 800-759-2979 ■ *Web:* www.paclease.com

Rush Enterprises Inc
555 IH 35 S Ste 500 New Braunfels TX 78130 830-626-5200 626-5310
NASDAQ: RUSHA ■ *TF:* 800-973-7874 ■ *Web:* www.rushenterprises.com

Ryder System Inc 11690 NW 105th St Miami FL 33178 305-500-3726 500-4599
NYSE: R ■ *TF:* 800-297-9337 ■ *Web:* www.ryder.com

Star Leasing Co 4080 Business Pk Dr Columbus OH 43204 614-278-9999 340-3137
TF: 888-771-1004 ■ *Web:* www.starleasing.com

Star Truck Rentals Inc
3940 Eastern Ave SE Grand Rapids MI 49508 616-243-7033 243-7498
TF: 800-748-0468 ■ *Web:* startruckrentals.com

Superstition Trailers LLC 535 N 51st Ave Phoenix AZ 85043 602-415-0222
Web: www.stlaz.com

U-Haul International Inc 2727 N Central Ave Phoenix AZ 85004 800-528-0361 263-6772*
**Fax Area Code:* 602 ■ *TF:* 800-528-0361 ■ *Web:* www.uhaul.com

782 TRUCK TRAILERS

SEE ALSO Motor Vehicles - Commercial & Special Purpose p. 2773

Phone Fax

4-Star Trailers Inc 10000 NW Tenth St Oklahoma City OK 73127 405-324-7827 324-8423
TF: 800-848-3095 ■ *Web:* www.4startrailers.com

Alta-Fab Structures Ltd 504-13 Ave Nisku AB T9E7P6 780-955-7733
Web: www.altafab.com

American Carrier Equipment Trailer Sales LLC
2285 E Date Ave Fresno CA 93706 559-442-1500 442-3618
TF: 800-344-2174 ■ *Web:* www.americancarrierequipment.com

Arkansas Trailer Manufacturing Co
3200 S Elm St Little Rock AR 72204 501-666-5417 666-1787
TF: 800-666-5417 ■ *Web:* arkansastrailer.com

Austin-Westran LLC
602 E Blackhawk Dr PO Box 921 Byron IL 61010 815-234-2811 234-3009
Web: www.austinwestran.com

Barrett Trailers Inc 1831 Hardcastle Blvd Purcell OK 73080 405-527-5050 527-3206
Web: www.barrett-trailers.com

Beall Corp 9200 N Ramsey Blvd Portland OR 97203 855-219-5686 289-3528*
**Fax Area Code:* 503 ■ *TF:* 855-219-5686 ■ *Web:* www.bealltrailers.com

Brenner Tank LLC 450 Arlington Ave Fond du Lac WI 54935 920-922-5020 922-3303
TF: 800-558-9750 ■ *Web:* www.brennertank.com

Bri-Mar Mfg LLC 1080 S Main St Chambersburg PA 17201 717-263-6116 263-6479
TF: 800-732-5845 ■ *Web:* www.bri-mar.com

Circle J Trailers 312 W Simplot Blvd Caldwell ID 83605 208-459-0842 459-0106
TF: 800-247-2535 ■ *Web:* www.circlejtrailers.com

Clement Industries Inc PO Box 914 Minden LA 71058 318-377-2776 377-2776
TF Cust Svc: 800-562-5948 ■ *Web:* www.clementind.com

CM Trailers Inc 200 County Rd PO Box 680 Madill OK 73446 580-795-5536 795-7263
TF: 888-268-7577 ■ *Web:* www.cmtrailers.com

Cottrell Inc 2125 Candler Rd Gainesville GA 30507 770-532-7251 535-2831
TF Sales: 800-827-0132 ■ *Web:* www.cottrelltrailers.com

Dakota Mfg Company Inc 1909 S Rowley St Mitchell SD 57301 605-996-5571 996-5572
TF: 800-232-5682 ■ *Web:* traileze.com

Dexter Chassis Group 501 Miller Dr White Pigeon MI 49099 269-483-7681
Web: dexterchassisgroup.com

Doonan Trailer Corp 36 NE Hwy 156 Great Bend KS 67530 620-792-6222 792-3308
Web: www.doonan.com

East Mfg Corp 1871 State Rt 44 PO Box 277 Randolph OH 44265 330-325-9921 325-7851
TF: 888-405-3278 ■ *Web:* www.eastmfg.com

	City	State	Zip	Phone	Fax
Featherlite Trailers Hwy 63 & 9 PO Box 320 *TF:* 800-800-1230 ■ *Web:* www.fthr.com	Cresco	IA	52136	563-547-6000	547-6100
Fontaine Trailer Co 430 Letson Rd PO Box 619 *TF:* 800-821-6535 ■ *Web:* www.fontainetrailer.com	Haleyville	AL	35565	205-486-5251	
Great Dane Trailers Inc 602 E Lathrop Ave *Web:* greatdanetrailers.com	Savannah	GA	31415	912-644-2100	
Hesse Inc 6700 St John Ave *TF:* 800-821-5562 ■ *Web:* www.grouphesse.com	Kansas City	MO	64123	816-483-7808	241-9010
Holden Industries Inc 5624 S State Hwy 43 *Web:* www.holdentrailers.com	South West City	MO	64863	417-762-3218	
Hudson Bros Trailer Manufacturing Inc 1508 Hwy 218 W *Web:* www.hudsontrailers.com	Indian Trail	NC	28079	704-753-4723	753-2011
K-Dee Supply Inc 621 E Lake St *TF:* 800-268-3681 ■ *Web:* lake-mills-wi.opendi.us	Lake Mills	WI	53551	920-648-8202	648-2903
Kentucky Trailer 7201 Logistics Dr *TF:* 888-598-7245 ■ *Web:* www.kytrailer.com	Louisville	KY	40258	502-637-2551	636-3675
Kentucky Trailer Technologies 1240 N Pontiac Trial *TF:* 866-638-6080 ■ *Web:* www.kytrailers.com	Walled Lake	MI	48390	248-960-9700	960-7775
LBT Inc 11502 "I" St *TF:* 888-528-7278 ■ *Web:* www.lbt-inc.com	Omaha	NE	68137	402-333-4900	333-0685
Ledwell & Son Enterprises 3300 Waco St **Fax:* Sales ■ *TF:* 888-533-9355 ■ *Web:* www.ledwell.com	Texarkana	TX	75501	903-838-6531	831-2719*
Liberty Industries Inc 130 E Cemetery Rd *Web:* www.liberty-industries.com	Fillmore	IN	46128	765-246-4031	
Loadcraft Industries Inc 3811 N Bridge St *Web:* www.loadcraft.com	Brady	TX	76825	325-597-2911	
Lufkin Industries Inc 601 S Raguet St *NASDAQ: LUFK* ■ *Web:* www.lufkin.com	Lufkin	TX	75902	936-634-2211	637-5474
Mac Trailer Mfg Inc 14599 Commerce St NE *TF:* 800-795-8454 ■ *Web:* www.mactrailer.com	Alliance	OH	44601	330-823-9900	823-0232
Magic Tilt Trailers Inc 2161 Lions Club Rd *TF:* 800-998-8458 ■ *Web:* www.boattrailers.com	Clearwater	FL	33764	727-535-5561	539-8472
Maurer Mfg 1300 38th Ave W PO Box 160 *TF:* 888-274-6010 ■ *Web:* www.maurermfg.com	Spencer	IA	51301	712-262-2992	262-1022
MCT Industries Inc 7451 Pan American Fwy *TF:* 800-876-8651 ■ *Web:* www.mct-ind.com	Albuquerque	NM	87109	505-345-8651	345-2597
Merritt Equipment Co 9339 Hwy 85 *TF:* 800-634-3036 ■ *Web:* www.merrittequipment.com	Henderson	CO	80640	303-289-2286	288-6127
Mickey Truck Bodies Inc 1305 Trinity Ave PO Box 2044 *TF:* 800-334-9061 ■ *Web:* www.mickeybody.com	High Point	NC	27261	336-882-6806	889-6712
Midwest Systems 5911 Hall St *TF:* 800-383-6281 ■ *Web:* www.mwsystems.com	Saint Louis	MO	63147	314-389-6280	389-9443
Nu Van Technology Inc 2155 Hwy 1187	Mansfield	TX	76063	817-477-1734	
Performance Co, The 1263 US Hwy 59 N *Web:* www.performancetruck.com	Cleveland	TX	77328	281-593-8888	
Pitts Enterprises Inc 5734 Hwy 431 *Web:* www.pittstrailers.com	Pittsview	AL	36871	334-855-4754	
Polar Service Centers 7600 E Sam Houston Pkwy N *TF:* 800-955-8558 ■ *Web:* www.polartank.com	Houston	TX	77049	281-459-6400	
Polar Tank Trailer Inc 12810 County Rd 17 *TF:* 800-826-6589 ■ *Web:* www.polartank.com	Holdingford	MN	56340	320-746-2255	746-2937
Redneck Trailer Supplies 2100 NW By-Pass *TF:* 877-973-3632 ■ *Web:* www.redneck-trailer.com	Springfield	MO	65803	417-864-5210	864-7764
Rogers Bros Corp 100 Orchard St *TF:* 800-441-9880 ■ *Web:* www.rogerstrailers.com	Albion	PA	16401	814-756-4121	756-4830
Royal Camp Services Ltd 7111 - 67 St *Web:* www.royalcamp.com	Edmonton	AB	T6B3L7	780-463-8000	
Schutt Industries Inc 185 Industrial Ave *Web:* www.schuttindustries.com	Clintonville	WI	54929	715-823-8025	
Schwend Inc 28945 Johnston Rd *TF:* 800-243-7757 ■ *Web:* www.schwendinc.com	Dade City	FL	33523	352-588-2220	588-2221
Stoughton Trailers LLC 416 S Academy St *Web:* www.stoughtontrailers.com	Stoughton	WI	53589	608-873-2500	873-2575
Summit Trailer Sales Inc One Summit Plz *TF:* 800-437-3729 ■ *Web:* www.summittrailer.com	Summit Station	PA	17979	570-754-3511	754-7025
Superior Fabrication Inc 801 S Eastern Ave *Web:* www.superiorfab.com	Elk City	OK	73644	580-243-5693	
Timpte Inc 1827 Industrial Dr *TF:* 888-256-4884 ■ *Web:* www.timpte.com	David City	NE	68632	402-367-3056	367-4340
Towmaster Inc 61381 US Hwy 12 *TF:* 800-462-4517 ■ *Web:* towmaster.com	Litchfield	MN	55355	320-693-7900	693-7921
Trail King Industries Inc 147 Industrial Pk Rd *TF:* 800-545-1549 ■ *Web:* www.trailking.com	Brookville	PA	15825	814-849-2342	849-5063
Trailiner Corp PO Box 5270 *TF:* 800-833-8209 ■ *Web:* www.trailiner.com	Springfield	MO	65801	417-866-7258	866-1168
Trailstar Mfg Corp 20700 Harrisburg-Westville Rd PO Box 2086 *TF:* 800-235-5635 ■ *Web:* trailstarintl.com	Alliance	OH	44601	330-821-9900	821-6941
Travis Body & Trailer Inc 13955 FM529 *TF:* 800-535-4372 ■ *Web:* www.travistrailers.com	Houston	TX	77041	713-466-5888	466-3238
Trinity Trailer Manufacturing Inc 8200 S Eisenman Rd *TF:* 800-235-6577 ■ *Web:* www.trinitytrailer.com	Boise	ID	83716	208-336-3666	336-3741
Truck Equipment Service Co 800 Oak St *TF:* 800-869-0363 ■ *Web:* www.cornhusker800.com	Lincoln	NE	68521	402-476-3225	476-3726
Utility Tool & Trailer Co 151 E 16th St PO Box 360 *TF:* 800-874-6807 ■ *Web:* www.uttwi.com	Clintonville	WI	54929	715-823-3167	823-5274
Utility Trailer Mfg Co 17295 E Railroad St *TF:* 800-874-6807 ■ *Web:* www.utilitytrailer.com	City of Industry	CA	91748	626-965-1541	965-2790
Vanco USA Trailer Mfg 1170 Florence Rd PO Box 98 *Web:* www.vancotrailers.com	Florence	NJ	08518	609-499-4141	499-8865
Vantage Trailers Inc 29335 Hwy Blvd *TF:* 800-826-8245 ■ *Web:* www.vantagetrailer.com	Katy	TX	77494	281-391-2664	
VE Enterprises Inc PO Box 369 *Web:* www.veenterprises.com	Springer	OK	73458	580-653-2171	653-2773
Wabash National Corp 1000 Sagamore PkwyS PO Box 6129 *NYSE: WNC* ■ *TF Sales:* 800-937-4784 ■ *Web:* www.wabashnational.com	Lafayette	IN	47903	765-771-5300	771-5474
Wells Cargo Inc 1503 W McNaughton St *TF:* 800-348-7553 ■ *Web:* www.wellscargo.com	Elkhart	IN	46514	574-264-9661	264-5938
Western Trailer Co 251 W Gowen Rd *TF:* 888-344-2539 ■ *Web:* www.westerntrailer.com	Boise	ID	83716	208-344-2539	344-1521
Wilson Trailer Co 4400 S Lewis Blvd *TF:* 800-798-2002 ■ *Web:* www.wilsontrailer.com	Sioux City	IA	51106	712-252-6500	252-6510
Witzco Trailers Inc 6101 McIntosh Rd *TF:* 800-363-7237 ■ *Web:* www.witzco.com	Sarasota	FL	34238	941-922-5301	924-2402

783 TRUCKING COMPANIES

SEE ALSO Logistics Services (Transportation & Warehousing) p. 2673; Moving Companies p. 2778

	City	State	Zip	Phone	Fax
A & A Express Inc PO Box 707 *TF:* 800-658-3549 ■ *Web:* www.aaexpressinc.com	Brandon	SD	57005	605-582-2402	582-7300
AAA Cooper Transportation 1751 Kinsey Rd *TF:* 800-633-7571 ■ *Web:* www.aaacooper.com	Dothan	AL	36303	334-793-2284	794-3353
Aaa Moving & Storage Inc 747 E Ship Creek Ave *TF:* 866-641-4446 ■ *Web:* www.aaa-moving.com	Anchorage	AK	99501	907-276-3506	276-1986
ABF Freight Systems Inc 3801 Old Greenwood Rd **Fax:* Cust Svc ■ *TF:* 800-610-5544 ■ *Web:* www.abfs.com	Fort Smith	AR	72903	479-785-8913	785-8800*
Ace Doran Hauling & Rigging Co Inc 1601 Blue Rock St *TF:* 800-829-0929 ■ *Web:* www.acedoran.com	Cincinnati	OH	45223	513-681-7900	681-7908
Ace Relocation Systems Inc 5608 Eastgate Dr *TF:* 800-453-0964 ■ *Web:* www.acerelocation.com	San Diego	CA	92121	858-677-5500	677-5587
Acme Truck Line Inc 121 Pailet Dr *TF:* 800-825-6246 ■ *Web:* www.acmetruck.com	Harvey	LA	70058	504-368-2510	368-2510
Action Carrier Inc 1720 S Southeastern Ave Ste 220	Sioux Falls	SD	57103	605-335-5500	
Admiral-Merchants Motor Freight Inc 215 S 11th St	Minneapolis	MN	55403	612-332-4819	332-4765
Alabama Motor Express Inc 10720 E US Hwy 84 E **Fax Area Code:* 334 ■ *TF:* 800-633-7590 ■ *Web:* www.amxtrucking.com	Ashford	AL	36312	800-633-7590	899-2311*
Alan Ritchey Inc 740 S I-35 E Frontage Rd *TF:* 800-877-0273 ■ *Web:* www.alanritchey.com	Valley View	TX	76272	940-726-3276	726-5335
All American Moving Group LLC PO Box 271277 *TF:* 800-467-2900 ■ *Web:* www.allamericanmoving.com	Memphis	TN	38167	901-353-3900	353-4113
All Freight Systems Inc PO Box 5279 *TF:* 800-377-7575 ■ *Web:* www.allfreightsystems.com	Kansas City	KS	66119	913-281-1203	281-5741
Allegheny Design Management Inc 1154 Parks Industrial Dr *TF:* 800-927-2611 ■ *Web:* www.alleghenydesignmgmt.com	Vandergrift	PA	15690	724-845-7336	845-9889
Allied Automotive Group 2302 ParkLake Dr Bldg 15 Ste 600 **Fax Area Code:* 404 ■ *TF:* 800-476-2058 ■ *Web:* www.alliedautomotive.com	Atlanta	GA	30345	800-476-2058	373-4285*
Ameril-Co Carriers Inc 1702 E Overland PO Box 1649 *TF:* 800-445-5400 ■ *Web:* www.americo-carriers.com	Scottsbluff	NE	69361	308-635-3157	635-1447
Amstan Logistics 101 Knightsbridge Dr *TF:* 800-322-5546 ■ *Web:* www.amstan.com	Hamilton	OH	45011	513-863-4627	863-0866
Anderson Trucking Service Inc 725 Opportunity St PO Box 1377 *TF:* 800-328-2316 ■ *Web:* www.atsinc.com	Saint Cloud	MN	56301	320-255-7400	255-7494
Anson County School District 320 Camden Rd *Web:* www.ansonschools.org	Wadesboro	NC	28170	704-694-4417	694-7479
Apgar Brothers Trucking Co 200 Apgar Dr	Somerset	NJ	08873	732-356-3900	
Ards Trucking Company Inc 1702 N Gov Williams Hwy *TF:* 800-845-7462 ■ *Web:* www.ardtrucking.com	Darlington	SC	29540	843-393-5101	393-6080
ARG Trucking Corp 369 Bostwick Rd **Fax:* Hum Res ■ *TF:* 800-334-1314 ■ *Web:* www.wadhams.com	Phelps	NY	14532	315-789-8871	789-8879*
Arkansas Best Corp (ABC) 3801 Old Greenwood Rd PO Box 10048 *NASDAQ: ARCB* ■ *Web:* arcb.com/	Fort Smith	AR	72903	479-785-6000	785-8927
Arlo G. Lott Trucking Inc 257 S 100 E *TF:* 800-443-5688 ■ *Web:* arloglotttrucking.com	Jerome	ID	83338	208-324-5053	324-8668
Armellini Express Lines Inc 3446 SW Armellini Ave **Fax:* Cust Svc ■ *TF:* 800-327-7887 ■ *Web:* www.armellini.com	Palm City	FL	34990	772-287-0575	221-3284*
Arnold Transportation Services Inc 9523 Florida Mining Blvd *TF:* 800-846-4321 ■ *Web:* www.arnoldtrans.com	Jacksonville	FL	32257	972-986-3154	
Associated Petroleum Carriers Inc PO Box 2808 *TF Cust Svc:* 800-573-9301 ■ *Web:* www.apccorporate.com	Spartanburg	SC	29304	864-573-9301	573-9305
Atkinson Freight Lines Co 2950 State Rd	Bensalem	PA	19020	215-638-1130	
Autolog Corp 401 Commerce Rd *TF:* 800-526-6078 ■ *Web:* www.autolog.net	Linden	NJ	07036	800-526-6078	
Averitt Express Inc 1415 Neal St **Fax Area Code:* 931 ■ *TF:* 800-283-7488 ■ *Web:* www.averittexpress.com	Cookeville	TN	38501	800-283-7488	528-7804*
B-D-R Transport Inc 7994 US Rt 5 *TF:* 800-421-0126 ■ *Web:* www.bdrtransport.com	Westminster	VT	05158	802-463-0606	463-0608
Baggett Transportation Co 2 S 32nd St **Fax Area Code:* 205 ■ *TF:* 800-633-8982 ■ *Web:* www.baggetttransport.com	Birmingham	AL	35233	888-224-4388	320-2329*

	City	State	Zip	Phone	Fax
Bailey's Express Inc 61 Industrial Pk Rd	Middletown	CT	06457	860-632-0388	632-9089
TF: 800-523-3758 ■ *Web:* www.baileysxpress.com					
Barlow 1305 Grand Dd SE	Faucett	MO	64448	816-238-3373	238-1481
TF: 800-688-1202 ■ *Web:* www.barlowtruckline.com					
Bastian Trucking Inc 440 South Main	Aurora	UT	84620	435-529-7453	529-7137
TF: 800-452-5126 ■ *Web:* www.bastiantrucking.com					
Baylor Trucking Inc 9269 E State Rd 48	Milan	IN	47031	812-623-2020	
TF: 800-322-9567 ■ *Web:* www.baylortrucking.com					
Bayshore Transportation System Inc					
901 Dawson Dr	Newark	DE	19713	302-366-0220	366-8085
TF: 800-523-3319 ■ *Web:* www.bayshoreallied.com					
Beam Mack Sales & Service Inc					
2674 W Henrietta Rd	Rochester	NY	14623	585-424-4860	272-8851
TF: 877-650-8789 ■ *Web:* www.beammack.com					
Beaver Express Service LLC					
4310 Oklahoma Ave PO Box 1147	Woodward	OK	73802	580-256-6460	256-6239
TF: 800-593-2328 ■ *Web:* www.beaverexpress.com					
Bee Trucking Inc 9540 Ball St	San Antonio	TX	78217	210-646-7211	646-6218
Beelman Truck Co One Racehorse Dr	East Saint Louis	IL	62205	618-646-5300	646-5400
TF Sales: 800-541-5918 ■ *Web:* www.beelman.com					
Beeville Independent School District					
201 N St Marys St	Beeville	TX	78102	361-358-7111	358-7837
Web: www.beevilleisd.net					
Benton Express Inc					
1045 S River Industrial Blvd SE	Atlanta	GA	30315	404-267-2200	267-2201
TF: 888-423-6866					
Besl Transfer Co 5700 Este Ave	Cincinnati	OH	45232	513-242-3456	242-4013
TF: 800-456-2375 ■ *Web:* www.besl.com					
Bestway Enterprises Inc 3877 Luker Rd	Cortland	NY	13045	607-753-8261	753-9948
Web: www.bestwaylumber.com					
Big G Express Inc PO Box 1650	Shelbyville	TN	37162	800-684-9140	
TF: 800-955-9140 ■ *Web:* www.biggexpress.com					
Bilkays Express Co 2400 Bedle Place	Linden	NJ	07036	908-289-2400	289-6364
TF: 800-526-4006 ■ *Web:* Www.bilkays.com					
Bob's Transport & Storage Company Inc					
7980 Tar Bay Dr PO Box 1305	Jessup	MD	20794	410-799-0832	799-0951
Web: www.bobstransport.com					
Boyd Bros Transportation Inc 3275 Alabama 30	Clayton	AL	36016	334-775-1400	775-1433
TF: 800-700-2693 ■ *Web:* www.boydbros.com					
Britt Trucking & Construction Co					
1900 Seminole Rd	Lamesa	TX	79331	806-872-3353	
Brooke County Schools 1201 Pleasant Ave	Wellsburg	WV	26070	304-737-3481	737-3480
Web: www.edline.net/pages/brookecountyschools					
Brph Cos Inc					
5700 N Harbor City Blvd Ste 400	Melbourne	FL	32940	321-254-7666	259-4703
Web: www.brph.com					
Bryan Construction Co					
1007 N Earl Rudder Fwy PO Box 4087	Bryan	TX	77805	979-776-6000	776-6008
Web: www.bryan-construction-co.com					
Bryan Systems 14020 US 20A Hwy	Montpelier	OH	43543	800-745-2796	485-6653*
**Fax Area Code:* 419 ■ *TF:* 800-745-2796 ■ *Web:* www.bryansystems.com					
Buchanan Hauling & Rigging					
4625 Industrial Rd	Fort Wayne	IN	46825	260-471-1877	471-8878
TF: 888-544-4285 ■ *Web:* www.buchananhauling.com					
Buddy Moore Trucking Inc PO Box 10047	Birmingham	AL	35202	205-949-2260	327-5178
TF: 866-704-1598 ■ *Web:* www.buddymooretrucking.com					
Bulk Transit Corp 7177 Industrial Pkwy	Plain City	OH	43064	614-873-4632	873-3393
TF: 800-345-2855 ■ *Web:* www.bulktransit.com					
Bulkmatic Transport Co 2001 N Cline Ave	Griffith	IN	46319	800-535-8505	972-7655*
**Fax Area Code:* 219 ■ *TF:* 800-535-8505 ■ *Web:* www.bulkmatic.com					
Burnet Consolidated Independent School District					
208 E Brier Ln	Burnet	TX	78611	512-756-2124	756-7498
Web: www.burnet.txed.net					
Burns Motor Freight Inc 500 Seneca Trl N	Marlinton	WV	24954	304-799-6106	799-4257
TF: 800-598-5674 ■ *Web:* www.burnsmotorfreight.com					
Butler Transport Inc 347 N James St	Kansas City	KS	66118	913-321-0047	342-5725
TF: 800-345-8158 ■ *Web:* www.butlertransport.com					
Cal-ark Inc PO Box 990	Mabelvale	AR	72103	501-455-3399	455-5962
Web: www.calark.com					
Calex Express Inc 58 Pittston Ave	Pittston	PA	18640	570-603-0180	603-0940
TF: 800-292-2539 ■ *Web:* www.calexlogistics.com					
California Cartage Company Inc					
2931 Redondo Ave	Long Beach	CA	90806	888-537-1432	427-6855*
**Fax Area Code:* 562 ■ *TF:* 888-537-1432 ■ *Web:* www.calcartage.com					
Cardinal Transport Inc 7180 E Reed Rd	Coal City	IL	60416	815-634-4443	634-8267
TF: 800-435-9302 ■ *Web:* www.cardinaltransport.com					
Cargo Transporters Inc					
3390 N Oxford St PO Box 850	Claremont	NC	28610	828-459-3282	459-3292
Web: www.cargotransporters.com					
Carroll Fulmer Logistics Corp					
8340 American Way	Groveland	FL	34736	352-429-5000	429-0350*
**Fax:* Mktg ■ *Web:* www.cfulmer.com					
Cassens Transport Co 145 N Kansas St	Edwardsville	IL	62025	618-656-3006	692-7316
Web: www.cassens.com/transport					
Cedar Rapids Truck Ctr Inc					
9201 Sixth St SW	Cedar Rapids	IA	52404	319-848-6230	848-4302
TF: 866-602-1597 ■ *Web:* www.cedarrapidstruckcenter.com					
Celadon Trucking Services Inc					
9503 E 33rd St	Indianapolis	IN	46235	317-972-7000	890-9428
TF: 800-235-2366 ■ *Web:* www.celadontrucking.com					
Centra Financial Holdings Inc					
101 Venture Dra	Morgantown	WV	26508	304-598-2000	
Web: www.bankwithunited.com					
Central Freight Lines Inc PO Box 2638	Waco	TX	76702	800-782-5036	741-5370*
**Fax Area Code:* 254 ■ *TF:* 800-782-5036 ■ *Web:* www.centralfreight.com					
Central Petroleum Transport Inc (CPT)					
6115 Mitchell St	Sioux City	IA	51111	712-258-6357	258-8592
TF: 800-798-6357 ■ *Web:* www.cptrans.com					
Central Refrigerated Service Inc					
5175 W 2100 S	West Valley City	UT	84120	801-924-7000	924-7142
TF: 800-777-0069					
Chadderton Trucking Inc 40 Stewart Way	Sharon	PA	16146	724-981-5050	981-1615
TF: 800-327-6868 ■ *Web:* www.chaddertontrucking.com					
Charles G Lawson Trucking 7815 Mobile Hwy	Hope Hull	AL	36043	334-284-3220	281-4672
Chester Bross Construction Co 6739 CR 423	Palmyra	MO	63461	573-221-5958	221-1892
Web: www.cbrossgroup.com					
Christenson Transportation Inc					
2001 W Old Rt 66	Strafford	MO	65757	417-866-5993	447-0864
TF: 800-880-6711 ■ *Web:* www.christensontrans.com					
Clipper Americas Inc 2500 City W Blvd Ste 500	Houston	TX	77042	713-953-2200	953-2201
Web: www.clipper-group.com					
Coastal Transport Co Inc					
1603 Ackerman Rd	San Antonio	TX	78219	210-661-4287	661-9368*
**Fax:* Cust Svc ■ *TF:* 800-523-8612 ■ *Web:* coastaltransport.com/					
Coleman American Moving Services Inc					
PO Box 960	Midland City	AL	36350	866-929-1482	
TF: 877-693-7060 ■ *Web:* www.colemanallied.com					
Colonial Freight Systems Inc					
10924 McBride Ln	Knoxville	TN	37932	865-966-9711	966-3649
TF: 800-826-1402 ■ *Web:* www.cfsi.com					
Colonial Truck Co 1833 Commerce Rd	Richmond	VA	23224	804-232-3492	230-1932
TF: 800-234-8782 ■ *Web:* www.colonialtruck.com					
Combined Transport Inc					
5656 Crater Lake Ave	Central Point	OR	97502	541-734-7418	826-2001
TF: 800-547-2870 ■ *Web:* www.combinedtransport.com					
Comcar Industries Inc 502 E Bridgers Ave	Auburndale	FL	33823	863-967-1101	965-1023
TF Cust Svc: 800-524-1101 ■ *Web:* www.comcar.com					
Commercial Storage & Distribution Co					
432 Richmond Rd	Texarkana	TX	75503	903-794-2202	
Con-way Freight 2211 Old Earhart Rd	Ann Arbor	MI	48105	734-994-6600	
TF: 800-755-2728 ■ *Web:* www.con-way.com/en/aboutcts/ccx.html					
Con-way Inc 2855 Campus Dr Ste 300	San Mateo	CA	94403	650-378-5200	357-9160
NYSE: CNW ■ *TF:* 800-755-2728 ■ *Web:* www.con-way.com					
Con-Way Transportation Services Inc					
110 Parkland Plz	Ann Arbor	MI	48103	734-769-0203	214-5650
Web: www.con-way.com					
Container Port Group 1340 Depot St Ste 103	Cleveland	OH	44116	440-333-1330	333-1520
Web: www.containerport.com					
Cooke Trucking Co Inc					
1759 S Andy Griffith Pkwy	Mount Airy	NC	27030	336-786-5181	789-7132
TF: 800-888-9502 ■ *Web:* www.cooketrucking.com					
Corvallis School District 509 J					
1555 SW 35th St PO Box 3509J	Corvallis	OR	97333	541-757-5811	
Web: www.csd509j.net					
Covenant Transport Inc					
400 Birmingham Hwy	Chattanooga	TN	37419	423-821-1212	821-5442
NASDAQ: CVTI ■ *TF:* 800-334-9686 ■ *Web:* www.covenanttransport.com					
Cox Transportation Services Inc					
10448 Dow Gil Rd	Ashland	VA	23005	804-798-1477	798-1299
TF: 800-288-8118 ■ *Web:* www.truckingforamerica.com					
CR England & Sons Inc					
4701 West 2100 South	Salt Lake City	UT	84120	801-972-2712	
TF: 800-453-8826 ■ *Web:* www.crengland.com					
Craig Transportation Co 26699 Eckel Rd	Perrysburg	OH	43551	419-872-3333	874-9372
TF: 800-521-9119 ■ *Web:* www.craigtransportation.com					
Cresco Lines Inc 15220 S Halsted St	Harvey	IL	60426	708-339-1186	339-1186
TF: 800-323-4476 ■ *Web:* www.crescolines.com					
Crete Carrier Corp					
400 NW 56th St PO Box 81228	Lincoln	NE	68528	402-475-9521	479-2073*
**Fax:* Mktg ■ *TF Cust Svc:* 800-998-4095 ■ *Web:* www.cretecarrier.com					
Crook County School District 1					
108 N Fourth St PO Box 830	Sundance	WY	82729	307-283-2299	283-1810
Web: www.crook1.com					
Crossett Inc PO Box 946	Warren	PA	16365	800-876-2778	
TF General: 800-876-2778 ■ *Web:* www.crossettinc.com					
CRST International Inc					
3930 16th Ave SW PO Box 68	Cedar Rapids	IA	52406	800-736-2778	390-2649*
**Fax Area Code:* 319 ■ **Fax:* Sales ■ *TF:* 800-736-2778 ■ *Web:* www.crst.com					
Crysteel Truck Equipment Inc					
55248 Ember Rd	Lake Crystal	MN	56055	507-726-6041	726-2984
TF General: 800-722-0588 ■ *Web:* www.crysteeltruckequipment.com					
CTI Inc 11105 Norrth Casa Grande Hwy	Rillito	AZ	85654	520-624-2348	682-3509
TF: 800-362-4952 ■ *Web:* www.cti-az.com					
CTL Distribution Inc 4201 Bonnie Mine Rd	Mulberry	FL	33860	863-428-2373	428-1731
TF: 800-237-9088 ■ *Web:* www.drivectl.com					
Curtiss Arlin Trucking Inc					
582 SW First St Ste 1	Montevideo	MN	56265	320-269-5581	269-9417
D M Bowman Inc					
10226 Governor Ln Blvd Ste 4009	Williamsport	MD	21795	301-582-2784	223-5968
TF: 800-326-3274 ■ *Web:* www.dmbowman.com					
D&D Sexton Inc PO Box 156	Carthage	MO	64836	417-358-8727	358-5669
TF: 800-743-0265 ■ *Web:* www.ddsextoninc.com					
D. P. Curtis Trucking Inc					
1450 South Hwy 118	Richfield	UT	84701	800-257-9151	896-6553*
**Fax Area Code:* 435 ■ *TF:* 800-257-9151 ■ *Web:* www.dpcurtis.com					
Daggett Truck Line Inc 32717 County Rd 10	Frazee	MN	56544	218-334-3711	334-2566
TF: 800-262-9393 ■ *Web:* daggetttruck.com					
Dahlsten Truck Line Inc					
101 W Edgar PO Box 95	Clay Center	NE	68933	402-762-3511	762-3592
TF: 800-228-4313 ■ *Web:* www.dahlsten.com					
Daily Express Inc 1072 Harrisburg Pk	Carlisle	PA	17013	717-243-5757	240-2103
TF: 800-735-3136 ■ *Web:* www.dailyexp.com					
Dakota Line Inc PO Box 476	Vermillion	SD	57069	605-624-5228	624-5338
TF: 800-532-5682 ■ *Web:* www.dakotalines.com					
Dana Transport Inc 210 Essex Ave E	Avenel	NJ	07001	732-750-9100	636-7441
TF: 800-733-3262 ■ *Web:* www.danacompanies.com					
Davis Express Inc PO Box 1276	Starke	FL	32091	800-874-4270	
TF: 800-874-4270 ■ *Web:* www.davis-express.com					
Daylight Transport 1501 Hughes Way Ste 200	Long Beach	CA	90810	800-468-9999	
TF: 800-468-9999 ■ *Web:* dylt.com					
Deboer Transportation Inc PO Box 145	Blenker	WI	54415	715-652-2911	652-2830
Web: www.deboertrans.com					
Decker Truck Line Inc 4000 Fifth Ave S	Fort Dodge	IA	50501	515-576-4141	
TF: 800-247-2537 ■ *Web:* www.deckercompanies.com					

Company / Address	City	State	ZIP	Phone	Fax
Dejana Truck & Utility Equipment Company Inc 490 Pulaski Rd *TF:* 877-335-2621 ■ *Web:* www.dejana.com	Kings Park	NY	11754	631-544-9000	544-0942
Devine Intermodal 3870 Ch Dr *Web:* www.devineintermodal.com	West Sacramento	CA	95691	916-371-4430	371-0355
Diamond Transportation System Inc 5021 21st St *TF:* 800-927-5702 ■ *Web:* diamondtrans.net	Racine	WI	53406	262-554-5400	
Dick Lavy Trucking Inc 8848 State Rt 121 *TF:* 800-345-5289 ■ *Web:* www.dicklavytrucking.com	Bradford	OH	45308	937-448-2104	448-2312
Dilmar Oil Company Inc 1951 W Darlington St PO Box 5629 *TF:* 800-922-5823 ■ *Web:* www.dilmar.com	Florence	SC	29501	800-922-5823	
Dino's Trucking Inc 9615 Continental Indus Dr *TF:* 800-771-7805 ■ *Web:* www.dinoslogistics.com	Saint Louis	MO	63123	314-631-3001	638-3562
Dircks Moving Services Inc 4340 W Mohave St *TF:* 800-523-5038 ■ *Web:* www.dircks.com	Phoenix	AZ	85043	602-267-9401	267-8188
DistTech Inc 4366 Mt. Pleasant St NW *TF:* 800-969-5419 ■ *Web:* www.disttech.com	North Canton	OH	44720	800-969-5419	
Don Hummer Trucking Corp 1486 Hwy 6 NW PO Box 310 *TF:* 888-642-7249 ■ *Web:* www.donhummertrucking.com	Oxford	IA	52322	319-828-2000	828-2105
Dts Cos Inc 1640 Monad Rd *TF:* 877-896-3420 ■ *Web:* www.dtsb.com	Billings	MT	59101	406-245-4695	245-5404
Dun Transportation & Stringing Inc 304 Reynolds Ln *Web:* www.duntrans.com	Sherman	TX	75092	903-891-9660	891-9660
Duncan & Son Lines Inc 23860 W US Hwy 85 *TF:* 800-528-4283 ■ *Web:* www.duncanandson.com	Buckeye	AZ	85326	623-386-4511	386-3656
Duncan Machinery Movers Inc 2004 Duncan Machinery Dr *Web:* www.dmmlex.com	Lexington	KY	40504	859-233-7333	233-7365
Eagle Express Lines Inc 715 W 172nd St PO Box 348 *TF:* 888-868-2501 ■ *Web:* www.eagleexpresslines.com	South Holland	IL	60473	708-333-8400	333-4747
Eagle Transport Corp 300 S Wesleyan Blvd Ste 202 *TF:* 800-776-9937 ■ *Web:* www.eagletransportcorp.com	Rocky Mount	NC	27804	252-937-2464	937-2198
Earl L Henderson Trucking Inc 206 W Main St *TF:* 800-447-8084 ■ *Web:* www.hendersontrucking.com	Salem	IL	62881	618-548-4667	548-6204
Epes Carriers Inc 3400 Edgefield Ct *TF:* 800-869-3737 ■ *Web:* www.epestransport.com	Greensboro	NC	27409	336-668-3358	668-7008
Equity Transportation Company Inc 3685 Dykstra Dr NW *Web:* equityinc.com	Grand Rapids	MI	49544	616-785-3800	785-0999
Erickson Transport Corp 2255 N Packer Rd *TF:* 800-641-4595 ■ *Web:* bulktransporter.com	Springfield	MO	65803	417-862-6741	862-0561
Essex County Public Schools 109 Cross St PO Box 756 *Web:* www.essex.k12.va.us	Tappahannock	VA	22560	804-443-4366	443-4498
Estes Express Lines Inc 3901 W Broad St PO Box 25612 **Fax:* Sales ■ *Web:* www.estes-express.com	Richmond	VA	23230	804-353-1900	353-8001*
Evans Dedicated Systems Inc PO Box 9 *TF:* 800-427-6387 ■ *Web:* www.evansdedicated.com	Maywood	CA	90270	323-725-2928	726-0796
EW Wylie Corp 1520 Second Ave NW *TF Cust Svc:* 800-437-4132 ■ *Web:* www.wylietrucking.com	West Fargo	ND	58078	701-282-5550	281-0415
Falcon Express Inc 2250 E Church St PO Box 4897 *TF:* 800-544-6566 ■ *Web:* www.falconexp.com	Philadelphia	PA	19124	215-992-3140	992-3150
Fauquier County Public Schools 320 Hospital Dr Ste 40 *Web:* www.schoolcenter.fcps1.org	Warrenton	VA	20186	540-422-7017	
FedEx Freight East 942 S Shady Grove Rd *Web:* www.fedex.com	Memphis	TN	38120	901-818-7500	
Fenix Constructors Inc 215 Drew St SW *Web:* www.fenixci.com	Ardmore	OK	73401	580-223-4313	223-4315
FFE Transportation Inc 1145 Empire Central Pl *TF:* 800-569-9200 ■ *Web:* www.ffeinc.com	Dallas	TX	75247	214-630-8090	819-5625
First Class Services Inc 9355 US Hwy 60 E *TF General:* 800-467-8684 ■ *Web:* www.firstclassservices.com	Lewisport	KY	42351	270-295-3746	
Firstexpress Inc 1135 Freightliner Dr **Fax Area Code:* 615 ■ *TF:* 800-848-9203 ■ *Web:* firstexpress.com/	Nashville	TN	37210	800-848-9203	244-1448*
Five Star Trucking Inc 4380 Glenbrook Rd *TF:* 800-321-3658 ■ *Web:* www.fivestartrucking.com	Willoughby	OH	44094	440-953-9300	953-1863
Fort Edward Express Company Inc 1402 Rt 9 *TF:* 800-342-1233 ■ *Web:* bulktransporter.com	Fort Edward	NY	12828	518-792-6571	
Forward Air Corp 430 Airport Rd PO Box 1058 *NASDAQ: FWRD* ■ *TF:* 800-726-6654 ■ *Web:* www.forwardair.com	Greeneville	TN	37744	423-636-7100	636-7221
Frank C. Alegre Trucking Inc PO Box 1508 *TF:* 800-769-2440 ■ *Web:* www.alegretrucking.com	Lodi	CA	95241	209-334-2112	367-0572
Fry-Wagner Moving & Storage Co 3700 Rider Trl S *TF:* 800-899-4035 ■ *Web:* www.fry-wagner.com	Earth City	MO	63045	314-291-4100	291-1263
Gabler Trucking Inc 5195 Technology Ave *Web:* www.hcgabler.com	Chambersburg	PA	17201	717-261-1492	709-0017
Godfrey Trucking Inc 6173 West 2100 South *TF:* 800-444-7669 ■ *Web:* www.godfreytrucking.com	West Valley City	UT	84128	801-972-0660	972-0709
Gordon Trucking Inc 151 Stewart Rd SW *TF:* 800-426-8486 ■ *Web:* www.gordontrucking.com	Pacific	WA	98047	253-863-7777	863-5328
Grammer Industries Inc 18375 E 345 S *TF:* 800-333-7410 ■ *Web:* www.grammerindustries.com	Grammer	IN	47236	812-579-5655	579-5643
Greatwide Logistics Services LLC 12404 Pk Central Dr Ste 300S *Web:* www.greatwide.com	Dallas	TX	75251	972-228-7300	228-7328
Green Transfer & Storage Co 10099 N Portland Rd *Web:* greentransfer.com	Portland	OR	97203	503-286-0673	286-0676
Groendyke Transport Inc 2510 Rock Island Blvd *TF:* 800-843-2103 ■ *Web:* www.groendyke.com	Enid	OK	73701	580-234-4663	234-1216
Gully Transportation Inc 3820 Wismann Ln *Web:* www.gullyicx.com	Quincy	IL	62305	217-224-0770	224-9885
Guy M Turner Inc 4514 S Holden Rd PO Box 7776 *TF:* 800-432-4859 ■ *Web:* www.guymturner.com	Greensboro	NC	27406	336-294-4660	294-6668
H & M International Transportation Inc 485B Rt 1 S *TF:* 800-446-4685 ■ *Web:* www.hmit.net	Iselin	NJ	08830	732-510-4640	510-4697
H & W Trucking Company Inc 1772 N Andy Griffith Pkwy PO Box 1545 *TF:* 800-334-9181 ■ *Web:* www.hwtrucking.com	Mount Airy	NC	27030	336-789-2188	789-7973
H O Wolding Inc PO Box 217 *TF:* 800-950-0054 ■ *Web:* www.howolding.com	Amherst	WI	54406	715-824-5513	824-5018
H. F. Campbell & Son PO Box 260 *TF:* 800-233-7112 ■ *Web:* www.camel-express.com	Millerstown	PA	17062	717-589-3194	589-7356
Hallamore Motor Transportation Inc 795 Plymouth St **Fax Area Code:* 920 ■ *TF:* 800-242-1300 ■ *Web:* www.hallamore.com	Holbrook	MA	02343	781-767-2000	683-6277*
Harbor Express Inc 501 Quay Ave *Web:* harbor-express.com	Wilmington	CA	90744	310-513-6478	835-3794
Harrisonburg City Public Schools (HCPS) 317 S Main St *Web:* www.harrisonburg.k12.va.us	Harrisonburg	VA	22801	540-434-9916	434-5196
Hazen Transport Inc 27050 Wick Rd **Fax Area Code:* 734 ■ *TF:* 800-251-2120 ■ *Web:* www.hazentransport.com	Taylor	MI	48180	313-292-2120	946-4452*
Heartland Express Inc 901 N Kansas Ave *NASDAQ: HTLD* ■ **Fax Area Code:* 319 ■ *TF:* 800-654-1175 ■ *Web:* www.heartlandexpress.com	North Liberty	IA	52317	800-654-1175	626-3311*
High Country Transportation Inc PO Box 700 *TF:* 800-635-7687 ■ *Web:* www.highcountrytrans.com	Cortez	CO	81321	800-635-7687	
Highway Transport Logistics Inc (HTL) 6420 Baum Dr *Web:* www.hytt.com	Knoxville	TN	37919	865-584-8631	
Hirschbach Motor Lines Inc 18355 US Hwy 20 **Fax Area Code:* 800 ■ *TF:* 800-554-2969 ■ *Web:* www.hirschbach.com	East Dubuque	IL	61025	402-494-5000	772-2500*
Hodges Trucking Co LLC 4050 W I-40 **Fax Area Code:* 817 ■ *TF:* 888-829-1370 ■ *Web:* www.hodgestruckingcompany.com	Oklahoma City	OK	73108	405-947-7764	783-3248*
Holman Transportation Services Inc 1010 Holman Ct *TF:* 800-375-2416 ■ *Web:* holmantransport.com	Caldwell	ID	83605	208-454-0779	454-2226
Hot-Line Freight System Inc PO Box 205 *TF:* 800-468-4686 ■ *Web:* www.hotlinefreight.com	West Salem	WI	54669	608-486-1600	486-1601
Houff Transfer Inc 46 Houff Rd *TF:* 800-476-4683 ■ *Web:* www.houff.com	Weyers Cave	VA	24486	540-234-9233	234-9011
Howard F Baer Inc 1301 Foster Ave *TF:* 800-447-7430 ■ *Web:* hbitransport.com	Nashville	TN	37210	615-255-7351	726-1529
Howard Sheppard Inc PO Box 797 *Web:* www.howardsheppard.com	Sandersville	GA	31082	478-552-5127	552-6973
Howell's Motor Freight Inc PO Box 12308 *TF:* 800-444-0585 ■ *Web:* www.howellsmotor.com	Roanoke	VA	24024	540-966-3200	966-3202
Hribar Trucking Inc 1521 Waukesha Rd *Web:* hribarlogistics.com	Caledonia	WI	53108	262-835-4401	
HVH Transportation Inc 181 E 56th Ave Ste 200 *TF:* 800-525-4844 ■ *Web:* www.hvhtransportation.com	Denver	CO	80216	303-292-3656	292-9713
Indian River Transport Co 2580 Executive Rd *TF:* 800-877-2430 ■ *Web:* www.indianrivertransport.com	Winter Haven	FL	33884	863-324-2430	326-9702
Interstate Distributor Co 11707 21st Ave S **Fax Area Code:* 253 ■ *TF:* 800-426-8560 ■ *Web:* www.intd.com	Tacoma	WA	98444	800-426-8560	538-4430*
Irvin Dick Inc 475 Wilson Ave	Shelby	MT	59474	406-434-5862	
J & J Motor Service Inc 2338 S Indiana Ave *Web:* jjexhibitors.com	Chicago	IL	60616	312-225-3323	225-9873
J A T of Fort Wayne Inc 5031 Industrial Rd *TF:* 800-522-3306 ■ *Web:* www.jatoffortwayne.com	Fort Wayne	IN	46825	260-482-8447	482-9990
J M Turner & Co Inc 130 Church Ave PO Box 2140 *Web:* www.jmturner.com	Roanoke	VA	24011	540-343-6749	343-6031
J P Noonan Transportation Inc 415 W St *TF:* 800-922-8026 ■ *Web:* www.jpnoonan.com	West Bridgewater	MA	02379	508-583-2880	587-0317
J R C Transportation Inc 47 Maple Ave PO Box 366 *TF General:* 800-346-3250 ■ *Web:* www.jrctransportation.com	Thomaston	CT	06787	860-283-0207	742-9379
J-Mar Enterprises Inc PO Box 4143 *TF:* 800-446-8283 ■ *Web:* www.j-mar-enterprises.com	Bismarck	ND	58502	701-222-4518	255-7587
Jack B Kelley Inc 801 S Fillmore St Ste 505 *TF:* 800-225-5525 ■ *Web:* www.jackbkelley.com	Amarillo	TX	79101	806-353-3553	356-9327
Jack Cooper Transport Co Inc 1100 Walnut St Ste 2400 *TF:* 866-449-6388 ■ *Web:* www.jackcooper.com	Kansas City	MO	64106	816-983-4000	983-5000
Jack Gray Transport Inc 4600 E 15th Ave	Gary	IN	46403	219-938-7020	938-0127
Jaro Transportation Services Inc 975 Post Rd PO Box 1890 *TF:* 800-451-3447 ■ *Web:* www.jarotrans.com	Warren	OH	44483	330-393-5659	393-5906
Jerry Lipps Inc 3888 Nash Rd PO Box F *TF:* 800-325-3331 ■ *Web:* www.jerrylippsinc.com	Cape Girardeau	MO	63702	573-335-8204	335-4483
Jet Star Inc 10825 Andrade Dr *TF:* 800-969-4222 ■ *Web:* www.jetstarinc.com	Zionsville	IN	46077	317-873-4222	873-4361
JH Walker Trucking Company Inc 152 N Hollywood Rd *TF:* 800-535-5992 ■ *Web:* www.jhwalkertrucking.com	Houma	LA	70364	985-868-8330	873-5210
Jim Palmer Trucking Inc 9730 Derby Dr *TF:* 888-698-3422 ■ *Web:* www.jimpalmertrucking.com	Missoula	MT	59801	406-721-5151	829-6271
JNJ Express Inc 3935 Old Getwell Rd PO Box 30983 *TF:* 888-383-7157 ■ *Web:* www.jnjexpress.com	Memphis	TN	38130	901-362-3444	362-2331
Johnson Carlier Inc 738 S 52nd St **Fax Area Code:* 480 ■ *Web:* www.johnsoncarlier.com	Tempe	AZ	85281	602-275-2222	921-9255*

Company	City	State	Zip	Phone	Fax
Jones Motor Company Inc 900 W Bridge St PO Box 137	Spring City	PA	19475	610-948-7900	948-5660
TF: 800-825-6637 ■ *Web:* www.jonesmotor.com					
KAG West 4076 Seaport Blvd	West Sacramento	CA	95691	916-371-8241	372-1760
TF: 800-547-1587 ■ *Web:* www.thekag.com					
Kahului Trucking & Storage Inc 140 Hobron Ave	Kahului	HI	96732	808-877-5001	877-0572
Web: kahuluitrucking.com					
Kaplan Trucking Co 6600 Bessemer Ave	Cleveland	OH	44127	216-341-3322	341-3348
Web: www.kaplantrucking.com					
Kauai Commercial Company Inc 1811 Leleiona St	Lihue	HI	96766	808-245-1985	245-2079
Web: kauaicommercialcompany.com					
Keim T S Inc 1249 N Ninth St PO Box 226	Sabetha	KS	66534	800-255-2450	942-4148*
**Fax Area Code:* 423 ■ *TF:* 800-255-2450 ■ *Web:* keimts.com					
Keith Titus Corp PO Box 920	Weedsport	NY	13166	315-834-6681	834-9687
TF: 800-233-2126 ■ *Web:* www.pagetrucking.com					
Kenan Advantage Group Inc (KAG) 4366 Mt Pleasant St NW	North Canton	OH	44720	330-491-0474	409-2786
TF: 800-969-5419 ■ *Web:* www.thekag.com					
Kenan Transport Co 100 Europa Ctr Ste 320	Chapel Hill	NC	27517	919-967-8221	929-5295
TF: 866-821-3444 ■ *Web:* thekag.com					
Kenworth Sales Co 2125 Constitution Blvd	West Valley City	UT	84119	801-487-4161	467-3820
TF General: 800-222-7831 ■ *Web:* www.kenworthsalesco.com					
Key Energy 2210 W Broadway	Sweetwater	TX	79556	325-236-6611	236-6106
Web: www.keyenergy.com					
Kildeer Countryside Community Consolidated School District 96 1050 Ivy Hall Ln	Buffalo Grove	IL	60089	847-459-4260	459-2344
Web: www.kcsd96.org					
KLLM Inc 135 Riverview Dr	Richland	MS	39218	800-925-1000	
TF: 800-925-5556 ■ *Web:* www.kllm.com					
Knight Transportation Inc 5601 W Buckeye Rd	Phoenix	AZ	85043	602-269-2000	269-8409
NYSE: KNX ■ *TF:* 800-489-2000 ■ *Web:* www.knighttrans.com					
Kruepke Trucking Inc 2881 Hwy P	Jackson	WI	53037	262-677-3155	677-3206
TF Cust Svc: 800-798-5000 ■ *Web:* kruepketrucking.com					
Kuntzman Trucking Inc 13515 Oyster Rd	Alliance	OH	44601	330-821-9160	821-9163
TF: 800-362-9779 ■ *Web:* www.kmantrucking.com					
La Rosa Del Monte Express Inc 1133-35 Tiffany St	Bronx	NY	10459	718-991-3300	893-1948
TF: 800-452-7672 ■ *Web:* www.larosadelmonte.com					
Land Span Inc 1120 Griffin Rd	Lakeland	FL	33805	863-686-6872	683-4677
TF: 800-248-4847 ■ *Web:* www.landspan.com					
Landair Corp 1110 Myers St	Greeneville	TN	37743	888-526-3247	
TF: 888-526-3247 ■ *Web:* www.landair.com					
Landmark Construction Group Inc 300 NW 61st St Ste 100	Oklahoma City	OK	73118	405-843-8041	
Web: landmarkokc.com					
Landmark International Trucks Inc 4550 Rutledge Pk	Knoxville	TN	37914	865-637-4881	522-0865
TF: 800-968-9999 ■ *Web:* www.landmarktrucks.com					
Landstar Express America Inc 13410 Sutton Pk Dr S	Jacksonville	FL	32224	904-398-9400	398-9400*
**Fax:* Hum Res ■ *TF:* 800-872-9400 ■ *Web:* www.Landstar.com					
Landstar Gemini Inc 13410 Sutton Pk Dr S	Jacksonville	FL	32224	262-250-7582	
TF: 800-872-9400 ■ *Web:* landstar.com					
Landstar Inway Inc 1000 Simpson Rd	Rockford	IL	61102	815-972-5000	*
**Fax:* Hum Res ■ *TF:* 800-435-7352 ■ *Web:* landstar.com					
Landstar Ligon Inc 13410 Sutton Pk Dr S	Jacksonville	FL	32224	262-250-7582	
Web: www.landstar.com					
Landstar Ranger Inc 13410 Sutton Pk Dr S	Jacksonville	FL	32224	904-398-9400	
TF: 800-872-9400 ■ *Web:* www.landstar.com					
Landstar System Inc 13410 Sutton Pk Dr S	Jacksonville	FL	32224	904-398-9400	390-1437
NASDAQ: LSTR ■ *TF:* 800-872-9400 ■ *Web:* www.landstar.com					
Lanter Delivery Systems Inc One Caine Dr	Madison	IL	62060	618-452-5300	452-5931
Web: www.lanterdeliverysystems.com					
Lawrence Companies (LTS) 872 Lee Hwy PO Box 7667	Roanoke	VA	24019	540-966-4000	966-4555
TF: 800-336-9626 ■ *Web:* www.lawrencetransportation.com					
LCT Transportation Services 26444 County Rd 33	Okahumpka	FL	34762	352-326-8900	365-1181
Web: citysearch.com/guide/orlando-fl-metro					
Liberty Moving & Storage Inc 350 Moreland Rd	Commack	NY	11725	631-234-3000	234-3639
Web: www.libertymoving.com					
Lightning Transportation Inc 16820 Blake Rd	Hagerstown	MD	21740	301-582-5700	582-5898
TF: 800-233-0624 ■ *Web:* www.lightningtrans.com					
Linden Bulk Transportation Company Inc 4200 Tremley Pt Rd	Linden	NJ	07036	908-862-3883	
Web: www.lindenbulk.com					
Linden Warehouse & Distribution Co Inc 1300 Lower Rd	Linden	NJ	07036	908-862-1400	862-7539
TF: 800-333-2855 ■ *Web:* www.lindencompanies.com					
Liquid Transport Corp 8470 Allison Pt Blvd Ste 400	Indianapolis	IN	46250	317-841-4200	841-8259
TF: 800-942-3175 ■ *Web:* www.liquidtransport.com					
Lisa Motor Lines 1145 Empire Central Pl PO Box 655888	Dallas	TX	75247	214-630-8090	
TF: 800-569-9200 ■ *Web:* www.ffeinc.com					
LL Smith Trucking Inc 711 Rail Rd	Riverton	WY	82501	307-856-2491	
Lockwood Bros Inc 220 Salters Creek Rd	Hampton	VA	23661	757-722-1946	
Web: www.lockwoodbros.com					
Lynden Transport Inc 3027 Rampart Dr	Anchorage	AK	99501	800-327-9390	257-5155*
**Fax Area Code:* 907 ■ *TF:* 800-327-9390 ■ *Web:* www.lynden.com					
Mail Contractors of America 3809 Roundtop Dr N	Little Rock	AR	72212	501-280-0500	280-0111
Market Transport Ltd 110 N Marine Dr	Portland	OR	97217	503-283-2405	289-3567
TF: 800-547-0781 ■ *Web:* markettransport.com					
Marten Transport Ltd 129 Marten St	Mondovi	WI	54755	715-926-4216	926-5609
NASDAQ: MRTN ■ *TF:* 800-395-3000 ■ *Web:* www.marten.com					
Martin Enterprises Inc 4315 Meyer Rd	Fort Wayne	IN	46806	260-447-5591	447-4026
TF: 800-348-4759 ■ *Web:* truckdriver.com					
Martin Trucking Inc 1015 W City Limits St	Hugoton	KS	67951	620-544-4920	
Mason City School District 211 NE St	Mason	OH	45040	513-398-0474	
Web: www.masonohioschools.com					
Matheson Trucking Inc 9785 Goethe Rd	Sacramento	CA	95827	916-685-2330	685-8875*
**Fax Area Code:* 919 ■ *TF:* 800-455-7678 ■ *Web:* www.mathesoninc.com					
Maverick USA Inc 13301 Valentine Rd	North Little Rock	AR	72117	501-955-1255	955-4670
TF: 800-289-6600 ■ *Web:* www.maverickusa.com					
Mawson & Mawson Inc 1800 Old Lincoln Hwy PO Box 248	Langhorne	PA	19047	215-750-1100	750-0396
TF: 800-262-9766 ■ *Web:* www.mawsonandmawson.com					
May Trucking Co 4185 Brooklake Rd PO Box 9039	Salem	OR	97305	800-547-9169	390-8836*
**Fax Area Code:* 503 ■ *TF:* 800-547-9169 ■ *Web:* www.maytrucking.com					
Mayfield Transfer Company Inc 3200 W Lake St	Melrose Park	IL	60160	708-681-4440	681-4483
TF: 800-222-2959 ■ *Web:* www.mfld.net					
McC Construction Corp 5990 Greenwood Plaza Blvd Ste 205	Greenwood	CO	80111	303-741-0404	741-0505
Web: catamountinc.com/mcc_construction					
McKenzie Tank Lines Inc 975 Appleyard Dr	Tallahassee	FL	32304	850-576-1221	574-2351
TF: 800-828-6495 ■ *Web:* www.mckenzietank.com					
MCT Transportation LLC 1600 E Benson Rd	Sioux Falls	SD	57104	605-339-8400	339-8407
TF Cust Svc: 800-843-9904 ■ *Web:* mcttrans.com/					
Melloul-Blamey Construction Ltd 55 Commerce Ctr	Greenville	SC	29615	864-627-0302	627-0804
Web: www.melloul.com					
Melton Truck Lines Inc 808 N 161 E Ave	Tulsa	OK	74116	918-234-8000	270-9401
TF General: 800-545-6651 ■ *Web:* www.meltontruck.com					
Mercer County State Bancorp Inc 3279 S Main St	Sandy Lake	PA	16145	724-376-7015	
Web: www.mcsbank.com					
Mercer Transportation Co 1128 W Main St PO Box 35610	Louisville	KY	40232	502-584-2301	
TF: 800-626-5375 ■ *Web:* www.mercer-trans.com					
Mergenthaler Transfer & Storage 1414 N Montana Ave	Helena	MT	59601	406-442-9470	442-4340
TF General: 800-826-5463 ■ *Web:* www.mergenthaler.net					
Mid Seven Transportation Co 2323 Delaware Ave	Des Moines	IA	50317	515-266-5181	266-1457
TF: 800-247-7448 ■ *Web:* www.mid7.com					
Middlesboro Independent School District 220 N 20th St PO Box 959	Middlesboro	KY	40965	606-242-8800	242-8805
Web: mboro.k12.ky.us					
Midwest Motor Express Inc 5015 E Main Ave	Bismarck	ND	58502	701-223-1880	224-1405
TF: 800-741-4097 ■ *Web:* www.mmeinc.com					
Milan Express Company Inc 1091 Kefauver Dr PO Box 699	Milan	TN	38358	731-686-7428	686-8829
TF: 800-231-7303 ■ *Web:* www.milanexpress.com					
Miller Transporters Inc 5500 Hwy 80 W	Jackson	MS	39209	601-922-8331	923-2535
TF Cust Svc: 800-645-5378 ■ *Web:* www.millert.com					
Milton Transportation Inc 5505 State Rt 405 PO Box 355	Milton	PA	17847	570-742-8774	742-2856
TF: 800-776-1150 ■ *Web:* www.miltontrans.com					
Minuteman Trucks Inc 2181 Providence Hwy	Walpole	MA	02081	508-668-3112	668-8466
TF: 800-231-8458 ■ *Web:* www.minutemantrucks.com					
Morris School District 54 54 White Oak Dr	Morris	IL	60450	815-942-0056	942-0240
Web: www.morris54.org					
Morristown Drivers Service Inc PO Box 2158	Morristown	TN	37816	423-581-6048	581-9696
Web: www.mdstrucking.com					
Murrows Transfer Inc PO Box 4095	High Point	NC	27263	336-475-6101	475-1240
TF Cust Svc: 800-669-2928 ■ *Web:* www.murrows.com					
National Carriers Inc 1501 E Eigth St	Liberal	KS	67901	620-624-1621	
TF: 800-835-9180 ■ *Web:* www.nationalcarriers.com					
National Highway Express Co 971 Old Henderson St PO Box 20262	Columbus	OH	43220	614-459-4900	
TF: 800-837-5700 ■ *Web:* www.nationalhighwayexpress.com					
Nationwide Truck Brokers Inc (NTB) 4203 Roger B Chaffee Memorial Blvd SE Ste 2	Grand Rapids	MI	49548	616-878-5554	878-5569
TF: 800-446-0682 ■ *Web:* www.ntbtrk.com					
Navajo Express Inc 1400 W 64 Ave	Denver	CO	80221	303-287-3800	286-9661*
**Fax:* Sales ■ *TF:* 800-525-1969 ■ *Web:* www.navajo.com					
NE Finch Co 1925 S Darst St PO Box 5187	Peoria	IL	61607	309-671-1433	671-1449
Web: nefinch.com					
New England Motor Freight Inc 1-71 N Ave E	Elizabeth	NJ	07201	908-965-0100	965-0795
New Penn Motor Express Inc 625 S Fifth Ave	Lebanon	PA	17042	717-274-2521	274-5593
TF Cust Svc: 800-285-5000 ■ *Web:* www.newpenn.com					
Newark School District 100 E Miller St 4th Fl	Newark	NY	14513	315-332-3230	332-3517
TF: 877-789-2613 ■ *Web:* www.newarkcsd.org					
Newton Independent School District 414 Main St	Newton	TX	75966	409-379-8137	379-2189
Web: www.newtonisd.net					
Nick Strimbu Inc 3500 PkwyRd	Brookfield	OH	44403	330-448-4046	448-4106
TF: 800-446-8785 ■ *Web:* www.nickstrimbu.com					
North Park Transportation Co 5150 Columbine St	Denver	CO	80216	303-295-0300	295-6244
Web: www.nopk.com					
North Shore Central Illinois Freight Co 5101 S Lawndale Ave	Summit	IL	60501	708-496-8222	496-8449
Web: www.northshorelogistics.net					
Northland Trucking Inc 1515 S 22nd Ave	Phoenix	AZ	85009	602-254-0007	254-0455
TF: 800-214-5564 ■ *Web:* www.northlandtrucking.com					
Nussbaum Trucking Inc 19336 N 1425 East Rd	Normal	IL	61748	309-452-4426	452-4431
TF: 800-322-7305 ■ *Web:* www.nussbaum.com					
O & S Trucking Inc 3769 E Evergreen St	Springfield	MO	65803	417-864-4780	
TF: 800-509-2021 ■ *Web:* www.oandstrucking.com					
Old Dominion Freight Line Inc 500 Old Dominion Way	Thomasville	NC	27360	336-889-5000	802-5229
NASDAQ: ODFL ■ *TF:* 800-432-6335 ■ *Web:* www.odfl.com					
Oliver Construction Co 1770 Executive Dr PO Box 65	Oconomowoc	WI	53066	262-567-6677	567-4676
Web: www.oliverconstruction.com					

Company	City	State	ZIP	Phone	Fax
Oliver Trucking Corp 1101 Harding Ct *TF:* 888-561-4449 ■ *Web:* www.oltg.com	Indianapolis	IN	46217	317-787-1101	787-1102
Online Transport System Inc 6311 W Stoner Dr *TF:* 866-543-1235 ■ *Web:* www.onlinetransport.com	Greenfield	IN	46140	317-894-2159	894-2160
Orcutt Union School District 500 Dyer St *Web:* www.orcutt-schools.net	Orcutt	CA	93455	805-938-8900	938-8919
Ormsby Trucking Inc 888 W Railroad St PO Box 67 *Web:* www.ormtrk.com	Uniondale	IN	46791	260-543-2233	543-2842
Osborn Transportation Inc 1245 West Grand Ave *TF:* 866-215-3659 ■ *Web:* www.osborntransportation.com	Rainbow City	AL	35902	256-442-2514	413-0002
Otto Trucking Inc 4220 E McDowell Ste 108 *Web:* www.ottotrucking.com	Mesa	AZ	85215	480-641-3500	641-3550
Overland Express Co 5539 Harvey Wilson PO Box 262322 *TF:* 800-929-7402 ■ *Web:* www.overlandexp.com	Houston	TX	77207	713-672-6161	672-5040
Ozark Motor Lines Inc 3934 Homewood Rd *TF:* 800-264-4100 ■ *Web:* www.ozark.com	Memphis	TN	38118	901-251-9711	375-8661
P J Hoerr Inc 107 Commerce Pl *Web:* www.pjhoerr.com	Peoria	IL	61604	309-688-9567	688-9556
Palmetto State Transportation Company Inc 1050 Pk W Blvd *TF:* 800-269-0175 ■ *Web:* www.palmettostatetrans.com	Greenville	SC	29611	864-672-3800	672-3810
PAM Transportation Services Inc 297 W Henri De Tonti Blvd *NASDAQ: PTSI* ■ *TF:* 800-879-7261 ■ *Web:* www.pamt.com	Tontitown	AR	72770	479-361-9111	361-5338
Pan Western Corp 4910 Donovan Way Ste A *TF:* 800-443-1560 ■ *Web:* www.panwestern.com	North Las Vegas	NV	89081	702-632-2931	632-2956
Paper Transport Inc 2701 Executive Dr **Fax Area Code:* 920 ■ *TF:* 800-317-3650 ■ *Web:* www.papertransport.com	Green Bay	WI	54304	800-317-3650	497-6230*
Patriot Transportation Holding Inc 501 Riverside Ave Ste 500 *NASDAQ: PATI* ■ *TF:* 877-704-1776 ■ *Web:* www.patriottrans.com	Jacksonville	FL	32202	904-396-5733	
Peet Frate Line Inc 650 S Eastwood Dr PO Box 1129 *TF:* 800-435-6909 ■ *Web:* www.peetfrateline.com	Woodstock	IL	60098	815-338-5500	338-1052
Penn's Best Inc PO Box 128 **Fax Area Code:* 570 ■ *TF:* 800-852-3243 ■ *Web:* www.pennsbest.net	Meshoppen	PA	18630	800-852-3243	833-5902*
Peoples Bancshares-Pnt Coupee 805 Hospital Rd PO Box 747 *Web:* www.thefriendlybank.com	New Roads	LA	70760	225-638-3713	638-6772
Phoenix Transportation Services LLC 335 E Yusen Dr *TF:* 800-860-0889 ■ *Web:* www.phoenix-transportation.net	Georgetown	KY	40324	502-863-0108	863-0029
Pitt Ohio Express 15 27th St *TF Cust Svc:* 800-366-7488 ■ *Web:* works.pittohio.com	Pittsburgh	PA	15222	412-232-3015	232-0944
Pleasant Trucking Inc 2250 Industrial Dr PO Box 778 **Fax Area Code:* 724 ■ *TF:* 800-245-2402 ■ *Web:* www.pleasanttrucking.com	Connellsville	PA	15425	800-245-2402	628-5868*
Pozas Bros Trucking Company Inc 8130 Enterprise Dr *TF:* 800-874-8383 ■ *Web:* pozasbros.com	Newark	CA	94560	510-742-9939	742-9979
Predator Trucking Co 3181 Trumbull Ave *TF:* 888-773-3875 ■ *Web:* www.predatortrucking.com	McDonald	OH	44437	888-773-3875	
Prestera Trucking 19129 US Rt 52 *TF:* 855-761-7943 ■ *Web:* www.prestera.com	South Point	OH	45680	740-894-4770	
Pride Transport Inc 5499 W 2455 S *TF:* 800-877-1320 ■ *Web:* pridetransport.com	Salt Lake City	UT	84120	801-972-8890	972-1450
Prime Inc PO Box 4208 **Fax:* Sales ■ *TF Cust Svc:* 800-848-4560 ■ *Web:* w3.primeinc.com	Springfield	MO	65808	417-866-0001	521-6850*
Pritchett Trucking Inc 1050 SE Sixth St PO Box 311 *TF:* 800-486-7504 ■ *Web:* www.pritchetttrucking.com	Lake Butler	FL	32054	386-496-2630	496-2883
Q Carriers Inc 1415 Maras St *TF:* 800-800-4755 ■ *Web:* www.qcarriers.com	Shakopee	MN	55379	952-445-8718	445-8794
Quality Distribution Inc 4041 Pk Oaks Blvd Ste 200 *NASDAQ: QLTY* ■ *TF:* 800-282-2031 ■ *Web:* www.qualitydistribution.com	Tampa	FL	33610	800-282-2031	
Queensboro Co 113 E Broad St PO Box 467 *TF:* 800-236-2442 ■ *Web:* www.qnbtrust.com	Louisville	GA	30434	478-625-2000	625-2008
R & R Trucking Inc 302 Thunder Rd PO Box 545 *TF:* 800-625-6885 ■ *Web:* www.randrtruck.com	Duenweg	MO	64841	417-623-6885	623-6479
Ralph Moyle Inc (RMI) 55475 N Main St	Mattawan	MI	49071	269-668-4531	
RAM Nationwide Inc 240 W N Bend Rd *TF:* 800-837-0110 ■ *Web:* www.ramnationwide.com	Cincinnati	OH	45216	513-821-0010	761-4632
Raven Transport Company Inc 6800 Broadway Ave *Web:* www.idriveraven.com	Jacksonville	FL	32254	904-880-1515	880-1913
Rbx Inc PO Box 2118 **Fax Area Code:* 417 ■ *TF:* 877-450-2200 ■ *Web:* www.rbxinc.com	Springfield	MO	65802	800-245-5507	862-5428*
Redwood Coast Trucking 2210 Peninsula Dr	Arcata	CA	95521	707-443-0857	
Refrigerated Food Express Inc 57 Littlefield St *TF:* 800-342-8822 ■ *Web:* www.rfxinc.com	Avon	MA	02322	508-587-4600	588-9655
Relco Systems Inc 7310 Chestnut Ridge Rd *TF:* 800-262-1020 ■ *Web:* www.relcosystems.com	Lockport	NY	14094	716-434-8100	434-7229
Riechmann Transport Inc 3328 W Chain of Rocks Rd *TF:* 800-844-4225 ■ *Web:* www.riechmanntransport.com	Granite City	IL	62040	618-797-6700	931-4246
River City Petroleum Inc 840 Delta Ln *Web:* rcpfuel.com	West Sacramento	CA	95691	916-371-4960	
River Forest Public Schools 90 7776 Lake St *Web:* www.district90.org	River Forest	IL	60305	708-771-8282	771-8291
Roadtex Transportation Corp 13 Jensen Dr *TF:* 800-762-3839 ■ *Web:* www.roadtex.com	Somerset	NJ	08873	800-762-3839	
Robert Bearden Inc 2601 Industrial Pk Dr PO Box 870 *TF:* 888-298-6928 ■ *Web:* www.rbitrucking.com	Cairo	GA	39828	229-377-6928	377-2880
Robert Heath Trucking Inc 1201 E 40th St *Web:* www.robertheath.com	Lubbock	TX	79404	806-747-1651	747-0339
Roehl Transport Inc 1916 E 29th St PO Box 750 *TF:* 800-826-8367 ■ *Web:* www.roehl.net	Marshfield	WI	54449	715-591-3795	387-1942
Roger Ward Inc 17275 Green Mtn Rd *TF General:* 888-909-3147 ■ *Web:* www.wardnorthamerican.com	San Antonio	TX	78247	210-655-8623	653-0919
Ross Neely Systems Inc 1500 Second St *Web:* www.rossneely.com	Birmingham	AL	35214	205-798-1137	798-0751
Rountree Transport & Rigging Inc 2640 N Ln Ave *TF:* 800-342-5036 ■ *Web:* rountreetransport.com	Jacksonville	FL	32254	904-781-1033	786-6229
Roy Bros Inc 764 Boston Rd *TF Cust Svc:* 800-225-0830 ■ *Web:* www.roybrosinc.com	Billerica	MA	01821	978-667-1921	667-5091
Royal Trucking Co 1323 Eshman Ave N PO Box 387 *TF:* 800-321-1293 ■ *Web:* www.royaltruck.com	West Point	MS	39773	662-494-1637	495-1066
RWH Trucking Inc 2970 Old Oakwood Rd **Fax Area Code:* 770 ■ *TF:* 800-256-8119 ■ *Web:* www.rwhtrucking.com	Oakwood	GA	30566	800-256-8119	287-7912*
S & S Transport Inc PO Box 12579 **Fax Area Code:* 701 ■ *TF:* 800-726-8022 ■ *Web:* www.sstransport.com	Grand Forks	ND	58208	800-726-8022	746-5665*
S T Bunn Construction 1904 University Blvd PO Box 20109 *TF:* 800-297-6302 ■ *Web:* www.stbunn.com	Tuscaloosa	AL	35401	205-752-8195	349-4288
S-j Transportation Co Inc PO Box 169 *TF:* 800-524-2552 ■ *Web:* www.sjtransportation.com	Woodstown	NJ	08098	856-769-2741	769-9811
Salida Union School District 4801 Sisk Rd PO Box 1329 *Web:* stancoe.org/scoe/districts/salida/	Salida	CA	95368	209-545-0339	545-2270
Sammons Trucking 3665 W Broadway *TF:* 800-548-9276 ■ *Web:* www.sammonstrucking.com	Missoula	MT	59808	406-728-2600	549-4989
Schilli Transportation Services Inc 6358 W US Hwy 24 *TF:* 800-759-2101 ■ *Web:* www.schilli.com	Remington	IN	47977	219-261-2100	
Security Van Lines LLC 100 W Airline Dr PO Box 830 **Fax Area Code:* 504 ■ *TF:* 800-218-6915 ■ *Web:* securitymayflower.com	Kenner	LA	70062	800-794-5961	464-1818*
Selland Auto Transport Inc 615 S 96th St *Web:* www.sellandauto.com	Seattle	WA	98108	206-767-5960	767-0604
Seward Motor Freight Inc PO Box 126 *TF:* 800-786-4468 ■ *Web:* www.sewardmotor.com	Seward	NE	68434	402-643-4503	643-3199
Shaffer Trucking Inc 49 E Main St PO Box 418 *TF Cust Svc:* 800-742-3337 ■ *Web:* www.shaffertrucking.com	New Kingstown	PA	17072	717-766-4708	795-5550
Sheedy Drayage Company Inc 1215 Michigan St *Web:* sheedydrayage.com	San Francisco	CA	94107	415-648-7171	648-1535
Shelba D. Johnson Trucking Inc PO Box 7287 *Web:* www.sdjtrucking.com	High Point	NC	27264	336-476-2000	476-0187
Sherman Bros Trucking 32921 Diamond Hill Dr PO Box 706 *TF:* 800-547-8980 ■ *Web:* www.sbht.com	Harrisburg	OR	97446	541-995-7751	995-7742
Shetler Moving & Storage Inc 1253 E Diamond Ave *TF:* 800-321-5069 ■ *Web:* www.shetlermoving.com	Evansville	IN	47711	812-421-7750	421-7759
Shippers Express Co 1651 Kerr Dr *TF:* 800-647-2480 ■ *Web:* shippersexpressinc.com	Jackson	MS	39204	601-948-4251	948-5232
Short Freight Lines Inc 459 S River Rd PO Box 357 *TF:* 800-248-0625 ■ *Web:* www.shortfreightlines.com	Bay City	MI	48707	989-893-3505	893-3151
Shuster's Transportation Inc 750 E Valley St	Willits	CA	95490	707-459-4131	459-1855
Simons Trucking Inc 920 Simon Dr PO Box 8 *TF:* 800-373-2580 ■ *Web:* www.simonstrucking.com	Farley	IA	52046	563-744-3304	744-3726
Skinner Transfer Corp PO Box 438 *TF:* 800-356-9350 ■ *Web:* www.skinnertransfer.com	Reedsburg	WI	53959	608-524-2326	524-9660
South Shore Transportation Inc 4010 Columbus Ave *TF:* 888-428-0879 ■ *Web:* www.sshoretrans.com	Sandusky	OH	44870	419-626-6267	626-9640
Southeastern Freight Lines Inc 420 Davega Rd **Fax:* Cust Svc ■ *TF:* 800-637-7335 ■ *Web:* www.sefl.com	Lexington	SC	29073	803-794-7300	939-3462*
Southern Pan Services Co (SPS) 2385 Lithonia Industrial Blvd PO Box 679 *TF:* 800-334-9145 ■ *Web:* www.southernpan.com	Lithonia	GA	30058	678-301-2400	301-2439
Southwest Freightlines 11991 Transpark Dr Horizon City *TF General:* 800-776-5799 ■ *Web:* www.swflines.com	El Paso	TX	79927	915-860-8592	860-9606
Southwestern Motor Transport Inc 4600 Goldfield *TF:* 800-531-1071 ■ *Web:* www.smtlines.com	San Antonio	TX	78218	210-661-6791	662-3295
Spectraserv Inc 75 Jacobus Ave *TF:* 800-445-4436 ■ *Web:* www.spectraserv.com	South Kearny	NJ	07032	973-589-0277	589-0415
Stahly Cartage Co 119 S Main St	Edwardsville	IL	62025	618-656-5070	656-0293
Star Fleet Inc PO Box 769 **Fax Area Code:* 574 ■ *TF:* 877-805-9547 ■ *Web:* www.starfleettrucking.com	Goshen	IN	46527	888-281-8727	825-9700*
Star Transportation Inc PO Box 100925 **Fax:* Cust Svc ■ *TF Cust Svc:* 800-333-3060 ■ *Web:* www.startransportation.com	Nashville	TN	37224	615-256-4336	255-9013*
Steelman Transportation 2160 N Burton *TF:* 800-488-6287 ■ *Web:* www.steelmantransport.com	Springfield	MO	65803	417-831-6300	
Stevens Transport PO Box 279010 **Fax Area Code:* 214 ■ *TF:* 800-233-9369 ■ *Web:* www.stevenstransport.com	Dallas	TX	75227	866-551-0337	647-3940*
Styer Transportation Co 7870 215th St W *TF:* 800-548-9149 ■ *Web:* www.styertrans.com	Lakeville	MN	55044	952-469-4491	469-3422
Summitt Trucking LLC 1800 Progress Way *TF:* 866-999-7799 ■ *Web:* www.summitttrucking.com	Clarksville	IN	47129	812-285-7777	285-8949
Sunbelt Furniture Express Inc PO Box 487 *TF:* 800-766-1117 ■ *Web:* www.sbfx.us	Hickory	NC	28603	828-464-7240	465-3560
Sunco Carriers Inc 1025 N Chestnut Rd *TF:* 800-237-8288 ■ *Web:* www.suncocarriers.com	Lakeland	FL	33805	863-688-1948	680-1759
Superior Carriers Inc 711 Jory Blvd Ste 101-N *TF:* 800-654-7707 ■ *Web:* www.superior-carriers.com	Oak Brook	IL	60523	630-573-2555	573-2570

Phone Fax

Sweetwater County School District 1 (SCSD)
3550 Foothill Blvd PO Box 1089 ... Rock Springs WY 82901 307-352-3400 352-3411
Web: www.sweetwater1.org

Swift Transportation Company Inc
2200 S 75th Ave ... Phoenix AZ 85043 602-269-9700 907-7380*
NYSE: SWFT ■ **Fax Area Code:* 623 ■ *TF:* 800-800-2200 ■ *Web:* www.swifttrans.com

Swing Transport Inc 1405 N Salisbury Ave ... Salisbury NC 28144 704-633-3567 636-2160
Web: www.swingtransport.com

T & T Trucking Inc 11396 N Hwy 99 ... Lodi CA 95240 209-931-6000 931-6156
TF Cust Svc: 800-692-3457 ■ *Web:* www.tttrucking.com

T-w Transport Inc 7405 S Hayford Rd ... Cheney WA 99004 509-623-4004 623-4069
TF: 800-356-4070 ■ *Web:* www.twtrans.com

TanTara Transportation Corp
2420 Stewart Rd ... Muscatine IA 52761 563-262-8621 264-8998
TF: 800-650-0292 ■ *Web:* www.tantara.us

Taylor Made Transportation Services Inc
2901 Druid Pk Dr Ste 206 ... Baltimore MD 21215 410-728-1951
Web: www.tmtransportation.com

Taylor Truck Line Inc
31485 Northfield Blvd ... Northfield MN 55057 507-645-4531 645-9722
TF: 800-962-5994 ■ *Web:* www.taylortruckline.com

Teal's Express Inc
22411 Teal Dr PO Box 6010 ... Watertown NY 13601 315-788-6437 788-5060
TF: 800-836-0369 ■ *Web:* www.teals.com

Telfer Oil Co 211 Foster St ... Martinez CA 94553 925-228-1515 229-3955
Web: telfercompanies.com

Tennessee Steel Haulers Inc PO Box 78189 ... Nashville TN 37207 615-271-2400 271-2450
TF: 800-776-4004 ■ *Web:* www.tenh.com

Teresi Trucking Inc 900 1/2 Victor Rd ... Lodi CA 95240 209-368-2472 369-2830
Web: www.teresitrucking.com

Texas Transeastern Inc PO Box 5339 ... Pasadena TX 77508 281-604-3100 648-0654*
**Fax Area Code:* 210 ■ *TF:* 800-866-8579 ■ *Web:* www.texastranseastern.com

Tiger Lines LLC Lodi 927 Black Diamond Way ... Lodi CA 95241 209-334-4100 333-3725
TF: 800-967-8443 ■ *Web:* www.tigerlines.com

Total Package Express Inc 5871 Cheviot Rd ... Cincinnati OH 45247 513-741-5500 741-5505
TF: 800-420-5505 ■ *Web:* tp-exp.com

TP Trucking LLC 5630 Table Rock Rd ... Central Point OR 97502 541-664-4776 664-5070
TF: 800-777-1121 ■ *Web:* www.tptrucking.com

Trailer Bridge Inc
10405 New Berlin Rd E ... Jacksonville FL 32226 904-751-7100 751-7444
OTC: TRBRQ ■ *TF:* 800-554-1589 ■ *Web:* www.trailerbridge.com

Trailer Transit Inc 1130 E US 20 ... Porter IN 46304 219-926-2111 859-1191*
**Fax Area Code:* 877 ■ *TF:* 800-423-3647 ■ *Web:* www.trailertransit.com

Trans-Carriers Inc 5135 US Hwy 78 ... Memphis TN 38118 901-368-2900 368-0336
TF: 800-999-7383 ■ *Web:* www.transcarriers.com

Trans-Phos Inc PO Box 9004 ... Bartow FL 33831 863-534-1575 534-3200
TF: 800-940-1575 ■ *Web:* www.transphos.com

TransAm Trucking Inc 15910 S 169th Hwy ... Olathe KS 66062 913-782-5300 324-7063
TF: 800-800-5945 ■ *Web:* www.transamtruck.com

Transport Corp of America Inc
1715 Yankee Doodle Rd ... Eagan MN 55121 651-686-2500 686-2566
TF: 800-328-3927 ■ *Web:* www.transportamerica.com

Transport Distribution Co PO Box 306 ... Joplin MO 64802 417-624-3814 624-9767
TF: 800-866-7709 ■ *Web:* www.gotdc.com

Transport Inc 2225 Main Ave SE ... Moorhead MN 56560 218-236-6300 236-0227
TF: 800-598-7267 ■ *Web:* www.transport-inc.com

Transport Service Co 2001 Spring Rd Ste 400 ... Oak Brook IL 60523 630-472-5900 472-0708
TF Sales: 800-323-5561 ■ *Web:* www.transportserviceco.com

TransWood Carriers Inc PO Box 189 ... Omaha NE 68101 888-346-8092 341-2112*
**Fax Area Code:* 402 ■ *TF:* 888-346-8092 ■ *Web:* www.transwood.com

Tri Star Freight System Inc 5407 Mesa Dr ... Houston TX 77028 713-631-1095 631-1099
TF: 800-229-1095 ■ *Web:* www.tristarfreightsys.com

Triad Transport Inc PO Box 818 ... McAlester OK 74502 918-426-4751 426-4770
TF: 800-324-1139 ■ *Web:* www.triadtransport.com

Trinity Logistics Group Inc 4001 Irving Blvd ... Dallas TX 75247 214-589-7505 589-7529
Web: www.trinitytrucking.com

Triple Crown Services
2720 Dupont Commerce Ct Ste 200 ... Fort Wayne IN 46825 260-416-3600 416-3771
TF: 800-325-6510 ■ *Web:* www.triplecrownsvc.com

Truline Corp 9390 Redwood St ... Las Vegas NV 89139 702-362-7495 362-3215
TF: 800-634-6489 ■ *Web:* www.trulinecorp.com

Tryon Trucking Inc PO Box 68 ... Fairless Hills PA 19030 215-295-6622 295-7168
TF: 800-523-5254 ■ *Web:* www.tryontrucking.com

Underwood Transfer Company LLC
940 W Troy Ave ... Indianapolis IN 46225 317-783-9235 782-2769
TF: 800-428-2372 ■ *Web:* www.underwoodcompanies.com

United Road Services Inc 10701 Middlebelt Rd ... Romulus MI 48174 734-947-7900
TF: 866-470-0036 ■ *Web:* www.unitedroad.com

Universal Truckload Services Inc
12755 E Nine Mile Rd ... Warren MI 48089 586-920-0100 920-0258
NASDAQ: UACL ■ *TF:* 800-233-9445 ■ *Web:* www.goutsi.com

Upper Township School District 525 Perry Rd ... Woodbine NJ 08270 609-628-3500 628-2002
Web: www.upperschools.org

US Xpress Enterprises Inc
4080 Jenkins Rd ... Chattanooga TN 37421 423-510-3000 510-4006
TF: 800-251-6291 ■ *Web:* www.usxpress.com

USA Truck Inc 3200 Industrial Pk Rd ... Van Buren AR 72956 479-471-2500 500-5118*
NASDAQ: USAK ■ **Fax Area Code:* 800 ■ *TF:* 800-643-9691 ■ *Web:* www.usa-truck.com

USF Holland Inc 750 E 40th St ... Holland MI 49423 616-395-5000 392-3104
Web: www.yrcregional.com

V & S Midwest Carriers Corp
2001 Hyland Ave PO Box 107 ... Kaukauna WI 54130 920-766-9696 766-1772
TF: 800-876-4330 ■ *Web:* www.vsmidwest.com

Van Eerden Foodservice Co
650 Ionia Ave SW ... Grand Rapids MI 49503 616-475-0900 475-0990
TF: 800-833-7374 ■ *Web:* www.vaneerden.com

Van Wyk Freight Lines Inc PO Box 70 ... Grinnell IA 50112 641-236-7551 236-4247
TF: 800-362-2595 ■ *Web:* www.middlewest.com

Venezia Transport Service Inc PO Box 909 ... Royersford PA 19468 610-495-5200 495-5086
Web: www.veneziainc.com

Vitran Express Canada Inc
1201 Creditstone Rd ... Concord ON L4K0C2 416-798-4965 798-4753
NASDAQ: VTNC ■ *TF:* 800-263-9588 ■ *Web:* www.vitran.com

Phone Fax

Vitran Express Inc 1600 W Oliver Ave ... Indianapolis IN 46221 317-803-4000 321-4629
TF: 800-366-0150 ■ *Web:* www.vitranexpress.com

Volume Transportation Inc
6575 Marshall Blvd ... Lithonia GA 30058 770-482-1400 482-4817
TF: 800-879-5565 ■ *Web:* www.volinc.com

Waggoners Trucking 5220 Midland Rd ... Billings MT 59101 406-248-1919 259-6924
TF: 800-999-9097 ■ *Web:* www.waggonerstrucking.com

Waller Truck Company Inc
400 S McCleary Rd ... Excelsior Springs MO 64024 816-629-3400 629-3460
TF: 800-821-2196 ■ *Web:* www.wallertruck.com

Walpole Inc PO Box 1177 ... Okeechobee FL 34973 863-763-5593 763-7874
TF: 800-741-6500 ■ *Web:* www.walpoleinc.com

Ward Trucking Corp PO Box 1553 ... Altoona PA 16603 814-944-0803 944-2369
TF: 800-458-3625 ■ *Web:* www.wardtrucking.com

Warren Transport Inc 210 Beck Ave ... Waterloo IA 50701 319-233-6113 235-6555
TF General: 800-553-2007 ■ *Web:* www.warrentransport.com

Watsontown Trucking Company Inc
60 Belford Blvd ... Milton PA 17847 570-522-9820 538-0254
TF: 800-344-0313 ■ *Web:* www.watsontowntrucking.com

WC McQuaide Inc 153 Macridge Rd ... Johnstown PA 15904 814-269-6000 269-6092
TF: 800-456-0292 ■ *Web:* www.mcquaide.com

Weaver Bros Inc 2230 Spar Ave ... Anchorage AK 99501 907-278-4526 276-4316
Web: weaverbrothersinc.com

Wel Companies Inc 1625 S Broadway PO Box 5610 ... De Pere WI 54115 920-339-0110 983-2139
TF: 800-333-4415 ■ *Web:* www.welcompanies.com

Werner Enterprises Inc 14507 Frontier Rd ... Omaha NE 68138 402-895-6640 894-3927*
NASDAQ: WERN ■ **Fax:* Hum Res ■ *TF:* 800-228-2240 ■ *Web:* www.werner.com

Western Co-op Transport Assn
4501 72nd St SW ... Montevideo MN 56265 320-269-5531 269-5532
TF: 800-992-8817 ■ *Web:* www.westernco-op.com

Western Express Inc 7135 Centennial Pl ... Nashville TN 37209 615-259-9920 350-9957
TF: 800-316-7160 ■ *Web:* westernexpress.publishpath.com/

Westwood Contractors Inc 951 W Seventh St ... Fort Worth TX 76102 817-877-3800 877-4731
Web: www.westwoodcontractors.com

White Bros Trucking Co 4N793 School Rd ... Wasco IL 60183 630-584-3810
TF: 800-323-4762 ■ *Web:* whitebrotherstrucking.com

White River Paper Co 1118 Rt 14 ... Hartford VT 05047 802-281-4501 721-9951*
**Fax Area Code:* 705 ■ *TF:* 800-461-7695 ■ *Web:* www.wrpaper.com

White Settlement Independent School District
401 S Cherry Ln PO Box 150187 ... Fort Worth TX 76108 817-367-1300 367-1351
Web: www.wsisd.com

Whitefish Bay Schools
1200 E Fairmount Ave ... Whitefish Bay WI 53217 414-963-3901
Web: www.wfbschools.com

Wildwood Express Trucking
12416 E Swanson Ave ... Kingsburg CA 93631 559-897-1035 897-1038
Web: wildwoodex.com

Wilhelm Trucking & Rigging Co
3250 NW St Helens Rd PO Box 10363 ... Portland OR 97210 503-227-0561 241-4913
TF Cust Svc: 800-873-4285 ■ *Web:* www.wilhelmtruck.com

Willis Shaw Express Inc 201 N Elm St ... Elm Springs AR 72728 479-248-7261
TF: 800-843-9904 ■ *Web:* mcttrans.com/

Wilson Lines of Minnesota Inc
2131 Second Ave ... Newport MN 55055 651-459-2384 769-3050
TF General: 800-525-3333 ■ *Web:* www.wilsonlines.com

Wilson Trucking Corp 137 Wilson Blvd ... Fishersville VA 22939 540-949-3200 949-3205
TF: 866-645-7405 ■ *Web:* www.wilsontrucking.com

Wiseway Motor Freight Inc PO Box 838 ... Hudson WI 54016 800-876-1660 381-3197*
**Fax Area Code:* 715 ■ *TF:* 800-876-1660 ■ *Web:* www.wiseway.com

Woodruff Construction LLC 1890 Kountry Ln ... Fort Dodge IA 50501 515-576-1118 955-2170
Web: www.woodruffcompanies.com

Woody Bogler Trucking Co PO Box 229 ... Rosebud MO 63091 573-764-3700 764-4200
TF: 800-899-4120 ■ *Web:* www.woodybogler.com

Wragtime Air Freight Inc 596 W 135th St ... Gardena CA 90248 800-586-9701
TF: 800-586-9701 ■ *Web:* www.visionexpressltl.com

Wright Transportation Inc
2333 Dauphin Island Pkwy ... Mobile AL 36605 251-432-6390 300-2930
TF: 800-342-4598 ■ *Web:* www.wrighttrans.com

Wyatt Transfer Inc
3035 Bells Rd PO Box 24326 ... Richmond VA 23224 804-743-3800 271-9598*
**Fax:* Administration ■ *TF:* 800-552-5708 ■ *Web:* www.wyatttransferinc.com

Wynne Transport Service Inc 2222 N 11th St ... Omaha NE 68108 402-342-4001 342-4608
TF: 800-383-9330 ■ *Web:* www.wynnetr.com

Yorkville Community Unit School District 115
602A Ctr Pkwy PO Box 579 ... Yorkville IL 60560 630-553-4382 553-4398
Web: www.y115.org

Young's Commercial Transfer
2075 W Scranton Ave PO Box 871 ... Porterville CA 93257 559-784-6651 784-5280
TF: 800-289-1639 ■ *Web:* www.yctinc.com

Yourga Trucking Inc 100 Shenango St ... Wheatland PA 16161 724-981-3600 981-3603
TF: 800-245-1722 ■ *Web:* www.yourga.com

784 TYPESETTING & RELATED SERVICES

SEE ALSO Graphic Design p. 2437; Printing Companies - Commercial Printers p. 2965

Phone Fax

A A Blueprint Company Inc 2757 Gilchrist Rd ... Akron OH 44305 330-794-8803
Web: aablueprint.com

Adflex Corp 300 Ormond St ... Rochester NY 14605 585-454-2950
Web: www.adflexcorp.com

Allied Bindery LLC 32451 N Avis Dr ... Madison Heights MI 48071 248-588-5990
Web: www.alliedbindery.com

Ano-Coil Corp 60 E Main St ... Rockville CT 06066 860-871-1200 872-0534
TF: 800-492-7286 ■ *Web:* www.anocoil.com

Aptara Inc 3110 Fairview Pk Dr ... Falls Church VA 22042 703-352-0001 352-8862
Web: www.aptaracorp.com

ARC Document Solutions (ARC)
ARC 1981 N Broadway Ste 385 ... Walnut Creek CA 94596 925-949-5100 949-5101
NYSE: ARC ■ *Web:* www.e-arc.com

	City	State	ZIP	Phone	Fax
Artisan Colour Inc 8970 E Bahia Dr Ste 100 *Web:* www.artisancaptures.com	Scottsdale	AZ	85260	480-948-0009	
As Soon As Possible Inc 3000 France Ave South *Web:* www.asap.net	Minneapolis	MN	55416	952-564-2727	
Auto-Graphics Inc 430 N Vineyard Ave *TF:* 800-776-6939 ■ *Web:* www4.auto-graphics.com	Ontario	CA	91764	909-595-7004	595-3506
Bacompt Systems Inc 12742 Hamilton Crossing Blvd *Web:* www.bacompt.com	Carmel	IN	46032	317-574-7474	
Bank-A-Count Corp 1666 Main St *Web:* www.bank-a-count.com	Rudolph	WI	54475	715-435-3131	
Bell Litho Inc 370 Crossen Ave *Web:* www.bell-litho.com	Elk Grove Village	IL	60007	847-952-3300	
Blanks Printing & Imaging Inc 2343 N Beckley Ave *TF:* 800-325-7651 ■ *Web:* www.blanks.com	Dallas	TX	75208	214-741-3905	741-6105
Boston Color Graphics LLC 755 Middlesex Tpke *Web:* www.bostoncolorgraphics.com	Billerica	MA	01821	978-528-7999	
Carey Digital 1718 Central Pkwy *TF:* 800-767-6071 ■ *Web:* www.careydigital.com	Cincinnati	OH	45214	513-241-5210	241-2205
Cohber Press PO Box 93100 *Web:* www.cohber.com	Rochester	NY	14692	585-475-9100	475-9406
Color Communication Inc 4000 W Fillmore St **Fax Area Code:* 773 ■ *TF:* 800-458-5743 ■ *Web:* www.ccicolor.com	Chicago	IL	60624	800-458-5743	638-0887*
Color House Graphics Inc 3505 Eastern Ave SE *Web:* www.colorhousegraphics.com	Grand Rapids	MI	49508	616-241-1916	
Color Technology 2455 NW Nicolai St *Web:* www.colortechnology.com	Portland	OR	97210	503-294-0393	
Computer Composition Corp 1401 W Girard Ave *Web:* www.computercomposition.com	Madison Heights	MI	48071	248-545-4330	544-1611
Container Graphics Corp 114 Edinburgh S Dr Ste 104 *Web:* www.containergraphics.com	Cary	NC	27511	919-481-4200	469-4897
Continental Colorcraft 1166 W Garvey Ave *Web:* www.continentalcolorcraft.com	Monterey Park	CA	91754	323-283-3000	283-3206
Dixie Graphics Co 636 Grassmere Pk *Web:* www.dixiegraphics.com	Nashville	TN	37211	615-832-7000	832-7621
eBlueprint Holdings Inc 3666 Carnegie Ave *Web:* www.eblueprint.com	Cleveland	OH	44115	216-281-1234	
ET Lowe Publishing Co 2920 Sidco Dr *Web:* www.etlowe.com	Nashville	TN	37204	615-254-8866	254-8867
GGS Technical Publications Services 3265 Farmtrail Rd *TF:* 800-927-4474 ■ *Web:* ggsinc.com/	York	PA	17406	717-764-2222	767-0027
Global Fulfillment Four S Idaho St *Web:* www.gloful.com	Seattle	WA	98134	206-405-3350	
GotPrint 7625 N San Fernando Rd *Web:* gotprint.com	Burbank	CA	91505	818-252-3000	
Graphic Solutions Group Inc 8575 Cobb Intl Blvd Nw *Web:* www.gsghome.com	Kennesaw	GA	30152	770-424-2300	
Graphics Group 2800 Taylor St *Web:* www.graphicsgroup.com	Dallas	TX	75226	214-749-2222	749-2252
Imtech Graphics Inc 545 Dell Rd *Web:* imtechgraphics.com	Carlstadt	NJ	07072	201-933-8002	
Jackson Typesetting Company Inc 1820 W Ganson St	Jackson	MI	49202	517-784-0576	784-1200
Kramer Graphics Inc 2408 W Dorothy Ln *Web:* www.kramergraphics.com	Dayton	OH	45439	937-296-9600	
Lancaster Ultra Graphics Inc 1900 McFarland Dr *Web:* www.ultragraphics.com	Landisville	PA	17538	717-898-9700	
Lasergraphics Inc Four Squire Rd *Web:* www.laserg.com	Revere	MA	02151	781-289-2022	289-2027
Ligature, The 4909 Alcoa Ave *TF:* 800-944-5440 ■ *Web:* www.theligature.com	Los Angeles	CA	90058	323-585-6000	585-1737
Luminite Products Corp 148 Commerce Dr *Web:* luminite.com	Bradford	PA	16701	814-817-1420	
Mark Trece Inc 2001 Stockton Rd *Web:* www.marktrece.com	Joppa	MD	21085	410-879-0060	879-3438
Maryland Composition Co 14880 Sweitzer Rd *Web:* ags.com	Laurel	MD	20707	240-295-5674	
MATRIX Publishing Co 36 N Highland Ave *Web:* matrix508.com	York	PA	17404	717-764-9673	764-9672
New England Typographic Service Inc 206 W Newberry Rd *Web:* www.netype.com	Bloomfield	CT	06002	860-242-2251	242-9350
Newtype Inc 447 Rte 10 E Ste 14 *Web:* www.newtypeinc.com	Randolph	NJ	07869	973-361-6000	361-6005
Pacific Digital Image 333 Broadway *Web:* www.pacdigital.com	San Francisco	CA	94133	415-576-0206	
Para Plate 15910 Shoemaker Ave *Web:* paraplate.com	Cerritos	CA	90703	562-404-3434	
Plastikoil of Pennsylvania Inc 230 W Kensinger Dr *Web:* plastikoilofpa.com	Cranberry Township	PA	16066	724-935-9190	
Presstek Inc 55 Executive Dr *NASDAQ: PRST* ■ *TF:* 800-422-3616 ■ *Web:* www.presstek.com	Hudson	NH	03051	603-595-7000	546-4234
Printing Prep Inc 12 E Tupper St *TF:* 877-878-7114 ■ *Web:* www.printleader.us	Buffalo	NY	14203	716-852-5011	852-3150
Progressive Information Technologies 315 Busser Rd *Web:* www.pit-magnus.com	Emigsville	PA	17318	717-764-5908	767-4092
Quintessence Publishing Co 4350 Chandler Dr *Web:* www.quintpub.com	Hanover Park	IL	60133	630-736-3600	
Reed Technology & Information Services Inc Seven Walnut Grove Dr *Web:* www.reedtech.com	Horsham	PA	19044	215-441-6400	
Regency Infographics Inc (SED) 2867 E Allegheny Ave *TF:* 800-829-0020 ■ *Web:* www.sed.com/desktop-publishing.html	Philadelphia	PA	19134	215-425-8800	425-9715
Richards Graphic Communications Inc 2700 Van Buren St *TF:* 866-827-3686 ■ *Web:* www.rgcnet.com	Bellwood	IL	60104	708-547-6000	547-6044
Rpr Graphics Inc 1136 US Hwy 22 *Web:* www.rprgraphicsinc.com	Mountainside	NJ	07092	908-654-8080	
Southern Graphic Systems Inc 502 N Willow Ave *TF:* 800-777-6789 ■ *Web:* www.sgsintl.com	Tampa	FL	33606	813-253-3427	254-2112
Southern Graphics Systems 7435 Empire Dr *TF:* 800-777-6789 ■ *Web:* sgsintl.com	Florence	KY	41042	859-525-1190	647-8205
Spectragraphic Inc Four Brayton Ct *Web:* www.spectragraphic.com	Commack	NY	11725	631-499-3100	499-5255
Spry Enterprises Inc 53 Loveton Cir Ste 207 *Web:* www.spryinc.com	Sparks	MD	21152	443-212-5072	
ST Assoc Inc One Teal Rd *Web:* www.stassoc.com	Wakefield	MA	01880	781-246-4700	246-4218
State & Federal Communications Inc 80 S Summit St *Web:* stateandfed.com	Akron	OH	44308	330-761-9960	
Stevenson The Color Company Inc 535 Wilmer Ave *Web:* www.stevensoncolor.com	Cincinnati	OH	45226	513-321-7500	321-7502
Sunrise Hitek Service Inc 5915 N Northwest Hwy *Web:* www.sunrisehitek.com	Chicago	IL	60631	773-792-8880	
Techniprint Co 2545 N Seventh St *Web:* www.techniprintaz.com	Phoenix	AZ	85006	602-257-0686	
Total Works Inc 2240 N Elston Ave *Web:* www.totalworks.net	Chicago	IL	60614	773-489-4313	489-0482
Typesetting Inc 1144 S Robertson Blvd *Web:* local.latimes.com	Los Angeles	CA	90035	310-273-3330	273-0733
VT Graphics Inc 465 Penn St PO Box 5334 *Web:* www.vtgraph.com	Yeadon	PA	19050	610-259-4090	259-7235
West Essex Graphics Inc (WEG) 305 Fairfield Ave **Fax Area Code:* 973 ■ *TF:* 800-221-5859 ■ *Web:* www.westessexgraphics.com	Fairfield	NJ	07004	800-221-5859	227-2906*

785 ULTRASONIC CLEANING EQUIPMENT

SEE ALSO Dental Equipment & Supplies - Mfr p. 2196

	City	State	ZIP	Phone	Fax
Branson Ultrasonics Corp 41 Eagle Rd *Web:* www.emersonindustrial.com	Danbury	CT	06813	203-796-0400	
Crest Ultrasonics Corp 10 Grumman Ave *TF:* 800-992-7378 ■ *Web:* www.crest-ultrasonics.com	Trenton	NJ	08628	609-883-4000	883-6452
L & R Manufacturing Co 577 Elm St *Web:* www.lrultrasonics.com	Kearny	NJ	07032	201-991-5330	991-5870
Sonicor Inc 82 Otis St *TF:* 800-864-5022 ■ *Web:* www.sonicor.com	West Babylon	NY	11704	631-920-6555	920-6080
Sonics & Materials Inc 53 Church Hill Rd *OTC: SIMA* ■ *TF:* 800-745-1105 ■ *Web:* www.sonicsandmaterials.com	Newtown	CT	06470	203-270-4600	270-4610
Sterigenics 2015 Spring Rd Ste 650 *TF:* 800-472-4508 ■ *Web:* www.sterigenics.com	Oak Brook	IL	60523	630-928-1700	928-1701

786 UNITED NATIONS AGENCIES, ORGANIZATIONS, PROGRAMS

	City	State	ZIP	Phone	Fax
United Nations UN Plz Rm DC2-2220 **Fax:* PR ■ *Web:* www.un.org	New York	NY	10017	212-963-1234	963-4260*
Inter-American Development Bank 1300 New York Ave NW *TF:* 877-782-7432 ■ *Web:* www.iadb.org	Washington	DC	20577	202-623-1000	623-3096
International Atomic Energy Agency (IAEA) One UN Plz Rm DC1-1155 **Fax Area Code:* 917 ■ *Web:* www.iaea.org	New York	NY	10017	212-963-6010	367-4046*
International Fund for Agricultural Development (IFAD) 1775 K St NW Ste 410 *Web:* www.ifad.org	Washington	DC	20006	202-331-9099	331-9366
International Labour Organization (ILO) 220 E 42nd St Ste 3101 *Web:* www.ilo.org	New York	NY	10017	212-697-0150	697-5218
International Monetary Fund (IMF) 700 19th St NW *Web:* www.imf.org	Washington	DC	20431	202-623-7000	623-4661
International Tsunami Information Ctr 737 Bishop St Ste 2200 *Web:* itic.ioc-unesco.org	Honolulu	HI	96813	808-532-6422	532-5576
United Nations Children's Fund (UNICEF) Three United Nations Plz *Web:* www.unicef.org	New York	NY	10017	212-326-7000	888-7465
United Nations Development Programme One UN Plz *Web:* www.undp.org	New York	NY	10017	212-906-5000	906-5364
United Nations Educational Scientific & Cultural Organization (UNESCO) Two UN Plz Ste 900 *Web:* en.unesco.org	New York	NY	10017	212-963-5995	963-8014
United Nations Environment Programme (UNEP) 900 17th St NW Ste 506 *Web:* www.rona.unep.org	Washington	DC	20006	202-785-0465	785-2096
United Nations Industrial Development Organization (UNIDO) One UN Plz Ste DC1-1110 *Web:* www.unido.org	New York	NY	10017	212-963-6890	963-7904
World Bank Group, The (WBG) 1818 H St NW *Web:* www.worldbank.org	Washington	DC	20433	202-473-1000	477-6391

	City	State	ZIP	Phone	Fax
World Intellectual Property Organization (WIPO) Two UN Plz Rm 2525	New York	NY	10017	212-963-6813	963-4801
Web: www.wipo.int					

787 UNITED NATIONS MISSIONS

SEE ALSO Embassies & Consulates - Foreign, in the US p. 2245

All of the missions listed here are permanent missions except the Holy See, which has the status of Permanent Observer Mission to the UN. Two member states, Kiribati and Palau, are not listed because they do not maintain offices in New York. Another member state, Guinea Bissau, has a New York office but is excluded from this list because no telephone number was available for it.

	City	State	ZIP	Phone	Fax
Afghanistan 633 Third Ave 27A Fl	New York	NY	10017	212-972-1212	972-1216
Web: www.afghanistan-un.org					
Albania 320 E 79th St	New York	NY	10075	212-249-2059	535-2917
Algeria 326 E 48th St	New York	NY	10017	212-750-1960	759-9538
Web: www.algeria-un.org					
Angola 820 Second Ave 12th Fl	New York	NY	10017	212-861-5656	861-9295
Web: www.un.int					
Antigua & Barbuda 305 E 47th St Sixth Fl	New York	NY	10017	212-541-4117	757-1607
Web: antigua-barbuda.org					
Armenia 119 E 36th St	New York	NY	10016	212-686-9079	686-3934
Web: www.un.int					
Austria 600 Third Ave 31st Fl	New York	NY	10016	917-542-8400	949-1840*
**Fax Area Code:* 212 ■ *Web:* advantageaustria.org					
Azerbaijan 866 UN Plz Ste 560	New York	NY	10017	212-371-2559	371-2784
Web: www.un.int					
Bahrain 866 Second Ave 14th & 15th Fls	New York	NY	10017	212-223-6200	
Bangladesh Mission To the UN 227 E 45th St 14th Fl	New York	NY	10017	212-867-3434	972-4038
Web: www.un.int					
Belarus 136 E 67th St Fourth Fl	New York	NY	10021	212-535-3420	734-4810
Web: www.un.int					
Belize 675 Third Ave Ste 1911	New York	NY	10017	212-986-1240	593-0932
Web: www.belizemission.com					
Benin 125 E 38th St	New York	NY	10016	212-684-1339	684-2058
Web: www.un.int					
Bolivia 801 Second Ave 4th Fl, Rm 42	New York	NY	10017	212-682-8132	
Botswana 154 E 46th St	New York	NY	10017	212-889-2277	725-5061
Web: botswanaun.org					
Brazil 747 Third Ave 9th Fl	New York	NY	10017	212-372-2600	371-5716
Web: www.un.int					
Bulgaria 11 E 84th St	New York	NY	10028	212-737-4790	472-9865
Burkina Faso 866 UN Plz Ste 326	New York	NY	10017	212-308-4720	308-4690
Web: www.burkina-onu.org					
Burundi 336 E 45th St 12th Fl	New York	NY	10017	212-499-0001	499-0006
Web: burundi-un.org					
Cameroon 22 E 73rd St	New York	NY	10021	212-794-2295	249-0533
Web: www.delecam.us					
Cape Verde 27 E 69th St	New York	NY	10021	212-472-0333	794-1398
Chad Mission 129 E 36th St	New York	NY	10016	212-986-0980	
Chile Mission 885 Second Ave 40th Fl	New York	NY	10017	917-322-6800	832-0236*
**Fax Area Code:* 212					
China 350 E 35th St	New York	NY	10016	212-655-6100	634-7626
Web: www.china-un.org					
Colombia 140 E 57th St	New York	NY	10022	212-355-7776	355-7776
Web: www.colombiaun.org					
Comoros 866 UN Plz Ste 418	New York	NY	10017	212-750-1637	750-1657
Web: www.un.int					
Consulate General of Liberia 866 UN Plz Ste 480	New York	NY	10017	212-687-1033	687-1035
Web: www.liberianconsulate-ny.com					
Cuba 315 Lexington Ave	New York	NY	10016	212-689-7215	689-9073
TF General: 800-553-3210 ■ *Web:* un.org					
Cyprus 13 E 40th St	New York	NY	10016	212-481-6023	685-7316
Web: www.un.int					
Democratic People's Republic of Korea 820 Second Ave 13th Fl	New York	NY	10017	212-972-3105	972-3154
Web: www.un.org					
Egypt 304 E 44th St	New York	NY	10017	212-503-0300	949-5999
Web: egyptembassy.net					
Eritrea 800 Second Ave 18th Fl	New York	NY	10017	212-687-3390	687-3138
Web: www.eritrea-unmission.org					
Estonia 305 E 47th St Sixth Fl	New York	NY	10017	212-883-0640	514-0099*
**Fax Area Code:* 646 ■ *Web:* www.un.estemb.org					
Ethiopia 866 Second Ave Third Fl	New York	NY	10017	212-421-1830	754-0360
Web: un.int/wcm/content/site/bangladesh/					
France 1 Dag Hammarskjold Plaza # 36	New York	NY	10017	212-937-0564	421-6889
Web: www.un.int					
Gambia 800 Second Ave Rm 400F	New York	NY	10017	212-949-6640	856-9820
Web: un.int					
German Marshall Fund of the United States 1744 R St NW	Washington	DC	20009	202-745-3950	
Web: www.gmfus.org					
Ghana 19 E 47th St	New York	NY	10017	212-832-1300	751-6743
Web: www.un.int/ghana					
Greece 866 Second Ave 13th Fl	New York	NY	10017	212-888-6900	888-4440
Web: www.mfa.gr					
Guatemala 57 Pk Ave	New York	NY	10016	212-679-4760	685-8741
Web: www.un.int					
Guinea 140 E 39th St	New York	NY	10016	212-687-8115	687-8248
Web: www.un.int					
Hungary 223 E 52nd St	New York	NY	10022	212-752-0209	
Web: www.un.int					
Indonesia 325 E 38th St	New York	NY	10016	212-972-8333	972-9780
Web: www.indonesiamission-ny.org					
Iran 622 Third Ave 34th Fl	New York	NY	10017	212-687-2020	867-7086
Web: www.un.int					
Ireland One Dag Hammarskjold Plz # 885	New York	NY	10017	212-421-6934	752-4726
Web: www.un.int					
Jamaica 767 Third Ave Ninth Fl	New York	NY	10017	212-935-7509	935-7607
Web: www.un.int					
Kenya 866 UN Plaza Rm 304	New York	NY	10017	212-421-4740	486-1985
TF: 866-445-3692 ■ *Web:* www.kenyaun.org					
Kuwait 321 E 44th St	New York	NY	10017	212-973-4300	370-1733
Web: www.kuwaitmission.com					
Lao People's Democratic Republic 317 E 51st St	New York	NY	10022	212-832-2734	750-0039
Web: www.un.int					
Latvia 333 E 50th St	New York	NY	10022	212-838-8877	838-8920
Web: mfa.gov.lv					
Lebanon 866 UN Plz Rm 531-533	New York	NY	10017	212-355-5460	838-2819
Web: www.un.int/wcm/content/site/lebanon					
Lesotho 204 E 39th St	New York	NY	10016	212-661-1690	682-4388
Web: www.un.int					
Libyan Arab Jamahiriya 309-315 E 48th St	New York	NY	10017	212-752-5775	593-4787
TF: 800-253-9646 ■ *Web:* www.un.org					
Madagascar 820 Second Ave Ste 800	New York	NY	10017	212-986-9491	986-6271
Web: un.int					
Malawi 866 UN Plz Ste 486	New York	NY	10017	212-317-8738	317-8729
Web: www.un.int/wcm/content/site/malawi					
Maldives 800 Second Ave Ste 400-E	New York	NY	10017	212-599-6194	661-6405
Mali 111 E 69th St	New York	NY	10021	212-737-4150	472-3778
Web: un.int					
Malta 249 E 35th St	New York	NY	10016	212-725-2345	779-7097
Web: www.foreign.gov.mt					
Marshall Islands 800 Second Ave 18th Fl	New York	NY	10017	212-983-3040	
Mauritania 116 E 38th St	New York	NY	10016	212-252-0113	252-0175
Web: www.un.int					
Mauritius 211 E 43rd St 22nd Fl	New York	NY	10017	212-949-0190	
Web: mfa.govmu.org					
Mission-Andorra To the UN Two UN Plz 27th Fl	New York	NY	10017	212-750-8064	750-6630
Monaco 866 UN Plaza Ste 520	New York	NY	10017	212-832-0721	832-5358
Web: www.monaco-un.org					
Mongolia Six E 77th St	New York	NY	10075	212-861-9460	861-9464
Web: www.un.int/mongolia					
Mozambique 420 E 50th St	New York	NY	10022	212-644-6800	644-5972
Web: www.un.int					
Nepal 820 Second Ave Ste 17B	New York	NY	10017	212-370-3988	953-2038
Nicaragua 820 Second Ave Ste 801	New York	NY	10017	212-490-7997	286-0815
Web: www.un.int					
Niger 417 E 50th St	New York	NY	10022	212-421-3260	753-6931
Web: www.un.int					
Norway 825 Third Ave 39th Fl	New York	NY	10022	646-430-7510	
Web: www.norway-un.org					
Oman 305 E 47th St 12th Fl	New York	NY	10017	212-355-3505	644-0070
Web: www.un.int/wcm/content/site/oman					
Paraguay 801 Second Ave Ste 702	New York	NY	10017	212-687-3490	818-1282
Web: www.paraguayun.com					
Permanent Mission of Cambodia 327 E 58th St	New York	NY	10022	212-336-0777	759-7672
Permanent Mission of Macedonia 866 UN Plaza	New York	NY	10017	646-524-5750	
Web: www.macedonianembassy.org					
Permanent Mission of Solomon Islands to the United Nations 800 Second Ave Ste 400L	New York	NY	10017	212-599-6192	661-8925
Web: www.un.int/wcm/content/site/solomonislands					
Permanent Mission of Sweden to the United Nations 885 Second Ave Fl 46 1 Dag Hammarskjold Plz	New York	NY	10017	212-583-2500	583-2549
Web: www.swedenabroad.com					
Permanent Mission of the Netherlands to the UN in New York United States 666 Third Ave 19th Fl	New York	NY	10017	212-519-9500	370-1954
Web: www.netherlandsmission.org					
Permanent Mission of the Republic of Seychelles to the United Nations 800 Second Ave Ste 400C	New York	NY	10017	212-972-1785	972-1786
Web: www.un.int/wcm/content/site/seychelles					
Permanent Mission of the Republic of the Union of Myanmar 10 E 77th St	New York	NY	10075	212-744-1271	744-1290
Web: mmnewyork.org/					
Philippines 556 Fifth Ave Fifth Fl	New York	NY	10036	212-764-1300	840-8602
Web: www.un.int					
Qatar 809 UN Plz Fourth Fl	New York	NY	10017	212-486-9335	758-4952
Web: www.un.org					
Romania 573-577 Third Ave	New York	NY	10016	212-682-3273	
Web: www.un.int					
Rwanda 124 E 39th St	New York	NY	10016	212-679-9010	679-9133
Saint Kitts & Nevis 414 E 75th St 5th Fl	New York	NY	10021	212-535-1234	535-6854
Web: www.stkittsnevis.org					
Saint Lucia 800 Second Ave Ninth Fl	New York	NY	10017	212-697-9360	697-4993
Web: www.un.int/stlucia					
San Marino 327 E 50th St	New York	NY	10022	212-751-1234	751-1436
Senegal 238 E 68th St	New York	NY	10065	212-517-9030	517-3032
Web: www.un.int					
Sierra Leone 245 E 49th St	New York	NY	10017	212-688-1656	688-4924
Web: www.un.int/sierraleone					
Slovakia 801 Second Ave 12th Fl	New York	NY	10017	212-286-8434	286-8439
Web: www.mzv.sk/nyc					
Somalia 425 E 61st St Ste 702	New York	NY	10065	212-688-9410	
Web: un.int					
South Africa 333 E 38th St Ninth Fl	New York	NY	10016	212-213-5583	692-2498
Web: www.southafrica-newyork.net					
Sudan 305 E 47th St Fourth Fl	New York	NY	10017	212-573-6033	573-6160
Web: un.int					
Suriname 866 UN Plaza Ste 320	New York	NY	10017	212-826-0660	980-7029
Web: www.un.int					
Syria 820 Second Ave 15th Fl	New York	NY	10017	212-661-1313	983-4439
Web: un.int					
Tanzania 307 East 53rd Street 4th Floor	New York	NY	10022	212-697-3612	697-3618
Web: www.tanzania-un.org					
Thailand 351 E 52nd St	New York	NY	10022	212-754-2230	688-3029
Web: un.int					
Tunisia 31 Beekman Pl	New York	NY	10022	212-751-7503	751-0569
Turkey 821 UN Plz 10th Fl	New York	NY	10017	212-949-0150	949-0086
Web: www.un.int/turkey					

	City	State	Zip	Phone	Fax
Uganda 336 E 45th St	New York	NY	10017	212-949-0110	687-4517
Web: ugandamissionunny.net					
Ukraine 220 E 51st St	New York	NY	10022	212-759-7003	355-9455
UN Mission of Iraq 14 E 79th St	New York	NY	10075	212-737-4433	
United Arab Emirates 305 E 47th St Seventh Fl	New York	NY	10017	212-371-0480	371-4923
Web: www.un.int/wcm/content/site/uae					
United States of America 799 United Nations Plz	New York	NY	10017	212-415-4000	415-4443
Web: www.un.int					
Uruguay 866 UN Plz Ste 322	New York	NY	10017	212-752-8240	593-0935
Web: www.un.int/uruguay					
Vanuatu 800 E Second Ave	New York	NY	10017	212-661-4303	422-3427
Web: www.un.int					
Venezuela 335 E 46th St	New York	NY	10017	212-557-2055	557-3528
Web: www.un.int					
Zambia 237 E 52nd St	New York	NY	10022	212-888-5770	888-5213
Web: www.un.int					
Zimbabwe 128 E 56th St	New York	NY	10022	212-980-9511	308-6705

788 UNIVERSITIES - CANADIAN

	City	Prov	Postal Code	Phone	Fax
Acadia University 15 University Ave	Wolfville	NS	B4P2R6	902-542-2201	585-1081
TF: 877-585-1121 ■ *Web:* www2.acadiau.ca					
Alberta College of Art & Design 1407 14th Ave NW	Calgary	AB	T2N4R3	403-284-7600	289-6682
TF: 800-251-8290 ■ *Web:* www.acad.ca					
Athabasca University One University Dr	Athabasca	AB	T9S3A3	780-675-6111	675-6174
TF: 800-788-9041 ■ *Web:* www.athabascau.ca					
Bethany Bible College 26 Western St	Sussex	NB	E4E1E6	506-432-4400	432-4425
TF: 888-432-4444 ■ *Web:* www.kingswood.edu					
Bishop's University 2600 College St	Sherbrooke	QC	J1M0C8	819-822-9600	822-9661
TF: 800-567-2792 ■ *Web:* www.ubishops.ca					
Brandon University 270 18th St	Brandon	MB	R7A6A9	204-728-9520	728-7346
Web: www.brandonu.ca					
Brescia University College 1285 Western Rd	London	ON	N6G1H2	519-432-8353	858-5137
Web: www.brescia.uwo.ca					
Brock University 500 Glenridge Ave	Saint Catharines	ON	L2S3A1	905-688-5550	988-5488
Web: www.brocku.ca					
Campion College at the University of Regina 3737 Wascana Pkwy	Regina	SK	S4S0A2	306-586-4242	359-1200
TF: 800-667-7282 ■ *Web:* www.campioncollege.sk.ca					
Canadian College of Naturopathic Medicine 1255 Sheppard Ave E	Toronto	ON	M2K1E2	416-498-1255	498-1576
TF: 866-241-2266 ■ *Web:* www.ccnm.edu					
Canadian Memorial Chiropractic College 6100 Leslie St	Toronto	ON	M2H3J1	416-482-2340	482-9745
Web: www.cmcc.ca					
Cape Breton University 1250 Grand Lk Rd	Sydney	NS	B1P6L2	902-539-5300	562-0119
TF: 888-959-9995 ■ *Web:* www.cbu.ca					
Carleton University 1125 Colonel By Dr	Ottawa	ON	K1S5B6	613-520-7400	520-3847
TF: 888-354-4414 ■ *Web:* www.carleton.ca					
Columbia Bible College 2940 Clearbrook Rd	Abbotsford	BC	V2T2Z8	604-853-3358	853-3063
Web: www.columbiabc.edu					
Concordia University 1455 de Maisonneuve Blvd W	Montreal	QC	H3G1M8	514-848-2424	848-2621
Web: www.concordia.ca					
Concordia University College of Alberta 7128 Ada Blvd NW	Edmonton	AB	T5B4E4	780-479-9220	378-8460
TF: 866-479-5200 ■ *Web:* www.concordia.ab.ca					
Crandall University 333 Gorge Rd	Moncton	NB	E1G3H9	506-858-8970	858-9694
TF: 888-968-6228 ■ *Web:* crandallu.ca					
Dalhousie University 6299 S St Rm 125 Henry Hicks A&A Bldg	Halifax	NS	B3H4R2	902-494-3998	494-2839
Web: www.dal.ca					
Dominican University College 96 Empress Ave	Ottawa	ON	K1R7G3	613-233-5696	233-6064
Web: udominicaine.ca/					
Emmanuel Bible College 100 Fergus Ave	Kitchener	ON	N2A2H2	519-894-8900	894-5331
Web: emmanuelbiblecollege.ca					
Northern 1301 Central Ave	Prince Albert	SK	S6V4W1	306-765-3333	765-3330
TF: 800-267-6303					
First Nations University of Canada *Saskatoon* 226 20th St E	Saskatoon	SK	S7K0A6	306-931-1800	
TF: 800-267-6303 ■ *Web:* fnuniv.ca					
Heritage College & Seminary 175 Holiday Inn Dr	Cambridge	ON	N3C3T2	519-651-2869	651-2870
TF: 800-465-1961 ■ *Web:* heritagecambridge.com/					
Huron University College 1349 Western Rd	London	ON	N6G1H3	519-438-7224	438-3938
Web: www.huronuc.on.ca					
Chicago One N State St Ste 500	Chicago	IL	60602	312-386-7681	
TF: 888-318-6111 ■ *Web:* www.iadt.edu					
Toronto 1835 Yonge St Second Fl	Toronto	ON	M4S1X8	866-838-6542	695-1389*
**Fax Area Code:* 905 ■ *TF General:* 866-838-6542 ■ *Web:* www.aodt.ca					
King's University College 9125 50th St	Edmonton	AB	T6B2H3	780-465-3500	465-3534
TF: 800-661-8582 ■ *Web:* kingsu.ca					
Lakehead University 955 Oliver Rd	Thunder Bay	ON	P7B5E1	807-343-8110	343-8023
Web: www.lakeheadu.ca					
Laurentian University 935 Ramsey Lake Rd	Sudbury	ON	P3E2C6	705-675-1151	675-4838
TF: 800-461-4030 ■ *Web:* www.laurentian.ca					
Laval University 2325 Rue University	Quebec	QC	G1V0A6	418-656-2131	656-5216
TF: 877-785-2825 ■ *Web:* www2.ulaval.ca					
McGill University 845 Sherbrooke St W	Montreal	QC	H3A2T5	514-398-4455	398-8939*
**Fax:* Admissions ■ *Web:* www.mcgill.ca					
McMaster University 1280 Main St W	Hamilton	ON	L8S4L8	905-525-9140	527-1105
Web: www.mcmaster.ca					
Mount Allison University 62 York St	Sackville	NB	E4L1E2	506-364-2269	364-2272
Web: www.mta.ca					
Mount Royal College 4825 Mt Royal Gate SW	Calgary	AB	T3E6K6	403-440-6111	440-6339
TF: 877-440-5001 ■ *Web:* www.mtroyal.ca					
Mount Saint Vincent University 166 Bedford Hwy	Halifax	NS	B3M2J6	902-457-6117	457-6498
TF: 877-733-6788 ■ *Web:* www.msvu.ca					
Nipissing University 100 College Dr PO Box 5002	North Bay	ON	P1B8L7	705-474-3450	495-1772
Web: nipissingu.ca/					
Brantford 67 Darling St	Brantford	ON	N3T2K6	519-756-8228	720-9996
Web: www.nipissingu.ca					
NSCAD University 5163 Duke St	Halifax	NS	B3J3J6	902-444-9600	425-2420
Web: www.nscad.ca					
Ontario College of Art & Design 100 McCaul St	Toronto	ON	M5T1W1	416-977-6000	977-6006
Web: www.ocad.on.ca					
Prairie Bible Institute 330 Fifth Ave NE PO Box 4000	Three Hills	AB	T0M2N0	403-443-5511	443-5540
TF: 800-661-2425 ■ *Web:* www.prairie.edu					
Queen's University 99 University Ave	Kingston	ON	K7L3N6	613-533-2000	533-2068
Web: www.queensu.ca					
Redeemer University College 777 Garner Rd E	Ancaster	ON	L9K1J4	905-648-2131	648-2134
TF: 877-779-0913 ■ *Web:* www.redeemer.ca					
Royal Military College of Canada Stn Forces PO Box 17000	Kingston	ON	K7K7B4	613-541-6000	541-6599
Web: www.rmc.ca					
Royal Roads University 2005 Sooke Rd	Victoria	BC	V9B5Y2	250-391-2511	391-2500
TF: 800-788-8028 ■ *Web:* www.royalroads.ca					
Ryerson University 350 Victoria St	Toronto	ON	M5B2K3	416-979-5000	979-5170
TF: 866-592-8882 ■ *Web:* www.ryerson.ca					
Saint Francis Xavier University PO Box 5000	Antigonish	NS	B2G2W5	902-863-3300	867-2329*
**Fax:* Admissions ■ *TF Admissions:* 877-867-7839 ■ *Web:* www.stfx.ca					
Saint Jerome's University 290 Westmount Rd N	Waterloo	ON	N2L3G3	519-884-8110	884-5759
Web: www.sju.ca					
Saint Mary's University 923 Robie St	Halifax	NS	B3H3C3	902-420-5756	420-5141
Web: www.smu.ca					
Saint Paul University 223 Main St	Ottawa	ON	K1S1C4	613-236-1393	782-3014
TF: 800-637-6859 ■ *Web:* www.ustpaul.ca					
Simon Fraser University (SFU) *Burnaby* 8888 University Dr MBC 1150	Burnaby	BC	V5A1S6	778-782-2667	782-5496
Web: www.sfu.ca					
Harbour Centre 515 W Hastings St	Vancouver	BC	V6B5K3	778-782-5000	782-5219
Web: www.sfu.ca					
Surrey 250 - 13450 102 Ave	Surrey	BC	V3T0A3	778-782-7400	782-7403
Web: www.surrey.sfu.ca					
Taylor University College & Seminary 11525 23rd Ave	Edmonton	AB	T6J4T3	780-431-5200	436-9416
TF: 800-567-4988 ■ *Web:* www.taylor-edu.ca					
Thompson Rivers University 900 McGill Rd PO Box 3010	Kamloops	BC	V2C5N3	250-828-5000	371-5960*
**Fax:* Admissions ■ *TF:* 800-663-1663 ■ *Web:* www.tru.ca					
Thorneloe University 935 Ramsey Lake Rd	Sudbury	ON	P3E2C6	705-673-1730	673-4979
TF General: 800-461-4030 ■ *Web:* thorneloe.laurentian.ca					
Toronto Baptist Seminary & Bible College 130 Gerrard St E	Toronto	ON	M5A3T4	416-925-3263	925-8305
Web: www.tbs.edu					
Toronto School of Theology 47 Queen's Pk Crescent E	Toronto	ON	M5S2C3	416-978-4039	978-7821
Web: www.tst.edu					
Trent University 1600 W Bank Dr	Peterborough	ON	K9J7B8	705-748-1011	748-1629
TF: 888-739-8885 ■ *Web:* www.trentu.ca					
Trinity Western University 7600 Glover Rd	Langley	BC	V2Y1Y1	604-888-7511	513-2064*
**Fax:* Admissions ■ *TF:* 888-468-6898 ■ *Web:* www.twu.ca					
Universite de Moncton *Campus Shippagan* 218 Blvd JD Gauthier	Shippagan	NB	E8S1P6	506-336-3400	336-3604
TF: 800-363-8336 ■ *Web:* www.umoncton.ca					
Edmundston 165 Blvd Hebert	Edmundston	NB	E3V2S8	506-737-5051	737-5373
TF: 888-736-8623 ■ *Web:* www.umoncton.ca					
Universite de Montreal CP 6128 Succursale Centre Ville	Montreal	QC	H3C3J7	514-343-6111	343-5788*
**Fax:* Admissions ■ *Web:* www.umontreal.ca					
Universite de Sherbrooke 2500 boul de l'Universite	Sherbrooke	QC	J1K2R1	819-821-8000	821-7966
Web: www.usherbrooke.ca					
Universite du Quebec 475 Rue du Parvis	Quebec	QC	G1K9H7	418-657-3551	657-2132
Web: www.uquebec.ca					
Universite du Quebec a Trois-Rivieres 3351 Boul des Forges CP 500	Trois-Rivieres	QC	G9A5H7	819-376-5011	376-5210
Web: www.uqtr.ca					
Universite Sainte Anne 1695 Rt 1	Pointe-de-l'Eglise	NS	B0W1M0	902-769-2114	769-2930
Web: www.usainteanne.ca					
University of Alberta 116 St & 85 Ave	Edmonton	AB	T6G2R3	780-492-3111	
Web: www.ualberta.ca					
Augustana 4901-46th Ave	Camrose	AB	T4V2R3	780-679-1100	679-1129
TF: 800-661-8714 ■ *Web:* www.augustana.ualberta.ca					
University of British Columbia 2016-1874 E Mall	Vancouver	BC	V6T1Z1	604-822-9836	822-3599
TF: 877-272-1422 ■ *Web:* www.ubc.ca					
Okanagan 3333 University Way	Kelowna	BC	V1V1V7	250-807-8000	
Web: ok.ubc.ca					
University of Calgary 2500 University Dr NW	Calgary	AB	T2N1N4	403-220-5110	282-7298
Web: www.ucalgary.ca					
University of Guelph 50 Stone Rd E	Guelph	ON	N1G2W1	519-824-4120	766-9481
Web: www.uoguelph.ca					
University of Lethbridge 4401 University Dr	Lethbridge	AB	T1K3M4	403-329-2111	329-5159*
**Fax:* Admissions ■ *Web:* www.uleth.ca					
University of Manitoba 65 Chancellors Cir 424 University Ctr	Winnipeg	MB	R3T2N2	204-474-8880	474-7554
TF Admissions: 800-224-7713 ■ *Web:* www.umanitoba.ca					
University of New Brunswick *Saint John* 100 Tucker Pk Rd PO Box 5050	Saint John	NB	E2L4L5	506-648-5500	648-5528
Web: www.unb.ca					

	City	State	Zip	Phone	Fax
University of Northern British Columbia 3333 University Way *Web:* www.unbc.ca	Prince George	BC	V2N4Z9	250-960-5555	960-6330
University of Ottawa 550 Cumberland St. *TF:* 877-868-8292 ■ *Web:* www.uottawa.ca	Ottawa	ON	K1N6N5	613-562-5800	562-5323
University of Regina					
Luther College 3737 Wascana Pkwy *Web:* www.luthercollege.edu	Regina	SK	S4S0A2	306-585-5333	585-5267
Saint Thomas More College 1437 College Dr *TF:* 800-667-2019 ■ *Web:* www.stmcollege.ca	Saskatoon	SK	S7N0W6	306-966-8900	966-8904
University of Toronto					
Mississauga 3359 Mississauga Rd N *Web:* www.utm.utoronto.ca	Mississauga	ON	L5L1C6	905-828-5399	569-4301
Scarborough 1265 Military Trl *Web:* www.utsc.utoronto.ca	Toronto	ON	M1C1A4	416-287-8872	978-7022
University of Trinity College Six Hoskin Ave *Web:* www.trinity.utoronto.ca	Toronto	ON	M5S1H8	416-978-2522	978-2797
Victoria University 140 Charles St *Web:* www.vicu.utoronto.ca	Toronto	ON	M5S1K9	416-585-4524	585-4524
University of Victoria 3800 Finnerty Rd Stn CSC PO Box 1700 *Web:* www.uvic.ca	Victoria	BC	V8P5C2	250-472-5416	472-5477
University of Waterloo 200 University Ave W *Web:* uwaterloo.ca	Waterloo	ON	N2L3G1	519-888-4567	746-3242
University of Western Ontario					
King's University College 266 Epworth Ave *TF:* 800-265-4406 ■ *Web:* www.uwo.ca	London	ON	N6A2M3	519-433-3491	433-2227
University of Windsor 401 Sunset Ave. *Web:* www.uwindsor.ca	Windsor	ON	N9B3P4	519-253-3000	973-7070
University of Winnipeg 515 Portage Ave *Web:* www.uwinnipeg.ca	Winnipeg	MB	R3B2E9	204-786-9914	783-8910
Wilfrid Laurier University 75 University Ave W *Web:* www.wlu.ca	Waterloo	ON	N2L3C5	519-884-1970	886-9351
York University 4700 Keele St *TF:* 800-426-2255 ■ *Web:* www.yorku.ca	Toronto	ON	M3J1P3	416-736-2100	736-5536

789 UNIVERSITY SYSTEMS

Listings are organized by state names.

	City	State	Zip	Phone	Fax
Alabama Higher Education Commission 100 N Union St PO Box 302000 *Web:* www.ache.state.al.us	Montgomery	AL	36130	334-242-1998	242-0268
University of Alabama System 401 Queen City Ave *TF:* 800-638-6420 ■ *Web:* www.uasystem.ua.edu	Tuscaloosa	AL	35401	205-348-5861	348-6301
University of Alaska System 910 Yukon Dr PO Box 775000 *Web:* www.alaska.edu	Fairbanks	AK	99775	907-450-8000	450-8012
Arakansas Higher Education Dept (ADHE) 423 Main St Ste 400 *Web:* www.adhe.edu	Little Rock	AR	72201	501-371-2000	371-2001
California State University 401 Golden Shore *TF:* 800-325-4000 ■ *Web:* www.calstate.edu	Long Beach	CA	90802	562-951-4000	951-4899
University of California System 1111 Franklin St 12th Fl *Web:* www.ucop.edu	Oakland	CA	94607	510-987-9074	987-9086
Colorado State University System 410 17th St Ste 2440 *Web:* www.csusystem.edu	Denver	CO	80202	303-534-6290	534-6298
University of Colorado System 1800 Grant St Ste 800 *Web:* www.cu.edu	Denver	CO	80203	303-860-5600	860-5610
Connecticut State University System 39 Woodland St *Web:* www.ct.edu	Hartford	CT	06105	860-493-0000	493-0085
Delaware Higher Education Commission 401 Federal St Ste 2 *Web:* www.doe.state.de.us	Dover	DE	19901	302-735-4000	
State University System of Florida 325 W Gaines St Ste 1614 *Web:* flbog.org	Tallahassee	FL	32399	850-245-0466	245-9685
University System of Georgia 270 Washington St SW *Web:* www.usg.edu	Atlanta	GA	30334	404-656-2250	657-6979
University of Hawaii System 2500 Campus Rd *Web:* www.hawaii.edu	Honolulu	HI	96822	808-956-8111	956-3952
Illinois Higher Education Board 431 E Adams St 2nd Fl *Web:* www.ibhe.org	Springfield	IL	62701	217-782-2551	782-8548
University of Illinois System 506 S Wright St Ste 352 *Web:* www.uillinois.edu	Urbana	IL	61801	217-333-1920	244-2282
Louisiana State University System 125 E Boyd Dr *TF:* 800-227-3002	Baton Rouge	LA	70803	225-578-3357	
Southern University System JS Clark Administrative Bldg Fourth Fl *Web:* www.sus.edu	Baton Rouge	LA	70813	225-771-4500	771-5522
University of Louisiana System 1201 N Third St Ste 7-300 *Web:* www.ulsystem.net	Baton Rouge	LA	70802	225-342-6950	342-6473
University of Maine System 16 Central St *Web:* www.maine.edu	Bangor	ME	04401	207-973-3200	973-3296
University System of Maryland 3300 Metzerott Rd *Web:* www.ums.edu	Adelphi	MD	20783	301-445-2740	445-1931
Massachusetts Higher Education Board 1 Ashburton Pl Rm 1401 *Web:* www.mass.edu	Boston	MA	02108	617-994-6950	727-6397
University of Massachusetts System 225 Franklin St 33rd Fl *Web:* www.massachusetts.edu	Boston	MA	02110	617-287-7050	287-7044
University of Missouri System 321 University Hall *TF:* 800-225-6075 ■ *Web:* www.umsystem.edu	Columbia	MO	65211	573-882-2011	882-2721
Montana University System 2500 E Broadway St *Web:* www.montana.edu	Helena	MT	59601	406-444-6570	444-1469
Nebraska State College System 1115 K St Ste 102 *Web:* www.nscs.edu	Lincoln	NE	68508	402-471-2505	471-2669
University of Nebraska System 3835 Holdrege St Varner Hall *TF:* 800-542-1602 ■ *Web:* www.nebraska.edu	Lincoln	NE	68583	402-472-2111	472-1237
Nevada System of Higher Education 2601 Enterprise Rd *Web:* system.nevada.edu	Reno	NV	89512	775-784-4905	784-1127
New Jersey Higher Education Commission 20 W State St PO Box 542 *Web:* www.state.nj.us	Trenton	NJ	08625	609-292-4310	292-7225
New Mexico Higher Education Dept 2048 Galisteo St *TF:* 800-279-9777 ■ *Web:* www.hed.state.nm.us	Santa Fe	NM	87505	505-476-8400	476-8453
City University of New York (CUNY) 535 E 80th St *TF:* 877-769-7441 ■ *Web:* www.cuny.edu	New York	NY	10075	212-794-5555	794-5397
New York State Education Dept 89 Washington Ave 5N EB *Web:* www.highered.nysed.gov	Albany	NY	12234	518-474-3901	
State University of New York, The (SUNY) State University Plz *TF:* 800-342-3811 ■ *Web:* www.suny.edu	Albany	NY	12246	518-320-1888	443-5322
North Carolina Community College System 200 W Jones St *Web:* nccommunitycolleges.edu	Raleigh	NC	27603	919-807-7100	807-7164
North Dakota University System 600 E Blvd Ave Dept 215 10th Fl *Web:* www.ndus.edu	Bismarck	ND	58505	701-328-2960	328-2961
Ohio State University System 190 N Oval Mall 205 Bricker Hall *Web:* www.osu.edu	Columbus	OH	43210	614-292-2424	292-1231
Oklahoma State System of Higher Education 655 Research Pkwy Ste 200 *Web:* www.okhighered.org	Oklahoma City	OK	73104	405-225-9120	225-9235
Pennsylvania State System of Higher Education 2986 N Second St *TF:* 800-732-0999 ■ *Web:* www.passhe.edu	Harrisburg	PA	17110	717-720-4000	720-4011
South Carolina Commission on Higher Education 1122 Lady St Ste 300 *Web:* www.che.sc.gov	Columbia	SC	29201	803-737-2260	737-2297
University of South Dakota Foundation 1110 N Dakota St PO Box 5555 *TF:* 800-521-3575 ■ *Web:* www.onwardsd.org	Vermillion	SD	57069	605-677-6703	677-6717
Tennessee Higher Education Commission 404 James Robertson Pkwy Ste 1900 *Web:* www.state.tn.us	Nashville	TN	37243	615-741-3605	741-6230
University of Tennessee System 800 Andy Holt Tower Eighth Fl *Web:* www.tennessee.edu	Knoxville	TN	37996	865-974-2241	974-3753
Texas A & M University System, The 200 Technology Way Ste 2043 *Web:* www.tamus.edu	College Station	TX	77845	979-458-6000	458-6044
Texas State University System (TSUS) 208 E Tenth St Ste 600 *Web:* www.tsus.edu	Austin	TX	78701	512-463-1808	463-1816
Texas Tech University System 124 Admin Bldg PO Box 42013 *Web:* www.texastech.edu	Lubbock	TX	79409	806-742-0012	742-8050
University of Texas System 601 Colorado St *TF:* 866-882-2034 ■ *Web:* www.utsystem.edu	Austin	TX	78701	512-499-4200	499-4215
Utah System of Higher Education 60 South 400 West *Web:* www.higheredutah.org	Salt Lake City	UT	84101	801-321-7101	366-8405
Vermont State Colleges 575 Stone Cutters Way *Web:* vsc.edu	Montpelier	VT	05601	802-224-3000	224-3035
Virginia Community College System 101 N 14th St 15th Fl *Web:* www.vccs.edu	Richmond	VA	23219	804-819-4901	819-4766
Washington Higher Education Coordinating Board 917 Lakeridge Way PO Box 43430 *Web:* www.wsac.wa.gov	Olympia	WA	98504	360-753-7800	753-7808
West Virginia Higher Education Policy Commission 1018 Kanawha Blvd E Ste 700 *TF:* 888-825-5707 ■ *Web:* wvhepc.com	Charleston	WV	25301	304-558-2101	
University of Wisconsin System 1220 Linden Dr 1720 Van Hise Hall *TF:* 800-442-6461 ■ *Web:* www.uwsa.edu	Madison	WI	53706	608-262-2321	262-3985
Wyoming Community College Commission 2300 Capitol Ave Fl 5 Ste B *Web:* communitycolleges.wy.edu	Cheyenne	WY	82002	307-777-7763	777-6567

790 UTILITY COMPANIES

SEE ALSO Electric Companies - Cooperatives (Rural) p. 2212; Gas Transmission - Natural Gas p. 2355
Types of utilities included here are electric companies, water supply companies, and natural gas companies.

	Phone	Fax

6D Global Technologies Inc
17 State St Ste 2550 New York NY 10004 646-681-4900
Web: www.6dglobal.com

889 Global Solutions 2501 Brookwood Rd Columbus OH 43209 614-235-8889
Web: www.889globalsolutions.com

A New Path 2527 Doubletree Rd Spring Valley CA 91978 619-670-1184
Web: anewpathsite.org

Acorn Energy Inc 3903 Centerville Rd Wilmington DE 19807 302-656-1708
Web: www.acornenergy.com

AES Corp 4300 Wilson Blvd 11th Fl Arlington VA 22203 703-522-1315 528-4510
NYSE: AES ■ *Web:* www.aes.com

AGL Resources Inc 10 Peachtree Pl PO Box 4569 Atlanta GA 30309 404-584-4000 *
NYSE: GAS ■ **Fax:* Hum Res ■ *Web:* www.aglresources.com

Alabama Gas Corp (Alagasco)
605 Richard Arrington Jr Blvd N Birmingham AL 35203 205-326-8100 326-2617
TF: 800-292-4005 ■ *Web:* www.alagasco.com

Alameda County Water District
43885 S Grimmer Blvd Fremont CA 94537 510-668-4200 770-1793
TF: 866-275-3772 ■ *Web:* www.acwd.org

Alaska Power & Telephone Co
193 Otto St PO Box 3222 Port Townsend WA 98368 360-385-1733 385-5177
OTC: APTL ■ *TF Cust Svc:* 800-982-0136 ■ *Web:* www.aptalaska.com

Allegheny Power 800 Cabin Hill Dr Greensburg PA 15601 724-837-3000
TF Cust Svc: 800-255-3443 ■ *Web:* www.firstenergycorp.com

Alliant Energy Corp
4902 N Biltmore Ln Ste 1000 Madison WI 53718 800-255-4268 458-0100*
NYSE: LNT ■ **Fax Area Code:* 608 ■ *TF:* 800-255-4268 ■ *Web:* www.alliantenergy.com

Alsco Inc 505 East South Temple Salt Lake City UT 84102 801-328-8831
Web: www.alsco.com

Ambit Energy LP 1801 N Lamar St Ste 200 Dallas TX 75202 214-270-1770
Web: ww2.ambitenergy.com

American Consumer Industries Inc (ACI)
1105 N Market St Ste 1150 Wilmington DE 19801 303-495-2665
Web: www.aciinc.net

American Emo Trans Inc PO Box 19030 Charlotte NC 28219 704-359-0045
Web: americanemotrans.com

American Municipal Power Inc
1111 Schrock Rd Ste 100 Columbus OH 43229 614-540-1111 540-1113
Web: www.amppartners.org

Aqua America Inc 762 W Lancaster Ave Bryn Mawr PA 19010 877-987-2782
NYSE: WTR ■ *TF:* 877-987-2782 ■ *Web:* www.aquaamerica.com

Aquarion Co 835 Main St Bridgeport CT 06604 203-336-7662 336-7775
TF: 800-732-9678 ■ *Web:* www.aquarion.com

AREVA Inc 4800 Hampden Ln Ste 1100 Bethesda MD 20814 301-841-1600 652-5691
Web: www.areva.com

Arizona Public Service Co (APS)
400 N Fifth St PO Box 53999 Phoenix AZ 85004 602-371-7171
TF: 800-253-9405 ■ *Web:* www.aps.com

ATCO Gas & Pipelines Ltd 10035 - 105 St Edmonton AB T5J2V6 780-424-5222
Web: www.atcogas.com

ATCO Ltd 700 909 11th Ave SW Calgary AB T2R1N6 403-292-7500 292-7532
TSE: ACO/X ■ *TF:* 800-242-3447 ■ *Web:* www.atco.com

Austin Tape & Label Inc 3350 Cavalier Trl Stow OH 44224 330-928-7999
Web: www.austintape.com

Avista Corp 1411 E Mission St Spokane WA 99202 509-489-0500
NYSE: AVA ■ *TF:* 800-936-6629 ■ *Web:* www.avistacorp.com

Avista Utilities 1411 E Mission St Spokane WA 99252 800-227-9187 495-8725*
**Fax Area Code:* 509 ■ *TF:* 800-227-9187 ■ *Web:* www.avistautilities.com

Baltimore Gas & Electric Co
110 W Fayette St P.O. Box 1475 Baltimore MD 21201 410-470-7433 234-7406
TF: 800-685-0123 ■ *Web:* www.bge.com

Bangor Hydro Electric Co PO Box 932 Bangor ME 04402 207-945-5621 990-6954
TF: 800-499-6600 ■ *Web:* emeramaine.com/

BCE Inc One CARREFOUR ALEXANDER-GRAHAM-BELL Verdun QC H3E3B3 514-786-3891
Web: www.bce.ca

Berkshire Gas Company Inc 115 Cheshire Rd Pittsfield MA 01201 413-442-1511 443-0546
TF: 800-292-5012 ■ *Web:* www.berkshiregas.com

Brownstown Electric Supply Company Inc
690 E State Rd 250 PO Box L Brownstown IN 47220 812-358-4555 358-2484
TF: 800-742-8492 ■ *Web:* www.brownstown.com

Cabot Oil & Gas Corp 840 Gessner Rd Ste 1200 Houston TX 77024 281-848-2799 589-4653*
NYSE: COG ■ **Fax:* Hum Res ■ *TF:* 800-434-3985 ■ *Web:* cabotog.com

Cadiz Inc 550 S Hope St Ste 2850 Los Angeles CA 90071 213-271-1600 271-1614
NASDAQ: CDZI ■ *Web:* www.cadizinc.com

Caithness Corp 565 Fifth Ave 29Fl New York NY 10017 212-921-9099 921-9239
Web: www.caithnessdevelopment.com

California ISO
151 Blue Ravine Rd PO Box 639014 Folsom CA 95630 916-351-4400 608-7222
TF: 800-220-4907 ■ *Web:* www.caiso.com

California Water Service Group
1720 N First St San Jose CA 95112 408-367-8200 367-8430
NYSE: CWT ■ *TF:* 800-750-8200 ■ *Web:* www.calwater.com

Calpine Corp 717 Texas Ave Ste 1000 Houston TX 77002 713-830-2000 830-2001
NYSE: CPN ■ *TF:* 800-367-5690 ■ *Web:* www.calpine.com

Canadian Utilities Ltd
1400 909 - 11th Ave SW Calgary AB T2R1N6 403-292-7500 292-7532
TSE: CU ■ *Web:* www.canadianutilities.com

Carthage Water & Electric Plant PO Box 611 Carthage MO 64836 417-237-7300 237-7310
Web: www.cwepnet.com

Cascade Natural Gas Corp (CNGC)
8113 W Grandridge Blvd Kennewick WA 99336 206-624-3900 624-7215
TF: 888-522-1130 ■ *Web:* www.cngc.com

	Phone	Fax

Central Hudson Gas & Electric Corp
284 S Ave Poughkeepsie NY 12601 845-452-2700 486-5415*
**Fax:* Hum Res ■ *TF:* 800-527-2714 ■ *Web:* www.centralhudson.com

Central Iowa Power Cooperative
1400 Hwy 13 SE Cedar Rapids IA 52403 319-366-8011
Web: www.cipco.net

Central Maine Power Co 83 Edison Dr Augusta ME 04336 207-623-3521 621-4778
TF: 800-565-0121 ■ *Web:* www.cmpco.com

Central Vermont Public Service Corp
77 Grove St Rutland VT 05701 800-649-2877 747-2199*
**Fax Area Code:* 802 ■ *TF:* 800-649-2877 ■ *Web:* www.greenmountainpower.com

Chesapeake Utilities Corp 909 Silver Lk Blvd Dover DE 19904 302-734-6799 734-6750
NYSE: CPK ■ *Web:* www.chpk.com

Cheyenne Light Fuel & Power Co
108 W 18th St Cheyenne WY 82001 307-638-3361 778-2106
Web: www.cheyennelight.com

Chickasaw Holding Co 124 W Vinita Sulphur OK 73086 580-622-2111
Web: www.chickasawholding.com

Chorus Aviation Inc Three Spectacle Lk Dr Dartmouth NS B3B1W8 902-873-5000
Web: www.flyjazz.ca

Chubu Electric Power Co Inc
900 17th St NW Ste 1220 Washington DC 20006 202-775-1960 331-9256
Web: www.chuden.co.jp

CI Financial Corp Twentieth 2 Queen St E Fl Toronto ON M5C3G7 416-364-1145
Web: www.globeinvestor.com

Citizens Gas & Coke Utility
2020 N Meridian St Indianapolis IN 46202 317-924-3311 927-4395
TF: 800-427-4217 ■ *Web:* www.citizensenergygroup.com

City Public Service Board PO Box 1771 San Antonio TX 78296 210-353-2222
TF: 800-870-1006 ■ *Web:* www.cpsenergy.com

Cleco Corp 2030 Donahue Ferry Rd Pineville LA 71361 318-484-7400 *
**Fax:* Hum Res ■ *TF Cust Svc:* 800-622-6537 ■ *Web:* cleco.com

Colorado Springs Utilities
111 S Cascade Ave PO Box 1103 Colorado Springs CO 80903 719-448-4800 668-7288
TF: 800-238-5434 ■ *Web:* www.csu.org

Columbia Gas of Ohio Inc 200 Civic Ctr Dr Columbus OH 43215 614-460-6000
TF: 800-807-9781 ■ *Web:* columbiagasohio.com

Columbia Gas of Virginia Inc 8063 Cedon Rd Woodford VA 22580 800-543-8911
TF Cust Svc: 800-543-8911 ■ *Web:* www.columbiagasva.com

Commissioners of Public Works
121 W Ct Ave PO Box 549 Greenwood SC 29649 864-942-8100 942-8114
Web: www.greenwoodcpw.com

Conergy Inc 2460 W 26th Ave Ste 280C Denver CO 80211 888-396-6611 473-3830*
**Fax Area Code:* 505 ■ *TF:* 888-396-6611 ■ *Web:* www.conergy.us

Connecticut Light & Power Co 107 Selden St Berlin CT 06037 860-665-5000 665-2032*
**Fax:* PR ■ *TF Cust Svc:* 800-286-2000 ■ *Web:* www.cl-p.com

Connecticut Natural Gas Corp (CNG)
76 Meadow St East Hartford CT 06108 860-727-3000
Web: www.cngcorp.com

Consumers Energy Co One Energy Plz Jackson MI 49201 517-788-0550 788-2451*
**Fax:* Hum Res ■ *TF Cust Svc:* 800-477-5050 ■ *Web:* www.consumersenergy.com

Coulson Group of Companies
4890 Cherry Creek Rd Port Alberni BC V9Y8E9 250-723-8118
Web: www.coulsongroup.com

Covanta Energy Corp 445 South Street Morristown NJ 07960 862-345-5000
NYSE: CVA ■ *Web:* covanta.com/

Cupric Canyon Capital LLC
7373 E Doubletree Ranch Rd Ste 200 Scottsdale AZ 85258 480-607-6771
Web: www.cupriccanyon.com

Dakota Gasification Co PO Box 5540 Bismarck ND 58506 701-221-4400 557-5336
TF: 800-759-0555 ■ *Web:* www.dakotagas.com

Dayton Power & Light Co PO Box 1247 Dayton OH 45401 937-331-3900 331-3900
TF: 800-433-8500 ■ *Web:* www.dpandl.com

Delmarva Power PO Box 231 Wilmington DE 19899 800-898-8042
TF Cust Svc: 800-898-8042 ■ *Web:* www.delmarva.com

Delta Natural Gas Co Inc
3617 Lexington Rd Winchester KY 40391 859-744-6171 744-3623
NASDAQ: DGAS ■ *TF:* 800-262-2012 ■ *Web:* www.deltagas.com

Dominion East Ohio PO Box 26532 Richmond VA 23261 800-362-7557
TF Cust Svc: 800-362-7557 ■ *Web:* www.dom.com

Dominion Hope 701 E Cary St Richmond VA 23219 888-366-8280
TF: 866-366-4357 ■ *Web:* www.dom.com/dominion-hope

Dominion North Carolina Power 701 E Cary St Richmond VA 23219 757-857-2112
TF: 888-667-3000 ■ *Web:* www.dom.com

Dominion Virginia Power 120 Tredegar St Richmond VA 23219 800-688-4673
TF: 800-688-4673 ■ *Web:* www.dom.com

Duquesne Light Co 411 Seventh Ave Pittsburgh PA 15219 412-393-7000 393-7000
TF Cust Svc: 888-393-7000 ■ *Web:* www.duquesnelight.com

Dynasty Import Co 2765 16th St San Francisco CA 94103 415-864-5084
Web: m.dynastygallery.com

Eastern Shore Natural Gas Co
1110 Forest Ave Ste 201 Dover DE 19904 302-734-6720
TF: 877-650-1257 ■ *Web:* www.esng.com

El Paso Electric Co
100 N Stanton Stanton Tower El Paso TX 79901 915-543-5711 521-4766
NYSE: EE ■ *TF:* 800-351-1621 ■ *Web:* www.epelectric.com

Elizabethtown Gas Co One Elizabethtown Plz Union NJ 07083 908-289-5000 859-5307
TF: 800-242-5830 ■ *Web:* www.elizabethtowngas.com

Emerald Coast Utilities Authority (ECUA)
9255 Sturdevant St PO Box 15311 Pensacola FL 32514 850-476-0480
Web: www.ecua.fl.gov

Empire District Electric Co, The
602 Joplin St PO Box 127 Joplin MO 64802 417-625-5100 625-5146*
NYSE: EDE ■ **Fax:* Hum Res ■ *TF:* 800-206-2300 ■ *Web:* www.empiredistrict.com

Energy West Inc 1 First Ave S Great Falls MT 59401 406-791-7500 791-7560
TF: 800-570-5688 ■ *Web:* www.ewst.com

ENMAX Corp 141 50 Ave SE Calgary AB T2G4S7 403-514-3000
Web: www.enmax.com

Enpower Corp 2420 Camino Ramon Ste 101 San Ramon CA 94583 925-244-1100
Web: www.enpowercorp.com

ENSTAR Natural Gas Co
401 E International Airport Rd Anchorage AK 99518 907-277-5551 276-6696
Web: www.enstargas.com

				Phone	Fax
Entergy Arkansas Inc 425 W Capitol Ave *TF:* 800-368-3749 ■ *Web:* www.entergy-arkansas.com	Little Rock	AR	72201	800-368-3749	
Entergy Louisiana Inc 639 Loyola Ave *TF Cust Svc:* 800-368-3749 ■ *Web:* www.entergy.com	New Orleans	LA	70113	504-576-6116	
Entergy Mississippi Inc PO Box 1640 *Web:* www.entergy-mississippi.com	Jackson	MS	39215	601-969-2440	
Entergy New Orleans Inc 639 Loyola Ave *TF Cust Svc:* 800-368-3749 ■ *Web:* www.entergy-neworleans.com	New Orleans	LA	70113	800-368-3749	
Entergy Texas Inc 350 Pine St *TF:* 800-368-3749 ■ *Web:* www.entergy-texas.com	Beaumont	TX	77701	409-981-3245	981-2317
EQT Corp 625 Liberty Ave Ste 1700 *NYSE: EQT* ■ *TF:* 800-242-1776 ■ *Web:* www.eqt.com	Pittsburgh	PA	15222	412-553-5700	
Equitable Gas Co PO Box 6766 *TF:* 800-654-6335 ■ *Web:* www.equitablegas.com	Pittsburgh	PA	15212	800-654-6335	
Erie County Water Authority (ECWA) 295 Main St Rm 350 *TF:* 855-748-1076 ■ *Web:* www.ecwa.org	Buffalo	NY	14203	716-849-8484	849-8467
Eversource 1 Nstar Way NW200 *TF Cust Svc:* 800-592-2000 ■ *Web:* nstar.com	Westwood	MA	02090	781-441-8011	441-8167
Far Bank Enterprises Inc 8500 NE Day Rd *Web:* www.farbank.com	Bainbridge Island	WA	98110	206-780-8767	
First Surgical Partners Inc 411 First St *Web:* www.firstsurgical.com	Bellaire	TX	77401	713-665-1111	
Florida City Gas (FCG) 955 E 25th St *TF:* 800-993-7546 ■ *Web:* www.floridacitygas.com	Hialeah	FL	33013	305-691-8710	
Florida Power & Light Co (FPL) 700 Universe Blvd *Web:* www.fpl.com	Juno Beach	FL	33408	561-697-8000	691-7177
Florida Public Utilities Co (FPUC) 401 S Dixie Hwy **Fax Area Code:* 561 ■ *TF:* 800-427-7712 ■ *Web:* www.fpuc.com	West Palm Beach	FL	33401	800-427-7712	833-0151*
Garvey Group LLC, The 7400 N Lehigh Ave *Web:* www.thegarveygroup.com	Niles	IL	60714	847-647-1900	
Gas Co, The 515 Kamake'e St *TF:* 866-499-3941 ■ *Web:* www.hawaiigas.com	Honolulu	HI	96814	808-535-5933	535-5934
Gatco Inc 1550 Factor Ave *Web:* www.gatco-inc.com	San Leandro	CA	94577	510-352-8770	
Georgia Power Co 241 Ralph McGill Blvd NE *TF Cust Svc:* 866-506-5333 ■ *Web:* www.southernco.com	Atlanta	GA	30308	404-506-5000	
Ges USA Inc 101 W Elm St Ste 550 *Web:* services-ges.com	Conshohocken	PA	19428	610-940-6088	
Globalscale Technologies Inc 1200 N Van Buren St Ste D *Web:* globalscaletechnologies.com	Anaheim	CA	92807	714-632-9239	
Goleta Water District 4699 Hollister Ave *Web:* www.goletawater.com	Goleta	CA	93110	805-964-6761	879-4609
Green Brick Partners Inc 2805 Dallas Pkwy Ste 400 *Web:* www.bfenergy.com	Plano	TX	75093	469-573-6763	
Green Mountain Energy Co PO Box 689008 *Web:* greenmountainenergy.com/	Austin	TX	78768	512-691-6100	691-6151
Green Mountain Power Corp 163 Acorn Ln *TF:* 888-835-4672 ■ *Web:* www.greenmountainpower.com	Colchester	VT	05446	802-864-5731	655-8419
GridPoint Inc 2801 Clarendon Blvd Ste 100 *Web:* www.gridpoint.com	Arlington	VA	22201	703-667-7000	667-7001
HaloSource Inc 1631 220th St SE Ste 100 *Web:* www.halosource.com	Bothell	WA	98021	425-881-6464	882-2476
Harris, Harris, Bauerle & Sharma PA 1201 E Robinson St *Web:* www.hhbslaw.com	Orlando	FL	32801	407-843-0404	
Hawaiian Electric Industries Inc 1001 Bishop St Ste 2900 *Web:* www.hei.com	Honolulu	HI	96813	808-543-5662	
Hawaiian Telcom Holdco Inc 1177 Bishop St *Web:* www.hawaiiantel.com	Honolulu	HI	96813	808-546-4511	
Hazelett Strip-Casting Corp 135 W Lakeshore Dr PO Box 600 *Web:* www.hazelett.com	Colchester	VT	05446	802-863-6376	
Home Meridian International Inc 3980 Premier Dr Ste 310 *Web:* www.homemeridian.com	High Point	NC	27265	336-819-7200	
Hydro One Inc 483 Bay St 15th Fl *TF:* 888-664-9376 ■ *Web:* www.hydroone.com	Toronto	ON	M5G2P5	416-345-5000	345-6060
I.D.S. Intelligent Data Systems (Canada) Inc 6790 Kitimat Rd Unit 6 *Web:* idscdn.com	Mississauga	ON	L5N5L9	905-826-6852	
Idaho Power Co 1221 W Idaho St **Fax:* Hum Res ■ *TF:* 800-488-6151 ■ *Web:* www.idahopower.com	Boise	ID	83702	208-388-2200	388-6695*
Indianapolis Power & Light Co One Monument Cir *Web:* www.iplpower.com	Indianapolis	IN	46204	317-261-8261	
Intermountain Gas Co Inc 555 S Cole Rd *TF Cust Svc:* 800-548-3679 ■ *Web:* www.intgas.com	Boise	ID	83709	208-377-6840	377-6081
Inuvialuit Regional Corp Bag Service #21 *Web:* www.irc.inuvialuit.com	Inuvik	NT	X0E0T0	867-777-2737	
Jackson Energy Authority 119 E College St *Web:* www.jaxenergy.com	Jackson	TN	38301	731-422-7500	422-7307
Kansas City Power & Light Co 1200 Main *TF:* 888-471-5275 ■ *Web:* www.kcpl.com	Kansas City	MO	64141	816-556-2200	654-1125
Kansas Gas Service 7421 W 129th St *TF:* 888-482-4950 ■ *Web:* www.kansasgasservice.com	Overland Park	KS	66213	888-482-4950	
Kimble Companies Inc 3596 State Rt 39 NW *Web:* www.kimblecompanies.com	Dover	OH	44622	330-343-1226	
Kinder Morgan Inc KN Energy Retail Div 370 Van Gordon St *TF:* 800-232-1627 ■ *Web:* www.kindermorgan.com	Lakewood	CO	80228	303-989-1740	
Kissimmee Utility Authority Inc (KUA) 1701 W Carroll St *TF:* 877-582-7700 ■ *Web:* www.kua.com	Kissimmee	FL	34741	407-933-7777	933-7715
Laclede Gas Co 720 Olive St **Fax:* Hum Res ■ *TF:* 800-887-4173 ■ *Web:* www.lacledegas.com	Saint Louis	MO	63101	314-342-0500	588-0615*

				Phone	Fax
Lad Global Enterprises Inc 1309 S Fountain Dr *Web:* www.lad-global.com	Olathe	KS	66061	913-768-0888	
Lake Haven Utility District 31627-1st Ave S PO Box 4249 *Web:* www.lakehaven.org	Federal Way	WA	98063	253-941-1516	
Lampton-Love Inc PO Box 1607 *Web:* www.lamptonlove.com	Jackson	MS	39215	601-939-8304	939-8309
Laney's Inc 55 27 St S PO Box 2562 *Web:* www.laneysinc.com	Fargo	ND	58103	701-237-0543	
Lightyear Network Solutions LLC 1901 Eastpoint Pkwy *Web:* www.lightyear.net	Louisville	KY	40223	502-244-6666	
Lineage Power Corp 601 Shiloh Rd *TF:* 877-546-3243 ■ *Web:* geindustrial.com/products/critical-power	Plano	TX	75074	972-244-9288	
Long Island Power Authority 333 Earle Ovington Blvd Ste 403 *TF Cust Svc:* 877-275-5472 ■ *Web:* www.lipower.org	Uniondale	NY	11553	516-222-7700	222-9137
Lord Electric Co Of Puerto Rico Inc 8 Simon Madera *Web:* www.lordelectric.com	San Juan	PR	00924	787-758-4040	763-3320
Lyondellbasell Industries Inc 1221 McKinney St LyondellBasell Tower Ste 700 *Web:* www.lyondellbasell.com	Houston	TX	77010	713-309-7200	
Madison Gas & Electric Co 133 S Blair St *TF:* 800-245-1125 ■ *Web:* www.mge.com	Madison	WI	53703	608-252-7000	252-7098
Marts & Lundy Inc 1200 Wall St W *TF:* 800-526-9005 ■ *Web:* www.martsandlundy.com	Lyndhurst	NJ	07071	201-460-1660	460-0680
MEAG Power 1470 Riveredge Pkwy NW *TF:* 800-333-6324 ■ *Web:* www.meagpower.org	Atlanta	GA	30328	770-563-0300	563-0004
Medley Communications Inc 560-6 Birch St **Fax Area Code:* 866 ■ *TF:* 888-551-7208 ■ *Web:* medleycom.net	Lake Elsinore	CA	92530	951-245-5200	241-3539*
Mel-Kay Electric Company Inc 1511 N Garvin St *Web:* www.mel-kayelectric.com	Evansville	IN	47711	812-423-1128	423-5117
Memphis Light Gas & Water (MLGW) 220 S Main St PO Box 430 *Web:* www.mlgw.com	Memphis	TN	38101	901-528-4011	528-4296
Menasha Utilities 321 Milwaukee St PO Box 340 *Web:* www.menashautilities.com	Menasha	WI	54952	920-967-3400	967-3441
Merrithew Corp 2200 Yonge St Ste 500 *Web:* www.merrithew.com	Toronto	ON	M4S2C6	416-482-4050	
Meruelo Construction 9550 Firestone Blvd Ste 105 *Web:* merueloenterprises.com	Downey	CA	90241	562-745-2345	
Metromedia Energy Inc 6 Industrial Way W *TF:* 800-828-9427 ■ *Web:* www.metromediaenergy.com	Eatontown	NJ	07724	732-542-7575	542-8655
Michael W Middleton PC (MWMPC) 3330 Longmire Dr *Web:* www.mwmpc.com	College Station	TX	77845	979-695-2726	695-2754
Middle Tennessee Natural Gas Utility District (MTNG) 1036 W Broad St PO Box 670 *TF:* 800-880-6373 ■ *Web:* www.mtng.com	Smithville	TN	37166	615-597-4300	597-6331
Middlesex County Utilities Authority Inc (MCUA) 2571 Main St PO Box 159 *Web:* www.mcua.com	Sayreville	NJ	08872	732-721-3800	721-0206
Middlesex Water Co 1500 Ronson Rd PO Box 1500 *NASDAQ: MSEX* ■ *TF:* 800-549-3802 ■ *Web:* middlesexwater.com	Iselin	NJ	08830	732-634-1500	638-7515
Miller-Eads Company Inc 4125 N Keystone Ave PO Box 55234 *TF:* 800-530-0684 ■ *Web:* www.miller-eads.com	Indianapolis	IN	46205	317-545-7101	545-4660
Minnesota Power 30 W Superior St *TF:* 800-228-4966 ■ *Web:* www.mnpower.com	Duluth	MN	55802	218-722-2625	720-2795
Missouri Gas Energy 3420 Broadway *TF:* 800-582-1234 ■ *Web:* www.missourigasenergy.com	Kansas City	MO	64111	816-756-5252	756-0595
Mobile Gas Service Corp 2828 Dauphin St **Fax:* Mktg ■ *Web:* www.mobile-gas.com	Mobile	AL	36606	251-476-2720	471-2588*
Monroe County Water Authority 475 Norris Dr PO Box 10999 *TF:* 866-426-6292 ■ *Web:* www.mcwa.com	Rochester	NY	14610	585-442-2000	442-0220
Montana-Dakota Utilities Co (MDU) 400 N Fourth St *TF:* 800-638-3278 ■ *Web:* www.montana-dakota.com	Bismarck	ND	58501	701-222-7900	
Morgan-McClure Motorsports Inc 26502 Newbanks Rd *Web:* www.morgan-mcclure.com	Abingdon	VA	24210	276-628-3683	
Morris Products Inc 53 Carey Rd *Web:* www.morrisproducts.com	Queensbury	NY	12804	518-743-0523	
Morristown Utility Systems PO Box 667 *Web:* www.morristownutilities.org	Morristown	TN	37815	423-586-4121	587-6590
Mount Carmel Public Utility Co 316 Market St PO Box 220 *TF:* 877-262-7036 ■ *Web:* www.mtcpu.com/home.php	Mount Carmel	IL	62863	618-262-5151	
MRC Global Inc Two Houston Ctr *TF:* 877-294-7574 ■ *Web:* www.mrcpvf.com	Houston	TX	77010	877-294-7574	
National Fuel Gas Distribution Corp 6363 Main St *TF:* 800-365-3234 ■ *Web:* nationalfuelgas.com	Williamsville	NY	14221	716-857-7000	857-7310
National Fuel Gas Supply Corp 6363 Main St *TF Cust Svc:* 800-365-3234 ■ *Web:* nationalfuelgas.com	Williamsville	NY	14221	716-857-7000	857-7206
National Fuel Resources Inc 165 Lawrence Bell Dr Ste 120 *TF:* 800-839-9993 ■ *Web:* www.nfrinc.com	Williamsville	NY	14221	716-630-6778	630-6798
Neal Electri Corp 13250 Kirkham Way *Web:* www.nealelectric.com	Poway	CA	92064	858-513-2525	513-9488
Nevada Irrigation District (NID) 1036 W Main St *TF:* 800-222-4102 ■ *Web:* nidwater.com/	Grass Valley	CA	95945	530-273-6185	271-6838
Nevada Power Co 6226 W Sahara Ave *NYSE: NVE* ■ *TF Cust Svc:* 800-331-3103 ■ *Web:* www.nvenergy.com	Las Vegas	NV	89146	702-367-5000	367-5535

Phone Fax

New York Power Authority
123 Main St Ste 10-H ... White Plains NY 10601 914-681-6200 681-6949
Web: www.nypa.gov

New York State Electric & Gas Corp
Corporate Dr PO Box 5240 ... Binghamton NY 13902 800-572-1111
TF: 800-572-1111 ■ *Web:* www.nyseg.com

NextEra Energy Resources LLC
NextEra Energy Resources LLC
700 Universe Blvd PO Box 14000 ... Juno Beach FL 33408 561-691-7171 691-7177
TF: 888-867-3050 ■ *Web:* www.nexteraenergyresources.com

Nicor Gas 1844 Ferry Rd ... Naperville IL 60563 630-983-8888 983-6755
TF: 888-642-6748

Nippon Kodo Inc 2771 Plz Del Amo Ste 805 ... Torrance CA 90503 310-320-8881
Web: www.nipponkodo.com

North Shore Gas Co 3001 Grand Ave ... Waukegan IL 60085 847-263-3200 336-8815*
**Fax:* Mktg ■ *TF:* 866-556-6004 ■ *Web:* northshoregasdelivery.com

Northern Electric Inc 1275 W 124th Ave ... Denver CO 80234 303-428-6969 428-6669
TF: 877-265-0794 ■ *Web:* www.northernelec.com

Northern Kentucky Water District
2835 Crescent Springs Rd PO Box 18640 ... Erlanger KY 41018 859-578-9898 578-5456
TF: 800-772-4636 ■ *Web:* www.nkywater.org

Northwest Natural Gas Co 220 NW Second Ave ... Portland OR 97209 503-226-4211 220-2584
NYSE: NWN ■ *TF:* 800-422-4012 ■ *Web:* www.nwnatural.com

Nova Scotia Power Inc PO Box 910 ... Halifax NS B3J2W5 902-428-6230 428-6108
TF: 800-428-6230 ■ *Web:* www.nspower.ca

NRG Energy Inc 211 Carnegie Ctr ... Princeton NJ 08540 609-524-4500 524-4501
NYSE: NRG ■ *TF:* 866-735-1214 ■ *Web:* nrg.com

NSTAR Gas One N Star Way ... Westwood MA 02090 800-592-2000
TF: 800-592-2000 ■ *Web:* nstar.com

Ocean Embassy Panama Inc
6426 Milner Blvd Ste 101 ... Orlando FL 32809 407-852-9129
Web: www.oceanembassy.com

OG & E Electric Services PO Box 24990 ... Oklahoma City OK 73124 405-553-3000 553-3165
TF: 800-272-9741 ■ *Web:* www.oge.com

Ohio Edison Co 76 S Main St PO Box 3637 ... Akron OH 44308 800-736-3402 384-3866*
**Fax Area Code:* 330 ■ *TF:* 800-736-3402 ■ *Web:* firstenergycorp.com

Oklahoma Natural Gas Co
401 N Harvey PO Box 401 ... Oklahoma City OK 73101 800-664-5463 551-6610*
**Fax Area Code:* 405 ■ *TF:* 800-664-5463 ■ *Web:* www.oklahomanaturalgas.com

Olympia Financial Group Inc
Ste 2300 125 - 9 Ave SE ... Calgary AB T2G0P6 403-261-0900
Web: www.olympiatrust.com

Oncor 1616 Woodall Rodgers Fwy Ste 2M-012 ... Dallas TX 75202 214-486-2000 486-2175
TF: 888-313-6862 ■ *Web:* www.oncor.com

Orange & Rockland Utilities Inc
One Blue Hill Plz ... Pearl River NY 10965 877-434-4100 577-2958*
**Fax Area Code:* 845 ■ *TF Cust Svc:* 877-434-4100 ■ *Web:* www.oru.com

Orange Water & Sewer Authority (Inc)
400 Jones Ferry Rd PO Box 366 ... Carrboro NC 27510 919-968-4421 968-4464
Web: www.owasa.org

Osaka Gas Energy America Corp
1 N Lexington Ave Ste 504 ... White Plains NY 10601 914-253-5500 328-4430
Web: www.osakagas.co.jp

Otter Tail Power Co 215 S Cascade St ... Fergus Falls MN 56537 218-739-8200 751-5151
TF: 800-257-4044 ■ *Web:* www.otpco.com

Pacific Data Electric Inc (PDE)
9970 Bell Ranch Dr Ste 109 ... Santa Fe Springs CA 90670 562-204-3550 204-0380
Web: www.pdeinc.com

Pacific Gas & Electric Co 77 Beale St ... San Francisco CA 94105 415-973-7000
TF Cust Svc: 800-743-5000 ■ *Web:* www.pge.com

Pacific Power & Light 825 NE Multnomah St ... Portland OR 97232 503-813-7100 800-2851*
**Fax Area Code:* 888 ■ **Fax:* Cust Svc ■ *TF Cust Svc:* 888-221-7070 ■ *Web:* www.pacificpower.net

PacifiCorp 825 NE Multnomah St ... Portland OR 97232 503-813-5000 813-6659*
**Fax:* Hum Res ■ *TF:* 888-221-7070 ■ *Web:* www.pacificorp.com

Paducah Power System 1500 Broadway PO Box 180 ... Paducah KY 42002 270-575-4000 575-4027
Web: www.paducahpower.com

Park Water Co 9750 Washburn Rd ... Downey CA 90241 562-923-0711 861-5902
TF: 800-727-5987 ■ *Web:* www.parkwater.com

Parkway Electric Inc 11952 James St ... Holland MI 49424 616-392-2788 392-6880
TF: 800-574-9553 ■ *Web:* www.parkwayelectric.com

Passaic Valley Water Commission
1525 Main Ave ... Clifton NJ 07011 973-340-4300 340-5598
TF: 877-772-7077 ■ *Web:* www.pvwc.com

Pennichuck Corp 25 Manchester St ... Merrimack NH 03054 603-882-5191 913-2362
NASDAQ: PNNW ■ *TF:* 800-553-5191 ■ *Web:* www.pennichuck.com

Peoples Gas Light & Coke Co
130 E Randolph Dr ... Chicago IL 60601 312-240-4000 240-4120
TF Cust Svc: 866-556-6001 ■ *Web:* northshoregasdelivery.com

Pepco Energy Services Inc
1300 N 17th St Ste 1600 ... Arlington VA 22209 703-253-1800 967-5820*
**Fax Area Code:* 301 ■ *TF:* 800-424-8028 ■ *Web:* www.pepco.com

Pepco Holdings Inc 701 Ninth St NW ... Washington DC 20068 202-872-2000
NYSE: POM ■ *Web:* www.pepcoholdings.com

PFB Corp 100-2886 Sunridge Way NE ... Calgary AB T1Y7H9 403-569-4300
Web: www.pfbcorp.com

Phalcon Ltd 505 Main St ... Farmington CT 06032 860-677-9797
Web: phalconusa.com

Philadelphia Gas Works (PGW)
800 W Montgomery Ave PO Box 3500 ... Philadelphia PA 19122 215-235-1000 684-6500*
**Fax:* Hum Res ■ *Web:* www.pgworks.com

Phillips 66 3010 Briarpark Dr ... Houston TX 77042 281-293-6600
Web: www.phillips66.com

Piedmont Natural Gas
4720 Piedmont Row Dr PO Box 33068 ... Charlotte NC 28210 704-364-3120 365-3849
NYSE: PNY ■ *TF:* 800-752-7504 ■ *Web:* www.piedmontng.com

Pinnacle Gas Resources Inc One E Aalger St ... Sheridan WY 82801 307-673-9710

Placer County Water Agency
144 Ferguson Rd PO Box 6570 ... Auburn CA 95604 530-823-4850
Web: www.pcwa.net

Portland General Electric 121 SW Salmon St ... Portland OR 97204 503-464-8000 464-2676*
NYSE: POR ■ **Fax:* Hum Res ■ *TF:* 800-542-8818 ■ *Web:* www.portlandgeneral.com

Phone Fax

Portland Water District
225 Douglass St PO Box 3553 ... Portland ME 04104 207-761-8310 761-8307
Web: www.pwd.org

Power Marketing Administrations
Bonneville Power Administration
905 NE 11th Ave ... Portland OR 97232 503-230-3000
Web: www.bpa.gov

PowerSecure International Inc
1609 Heritage Commerce Ct ... Wake Forest NC 27587 919-556-3056 556-3596
NYSE: POWR ■ *TF:* 866-347-5455 ■ *Web:* www.powersecure.com

PPL Electric Utilities Corp Two N Ninth St ... Allentown PA 18101 610-774-5151 774-5408*
**Fax:* Cust Svc ■ *TF Cust Svc:* 800-342-5775 ■ *Web:* www.pplweb.com

PPL Global LLC Two N Ninth St ... Allentown PA 18101 610-774-5151
NYSE: PPL ■ *TF:* 800-342-5775 ■ *Web:* www.pplweb.com

Pratt Communications 2913 Tech Ctr ... Santa Ana CA 92705 714-540-6840
TF General: 800-980-2323 ■ *Web:* www.prattcommunications.com

PS Energy Group Inc 2987 Clairmont Rd Ste 500 ... Atlanta GA 30329 404-321-5711 321-3938
TF: 800-334-7548 ■ *Web:* www.psenergy.com

PSEG Power LLC 80 Pk Plz ... Newark NJ 07101 973-430-7000
TF: 800-436-7734 ■ *Web:* www.pseg.com

Public Service of New Hampshire
780 N Commercial St ... Manchester NH 03105 603-669-4000
TF: 800-662-7764 ■ *Web:* www.psnh.com

Public Works Commission of The City of Fayetteville North Carolina
955 Old Wilmington Rd PO Box 1089 ... Fayetteville NC 28301 910-483-1382
TF: 877-687-7921 ■ *Web:* www.faypwc.com

Puget Sound Energy Inc 10885 NE Fourth St ... Bellevue WA 98004 425-452-1234 424-6537
TF: 888-225-5773 ■ *Web:* www.pse.com

Quantum Utility Generation LLC
1401 McKinney St Ste 1800 ... Houston TX 77010 713-485-8600
Web: www.quantumug.com

Questar Gas Co PO Box 45841 ... Salt Lake City UT 84139 801-324-5111 324-5483
TF: 800-323-5517 ■ *Web:* questargas.com

Reliant Energy Retail Services LLC
1201 Fannin St ... Houston TX 77002 866-222-7100 488-4422*
**Fax Area Code:* 713 ■ *TF:* 866-660-4900 ■ *Web:* www.reliant.com

RF Fisher Electric Co LLC
1707 W 39th Ave ... Kansas City KS 66103 913-384-1500 384-1503
Web: rffisher.com

Roanoke Gas Co 519 Kimball Rd ... Roanoke VA 24030 540-777-4427 777-7952
Web: www.roanokegas.com

Rochester Gas & Electric Corp 89 E Ave ... Rochester NY 14649 800-743-2110 724-8432*
**Fax Area Code:* 716 ■ *TF:* 800-743-2110 ■ *Web:* www.rge.com

Roland's Electric Inc
307 Suburban Ave Ste A ... Deer Park NY 11729 631-242-8080 242-6392
TF: 800-981-8010 ■ *Web:* www.rolandselectric.com

S&W Contracting Company Inc
952 New Salem Rd ... Murfreesboro TN 37129 615-893-2511 895-2030
Web: www.sandwcontracting.com

Salt River Project (SRP) 1521 N Project Dr ... Tempe AZ 85281 602-236-5900 236-2442
TF: 800-258-4777 ■ *Web:* www.srpnet.com

San Diego Gas & Electric Co 101 Ash St ... San Diego CA 92101 619-696-2000 654-1755*
**Fax Area Code:* 858 ■ **Fax:* Cust Svc ■ *TF:* 800-411-7343 ■ *Web:* www.sdge.com

San Jacinto River Authority 1577 Dam Site Rd ... Conroe TX 77304 936-588-1111 588-3043
Web: www.sanjacintoriverauthority.com

SCANA Energy Marketing Inc
220 Operation Way MC 092 ... Cayce SC 29033 803-217-9000 217-7344
TF: 800-472-1051 ■ *Web:* www.scana.com

SemCAMS 521 Third Ave SW Ste 1200 ... Calgary AB T2P3T3 403-536-3000
Web: semcams.com

SETEL UC 5121 Maryland Way Ste 300 ... Brentwood TN 37027 615-874-6000
TF: 800-743-1340 ■ *Web:* www.setelecom.com

Shell Trading 909 Fannin St Plz Level 1 ... Houston TX 77010 713-767-5400
Web: www.shell.us

Sid Richardson Carbon & Energy Cos
201 Main St ... Fort Worth TX 76102 817-390-8600
Web: www.sidrich.com

Sims Recycling Solutions Holdings Inc
1600 Harvester Rd ... West Chicago IL 60185 630-231-6060
Web: www.simsrecycling.com

SourceGas 655 E Millsap Dr ... Fayetteville AR 72703 800-563-0012
TF: 800-563-0012 ■ *Web:* www.sourcegasarkansas.com

South Carolina Electric & Gas Co
PO Box 100255 ... Columbia SC 29202 803-635-4444
TF: 800-251-7234 ■ *Web:* www.sceg.com

South Coast Water District 31592 W St ... Laguna Niguel CA 92651 949-499-4555 499-4256
Web: www.scwd.org

Southern California Edison Co
2244 Walnut Grove Ave ... Rosemead CA 91770 626-302-1212 302-8984
TF: 800-655-4555 ■ *Web:* www.sce.com

Southern California Gas Co
555 W Fifth St ... Los Angeles CA 90013 562-733-1852 244-8293*
**Fax Area Code:* 213 ■ *TF:* 800-427-2200 ■ *Web:* www.socalgas.com

Southern California Public Power Authority (SCPPA)
225 S Lake Ave Ste 1250 ... Pasadena CA 91101 626-793-9364 793-9461
Web: www.scppa.org

Southern Connecticut Gas (SCG) 60 Marsh Hill Rd ... Orange CT 06477 866-268-2887 795-7923*
**Fax Area Code:* 203 ■ *TF:* 866-268-2887 ■ *Web:* www.soconngas.com

Southwest Gas Corp
5241 Spring Mtn Rd PO Box 98510 ... Las Vegas NV 89193 702-876-7237 876-7037
NYSE: SWX ■ *TF:* 800-748-5539 ■ *Web:* www.swgas.com

Southwest Gas Corp Northern Nevada Div
400 Eagle Stn Ln ... Carson City NV 89701 877-860-6020 884-3027*
**Fax Area Code:* 775 ■ *TF:* 877-860-6020 ■ *Web:* www.swgas.com

Southwest Gas Corp Southern Arizona Div
3401 E Gas Rd ... Tucson AZ 85714 877-860-6020 295-1991*
**Fax Area Code:* 520 ■ *TF:* 877-860-6020 ■ *Web:* www.swgas.com

Southwest Gas Corp Southern California Div
13471 Mariposa Rd ... Victorville CA 92395 877-860-6020
TF: 877-860-6020 ■ *Web:* www.swgas.com

Southwest Gas Corp Southern Nevada Div
5241 Spring Mtn Rd ... Las Vegas NV 89150 702-876-7011
TF: 877-860-6020 ■ *Web:* www.swgas.com

				Phone	Fax
Southwest Water Co 12535 Reed Rd. . . . Web: www.swwc.com	Sugar Land	TX	77478	281-207-5800	
Southwestern Energy Co 2350 N Sam Houston Pkwy E Ste 300 . . . NYSE: SWN ■ TF: 866-322-0801 ■ Web: www.swn.com	Houston	TX	77032	832-796-1000	796-4818
Spectra Energy Corp 5400 Westheimer Ct . . . TF: 800-700-8744 ■ Web: m.duke-energy.com	Houston	TX	77056	713-627-5400	
Spectra Plus Inc 638 Goodwin Dr. . . . Web: spectra-plus-inc.hub.biz	Richardson	TX	75081	214-437-5705	
Star Group Inc, The 220 Laurel Rd Voorhees Town Center. . . . Web: www.starnj.com	Voorhees	NJ	08043	856-782-7000	
Stream Gas & Electric Ltd 1950 Stemmons Fwy Ste 3000. . . . TF: 866-447-8732 ■ Web: mystream.com	Dallas	TX	75207	866-447-8732	
Summer Infant Inc 1275 Park E Dr. . . . Web: www.summerinfant.com	Woonsocket	RI	02895	401-334-9966	
Superior Water Light & Power 2915 Hill Ave PO Box 519 . . . TF: 800-227-7957 ■ Web: www.swlp.com	Superior	WI	54880	715-394-2200	
Sweetwater Authority PO Box 2328 . . . TF: 866-275-3772 ■ Web: www.sweetwater.org	Chula Vista	CA	91912	619-420-1413	425-7469
SWEPCo One Riverside Plz . . . TF: 888-216-3523 ■ Web: www.swepco.com	Columbus	OH	43215	888-216-3523	
Synex International Inc Ste 400 1444 Alberni St . . . Web: www.synex.com	Vancouver	BC	V6G2Z4	604-688-8271	
System Engineering International Inc (SEI) 5115 Pegasus Ct Ste Q. . . . TF: 800-765-4734 ■ Web: www.seipower.com	Frederick	MD	21704	301-694-9601	694-9608
Tallgrass Energy Partners LP 6640 W 143rd St Ste 200. . . . Web: www.tallgrassenergylp.com	Overland Park	KS	66223	303-763-2950	
Telemark Diversified Graphics 411 Mckee St . . . Web: www.telemarkcorp.com	Sturgis	MI	49091	269-651-7876	
Texarkana Water Utilities 801 Wood St. . . . Web: txkusa.org	Texarkana	TX	75501	903-798-3800	791-0724
Texas Gulf Supply Corp 10420 Rockley Rd. . . . Web: www.texasgulfsupply.com	Houston	TX	77099	281-495-5500	
Texas-New Mexico Power Co (TNMP) 577 N Garden Ridge Blvd . . . TF: 888-866-7456 ■ Web: www.tnmp.com	Lewisville	TX	75067	972-420-4189	737-1392
Thompson Electric Co (TEC) 2300 Seventh St PO Box 207 . . . TF: 800-832-2936 ■ Web: www.thompsonelectriccompany.com	Sioux City	IA	51105	712-252-4221	
Tile Shop Holdings Inc 14000 Carlson Pkwy . . . Web: www.tileshop.com	Plymouth	MN	55441	763-852-2978	
Tokyo Electric Power Company Inc 1901 L St NW Ste 720 . . . Web: www.tepco.co.jp	Washington	DC	20036	202-457-0790	457-0810
Toledo Edison Co PO Box 3687. . . . TF: 800-447-3333 ■ Web: www.firstenergycorp.com/content/customer/toledo_edison	Akron	OH	44309	800-447-3333	
Trans-Tel Central Inc (TTC) 2805 Broce Dr. . . . TF: 800-729-4636 ■ Web: www.trans-tel.com	Norman	OK	73072	405-447-5025	447-5029
TransAlta Corp 110 12th Ave SW PO Box 1900 Stn M . . . TSE: TA ■ Web: www.transalta.com	Calgary	AB	T2P2M1	403-267-7110	
Travel Leaders Group LLC 3033 Campus Dr Ste W320 . . . Web: www.travelleadersgroup.com	Plymouth	MN	55441	763-744-3700	
Tricomm Services Corp 1247 N Church St Ste 8 . . . TF: 800-872-2401 ■ Web: www.tricommcorp.com	Moorestown	NJ	08057	856-914-9001	914-9065
Triple Peaks LLC 77 Okemo Heights . . . Web: www.okemo.com	Ludlow	VT	05149	802-228-1947	
Trivascular Technologies Inc 3910 Brickway Blvd . . . Web: www.trivascular.com	Santa Rosa	CA	95403	707-543-8800	
Tucker Technology Inc 300 Frank H Ogawa Plaza Ste 235 . . . Web: www.tuckertech.com	Oakland	CA	94612	510-836-0422	836-2625
Tucson Electric Power Co 1 S Church Ave Ste 100 . . . TF: 800-430-4046 ■ Web: www.tep.com	Tucson	AZ	85701	520-571-4000	
TXU Electric 1601 Bryan St. . . . TF: 800-242-9113 ■ Web: www.txu.com/us/ourbus/elecgas	Dallas	TX	75201	214-486-2534	812-2488
Underground Specialists Inc (USI) 570 SW 16th Terr Bldg 1500 . . . Web: www.usicable.com	Pompano Beach	FL	33069	954-782-8740	782-1919
United Electric Supply Inc 10 Bellecor Dr. . . . TF: 800-322-3374 ■ Web: www.unitedelectric.com	New Castle	DE	19720	302-322-3333	324-3333
United Illuminating Co 157 Church St. . . . *Fax: Hum Res ■ TF Cust Svc: 800-722-5584 ■ Web: www.uinet.com	New Haven	CT	06510	203-499-2000	499-5973*
United States Information Systems Inc (USIS) 35 W Jefferson Ave. . . . TF: 866-222-3778 ■ Web: www.usis.net	Pearl River	NY	10965	845-358-7755	358-7882
Upper Trinity Regional Water District 900 N Kealy St PO Box 305 . . . Web: www.utrwd.com	Lewisville	TX	75067	972-219-1228	221-9896
USlegal Inc 3720 Flowood Dr. . . . Web: www.uslegal.com	Jackson	MS	39232	601-896-0180	
Virginia American Water Co (VAWC) 2223 Duke St . . . Web: www.amwater.com	Alexandria	VA	22314	703-706-3879	
Virginia Natural Gas Inc AGL Resources Inc PO Box 4569 . . . *Fax Area Code: 484 ■ TF: 800-633-4236 ■ Web: www.aglresources.com/	Atlanta	GA	30302	404-584-4000	281-3184*
Volaris Group Inc 5800 Explorer Dr Fifth Fl . . . Web: www.volarisgroup.com	Mississauga	ON	L4W5K9	905-267-5400	
W Bradley Electric Inc 90 Hill Rd. . . . Web: www.wbeinc.com	Novato	CA	94945	415-898-1400	898-5991
Wachter Inc 16001 W 99th St . . . TF: 800-462-9638 ■ Web: www.wachter.com	Lenexa	KS	66219	913-541-2500	541-2529
Walter Stern Inc 68 Sintsink Dr E . . . Web: www.altersterninc.com	Port Washington	NY	11050	516-883-9100	
Wang Electric Inc 4107 E Winslow Ave Ste C. . . . Web: www.wangelectric.com	Phoenix	AZ	85040	602-324-5350	324-5360
Ward's Marine Electric Inc 617 SW Third Ave. . . . TF: 800-545-9273 ■ Web: www.wardsmarine.com	Fort Lauderdale	FL	33315	954-523-2815	523-1967
Washington Gas & Light Co 6801 Industrial Rd . . . *Fax Area Code: 202 ■ TF: 800-752-7520 ■ Web: www.washgas.com	Springfield	VA	22151	703-750-4440	624-6010*
Washington Gas Energy Services Inc (WGES) 13865 Sunrise Vly Dr Ste 200 . . . TF: 888-884-9437 ■ Web: www.wges.com	Herndon	VA	20171	703-793-7500	
We Energies 231 W Michigan St PO Box 2046. . . . *Fax: Mktg ■ TF: 800-242-9137 ■ Web: www.we-energies.com	Milwaukee	WI	53203	414-221-2345	221-3853*
Weber Basin Water Conservancy District 2837 East Hwy 193. . . . Web: www.weberbasin.com	Layton	UT	84040	801-771-1677	
Westar Energy PO Box 758500 . . . TF: 800-544-4857 ■ Web: www.westarenergy.com	Topeka	KS	66675	785-575-6300	575-1796
Western Massachusetts Electric Co 1 Federal St Bldg 111-4 . . . TF: 800-286-2000 ■ Web: www.wmeco.com	Springfield	MA	01105	413-785-5871	
Western Water Co 705 Mission Ave Ste 200 . . .	San Rafael	CA	94901	415-256-8800	256-8803
Wisconsin Power & Light Co 4902 N Biltmore Ln PO Box 77007. . . . TF: 800-255-4268 ■ Web: www.alliantenergy.com	Madison	WI	53718	800-255-4268	
Wisconsin Public Service Corp PO Box 19001 . . . *Fax Area Code: 920 ■ *Fax: Mktg ■ TF: 800-450-7260 ■ Web: www.wisconsinpublicservice.com	Green Bay	WI	54307	800-450-7260	433-1527*
Worldwide Energy & Mfg USA Inc 408 N Canal St Ste A&B. . . . OTC: WEMU ■ Web: www.wwmusa.com	South San Francisco	CA	94080	650-794-9888	794-9878
Xcel Energy Inc PO Box 840 . . . NYSE: XEL ■ TF: 877-322-8228 ■ Web: www.xcelenergy.com	Denver	CO	80201	303-571-7511	
Y Ss Group Inc 8612 Nw 70th St. . . . Web: yssgroup.com	Miami	FL	33166	305-436-7371	
Yankee Gas Services Co 107 Selden St. . . . TF: 800-989-0900 ■ Web: www.yankeegas.com	Berlin	CT	06037	800-989-0900	841-8684
York Water Co, The 130 E Market St PO Box 15089. . . . NASDAQ: YORW ■ TF: 800-750-5561 ■ Web: www.yorkwater.com	York	PA	17405	717-845-3601	845-3792
Yucaipa Valley Water District PO Box 730 . . . TF: 800-272-8869 ■ Web: www.yvwd.dst.ca.us	Yucaipa	CA	92399	909-797-5117	797-6381

791 VACUUM CLEANERS - HOUSEHOLD

SEE ALSO Appliances - Small - Mfr p. 1744

				Phone	Fax
Beam Industries 1700 W Second St . . . TF: 800-369-2326 ■ Web: www.beamvac.com	Webster City	IA	50595	515-832-4620	832-6659
Bissell Inc 2345 Walker NW. . . . *Fax: Hum Res ■ Web: www.bissell.com	Grand Rapids	MI	49544	616-453-4451	791-0662*
CentralVac International 23455 Hellman Ave PO Box 259. . . . TF: 800-666-3133 ■ Web: www.centralvac.com	Dollar Bay	MI	49922	800-666-3133	
Electrolux Home Care Products Inc PO Box 3900 . . . TF Cust Svc: 800-282-2886 ■ Web: www.eureka.com	Peoria	IL	61612	800-282-2886	
Kirby Co 1920 W 114th St . . . TF: 800-437-7170 ■ Web: www.kirby.com	Cleveland	OH	44102	216-228-2400	529-6146
Lindsay Manufacturing Inc PO Box 1708. . . . TF: 800-546-3729 ■ Web: www.lindsaymfg.com	Ponca City	OK	74602	580-762-2457	762-9547
Metropolitan Vacuum Cleaner Co Inc one Ramapo Ave PO Box 149. . . . TF: 800-822-1602 ■ Web: www.metrovacworld.com	Suffern	NY	10901	845-357-1600	357-1640
Oreck Corp 1400 Salem Rd. . . . TF: 800-289-5888 ■ Web: www.oreck.com	Cookeville	TN	38506	800-289-5888	
Rexair Inc 50 W Big Beaver Rd Ste 350 . . . Web: www.rainbowsystem.com	Troy	MI	48084	248-643-7222	643-7676
Sanyo Fisher Co 21605 Plummer St . . . Web: us.sanyo.com	Chatsworth	CA	91311	818-998-7322	
Sequoia Vacuum Systems Inc 164 Jefferson Dr. . . .	Menlo Park	CA	94025	800-994-0494	

792 VALVES - INDUSTRIAL

				Phone	Fax
Alkon Corp 728 Graham Dr. . . . Web: www.alkoncorp.com	Fremont	OH	43420	419-333-7000	
American Cast Iron Pipe Co (ACIPCO) 1501 31st Ave N. . . . TF: 800-442-2347 ■ Web: www.american-usa.com	Birmingham	AL	35207	205-325-7701	
American Valve & Hydrant Manufacturing Company LP 3525 Hollywood St. . . . Web: www.avhmc.com	Beaumont	TX	77701	409-832-7721	
Anderson Brass Co 1629 W Bobo Newsome Hwy. . . . TF: 800-476-9876 ■ Web: www.andersonbrass.com	Hartsville	SC	29550	843-332-4111	332-3752
Armstrong International Inc 2081 SE Ocean Blvd 4th Fl. . . . TF: 866-738-5125 ■ Web: www.armstronginternational.com	Stuart	FL	34996	772-286-7175	286-1001
Automatic Valve Corp 41144 Vincenti Ct. . . . Web: www.automaticvalve.com	Novi	MI	48375	248-474-6700	474-6732
Balon Corp 3245 S Hattie Ave. . . . Web: www.balon.com	Oklahoma City	OK	73129	405-677-3321	
Barksdale Inc 3211 Fruitland Ave . . . TF: 800-835-1060 ■ Web: www.barksdale.com	Los Angeles	CA	90058	323-589-6181	589-3463
Bray International Inc 13333 Westland E Blvd. . . . Web: www.bray.com	Houston	TX	77041	281-894-5454	
BS&B Safety Systems LLC 7455 E 46th St. . . . Web: www.bsbsystems.com	Tulsa	OK	74145	918-622-5950	

Phone Fax

C & D Valve Manufacturing Co
201 Nw 67th St................................Oklahoma City OK 73116 405-843-5621
Web: www.cdvalve.com

Campbell Sevey Inc 15350 Minnetonka Blvd........Minnetonka MN 55345 952-935-2345
Web: www.campbell-sevey.com

Cash Acme Inc 2400 Seventh Ave Sw.................Cullman AL 35055 256-775-8200
Web: www.cashacme.com

Circle Seal Controls Inc 2301 Wardlow Cir............Corona CA 92880 951-270-6200 270-6201
TF: 800-991-2726 ■ Web: www.circle-seal.com

Clow Valve Co 902 S Second St....................Oskaloosa IA 52577 641-673-8611 673-8269
TF: 800-829-2569 ■ Web: www.clowvalve.com

Continental Disc Corp 3160 W Heartland Dr............Liberty MO 64068 816-792-1500 792-2277
Web: www.contdisc.com

Control Components Inc
22591 Avenida Empresa...............Rancho Santa Margarita CA 92688 949-858-1877 858-1878
Web: www.ccivalve.com

Conval Inc 265 Field Rd..........................Somers CT 06071 860-749-0761 763-3557
Web: www.conval.com

Crane Co 100 First Stamford Pl Fourth Fl..............Stamford CT 06902 203-363-7300 363-7295
NYSE: CR ■ Web: www.craneco.com

Crane Company Stockham Div 2129 Third Ave SE......Cullman AL 35055 256-775-3800 775-3860
TF: 800-786-2542 ■ Web: www.cranecpe.com

Curtiss-Wright Flow Control Target Rock Div
1966 Broadhollow Rd..........................Farmingdale NY 11735 631-293-3800 293-6144
Web: www.curtisswright.com

DeZurik Water Controls 250 Riverside Ave N............Sartell MN 56377 320-259-2000 259-2227
Web: www.dezurik.com

DFT Inc 140 Sheree Blvd..........................Exton PA 19341 610-363-8903
Web: www.dft-valves.com

Dynex Rivett Inc 770 Capitol Dr...................Pewaukee WI 53072 262-691-0300 691-0312
Web: www.dynexhydraulics.com

Engineered Controls International Inc (ECII)
100 Rego Dr PO Box 247..............................Elon NC 27244 336-449-7707 449-6594
TF: 800-650-0061 ■ Web: www.regoproducts.com

Equilibar LLC 320 Rutledge Rd.......................Fletcher NC 28732 828-650-6590
Web: www.equilibar.com

Fike Corp 704 SW Tenth St.......................Blue Springs MO 64015 816-229-3405 228-9277
TF: 877-342-3453 ■ Web: www.fike.com

Fisher Controls International Inc
205 S Ctr St PO Box 190......................Marshalltown IA 50158 641-754-3011 754-2830
Web: www2.emersonprocess.com/en-us/brands/fisher

Flowserve Corp 5215 N O'Connor Blvd Ste 2300..........Irving TX 75039 972-443-6500 443-6800
NYSE: FLS ■ TF: 800-350-1082 ■ Web: www.flowserve.com

Fluid Flow Products Inc 2108 Crown View Dr.........Charlotte NC 28227 704-847-4464
Web: www.fluidflow.com

FMC Technologies Inc 1803 Gears Rd..................Houston TX 77067 281-591-4000 591-4102
NYSE: FTI ■ TF: 800-356-4898 ■ Web: www.fmctechnologies.com

GA Industries Inc
9025 Marshall Rd........................Cranberry Township PA 16066 724-776-1020 776-1254
Web: www.gaindustries.com

Gemini Valve Two Otter Ct...........................Raymond NH 03077 603-895-4761 895-6785
TF: 800-370-0936 ■ Web: www.geminivalve.com

Gemu Valves Inc 3800 Camp Creek Pkwy SW............Atlanta GA 30331 678-553-3400 344-9350*
*Fax Area Code: 404 ■ Web: www.gemu.com

Girard Equipment Inc 531 Hwy 146 N ....La Porte TX 77571 281-842-7500
Web: www.girardequip.com

Gonzales Inquirer, The
1000 Civic Ctr Loop...............................San Marcos TX 78666 830-672-2861 672-7029
Web: gonzalesinquirer.com

Goulds Pumps Inc Goulds Water Technologies Group
240 Fall St.......................................Seneca Falls NY 13148 315-568-2811 568-2418
TF: 800-327-7700 ■ Web: www.gouldspumps.com

Groth Corp 13650 N Promenade Blvd..................Stafford TX 77477 281-295-6800 295-6999
TF: 800-354-7684 ■ Web: www.grothcorp.com

High Vacuum Apparatus LLC (HVA) 12880 Moya Blvd.....Reno NV 89506 775-359-4442 359-1369
TF: 800-551-4422 ■ Web: www.highvac.com

Hilton Valve 14520 NE 91st Ct......................Redmond WA 98052 425-883-7000
Web: www.dezurik.com

Hoerbiger Corp of America Inc
3350 Gateway Dr ....Pompano Beach FL 33069 954-974-5700 974-0964
TF: 800-327-8961 ■ Web: hoerbiger.com

Hudson Valve Company Inc
5301 Office Pk Dr Ste 330 ....Bakersfield CA 93309 661-869-1126 607-8731*
*Fax Area Code: 800 ■ TF: 800-748-6218 ■ Web: www.hudsonvalve.com

Humphrey Products Co
5070 E N Ave PO Box 2008.........................Kalamazoo MI 49048 269-381-5500 381-4113
TF: 800-477-8707 ■ Web: www.humphrey-products.com

Hunt Valve Company Inc 1913 E State St..............Salem OH 44460 330-337-9535 337-3754
Web: www.huntvalve.com

Hydroseal Valve Co Inc 1500 SE 89th St.........Oklahoma City OK 73149 405-631-1533 778-1072*
*Fax Area Code: 800 ■ TF: 800-398-2493 ■ Web: circorenergy.com

ITT Goulds Pumps Industries/Goulds Industrial Pumps Group
240 Fall St ....Seneca Falls NY 13148 315-568-2811 568-2418
TF: 800-327-7700 ■ Web: www.gouldspumps.com

ITT Industries Inc Engineered Valves Div
33 Centerville Rd ....Lancaster PA 17603 717-509-2200 509-2336
TF: 800-366-1111 ■ Web: www.engvalves.com

Jarecki Valves 6910 W Ridge Rd.....................Fairview PA 16415 814-474-2666 474-3645
Web: jareckivalves.net

John C Kupferle Foundry Co
2511 N Ninth St ....Saint Louis MO 63102 314-231-8738
Web: hydrants.com

Kennedy Valve 1021 E Water St........................Elmira NY 14902 607-734-2211 734-3288
TF: 800-782-5831 ■ Web: www.kennedyvalve.com

KF Industries Inc 1500 SE 89th St.............Oklahoma City OK 73149 405-631-1533 631-5034
TF: 800-654-4842 ■ Web: circorenergy.com

Kraft Fluid Systems Inc
14300 Foltz Pkwy..............................Strongsville OH 44149 440-238-5545 238-5266
TF: 800-257-1155 ■ Web: www.kraftfluid.com

Lee Co Two Pellitaug Rd PO Box 424.................Westbrook CT 06498 860-399-6281 399-7058*
*Fax: Sales ■ Web: www.theleeco.com

Leonard Valve Co 1360 Elmwood Ave...................Cranston RI 02910 401-461-1200 941-5310
TF: 800-222-1208 ■ Web: www.leonardvalve.com

Leslie Controls Inc 12501 Telecom Dr...................Tampa FL 33637 813-978-1000 978-0984
TF: 800-323-8366 ■ Web: www.lesliecontrols.com

Lourdes Industries Inc 65 Hoffman Ave............Hauppauge NY 11788 631-234-6600
Web: www.lourdesinc.com

Mac Valves Inc 30569 Beck Rd ....Wixom MI 48393 248-624-7700 624-0549
TF: 800-622-8587 ■ Web: www.macvalves.com

Marotta Controls Inc
78 Boonton Ave PO Box 427 ....Montville NJ 07045 973-334-7800 334-1219
TF: 888-627-6882 ■ Web: www.marotta.com

Maxon Corp 201 E 18th St PO Box 2068 ....Muncie IN 47307 765-284-3304 286-8394
Web: www.maxoncorp.com

McDantim Inc 3730 N Montana Ave ....Helena MT 59602 406-442-5153
Web: mcdantim.com

McKenzie Valve & Machining Co
145 Airport Rd ....McKenzie TN 38201 731-352-5027 352-3029
Web: www.mckenzievalve.com

McWane Inc 2900 Hwy 280 Ste 300 ....Birmingham AL 35223 205-414-3100 414-3170
TF: 877-231-0904 ■ Web: www.mcwane.com

Milwaukee Valve Company Inc
16550 W Stratton Dr.............................New Berlin WI 53151 262-432-2800 432-2801
TF: 800-348-6544 ■ Web: www.milwaukeevalve.com

Mueller Co 500 W Eldorado St.......................Decatur IL 62522 217-423-4471 425-7537*
*Fax: Cust Svc ■ TF: 800-423-1323 ■ Web: www.muellerflo.com

Mueller Refrigeration Co Inc
121 Rogers St....................................Hartsville TN 37074 615-374-2124 374-2080
TF Cust Svc: 800-937-5449 ■ Web: www.muellerrefrigeration.com

Newdell Co, The 13750 Hollister Rd ....Houston TX 77086 713-590-1312
Web: www.newdellco.com

Newport News Industrial Corp
182 Enterprise Dr............................Newport News VA 23603 757-380-7053 688-3841
TF: 800-627-0353 ■ Web: nni.huntingtoningalls.com

NIBCO Inc 1516 Middlebury St.........................Elkhart IN 46515 574-295-3000 295-3307
TF: 800-234-0227 ■ Web: www.nibco.com

Noranco Inc 1842 Clements Rd ....Pickering ON L1W3R8 905-831-0100
Web: www.noranco.com

Ogontz Corp 2835 Terwood Rd..................Willow Grove PA 19090 215-657-4770 657-0460
TF: 800-523-2478 ■ Web: www.ogontz.com

Parker Hannifin Corp Hydraulic Valve Div
520 Ternes Ave...Elyria OH 44035 440-366-5200 366-5253*
*Fax: Sales ■ TF: 800-272-7537 ■ Web: www.parker.com

Parker Hannifin Corp Sporlan Div
711 Industrial Ave.................................Washington MO 63090 636-239-6524 239-5042
Web: parker.com

Parker Instrumentation Group
6035 Parkland Blvd ....Cleveland OH 44124 216-896-3000 896-4022
TF: 800-272-7537 ■ Web: parker.com

Peter Paul Electronics Co Inc
480 John Downey Dr ....New Britain CT 06051 860-229-4884 223-1734
TF: 800-825-8377 ■ Web: peterpaul.com

PGI International 16101 Vallen Dr...................Houston TX 77041 713-466-0056 744-9892
TF: 800-231-0233 ■ Web: www.pgiint.com

Plast-O-Matic Valves Inc
1384 Pompton Ave...........................Cedar Grove NJ 07009 973-256-3000 256-4745
TF: 800-323-2710 ■ Web: www.plastomatic.com

Plattco Corp 7 White St........................Plattsburgh NY 12901 518-563-4640 563-4892
TF: 800-352-1731 ■ Web: www.plattco.com

Primore Inc 2304 W Beecher Rd.......................Adrian MI 49221 517-263-2220 265-6160
Web: www.primore.com

Red Valve Company Inc 600 N Bell Ave Bldg. 2........Carnegie PA 15106 412-279-0044
Web: www.redvalve.com

Richards Industries Inc 3170 Wasson Rd...........Cincinnati OH 45209 513-533-5600 871-0105*
*Fax: Sales ■ TF Cust Svc: 800-543-7311 ■ Web: www.richardsind.com

Robert H Wager Co 570 Montroyal Rd ....Rural Hall NC 27045 336-969-6909 969-6375
TF: 800-562-7024 ■ Web: www.wagerusa.com

Rocker Solenoid Co 1500 W 240th St.............Harbor City CA 90710 310-534-5660
Web: www.rockerindustries.com

Salina Vortex Corp 1725 Vortex Ave....................Salina KS 67401 785-825-7177
Web: www.vortexvalves.com

Sealant Equipment & Engineering Inc
45677 Helm St PO Box 701460 ....Plymouth MI 48170 734-459-8600
Web: www.sealantequipment.com

Sedco 2304 W Beecher Rd PO Box 624..................Adrian MI 49221 517-263-2220 265-6160
Web: www.sedco-prv.com

Servotronics Inc 1110 Maple St PO Box 300.............Elma NY 14059 716-655-5990 655-6012
NYSE: SVT ■ Web: www.servotronics.com

Shan-Rod Inc 7308 Driver Rd..................Berlin Heights OH 44814 419-588-2066
Web: shanrodinc.com

Sherwood 2200 North Main St....................Washington PA 15301 724-225-8000 225-6188
TF: 888-508-2583 ■ Web: www.sherwoodvalve.com

Snap-Tite Inc 8325 Hessinger Dr.........................Erie PA 16509 814-838-5700 833-0145
Web: www.snap-tite.com

Spence Engineering Company Inc
150 Coldenham Rd..................................Walden NY 12586 845-778-5566 778-1072
Web: www.spenceengineering.com

Tapco International Inc 990 W 15th St...........Riviera Beach FL 33404 561-844-2502 845-2410

Taylor Valve Technology Inc
8300 SW 8th....................................Oklahoma City OK 73128 405-787-0145
Web: www.taylorvalve.com

Transtech Industries Inc 2025 Delsea Dr ....Sewell NJ 08080 856-481-4214 227-6578
OTC: TRTI ■ Web: www.transtechindustries.com

Triangle Process Equipment Inc
2307 Industrial Park Dr Se..........................Wilson NC 27893 252-246-1089
Web: www.4tpe.com

Tru Tech Valve LLC 577 W Pike St................Canonsburg PA 15317 724-916-4805
Web: www.ttvlv.com

United Brass Works Inc 714 S Main St ....Randleman NC 27317 336-498-2661 498-4267
TF: 800-334-3035 ■ Web: www.ubw.com

Valcor Engineering Corp Two Lawrence Rd..........Springfield NJ 07081 973-467-8400 467-8382
Web: www.valcor.com

Valvtechnologies Inc 5904 Bingle Rd................Houston TX 77092 713-860-0400 860-0499
Web: www.valv.com

Velan Inc 7007 Cote de Liesse ....Montreal QC H4T1G2 514-748-7743 748-8635
TSE: VLN ■ Web: www.velan.com

	City	State	ZIP	Phone	Fax
Watts Water Technologies Inc 815 Chestnut St *NYSE: WTS* ■ *Web:* www.wattswater.com	North Andover	MA	01845	978-688-1811	794-1848
Zimmermann & Jansen Inc 4525 Kennedy Commerce Dr *Web:* www.zjinc.com	Houston	TX	77032	281-446-8000	446-8126

793 VALVES & HOSE FITTINGS - FLUID POWER

SEE ALSO Carburetors, Pistons, Piston Rings, Valves p. 1902

	City	State	ZIP	Phone	Fax
Aero Kool Corp 1495 SE Tenth Ave *Web:* www.aerokool.com	Hialeah	FL	33010	305-887-6912	
Aero-craft Hydraulics Inc 392 N Smith Ave *Web:* www.aero-craft.com	Corona	CA	92880	951-736-4690	
Air-Way Manufacturing Co 586 N Main St *TF Cust Svc:* 800-253-1036 ■ *Web:* www.air-way.com	Olivet	MI	49076	269-749-2161	749-3161
Allen Orton LLC 3180 Reps Miller Rd Ste 200 *Web:* www.ortondirect.com	Norcross	GA	30071	770-986-9999	
Arkwin Industries Inc 686 Main St **Fax:* Sales ■ *TF:* 800-284-2551 ■ *Web:* www.arkwin.com	Westbury	NY	11590	516-333-2640	334-6786*
Bosch Rexroth PO Box 394 *TF:* 800-739-7684 ■ *Web:* www.boschrexroth-us.com	Wooster	OH	44691	330-263-3300	263-3333
Bosch Rexroth Corp 5150 Prairie Stone Pkwy *TF:* 800-860-1055 ■ *Web:* www.boschrexroth-us.com	Hoffman Estates	IL	60192	847-645-3600	645-6201
Brand Hydraulics Company Inc 2332 S 25th St *Web:* www.brand-hyd.com	Omaha	NE	68106	402-344-4434	
Cameron Valves & Measurement 3250 Briarpark Dr Ste 300 *Web:* www.c-a-m.com	Houston	TX	77042	281-499-8511	261-3588
Carten Controls 604 W Johnson Ave *Web:* www.cartenus.com	Cheshire	CT	06410	203-699-2100	
Cashco Inc 607 W 15th St *Web:* www.cashco.com	Ellsworth	KS	67439	785-472-4461	472-3539
Civacon 4304 N Mattox Rd *TF Sales:* 888-526-5657 ■ *Web:* www.civacon.com	Kansas City	MO	64150	816-741-6600	741-1061
Clippard Instrument Lab 7390 Colerain Ave *TF:* 877-245-6247 ■ *Web:* www.clippard.com	Cincinnati	OH	45239	513-521-4261	521-4464
Control Flow Inc 9201 Fairbanks N Houston Rd *TF:* 800-231-9922 ■ *Web:* www.controlflow.com	Houston	TX	77064	281-890-8300	890-3947
Crissair Inc 28909 Avenue Williams *Web:* www.crissair.com	Valencia	CA	91355	661-367-3300	273-1280
Daman Products Co Inc 1811 N Home St *TF:* 800-959-7841 ■ *Web:* www.damanifolds.com	Mishawaka	IN	46545	574-259-7841	259-7665
Delta Power Co 4484 Boeing Dr *Web:* www.delta-power.com	Rockford	IL	61109	815-397-6628	397-2526
Deltrol Fluid Products 3001 Grant Ave **Fax:* Sales ■ *TF:* 800-477-9772 ■ *Web:* www.deltrolfluid.com	Bellwood	IL	60104	708-547-0500	547-6881*
Dynaquip Controls 10 Harris Industrial Pk *TF:* 800-545-3636 ■ *Web:* www.dynaquip.com	Saint Clair	MO	63077	636-629-3700	629-5528
E H Lynn Industries Incoporated 524 Anderson Dr *Web:* www.ehlynn.com	Romeoville	IL	60446	815-328-8800	
EA Patten Co 303 Wetherell St *Web:* eapatten.com	Manchester	CT	06040	860-649-2851	649-6230
EDN Aviation Inc 6720 Valjean Ave *Web:* www.ednaviation.com	Van Nuys	CA	91406	818-988-8826	904-6799
Faber Enterprises Inc 6606 Variel Ave *Web:* www.faberent.com	Canoga Park	CA	91303	818-999-1300	
Fresno Valves & Castings Inc 7736 E Springfield Ave PO Box 40 *TF:* 800-333-1658 ■ *Web:* www.fresnovalves.com	Selma	CA	93662	559-834-2511	834-2017
Gar-KenyonTechnologies 238 Water St PO Box 559 *Web:* www.garkenyon.com	Naugatuck	CT	06770	203-729-4900	729-4950
Hays Fluid Controls 114 Eason Rd *TF:* 800-354-4297 ■ *Web:* www.haysfluidcontrols.com	Dallas	NC	28034	704-922-9565	922-9595
Henry Pratt Co 401 S Highland Ave *TF:* 877-436-7977 ■ *Web:* www.henrypratt.com	Aurora	IL	60506	630-844-4000	844-4124
Hoke Inc 405 Centura Ct PO Box 4866 *Web:* www.hoke.com	Spartanburg	SC	29305	864-574-7966	574-0998
Hose Master LLC 1233 E 222nd St *Web:* www.hosemaster.com	Cleveland	OH	44117	216-481-2020	
Hunt Valve Company Inc 1913 E State St *Web:* www.huntvalve.com	Salem	OH	44460	330-337-9535	337-3754
HUSCO International Inc 2239 Pewaukee Rd *Web:* www.huscointl.com	Waukesha	WI	53188	262-513-4200	513-4514
Hydraforce Inc 500 Barclay Blvd *TF:* 877-237-9101 ■ *Web:* www.hydraforce.com	Lincolnshire	IL	60069	847-793-2300	793-0087
Hyson Products 10367 Brecksville Rd *TF:* 800-876-4976 ■ *Web:* hysonproducts.com	Brecksville	OH	44141	440-526-5900	838-7684
ITT Aerospace Controls 28150 Industry Dr *TF:* 866-294-8691 ■ *Web:* www.ittaerospace.com	Valencia	CA	91355	661-295-4000	294-1750
ITT Industries Inc 1133 Westchester Ave *NYSE: ITT* ■ *TF:* 800-254-2823 ■ *Web:* www.itt.com	White Plains	NY	10604	914-641-2000	696-2950
JD Gould Co Inc 4707 Massachusetts Ave **Fax Area Code:* 317 ■ *TF:* 800-634-6853 ■ *Web:* www.gouldvalve.com	Indianapolis	IN	46218	800-634-6853	547-5234*
Jetstream of Houston LLP 4930 Cranswick *TF:* 800-231-8192 ■ *Web:* www.waterblast.com	Houston	TX	77041	713-462-7000	462-5387
Kepner Products Co 995 N Ellsworth Ave *Web:* www.kepner.com	Villa Park	IL	60181	630-279-1550	279-9669
Kimray Inc 52 NW 42nd St *TF:* 866-586-7233 ■ *Web:* www.kimray.com	Oklahoma City	OK	73118	405-525-6601	525-7520
LDI Industries Inc 1864 Nage Ave PO Box 1810 *Web:* www.ldi-industries.com	Manitowoc	WI	54221	920-682-6877	684-7210
Long Beach Hose & Coupling Coinc 1265 W 16th St *Web:* www.lbhose.com	Long Beach	CA	90813	562-901-2970	
McTurbine Inc 401 Junior Beck Dr *Web:* www.mcturbine.com	Corpus Christi	TX	78405	361-851-1290	
Mead Fluid Dynamics Inc 4114 N Knox Ave *TF Cust Svc:* 877-632-3872 ■ *Web:* www.mead-usa.com	Chicago	IL	60641	773-685-6800	685-7002
Midland Manufacturing Corp 7733 Gross Pt Rd *Web:* www.midlandmfg.com	Skokie	IL	60077	847-677-0333	
Morrison Bros Co 570 E Seventh St *TF:* 800-553-4840 ■ *Web:* www.morbros.com	Dubuque	IA	52001	563-583-5701	583-5028
Norgren 5400 S Delaware St **Fax:* Mktg ■ *TF:* 800-514-0129 ■ *Web:* norgren.com/us	Littleton	CO	80120	303-794-5000	795-9487*
Oilgear Co 2300 S 51st St PO Box 343924 *Web:* www.oilgear.com	Milwaukee	WI	53219	414-327-1700	327-0532
Omega Flex Inc 451 Creamery Way *NASDAQ: OFLX* ■ *TF:* 800-355-1039 ■ *Web:* www.omegaflex.com	Exton	PA	19341	610-524-7272	524-7282
Ontic Engineering & Manufacturing Inc 4150 N Sam Houston E Pkwy *Web:* www.ontic.com	Houston	TX	77032	281-590-1431	
Parker Fluid Connectors Group 6035 Parkland Blvd *TF General:* 800-272-7537 ■ *Web:* parker.com	Cleveland	OH	44124	216-896-3000	896-4000
Parker Hannifin Corp 6035 Parkland Blvd *Web:* parker.com	Cleveland	OH	44124	216-896-3000	514-6738
Parker Hannifin Corp Brass Products Div 100 Parker Dr *TF:* 800-272-7537 ■ *Web:* www.parker.com	Otsego	MI	49078	269-694-9411	694-4614
Parker Hannifin Corp General Valve Div 26 Clinton Dr Unit 103 **Fax Area Code:* 603 ■ *TF:* 800-272-7537 ■ *Web:* www.parker.com	Hollis	NH	03049	800-272-7537	585-8080*
Parker Hannifin Corp Instrumentation Pneutronics Div 26 Clinton Dr Ste 103 *Web:* www.parker.com	Hollis	NH	03049	603-595-1500	595-8080
Parker Hannifin Corp Pneumatic Div 8676 E M 89 *Web:* www.parker.com	Richland	MI	49083	269-629-5000	629-5385
Parker Hannifin Corp Skinner Valve Div 95 Edgewood Ave *TF:* 800-825-8305 ■ *Web:* www.parker.com	New Britain	CT	06051	860-827-2300	827-2384
PBM Inc 1070 Sandy Hill Rd *TF:* 800-967-4726 ■ *Web:* www.pbmvalve.com	Irwin	PA	15642	724-863-0550	864-9255
PerkinElmer Inc 940 Winter St *NYSE: PKI* ■ *Web:* www.perkinelmer.com	Waltham	MA	02451	203-925-4602	944-4904
Pima Valve Inc 6525 W Allison Rd *Web:* www.pimavalve.com	Chandler	AZ	85226	520-796-1095	796-4012
Plattco Corp 7 White St *TF:* 800-352-1731 ■ *Web:* www.plattco.com	Plattsburgh	NY	12901	518-563-4640	563-4892
Precision Sensors Inc 50 Seemans Ln *Web:* www.precisionsensors.com	Milford	CT	06460	203-877-2795	
Rexarc Inc PO Box 7 *Web:* www.rexarc.com	West Alexandria	OH	45381	937-839-4604	839-5897
Richards Industries Inc 3170 Wasson Rd **Fax:* Sales ■ *TF Cust Svc:* 800-543-7311 ■ *Web:* www.richardsind.com	Cincinnati	OH	45209	513-533-5600	871-0105*
Ritter Technology LLC 100 Williams Dr *Web:* www.ritter1.com	Zelienople	PA	16063	724-452-6000	452-0766
Ross Controls 1250 Stephenson Hwy *TF:* 800-438-7677 ■ *Web:* www.rosscontrols.com	Troy	MI	48083	248-764-1800	764-1850
Rupe's Hydraulics Sales & Service 725 N Twin Oaks Vly Rd *Web:* rupeshydraulics.com	San Marcos	CA	92069	760-744-9350	
Sedco 2304 W Beecher Rd PO Box 624 *Web:* www.sedco-prv.com	Adrian	MI	49221	517-263-2220	265-6160
SH Leggitt Co 1000 Civic Ctr Loop *Web:* shleggitt.com	San Marcos	TX	78666	512-396-2257	396-3064
Specialty Manufacturing Co 5858 Centerville Rd *Web:* www.specialtymfg.com	Saint Paul	MN	55127	651-653-0599	653-0989
Sun Hydraulics Corp 1500 W University Pkwy *NASDAQ: SNHY* ■ *Web:* www.sunhydraulics.com	Sarasota	FL	34243	941-362-1200	355-4497
Universal Valve Company Inc 478 Schiller St *Web:* www.universalvalve.com	Elizabeth	NJ	07206	908-351-0606	
Versa Products Co Inc 22 Spring Valley Rd *Web:* versa-valves.com	Paramus	NJ	07652	201-843-2400	843-2931
Watts Fluidair Inc Nine Cutts Rd **Fax:* Cust Svc ■ *TF:* 877-467-4323 ■ *Web:* www.wattsfluidair.com	Kittery	ME	03904	207-439-9511	475-4010*
Watts Regulator Co 815 Chestnut St *Web:* www.watts.com	North Andover	MA	01845	978-688-1811	794-1848
Whitco Supply LLC 200 N Morgan Ave *Web:* www.whitcosupply.com	Broussard	LA	70518	337-837-2440	
Young & Franklin Inc (Y&F) 942 Old Liverpool Rd *Web:* www.yf.com	Liverpool	NY	13088	315-457-3110	457-9204

794 VARIETY STORES

	City	State	ZIP	Phone	Fax
99 Cents Only Stores 4000 Union Pacific Ave *TF:* 888-582-5999 ■ *Web:* www.99only.com	Commerce	CA	90023	323-980-8145	980-8160
AC Doctor LLC 2151 W Hillsboro Blvd Ste 400 *TF:* 866-264-1479 ■ *Web:* www.acdoctor.com	Deerfield Beach	FL	33442	866-264-1479	
Alaska Textiles Inc 620 W Fireweed Ln *Web:* www.alaskatextiles.com	Anchorage	AK	99503	907-265-4880	
Albuquerque Winnelson Co 3545 Princeton Dr NE *Web:* www.bristolwinnelson.com	Albuquerque	NM	87107	505-884-1553	
All Graphic Supplies 6691 Edwards Blvd *Web:* www.allgraphicsupplies.com	Mississauga	ON	L5T2H8	905-795-2610	
Allen Tel Products Inc 30 TV5 Dr *Web:* www.allentel.com	Henderson	NV	89014	702-855-5700	
American Eagle Steel Corp 716 Giddings Ave *Web:* www.americaneaglesteel.com	Annapolis	MD	21401	410-573-0335	

Phone Fax

American Key Products Inc One Reuten Dr ....Closter NJ 07624 201-767-8022
Web: www.akfponline.com

American Muscle 7 Lee Blvd ....Malvern PA 19355 610-251-2397
TF: 888-332-7930 ■ *Web:* www.americanmuscle.com

Andersons Inc Retail Group
480 W Dussel Dr PO Box 119.......................Maumee OH 43537 419-893-5050
TF: 800-537-3370 ■ *Web:* www.andersonsinc.com

APEL International Inc 11201 Ampere Ct.............Louisville KY 40299 502-240-0443
Web: www.apelfilters.com

Arctic Co-Operatives Ltd 1645 Inkster Blvd...........Winnipeg MB R2X2W7 204-697-1625
Web: www.arcticco-op.com

Armature Dns 2000 Inc 11001 Jean Meunier..........Montreal QC H1G4S7 514-324-1141 324-1402
TF: 800-363-7996 ■ *Web:* www.dns-2000.com

AutoTruckToys.com 2814 W Wood St..................Paris TN 38242 731-642-3535
Web: www.autotrucktoys.com

B & B Discount Sales Co 712 S Broadway ....Oklahoma City OK 73109 405-232-3578 232-2848

Bearing Service & Supply Inc
1327 N Market ....Shreveport LA 71107 318-424-1447
Web: www.bearserco.com

Beere Precision Products Inc 4915 21st St............Racine WI 53406 262-632-0472
Web: www.beere.com

Best Impressions Catalog Co 345 N Lewis Ave.........Oglesby IL 61348 815-883-3532
Web: www.bestimpressions.com

Big Lots Inc (BLI) 300 Phillipi Rd...................Columbus OH 43228 614-278-6800 278-8322
NYSE: BIG ■ *TF:* 877-998-1697 ■ *Web:* www.biglots.com

Black Forest Decor LLC PO Box 297 ....Jenks OK 74037 800-605-0915
TF: 800-605-0915 ■ *Web:* www.blackforestdecor.com

Blocker & Wallace Service LLC
1472 Rogers Ave.................................Memphis TN 38114 901-274-0708
Web: www.blockerandwallace.com

Bobcat of Atlanta 6972 Best Friend Rd.................Atlanta GA 30340 770-242-6500
Web: www.bobcatofatlanta.com

Bobcat of Boston Inc 20 Concord St ....North Reading MA 01864 978-664-3727
Web: www.bobcatboston.com

Bomgaars 1805 Zenith ....Sioux City IA 51103 712-277-2000 277-1247
Web: www.bomgaars.com

Boscogen Inc Four Vanderbilt Ste B ....Irvine CA 92618 949-380-4317
Web: www.boscogen.com

Building 19 Inc 319 Lincoln St ....Hingham MA 02043 781-749-6900
TF: 800-225-5061 ■ *Web:* www.building19.com

Busch Electronics 2306 Robbins St................Saint Paul MN 55114 651-288-2580
Web: www.buschelectronics.com

C W Rod Tool Company Inc 15050 Northgreen Dr ....Houston TX 77032 281-449-0881
Web: www.cwrodtool.com

Camping World RV Sales 8155 Rivers Ave ....Charleston SC 29406 888-586-5446
Web: www.campingworldofcharleston.com

CBS Builders Supply Inc 1000 Carroll St.............Clermont FL 34711 352-394-2116
Web: www.cbsbuilderssupply.com

Churchville Fire Equipment Corp
340 Sanford Rd S..............................Churchville NY 14428 585-293-1688
Web: www.churchvillefire.com

Clubfurniture.com
11535 Carmel Commons Blvd Ste 202................Charlotte NC 28226 888-378-8383
TF: 888-378-8383 ■ *Web:* www.clubfurniture.com

Coast Guard Exchange System
510 Independence Pkwy Ste 500 ....Chesapeake VA 23320 757-420-2480
Web: www.cg-exchange.com

Conserv FS Inc 1110 McConnell Rd ....Woodstock IL 60098 815-334-5950
Web: www.conservfs.com

CoolTronics 220 E Madison St Ste 1220 ....Tampa FL 33602 813-259-4407
Web: www.cooltronics.com

Dana Safety Supply Inc 5221 W Market St..........Greensboro NC 27409 336-854-5536
Web: www.danasafetysupply.com

DeMesy & Company Ltd 300 Crescent Ct ....Dallas TX 75201 214-855-8777
Web: www.demesy.com

Dempsey Corp 47 Davies Ave..........................Toronto ON M4M2A9 416-461-0844
Web: www.dempseycorporation.com

Diamond Attachments LLC 2801A S Mississippi ....Atoka OK 74525 580-889-6202
Web: www.diamondattachments.com

Dixie Aerospace Inc 473 Dividend Dr............Peachtree City GA 30269 678-490-0140
Web: www.dixieaerospace.com

Dollar General Corp 100 Mission Ridge ....Goodlettsville TN 37072 615-855-4000
NYSE: DG ■ *TF:* 800-777-1410 ■ *Web:* www.dollargeneral.com

Dollar Tree Stores Inc 500 Volvo Pkwy ....Chesapeake VA 23320 877-530-8733
NASDAQ: DLTR ■ *TF:* 877-530-8733 ■ *Web:* www.dollartree.com

Drury Capital Inc 47 Hulfish St Ste 340..............Princeton NJ 08542 609-252-1230
Web: www.drurycapital.com

Dueber's Inc
300 Industrial Blvd...................Norwood Young America MN 55397 952-467-3085 467-3001

Easy Ice LLC 925 W Washington St Ste 100..........Marquette MI 49855 866-327-9423
TF: 866-327-9423 ■ *Web:* www.easyice.com

Echo Engineering & Production Supplies Inc
5406 W 78th St................................Indianapolis IN 46268 317-876-8848
Web: www.echosupply.com

Emitations.com 6162 Mission Gorge Rd Ste G ....San Diego CA 92120 619-528-9100
Web: www.emitations.com

Employee Owned Holdings Inc
5500 N Sam Houston Pkwy W Ste 100.................Houston TX 77086 281-569-7000
Web: www.eoh-inc.com

Exchange, The 3911 S Walton Walker Blvd.............. Dallas TX 75236 214-312-2011 446-0163*
**Fax Area Code: 800* ■ *TF:* 800-527-2345 ■ *Web:* www.shopmyexchange.com

Exporting Commodities International Inc
12000 Lincoln Dr W Ste 108 ....Marlton NJ 08053 856-797-2004
Web: www.eci-coal.com

Fabric Images Inc 325 Corporate Dr.....................Elgin IL 60123 847-488-9877
Web: www.fabricimages.com

Family Dollar Stores Inc PO Box 1017 ....Charlotte NC 28201 704-847-6961
NYSE: FDO ■ *TF:* 866-377-6420 ■ *Web:* www.familydollar.com

Fertilizer Company of Arizona Inc
2850 S Peart Rd...............................Casa Grande AZ 85293 520-836-7477
Web: www.comptonag.com

Phone Fax

Filtration Lab Inc
193 Rang De L Eglise..........................Saint Ligouri QC J0K2X0 450-754-4222
Web: www.filtrationlab.com

Fortune Metals Inc 330 Hwy 7 E Ste 201.........Richmond Hill ON L4B3P8 905-707-0786
Web: www.fortunemetals.com

Fusion Tech 218 20th Ave..........................Roseville IL 61473 309-774-4275
Web: www.ftiinc.org

Ghost Armor LLC 1470 N Horne St....................Gilbert AZ 85233 480-921-3161
Web: www.ghost-armor.com

GK TechStar LLC 802 W 13th St.....................Deer Park TX 77536 281-542-0205
Web: www.techstaris.com

Great Canadian Dollar Store (1993) Ltd
2957 Jutland Rd Ste 101 ....Victoria BC V8T5J9 250-388-0123 388-9763
Web: www.dollarstores.com

Greatlookz 4635 N Black Canyon Hwy.................Phoenix AZ 85015 602-218-5976
Web: www.greatlookz.com

Gulf States Engineering Inc 4110 Moffett Rd ....Mobile AL 36618 251-460-4646
Web: www.gseeng.com

Hanwha International LLC 2559 Rt 130..............Cranbury NJ 08512 609-655-2500
Web: www.hanwha-usa.com

Herman Strauss Inc 35th & McColloch St ....Wheeling WV 26003 304-748-0699
Web: www.strauss-ind.com

Home Furniture Mart 5301 Sheila St ....Commerce CA 90040 323-267-0802
Web: www.homefurnituremart.com

Howell Tractor & Equipment LLC 480 Blaine St...........Gary IN 46406 800-852-8816
TF: 800-852-8816 ■ *Web:* www.howelltractor.com

Hubbard`s Impala Parts Inc
1676 Anthony Rd ....Burlington NC 27215 336-227-1589
Web: www.impalaparts.com

Intrepid Aviation Group Holdings LLC
263 Tresser Blvd One Stamford Plz...................Stamford CT 06901 203-905-4220
Web: www.intrepidaviation.com

JD Fields & Company Inc 55 Waugh Dr Ste 1250 ....Houston TX 77007 281-558-7199
Web: www.jdfields.com

K&D Pratt Group Inc
55 Akerley Blvd Burnside Industrial Park ....Dartmouth NS B3B1M3 902-468-1955
Web: www.kdpratt.com

Karl Chevrolet Accessories
1101 Se Oralabor Rd ....Ankeny IA 50021 515-299-4300
Web: www.karlchevrolet.com

Kataman Metals LLC
7733 Forsyth Blvd Ste 300..........................St. Louis MO 63105 314-863-6699
Web: www.katamanmetals.com

Keenpac North America Ltd 25 Main St Ste 3 ....Goshen NY 10924 845-291-8680
Web: keenpac.com

Kelloggauto Supply 502 S Edgemoor St ....Wichita KS 67218 316-682-4525
Web: www.poormanautosupply.com

Kerley & Sears Inc 4331 Cement Vly Rd.............Midlothian TX 76065 972-775-3902
Web: www.kerleyandsears.net

Keystone Archery Inc 186 Path Vly Rd ....Fort Loudon PA 17224 717-369-2970
Web: www.keystonecountrystore.com

Kryptonite Kollectibles
1441 Plainfield Ave...............................Janesville WI 53545 877-646-1728
TF: 877-646-1728 ■ *Web:* www.kryptonitekollectibles.com

Leeco Steel LLC 1011 Warrenville Rd Ste 500............. Lisle IL 60532 630-427-2100
Web: www.leecosteel.com

Little General Store Inc 17 Yellow Wood Way.......... Beckley WV 25801 304-253-9592
Web: www.lgstores.com

Lynch Metals Inc 1075 Lousons Rd .... Union NJ 07083 908-686-8401
Web: www.lynchmetals.com

Lynn Roberts International Inc 9100 F St.............Omaha NE 68127 402-331-5400
Web: www.golynnroberts.com

Mallory Sonalert Products Inc
4411 S High School Rd ....Indianapolis IN 46241 317-821-0370
Web: www.mallory-sonalert.com

Marden's 458 Kennedy Memorial Dr................ Waterville ME 04901 207-873-6112 680-2229
Web: www.mardenssurplus.com

Materials Innovation Technologies LLC
320 Rutledge Rd...................................Fletcher NC 28732 828-651-9646
Web: www.emergingmit.com

McVean Trading & Investments LLC
850 Ridge Lk Blvd Ste One.........................Memphis TN 38120 901-761-8400
Web: www.mcvean.com

Middlesex Gases & Technologies Inc
292 Second St PO Box 490249 ....Everett MA 02149 617-387-5050
Web: www.middlesexgases.com

Midwest Manufacturing Resources Inc
1993 Case Pkwy N ....Twinsburg OH 44087 330-405-4227
Web: www.hfomidwest.com

Nashville Rubber & Gasket Company Inc
1900 Elm Tree Dr ....Nashville TN 37210 615-883-0030
Web: www.nashvillerubber.com

Navy Exchange Service Command (NEXCOM)
3280 Virginia Beach Blvd.....................Virginia Beach VA 23452 757-463-6200
TF: 800-628-3924 ■ *Web:* www.mynavyexchange.com

NeedleTech Products Inc
452 John L Dietsch Blvd.....................North Attleboro MA 02760 508-431-4000
Web: www.needletech.com

Net Worth Solutions Inc
1410 Broadway 34th Fl.............................New York NY 10018 212-278-8200
Web: www.networthsolutionsinc.com

New Vitality 260 Smith St...................... Farmingdale NY 11735 888-997-2941
TF: 888-997-2941 ■ *Web:* www.newvitality.com

Norquist Salvage Corp
2151 Professional Dr Ste 200.......................Roseville CA 95661 916-787-1070
Web: www.thrifttown.com

Ocean State Jobbers Inc
375 Commerce Pk Rd......................North Kingstown RI 02852 401-295-2672 885-0359
Web: www.oceanstatejoblot.com

Ollie's Bargain Outlet Inc
6295 Allentown Blvd Ste 1 ....Harrisburg PA 17112 717-657-2300
Web: www.olliesbargainoutlet.com

Company	City	State	ZIP	Phone	Fax
Overstock.com Inc 6350 South 3000 East *NASDAQ:* OSTK ■ *TF Cust Svc:* 800-843-2446 ■ *Web:* www.overstock.com	Salt Lake City	UT	84121	801-947-3100	944-4629
Palay Display Industries Inc 10901 Louisiana Ave S Ste 106 *Web:* www.palaydisplay.com	Bloomington	MN	55438	952-983-2026	
PB Hoidale Company Inc 3801 W Harry *Web:* www.hoidale.com	Wichita	KS	67213	316-942-1361	
Peach Trader Inc 6286 Dawson Blvd *Web:* www.acitydiscount.com	Norcross	GA	30093	404-752-6715	
Pet Supplies Inc Customer Service Return Ctr 1 Maplewood Dr *TF:* 800-738-7877 ■ *Web:* www.petsupplies.com	Hazleton	PA	18202	800-738-7877	
Playscripts 450 Seventh Ave Ste 809 *TF:* 866-639-7529 ■ *Web:* www.playscripts.com	New York	NY	10123	866-639-7529	
PLH Products Inc 6655 Knott Ave *Web:* www.healthmatesauna.com	Buena Park	CA	90620	714-739-6600	
Polyform Products Co 1901 Estes Ave *Web:* sculpey.com	Elk Grove Village	IL	60007	847-427-0020	
Premier Elevator Company Inc 230 Andrew Dr *Web:* www.premier-elevator.com	Stockbridge	GA	30281	770-389-4951	
Pride Products Corp 4333 Veterans Memorial Hwy *Fax Area Code: 877 ■ *TF:* 800-898-5550 ■ *Web:* www.prideproducts.com	Ronkonkoma	NY	11779	631-737-4444	729-4749*
Pro Athlete Inc 10800 N Pomona Ave *Web:* www.beapro.com	Kansas City	MO	64153	816-587-6050	
Promoshop Inc 5420 McConnell Ave *Web:* www.promoshopinc.com	Los Angeles	CA	90066	310-821-1780	
Protective Group Inc, The 14100 NW 58th Ct *Web:* www.protectivegroup.com	Miami Lakes	FL	33014	305-820-4270	
Quadratec Inc 1028 Saunders Ln *Web:* www.acmejeepparts.com	West Chester	PA	19380	610-701-3336	
R J Schinner Company Inc 16950 W Lincoln Ave PO Box 510470 *TF:* 800-234-1460 ■ *Web:* www.rjschinner.com	New Berlin	WI	53151	262-797-7180	797-7190
Rack Attack-car Rack & Hitch Center 745 Worcester Rd *Web:* www.rackattack.com	Framingham	MA	01701	508-879-1444	
Rakuten.com Shopping 85 Enterprise St *Web:* www.rakuten.com	Aliso Viejo	CA	92656	949-389-2000	389-2800
Rally House & Kansas Sampler 9750 Quivira Rd *TF:* 800-645-5394 ■ *Web:* www.rallyhouse.com	Lenexa	KS	66215	800-645-5394	
Regal Mold and Die 25208 Leer Dr *Web:* www.regalmold.com	Elkhart	IN	46514	574-262-4110	
Reliance Parts Corp 2535 Business Pkwy *Web:* www.relianceparts.com	Minden	NV	89423	800-776-3113	
Rennco LLC 300 Elm St *TF:* 800-409-5225 ■ *Web:* www.rennco.com	Homer	MI	49245	800-409-5225	
River Trading Company LTD 10900 89th Ave N *Web:* www.rivertradingcompany.com	Maple Grove	MN	55369	763-463-3400	
Rogers Stereo Inc 525 Woodruff Rd *Web:* www.rogersstereo.com	Greenville	SC	29607	864-288-9999	
Sawyer Products Inc 605 Seventh Ave N *Web:* www.sawyer.com	Safety Harbor	FL	34695	727-725-1177	
Schwing Bioset Inc 350 SMC Dr *Web:* www.schwingbioset.com	Somerset	WI	54025	715-247-3433	
Scout Stuff PO Box 7143 *TF:* 800-323-0736 ■ *Web:* www.scoutstuff.org	Charlotte	NC	28241	800-323-0736	
SDB Trade International LP 817 Southmore Ave Ste 301 *Web:* thesdbgroup.com	Houston	TX	77502	713-475-0048	
SelecTransportation Resources LLC 9550 N Loop E *Web:* www.selectransportation.com	Houston	TX	77029	713-672-4115	
Shoplet.com 39 Broadway Ste 2030 *TF:* 800-757-3015 ■ *Web:* www.shoplet.com	New York	NY	10006	212-619-3353	617-3389
Skycraft Parts & Surplus Inc 2245 W Fairbanks Ave *Web:* www.skycraftsurplus.com	Winter Park	FL	32789	407-628-5634	
Slack Auto Parts 404 Main St Sw *Web:* www.slackautoparts.com	Gainesville	GA	30501	770-535-6000	
Southern Company of NLR Inc, The 1201 Cypress St *Web:* www.thesoco.com	North Little Rock	AR	72114	501-376-6333	
Speedway Motors 340 Victory Ln PO Box 81906 *Web:* www.speedwaymotors.com	Lincoln	NE	68528	402-323-3200	
Spot Trading LLC 440 S LaSalle St Ste 2800 *Web:* www.spottradingllc.com	Chicago	IL	60605	312-362-4550	
Stahl Peterbilt Inc 18020-118 Ave *Web:* www.stahlpeterbilt.com	Edmonton	AB	T5S2G2	780-483-6666	
SteelCon Supply Co 265 Industrial Dr *Web:* www.steelconsupply.com	Beckley	WV	25801	304-255-1416	
Store Supply Warehouse LLC 9801 Page Ave *Web:* www.storesupply.com	St Louis	MO	63132	314-427-8887	
Store51 3653 Regent Blvd Ste 606 *Web:* www.store51.com	Jacksonville	FL	32224	904-998-2222	
Stowers Rental & Supply Inc 10644 Lexington Dr *Web:* www.stowerscat-inventory.com	Knoxville	TN	37932	865-218-8800	
Strato Inc 100 New England Ave *Web:* www.stratoinc.com	Piscataway	NJ	08854	732-981-1515	
Stratum Energy Systems LLC 1791 E 40th St *Web:* stratumenergy.com	Cleveland	OH	44103	216-432-9850	
Stylin Online 81900 Main St *Web:* www.stylinonline.com	Memphis	MI	48041	586-270-1086	
Sun Machinery Company Inc PO Box 789 *Web:* www.sunmachineryco.com	Lexington	SC	29071	803-359-1000	
Supply Chain Equity Partners 1300 East Ninth St *Web:* www.supplychainequity.com	Cleveland	OH	44199	216-925-4184	
Swain's General Store Inc 602 E First St *Web:* www.swainsinc.com	Port Angeles	WA	98362	360-452-2357	452-7561
Third Door Media Inc 279 Newtown Tpke *Web:* www.thirddoormedia.com	Redding	CT	06896	203-664-1350	
Tiger Supplies Inc 27 Selvage St *Web:* www.tigersupplies.com	Irvington	NJ	07111	973-854-8636	
Trydor Industries (Canada) Ltd 19275 - 25th Ave *Web:* www.trydor.com	Surrey	BC	V3S3X1	604-542-4773	542-4776
Turbo International Inc 2151 Las Palmas Dr Ste E *Web:* www.turbointernational.com	Carlsbad	CA	92011	760-476-1444	
U-line Corp PO Box 245040 *TF:* 800-779-2547 ■ *Web:* www.u-line.com	Milwaukee	WI	53224	414-354-0300	354-0349
Unclaimed Baggage Ctr 509 W Willow St *Web:* unclaimedbaggage.com	Scottsboro	AL	35768	256-259-1525	
URELL Inc 86 Coolidge Ave *Web:* www.urell.com	Watertown	MA	02471	617-923-9500	
US-Japan High-Speed Rail LLC 1212 New York Ave NW Ste 700 *Web:* www.usjhsr.com	Washington	DC	20005	202-403-0437	
Valterra Products Inc 15230 San Fernando Mission Blvd Ste 107 *Web:* www.valterra.com	Mission Hills	CA	91345	818-898-1671	
Vanguard Steel Ltd 2160 Meadowpine Blvd *Web:* www.vanguardsteel.com	Mississauga	ON	L5N6H6	905-821-1100	
Vermeer Mid Atlantic Inc 10900 Carpet St *Web:* www.vermeermidatlantic.com	Charlotte	NC	28273	704-588-3238	
Vermeer Southeast Sales & Service Inc 4559 Old Winter Garden Rd *Web:* www.vermeersoutheast.com	Orlando	FL	32811	407-295-2020	
Waterfront Container Leasing Company Inc 888 N Point St *Web:* www.waterfrontcontainer.com	San Francisco	CA	94109	415-788-5667	
Weir Canada Inc 2360 Millrace Ct *Web:* www.weirpowerindustrial.com	Mississauga	ON	L5N1W2	905-812-7100	
West Springfield Auto Parts 92 Blandin Ave Ste C *Web:* www.wsaparts.com	Framingham	MA	01702	508-879-6932	
Western States Truck Centers LLC 3790 N Reserve St *Web:* www.westernstatestruckcenters.com	Missoula	MT	59808	406-543-3196	
Western United Electric Supply Corp 100 Bromley Business Pkwy *Web:* www.wue.coop	Brighton	CO	80603	303-659-2356	
Wild Bird Centers of America 4046 W 83rd St *Web:* www.wildbird.com	Prairie Village	KS	66208	913-381-5633	
World Trade Service Inc 1050 Nine N Dr Ste A *Web:* www.worldtradeservice.com	Alpharetta	GA	30004	770-521-0124	
WristWatch 109 S Main St *Web:* www.wristwatch.com	Mcallen	TX	78501	956-682-7132	682-1528
Yale Materials Handling-Green Bay Inc 2140 Hutson Rd *Web:* www.yalegb.com	Green Bay	WI	54303	920-494-8726	

795 VENTURE CAPITAL FIRMS

Companies listed here are investors, not lenders.

Company	City	State	ZIP	Phone	Fax
AAVIN Equity Partners LP 118 Third Ave SE Ste 630 *Web:* www.aavin.com	Cedar Rapids	IA	52401	319-247-1072	363-9519
Aberdare Ventures One Embarcadero Ctr Ste 4000 *Web:* www.aberdare.com	San Francisco	CA	94111	415-392-7442	392-4264
ABS Capital Partners 400 E Pratt St Ste 910 *Web:* www.abscapital.com	Baltimore	MD	21202	410-246-5600	246-5606
ABS Ventures 950 Winter St Ste 2600 *Web:* www.absventures.com	Waltham	MA	02451	781-250-0400	250-0345
Accel Partners 428 University Ave *Web:* www.accel.com	Palo Alto	CA	94301	650-614-4800	614-4880
Adams Capital Management Inc 500 Blackburn Ave *Web:* www.acm.com	Sewickley	PA	15143	412-749-9454	749-9459
Adams Harkness Techventures 60 State St	Boston	MA	02109	617-788-1670	788-1663
Adams Street Partners LLC One N Wacker Dr Ste 2200 *Web:* www.adamsstreetpartners.com	Chicago	IL	60606	312-553-7890	553-7891
Adena Ventures 20 E Cir Dr Ste 143	Athens	OH	45701	740-597-1470	
Adobe Ventures LP 345 Pk Ave *TF:* 877-722-7088 ■ *Web:* www.adobe.com	San Jose	CA	95110	408-536-6000	537-6000
Advanced Technology Ventures 500 Boylston St Ste 1380 *Web:* www.atvcapital.com	Boston	MA	02116	617-850-9700	850-9750
Advantage Capital Partners c/o Eastside Partners 207 E Side Sq *Web:* www.advantagecap.com	Huntsville	AL	35801	256-883-8711	883-8558
Advent International Corp 75 State St 29th Fl *Web:* www.adventinternational.com	Boston	MA	02109	617-951-9400	951-0566
Alerion Partners 23 Old Kings Hwy S *Web:* www.alerionpartners.com	Darien	CT	06820	203-202-9900	202-9906
Alexander Hutton Venture Partners 1215 Fourth Ave Ste 900 *Web:* www.ahvp.com	Seattle	WA	98161	206-341-9800	341-9810

Firm	City	State	Zip	Phone	Fax
Allegis Capital 130 Lytton Ave Ste 210 *Web:* www.allegiscapital.com	Palo Alto	CA	94301	650-687-0500	687-0234
Alloy Ventures 400 Hamilton Ave Fourth Fl *Web:* www.alloyventures.com	Palo Alto	CA	94301	650-687-5000	687-5010
Alpha Capital Partners Ltd 122 S Michigan Ave Ste 1700 *Web:* www.alphacapital.com	Chicago	IL	60603	312-322-9800	322-9808
Alta Communications 1000 Winter St S Entrance Ste 3500 *Web:* www.altacomm.com	Waltham	MA	02451	617-956-1325	262-9779
Alta Partners One Embarcadero Ctr 37th Fl *Web:* www.altapartners.com	San Francisco	CA	94111	415-362-4022	362-6178
Altira Group LLC 1675 Broadway Ste 2400 *Web:* www.altiragroup.com	Denver	CO	80202	303-592-5500	592-5519
Altos Ventures 2882 Sand Hill Rd Ste 100 *Web:* www.altosventures.com	Menlo Park	CA	94025	650-234-9771	233-9821
Altotech Ventures LLC 205 De Anza Blvd Ste 14 *Web:* www.altotechventures.com	San Mateo	CA	94402	650-574-1870	574-1870
AM Pappas & Assoc 2520 Meridian Pkwy *Web:* www.pappasventures.com	Durham	NC	27713	919-998-3300	998-3301
American Bullion Inc 12301 Wilshire Blvd Ste 650 *TF:* 800-326-9598 ■ *Web:* www.americanbullion.com	Los Angeles	CA	90025	310-689-7720	
American Capital Group Inc 8105 Irvine Ctr Dr Ste 250 *TF:* 877-814-6871 ■ *Web:* www.acgcapital.com	Irvine	CA	92618	949-485-3005	271-5850
American River Ventures 2270 Douglas Blvd Ste 212 *Web:* www.arventures.com	Roseville	CA	95661	916-780-2828	780-5443
Ampersand Capital Partners 55 William St Ste 240 *TF:* 800-477-6834 ■ *Web:* www.ampersandcapital.com	Wellesley	MA	02481	781-239-0700	239-0824
Aperture Venture Partners 645 Madison Ave 20th Fl *Web:* www.aperturevp.com	New York	NY	10022	212-758-7325	319-8779
Apex Venture Partners 225 W Washington St Ste 1500 *Web:* www.apexvc.com	Chicago	IL	60606	312-857-2800	857-1800
Arbor Partners LLC 130 S First St *Web:* www.arborpartners.com	Ann Arbor	MI	48104	734-668-9000	669-4195
Arboretum Ventures 303 Detroit St *Web:* www.arboretumvc.com	Ann Arbor	MI	48104	734-998-3688	998-3689
ARCH Venture Partners 8725 W Higgins Rd Ste 290 *Web:* www.archventure.com	Chicago	IL	60631	773-380-6600	380-6606
Arete Corp PO Box 1299 *Web:* www.arete-microgen.com	Center Harbor	NH	03226	603-253-9797	253-9799
Ascension Health Ventures LLC 11775 Borman Dr Ste 310 *Web:* ascensionventures.org/	Saint Louis	MO	63146	314-733-8100	733-8678
Ascent Venture Partners 255 State St Fifth Fl *Web:* www.ascentvp.com	Boston	MA	02109	617-720-9400	720-9401
Asset Management Ventures 2100 Geng Rd Ste 200 *Web:* www.assetman.com	Palo Alto	CA	94303	650-621-8808	856-1826
Associated Venture Investors Management 130 Lytton Ave Ste 210 *Web:* pinnacleven.com	Palo Alto	CA	94301	650-687-0235	687-0234
ATA Ventures 4300 El Camino Real Ste 205 *Web:* www.ataventures.com	Los Altos	CA	94022	650-594-0189	594-0257
Atlas Venture 25 First St Ste 303 *Web:* www.atlasventure.com	Cambridge	MA	02141	617-588-2600	
August Capital 2480 Sand Hill Rd Ste 101 *Web:* www.augustcap.com	Menlo Park	CA	94025	650-234-9900	234-9910
Aurora Funds 3100 Tower Blvd *Web:* www.aurorafunds.com	Durham	NC	27707	919-484-0400	484-0444
Austin Ventures 300 W Sixth St Ste 2300 *Web:* www.austinventures.com	Austin	TX	78701	512-485-1900	651-8500
Avansis Ventures LLC 12710 Popes Head Rd *Web:* www.avansis.com	Clifton	VA	20124	703-796-0222	935-0574
Bain Capital Inc 200 Clarendon St *Web:* baincapital.com	Boston	MA	02116	617-516-2000	516-2010
Battelle Ventures 100 Princeton S Corp Ctr Ste 150 *Web:* www.battelleventures.com	Ewing	NJ	08628	609-921-1456	921-8703
Battery Ventures One Marina Pk Dr Ste 1100 *Web:* www.battery.com	Boston	MA	02210	617-948-3600	948-3601
Bay Partners 10600 N De Anza Blvd Ste 100 *Web:* www.baypartners.com	Cupertino	CA	95014	408-725-2444	446-4502
BCM Technologies 1709 Dryden Rd Ste 1790 *Web:* www.bcmtechnologies.com	Houston	TX	77030	713-795-0105	795-4602
Beecken Petty O'Keefe & Co 131 S Dearborn St Ste 2800 *Web:* www.beeckenpetty.com	Chicago	IL	60603	312-435-0300	435-0371
Beringea LLC 32330 W 12 Mile Rd *Web:* www.beringea.com	Farmington Hills	MI	48334	248-489-9000	489-8819
Berkeley International Capital Corp 650 California St 26th Fl *Web:* www.berkeleyvc.com	San Francisco	CA	94108	415-249-0450	
BioAdvance 3711 Market St Fl 8 *Web:* www.bioadvance.com	Philadelphia	PA	19104	215-966-6214	966-6215
Bioventures Investors 70 Walnut St Ste 302 *Web:* www.bioventuresinvestors.com	Wellesley	MA	02481	617-252-3443	621-7993
Black River Asset Management LLC 9320 Excelsior Blvd *Web:* www.black-river.com	Hopkins	MN	55343	952-984-3863	
Blue Chip Venture Co 312 Walnut St Ste 1120 *TF:* 800-775-1812 ■ *Web:* www.bcvc.com	Cincinnati	OH	45202	513-723-2300	723-2306
Blueprint Ventures 601 Gateway Blvd Ste 1140 *Web:* www.blueprintventures.com	South San Francisco	CA	94080	415-901-4000	
BlueRun Ventures 545 Middlefield Rd Ste 250 *Web:* brv.com	Menlo Park	CA	94025	650-462-7250	462-7252
Boldcap Ventures LLC 750 Lexington Ave Sixth Fl **Fax Area Code:* 917 ■ *Web:* www.boldcap.com	New York	NY	10022	212-730-5498	591-0880*
Borealis Ventures 10 Allen St *Web:* www.borealisventures.com	Hanover	NH	03755	603-643-1500	643-7600
Boston Capital Ventures 84 State St Ste 320	Boston	MA	02109	617-227-6550	227-3847
Boston Millennia Partners 30 Rowes Wharf Ste 400 *Web:* www.bostonmillenniapartners.com	Boston	MA	02110	617-428-5150	428-5160
Brantley Partners 3550 Lander Rd Ste 300	Cleveland	OH	44124	216-464-8400	464-8405
BTG International Inc 300 Barr Harbor Dr Seventh Fl *Web:* www.btgplc.com	West Conshohocken	PA	19428	610-278-1660	278-1605
Burrill & Co 1 Embarcadero Ctr Ste 2700	San Francisco	CA	94111	415-591-5400	591-5401
BV Cornerstone Ventures LP 385 Interlocken Crescent Ste 250 *Web:* www.bvcv.com	Broomfield	CO	80021	303-410-2510	
Cambridge Innovations Inc *Cambridge Innovation Ctr* One Broadway 14th Fl *Web:* cic.us	Cambridge	MA	02142	617-758-4200	758-4101
Camp Ventures LLC 280 Second St Ste 280 *Web:* www.campventures.com	Los Altos	CA	94022	650-949-0804	618-1719
Capital Network Inc, The 30 Washington St *Web:* www.thecapitalnetwork.org	Wellesley	MA	02481	781-591-0291	
Capital Resource Partners 31 State St 6th Fl *TF:* 800-623-2880 ■ *Web:* www.crp.com	Boston	MA	02109	617-478-9600	478-9605
Capital Southwest Corp 12900 Preston Rd Ste 700 *NASDAQ: CSWC* ■ *TF:* 877-870-5176 ■ *Web:* www.capitalsouthwest.com	Dallas	TX	75230	972-233-8242	233-7362
Cardinal Partners 230 Nassau St *Web:* www.cardinalpartners.com	Princeton	NJ	08542	609-924-6452	683-0174
Cardinal Venture Capital 325 Sharon Pk Dr Ste 107 *Web:* www.cardinalvc.com	Menlo Park	CA	94025	650-289-4700	614-4865
Castile Ventures 65 William St Ste 205 *Web:* www.castileventures.com	Wellesley	MA	02481	781-890-0060	890-0065
Catamount Ventures 400 Pacific Ave Third Fl *Web:* www.catamountventures.com	San Francisco	CA	94133	415-277-0300	277-0301
Catterton 599 W Putnam Ave *Web:* www.cpequity.com	Greenwich	CT	06830	203-629-4901	629-4903
CEI Ventures Inc 2 Portland Fish Pier Ste 206 *Web:* www.ceiventures.com	Portland	ME	04101	207-772-5356	772-5503
CenterPoint Ventures 6300 Bridge Pt Pkwy Bldg 1 Ste 500 *Web:* www.cpventures.com	Austin	TX	78730	512-795-5800	795-5849
Charles River Ventures One Broadway 15th Fl *Web:* www.crv.com	Cambridge	MA	02142	781-768-6000	768-6100
Charter Venture Capital 525 University Ave Ste 1400 *Web:* www.charterventures.com	Palo Alto	CA	94301	650-325-6953	
Cherry Tree Investment Co 301 Carlson Pkwy Ste 103 *Web:* www.cherrytree.com	Minnetonka	MN	55305	952-893-9012	893-9036
Chevron Technology Ventures (CTV) 6001 Bollinger Canyon Rd *NYSE: CVX* ■ *Web:* www.chevron.com/technologyventures	San Ramon	CA	94583	925-842-1000	
CHL Medical Partners 1055 Washington Blvd Sixth Fl *Web:* www.chlmedical.com	Stamford	CT	06901	203-324-7700	324-3636
Chrysalis Ventures 101 S Fifth St Ste 1650 *Web:* www.chrysalisventures.com	Louisville	KY	40202	502-583-7644	583-7648
CIBC Wood Gundy Capital 425 Lexington Ave *TF:* 800-999-6726 ■ *Web:* www.cibcwm.com	New York	NY	10017	212-856-4000	
CID Capital Inc 201 W 103rd St Ste 200 *Web:* www.cidcap.com	Indianapolis	IN	46290	317-818-5030	644-2914
CIVC Partners 191 N Wacker Dr Ste 1100 *Web:* www.civc.com	Chicago	IL	60606	312-873-7300	873-7300
Clearstone Venture Partners 1351 Fourth St 4th Fl *Web:* www.clearstone.com	Santa Monica	CA	90401	310-460-7900	460-7901
Code Hennessy & Simmons Inc 10 S Wacker Dr Ste 3175 *TF:* 888-603-5847 ■ *Web:* www.chsonline.com	Chicago	IL	60606	312-876-1840	876-3854
Columbia Capital 204 S Union St Ste 300 *Web:* www.colcap.com	Alexandria	VA	22314	703-519-2000	519-5870
Commons Capital LP 320 Washington St Fourth Fl *Web:* www.commonscapital.com	Brookline	MA	02445	617-739-3500	
Commonwealth Capital Ventures 400 Cummings Park Dr Ste 1725 *Web:* www.commonwealthvc.com	Woburn	MA	01801	781-890-5554	
Connecticut Innovations Inc 865 Brook St Third Fl *TF:* 800-733-4763 ■ *Web:* www.ctinnovations.com	Rocky Hill	CT	06067	860-563-5851	563-4877
Cordova Ventures 4080 McGinnis Ferry Rd Ste 1201 *Web:* www.cordovaventures.com	Alpharetta	GA	30005	678-942-0300	942-0301
Cornerstone Equity Investors LLC 281 Tresser Blvd 12th Fl *TF:* 800-438-7465 ■ *Web:* www.cornerstone-equity.com	Stamford	CT	06901	212-753-0901	826-6798
Court Square Ventures 455 Second St SE Ste 401 *Web:* courtsquareventures.com	Charlottesville	VA	22902	434-817-3300	817-3299

Firm	City	State	ZIP	Phone	Fax
Covera Ventures 6836 Bee Caves Road Ste275 *Web:* www.coveraventures.com	Austin	TX	78746	512-795-5870	
Crescendo Ventures 600 Hansen Way *Web:* www.crescendoventures.com	Palo Alto	CA	94304	650-470-1200	470-1201
Cross Atlantic Capital Partners Five Radnor Corporate Ctr 100 Matsonford Rd Ste 555 *Web:* www.xacp.com	Radnor	PA	19087	610-995-2650	971-2062
Crosslink Capital Two Embarcadero Ctr Ste 2200 *Web:* www.crosslinkcapital.com	San Francisco	CA	94111	415-617-1800	
Crosspoint Venture Partners 670 Woodside Rd *Web:* www.cpvp.com	Redwood City	CA	94061	650-851-7600	851-7600
Cutlass Capital LLC 229 Marlborough St *Web:* www.cutlasscapital.com	Boston	MA	02116	617-867-0820	624-9669
Davis Tuttle Venture Partners LP 110 W Seventh St *Web:* www.davistuttle.com	Tulsa	OK	74103	918-584-7272	582-3404
Defta Partners 111 Pine St *Web:* www.deftapartners.com	San Francisco	CA	94111	415-433-2262	433-2264
Delphi Ventures 3000 Sand Hill Rd Bldg 1 Ste 135 *Web:* www.delphiventures.com	Menlo Park	CA	94025	650-854-9650	854-2961
Digital Power Capital 411 W Putnam Ave	Greenwich	CT	06830	203-862-7040	
Doll Capital Management 2420 Sand Hill Rd Ste 200 *Web:* www.dcm.com	Menlo Park	CA	94025	650-233-1400	854-9159
Dolphin Equity Partners 330 Madison Ave 9th Fl	New York	NY	10017	212-446-1600	
Domain Assoc 1 Palmer Sq Ste 515 *TF:* 866-803-9204 ■ *Web:* www.domainvc.com	Princeton	NJ	08542	609-683-5656	683-9789
Dominion Ventures 1646 N California Blvd *Web:* www.dominion.com	Walnut Creek	CA	94596	925-280-6338	
Draper Fisher Jurvetson (DFJ) 2882 Sand Hill Rd Ste 150 *Web:* www.dfj.com	Menlo Park	CA	94025	650-233-9000	233-9233
East Gate Capital Management 5050 El Camino Real Ste 104 *Web:* www.eg-group.com	Los Altos	CA	94022	650-584-3078	325-5072
Edelson Technology Partners 300 Tice Blvd *Web:* www.edelsontech.com	Woodcliff Lake	NJ	07677	201-930-9898	930-8899
EDF Ventures 425 N Main St *Web:* www.edfvc.com	Ann Arbor	MI	48104	734-663-3213	663-7358
Edison Venture Fund 1009 Lenox Dr Ste 4 *Web:* edisonpartners.com	Lawrenceville	NJ	08648	609-896-1900	
EGL Holdings 3495 Piedmont Rd 11 Piedmont Ctr Ste 412 *Web:* www.eglholdings.com	Atlanta	GA	30305	404-949-8300	949-8311
El Dorado Ventures 850 Oak Grove Ave *Web:* www.eldorado.com	Menlo Park	CA	94025	650-854-1200	854-1202
EnerTech Capital 625 W Ridge Pk Bldg D Ste 105 *Web:* www.enertechcapital.com	Conshohocken	PA	19428	484-539-1860	539-1870
Enterprise Partners Venture Capital (EPVC) 2223 Avenida de la Playa Ste 300	La Jolla	CA	92037	858-731-0300	
Entrepia Ventures Inc 2975 Bowers Ave Ste 223 *Web:* www.entrepia.com	Santa Clara	CA	95051	408-492-9040	492-9540
Envest Ventures 2101 Parks Ave Ste 401 *Web:* www.envestventures.com	Virginia Beach	VA	23451	757-437-3000	437-3884
EQUUS Total Return Inc 700 Louisiana St 48th Fl **Fax Area Code:* 212 ■ *TF:* 888-323-4533 ■ *Web:* www.equuscap.com	Houston	TX	77002	888-323-4533	671-1534*
Euclid SR Partners 45 Rockefeller Plaza Ste 1910	New York	NY	10111	212-218-6880	218-6877
Ferrer Freeman & Company LLC 10 Glenville St The Mill *Web:* www.ffandco.com	Greenwich	CT	06831	203-532-8011	532-8016
First Analysis Corp One S Wacker Dr Ste 3900 *Web:* firstanalysis.com	Chicago	IL	60606	312-258-1400	258-0334
Fisher Lynch Capital 2929 Campus Dr Ste 420 *Web:* www.fisherlynch.com	San Mateo	CA	94403	650-287-2700	287-2701
FLAG Capital Management LLC 1266 E Main St Fifth Fl *Web:* www.flagcapital.com	Stamford	CT	06902	203-352-0440	352-0441
Flagship Ventures One Memorial Dr Seventh Fl *Web:* www.flagshipventures.com	Cambridge	MA	02142	617-868-1888	868-1115
Fletcher Spaght Inc 222 Berkeley St 20th Fl *Web:* www.fletcherspaght.com	Boston	MA	02116	617-247-6700	247-7757
Focus Ventures 525 University Ave Ste 225 *Web:* www.focusventures.com	Palo Alto	CA	94301	650-325-7400	325-8400
Forward Ventures 9393 Towne Centre Dr Ste 200 *Web:* www.forwardventures.com	San Diego	CA	92121	858-677-6077	964-5028
Foundation Capital 250 Middlefield Rd *Web:* www.foundationcapital.com	Menlo Park	CA	94025	650-614-0500	
Foundation Medical Partners 105 Rowayton Ave *Web:* www.foundmed.com	Rowayton	CT	06853	203-851-3900	831-8289
Frazier Healthcare 601 Union 2 Union Sq Ste 3200 *TF:* 800-638-4817 ■ *Web:* www.frazierco.com	Seattle	WA	98101	206-621-7200	621-1848
Frontenac Co 135 S La Salle St Ste 3800 *TF:* 800-368-3681 ■ *Web:* www.frontenac.com	Chicago	IL	60603	312-368-0044	368-9520
G-51 Capital Management 900 S Capital of Texas Hwy Ste 151 *Web:* www.g51.com	Austin	TX	78746	512-929-5151	732-0886
Gabriel Venture Partners 999 Baker Way Ste 400 *Web:* www.gabrielvp.com	San Mateo	CA	94404	650-551-5000	551-5001
Gazelle Techventures 11611 N Meridian St Ste 310 *Web:* allosventures.com	Carmel	IN	46032	317-275-6800	275-1100
General Atlantic LLC 600 Steamboat Rd Ste 105 *Web:* www.generalatlantic.com	Greenwich	CT	06830	203-629-8600	622-8818
Geocapital Partners 1 Executive Dr Ste 160	Fort Lee	NJ	07024	201-461-9292	461-7793
GFI Energy Ventures LLC 333 S Grand Ave 28 Fl *Web:* www.oaktreecapital.com	Los Angeles	CA	90071	213-830-6300	830-6293
Globespan Capital Partners One Boston Pl Ste 2810 *Web:* www.globespancapital.com	Boston	MA	02108	617-305-2300	305-2301
GrandBanks Capital 65 William St Ste 330 *Web:* www.grandbankscapital.com	Wellesley	MA	02481	781-997-4300	997-4301
Great Hill Partners LLC One Liberty Sq *Web:* www.greathillpartners.com	Boston	MA	02109	617-790-9400	790-9401
Greenspring Assoc Inc 100 Painters Mill Rd Ste 700 *Web:* greenspringassociates.com	Owings Mills	MD	21117	410-363-2725	
Greer Capital Advisors LLC 2200 Woodcrest Pl Ste 309 *Web:* www.greercap.com	Birmingham	AL	35209	205-445-0800	445-1013
Grosvenor Funds 888 17th St NW *Web:* www.grosvenorfund.com	Washington	WA	20006	202-861-5650	861-5653
Grove Street Advisors 20 William St Ste 230 *Web:* grovestreet.com/	Wellesley	MA	02481	781-263-6100	263-6101
GTCR Golder Rauner LLC 300 N Lasalle Ste 5600 *Web:* www.gtcr.com	Chicago	IL	60654	312-382-2200	382-2201
Hamilton BioVentures 990 Highland Dr Ste 302	Solana Beach	CA	92075	858-314-2350	314-2355
HarbourVest Partners LLC 1 Financial Ctr *Web:* www.harbourvest.com	Boston	MA	02111	617-348-3707	350-0305
Harvard Management Company Inc 600 Atlantic Ave *Web:* www.hmc.harvard.edu	Boston	MA	02210	617-523-4400	
Harvest Partners 280 Pk Ave 25th Fl *TF:* 866-771-1000 ■ *Web:* harvestpartners.com/	New York	NY	10017	212-599-6300	812-0100
HC Wainwright & Co Inc 430 Park Ave 4th Fl *Web:* www.hcwainwright.com	New York	NY	10022	212-356-0500	
Hercules Technology Growth Capital Inc 400 Hamilton Ave Ste 310 *NYSE: HTGC* ■ *Web:* htgc.com/	Palo Alto	CA	94301	650-289-3060	473-9194
Highland Capital Partners 92 Hayden Ave *Web:* www.hcp.com	Lexington	MA	02421	781-861-5500	
HLM Venture Partners 222 Berkeley St 20th Fl *Web:* www.hlmvp.com	Boston	MA	02116	617-266-0030	
HMS Hawaii 841 Bishop St Ste 860 *Web:* www.hmshawaii.com	Honolulu	HI	96813	808-545-3755	546-2211
HO2 Partners 13455 Noel Rd 2 Galleria Tower Ste 1670 *Web:* www.ho2.com	Dallas	TX	75240	972-702-1107	702-8234
Housatonic Partners 800 Boylston St Ste 2220 *Web:* www.housatonicpartners.com	Boston	MA	02199	617-399-9200	267-5565
Hummer Winblad Venture Partners Pier 33 S, The Embarcadero Ste 300 *Web:* hwvp.com	San Francisco	CA	94111	415-979-9600	979-9601
Icon Ventures 505 Hamilton Ave Ste 310 *Web:* www.jafco.com	Palo Alto	CA	94301	650-463-8800	463-8801
Idealab 130 W Union St *Web:* www.idealab.com	Pasadena	CA	91103	626-585-6900	535-2701
IDG Ventures 1 Letterman Dr *Web:* www.idgvsf.com	San Francisco	CA	94129	415-439-4420	439-4428
IGNITE Group 255 Shoreline Dr	Redwood City	CA	94065	650-622-2005	
In-Q-Tel PO Box 749 *Web:* www.iqt.org	Arlington	VA	22216	703-248-3000	248-3001
Inflection Point Ventures (IPV) 1 Innovation Way Ste 302 *Web:* www.inflectpoint.com	Newark	DE	19711	302-452-1120	452-1122
InnoCal LP 650 Town Ctr Dr Ste 770 *Web:* www.innocal.com	Costa Mesa	CA	92626	714-850-6784	850-6798
Innovation Works Inc 2000 Technology Dr Ste 250 *Web:* www.innovationworks.org	Pittsburgh	PA	15219	412-681-1520	681-2625
Institutional Venture Partners 3000 Sand Hill Rd Bldg 2 Ste 250 *Web:* www.ivp.com	Menlo Park	CA	94025	650-854-0132	854-2009
Intelligent Systems Corp 4355 Shackleford Rd *NYSE: INS* ■ *Web:* www.intelsys.com	Norcross	GA	30093	770-381-2900	381-2808
InterWest Partners 2710 Sand Hill Rd 2nd Fl *TF:* 866-803-9204 ■ *Web:* www.interwest.com	Menlo Park	CA	94025	650-854-8585	854-4706
INVESCO Private Capital Inc 1166 Ave of the Americas 26th Fl *TF:* 800-959-4246 ■ *Web:* www.invesco.com	New York	NY	10036	212-278-9000	278-9822
Ironside Capital 945 Concord St *Web:* www.ironsidecapital.com	Framingham	MA	01701	781-622-5800	
iSherpa Capital LLC 6400 S Fiddlers Green Cir *Web:* isherpa.com	Greenwood Village	CO	80111	303-645-0500	645-0501
JatoTech Ventures 6300 Bridgepoint Pkwy Bldg 1 Ste 500 *TF:* 800-626-4686 ■ *Web:* www.jatotech.com	Austin	TX	78730	512-795-5860	692-2868
JEGI Capital LLC 150 E 52nd St 18th Fl *Web:* www.jegi.com	New York	NY	10022	212-754-0710	754-0337
JH Whitney & Co 130 Main St *Web:* www.whitney.com	New Canaan	CT	06840	203-716-6100	716-6122
JK&B Capital 180 N Stetson Ave Ste 4500 *Web:* www.jkbcapital.com	Chicago	IL	60601	312-946-1200	946-1103

Firm	City	State	Zip	Phone	Fax
Johnson & Johnson Development Corp					
One Johnson & Johnson Plz	New Brunswick	NJ	08933	732-524-0400	
NYSE: JNJ ■ *Web:* www.jnj.com					
KB Partners LLC 600 Central Ave Ste 390	Highland Park	IL	60035	847-681-1270	681-1370
Web: www.kbpartners.com					
KBL Healthcare Ventures 52 E 72nd St-PH	New York	NY	10021	212-319-5555	319-5591
Web: www.kblvc.com					
Kirtland Capital Partners					
3201 Enterprise Pkwy Ste 200	Beachwood	OH	44122	216-593-0100	593-0240
Web: www.kirtlandcapital.com					
Kleiner Perkins Caufield & Byers (KPCB)					
2750 Sand Hill Rd	Menlo Park	CA	94025	650-233-2750	233-0300
TF: 877-312-5521 ■ *Web:* www.kpcb.com					
Kodiak Venture Partners					
1000 Winter St Ste 3800	Waltham	MA	02451	781-672-2500	672-2501
Web: www.kodiakvp.com					
Labrador Ventures					
101 University Ave Fourth Fl	Palo Alto	CA	94301	650-366-6000	366-6430
Web: www.labrador.com					
Lancet Capital 245 First St Ste 1800	Cambridge	MA	02142	617-444-8582	444-8405
Web: www.lancetcapital.com					
Lee Munder Capital Group 200 Clarendon St	Boston	MA	02116	617-380-5600	380-5601
Web: www.leemunderpim.com					
Legacy Venture 180 Lytton Ave Second Fl	Palo Alto	CA	94301	650-324-5980	324-5982
Web: www.legacyventure.com					
Life Sciences Greenhouse					
225 Market St Ste 500	Harrisburg	PA	17101	717-635-2100	635-2010
Web: www.lsgpa.com					
Lightspeed Venture Partners					
2200 Sand Hill Rd Ste 100	Menlo Park	CA	94025	650-234-8300	234-8333
Web: lsvp.com					
Lilly Ventures 115 W Washington St	Indianapolis	IN	46204	317-429-0140	759-2819
Web: www.lillyventures.com					
Lubar & Co 700 N Water St Ste 1200	Milwaukee	WI	53202	414-291-9000	291-9061
Web: www.lubar.com					
Madison Dearborn Partners LLC (MDP)					
70 W Madison Ste 4600	Chicago	IL	60602	312-895-1000	895-1001
Web: www.mdcp.com					
Markpoint Venture Partners					
15770 Dallas Pkwy Ste 800	Dallas	TX	75248	972-490-1976	490-1980
Web: www.markpt.com					
Mason Wells Biomedical Fund					
411 E Wisconsin Ave Ste 1280	Milwaukee	WI	53202	414-727-6400	727-6410
Web: www.masonwells.com					
Massachusetts Capital Resource Co					
420 Boylston St 5th Fl	Boston	MA	02116	617-536-3900	536-7930
Web: www.masscapital.com					
Massachusetts Growth Capital Corp (MGCC)					
529 Main St Schrafft Ctr Ste 1M10	Charlestown	MA	02129	617-523-6262	523-7676
Web: www.mcdfc.com					
Matrix Partners					
1000 Winter St					
Bay Colony Corporate Ctr Ste 4500	Waltham	MA	02451	781-890-2244	890-2288
Web: www.matrixpartners.com					
Maveron LLC 411 First Ave S Ste 600	Seattle	WA	98104	206-288-1700	288-1777
Web: www.maveron.com					
Mayfield Fund					
2484 Sand Hill Rd Quadrus Complex Bldg 4	Menlo Park	CA	94025	650-854-5560	854-5712
Web: www.mayfield.com					
MCG Capital Corp 1100 Wilson Blvd Ste 3000	Arlington	VA	22209	703-247-7500	247-7505
NASDAQ: MCGC ■ *TF:* 888-748-3526 ■ *Web:* www.mcgcapital.com					
McKellar & Co 311 E Rose Ln	Phoenix	AZ	85012	602-277-1800	277-0429
Web: mckellarandcompany.com					
MDT Advisors Inc					
125 High St Oliver St Tower Fl 21	Boston	MA	02110	617-235-7100	235-7199
Web: www.federatedinvestors.com					
Menlo Ventures					
3000 Sand Hill Rd Bldg 4 Ste 100	Menlo Park	CA	94025	650-854-8540	854-7059
Web: www.menloventures.com					
Mesirow Financial Private Equity					
350 N Clark St	Chicago	IL	60610	312-595-6000	595-4246
TF: 800-453-0600 ■ *Web:* www.mesirowfinancial.com					
MidCoast Capital					
259 N Radnor-Chester Rd Ste 210	Radnor	PA	19087	610-687-8580	971-2154
Web: www.midcoastcapital.com					
Milestone Venture Partners					
551 Madison Ave Seventh Fl	New York	NY	10022	212-223-7400	223-0315
Web: www.milestonevp.com					
Mission Ventures					
3570 Carmel Mountain Rd Ste 200	San Diego	CA	92130	858-350-2100	350-2101
Web: www.missionventures.com					
Mohr Davidow Ventures					
3000 Sand Hill Rd Bldg 3 Ste 290	Menlo Park	CA	94025	650-854-7236	854-7365
Web: www.mdv.com					
Montlake Capital 1200 Fifth Ave Ste 1800	Seattle	WA	98101	206-956-0898	956-0863
Web: montlakecapital.com					
Morgan Stanley Venture Partners					
1585 Broadway 38th Fl	New York	NY	10036	212-761-4000	761-9606
TF: 866-722-7310 ■					
Web: www.morganstanley.com/institutional/venturepartners					
Morgenthaler 2710 Sand Hill Rd Ste 100	Menlo Park	CA	94025	650-388-7600	388-7601
Web: www.morgenthaler.com					
Morgenthaler Ventures 50 Public Sq Ste 2700	Cleveland	OH	44113	216-416-7500	416-7501
Web: www.morgenthaler.com					
Mountaineer Capital LP					
107 Capital St Ste 300	Charleston	WV	25301	304-347-7519	347-0072
Web: www.mtncap.com					
MPM Capital Offices 200 Clarendon St 54th Fl	Boston	MA	02116	617-425-9200	425-9201
TF: 888-286-8010 ■ *Web:* www.mpmcapital.com					
MRV Communications Inc 20415 Nordhoff St	Chatsworth	CA	91311	818-773-0900	773-0906
OTC: MRVC ■ *TF Sales:* 800-338-5316 ■ *Web:* www.mrv.com					
MVC Capital Inc 287 Bowman Ave 2nd Fl	Purchase	NY	10577	914-510-9400	701-0315
NYSE: MVC ■ *TF:* 800-322-2885 ■ *Web:* www.mvccapital.com					
Nautic Partners LLC 50 Kennedy Plz 12th Fl	Providence	RI	02903	401-278-6770	278-6387
Web: www.nautic.com					
NCA Partners Inc 1200 Westlake Ave N Ste 600	Seattle	WA	98109	206-689-5615	689-5614
Web: www.nwcap.com					
NCIC Capital Fund 900 Kettering Tower	Dayton	OH	45423	937-222-4422	222-1323
Web: www.ncicfund.com					
Needham Capital Partners 445 Pk Ave	New York	NY	10022	212-371-8300	371-2311
TF: 800-625-7071 ■ *Web:* www.needhamcapital.com					
NeuroVentures Capital LLC Zero Ct Sq	Charlottesville	VA	22902	434-297-1000	297-1001
Web: www.neuroventures.com					
New Venture Partners LLC (NVP)					
430 Mountain Ave Ste 404	Murray Hill	NJ	07974	908-464-0900	464-8131
Web: www.nvpllc.com					
New York Life Capital Partners					
51 Madison Ave	New York	NY	10010	212-576-7000	
Web: newyorklife.com					
NewSpring Capital 555 E Lancaster Ave Ste 520	Radnor	PA	19087	610-567-2380	567-2388
Web: www.newspringcapital.com					
Newtek Business Services Inc					
1440 Broadway 17th Fl	New York	NY	10018	212-356-9500	273-8252
NASDAQ: NEWT ■ *TF Sales:* 866-820-8902 ■ *Web:* www.thesba.com					
Newton Technology Partners 550 Bryant St	Palo Alto	CA	94301	650-331-3992	
NGEN Partners LLC 1114 State St Ste 247	Santa Barbara	CA	93101	805-564-3156	564-1669
Web: www.ngenpartners.com					
NJTC Venture Fund 1001 Briggs Rd Ste 280	Mount Laurel	NJ	08054	856-273-6800	787-9800
Web: www.njtcvc.com					
Noro-Moseley Partners					
3284 Northside Pkwy NW Ste 525	Atlanta	GA	30327	404-233-1966	239-9280
Web: www.noromoseley.com					
North Atlantic Capital Two City Ctr Fifth Fl	Portland	ME	04101	207-772-4470	772-3257
Web: www.northatlanticcapital.com					
North Bridge Venture Partners					
950 Winter St Ste 4600	Waltham	MA	02451	781-290-0004	290-0999
Web: www.nbvp.com					
North Hill Ventures 535 Boylston St 6th Fl	Boston	MA	02116	617-600-7050	788-2152
Web: www.northhillventures.com					
Northleaf Capital Partners					
79 Wellington St W Sixth Fl PO Box 120	Toronto	ON	M5K1N9	866-964-4141	304-0195*
**Fax Area Code:* 416 ■ *TF:* 866-964-4141 ■ *Web:* www.northleafcapital.com					
Northwood Ventures 485 Underhill Blvd Ste 205	Syosset	NY	11791	516-364-5544	364-0879
Web: www.northwoodventures.com					
Norwest Equity Partners					
80 S Eigth St Ste 3600	Minneapolis	MN	55402	612-215-1600	215-1601
Web: www.nep.com					
Norwest Venture Partners					
525 University Ave Ste 800	Palo Alto	CA	94301	650-321-8000	321-8010
Web: www.nvp.com					
Novak Biddle Venture Partners					
7501 Wisconsin Ave E Tower Ste 1380	Bethesda	MD	20814	240-497-1910	223-0255
Web: www.novakbiddle.com					
Noventi Ventures 8100 Jarvis Ave Ste 110	Newark	CA	94560	650-325-6699	325-7799
Web: www.noventivc.com					
NTH Power Technologies Inc					
One Embarcadero Ctr Ste 1550	San Francisco	CA	94111	415-983-9983	983-9984
Web: www.nthpower.com					
OCA Ventures 351 W Hubbard St Ste 600	Chicago	IL	60654	312-327-8400	542-8952
Web: www.ocaventures.com					
Olympic Venture Partners 1010 Market St	Kirkland	WA	98033	425-889-9192	
Web: www.ovp.com					
Olympus Partners 1 Stn Pl Ste 1	Stamford	CT	06902	203-353-5900	353-5910
Web: www.olympuspartners.com					
ONCAP 161 Bay St 48th Fl	Toronto	ON	M5J2S1	416-214-4300	216-1834
Web: www.oncap.com					
Onset Ventures 2490 Sand Hill Rd	Menlo Park	CA	94025	650-529-0700	529-0777
Web: www.onset.com					
Osprey Ventures LP 502 Waverley St	Palo Alto	CA	94301	650-473-9250	
Pacific Horizon Ventures					
800 Fifth Ave Ste 4120	Seattle	WA	98104	206-682-1181	682-8077
Web: www.pacifichorizon.com					
Palomar Ventures					
233 Wilshire Blvd Ste 900	Santa Monica	CA	90401	310-260-6050	656-4150
Web: www.palomarventures.com					
Pappajohn Capital Resources 666 Walnut St	Des Moines	IA	50309	515-244-5746	
Web: www.pappajohn.com					
Partech International					
50 California St Ste 3200	San Francisco	CA	94111	415-788-2929	788-6763
Web: www.partechventures.com					
Paul Capital Partners					
575 Market St Ste 2500	San Francisco	CA	94105	415-283-4300	283-4301
Web: www.paulcapital.com					
Peck's Management Partners Ltd					
One Rockefeller Plz Ste 1427	New York	NY	10020	212-332-1333	332-1334
Web: www.pecks.com					
Pfingsten Partners LLC					
300 N LaSalle St Ste 5400	Chicago	IL	60654	312-222-8707	222-8708
Web: www.pfingsten.com					
Pitango Venture Capital					
540 Cowper St Suite 200	Palo Alto	CA	94301	650-322-2201	
Web: www.pitango.com					
Pomona Capital 780 Third Ave 46th Fl	New York	NY	10017	212-593-3639	593-3987
Web: www.pomonacapital.com					
Primus Venture Partners					
5900 Landerbrook Dr Ste 200	Cleveland	OH	44124	440-684-7300	684-7342
Web: www.primuscapital.com					
Prince Ventures 6475 Bold Venture Tr	Tallahassee	FL	32309	850-321-3353	668-7223
Web: www.princeventures.com					
Prism Venture Management LLC					
117 Kendrick St Ste 200	Needham	MA	02494	781-302-4000	302-4040
Web: www.prismventure.com					
Private Capital Management					
8889 Pelican Bay Blvd Ste 500	Naples	FL	34108	239-254-2500	254-2557
TF: 800-763-0337 ■ *Web:* www.private-cap.com					

Firm / Address	City	State	ZIP	Phone	Fax
Prolog Ventures LLC 7701 Forsyth Blvd Ste 1095 *Web:* www.prologventures.com	Saint Louis	MO	63105	314-743-2400	743-2403
Prospect Venture Partners 435 Tasso St Ste 200 *Web:* www.prospectventures.com	Palo Alto	CA	94301	650-327-8800	324-8838
Provco Group 795 E Lancaster Ave Ste 200 *Web:* provcogroup.com	Villanova	PA	19085	610-520-2010	520-1905
Providence Equity Partners LLC 50 Kennedy Plz 18th Fl *Web:* www.provequity.com	Providence	RI	02903	401-751-1700	751-1790
Psilos Group Managers LLC 140 Broadway 51st Fl *Web:* www.psilos.com	New York	NY	10005	212-242-8844	242-8855
PureTech Ventures 500 Boylston St Ste 1600 *Web:* www.puretechventures.com	Boston	MA	02116	617-482-2333	482-3337
Quaker BioVentures 2929 Arch St Cira Ctr *Web:* www.quakerbio.com	Philadelphia	PA	19104	215-988-6800	988-6801
Radius Ventures LLC 400 Madison Ave Eighth Fl *Web:* www.radiusventures.com	New York	NY	10017	212-897-7778	397-2656
Rembrandt Venture Partners 600 Montgomery St 44th Fl **Fax Area Code:* 415 ■ *Web:* www.rembrandtvc.com	San Francisco	CA	94111	650-326-7070	528-2901*
Research Corp Technologies 101 N Wilmot Rd Ste 600 *Web:* www.rctech.com	Tucson	AZ	85711	520-748-4400	748-0025
Reynolds De Witt Securities 300 Main St	Cincinnati	OH	45202	513-241-8716	
Rho Capital Partners Inc 152 W 57th St 23rd Fl *Web:* www.rhoventures.com	New York	NY	10019	212-751-6677	751-3613
Richland Ventures 1201 16th Ave S	Nashville	TN	37212	615-383-8030	
Riordan Lewis & Haden 10900 Wilshire Blvd Ste 850 *Web:* www.rlhinvestors.com	Los Angeles	CA	90024	310-405-7200	405-7222
Rockport Capital Partners 160 Federal St 18th Fl *Web:* www.rockportcap.com	Boston	MA	02110	617-912-1420	912-1449
Rosewood Capital One Maritime Plz Ste 1575 *Web:* www.rosewoodcap.com	San Francisco	CA	94111	415-362-5526	362-1192
RRE Ventures LLC 130 E 59th St 17th Fl *Web:* www.rre.com	New York	NY	10022	212-418-5100	
Rustic Canyon Partners 100 Wilshire Blvd Ste 200 *Web:* rusticcanyon.com	Santa Monica	CA	90401	310-998-8000	
Safeguard Scientifics Inc 435 Devon Pk Dr Ste 800 *NYSE: SFE* ■ *TF:* 877-506-7371 ■ *Web:* www.safeguard.com	Wayne	PA	19087	610-293-0600	293-0601
Sail Venture Partners LP 3161 Michelson Dr Ste 750 *Web:* www.sailcapital.com	Irvine	CA	92612	949-398-5100	398-5101
Saints Ventures LLC 2020 Union St *Web:* www.saintscapital.com	San Francisco	CA	94123	415-773-2080	835-5970
Sanderling 400 S El Camino Real Ste 1200 *Web:* www.sanderling.com	San Mateo	CA	94402	650-401-2000	375-7077
Sapient Capital Management LLC 4020 Lk Creek Dr PO Box 1590 *Web:* www.sapientcapital.com	Wilson	WY	83014	307-733-3806	733-4630
Saugatuck Capital Co 187 Danbury Rd *Web:* www.saugatuckcapital.com	Wilton	CT	06897	203-348-6669	324-6995
Scale Venture Partners 950 Tower Ln Ste 700 *Web:* www.scalevp.com	Foster City	CA	94404	650-378-6000	378-6040
Selby Venture Partners 3500 Alameda de las Pulgas Ste 200 *Web:* selbyventures.com/	Menlo Park	CA	94025	650-854-7399	
Sequel Venture Partners 4430 Arapahoe Ave Ste 220 *Web:* www.sequelvc.com	Boulder	CO	80303	303-546-0400	546-9728
Sequoia Capital 2800 Sand Hill Rd Ste 101 *Web:* www.sequoiacap.com	Menlo Park	CA	94025	650-854-3927	
Sevin Rosen Funds 13455 Noel Rd Ste 1670 *Web:* www.srfunds.com	Dallas	TX	75240	972-702-1100	702-1103
Shasta Ventures 2440 Sand Hill Rd Ste 300 *Web:* www.shastaventures.com	Menlo Park	CA	94025	650-543-1700	543-1799
Shepherd Ventures 11696 Sorrento Valley Rd Ste 203 *Web:* www.shepherdventures.com	San Diego	CA	92121	858-509-4744	509-3662
Sierra Ventures 1400 Fashion Island Blvd Ste 1010 *Web:* www.sierraventures.com	San Mateo	CA	94404	650-854-1000	854-5593
Sigma Partners 156 Diablo Rd Ste 320 *Web:* www.sigmapartners.com	Danville	CA	94526	650-853-1700	853-1717
Signal Peak 2795 E Cottonwood Pkwy Ste 360 *Web:* www.signalpeak.com/	Salt Lake City	UT	84121	801-942-8999	942-1636
Signature Capital LLC 100 Commercial St *Web:* www.signaturecapital.com	Portland	ME	04101	207-773-8123	
Siguler Guff & Co LLC 825 Third Ave 10th Fl *Web:* www.sigulerguff.com	New York	NY	10022	212-332-5100	332-5120
SmartForest Ventures 319 SW Washington St Ste 720 *Web:* www.smartforest.com	Portland	OR	97204	503-222-2552	222-2834
Sofinnova Ventures Inc 3000 Sand Hill Rd Bldg 4 Ste 250 *Web:* www.sofinnova.com	Menlo Park	CA	94025	650-681-8420	322-2037
SOFTBANK Inc 38 Glen Ave *Web:* www.softbank.com	Newton	MA	02459	617-928-9300	928-9304
Solstice Capital 81 Washington St Ste 303 *Web:* www.solcap.com	Salem	MA	01970	617-523-7733	
South Atlantic Capital Inc 614 W Bay St *Web:* www.southatlantic.com	Tampa	FL	33606	813-253-2500	253-2360
Spectrum Equity Investors LP 1 International Pl 35th Fl *Web:* www.spectrumequity.com	Boston	MA	02110	617-464-4600	464-4601
Split Rock Partners 1600 El Camino Real Ste 290 *Web:* www.splitrock.com	Menlo Park	CA	94025	650-617-1500	617-1510
Sprout Group 11 Madison Ave 13th Fl *Web:* www.sproutgroup.com	New York	NY	10010	212-538-3600	538-8245
Steamboat Ventures 3601 W Olive Ave Ste 650 *Web:* steamboatvc.com	Burbank	CA	91505	818-566-7400	566-7490
Sterling Venture Partners 650 S Exeter St # 10 *Web:* www.sterlingpartners.com	Baltimore	MD	21202	443-703-1700	703-1750
Storm Ventures 2440 Sand Hill Rd Ste 301 *Web:* www.stormventures.com	Menlo Park	CA	94025	650-926-8800	926-8888
Strategic Investments & Holdings Inc (SIHI) 50 Fountain Plz Ste 1350 *Web:* www.sihi.net	Buffalo	NY	14202	716-857-6000	857-6490
Summit Partners 222 Berkeley St 18th Fl *TF:* 800-503-4611 ■ *Web:* www.summitpartners.com	Boston	MA	02116	617-824-1000	824-1100
Sutter Hill Ventures 755 Page Mill Rd Ste A-200 *Web:* www.shv.com	Palo Alto	CA	94304	650-493-5600	858-1854
SV Life Sciences (SVLS) 201 Washington St Ste 3900 *Web:* www.svlsa.com	Boston	MA	02108	617-367-8100	367-1590
TA Assoc Inc 200 Clarendon St 56th Fl *TF:* 800-836-8873 ■ *Web:* www.ta.com	Boston	MA	02116	617-574-6700	574-6728
TDF Ventures (TDF) Two Wisconsin Cir Ste 920 **Fax Area Code:* 301 ■ *Web:* www.tdfventures.com	Chevy Chase	MD	20815	240-483-4286	907-8850*
Technology Crossover Ventures 528 Ramona St *Web:* www.tcv.com	Palo Alto	CA	94301	650-614-8200	614-8222
Technology Funding Inc 460 St Michael's Dr Ste 1000 *TF:* 800-821-5323 ■ *Web:* www.techfunding.com	Santa Fe	NM	87505	800-821-5323	
Technology Partners 550 University Ave *TF:* 800-747-3924 ■ *Web:* www.technologypartners.com	Palo Alto	CA	94301	650-289-9000	289-9001
TeleSoft Partners 950 Tower Ln Ste 1600 *Web:* www.telesoftvc.com	Foster	CA	94404	650-358-2500	358-2501
TEOCO Corp 12150 Monument Dr Ste 400 *TF:* 888-868-3626 ■ *Web:* www.teoco.com	Fairfax	VA	22033	703-322-9200	322-9133
Texas Growth Fund 900 S Capital of Texas Hwy Ste 430 *Web:* www.tgfmanagement.com	Austin	TX	78746	512-322-3100	322-3101
TGap Ventures LLC 7171 Stadium Dr *Web:* www.tgapventures.com	Kalamazoo	MI	49009	269-217-1999	381-7620
Thoma Cressey Bravo Inc 600 Montgomery St 32nd Fl *Web:* www.thomabravo.com	San Francisco	CA	94111	415-263-3660	392-6480
Thomas McNerney & Partners One Landmark Sq Ste 1920 *Web:* www.tm-partners.com	Stamford	CT	06901	203-978-2000	978-2005
Thomas Weisel Partners Group LLC One Montgomery St *TF:* 888-267-3700 ■ *Web:* www.tweisel.com	San Francisco	CA	94104	415-364-2500	364-2695
TL Ventures 435 Devon Pk Dr *Web:* www.tlventures.com	Wayne	PA	19087	610-971-1515	975-9330
Topspin Partners LP 3 Expy Plaza *Web:* www.topspinpartners.com	Roslyn Heights	NY	11577	516-625-9400	625-9499
Tortoise Energy Capital Corp 11550 Ash St Ste 300 *NYSE: TYY* ■ *TF:* 866-362-9331 ■ *Web:* www.tortoiseadvisors.com	Leawood	KS	66211	913-981-1020	981-1021
Trelys Funds PO Box 5066 *Web:* www.trelys.com	Cary	NC	27512	919-459-4650	459-4670
Triathlon Medical Ventures (TMVP) 300 E Business Way Ste 200 *Web:* www.tmvp.com	Cincinnati	OH	45241	513-723-2600	247-6122
Trident Capital 505 Hamilton Ave Ste 200 *Web:* www.tridentcap.com	Palo Alto	CA	94301	650-289-4400	289-4444
Trillium Group LLC 1221 Pittsford Victor Rd *Web:* www.trillium-group.com	Pittsford	NY	14534	585-383-5680	383-0042
Trinity Ventures 3000 Sand Hill Rd Bldg 4 Ste 160 *Web:* trinityventures.com	Menlo Park	CA	94025	650-854-9500	854-9501
Triton Ventures 6300 Bridge Pt Pkwy Bldg 1 Ste 500 *Web:* www.tritonventures.com	Austin	TX	78730	512-795-5820	795-5828
TVM Capital 101 Arch St Ste 1950 *Web:* www.tvm-capital.com	Boston	MA	02110	617-345-9320	
Union Square Ventures 915 Broadway 19th Fl *Web:* www.usv.com	New York	NY	10010	212-994-7880	994-7399
UPS Strategic Enterprise Fund 55 Glenlake Pkwy NE Bldg 1 4th Fl **Fax Area Code:* 404 ■ *TF:* 800-742-5877 ■ *Web:* www.ups.com/sef	Atlanta	GA	30328	800-742-5877	828-8088*
US Venture Partners (USVP) 2735 Sand Hill Rd Ste 300 *Web:* www.usvp.com	Menlo Park	CA	94025	650-854-9080	854-3018
Valhalla Partners 8000 Towers Crescent Dr Ste 1050 *Web:* www.valhallapartners.com	Vienna	VA	22182	703-448-1400	448-1441
VantagePoint Venture Partners 1001 Bayhill Dr Ste 300 *Web:* www.vpcp.com	San Bruno	CA	94066	650-866-3100	869-6078
Vector Capital One Matket St Steuart Tower 23rd Fl *Web:* www.vectorcapital.com	San Francisco	CA	94105	415-293-5000	293-5100
Venrock Assoc 3340 Hillview Ave *Web:* www.venrock.com	Palo Alto	CA	94304	650-561-9580	561-9180
Venture Capital Fund of America 509 Madison Ave Ste 14 *Web:* www.vcfa.com	New York	NY	10022	212-838-5577	838-7614

	City	State	Zip	Phone	Fax
Venture Investors LLC 505 S Rosa Rd Ste 201 *Web:* www.ventureinvestors.com	Madison	WI	53719	608-441-2700	441-2727
Vertical Group 25 DeForest Ave *Web:* www.vertical-group.com	Summit	NJ	07901	908-277-3737	273-9434
Vesbridge Partners 601 Carlson Pkwy Ste 1160 *Web:* www.vesbridge.com	Minnetonka	MN	55305	952-995-7499	995-7493
Village Ventures Inc One Bank St Ste2 *Web:* villageventures.com	Williamstown	MA	01267	413-458-1100	458-0338
VIMAC Ventures LLC 177 Milk St *Web:* www.vimac.com	Boston	MA	02109	617-350-9800	350-9899
Vision Capital 700 Airport Blvd Ste 370 *Web:* www.visioncap.com	Burlingame	CA	94010	650-373-2720	373-2727
VSP Capital 201 Post St Ste 1100	San Francisco	CA	94108	415-558-8600	
Walden Venture Capital 750 Battery St Ste 700 *Web:* www.waldenvc.com	San Francisco	CA	94111	415-391-7225	391-7262
Warburg Pincus Ventures Co Inc 450 Lexington Ave *Web:* www.warburgpincus.com	New York	NY	10017	212-878-0600	878-9351
Washington Research Foundation 2815 Eastlake Ave E Ste 300 *Web:* www.wrfcapital.com	Seattle	WA	98102	206-336-5600	336-5615
WayPoint Ventures *RPM Ventures* 320 N Main St Ste 400 *Web:* www.rpmvc.com	Ann Arbor	MI	48104	734-332-1700	332-1900
Western Technology Investment (WTI) 104 La Mesa Dr Ste 102 *Web:* www.westerntech.com	Portola Valley	CA	94028	650-234-4300	234-4343
Wicks Group of Cos LLC 405 Pk Ave Ste 702 *Web:* www.wicksgroup.com	New York	NY	10022	212-838-2100	223-2109
Wind Point Partners 676 N Michigan Ave Ste 3700 *Web:* www.wppartners.com	Chicago	IL	60611	312-255-4800	255-4820
Windjammer Capital Investors 610 Newport Ctr Dr Ste 1100 *Web:* www.windjammercapital.com	Newport Beach	CA	92660	949-721-9944	720-4222
Windspeed Ventures 52 Waltham St *Web:* www.wsventures.com	Lexington	MA	02421	781-860-8888	860-0493
Woodside Fund 303 Twin Dolphin Dr Ste 600 *TF:* 888-368-5545 ■ *Web:* www.woodsidefund.com	Redwood Shores	CA	94065	650-610-8050	610-8051
Zanett Inc 635 Madison Ave 15th Fl *OTC: ZANE* ■ *Web:* www.zanett.com	New York	NY	10022	212-583-0300	583-0221
Zon Capital Partners Five Vaughn Dr Ste 302 *Web:* www.zoncapital.com	Princeton	NJ	08540	609-452-1653	452-1693
ZS Fund LP 1133 Ave of the Americas *Web:* www.zsfundlp.com	New York	NY	10036	212-398-6200	398-1808

796 VETERANS NURSING HOMES - STATE

SEE ALSO Veterans Hospitals p. 2523

	City	State	Zip	Phone	Fax
Arizona State Veterans Home 4141 N Third St *Web:* azdvs.gov	Phoenix	AZ	85012	602-248-1550	222-6687
Arkansas State Veterans Home 4701 W 20th St	Little Rock	AR	72204	501-296-1885	
Baldomero Lopez State Veterans' Nursing Home 6919 Pkwy Blvd *Web:* floridavets.org	Land O'Lakes	FL	34639	813-558-5000	558-5021
Barboursville Veterans Home 512 Water St *Web:* veterans.wv.gov	Barboursville	WV	25504	304-736-1027	736-1093
Charlotte Hall Veterans Home 29449 Charlotte Hall Rd *Web:* charhall.org	Charlotte Hall	MD	20622	301-884-8171	884-4964
Chelsea Soldiers Home 91 Crest Ave *Web:* mass.gov	Chelsea	MA	02150	617-884-5660	884-1162
Colorado State Veterans Nursing Home-Rifle 851 E Fifth St *Web:* colorado.gov	Rifle	CO	81650	970-625-0842	625-3706
DJ Jacobetti Home for Veterans 425 Fisher St *TF:* 800-433-6760 ■ *Web:* michigan.gov	Marquette	MI	49855	906-226-3576	226-2380
Eastern Nebraska Veterans Home 12505 S 40th St *Web:* dhhs.ne.gov	Bellevue	NE	68123	402-595-2180	595-2234
Emory L Bennett Memorial Veterans' Nursing Home 1920 Mason Ave	Daytona Beach	FL	32117	386-274-3460	274-3487
Floyd E Tut Fann State Veterans Home 2701 Meridian St *TF:* 855-212-8028 ■ *Web:* www.va.state.al.us	Huntsville	AL	35811	256-851-2807	851-2967
Georgia War Veterans Nursing Home 1101 15th St	Augusta	GA	30901	706-721-2824	721-3892
Grand Island Veterans' Home 2300 W Capital Ave **Fax:* Acctg ■ *TF:* 800-358-8802 ■ *Web:* dhhs.ne.gov	Grand Island	NE	68803	308-385-6252	385-6257*
Hastings Veterans Home 1200 E 18th St *TF:* 877-838-3803 ■ *Web:* mn.gov	Hastings	MN	55033	651-438-8500	437-2012
Hollidaysburg Veterans Home PO Box 319 *Web:* www.portal.state.pa.us	Hollidaysburg	PA	16648	814-696-5201	
Holyoke Soldiers Home 110 Cherry St *Web:* mass.gov	Holyoke	MA	01040	413-532-9475	538-7968
Idaho State Veterans Home-Boise 320 Collins Rd *Web:* veterans.idaho.gov	Boise	ID	83702	208-334-5000	334-4753
Idaho State Veterans Home-Lewiston 821 21st Ave *TF:* 877-222-8387 ■ *Web:* veterans.idaho.gov	Lewiston	ID	83501	208-799-3422	799-3414
Idaho State Veterans Home-Pocatello 1957 Alvin Ricken Dr *TF:* 877-222-8387 ■ *Web:* veterans.idaho.gov	Pocatello	ID	83201	208-236-6340	236-6343
Illinois Veterans Home-Anna 792 N Main St *TF:* 888-261-3336 ■ *Web:* illinois.gov	Anna	IL	62906	618-833-6302	833-3603
Illinois Veterans Home-La Salle 1015 O'Connor Ave *Web:* www.vfwil.org/lasalle.asp	La Salle	IL	61301	815-223-0303	
Illinois Veterans Home-Manteno One Veterans Dr *Web:* vfwil.org	Manteno	IL	60950	815-468-6581	468-7001
Illinois Veterans Home-Quincy 1707 N 12th St *Web:* quincyivh.org	Quincy	IL	62301	217-222-8641	222-9621
Indiana Veterans Home 3851 N River Rd *Web:* in.gov	West Lafayette	IN	47906	765-463-1502	497-8568
Iowa Veterans Home 1301 Summit St Bldg 3465 *TF:* 800-838-4692 ■ *Web:* va.iowa.gov/	Marshalltown	IA	50131	515-252-4698	727-3713
Long Island State Veterans Home 100 Patriots Rd	Stony Brook	NY	11790	631-444-8387	
Louisiana War Veterans' Home 4739 Hwy 10 *Web:* wwwprd.doa.louisiana.gov	Jackson	LA	70748	225-634-5265	634-4057
Luverne Veterans Home 1300 N Kniss Ave *Web:* mn.gov	Luverne	MN	56156	507-283-1100	283-1127
Maine Veterans Home-Augusta 310 Cony Rd *TF:* 888-684-4664 ■ *Web:* www.maineveteranshomes.org	Augusta	ME	04330	888-684-4664	
Maine Veterans Home-Bangor 44 Hogan Rd *TF:* 888-684-4665 ■ *Web:* www.maineveteranshomes.org	Bangor	ME	04401	207-942-2333	942-4810
Maine Veterans Home-Caribou 163 Van Buren Rd Ste 2 *TF:* 888-684-4667 ■ *Web:* www.maineveteranshomes.org	Caribou	ME	04736	207-498-6074	498-3037
Maine Veterans Home-Scarborough 290 US Rt 1 *TF:* 888-684-4666 ■ *Web:* www.maineveteranshomes.org	Scarborough	ME	04074	207-883-7184	883-7852
Maine Veterans Home-South Paris 477 High St *TF:* 888-684-4668 ■ *Web:* www.maineveteranshomes.org	South Paris	ME	04281	207-743-6300	743-7595
Military Affairs 3000 Monroe Ave NW	Grand Rapids	MI	49505	616-364-5300	364-5397*
Minnesota Veterans Home-Fergus Falls 1821 N Pk St *Web:* mn.gov	Fergus Falls	MN	56537	218-736-0400	739-7686
Minnesota Veterans Home-Minneapolis 5101 Minnehaha Ave S *TF:* 877-838-6757 ■ *Web:* mn.gov	Minneapolis	MN	55407	612-721-0600	721-0604
Minnesota Veterans Home-Silver Bay 45 Banks Blvd *TF:* 877-729-8387 ■ *Web:* mn.gov	Silver Bay	MN	55614	218-226-6300	226-6336
Mississippi State Veterans Home 120 Veterans Dr *Web:* caremississippi.org	Oxford	MS	38655	662-236-7641	
Mississippi State Veterans' Home Collins 3261 Hwy 49 S *TF:* 877-203-5632 ■ *Web:* www.vab.ms.gov	Collins	MS	39428	601-765-0403	
Mississippi State Veterans' Home Kosciusko 310 Autumn Ridge Dr **Fax Area Code:* 601 ■ *TF:* 877-203-5632	Kosciusko	MS	39090	662-289-7044	576-4868*
Missouri Veterans Home-Cape Girardeau 2400 Veterans Memorial Dr *TF:* 800-392-0210 ■ *Web:* www.mo.gov	Cape Girardeau	MO	63701	573-290-5870	290-5909
Missouri Veterans Home-Mount Vernon 1600 S Hickory *Web:* mvc.dps.mo.gov	Mount Vernon	MO	65712	417-466-7103	466-4040
Missouri Veterans Home-Saint James 620 N Jefferson St	Saint James	MO	65559	573-265-3271	265-5771
Missouri Veterans Home-Saint Louis 10600 Lewis & Clark Blvd *Web:* mvc.dps.mo.gov	Saint Louis	MO	63136	314-340-6389	340-6379
Montana Veterans Home 400 Veterans Dr *TF:* 888-279-7532 ■ *Web:* dphhs.mt.gov	Columbia Falls	MT	59912	406-892-3256	892-0256
New Hampshire Veterans Home 139 Winter St *TF:* 800-735-2964 ■ *Web:* www.nh.gov/veterans	Tilton	NH	03276	603-527-4400	527-4402
New Mexico State Veterans Ctr 992 S Broadway St *TF:* 800-964-3976 ■ *Web:* www.nmstateveteranshome.org	Truth or Consequences	NM	87901	575-894-4200	894-4270
New York State Veterans Home at Batavia 220 Richmond Ave *Web:* www.nysvets.org	Batavia	NY	14020	585-345-2000	345-9030
New York State Veterans Home at Oxford 4207 New York 220	Oxford	NY	13830	607-843-3100	843-3194
New York State Veterans Home at Saint Albans 178-50 Linden Blvd *Web:* veterans.ny.gov	Jamaica	NY	11434	718-990-0353	
NJ State Veteran's Memorial Home 132 Evergreen Rd PO Box 3013 *Web:* nj.gov	Edison	NJ	08837	732-452-4100	
Norfolk Veterans Home 600 E Benjamin Ave *Web:* nebraska.gov	Norfolk	NE	68701	402-370-3330	370-3190
North Dakota Veterans Home 1600 Veterans Dr *Web:* www.nd.gov	Lisbon	ND	58054	701-683-6500	683-6550
Ohio Veterans Home 3416 Columbus Ave *TF Admissions:* 800-572-7934 ■ *Web:* dvs.ohio.gov	Sandusky	OH	44870	419-625-2454	
Oklahoma Veterans Ctr Ardmore 1015 S Commerce *TF:* 800-941-2160 ■ *Web:* www.ok.gov	Ardmore	OK	73401	580-223-2266	221-5606
Oklahoma Veterans Ctr Claremore PO Box 988 *Web:* www.ok.gov	Claremore	OK	74018	918-342-5432	342-0835
Oklahoma Veterans Ctr Clinton PO Box 1209 *Web:* www.ok.gov	Clinton	OK	73601	580-331-2200	323-4834
Oklahoma Veterans Ctr Norman 1776 E Robinson St *TF:* 800-782-5218 ■ *Web:* www.ok.gov/	Norman	OK	73071	405-360-5600	
Oklahoma Veterans Ctr Sulphur 200 E Fairlane *Web:* www.ok.gov	Sulphur	OK	73086	580-622-2144	
Oklahoma Veterans Ctr Talihina 10014 SE 1138th Ave PO Box 1168 *TF:* 800-941-2160 ■ *Web:* www.ok.gov	Talihina	OK	74571	918-567-2251	567-2950

	City	State	Zip	Phone	Fax
Oregon Veterans' Home 700 Veterans Dr *TF:* 800-846-8460 ■ *Web:* oregon.gov	The Dalles	OR	97058	541-296-7190	296-7862
Rhode Island Veterans' Home 480 Metacom Ave	Bristol	RI	02809	401-253-8000	254-1340
Richard M Campbell Veterans Home 4605 Belton Hwy	Anderson	SC	29621	864-261-6734	261-0453
Rocky Hill Veterans Home & Healthcare Ctr 287 W St *Web:* www.ct.gov/ctva/cwp/view.asp?a=2005&q=482380	Rocky Hill	CT	06067	860-721-5891	721-5904
Tennessee State Veterans Home-Murfreesboro 345 Compton Rd *Web:* tsvh.org	Murfreesboro	TN	37130	615-895-8850	895-5091
Thomson-Hood Veterans Ctr 100 Veterans Dr *TF:* 800-928-4838 ■ *Web:* www.thvc.ky.gov	Wilmore	KY	40390	859-858-2814	858-4039
Vermont Veterans Home 325 N St *Web:* www.vvh.vermont.gov	Bennington	VT	05201	802-442-6353	447-6466
Veterans Care Ctr 4550 Shenandoah Ave *Web:* www.dvs.virginia.gov	Roanoke	VA	24017	540-982-2860	982-8667
Veterans Home of California-Barstow 100 E Veterans Pkwy *TF:* 800-746-0606 ■ *Web:* www.calvet.ca.gov/vethomes/barstow.aspx	Barstow	CA	92311	760-252-6200	
Veterans Home of California-Chula Vista 700 E Naples Ct **Fax Area Code:* 619 ■ *TF:* 800-952-5626 ■ *Web:* www.calvet.ca.gov/	Chula Vista	CA	91911	800-952-5626	205-1903*
Veterans Home of California-Yountville 1227 O St **Fax Area Code:* 707 ■ *TF:* 800-952-5626 ■ *Web:* www.calvet.ca.gov/vethomes/yountville.aspx	Sacramento	CA	95814	800-952-5626	944-4542*
Washington Veterans Home 1141 Beach Dr PO Box 698 *Web:* www.dva.wa.gov	Retsil	WA	98378	360-895-4700	
Wisconsin Veterans Home N2665 County Rd QQ *TF:* 877-944-6667 ■ *Web:* www.dva.state.wi.us	King	WI	54946	715-258-5586	256-3207

797 VETERINARY HOSPITALS

	City	State	Zip	Phone	Fax
Abita Trace Animal Clinic 69142 Hwy 59 Ste E *Web:* www.medi-vet.com	Mandeville	LA	70471	985-892-5656	
Alameda Animal Hospital 431 12th Ave Ne *Web:* www.myvetonline.com	Norman	OK	73071	405-360-0045	
All Creatures Animal Hospital 1894 State Rt 125 *Web:* www.all-creatures.com	Amelia	OH	45102	513-797-7387	
American Animal Care Center Salwan Shanima Dvm 37177 Fremont Blvd *Web:* www.americananimalcare.com	Fremont	CA	94536	510-791-0464	
Amherst Veterinary Hospital 313 Us Hwy 10 *Web:* wi-net.com	Amherst	WI	54406	715-824-2545	
Anchor Animal Hospital Inc 750 State Rd *Web:* anchoranimalhospital.com	North Dartmouth	MA	02747	508-996-3731	
Anchor Bay Veterinary Center PC 36755 Green St *Web:* www.anchorbayvetcenter.com	Anchor Bay	MI	48047	586-725-7700	
Animal Ark Veterinary Clinic Pc 3235 N Kedzie Ave *Web:* www.animalark.us	Chicago	IL	60618	773-442-6500	
Animal Eye Specialty Clinic 2239 S Kanner Hwy *Web:* www.animaleyedocs.com	Stuart	FL	34994	772-220-8485	
Animal Hospital Inc 5001 N 12th Ave *Web:* www.petcarehospital.com	Pensacola	FL	32504	850-479-2900	479-3322
Animal Hospital of Pittsford PC 2816 Monroe Ave Ste 2 *Web:* www.pittsfordvet.com	Rochester	NY	14618	585-271-7700	
Animal Medical Center of Somerset County Inc 1911 N Center Ave *Web:* www.amcdocs.com	Somerset	PA	15501	814-443-6979	
Animal Medical Center, The 510 E 62nd St Fl 2 *Web:* www.amcny.org	New York	NY	10065	212-838-8100	
Animal Welfare Association 509 Centennial Blvd *Web:* www.awanj.org	Voorhees	NJ	08043	856-424-2288	
ARC Medical Devices Inc 2386 E Mall Ste 102 *Web:* arcmedicaldevices.com	Vancouver	BC	V6T1Z3	604-222-9577	
Aston Veterinarian Hospital 5200 Pennell Rd *Web:* www.astonvet.com	Media	PA	19063	610-494-5800	
Banfield the Pet Hospital 8000 NE Tillamook St **Fax Area Code:* 503 ■ *TF:* 866-894-7927 ■ *Web:* www.banfield.com	Portland	OR	97213	866-894-7927	922-5000*
Barton Heights Veterinary Hospital 117 Terrace Dr *Web:* www.bartonheights.com	Stroudsburg	PA	18360	570-424-6773	
Bay Glen Animal Hospital P C 1616 Clear Lk City Blvd *Web:* www.bayglenvet.com	Houston	TX	77062	281-480-8800	
Best Friends Pet Care Inc 520 Main Ave *Web:* www.bestfriendspetcare.com	Norwalk	CT	06851	203-846-3360	
Best Friends Veterinary Center 2082 Cheyenne Ct *Web:* www.bestfriendsvet.com	Grafton	WI	53024	262-375-0130	
Bio Agri Mix LP 11 Ellens St *Web:* www.bioagrimix.com	Mitchell	ON	N0K1N0	519-348-9865	
BluePearl Veterinary Partners LLC 3000 Busch Lk Blvd *Web:* bluepearlvet.com	Tampa	FL	33614	813-933-8944	
Brook Farm Veterinary Center 2371 Route 22 *Web:* www.brookfarmveterinarycenter.com	Patterson	NY	12563	845-878-4833	
Burnham Park Animal Hospital 1025 S State St *Web:* www.chicagovet.net	Chicago	IL	60605	312-663-9200	
Canine Country Club Kennel & Pet Resort, The 33306 Tract 43 Rd *Web:* www.caninecountryclub.com	Los Fresnos	TX	78566	956-233-1746	
Caring Hands Animal Hospital of Arlington LLC 5659 Stone Rd *Web:* caringhandsvet.com	Centreville	VA	20120	703-830-5700	
Carolina Veterinary Specialists 2225 Township Rd *Web:* www.carolinavet.com	Charlotte	NC	28273	704-588-7015	
Carthage Veterinary Service Ltd 34 W Main St *Web:* www.hogvet.com	Carthage	IL	62321	217-357-2811	
Cat Doctor, The 535 N 22nd St *Web:* www.thecatdr.com	Philadelphia	PA	19130	215-561-7668	
Claremont Animal Hospital Inc 446 Charlestown Rd *Web:* www.claremontanimalhospital.com	Claremont	NH	03743	603-543-0117	
Clemson Univ Service 605 W Main St Ste 109	Lexington	SC	29072	803-785-8515	
Colorado River Animal Medical Center Inc 2079 Hwy 95 *Web:* www.cramcvet.com	Bullhead City	AZ	86442	928-763-7387	
Cresskill Animal Hospital 39 Spring St *Web:* www.cresskillanimalhosp.com	Cresskill	NJ	07626	201-568-7700	
Crysler Animal Hospital DVM Becky Voth 12440 E New 40 Hwy *Web:* www.crysleranimalhospital.com	Independence	MO	64055	816-358-2857	
Dove Lewis Emergency Animal Hospital Inc 1945 Nw Pettygrove St *Web:* www.dovelewis.org	Portland	OR	97209	503-228-7281	
Emergency Animal Clinic Properties Ltd 2260 W Glendale Ave *Web:* www.eac-az.com	Phoenix	AZ	85021	602-995-3757	
Family Friends Veterinary Hospital & Kennel 864 Massachusetts Ave *Web:* www.familyfriendsvetandkennel.com	Boxborough	MA	01719	978-263-3412	
Family Pet Animal Hospital 1401 W Webster Ave *Web:* familypetanimalhospital.com	Chicago	IL	60614	773-935-2311	
Five Mile Pet Clinic Ps 6825 N Country Homes Blvd *Web:* www.healthypets.com	Spokane	WA	99208	509-326-3465	
Forest Valley Veterinary Clinic 2555 Mosby Creek Rd *Web:* fvvet.com	Cottage Grove	OR	97424	541-942-9132	
Friedman Deborah s Dvm 1612 Washington Blvd *Web:* www.animaleyecare.com	Fremont	CA	94539	510-623-0444	
Friendship Hospital for Animals 4105 Brandywine St Nw *Web:* www.friendshiphospital.com	Washington	DC	20016	202-363-7300	
Garden District Animal Hospital, The 1302 Perkins Rd *Web:* www.cjbrown.com	Baton Rouge	LA	70806	225-381-9661	
Gold Coast Animal Hospital 225 W Division St *Web:* www.goldcoastah.com	Chicago	IL	60610	312-337-7387	
Greenbriar Animal Hospital LLC 4307 N Green River Rd *Web:* www.greenbrieranimalhospital.com	Evansville	IN	47715	812-479-0867	
Gulf Coast Veterinary Avian 1111 W Loop S Ste 120 *Web:* www.gcvs.com	Houston	TX	77027	713-693-1133	
Hawthorne Animal Hospital 1516 Alarth Dr *Web:* glencarbonhawthorne.com	Troy	IL	62294	618-667-4900	
Healthy Pets of Westgate Inc 3588 W Broad St *Web:* healthypetsofohio.com	Columbus	OH	43228	614-279-8415	
Hickory Veterinary Hospital 2303 Hickory Rd *Web:* hickoryvet.com	Plymouth Meeting	PA	19462	610-828-3054	
Hopewell Veterinary Group Inc 230 Hopewell Pennington Rd *Web:* saintsbury.com	Hopewell	NJ	08525	609-466-0131	
Imex Veterinary Inc 1001 Mckesson Dr *Web:* www.imexvet.com	Longview	TX	75604	903-295-2196	
Janssen Clinic for Animals 1624 N High Point Rd *Web:* www.janssenclinic.com	Middleton	WI	53562	608-836-0600	
John Paul Pet Salon 317 Marshall Plz *Web:* johnpaulpetsalon.com	Grand Prairie	TX	75051	972-264-4559	
Look Ahead Veterinary Services 1451 Clark Rd *Web:* www.lookaheadvet.net	Oroville	CA	95965	530-534-0722	
Lyon Veterinary Clinic 21188 Pontiac Trl *Web:* lyonveterinaryclinic.com	South Lyon	MI	48178	248-486-8800	
Millburn Veterinary Hospital 147 Millburn Ave *Web:* millburnvet.com	Millburn	NJ	07041	973-467-1700	
Millhopper Veterinary Medical Center 4209 Northwest 37Th Pl *Web:* millhoppervet.com	Gainesville	FL	32606	352-373-8055	
Moore Lane Veterinary Hospital 30 Moore Ln *Web:* www.yellowstonevalleyvet.com	Billings	MT	59101	406-252-4159	
Mspca Animal Shelter 1577 Falmouth Rd *Web:* www.mspca.org	Centerville	MA	02632	508-775-0940	
National Veterinary Associates Inc 29229 Canwood St Ste 100 *Web:* www.nvaonline.com	Agoura Hills	CA	91301	805-777-7722	
Noah's Animal Hospitals 5510 Millersville Rd *Web:* noahsanimalhospital.com	Indianapolis	IN	46226	317-244-7738	
Noah's Ark Starr Animal Hospital Inc 422 Noth Euclid St *Web:* www.noahsarkfullerton.com	Fullerton	CA	92832	714-525-2202	

				Phone	Fax
North Las Vegas Animal Hospital 2437 E Cheyenne Ave *Web:* www.huntco.com	North Las Vegas	NV	89030	702-642-5353	
Northgate Animal Hospital PA 2921 Ramsey St *Web:* www.northgateanimalhosp.com	Fayetteville	NC	28301	910-822-3141	
Oak Knoll Animal Hospital Ltd 3113 41st St *Web:* oakknollanimalhospital.com	Moline	IL	61265	309-762-9474	
Ocean City Animal Hospital 11843 Ocean Gtwy *Web:* oceancityvet.com	Ocean City	MD	21842	410-213-1170	
Ocean State Veterinary Specialists Ltd 1480 S County Trl *Web:* www.osvs.net	East Greenwich	RI	02818	401-886-6787	
Oradell Animal Hospital Inc 580 Winters Ave *Web:* www.oradell.com	Paramus	NJ	07652	201-262-0010	
Parkside Animal Hospital 12962 Publishers Dr *Web:* parksidepets.com	Fishers	IN	46038	317-849-1440	
Penn Veterinary Supply Inc 53 Industrial Cir *Web:* pennvet.com	Lancaster	PA	17601	717-656-4121	
Perry Veterinary Clinic PLLC 3180 Rt 246 Perry *Web:* www.perryvet.com	New York	NY	14530	585-237-5550	
Pet Adoption Network, The 4261 Culver Rd *Web:* www.petadoptionnetwork.org	Rochester	NY	14622	585-338-9175	
Pet Vet Animal Hospitals 6763 Hwy 6 S Bellaire Blvd Ste 1800 **Fax Area Code:* 713 ■ *Web:* www.petvethospitals.com	Houston	TX	77083	281-561-0276	629-7737*
Peterson & Smith Equine Hospital LLC 4747 SW 60th Ave *Web:* www.petersonsmith.com	Ocala	FL	34474	352-237-6151	
Petlovers Animal Hospital 6425 E Livingston Ave *Web:* petloversah.com	Reynoldsburg	OH	43068	614-866-1912	
Pipestone Veterinary Clinic LLC 1300 Hwy 75 S PO Box 188 *TF:* 800-658-2523 ■ *Web:* www.pipevet.com	Pipestone	MN	56164	507-825-4211	
Radiocat 32-A Mellor Ave **Fax Area Code:* 866 ■ *TF:* 800-323-9729 ■ *Web:* www.radiocat.com	Baltimore	MD	21228	800-323-9729	788-5201*
Ridgeview Animal Hospital 18146 Wright St *Web:* www.ridgeviewanimalhosp.com	Omaha	NE	68130	402-333-3366	
Rood Riddle & Partners PSC 2150 Georgetown Rd *Web:* www.roodandriddle.com	Lexington	KY	40511	859-233-0371	
Sage Centers 1410 Monument Blvd Ste 100 *Web:* sagecenters.com	Concord	CA	94520	925-627-7243	
Schafer Veterinary Consultants LLC 800 Helena Ct *Web:* schaferveterinary.com	Fort Collins	CO	80524	970-224-5103	
Spring Creek Animal Hospital 101 Saint John Church Rd *Web:* springcreekvet.com	Goldsboro	NC	27534	919-778-4260	
Stone Mountain Pet Lodge 9935 Radisson Rd Ne *Web:* stonemountainpetlodge.com	Minneapolis	MN	55449	763-792-8929	
Summit Pet Product Distributors Inc 420 N Chimney Rock Rd *TF:* 800-323-2963 ■ *Web:* www.summitpet.com	Greensboro	NC	27410	336-294-3200	
Surrey Veterinary Clinic 5957 E Surrey Rd *Web:* www.surreyvetclinic.com	Clare	MI	48617	989-386-9200	
Tewksbury Animal Hospital 1098 Main St *Web:* tewksburyanimalhospital.com	Tewksbury	MA	01876	978-851-3626	
Trans Ova Genetics LC 2938 380th St *Web:* www.transova.com	Sioux Center	IA	51250	712-722-3586	
Tri-city Veterinary Clinic Inc 1929 W Vista Way *Web:* www.tricityvet.com	Vista	CA	92083	760-758-2091	
Twin City Animal Hospital 869 South St *Web:* www.lid.com	Fitchburg	MA	01420	978-343-3049	
United Pet Care LLC 6232 N Seventh St Ste 202 *Web:* www.unitedpetcare.com	Phoenix	AZ	85014	602-266-5303	
Valley Cottage Animal Hospital Inc 202 Rt 303 *Web:* www.valleycottageanimalhospital.com	Valley Cottage	NY	10989	845-268-9263	268-0516
VCA Antech Inc 12401 W Olympic Blvd *NASDAQ: WOOF* ■ *TF:* 800-966-1822 ■ *Web:* www.vcaantech.com	Los Angeles	CA	90064	310-571-6500	571-6700
VCA Boston Road Animal Hospital 1235 Boston Rd *Web:* www.vcahospitals.com	Springfield	MA	01119	413-783-1203	
VDx Veterinary Diagnostics Inc 2019 Anderson Rd Ste C *Web:* vdxpathology.com	Davis	CA	95616	530-753-4285	
Vedco Inc 5503 Corporate Dr *Web:* www.vedco.com	Saint Joseph	MO	64507	816-238-8840	
Vet Clinic of Palm Harbor Inc, The 35891 Us Hwy 19 N *Web:* thevetclinic.com	Palm Harbor	FL	34684	727-781-7704	
Vet Path Services Inc 6450 Castle Dr *Web:* www.vetpathservicesinc.com	Mason	OH	45040	513-469-0777	
Vet-Stem Inc 12860 Danielson Court Ste B *Web:* www.vet-stem.com	Poway	CA	92064	858-748-2004	
VetCor Inc 350 Lincoln Pl *Web:* www.vetcor.com	Hingham	MA	02043	781-749-8151	
Veterinary Specialists of the Southeast (CCVS) 3163 W Montague Ave *Web:* www.ccvsllc.com	North Charleston	SC	29418	843-747-1507	747-7920
Veterinary Specialty and Emergency Hospital 3550 S Jason St *Web:* www.vrcc.com	Englewood	CO	80110	303-874-7387	
Veterinary Specialty Hospital of The Carolinas 6405 Tryon Rd Ste 100 *Web:* www.vshcarolinas.com	Cary	NC	27518	919-233-4911	
Veterinary Surgical Associates 1410 Monument Blvd Ste 100 *Web:* www.ccvec.com	Concord	CA	94520	925-827-1777	
Veterinary Transplant Services Inc 215 E Titus St *Web:* www.vtsonline.com	Kent	WA	98032	253-520-0771	
Vets & Pets 3345 El Camino Real *Web:* www.vcai.com	Santa Clara	CA	95051	408-246-1893	
VetSelect Animal Hospital 2150 Old Novi Rd *TF:* 800-462-8749 ■ *Web:* www.vetselect.com	Novi	MI	48377	248-624-1100	624-6542
Villa La PAWS LLC 3618 W Bell Rd Ste B1 *Web:* www.villalapaws.com	Glendale	AZ	85308	602-588-7833	
Western Veterinary Conference 2425 E Oquendo Rd *Web:* www.wvc.org	Las Vegas	NV	89120	702-739-6698	
Westfield Veterinary Hospital Pc 8789 Nw 54th Ave *Web:* www.westfieldvet.com	Johnston	IA	50131	515-986-5738	
Wild Animal Sanctuary, The 1946 County Rd 53 *Web:* www.wildanimalsanctuary.org	Keenesburg	CO	80643	303-536-0118	

798 VETERINARY MEDICAL ASSOCIATIONS - STATE

				Phone	Fax
Alabama Veterinary Medical Assn 8116 Old Federal Rd Ste C *Web:* www.alvma.com	Montgomery	AL	36117	334-395-0086	270-3399
Alaska State Veterinary Medical Assn (AKVMA) 1731 Bragaw St *Web:* www.akvma.org	Anchorage	AK	99508	907-563-3701	
Arizona Veterinary Medical Assn 100 W Coolidge St *Web:* www.azvma.org	Phoenix	AZ	85013	602-242-7936	249-3828
Arkansas Veterinary Medical Assn PO Box 17687 *Web:* www.arkvetmed.org	Little Rock	AR	72222	501-868-3036	868-3034
Colorado Veterinary Medical Assn 191 Yuma St *TF:* 800-228-5429 ■ *Web:* colovma.org/?	Denver	CO	80223	303-318-0447	318-0450
Connecticut Veterinary Medical Assn PO Box 1058 *Web:* www.ctvet.org	Glastonbury	CT	06033	860-635-7770	659-8772
Delaware Veterinary Medical Assn 937 Monroe Terr *Web:* www.devma.org	Dover	DE	19904	302-242-7014	674-8581
District of Columbia Academy of Veterinary Medicine PO Box 710477 *Web:* www.dcavm.org	Herndon	VA	20171	703-733-0556	742-8745
Georgia Veterinary Medical Assn 233 Peachtree St NE Ste 2205 *TF:* 800-853-1625 ■ *Web:* www.gvma.net	Atlanta	GA	30303	678-309-9800	309-3361
Idaho Veterinary Medical Assn (IVMA) 1841 W Secluded Ct *Web:* www.ivma.org	Kuna	ID	83634	208-922-9431	922-9435
Illinois State Veterinary Medical Assn 1121 Chatham Rd *Web:* www.isvma.org	Springfield	IL	62704	217-546-8381	546-5633
Indiana Veterinary Medical Assn 201 S Capitol Ave Ste 405 *TF:* 800-270-0747 ■ *Web:* www.invma.org	Indianapolis	IN	46225	317-974-0888	974-0985
Iowa Veterinary Medical Assn 1605 N Ankeny Blvd Ste 110 *TF:* 800-369-9564 ■ *Web:* www.iowavma.org	Ankeny	IA	50023	515-965-9237	965-9239
Kansas Veterinary Medical Assn 816 SW Tyler St Ste 200 *TF:* 888-545-5862 ■ *Web:* www.ksvma.org	Topeka	KS	66612	785-233-4141	233-2534
Kentucky Veterinary Medical Assn 108 Consumer Ln *TF:* 800-552-5862 ■ *Web:* www.kvma.org	Frankfort	KY	40601	502-226-5862	226-6177
Louisiana Veterinary Medical Assn 8550 United Plz Blvd Ste 1001 *TF:* 800-524-2996 ■ *Web:* www.lvma.org	Baton Rouge	LA	70809	225-928-5862	408-4422
Maine Veterinary Medical Assn (MVMA) 97A Exchange St Ste 305 **Fax Area Code:* 888 ■ *TF:* 800-448-2772 ■ *Web:* netforum.avectra.com	Portland	ME	04101	800-448-2772	612-0941*
Maryland Veterinary Medical Assn 8015 Corporate Dr Ste A *TF:* 888-884-6862 ■ *Web:* www.mdvma.org	Baltimore	MD	21236	410-931-3332	931-2060
Massachusetts Veterinary Medical Assn 163Lakeside Ave *Web:* www.massvet.org	Marlborough	MA	01752	508-460-9333	460-9969
Michigan Veterinary Medical Assn (MVMA) 2144 Commons Pkwy *Web:* www.michvma.org	Okemos	MI	48864	517-347-4710	347-4666
Minnesota Veterinary Medical Assn 101 Bridgepoint Way Ste 100 *TF:* 888-933-5363 ■ *Web:* www.mvma.org	South Saint Paul	MN	55075	651-645-7533	645-7539
Missouri Veterinary Medical Assn 2500 Country Club Dr *TF:* 800-632-6900 ■ *Web:* movma.org	Jefferson City	MO	65109	573-636-8612	659-7175
Montana Veterinary Medical Assn PO Box 6322 *Web:* www.mtvma.org	Helena	MT	59604	406-447-4259	442-8018
Nebraska Veterinary Medical Assn 2727 W Second St Ste 227 *Web:* www.nvma.org	Hastings	NE	68901	402-463-4704	463-4705
Nevada Veterinary Medical Assn PO Box 34420 *Web:* www.nevadavma.org	Reno	NV	89533	775-324-5344	
New Jersey Veterinary Medical Assn 390 Amwell Rd Ste 402 *Web:* www.njvma.org	Hillsborough	NJ	08844	908-281-0918	450-1286

	City	State	Zip	Phone	Fax
New Mexico Veterinary Medical Assn 60 Placitas Trls Rd *Web:* www.nmvma.org	Placitas	NM	87043	505-867-6373	771-8963
New York State Veterinary Medical Society 100 Great Oaks Blvd Ste 127 *TF:* 800-876-9867 ■ *Web:* www.nysvms.org/	Albany	NY	12203	518-869-7867	869-7868
North Carolina Veterinary Medical Assn (NCVMA) 1611 Jones Franklin Rd Ste 108 *TF:* 800-446-2862 ■ *Web:* www.ciclt.net	Raleigh	NC	27606	919-851-5850	851-5859
North Dakota Veterinary Medical Assn 921 S Ninth St Ste 120 *Web:* www.ndvma.com	Bismarck	ND	58504	701-221-7740	258-9005
Ohio Veterinary Medical Assn (OVMA) 3168 Riverside Dr *TF:* 800-662-6862 ■ *Web:* www.ohiovma.org	Columbus	OH	43221	614-486-7253	486-1325
Oklahoma Veterinary Medical Assn PO Box 14521 *TF:* 800-248-2862 ■ *Web:* www.okvma.org	Oklahoma City	OK	73113	405-478-1002	478-7193
Oregon Veterinary Medical Assn 1880 Lancaster Dr NE Ste 118 *TF:* 800-235-3502 ■ *Web:* www.oregonvma.org	Salem	OR	97305	503-399-0311	363-4218
Puerto Rico Veterinary Medical Assn 352 San Claudio Ave Ste 248 *TF:* 888-791-1856 ■ *Web:* www.cmvpr.org	San Juan	PR	00926	787-283-0565	761-3440
Rhode Island Veterinary Medical Assn 302 Pearl St Ste 108 *Web:* www.rivma.org	Providence	RI	02907	401-751-0944	780-0940
South Carolina Assn of Veterinarians PO Box 11766 *TF:* 800-441-7228 ■ *Web:* www.scav.org	Columbia	SC	29211	803-254-1027	254-3773
Tennessee Veterinary Medical Assn PO Box 803 *TF:* 800-697-3587 ■ *Web:* www.tvmanet.org	Fayetteville	TN	37334	931-438-0070	433-6289
Texas Veterinary Medical Assn 8104 Exchange Dr *TF:* 800-711-0023 ■ *Web:* www.tvma.org	Austin	TX	78754	512-452-4224	452-6633
Vermont Veterinary Medical Assn 88 Beech St *Web:* www.vtvets.org	Essex Junction	VT	05452	802-878-6888	878-2871
Virginia Veterinary Medical Assn (VVMA) 3801 Westerre Pkwy Ste D *TF:* 800-937-8862 ■ *Web:* www.vvma.org	Henrico	VA	23233	804-346-2611	346-2655
Washington State Veterinary Medical Assn 8024 Bracken Pl SE *TF:* 800-399-7862 ■ *Web:* www.wsvma.org	Snoqualmie	WA	98065	425-396-3191	454-8382
West Virginia Veterinary Medical Assn (WVVMA) 3801 Westerre Pkwy Ste D *Web:* www.wvvma.org	Henrico	VA	23233	804-346-2611	346-2655
Wisconsin Veterinary Medical Assn (WVMA) 2801 Crossroads Dr Ste 1200 *TF:* 888-254-5202 ■ *Web:* www.wvma.org	Madison	WI	53718	608-257-3665	257-8989
Wyoming Veterinary Medical Assn (WVMA) 1841 W Secluded Ct *TF:* 800-272-1813 ■ *Web:* www.wyvma.org	Kuna	ID	83634	208-922-9431	922-9435

799 VIATICAL SETTLEMENT COMPANIES

A viatical settlement is the sale of an existing life insurance policy by a terminally ill person to a third party in return for a percentage of the face value of the policy paid immediately.

	City	State	Zip	Phone	Fax
Altrius Capital Management Inc 1323 Commerce Dr *Web:* www.altrius-capital.com	New Bern	NC	28562	252-638-7598	
Angel Baby Brokerage 26 Red Ball Trl *Web:* www.angelbabybrokerage.com	Coffeen	IL	62017	217-534-2557	
BRC Investment Management LLC 8400 E Prentice Ave Ste 1401 *Web:* www.brcinvest.com	Greenwood Village	CO	80111	303-414-1100	
Century Capital Management LLC 100 Federal St 29th Fl *Web:* www.centurycap.com	Boston	MA	02110	617-482-3060	
Chestnut Investment Advisory 402 Bethlehem Pk *Web:* www.regardingyourmoney.com	Glenside	PA	19038	215-836-4880	
CMG Surety LLC 1016 Collier Ctr Way Ste 100 *Web:* www.cmgsurety.com	Naples	FL	34110	239-597-0128	597-1977
Cockrell Investment Group 6138 Orange Ave Ste 103 *Web:* cockrell-investment-group.hub.biz	Long Beach	CA	90805	562-984-7176	
Coventry First LLC 7111 Vly Green Rd **Fax Area Code:* 215 ■ *TF:* 877-836-8300 ■ *Web:* www.coventry.com	Fort Washington	PA	19034	877-836-8300	233-3201*
Crystal Wealth Management System Ltd 3385 Harvester Rd Ste 200 *Web:* www.crystalwealth.com	Burlington	ON	L7N3N2	905-332-4414	
Excel Funds Management Inc 2810 Matheson Blvd E Ste 800 *Web:* www.excelfunds.com	Mississauga	ON	L4W4X7	905-813-7111	
Founders Financial Inc 1020 Cromwell Bridge Rd *Web:* www.foundersfinancial.com	Towson	MD	21286	410-308-9988	
Francis Investment Counsel LLC 21180 W Capitol Dr *TF:* 866-232-6457 ■ *Web:* www.francisinvco.com	Pewaukee	WI	53072	866-232-6457	
GlassRatner Advisory & Capital Group LLC Monarch Tower 3424 Peachtree Rd Ste 2150 *Web:* www.glassratner.com	Atlanta	GA	30326	678-904-1990	
Habersham Funding LLC 415 E Paces Ferry Rd NE Terr Level *TF:* 888-874-2402 ■ *Web:* www.habershamfunding.com	Atlanta	GA	30305	404-233-8275	233-9394
Indiana Trust & Investment Management Co 4045 Edison Lakes Pkwy Ste 100 *Web:* www.indtrust.com	Mishawaka	IN	46545	574-271-0374	
Interis Consulting Inc 275 Slater St 20th Fl *Web:* www.interis.ca	Ottawa	ON	K1P5H9	613-237-9331	
Legacy Benefits Corp 350 Fifth Ave Ste 4320 **Fax Area Code:* 212 ■ *TF:* 800-875-1000 ■ *Web:* www.legacybenefits.com	New York	NY	10118	800-875-1000	643-1180*
Life Equity LLC 5611 Hudson Dr # 100 *Web:* www.lifeequity.net	Hudson	OH	44236	330-342-7772	342-7782
Life Partners Inc (LPI) 204 Woodhew Dr *TF:* 800-368-5569 ■ *Web:* www.lifepartnersinc.com	Waco	TX	76712	254-751-7797	751-1025
Life Settlement Solutions Inc 9201 Spectrum Ctr Blvd Ste 105 *TF:* 800-762-3387 ■ *Web:* www.lss-corp.com	San Diego	CA	92123	858-576-8067	576-9329
Life Trust LLC 330 Madison Ave Sixth Fl *Web:* www.life-trust.net	New York	NY	10017	212-653-0840	653-0844
Lombardia Capital Partners LLC 55 S Lk Ave Ste 200 *Web:* www.lombardiacapital.com	Pasadena	CA	91101	626-568-2792	
Long Point Capital Inc 26700 Woodward Ave *Web:* www.longpointcapital.com	Royal Oak	MI	48067	248-591-6000	
Mcube Investment Technologies LLC 5240 Tennyson Pkwy Ste 102 *Web:* www.mcubeit.com	Plano	TX	75024	972-608-9919	
Meketa Investment Group 100 Lowder Brook Dr Ste 1100 *Web:* www.meketagroup.com	Westwood	MA	02090	781-471-3500	
Mercom Capital Group LLC 6836 Bee Cave Rd Ste 238 *Web:* www.mercomcapital.com	Austin	TX	78746	512-215-4452	
Nicola Wealth Management Ltd 1508 W Broadway Fifth Fl *Web:* www.nicolawealth.com	Vancouver	BC	V6J1W8	604-739-6450	
Pabrai Investment Funds 1220 Roosevelt Ste 200 *Web:* www.pabraifunds.com	Irvine	CA	92620	949-453-0609	
Page & Assoc Inc 1979 Lakeside Pkwy Ste 200 **Fax Area Code:* 770 ■ *TF:* 800-252-5282 ■ *Web:* www.thelifeline.com	Tucker	GA	30084	800-252-5282	724-7373*
Pembroke Management Ltd 1002 Sherbrooke St W Ste 1700 *Web:* www.pml.ca	Montreal	QC	H3A3S4	514-848-1991	
Red Barn Investments 5215 Old Orchard Rd Ste 675 *Web:* www.redbarnllc.com	Skokie	IL	60077	847-920-7100	
Reilly Financial Advisors 7777 Alvarado Rd Ste 116 *Web:* www.rfadvisors.com	La Mesa	CA	91942	619-698-0794	
Sandalwood Securities Inc 101 Eisenhower Pkwy *Web:* www.sandalwoodsecurities.com	Roseland	NJ	07068	973-228-5466	
SDR Ventures Inc 5613 DTC Pkwy Ste 830 *Web:* sdrventures.com	Greenwood Village	CO	80111	720-221-9220	
Senior Settlements LLC 1000 S Lenola Rd Bldg 1 Ste 202 *TF:* 800-834-0628 ■ *Web:* www.seniorsettlementsllc.com	Maple Shade	NJ	08052	856-235-2133	235-1294
Tolleson Wealth Management Inc 5500 Preston Rd Ste 250 *Web:* www.tollesonwealth.com	Dallas	TX	75205	214-252-3250	
Vega Capital Group LLC 100 Bush St Ste 1428 *Web:* www.vegacapital.com	San Francisco	CA	94104	415-318-8740	
Venturehouse Group 509 Seventh St Nw Ste 3 *Web:* www.venturehousegroup.com	Washington	DC	20004	202-654-7000	
Verge Fund 317 Commercial St NE Third Fl *Web:* vergefund.com	Albuquerque	NM	87102	505-247-1038	
Weik Investment Services Inc 1075 Berkshire Blvd Ste 825 *Web:* weikinvest.com	Wyomissing	PA	19610	610-376-2240	
Winfield Associates Inc 700 W St Clair Ave Ste 404 *Web:* www.winfieldinc.com	Cleveland	OH	44113	216-241-2575	
Wright Investment Properties Inc 277 German Oak Dr *Web:* wrightinvestments.com	Cordova	TN	38018	901-755-9501	
Zesiger Capital Group LLC 460 Park Ave 22nd Fl *Web:* www.zcgllc.com	New York	NY	10022	212-508-6300	

800 VIDEO STORES

SEE ALSO Book, Music, Video Clubs p. 1877

	City	State	Zip	Phone	Fax
Amazon.com Inc 1200 12th Ave S Ste 1200 *NASDAQ: AMZN* ■ **Fax:* Hum Res ■ *TF Cust Svc:* 800-201-7575 ■ *Web:* www.amazon.com	Seattle	WA	98144	206-266-1000	266-7601*
Best Buy Company Inc 7601 Penn Ave S *NYSE: BBY* ■ **Fax:* Cust Svc ■ *TF:* 888-237-8289 ■ *Web:* www.bestbuy.com	Minneapolis	MN	55423	612-291-1000	292-2323*
DVD Empire 2140 Woodland Rd *TF:* 888-383-1880 ■ *Web:* www.dvdempire.com	Warrendale	PA	15086	888-383-1880	
Facets Multimedia Inc 1517 W Fullerton Ave *TF Cust Svc:* 800-331-6197 ■ *Web:* www.facets.org	Chicago	IL	60614	773-281-9075	929-5437
Family Video 2500 Lehigh Ave *TF:* 888-332-6843 ■ *Web:* www.familyvideo.com	Glenview	IL	60026	847-904-9000	904-9009
NetFlix Inc 100 Winchester Cir *NASDAQ: NFLX* ■ *TF:* 800-290-8191 ■ *Web:* netflix.com/	Los Gatos	CA	95032	408-540-3700	540-3737
Rainbo Record Manufacturing Corp 8960 Eton Ave *Web:* www.rainborecords.com	Canoga Park	CA	91304	818-280-1100	
Ross Video Ltd Eight John St *Web:* www.rossvideo.com	Iroquois	ON	K0E1K0	613-652-4886	
Videoflicks Canada 1701 Ave Rd *Web:* www.myvideoflicks.ca	Toronto	ON	M5M3Y3	416-782-1883	782-1265

801 VISION CORRECTION CENTERS

				Phone	Fax
Barnet-Dulaney Eye Ctr 4800 N 22nd St *TF:* 866-742-6581 ■ *Web:* www.goodeyes.com	Phoenix	AZ	85016	602-955-1000	508-4700
Carolina Eye Assoc PA 2170 Midland Rd. *Web:* www.carolinaeye.com	Southern Pines	NC	28387	910-295-2100	295-5339
Center for Lasik Ophthalmology Consultants, The 5800 Colonial Dr Ste 103 *TF:* 800-448-8770 ■ *Web:* www.bestvision.com	Margate	FL	33063	954-969-0090	977-8774
Chicago Cornea Consultants Ltd 806 S Central Ave Ste 300 *Web:* www.chicagocornea.com	Highland Park	IL	60035	847-882-5900	882-6028
Eye Centers of Florida (ECOF) 4101 Evans Ave. *TF:* 888-393-2455 ■ *Web:* www.ecof.com	Fort Myers	FL	33901	239-939-3456	936-8776
Gordon Binder Vision Institute 8910 University Ctr Ln Ste 800	San Diego	CA	92122	858-455-6800	455-0244
John-Kenyon Eye Ctr 1305 Wall St Ste 200 **Fax Area Code:* 812 ■ *TF:* 800-342-5393 ■ *Web:* www.johnkenyon.com	Jeffersonville	IN	47130	800-342-5393	288-7479*
Jones Eye Clinic 4405 Hamilton Blvd PO Box 3246 *TF:* 800-334-2015 ■ *Web:* joneseye.com	Sioux City	IA	51104	712-239-3937	239-1305
LaserVue Eye Ctr 3540 Mendocino Ave Ste 200 *TF:* 888-527-3745 ■ *Web:* www.laservue.com	Santa Rosa	CA	95403	707-522-6200	
LCA-Vision Inc 7840 Montgomery Rd *NASDAQ: LCAV* ■ *TF:* 800-688-4550 ■ *Web:* www.lasikplus.com	Cincinnati	OH	45236	513-792-9292	792-5620
Minnesota Eye Consultants PA 710 E 24th St Ste 100 *TF:* 800-526-7632 ■ *Web:* www.mneye.com	Minneapolis	MN	55404	612-813-3600	813-3601
Pacific Cataract & Laser Institute 2517 NE Kresky Ave *TF:* 800-888-9903 ■ *Web:* www.pcli.com	Chehalis	WA	98532	360-748-8632	748-3869
Prado Vision & Lasik Ctr 7522 N Himes Ave *Web:* www.pradovision.com	Tampa	FL	33614	813-931-0500	935-4055
South Penn Eye Care (SPECS) 250 E Walnut St. *Web:* www.southpenneyecare.com	Hanover	PA	17331	717-632-6063	
Southwestern Eye Ctr 2610 E University Dr *TF General:* 800-224-3339 ■ *Web:* www.sweye.com	Mesa	AZ	85213	480-892-8400	892-9533
TLC Vision Corp 50 Burnhamthorpe Rd W Ste 101 **Fax Area Code:* 905 ■ *TF:* 877-852-2020 ■ *Web:* www.tlcvision.com	Mississauga	ON	L5B3C2	877-852-2020	602-2025*
Will Vision & Laser Centers 8100 NE Pkwy Dr Ste 125 *TF:* 877-542-3937 ■ *Web:* www.willvision.com	Vancouver	WA	98662	360-885-1327	885-1333

802 VITAMINS & NUTRITIONAL SUPPLEMENTS

SEE ALSO Diet & Health Foods p. 2301; Medicinal Chemicals & Botanical Products p. 2736; Pharmaceutical Companies p. 2921; Pharmaceutical Companies - Generic Drugs p. 2924

				Phone	Fax
ADM Natural Health & Nutrition *Archer Daniels Midland Co* 4666 Faries Pkwy **Fax:* PR ■ *TF:* 800-637-5843 ■ *Web:* www.adm.com	Decatur	IL	62526	217-451-7231	451-4510*
Afexa Life Sciences 9604 20th Ave *TF:* 888-280-0022 ■ *Web:* www.afexa.com	Edmonton	AB	T6N1G1	780-432-0022	432-7772
AST Sports Science Inc 120 Capitol Dr *TF:* 800-627-2788 ■ *Web:* www.ast-ss.com	Golden	CO	80401	303-278-1420	278-1417
Atkins Nutritionals Inc 1050 17th St Ste 1000 *TF:* 800-628-5467 ■ *Web:* www.atkins.com	Denver	CO	80265	303-633-2840	633-2860
Beehive Botanicals Inc 16297 W Nursery Rd *TF:* 800-233-4483 ■ *Web:* www.beehivebotanicals.com	Hayward	WI	54843	715-634-4274	634-3523
Cc Pollen Co 3627 E Indian School Rd Ste 209 *TF:* 800-875-0096 ■ *Web:* www.ccpollen.com	Phoenix	AZ	85018	602-957-0096	381-3130
Celex Laboratories Inc #115-21600 Westminster Hwy *Web:* www.celexlaboratories.com	Richmond	BC	V6V0A2	604-231-6077	231-6078
Chattem Inc 1715 W 38th St PO Box 2219 *Web:* www.chattem.com	Chattanooga	TN	37409	423-821-4571	821-0395
CytoSport Inc 4795 Industrial Way. *TF:* 888-313-1922 ■ *Web:* www.cytosport.com	Benicia	CA	94510	707-751-3942	748-5732
Douglas Laboratories Inc 600 Boyce Rd *TF:* 800-245-4440 ■ *Web:* www.douglaslabs.com	Pittsburgh	PA	15205	412-494-0122	494-0155
Edom Laboratories Inc 100 E Jefryn Blvd Ste M *Web:* www.edomlaboratories.com	Deer Park	NY	11729	631-586-2266	
Enzymatic Therapy 825 Challenger Dr *TF:* 800-783-2286 ■ *Web:* www.enzymatictherapy.com	Green Bay	WI	54311	920-469-1313	469-4444
Foodscience Corp 20 New England Dr Ste 10 *TF:* 800-451-5190 ■ *Web:* www.foodsciencecorp.com	Essex Junction	VT	05452	802-878-5508	878-0549
Fruitful Yield Inc 395 Glen Ellyn Rd *Web:* www.nowfoods.com	Bloomingdale	IL	60108	630-545-9098	790-8019
Futurebiotics LLC 70 Commerce Dr *TF:* 800-645-1721 ■ *Web:* www.futurebiotics.com	Hauppauge	NY	11788	631-273-6300	273-1165
Garden of Life Inc 5500 Village Blvd Ste 102 **Fax Area Code:* 561 ■ *TF:* 866-465-0051 ■ *Web:* www.gardenoflife.com	West Palm Beach	FL	33407	866-465-0051	472-9298*
GNC Inc 300 Sixth Ave 14th Fl *NYSE: GNC* ■ *TF:* 877-462-4700 ■ *Web:* www.gnc.com	Pittsburgh	PA	15222	877-462-4700	
Hammer Nutrition Ltd 4952 Whitefish Stage Rd *TF Cust Svc:* 800-336-1977 ■ *Web:* www.hammernutrition.com	Whitefish	MT	59937	406-862-1877	862-4543
Health Products Corp 1060 Nepperhan Ave *Web:* www.hpc7.com	Yonkers	NY	10703	914-423-2900	963-6001
Herbalist, The 2106 NE 65th St *TF:* 800-694-3727 ■ *Web:* store.theherbalist.com	Seattle	WA	98115	206-523-2600	522-3253
Integrated BioPharma Inc 225 Long Ave *OTC: INBP* ■ *TF:* 888-319-6962 ■ *Web:* www.chemintl.com	Hillside	NJ	07205	973-926-0816	926-1735
Irwin Naturals 5310 Beethoven St *TF:* 800-297-3273 ■ *Web:* www.appliednutrition.com	Los Angeles	CA	90066	310-306-3636	301-1546
Jarrow Formulas Inc 1824 S Robertson Blvd *TF:* 800-726-0886 ■ *Web:* www.jarrow.com	Los Angeles	CA	90035	310-204-6936	204-2520
Labrada Nutrition 403 Century Plz Dr Ste 440 **Fax Area Code:* 281 ■ *TF:* 800-832-9948 ■ *Web:* www.labrada.com	Houston	TX	77073	800-832-9948	209-2135*
Maximum Human Performance Inc (MHP Inc) 21 Dwight Pl *TF:* 888-783-8844 ■ *Web:* www.maxperformance.com	Fairfield	NJ	07004	973-785-9055	785-9159
Mega-Pro International Inc 251 W Hilton Dr *TF:* 800-541-9469 ■ *Web:* www.mega-pro.com	Saint George	UT	84770	435-673-1001	673-1007
Natrol Inc 21411 Prairie St *Web:* www.natrol.com	Chatsworth	CA	91311	818-739-6000	
Naturade Products Inc 2030 Main St Ste 630 **Fax Area Code:* 714 ■ *TF:* 800-421-1830 ■ *Web:* www.naturade.com	Irvine	CA	92614	800-421-1830	935-9837*
Natural Alternatives International Inc 1185 Linda Vista Dr *NASDAQ: NAII* ■ *TF:* 800-848-2646 ■ *Web:* www.nai-online.com	San Marcos	CA	92078	760-744-7340	744-9589
Natural Factors Nutritional Products Ltd 1550 United Blvd **Fax Area Code:* 800 ■ *TF:* 800-663-8900 ■ *Web:* www.naturalfactors.com	Coquitlam	BC	V3K6Y7	604-777-1757	663-2115*
Natural Organics Inc 548 Broadhollow Rd **Fax Area Code:* 631 ■ *TF:* 800-645-9500 ■ *Web:* www.naturesplus.com	Melville	NY	11747	800-645-9500	980-9612*
Naturally Vitamins 4404 E Elwood St *TF:* 800-899-4499 ■ *Web:* www.naturally.com	Phoenix	AZ	85040	480-991-0200	991-0551
Nature's Way Products Inc 3051 W Maple Loop Dr Ste 125 *TF:* 800-962-8873 ■ *Web:* www.naturesway.com	Lehi	UT	84043	800-962-8873	688-3303
NBTY Inc 2100 Smithtown Ave *Web:* www.nbty.com	Ronkonkoma	NY	11779	631-200-2000	
Nickers International Ltd PO Box 50066 *TF:* 800-642-5377 ■ *Web:* www.nickersinternational.com	Staten Island	NY	10305	718-448-6283	448-6298
Nutraceutical International Corp 1400 Kearns Blvd *NASDAQ: NUTR* ■ **Fax Area Code:* 800 ■ *TF:* 800-669-8877 ■ *Web:* www.nutraceutical.com	Park City	UT	84060	435-655-6000	767-8541*
Nutrilite Products Inc 5600 Beach Blvd PO Box 5940 *Web:* www.nutrilite.com	Buena Park	CA	90621	714-562-6200	736-7610
Pacific Health Laboratories Inc 100 Matawan Rd Ste 150 *TF General:* 877-363-8769 ■ *Web:* www.pacifichealthlabs.com	Matawan	NJ	07747	732-739-2900	739-4360
Paragon Laboratories 20433 Earl St *TF:* 800-231-3670 ■ *Web:* www.paragonlabsusa.com	Torrance	CA	90503	310-370-1563	
Peak Nutrition Inc 1097 11th St PO Box 87 *TF Sales:* 800-600-2069 ■ *Web:* www.peaknutrition.com	Syracuse	NE	68446	402-269-2825	269-2649
Perrigo Co 515 Eastern Ave. *NYSE: PRGO* ■ *TF:* 800-719-9260 ■ *Web:* www.perrigo.com	Allegan	MI	49010	269-673-8451	673-9128
Phibro Animal Health Corp 300 Frank W Burr Blvd Ste 21 *TF:* 800-223-0434 ■ *Web:* www.phibrochem.com	Teaneck	NJ	07660	201-329-7300	329-7399
Power Organics 301 S Old Stage Rd *TF:* 866-277-3420 ■ *Web:* www.klamathbluegreen.com	Mount Shasta	CA	96067	530-926-6684	
Prolab Nutrition 21411 Prairie St *TF:* 800-776-5221 ■ *Web:* www.prolab.com	Chatsworth	CA	91311	818-739-6000	739-6001
Robinson Pharma Inc 3330 S Harbor Blvd *Web:* www.robinsonpharma.com	Santa Ana	CA	92704	714-241-0235	751-6066
Santa Cruz Nutritionals 2200 Delaware Ave **Fax:* Sales ■ *Web:* www.santacruznutritionals.com	Santa Cruz	CA	95060	831-457-3200	454-0915*
Sportika Export Inc 225 Episcopal Rd *Web:* www.sportika.com	Berlin	CT	06037	860-828-9000	828-5962
SportPharma Inc Three Terminal Rd *TF:* 800-872-0101 ■ *Web:* www.sportpharma.com	New Brunswick	NJ	08901	732-545-3130	509-0458
Swanson Health Products Inc PO Box 2803 *TF:* 800-824-4491 ■ *Web:* www.swansonvitamins.com	Fargo	ND	58108	701-356-2700	356-2708
Synutra International Inc 2275 Research Blvd Ste 500 *NASDAQ: SYUT* ■ *TF:* 866-405-2350 ■ *Web:* www.synutra.com	Rockville	MD	20850	301-840-3888	
Thayers Natural Pharmaceuticals Inc PO Box 56 **Fax Area Code:* 203 ■ *TF:* 888-842-9371 ■ *Web:* www.thayers.com	Westport	CT	06881	888-842-9371	227-8183*
Tishcon Corp 50 Sylvester St *TF:* 800-848-8442 ■ *Web:* www.tishcon.com	Westbury	NY	11590	516-333-3050	997-1052
Twinlab 600 E Quality Dr **Fax Area Code:* 800 ■ *TF:* 800-645-5626 ■ *Web:* www.twinlab.com	American Fork	UT	84003	801-763-0700	723-5837*
Ultra-Lab Nutrition Inc 3100 NW Boca Raton Blvd *Web:* www.ultralab.com	Boca Raton	FL	33431	561-367-1474	
USANA Health Sciences Inc 3838 West PkwyBlvd *NYSE: USNA* ■ *TF:* 888-950-9595 ■ *Web:* www.usana.com	Salt Lake City	UT	84120	801-954-7100	954-7300
Vitamins Inc 315 E Fullerton Ave *Web:* www.prinovausa.com	Carol Stream	IL	60188	312-861-0700	
Wachters' Organic Sea Products Corp 550 Sylvan St *TF:* 800-682-7100 ■ *Web:* www.wachters.com	Daly City	CA	94014	650-757-9851	757-9858
Wakunaga of America Company Ltd 23501 Madero *TF:* 800-421-2998 ■ *Web:* www.kyolic.com	Mission Viejo	CA	92691	949-855-2776	458-2764
Windmill Health Products Six Henderson Dr *TF:* 800-822-4320 ■ *Web:* www.windmillvitamins.com	West Caldwell	NJ	07006	973-575-6591	882-3256
Young Living Essential Oils 3125 Executive Pkwy *TF:* 866-203-5666 ■ *Web:* www.youngliving.com	Lehi	UT	84043	801-418-8900	418-8800

803 VOCATIONAL & TECHNICAL SCHOOLS

SEE ALSO Children's Learning Centers p. 1948; Colleges - Community & Junior p. 1961; Colleges - Culinary Arts p. 1976; Colleges - Fine Arts p. 1977; Colleges & Universities - Four-Year p. 1980; Language Schools p. 2620; Military Service Academies p. 2760; Universities - Canadian p. 3268

Listings in this category are organized alphabetically by states.

Phone | Fax

Enterprise-Ozark Community College 1975 Ave C ..... Mobile AL 36615 251-438-2816 438-2816
TF: 877-701-0033 ■ Web: escc.edu

Herzing College Birmingham
280 W Valley Ave ..... Birmingham AL 35209 205-916-2800 916-2807*
*Fax: Admissions ■ TF: 800-425-9432 ■ Web: www.herzing.edu/birmingham

ITT Technical Institute Birmingham
6270 Pk S Dr ..... Bessemer AL 35022 205-497-5700 497-5799
TF: 800-488-7033 ■ Web: www.itt-tech.edu

JF Drake State Technical College
3421 Meridian St N ..... Huntsville AL 35811 256-539-8161 551-3142
TF: 888-413-7253 ■ Web: www.drakestate.edu

Lawson State Community College
Bessemer 1100 Ninth Ave SW ..... Bessemer AL 35022 205-925-2515 929-3598
TF: 800-373-4879 ■ Web: www.lawsonstate.edu

Lurleen B Wallace Community College
Andalusia 1000 Dannelly Blvd PO Box 1418 ..... Andalusia AL 36420 334-222-6591 881-2201*
*Fax: Admissions ■ TF: 877-382-4357 ■ Web: www.lbwcc.edu
MacAurthur 1708 N Main St PO Box 910 ..... Opp AL 36467 334-493-3573 493-7003
TF: 877-382-4357 ■ Web: www.lbwcc.edu

Trenholm State Technical College
1225 Air Base Blvd ..... Montgomery AL 36108 334-420-4200 420-4206
TF: 800-917-2081 ■ Web: www.trenholmstate.edu/

Virginia College
Birmingham 488 Palisades Blvd ..... Birmingham AL 35209 205-802-1200
Web: www.vc.edu
Huntsville 2021 Drake Ave SW ..... Huntsville AL 35801 256-533-7387 533-7785
Web: www.vc.edu

Wallace Community College Selma
3000 Earl Goodwin Pkwy ..... Selma AL 36703 334-876-9227 876-9250
TF: 855-428-8313 ■ Web: www.wccs.edu
Calgary 2700 Third Ave SE ..... Calgary AB T2A7W4 403-235-3450
TF General: 800-363-5558 ■ Web: www.cal.devry.edu

Brown Mackie College Tucson
4585 E Speedway Blvd Ste 204 ..... Tucson AZ 85712 520-319-3300
Web: www.brownmackie.edu

DeVry University Phoenix 2149 W Dunlap Ave ..... Phoenix AZ 85021 602-870-9222 331-1494
TF Cust Svc: 800-528-0250 ■ Web: www.phx.devry.edu

ITT Technical Institute Tempe
5005 S Wendler Dr ..... Tempe AZ 85282 602-437-7500 437-7505
TF: 800-879-4881 ■ Web: www.itt-tech.edu

ITT Technical Institute Tucson
1455 W River Rd ..... Tucson AZ 85704 520-408-7488 292-9899
TF: 800-870-9730 ■ Web: www.itt-tech.edu

Southwest Institute of Healing Arts
1100 E Apache Blvd ..... Tempe AZ 85281 480-994-9244 994-3228
TF: 888-504-9106 ■ Web: www.swiha.edu

Remington College
Little Rock 19 Remington Rd ..... Little Rock AR 72204 501-312-0007 225-3819
Web: www.remingtoncollege.edu

Concorde Career Colleges Inc
San Bernardino 201 E Airport Dr ..... San Bernardino CA 92408 909-884-8891 384-1768
TF: 800-852-8434 ■ Web: www.concorde.edu
San Diego 4393 Imperial Ave Ste 100 ..... San Diego CA 92113 619-688-0800 220-4177
Web: www.concorde.edu

DeVry University Fremont 6600 Dumbarton Cir ..... Fremont CA 94555 510-574-1200 284-1805*
*Fax: Admissions ■ TF: 800-363-5558 ■ Web: www.fre.devry.edu

DeVry University Long Beach
3880 Kilroy Airport Way ..... Long Beach CA 90806 562-997-5300
TF: 800-597-1333 ■ Web: www.lb.devry.edu

DeVry University Pomona 901 Corporate Ctr Dr ..... Pomona CA 91768 909-622-8866
TF: 800-243-3660 ■ Web: www.pom.devry.edu

DeVry University Sherman Oaks
15301 Ventura Blvd Bldg D-100 ..... Sherman Oaks CA 91403 818-713-8111 713-8118
Web: www.devry.edu

Everest College Alhambra 2215 W Mission Rd ..... Alhambra CA 91803 626-979-4940 979-4960
TF: 888-223-8556 ■ Web: www.everest.edu

Everest College Anaheim
511 N Brookhurst Ste 300 ..... Anaheim CA 92801 714-953-6500 953-4163
TF: 888-224-6684 ■ Web: www.everest.edu

Everest College City of Industry
12801 Crossroads Pkwy S ..... City of Industry CA 91746 562-908-2500 908-7656
TF: 888-224-6684 ■ Web: www.everest.edu

Everest College Los Angeles
3000 S Robertson Blvd Ste 300 ..... Los Angeles CA 90034 310-840-5777 287-2344
Web: www.everest.edu

Everest College San Bernardino
217 E Club Ctr Dr Ste A ..... San Bernardino CA 92408 909-777-3300 777-3313
TF: 888-224-6684 ■ Web: www.everest.edu

Everest College San Jose
1245 S Winchester Blvd Ste 102 ..... San Jose CA 95128 408-246-4171 557-9874
TF: 888-223-8556 ■ Web: www.everest.edu

Everest Institute Long Beach
2161 Technology Pl ..... Long Beach CA 90810 562-624-9530 437-8111
TF: 888-223-8556 ■ Web: www.everest.edu
Roseville Seven Sierra Gate Plz Ste 101 ..... Roseville CA 95678 916-648-1446
Web: www.ggu.edu

Golden Gate University
San Francisco 536 Mission St ..... San Francisco CA 94105 415-442-7000 442-7807*
*Fax: Admissions ■ TF: 800-448-4968 ■ Web: www.ggu.edu
Concord 5130 Commercial Cir ..... Concord CA 94520 925-288-5800 288-5896

Heald College
Fresno 255 W Bullard Ave ..... Fresno CA 93704 559-438-4222 437-4184*
Hayward 25500 Industrial Blvd ..... Hayward CA 94545 510-783-2100 783-3287
Rancho Cordova 2910 Prospect Pk Dr ..... Rancho Cordova CA 95670 916-638-1616 414-2676
Salinas 1450 N Main St ..... Salinas CA 93906 831-443-1700 443-1050
San Jose 341 Great Mall Pkwy ..... Milpitas CA 95035 408-934-4900 808-3005*
*Fax Area Code: 415
Stockton 1605 E March Ln ..... Stockton CA 95210 209-473-5200 477-2739

ITT Technical Institute
Lathrop 16916 S Harlan Rd ..... Lathrop CA 95330 209-858-0077 858-0277
TF: 800-346-1786 ■ Web: www.itt-tech.edu
Oxnard 2051 Solar Dr Ste 150 ..... Oxnard CA 93036 805-988-0143 988-1813
TF: 800-530-1582 ■ Web: www.itt-tech.edu
Rancho Cordova 10863 Gold Ctr Dr ..... Rancho Cordova CA 95670 916-851-3900 851-9225
TF: 800-488-8466 ■ Web: www.itt-tech.edu
San Bernardino 670 Carnegie Dr ..... San Bernardino CA 92408 909-806-4600 806-4699
TF: 800-888-3801 ■ Web: www.itt-tech.edu
San Dimas 650 W Cienega Ave ..... San Dimas CA 91773 909-971-2300 971-2350
TF: 800-414-6522 ■ Web: www.itt-tech.edu
Sylmar 12669 Encinitas Ave ..... Sylmar CA 91342 818-364-5151 364-5150
TF: 800-363-2086 ■ Web: www.itt-tech.edu
Torrance 2555 W 190th St Ste 125 ..... Torrance CA 90504 310-965-5900
Web: www.itt-tech.edu

Shasta College
11555 Old Oregon Trl PO Box 496006 ..... Redding CA 96049 530-242-7500 225-4896
Web: www.shastacollege.edu

West Orange College
12541 Brookhurst St Ste 100 ..... Garden Grove CA 92840 714-530-5000

Westwood College Inland Empire
20 W Seventh St ..... Upland CA 91786 909-931-7550
TF: 866-221-5632 ■ Web: www.westwood.edu

Westwood College Los Angeles
3250 Wilshire Blvd Ste 400 ..... Los Angeles CA 90010 213-739-9999 382-2468*
*Fax: Admissions ■ TF: 866-930-9256 ■ Web: www.westwood.edu

Wyotech Fremont 200 Whitney Pl ..... Fremont CA 94539 510-490-6900 490-8599
Web: www.wyotech.edu

Wyotech Sacramento
980 Riverside Pkwy ..... West Sacramento CA 95605 916-376-8888 721-4854*
*Fax Area Code: 307 ■ *Fax: Admissions ■ TF: 888-308-7158 ■ Web: www.wyotech.edu

Bel-Rea Institute of Animal Technology
1681 S Dayton St ..... Denver CO 80247 303-751-8700 751-9969
TF: 800-950-8001 ■ Web: belrea.edu

Colorado Technical University Denver
1865 W 121st Ave Bldg C Ste 100 ..... Westminster CO 80234 303-362-2900
TF: 877-250-9372 ■ Web: www.coloradotech.edu/denver

Concorde Career Colleges Inc Denver
111 N Havana St ..... Aurora CO 80010 303-861-1151 839-5478
Web: www.concorde.edu

Denver Academy of Court Reporting
9051 Harlan St Ste 20 ..... Westminster CO 80031 303-427-5292 427-5383
TF: 866-712-2425 ■ Web: www.princeinstitute.edu
Colorado Springs
1175 Kelly Johnson Blvd ..... Colorado Springs CO 80920 719-632-3000 866-6770
TF Help Line: 877-784-1997 ■ Web: www.devry.edu

DeVry University
Denver
6312 S Fiddlers Green Cr Ste 150E ..... Greenwood Village CO 80111 303-329-3000
Web: www.wes.devry.edu

Everest College Aurora
14280 E Jewell Ave Ste 100 ..... Aurora CO 80012 303-745-6244 745-6245
TF: 888-223-8556 ■ Web: www.everest.edu

Everest College Thornton 9065 Grant St ..... Thornton CO 80229 303-457-2757 457-4030
TF: 888-223-8556 ■ Web: www.everest.edu

Jones International University Ltd
9697 E Mineral Ave ..... Centennial CO 80112 303-784-8904 799-0966*
*Fax: Admissions ■ TF: 800-811-5663 ■ Web: www.jiu.edu

Redstone College
Denver 10851 W 120th Ave ..... Broomfield CO 80021 303-466-1714
TF: 800-888-3995 ■ Web: www.redstone.edu

Westwood College
Denver 7350 N Broadway ..... Denver CO 80221 303-650-5050 487-0214
TF: 800-281-2978 ■ Web: www.westwood.edu

Delaware Technical & Community College
Owens 18800 Seashore Hwy PO Box 610 ..... Georgetown DE 19947 302-856-5400
Web: www.dtcc.edu
Stanton 400 Stanton-Christiana Rd ..... Newark DE 19713 302-454-3900 292-3816*
*Fax: Admissions ■ Web: www.dtcc.edu
Terry 100 Campus Dr ..... Dover DE 19904 302-857-1000 857-1004
Web: www.dtcc.edu/terry

Acupuncture & Massage College
10506 N Kendall Dr ..... Miami FL 33176 305-595-9500 595-2622*
*Fax: Admissions ■ Web: www.amcollege.edu

Brown Mackie College Miami 3700 Lakeside Dr ..... Miramar FL 33132 305-341-6600 428-5836*
*Fax: Admissions ■ TF: 866-505-0335 ■ Web: www.brownmackie.edu

Concorde Career Colleges inc Miramar
10933 Marks Way ..... Miramar FL 33025 954-731-8880
TF: 800-693-7010 ■ Web: www.concorde.edu

DeVry University Miramar 2300 SW 145th Ave ..... Miramar FL 33027 954-499-9800
Web: www.devry.edu

DeVry University Orlando 4000 Millenia Blvd ..... Orlando FL 32839 407-345-2800 370-3198*
*Fax: Admissions ■ TF: 888-857-5757 ■ Web: www.devry.edu
Brandon 3924 Coconut Palm Dr ..... Tampa FL 33619 813-621-0041 628-0919*
*Fax: Admissions ■ TF Cust Svc: 877-439-0003 ■ Web: www.everest.edu
Jacksonville 8226 Phillips Hwy ..... Jacksonville FL 32256 904-731-4949 731-0599
TF: 800-611-2101 ■ Web: www.everest.edu
Lakeland 995 E Memorial Blvd Ste 110 ..... Lakeland FL 33801 863-686-1444 682-1077
TF: 888-223-8556 ■ Web: www.everest.edu
Largo 1199 E Bay Dr ..... Largo FL 33770 727-725-2688 373-4412
TF: 888-223-8556 ■ Web: www.everest.edu

Everest University
North Orlando 5421 Diplomat Cir ..... Orlando FL 32810 407-628-5870 628-1344*
*Fax: Admissions ■ TF: 888-223-8556 ■ Web: www.everest.edu
Orange Park 805 Wells Rd ..... Orange Park FL 32073 904-264-9122 264-9952
TF: 888-223-8556 ■ Web: www.everest.edu

Name / Address	City	State	Zip	Phone	Fax
Pompano Beach 225 N Federal Hwy	Pompano Beach	FL	33062	954-783-7339	783-7964
TF: 888-223-8556 ■ *Web:* www.everest.edu					
South Orlando 9200 Southpark Ctr Loop	Orlando	FL	32819	407-851-2525	851-1477
TF: 800-611-2101 ■ *Web:* www.everest.edu					
Tampa 3319 W Hillsborough Ave	Tampa	FL	33614	813-879-6000	871-2483
TF: 888-223-8556 ■ *Web:* www.everest.edu					
Florida Technical College					
12900 Challenger Pkwy Ste 130	Orlando	FL	32826	407-447-7300	447-7301
TF General: 888-678-2929 ■ *Web:* www.ftccollege.edu					
Full Sail University					
3300 University Blvd Ste 160	Winter Park	FL	32792	407-679-6333	678-0070
TF: 800-226-7625 ■ *Web:* www.fullsail.edu					
ITT Technical Institute Fort Lauderdale					
3401 S University Dr	Fort Lauderdale	FL	33328	954-476-9300	476-6889
TF: 800-488-7797 ■ *Web:* www.itt-tech.edu					
ITT Technical Institute Jacksonville					
7011 AC Skinner Pkwy Ste 140	Jacksonville	FL	32256	904-573-9100	573-0512
TF: 800-318-1264 ■ *Web:* www.itt-tech.edu					
ITT Technical Institute Miami					
7955 NW 12th St Ste 119	Miami	FL	33126	305-477-3080	477-7561*
**Fax:* Admissions ■ *Web:* www.itt-tech.edu					
ITT Technical Institute Tampa					
4809 Memorial Hwy	Tampa	FL	33634	813-885-2244	888-8451
TF: 800-825-2831 ■ *Web:* www.itt-tech.edu					
Kaplan University					
6301 Kaplan University Ave	Fort Lauderdale	FL	33309	954-515-4015	588-4127*
**Fax Area Code:* 800 ■ *TF:* 866-522-7747 ■ *Web:* www.kaplanuniversity.edu					
Keiser University					
Daytona Beach 1800 Business Pk Blvd	Daytona Beach	FL	32114	386-274-5060	274-2725
Web: www.keiseruniversity.edu					
Fort Lauderdale 1500 W Commercial Blvd	Fort Lauderdale	FL	33309	954-776-4456	771-4894
TF: 800-749-4456 ■ *Web:* www.keiseruniversity.edu					
Melbourne 900 S Babcock St	Melbourne	FL	32901	321-409-4800	725-3766
Web: www.keiseruniversity.edu					
Sarasota 6151 Lk Osprey Dr	Sarasota	FL	34240	941-907-3900	907-2016
TF: 866-534-7372 ■ *Web:* www.keiseruniversity.edu					
Remington College Largo					
6302 E Dr Martin Luther King Jr Blvd Ste 400	Tampa	FL	33619	800-560-6192	
TF: 800-560-6192 ■ *Web:* www.remingtoncollege.edu					
Remington College Tampa 6302 E MLK Blvd Ste 400	Tampa	FL	33619	813-935-5700	935-7415
TF General: 800-323-8122 ■ *Web:* www.remingtoncollege.edu					
Stenotype Institute of Jacksonville					
3563 Phillips Hwy Bldg E Ste 501	Jacksonville	FL	32207	904-398-4141	398-7878
TF: 800-273-5090 ■ *Web:* www.stenotype.edu					
Athens Technical College (ATC) 800 US Hwy 29 N	Athens	GA	30601	706-355-5000	369-5756
Web: athenstech.edu					
Augusta Technical College					
3200 Augusta Tech Dr	Augusta	GA	30906	706-771-4000	771-4034*
**Fax:* Admissions ■ *Web:* www.augustatech.edu					
Bauder College 384 N Yards Blvd NW Ste 190	Atlanta	GA	30313	404-237-7573	237-1619*
**Fax:* Admissions ■ *TF:* 800-935-1857 ■ *Web:* www.bauder.edu					
Brown College of Court Reporting & Medical Transcription (BCCR)					
1900 Emery St NW Ste 200	Atlanta	GA	30318	404-876-1227	876-4415
TF: 800-849-0703 ■ *Web:* www.bccr.edu					
Brown Mackie College Atlanta					
4370 Peachtree Rd NE	Atlanta	GA	30319	404-799-4500	
TF: 877-479-8419 ■ *Web:* www.brownmackie.edu					
Central Georgia Technical College					
3300 Macon Tech Dr	Macon	GA	31206	478-757-3400	757-3454
TF: 866-430-0135 ■ *Web:* centralgatech.edu					
Columbus Technical College					
928 Manchester Expy	Columbus	GA	31904	706-649-1800	649-1804
Web: www.columbustech.edu					
Gupton-Jones College of Funeral Service					
5141 Snapfinger Woods Dr	Decatur	GA	30035	770-593-2257	593-1891
TF: 800-848-5352 ■ *Web:* www.gupton-jones.edu					
Herzing College					
Atlanta 3393 Peachtree Rd Ste 1003	Atlanta	GA	30326	404-816-4533	816-5576
TF: 800-573-4533 ■ *Web:* www.herzing.edu/atlanta					
Imedex Inc 4325 Alexander Dr	Alpharetta	GA	30022	770-751-7332	751-7334
TF: 800-243-6969 ■ *Web:* www.imedex.com					
ITT Technical Institute Kennesaw					
2065 Baker Rd NW	Kennesaw	GA	30144	770-426-2300	706-3040*
**Fax Area Code:* 317 ■ *TF:* 800-564-9771 ■ *Web:* www.itt-tech.edu					
Savannah Technical College					
5717 White Bluff Rd	Savannah	GA	31405	912-443-5700	443-5705
TF: 800-769-6362 ■ *Web:* www.savannahtech.edu					
Westwood College Atlanta Northlake					
2309 Parklake Dr NE	Atlanta	GA	30345	770-743-3000	
TF: 866-821-6145 ■ *Web:* www.westwood.edu					
Argosy University Hawaii					
400 ASB Tower 1001 Bishop St	Honolulu	HI	96813	808-536-5555	536-5505
TF: 888-323-2777 ■ *Web:* www.argosy.edu					
Remington College Honolulu					
1111 Bishop St Ste 400	Honolulu	HI	96813	808-772-5978	533-3064
Web: www.remingtoncollege.edu					
Eastern Idaho Technical College					
1600 S 25th E	Idaho Falls	ID	83404	208-524-3000	525-7026
TF: 800-662-0261 ■ *Web:* www.eitc.edu					
ITT Technical Institute Boise					
12302 W Explorer Dr	Boise	ID	83713	208-322-8844	322-0173
TF: 800-666-4888 ■ *Web:* www.itt-tech.edu					
DeVry University Addison 1221 N Swift Rd	Addison	IL	60101	630-953-1300	543-2196
TF: 800-346-5420 ■ *Web:* www.devry.edu					
DeVry University Chicago 3300 N Campbell Ave	Chicago	IL	60618	773-929-8500	697-2710*
**Fax:* Admissions ■ *Web:* www.chi.devry.edu					
DeVry University Tinley Park					
18624 W Creek Dr	Tinley Park	IL	60477	708-342-3300	342-3505
Web: www.devry.edu					
Gem City College 700 State St	Quincy	IL	62301	217-222-0391	222-1557
Web: www.gemcitycollege.com					
ITT Technical Institute Mount Prospect					
3800 N Wilke RD	Arlington Heights	IL	60004	847-454-1800	375-9022
Web: www.itt-tech.edu					
ITT Technical Institute Orland Park					
11551 184th Pl	Orland Park	IL	60467	708-326-3200	326-3250
Web: www.itt-tech.edu					
Lexington College 310 S Peoria St Ste 512	Chicago	IL	60607	312-226-6294	226-6405*
**Fax:* Admissions ■ *Web:* www.lexingtoncollege.edu					
MacCormac College 29 E Madison St	Chicago	IL	60602	312-922-1884	922-4286
Web: www.maccormac.edu					
Midstate College 411 W Northmoor Rd	Peoria	IL	61614	309-692-4092	692-3893
TF: 800-251-4299 ■ *Web:* www.midstate.edu					
Morrison Institute of Technology					
701 Portland Ave	Morrison	IL	61270	815-772-7218	772-7584
Web: morrisontech.edu					
Northwestern College Chicago Campus					
4829 N Lipps Ave	Chicago	IL	60630	773-777-4220	
TF: 888-205-2283 ■ *Web:* www.northwesterncollege.edu					
Westwood College O'Hare Airport					
8501 W Higgins Rd Ste 100	Chicago	IL	60631	773-380-6800	
TF: 866-235-2457 ■ *Web:* www.westwood.edu					
Westwood College River Oaks					
80 River Oaks Ctr Ste 111	Calumet City	IL	60409	708-832-1988	832-9623
TF: 888-549-4960 ■ *Web:* www.westwood.edu					
Worsham College of Mortuary Science					
495 Northgate Pkwy	Wheeling	IL	60090	847-808-8444	808-8493
Web: www.worshamcollege.com					
Fort Wayne 3000 E Coliseum Blvd	Fort Wayne	IN	46805	260-484-4400	484-2678
TF General: 866-433-2289 ■ *Web:* www.brownmackie.edu					
Merrillville 1000 E 80th Pl Ste 101N	Merrillville	IN	46410	219-769-3321	738-1076
TF: 800-258-3321 ■ *Web:* www.brownmackie.edu					
Brown Mackie College					
Michigan City 1001 E US Hwy 20	Michigan City	IN	46360	219-877-3100	
TF: 800-519-2416 ■ *Web:* www.brownmackie.edu					
South Bend 3454 Douglas Rd	South Bend	IN	46635	574-237-0774	237-3585
TF: 800-743-2447 ■ *Web:* www.brownmackie.edu					
College of Court Reporting Inc					
111 W Tenth St Ste 111	Hobart	IN	46342	219-942-1459	942-1631
TF: 866-294-3974 ■ *Web:* www.ccr.edu					
International Business College					
5699 Coventry Ln	Fort Wayne	IN	46804	260-459-4500	436-1896
TF: 800-589-6363 ■ *Web:* www.ibcfortwayne.edu					
ITT Technical Institute Fort Wayne					
2810 Dupont Commerce Ct	Fort Wayne	IN	46825	260-497-6200	497-6299
TF: 800-866-4488 ■ *Web:* www.itt-tech.edu					
ITT Technical Institute Indianapolis					
9511 Angola Ct	Indianapolis	IN	46268	317-875-8640	875-8641
TF: 800-937-4488 ■ *Web:* www.itt-tech.edu					
ITT Technical Institute Newburgh					
10999 Stahl Rd	Newburgh	IN	47630	812-858-1600	858-0646
TF: 800-832-4488 ■ *Web:* www.itt-tech.edu					
Ivy Tech Columbus College					
Columbus 4475 Central Ave	Columbus	IN	47203	812-372-9925	372-0311
TF: 800-922-4838 ■ *Web:* www.ivytech.edu/columbus					
Bloomington 200 Daniels Way	Bloomington	IN	47404	812-330-6137	330-6140
TF: 866-447-0700 ■ *Web:* www.ivytech.edu					
Ivy Tech Community College					
Central Indiana 50 W Fall Creek Pkwy N Dr	Indianapolis	IN	46208	317-921-4800	921-4753
TF: 888-489-5463 ■ *Web:* www.ivytech.edu/indianapolis					
Kokomo 1815 E Morgan St	Kokomo	IN	46901	765-459-0561	454-5111
TF: 800-459-0561 ■ *Web:* www.ivytech.edu/kokomo					
Muncie 4301 S Cowan Rd	Muncie	IN	47302	765-289-2291	289-2292
TF: 800-589-8324 ■ *Web:* www.ivytech.edu/eastcentral					
North Central 220 Dean Johnson Blvd	South Bend	IN	46601	574-289-7001	236-7177
TF: 888-489-3478 ■ *Web:* www.ivytech.edu					
Northwest 1440 E 35th Ave	Gary	IN	46409	219-981-1111	981-4415
Web: www.ivytech.edu					
Richmond 2357 Chester Blvd	Richmond	IN	47374	765-966-2656	962-8741
TF: 800-659-4562 ■ *Web:* www.ivytech.edu					
Southeast 590 Ivy Tech Dr	Madison	IN	47250	812-265-2580	265-4028
TF: 800-403-2190 ■ *Web:* www.ivytech.edu					
Southern Indiana 8204 old Indiana 311	Sellersburg	IN	47172	812-246-3301	246-9905
TF: 800-321-9021 ■ *Web:* www.ivytech.edu					
Southwest Indiana 3501 N First Ave	Evansville	IN	47710	812-426-2865	429-9878
Web: www.ivytech.edu					
Wabash Valley 8000 S Education Dr	Terre Haute	IN	47802	812-298-2293	298-2294
Web: www.ivytech.edu					
Lincoln College of Technology					
7225 Winton Dr Bldg 128	Indianapolis	IN	46268	317-632-5553	245-3238*
**Fax Area Code:* 850 ■ *TF:* 800-228-6232 ■ *Web:* www.lincolnedu.com					
Mid-America College of Funeral Science (MACFS)					
3111 Hamburg Pk	Jeffersonville	IN	47130	812-288-8878	288-5942
TF: 800-221-6158 ■ *Web:* www.mid-america.edu					
AIB College of Business 2500 Fleur Dr	Des Moines	IA	50321	515-244-4221	244-6773
TF: 800-444-1921 ■ *Web:* www.aib.edu					
Brown Mackie College Bettendorf					
2119 E Kimberly Rd	Bettendorf	IA	52722	563-344-1500	
TF: 888-420-1652 ■ *Web:* www.brownmackie.edu					
Des Moines Unviersity 3200 Grand Ave	Des Moines	IA	50312	515-271-1400	
Web: www.dmu.edu					
Western Iowa Tech Community College					
4647 Stone Ave	Sioux City	IA	51102	712-274-6400	274-6412
TF: 800-352-4649 ■ *Web:* witcc.edu					
Brown Mackie College Lenexa 9705 Lenexa Dr	Lenexa	KS	66215	913-768-1900	495-9555
TF: 800-635-9101 ■ *Web:* www.brownmackie.edu					
Brown Mackie College Salina 2106 S Ninth St	Salina	KS	67401	785-825-5422	
TF: 800-365-0433 ■ *Web:* www.brownmackie.edu/salina.aspx					
Concorde Career Colleges					
5800 Foxridge Dr Ste 500	Mission	KS	66202	913-831-9977	831-6556
TF: 800-693-7010 ■ *Web:* www.concorde.edu					

	City	State	ZIP	Phone	Fax
Wichita Area Technical College					
301 S Grove St Bldg A	Wichita	KS	67211	316-677-9400	677-9555
TF: 866-296-4031 ■ *Web:* www.watc.edu					
Bowling Green Technical College					
1845 Loop Dr	Bowling Green	KY	42101	270-901-1000	901-1144
TF: 866-590-9238 ■ *Web:* www.bowlinggreen.kctcs.edu					
Brown Mackie College Hopkinsville					
4001 Ft Campbell Blvd	Hopkinsville	KY	42240	270-886-1302	886-3544
TF: 800-359-4753 ■ *Web:* www.brownmackie.edu					
Brown Mackie College Louisville					
3605 Fern Vly Rd	Louisville	KY	40219	502-968-7191	357-9956
TF: 800-999-7387 ■ *Web:* www.brownmackie.edu					
Brown Mackie College Northern Kentucky					
309 Buttermilk Pk	Fort Mitchell	KY	41017	859-341-5627	341-6483
TF: 800-888-1445 ■ *Web:* www.brownmackie.edu					
Daymar College 3361 Buckland Sq	Owensboro	KY	42301	270-926-4040	685-4090
Web: daymarcollege.edu					
Gateway Community & Technical College (GCTC)					
1025 Amsterdam Rd	Covington	KY	41011	859-441-4500	292-6415
TF: 855-346-4282 ■ *Web:* www.gateway.kctcs.edu					
ITT Technical Institute Lexington					
2473 Fortune Dr Ste 180	Lexington	KY	40509	859-246-3300	246-3350
Web: www.itt-tech.edu					
ITT Technical Institute Louisville					
9500 Ormsby Stn Rd Ste 100	Louisville	KY	40223	502-327-7424	327-7624
TF: 888-790-7427 ■ *Web:* www.itt-tech.edu					
Louisville Technical Institute					
Sullivan College of Technology & Design					
3901 Atkinson Sq Dr	Louisville	KY	40218	502-456-6509	456-2341
TF: 800-844-6528 ■ *Web:* www.sctd.edu					
National College					
Lexington 2376 Sir Barton Way	Lexington	KY	40509	859-253-0621	254-7664
Web: national-college.edu					
National College of Business & Technology Danville					
115 E Lexington Ave	Danville	KY	40422	859-236-6991	236-1063
Web: national-college.edu					
National College of Business & Technology Florence					
8095 Connector Dr	Florence	KY	41042	859-525-6510	525-8961
TF: 888-956-2732 ■ *Web:* www.national-college.edu					
National College of Business & Technology Pikeville					
50 National College Blvd	Pikeville	KY	41501	606-478-7200	478-7209
TF: 800-664-1886 ■ *Web:* national-college.edu					
National College of Business & Technology Richmond					
125 S Killarney Ln	Richmond	KY	40475	859-623-8956	624-5544
Web: national-college.edu					
Owensboro Community & Technical College					
4800 New Hartford Rd	Owensboro	KY	42303	270-686-4400	686-4496
TF: 866-755-6282 ■ *Web:* www.octc.kctcs.edu					
Remington College Lafayette					
303 Rue Louis XIV	Lafayette	LA	70508	337-981-4010	983-7130
Web: www.remingtoncollege.edu					
Andover College 265 Western Ave	South Portland	ME	04106	207-774-6126	774-1715
TF: 800-639-3110 ■ *Web:* kaplanuniversity.edu					
Beal College 99 Farm Rd	Bangor	ME	04401	207-947-4591	947-0208
TF: 800-660-7351 ■ *Web:* www.bealcollege.edu					
Central Maine Community College					
1250 Turner St	Auburn	ME	04210	207-755-5100	755-5493
TF Admissions: 800-891-2002 ■ *Web:* www.cmcc.edu					
Central Maine Medical Ctr School of Nursing					
70 Middle St	Lewiston	ME	04240	207-795-2840	795-2849
Web: mchp.edu/					
Eastern Maine Community College 354 Hogan Rd	Bangor	ME	04401	207-974-4600	974-4608
TF: 800-286-9357 ■ *Web:* www.emcc.edu					
Northern Maine Community College (NMCC)					
33 Edgemont Dr	Presque Isle	ME	04769	207-768-2700	768-2848
Web: nmcc.edu					
Southern Maine Community College (SMCC)					
Two Ft Rd	South Portland	ME	04106	207-741-5500	741-5760
TF: 877-282-2182 ■ *Web:* www.smccme.edu					
ITT Technical Institute Owings Mills					
11301 Red Run Blvd	Owings Mills	MD	21117	443-394-7115	394-7715
TF: 877-411-6782 ■ *Web:* www.itt-tech.edu					
Maryland Bartending Academy					
209 New Jersey Ave NE	Glen Burnie	MD	21060	410-787-0020	787-0402
Web: www.marylandbartending.com					
National Labor College					
10000 New Hampshire Ave	Silver Spring	MD	20903	301-431-6400	431-5411
TF: 888-427-8100 ■ *Web:* www.nlc.edu					
Bay State College 122 Commonwealth Ave	Boston	MA	02116	617-217-9000	249-0400
TF: 800-815-3276 ■ *Web:* www.baystate.edu					
Benjamin Franklin Institute of Technology					
41 Berkeley St	Boston	MA	02116	617-423-4630	482-3706
TF: 877-400-2348 ■ *Web:* www.bfit.edu					
Boston Architectural College 320 Newbury St	Boston	MA	02115	617-262-5000	585-0100*
**Fax:* Admissions ■ *TF:* 877-585-0100 ■ *Web:* www.the-bac.edu					
Cambridge College Inc 1000 Mass Ave Ste 31	Cambridge	MA	02138	617-868-1000	349-3545
TF: 800-829-4723 ■ *Web:* www.cambridgecollege.edu					
FINE Mortuary College LLC 150 Kerry Pl	Norwood	MA	02062	781-762-1211	762-7177
Web: www.fine-ne.com					
ITT Technical Institute Wilmington					
200 Ballardvale St Ste 200	Wilmington	MA	01887	978-658-2636	
TF: 800-430-5097 ■ *Web:* www.itt-tech.edu					
Laboure College 303 Adams St	Milton	MA	02186	617-379-1249	690-3730
Web: www.laboure.edu					
National Aviation Academy 150 Hanscom Dr	Bedford	MA	01730	781-274-8448	274-8490
TF: 800-659-2080 ■ *Web:* www.naa.edu					
New England College of Business & Finance					
10 High St Ste 204	Boston	MA	02110	617-951-2350	951-2533
TF: 888-357-7332 ■ *Web:* www.necb.edu					
Sanford-Brown College					
Boston 126 Newbury St	Boston	MA	02116	617-578-7100	
TF: 877-809-2444 ■ *Web:* www.sanfordbrown.edu					
Academy of Court Reporting					
Clawson 1055 W Maple Rd	Clawson	MI	48017	888-314-7780	435-8570*
**Fax Area Code:* 248 ■ *TF:* 888-314-7780 ■ *Web:* www.acr.edu					
Cleary University 3601 Plymouth Rd	Ann Arbor	MI	48105	734-332-4477	332-4646
TF: 800-686-1883 ■ *Web:* www.cleary.edu					
Livingston 3750 Cleary Dr	Howell	MI	48843	517-548-3670	552-7805
TF: 800-686-1883 ■ *Web:* www.cleary.edu					
ITT Technical Institute Canton					
1905 S Haggerty Rd	Canton	MI	48188	734-397-7800	397-1945
TF: 800-247-4477 ■ *Web:* www.itt-tech.edu					
ITT Technical Institute Grand Rapids					
1980 Metro Ct SW	Wyoming	MI	49519	616-406-1200	406-1250
TF: 800-632-4676 ■ *Web:* www.itt-tech.edu					
ITT Technical Institute Troy					
1522 E Big Beaver Rd	Troy	MI	48083	248-524-1800	524-1965
TF: 800-832-6817 ■ *Web:* www.itt-tech.edu					
Anoka Technical College 1355 W Hwy 10	Anoka	MN	55303	763-433-1100	576-7701*
**Fax:* Admissions ■ *TF:* 800-627-3529 ■ *Web:* www.anokatech.edu					
Brown College					
1345 Mendota Heights Rd	Mendota Heights	MN	55120	651-905-3400	905-3540
TF: 888-574-3777 ■ *Web:* www.browncollege.edu					
Dakota County Technical College					
1300 E 145th St	Rosemount	MN	55068	651-423-8301	423-8775
TF: 877-937-3282 ■ *Web:* www.dctc.edu					
Duluth Business University (DBU)					
4724 Mike Colalilo Dr	Duluth	MN	55807	218-722-4000	628-2127
TF: 800-777-8406 ■ *Web:* www.dbumn.edu					
Dunwoody College of Technology					
818 Dunwoody Blvd	Minneapolis	MN	55403	612-374-5800	374-4128
TF: 800-292-4625 ■ *Web:* www.dunwoody.edu					
Hennepin Technical College					
9000 Brooklyn Blvd	Brooklyn Park	MN	55445	952-995-1300	488-2944*
**Fax Area Code:* 763 ■ *TF:* 800-345-4655 ■ *Web:* www.hennepintech.edu					
Northwest Technical Institute					
950 Blue Gentian Rd Ste 500	Eagan	MN	55121	952-944-0080	
Web: www.nti.edu					
Ridgewater College					
Hutchinson Two Century Ave SE	Hutchinson	MN	55350	320-234-8500	587-9019*
**Fax:* Admissions ■ *TF:* 800-722-1151 ■ *Web:* www.ridgewater.edu					
Willmar 2101 15th Ave NW PO Box 1097	Willmar	MN	56201	320-222-5200	222-5216*
**Fax:* Admissions ■ *TF:* 800-722-1151 ■ *Web:* www.ridgewater.edu					
Saint Cloud Technical & Community College					
1540 Northway Dr	Saint Cloud	MN	56303	320-308-5089	308-5981
TF: 800-222-1009 ■ *Web:* www.sctcc.edu					
Saint Paul College 235 Marshall Ave	Saint Paul	MN	55102	651-846-1600	846-1703
TF: 800-227-6029 ■ *Web:* www.saintpaul.edu					
Virginia College Gulf Coast 920 Cedar Lk Rd	Biloxi	MS	39532	228-392-2994	392-2039
Web: www.vc.edu					
Virginia College Jackson 5841 Ridgewood Rd	Jackson	MS	39211	601-977-0960	
Web: www.vc.edu					
Concorde Career Colleges inc Kansas City					
3239 Broadway	Kansas City	MO	64111	816-531-5223	756-3231
Web: www.concorde.edu					
DeVry University Kansas City					
11224 Holmes Rd	Kansas City	MO	64131	816-941-0430	943-7551
TF: 800-821-3766 ■ *Web:* www.kc.devry.edu					
Everest College 1010 W Sunshine St	Springfield	MO	65807	417-864-7220	864-5697
TF: 888-223-8556 ■ *Web:* www.everest.edu					
ITT Technical Institute Arnold					
1930 Meyer Drury Dr	Arnold	MO	63010	636-464-6600	464-6611
TF: 888-488-1082 ■ *Web:* www.itt-tech.edu					
ITT Technical Institute Earth City					
3640 Corporate Trl Dr	Earth City	MO	63045	314-298-7800	513-5750
TF: 800-235-5488 ■ *Web:* www.itt-tech.edu					
ITT Technical Institute Kansas City					
9150 E 41st Terr	Kansas City	MO	64133	816-276-1400	276-1410
TF: 877-488-1442 ■ *Web:* www.itt-tech.edu					
Vatterott College Berkeley 8580 Evans Ave	Berkeley	MO	63134	314-264-1000	
TF: 888-202-2636 ■ *Web:* www.vatterott.edu					
Vatterott College Joplin 809 Illinois Ave	Joplin	MO	64801	417-781-5633	781-6437
Web: www.vatterott.edu					
Vatterott College South County					
12970 Maurer Industrial Dr	Saint Louis	MO	63127	314-843-4200	843-1709
TF: 866-312-8276 ■ *Web:* www.vatterott.edu					
Vatterott College Springfield					
3850 S Campbell	Springfield	MO	65807	417-831-8116	831-5099*
**Fax:* Admissions ■ *TF:* 844-244-3304 ■ *Web:* www.vatterott.edu					
University of Montana					
College of Technology 909 S Ave W	Missoula	MT	59801	406-243-7852	243-7899
TF: 800-542-6882 ■ *Web:* www.mc.umt.edu					
Helena College of Technology					
1115 N Roberts St	Helena	MT	59601	406-444-6800	444-6892
TF: 800-827-1000 ■ *Web:* www.umhelena.edu					
ITT Technical Institute Omaha					
1120 N 103rd Plz Ste 200	Omaha	NE	68114	402-331-2900	452-3512
TF: 800-677-9260 ■ *Web:* www.itt-tech.edu					
Kaplan University Lincoln 1821 K St	Lincoln	NE	68508	800-987-7734	
Web: www.kaplanuniversity.edu					
Kaplan University Omaha 5425 N 103rd St	Omaha	NE	68134	402-572-8500	573-6482
TF: 800-987-7734 ■ *Web:* www.kaplanuniversity.edu					
Nebraska College of Technical Agriculture					
404 E 7th	Curtis	NE	69025	308-367-4124	367-5203
TF: 800-328-7847 ■ *Web:* www.ncta.unl.edu					
Beatrice 4771 W Scott Rd	Beatrice	NE	68310	402-228-3468	228-2218*
**Fax:* Admissions ■ *TF:* 800-233-5027 ■ *Web:* www.southeast.edu					
Milford 600 State St	Milford	NE	68405	402-761-2131	761-2324
TF: 800-933-7223 ■ *Web:* www.southeast.edu					
Vatterott College					
Omaha 11818 I St	Omaha	NE	68137	402-891-9411	
Web: www.vatterott.edu					
ITT Technical Institute Henderson					
168 Gibson Rd	Henderson	NV	89014	702-558-5404	558-5412
TF: 800-488-8459 ■ *Web:* www.itt-tech.edu					

Name / Address	City	State	Zip	Phone	Fax
Garrett Mountain 44 Rifle Camp Rd	Woodland Park	NJ	07424	973-278-5400	278-9141
TF: 800-446-5400 ■ *Web:* www.berkeleycollege.edu					
Berkeley College					
Paramus 64 E Midland Ave	Paramus	NJ	07652	201-967-9667	265-6446
TF: 800-446-5400 ■ *Web:* www.berkeleycollege.edu					
Woodbridge 430 Rahway Ave	Woodbridge	NJ	07095	732-750-1800	750-0652
TF: 800-446-5400 ■ *Web:* www.berkeleycollege.edu					
DeVry University North Brunswick 630 US Hwy 1	North Brunswick	NJ	08902	800-333-3879	729-3965*
**Fax Area Code:* 732 ■ **Fax:* Admissions ■ *TF:* 800-333-3879 ■ *Web:* www.nj.devry.edu					
Divers Academy International 1500 Liberty Pl	Erial	NJ	08081	800-238-3483	
TF: 800-238-3483 ■ *Web:* www.diversacademy.edu					
Central New Mexico Community College 10549 Universe Blvd NW	Albuquerque	NM	87114	505-224-3000	224-3237
Web: www.cnm.edu					
ITT Technical Institute Albuquerque 5100 Masthead St NE	Albuquerque	NM	87109	505-828-1114	828-1849
TF: 800-636-1114 ■ *Web:* www.itt-tech.edu					
Navajo Technical College PO Box 849	Crownpoint	NM	87313	505-786-4100	786-5644
Web: www.navajotech.edu					
Southwestern Indian Polytechnic Institute 9169 Coors Blvd NW PO Box 10146	Albuquerque	NM	87120	505-346-2306	346-2311
TF: 800-586-7474 ■ *Web:* www.sipi.edu					
American Academy McAllister Institute of Funeral Service 619 W 54th St 2nd Fl	New York	NY	10019	212-757-1190	765-5923
TF: 866-932-2264 ■ *Web:* www.funeraleducation.org					
Berkeley College New York City Three E 43rd St	New York	NY	10017	212-986-4343	818-1079
TF: 800-446-5400 ■ *Web:* www.berkeleycollege.edu					
Berkeley College White Plains 99 Church St	White Plains	NY	10601	914-694-1122	328-9469
TF: 800-446-5400 ■ *Web:* www.berkeleycollege.edu					
Bramson ORT College 69-30 Austin St	Forest Hills	NY	11375	718-261-5800	575-5119
Web: www.bramsonort.org					
Bryant & Stratton College Albany 1259 Central Ave	Albany	NY	12205	518-437-1802	437-1048
Web: www.bryantstratton.edu					
Bryant & Stratton College Amherst 3650 Millersport Hwy	Getzville	NY	14068	716-625-6300	
Web: www.bryantstratton.edu					
Bryant & Stratton College Buffalo 465 Main St Ste 400	Buffalo	NY	14203	716-884-9120	884-0091
Web: www.bryantstratton.edu					
Bryant & Stratton College Greece 150 Bellwood Dr	Rochester	NY	14606	585-720-0660	585-9226
Web: www.bryantstratton.edu					
Bryant & Stratton College Henrietta 1225 Jefferson Rd	Rochester	NY	14623	585-292-5627	292-6015
Web: www.bryantstratton.edu					
Bryant & Stratton College Southtowns 200 Red Tail	Orchard Park	NY	14127	716-677-9500	677-9599
Web: www.bryantstratton.edu					
Bryant & Stratton College Syracuse 953 James St	Syracuse	NY	13203	315-472-6603	474-4383
Web: www.bryantstratton.edu					
Bryant & Stratton College Syracuse North 8687 Carling Rd	Liverpool	NY	13090	315-652-6500	652-5500
Web: www.bryantstratton.edu					
Champlain Valley Educational Services PO Box 455	Plattsburgh	NY	12901	518-561-0100	
Web: www.cves.org					
Cochran School of Nursing 967 N Broadway	Yonkers	NY	10701	914-964-4444	964-4796
Web: www.riversidehealth.org					
College of Westchester (CW) 325 Central Ave	White Plains	NY	10606	800-660-7093	948-5441*
**Fax Area Code:* 914 ■ **Fax:* Admissions ■ *TF:* 800-660-7093 ■ *Web:* www.cw.edu					
Commercial Driver Training 600 Patton Ave	West Babylon	NY	11704	631-249-1330	
TF: 800-649-7447 ■ *Web:* www.cdtschool.com					
DeVry University Long Island City 3020 Thomson Ave	Long Island City	NY	11101	718-472-2728	269-4432*
**Fax:* Admissions ■ *TF:* 888-713-3879 ■ *Web:* www.devry.edu					
Helene Fuld College of Nursing 24 E 120th St	New York	NY	10035	212-616-7200	616-7299
Web: www.helenefuld.edu					
Institute of Design & Construction (IDC) 141 Willoughby St	Brooklyn	NY	11201	718-855-3661	852-5889
Web: www.idc.edu					
ITT Technical Institute Albany 13 Airline Dr	Albany	NY	12205	518-452-9300	452-9393
TF: 800-489-1191 ■ *Web:* www.itt-tech.edu					
ITT Technical Institute Getzville 2295 Millersport Hwy	Getzville	NY	14068	716-689-2200	689-2828
TF: 800-469-7593 ■ *Web:* www.itt-tech.edu					
ITT Technical Institute Liverpool 235 Greenfield Pkwy	Liverpool	NY	13088	315-461-8000	461-8008
TF: 877-488-0011 ■ *Web:* www.itt-tech.edu					
Jamestown Business College Seven Fairmount Ave PO Box 429	Jamestown	NY	14702	716-664-5100	664-3144
Web: www.jamestownbusinesscollege.edu					
Monroe College 2501 Jerome Ave	Bronx	NY	10468	718-933-6700	364-3552*
**Fax:* Admissions ■ *TF:* 800-556-6676 ■ *Web:* www.monroecollege.edu					
New York Career Institute 11 Pk Pl Fourth Fl	New York	NY	10007	212-962-0002	385-7574
Web: www.nyci.edu					
Phillips Beth Israel School of Nursing 776 Ave of the Americas Fourth Fl	New York	NY	10001	212-614-6110	614-6109
Web: pbisn.edu					
Plaza College 74-09 37th Ave	Jackson Heights	NY	11372	718-779-1430	779-7423
Web: www.plazacollege.edu					
Simmons Institute of Funeral Service 1828 S Ave	Syracuse	NY	13207	315-475-5142	475-3817
Web: www.simmonsinstitute.com					
TCI College of Technology 320 W 31st St	New York	NY	10001	212-594-4000	330-0891
TF: 800-878-8246 ■ *Web:* www.tcicollege.edu					
Utica School of Commerce 201 Bleecker St	Utica	NY	13501	315-733-2307	733-9281
TF: 800-321-4872 ■ *Web:* www.uscny.edu					
Wood Tobe-Coburn School Eight E 40th St	New York	NY	10016	212-686-9040	686-9171
TF: 800-394-9663 ■ *Web:* www.woodtobecoburn.edu					
Forsyth Technical Community College 2100 Silas Creek Pkwy	Winston-Salem	NC	27103	336-723-0371	761-2399
TF: 800-870-3676 ■ *Web:* www.forsythtech.edu					
ITT Technical Institute High Point 4050 Piedmont Pkwy	High Point	NC	27265	336-819-5900	819-5950
TF: 877-536-5231 ■ *Web:* www.itt-tech.edu					
South College-Asheville 140 Sweeten Creek Rd	Asheville	NC	28803	828-398-2500	
Web: www.southcollegenc.edu					
Stanly Community College 141 College Dr	Albemarle	NC	28001	704-982-0121	982-0819
TF: 877-275-4219 ■ *Web:* www.stanly.edu					
United Tribes Technical College 3315 University Dr	Bismarck	ND	58504	701-255-3285	530-0640
Web: www.uttc.edu					
Academy of Court Reporting Cleveland 2044 Euclid Ave	Cleveland	OH	44115	888-314-7780	861-4517*
**Fax Area Code:* 216 ■ *TF:* 888-314-7780 ■ *Web:* www.acr.edu					
Academy of Court Reporting Columbus 150 E Gay St	Columbus	OH	43215	614-221-7770	221-8429
TF: 866-865-8067 ■ *Web:* www.miamijacobs.edu					
Bradford School 2469 Stelzer Rd	Columbus	OH	43219	614-416-6200	416-6210*
**Fax:* Admissions ■ *TF:* 800-678-7981 ■ *Web:* www.bradfordschoolcolumbus.edu					
Brown Mackie College Akron 755 White Pond Dr	Akron	OH	44320	330-869-3600	869-3650
Web: www.brownmackie.edu					
Brown Mackie College Canton 4300 Munson Ave NW	North Canton	OH	44718	330-494-1214	494-8112
Web: www.brownmackie.edu					
Brown Mackie College Cincinnati 1011 Glendale-Milford Rd	Cincinnati	OH	45215	513-771-2424	771-3413
Web: www.brownmackie.edu					
Brown Mackie College Findlay 1700 Fostoria Ave Ste 100	Findlay	OH	45840	419-423-2211	423-0725
TF: 800-842-3687 ■ *Web:* www.brownmackie.edu					
Bryant & Stratton College					
Cleveland 3121 Euclid Ave	Cleveland	OH	44115	216-771-1700	771-7787
TF: 866-948-0571 ■ *Web:* www.bryantstratton.edu					
Eastlake 35350 Curtis Blvd	Eastlake	OH	44095	440-510-1112	306-2015
Web: www.bryantstratton.edu					
Parma 12955 Snow Rd	Parma	OH	44130	216-265-3151	265-0325
Web: www.bryantstratton.edu					
Central Ohio Technical College 1179 University Dr	Newark	OH	43055	740-366-9494	
Web: www.cotc.edu					
Cincinnati College of Mortuary Science 645 W N Bend Rd	Cincinnati	OH	45224	513-761-2020	761-3333
TF: 888-377-8433 ■ *Web:* www.ccms.edu					
Cleveland Institute of Electronics 1776 E 17th St	Cleveland	OH	44114	216-781-9400	781-0331
TF: 800-243-6446 ■ *Web:* www.cie-wc.edu					
Davis College 4747 Monroe St	Toledo	OH	43623	419-473-2700	473-2472
TF: 800-477-7021 ■ *Web:* www.daviscollege.edu					
DeVry University Dayton 3610 Pentagon Blvd Ste 100	Dayton	OH	45431	937-320-3200	320-9380
Web: www.devry.edu					
Eastern Gateway Community College 4000 Sunset Blvd	Steubenville	OH	43952	740-264-5591	264-1338
TF: 800-682-6553 ■ *Web:* egcc.edu					
ETI Technical College of Niles 2076 Youngstown-Warren Rd	Niles	OH	44446	330-652-9919	652-4399
Web: www.eticollege.edu					
Hocking College 3301 Hocking Pkwy	Nelsonville	OH	45764	740-753-3591	753-7065
TF: 877-462-5464 ■ *Web:* www.hocking.edu					
ITT Technical Institute Dayton 3325 S- Eight Rd	Dayton	OH	45414	937-264-7700	264-7799
TF: 800-568-3241 ■ *Web:* www.itt-tech.edu					
ITT Technical Institute Norwood 4750 Wesley Ave	Norwood	OH	45212	513-531-8300	531-8368
TF: 800-314-8324 ■ *Web:* www.itt-tech.edu					
ITT Technical Institute Strongsville 14955 Sprague Rd	Strongsville	OH	44136	440-234-9091	234-7694
TF: 800-331-1488 ■ *Web:* www.itt-tech.edu					
ITT Technical Institute Warrensville Heights 4700 Richmond Rd	Warrensville Heights	OH	44128	216-896-6500	896-6599
TF: 800-741-3494 ■ *Web:* www.itt-tech.edu					
ITT Technical Institute Youngstown 1030 N Meridian Rd	Youngstown	OH	44509	330-270-1600	270-8333
TF: 800-832-5001 ■ *Web:* www.itt-tech.edu					
James A Rhodes State College 4240 Campus Dr	Lima	OH	45804	419-995-8320	995-8098*
**Fax:* Admissions ■ *TF:* 866-498-4968 ■ *Web:* www.rhodesstate.edu					
Marion Technical College 1467 Mt Vernon Ave	Marion	OH	43302	740-389-4636	389-6136
TF: 800-772-1213 ■ *Web:* www.mtc.edu					
North Central State College 2441 Kenwood Cir	Mansfield	OH	44906	419-755-4800	755-4750
TF: 888-755-4899 ■ *Web:* www.ncstatecollege.edu					
Northwest State Community College 22600 SR-34	Archbold	OH	43502	419-267-5511	267-3688
Web: www.northweststate.edu					
Remington College Cleveland 14445 Broadway Ave	Cleveland	OH	44125	216-475-7520	475-6055
Web: www.remingtoncollege.edu					
Stark State College of Technology 6200 Frank Ave NW	North Canton	OH	44720	330-494-6170	497-6313
TF: 800-797-8275 ■ *Web:* www.starkstate.edu					
University of Northwestern Ohio 1441 N Cable Rd	Lima	OH	45805	419-998-3120	998-3139
Web: www.unoh.edu					
Zane State College 1555 Newark Rd	Zanesville	OH	43701	740-454-2501	454-0035
TF: 800-686-8324 ■ *Web:* www.zanestate.edu					

	City	State	ZIP	Phone	Fax
Indian Capital Technology Ctr 2403 N 41st St E	Muskogee	OK	74403	918-687-6383	
TF: 800-757-0877 ■ *Web:* www.ictctech.com					
Oklahoma State University 219 Student Union Bldg	Stillwater	OK	74078	405-744-5000	744-7092
TF: 800-852-1255 ■ *Web:* www.okstate.edu					
Okmulgee 1801 E Fourth St	Okmulgee	OK	74447	918-293-4678	293-4650
TF: 800-722-4471 ■ *Web:* go.osuit.edu					
Spartan College of Aeronautics & Technology 8820 E Pine St PO Box 582833	Tulsa	OK	74115	918-836-6886	831-5287
TF Admissions: 800-331-1204 ■ *Web:* www.spartan.edu					
ITT Technical Institute Portland 9500 NE Cascades Pkwy	Portland	OR	97220	503-255-6500	
TF: 800-234-5488 ■ *Web:* www.itt-tech.edu					
American College 270 S Bryn Mawr Ave	Bryn Mawr	PA	19010	610-526-1000	526-1300*
**Fax:* Admissions ■ *TF:* 888-263-7265 ■ *Web:* www.theamericancollege.edu					
Aviation Institute of Maintenance 3001 Grant Ave	Philadelphia	PA	19114	215-676-7700	671-0566
Web: www.aviationmaintenance.edu					
Cambria-Rowe Business College (CRBC) 221 Central Ave	Johnstown	PA	15902	814-536-5168	
TF: 800-639-2273 ■ *Web:* www.crbc.net					
Central Pennsylvania College 600 Valley Rd PO Box 309	Summerdale	PA	17093	717-732-0702	732-5254
TF: 800-759-2727 ■ *Web:* www.centralpenn.edu					
Dean Institute of Technology 1501 W Liberty Ave	Pittsburgh	PA	15226	412-531-4433	531-4435
Web: www.deantech.edu					
DeVry University Fort Washington 1140 Virginia Dr	Fort Washington	PA	19034	215-591-5700	591-5745
Web: www.devry.edu					
DuBois Business College 1 Beaver Dr	Du Bois	PA	15801	814-371-6920	371-3974
TF: 800-692-6213 ■ *Web:* www.dbcollege.com					
Erie Business Ctr *Erie* 246 W Ninth St	Erie	PA	16501	814-456-7504	456-4882
ITT Technical Institute Harrisburg 449 Eisenhower Blvd Ste 100	Harrisburg	PA	17111	717-565-1700	565-1750
TF: 800-847-4756 ■ *Web:* www.itt-tech.edu					
Johnson College 3427 N Main Ave	Scranton	PA	18508	570-342-6404	348-2181*
**Fax:* Admissions ■ *TF:* 800-293-9675 ■ *Web:* www.johnson.edu					
Kaplan Career Institute 5650 Derry St	Harrisburg	PA	17111	717-564-4112	
Web: kaplancareerinstitute.com					
Franklin Mills 177 Franklin Mills Blvd	Philadelphia	PA	19154	215-612-6600	
TF: 800-935-1857 ■ *Web:* www.kaplancareerinstitute.com					
Lansdale School of Business 290 Wissahickon Ave	North Wales	PA	19454	215-699-5700	699-8770
Web: www.lsb.edu					
Lincoln Technical Institute 9191 Torresdale Ave	Philadelphia	PA	19136	215-335-0800	335-1443
Web: www.lincolnedu.com					
Mixology Wine Institute 77 W Broad St	Bethlehem	PA	18018	610-814-2900	
Web: mixologywine.com					
Penn Commercial Inc 242 Oak Spring Rd	Washington	PA	15301	724-222-5330	222-4722
TF: 888-309-7484 ■ *Web:* www.penncommercial.edu					
Penn Foster Career School 925 Oak St	Scranton	PA	18515	570-342-7701	
Web: pennfoster.edu					
Pennco Tech 3815 Otter St	Bristol	PA	19007	215-785-0111	
TF General: 844-226-0975 ■ *Web:* www.penncotech.com					
Pennsylvania College of Technology One College Ave	Williamsport	PA	17701	570-326-3761	321-5551
TF Admissions: 800-367-9222 ■ *Web:* www.pct.edu					
Pennsylvania Institute of Technology (PIT) 800 Manchester Ave	Media	PA	19063	610-892-1500	892-1533*
**Fax:* Admissions ■ *TF Admissions:* 800-422-0025 ■ *Web:* www.pit.edu					
Philadelphia College of Osteopathic Medicine (PCOM) 4170 City Ave	Philadelphia	PA	19131	215-871-6100	
TF Admissions: 800-999-6998 ■ *Web:* www.pcom.edu					
Pittsburgh Institute of Aeronautics (PIA) Five Allegheny County Airport	West Mifflin	PA	15122	412-346-2100	346-2170
TF: 800-444-1440 ■ *Web:* www.pia.edu					
Pittsburgh Institute of Mortuary Science Inc 5808 Baum Blvd	Pittsburgh	PA	15206	412-362-8500	362-1684
TF: 800-933-5808 ■ *Web:* www.pims.edu					
Pittsburgh Technical Institute (PTI) 1111 McKee Rd	Oakdale	PA	15071	412-809-5100	809-5121*
**Fax:* Admissions ■ *TF:* 800-784-9675 ■ *Web:* www.pti.edu					
Thaddeus Stevens College of Technology (TSCT) 750 E King St	Lancaster	PA	17602	717-299-7701	391-6929
TF: 800-842-3832 ■ *Web:* www.stevenstech.org					
Triangle Tech Inc *Du Bois* PO Box 551	Du Bois	PA	15801	814-371-2090	371-9227
TF: 800-874-8324 ■ *Web:* www.triangle-tech.edu					
Erie 2000 Liberty St	Erie	PA	16502	814-453-6016	454-2818
TF: 800-874-8324 ■ *Web:* www.triangle-tech.edu					
Greensburg 222 E Pittsburgh St	Greensburg	PA	15601	724-832-1050	834-0325
TF: 800-874-8324 ■ *Web:* www.triangle-tech.edu					
Welder Training & Testing Institute 1144 N Graham St	Allentown	PA	18109	610-820-9551	820-0271
TF: 800-223-9884 ■ *Web:* www.welderinstitute.com					
Williamson Free School of Mechanical Trades, The 106 S New Middletown Rd	Media	PA	19063	610-566-1776	566-6502
TF: 888-565-1095 ■ *Web:* www.williamson.edu					
Wyotech Blairsville 500 Innovation Dr	Blairsville	PA	15717	724-459-9500	459-6499
Web: www.wyotech.edu					
New England Institute of Technology 2500 Post Rd	Warwick	RI	02886	401-467-7744	738-5122
TF: 800-736-7744 ■ *Web:* www.neit.edu					
Central Carolina Technical College 506 N Guignard Dr	Sumter	SC	29150	803-778-1961	778-6696
Web: www.sum.tec.sc.us					
Denmark Technical College 1126 Solomon Blatt Blvd PO Box 327	Denmark	SC	29042	803-793-5176	793-5942*
**Fax:* Admissions ■ *Web:* www.denmarktech.edu					
Florence-Darlington Technical College 2715 W Lucas St	Florence	SC	29502	843-661-8324	661-8041
TF: 800-228-5745 ■ *Web:* www.fdtc.edu					
Horry-Georgetown Technical College 2050 E Hwy 501	Conway	SC	29526	843-347-3186	347-4207
Web: www.hgtc.edu					
Grand Strand Campus 743 Hemlock Ave	Myrtle Beach	SC	29577	843-477-0808	477-0775
TF: 855-544-4482 ■ *Web:* www.hgtc.edu					
ITT Technical Institute Greenville Six Independence Pointe Independence Corporate Pk	Greenville	SC	29615	864-288-0777	297-0930
TF: 800-932-4488 ■ *Web:* www.itt-tech.edu					
Piedmont Technical College 620 N Emerald Rd	Greenwood	SC	29646	864-941-8324	941-8555
TF: 800-868-5528 ■ *Web:* www.ptc.edu					
Spartanburg Community College 800 Brisack Rd PO Box 4386	Spartanburg	SC	29305	864-592-4800	592-4564
TF: 866-591-3700 ■ *Web:* www.sccsc.edu					
Tri-County Technical College 7900 Hwy 76	Pendleton	SC	29670	864-646-8361	646-1890
TF: 866-269-5677 ■ *Web:* www.tctc.edu					
Trident Technical College (TTC) 7000 Rivers Ave PO Box 118067	North Charleston	SC	29406	843-574-6111	574-6483*
**Fax:* Admissions ■ *TF:* 877-349-7184 ■ *Web:* www.tridenttech.edu					
Southeast Technical Institute 2320 N Career Ave	Sioux Falls	SD	57107	605-367-8355	367-4372*
**Fax:* Hum Res ■ *TF:* 800-247-0789 ■ *Web:* www.southeasttech.edu					
Draughons Junior College 340 Plus Pk Blvd	Nashville	TN	37217	615-361-7555	367-2736
TF: 877-849-7921 ■ *Web:* daymarinstitute.edu					
Fountainhead College of Technology 3203 Tazewell Pk	Knoxville	TN	37918	865-688-9422	688-2419
TF: 888-218-7335 ■ *Web:* www.fountainheadcollege.edu					
ITT Technical Institute Cordova 7260 Goodlett Farms Pkwy	Cordova	TN	38016	901-381-0200	381-0299
TF: 866-444-5141 ■ *Web:* www.itt-tech.edu					
ITT Technical Institute Nashville 2845 Elm Hill Pk	Nashville	TN	37214	615-889-8700	872-7209
TF: 800-331-8386 ■ *Web:* www.itt-tech.edu					
John A Gupton College 1616 Church St	Nashville	TN	37203	615-327-3927	321-4518
Web: guptoncollege.edu					
Nashville State Community College (NSCC) 120 White Bridge Rd	Nashville	TN	37209	615-353-3333	353-3243*
**Fax:* Admissions ■ *TF:* 800-272-7363 ■ *Web:* www.nscc.edu					
National College of Business & Technology Bristol 1328 Hwy 11 W	Bristol	TN	37620	423-878-4440	
TF: 888-956-2732 ■ *Web:* www.national-college.edu					
National College of Business & Technology Nashville 1638 Bell Rd	Nashville	TN	37211	615-333-3344	
TF: 855-800-1715 ■ *Web:* national-college.edu					
Northeast State Technical Community College 2425 Hwy 75 PO Box 246	Blountville	TN	37617	423-323-3191	323-0217
TF: 800-836-7822 ■ *Web:* www.northeaststate.edu					
Remington College Memphis 2710 Nonconnah Blvd	Memphis	TN	38132	901-345-1000	396-8310
Web: www.remingtoncollege.edu					
South College 3904 Lonas Dr	Knoxville	TN	37909	865-251-1800	584-7339
TF: 877-557-2575 ■ *Web:* www.southcollegetn.edu					
Aviation Institute of Maintenance Houston 7651 Airport Blvd	Houston	TX	77061	713-644-7777	644-0902
TF: 888-349-5387 ■ *Web:* www.aviationmaintenance.edu					
Court Reporting Institute of Dallas 1341 W Mockingbird Ln Ste 200-E	Dallas	TX	75247	214-350-9722	631-0143
TF: 866-382-1284 ■ *Web:* www.cri.edu					
Court Reporting Institute of Houston 13101 NW Fwy Ste 100	Houston	TX	77040	713-996-8300	
TF: 866-996-8300 ■ *Web:* www.cri.edu					
Dallas Institute of Funeral Service 3909 S Buckner Blvd	Dallas	TX	75227	214-388-5466	388-0316
TF: 800-235-5444 ■ *Web:* www.dallasinstitute.edu					
DeVry University Houston 11125 Equity Dr	Houston	TX	77041	713-973-3100	896-7650
TF: 866-703-3879 ■ *Web:* www.devry.edu					
DeVry University Irving 4800 Regent Blvd	Irving	TX	75063	972-929-6777	929-6778
TF: 800-633-3879 ■ *Web:* www.dal.devry.edu					
Everest Institute San Antonio 6550 First Pk Ten Blvd	San Antonio	TX	78213	210-732-7800	731-9313
Web: www.everest.edu					
ITT Technical Institute Arlington 551 Ryan Plz Dr	Arlington	TX	76011	817-794-5100	275-8446*
**Fax:* Admissions ■ *TF:* 888-288-4950 ■ *Web:* www.itt-tech.edu					
ITT Technical Institute Austin 6330 Hwy 290 E Ste 150	Austin	TX	78723	512-467-6800	467-7656
TF: 800-431-0677 ■ *Web:* www.itt-tech.edu					
ITT Technical Institute Houston 15651 N Fwy	Houston	TX	77090	281-873-0512	873-0518*
**Fax:* Admissions ■ *TF:* 800-879-6486 ■ *Web:* www.itt-tech.edu					
ITT Technical Institute Richardson 2101 Waterview Pkwy	Richardson	TX	75080	972-690-9100	690-0853
TF: 888-488-5761 ■ *Web:* www.itt-tech.edu					
ITT Technical Institute San Antonio 5700 NW Pkwy	San Antonio	TX	78249	210-694-4612	694-4651*
**Fax:* Admissions ■ *TF:* 800-880-0570 ■ *Web:* www.itt-tech.edu					
Remington College Dallas 1800 Eastgate Dr	Garland	TX	75041	972-686-7878	686-5116
Web: www.remingtoncollege.edu					
Wade College 1950 N Stemmons Fwy Ste 2026	Dallas	TX	75207	214-637-3530	637-0827
TF: 800-624-4850 ■ *Web:* www.wadecollege.edu					
Westwood College Dallas 8390 LBJ Fwy Ste 100 Executive Ctr 1	Dallas	TX	75243	800-281-2978	756-6979*
**Fax Area Code:* 214 ■ **Fax:* Admissions ■ *TF:* 800-331-4879 ■ *Web:* www.westwood.edu					
ITT Technical Institute Murray 920 Levoy Dr	Murray	UT	84123	801-263-3313	263-3497
TF: 800-365-2136 ■ *Web:* www.itt-tech.edu					
Latter Day Saints Business College 95 North 300 West	Salt Lake City	UT	84101	801-524-8100	524-1900
TF: 800-999-5767 ■ *Web:* www.ldsbc.edu					
Sterling College PO Box 72	Craftsbury Common	VT	05827	802-586-7711	586-2596
TF: 800-648-3591 ■ *Web:* www.sterlingcollege.edu					

	City	State	Zip	Phone	Fax
Vermont Technical College PO Box 500 *TF:* 800-442-8821 ■ *Web:* www.vtc.edu	Randolph Center	VT	05061	802-728-1000	728-1321
Bryant & Stratton College Richmond 8141 Hull St Rd *TF:* 866-948-0571 ■ *Web:* www.bryantstratton.edu	Richmond	VA	23235	804-745-2444	745-6884
Bryant & Stratton College Virginia Beach 301 Ctr Pt Dr *Web:* www.bryantstratton.edu	Virginia Beach	VA	23462	757-499-7900	499-9977
DeVry University Crystal City 2450 Crystal Dr *Web:* www.devry.edu	Arlington	VA	22202	703-414-4000	414-4040
ITT Technical Institute Norfolk 5425 Robin Hood Rd Ste 100 *TF:* 888-253-8324 ■ *Web:* www.itt-tech.edu	Norfolk	VA	23513	757-466-1260	466-7630
ITT Technical Institute Richmond 300 Gateway Centre Pkwy *TF:* 888-330-4888 ■ *Web:* www.itt-tech.edu	Richmond	VA	23235	804-330-4992	330-4993
ITT Technical Institute Springfield 7300 Boston Blvd *TF:* 866-817-8324 ■ *Web:* www.itt-tech.edu	Springfield	VA	22153	703-440-9535	440-9561
Jefferson College of Health Sciences 101 Elm Ave SE *TF:* 888-985-8483 ■ *Web:* www.jchs.edu	Roanoke	VA	24031	540-985-8483	224-6703
Charlottesville 3926 Seminole Trl *Web:* national-college.edu	Charlottesville	VA	22911	434-295-0136	979-8061
Danville 336 Old Riverside Dr *Web:* www.national-college.edu	Danville	VA	24541	434-793-6822	793-3634
Harrisonburg 1515 Country Club Rd *Web:* an.edu	Harrisonburg	VA	22802	540-432-0943	
National College of Business & Technology *Lynchburg* 104 Candlewood Ct *Web:* national-college.edu	Lynchburg	VA	24502	434-239-3500	239-3948
Martinsville 905 N Memorial Blvd *Web:* www.national-college.edu	Martinsville	VA	24112	276-632-5621	632-7915
Roanoke Valley 1813 E Main St *TF:* 800-664-1886 ■ *Web:* www.national-college.edu	Salem	VA	24153	540-986-1800	
Westwood College Arlington Ballston 4300 Wilson Blvd Ste 200 *Web:* www.westwood.edu	Arlington	VA	22203	703-243-3900	243-3992
DeVry University Federal Way 3600 S 344th Way **Fax:* Admissions ■ *TF:* 877-923-3879 ■ *Web:* www.devry.edu	Federal Way	WA	98001	253-943-2800	943-3291*
Highline Community College 2400 S 240th St *Web:* www.highline.edu	Des Moines	WA	98198	206-878-3710	870-4855
ITT Technical Institute Seattle 12720 Gateway Dr Ste 100 *TF:* 800-422-2029 ■ *Web:* www.itt-tech.edu	Seattle	WA	98168	206-244-3300	246-7635
Everest Institute 5514 Big Tyler Rd *Web:* www.everest.edu	Cross Lanes	WV	25313	304-776-6290	776-6262
Huntington Junior College 900 Fifth Ave *TF:* 800-344-4522 ■ *Web:* www.huntingtonjuniorcollege.com	Huntington	WV	25701	304-697-7550	697-7554
West Virginia Junior College *Charleston* 1000 Virginia St E *TF:* 800-924-5208 ■ *Web:* www.wvjc.edu	Charleston	WV	25301	304-345-2820	345-1425
Morgantown 148 Willey St *Web:* www.wvjc.edu	Morgantown	WV	26505	304-296-8282	581-6990
West Virginia Junior College - Bridgeport 176 Thompson Dr *TF:* 800-470-5627 ■ *Web:* www.wvjc.edu	Bridgeport	WV	26330	304-842-4007	842-8191
Blackhawk Technical College 6004 S County Rd G *TF:* 800-498-1282 ■ *Web:* www.blackhawk.edu	Janesville	WI	53546	608-758-6900	743-4407
Bryant & Stratton College Milwaukee 310 W Wisconsin Ave Ste 500-E *TF:* 866-948-0571 ■ *Web:* www.bryantstratton.edu	Milwaukee	WI	53203	414-276-5200	276-3930
Chippewa Valley Technical College 620 W Clairemont Ave *TF:* 800-547-2882 ■ *Web:* www.cvtc.edu	Eau Claire	WI	54701	715-833-6200	833-6470
Fox Valley Technical College 1825 N Bluemound Dr PO Box 2277 *TF:* 800-735-3882 ■ *Web:* www.fvtc.edu	Appleton	WI	54912	920-735-5600	735-2484
Gateway Technical College 3520 30th Ave *TF:* 800-247-7122 ■ *Web:* www.gtc.edu	Kenosha	WI	53144	262-564-2200	564-2201
Herzing College Madison 5218 E Terr Dr *TF:* 800-582-1227 ■ *Web:* www.herzing.edu	Madison	WI	53718	608-249-6611	249-8593
ITT Technical Institute Greenfield 6300 W Layton Ave *Web:* www.itt-tech.edu	Greenfield	WI	53220	414-282-9494	282-9698
Lakeshore Technical College 1290 N Ave *TF:* 888-468-6582 ■ *Web:* www.gotoltc.com	Cleveland	WI	53015	920-693-1000	693-3561
Madison Area Technical College 1701 Wright St *Web:* www.madisoncollege.edu	Madison	WI	53704	608-246-6100	246-6880
Milwaukee Area Technical College 700 W State St *TF:* 866-211-3380 ■ *Web:* www.matc.edu	Milwaukee	WI	53233	414-297-6600	297-6496
Moraine Park Technical College 235 N National Ave *TF:* 800-472-4554 ■ *Web:* www.morainepark.edu	Fond du Lac	WI	54935	920-922-8611	924-3421
Northcentral Technical College 1000 W Campus Dr *TF:* 888-682-7144 ■ *Web:* www.ntc.edu	Wausau	WI	54401	715-675-3331	675-9776
Northeast Wisconsin Technical College PO Box 19042 *TF:* 800-422-6982 ■ *Web:* www.nwtc.edu	Green Bay	WI	54307	920-498-5400	498-6882
Southwest Wisconsin Technical College (SWTC) 1800 Bronson Blvd *TF:* 800-362-3322 ■ *Web:* www.swtc.edu	Fennimore	WI	53809	608-822-3262	822-6019
Waukesha County Technical College 800 Main St *Web:* www.wctc.edu	Pewaukee	WI	53072	262-691-5566	
Western Technical College 400 Seventh St N *TF:* 800-322-9982 ■ *Web:* www.westerntc.edu	La Crosse	WI	54601	608-785-9200	789-6206
Wisconsin Indianhead Technical College *New Richmond Campus* 1019 S Knowles Ave *TF:* 800-243-9482 ■ *Web:* www.witc.edu	New Richmond	WI	54017	715-246-6561	246-2777
Rice Lake Campus 1900 College Dr *TF:* 800-243-9482 ■ *Web:* www.witc.edu	Rice Lake	WI	54868	715-234-7082	234-5172
Superior Campus 600 N 21 St *TF:* 800-243-9482 ■ *Web:* www.witc.edu	Superior	WI	54880	715-394-6677	394-3771
WyoTech 4373 N Third St *Web:* www.wyotech.com	Laramie	WY	82072	307-742-3776	

804 VOTING SYSTEMS & SOFTWARE

	City	State	Zip	Phone	Fax
Avante International Technology Inc (AIT) 70 Washington Rd *TF:* 800-735-5040 ■ *Web:* www.aitechnology.com	Princeton Junction	NJ	08550	609-799-9388	799-9308
Diebold Inc 5995 Mayfair Rd *NYSE:* DBD ■ *TF:* 800-999-3600 ■ *Web:* www.diebold.com	North Canton	OH	44720	330-490-4000	
Dynapar 1675 Delany Rd *TF General:* 800-873-8731 ■ *Web:* www.dynapar.com	Gurnee	IL	60031	800-873-8731	
Election Data Corp 29751 Vly Ctr Rd *Web:* www.electiondata.com	Valley Center	CA	92082	760-751-1131	751-1141
Election Services Corp 70 Trade Zone Ct *Web:* electionservicescorp.com	Ronkonkoma	NY	11779	516-248-4200	248-4770
Election Systems & Software Inc 11208 John Galt Blvd *TF General:* 877-377-8683 ■ *Web:* essvote.com	Omaha	NE	68137	402-593-0101	593-8107
Elections USA Inc 1927 E Saw Mill Rd *TF:* 800-789-8683 ■ *Web:* www.electionsusainc.com	Quakertown	PA	18951	215-538-0779	538-3283
Hart InterCivic 15500 Wells Port Dr PO Box 80649 *TF:* 800-223-4278 ■ *Web:* www.hartintercivic.com	Austin	TX	78708	512-252-6400	252-6466
MicroVote General Corp 6366 Guilford Ave *TF:* 800-257-4901 ■ *Web:* www.microvote.com	Indianapolis	IN	46220	317-257-4900	254-3269
UniLect Corp PO Box 3026 *TF:* 888-864-5328 ■ *Web:* www.unilect.com	Danville	CA	94526	925-833-8660	833-8874

805 WALLCOVERINGS

	City	State	Zip	Phone	Fax
Blonder Home Accents 3950 Prospect Ave	Cleveland	OH	44115	216-431-3561	431-4748
Blue Mountain Wallcoverings Inc 15 Akron Rd *TF:* 866-563-9872 ■ *Web:* www.blmtn.com	Etobicoke	ON	M8W1T3	416-251-1678	
Butler/Newco Printing & Laminating Inc 250 Hamburg Tpke *Web:* www.butlerprinting.com	Butler	NJ	07405	973-838-8550	838-1767
Fashion Wallcoverings 4005 Carnegie Ave *TF Orders:* 800-362-9930 ■ *Web:* www.fashionwallcoverings.com	Cleveland	OH	44103	216-432-1600	432-0800
Goldcrest Wallcoverings PO Box 245 *TF:* 800-535-9513 ■ *Web:* www.wallcovering.com	Slingerlands	NY	12159	518-478-7214	478-7216
J Josephson Inc 35 Horizon Blvd **Fax:* Cust Svc ■ *Web:* www.jjosephson.com	South Hackensack	NJ	07606	201-440-7000	440-7109*
Thibaut Inc 480 Frelinghuysen Ave *TF:* 800-223-0704 ■ *Web:* www.thibautdesign.com	Newark	NJ	07114	973-643-1118	643-3050
York Wallcoverings Inc 750 Linden Ave PO Box 5166 *TF:* 800-375-9675 ■ *Web:* www.yorkwall.com	York	PA	17405	717-846-4456	843-5624

806 WAREHOUSING & STORAGE

SEE ALSO Logistics Services (Transportation & Warehousing) p. 2673

806-1 Commercial Warehousing

	City	State	Zip	Phone	Fax
Acme Distribution Centers Inc 18101 E Colfax Ave *TF:* 800-444-3614 ■ *Web:* www.acmedistribution.com	Aurora	CO	80011	303-340-2100	340-2424
Action Warehouse Company Ltd 1500 Delaware Ave *Web:* www.actionwarehouse.com	Des Moines	IA	50317	515-265-2099	
All Source Security Container Mfg Corp 40 Mills Rd *TF:* 866-526-4579 ■ *Web:* www.allsourcemfg.com	Barrie	ON	L4N6H4	705-726-6460	726-5017
American Warehouses Inc 1918 Collingsworth St *Web:* www.americanwarehouses.com	Houston	TX	77009	713-228-6381	228-5913
ASW Global LLC 3375 Gilchrist Rd *TF:* 888-826-5087 ■ *Web:* www.aswglobal.com	Mogadore	OH	44260	330-733-6291	
ATCO Industries Inc 7300 Fifteen Mile Rd *Web:* www.atcoindustries.com	Sterling Heights	MI	48312	586-795-9595	
Automated Records Management Systems Inc 1850 Enterprise Dr *Web:* www.arms4rim.com	De Pere	WI	54115	920-339-0135	
Barrett Distribution Centers Inc 15 Freedom Way *Web:* www.barrettdistribution.com	Franklin	MA	02038	508-553-8800	
Bay Logistics Inc 1202 Pontaluna Rd *Web:* www.baylogistics.com	Spring Lake	MI	49456	231-799-1015	
Brundage Management Co Inc 254 Spencer Ln *TF:* 800-531-7652 ■ *Web:* www.brundagemgt.com	San Antonio	TX	78201	210-735-9393	735-2061
Case Systems Inc 2700 James Savage Rd *Web:* www.casesystems.com	Midland	MI	48642	989-496-9510	

Company	City	State	Zip	Phone	Fax
Customized Distribution Services Inc 20 Harry Shupe Blvd. *Web:* www.dsdcds.com	Wharton	NJ	07885	973-366-5090	
D & D Distribution Services Inc 789 Kings Mill Rd. *Web:* www.dd-dist.com	York	PA	17403	717-845-1646	846-0414
Dart Entities 1430 S Eastman Ave *Web:* www.dartentities.com	Los Angeles	CA	90023	323-264-1011	264-6925
Datalok Co 5990 Malburg Way *TF:* 800-232-8256 ■ *Web:* www.datalok.com	Los Angeles	CA	90058	323-582-6100	581-8285
DD Jones Transfer & Warehouse Co Inc 2121 Old Greenbrier Rd *TF:* 800-335-4787 ■ *Web:* www.ddjones.com	Chesapeake	VA	23320	757-494-0225	494-0291
Derby Industries LLC 4451 Robards Ln. *TF:* 800-569-4812 ■ *Web:* www.derbyllc.com	Louisville	KY	40218	502-451-7373	451-6330
Distribution Technology Inc 1701 Continental Blvd *Web:* www.distributiontechnology.com	Charlotte	NC	28273	704-587-5587	587-5591
E L Hamm Assoc Inc 4801 Columbus St Ste 400. *Web:* www.elhamm.com	Virginia Beach	VA	23462	757-497-5000	497-5707
Evans Distribution Systems 18765 Seaway Dr *TF:* 800-653-8267 ■ *Web:* www.evansdist.com	Melvindale	MI	48122	313-388-3200	388-0136
Federal Compress & Warehouse Company Inc (FCWI) 6060 Primacy Pkwy Ste 400. *Web:* www.federalcompress.com	Memphis	TN	38119	901-524-4000	524-4050
GSC Logistics Inc 530 Water St Fifth Fl *Web:* www.gschq.com	Oakland	CA	94607	510-844-3700	
Gulf Compress 201 N 19th St PO Box 1378 *Web:* www.gulfcompress.com	Corpus Christi	TX	78408	361-882-5489	882-8081
Gulf Winds International Inc 411 Brisbane St. *TF:* 866-238-4909 ■ *Web:* www.gwii.com	Houston	TX	77061	713-747-4909	747-5330
Habco Beverage Systems Inc 501 Gordon Baker Rd *TF:* 800-448-0244 ■ *Web:* www.habcotech.com	Toronto	ON	M2H2S6	416-491-6008	491-6982
Harley Marine Services Inc 910 SW Spokane St *Web:* www.harleymarine.com	Seattle	WA	98134	206-628-0051	
Holman Distribution Ctr of Oregon Inc 2300 SE Beta St *Web:* holmanusa.com	Milwaukie	OR	97222	503-652-1912	
Hyperlogistics Group Inc 9301 Intermodal Ct N Rickenbacker Global Logistics Pk *Web:* www.hyperlog.com	Columbus	OH	43217	614-497-0800	
Iron Mountain 745 Atlantic Ave *NYSE: IRM* ■ *TF:* 800-899-4766 ■ *Web:* www.ironmountain.com	Boston	MA	02111	617-535-4766	350-7881
Kenco Group Inc 2001 Riverside Dr. **Fax Area Code: 423* ■ *TF:* 800-758-3289 ■ *Web:* www.kencogroup.com	Chattanooga	TN	37406	800-758-3289	643-3500*
Longistics Transportation Inc 10900 World Trade Blvd *TF:* 800-289-0082 ■ *Web:* www.longistics.com	Raleigh	NC	27617	919-872-7626	872-2883
Mackinnon Transport Inc 405 Laird Rd *TF:* 800-265-9394 ■ *Web:* www.mackinnontransport.com	Guelph	ON	N1G4P7	519-821-2311	821-1834
Mid-West Terminal Warehouse Company Inc 1700 Universal Ave. *Web:* www.mwtco.com	Kansas City	MO	64120	816-231-8811	231-0020
Monsoon Commerce Solutions Inc 1250 45th St Ste 100 *TF:* 800-520-2294 ■ *Web:* www.monsooncommerce.com	Emeryville	CA	94608	510-594-4500	652-2403
MSI General Corp PO Box 7 *Web:* www.msigeneral.com	Oconomowoc	WI	53066	262-367-3661	367-7390
Murphy Warehouse Co 701 24th Ave SE *Web:* www.murphywarehouse.com	Minneapolis	MN	55414	612-623-1200	623-9108
Offshore International Inc 8350 E Old Vail Rd *Web:* www.offshoregroup.com	Tucson	AZ	85747	520-889-0022	
Oilseeds International Ltd Eight Jackson St *Web:* www.oilseedssf.com	San Francisco	CA	94111	415-956-7251	
Pacific Storage Co PO Box 334 *TF:* 888-823-5467 ■ *Web:* www.pacificstorage.com	Stockton	CA	95201	209-320-6600	465-9533
PenserSC 11001 Pritchard Rd. *Web:* www.pensersc.com	Jacksonville	FL	32219	904-786-1811	
Quality Logistics Systems Inc PO Box 5637 *Web:* www.qualitylogistics.com	Meridian	MS	39302	601-483-0265	483-7928
Recall Inc 180 Technology Pkwy NW 180 Technology Pkwy. *TF:* 888-732-2556 ■ *Web:* www.recall.com	Norcross	GA	30092	888-732-2556	
Robinson Terminal Warehouse Corp 1 Oronoco St *Web:* www.robinsonterminal.com	Alexandria	VA	22314	703-836-8300	836-8307
Security Storage Co 1701 Florida Ave NW. *TF:* 800-736-6825 ■ *Web:* www.secor-group.com	Washington	DC	20009	202-234-5600	234-3513
SFI of Tennessee LLC 4768 Hungerford Rd. *Web:* www.sfifab.com	Memphis	TN	38118	901-363-1571	
Shippers Group, The 8901 Forney Rd. *Web:* www.shipperswarehouse.com	Dallas	TX	75227	214-381-5050	
Smart Warehousing LLC 18905 Kill Creek Rd *Web:* www.smartwarehousing.com	Edgerton	KS	66021	913-888-3222	888-6322
SOPAKCO Inc 118 S Cypress St *Web:* www.sopakco.com	Mullins	SC	29574	843-464-7851	464-2096
Southern Warehousing & Distribution Inc 3232 N Pan Am Expy *Web:* www.southernwd.com	San Antonio	TX	78219	210-224-7771	226-9485
SRC Logistics Inc 2065 E Pythian *Web:* www.srclogisticsinc.com	Springfield	MO	65802	417-864-4946	
States Logistics Services Inc 5650 Dolly Ave. *Web:* www.stateslogistics.com	Buena Park	CA	90621	714-521-6520	
Tejas Logistics System PO Box 1339. *TF:* 800-535-9786 ■ *Web:* www.tejaswarehouse.com	Waco	TX	76703	254-753-0301	752-4452
Tri Union Express Inc 1939 N Lafayette Ct. *TF:* 800-228-9098 ■ *Web:* www.triunion.com	Griffith	IN	46319	219-838-5400	838-1680
Triad Manufacturing Inc 4321 Semple Ave *Web:* www.triadmfg.com	Saint Louis	MO	63120	314-381-5280	381-7786
Vanderpol's Eggs Ltd 3911 Mt Lehman Rd *Web:* www.vanderpolseggs.com	Abbotsford	BC	V4X2N1	604-856-4127	
Verst Group Logistics Inc 300 Shorland Dr. *Web:* www.verstgroup.com	Walton	KY	41094	859-485-1212	
W O W Logistics Co 3040 W Wisconsin Ave *TF:* 800-236-3565 ■ *Web:* www.wowlogistics.com	Appleton	WI	54914	920-734-9924	734-2697
Willis Day Storage Co 4100 Bennett Rd PO Box 676 *Web:* willisday.com	Toledo	OH	43697	419-476-8000	476-1087

806-2 Refrigerated Storage

Company	City	State	Zip	Phone	Fax
American Growers Cooling Co 1225 Abbott St.	Salinas	CA	93901	831-753-6555	
Berkshire Refrigerated Warehousing 4550 S Packers Ave	Chicago	IL	60609	773-254-2424	
Burris Logistics 501 SE Fifth St PO Box 219. *TF:* 800-805-8135 ■ *Web:* www.burrislogistics.com	Milford	DE	19963	302-839-5157	839-5175
MTC Logistics 4851 Holabird Ave *Web:* mtccold.com	Baltimore	MD	21224	410-342-9300	522-1163
New Orleans Cold Storage & Warehouse Company Inc (NOCS) 3411 JouRdan Rd. *TF:* 800-782-2653 ■ *Web:* www.nocs.com	New Orleans	LA	70126	504-944-4400	
Perley-Halladay Assn Inc 1037 Andrew Dr *TF:* 800-248-5800 ■ *Web:* www.perleyhalladay.com	West Chester	PA	19380	610-296-5800	647-1711
United Freezer & Storage Co 650 N Meridian Rd PO Box 2446 *TF:* 800-716-1416 ■ *Web:* www.unitedfreezer.com	Youngstown	OH	44509	330-792-1739	792-2299
US Cold Storage Inc 201 Laurel Rd Ste 400 4 Echelon Plz *Web:* www.uscoldstorage.com	Voorhees	NJ	08043	856-354-8181	772-1876

806-3 Self-Storage Facilities

Company	City	State	Zip	Phone	Fax
A-American Self Storage Management Co Inc 11560 Tennessee Ave. *TF:* 888-333-6479 ■ *Web:* www.aamericanselfstorage.com	Los Angeles	CA	90064	310-914-4022	914-4042
Derrel's Mini Storage 3265 W Ashlan Ave. *Web:* www.derrels.com	Fresno	CA	93722	559-224-9900	224-1884
Devon Self Storage Holdings LLC 2000 Powell St Ste 1240 *TF:* 800-326-3199 ■ *Web:* www.devonselfstorage.com	Emeryville	CA	94608	510-450-1300	450-1325
Executive Self Storage Assoc Inc 5353 W Dartmouth Ave Ste 401 *Web:* www.executiveselfstorage.com	Denver	CO	80227	303-703-1289	703-1289
Hammond North Condominium Assn 5300 Hamilton Ave.	Cincinnati	OH	45224	513-541-5252	
Lock Up Self Storage, The 800 Frontage Rd *Web:* www.thelockup.com	Northfield	IL	60093	847-441-7477	441-7732
Metro Storage LLC 13528 Boulton Blvd *TF Cust Svc:* 888-498-1660 ■ *Web:* www.metrostorage.com	Lake Forest	IL	60045	847-235-8900	235-8901
Olson Bros Contractors Inc 829 Chambers St	South Haven	MI	49090	269-637-4494	
Public Storage Inc 701 Western Ave. *NYSE: PSA* ■ **Fax:* Mail Rm ■ *TF Cust Svc:* 800-567-0759 ■ *Web:* www.publicstorage.com	Glendale	CA	91201	818-244-8080	291-1015*
Shader Bros Corp 6325 Edgewater Dr *Web:* www.personalministorage.com	Orlando	FL	32810	407-297-3683	578-0400
Sovran Self Storage Inc 6467 Main St. *NYSE: SSS* ■ *TF:* 800-242-1715 ■ *Web:* www.unclebobs.com	Buffalo	NY	14221	716-633-1850	633-3397
Stor-All Storage 1375 W Hillsboro Blvd *TF:* 877-786-7255 ■ *Web:* www.stor-all.com	Deerfield Beach	FL	33442	954-421-7888	426-1108

807 WASTE MANAGEMENT

SEE ALSO Recyclable Materials Recovery p. 3046; Remediation Services p. 3048

Company	City	State	Zip	Phone	Fax
Allied Waste Bettendorf 6449 Valley Dr *Web:* www.republicservices.com	Bettendorf	IA	52722	563-332-0050	332-4464
ARC Disposal & Recycling Company Inc 2101 S Busse Rd *Web:* www.republicservices.com	Mount Prospect	IL	60056	847-981-0091	981-9180
Aspen Waste Systems Inc 2951 Weeks Ave SE *Web:* www.aspenwaste.com	Minneapolis	MN	55414	612-884-8000	884-8010
Athens Services 14048 Valley Blvd. *TF:* 888-336-6100 ■ *Web:* www.athensservices.com	La Puente	CA	91746	626-336-3636	330-4686
Avalon Holdings Corp One American Way *NYSE: AWX* ■ *Web:* www.avalonholdings.com	Warren	OH	44484	330-856-8800	856-8480
Basin Disposal Inc 2021 N Commercial Ave. *TF:* 800-642-6447 ■ *Web:* www.basindisposal.com	Pasco	WA	99301	509-547-2476	547-8617
Bend Garbage & Recycling Inc 20835 NE Montana St PO Box 504. *Web:* www.bendgarbage.com	Bend	OR	97709	541-382-2263	383-3640
Bluebonnet Waste Control PO Box 223845 *Web:* www.bluebonnetwaste.com	Dallas	TX	75222	214-748-5221	748-6886
Boston Harbor Association, The 374 Congress St Ste 307 *Web:* www.tbha.org	Boston	MA	02210	617-482-1722	
Burrtec Waste Industries Inc 9890 Cherry Ave *TF:* 888-287-7832 ■ *Web:* www.burrtec.com	Fontana	CA	92335	909-429-4200	429-4291
CalMet Services Inc 9821 Downey Norwalk Rd *Web:* www.calmetservices.com	Downey	CA	90241	562-869-0901	529-7958

Phone Fax

Casella Waste Systems Inc 25 Greens Hill Ln .... Rutland VT 05701 802-775-0325
NASDAQ: CWST ■ *TF:* 800-227-3552 ■ *Web:* www.casella.com

Catalytic Products International Inc
980 Ensell Rd .... Lake Zurich IL 60047 847-438-0334
Web: www.cpilink.com

Coalition for Buzzards Bay Inc, The
114 Front St .... New Bedford MA 02740 508-999-6363
Web: www.savebuzzardsbay.org

Community Waste Disposal Inc
2010 California Crossing .... Dallas TX 75220 972-392-9300 392-9301
Web: www.communitywastedisposal.com

Consolidated Disposal Services Inc
12949 Telegraph Rd .... Santa Fe Springs CA 90670 800-299-4898 347-4051*
**Fax Area Code:* 562 ■ *TF:* 800-299-4898 ■ *Web:* republicservices.com

Curtis Bay Energy 3200 Hawkins Pt Rd .... Baltimore MD 21226 410-354-3228 354-3591
Web: curtisbaymws.com/

Deffenbaugh Industries Inc
2601 Midwest Dr .... Kansas City KS 66111 913-631-3300 667-8798
TF: 800-631-3301 ■ *Web:* deffenbaughinc.com

Dolphins Plus Inc 31 Corrine Pl .... Key Largo FL 33037 305-451-1993
Web: dolphinsplus.com

Duncan Disposal Co
Arlington 1212 Harrison Ave .... Arlington TX 76011 817-317-2000 860-0330
Web: www.republicservices.com

E J Harrison & Sons PO Box 4009 .... Ventura CA 93007 805-647-1414 644-7751
TF: 800-418-7274 ■ *Web:* www.ejharrison.com

Edco Disposal Corp 6670 Federal Blvd .... Lemon Grove CA 91945 619-287-7555 287-4073
Web: www.edcodisposal.com

EL Harvey & Sons Inc 68 Hopkinton Rd. .... Westborough MA 01581 508-836-3000 836-3040
TF: 800-321-3002 ■ *Web:* www.elharvey.com

EnergySolutions LLC
423 West Broadway Ste 200 .... Salt Lake City UT 84101 801-649-2000 321-0453
Web: www.energysolutions.com

Exp Pharmaceutical Services Corp
48021 Warm Springs Blvd .... Fremont CA 94539 510-476-0909 933-1470
TF: 800-350-0397 ■ *Web:* www.expworld.com

Gilton Solid Waste Management
755 S Yosemite Ave .... Oakdale CA 95361 209-527-3781 527-0422
TF: 800-894-8980 ■ *Web:* www.gilton.com

Headwaters Inc
10653 Riverfront Pkwy Ste 300. .... South Jordan UT 84095 801-984-9400 984-9410
NYSE: HW ■ *Web:* www.headwaters.com

Health & Environment Dept
130 S Market St Ste 6050 .... Wichita KS 67202 316-337-6020
Web: www.kdhe.state.ks.us

Heritage Environmental Services Inc
7901 W Morris St .... Indianapolis IN 46231 317-243-0811 486-5085
Web: www.heritage-enviro.com

Homewood Disposal Service Inc
1501 W 175th St. .... Homewood IL 60430 708-798-1004 798-7193
Web: www.homewooddisposal.com

K B Recycling Inc PO Box 550 .... Canby OR 97013 503-266-7903 263-6477
Web: www.kbrecycling.com

Kaiser Ventures LLC
3633 Inland Empire Blvd Ste 480 .... Ontario CA 91764 909-483-8500

Knox County Health Dept
11660 Upper Gilchrist Rd .... Mount Vernon OH 43050 740-392-2200
Web: www.knoxhealth.com

Land-municipal Solid Waste
4244 International Pkwy Ste 104 .... Atlanta GA 30354 404-362-2692
Web: www.dnr.state.ga.us

Little Rock Wastewater 11 Clearwater Dr .... Little Rock AR 72204 501-376-2903 688-1409
Web: www.lrwu.com

Maine Coast Heritage Trust
One Bowdoin Mill Island Ste 201 .... Topsham ME 04086 207-729-7366
Web: www.mcht.org

Metro Waste Authority
300 E Locust St Ste 100 .... Des Moines IA 50309 515-244-0021 244-9477
Web: www.mwatoday.com

Modern Corp 4746 Model City Rd .... Model City NY 14107 716-754-8226 754-8964
TF: 800-662-0012 ■ *Web:* www.moderncorporation.com

N-Viro International Corp 2254 Centennial Rd .... Toledo OH 43606 419-535-6374 535-7008
OTC: NVIC ■ *TF:* 800-336-2225 ■ *Web:* www.nviro.com

Napa Recycling & Waste Services (NRWS)
820 Levitin Way PO Box 239 .... Napa CA 94559 707-256-3500 256-3565
Web: www.naparecycling.com

National Serv-All Inc 6231 McBeth Rd. .... Fort Wayne IN 46809 260-747-4117 478-4903
TF: 800-876-9001 ■ *Web:* servall.com

Natural Capitalism Solutions Inc
11823 N 75th St .... Longmont CO 80503 720-684-6580
Web: www.natcapsolutions.org

Oakleaf Waste Management LLC 415 Day Hill Rd. ...... Windsor CT 06095 713-512-6200 290-1251*
**Fax Area Code:* 860 ■ *TF:* 888-625-5323 ■ *Web:* wmsbs.wm.com/

Oregon Environmental Council
222 Nw Davis St Ste 309 .... Portland OR 97209 503-222-1963
Web: www.oeconline.org

Palm Springs Disposal Services
4690 E Mesquite Ave .... Palm Springs CA 92264 760-327-1351 323-5132
Web: www.palmspringsdisposal.com

Republic Services 1131 N Blue Gum St .... Anaheim CA 92806 714-238-3300 238-3304*
**Fax:* Hum Res ■ *Web:* republicservices.com/

Republic Services Inc 18500 N Allied .... Phoenix AZ 85054 480-627-2700
NYSE: RSG ■ *Web:* www.republicservices.com

Republic Services of Southern Nevada
770 E Sahara Ave .... Las Vegas NV 89193 702-735-5151
TF: 800-752-4092 ■ *Web:* www.republicservices.com

Rubatino Refuse Removal Inc 2812 Hoyt Ave .... Everett WA 98201 425-259-0044 339-4196
Web: www.rubatino.com

Rumpke 10795 Hughes Rd .... Cincinnati OH 45251 800-582-3107 742-2900*
**Fax Area Code:* 513 ■ *TF:* 800-582-3107 ■ *Web:* www.rumpke.com

San Luis Garbage Co
2945 McMillan St Ste 136 .... San Luis Obispo CA 93401 805-543-0875 543-0620
Web: wasteconnections.com

Phone Fax

Sanitary Services Co Inc
21 Bellwether Way Ste 404 .... Bellingham WA 98225 360-734-3490 671-0239
TF: 888-333-9882 ■ *Web:* www.ssc-inc.com

Sanitation District 1 of Northern Kentucky
1045 Eaton Dr. .... Fort Wright KY 41017 859-578-7450
Web: www.sd1.org

Sewerage & Water Board of New Orleans
625 Saint Joseph St Rm 140 .... New Orleans LA 70165 504-529-2837
Web: www.swbno.org

South Tahoe Refuse Co 2140 Ruth Ave .... South Lake Tahoe CA 96150 530-541-5105 544-2608
Web: www.southtahoerefuse.com

Spirit Lake Tribe (SLT) PO Box 359. .... Fort Totten ND 58335 701-766-4221 766-4126
Web: www.spiritlakenation.com

Stericycle Inc 28161 N Keith Dr .... Lake Forest IL 60045 847-367-5910 367-9493
NASDAQ: SRCL ■ *TF:* 866-783-7422 ■ *Web:* www.stericycle.com

Sudbury Valley Trustees Inc 18 Wolbach Rd .... Sudbury MA 01776 978-443-5588
Web: www.sudburyvalleytrustees.org

Sunset Scavenger Co
250 Executive Pk Ste 2100 .... San Francisco CA 94134 415-330-1300 330-1338
Web: www.sunsetscavenger.com

Synagro Technologies Inc
435 Williams Ct Ste 100. .... Baltimore MD 21220 443-489-9017 284-9220*
**Fax Area Code:* 410 ■ *TF:* 800-370-0035 ■ *Web:* www.synagro.com

Tahoe Truckee Disposal Co
645 W Lk Blvd Sunnyside. .... Tahoe City CA 96145 530-583-0148
Web: waste101.com

Texas Disposal Systems Inc (TDS)
12200 Carl Rd .... Creedmoor TX 78610 512-421-1300 243-4123
TF: 800-375-8375 ■ *Web:* www.texasdisposal.com

Triumvirate Environmental 61 Innerbelt Rd .... Somerville MA 02143 617-628-8098 628-8099
TF: 800-966-9282 ■ *Web:* www.triumvirate.com

Union Sanitary District (USD)
5072 Benson Rd PO Box 5050 .... Union City CA 94587 510-477-7500 477-7501
Web: www.unionsanitary.com

Urban Services Systems
212 Van Buren St NW .... Washington DC 20012 202-543-2000 547-0159
Web: www.urbanssc.com

Vallejo Sanitation & Flood Control District Financing Corp
450 Ryder St. .... Vallejo CA 94590 707-644-8949
Web: www.vsfcd.com

Veolia Environmental Services
1980 N Hwy 146 .... La Porte TX 77571 713-307-2100
Web: www.veoliaes.com

Waste Industries USA Inc
3301 Benson Dr Ste 601. .... Raleigh NC 27609 919-325-3000 872-1471*
**Fax:* Mktg ■ *TF:* 800-647-9946 ■ *Web:* www.wasteindustries.com

Waste Management Inc 1001 Fannin St Ste 4000. ...... Houston TX 77002 713-512-6200 512-6299
NYSE: WM ■ *TF:* 800-633-7871 ■ *Web:* www.wm.com

Waste Services Inc
1122 International Blvd Ste 601 .... Burlington ON L7L6Z8 905-319-1237 319-9050
Web: www.wasteservicesinc.com

WCA Waste Corp 1330 Post Oak Blvd 30th Fl .... Houston TX 77056 713-292-2400 292-2455
NASDAQ: WCAA ■ *Web:* www.wcawaste.com

Wheelabrator Technologies Inc 4 Liberty Ln W ...... Hampton NH 03842 603-929-3000 929-3139
TF: 800-682-0026 ■ *Web:* www.wheelabratortechnologies.com

York Waste Disposal Inc 3730 Sandhurst Dr. .... York PA 17406 717-845-1557 764-1944
Web: yorkwaste.com

808 WATER - BOTTLED

Phone Fax

Absopure Water Co 8835 General Dr .... Plymouth MI 48170 313-898-1200 *
**Fax:* Cust Svc ■ *TF:* 800-422-7678 ■ *Web:* www.absopure.com

Calistoga Beverage Co 865 Silverado Trl .... Calistoga CA 94515 800-365-4446
TF: 800-365-4446 ■ *Web:* www.calistogawater.com

Carolina Mountain Water Co
150 Central Ave .... Hot Springs AR 71902 800-828-0836
TF: 800-828-0836 ■ *Web:* www.mountainvalleyspring.com

Chester Water Authority PO Box 467 .... Chester PA 19016 610-876-8185
TF: 800-793-2323 ■ *Web:* www.chesterwater.com

Coca-Cola Enterprises Inc
2500 Windy Ridge Pkwy .... Atlanta GA 30339 770-989-3000 989-3597
NYSE: CCE ■ *Web:* www.cokecce.com

Coca-Cola Export Corp, The
One Coca Cola Plz Nw .... Atlanta GA 30313 404-676-2121
Web: www.coca-colacompany.com

Culligan International Co
9399 W Higgins Rd Ste 1100 .... Rosemont IL 60018 847-430-2800
TF: 800-285-5442 ■ *Web:* www.culligan.com

Distillata Co 1608 E 24th St. .... Cleveland OH 44114 216-771-2900 771-1672
TF Cust Svc: 800-999-2906 ■ *Web:* www.distillata.com

DS Waters of America Inc
5660 New Northside Dr Ste 500 .... Atlanta GA 30328 800-201-6218 965-5011*
**Fax Area Code:* 770 ■ *TF Cust Svc:* 800-201-6218 ■ *Web:* www.water.com

Glacier Clear Enterprises Inc
3291 Thomas St .... Innisfil ON L9S3W3 705-436-6363 436-4949
TF Cust Svc: 800-668-5118 ■ *Web:* www.glacierclear.com

Mountain Valley Spring Co
150 Central Ave .... Hot Springs AR 71901 501-624-1635 623-5135
TF: 800-828-0836 ■ *Web:* www.mountainvalleyspring.com

Natural Springs Water Group
128 LP Auer Rd .... Johnson City TN 37604 423-926-7905 926-8210

Polar Beverages Inc 1001 Southbridge St .... Worcester MA 01610 508-753-4300 793-0813
TF Cust Svc: 800-734-9800 ■ *Web:* www.polarbev.com

Pure-Flo Water Co 7737 Mission Gorge Rd .... Santee CA 92071 619-448-5120 596-4154
TF Cust Svc: 800-787-3356 ■ *Web:* www.pureflo.com

Temple Bottling Company Ltd
3510 Pkwy Dr PO Box 308 .... Temple TX 76501 254-773-3376 778-5414
Web: www.templebot.com

809 WATER TREATMENT & FILTRATION PRODUCTS & EQUIPMENT

Company	City	State	Zip	Phone	Fax
Aqua-Aerobic Systems Inc 6306 N Alpine Rd TF: 800-940-5008 ■ Web: www.aqua-aerobic.com	Loves Park	IL	61111	815-654-2501	654-2508
Aquion Water Treatment Products LLC 2080 E Lunt Ave Web: aquion.com	Elk Grove Village	IL	60007	847-437-9400	437-1594
Aquion Water Treatment Products LLC Rainsoft Div 2080 E Lunt Ave TF: 800-860-7638 ■ Web: www.rainsoft.com	Elk Grove Village	IL	60007	847-437-9400	437-5539
Atlas Water Systems Inc 301 Second Ave *Fax Area Code: 617 ■ TF: 888-877-0561 ■ Web: atlaswater.com/	Waltham	MA	02451	781-373-4700	244-5141*
Beaufort-Jasper Water & Sewer Authority Six Skake Rd Web: www.bjwsa.org	Okatie	SC	29909	843-987-9200	
Brentwood Industries Inc Polychem Systems Div 621 Brentwood Dr *Fax Area Code: 484 ■ Web: brentwoodindustries.com/products/clarification/sludge-collectors/	Reading	PA	19611	610-374-5109	651-1499*
Brita Products Co 1221 Broadway PO Box 24305 TF: 800-242-7482 ■ Web: www.brita.com	Oakland	CA	94612	510-271-7000	832-1463
Bucks County Water & Sewer Authority (BCWSA) 1275 Almshouse Rd *Fax Area Code: 267 ■ TF: 800-222-2068 ■ Web: www.bcwsa.net	Warrington	PA	18976	215-343-2538	200-0339*
Carolina Filters Inc 109 E Newberry Ave PO Box 716 TF: 800-849-5646 ■ Web: www.carolinafilters.com	Sumter	SC	29151	803-773-6842	775-6190
Clack Corp 4462 Duraform Ln Web: www.clackcorp.com	Windsor	WI	53598	608-846-3010	846-2586
Court Thomas Wingert 11800 Monarch St PO Box 6207 Web: www.jlwingert.com	Garden Grove	CA	92841	714-379-5519	379-5549
Culligan International Co 9399 W Higgins Rd Ste 1100 TF: 800-285-5442 ■ Web: www.culligan.com	Rosemont	IL	60018	847-430-2800	
Deepwater Chemicals Inc 1210 Airpark Rd TF: 800-854-4064 ■ Web: www.deepwaterchemicals.com	Woodward	OK	73801	580-256-0500	256-0575
Dow Liquid Separations PO Box 1206 TF: 800-447-4369 ■ Web: dow.com	Midland	MI	48642	989-636-1000	832-1465
East Valley Water District 3654 E Highland Ave Ste 18 TF: 866-275-3772 ■ Web: www.eastvalley.org	Highland	CA	92346	909-889-9501	889-5732
Energy Recovery Inc 1717 Doolittle Dr NASDAQ: ERII ■ TF: 888-455-2263 ■ Web: www.energyrecovery.com	San Leandro	CA	94577	510-483-7370	483-7371
Everpure LLC 1040 Muirfield Dr TF: 800-323-7873 ■ Web: www.everpure.com	Hanover Park	IL	60133	630-307-3000	307-3030
Filterspun 624 N Fairfield St TF: 800-323-5431 ■ Web: www.serfilco.com	Amarillo	TX	79107	806-383-3840	383-3842
Filtra-Systems Co 23900 Haggerty Rd Web: www.filtrasystems.com	Farmington Hills	MI	48335	248-427-9090	427-9895
GE Water & Process Technologies 4636 Somerton Rd TF: 866-439-2837 ■ Web: www.gewater.com	Trevose	PA	19053	215-355-3300	
Graver Technologies LLC 200 Lake Dr TF: 800-249-1990 ■ Web: www.gravertech.com	Newark	DE	19702	302-731-1700	731-1707
Graver Water Systems 675 Central Ave Ste 3 TF: 877-472-8379 ■ Web: www.graver.com	New Providence	NJ	07974	908-516-1400	516-1401
Hungerford & Terry Inc 226 N Atlantic Ave Web: www.hungerfordterry.com	Clayton	NJ	08312	856-881-3200	881-6859
Infilco Degremont Inc 8007 Discovery Dr PO Box 71390 Web: www.degremont-technologies.com	Richmond	VA	23255	804-756-7600	756-7643
Kinetico Inc 10845 Kinsman Rd *Fax Area Code: 440 ■ TF: 800-944-9283 ■ Web: www.kinetico.com	Newbury	OH	44065	800-944-9283	564-9541*
KX Technologies LLC 55 Railroad Ave Web: www.kxtech.com	West Haven	CT	06516	203-799-9000	799-7000
Lancaster Pump Co 1340 Manheim Pk Web: www.lancasterpump.com	Lancaster	PA	17601	717-397-3521	392-0266
Macon Water Authority 790 Second St PO Box 108 Web: www.maconwater.org	Macon	GA	31202	478-464-5600	741-9146
Met-Pro Corp Systems Div 160 Cassell Rd PO Box 144 TF: 800-621-0734 ■ Web: www.mpeas.com	Harleysville	PA	19438	215-723-9300	723-8501
MSC Filtration Technologies 198 Freshwater Blvd TF Cust Svc: 800-237-7359 ■ Web: www.mscfiltertech.com	Enfield	CT	06082	860-745-7475	745-7477
National Water Purifiers Corp 1065 E 14th St	Hialeah	FL	33010	305-887-7065	887-6209
Pall Corp 2200 Northern Blvd NYSE: PLL ■ TF: 800-645-6532 ■ Web: www.pall.com	East Hills	NY	11548	516-484-5400	801-9754
Pentair Inc 5500 Wayzata Blvd Ste 800 NYSE: PNR ■ Web: www.pentair.com	Minneapolis	MN	55416	763-545-1730	656-5400
PEP Filters Inc 322 Rolling Hill Rd TF: 800-243-4583 ■ Web: www.pepfilters.com	Mooresville	NC	28117	704-662-3133	662-3155
Polaris Pool Systems Inc 2620 Commerce Way TF: 800-822-7933 ■ Web: www.polarispool.com	Vista	CA	92081	760-599-9600	597-1235
Pro Products LLC 7201 Engle Rd TF: 866-357-5063 ■ Web: www.proproducts.com	Fort Wayne	IN	46804	260-490-5970	490-9431
Pure & Secure LLC 4120 NW 44th St *Fax Area Code: 800 ■ TF Cust Svc: 800-875-5915 ■ Web: www.mypurewater.com	Lincoln	NE	68524	402-467-9300	659-2939*
Schreiber LLC 100 Schreiber Dr Web: www.schreiberwater.com	Trussville	AL	35173	205-655-7466	655-7669
Severn Trent Services 580 Virginia Dr Ste 300 TF: 866-646-9201 ■ Web: www.severntrentservices.com	Fort Washington	PA	19034	215-646-9201	
Sharp Water Culligan 129 Columbia Rd TF: 800-439-3853 ■ Web: www.sharpwaterculligan.com	Salisbury	MD	21801	410-742-3333	
Siemens Water Technologies 181 Thorn Hill Rd TF: 800-424-9300	Warrendale	PA	15086	724-772-0044	772-1300
Sydnor Hydro Inc 2111 Magnolia St PO Box 27186 TF: 800-552-7714 ■ Web: www.sydnorhydro.com	Richmond	VA	23261	804-643-2725	788-9058
Taylor Technologies Inc 31 Loveton Cir TF Cust Svc: 800-837-8548 ■ Web: www.taylortechnologies.com	Sparks	MD	21152	410-472-4340	771-4291
Tomco2 Equipment Co 3340 Rosebud Rd TF: 800-832-4262 ■ Web: www.tomcosystems.com	Loganville	GA	30052	770-979-8000	985-9179
Walker Process Equipment 840 N Russell Ave TF: 800-992-5537 ■ Web: www.walker-process.com	Aurora	IL	60506	630-892-7921	892-7951
Waterco USA Inc 1864 Tobacco Rd TF General: 800-277-4150 ■ Web: www.waterco.com.au	Augusta	GA	30906	706-793-7291	790-5688
Westech Engineering Inc 3665 SW Temple Web: www.westech-inc.com	Salt Lake City	UT	84115	801-265-1000	265-1080
Xylem Inc 227 S Div St Web: www.fbleopold.com	Zelienople	PA	16063	724-452-6300	452-1377
Zodiac Pool Systems Inc 2620 Commerce Way TF: 800-822-7933 ■ Web: www.zodiacpoolsystems.com	Vista	CA	92081	800-822-7933	479-8324

810 WEAPONS & ORDNANCE (MILITARY)

SEE ALSO Firearms & Ammunition (Non-Military) p. 2289; Missiles, Space Vehicles, Parts p. 2764; Simulation & Training Systems p. 3175

Company	City	State	Zip	Phone	Fax
Adams Arms Inc 612 Florida Ave Web: www.adamsarms.net	Palm Harbor	FL	34683	727-853-0550	
Addison Clark Management LLC 10 Wright St Ste 100 Web: www.leask.com	Westport	CT	06880	203-222-4000	
Amron LLC 920 Amron Ave *Fax Area Code: 608 ■ Web: amteccorp.net	Antigo	WI	54409	715-623-4176	752-2544*
ArmaLite Inc 745 S Hanford St Web: www.armalite.com	Geneseo	IL	61254	309-944-6939	
Armtec Defense Products Co 85-901 Ave 53 Web: esterline.com	Coachella	CA	92236	760-398-0143	398-3896
Cammenga Company LLC 2011 Bailey St Web: www.cammenga.com	Dearborn	MI	48124	313-914-7160	
Colt Defense LLC 547 New Pk Ave Web: www.colt.com	West Hartford	CT	06110	860-232-4489	244-1442
Dillon Aero Inc 8009 E Dillons Way Web: www.dillonaero.com	Scottsdale	AZ	85260	480-444-2919	
Essex Industries Inc 7700 Gravois Rd Web: essexindustries.com	Saint Louis	MO	63123	314-832-4500	832-1633
FN America LLC 797 Old Clemson Rd Web: www.fnmfg.com	Columbia	SC	29229	803-736-0522	
General Dynamics Corp 2941 Fairview Pk Dr Ste 100 NYSE: GD ■ Web: www.generaldynamics.com	Falls Church	VA	22042	703-876-3000	876-3125
Kaman Aerospace Corp Old Windsor Rd PO Box 2 Web: www.kaman.com	Bloomfield	CT	06002	860-242-4461	243-7514
Keystone Sporting Arms LLC 155 Sodom Rd Web: www.keystonesportingarmsllc.com	Milton	PA	17847	570-742-2777	
Knight's Armament Co 701 Columbia Blvd Web: www.knightarmco.com	Titusville	FL	32780	321-607-9900	
Lilja Precision Rifle Barrel 81 Lower Lynch Creek Rd Web: www.riflebarrels.com	Plains	MT	59859	406-826-3084	
Magpul Industries Corp 400 Young Court Unit 1 Web: www.magpul.com	Erie	CO	80516	303-828-3460	
Manroy USA LLC 201 Lonnie E Crawford Blvd Web: www.manroy-usa.com	Scottsboro	AL	35769	256-259-9800	
Marvin Engineering Co 261 W Beach Ave Web: www.marvingroup.com	Inglewood	CA	90302	310-674-5030	673-9472
NAPCO International Inc 11055 Excelsior Blvd Web: www.napcointl.com	Hopkins	MN	55343	952-931-2400	931-2402
North American Arms Inc 2150 South 950 East Web: www.naaminis.com	Provo	UT	84606	801-374-9990	
Rock River Arms Inc 1042 Cleveland Rd Web: www.rockriverarms.com	Colona	IL	61241	309-792-5780	
Sai Industries Inc 631 Allen Ave Web: www.standardarmament.com	Glendale	CA	91201	818-842-6144	
Silencerco LLC 5511 South 6055 West Web: www.silencerco.com	West Valley City	UT	84118	801-417-5384	
Textron Systems Corp 201 Lowell St Web: textron.com	Wilmington	MA	01887	978-657-5111	657-6644
US Ordnance Inc 300 Sydney Dr Web: www.usord.com	Mccarran	NV	89434	775-343-1320	

811 WEB HOSTING SERVICES

SEE ALSO Internet Service Providers (ISPs) p. 2589

Companies listed here are engaged primarily in hosting web sites for companies and individuals. Although many Internet Service Providers (ISPs) also provide web hosting services, they are not included among these listings.

Company	City	State	Zip	Phone	Fax
Baillio's Inc 5301 Menaul Blvd NE TF: 800-540-7511 ■ Web: baillios.com	Albuquerque	NM	87110	505-883-7511	
Catalog.com Inc 14000 Quail Springs Pkwy Ste 3600 TF: 888-932-4376 ■ Web: www.webhero.com	Oklahoma City	OK	73134	405-753-9300	753-9353
CBS Interactive Inc 235 Second St Web: www.cbsinteractive.com/	San Francisco	CA	94105	415-344-2000	
Classified Ventures LLC 175 W Jackson Blvd Ste 800 Eighth Fl Web: www.classifiedventures.com	Chicago	IL	60604	312-601-5000	
Coronado Unified School District 201 Sixth St Web: www.edline.net	Coronado	CA	92118	619-522-8900	

Company	Address	City	State	Zip	Phone	Fax
Cuadra Assoc Inc	3415 S Sepulveda Blvd Ste 210	Los Angeles	CA	90034	310-591-2490	591-2488
Web: www.cuadra.com						
DataPipe	10 Exchange Pl	Jersey City	NJ	07302	201-792-4847	749-5821*
**Fax Area Code:* 888 ■ *TF:* 877-773-3306 ■ *Web:* www.datapipe.com						
Datarealm Internet Services Inc	PO Box 1616	Hudson	WI	54016	877-227-3783	850-3660*
**Fax Area Code:* 602 ■ *TF:* 877-227-3783 ■ *Web:* www.datarealm.com						
Fortress Integrated Technologies	100 Delawanna Ave	Clifton	NJ	07014	973-572-1070	572-1061
TF: 888-734-9320 ■ *Web:* www.fortressitx.com						
Freeservers.com	1253 N Research Way Ste Q-2500	Orem	UT	84097	800-396-1999	
TF: 800-396-1999 ■ *Web:* www.freeservers.com						
Global Knowledge Group Inc (GKG)	302 N Bryan Ave	Bryan	TX	77803	866-776-7584	694-7060*
**Fax Area Code:* 979 ■ *TF:* 866-776-7584 ■ *Web:* www.gkg.net						
Homestead Technologies Inc	180 Jefferson Dr	Menlo Park	CA	94025	650-944-3100	364-7329
TF: 800-797-2958 ■ *Web:* www.homestead.com						
Host Depot Inc	2455 Paces Ferry Rd NW	Atlanta	GA	30339	770-433-8211	340-3539*
**Fax Area Code:* 954 ■ *TF:* 888-340-3527 ■ *Web:* www.hostdepot.com						
Hostcentric Inc	70 BlanchaRd Rd 3rd Fl	Burlington	MA	01803	602-716-5396	998-8277*
**Fax Area Code:* 781 ■ *TF Tech Supp:* 866-897-5418 ■ *Web:* www.hostcentric.com						
Hostedware Corp	16 Technology Dr Ste 116	Irvine	CA	92618	949-585-1500	
TF: 800-211-6967 ■ *Web:* www.hostedware.com						
Hostway Corp	100 N Riverside Plaza 8th Fl	Chicago	IL	60606	312-238-0125	236-1958
TF: 866-467-8929 ■ *Web:* www.hostway.com						
Hurricane Electric Internet Services	760 Mission Ct	Fremont	CA	94539	510-580-4100	580-4151
Web: www.he.com						
INetU Inc	744 Roble Rd Ste 70	Allentown	PA	18109	610-266-7441	266-7434
TF: 888-664-6388 ■ *Web:* www.inetu.net						
LightEdge Solutions Inc	215 10th St Ste 1000	Des Moines	IA	50309	515-471-1000	471-1112
TF: 877-771-3343 ■ *Web:* www.lightedge.com						
Media3 Technologies LLC	33 Riverside Dr N River Commerce Pk	Pembroke	MA	02359	781-826-1213	996-4971
TF: 800-903-9327 ■ *Web:* www.media3.net						
Microserve	276 Fifth Ave Ste 1011	New York	NY	10001	212-683-2811	
Web: www.mserve.com						
NetNation Communications Inc	550 Burrard St Ste 200	Vancouver	BC	V6C2B5	604-688-8946	688-8934
TF: 888-277-0000 ■ *Web:* www.netnation.com						
OLM LLC	Four Trefoil Dr	Trumbull	CT	06611	203-445-7700	
TF: 800-741-6813 ■ *Web:* olm.net						
Opsource Inc	5201 Great America Pkwy Ste 120	Santa Clara	CA	95054	408-567-2000	982-8902
TF: 800-664-9973 ■ *Web:* cloud.dimensiondata.com/saas-solutions/						
Pacific Internet	105 W Clay St	Ukiah	CA	95482	707-468-1005	468-5822
TF: 888-722-8638 ■ *Web:* www.pacific.net						
Power Surge Web Solutions	1171 South Robertson Blvd Ste 194	Los Angeles	CA	90035	312-492-4053	224-8428
TF: 800-867-5055 ■ *Web:* www.powersurge.net						
Radiant Communications Corp	1600-1050 W Pender St	Vancouver	BC	V6E4T3	888-219-2111	
CVE: RCN ■ *TF:* 888-219-2111 ■ *Web:* www.radiant.net						
Salon Media Group Inc	101 Spear St Ste 203	San Francisco	CA	94105	415-645-9200	307-5226*
**Fax Area Code:* 212 ■ *TF:* 800-257-8650 ■ *Web:* www.salon.com						
SilverSky	440 Wheelers Farms Rd Ste 202	Milford	CT	06461	800-234-2175	
TF: 800-234-2175 ■ *Web:* www.silversky.com						
Superb Internet Corp	999 Bishop St Ste 1850	Honolulu	HI	96813	808-544-0387	441-0952
TF: 888-354-6128 ■ *Web:* www.superb.net						
Telus	1000 Rue de Serigny	Longueuil	QC	J4K5B1	450-928-6000	928-6344
TF: 888-709-8759 ■ *Web:* www.telushealth.com						
TierraNet Inc	14284 Dani Elson St	Poway	CA	92064	858-560-9416	560-9417
TF: 877-843-7721 ■ *Web:* www.tierra.net						
Verio Inc	8005 S Chester St Ste 200	Centennial	CO	80112	561-912-2555	
TF Sales: 800-438-8374 ■ *Web:* www.verio.com						
VPOP Technologies Inc	1772J Avenida de los Arboles PO Box 372	Thousand Oaks	CA	91362	805-529-9374	
TF Sales: 888-811-8767 ■ *Web:* www.vpop.net						
WorldPost Technologies Inc	5886 De Zavala Rd Ste 102/535	San Antonio	TX	78249	210-212-5600	212-5800
Web: www.worldpost.com						

812 WEB SITE DESIGN SERVICES

SEE ALSO Computer Systems Design Services p. 2054; Advertising Agencies p. 1705; Advertising Services - Online p. 1715

Company	Address	City	State	Zip	Phone	Fax
415 Productions Inc	2507 Bryant St	San Francisco	CA	94110	415-642-4200	642-4210
Web: www.415.com						
Acro Media Inc	2303 Leckie Rd Ste 103	Kelowna	BC	V1X6Y5	250-763-8884	763-6936
TF: 877-763-8844 ■ *Web:* acromediainc.com/						
Bixler Inc	1600 Tysons Blvd Ste 800	McLean	VA	22102	703-894-3000	894-3001
Web: www.bixler.com						
bx.com Inc	1 W Exchange St	Providence	RI	02903	401-274-8991	
TF: 877-447-2355 ■ *Web:* www.bx.com						
Cramer	425 University Ave	Norwood	MA	02062	781-278-2300	278-8464
Web: www.cramer.com						
Digital West Media Inc	PO Box 270219	San Diego	CA	92198	760-740-1787	257-0042*
**Fax Area Code:* 310 ■ *Web:* www.dwmi.com						
Forum One Communications Corp	2200 Mt Vernon Ave	Alexandria	VA	22301	703-548-1855	995-4937
Web: www.forumone.com						
Fusebox Inc	36 W 20th St	New York	NY	10011	212-929-7644	929-7947
Web: www.fusebox.com						
Genex Interactive	800 Corporate Pointe	Culver City	CA	90230	424-672-9500	
Web: meredithxceleratedmarketing.com/						
GotData.com Inc	25431 Cabot Rd Ste 202	Laguna Hills	CA	92653	949-716-7500	269-9161
Web: www.gotdata.com						

Company	Address	City	State	Zip	Phone	Fax
Headquarters.Com Inc	625 Walnut Ridge Dr Ste 108	Hartland	WI	53029	262-369-0600	369-0800
Paloma Systems Inc	11250 Waples Mill Rd	Fairfax	VA	22030	703-626-5024	591-0985
TF: 855-300-2686 ■ *Web:* www.palomasys.com						
Patel Consultants Corp	1525 Morris Ave	Union	NJ	07083	908-964-7575	964-3176
Web: www.patelcorp.com						
Sapient Corp	131 Dartmouth St 3rd Fl	Boston	MA	02116	617-621-0200	621-1300
NASDAQ: SAPE ■ *TF:* 866-796-6860 ■ *Web:* www.sapient.com						
Web.com	12808 Grand Bay Pkwy W	Jacksonville	FL	32258	904-680-6600	880-0350
TF: 800-338-1771 ■ *Web:* www.web.com						

813 WEIGHT LOSS CENTERS & SERVICES

SEE ALSO Health & Fitness Centers p. 2451; Spas - Health & Fitness p. 3176

Company	Address	City	State	Zip	Phone	Fax
American Laser Skincare	24555 Hallwood Ct	Farmington Hills	MI	48335	248-426-8250	426-0129
TF: 877-252-2010 ■ *Web:* www.americanlaser.com						
Barix Clinics	135 S Prospect St	Ypsilanti	MI	48198	734-547-4700	547-1281
TF: 800-282-0066 ■ *Web:* www.barixclinics.com						
Companions & Homemakers Inc	613 New Britain Ave	Farmington	CT	06032	860-677-4948	
TF: 800-348-4663 ■ *Web:* www.companionsandhomemakers.com						
Fit America MD	4864 Arthur Kill Rd	Staten Island	NY	10309	718-227-4980	
TF: 800-940-7546 ■ *Web:* fitamerica.com/						
Fuze Fit for a Kid	15405 Los Gatos Blvd Ste 103	Los Gatos	CA	95032	408-358-7529	
Web: www.fuzefit.com						
Greenpath Inc	38505 Country Club Dr	Farmington Hills	MI	48331	248-553-5400	699-1613
TF: 800-550-1961 ■ *Web:* www.greenpath.com						
Indigo Integrative Studio	1304 Eighth Ave	Brooklyn	NY	11215	718-832-3464	
Web: www.indigo-pilates.com						
Jazzercise Inc	2460 Impala Dr	Carlsbad	CA	92010	760-476-1750	602-7180
TF Cust Svc: 800-348-4748 ■ *Web:* www.jazzercise.com						
Jenny Craig International Inc	5770 Fleet St	Carlsbad	CA	92008	760-696-4000	696-4506
TF: 800-443-2331 ■ *Web:* www.jennycraig.com						
JumpstartMD	595 Price Ave Ste 200	Redwood City	CA	94063	650-241-6550	
Web: www.jumpstartmd.com						
Maria Paonessa Moda 2000	1500 N Wells St 2	Chicago	IL	60610	312-994-6747	
NutriSystem Inc	300 Welsh Rd Bldg 1	Horsham	PA	19044	215-706-5300	706-5388
NASDAQ: NTRI ■ *TF:* 800-585-5483 ■ *Web:* www.nutrisystem.com						
Physicians Weight Loss Centers of America Inc	395 Springside Dr	Akron	OH	44333	330-666-7952	666-2197
TF: 800-205-7887 ■ *Web:* www.pwlc.com						
Primescape Solutions Inc	13221 Wdlnd Pk Dr Ste 300	Herndon	VA	20171	703-650-1900	650-1901
Web: www.primescape.net						
Weight Management Centers	2605 W Swann Ave Ste 600	Tampa	FL	33609	813-876-7073	877-1277
Web: www.weightmanagement.com						

814 WELDING & SOLDERING EQUIPMENT

Company	Address	City	State	Zip	Phone	Fax
Acro Automation Systems Inc	2900 W Green Tree Rd	Milwaukee	WI	53209	414-352-4540	352-1609
Web: www.acro.com						
AGM Industries Inc	16 Jonathan Dr	Brockton	MA	02301	508-587-3900	587-3283
TF: 800-225-9990 ■ *Web:* www.agmind.com						
Alliance Winding Equipment Inc	3939 Vanguard Dr	Fort Wayne	IN	46809	260-478-2200	
Web: www.alliance-winding.com						
American Ultraviolet Co	40 Morristown Rd	Bernardsville	NJ	07924	908-696-1130	696-1131
TF: 800-288-9288 ■ *Web:* www.americanultraviolet.com						
Applied Fusion Inc	1915 Republic Ave	San Leandro	CA	94577	510-351-4511	351-0692
Web: appliedfusioninc.com						
Arc Machines Inc	10500 Orbital Way	Pacoima	CA	91331	818-896-9556	890-3724
Web: www.arcmachines.com						
Arcos Industries	One Arcos Dr	Mount Carmel	PA	17851	570-339-5200	339-5206
TF: 800-233-8460 ■ *Web:* www.arcos.us						
Argus International Ltd	108 Whispering Pines Dr Ste 110	Scotts Valley	CA	95066	831-461-4700	
TF: 800-862-7487 ■ *Web:* www.argusinternational.com						
Aro Welding	48500 Structural Dr	Chesterfield	MI	48051	586-949-9353	949-4493
Web: www.arotechnologies.com						
Automation International Inc	1020 Bahls St	Danville	IL	61832	217-446-9500	446-6855
Web: www.automation-intl.com						
Banner Welder Inc	N 117 W 18200 Fulton Dr	Germantown	WI	53022	262-253-2900	253-2917*
**Fax:* Cust Svc ■ *Web:* www.bannerweld.com						
Bernard Welding Equipment	449 W Corning Rd	Beecher	IL	60401	708-946-2281	
Web: www.bernardwelds.com						
Bonal Technologies Inc	1300 N Campbell Rd	Royal Oak	MI	48067	248-582-0900	
Web: www.bonal.com						
BUG-O Systems Inc	161 Hillpointe Dr	Canonsburg	PA	15317	412-331-1776	331-0383
TF: 800-245-3186 ■ *Web:* www.bugo.com						
CK Worldwide Inc	3501 C St NE	Auburn	WA	98002	253-854-5820	939-1746
TF: 800-426-0877 ■ *Web:* www.ckworldwide.com						
Esab Welding & Cutting Products Inc	411 S Ebenezer Rd PO Box 100545	Florence	SC	29501	843-669-4411	664-4258*
**Fax:* Hum Res ■ *TF:* 800-372-2123 ■ *Web:* www.esabna.com						
Eureka Welding Alloys Inc	2000 E Avis Dr	Madison Heights	MI	48071	248-588-0001	585-7711
TF: 800-962-8560 ■ *Web:* www.eurekaweldingalloys.com						
Eutectic Corp	N 94 W 14355 Garwin Mace Dr	Menomonee Falls	WI	53051	262-532-4677	255-5542
TF: 800-558-8524 ■ *Web:* www.eutectic-na.com						
Forney Industries Inc	1830 LaPorte Ave	Fort Collins	CO	80521	800-521-6038	
TF: 800-521-6038 ■ *Web:* www.forneyind.com						

Phone Fax

Gapco Inc 2151 Centennial Dr ....Gainesville GA 30504 770-534-7928
Web: www.gapco.com
Goss Inc 1511 William Flynn Hwy ....Glenshaw PA 15116 412-486-6100 486-6844
TF: 800-367-4677 ■ *Web:* www.gossonline.com
Grossel Tool Co 34190 Doreka........................ Fraser MI 48026 586-294-3660 294-7134
Web: www.grosseltool.com
Harris Products Group 4501 Quality Pl.................Mason OH 45040 513-754-2000 754-8778*
**Fax:* Sales ■ *TF:* 800-733-4043 ■ *Web:* www.harrisproductsgroup.com
Hobart Bros Co 101 Trade Sq E .... Troy OH 45373 937-332-4000 332-5178
Web: www.hobartbrothers.com
Indalco Alloys Inc 939 Gana Ct.................. Mississauga ON L5S1N9 905-564-1151 564-1405
Web: www.indalco.com
Industrial Welders & Machinists Inc
610 Opperman Dr.................................. Eagan MN 55123 800-455-4565
TF: 800-455-4565 ■ *Web:* caselaw.findlaw.com
Jetline Engineering 15 Goodyear St....................Irvine CA 92618 949-951-1515 951-9237
Web: www.jetline.com
JWF Industries 84 Iron St PO Box 1286.............Johnstown PA 15907 814-539-6922
TF: 800-225-9359 ■ *Web:* www.jwfi.com
Lincoln Electric Co 22801 St Clair Ave............. Cleveland OH 44117 216-481-8100 486-1751
TF: 888-935-3878 ■ *Web:* www.lincolnelectric.com
M K Products Inc 16882 Armstrong Ave ....Irvine CA 92606 949-863-1234 474-1428
TF: 800-787-9707 ■ *Web:* www.mkprod.com
Maine Oxy 22 Albiston Way.......................... Auburn ME 04210 207-784-5788 784-5383
TF: 800-639-1108 ■ *Web:* www.maineoxy.com
Manufacturing Technology Inc (MTI)
1702 W Washington St..........................South Bend IN 46628 574-233-9490 233-9489
Web: www.mtiwelding.com
Merrill Mfg Corp 236 S Genesee St....................Merrill WI 54452 715 536 5533 536 5590
TF: 800-831-6962 ■ *Web:* www.merrill-mfg.com
Milco Manufacturing Co 2147 E 10-Mile Rd............Warren MI 48091 586-755-7320 755-7442
Web: www.milcomfg.com
Miller Electric Mfg Co 1635 W Spencer St .... Appleton WI 54914 920-734-9821 735-4134*
**Fax:* Sales ■ *TF:* 888-843-7693 ■ *Web:* www.millerwelds.com
NLC Inc 319 W Main St ....Jackson MO 63755 573-243-3141 232-3046*
**Fax Area Code:* 800 ■ *TF Sales:* 800-594-3958 ■ *Web:* profaxlenco.com
Northern Stamping Corp 6600 Chapek Pkwy......... Cleveland OH 44125 216-883-8888 883-8237
Web: northernstamping.com
Ogden Welding Systems Inc 372 Div St ....Schererville IN 46375 219-322-5252 865-1825
Web: www.ogdenwelding.com
Palomar Technologies 2728 Loker Ave W............ Carlsbad CA 92010 760-931-3600 931-5191
TF: 800-854-3467 ■ *Web:* www.palomartechnologies.com
Pandjiris Inc 5151 Northrup Ave .... Saint Louis MO 63110 314-776-6893 776-8763
Web: www.pandjiris.com
Pia Group Inc 3520 Ibsen Ave...................... Cincinnati OH 45209 513-351-3300
Web: www.piagroup.com
Research Inc 7128 Shady Oak Rd ....Eden Prairie MN 55344 952-941-3300 941-3628
Web: pcscontrols.com/
RoMan Manufacturing Inc 861 47th St SW ....Grand Rapids MI 49509 616-530-8641 530-8953
Web: www.romanmfg.com
RWC Inc 2105 S Euclid Ave ....Bay City MI 48706 989-684-4030 684-3960
Web: www.rwcinc.com
Sciaky Inc 4915 W 67th St ....Chicago IL 60638 708-594-3800 594-9213
Web: www.sciaky.com
Smith Equipment Mfg Co 2601 Lockheed Ave........ Watertown SD 57201 605-882-3200 882-2100
TF Cust Svc: 866-931-9730 ■ *Web:* www.smithequipment.com
Sonobond Ultrasonics Inc
1191 McDermott Dr ....West Chester PA 19380 610-696-4710 692-0674
TF: 800-323-1269 ■ *Web:* sonobondultrasonics.com/
Systematics Inc
1025 Saunders Ln PO Box 2429.................West Chester PA 19380 610-696-9040 430-8714
TF: 800-222-9353 ■ *Web:* 800abcweld.com
Taylor-Winfield Inc PO Box 779.................Youngstown OH 44509 330-259-8500 259-8538
TF: 800-523-4899 ■ *Web:* www.taylor-winfield.com
Thermatool Corp
31 Commerce St PO Box 120769...................East Haven CT 06512 203-468-4100 468-4281*
**Fax:* Cust Svc ■ *Web:* www.thermatool.com
Tuffaloy Products Inc 1400 S Batesville Rd..............Greer SC 29650 864-879-0763 877-2212
TF: 800-521-3722 ■ *Web:* www.tuffaloy.com
Unitek Miyachi Corp 1820 S Myrtle Ave.............Monrovia CA 91017 626-303-5676 358-8048
TF: 866-751-7378 ■ *Web:* www.miyachiamerica.com
Uniweld Products Inc
2850 Ravenswood Rd........................Fort Lauderdale FL 33312 954-584-2000 587-0109
TF: 800-323-2111 ■ *Web:* www.uniweld.com
Vitronics Soltec Inc Two Marin Way .... Stratham NH 03885 603-772-7778 772-9340
Web: www.vitronics-soltec.com
Weld Mold Co 750 Rickett Rd....................... Brighton MI 48116 810-229-9521 229-9580
TF: 800-521-9755 ■ *Web:* www.weldmold.com
Western Enterprises Inc 875 Bassett Rd............ Westlake OH 44145 800-783-7890 835-8283*
**Fax Area Code:* 440 ■ *TF:* 800-783-7890 ■ *Web:* www.westernenterprises.com

815 WHOLESALE CLUBS

Phone Fax

Costco Wholesale Corp 999 Lake Dr................ Issaquah WA 98027 425-313-8100 313-8103
NASDAQ: COST ■ *TF Cust Svc:* 800-774-2678 ■ *Web:* www.costco.com
Marukai Wholesale Mart 2310 Kamehameha Hwy ..... Honolulu HI 96819 808-845-5051 841-2379
Web: www.marukaihawaii.com
PriceSmart Inc 9740 Scranton Rd.................. San Diego CA 92121 858-404-8800
NASDAQ: PSMT ■ *Web:* www.pricesmart.com

816 WIRE & CABLE

Phone Fax

Ace Wire & Cable Co Inc 7201 51st Ave .... Woodside NY 11377 718-458-9200 335-6340
TF: 800-225-2354 ■ *Web:* www.acewireco.com
AFC Cable Systems Inc 272 Duchaine Blvd .... New Bedford MA 02745 508-998-1131 998-1447
TF: 800-757-6996 ■ *Web:* www.afcweb.com
Alcan Cable 3 Ravinia Dr Ste 1600.......................Atlanta GA 30346 770-394-9886 395-9053
TF: 800-347-0571 ■ *Web:* www.stabiloy.com

Phone Fax

Allwire Inc 16395 Ave 24 1/2 PO Box 1000 .... Chowchilla CA 93610 559-665-4893 665-7389
TF: 800-255-3828 ■ *Web:* www.allwire.com
AmerCable Inc 350 Bailey Rd .... El Dorado AR 71730 870-862-4919 862-9613
TF: 800-643-1516 ■ *Web:* www.amercable.com
Astro Industries Inc 4403 Dayton-Xenia Rd ....Dayton OH 45432 937-429-5900 429-4054*
**Fax:* Sales ■ *TF:* 800-543-5810 ■ *Web:* www.astro-ind.com
Bekaert Corp 3200 W Market St Ste 303 ....Akron OH 44333 330-867-3325 873-3424
Web: www.bekaert.com
Cerro Wire & Cable Company Inc
1099 Thompson Rd SE........................... Hartselle AL 35640 256-773-2522
TF: 800-523-3869 ■ *Web:* www.cerrowire.com
Charter Wire 3700 W Milwaukee Rd.................Milwaukee WI 53208 414-390-3000 390-3031
TF: 800-436-9074 ■ *Web:* www.charterwire.com
Cooner Wire Co 9265 Owensmouth Ave............. Chatsworth CA 91311 818-882-8311 709-8281
Web: www.coonerwire.com
Cove West 195 E Merrick Rd.........................Freeport NY 11520 516-379-4232 525-2928*
**Fax Area Code:* 714 ■ *Web:* www.covefour.com
Draka Cableteq USA 22 Warner Blvd .... North Dighton MA 02764 508-822-5444 201-8280*
**Fax Area Code:* 888 ■ *Web:* drakausa.com
Elektrisola Inc 126 High St...................... Boscawen NH 03303 603-796-2114
TF: 800-325-2022 ■ *Web:* www.elektrisola.com
Encore Wire Corp 1329 Millwood Rd .... McKinney TX 75069 972-562-9473 562-3644
NASDAQ: WIRE ■ *TF:* 800-962-9473 ■ *Web:* www.encorewire.com
Eubanks Engineering Co
3022 Inland Empire Blvd .... Ontario CA 91764 909-483-2456 483-2498
TF: 800-729-4208 ■ *Web:* www.eubanks.com
Fiberwave Corp 140 58th St Bldg B Unit 6E........... Brooklyn NY 11220 718-802-9011 802-0116
TF: 800-280-9011 ■ *Web:* www.fiberwave.com
Foerster Instruments Inc 140 Industry Dr........... Pittsburgh PA 15275 412-788-8976 788-8984
Web: www.foerstergroup.com
Gehr Industries 7400 E Slauson Ave ....Los Angeles CA 90040 323-728-5558 728-1983
TF: 800-688-6606 ■ *Web:* gehr.com
Hendrix Wire & Cable Inc 53 Old Wilton Rd .... Milford NH 03055 603-673-2040 673-1497
Web: www.hendrix-wc.com
Insteel Industries Inc 1373 Boggs Dr .... Mount Airy NC 27030 336-786-2141 786-2144
NASDAQ: IIIN ■ *TF:* 800-334-9504 ■ *Web:* www.insteel.com
Inter-Wire Products (IWP) 355 Main St .... Armonk NY 10504 914-273-6633 273-6848
Web: www.interwiregroup.com
Kalas Manufacturing Inc 167 Greenfield Rd ....Lancaster PA 17601 717-336-5575 945-1002
Web: www.kalaswire.com
Kerite Co 49 Day St............................... Seymour CT 06483 203-888-2591 888-1987
TF: 800-777-7483 ■ *Web:* www.kerite.com
Keystone Consolidated Industries Inc
7000 SW Adams St.................................. Peoria IL 61641 800-447-6444 697-7120*
**Fax Area Code:* 309 ■ *TF Sales:* 800-447-6444 ■ *Web:* www.redbrand.com
Leggett Wire Co One Leggett Rd .... Carthage MO 64836 417-358-8131 358-6996
TF: 800-888-4569 ■ *Web:* www.leggett.com
Leoni Wiring Systems Inc
2861 N Flowing Wells Rd Ste 121 ....Tucson AZ 85705 520-741-0895 741-0864
Web: www.leoni.com
Major Custom Cable Inc 281 Lotus Dr.................Jackson MO 63755 800-455-6224 243-1365*
**Fax Area Code:* 573 ■ *TF:* 800-455-6224 ■ *Web:* www.majorcustomcable.com
Mercury Wire Products Inc One Mercury Dr ....Spencer MA 01562 508-885-6363 885-3316
Web: www.mercurywire.com
Mid-South Wire Company Inc 1070 Visco Dr......... Nashville TN 37210 615-743-2850 256-5836
TF: 800-714-7800 ■ *Web:* www.midsouthwire.com
Mount Joy Wire Corp 1000 E Main St...............Mount Joy PA 17552 717-653-1461 653-0221
TF: 800-321-2305 ■ *Web:* www.mjwire.com
Nichols Wire 1547 Helton Dr .... Florence AL 35630 256-764-4271 767-5152
TF: 800-633-3156 ■ *Web:* investors.kaiseraluminum.com
Okonite Co 102 Hilltop Rd .... Ramsey NJ 07446 201-825-0300 825-3524
Web: www.okonite.com
Owl Wire & Cable Inc 3127 Seneca Tpke .... Canastota NY 13032 315-697-2011 697-2123
TF: 800-765-9473 ■ *Web:* www.owlwire.com
Rea Magnet Wire Company Inc
3600 E Pontiac St............................. Fort Wayne IN 46803 260-421-7321
TF: 800-732-9473 ■ *Web:* www.reawire.com
Ribbon Technology Corp
825 Taylor Stn Rd PO Box 30758 .... Gahanna OH 43230 614-864-5444 864-5305
TF: 800-848-0477 ■ *Web:* www.ribtec.com
S & S Industries Inc Five Odell Plz .... Yonkers NY 10701 914-885-1500 885-1488
Web: www.sandsindustries.com
Seneca Wire & Manufacturing Co
319 S Vine St.....................................Fostoria OH 44830 419-435-9261 435-9265
Shaped Wire Inc 30000 Solon Rd......................Solon OH 44139 440-248-7600 248-5491
Web: www.shapedwire.com
Sivaco Wire Group 800 Rue Ouellette .... Marieville QC J3M1P5 450-658-8741 460-2744
TF: 800-876-9473 ■ *Web:* www.sivaco.com
Southwestern Wire Inc PO Box CC.................Norman OK 73070 405-447-6900 447-2830
TF: 800-348-9473 ■ *Web:* www.southwesternwire.com
Southwire Co 1 Southwire Dr...................... Carrollton GA 30119 770-832-4242 832-4406
TF: 800-444-1700 ■ *Web:* www.southwire.com
Spotnails 1100 Hicks Rd.........................Rolling Meadows IL 60008 847-259-1620 259-9236
TF: 800-873-2239 ■ *Web:* www.spotnails.com
Sumitomo Electric USA Inc
21241 S Western Ave Ste 120...................... Torrance CA 90501 310-782-0227 782-0211
Web: www.sumitomoelectricusa.com
Superior Essex Inc Magnet Wire/Winding Wire Div
1601 Wall St PO Box 1601....................... Fort Wayne IN 46802 260-461-4550 461-4690
TF: 800-551-8948 ■ *Web:* www.superioressex.com
TE's Rochester Wire & Cable product line
751 Old Brandy Rd .... Culpeper VA 22701 540-825-2111 825-2238
Web: www.rochestercables.com
Techalloy Company Inc Baltimore Wire Div
2310 Chesapeake Ave............................Baltimore MD 21222 410-633-9300 633-2033
TF: 800-638-1458 ■ *Web:* www.techalloy.com
Times Fiber Communications Inc
358 Hall Ave PO Box 384....................... Wallingford CT 06492 203-265-8500 265-8422
TF: 800-677-2288 ■ *Web:* www.timesfiber.com
Tokusen USA Inc 1500 Amity Rd PO Box 1150.......... Conway AR 72033 501-327-6800 327-0231
Web: www.tokusenusa.com

Phone Fax

Tree Island Steel 12459 Arrow Rt .... Rancho Cucamonga CA 91739 909-594-7511 595-0439
TF: 800-255-6974 ■ *Web:* treeisland.com/brands/tree-island

WireCo WorldGroup 12200 NW Ambassador Dr ...... Kansas City MO 64163 816-270-4700 270-4707
Web: www.wirecoworldgroup.com

Wirerope Works Inc 100 Maynard St .... Williamsport PA 17701 570-326-5146 327-4274
TF Cust Svc: 800-541-7673 ■ *Web:* www.wwrope.com

Wrap-On Company Inc 5550 W 70th Pl .... Chicago IL 60638 708-496-2150 496-2154
TF: 800-621-6947 ■ *Web:* wrap-on.com

817 WIRE & CABLE - ELECTRONIC

Phone Fax

Alpha Wire Co 711 Lidgerwood Ave.................. Elizabeth NJ 07207 908-925-8000 925-5411
TF: 800-522-5742 ■ *Web:* www.alphawire.com

Belden Inc Americas Div
2200 US Hwy 27 S PO Box 1980 .... Richmond IN 47375 765-983-5200 983-5294
TF: 800-235-3362 ■ *Web:* www.belden.com

C & M Corp 349 Lake Rd PO Box 348 .... Dayville CT 06241 860-774-4812 779-4330
Web: www.cmcorporation.com

Cable USA LLC 2584 S Horseshoe Dr................... Naples FL 34104 239-643-6400 643-4230
Web: www.cableusa.cc

Cables to Go Inc 3599 Dayton Pk Dr.................. Dayton OH 45414 937-224-8646 496-2666
TF: 800-826-7904 ■ *Web:* www.cablestogo.com

Champlain Cable Corp 175 Hercules Dr .... Colchester VT 05446 800-451-5162 654-4224*
*Fax Area Code: 802 ■ *Fax: Sales ■ *TF:* 800-451-5162 ■ *Web:* www.champcable.com

Cicoil Corp 24960 Ave Tibbitts .... Valencia CA 91355 661-295-1295 295-0813
Web: www.cicoil.com

CommScope Inc 1100 Commscope Pl SE PO Box 339.... Hickory NC 28603 828-324-2200 328-3400*
*Fax: Cust Svc ■ *TF:* 800-982-1708 ■ *Web:* www.commscope.com

Compulink Inc 1205 Gandy Blvd N .... Saint Petersburg FL 33702 727-579-1500 578-8420
TF: 800-231-6685 ■ *Web:* www.compulink.com

Comtran Corp 330A Turner St .... Attleboro MA 02703 508-399-7004 399-8839
Web: comtrancorp.com

Consolidated Electronic Wire & Cable Co
11044 King St................................. Franklin Park IL 60131 847-455-8830 455-8837
TF: 800-621-4278 ■ *Web:* www.conwire.com

Corning Cable Systems 800 17th St NW .... Hickory NC 28603 828-901-5000 325-5060
TF: 800-743-2671 ■ *Web:* www.corning.com

CXtec 5404 S Bay Rd PO Box 4799 .... Syracuse NY 13212 315-476-3000 455-1800
TF Orders: 800-767-3282 ■ *Web:* www.cxtec.com

DC Electronics 1870 Little Orchard St .... San Jose CA 95125 408-947-4500 947-4510
Web: www.dcelectronics.com

Dekoron Wire & Cable
1300 Industrial Blvd .... Mount Pleasant TX 75455 903-572-3475 572-6153*
*Fax: Cust Svc ■ *Web:* www.dekoroncable.com

Draka Comteq Americas 2512 Penny Rd............ Claremont NC 28610 828-459-9821
TF: 800-879-9862 ■ *Web:* prysmiangroup.com

Fargo Assembly Co (FAC)
3300 Seventh Ave N PO Box 2340 .... Fargo ND 58102 701-298-3803 298-3806
Web: www.facnd.com

Gallant & Wein Corp 11-20 43Rd Rd .... Long Island City NY 11101 718-784-5210 937-6426
Web: www.galwein.com

General Cable Corp
Four Tesseneer Dr......................... Highland Heights KY 41076 859-572-8000 547-8072
NYSE: BGC ■ *TF:* 800-572-8000 ■ *Web:* www.generalcable.com

Harbour Industries Inc
4744 Shelburne Rd PO Box 188.................... Shelburne VT 05482 802-985-3311 985-9534
TF: 800-659-4733 ■ *Web:* www.harbourind.com

Judd Wire Inc 124 Tpke Rd........................ Turners Falls MA 01376 413-863-4357 863-2305
TF Cust Svc: 800-545-5833 ■ *Web:* www.juddwire.com

Lynn Products Inc 2645 W 237th St .... Torrance CA 90505 310-530-5966 530-8426
Web: www.lynnprod.com

Madison Cable Corp 125 Goddard Memorial Dr....... Worcester MA 01603 508-752-2884 752-4230
TF: 877-623-4766 ■ *Web:* www.te.com

National Wire & Cable Corp
136 N San Fernando Rd .... Los Angeles CA 90031 323-225-5611 225-4630
Web: www.nationalwire.com

Nehring Electric Works Inc 1005 E Locust St........... DeKalb IL 60115 815-756-2741 756-7048
TF: 800-435-4481 ■ *Web:* www.nehringwire.com

Oleco Inc 18683 Trimble Ct PO Box 463............ Spring Lake MI 49456 616-842-6790 842-5886
Web: globaltec.com

Optical Cable Corp (OCC) 5290 Concourse Dr......... Roanoke VA 24019 540-265-0690 265-0724
NASDAQ: OCC ■ *TF:* 800-622-7711 ■ *Web:* www.occfiber.com

Parlex Corp One Parlex Pl.......................... Methuen MA 01844 978-685-4341
Web: www.parlex.com

Prestolite Wire Corp
200 Galleria Officentre Ste 212..................... Southfield MI 48034 248-355-4422 386-4462
TF: 800-498-3132 ■ *Web:* www.prestolitewire.com

Rockbestos-Surprenant Cable Corp
20 Bradley Pk Rd .... East Granby CT 06026 860-653-8300 653-8410
Web: www.r-scc.com

Siemon Co 101 Siemon Co Dr...................... Watertown CT 06795 860-945-4200 945-4225
TF: 866-548-5814 ■ *Web:* www.siemon.com

Superior Essex Inc
6120 Powers Ferry Rd Ste 150 .... Atlanta GA 30339 770-657-6000 303-8883
NASDAQ: SPSX ■ *TF:* 800-551-8948 ■ *Web:* www.superioressex.com

Trilogy Communications Inc 2910 Hwy 80 E .... Pearl MS 39208 601-932-4461 939-6637
TF: 888-713-1414 ■ *Web:* www.trilogycoax.com

Tyco Telecommunications 60 Columbia Rd .... Morristown NJ 07960 973-656-8000
Web: www.tycotelecom.com

818 WIRING DEVICES - CURRENT-CARRYING

Phone Fax

360 Electrical LLC
3165 E Millrock Dr Ste 340 .... Salt Lake City UT 84121 801-364-4900
Web: www.360electrical.com

Aerospace Optics Inc 3201 Sandy Ln .... Fort Worth TX 76112 817-451-1141 654-3405
TF: 888-848-4786 ■ *Web:* www.vivisun.com

American Superconductor Corp 64 Jackson Rd .... Devens MA 01434 978-842-3000
Web: www.amsc.com

Amphenol Corp 358 Hall Ave...................... Wallingford CT 06492 203-265-8900 265-8628
NYSE: APH ■ *TF:* 877-267-4366 ■ *Web:* www.amphenol.com

AVA Electronics Corp 4000 Bridge St.............. Drexel Hill PA 19026 610-284-2500 259-8379

Backer Springfield Inc
4700 John Bragg Hwy .... Murfreesboro TN 37127 615-907-6900 739-3809*
*Fax Area Code: 413 ■ *Web:* backer-springfield.com

Bizlink Technology Inc 3400 Gateway Blvd .... Fremont CA 94538 510-252-0786 252-1178
TF: 800-326-4193 ■ *Web:* www.bizlinktech.com

Brainin Advance Industries Inc
48 Frank Mossberg Dr........................... Attleboro MA 02703 508-226-1200 226-8703
Web: www.pepbrainin.com

Burndy LLC 47 E Industrial Park Dr................ Manchester NH 03109 800-346-4175
TF: 800-346-4175 ■ *Web:* www.burndy.com

Carbide Probes Inc 1328 Research Park Dr .... Dayton OH 45432 937-429-9123
Web: www.carbideprobes.com

Carling Technologies Inc 60 Johnson Ave .... Plainville CT 06062 860-793-9281 793-9231
TF: 800-243-8556 ■ *Web:* www.carlingtech.com

Charles E Gillman Co 907 E Frontage Rd .... Rio Rico AZ 85648 520-281-1141 281-1372
Web: www.gillman.com

Checon Corp 30 Larsen Way................... North Attleboro MA 02763 508-809-5100 809-5163
Web: www.checon.com

Cherry Corp 11200 88th Ave................. Pleasant Prairie WI 53158 262-942-6500 942-6566
TF: 800-510-1689 ■ *Web:* www.cherrycorp.com

Cinch Connectors Inc 1700 Findley Rd .... Lombard IL 60148 630-705-6000 705-6055
TF: 800-323-9612 ■ *Web:* www.cinch.com

Cole Hersee Co 20 Old Colony Ave .... Boston MA 02127 617-268-2100 268-9490
TF: 800-365-2653 ■ *Web:* www.colehersee.com

Component Enterprises Co Inc
235 E Penn St PO Box 189 .... Norristown PA 19401 877-232-7253 272-7040*
*Fax Area Code: 610 ■ *TF:* 877-232-7253 ■ *Web:* componententerprises.com

Connector Manufacturing Co 3501 Symmes Rd ...... Hamilton OH 45015 513-860-4455 860-6114
Web: www.cmclugs.com

Cooper Bussmann Inc 114 Old State Rd............... Ellisville MO 63021 636-394-2877 394-2877*
*Fax: Cust Svc ■ *TF:* 855-287-7626 ■
Web: www.cooperindustries.com/content/public/en/bussmann.html

Cooper Crouse-Hinds 1201 Wolf St .... Syracuse NY 13208 315-477-5531 477-5531
TF: 866-764-5454 ■ *Web:* www.cooperindustries.com

Cooper Industries 600 Travis St Ste 5400............. Houston TX 77002 713-209-8400 209-8995
NYSE: ETN ■ *TF:* 866-853-4293 ■ *Web:* www.cooperindustries.com

Cooper Wiring Devices Inc
203 Cooper Cir............................. Peachtree City GA 30269 770-631-2100 631-2100
TF Cust Svc: 866-853-4293 ■ *Web:* www.cooperindustries.com

Cord Sets Inc 1015 Fifth St N .... Minneapolis MN 55411 612-337-9700 337-0800
TF: 800-752-0580 ■ *Web:* www.cordsetsinc.com

Cord Specialties Co 10632 Grand Ave .... Franklin Park IL 60131 847-455-3503 455-0916
Web: www.cordspecialties.com

Cristek Interconnects Inc 5395 E Hunter Ave......... Anaheim CA 92807 714-696-5200 696-5225
TF: 888-265-9162 ■ *Web:* www.cristek.com

Curtis Industries Inc
2400 S 43rd St PO Box 343925 .... Milwaukee WI 53219 414-649-4200 649-4279
TF: 800-657-0853 ■ *Web:* www.curtisind.com

Ddh Enterprise Inc 2220 Oak Ridge Way................ Vista CA 92081 760-599-0171 599-9397
Web: www.ddhent.com

Edwin Gaynor Corp 200 Charles St .... Stratford CT 06615 203-378-5545 381-9019
TF: 800-342-9667 ■ *Web:* www.egaynor.com

EECO Switch 880 Columbia St .... Brea CA 92821 714-835-6000 482-9429
TF: 800-854-3808 ■ *Web:* www.eecoswitch.com

Electri-Cord Mfg Co Inc 312 E Main St............. Westfield PA 16950 814-367-2265 367-2314
TF: 888-278-8253 ■ *Web:* www.electri-cord.com

Electro Adapter Inc 20640 Nordhoff St .... Chatsworth CA 91311 818-998-1198
Web: www.electro-adapter.com

Electronic Systems Packaging LLC (ESP)
1175 W Victoria St .... Rancho Dominguez CA 90220 310-639-2535 632-6666
Web: www.espbus.com

Electroswitch 2010 Yonkers Rd .... Raleigh NC 27604 919-833-0707 833-8016
TF: 888-768-2797 ■ *Web:* www.electro-nc.com

ERICO Products Inc 34600 Solon Rd .... Solon OH 44139 440-248-0100 248-0723
TF: 800-813-3378 ■ *Web:* www.erico.com

ETCO Inc 25 Bellows St .... Warwick RI 02888 401-467-2400 467-9230
TF: 800-689-3826 ■ *Web:* www.etco.com

Eureka Electrical Products Inc 79 Clay St.......... North East PA 16428 814-725-9638 725-3670

Fastron Company Inc, The
11800 Franklin Ave........................... Franklin Park IL 60131 630-766-5000
Web: www.fastron.com

FTZ Industries Inc 515 Palmetto Dr............... Simpsonville SC 29681 864-963-5000 963-5352
Web: www.ftzind.com

Glenair Inc 1211 Air Way .... Glendale CA 91201 818-247-6000 500-9912
TF: 888-465-4094 ■ *Web:* www.glenair.com

Group Dekko Services LLC 2505 Dekko Dr .... Garrett IN 46738 260-357-3621 357-4293
TF: 800-829-3101 ■ *Web:* www.dekko.com

Harger Inc 301 Ziegler Dr .... Grayslake IL 60030 847-548-8700
Web: www.harger.com

Hi Rel Connectors Inc 760 Wharton Dr............. Claremont CA 91711 909-626-1820 399-0626
Web: www.hirelco.net

Hi-Stat Mfg Company Inc 345 S Mill St............. Lexington OH 44904 419-884-1219 884-4196
Web: www.stoneridge.com

Hoffman Products 9600 Vly View Rd .... Macedonia OH 44056 216-525-4320 896-3017*
*Fax Area Code: 866 ■ *TF:* 800-645-2014 ■ *Web:* www.tpcwire.com

Hubbell Premise Wiring Inc 23 Clara Dr............. Mystic CT 06355 800-626-0005 535-8328*
*Fax Area Code: 860 ■ *TF:* 800-626-0005 ■ *Web:* www.hubbell-premise.com

Hubbell Wiring Device-Kellems
40 Waterview Dr................................ Shelton CT 06484 203-882-4800 882-4852*
*Fax: Tech Supp ■ *TF Cust Svc:* 800-288-6000 ■ *Web:* www.hubbell-wiring.com

ILSCO 4730 Madison Rd.......................... Cincinnati OH 45227 513-533-6200 533-6274
TF Sales: 800-776-9775 ■ *Web:* www.ilsco.com

Independent Protection Company Inc
1607 S Main St.................................. Goshen IN 46526 574-533-4116 534-3719
TF: 800-860-8388 ■ *Web:* www.ipclp.com

	City	State	Zip	Phone	Fax
JB Nottingham & Company Inc Duraline Div 75 Hoffman Ln *Web:* store.jbn-duraline.com	Islandia	NY	11749	631-234-2002	234-2360
Kemlon Products & Development Co 1424 N Main St *Web:* www.kemlon.com	Pearland	TX	77581	281-997-3300	997-1300
Keystone Cable Corp 8200 Lynch Rd *Web:* www.keystonecable.net	Detroit	MI	48234	313-924-9720	924-0050
LL Rowe Co 66 Holton St *Web:* www.llrowe.com	Woburn	MA	01801	781-729-7860	721-7264
Lumens Light & Living 2028 K St *TF:* 877-445-4486 ■ *Web:* www.lumens.com	Sacramento	CA	95811	916-444-5585	
Marinco 2655 Napa Valley Corp Dr *TF:* 800-307-6702 ■ *Web:* www.marinco.com	Napa	CA	94558	707-226-9600	226-9670
McGill Electrical Product Group 9377 W Higgins Rd **Fax Area Code:* 800 ■ *TF:* 800-621-1506 ■ *Web:* www.emersonindustrial.com	Rosemont	IL	60018	847-268-6000	356-4714*
Metalor Electrotechnics 1003 Corporate Ln *Web:* www.metalor.com	Export	PA	15632	724-733-8332	733-8341
Midwest Manufacturing Inc 5311 Kane Rd *Web:* www.midwestmanufacturing.com	Eau Claire	WI	54703	715-876-5555	
Mill-Max Mfg Corp 190 Pine Hollow Rd *TF:* 800-333-4237 ■ *Web:* www.mill-max.com	Oyster Bay	NY	11771	516-922-6000	922-9253
Minnesota Wire & Cable Co 1835 Energy Pk Dr *TF:* 800-258-6922 ■ *Web:* www.mnwire.com	Saint Paul	MN	55108	651-642-1800	642-9286
Nexus Inc 50 Sunnyside Ave *Web:* www.nexus.com	Stamford	CT	06902	203-327-7300	324-7623
Ohio Associated Enterprises LLC 1382 W Jackson St *TF:* 888-637-4832 ■ *Web:* www.meritec.com	Painesville	OH	44077	440-354-3148	354-0687
Omnetics Connector Corp 7260 Commerce Cir E *TF Cust Svc:* 800-343-0025 ■ *Web:* www.omnetics.com	Minneapolis	MN	55432	763-572-0656	572-3925
Panduit Corp 17301 Ridgeland Ave *TF:* 888-506-5400 ■ *Web:* www.panduit.com	Tinley Park	IL	60477	708-532-1800	532-1811
Pass & Seymour Inc 50 Boyd Ave PO Box 4822 *Web:* www.passandseymour.com	Syracuse	NY	13221	315-468-6211	
Penn-Union Corp 229 Waterford St *Web:* www.penn-union.com	Edinboro	PA	16412	814-734-1631	734-4946
Phoenix Co of Chicago Inc 555 Pond Dr *Web:* www.phoenixofchicago.com	Wood Dale	IL	60191	630-595-2300	595-6579
Preformed Line Products 660 Beta Dr *NASDAQ: PLPC* ■ *TF:* 800-622-6757 ■ *Web:* www.preformed.com	Cleveland	OH	44143	440-461-5200	442-8816
Shape LLC 2105 Corporate Dr *TF:* 800-367-5811 ■ *Web:* www.shapellc.com	Addison	IL	60101	630-620-8394	620-0784
Special Mine Services Inc PO Box 188 *Web:* www.smsconnectors.com	West Frankfort	IL	62896	618-932-2151	937-2715
State Tool & Manufacturing Co 1650 E Empire Ave *Web:* www.statetool.com	Benton Harbor	MI	49022	269-927-3153	927-4230
Tower Manufacturing Corp 25 Reservoir Ave *Web:* www.towermfg.com	Providence	RI	02907	401-467-7550	461-2710
Tripp Lite Inc 1111 W 35th St *Web:* www.tripplite.com	Chicago	IL	60609	773-869-1111	869-1329
Unlimited Services of Wisconsin Inc 170 Evergreen Rd *Web:* www.us-wire-harness.com	Oconto	WI	54153	920-834-4418	
Veetronix Inc 1311 W Pacific Ave *TF General:* 800-445-0007 ■ *Web:* www.veetronix.com	Lexington	NE	68850	308-324-6661	324-4985
Volex Inc 915 Tate Blvd SE Ste 130 *Web:* www.volex.com	Hickory	NC	28602	828-485-4500	485-4501
Weidmuller Inc 821 Southlake Blvd *TF Cust Svc:* 800-849-9343 ■ *Web:* www.weidmuller.com	Richmond	VA	23236	804-794-2877	379-2593
Zierick Manufacturing Corp 131 Radio Cr *TF:* 800-882-8020 ■ *Web:* www.zierick.com	Mount Kisco	NY	10549	914-666-2911	666-0216

819 WIRING DEVICES - NONCURRENT-CARRYING

	City	State	Zip	Phone	Fax
Adalet 4801 W 150th St **Fax:* Sales ■ *Web:* www.adalet.com	Cleveland	OH	44135	216-267-9000	267-1681*
Allied Moulded Products Inc 222 N Union St *TF:* 800-722-2679 ■ *Web:* www.alliedmoulded.com	Bryan	OH	43506	419-636-4217	636-2450
Aluma-Form Inc 3625 Old Getwell Rd *Web:* www.alumaform.com	Memphis	TN	38118	901-362-0100	794-9515
Bedford Materials Co Inc 7676 Allegheny Rd **Fax Area Code:* 814 ■ *TF:* 800-773-4276 ■ *Web:* www.bedfordmaterials.com	Manns Choice	PA	15550	800-773-4276	623-9199*
Bridgeport Fittings Inc 705 Lordship Blvd *Web:* www.bptfittings.com	Stratford	CT	06615	203-377-5944	381-3488
Chalfant Manufacturing Co 11525 Madison Ave *Web:* www.chalfantcabletray.com	Cleveland	OH	44102	216-521-7922	521-6854
Chase & Sons Inc 295 University Ave *TF:* 800-323-4182 ■ *Web:* www.chasecorp.com	Westwood	MA	02090	781-332-0700	963-9584
Conduit Pipe Products Co 1501 W Main St *TF:* 800-848-6125 ■ *Web:* www.conduitpipe.com	West Jefferson	OH	43162	614-879-9114	879-5185
Cooper B-Line Inc 509 W Monroe St **Fax Area Code:* 800 ■ *TF:* 800-851-7415 ■ *Web:* www.cooperindustries.com	Highland	IL	62249	618-654-2184	356-1438*
Cottrell Paper Company Inc 1135 Rock City Rd PO Box 35 *TF:* 800-948-3559 ■ *Web:* www.cottrellpaper.com	Rock City Falls	NY	12863	518-885-1702	885-1702
Durham Co 722 Durham Rd *Web:* www.durhamcompany.com	Lebanon	MO	65536	417-532-7121	532-2366
EGS Electrical Group LLC 9377 W Higgins Rd *TF:* 800-621-1506 ■ *Web:* www.emersonindustrial.com	Rosemont	IL	60018	847-268-6000	268-6011
Electri-Flex Co 222 Central Ave *TF:* 800-323-6174 ■ *Web:* www.electriflex.com	Roselle	IL	60172	630-529-2920	529-0482
Flex-Cable Inc 5822 N Henkel Rd *TF:* 800-245-3539 ■ *Web:* www.flexcable.com	Howard City	MI	49329	231-937-8000	937-8091
Gaylord Manufacturing Co 1088 Montclaire Dr *TF:* 800-375-0091 ■ *Web:* www.gaylordmfg.com	Ceres	CA	95307	209-538-3313	
Gund Co 2121 Walton Rd *Web:* www.thegundcompany.com	Saint Louis	MO	63114	314-423-5200	423-9009
Hubbell Premise Wiring Inc 23 Clara Dr **Fax Area Code:* 860 ■ *TF:* 800-626-0005 ■ *Web:* www.hubbell-premise.com	Mystic	CT	06355	800-626-0005	535-8328*
Hubbell RACO 3902 W Sample St **Fax Area Code:* 800 ■ *TF:* 800-722-6437 ■ *Web:* www.hubbell-raco.com	South Bend	IN	46619	574-234-7151	722-6462*
Hubbell Wiegmann 501 W Apple St *Web:* www.hubbell-wiegmann.com	Freeburg	IL	62243	618-539-3193	539-5794
Hughes Bros Inc 210 N 13th St PO Box 159 *TF:* 800-869-0359 ■ *Web:* www.hughesbros.com	Seward	NE	68434	402-643-2991	643-2149
ICO-RALLY Corp 2575 E Bayshore Rd **Fax Area Code:* 800 ■ *Web:* www.icorally.com	Palo Alto	CA	94303	650-856-9900	856-2006*
Ideal Industries Inc 1000 Pk Ave *TF:* 800-435-0705 ■ *Web:* www.idealindustries.com	Sycamore	IL	60178	815-895-5181	899-7712
Joslyn Sunbank Co LLC 1740 Commerce Way **Fax:* Cust Svc ■ *TF:* 800-523-0727 ■ *Web:* www.sunbankcorp.com	Paso Robles	CA	93446	805-238-2840	238-0241*
Kortick Manufacturing Co 2230 Davis Ct *Web:* www.kortick.com	Hayward	CA	94545	510-856-3600	856-3606
LoDan Electronics Inc 3311 N Kennicott Ave *TF:* 800-401-4995 ■ *Web:* www.lodanelectronics.com	Arlington Heights	IL	60004	847-398-5311	398-5340
MacLean Power Systems 11411 Addison St **Fax:* Sales ■ *TF:* 855-677-7447 ■ *Web:* www.macleanpower.com	Franklin Park	IL	60131	847-455-0014	455-0029*
Monti Inc 333 W Seymour Ave *Web:* www.monti-inc.com	Cincinnati	OH	45216	513 761 7775	948 6858
MP Husky Corp 204 Old Piedmont Hwy PO Box 16749 *TF:* 800-277-4810 ■ *Web:* www.mphusky.com	Greenville	SC	29605	864-234-4800	234-4822
Mulberry Metal Products Inc 2199 Stanley Terr *Web:* www.mulberrymetal.com	Union	NJ	07083	908-688-8850	688-7294
Ngk-locke Polymer Insulators Inc 1609 Diamond Springs Rd *Web:* www.ngk-polymer.com	Virginia Beach	VA	23455	757-460-3649	460-3550
O-Z/Gedney 9377 W Higgins Rd **Fax Area Code:* 800 ■ *TF:* 800-621-1506 ■ *Web:* www.emersonindustrial.com	Rosemont	IL	60018	847-268-6000	356-4714*
Ohio Brass Co 1850 Richland Ave E *Web:* www.hubbellpowersystems.com	Aiken	SC	29801	803-648-8386	642-2959
Opti-Com Mfg Network Co Inc 259 Plauche St *TF:* 800-345-8774 ■ *Web:* opti-com.info	New Orleans	LA	70123	504-736-0331	733-9046
Rittal Corp One Rittal Pl *TF:* 800-477-4000 ■ *Web:* www.rittal.us	Springfield	OH	45504	937-399-0500	390-5599
Saginaw Control & Engineering Inc 95 Midland Rd *TF:* 800-234-6871 ■ *Web:* www.saginawcontrol.com	Saginaw	MI	48638	989-799-6871	799-4524
TJ Cope Inc 11500 Norcom Rd *TF:* 800-483-3473 ■ *Web:* copecabletray.com/	Philadelphia	PA	19154	215-961-2570	961-2580
Varflex Corp 512 W Ct St *TF:* 800-648-4014 ■ *Web:* www.varflex.com	Rome	NY	13440	315-336-4400	336-0005
Virginia Plastics Co Inc 3453 Aerial Way Dr PO Box 4577 *TF:* 877-351-1699 ■ *Web:* www.vaplastics.com	Roanoke	VA	24018	540-981-9700	981-2022
Weidmann Electrical Technology 1 Gordon Mills Way PO Box 903 *TF:* 800-242-6748 ■ *Web:* weidmann-electrical.com	Saint Johnsbury	VT	05819	802-748-8106	748-8630

820 WOOD MEMBERS - STRUCTURAL

	City	State	Zip	Phone	Fax
Alpine Engineered Products Inc 1100 Pk Central Blvd S PO Box 2225 *TF General:* 800-786-6086 ■ *Web:* www.alpeng.com	Pompano Beach	FL	33064	954-781-3333	973-2644
American Laminators 600 Applegate St PO Box 297 *Web:* www.americanlaminators.com	Drain	OR	97435	541-836-2000	836-7144
Armstrong Lumber Co Inc 2709 Auburn Way N *TF:* 800-868-9066 ■ *Web:* www.armstrong-homes.com	Auburn	WA	98002	253-833-6666	833-5878
Automated Bldg Components Inc 2359 Grant Rd *TF:* 800-837-2152 ■ *Web:* www.abctruss.com	North Baltimore	OH	45872	419-257-2152	257-2779
Automated Products Inc 1812 Karau Dr *Web:* apiebs.com	Marshfield	WI	54449	715-387-3426	387-6588
Buettner Bros Lumber Co 700 Seventh Ave SW *TF:* 800-500-0669 ■ *Web:* bblumber.net	Cullman	AL	35055	256-734-4221	737-8102
California Truss Co 23665 Cajalco Rd *Web:* caltrusframe.com	Perris	CA	92570	951-657-7491	
Chantiers Chibougamau Ltd 521 Chemin Merrill PO 216 *Web:* www.chibou.com	Chibougamau	QC	G8P2K7	418-748-6481	
Columbia Forest Products Inc 7900 Triad Ctr Dr Ste 200 *TF:* 800-637-1609 ■ *Web:* www.columbiaforestproducts.com	Greensboro	NC	27409	336-291-5905	
East Coast Lumber & Supply Co 308 Ave A **Fax Area Code:* 772 ■ *Web:* www.eastcoastlumber.com	Fort Pierce	FL	34950	321-636-0411	465-8678*
Enwood Structures Inc 5724 McCrimmon Pkwy PO Box 2002 *TF:* 800-777-8648 ■ *Web:* www.enwood.com	Morrisville	NC	27560	919-518-0464	469-2536
Fullerton Bldg Systems Inc (FBS) 34620 250th St PO Box 308 *TF:* 800-450-9782 ■ *Web:* www.fullertonbuildingsystems.com	Worthington	MN	56187	507-376-3128	376-9530
Giddings Manufacturing Company Inc 1426 Us Route 7 *Web:* giddingsvt.com	Pittsford	VT	05763	802-483-2292	
Giles & Kendall Inc 3470 Maysville Rd Ne *Web:* www.cedarsafeclosets.com	Huntsville	AL	35811	256-776-2979	
Goodfellow Inc 225 Goodfellow St *Web:* www.goodfellowinc.com	Delson	QC	J5B1V5	450-635-6511	635-3729

Phone Fax

HM Stauffer & Sons Inc 33 Glenola Dr PO Box 567 .... Leola PA 17540 717-656-2811 656-4392
TF: 800-662-2226 ■ *Web:* hmstauffer.com

J C Snavely & Sons Inc 150 Main St .... Landisville PA 17538 717-898-2241 898-5208
Web: www.jcsnavely.com

Laminate Technologies Inc 161 Maule Rd .... Tiffin OH 44883 800-231-2523 448-0811*
**Fax Area Code:* 419 ■ *TF:* 800-231-2523 ■ *Web:* www.lamtech.net

Laminated Wood Systems Inc (LWS)
1327 285th Rd PO Box 386 .... Seward NE 68434 402-643-4708 643-4374
TF: 800-949-3526 ■ *Web:* www.lwsinc.com

Laminators Inc 3255 Penn St .... Hatfield PA 19440 215-723-8107 721-4669
TF: 877-663-4277 ■ *Web:* www.laminatorsinc.com

Molpus Co, The 502 Vly View Dr PO Box 59 .... Philadelphia MS 39350 601-656-3373 656-4947
TF: 800-535-5434 ■ *Web:* www.molpus.com

Montgomery Truss & Panel Inc
803 W Main St .... Grove City PA 16127 724-458-7500 458-0765
TF: 800-942-8010 ■ *Web:* montgomerytruss.com

Okaw Truss Inc 368 E St Rt 133 .... Arthur IL 61911 217-543-3371 543-3376
Web: www.okawtruss.com

RedBuilt LLC 200 E Mallard Dr .... Boise ID 83706 208-364-1316
Web: www.redbuilt.com

Robbins Mfg Co 13001 N Nebraska Ave .... Tampa FL 33612 813-971-3030 972-3980
TF: 888-558-8199 ■ *Web:* www.robbinslumber.com

Roof Structures Inc 3333 Yale Way .... Fremont CA 94538 510-226-7171 226-8989
Web: www.roofstructures.com

Sentinel Structures Inc 477 S Peck Ave .... Peshtigo WI 54157 715-582-4544 582-4932
Web: www.sentinelstructures.com

Shook Builder Supply Co 1400 16th St NE .... Hickory NC 28601 828-328-2051 328-2425
TF: 800-968-0758 ■ *Web:* shookbuildersupply.com

Southern Components Inc
7360 Julie Frances Dr PO Box 29010 .... Shreveport LA 71129 318-687-3330 686-5159
TF: 800-256-2144 ■ *Web:* www.socomp.com

Stow Co, The 3311 Windquest Dr .... Holland MI 49424 616-399-3311 399-8784
TF: 800-562-4257 ■ *Web:* www.windquestco.com

Structural Wood Corp 4000 Labore Rd .... Saint Paul MN 55110 651-426-8111 426-6859
TF: 800-652-9058 ■ *Web:* www.structural-wood.com

Structural Wood Systems 321 Dohrimier St .... Greenville AL 36037 334-382-6534 382-4260
Web: www.structuralwood.com

Tacoma Truss Systems Inc 20617 Mtn Hwy E .... Spanaway WA 98387 253-847-2204 847-2207
Web: www.tacomatruss.com

Trusco Inc 12527 Porr Rd .... Doylestown OH 44230 330-658-2027 658-4979
Web: www.truscoinc.com

Trussway Ltd 9411 Alcorn Rd .... Houston TX 77093 713-691-6900 691-2064
Web: www.trussway.com

Valley Best-Way Bldg Supply 118 S Union Rd .... Spokane WA 99206 509-924-1250 922-5420

Villaume Industries Inc 2926 Lone Oak Cir .... Saint Paul MN 55121 651-454-3610 454-8556
TF Cust Svc: 800-488-3610 ■ *Web:* www.villaume.com

821 WOOD PRESERVING

Phone Fax

Appalachian Timber Services Inc
393 EDGAR Givens Pkwy Ste 100 .... Sutton WV 26601 304-765-7393 321-2520*
**Fax Area Code:* 770 ■ *Web:* www.atstimber.com

Bell Lumber & Pole Co
778 First St NW PO Box 120786 .... New Brighton MN 55112 651-633-4334 633-8852
TF: 877-633-4334 ■ *Web:* www.blpole.com

Biewer Lumber LLC 812 S Riverside .... Saint Clair MI 48079 810-329-4789
Web: www.biewerlumber.com

Brooks Mfg Co 2120 Pacific St PO Box 7 .... Bellingham WA 98229 360-733-1700 734-6668
Web: www.brooksmfg.com

Brown Wood Preserving Company Inc
6201 Camp Ground Rd .... Louisville KY 40216 502-448-2337 448-9944
TF: 800-537-1765 ■ *Web:* brownwoodpoles.com

Building Products Plus 12317 Almeda Rd .... Houston TX 77045 800-460-8627 433-7068*
**Fax Area Code:* 713 ■ *TF:* 800-460-8627 ■ *Web:* www.buildingproductsplus.com

Conrad Forest Products 68765 Wildwood Dr .... North Bend OR 97459 800-356-7146 756-0131*
**Fax Area Code:* 541 ■ *TF:* 800-356-7146 ■ *Web:* www.conradfp.com

Cox Industries Inc
860 Cannon Bridge Rd PO Box 1124 .... Orangeburg SC 29116 803-534-7467 534-1410
TF: 800-476-4401 ■ *Web:* www.coxwood.com

Culpeper Wood Preservers Inc
15487 Braggs Corner Rd PO Box 1148 .... Culpeper VA 22701 540-825-5201
Web: www.culpeperwood.com

Elder Wood Preserving Co Inc
334 Elder Wood Rd .... Mansura LA 71350 318-964-2196 964-5276
TF: 800-467-8018 ■ *Web:* greatsouthernwood.com

Exterior Wood Inc 2685 Index St .... Washougal WA 98671 360-835-8561
Web: www.exteriorwood.com

Great Southern Wood Preserving Inc
1100 US Hwy 431 N .... Abbeville AL 36310 334-585-2291 585-4353
TF: 800-633-7539 ■ *Web:* www.greatsouthernwood.com

Hoover Treated Wood Products Inc 154 Wire Rd ..... Thomson GA 30824 706-595-1264 595-8462
Web: www.frtw.com

JH Baxter & Co PO Box 5902 .... San Mateo CA 94402 650-349-0201 570-6878
TF: 800-556-1098 ■ *Web:* www.jhbaxter.com

Koppers Inc 436 Seventh Ave .... Pittsburgh PA 15219 412-227-2001 227-2333
NYSE: KOP ■ *TF:* 800-321-9876 ■ *Web:* www.koppers.com

Madison Wood Preservers Inc 216 Oak Park Rd ...... Madison VA 22727 540-948-6801
Web: www.madwood.com

McFarland Cascade 1640 E Marc St PO Box 1496 ...... Tacoma WA 98421 253-572-3033 627-0764
TF Cust Svc: 800-426-8430 ■ *Web:* www.ldm.com

Osmose Inc 980 Ellicott St .... Buffalo NY 14209 716-882-5905 882-5139
TF: 800-877-7653 ■ *Web:* www.osmose.com

Perma Treat Corp 74 Airline Dr .... Durham CT 06422 860-349-1133 349-1365

Professional Coaters Inc
2148 Port of Tacoma Rd .... Tacoma WA 98421 253-627-1141 627-1150
Web: www.procoatinc.com

Robbins Mfg Co 13001 N Nebraska Ave .... Tampa FL 33612 813-971-3030 972-3980
TF: 888-558-8199 ■ *Web:* www.robbinslumber.com

Shenandoah Wood Preserving Inc
301 E 16th St .... Scotland Neck NC 27874 252-826-4151

Phone Fax

Western Wood Preserving Co
1310 Zehnder St PO Box 1250 .... Sumner WA 98390 253-863-8191 863-9129
TF: 800-472-7714 ■ *Web:* www.westernwoodpreserving.com

Wood Preservers Inc
15939 Historyland Hwy PO Box 158 .... Warsaw VA 22572 804-333-4022 333-9269
TF: 800-368-2536 ■ *Web:* www.woodpreservers.com

822 WOOD PRODUCTS - RECONSTITUTED

Phone Fax

Aya Kitchens & Baths Ltd
1551 Caterpillar Rd .... Mississauga ON L4X2Z6 905-848-1999 848-5127
Web: www.ayakitchens.com

Cabinet Tronix LLC 290 Trousdale Dr Ste A .... Chula Vista CA 91910 866-876-6199
TF: 866-876-6199 ■ *Web:* www.cabinet-tronix.com

Duraflame Inc 2894 Mt Diablo Ave PO Box 1230 .... Stockton CA 95201 209-461-6600 462-9412
Web: www.duraflame.com

Geo Products LLC 8615 Golden Spike Ln .... Houston TX 77086 281-820-5493
TF: 800-434-4743 ■ *Web:* www.geoproducts.org

Homasote Co
932 Lower Ferry Rd PO Box 7240 .... West Trenton NJ 08628 609-883-3300 883-3497
OTC: HMTC ■ *TF:* 800-257-9491 ■ *Web:* www.homasote.com

Liberty Wood Products 874 Iotla Church Rd .... Franklin NC 28734 828-524-7958 369-7652
Web: www.libertywoodproducts.net

Panel Processing Inc 120 N Industrial Hwy .... Alpena MI 49707 989-356-9007 356-9000
TF: 800-433-7142 ■ *Web:* www.panel.com

Panolam Industries International Inc
20 Progress Dr .... Shelton CT 06484 203-925-1556 225-0051
TF: 800-672-6652 ■ *Web:* www.panolam.com

Pasquier Panel Products Inc
1510 Puyallup St PO Box 1170 .... Sumner WA 98390 253-863-6323 891-7993
Web: www.pasquierpanel.com

Potlatch Corp 601 W First Ave Ste 1600 .... Spokane WA 99201 509-835-1500 835-1555
NASDAQ: PCH ■ *Web:* www.potlatchcorp.com

Potlatch Corp Wood Products Div
805 Mill Rd PO Box 1388 .... Lewiston ID 83501 509-835-1500 799-1918*
**Fax Area Code:* 208 ■ *Web:* www.potlatchcorp.com

Rex Lumber Co 840 Main St .... Acton MA 01720 978-263-0055 263-9806
TF: 800-343-0567 ■ *Web:* www.rexlumber.com

Tectum Inc 105 S Sixth St .... Newark OH 43055 740-345-9691 349-9305
TF: 888-977-9691 ■ *Web:* www.tectum.com

823 WOOD PRODUCTS - SHAPED & TURNED

Phone Fax

A&M Supply Corp 6701 90th Ave N .... Pinellas Park FL 33782 727-541-6631 546-3617
TF: 800-877-8551

American Wood Fibers Inc
9841 Broken Land Pkwy Ste 302 .... Columbia MD 21046 410-290-8700
Web: www.awf.com

Amorim Industrial Solutions Inc
26112 110th St .... Trevor WI 53179 262-862-2311
Web: www.amorimusa.com

Art Connection Inc 2860 Ctr Port Cir .... Pompano Beach FL 33064 954-977-8177
Web: www.artconnectionusa.com

Art for Everyday Inc 420 Canarctic Dr .... Toronto ON M3J2V3 416-645-5120 645-5121
Web: www.afe-inc.com

Baker McMillen Co 3688 Wyoga Lk Rd .... Stow OH 44224 330-923-8300
Web: www.baker-mcmillen.com

Banks Hardwoods Inc 69937 M-103 .... White Pigeon MI 49099 269-483-2323
Web: www.bankshardwoods.com

Brown Wood Products Co
7040 N Lawndale Ave .... Lincolnwood IL 60712 800-328-5858 884-0423
TF: 800-328-5858 ■ *Web:* www.brownwoodinc.com

Burroughs-Ross-Colville Co 301 Depot St .... McMinnville TN 37110 931-473-2111 473-5350
Web: www.brclumber.com

Carriage Works Inc 1877 Mallard Ln .... Klamath Falls OR 97601 541-882-0700
Web: www.carriageworks.com

Chicago Dowel Company Inc 4700 W Grand Ave .... Chicago IL 60639 773-622-2000 622-2047
TF: 800-333-6935 ■ *Web:* www.chicagodowel.com

Circular Technologies 3275 Prairie Ave .... Boulder CO 80301 303-443-8512
Web: www.circulartech.com

Cochran Forest Products Inc
702 NE Okinawa St .... Lake City FL 32055 386-752-0335 755-5561
Web: www.cochranforestproducts.com

Confluence Energy LLC 1809 Hwy 9 .... Kremmling CO 80459 970-724-9839
Web: www.confluenceenergy.com

Davidson Plyforms Inc 5505 33rd St SE .... Grand Rapids MI 49512 616-956-0033 956-0041
TF: 800-505-4732 ■ *Web:* www.lpofficefurnituregroup.com

Del-Tin Fiber LLC 757 Del-Tin Hwy .... El Dorado AR 71730 870-309-3100
Web: www.deltinfiber.com

Dry Creek Products Inc 51 Edward St .... Arcade NY 14009 585-492-2990
Web: www.drycreekproducts.com

Empire Architectural 409 N Main St .... Freeport NY 11520 516-377-8545
Web: www.empirearchitecturalproducts.com

Enviva Lp 7200 Wisconsin Ave Ste 1100 .... Bethesda MD 20814 301-657-5560
Web: www.envivabiomass.com

Flakeboard America Ltd
515 River Crossing Dr Ste 110 .... Fort Mill SC 29715 905-475-9686
Web: www.flakeboard.com

Fox Lumber Sales Inc Two Riverbend Ct .... Hamilton MT 59840 406-363-5140
Web: www.foxlumber.com

Frank Edmunds & Co 6111 S Sayre .... Chicago IL 60638 773-586-2772 586-2783
TF: 800-447-3516 ■ *Web:* www.frankedmunds.com

Garick Corp 13600 Broadway Ave .... Cleveland OH 44125 216-581-0100
Web: www.garick.com

Geneva Wood Fuels LLC 30 Norton Hill Rd .... Strong ME 04983 617-934-6512
Web: www.genevapellets.com

Groupe de Scieries GDS Inc 207 Rt 295 .... Degelis QC G5T1R1 418-853-2566
Web: www.groupgds.com

	City	State	ZIP	Phone	Fax
Harbortown Industries Inc 28477 N Ballard Dr *Web:* www.harbortown.net	Lake Forest	IL	60045	847-327-9900	
Highwood USA LLC 87 Tide Rd *Web:* www.highwood-usa.com	Tamaqua	PA	18252	570-668-6113	
Horton Components 117 Milledgeville Rd *Web:* www.hortoncomponents.com	Eatonton	GA	31024	706-485-5480	
Humboldt Redwood Company LLC 108 Main St PO Box 565 *Web:* www.getredwood.com	Scotia	CA	95565	707-764-4472	
Idaho Cedar Sales LLC 221 Main St *Web:* www.cedar.idahotimber.com	Troy	ID	83871	208-835-2161	
Intermountain Wood Products Inc 1948 SW Temple *Web:* www.intermountainwood.com	Salt Lake City	UT	84115	801-486-5414	466-0428
Jarden Home Brands 14611 W Commerce Rd *TF Cust Svc:* 800-240-3340 ■ *Web:* www.jardenhomebrands.com	Daleville	IN	47334	765-557-3000	
Lexington Manufacturing Inc 1330 115th Ave NW *Web:* www.lexingtonmfg.com	Minneapolis	MN	55448	763-754-9055	
Maine Wood Concepts Inc 1687 New Vineyard Rd *Web:* www.mainewoodconcepts.com	New Vineyard	ME	04956	207-652-2441	
Michigan Maple Block Co 1420 Standish Ave **Fax Area Code:* 519	Petoskey	MI	49770	231-347-4170	880-1201*
New Century Picture Corp 2737 W Fulton St *Web:* newcenturybk.com	Chicago	IL	60612	773-638-8888	
Nomacorc LLC 400 Vintage Park Dr *Web:* www.nomacorc.com	Zebulon	NC	27597	919-460-2200	
Owens Handle Company Inc 4200 N Frazier St	Conroe	TX	77303	936-856-2981	856-2260
Pallet Logistics of America LLC 4100 Platinum Way *Web:* www.plofa.com	Dallas	TX	75237	972-850-5000	
Paramount Pallet Inc 1330 Martin Grove Rd *Web:* www.paramountpallet.com	Toronto	ON	M9W4X3	416-742-6006	
Price Companies Inc, The 218 Midway Route *Web:* www.thepricecompanies.com	Monticello	AR	71655	870-367-9751	
Rochester Shoe Tree Co One Cedar Ln *Web:* www.rstco.com	Ashland	NH	03217	603-968-3301	
Saunders Bros LLC 256 Main St *Web:* www.saundersbros.com	Locke Mills	ME	04255	207-875-2853	875-2857
Sharut Furniture Inc 220 Passaic St *Web:* www.furnitureinmotion.com	Passaic	NJ	07055	973-473-1000	
Southern Filter Media LLC 2735 Kanasita Dr Ste A *Web:* www.southernfiltermedia.com	Hixson	TN	37343	423-698-8988	
TrimJoist Corp 5146 Hwy 182 E *Web:* www.trimjoist.com	Columbus	MS	39704	662-327-7950	
US Joiner LLC 5690 Three Notched Rd Crozet Commons Ste 200 *Web:* www.usjoiner.com	Crozet	VA	22932	434-220-8500	
Wayne Kiltz 240 S Main St Ste A *Web:* www.africaimports.com	South Hackensack	NJ	07606	201-457-1995	
Western Excelsior Corp 901 Grand Ave *Web:* www.westernexcelsior.com	Mancos	CO	81328	970-533-7412	
Willi Hahn Corp - Wiha Tools 1348 Dundas Cir *Web:* www.wihatools.com	Monticello	MN	55362	763-295-6591	
WJ Cowee LLC 28 Taylor Ave PO Box 248 *Web:* www.cowee.com	Berlin	NY	12022	518-658-2233	658-2246

824 WOODWORKING MACHINERY

	City	State	ZIP	Phone	Fax
Acrowood Corp 4425 S Third Ave PO Box 1028 *Web:* www.acrowood.com	Everett	WA	98203	425-258-3555	252-7622
Baker Products 55480 Hwy 21 N PO Box 128 *TF:* 800-548-6914 ■ *Web:* www.baker-online.com	Ellington	MO	63638	573-663-7711	663-2787
Capital Machine Company Inc 2801 Roosevelt Ave *Web:* www.capitalmachineco.com	Indianapolis	IN	46218	317-638-6661	636-5122
Corley Manufacturing Co PO Box 471 *Web:* www.corleymfg.com	Chattanooga	TN	37401	423-698-0284	622-3258
Diehl Woodworking Mach Inc 981 S Wabash St PO Box 465 *Web:* diehlmachines.com	Wabash	IN	46992	260-563-2102	563-0206
HMC Corp 284 Maple St *Web:* www.hmccorp.com	Contoocook	NH	03229	603-746-4691	746-4819
James L. Taylor Manufacturing Co 108 Parker Ave *TF:* 800-952-1320 ■ *Web:* www.jamesltaylor.com	Poughkeepsie	NY	12601	845-452-3780	452-0764
Jenkins Systems LLC 4336 Gateway Dr *Web:* www.jenkins-systems.com	Sheboygan	WI	53081	920-452-2110	452-2338
Kimwood Corp 77684 Oregon 99 *TF:* 800-942-4401 ■ *Web:* www.kimwood.com	Cottage Grove	OR	97424	541-942-4401	942-0719
KVAL Inc 825 Petaluma Blvd S *TF:* 800-553-5825 ■ *Web:* www.kvalinc.com	Petaluma	CA	94952	707-762-7367	762-0621
McDonough Manufacturing Co 2320 Melby St PO Box 510 *Web:* www.mcdonough-mfg.com	Eau Claire	WI	54702	715-834-7755	834-3968
Memphis Machinery & Supply Co Inc 2881 Directors Cove *TF:* 800-388-4485 ■ *Web:* machinery-sales.com	Memphis	TN	38131	901-527-4443	526-2339
Mereen-Johnson Machine Co 4401 Lyndale Ave N *TF:* 888-465-7297 ■ *Web:* www.mereen-johnson.com	Minneapolis	MN	55412	612-529-7791	529-0120
Michael Weining Inc 124 Crosslake Pk Dr PO Box 3158 *TF:* 877-548-0929 ■ *Web:* www.weinigusa.com	Mooresville	NC	28117	704-799-0100	799-7400
Oliver Machinery Co 6902 S 194th St *TF:* 800-559-5065 ■ *Web:* www.olivermachinery.net	Kent	WA	98032	253-867-0334	867-0387
Pendu Manufacturing Inc 718 N Shirk Rd *TF:* 800-233-0471 ■ *Web:* www.pendu.com	New Holland	PA	17557	717-354-4348	355-2148
Premier Gear & Machine Works Inc 1700 NW Thurman St *Web:* www.premier-gear.com	Portland	OR	97209	503-227-3514	227-1611
Safety Speed Cut Mfg Co Inc 13943 Lincoln St NE *TF:* 800-772-2327 ■ *Web:* www.safetyspeed.com	Ham Lake	MN	55304	763-755-1600	755-6080
Schutte Lumber Co 3001 SW Blvd *Web:* www.schuttelumber.com	Kansas City	MO	64108	816-753-6262	753-7935
Selway Corp PO Box 287 *Web:* www.selwaycorp.com	Stevensville	MT	59870	406-777-5471	777-5473
Thermwood Corp 904 Buffaloville Rd *OTC:* TOOD ■ *TF Mktg:* 800-533-6901 ■ *Web:* www.thermwood.com	Dale	IN	47523	812-937-4476	937-2956
USNR 1981 Schurman Way PO Box 310 *TF:* 800-289-8767 ■ *Web:* www.coemfg.com	Woodland	WA	98674	360-225-8267	225-8017
USNR Inc 558 Robinson Rd PO Box 310 *TF:* 800-289-8767 ■ *Web:* www.usnr.com	Woodland	WA	98674	360-225-8267	225-8017
Viking Engineering & Development Inc 5750 Main St NE *TF Sales:* 800-328-2403 ■ *Web:* www.vikingeng.com	Fridley	MN	55432	763-571-2400	586-1319
Voorwood Co 2350 Barney St PO Box 1127 *TF:* 800-826-0089 ■ *Web:* www.voorwood.com	Anderson	CA	96007	530-365-3311	365-3315
Yates-American Machine Company Inc 2880 Kennedy Dr *TF:* 800-752-6377 ■ *Web:* www.yatesamerican.com	Beloit	WI	53511	608-364-6333	

825 WORLD TRADE CENTERS

	City	State	ZIP	Phone	Fax
Houston World Trade Ctr Greater Houston Partnership 1200 Smith St Ste 700 *Web:* www.houston.org	Houston	TX	77002	713-844-3600	
Messe Frankfurt Inc 1600 Parkwood Cir Ste 615 *Web:* us.messefrankfurt.com	Atlanta	GA	30339	770-984-8016	984-8023
Montana World Trade Ctr Gallagher Business Bldg University of Montana Ste 257 *TF:* 888-442-6668 ■ *Web:* www.mwtc.org	Missoula	MT	59812	406-243-6982	243-5259
Northern California World Trade Ctr One Capitol Mall Ste 300 **Fax Area Code:* 916 ■ *TF:* 855-667-2259 ■ *Web:* www.norcalwtc.org	Sacramento	CA	95814	855-667-2259	443-2672*
Ronald Reagan Bldg & International Trade Ctr 1300 Pennsylvania Ave NW *TF:* 800-734-7393 ■ *Web:* www.itcdc.com	Washington	DC	20004	202-312-1300	312-1310
San Diego World Trade Ctr 2980 Pacific Hwy *Web:* wtcsd.org	San Diego	CA	92101	619-615-0868	615-0876
Seaport World Trade Ctr Boston 200 Seaport Blvd **Fax:* Sales ■ *TF:* 800-440-3318 ■ *Web:* www.seaportboston.com	Boston	MA	02210	617-385-4212	385-5090*
State of Hawaii World Trade Ctr 250 S Hotel St PO Box 2359 *Web:* hawaii.gov	Honolulu	HI	96813	808-587-2750	586-2589
World Trade Ctr 101 W Main St	Norfolk	VA	23510	757-627-9440	627-1548
World Trade Ctr Alaska 431 W Seventh Ave Ste 108 *Web:* www.wtcak.org	Anchorage	AK	99501	907-278-7233	278-2982
World Trade Ctr Assn Los Angeles-Long Beach 350 S Figueroa St Ste 272 *Web:* laedc.org/wtc	Los Angeles	CA	90071	213-680-1888	680-1878
World Trade Ctr Baltimore 401 E Pratt St Ste 232 *Web:* www.wtci.org	Baltimore	MD	21202	410-576-0022	576-0751
World Trade Ctr Delaware 802 NW St *Web:* www.wtcde.com	Wilmington	DE	19801	302-656-7905	656-7956
World Trade Ctr Denver 1625 Broadway Ste 680 *Web:* wtcdenver.org	Denver	CO	80202	303-592-5760	592-5228
World Trade Ctr Detroit/Windsor 1200 Sixth St *Web:* www.wtcdw.com	Detroit	MI	48226	313-962-2345	962-9945
World Trade Ctr Miami 1007 N America Way Ste 500 *Web:* worldtrade.org	Miami	FL	33132	305-871-7910	871-7904
World Trade Ctr Montreal 380 St Antoine St W Ste 6000 *Web:* www.ccmm.qc.ca	Montreal	QC	H2Y3X7	514-871-4000	871-1255
World Trade Ctr of New Orleans 365 Canal St Ste 1120 *Web:* wtcno.org	New Orleans	LA	70130	504-529-1601	529-1691
World Trade Ctr Orlando 1600 E Amelia St *Web:* www.worldtradecenterorlando.org	Orlando	FL	32803	407-894-5740	894-5740
World Trade Ctr Palm Beach 777 S Flagler Dr Ste 800-W *Web:* www.wtcpalmbeach.com	West Palm Beach	FL	33401	561-712-1443	712-1445
World Trade Ctr Portland 121 SW Salmon St Ste 1350 *Web:* www.wtcpd.com	Portland	OR	97204	503-464-8688	464-2300
World Trade Ctr Saint Louis 121 S Meramec Ave Ste 1111 *Web:* www.worldtradecenter-stl.com	Saint Louis	MO	63105	314-615-8141	615-8140
World Trade Ctr Seattle 2200 Alaskan Way Ste 410 *Web:* www.wtcseattle.com	Seattle	WA	98121	206-441-5144	770-7923
World Trade Ctr Tacoma 950 Pacific Ave Ste 310 *Web:* www.wtcta.org	Tacoma	WA	98402	253-396-1022	396-1033
World Trade Ctr Tampa Bay 1101 Channelside Dr *Web:* www.wtctampa.com	Tampa	FL	33602	813-864-3000	
World Trade Ctr Wisconsin 750 N Lincoln Memorial Dr *Web:* www.wistrade.org	Milwaukee	WI	53202	414-274-3840	

826 ZOOS & WILDLIFE PARKS

SEE ALSO Aquariums - Public p. 1746; Botanical Gardens & Arboreta p. 1880

Name / Address	City	State	Zip	Phone	Fax
Abilene Zoological Gardens 2070 Zoo Ln Nelson Pk	Abilene	TX	79602	325-676-6085	676-6084
Web: www.abilenetx.com					
African Lion Safari & Game Farm RR 1	Cambridge	ON	N1R5S2	519-623-2620	623-9542
TF: 800-461-9453 ■ *Web:* www.lionsafari.com					
African Safari Wildlife Park 267 S Lightner Rd	Port Clinton	OH	43452	419-732-3606	734-1919
TF: 800-521-2660 ■ *Web:* www.africansafariwildlifepark.com					
Akron Zoological Park 500 Edgewood Ave	Akron	OH	44307	330-375-2550	375-2575
Web: www.akronzoo.org					
Alabama Gulf Coast Zoo, The 1204 Gulf Shores Pkwy	Gulf Shores	AL	36542	251-968-5732	
Web: alabamagulfcoastzoo.org					
Alaska Wildlife Conservation Ctr Mile 79 Seward Hwy PO Box 949	Portage	AK	99587	907-783-2025	783-2370
Web: www.alaskawildlife.org					
Alaska Zoo 4731 O'Malley Rd	Anchorage	AK	99507	907-346-3242	346-2673
Web: www.alaskazoo.org					
Alexandria Zoological Park 3016 Masonic Dr	Alexandria	LA	71301	318-441-6810	473-1149
Web: www.thealexandriazoo.com					
Alligator Adventure 4604 Hwy 17 S Barefoot Landing	North Myrtle Beach	SC	29582	843-361-0789	
Web: www.alligatoradventure.com					
Amarillo Zoo NE 24 Ave & Dumas Hwy Thompson Pk	Amarillo	TX	79105	806-381-7911	381-7901
Web: www.amarillozoo.org					
Animal Ark Wildlife Sanctuary & Nature Ctr 1265 Deerlodge Rd	Reno	NV	89508	775-970-3111	366-5771*
**Fax Area Code:* 866 ■ *Web:* www.animalark.org					
Arkansas Alligator Farm & Petting Zoo 847 Whittington Ave	Hot Springs	AR	71901	501-623-6172	
TF: 800-750-7891 ■ *Web:* www.arkansasalligatorfarm.net					
Assiniboine Park Zoo 55 Pavilion Crescent	Winnipeg	MB	R3P2N6	204-927-8080	
TF: 877-927-6006 ■ *Web:* www.zoosociety.com					
Audubon Zoo 6500 Magazine St	New Orleans	LA	70118	504-581-4629	
TF: 800-774-7394 ■ *Web:* www.auduboninstitute.org					
Austin Zoo 10807 Rawhide Trail	Austin	TX	78736	512-288-1490	288-3972
Web: www.austinzoo.org					
Beardsley Zoo 1875 Noble Ave	Bridgeport	CT	06610	203-394-6565	394-6566
Web: www.beardsleyzoo.org					
Bergen County Zoological Park 216 Forest Ave	Paramus	NJ	07652	201-262-3771	986-1788
Web: co.bergen.nj.us					
Binder Park Zoo 7400 Div Dr	Battle Creek	MI	49014	269-979-1351	979-8834
Web: www.binderparkzoo.org					
Binghampton Zoo at Ross Park 60 Morgan Rd	Binghamton	NY	13903	607-724-5461	724-5454
Web: www.rossparkzoo.com					
Birmingham Zoo 2630 Cahaba Rd	Birmingham	AL	35223	205-879-0409	879-9426
Web: www.birminghamzoo.com					
Blank Park Zoo 7401 SW Ninth St	Des Moines	IA	50315	515-285-4722	
Web: www.blankparkzoo.com					
Bolsa Chica Ecological Reserve 3842 Warner Ave	Huntington Beach	CA	92649	714-846-1114	846-4065
Web: www.bolsachica.org					
Bowmanville Zoological Park Ltd 340 King St E	Bowmanville	ON	L1C3K5	905-623-5655	623-0957
Web: www.bowmanvillezoo.com					
Bramble Park Zoo 800 Tenth St NW PO Box 910	Watertown	SD	57201	605-882-6269	882-5232
Web: www.brambleparkzoo.com					
Brandywine Zoo 1001 N Pk Dr	Wilmington	DE	19802	302-571-7747	571-7787
Web: www.brandywinezoo.org					
BREC's Baton Rouge Zoo 3601 Thomas Rd	Baton Rouge	LA	70807	225-775-3877	775-3931
Web: www.brzoo.org					
Brevard Zoo 8225 N Wickham Rd	Melbourne	FL	32940	321-254-9453	259-5966
TF: 800-435-7352 ■ *Web:* brevardzoo.org					
British Columbia Wildlife Park 9077 Dallas Dr	Kamloops	BC	V2C6V1	250-573-3242	573-2406
Web: www.bczoo.org					
Bronx Zoo 2300 Southern Blvd	Bronx	NY	10460	718-220-5100	
TF: 800-433-4149 ■ *Web:* www.bronxzoo.com					
Brookfield Zoo 3300 Golf Rd	Brookfield	IL	60513	708-688-8317	
Web: www.brookfieldzoo.org					
Buffalo Zoological Gardens 300 Parkside Ave	Buffalo	NY	14214	716-837-3900	837-0738
Web: www.buffalozoo.org					
Busch Gardens Williamsburg 1 Busch Gardens Blvd	Williamsburg	VA	23185	800-343-7946	253-3399*
**Fax Area Code:* 757 ■ **Fax:* Mktg ■ *TF:* 800-343-7946 ■ *Web:* www.buschgardens.com					
Butterfly Pavilion & Insect Ctr 6252 W 104th Ave	Westminster	CO	80020	303-469-5441	657-5944
Web: www.butterflies.org					
Buttonwood Park Zoo 425 Hawthorn St	New Bedford	MA	02740	508-991-6178	979-1731
Web: www.bpzoo.org					
Caldwell Zoo 2203 ML King Blvd	Tyler	TX	75702	903-593-0121	595-5083
Web: www.caldwellzoo.org					
Calgary Zoo Botanical Garden & Prehistoric Park 1300 Zoo Rd NE	Calgary	AB	T2E7V6	403-232-9300	237-7582
TF: 800-588-9993 ■ *Web:* www.calgaryzoo.com					
Cameron Park Zoo 1701 N Fourth St	Waco	TX	76707	254-750-8400	750-8430
Web: www.cameronparkzoo.com					
Capron Park Zoo 201 County St	Attleboro	MA	02703	508-222-3047	223-2208
Web: www.capronparkzoo.com					
Caribbean Gardens 1590 Goodlette-Frank Rd	Naples	FL	34102	239-262-5409	262-6866
TF: 888-520-3756 ■ *Web:* napleszoo.com					
Cat Tales Zoological Park 17020 Newport Hwy	Mead	WA	99021	509-238-4126	238-4126
Web: www.cattales.org					
Central Florida Zoological Park 3755 NW Hwy 17-92 & I-4 PO Box 470309	Lake Monroe	FL	32747	407-323-4450	321-0900
TF: 800-435-7352 ■ *Web:* www.centralfloridazoo.org					
Central Park Zoo Fifth Ave & 64th St	New York	NY	10065	212-439-6500	988-0286
Web: www.centralparkzoo.org					
Chahinkapa Zoo Park & Carousel 1004 RJ Hughes Dr	Wahpeton	ND	58075	701-642-8709	642-9285
Web: www.wahpetonpark.com					
Charles Paddock Zoo 9305 Pismo Ave	Atascadero	CA	93422	805-461-5080	
Web: www.charlespaddockzoo.org					
Chattanooga Zoo 301 N Holltzclaw Ave	Chattanooga	TN	37404	423-697-1322	697-1329
Web: chattzoo.org					
Cherry Brook Zoo Inc 901 Foster Thurston Dr	Saint John	NB	E2K5H9	506-634-1440	634-0717
Web: www.cherrybrookzoo.com					
Cheyenne Mountain Zoological Park 4250 Cheyenne Mtn Zoo Rd	Colorado Springs	CO	80906	719-633-9925	633-2254
Web: www.cmzoo.org					
Cincinnati Zoo & Botanical Garden 3400 Vine St	Cincinnati	OH	45220	513-281-4700	559-7790
TF: 800-944-4776 ■ *Web:* www.cincinnatizoo.org					
Claws 'n' Paws Wild Animal Park 1475 Ledgedale Rd	Lake Ariel	PA	18436	570-698-6154	
Web: www.clawsnpaws.com					
Cleveland Metroparks Zoo 3900 Wildlife Way	Cleveland	OH	44109	216-661-6500	
Web: clevelandmetroparks.com/zoo/zoo.aspx					
Clyde Peeling's Reptiland 18628 US Rt 15	Allenwood	PA	17810	800-737-8452	
TF: 800-737-8452 ■ *Web:* www.reptiland.com					
Columbian Park Zoo 1915 Scott St	Lafayette	IN	47904	765-807-1540	807-1547
TF: 800-438-9926 ■ *Web:* www.lafayette.in.gov					
Columbus Zoo & Aquarium 4850 W Powell Rd	Powell	OH	43065	614-645-3400	645-3465
TF: 800-945-3543 ■ *Web:* columbuszoo.org					
Como Zoo & Conservatory 1225 Estabrook Dr	Saint Paul	MN	55103	651-487-8200	487-8254
Web: comozooconservatory.org					
Cosley Zoo 1356 N Gary Ave	Wheaton	IL	60187	630-665-5534	260-6408
Web: www.cosleyzoo.org					
Cougar Mountain Zoo 19525 SE 54th St	Issaquah	WA	98027	425-392-6278	392-1076
Web: www.cougarmountainzoo.org					
Dakota Zoo 602 Riverside Pk Rd	Bismarck	ND	58504	701-223-7543	258-8350
Web: www.dakotazoo.org					
David Traylor Zoo of Emporia 75 Soden Rd	Emporia	KS	66801	620-341-4365	
Web: www.emporiazoo.org					
Denver Zoo 2300 Steele St	Denver	CO	80205	303-376-4800	376-4801
Web: www.denverzoo.org					
Detroit Zoological Institute 8450 W Ten-Mile Rd	Royal Oak	MI	48067	248-541-5717	541-0344
Web: www.detroitzoo.org					
Dickerson Park Zoo 3043 N Ft	Springfield	MO	65803	417-833-1570	833-4459
Web: www.dickersonparkzoo.org					
Discovery Cove 6000 Discovery Cove Way Ste B	Orlando	FL	32821	407-370-1280	586-8046
TF: 877-434-7268 ■ *Web:* www.discoverycove.com					
Ecomuseum 21125 Ch Sainte-Marie	Sainte-Anne-de-Bellevue	QC	H9X3Y7	514-457-9449	457-0769
Web: www.ecomuseum.ca					
El Paso Zoo 4001 E Paisano Dr	El Paso	TX	79905	915-521-1850	521-1857
Web: www.elpasozoo.org					
Ellen Trout Zoo 402 Zoo Cir	Lufkin	TX	75904	936-633-0399	633-0311
Web: cityoflufkin.com/zoo					
Elmwood Park Zoo 1661 Harding Blvd	Norristown	PA	19401	610-277-3825	292-0332
Web: www.elmwoodparkzoo.org					
Erie Zoo 423 W 38th St	Erie	PA	16508	814-864-4091	864-1140
TF: 877-371-5422 ■ *Web:* www.eriezoo.org					
Everglades Alligator Farm 40351 SW 192nd Ave	Homestead	FL	33034	305-247-2628	248-9711
Web: www.everglades.com					
Everglades Safari Park 26700 SW 8th St	Miami	FL	33194	305-226-6923	554-5666
Web: www.evergladessafaripark.com					
Felix Neck Wildlife Sanctuary 100 Felix Neck Dr	Edgartown	MA	02539	508-627-4850	627-6052
TF: 866-627-2267 ■ *Web:* massaudubon.org					
For-Mar Nature Preserve & Arboretum 2142 N Genesee Rd	Burton	MI	48509	810-789-8567	
Web: www.geneseecountyparks.org					
Fort Wayne Children's Zoo 3411 Sherman Blvd	Fort Wayne	IN	46808	260-427-6800	427-6820
Web: kidszoo.org					
Fossil Rim Wildlife Ctr 2155 CR 2008	Glen Rose	TX	76043	254-897-2960	897-3785
Web: www.fossilrim.com					
Franklin Park Zoo One Franklin Pk Rd	Boston	MA	02121	617-541-5466	989-2025
Web: www.zoonewengland.org					
Fresno Chaffee Zoo 894 W Belmont Ave	Fresno	CA	93728	559-498-5910	264-9226
Web: www.fresnochaffeezoo.org					
Gator Park 24050 SW Eigth St	Miami	FL	33187	305-559-2255	
TF: 800-559-2205 ■ *Web:* www.gatorpark.com					
Gatorland 14501 S Orange Blossom Trl	Orlando	FL	32837	407-855-5496	
TF: 800-393-5297 ■ *Web:* www.gatorland.com					
Gibbon Conservation Ctr 19100 Esguerra Rd	Santa Clarita	CA	91350	661-296-2737	
Web: www.gibboncenter.org					
Gladys Porter Zoo 500 Ringgold St	Brownsville	TX	78520	956-546-7187	541-4940
TF: 800-424-8802 ■ *Web:* www.gpz.org					
Glen Oak Park 2218 N Prospect Rd	Peoria	IL	61603	309-686-3365	685-6240
Web: www.peoriazoo.org					
Global Wildlife Ctr 26389 Hwy 40	Folsom	LA	70437	985-796-3585	796-9487
Web: www.globalwildlife.com					
Good Zoo & Benedum Planetarium Rt 88 N Oglebay Pk	Wheeling	WV	26003	304-243-4030	243-4110
TF: 800-624-6988 ■ *Web:* www.oglebay-resort.com/goodzoo					
Great Plains Zoo 805 S Kiwanis Ave	Sioux Falls	SD	57104	605-367-7059	367-8340
Web: www.greatzoo.org					
Greenville Zoo 150 Cleveland Pk Dr	Greenville	SC	29601	864-467-4300	467-4314
TF: 800-877-8339 ■ *Web:* www.greenvillezoo.com					

Name	Address	City	State	ZIP	Phone	Fax
Grizzly & Wolf Discovery Ctr	201 S Canyon St *TF:* 800-257-2570 ■ *Web:* www.grizzlydiscoveryctr.com	West Yellowstone	MT	59758	406-646-7001	646-7004
Happy Hollow Park & Zoo	1300 Senter Rd Kelley Pk *Web:* www.hhpz.org	San Jose	CA	95112	408-794-6400	
Harmony Park Safari	431 Clouds Cove Rd SE	Huntsville	AL	35803	256-723-3880	
Hattiesburg Zoo	107 S 17th Ave Kamper Pk *Web:* www.hattiesburgms.com	Hattiesburg	MS	39401	601-545-4576	
Henry Doorly Zoo	3701 S Tenth St *Web:* www.omahazoo.com	Omaha	NE	68107	402-733-8401	733-7868
Henry Vilas Park Zoo	702 S Randall Ave *Web:* www.vilaszoo.org	Madison	WI	53715	608-266-4732	266-5923
Henson Robinson Zoo	1100 E Lake Dr *Web:* www.hensonrobinsonzoo.org	Springfield	IL	62712	217-585-1821	529-8748
Honolulu Zoo	151 Kapahulu Ave *Web:* www.honoluluzoo.org	Honolulu	HI	96815	808-971-7171	971-7173
Houston Zoo Inc	1513 Cambridge *Web:* www.houstonzoo.org	Houston	TX	77030	713-533-6500	533-6755
Hutchinson Zoo	6 Emerson Loop E Carey Pk *TF:* 800-362-3247 ■ *Web:* hutchgov.com	Hutchinson	KS	67501	620-694-2693	694-1980
Indianapolis Zoo	1200 W Washington St *Web:* www.indianapoliszoo.com	Indianapolis	IN	46222	317-630-2001	630-5153
International Exotic Feline Sanctuary	PO Box 637 *Web:* www.bigcat.org	Boyd	TX	76023	940-433-5091	433-5092
Jackson Zoological Park	2918 W Capitol St *Web:* www.jacksonzoo.org	Jackson	MS	39209	601-352-2580	352-2594
Jacksonville Zoo & Gardens	370 Zoo Pkwy *Web:* www.jacksonvillezoo.org	Jacksonville	FL	32218	904-757-4463	757-4315
John Ball Zoological Garden	1300 W Fulton St *Web:* www.johnballzoosociety.org	Grand Rapids	MI	49504	616-336-4301	336-3907
Jungle Adventures	26205 E Colonial Dr *TF:* 877-424-2867 ■ *Web:* www.jungleadventures.com	Christmas	FL	32709	407-568-2885	568-0038
Jungle Cat World Inc	3667 Concession Rd 6 *Web:* www.junglecatworld.com	Orono	ON	L0B1M0	905-983-5016	983-9858
Jungle Island	1111 Parrot Jungle Trl *Web:* www.jungleisland.com	Miami	FL	33132	305-400-7000	400-7290
Kansas City Zoo	6800 Zoo Dr *Web:* www.kansascityzoo.org	Kansas City	MO	64132	816-595-1234	513-5850
Kentucky Horse Park	4089 Iron Works Pkwy *TF:* 800-678-8813 ■ *Web:* www.kyhorsepark.com	Lexington	KY	40511	859-233-4303	254-0253
Kisma Preserve	PO Box 84 *Web:* www.kismapreserve.org	Mount Desert	ME	04660	207-667-3244	
Knoxville Zoological Gardens Inc	3500 Knoxville Zoo Dr PO Box 6040 *Web:* www.knoxville-zoo.org	Knoxville	TN	37914	865-637-5331	637-1943
Lake Superior Zoo	7210 Fremont St *Web:* lszooduluth.org/	Duluth	MN	55807	218-730-4500	723-3750
Lee Richardson Zoo	312 E Finnup Dr *Web:* leerichardsonzoo.org	Garden City	KS	67846	620-276-1250	276-1259
Lincoln Children's Zoo	1222 S 27th St *Web:* www.lincolnzoo.org	Lincoln	NE	68502	402-475-6741	475-6742
Lincoln Park Zoo	2001 N Clark St PO Box 14903 *Web:* www.lpzoo.org	Chicago	IL	60614	312-742-2000	742-2299
Lion Country Safari	2003 Lion Country Safari Rd *Web:* www.lioncountrysafari.com	Loxahatchee	FL	33470	561-793-1084	793-9603
Little Rock Zoo	One Jonesboro Dr *Web:* www.littlerockzoo.com	Little Rock	AR	72205	501-666-2406	666-7040
Living Desert Zoo & Gardens	47900 Portola Ave *Web:* www.livingdesert.org	Palm Desert	CA	92260	760-346-5694	568-9685
Los Angeles Zoo & Botanical Gardens	5333 Zoo Dr *Web:* www.lazoo.org	Los Angeles	CA	90027	323-644-4200	662-9786
Louisville Zoo	1100 Trevilian Way *TF:* 866-229-0502 ■ *Web:* www.louisvillezoo.org	Louisville	KY	40213	502-459-2181	459-2196
Lowry Park Zoo	1101 W Sligh Ave *Web:* www.lowryparkzoo.com	Tampa	FL	33604	813-935-8552	935-9486
Maryland Zoo in Baltimore	1876 Mansion House Dr *Web:* marylandzoo.org	Baltimore	MD	21217	410-396-7102	396-6464
Maymont	2201 Shields Dr *Web:* www.maymont.org	Richmond	VA	23220	804-358-7166	358-9994
Memphis Zoo	2000 Prentiss Pl *Web:* www.memphiszoo.org	Memphis	TN	38112	901-333-6500	333-6501
Mesker Park Zoo	1545 Mesker Pk Dr *Web:* meskerparkzoo.com	Evansville	IN	47720	812-435-6143	435-6140
Micke Grove Zoo	11793 N Micke Grove Rd *Web:* www.co.san-joaquin.ca.us/mgzoo	Lodi	CA	95240	209-953-8840	331-7271
Minnesota Zoo	13000 Zoo Blvd *TF:* 800-366-7811 ■ *Web:* www.mnzoo.com	Apple Valley	MN	55124	952-431-9200	431-9300
Mobile Zoo	15161 WaRd Rd W *Web:* www.mobilezoo.cc	Wilmer	AL	36587	251-649-1845	649-0434
Monkey Jungle	14805 SW 216th St *Web:* www.monkeyjungle.com	Miami	FL	33170	305-235-1611	235-4253
Montgomery Zoo	2301 Coliseum Pkwy *Web:* www.montgomeryzoo.com	Montgomery	AL	36110	334-240-4900	240-4916
Nashville Zoo	3777 Nolensville Rd *Web:* www.nashvillezoo.org	Nashville	TN	37211	615-833-1534	333-0728
National Zoological Park (Smithsonian Institution)	3001 Connecticut Ave NW *Web:* www.nationalzoo.si.edu	Washington	DC	20008	202-633-4800	673-4836
Natural Bridge Wildlife Ranch	26515 Natural Bridge Caverns Rd *Web:* www.wildliferanchtexas.com	San Antonio	TX	78266	830-438-7400	438-3494
New York State Zoo	One Thompson Pk *Web:* www.nyszoo.org	Watertown	NY	13601	315-782-6180	782-6192
North Carolina Zoological Park	4401 Zoo Pkwy *TF:* 800-488-0444 ■ *Web:* www.nczoo.org	Asheboro	NC	27205	336-879-7000	879-2891
Northeastern Wisconsin Zoo	305 E Walnut St Rm 102 PO Box 23600 *TF:* 888-844-8070 ■ *Web:* co.brown.wi.us/departments	Green Bay	WI	54301	920-448-6242	448-4054
Northwest Trek Wildlife Park	11610 Trek Dr E *Web:* www.nwtrek.org	Eatonville	WA	98328	360-832-6117	832-6118
Oakland Zoo	9777 Golf Links Rd *Web:* www.oaklandzoo.org	Oakland	CA	94605	510-632-9525	635-5719
Oklahoma City Zoological Park & Botanical Gardens	2101 NE 50th St *TF:* 800-891-2917 ■ *Web:* www.okczoo.com	Oklahoma City	OK	73111	405-424-3344	425-0297
Orange County Zoo	1 Irvine Pk Rd *Web:* www.ocparks.com	Orange	CA	92869	714-973-6847	
Oregon Zoo	4001 SW Canyon Rd *Web:* www.oregonzoo.org	Portland	OR	97221	503-226-1561	226-6836
Out of Africa Wildlife Park	4020 N Cherry Rd *Web:* www.outofafricapark.com	Camp Verde	AZ	86322	928-567-2840	567-2839
Oxbow Park	5731 County Rd 105 NW	Byron	MN	55920	507-775-2451	775-2544
Palm Beach Zoo at Dreher Park	1301 Summit Blvd *Web:* www.palmbeachzoo.org	West Palm Beach	FL	33405	561-533-0887	585-6085
Parc Safari	280 Rang Roxham *Web:* www.parcsafari.com	Saint-Bernard-de-Lacolle	QC	J0L1H0	450-247-2727	247-3563
Parks at Chehaw	105 Chehaw Pk Rd *Web:* www.chehaw.org	Albany	GA	31701	229-430-5275	430-3035
Philadelphia Zoo	3400 W Girard Ave *Web:* www.philadelphiazoo.org	Philadelphia	PA	19104	215-243-1100	243-5385
Phoenix Zoo	455 N Galvin Pkwy *Web:* www.phoenixzoo.org	Phoenix	AZ	85008	602-273-1341	273-7078
Pittsburgh Zoo & PPG Aquarium	1 Wild Pl *TF:* 800-732-0999 ■ *Web:* pittsburghzoo.com	Pittsburgh	PA	15206	412-665-3640	665-3661
Pocatello Zoo	2900 S Second Ave *Web:* www.pocatellozoo.org	Pocatello	ID	83204	208-234-6264	234-6265
Point Defiance Zoo & Aquarium	5400 N Pearl St *Web:* www.pdza.org	Tacoma	WA	98407	253-591-5337	591-5448
Potter Park Zoo	1301 S Pennsylvania Ave *Web:* www.potterparkzoo.org	Lansing	MI	48912	517-483-4222	316-3894
Provincial Wildlife Park	149 Creighton Rd PO Box 299 *Web:* wildlifepark.novascotia.ca	Shubenacadie	NS	B0N2H0	902-758-2040	758-7011
Pueblo Zoo	3455 Nuckolls Ave *Web:* www.pueblozoo.org	Pueblo	CO	81005	719-561-1452	561-8686
Queens Zoo	53-51 111th St *Web:* www.wcs.org	Flushing	NY	11368	718-271-1500	
Racine Zoo	200 Goold St *Web:* www.racinezoo.org	Racine	WI	53402	262-636-9189	636-9307
Red River Zoo	4255 23rd Ave S *Web:* www.redriverzoo.org	Fargo	ND	58104	701-277-9240	277-9238
Reid Park Zoo	1100 S Randolph Way *Web:* reidparkzoo.org	Tucson	AZ	85716	520-791-3204	791-5378
Riverbanks Zoo & Botanical Garden	500 Wildlife Pkwy *Web:* www.riverbanks.org	Columbia	SC	29210	803-779-8717	253-6381
Riverside Zoo	1600 S Beltline Hwy W	Scottsbluff	NE	69361	308-630-6236	
Roger Williams Park Zoo	1000 Elmwood Ave *Web:* rwpzoo.org	Providence	RI	02907	401-785-3510	941-3988
Rolling Hills Wildlife Adventure	625 N Hedville Rd *Web:* www.rollinghillswildlife.com	Salina	KS	67401	785-827-9488	827-3738
Roosevelt Park Zoo	1219 Burdick Expy *Web:* www.rpzoo.com	Minot	ND	58701	701-857-4166	857-4169
Rosamond Gifford Zoo at Burnet Park	1 Conservation Pl *TF:* 800-724-5006 ■ *Web:* rosamondgiffordzoo.org	Syracuse	NY	13204	315-435-8511	435-8517
Sacramento Zoo	3930 W Land Pk Dr *Web:* www.saczoo.org	Sacramento	CA	95822	916-808-5888	
Safari West Wildlife Preserve & Tent Camp	3115 Porter Creek Rd *TF:* 800-616-2695 ■ *Web:* www.safariwest.com	Santa Rosa	CA	95404	707-579-2551	579-8777
Saint Augustine Alligator Farm	999 Anastasia Blvd *Web:* www.alligatorfarm.com	Saint Augustine	FL	32080	904-824-3337	829-6677
Saint Louis Zoological Park	One Government Dr *Web:* www.stlzoo.org	Saint Louis	MO	63110	314-781-0900	647-7969
Salisbury Zoological Park	755 S Pk Dr *Web:* www.salisburyzoo.org	Salisbury	MD	21804	410-548-3188	860-0919
Salmonier Nature Park	PO Box 190 *Web:* www.env.gov.nl.ca	Holyrood	NL	A0A2R0	709-229-3915	229-7078
San Antonio Zoological Gardens & Aquarium	3903 N St Mary's St *Web:* www.sazoo-aq.org	San Antonio	TX	78212	210-734-7184	734-7291
San Diego Zoo	2920 Zoo Dr *Web:* www.sandiegozoo.org	San Diego	CA	92101	619-231-1515	231-0249
San Diego Zoo Safari Park	15500 San Pasqual Valley Rd *TF Cust Svc:* 877-363-6237 ■ *Web:* www.sdzsafaripark.org	Escondido	CA	92027	760-747-8702	738-5023
San Francisco Zoo	One Zoo Rd *Web:* www.sfzoo.org	San Francisco	CA	94132	415-753-7080	681-2039
Santa Ana Zoo	1801 E Chestnut Ave *Web:* www.santaanazoo.org	Santa Ana	CA	92701	714-835-7484	550-0346
Santa Barbara Zoological Gardens	500 Ninos Dr *Web:* www.sbzoo.org	Santa Barbara	CA	93103	805-962-5339	962-1673
Santa Fe Community College Teaching Zoo	3000 NW 83rd St *Web:* www.sfcollege.edu/zoo	Gainesville	FL	32606	352-395-5604	
Sarasota Jungle Gardens	3701 Bay Shore Rd *TF:* 877-681-6547 ■ *Web:* www.sarasotajunglegardens.com	Sarasota	FL	34234	941-355-5305	355-1222

Name / Address	City	State	Zip	Phone	Fax
Scovill Zoo 71 S Country Club Rd *Web:* www.decatur-parks.org	Decatur	IL	62521	217-421-7435	422-7330
Sedgwick County Zoo 5555 W Zoo Blvd *Web:* www.scz.org	Wichita	KS	67212	316-660-9453	942-3781
Seneca Park Zoo 2222 St Paul St *Web:* www.senecaparkzoo.org	Rochester	NY	14621	585-336-7200	342-1477
Sequoia Park Zoo 3414 W St *Web:* www.sequoiaparkzoo.net	Eureka	CA	95503	707-441-4263	442-5841
Sierra Safari Zoo 10200 N Virginia St *Web:* www.sierrasafarizoo.com	Reno	NV	89506	775-677-1101	
Smithsonian National Zoological Park 3001 Connecticut Ave NW *Web:* nationalzoo.si.edu	Washington	DC	20008	202-633-4888	
Spring River Park & Zoo 1306 E College Blvd PO Box 1838 *Web:* www.museumsusa.org	Roswell	NM	88201	575-624-6760	
Staten Island Zoo 614 Broadway *Web:* www.statenislandzoo.org	Staten Island	NY	10310	718-442-3101	981-8711
Sunset Zoo 2333 Oak St *Web:* www.ci.manhattan.ks.us	Manhattan	KS	66502	785-587-2737	587-2730
Tautphaus Park Zoo 308 Constitution Way *Web:* www.idahofallsidaho.gov	Idaho Falls	ID	83402	208-612-8100	528-6256
Texas Zoo 110 Memorial Dr *Web:* www.texaszoo.org	Victoria	TX	77901	361-573-7681	576-1094
Toledo Zoo 2700 Broadway *TF:* 866-900-1146 ■ *Web:* www.toledozoo.org	Toledo	OH	43609	419-385-5721	389-8670
Topeka Zoological Park 635 SW Gage Blvd *Web:* topekazoo.org	Topeka	KS	66606	785-368-9180	368-9152
Toronto Zoo 361-A Old Finch Ave *Web:* www.torontozoo.com	Toronto	ON	M1B5K7	416-392-5900	392-5934
Tracy Aviary 589 East 1300 South *Web:* www.tracyaviary.org	Salt Lake City	UT	84105	801-596-8500	596-7325
Trevor Zoo 131 Millbrook School Rd *Web:* trevorzoo.org	Millbrook	NY	12545	845-677-3704	
Tulsa Zoo 6421 E 36th St N *Web:* www.tulsazoo.com	Tulsa	OK	74115	918-669-6600	669-6610
Tupelo Buffalo Park & Zoo 2272 N Coley Rd *TF:* 866-272-4766 ■ *Web:* www.tupelobuffalopark.com	Tupelo	MS	38803	662-844-8709	844-8850
Utah's Hogle Zoo 2600 E Sunnyside Ave *Web:* www.hoglezoo.org	Salt Lake City	UT	84108	801-582-1631	584-1770
Utica Zoo 99 Steele Hill Rd *Web:* www.uticazoo.org	Utica	NY	13501	315-738-0472	738-0475
Virginia Zoological Park 3500 Granby St *Web:* www.virginiazoo.org	Norfolk	VA	23504	757-441-2374	441-5408
Waccatee Zoological Farm 8500 Enterprise Rd *Web:* www.waccateezoo.com	Myrtle Beach	SC	29588	843-650-8500	
West Virginia State Wildlife Ctr PO Box 38 Web: www.wvdnr.gov/wildlife/wildlifecenter.shtm	French Creek	WV	26218	304-924-6211	
Wild Animal Safari 1300 Oak Grove Rd *TF:* 800-367-2751 ■ *Web:* www.animalsafari.com	Pine Mountain	GA	31822	706-663-8744	663-8880
Wildlife Sanctuary of Northwest Florida PO Box 1092 *Web:* www.pensacolawildlife.com	Pensacola	FL	32591	850-433-9453	438-6168
Wildlife West Nature Park 87 N Frontage Rd *Web:* www.wildlifewest.org	Edgewood	NM	87015	505-281-7655	281-7170
Wildlife World Zoo 16501 W Northern Ave *Web:* www.wildlifeworld.com	Litchfield Park	AZ	85340	623-935-9453	935-7499
Wilds, The 14000 International Rd *Web:* www.thewilds.org	Cumberland	OH	43732	740-638-5030	638-2287
Wonders of Wildlife 500 W Sunshine St *TF:* 877-245-9453 ■ *Web:* www.wondersofwildlife.org	Springfield	MO	65807	417-890-9453	890-9278
Woodland Park Zoo 601 N 59th St *Web:* www.zoo.org	Seattle	WA	98103	206-548-2500	548-1536
World of Reptiles & Birds Park Edgartown-VineyaRd Haven Rd *Web:* www.reptilesandbirds.com	Edgartown	MA	02539	508-627-5634	
Zoo Atlanta 800 Cherokee Ave SE *Web:* www.zooatlanta.org	Atlanta	GA	30315	404-624-5600	627-7514
Zoo Boise 355 Julia Davis Dr *Web:* zooboise.org	Boise	ID	83702	208-384-4260	384-4194
Zoo in Forest Park, The 302 Sumner Ave PO Box 80295 *Web:* www.forestparkzoo.org	Springfield	MA	01138	413-733-2251	733-2330
Zoo of Acadiana 5601 Hwy 90 E *Web:* www.zooofacadiana.org	Broussard	LA	70518	337-837-4325	837-4253
Zoo, The 5701 Gulf Breeze Pkwy *Web:* gulfbreezezoo.org	Gulf Breeze	FL	32563	850-932-2229	
ZooAmerica North American Wildlife Park 100 W Hersheypark Dr *Web:* www.zooamerica.com	Hershey	PA	17033	717-534-3900	534-3151
ZooMontana & Botanical Gardens 2100 S Shiloh Rd *Web:* www.zoomontana.org	Billings	MT	59106	406-652-8100	652-9281

Area Code and Zip Code Guide

The information provided in this Guide is organized **alphabetically by city name,** with area code(s) and zip code(s) shown to the right of the city name.

A

City	Area Code(s)	Zip Code(s)
Abbeville, AL	334	36310
Abbeville, GA	229	31001
Abbeville, LA	337	70510-70511
Abbeville, SC	864	29620
Abbotsford, WI	715, 534	54405
Abbott Park, IL	224, 847	60064
Aberdeen, ID	208	83210
Aberdeen, MD	410	21001
Aberdeen, MS	662	39730
Aberdeen, NC	910	28315
Aberdeen, SD	605	57401-57402
Aberdeen, WA	360	98520
Aberdeen Proving Ground, MD	410	21005, 21010
Abernathy, TX	806	79311
Abilene, KS	785	67410
Abilene, TX	915	79601-79608, 79697-79699
Abingdon, VA	276	24210-24212
Abington, MA	339, 781	02351
Abington, PA	215, 267	19001
Accident, MD	301	21520
Accokeek, MD	301	20607
Accomac, VA	757	23301
Accord, NY	845	12404
Ackerman, MS	662	39735
Acme, MI	231	49610
Acton, MA	351, 978	01718-01720
Acworth, GA	470, 770	30101-30102
Ada, MI	616	49301, 49355-49357
Ada, MN	218	56510
Ada, OH	419, 567	45810
Ada, OK	580	74820-74821
Adairsville, GA	470, 770	30103
Adams, MA	413	01220
Adams, OR	541, 458	97810
Adamstown, MD	301	21710
Adamstown, PA	717	19501
Adamsville, TN	731	38310
Addison, AL	256	35540
Addison, IL	331, 630	60101
Addison, TX	469, 972	75001
Addison, VT	802	05491
Adel, GA	229	31620
Adel, IA	515	50003
Adelanto, CA	760, 442	92301
Adelphi, MD	301	20783, 20787
Adrian, GA	478	31002
Adrian, MI	517	49221
Advance, NC	336	27006
Affton, MO	314	63123
Afton, OK	918	74331
Afton, WY	307	83110
Agawam, MA	413	01001
Agoura Hills, CA	818	91301, 91376-91377
Aguadilla, PR	787, 939	00603-00605
Ahoskie, NC	252	27910
Aiea, HI	808	96701
Aiken, SC	803	29801-29808
Ainsworth, NE	402	69210
Airway Heights, WA	509	99001
Aitkin, MN	218	56431
Ajo, AZ	520	85321
Akron, CO	970	80720
Akron, IN	574	46910
Akron, NY	585	14001
Akron, OH	234, 330	44301-44328, 44333-44334*
Akron, PA	717	17501
Alabaster, AL	205	35007, 35144
Alachua, FL	386	32615-32616
Alamance, NC	336	27201
Alameda, CA	510	94501-94502
Alamo, CA	925	94507
Alamo, GA	912	30411
Alamo, TN	731	38001
Alamo, TX	956	78516
Alamogordo, NM	505	88310-88311
Alamosa, CO	719	81101-81102
Albany, CA	510	94706, 94710
Albany, GA	229	31701-31708
Albany, KY	606	42602
Albany, MN	320	56307
Albany, MO	660	64402
Albany, NY	518	12201-12214, 12220-12262*
Albany, OR	541, 458	97321
Albany, TX	915	76430
Albemarle, NC	704, 980	28001-28002
Albert Lea, MN	507	56007
Alberta, VA	434	23821
Albertson, NY	516	11507
Albertville, AL	256	35950-35951
Albia, IA	641	52531
Albion, IL	618	62806
Albion, IN	260	46701
Albion, MI	517	49224
Albion, NE	402	68620
Albion, NY	585	14411
Albion, PA	814	16401, 16475
Albuquerque, NM	505	87101-87125, 87131, 87153*
Alcoa, TN	865	37701
Alcorn State, MS	601, 769	39096
Alden, NY	585	14004
Alderson, WV	304	24910
Aledo, IL	309	61231
Alexander, AR	501	72002
Alexander, IA	641	50420
Alexander, NY	585	14005
Alexander City, AL	256	35010-35011
Alexandria, AL	256	36250
Alexandria, IN	765	46001
Alexandria, LA	318	71301-71309, 71315
Alexandria, MN	320	56308
Alexandria, SD	605	57311
Alexandria, TN	615	37012
Alexandria, VA	571, 703	22301-22315, 22320-22321*
Alexandria Bay, NY	315	13607
Alfred, ME	207	04002
Alfred, NY	607	14802
Algoma, WI	920	54201
Algona, IA	515	50511
Algona, WA	253	98001
Algonquin, IL	224, 847	60102, 60156
Alhambra, CA	626	91801-91804, 91841, 91896*
Alice, TX	361	78332-78333, 78342
Aliceville, AL	205	35442
Aliquippa, PA	724, 878	15001
Aliso Viejo, CA	949	92653-92656, 92698
Alledonia, OH	740	43902
Allegan, MI	616	49010
Allen, TX	469, 972	75002, 75013
Allen Park, MI	313	48101
Allendale, MI	616	49401
Allendale, NJ	201, 551	07401
Allendale, SC	803	29810
Allenhurst, NJ	732, 848	07709-07711
Allenstown, NH	603	03275
Allentown, NJ	609	08501
Allentown, PA	484, 610	18101-18109, 18175, 18195
Allenwood, NJ	732, 848	08720
Allenwood, PA	570	17810
Allgood, AL	205	35013
Alliance, NE	308	69301
Alliance, OH	234, 330	44601
Allison, IA	319	50602
Allison Park, PA	412, 878	15101
Allston, MA	617, 857	02134
Alma, GA	912	31510
Alma, KS	785	66401, 66501
Alma, MI	989	48801-48802
Alma, NE	308	68920
Alma, WI	608	54610
Almena, WI	715, 534	54805
Almo, ID	208	83312
Almont, MI	810	48003
Alpena, MI	989	49707
Alpha, NJ	908	08865
Alpharetta, GA	470, 678, 770	30004-30005, 30009, 30022*
Alpine, CA	619	91901-91903
Alpine, TX	915	79830-79832
Alpine, UT	801, 385	84004
Alsip, IL	708	60803
Alta, UT	801, 385	84092
Altadena, CA	626	91001-91003
Altamahaw, NC	336	27202
Altamont, KS	620	67330
Altamont, TN	931	37301
Altamonte Springs, FL	321, 407	32701, 32714-32716
Altavista, VA	434	24517
Alto, GA	706, 762	30510, 30596
Alton, IL	618	62002
Alton, MO	417	65606
Altona, NY	518	12910
Altoona, IA	515	50009
Altoona, PA	814	16601-16603
Alturas, CA	530	96101
Altus, OK	580	73521-73523
Altus AFB, OK	580	73523
Alva, OK	580	73717
Alvarado, TX	682, 817	76009
Alvin, TX	281, 832	77511-77512
Alviso, CA	408	95002
Amado, AZ	520	85640, 85645
Amana, IA	319	52203-52204
Amarillo, TX	806	79101-79124, 79159, 79163*
Ambler, PA	215, 267	19002
Amboy, IL	815	61310
Amboy, WA	360	98601
Ambridge, PA	724, 878	15003
Amelia Court House, VA	804	23002
Amelia Island, FL	904	32034
American Falls, ID	208	83211
American Fork, UT	801, 385	84003
Americus, GA	229	31709-31710
Ames, IA	515	50010-50014
Amesbury, MA	351, 978	01913
Amherst, MA	413	01002-01004, 01059
Amherst, NH	603	03031
Amherst, NY	716	14051, 14068, 14221, 14226*
Amherst, TX	806	79312
Amherst, VA	434	24521
Amidon, ND	701	58620
Amite, LA	985	70422
Amityville, NY	631	11701, 11708
Amlin, OH	614	43002
Amory, MS	662	38821
Amsterdam, NY	518	12010
Anaconda, MT	406	59711
Anacortes, WA	360	98221-98222
Anadarko, OK	405	73005
Anaheim, CA	714	92801-92817, 92825, 92850*
Anaheim Hills, CA	714	92807-92809, 92817
Anahuac, TX	409	77514
Analomink, PA	570	18320
Anamosa, IA	319	52205
Anchorage, AK	907	99501-99524, 99540, 99599*
Ancora, NJ	609	08037
Andalusia, AL	334	36420
Anderson, CA	530	96007
Anderson, IN	765	46011-46018
Anderson, MO	417	64831
Anderson, SC	864	29621-29626
Anderson, TX	936	77830, 77875
Andersonville, GA	229	31711
Andover, KS	316	67002
Andover, ME	207	04216

*Partial list of zip codes, including main range

City	Area Code(s)	Zip Code(s)
Andover, MA	351, 978	01810-01812, 01899, 05501*
Andover, NJ	862, 973	07821
Andover, OH	440	44003
Andrews, TX	915	79714
Andrews AFB, MD	240, 301	20762
Angel Fire, NM	505	87710
Angels Camp, CA	209	95221-95222
Angie, LA	985	70426, 70467
Angleton, TX	979	77515-77516
Angola, IN	260	46703
Angola, LA	225	70712
Angoon, AK	907	99820
Angwin, CA	707	94508, 94576
Ankeny, IA	515	50015, 50021
Ann Arbor, MI	734	48103-48109, 48113
Anna, IL	618	62906
Annandale, MN	320	55302
Annandale, NJ	908	08801
Annandale, VA	571, 703	22003
Annapolis, MD	410, 443	21401-21405, 21411-21412
Annapolis Junction, MD	301	20701
Anniston, AL	256	36201-36207
Annona, TX	903	75550
Annville, PA	717	17003
Anoka, MN	763	55303-55304
Anson, TX	915	79501
Ansonia, CT	203	06401
Ansonia, OH	937	45303
Ansted, WV	304	25812
Anthony, KS	620	67003
Anthony, TX	915	79821
Antigo, WI	715, 534	54409
Antioch, CA	925	94509, 94531
Antioch, IL	224, 847	60002
Antioch, TN	615	37011-37013
Antlers, OK	580	74523
Antonito, CO	719	81120
Antrim, NH	603	03440
Anza, CA	951	92539
Apache, OK	580	73006
Apache Junction, AZ	480	85217-85220, 85278, 85290
Apalachicola, FL	850	32320, 32329
Apex, NC	919	27502
Apopka, FL	321, 407	32703-32704, 32712
Apple Valley, CA	760, 442	92307-92308
Apple Valley, MN	952	55124
Appleton, WI	920	54911-54915, 54919
Appomattox, VA	434	24522
Aptos, CA	831	95001-95003
Aquebogue, NY	631	11931
Arab, AL	256	35016
Arapaho, OK	580	73620
Arbor Vitae, WI	715, 534	54568
Arbuckle, CA	530	95912
Arcade, NY	585	14009
Arcadia, CA	626	91006-91007, 91066, 91077
Arcadia, FL	863	34265-34269
Arcadia, LA	318	71001
Arcadia, SC	864	29320
Arcadia, WI	608	54612
Arcata, CA	707	95518-95521
Archbold, OH	419, 567	43502
Archdale, NC	336	27263
Archer, FL	352	32618
Archer City, TX	940	76351
Arco, ID	208	83213
Arcola, IL	217	61910
Arcola, TX	281, 832	77583
Arden, NC	828	28704
Arden Hills, MN	651	55112
Ardmore, OK	580	73401-73403
Ardmore, PA	484, 610	19003
Ardsley, NY	914	10502
Arecibo, PR	787, 939	00612-00614
Argonne, IL	331, 630	60439
Argyle, MN	218	56713
Arkadelphia, AR	870	71923, 71998-71999
Arkansas City, AR	870	71630
Arkansas City, KS	620	67005
Arlington, MA	339, 781	02474-02476
Arlington, MN	507	55307
Arlington, TN	901	38002
Arlington, TX	682, 817	76001-76019, 76094-76096
Arlington, VT	802	05250
Arlington, VA	571, 703	22201-22230, 22234, 22240*
Arlington, WA	360	98223
Arlington Heights, IL	224, 847	60004-60006
Armada, MI	586	48005
Armonk, NY	914	10504
Armour, SD	605	57313
Armstrong, IA	712	50514
Arnett, OK	580	73832
Arnold, MD	410	21012
Arnold, MO	636	63010
Arnold, PA	724, 878	15068
Arnold AFB, TN	931	37389
Aromas, CA	831	95004
Arroyo Grande, CA	805	93420-93421
Artesia, CA	562	90701-90703
Artesia, NM	505	88210-88211
Artesian, SD	605	57314
Arthur, IL	217	61911
Arthur, NE	308	69121
Arthurdale, WV	304	26520
Arvada, CO	303, 720	80001-80007, 80021, 80403
Arvilla, ND	701	58214
Arvin, CA	661	93203
Arvonia, VA	434	23004
Asbury, NJ	908	08802
Asbury Park, NJ	732, 848	07712
Ash Flat, AR	870	72513
Ashaway, RI	401	02804
Ashburn, GA	229	31714
Ashburn, VA	571, 703	20146-20149, 22093
Ashdown, AR	870	71822
Asheboro, NC	336	27203-27205
Asheville, NC	828	28801-28806, 28810-28816
Ashford, AL	334	36312
Ashford, WA	360	98304
Ashippun, WI	920	53003
Ashland, AL	256	36251
Ashland, KS	620	67831
Ashland, KY	606	41101-41105, 41114
Ashland, ME	207	04732, 04737, 04759
Ashland, MA	508, 774	01721
Ashland, MS	662	38603
Ashland, MT	406	59003-59004
Ashland, NE	402	68003
Ashland, NH	603	03217
Ashland, OH	419, 567	44805
Ashland, OR	541, 458	97520
Ashland, PA	570	17921
Ashland, VA	804	23005
Ashland, WI	715, 534	54806
Ashland City, TN	615	37015
Ashley, ND	701	58413
Ashtabula, OH	440	44004-44005
Ashton, ID	208	83420, 83447
Ashton, IL	815	61006
Ashville, AL	205	35953
Ashville, NY	716	14710
Ashville, OH	740	43103
Asotin, WA	509	99402
Aspen, CO	970	81611-81612
Aspermont, TX	940	79502
Assumption, IL	217	62510
Aston, PA	484, 610	19014
Astoria, NY	347, 718	11101-11106
Astoria, OR	503	97103
Atascadero, CA	805	93422-93423
Atchison, KS	913	66002
Atco, NJ	856	08004
Atglen, PA	484, 610	19310
Athens, AL	256	35611-35614
Athens, GA	706, 762	30601-30612
Athens, OH	740	45701
Athens, TN	423	37303, 37371
Athens, TX	903	75751-75752
Athens, WV	304	24712
Atherton, CA	650	94027
Athol, ID	208	83801
Athol, MA	351, 978	01331, 01368
Atkinson, NH	603	03811
Atlanta, GA	404, 470, 678	30301-30380, 30384-30399*
Atlanta, MI	989	49709
Atlanta, TX	903	75551
Atlantic, IA	712	50022
Atlantic, NC	252	28511
Atlantic Beach, FL	904	32224, 32233
Atlantic Beach, NC	252	28512
Atlantic City, NJ	609	08400-08406
Atmore, AL	251	36502-36504
Atoka, OK	580	74525, 74542
Attalla, AL	256	35954
Attica, IN	765	47918
Attica, NY	585	14011
Attica, OH	419, 567	44807
Attleboro, MA	508, 774	02703
Attleboro Falls, MA	508, 774	02763
Atwater, CA	209	95301, 95342
Atwood, KS	785	67730
Au Gres, MI	989	48703
Auburn, AL	334	36830-36832
Auburn, CA	530	95602-95604
Auburn, IL	217	62615
Auburn, IN	219	46706
Auburn, KY	270	42206
Auburn, ME	207	04210-04212
Auburn, MA	508, 774	01501
Auburn, NE	402	68305
Auburn, NY	315	13021-13024
Auburn, WA	253	98001-98003, 98023, 98047*
Auburn University, AL	334	36849
Auburndale, FL	863	33823
Auburndale, MA	617, 857	02466
Audubon, IA	712	50025
Audubon, PA	484, 610	19403, 19407
Augusta, AR	870	72006
Augusta, GA	706, 762	30901-30919, 30999
Augusta, KS	316	67010
Augusta, ME	207	04330-04338
Augusta, MI	616	49012
Augusta, MT	406	59410
Auke Bay, AK	907	99821
Aumsville, OR	503, 971	97325
Aurora, CO	303, 720	80002, 80010-80019, 80040*
Aurora, IL	331, 630	60504-60507, 60568, 60572*
Aurora, IN	812	47001
Aurora, MN	218	55705
Aurora, MO	417	65605
Aurora, NE	402	68818
Aurora, NY	315	13026
Aurora, OH	234, 330	44202
Aurora, OR	503, 971	97002
Austell, GA	470, 770	30106, 30168
Austin, IN	812	47102
Austin, MN	507	55912
Austin, PA	814	16720
Austin, TX	512	73301, 73344, 78701-78774*
Austinburg, OH	440	44010
Autaugaville, AL	334	36003
Ava, MO	417	65608
Avalon, CA	310, 424	90704
Avenal, CA	559	93204
Avenel, NJ	732, 848	07001
Aventura, FL	305, 786	33160, 33180, 33280
Avery Island, LA	337	70513
Avoca, PA	570	18641
Avon, CO	970	81620
Avon, CT	860	06001
Avon, MA	508, 774	02322
Avon, MN	320	56310
Avon, OH	440	44011
Avon Lake, OH	440	44012
Avon Park, FL	863	33825-33826
Avondale, AZ	623	85323
Avondale, PA	484, 610	19311
Axis, AL	251	36505
Axtell, KS	785	66403
Axtell, NE	308	68924
Ayer, MA	351, 978	01432
Azle, TX	682, 817	76020, 76098
Aztec, NM	505	87410
Azusa, CA	626	91702

B

City	Area Code(s)	Zip Code(s)
Babson Park, FL	863	33827

*Partial list of zip codes, including main range

City	Area Code(s)	Zip Code(s)
Babson Park, MA	339, 781	02457
Babylon, NY	631	11702-11707
Bad Axe, MI	989	48413
Bagdad, KY	502	40003
Bagley, MN	218	56621
Baileys Harbor, WI	920	54202
Bainbridge, GA	229	31717-31718
Bainbridge Island, WA	206	98110
Baird, TX	915	79504
Baker, LA	225	70704, 70714
Baker, MT	406	59313, 59354
Baker, NV	775	89311
Baker City, OR	541, 458	97814
Bakersfield, CA	661	93301-93313, 93380-93390
Bakerstown, PA	724, 878	15007
Bakersville, NC	828	28705
Bal Harbour, FL	305, 786	33154
Bala Cynwyd, PA	484, 610	19004
Baldwin, GA	706, 762	30511
Baldwin, LA	337	70514
Baldwin, MI	231	49304
Baldwin, NY	516	11510
Baldwin, WI	715, 534	54002
Baldwin City, KS	785	66006
Baldwin Park, CA	626	91706
Baldwinsville, NY	315	13027
Ball Ground, GA	470, 770	30107
Ballinger, TX	915	76821
Ballston Spa, NY	518	12020
Ballwin, MO	636	63011, 63021-63024
Bally, PA	484, 610	19503
Balsam Lake, WI	715, 534	54810
Baltimore, MD	410, 443	21075, 21201-21244, 21250*
Bamberg, SC	803	29003
Bandera, TX	830	78003
Bangor, ME	207	04401-04402
Bangor, PA	484, 610	18010-18013, 18050
Bangor, WI	608	54614
Banner Elk, NC	828	28604, 28691
Banning, CA	951	92220
Bannock, OH	740	43972
Bannockburn, IL	224, 847	60015
Bar Harbor, ME	207	04609
Baraboo, WI	608	53913
Baraga, MI	906	49908
Barberton, OH	234, 330	44203
Barboursville, WV	304	25504
Barbourville, KY	606	40906
Bardstown, KY	502	40004
Bardwell, KY	270	42023
Barker, NY	716	14012
Barksdale AFB, LA	318	71110
Barnard, VT	802	05031
Barnardsville, NC	828	28709
Barnesville, GA	470, 770	30204
Barneveld, NY	315	13304
Barnstable, MA	508, 774	02630, 02634
Barnwell, SC	803	29812-29813
Barre, MA	351, 978	01005
Barre, VT	802	05641
Barrington, IL	224, 847	60010-60011
Barrington, NH	603	03825
Barrington, NJ	856	08007
Barron, WI	715, 534	54812
Barrow, AK	907	99723, 99734, 99759, 99789*
Barstow, CA	760, 442	92310-92312
Bartlesville, OK	918	74003-74006
Bartlett, IL	331, 630	60103, 60108, 60133
Bartlett, NE	308	68622
Bartlett, TN	901	38133-38135, 38184
Bartlett, TX	254	76511
Bartow, FL	863	33830-33831
Basalt, CO	970	81621
Basin, WY	307	82410
Basking Ridge, NJ	908	07920, 07939
Bassett, NE	402	68714
Bassett, VA	276	24055
Bastrop, LA	318	71220-71221
Bastrop, TX	512	78602
Batavia, IL	331, 630	60510, 60539
Batavia, NY	585	14020-14021
Batavia, OH	513	45103
Batesburg, SC	803	29006
Batesville, AR	870	72501-72503
Batesville, IN	812	47006
Batesville, MS	662	38606
Bath, ME	207	04530
Bath, NY	607	14810
Bath, OH	234, 330	44210
Bath, PA	484, 610	18014
Bath, SD	605	57427
Baton Rouge, LA	225	70801-70827, 70831-70837*
Battle Creek, MI	616	49014-49018
Battle Creek, NE	402	68715
Battle Ground, WA	360	98604
Battle Mountain, NV	775	89820
Baudette, MN	218	56623
Baxley, GA	912	31513-31515
Bay City, MI	989	48706-48708
Bay City, TX	979	77404, 77414
Bay Harbor, MI	231	49770
Bay Harbor Islands, FL	305, 786	33154
Bay Minette, AL	251	36507
Bay Pines, FL	727	33744
Bay Saint Louis, MS	228	39520-39521, 39525
Bay Shore, NY	631	11706
Bay Springs, MS	601, 769	39422
Bay Village, OH	440	44140
Bayamon, PR	787, 939	00956-00961
Bayard, NE	308	69334
Bayboro, NC	252	28515
Bayfield, WI	715, 534	54814
Bayonne, NJ	201, 551	07002
Bayou La Batre, AL	251	36509
Bayport, MN	651	55003
Bayport, NY	631	11705
Bayside, NY	347, 718	11359-11361
Baytown, TX	281, 832	77520-77522
Bayville, NJ	732, 848	08721
Beach, ND	701	58621
Beach Lake, PA	570	18405
Beachwood, OH	216	44122
Beacon, NY	845	12508
Beale AFB, CA	530	95903
Bean Station, TN	865	37708
Bear Creek, WI	715, 534	54922
Bear Mountain, NY	845	10911
Bearden, AR	870	71720
Beatrice, NE	402	68310
Beattyville, KY	606	41311
Beaufort, NC	252	28516
Beaufort, SC	843	29901-29906
Beaumont, CA	951	92223
Beaumont, TX	409	77657, 77701-77713, 77720*
Beaumont, VA	804	23014
Beaver, OK	580	73932
Beaver, PA	724, 878	15009
Beaver, UT	435	84713
Beaver, WV	304	25813
Beaver City, NE	308	68926
Beaver Creek, CO	970	81620
Beaver Dam, KY	270	42320
Beaver Dam, WI	920	53916-53917
Beaver Dams, NY	607	14812
Beaver Falls, NY	315	13305
Beaver Falls, PA	724, 878	15010
Beavercreek, OH	937	45410, 45430-45434, 45440
Beaverton, OR	503, 971	97005-97008, 97075-97078
Bechtelsville, PA	484, 610	19505
Beckley, WV	304	25801-25802, 25926
Bedford, IN	812	47421
Bedford, IA	712	50833
Bedford, KY	502	40006
Bedford, MA	339, 781	01730-01731
Bedford, NH	603	03110
Bedford, OH	440	44146
Bedford, PA	814	15522
Bedford, TX	682, 817	76021-76022, 76095
Bedford, VA	540	24523
Bedford Heights, OH	216	44128, 44146
Bedford Hills, NY	914	10507
Bedford Park, IL	708	60455-60459, 60499-60501*
Bedminster, NJ	908	07921
Beebe, AR	501	72012
Beech Creek, PA	570	16822
Beech Grove, IN	317	46107
Beeville, TX	361	78102-78104
Bel Air, MD	410	21014-21015
Belcamp, MD	410	21017
Belcourt, ND	701	58316
Belding, MI	616	48809, 48887
Belfast, ME	207	04915
Belgrade, MT	406	59714
Belhaven, NC	252	27810
Bell, CA	323	90201-90202, 90270
Bell Gardens, CA	562	90201-90202
Bella Vista, AR	479	72714-72715
Bellaire, MI	231	49615
Bellaire, TX	713, 832	77401-77402
Belle Chasse, LA	504	70037
Belle Fourche, SD	605	57717
Belle Glade, FL	561	33430
Belle Mead, NJ	908	08502
Belle Plaine, MN	952	56011
Belle Vernon, PA	724, 878	15012
Bellefontaine, OH	937	43311
Bellefonte, PA	814	16823
Bellerose, NY	347, 718	11426
Belleview, FL	352	34420-34421
Belleville, IL	618	62220-62226
Belleville, KS	785	66935
Belleville, MI	734	48111-48112
Belleville, NJ	862, 973	07109
Belleville, PA	717	17004
Belleville, WI	608	53508
Bellevue, IA	563	52031
Bellevue, NE	402	68005, 68123, 68147, 68157
Bellevue, OH	419, 567	44811
Bellevue, WA	425	98004-98009, 98015
Bellflower, CA	562	90706-90707
Bellingham, MA	508, 774	02019
Bellingham, WA	360	98225-98228
Bellmawr, NJ	856	08031, 08099
Bellmore, NY	516	11710
Bellows Falls, VT	802	05101
Bellport, NY	631	11713
Bells, TN	731	38006
Bellville, OH	419, 567	44813
Bellville, TX	979	77418
Bellvue, CO	970	80512
Bellwood, IL	708	60104
Bellwood, PA	814	16617
Belmont, CA	650	94002-94003
Belmont, MA	617, 857	02478-02479
Belmont, MS	662	38827
Belmont, NH	603	03220
Belmont, NY	585	14813
Belmont, NC	704, 980	28012
Beloit, KS	785	67420
Beloit, WI	608	53511-53512
Belpre, OH	740	45714
Belton, SC	864	29627
Belton, TX	254	76513
Beltsville, MD	301	20704-20705
Belvidere, IL	815	61008
Belvidere, NJ	908	07823
Belzoni, MS	662	39038
Bemidji, MN	218	56601, 56619
Bend, OR	541, 458	97701-97702, 97707-97709
Benicia, CA	707	94510
Benjamin, TX	940	79505
Benkelman, NE	308	69021
Bennettsville, SC	843	29512
Bennington, NH	603	03442
Bennington, VT	802	05201
Bensalem, PA	215, 267	19020-19021
Bensenville, IL	331, 630	60105-60106, 60399
Benson, AZ	520	85602
Benson, MN	320	56215
Benson, NC	919	27504
Benton, AR	501	72015-72018, 72022, 72158
Benton, IL	618	62812
Benton, KY	270	42025
Benton, LA	318	71006
Benton, MO	573	63736
Benton, PA	570	17814
Benton, TN	423	37307
Benton Harbor, MI	616	49022-49023
Bentonville, AR	479	72712, 72716
Berea, KY	859	40403-40404
Berea, OH	440	44017
Bergenfield, NJ	201, 551	07621
Berkeley, CA	510	94701-94712, 94720
Berkeley, IL	708	60163
Berkeley, MO	314	63134, 63140

*Partial list of zip codes, including main range

City	Area Code(s)	Zip Code(s)
Berkeley Heights, NJ	908	07922
Berkeley Springs, WV	304	25411
Berlin, CT	860	06037
Berlin, MD	410	21811
Berlin, NH	603	03570
Berlin, NJ	856	08009
Berlin, NY	518	12022
Berlin, OH	234, 330	44610
Berlin, PA	814	15530
Berlin, WI	920	54923
Berlin Heights, OH	419, 567	44814
Bernalillo, NM	505	87004
Bernardsville, NJ	908	07924
Berne, IN	260	46711, 46769
Berrien Springs, MI	616	49103-49104
Berryville, AR	870	72616
Berryville, VA	540	22611
Berwick, PA	570	18603
Berwyn, IL	708	60402
Berwyn, PA	484, 610	19312
Beryl, UT	435	84714
Bessemer, AL	205	35020-35023
Bessemer, MI	906	49911
Bessemer City, NC	704, 980	28016
Bethany, CT	203	06524
Bethany, MO	660	64424
Bethany, OK	405	73008
Bethany, WV	304	26032
Bethany Beach, DE	302	19930
Bethel, AK	907	99559, 99637, 99679-99680*
Bethel, CT	203	06801
Bethel, ME	207	04217, 04286
Bethel, MN	763	55005
Bethel, VT	802	05032
Bethel Park, PA	412, 878	15102
Bethesda, MD	240, 301	20810-20817, 20824-20827*
Bethlehem, GA	470, 770	30620
Bethlehem, PA	484, 610	18015-18020, 18025
Bethpage, NY	516	11714
Bettendorf, IA	563	52722
Beulah, MI	231	49617
Beulah, ND	701	58523
Beverly, MA	351, 978	01915
Beverly, NJ	609	08010
Beverly, OH	740	45715, 45721
Beverly Hills, CA	310, 323, 424	90209-90213
Bexley, OH	614	43209
Biddeford, ME	207	04005-04007
Big Bear Lake, CA	909	92315
Big Bend National Park, TX	915	79834
Big Cabin, OK	918	74332
Big Island, VA	434	24526
Big Lake, AK	907	99652
Big Lake, MN	763	55309
Big Lake, TX	915	76932
Big Pine Key, FL	305, 786	33043
Big Rapids, MI	231	49307
Big Rock, IL	331, 630	60511
Big Sky, MT	406	59716
Big Spring, TX	915	79720-79721
Big Stone Gap, VA	276	24219
Big Sur, CA	831	93920
Big Timber, MT	406	59011
Bigfork, MN	218	56628, 56639
Bigfork, MT	406	59911
Biglerville, PA	717	17307
Billerica, MA	351, 978	01821-01822, 01862
Billings, MT	406	59101-59117
Billings, OK	580	74630
Biloxi, MS	228	39530-39535, 39540
Bingen, WA	509	98605
Binger, OK	405	73009
Bingham Farms, MI	248, 947	48025
Binghamton, NY	607	13901-13905
Bird-in-Hand, PA	717	17505
Birdsboro, PA	484, 610	19508
Birmingham, AL	205	35201-35249, 35253-35255*
Birmingham, MI	248, 947	48009-48012
Birmingham, NJ	609	08011
Bisbee, AZ	520	85603
Biscoe, NC	910	27209
Bishop, CA	760, 442	93512-93515
Bishopville, SC	803	29010
Bismarck, ND	701	58501-58507
Bison, SD	605	57620
Bixby, OK	918	74008
Black Butte Ranch, OR	541, 458	97759
Black Creek, NC	252	27813
Black Earth, WI	608	53515
Black Hawk, CO	303, 720	80403, 80422
Black Mountain, NC	828	28711
Black River Falls, WI	715, 534	54615
Blackfoot, ID	208	83221
Blacksburg, SC	864	29702
Blacksburg, VA	540	24060-24063
Blackshear, GA	912	31516
Blackwell, OK	580	74631
Blackwood, NJ	856	08012
Bladensburg, MD	301	20710
Blaine, MN	763	55014, 55434, 55449
Blaine, WA	360	98230-98231
Blair, NE	402	68008-68009
Blairsville, GA	706, 762	30512-30514
Blairsville, PA	724, 878	15717
Blakely, GA	229	31723
Blakeslee, PA	570	18610
Blanchester, OH	937	45107
Bland, VA	276	24315
Blanding, UT	435	84511
Blandon, PA	484, 610	19510
Blasdell, NY	716	14219
Blauvelt, NY	845	10913
Blissfield, MI	517	49228
Blomkest, MN	320	56216
Bloomfield, CT	860	06002
Bloomfield, IN	812	47424
Bloomfield, IA	641	52537-52538
Bloomfield, MO	573	63825
Bloomfield, NJ	862, 973	07003
Bloomfield Hills, MI	248, 947	48301-48304
Bloomingdale, IL	331, 630	60108, 60117
Bloomingdale, IN	765	47832
Bloomington, CA	909	92316
Bloomington, IL	309	61701-61704, 61709-61710*
Bloomington, IN	812	47401-47408, 47490
Bloomington, MN	952	55420, 55425, 55431, 55435*
Bloomsburg, PA	570	17815, 17839
Bloomsbury, NJ	908	08804
Blountstown, FL	850	32424
Blountville, TN	423	37617
Blowing Rock, NC	828	28605
Blue Anchor, NJ	609	08037
Blue Ash, OH	513	45242
Blue Ball, PA	717	17506
Blue Bell, PA	215	19422-19424
Blue Earth, MN	507	56013
Blue Hill, ME	207	04614
Blue Island, IL	708	60406, 60827
Blue Mounds, WI	608	53517
Blue Mountain, MS	662	38610
Blue Ridge, GA	706, 762	30513
Blue Springs, MO	816	64013-64015
Bluefield, VA	276	24605
Bluefield, WV	304	24701
Bluegrove, TX	940	76352
Bluffton, IN	260	46714
Bluffton, OH	419, 567	45817
Bluffton, SC	843	29910
Blunt, SD	605	57522
Blythe, CA	760, 442	92225-92226, 92280
Blytheville, AR	870	72315-72319
Blythewood, SC	803	29016
Boardman, OH	234, 330	44512-44513
Boardman, OR	541, 458	97818
Boaz, AL	256	35956-35957
Boca Raton, FL	561	33427-33434, 33464, 33481*
Bodega Bay, CA	707	94923
Boerne, TX	830	78006, 78015
Bogalusa, LA	985	70427-70429
Bogart, GA	706, 762	30622
Bogota, NJ	201, 551	07603
Bohemia, NY	631	11716
Boiling Springs, NC	704, 980	28017
Boise, ID	208	83701-83735, 83744, 83756*
Boise City, OK	580	73933
Boley, OK	918	74829
Bolingbrook, IL	331, 630	60439-60440, 60490
Bolivar, MO	417	65613, 65727
Bolivar, TN	731	38008, 38074
Bolivia, NC	910	28422
Bolton, CT	860	06043
Bolton, MA	351, 978	01740
Bolton Landing, NY	518	12814
Bon Air, VA	804	23235
Bon Secour, AL	251	36511
Bon Wier, TX	409	75928
Bonham, TX	903	75418
Bonifay, FL	850	32425
Bonita, CA	619	91902, 91908
Bonita Springs, FL	239	34133-34136
Bonner Springs, KS	913	66012
Bonners Ferry, ID	208	83805
Bono, AR	870	72416
Boone, IA	515	50036-50037
Boone, NC	828	28607-28608
Booneville, AR	479	72927
Booneville, KY	606	41314
Booneville, MS	662	38829
Boonton, NJ	862, 973	07005
Boonville, IN	812	47601
Boonville, MO	660	65233
Boothbay Harbor, ME	207	04536-04538, 04570
Boothwyn, PA	484, 610	19061
Borden, IN	812	47106
Bordentown, NJ	609	08505
Borger, TX	806	79007-79008
Boring, OR	503, 971	97009
Borrego Springs, CA	760, 442	92004
Boscawen, NH	603	03303
Boscobel, WI	608	53805
Bossier City, LA	318	71111-71113, 71171-71172
Boston, MA	617, 857	02101-02137, 02163, 02196*
Bothell, WA	425	98011-98012, 98021, 98028*
Botkins, OH	937	45306
Bottineau, ND	701	58318
Bouckville, NY	315	13310
Boulder, CO	303, 720	80301-80310, 80314, 80321*
Boulder, MT	406	59632
Boulder City, NV	702	89005-89006
Bound Brook, NJ	732, 848	08805
Bountiful, UT	801, 385	84010-84011
Bourbon, MO	573	65441
Bourbonnais, IL	815	60914
Bovey, MN	218	55709
Bow, NH	603	03304
Bow, WA	360	98232
Bowbells, ND	701	58721
Bowdon, GA	470, 770	30108
Bowerston, OH	740	44695
Bowie, AZ	520	85605
Bowie, MD	301	20715-20721
Bowie, TX	940	76230
Bowling Green, FL	863	33834
Bowling Green, KY	270	42101-42104
Bowling Green, MO	573	63334
Bowling Green, OH	419, 567	43402-43403
Bowling Green, VA	804	22427-22428
Bowman, ND	701	58623
Bowmansville, NY	716	14026
Box Elder, MT	406	59521
Boxborough, MA	351, 978	01719
Boyden, IA	712	51234
Boydton, VA	434	23917
Boyertown, PA	484, 610	19512
Boylston, MA	508, 774	01505
Boyne Falls, MI	231	49713
Boynton Beach, FL	561	33424-33426, 33435-33437*
Boys Town, NE	402	68010
Bozeman, MT	406	59715-59719, 59771-59773
Bozrah, CT	860	06334
Brackenridge, PA	724, 878	15014
Brackettville, TX	830	78832
Bradbury, CA	626	91010
Braddock, PA	412, 878	15104
Bradenton, FL	941	34201-34212, 34280-34282
Bradford, PA	814	16701
Bradford, VT	802	05033
Bradley, IL	815	60915
Bradley, ME	207	04411
Bradley, WV	304	25818
Brady, TX	915	76825
Braham, MN	320	55006
Braidwood, IL	815	60408
Brainard, NE	402	68626

**Partial list of zip codes, including main range*

City	Area Code(s)	Zip Code(s)
Brainerd, MN	218	56401, 56425
Braintree, MA	339, 781	02184-02185
Braithwaite, LA	504	70040, 70046
Branchburg, NJ	908	08876
Branchville, NJ	862, 973	07826-07827, 07890
Brandenburg, KY	270	40108
Brandon, FL	813	33508-33511
Brandon, MS	601, 769	39042-39043, 39047, 39232
Brandon, VT	802	05733
Branford, CT	203	06405
Branson, MO	417	65615-65616
Braselton, GA	470, 678, 770	30517
Brattleboro, VT	802	05301-05304
Brawley, CA	760, 442	92227
Braymer, MO	660	64624
Brazil, IN	812	47834
Brea, CA	714	92821-92823
Breckenridge, CO	970	80424
Breckenridge, MN	218	56520
Breckenridge, TX	254	76424
Brecksville, OH	440	44141
Breese, IL	618	62230
Breezy Point, MN	218	56472
Bremen, GA	470, 770	30110
Bremen, IN	574	46506
Bremen, OH	740	43107
Bremerton, WA	360	98310-98314, 98337
Brenham, TX	979	77833-77834
Brent, AL	205	35034
Brentwood, NH	603	03833
Brentwood, NY	631	11717
Brentwood, TN	615	37024-37027
Bretton Woods, NH	603	03575
Brevard, NC	828	28712
Brewer, ME	207	04412
Brewerton, NY	315	13029
Brewster, MA	508, 774	02631
Brewster, NE	308	68821
Brewster, NY	845	10509
Brewster, OH	234, 330	44613
Brewster, WA	509	98812
Brewton, AL	251	36426-36427
Briarcliff Manor, NY	914	10510
Briarwood, NY	347, 718	11435
Brick, NJ	732, 848	08723-08724
Brickeys, AR	870	72320
Bridgeport, AL	256	35740
Bridgeport, CA	760, 442	93517
Bridgeport, CT	203	06601-06615, 06650, 06673*
Bridgeport, NE	308	69336
Bridgeport, NJ	856	08014
Bridgeport, PA	484, 610	19405
Bridgeport, WV	304	26330
Bridgeton, MO	314	63044-63045
Bridgeton, NJ	856	08302
Bridgeview, IL	708	60455
Bridgeville, PA	412, 878	15017
Bridgewater, MA	508, 774	02324-02325
Bridgewater, NJ	908	08807
Bridgewater, VA	540	22812
Bridgewater Corners, VT	802	05035
Bridgman, MI	616	49106
Bridgton, ME	207	04009
Brigantine, NJ	609	08203
Brigham City, UT	435	84302
Brighton, CO	303, 720	80601-80603
Brighton, MA	617, 857	02135
Brighton, MI	810	48114-48116
Brighton, UT	801, 385	84121
Brillion, WI	920	54110
Brimfield, IL	309	61517
Brinkley, AR	870	72021
Brinson, GA	229	31725
Brisbane, CA	415, 650	94005
Bristol, CT	860	06010-06011
Bristol, FL	850	32321
Bristol, IN	574	46507
Bristol, PA	215, 267	19007
Bristol, RI	401	02809
Bristol, TN	423	37620-37621, 37625
Bristol, VT	802	05443
Bristol, VA	276	24201-24203, 24209
Bristol, WI	262	53104
Britton, SD	605	57430
Broadalbin, NY	518	12025
Broadus, MT	406	59317
Broadview, IL	708	60153-60155
Broadview Heights, OH	440	44147
Broadway, VA	540	22815
Brockport, NY	585	14420
Brockton, MA	508, 774	02301-02305
Brockway, PA	814	15824
Brocton, NY	716	14716
Brodhead, WI	608	53520
Brodnax, VA	434	23920
Broken Arrow, OK	918	74011-74014
Broken Bow, NE	308	68822
Broken Bow, OK	580	74728
Bronson, FL	352	32621
Bronwood, GA	229	31726
Bronx, NY	347, 718	10451-10475, 10499
Bronxville, NY	914	10708
Brook Park, OH	216	44142
Brookfield, CT	203	06804
Brookfield, IL	708	60513
Brookfield, MO	660	64628
Brookfield, OH	234, 330	44403
Brookfield, WI	262	53005-53008, 53045
Brookhaven, MS	601, 769	39601-39603
Brookhaven, PA	484, 610	19015
Brookings, OR	541, 458	97415
Brookings, SD	605	57006-57007
Brookline, MA	617, 857	02445-02447
Brooklyn, CT	860	06234
Brooklyn, IA	641	52211
Brooklyn, MI	517	49230
Brooklyn, NY	347, 718	11201-11256
Brooklyn Center, MN	763	55428-55430, 55443-55444
Brooklyn Heights, OH	216	44109, 44131
Brooklyn Park, MN	763	55428-55429, 55443-55445
Brooks AFB, TX	210	78235
Brookshire, TX	281, 832	77423
Brooksville, FL	352	34601-34614
Brooksville, KY	606	41004
Brookville, IN	765	47012
Brookville, OH	937	45309
Brookville, PA	814	15825
Brookwood, AL	205	35444
Broomall, PA	484, 610	19008
Broomfield, CO	303, 720	80020-80021, 80038, 80234
Broussard, LA	337	70518
Brown Deer, WI	414	53209, 53223
Brownfield, TX	806	79316, 79376
Browning, MT	406	59417
Browns Mills, NJ	609	08015
Brownsboro, AL	256	35741
Brownsburg, IN	317	46112
Brownstown, IN	812	47220
Brownsville, KY	270	42210
Brownsville, PA	724, 878	15417
Brownsville, TN	731	38012
Brownsville, TX	956	78520-78526
Brownsville, VT	802	05037
Brownsville, WI	920	53006
Brownville, NY	315	13615
Brownwood, TX	915	76801-76804
Bruce, SD	605	57220
Bruceton Mills, WV	304	26525
Brunswick, GA	912	31520-31527, 31561
Brunswick, ME	207	04011, 04053
Brunswick, NC	910	28424
Brunswick, OH	234, 330	44212
Brush, CO	970	80723
Brusly, LA	225	70719
Bryan, OH	419, 567	43506
Bryan, TX	979	77801-77808
Bryantown, MD	301	20617
Bryce Canyon, UT	435	84717
Bryn Athyn, PA	215, 267	19009
Bryn Mawr, PA	484, 610	19010
Bryson City, NC	828	28713
Buchanan, GA	470, 770	30113
Buchanan, MI	616	49107
Buchanan, VA	540	24066
Buckeye, AZ	623	85326
Buckhannon, WV	304	26201
Buckingham, VA	434	23921
Bucyrus, OH	419, 567	44820
Buda, TX	512	78610
Budd Lake, NJ	862, 973	07828
Buellton, CA	805	93427
Buena, NJ	856	08310
Buena Park, CA	714	90620-90624
Buena Vista, CO	719	81211
Buena Vista, GA	229	31803
Buena Vista, VA	540	24416
Buffalo, MN	763	55313
Buffalo, MO	417	65622
Buffalo, NY	716	14201-14233, 14240-14241*
Buffalo, OK	580	73834
Buffalo, SD	605	57720
Buffalo, WY	307	82834, 82840
Buffalo Gap, TX	915	79508
Buffalo Grove, IL	224, 847	60089
Buford, GA	470, 678, 770	30515-30519
Buhl, ID	208	83316
Buies Creek, NC	910	27506
Bullhead City, AZ	928	86426-86430, 86439-86442*
Bunker Hill, IN	765	46914
Bunker Hill, KS	785	67626
Bunn, NC	919	27508
Bunnell, FL	386	32110
Buras, LA	504	70041
Burbank, CA	818	91501-91510, 91521-91526
Burbank, IL	708	60459
Burgaw, NC	910	28425
Burgettstown, PA	724, 878	15021
Burien, WA	206	98146-98148, 98166-98168
Burke, SD	605	57523
Burke, VA	571, 703	22009, 22015
Burkesville, KY	270	42717
Burkeville, VA	434	23922
Burleigh, NJ	609	08210
Burleson, TX	682, 817	76028, 76097
Burley, ID	208	83318
Burlingame, CA	650	94010-94012
Burlington, CO	719	80807
Burlington, IL	224, 847	60109
Burlington, IA	319	52601
Burlington, KS	620	66839
Burlington, KY	859	41005
Burlington, MA	339, 781	01803-01805
Burlington, NJ	609	08016
Burlington, NC	336	27215-27220
Burlington, VT	802	05401-05407
Burlington, WA	360	98233
Burlington, WI	262	53105
Burnet, TX	512	78611
Burnham, PA	717	17009
Burns, OR	541, 458	97710, 97720
Burnsville, MN	952	55306, 55337
Burnsville, NC	828	28714
Burr Ridge, IL	331, 630	60525-60527
Burton, MI	810	48509, 48519, 48529
Burton, OH	440	44021
Burtonsville, MD	301	20866
Burwell, NE	308	68823
Bushkill, PA	570	18324, 18371-18373
Bushnell, FL	352	33513
Bushnell, IL	309	61422
Butler, AL	205	36904
Butler, GA	478	31006
Butler, IN	260	46721
Butler, MD	410	21023
Butler, MO	660	64730
Butler, NJ	862, 973	07405
Butler, PA	724, 878	16001-16003
Butler, WI	262	53007
Butner, NC	919	27509
Butte, MT	406	59701-59703, 59707, 59750
Butte, NE	402	68722
Butterfield, MN	507	56120
Buxton, NC	252	27920
Buzzards Bay, MA	508, 774	02532, 02542
Byfield, MA	351, 978	01922
Byhalia, MS	662	38611
Byrdstown, TN	931	38549
Byron, IL	815	61010
Byron, MN	507	55920
Byron Center, MI	616	49315

*Partial list of zip codes, including main range

C

City	Area Code(s)	Zip Code(s)
Cabazon, CA	951	92230, 92282
Cabot, AR	501	72023
Cabot, PA	724, 878	16023
Cadillac, MI	231	49601
Cadiz, KY	270	42211
Cadiz, OH	740	43907
Cahokia, IL	618	62206
Cairo, GA	229	31728
Cairo, IL	618	62914
Calabasas, CA	818	91301-91302, 91372
Calabasas Hills, CA	818	91301
Calais, ME	207	04619
Caldwell, ID	208	83605-83607
Caldwell, NJ	862, 973	07006-07007
Caldwell, OH	740	43724
Caldwell, TX	979	77836
Caledonia, MN	507	55921
Caledonia, NY	585	14423
Caledonia, WI	262	53108
Calexico, CA	760, 442	92231-92232
Calhoun, GA	706, 762	30701-30703
Calhoun, KY	270	42327
Calhoun, TN	423	37309
Calhoun City, MS	662	38916, 38955
Calico Rock, AR	870	72519
California, MD	301	20619
California, MO	573	65018, 65042
California, PA	724, 878	15419
Calipatria, CA	760, 442	92233
Calistoga, CA	707	94515
Callery, PA	724, 878	16024
Callicoon, NY	845	12723
Calmar, IA	563	52132
Calumet, MI	906	49913, 49918, 49942
Calumet City, IL	708	60409
Calumet Park, IL	708	60643, 60827
Camarillo, CA	805	93010-93012
Camas, WA	360	98607
Cambria, CA	805	93428
Cambridge, IL	309	61238
Cambridge, MD	410	21613
Cambridge, MA	617, 857	02138-02142, 02163, 02238*
Cambridge, MN	763	55008
Cambridge, NE	308	69022
Cambridge, OH	740	43725, 43750
Cambridge, WI	608	53523
Cambridge City, IN	765	47327
Cambridge Springs, PA	814	16403
Camden, AL	334	36726
Camden, AR	870	71701, 71711
Camden, DE	302	19934
Camden, IN	574	46917
Camden, ME	207	04843, 04847
Camden, MI	517	49232
Camden, NJ	856	08100-08110
Camden, NY	315	13316
Camden, NC	252	27921
Camden, SC	803	29020
Camden, TN	731	38320
Camdenton, MO	573	65020
Cameron, LA	337	70631
Cameron, MO	816	64429
Cameron, MT	760, 442	59720
Cameron, TX	254	76520
Cameron Park, CA	530	95682
Camilla, GA	229	31730
Camillus, NY	315	13031
Camp Douglas, WI	608	54618, 54637
Camp Hill, PA	717	17001, 17011-17012, 17089*
Camp Lejeune, NC	910	28542, 28547
Camp Pendleton, CA	760, 442	92054-92055
Camp Point, IL	217	62320
Camp Shelby, MS	601, 769	39401, 39407
Camp Springs, MD	301	20746-20748
Camp Verde, AZ	928	86322
Campbell, CA	408	95008-95011
Campbell Hall, NY	845	10916
Campbellsville, KY	270	42718-42719
Campton, KY	606	41301, 41342
Canadian, TX	806	79014
Canal Winchester, OH	614	43110
Canandaigua, NY	585	14424-14425
Canastota, NY	315	13032
Candler, NC	828	28715
Cando, ND	701	58324
Candor, NC	910	27229
Canfield, OH	234, 330	44406
Cannon AFB, NM	505	88101-88103
Cannon Beach, OR	503	97110
Cannon Falls, MN	507	55009
Canoga Park, CA	818	91303-91309, 91396
Canon City, CO	719	81212-81215, 81246
Canonsburg, PA	724, 878	15317
Canterbury, NH	603	03224
Canton, GA	470, 770	30114-30115
Canton, IL	309	61520
Canton, MA	339, 781	02021
Canton, MI	734	48187-48188
Canton, MS	601, 769	39046
Canton, MO	573	63435
Canton, NY	315	13617
Canton, OH	234, 330	44701-44714, 44718-44721*
Canton, PA	570	17724, 17743
Canton, SD	605	57013
Canton, TX	903	75103
Canyon, TX	806	79015-79016
Canyon City, OR	541, 458	97820
Canyonville, OR	541, 458	97417
Cape Canaveral, FL	321	32920
Cape Charles, VA	757	23310
Cape Coral, FL	239	33904, 33909-33910, 33914*
Cape Elizabeth, ME	207	04107
Cape Girardeau, MO	573	63701-63705
Cape May, NJ	609	08204
Cape May Court House, NJ	609	08210
Cape Vincent, NY	315	13618
Capitol Heights, MD	301	20731, 20743, 20753, 20790*
Capitola, CA	831	95010, 95062
Capron, VA	434	23829
Captain Cook, HI	808	96704
Captiva, FL	239	33924
Capulin, NM	505	88414
Carbondale, IL	618	62901-62903
Carbondale, PA	570	18407
Carefree, AZ	480	85377
Carey, OH	419, 567	43316
Caribou, ME	207	04736
Carle Place, NY	516	11514
Carlinville, IL	217	62626
Carlisle, IN	812	47838
Carlisle, KY	859	40311, 40350
Carlisle, PA	717	17013
Carlisle, SC	864	29031
Carlsbad, CA	760, 442	92008-92009, 92013, 92018
Carlsbad, NM	505	88220-88221
Carlstadt, NJ	201, 551	07072
Carlton, MN	218	55718
Carlyle, IL	618	62231
Carmel, CA	831	93921-93923
Carmel, IN	317	46032-46033, 46082
Carmel, NY	845	10512
Carmel Valley, CA	831	93924
Carmi, IL	618	62821
Carmichael, CA	916	95608-95609
Carnegie, PA	412, 878	15106
Carnesville, GA	706, 762	30521
Carneys Point, NJ	856	08069
Caro, MI	989	48723
Carol Stream, IL	331, 630	60116, 60125-60128, 60132*
Carolina, PR	787, 939	00979-00988
Carpentersville, IL	224, 847	60110
Carpinteria, CA	805	93013-93014
Carrabassett Valley, ME	207	04947
Carrington, ND	701	58421
Carrizo Springs, TX	830	78834
Carrizozo, NM	505	88301
Carroll, IA	712	51401
Carroll Valley, PA	717	17320
Carrollton, AL	205	35447
Carrollton, GA	470, 770	30112, 30116-30119
Carrollton, IL	217	62016
Carrollton, KY	502	41008, 41045
Carrollton, MS	662	38917
Carrollton, MO	660	64633
Carrollton, OH	234, 330	44615
Carrollton, TX	469, 972	75006-75011
Carson, CA	310, 424	90745-90749, 90810
Carson, ND	701	58529
Carson City, MI	989	48811
Carson City, NV	775	89701-89706, 89711-89714*
Carter Lake, IA	712	51510
Carteret, NJ	732, 848	07008
Cartersville, GA	470, 770	30120-30121
Carterville, IL	618	62918
Carthage, IL	217	62321
Carthage, MS	601, 769	39051
Carthage, MO	417	64836
Carthage, NC	910	28327
Carthage, TN	615	37030
Carthage, TX	903	75633
Caruthersville, MO	573	63830
Carver, MA	508, 774	02330, 02355, 02366
Cary, IL	224, 847	60013
Cary, NC	919	27511-27513, 27518-27519
Casa Grande, AZ	520	85222, 85230
Cascade, ID	208	83611
Cascade Locks, OR	509	97014
Casey, IL	217	62420
Cashiers, NC	828	28717
Cashmere, WA	509	98815
Casper, WY	307	82601-82605, 82609, 82615*
Casselberry, FL	321, 407	32707-32708, 32718-32719*
Cassopolis, MI	616	49031
Cassville, MO	417	65623-65625
Castaic, CA	661	91310, 91384
Castine, ME	207	04420-04421
Castle Dale, UT	435	84513
Castle Point, NY	845	12511
Castle Rock, CO	303, 720	80104
Castleton, VT	802	05735
Castro Valley, CA	510	94546, 94552
Castroville, CA	831	95012
Catalina, AZ	520	85738-85739
Catasauqua, PA	484, 610	18032
Catawba, VA	540	24070
Catawissa, PA	570	17820
Cathedral City, CA	760, 442	92234-92235
Cathlamet, WA	360	98612
Catlettsburg, KY	606	41129
Catonsville, MD	410	21228
Catoosa, OK	918	74015
Catskill, NY	518	12414
Cavalier, ND	701	58220
Cave Junction, OR	541, 458	97523, 97531
Cayce, SC	803	29033
Cazenovia, NY	315	13035
Cedar City, UT	435	84720-84721
Cedar Crest, NM	505	87008
Cedar Falls, IA	319	50613-50614
Cedar Falls, NC	336	27230
Cedar Grove, NJ	862, 973	07009
Cedar Grove, WI	920	53013
Cedar Hill, TX	469, 972	75104-75106
Cedar Knolls, NJ	862, 973	07927
Cedar Park, TX	512	78613, 78630
Cedar Rapids, IA	319	52401-52411, 52497-52499
Cedar Springs, GA	229	31732
Cedar Springs, MI	616	49319
Cedar Vale, KS	620	67024
Cedarburg, WI	262	53012
Cedartown, GA	470, 770	30125
Cedarville, OH	937	45314
Celebration, FL	321, 407	34747
Celina, OH	419, 567	45822, 45826
Celina, TN	931	38551
Centennial, CO	303, 720	80015-80016, 80111-80112*
Center, NE	402	68724
Center, ND	701	58530
Center, TX	936	75935
Center City, MN	651	55002, 55012
Center Hill, FL	352	33514
Center Line, MI	586	48015
Center Moriches, NY	631	11934
Center Point, TX	830	78010
Center Valley, PA	484, 610	18034
Centerburg, OH	740	43011
Centerport, NY	631	11721
Centerville, IA	641	52544
Centerville, MA	508, 774	02632-02636

*Partial list of zip codes, including main range

City	Area Code(s)	Zip Code(s)
Centerville, MO	573	63633
Centerville, OH	937	45458-45459
Centerville, TN	931	37033
Centerville, TX	903	75833
Centerville, UT	801, 385	84014
Central, SC	864	29630
Central City, CO	303, 720	80427
Central City, KY	270	42330
Central City, NE	308	68826
Central Falls, RI	401	02863
Central Islip, NY	631	11722, 11749, 11760
Central Point, OR	541, 458	97502
Centralia, IL	618	62801
Centralia, MO	573	65240
Centralia, WA	360	98531
Centre, AL	256	35960
Centre Hall, PA	814	16828
Centreville, AL	205	35042
Centreville, IL	618	62207
Centreville, MD	410	21617
Centreville, MI	616	49032
Centreville, MS	601, 769	39631
Centreville, VA	571, 703	20120-20122
Centuria, WI	715, 534	54824
Century, FL	850	32535
Ceres, CA	209	95307
Cerritos, CA	562	90701-90703
Chadds Ford, PA	484, 610	19317
Chadron, NE	308	69337
Chaffee, NY	585	14030
Chagrin Falls, OH	440	44022-44023
Chalfont, PA	215, 267	18914
Challis, ID	208	83226-83229
Chalmette, LA	504	70043-70044
Chama, NM	505	87520
Chamberlain, SD	605	57325-57326
Chambersburg, PA	717	17201
Chamblee, GA	470, 770	30341, 30366
Champaign, IL	217	61820-61826
Champion, PA	814	15622
Chandler, AZ	480	85224-85226, 85244-85249
Chandler, IN	812	47610
Chandler, OK	405	74834
Chandlerville, IL	217	62627
Chanhassen, MN	952	55317
Channahon, IL	815	60410
Channelview, TX	281, 832	77530
Channing, TX	806	79018, 79058
Chantilly, VA	571, 703	20151-20153
Chanute, KS	620	66720
Chapel Hill, NC	919	27514-27517, 27599
Chapin, SC	803	29036
Chapmanville, WV	304	25508
Chappell, NE	308	69129
Chardon, OH	440	44024
Chariton, IA	641	50049
Charleroi, PA	724, 878	15022
Charles City, IA	641	50616, 50620
Charles City, VA	804	23030
Charles Town, WV	304	25414
Charleston, IL	217	61920
Charleston, ME	207	04422
Charleston, MS	662	38921, 38958
Charleston, MO	573	63834
Charleston, SC	843	29401-29425, 29492
Charleston, WV	304	25301-25339, 25350, 25356*
Charleston AFB, SC	843	29404
Charlestown, IN	812	47111
Charlestown, MA	617, 857	02129
Charlestown, NH	603	03603
Charlevoix, MI	231	49711, 49720
Charlotte, MI	517	48813
Charlotte, NC	704, 980	28201-28290, 28296-28299
Charlotte, TN	615	37036
Charlotte, VT	802	05445
Charlotte Court House, VA	434	23923
Charlotte Hall, MD	301	20622
Charlottesville, VA	434	22901-22911
Charlton City, MA	508, 774	01508
Chase City, VA	434	23924
Chaska, MN	952	55318
Chateaugay, NY	518	12920
Chatfield, MN	507	55923
Chatham, IL	217	62629
Chatham, MA	508, 774	02633
Chatham, NJ	862, 973	07928
Chatham, NY	518	12037
Chatham, VA	434	24531
Chatom, AL	251	36518
Chatsworth, CA	818	91311-91313
Chatsworth, GA	706, 762	30705
Chatsworth, IL	815	60921
Chattahoochee, FL	850	32324
Chattanooga, TN	423	37343, 37401-37424, 37450
Chautauqua, NY	716	14722
Chauvin, LA	985	70344
Cheboygan, MI	231	49721
Checotah, OK	918	74426
Cheektowaga, NY	716	14043, 14206, 14211-14215*
Chehalis, WA	360	98532
Chelan, WA	509	98816
Chelmsford, MA	351, 978	01824
Chelsea, MA	617, 857	02150
Chelsea, MI	734	48118
Chelsea, VT	802	05038
Cheltenham, PA	215, 267	19012
Cheney, KS	316	67025
Cheney, WA	509	99004
Cheraw, SC	843	29520
Cherokee, IA	712	51012
Cherokee, NC	828	28719
Cherokee, OK	580	73728
Cherry Hill, NJ	856	08002-08003, 08034
Cherry Point, NC	252	28533
Cherry Valley, IL	815	61016
Cherry Valley, MA	508, 774	01611
Cherryfield, ME	207	04622
Cherryville, NC	704, 980	28021
Chesapeake, VA	757	23320-23328
Chesapeake City, MD	410	21915
Cheshire, CT	203	06408-06411
Chester, CT	860	06412
Chester, GA	478	31012
Chester, IL	618	62233
Chester, MD	410	21619
Chester, MT	406	59522
Chester, NH	603	03036
Chester, NJ	908	07930
Chester, NY	845	10918
Chester, PA	484, 610	19013-19016, 19022
Chester, SC	803	29706
Chester, VA	804	23831, 23836
Chester, WV	304	26034
Chester Springs, PA	484, 610	19425
Chesterbrook, PA	484, 610	19087
Chesterfield, MI	586	48047, 48051
Chesterfield, MO	314, 636	63005-63006, 63017
Chesterfield, SC	843	29709
Chesterfield, VA	804	23832, 23838
Chesterfield Township, MI	586	48047, 48051
Chesterland, OH	440	44026
Chesterton, IN	219	46304
Chestertown, MD	410	21620, 21690
Chestertown, NY	518	12817
Chestnut Hill, MA	617, 857	02467
Chestnut Ridge, NY	845	10952, 10965, 10977
Cheswick, PA	724, 878	15024
Cheverly, MD	301	20781-20785
Chevy Chase, MD	301	20813-20815, 20825
Cheyenne, OK	580	73628
Cheyenne, WY	307	82001-82010
Cheyenne Wells, CO	719	80810
Cheyney, PA	484, 610	19319
Chicago, IL	312, 773	60601-60701, 60706-60707*
Chicago Heights, IL	708	60411-60412
Chickamauga, GA	706, 762	30707
Chickasaw, AL	251	36611
Chickasha, OK	405	73018, 73023
Chico, CA	530	95926-95929, 95973-95976
Chicopee, MA	413	01013-01014, 01020-01022
Chiefland, FL	352	32626, 32644
Childersburg, AL	256	35044
Childress, TX	940	79201
Chillicothe, IL	309	61523
Chillicothe, MO	660	64601
Chillicothe, OH	740	45601
Chilton, WI	920	53014
Chincoteague Island, VA	757	23336-23337
Chinle, AZ	928	86503, 86507, 86538, 86545*
Chino, CA	909	91708-91710
Chinook, MT	406	59523, 59535
Chipley, FL	850	32428
Chippewa Falls, WI	715, 534	54729, 54774
Chisholm, MN	218	55719
Chocorua, NH	603	03817
Choteau, MT	406	59422
Chowchilla, CA	559	93610
Christiana, PA	484, 610	17509
Christiansburg, VA	540	24068, 24073
Christmas, FL	321, 407	32709
Chuckey, TN	423	37641
Chula Vista, CA	619	91909-91915, 91921
Cicero, IL	708	60804
Cimarron, KS	620	67835
Cincinnati, OH	513	45201-45258, 45262-45280*
Cinnaminson, NJ	856	08077
Circle, MT	406	59215
Circle Pines, MN	763	55014
Circleville, OH	740	43113
Cisco, TX	254	76437
Citrus Heights, CA	916	95610-95611, 95621, 95662
City of Commerce, CA	323	90040, 90091
City of Industry, CA	626	90601, 91714-91716, 91732*
Clackamas, OR	503, 971	97015
Clairton, PA	412, 878	15025
Clallam Bay, WA	360	98326
Clanton, AL	205	35045-35046
Clare, MI	989	48617
Claremont, CA	909	91711
Claremont, NH	603	03743
Claremont, NC	828	28610
Claremore, OK	918	74017-74018
Clarence, NY	716	14031, 14221
Clarendon, AR	870	72029
Clarendon, TX	806	79226
Clarendon Hills, IL	331, 630	60514, 60527
Clarinda, IA	712	51632
Clarion, IA	515	50525-50526
Clarion, PA	814	16214
Clarissa, MN	218	56440
Clark, CO	970	80428
Clark, NJ	732, 848	07066
Clark, SD	605	57225
Clarkdale, AZ	928	86324
Clarkesville, GA	706, 762	30523
Clarks Summit, PA	570	18411
Clarksburg, MD	240, 301	20871
Clarksburg, WV	304	26301-26302, 26306, 26461
Clarksdale, MS	662	38614, 38669
Clarkston, MI	248, 947	48346-48348
Clarksville, AR	479	72830
Clarksville, IN	812	47129-47131
Clarksville, TN	931	37040-37044
Clarksville, TX	903	75426
Claude, TX	806	79019
Clawson, MI	248, 947	48017, 48398
Claxton, GA	912	30414-30417, 30438
Clay, WV	304	25043
Clay Center, KS	785	67432
Clay Center, NE	402	68933
Claymont, DE	302	19703
Clayton, AL	334	36016
Clayton, CA	925	94517
Clayton, DE	302	19938
Clayton, GA	706, 762	30525
Clayton, MO	314	63105, 63124
Clayton, NJ	856	08312
Clayton, NM	505	88415
Clayton, NC	919	27520
Clear Brook, VA	540	22624
Clear Creek, IN	812	47426
Clear Lake, IA	641	50428
Clear Lake, SD	605	57226
Clearfield, PA	814	16830
Clearfield, UT	801, 385	84015-84016, 84089
Clearwater, FL	727	33755-33769
Clearwater Beach, FL	727	33767
Cleburne, TX	682, 817	76031-76033
Cleghorn, IA	712	51014
Clementon, NJ	856	08021
Clements, CA	209	95227
Clements, MN	507	56224
Clemson, SC	864	29631-29634
Clermont, FL	352	34711-34713
Cleveland, GA	706, 762	30528
Cleveland, MS	662	38732-38733

*Partial list of zip codes, including main range

City	Area Code(s)	Zip Code(s)
Cleveland, OH	216, 440	44101-44149, 44177-44199
Cleveland, OK	918	74020
Cleveland, TN	423	37311-37312, 37320-37323*
Cleveland, TX	281, 832	77327-77328
Cleveland, WI	920	53015
Cleveland Heights, OH	216	44106, 44112, 44118-44121
Clewiston, FL	863	33440
Clifford, PA	570	18413
Cliffside, NC	828	28024
Cliffside Park, NJ	201, 551	07010
Cliffwood Beach, NJ	732, 848	07735
Clifton, AZ	928	85533
Clifton, KS	785	66937
Clifton, NJ	862, 973	07011-07015
Clifton, TN	931	38425
Clifton, TX	254	76634, 76644
Clifton Forge, VA	540	24422
Clifton Heights, PA	484, 610	19018
Clifton Park, NY	518	12065
Clifton Springs, NY	315	14432
Clines Corners, NM	505	87070
Clinton, AR	501	72031
Clinton, CT	860	06413
Clinton, IL	217	61727
Clinton, IN	765	47842
Clinton, IA	563	52732-52736, 52771
Clinton, KY	270	42031
Clinton, LA	225	70722
Clinton, ME	207	04927
Clinton, MD	301	20735
Clinton, MA	351, 978	01510
Clinton, MI	517	49236
Clinton, MN	320	56225
Clinton, MS	601, 769	39056-39060
Clinton, MO	660	64735
Clinton, NJ	908	08809
Clinton, NY	315	13323
Clinton, NC	910	28328-28329
Clinton, OK	580	73601
Clinton, SC	864	29325
Clinton, TN	865	37716-37717
Clinton Township, MI	586	48035-48038
Clintonville, WI	715, 534	54929
Clintwood, VA	276	24228
Clio, MI	810	48420
Clive, IA	515	50325
Cloquet, MN	218	55720
Closter, NJ	201, 551	07624
Cloudcroft, NM	505	88317, 88350
Clover, SC	803	29710
Clover, VA	434	24534
Cloverdale, VA	540	24077
Clovis, CA	559	93611-93613
Clovis, NM	505	88101-88103
Clute, TX	979	77531
Clyde, NY	315	14433
Clyde, NC	828	28721
Clyde Park, MT	406	59018
Coachella, CA	760, 442	92236
Coal Township, PA	570	17866
Coalgate, OK	580	74538
Coalinga, CA	559	93210
Coalmont, TN	931	37313
Coalville, UT	435	84017
Coatesville, PA	484, 610	19320
Cobleskill, NY	518	12043
Coburg, OR	541, 458	97408
Cochran, GA	478	31014
Cochranton, PA	814	16314
Cockeysville, MD	410	21030-21031
Cocoa, FL	321	32922-32927
Cocoa Beach, FL	321	32931-32932
Coconut Creek, FL	754, 954	33063-33066, 33073, 33097
Coconut Grove, FL	305, 786	33133-33134, 33146
Cody, WY	307	82414
Coeburn, VA	276	24230
Coeur d'Alene, ID	208	83814-83816
Coffeyville, KS	620	67337
Cogan Station, PA	570	17728
Cohasset, MA	339, 781	02025
Cohoes, NY	518	12047
Cokato, MN	320	55321
Coker, AL	205	35452
Colby, KS	785	67701
Colchester, CT	860	06415, 06420
Colchester, IL	309	62326
Colchester, VT	802	05439, 05446-05449
Cold Spring, KY	859	41076
Cold Spring, MN	320	56320
Cold Spring, NY	845	10516
Cold Spring Harbor, NY	516	11724
Cold Springs, NV	775	89506
Coldspring, TX	936	77331
Coldwater, KS	620	67029
Coldwater, MI	517	49036
Coldwater, OH	419, 567	45828
Coleman, FL	352	33521
Coleman, MI	989	48618
Coleman, OK	580	73432
Coleman, TX	915	76834
Colfax, IA	515	50054
Colfax, LA	318	71417
Colfax, WA	509	99111
College Corner, OH	513	45003
College Park, GA	404, 470	30337
College Park, MD	301	20740-20742
College Place, WA	509	99324
College Point, NY	347, 718	11356
College Station, TX	979	77840-77845
Collegedale, TN	423	37315
Collegeville, MN	320	56321
Collegeville, PA	484, 610	19426, 19473
Colleyville, TX	682, 817	76034
Collierville, TN	901	38017, 38027
Collingswood, NJ	856	08108
Collins, MS	601, 769	39428
Collins, NY	716	14034
Collinsville, IL	618	62234
Collinsville, OK	918	74021
Collinsville, VA	276	24078
Collinwood, TN	931	38450
Colman, SD	605	57017
Colmar, PA	215, 267	18915
Coloma, CA	530	95613
Coloma, MI	616	49038-49039
Colon, MI	616	49040
Colonial Heights, VA	804	23834
Colorado City, AZ	928	86021
Colorado City, TX	915	79512
Colorado Springs, CO	719	80901-80950, 80960-80962*
Colquitt, GA	229	31737
Colstrip, MT	406	59323
Colt, AR	870	72326
Colton, CA	909	92313, 92324
Columbia, IL	618	62236
Columbia, KY	270	42728, 42735
Columbia, LA	318	71418
Columbia, MD	410, 443	21044-21046
Columbia, MS	601, 769	39429
Columbia, MO	573	65201-65205, 65211-65218*
Columbia, NC	252	27925
Columbia, PA	717	17512
Columbia, SC	803	29201-29230, 29240, 29250*
Columbia, TN	931	38401-38402
Columbia City, IN	260	46725
Columbia Falls, MT	406	59912
Columbia Heights, MN	763	55421
Columbia Station, OH	440	44028
Columbiana, AL	205	35051
Columbiana, OH	234, 330	44408
Columbus, GA	706, 762	31829, 31901-31909, 31914*
Columbus, IN	812	47201-47203
Columbus, KS	620	66725
Columbus, MS	662	39701-39705, 39710
Columbus, MT	406	59019
Columbus, NE	402	68601-68602
Columbus, NC	828	28722
Columbus, ND	701	58727
Columbus, OH	614	43085, 43201-43236, 43240*
Columbus, TX	979	78934
Columbus, WI	920	53925
Columbus AFB, MS	662	39701
Columbus Grove, OH	419, 567	45830
Colusa, CA	530	95932
Colville, WA	509	99114
Comanche, TX	915	76442
Combined Locks, WI	920	54113
Commack, NY	631	11725
Commerce, CA	323	90040, 90091
Commerce, GA	706, 762	30529-30530, 30599
Commerce, TX	903	75428-75429
Commerce City, CO	303, 720	80022, 80037
Commerce Township, MI	248, 947	48382, 48390
Compton, CA	310, 424	90220-90224
Comstock, NY	518	12821
Comstock Park, MI	616	49321
Conception, MO	660	64433
Concord, CA	925	94518-94529
Concord, MA	351, 978	01742
Concord, NH	603	03301-03305
Concord, NC	704, 980	28025-28027
Concord, OH	440	44060, 44077
Concordia, KS	785	66901
Concordville, PA	484, 610	19331, 19339-19340
Condon, OR	541, 458	97823
Conejos, CO	719	81129
Conestoga, PA	717	17516
Congers, NY	845	10920
Conklin, NY	607	13748
Conneaut, OH	440	44030
Connell, WA	509	99326
Connellsville, PA	724, 878	15425
Connersville, IN	765	47331
Conover, NC	828	28613
Conrad, IA	641	50621
Conrad, MT	406	59425
Conroe, TX	936	77301-77306, 77384-77385
Conshohocken, PA	484, 610	19428-19429
Contoocook, NH	603	03229
Convent, LA	225	70723
Conway, AR	501	72032-72035
Conway, NH	603	03818
Conway, SC	843	29526-29528
Conyers, GA	470, 770	30012-30013, 30094
Cook, MN	218	55723
Cookeville, TN	931	38501-38506
Coolidge, AZ	520	85228
Coolidge, GA	229	31738
Coolidge, TX	254	76635
Coon Rapids, MN	763	55433, 55448
Cooper, TX	903	75432
Cooper City, FL	754, 954	33024-33026, 33328-33330
Coopersburg, PA	484, 610	18036
Cooperstown, NY	607	13326
Cooperstown, ND	701	58425
Coopersville, MI	616	49404
Coos Bay, OR	541, 458	97420
Copiague, NY	631	11726
Copley, OH	234, 330	44321
Coppell, TX	469, 972	75019, 75099
Copper Center, AK	907	99573
Copper Mountain, CO	970	80443
Copperas Cove, TX	254	76522
Coquille, OR	541, 458	97423
Cora, WY	307	82925
Coral Gables, FL	305, 786	33114, 33124, 33133-33134*
Coral Springs, FL	754, 954	33065-33067, 33071, 33075*
Coralville, IA	319	52241
Coraopolis, PA	412, 878	15108
Corbett, OR	503, 971	97019
Corbin, KY	606	40701-40702
Corcoran, CA	559	93212, 93282
Cordele, GA	229	31010, 31015
Cordell, OK	580	73632
Cordova, AK	907	99574, 99677
Cordova, TN	901	38016-38018, 38088
Core, WV	304	26529
Corinne, UT	435	84307
Corinth, MS	662	38834-38835
Corinth, TX	940	76208-76210
Cornelia, GA	706, 762	30531
Cornelius, NC	704, 980	28031
Cornelius, OR	503, 971	97113
Cornell, WI	715, 534	54732
Corning, AR	870	72422
Corning, CA	530	96021, 96029
Corning, IA	712	50841
Corning, NY	607	14830-14831
Cornish, NH	603	03745
Cornville, AZ	928	86325
Cornwall, NY	845	12518
Cornwall Bridge, CT	860	06754

Partial list of zip codes, including main range

City	Area Code(s)	Zip Code(s)
Corona, CA	951	92877-92883
Corona, NY	347, 718	11368
Corona del Mar, CA	949	92625
Coronado, CA	619	92118, 92178
Corpus Christi, TX	361	78350, 78401-78419, 78426*
Corry, PA	814	16407
Corsicana, TX	903	75109-75110, 75151
Corte Madera, CA	415	94925, 94976
Cortez, CO	970	81321
Cortland, NY	607	13045
Cortlandt Manor, NY	845	10567
Corunna, MI	989	48817
Corvallis, MT	406	59828
Corvallis, OR	541, 458	97330-97333, 97339
Corydon, IN	812	47112
Corydon, IA	641	50060
Cos Cob, CT	203	06807
Coshocton, OH	740	43812
Costa Mesa, CA	714, 949	92626-92628
Cotati, CA	707	94926-94931
Cottage Grove, OR	541, 458	97424, 97472
Cottonport, LA	318	71327
Cottonwood, AZ	928	86326
Cottonwood, CA	530	96022
Cottonwood, ID	208	83522, 03533
Cottonwood, MN	507	56229
Cottonwood Falls, KS	620	66845
Cotuit, MA	508, 774	02635
Cotulla, TX	830	78001, 78014
Coudersport, PA	814	16915
Coulee City, WA	509	99115
Coulee Dam, WA	509	99116
Council, ID	208	83612
Council Bluffs, IA	712	51501-51503
Council Grove, KS	620	66846, 66873
Countryside, IL	708	60525
Coupeville, WA	360	98239
Courtland, VA	757	23837
Coushatta, LA	318	71019
Coventry, RI	401	02816
Covina, CA	626	91722-91724
Covington, GA	470, 770	30014-30016
Covington, IN	765	47932
Covington, KY	859	41011-41019
Covington, LA	985	70433-70435
Covington, TN	901	38019
Covington, VA	540	24426
Cowiche, WA	509	98923
Coxsackie, NY	518	12051, 12192
Cozad, NE	308	69130
Craftsbury Common, VT	802	05827
Craig, CO	970	81625-81626
Craigsville, VA	540	24430
Cranberry Township, PA	724, 878	16066
Cranbury, NJ	609	08512, 08570
Crandall, TX	469, 972	75114
Crandon, WI	715, 534	54520
Crane, TX	915	79731
Cranford, NJ	908	07016
Cranston, RI	401	02823, 02905-02910, 02920*
Craryville, NY	518	12521
Crater Lake, OR	541, 458	97604
Crawfordsville, IN	765	47933-47939
Crawfordville, FL	850	32326-32327
Crawfordville, GA	706, 762	30631
Crazy Horse, SD	605	57730
Creede, CO	719	81130
Creedmoor, NC	919	27522, 27564
Creighton, NE	402	68729
Crescent City, CA	707	95531-95532, 95538
Crescent Springs, KY	859	41017
Cresco, IA	563	52136
Cresco, PA	570	18326
Cresskill, NJ	201, 551	07626
Cresson, PA	814	16630, 16699
Cresson, TX	682, 817	76035
Cressona, PA	570	17929
Creston, IA	641	50801
Crestview, FL	850	32536-32539
Crestview Hills, KY	859	41017
Creswell, OR	541, 458	97426
Crete, IL	708	60417
Crete, NE	402	68333
Creve Coeur, IL	309	61610
Creve Coeur, MO	314	63141
Crewe, VA	434	23930
Cripple Creek, CO	719	80813
Crisfield, MD	410	21817
Crockett, CA	510	94525
Crockett, TX	936	75835
Crofton, MD	410	21114
Cromwell, CT	860	06416
Crookston, MN	218	56716
Crosby, ND	701	58730
Crosbyton, TX	806	79322
Cross City, FL	352	32628
Cross Lanes, WV	304	25313, 25356
Cross Plains, WI	608	53528
Crossett, AR	870	71635
Crossville, TN	931	38555-38558, 38571-38572
Croswell, MI	810	48422
Crow Agency, MT	406	59022
Crowell, TX	940	79227
Crowley, CO	719	81033-81034
Crowley, LA	337	70526-70527
Crown Point, IN	219	46307-46308
Crownsville, MD	410	21032
Croydon, PA	215, 267	19021
Crum Lynne, PA	484, 610	19022
Crystal, MN	763	55422, 55427-55429
Crystal Bay, NV	775	89402
Crystal City, MO	636	63019
Crystal City, TX	830	78839
Crystal Falls, MI	906	49920
Crystal Lake, IL	815	60012-60014, 60039
Crystal River, FL	352	34423, 34428-34429
Crystal Springs, MS	601, 769	39059
Cuba, NY	585	14727
Cudahy, CA	323	90201
Cudahy, WI	414	53110
Cuddy, PA	412, 878	15031
Cuero, TX	361	77954
Cullman, AL	256	35055-35058
Cullowhee, NC	828	28723
Culpeper, VA	540	22701
Culver, OR	541, 458	97734
Culver City, CA	310, 424	90230-90233
Cumberland, KY	606	40823
Cumberland, MD	301	21501-21505
Cumberland, OH	740	43732
Cumberland, RI	401	02864
Cumberland, VA	804	23040
Cumberland Gap, TN	423	37724, 37752
Cumming, GA	470, 770	30028, 30040-30041
Cupertino, CA	408	95014-95015
Currie, NC	910	28435
Currituck, NC	252	27929
Curtis, NE	308	69025
Cushing, OK	918	74023
Cusick, WA	509	99119
Cusseta, GA	706, 762	31805
Custer, SD	605	57730
Cut Bank, MT	406	59427
Cuthbert, GA	229	31740
Cuyahoga Falls, OH	234, 330	44221-44224
Cuyahoga Heights, OH	216	44105, 44125-44127
Cynthiana, KY	859	41031
Cypress, CA	714	90630
Cypress, TX	281, 832	77410, 77429, 77433

D

City	Area Code(s)	Zip Code(s)
Dade City, FL	352	33523-33526
Dadeville, AL	256	36853
Dafter, MI	906	49724
Dahlgren, VA	540	22448
Dahlonega, GA	706, 762	30533, 30597
Daingerfield, TX	903	75638
Dakota, IL	815	61018
Dakota City, IA	515	50529
Dakota City, NE	402	68731
Dakota Dunes, SD	605	57049
Dale, IN	812	47523
Dalhart, TX	806	79022
Dallas, GA	470, 770	30132, 30157
Dallas, NC	704, 980	28034
Dallas, OR	503, 971	97338
Dallas, PA	570	18612, 18690
Dallas, TX	214, 469, 972	75201-75254, 75258-75270*
Dallastown, PA	717	17313
Dalton, GA	706, 762	30719-30722
Dalton, MA	413	01226-01227
Dalton, OH	234, 330	44618
Daly City, CA	650	94013-94017
Damariscotta, ME	207	04543
Dammeron Valley, UT	435	84783
Dana Point, CA	949	92624, 92629
Danboro, PA	215, 267	18916
Danbury, CT	203	06810-06817
Danbury, NC	336	27016
Dandridge, TN	865	37725
Dania Beach, FL	754, 954	33004, 33312
Daniel, WY	307	83115
Danielson, CT	860	06239
Danielsville, GA	706, 762	30633
Dannemora, NY	518	12929
Danube, MN	320	56230
Danvers, MA	351, 978	01923
Danville, AR	479	72833
Danville, CA	925	94506, 94526
Danville, IL	217	61832-61834
Danville, IN	317	46122
Danville, IA	319	52623
Danville, KY	859	40422-40423
Danville, PA	570	17821-17822
Danville, VA	434	24540-24544
Daphne, AL	251	36526
Darby, MT	406	59829
Dardanelle, AR	479	72834
Darien, CT	203	06820
Darien, GA	912	31305
Darien, IL	331, 630	60561
Darien Center, NY	585	14040
Darlington, SC	843	29532, 29540
Darlington, WI	608	53530
Darrow, LA	225	70725
Dartmouth, MA	508, 774	02714, 02747-02748
Dassel, MN	320	55325
Dauphin Island, AL	251	36528
Davenport, FL	863	33836-33837, 33896-33897
Davenport, IA	563	52801-52809
Davenport, WA	509	99122
David City, NE	402	68632
Davidson, NC	704, 980	28035-28036
Davie, FL	754, 954	33024, 33312-33317, 33324*
Davis, CA	530	95616-95618
Davis, WV	304	26260
Davison, MI	810	48423
Daviston, AL	256	36256
Davisville, WV	304	26142
Dawson, GA	229	31742
Dawsonville, GA	706, 762	30534
Dayton, IA	515	50530
Dayton, NV	775	89403
Dayton, NJ	732, 848	08810
Dayton, OH	937	45390, 45401-45441, 45448*
Dayton, TN	423	37321
Dayton, TX	936	77535
Dayton, WA	509	99328
Daytona Beach, FL	386	32114-32129, 32198
Daytona Beach Shores, FL	386	32116
Dayville, CT	860	06241
De Funiak Springs, FL	850	32433-32435
De Kalb, MS	601, 769	39328
De Pere, WI	920	54115
De Queen, AR	870	71832
De Smet, SD	605	57231
De Witt, AR	870	72042
De Witt, IA	563	52742
Deadwood, SD	605	57732
Dearborn, MI	313	48120-48128
Dearborn Heights, MI	313	48125-48127
Death Valley, CA	760, 442	92328
Decatur, AL	256	35601-35603, 35609, 35699
Decatur, AR	479	72722
Decatur, GA	404, 470	30030-30037
Decatur, IL	217	62521-62527
Decatur, IN	260	46733
Decatur, MS	601, 769	39327
Decatur, TN	423	37322
Decatur, TX	940	76234
Decaturville, TN	731	38329
Deckerville, MI	810	48427
Declo, ID	208	83323

*Partial list of zip codes, including main range

City	Area Code(s)	Zip Code(s)
Decorah, IA	563	52101
Dedham, MA	339, 781	02026-02027
Deer Harbor, WA	360	98243
Deer Lodge, MT	406	59722
Deer Park, CA	707	94576
Deer Park, NY	631	11729
Deer Park, TX	281, 832	77536
Deer River, MN	218	56636
Deerfield, IL	224, 847	60015
Deerfield, MA	413	01342
Deerfield, WI	608	53531
Deerfield Beach, FL	754, 954	33064, 33441-33443
Deerwood, MN	218	56444
Defiance, OH	419, 567	43512
DeForest, WI	608	53532
DeGraff, OH	937	43318
DeKalb, IL	815	60115
Del City, OK	405	73115, 73135, 73165
Del Mar, CA	858	92014
Del Norte, CO	719	81132
Del Rey, CA	559	93616
Del Rio, TX	830	78840-78843, 78847
Delair, NJ	856	08110
Delanco, NJ	856	08075
DeLand, FL	386	32720-32724
Delano, CA	661	93215-93216
Delano, MN	763	55328
Delavan, MN	507	56023
Delavan, WI	262	53115
Delaware, OH	740	43015
Delaware City, DE	302	19706
Delaware Water Gap, PA	570	18327
Delbarton, WV	304	25670
DeLeon Springs, FL	386	32130
Delhi, NY	607	13753
Dellroy, OH	234, 330	44620
Delmar, MD	410	21875
Delmar, NY	518	12054
Delmont, NJ	856	08314
Delmont, PA	724, 878	15626
Delphi, IN	765	46923
Delphos, OH	419, 567	45833
Delray Beach, FL	561	33444-33448, 33482-33484
Delta, CO	970	81416
Delta, UT	435	84624
Deming, NM	505	88030-88031
Demopolis, AL	334	36732
Demorest, GA	706, 762	30535, 30544
Demotte, IN	219	46310
Denham Springs, LA	225	70706, 70726-70727
Denison, IA	712	51442
Denison, TX	903	75020-75021
Denmark, SC	803	29042
Denmark, WI	920	54208
Denton, MD	410	21629
Denton, NC	336	27239
Denton, TX	940	76201-76210
Denver, CO	303, 720	80002, 80010-80014, 80022*
Denver, IA	319	50622
Denver, NC	704, 980	28037
Denver, PA	717	17517
Denville, NJ	862, 973	07834
Depew, NY	716	14043
Depoe Bay, OR	541, 458	97341
Deposit, NY	607	13754
Dequincy, LA	337	70633
Derby, CT	203	06418
Derby, KS	316	67037
Derby, NY	716	14047
DeRidder, LA	337	70634
Dermott, AR	870	71638
Derry, NH	603	03038
Derwent, OH	740	43733
Des Allemands, LA	504	70030
Des Arc, AR	870	72040
Des Moines, IA	515	50301-50340, 50347-50350*
Des Moines, WA	206	98148, 98198
Des Plaines, IL	224, 847	60016-60019
Descanso, CA	760, 442	91916
Desert Hot Springs, CA	760, 442	92240-92241
Deshler, NE	402	68340
DeSoto, KS	913	66018
DeSoto, TX	469, 972	75115, 75123
Destin, FL	850	32540-32541, 32550
Destrehan, LA	985	70047
Detroit, MI	313, 734	48201-48244, 48255, 48260*
Detroit, OR	503, 971	97342
Detroit Lakes, MN	218	56501-56502
Devault, PA	484, 610	19432
Devens, MA	351, 978	01432
Devils Lake, ND	701	58301
Devils Tower, WY	307	82714
Devon, PA	484, 610	19333
Dewey, OK	918	74029
Dewey Beach, DE	302	19971
DeWitt, NY	315	13214
Dexter, MI	734	48130
Dexter, MO	573	63841
Diamond, MO	417	64840
Diamond Bar, CA	909	91765
Diamond Point, NY	518	12824
Diboll, TX	936	75941
Dickens, TX	806	79229
Dickinson, ND	701	58601-58602
Dickinson, TX	281, 832	77539
Dickson, TN	615	37055-37056
Dighton, KS	620	67839
Dighton, MA	508, 774	02715
Dillingham, AK	907	99576
Dillon, MT	406	59725
Dillon, SC	843	29536
Dillwyn, VA	434	23936
Dimmitt, TX	806	79027
Dinosaur, CO	970	81610, 81633
Dinuba, CA	559	93618
Dinwiddie, VA	804	23841
Dix Hills, NY	631	11746
Dixie, GA	229	31629
Dixmoor, IL	708	60406, 60426
Dixon, CA	707	95620
Dixon, IL	815	61021
Dixon, KY	270	42409
Dixon, MO	573	65459
Dobbs Ferry, NY	914	10522
Dobson, NC	336	27017
Dodge Center, MN	507	55927
Dodge City, KS	620	67801
Dodgeville, WI	608	53533, 53595
Dolgeville, NY	315	13329
Dolton, IL	708	60419
Donaldson, IN	574	46513
Donaldsonville, LA	225	70346
Donalsonville, GA	229	31745
Dongola, IL	618	62926
Doniphan, MO	573	63935
Dorado, PR	787, 939	00646
Doraville, GA	470, 770	30340, 30360-30362
Dorchester, MA	617, 857	02121-02125
Dorchester, NE	402	68343
Doswell, VA	804	23047
Dothan, AL	334	36301-36305
Double Springs, AL	205	35553
Douglas, AK	907	99824
Douglas, AZ	520	85607-85608, 85655
Douglas, GA	912	31533-31535
Douglas, MI	616	49406
Douglas, WY	307	82633
Douglassville, PA	484, 610	19518
Douglassville, TX	903	75560
Douglaston, NY	347, 718	11362-11363
Douglasville, GA	470, 770	30133-30135, 30154
Dove Creek, CO	970	81324
Dover, DE	302	19901-19906
Dover, FL	813	33527
Dover, NH	603	03820-03822
Dover, NJ	862, 973	07801-07806, 07869
Dover, OH	234, 330	44622
Dover, TN	931	37058
Dover AFB, DE	302	19902
Dover Plains, NY	845	12522
Dowagiac, MI	616	49047
Downers Grove, IL	331, 630	60515-60517
Downey, CA	562	90239-90242
Downieville, CA	530	95936
Downingtown, PA	484, 610	19335, 19372
Doylestown, OH	234, 330	44230
Doylestown, PA	215, 267	18901, 18933
Doyline, LA	318	71023
Dracut, MA	351, 978	01826
Dragoon, AZ	520	85609
Drain, OR	541, 458	97435
Draper, UT	801, 385	84020
Dravosburg, PA	412, 878	15034
Dresden, TN	731	38225
Dresher, PA	215, 267	19025
Dresser, WI	715, 534	54009
Drexel Hill, PA	484, 610	19026
Driggs, ID	208	83422
Drummond Island, MI	906	49726
Dry Ridge, KY	859	41035
Dryden, NY	607	13053
Du Bois, PA	814	15801
Duarte, CA	626	91009-91010
Dublin, CA	925	94568
Dublin, GA	478	31021, 31027, 31040
Dublin, NH	603	03444
Dublin, NC	910	28332
Dublin, OH	614	43016-43017
Dublin, VA	540	24084
Dubois, ID	208	83423, 83446
Dubois, WY	307	82513
Dubuque, IA	563	52001-52004, 52099
Duchesne, UT	435	84021
Duck, NC	252	27949
Duck Hill, MS	662	38925
Duck Key, FL	305, 786	33050
Dudley, GA	478	31022
Dudley, MA	508, 774	01571
Dudley, MO	573	63936
Dudley, NC	919	28333
Due West, SC	864	29639
Dugway, UT	435	84022
Dulles, VA	571, 703	20101-20104, 20163-20166*
Duluth, GA	470, 678, 770	30026-30029, 30095-30099
Duluth, MN	218	55701, 55801-55816
Dumas, TX	806	79029
Dunbar, PA	724, 878	15431
Dunbar, WV	304	25064
Dunbar, WI	715, 534	54119
Dunbridge, OH	419, 567	43414
Duncan, AZ	928	85534
Duncan, OK	580	73533-73536, 73575
Duncan, SC	864	29334, 29390-29391
Duncannon, PA	717	17020
Duncansville, PA	814	16635
Duncanville, TX	469, 972	75116, 75137-75138
Dundalk, MD	410	21222
Dundee, FL	863	33838
Dundee, IL	224, 847	60118
Dundee, NY	607	14837
Dundee, OR	503, 971	97115
Dunedin, FL	727	34697-34698
Dunkirk, IN	765	47336
Dunkirk, MD	301	20754
Dunkirk, NY	716	14048, 14166
Dunlap, IL	309	61525
Dunlap, TN	423	37327
Dunmore, PA	570	18509-18512
Dunn, NC	910	28334-28335
Dunnell, MN	507	56127
Dunnellon, FL	352	34430-34434
Dunning, NE	308	68833
Dunseith, ND	701	58329
Dupont, WA	253	98327
Dupree, SD	605	57623
DuQuoin, IL	618	62832
Durand, MI	989	48429
Durand, WI	715, 534	54736
Durango, CO	970	81301-81303
Durant, OK	580	74701-74702
Durham, CT	860	06422
Durham, NH	603	03824
Durham, NC	919	27701-27717, 27722
Duryea, PA	570	18642
Dushore, PA	570	18614
Duxbury, MA	339, 781	02331-02332
Dwight, IL	815	60420
Dyer, NV	760, 442	89010
Dyersburg, TN	731	38024-38025
Dyersville, IA	563	52040
Dyess AFB, TX	915	79607

Partial list of zip codes, including main range

E

City	Area Code(s)	Zip Code(s)
Eads, CO	719	81036
Eagan, MN	651	55120-55123
Eagle, CO	970	81631
Eagle, WI	262	53119
Eagle Creek, OR	503, 971	97022
Eagle Grove, IA	515	50533
Eagle Nest, NM	505	87710, 87718
Eagle Pass, TX	830	78852-78853
Eagle River, AK	907	99577
Eagle River, MI	906	49950
Eagle River, WI	715, 534	54521
Eagle Rock, CA	323	90041
Eagleville, PA	484, 610	19403, 19408, 19415
Earle, AR	870	72331
Earlville, IL	815	60518
Early Branch, SC	803	29916
Earth City, MO	314	63045
Easley, SC	864	29640-29642
East Alton, IL	618	62024
East Amherst, NY	716	14051
East Aurora, NY	585	14052
East Bend, NC	336	27018
East Berlin, CT	860	06023
East Bernstadt, KY	606	40729
East Bloomfield, NY	585	14443, 14469
East Boston, MA	617, 857	02128, 02228
East Brunswick, NJ	732, 848	08816
East Canton, OH	234, 330	44730
East Chicago, IN	219	46312
East Cleveland, OH	216	44110-44112, 44118
East Derry, NH	603	03041
East Dubuque, IL	815	61025
East Dundee, IL	224, 847	60118
East Durham, NY	518	12423
East Earl, PA	717	17519
East Elmhurst, NY	347, 718	11369-11371
East Falmouth, MA	508, 774	02536
East Farmingdale, NY	631	11735
East Granby, CT	860	06026
East Grand Forks, MN	218	56721
East Grand Rapids, MI	616	49506, 49546
East Greenville, PA	215, 267	18041
East Greenwich, RI	401	02818
East Haddam, CT	860	06423
East Hampstead, NH	603	03826
East Hampton, CT	860	06424, 06447
East Hampton, NY	631	11937
East Hanover, NJ	862, 973	07936
East Hartford, CT	860	06108, 06118, 06128, 06138
East Haven, CT	203	06512-06513
East Hazel Crest, IL	708	60429
East Hills, NY	516	11548, 11576-11577
East Jordan, MI	231	49727
East Lansing, MI	517	48823-48826
East Liberty, OH	937	43074, 43319
East Liverpool, OH	234, 330	43920
East Longmeadow, MA	413	01028, 01116
East Meadow, NY	516	11554
East Millstone, NJ	732, 848	08873-08875
East Moline, IL	309	61244
East Montpelier, VT	802	05651
East New Market, MD	410	21631
East Northport, NY	631	11731
East Norwalk, CT	203	06855
East Orange, NJ	862, 973	07017-07019
East Palatka, FL	386	32131
East Palestine, OH	234, 330	44413
East Palo Alto, CA	650	94303
East Pembroke, NY	585	14056
East Peoria, IL	309	61611
East Petersburg, PA	717	17520
East Point, GA	404, 470	30344, 30364
East Providence, RI	401	02914-02916
East Rochester, NH	603	03868
East Rutherford, NJ	201, 551	07073
East Saint Louis, IL	618	62201-62208
East Stroudsburg, PA	570	18301
East Syracuse, NY	315	13057
East Taunton, MA	508, 774	02718
East Tawas, MI	989	48730
East Templeton, MA	351, 978	01438
East Texas, PA	484, 610	18046
East Troy, WI	262	53120
East Walpole, MA	508, 774	02032
East Weymouth, MA	339, 781	02189
East Windsor, CT	860	06016, 06088
East Windsor, NJ	609	08512, 08520
Eastaboga, AL	256	36260
Easthampton, MA	413	01027
Eastlake, MI	231	49626
Eastlake, OH	440	44095-44097
Eastland, TX	254	76448
Eastman, GA	478	31023
Easton, MD	410	21601, 21606
Easton, PA	484, 610	18040-18045
Eastpointe, MI	586	48021
Eastport, ME	207	04631
Eastsound, WA	360	98245
Eastville, VA	757	23347
Eaton, CO	970	80615
Eaton, IN	765	47338
Eaton, OH	937	45320
Eaton Rapids, MI	517	48827
Eatonton, GA	706, 762	31024
Eatontown, NJ	732, 848	07724, 07799
Eatonville, WA	360	98328
Eau Claire, WI	715, 534	54701-54703
Ebensburg, PA	814	15931
Edcouch, TX	956	78538
Eddyville, KY	270	42038
Eden, NC	336	27288-27289
Eden Prairie, MN	952	55343-55347
Edenton, NC	252	27932
Edgartown, MA	508, 774	02539
Edgefield, SC	803	29824
Edgeley, ND	701	58433
Edgerton, MN	507	56128
Edgerton, OH	419, 567	43517
Edgerton, WI	608	53534
Edgewater, FL	386	32132, 32141
Edgewater, MD	410, 443	21037
Edgewater, NJ	201, 551	07020
Edgewood, IA	563	52042-52044
Edgewood, MD	410	21040
Edgewood, NY	631	11717
Edgewood, WA	253	98371-98372, 98390
Edina, MN	952	55343, 55410, 55416, 55424*
Edina, MO	660	63537
Edinboro, PA	814	16412, 16444
Edinburg, TX	956	78539-78540
Edinburg, VA	540	22824
Edinburgh, IN	812	46124
Edison, CA	661	93220
Edison, NJ	732, 848	08817-08820, 08837, 08899
Edisto Beach, SC	843	29438
Edmeston, NY	607	13335
Edmond, OK	405	73003, 73013, 73034, 73083
Edmonds, WA	425	98020, 98026
Edmonton, KY	270	42129
Edmore, MI	989	48829
Edna, TX	361	77957
Edon, OH	419, 567	43518
Edwards, CA	661	93523-93524
Edwards, CO	970	81632
Edwardsburg, MI	616	49112, 49130
Edwardsville, IL	618	62025-62026
Edwardsville, KS	913	66111-66113
Edwardsville, PA	570	18704
Effingham, IL	217	62401
Egg Harbor, WI	920	54209
Egg Harbor City, NJ	609	08215
Egg Harbor Township, NJ	609	08234
Eglin AFB, FL	850	32542
Eielson AFB, AK	907	99702
Eighty Four, PA	724, 878	15330
Ekalaka, MT	406	59324
El Cajon, CA	619	92019-92022, 92090
El Campo, TX	979	77437
El Centro, CA	760, 442	92243-92244
El Cerrito, CA	510	94530
El Dorado, AR	870	71730-71731, 71768
El Dorado, KS	316	67042
El Dorado Hills, CA	916	95762
El Dorado Springs, MO	417	64744
El Monte, CA	626	91731-91735
El Paso, IL	309	61738
El Paso, TX	915	79821, 79901-79961, 79966*
El Reno, OK	405	73036
El Segundo, CA	310, 424	90245
El Sobrante, CA	510	94803, 94820
Elba, AL	334	36323
Elba, NY	585	14058
Elberfeld, IN	812	47613
Elberton, GA	706, 762	30635
Elbow Lake, MN	218	56531
Eldora, IA	641	50627
Eldorado, IL	618	62930
Eldorado, TX	915	76936
Eldorado Springs, CO	303, 720	80025
Eldridge, CA	707	95431
Eldridge, IA	563	52748
Eleele, HI	808	96705
Elephant Butte, NM	505	87935
Elgin, IL	224, 847	60120-60123
Elgin, SC	803	29045
Elizabeth, IL	815	61028
Elizabeth, IN	812	47117
Elizabeth, NJ	908	07201-07202, 07206-07208
Elizabeth, PA	412, 878	15037
Elizabeth, WV	304	26143
Elizabeth City, NC	252	27906-27909
Elizabethton, TN	423	37643-37644
Elizabethtown, IL	618	62931
Elizabethtown, KY	270	42701-42702
Elizabethtown, NY	518	12932
Elizabethtown, NC	910	28337
Elizabethtown, PA	717	17022
Elizabethville, PA	717	17023
Elk City, OK	580	73644, 73648
Elk Grove, CA	916	95624, 95758-95759
Elk Grove Village, IL	224, 847	60007-60009
Elk Point, SD	605	57025
Elk Rapids, MI	231	49629
Elk River, MN	763	55330
Elkader, IA	563	52043
Elkhart, IN	574	46514-46517
Elkhart, KS	620	67950
Elkhart Lake, WI	920	53020
Elkhorn, NE	402	68022
Elkhorn, WI	262	53121
Elkin, NC	336	28621
Elkins, WV	304	26241
Elkins Park, PA	215, 267	19027
Elkland, PA	814	16920
Elko, MN	952	55020
Elko, NV	775	89801-89803, 89815
Elkridge, MD	410	21075
Elkton, KY	270	42220
Elkton, MD	410	21921-21922
Elkton, OH	234, 330	44415
Ellaville, GA	229	31806
Ellendale, ND	701	58436
Ellensburg, WA	509	98926, 98950
Ellenville, NY	845	12428
Ellenwood, GA	404, 470	30294
Ellettsville, IN	812	47429
Ellicott City, MD	410	21041-21043
Ellicottville, NY	716	14731
Ellijay, GA	706, 762	30540
Ellington, CT	860	06029
Ellinwood, KS	620	67526
Ellis, KS	785	67637
Ellisville, MS	601, 769	39437
Ellisville, MO	636	63011, 63021, 63038
Ellsworth, KS	785	67439
Ellsworth, ME	207	04605
Ellsworth, WI	715, 534	54003, 54010-54011
Ellsworth AFB, SD	605	57706
Ellwood City, PA	724, 878	16117
Elm Grove, WI	262	53122
Elm Springs, AR	479	72728
Elma, NY	585	14059
Elma, WA	360	98541
Elmendorf AFB, AK	907	99505-99506
Elmer, NJ	856	08318
Elmhurst, IL	331, 630	60126
Elmhurst, NY	347, 718	11373, 11380
Elmira, NY	607	14901-14905, 14925
Elmira, OR	541, 458	97437
Elmira Heights, NY	607	14903
Elmont, NY	516	11003
Elmore, AL	334	36025
Elmore, OH	419, 567	43416
Elmsford, NY	914	10523

*Partial list of zip codes, including main range

City	Area Code(s)	Zip Code(s)
Elmwood, CT	860	06110, 06133
Elmwood Park, IL	708	60707
Elmwood Park, NJ	201, 551	07407
Elon, NC	336	27244
Elsah, IL	618	62028
Elsmere, KY	859	41018
Elverson, PA	484, 610	19520
Elwood, IN	765	46036
Elwood, NE	308	68937
Ely, MN	218	55731
Ely, NV	775	89301, 89315
Elyria, OH	440	44035-44039
Elysburg, PA	570	17824
Emerado, ND	701	58228
Emeryville, CA	510	94608, 94662
Emigrant, MT	406	59027
Emigsville, PA	717	17318
Eminence, KY	502	40019
Eminence, MO	573	65466
Emlenton, PA	724, 878	16373
Emmaus, PA	484, 610	18049, 18098-18099
Emmetsburg, IA	712	50536
Emmett, ID	208	83617
Emmitsburg, MD	301	21727
Emory, TX	903	75440
Emory, VA	276	24327
Empire, MI	231	49630
Emporia, KS	620	66801
Emporia, VA	434	23847
Emporium, PA	814	15834
Encinitas, CA	760, 442	92023-92024
Encino, CA	818	91316, 91335, 91416, 91426*
Endicott, NY	607	13760-13763
Enfield, CT	860	06082-06083
Enfield, NH	603	03748
Enfield, NC	252	27823
Engelhard, NC	252	27824
England, AR	501	72046
Englewood, CO	303, 720	80110-80112, 80150-80155*
Englewood, FL	941	34223-34224, 34295
Englewood, NJ	201, 551	07631-07632
Englewood, OH	937	45315, 45322
Englewood Cliffs, NJ	201, 551	07632
English, IN	812	47118
Englishtown, NJ	732, 848	07726
Enid, OK	580	73701-73706
Ennis, MT	406	59729
Ennis, TX	469, 972	75119-75120
Enola, PA	717	17025
Enon, OH	937	45323
Enoree, SC	864	29335
Enosburg Falls, VT	802	05450
Enterprise, AL	334	36330-36331
Enterprise, OR	541, 458	97828
Enumclaw, WA	360	98022
Ephraim, UT	435	84627
Ephrata, PA	717	17522
Ephrata, WA	509	98823
Epping, NH	603	03042
Epps, LA	318	71237
Epworth, IA	563	52045
Erdenheim, PA	215, 267	19038
Erie, CO	303, 720	80516
Erie, IL	309	61250
Erie, KS	620	66733
Erie, MI	734	48133
Erie, PA	814	16501-16515, 16522, 16530*
Erin, TN	931	37061
Erlanger, KY	859	41017-41018
Erving, MA	351, 978	01344
Erwin, TN	423	37650
Escalon, CA	209	95320
Escanaba, MI	906	49829
Escondido, CA	760, 442	92025-92033, 92046
Esopus, NY	845	12429
Espanola, NM	505	87532-87533
Essex, CT	860	06426
Essex, MD	410	21221
Essex Junction, VT	802	05451-05453
Essexville, MI	989	48732
Essington, PA	484, 610	19029
Estancia, NM	505	87009, 87016
Estero, FL	239	33928
Estes Park, CO	970	80511, 80517
Estherville, IA	712	51334
Estill, SC	803	29918, 29939
Euclid, OH	216	44117-44119, 44123, 44132*
Eudora, AR	870	71640
Eufaula, AL	334	36027, 36072
Eufaula, OK	918	74432, 74461
Eugene, OR	541, 458	97401-97408, 97412, 97440*
Euless, TX	682, 817	76039-76040
Eunice, LA	337	70535
Eureka, CA	707	95501-95503, 95534
Eureka, IL	309	61530
Eureka, KS	620	67045
Eureka, MO	636	63025
Eureka, MT	406	59917
Eureka, NV	775	89316
Eureka Springs, AR	479	72631-72632
Eustis, FL	352	32726-32727, 32736
Eutaw, AL	205	35462
Evans, GA	706, 762	30809
Evans City, PA	724, 878	16033
Evanston, IL	224, 847	60201-60204, 60208-60209
Evanston, WY	307	82930-82931
Evansville, IN	812	47701-47750
Evansville, WI	608	53536
Evansville, WY	307	82636
Eveleth, MN	218	55734
Everett, MA	617, 857	02149
Everett, PA	814	15537
Everett, WA	425	98201-98208
Evergreen, AL	251	36401
Evergreen, CO	303, 720	80437-80439
Evergreen Park, IL	708	60805
Ewa Beach, HI	808	96706
Ewing, NJ	609	08618, 08628, 08638
Excelsior, MN	952	55331
Excelsior Springs, MO	816	64024
Exeter, CA	559	93221
Exeter, NH	603	03833
Exeter, PA	570	18643
Exeter, RI	401	02822
Export, PA	724, 878	15632
Exton, PA	484, 610	19341, 19353
Eynon, PA	570	18403

F

City	Area Code(s)	Zip Code(s)
Fabens, TX	915	79838
Fair Haven, VT	802	05731, 05743
Fair Lawn, NJ	201, 551	07410
Fair Oaks, CA	916	95628
Fairbanks, AK	907	99701-99716, 99767, 99775*
Fairborn, OH	937	45324, 45431
Fairburn, GA	470, 770	30213
Fairbury, NE	402	68352
Fairchild AFB, WA	509	99011
Fairfax, SC	803	29827
Fairfax, VA	571, 703	20151-20153, 22030-22039
Fairfax Station, VA	571, 703	22039
Fairfield, AL	205	35064
Fairfield, CA	707	94533-94535, 94585
Fairfield, CT	203	06430-06432
Fairfield, ID	208	83322, 83327
Fairfield, IL	618	62837
Fairfield, IA	641	52556-52557
Fairfield, ME	207	04937
Fairfield, MT	406	59436
Fairfield, NJ	862, 973	07004
Fairfield, OH	513	45011-45014, 45018
Fairfield, PA	717	17320
Fairfield, TX	903	75840
Fairfield, VT	802	05455
Fairfield Glade, TN	931	38555-38558
Fairgrove, MI	989	48733
Fairhaven, MA	508, 774	02719
Fairhope, AL	251	36532-36533
Fairlawn, OH	234, 330	44313, 44333-44334
Fairlee, VT	802	05045
Fairless Hills, PA	215, 267	19030
Fairmont, MN	507	56031, 56075
Fairmont, MT	406	59711
Fairmont, WV	304	26554-26555
Fairplay, CO	719	80432, 80440, 80456
Fairport, NY	585	14450
Fairport Harbor, OH	440	44077
Fairton, NJ	856	08320
Fairview, NJ	201, 551	07022
Fairview, OK	580	73737
Fairview, OR	503, 971	97024
Fairview, PA	814	16415
Fairview Heights, IL	618	62208, 62232
Fairview Park, OH	440	44126
Fairview Village, PA	484, 610	19409
Fajardo, PR	787, 939	00738
Falconer, NY	716	14733
Falfurrias, TX	361	78355
Fall Creek, WI	715, 534	54742
Fall River, MA	508, 774	02720-02726
Fall River, WI	920	53932
Fallbrook, CA	760, 442	92028, 92088
Fallon, NV	775	89406-89407, 89496
Falls Church, VA	571, 703	22040-22047
Falls City, NE	402	68355
Fallsburg, NY	845	12733
Fallston, MD	410	21047
Falmouth, KY	859	41040
Falmouth, ME	207	04105
Falmouth, MA	508, 774	02540-02543
Fanwood, NJ	908	07023
Far Hills, NJ	908	07931
Far Rockaway, NY	347, 718	11096, 11690-11697
Fargo, ND	701	58102-58109, 58121-58126
Faribault, MN	507	55021
Farina, IL	618	62838
Farmers Branch, TX	469, 972	75234, 75244
Farmerville, LA	318	71241
Farmingdale, NJ	732, 848	07727
Farmingdale, NY	631	11735-11737, 11774
Farmington, CT	860	06030-06034, 06085
Farmington, ME	207	04911, 04938
Farmington, MI	248, 947	48331-48336
Farmington, MN	651	55024
Farmington, MO	573	63640
Farmington, NH	603	03835
Farmington, NM	505	87401-87402, 87499
Farmington, NY	585	14425
Farmington, PA	724, 878	15437
Farmington, UT	801, 385	84025
Farmington Hills, MI	248, 947	48331-48336
Farmingville, NY	631	11738
Farmville, NC	252	27828
Farmville, VA	434	23901, 23909, 23943
Farnhamville, IA	515	50538
Farragut, TN	865	37922
Farwell, TX	806	79325
Faulkner, MD	301	20632
Faulkton, SD	605	57438
Fayette, AL	205	35555
Fayette, IA	563	52142
Fayette, MS	601, 769	39069, 39081
Fayette, MO	660	65248
Fayetteville, AR	479	72701-72704
Fayetteville, GA	470, 770	30214-30215, 30232
Fayetteville, NY	315	13066
Fayetteville, NC	910	28301-28314
Fayetteville, PA	717	17222
Fayetteville, TN	931	37334
Fayetteville, WV	304	25840
Feasterville, PA	215, 267	19053
Federal Way, WA	253	98001-98003, 98023, 98063*
Federalsburg, MD	410	21632
Feeding Hills, MA	413	01030
Felton, DE	302	19943
Fennimore, WI	608	53809
Fenton, MI	810	48430
Fenton, MO	636	63026, 63099
Fenwick, WV	304	26202
Ferdinand, IN	812	47532
Fergus Falls, MN	218	56537-56538
Ferguson, MO	314	63135-63136, 63145
Fernandina Beach, FL	904	32034-32035
Ferndale, CA	707	95536
Ferndale, MI	248, 947	48220
Ferndale, WA	360	98248
Ferriday, LA	318	71334
Ferrisburg, VT	802	05456
Ferrum, VA	540	24088
Ferrysburg, MI	616	49409
Fessenden, ND	701	58438

*Partial list of zip codes, including main range

City	Area Code(s)	Zip Code(s)
Festus, MO	636	63028
Fillmore, UT	435	84631
Fincastle, VA	540	24090
Findlay, OH	419, 567	45839-45840
Finksburg, MD	410	21048
Finley, ND	701	58230
Finleyville, PA	724, 878	15332
Firebaugh, CA	559	93622
Firth, ID	208	83236
Fisher Island, FL	305, 786	33109, 33139
Fishers, IN	317	46038
Fishersville, VA	540	22939
Fishkill, NY	845	12524
Fiskeville, RI	401	02823
Fitchburg, MA	351, 978	01420
Fitzgerald, GA	229	31750
Flagler Beach, FL	386	32136, 32151
Flagstaff, AZ	928	86001-86004, 86011, 86015*
Flanders, NJ	862, 973	07836
Flandreau, SD	605	57028
Flasher, ND	701	58535
Flat Rock, NC	828	28731
Flatonia, TX	361	78941
Fleetwood, PA	484, 610	19522
Flemingsburg, KY	606	41041
Flemington, NJ	908	08822
Fletcher, NC	828	28732
Fletcher, OH	937	45326
Flint, MI	810	48501-48509, 48519, 48529*
Flintstone, GA	706, 762	30725
Flippin, AR	870	72634
Flora, IL	618	62839
Flora, MS	601, 769	39071
Floral Park, NY	516	11001-11005
Florence, AL	256	35630-35634
Florence, AZ	520	85232, 85279
Florence, CO	719	81226, 81290
Florence, KY	859	41022, 41042
Florence, MA	413	01062
Florence, MS	601, 769	39073
Florence, NJ	609	08518
Florence, OR	541, 458	97439
Florence, SC	843	29501-29506
Florence, WI	715, 534	54121
Floresville, TX	830	78114
Florham Park, NJ	862, 973	07932
Florida, NY	845	10921
Florida City, FL	305, 786	33034
Florien, LA	318	71429
Florissant, CO	719	80816
Florissant, MO	314	63031-63034
Flourtown, PA	215, 267	19031
Flower Mound, TX	469, 972	75022, 75027-75028
Flowery Branch, GA	470, 770	30542
Flowood, MS	601, 769	39208, 39232
Floyd, VA	540	24091
Floydada, TX	806	79235
Flushing, MI	810	48433
Flushing, NY	347, 718	11351-11381, 11385-11386*
Fogelsville, PA	484, 610	18051
Folcroft, PA	484, 610	19032
Foley, AL	251	36535-36536
Foley, MN	320	56329, 56357
Folkston, GA	912	31537
Folsom, CA	916	95630, 95762-95763
Folsom, LA	985	70437
Folsom, NJ	609	08037
Fond du Lac, WI	920	54935-54937
Fonda, NY	518	12068
Fontana, CA	951	92334-92337
Fontana, WI	262	53125
Fontana Dam, NC	828	28733
Foothill Ranch, CA	949	92610
Ford, KS	620	67842
Fordland, MO	417	65652
Fords, NJ	732, 848	08863
Fordyce, AR	870	71742
Forest, MS	601, 769	39074
Forest, OH	419, 567	45843
Forest, VA	434	24551
Forest City, IA	641	50436
Forest City, NC	828	28043
Forest City, PA	570	18421
Forest Grove, OR	503, 971	97116
Forest Hill, MD	410	21050

City	Area Code(s)	Zip Code(s)
Forest Hills, NY	347, 718	11375
Forest Lake, MN	651	55025
Forest Park, GA	404, 470	30297-30298
Forest Park, IL	708	60130
Forestville, CA	707	95436
Forestville, CT	860	06010
Forked River, NJ	609	08731
Forks, WA	360	98331
Forksville, PA	570	18616
Forman, ND	701	58032
Forrest City, AR	870	72335-72336
Forsyth, GA	478	31029
Forsyth, MO	417	65653
Forsyth, MT	406	59327
Fort Atkinson, WI	920	53538
Fort Belvoir, VA	571, 703	22060
Fort Benning, GA	706, 762	31905, 31995
Fort Benton, MT	406	59442
Fort Bliss, TX	915	79906-79908, 79916-79918
Fort Bragg, CA	707	95437, 95488
Fort Bragg, NC	910	28307-28310
Fort Buchanan, PR	787, 939	00920-00922, 00934-00936
Fort Calhoun, NE	402	68023
Fort Campbell, KY	270	42223
Fort Carson, CO	719	80913
Fort Collins, CO	970	80521-80528, 80553
Fort Davis, TX	915	79734
Fort Defiance, AZ	928	86504, 86549
Fort Deposit, AL	334	36032
Fort Dix, NJ	609	08640
Fort Dodge, IA	515	50501
Fort Dodge, KS	620	67801
Fort Drum, NY	315	13602-13603
Fort Edward, NY	518	12828
Fort Eustis, VA	757	23604
Fort Gaines, GA	229	31751
Fort Gibson, OK	918	74434
Fort Gordon, GA	706, 762	30905
Fort Harrison, MT	406	59636
Fort Hood, TX	254	76544
Fort Huachuca, AZ	520	85613, 85670
Fort Irwin, CA	760, 442	92310
Fort Jackson, SC	803	29207
Fort Jones, CA	530	96032
Fort Kent, ME	207	04741-04743
Fort Knox, KY	502	40121
Fort Laramie, WY	307	82212
Fort Lauderdale, FL	754, 954	33301-33340, 33345-33351*
Fort Leavenworth, KS	913	66027
Fort Lee, NJ	201, 551	07024
Fort Lee, VA	804	23801
Fort Leonard Wood, MO	573	65473
Fort Lewis, WA	253	98433
Fort Loramie, OH	937	45845
Fort Madison, IA	319	52627
Fort McPherson, GA	404, 470	30310, 30330
Fort Meade, MD	301	20755
Fort Meade, SD	605	57741
Fort Mill, SC	803	29708, 29715-29716
Fort Mitchell, KY	859	41017
Fort Monmouth, NJ	732, 848	07703
Fort Monroe, VA	757	23651
Fort Morgan, CO	970	80701, 80705, 80742
Fort Myer, VA	571, 703	22211
Fort Myers, FL	239	33901-33919, 33965, 33994
Fort Myers Beach, FL	239	33931-33932
Fort Oglethorpe, GA	706, 762	30742
Fort Payne, AL	256	35967-35968
Fort Pierce, FL	772	34945-34954, 34979-34988
Fort Pierre, SD	605	57532
Fort Polk, LA	337	71459
Fort Recovery, OH	419, 567	45846
Fort Richardson, AK	907	99504-99505
Fort Riley, KS	785	66442
Fort Rucker, AL	334	36362
Fort Sam Houston, TX	210	78234
Fort Scott, KS	620	66701
Fort Shafter, HI	808	96858
Fort Sill, OK	580	73503
Fort Smith, AR	479	72901-72908, 72913-72919
Fort Smith, MT	406	59035
Fort Snelling, MN	612	55111
Fort Stewart, GA	912	31313-31315
Fort Stockton, TX	915	79735

City	Area Code(s)	Zip Code(s)
Fort Story, VA	757	23459
Fort Sumner, NM	505	88119
Fort Supply, OK	580	73841
Fort Thomas, KY	859	41075
Fort Totten, ND	701	58335
Fort Valley, GA	478	31030
Fort Wainwright, AK	907	99703
Fort Walton Beach, FL	850	32547-32549
Fort Washington, MD	301	20744, 20749-20750
Fort Washington, PA	215, 267	19034, 19048-19049
Fort Wayne, IN	260	46801-46809, 46814-46819*
Fort Worth, TX	682, 817	76101-76140, 76147-76150*
Fort Yates, ND	701	58538
Fortine, MT	406	59918
Fortuna, CA	707	95540
Forty Fort, PA	570	18704
Fossil, OR	541, 458	97830
Foster City, CA	650	94404
Fostoria, OH	419, 567	44830
Fountain Hills, AZ	480	85268-85269
Fountain Inn, SC	864	29644
Fountain Valley, CA	714	92708, 92728
Four Oaks, NC	919	27524
Fowler, CA	559	93625
Fowler, IN	765	47944, 47984-47986
Fowlerville, MI	517	48836
Fox Lake, WI	920	53933
Foxboro, MA	508, 774	02035
Foxborough, MA	508, 774	02035
Frackville, PA	570	17931-17932
Framingham, MA	508, 774	01701-01705
Francesville, IN	219	47946
Frankenmuth, MI	989	48734, 48787
Frankfort, IL	815	60423
Frankfort, IN	765	46041
Frankfort, KY	502	40601-40604, 40618-40622
Frankfort, MI	231	49635
Frankfort, NY	315	13340
Franklin, GA	706, 762	30217
Franklin, ID	208	83237
Franklin, IN	317	46131
Franklin, KY	270	42134-42135
Franklin, LA	337	70538
Franklin, MA	508, 774	02038
Franklin, NE	308	68939
Franklin, NH	603	03235
Franklin, NJ	862, 973	07416
Franklin, NC	828	28734, 28744
Franklin, OH	513	45005, 45342
Franklin, PA	814	16323
Franklin, TN	615	37064-37069
Franklin, TX	979	77856
Franklin, VA	757	23851
Franklin, WV	304	26807
Franklin, WI	414	53132
Franklin Furnace, OH	740	45629
Franklin Lakes, NJ	201, 551	07417
Franklin Park, IL	224, 847	60131, 60398
Franklin Springs, GA	706, 762	30639
Franklin Square, NY	516	11010
Franklinton, LA	985	70438
Franklinton, NC	919	27525
Franklinville, NY	585	14737
Franksville, WI	262	53126
Frankton, IN	765	46044
Franktown, CO	303, 720	80116
Fraser, MI	586	48026
Frazee, MN	218	56544
Frazer, PA	484, 610	19355
Frazeysburg, OH	740	43822
Frederic, MI	989	49733
Frederica, DE	302	19946
Frederick, CO	303, 720	80504, 80516, 80530
Frederick, MD	301	21701-21705, 21709
Frederick, OK	580	73542
Fredericksburg, PA	717	17026
Fredericksburg, TX	830	78624
Fredericksburg, VA	540	22401-22408, 22412
Fredericktown, MO	573	63645
Fredericktown, OH	740	43019
Fredonia, AZ	928	86022, 86052
Fredonia, KS	620	66736
Fredonia, NY	716	14063
Fredonia, WI	262	53021
Freeburg, IL	618	62243

*Partial list of zip codes, including main range

City	Area Code(s)	Zip Code(s)
Freeburg, MO	573	65035
Freedom, WY	307	83120
Freehold, NJ	732, 848	07728
Freeland, MI	989	48623
Freeland, PA	570	18224
Freeland, WA	360	98249
Freeport, IL	815	61032
Freeport, ME	207	04032-04034
Freeport, MI	616	49325
Freeport, NY	516	11520
Freeport, PA	724, 878	16229
Freeport, TX	979	77541-77542
Fremont, CA	510	94536-94539, 94555
Fremont, IN	260	46737
Fremont, MI	231	49412-49413
Fremont, NE	402	68025-68026
Fremont, OH	419, 567	43420
French Camp, CA	209	95231
French Creek, WV	304	26218-26219
French Lick, IN	812	47432
Frenchburg, KY	606	40322
Frenchtown, NJ	908	08825
Fresh Meadows, NY	347, 718	11365-11366
Fresno, CA	559	93650, 93701-93729, 93740*
Friday Harbor, WA	360	98250
Fridley, MN	763	55421, 55432
Friendship, WI	608	53927, 53934
Friendswood, TX	281, 832	77546-77549
Friona, TX	806	79035
Frisco, CO	970	80443
Frisco, TX	469, 972	75034-75035
Fritch, TX	806	79036
Front Royal, VA	540	22630
Frostburg, MD	301	21532
Frostproof, FL	863	33843
Fruita, CO	970	81521
Fruitland, ID	208	83619
Fruitport, MI	231	49415
Fullerton, CA	714	92831-92838
Fullerton, NE	308	68638
Fulton, AL	334	36446
Fulton, IL	815	61252
Fulton, MS	662	38843
Fulton, MO	573	65251
Fulton, NY	315	13069
Fultonville, NY	518	12016, 12072
Fuquay-Varina, NC	919	27526

G

City	Area Code(s)	Zip Code(s)
Gabriels, NY	518	12939
Gadsden, AL	256	35901-35907
Gaffney, SC	864	29340-29342
Gahanna, OH	614	43230
Gail, TX	806	79738
Gainesboro, TN	931	38562
Gainesville, FL	352	32601-32614, 32627, 32635*
Gainesville, GA	470, 678, 770	30501-30507
Gainesville, MO	417	65655
Gainesville, TX	940	76240-76241
Gaithersburg, MD	240, 301	20877-20886, 20898-20899
Galax, VA	276	24333
Galena, IL	815	61036
Galena, KS	620	66739
Galena, MD	410	21635
Galena, MO	417	65624, 65656
Galena Park, TX	713, 832	77547
Galesburg, IL	309	61401-61402
Galesburg, KS	620	66740
Galion, OH	419, 567	44833
Gallatin, MO	660	64640
Gallatin, TN	615	37066
Gallatin Gateway, MT	406	59730
Gallaway, TN	901	38036
Galliano, LA	985	70354
Gallipolis, OH	740	45631
Gallitzin, PA	814	16641
Galloway, NJ	609	08201, 08205
Gallup, NM	505	87301-87305, 87310, 87317*
Galt, CA	209	95632
Galveston, TX	409	77550-77555
Gambier, OH	740	43022
Ganado, AZ	928	86505, 86540
Gann Valley, SD	605	57341
Gap, PA	717	17527
Garden City, GA	912	31405-31408, 31415-31418
Garden City, KS	620	67846, 67868
Garden City, MI	734	48135-48136
Garden City, NY	516	11530-11531, 11535-11536*
Garden City, TX	915	79739
Garden City Park, NY	516	11040
Garden Grove, CA	714	92840-92846
Gardena, CA	310, 323, 424	90247-90249
Gardiner, ME	207	04345
Gardner, IL	815	60424
Gardner, KS	913	66030-66031
Gardner, MA	351, 978	01440
Gardners, PA	717	17324
Gardnerville, NV	775	89410
Garfield, NJ	862, 973	07026
Garfield Heights, OH	216	44105, 44125-44128
Garland, NC	910	28441
Garland, TX	469, 972	75040-75049
Garner, IA	641	50438
Garner, NC	919	27529
Garnett, KS	785	66032
Garretson, SD	605	57030
Garrett, IN	260	46738
Garrettsville, OH	234, 330	44231
Garrison, NY	845	10524
Garrison, ND	701	58540
Garwood, NJ	908	07027
Gary, IN	219	46401-46411
Garyville, LA	985	70051, 70076
Gaston, OR	503, 971	97119
Gastonia, NC	704, 980	28052-28056
Gate City, VA	276	24251
Gatesville, NC	252	27938
Gatesville, TX	254	76528, 76596-76599
Gatlinburg, TN	865	37738
Gautier, MS	228	39553
Gaylord, MI	989	49734-49735
Gaylord, MN	507	55334
Gearhart, OR	503, 971	97138
Geismar, LA	225	70734
Geneseo, IL	309	61254
Geneseo, NY	585	14454
Geneva, AL	334	36340
Geneva, IL	331, 630	60134
Geneva, NE	402	68361
Geneva, NY	315	14456
Geneva, OH	440	44041
Genoa, OH	419, 567	43430
Genoa City, WI	262	53128
Gentry, AR	479	72734
George, IA	712	51237
George West, TX	361	78022
Georgetown, CO	303, 720	80444
Georgetown, DE	302	19947
Georgetown, GA	229	31754
Georgetown, KY	502	40324
Georgetown, MA	351, 978	01833
Georgetown, NY	315	13072, 13129
Georgetown, OH	937	45121
Georgetown, SC	843	29440-29442
Georgetown, TX	512	78626-78628
Gering, NE	308	69341
Germantown, MD	301	20874-20876
Germantown, OH	937	45325-45327
Germantown, TN	901	38138-38139, 38183
Germantown, WI	262	53022
Gervais, OR	503, 971	97026
Gettysburg, PA	717	17325-17326
Gettysburg, SD	605	57442
Getzville, NY	716	14068
Geyserville, CA	707	95441
Gibbon, MN	507	55335
Gibbon, NE	308	68840
Gibbsboro, NJ	856	08026
Gibbstown, NJ	856	08027
Gibson, GA	706, 762	30810
Gibson City, IL	217	60936
Gibsonia, PA	724, 878	15044
Gibsonville, NC	336	27249
Giddings, TX	979	78942
Gig Harbor, WA	253	98329-98335
Gilbert, AZ	480	85233-85234, 85296-85299
Gilbertsville, KY	270	42044
Gilford, NH	603	03247-03249
Gillett, AR	870	72055
Gillette, WY	307	82716-82718, 82731-82732
Gilman, CT	860	06336
Gilmer, TX	903	75644-75645
Gilmore City, IA	515	50541
Gilroy, CA	408	95020-95021
Girard, KS	620	66743
Girard, OH	234, 330	44420
Girard, PA	814	16417
Girdwood, AK	907	99587, 99693
Gladstone, MI	906	49837
Gladstone, MO	816	64116-64119, 64155-64156*
Gladstone, NJ	908	07934
Gladwin, MI	989	48624
Gladwyne, PA	484, 610	19035
Glasgow, KY	270	42141-42142, 42156
Glasgow, MT	406	59230-59231
Glassboro, NJ	856	08028
Glassport, PA	412, 878	15045
Glastonbury, CT	860	06033
Glen Allen, VA	804	23058-23060
Glen Arbor, MI	231	49636
Glen Arm, MD	410	21057
Glen Burnie, MD	410	21060-21062
Glen Cove, NY	516	11542
Glen Dale, WV	304	26038
Glen Echo, MD	301	20812
Glen Ellen, CA	707	95442
Glen Ellyn, IL	331, 630	60137-60138
Glen Gardner, NJ	908	08826
Glen Head, NY	516	11545
Glen Jean, WV	304	25846
Glen Lyn, VA	540	24093
Glen Raven, NC	336	27215
Glen Riddle, PA	484, 610	19037, 19063
Glen Ridge, NJ	862, 973	07028
Glen Rock, NJ	201, 551	07452
Glen Rock, PA	717	17327
Glen Rose, TX	254	76043
Glencoe, IL	224, 847	60022
Glencoe, MN	320	55336
Glendale, AZ	623	85301-85313, 85318
Glendale, CA	818	91201-91210, 91214, 91221*
Glendale, CO	303, 720	80246
Glendale, NY	347, 718	11385
Glendale, WI	414	53209-53212, 53217
Glendale Heights, IL	331, 630	60139
Glendive, MT	406	59330
Glendora, CA	626	91740-91741
Glendora, NJ	856	08029
Gleneden Beach, OR	541, 458	97388
Glenelg, MD	410	21737
Glenmont, OH	234, 330	44628
Glenmoore, PA	484, 610	19343
Glennallen, AK	907	99588
Glennville, GA	912	30427
Glens Falls, NY	518	12801-12804
Glenshaw, PA	412, 878	15116
Glenside, PA	215, 267	19038
Glenview, IL	224, 847	60025-60026
Glenville, NY	518	12302, 12325
Glenville, WV	304	26351
Glenwillow, OH	440	44139
Glenwood, IL	708	60425
Glenwood, IA	712	51534
Glenwood, MN	320	56334
Glenwood Springs, CO	970	81601-81602
Glidden, IA	712	51443
Glide, OR	541, 458	97443
Globe, AZ	928	85501-85502
Glorieta, NM	505	87535
Gloucester, MA	351, 978	01930-01931
Gloucester, NJ	856	08030-08031
Gloucester, VA	804	23061
Gloucester Point, VA	804	23062
Gloversville, NY	518	12078
Gnadenhutten, OH	740	44629
Godfrey, IL	618	62035
Godwin, NC	910	28344
Goffstown, NH	603	03045-03046
Golconda, IL	618	62938
Golconda, NV	480	89414
Gold Beach, OR	541, 458	97444
Gold Canyon, AZ	480	85218-85219

*Partial list of zip codes, including main range

City	Area Code(s)	Zip Code(s)
Gold Hill, NV	775	89440
Gold Hill, OR	541, 458	97525
Gold River, CA	916	95670
Golden, CO	303, 720	80401-80403, 80419
Golden, MS	662	38847
Golden Valley, MN	763	55416, 55422, 55426-55427
Goldendale, WA	509	98620
Goldfield, NV	775	89013
Goldsboro, NC	919	27530-27534
Goldthwaite, TX	915	76844
Goleta, CA	805	93110-93111, 93116-93118*
Golf, IL	224, 847	60029
Goliad, TX	361	77963
Gonzales, CA	831	93926
Gonzales, LA	225	70707, 70737
Gonzales, TX	830	78629
Goochland, VA	804	23063
Goodfellow AFB, TX	915	76908
Goodfield, IL	309	61742
Gooding, ID	208	83330
Goodland, KS	785	67735
Goodlettsville, TN	615	37070-37072
Goodman, MS	662	39079
Goodrich, MI	810	48438
Goodwell, OK	580	73939
Goodyear, AZ	623	85338
Gordo, AL	205	35466
Gordon, NE	308	69343
Gordonsville, VA	540	22942
Gordonville, TX	903	76245
Gore, OK	918	74435
Gorham, ME	207	04038
Gorham, NH	603	03581
Goshen, IN	574	46526-46528
Goshen, NY	845	10924
Goulds, FL	305, 786	33170
Gouverneur, NY	315	13642
Gove, KS	785	67736
Gowanda, NY	716	14070
Grabill, IN	260	46741
Graceville, FL	850	32440
Gracewood, GA	706, 762	30812
Grady, AR	870	71644
Grafton, IL	618	62037
Grafton, MA	508, 774	01519
Grafton, ND	701	58237
Grafton, OH	440	44044
Grafton, WV	304	26354
Grafton, WI	262	53024
Graham, NC	336	27253
Graham, TX	940	76450
Grain Valley, MO	816	64029
Grambling, LA	318	71245
Gramercy, LA	225	70052
Gramling, SC	864	29348
Grampian, PA	814	16838
Granada Hills, CA	818	91344, 91394
Granbury, TX	682, 817	76048-76049
Granby, CO	970	80446
Granby, CT	860	06035, 06090
Grand Blanc, MI	810	48439
Grand Canyon, AZ	928	86023
Grand Chenier, LA	337	70643
Grand Forks, ND	701	58201-58208
Grand Forks AFB, ND	701	58204-58205
Grand Haven, MI	616	49417
Grand Island, NE	308	68801-68803
Grand Island, NY	716	14072
Grand Junction, CO	970	81501-81506
Grand Junction, MI	616	49056
Grand Ledge, MI	517	48837
Grand Marais, MN	218	55604
Grand Marsh, WI	608	53936
Grand Portage, MN	218	55605
Grand Prairie, TX	469, 972	75050-75054
Grand Rapids, MI	616	49501-49518, 49523-49525*
Grand Rapids, MN	218	55730, 55744-55745
Grand Rapids, OH	419, 567	43522
Grand Terrace, CA	909	92313, 92324
Grandview, MO	816	64030
Grandview, WA	509	98930
Grandville, MI	616	49418, 49468
Granger, IN	574	46530
Granger, WA	509	98932
Grangeville, ID	208	83530-83531
Granite, OK	580	73547
Granite City, IL	618	62040
Granite Falls, MN	320	56241
Granite Falls, NC	828	28630
Granite Quarry, NC	704, 980	28072
Graniteville, SC	803	29829
Graniteville, VT	802	05654
Grant, CO	303, 720	80448
Grant, MI	231	49327
Grant, NE	308	69140
Grant City, MO	660	64456
Grantham, PA	717	17027
Grants, NM	505	87020
Grants Pass, OR	541, 458	97526-97528, 97543
Grantsboro, NC	252	28529
Grantsburg, WI	715, 534	54840
Grantsville, MD	301	21536
Grantsville, WV	304	26147
Grantville, PA	717	17028
Granville, IL	815	61326
Granville, MA	413	01034
Granville, NY	518	12832
Granville, OH	740	43023
Grapevine, TX	682, 817	76051, 76092, 76099
Grass Valley, CA	530	95945, 95949
Graterford, PA	484, 610	19426
Gratz, PA	717	17030
Grawn, MI	231	49637
Gray, GA	478	31032
Gray, KY	606	40734
Gray, LA	985	70359
Grayling, MI	989	49738-49739
Grayslake, IL	224, 847	60030
Grayson, KY	606	41143
Grayville, IL	618	62844
Great Barrington, MA	413	01230
Great Bend, KS	620	67530
Great Falls, MT	406	59401-59406
Great Falls, VA	571, 703	22066
Great Lakes, IL	224, 847	60088
Great Neck, NY	516	11020-11027
Greeley, CO	970	80631-80634, 80638-80639
Greeley, NE	308	68842
Green Bay, WI	920	54301-54313, 54324, 54344
Green Brook, NJ	732, 848	08812
Green Cove Springs, FL	904	32043
Green Forest, AR	870	72638
Green Island, NY	518	12183
Green Lake, WI	920	54941
Green Lane, PA	215, 267	18054
Green Pond, AL	205	35074
Green River, UT	435	84515, 84525, 84540
Green River, WY	307	82935-82938
Green Springs, OH	419, 567	44836
Green Valley, AZ	520	85614, 85622
Greenbelt, MD	301	20768-20771
Greenbrae, CA	415	94904, 94914
Greencastle, IN	765	46135
Greencastle, PA	717	17225
Greendale, WI	414	53129
Greene, NY	607	13778
Greeneville, TN	423	37743-37745
Greenfield, IN	317	46140
Greenfield, IA	641	50849
Greenfield, MA	413	01301-01302
Greenfield, MO	417	65661
Greenfield, NH	603	03047
Greenfield, OH	937	45123, 45165
Greenfield, WI	414	53219-53221, 53227-53228
Greenland, NH	603	03840
Greenlawn, NY	631	11740
Greenport, NY	631	11944
Greens Farms, CT	203	06436
Greensboro, AL	334	36744
Greensboro, GA	706, 762	30642
Greensboro, NC	336	27401-27420, 27425-27429*
Greensburg, IN	812	47240
Greensburg, KS	620	67054
Greensburg, KY	270	42743
Greensburg, LA	225	70441
Greensburg, PA	724, 878	15601, 15605-15606
Greenup, KY	606	41144
Greenvale, NY	516	11548
Greenville, AL	334	36037
Greenville, DE	302	19807
Greenville, GA	706, 762	30222
Greenville, IL	618	62246
Greenville, KY	270	42345
Greenville, MI	616	48838
Greenville, MS	662	38701-38704, 38731
Greenville, MO	573	63944
Greenville, NC	252	27833-27836, 27858
Greenville, OH	937	45331
Greenville, PA	724, 878	16125
Greenville, RI	401	02828
Greenville, SC	864	29601-29617, 29698
Greenville, TX	903	75401-75404
Greenwell Springs, LA	225	70739
Greenwich, CT	203	06830-06832, 06836
Greenwood, AR	479	72936
Greenwood, DE	302	19950
Greenwood, IN	317	46142-46143
Greenwood, MS	662	38930, 38935
Greenwood, SC	864	29646-29649
Greenwood, WI	715, 534	54437
Greenwood Village, CO	303, 720	80110-80112, 80121, 80150*
Greer, SC	864	29650-29652
Gregory, SD	605	57533
Grenada, MS	662	38901-38902
Grenloch, NJ	856	08032
Gresham, OR	503, 971	97030, 97080
Gretna, LA	504	70053-70056
Gretna, NE	402	68028
Gretna, VA	434	24557
Greybull, WY	307	82426
Greystone Park, NJ	862, 973	07950
Griffin, GA	470, 770	30223-30224
Griffith, IN	219	46319
Griggsville, IL	217	62340
Grinnell, IA	641	50112, 50177
Groesbeck, TX	254	76642
Grosse Pointe, MI	313	48224, 48230, 48236
Grosse Pointe Farms, MI	313	48230, 48236
Grosse Pointe Park, MI	313	48215, 48224, 48230, 48236
Grosse Pointe Shores, MI	313	48230, 48236
Groton, CT	860	06340, 06349
Groton, MA	351, 978	01450, 01470-01471
Groton, VT	802	05046
Grove, OK	918	74344-74345
Grove City, OH	614	43123
Grove City, PA	724, 878	16127
Grove Hill, AL	251	36451
Groveland, FL	352	34736
Groveport, OH	614	43125, 43195-43199
Grover, NC	704, 980	28073
Grover Beach, CA	805	93433, 93483
Groves, TX	409	77619
Groveton, TX	936	75845
Grovetown, GA	706, 762	30813
Grundy, VA	276	24614
Grundy Center, IA	319	50638
Gruver, TX	806	79040
Guayama, PR	787, 939	00784-00785
Guerneville, CA	707	95446
Guilderland, NY	518	12084
Guildhall, VT	802	05905
Guilford, CT	203	06437
Guilford, ME	207	04443
Guin, AL	205	35563
Gulf Breeze, FL	850	32561-32566
Gulf Shores, AL	251	36542, 36547
Gulfport, FL	727	33707, 33711, 33737
Gulfport, MS	228	39501-39507
Gun Barrel City, TX	903	75147
Gunnison, CO	970	81230-81231, 81247
Gunnison, UT	435	84634
Guntersville, AL	256	35976
Guntown, MS	662	38849
Gurdon, AR	870	71743
Gurnee, IL	224, 847	60031
Gustavus, AK	907	99826
Guthrie, OK	405	73044
Guthrie, TX	806	79236
Guthrie Center, IA	641	50115
Guymon, OK	580	73942
Gwynedd, PA	215, 267	19436
Gwynedd Valley, PA	215, 267	19437

Partial list of zip codes, including main range

H

City	Area Code(s)	Zip Code(s)
Hackensack, NJ	201, 551	07601-07602
Hackettstown, NJ	908	07840
Haddam, CT	860	06438
Haddonfield, NJ	856	08033
Hadley, MA	413	01035
Hagerman, ID	208	83332
Hagerman, NM	505	88232
Hagerstown, MD	240, 301	21740-21742, 21746-21749
Hahnville, LA	985	70057
Hailey, ID	208	83333
Haines, AK	907	99827
Haines City, FL	863	33844-33845
Hainesport, NJ	609	08036
Haledon, NJ	862, 973	07508, 07538
Hales Corners, WI	414	53130-53132
Haleyville, AL	205	35565
Half Moon Bay, CA	650	94019
Halifax, MA	339, 781	02338
Halifax, NC	252	27839
Halifax, PA	717	17032
Halifax, VA	434	24558
Hall, NY	585	14463
Hallandale, FL	754, 954	33008-33009
Hallettsville, TX	361	77964
Hallock, MN	218	56728, 56740, 56755
Hallowell, ME	207	04347
Halls, TN	731	38040
Halstad, MN	218	56548
Halstead, KS	316	67056
Haltom City, TX	682, 817	76111, 76117, 76137, 76148*
Ham Lake, MN	763	55304
Hamburg, AR	870	71646
Hamburg, NJ	862, 973	07419
Hamburg, NY	716	14075, 14219
Hamburg, PA	484, 610	19526
Hamden, CT	203	06514-06518
Hamel, MN	763	55340
Hamer, ID	208	83425
Hamilton, AL	205	35570
Hamilton, GA	706, 762	31811
Hamilton, IL	217	62341
Hamilton, MT	406	59840
Hamilton, NJ	609	08609-08611, 08619-08620*
Hamilton, NY	315	13346
Hamilton, OH	513	45011-45026
Hamilton, TX	254	76531
Hamilton Square, NJ	609	08690
Hamlet, NC	910	28345
Hamlin, NY	585	14464
Hamlin, TX	915	79520
Hamlin, WV	304	25523
Hammond, IN	219	46320-46327
Hammond, LA	985	70401-70404
Hammond, WI	715, 534	54002, 54015
Hammondsport, NY	607	14840
Hammonton, NJ	609	08037
Hampden-Sydney, VA	434	23943
Hampshire, IL	224, 847	60140
Hampstead, MD	410	21074
Hampstead, NH	603	03841
Hampton, AR	870	71744
Hampton, GA	470, 770	30228
Hampton, IA	641	50441
Hampton, NH	603	03842-03843
Hampton, SC	803	29913, 29924
Hampton, VA	757	23605, 23630-23631, 23651*
Hampton Falls, NH	603	03844
Hamptonville, NC	336	27020
Hamtramck, MI	313	48211-48212
Hana, HI	808	96713
Hanahan, SC	843	29406, 29410
Hanceville, AL	256	35077
Hancock, MI	906	49930
Hancock, MN	320	56244
Hancock, WI	715, 534	54943
Hanford, CA	559	93230-93232
Hannibal, MO	573	63401
Hannibal, OH	740	43931
Hanover, IN	812	47243
Hanover, MD	410	21075-21076, 21098
Hanover, NH	603	03755
Hanover, PA	717	17331-17334
Hanover, VA	804	23069
Hanover Park, IL	331, 630	60108, 60133
Hanscom AFB, MA	339, 781	01731
Hanson, MA	339, 781	02341, 02350
Harahan, LA	504	70123
Harbor Beach, MI	989	48441
Harbor City, CA	310, 424	90710
Harbor Springs, MI	231	49737-49740
Harborcreek, PA	814	16421
Harcourt, IA	515	50544
Hardin, IL	618	62047
Hardin, MT	406	59034
Hardinsburg, KY	270	40143
Hardwick, GA	478	31034
Hardwick, VT	802	05843
Hardy, VA	540	24101
Harkers Island, NC	252	28531
Harlan, IA	712	51537, 51593
Harlan, KY	606	40831, 40840
Harlem, GA	706, 762	30814
Harlem, MT	406	59526
Harleysville, PA	215, 267	19438-19441
Harlingen, TX	956	78550-78553
Harlowton, MT	406	59036
Harpers Ferry, IA	563	52146
Harpers Ferry, WV	304	25425
Harrells, NC	910	28444
Harriman, NY	845	10926
Harriman, TN	865	37748
Harrington, DE	302	19952
Harrington Park, NJ	201, 551	07640
Harris, MN	651	55032
Harris, NY	845	12742
Harrisburg, AR	870	72432
Harrisburg, IL	618	62946
Harrisburg, NE	308	69345
Harrisburg, NC	704, 980	28075
Harrisburg, PA	717	17101-17113, 17120-17130*
Harrison, AR	870	72601-72602
Harrison, ID	208	83833, 83842
Harrison, MI	989	48625
Harrison, NE	308	69346
Harrison, NJ	862, 973	07029
Harrison, NY	914	10528
Harrison, OH	513	45030
Harrison Township, MI	586	48045
Harrisonburg, LA	318	71340
Harrisonburg, VA	540	22801-22803, 22807
Harrisonville, MO	816	64701
Harrisville, MI	989	48740
Harrisville, WV	304	26362
Harrodsburg, KY	859	40330
Harrogate, TN	423	37707, 37752
Hart, MI	231	49420
Hartford, AL	334	36344
Hartford, CT	860	06101-06156, 06160-06161*
Hartford, KY	270	42347
Hartford, WI	262	53027
Hartford City, IN	765	47348
Hartington, NE	402	68739
Hartland, ME	207	04943
Hartland, WI	262	53029
Hartsdale, NY	914	10530
Hartselle, AL	256	35640
Hartsville, SC	843	29550-29551
Hartsville, TN	615	37074
Hartville, MO	417	65667
Hartville, OH	234, 330	44632
Hartwell, GA	706, 762	30643
Hartwick, NY	607	13348
Harvard, IL	815	60033
Harvey, IL	708	60426
Harvey, LA	504	70058-70059
Harwich, MA	508, 774	02645
Harwood Heights, IL	708	60656, 60706
Hasbrouck Heights, NJ	201, 551	07604
Haskell, NJ	862, 973	07420
Haskell, TX	940	79521
Hastings, MI	616	49058
Hastings, MN	651	55033
Hastings, NE	402	68901-68902
Hastings-on-Hudson, NY	914	10706
Hatboro, PA	215, 267	19040
Hatfield, MA	413	01038
Hatfield, PA	215, 267	19440
Hato Rey, PR	787, 939	00917-00919
Hattiesburg, MS	601, 769	39401-39407
Haughton, LA	318	71037
Hauppauge, NY	631	11749, 11760, 11788
Havana, IL	309	62644
Haverford, PA	484, 610	19041
Haverhill, MA	351, 978	01830-01835
Haverstraw, NY	845	10927
Havertown, PA	484, 610	19083
Haviland, KS	620	67059
Havre, MT	406	59501
Havre de Grace, MD	410	21078
Haw River, NC	336	27258
Hawaii National Park, HI	808	96718
Hawaiian Gardens, CA	562	90716
Hawesville, KY	270	42348
Hawkins, TX	903	75765
Hawkins, WI	715, 534	54530
Hawkinsville, GA	478	31036
Hawthorn Woods, IL	224, 847	60047
Hawthorne, CA	310, 424	90250-90251
Hawthorne, NV	775	89415
Hawthorne, NJ	862, 973	07506-07507
Hawthorne, NY	914	10532
Hay Springs, NE	308	69347, 69367
Hayden, AZ	520	85235
Hayden, ID	208	83835
Hayden Lake, ID	208	83835
Hayes Center, NE	308	69032
Hayesville, NC	828	28904
Hayesville, OH	419, 567	44838
Haynesville, VA	804	22472
Hayneville, AL	334	36040
Hays, KS	785	67601, 67667
Haysville, KS	316	67060
Hayti, MO	573	63851
Hayti, SD	605	57241
Hayward, CA	510	94540-94546, 94552, 94557
Hayward, WI	715, 534	54843
Hazard, KY	606	41701-41702
Hazel Crest, IL	708	60429
Hazel Park, MI	248, 947	48030
Hazelwood, MO	314	63042-63045, 63135
Hazen, ND	701	58545
Hazlehurst, GA	912	31539
Hazlehurst, MS	601, 769	39083
Hazlet, NJ	732, 848	07730
Hazleton, PA	570	18201-18202
Healdsburg, CA	707	95448
Healy, AK	907	99743, 99755
Healy, KS	620	67850
Heartwell, NE	308	68945
Heath, OH	740	43056
Heathrow, FL	321, 407	32746
Heathsville, VA	804	22473
Hebbronville, TX	361	78361
Heber, CA	760, 442	92249
Heber City, UT	435	84032
Heber Springs, AR	501	72543-72545
Hebron, IL	815	60034
Hebron, KY	859	41048
Hebron, NE	402	68370
Hebron, OH	740	43025, 43098
Hector, MN	320	55342
Hedgesville, WV	304	25427
Heflin, AL	256	36264
Helen, GA	706, 762	30545
Helena, AL	205	35080
Helena, AR	870	72342
Helena, GA	229	31037
Helena, MT	406	59601-59604, 59620-59626
Helena, OK	580	73741
Helenwood, TN	423	37755
Hellertown, PA	484, 610	18055
Hemet, CA	951	92543-92546
Hemphill, TX	409	75948
Hempstead, NY	516	11549-11551
Hempstead, TX	979	77445
Henderson, CO	303, 720	80640
Henderson, KY	270	42419-42420
Henderson, NE	402	68371
Henderson, NV	702	89009-89016, 89052-89053*
Henderson, NC	252	27536-27537
Henderson, TN	731	38340
Henderson, TX	903	75652-75654, 75680
Hendersonville, NC	828	28739, 28791-28793

**Partial list of zip codes, including main range*

City	Area Code(s)	Zip Code(s)
Hendersonville, TN	615	37075-37077
Hennepin, IL	815	61327
Henniker, NH	603	03242
Henning, TN	731	38041
Henrietta, NY	585	14467
Henrietta, TX	940	76365
Henry, TN	731	38231
Henryetta, OK	918	74437
Henryville, IN	812	47126
Heppner, OR	541, 458	97836
Hercules, CA	510	94547
Hereford, AZ	520	85615
Hereford, TX	806	79045
Herkimer, NY	315	13350
Hermann, MO	573	65041
Hermiston, OR	541, 458	97838
Hermitage, MO	417	65668
Hermitage, PA	724, 878	16148
Hermitage, TN	615	37076
Hermleigh, TX	915	79526
Hermon, ME	207	04401
Hermosa, SD	605	57744
Hernando, FL	352	34442
Hernando, MS	662	38632
Herndon, PA	570	17830
Herndon, VA	571, 703	20170-20172, 20190-20195*
Herrin, IL	618	62948
Hershey, PA	717	17033
Hertford, NC	252	27930, 27944
Hesperia, CA	760, 442	92340, 92345
Hesston, KS	620	67062
Hettinger, ND	701	58639
Heuvelton, NY	315	13654
Hewitt, NJ	862, 973	07421
Hewitt, TX	254	76643
Heyburn, ID	208	83336
Hialeah, FL	305, 786	33002, 33010-33018, 33054
Hialeah Gardens, FL	305, 786	33010, 33016-33018
Hiawassee, GA	706, 762	30546
Hiawatha, IA	319	52233
Hiawatha, KS	785	66434
Hibbing, MN	218	55746-55747
Hickam AFB, HI	808	96853
Hickman, KY	270	42050
Hickory, KY	270	42051
Hickory, NC	828	28601-28603
Hicksville, NY	516	11801-11804, 11815, 11819*
Hidden Valley, PA	814	15502
Higginsville, MO	660	64037
High Point, NC	336	27260-27265
High Ridge, MO	636	63049
High Shoals, GA	706, 762	30645
Highgate Springs, VT	802	05460
Highland, CA	909	92346
Highland, IL	618	62249
Highland, IN	219	46322, 47854
Highland, KS	785	66035
Highland, NY	845	12528
Highland Heights, KY	859	41076
Highland Heights, OH	440	44143
Highland Hills, OH	216	44122, 44128
Highland Park, IL	224, 847	60035-60037
Highland Park, MI	313	48203
Highland Springs, VA	804	23075
Highlands, NJ	732, 848	07732
Highlands Ranch, CO	303, 720	80124-80130, 80163
Highmore, SD	605	57345
Hightstown, NJ	609	08520
Hildebran, NC	828	28637
Hill AFB, UT	801, 385	84056
Hill City, KS	785	67642
Hill City, SD	605	57745
Hilliard, OH	614	43026
Hillsboro, IL	217	62049
Hillsboro, KS	620	67063
Hillsboro, MO	636	63050
Hillsboro, NH	603	03244
Hillsboro, ND	701	58045
Hillsboro, OH	937	45133
Hillsboro, OR	503, 971	97123-97124
Hillsboro, TX	254	76645
Hillsboro, WV	304	24946
Hillsboro, WI	608	54634
Hillsboro Beach, FL	754, 954	33062
Hillsborough, NJ	908	08844
Hillsborough, NC	919	27278
Hillsdale, MI	517	49242
Hillsdale, NJ	201, 551	07642, 07676
Hillsgrove, PA	570	18619
Hillside, IL	708	60162-60163
Hillside, NJ	973	07205
Hillsville, VA	276	24343
Hilmar, CA	209	95324
Hilo, HI	808	96720-96721
Hilton, NY	585	14468
Hilton Head Island, SC	843	29915, 29925-29928, 29938
Hinckley, MN	320	55037
Hinckley, OH	234, 330	44233
Hindman, KY	606	41822
Hines, IL	708	60141
Hinesville, GA	912	31310-31315
Hingham, MA	339, 781	02018, 02043-02044
Hinsdale, IL	331, 630	60521-60523, 60570
Hinsdale, NH	603	03451
Hinton, OK	405	73047
Hinton, WV	304	25951
Hiram, OH	234, 330	44234
Hixson, TN	423	37343
Hobart, IN	219	46342
Hobart, OK	580	73651
Hobbs, IN	765	46047
Hobbs, NM	505	88240-88244
Hobe Sound, FL	772	33455, 33475
Hoboken, NJ	201, 551	07030
Hockessin, DE	302	19707
Hodgenville, KY	270	42748
Hodgkins, IL	708	60525
Hoffman, NC	910	28347
Hoffman Estates, IL	224, 847	60173, 60179, 60192-60195
Hohenwald, TN	931	38462
Hoisington, KS	620	67544
Holbrook, AZ	928	86025-86031
Holbrook, MA	339, 781	02343
Holbrook, NY	631	11741
Holden, MA	508, 774	01520
Holdenville, OK	405	74848
Holdingford, MN	320	56340
Holdrege, NE	308	68949, 68969
Holland, IN	812	47541
Holland, MI	616	49422-49424
Holland, NY	716	14080
Holland, OH	419, 567	43528
Hollandale, MS	662	38748
Hollidaysburg, PA	814	16648
Hollis, NH	603	03049
Hollis, OK	580	73550
Hollister, CA	831	95023-95024
Hollister, MO	417	65672-65673
Holliston, MA	508, 774	01746
Holloman AFB, NM	505	88330
Hollsopple, PA	814	15935
Holly, MI	248, 947	48442
Holly Hill, FL	386	32117
Holly Springs, MS	662	38634-38635, 38649
Hollywood, CA	323	90027-90028, 90038, 90068*
Hollywood, FL	754, 954	33019-33029, 33081-33084*
Holmdel, NJ	732, 848	07733, 07777
Holmen, WI	608	54636
Holstein, IA	712	51025
Holt, MI	517	48842
Holton, KS	785	66436
Holtsville, NY	631	00501, 00544, 11742
Holyoke, CO	970	80734
Holyoke, MA	413	01040-01041
Homer, AK	907	99603
Homer, GA	706, 762	30547
Homer, LA	318	71040
Homerville, GA	912	31634
Homestead, FL	305, 786	33030-33035, 33039, 33090*
Homestead, PA	412, 878	15120
Homewood, AL	205	35209, 35219, 35259
Homewood, IL	708	60430
Hominy, OK	918	74035
Homosassa Springs, FL	352	34447
Honaunau, HI	808	96726
Hondo, TX	830	78861
Honea Path, SC	864	29654
Honeoye, NY	585	14471
Honesdale, PA	570	18431
Honolulu, HI	808	96801-96830, 96835-96850
Hood River, OR	541, 458	97031
Hooker, OK	580	73945
Hooper, NE	402	68031
Hoosick Falls, NY	518	12090
Hoover, AL	205	35216, 35226, 35236, 35244
Hopatcong, NJ	862, 973	07843
Hope, AK	907	99605
Hope, AR	870	71801-71802
Hope Hull, AL	334	36043
Hope Valley, RI	401	02832
Hopedale, MA	508, 774	01747
Hopewell, VA	804	23860
Hopewell Junction, NY	845	12533
Hopkins, MI	616	49328
Hopkins, MN	952	55305, 55343-55345
Hopkins, SC	803	29061
Hopkinsville, KY	270	42240-42241
Hopkinton, MA	508, 774	01748
Hopkinton, NH	603	03229
Hopland, CA	707	95449
Hoquiam, WA	360	98550
Horn Lake, MS	662	38637
Hornell, NY	607	14843
Hornick, IA	712	51026
Horse Cave, KY	270	42749
Horseheads, NY	607	14844-14845
Horseshoe Bay, TX	830	78654-78657
Horsham, PA	215, 267	19044
Horton, KS	785	66439
Hot Springs, AR	501	71901-71903, 71909-71914
Hot Springs, SD	605	57747
Hot Springs, VA	540	24445
Hot Springs National Park, AR	501	71901-71903, 71909-71914*
Hot Sulphur Springs, CO	970	80451
Houghton, IA	319	52631
Houghton, MI	906	49921, 49931
Houghton, NY	585	14744
Houghton Lake, MI	989	48629
Houlka, MS	662	38850
Houlton, ME	207	04730, 04761
Houma, LA	985	70360-70364
Houston, MS	662	38851
Houston, MO	417	65483
Houston, TX	281, 713, 832	77001-77099, 77201-77293*
Houtzdale, PA	814	16651, 16698
Howard, KS	620	67349
Howard, SD	605	57349
Howard Lake, MN	320	55349, 55575
Howell, MI	517	48843-48844, 48863
Howell, NJ	732, 848	07731
Howes Cave, NY	518	12092
Howey in the Hills, FL	352	34737
Hoxie, KS	785	67740
Hubbard, OR	503, 971	97032
Huber Heights, OH	937	45424
Hudson, FL	727	34667-34669, 34674
Hudson, KS	620	67545
Hudson, MA	351, 978	01749
Hudson, MI	517	49247
Hudson, NH	603	03051
Hudson, NY	518	12534
Hudson, NC	828	28638
Hudson, OH	234, 330	44236-44238
Hudson, WI	715, 534	54016, 54082
Hudson Falls, NY	518	12839
Hueytown, AL	205	35022-35023
Hughesville, MD	301	20637
Hughson, CA	209	95326
Hugo, CO	719	80821
Hugo, MN	651	55038
Hugo, OK	580	74743
Hugoton, KS	620	67951
Hulbert, OK	918	74441
Hull, IA	712	51239
Hull, MA	339, 781	02045
Humacao, PR	787, 939	00791-00792
Humble, TX	281, 832	77325, 77338-77339, 77345*
Humboldt, IA	515	50548
Humboldt, KS	620	66748
Humboldt, TN	731	38343
Hummelstown, PA	717	17036

Partial list of zip codes, including main range

City	Area Code(s)	Zip Code(s)
Hunlock Creek, PA	570	18621
Hunt, TX	830	78024
Hunt Valley, MD	410	21030-21031, 21065
Hunter, NY	518	12442
Huntersville, NC	704, 980	28070, 28078
Huntertown, IN	260	46748
Huntingburg, IN	812	47542
Huntingdon, PA	814	16652-16654
Huntingdon, TN	731	38344
Huntingdon Valley, PA	215, 267	19006
Huntington, IN	260	46750
Huntington, NY	631	11743
Huntington, UT	435	84528
Huntington, VT	802	05462
Huntington, WV	304	25701-25729, 25755, 25770*
Huntington Beach, CA	714	92605, 92615, 92646-92649
Huntington Park, CA	323	90255
Huntington Station, NY	631	11746-11750
Huntley, IL	224, 847	60142
Huntley, MT	406	59037
Huntsville, AL	256	35801-35816, 35824, 35893*
Huntsville, AR	479	72740
Huntsville, MO	660	65259
Huntsville, TN	423	37756
Huntsville, TX	936	77320, 77340-77344, 77348*
Hurley, WI	715, 534	54534, 54565
Huron, CA	559	93234
Huron, OH	419, 567	44839
Huron, SD	605	57350, 57399
Hurricane, WV	304	25526
Hurst, TX	682, 817	76053-76054
Hutchins, TX	469, 972	75141
Hutchinson, KS	620	67501-67505
Hutchinson, MN	320	55350
Huttonsville, WV	304	26273
Hyannis, MA	508, 774	02601
Hyannis, NE	308	69350
Hyattsville, MD	301	20781-20788
Hydaburg, AK	907	99922
Hyde Park, MA	617, 857	02136-02137
Hyde Park, NY	845	12538
Hyde Park, VT	802	05655
Hyden, KY	606	41749, 41762
Hyrum, UT	435	84319
Hysham, MT	406	59038, 59076

I

City	Area Code(s)	Zip Code(s)
Ida Grove, IA	712	51445
Idabel, OK	580	74745
Idaho City, ID	208	83631
Idaho Falls, ID	208	83401-83406, 83415
Idaho Springs, CO	303, 720	80452
Idyllwild, CA	951	92549
Imlay City, MI	810	48444
Immaculata, PA	484, 610	19345
Immokalee, FL	239	34142-34143
Imperial, CA	760, 442	92251
Imperial, MO	636	63052-63053
Imperial, NE	308	69033
Imperial Beach, CA	619	91932-91933
Ina, IL	618	62846
Incline Village, NV	775	89450-89452
Independence, CA	760, 442	93526
Independence, IA	319	50644
Independence, KS	620	67301
Independence, KY	859	41051
Independence, MO	816	64050-64058
Independence, OH	216	44131
Independence, OR	503, 971	97351
Independence, VA	276	24348
Indian, AK	907	99540
Indian Orchard, MA	413	01151
Indian Springs, NV	702	89018, 89070
Indian Trail, NC	704, 980	28079
Indian Wells, CA	760, 442	92210
Indiana, PA	724, 878	15701, 15705
Indianapolis, IN	317	46201-46260, 46266-46268*
Indianola, IA	515	50125
Indianola, MS	662	38749-38751
Indianola, PA	412, 878	15051
Indiantown, FL	772	34956
Indio, CA	760, 442	92201-92203
Inez, KY	606	41224
Ingalls, KS	620	67853
Inglewood, CA	310, 424	90301-90313, 90397-90398
Ingomar, PA	412, 878	15127
Inkster, MI	313	48141
Inman, SC	864	29349
Institute, WV	304	25112
Intercourse, PA	717	17534
Interior, SD	605	57750
Interlochen, MI	231	49643
International Falls, MN	218	56649
Inver Grove Heights, MN	651	55076-55077
Inverness, FL	352	34450-34453
Inwood, NY	516	11096
Iola, KS	620	66749
Iola, WI	715, 534	54945, 54990
Ione, CA	209	95640
Ionia, MI	616	48846
Iowa City, IA	319	52240-52246
Iowa Falls, IA	641	50126
Ipswich, MA	351, 978	01938
Ipswich, SD	605	57451
Irma, WI	715, 534	54442
Irmo, SC	803	29063
Iron Mountain, MI	906	49801-49802, 49831
Iron River, WI	715, 534	54847
Irondale, AL	205	35210
Ironton, MO	573	63650
Ironton, OH	740	45638
Ironwood, MI	906	49938
Irvine, CA	949	92602-92606, 92612-92623*
Irvine, KY	606	40336, 40472
Irvine, PA	814	16329
Irving, TX	214, 469, 972	75014-75017, 75037-75039*
Irvington, NJ	862, 973	07111
Irvington, NY	914	10533
Irvington, VA	804	22480
Irwin, PA	724, 878	15642
Irwindale, CA	626	91706
Irwinton, GA	478	31042
Iselin, NJ	732, 848	08830
Ishpeming, MI	906	49849, 49865
Islamorada, FL	305, 786	33036, 33070
Islandia, NY	631	11749, 11760
Isle of Palms, SC	843	29451
Isle of Wight, VA	757	23397
Islip, NY	631	11751
Isola, MS	662	38754
Issaquah, WA	425	98027-98029, 98075
Itasca, IL	331, 630	60143
Itasca, TX	254	76055
Ithaca, MI	989	48847
Ithaca, NY	607	14850-14853, 14882
Itta Bena, MS	662	38941
Iuka, MS	662	38852
Ivanhoe, CA	559	93235
Ivanhoe, MN	507	56142
Ivel, KY	606	41642
Ivins, UT	435	84738
Ivoryton, CT	860	06442
Ivyland, PA	215, 267	18974
Ixonia, WI	920	53036

J

City	Area Code(s)	Zip Code(s)
Jackman, ME	207	04945
Jackpot, NV	775	89825
Jacksboro, TN	423	37757
Jacksboro, TX	940	76458
Jackson, AL	251	36501, 36515, 36545
Jackson, CA	209	95642, 95654
Jackson, GA	470, 770	30233
Jackson, KY	606	41307, 41339
Jackson, LA	225	70748
Jackson, MI	517	49201-49204
Jackson, MN	507	56143
Jackson, MS	601, 769	39201-39218, 39225, 39232*
Jackson, MO	573	63755
Jackson, NH	603	03846
Jackson, NJ	732, 848	08527
Jackson, NC	252	27845
Jackson, OH	740	45640
Jackson, SC	803	29831
Jackson, TN	731	38301-38308, 38314
Jackson, WI	262	53037
Jackson, WY	307	83001-83002, 83025
Jackson Center, OH	937	45334
Jackson Heights, NY	347, 718	11372
Jackson Hole, WY	307	83001-83002
Jacksonville, AL	256	36265
Jacksonville, AR	501	72076-72078
Jacksonville, FL	904	32099, 32201-32250, 32254*
Jacksonville, IL	217	62650-62651
Jacksonville, NC	910	28540-28546
Jacksonville, TX	903	75766
Jacksonville Beach, FL	904	32227, 32240, 32250
Jaffrey, NH	603	03452
Jamaica, NY	347, 718	11405, 11411-11439, 11451*
Jamaica Plain, MA	617, 857	02130
Jamesburg, NJ	732, 848	08831
Jamestown, CA	209	95327
Jamestown, KY	270	42629
Jamestown, NY	716	14701-14704
Jamestown, NC	336	27282
Jamestown, ND	701	58401-58405
Jamestown, OH	937	45335
Jamestown, RI	401	02835
Jamestown, SC	843	29453
Jamestown, TN	931	38556
Janesville, IA	319	50647
Janesville, WI	608	53545-53547
Jarratt, VA	434	23867-23870
Jasper, AL	205	35501-35504
Jasper, AR	870	72641
Jasper, FL	386	32052
Jasper, GA	706, 762	30143
Jasper, IN	812	47546-47549
Jasper, MN	507	56144
Jasper, TN	423	37347
Jasper, TX	409	75951
Jay, FL	850	32565
Jay, ME	207	04239, 04262
Jay, OK	918	74346
Jay, VT	802	05859
Jayton, TX	806	79528
Jean, NV	702	89019, 89026
Jeanerette, LA	337	70544
Jeannette, PA	724, 878	15644
Jefferson, AR	870	72079
Jefferson, GA	706, 762	30549
Jefferson, IA	515	50129
Jefferson, LA	504	70121
Jefferson, NC	336	28640
Jefferson, OH	440	44047
Jefferson, OR	541, 458	97352
Jefferson, SD	605	57038
Jefferson, TX	903	75657
Jefferson, WI	920	53549
Jefferson City, MO	573	65101-65111
Jefferson City, TN	865	37760
Jefferson Valley, NY	914	10535
Jeffersontown, KY	502	40269, 40299
Jeffersonville, GA	478	31044
Jeffersonville, IN	812	47129-47134, 47144, 47199
Jeffersonville, NY	845	12748
Jeffersonville, OH	740	43128
Jekyll Island, GA	912	31527
Jelm, WY	970	82063, 82070-82072
Jena, LA	318	71342
Jenison, MI	616	49428-49429
Jenkintown, PA	215, 267	19046
Jenks, OK	918	74037
Jennerstown, PA	814	15547
Jennings, LA	337	70546
Jericho, NY	516	11753, 11853
Jermyn, PA	570	18433
Jerome, ID	208	83338
Jersey City, NJ	201, 551	07097, 07302-07311, 07399
Jerseyville, IL	618	62052
Jessup, MD	410, 443	20794
Jesup, GA	912	31545-31546, 31598-31599
Jetersville, VA	804	23083
Jetmore, KS	620	67854
Jewell, IA	515	50130
Jewett, TX	903	75846
Jim Thorpe, PA	570	18229

**Partial list of zip codes, including main range*

City	Area Code(s)	Zip Code(s)
Johnson, KS	620	67855
Johnson, VT	802	05656
Johnson City, NY	607	13790
Johnson City, TN	423	37601-37605, 37614-37615
Johnson City, TX	830	78636
Johnston, IA	515	50131
Johnston, RI	401	02919
Johnston, SC	803	29832
Johnston City, IL	618	62951
Johnstown, NY	518	12095
Johnstown, OH	740	43031
Johnstown, PA	814	15901-15909, 15915, 15945
Joliet, IL	815	60431-60436
Jonesboro, AR	870	72401-72404
Jonesboro, GA	470, 770	30236-30238
Jonesboro, IL	618	62952
Jonesboro, LA	318	71251
Jonesborough, TN	423	37659
Jonesburg, MO	636	63351
Jonestown, MS	662	38639
Jonesville, LA	318	71343, 71377
Jonesville, VA	276	24263
Joplin, MO	417	64801-64804
Joppa, MD	410	21085
Jordan, MN	952	55352, 56071
Jordan, MT	406	59337
Jordan, NY	315	13080
Joshua Tree, CA	760, 442	92252
Jourdanton, TX	830	78026
Julesburg, CO	970	80737
Junction, TX	915	76849
Junction, UT	435	84740
Junction City, KS	785	66441-66442
Junction City, OR	541, 458	97448
Juneau, AK	907	99801-99803, 99811, 99821*
Juneau, WI	920	53039
Juno Beach, FL	561	33408
Jupiter, FL	561	33458, 33468-33469, 33477*

K

City	Area Code(s)	Zip Code(s)
Kadoka, SD	605	57543
Kahoka, MO	660	63445
Kahuku, HI	808	96731
Kahului, HI	808	96732-96733
Kailua, HI	808	96734
Kailua-Kona, HI	808	96739-96740, 96745
Kaiser, MO	573	65047
Kalaheo, HI	808	96741
Kalama, WA	360	98625
Kalamazoo, MI	616	49001-49009, 49019, 49024*
Kalaupapa, HI	808	96742
Kalida, OH	419, 567	45853
Kalispell, MT	406	59901-59904
Kalkaska, MI	231	49646
Kalona, IA	319	52247
Kamuela, HI	808	96743
Kanab, UT	435	84741
Kanawha, IA	641	50447
Kane, PA	814	16735
Kaneohe, HI	808	96744
Kankakee, IL	815	60901-60902
Kannapolis, NC	704, 980	28081-28083
Kansas City, KS	913	66101-66119, 66160
Kansas City, MO	816	64101-64173, 64179-64199*
Kapaa, HI	808	96746
Kapolei, HI	808	96707-96709
Karnes City, TX	830	78118
Karthaus, PA	814	16845
Kasson, MN	507	55944
Katonah, NY	914	10536
Katy, TX	281, 832	77449-77450, 77491-77494
Kaufman, TX	469, 972	75142
Kaukauna, WI	920	54130-54131
Kaumakani, HI	808	96747
Keaau, HI	808	96749
Kealakekua, HI	808	96750
Kearney, MO	816	64060
Kearney, NE	308	68845-68849
Kearneysville, WV	304	25429-25430
Kearny, NJ	201, 551	07032, 07099
Keene, CA	661	93531
Keene, NH	603	03431, 03435
Keene, TX	682, 817	76059
Keesler AFB, MS	228	39534
Keizer, OR	503, 971	97303, 97307
Keller, TX	682, 817	76244, 76248
Kellogg, ID	208	83837
Kelly, WY	307	83011
Kelseyville, CA	707	95451
Kelso, WA	360	98626
Kemmerer, WY	307	83101
Kenai, AK	907	99611, 99635
Kenansville, NC	910	28349
Kendall, FL	305, 786	33156-33158, 33173-33176*
Kendallville, IN	260	46720, 46755
Kenedy, TX	830	78119, 78125
Kenilworth, NJ	908	07033
Kenmare, ND	701	58746
Kenmore, NY	716	14217, 14223
Kenmore, WA	425	98028
Kennebec, SD	605	57544
Kennebunk, ME	207	04043
Kennebunkport, ME	207	04046
Kennedy Space Center, FL	321	32815
Kenner, LA	504	70062-70065
Kennesaw, GA	470, 770	30144, 30152, 30156, 30160
Kennett, MO	573	63857
Kennett Square, PA	484, 610	19348
Kennewick, WA	509	99336-99338
Kenosha, WI	262	53140-53144, 53158
Kenova, WV	304	25530
Kensington, CT	860	06037
Kensington, MD	301	20891, 20895
Kent, CT	860	06757
Kent, OH	234, 330	44240-44243
Kent, WA	253	98031-98035, 98042, 98064
Kentfield, CA	415	94904, 94914
Kentland, IN	219	47951
Kenton, OH	419, 567	43326
Kentwood, MI	616	49506-49508, 49512, 49518*
Kenwood, CA	707	95452
Kenyon, MN	507	55946
Keokuk, IA	319	52632
Keosauqua, IA	319	52565
Kermit, TX	915	79745
Kernersville, NC	336	27284-27285
Kernville, CA	760, 442	93238
Kerrville, TX	830	78028-78029
Kershaw, SC	803	29067
Keshena, WI	715, 534	54135
Keswick, VA	434	22947
Ketchikan, AK	907	99901-99903, 99918-99919*
Ketchum, ID	208	83340
Kettering, OH	937	45409, 45419-45420, 45429*
Keuka Park, NY	315	14478
Kew Gardens, NY	347, 718	11415-11418
Kewanee, IL	309	61443
Kewanna, IN	574	46935, 46939
Kewaskum, WI	262	53040
Kewaunee, WI	920	54216
Key Biscayne, FL	305, 786	33149
Key Largo, FL	305, 786	33037
Key West, FL	305, 786	33040-33041, 33045
Keyser, WV	304	26726
Keystone, CO	970	80435
Keystone, SD	605	57751
Keystone Heights, FL	352	32656
Keytesville, MO	660	65261
Kiamesha Lake, NY	845	12751
Kiawah Island, SC	843	29455
Kidron, OH	234, 330	44636
Kiel, WI	920	53042
Kihei, HI	808	96753
Kilgore, TX	903	75662-75663
Kill Devil Hills, NC	252	27948
Killbuck, OH	234, 330	44637
Killeen, TX	254	76540-76549
Killington, VT	802	05751
Kimball, NE	308	69145
Kimberly, OR	541, 458	97848
Kimberly, WI	920	54136
Kincheloe, MI	906	49784-49788
Kinder, LA	337	70648
Kinderhook, NY	518	12106
Kindred, ND	701	58051
King, NC	336	27021
King, WI	715, 534	54946
King City, CA	831	93930
King Ferry, NY	315	13081
King George, VA	540	22485
King of Prussia, PA	484, 610	19406, 19487
King Salmon, AK	907	99549, 99613
King William, VA	804	23086
Kingfisher, OK	405	73750
Kingman, AZ	928	86401-86402, 86411-86413*
Kingman, KS	620	67068
Kings Bay, GA	912	31547
Kings Mountain, NC	704, 980	28086
Kings Point, NY	516	11024
Kingsburg, CA	559	93631
Kingsford, MI	906	49801-49802
Kingsport, TN	423	37660-37665, 37669
Kingston, MA	339, 781	02364
Kingston, MO	816	64650
Kingston, NJ	609	08528
Kingston, NY	845	12401-12402
Kingston, OK	580	73439
Kingston, PA	570	18704
Kingston, RI	401	02881
Kingston, TN	865	37763
Kingston, WA	360	98346
Kingstree, SC	843	29556
Kingsville, MD	410	21087
Kingsville, MO	816	64061
Kingsville, TX	361	78363-78364
Kingwood, TX	281, 832	77325, 77339, 77345-77346
Kingwood, WV	304	26519, 26537
Kinnelon, NJ	862, 973	07405
Kinsale, VA	804	22488
Kinsley, KS	620	67547
Kinsman, OH	234, 330	44428
Kinston, NC	252	28501-28504
Kiowa, CO	303, 720	80117
Kirbyville, TX	409	75956
Kirkland, WA	425	98033-98034, 98083
Kirksville, MO	660	63501
Kirkville, NY	315	13082
Kirkwood, MO	314	63122
Kirtland, OH	440	44094
Kirtland AFB, NM	505	87116-87118
Kissimmee, FL	321, 407	34741-34747, 34758-34759
Kittanning, PA	724, 878	16201, 16215
Kittery, ME	207	03904
Klamath Falls, OR	541, 458	97601-97603, 97625
Knights Landing, CA	530	95645
Knightstown, IN	765	46148
Knox, IN	574	46534
Knoxville, IA	641	50138, 50197-50198
Knoxville, TN	865	37901-37902, 37909-37933*
Kodiak, AK	907	99615, 99619, 99697
Kohler, WI	920	53044
Kokomo, IN	765	46901-46904
Koloa, HI	808	96756
Kosciusko, MS	662	39090
Koshkonong, MO	417	65692
Kotzebue, AK	907	99752
Kountze, TX	409	77625
Kreamer, PA	570	17833
Kula, HI	808	96790
Kulpsville, PA	215, 267	19443
Kuna, ID	208	83634
Kurten, TX	979	77862
Kutztown, PA	484, 610	19530

L

City	Area Code(s)	Zip Code(s)
La Belle, FL	863	33935
La Canada, CA	818	91011-91012
La Conner, WA	360	98257
La Crescenta, CA	818	91214, 91224
La Crosse, KS	785	67548, 67553
La Crosse, WI	608	54601-54603
La Fayette, GA	706, 762	30728
La Follette, TN	423	37729, 37766
La France, SC	864	29656
La Grande, OR	541, 458	97850
La Grange, IL	708	60525
La Grange, TX	979	78945

*Partial list of zip codes, including main range

City	Area Code(s)	Zip Code(s)
La Grange Park, IL	708	60526
La Habra, CA	562	90631-90633
La Jolla, CA	858	92037-92039, 92092-92093
La Junta, CO	719	81050
La Mesa, CA	619	91941-91944
La Mesa, NM	505	88044
La Mirada, CA	562, 714	90637-90639
La Moure, ND	701	58458
La Palma, CA	714	90623
La Pine, OR	541, 458	97739
La Plata, MD	301	20646
La Plume, PA	570	18440
La Porte, IN	574	46350-46352
La Porte, TX	281, 832	77571-77572
La Puente, CA	626	91744-91749
La Quinta, CA	760, 442	92253
La Rue, OH	740	43332
La Salle, IL	815	61301
La Union, NM	505	88021
La Vergne, TN	615	37086-37089
La Verne, CA	909	91750
La Veta, CO	719	81055
Lac du Flambeau, WI	715, 534	54538
Lacey, WA	360	98503-98509, 98513-98516
Lackawanna, NY	716	14218
Lackland AFB, TX	210	78236
Laclede, ID	208	83841
Lacon, IL	309	61540
Laconia, NH	603	03246-03249
Ladd, IL	815	61329
Ladysmith, WI	715, 534	54848
Lafayette, AL	334	36862
Lafayette, CA	925	94549, 94596
Lafayette, CO	303, 720	80026
Lafayette, IN	765	47901-47909, 47996
Lafayette, LA	337	70501-70509, 70593-70598
Lafayette, NJ	862, 973	07848
Lafayette, TN	615	37083
LaFox, IL	331, 630	60147
Lago Vista, TX	512	78645
LaGrange, GA	706, 762	30240-30241, 30261
LaGrange, IN	260	46761
LaGrange, KY	502	40031
Lagrangeville, NY	845	12540
Laguna Beach, CA	949	92607, 92637, 92651-92656*
Laguna Hills, CA	949	92637, 92653-92656
Laguna Niguel, CA	949	92607, 92677
Lahaina, HI	808	96761, 96767
Laie, HI	808	96762
Lake Alfred, FL	863	33850
Lake Andes, SD	605	57356
Lake Ariel, PA	570	18436
Lake Bluff, IL	224, 847	60044
Lake Buena Vista, FL	321, 407	32830
Lake Butler, FL	386	32054
Lake Charles, LA	337	70601-70616, 70629
Lake City, CO	970	81235
Lake City, FL	386	32024-32025, 32055-32056
Lake City, IA	712	51449
Lake City, MI	231	49651
Lake City, MN	651	55041
Lake City, PA	814	16423
Lake City, SC	843	29560
Lake Crystal, MN	507	56055
Lake Dallas, TX	940	75065
Lake Delton, WI	608	53940
Lake Elsinore, CA	951	92530-92532
Lake Forest, CA	949	92609, 92630
Lake Forest, IL	224, 847	60045
Lake Geneva, WI	262	53147
Lake George, CO	719	80827
Lake George, NY	518	12845
Lake Grove, NY	631	11755
Lake Harmony, PA	570	18624
Lake Havasu City, AZ	928	86403-86406
Lake Helen, FL	386	32744
Lake Hiawatha, NJ	862, 973	07034
Lake Isabella, CA	760, 442	93240
Lake Jackson, TX	979	77566
Lake Junaluska, NC	828	28745
Lake Lillian, MN	320	56253
Lake Lure, NC	828	28746
Lake Mary, FL	321, 407	32746, 32795
Lake Mills, WI	920	53551
Lake Monroe, FL	321, 407	32747
Lake Odessa, MI	616	48849
Lake Orion, MI	248, 947	48359-48362
Lake Oswego, OR	503, 971	97034-97035
Lake Ozark, MO	573	65049
Lake Park, GA	229	31636
Lake Placid, FL	863	33852, 33862
Lake Placid, NY	518	12946
Lake Pleasant, NY	518	12108
Lake Powell, UT	435	84533
Lake Providence, LA	318	71254
Lake Saint Louis, MO	636	63367
Lake Stevens, WA	425	98258
Lake Success, NY	516	11020, 11042
Lake Toxaway, NC	828	28747
Lake View, SC	843	29563
Lake Village, AR	870	71653
Lake Wales, FL	863	33853-33859, 33867, 33898
Lake Worth, FL	561	33454, 33460-33467
Lake Zurich, IL	224, 847	60047
Lakehurst, NJ	732, 848	08733, 08755, 08759
Lakeland, FL	863	33801-33815
Lakeland, GA	229	31635
Lakeland, LA	225	70752
Lakeport, CA	707	95453
Lakeside, AZ	928	85929
Lakeside, CA	619	92040
Laketon, IN	260	46943
Lakeview, AR	870	72642
Lakeview, CA	909	92567
Lakeview, OR	541, 458	97630
Lakeville, CT	860	06039
Lakeville, MN	952	55044
Lakeville, PA	570	18438
Lakeway, TX	512	78734, 78738
Lakewood, CA	562	90711-90716, 90805
Lakewood, CO	303, 720	80033, 80123, 80214-80215*
Lakewood, NJ	732, 848	08701
Lakewood, NY	716	14750
Lakewood, OH	216	44107
Lakewood, WA	253	98439, 98492, 98497-98499
Lakin, KS	620	67860
Lakota, ND	701	58344
Lamar, CO	719	81052
Lamar, MO	417	64759
Lamberton, MN	507	56152
Lambertville, NJ	609	08530
Lame Deer, MT	406	59043
Lamesa, TX	806	79331
Lamoni, IA	641	50140
Lamont, CA	661	93241
Lampasas, TX	512	76550
Lanai City, HI	808	96763
Lanark, IL	815	61046
Lancaster, CA	661	93534-93539, 93584-93586
Lancaster, KY	859	40444-40446
Lancaster, MO	660	63548
Lancaster, NH	603	03584
Lancaster, NY	716	14043, 14086
Lancaster, OH	740	43130
Lancaster, PA	717	17601-17608, 17699
Lancaster, SC	803	29720-29722
Lancaster, TX	469, 972	75134, 75146
Lancaster, VA	804	22503
Lancaster, WI	608	53813
Lander, WY	307	82520
Landisburg, PA	717	17040
Landisville, PA	717	17538
Landover, MD	301	20785
Landrum, SC	864	29356
Lanett, AL	334	36863
Langdon, ND	701	58249
Langhorne, PA	215, 267	19047, 19053
Langley, WA	360	98260
Langley AFB, VA	757	23665
Langston, OK	405	73050
Lanham, MD	301	20703-20706, 20784
Lanham Seabrook, MD	301	20703-20706
Lansdale, PA	215, 267	19446
Lansdowne, PA	484, 610	19050
L'Anse, MI	906	49946
Lansford, PA	570	18232
Lansing, IL	708	60438
Lansing, KS	913	66043
Lansing, MI	517	48901, 48906-48924, 48929*
Lantana, FL	561	33460-33465
Lapeer, MI	810	48446
LaPlace, LA	985	70068-70069
Laporte, PA	570	18626
Laramie, WY	307	82051, 82063, 82070-82073
Larchmont, NY	914	10538
Laredo, TX	956	78040-78049
Largo, FL	727	33770-33779
Largo, MD	301	20774
Larkspur, CA	415	94939, 94977
Larned, KS	620	67550
Larose, LA	985	70373-70374
Las Animas, CO	719	81054
Las Cruces, NM	505	88001-88006, 88011-88012
Las Vegas, NV	702	89101-89164, 89170-89173*
Las Vegas, NM	505	87701, 87745
Latham, NY	518	12110-12111, 12128
Lathrop, CA	209	95330
Latrobe, PA	724, 878	15650
Latta, SC	843	29565
Latty, OH	419, 567	45855
Lauderdale-by-the-Sea, FL	754, 954	33062, 33308
Lauderhill, FL	754, 954	33311-33313, 33319-33321*
Laughlin, NV	702	89028-89029
Laughlin AFB, TX	830	78840-78843
Laurel, MD	240, 301	20707-20709, 20723-20726
Laurel, MS	601, 769	39440-39443
Laurel Hill, NC	910	28351
Laurelton, NY	347, 718	11413
Laurens, IA	712	50554
Laurens, SC	864	29360
Laurinburg, NC	910	28352-28353
Lava Hot Springs, ID	208	83246
LaVale, MD	301	21502-21504
Lawndale, CA	310, 424	90260-90261
Lawrence, KS	785	66044-66049
Lawrence, MA	351, 978	01840-01843
Lawrence, MI	616	49064
Lawrence, NY	516	11559
Lawrence, PA	724, 878	15055
Lawrenceburg, IN	812	47025
Lawrenceburg, KY	502	40342
Lawrenceburg, TN	931	38464
Lawrenceville, GA	470, 678, 770	30042-30049
Lawrenceville, IL	618	62439
Lawrenceville, NJ	609	08648
Lawrenceville, VA	434	23868
Lawton, MI	616	49065
Lawton, OK	580	73501-73507, 73558
Layton, NJ	862, 973	07851
Layton, UT	801, 385	84040-84041
Le Center, MN	507	56057
Le Grand, IA	641	50142
Le Mars, IA	712	51017, 51031
Le Roy, NY	585	14482
Le Sueur, MN	507	56058
Lead, SD	605	57754
Leadville, CO	719	80429, 80461
League City, TX	281, 832	77573-77574
Leakesville, MS	601, 769	39451
Leakey, TX	830	78873
Leander, TX	512	78641, 78645-78646
Leavenworth, KS	913	66043, 66048
Leavittsburg, OH	234, 330	44430
Leawood, KS	913	66206-66211, 66224
Lebanon, CT	860	06249
Lebanon, IL	618	62254
Lebanon, IN	765	46052
Lebanon, KY	270	40033
Lebanon, MO	417	65536
Lebanon, NH	603	03756, 03766
Lebanon, NJ	908	08833
Lebanon, OH	513	45036
Lebanon, OR	541, 458	97355
Lebanon, PA	717	17042, 17046
Lebanon, TN	615	37087-37090
Lebanon, VA	276	24266
Lebec, CA	661	93243
Lecanto, FL	352	34460-34461
Lee, MA	413	01238, 01264
Leechburg, PA	724, 878	15656
Leeds, AL	205	35094
Leeds, MA	413	01053
Lee's Summit, MO	816	64063-64065, 64081-64082*
Leesburg, FL	352	34748-34749, 34788-34789

*Partial list of zip codes, including main range

City	Area Code(s)	Zip Code(s)
Leesburg, GA	229	31763
Leesburg, NJ	856	08327
Leesburg, VA	571, 703	20175-20178
Leesville, LA	337	71446, 71459, 71496
Leesville, SC	803	29070
Lehi, UT	801, 385	84043
Lehigh Acres, FL	239	33936, 33970-33972
Lehigh Valley, PA	484, 610	18001-18003
Lehighton, PA	484, 610	18235
Lehman, PA	570	18627
Leicester, MA	508, 774	01524
Leicester, NY	585	14481
Leitchfield, KY	270	42754-42755
Leland, MI	231	49654
Leland, NC	910	28451
Lemmon, SD	605	57638
Lemon Grove, CA	619	91945-91946
Lemont, IL	331, 630	60439-60440, 60490
Lemoore, CA	559	93245-93246
Lemoyne, PA	717	17043
Lena, IL	815	61048
Lenexa, KS	913	66210-66220, 66227, 66285*
Lenni, PA	484, 610	19052
Lenoir, NC	828	28633, 28645
Lenoir City, TN	865	37771-37772
Lenox, MA	413	01240
Leola, PA	717	17540
Leola, SD	605	57456
Leominster, MA	351, 978	01453
Leon, IA	641	50144
Leonardtown, MD	301	20650
Leonia, NJ	201, 551	07605
Leoti, KS	620	67861
Lester, PA	484, 610	19029, 19113
Lester Prairie, MN	320	55354
Levelland, TX	806	79336-79338
Leverett, MA	413	01054
Levittown, NY	516	11756
Levittown, PA	215, 267	19054-19059
Lewes, DE	302	19958
Lewis Center, OH	740	43035
Lewis Run, PA	814	16738
Lewisberry, PA	717	17339
Lewisburg, PA	570	17837
Lewisburg, TN	931	37091
Lewisburg, WV	304	24901
Lewiston, ID	208	83501
Lewiston, ME	207	04240-04243
Lewiston, MI	989	49756
Lewiston, MN	507	55952
Lewiston, NY	716	14092
Lewiston, NC	252	27849
Lewistown, IL	309	61542
Lewistown, MO	573	63452
Lewistown, MT	406	59457
Lewistown, PA	717	17044
Lewisville, AR	870	71845
Lewisville, ID	208	83431
Lewisville, NC	336	27023
Lewisville, TX	469, 972	75022, 75027-75029, 75056*
Lexington, GA	706, 762	30648
Lexington, KY	859	40502-40517, 40522-40526*
Lexington, MA	339, 781	02420-02421
Lexington, MI	810	48450
Lexington, MS	662	39095
Lexington, MO	660	64067
Lexington, NE	308	68850
Lexington, NC	336	27292-27295
Lexington, OH	419, 567	44904
Lexington, OK	405	73051
Lexington, SC	803	29071-29073
Lexington, TN	731	38351
Lexington, VA	540	24450
Lexington Park, MD	301	20653
Libby, MT	406	59923
Liberal, KS	620	67901, 67905
Liberty, IN	765	47353
Liberty, KY	606	42539
Liberty, MS	601, 769	39645
Liberty, MO	816	64068-64069, 64087
Liberty, NC	336	27298
Liberty, SC	864	29657
Liberty, TX	936	77575
Liberty Corner, NJ	908	07938
Liberty Lake, WA	509	99019

City	Area Code(s)	Zip Code(s)
Libertyville, IL	224, 847	60048, 60092
Licking, MO	573	65542
Lightfoot, VA	757	23090
Lighthouse Point, FL	754, 954	33064, 33074
Ligonier, PA	724, 878	15658
Lihue, HI	808	96766
Lilburn, GA	470, 770	30047-30048
Lillington, NC	910	27546
Lima, NY	585	14485
Lima, OH	419, 567	45801-45809, 45819, 45854
Lima, PA	484, 610	19037
Limerick, PA	484, 610	19468
Limon, CO	719	80826-80828
Lincoln, CA	916	95648
Lincoln, IL	217	62656
Lincoln, KS	785	67455
Lincoln, ME	207	04457
Lincoln, MA	339, 781	01773
Lincoln, MI	989	48742
Lincoln, NE	402	68501-68532, 68542, 68583*
Lincoln, RI	401	02802, 02865
Lincoln City, IN	812	47552
Lincoln City, OR	541, 458	97367
Lincoln Park, MI	313	48146
Lincoln Park, NJ	862, 973	07035
Lincoln University, PA	484, 610	19352
Lincolnshire, IL	224, 847	60069
Lincolnton, GA	706, 762	30817
Lincolnton, NC	704, 980	28092-28093
Lincolnwood, IL	224, 847	60645-60646, 60659, 60712
Lincroft, NJ	732, 848	07738
Linden, AL	334	36748
Linden, IN	765	47955
Linden, NJ	908	07036
Linden, TN	931	37096
Linden, TX	903	75563
Lindenhurst, NY	631	11757
Lindenwood, IL	815	61049
Lindon, UT	801, 385	84042
Lindsay, CA	559	93247
Lindsay, NE	402	68644
Lindsay, OK	405	73052
Lindsborg, KS	785	67456
Lindstrom, MN	651	55045
Linesville, PA	814	16424
Lingle, WY	307	82223
Linn, MO	573	65051
Linneus, MO	660	64653
Lino Lakes, MN	651	55014, 55038, 55110, 55126
Linthicum, MD	410	21090
Linthicum Heights, MD	410	21090
Linton, IN	812	47441
Linton, ND	701	58552
Linville, NC	828	28646
Linwood, KS	913	66052
Linwood, NJ	609	08221
Linwood, PA	484, 610	19061
Lionville, PA	484, 610	19353
Lipscomb, TX	806	79056
Lisbon, NH	603	03585
Lisbon, ND	701	58054
Lisbon, OH	234, 330	44432
Lisbon Falls, ME	207	04252
Lisle, IL	331, 630	60532
Litchfield, CT	860	06750, 06759
Litchfield, IL	217	62056
Litchfield, MI	517	49252
Litchfield, MN	320	55355
Litchfield Park, AZ	623	85340
Lithia, FL	813	33547
Lithia Springs, GA	470, 770	30122
Lithonia, GA	470, 770	30038-30039, 30058
Lititz, PA	717	17543
Little Chute, WI	920	54140
Little Compton, RI	401	02801, 02837
Little Elm, TX	469, 972	75068
Little Falls, MN	320	56345
Little Falls, NJ	862, 973	07424
Little Falls, NY	315	13365
Little Ferry, NJ	201, 551	07643
Little Neck, NY	347, 718	11362-11363
Little River, SC	843	29566
Little Rock, AR	501	72201-72227, 72231, 72260*
Little Rock AFB, AR	501	72076

City	Area Code(s)	Zip Code(s)
Little Silver, NJ	732, 848	07739
Little Torch Key, FL	305, 786	33042
Little Valley, NY	716	14755
Littlefield, TX	806	79339
Littlerock, WA	360	98556
Littlestown, PA	717	17340
Littleton, CO	303, 720	80120-80130, 80160-80166
Littleton, MA	351, 978	01460
Live Oak, CA	530	95953
Live Oak, FL	386	32060, 32064
Livermore, CA	925	94550-94551
Livermore, CO	970	80536
Liverpool, NY	315	13088-13090
Livingston, AL	205	35470
Livingston, CA	209	95334
Livingston, LA	225	70754
Livingston, MT	406	59047
Livingston, NJ	862, 973	07039
Livingston, TN	931	38570
Livingston, TX	936	77351, 77399
Livingston Manor, NY	845	12758
Livonia, MI	734	48150-48154
Llano, TX	915	78643
Loa, UT	435	84747
Loch Sheldrake, NY	845	12759
Lock Haven, PA	570	17745
Lockhart, TX	512	78644
Lockport, IL	815	60441, 60446
Lockport, LA	985	70374
Lockport, NY	716	14094-14095
Locust Grove, VA	540	22508
Lodi, CA	209	95240-95242
Lodi, NJ	862, 973	07644
Logan, IA	712	51546, 51550
Logan, OH	740	43138
Logan, UT	435	84321-84323, 84341
Logan, WV	304	25601
Logansport, IN	574	46947
Loganville, GA	470, 770	30052
Loma Linda, CA	909	92350, 92354-92357
Lombard, IL	331, 630	60148
Lompoc, CA	805	93436-93438
London, KY	606	40741-40745
London, OH	740	43140
Londonderry, NH	603	03053
Lone Tree, CO	303, 720	80112, 80124
Lone Tree, IA	319	52755
Lone Wolf, OK	580	73655
Long Beach, CA	562	90745-90749, 90801-90815*
Long Beach, MS	228	39560
Long Beach, NY	516	11561
Long Beach, WA	360	98631
Long Branch, NJ	732, 848	07740
Long Grove, IL	224, 847	60047-60049
Long Island City, NY	347, 718	11101-11109, 11120
Long Pond, PA	570	18334
Long Prairie, MN	320	56347
Long Valley, NJ	908	07853
Longboat Key, FL	941	34228
Longmeadow, MA	413	01106, 01116
Longmont, CO	303, 720	80501-80504
Longview, TX	903	75601-75608, 75615
Longview, WA	360	98632
Longwood, FL	321, 407	32750-32752, 32779, 32791
Lonoke, AR	501	72086
Lookout Mountain, GA	706, 762	30750
Lookout Mountain, TN	423	37350
Loomis, CA	916	95650
Lorain, OH	440	44052-44055
Lordsburg, NM	505	88009, 88045, 88055
Lorenzo, TX	806	79343
Loretto, KY	270	40037
Loretto, PA	814	15940
Loretto, TN	931	38469
Loris, SC	843	29569
Lorman, MS	601, 769	39096
Lorton, VA	571, 703	22079, 22199
Los Alamitos, CA	562, 714	90720-90721
Los Alamos, NM	505	87544-87545
Los Altos, CA	650	94022-94024
Los Altos Hills, CA	650	94022-94024
Los Angeles, CA	213, 310, 323, 424	90001-90103, 90174, 90185*
Los Angeles AFB, CA	310, 424	90009

Partial list of zip codes, including main range

City	Area Code(s)	Zip Code(s)
Los Banos, CA	209	93635
Los Gatos, CA	408	95030-95033
Los Lunas, NM	505	87031
Lostine, OR	541, 458	97857
Lotus, CA	530	95651
Loudon, NH	603	03307
Loudon, TN	865	37774
Loudonville, NY	518	12211
Loudonville, OH	419, 567	44842
Louisa, KY	606	41201, 41230
Louisa, VA	540	23093
Louisburg, NC	919	27549
Louisville, CO	303, 720	80027-80028
Louisville, GA	478	30434
Louisville, IL	618	62858
Louisville, KY	502	40201-40233, 40241-40245*
Louisville, MS	662	39339
Louisville, OH	234, 330	44641
Louisville, TN	865	37777
Loup City, NE	308	68853
Loveland, CO	970	80537-80539
Loveland, OH	513	45111, 45140
Lovell, WY	307	82431
Lovelock, NV	775	89419
Loves Park, IL	815	61111, 61130-61132
Lovingston, VA	434	22949
Lovington, NM	505	88260
Low Moor, VA	540	24457
Lowell, AR	479	72745
Lowell, FL	352	32663
Lowell, IN	219	46356
Lowell, MA	351, 978	01850-01854
Lowell, MI	616	49331
Lowellville, OH	234, 330	44436
Lower Burrell, PA	724, 878	15068
Lower Gwynedd, PA	215, 267	19002
Lower Waterford, VT	802	05848
Lowville, NY	315	13367
Loxahatchee, FL	561	33470
Loysville, PA	717	17047
Lubbock, TX	806	79401-79416, 79423-79424*
Lubec, ME	207	04652
Lucas, KY	270	42156
Lucasville, OH	740	45648, 45699
Lucedale, MS	601, 769	39452
Ludington, MI	231	49431
Ludlow, MA	413	01056
Ludlow, VT	802	05149
Ludowici, GA	912	31316
Lufkin, TX	936	75901-75904, 75915
Lugoff, SC	803	29078
Luke AFB, AZ	623	85307-85309
Lula, MS	662	38644
Luling, LA	985	70070
Lumber Bridge, NC	910	28357
Lumberton, NJ	856	08048
Lumberton, NC	910	28358-28360
Lumberton, TX	409	77657
Lumpkin, GA	229	31815
Lunenburg, MA	351, 978	01462
Lunenburg, VT	802	05906
Lunenburg, VA	434	23952
Luray, VA	540	22835
Lusk, WY	307	82225
Lutherville, MD	410	21093-21094
Lutsen, MN	218	55612
Luttrell, TN	865	37779
Luverne, AL	334	36049
Luverne, MN	507	56156
Luxemburg, WI	920	54217
Lykens, PA	717	17048
Lyman, SC	864	29365
Lyme, NH	603	03768
Lynbrook, NY	516	11563-11564
Lynchburg, TN	931	37352
Lynchburg, VA	434	24501-24506, 24512-24515
Lyndhurst, NJ	201, 551	07071
Lyndon, KS	785	66451
Lyndonville, NY	585	14098
Lyndonville, VT	802	05851
Lynn, IN	765	47355
Lynn, MA	339, 781	01901-01905, 01910
Lynn Haven, FL	850	32444
Lynnfield, MA	339, 781	01940
Lynnwood, WA	425	98036-98037, 98046
Lynwood, CA	310, 424	90262
Lyon, MS	662	38645
Lyon Mountain, NY	518	12952-12955
Lyon Station, PA	484, 610	19536
Lyons, CO	303, 720	80540
Lyons, GA	912	30436
Lyons, KS	620	67554
Lyons, NJ	908	07939
Lyons, NY	315	14489
Lyons, OR	503, 971	97358

M

City	Area Code(s)	Zip Code(s)
Mableton, GA	404, 470	30126
Macclenny, FL	386	32063
MacDill AFB, FL	813	33608
Macedon, NY	315	14502
Macedonia, OH	234, 330	44056
Machesney Park, IL	815	61115
Machias, ME	207	04654, 04686
Machiasport, ME	207	04655
Mackay, ID	208	83251
Mackinac Island, MI	906	49757
Mackinaw City, MI	231	49701
Macomb, IL	309	61455
Macomb, MI	586	48042-48044
Macomb Township, MI	586	48042-48044
Macon, GA	478	31201-31221, 31294-31299
Macon, MS	662	39341
Macon, MO	660	63552
Macungie, PA	484, 610	18062
Macy, IN	574	46951
Macy, NE	402	68039
Maddock, ND	701	58348
Madeira Beach, FL	727	33708, 33738
Madelia, MN	507	56062
Madera, CA	559	93637-93639
Madill, OK	580	73446
Madison, AL	256	35756-35758
Madison, CT	203	06443
Madison, FL	850	32340-32341
Madison, GA	706, 762	30650
Madison, IL	618	62060
Madison, IN	812	47250
Madison, ME	207	04950
Madison, MN	320	56256
Madison, MS	601, 769	39110, 39130
Madison, NE	402	68748
Madison, NJ	862, 973	07940
Madison, NC	336	27025
Madison, OH	440	44057
Madison, SD	605	57042
Madison, TN	615	37115-37116
Madison, VA	540	22719, 22727
Madison, WV	304	25130
Madison, WI	608	53562, 53593, 53701-53719*
Madison Heights, MI	248, 947	48071
Madisonville, KY	270	42431
Madisonville, LA	985	70447
Madisonville, TN	423	37354
Madisonville, TX	936	77864
Madras, OR	541, 458	97741
Maggie Valley, NC	828	28751
Magna, UT	801, 385	84044
Magnolia, AR	870	71753-71754
Magnolia, MS	601, 769	39652
Mahanoy City, PA	570	17948
Mahnomen, MN	218	56557
Mahomet, IL	217	61853
Mahopac, NY	845	10541
Mahwah, NJ	201, 551	07430, 07495-07498
Maiden, NC	828	28650
Maiden Rock, WI	715, 534	54750
Maitland, FL	321, 407	32751, 32794
Makanda, IL	618	62958
Makawao, HI	808	96768
Malad City, ID	208	83252
Malden, MA	339, 781	02148
Malden, MO	573	63863
Malibu, CA	310, 424	90263-90265
Malinta, OH	419, 567	43535
Malone, FL	850	32445
Malone, NY	518	12953
Malta, ID	208	83342
Malta, IL	815	60150
Malta, MT	406	59538
Malta, NY	518	12020
Malvern, AR	501	72104-72105
Malvern, OH	234, 330	44644
Malvern, PA	484, 610	19355
Malverne, NY	516	11565
Mamaroneck, NY	914	10543
Mammoth Cave, KY	270	42259
Mammoth Lakes, CA	760, 442	93546
Mamou, LA	337	70554
Manahawkin, NJ	609	08050
Manalapan, FL	561	33462
Manalapan, NJ	732, 848	07726
Manasquan, NJ	732, 848	08736
Manassas, VA	571, 703	20108-20113
Manassas Park, VA	571, 703	20111
Manawa, WI	920	54949
Manchester, CT	860	06040-06045
Manchester, IA	563	52057
Manchester, KY	606	40962
Manchester, ME	207	04351
Manchester, MI	734	48158
Manchester, NH	603	03101-03111
Manchester, TN	931	37349, 37355
Manchester, VT	802	05254
Manchester Center, VT	802	05255
Manchester Village, VT	802	05254
Mancos, CO	970	81328
Mandan, ND	701	58554
Mandeville, LA	985	70448, 70470-70471
Mangum, OK	580	73554
Manhasset, NY	516	11030
Manhattan, KS	785	66502-66506
Manhattan Beach, CA	310, 424	90266-90267
Manheim, PA	717	17545
Manila, UT	435	84046
Manistee, MI	231	49660
Manistique, MI	906	49854
Manitou, OK	580	73555
Manitou Springs, CO	719	80829
Manitowoc, WI	920	54220-54221
Mankato, KS	785	66956
Mankato, MN	507	56001-56006
Manlius, NY	315	13104
Manning, IA	712	51455
Manning, ND	701	58642
Manning, SC	803	29102
Manor, TX	512	78653
Mansfield, AR	479	72944
Mansfield, CT	860	06250, 06268
Mansfield, LA	318	71052
Mansfield, MA	508, 774	02031, 02048
Mansfield, MO	417	65704
Mansfield, OH	419, 567	44901-44907, 44999
Mansfield, PA	570	16933
Mansfield, TX	682, 817	76063
Manson, NC	252	27553
Manteca, CA	209	95336-95337
Manteno, IL	815	60950
Manteo, NC	252	27954
Manti, UT	435	84642
Mantorville, MN	507	55955
Mantua, NJ	856	08051
Mantua, OH	234, 330	44255
Many, LA	318	71449
Maple Glen, PA	215, 267	19002
Maple Grove, MN	763	55311, 55369, 55569
Maple Heights, OH	216	44137
Maple Park, IL	331, 630	60151
Maple Plain, MN	763	55348, 55359, 55393, 55570*
Maple Shade, NJ	856	08052
Maple Valley, WA	425	98038
Mapleton, OR	541, 458	97453
Mapleville, RI	401	02839
Maplewood, MN	651	55109, 55117-55119
Maplewood, NJ	862, 973	07040
Maplewood, NY	518	12189
Mappsville, VA	757	23407
Maquoketa, IA	563	52060
Marana, AZ	520	85653
Marathon, FL	305, 786	33050-33052
Marathon, WI	715, 534	54448
Marble City, OK	918	74945
Marble Falls, TX	830	78654-78657
Marblehead, MA	339, 781	01945
Marblehead, OH	419, 567	43440

*Partial list of zip codes, including main range

City	Area Code(s)	Zip Code(s)
Marceline, MO	660	64658
Marcellus, NY	315	13108
Marco Island, FL	239	34145-34146
Marcus, IA	712	51035
Marcy, NY	315	13403
Marengo, IL	815	60152
Marengo, IA	319	52301
Marfa, TX	915	79843
Margate, FL	754, 954	33063-33068, 33073, 33093
Marianna, AR	870	72360
Marianna, FL	850	32446-32448
Maricopa, AZ	520	85239
Marietta, GA	470, 678, 770	30006-30008, 30060-30069*
Marietta, OH	740	45750
Marietta, OK	580	73448
Marietta, PA	717	17547
Marina, CA	831	93933
Marina del Rey, CA	310, 424	90291-90295
Marine City, MI	810	48039
Marinette, WI	715, 534	54143
Marion, AL	334	36756
Marion, AR	870	72364
Marion, IL	618	62959
Marion, IN	765	46952-46953
Marion, IA	319	52302
Marion, KS	620	66861
Marion, KY	270	42064
Marion, MA	508, 774	02738
Marion, NY	315	14505
Marion, NC	828	28737, 28752
Marion, OH	740	43301-43302, 43306-43307
Marion, SC	843	29571
Marion, SD	605	57043
Marion, VA	276	24354
Marion, WI	715, 534	54950
Mariposa, CA	209	95338
Marissa, IL	618	62257
Marked Tree, AR	870	72365
Markham, IL	708	60426
Markle, IN	260	46770
Markleeville, CA	530	96120
Marks, MS	662	38646
Marksville, LA	318	71351
Marlboro, NJ	732, 848	07746
Marlboro, VT	802	05344
Marlborough, MA	508, 774	01752
Marlin, TX	254	76661
Marlinton, WV	304	24954
Marlow Heights, MD	301	20746-20748
Marlton, NJ	856	08053
Marquette, MI	906	49855
Marrero, LA	504	70072-70073
Marriottsville, MD	410	21104
Mars, PA	724, 878	16046
Mars Hill, NC	828	28754
Marshall, AR	870	72650
Marshall, IL	217	62441
Marshall, MI	616	49068-49069
Marshall, MN	507	56258
Marshall, MO	660	65340
Marshall, NC	828	28753
Marshall, TX	903	75670-75672
Marshall, WI	608	53559
Marshalls Creek, PA	570	18335
Marshalltown, IA	641	50158
Marshfield, MA	339, 781	02020, 02041, 02047-02051*
Marshfield, MO	417	65706
Marshfield, WI	715, 534	54404, 54441, 54449, 54472
Marshville, NC	704, 980	28103
Marstons Mills, MA	508, 774	02648
Martin, SD	605	57551
Martin, TN	731	38237-38238
Martinez, CA	925	94553
Martinez, GA	706, 762	30907
Martins Ferry, OH	740	43935
Martinsburg, WV	304	25401-25402
Martinsdale, MT	406	59053
Martinsville, IN	765	46151
Martinsville, VA	276	24112-24115
Maryland Heights, MO	314	63043
Marylhurst, OR	503, 971	97036
Marysville, CA	530	95901-95903
Marysville, KS	785	66508, 66555
Marysville, MI	810	48040
Marysville, OH	937	43040-43041
Marysville, PA	717	17053
Marysville, WA	360	98270-98271
Maryville, IL	618	62062
Maryville, MO	660	64468
Maryville, TN	865	37801-37804
Mascot, TN	865	37806
Mashantucket, CT	860	06339
Mashpee, MA	508, 774	02649
Mason, MI	517	48854
Mason, OH	513	45040
Mason, TX	915	76856
Mason City, IA	641	50401-50402, 50467
Maspeth, NY	347, 718	11378
Massapequa, NY	516	11758
Massena, IA	712	50853
Massena, NY	315	13662
Massillon, OH	234, 330	44646-44648
Matador, TX	806	79244
Matawan, NJ	732, 848	07747
Mather, CA	916	95655
Mathews, LA	985	70375
Mathews, VA	804	23109
Matteson, IL	708	60443
Matthews, NC	704, 980	28104-28106
Mattoon, IL	217	61938
Mattoon, WI	715, 534	54450
Mauldin, SC	864	29662
Maumee, OH	419, 567	43537
Maumelle, AR	501	72113, 72118
Maunaloa, HI	808	96770
Maury, NC	252	28554
Mauston, WI	608	53948
Maxton, NC	910	28364
Maxwell AFB, AL	334	36112-36113
Mayaguez, PR	787, 939	00680-00682
Maybrook, NY	845	12543
Mayersville, MS	662	39113
Mayetta, KS	785	66509
Mayfield, KY	270	42066
Mayfield, PA	570	18433
Mayfield Heights, OH	440	44124
Mayfield Village, OH	440	44143
Mayhill, NM	505	88339
Maynard, IA	563	50655
Maynard, MA	351, 978	01754
Maynardville, TN	865	37807
Mayo, FL	386	32066
Mayport, FL	904	32227-32228
Mays Landing, NJ	609	08330
Maysville, KY	606	41056
Maysville, MO	816	64469
Mayville, NY	716	14757
Mayville, ND	701	58257
Mayville, WI	920	53050
Maywood, CA	323	90270
Maywood, IL	708	60153-60155
Maywood, NE	308	69038
Maywood, NJ	201, 551	07607
Mazama, WA	509	98833
Mazomanie, WI	608	53560
McAdenville, NC	704, 980	28101
McAfee, NJ	862, 973	07428
McAlester, OK	918	74501-74502
McAllen, TX	956	78501-78505
McArthur, OH	740	45651
McBee, SC	843	29101
McCall, ID	208	83635-83638
McCalla, AL	205	35111
McCaysville, GA	706, 762	30555
McChord AFB, WA	253	98438-98439, 98499
McClelland, IA	712	51548
McCloud, CA	530	96057
McClusky, ND	701	58463
McComb, MS	601, 769	39648-39649
McComb, OH	419, 567	45858
McConnell AFB, KS	316	67221
McConnellsburg, PA	717	17233
McConnellsville, NY	315	13401
McConnelsville, OH	740	43756
McCook, IL	708	60525
McCook, NE	308	69001
McCordsville, IN	317	46055
McCormick, SC	864	29835
McDermott, OH	740	45652
McDonough, GA	470, 770	30252-30253
McEwen, TN	931	37101
McFarland, WI	608	53558
McGraw, NY	607	13101
McGregor, IA	563	52157
McGregor, MN	218	55760
McGregor, TX	254	76657
McGuire AFB, NJ	609	08641
McHenry, IL	815	60050-60051
McHenry, MD	301	21541
McIntosh, SD	605	57641
McKee, KY	606	40447
McKees Rocks, PA	412, 878	15136
McKeesport, PA	412, 878	15130
McKenzie, TN	731	38201
McKinleyville, CA	707	95519-95521
McKinney, TX	469, 972	75069-75071
McLean, TX	806	79057
McLean, VA	571, 703	22101-22106
McLeansboro, IL	618	62859
McLeansville, NC	336	27301
McLeod, MT	406	59052
McLoud, OK	405	74851
McLouth, KS	913	66054
McMinnville, OR	503, 971	97128
McMinnville, TN	931	37110-37111
McMurray, PA	724, 878	15317
McPherson, KS	620	67460
McRae, GA	229	31055
McShan, AL	205	35471
McSherrystown, PA	717	17344
Mead, WA	509	99021
Meade, KS	620	67864
Meadow Lands, PA	724, 878	15347
Meadowbrook, PA	215, 267	19046
Meadville, MS	601, 769	39653
Meadville, PA	814	16335, 16388
Mebane, NC	919	27302
Mechanicsburg, IL	217	62545
Mechanicsburg, PA	717	17050, 17055
Mechanicsville, VA	804	23111, 23116
Mechanicville, NY	518	12118
Medaryville, IN	219	47957
Medfield, MA	508, 774	02052
Medford, MA	339, 781	02153-02156
Medford, NJ	609	08055
Medford, NY	631	11763
Medford, OK	580	73759
Medford, OR	541, 458	97501-97504
Medford, WI	715, 534	54451
Media, PA	484, 610	19037, 19063-19065, 19086*
Medical Lake, WA	509	99022
Medicine Lake, MT	406	59247
Medicine Lodge, KS	620	67104
Medina, MN	763	55340, 55357-55359
Medina, NY	585	14103
Medina, OH	234, 330	44215, 44256-44258
Medley, FL	305, 786	33166, 33178
Medora, ND	701	58645
Medway, MA	508, 774	02053
Meeker, CO	970	81641
Mehoopany, PA	570	18629
Melba, ID	208	83641
Melbourne, AR	870	72556
Melbourne, FL	321	32901-32912, 32919, 32934*
Melbourne Beach, FL	321	32951
Melfa, VA	757	23410
Melrose, MA	339, 781	02176-02177
Melrose, MN	320	56352
Melrose Park, IL	708	60160-60165
Melrose Park, PA	215, 267	19027
Melville, NY	516, 631	11747, 11775
Melvin, IL	217	60952
Melvindale, MI	313	48122
Memphis, MO	660	63555
Memphis, TN	901	37501, 38101-38152, 38157*
Memphis, TX	806	79245
Mena, AR	479	71953
Menahga, MN	218	56464
Menan, ID	208	83434
Menard, IL	618	62259
Menard, TX	915	76859
Menasha, WI	920	54952
Mendenhall, MS	601, 769	39114

*Partial list of zip codes, including main range

City	Area Code(s)	Zip Code(s)
Mendham, NJ	862, 973	07945
Mendocino, CA	707	95460
Mendon, IL	217	62351
Mendon, MA	508, 774	01756
Mendota, CA	559	93640
Mendota, IL	815	61342
Mendota Heights, MN	651	55118-55120
Menlo, GA	706, 762	30731
Menlo Park, CA	650	94025-94029
Menominee, MI	906	49858
Menomonee Falls, WI	262	53051-53052
Menomonie, WI	715, 534	54751
Mentone, CA	909	92359
Mentone, IN	574	46539
Mentone, TX	915	79754
Mentor, OH	440	44060-44061
Mequon, WI	262	53092, 53097
Merced, CA	209	95340-95344, 95348
Mercedes, TX	956	78570
Mercer, PA	724, 878	16137
Mercer Island, WA	206	98040
Mercersburg, PA	717	17236
Mercerville, NJ	609	08619
Meredith, NH	603	03253
Meriden, CT	203	06450-06454
Meridian, GA	912	31319
Meridian, ID	208	83642, 83680
Meridian, MS	601, 769	39301-39309
Meridian, TX	254	76665
Merion, PA	484, 610	19066
Merkel, TX	915	79536
Merriam, KS	913	66202-66204
Merrick, NY	516	11566
Merrifield, VA	571, 703	22081-22082, 22116-22120
Merrill, MI	989	48637
Merrill, WI	715, 534	54452
Merrillville, IN	219	46410-46411
Merrimac, MA	351, 978	01860
Merrimac, WI	608	53561
Merrimack, NH	603	03054
Merritt Island, FL	321	32952-32954
Mertzon, TX	915	76941
Mertztown, PA	484, 610	19539
Mesa, AZ	480	85201-85216, 85274-85277
Mesa Verde National Park, CO	970	81330
Mesilla Park, NM	505	88047
Mesquite, NV	702	89024-89027
Mesquite, TX	469, 972	75149-75150, 75180-75187
Metairie, LA	504	70001-70011, 70033, 70055*
Metamora, IL	309	61548
Metcalf, GA	229	31792
Methuen, MA	351, 978	01844
Metlakatla, AK	907	99926
Metropolis, IL	618	62960
Metter, GA	912	30439
Metuchen, NJ	732, 848	08840
Mexia, TX	254	76667
Mexico, MO	573	65265
Mexico, NY	315	13114
Meyersdale, PA	814	15552
Miami, FL	305, 786	33010-33018, 33054-33056*
Miami, OK	918	74354-74355
Miami, TX	806	79059
Miami Beach, FL	305, 786	33109, 33119, 33139-33141*
Miami Lakes, FL	305, 786	33014-33018
Miami Shores, FL	305, 786	33138, 33150-33153, 33161*
Miami Springs, FL	305, 786	33166, 33266
Miamisburg, OH	937	45342-45343
Micanopy, FL	352	32667
Micaville, NC	828	28755
Michigan City, IN	219	46360-46361
Middle Granville, NY	518	12849
Middle Island, NY	631	11953
Middle River, MD	410	21220
Middle Village, NY	347, 718	11379
Middleboro, MA	508, 774	02344-02349
Middlebourne, WV	304	26149
Middleburg, PA	570	17842
Middleburg, VA	540	20117-20118
Middleburg Heights, OH	440	44130
Middlebury, CT	203	06762
Middlebury, IN	574	46540
Middlebury, VT	802	05753
Middlefield, CT	860	06455
Middlefield, OH	440	44062
Middleport, NY	585	14105
Middlesboro, KY	606	40965
Middlesex, NJ	732, 848	08846
Middleton, MA	351, 978	01949
Middleton, NH	603	03887
Middleton, WI	608	53562
Middletown, CA	707	95461
Middletown, CT	860	06457-06459
Middletown, DE	302	19709
Middletown, NJ	732, 848	07748
Middletown, NY	845	10940-10943
Middletown, OH	513	45042-45044
Middletown, PA	717	17057
Middletown, RI	401	02840-02842
Middletown, VA	540	22645, 22649
Midland, GA	706, 762	31820
Midland, MI	989	48640-48642, 48667-48670*
Midland, NC	704, 980	28107
Midland, TX	915	79701-79712
Midland, VA	540	22728
Midland Park, NJ	201, 551	07432
Midlothian, IL	708	60445
Midlothian, TX	469, 972	76065
Midlothian, VA	804	23112-23114
Midvale, UT	801, 385	84047
Midway, FL	850	32343
Midway, GA	912	31320
Midway, KY	859	40347
Midway, UT	435	84049
Midwest City, OK	405	73110, 73130, 73140, 73145
Mifflinburg, PA	570	17844
Mifflintown, PA	717	17059
Milaca, MN	320	56353
Milan, GA	229	31060
Milan, IL	309	61264
Milan, MI	734	48160
Milan, MO	660	63556
Milan, OH	419, 567	44846
Milan, TN	731	38358
Milbank, SD	605	57252-57253
Milbridge, ME	207	04658
Miles City, MT	406	59301
Milford, CT	203	06460
Milford, DE	302	19963
Milford, IN	574	46542
Milford, IA	712	51351
Milford, MA	508, 774	01757
Milford, MI	248, 947	48380-48381
Milford, NE	402	68405
Milford, NH	603	03055
Milford, OH	513	45150
Milford, PA	570	18337
Mililani, HI	808	96789
Mill City, OR	503, 971	97360
Mill Run, PA	724, 878	15464
Mill Valley, CA	415	94941-94942
Millboro, VA	540	24460
Millbrae, CA	650	94030-94031
Millbrook, NY	845	12545
Millburn, NJ	862, 973	07041
Millbury, MA	508, 774	01527, 01586
Millbury, OH	419, 567	43447
Milldale, CT	860	06467
Milledgeville, GA	478	31059-31062
Millen, GA	478	30442
Miller, SD	605	57362
Millersburg, OH	234, 330	44654
Millersburg, PA	717	17061
Millersville, MD	410	21108
Millersville, PA	717	17551
Millersville, TN	615	37072
Millerton, NY	518	12546
Milligan College, TN	423	37682
Millington, TN	901	38053-38055, 38083
Millinocket, ME	207	04462
Millis, MA	508, 774	02054
Mills, WY	307	82604, 82644
Millville, NJ	856	08332
Millwood, VA	540	22646
Milpitas, CA	408	95035-95036
Milroy, IN	765	46156
Milton, FL	850	32570-32572, 32583
Milton, MA	617, 857	02186
Milton, NY	845	12547
Milton, PA	570	17847
Milton, WV	304	25541
Milton, WI	608	53563
Milton-Freewater, OR	541, 458	97862
Milwaukee, WI	414	53201-53228, 53233-53237*
Milwaukie, OR	503, 971	97222, 97267-97269
Minden, LA	318	71055-71058
Minden, NE	308	68959
Minden, NV	775	89423
Mineola, NY	516	11501
Mineral, CA	530	96061-96063
Mineral Point, MO	573	63660
Mineral Wells, TX	940	76067-76068
Mineral Wells, WV	304	26120-26121, 26150
Minersville, PA	570	17954
Minerva, OH	234, 330	44657
Mineville, NY	518	12956
Mingo Junction, OH	740	43938
Minneapolis, KS	785	67467
Minneapolis, MN	612, 763, 952	55401-55450, 55454-55460*
Minnesota Lake, MN	507	56068
Minnetonka, MN	763, 952	55305, 55343-55345
Minnewaukan, ND	701	58351
Minonk, IL	309	61760
Minooka, IL	815	60447
Minot, ND	701	58701-58707, 58768
Minot AFB, ND	701	58704-58705
Minster, OH	419, 567	45865
Mio, MI	989	48647
Mira Loma, CA	951	91752
Miramar, FL	754, 954	33023-33029, 33083
Misenheimer, NC	704, 980	28109
Mishawaka, IN	574	46544-46546
Mishicot, WI	920	54228
Mission, KS	913	66201-66205, 66222
Mission, SD	605	57555
Mission, TX	956	78572-78573
Mission Hills, CA	818	91345-91346, 91395
Mission Viejo, CA	949	92675, 92690-92694
Mission Woods, KS	913	66205
Mississippi State, MS	662	39762
Missoula, MT	406	59801-59808, 59812
Missouri City, TX	281, 832	77459, 77489
Mitchell, IN	812	47446
Mitchell, NE	308	69357
Mitchell, SD	605	57301
Mitchells, VA	540	22729
Mitchellville, IA	515	50169
Mitchellville, MD	301	20716-20717, 20721
Moab, UT	435	84532
Moberly, MO	660	65270
Mobile, AL	251	36601-36633, 36640-36644*
Mocksville, NC	336	27028
Model City, NY	716	14107
Modesto, CA	209	95350-95358, 95397
Moffett Field, CA	650	94035
Mogadore, OH	234, 330	44260
Mohall, ND	701	58761
Mohawk, NY	315	13407
Mohnton, PA	484, 610	19540
Mojave, CA	661	93501-93502, 93519
Mokena, IL	708	60448
Molalla, OR	503, 971	97038
Moline, IL	309	61265-61266
Monaca, PA	724, 878	15061
Monahans, TX	915	79756
Monarch, CO	719	81227
Moncks Corner, SC	843	29430, 29461
Mondovi, WI	715, 534	54755, 54764
Monee, IL	708	60449
Monessen, PA	724, 878	15062
Monett, MO	417	65708
Monitor, WA	509	98836
Monmouth, IL	309	61462
Monmouth, OR	503, 971	97361
Monmouth Junction, NJ	732, 848	08852
Monona, IA	563	52159
Monongahela, PA	724, 878	15063
Monroe, CT	203	06468
Monroe, GA	470, 770	30655-30656
Monroe, IA	641	50170
Monroe, LA	318	71201-71203, 71207-71213
Monroe, MI	734	48161-48162

*Partial list of zip codes, including main range

City	Area Code(s)	Zip Code(s)
Monroe, NC	704, 980	28110-28112
Monroe, OH	513	45050, 45073, 45099
Monroe, WA	360	98272
Monroe, WI	608	53566
Monroe Township, NJ	609	08831
Monroeville, AL	251	36460-36462
Monroeville, PA	412, 878	15140, 15146
Monrovia, CA	626	91016-91017
Monsey, NY	845	10952
Mont Alto, PA	717	17237
Montague, MI	231	49437
Montague, TX	940	76251
Montauk, NY	631	11954
Montclair, CA	909	91763
Montclair, NJ	862, 973	07042-07043
Monte Vista, CO	719	81135, 81144
Montebello, CA	323	90640
Montebello, NY	845	10901
Montecito, CA	805	93108, 93150
Montello, WI	608	53949
Monterey, CA	831	93940-93944
Monterey, VA	540	24465
Monterey Park, CA	323, 626	91754-91756
Montesano, WA	360	98563
Montevallo, AL	205	35115
Montevideo, MN	320	56265
Montezuma, IA	641	50171
Montezuma, KS	620	67867
Montgomery, AL	334	36101-36125, 36130-36135*
Montgomery, IL	331, 630	60538
Montgomery, NY	845	12549
Montgomery, PA	570	17752
Montgomery, TX	936	77316, 77356
Montgomery, WV	304	25136
Montgomery City, MO	573	63361
Montgomery Village, MD	301	20877-20879, 20886
Montgomeryville, PA	215, 267	18936
Monticello, AR	870	71655-71657
Monticello, FL	850	32344-32345
Monticello, GA	706, 762	31064
Monticello, IL	217	61856
Monticello, IN	574	47960
Monticello, IA	319	52310
Monticello, KY	606	42633
Monticello, MN	763	55362-55365, 55561-55565*
Monticello, MS	601, 769	39654
Monticello, MO	573	63457
Monticello, NY	845	12701, 12777
Monticello, UT	435	84535
Montour Falls, NY	607	14865
Montoursville, PA	570	17754
Montpelier, IN	765	47359
Montpelier, OH	419, 567	43543
Montpelier, VT	802	05601-05604, 05609, 05620*
Montreat, NC	828	28757
Montrose, CA	818	91020-91021
Montrose, CO	970	81401-81402
Montrose, MI	810	48457
Montrose, NY	845	10548
Montrose, PA	570	18801
Montross, VA	804	22520
Montvale, NJ	201, 551	07645
Montville, NJ	862, 973	07045
Monument, OR	541, 458	97864
Moodus, CT	860	06469
Moody, AL	205	35004
Moon Township, PA	412, 878	15108
Moonachie, NJ	201, 551	07074
Moore, OK	405	73153, 73160, 73170
Moore Haven, FL	863	33471
Moorefield, WV	304	26836
Moorestown, NJ	856	08057
Mooresville, IN	317	46158
Mooresville, NC	704, 980	28115-28117
Moorhead, MN	218	56560-56563
Moorhead, MS	662	38761
Moorpark, CA	805	93020-93021
Moose, WY	307	83012
Moose Lake, MN	218	55767
Mooseheart, IL	331, 630	60539
Moosic, PA	570	18507
Moosup, CT	860	06354
Mora, MN	320	55051
Mora, NM	505	87732
Moraga, CA	925	94556, 94570, 94575
Moran, WY	307	83013
Moravia, NY	315	13118
Morehead, KY	606	40351
Morehead City, NC	252	28557
Morenci, AZ	928	85540
Morenci, MI	517	49256
Moreno Valley, CA	951	92551-92557
Morgan, GA	229	31766
Morgan, MN	507	56266
Morgan, UT	801, 385	84050
Morgan City, LA	985	70380-70381
Morgan Hill, CA	408	95037-95038
Morganfield, KY	270	42437
Morganton, NC	828	28655, 28680
Morgantown, KY	270	42261
Morgantown, PA	484, 610	19543
Morgantown, WV	304	26501-26508
Moro, OR	541, 458	97039
Moroni, UT	435	84646
Morrilton, AR	501	72110
Morris, AL	205	35116
Morris, IL	815	60450
Morris, MN	320	56267
Morris Plains, NJ	862, 973	07950
Morrison, CO	303, 720	80465
Morrison, IL	815	61270
Morristown, IN	765	46161
Morristown, NJ	862, 973	07960-07963
Morristown, OH	740	43759
Morristown, TN	423	37813-37816
Morrisville, NY	315	13408
Morrisville, NC	919	27560
Morrisville, PA	215, 267	19067
Morrisville, VT	802	05657, 05661
Morro Bay, CA	805	93442-93443
Morrow, GA	470, 770	30260, 30287
Morton, IL	309	61550
Morton, MN	507	56270
Morton, MS	601, 769	39117
Morton, TX	806	79346
Morton Grove, IL	224, 847	60053
Mosca, CO	719	81146
Moscow, ID	208	83843-83844
Moscow, TN	901	38057
Moselle, MS	601, 769	39459
Moses Lake, WA	509	98837
Mosinee, WI	715, 534	54455
Mosquero, NM	505	87733
Moss Beach, CA	650	94038
Moss Landing, CA	831	95039
Moss Point, MS	228	39562-39563, 39581
Motley, MN	218	56466
Mott, ND	701	58646
Moulton, AL	256	35650
Moultrie, GA	229	31768, 31776
Mound City, IL	618	62963
Mound City, KS	913	66056
Mound City, SD	605	57646
Moundridge, KS	620	67107
Mounds View, MN	763	55112
Moundsville, WV	304	26041
Mount Airy, NC	336	27030-27031
Mount Angel, OR	503, 971	97362
Mount Arlington, NJ	862, 973	07856
Mount Ayr, IA	641	50854
Mount Berry, GA	706, 762	30149
Mount Carmel, IL	618	62863
Mount Carmel, PA	570	17851
Mount Carroll, IL	815	61053
Mount Clemens, MI	586	48043-48046
Mount Crawford, VA	540	22841
Mount Crested Butte, CO	970	81225
Mount Dora, FL	352	32756-32757
Mount Freedom, NJ	862, 973	07970
Mount Gay, WV	304	25637
Mount Gilead, NC	910	27306
Mount Gilead, OH	419, 567	43338
Mount Holly, NJ	609	08060
Mount Holly, NC	704, 980	28120
Mount Hope, OH	234, 330	44660
Mount Ida, AR	870	71957
Mount Jackson, VA	540	22842
Mount Joy, PA	717	17552
Mount Juliet, TN	615	37121-37122
Mount Kisco, NY	914	10549
Mount Laurel, NJ	856	08054
Mount Lebanon, PA	412, 878	15228
Mount Marion, NY	845	12456
Mount Meigs, AL	334	36057
Mount Morris, IL	815	61054
Mount Morris, NY	585	14510
Mount Olive, MS	601, 769	39119
Mount Olive, NJ	862, 973	07828
Mount Olive, NC	919	28365
Mount Olive, WV	304	25185
Mount Olivet, KY	606	41064
Mount Pleasant, IA	319	52641
Mount Pleasant, MI	989	48804, 48858-48859
Mount Pleasant, NC	704, 980	28124
Mount Pleasant, PA	724, 878	15666
Mount Pleasant, SC	843	29464-29466
Mount Pleasant, TN	931	38474
Mount Pleasant, TX	903	75455-75456
Mount Pocono, PA	570	18344
Mount Prospect, IL	224, 847	60056
Mount Pulaski, IL	217	62548
Mount Royal, NJ	856	08061
Mount Shasta, CA	530	96067
Mount Solon, VA	540	22843
Mount Sterling, IL	217	62353
Mount Sterling, KY	859	40353
Mount Sterling, OH	740	43143
Mount Vernon, AL	251	36560
Mount Vernon, GA	912	30445
Mount Vernon, IL	618	62864
Mount Vernon, IN	812	47620
Mount Vernon, IA	319	52314
Mount Vernon, KY	606	40456
Mount Vernon, MO	417	65712
Mount Vernon, NY	914	10550-10553, 10557-10558
Mount Vernon, OH	740	43050
Mount Vernon, TX	903	75457
Mount Vernon, VA	571, 703	22121
Mount Vernon, WA	360	98273-98274
Mount Washington, KY	502	40047
Mount Wolf, PA	717	17347
Mountain City, TN	423	37683
Mountain Grove, MO	417	65711
Mountain Home, AR	870	72653-72654
Mountain Home, ID	208	83647
Mountain Home, TN	423	37684
Mountain Home AFB, ID	208	83648
Mountain Lakes, NJ	862, 973	07046
Mountain Pass, CA	760, 442	92366
Mountain Pine, AR	501	71956
Mountain Top, PA	570	18707
Mountain View, AR	870	72533, 72560
Mountain View, CA	650	94035, 94039-94043
Mountain View, MO	417	65548
Mountain View, WY	307	82939
Mountainair, NM	505	87036
Mountainside, NJ	908	07092
Mountlake Terrace, WA	425	98043
Moville, IA	712	51039
Moxee, WA	509	98936
Muenster, TX	940	76252
Mukilteo, WA	425	98275
Mukwonago, WI	262	53149
Mulberry, FL	863	33860
Muleshoe, TX	806	79347
Mullen, NE	308	69152
Mullica Hill, NJ	856	08062
Muncie, IN	765	47302-47308
Muncy, PA	570	17756
Mundelein, IL	224, 847	60060
Munfordville, KY	270	42765
Munhall, PA	412, 878	15120
Munising, MI	906	49862
Munroe Falls, OH	234, 330	44262
Munster, IN	219	46321
Murdo, SD	605	57559
Murdock, NE	402	68407
Murfreesboro, AR	870	71958
Murfreesboro, NC	252	27855
Murfreesboro, TN	615	37127-37133
Murphy, ID	208	83650
Murphy, NC	828	28906
Murphysboro, IL	618	62966
Murray, KY	270	42071
Murray, UT	801, 385	84107, 84117, 84121-84123*
Murray Hill, NJ	908	07974
Murrells Inlet, SC	843	29576

Partial list of zip codes, including main range

City	Area Code(s)	Zip Code(s)
Murrieta, CA	951	92562-92564
Murrysville, PA	724, 878	15668
Muscatine, IA	563	52761
Muscle Shoals, AL	256	35661-35662
Muskego, WI	262	53150
Muskegon, MI	231	49440-49445
Muskegon Heights, MI	231	49444
Muskogee, OK	918	74401-74403
Mustang, OK	405	73064
Myerstown, PA	717	17067
Myrtle Beach, SC	843	29572-29579, 29587-29588
Mystic, CT	860	06355, 06388

N

City	Area Code(s)	Zip Code(s)
Nacogdoches, TX	936	75961-75965
Nageezi, NM	505	87037
Nags Head, NC	252	27959
Nahunta, GA	912	31553
Naknek, AK	907	99633
Nampa, ID	208	83651-83653, 83686-83687
Nanticoke, MD	410	21840
Nanticoke, PA	570	18634
Nantucket, MA	508, 774	02554, 02564, 02584
Nanuet, NY	845	10954
Napa, CA	707	94558-94559, 94581
Napanoch, NY	845	12458
Naperville, IL	331, 630	60540, 60563-60567
Naples, FL	239	34101-34120
Naples, NY	585	14512
Napoleon, ND	701	58561
Napoleon, OH	419, 567	43545
Napoleonville, LA	985	70390
Nappanee, IN	574	46550
Narberth, PA	484, 610	19072
Narragansett, RI	401	02874, 02879-02882
Naselle, WA	360	98638
Nashotah, WI	262	53058
Nashua, NH	603	03060-03064
Nashville, AR	870	71852
Nashville, GA	229	31639
Nashville, IL	618	62263
Nashville, IN	812	47448
Nashville, NC	252	27856
Nashville, TN	615	37201-37250
Nassau, NY	518	12123
Nassau Bay, TX	281, 832	77058, 77258
Nassawadox, VA	757	23413
Natchez, MS	601, 769	39120-39122
Natchitoches, LA	318	71457-71458, 71497
Nathrop, CO	719	81236
Natick, MA	508, 774	01760
National City, CA	619	91950-91951
Natrona Heights, PA	724, 878	15065
Natural Bridge Station, VA	540	24579
Naugatuck, CT	203	06770
Navarre, MN	952	55392
Navarre, OH	234, 330	44662
Navasota, TX	936	77868-77869
Navesink, NJ	732, 848	07752
Nazareth, PA	484, 610	18064
Nebo, NC	828	28761
Nebraska City, NE	402	68410
Nederland, TX	409	77627
Nedrow, NY	315	13120
Needham, MA	339, 781	02492-02494
Needham Heights, MA	339, 781	02494
Neenah, WI	920	54956-54957
Neillsville, WI	715, 534	54456
Neligh, NE	402	68756
Nellis AFB, NV	702	89191
Nelson, NE	402	68961
Nelsonville, OH	740	45764
Neodesha, KS	620	66757
Neosho, MO	417	64850-64853
Nephi, UT	435	84648
Neponset, IL	309	61345
Neptune, NJ	732, 848	07753-07754
Neptune Beach, FL	904	32266
Nespelem, WA	509	99155
Nesquehoning, PA	570	18240
Ness City, KS	785	67560
Netcong, NJ	862, 973	07857
Nettleton, MS	662	38858

City	Area Code(s)	Zip Code(s)
Nevada, IA	515	50201
Nevada, MO	417	64772
Nevada City, CA	530	95959
Neversink, NY	845	12765
New Albany, IN	812	47150-47151
New Albany, MS	662	38652
New Albany, OH	614	43054
New Augusta, MS	601, 769	39462
New Baltimore, MI	586	48047, 48051
New Bedford, MA	508, 774	02740-02746
New Berlin, NY	607	13411
New Berlin, WI	262	53146, 53151
New Bern, NC	252	28560-28564
New Bethlehem, PA	814	16242
New Bloomfield, PA	717	17068
New Boston, TX	903	75570
New Braunfels, TX	830	78130-78135
New Bremen, OH	419, 567	45869
New Brighton, MN	651	55112
New Brighton, PA	724, 878	15066
New Britain, CT	860	06050-06053
New Brunswick, NJ	732, 848	08901-08906, 08922, 08933*
New Canaan, CT	203	06840-06842
New Carlisle, IN	574	46552
New Carlisle, OH	937	45344
New Castle, CO	970	81647
New Castle, DE	302	19720-19721
New Castle, IN	765	47362
New Castle, KY	502	40050
New Castle, PA	724, 878	16101-16108
New Castle, VA	540	24127
New Century, KS	913	66031
New City, NY	845	10956
New Columbia, PA	570	17856
New Concord, OH	740	43762
New Cumberland, PA	717	17070
New Cumberland, WV	304	26047
New England, ND	701	58647
New Enterprise, PA	814	16664
New Era, MI	231	49446
New Fairfield, CT	203	06812
New Freedom, PA	717	17349
New Glarus, WI	608	53574
New Gretna, NJ	609	08224
New Hampton, IA	641	50659-50661
New Hampton, NY	845	10958
New Harbor, ME	207	04554, 04558
New Hartford, CT	860	06057
New Hartford, NY	315	13413
New Haven, CT	203	06501-06525, 06530-06540
New Haven, IN	260	46774
New Haven, MI	586	48048-48050
New Hill, NC	919	27562
New Holland, PA	717	17557
New Hope, MN	763	55427-55428
New Hope, PA	215, 267	18938
New Hyde Park, NY	516	11040-11044, 11099
New Iberia, LA	337	70560-70563
New Kensington, PA	724, 878	15068-15069
New Kent, VA	804	23124
New Kingstown, PA	717	17072
New Knoxville, OH	419, 567	45871
New Lebanon, NY	518	12125
New Lenox, IL	815	60451
New Lexington, OH	740	43764
New Lisbon, NJ	609	08064
New Lisbon, WI	608	53950
New London, CT	860	06320
New London, IA	319	52645
New London, MO	573	63459
New London, NH	603	03257
New London, OH	419, 567	44851
New London, WI	920	54961
New Madrid, MO	573	63869
New Market, VA	540	22844
New Martinsville, WV	304	26155
New Milford, CT	860	06776
New Milford, NJ	201, 551	07646
New Orleans, LA	504	70112-70131, 70139-70190*
New Oxford, PA	717	17350
New Paltz, NY	845	12561
New Paris, IN	574	46553
New Philadelphia, OH	234, 330	44663
New Port Richey, FL	727	34652-34656
New Providence, NJ	908	07974

City	Area Code(s)	Zip Code(s)
New Richmond, OH	513	45157
New Richmond, WI	715, 534	54017
New Roads, LA	225	70760
New Rochelle, NY	914	10801-10805
New Rockford, ND	701	58356
New Sharon, IA	641	50207
New Smyrna Beach, FL	386	32168-32170
New Springfield, OH	234, 330	44443
New Tazewell, TN	423	37824-37825
New Town, ND	701	58763
New Ulm, MN	507	56073
New Wilmington, PA	724, 878	16142, 16172
New Windsor, MD	410	21776
New Windsor, NY	845	12553
New York, NY	212, 646, 917	10001-10048, 10055, 10060*
New York Mills, MN	218	56567
New York Mills, NY	315	13417
Newark, CA	510	94560
Newark, DE	302	19702, 19711-19718, 19725*
Newark, NJ	862, 973	07101-07108, 07112-07114*
Newark, NY	315	14513
Newark, OH	740	43055-43058, 43093
Newaygo, MI	231	49337
Newberg, OR	503, 971	97132
Newberry, MI	906	49868
Newberry, SC	803	29108
Newburg, WI	262	53060
Newburgh, IN	812	47629-47630
Newburgh, NY	845	12550-12555
Newbury, OH	440	44065
Newbury Park, CA	805	91319-91320
Newburyport, MA	351, 978	01950-01951
Newcastle, WY	307	82701, 82715
Newcomerstown, OH	740	43832
Newell, SD	605	57760
Newell, WV	304	26050
Newfane, VT	802	05345
Newhall, CA	661	91321-91322, 91381-91382
Newington, CT	860	06111, 06131
Newington, NH	603	03801
Newington, VA	571, 703	22122
Newkirk, OK	580	74647
Newland, NC	828	28657
Newman Grove, NE	402	68758
Newnan, GA	470, 678, 770	30263-30265, 30271
Newport, AR	870	72112
Newport, DE	302	19804
Newport, IN	765	47966
Newport, KY	859	41071-41076, 41099
Newport, MN	651	55055
Newport, NH	603	03773
Newport, NC	252	28570
Newport, OR	541, 458	97365-97366
Newport, RI	401	02840-02841
Newport, TN	423	37821-37822
Newport, VT	802	05855
Newport, WA	509	99156
Newport Beach, CA	949	92657-92663
Newport News, VA	757	23600-23612, 23628
Newton, GA	229	31770
Newton, IL	618	62448
Newton, IA	641	50208
Newton, KS	316	67114-67117
Newton, MA	617, 857	02456-02468, 02495
Newton, NJ	862, 973	07860
Newton, NC	828	28658
Newton, TX	409	75966
Newton Center, MA	617, 857	02459
Newton Falls, OH	234, 330	44444
Newton Grove, NC	910	28366
Newton Upper Falls, MA	617, 857	02464
Newtonville, NY	518	12110, 12128
Newtown, CT	203	06470
Newtown, PA	215, 267	18940
Newtown Square, PA	484, 610	19073
Nezperce, ID	208	83543
Niagara Falls, NY	716	14301-14305
Niagara University, NY	716	14109
Niantic, CT	860	06357
Niceville, FL	850	32578, 32588
Nicholasville, KY	859	40340, 40356
Niles, IL	224, 847	60714
Niles, MI	616	49120-49121

**Partial list of zip codes, including main range*

City	Area Code(s)	Zip Code(s)
Niles, OH	234, 330	44446
Ninety Six, SC	864	29666
Niota, TN	423	37826
Nipomo, CA	805	93444
Niskayuna, NY	518	12309
Nisswa, MN	218	56468
Nixon, TX	830	78140
Noble, OK	405	73068
Noblesville, IN	317	46060-46061
Nocona, TX	940	76255
Nogales, AZ	520	85621, 85628, 85648, 85662
Nokomis, FL	941	34274-34275
Nome, AK	907	99762
Norco, CA	951	92860
Norcross, GA	470, 678, 770	30003, 30010, 30071, 30091*
Norfolk, CT	860	06058
Norfolk, MA	508, 774	02056
Norfolk, NE	402	68701-68702
Norfolk, VA	757	23500-23523, 23529-23530*
Normal, AL	256	35762
Normal, IL	309	61761, 61790
Norman, OK	405	73019, 73026, 73069-73072
Norridge, IL	708	60634, 60656, 60706
Norristown, PA	484, 610	19401-19409, 19488-19489
North Adams, MA	413	01247
North Amityville, NY	631	11701
North Andover, MA	351, 978	01845
North Anson, ME	207	04958
North Attleboro, MA	508, 774	02760-02763
North Augusta, SC	803	29841-29842, 29860-29861
North Aurora, IL	331, 630	60542
North Babylon, NY	631	11703
North Baltimore, OH	419, 567	45872
North Barrington, IL	224, 847	60010
North Bay Village, FL	305, 786	33141
North Bend, OR	541, 458	97459
North Bend, WA	425	98045
North Bergen, NJ	201, 551	07047
North Berwick, ME	207	03906
North Billerica, MA	351, 978	01862
North Branch, MN	651	55056
North Branch, NJ	908	08876
North Branford, CT	203	06471
North Brookfield, MA	508, 774	01535
North Brunswick, NJ	732, 848	08902
North Canton, OH	234, 330	44709, 44720
North Charleston, SC	843	29405-29406, 29410, 29415*
North Chelmsford, MA	351, 978	01863
North Chicago, IL	224, 847	60064, 60086-60088
North Chili, NY	585	14514
North Clarendon, VT	802	05759
North Conway, NH	603	03860
North Dartmouth, MA	508, 774	02747
North Dighton, MA	508, 774	02764
North East, MD	410	21901
North East, PA	814	16428
North Easton, MA	508, 774	02356-02357
North Falmouth, MA	508, 774	02556, 02565
North Fort Myers, FL	239	33903, 33917-33918
North Grafton, MA	508, 774	01536
North Grosvenordale, CT	860	06255
North Haledon, NJ	862, 973	07508, 07538
North Haven, CT	203	06473
North Haverhill, NH	603	03774
North Hero, VT	802	05474
North Highlands, CA	916	95660
North Hills, CA	818	91343, 91393
North Hollywood, CA	818	91601-91618
North Huntingdon, PA	724, 878	15642
North Judson, IN	574	46366
North Kansas City, MO	816	64116
North Kingstown, RI	401	02852-02854, 02874
North Kingsville, OH	440	44068
North Lake, WI	262	53064
North Las Vegas, NV	702	89030-89036, 89084-89086
North Liberty, IA	319	52317
North Lima, OH	234, 330	44452
North Little Rock, AR	501	72113-72120, 72124, 72190*
North Logan, UT	435	84341
North Manchester, IN	260	46962
North Mankato, MN	507	56002-56003
North Miami, FL	305, 786	33161-33162, 33167-33169*
North Miami Beach, FL	305, 786	33160-33162, 33169, 33179*
North Monmouth, ME	207	04265
North Myrtle Beach, SC	843	29582, 29597-29598
North Newton, KS	316	67117
North Olmsted, OH	440	44070
North Palm Beach, FL	561	33403, 33408-33410
North Pekin, IL	309	61554
North Plains, OR	503, 971	97133
North Platte, NE	308	69101-69103
North Providence, RI	401	02904, 02908-02911
North Quincy, MA	617, 857	02171
North Redington Beach, FL	727	33708
North Richland Hills, TX	682, 817	76118, 76180-76182
North Ridgeville, OH	440	44035, 44039
North Riverside, IL	708	60546
North Royalton, OH	440	44133
North Saint Paul, MN	651	55109
North Salt Lake, UT	801, 385	84054
North Scituate, RI	401	02857
North Sioux City, SD	605	57049
North Smithfield, RI	401	02824, 02896
North Springfield, VT	802	05150
North Stonington, CT	860	06359
North Syracuse, NY	315	13212
North Tonawanda, NY	716	14120
North Vernon, IN	812	47265
North Versailles, PA	412, 878	15137
North Wales, PA	215, 267	19436, 19454-19455, 19477
North Warren, PA	814	16365
North Webster, IN	574	46555
North White Plains, NY	914	10603
North Wilkesboro, NC	336	28656-28659, 28674
Northampton, MA	413	01060-01063
Northampton, PA	484, 610	18067
Northborough, MA	508, 774	01532
Northbrook, IL	224, 847	60062-60065
Northeast Harbor, ME	207	04662
Northfield, IL	224, 847	60093
Northfield, MN	507	55057
Northfield, NJ	609	08225
Northfield, OH	234, 330	44056, 44067
Northfield, VT	802	05663
Northford, CT	203	06472
Northlake, IL	708	60164
Northport, AL	205	35473-35476
Northport, NY	631	11768
Northridge, CA	818	91324-91330, 91343
Northumberland, PA	570	17857
Northvale, NJ	201, 551	07647
Northville, MI	248	48167
Northwood, IA	641	50459
Northwood, OH	419, 567	43605, 43619
Norton, KS	785	67654
Norton, MA	508, 774	02766
Norton, OH	234, 330	44203
Norton, VA	276	24273
Norton Shores, MI	231	49441
Norwalk, CA	562	90650-90652, 90659
Norwalk, CT	203	06850-06860
Norwalk, OH	419, 567	44857
Norway, IA	319	52318
Norwell, MA	339, 781	02018, 02061
Norwich, CT	860	06351, 06360, 06365
Norwich, KS	620	67118
Norwich, NY	607	13815
Norwich, OH	740	43767
Norwood, MA	339, 781	02062
Norwood, MN	952	55368, 55383, 55554, 55583
Norwood, NJ	201, 551	07648
Norwood, NC	704, 980	28128
Norwood, OH	513	45207, 45212
Notre Dame, IN	574	46556
Nottingham, PA	484, 610	19362
Nottoway, VA	434	23955
Novato, CA	415	94945-94949, 94998
Novi, MI	248, 947	48374-48377
Nowata, OK	918	74048
Nucla, CO	970	81424
Nuevo, CA	951	92567
Nutley, NJ	862, 973	07110
Nyack, NY	845	10960
Nyssa, OR	541, 458	97913

O

City	Area Code(s)	Zip Code(s)
Oak Brook, IL	331, 630	60521-60523, 60527, 60561
Oak Creek, WI	414	53154
Oak Forest, IL	708	60452
Oak Grove, LA	318	71263
Oak Grove, OR	503, 971	97222, 97267-97268
Oak Grove, VA	804	22443
Oak Harbor, WA	360	98277-98278
Oak Hill, WV	304	25901
Oak Lawn, IL	708	60453-60459
Oak Park, IL	708	60301-60304
Oak Park, MI	248, 947	48237
Oak Ridge, NJ	862, 973	07438
Oak Ridge, TN	865	37830-37831
Oakbrook Terrace, IL	331, 630	60181
Oakdale, CA	209	95361
Oakdale, LA	318	71463
Oakdale, MN	651	55042, 55128
Oakdale, NY	631	11769
Oakdale, PA	412, 878	15071
Oakdale, WI	608	54649
Oakham, MA	508, 774	01068
Oakhurst, CA	559	93644
Oakhurst, NJ	732, 848	07755
Oakland, CA	510	94601-94627, 94643, 94649*
Oakland, MD	301	21550
Oakland, NJ	201, 551	07436
Oakland, TN	901	38060
Oakland City, IN	812	47660
Oakland Park, FL	754, 954	33304-33311, 33334
Oakley, CA	925	94513, 94561
Oakley, KS	785	67748
Oakmont, PA	412, 878	15139
Oaks, PA	484, 610	19456
Oakton, VA	571, 703	22124
Oakville, CA	707	94562
Oakville, IA	319	52646
Oakwood, GA	470, 770	30502, 30566
Oakwood, OH	419, 567	45409, 45419, 45873
Oakwood, VA	276	24631
Oakwood Village, OH	440	44146
Oberlin, KS	785	67749
Oberlin, LA	337	70655
Oberlin, OH	440	44074
Oblong, IL	618	62449
Ocala, FL	352	34470-34483
Ocean, NJ	732, 848	07712
Ocean City, MD	410	21842-21843
Ocean City, NJ	609	08226
Ocean Shores, WA	360	98569
Ocean Springs, MS	228	39564-39566
Oceano, CA	805	93445
Oceanport, NJ	732, 848	07757
Oceanside, CA	760, 442	92049-92058
Oceanside, NY	516	11572
Oceanville, NJ	609	08231
Ochopee, FL	239	34141
Ocilla, GA	229	31774
Ocoee, FL	321, 407	34761
Oconomowoc, WI	262	53066
Oconto, WI	920	54153
Oconto Falls, WI	920	54154
Odenton, MD	410	21113
Odessa, FL	813	33556
Odessa, MO	816	64076
Odessa, TX	915	79760-79769
Odessa, WA	509	99144, 99159
Odon, IN	812	47562
Odum, GA	912	31555
Oelwein, IA	319	50662
O'Fallon, MO	636	63366-63367
Offutt AFB, NE	402	68113
Ogallala, NE	308	69153
Ogden, UT	801, 385	84201, 84244, 84401-84415
Ogdensburg, NY	315	13669
Oglesby, IL	815	61348
Oglethorpe, GA	478	31068
Ogunquit, ME	207	03907
Oil City, PA	814	16301
Ojai, CA	805	93023-93024
Ojo Caliente, NM	505	87549
Ojus, FL	305, 786	33163, 33180

*Partial list of zip codes, including main range

City	Area Code(s)	Zip Code(s)
Okahumpka, FL	352	34762
Okanogan, WA	509	98840
Okarche, OK	405	73762
Okeechobee, FL	863	34972-34974
Okemah, OK	918	74859
Okemos, MI	517	48805, 48864
Oklahoma City, OK	405	73101-73173, 73177-73180*
Okmulgee, OK	918	74447
Olathe, KS	913	66051, 66061-66063
Old Bethpage, NY	631	11804
Old Bridge, NJ	732, 848	08857
Old Brookville, NY	516	11545-11548
Old Chatham, NY	518	12136
Old Forge, PA	570	18518
Old Fort, NC	828	28762
Old Greenwich, CT	203	06870
Old Hickory, TN	615	37138
Old Lyme, CT	860	06371
Old Orchard Beach, ME	207	04064
Old Saybrook, CT	860	06475
Old Town, ME	207	04468
Old Westbury, NY	516	11568
Oldwick, NJ	908	08858
Olean, NY	585	14760
Olive Branch, MS	662	38654
Olive Hill, KY	606	41164
Olivet, MI	616	49076
Olivet, SD	605	57052
Olivia, MN	320	56277
Olney, IL	618	62450
Olney, MD	301	20830-20832
Olney, TX	940	76374
Olustee, FL	386	32072
Olympia, WA	360	98501-98516, 98599
Olympia Fields, IL	708	60461
Olympic Valley, CA	530	96146
Olyphant, PA	570	18447-18448
Omaha, NE	402	68046, 68101-68147, 68152*
Omak, WA	509	98841
Onalaska, WI	608	54650
Onamia, MN	320	56359
Onawa, IA	712	51040
Onaway, MI	989	49765
Oneida, NY	315	13421
Oneida, TN	423	37841
Oneida, WI	920	54155
O'Neill, NE	402	68763
Oneonta, AL	205	35121
Oneonta, NY	607	13820
Onida, SD	605	57564
Onley, VA	757	23418
Only, TN	931	37140
Onsted, MI	517	49265
Ontario, CA	909	91758-91764, 91798
Ontario, NY	585	14519
Ontario, OR	541, 458	97914
Ontonagon, MI	906	49953
Ooltewah, TN	423	37363
Opa Locka, FL	305, 786	33014, 33054-33056
Opelika, AL	334	36801-36804
Opelousas, LA	337	70570-70571
Opheim, MT	406	59250
Opp, AL	334	36467
Oquawka, IL	309	61469
Oracle, AZ	520	85623
Oradell, NJ	201, 551	07649
Orange, CA	714	92856-92869
Orange, CT	203	06477
Orange, MA	351, 978	01355, 01364, 01378
Orange, NJ	862, 973	07050-07051
Orange, TX	409	77630-77632
Orange, VA	540	22960
Orange Beach, AL	251	36561
Orange City, IA	712	51041
Orange Cove, CA	559	93646, 93675
Orange Park, FL	904	32003-32006, 32065-32067*
Orange Village, OH	216	44022, 44122, 44128, 44146
Orangeburg, NY	845	10962
Orangeburg, SC	803	29115-29118
Orangevale, CA	916	95662
Orchard Lake, MI	248, 947	48323-48324
Orchard Park, NY	716	14127
Ord, NE	308	68862
Ordway, CO	719	81063
Orefield, PA	484, 610	18069
Oregon, IL	815	61061
Oregon, MO	660	64473
Oregon, OH	419, 567	43605, 43616-43618
Oregon, WI	608	53575
Oregon City, OR	503, 971	97045
Orem, UT	801, 385	84057-84059, 84097
Orestes, IN	765	46063
Orient, OH	614	43146
Oriental, NC	252	28571
Orinda, CA	925	94563
Orion, MI	248, 947	48359-48362
Oriskany, NY	315	13424
Orland, CA	530	95963
Orland Park, IL	708	60462, 60467
Orlando, FL	321, 407	32801-32839, 32853-32862*
Orleans, IN	812	47452
Orleans, MA	508, 774	02653
Ormond Beach, FL	386	32173-32176
Orofino, ID	208	83544
Orondo, WA	509	98843
Orono, ME	207	04469, 04473
Orosi, CA	559	93647
Oroville, CA	530	95915, 95940, 95965-95966*
Orrtanna, PA	717	17353
Orrville, OH	234, 330	44667
Ortonville, MI	248, 947	48462
Ortonville, MN	320	56278
Orwigsburg, PA	570	17961
Osage, IA	641	50454, 50461
Osage Beach, MO	573	65065
Osage City, KS	785	66523
Osawatomie, KS	913	66064
Osborne, KS	785	67473
Osceola, AR	870	72370
Osceola, IA	641	50213
Osceola, MO	417	64776
Osceola, NE	402	68651
Osceola, WI	715, 534	54020
Osceola Mills, PA	814	16666
Oscoda, MI	989	48750
Osgood, IN	812	47037
Osgood, OH	419, 567	45351
Oshkosh, NE	308	69154, 69190
Oshkosh, WI	920	54901-54906
Oskaloosa, IA	641	52577
Oskaloosa, KS	785	66066
Osseo, MN	763	55311, 55369, 55569
Ossining, NY	914	10562
Ossipee, NH	603	03864
Osterville, MA	508, 774	02655
Oswego, IL	331, 630	60543
Oswego, KS	620	67356
Oswego, NY	315	13126
Otisville, NY	845	10963
Otsego, MI	616	49078
Ottawa, IL	815	61350
Ottawa, KS	785	66067
Ottawa, OH	419, 567	45875
Ottawa Lake, MI	734	49267
Otter River, MA	351, 978	01436
Otter Rock, OR	541, 458	97369
Ottsville, PA	484, 610	18942
Ottumwa, IA	641	52501
Ouray, CO	970	81427
Overland Park, KS	913	66202-66215, 66221-66225*
Overton, NV	702	89040
Oviedo, FL	321, 407	32762-32766
Owasso, OK	918	74055, 74073
Owatonna, MN	507	55060
Owego, NY	607	13827
Owen, WI	715, 534	54460
Owensboro, KY	270	42301-42304
Owensville, MO	573	65066
Owenton, KY	502	40359
Owings Mills, MD	410	21117
Owingsville, KY	606	40360
Owosso, MI	989	48841, 48867
Oxford, AL	256	36203
Oxford, CT	203	06478
Oxford, GA	470, 770	30054
Oxford, ME	207	04270
Oxford, MI	248, 947	48370-48371
Oxford, MS	662	38655
Oxford, NY	607	13830
Oxford, NC	919	27565
Oxford, OH	513	45056
Oxford, PA	484, 610	19363
Oxford, WI	608	53952
Oxnard, CA	805	93030-93035
Oyster Bay, NY	516	11771
Ozark, AL	334	36360-36361
Ozark, AR	479	72949
Ozark, MO	417	65721
Ozawkie, KS	785	66070
Ozona, TX	915	76943
Ozone Park, NY	347, 718	11416-11417

P

City	Area Code(s)	Zip Code(s)
Pablo, MT	406	59855
Pace, FL	850	32571
Pacheco, CA	925	94553
Pacific, MO	636	63069
Pacific, WA	253	98047
Pacific Beach, CA	858	92109
Pacific Grove, CA	831	93950
Pacific Palisades, CA	310, 424	90272
Pacifica, CA	650	94044-94045
Packwood, IA	319	52580
Pacoima, CA	818	91331-91334
Paden City, WV	304	26159
Paducah, KY	270	42001-42003
Paducah, TX	806	79248
Page, AZ	928	86036, 86040
Pageland, SC	843	29728
Pagosa Springs, CO	970	81147, 81157
Pahoa, HI	808	96778
Pahokee, FL	561	33476
Pahrump, NV	775	89041, 89048, 89060-89061
Paicines, CA	831	95043
Paincourtville, LA	985	70391
Painesville, OH	440	44077
Paint Rock, TX	915	76866
Painted Post, NY	607	14870
Paintsville, KY	606	41240
Palatine, IL	224, 847	60038, 60055, 60067, 60074*
Palatine Bridge, NY	518	13428
Palatka, FL	386	32177-32178
Palestine, TX	903	75801-75803, 75882
Palisade, NE	308	69040
Palisades, NY	845	10964
Palisades Park, NJ	201, 551	07650
Palm Bay, FL	321	32905-32911
Palm Beach, FL	561	33480
Palm Beach Gardens, FL	561	33403, 33408-33412, 33418*
Palm Beach Shores, FL	561	33404
Palm City, FL	772	34990-34991
Palm Coast, FL	386	32135-32137, 32142, 32164
Palm Desert, CA	760, 442	92210-92211, 92255, 92260*
Palm Harbor, FL	727	34682-34685
Palm Springs, CA	760, 442	92262-92264, 92292
Palmdale, CA	661	93550-93552, 93590-93591*
Palmer, AK	907	99645
Palmer, MA	413	01069
Palmerton, PA	484, 610	18071
Palmetto, FL	941	34220-34221
Palmetto, GA	470, 770	30268
Palmyra, IN	812	47164
Palmyra, MO	573	63461
Palmyra, NJ	856	08065
Palmyra, NY	315	14522
Palmyra, PA	717	17078
Palmyra, VA	434	22963
Palmyra, WI	262	53156
Palo Alto, CA	650	94301-94310
Palo Pinto, TX	940	76484
Palos Heights, IL	708	60463
Palos Hills, IL	708	60465
Palos Verdes Peninsula, CA	310, 424	90274-90275
Pampa, TX	806	79065-79066
Pana, IL	217	62557
Panama City, FL	850	32401-32413, 32417, 32461
Panama City Beach, FL	850	32401, 32407-32408, 32413*
Panguitch, UT	435	84759
Panhandle, TX	806	79068
Panorama City, CA	818	91402, 91412
Pantego, NC	252	27860
Paola, KS	913	66071

**Partial list of zip codes, including main range*

City	Area Code(s)	Zip Code(s)
Paoli, IN	812	47454
Paoli, PA	484, 610	19301
Paonia, CO	970	81428
Papaikou, HI	808	96781
Papillion, NE	402	68046, 68133, 68157
Paradise, CA	530	95967-95969
Paradise, PA	717	17562
Paragould, AR	870	72450-72451
Paramount, CA	562	90723
Paramus, NJ	201, 551	07652-07653
Parchman, MS	662	38738
Paris, ID	208	83261, 83287
Paris, IL	217	61944
Paris, KY	859	40361-40362
Paris, MO	660	65275
Paris, TN	731	38242
Paris, TX	903	75460-75462
Park City, KY	270	42160
Park City, UT	435	84060, 84068, 84098
Park Falls, WI	715, 534	54552
Park Forest, IL	708	60466
Park Hill, OK	918	74451
Park Hills, MO	573	63601, 63653
Park Rapids, MN	218	56470
Park Ridge, IL	224, 847	60068
Park Ridge, NJ	201, 551	07656
Parker, AZ	928	85344
Parker, CO	303, 720	80134, 80138
Parker, SD	605	57053
Parker, WA	509	98939
Parker City, IN	765	47368
Parker Ford, PA	484, 610	19457
Parkersburg, WV	304	26101-26106
Parksley, VA	757	23421
Parkville, MO	816	64151-64152
Parlier, CA	559	93648
Parlin, NJ	732, 848	08859
Parma, ID	208	83660
Parma, OH	216, 440	44129-44134
Parowan, UT	435	84761
Parshall, CO	970	80468
Parsippany, NJ	862, 973	07054
Parsons, KS	620	67357
Parsons, TN	731	38363
Parsons, WV	304	26287
Pasadena, CA	626	91050-91051, 91101-91110*
Pasadena, MD	410	21122-21123
Pasadena, TX	281, 713, 832	77501-77508
Pascagoula, MS	228	39562-39563, 39567-39569*
Pasco, WA	509	99301-99302
Pascoag, RI	401	02859
Paso Robles, CA	805	93446-93447
Passaic, NJ	862, 973	07055
Patagonia, AZ	520	85624
Patchogue, NY	631	11772
Paterson, NJ	862, 973	07501-07514, 07522-07524*
Paterson, WA	509	99345
Patrick AFB, FL	321	32925
Patterson, CA	209	95363
Patterson, GA	912	31557
Patterson, LA	985	70392
Patterson, NY	845	12563
Patton, CA	909	92369
Patuxent River, MD	301	20670
Paul, ID	208	83347
Paulding, OH	419, 567	45879
Pauls Valley, OK	405	73075
Paw Paw, MI	616	49079
Pawcatuck, CT	860	06379
Pawhuska, OK	918	74009, 74056
Pawleys Island, SC	843	29585
Pawling, NY	845	12564
Pawnee, OK	918	74058
Pawnee City, NE	402	68420
Pawtucket, RI	401	02860-02862
Paxton, IL	217	60957
Paxton, MA	508, 774	01612
Payette, ID	208	83661
Paynesville, MN	320	56362
Payson, AZ	928	85541, 85547
Payson, UT	801, 385	84651
Peabody, MA	351, 978	01960-01961
Peace Dale, RI	401	02879, 02883
Peach Glen, PA	717	17375
Peachtree City, GA	470, 770	30269
Peapack, NJ	908	07977
Pearce, AZ	520	85625
Pearisburg, VA	540	24134
Pearl, MS	601, 769	39208, 39218, 39232, 39288
Pearl City, HI	808	96782
Pearl Harbor, HI	808	96860
Pearl River, NY	845	10965
Pearland, TX	281, 832	77581-77584, 77588
Pearsall, TX	830	78061
Pearson, GA	912	31642
Pebble Beach, CA	831	93953
Pecos, NM	505	87552
Pecos, TX	915	79772
Peculiar, MO	816	64078
Peekskill, NY	845	10566
Pekin, IL	309	61554-61558
Pekin, IN	812	47165
Pelham, AL	205	35124
Pelham, GA	229	31779
Pelham, NH	603	03076
Pelham, NY	845	10803
Pelham Manor, NY	845	10803
Pelican Rapids, MN	218	56572
Pell City, AL	205	35125-35128
Pella, IA	641	50219
Pelzer, SC	864	29669
Pemberton, NJ	609	08068
Pembroke, GA	912	31321
Pembroke, MA	339, 781	02327, 02358-02359
Pembroke, NH	603	03275
Pembroke, NC	910	28372
Pembroke, VA	540	24136
Pembroke Park, FL	754, 954	33009, 33021-33023
Pembroke Pines, FL	754, 954	33019-33029, 33081-33084*
Pen Argyl, PA	484, 610	18072
Penacook, NH	603	03303
Penasco, NM	505	87553
Pender, NE	402	68047
Pendergrass, GA	706, 762	30567
Pendleton, IN	765	46064
Pendleton, OR	541, 458	97801
Pendleton, SC	864	29670
Penfield, NY	585	14526
Penfield, PA	814	15849
Peninsula, OH	234, 330	44264
Penland, NC	828	28765
Penn Yan, NY	315	14527
Penndel, PA	215, 267	19047
Pennington, NJ	609	08534
Pennsauken, NJ	856	08109-08110
Pennsburg, PA	215, 267	18073
Pennsville, NJ	856	08070
Penrose, CO	719	81240
Pensacola, FL	850	32501-32516, 32520-32526*
Pensacola Beach, FL	850	32561
Pentwater, MI	231	49449
Peoria, AZ	623	85345, 85380-85385
Peoria, IL	309	61601-61616, 61625-61644*
Peoria Heights, IL	309	61614-61616
Peosta, IA	563	52068
Peotone, IL	708	60468
Pepper Pike, OH	216	44122-44124
Pequannock, NJ	862, 973	07440
Perdue Hill, AL	251	36470
Perham, MN	218	56573
Perkasie, PA	215, 267	18944
Perkinston, MS	601, 769	39573
Perris, CA	951	92570-92572, 92599
Perry, FL	850	32347-32348
Perry, GA	478	31069
Perry, IA	515	50220
Perry, KS	785	66073
Perry, OH	440	44081
Perry, OK	580	73077
Perrysburg, OH	419, 567	43551-43552
Perrysville, OH	419, 567	44864
Perryton, TX	806	79070
Perryville, AR	501	72126
Perryville, MO	573	63747, 63775-63776, 63783
Perth Amboy, NJ	732, 848	08861-08863
Peru, IL	815	61354
Peru, IN	765	46970-46971
Peru, NE	402	68421
Pescadero, CA	650	94060
Peshastin, WA	509	98847
Peshtigo, WI	715, 534	54157
Petal, MS	601, 769	39465
Petaluma, CA	707	94952-94955, 94975, 94999
Peterborough, NH	603	03458
Petersburg, AK	907	99833
Petersburg, IL	217	62659, 62675
Petersburg, IN	812	47567
Petersburg, TX	806	79250
Petersburg, VA	804	23801-23806
Petersburg, WV	304	26847
Petersburgh, NY	518	12138
Peterson AFB, CO	719	80914
Petoskey, MI	231	49770
Pewaukee, WI	262	53072
Pewee Valley, KY	502	40056
Pflugerville, TX	512	78660, 78691
Pharr, TX	956	78577
Phelps, NY	315	14532
Phenix City, AL	334	36867-36870
Phil Campbell, AL	256	35581
Philadelphia, MS	601, 769	39350
Philadelphia, PA	215, 267	19019, 19092-19093, 19099*
Philip, SD	605	57567
Philippi, WV	304	26416
Philipsburg, MT	406	59858
Philipsburg, PA	814	16866
Phillips, WI	715, 534	54555
Phillipsburg, KS	785	67661
Phillipsburg, NJ	908	08865
Philmont, NY	518	12565
Philomath, OR	541, 458	97370
Philpot, KY	270	42366
Phoenix, AZ	480, 602	85001-85055, 85060-85087*
Phoenix, OR	541, 458	97535
Phoenixville, PA	484, 610	19453, 19460
Picayune, MS	601, 769	39466
Pickens, SC	864	29671
Pickerington, OH	614	43147
Pico Rivera, CA	562	90660-90665
Piedmont, AL	256	36272
Pierce, NE	402	68767
Pierre, SD	605	57501
Pierz, MN	320	56364
Piffard, NY	585	14533
Pigeon, MI	989	48755
Pigeon Forge, TN	865	37862-37864, 37868, 37876
Piggott, AR	870	72454
Pikesville, MD	410	21208, 21282
Pikeville, KY	606	41501-41502
Pikeville, TN	423	37367
Pilot Grove, IA	319	52648
Pima, AZ	928	85535, 85543
Pinckneyville, IL	618	62274
Pinconning, MI	989	48650
Pine Bluff, AR	870	71601-71603, 71611-71613
Pine Bluffs, WY	307	82082
Pine Brook, NJ	862, 973	07058
Pine City, MN	320	55063
Pine City, NY	607	14871
Pine Island, MN	507	55963
Pine Mountain, GA	706, 762	31822
Pine Plains, NY	518	12567
Pine River, MN	218	56456, 56474
Pinedale, WY	307	82941
Pinehurst, NC	910	28370, 28374
Pinellas Park, FL	727	33780-33782
Pinetops, NC	252	27864
Pineville, KY	606	40977
Pineville, LA	318	71359-71361
Pineville, MO	417	64856
Pineville, NC	704, 980	28134
Pineville, WV	304	24859, 24874
Piney Flats, TN	423	37686, 37699
Pinole, CA	510	94564
Pioche, NV	775	89043
Pioneer, OH	419, 567	43554
Pipersville, PA	215, 267	18947
Pipestem, WV	304	25979
Pipestone, MN	507	56164
Pippa Passes, KY	606	41844
Piqua, OH	937	45356
Piru, CA	805	93040

**Partial list of zip codes, including main range*

City	Area Code(s)	Zip Code(s)
Piscataway, NJ	732, 848	08854-08855
Pismo Beach, CA	805	93420, 93433, 93448-93449
Pitman, NJ	856	08071
Pittsboro, MS	662	38951
Pittsboro, NC	919	27228, 27312
Pittsburg, CA	925	94565
Pittsburg, KS	620	66762-66763
Pittsburg, TX	903	75686
Pittsburgh, PA	412, 878	15122-15123, 15201-15244*
Pittsfield, IL	217	62363
Pittsfield, ME	207	04967
Pittsfield, MA	413	01201-01203
Pittsfield, NH	603	03263
Pittsford, NY	585	14534
Pittston, PA	570	18640-18644
Pittstown, NJ	908	08867
Pittsville, WI	715, 534	54466
Placentia, CA	714	92870-92871
Placerville, CA	530	95667
Plain, WI	608	53577
Plain City, OH	614	43064
Plainfield, IL	815	60544
Plainfield, IN	317	46168
Plainfield, NJ	908	07060-07063, 07069
Plainfield, VT	802	05667
Plainfield, WI	715, 534	54966
Plains, GA	229	31780
Plains, PA	570	18702-18705
Plains, TX	806	79355
Plainsboro, NJ	609	08536
Plainview, MN	507	55964
Plainview, NY	516	11803
Plainview, TX	806	79072-79073
Plainville, CT	860	06062
Plainville, KS	785	67663
Plainville, MA	508, 774	02762
Plainville, NY	315	13137
Plainwell, MI	616	49080
Plankinton, SD	605	57368
Plano, IL	331, 630	60545
Plano, TX	469, 972	75023-75026, 75074-75075*
Plant City, FL	813	33564-33567
Plantation, FL	754, 954	33311-33313, 33317-33318*
Plantsville, CT	860	06479
Plaquemine, LA	225	70764-70765
Plato, MN	320	55370
Platte City, MO	816	64079
Platteville, WI	608	53818
Plattsburg, MO	816	64477
Plattsburgh, NY	518	12901-12903
Plattsmouth, NE	402	68048
Pleasant Gap, PA	814	16823
Pleasant Grove, UT	801, 385	84062
Pleasant Hill, CA	925	94523
Pleasant Plains, IL	217	62677
Pleasant Prairie, WI	262	53142-53143, 53158
Pleasant Valley, NY	845	12569
Pleasanton, CA	925	94566-94568, 94588
Pleasanton, TX	830	78064
Pleasantville, NJ	609	08232-08234
Pleasantville, NY	914	10570-10572
Plentywood, MT	406	59254
Plover, WI	715, 534	54467
Plymouth, IN	574	46563
Plymouth, MA	508, 774	02345, 02360-02362
Plymouth, MI	734	48170
Plymouth, MN	763	55441-55442, 55447
Plymouth, NH	603	03264
Plymouth, NC	252	27962
Plymouth, VT	802	05056
Plymouth, WI	920	53073
Plymouth Meeting, PA	484, 610	19462
Pocahontas, AR	870	72455
Pocahontas, IA	712	50574
Pocatello, ID	208	83201-83209
Pocomoke City, MD	410	21851
Pocono Manor, PA	570	18349
Point Clear, AL	334	36564
Point Comfort, TX	361	77978
Point Lookout, MO	417	65726
Point Lookout, NY	516	11569
Point Marion, PA	724, 878	15474
Point of Rocks, MD	301	21777
Point Pleasant, WV	304	25550
Point Pleasant Beach, NJ	732, 848	08742
Point Richmond, CA	510	94801
Poland, OH	234, 330	44514
Polk City, FL	863	33868
Polk City, IA	515	50226
Polkton, NC	704, 980	28135
Pollocksville, NC	252	28573
Polson, MT	406	59860
Pomeroy, OH	740	45769
Pomeroy, WA	509	99347
Pomfret, CT	860	06258
Pomfret Center, CT	860	06259
Pomona, CA	909	91765-91769, 91797-91799
Pomona, NJ	609	08240
Pomona, NY	845	10970
Pompano Beach, FL	754, 954	33060-33077, 33093, 33097
Pompton Lakes, NJ	862, 973	07442
Pompton Plains, NJ	862, 973	07444
Ponca, NE	402	68770
Ponca City, OK	580	74601-74604
Ponce Inlet, FL	386	32127
Ponchatoula, LA	985	70454
Ponte Vedra Beach, FL	904	32004, 32082
Pontiac, IL	815	61764
Pontiac, MI	248, 947	48340-48343
Pontotoc, MS	662	38863
Pooler, GA	912	31322
Pope AFB, NC	910	28308
Poplar, MT	406	59255
Poplar Bluff, MO	573	63901-63902
Poplarville, MS	601, 769	39470
Poquoson, VA	757	23662
Port Allen, LA	225	70767
Port Angeles, WA	360	98362-98363
Port Aransas, TX	361	78373
Port Arthur, TX	409	77640-77643
Port Charlotte, FL	941	33948-33954, 33980-33983
Port Chester, NY	914	10573
Port Clinton, OH	419, 567	43452
Port Ewen, NY	845	12466
Port Gibson, MS	601, 769	39150
Port Hueneme, CA	805	93041-93044
Port Huron, MI	810	48060-48061
Port Isabel, TX	956	78578, 78597
Port Jefferson, NY	631	11777
Port Jefferson Station, NY	631	11776-11777
Port Jervis, NY	845	12771, 12785
Port Lavaca, TX	361	77972, 77979
Port Ludlow, WA	360	98365
Port Neches, TX	409	77651
Port Orange, FL	386	32118-32119, 32124-32129
Port Orchard, WA	360	98366-98367
Port Orford, OR	541, 458	97465
Port Saint Joe, FL	850	32410, 32456-32457
Port Saint Lucie, FL	772	34952-34953, 34983-34988
Port Sulphur, LA	504	70083
Port Tobacco, MD	301	20677
Port Townsend, WA	360	98368
Port Washington, NY	516	11050-11055
Port Washington, WI	262	53074
Portage, IN	219	46368
Portage, MI	616	49002, 49024, 49081
Portage, WI	608	53901
Portageville, MO	573	63873
Portales, NM	505	88123, 88130
Porter, IN	219	46304
Porterville, CA	559	93257-93258
Portland, AR	870	71663
Portland, CT	860	06480
Portland, IN	260	47371
Portland, ME	207	04101-04112, 04116, 04122*
Portland, MI	517	48875
Portland, OR	503, 971	97201-97242, 97251-97259*
Portland, TN	615	37148
Portola, CA	530	96122, 96129
Portola Valley, CA	650	94028
Portsmouth, NH	603	03801-03804
Portsmouth, OH	740	45662-45663
Portsmouth, RI	401	02871-02872
Portsmouth, VA	757	23701-23709
Portville, NY	585	14770
Post, TX	806	79356
Post Falls, ID	208	83854, 83877
Post Mills, VT	802	05058
Postville, IA	563	52162
Poteau, OK	918	74953
Potomac, MD	301	20854, 20859
Potosi, MO	573	63664
Potsdam, NY	315	13676, 13699
Pottsboro, TX	903	75076
Pottstown, PA	484, 610	19464-19465
Pottsville, PA	570	17901
Poughkeepsie, NY	845	12601-12604
Poughquag, NY	845	12570
Poulsbo, WA	360	98370
Poultney, VT	802	05741, 05764
Pound, VA	276	24279
Poway, CA	858	92064, 92074
Powderhorn, CO	970	81243
Powell, OH	614	43065
Powell, TN	865	37849
Powell, WY	307	82435
Powhatan, VA	804	23139
Prairie City, IL	309	61470
Prairie du Chien, WI	608	53821
Prairie du Sac, WI	608	53578
Prairie Grove, IL	815	60012, 60050
Prairie View, TX	936	77446
Prairie Village, KS	913	66202-66208
Prairieville, LA	225	70769
Pratt, KS	620	67124
Prattville, AL	334	36066-36068
Preble, IN	260	46782
Prentiss, MS	601, 769	39474
Prescott, AZ	928	86301-86305, 86313, 86330
Prescott, AR	870	71857
Prescott, WA	509	99348
Prescott, WI	715, 534	54021
Prescott Valley, AZ	928	86312-86314
Presidio of San Francisco, CA	415	94129
Presque Isle, ME	207	04769
Preston, GA	229	31824
Preston, ID	208	83263
Preston, MN	507	55965
Preston, WA	425	98050
Prestonsburg, KY	606	41653
Price, UT	435	84501
Prichard, AL	251	36610, 36617
Prides Crossing, MA	617, 857	01965
Primghar, IA	712	51245
Primm, NV	702	89019
Primos, PA	484, 610	19018
Prince Frederick, MD	410	20678
Prince George, VA	804	23875
Prince William, VA	571, 703	22193
Princess Anne, MD	410	21853
Princeton, ID	208	83857
Princeton, IL	815	61356
Princeton, IN	812	47670
Princeton, KY	270	42445
Princeton, MN	763	55371
Princeton, MO	660	64673
Princeton, NJ	609	08540-08544
Princeton, WV	304	24740
Princeton Junction, NJ	609	08550
Princeville, HI	808	96714, 96722
Princeville, IL	309	61559
Prineville, OR	541, 458	97754
Prinsburg, MN	320	56281
Prior Lake, MN	952	55372
Proctor, MN	218	55810
Proctor, VT	802	05765
Prophetstown, IL	815	61277
Prospect, CT	203	06712
Prospect, ME	207	04981
Prospect Harbor, ME	207	04669
Prospect Heights, IL	224, 847	60070
Prospect Hill, NC	336	27314
Prosperity, SC	803	29127
Prosser, WA	509	99350
Providence, RI	401	02901-02912, 02918, 02940
Provincetown, MA	508, 774	02657
Provo, UT	801, 385	84601-84606
Pryor, OK	918	74361-74362
Pueblo, CO	719	81001-81015
Pueblo West, CO	719	81007
Puerto Nuevo, PR	787, 939	00920-00921
Pulaski, NY	315	13142
Pulaski, TN	931	38478

**Partial list of zip codes, including main range*

City	Area Code(s)	Zip Code(s)
Pulaski, VA	540	24301
Pulaski, WI	920	54162
Pullman, WA	509	99163-99165
Punta Gorda, FL	941	33950-33951, 33955, 33980*
Punxsutawney, PA	814	15767
Purcell, OK	405	73080
Purcellville, VA	540	20132-20134, 20160
Purchase, NY	914	10577
Purvis, MS	601, 769	39475
Put-in-Bay, OH	419, 567	43456
Putnam, CT	860	06260
Putney, VT	802	05346
Puunene, HI	808	96784
Puyallup, WA	253	98371-98375
Pyote, TX	915	79777

Q

City	Area Code(s)	Zip Code(s)
Quakertown, PA	215, 267	18951
Quanah, TX	940	79252
Quantico, VA	571, 703	22134-22135
Quapaw, OK	918	74363
Quarryville, PA	717	17566
Queens Village, NY	347, 718	11427-11429
Queensbury, NY	518	12801-12804
Queenstown, MD	410	21658
Quimby, IA	712	51049
Quinault, WA	360	98575
Quincy, CA	530	95971
Quincy, FL	850	32351-32353
Quincy, IL	217	62301, 62305-62306
Quincy, MA	617, 857	02169-02171, 02269
Quincy, PA	717	17247
Quincy, WA	509	98848
Quinlan, TX	903	75474
Quinter, KS	785	67752
Quitman, GA	229	31643
Quitman, MS	601, 769	39355
Quitman, TX	903	75783

R

City	Area Code(s)	Zip Code(s)
Racine, WI	262	53401-53408, 53490
Radcliff, KY	270	40159-40160
Radcliffe, IA	515	50230
Radford, VA	540	24141-24143
Radisson, WI	715, 534	54867
Radnor, PA	484, 610	19087
Raeford, NC	910	28361, 28376
Rahway, NJ	732, 848	07065
Raiford, FL	386, 904	32026, 32083
Rainsville, AL	256	35986
Raleigh, MS	601, 769	39153
Raleigh, NC	919	27601-27629, 27634-27636*
Ralls, TX	806	79357
Ralston, IA	712	51459
Ralston, NE	402	68127
Ramah, NM	505	87321, 87357
Ramona, CA	760, 442	92065
Ramona, OK	918	74061
Ramseur, NC	336	27316
Ramsey, MN	763	55303
Ramsey, NJ	201, 551	07446
Rancho Cordova, CA	916	95670, 95741-95743
Rancho Cucamonga, CA	909	91701, 91729-91730, 91737*
Rancho Dominguez, CA	310, 424	90220, 90224
Rancho Mirage, CA	760, 442	92270
Rancho Palos Verdes, CA	310, 424	90275
Rancho Santa Fe, CA	858	92067, 92091
Rancho Santa Margarita, CA	949	92688
Rancho Viejo, TX	956	78575
Rancocas, NJ	609	08073
Randallstown, MD	410	21133
Randleman, NC	336	27317
Randolph, MA	339, 781	02368
Randolph, NJ	862, 973	07869
Randolph, UT	435	84064
Randolph, VT	802	05060
Randolph, WI	920	53956-53957
Randolph AFB, TX	210	78148-78150
Randolph Center, VT	802	05061
Random Lake, WI	920	53075
Rangely, CO	970	81648
Ranger, TX	254	76470
Rankin, PA	412, 878	15104
Rankin, TX	915	79778
Rantoul, IL	217	61866
Rapid City, SD	605	57701-57703, 57709
Rapidan, VA	540	22733
Raritan, NJ	908	08869, 08896
Raton, NM	505	87740
Ravenna, MI	231	49451
Ravenna, OH	234, 330	44266
Ravenswood, WV	304	26164
Rawlins, WY	307	82301, 82310
Ray Brook, NY	518	12977
Raymond, ME	207	04071
Raymond, MS	601, 769	39154
Raymond, NH	603	03077
Raymond, WA	360	98577
Raymondville, TX	956	78580, 78598
Raymore, MO	816	64083
Rayne, LA	337	70578
Raynham, MA	508, 774	02767
Raytown, MO	816	64129, 64133, 64138
Rayville, LA	318	71269
Readfield, ME	207	04355
Reading, MA	339, 781	01867
Reading, PA	484, 610	19601-19612, 19640
Readville, MA	617, 857	02136-02137
Reamstown, PA	717	17567
Red Bank, NJ	732, 848	07701-07704
Red Bay, AL	256	35582
Red Bluff, CA	530	96080
Red Bud, IL	618	62278
Red Cloud, NE	402	68970
Red Feather Lakes, CO	970	80536, 80545
Red Hill, PA	215, 267	18073-18076
Red Lake Falls, MN	218	56750
Red Lion, PA	717	17356
Red Lodge, MT	406	59068
Red Oak, IA	712	51566, 51591
Red River, NM	505	87558
Red Rock, AZ	520	85245
Red Springs, NC	910	28377
Red Wing, MN	651	55066
Redding, CA	530	96001-96003, 96049, 96099
Redding, CT	203	06896
Redfield, SD	605	57469
Redford, MI	313	48239-48240
Redlands, CA	909	92373-92375
Redmond, OR	541, 458	97756
Redmond, WA	425	98052-98053, 98073-98074
Redondo Beach, CA	310, 424	90277-90278
Redstone, CO	970	81623
Redstone Arsenal, AL	256	35808-35809
Redwood, NY	315	13679
Redwood City, CA	650	94059-94065
Redwood Falls, MN	507	56283
Reed City, MI	231	49677
Reedley, CA	559	93654
Reedsburg, WI	608	53958-53959
Refugio, TX	361	78377
Rego Park, NY	347, 718	11374
Rehoboth Beach, DE	302	19971
Reidsville, GA	912	30453, 30499
Reidsville, NC	336	27320-27323
Reinbeck, IA	319	50669
Reisterstown, MD	410	21071, 21136
Rembert, SC	803	29128
Remington, IN	219	47977
Remus, MI	989	49340
Renick, WV	304	24966
Reno, NV	775	89501-89515, 89520-89523*
Rensselaer, IN	219	47978
Rensselaer, NY	518	12144
Renton, WA	425	98055-98059
Renville, MN	320	56284
Represa, CA	916	95671
Republic, MO	417	65738
Republic, WA	509	99166
Research Triangle Park, NC	919	27709
Reseda, CA	818	91335-91337
Reserve, NM	505	87830
Reston, VA	571, 703	20190-20196, 22096
Retsil, WA	360	98378
Revere, MA	339, 781	02151
Rexburg, ID	208	83440-83441, 83460
Reynolds, GA	478	31076
Reynoldsburg, OH	614	43068
Rhinebeck, NY	845	12572
Rhinelander, WI	715, 534	54501
Rhodes, MI	989	48652
Rialto, CA	909	92376-92377
Rice Lake, WI	715, 534	54868
Riceboro, GA	912	31323
Rich Square, NC	252	27869
Richardson, TX	214, 469, 972	75080-75085
Richfield, MN	612	55423
Richfield, OH	234, 330	44286
Richfield, UT	435	84701
Richfield, WI	414	53076
Richland, MI	616	49083
Richland, MS	601, 769	39208, 39218, 39232
Richland, PA	717	17087
Richland, WA	509	99352-99353
Richland Center, WI	608	53581
Richland Hills, TX	682, 817	76118, 76180
Richlands, VA	276	24641
Richmond, CA	510	94801-94808, 94820, 94850
Richmond, IL	815	60071
Richmond, IN	765	47374-47375
Richmond, KY	859	40475-40476
Richmond, MO	816	64085
Richmond, TX	281, 832	77406, 77469
Richmond, VA	804	23173, 23218-23242, 23249*
Richmond Heights, MO	314	63117
Richmond Heights, OH	216	44143
Richmond Hill, NY	347, 718	11418
Richvale, CA	530	95974
Rickreall, OR	503, 971	97371
Riddle, OR	541, 458	97469
Riderwood, MD	410	21139
Ridge, NY	631	11961
Ridge Spring, SC	803	29129
Ridgecrest, CA	760, 442	93555-93556
Ridgedale, MO	417	65739
Ridgefield, CT	203	06877-06879
Ridgefield, NJ	201, 551	07657
Ridgefield Park, NJ	201, 551	07660
Ridgeland, MS	601, 769	39157-39158
Ridgeland, SC	843	29912, 29936
Ridgeville, SC	843	29472
Ridgeway, SC	803	29130
Ridgeway, VA	276	24148
Ridgewood, NJ	201, 551	07450-07452
Ridgewood, NY	347, 718	11385-11386
Ridgway, CO	970	81432
Ridgway, PA	814	15853
Ridley Park, PA	484, 610	19078
Rifle, CO	970	81650
Rigby, ID	208	83442
Rillito, AZ	520	85654
Rindge, NH	603	03461
Ringgold, GA	706, 762	30736
Ringoes, NJ	908	08551
Ringwood, NJ	862, 973	07456
Rio, WI	920	53960
Rio Grande, NJ	609	08242
Rio Grande, OH	740	45674
Rio Grande City, TX	956	78582
Rio Rancho, NM	505	87124, 87174
Rio Rico, AZ	520	85648
Rio Verde, AZ	480	85263
Rio Vista, CA	707	94571
Ripley, MS	662	38663
Ripley, TN	731	38063
Ripley, WV	304	25271
Ripon, CA	209	95366
Ripon, WI	920	54971
Ririe, ID	208	83443
Rising Sun, IN	812	47040
Rising Sun, MD	410	21911
Rison, AR	870	71665
Ritzville, WA	509	99169
River Edge, NJ	201, 551	07661
River Falls, WI	715, 534	54022
River Forest, IL	708	60305
River Grove, IL	708	60171
River Rouge, MI	313	48218
Riverbank, CA	209	95367, 95390
Riverdale, GA	470, 770	30274, 30296
Riverdale, IL	708	60827

*Partial list of zip codes, including main range

City	Area Code(s)	Zip Code(s)
Riverdale, MD	301	20737-20738
Riverdale, NJ	862, 973	07457
Riverdale, NY	347, 718	10463, 10471
Riverdale, UT	801, 385	84405
Riverhead, NY	631	11901
Riverside, CA	951	92501-92509, 92513-92522
Riverside, MI	616	49084
Riverside, MO	816	64150-64151, 64168
Riverside, NJ	856	08075
Riverton, NJ	856	08076-08077
Riverton, UT	801, 385	84065, 84095
Riverton, WY	307	82501
Riverview, FL	813	33568-33569
Riverwoods, IL	224, 847	60015
Riviera Beach, FL	561	33403-33407, 33418-33419
Roanoke, IN	260	46783
Roanoke, VA	540	24001-24050
Roanoke Rapids, NC	252	27870
Roaring Spring, PA	814	16673
Robbins, NC	910	27325
Robbinsdale, MN	763	55422
Robbinsville, NJ	609	08691
Robbinsville, NC	828	28771
Robert Lee, TX	915	76945
Roberta, GA	478	31078
Roberts, IL	217	60962
Robertsdale, AL	251	36567, 36574
Robesonia, PA	484, 610	19551
Robins AFB, GA	478	31098
Robinson, IL	618	62454
Robinsonville, MS	662	38664
Robstown, TX	361	78380
Roby, TX	915	79543
Rochdale, MA	508, 774	01542
Rochelle, IL	815	61068
Rochelle Park, NJ	201, 551	07662
Rochester, IN	574	46975
Rochester, MI	248, 947	48306-48309
Rochester, MN	507	55901-55906
Rochester, NH	603	03839, 03866-03868
Rochester, NY	585	14601-14627, 14638-14653*
Rochester, PA	724, 878	15074
Rochester, VT	802	05767
Rochester, WA	360	98579
Rochester, WI	262	53167
Rochester Hills, MI	248, 947	48306-48309
Rock City Falls, NY	518	12863
Rock Creek, OH	440	44084
Rock Falls, IL	815	61071
Rock Hill, NY	845	12775
Rock Hill, SC	803	29730-29734
Rock Island, IL	309	61201-61204, 61299
Rock Port, MO	660	64482
Rock Rapids, IA	712	51246
Rock Spring, GA	706, 762	30739
Rock Springs, WY	307	82901-82902, 82942
Rockaway, NJ	862, 973	07866
Rockaway Beach, NY	347, 718	11693
Rockaway Park, NY	347, 718	11694
Rockford, AL	256	35136
Rockford, IL	815	61101-61114, 61125-61126
Rockford, MI	616	49341, 49351
Rockford, MN	763	55373
Rockford, TN	865	37853
Rockingham, NC	910	28379-28380
Rockland, ME	207	04841
Rockland, MA	339, 781	02370
Rockledge, FL	321	32955-32956
Rockleigh, NJ	201, 551	07647
Rocklin, CA	916	95677, 95765
Rockmart, GA	470, 770	30153
Rockport, IN	812	47635
Rockport, ME	207	04856
Rockport, MA	351, 978	01966
Rockport, TX	361	78381-78382
Rocksprings, TX	830	78880
Rockton, IL	815	61072
Rockville, CT	860	06066
Rockville, IN	765	47872
Rockville, MD	240, 301	20847-20859
Rockville Centre, NY	516	11570-11572, 11592
Rockwall, TX	469, 972	75032, 75087
Rockwell, NC	704, 980	28138
Rockwell City, IA	712	50579
Rockwood, MI	734	48173
Rocky Ford, CO	719	81067

City	Area Code(s)	Zip Code(s)
Rocky Hill, CT	860	06067
Rocky Mount, NC	252	27801-27804
Rocky Mount, VA	540	24151
Roebuck, SC	864	29376
Rogers, AR	479	72756-72758
Rogers, CT	860	06263
Rogers City, MI	989	49779
Rogersville, AL	256	35652
Rogersville, TN	423	37857
Rogue River, OR	541, 458	97537
Rohnert Park, CA	707	94927-94928
Roland, AR	501	72135
Roland, IA	515	50236
Rolla, MO	573	65401-65402, 65409
Rolla, ND	701	58367
Rolling Fork, MS	662	39159
Rolling Hills Estates, CA	310, 424	90274-90275
Rolling Meadows, IL	224, 847	60008
Rome, GA	706, 762	30149, 30161-30165
Rome, NY	315	13440-13442, 13449
Romeo, MI	586	48065
Romeoville, IL	815	60441, 60446
Romney, WV	304	26757
Romulus, MI	734	48174
Romulus, NY	315	14541
Ronceverte, WV	304	24970
Ronkonkoma, NY	631	11749, 11779
Roodhouse, IL	217	62082
Roosevelt, AZ	928	85545
Roosevelt, UT	435	84066
Rootstown, OH	234, 330	44272
Rosamond, CA	661	93560
Roscoe, IL	815	61073
Roscoe, PA	412, 878	15477
Roscommon, MI	989	48653
Rose Hill, NC	910	28458
Roseau, MN	218	56751
Rosebud, TX	254	76570
Roseburg, OR	541, 458	97470
Rosedale, MS	662	38769
Roseland, NJ	862, 973	07068
Roselle, IL	331, 630	60172
Roselle, NJ	908	07203
Roselle Park, NJ	908	07204
Rosemead, CA	626	91770-91772
Rosemont, IL	224, 847	60018
Rosemont, PA	484, 610	19010
Rosemount, MN	651	55068
Rosenberg, TX	281, 832	77471
Rosendale, WI	920	54974
Rosenhayn, NJ	856	08352
Roseville, CA	916	95661, 95678, 95746-95747
Roseville, MI	586	48066
Roseville, MN	651	55112-55113, 55126
Roseville, OH	740	43777
Rosiclare, IL	618	62982
Roslindale, MA	617, 857	02131
Roslyn, NY	516	11576
Roslyn Heights, NY	516	11577
Rosman, NC	828	28772
Rosslyn, VA	571, 703	22209
Rossville, GA	706, 762	30741-30742
Roswell, GA	470, 678, 770	30075-30077
Roswell, NM	505	88201-88203
Rothschild, WI	715, 534	54474
Round Lake, IL	224, 847	60073
Round Rock, TX	512	78664, 78680-78683
Roundup, MT	406	59072-59073
Rouses Point, NY	518	12979
Rowayton, CT	203	06853
Rowe, MA	413	01367
Rowlett, TX	469, 972	75030, 75088-75089
Rowley, MA	351, 978	01969
Roxboro, NC	336	27573
Roxbury, MA	617, 857	02118-02120
Roxbury Crossing, MA	617, 857	02120
Roy, NM	505	87743
Roy, UT	801, 385	84067
Roy, WA	360	98580
Royal Oak, MI	248, 947	48067-48068, 48073
Royal Palm Beach, FL	561	33411-33412, 33421
Royersford, PA	484, 610	19468
Rugby, ND	701	58368
Ruidoso Downs, NM	505	88346
Rumford, RI	401	02916

City	Area Code(s)	Zip Code(s)
Running Springs, CA	909	92382
Rupert, ID	208	83343, 83350
Rural Hall, NC	336	27045, 27094, 27098-27099
Rush, NY	585	14543
Rush City, MN	320	55067-55069
Rushford, MN	507	55971
Rushville, IL	217	62681
Rushville, IN	765	46173
Rushville, NE	308	69360
Rusk, TX	903	75785
Ruskin, FL	813	33570-33573
Russell, KS	785	67665
Russellville, AL	256	35653-35654
Russellville, AR	479	72801-72802, 72811-72812
Russellville, KY	270	42276
Russia, OH	937	45363
Rustburg, VA	434	24588
Ruston, LA	318	71270-71273
Rutherford, CA	707	94573
Rutherford, NJ	201, 551	07070
Rutherfordton, NC	828	28139
Rutland, MA	508, 774	01543
Rutland, VT	802	05701-05702
Rutledge, TN	865	37861
Rydal, PA	215, 267	19046
Rye, NY	914	10580
Rye Brook, NY	914	10573
Ryegate, MT	406	59074

S

City	Area Code(s)	Zip Code(s)
Sabetha, KS	785	66534
Sac City, IA	712	50583
Saco, ME	207	04072
Sacramento, CA	916	94203-94211, 94229-94263*
Saddle Brook, NJ	201, 551	07663
Saegertown, PA	814	16433
Safety Harbor, FL	727	34695
Safford, AZ	928	85546-85548
Sag Harbor, NY	631	11963
Saginaw, MI	989	48601-48609, 48663
Sagle, ID	208	83809, 83860
Saguache, CO	719	81149
Sahuarita, AZ	520	85629
Saint Albans, VT	802	05478-05479
Saint Albans, WV	304	25177
Saint Ann, MO	314	63074
Saint Ansgar, IA	641	50472, 50481
Saint Anthony, ID	208	83445
Saint Anthony, MN	612	55418-55421
Saint Augustine, FL	904	32080, 32084-32086, 32092*
Saint Bonaventure, NY	585	14778
Saint Bonifacius, MN	952	55375
Saint Catharine, KY	859	40061
Saint Charles, IL	331, 630	60174-60175
Saint Charles, MI	989	48655
Saint Charles, MO	636	63301-63304
Saint Clair, MI	810	48079
Saint Clair, MN	507	56080
Saint Clair, MO	636	63077
Saint Clair, PA	570	17970
Saint Clair Shores, MI	586	48080-48082
Saint Clairsville, OH	740	43950
Saint Cloud, FL	321, 407	34769-34773
Saint Cloud, MN	320	56301-56304, 56372, 56387*
Saint Croix Falls, WI	715, 534	54024
Saint Davids, PA	484, 610	19087
Saint Francis, KS	785	67756
Saint Francis, WI	414	53207, 53235
Saint Francisville, IL	618	62460
Saint Francisville, LA	225	70775
Saint Gabriel, LA	225	70776
Saint George, SC	843	29477
Saint George, UT	435	84770-84771, 84782-84783*
Saint Helena, CA	707	94574
Saint Helena Island, SC	843	29920
Saint Helens, OR	503, 971	97051
Saint Henry, OH	419, 567	45883
Saint Hilaire, MN	218	56754
Saint Ignace, MI	906	49781
Saint James, LA	225	70086
Saint James, MN	507	56081
Saint James, MO	573	65559
Saint James, NY	631	11780

Partial list of zip codes, including main range

City	Area Code(s)	Zip Code(s)
Saint Joe, IN	260	46785
Saint John, KS	620	67576
Saint Johns, AZ	928	85936
Saint Johns, MI	989	48879
Saint Johnsbury, VT	802	05819
Saint Joseph, LA	318	71366
Saint Joseph, MI	616	49085
Saint Joseph, MN	320	56374-56375
Saint Joseph, MO	816	64501-64508
Saint Leo, FL	352	33574
Saint Louis, MI	989	48880
Saint Louis, MO	314	63101-63151, 63155-63171*
Saint Louis Park, MN	952	55416, 55424-55426, 55436
Saint Maries, ID	208	83861
Saint Martin, OH	513	45118
Saint Martinville, LA	337	70582
Saint Marys, GA	912	31558
Saint Marys, OH	419, 567	45885
Saint Marys, PA	814	15857
Saint Marys, WV	304	26170
Saint Matthews, SC	803	29135
Saint Meinrad, IN	812	47577
Saint Michael, MN	763	55376
Saint Michaels, MD	410	21624, 21647, 21663
Saint Nazianz, WI	920	54232
Saint Paul, MN	651	55101-55129, 55133, 55144*
Saint Paul, NE	308	68873
Saint Pauls, NC	910	28384
Saint Pete Beach, FL	727	33706, 33736
Saint Peter, MN	507	56082
Saint Peters, MO	636	63303-63304, 63376
Saint Petersburg, FL	727	33701-33716, 33728-33743*
Saint Rose, LA	504	70087
Saint Simons Island, GA	912	31522
Sainte Genevieve, MO	573	63670
Salamanca, NY	716	14779
Salem, AR	870	72576
Salem, IL	618	62881
Salem, IN	812	47167
Salem, MA	351, 978	01970-01971
Salem, MO	573	65560
Salem, NH	603	03079
Salem, NJ	856	08079
Salem, OH	234, 330	44460
Salem, OR	503, 971	97301-97314
Salem, SC	864	29676
Salem, SD	605	57058
Salem, VA	540	24153-24157
Salem, WV	304	26426
Salida, CA	209	95368
Salida, CO	719	81201, 81227-81228, 81237*
Salina, KS	785	67401-67402
Salinas, CA	831	93901-93908, 93912-93915*
Saline, MI	734	48176
Salineville, OH	234, 330	43945
Salisbury, CT	860	06068, 06079
Salisbury, MD	410	21801-21804
Salisbury, MA	351, 978	01952
Salisbury, NC	704, 980	28144-28147
Sallisaw, OK	918	74955
Salmon, ID	208	83467
Salt Flat, TX	915	79847
Salt Lake City, UT	801, 385	84101-84153, 84157-84158*
Saltillo, MS	662	38866
Saltsburg, PA	724, 878	15681
Saluda, SC	864	29138
Saluda, VA	804	23149
Salyersville, KY	606	41465
San Andreas, CA	209	95249-95250
San Angelo, TX	915	76901-76909
San Anselmo, CA	415	94960, 94979
San Antonio, FL	352	33576
San Antonio, TX	210	78201-78270, 78275-78299
San Augustine, TX	936	75972
San Benito, TX	956	78586
San Bernardino, CA	909	92401-92427
San Bruno, CA	650	94066-94067, 94096-94098
San Carlos, CA	650	94070-94071
San Clemente, CA	949	92672-92674
San Diego, CA	619, 858	92101-92199
San Dimas, CA	909	91773
San Fernando, CA	818	91340-91346
San Francisco, CA	415	94101-94177, 94188
San Gabriel, CA	626	91775-91778
San Gregorio, CA	650	94074
San Jacinto, CA	951	92581-92583
San Joaquin, CA	559	93660
San Jose, CA	408	95101-95142, 95148-95164*
San Juan, PR	787, 939	00901-00902, 00906-00940*
San Juan Bautista, CA	831	95045
San Juan Capistrano, CA	949	92675, 92690-92694
San Leandro, CA	510	94577-94579
San Lorenzo, CA	510	94580
San Luis, CO	719	81134, 81152
San Luis Obispo, CA	805	93401-93412
San Marcos, CA	760, 442	92069, 92078-92079, 92096
San Marcos, TX	512	78666-78667
San Marino, CA	626	91108, 91118
San Mateo, CA	650	94401-94409, 94497
San Pablo, CA	510	94806
San Pedro, CA	310, 424	90731-90734
San Quentin, CA	415	94964, 94974
San Rafael, CA	415	94901-94904, 94912-94915
San Ramon, CA	925	94583
San Saba, TX	915	76877
San Ysidro, CA	619	92143, 92173
Sanborn, NY	716	14132
Sand Point, AK	907	99661
Sand Springs, OK	918	74063
Sanderson, FL	386	32087
Sanderson, TX	915	79848
Sandersville, GA	478	31082
Sandia Park, NM	505	87047
Sandpoint, ID	208	83862-83864, 83888
Sandston, VA	804	23150
Sandstone, MN	320	55072
Sandusky, MI	810	48471
Sandusky, OH	419, 567	44870-44871
Sandwich, MA	508, 774	02563, 02644
Sandy, UT	801, 385	84070, 84090-84094
Sandy Hook, CT	203	06482
Sandy Hook, KY	606	41171
Sandy Lake, PA	724, 878	16145
Sandy Spring, MD	301	20860
Sanford, FL	321, 407	32771-32773
Sanford, ME	207	04073
Sanford, NC	919	27237, 27330-27332
Sanger, CA	559	93657
Sangerfield, NY	315	13455
Sanibel, FL	239	33957
Santa Ana, CA	714, 949	92701-92712, 92725-92728*
Santa Ana Pueblo, NM	505	87004
Santa Barbara, CA	805	93101-93111, 93116-93121*
Santa Clara, CA	408	95050-95056
Santa Clarita, CA	661	91310, 91321-91322, 91350*
Santa Claus, IN	812	47579
Santa Cruz, CA	831	95060-95067
Santa Cruz, NM	505	87567
Santa Fe, NM	505	87500-87509, 87592-87594
Santa Fe Springs, CA	562	90605, 90670-90671
Santa Maria, CA	805	93454-93458
Santa Monica, CA	310, 424	90401-90411
Santa Paula, CA	805	93060-93061
Santa Rosa, CA	707	95401-95409
Santa Rosa, NM	505	88435
Santa Rosa, TX	956	78593
Santa Rosa Beach, FL	850	32459
Santa Teresa, NM	505	88008, 88063
Santa Ynez, CA	805	93460
Santee, CA	619	92071-92072
Santurce, PR	787, 939	00907-00916, 00936, 00940
Sapulpa, OK	918	74066-74067
Saraland, AL	251	36571
Saranac Lake, NY	518	12983
Sarasota, FL	941	34230-34243, 34260, 34276*
Saratoga, CA	408	95070-95071
Saratoga, WY	307	82331
Saratoga Springs, NY	518	12866
Sardinia, OH	937	45171
Sardis, MS	662	38666
Sarita, TX	361	78385
Sartell, MN	320	56377
Sasabe, AZ	520	85633
Satanta, KS	620	67870
Satsuma, AL	251	36572
Saugerties, NY	845	12477
Sauget, IL	618	62201
Saugus, CA	661	91350, 91390
Saugus, MA	339, 781	01906
Sauk Centre, MN	320	56378, 56389
Sauk City, WI	608	53583
Sauk Rapids, MN	320	56379
Saukville, WI	262	53080
Sault Sainte Marie, MI	906	49783, 49788
Sausalito, CA	415	94965-94966
Savage, MD	410, 443	20763
Savage, MN	952	55378
Savanna, IL	815	61074
Savannah, GA	912	31401-31422, 31498-31499
Savannah, MO	816	64485
Savannah, TN	731	38372
Savoy, IL	217	61874
Saxonburg, PA	724, 878	16056
Sayre, OK	580	73662
Sayre, PA	570	18840
Sayreville, NJ	732, 848	08871-08872
Scandia, KS	785	66966
Scandinavia, WI	715, 534	54977
Scappoose, OR	503, 971	97056
Scarborough, ME	207	04070, 04074
Scarsdale, NY	914	10583
Schaefferstown, PA	717	17088
Schaumburg, IL	224, 847	60159, 60168, 60173, 60192*
Schenectady, NY	518	12008, 12301-12309, 12325*
Schererville, IN	219	46375
Schertz, TX	210	78154
Schiller Park, IL	224, 847	60176
Schnecksville, PA	484, 610	18078
Schofield, WI	715, 534	54476
Schoharie, NY	518	12157
Schoolcraft, MI	616	49087
Schuyler, NE	402	68661
Schuylkill Haven, PA	570	17972
Schwertner, TX	254	76573
Scituate, MA	339, 781	02040, 02055, 02060, 02066
Scobey, MT	406	59263
Scooba, MS	662	39358
Scotch Plains, NJ	908	07076
Scotia, CA	707	95565
Scotia, NY	518	12302
Scotland Neck, NC	252	27874
Scotrun, PA	570	18355
Scott, AR	501	72142
Scott, LA	337	70583
Scott, MS	662	38772
Scott AFB, IL	618	62225
Scott City, KS	620	67871
Scott City, MO	573	63780
Scott Depot, WV	304	25560
Scottdale, GA	404, 470	30079
Scottdale, PA	724, 878	15683
Scotts Valley, CA	831	95060, 95066-95067
Scottsbluff, NE	308	69361-69363
Scottsboro, AL	256	35768-35769
Scottsburg, IN	812	47170
Scottsdale, AZ	480	85250-85271
Scottsville, KY	270	42164
Scottsville, NY	585	14546
Scottsville, TX	903	75688
Scottville, MI	231	49454
Scranton, PA	570	18501-18522, 18540, 18577
Sea Island, GA	912	31561
Seabrook, NH	603	03874
Seabrook, NJ	856	08302
Seabrook, TX	281, 832	77586
Seabrook Island, SC	843	29455
Seaford, DE	302	19973
Seagoville, TX	469, 972	75159
Seal Beach, CA	562	90740
Seale, AL	334	36875
Searcy, AR	501	72143-72145, 72149
Searsmont, ME	207	04973
Searsport, ME	207	04974
Seaside, CA	831	93955
Seaside, OR	503	97138
Seaside Heights, NJ	732, 848	08751
Seattle, WA	206	98101-98138, 98144-98191*
Sebastian, FL	772	32958, 32976-32978
Sebastopol, CA	707	95472-95473
Sebastopol, MS	601, 769	39359
Sebring, FL	863	33870-33876

Partial list of zip codes, including main range

City	Area Code(s)	Zip Code(s)
Sebring, OH	234, 330	44672
Secaucus, NJ	201, 551	07094-07096
Sedalia, CO	303, 720	80135
Sedalia, MO	660	65301-65302
Sedalia, NC	336	27342
Sedan, KS	620	67361
Sedona, AZ	928	86336-86341, 86351
Sedro Woolley, WA	360	98284
Seeley Lake, MT	406	59868
Seffner, FL	813	33583-33584
Seguin, TX	830	78155-78156
Selah, WA	509	98942
Selby, SD	605	57472
Selden, NY	631	11784
Selinsgrove, PA	570	17870
Selkirk, NY	518	12158
Sellersburg, IN	812	47172
Sellersville, PA	215, 267	18960
Sells, AZ	520	85634
Selma, AL	334	36701-36703
Selma, CA	559	93662
Selma, TX	210	78154
Selmer, TN	731	38375
Seminole, FL	727	33772-33778
Seminole, OK	405	74818, 74868
Seminole, TX	915	79360
Semmes, AL	251	36575
Senatobia, MS	662	38665-38668
Seneca, KS	785	66538
Seneca, SC	864	29672, 29678-29679
Seneca Falls, NY	315	13148
Sequatchie, TN	423	37374
Seven Hills, OH	216	44131
Severn, MD	410	21144
Severn, NC	252	27877
Severna Park, MD	410	21146
Sevierville, TN	865	37862-37864, 37868, 37876
Seville, OH	234, 330	44273
Sewanee, TN	931	37375, 37383
Seward, AK	907	99664
Seward, NE	402	68434
Sewell, NJ	856	08080
Sewickley, PA	412, 878	15143, 15189
Seymour, CT	203	06478, 06483
Seymour, IN	812	47274
Seymour, TX	940	76380
Seymour Johnson AFB, NC	919	27531
Shady Grove, PA	717	17256
Shadyside, OH	740	43947
Shafter, CA	661	93263
Shaftsbury, VT	802	05262
Shaker Heights, OH	216	44118-44122
Shakopee, MN	952	55379
Shallotte, NC	910	28459, 28467-28470
Shamokin, PA	570	17872
Shamokin Dam, PA	570	17876
Shannock, RI	401	02875
Sharon, CT	860	06069
Sharon, MA	339, 781	02067
Sharon, PA	724, 878	16146-16148
Sharon, WI	262	53585
Sharon Center, OH	234, 330	44274
Sharon Springs, KS	785	67758
Sharonville, OH	513	45241
Sharpsburg, MD	301	21782
Sharpsville, PA	724, 878	16150
Sharptown, MD	410	21861
Shavertown, PA	570	18708
Shaw AFB, SC	803	29152
Shawano, WI	715, 534	54166
Shawnee, CO	303, 720	80448, 80475
Shawnee, KS	913	66203, 66214-66220, 66226*
Shawnee, OK	405	74801-74804
Shawnee Mission, KS	913	66201-66227, 66250, 66276*
Shawnee on Delaware, PA	570	18356
Shawneetown, IL	618	62984
Sheboygan, WI	920	53081-53083
Sheboygan Falls, WI	920	53085
Sheffield, AL	256	35660
Sheffield, IA	641	50475
Sheffield, MA	413	01257
Sheffield, PA	814	16347
Sheffield, TX	915	79781
Shelbina, MO	573	63468
Shelburne, VT	802	05482
Shelburne Falls, MA	413	01370
Shelby, MI	231	49455
Shelby, MT	406	59474
Shelby, NE	402	68662
Shelby, NC	704, 980	28150-28152
Shelby, OH	419, 567	44875
Shelby Township, MI	586	48315-48318
Shelbyville, IL	217	62565
Shelbyville, IN	317	46176
Shelbyville, KY	502	40065-40066
Shelbyville, MO	573	63469
Shelbyville, TN	931	37160-37162
Sheldon, IA	712	51201
Shell, WY	307	82441
Shell Lake, WI	715, 534	54871
Shelley, ID	208	83274
Shellman, GA	229	31786
Shelocta, PA	724, 878	15774
Shelton, CT	203	06484
Shelton, NE	308	68876
Shelton, WA	360	98584
Shenandoah, IA	712	51601-51603
Shenandoah, PA	570	17976
Shepherdstown, WV	304	25443
Shepherdsville, KY	502	40165
Sheppard AFB, TX	940	76311
Sherburne, NY	607	13460
Sheridan, AR	870	72150
Sheridan, IN	317	46069
Sheridan, MI	989	48884
Sheridan, OR	503, 971	97378
Sheridan, WY	307	82801
Sherman, MS	662	38869
Sherman, TX	903	75090-75092
Sherman Oaks, CA	818	91401-91403, 91411-91413*
Sherwood, AR	501	72116-72120, 72124
Sherwood, OR	503, 971	97140
Shickshinny, PA	570	18655
Shillington, PA	484, 610	19607
Shiloh, OH	419, 567	44878
Shiloh, TN	731	38376
Shiner, TX	361	77984
Ship Bottom, NJ	609	08008
Shippensburg, PA	717	17257
Shippenville, PA	814	16254
Shiprock, NM	505	87420, 87461
Shipshewana, IN	260	46565
Shirley, MA	351, 978	01464
Shirley, NY	631	11967
Shoals, IN	812	47581
Shoemakersville, PA	484, 610	19555
Shoreline, WA	206	98133, 98155, 98177
Shoreview, MN	651	55126
Shorewood, IL	815	60431, 60435-60436
Short Hills, NJ	862, 973	07078
Shoshone, ID	208	83324, 83352
Show Low, AZ	928	85901-85902, 85911
Shreveport, LA	318	71101-71110, 71115-71120*
Shrewsbury, MA	508, 774	01545-01546
Shrewsbury, NJ	732, 848	07702
Shrub Oak, NY	914	10588
Sibley, IA	712	51249
Sibley, MO	816	64088
Sidney, IA	712	51652
Sidney, MI	989	48885
Sidney, MT	406	59270
Sidney, NE	308	69160-69162
Sidney, NY	607	13838
Sidney, OH	937	45365-45367
Sierra Blanca, TX	915	79851
Sierra Madre, CA	626	91024-91025
Sierra Vista, AZ	520	85613, 85635-85636, 85650*
Signal Hill, CA	562	90804-90807
Signal Mountain, TN	423	37377
Sigourney, IA	641	52591
Sikeston, MO	573	63801
Siler City, NC	919	27344
Siloam Springs, AR	479	72761
Silsbee, TX	409	77656
Silver Bay, MN	218	55614
Silver City, NM	505	88022, 88036, 88053, 88061*
Silver Creek, NE	308	68663
Silver Creek, NY	716	14136
Silver Lake, IN	260	46982
Silver Lake, NH	603	03875
Silver Spring, MD	301	20901-20918, 20997
Silver Spring, PA	717	17575
Silver Springs, FL	352	34488-34489
Silverdale, WA	360	98315, 98383
Silverton, CO	970	81433
Silverton, OH	513	45236
Silverton, OR	503, 971	97381
Silverton, TX	806	79257
Silvis, IL	309	61282
Simi Valley, CA	805	93062-93065, 93093-93094*
Simpson, PA	570	18407
Simpsonville, KY	502	40067
Simpsonville, SC	864	29680-29681
Simsbury, CT	860	06070, 06081, 06089-06092
Singer Island, FL	561	33404
Sinking Spring, PA	484, 610	19608
Sinton, TX	361	78387
Sioux Center, IA	712	51250
Sioux City, IA	712	51101-51111
Sioux Falls, SD	605	57101-57110, 57117-57118*
Siren, WI	715, 534	54872
Sisseton, SD	605	57262
Sisters, OR	541, 458	97759
Sitka, AK	907	99835-99836
Skagway, AK	907	99840
Skaneateles Falls, NY	315	13119, 13153
Skillman, NJ	908	08558
Skokie, IL	224, 847	60076-60077
Skowhegan, ME	207	04976
Sky Valley, GA	706, 762	30537
Skytop, PA	570	18357
Slater, CO	970	81653
Slater, IA	515	50244
Slatersville, RI	401	02876
Slaton, TX	806	79364
Slayton, MN	507	56172
Sleepy Eye, MN	507	56085
Slidell, LA	985	70458-70461, 70469
Slippery Rock, PA	724, 878	16057
Smackover, AR	870	71762
Smethport, PA	814	16749
Smith Center, KS	785	66967
Smithfield, NC	919	27577
Smithfield, RI	401	02828, 02917
Smithfield, VA	757	23430-23431
Smithland, KY	270	42081
Smithton, PA	724, 878	15479
Smithtown, NY	631	11745, 11787-11788
Smithville, MO	816	64089
Smithville, OH	234, 330	44677
Smithville, TN	615	37166
Smithville, TX	512	78957
Smyrna, DE	302	19977
Smyrna, GA	404, 770	30080-30082, 30339
Smyrna, TN	615	37167
Sneads, FL	850	32460
Sneedville, TN	423	37869
Snellville, GA	770	30039, 30078
Snohomish, WA	360	98290-98291, 98296
Snoqualmie, WA	425	98065-98068
Snow Hill, MD	410	21863
Snow Hill, NC	252	28580
Snowbird, UT	801, 385	84092
Snowflake, AZ	928	85937, 85942
Snowmass Village, CO	970	81615
Snowshoe, WV	304	26209
Snyder, NE	402	68664
Snyder, TX	915	79549-79550
Social Circle, GA	470, 770	30025
Socorro, NM	505	87801
Soda Springs, ID	208	83230, 83276, 83285
Sodus, NY	315	14551
Solana Beach, CA	858	92075
Soldotna, AK	907	99669
Soledad, CA	831	93960
Solitude, UT	801, 385	84121
Solomon, KS	785	67480
Solomons, MD	410	20688
Solon, OH	440	44139
Solvang, CA	805	93463-93464
Somers, CT	860	06071
Somers, NY	914	10589
Somers Point, NJ	609	08244
Somerset, KY	606	42501-42503, 42564
Somerset, MA	508, 774	02725-02726
Somerset, NJ	732, 848	08873-08875
Somerset, PA	814	15501, 15510
Somerton, AZ	928	85350

**Partial list of zip codes, including main range*

City	Area Code(s)	Zip Code(s)
Somerville, MA	617, 857	02143-02145
Somerville, NJ	908	08876
Somerville, TN	901	38060, 38068
Sonoita, AZ	520	85637
Sonoma, CA	707	95476
Sonora, CA	209	95370-95373
Sonora, TX	915	76950
Sonyea, NY	585	14556
Soperton, GA	912	30457
Sorrento, LA	225	70778
Souderton, PA	215, 267	18964
South Attleboro, MA	508, 774	02703
South Barre, VT	802	05670
South Barrington, IL	224, 847	60010
South Bay, FL	561	33493
South Beloit, IL	815	61080
South Bend, IN	574	46601-46604, 46612-46620*
South Bend, WA	360	98586
South Boston, VA	434	24592
South Brunswick, NJ	732, 848	08810
South Burlington, VT	802	05401-05407
South Canaan, PA	570	18459
South Carver, MA	508, 774	02366
South Casco, ME	207	04077
South Charleston, WV	304	25303, 25309
South Chicago Heights, IL	708	60411
South Deerfield, MA	413	01373
South Easton, MA	508, 774	02375
South El Monte, CA	626	91733
South Elgin, IL	224, 847	60177
South Euclid, OH	216	44118-44121
South Fallsburg, NY	845	12779
South Fork, PA	814	15956
South Fulton, TN	731	38257
South Gate, CA	323, 562	90280
South Hackensack, NJ	201, 551	07606
South Hadley, MA	413	01075
South Haven, MI	616	49090
South Hill, VA	434	23970
South Holland, IL	708	60473
South Houston, TX	713, 832	77587
South Jordan, UT	801, 385	84065, 84095
South Kearny, NJ	862, 973	07032
South Laguna, CA	949	92651
South Lake Tahoe, CA	530	96150-96158
South Lancaster, MA	351, 978	01561
South Lee, MA	413	01260
South Lyon, MI	248, 947	48178
South Miami, FL	305, 786	33143-33146, 33155-33156*
South Milwaukee, WI	414	53172
South Mountain, PA	717	17261
South Natick, MA	508, 774	01760
South Norwalk, CT	203	06854
South Orange, NJ	862, 973	07079
South Otselic, NY	315	13155
South Padre Island, TX	956	78597
South Paris, ME	207	04281
South Pasadena, CA	626	91030-91031
South Pittsburg, TN	423	37380
South Plainfield, NJ	908	07080
South Plymouth, NY	607	13844
South Point, OH	740	45680
South Portland, ME	207	04106, 04116
South River, NJ	732, 848	08877, 08882
South Saint Paul, MN	651	55075-55077
South Salt Lake, UT	801, 385	84107, 84115, 84119, 84123*
South San Francisco, CA	650	94080-94083, 94099
South Sioux City, NE	402	68776
South Weymouth, MA	339, 781	02190
South Whitley, IN	260	46787
South Williamson, KY	606	41503
South Williamsport, PA	570	17702
South Windham, CT	860	06266
South Windham, ME	207	04082
South Windsor, CT	860	06074
South Yarmouth, MA	508, 774	02664, 02673
Southampton, NY	631	11968-11969
Southampton, PA	215, 267	18954, 18966
Southaven, MS	662	38671-38672
Southborough, MA	508, 774	01745, 01772
Southbridge, MA	508, 774	01550
Southbury, CT	203	06488
Southern Pines, NC	910	28387-28388
Southfield, MI	248, 947	48034-48037, 48075-48076*
Southgate, MI	734	48195
Southington, CT	860	06489
Southlake, TX	682, 817	76092
Southold, NY	631	11971
Southport, CT	203	06490
Southport, NC	910	28461, 28465
Southwest Harbor, ME	207	04656, 04679
Southwick, MA	413	01077
Spalding, ID	208	83540, 83551
Spanaway, WA	253	98387
Spanish Fort, AL	251	36527, 36577
Sparkill, NY	845	10976
Sparks, MD	410	21152
Sparks, NV	775	89431-89436
Sparta, GA	706, 762	31087
Sparta, MI	616	49345
Sparta, NJ	862, 973	07871
Sparta, NC	336	28675
Sparta, TN	931	38583
Sparta, WI	608	54656
Spartanburg, SC	864	29301-29307, 29316-29319
Spearfish, SD	605	57783, 57799
Spearman, TX	806	79081
Spearville, KS	620	67876
Speedway, IN	317	46224
Spencer, IN	812	47460
Spencer, IA	712	51301, 51343
Spencer, MA	508, 774	01562
Spencer, NY	607	14883
Spencer, NC	704, 980	28159
Spencer, TN	931	38585
Spencer, WV	304	25276
Spencerport, NY	585	14559
Spencerville, OH	419, 567	45887
Spiceland, IN	765	47385
Spindale, NC	828	28160
Spirit Lake, IA	712	51360
Spokane, WA	509	99201-99224, 99228, 99251*
Spotsylvania, VA	540	22553
Spring, TX	281, 832	77373, 77379-77393
Spring Arbor, MI	517	49283
Spring City, PA	484, 610	19475
Spring City, UT	435	84662
Spring Green, WI	608	53588
Spring Grove, IL	815	60081
Spring Hill, FL	352	34604-34611
Spring Hill, TN	931	37174
Spring Hope, NC	252	27882
Spring House, PA	215, 267	19477
Spring Lake, MI	231, 616	49456
Spring Lake, NJ	732, 848	07762
Spring Lake Park, MN	612, 763	55432
Spring Mills, PA	814	16875
Spring Valley, CA	619	91976-91979
Spring Valley, IL	815	61362
Spring Valley, MN	507	55975
Spring Valley, NY	845	10977
Spring Valley, WI	715, 534	54767
Springboro, OH	513	45066
Springdale, AR	479	72762-72766
Springdale, OH	513	45246
Springdale, PA	724, 878	15144
Springdale, UT	435	84767, 84779
Springer, NM	505	87729, 87747
Springer, OK	580	73458
Springfield, CO	719	81073
Springfield, GA	912	31329
Springfield, IL	217	62701-62709, 62713-62726*
Springfield, KY	859	40069
Springfield, MA	413	01101-01119, 01128-01129*
Springfield, MN	507	56087
Springfield, MO	417	65721, 65742, 65801-65810*
Springfield, NJ	862, 973	07081
Springfield, OH	937	45501-45506
Springfield, OR	541, 458	97477-97478, 97482
Springfield, PA	484, 610	19064, 19118
Springfield, SD	605	57062
Springfield, TN	615	37172
Springfield, VT	802	05156
Springfield, VA	571, 703	22009, 22015, 22150-22161
Springfield Gardens, NY	347, 718	11413
Springs, PA	814	15562
Springtown, TX	682, 817	76082
Springvale, ME	207	04083
Springview, NE	402	68778
Springville, AL	205	35146
Springville, UT	801, 385	84663
Spruce Pine, NC	828	28777
Stafford, TX	281, 832	77477, 77497
Stafford, VA	540	22554-22555
Stafford Springs, CT	860	06076
Stamford, CT	203	06901-06914, 06920-06928
Stamford, NY	607	12167
Stamps, AR	870	71860
Stanardsville, VA	434	22973
Stanberry, MO	660	64489
Standish, ME	207	04084
Standish, MI	989	48658
Stanfield, AZ	520	85272
Stanford, CA	650	94305, 94309
Stanford, KY	606	40484
Stanford, MT	406	59479
Stanhope, NJ	862, 973	07874
Stanley, NC	704, 980	28164
Stanley, ND	701	58784
Stanleytown, VA	276	24168
Stanton, CA	714	90680
Stanton, KY	606	40380
Stanton, MI	989	48888
Stanton, NE	402	68779
Stanton, ND	701	58571
Stanton, TX	915	79782
Stanwood, WA	360	98282, 98292
Staples, MN	218	56479
Stapleton, NE	308	69163
Star, NC	910	27356
Star City, AR	870	71667
Starbuck, MN	320	56381
Starke, FL	904	32091
Starkville, MS	662	39759-39760
State Center, IA	641	50247
State College, PA	814	16801-16805
State Farm, VA	804	23160
State University, AR	870	72467
Stateline, NV	775	89449
Staten Island, NY	347, 718	10301-10314
Statenville, GA	229	31648
Statesboro, GA	912	30458-30461
Statesville, NC	704, 980	28625, 28677, 28687
Staunton, VA	540	24401-24402, 24407
Stayton, OR	503, 971	97383
Steamboat Springs, CO	970	80477, 80487-80488
Stearns, KY	606	42647
Steele, ND	701	58482
Steeleville, IL	618	62288
Steelville, MO	573	65565-65566
Steilacoom, WA	253	98388
Stennis Space Center, MS	228	39522, 39529
Stephenville, TX	254	76401-76402
Sterling, CO	970	80751
Sterling, IL	815	61081
Sterling, KS	620	67579
Sterling, VA	571, 703	20163-20167
Sterling City, TX	915	76951
Sterling Heights, MI	586	48310-48314
Steubenville, OH	740	43952-43953
Stevens Point, WI	715, 534	54481, 54492
Stevensburg, VA	540	22741
Stevenson, AL	256	35772
Stevenson, CT	203	06491
Stevenson, MD	410	21153
Stevenson, WA	509	98648
Stevensville, MD	410	21666
Stevensville, MI	616	49127
Stewart, MN	320	55385
Stewartville, MN	507	55976
Stigler, OK	918	74462
Stillwater, ME	207	04489
Stillwater, MN	651	55082-55083
Stillwater, NY	518	12170
Stillwater, OK	405	74074-74078
Stilwell, OK	918	74960
Stinnett, TX	806	79083
Stirling, NJ	908	07980
Stockbridge, GA	470, 770	30281
Stockbridge, MA	413	01262-01263
Stockton, CA	209	95201-95215, 95219, 95267*
Stockton, KS	785	67669
Stockton, MO	417	65785

*Partial list of zip codes, including main range

City	Area Code(s)	Zip Code(s)
Stockville, NE	308	69042
Stone Creek, OH	234, 330	43840
Stone Mountain, GA	470, 770	30083-30088
Stone Ridge, NY	845	12484
Stoneham, MA	339, 781	02180
Stoneville, MS	662	38776
Stonington, CT	860	06378
Stony Brook, NY	631	11790, 11794
Stony Creek, VA	434	23882
Stony Point, NY	845	10980
Storm Lake, IA	712	50588
Stormville, NY	845	12582
Storrs, CT	860	06268
Stoughton, MA	339, 781	02072
Stoughton, WI	608	53589
Stow, OH	234, 330	44224
Stowe, PA	484, 610	19464
Stowe, VT	802	05672
Stoystown, PA	814	15563
Strafford, MO	417	65757
Strasburg, CO	303, 720	80136
Strasburg, OH	234, 330	44680
Strasburg, VA	540	22641, 22657
Stratford, CA	559	93266
Stratford, CT	203	06497, 06614-06615
Stratford, NJ	856	08084
Stratford, TX	806	79084
Stratford, WI	715, 534	54484
Stratham, NH	603	03885
Stratton, CO	719	80836
Stratton Mountain, VT	802	05155
Strausstown, PA	484, 610	19559
Strawberry Point, IA	563	52076
Streamwood, IL	331, 630	60107
Streator, IL	815	61364
Streetsboro, OH	234, 330	44241
Stringtown, OK	580	74569
Stromsburg, NE	402	68666
Strongsville, OH	440	44136, 44149
Stroudsburg, PA	570	18360
Stryker, OH	419, 567	43557
Stuart, FL	772	34994-34997
Stuart, VA	276	24171
Stuarts Draft, VA	540	24477
Studio City, CA	818	91602-91607, 91614
Sturbridge, MA	508, 774	01518, 01566
Sturgeon Bay, WI	920	54235
Sturgis, MI	616	49091
Sturgis, SD	605	57785
Sturtevant, WI	262	53177
Stuttgart, AR	870	72160
Subiaco, AR	479	72865
Sublette, KS	620	67877
Sublimity, OR	503, 971	97385
Succasunna, NJ	862, 973	07876
Sudbury, MA	351, 978	01776
Suffern, NY	845	10901
Suffield, CT	860	06078-06080, 06093
Suffolk, VA	757	23432-23439
Sugar Grove, IL	331, 630	60554
Sugar Land, TX	281, 832	77478-77479, 77487, 77496
Sugar Valley, GA	706, 762	30746
Sugarcreek, OH	234, 330	44681
Suitland, MD	301	20746, 20752
Sullivan, IL	217	61951
Sullivan, IN	812	47864, 47882
Sullivan, MO	573	63080
Sullivans Island, SC	843	29482
Sulphur, LA	337	70663-70665
Sulphur, OK	580	73086
Sulphur Springs, TX	903	75482-75483
Sultan, WA	360	98294
Summerdale, AL	251	36580
Summerdale, PA	717	17093
Summersville, WV	304	26651
Summerville, GA	706, 762	30747
Summerville, SC	843	29483-29485
Summit, IL	708	60501
Summit, MS	601, 769	39666
Summit, NJ	908	07901-07902
Summit, NY	518	12175
Summit Station, PA	570	17979
Summitville, OH	234, 330	43962
Sumner, WA	253	98352, 98390
Sumter, SC	803	29150-29154
Sumterville, FL	352	33585
Sun City, AZ	623	85351, 85372-85379, 85387
Sun City, CA	951	92584-92587
Sun City, FL	813	33586
Sun City Center, FL	813	33570-33573
Sun City West, AZ	623	85374-85379, 85387
Sun Lakes, AZ	480	85248
Sun Prairie, WI	608	53590-53591, 53596
Sun Valley, CA	818	91352-91353
Sun Valley, ID	208	83353-83354
Sunbury, OH	740	43074
Sunbury, PA	570	17801, 17877
Suncook, NH	603	03275
Sundance, WY	307	82729
Sunland, CA	818	91040-91041
Sunland Park, NM	505	88008, 88063
Sunman, IN	812	47041
Sunny Isles Beach, FL	305, 786	33160
Sunnyside, NY	347, 718	11104
Sunnyside, WA	509	98944
Sunnyvale, CA	408	94085-94090
Sunnyvale, TX	469, 972	75182
Sunrise, FL	754, 954	33304, 33313, 33319-33326*
Sunriver, OR	541, 458	97707
Superior, AZ	520	85273
Superior, MT	406	59872
Superior, WI	715, 534	54880
Supply, NC	910	28462
Surfside, FL	305, 786	33154
Surfside Beach, SC	843	29575, 29587
Surgoinsville, TN	423	37873
Surry, VA	757	23883
Susanville, CA	530	96127-96130
Sussex, NJ	862, 973	07461
Sussex, VA	434	23884
Sussex, WI	262	53089
Sutherlin, OR	541, 458	97479
Sutter, CA	530	95982
Sutton, MA	508, 774	01590
Sutton, WV	304	26601
Suttons Bay, MI	231	49682
Suwanee, GA	470, 678, 770	30024
Swainsboro, GA	478	30401
Swampscott, MA	339, 781	01907
Swannanoa, NC	828	28778
Swanquarter, NC	252	27885
Swansea, IL	618	62220-62226
Swansea, MA	508, 774	02777
Swanton, OH	419, 567	43558
Swanton, VT	802	05488
Swarthmore, PA	484, 610	19081
Swartz Creek, MI	810	48473
Swea City, IA	515	50590
Swedesboro, NJ	856	08085
Sweet Briar, VA	434	24595
Sweet Home, OR	541, 458	97386
Sweetwater, TN	423	37874
Sweetwater, TX	915	79556
Swepsonville, NC	336	27359
Swiftwater, PA	570	18370
Swissvale, PA	412, 878	15218
Swords Creek, VA	276	24649
Swoyersville, PA	570	18704
Sycamore, AL	256	35149
Sycamore, IL	815	60178
Sykesville, MD	410	21784
Sylacauga, AL	256	35150-35151
Sylmar, CA	818	91342, 91392
Sylva, NC	828	28779
Sylvania, GA	912	30467
Sylvania, OH	419, 567	43560
Sylvester, GA	229	31791
Syosset, NY	516	11773, 11791
Syracuse, IN	574	46567
Syracuse, KS	620	67878
Syracuse, NE	402	68446
Syracuse, NY	315	13201-13225, 13235, 13244*

T

City	Area Code(s)	Zip Code(s)
Tabor, SD	605	57063
Tabor City, NC	910	28463
Tacoma, WA	253	98401-98424, 98431-98433*
Taft, CA	661	93268
Taft, OK	918	74463
Taftville, CT	860	06380
Tahlequah, OK	918	74464-74465
Tahoe City, CA	530	96145-96146
Tahoka, TX	806	79373
Takoma Park, MD	301	20903, 20912-20913
Talbotton, GA	706, 762	31827
Talihina, OK	918	74571
Talladega, AL	256	35160-35161
Tallahassee, FL	850	32301-32318, 32395, 32399
Tallapoosa, GA	470, 770	30176
Tallassee, AL	334	36023, 36045, 36078
Tallevast, FL	941	34270
Tallmadge, OH	234, 330	44278
Tallulah, LA	318	71282-71284
Talmage, PA	717	17580
Taloga, OK	580	73667
Tama, IA	641	52339
Tamaqua, PA	570	18252
Tamarac, FL	754, 954	33309, 33319-33323, 33351*
Tamiment, PA	570	18371
Tamms, IL	618	62988, 62993
Tampa, FL	813	33601-33637, 33647-33651*
Taneytown, MD	410	21787
Tangent, OR	541, 458	97389
Tannersville, PA	570	18372
Taos, NM	505	87571
Tappahannock, VA	804	22560
Tarboro, NC	252	27886
Tarentum, PA	724, 878	15084
Tarpon Springs, FL	727	34688-34691
Tarrytown, NY	914	10591
Tarzana, CA	818	91335, 91356-91357
Taunton, MA	508, 774	02718, 02780-02783
Tavares, FL	352	32778
Tavernier, FL	305, 786	33070
Tawas City, MI	989	48763-48764
Taylor, MI	313, 734	48180
Taylor, NE	308	68879
Taylor, PA	570	18517
Taylor, TX	512	76574
Taylors, SC	864	29687
Taylorsville, KY	502	40071
Taylorsville, MS	601, 769	39168
Taylorsville, NC	828	28681
Taylorville, IL	217	62568
Tazewell, TN	423	37879
Tazewell, VA	276	24608, 24651
Teaneck, NJ	201, 551	07666
Teays, WV	304	25569
Tecumseh, MI	517	49286
Tecumseh, NE	402	68450
Tecumseh, OK	405	74873
Tehachapi, CA	661	93561, 93581
Tekamah, NE	402	68061
Telford, PA	215, 267	18969
Tell City, IN	812	47586
Telluride, CO	970	81435
Temecula, CA	951	92589-92593
Tempe, AZ	480, 602	85280-85289
Temperance, MI	734	48182
Temple, PA	484, 610	19560
Temple, TX	254	76501-76508
Temple City, CA	626	91780
Temple Hills, MD	301	20748, 20752, 20757, 20762
Temple Terrace, FL	813	33617, 33637, 33687
Templeton, CA	805	93465
Tenafly, NJ	201, 551	07670
Tenino, WA	360	98589
Tenstrike, MN	218	56683
Tequesta, FL	561	33469
Terminal Island, CA	310, 424	90731
Terra Bella, CA	559	93270
Terre Haute, IN	812	47801-47814
Terrell, TX	469, 972	75160-75161
Terry, MT	406	59349
Terryville, CT	860	06786
Teterboro, NJ	201, 551	07608
Teton Village, WY	307	83025
Teutopolis, IL	217	62467
Tewksbury, MA	351, 978	01876
Texarkana, AR	870	71854
Texarkana, TX	903	75501-75507, 75599

Partial list of zip codes, including main range

City	Area Code(s)	Zip Code(s)
Texas City, TX	409	77590-77592
Thatcher, AZ	928	85552
The Colony, TX	469, 972	75034, 75056
The Dalles, OR	541, 458	97058
The Sea Ranch, CA	707	95445, 95497
The Villages, FL	352	32159-32162
The Woodlands, TX	281, 832	77380-77387, 77393
Thedford, NE	308	69166
Theodore, AL	251	36582, 36590, 36619
Thermopolis, WY	307	82443
Thibodaux, LA	985	70301-70302, 70310
Thief River Falls, MN	218	56701
Thiensville, WI	262	53092, 53097
Thomaston, CT	860	06778, 06787
Thomaston, GA	706, 762	30286
Thomaston, ME	207	04861
Thomasville, AL	334	36762, 36784
Thomasville, GA	229	31757-31758, 31792, 31799
Thomasville, NC	336	27360-27361
Thomasville, PA	717	17364
Thompson, CT	860	06277
Thompson, IA	641	50478
Thompson Falls, MT	406	59873
Thompsons Station, TN	615	37179
Thompsonville, MI	231	49683
Thomson, GA	706, 762	30824
Thorndale, PA	484, 610	19372
Thornton, CO	303, 720	80020, 80221, 80229, 80233*
Thornton, IL	708	60476
Thornville, OH	740	43076
Thornwood, NY	914	10594
Thorofare, NJ	856	08086
Thousand Oaks, CA	805	91319-91320, 91358-91362
Three Lakes, WI	715, 534	54562
Three Rivers, CA	559	93271
Three Rivers, MI	616	49093
Three Rivers, TX	361	78060, 78071
Throckmorton, TX	940	76483
Thurmont, MD	301	21788
Tiburon, CA	415	94920
Tie Siding, WY	307	82084
Tierra Amarilla, NM	505	87575
Tierra Verde, FL	727	33715
Tiffin, OH	419, 567	44883
Tifton, GA	229	31793-31794
Tigard, OR	503, 971	97223-97224, 97281
Tigerville, SC	864	29688
Tilden, TX	361	78072
Tillamook, OR	503	97141
Tillery, NC	252	27887
Tilton, NH	603	03276, 03298-03299
Timber Lake, SD	605	57656
Timberline Lodge, OR	503, 971	97028
Timmonsville, SC	843	29161
Timonium, MD	410	21093-21094
Tinker AFB, OK	405	73145
Tinley Park, IL	708	60477
Tinton Falls, NJ	732, 848	07724
Tionesta, PA	814	16353
Tipp City, OH	937	45371
Tipton, IN	765	46072
Tipton, IA	563	52772
Tipton, MO	660	65081
Tipton, OK	580	73570
Tipton, PA	814	16684
Tiptonville, TN	731	38079
Tishomingo, OK	580	73460
Titusville, FL	321	32780-32783, 32796
Titusville, NJ	609	08560
Titusville, PA	814	16354
Toa Baja, PR	787, 939	00949-00951
Toccoa, GA	706, 762	30577
Toccoa Falls, GA	706, 762	30598
Togo, MN	218	55723
Tok, AK	907	99776-99780
Tokeland, WA	360	98590
Toledo, IL	217	62468
Toledo, IA	641	52342
Toledo, OH	419, 567	43601-43624, 43635, 43652*
Tolland, CT	860	06084
Tolleson, AZ	623	85353
Tollhouse, CA	559	93667
Tolono, IL	217	61880
Toluca, IL	815	61369
Tomah, WI	608	54660
Tomball, TX	281, 832	77337, 77375-77377
Tombstone, AZ	520	85638
Tompkinsville, KY	270	42167
Toms River, NJ	732, 848	08753-08757
Tonalea, AZ	928	86044, 86053-86054
Tonawanda, NY	716	14150-14151, 14217, 14223
Tonkawa, OK	580	74653
Tonopah, NV	775	89049
Tontitown, AR	479	72770
Tooele, UT	435	84074
Topeka, IN	260	46571
Topeka, KS	785	66601-66629, 66634-66638*
Toppenish, WA	509	98948
Topsfield, MA	351, 978	01983
Topsham, ME	207	04086
Topton, PA	484, 610	19562
Torrance, CA	310, 424	90501-90510
Torrance, PA	724, 878	15779
Torrey, UT	435	84775
Torrington, CT	860	06790-06791
Torrington, WY	307	82240
Totowa, NJ	862, 973	07511-07512
Tougaloo, MS	601, 769	39174
Toulon, IL	309	61483
Toutle, WA	360	98645, 98649
Towaco, NJ	862, 973	07082
Towanda, PA	570	18848
Towner, ND	701	58788
Townsend, MA	351, 978	01469, 01474
Townsend, MT	406	59644
Townsend, TN	865	37882
Towson, MD	410	21204, 21284-21286
Tracy, CA	209	95304, 95376-95378, 95385*
Travelers Rest, SC	864	29690
Traverse City, MI	231	49684-49686, 49696
Travis AFB, CA	707	94535
Tremonton, UT	435	84337
Trenton, FL	352	32693
Trenton, GA	706, 762	30752
Trenton, ME	207	04605
Trenton, MI	734	48183
Trenton, MO	660	64683
Trenton, NE	308	69044
Trenton, NJ	609	08601-08611, 08618-08620*
Trenton, NC	252	28585
Trenton, OH	513	45067
Trenton, SC	803	29847
Trenton, TN	731	38382
Trevor, WI	262	53102, 53179
Trevose, PA	215, 267	19053
Triangle, VA	571, 703	22172
Tribune, KS	620	67879
Trinidad, CO	719	81074, 81082
Trinity, AL	256	35673
Trinity, NC	336	27370
Trinity Center, CA	530	96091
Trion, GA	706, 762	30753
Trotwood, OH	937	45406, 45415-45418, 45426*
Troutdale, OR	503, 971	97060
Troy, AL	334	36079-36082
Troy, ID	208	83871
Troy, IL	618	62294
Troy, KS	785	66087
Troy, MI	248, 947	48007, 48083-48085, 48098*
Troy, MO	636	63379
Troy, NY	518	12179-12183
Troy, NC	910	27371
Troy, OH	937	45373-45374
Troy, VA	434	22974
Truckee, CA	530	96160-96162
Truman, MN	507	56088
Trumann, AR	870	72472
Trumbauersville, PA	215, 267	18970
Trumbull, CT	203	06611
Trussville, AL	205	35173
Truth or Consequences, NM	505	87901
Tryon, NE	308	69167
Tryon, NC	828	28782
Tsaile, AZ	928	86556
Tualatin, OR	503, 971	97062
Tuba City, AZ	928	86045
Tuckahoe, NY	914	10707
Tucker, AR	501	72168
Tucker, GA	470, 678, 770	30084-30085
Tucson, AZ	520	85701-85754, 85775-85777
Tucumcari, NM	505	88401, 88416
Tukwila, WA	206, 425	98108, 98138, 98168, 98178*
Tulare, CA	559	93274-93275
Tulelake, CA	530	96134
Tulia, TX	806	79088
Tullahoma, TN	931	37388-37389
Tullytown, PA	215, 267	19007
Tulsa, OK	918	74101-74121, 74126-74137*
Tumacacori, AZ	520	85640, 85645-85646
Tumwater, WA	360	98501, 98511-98512
Tunica, MS	662	38676
Tunkhannock, PA	570	18657
Tupelo, MS	662	38801-38804
Turbeville, SC	843	29162
Turlock, CA	209	95380-95382
Turner, OR	503, 971	97359, 97392
Turners Falls, MA	413	01349, 01376
Turnersville, NJ	856	08012
Turpin, OK	580	73950
Turtle Creek, PA	412, 878	15145
Turtle Lake, WI	715, 534	54004, 54889
Tuscaloosa, AL	205	35401-35407, 35485-35487
Tuscola, IL	217	61953
Tuscola, TX	915	79562
Tuscumbia, AL	256	35674
Tuscumbia, MO	573	65082
Tuskegee, AL	334	36083
Tuskegee Institute, AL	334	36083, 36087-36088
Tustin, CA	714	92780-92782
Twentynine Palms, CA	760, 442	92277-92278
Twin Bridges, MT	406	59754
Twin Falls, ID	208	83301-83303
Twinsburg, OH	234, 330	44087
Two Harbors, MN	218	55616
Two Rivers, WI	920	54241
Tybee Island, GA	912	31328
Tyler, MN	507	56178
Tyler, TX	903	75701-75713, 75798-75799
Tylertown, MS	601, 769	39667
Tyndall, SD	605	57066
Tyndall AFB, FL	850	32403
Tyngsboro, MA	351, 978	01879
Tyrone, GA	470, 770	30290
Tyrone, PA	814	16686

U

City	Area Code(s)	Zip Code(s)
Ubly, MI	989	48475
Uhrichsville, OH	740	44683
Ukiah, CA	707	95418, 95482
Ullin, IL	618	62992
Ulm, MT	406	59485
Ulysses, KS	620	67880
Umatilla, OR	541, 458	97882
Una, SC	864	29378
Unadilla, GA	478	31091
Unadilla, NY	607	13849
Unalakleet, AK	907	99684
Unalaska, AK	907	99547, 99685, 99692
Uncasville, CT	860	06382
Union, IL	815	60180
Union, MO	636	63084
Union, NJ	908	07083
Union, SC	864	29379
Union, WA	360	98592
Union, WV	304	24983
Union City, CA	510	94587
Union City, GA	470, 770	30291
Union City, IN	765	47390
Union City, NJ	201, 551	07086-07087
Union City, PA	814	16438
Union City, TN	731	38261, 38281
Union Gap, WA	509	98901-98903
Union Grove, WI	262	53182
Union Lake, MI	248, 947	48387
Union Springs, AL	334	36089
Uniondale, NY	516	11553-11556, 11588
Uniontown, AL	334	36786
Uniontown, OH	234, 330	44685
Uniontown, PA	724, 878	15401

*Partial list of zip codes, including main range

City	Area Code(s)	Zip Code(s)
Unionville, MO	660	63565
Unity, ME	207	04988
Universal City, CA	818	91608, 91618
Universal City, TX	210	78148-78150
University, MS	662	38677
University Center, MI	989	48710
University City, MO	314	63124, 63130
University Heights, OH	216	44118, 44122
University of Richmond, VA	804	23173
University Park, IL	708	60466
University Park, IA	641	52595
University Park, PA	814	16802
Upland, CA	909	91784-91786
Upland, IN	765	46989
Upland, PA	484, 610	19013-19015
Upper Arlington, OH	614	43220-43221
Upper Black Eddy, PA	484, 610	18972
Upper Marlboro, MD	301	20772-20775, 20792
Upper Montclair, NJ	862, 973	07043
Upper Saddle River, NJ	201, 551	07458
Upper Saint Clair, PA	724, 878	15241
Upper Sandusky, OH	419, 567	43351
Upperville, VA	540	20184-20185
Upton, MA	508, 774	01568
Upton, NY	631	11973
Urbana, IL	217	61801-61803
Urbana, IN	260	46990
Urbana, IA	319	52345
Urbana, OH	937	43078
Urbandale, IA	515	50322-50323
Ursa, IL	217	62376
USAF Academy, CO	719	80841
Utica, MI	586	48315-48318
Utica, MS	601, 769	39175
Utica, NY	315	13501-13505, 13599
Uvalde, TX	830	78801-78802

V

City	Area Code(s)	Zip Code(s)
Vacaville, CA	707	95687-95688, 95696
Vail, CO	970	81657-81658
Valdese, NC	828	28690
Valdez, AK	907	99686
Valdosta, GA	229	31601-31606, 31698-31699
Vale, OR	541, 458	97918
Valencia, CA	661	91354-91355, 91380, 91385
Valencia, PA	724, 878	16059
Valentine, NE	402	69201
Valhalla, NY	914	10595
Vallejo, CA	707	94503, 94589-94592
Valley, AL	334	36854, 36872
Valley Center, CA	760, 442	92082
Valley Center, KS	316	67147
Valley City, ND	701	58072
Valley City, OH	234, 330	44280
Valley Cottage, NY	845	10989
Valley Falls, NY	518	12185
Valley Forge, PA	484, 610	19481-19485, 19493-19496
Valley Park, MO	636	63088
Valley Stream, NY	516	11580-11583
Valley View, OH	216	44125, 44131
Valley View, TX	940	76272
Valley Village, CA	818	91607, 91617
Valparaiso, IN	219	46383-46385
Valyermo, CA	661	93563
Van Alstyne, TX	903	75495
Van Buren, AR	479	72956-72957
Van Buren, MO	573	63965
Van Horn, TX	915	79855
Van Nuys, CA	818	91316, 91388, 91401-91416*
Van Wert, OH	419, 567	45891
Vanceburg, KY	606	41179
Vancouver, WA	360	98660-98668, 98682-98687
Vandalia, IL	618	62471
Vandalia, OH	937	45377
Vandenberg AFB, CA	805	93437
Vanderbilt, MI	989	49795
Vandergrift, PA	724, 878	15690
Vansant, VA	276	24656
Vashon, WA	206	98013, 98070
Vassar, MI	989	48768-48769
Vega, TX	806	79092
Vega Alta, PR	787, 939	00692
Velva, ND	701	58790
Venice, CA	310, 424	90291-90296
Venice, FL	941	34284-34293
Ventura, CA	805	93001-93009
Verdi, NV	775	89439
Vergennes, VT	802	05491
Vermillion, SD	605	57069
Vernal, UT	435	84078-84079
Vernon, AL	205	35592
Vernon, CA	323	90058
Vernon, CT	860	06066
Vernon, IN	812	47282
Vernon, NJ	862, 973	07462
Vernon, NY	315	13476
Vernon, TX	940	76384-76385
Vernon Hills, IL	224, 847	60061
Vernonia, OR	503, 971	97064
Vero Beach, FL	772	32960-32969
Verona, MS	662	38879
Verona, NY	315	13478
Verona, PA	412, 878	15147
Verona, VA	540	24482
Verona, WI	608	53593
Versailles, IN	812	47042
Versailles, KY	859	40383-40386
Versailles, MO	573	65084
Vesta, VA	276	24177
Vestal, NY	607	13850-13851
Vevay, IN	812	47043
Vicksburg, MI	616	49097
Vicksburg, MS	601, 769	39180-39183
Victor, ID	208	83455
Victor, NY	585	14564
Victoria, MN	952	55386
Victoria, TX	361	77901-77905
Victoria, VA	434	23974
Vidalia, GA	912	30474-30475
Vidalia, LA	318	71373
Vienna, GA	229	31092
Vienna, IL	618	62995
Vienna, MO	573	65582
Vienna, OH	234, 330	44473
Vienna, VA	571, 703	22027, 22124, 22180-22185
Vienna, WV	304	26101, 26105
Viera, FL	321	32940, 32955
Villa Park, IL	331, 630	60181
Villanova, PA	484, 610	19085
Ville Platte, LA	337	70586
Vinalhaven, ME	207	04863
Vincennes, IN	812	47591
Vincent, AL	205	35178
Vineland, NJ	856	08360-08362
Vineyard Haven, MA	508, 774	02568, 02573
Vinita, OK	918	74301
Vinton, IA	319	52349
Vinton, LA	337	70668
Vinton, VA	540	24179
Virginia, IL	217	62691
Virginia, MN	218	55777, 55792
Virginia Beach, VA	757	23450-23471, 23479
Virginia City, MT	406	59755
Virginia City, NV	775	89440
Viroqua, WI	608	54665
Visalia, CA	559	93277-93279, 93290-93292
Vista, CA	760, 442	92083-92085
Vivian, LA	318	71082
Vonore, TN	423	37885
Voorhees, NJ	856	08043
Voorheesville, NY	518	12186

W

City	Area Code(s)	Zip Code(s)
Wabash, IN	260	46992
Wabasha, MN	651	55981
Wabasso, FL	772	32970
Waco, TX	254	76701-76716, 76795-76799
Waconia, MN	952	55375, 55387
Waddington, NY	315	13694
Wadena, MN	218	56482
Wadesboro, NC	704, 980	28170
Wadley, AL	256	36276
Wadley, GA	478	30477
Wadsworth, OH	234, 330	44281-44282
Wagoner, OK	918	74467, 74477
Wahoo, NE	402	68066
Wahpeton, ND	701	58074-58076
Waianae, HI	808	96792
Waikoloa, HI	808	96738
Wailea, HI	808	96753
Wailuku, HI	808	96793
Waimanalo, HI	808	96795
Waipahu, HI	808	96797
Waite Park, MN	320	56387-56388
Wakarusa, IN	574	46573
Wake Forest, NC	919	27587-27588
WaKeeney, KS	785	67672
Wakefield, MA	339, 781	01880
Wakefield, MI	906	49968
Wakefield, RI	401	02879-02883
Wakulla Springs, FL	850	32327
Walbridge, OH	419, 567	43465
Walcott, IA	563	52773
Walden, CO	970	80430, 80480
Walden, NY	845	12586
Waldorf, MD	301	20601-20604
Waldron, AR	479	72924, 72958
Wales, WI	262	53183
Waleska, GA	470, 770	30183
Walhalla, SC	864	29691
Walker, MI	616	49544
Walker, MN	218	56484
Walkerton, IN	574	46574
Wall, NJ	732, 848	07719
Wall, SD	605	57790
Walla Walla, WA	509	99362
Wallace, ID	208	83873-83874
Wallace, NC	910	28466
Wallace, SC	843	29596
Walland, TN	865	37886
Walled Lake, MI	248, 947	48390-48391
Waller, TX	281, 832	77484
Wallingford, CT	203	06492-06495
Wallingford, PA	484, 610	19086
Wallington, NJ	862, 973	07057
Wallkill, NY	845	12589
Walls, MS	662	38680, 38686
Walnut, CA	909	91788-91789, 91795
Walnut, IL	815	61376
Walnut Creek, CA	925	94595-94598
Walnut Creek, OH	234, 330	44687
Walnut Ridge, AR	870	72476
Walpole, MA	508, 774	02032, 02071, 02081
Walpole, NH	603	03608
Walsenburg, CO	719	81089
Walstonburg, NC	252	27888
Walterboro, SC	843	29488
Walters, OK	580	73572
Walthall, MS	662	39771
Waltham, MA	339, 781	02451-02455
Walthourville, GA	912	31333
Walton, IN	574	46994
Walton Hills, OH	440	44146
Walworth, WI	262	53184
Wamego, KS	785	66547
Wampsville, NY	315	13163
Wanamingo, MN	507	55983
Wanatah, IN	219	46390
Wantagh, NY	516	11793
Wapakoneta, OH	419, 567	45819, 45895
Wapato, WA	509	98951
Wapello, IA	319	52653
Wapiti, WY	307	82450
Wappingers Falls, NY	845	12590
Ward, CO	303, 720	80481
Ward Hill, MA	351, 978	01835
Warden, WA	509	98857
Ware, MA	413	01082
Wareham, MA	508, 774	02571
Warfordsburg, PA	301	17267
Warm Springs, GA	706, 762	31830
Warm Springs, MT	406	59756
Warm Springs, OR	541, 458	97761
Warm Springs, VA	540	24484
Warminster, PA	215, 267	18974, 18991
Warner, NH	603	03278
Warner, OK	918	74469
Warner Robins, GA	478	31088, 31093-31099
Warren, AR	870	71671
Warren, MI	586	48088-48093, 48397

Partial list of zip codes, including main range

City	Area Code(s)	Zip Code(s)
Warren, MN	218	56762
Warren, NJ	908	07059
Warren, OH	234, 330	44481-44488
Warren, PA	814	16365-16369
Warren, RI	401	02885
Warren, VT	802	05674
Warrendale, PA	724, 878	15086, 15095-15096
Warrensburg, MO	660	64093
Warrensville Heights, OH	216	44122, 44128
Warrenton, GA	706, 762	30828
Warrenton, MO	636	63383
Warrenton, NC	252	27589
Warrenton, OR	503	97146
Warrenton, VA	540	20186-20188
Warrenville, IL	331, 630	60555
Warrington, PA	215, 267	18976
Warrior, AL	205	35180
Warroad, MN	218	56741, 56763
Warsaw, IN	574	46580-46582
Warsaw, KY	859	41095
Warsaw, MO	660	65355
Warsaw, NY	585	14569
Warsaw, NC	910	28398
Warsaw, VA	804	22572
Wartburg, TN	423	37887
Warwick, NY	845	10990
Warwick, RI	401	02818, 02886-02889
Wasco, IL	331, 630	60183
Waseca, MN	507	56093
Washburn, MO	417	65772
Washburn, ND	701	58577
Washburn, WI	715, 534	54891
Washington, CT	860	06777, 06793-06794
Washington, DC	202	20001-20020, 20024-20082*
Washington, GA	706, 762	30673
Washington, IL	309	61571
Washington, IN	812	47501
Washington, IA	319	52353
Washington, KS	785	66968
Washington, MO	636	63090
Washington, NJ	908	07882
Washington, NC	252	27889
Washington, PA	724, 878	15301
Washington, VA	540	22747
Washington, WV	304	26181
Washington Court House, OH	740	43160
Washington Green, CT	860	06793
Washington Island, WI	920	54246
Washington Navy Yard, DC	202	20374-20376, 20388-20391*
Washingtonville, NY	845	10992
Washougal, WA	360	98671
Wasilla, AK	907	99652-99654, 99687, 99694
Wassaic, NY	845	12592
Watauga, TX	682, 817	76148
Water Valley, MS	662	38965
Waterbury, CT	203	06701-06712, 06716, 06720*
Waterbury, VT	802	05671, 05676
Waterbury Center, VT	802	05677
Waterford, CT	860	06385-06386
Waterford, MI	248, 947	48327-48330
Waterford, NY	518	12188
Waterford, PA	814	16441
Waterford, WI	262	53185
Waterloo, IL	618	62298
Waterloo, IN	260	46793
Waterloo, IA	319	50701-50707, 50799
Waterloo, NY	315	13165
Waterloo, WI	920	53594
Watertown, CT	860	06779, 06795
Watertown, MA	617, 857	02471-02472, 02477
Watertown, MN	952	55388
Watertown, NY	315	13601-13603
Watertown, SD	605	57201
Watertown, WI	920	53094, 53098
Waterville, ME	207	04901-04903
Waterville, OH	419, 567	43566
Waterville, WA	509	98858
Waterville Valley, NH	603	03215
Watervliet, NY	518	12189
Watford City, ND	701	58854
Watkins Glen, NY	607	14891
Watkinsville, GA	706, 762	30677
Watonga, OK	580	73772
Watrous, NM	505	87750-87753
Watseka, IL	815	60970
Watsonville, CA	831	95076-95077

City	Area Code(s)	Zip Code(s)
Wauchula, FL	863	33873
Waucoma, IA	563	52171
Wauconda, IL	224, 847	60084
Waukegan, IL	224, 847	60079, 60085-60087
Waukesha, WI	262	53146, 53151, 53186-53189
Waukon, IA	563	52172
Waunakee, WI	608	53597
Waupaca, WI	715, 534	54981
Waupun, WI	920	53963
Wauregan, CT	860	06387
Waurika, OK	580	73573
Wausau, WI	715, 534	54401-54403
Wauseon, OH	419, 567	43567
Wautoma, WI	920	54982
Wauwatosa, WI	414	53210-53213, 53222, 53226
Waverly, FL	863	33877
Waverly, IA	319	50677
Waverly, OH	740	45690
Waverly, TN	931	37185
Waverly, VA	804	23890-23891
Wawaka, IN	260	46794
Waxahachie, TX	469, 972	75165-75168
Waycross, GA	912	31501-31503
Wayland, MA	508, 774	01778
Wayland, MI	616	49348
Wayland, NY	585	14572
Waymart, PA	570	18472
Wayne, MI	734	48184
Wayne, NE	402	68787
Wayne, NJ	862, 973	07470, 07474-07477
Wayne, PA	484, 610	19080, 19087-19089
Wayne, WV	304	25570
Waynesboro, GA	706, 762	30830
Waynesboro, MS	601, 769	39367
Waynesboro, PA	717	17268
Waynesboro, TN	931	38485
Waynesboro, VA	540	22980
Waynesburg, PA	724, 878	15370
Waynesville, MO	573	65583
Waynesville, NC	828	28738, 28785-28786
Wayzata, MN	763, 952	55391
Weatherford, OK	580	73096
Weatherford, TX	682, 817	76085-76088
Weaverville, CA	530	96093
Weaverville, NC	828	28787
Webb City, MO	417	64870
Webberville, MI	517	48892
Webster, MA	508, 774	01570
Webster, NY	585	14580
Webster, SD	605	57274
Webster, TX	281, 832	77598
Webster City, IA	515	50595
Webster Groves, MO	314	63119
Webster Springs, WV	304	26288
Wedowee, AL	256	36278
Weed, CA	530	96094
Weehawken, NJ	201, 551	07086-07087
Weidman, MI	989	48893
Weimar, CA	530	95736
Weirsdale, FL	352	32195
Weirton, WV	304	26062
Weiser, ID	208	83672
Welch, WV	304	24801
Welches, OR	503, 971	97067
Weldon, NC	252	27890
Wellesley, MA	339, 781	02457, 02481-02482
Wellesley Hills, MA	339, 781	02481
Wellesley Island, NY	315	13640
Wellfleet, MA	508, 774	02667
Wellington, CO	970	80549
Wellington, FL	561	33414, 33421, 33467
Wellington, KS	620	67152
Wellington, OH	440	44090
Wellington, TX	806	79095
Wells, ME	207	04090
Wells, MN	507	56097
Wells, NV	775	89835
Wellsboro, PA	570	16901
Wellsburg, NY	570	14894
Wellsburg, WV	304	26070
Wellsville, NY	585	14895
Wellsville, OH	234, 330	43968
Wellton, AZ	928	85356
Wenatchee, WA	509	98801-98802, 98807
Wendell, NC	919	27591
Wenham, MA	351, 978	01984

City	Area Code(s)	Zip Code(s)
Wentworth, NC	336	27375
Wernersville, PA	484, 610	19565
Weslaco, TX	956	78596-78599
Wesley Chapel, FL	813	33543-33544
Wessington Springs, SD	605	57382
Wesson, MS	601, 769	39191
West Alexandria, OH	937	45381
West Allis, WI	414	53214, 53219, 53227
West Atlantic City, NJ	609	08232
West Babylon, NY	631	11704-11707
West Barnstable, MA	508, 774	02668
West Bath, ME	207	04530
West Belmar, NJ	732, 848	07719
West Bend, IA	515	50597
West Bend, WI	262	53090, 53095
West Bethesda, MD	301	20817, 20827
West Bloomfield, MI	248, 947	48322-48325
West Boylston, MA	508, 774	01583
West Branch, IA	319	52358
West Branch, MI	989	48661
West Brentwood, NY	631	11717
West Bridgewater, MA	508, 774	02379
West Burlington, IA	319	52655
West Caldwell, NJ	862, 973	07006-07007
West Carrollton, OH	937	45439, 45449
West Chester, OH	513	45069-45071
West Chester, PA	484, 610	19380-19383
West Chicago, IL	331, 630	60185-60186
West Columbia, SC	803	29033, 29169-29172
West Columbia, TX	979	77486
West Conshohocken, PA	484, 610	19428
West Covina, CA	626	91790-91793
West Deptford, NJ	856	08066
West Des Moines, IA	515	50265-50266, 50398
West Dover, VT	802	05351, 05356
West Dundee, IL	224, 847	60118
West Falmouth, MA	508, 774	02574
West Fargo, ND	701	58078
West Frankfort, IL	618	62896
West Franklin, NH	603	03235
West Glacier, MT	406	59921, 59936
West Greenwich, RI	401	02817
West Grove, PA	484, 610	19390
West Hartford, CT	860	06107-06110, 06117-06119*
West Haven, CT	203	06516
West Haverstraw, NY	845	10993
West Hazleton, PA	570	18202
West Helena, AR	870	72390
West Hempstead, NY	516	11552
West Henrietta, NY	585	14586
West Hills, CA	818	91304-91308
West Hollywood, CA	310, 323, 424	90038, 90046-90048, 90069
West Homestead, PA	412, 878	15120
West Hurley, NY	845	12491
West Islip, NY	631	11795
West Jefferson, OH	614	43162
West Jordan, UT	801, 385	84084, 84088
West Kennebunk, ME	207	04094
West Kingston, RI	401	02892
West Lafayette, IN	765	47906-47907, 47996
West Lafayette, OH	740	43845
West Lebanon, IN	765	47991
West Lebanon, NH	603	03784
West Liberty, IA	319	52776
West Liberty, KY	606	41472
West Liberty, WV	304	26074
West Long Branch, NJ	732, 848	07764
West Los Angeles, CA	310, 424	90025
West Mansfield, OH	937	43358
West Melbourne, FL	321	32904, 32912
West Memphis, AR	870	72301-72303
West Middlesex, PA	724, 878	16159
West Mifflin, PA	412, 878	15122-15123, 15236
West Milford, NJ	862, 973	07480
West Monroe, LA	318	71291-71294
West New York, NJ	201, 551	07093
West Nyack, NY	845	10994
West Olive, MI	616	49460
West Orange, NJ	862, 973	07052
West Palm Beach, FL	561	33401-33422
West Park, NY	845	12493
West Paterson, NJ	862, 973	07424
West Pittsburg, PA	724, 878	16160
West Plains, MO	417	65775-65776
West Point, GA	706, 762	31833

**Partial list of zip codes, including main range*

City	Area Code(s)	Zip Code(s)
West Point, MS	662	39773
West Point, NE	402	68788
West Point, NY	845	10996-10997
West Point, PA	215, 267	19486
West Point, VA	804	23181
West Redding, CT	203	06896
West Roxbury, MA	617, 857	02132
West Sacramento, CA	916	95605, 95691, 95798-95799
West Saint Paul, MN	651	55107, 55118
West Salem, OH	419, 567	44287
West Salem, WI	608	54669
West Sayville, NY	631	11796
West Seneca, NY	716	14206, 14210, 14218-14220*
West Springfield, MA	413	01089-01090
West Tawakoni, TX	903	75474
West Terre Haute, IN	812	47885
West Trenton, NJ	609	08628
West Union, IA	563	52175
West Union, OH	937	45693
West Union, WV	304	26456
West Valley, NY	716	14171
West Valley City, UT	801, 385	84118-84120, 84128
West Warren, MA	413	01092
West Warwick, RI	401	02893
West Yellowstone, MT	406	59758
Westampton, NJ	609	08060
Westborough, MA	508, 774	01580-01582
Westbrook, CT	860	06498
Westbrook, ME	207	04092, 04098
Westbury, NY	516	11568, 11590-11597
Westby, WI	608	54667
Westchester, IL	708	60154
Westcliffe, CO	719	81252
Westerlo, NY	518	12055, 12193
Westerly, RI	401	02808, 02891
Westerville, OH	614	43081-43082, 43086
Westfield, IN	317	46074
Westfield, MA	413	01085-01086
Westfield, NJ	908	07090-07091
Westfield, NY	716	14787
Westfield, PA	814	16927, 16950
Westfield, VT	802	05874
Westfield Center, OH	234, 330	44251
Westford, MA	351, 978	01886
Westhampton Beach, NY	631	11978
Westlake, LA	337	70669
Westlake, OH	440	44145
Westlake, TX	682, 817	76262
Westlake Village, CA	805, 818	91359-91363
Westland, MI	734	48185-48186
Westminster, CA	714	92683-92685
Westminster, CO	303, 720	80003-80005, 80020-80021*
Westminster, MD	410	21157-21158
Westminster, MA	351, 978	01441, 01473
Westminster Station, VT	802	05159
Westmont, IL	331, 630	60559-60561
Westmont, NJ	856	08108
Westmoreland, KS	785	66426, 66549
Weston, CT	203	06883
Weston, FL	754, 954	33326-33327, 33331-33332
Weston, MA	339, 781	02493
Weston, MO	816	64098
Weston, WV	304	26452
Westover, MD	410	21871, 21890
Westport, CT	203	06880-06881, 06888-06889
Westport, MA	508, 774	02790
Westport, WA	360	98595
Westville, IN	574	46391
Westwego, LA	504	70094-70096
Westwood, KS	913	66205
Westwood, MA	339, 781	02090
Westwood, NJ	201, 551	07675-07677
Wethersfield, CT	860	06109, 06129
Wetumpka, AL	334	36092-36093
Wewahitchka, FL	850	32465
Wewoka, OK	405	74884
Wexford, PA	724, 878	15090
Weyers Cave, VA	540	24486
Weymouth, MA	339, 781	02188-02191
Wharton, TX	979	77488
Whately, MA	413	01093, 01373
Wheat Ridge, CO	303, 720	80002, 80033-80034, 80212*
Wheatland, IA	563	52777
Wheatland, PA	724, 878	16161
Wheatland, WY	307	82201
Wheaton, IL	331, 630	60187-60189
Wheaton, MD	301	20902, 20906, 20915
Wheaton, MN	320	56296
Wheeler, TX	806	79096
Wheeling, IL	224, 847	60090
Wheeling, WV	304	26003
Whippany, NJ	862, 973	07981-07983, 07999
Whiskeytown, CA	530	96095
White Bear Lake, MN	651	55110, 55115
White Castle, LA	225	70788
White City, OR	541, 458	97503
White Cloud, MI	231	49349
White Deer, PA	570	17887
White Haven, PA	570	18661
White Lake, MI	248, 947	48383-48386
White Oak, PA	412, 878	15131
White Oak, TX	903	75693
White Pigeon, MI	616	49099
White Plains, NY	914	10601-10610, 10650
White River, SD	605	57579
White River Junction, VT	802	05001, 05009
White Sands, NM	505	88002
White Sands Missile Range, NM	505	88002
White Stone, VA	804	22578
White Sulphur Springs, MT	406	59645
White Sulphur Springs, WV	304	24986
Whitefish, MT	406	59937
Whitehall, MI	231	49461-49463
Whitehall, PA	484, 610	18052
Whitehall, WI	715, 534	54773
Whitehouse, NJ	908	08888
Whitehouse, OH	419, 567	43571
Whitehouse Station, NJ	908	08889
Whitesburg, KY	606	41858
Whitestone, NY	347, 718	11357
Whiteville, NC	910	28472
Whiteville, TN	901	38075
Whitewater, WI	262	53190
Whitfield, MS	601, 769	39193
Whiting, IN	219	46394
Whiting, NJ	732, 848	08759
Whitinsville, MA	508, 774	01588
Whitley City, KY	606	42653
Whitsett, NC	336	27377
Whittier, AK	907	99693
Whittier, CA	562	90601-90612
Wibaux, MT	406	59353
Wichita, KS	316	67201-67236, 67251, 67256*
Wichita Falls, TX	940	76301-76311
Wickenburg, AZ	928	85358, 85390
Wickliffe, KY	270	42087
Wickliffe, OH	440	44092
Wiggins, MS	601, 769	39577
Wilber, NE	402	68465
Wilberforce, OH	937	45384
Wilbraham, MA	413	01095
Wilburton, OK	918	74578
Wilder, KY	859	41071, 41076
Wilder, VT	802	05088
Wildomar, CA	951	92595
Wildorado, TX	806	79098
Wildwood, FL	352	34785
Wildwood, NJ	609	08260
Wildwood Crest, NJ	609	08260
Wilkes-Barre, PA	570	18701-18711, 18761-18769*
Wilkesboro, NC	336	28697
Willard, OH	419, 567	44888-44890
Willard, UT	435	84340
Willcox, AZ	520	85643-85644
Williams Bay, WI	262	53191
Williamsburg, IA	319	52361
Williamsburg, KY	606	40769
Williamsburg, OH	513	45176
Williamsburg, PA	814	16693
Williamsburg, VA	757	23081, 23185-23188
Williamson, WV	304	25661
Williamsport, IN	765	47993
Williamsport, MD	301	21795
Williamsport, PA	570	17701-17705
Williamston, MI	517	48895
Williamston, NC	252	27892
Williamstown, KY	859	41097
Williamstown, MA	413	01267
Williamstown, NJ	856	08094
Williamstown, WV	304	26187
Williamsville, NY	716	14221, 14231
Willimantic, CT	860	06226
Willingboro, NJ	609	08046
Willis, TX	936	77318, 77378
Williston, FL	352	32696
Williston, ND	701	58801-58802
Williston, SC	803	29853
Williston, VT	802	05495
Willits, CA	707	95429, 95490
Willmar, MN	320	56201
Willoughby, OH	440	44094-44097
Willow Grove, PA	215, 267	19090
Willow Springs, MO	417	65793
Willow Street, PA	717	17584
Willowbrook, IL	331, 630	60527
Willows, CA	530	95988
Willsboro, NY	518	12996
Wilmerding, PA	412, 878	15148
Wilmette, IL	224, 847	60091
Wilmington, CA	310, 424	90744, 90748
Wilmington, DE	302	19801-19810, 19850, 19880*
Wilmington, MA	978	01887
Wilmington, NC	910	28401-28412
Wilmington, OH	937	45177
Wilmore, KY	859	40390
Wilson, NY	716	14172
Wilson, NC	252	27893-27896
Wilson, WY	307	83014
Wilsonville, OR	503, 971	97070
Wilton, CT	203	06897
Wilton, IA	563	52778
Wilton, ME	207	04294
Wilton, NH	603	03086
Wilton, NY	518	12831
Wimberley, TX	512	78676
Winamac, IN	574	46996
Winchester, IL	217	62694
Winchester, IN	765	47394
Winchester, KY	859	40391-40392
Winchester, MA	339, 781	01890
Winchester, NH	603	03470
Winchester, TN	931	37398
Winchester, VA	540	22601-22604, 22638
Wind Gap, PA	484, 610	18091
Windber, PA	814	15963
Winder, GA	470, 770	30680
Windermere, FL	321, 407	34786
Windham, NH	603	03087
Windom, MN	507	56101, 56118
Window Rock, AZ	928	86515
Windsor, CA	707	95492
Windsor, CT	860	06006, 06095
Windsor, NC	252	27983
Windsor, VT	802	05089
Windsor, VA	757	23487
Windsor, WI	608	53598
Windsor Locks, CT	860	06096
Winfield, AL	205	35594
Winfield, IL	331, 630	60190
Winfield, KS	620	67156
Winfield, WV	304	25213
Wingate, NC	704, 980	28174
Winlock, WA	360	98596
Winn, ME	207	04495
Winnebago, WI	920	54985
Winneconne, WI	920	54986
Winnemucca, NV	775	89445-89446
Winner, SD	605	57580
Winnetka, CA	818	91306, 91396
Winnett, MT	406	59084-59087
Winnfield, LA	318	71483
Winnsboro, LA	318	71295
Winnsboro, SC	803	29180
Winona, MN	507	55987-55988
Winona, MS	662	38967
Winona, MO	573	65588
Winona Lake, IN	219	46590
Winooski, VT	802	05404
Winslow, AZ	928	86047
Winslow, ME	207	04901
Winslow, NJ	609	08095
Winsted, CT	860	06063, 06094, 06098
Winston, OR	541, 458	97496
Winston-Salem, NC	336	27101-27109, 27113-27117*

Partial list of zip codes, including main range

City	Area Code(s)	Zip Code(s)
Winter Garden, FL	321, 407	34777-34778, 34787
Winter Haven, FL	863	33880-33888
Winter Park, CO	970	80482
Winter Park, FL	321, 407	32789-32793
Winters, CA	530	95694
Winters, TX	915	79567
Winterset, IA	515	50273
Wintersville, OH	740	43952-43953
Winterthur, DE	302	19735
Winthrop, ME	207	04364
Winthrop, WA	509	98862
Winton, NC	252	27986
Wiscasset, ME	207	04578
Wisconsin Dells, WI	608	53965
Wisconsin Rapids, WI	715, 534	54494-54495
Wisdom, MT	406	59761
Wise, VA	276	24293
Wixom, MI	248, 947	48393
Woburn, MA	781	01801, 01806-01808, 01813*
Wolcott, CT	203	06716
Wolcott, IN	219	47995
Wolcott, NY	315	14590
Wolf, WY	307	82844
Wolf Point, MT	406	59201
Wolfe City, TX	903	75496
Wolfeboro, NH	603	03894
Womelsdorf, PA	484, 610	19567
Wood Dale, IL	331, 630	60191
Wood River, IL	618	62095
Woodbine, GA	912	31569
Woodbine, IA	712	51579
Woodbine, MD	301	21797
Woodbourne, NY	845	12788
Woodbridge, CT	203	06525
Woodbridge, NJ	732, 848	07095
Woodbridge, VA	571, 703	22191-22195
Woodburn, IN	260	46797
Woodburn, OR	503, 971	97071
Woodbury, CT	203	06798
Woodbury, MN	651	55125, 55129
Woodbury, NJ	856	08096-08097
Woodbury, NY	516	11797
Woodbury, TN	615	37190
Woodcliff Lake, NJ	201, 551	07677
Woodhaven, MI	734	48183
Woodhaven, NY	347, 718	11421
Woodinville, WA	425	98072
Woodland, CA	530	95695, 95776
Woodland, PA	814	16881
Woodland, WA	360	98674
Woodland Hills, CA	818	91302-91303, 91364-91367*
Woodridge, IL	331, 630	60517, 60540
Woodruff, SC	864	29388
Woodruff, WI	715, 534	54568
Woods Cross, UT	801, 385	84010, 84087
Woods Hole, MA	508, 774	02543
Woodsfield, OH	740	43793
Woodside, CA	650	94062
Woodside, NY	347, 718	11377
Woodstock, CT	860	06281
Woodstock, GA	470, 770	30188-30189
Woodstock, IL	815	60098
Woodstock, NY	845	12498
Woodstock, VT	802	05091
Woodstock, VA	540	22664
Woodstown, NJ	856	08098
Woodville, MS	601, 769	39669
Woodville, OH	419, 567	43469
Woodville, TX	409	75979, 75990
Woodville, WI	715, 534	54028
Woodward, IA	515	50276
Woodward, OK	580	73801-73802
Woolrich, PA	570	17779
Woonsocket, RI	401	02895
Woonsocket, SD	605	57385
Wooster, OH	234, 330	44691
Worcester, MA	508, 774	01601-01615, 01653-01655
Worcester, PA	484, 610	19490
Worland, WY	307	82401, 82430
Wormleysburg, PA	717	17043
Worth, IL	708	60482
Worthington, MN	507	56187
Worthington, OH	614	43085
Wrangell, AK	907	99929
Wray, CO	970	80758
Wrens, GA	706, 762	30818, 30833
Wrentham, MA	508, 774	02070, 02093
Wright, WY	307	82732
Wright City, MO	636	63390
Wright-Patterson AFB, OH	937	45433
Wrightstown, NJ	609	08562
Wrightsville, AR	501	72183
Wrightsville, GA	478	31096
Wrightsville, PA	717	17368
Wrightsville Beach, NC	910	28480
Wyalusing, PA	570	18853
Wyandanch, NY	631	11798
Wyandotte, MI	734	48192
Wyckoff, NJ	201, 551	07481
Wye Mills, MD	410	21679
Wylliesburg, VA	434	23976
Wyncote, PA	215, 267	19095
Wyndmoor, PA	215, 267	19038
Wynne, AR	870	72396
Wynnewood, PA	484, 610	19096
Wyoming, MI	616	49418, 49508-49509, 49548
Wyoming, MN	651	55092
Wyoming, PA	570	18644
Wyomissing, PA	484, 610	19610
Wysox, PA	570	18854
Wytheville, VA	276	24382

X

City	Area Code(s)	Zip Code(s)
Xenia, OH	937	45385

Y

City	Area Code(s)	Zip Code(s)
Yabucoa, PR	787, 939	00767
Yacolt, WA	360	98675
Yadkinville, NC	336	27055
Yakima, WA	509	98901-98909
Yakutat, AK	907	99689
Yale, IA	641	50277
Yanceyville, NC	336	27379
Yankton, SD	605	57078-57079
Yardley, PA	215, 267	19067
Yardville, NJ	609	08620
Yarmouth, ME	207	04096
Yates Center, KS	620	66783
Yazoo City, MS	662	39194
Yeadon, PA	484, 610	19050
Yellow Springs, OH	937	45387
Yellowstone National Park, WY	307	82190
Yellville, AR	870	72687
Yelm, WA	360	98597
Yerington, NV	775	89447
Yoakum, TX	361	77995
Yonkers, NY	914	10701-10710
Yorba Linda, CA	714	92885-92887
York, AL	205	36925
York, NE	402	68467
York, PA	717	17315, 17401-17407, 17415
York, SC	803	29745
York Harbor, ME	207	03910-03911
York Haven, PA	717	17370
York Springs, PA	717	17372
Yorktown, VA	757	23690-23693
Yorktown Heights, NY	914	10598
Yorkville, IL	331, 630	60560
Yorkville, NY	315	13495
Young America, MN	952	55394-55399, 55473, 55550*
Young Harris, GA	706, 762	30582
Youngstown, OH	234, 330	44501-44515, 44555, 44598*
Youngsville, LA	337	70592
Youngsville, NC	919	27596
Youngsville, PA	814	16371
Youngwood, PA	724, 878	15697
Yountville, CA	707	94599
Ypsilanti, MI	734	48197-48198
Yreka, CA	530	96097
Yuba City, CA	530	95991-95993
Yucaipa, CA	909	92399
Yucca Valley, CA	760, 442	92284-92286
Yukon, OK	405	73085, 73099
Yuma, AZ	928	85364-85369
Yuma, CO	970	80759

Z

City	Area Code(s)	Zip Code(s)
Zachary, LA	225	70791
Zachow, WI	715, 534	54182
Zanesville, OH	740	43701-43702
Zapata, TX	956	78076
Zebulon, GA	470, 770	30295
Zebulon, NC	919	27597
Zeeland, MI	616	49464
Zelienople, PA	724, 878	16063
Zellwood, FL	321, 407	32798
Zenda, WI	262	53195
Zephyrhills, FL	813	33539-33544
Zillah, WA	509	98953
Zion, IL	224, 847	60099
Zionsville, IN	317	46077
Zionsville, PA	484, 610	18092
Zolfo Springs, FL	863	33890
Zumbrota, MN	507	55992

**Partial list of zip codes, including main range*

Index to Classified Headings

Citations given in this index refer to the subject headings under which listings are organized in the Classified Section. The page numbers given for each citation refer to the page on which a particular subject category begins rather than to a specific company or organization name. "See" and "See also" references are included to help in the identification of appropriate subject categories.

A

B

C

E

F

G

H

I

J

K

L

M

N

O

Q

R

S

T

U

V

W

X

Y

Z

How To Use This Directo

Illustrated here are the various symbols, terms, and other features typically found on the pages of this directory,
concise explanations of what those features represent. For more detailed information about what's included in
please refer to the introductory section also titled "How To Use This Directory."

PLEASE NOTE: Listing data printed here are for sample purposes only. Consult directory for actual entries.

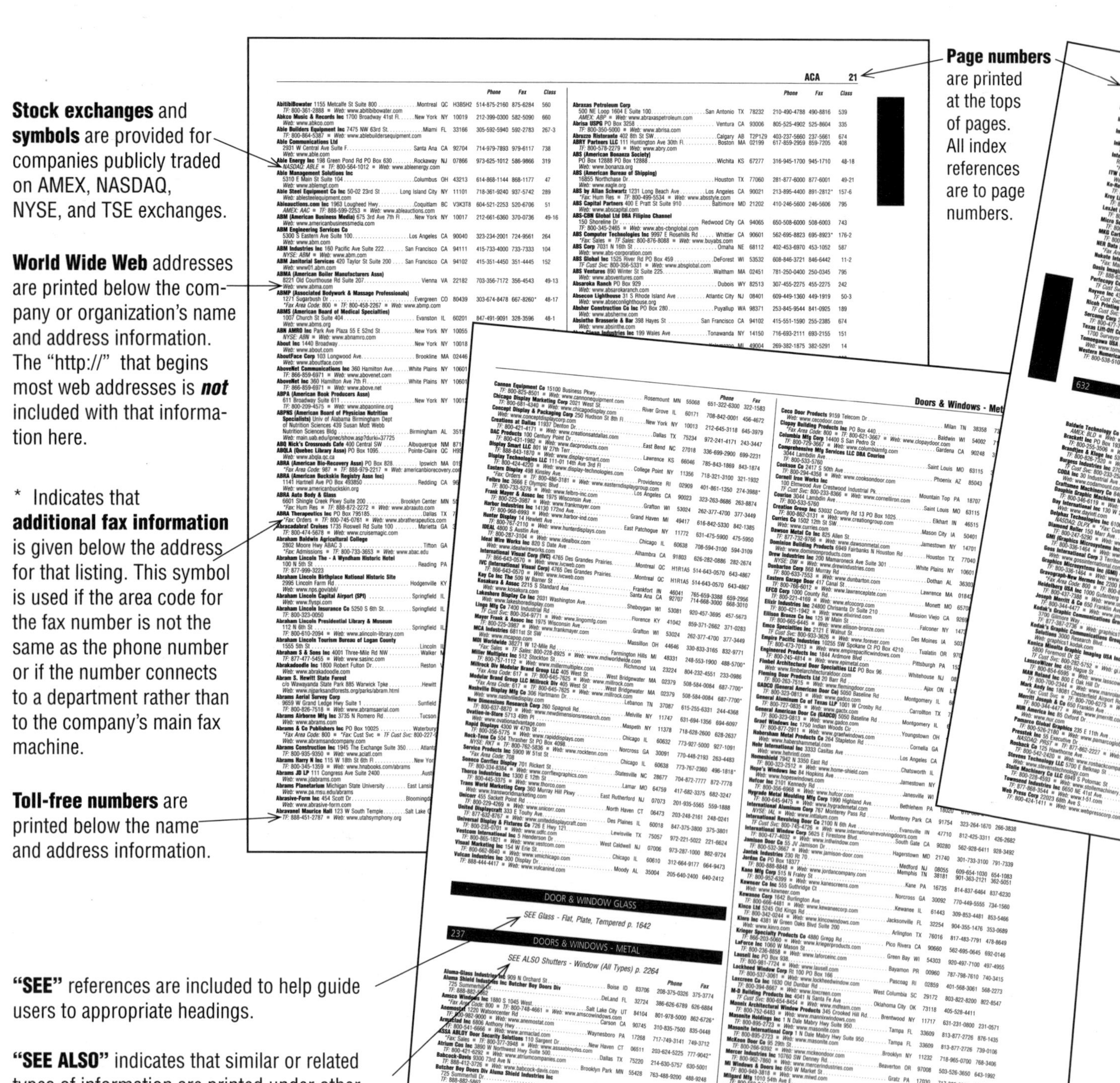

Stock exchanges and **symbols** are provided for companies publicly traded on AMEX, NASDAQ, NYSE, and TSE exchanges.
World Wide Web addresses are printed below the company or organization's name and address information. The "http://" that begins most web addresses is ***not*** included with that information here.
* Indicates that **additional fax information** is given below the address for that listing. This symbol is used if the area code for the fax number is not the same as the phone number or if the number connects to a department rather than to the company's main fax machine.
Toll-free numbers are printed below the name and address information.
"SEE" references are included to help guide users to appropriate headings.
"SEE ALSO" indicates that similar or related types of information are printed under other classified headings.
Page numbers are printed at the tops of pages. All index references are to page numbers.